American Men & Women of Science

1998-99 • 20th Edition

The 20th edition of *AMERICAN MEN & WOMEN OF SCIENCE* was prepared by the R.R. Bowker Database Publishing Group in collaboration with the Publication Systems Department.

Senior Staff of the Database Publishing Group includes:

Senior Vice President & Chief Operating Officer, R.R. Bowker
Neal Goff

Publisher
Nan Hudes

Vice President, Database Publishing
Leigh Yuster-Freeman

Editorial:
Director: *Owen O'Donnell*
Managing Editor: *Karen Hallard*
Senior Editor: *Alison J. Butkiewicz*
Associate Editors: *Angela Krakow*
Elizabeth McCarthy

Research:
Director: *Judy Redel*
Senior Managing Editor: *Tanya Hurst*
Senior Editor: *Beverly Heath*

Tampa Division:
Director: *Valerie Harris*
Production Manager: *Debra Wilson*
Associate Coordinator: *Jennifer Rodgers*

American Men & Women of Science

1998-99 • 20th Edition

A Biographical Directory of Today's Leaders in Physical, Biological and Related Sciences.

Volume 1 • A-B

R.R. BOWKER
A Unit of Reed Elsevier Business Information
New Providence, New Jersey

Published by R.R. Bowker, A Unit of Reed Elsevier Business Information

International Standard Book Number
Set: 0-8352-3748-6
Volume 1: 0-8352-3749-4
Volume 2: 0-8352-3775-3
Volume 3: 0-8352-3776-1
Volume 4: 0-8352-3778-8
Volume 5: 0-8352-3779-6
Volume 6: 0-8352-3781-8
Volume 7: 0-8352-3782-6
Volume 8: 0-8352-3783-4

International Standard Serial Number: 0192-8570
Library of Congress Catalog Card Number: 6-7326
Printed and bound in the United States of America.

8 Volume Set

ISBN 0-8352-3748-6

9 780835 237482

Contents

Advisory Committee

Dr. Charles Henderson Dickens
Former Executive Secretary, Federal Coordinating Council for Science, Engineering & Technology
Office of Science & Technology Policy

Dr. Oscar Nicolas Garcia
NCR Distinguished Professor & Chair, Department of Computer Science & Engineering
Wright State University

Dr. Michael J. Jackson
Executive Director
Federation of American Societies for Experimental Biology

Dr. Shirley Mahaley Malcom
Head, Directorate for Education and Human Resources Programs
American Association for the Advancement of Science

Ms. Beverly Fearn Porter
Assistant to the Executive Director for Society Relations
American Institute of Physics

Dr. William Eldon Splinter
Former Vice Chancellor for Research
University of Nebraska-Lincoln

Dr. Dael Lee Wolfle
Professor Emeritus, Graduate School of Public Affairs
University of Washington

Dr. Ahmed H. Zewail
Linus Pauling Professor of Chemistry & Physics
California Institute of Technology

Preface

American Men and Women of Science remains without peer as a chronicle of North American and Canadian scientific endeavor and achievement. The present work is the twentieth edition since it was first compiled as *American Men of Science* by J. McKeen Cattell in 1906. In its ninety-two year history, *American Men and Women of Science* has profiled the careers of over 300,000 scientists and engineers. Since the first edition, the number of American scientists and the fields they pursue has grown immensely. This edition alone lists full biographies for 119,618 engineers and scientists, 4184 of which are listed for the first time. Although the book has grown, our stated purpose is the same as when Dr. Cattell first undertook the task of producing a biographical directory of active American scientists. It was his intention to record educational, personal and career data which would make "a contribution to the organization of science in America" and "make men [and women] of science acquainted with one another and with one another's work." It is our hope that this edition will fulfill these goals.

The biographies of engineers and scientists constitute seven of the eight volumes and provide birthdate, birthplace, field of specialty, education, honorary degrees, current position, professional and concurrent experience, awards, memberships, research information and addresses for each entrant when applicable. The eighth volume, the discipline index, organizes biographees by field of activity. This index, adapted from the National Science Foundation's Taxonomy of Degree and Employment Specialties, classifies entrants by 192 subject specialties listed in the table of contents of Volume 8. The index lists scientists and engineers by state within each subject specialty, allowing the user to easily locate a scientist in a given area. Also included are statistical information and charts showing the distribution of *AMWS* listees by age and discipline and and annotated listing of the recipients of the Nobel Prizes, the Craaford Prize, the Charles Stark Draper Prize, the National Medals of Science and Technology, the Fields Medal and the Alan T. Waterman Award since the last edition.

While the scientific fields covered by *American Men and Women of Science* are comprehensive, no attempt has been made to include all American scientists. Entrants are meant to be limited to those who have made significant contributions in their field. The names of new entrants were submitted for consideration at the editors' request by current entrants and by leaders of academic, government and private research programs and associations. Those included met the following criteria:

1. Distinguished achievement, by reason of experience, training or accomplishment, including contributions to literature, coupled with continuing activity in scientific work;

   or

2. Research activity of high quality in science as evidenced by publication in reputable scientific journals; or, for those whose work cannot be published due to governmental or industrial security, research activity of high quality in science as evidenced by the judgement of the individual's peers;

   or

3. Attainment of a position of substantial responsibility requiring scientific training and experience.

This edition profiles living scientists in the physical and biological fields, as well as public health scientists, engineers, mathematicians, statisticians, and computer scientists. The information is collected by means of direct communication whenever possible. All entrants receive forms for corroboration and updating. New entrants receive questionaires and verification proofs before publication. The information submitted by entrants is included as completely as possible within the boundaries of editorial and space restrictions. If an entrant does not return the form and his or her current location can be verified in secondary sources, the full entry is repeated. References to the previous edition are given for those who do not return forms and cannot be located, but who are presumed to be still active in science or engineering. Entrants known to be deceased are noted as such and a reference to the previous edition is given. Scientists and engineers who are not citizens of the United States or Canada are included if a significant portion of their work was performed in North America.

The information in *American Men & Women of Science* is available on magnetic tape. For information, contact Bowker Electronic Publishing (888-BOWKER-2). *American Men and Women of Science* is also available for online searching through Lexis®-Nexis® (800-227-4908) and through DIALOG, a service of Knight-Ridder Information, Inc. (800-334-2564). The online products allow fielded as well as key word searches of all elements of a record, including field of interest, experience, and location. An ERL-compliant CD-ROM is available through SilverPlatter Information (800-343-0064). Mailing lists are available through Reed Elsevier Business Information Lists (John Panza, Account Manager, Bowker Files, 245 W 17th St, New York, NY, 10011; 212-337-7164).

A project as large as publishing *American Men and Women of Science* involves the efforts of a great many people. The editors take this opportunity to thank the twentieth edition advisory committee for their guidance, encouragement and support. Appreciation is also expressed to the many scientific societies who provided their membership lists for the purpose of locating former entrants whose addresses had changed, and to the tens of thousands of scientists across the country who took time to provide us with biographical information. We also wish to thank Donna Brinkmann and Carol Carr of Reed Technology & Information Services, Inc. for their assistance in the successful production of this directory.

Comments, suggestions and nominations for the twenty-first edition are encouraged and should be directed to The Editors, *American Men and Women of Science*, R.R. Bowker, 121 Chanlon Road, New Providence, New Jersey, 07974.

Karen Hallard
Managing Editor

Major Honors & Awards

Nobel Prizes

Nobel Foundation, Royal Swedish Academy of Sciences & Nobel Assembly of the Karolinska

The Nobel Prizes were established in 1900 (and first awarded in 1901) to recognize those people who "have conferred the greatest benefit on mankind."

1995 Recipients

Chemistry:
Paul Josef Crutzen, Mario Jose Molina & Frank Sherwood Rowland
Awarded "for their work in atmospheric chemistry, particularly concerning the formation and decomposition of ozone."

Physics:
Martin Lewis Perl
Frederick Reines
Awarded to Perl "for the discovery of the tau lepton" and to Reines "for the detection of the nutrino."

Physiology or Medicine:
Edward B. Lewis, Christiane Nusslein-Volhard & Eric F. Wieschaus
Awarded "for their discoveries concerning the genetic control of early embryonic development."

1996 Recipients

Chemistry:
Robert Floyd Curl, Harold Walter Kroto & Richard Errett Smalley
Awarded "for their discovery of fullerenes, carbon atoms bound in the form of a ball."

Physics:
David Morris Lee, Douglas Dean Osheroff & Robert Coleman Richardson
Awarded "for their discovery of superfluidity in helium-3."

Physiology or Medicine:
Peter Charles Doherty & Rolf Martin Zinkernagel
Awarded "for their discoveries of how the immune system recognizes virus-infected cells."

1997 Recipients

Chemistry:
Paul Delos Boyer, Jens Christian Skou & John Ernest Walker
Awarded to Boyer & Walker "for their elucidation of the enzymatic mechanism underlying the synthesis of adenosine triphosphate (ATP)" and to Skou "for the first discovery of an ion-transporting enzyme, NA^{+}, K^{+}-ATPase."

Physics:
Claude Nessin Cohen-Tannoudji, Steven Chu & William Daniel Phillips
Awarded "for their development of methods to cool and trap atoms with laser light."

Physiology or Medicine:
Stanley Ben Prusiner
Awarded to Prusiner for his discovery of prions, a new genre of infectious agents.

Crafoord Prize

Royal Swedish Academy of Sciences

The Crafoord Prize was introduced in 1982 to award scientists in disciplines not covered by the Nobel Prize, namely mathematics, astronomy, geosciences and biosciences.

1995 Recipients

Willi Dansgaard & Nicholas John Shackleton
Awarded "for their fundamental work on developing and applying isotope geological analysis methods for the study of climatic variations during the Quaternary period."

1996 Recipient

Robert McRedie May
Awarded to May "for his pioneering ecological research concerning theoretical analysis of the dynamics of populations, communities and ecosystems."

1997 Recipients

Fred Hoyle & Edwin Ernest Salpeter
Awarded "for their pioneering contributions involving the study of nuclear reactions in stars and stars' development."

Charles Stark Draper Prize

National Academy of Engineering

The Draper Prize, awarded biennially, was introduced in 1989 to recognize engineering achievement.

1995 Recipients

John Robinson Pierce & Harold A. Rosen
Awarded for developing communications satellite technology.

1997 Recipients

Vladimir Haensel
Awarded to Haensel for inventing "Platforming" — platinum reforming to convert petroleum into high-performance fuels.

National Medal of Science

National Science Foundation

The National Medals of Science were established by the United States Congress in 1959 and have been awarded by the President of the United States since 1962. The National Science Foundation's selection criteria are based on the "total impact of an individual's work on the present state of physical, biological, mathematical, engineering, behavioral, or social sciences."

1995 Recipients

Thomas Robert Cech
Hans Georg Dehmelt
Peter Goldreich
Hermann A(nton) Haus
Isabella Lugoski Karle
Louis Nirenberg
Alexander Rich
Roger N. Shepard

1996 Recipients

Wallace Broecker
Norman Ralph Davidson
James L(oton) Flanagan
Richard M. Karp
Chandra Kumar Naranbhai Patel
Ruth Patrick
Paul Anthony Samuelson
Stephen Smale

1997 Recipients

William K. Estes
Darleane Christian Hoffman
Harold Sledge Johnston
Marshall N. Rosenbluth
Martin Schwarzschild (deceased)
James Dewey Watson
Robert A. Weinberg
George West Wetherill
Shing-Tung Yau

Fields Medal

International Mathematical Union

The Fields Medals were established in 1936 by Canadian mathematician John Fields to acknowledge outstanding research by young mathematicians. The medals are awarded every four years at the International Congress of Mathematicians.

1994 Recipients

Jean Bourgain
Pierre Louis Lions
Jean-Christophe Yoccoz
Efim Isaakovich Zelmanof

Awarded to Bourgain for his insights into the geometry of infinite dimensional spaces. Awarded to Lions for advances in non-linear partial differential equations. Awarded to Yoccoz for analyzing the end results of complicated sequences of circle maps. Awarded to Zelmanov for solving the unrestricted Burnside problem.

National Medal of Technology

U.S. Department of Commerce

The National Medals of Technology were created as part of the 1980 Stevenson-Wydler Technology Innovation Act and were first awarded in 1985. They are bestowed by the President of the United States to recognize individuals and companies for their development or commercialization of technology or for their contributions to the establishment of a technologically-trained workforce.

1995 Recipients

Praveen Chaudhari
Jerome John Cuomo
Richard Joseph Gambino
Edward R. McCracken
Sam B. Williams
Alejandro Zaffaroni
Procter & Gamble Company
3M

1996 Recipients

Charles Huron Kaman
Stephanie Louise Kwolek
James C. Morgan
Peter Henry Rose
Johnson & Johnson

1997 Recipients

Norman R. Augustine
Vinton Gray Cerf
Ray Milton Dolby
Robert Elliot Kahn
Robert Steven Ledley

Alan T. Waterman Award

National Science Foundation & National Science Board

Established by the United States Congress in 1975, the Waterman Award is given annually to an outstanding researcher, aged 35 or younger, in any field of science or engineering supported by the National Science Foundation.

1995 Recipient

Matthew P.A. Fisher
Awarded to Fisher "for his pioneering contributions to the theory of disordered superconductors."

1996 Recipient

Robert Mebane Waymouth
Awarded to Waymouth for discovering new ways to make polymers.

1997 Recipient

Eric Allin Cornell
Awarded to Cornell for creation of Bose-Einstein condensate (BEC).

Statistics

Statistical distribution of entrants in *American Men & Women of Science* with U.S. mailing addresses is illustrated on the following five pages. The regional scheme for geographical analysis is diagrammed in the map below. A table enumerating the geographic distribution can be found on page xvi, following the charts. The statistics are compiled by tallying all occurrences of a major index subject. Each scientist may choose to be indexed under as many as four categories; thus, the total number of subject references is greater than the number of entrants in *AMWS.*

All Disciplines

	Number	Percent
Northeast	56,006	34%
Southeast	41,313	25%
North Central	19,699	12%
South Central	12,169	7%
Mountain	11,675	7%
Pacific	25,703	15%
TOTAL	**166,565**	**100%**

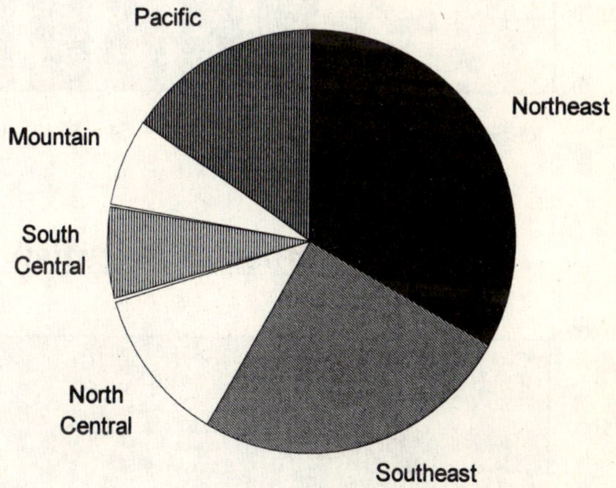

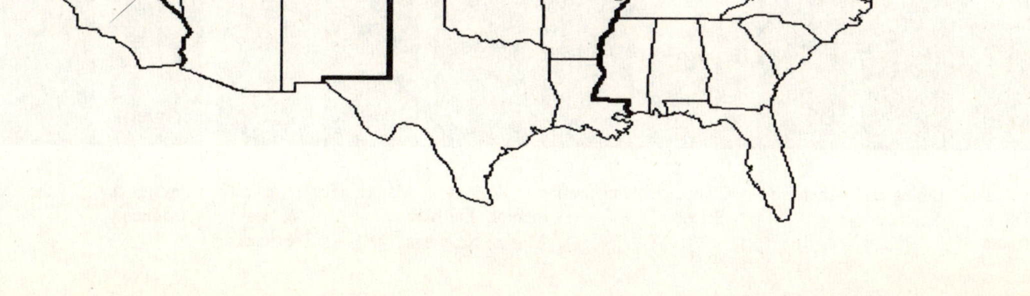

Age Distribution of American Men & Women of Science

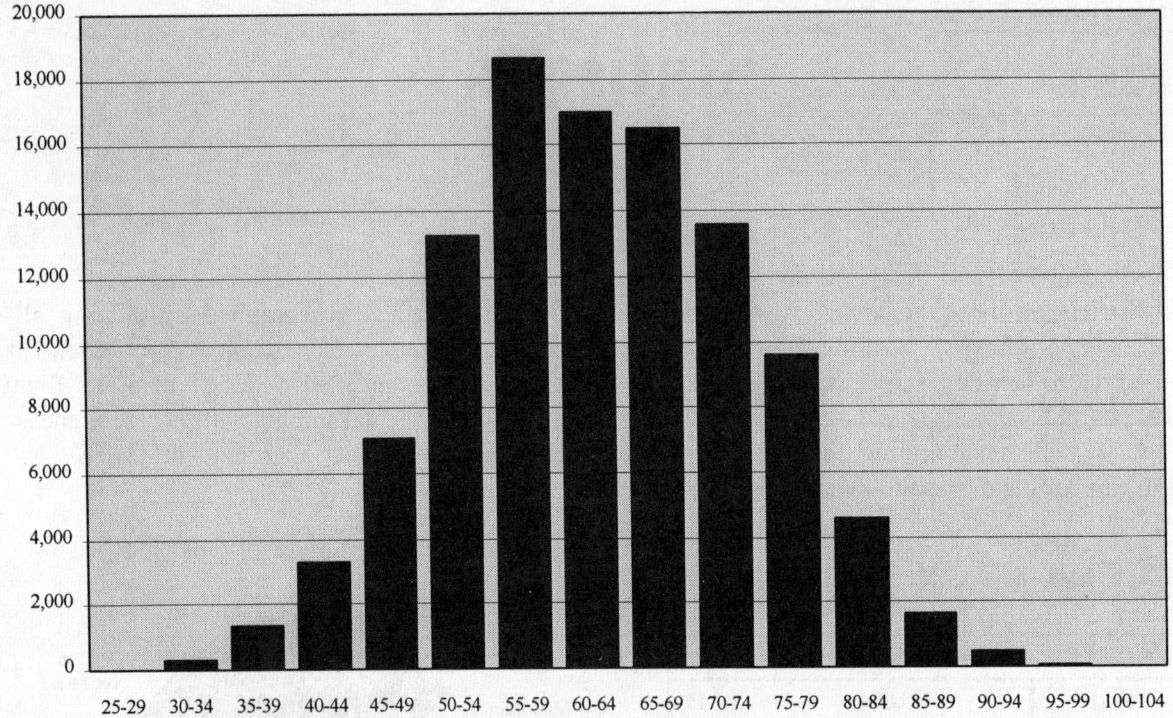

Number of Scientists in Each Discipline of Study

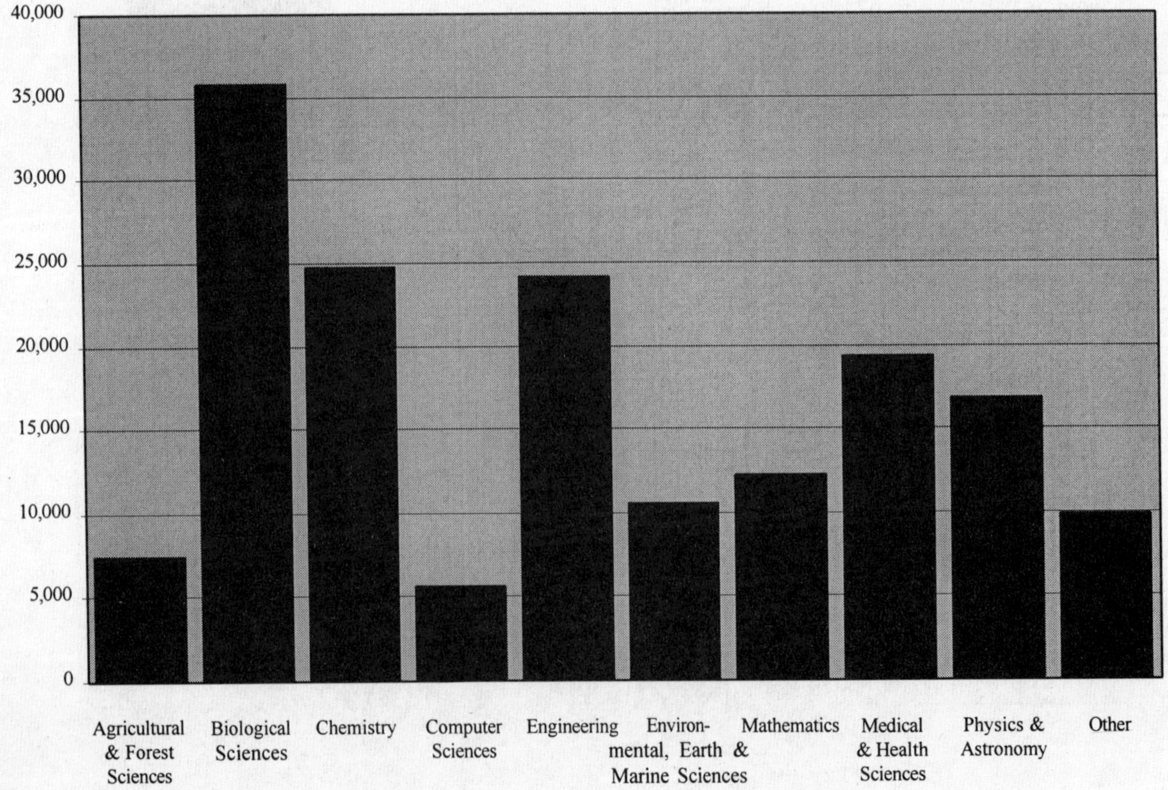

Agricultural & Forest Sciences

	Number	Percent
Northeast	1,585	21%
Southeast	2,053	27%
North Central	1,171	16%
South Central	635	8%
Mountain	739	10%
Pacific	1,305	17%
TOTAL	**7,488**	**100%**

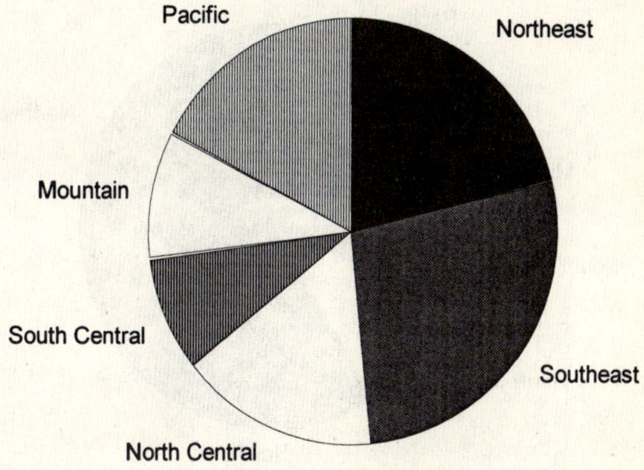

Biological Sciences

	Number	Percent
Northeast	11,671	33%
Southeast	9,045	25%
North Central	4,918	14%
South Central	2,741	8%
Mountain	2,125	6%
Pacific	5,277	15%
TOTAL	**35,777**	**100%**

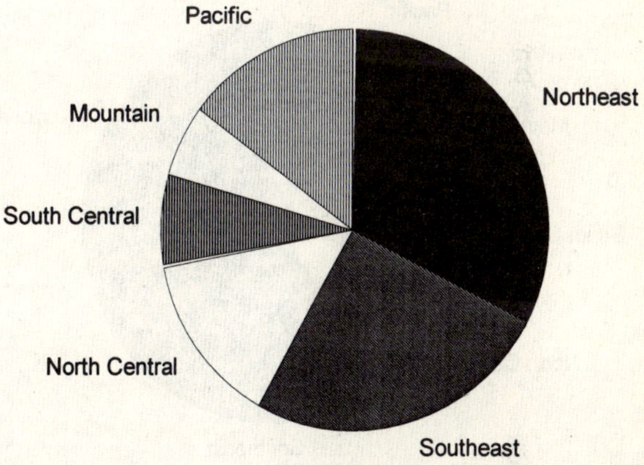

Chemistry

	Number	Percent
Northeast	9,296	38%
Southeast	6,196	25%
North Central	2,964	12%
South Central	1,724	7%
Mountain	1,381	6%
Pacific	3,139	13%
TOTAL	**24,700**	**100%**

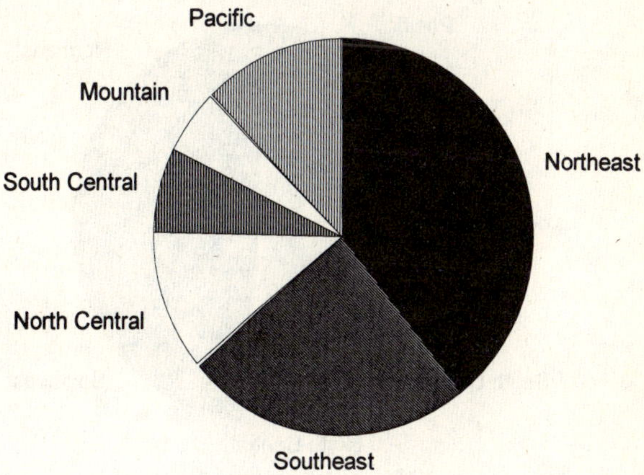

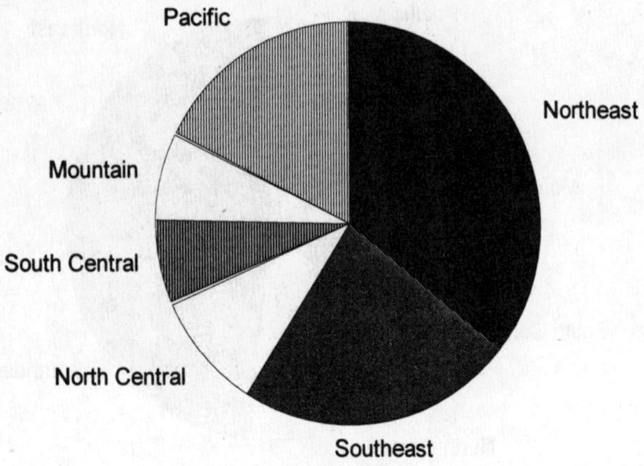

Computer Sciences

	Number	Percent
Northeast	1,983	35%
Southeast	1,278	23%
North Central	556	10%
South Central	378	7%
Mountain	423	7%
Pacific	1,034	18%
TOTAL	**5,652**	**100%**

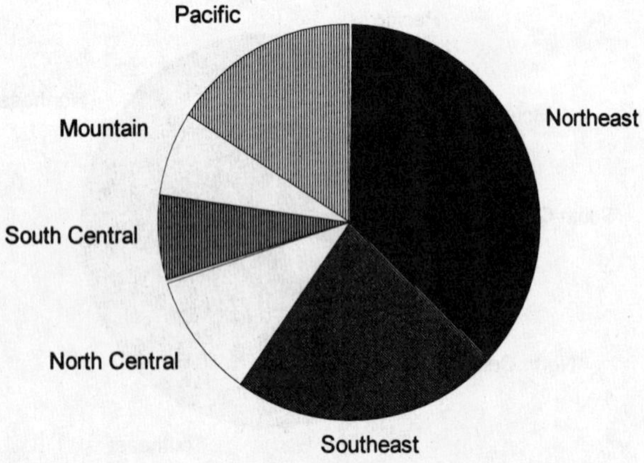

Engineering

	Number	Percent
Northeast	8,780	36%
Southeast	5,487	23%
North Central	2,501	10%
South Central	1,742	7%
Mountain	1,760	7%
Pacific	3,883	16%
TOTAL	**24,153**	**100%**

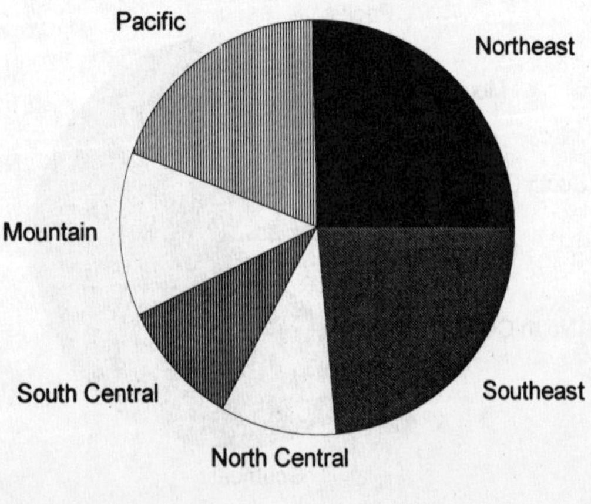

Environmental, Earth & Marine Sciences

	Number	Percent
Northeast	2,654	25%
Southeast	2,507	24%
North Central	984	9%
South Central	1,008	10%
Mountain	1,365	13%
Pacific	2,008	19%
TOTAL	**10,526**	**100%**

Mathematics

	Number	Percent
Northeast	4,292	35%
Southeast	2,865	23%
North Central	1,552	13%
South Central	933	8%
Mountain	760	6%
Pacific	1,901	15%
TOTAL	**12,303**	**100%**

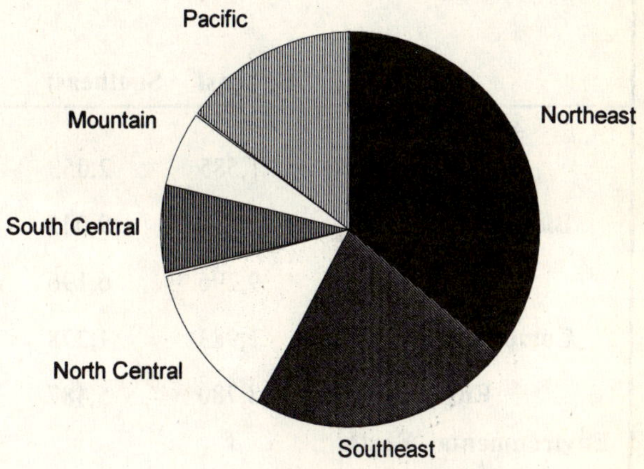

Medical & Health Sciences

	Number	Percent
Northeast	6,883	36%
Southeast	5,139	27%
North Central	2,471	13%
South Central	1,494	8%
Mountain	804	4%
Pacific	2,501	13%
TOTAL	**19,292**	**100%**

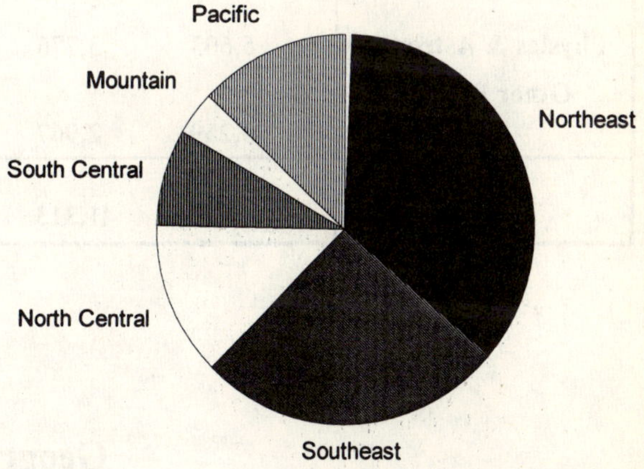

Physics & Astronomy

	Number	Percent
Northeast	5,603	33%
Southeast	3,776	22%
North Central	1,545	9%
South Central	904	5%
Mountain	1,674	10%
Pacific	3,307	20%
TOTAL	**16,809**	**100%**

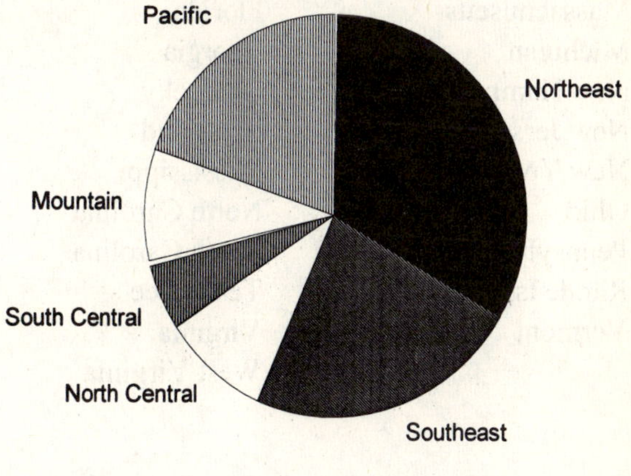

Geographic Distribution of Scientists by Discipline

	Northeast	Southeast	North Central	South Central	Mountain	Pacific	TOTAL
Agricultural & Forest Sciences	1,585	2,053	1,171	635	739	1,305	**7,488**
Biological Sciences	11,671	9,045	4,918	2,741	2,125	5,277	**35,777**
Chemistry	9,296	6,196	2,964	1,724	1,381	3,139	**24,700**
Computer Sciences	1,983	1,278	556	378	423	1,034	**5,652**
Engineering	8,780	5,487	2,501	1,742	1,760	3,883	**24,153**
Environmental, Earth & Marine Sciences	2,654	2,507	984	1,008	1,365	2,008	**10,526**
Mathematics	4,292	2,865	1,552	933	760	1,901	**12,303**
Medical & Health Sciences	6,883	5,139	2,471	1,494	804	2,501	**19,292**
Physics & Astronomy	5,603	3,776	1,545	904	1,674	3,307	**16,809**
Other Professional Fields	3,259	2,967	1,037	610	644	1,348	**9,865**
TOTAL	**56,006**	**41,313**	**19,699**	**12,169**	**11,675**	**25,703**	**166,565**

Geographic Definitions

Northeast
Connecticut
Indiana
Maine
Massachusetts
Michigan
New Hampshire
New Jersey
New York
Ohio
Pennsylvania
Rhode Island
Vermont

Southeast
Alabama
Delaware
District of Columbia
Florida
Georgia
Kentucky
Maryland
Mississippi
North Carolina
South Carolina
Tennessee
Virginia
West Virginia

North Central
Illinois
Iowa
Kansas
Minnesota
Missouri
Nebraska
North Dakota
South Dakota
Wisconsin

South Central
Arkansas
Louisiana
Texas
Oklahoma

Mountain
Arizona
Colorado
Idaho
Montana
Nevada
New Mexico
Utah
Wyoming

Pacific
Alaska
California
Hawaii
Oregon
Washington

Sample Entry

American Men & Women of Science (AMWS) is an extremely useful reference tool. The book is most often used in two ways: to find more information about a particular scientist and to locate a scientist in a specific field.

To locate information about an individual, the biographical section is most helpful. It encompasses the first seven volumes and lists scientists and engineers alphabetically by last name. The fictitious biographical listing shown below illustrates every type of information an entry may include.

The Discipline Index, volume 8, can be used to easily find a scientist in a specific subject specialty. This index is first classified by area of study; within each specialty entrants are divided further by state of residence.

REED, SAMANTHA J(EAN), OCEANOGRAPHY, MARINE BIOLOGY. *Current Pos:* SR ASSOC OCEANOGRAPHER, DEPT NAVY, 86- *Personal Data:* b Brooklyn, NY, Nov 9, 42; m 67, James A. Mayer; c Steven C & Lillian M. *Educ:* Univ Notre Dame, BS, 63, MS, 65, Fla State Univ, PhD(oceanog), 70. *Hon Degrees:* DSc, Univ Calif, Davis, 79. *Honors & Awards:* Henry Bryant Bigelow Medal, Oceanog, 92; *Prof Exp:* Asst prof oceanog, 71-73, assoc prof oceanog & biol, Harvard Univ, 73-75. *Concurrent Pos:* Consult, New England Aquarium, 74-78; vis lect, Wash Univ, 77. *Mem:* AAAS, Am Soc Naval Engrs, Sigma Xi, Oceanog Soc (vpres 82-83). *Res:* Ocean pollution prevention, water treatment and analysis, ecology of marine plankton and sponges, author of 13 publications. *Mailing Address:* 121102 Smithfield Way, Boca Raton, FL 33431. *Fax:* 407-555-5939; *E-Mail:* sreed@usnavy.mil.fla

Name
Birthdate
Children's Name(s)
Honors & Awards
Concurrent Experience
Memberships
E-Mail Address
Field of Specialty
Current Position
Marriage/Spouse data
Education
Honorary Degrees
Professional Experience
Research and Publications
Mailing Address
Fax Number

Abbreviations

AAAS—American Association for the Advancement of Science
abnorm—abnormal
abstr—abstract
acad—academic, academy
acct—account, accountant, accounting
acoust—acoustic(s), acoustical
ACTH—adrenocorticotrophic hormone
actg—acting
activ—activities, activity
addn—addition(s), additional
Add—Address
adj—adjunct, adjutant
adjust—adjustment
Adm—Admiral
admin—administration, administrative
adminr—administrator(s)
admis—admission(s)
adv—adviser(s), advisory
advan—advance(d), advancement
advert—advertisement, advertising
AEC—Atomic Energy Commission
aerodyn—aerodynamic
aeronaut—aeronautic(s), aeronautical
aerophys—aerophysical, aerophysics
aesthet—aesthetic
AFB—Air Force Base
affil—affiliate(s), affiliation
agr—agricultural, agriculture
agron—agronomic, agronomical, agronomy
agrost—agrostologic, agrostological, agrostology
agt—agent
AID—Agency for International Development
Ala—Alabama
allergol—allergological, allergology
alt—alternate
Alta—Alberta
Am—America, American
AMA—American Medical Association
anal—analysis, analytic, analytical
analog—analogue
anat—anatomic, anatomical, anatomy
anesthesiol—anesthesiology
angiol—angiology
Ann—Annal(s)
ann—annual
anthrop—anthropological, anthropology
anthropom—anthropometric, anthropometrical, anthropometry
antiq—antiquary, antiquities, antiquity
antiqn—antiquarian
apicult—apicultural, apiculture
APO—Army Post Office
app—appoint, appointed
appl—applied
appln—application
approx—approximate(ly)
Apr—April
apt—apartment(s)
aquacult—aquaculture
arbit—arbitration
arch—archives
archaeol—archaeological, archaeology
archit—architectural, architecture
Arg—Argentina, Argentine
Ariz—Arizona
Ark—Arkansas
artil—artillery
asn—association
assoc(s)—associate(s), associated
asst(s)—assistant(s), assistantship(s)
assyriol—Assyriology
astrodyn—astrodynamics
astron—astronomical, astronomy
astronaut—astronautical, astronautics
astronr—astronomer
astrophys—astrophysical, astrophysics
attend—attendant, attending
atty—attorney
audiol—audiology
Aug—August
auth—author
AV—audiovisual
Ave—Avenue
avicult—avicultural, aviculture

b—born
bact—bacterial, bacteriologic, bacteriological, bacteriology
BC—British Colombia
bd—board
behav—behavior(al)
Belg—Belgian, Belgium
Bibl—Biblical
bibliog—bibliographic, bibliographical, bibliography
bibliogr—bibliographer
biochem—biochemical, biochemistry
biog—biographical, biography
biol—biological, biology
biomed—biomedical, biomedicine
biomet—biometric(s), biometrical, biometry
biophys—biophysical, biophysics
bk(s)—book(s)
bldg—building
Blvd—Boulevard
Bor—Borough
bot—botanical, botany
br—branch(es)
Brig—Brigadier
Brit—Britain, British
Bro(s)—Brother(s)
byrol—byrology
bull—Bulletin
bur—bureau
bus—business
BWI—British West Indies

c—children
Calif—California
Can—Canada, Canadian
cand—candidate
Capt—Captain
cardiol—cardiology
cardiovasc—cardiovascular
cartog—cartographic, cartographical, cartography
cartogr—cartographer
Cath—Catholic
CEngr—Corp of Engineers
cent—central
Cent Am—Central American
cert—certificate(s), certification, certified
chap—chapter
chem—chemical(s), chemistry
chemother—chemotherapy
chg—change
chmn—chairman
citricult—citriculture
class—classical
climat—climatological, climatology
clin(s)—clinic(s), clinical
cmndg—commanding
Co—County
Co—Companies, Company
co-auth—co-author
co-dir—co-director
co-ed—co-editor
co-educ—co-education, co-educational
col(s)—college(s), collegiate, colonel
collab—collaboration, collaborative
collabr—collaborator

Colo—Colorado
com—commerce, commercial
Comdr—Commander
commun—communicable, communication(s)
comn(s)—commission(s), commissioned
comndg—commanding
comnr—commissioner
comp—comparitive
compos—composition
comput—computation, computer(s), computing
comt(s)—committee(s)
conchol—conchology
conf—conference
cong—congress, congressional
Conn—Connecticut
conserv—conservation, conservatory
consol—consolidated, consolidation
const—constitution, constitutional
construct—construction, constructive
consult(s)—consult, consultant(s), consultantship(s), consultation, consulting
contemp—contemporary
contrib—contribute, contributing, contribution(s)
contribr—contributor
conv—convention
coop—cooperating, cooperation, cooperative
coord—coordinate(d), coordinating, coordination
coordr—coordinator
corp—corporate, corporation(s)
corresp—correspondence, correspondent, corresponding
coun—council, counsel, counseling
counr—councilor, counselor
criminol—criminological, criminology
cryog—cryogenic(s)
crystallog—crystallographic, crystallographical, crystallography
crystallogr—crystallographer
Ct—Court
Ctr—Center
cult—cultural, culture
cur—curator
curric—curriculum
cybernet—cybernetic(s)
cytol—cytological, cytology
Czech—Czechoslovakia, Czech Republic

DC—District of Columbia
Dec—December
Del—Delaware
deleg—delegate, delegation
delinq—delinquency, delinquent
dem—democrat(s), democratic
demog—demographic, demography
demogr—demographer
demonstr—demontrator
dendrol—dendrologic, dendrological, dendrology
dent—dental, dentistry
dep—deputy
dept—department
dermat—dermatologic, dermatological, dermatology
develop—developed, developing, development, developmental
diag—diagnosis, diagnostic
dialectol—dialectological, dialectology
dict—dictionaries, dictionary
Dig—Digest
dipl—diploma, diplomate
dir(s)—director(s), directories, directory
dis—disease(s), disorders
Diss Abst—Dissertation Abstracts
dist—district
distrib—distributed, distribution, distributive
distribr—distributor(s)
div—division, divisional, divorced
DNA—deoxyribonucleic acid
doc—document(s), documentary, documentation
Dom—Dominion
Dr—Drive

E—East
ecol—ecological, ecology
econ(s)—economic(s), economical, economy
economet—econometric(s)
ECT—electroconvulsive or electroshock therapy
ed—edition(s), editor(s), editorial
ed bd—editorial board
educ—education, educational
educr—educator(s)
EEG—electroencephalogram, electroencephalographic, electroencephalography
Egyptol—Egyptology
EKG—electrocardiogram
elec—electric, electrical, electricity
electrochem—electrochemical, electrochemistry
electroph—electrophysical, electrophysics
elem—elementary
embryol—embryologic, embryological, embryology
emer—emeriti, emeritus
employ—employment
encour—encouragement
encycl—encyclopedia
endocrinol—endocrinologic, endocrinology
eng—engineering
Eng—England, English
engr(s)—engineer(s)
enol—enology
Ens—Ensign
entom—entomological, entomology
environ—environment(s), environmental
enzym—enzymology
epidemiol—epidemiologic, epidemiological, epidemiology
equip—equipment
ERDA—Energy Research & Development Administration
ESEA—Elementary & Secondary Education Act
espec—especially
estab—established, establishment(s)
ethnog—ethnographic, ethnographical, ethnography
ethnogr—ethnographer
ethnol—ethnologic, ethnological, ethnology
Europ—European
eval—evaluation
Evangel—Evangelical
eve—evening
exam—examination(s), examining
examr—examiner
except—exceptional
exec(s)—executive(s)
exeg—exegeses, exegesis, exegetic, exegetical
exhib(s)—exhibition(s), exhibit(s)
exp—experiment, experimental
exped(s)—expedition(s)
explor—exploration(s), exploratory
expos—exposition
exten—extension

fac—faculty
facil—facilities, facility
Feb—February
fed—federal
fedn—federation
fel(s)—fellow(s), fellowship(s)
fermentol—fermentology
fertil—fertility, fertilization
Fla—Florida
floricult—floricultural, floriculture
found—foundation
FPO—Fleet Post Office
Fr—French
Ft—Fort

Ga—Georgia
gastroenterol—gastroenterological, gastroenterology
gen—general
geneal—genealogical, genealogy
geod—geodesy, geodetic
geog—geographic, geographical, geography
geogr—geographer
geol—geologic, geological, geology
geom—geometric, geometrical, geometry
geomorphol—geomorphologic, geomorphology
geophys—geophysical, geophysics
Ger—German, Germanic, Germany
geriat—geriatric
geront—gerontological, gerontology
Ges—Gesellschaft
glaciol—glaciology
gov—governing, governor(s)
govt—government, governmental
grad—graduate(d)
Gt Brit—Great Britain
guid—guidance
gym—gymnasium
gynec—gynecologic, gynecological, gynecology

handbk(s)—handbook(s)
helminth—helminthology
hemat—hematologic, hematological, hematology
herpet—herpetologic, herpetological, herpetology
HEW—Department of Health, Education & Welfare

Hisp—Hispanic, Hispania
hist—historic, historical, history
histol—histological, histology
HM—Her Majesty
hochsch—hochschule
homeop—homeopathic, homeopathy
hon(s)—honor(s), honorable, honorary
hort—horticultural, horticulture
hosp(s)—hospital(s), hospitalization
hq—headquarters
HumRRO—Human Resources Research Office
husb—husbandry
Hwy—Highway
hydraul—hydraulic(s)
hydrodyn—hydrodynamic(s)
hydrol—hydrologic, hydrological, hydrologics
hyg—hygiene, hygienic(s)
hypn—hypnosis

ichthyol—ichthyological, ichthyology
Ill—Illinois
illum—illuminating, illumination
illus—illustrate, illustrated, illustration
illusr—illustrator
immunol—immunologic, immunological, immunology
Imp—Imperial
improv—improvement
Inc—Incorporated
in-chg—in charge
incl—include(s), including
Ind—Indiana
indust(s)—industrial, industries, industry
Inf—Infantry
info—information
inorg—inorganic
ins—insurance
inst(s)—institute(s), institution(s)
instnl—institutional(ized)
instr(s)—instruct, instruction, instructor(s)
instrnl—instructional
int—international
intel—intellligence
introd—introduction
invert—invertebrate
invest(s)—investigation(s)
investr—investigator
irrig—irrigation
Ital—Italian

J—Journal
Jan—January
Jct—Junction
jour—journal, journalism
jr—junior
jurisp—jurisprudence
juv—juvenile

Kans—Kansas
Ky—Kentucky

La—Louisiana
lab(s)—laboratories, laboratory
lang—language(s)
laryngol—larygological, laryngology
lect—lecture(s)
lectr—lecturer(s)
legis—legislation, legislative, legislature
lett—letter(s)
lib—liberal
libr—libraries, library
librn—librarian
lic—license(d)
limnol—limnological, limnology
ling—linguistic(s), linguistical
lit—literary, literature
lithol—lithologic, lithological, lithology
Lt—Lieutenant
Ltd—Limited
m—married
mach—machine(s), machinery
mag—magazine(s)
maj—major
malacol—malacology
mammal—mammalogy
Man—Manitoba
Mar—March
Mariol—Mariology
Mass—Massechusetts
mat—material(s)
mat med—materia medica
math—mathematic(s), mathematical
Md—Maryland
mech—mechanic(s), mechanical
med—medical, medicinal, medicine
Mediter—Mediterranean
Mem—Memorial
mem—member(s), membership(s)
ment—mental(ly)
metab—metabolic, metabolism
metall—metallurgic, metallurgical, metallurgy
metallog—metallographic, metallography
metallogr—metallographer
metaphys—metaphysical, metaphysics
meteorol—meteorological, meteorology
metrol—metrological, metrology
metrop—metropolitan
Mex—Mexican, Mexico
mfg—manufacturing
mfr—manufacturer
mgr—manager
mgt—management
Mich—Michigan
microbiol—microbiological, microbiology
micros—microscopic, microscopical, microscopy
mid—middle
mil—military
mineral—mineralogical, mineralogy
Minn—Minnesota
Miss—Mississippi
mkt—market, marketing
Mo—Missouri
mod—modern
monogr—monograph
Mont—Montana
morphol—morphological, morphology
Mt—Mount
mult—multiple
munic—municipal, municipalities
mus—museum(s)
musicol—musicological, musicology
mycol—mycologic, mycology
N—North
NASA—National Aeronautics & Space Administration
nat—national, naturalized
NATO—North Atlantic Treaty Organization
navig—navigation(al)
NB—New Brunswick
NC—North Carolina
NDak—North Dakota
NDEA—National Defense Education Act
Nebr—Nebraska
nematol—nematological, nematology
nerv—nervous
Neth—Netherlands
neurol—neurological, neurology
neuropath—neuropathological, neuropathology
neuropsychiat—neuropsychiatric, neuropsychiatry
neurosurg—neurosurgical, neurosurgery
Nev—Nevada
New Eng—New England
New York—New York City
Nfld—Newfoundland
NH—New Hampshire
NIH—National Institute of Health
NIMH—National Institute of Mental Health
NJ—New Jersey
NMex—New Mexico
No—Number
nonres—nonresident
norm—normal
Norweg—Norwegian
Nov—November
NS—Nova Scotia
NSF—National Science Foundation
NSW—New South Wales
numis—numismatic(s)
nutrit—nutrition, nutritional
NY—New York State
NZ—New Zealand

observ—observatories, observatory
obstet—obstetric(s), obstetrical
occas—occasional(ly)
occup—occupation, occupational
oceanog—oceanographic, oceanographical, oceanography
oceanogr—oceanographer
Oct—October
odontol—odontology
OEEC—Organization for European Economic Cooperation
off—office, official
Okla—Oklahoma
olericult—olericulture
oncol—oncologic, oncology
Ont—Ontario
oper(s)—operation(s), operational, operative
ophthal—ophthalmologic, ophthalmological, ophthalmology
optom—optometric, optometrical, optometry
ord—ordnance
Ore—Oregon
org—organic

orgn—organization(s), organizational
orient—oriental
ornith—ornithological, ornithology
orthod—orthodontia, orthodontic(s)
orthop—orthopedic(s)
osteop—osteopathic, osteopathy
otol—otological, otology
otolaryngol—otolaryngological, otolaryngology
otorhinol—otorhinologic, otorhinology

Pa—Pennsylvania
Pac—Pacific
paleobot—paleobotanical, paleobotany
paleont—paleontology
Pan-Am—Pan-American
parasitol—parasitology
partic—participant, participating
path—pathologic, pathological, pathology
pedag—pedagogic(s), pedagogical, pedagogy
pediat—pediatric(s)
PEI—Prince Edward Islands
penol—penological, penology
periodont—periodontal, periodontic(s)
petrog—petrographic, petrographical, petrography
petrogr—petrographer
petrol—petroleum, petrologic, petrological, petrology
pharm—pharmacy
pharmaceut—pharmaceutic(s), pharmaceutical(s)
pharmacog—pharmacognosy
pharamacol—pharmacologic, pharmacological, pharmacology
phenomenol—phenomenologic(al), phenomenology
philol—philological, philology
philos—philosophic, philosophical, philosophy
photog—photographic, photography
photogeog—photogeographic, photogeography
photogr—photographer(s)
photogram—photogrammetric, photogrammetry
photom—photometric, photometrical, photometry
phycol—phycology
phys—physical
physiog—physiographic, physiographical, physiography
physiol—physiological, phsysiology
Pkwy—Parkway
Pl—Place
polit—political, politics
polytech—polytechnic(s)
pomol—pomological, pomology
pontif—pontifical
pop—population
Port—Portugal, Portuguese
Pos—Position
postgrad—postgraduate
PQ—Province of Quebec
PR—Puerto Rico
pract—practice
practr—practitioner
prehist—prehistoric, prehistory
prep—preparation, preparative, preparatory
pres—president
Presby—Presbyterian
preserv—preservation
prev—prevention, preventive
prin—principal
prob(s)—problem(s)
proc—proceedings
proctol—proctologic, proctological, proctology
prod—product(s), production, productive
prof—professional, professor, professorial
Prof Exp—Professional Experience
prog(s)—program(s), programmed, programming
proj—project(s), projection(al), projective
prom—promotion
protozool—protozoology
Prov—Province, Provincial
psychiat—psychiatric, psychiatry
psychoanal—psychoanalysis, psychoanalytic, psychoanalytical
psychol—psychological, psychology
psychomet—psychometric(s)
psychopath—psychopathologic, psychopathology
psychophys—psychophysical, psychophysics
psychophysiol—psychophysiological, psychophysiology
psychosom—psychosomatic(s)
psychother—psychoterapeutic(s), psychotherapy
Pt—Point
pub—public
publ—publication(s), publish(ed), publisher, publishing
pvt—private

Qm—Quartermaster
Qm Gen—Quartermaster General
qual—qualitative, quality
quant—quantitative
quart—quarterly
Que—Quebec

radiol—radiological, radiology
RAF—Royal Air Force
RAFVR—Royal Air Force Volunteer Reserve
RAMC—Royal Army Medical Corps
RAMCR—Royal Army Medical Corps Reserve
RAOC—Royal Army Ordnance Corps
RASC—Royal Army Service Corps
RASCR—Royal Army Service Corps Reserve
RCAF—Royal Canadian Air Force
RCAFR—Royal Canadian Air Force Reserve
RCAFVR—Royal Canadian Air Force Volunteer Reserve
RCAMC—Royal Canadian Army Medical Corps
RCAMCR—Royal Canadian Army Medical Corps Reserve
RCASC—Royal Canadian Army Service Corps
RCASCR—Royal Canadian Army Service Corps Reserve
RCEME—Royal Canadian Electrical & Mechanical Engineers
RCN—Royal Canadian Navy
RCNR—Royal Canadian Naval Reserve
RCNVR—Royal Canadian Naval Volunteer Reserve
Rd—Road
RD—Rural Delivery
rec—record(s), recording
redevelop—redevelopment
ref—reference(s)
refrig—refrigeration
regist—register(ed), registration
registr—registrar
regt—regiment(al)
rehab—rehabilitation
rel(s)—relation(s), relative
relig—religion, religious
REME—Royal Electrical & Mechanical Engineers
rep—represent, representative
Repub—Republic
req—requirements
res—research, reserve
rev—review, revised, revision
RFD—Rural Free Delivery
rhet—rhetoric, rhetorical
RI—Rhode Island
Rm—Room
RM—Royal Marines
RN—Royal Navy
RNA—ribonucleic acid
RNR—Royal Naval Reserve
RNVR—Royal Naval Volunteer Reserve
roentgenol—roentgenologic, roentgenological, roentgenology
RR—Railroad, Rural Route
Rte—Route
Russ—Russian
rwy—railway

S—South
SAfrica—South Africa
SAm—South America, South American
sanit—sanitary, sanitation
Sask—Saskatchewan
SC—South Carolina
Scand—Scandinavia(n)
sch(s)—school(s)
scholar—scholarship
sci—science(s), scientific
SDak—South Dakota
SEATO—Southeast Asia Treaty Organization
sec—secondary
sect—section
secy—secretary
seismog—seismograph, seismographic, seismography
seismogr—seismographer
seismol—seismological, seismology
sem—seminar, seminary
Sen—Senator, Senatorial
Sept—September
ser—serial, series
serol—serologic, serological, serology
serv—service(s), serving

silvicult—silvicultural, silviculture
soc(s)—societies, society
soc sci—social science
sociol—sociologic, sociological, sociology
Span—Spanish
spec—special
specif—specification(s)
spectrog—spectrograph, spectrographic, spectrography
spectrogr—spectrographer
spectrophotom—spectrophotometer, spectrophotometric, spectrophotometry
spectros—spectroscopic, spectroscopy
speleol—speleological, speleology
Sq—Square
sr—senior
St—Saint, Street(s)
sta(s)—station(s)
stand—standard(s), standardization
statist—statistical, statistics
Ste—Sainte
steril—sterility
stomatol—stomatology
stratig—stratigraphic, stratigraphy
stratigr—stratigrapher
struct—structural, structure(s)
stud—student(ship)
subcomt—subcommittee
subj—subject
subsid—subsidiary
substa—substation
super—superior
suppl—supplement(s), supplemental, supplementary
supt—superintendent
supv—supervising, supervision
supvr—supervisor
supvry—supervisory
surg—surgery, surgical
surv—survey, surveying
survr—surveyor
Swed—Swedish
Switz—Switzerland
symp—symposia, symposium(s)
syphil—syphilology
syst(s)—system(s), systematic(s), systematical

taxon—taxonomic, taxonomy
tech—technical, technique(s)
technol—technologic(al), technology
tel—telegraph(y), telephone
temp—temporary
Tenn—Tennessee
Terr—Terrace
Tex—Texas
textbk(s)—textbook(s)
text ed—text edition
theol—theological, theology
theoret—theoretic(al)
ther—therapy
therapeut—therapeutic(s)
thermodyn—thermodynamic(s)
topog—topographic, topographical, topography
topogr—topographer
toxicol—toxicologic, toxicological, toxicology
trans—transaction(s)
transl—translated, translation(s)
translr—translator(s)
transp—transport, transportation
treas—treasurer, treasury
treat—treatment
trop—tropical
tuberc—tuberculosis
TV—television
Twp—Township

UAR—United Arab Republic
UK—United Kingdom
UN—United Nations
undergrad—undergraduate
unemploy—unemployment
UNESCO—United Nations Educational Scientific & Cultural Organization
UNICEF—United Nations International Childrens Fund
univ(s)—universities, university
UNRRA—United Nations Relief & Rehabilitation Administration
UNRWA—United Nations Relief & Works Agency
urol—urologic, urological, urology
US—United States
USAAF—US Army Air Force
USAAFR—US Army Air Force Reserve
USAF—US Air Force
USAFR—US Air Force Reserve
USAID—US Agency for International Development
USAR—US Army Reserve
USCG—US Coast Guard
USCGR—US Coast Guard Reserve
USDA—US Department of Agriculture
USMC—US Marine Corps
USMCR—US Marine Corps Reserve
USN—US Navy
USNAF—US Naval Air Force
USNAFR—US Naval Air Force Reserve
USNR—US Naval Reserve
USPHS—US Public Health Service
USPHSR—US Public Health Service Reserve
USSR—Union of Soviet Socialist Republics

Va—Virginia
var—various
veg—vegetable(s), vegetation
vent—ventilating, ventilation
vert—vertebrate
Vet—Veteran(s)
vet—veterinarian, veterinary
VI—Virgin Islands
vinicult—viniculture
virol—virological, virology
vis—visiting
voc—vocational
vocab—vocabulary
vol(s)—voluntary, volunteer(s), volume(s)
vpres—vice president
vs—versus
Vt—Vermont

W—West
Wash—Washington
WHO—World Health Organization
WI—West Indies
wid—widow, widowed, widower
Wis—Wisconsin
WVa—West Virginia
Wyo—Wyoming

Yearbk(s)—Yearbook(s)
YMCA—Young Men's Christian Association
YMHA—Young Men's Hebrew Association
Yr(s)—Year(s)
YT—Yukon Territory
YWCA—Young Women's Christian Association
YWHA—Young Women's Hebrew Association

zool—zoological, zoology

AMERICAN MEN & WOMEN OF SCIENCE

A

AABOE, ASGER (HARTVIG), MATH, HISTORY & PHILOSOPHY OF SCIENCE. *Current Pos:* assoc prof, 62-67, chmn Dept Hist Sci & Med, 68-71, PROF MATH & HIST SCI & MED, 67-, PROF NEAR EASTERN LANG & LITS, YALE UNIV, 77- *Personal Data:* b Copenhagen, Denmark, Apr 26, 22; m 50; c 4. *Educ:* Brown Univ, PhD(hist math), 57. *Prof Exp:* Vis lectr math, Wash Univ, 47-48; adj, Birkerod State Sch, Denmark, 48-52; from instr to assoc prof, Tufts Univ, 52-62. *Concurrent Pos:* Vis assoc prof, Yale Univ, 61-62. *Mem:* Royal Danish Soc. *Res:* History of mathematics and mathematical astronomy. *Mailing Add:* PO Box 208274 Yale Univ New Haven CT 06520-8274

AAGAARD, GEORGE NELSON, INTERNAL MEDICINE, CLINICAL PHARMACOLOGY. *Current Pos:* dean sch med, 54-64, ombudsman, 69-70, prof med & head, Div Clin Pharmacol, 64-79, first distinguished prof, 78-84, EMER PROF MED & PHARMACOL, SCH MED, UNIV WASH, 84- *Personal Data:* b Minneapolis, Minn, Aug 16, 13; m 39; c 5. *Educ:* Univ Minn, BS, 34, BMed, 36, MD, 37. *Honors & Awards:* Elliott Award, Am Soc Clin Pharmacol & Therapeut. *Prof Exp:* Instr internal med, Univ Minn, 42-45, asst prof, 45-48, assoc prof & dir postgrad med educ, 48-51; prof med & dean, Univ Tex Southwestern Med Sch Dallas, 52-54. *Concurrent Pos:* Fel internal med, Univ Minn, 41-47; mem health res facil adv coun, NIH, 56-58; mem nat adv coun, Nat Heart Inst, 61-65; mem bd dirs, Am Heart Asn, 58; mem spec med adv group, Vet Admin, 70-74; mem sci adv comt, Pharmaceut Mfg Asn Found, 67-74. *Mem:* AMA; Am Heart Asn; Am Pub Health Asn; Am Col Physicians; Asn Am Med Col (pres, 60-61); Am Soc Clin Pharmacol & Therapeut (pres, 77). *Res:* Medical education; hypertension; clinical pharmacology. *Mailing Add:* Sch Med RG-23 Univ Wash Seattle WA 98195. *Fax:* 206-543-3947; *E-Mail:* gnaagaar@w.washington.edu

AAGAARD, JAMES S(TUART), COMPUTER SCIENCE. *Current Pos:* From asst prof to assoc prof elec eng, 57-70, assoc prof elec eng & comput sci, 70-76, PROF ELEC ENG & COMPUT SCI, NORTHWESTERN UNIV, EVANSTON, 76-, HEAD INFO SYSTS DEVELOP LIBR, 72- *Personal Data:* b Lake Forest, Ill, July 20, 30; m 63. *Educ:* Northwestern Univ, BS, 53, MS, 55, PhD(elec eng), 57. *Honors & Awards:* Lita/Gaylord Award for Achievement in Libr & Info Technol, Am Lib Asn, 85. *Concurrent Pos:* Mem bd dirs, Nat Electronics Conf, 58-66. *Mem:* Fel AAAS; Inst Elec & Electronics Engrs; Asn Comput Mach; Am Soc Eng Educ; Am Soc Info Sci. *Res:* Computer software; electronic circuits; communications theory. *Mailing Add:* 744 Lenox Lane Glenview IL 60025-4438

AAGAARD, KNUT, PHYSICAL OCEANOGRAPHY. *Current Pos:* PRIN OCEANOGRAPHER, UNIV WASH, 93- *Personal Data:* b Brooklyn, NY, Feb 5, 39; m 63; c 3. *Educ:* Oberlin Col, AB, 61; Univ Wash, MS, 64, PhD(phys oceanog), 66. *Prof Exp:* Res assoc phys oceanog, Univ Wash, 66; Nat Acad Sci-US Air Force Off Sci Res, res assoc, Geophys Inst, Univ Bergen, 67; res asst prof, Univ Wash, 68-73, res assoc prof, 73-78, res prof phys oceanog, 78-86; oceanographer, NOAA, 86-93. *Concurrent Pos:* Mem various int comts & working groups. *Mem:* AAAS; fel Arctic Inst NAm; Am Geophys Union. *Res:* Arctic oceanography, current measurements, general physical oceanography, climate. *Mailing Add:* Appl Physics Lab Univ Wash 1013 NE 40th St Seattle WA 98105-6698

AALDERS, LEWIS ELDON, SCIENCE EDUCATION. *Current Pos:* RETIRED. *Personal Data:* b Kentville, NS, July 19, 33; div. *Educ:* Acadia Univ, BSc, 52, MSc, 53; Cornell Univ, PhD(cytogenetics), 57. *Prof Exp:* Horticulturist plant breeding, Res Sta, Can Dept Agr, 53-67, res scientist, 67-82. *Mem:* Sigma Xi; AAAS. *Res:* Effect of quality of family ties on the progressive attraction to religious versus scientific principles. *Mailing Add:* 83 Elm Ave Kentville NS B4N 1Z3 Can

AAMODT, RICHARD E, PHYSICS, PLASMA PHYSICS. *Current Pos:* PRES, LODESTAR RES CORP, 87- *Personal Data:* b St Paul, Minn, Nov 22, 36; div; c Eric, Kirsten & Andrea. *Educ:* Univ Mich, BSE, 58, MS, 59, PhD(physics), 63. *Prof Exp:* Staff assoc plasma physics, Gen Atomic Div, Gen Dynamics Corp, 62-64, staff mem, 64-65; from asst prof to assoc prof physics, Univ Tex, Austin, 65-69; vis assoc prof astro-geophys, Univ Colo, 69-70, from assoc prof to prof, 70-75; sr staff scientist, 75-79, dir, Plasma Res Inst, Sci Appln Intl Corp, 79-87. *Concurrent Pos:* Consult, Lawrence Radiation Lab, Univ Calif, 66-85, Boeing Sci Res Lab, 66-70; vis staff mem, Los Alamos Sci Lab, 69-93; res physicist, Naval Res Lab, 74. *Mem:* Fel Am Phys Soc. *Res:* Theoretical plasma physics; transport theory. *Mailing Add:* Lodestar Res Corp 2400 Central Ave Boulder CO 80301

AAMODT, ROGER LOUIS, CANCER DIAGNOSIS, RADIATION BIOLOGY. *Current Pos:* sect chief tracer metab, Dept Nuclear Med, Clin Ctr, NIH, 71-83, grants assoc, Off of Dir, 83-84, prog dir, Cancer Diag Br, DCBDC, 84-96, ACTG CHIEF, RESOURCES DEVELOP BR, CDP, DCTDC, NAT CANCER INST, NIH, ROCKVILLE, MD, 96- *Personal Data:* b San Francisco, Calif, Dec 9, 41; div; c 2. *Educ:* Univ Utah, BS, 66; Univ Rochester, PhD(radiation biol), 72. *Prof Exp:* Res asst health physics, Dept Radiol Health, Univ Utah, 65-66. *Mem:* Am Soc Invest Pathol; Sigma Xi; Int Soc Anal Cytol; AAAS. *Res:* Cancer diagnosis; research resources; human subjects rules; bioethics; informatics; data privacy; access to human tissue and data for research. *Mailing Add:* Cancer Diag Br DCBDC Nat Cancer Inst NIH EPN Rm 700 6130 Executive Blvd Rockville MD 20892. *Fax:* 301-402-1037

AARON, CHARLES SIDNEY, MOLECULAR GENETICS, MUTAGENESIS. *Current Pos:* sr res scientist, genetic toxicol res, 85-89, DIR, INVESTIGATIVE TOXICOL, UPJOHN CO, KALAMAZOO, MICH, 89- *Personal Data:* b Jonesboro, La, Feb 17, 43; m 87; c 2. *Educ:* La Tech Univ, BS, 68; La State Univ, Baton Rouge, PhD(biochem), 72; Am Bd Toxicol, dipl. *Prof Exp:* Teacher chem, Episcopal High Sch, Baton Rouge, 71-72; res assoc chem mutagenesis, La State Univ, Baton Rouge, 72- 76; mgr, analytical & biochem toxicol, Allied Corp, 80-84. *Concurrent Pos:* Res scientist, Dept Radiation Genetics & Chem Mutagenesis, State Univ, Leiden, Neth, 76-79; genetics & reproduction team leader, Off Toxic Sub, US Environ Protection Agency, Washington, DC, 79-80; mem coun, Environ Mutagen Soc. *Mem:* Am Chem Soc; Sigma Xi; Environ Mutagen Soc; Soc Risk Anal; Int Soc Study Xenobiotics; fel Environ Health Inst. *Res:* Molecular dosimetry of chemical mutagens in in vitro test systems; molecular mechanisms of mutagenesis; quantitive risk assessment; structure activity correlations; non-genotoxic carcinogens. *Mailing Add:* Pharmacia Upjohn Inc 7000 Portage Rd Kalamazoo MI 49001

AARON, HENRY JACOB, ECONOMICS EDUCATION. *Current Pos:* asst secy planning & eval, 77 & 78, DIR ECON STUDIES, HEW, WASHINGTON, 90-, SR FEL, BROOKINGS INST, 96- *Personal Data:* b Chicago, Ill, June 16, 36; m 63, Ruth Kotell; c Jeffrey & Melissa. *Educ:* Univ Calif, Los Angeles, AB, 58; Harvard Univ, MA, 60, PhD, 63. *Prof Exp:* Assoc prof econ, Univ Md, 67-75, prof, 75-77 & 79-89. *Concurrent Pos:* Sr staff economist, Pres Coun Econ Advs, 68-75; mem, Comn Behav & Social Sci Edic, Nat Res Coun, 83-86; sr fel, Brookings Inst, 68-78, dir econ studies, 90-96; vis prof econ, Harvard Univ, 74 & 85-89; trustee, Teachers Ins & Annuity Asn, 84-87; vpres, Nat Acad Social Ins, 86-; assoc ed, J Econ Perspectives, J Pub Econs & J Health Econs; mem bd dirs, Georgetown Univ, Abt Assocs, Ctr Budget & Policy Priorities, 94; Guggenheim fel, 96-; fel, Ctr Adv Study in Behav Sci, 96- *Mem:* Inst Med-Nat Acad Sci; Nat Acad Social Ins (pres, 86); AAAS; Am Econ Asn (vpres, 91); Am Acad Arts & Sci. *Mailing Add:* 1775 Massachusetts Ave NW Washington DC 20036-2188

AARON, HERBERT SAMUEL, ORGANOPHOSPHORUS CHEMISTRY, STEREOCHEMISTRY. *Current Pos:* CHEMIST, CHEM RES LABS, EDGEWOOD ARSENAL-ABERDEEN PROVING GROUND, 54- *Personal Data:* b Minneapolis, Minn, Jan 12, 29; m 59; c 2. *Educ:* Univ Minn, BS, 49; Univ Calif, Los Angeles, PhD(chem), 53. *Prof Exp:* Res chemist, Yerkes Res Lab, E I du Pont de Nemours & Co, 53-54. *Mem:* Am Chem Soc. *Res:* Stereochemistry; conformational analysis; organo-phosphorus chemistry. *Mailing Add:* 7412 Kathydale Rd Baltimore MD 21208-5735

AARON, HOWARD BERTON, physical metallurgy, materials science, for more information see previous edition

AARON, M ROBERT, ELECTRICAL ENGINEERING, COMMUNICATIONS. *Current Pos:* CONSULT, 89- *Personal Data:* b Philadelphia, Pa, Aug 21, 22; m 44; c Richard & James. *Educ:* Univ Pa, BS, 49, MS, 51. *Honors & Awards:* Alexander Graham Bell Medal, Inst Elec & Electronics Engrs, 78, Centennial Medal, 84, Donald W McLellan Award, 85; C & C Prize, C & C Found, Japan, 88. *Prof Exp:* Res engr, Res Labs, Franklin Inst, 49-51 & Leeds & Northrup Co, 51; mem tech staff, Bell Tel Labs, Inc, 51-54, supvr, 54-69, head, Dept Digital Tech, AT&T Bell Labs, 69-88. *Concurrent Pos:* Consult, Contemplating Consult; pres, Circuits & Systs Soc, Inst Elec & Electronics Engrs, 73 & Tech Comts. *Mem:* Nat Acad Eng; fel Inst Elec & Electronics Engrs; Soc Cable & TV Engrs. *Res:* Digital communications systems, especially pulse code modulation; broadband ISDN; digital signal processing; technology forecasting; strategic planning; more than 12 patents. *Mailing Add:* 1700 Presidential Way Apt 203 West Palm Beach FL 33401. *Fax:* 561-687-8739; *E-Mail:* b.aaron@ieee.org; aaronb@ccgate.ml.nec.com

AARON, RONALD, THEORETICAL PHYSICS. *Current Pos:* asst prof physics, 63-72, PROF PHYSICS, NORTHEASTERN UNIV, 72- *Personal Data:* b Philadelphia, Pa, June 14, 35; m 62; c 2. *Educ:* Temple Univ, AB, 56; Univ Pa, PhD(physics), 61. *Prof Exp:* Res assoc physics, Univ Md, 61-62; res assoc, Ind Univ, 62-63; physicist, Goddard Space Ctr, NASA, 63. *Concurrent Pos:* Consult, Lawrence Radiation Lab, Univ Calif, Livermore, 64-67; vis staff mem, Los Alamos Sci Lab, NMex, 67-74; Med Physics, The Gordon Inst, 86- *Mem:* Am Phys Soc. *Res:* Theoretical high energy physics and scattering theory. *Mailing Add:* Dept Physics Northeastern Univ Boston MA 02115

AARONOFF, BURTON ROBERT, ORGANIC CHEMISTRY. *Current Pos:* REG ASSOC, FOREST LABS, 93- *Personal Data:* b Brooklyn, NY, July 4, 35; m 66, Barbara When; c Michael & David. *Educ:* Brooklyn Col, BS, 56; Johns Hopkins Univ, MA, 59, PhD(chem), 62. *Prof Exp:* Res assoc chem, Lever Bros Co, 62-63; sr chemist, Merck, Sharp & Dohme Labs, 63-66; asst to vpres res & develop, Block Drug Co, 66-68, assoc res dir, 68-73; dir explor res, Pfizer Consumer Prod Div, 73-84; pharm consult, 85-88; mgr reg affairs, Zenith Labs, 89-93. *Mem:* Am Chem Soc; Am Pharmaceut Asn; Regulatory Affairs Prof Soc. *Res:* Organic and medicinal chemistry; proprietary drugs and toiletries; pharmaceutical dosage forms; research administration; regulatory affairs. *Mailing Add:* 232 Riveredge Dr 909 Third Ave Chatham NJ 07928. *Fax:* 212-750-9152

AARONS, JULES, IONOSPHERIC PHYSICS. *Current Pos:* RES PROF ASTRON & SPACE SCI, BOSTON UNIV, 81- *Personal Data:* b New York, NY, Oct 3, 21; c 2. *Educ:* City Col, NY, BS, 42; Boston Univ, MA, 49; Univ Paris, PhD, 54. *Honors & Awards:* Harry Diamond Award, Inst Elec & Electronics Engrs, 82. *Prof Exp:* Physicist, Air Force Cambridge Res Labs, 46-55, chief radio astron br, 55-72, chief trans-ionospheric propagation br & sr scientist, Space Physics Lab, Air Force Geophys Lab, 72-81. *Concurrent Pos:* Chmn electromagnetic propagation panel, Adv Group Aerospace Res & Develop, 73-75; int chmn comn G, Int Sci Radio Union. *Mem:* Fel Inst Elec & Electronics Engrs; Am Geophys Union. *Res:* Upper atmosphere physics; ionospheric propagation, solar terestrial relationships. *Mailing Add:* Ctr Space Physics Boston Univ 725 Commonwealth Ave Boston MA 02215

AARONSON, HUBERT IRVING, NUCLEATION KINETICS, GROWTH KINETICS IN SOLID-SOLID TRANSFORMATIONS IN METALS. *Current Pos:* RF Mehl prof mats sci & eng, 79-92, RF MEHL EMER PROF, CARNEGIE MELLON UNIV, 92- *Personal Data:* b New York, NY, July 10, 24. *Educ:* Carnegie Inst Technol, BS, 48, MS & PhD(metall eng), 54. *Honors & Awards:* Champion H Mathewson Gold Medal, Metall Soc, 68; Albert Sauveur Achievement Award, Am Soc Metals, 87; R F Mehl Lectr, Metall Soc, 90. *Prof Exp:* Res metallurgist, Carnegie Inst Technol, 53-57; prin res scientist, Sci Lab, Ford Motor Co, 58-72; prof metall eng, Mich Technol Univ, 72-79. *Concurrent Pos:* Chmn bd, Tech Div, Am Soc Metals, 70-72; sr res fel, Univ Manchester, UK, 72; scientist III Naval Res Lab (Geo Ctr Inc), 92-96. *Mem:* Nat Acad Eng; fel Am Soc Metals; fel Metall Soc; Inst Mats; Sigma Xi; Int Metallog Soc. *Res:* Morphology, kinetics and mechanism of diffusional nucleation and diffusional growth in metallic alloys. *Mailing Add:* 5700 Bunker Hill St Apt 2107 Pittsburgh PA 15206-1168. *Fax:* 412-268-1513; *E-Mail:* aaronsont@cmv.andrew.edu

AARONSON, SHELDON, MICROBIAL BIOCHEMISTRY. *Current Pos:* from instr to prof, 53-95, EMER PROF BIOL, QUEENS COL, NY, 95- *Personal Data:* b New York, NY, Oct 9, 22; m 48; c 4. *Educ:* City Col New York, BS, 44; Univ Pa, MA, 48; NY Univ, PhD(protistology), 53. *Prof Exp:* Lectr biol, City Col New York, 48-53. *Concurrent Pos:* Res assoc, Haskins Labs, Inc, 49-65, sr staff mem, 65-68; pres fel, Am Soc Microbiol, 57; guest res collabr, biol dept, Brookhaven Nat Lab, 57-58; NSF sci fac fel, 59-60; guest collab scientist, Dept Physiol & Anat, Univ Calif, Berkeley, 63; vis scientist, Biochem Dept, Weizmann Inst, 75; vis prof, Biol Dept, Ben Gurion Univ Negev, 75; lectr, UNEP/UNESCO/ICRO, Nairobi, Kenya, 76; Mellon Fel, Queens Col, 82-84; Fulbright sr med lectr, Hacettepe Med Sch, Turkey, 86-87. *Mem:* Fel AAAS; Am Soc Microbiol; Soc Protozool; Soc Gen Microbiol; Phycol Soc Am; Biochem Soc; fel Am Acad Microbiol. *Res:* Biochemistry of microorganisms; biochemical phylogeny; cellular action of drugs; microbial ecology; ethnomicrobiology. *Mailing Add:* Dept Biol Queens Col Flushing NY 11367. *Fax:* 718-997-3445

AARONSON, STUART A, VIRAL ONCOLOGY, CELL BIOLOGY. *Current Pos:* DIR, DERALD H RUTTENBERG CANCER CTR, 93- *Personal Data:* b Mt Clemens, Mich, Feb 28, 42; m 71; c 3. *Educ:* Univ Calif, Berkeley, BS, 62, MS, 65, San Francisco, MD, 66. *Honors & Awards:* Rhoads Mem Award, Am Asn Cancer Res, 82. *Prof Exp:* Staff assoc, Viral Carcinogenesis Br, Nat Cancer Inst, 67-69, sr staff fel, 69-70, head, Molecular Biol Sect, 70-77, chief, Lab Cellular & Molecular Biol, 77-93. *Concurrent Pos:* Assoc ed, J Nat Cancer Inst, 77- & Cancer Res, 81-; mem, Sci Adv Comt, Am Cancer Soc, 84-87, Mott Selection Comt, Gen Motors Cancer Res Found, 84-; counr, Soc Exp Biol & Med, 84-89. *Mem:* Am Soc Microbiol; AAAS; Fedn Am Soc Exp Biol; Am Asn Cancer Res; Am Soc Virol. *Res:* Cell biology and molecular genetics of cancer; growth factor signal transduction; retroviruses. *Mailing Add:* Mt Sinai Med Center 1 Gustave L Levy Pl Box 1130 New York NY 10029-6574

AASE, JAN KRISTIAN, SOIL SCIENCE. *Current Pos:* RES SOIL SCIENTIST, NORTHERN PLAINS SOIL & WATER RES CTR, AGR RES SERV, USDA, 67-, RES LEADER, 82- *Personal Data:* b Stavanger, Norway, Nov 21, 35; US citizen; m 65, Janet Peterson; c Erik, Arvid, Jared, Jason & Janelle. *Educ:* Brigham Young Univ, BA, 58; Univ Minn, MS, 60; Colo State Univ, PhD(soil physics), 67. *Concurrent Pos:* Sr res assoc & adj prof, Mont State Univ; location coordr, Agr Res Serv, USDA, 83- *Mem:* Am Soc Agron; Soil Sci Soc Am; Int Soil Sci Soc; Soil Conserv Soc Am; Sigma Xi. *Res:* Soil-plant-water relations; plant water use efficiency and microclimatological research on agronomic crops and native rangeland and remote sensing. *Mailing Add:* US Dept Agr 3793 N 3600 E Kimberly ID 83341

AASLESTAD, HALVOR GUNERIUS, VIROLOGY. *Current Pos:* RETIRED. *Personal Data:* b Birmingham, Ala, Sept 6, 37; m 60, Barbara Wohn; c Katherine, Karen, Peter & Lauren. *Educ:* La State Univ, BS, 60, PhD(microbiol), 65; Pa State Univ, MS, 61. *Prof Exp:* Nat Acad Sci-Nat Res Coun fel, US Army Biol Ctr, 65-66, prin investr microbiol, 66-68; asst prof, Univ Ga, 68-70; asst prof, Wistar Inst, 70-73; sr scientist, Cancer Res Ctr, Nat Cancer Inst, Frederick, Md, 73-76; exec secy, NIH, 76-81, asst br chief, Div Res Grants, 81-85; dir res grants, Sch Med, Yale Univ, 85-95, assoc dean, 89-96. *Res:* Administration of biomedical research personnel funds, space and resources; regulatory issues and technology transfer. *Mailing Add:* 21 Pine Hollow Rd North Branford CT 06471. *E-Mail:* aaslestad@worldnet.att.net

ABADI, DJAHANGUIR M, CLINICAL CHEMISTRY. *Current Pos:* CLIN CHEMIST, VET ADMIN HOSP, IOWA CITY, 64- *Personal Data:* b Tehran, Iran, Sept 1, 29; US citizen; m 60; c 2. *Educ:* Doane Col, BA, 52; Univ Nebr, MS, 55; Univ Wash, PhD(biochem), 58; Am Bd Clin Chem, dipl. *Prof Exp:* Biochemist, Swed Hosp, Seattle, Wash, 59-61; clin chemist, Good Samaritan Hosp, Portland, Ore, 61-64. *Mem:* Fel Am Asn Clin Chemists. *Res:* Proteolytic enzymes; protein chemistry. *Mailing Add:* Vet Med Ctr Path & Lab Med Servs, 113 Hwy 6 W Iowa City IA 52246

ABADIE, STANLEY HERBERT, MEDICAL PARASITOLOGY, MEDICAL EDUCATION. *Current Pos:* Grad asst med microbiol & parasitol, 56-58, from instr to assoc prof med parasitol, 58-72, MEM GRAD FAC MED PARASITOL, LA STATE UNIV MED CTR, 60-, PROF MED PARASITOL & MICROBIOL, 72-, DEAN, SCH ALLIED HEALTH PROFESSIONS, 75- *Personal Data:* b New Orleans, La, Nov 13, 25; m 62; c 2. *Educ:* Loyola Univ, La, BS, 55; La State Univ, New Orleans, MS, 58, PhD(med parasitol), 63. *Concurrent Pos:* La State Univ Interam Training Prog fel trop med, Costa Rica, 64; Schlieder Educ Found res grant Chagas' dis, 74-77; consult mycol, Touro Infirm, New Orleans, 63-64; scientist, Vis Staff, Charity Hosp, New Orleans, 63-; consult parasitol, Vet Admin Hosp, New Orleans, 70-; lectr parasitic dis, Sch Dent, La State Univ, New Orleans, 71-; contribr, Manual of Microbiol & Manual of Trop Med. *Mem:* AAAS; Am Soc Trop Med & Hyg; Am Soc Parasitol; Am Soc Allied Health. *Res:* Hookworm disease; heartworm; filarial infections. *Mailing Add:* 8433 Oakbrook Dr Baton Rouge LA 70810

ABAJIAN, PAUL G, WATER ANALYSIS, PHYSICAL CHEMISTRY. *Current Pos:* asst prof, Johnston State Col, 69-77, assoc dean, 81, assoc prof chem, 77-89, PROF CHEM, JOHNSON STATE COL, 89-, ACTG DEAN, ACAD AFFAIRS, 90- *Personal Data:* b Framingham, Mass, Aug 4, 41; div; c 4. *Educ:* Worcester Polytech Inst, BS, 63; Univ Vt, PhD(chem), 67. *Prof Exp:* Asst anal chem, Univ Vt, 63-67; asst prof chem, Southern Conn State Col, 67-69. *Res:* Solution calorimetry of transition metal compounds and also polarographic studies of rare earth metals; correlation of metals in water and neurological disorders. *Mailing Add:* Dept Environ Sci Johnson State Col Johnson VT 05656-9405

ABARBANEL, HENRY D I, THEORETICAL PHYSICS. *Current Pos:* PROF PHYSICS, UNIV CALIF, SAN DIEGO, 83-, DIR, INST NONLINEAR SCI, 86-; RES PHYSICIST, SCRIPPS INST OCEANOG, 83- *Personal Data:* b Washington, DC, May 31, 43; m 82, Beth Levine; c Brett & Sara. *Educ:* Princeton Univ, PhD(physics), 66. *Prof Exp:* Res assoc physics, Princeton Univ, 66, vis fel, 66-67; res assoc, Stanford Linear Accelerator Ctr, 67-68; asst prof, Princeton Univ, 68-72; physicist, Fermi Nat Accelerator Lab, 72-80; physicist, Lawrence Berkeley Lab, Univ Calif, 80-83. *Concurrent Pos:* NSF fel, Princeton Univ, 67-68, A P Sloan res fel, 69-72; adj prof physics & astron, Northwestern Univ, 77-79; chair, activ group dynamical systs, Soc Indust & Appl Math, 88-90. *Mem:* Fel Am Phys Soc; Am Geophys Union. *Res:* Communications using nonlinear dynamics; nonlinear dynamics of neurons; classical dynamics of nonlinear stochastic systems. *Mailing Add:* Scripps Inst Oceanog Univ Calif San Diego La Jolla CA 92093-0402. *Fax:* 619-534-7664; *E-Mail:* hdia@hamilton.ucsd.edu

ABASHIAN, ALEXANDER, ELEMENTARY PARTICLE PHYSICS. *Current Pos:* head, Physics Dept, 80-82, dir, Inst High Energy Physics, 87-90, PROF PHYSICS, VA POLYTECH INST, 80-; CONSULT, 90- *Personal Data:* b Binghamton, NY, Mar 11, 30; m 57; c 4. *Educ:* Purdue Univ, BS, 52; Johns Hopkins Univ, PhD, 57. *Prof Exp:* Tech engr, IBM, 52; jr instr physics, Johns Hopkins Univ, 52-55; jr res assoc high energy physics, Brookhaven Cosmotron, 55-57; instr physics, Univ Rochester, 57-59; res assoc, Radiation Lab, Univ Calif, 59-61; from asst prof to prof, Univ Ill, Urbana-Champaign, 61-74; prog dir elem particle physics, NSF, 72-80. *Concurrent Pos:* Vis prof, Univ Hamburg, Ger, 78-79; vis staff, Nat Lab H E Physics (KEK), Japan, 86-87. *Mem:* Fel AAAS; fel Am Phys Soc. *Res:* Pion interactions; nuclear polarization; invariance tests; weak interactions; instrumentation; muon scattering; neutrino interactions; electron-positron interactions. *Mailing Add:* Dept Physics Va Polytech Inst & State Univ Blacksburg VA 24061

ABATE, KENNETH, SILICONE CHEMISTRY & PHOTOCHEMICAL ETCHING. *Current Pos:* VPRES WORLDWIDE TECHNOL, BMC IND, MASK GROUP, 93- *Personal Data:* b Detroit, Mich, Jan 9, 44; m 73; c 2. *Educ:* Wayne State Univ, BS, 65; Mich Tech Univ, MS, 67; Univ Fla, PhD(chem), 71. *Prof Exp:* Postdoctoral fel pharm, Col Pharm, Univ Fla, 71-72; group leader, Conchemco, 72-73; res chemist, Celanese, 73-76; vpres chem tech, H H Robertson Co, 76-90; assoc dir specialty chem, PPG Ind, 90-92; Sr vpres, MVS, 92-93. *Mem:* Am Chem Soc; Am Inst Chemists; Nat Asn Corrosion Engrs; Fedn Soc Coatings Technologies. *Res:* Corrosion prevention, coatings, polymers, paint manufacture, surfactants and speciality monomers, metal pretreating and coatings application methods; silicones; liposomes; photochemical etching. *Mailing Add:* BMC Industs Inc PO Box 189 Cortland NY 13045. *Fax:* 607-753-6258; *E-Mail:* abatek@bmcmask.com

ABAYEV, MICHAEL, AGRICULTURAL CHEMISTRY, TECHNOLOGY & SELECTION SUBTROPICAL CULTURES. *Current Pos:* CLIN LAB TECH, LENOX HILL HOSP, 93- *Personal Data:* b Dushanbe, Tajicistan, Apr 8, 42; m 65, Dora; c Natella, Regina, Irina & Inessa. *Educ:* Tajic State Univ, BS, 63; Acad Sci Tadzhik, PhD(biol), 72. *Honors & Awards:* Gold Medal, Exhib Nat Econ Achievement, 83, Bronz Medal, 87; Medal Mendeleev, Nat Orgn, USSR, 88. *Prof Exp:* Res scientist, Bot Garden, 63-68; researcher, Tajic Agr Inst, 68-73; sr res scientist, Vahshskaya Exp Sta, 73-75, Forest Exp Station, 75-79 & Hort Inst, Tajicistan, 79-89. *Res:* Designed effect of mineral fertilizers on productivity of citrus plants and on development of rest systems; designed introduction of plants of new kinds in the dryconditions of Central Asia; designed the mathematical model influences of microclouegtes on productivity of trees. *Mailing Add:* 108-21 65th Ave Queens NY 11375

ABBAS, DANIEL CORNELIUS, ELECTRONIC IMAGING SYSTEMS. *Current Pos:* res physicist solid state light emitters, 77-86, LAB HEAD, EASTMAN KODAK CO, 86- *Personal Data:* b Cincinnati, Ohio, Nov 30, 47; m 69, Elizabeth Keutgen; c Erika & Geoffrey. *Educ:* Calvin Col, AB, 69; Univ Ill, MS, 70, PhD(physics), 77. *Prof Exp:* Phys sci asst, Vehicle Signature Study, US Army, 71-72, res physicist automotive diag equip, 72-74. *Concurrent Pos:* Instr, Wayne Co Community Col, 71-72; adj prof, State Univ NY, Buffalo, 89-90. *Mem:* Am Phys Soc; Inst Elec & Electronics Engrs. *Res:* Solid state light emitters. *Mailing Add:* 1216 Stockbridge Rd Webster NY 14580. *E-Mail:* abbas@eslsrv.kodak.com

ABBAS, HAMED K, BIOLOGICAL WEED CONTROL, MYCOTOXINS PHYTOTOXINS & NATURAL PRODUCTS. *Current Pos:* RES, PLANT PATHOLOGIST, SOUTHERN WEED SCI LAB, USDA AGR RES SERV, 90- *Personal Data:* b Baghdad, Iraq, July 1, 50; US citizen; m 84, Jean M Barker; c Noah H, Samuel H & Alia J. *Educ:* Univ Baghdad, Iraq, BSc, 74, MS, 77; Univ Minn, PhD(mycotoxins), 88. *Prof Exp:* Res specialist plant path, Univ Minn, 87-90. *Mem:* Sigma Xi; Am Phytopath Soc; Weed Sci Soc Am. *Res:* Biological weed control by pathogens, particularly fungi and their secondary metabolites; investigation and analysis of their mechanisms of action. *Mailing Add:* 1545 Woodcrest Cove Greenville MS 38701. *Fax:* 601-686-5422

ABBAS, MIAN MOHAMMAD, ATMOSPHERIC PHYSICS, ASTROPHYSICS. *Current Pos:* ASTROPHYSICIST, NASA/MARSHALL SPACE FLIGHT CTR, 87- *Personal Data:* b Pakistan, June 22, 33; US citizen; m 60; c 4. *Educ:* Panjab Univ, BS, 55; Laval Univ, MS, 60; Univ RI, PhD, 67. *Prof Exp:* Res fel, Univ RI, 64-68; asst prof, Ohio Univ, 68-70; assoc prof, Univ Ky, Lexington, 70-74; Nat Acad Sci sr res assoc, Goddard Space Flight Ctr, NASA, 74-80; assoc prof, Dept Physics, Drexel Univ, 80-87. *Concurrent Pos:* Sr res assoc, Astron Prog, Univ Md. *Mem:* Am Geophys Union. *Res:* Infrared astronomy; planetary atmospheres; stratosphere. *Mailing Add:* ES83 Space Sci Lab NASA/Marshall Space Flight Ctr Huntsville AL 35812

ABBASABADI, ALIREZA, FIELD THEORY. *Current Pos:* asst prof, 88-93, ASSOC PROF PHYSICS, FERRIS STATE UNIV, 93- *Personal Data:* b Gorgan, Iran, Jan 18, 50. *Educ:* Tehran Univ, BS, 73, MS, 75; Mich State Univ, PhD(physics), 85. *Prof Exp:* Instr physics, Aborihan Univ, 75-78; vis asst prof, Mich State Univ, 85-88. *Mem:* Am Phys Soc. *Res:* Quantum electrodynamics and study of various implications and phenomenology of the standard model of electroweak and strong interactions. *Mailing Add:* Physics Sci Dept Ferris State Univ Big Rapids MI 49307

ABBASCHIAN, REZA, MATERIALS SCIENCE ENGINEERING. *Current Pos:* assoc prof, 80-83, PROF MAT SCI & ENG, UNIV FLA, 83-, CHMN, 86- *Personal Data:* b Zanjan, Iran, Jan 23, 44; US citizen; m 73, Janette S Johnson; c Lara S & Cyrus E. *Educ:* Univ Theran, Iran, BS, 65; Mich Technol Univ, MS, 68; Univ Calif, Berkeley, PhD(mat sci & eng), 71. *Prof Exp:* From asst prof to assoc prof, Dept Mat Sci & Eng, Shiraz Univ, Iran, 72-80, chmn, 74-76; vis assoc prof metall & mining eng, Univ Ill, Urbana, 76-78. *Concurrent Pos:* Vis scientist, Mass Inst Technol, 80, NASA Space Proc Lab, Marshall Space Flight Ctr, 81; res creativity award, NSF, 84-86; vchmn, Am Soc Mat, 86-88, chmn, 88-90; mem acad affairs comt, Mat Res Soc, 91-; bd dirs, Minerals Metals & Mat Soc, 93- *Mem:* Mat Res Soc; Am Soc Mat. *Res:* Solidification processing and properties of advanced materials and composites; high temperature intermetallics; crystal growth and space processing; granted 4 US patents; author of 10 publications. *Mailing Add:* 2630 NW 27th Terr Gainesville FL 32605. *Fax:* 352-392-6359; *E-Mail:* rabba@mse.ufl.edu

ABBATIELLO, MICHAEL JAMES, zoology, biology, for more information see previous edition

ABBE, WINFIELD JONATHAN, THEORETICAL HIGH ENERGY PHYSICS. *Current Pos:* CONSULT, 80- *Personal Data:* b Cleveland, Ohio, Feb 27, 39; m 66; c 1. *Educ:* Univ Calif, Berkeley, AB, 61; Calif State Col, Los Angeles, MS, 62; Univ Calif, Riverside, PhD(physics), 66. *Prof Exp:* From asst prof to assoc prof physics, Univ Ga, 66-80. *Concurrent Pos:* Res fel, Univ Mich, 66-67. *Res:* Elementary particle theory; S-matrix theory of strong interactions; Regge Pole theory; dispersion relations. *Mailing Add:* 150 Raintree Ct Athens GA 30607

ABBEY, HELEN, BIOSTATISTICS. *Current Pos:* From instr to assoc prof, 51-69, PROF BIOSTATIST, JOHNS HOPKINS UNIV, 69- *Personal Data:* b Ann Arbor, Mich, Sept 1, 20. *Educ:* Battle Creek Col, BS, 40; Univ Mich, MA, 42; Johns Hopkins Univ, ScD, 51. *Concurrent Pos:* Mem epidemiol & dis control study sect, Div Res Grants, NIH, 72-76. *Mem:* Fel Am Statist Asn; Pop Asn Am; Am Soc Human Genetics; Am Pub Health Asn; Biomet Soc; Sigma Xi. *Res:* Application of statistics in medicine; biological sciences; epidemiology; human genetics; demography. *Mailing Add:* Sch Hyg & Pub Health Dept 615 N Wolfe St Baltimore MD 21205

ABBEY, KATHLEEN MARY KYBURZ, ELECTROCHEMISTRY, LASER LIGHT SCATTERING. *Current Pos:* CONSULT, 88-; PRIN, CARY TECH INC, 89- *Personal Data:* b Oak Park, Ill, Feb 28, 50; c Ralph. *Educ:* Rockford Col, BS, 72; Georgetown Univ, PhD(phys chem), 77, Mass Inst Technol, MS, 97. *Prof Exp:* Res fel laser light scattering, State Univ NY, Stony Brook, 76-80; res chemist, Lewis Res Ctr, NASA, Cleveland, 80-84; polymer chemist, Therm-O-Disc Div, Emerson Elec, 84-86, consult, 86-88. *Concurrent Pos:* Co-ed, Membranes & Ionic & Elec Conducting Polymers, Electrochem Soc, 72; comput software consult, Malvern Sci, Inc, 80; tech adv, Shuttle Stud Involvment Proj, NASA, 83-84; chmn, Ohio Sect, Electrochem Soc, 84-86; staff mem, Amp Inc, 88. *Mem:* Electrochem Soc; Am Inst Aeronaut & Astronaut; Am Phys Soc. *Res:* Laser light scattering and instrumentation with emphasis on computer interfacing; electrochemical storage systems and fuel cells; polymeric devices for energy storage and electrical switching; colloidal interaction in solution; physical chemistry; aeronautical and astronautical engineering; computer software and hardware; nuclear reactor modelling. *Mailing Add:* PO Box 5527 Cary NC 27512-5527

ABBEY, KIRK J, ADHESIVES, COATINGS. *Current Pos:* staff scientist, 86-93, SR STAFF SCIENTIST, LORD CORP, 93- *Personal Data:* b Monmouth, Ill, Aug, 19, 49; m, Kathleen M Kyburz. *Educ:* Rockford Col, BA, 71; Johns Hopkins Univ, MS, 76, PhD(org chem), 77. *Prof Exp:* Scientist, Glidden Coatings & Resins, Div SCM Corp, 76-86. *Concurrent Pos:* Chmn, Akron Polymer Lect Group, 83-84, chmn-elect, Polymer Group, NC Sect, Am Chem Soc, 90-91. *Mem:* Am Chem Soc; Adhesion Soc. *Res:* Polymer chemistry and engineering with emphasis on oligomer synthesis and cure chemistry; emulsion polymerization; coatings and adhesives with a focus on polymer and olizomer synthesis, cure studies and computational modeling of cure reactions; granted 21 patents. *Mailing Add:* Lord Corp 405 Greyson Dr Cary NC 27511. *E-Mail:* kirk_abbey@lord.com

ABBEY, ROBERT FRED, JR, MARINE METEOROLOGY. *Current Pos:* DIR MARINE METEOROL RES PROG, OFF NAVAL RES, US NAVY, 83- *Personal Data:* b Klamath Falls, Ore, May 27, 47; m 68; c 5. *Educ:* Univ Ore, BS & BA, 69, MA, 71; Colo State Univ, MS, 72, PhD(atmospheric sci), 82; Univ Southern Calif, MPA, 83, DPA, 85. *Prof Exp:* Res assoc physics, Southwestern Ore Community Col, 66-67; res asst atmospheric sci, Colo State Univ, 69-72; sr environ scientist meteorol, Atomic Energy Comn, 72-75; dir, Meteorol Res Prog, US Nuclear Regulatory Comn, 75-83. *Concurrent Pos:* Mem, Standards Comn Tornadoes & Extreme Winds, Am Nuclear Soc, 76- & Fed Comn Meteorol Serv & Supporting Res, 79-83; Comt Wind Effects on Structures, Am Soc Civil Engrs, 79-85, Turbulence, 81-; vis prof, Univ Md, 81-83; chmn, Severe Local Storms, Am Meteorol Soc, 76-77, Fed Working Group Atmospheric Transport Models, 80-83; consult, Time Life, Nat Geographic, Univ Chicago Press, GEO Magazine; cert consult meteorologist, Am Meteorol Soc, 81-; adj prof, Montgomery Col, 83-; exec secy, Tropical Cyclone Steering Comt, Dept Defense, 85-; adjunct prof, Montgomery Col, Southern Univ, Univ Southern Calif. *Mem:* Fel Am Meteorol Soc; Am Soc Civil Engrs; AAAS. *Res:* Theoretical and empirical studies in atmospheric transport and diffusion of airborne effluents, severe storm (tornado, hurricane and lightning) characterization, probabilistic hazard modeling and climatology; author or coauthor of over 100 papers in technical journals, conference proceedings and chapters in books. *Mailing Add:* 5815 Ogden Ct Bethesda MD 20816

ABBOTT, A(NTON) DWIGHT, SPACE SYSTEMS ENGINEERING, SPACE TECHNOLOGY APPLICATIONS. *Current Pos:* mem tech staff, Systs Res & Planning Div, Aerospace Corp, 60-70, dir advan projs, Develop Planning Div, 70-75, prin dir, Environ & Conserv Directorate, 75-82, Space Transp Develop, 84-90, Design Eng Subdiv, 90-92, prin engr shuttle develop & applns, 82-84, gen mgr space technol applns, 92-97, GEN MGR, SYSTS ENG DIV, AEROSPACE CORP, 97- *Personal Data:* b Indianapolis, Ind, Aug 28, 36; m 64, Janet Kyseth; c Steven D & Douglas D. *Educ:* Purdue Univ, BS, 58, MS, 65. *Prof Exp:* Engr fluid dynamics, Northrop Corp, 58-59; mem tech staff, Propulsion Dept, Space Technol Labs, 59-60. *Mem:* Assoc fel Am Inst Aeronaut & Astronaut; AAAS. *Res:* Space systems architect-engineering including advanced technology applications, development planning, design engineering and program management. *Mailing Add:* 1825 Via Estudillo Palos Verdes Estates CA 90274

ABBOTT, ANDREW DOYLE, physical chemistry, for more information see previous edition

ABBOTT, BARBARA D, TOXICOLOGY, DEVELOPMENTAL TOXICOLOGY. *Current Pos:* RESEARCHER DEVELOP TOXICOL DIV, US ENVIRON PROTECTION AGENCY, 90- *Personal Data:* b Waynesville, NC, Sept 8, 44. *Educ:* Northeastern Ill Univ, BS, 79; NC State, MS, 82, PhD(genetic res), 85. *Prof Exp:* Fel, Nat Inst Environ Health Sci, 85-87 & Nat Res Serv Award, 87-90. *Mem:* Teratology Soc; Am Soc Cell Biol. *Mailing Add:* Develop Toxicol Div MD67 Environ Protection Agency Health Effects Res Lab Research Triangle Park NC 27711

ABBOTT, BERNARD C, BIOPHYSICS. *Current Pos:* prof physiol, Sch Med, chmn, Dept Biol Sci, dir, Allan Hancock Found, 68-81, prof, 81-85, EMER PROF BIOL, UNIV SOUTHERN CALIF, 85- *Personal Data:* b Yeovil, Eng, Oct 13, 20; m 44; c 1. *Educ:* Univ London, BSc, 41 & 48, PhD(biophys), 50. *Prof Exp:* Lectr biophys, Univ Col, Univ London, 46-53; prin sci officer, Marine Biol Asn, UK, 53-57; assoc res zoologist, Univ Calif, Los Angeles, 57-58, assoc prof zool, 58-62; prof biophys & physiol, Univ Ill, Urbana, 62-68. *Mem:* Am Physiol Soc; Biophys Soc; Soc Gen Physiol; Am Soc Zoologists; NY Acad Sci; Sigma Xi. *Res:* Muscle physiology; thermodynamics of bioelectric phenomena; toxins present in poisonous red tides. *Mailing Add:* 2025 Fair Oaks Ave South Pasadena CA 91030-4605

ABBOTT, BETTY JANE, CANCER, AIDS. *Current Pos:* RETIRED. *Personal Data:* b Roanoke, Va, Oct 13, 31. *Educ:* Radford Col, BS, 52; Va Polytech Inst, MS, 55. *Prof Exp:* Instr high schs, Va, 52-57, chmn dept biol, 53-57; asst biol, Va Polytech Inst, 57-59; biologist, Va Agr Res Sta, Agr Res Serv, USDA, 59-60; biologist, 60-67, head screening sect, biol testing br, develop therapeut prog, Nat Cancer Inst, 67-90. *Mem:* AAAS; Am Asn Cancer Res; NY Acad Sci. *Res:* Development and selection of new drugs for trial as potential cancer chemotherapeutic agents or AIDS; ways to increase effectiveness of agents of established clinical usefulness. *Mailing Add:* Rte 2 Box 1081 Newcastle VA 24127-9418

ABBOTT, DAVID MICHAEL, DENTISTRY, PERIODONTOLOGY. *Current Pos:* ASSOC PROF PERIODONT & OCCLUSION, MED COL, VA COMMONWEALTH UNIV, 75- *Personal Data:* b Kansas City, Mo, Dec 29, 45; m 71; c 2. *Educ:* James Madison Univ, BS, 68; Univ NC, DDS, 72; Univ Minn, MS, 75. *Prof Exp:* Instr dent, Univ NC, 72-73; clin instr periodont, Univ Minn, 74-75. *Mem:* Sigma Xi; Am Acad Periodont; Int Asn Dent; Am Dent Asn; Am Asn Dent Schs. *Res:* Microbiology of periodontal disease; biofeedback in dentistry; chronic facial pain. *Mailing Add:* 521 N 11th St Richmond VA 23298

ABBOTT, DEAN WILLIAM, SIGNAL PROCESSING, CONTROL SYSTEMS. *Current Pos:* SR RES SCIENTIST, ELDER RES. *Personal Data:* b Oak Park, Ill, Nov 28, 63; US citizen; m 88. *Educ:* Rensselaer Polytechnic Institute, BS, 85; Univ Va, MAM, 87. *Prof Exp:* Assoc Engr, Sperry Marine, Sys Div, 86; res scientist, Barron Assoc Inc, 87-91; res scientist, Martin Marietta, 91- *Res:* Extentions of traditional calculus of variations to optimally guide tactical weapons to fixed or moving targets. *Mailing Add:* 3443 Villanova Ave San Diego CA 92122

ABBOTT, DONALD CLAYTON, BIOCHEMISTRY, CEREAL CHEMISTRY. *Current Pos:* RETIRED. *Personal Data:* b Lincoln, Kans, Nov 11, 23; m 45; c 3. *Educ:* Kans State Univ, BS, 49, MS, 51, PhD, 64. *Prof Exp:* Asst to head, Exp Baking Lab, Fleischman Labs, Stand Brands, Inc, NY, 51; cereal technologist, Soft Wheat Qual Lab, Ohio Agr Exp Sta, 51-54; prof biochem, Okla State Univ, 54-86. *Mem:* Am Asn Cereal Chem; Am Chem Soc. *Res:* Baking quality of wheat varieties; immunological properties of wheat proteins; development of wheat proteins during maturation. *Mailing Add:* 924 W Liberty Lane Stillwater OK 74075

ABBOTT, DOUGLAS E(UGENE), FLUID MECHANICS, APPLIED MATHEMATICS. *Current Pos:* ASSOC VCHANCELLOR FOR COMPUT & INFO SYSTS, UNIV MASS, AMHERST, 85- *Personal Data:* b Glendale, Calif, Apr 20, 34; m 56; c 4. *Educ:* Stanford Univ, BS, 56, MS, 57, PhD(mech eng), 61. *Prof Exp:* Asst head fluid mech sect, Vidya Div, Itek Corp, 60-64; from assoc to prof fluid mech, Purdue Univ, 64-77, dir, Thermal Sci & Propulsion Ctr, 72-77; prof mech eng & chmn dept, Lehigh Univ, 77-85. *Concurrent Pos:* Lectr mech eng, Stanford Univ, 63-64; staff consult, Midwest Appl Sci Corp, 64-72, Energy Controls Div, Bendix Corp, 67-75 & Westinghouse Elec Corp, 70-75; hon res fel, Sci Res Coun, UK, 71-72; chmn air breathing propulsion adv comt, Air Force Off Sci Res, 73-83; dir, Comput-Aided Design/Comput Aided Mfg Educ Prog & chmn, Comt Interactive Graphics Educ & Res, Lehigh Univ, 81-83; vice provost, Comput & Info Serv, Lehigh Univ, 83-85. *Mem:* NY Acad Sci; Am Inst Aeronaut & Astronaut; Am Soc Mech Engrs; Am Soc Eng Educ; AAAS; fel Am Asn Adv Sci; fel Am Phys Soc. *Res:* Analytical fluid mechanics; subsonic and supersonic viscous flows; inviscid transonic and hypersonic flows; experimental and theoretical investigations of fluid mechanics of biological systems. *Mailing Add:* Univ Mass Whitmore Admin Bldg Amherst MA 01003

ABBOTT, EDWIN HUNT, INORGANIC CHEMISTRY. *Current Pos:* prof chem & head dept, 77-91, PROF, MONT STATE UNIV, 77- *Personal Data:* b New York, NY, Dec 28, 41; c 2. *Educ:* Tufts Univ, BS, 64; Tex A&M Univ, PhD(chem), 69. *Prof Exp:* Fel chem, Tex A&M Univ, 69-70; from asst prof to assoc prof, Hunter Col, 74-77. *Concurrent Pos:* Mem doctoral fac, City Univ New York, 70-77; proj dir, Exp Prog Stimulate Competitive Res, NSF, 91- *Mem:* Am Chem Soc; fel NY Acad Sci; Sigma Xi. *Res:* Coordination chemistry; bioinorganic chemistry; nuclear magnetic resonance. *Mailing Add:* Dept Chem Mont State Univ Bozeman MT 59717. *Fax:* 406-994-5407; *E-Mail:* uchea@earth.oscs.montana.edu

ABBOTT, HERSCHEL GEORGE, FORESTRY. *Current Pos:* from instr to assoc prof, 53-70, PROF FORESTRY, UNIV MASS, AMHERST, 70- *Personal Data:* b Woodstock, Maine, May 4, 21; m 43. *Educ:* Univ Maine, BS, 43; Harvard Univ, MF, 52, MA, 59. *Prof Exp:* Forester, Chadbourne Lumber Co, Maine, 46-50. *Concurrent Pos:* Vpres & treas, Rich Tree Farms & Forestry Corp, 64- *Mem:* Soc Am Foresters. *Res:* Silviculture. *Mailing Add:* 78 Montague Rd Leverett MA 01054

ABBOTT, ISABELLA AIONA, PHYCOLOGY, MARINE BIOLOGY. *Current Pos:* WILDER PROF BOT, UNIV HAWAII, 78- *Personal Data:* b Hana, Hawaii, June 20, 19; m 43, Donald P; c Ann K (Forester). *Educ:* Univ Hawaii, AB, 41; Univ Mich, MS, 42; Univ Calif, Berkeley, PhD(bot), 50. *Honors & Awards:* Darbaker Award, Bot Soc Am, 69; Smith Medal, Nat Acad Sci, 97. *Prof Exp:* Lectr bot, Univ Hawaii, 43-46; res assoc & lectr phycol, 60-70, prof biol, Stanford Univ, 71-82. *Mem:* Int Phycol Soc (treas, 67-71); Phycol Soc Am; Bot Soc Am; Brit Phycol Soc; Sigma Xi; fel AAAS. *Res:* Life histories, development and systematics of marine red algae, particularly Pacific marine algae. *Mailing Add:* Dept Bot Univ Hawaii 3190 Maile Way Honolulu HI 96822. *Fax:* 808-956-3923

ABBOTT, JAMES H, MATHEMATICS STATISTICS, INFORMATION THEORY. *Current Pos:* RETIRED. *Personal Data:* b San Miguel, NMex, Aug 19, 24. *Educ:* Univ Colo, BS, 46; SMU, MS, 49, Univ Ill, PhD(math), 59. *Prof Exp:* Instr math, SMU, 47-49; instr math, Tex A&M Univ, 49-51; asst prof math, Purdue Univ, 57-60; assoc prof math, NMex Univ, 60-64; prof math, Univ New Orleans, 65-84, chmn dept, 65-67. *Mem:* Am Math Soc; Am Math Asn; Inst Elec & Electronics Engrs. *Mailing Add:* 2334 New York St New Orleans LA 70122-5657

ABBOTT, JOAN, CELL DIFFERENTIATION. *Current Pos:* sr res scientist, 83-84, RES DIR, ELECTRO-BIOL INC, 84- *Personal Data:* b Newton, Mass, Aug 5, 32. *Educ:* Conn Col, BA, 54; Wash Univ, MA, 57; Univ Pa, PhD(develop biol), 65. *Prof Exp:* Asst prof biol, Barnard Col, Columbia Univ, 65-67, asst prof dept biol sci, Columbia Univ, 67-72; assoc, Mem Sloan-Kettering Cancer Ctr, 72-83, asst prof biol, Sloan-Kettering Div, Grad Sch Med Sci, Cornell Univ, 73-84. *Mem:* AAAS; Am Soc Cell Biol; Orthop Res Soc; NY Acad Sci. *Res:* Effects of electromagnetic fields on biological systems. *Mailing Add:* Electro Biol Inc Six Upper Pond Rd Parsippany NJ 07054

ABBOTT, JOHN S, GEOMETRY. *Current Pos:* SR PROJ ENGR, CORNING GLASS WORKS, 78- *Personal Data:* b Denver, Colo, April 23, 52. *Educ:* Univ Colo, BA, 76; Univ Denver, PhD(math), 79. *Mailing Add:* Corning Inc HP-ME-01-024 Corning NY 14831-0001

ABBOTT, LAURENCE FREDERIC, COMPUTATIONAL NEUROSCIENCE. *Current Pos:* PROF BIOL, BRANDEIS UNIV, 79- *Personal Data:* b Toronto, Ont, May 15, 50; m 74; c 2. *Educ:* Brandeis Univ, PhD(physics), 77. *Prof Exp:* Res assoc physics, Stanford Linear Accelerator Ctr, 77-79. *Concurrent Pos:* Elec engr, Honeywell Comput Div, Gilford Instruments, Teredyne Inc; sci assoc, Europ Orgn Nuclear Res, 80-81; Alfred P Sloan Found fel, 83. *Mem:* Soc Neurosci. *Res:* Computational and mathematical modeling of neurons and neural networks including central pattern generators, and visual and other cortical areas. *Mailing Add:* Brandeis Univ Volen Ctr Waltham MA 02254

ABBOTT, LOUISE C, VETERINARY ANATOMY. *Current Pos:* ASST PROF, DEPT VET ANAT & PUB HEALTH, TEX A&M UNIV, 94-, FAC MEM, NEUROSCI PROG & TOXICOL PROG, 95- *Personal Data:* b Ft Monroe, Va, Sept 8, 53. *Educ:* Whitman Col, BA, 75; Univ Wash, PhD, 82; Wash State Univ, DVM, 88. *Prof Exp:* Postdoctoral res assoc, Dept Vet & Comp Anat, Pharmacol & Physiol, Col Vet Med, Wash State Univ, 78-81, asst prof, 83-88; vis asst prof, Dept Vet Biosci, Col Med, Univ Ill, 88-89, mem neurosci fac, 88-94, asst prof, 89-94. *Concurrent Pos:* Fulbright res scholar, Paris, 94. *Mem:* AAAS; Am Vet Med Asn; Am Asn Vet Anatomists; Soc Neurosci. *Mailing Add:* Dept Vet Anat & Pub Health Col Vet Med Tex A&M Univ College Station TX 77843-4458

ABBOTT, LYNN DE FORREST, JR, BIOCHEMISTRY. *Current Pos:* res assoc, 40-43, from asst prof to prof, 43-76, chmn dept, 62-76, EMER PROF BIOCHEM, MED COL VA, 76- *Personal Data:* b Ithaca, NY, Nov 23, 13; m 40, Hester M Easton; c Lynn D III, James E & William L. *Educ:* Wayne Univ, BS, 36, MS, 37; Univ Mich, PhD(biochem), 40. *Prof Exp:* Asst chem, Wayne Univ, 35-36, asst biochem, 36-37; asst, Univ Mich, 37-40. *Concurrent Pos:* Ed, Va J Sci, 68-73. *Mem:* Fel AAAS; Am Chem Soc; Am Soc Biochem; Am Inst Nutrit; Am Soc Clin Nutrit. *Res:* Blood chemistry and amino acid metabolism; enzyme chemistry; isotopic nitrogen in metabolism. *Mailing Add:* 607 Horsepen Rd Richmond VA 23229

ABBOTT, MICHAEL MCFALL, THERMODYNAMICS. *Current Pos:* res assoc fluid, chem & thermal processes, 69-76, ASSOC PROF CHEM ENG, RENSSELAER POLYTECH INST, 76- *Personal Data:* b Niagara Falls, NY, Oct 3, 38; m 62; c 1. *Educ:* Rensselaer Polytech Inst, BChE, 61, PhD(thermodyn), 65. *Prof Exp:* Chem engr, Esso Res & Eng Co, Stand Oil Co, NJ, 65-67, res engr, 67-69. *Mem:* Am Inst Chem Engrs. *Res:* Thermodynamics and phase equilibria; conductivities of heterogeneous systems; electrochemical engineering. *Mailing Add:* Rensselaer Polytech Inst 110 Eighth St Troy NY 12180-3522

ABBOTT, MITCHEL THEODORE, BIOCHEMISTRY. *Current Pos:* asst prof, 64-71, PROF BIOCHEM, SAN DIEGO STATE UNIV, 71- *Personal Data:* b Los Angeles, Calif, June 6, 30; m 62; c 3. *Educ:* Univ Calif, Los Angeles, BS, 57, PhD(biochem), 63. *Prof Exp:* Fel biochem, Sch Med, NY Univ, 62-64. *Concurrent Pos:* Vis scientist, Roche Inst Molecular Biol, 72-73; NSF & NIH basic res grants. *Mem:* Am Soc Biol Chem; AAAS; Protein Soc. *Res:* Enzymology and regulation of pyrimidine metabolism; processing of small nuclear RNA. *Mailing Add:* Dept Chem San Diego State Univ San Diego CA 92182-0328

ABBOTT, NORMAN JOHN, TEXTILE PHYSICS. *Current Pos:* CONSULT, 88- *Personal Data:* b Toronto, Ont, Nov 14, 18; m 44; c 3. *Educ:* Univ Toronto, BA, 40. *Honors & Awards:* Harold DeWitt Smith Mem Medal, Am Soc Testing & Mat, 87- *Prof Exp:* Elec engr, Amalgamated Elec Corp, 40-41; spec instr armed forces, Dept Physics, Univ Toronto, 41-43; tech writer, Radar Div, Res Enterprises Ltd, 43-45; fel, Textile Dept, Ont Res Found, 45-57; from asst dir to assoc dir appl physics, Albany Int Res Co, 57-87. *Mem:* Fiber Soc; fel Brit Textile Inst; Sigma Xi; Tech Asn Pulp & Paper Indust. *Res:* Mechanical properties of textile structures; behavior of textiles under extreme conditions; coated fabric mechanics; characterization, utilization of high temperature, high performance, nonflammable fibers; design of mechanical structures containing such fibers. *Mailing Add:* 102 Blake St Needham MA 02192

ABBOTT, PATRICK LEON, SEDIMENTOLOGY, ENVIRONMENTAL GEOLOGY. *Current Pos:* Lectr geol, 68-69, from asst prof to assoc prof, 71-76, PROF GEOL, SAN DIEGO STATE UNIV, 76-, CHMN, 80- *Personal Data:* b San Diego, Calif, Sept 30, 40; div; c 3. *Educ:* San Diego State Col, BS, 63; Univ Tex, Austin, MA, 65, PhD(geol), 73. *Concurrent Pos:* Vis prof, Univ Canterbury, NZ, 84. *Mem:* AAAS; Geol Soc Am; Soc Econ Paleontologists & Mineralogists; Am Asn Petrol Geologists; Int Asn Sedimentologists. *Res:* Interaction of humankind and the earth; sedimentology and tectonics of Mesozoic and Cenozoic rocks, southwestern United States and northwestern Mexico; geologic hazards. *Mailing Add:* Dept Geol Sci San Diego State Univ San Diego CA 92182-1020

ABBOTT, RICHARD NEWTON, JR, CRYSTAL-CHEMISTRY. *Current Pos:* from asst prof to assoc prof, 79-89, PROF GEOL, APPALACHIAN STATE UNIV, 89- *Personal Data:* b Newton, Mass, Jan 12, 49; m 71, Lesley MacVane; c Andrew M, Tyson W & Paige W. *Educ:* Bowdoin Col, BA, 71; Univ Maine, Orono, MSc, 73; Harvard Univ, PhD(geol), 77. *Honors & Awards:* Hawley Award, Mineral Asn Can, 79. *Prof Exp:* Fel, Dalhousie Univ, 77-79. *Concurrent Pos:* Postdoctoral Fel, Harvard Univ, 87. *Mem:* Mineral Asn Can; Mineral Soc Am; Sigma Xi; Am Geophys Union; Clay Minerals Soc. *Res:* Crystal-chemistry; phase relationships of igneous and metamorphic rocks. *Mailing Add:* Dept Geol Appalachian State Univ Boone NC 28607. *Fax:* 704-262-2127

ABBOTT, ROBERT CLASSIE, COMPUTER SCIENCES, STATISTICAL ANALYSIS. *Current Pos:* RETIRED. *Personal Data:* b Syracuse, NY, June 7, 26; m 62; c 2. *Educ:* Syracuse Univ, BEE, 50, MS, 58, PhD(physics), 59. *Prof Exp:* Elec engr, Wright Air Develop Ctr, Ohio, 50 & Navy Ord Div Eastman Kodak Co, NY, 50-51; asst physics, Syracuse Univ, 51-59; res physicist, Cornell Aeronaut Lab, Inc, 59-61, prin physicist, 61-62, head, Solid State Physics Sect, 62-66; assoc prof fac eng & appl sci, State Univ NY, Buffalo, 66-73; vpres res, Multitech Res & Invest Corp, 73-78; res asst prof, Biophys Dept, State Univ NY, Buffalo, 78-82; tech staff, Mitre Corp, Boston, 84-93. *Mem:* Am Phys Soc. *Res:* Surface physics and biophysics; ion-metal surface interactions; metallic adsorption systems; macromolecular information storage mechanisms; digital signal processing for biological and economic systems; artificial intelligence-expert systems techniques applied to decision aids and simulations. *Mailing Add:* 12 Highbridge Hill Nashua NH 03063. *E-Mail:* abbott@msn.com

ABBOTT, ROBINSON S, ECOLOGY. *Current Pos:* from asst prof to prof, 61-91, chmn div sci & math, 64-68, EMER PROF BIOL, UNIV MINN, MORRIS, 91- *Personal Data:* b Philadelphia, Pa, June 23, 26; m 56, Rosemarie H Savelkoul; c Rodman P, Jane P, Bartram S & Braden K. *Educ:* Bucknell Univ, BS, 49; Cornell Univ, PhD(biol), 56. *Prof Exp:* Teacher pub sch, LI, 50-51; asst bot, Cornell Univ, 53; asst, Wiegand Herbarium, 53-54, econ bot, 55-56; instr bot, Smith Col, 56-61. *Concurrent Pos:* Vis researcher, Padre Island Nat Seashore, Tex, 81-82, Radioecol Inst, NSF & Oak Ridge Inst Nuclear Studies, Oak Ridge, Tenn, 64. *Mem:* Bot Soc Am; Ecol Soc Am; Phycol Soc Am; Int Phycol Soc. *Res:* General ecology, especially beach and salt marsh ecology; use of filamentous algae as ecological indicators; environmental effects of the growth and development of algae; ecology and population dynamics of Desmanthus illinoensis. *Mailing Add:* 205 E Sixth St Morris MN 56267-1212. *E-Mail:* abbottr@caa.mrs.umn.edu

ABBOTT, ROSE MARIE SAVELKOUL, PLANT MORPHOLOGY. *Current Pos:* RETIRED. *Personal Data:* b Chaska, Minn, Feb 7, 31; m 56, Robinson S; c Rodman P, Jane P, Bartram S & Braden K. *Educ:* Univ Minn, BA, 53, MS, 55; Cornell Univ, PhD(plant morphol), 59. *Prof Exp:* Instr biol, Smith Col, 57-58; instr plant morphol, Univ Minn, Morris, 64-66, instr genetics, 66-77, asst prof biol, 77-90. *Concurrent Pos:* Fel, NSF, 56-57 & 57-58. *Mem:* Bot Soc Am. *Res:* Developmental anatomy of primary xylem elements; development of shoot apices; developmental anatomy of Berberidaceae. *Mailing Add:* Dept Biol Univ Minn Morris MN 56267. *E-Mail:* abbottr@caa.mrs.umn.edu

ABBOTT, SETH R, CHEMICAL INSTRUMENTATION, SPECTROSCOPY. *Current Pos:* sr res chemist, Varian Assocs, 72-79, mgr res, 79-85, mgr mkt, 88-93, MGR RES & ENG, VARIAN ASSOCS, 85-87 & 94- *Personal Data:* b Brooklyn, NY, Mar 14, 44; m 96, Margaret June Roberts; c Jason & Jessica. *Educ:* Brooklyn Col, BS, 64; Mass Inst Technol, PhD(chem), 69. *Prof Exp:* Res chemist analysis & polmer chem, Memorex Corp, 69-72. *Concurrent Pos:* Lectr liquid chromatography, Am Chem Soc. *Mem:* Am Chem Soc. *Res:* Liquid chromatography; emission and Raman spectroscopy; mass spectroscopy; artificial intelligence; gas chromatography. *Mailing Add:* 5308 Lightwood Dr Concord CA 94521-3711. *Fax:* 510-945-2334; *E-Mail:* seth.abbott@csb.varian.com

ABBOTT, STEPHEN DUDLEY, OPERATIONS RESEARCH. *Current Pos:* ASST PROF MATH, MIDDLEBURY COL, 93- *Personal Data:* b Davidson, NC, Oct 8, 64. *Educ:* Colgate Univ, BA, 86; Va Univ, MA, 88. *Prof Exp:* Prof math, Univ Va, 87-92. *Mem:* Am Math Asn. *Mailing Add:* Middlebury Col Middlebury VT 05753

ABBOTT, THOMAS B, SPEECH PATHOLOGY. *Current Pos:* asst prof speech path & head speech & hearing clin, 63-66, assoc prof speech path & dir div, 66-78, prof & chmn, Dept Speech, 78-86, EMER PROF, UNIV FLA, 86- *Personal Data:* b Pa, June 27, 21; m 45; c 2. *Educ:* Muskingum Col, BA, 43; Case-Western Res Univ, MA, 48; Univ Fla, PhD, 57. *Prof Exp:* Asst prof speech & hearing, St Cloud State Col, 49-53; instr, Univ Fla, 54-57; dir speech ther prog, Los Angeles Co Soc Crippled Children, 57-58; from assoc prof to prof speech path, Baylor Univ, 58-63, dir, Speech Clin, 58-63; consult, Kuwait Univ, 88-89. *Concurrent Pos:* Lectr, Univ Southern Calif, 57-58. *Mem:* Fel Am Speech-Lang-Hearing Asn; Speech Asn Am. *Res:* Stuttering; language. *Mailing Add:* 1502 NW 31st Gainesville FL 32605

ABBOTT, THOMAS PAUL, POLYMER CHEMISTRY. *Current Pos:* res chemist elastomers & plastics, 71-80, res chemist natural polymers, 81-85, RES CHEMIST AGR PROD, USDA, 85- *Personal Data:* b Akron, Ohio, Sept 26, 42; m 61; c 3. *Educ:* Univ Akron, BS, 64, MS, 68, PhD(polymer chem), 72. *Prof Exp:* Chemist polymer analysis, Cent Res, Gen Tire & Rubber Co, 64-69. *Concurrent Pos:* Lectr, Ill Cent Col, 87. *Mem:* Am Chem Soc. *Res:* Lignin chemistry and natural products chemistry; detoxification of oilseed meals. *Mailing Add:* 2016 Del Ray Peoria IL 61614-3306

ABBOTT, URSULA K, DEVELOPMENTAL GENETICS. *Current Pos:* prin lab tech, 54-55, lectr & asst specialist, 55-56, instr & jr poultry geneticist, 56-57, from asst prof & asst geneticist to assoc prof & assoc geneticist, 57-67, PROF AVIAN SCI & GENETICIST, UNIV CALIF, DAVIS, 67- *Personal Data:* b Chilliwack, BC, July 30, 27; m 54; c 2. *Educ:* Univ BC, BSA, 49, MSA, 50; Univ Calif, PhD(genetics), 55. *Prof Exp:* Asst poultry, Univ BC, 48-50; res asst poultry genetics, Univ Calif, Berkeley, 50-54. *Concurrent Pos:* Guggenheim fel, 60-61; prof dir develop biol, NSF, 68-69; Hon prof, Univ BC, 67. *Mem:* Am Genetic Asn; Poultry Sci Asn; Int Soc Develop Biol; Soc Develop Biol; Am Soc Naturalists. *Res:* Developmental genetics; experimental embryology and teratology. *Mailing Add:* Dept Avian Sci Univ Calif Davis CA 95616

ABBOTT, WILLIAM ASHTON, chemical biology, biochemical toxicology, for more information see previous edition

ABBOTT, WILLIAM M, VASCULAR SURGERY. *Current Pos:* PROF SURG, HARVARD UNIV, 76-; CHIEF VASCULAR SURG, MASS GEN HOSP, 78- *Personal Data:* b San Francisco, Calif, Apr 14, 36; c 2. *Educ:* Stanford Univ, MD, 61. *Mem:* Am Col Surgeons; Am Surg Asn; Soc Vascular Surg. *Mailing Add:* Mass Gen Hosp Dept Surg 15 Parkman St Boston MA 02114

ABBOTT, WILTON R(OBERT), ELECTRICAL ENGINEERING, SYSTEMS ENGINEERING. *Current Pos:* mgr satellite syst integration, Missile & Space Systs Div, Lockheed Aircraft Corp, 57-63, consult spacecraft scientist, 63-68, spec asst to vpres & gen mgr, Space Systs Div, 68-74, SR CONSULT ENGR, LOCKHEED AIRCRAFT CORP, 74- *Personal Data:* b Campbell, Calif, Jan 19, 16; m 38; c 3. *Educ:* Univ Calif, BS, 37; Iowa State Col, MS, 42, PhD(elec eng), 45. *Prof Exp:* Asst instruction & res, Stanford

Univ, 37-38; asst eng, Remler Co, Ltd, Calif, 38-39 & Gen Elec Co, 39-40; from instr to assoc prof elec eng, Iowa State Col, 40-47; asst prof, Univ Calif, 47-52; sr res engr & res specialist, NAm Aviation Co, 52-57. *Concurrent Pos:* Asst prof continuing educ, San Jose State Univ; trustee, Linfield Col, McMinnville, Ore. *Mem:* Inst Elec & Electronics Engrs. *Res:* Transient and steady state analysis of electrical circuits containing vacuum tubes; numerical machine tool control; spacecraft systems. *Mailing Add:* 27899 Via Ventana Los Altos Hills CA 94022-3224

ABBOUD, FRANCOIS MITRY, INTERNAL MEDICINE. *Current Pos:* adv res fel cardiol, Cardiovasc Res Labs, Univ Iowa, 60-61, from asst prof to assoc prof internal med, 61-68, dir, Cardiovasc Div, Dept Internal Med, 70-76, PROF MED, UNIV IOWA, 68-, PROF PHYSIOL & BIOPHYS & DIR, CARDIOVASC CTR, 75-, CHMN, DEPT INTERNAL MED, 76-, EDITH KING PEARSON PROF CARDIOVASC RES, 88- *Personal Data:* b Cairo, Egypt, Jan 5, 31; US citizen; m 55; c 4. *Educ:* Ain Shams Univ, Cairo, MB, BCh, 55; Am Bd Internal Med, cert, 64, Am Bd Cardiovascular Dis, cert, 72. *Hon Degrees:* Dr, Univ Lyon, 91; DSc, Med Col Wis, 94. *Honors & Awards:* Award for Exp Therapeut, Am Soc Pharmacol & Exp Therapeut, 72; R T Hall Lectr, Cardiac Soc Australia & NZ, 89; CIBA Award, Am Heart Asn, 90, Gold Heart Award, 95; Distinguished Serv Award, Cent Soc Clin Res, 92; Robert H Williams Distinguished Chmn Med Award, Asn Profs Med, 93; Merck Sharp & Dohme Int Award, Int Soc Hypertension, 94; Wiggers Award, Cardiovasc Sect, Am Physiol Soc. *Prof Exp:* Intern, Demerdash Govt Hosp, Cairo, 55; resident, Milwaukee County Hosp, Wis, 55-58; res assoc & instr med & cardiol, Marquette Univ, 58-60. *Concurrent Pos:* Am Heart Asn res fel, Cardiovasc Lab, Sch Med, Marquette Univ, 58-60, advan res fel, 60-62; USPHS res career develop award, 62-71; chmn, Coun Circulation, Am Heart Asn, 77-80, ed-in-chief, Circulation Res, 81-86, assoc ed, Hypertension, 89-90; ed, Circulation Res, 81-86; chmn, Syntex Scholars Prog Adv Comt, 84-90; pres, Cent Soc Clin Res, 85-86; bd mem, Am Bd Internal Med, 87-93. *Mem:* Inst Med-Nat Acad Sci; Am Heart Asn (pres-elect, 89-90, pres, 90-91); AMA; Am Physiol Soc; Soc Exp Biol & Med; Am Soc Clin Invest; master Am Col Physicians; Asn Univ Cardiologists; Asn Am Physicians (treas, 79-84, pres, 90-91); Sigma Xi; NY Acad Sci; fel Am Col Cardiologists; Soc Neurosci; Asn Profs Med. *Res:* Cardiovascular physiology and pharmacology; peripheral circulation; neurogenic control of the circulation; interaction of cardiovascular reflex; baroreflex in hypertension; regulation of the circulation in pathological states; mechanisms of resetting of arterial baroreceptors; control of sympathetic activity in humans-role of sensory receptors. *Mailing Add:* 24 Kennedy Pkwy Iowa City IA 52240

ABBOUD, HANNA E, NEPHROLOGY, RENAL DISEASES. *Current Pos:* PROF MED, HEALTH SC CTR, UNIV TEX, 90- *Personal Data:* b Amman, Jordan, Sept 5, 47. *Res:* Nephrology; renal diseases. *Mailing Add:* Univ Tex Health Sci Ctr 7703 Floyd Curl Dr San Antonio TX 78284-7882

ABBRECHT, PETER H, RESPIRATORY PHYSIOLOGY, PULMONARY MEDICINE. *Current Pos:* PROF PHYSIOL & MED, UNIFORMED SERV UNIV HEALTH SCI, 80-, CHMN PHYSIOL, 87-; CONSULT & ATTEND PHYSICIAN, WALTER REED ARMY MED CTR, 80- *Personal Data:* b Toledo, Ohio, Nov 27, 30; m 57; c 2. *Educ:* Purdue Univ, BS, 52; Univ Mich, MS, 53, PhD(chem eng), 57, MD, 62. *Prof Exp:* Sr chem engr, Minn Mining & Mfg Co, 56-58; intern med, Univ Calif Hosp, Los Angeles, 62-63; from asst prof to prof physiol, Univ Mich, Ann Arbor, 63-80, resident internal med, 70-72, chmn bioeng prog, 72-78, prof internal med, 75-80. *Concurrent Pos:* NIH career develop award, 69-73; vis prof bioeng, Univ Calif, San Diego, 73; fel pulmonary dis, Med Ctr, Univ Mich, Ann Arbor, 74-75; instr, Wayne State Univ, 57-58; actg dir, Physiol & Biomed Eng Prog, Nat Inst Gen Med Sci, NIH, 77-78. *Mem:* Am Physiol Soc; fel Am Col Physicians; fel Am Col Chest Physicians; Biomed Eng Soc; Am Thoracic Soc; AAAS. *Res:* Cardiopulmonary physiology and modeling; use of systems theory in medical diagnosis and therapy; biomechanics of injury causation. *Mailing Add:* Dept Physiol & Med Uniformed Serv Univ Health Sci 4301 Jones Bridge Rd Bethesda MD 20814-4799. *Fax:* 301-295-3566; *E-Mail:* pabbrech@usuhs.mil

ABBUNDI, RAYMOND JOSEPH, LUMINESCENCE, MAGNETO-ELASTIC EFFECTS. *Current Pos:* res physicist, Solid State Br, 76-85, RES PHYSICIST, NUCLEAR BR, US NAVAL SURFACE WEAPONS CTR, 85- *Personal Data:* b New York, NY, Aug 14, 49. *Educ:* Am Univ, BS, 71, MS, 73, PhD(physics), 76. *Prof Exp:* Res asst physics, Am Univ, 73-75. *Concurrent Pos:* Lectr physics, Am Univ, 73-74; NAS-Nat Res Coun res assoc, US Naval Surface Weapons Ctr, 76-77. *Res:* Magnetic and magnetoelastic properties of rare earth compounds; magnetostriction of rare earth-iron intermetallic compounds; luminescence and optical properties of phosphors for personnel dosimetry. *Mailing Add:* 10103 Ridgeline Dr Gaithersburg MD 20879

ABDALI, SYED KAMAL, SYMBOLIC & ALGEBRAIC COMPUTATION. *Current Pos:* PROG DIR, NSF, 88- *Personal Data:* b Patna, India, Mar 10, 40; US citizen; m 65, Rehana; c 2. *Educ:* Am Univ Beirut, BE, 63; Univ Montreal, MSc, 68; Univ Wis-Madison, PhD(comput sci), 74. *Prof Exp:* Lectr elec eng, Govt Eng Col, Karachi, Pakistan, 63-64; jr engr, Tel Indust Pakistan, Haripur, 64-65; design engr, IT&T, Montreal, 65-66; consult, All-Tech Assocs, Montreal, 66-67; teaching asst comput sci, Univ Wis, 68-71; asst prof, NY Univ, 71-73; from asst prof to assoc prof math sci, Rensselaer Polytech Inst, 73-83; prin comput scientist, Tektronic Comput Res Lab, 83-88. *Concurrent Pos:* Adj assoc prof to adj prof, Comput Sci & Eng, Ore Grad Inst, 84-88; adj prof, Comput & Info Sci, Univ Del, 89, 92. *Mem:* Asn Comput Mach; Inst Elec & Electronics Engrs Comput Soc. *Res:* Semantics of programming languages; combinatory logic; computer algebra; parallel symbolic computations. *Mailing Add:* NSF 4201 Wilson Blvd Rm 1145 Arlington VA 22230. *E-Mail:* kabdali@nsf.gov

ABDALLAH, ABDULMUNIEM HUSEIN, pharmacology, biochemistry, for more information see previous edition

ABDALLAH, CHAOUKI TANIOS, CONTROL SYSTEMS, COMMUNICATIONS. *Current Pos:* asst prof, 88-94, ASSOC PROF ELEC ENG, UNIV NMEX, 94- *Personal Data:* b Rachana, Lebanon, July 4, 59; US citizen; m 90, Catherine Cooper. *Educ:* Youngstown State Univ, BE, 81; Ga Tech, MS, 82, PhD(elec eng), 88. *Prof Exp:* Proj mgr & engr, Sawtech, 84-85. *Concurrent Pos:* Co-prin investr, Boeing Comput Serv, 94-97, AFOSR, 94-, Los Alamos Nat Labs, 94-95; vchmn, Albuquerque Sect, Inst Elec & Electronics Engrs, 94-95, chmn, 95-96; prin investr, Chadwick-Helmuth, 96. *Mem:* Sr mem Inst Elec & Electronics Engrs. *Res:* Nonlinear systems and their applications in control, signal processing, communications and computer engineering; control and identification of physical systems; neural network applications in control. *Mailing Add:* EECE Dept Univ NMex Albuquerque NM 87131. *E-Mail:* chaouki@eece.unm.edu

ABDELAL, AHMED T, BACTERIOLOGY. *Current Pos:* DEAN, COL ARTS & SCI & PROF BIOL, GA STATE UNIV, 92- *Personal Data:* b Ciaro, Egypt. *Res:* Bacteriology. *Mailing Add:* Ga State Univ Univ Plaza Suite 741GCB Atlanta GA 30303-3083

ABDEL-BASET, MAHMOUD B, COAL CHEMISTRY, PETROLEUM CHEMISTRY. *Current Pos:* AT KUWAIT INST SCI RES. *Personal Data:* b 1944. *Educ:* Cairo Univ, BS, 65; Ain Shams Univ, MS, 69; Univ Tex, PhD(chem), 73. *Prof Exp:* Res asst petrol chem, Nat Res Ctr, Cairo, 66-69; teaching asst, Univ Tex, 69-71; res assoc coal sci, Pa State Univ, 73-77; res chemist, Allied Chem Corp, 77-80; staff chemist coal res, Exxon Res & Eng, 80- *Mem:* Am Chem Soc. *Res:* Physical organic chemistry; hydrocarbons and carbonium ions reactions and mechanism; coal chemistry and coal conversion processes. *Mailing Add:* 20641 Camino De Los Cantos Yorba Linda CA 92686

ABDEL-GHAFFAR, AHMED MANSOUR, EARTHQUAKE ENGINEERING, STRUCTURAL DYNAMICS. *Current Pos:* PROF & CO-DIR CTR RES EARTHQUAKE & CONSTRUCT ENG, UNIV SOUTHERN CALIF, 88- *Personal Data:* b Egypt, Apr 30, 47; US citizen; m 75; c Samy, Tarek & Sarah. *Educ:* Fac Eng, Cairo Univ, BSc, 70; Calif Inst Technol, MSc, 73, PhD(civil eng), 76. *Honors & Awards:* Raymond C Reese Res Prize & Thomas A Middlebrooks Award, Am Soc Civil Engrs, 82 & Huber Res Award, 89; Rheinstein Fac Res Award, Princeton Univ, 81, Norman Sollenberger Fac Award, 85. *Prof Exp:* Instr struct eng, Fac Eng, Cairo Univ, 70-72; res fel civil eng, Calif Inst Technol, 76-78; asst prof, Univ Ill, Chicago Circle, 78-79; from asst prof to assoc prof struct eng, Princeton Univ, 79-88, prof civil eng, 84-86. *Concurrent Pos:* Struct engr, Bakhoum & Moharram Consult, Egypt, 71-72; assoc ed, Intern J Soil Dynamics & Earthquake Eng, 82-86; mem, Wind Eng Res Coun; vis prof struct & earthquake eng, Kyoto Univ, Japan, 86. *Mem:* Am Soc Civil Engrs; Am Acad Mech; Earthquake Eng Res Inst; Int Soc Soil Mech & Found Eng; Int Asn Bridge Struct & Struct Eng; Int Asn Safety & Reliability Struct; fel Japan Soc Prom Sci. *Res:* Structural dynamics and earthquake-response analysis and design of large civil engineering structures such as long-span cable supported bridges, buildings, and earth dams and the full scale dynamic testings of these structures; dynamic structural control and seismic performance evaluation of suspension and cable-stayed bridges. *Mailing Add:* Civil Eng Dept Univ Southern Calif Los Angeles CA 90089-2531

ABDEL-HADY, M(OHAMED) A(HMED), CIVIL & HIGHWAY ENGINEERING. *Current Pos:* RETIRED. *Personal Data:* b Cairo, Egypt, Feb 15, 34; m 66; c 3. *Educ:* Ain-Shams Univ, Cairo, BS, 56; Univ Ill, MS, 61, PhD(civil eng), 63. *Honors & Awards:* Presidential Citation of Accomplishments, President Sadat, Egypt. *Prof Exp:* Res engr, Bldg Res Ctr, Cairo, 56-57; instr civil eng, Col Eng, Ain-Shams Univ, Cairo, 57-59; from asst prof to prof civil eng, Okla State Univ, 63-91. *Concurrent Pos:* Spec lectr, US Army CEngrs, 66-68, consult, 67-; dir, NSF-Okla State Univ Remote Sensing Ctr, Cairo, Egypt, 72-75; bd adv, President Sadat, Egypt, 79-80; pres, Acad Sci Res, Cairo, Egypt, 86-88; consult, Wibur Smith & Assoc, US AID, Cairo proj, World Bank & Cairo Govt for Transp Studies; co-chmn, Int Conf Remote Sensing, Cairo, 81; auth & co-auth of four bks in civil eng, remote sensing & outer space; pres, Acad Sci & Technology, Egypt, 86-87; chmn bd, Nat Authority Remote Sensing & Space Sci, 87- *Mem:* Soc Am Mil Engrs; Am Soc Civil Engrs; Am Soc Photogram; Int Astronaut Acad. *Res:* Highway and transportation engineering; aerial photographic interpretation and remote sensing; engineering geology and rock engineering. *Mailing Add:* Sch Civil Eng Okla State Univ Stillwater OK 74074

ABDELHAK, SHERIF SAMY, HEALTH SCIENCE. *Current Pos:* consult, 85-86, PRES & CHIEF EXEC OFFICER, ALLEGHENY HEALTH EDUC & RES FOUND, PITTSBURGH, 86- *Personal Data:* b Cairo Egypt, Mar 14, 46; m, Marlynn Singleton; c S Jonathan, Matthew H, Derek A & Aaron W. *Educ:* Am Univ Cairo, BA, 68; Univ Pittsburgh, MBA, 76. *Prof Exp:* Pres & chief exec officer, Greater Canonsburg Health Syst, Pa, 82-86. *Concurrent Pos:* Adj prof, Univ Pittsburgh, 77-89; consult, Price Waterhouse Health Care Div, Pittsburgh, 85-87; bd dirs, Vol Hosps Am, Dallas, 86- Juv Diabetes Found, 87- & Hosp Co Western Pa, 87-; chmn, Hosp Trustee Forum Prudent Buyer Co, 89- *Res:* Health science. *Mailing Add:* Alleghany Health Educ Res 120 Fifth Ave Suite 2900 Pittsburgh PA 15222

ABDELHAMIED, KADRY A, biomedical engineering, for more information see previous edition

ABDEL-KHALIK, SAID IBRAHIM, NUCLEAR ENGINEERING, MECHANICAL ENGINEERING. *Current Pos:* GEORGIA POWER DISTINGUISHED PROF, NUCLEAR ENG, GEORGIA INST TECHNOL, 87-, ASSOC DIR, SCH MECH ENG, 90- *Personal Data:* b Alexandria, Egypt, Aug 9, 48. *Educ:* Alexandria Univ, Egypt, BS, 67; Univ Wis-Madison, MS, 71, PhD(mech eng), 73. *Prof Exp:* Instr mech eng, Alexandria Univ, Egypt, 67-69; vis asst prof chem eng, Univ Wis-Madison, 74-75; sr engr nuclear eng, Babcock & Wilcox Co, 75; from asst prof to assoc prof, 76-82, prof nuclear eng, Univ Wis-Madison, 82-87. *Concurrent Pos:* Fel, Rheol Res Ctr, Univ Wis-Madison, 73-74 & Solar Energy Lab, 74-75; consult, Los Alamos Sci Lab, 77, EG&G Idaho, 77-, Elec Power Res Inst, 81, Dept Energy, Sandia Labs, 81-82, adv comt Reactor Safeguards, 82-83 & Kewaunee Nuclear Power Plant, 83-, United Energy Serv Corp, 90 & Westinghouse Savannah River Co, 90-; vis res scientist, Nuclear Res Ctr, Karlsruhe, WGer, 79; invited prof, Ecole Polytechnique Federale de Lausanne, Switz. *Mem:* Am Inst Physics; Am Nuclear Soc; Solar Energy Soc; Combustion Inst; Sigma Xi. *Res:* Fission reactor operations; fission reactor safety; transport phenomena. *Mailing Add:* Nuclear Eng Prog Ga Inst Technol Atlanta GA 30332

ABDELLA, KENZU, COMPUTATIONAL & THEORETICAL FLUID DYNAMICS, APPLIED MATHEMATICS. *Current Pos:* RES SCIENTIST, CAN CTR CLIMATE MODELING & ANALYSIS, 94- *Personal Data:* b Ethiopia, Oct 16, 64; Can citizen; m 91; c 1. *Educ:* Trent Univ, BSc, 87; Univ Alta, MSc, 89; Univ Western Ont, PhD(appl math), 93. *Prof Exp:* lectr, Univ Western Ont, 92-94. *Res:* Parameterization of physical processes in the atmosphere boundary layer and surface layer, including lower level clouds. *Mailing Add:* Can Ctr Climate Modeling & Anal PO Box 1700 Victoria BC V8W 2Y2 Can

ABDELLAH, FAYE G, MEDICAL ADMINISTRATION. *Current Pos:* DEAN & PROF, GRAD SCH NURSING, UNIFORMED SERVS, UNIV HEALTH SCIS, 93- *Personal Data:* b New York, NY, Mar 13. *Educ:* Columbia Univ, BS, 45, MA, 47, EdD, 55. *Hon Degrees:* Var from US univs, 67-90. *Honors & Awards:* Nat Defense Serv Medal, 70; Nickolai Ivanovich Pirogov Medal, Acad Sci, USSR, 70; Distinguished Serv Award, Am Pub Health Asn, 78; Mary Adelaide Nursing Award, 83; Gustav O Liehard Award, Inst Med-Nat Acad Sci, 92. *Prof Exp:* Nurse consult, Div Nursing Resources, Bur State Serv, USPHS, 49-54, sr consult, 55-58, asst chief, Res Grants Br, 60-61, chief, Bur Health Manpower Educ, NIH, 61-68, dir, Off Res Training, 69-70, asst surgeon gen & chief nurse officer, 70-87, dep surgeon gen, 82-89; prof nursing, Univ SC, 90-91. *Concurrent Pos:* Consult, WHO, 74, Port Govt, 76, Tel Aviv Univ, 76 & Japanese Nursing Assoc; mem, Coun Cardiovasc Nursing, Am Heart Asn & Subcomt Preparing & Estab Criteria Res; bd trustees, Am Nurses Found; mem bd regents, Nat Libr Med; vis prof, Univ Colo, Univ Wash & Univ Minn; dir, Off Long Term Care, Off Asst Secy Health, USPHS, HEW, 76-77, from chief adv Long Term Care Policy to dep asst secy health policy, res & statist, 77-79, health planning & eval, 79-80. *Mem:* Inst Med-Nat Acad Sci; AAAS; Am Heart Asn; fel Am Acad Nursing; NY Acad Sci; Am Pub Health Asn; fel Am Psychol Asn; Am Nurses Asn; Geront Soc. *Res:* Published numerous articles in various journals. *Mailing Add:* 3713 Chanel Rd Annandale VA 22003

ABDEL-LATIF, ATA A, BIOCHEMISTRY, NEUROCHEMISTRY. *Current Pos:* from assoc prof to prof, 67-87, REGENTS PROF, BIOCHEM & MOLECULAR BIOL, MED COL GA, 87- *Personal Data:* b Beitunia, Ramallah, Palestine, Jan 22, 33; US citizen; m 57, Iris K Graham; c Rhonda, David, Joseph & Rhadi. *Educ:* DePaul Univ, BS, 55, MS, 58; Ill Inst Technol, PhD(biochem, physiol), 63. *Honors & Awards:* Merit Award, NIH, 89; Vision Res Award, Alcon Res Inst, 90. *Prof Exp:* Control chemist, Ninol Chem Labs, 55-56; med res assoc, State Ill Pediat Inst, 63-67. *Concurrent Pos:* Res assoc psychiat, Col Med, Univ Ill, 63-67; NIH grants, 65-; vis prof, Univ Nottingham, 75-76. *Mem:* AAAS; Am Soc Biol Chemists; Am Physiol Soc; Int Soc Eye Res; Am Soc Neurochem; Am Soc Pharmacol Exp Ther; Int Soc Neurochem; Soc Exp Biol & Med; Asn Res Vision & Ophthal. *Res:* Experimental therapeutics; role of phosphoinositides in adrenergic and cholinergic muscarinic receptor function in nerve and muscle; glycerolipids and prostaglandin synthesis in ocular tissues. *Mailing Add:* Dept Biochem & Molecular Biol Med Col Ga Augusta GA 30912-2100. *Fax:* 706-721-6608

ABDELMALEK, NABIH N, MATHEMATICS. *Current Pos:* RETIRED. *Personal Data:* b Egypt, 29. *Educ:* Cairo Univ, BSc, 54; Manchester Univ, PhD(theoret physics), 58. *Prof Exp:* Teacher, Cairo Univ, 52-65; researcher, Comput Ctr, Bell Northern Res, 65-67, researcher numerical analytic technol, 67-76; mem staff, Elec Eng Div, Nat Res Coun Can, 76-91. *Mem:* Am Math Soc; Can Math Soc; Can Image Processing Soc. *Mailing Add:* 788 E Vale Dr Gloucester ON K1J 7A1 Can. *Fax:* 613-745-5851

ABDEL-MONEM, MAHMOUD MOHAMED, MEDICINAL CHEMISTRY. *Current Pos:* from asst prof to assoc prof, 71-80, asst dean, Col Pharm, 80-87, PROF MED CHEM, UNIV MINN, MINNEAPOLIS, 80-, DEAN, COL PHARM, 87- *Personal Data:* b Cairo, Egypt, June 7, 38; m 64. *Educ:* Cairo Univ, BS, 59; Univ Minn, Minneapolis, PhD(med chem), 66. *Prof Exp:* Instr plant chem, Cairo Univ, 60-61; head res, Nile Co Pharmaceut, Cairo, 65-68; res specialist med chem, Univ Minn, Minneapolis, 68-70; asst prof, Med Ctr, Univ Ill, Chicago, 70-71. *Concurrent Pos:* Assoc ed, J Med Chem, 72-; consult, Zinpro Corp, Excelsior, Minn, 72- *Res:* Study of distribution and metabolism of drugs; structure activity correlation and chemical mechanisms in drug metabolism. *Mailing Add:* Wash State Univ Pullman WA 99164-6510

ABDELNOOR, ALEXANDER MICHAEL, CELLULAR ANTIGENS, TISSUE TYPING. *Current Pos:* from asst prof to assoc prof, 77-84, PROF, AM UNIV BEIRUT, 84- *Personal Data:* b New York, NY, Jan 18, 41; m 70; c 3. *Educ:* Am Univ Beirut, BS, 64, MS, 66; Univ Mich, PhD(microbiol), 69. *Prof Exp:* Postdoctoral res, Univ Mich, 69-70 & Temple Univ, 70-72; lab dir res, Fanar Res Inst, 73-76; vis researcher, Temple Univ, 76-77. *Concurrent Pos:* Guest prof, Yale Univ, 83, Univ Pa, 89. *Mem:* Am Asn Immunologists; Am Soc Microbiol; NY Acad Sci; Int Endotoxin Soc; Soc Exp Biol & Med; Am Soc Histocompatibility & Immunogenetics. *Res:* Structure-function relationship of bacterial endotoxins; human leucocyte antigens, transplantation and disease associations; epidemiological study of HIV in Lebanon. *Mailing Add:* Am Univ Beirut 850 Third Ave New York NY 10022-6297

ABDEL-RAHMAN, MOHAMED SHAWKY, DRUG-DRUG INTERACTION, CLINICAL & ENVIRONMENTAL TOXICOLOGY. *Current Pos:* from asst prof to assoc prof pharmacol, 80-87, DIR TOXICOL, UNIV MED & DENT NJ, 81-, PROF PHARMACOL, 87- *Personal Data:* b Mansoura, Egypt, Aug 27, 38; US citizen; m, Rita M Turkall. *Educ:* Alexandria Univ, Egypt, BSc, 61; Ohio State Univ, MS, 75, PhD(pharmacol & toxicol), 79. *Honors & Awards:* Fulbright Award, 89. *Prof Exp:* Biol teacher, Mansoura High Sch, 61-70; technologist, Ohio State Univ, 71-73, supvr, 76-78, asst dir, 78-79; technologist, Consol Biomed Lab, 73-75. *Concurrent Pos:* Mem, NJ Poison Info & Educ Servs, 81-; dir, Hazardous Sub Mgt Res Ctr, Health Effects Div, 84-; consult, Am Cyanamid Co, 90-91; study sect mem, Nat Inst Allergy & Infectious Dis, NIH, 92; lectr, Citizen Ambassador Prog, 93. *Mem:* Soc Toxicol; Am Col Toxicol; Am Soc Pharmacol & Exp Therapeut; Am Conf Govt Indust Hygientists; Am Col Clin Pharmacol; Int Soc Occup Med & Toxicol. *Res:* Mechanism of acrion of drug action and reaction; toxicity profile of drug toxicity; pharmacokinetics of drugs and chemicals. *Mailing Add:* Univ Med & Dent NJ-NJ Med Sch 185F5 Orange Ave Rm I0665 Newark NJ 07103-2714. *Fax:* 973-982-4554

ABDOU, HAMED M, PHARMACEUTICAL MANUFACTURING & ANALYSIS. *Current Pos:* VPRES PHARMACEUT TECH OPERS, E R SQUIBB & SON, NJ, 69- *Personal Data:* b Cairo, Egypt, Feb 2, 41; US citizen; m 70; c 1. *Educ:* Univ Cairo, BSc, 61, MSc, 66; Rutgers Univ, PhD(pharmaceut chem), 77. *Prof Exp:* Head, Qual Control Dept, El-Kahira Pharmaceut & Chem, Cairo, 67-69. *Concurrent Pos:* Adj prof, Col Pharm, Rutgers Univ, 78- *Mem:* Am Pharmaceut Asn; Am Chem Soc; Sigma Xi. *Res:* Separation sciences; hydrazine chemistry; automation in pharmaceutical analysis; dissolution kinetics and bioavailability. *Mailing Add:* 994 Stuart Rd Princeton NJ 08540-1213

ABDOU, NABIH I, MEDICINE, IMMUNOLOGY. *Current Pos:* AT CTR RHEUMATIC DIS, 89- *Personal Data:* b Cairo, Egypt, Oct 11, 34; m 67; c 2. *Educ:* Cairo Univ, MD, 59; Univ Pa, MSc, 67; McGill Univ, PhD(immunol), 69. *Prof Exp:* Form asst prof to assoc prof med, Univ Pa, 69-78; prof med, Univ Kans, 78-88. *Mem:* Am Asn Immunol; Am Acad Allergy; Transplantation Am Rheumatism Asn; Cent Soc Clin Res; Am Col Physicians. *Res:* Cellular immunology. *Mailing Add:* St Lukes Hosp Ctr Rheumatol Dis Allergy & Immunol Med Plaza II Kansas City MO 64111

ABDULLA, RIAZ FAZAL, CHEMISTRY, SUPER-COMPUTER. *Current Pos:* sr scientist, Eli Lilly & Co, 73-77, res scientist, 77-84, res assoc, 84-, mgr supercomput appln, 88-, SR INFO OFFICER, ELI LILLY & CO. *Personal Data:* b Calcutta, India, Mar 24, 43; US citizen; m 68; c 2. *Educ:* Calcutta Univ, BS, 65; Indian Inst Technol, MS, 66, PhD(chem), 70. *Prof Exp:* Vis Damon Runyon res fel chem, Princeton Univ, 71-73. *Mem:* Fel Am Inst Chemists; Am Chem Soc. *Res:* Synthesis and design of herbicides and plant bioregulators; synthesis of new heterocyclic compounds. *Mailing Add:* Lilly Corp Ctr Drop Code 1513 Indianapolis IN 46285

ABDULLAH, MUNIR, CELLULAR & MOLECULAR PHARMACOLOGY. *Current Pos:* SR STAFF FEL, LAB CELLULAR & MOLECULAR PHARMACOL, NAT INST ENVIRON HEALTH SCI, 90- *Educ:* Univ Karachi, Pakistan, MS, 74; Queen's Univ Belfast, PhD(biochem), 84. *Prof Exp:* Postdoctoral fel, Dept Biochem & Oncol, Queen's Univ Belfast, 84 & Dept Cell Biol & Anat, Univ NC, Chapel Hill, 84-87; res assoc, Dept Cell Biol & Anat, Univ NC, 87-90. *Mem:* Fedn Am Socs Exp Biol. *Res:* Author of 18 technical publications. *Mailing Add:* Dept Regulatory Affairs Glaxo Res Inst 5 Moore Dr Research Triangle Park NC 27709

ABDULRAHMAN, MUSTAFA SALIH, CIVIL ENGINEERING, THEORETICAL MECHANICS. *Current Pos:* asst prof, 65-70, ASSOC PROF CIVIL ENG, UNIV MISS, 70- *Personal Data:* b Sulaimaniah, Iraq, June 15, 30. *Educ:* Univ Baghdad, BS, 52; Rutgers Univ, MS, 58; Iowa State Univ, PhD(civil eng), 64. *Prof Exp:* Chief engr admin, Univ Baghdad, 64-65. *Concurrent Pos:* Dir, Abdulrahman & Assoc, & Consult Engrs & Land Surveyors, Oxford, Miss. *Res:* Effect of ions in solution on the permeability of filter aids; computer applied matrix methods of structural analysis. *Mailing Add:* 2204 Church St Oxford MS 38655. *Fax:* 601-232-7191

ABE, RYO, IMMUNOLOGY. *Current Pos:* vis fel, 85-88, vis assoc, 88-89, INVESTR, EXP IMMUNOL BR, DCBD, NAT CANCER INST, NIH, 89- *Personal Data:* b Tokyo, Japan, Dec, 24, 51; c 2. *Educ:* Teikyo Univ, MD, 78; Univ Tokyo, DrMedSci, 83. *Prof Exp:* Physician, Kawakita Gen Hosp, 78-79; asst prof, Dept Immunol, Fac Med, Univ Tokyo, 83-85. *Mem:* Japanese Soc Immunol; Am Asn Immunologists. *Res:* Author or co-author of over 40 publications. *Mailing Add:* Immunol Cell Bio Prog Code 0613 Naval Med Res Inst 8901 Wisconsin Ave Bldg 1 Rm 163 Bethesda MD 20889-5607. *Fax:* 301-295-6857

ABED, EYAD HUSNI, NON-LINEAR CONTROL SYSTEMS, AEROSPACE CONTROL SYSTEMS. *Current Pos:* asst prof, 83-87, ASSOC PROF ELEC ENG, UNIV MD, COL PARK, 87- *Personal Data:* b Jordan, Jan 24, 59; US citizen; m 82; c 3. *Educ:* Mass Inst Technol, SB, 79; Univ Calif, Berkeley, MS, 81, PhD(elec eng), 82. *Prof Exp:* Res asst elec eng, Univ Calif, Berkeley, 80-82. *Concurrent Pos:* Consult, Naval Res Lab, 86-, Gen Elec Co, 87-, BDM Int, 88-; pres young investr award, NSF, 87; assoc ed, Inst Elec & Electronics Engrs Trans Automatic Control, 90- *Mem:* Inst Elec & Electronics Engrs; Soc Indust & Appl Math; Am Inst Aeronaut & Astronaut. *Res:* Theory and application of non-linear control systems; bifurcation analysis, singular perturbations, robust stability, power system dynamics; advanced aircraft control, radar systems, satellite control and jet engine dynamics and control. *Mailing Add:* Elec Eng Dept Univ Md College Park MD 20742

ABEDI, FARROKH, PROGRAMMING. *Current Pos:* ASSOC PROF MATH, UNIV ARK, MONTICELLO, 82- *Personal Data:* b Tehran, Iran, Aug 20, 49. *Educ:* Okla State Univ, PhD(math), 83. *Mem:* Am Math Asn. *Mailing Add:* Dept Math & Sci Univ Ark PO Box 3469 Monticello AR 71656

ABEGG, CARL F(RANK), SCIENCE EDUCATION. *Current Pos:* PROF CHEM ENG, ROSE HULMAN INST TECHNOL, 84- *Personal Data:* b Peoria, Ill, June 5, 39; m 64; c 2. *Educ:* Univ Ill, BS, 62; Iowa State Univ, MS, 63, PhD(chem eng), 66. *Prof Exp:* Asst prof chem eng, Univ Cincinnati, 66-73; proj engr, Corning Glass Works, 73-76; mgr eng res, O M Scott & Sons, 76-84. *Concurrent Pos:* Consult, Eli Lilly & Co, 85-, Stauffer Chem Co, 85-86, LESCO Inc, 86. *Mem:* Am Inst Chem Engrs; Am Chem Soc. *Res:* Crystallization from solution; controlled release nitrogen fertilizer technology; chemical reaction engineering. *Mailing Add:* Rose Hulman Inst Technol Box 50 5500 Wabash Ave Terre Haute IN 47803-3999

ABEGG, VICTOR PAUL, ORGANIC CHEMISTRY, HISTORY OF SCIENCE. *Current Pos:* asst prof, 76-80, ASSOC PROF CHEM, CALIF STATE POLYTECH UNIV, POMONA, 80-, ASSOC DEAN, COL SCI, 85- *Personal Data:* b Torrance, Calif, Feb 14, 45. *Educ:* Loyola Univ Chicago, AB, 67; Mass Inst Technol, PhD(chem), 70; Univ Toronto, MDiv, 73. *Prof Exp:* Teaching fel, 74-75, sessional lectr chem, York Univ, 75-76. *Mem:* AAAS; Am Chem Soc. *Res:* An examination of new synthetic pathways to small-ring carbon compounds is continuing with emphasis on photochemical methods; syntheses leading to steroids and chrysenes are being tested; subsequently subjected to strong-acid-catalyzed rearrangement and product amidine sensitivity to oxidation; ethics. *Mailing Add:* Deans Off Col Sci Calif State Polytech Univ 3801 W Temple Ave Pomona CA 91768

ABEL, ALAN WILSON, PHYSICAL CHEMISTRY. *Current Pos:* RETIRED. *Personal Data:* b Wilkinsburg, Pa, Mar 7, 39. *Educ:* Univ Pittsburgh, BS, 61, PhD(chem), 67. *Prof Exp:* Asst ed, Chem Abstr Serv, 67-69, assoc indexer, 69-70, sr assoc ed, 70-87, sr ed Phys-Inorg-Anal Dept, 87-94. *Mem:* Am Chem Soc. *Res:* Indexing of chemical literature; magnetic properties of metals, alloys and intermetallic compounds; gas-metal reactions. *Mailing Add:* 3015 Stadium Dr Apt 2 Columbus OH 43202

ABEL, CARLOS ALBERTO, IMMUNOCHEMISTRY, LECTINS. *Current Pos:* CONSULT BIOTECHNOL, 92- *Personal Data:* b Buenos Aires, Arg, May 7, 30; US citizen; m 59, Amalia Minieri. *Educ:* M Belgrano Col, Arg, BS, 49; Univ Buenos Aires, Arg, MD, 57. *Prof Exp:* Physician, Pediat Sect, Childrens Hosp, Buenos Aires, 57-59; intern, St Joseph's Hosp, Providence, RI, 59-60; fel pediat, Univ Md Hosp, Baltimore, 60-64, resident, 64-66; res fel immunol, Scripps Clin, La Jolla, Calif, 66-69; vis scientist, Univ Oxford, Eng, 69-70; from asst prof to assoc prof biophys & genetics, Univ Colo Med Ctr, 70-84, assoc prof med, 79-84; sr scientist, GBCRI, Med Res Inst, San Francisco, 84-92. *Concurrent Pos:* Fel, Arthritis Found, NY & Wellcome Trust, Eng, 69; mem, Immunol Sect, Nat Jewish Hosp, Denver, Colo, 70-84; vis scholar immunol, Dept Microbiol, Univ Calif, Berkeley, 82. *Mem:* Am Asn Immunologists; Am Soc Path; Latin Am Soc Immunol; Arg Asn Immunologists; AAAS. *Res:* Isolation, purification and characterization of oligosaccharide moieties from glycoproteins and relationships of the structures of these components with various immunological functions; biology of HIV infection. *Mailing Add:* 523 Cragmont Ave Berkeley CA 94708

ABEL, ERNEST LAWRENCE, TERATOLOGY, TOXICOLOGY. *Current Pos:* prof psychol, obstet & gynecol & dir oper, 85-89, DIR, MOTT CTR HUMAN GROWTH & DEVELOP, WAYNE STATE UNIV, 89- *Personal Data:* b Toronto, Ont, Feb 10, 43; m 71, Barbara Buckley; c Jason & Rebecca. *Educ:* Univ Toronto, BA, 65, MA, 67, PhD(psychol), 71. *Honors & Awards:* Henry Rosett Award fetal Alcohol Res, 95. *Prof Exp:* Actg dep dir, Res Inst Alcoholism, NY State Dept Ment Hyg, 84-85. *Concurrent Pos:* Pres, Behav Teratal Soc, 84-85; pres, Fetal Alcohol Study Group, Res Soc Alcohol, 85-86. *Mem:* Behav Teratology Soc (pres, 84-85); fel Sigma Xi. *Res:* Consequences of exposure to alcohol/drugs during pregnancy. *Mailing Add:* Mott Ctr Human Growth & Develop 275 E Hancock Detroit MI 48201

ABEL, FRANCIS LEE, CARDIOVASCULAR PHYSIOLOGY. *Current Pos:* chmn, Dept Physiol & Pharmacol, 75-78, interim dean, 76, CHMN & PROF PHYSIOL, SCH MED, UNIV SC, 75- *Personal Data:* b Iowa City, Iowa, Apr 12, 31; m 74, Anne Sutherland; c Wanda, Donna, Carolyn & Jonathan. *Educ:* Univ Kans, BA, 52; Harvard Med Sch, MD, 57; Univ Wis, PhD(physiol), 60. *Prof Exp:* Intern pediat, Children's Hosp, Los Angeles, 60-61; res instr, Univ Wash, 61-62; from asst prof to prof physiol, Sch Med, Ind Univ, Indianapolis, 62-75. *Concurrent Pos:* USPHS trainee physiol, Univ Wis, 59-60; vis prof, Ind Univ-USAID at Jinnah Postgrad Med Ctr, Karachi, 64-65, Univ Calif, 70 & Simon Fraser, Vancouver, BC, 82, Univ Limburg, Meastricht, Neth, 89-90; NIH career develop award, 68-73, Nat Res Serv Award, 89-90. *Mem:* Biomed Eng Soc; Inst Elec & Electronics Engrs; Am Physiol Soc; Am Heart Asn; Shock Soc. *Res:* Cardiovascular physiology; biophysical instrumentation; blood flow studies; reactions to hemorrhage; electro-magnetic flowmeters; shock; venous return; arterial pressure; regulation; cardiac function; coronary blood flow. *Mailing Add:* Dept Physiol Sch Med Univ SC Columbia SC 29208. *Fax:* 803-733-1523; *E-Mail:* abel@dcsmserver.med.scarolina.edu

ABEL, HAROLD, EDUCATION ADMINISTRATION. *Current Pos:* pres, 93-95, CHANCELLOR, GRAD SCH AM, MINNEAPOLIS, MINN, 95- *Personal Data:* b New York, NY, July 31, 26; m 49, Iris Tash; c Lawrence William & Matthew Robert. *Educ:* Syracuse Univ, AB, 49, MA, 51, PhD, 58. *Hon Degrees:* DLitt, Hanyang Univ, Repub Korea, 79. *Prof Exp:* Teacher ment retarded, Syracuse & Rochester, NY, 50-52; asst instr, Syracuse Univ, 52-56; from assoc prof to prof, Depts Psychol & Home Econs, dir, Child Develop Lab, Univ Nebr, 56-65, chmn, Dept Human Develop, 63-65; prof educ & dir, Div Psychol-Educ Studies, Univ Ore, 65-68, assoc dean & prof, Educ Psychol, Col Educ, 68-70; pres, Castleton State Col, 70-75; pres, Cent Mich Univ, 75-85, prof, Psychol & Educ Admin, 85-93; pres, Walden Univ, Minneapolis, Minn, 88-91. *Mem:* AAAS; Am Psychol Asn; Sigma Xi; Soc Res Child Develop. *Mailing Add:* 1150 Hennepin Ave Apt 1803 Minneapolis MN 55403-1721

ABEL, JOHN FREDRICK, CIVIL & STRUCTURAL ENGINEERING. *Current Pos:* from asst prof to assoc prof, 74-82, PROF CIVIL ENG, CORNELL UNIV, 82- *Personal Data:* b Brooklyn, NY, Oct 24, 40; m 64; c 2. *Educ:* Cornell Univ, BCE, 63; Stanford Univ, MS, 64; Univ Calif, Berkeley, PhD(civil eng), 68. *Prof Exp:* Res assoc civil eng, Princeton Univ, 70-74, lectr archit, 73-74. *Concurrent Pos:* Prin, 3D-Eye Inc, Ithaca, 81. *Mem:* Am Soc Civil Engrs; Int Asn Bridge & Struct Engrs; Am Concrete Inst; Int Assoc Shell & Spatial Structures. *Res:* Numerical methods in structural engineering, structural mechanics and civil engineering; computer graphics and computer-aided design in civil engineering; behavior and analysis of large frames and shells; structural dynamics and earthquake engineering. *Mailing Add:* Dept Civil Eng Hollister Hall Cornell Univ Ithaca NY 14853

ABEL, JOHN H, JR, CELL BIOLOGY. *Current Pos:* PROF & HEAD DEPT ZOOL, UNIV TENN, 80- *Personal Data:* b Painesville, Ohio, Feb 25,37; m 58; c 3. *Educ:* Col Wooster, BA, 59; Brown Univ, MA, 64; PhD(cell biol), 66. *Honors & Awards:* Sr US Scientist Award for Res & Teaching, Alexander von Humboldt Stiftung, Fed Repub Ger, 73. *Prof Exp:* Chmn dept high sch, Ohio, 59-61; teacher high sch, Ill, 61-62; instr cell biol, NY Med Col, 66-67; from asst prof to prof cell biol, Colo State Univ, 67-80. *Concurrent Pos:* Consult, Ciba Chem & Dye Co, 66-68; ed consult, McGraw-Hill Bk Co, 66-; guest prof, Univ Bonn, Fed Repub Ger, 74-75. *Mem:* Am Soc Cell Biol; Am Asn Anatomists; NY Acad Sci; Soc Study Reproduction & Fertil; AAAS. *Res:* Endocrine and neuroendocrine control of ovarian and adrenal function; osmoregulation in euryhaline birds. *Mailing Add:* Dept Biol Lehigh Univ 27 Memorial Dr W Bethlehem PA 18015-3044

ABEL, LARRY ALLEN, BIOENGINEERING, ELECTRICAL ENGINEERING. *Current Pos:* STAFF MEM, SCH ORTHOPTICS, LATROBE UNIV, 96- *Personal Data:* b Pittsburgh, Pa, Dec 21, 49. *Educ:* Carnegie-Mellon Univ, BS, 71, MS, 72, PhD(elec eng, bioeng), 76. *Prof Exp:* Res assoc neurol, Sch Med, Univ Pittsburgh, 78-80; asst prof, Univ Hosp, Case-Western Res Univ, 80-86; assoc prof biomed eng, Univ Akron, 86-90; assoc prof ophthal, Ind Univ, Indianapolis, 90-96. *Concurrent Pos:* Res fel, Bascom Palmer Eye Inst, Sch Med, Univ Miami, 76-78. *Mem:* Asn Res Vision & Ophthal; Inst Elec & Electronics Engrs. *Res:* Ocular motility; visual perception; electrophysiology; neural control systems. *Mailing Add:* Sch Orthoptics Fac Health Sci Latrobe Univ Bundoora Victoria 3083 Australia. *Fax:* 61 3-9479-3692; *E-Mail:* l.abel@latrobe.edu.au

ABEL, PETER WILLIAM, VASCULAR SMOOTH MUSCLE, ELECTROPHYSIOLOGY. *Current Pos:* ASSOC PROF DEPT PHARMACOL, CREIGHTON UNIV, 88- *Personal Data:* b Milwaukee, Wis, June 23, 49; m 73; c 2. *Educ:* Univ Wis-Madison, BS, 73; WVa Univ, PhD(pharmacol), 78. *Prof Exp:* Fel pharmacol, Univ Iowa, 78-80, res scientist, Div Neurosurg, 81; asst prof pharmacol, Emory Univ, 82-87. *Res:* Factors which regulate the sensitivity of cardiac and smooth muscle to drugs; correlation of electrophysiological changes in muscle cells with altered sensitivity; role of altered vascular sensitivity in hypertension and cerebrovasospasm; adrenergic receptors and neuropeptides in smooth muscle. *Mailing Add:* Dept Pharmacol Creighton Univ Sch Med 2500 California Plaza Omaha NE 68178-0225

ABEL, ROBERT BERGER, MANAGEMENT OF INTERNATIONAL PROGRAMS IN OCEAN SCIENCE & ENGINEERING, COORDINATION OF REGIONAL & INTERNATIONAL ACTIVITIES IN BEACH PROTECTION-MARICULTURE & AIR-SEA ENERGY EXCHANGE. *Current Pos:* asst vpres, 77-80, prof marine resources mgt, 77-78, RES PROF, TEX A&M UNIV, 93-; SR SCIENTIST, STEVENS INST TECHNOL, 93- *Personal Data:* b Providence, RI, July 21, 26; m 54, Nancy Klein; c Alan & Deborah (Glazer). *Educ:* Brown Univ, BS, 47; George Washington Univ, MEA, 62; Am Univ, PhD(polit sci), 72. *Honors & Awards:* Compass Award, Marine Technol Soc, 87; Distinguished Serv Award, Egyptian Nat Inst Oceanog & Fisheries, 90. *Prof Exp:* Chem oceanogr, Woods Hole Oceanog Inst, 47-50; dir, Oceanog Surv Br, US Naval Hydrographic Off, 50-55, asst to dir, 55-60; asst res coord, Off Naval Res, 60-67; dir, Nat Sea Grant Prog, US Dept Com, Nat Oceanog & Atmospheric Admin, 70-77. *Concurrent Pos:* Instr oceanog, Naval Res Officers Sch, 60-66;

exec secy, Interagency Comt Oceanog, 60-67; adj prof oceanog, Fairleigh Dickinson Univ, 67-81; adj instr ocean law & policy, Univ Va, 75-77; dir, Ctr Ocean Policy & Law, 75-; pres, NJ Marine Sci Consortium, 80-93; dir, Coop Marine Technol Prog Mid East, 79-, mgr, 80-; adj prof ocean mgt, Rutgers Univ, 80-85. *Mem:* Marine Technol Soc (pres, 73-74); Ctr Ocean Policy & Law; NY Acad Sci. *Mailing Add:* 55 Queen Anne Dr Shrewsbury NJ 07702. *Fax:* 201-216-8214; *E-Mail:* babel@sitvastevens-tech.edu

ABEL, WILLIAM T, FUEL SCIENCE, PHYSICAL CHEMISTRY. *Current Pos:* RETIRED. *Personal Data:* b Marion, Ind, Feb 16, 22; m 49, Marguerite Emerson; c William F, Richard E, Kathleen (McLaughlin) & Gary S. *Educ:* Franklin Col, BA, 44; Univ Ill, Urbana, MS, 47. *Prof Exp:* Res asst chem, Ill Geol Surv, 44-47; res asst, Mound Lab, Ohio, 47-53; chemist, Dowell Inc, Okla, 53-56; chemist, Elec Auto-Lite Co, 56-58; supvy chemist, US Bur Mines, 58-60, chem res engr, 60-74; chem engr, Energy Res Develop Admin, Dept Energy, 74-78, chem engr, 78-83. *Concurrent Pos:* Chem engr, Resource Technol Group, Inc, WVa, 86-88. *Mem:* AAAS; Am Chem Soc. *Res:* Corrosion inhibition; gas-solid reaction; dry processes for removal of pyrite from coal; coal liquefaction; fluidized bed combustion. *Mailing Add:* 564 Killarney Dr Morgantown WV 26505

ABELE, LAWRENCE GORDON, ECOLOGY, SYSTEMATICS. *Current Pos:* asst prof, Int Progs, 73-74, from asst prof to prof, Dept Biol Sci, 74-91, dean, Col Arts & Sci, 91-94, PROVOST & VPRES, ACAD AFFAIRS, FLA STATE UNIV, 94- *Personal Data:* b Baltimore, Md, Mar 01, 46; m 66; c 2. *Educ:* Fla State Univ, BS, 68, MS, 70; Univ Miami, PhD(biol), 72. *Prof Exp:* Fel trop biol, Smithsonian Trop Res Inst, 72-73. *Mem:* Crustacean Soc; Soc Syst Zool; fel AAAS. *Res:* Systematics ecology and systematics of decapod crustaceans; community ecology; island biogeography; quantitative morphology of invertebrates. *Mailing Add:* Provost & Vpres Acad Affairs Fla State Univ 212 Westcott Tallahassee FL 32306-3020

ABELES, BENJAMIN, SOLID STATE PHYSICS. *Current Pos:* MEM STAFF, EXXON RES & ENG CO, 77- *Personal Data:* b; m 58; c 1. *Educ:* Prague Univ, MS, 49; Hebrew Univ, Israel, PhD, 56. *Honors & Awards:* Franklin Inst Medal. *Prof Exp:* Res tech, Meteorol Serv, Israel, 49-51; researcher, Weizmann Inst, Israel, 51-56 & Radio Corp Am, 56-77. *Mem:* Fel Am Phys Soc. *Res:* Solar cells; plasma chemistry. *Mailing Add:* Exxon Res & Eng Co Annandale NJ 08801. *Fax:* 908-730-3042

ABELES, FRANCINE, COMPUTER INFORMATION & OPERATING SYSTEMS. *Current Pos:* from asst prof to assoc prof, 64-72, PROF MATH, KEAN COL NJ, 72-, HEAD GRAD PROG MATH & COMPUT SCI, 74- *Personal Data:* b New York, NY, Oct 19, 35; m 57; c 3. *Educ:* Barnard Col, Columbia Univ, AB, 57; Columbia Univ, MA, 59, EdD(math), 64; Stevens Inst of Technol, MS, 86. *Prof Exp:* Teacher high schs, NY & Ger, 57-63. *Concurrent Pos:* Vis mem, Courant Inst Math Sci, NY Univ, 76-77; ed, Math Pamphlets Lewis Carroll, Univ Va Press, 87-; referee, Math Mag; res grant, Am Philos Soc, 91; rev ed, Modern Logic, 91- *Mem:* Am Math Soc; Math Asn Am; Lewis Carroll Soc (treas, 90-); Can Soc Hist & Philos of Math; Asn Symbolic Logic; Asn Comput Mach. *Res:* Geometry; Lewis Carroll; 19th century mathematics; databases; ciphers; linear algebra; logic. *Mailing Add:* Kean Col NJ Morris Ave Union NJ 07083-7131

ABELES, JOSEPH HY, OPTICAL SEMICONDUCTOR DEVICES,. *Current Pos:* MECH TECH STAFF, BELL COMMUN RES, 82- *Personal Data:* b Brooklyn, NY, Apr 14, 55. *Educ:* Mass Inst Technol, BS, 76; Princeton Univ, PhD(physics), 82. *Mem:* Am Phys Soc; Inst Elec & Electronic Engrs. *Mailing Add:* David Sarnoff Res Ctr 201 Washington Rd Princeton NJ 08543

ABELES, ROBERT HEINZ, BIOCHEMISTRY. *Current Pos:* assoc prof, 64-67, chmn, Grad Dept, 73-88, PROF BIOCHEM, BRANDEIS UNIV, 67- *Personal Data:* b Vienna, Austria, Jan 14, 26; nat US; m 48; c 2. *Educ:* Univ Chicago, MS, 50; Univ Colo, PhD(biochem), 55. *Hon Degrees:* DSc, Univ Chicago. *Honors & Awards:* Steenbock Lectr, 84; Edward E Smissman-Bristol Myers Award Med Chem, 87; Repligen Award Biol Chem, 88; Alfred E Bader Award, 90; Rose Award, 94. *Prof Exp:* Asst, Dept Pediat, Univ Chicago, 50-51; fel, Nat Found Infantile Paralysis, 55-56; fel chem, Harvard Univ, 56-57; asst prof chem, Ohio State Univ, 57-60; from asst prof to assoc prof biochem, Univ Mich, 60-64. *Concurrent Pos:* Ed, J Biol Chem, Am Soc Biol Chem, 67-72; mem coun, Am Cancer Soc, 77; Shen vis prof, Mass Inst Technol, 83; Burroughs Welcome prof, 83. *Mem:* Nat Acad Sci; Am Chem Soc; Am Soc Biol Chem; Am Acad Arts & Sci; Fedn Am Soc Exp Biol. *Res:* Mechanism of enzyme action; biological oxidations. *Mailing Add:* Dept Biochem Brandeis Univ Waltham MA 02254

ABELES, RONALD P, SOCIAL PSYCHOLOGY. *Current Pos:* dep assoc dir behav & social res, 80-91, actg dir, 91-94, ASSOC DIR, NAT INST AGING, NIH, 94- *Personal Data:* b New York, NY, Dec 12, 44. *Educ:* Univ Calif, Los Angeles, BA, 66; Harvard Univ, MA, 68, PhD(social psychol), 71. *Prof Exp:* Postdoctoral fel polit sci & psychol, Yale Univ, 71-72; assoc prof psychol, Dept Psychol, Boston Univ, 72-74; staff assoc soc sci, Res Coun NY, 74-78; res scientist, Am Inst Res Behav Sci, 78-80. *Concurrent Pos:* Ed, Am Sociol Newslett, 80-; secy & treas, Sect Aging, Am Sociol Asn, 81-91; vis scientist, Max Planck Inst Educ & Human Develop, 87; secy, Div Adult Develop & Aging, Am Psychol Asn, 94-96. *Mem:* Fel Am Psychol Asn; Am Sociol Asn; Geront Soc Am; Soc Behav Med. *Mailing Add:* Nat Inst Aging NIH Gateway Bldg Suite 533 7201 Wisconsin Ave MSC 9205 Bethesda MD 20892-9205. *Fax:* 301-402-0051; *E-Mail:* ronald_abele@nih.gov

ABELES, TOM P, APPLICATIONS OF COMPLEX DYNAMICS TO PLANNING & MANAGEMENT, SUSTAINABLE AGRICULTURE & ENVIRONMENTAL ISSUES. *Current Pos:* PRES, SAGACITY, INC, 76- *Personal Data:* B Louisville, Ky, Feb 25, 41; m 80, Ruth E Brink; c Christopher & Katrina V. *Educ:* Wilmington Col, Ohio, BS, 63; Univ Louisville, PhD(chem), 69. *Prof Exp:* Fel chem, Va Polytech Inst & State Univ, 68-70; assoc prof environ sci, Univ Wis, Green Bay, 70-76. *Concurrent Pos:* Community fac, Metropolitan State Univ. *Mem:* Sigma Xi. *Res:* Application of complex dynamics to futures-forecasting, sustainable agriculture, environment and business management; application of chemistry and environmental sciences to sustainable agriculture and environmental issues; construction of virtual conference centers on the internet. *Mailing Add:* Sagacity Inc 3704 11th Ave S Minneapolis MN 55407. *Fax:* 612-825-6865; *E-Mail:* tabeles@tmn.com

ABELEV, GARRI IZRAILEVICH, IMMUNOCHEMISTRY, CANCER IMMUNOLOGY. *Current Pos:* HEAD LAB CANCER IMMUNOCHEM, CANCER RES CTR USSR, ACAD MED SCI, 77- *Personal Data:* b Moscow, USSR, Jan 10, 28; m 49; c 2. *Educ:* Moscow State Univ, dipl biol, 50; Acad Med Sci, PhD(biochem), 55, DSc, 63. *Honors & Awards:* USSR State Award, 78; Abbot Award, 91. *Prof Exp:* Sr technician biochem cancer, NF Gamaleya Inst Epidemiol & Microbiol, USSR Acad Med Sci, 50-55, jr res worker, 55-59, sr res worker, 59-61, head lab cancer immunochem, 61, head lab dept cancer virol & immunol, 66-77. *Concurrent Pos:* Lectr immunochem, Moscow State Univ, 64-; prin investr, Coop Ref Ctr, WHO, 66-85; mem, comt tumor immunodiag, Int Union Against Cancer, adv bd develop biol, USSR Acad Med Sci, 75-, adv bd malignant tumors, 80- *Mem:* USSR Asn Immunologist; hon mem Am Asn Immunologists; Int Soc Oncodevelop Biol & Med; corresp mem USSR Acad Sci; hon mem Europ Asn Cancer Res. *Res:* Cancer immunology and immunodiagnosis; carcino-embryonic proteins, their finding, characterization and use in cancer diagnosis; antigenic structure of virus-induced experimental leukoses; development of new techniques of protein immunochemistry. *Mailing Add:* Cancer Res Ctr Kashirskoye Shosse 24 Moscow 115478 Russia

ABELING, EDWIN JOHN, FOOD SCIENCE & TECHNOLOGY. *Current Pos:* RETIRED. *Personal Data:* b Amsterdam, NY, Oct 4, 15; m 45, Polly Eldridge; c Michael, Steven & Jeffrey. *Educ:* Univ Ky, BS, 44. *Prof Exp:* Med technologist, Montgomery County Lab, NY, 39-41, St Joseph's Hosp, Lexington, Ky, 41-44; bacteriologist, Beech-Nut Packing Co, NY, 44-47, head, San Jose Lab, Calif, 47-50, food lab, Canajoharie, NY, 50-54, assoc dir res, Beech-Nut Life Savers, 54-57, dir res & develop, Quality Control, 57-61; dir, Peter Paul, Inc, 61-68, vpres, res & develop, 68-81. *Concurrent Pos:* Mem, Exec Prog Bus Admin, Grad Sch Bus, Columbia Univ, 60. *Mem:* Inst Food Technologists. *Res:* Development of new products; food, packaging and market research; quality control; bacteriology. *Mailing Add:* 162 Ansonia Rd Woodbridge CT 06525

ABELL, CREED WILLS, BIOCHEMISTRY, ONCOLOGY. *Current Pos:* PROF HUMAN BIOL CHEM & GENETICS, UNIV TEX MED BR, GALVESTON, 72-, DIR, DIV BIOCHEM, 78- *Personal Data:* b Charlottesville, Va, July 8, 34; m 56; c 2. *Educ:* Va Mil Inst, BS, 56; Purdue Univ, MS, 58; Univ Wis, PhD(oncol), 62. *Prof Exp:* Chemist, Chem Sect, Carcinogenesis Studies Br, Nat Cancer Inst, 62-67; from assoc prof to prof biochem & molecular biol, Sch Med, Univ Okla, 67-72. *Mem:* Am Asn Cancer Res; Am Soc Biol Chemists; Sigma Xi; AAAS; NY Acad Sci. *Res:* Regulation of division of normal and leukemic lymphocytes, enzyme therapy of neoplasia biosynthesis and degradation of neurotransmitters. *Mailing Add:* Col Pharm Div Med Chem PHR 2222 Univ Tex Austin TX 78712-1074

ABELL, JARED, ORGANIC CHEMISTRY. *Current Pos:* RETIRED. *Personal Data:* b Los Angeles, Calif, Sept 5, 28; m 50; c 3. *Educ:* Calif Inst Technol, BS, 50; Univ Calif, Los Angeles, PhD(org chem), 54. *Prof Exp:* Sr res chemist, Chevron Res Co, 54-66; res chemist, Ortho Div, Chevron Chem Co, 66-68, mgr prod res & serv, Div Res & Develop, 68-83, supt, residue metab & environ fate of pesticides, 83-86. *Mem:* Am Chem Soc. *Res:* Formulation, residue, metabolism, environmental fate of pesticides and agricultural chemicals in general. *Mailing Add:* 517 Allegheny Dr Walnut Creek CA 94598

ABELL, LIESE LEWIS, BIOCHEMISTRY. *Current Pos:* RETIRED. *Personal Data:* b Frankfurt, Ger, Aug 17, 09; nat US. *Educ:* Univ Frankfurt, PhD, 35. *Prof Exp:* Chemist, Flower & Fifth Ave Hosp, New York Med Col, 40-42; chemist, Wyeth Inst Appl Biochem, Pa, 45-47; asst prof biochem, Columbia Univ, 47-68; sr res scientist, Bur Labs, Pub Health Labs, New York City Dept Health, 68-74; asst to ed, J Lipid Res, 75-78; coordr clin trial, Med Sch, Cornell Univ, 79-81. *Concurrent Pos:* Res fel, Columbia Univ, 38-40 & 42-45. *Mem:* AAAS; Am Soc Biol Chemists. *Res:* Lipid metabolism in connection with arteriosclerosis. *Mailing Add:* 7 Peter Cooper Rd New York NY 10010-6601

ABELL, MURRAY RICHARDSON, MEDICINE, PATHOLOGY. *Current Pos:* EXEC DIR, AM BD PATH. *Personal Data:* b Aylmer, Ont, Oct 14, 20; nat US; m 44; c 4. *Educ:* Univ Western Ont, MD, 44, PhD(path), 51; Am Bd Path, dipl; FRCPS(C). *Prof Exp:* From instr to assoc prof, Univ Mich, Ann Arbor, 52-59, prof path, 59- *Concurrent Pos:* Trustee, Am Bd Path. *Mem:* Am Asn Pathologists; Col Am Pathologists; Int Acad Path; Am Soc Clin Path. *Res:* Hepatic disease; mediastinal tumors; neoplasms of female reproductive tract; antigen-antibody reactions in tissues; testicular neoplasms. *Mailing Add:* Lincoln Ctr 3601 Hudson Tampa FL 33622

ABELL, PAUL IRVING, ORGANIC CHEMISTRY, GEOCHEMISTRY. *Current Pos:* From instr to assoc prof, 51-64, PROF ORG CHEM, UNIV RI, 64- *Personal Data:* b Pelham, Mass, July 24, 23; m 51, 80; c Susan E, Erin G & Octavia. *Educ:* Univ NH, BS, 48; Univ Wis, PhD(chem), 51. *Concurrent Pos:* Petrol Res Fund Int Award, Univ Wales, 60-61 & Univ Bristol, 69-70; Fulbright lectr, UAR, 65-66; mem, Omo River Res Exped, 67 & Lake Rudolf Res Expeds, 68-74. *Mem:* Am Chem Soc; Geochem Soc; Brit Chem Soc; Faraday Soc; Sigma Xi. *Res:* Stereochemistry and kinetics of free radical reactions; organic geochemistry; paleontology; fate of organic pollutants in groundwater pollution. *Mailing Add:* 1236 Stony Fort Rd West Kingston RI 02892-1210. *Fax:* 401-789-8086

ABELLA, ISAAC D, EXPERIMENTAL PHYSICS, QUANTUM OPTICS. *Current Pos:* from asst prof to assoc prof, 65-86, RESIDENT MASTER, UNIV CHICAGO, 85- PROF PHYSICS, 86- *Personal Data:* b Toronto, Ont, June 20, 34; m 66; c 2. *Educ:* Univ Toronto, BA, 57; Columbia Univ, MA, 59, PhD(physics), 63. *Prof Exp:* Asst physics, Columbia Univ, 57-63, res assoc, 63-65. *Concurrent Pos:* Mem laser apparatus comt, Am Inst Physics, 65, vis scientist, 66-71; consult, Mithras, Inc, Mass, 65-70 & Sanders Assoc, NH, 70-; mem laser adv comt, Ill Dept Pub Health, 68-72; vis fel, Joint Inst Lab Astrophys, Univ Colo, Boulder, 72-73; vis scientist, Naval Res Lab, Washington, DC, 81-82; mem, US Nat Comt Int Comn Optics, 82-84; consult, Physics Div, Atgonne Nat Lab, 82-88, vis fac, 83; Am Soc Eng Educ fac scientist optical sci, Naval Res Lab, 85-89; chair, Educ Comt, Laser Sci Tech Group, Am Phys Soc, 88-90; mem, Nat Educ Comt, Am Phys Soc & Isaicson Prize Comt, Am Phys Soc, 91-93; mem, Comt Undergrad Sci Educ, Nat Acad Sci, 93- *Mem:* AAAS; fel Am Phys Soc; fel Optical Soc Am. *Res:* Experimental physics, especially non-linear optics, photon echoes, quantum beats, atomic physics and lasers; energy transfer; rare-earth materials. *Mailing Add:* 5454 South Shore Dr Chicago IL 60615. *E-Mail:* asea@midway.uchicago.edu

ABELMANN, WALTER H, MEDICINE, CARDIOLOGY. *Current Pos:* Asst, Harvard Med Sch, 51-53, instr, 53-55, assoc, 55-58, asst prof, 58-64, assoc clin prof, 64-69, from assoc prof to prof, 69-91, EMER PROF MED, HARVARD MED SCH, 91- *Personal Data:* b Frankfurt, Ger, May 16, 21; nat US; m 58, Rena White; c 5. *Educ:* Harvard Univ, AB, 43; Univ Rochester, MD, 46. *Concurrent Pos:* Res fel, Thorndike Mem Lab, Boston City Hosp, 51- & Am Heart Asn, 53-55; estab investr, Am Heart Asn, 55-60; sr physician, Beth Israel Hosp. *Mem:* AAAS; Am Fedn Clin Res; Am Heart Asn; Asn Univ Cardiol; Am Soc Clin Invest; Am Col Cardiol; Asn Am Physicians. *Res:* Cardiovascular pathophysiology. *Mailing Add:* 330 Brookline Ave Boston MA 02215. *Fax:* 617-667-4833

ABELSON, JOHN NORMAN, MOLECULAR BIOLOGY, MOLECULAR GENETICS. *Current Pos:* chmn, Div Biol, 89-95, PROF BIOL, CALIF INST TECHNOL, 82- *Personal Data:* b Grand Coulee Dam, Wash, Oct 19, 38. *Educ:* Wash State Univ, BS, 60; Johns Hopkins Univ, PhD(biophys), 65. *Prof Exp:* Fel, Lab Molecular Biol, Cambridge Univ, Eng, 65-68; from asst prof to prof chem, Univ Calif, San Diego, 68-82. *Concurrent Pos:* John Simon Guggenheim Mem Found fel, 80-81; mem, Rev Comt Biol, Univ Calif, Santa Cruz, 85 & Adv Comt Molecular Biol, Am Cancer Soc, 85-88; chmn, Sci Adv Bd, Agooron Pharmaceut, Inc, 84-; chmn, Comt to Visit Dept Biochem & Molecular Biol, Bd Overseers Harvard Col, 87-; lectr, Harvey Soc, 89. *Mem:* Nat Acad Sci; Am Soc Biol Chemists; Am Chem Soc; Am Acad Arts & Sci; Protein Soc. *Res:* Genetic control mechanisms; nucleotide sequences of DNA and RNA; RNA synthesis and post-transcriptional processing; author of numerous technical publications. *Mailing Add:* Div Biol Calif Inst Technol Mail Code 147-75 Pasadena CA 91125

ABELSON, PHILIP HAUGE, ORGANIC GEOCHEMISTRY. *Current Pos:* ed, Sci, 61-84, dep ed Sci & Scholar in Residence, Resources for Future Sci, 85-88, SCI ADV, AAAS, 85- *Personal Data:* b Tacoma, Wash, Apr 27, 13; m 36; c 1. *Educ:* Wash State Univ, BS, 33, MS, 35; Univ Calif, PhD(nuclear physics), 39. *Hon Degrees:* DSc, Yale Univ, 64, Southern Methodist Univ, 69, Tufts Univ,76, Duke Univ, 81, Univ Pittsburgh, 82; DHL, Univ Puget Sound, 68. *Honors & Awards:* Mod Med Award, 67; Kalinga Prize, UNESCO, 73; Sci Achievement Award, AMA, 74; President's Nat Medal Sci; Pub Welfare Award, Nat Acad Sci, 94; Vannevar Bush Award, NSF, 96. *Prof Exp:* Asst physics, Wash State Univ, 33-35; asst, Univ Calif, 35-38, asst, Radiation Lab, 38-39; asst physicist, Carnegie Inst, 39-41; from assoc physicist to prin physicist, Naval Res Lab, 41-45; chmn, Biophys Sect, Dept Terrestrial Magnetism, Carnegie Inst, 46-53, dir, Geophys Lab, 53-71, pres, 71-78. *Concurrent Pos:* Mem, Nat Defense Res Comt, 40-42; chmn, Radiation Cataract Comt, Nat Res Coun, 49-57; mem, Biophys & Biophys Chem Study Sect, NIH, 56-59, Phys Biol Training Grants Comt, 58-60; co-ed, J Geophys Res, 58-64; mem, Plowshare Adv Comt, AEC, 59-63, gen adv comt, 60-63; sci counr, Nat Inst Arthritis & Metab Dis, 60-63; mem coun, Nat Acad Sci, 78-81; bd dirs, Chem Indust Inst Toxicol, 85-; mem, Space Studies Bd, 87- *Mem:* Nat Acad Sci; Int Union Geol Sci (pres, 72-76); fel Am Geophys Union (pres, 72-74); fel Am Phys Soc; fel Am Acad Arts & Sci; fel Geol Soc Am; fel Mineral Soc Am; Seismol Soc Am; Am Chem Soc; Soc Am Bacteriologists; Am Asn Petrol Geol; Sigma Xi; AAAS. *Res:* Nuclear physics; radioactive tracers; fission products of uranium; characteristic x-rays emitted by radioactive substances; neptunium; separation of uranium isotopes; mechanisms of ion transport into living matter; biosynthesis in microorganisms; plasma volume expanders; petrology; paleobiochemistry; geochemistry; 400 articles and editorials published. *Mailing Add:* AAAS 1200 New York Ave NW Washington DC 20005

ABEND, KENNETH, SIGNAL PROCESSING, INFORMATION SCIENCE. *Current Pos:* DIR, ADVAN SIGNAL PROCESSING LAB, GORCA SYSTS INC, 91- *Personal Data:* b New York, NY, Jan 14, 36; m 66, Judith Segal; c Cary, Illysa, Debra & Lori. *Educ:* City Col New York, BEE, 58; Univ Pa, MSE, 63, PhD(elec eng), 66. *Honors & Awards:* Spec 50th Anniversary Commemoration Medal Award, Outstanding Young Engr, City Col New York, 69. *Prof Exp:* Elec eng trainee, Rome Air Develop Ctr, NY, 56; eng aid, Bell Aircraft Corp, 57; jr engr res lab, Philco-Ford Corp, Ford Motor Co, 58-59, engr, 59-60, sr res engr, 60-63, proj engr, 64-65, eng res specialist, 65-68, sr eng specialist, Commun & Tech Serv Div, 68-76; prin mem eng staff, missile & surface radar systs eng, RCA Govt Systs Div, 76-84; mgr, Advan Signal Processing, Interspec Inc, 84-91. *Concurrent Pos:* Inst Elec & Electronics Engrs, PR, 66; Partic pattern recognition workshop, lectr, Grad Ctr, Pa State Univ, 67-; lectr systs eng dept, Univ Pa, 72- *Mem:* Sr mem Inst Elec & Electronics Engrs; Sigma Xi. *Res:* Development and analysis of statistical techniques for communications, radar and pattern classification; adaptive sampled data detector for channels with intersymbol interference; compound decision techniques for pattern recognition using context; modern spectral estimation for radar imaging; adaptive processing for phased array radars; automatic motion compensation for synthetic apertures. *Mailing Add:* 623 Killdeer Lane Huntingdon Valley PA 19006. *E-Mail:* Knabend@gorca.com

ABENDROTH, REINHARD P(AUL), glass technology; deceased, see previous edition for last biography

ABENES, FIORELLO BIGORNIA, SWINE PRODUCTION SYSTEMS, COMPUTER APPLICATIONS IN AGRICULTURE. *Current Pos:* PROF ANIMAL SCI, CALIF STATE POLYTECH UNIV, 86- *Personal Data:* b Naguilian, La Union, Philippines, Dec 10, 46; Can citizen; m 71; c 2. *Educ:* Cent Luzon State Univ, BS, 69; Univ Conn, MS, 71, PhD(physiol), 75. *Prof Exp:* Asst prof animal sci, Univ Philippines, 75-77; swine specialist, Alta Agr, 79-84; prof animal sci, Olds Col, 84-86. *Concurrent Pos:* Prin investr, Sustainable Agr Prog, Calif State Polytech Univ, Pomona. *Mem:* Am Soc Animal Sci; Sigma Xi. *Res:* Developing ecologically responsible ways of producing foods & fiber. *Mailing Add:* Dept Animal Sci Calif State Polytech Univ 3801 W Temple Ave Pomona CA 91768-4045

ABER, JAMES SANDUSKY, GEOMORPHOLOGY, REMOTE SENSING. *Current Pos:* from asst prof, to assoc prof, 80-91, PROF GEOL, EMPORIA STATE UNIV, KANS, 91- *Personal Data:* b Kansas City, Mo, Apr 25, 52; m 77, Susan Ward; c 2. *Educ:* State Univ NY Binghamton, BS, 74; Univ Kans, MS, 76, PhD(geol), 78. *Prof Exp:* Asst prof geol, Chadron State Col, Nebr, 78-80. *Concurrent Pos:* Fulbright-Hays fel, Inst Gen Geol, Univ Copenhagen, 79; fac exchange, Univ Regina, Can, 84; Marshall Fund fel, Univ Bergen, Norway, 87; Fulbright scholar, Poland, 93. *Mem:* Geol Soc Am; Geol Soc Denmark; Sigma Xi. *Res:* Glaciation, glacial stratigraphy, glaciotectonics and Quaternary environments of central North America and northern Europe. *Mailing Add:* Dept Earth Sci Emporia State Univ 1200 Commercial St Emporia KS 66801

ABERCROMBIE, CLARENCE LEWIS, sustained-yield harvest of wildlife resources, populatio dynamics of long-lived vertebrates, for more information see previous edition

ABERCROMBIE, RONALD FORD, BIOPHYSICS, CELL PHYSIOLOGY. *Current Pos:* asst prof, 82-88, ASSOC PROF PHYSIOL, SCH MED, EMORY UNIV, 88- *Personal Data:* b Greenville, SC, June 10, 46; m 69, Janice Nale. *Educ:* Univ NC, Chapel Hill, BS, 68; Univ Md, College Park, MS, 72; Univ Md, Baltimore City, PhD(biophys), 77. *Prof Exp:* asst prof biophys, Sch Med, Univ Md, 76-80; res assoc, Dept Physiol, Sch Med, Wash Univ, 80-82. *Concurrent Pos:* Grass Found fel, 76; secy/treas, Membrain Biophys Group, Biophys Soc, 91-94. *Mem:* Biophys Soc; Am Asn Physics Teachers; NY Acad Sci; Soc Gen Physiol. *Res:* Ion transport mechanisms; active membrane transport; regulation of intracellular ionic environment; the diffusion and buffering of calcium and the interaction between calcium and hydrogen in the intracellular environment. *Mailing Add:* Dept Physiol Emory Univ Sch Med Atlanta GA 30322-0311

ABERE, JOSEPH FRANCIS, POLYMER CHEMISTRY. *Current Pos:* res chemist, Minn Mining & Mfg Co, 48-53, head, Appl Res Sect, Cent Res, 53-57, proj mgr, Chem Div, 57-62, assoc mgr tape res, 62-67, mgr pioneering res, Indust Spec Prod Dept, 67-72, tech mgr composites, 70-72, tech mgr overseas opers, 72-78, CORP SCIENTIST, MINN MINING & MFG CO, 78- *Personal Data:* b New York, NY, Mar 30, 20; m 44; c 7. *Educ:* Queens Col, NY, BS, 41; Polytech Inst Brooklyn, MS, 43, PhD(high polymers), 48. *Honors & Awards:* Best Symp, Rubber Div, Am Chem Soc, 84. *Prof Exp:* Tutor chem, Queens Col, NY, 43-44, instr, 46-47. *Mem:* AAAS; Am Chem Soc; Am Inst Chemists; Am Inst Aeronaut & Astronaut; Sigma Xi. *Res:* High polymers; fluorine containing polymers; vulcanization; adhesives and adhesion; resins; plastics; chemical development; imine chemistry; composites; reinforced plastics; irradiation chemistry; polymeric light fibers. *Mailing Add:* 3M Ctr Bldg 201-2S-05 St Paul MN 55144-1000

ABERGEL, CHANTEL, CRYSTALLOGRAPHY, BIOCHEMISTRY. *Current Pos:* RESEARCHER CRYSTALLOG & BIOCHEM RES, NIH, 90- *Personal Data:* b Marseilles, France, Dec 1, 61. *Educ:* Univ Marseilles, BS, 83, MS, 84, PhD(Sci), 90. *Mailing Add:* La Pauline 19A 1309 Marseille France. *E-Mail:* chantal@dali.chrs-mrs.fr

ABERHART, DONALD JOHN, BIOCHEMISTRY. *Current Pos:* SR STAFF CHEMIST, CAMBRIDGE ISOTOPE LABS, 92- *Personal Data:* b St John, NB, Oct 20, 41. *Educ:* Univ Western Ont, BSc, 63, PhD(org chem), 67. *Prof Exp:* NATO sci fel, Glasgow Univ, 67-68; fel, Worcester Found Exp Biol, 69-70; res assoc, Mass Inst Technol, 70-71; from asst prof to assoc prof chem, Cath Univ Am, 71-77; sr scientist, Worcester Found Exp Biol, 77-92. *Mem:* AAAS; Am Chem Soc. *Res:* Enzyme chemistry; biosynthetic studies. *Mailing Add:* Cambridge Isotope Labs 50 Frontage Rd Andover MA 01810-5413

ABERLE, ELTON D, MEAT SCIENCE, FOOD SCIENCE. *Current Pos:* PROF ANIMAL SCI & HEAD DEPT, UNIV NEBR, 83- *Personal Data:* b Sabetha, Kans, Aug 30, 40; m 65; c 2. *Educ:* Kans State Univ, BS, 62; Mich State Univ, MS, 65, PhD(food sci), 67. *Honors & Awards:* Meat Res Award, Am Soc Animal Sci, 82; Distinguished Res Award, Am Meat Sci Asn, 86. *Prof Exp:* From asst prof to prof animal sci, Purdue Univ, 67-83. *Concurrent Pos:* Mem NC-91, Tech Comt Regional Res Proj, Agr Res Serv, USDA, 68-74, NC-131, 75-83, NCA-6, 7, 8, 83-; assoc, Univ Minn, 75. *Mem:* Am Soc Animal Sci; Inst Food Tech; Am Meat Sci Asn; AAAS. *Res:* Muscle biochemistry and physiology and muscle growth and differentiation in meat animals relating to use of muscle as food; adipose tissue growth in animals; meat processing. *Mailing Add:* Univ Nebr Dept Animal Sci Univ NE East Campus PO Box 830908 Lincoln NE 68583-0908

ABERLE, SOPHIE D, nutrition; deceased, see previous edition for last biography

ABERMAN, HAROLD MARK, ANIMAL MODELS, SAFETY & EFFECTIVENESS OF ORTHOPAEDIC MATERIALS & DEVICES. *Current Pos:* DIR RES & DEVELOP, HOWMEDICA, INC, 87- *Personal Data:* b Chicago, Ill, Aug 5, 56. *Educ:* Purdue Univ, BS, 79, DVM, 83, BSE, 86, MS, 87. *Prof Exp:* Fel, NIH-Purdue Univ, 83-87. *Concurrent Pos:* Adj prof, NC State Univ, 88-, Miss State Univ, 89-, Purdue Univ, 90- *Mem:* Orthop Res Soc; Am Vet Med Asn; Soc Biomech; Am Animal Health Asn; Nat Soc Histotechnol; Acad Surg Res. *Res:* Testing new materials for safety and effectiveness as orthopaedic implants; toxicology; animal model development; biomechanics; undecalcified histology; tissue engineering. *Mailing Add:* 28 Glen Rd Ringwood NJ 07456

ABERNATHY, A(TWELL) RAY, ENVIRONMENTAL BIOLOGY, ENVIRONMENTAL CHEMISTRY. *Current Pos:* From asst prof civil eng to assoc prof environ systs eng, 62-73, PROF ENVIRON SYSTS ENG, CLEMSON UNIV, 73- *Personal Data:* b Hiddenite, NC, May 29, 30; m 55; c 2. *Educ:* Lenoir-Rhyne Col, AB, 53; Univ NC, MSPH, 59, PhD(environ sci), 63. *Honors & Awards:* Arthur Sidney Bedell Award, Water Pollution Control Fedn, 75; W T Linton Award, Water & Pollution Control Asn SC, 77. *Concurrent Pos:* Fel, Univ Wash, 67-68. *Mem:* Water Pollution Control Fedn; Am Soc Limnol & Oceanog; Sigma Xi. *Res:* Water pollution control; fate of heavy metals in wastewater discharges; nonpoint source pollution control. *Mailing Add:* Dept Environ Systs Eng Clemson Univ 501 Rhodes Ctr Clemson SC 29632-0001

ABERNATHY, BOBBY F, RESERVOIR ENGINEERING, ENHANCED RECOVERY. *Current Pos:* RETIRED. *Personal Data:* b Athens, Tex, June 25, 33; m 63, Donna J Childers; c Julie A & Scott F. *Educ:* Univ Tex Austin, BS, 55. *Honors & Awards:* Cedrick Ferguson Medal, Soc Petrol Engrs. *Prof Exp:* Engr, Amoco Prod Co, 55-68; chief engr, Amoco Can Petrol Ltd, 68-72; vpres, Am Quasar Petrol, 72-76; sr vpres explor & prod & dir, Champlin Petrol, Co, 76-81; owner, Abernathy Explor Co, 81-95. *Concurrent Pos:* Exec vpres, Quasar Petrol Co, 72-76; pres, Quasar Energy Inc, 74-76; exec comt, Independent Petrol Asn Am. *Mem:* Am Inst Mining Metall & Petrol Engrs. *Res:* Study of reservoir mechanics, fragile environment of arctic areas, ice mechanics. *Mailing Add:* 2005 Mount Royal Terr 307 W Seventh Ft Worth TX 76107

ABERNATHY, CHARLES OWEN, TOXICOLOGY. *Current Pos:* TOXICOLOGIST, OFFICE WATER, US ENVIRON PROTECTION AGENCY, WASHINGTON, DC, 83- *Personal Data:* b Brunswick, Ga, Nov 18, 41; m 72, Mella Dees. *Educ:* Asbury Col, AB, 64; Univ Ky, MS, 67; NC State Univ, PhD(physiol), 70. *Prof Exp:* Res asst entom, Univ Ky, 64-66; USPHS trainee toxicol, NC State Univ, 67-70; researcher, Univ Calif, Berkeley, 70-73; pharmacologist, Liver Res Unit, Vet Admin Hosp, Washington, DC, 73-83. *Mem:* Soc Toxicol; NY Acad Sci; Soc Exp Biol & Med; Soc Environ Geochem Health; Int Soc Study Xenobiotics. *Res:* Risk assessment of chemicals found in drinking water. *Mailing Add:* HECD (4304) Environ Protection Agency 401 M St SW Washington DC 20460-0001. *Fax:* 202-260-1036; *E-Mail:* abernathy.charles@epamail.epa.gov

ABERNATHY, FREDERICK HENRY, FLUID MECHANICS, NUCLEAR ENGINEERING. *Current Pos:* lectr eng, 59, from asst prof to assoc prof, 59-67, assoc dean eng & appl physics, 67-69, GORDON McKAY PROF MECH ENG, HARVARD UNIV, 67- *Personal Data:* b Denver, Colo, June 19, 30; m 61; c 3. *Educ:* Newark Col Eng, BS, 51; Harvard Univ, SM, 54, PhD, 59. *Prof Exp:* Develop engr, Oak Ridge Nat Lab, 52-54; asst, Los Alamos Sci Lab, 55; dir, Textile/Clothing Technol Corp, 85-87. *Concurrent Pos:* Consult, Reactor Proj Div, Oak Ridge Nat Lab, 59, Arthur D Little Co, Mass, 63-, Inst Defense Anal, 66- & NSF, 71-; NSF fel, 62-63; mem, Nat Comt Fluid Mech Films, 65-, chmn, 69-71; master South House, Harvard-Radcliffe Cols, 69-71. *Mem:* Am Soc Mech Engrs; Sigma Xi. *Res:* Incompressible wakes of bluff bodies; forced convection film boiling; nuclear reactor kinetics. *Mailing Add:* 326 Pierce Hall Harvard Univ Cambridge MA 02138

ABERNATHY, GEORGE HENRY, AGRICULTURAL ENGINEERING. *Current Pos:* RETIRED. *Personal Data:* b West Newton, Pa, Nov 9, 29; m 55; c 4. *Educ:* NMex State Univ, BS, 52; Univ Calif, ME, 56; Okla State Univ, PhD(soil tillage), 67. *Prof Exp:* Jr res specialist, Univ Calif, 55-57; from asst prof to prof agr eng, NMex State Univ, 57-87, head, Dept Agr Eng, 80-87. *Mem:* Am Soc Agr Engrs. *Res:* Mechanization of agricultural activities. *Mailing Add:* Star RR Box 30 Mesilla Park NM 88047

ABERNATHY, HENRY HERMAN, POLYMER CHEMISTRY. *Current Pos:* RETIRED. *Personal Data:* b Vidalia, Ga, Oct 7, 13; m 41; c Henry H Jr, Janet A (Robertson), Martha W (Guichard) & Ann K (Stetson). *Educ:* Emory Univ, AB, 38, MS, 39. *Prof Exp:* Analytical chemist, Jackson Lab, E I DuPont de Nemours & Co Inc, 39-40, rubber chemist, Rubber Lab, 40-52, tech mgr, Rubber Chem Div, 54-57, mgr mkt develop, Elastomer Chem Dept, 57-64, dir & mkt adv, DuPont Far East, Inc, Showa Neoprene KK, Tokyo, 64-65, mgr planning & eng, Elastomer Chem Dept, 65-78, consult, 78-81; consult, 78-81. *Mem:* Am Chem Soc. *Res:* Synthetic rubber and latices. *Mailing Add:* 402 Country Club Dr Woodbrook Wilmington DE 19803-2921

ABERNATHY, JAMES RALPH, BIOSTATISTICS. *Current Pos:* res assoc, 64-65, from asst prof to assoc prof, 65-75, PROF BIOSTATIST, UNIV NC, CHAPEL HILL, 75- *Personal Data:* b Dadeville, Ala, Jan 8, 26; m 55; c 4. *Educ:* Samford Univ, BS, 51; Univ NC, MSPH, 53, PhD(biostatist), 65. *Prof Exp:* Statistician, Jeffer Co Bd Health, Ala, 52-59; biostatistician, NC State Bd Health, 59-61. *Mem:* Fel Am Pub Health Asn; fel Am Statist Asn; Pop Asn Am. *Res:* Statistical methodology in perinatal mortality and morbidity; demography and life tables; demographic surveys in developing countries. *Mailing Add:* 110 Virginia Dr Chapel Hill NC 27514

ABERNATHY, RICHARD PAUL, NUTRITION. *Current Pos:* HEAD DEPT FOODS & NUTRIT, PURDUE UNIV, 74- *Personal Data:* b McCaysville, Ga, Mar 22, 32; m 57; c 3. *Educ:* Berry Col, BSA, 52; Univ Ga, MS, 57; Cornell Univ, PhD(animal nutrit), 60. *Prof Exp:* Asst prof & nutritionist, Ga Exp Sta, 60-66; from assoc prof to prof nutrit, Va Polytech Inst & State Univ, 66-74. *Mem:* Am Inst Nutrit; Inst Food Technol. *Res:* Metabolic studies and nutrient requirements of preadolescent children. *Mailing Add:* Dept Foods & Nutrit Purdue Univ 1264 Stone Hall West Lafayette IN 47907-1264

ABERNATHY, ROBERT O, mathematics; deceased, see previous edition for last biography

ABERNATHY, ROBERT SHIELDS, MEDICINE, MICROBIOLOGY. *Current Pos:* from asst prof to assoc prof, UNiv Ark, 57-67, head, Dept Med, 67-76, dir, Div Infectious Dis, 76-86, PROF MED & MICROBIOL, UNIV ARK, LITTLE ROCK, 67- *Personal Data:* b Gastonia, NC, Nov 18, 23; m 49; c 5. *Educ:* Duke Univ, BS & MD, 49; Univ Minn, PhD, 57. *Prof Exp:* From intern to resident med, Univ Minn, 49-54, instr med & microbiol, 55-57. *Mem:* Am Fedn Clin Res; Am Col Physicians; Infectious Dis Soc Am. *Res:* Infectious disease. *Mailing Add:* Dept Med Slot 640 Univ Ark Med Sci 230 Kingsrow Dr Little Rock AR 72205-7249

ABERNETHY, JOHN LEO, bio-organic chemistry, for more information see previous edition

ABERNETHY, VIRGINIA DEANE, POPULATION ANTHROPOLOGY. *Current Pos:* from asst prof to assoc prof, 75-80, PROF PSYCHIAT, SCH MED, VANDERBILT UNIV, 80- *Personal Data:* b Havana, Cuba, Oct 4, 34; US citizen; m 80, C Gregory Smith; c Hugh, John B, Elena K (Campbell) & Diana K (Untermeyer). *Educ:* Wellesley Col, BA, 55; Harvard Univ, MA, 68, PhD(anthrop), 70; Vanderbilt Univ, MBA, 81. *Prof Exp:* Fel social psychiat, Med Sch, Harvard Univ, 70-72, res assoc anthrop, Dept Psychiat, 72, assoc, 72-75. *Concurrent Pos:* Ed, Population & Environment. *Mem:* Am Anthrop Asn; AAAS. *Res:* Links between population and environment; economic and cultural determinants of change in fertility. *Mailing Add:* 6501 Grayson Ct Nashville TN 37205-3033. *Fax:* 615-343-8639

ABERS, ERNEST S, PHYSICS. *Current Pos:* from asst prof to assoc prof, 65-74, PROF PHYSICS, UNIV CALIF, LOS ANGELES, 74- *Personal Data:* b San Mateo, Calif, Dec 31, 36; m 60; c 1. *Educ:* Harvard Univ, AB, 58; Univ Calif, Berkeley, PhD(physics), 63. *Prof Exp:* Res fel physics, Calif Inst Technol, 63-64; vis scientist, Europ Orgn Nuclear Res, Switz, 64-65. *Concurrent Pos:* Visitor, Ctr Theoret Physics, Mass Inst Technol, 68-69; Alfred P Sloan Found fel, 68-70. *Mem:* Am Phys Soc. *Res:* Theoretical elementary particle physics. *Mailing Add:* 2211 Kelton Ave Univ Calif Los Angeles CA 90064

ABERTH, OLIVER GEORGE, MATHEMATICS. *Current Pos:* PROF MATH, TEX A&M UNIV, 70- *Personal Data:* b Akron, Ohio, July 23, 29; m 58; c 3. *Educ:* City Col New York, BS, 50; Mass Inst Technol, MS, 51; Univ Pa, PhD(math), 62. *Prof Exp:* Engr, Remington Rand Univac Div, Sperry Rand Corp, 51-53 & 56-58; instr math, Swarthmore Col, 60-62; asst prof, Univ Ill, 62-66; assoc prof, Rutgers Univ, 66-69; lectr, City Col New York, 69-70. *Mem:* Am Math Soc; Soc Indust & Appl Math. *Res:* Constructive analysis; geometry; tensor analysis; numerical analysis. *Mailing Add:* Dept of Math Tex A&M Univ College Station TX 77843

ABERTH, WILLIAM H, MASS SPECTROMETRY. *Current Pos:* RES PHYSICIST, MASS SPECTRUM FAC, UNIV CALIF, SAN FRANCISCO, 82- *Personal Data:* b Los Angeles, Calif, Jan 4, 33; m 54; c 3. *Educ:* City Col New York, BS, 54; Columbia Univ, MA, 57; NY Univ, PhD(physics), 63. *Prof Exp:* Lectr physics, City Col New York, 57-60; res fel, 63-65, physicist, Stanford Res Inst, 65-69; assoc prof physics, Sonoma State Col, 69-70; sr physicist, Stanford Res Inst Int, 70-72, asst mgr, Mass Spectrom Res Ctr, 72-75; res assoc, Space Sci Lab, Univ Calif, Berkeley, 75-76; assoc res prof, Linus Pauling Inst Sci & Med, 76-82. *Mem:* Am Phys Soc; Am Soc Mass Spectrom. *Res:* Electron scattering; atomic beams; universal detectors; ionic and atomic collisions; ultra high vacuum techniques; mass spectrometer development; ion source development. *Mailing Add:* 3146 Manchester Ct Palo Alto CA 94303

ABETTI, PIER ANTONIO, TECHNOLOGICAL INNOVATION & ENTREPRENEURSHIP, TECHNOLOGY STRATEGY & PLANNING. *Current Pos:* PROF MGT TECHNOL & ENTREPRENEURSHIP, SCH MGT, RENSSELAER POLYTECH INST, 82-, CONSULT, TECHNOL ASSESSMENT GROUP, 82- *Personal Data:* b Florence, Italy, Feb 7, 21; US citizen; m 48, Elizabeth B Nelson; c George E & Frank A. *Educ:* Univ Pisa, Italy, Dr Ing(indust eng), 46; Ill Inst Technol, MS, 48, PhD(elec eng), 53. *Honors & Awards:* Coffin Award, Gen Elec Co, 52. *Prof Exp:* Adv develop engr, power transformer div, Gen Elec Co, 48-56, mgr, Proj Extra-High-Voltage, 57-60, Advan Technol Elec & Info Labs, 61-62, Large Comput Systs, 65-66, Data Commun Prods, 67-70, Pvt Tel Systs, 70-73 & Europe Strategic Planning, 74-79, consult res & develop, Tech Systs, 80-81; asst mgr dir, Univac Div, Sperry Rand Int, 63-64. *Concurrent Pos:* Instr, Mass Inst Technol, 50-57; adj prof, Berkshire Community Col, 58-60; vis prof, Technol Univ Compliegne, France, 88-91, Elec Res Inst, Mexico, 89-90 & Int Univ Japan, 91-93; Helsinki Sch Econ, Finland, 94-, Lectr, Korean Advanc/ Inst & Sci Tech, 95-, mem, Am Mgt Asn Res & Develop Coun, 90-95; non-resident prof, Gordon Inst, Tufts Univ, 87- *Mem:* Fel Inst Elec & Electronics Engrs. *Res:* Creation of new high-technology entrepreneurial ventures; innovation and entrepreneurship in large and small companies; technological strategies and diversification; technological innovation and new product development; technological intrepreneurship and intrapreneurship. *Mailing Add:* 1026 Mohegan Rd Schenectady NY 12309. *Fax:* 518-276-8661

ABEY, ALBERT EDWARD, SOLID MECHANICS. *Current Pos:* PHYSICIST, LAWRENCE RADIATION LAB, 67- *Personal Data:* b Spokane, Wash, Aug 12, 35; m 57; c 2. *Educ:* Wash State Univ, BS, 58; Univ Wash, MS, 60; Univ Ariz, PhD(physics), 64. *Prof Exp:* Res assoc physics, Univ Ariz, 64; res assoc, Advan Mat Res & Develop Lab, Pratt & Whitney Aircraft, 64-67. *Mem:* Am Phys Soc. *Res:* High hydrostatic and nearly hydrostatic pressure studies of solid state physics, particularly ionic conductivity; elastic and plastic properties of materials; surface physics in connection with thermionics. *Mailing Add:* 1763 Buena Vista Ave Livermore CA 94550

ABHYANKAR, SHREERAM, MATHEMATICS. *Current Pos:* prof, 63-67, MARSHALL DISTINGUISHED PROF MATH, PURDUE UNIV, 67-, PROF INDUST ENG & COMPUT SCI, 87- *Personal Data:* b Ujjain, India, July 22, 30; m 58, Yvonne Margit Kraft; c Hari & Kashi. *Educ:* Inst Sci, India, BSc, 51; Harvard Univ, AM, 52, PhD(math), 55. *Honors & Awards:* Chauvenet Award, Math Asn Am, 78. *Prof Exp:* Res fel math, Harvard Univ, 54-55; res assoc, Columbia Univ, 55-56, vis asst prof, 56-57; asst prof, Cornell Univ, 57-58; vis asst prof, Princeton Univ, 58-59; assoc prof, Johns Hopkins Univ, 59-63. *Concurrent Pos:* Sloan Found fel, 58- *Mem:* Am Math Soc. *Res:* Algebraic geometry; algebra; several complex variables; circuit and invariant theory; quantum electrodynamics; combinatorics; computer aided design and robotics. *Mailing Add:* Div Math Sci Purdue Univ West Lafayette IN 47907-1968

ABIAN, ALEXANDER, PURE MATHEMATICS. *Current Pos:* PROF MATH, IOWA STATE UNIV, 67- *Personal Data:* b Tabriz, Iran, Jan 1, 25; US citizen; m 59; c 3. *Educ:* Univ Tehran, BS, 46; Univ Chicago, MS, 54; Univ Cincinnati, PhD(math), 56. *Prof Exp:* Asst prof math, Univ Tenn, 56-57, Queens Col, 57-59 & Univ Pa, 59-62; assoc prof, Ohio State Univ, 62-67. *Mem:* Am Math Soc. *Res:* Theory of sets, analysis and mathematical logic. *Mailing Add:* Dept Math Iowa State Univ Ames IA 50011-0001

ABIKOFF, WILLIAM, GEOMETRY, ANALYSIS. *Current Pos:* PROF, DEPT MATH, UNIV CONN, 81- *Personal Data:* b New York, NY, Aug 18, 44; div. *Educ:* Polytech Inst Brooklyn, BS, 65, MS, 66, PhD(math), 71. *Prof Exp:* Mem tech staff, Bell Tel Labs, Inc, 65-70; instr math, Columbia Univ, 70-71; res fel, Mittag-Leffler Inst, Swed Royal Acad Sci, 71-72; asst prof, Columbia Univ, 72-75; from asst prof to assoc prof math, Univ Ill, Urbana, 75-81. *Concurrent Pos:* Res fel, Inst Higher Sci Studies, 76-77 & Sloan Fel; mem, Inst Adv Study, 89; Lady Davis fel & vis prof, Technion, 96-97; distinguished lectr, Sigma Xi, 97- *Mem:* Am Math Soc; Math Asn Am; Sigma Xi. *Res:* Complex analysis; hyperbolic geometry; Riemann surfaces; computation; mathematical physics. *Mailing Add:* Dept Math Box U-9 Univ Conn Storrs CT 06269-3009. *E-Mail:* abikoff@math.uconn.edu

ABILDGAARD, CHARLES FREDERICK, PEDIATRICS. *Current Pos:* PROF PEDIAT, SCH MED, UNIV CALIF, DAVIS, 68- *Personal Data:* b Winfield, Kans, Aug 10, 30; m; c 3. *Educ:* Stanford Univ, AB, 52, MD, 55; Am Bd Pediat, dipl, 59. *Prof Exp:* Intern, Boston City Hosp, 54-55; resident pediat, Stanford Univ Hosps, 55-57; pediatrician, Coco Solo Hosp, Cristobal, CZ, 59-60; from asst prof to assoc prof pediat, Col Med, Univ Ill, 61-68. *Concurrent Pos:* USPHS trainee hemat, Children's Mem Hosp, Chicago, 60-61. *Mem:* Am Soc Hemat; Am Pediat Soc; Soc Pediat Res; Am Acad Pediat; Am Physiol Soc. *Res:* Pediatric hematology, thrombopoiesis, hemostasis, hemophilia. *Mailing Add:* Dept Pediat Ticon II Bldg Univ Calif Sacramento CA 95817

ABILDSKOV, J(UNIOR) A, MEDICINE. *Current Pos:* PROF MED, UNIV UTAH, 68- *Personal Data:* b Salem, Utah, Sept 22, 23; m 44, Mary McKell; c Becky A, Alan, Mary K & Marilyn. *Educ:* Univ Utah, BA, 44, MD, 46. *Honors & Awards:* Cummings Humanitarian Award, Am Col Cardiol. *Prof Exp:* Instr internal med, Tulane Univ, 51-54; cardiologist & chief serv, William Beaumont Army Hosp, 54-56; from asst prof to prof med, State Univ NY Upstate Med Ctr, 56-68. *Concurrent Pos:* Fel internal med, Tulane Univ, 47-51. *Mem:* AAAS; Am Soc Clin Invest; Am Fedn Clin Res; Soc Exp Biol & Med; Asn Am Physicians. *Res:* Improved electrocardiographic examination; recognition of states at high risk of cardiac arrhythmias; physiologic basis of electrocardiographic waveform and disorders of cardiac rhythm. *Mailing Add:* Univ Utah CVRTI Bldg 100 Salt Lake City UT 84112. *Fax:* 801-581-3128

ABITBOL, CAROLYN LARKINS, PEDIATRIC NEPHROLOGY. *Current Pos:* ASST PROF PEDIAT, UNIV MIAMI, 83- *Personal Data:* b Quincy, Fla, Apr 8, 46; m 74; c 5. *Educ:* James Madison Univ, BS, 67; Univ VA, MD, 71. *Honors & Awards:* Ross Pediat Award, Ross Labs & Am Col Nutrit, 87. *Prof Exp:* Intern med & pediat, Emory Univ, 71-72, resident pediat 72-73; fel pediat nephrol, Univ Calif, San Francisco, 73-75; Fulbright Hays scholar, Hospital des Enfants Malades, Paris, France, 75-76; asst prof pediat, Cornell Med Col, 76-78; attending physician, Nassau Co Med Ctr, 78-83; asst prof pediat, Stonybrook Univ, 80-83. *Mem:* Am Col Nutrit; Am Acad Pediat; Am Soc Nephrol; Int Soc Nephrol; Int Soc Pediat Nephrol. *Res:* Problems of growth failure related to chronic renal failure in infants and children. *Mailing Add:* Dept Pediat Div Pediat Nephrotoxicol Univ Miami Sch Med PO Box 016960 R131 Miami FL 33101-6960

ABKOWITZ, MARTIN A(ARON), ocean engineering, naval architecture; deceased, see previous edition for last biography

ABKOWITZ, MARTIN ARNOLD, EXPERIMENTAL SOLID STATE PHYSICS. *Current Pos:* ASSOC LECTR PHYSICS, UNIV ROCHESTER, 69- *Personal Data:* b New York, NY, Feb 22, 36; m 57, Rollic Greenberg; c David B & Pamina A. *Educ:* City Col New York, BS, 57; Univ Rochester, MA, 59; Syracuse Univ, PhD(physics), 64. *Prof Exp:* Fel physics, Univ Pittsburgh, 64-65; scientist, 65-73, prin scientist, Xerox Webster Corp Res Lab, 73- *Concurrent Pos:* Adj prof physics, Univ Rochester, 66-67. *Mem:* Fel Am Phys Soc; Am Chem Soc. *Res:* Amorphous semiconductors; magnetic resonance; dielectric spectroscopy; charge generation and transport in disordered molecular solids; polymer physics. *Mailing Add:* 1198 Gatestone Circle Webster NY 14580

ABKOWITZ, STANLEY, POWDER METALLURGY, TITANIUM METALLURGY. *Current Pos:* PRES, DYNAMET TECHNOL, INC, 69- *Personal Data:* b Revere, Mass, Mar 17, 27; m 54; c 3. *Educ:* Mass Inst Technol, SB, 48. *Honors & Awards:* William Hunt Eisenman Award, Am Soc Metall, 93. *Prof Exp:* Mgr, Reactive Metals, Inc, 55-58 & Spec Metals, Inc, 60-62; dir res & develop, Nuclear Metals, Inc, 62-68. *Concurrent Pos:* Mem, Comt Export Admin, 88- *Mem:* Fel Am Soc Metals Int; Metall Soc; Metal Powder Industs Fedn; Titanium Develop Asn. *Res:* Titanium technology; development of alloys and processing techniques brought to commercial operation; isostatic pressing. *Mailing Add:* Dynamet Technol Eight A St Burlington MA 01803

ABLE, KENNETH PAUL, ANIMAL ORIENTATION & NAVIGATION. *Current Pos:* From asst prof to assoc prof, 71-84, PROF BIOL, STATE UNIV NY ALBANY, 84- *Personal Data:* b Louisville, Ky, Feb 5, 44; m 67, Mary Allen; c Joshua. *Educ:* Univ Louisville, BS, 66, MS, 68; Univ Ga, PhD(zool), 71. *Honors & Awards:* Brewster Medal, Am Ornithologists Union, 96. *Concurrent Pos:* NSF res grant, 74- *Mem:* Fel Animal Behav Soc; Am Soc Naturalists; fel Am Ornithologists Union (treas, 81-85); Int Soc Behav Ecol. *Res:* Migration and orientation of birds; ecology and evolution of animal migration. *Mailing Add:* Dept Biol Sci State Univ NY Albany NY 12222. *Fax:* 518-442-4767

ABLER, RONALD FRANCIS, HISTORY OF GEOGRAPHY. *Current Pos:* EXEC DIR, ASN AM GEOGR, 90- *Personal Data:* b Milwaukee, Wis, May 30, 39; m 81, Barbara Bailey; c 2. *Educ:* Univ Minn, BA, 63, MA, 66, PhD(geog), 68. *Honors & Awards:* Centenary Medal, Royal Scottish Geog Soc, 90; Victoria Medal, Royal Geog Soc Inst Brit Geog, 96. *Prof Exp:* Prof geog, Pa State Univ, 67-90. *Concurrent Pos:* Vis prof, Univ BC, 71, Univ Minn, 72-74 & Stockholm Sch Econ, 82-83; dir geog prog, NSF, 84-87. *Mem:* Fel AAAS; Asn Am Geogrs (pres, 85-86); Can Asn Geogrs; Am Geog Soc; Nat Coun Geog Educ. *Res:* Interpersonal communications technologies especially postal and telecommunications networks; urban geography; history of geography and history of science. *Mailing Add:* 1710 16th St NW Washington DC 20009. *Fax:* 202-234-2744; *E-Mail:* rabler@aag.org

ABLER, WILLIAM LEWIS, PALEOPSYCHOLOGY, COMPLEX SYSTEMS. *Current Pos:* SELF-EMPLOYED SCIENTIST, 80- *Personal Data:* b Chicago, Ill, Dec 6, 43; m 86, Patricia Ehlert; c Alice & Nicholas. *Educ:* Univ Pa, BA, 66, MA, 68, PhD(ling), 71. *Prof Exp:* Fel, Stanford Univ, 71-74; asst prof ling, Ill Inst Technol, 74-80. *Res:* Particulate principle of self-diversifying systems - the opposite material property from chaos and basis of biological inheritance, human language, arithmetic and chemical elements; serrated teeth of carnivorous dinosaurs - microanatomy and behavioral interpretation. *Mailing Add:* 411 N Harvey Ave Oak Park IL 60302

ABLES, ERNEST D, WILDLIFE ECOLOGY, ZOOLOGY. *Current Pos:* actg dean, 84-85, head, Fish & Wildlife Dept, 82-89, PROF WILDLIFE ECOL, UNIV IDAHO, 73-, ASSOC ACAD DEAN, COL FORESTRY, WILDLIFE & RANGE SCI, 74-82, 90- *Personal Data:* b Hugo, Okla, Jan 13, 34; m 60. *Educ:* Okla State Univ, BS, 61; Univ Wis, MS, 64, PhD(wildlife ecol), 68. *Prof Exp:* From asst prof to assoc prof ecol, Tex A&M Univ, 67-73. *Concurrent Pos:* Vis lectr wildlife ecol, Peoples Repub China, 80. *Mem:* Ecol Soc Am; Wildlife Soc; Am Soc Mammal; Am Inst Biol Sci; Wilderness Soc. *Res:* Home range and activity studies of red foxes by radio tracking; radio tracking studies of impala in Africa; ecology of exotic ungulates in Texas; ecological animal behavior. *Mailing Add:* Wildlife Mgmt Univ Idaho 375 S Line St Moscow ID 83843-4140

ABLES, HAROLD DWAYNE, astronomy, for more information see previous edition

ABLIN, RICHARD J, IMMUNOBIOLOGY, MEDICAL & SCIENCE EDUCATION. *Current Pos:* DIR, SCI INVEST, INNAPHARMA INC, UPPER SADDLE RIVER, NJ. *Personal Data:* b Chicago, Ill, May 15, 40; m 64, Linda L Lutwack; c Michael D. *Educ:* Lake Forest Col, AB, 62; State Univ NY, Buffalo, PhD(microbiol & immunol), 67. *Honors & Awards:* P D Agarwal Mem Award lect, Bhoruka Pub Welfare Trust, Calcutta, India, 88. *Prof Exp:* Lectr microbiol, Sch Med, State Univ NY, Buffalo, 66-68; dir immunol, Millard Fillmore Hosp, 68-70; head immunol, Mem Hosp Springfield, 70-73; dir immunobiol, Cook Co Hosp & Hektoen Inst Med Res, Chicago, Ill, 73-75, from sci officer to sr sci officer immunol, 76-83; dir & res assoc prof, Immunol Unit, Dept Urol, State Univ NY, Stony Brook Sch Med, 83-89. *Concurrent Pos:* Consult, Millard Fillmore Hosp, 70; consult med staff, Mem Hosp Springfield, 70-73 & St Johns Hosp, 71-73; asst prof, Sch Med, Southern Ill Univ, 71-73; assoc prof, Univ Health Sci/Chicago Med Sch, 73-74; clin instr, Dept Med Lab Technol, Cent YMCA Community Col & Malcolm Col, Chicago, Ill, 77-83; pres & dir, Robert Benjamin Ablin Found Cancer Res Inc, Skokie, Ill, 79- *Mem:* Am Col Cryosurg (vpres, 77-78 & 78-79); Am Asn Cancer Res; Am Asn Immunologists; Am Soc Microbiol; Int Soc Cryosurg (pres, 77-80, hon lifetime pres, 80); Soc Exp Biol & Med; Sigma Xi. *Res:* Immunobiology of genitourinary tumors, principally of the prostate, and of the knowledge derived thereof for the diagnosis, prognosis and treatment of diseases of the prostate. *Mailing Add:* Innapharma Inc 10 Mountainview Rd Suite 301 Upper Saddle River NJ 07458. *Fax:* 201-818-3388

ABLOW, CLARENCE MAURICE, MATHEMATICS. *Current Pos:* RETIRED. *Personal Data:* b New York, NY, Nov 6, 19; m 45. *Educ:* Univ Calif, Los Angeles, BA, 40, MA, 42; Brown Univ, PhD(appl math), 51. *Prof Exp:* Mathematician, Boeing Airplane Co, 51-55; mathematician, SRI Int, 55-84. *Mem:* Am Math Soc; Soc Indust & Appl Math; Math Asn Am. *Res:* Solution of differential equations. *Mailing Add:* 40 Los Altos Sq Los Altos CA 94022-1428

ABLOWITZ, MARK JAY, MATHEMATICAL PHYSICS. *Current Pos:* CHAIR & PROF, DEPT APPL MATH, UNIV COLO, BOULDER, 89- *Personal Data:* b New York, NY, June 5, 45; m 68, Enid M Bate; c Todd, Jacob & Stephanie. *Educ:* Univ Rochester, BS, 67; Mass Inst Technol, PhD(math), 71. *Honors & Awards:* Clarkson Graham Res Award, 76. *Prof Exp:* From asst prof to prof math, Clarkson Univ, 71-79, prof & chmn, Dept Math & Comput Sci, 79-85, dean sci, 85-89. *Concurrent Pos:* Teaching asst math, Mass Inst Technol, 67-71; vis prof appl math, Princeton Univ, 77-78 & 84; Sloan found fel, 75-77, John Simon Guggenheim Found fel, 84; Nat Acad Sci exchange visit, USSR, 84; assoc ed, J Math Physics, 76-79. *Mem:* Sigma Xi; Soc Indust & Appl Math; Math Asn Am; Am Math Soc. *Res:* Mathematical physics; author of over 150 technical publications and three books. *Mailing Add:* Dept Appl Math Univ Colo Box 526 Boulder CO 80309-0526. *Fax:* 303-492-4066; *E-Mail:* markjab@newton.colorado.edu

ABNEY, THOMAS SCOTT, plant pathology, mycology, for more information see previous edition

ABOLHASSNI, MOHSEN, MEDICINE. *Current Pos:* instr, 87-90, ASST PROF MED, DEPT MED, NY MED COL, VALHALLA, 90- *Personal Data:* b Nov 7, 47. *Educ:* Tehran Univ, BS, 70, MS, 76; Fla State Univ, PhD(immunol), 84. *Prof Exp:* Lab instr, Razapad Hosp, Maragheh, Iran, 70-72; lab technologist, Dept Immunol & Biochem, Pasteur Inst, 73-77; res asst, Dept Biol, Univ SFla, Tampa, 77-78, Dept Biol Sci, Fla State Univ, Tallahassee, 82-83; postdoctoral fel, Dept Large Animal Med, Univ Ga, Athens, 85-86. *Mem:* Am Asn Immunologists. *Mailing Add:* 15 Overlook Oval Peekskill NY 10566

ABOLINS, MARIS ARVIDS, ELEMENTARY PARTICLE PHYSICS. *Current Pos:* assoc prof, 68-72, PROF PHYSICS, MICH STATE UNIV, 72- *Personal Data:* b Liepaja, Latvia, Feb 5, 38; US citizen; m 59, Frances Deland; c 2. *Educ:* Univ Wash, BS, 60; Univ Calif, San Diego, MS, 62, PhD(physics), 65. *Prof Exp:* Res asst physics, Univ Calif, San Diego, 60-65; physicist, Lawrence Radiation Lab, Univ Calif, Berkeley, 65- 68. *Concurrent Pos:* Vis physicist, Europ Coun Nuclear Res, 76-77, Ctr Atomic Energy, Saclay, France, 77 & Fermi Nat Accelerator Lab, 90-92; chmn, Fermilab Users Orgn, 82-83, Exec Comt, Div Particles & Fields, 84-86, SSC Users Orgn, 89-91; consult, Dept Energy, 83- *Mem:* Fel Am Phys Soc; AAAS. *Res:* High energy physics research with electronic detectors; high energy instrumentation. *Mailing Add:* Dept Physics Mich State Univ East Lansing MI 48823. *Fax:* 517-355-6661; *E-Mail:* abolins@msupa.pa.msu.edu

ABOOD, LEO GEORGE, BIOCHEMISTRY. *Current Pos:* PROF BIOCHEM, UNIV ROCHESTER, 65-, PROF PHARMOCOL, 87-; DISTINGUISHED PROF NEUROSCI, UNIV TOLEDO, 87- *Personal Data:* b Erie, Pa, Jan 15, 22; m 47, Lois Wuchner; c George & Mary. *Educ:* Ohio State Univ, BS, 43; Univ Chicago, PhD(pharmacol), 50. *Prof Exp:* Instr physiol, Univ Chicago, 50-52; from asst prof to prof neurophysiol & biochem, Col Med, Univ Ill, 52-65, dir res labs, Dept Psychiat, 56-65. *Concurrent Pos:* Mem rev panel, NIH; mem var comts, Nat Res Coun; trustee, Brain Res Found, Univ Chicago. *Mem:* Am Physiol Soc; Am Chem Soc; Am Col Neuropsychopharmacol; Soc Neurosci; Int Soc Neurochem. *Res:* Chemistry and cellular physiology of nervous system; isolation and characterization of neurotransmitter receptors from mammalian brain, particularly the nicotinic, vasopressin and opioid receptors; brain sites and mechanisms of action of nicotine and vasopressin. *Mailing Add:* Dept Pharmacol Univ Rochester Med Ctr Rochester NY 14642

ABOU-DONIA, MOHAMED BAHIE, NEUROTOXICOLOGY. *Current Pos:* PROF PHARMACOL, MED CTR, DUKE UNIV, 73- *Educ:* Univ Calif, Berkeley, PhD(pharmacol), 67. *Mailing Add:* Dept Pharmacol Duke Univ Med Ctr PO Box 3813 Durham NC 27710-0001

ABOU-EL-SEOUD, MOHAMED OSMAN, MYCOLOGY. *Current Pos:* RETIRED. *Personal Data:* b Cairo, Egypt, Apr 6, 21; m 49; c 4. *Educ:* Cairo Univ, BSc, 43; Ain Shams Univ, Cairo, Dipl Educ, 59; Ohio State Univ, MSc, 62, PhD(mycol), 64. *Prof Exp:* Sec sch teacher, Egypt, 45-51; tech secy, Sci Div, Egyptian Ministry Educ, 51-54; asst prof bot, Teachers Col, Cairo, 54-60; res assoc, Southern Ill Univ, Carbondale, 64-65; prof, Ain Shams Univ, Cairo, 65-67; lectr, MIch State Univ, 68-69, asst prof, 69-71, assoc prof, 71-77, prof natural sci, 77. *Concurrent Pos:* Curric consult, King Abdulaziz Univ, Jedda, Saudi Arabia, 81-82. *Mem:* Am Inst Biol Sci. *Res:* Lipid and protein synthesis by fungi; light effect on sporulation and pigmentation of fungi. *Mailing Add:* 2827 Southwood Dr East Lansing MI 48823

ABOU-GHARBIA, MAGID, PHARMACY. *Current Pos:* sr res chemist, 82-84, supvr res, Wyeth Labs, 84-87, sect head, 87-89, assoc dir, 89-91, DIR, WYETH-AYERST RES, 91- *Personal Data:* b Cairo, Egypt, Dec 1, 49; US citizen; m 72; c 3. *Educ:* Cairo Univ, BSc, 71, MSc, 74; Univ Pa, PhD(org chem), 79. *Prof Exp:* Instr org chem, Cairo Univ, Egypt, 71-74; teaching fel chem, Univ Pa, 74-78; vis res fel med clin chem, Sch Pharm, Temple Univ, 78-79, NIH res fel, Fels Res Inst, 79-81. *Concurrent Pos:* Lectr, Univ Pa, 79-81. *Mem:* Am Chem Soc; fel Sigma Xi; Royal Inst Chem; Soc Neurosci. *Res:* Synthesis of biologically active compounds for the cardiovascular and central nervous systems; reaction mechanisms. *Mailing Add:* 26 Hawthorn Dr Princeton Junction NJ 08550

ABOUHALKAH, T A, PETROLEUM RESERVOIR ENGINEERING. *Current Pos:* CONSULT PETROL ENGR, 86- *Personal Data:* b Tripoli, Lebanon, May 31, 29; m 54, Susan Hanke; c 4. *Educ:* Univ Tex, BA & BS, 54. *Prof Exp:* Petrol Reservoir engr, Panhandle Eastern Pipe Line Co, 56-63, mgr reservoir eng, Underground Storage Div, 63-75; consult petrol engr, Miller & Lents Ltd, 75-86. *Concurrent Pos:* Expert witness, fed & state regulatory bodies. *Res:* Electric log interpretation; estimation, evaluation and economic studies of oil and gas reserves; well completion recommendation; design and development of underground gas storage reservoirs; fluid flow in porous rocks; well-test analyses. *Mailing Add:* 6522 Apple Valley Lane Houston TX 77069-2407

ABOU-KHALIL, SAMIR, BIOENERGETICS, COMPUTERS. *Current Pos:* PRES, EASYCOMP, COMPUTER EDUC & CONSULT, MIAMI, 89- *Personal Data:* b Lebanon, July 18, 43; US citizen; m 76, Wafa Hammoud; c Lara & Ronny. *Educ:* Lebanese Univ, Beirut, BS, 70; Claude Bernard Univ, Lyon, France, MS, 73, PhD(biochem), 75. *Prof Exp:* Res assoc plant biochem, Univ Ill, Urbana-Champaign, 76-79; res assoc, Sch Med, Univ Miami, 79-81, res asst prof med, 81-84, res assoc prof med, 85-88. *Concurrent Pos:* Res assoc biochem, Howard Hughes Med Inst, 79-81. *Mem:* Am Soc Biochem & Molecular Biol. *Res:* Exploration of cellular energy in normal and neoplastic tissues by investigating unusual mitochondrial functions in tumors; drug interactions and metabolism in human and animal tissues using state-of-the-art technology. *Mailing Add:* 9805 SW 125th Terr Miami FL 33176. *E-Mail:* samkii@aol.com

ABOUL-ELA, MOHAMED MOHAMED, PLANT PHYSIOLOGY. *Current Pos:* asst prof, 65-67, ASSOC PROF BIOL, TEX WOMAN'S UNIV, 67- *Personal Data:* b Damanhur, Egypt, Mar 10, 18; US citizen; m 51; c 6. *Educ:* Univ Cairo, BA, 40; Iowa State Univ, MS, 47, PhD(plant physiol), 50. *Prof Exp:* Teacher high sch, Damanhur, Egypt, 40-42; from instr to asst prof crops, Univ Alexandria, 42-55; assoc prof, Univ Bagdad, 55-56; assoc prof, Univ Alexandria, 56-62; fel plant sci, Tex A&M Univ, 62-65. *Concurrent Pos:* Consult, Agrarian Reform Ministry Egypt, 56-62. *Mem:* AAAS; Am Inst Biol Sci. *Res:* Effect of radiation on growing bean seedlings; cotton defoliation. *Mailing Add:* 1100 Mansell Dr Youngstown OH 44505

ABOU-SABE, MORAD A, MOLECULAR BIOLOGY. *Current Pos:* asst prof, 68-74, ASSOC PROF BACT, RUTGERS UNIV, 74- *Personal Data:* b Cairo, Egypt, Apr 3, 37; m 60; c 2. *Educ:* Univ Alexandria, BSc, 58; Univ Calif, Berkeley, MSc, 62; Univ Pittsburgh, PhD(bact), 65. *Prof Exp:* Instr agr, Univ Alexandria, 58-59; asst prof genetics, Cairo Univ, 66-68. *Mem:* Am Soc Microbiol; Genetics Soc Am; UAR Soc Microbiol. *Res:* Gene enzyme interactions; specific genetic control mechanism in bacteria; cyclic adenosine monophosphate regulation of cell growth and growth control. *Mailing Add:* Dept Biol Rutgers Univ New Brunswick NJ 08903

ABPLANALP, HANS, GENETICS. *Current Pos:* RETIRED. *Personal Data:* b Zurich, Switz, Apr 22, 25; m 54; c 3. *Educ:* Inst Technol, Zurich, Ing Agron, 49; Wash State Col, MS, 51; Univ Calif, PhD(genetics), 55. *Prof Exp:* Res asst genetics, Wash State Col, 49-51 & Univ Calif, 51-53; asst specialist statist & genetics, Div Poultry Husb, Univ Calif, Davis, 53-56, asst prof genetics, 56-59, prof avian sci & univ & poultry geneticist, Exp Sta, 69-91. *Mem:* Genetics Soc Am; Am Genetic Asn; Soc Study Evolution. *Res:* Population genetics; application to breeding; basic research in underlying genetic mechanisms. *Mailing Add:* 601 Tenth St Davis CA 95616

ABRAHAM, BERNARD M, CHEMISTRY. *Current Pos:* RES PROF, DEPT PHYSICS & ASTRON, NORTHWESTERN UNIV, 85- *Personal Data:* b Kansas City, Mo, Nov 21, 18; m 42; c 3. *Educ:* Univ Chicago, BS, 40, PhD(chem), 46. *Prof Exp:* Jr assoc, Univ Chicago, 41-42 & Northwestern Univ, 42; jr assoc & jr chemist, Univ Chicago, 42-45; sr chemist, Monsanto Chem Co, 45; Universal Oil Prod fel, Northwestern Univ, 46-47; assoc chemist, Argonne Nat Lab, 47-59, sr chemist & group leader, 59-85. *Concurrent Pos:* Guggenheim Mem fel, 59; Lady Davis fel, Technion, Haifa, Israel, 76; dir, Off Indust Coop, Univ Chicago, 76-78. *Mem:* AAAS; Am Chem Soc; fel Am Phys Soc. *Res:* Thermodynamic and transport properties of liquid helium-3 and liquid helium-4; thermal and magnetic measurements as very low temperatures; suspension of inorganic compounds in liquid metals; thermochemical water splitting cycles; surface chemistry; monomolecular films. *Mailing Add:* 1131 N Oak Park Oak Park IL 60302-1222

ABRAHAM, CARL J, ORGANIC CHEMISTRY. *Current Pos:* ASSOC DIR, SPORTS RECREATION & ATHLETICS DIV, INTER-CITY TESTING & CONSULT CORP, 70-, CHMN BD, 75- *Educ:* Hofstra Univ, BA, 59, ID, 79; Univ Pacific, MS, 61; Clayton Univ, PhD(chem), 75. *Prof Exp:* Res asst, Univ Ore, 59-60; res asst, Univ NC, 61-63; res engr & chemist, Aerojet Gen Corp, 63-65; mat specialist, Corp Res Lab, J P Stevens & Co, 65-66; dir res & develop, Mansol Ceramics Co, 66-67; vpres & tech dir, Polyphase Chem Serv, 67-69. *Concurrent Pos:* Chmn bd, Protective Devices Inc, 85-90, Chase-A-Way Inc, 93-; pres, Athletic Safety Prod, Inc, 83-; consult chem eng & safety eng, ABC & CBS News. *Mem:* Am Acad Environ Engrs; AAAS; fel Royal Soc Chem London; fel Textile Inst Eng; Nat Fire Protect Asn; Nat Soc Prof Engrs. *Res:* High temperature carbonaceous and siliceous materials; dental and medical fields; industrial formulations for air and water pollution fields; polymers and novel adhesives; formulations for cleaning industrial and consumer applications; glass and coating formulations; granted 5 US patents, 7 international patents; author of 52 publications. *Mailing Add:* Inter-City Testing & Consult 167 Willis Ave Mineola NY 11501

ABRAHAM, DONALD JAMES, ORGANIC CHEMISTRY, MEDICINAL CHEMISTRY. *Current Pos:* PROF MED CHEM & DEPT CHMN, MED COL VA, VA COMMONWEALTH UNIV, 88- *Personal Data:* b Greensburg, Pa, Nov 19, 36; m 62; c 1. *Educ:* Pa State Univ, BS, 58; Marshall Univ, MS, 59; Purdue Univ, PhD(org chem), 63. *Honors & Awards:* Sr US Scientist, Alexander von Humboldt Found, 74. *Prof Exp:* Res assoc med chem & fel, Univ Va, 63-64; res assoc, Univ Pittsburgh, 64-67, from assoc prof to prof med chem, 68-88, head dept, 68-88. *Concurrent Pos:* Mem preclin psychopharmacol study sect, NIMH, Alcohol & Drug Abuse Ment Health Admin, 73-77; vis scientist, MRC Lab Molecular Biol, Cambridge, Eng, 80-81. *Mem:* Am Chem Soc. *Res:* Antisickling agents and x-ray structures of complexes of antisickling agents and hemoglobin; structure elucidation of biologically important compounds; synthesis of medicinals; x-ray crystallography; molecular action of drug molecules; psychopharmacology research. *Mailing Add:* 3511 Buckhead Rd Midlothian VA 23113-1377

ABRAHAM, EDATHARA CHACKO, BIOCHEMISTRY. *Current Pos:* from asst prof to assoc prof, 74-86, PROF BIOCHEM, MED COL GA, 86- *Personal Data:* b Kottayam, India; m 63, Amminikutty; c Jacob, Mini (Panikar) & James. *Educ:* Univ Kerala, BS, 59; Univ Louisville, PhD(biochem), 71. *Prof Exp:* Clin biochemist, Christian Med Col, Vellore, India, 59-62, res biochemist, 63-67; res biochemist renal biochem, Univ Louisville Sch Med, 67-69, grad res asst biochem, 69-71. *Concurrent Pos:* Res assoc, Univ Louisville Sch Med, 72-73 & Med Col Ga, 73-74. *Mem:* Am Soc Hematol; Am Asn Clin Chem; Am Soc Human Genetics; NY Acad Sci; AAAS; Am Diabetes Asn; Geront Soc Am; Asn Res Vision Ophthal; Int Soc Eye Res. *Res:* Protein glycation in biological aging and in diabetes; glycation of lens crystallins in diabetic and senile cataractogenesis; protein engineering; site directed mutagenesis; expression systems; site specific glycation. *Mailing Add:* Dept Biochem & Molecular Biol Med Col Ga Augusta GA 30912. *Fax:* 706-721-6300; *E-Mail:* eabraham@mail.mcg.edu

ABRAHAM, EUGENE V, MANAGEMENT. *Current Pos:* CHMN & CHIEF EXEC OFFICER, SARGENT & LUNDY ENGRS, CHICAGO, ILL. *Honors & Awards:* James N Lardis Medal, Am Soc Mech Engrs, 95. *Mailing Add:* Sargent & Lundy Engrs 55 E Monroe St Chicago IL 60603-5702

ABRAHAM, FARID FADLOW, PHYSICS. *Current Pos:* staff mem, IBM Sci Ctr, 66-71, proj leader air qual dynamics group, 71-72, MEM STAFF, IBM RES LAB, 72- *Personal Data:* b Phoenix, Ariz, May 5, 37; m 59; c 4. *Educ:* Univ Ariz, BS, 59, PhD(physics), 62. *Prof Exp:* Res assoc high energy physics, Univ Chicago, 62-64; sr physicist, Lawrence Radiation Lab, Univ Calif, 64-66. *Mem:* Am Phys Soc. *Res:* Nucleation theory; phase stability, thermodynamics of nonuniform systems, statistical physics. *Mailing Add:* IBM Almaden Res Ctr 650 Harry Rd San Jose CA 95120

ABRAHAM, GEORGE, solid state electronics, for more information see previous edition

ABRAHAM, GEORGE N, BIOCHEMISTRY, MOLECULAR BIOLOGY. *Current Pos:* ASSOC PROF MED & MICROBIOL, SCH MED, UNIV ROCHESTER, 70- *Educ:* Univ Buffalo, MD, 63. *Res:* Immunology. *Mailing Add:* Ctr Aging Sch Med Univ Rochester Box 657 Rochester NY 14642-0001

ABRAHAM, IRENE, CELL BIOLOGY, SOMATIC CELL GENETICS. *Current Pos:* res scientist, 84-89, BIOLOGIST, CELL BIOL DEPT, UPJOHN CO, 84-, SR RES SCIENTIST, 89- *Personal Data:* b Chicago, Ill, Dec 12, 46; m 76; c 2. *Educ:* Univ Ill, Urbana, BS, 68; Univ NC, Chapel Hill, PhD(zool), 73. *Prof Exp:* Fel biol, Yale Univ, 73-75; asst prof, Emory Univ, 75-76; fel, Univ Berne, Switz, 76-78; biologist, Nat Cancer Inst, 79-84. *Mem:* Soc Develop Biol; Am Soc Cell Biol; Sigma Xi; Am Asn Cancer Res. *Res:* Gene regulation and developmental genetics of eukaryotes; cyclic adenosine monophosphate dependent protein kinase and the control of cell growth; the role of the cytoskeleton in cell growth and behavior; multidrug resistance. *Mailing Add:* Cell Biol Dept 7239-267-3 Kalamazoo MI 49008

ABRAHAM, JACOB A, COMPUTER ARCHITECTURE. *Current Pos:* from asst prof to assoc prof elec eng, 75-83, PROF ELEC ENG, UNIV ILL, URBANA, 83-, PROF COMPUT SCI, 84- *Personal Data:* b Tiruvalla, Kerala State, India, Dec 8, 48; US citizen; m 75; c 2. *Educ:* Univ Kerala, BSc, 70; Stanford Univ, MS, 71, PhD(elec eng & comput sci), 74. *Prof Exp:* Actg asst prof elec eng, Stanford Univ, 74-75. *Concurrent Pos:* Co-prin investr, Very High Speed Integrated Circuits Prog, Off Naval Res, 80-84; consult, Gen Elec Co, 83-, Gen Tel & Electronics, 84-, Gen Motors Res Labs, 85- & Gen Res Corp; assoc ed, Trans Comput-Aided Design of Integrated Circuits & Systs, Inst Elec & Electronics Engrs, 84-; sr prin investr, NASA, 85-; dir res prog, Semiconductor Res Corp, 85-; Beckman assoc, Ctr Advan Study, Univ Ill, 85-86. *Mem:* Fel Inst Elec & Electronics Engrs; Asn Comput Mach; Sigma Xi; Int Fedn Info Processing. *Res:* Functional-level testing of very-large-scale integration; design automation; design of testable systems and built-in tests; concurrent error detection; fault-tolerant computer; reconfiguration and recovery in distributed systems; high-performance computer architecture. *Mailing Add:* Univ Tex Austin Comput Eng Res Ctr ENS 433A Austin TX 78711

ABRAHAM, JERROLD L, ENVIRONMENTAL PATHOLOGY, PULMONARY PATHOLOGY. *Current Pos:* ASST PROF PATH, SCH MED, UNIV CALIF, SAN DIEGO, 75- *Personal Data:* b Los Angeles, Calif, Nov 5, 44; m 67; c 3. *Educ:* Mass Inst Technol, BS, 66; Univ Calif, San Francisco, MD, 70. *Prof Exp:* Pathologist, Appalachian Ctr Occup Safety & Health, USPHS, 72-74, chief path, 74-75. *Concurrent Pos:* Instr path, WVa Univ, 72-75. *Mem:* AAAS; Am Thoracic Soc; Int Acad Path; Soc Toxicol Path. *Res:* Diagnostic and investigational studies of environmental occupational disease, especially lung diseases caused by inorganic particulates; development and application of microanalytic techniques, electron probe, ion probe, to pathology of humans and animals. *Mailing Add:* Dept Path SUNY Health Sci Ctr 766 Irving Ave Syracuse NY 13210

ABRAHAM, JOHN, COMBUSTION, NUMERICAL METHODS. *Current Pos:* ASSOC PROF MECH ENG, PURDUE UNIV, 95- *Personal Data:* b Kerala, India, Dec 14, 56; m 86, Regi Sara. *Educ:* Indian Inst Technol, India, BTech, 81; Princeton Univ, MA, 84, PhD(mech & aerospace eng), 86. *Prof Exp:* Sr engr, Joh Deere Technologies Int, Deere & Co, 86-89; vis res collabr, Princeton Univ, 89-91, res staff, 92-93; asst prof mech eng, Univ Minn, 93-95. *Mem:* Am Soc Mech Engrs; Am Inst Aeronaut & Astronaut; Soc Automotive Engrs; Combustion Inst. *Res:* Combustion; numerical solution of reacting flow problems and fluid mechanics with specific interest in modeling and diagnostics of combustion in engines. *Mailing Add:* 1288 Mech Eng Bldg Purdue Univ West Lafayette IN 47907

ABRAHAM, L(EONARD) G(LADSTONE), JR, RADIO WAVE PROPAGATION,. *Current Pos:* RETIRED. *Personal Data:* b Brooklyn, NY, Mar 3, 26; m 50, 78; c 4. *Educ:* Cornell Univ, BEE, 49, MEE, 52, PhD(radiowave propagation), 53. *Prof Exp:* Res assoc, Gen Elec Res Lab, 53-60; sr eng specialist, Appl Res Lab, Sylvania Electronic Syst Div, 60-70, sr scientist, Gen Tel & Electronics Labs, Gen Tel & Electronics Corp, 70-84; lead engr, Mitre Corp, 84-89, prin scientist, 89-92. *Mem:* Inst Elec & Electronic Engrs; Sigma Xi. *Res:* Telephone systems, digital processing and transmission; communication systems, interactive terminals; radio wave propagation. *Mailing Add:* 195 Stebbins St Belchertown MA 01007-9702

ABRAHAM, MARVIN MEYER, PHYSICS, MAGNETIC RESONANCE OF RARE EARTH & ACTINIDE IONS. *Current Pos:* RES PHYSICIST, SOLID STATE DIV, OAK RIDGE NAT LAB, 63- *Personal Data:* b New York, NY, Dec 8, 30; m 58, Reeva Swidler; c Seth, Naomi & David. *Educ:* City Col New York, BS, 53; Univ Calif, Berkeley, MA, 54, PhD(physics), 58. *Honors & Awards:* IR-100 Award, 75 & 82. *Prof Exp:* Asst physics, Univ Calif, 54-58; Fulbright res fel, Clarendon Lab, Oxford Univ, 58-60; res physicist, Lawrence Radiation Lab, Univ Calif, Berkeley, 60-63. *Concurrent Pos:* Fulbright-Hays fel, Oxford Univ, 58-60, pressed steel fel, 59-60; Int Atomic Energy Auth vis prof, San Carlos de Bariloche Inst Physics, Arg, 62-63; OAS fel, UNAM, Mex, 74; vis fel, St Catherine's Col, Oxford Univ, UK, 89. *Mem:* Fel Am Phys Soc; fel Am Ceramic Soc. *Res:* Experimental solid state physics; electron paramagnetic resonance; nuclear magnetic resonance. *Mailing Add:* 102 Caldwell Dr Oak Ridge TN 37830

ABRAHAM, NEAL BROADUS, QUANTUM OPTICS, LASER PHYSICS. *Current Pos:* from asst prof to assoc prof, 80-87, chmn, 84-87, 91-93, PROF PHYSICS, BRYN MAWR COL, 87-, RACHEL C HALE PROF SCI & MATH, 88- *Personal Data:* b Hagerstown, MD, Dec 3, 50; m 89, Donna

Wiley. *Educ:* Dickinson Col, BS, 72; Bryn Mawr Col, PhD(physics), 77. *Prof Exp:* Instr, Dickinson Col, 71-72, Bryn Mawr Col, 76; asst prof physics, Swarthmore Col, 77-80; gov bd, Nat Conf Undergrad Res, 88-94, chair, 92-94. *Concurrent Pos:* Proj dir, Res Corp grant, 77-79; prin investr, NSF grants, 78-87; Alfred P Sloan res fel, 82-84; Int Conf Organizer, 83-85, 87, 90-92, 94-95 & 97-98; NATO grants, 84-94; vis prof, Univ Florence, 84, Polytech Torino, 88, Univ Lill, 88, Jilin Univ, 87, Univ Nice, 94-96, Univ Illes Balears, 95 & 97; prof dir, ARO Contract, 86-87; Alexander von Humboldt Fel, 87-88; Res Corp grants adv comt, 87-92; exec comt, Am Phys Soc, 91-94; Nat Res Ctr Comt, Undergrad Sci Educ, 93-96; pres, Coun Undergrad Res, 96-; Int Sci Found panel chair, 93-94; ed, Optics Commun, 90-95; div assoc ed, Phys Rev Lett, 92-95; assoc ed, Phys Rev E, 95- *Mem:* Fel Am Phys Soc; fel Optical Soc Am; Am Asn Physics Teachers; Sigma Xi; Coun Undergrad Res; AAAS. *Res:* High gain gas lasers and laser amplifiers; intensity fluctuations; descriptions of stimulated and spontaneous emission; nonlinear phenomena; optical chaos and dynamics; spatial pattern formation in lasers and nonlinear optics, optical turbulence. *Mailing Add:* Dept Physics Bryn Mawr Col 101 N Merion Ave Bryn Mawr PA 19010-2899. *Fax:* 610-526-7469; *E-Mail:* nabraham@brynmawr.edu

ABRAHAM, RAJENDER, ENVIRONMENTAL HEALTH, EXPERIMENTAL PATHOLOGY. *Current Pos:* PRES, ABRAHAM ASSOC LTD, 87- *Personal Data:* b Hyderabad, India, May 26, 32; US citizen; m 58; c 1. *Educ:* Osmania Univ, BSc, 52, MSc, 54, PhD(protozool), 57. *Prof Exp:* Prof toxicol, Sch Pub Health, State Univ NY, 84; prof pharmacol, 84-86, prof path & toxicol, Albany Med Col, 86-88. *Concurrent Pos:* Dir, Inst Exp Path & Toxicol, Albany Med Col, 81-86; vis prof, Russell Sage Col, Albany, NY, 75-77. *Mem:* Soc Toxicol; Path Soc Gt Brit & Ireland; Fel Royal Micros Soc; AAAS. *Res:* Toxicology; effects of chemicals on molecular mechanisms in carcinogenesis; chemical interfering with reproductive process. *Mailing Add:* 40 Marion Ave Albany NY 12203

ABRAHAM, RALPH HERMAN, MATHEMATICS. *Current Pos:* assoc prof, 68-80, PROF NATURAL SCI, UNIV CALIF, SANTA CRUZ, 80- *Personal Data:* b Burlington, Vt, July 4, 36; m 58; c 2. *Educ:* Univ Mich, BSE, 56, MS, 58, PhD(math), 60. *Prof Exp:* Lectr math, Univ Calif, Berkeley, 60-62; Off Naval Res res assoc, Columbia Univ, 62-63, asst prof, 63-64; asst prof, Princeton Univ, 64-68. *Mem:* Am Math Soc. *Res:* General relativity, qualitative theory of ordinary differential equations and mechanical systems; analysis on manifolds. *Mailing Add:* Univ Calif Santa Cruz CA 95064-1099

ABRAHAM, ROBERT THOMAS, CHEMICAL PHARMACOLOGY, DRUG METABOLISM. *Current Pos:* Res fel pharmacol, 81-91, ASST PROF & CONSULT, DEPT IMMUNOL & PHARMACOL, MAYO FOUND, 91- *Personal Data:* b Munhall, Pa, Oct 11, 52. *Educ:* Bucknell Univ, BS, 74; Univ Pittsburgh, PhD(pharmacol), 81. *Mem:* Am Soc Mass Spectrometry; AAAS. *Res:* Effects of xenobiotics on the immune system; the interplay between the drug metabolizing system of liver and other organs and the immunomodulatory activity of sulfhydryl containing drugs. *Mailing Add:* Dept Immunol & Pharmacol Mayo Clin 342B Guggenheim Bldg Rochester MN 55905-0001

ABRAHAM, SANDY, BIOCHEMISTRY, ENZYMOLOGY & CARCINOGENESIS. *Current Pos:* dir res, 66-82, RESEARCHER BIOCHEM, ENZYMOLOGY & CARCINOGENESIS, BRUCE LYONS MEM RES LAB, CHILDRENS HOSP NORTHERN CALIF, 86- *Personal Data:* b New York, NY, 1923. *Educ:* City Col New York, BS, 48; Univ Calif, Berkeley, PhD(comp biochem), 53. *Prof Exp:* Prof nutrit sci, Univ Calif, Berkeley, 66-86. *Mem:* Am Soc Biol Chem; Am Inst Nutrit. *Mailing Add:* 111 Highland Blvd Berkeley CA 94708

ABRAHAM, THOMAS, ADVANCE CERAMICS, HIGH-PERFORMANCE MATERIALS. *Current Pos:* proj analyst, 84-85, dir ceramics group, 86-90, DIR ADVAN MAT, BUS COMMUN CO, 91- *Personal Data:* b Pathanamthitta, Kerala, India, Sept 11, 48; m 80, Susy John; c Nitya E & Jay T. *Educ:* Rajasthan Univ, India, BTech, 71; Columbia Univ, MS, 75, DEng Sci, 81. *Honors & Awards:* Cert Appreciation, Am Ceramic Soc, 93. *Prof Exp:* Metallurgist, Alcobex Metals, India, 71-73; res metallurgist, Univ Denver, 81-84; asst metallurgist, Brookhaven Nat Lab, 85-86. *Mem:* Am Ceramic Soc; Metall Soc. *Res:* Conduct industry and market analysis of advanced ceramics, diamond and diamond products, high performance fibers, and magnetic materials; advanced glasses; thin films. *Mailing Add:* Bus Commun Co 25 Van Zant St Norwalk CT 06855. *E-Mail:* buscom2@ad.com

ABRAHAM, TIMOTHY WALTER, ORGANIC CHEMISTRY, NON-ISOTOPIC DETECTION OF NUCLEIC ACID. *Current Pos:* SR SCIENTIST, AMBION INC, 96- *Personal Data:* b Trinlomalee, Sri-Lanka, Sept 20, 58. *Educ:* Univ Colombo, Sri-Lanka, BS, 83; Univ Minn, PhD(org chem), 92. *Prof Exp:* Postdoctoral assoc, Dept Med Chem, Univ Minn, 92-95, res assoc, 95-96. *Mem:* Am Chem Soc. *Res:* Interface of organic chemistry and molecular biology; improving non-isotopic methods for analyzing nucleic acids; synthesis of prodrugs of anti-tumor nucleosides, haptens for catalytic antibodies and natural products. *Mailing Add:* 3111 Parker Lane No 237 Austin TX 78741

ABRAHAM, TONSON, WATER DISPERSIBLE POLYMERS. *Current Pos:* RES & DEVELOP ASSOC, B F GOODRICH CO, 87- *Personal Data:* b Bombay, India, Dec 21, 48; US citizen; m 78, Iona Joseph; c Akash & Kavi. *Educ:* Indian Inst Technol, Kanpur, BTech, 70; Cath Univ Am, PhD(chem), 76. *Prof Exp:* Res assoc, Nat Res Coun, 76-78; fel, Northern Ill Univ, 78-79; asst prof org chem, Ill State Univ, 79-80; assoc res & polymer chemist, Wright Res & Develop Lab, Wright-Patterson AFB, 80-85; sr scientist, Owens-Corning Fiberglass, 86. *Mem:* Fel Am Inst Chemists; Am Chem Soc. *Res:* Water soluble polymers; high temperature elastomers; homogeneous hydrogenation catalysts; matrix materials for aerospace structural components; chemistry of indoles. *Mailing Add:* B F Goodrich Res & Develop Ctr 9921 Brecksville Rd Brecksville OH 44141. *Fax:* 216-447-5544

ABRAHAM, VARGHESE K, QUALITY OF FRYING OILS IN FOODSERVICE INDUSTRIES, NEW METHODS OF FOOD PROCESSING. *Current Pos:* ASST VPRES RES, CARAVELLE FOODS, 93- *Personal Data:* b Kerala, India, Oct 11, 46; Can citizen; m 75, Blessy Mathew; c Arun & Anita. *Educ:* Kerala Univ, BSc, 68; Agra Univ, MSc, 71; Univ Guelph, PhD(food sci), 86. *Prof Exp:* Chem lectr, Ministry Educ, 71-81; asst mgr, Carson Foods, 86-87, dir res, 87-93. *Concurrent Pos:* Prin investr, Nat Res Coun, 87-90, Ont Ministry Agr Food & Rural Affairs, 92-; adj prof, Univ Guelph, 91-; mem, Expert Comt Fats Oils & Other Lipids, Govt Can, 91- *Mem:* Am Oil Chemists Soc; fel Am Inst Chem; fel Royal Soc Chemists; fel Chem Soc. *Res:* Extend the life of oils and fats and incorporate novel technologies to process the oil to provide better stability and nutritional characteristics. *Mailing Add:* 235 Nuggett Ct Brampton ON L6T 5H4 Can. *Fax:* 905-790-9202; *E-Mail:* abraham@globalserve.net

ABRAHAM, W(AYNE) G(ORDON), ELECTRONICS. *Current Pos:* RETIRED. *Personal Data:* b Durban, SAfrica, Mar 23, 21; US citizen; m 50; c 4. *Educ:* Calif Inst Technol, BS, 41; Stanford Univ, MS, 47, PhD(elec eng), 50. *Prof Exp:* Asst proj engr, Sperry Gyroscope Co, 41-44; res physicist, Naval Res Lab, 44-45; sr scientist, Varian Assocs, 48-87. *Mem:* Inst Elec & Electronics Engrs; Sigma Xi. *Res:* Electronics; velocity modulation tubes. *Mailing Add:* 12630 Corte Madera Lane Los Altos Hills CA 94022-2614

ABRAHAM, WILLIAM H, CHEMICAL ENGINEERING. *Current Pos:* RETIRED. *Personal Data:* b Englewood, NJ, May 20, 29; m 53; c 5. *Educ:* Cornell Univ, BChE, 52; Purdue Univ, PhD, 57. *Prof Exp:* Res engr, Eng Res Lab, E I du Pont de Nemours & Co, 57-62; from asst prof to prof chem eng, Iowa State Univ, 62-94. *Mem:* Am Inst Chem Engrs; Sigma Xi. *Res:* Chemical process dynamics; process control; thermodynamic measurements. *Mailing Add:* Dept Chem Eng Sweeney Hall Iowa State Univ Ames IA 50011

ABRAHAM, WILLIAM MICHAEL, ALLERGIC AIRWAY DISEASES, PULMONARY PHYSIOLOGY. *Current Pos:* Sr res assoc, div pulmonary dis, 81-83, ASSOC DIR RES, MT SINAI MED CTR, 83-, ADMIN, DEPT RES, 87- *Personal Data:* b Clifton Springs, NY, Nov 11, 49; m 72; c 2. *Educ:* Brown Univ, AB, 71; Univ Rochester, MS, 74, PhD(physiol), 76. *Mem:* NY Acad Sci; Am Physiol Soc; Am Thoracic Soc. *Res:* Respiratory physiology and pharmacology. *Mailing Add:* Dept Med Mt Sinai Med Ctr 4300 Alton Rd Miami Beach FL 33140-2849

ABRAHAMIAN, HRATCH A, DENTAL EDUCATION. *Current Pos:* RETIRED. *Prof Exp:* Assoc prof prosthodontics, Georgetown Univ Dent Sch. *Concurrent Pos:* Fulbright grantee med sci, Med Inst Yerevan, Armenia, 95-96. *Mailing Add:* Dept Prosthodont Dent Sch Georgetown Univ Washington DC 20007

ABRAHAMS, ATHOL DENIS, FLUVIAL GEOMORPHOLOGY, DESERT GEOMORPHOLOGY. *Current Pos:* assoc prof, 77-84, chmn dept, 88-91, PROF GEOG, STATE UNIV NY BUFFALO, 84- *Personal Data:* b New SWales, Australia, Mar 10, 46; m 76, H Lorraine Oak; c Geoffrey J. *Educ:* Univ Sydney, BA, 67 & PhD(geomorphol), 71. *Honors & Awards:* GK Gilbert Award, Asn Am Geogr, 85; Gladys W Cole Res Award, Geol Soc Am, 85, Asn Am Geog Hons, 92. *Prof Exp:* Fel geog, Univ Alta, 71-73; lectr geog, Univ New SWales, 73-77. *Concurrent Pos:* Vis mem staff, Univ Exeter, Eng, 77; assoc ed, Annals Asn Am Geogr, 82-87; secy-treas, Geomorphol Specialty Group, Asn Am Geogr, 84-85, chair, 85-86; proj dir, Nat Sci Found Grants, 85, 86, 88-90, 92-94; NATO grants, 85-89, 93-94; distinguished vis prof, Ariz State Univ, 87. *Mem:* Asn Am Geogr; Am Geophys Union; fel Geol Soc Am; Brit Geomorphol Res Group; Int Geog Union. *Res:* Hydraulics and erosion mechanics of overland flow on desert hillslopes; morphology and sedimentology of desert hillslopes; morphometry of channel networks; river channel morphology and processes. *Mailing Add:* Dept Geog State Univ NY PO Box 600001 Buffalo NY 14261-0001. *Fax:* 716-645-2329; *E-Mail:* geoada@ubvms.cc.buffalo.edu

ABRAHAMS, ELIHU, SUPERCONDUCTIVITY, QUANTUM STATISTICAL MECHANICS. *Current Pos:* from asst prof to assoc prof, 56-64, PROF PHYSICS, RUTGERS UNIV, NEW BRUNSWICK, 64- *Personal Data:* b Port Henry, NY, Apr 3, 27; m 53; c 2. *Educ:* Univ Calif, PhD(physics), 52. *Prof Exp:* Res assoc physics, Univ Calif, 52-53; res assoc, Univ Ill, 53-55, asst prof, 55-56. *Concurrent Pos:* Trustee, Aspen Ctr Physics, 76-82 & 92-, pres, 79-82. *Mem:* Nat Acad Sci; Am Phys Soc; AAAS. *Res:* Theoretical condensed matter physics; many body problem; critical phenomena; disordered systems; superconductivity. *Mailing Add:* Serin Phys Labs Rutgers Univ PO Box 849 Piscataway NJ 08855-0849

ABRAHAMS, M(ARVIN) S(IDNEY), MATERIALS SCIENCE. *Current Pos:* RETIRED. *Personal Data:* b New York, NY, Jan 5, 33; m 58; c 3. *Educ:* Columbia Univ, BS, 54, MS, 55, ScD(metall eng), 58. *Prof Exp:* Res assoc, Columbia Univ, 56-57; mem tech staff, Mat Res Lab, David Sarnoff Res Ctr, RCA Labs, 57-88; staff mem, Sensors Unlimited, 88-89. *Concurrent Pos:* Sr vis fel, Univ Oxford, Eng, 80. *Mem:* Am Phys Soc; Mat Anal Soc; Electron

Micros Soc Am; Electrochem Soc. *Res:* Plastic deformation of crystalline solids; brittle fracture of semiconductors; effect of structural imperfections on transport phenomena in semiconductors; defect origin, interactions and control in crystals; crystal growth of display phosphor. *Mailing Add:* 8 Evans Dr Cranbury NJ 08512

ABRAHAMS, MARK VIVIAN, BEHAVIORAL ECOLOGY, PREDATOR-PREY INTERACTIONS. *Current Pos:* ASST PROF, UNIV MAN, 89- *Personal Data:* m 83, Cheryl Cline; c Maxwell & Zea. *Educ:* Univ Western Ont, BSc, 80; Queen's Univ, MS, 82; Simon Fraser Univ, PhD(biol sci), 88. *Prof Exp:* Vis fel, Dept Fisheries & Oceans, Pac Biol Sta, 88-89. *Res:* Predator-prey interactions in aquatic communities and their impact on community structure. *Mailing Add:* Dept Zool Univ Man Winnipeg MB R3T 2N2 Can

ABRAHAMS, PAUL W, PROGRAMMING LANGUAGES, TEXT EDITING. *Current Pos:* CONSULT COMPUT SCI, 80- *Personal Data:* b Brooklyn, NY, Nov 17, 35; m 80; c 1. *Educ:* Mass Inst Technol, BS, 56; ScD(math), 63. *Prof Exp:* Sect supvr, ITT Data & Info Systs, 62-64; sr res scientist, Info Inst Inc, 64-64; assoc prof comput sci, NY Univ, 66-80. *Concurrent Pos:* Chmn, ACM Spec Interest Group Prog Languages, 78-80; vpres, assoc comput mach, 82-84, chmn, 84-86, pres, 86-88. *Mem:* Asn Comput Mach; Inst Elec & Electronics Engrs. *Res:* Programming language design, definition and implementation; text editing systems, technical writing. *Mailing Add:* 483 River Rd Deerfield MA 01342

ABRAHAMS, SIDNEY CYRIL, CRYSTALLOGRAPHY. *Current Pos:* ADJ PROF PHYSICS DEPT, SOUTHERN ORE STATE COL, 90- *Personal Data:* b London, Eng, May 28, 24; US citizen; m 50, Rhoda Banks; c David M, Peter B & Jennifer A. *Educ:* Glasgow Univ, BSc, 46, PhD, 49, DSc, 57. *Hon Degrees:* Fil Dr, Master Liberal Arts, Uppsala Univ, 82. *Honors & Awards:* Alexander Von Humboldt Found Award, 89. *Prof Exp:* Fel, Univ Minn, 49-50; mem staff, Div Indust Coop, Lab Insulation Res, Mass Inst Technol, 50-54; Imp chem indust fel, Univ Glasgow, 54-57; mem tech staff, AT&T Bell Labs, 57-82, distinguished mem tech staff, 82-88. *Concurrent Pos:* Guest scientist, Brookhaven Nat Lab, 57-, mem vis comt, 80-83, mem High Flux Reactor Adv Comt, 85-89; mem comn crystallog apparatus, Int Union Crystallog, 63-72, chmn, 72-75, chmn comn jour, 78-87, chmn comn crystallog nomenclature, 78-, mem finance comt, 81-87; mem, Nat Comt Crystallog, 66-79, chmn, 70-72; mem comt chem crystallog, Div Chem & Chem Technol, Nat Res Coun, 67-68, chmn, 68-76; mem publ policy comt, Am Inst Physics, 74-81, chmn, 81-91; vis prof, Univ Bordeaux, France, 79, 90 & 95, Univ Tuebingen, 95; mem, Numerical Data Adv Bd, Nat Res Coun, 87-89; Alexander von Humboldt Found Sr US Scientist, Inst Kristallographie, Univ Tuebingen, WGer, 89-90; founding pres, Southern Ore State Col, Sigma Xi chap, 93- *Mem:* Am Crystallog Asn (pres, 68); fel Am Phys Soc; Brit Royal Soc Chem; fel AAAS; Sigma Xi. *Res:* Crystal chemistry and solid state physics; dielectric, elastic, optical and magnetic properties in relation to atomic arrangement; crystallographic instrumentation, accuracy and automation. *Mailing Add:* Physics Dept Southern Ore State Col Ashland OR 97520-5074

ABRAHAMS, VIVIAN CECIL, NEUROPHYSIOLOGY. *Current Pos:* DIR, MED RES COUN CAN GROUP SENSORY-MOTOR PHYSIOL, 90- *Personal Data:* b London, Eng, Oct 19, 27; m 55; c 4. *Educ:* Univ Edinburgh, BSc, 52, PhD(physiol), 55, DSc, 78. *Honors & Awards:* Sarrazin lectr, Can Physiol Soc, 88. *Prof Exp:* Asst lectr physiol, Univ Edinburgh, 52-54, lectr, 54-55; vis instr, Univ Pa, 55-56; Beit fel med res, Nat Inst Med Res, Univ London, 56-59, mem sci staff, Med Res Coun, 59-63; assoc prof, 63-67, head dept, 76-88, prof physiol, Queens Univ, Ont, 67- *Concurrent Pos:* Med Res Coun vis scientist, Cerebral Functions Group, Dept Anat, Univ Col, Univ London, 70-71; bd mem, Biol Studies, Ont Grad Scholar Prog, chmn, 76-77; mem, Sci Policy Comt, Can Fedn Biol Socs, SCITEC Coun, Rep Can Physiol Soc, 76-, sci comt, Muscular Dystrophy Asn Can, 82-91, med res coun, Comt Neurosci, 82-85, finance comt, Soc Neurosci, 83-86, organizing comt, Int Union Physiol Sci, 84-86, med res coun, 84-89, standing comt on pub affairs, 85-89, med res coun, Working Group Res Involving Animals, 86-89, med res coun, Standing Comt Res & Personnel Funding, 87-89, nat organizing comt, Third IBRO/WFNS Cong, 87-91, Soc Neurosci, Govt & Pub Affairs Comt, 87-; chmn, Sci Policy Comt, Can Psychol Soc, Ont Grad Scholar Bd, 77-78; bd dirs, Sci Policy Comt, Can Fedn Biol Socs, 82-85 & vchmn, 83-85; counr, Interciencia Asn Sci Asn of Americas; vpres, Parliamentary & Sci Comt, 79-80; mem & vpres, Sci Side Comt Parliamentarians, Scientists & Engrs, 79-83; mem, Coun Scientists, Human Frontiers Sci Prog Orgn, 90-; prin investr, Network Centres Excellence for Neural Regeneration & Functional Recovery, 90- *Mem:* Am Physiol Soc; Can Physiol Soc (pres, 83-84); Asn Sci, Technol & Eng Commun Can (pres, 78-79); Soc Neurosci; Can Asn Neurosci (pres, 81-82); Can Fedn Biol Socs; Int Asn Study Pain; Physiol Soc. *Res:* Organization of sensory and effector systems in the brain stem. *Mailing Add:* 259 Fairway Hills Cres Kingston ON K7L 3N6 Can

ABRAHAMSEN, EILEEN PATRICIA, LEARNING DISBILITIES, AUTISM. *Current Pos:* ASSOC PROF SPEECH & LANG PATH, CHILD STUDY SPEC EDUC, OLD DOMINION UNIV, 79- *Personal Data:* b Englewood, NJ, June 14, 46. *Educ:* Elmira Col, BA, 68; State Univ NY, Albany, MS, 73; Columbia Univ, PhD(path), 80. *Prof Exp:* Clin supvr, Columbia Univ; speech pathologist, Helen Hayes Hosp, Haverstown, NY. *Concurrent Pos:* Fulbright scholar, Univ Malta, 95-96. *Mem:* Am Speech Lang & Hearing Asn. *Mailing Add:* 732 Maryland Ave Norfolk VA 23508. *E-Mail:* epa100@oduvm.ec.odu.edu

ABRAHAMSON, ADOLF AVRAHAM, THEORETICAL PHYSICS. *Current Pos:* Tutor physics, 57-60, from instr to assoc prof, 60-74, PROF PHYSICS, CITY COL NEW YORK, 74- *Personal Data:* b Berlin, Ger, Mar 14, 20; US citizen; m 51; c 1. *Educ:* NY Univ, BA, 50, MS, 54, PhD(physics), 60. *Concurrent Pos:* Consult, Brookhaven Nat Lab, 60-66; NASA res grant, 61-67; nat scientist personnel registr, Am Inst Physics, 63; Israel AEC fel, 64-65. *Mem:* Am Phys Soc; Am Asn Physics Teachers; NY Acad Sci. *Res:* Interatomic potentials at very small and intermediate separations; applications to radiation damage in solids; gas scattering; astrophysics; statistical model of the atom; three articles on math and eight articles on physics in Encyclopedia Britanica. *Mailing Add:* Dept Physics City Col NY Convent Ave & 138th St New York NY 10031. *Fax:* 212-650-6940

ABRAHAMSON, DALE RAYMOND, ELECTRON MICROSCOPY, IMMUNOCYTOCHEMISTRY. *Current Pos:* from asst prof to assoc prof, 83-92, PROF CELL BIOL, UNIV ALA, BIRMINGHAM, 92- *Personal Data:* b Washington, DC, June 18, 49; m 71, Susan Spell; c 1. *Educ:* Univ Va, BA, 71, PhD(cell biol), 81; George Mason Univ, BA, 76. *Honors & Awards:* Established Investr Am Heart Asn Merit Award, NIH. *Prof Exp:* Res fel, Med Sch, Harvard Univ, 80-83. *Concurrent Pos:* Res fel, Brigham & Women's Hosp, 80-83. *Mem:* AAAS; Am Asn Anatomists; Am Soc Cell Biol; Histochem Soc; Am Soc Nephrology; Micros Soc Am. *Res:* Use of labeled polyclonal and monoclonal antibodies against laminin, which is the primary noncollagenous glycoprotein of basement membranes, to determine the ultrastructural distribution of laminin with the normal glomerular basement membrane and in several experimental models of kidney disease; investigations of in vivo and in vitro development of nephrons; cloning of kidney basement membrane proteins. *Mailing Add:* Dept Cell Biol Univ Ala Univ Sta Box 302 Birmingham AL 35294-0019. *Fax:* 205-934-7029

ABRAHAMSON, DEAN EDWIN, FORENSIC SCIENCE, ENVIRONMENTAL SCIENCES. *Current Pos:* asst prof anat & lab med, Univ Minn, 67-70, assoc prof anat, lab med & physics & dir ctr studies phys environ, 70-72, assoc dean, Humphrey Inst, 82-84, PROF PUB AFFAIRS & CHMN ALL-UNIV COUN EN IRON QUAL, UNIV MINN, 72- *Personal Data:* b Hasty, Minn, Dec 21, 34; c 2. *Educ:* Gustavus Adolphus Col, BS, 55; Univ Nebr, MA, 58; Univ Minn, Minneapolis, MD & PhD, 67. *Prof Exp:* First asst physics, Royal Inst Technol, Sweden, 58; reactor physicist, Babcock & Wilcox Co, Va, 58-59; sr scientist, Honeywell Inc, Minn, 59-63. *Concurrent Pos:* Mem adv bd, Energy Pol Proj, Ford Found, 72-74; mem bd dirs, Natural Resources Defense Coun, 72-; mem, Resource Group Sociopolit Effects, Nat Res Coun Comt Nuclear & Alternative Energy Systs, Nat Acad Sci, 76-79; adv, Swedish Minister Energy, Stockholm, 77-78; vis prof, Inst Theoret Physics, Chalmers Tech Univ, Univ Gothenburg, Sweden, 77-78, Univ Iceland, 84-85, Lund Univ, Lund, Sweden, 90-94 & Inst Phys Resource Theory, Chalmers Univ Technol, Goteburg, Sweden, 94-; mem, Int Rev Group, Gorleben Nuclear Waste Storage & Reprocessing Ctr, Minister Social Affairs, Lower Saxony, 78-79; mem spec inquiry, Three Mile Island Nuclear Accident, Peer Rev Group, US Nuclear Regulatory Comn, 79-80; gov, Select Health Adv Comt, Dept Health, Pa, 82-87. *Mem:* Fel, Sci Inst Pub Info; fel AAAS; Am Geophys Union. *Res:* Technology assessment; energy policy with emphasis on nuclear issues; environmental implications of energy policies; policy relating to atmospheric buildup of carbon dioxide and climate change. *Mailing Add:* Humphrey Inst Pub Affairs Univ Minn 301 19th Ave S Minneapolis MN 55455

ABRAHAMSON, EARL ARTHUR, ANALYTICAL CHEMISTRY. *Current Pos:* RETIRED. *Personal Data:* b Aberdeen, SDak, June 5, 24; m 48, Dorothy Bergesen; c Kris L, Jill A & Kirsten L. *Educ:* Univ NDak, BS, 48; Univ Kans, PhD(chem), 51. *Prof Exp:* Analy res chemist, E I DuPont de Nemours & Co, Inc, 51-58, asst div head, phys & analy div, 58-69, mgr comput serv sect, Cent Res Dept, 69-83, res suprv, 83-85; staff market res environ field, Rolling Environ Co Inc, Du Pont, 86-96. *Mem:* AAAS; Am Chem Soc; Sigma Xi. *Res:* Analytical and physical chemistry; electrochemistry; on-line computer systems. *Mailing Add:* 1960 Superfine Lane No 85 Wilmington DE 19802

ABRAHAMSON, GEORGE R(AYMOND), ENGINEERING MECHANICS. *Current Pos:* RETIRED. *Personal Data:* b Painesville, Ohio, Aug 31, 27; m 48; c 4. *Educ:* Stanford Univ, BS, 55, MS, 56, PhD(eng mech), 58. *Prof Exp:* Machinist, SRI Int, 53-54, mech engr, 54-58, head, Explosives Eng Sect, 58-69, dir, Poulter Lab, 69-80, vpres, Phys Sci Div, 81-88, sr vpres sci groups, 88-92. *Concurrent Pos:* Consult, Norweg Defense Estab, 68-69, & US Air Force Sci Adv Bd, 85- *Mem:* Sigma Xi. *Res:* Nuclear weapons effects; dynamics of structures under pulse loads; simulation of pulse loads with explosives; properties of explosives; mechanics of penetration; precision explosive devices. *Mailing Add:* SRI Int 333 Ravens Wood Ave Menlo Park CA 94025

ABRAHAMSON, HARMON BRUCE, PHOTOCHEMISTRY, SPECTROSCOPY. *Current Pos:* asst prof to assoc prof, 84-95, PROF CHEM, UNIV NDAK, 95-, CHMN, 96- *Personal Data:* b Cokato, Minn, Aug 26, 52; m 82, Julie Conrad; c 3. *Educ:* Univ Minn, Minneapolis, BChem, 74; Mass Inst Technol, PhD(chem), 78. *Prof Exp:* Asst prof chem, Univ Okla, 78-84. *Concurrent Pos:* Vis assoc prof chem, Ohio State Univ, 91-92. *Mem:* Am Chem Soc; Sigma Xi; Inter-Am Photochem Soc. *Res:* Inorganic and organometallic photochemistry; spectroscopy of transition metal coordination complexes; coordination chemistry of small reactive molecules. *Mailing Add:* Dept Chem Univ NDak Box 9024 Grand Forks ND 58202-9024. *Fax:* 701-777-2331; *E-Mail:* habraham@plains.nodak.edu

ABRAHAMSON, JAMES ALAN, AIR TRAFFIC CONTROL SYSTEMS, GLOBAL CIVIL AVIATION. *Current Pos:* CHMN & CHIEF EXEC OFFICER, INT AIR SAFETY, 97- *Personal Data:* b Williston, NDak, May 19, 33; m 88, Susan Ragland Lewis; c Kelly Anne, James A, James W Lewis Jr, Jennifer Lewis & Christopher Lewis. *Educ:* Mass Inst Technol, BS, 55; Univ Okla, MS, 61. *Hon Degrees:* DEng, Rensselaer Polytech Inst, Utah State Univ & NY Univ. *Honors & Awards:* Aerospace Power Award, Air Force Asn; Von Karmen lectr astronaut, Am Inst Aeronaut & Astronaut, 93; Except Serv Medal, US Dept Energy; Order of King Olaf, Norway; Order of Orange, Netherlands; Order of King Leopold, Belg; Award, Daedalian Weapon Systs Mgt Asn. *Prof Exp:* Flight instr, Bryan AFB, Tex, USAF, 57-59; Spacecraft proj officer, Vela Nuclear Detection Satellite Prog, USAF, Los Angeles, 61-64; astronaut, USAF Manned Orbiting Lab, 67-69; mem staff, Nat Aeronaut & Space Coun, Exec Off Pres US, Washington, 69-71; prog dir, Maverick Missile Prog, 71-73; comdr 495th test wing, USAF, Wright Patterson AFB, 73-74; inspector gen, AF Systs Command, 74-76; syst prog dir, Multinat F-6 Prog, USAF, 76-80; dep chief staff systs, AF Syst Command, Andrews AFB, 80-81; assoc admin space flight, NASA, Washington, 81-84; dir, Pres Reagan's Strategic Defense Initiative, Pentagon, USAF, 84-89; pres transp sector & exec vpres develop, Hughes Aircraft Co, Los Angeles, 89-92; chmn bd, Oracle Corp, Redwood Shores, Calif, 92-95; investment banker, Int Air Safety LLC, 95-97; comnr, White House Comn Aviation Safety & Security, 96-97. *Mem:* Fel Am Inst Aeronaut & Astronaut. *Mailing Add:* Int Air Safety 1001 G St NW Suite 200 East Washington DC 20001. *E-Mail:* genabe@aol.com

ABRAHAMSON, SEYMOUR, GENETICS. *Current Pos:* from asst prof to assoc prof zool, 60-69, PROF ZOOL & GENETICS, UNIV WIS-MADISON, 69- *Personal Data:* b New York, NY, Nov 28, 27; m 53; c 1. *Educ:* Rutgers Univ, AB, 51; Ind Univ, PhD(genetics), 56. *Prof Exp:* USPHS fel, Univ Wis, 56-57; from instr to asst prof biol, Rutgers Univ, 57-60. *Concurrent Pos:* Mem, UN Sci Comt Effect of Atomic Radiation, 65-66 & 70; USPHS fel, Calif Inst Technol, 69; Ford Found biol adv, Agrarian Univ, Peru; mem radiation protection adv comt, Wis State Bd Health; mem, Nat Comt Radiation Protection & Measurements, adv comt biol effect of ionizing radiation, Nat Acad Sci & Comt, Int Comn Radiation Protection. *Mem:* Radiation Res Soc; Genetics Soc Am; Environ Mutagen Soc. *Res:* Radiation genetics; induced mutation by radiation and other environmental mutagens. *Mailing Add:* Zool 145 Noland Hall Univ Wis Madison 250 N Mills St Madison WI 53706-1794

ABRAHAMSON, WARREN GENE, II, PLANT ECOLOGY, INSECT HERBIVORY. *Current Pos:* from asst prof to assoc prof biol, 73-83, DAVID BURPEE PROF PLANT GENETICS, BUCKNELL UNIV, 83- *Personal Data:* b Ludington, Mich, Mar 26, 47; m 69, Christy Harmon; c Jill Raye. *Educ:* Univ Mich, Ann Arbor, BS, 69; Harvard Univ, AM, 71, PhD(biol), 73. *Honors & Awards:* Bradley-Moore Davis Award, Univ Mich, 69; Lindback Award for Distinguished Teaching, Bucknell Univ, 75; William Dutcher Award, Nat Audubon Soc, 84. *Prof Exp:* Res asst plant ecol, Univ Mich, 68-69; teaching asst biol, Harvard Univ, 69-72; tutor, 72-73. *Concurrent Pos:* Res assoc & res fel, Archbold Biol Sta, 76-; vis asst prof biol, Mich State Univ, 76; Colo Plateau Scholar-in-residence, Mus Northern Ariz & Northern Ariz Univ, 87-88. *Mem:* Ecol Soc Am; Soc Study Evolution; Sigma Xi; Bot Soc Am; Torrey Bot Club; AAAS. *Res:* Life history strategies of plants, vegetative and seed reproduction; environmental influences on life histories; effects of herbivorous insects on life history parameters of goldenrods; fire ecology of south central Florida. *Mailing Add:* Dept Biol Bucknell Univ Lewisburg PA 17837. *Fax:* 717-524-3537; *E-Mail:* abrahmsn@bucknell.edu

ABRAIRA, CARLOS, ENDOCRINOLOGY, DIABETES & NUTRITION. *Current Pos:* asst chief, 70-71, CHIEF ENDOCRINOL & DIABETES, HINES VET ADMIN HOSP, HINES, ILL, 72-; PROF MED, GRAD SCH MED, LOYOLA UNIV, 86- *Personal Data:* b Buenos Aires, Arg, Mar 25, 36; US citizen; m 63; c 2. *Educ:* Univ Buenos Aires Nat Col, Baccalaureate, 53; Univ Buenos Aires Med Sch, MD, 61; Am Bd Internal Med, dipl, 72. *Prof Exp:* Med internship, Inst Med Res, Univ Buenos Aires, 62-63; int med resident, Mt Sinai Hosp, Chicago, 64-66; clin asst med, Chicago Med Sch, 65-66; res fel med, Northwestern Univ-Evanston Hosp, 66-67; fel metab & endocrinol, Michael Reese Hosp, Chicago, 67-69, res assoc, 69-70, attend physician, dept med, 69-70; from asst prof to assoc prof med, Abraham Lincoln Sch, Univ Ill, 70-83,. *Concurrent Pos:* Lectr, Cook Ct Grad Sch Med, 75-77, Ill Acad Physicians, 85-86, Am Diabetes Asn, 84 & 94-95, Steno Inst, Denmark, 97 & Am Col Nutrit, 97; nat chmn, Vet Admin Coop Study Glycemic Control & Complications in Diabetes type II (CSDM), 89- *Mem:* Am Diabetes Asn; fel Am Col Physicians; Am Fedn Clin Res; Am Inst Nutrit; Am Soc Clin Nutrit; Endocrine Soc; fel Am Col Nutrit. *Res:* Carbohydrate metabolism; dietary influences on lipid metabolism in diabetes; drug treatment of diabetes and its complications. *Mailing Add:* Hines Vet Admin Hosp Med Serv 111A 12W Endocrinol-Diabetes Sect Hines IL 60141

ABRAM, JAMES BAKER, JR, ZOOLOGY, PARASITOLOGY. *Current Pos:* PROF, DEPT BIOL, LANGSTON UNIV, 92- *Personal Data:* b Tulsa, Okla, Dec 5, 37; m 61; c 2. *Educ:* Langston Univ, BS, 59; Okla State Univ, MS, 63, PhD(zool), 68. *Prof Exp:* Teacher high sch, Okla, 59-62; from instr to assoc prof biol, Md State Col, Princess Anne, 63-70; from assoc prof to prof, Hampton Inst, 73-82; asst dean, Sch Math & Sci, Cent State Univ, Edmond, Okla, 82-83; prof & chmn, Biol Dept, Norfolk State Univ, 83-88; prof, Dept Biol, Dillard Univ, 88-92. *Mem:* Am Soc Parasitol; Am Soc Mammal. *Res:* Helminths of muskrats; helminths of small mammals; ecological influences upon parasites. *Mailing Add:* Appl Sci Langston Univ Langston OK 73050

ABRAMOFF, PETER, ZOOLOGY, IMMUNOLOGY. *Current Pos:* CLIN PROF IMMUNOL, DEPT SURG, MED COL WIS, 72- *Personal Data:* b Montreal, Que, Dec 28, 27; nat US; m 52, 88; c 6. *Educ:* Univ Western Ont, BA, 50; Univ Detroit, MSc, 52; Univ Wis, PhD(zool), 55. *Prof Exp:* Asst, Univ Detroit, 50-52; from instr to prof biol, Marquette Univ, 55-78, chmn dept, 65-89, Wehr distinguished prof biol, Marquette Univ, 78- *Concurrent Pos:* Consult, Faust Sci Supply Co, 66-70, US Comn Undergrad Educ Biol Sci, 66-70, Educ Prods Div, 68-74, US Off Biol Educ, 70-78, NSF, 70-78, NIH Pulmonary Spec Ctr Res, 73-86 & Vet Admin Hosp, Wood, Wis, 74-86; sect ed, J Reticuloendothelial Soc, 77-87; pres, Int Union Reticuloendothelial Soc, 84-87; sr educ consult, Fotodyne, Inc, 89-; secy, Am Soc Zoologists, Div Comparative Immunol, 79-81. *Mem:* Am Asn Immunologists; Nat Asn Biol Teachers; Nat Sci Teachers Asn; Reticuloendothelial Soc (pres, 80); Int Soc Exp Hemat. *Res:* Immunobiology of the lung; hypersensitivity pneumonitis. *Mailing Add:* Fotodyne Inc 950 Walnut Ridge Dr Hartland WI 53029-9388

ABRAMOVITCH, RUDOLPH ABRAHAM HAIM, ORGANIC CHEMISTRY. *Current Pos:* prof chem & geol & head dept, 77-82, PROF CHEM, CLEMSON UNIV, 82- *Personal Data:* b Alexandria, Egypt, July 19, 30; m 52, 77. *Educ:* Univ London, BSc, 50, PhD(chem), 53, DSc, 64. *Honors & Awards:* Outstanding Res Scientist, Sigma Xi, 81. *Prof Exp:* Med Res Coun fel, Univ Exeter, 54; res chemist, Weizmann Inst Sci, Israel, 54-55; Imp Chem Indust res fel, King's Col, Univ London, 55-57; from asst prof to prof chem, Univ Sask, 57-67; prof, Univ Ala, 67-70, res prof chem, 70-77. *Concurrent Pos:* Chmn, Org Div, Chem Inst, Can, 66-67; Consult, Mead Johnson Res Ctr, 73-78; assoc prof, Marseille, France, 83, Fulbright grant, 83; Emilio Noelting chair, Mulhouse, France, 83-84; vis prof, Univ Autonoma Barcelona, 92; Fulbright lectr, Portugal, 92. *Mem:* Int Microwave Power Inst; Am Chem Soc; Chem Inst Can; Int Soc Heterocyclic Chem. *Res:* Reactive intermediates; heterocyclic chemistry; medicinal and agricultural chemistry; polymer chemistry; microwave chemistry. *Mailing Add:* Dept Chem Clemson Univ Clemson SC 29634-1905

ABRAMOVITZ, MAX, ARCHITECTURE. *Current Pos:* partner, Harrison & Abramovitz Archit, 45-76, Abramovitz-Harris-Kingsland Archit, 76-85, PARTNER, ABRAMOVITZ-KINGSLAND-SCHIFF, 85- *Personal Data:* b Chicago, Ill, May 23, 08; m 64, Anita Zeltner Brooks; c Michael John & Katherine Paul. *Educ:* Univ Ill, BS, 29; Columbia Univ, MS, 31. *Hon Degrees:* DFA, Univ Pittsburgh, 61, Univ Ill, 70. *Prof Exp:* Assoc prof, Yale Sch Fine Arts, 39-42. *Concurrent Pos:* Dep dir, UN Hq Planning Off, 47-52; consult, Brandies Univ & Univ Pittsburgh. *Mem:* Fel Am Inst Archit; Am Soc Civil Engrs. *Mailing Add:* 176 Honey Hollow Rd Pound Ridge NY 10576-1105

ABRAMOWICZ, DANIEL ALBERT, BIODEGRADATION & CHEMICAL BIOSYNTHESIS, ENZYMOLOGY. *Current Pos:* res chemist, Corp Res & Develop, Gen Elec, 84-88, mgr environ technol, 88-91, mgr bioremediation, 91-92, mgr, Environ Lab, 93-97, PROGS MGR INDUST BUS, GEN ELEC, 97- *Personal Data:* b Levittown, Pa, July 16, 57; m 83; c 2. *Educ:* St Francis Col, BS & BA, 79; Princeton Univ, MA, 81 PhD(phys chem), 84. *Prof Exp:* Comput programmer, Rohm & Haas, 79; instr chem, Princeton Univ, 81-84. *Concurrent Pos:* Adj prof biol, Rensselear Polytech Inst, 91- *Mem:* Am Chem Soc; AAAS; Am Soc Microbiol. *Res:* Use of microorganisms to degrade hazardous chemicals; application of enzymes to chemical synthesis; utilizing whole cells or immobilized enzymes. *Mailing Add:* Corp Res & Develop Gen Elec PO Box 8 Bldg DW Rm 286 Schenectady NY 12301. *Fax:* 518-387-7611

ABRAMOWITZ, STANLEY, CHEMICAL PHYSICS. *Current Pos:* Nat Acad Sci-Nat Res Coun fel, 62-64, PHYS CHEMIST, MOLECULAR SPECTROS, NAT BUR STANDARDS, 64- *Personal Data:* b Brooklyn, NY, Sept 18, 36; m 57; c 3. *Educ:* Brooklyn Col, BS, 57; Polytech Inst Brooklyn, PhD(phys chem), 63. *Prof Exp:* Asst chem, Polytech Inst Brooklyn, 57-59. *Res:* Molecular spectroscopy and structure. *Mailing Add:* Nat Inst of Standards Gaithersburg MD 20899-0001

ABRAMS, ADOLPH, BIOCHEMISTRY. *Current Pos:* actg chmn dept biochem, 73-78, from asst prof to prof, 54-90, EMER PROF BIOCHEM, SCH MED, UNIV COLO, DENVER, 90- *Personal Data:* b Springfield, Mass, Apr 30, 19; m 51; c 3. *Educ:* Univ Wis, PhD(biochem), 49. *Concurrent Pos:* Nat Res Coun fel, Cancer Soc, Carlsberg Lab & Copenhagen Univ, 49-50; Lilly fel biochem, Calif Inst Technol, 50-54. *Mem:* Am Chem Soc; Am Soc Biol Chemists. *Res:* Physical chemistry and biosynthesis of proteins; intermediary metabolism of amino and nucleic acids; chemistry and enzymology of bacterial cell membranes; relations between membranes, nucleic acids and protein synthesis; membrane permeability and active transport; bacterial membrane ATPase. *Mailing Add:* Dept Biochem Univ Colo Sch Med 13691 E marina Dr No 402 Aurora CO 80014-3739

ABRAMS, ALBERT, PHYSICAL CHEMISTRY, PETROLEUM ENGINEERING. *Current Pos:* chemist, 52-63, res chemist, 63-71, RES ASSOC, EXPLOR & PROD RES DIV, SHELL DEVELOP CO, 71- *Personal Data:* b St Joseph, La, Sept 2, 21; m 54; c 2. *Educ:* City Col NY, BS, 48; NY Univ, PhD(chem), 52. *Prof Exp:* Control chemist, Stauffer Chem Co, 48. *Mem:* Am Chem Soc; Am Inst Mining, Metall & Petrol Eng. *Res:* Fluid flow; transport phenomena; surface chemistry; flow of fluids through porous media; oil formation impairment; oil production problems. *Mailing Add:* 4630 O'Meara Dr Houston TX 77035

ABRAMS, ALBERT MAURICE, PATHOLOGY, ORAL PATHOLOGY. *Current Pos:* Instr periodont & oral path, 58-59, PROF PATH & CHMN ORAL PATH DEPT, SCH DENT, UNIV SOUTHERN CALIF, 65- *Personal Data:* b Los Angeles, Calif, June 7, 31; m 56; c 2. *Educ:* Univ Calif, DDS, 57; Univ Southern Calif, MS, 61. *Concurrent Pos:* Fel oral path, Armed Forces Inst Path, 62-64; mem attend staff, Dept Path, Los Angeles County Univ Southern Calif Med Ctr, 65-; consult, Long Beach Vet Hosp, 65-; Wadsworth Va Hosp, 79- *Mem:* Am Acad Oral Path (pres, 83); fel Am Col Dent; Am Soc Clin Path. *Res:* Clinical-pathological studies of odontogenic tumors, salivary gland diseases and fibro-osseous lesions. *Mailing Add:* 130 S Saltair Ave Los Angeles CA 90049

ABRAMS, CHARLIE FRANK, JR, AGRICULTURAL ENGINEERING, BIOENGINEERING. *Current Pos:* PROF BIOL & AGR ENG, NC STATE UNIV, 72- *Personal Data:* b Edgecombe Co, NC, June 3, 44; m 69; c 2. *Educ:* NC State Univ, BS, 66, MS, 69, PhD(bioeng & agr eng), 71. *Prof Exp:* Asst exten prof agr eng, Univ Ky, 71-72. *Mem:* Am Soc Agr Engrs; Am Soc Eng Educ; Sigma Xi; Eng Med Biol Soc of Inst Elec & Electronic Engrs; Biomed Eng Soc. *Res:* Mechanics of biological tissues as related to human and animal medicine; occupational biomechanics; agriculture. *Mailing Add:* NC State Univ PO Box 7101 Raleigh NC 27695-0001

ABRAMS, GERALD DAVID, PATHOLOGY. *Current Pos:* from asst prof to assoc prof, 63-69, dir anat path, 85-89, PROF PATH, MED SCH, UNIV MICH, ANN ARBOR, 69- *Personal Data:* b Detroit, Mich, Apr 27, 32; m 54, Gloria Turner; c Kathryn & Nancy. *Educ:* Wayne State Univ, AB, 51; Univ Mich, MD, 55. *Honors & Awards:* Kaiser Permanente Award, 78. *Prof Exp:* Instr path, Med Sch, Univ Mich, 59-60; asst chief, Dept Exp Path, Walter Reed Army Inst Res, 61-62. *Concurrent Pos:* Markle scholar acad med, 63-68; attend consult, Vet Admin Hosp, Ann Arbor, Mich, 63-; dep med examr, Washtenaw Co, Mich, 63- *Mem:* AAAS; Int Acad Path. *Res:* Pathologic anatomy; experimental pathology; gnotobiotics; effects of normal flora on host resistance; cardiovascular pathology. *Mailing Add:* Dept Path Rm 2G 332 Univ Hosp Univ Mich Med Sch Ann Arbor MI 48109-0054

ABRAMS, GERALD STANLEY, HIGH ENERGY PHYSICS. *Current Pos:* PHYSICIST, LAWRENCE BERKELEY LAB, 69- *Personal Data:* b New York, NY, May 30, 41; m 63, 80; c 2. *Educ:* Cornell Univ, BA, 62; Univ Md, PhD(physics), 67. *Prof Exp:* Res assoc physics, Univ Ill, Urbana, 67-69. *Concurrent Pos:* Guest physicist, Superconducting Super Collider Lab. *Mem:* Am Phys Soc. *Res:* Experimental high energy physics. *Mailing Add:* Lawrence Berkeley Lab MS 50A/2160 One Cyclotron Rd Berkeley CA 94720

ABRAMS, HERBERT L, DIAGNOSTIC RADIOLOGY. *Current Pos:* PROF RADIOL, SCH MED, STANFORD UNIV, 85- *Personal Data:* b New York, NY, Aug 16, 20; m 43; c 2. *Educ:* Cornell Univ, BA, 41; State Univ NY Downstate Med Ctr, MD, 46; Am Bd Radiol, cert, 51. *Hon Degrees:* MA, Harvard Univ, 67. *Honors & Awards:* Caldwell Lectr, Am Roentgen Ray Soc, 82; Dotter Lectr, Soc Cardiovasc & Interventional Radiol, 88; Hodes Lectr, Thomas Jefferson Univ, 88; Gold Medal, Radiol Soc NAm, 95. *Prof Exp:* Intern, Long Island Col Hosp, 46-47; resident, Montefiore Hosp, 47-48; resident radiol, Stanford Univ Hosp, 48-51; from instr to assoc prof radiol, Sch Med, Stanford Univ, 51-61, actg exec dir, Dept Radiol, 61-62, dir, Div Diag Roentgenol, 61-67, prof radiol, 62-67; Philip H Cook prof radiol & chmn dept, Harvard Med Sch, 67-85. *Concurrent Pos:* Nat Cancer res fel, 50; Nat Heart Inst spec res fel, Univ Lund, 60; mem radiation study sect, NIH, 63-67, exec comt, Coop Study Renovascular Hypertension; mem med adv bd, Coun High Blood Pressure Res, AHC, 66, chmn prog comt, Coun Cardiovasc Radiol, 72-75, mem exec comt, 74-; radiologist-in-chief, Peter Bent Brigham Hosp, 67-85 & Sidney Farber Cancer Inst, 74-; mem exec & adv comts, Inter-Soc Comn Heart Dis Resources, 70; mem, Joint Comn Accreditation Hosps, 72; NIH res fel, Cardiovasc Res Inst, Univ Calif, San Francisco, 73-74; consult surv renovascular hypertension, Nat Heart Inst; consult US Naval Hosp & Vet Admin, Calif & coun pharmacol & chem, AMA; mem overseas adv comt, Tel Aviv Univ Med Sch; mem, Int Blue Ribbon Panel Radiation Effects Res Found, Hiroshima & Nagasaki, 95-96. *Mem:* Inst Med-Nat Acad Sci; Asn Univ Radiol; AAAS; fel Am Col Radiol; Am Asn Cancer Res; hon fel Royal Soc Radiol, Eng; hon fel Royal Soc Surg, Ireland. *Res:* Cardiovascular radiology and physiology. *Mailing Add:* Dept Radiol Stanford Univ Sch Med Stanford CA 94305

ABRAMS, IRVING M, ION EXCHANGE, ULTRAPURE WATER. *Current Pos:* CONSULT & LECTR ION EXCHANGE, 82- *Personal Data:* b St Paul, Minn, Feb 25, 17; m 52, 78, Ann Goldstein; c Judith, Nicki & Stuart. *Educ:* Univ Minn, BCh, 38, PhD(biochem), 42. *Honors & Awards:* Award of Merit, Int Water Conf, 81. *Prof Exp:* Res chemist, Econ Lab, Inc, St Paul, 38-39; Bristol-Myers fel, Stanford Univ, 42-44, & Nat Adv Comt Aeronaut, 42-44; sr res chemist, Int Minerals & Chem Corp, Chicago, 44-47; lab dir, Chem Process Co, 47-55, assoc tech dir, 55-62; tech mgr, dept ion exchange, Duolite Int Inc, Subsid Diamond Shamrock Corp, 62-75, mgr tech develop, 75-82. *Concurrent Pos:* Instr human rels & effective speech, Simmons Inst, San Francisco & Los Angeles, 48-68; consult, Stanford Res Inst, 48, Aptech Eng Serv, Inc, 79-81, Balazs Anal Lab Inc, 84-91; mem adv comt, Int Water Conf, 62-83; chmn-elect, Gordon Res Conf Ion Exchange, 85. *Mem:* Emer mem Am Chem Soc; Am Soc Enologists; Am Soc Mech Engrs. *Res:* Anomalous osmosis and collodion membranes; foaming phenomena; chemistry of sugar beets; ion exchange resins; adsorption phenomena; water treatment and wastewater renovation; counter-current ion exchange; condensate polishing; production of ultrahigh purity water for semiconductor industry; wine and fruit juice chemistry. *Mailing Add:* 511 Castano Corte Los Altos CA 94022. *Fax:* 650-941-5640; *E-Mail:* abrams@ batnet.com

ABRAMS, ISRAEL JACOB, MARKET RESEARCH, APPLIED STATISTICS. *Current Pos:* VPRES, MRCA INFO SERV, 71- *Personal Data:* b Syracuse, NY, June 11, 26. *Educ:* Univ Calif, BA, 50, MA, 52, PhD(math statist), 57. *Prof Exp:* Asst, Univ Calif, 50-57; math statistician, Space Tech Labs, 57-61; vpres technol, Mkt Res Corp Am, 61-69; pres, Datanamics Corp Am, 69-71. *Concurrent Pos:* Lectr, Exten, Univ Calif, Los Angeles, 59-60; ed comput sect, J Mkt Res, 67-72. *Mem:* Am Mkt Asn; Inst Math Statist; Am Statist Asn; Inst Food Technologists. *Res:* Marketing research; applied statistics; computer systems design; operations research. *Mailing Add:* MRCA Info Serv 2720 River Rd Des Plaines IL 60018-4109

ABRAMS, JOEL IVAN, CIVIL ENGINEERING. *Current Pos:* RETIRED. *Personal Data:* b Baltimore, Md, Sept 7, 28; m 53; c 3. *Educ:* Johns Hopkins Univ, BS, 49, MS, 50, Dr Eng, 56. *Prof Exp:* Instr civil eng, Johns Hopkins Univ, 50-53, asst, 53-55, asst prof, 55-56; from asst prof to assoc prof, Yale Univ, 56-65; prof civil eng & chmn dept, Univ Pittsburgh, 65-92. *Concurrent Pos:* Consult, Am Mach & Foundry Co, 61- & Skorsky Aircraft Co, 62- *Mem:* Am Soc Civil Engrs; Am Soc Eng Educ; Am Concrete Inst; Int Asn Shell Struct. *Res:* Dynamics of structures; plate and shell structures; numerical methods. *Mailing Add:* 6141 Waldick Circle Delray Beach FL 33484

ABRAMS, JONATHAN, CARDIOLOGY. *Current Pos:* from asst prof to assoc prof, 70-80, PROF MED, SCH MED, UNIV NMEX, 81-, CHIEF, DIV CARDIOL, 73- *Personal Data:* b New York, NY, Feb 15, 39; m 62; c 2. *Educ:* Univ Calif, Berkeley, BA, 60; Univ Calif, San Francisco, MD, 64. *Prof Exp:* Physician internal med & cardiol, Sandia Base Army Hosp, Albuquerque, 68-70. *Concurrent Pos:* Staff cardiologist, Albuquerque Vet Admin Hosp, 70-71, actg chief cardiol, 71-72, chief cardiol sect, 72-74; trustee, Univ NMex Hosp, 79- *Mem:* Fel Am Col Physicians; fel Am Col Cardiol. *Mailing Add:* Dept Med Univ NMex Sch Med Albuquerque NM 87131

ABRAMS, LLOYD, THERMODYNAMICS & MATERIAL PROPERTIES. *Current Pos:* res chemist, Pigments Dept, Exp Sta, E I du Pont de Nemours & Co Inc, 68-72, sr res chemist, 72-75, res assoc, 75-79, staff scientist, cent res dept, exp sta, 79-91, SR RES ASSOC, E I DU PONT DE NEMOURS & CO, INC, 91- *Personal Data:* b New York, NY, June 9, 39; m 71, Virgina A Mai; c Elizabeth & Laura. *Educ:* City Col NY, BChE, 61; Rutgers Univ, PhD(phys chem), 67. *Prof Exp:* Analy engr, Conn Aircraft Nuclear Engine Lab, Pratt & Whitney Aircraft, 61, exp engr, Adv Powers Systs, Conn, 61-62, Apollo Proj, 62-63; teaching asst chem, Rutgers Univ, 63-64; res assoc, Brookhaven Nat Lab, 66-68. *Concurrent Pos:* Fel radiation chem, Brookhaven Nat Lab, 66-68; chmn, Gordon Res Conf, Chem of Interfaces, 87. *Mem:* AAAS; Am Chem Soc; Sigma Xi; Tech Asn Pulp & Paper Indust. *Res:* Gas-solid reactions; adsorption studies; phenomena in micropores; zeolites; solid state chemistry; oxides; porosimetry. *Mailing Add:* 555 Holly Knoll Hockessin DE 19707. *Fax:* 302-695-1351; *E-Mail:* abrams@esvax. dnet.dupont.com

ABRAMS, MARSHALL D, INFORMATION SECURITY. *Current Pos:* PRIN SCIENTIST, MITRE CORP, MCLEAN, VA, 81- *Personal Data:* b Jersey City, NJ, Nov 7, 40; m 62; c 2. *Educ:* Carnegie Inst Technol, BSEE, 62; Univ Pittsburgh, MSEE, 63, PhD(elec eng), 66. *Honors & Awards:* Appl res award, Nat Bur Standards, 79. *Prof Exp:* From asst prof to assoc prof elec eng, Univ Md, 66-76; mem prof staff, Nat Bur Standards, Inst Comput Sci & Technol, Washington, DC, 76-81. *Concurrent Pos:* Vis adj prof, George Mason Univ, 89-90. *Mem:* Inst Elec & Electronic Engrs; Asn Comput Mach. *Res:* Computer and network security; generalized framework for access control; security policy models. *Mailing Add:* 7525 Colshire Dr McLean VA 22102-3184

ABRAMS, MARVIN COLIN, PHYSICAL CHEMISTRY, SPECTROSCOPY. *Current Pos:* DIR SPONSORED RES & CHEM INSTR, CALIF STATE POLYTECH UNIV, 91- *Personal Data:* b Reno, Nev, Sept 6, 30; m 56; c Hal & Gale. *Educ:* Univ Nev, BS, 52, MS, 54; Wash State Univ, PhD(chem), 58. *Prof Exp:* Res chemist, AEC, Univ Nev, 52-54; asst chem, Wash State Univ, 54-58; staff scientist chem & physics, Gen Dynamics, Pomona, 59-67, sr staff scientist, 67-70, chief mfg technol, 70-79, mgr mfg technol, 79-85, chief scientist, Lockheed Air Craft Co, 86-91. *Mem:* Am Chem Soc; Combustion Inst; Sigma Xi; Spectros Soc. *Res:* Chemical mechanism and kinetics of combustion processes; spectroscopic studies of solids and reacting gaseous media; illumination. *Mailing Add:* 1989 Yorba Dr Pomona CA 91768. *Fax:* 909-869-4370

ABRAMS, MICHAEL J, GEOLOGY, REMOTE SENSING. *Current Pos:* SR SCIENTIST GEOL, JET PROPULSION LAB, NASA, 73- *Personal Data:* b Cleveland, Ohio, Mar 3, 48; m 73. *Educ:* Calif Inst Technol, BSc, 70, MSc, 73. *Prof Exp:* Jr chemist, Calif Inst Technol, 72. *Concurrent Pos:* Vpres consult, GeoImages, Inc, 74- *Mem:* Soc Econ Geol; Int Asn on Genesis Ore Deposits. *Res:* Mineral exploration. *Mailing Add:* 544 Prescott St Pasadena CA 91104

ABRAMS, RICHARD, BIOCHEMISTRY. *Current Pos:* prof biochem & nutrit & head dept, Grad Sch Pub Health, 65-70, PROF BIOCHEM & CHMN DEPT, FAC ARTS & SCI, UNIV PITTSBURGH, 70- *Personal Data:* b Chicago, Ill, Sept 19, 17; m 47; c 4. *Educ:* Univ Chicago, SB, 38, PhD(chem), 41. *Prof Exp:* Res instr chem, Univ Chicago, 41-42, group leader, Manhattan Proj, 42-46; Donner Found fel, Karolinska Inst, Sweden, 46; asst prof biochem, Inst Radiobiol & Biophys, Univ Chicago, 47-51; assoc dir inst res, Montefiore Hosp, 51-58, dir res, 58-65. *Mem:* AAAS; Am Chem Soc; Am Soc Biol Chemists; Sigma Xi. *Res:* Isolation and properties of respiratory enzymes; metabolism of fission products and transuranic elements; tracer studies of nucleic acid metabolism. *Mailing Add:* Dept Biol Sci Univ Pittsburgh Pittsburgh PA 15260-0001

ABRAMS, RICHARD LEE, APPLIED PHYSICS. *Current Pos:* sr staff physicist, Hughes Aircraft Co, 71-72, head Electro-Optics Sect, 72-75, mgr, Optical Physics Dept, 75-83, chief scientist, Govt Systs Div, 83-88, CHIEF SCIENTIST, RES LAB, HUGHES AIRCRAFT CO, 88-, CONSULT, HUGHES RES LAB. *Personal Data:* b Cleveland, Ohio, Apr 20, 41; m 62; c 2. *Educ:* Cornell Univ, BEP, 64, PhD(appl physics), 68. *Honors & Awards:* Centennial Medal, Inst Elec & Electronics Engrs. *Prof Exp:* Mem tech staff laser physics, Bell Tel Labs, 68-71. *Mem:* Fel Optical Soc Am (pres, 90); fel Inst Elec & Electronics Engrs (pres, 83); Quantrum Electronics & Applns Soc (pres, 83). *Res:* Quantum electronics; atomic physics; infrared physics; laser communications; nonlinear optics; electro-optics. *Mailing Add:* 922 Enchanted Way Pacific Palisades CA 90272. *Fax:* 310-317-5234; *E-Mail:* abrams@csfuax.hac.hrl.com

ABRAMS, ROBERT A, OPERATIONS RESEARCH, RESEARCH ADMINISTRATION. *Current Pos:* asst prof, Univ Ill, Urbana, 69-70, PROF & HEAD INFO & DECISION SCI, UNIV ILL, CHICAGO, 79- *Personal Data:* b 1939; m, Margery Lindewer; c Jonathan & Daniel. *Educ:* Mass Inst Technol, BA, 61; Northwestern Univ, MA, 65, PhD(indust eng), 69. *Prof Exp:* Assoc prof, oper res & mgt, Univ Chicago, 75-79 & Northwestern Univ, 70-75. *Concurrent Pos:* Pres, Opers Res Soc Am, 94. *Mem:* Soc Indust & Appl Math; Inst Opers Res & Mgt Sci. *Mailing Add:* Dept Info & Decision Sci Col Bus Admin 601 S Morgan St Chicago IL 60607-7124

ABRAMS, ROBERT JAY, EXPERIMENTAL HIGH ENERGY PHYSICS. *Current Pos:* asst prof, 70-74, ASSOC PROF PHYSICS, UNIV ILL, CHICAGO CIRCLE, 74- *Personal Data:* b Chicago, Ill, June 16, 38; m 66; c 3. *Educ:* Ill Inst Technol, BS, 59; Univ Ill, Urbana, MS, 61, PhD(physics), 66. *Prof Exp:* Res assoc physics, Brookhaven Nat Lab, 66-68, asst physicist, 68-70. *Mem:* Am Phys Soc. *Res:* High energy multiparticle reactions; K meson decays. *Mailing Add:* 1122 S Charles Ave Naperville IL 60540

ABRAMS, ROBERT MARLOW, PHYSIOLOGY. *Current Pos:* from asst prof to assoc prof, 69-86, PROF OBSTET & GYNEC, 86-, PROF PEDIAT, COL MED, UNIV FLA, 87- *Personal Data:* b Rome, NY, June 8, 31; m 57; c 4. *Educ:* Hamilton Col, AB, 53; Univ Pa, MS & DDS, 60, PhD(physiol), 63. *Prof Exp:* Asst prof pub health & epidemiol, Yale Univ, 68-69. *Concurrent Pos:* USPHS career develop award, 63-68; asst fel, John B Pierce Found Lab, Med Sch, Yale Univ, 63-69; mem study sect, Human Embryol & Develop, NIH, 75-78; Fogarty sr int fel, Clin Res Ctr, Harrow, UK, 78-79. *Mem:* Am Physiol Soc; Soc Gynecol Invest. *Res:* Reproductive physiology; reproduction. *Mailing Add:* Dept Obstet & Gynec Univ Fla Col Med Box 100294 JHMHC Gainesville FL 32610

ABRAMS, STEVEN ALLEN, CALCIUM METABOLISM, STABLE ISOTOPES. *Current Pos:* fel nutrit, 85-88, ASST PROF NUTRIT & NEONATOLOGY, CHILDREN'S NUTRIT RES CTR, AGR RES SERV, USDA, 91- *Personal Data:* b Columbus, Ohio, Dec 27, 57; m 87; c 2. *Educ:* Mass Inst Technol, BS, 79; Ohio State, MD, 82. *Prof Exp:* Resident pediat, Children's Hosp Akron, 82-85; fel neonatology, Baylor Col Med, 85-88; res fel nutrit, Nat Inst Child Health & Human Develop, 88-91. *Concurrent Pos:* Asst prof neonatology, George Washington Univ, 88-91. *Mem:* Am Inst Nutrit; Am Soc Clin Nutrit; Am Soc Bone & Mineral Res. *Res:* Assessment of nutritional needs especially calcium needs of infants and children using balance techniques; photon densitometry and stable isotopes; development of mathematical models of calcium disteasation in children and adults. *Mailing Add:* Childrens Nutrit Res Ctr 1100 Bates St Houston TX 77030

ABRAMS, SUZANNE ROBERTA, SYNTHETIC ORGANIC CHEMISTRY. *Current Pos:* res assoc, Nat Res Coun Can, 78-80, asst res officer to assoc res officer, Prairie Regional Lab, 80-90, SR RES OFFICER, PLANT BIOTECHNOL INST, NAT RES COUN CAN, 90- *Personal Data:* b Goderich, Ont, Apr 8, 47; m 81; c Thomas J & Margaret J. *Educ:* Carleton Univ, BSc, 72; Dalhousie Univ, PhD(org chem), 77. *Prof Exp:* Fel, Univ Alberta, 77-78. *Concurrent Pos:* Adj prof chem, Univ Sask, 88- *Mem:* Chem Inst Can. *Res:* Plant hormones; abscisic acid analogs, metabolism of abscisic acid in plants, structure/activity, jasmonic acid chemistry. *Mailing Add:* Plant Biotechnol Inst Nat Res Coun 110 Gymnasium Pl Saskatoon SK S7N 0W9 Can. *Fax:* 306-975-4839; *E-Mail:* sabrams@pbi.nrc.ca

ABRAMS, WILLIAM R, PROTEASE & PROTEASE INHIBITOR INTERACTIONS. *Current Pos:* res asst prof, Dept Med, Grad Hosp, 84-87, ASST PROF, UNIV PA SCH DENT MED, 87- *Personal Data:* b Philadelphia, Pa, May 7, 45. *Educ:* Univ Pa, PhD(biochem), 71. *Prof Exp:* Mem staff, Albert Einstein Med Ctr, 75-84; instr, Temple Univ, 81-84. *Mem:* AAAS; Am Asn Pathologists; Am Chem Soc; Protein Soc. *Res:* Connective tissue/elastin. *Mailing Add:* Dept Anat/Histology Univ Pa Sch Dent Med, 4001 Spruce St Philadelphia PA 19104-6003

ABRAMSON, ALLAN LEWIS, OTOLARYNGOLOGY. *Current Pos:* PROF & CHMN, DEPT OTOLARYNGOL, LONG ISLAND JEWISH MED CTR, 82- *Personal Data:* b New York, NY, Nov 8, 40; m 64; c 2. *Educ:* Colgate Univ, BA, 62; State Univ NY Downstate Med Ctr, MD, 67. *Prof Exp:* Resident otolaryngol, Mt Sinai Sch Med, 69-72; dir div otolaryngol, Naval Hosp, Camp LeJeune, NC, 72-74; assoc prof otolaryngol, State Univ NY, Stony Brook, 74-; dir otolaryngol, Long Island Jewish-Hillside Med Ctr, 74-; mem staff, Dept Otolaryngol, State Univ NY Health Sci Ctr, Stony Brook. *Mem:* Fel Am Col Surgeons; Am Broncho-Esophagol Soc; Am Acad Ophthal & Otolaryngol; Am Acad Facial Plastic & Reconstruct Surg. *Res:* Molecular and antibiotic transfer across normal and infected sinus membranes; bone grafting into the frontal sinus cavity. *Mailing Add:* Dept Otolaryngol Long Island Jewish Med Ctr New Hyde Park NY 11040

ABRAMSON, DAVID C, PEDIATRICS, NEONATOLOGY. *Current Pos:* CHMN, EMERGENCY MED, CAPITAL HILL HOSP; MED DIR, CHC INC. *Personal Data:* b Philadelphia, Pa, Mar 30, 38; m 60, Bonnie Nelson; c Maia, Gabrielle & Benjamin. *Educ:* Muhlenberg Col, BS, 60; Georgetown Univ, MD(med, physiol), 66. *Prof Exp:* Dir nurseries, Georgetown Univ Hosp, 69-77. *Concurrent Pos:* Consult, Columbia Hosp Women, Providence Hosp & Arlington Hosp, 68-77; prin investr, NIH, 68-; dir nurseries, Fairfax Co Hosp, 70-; consult med law, 76- *Mem:* Soc Obstet Anesthesia & Perinatology; Sigma Xi. *Res:* Placental transfer of iron; disseminated intravascular coagulation in the newborn; carbohydrate metabolism in the newborn; congenital heart disease; effect of microtransmitters on cerebral palsy; emergency medicine. *Mailing Add:* 4200 42nd St NW Washington DC 20016

ABRAMSON, DAVID IRVIN, CARDIOVASCULAR DISEASES. *Current Pos:* from asst prof to prof med, 46-72, prof phys med & rehab & head dept, 55-72, EMER PROF MED, COL MED, UNIV ILL, 72- *Personal Data:* b New York, NY, Oct 14, 05; m 40, Louise Felson; c Julie S & M Beth. *Educ:* Long Island Col Med, MD, 29; Am Bd Int Med Cardiovasc Dis, dipl, 46. *Honors & Awards:* Conrad Jobst Award Vascular Res, Am Cong Phys Med & Rehab, 70. *Prof Exp:* Asst physiol, Long Island Col Med, 28-29, instr physiol & pharm, 30-36; intern, Bushwick Hosp, Brooklyn, 29-30; dir cardiovasc res, May Inst Med Res, Jewish Hosp, Cincinnati, 37-42. *Concurrent Pos:* Fel, Michael Reese Hosp, Chicago, 36 & Mt Sinai Hosp, NY, 36-37; dir, Dept Electrocardiography, Jewish Hosp, Cincinnati, 38-42; instr, Sch Med, Univ Cincinnati, 38-42; attend physician, Hines Vet Hosp, Ill, 46-53, consult, 63-90; attend physician, W Side Vet Hosp, Chicago, 46-53, consult, 63-95; attend physician, Michael Reese Hosp, Chicago, 47-76 & Mt Sinai Hosp, 49-96. *Mem:* Fel Am Col Physicians; Am Soc Clin Invest; Soc Exp Biol & Med; Am Physiol Soc; Cent Soc Clin Res. *Res:* Physiology of peripheral circulation; peripheral vascular disorders; convalescence; rate of peripheral blood flow in man under normal and abnormal conditions and in various pathologic states, using the venous occlusion plethysmographic method. *Mailing Add:* 550 Sheridan Sq Evanston IL 60202

ABRAMSON, EDWARD, OPTICAL FIBER SYSTEMS. *Current Pos:* RETIRED. *Personal Data:* b Philadelphia, Pa, Mar 2, 33; m 76; c 3. *Educ:* Ursinus Col, BS, 54; Univ Pa, MS, 57, PhD(physics), 62. *Prof Exp:* Physicist, Cent Res Dept, EI DuPont de Nemours & Co, 62-67, res physicist, Org Chem Dept, 67-71, sr res physicist, Electronics Dept, 71-92. *Concurrent Pos:* Adj asst prof, Dept Physics & Astron, Univ Del; asst prof, Dept Physics, Millersville Univ, Pa. *Mem:* Optical Soc Am. *Res:* Ultraviolet sources and optics; photochemistry; optical imaging systems; applications of lasers; electrooptics and fiber optics; high speed electronic signal propagation. *Mailing Add:* 5 Woodcrest Way Landenberg PA 19350. *E-Mail:* abramson@dplus.net

ABRAMSON, EDWARD E, CLINICAL PSYCHOLOGY, HEALTH PSYCHOLOGY. *Current Pos:* From asst prof to assoc prof, 70-78, PROF PSYCHOL, CALIF STATE UNIV, CHICO, 78- *Personal Data:* b Brooklyn, NY, July 7, 44; m, Crystal Welton; c Anne K & Jeremy D. *Educ:* State Univ NY, Stony Brook, BA, 65; Catholic Univ, PhD(clin psychol), 71. *Concurrent Pos:* Clin psychologist, Sutter-Yuba Mental Health Serv, 73-75, York Clin, Guys Hosp Med Sch, London, 78, Alcohol Unit, Glen Gen Hosp, 81-83 & pvt pract, 85-; dir, Eating Disorders Ctr, 83-85, clin psychologist, N State Ctr Psychiat, Chico Community Hosp, 88-91; consult, Cypress Ctr, 85-88. *Mem:* Am Psychol Asn; Asn Advan Behav Therap. *Res:* Psychological variable affecting weight regulation, obesity and eating disorders; anxiety disorders; sexual dysfunction. *Mailing Add:* Dept Psychol Calif State Univ Chico CA 95929. *Fax:* 530-895-3365; *E-Mail:* eabramson@aavax.csuchico.edu

ABRAMSON, FRED PAUL, PHARMACOKINETICS, MASS SPECTROMETRY. *Current Pos:* PROF PHARMACOL, GEORGE WASHINGTON UNIV, 81- *Personal Data:* b Columbus, Ohio, 41; m 63; c 2. *Educ:* Ohio State Univ, PhD(chem), 65. *Mem:* Am Soc Pharmacol & Exp Therapeut; Am Soc Mass Spectrometry; AAAS. *Res:* Pharmacology. *Mailing Add:* Dept Pharmacol George Washington Univ 2300 Eye St NW Ross Hall No 611 Washington DC 20037-2803

ABRAMSON, FREDRIC DAVID, COMMUNICATION SYSTEMS, MANAGEMENT. *Current Pos:* PRES, HEALTH MGT SYSTS, INC, 75- *Personal Data:* b Philadelphia, Pa, Nov 9, 41; m 64, 79; c 5. *Educ:* Univ Pa, AB, 63; Univ Rochester, MS, 66; Univ Mich, PhD(genetics), 71; Mass Inst Technol, MSM, 77; Am Univ, JD, 77. *Prof Exp:* Genetic counr birth defects, Wayne State Univ, 71-72; asst prof community med, Col Med, Univ Ky, 72-75. *Concurrent Pos:* Consult, Gen Elec Co, 78-80 & Nuclear Regulatory Comn, 80-; adj prof mgt, Loyola Col, Baltimore, 80-81; bd trustees, N Charles Hosp, 82-; chmn, gov comn on workmen's comp laws, Md, 83-; adj prof mgt, Georgetown Univ, 83-84; assoc prof mgt, Col Bus, Am Univ, 83-85; adj prof technol, Johns Hopkins Univ, 95- *Res:* Development of decision support systems; recruitment and staffing; program planning and evaluation; basis of public policy formulation; strategic and long range planning systems; productivity management; performance evaluation; organization management; expert software systems; law & technology. *Mailing Add:* 21155 Woodfield Rd Gaithersburg MD 20882. *E-Mail:* fdabramson@compuserve.com

ABRAMSON, H(YMAN) NORMAN, ENGINEERING, MATHEMATICS. *Current Pos:* RETIRED. *Personal Data:* b San Antonio, Tex, Mar 4, 26; m 47, Idelle Ringel; c Phillip D & Mark D. *Educ:* Stanford Univ, BS, 50, MS, 52; Univ Tex, PhD(mech eng, math), 56. *Honors & Awards:* Distinguished Serv Award, Am Inst Aeronaut & Astronaut, 73,

Struct Dynamics & Mats Award, 94. *Prof Exp:* Proj anal engr, Chance-Vought Aircraft, 51-52; assoc prof aeronaut eng, Agr & Mech Col Tex, 52-56; dir, Dept Mech Sci, Southwest Res Inst, 56-72, vpres, Eng Sci Div, 72-85, exec vpres, 85-91. *Concurrent Pos:* Indust consult, 52-56; consult, govt agencies; assoc ed, Appl Mech Rev, 54-; vis prof, Incarnate Word Col, 58-61; adj prof mech eng, Univ Tex, Austin, 83- *Mem:* Nat Acad Eng; Am Soc Mech Engrs; Soc Exp Mech; Am Inst Aeronaut & Astronaut; Soc Naval Architects & Marine Engrs. *Res:* Applied mathematics and engineering mechanics; aerodynamics; fluid flow; shock and vibration; aeroelasticity; dynamics; nonlinear mechanics. *Mailing Add:* Southwest Res Inst PO Drawer 28510 San Antonio TX 78228-0510. *Fax:* 210-522-5122

ABRAMSON, HANLEY N, MEDICINAL CHEMISTRY. *Current Pos:* from asst prof to assoc prof, Wayne State Univ, 67-78, chair, Dept Pharmaceut Sci, 86-93, assoc provost, 91-95, PROF PHARMACEUT CHEM, COL PHARM & ALLIED HEALTH PROFESSIONS, WAYNE STATE UNIV, 78-, ASSOC DEAN, 96- *Personal Data:* b Detroit, Mich, June 10, 40; m 67, Young Hee Kim; c Nathan, Deborah & Stephen. *Educ:* Wayne State Univ, BS, 62; Univ Mich, MS, 63, PhD(pharmaceut chem), 66. *Prof Exp:* NSF fel, Hebrew Univ, Jerusalem, 66-67. *Concurrent Pos:* Interim dir, Inst Chem Toxicol, 86-88; interim dean, Col Pharm & Allied Health Profs, 87-88. *Mem:* Am Pharmaceut Asn; Am Chem Soc; Acad Pharmaceut Sci; Am Asn Col Pharm; Am Asn Pharmaceut Scientists. *Res:* Synthesis and biochemical pharmacology of natural products and their analogs. *Mailing Add:* Col Pharm & Allied Health Professions Wayne State Univ Shapero Hall Rm 125 Detroit MI 48202. *Fax:* 313-577-5589; *E-Mail:* hna@wizard.pharm.wayne.edu

ABRAMSON, I JEROME, MICROBIOLOGY, BACTERIOLOGY. *Current Pos:* sci reviewer, Div Clin Lab Device, Ctr Devices & Radiol, 78-88, eval antimicrobial agents, Ctr Drug Eval & Res, 88-93, ASST TO DIR & SUPVR MICROBIOLOGIST, OFF RES & TESTING, DIV RES & TEST, FOOD & DRUG ADMIN, 93- *Personal Data:* b Philadelphia, Pa, Aug 3; m, Barbara S Reikob; c Tammi R & Kim D. *Educ:* Pa State Univ, BS, 57; Va Polytech Inst & State Univ, PhD(microbiol), 71. *Honors & Awards:* US Pub Serv Award, 73. *Prof Exp:* Chief microbiol, Philadelphia Labs, Inc, 63-67; mgr, Fowl Cholera Vaccine Prod, VIPOL, 67; staff fel & res microbiologist, Baltimore Cancer Res Ctr, Nat Cancer Inst, 71-73; consult pharmaceut, 72-74 & 77-78; sr microbiologist, BBL Div, Becton Dickinson Corp, 73-77. *Concurrent Pos:* Consult anaerobe lab apparatus, Kontes Glass Co, 72-74; mem comt, Am Acad Microbiol, 78; mem, Task Force Vet Educ, Md, 78-81; subcomt anaerobic bacteria, Nat Comt Clin Lab Stand, 79-85; mid-level assoc, Mgt & Sci Training, Food & Drug Admin, 81-82; rep public policy, Am Soc Microbiol, 88- *Mem:* Am Soc Microbiol; fel Am Acad Microbiol; Sigma Xi. *Res:* Development, design and testing of media and devices for collection, transport, and isolation of anaerobic and aerobic microorganisms from a clinical specimen; investigation of methods to improve growth of anaerobes on commercial media; effect of antimicrobial agents on treponemes; veterinary research; inventions; patent, hormon assays. *Mailing Add:* 12405 Knollcrest Rd Reisterstown MD 21136-5609. *Fax:* 301-594-3037; *E-Mail:* abrahmson@cder.fda.gov

ABRAMSON, JON STUART, PEDIATRICS INFECTIOUS DISEASES. *Current Pos:* from asst prof to assoc prof, 81-90, vchmn, 91-96, PROF PEDIAT INFECTIOUS DIS & CROSS APPOINTMENT DEPT MICROBIOL & IMMUNOL, BOWMAN GRAY SCH MED, 90-, CHMN, DEPT PEDIAT, 96- *Personal Data:* b NY, NY Oct 31, 50; m 85; c 2. *Educ:* Boston Univ, BA, 72; Bowman Med Ctr, MD, 76. *Honors & Awards:* Res Career Develop Award, CNIAID. *Prof Exp:* Resident pediat, NC Baptist Hosp, 79. *Concurrent Pos:* Fel infectious dis, Univ Minn, 81-; prin investr, res career develop award, Nat Inst Allergy Infectious Dis, 85- & effect on influenza virus on neotrophils, NIH, 84- *Mem:* Am Soc Microbiol; Am Asn Immunologist; Fel Infectious Dis Soc Am; Soc Pediat Res (pres); Am Fedn Clin Res; Fel Acad Pediat. *Res:* Determine the mechanism by which viruses depress neutrophil function predisposing people to bacterial and fungal superinfections; pathogenesis of serious bacterial infections. *Mailing Add:* Dept Pediat Bowman Gray Sch Med Med Ctr Blvd Winston-Salem NC 27157. *Fax:* 910-716-7100; *E-Mail:* jabrams@bgsm.edu

ABRAMSON, LEE RICHARD, MATHEMATICAL STATISTICS. *Current Pos:* STATIST ADV, NUCLEAR REGULATORY COMN, 77- *Personal Data:* b New York, NY, May 19, 33; m 54; c 2. *Educ:* Columbia Univ, AB, 54, PhD(math statist), 63. *Prof Exp:* Sr res mathematician, Electronics Res Lab, Columbia Univ, 57-63, prin res mathematician, 64-67; mem res staff, Riverside Res Inst, 67-71; opers res analyst, Off Emergency Preparedness, 71-73; sr opers res analyst, AEC, 73-75; analyst, Energy Res & Develop Admin, 75-77. *Concurrent Pos:* Lectr, Sci Hons Prog, Columbia Univ, 64-69 & Math Prog High Sch Students, City Univ NY, 70-71; consult, Sandoz Pharmaceut, 69-71 & Schering Corp, 72-; prof lectr, Am Univ, 79- *Mem:* AAAS; Inst Math Statist; Am Math Soc; Opers Res Soc Am; Am Statist Asn; Sigma Xi. *Res:* General statistics; reliability. *Mailing Add:* Off Res T-10-E50 Nuclear Regulatory Comn Washington DC 20555-0001

ABRAMSON, MORRIS BARNET, PHYSICAL BIOCHEMISTRY, NEUROCHEMISTRY. *Current Pos:* Res assoc, 62-73, ASSOC PROF PHYS CHEM, DEPT NEUROL, ALBERT EINSTEIN COL MED, 73- *Personal Data:* b New York, NY, July 8, 10; m 38; c Edward & Robert. *Educ:* NY Univ, BS, 31, MS, 34, PhD(chem), 39. *Concurrent Pos:* Adj assoc prof, NY Univ, 42-; Sir Ernest Oppenheimer fel, Cambridge Univ, 61 & Polytech Inst Brooklyn, 63; NIH fel, 63; vis prof, Univ Fla, 82-84. *Mem:* Am Chem Soc. *Res:* Physical chemistry of lipids; surface chemistry of particles in aqueous media; model membrane systems; physical chemistry of neurotransmitters and enzymes acting on these. *Mailing Add:* 53-35 Hollis Ct Blvd Flushing NY 11365

ABRAMSON, N(ORMAN), COMMUNICATION THEORY, DATA NETWORKS. *Current Pos:* chmn, Info Sci Prog, 68-70, PROF ELEC ENG, UNIV HAWAII, 66-, PROF INFO SCI & DIR, ALOHA SYST, 68- *Personal Data:* b Boston, Mass, Apr 1, 32; m 54, Joan Freulich; c Mark & Carin. *Educ:* Harvard Univ, AB, 53; Univ Calif, Los Angeles, MA, 55; Stanford Univ, PhD(elec eng), 58. *Prof Exp:* Systs engr, Hughes Aircraft Co, 53-56; asst prof, Elec Eng, Stanford Univ, 59-62, assoc prof, 62-65; vis prof, Harvard Univ, 65-66. *Concurrent Pos:* Consult, indust & govt labs, 57, UN Develop Prog, 75- & IBM World Trade Corp, 76-; vis prof, Univ Calif, Berkeley, 64-65; pres, Systs Res Corp, Honolulu, 68-77; vis prof, Mass Inst Technol, 81; chmn bd, Technol Educ Assocs, Sydney, Australia, 80- *Mem:* AAAS; Inst Elec & Electronics Engrs. *Res:* Satellite communications; packet radio networks; digital networks; computer nets. *Mailing Add:* Dept Elec Eng Univ Hawaii Holmes Hall 436 Honolulu HI 96822. *Fax:* 808-926-5851; *E-Mail:* abramson@wiliki.eng.hawaii.edu

ABRAMSON, NORMAN JAY, FISHERIES, BIOMETRICS. *Current Pos:* RETIRED. *Personal Data:* b Los Angeles, Calif, May 4, 27; m 51; c 1. *Educ:* Univ Wash, BS, 55. *Prof Exp:* Marine biologist, Calif State Fisheries Lab, 55-57, head biomet anal sect, 57-70; surv biometrician, Nat Marine Fisheries Serv, 71-72; fishery biologist, Tiburon Lab, Southwest Fisheries Ctr, 72-74, dir, 74-87; fishery biologist, Calif Dept Fish & Game, Intergovermental Personnel Act, 88-92. *Concurrent Pos:* Consult, Fisheries Res Inst, Univ Wash, 69 & Food & Agr Orgn, UN, 70, 86; mem bd dir, Inst Biol Explor, 82- *Mem:* Am Inst Fishery Res Biologists. *Res:* Population dynamics of marine fishes and related statistical problems. *Mailing Add:* 397 Woodland Rd Kentfield CA 94904. *E-Mail:* normanjay2@msn.com

ABRAMSON, STANLEY L, PHYSICS, OPERATIONS RESEARCH. *Current Pos:* RETIRED. *Personal Data:* b Akron, Ohio, Mar 29, 25; m 49; c 3. *Educ:* Univ Akron, BS, 47, MS, 48. *Prof Exp:* Instr physics, Univ Akron, 46-49; asst prof, Nebr Wesleyan Univ, 49-50; chief, Ballistics Sect, US Army Chem Ctr, 50-53, mem opers res group, 53-55; sr engr, Air Arm Div, Westinghouse Elec Corp, 55-58; sr engr, Arma Div, Am Bosch Arma Corp, 58-60; adv engr, Res Lab, Westinghouse Elec Corp, 60-63, mgr tech utilization prog res & develop, Astronuclear Lab, 63-67, planning consult, Westinghouse Power Systs Planning, 67-69, consult, Westinghouse Nuclear Fuel Div, 69-78, sr consult technologist to corp staff, Corp Planning, Westinghouse Elec Corp, Pittsburgh, 78-90. *Concurrent Pos:* Adj prof, Carnegie-Mellon Univ, Grad Sch Indust Admin, 89-, Univ Pittsburgh, Katz Grad Sch Bus, 89. *Mem:* AAAS; Am Phys Soc; Inst Elec & Electronic Engrs. *Res:* Ballistics and aerodynamics of various blunt configurations; operations research applied to chemical, biological and radiological warfare and to selection of new products and new business ventures. *Mailing Add:* 1190 Colgate Dr Monroeville PA 15146

ABRAMSON, STEPHAN B, CLINICAL RESEARCH, PROTEIN CHEMISTRY. *Current Pos:* clin res assoc, Alpha Therapeut Corp, 86, clin proj mgr, 86-89, assoc dir, clin res, 89-92, ASSOC DIR, SCI EVAL, ALPHA THERAPEUT CORP, 91- *Personal Data:* b Newark, NJ, Aug 17, 45; m 84, Kathleen Oicles; c Michelle & Ryan. *Educ:* Calif Inst Technol, BS, 67; Harvard Univ, PhD(biochem), 75. *Prof Exp:* Teaching fel biol chem, Div Med Sci, Harvard Univ, 68-74; postdoctoral fel, Div Hemat-Oncol, Ctr Health Sci, Univ Calif, 75-77; postdoctoral res assoc biochem, Sect Gastroenterol, Sch Med, Univ Southern Calif, 77-81; investr biochem & cell biol, Huntington Med Res Insts, 81-86. *Concurrent Pos:* Postdoctoral fel, Nat Heart, Lung & Blood Inst, USPHS, 75-77. *Mem:* Sigma Xi; AAAS; Am Chem Soc; Am Soc Cell Biol; Am Soc Microbiol; NY Acad Sci. *Res:* Clinical and preclinical development of immunological and chemical cancer therapeutic entities and of clinically important plasmaproteins. *Mailing Add:* Dept Bus Develop Alpha Therapeut Corp 5555 Valley Blvd Los Angeles CA 90032. *Fax:* 213-227-7027; *E-Mail:* sb.abramson@altadena.worldnet.att.net

ABRASH, HENRY I, ORGANIC CHEMISTRY, BIOCHEMISTRY. *Current Pos:* from asst prof to assoc prof, 61-70, PROF CHEM, CALIF STATE UNIV, NORTHRIDGE, 70- *Personal Data:* b Paterson, NJ, Sept 27, 35; m 62, Barbara Miriom Cherne; c Ingrid. *Educ:* Harvard Univ, BA, 56; Calif Inst Technol, PhD(chem), 61. *Prof Exp:* Proj asst chem, Univ Wis, 60-61. *Concurrent Pos:* USPHS grant, 62-68; Hays-Fulbright travel grant, Carlsberg Labs, Copenhagen Univ, 68-69. *Mem:* Am Chem Soc; The Chem Soc; Sigma Xi. *Res:* Mechanism of enzyme action, particularly on hydrolytic enzymes; mechanism of hydrolytic reactions; proteins in solution; oxidation of polyphenols. *Mailing Add:* Northridge Chem Dept Calif State Univ 18111 Nordhoff St Northridge CA 91330-8262. *Fax:* 818-677-4068; *E-Mail:* henry.abrash@csun.edu

ABRASS, CHRISTINE K, IMMUNONEPHROLOGY. *Current Pos:* CHIEF IMMUNONEPHROLOGY & PROF MED & NEPHROLOGY, VET ADMIN MED CTR, 92- *Res:* Immunonephrology. *Mailing Add:* Div Nephrology Vet Admin Med Ctr 1660 S Columbian Way Seattle WA 98108

ABRELL, JOHN WILLIAM, BIOORGANIC CHEMISTRY, RESEARCH ADMINISTRATION. *Current Pos:* RETIRED. *Personal Data:* b Martinsburg, WVa, Aug 30, 36; m 67. *Educ:* Duke Univ, BS, 58; Dartmouth Col, MA, 60; Wash Univ, PhD(chem), 65. *Prof Exp:* NIH fel, 65-68; res chemist, Nat Inst Arthritis & Metab Dis, NIH, 68-71; biochemist, Litton-Bionetics, Inc, 71-74, sci adminr, Div Lung Dis, Nat Heart & Lung Inst, HIH, 74-76, Ctr Rev, Nat Inst Arthritis, Metab & Digestive Dis, 76-80, health scientist adminr, Grants Rev Br, Nat Cancer Inst, 80-97. *Mem:* Sigma Xi; Am Asn Cancer Res; AAAS; NY Acad Sci. *Res:* Enzymology; ribonuclease I from E coli; mechanism of action; nucleic acid metabolism, in particular DNA synthesis by the DNA polymerases found in RNA viruses; isolation and characterization of mammalian cellular DNA polymerases; biomedical research administration. *Mailing Add:* 2222 Pleasantview Rd Adamstown MD 21710

ABREMSKI, KENNETH EDWARD, SEQUENCE ANALYSIS, MOLECULAR BIOLOGY. *Current Pos:* PRIN INVESTR, DUPONT-MERCK PHARMACEUT, 91- *Personal Data:* b Baltimore, MD, Jan 3, 48. *Educ:* Loyola Col, MD, BS, 69; Univ MD, Med Sch, PhD(biochem), 77. *Prof Exp:* Fel NIH, Lab Molecular Biol, 77-80; scientist, Frederick Cancer Res Facil, 80-84; prin investr, E I DuPont & Co, 84-90. *Concurrent Pos:* Vis lectr, Hood Col, Frederick, MD, 83- *Mem:* Int Neural Network Soc; Asn Comput Mach. *Res:* Protein DNA interactions, computer analysis of DNA and protein sequences; neural networks. *Mailing Add:* 124 Wyeth Way Hockessin DE 19707

ABREU, SERGIO LUIS, BIOMATHEMATICS, INTELLIGENT SYSTEMS. *Current Pos:* Chmn dept, 86-90, ASSOC PROF BIOL SCI, FORDHAM UNIV, 79-, DIR GRAD PROGS, DEPT BIOL SCI, 90- *Personal Data:* b Habana, Cuba, Sept 9, 44. *Educ:* Long Island Univ, BS, 70, MS, 72; Univ Conn, PhD (biochem), 76. *Mem:* AAAS; Am Soc Microbiol; Am Soc Cell Biol; NY Acad Sci; Int Soc Differentiation. *Res:* Biology and biochemistry of differentiating systems; computer modeling of biological phenomena. *Mailing Add:* Dept Biol Sci Fordham Univ Bronx NY 10458-0001

ABRHAM, JAROMIR VACLAV, mathematics; deceased, see previous edition for last biography

ABRIKOSOV, ALEXEI ALEXEYEVICH, SUPERCONDUCTIVITY. *Current Pos:* DISTINGUISHED ARGONNE SCIENTIST & LEADER CONDENSED MATTER THEORY GROUP, ARGONNE NAT LAB, 91- *Personal Data:* b Moscow, USSR, June 25, 28; m 77, Svetlana Bun'kova; c Alexei, Michel & Natalia. *Educ:* Moscow State Univ, dipl, 48, Inst Phys Probs, Moscow, PhD(physics), 51, Dr habil, 55. *Hon Degrees:* DSc, Univ Lausanne, Switz, 75. *Honors & Awards:* Lenin Prize, USSR, 66; Fritz London Award, 72; State Prize, USSR, 82; Landau Prize, Acad Sci USSR, 89; John Bardeen Award, 91. *Prof Exp:* From jr scientist to sr scientist, Inst Phys Probs, Moscow, 51-65; dept head, Landau Inst Theoret Physics, Moscow, 65-88; dir, Inst High Pressure Physics, Troitsk, 88-91. *Concurrent Pos:* From asst prof to prof physics, Moscow State Univ, 51-76; vis prof, Univ Dehli, India, 66, Ecole Normale Superiore, France, 67, Univ Naples, Italy, 88, Univ Cologne, Ger, 89 & Oxford Univ, 89; chair theoret physics, Moscow Inst Steel & Alloys, 76-91. *Mem:* Russian Acad Sci; Am Acad Arts & Sci; Am Phys Soc. *Res:* Theoretical physics, quantum and electrodynamics; superconductors, semiconductors and semimetals; quantum fluids, statistical mechanics and physics; molecular physics, magnetism and astrophysics. *Mailing Add:* Bldg 223 Argonne Nat Lab 9700 S Cass Ave Argonne IL 60439. *Fax:* 630-252-7777; *E-Mail:* alex_abrikosov@gmgate.anl.gov

ABRIOLA, LINDA MARIE, SANITARY & ENVIRONMENTAL ENG, HYDROLOGY. *Current Pos:* asst prof, 84-90, ASSOC PROF CIVIL ENG, UNIV MICH, 90- *Personal Data:* b Philadelphia, Pa, Nov 17, 54. *Educ:* Drexel Univ, BS, 76; Princeton Univ, MS, 79, MA, 80, PhD(civil eng), 83. *Prof Exp:* Proj engr, Procter & Gamble Mfg Co, 76-78; researcher, Princeton Univ, 83-84. *Concurrent Pos:* Mem, Pub Info Comt, Am Geophys Union, 90-92, secy hydrol sect, 92-; mem, Environ Eng Comt, US Environ Protection Agency sci adv bd, 90-; mem bd dirs, Asn Environ Eng Professors, 90-93; vis assoc prof, Dept Petrol Eng, Univ Tex, Austin, 91; mem, Nat Res Coun Comt, groundwater clean-up alternatives, 91. *Mem:* Asn Environ Eng Professors; Am Geophys Union; Int Asn Hydrol Sci; Asn Ground Water Scientists & Engrs; Int Asn Hydraul Res; Asn Women Geoscientists. *Res:* Mathematical modeling of flow and transport in porous media, particularly the use of models to elucidate processes involved in the multiphase migration and transformation of organic chemical pollutants and in aquifer remediation. *Mailing Add:* PO Box 7775 Ann Arbor MI 48107-7775. *Fax:* 313-763-2275

ABROMSON-LEEMAN, SARA R, PATHOLOGY, IMMUNOLOGY. *Current Pos:* postdoctoral fel immunol, 85-88, INSTR, DEPT PATH, MED SCH, HARVARD UNIV, 88- *Educ:* Simmons Col, Boston, BS, 75; Harvard Univ, PhD(immunol), 82. *Prof Exp:* Postdoctoral fel immunol, Dana-Farber Cancer Inst, 82-84. *Concurrent Pos:* Cancer Res Inst fel, 84-87; ad hoc reviewer, J Immunol, 88- *Mem:* Am Asn Immunologists. *Res:* Immunology; pathology. *Mailing Add:* Dept Path Harvard Med Sch 200 Longwood Ave D-2 Rm 539 Boston MA 02115-5701

ABRUNA, HECTOR D, ELECTROCHEMISTRY. *Current Pos:* from asst prof to assoc prof, 83-91, PROF CHEM, CORNELL UNIV, 91- *Personal Data:* b Santurce, PR, Nov 8, 53; US citizen. *Educ:* Rensselaer Polytech Inst, BS, 75, MS, 76; Univ NC, Chapel Hill, PhD(chem), 80. *Honors & Awards:* Presidential Young Investr Award, NSF, 84; Tajima Prize, 87. *Prof Exp:* Fel, Univ Tex, Austin, 80-81; asst prof, Univ PR, Rio Piedras, 82-83. *Concurrent Pos:* Sloan Fel, 87; Guggenheim fel, 92. *Mem:* Am Chem Soc; Soc Electroanal Chem; Electrochem Soc. *Res:* Chemically modified electrodes; electrocatalysis; sensors; electrochemistry of transition metal complexes; x-ray techniques for the study of the electrode solution interface. *Mailing Add:* Dept Chem Cornell Univ Baker Lab Ithaca NY 14853-1301

ABRUTYN, DONALD, VETERINARY MEDICINE, TOXICOLOGY. *Current Pos:* ASSOC DIR TOXICOL, WARNER-LAMBERT CORP RES & DEVELOP, 90- *Personal Data:* b New York, NY, Nov 13, 34; m 64, Gesine Hildebrandt; c Kimberly, Scott, Karen & Lorraine. *Educ:* Univ Pa, VMD, 61. *Prof Exp:* Scientist toxicol, E R Squibb Corp, 65-67; res scientist, Bristol-Myers Corp, 67-68; sr res assoc, Warner-Lambert Corp, 68-77 & Pennwalt Corp, 77; group leader, Ortho Pharmaceut Corp, 78-81, sect head, 81-88, res mgr, 85-88; Dir, J J Res Found, 88-90. *Mem:* Am Vet Med Asn; Soc Comp Ophthal (secy-treas, 70-93); Indust Vet Asn Genetic Toxicol; Am Col Toxicol; Soc Toxicol. *Res:* Regulatory toxicology; ophthalmologic toxicology. *Mailing Add:* 102 Petticoat Lane Annandale NJ 08801. *Fax:* 973-540-4300

ABRUZZO, JOHN L, MEDICINE. *Current Pos:* from asst prof to assoc prof, 67-74, PROF MED, JEFFERSON MED COL, 74- *Personal Data:* b West New York, NJ, Apr 27, 31; m; c 7. *Educ:* St Peter's Col, NJ, BS, 53; Georgetown Univ, MD, 57. *Prof Exp:* Jr intern, Childrens Convalescent Hosp, DC, 56-57; med intern, Jersey City Med Ctr, NJ, 57-58; asst in med, Seton Hall Col Med, 58-60, instr, 63-64; asst prof, NJ Col Med, 64-67. *Concurrent Pos:* USPHS fel, Columbia-Presby Med Ctr, 60-61, vis fel, Col Physicians & Surgeons, 63-64; Arthritis Found fel, 63-66; NIH res grants, 64-70; from jr asst med resident to sr asst med resident, Jersey City Med Ctr, 58-60; spec investr, Arthritis Found, 66-67; asst ed, Annals Internal Med, 71-78, assoc ed, 78-; attend physician, Thomas Jefferson Univ Hosp. *Mem:* Am Fedn Clin Res; AMA; fel Am Col Physicians; Am Rheumatism Asn; Sigma Xi. *Mailing Add:* Med Rheumatol Jefferson Med Col 1025 Walnut St Philadelphia PA 19107-5001

ABSE, DAVID WILFRED, PSYCHIATRY, PSYCHOANALYSIS. *Current Pos:* prof psychiat, Sch Med, 62-87, EMER PROF, UNIV VA, 87- *Personal Data:* b Cardiff, Wales, Mar 15, 15; US citizen; c 2. *Educ:* Univ Wales, BSc, 35, MD, 48; Welsh Nat Sch Med, MB, BCh, 38; Univ London, DPM, 40. *Prof Exp:* Dep med supt, Monmouthshire Ment Hosp, Abergavenny, UK, 47-48; chief asst psychiatrist, Med Sch, Charing Cross Hosp, London, 49-51; clin dir, Dorothea Dix State Hosp, Raleigh, NC, 52-53; teaching analyst, Washington Psychoanal Inst, 62- & Washington Sch Psychiat, 71-73. *Concurrent Pos:* Lectr psychol, City Col, London, 50-51; lectr psychol & clin assoc prof psychiat, Univ NC, Chapel Hill, 52-53; from assoc prof to prof psychiat, Univ NC, Chapel Hill, 53-62. *Mem:* Fel Royal Soc Med; fel Am Psychiat Asn; Brit Med Asn; Am Psychoanal Asn; Int Psychoanal Asn. *Res:* Clinical evaluation of psychotropic drugs; psychiatric aspects of cancer; psychotherapy of schizophrenics; group analysis and cultural pathology; aystena and related mental disorders. *Mailing Add:* 1852 Winston Rd Charlottesville VA 22903

ABSHIER, CURTIS BRENT, DIGITAL SIGNAL PROCESSING, COMPUTER SYSTEM INTEGRATION. *Current Pos:* PRES, SOFTWARE SCI, INC, 90- *Personal Data:* b Tallapoosa, Mo, June 11, 45; m 78. *Educ:* Univ Mo, Rolla, BSEE, 70, MSEE, 71, PhD(elec eng), 76. *Prof Exp:* Geophysicist, Gulf Res & Develop, 76-80; sr res geophysicist, Cities Serv, 80-85; vpres, Mountain Systs Serv, 85-90. *Mem:* Inst Elec & Electronic Engrs; Soc Explor Geophysicists; Europ Asn Explor Geophysicists. *Res:* Adaptive filtering for the oil exploration industry. *Mailing Add:* 10196 Fillmore St Denver CO 80229

ABSOLON, KAREL B, THORACIC & CARDIOVASCULAR SURGERY, WRITER & PUBLISHER. *Current Pos:* CONSULT SURGEON, 85- *Personal Data:* b Brno, Czech, Mar 21, 26; US citizen; m 54; c 4. *Educ:* Masaryk Univ, BM, 48; Yale Univ, MD, 52; Univ Minn, MS & PhD(physiol & surg), 63; Am Bd Surg, dipl; Am Bd Thoracic Surg, dipl; Am Bd Cardiovasc Dis, dipl. *Prof Exp:* Asst prof surg, Med Col, Univ Minn, 63-69; asst prof, Univ Tex Health Sci Ctr Dallas, 69-70; assoc prof surg, Med Sch, George Washington Univ, 70-75 & chmn dept surg, Washington Hosp Ctr, 70-75; prof surg & acad chmn, Sch Med, Univ Ill, 75-80; expert appointment, Artificial Heart Prog, Nat Heart, Lung & Blood Inst, NIH, 80-84; publ & author, Kabel Publ, Rockville, Md, 85- *Concurrent Pos:* Am Cancer Soc fel, 54-56; USPHS trainee, 58-61, spec fel, 61-63; chg surg, Cardiopulmonary Inst, Methodist Hosp, Dallas, 69-70. *Mem:* Am Col Angiol; NY Acad Sci; Am Heart Asn; Am Col Surg. *Res:* Clinical and experimental surgery; experimental physiology and surgery; cardiovascular and pulmonary and hepatic physiology and surgery; history of surgical development. *Mailing Add:* 11225 Huntover Dr Rockville MD 20852

ABT, HELMUT ARTHUR, ASTRONOMY. *Current Pos:* assoc astronr, 59-63, ASTRONR, KITT PEAK NAT OBSERV, 63- *Personal Data:* b Helmstedt, Ger, May 26, 25; US citizen; c Daniel. *Educ:* Northwestern Univ, BS, 46, MS, 48; Calif Inst Technol, PhD(astron), 52. *Prof Exp:* Jr res astronr, Lick Observ, Univ Calif, 52-53; res assoc, Yerkes Observ, Univ Chicago, 53-55, asst prof, 55-59. *Concurrent Pos:* Assoc ed, Astron J, 67-69; consult, NASA, 67-; managing ed, Astrophys J, 71- *Mem:* Fel AAAS; Am Astron Soc; Astron Soc Pac (pres, 66-68); Int Astro; Int Coun Sci Unions. *Res:* Stellar spectroscopy and rotation; spectroscopic binaries; spectral classification; astrosociology. *Mailing Add:* Kitt Peak Nat Observ PO Box 26732 Tucson AZ 85726-6732. *Fax:* 520-318-8183; *E-Mail:* apj@moao.edu

ABU-ISA, ISMAT ALI, PHYSICAL CHEMISTRY, POLYMER CHEMISTRY. *Current Pos:* assoc sr res chemist, Gen Motors Corp, 67-69, sr res chemist, 69-77, staff res scientist, 77-80, sr staff res scientist, 80-87, prin res scientist, 87-93, RES FEL, RES & DEVELOP CTR, GEN MOTORS CORP, 93- *Personal Data:* b Tarshiha, Palestine, Dec 12, 38; m 77, Nahawand D Hammoda; c Gretta, Rima, Eyad & Nada. *Educ:* Am Univ Beirut, BSc, 59, MS, 61; Northwestern Univ, PhD(phys chem), 65. *Honors & Awards:* John M Campbell Award; Charles L McCuen Award. *Prof Exp:* Asst prof chem, P E I Univ, 64-67. *Concurrent Pos:* Nat Res Coun Can res awards, 65-67. *Mem:* Sigma Xi; Am Chem Soc. *Res:* Thermodynamic properties of polymers, oxidation and surface characteristics of polymers; processing and properties of polymers; permeation characteristics of polymer; flammability of polymers; polymer aging; polymer blends. *Mailing Add:* Polymers Dept Gen Motors NAO Res & Develop Ctr 30500 Mound Rd Warren MI 48090-9055. *Fax:* 810-986-8859; *E-Mail:* iabuisa@cmsa.gmr.com

ABUL-HAJJ, YUSUF J, BIOCHEMISTRY, ORGANIC CHEMISTRY. *Current Pos:* assoc prof, 68-80, actg chmn dept med chem & pharmacog, 84-87, PROF PHARMACOG, UNIV MINN, MINNEAPOLIS, 80- *Personal Data:* b Jerusalem, Palestine, Apr 3, 40; m 65; c 2. *Educ:* Am Univ, Beirut, BSc, 62, MSc, 64; Univ Wis-Madison, PhD(pharmaceut biochem), 68. *Prof Exp:* Asst chem, Am Univ, Beirut, 62-64; asst pharmaceut biochem, Univ Wis-Madison, 64-68. *Concurrent Pos:* Gustavus A Pfeiffer Mem Res fel, 84. *Mem:* AAAS; Am Asn Cancer Res; Am Soc Pharmacog; Sigma Xi. *Res:* Mechanisms of enzymic reactions; mechanisms in steroid metabolism; biotransformation of steroids and alkaloids; estrogen carcinogenesis, steroid metabolism in mammary tumors. *Mailing Add:* Col Pham Univ Minn Minneapolis MN 55455-0343

ABURDENE, MAURICE FELIX, ELECTRICAL ENGINEERING. *Current Pos:* prof, 81-90, T JEFFERSON MIERS PROF ELEC ENG, BUCKNELL UNIV, 90-, CHMN DEPT, 81- *Personal Data:* b Bethlehem, Palestine, May 22, 46; US citizen; c 2. *Educ:* Univ Conn, BSEE, 68, MSEE, 70, PhD(elec eng), 74. *Prof Exp:* Proj mgr, Bristol Div, Am Chain & Cable, 68-70; asst prof comput sci, State Univ NY, Oswego, 74-75; asst prof comput eng, Swarthmore Col, 75-81. *Concurrent Pos:* Electron engr, Rome Air Develop Ctr, 74 & 75; NASA/Am Soc Eng Educ fel, 77; vis scholar, Stanford Univ, 78; vis res assoc, Mass Inst Technol, 78-79; vis Dept Energy & Am Soc Eng Educ fel, Jet Propulsion Lab, Calif Inst Technol, 81; acad vis, Imperial Col, 87-88. *Mem:* Inst Elec & Electron Engrs; Asn Comput Mach; Am Soc Eng Educ; Sigma Xi. *Res:* Design and application of distributed algorithms for computer networks and graphics simulation for performance analyses; real time data acquistion; control of laboratory and industrial processes; parallel algorithms for signal processing. *Mailing Add:* Dept Elec Eng Bucknell Univ Lewisburg PA 17837

ABUSHANAB, ELIE, SYNTHETIC ORGANIC CHEMISTRY. *Current Pos:* asst prof, to assoc prof,70-79, PROF MED CHEM, UNIV RI, 79- *Personal Data:* b Damascus, Syria, Nov 6, 36; US citizen; m 65; c 3. *Educ:* Am Univ Beirut, BSc, 60; Univ Wis, MSc, 62, PhD(pharmaceut chem), 65. *Prof Exp:* Asst prof pharmaceut chem, Univ Md, Baltimore, 65-67; staff chemist, Chas Pfizer & Co, Inc, Conn, 67-70. *Mem:* Am Chem Soc; Sigma Xi; Cong Heterocycles Chem. *Res:* The use of carbohydrates as chiral templates for the synthesis of 1',2'-seco-nucleosites as inhibitors of target enzymes in cancer and viral chemotherapy; of interest are adenosien deaminase and purine and pyrimidine phosphorylase inhibitors. *Mailing Add:* 230 Fogarty Hall Col Pharm RI Univ Kingston RI 02881

ABU-SHUMAYS, IBRAHIM KHALIL, NUMERICAL ANALYSIS, APPLIED MATHEMATICS. *Current Pos:* SR FEL & ADV MATHEMATICIAN NUMERICAL ANALYST, BETTIS ATOMIC POWER LAB, 73- *Personal Data:* b Jaffa, Palestine, Feb 11, 37; m 68; c 2. *Educ:* Am Univ Beirut, BS, 60; Harvard Univ, PhD(physics), 66. *Prof Exp:* Res asst, Harvard Univ, 60-61, teaching fel, 61-64, Off Naval Res asst, 64-66; res assoc appl math, Argonne Nat Lab, 66-69, asst mathematician, Appl Math Div, 69-72; vis assoc prof eng sci dept, Northwestern Univ, 72-73. *Concurrent Pos:* Res fel, Harvard Univ, 67; vchmn & chmn, Math & Comput Div, Am Nuclear Soc, 85-87, chmn, Pittsburgh Sect, 86-87. *Mem:* Soc Indust & Appl Math; Am Nuclear Soc. *Res:* Reactor mathematics; mathematical analysis; differential equations; approximation theory; reactor science and engineering; numerical analysis; computational methods for supercomputers. *Mailing Add:* Bettis Atomic Power Lab Box 79 Lap 34DD West Mifflin PA 15122-0079

ABUZZAHAB, FARUK S, SR, PSYCHIATRY, PHARMACOLOGY. *Current Pos:* PRES, CLIN PSYCHOPHARMACOL CONSULTS, P A, 73- *Personal Data:* b Beirut, Lebanon, Oct 12, 32; m 62; c 4. *Educ:* Am Univ Beirut, BS, 55, MD, 59; Univ Minn, Minneapolis, PhD, 68. *Prof Exp:* Pharmaceut Mfr Asn Found fac career develop award & asst prof clin pharmacol, 67-69, asst clin prof psychiat & pharmacol, 69-73, assoc clin prof psychiat, Pharmacol & Family Pract, Univ Minn, 73- *Concurrent Pos:* Consult, Northern Pines Ment Health Clin, Turtle Lake, Wis, 63-70; chmn pharm subcomt, Hastings State Hosp, Minn, 64-78, chief psychiat, 70-78; clin dir, Clin Psychopharmacol Serv, Univ Minn Hosp, Minneapolis, 67-69; mem subcomt on alcoholism & drug abuse, Minn State Med Soc, 71-; consult polydrug abuse proj, Multi-Resource Ctr, 74- *Mem:* AMA; Am Psychiat Asn; Am Soc Clin Pharmacol & Therapeut; Int Col Neuropsychopharmacol; Sigma Xi. *Res:* Clinical psychopharmacology research in the area of psychoactive drugs mainly in depression, schizophrenia and memory; neurochemical correlates of behavior and drug action; toxicity of lithium carbonate in animals and man. *Mailing Add:* 701 25th Ave S Suite 303 Minneapolis MN 55454-1443

ABZUG, M(ALCOLM) J, FLIGHT MECHANICS. *Current Pos:* CONSULT, 76 - *Personal Data:* b New York, NY, Apr 13, 20; m 46; c 2. *Educ:* Mass Inst Technol, BS, 41; Univ Calif, Los Angeles, MS, 59, PhD(eng), 62. *Honors & Awards:* Douglas Aircraft Co Award, 57 & 64. *Prof Exp:* Asst aeronaut engr, Aircraft Lab, Aerodyn Br, US Air Corps, 41-43; proj engr, Flight Control Dept, Aeronaut Div, Sperry Gyroscope Co, 49-52; aeroodyn engr, Stability & Control Group, Aerodyn Sect, Douglas Co, 46-48, design specialist, 52-55, supvr, 55-62, chief, Astrodyn Br, Missile & Space Systs Div, Santa Monica, 63-64, chief engr, Flight Mech Dept, Res & Develop Directorate, 64-67; sr staff engr, TRW Systs, Inc, 67-72. *Concurrent Pos:* Consult, Cambridge Univ Press, 51-57; guest lectr, Univ Calif, Los Angeles, 58, lectr, 62-70; adj prof, Univ Southern Calif, 80-86. *Mem:* Nat Acad Eng; Fel Am Inst Aeronaut & Astronaut. *Res:* Flight mechanics of airplanes and other vehicles; fluid mechanics contributions; effects of automatic control and stabilization. *Mailing Add:* 14951 Camarosa Dr Pacific Palisades CA 90272

ACARA, MARGARET A, PHARMACOLOGY, PHYSIOLOGY. *Current Pos:* res asst med chem, 61-64, res asst biochem pharmacol, 64-67, fel & res assoc pharmacol, 73-74, from asst prof to assoc prof pharmacol, 74-90, PROF PHARMACOL, STATE UNIV NY, BUFFALO, 90- *Personal Data:* b Buffalo, NY, Jan 11, 34; m 57; c 4. *Educ:* D'Youville Col, BA, 55; State Univ NY, Buffalo, PhD(pharmacol), 71. *Prof Exp:* Prof & tech asst clin chem, Roswell Park Mem Inst, 55-57. *Concurrent Pos:* United Health Found fel, 71-73; Nat Women Sci grant-in-aid, 72; Pharmaceut Mfrs Asn Found award, 74. *Mem:* Am Soc Pharmacol & Exp Therapeut; Am Soc Nephrol; Am Chem Soc; Sigma Xi. *Res:* Renal transport and metabolism of organic cations; the role of choline and betaine in the kidney; effect of drugs on renal function. *Mailing Add:* Dept Pharmacol & Therapeut State Univ NY Sch Med Buffalo NY 14214. *Fax:* 716-829-2801; *E-Mail:* macara@ubmed.buffalo.edu

ACCIARRI, JERRY A(NTHONY), CHEMICAL ENGINEERING. *Current Pos:* RETIRED. *Personal Data:* b Filbert, Pa, Jan 6, 32; m 56; c 3. *Educ:* Pa State Univ, BS, 53, MS, 55, PhD(chem eng), 57. *Prof Exp:* From res chem engr to res group leader, 57-66, supvr petrochem process develop, 66-70, supvr fuels technol div, 70-73, cooke coordr, Worldwide Refining, Continental Oil Co, 73-93. *Concurrent Pos:* Fulbright lectr, Naples, 61-62. *Mem:* Am Chem Soc; Am Inst Chem Engrs. *Res:* Thermodynamics of vapor-liquid equilibria. *Mailing Add:* 4218 Forest Holly Humble TX 77345

ACEDO, GREGORIA N, MOLECULAR BIOLOGY, PLANT PATHOLOGY. *Current Pos:* FEL, GENETICS DEPT, NC STATE UNIV, RALEIGH, 88- *Personal Data:* b Albay, Philippines, Apr 24, 36; m 65; c 1. *Educ:* Univ Philippines, Los Banos, BSA, 59, MS, 65; Univ Mass, Amherst, PhD(plant path), 69. *Hon Degrees:* BSA Honor's Curriculum, 59. *Prof Exp:* Researcher plant path, Bur Plant Indust, Philippines, 59-62; res instr, Univ Philippines, 65-66; fel plant path, Univ Mo, Columbia, 70-71, res assoc, 73-85; scientist, Environ Protection Agency, Durham, NC, 85-87. *Concurrent Pos:* Nat Sci Develop Bd fel plant path, 62-64. *Mem:* Philippine Phytopath Soc; Environ Mutagenesis Soc. *Res:* Genetic aspect of disease resistance in plants; genetic control of flower differentiation; search for auxotrophs; tissue culture; mutagenicity testing; plant metabolic activation; down-regulation of nematode infection in transgenic plants by antisense RNA. *Mailing Add:* 22 Westridge Rd Durham NC 27713

ACERBO, SAMUEL NICHOLAS, ORGANIC CHEMISTRY. *Current Pos:* From instr to assoc prof, 58-70, PROF CHEM, IONA COL, 70- *Personal Data:* b Port Chester, NY, Jan 19, 29. *Educ:* Iona Col, BS, 55; Fordham Univ, MS, 57, PhD(org chem), 60. *Concurrent Pos:* NIH res grant, 61-62. *Mem:* Am Chem Soc. *Res:* Trace quantities of boron produce profound effects on plant growth; the use of C14 on cell wall formation in plants grown in media of varying boron content. *Mailing Add:* One Mitchell Pl Port Chester NY 10573-1804

ACETO, MARIO DOMENICO, CENTRAL NERVOUS SYSTEM PHARMACOLOGY, DRUG DEPENDENCE. *Current Pos:* assoc prof, 72-86, PROF PHARMACOL, MED COL VA, VA COMMONWEALTH UNIV, 86- *Personal Data:* b Providence, RI, Oct 26, 30; m 59, 82; c David & Steven. *Educ:* Univ RI, BS, 53; Univ Md, MS, 55; Univ Conn, PhD(pharmacol), 59. *Honors & Awards:* Honor Achievement Award, Am Col Angiol. *Prof Exp:* From instr to asst prof pharmacol, Sch Pharm, Univ Pittsburgh, 58-62; assoc res biologist, Sterling Winthrop Res Inst, 62, res biologist & group leader, 63-66, sr res biologist & head, Sect Pharmacol, 66-72, proj dir, 71-72. *Concurrent Pos:* Consult, Lederle Labs, 78, Key Pharmaceut, 84-86 & Biomet Res Inst, 90; mem, Drug Eval Comt, Col Probs Drug Dependence. *Mem:* Am Soc Pharmacol & Exp Therapeut; fel Am Col Angiol; Neuropharmacol Soc; Col Probs Drug Dependence. *Res:* Central nervous system pharmacology and drug dependence including opiates, nicotine and cocaine. *Mailing Add:* Dept Pharmacol Med Col Va Commonwealth Univ PO Box 980613 Richmond VA 23298-0613. *Fax:* 804-828-2117; *E-Mail:* maceto@gems.vcu.edu

ACHAR, B N NARAHARI, SOLID STATE PHYSICS, HISTORY OF ASTRONOMY. *Current Pos:* PROF, DEPT PHYSICS, UNIV MEMPHIS, 84- *Personal Data:* b India, Jan 5, 39; m 73, Kusuma Kongovi; c Pramod & Chandrika. *Educ:* Mysore Univ, BS, 60; Pa State Univ, MS, 65, PhD(solid state sci), 68. *Prof Exp:* Res assoc, Argonne Nat Lab, 69-72, Pa State Univ, 73-81; vis asst prof physics, Bucknell Univ, 81-84. *Mem:* Am Phys Soc. *Res:* Theory of superconductivity; ferroelectricity; ancient astronomies of India and Maya. *Mailing Add:* Dept Physics Univ Memphis Memphis TN 38152. *E-Mail:* nachar@memphis.edu

ACHARI, RAJA GOPAL, ORGANIC CHEMISTRY, ANALYTICAL CHEMISTRY. *Current Pos:* SECT HEAD ANALYTICAL CHEM, BRISTOL-MYERS PROD, 79- *Personal Data:* b West Bengal, India, Apr 22, 43; US citizen; m 71; c 1. *Educ:* Ranchi Univ, India, BSc, 61, MSc, 63; Bradford Univ, Eng, PhD(bioorg chem), 70. *Prof Exp:* Res asst org chem, Nottingham Univ, Eng, 66-67; res fel anal & org chem, Bradford Univ, Eng, 70-72; res assoc analytical chem, SC State Col, 73-74; group leader analytical chem, Cooper Labs, Inc, 74-79. *Mem:* Am Chem Soc; Royal Inst Chem London; Am Asn Pharm Scientists; Am Inst Chem. *Res:* Pharmaceutically active drugs in dosage forms and biological fluids; biosynthetic route of naturally occuring drugs and metabolism of various drugs. *Mailing Add:* Scherling-Plough Corp Galloping Hill Rd K-15-1 1945 Kenilworth NJ 07033

ACHARYA, SEETHARAMA A, PROTEIN CHEMISTRY. *Current Pos:* ASST PROF BIOCHEM, ROCKEFELLER UNIV, 78- *Personal Data:* b Ubipi, India, Aug 23, 41. *Educ:* India Inst Sci, Bangalore, PhD(biochem), 70. *Mailing Add:* Dept Med Albert Einstein Col Med 1300 Morris Park Ave Bronx NY 10461-1975

ACHE, HANS JOACHIM, radiochemistry, radiation chemistry, for more information see previous edition

ACHENBACH, JAN DREWES, APPLIED MECHANICS & MATHEMATICS, ULTRASONICS. *Current Pos:* from asst prof to assoc prof civil eng, 63-69, prof civil eng & appl math, 69-81, WALTER P MURPHY PROF CIVIL ENG, MECH ENG & APPL MATH, NORTHWESTERN UNIV, EVANSTON, 81-, MCCORMICK SCH PROF, 82-, DIR, CTR QUAL ENG & FAILURE PROTECTION, 85- *Personal Data:* b Leeuwarden, Neth, Aug 20, 35; m 61, Marcia Fee. *Educ:* Tech Univ Delft, Neth, MS, 59; Stanford Univ, PhD(aeronaut, astronaut), 62. *Honors & Awards:* C Gelderman Found Award, 70; C W McGraw Res Award, Am Soc Eng Educ, 75; Timoshenko Medal, Am Soc Mech Engrs, 92. *Prof Exp:* Preceptor civil eng, Columbia Univ, 62-63. *Concurrent Pos:* Vis assoc prof, Univ Calif, San Diego, 69; vis prof, Tech Univ Delft, 70-71; mem-at-large, US Nat Comt Theoret & Appl Mech, 72-78, 87-; consult prof, Huazhong Inst Sci & Technol, China, 81- *Mem:* Nat Acad Sci; Nat Acad Eng; fel Am Soc Mech Engrs; Am Geophys Union; Acoust Soc Am; fel Japanese Soc Adv Sci; Am Soc Nondestructive Testing; AAAS; fel Am Acad Mech (pres, 78-79). *Res:* Theoretical and applied mechanics and mathematics, particularly propagation of mechanical disturbances in solids, mechanics of fracture of solids, and quantitative non-destructive evaluation by ultrasonic wave-scattering techniques. *Mailing Add:* 711 Roslyn Terr Evanston IL 60201. *Fax:* 847-491-5227

ACHESON, DONALD THEODORE, METEOROLOGY, INSTRUMENTATION. *Current Pos:* PROJ MGR, SYST TECHNOL ASSOCS, 94- *Personal Data:* b Waltham, Mass, June 18, 35; m 61; c 2. *Educ:* Harvard Univ, BA, 57; Univ Md, MS, 65, PhD(meteorol), 74. *Prof Exp:* Gen engr physics, Engr Res & Develop Labs, Dept Army, 57-61; gen engr physics, Nat Weather Serv, Nat Oceanic & Atmospheric Admin, 61-72, gen engr physics & meteorol, Ctr Exp Design & Data Anal, 72-77, supvry electronics engr, 77-90. *Mem:* Am Meteorol Soc. *Res:* Origin and propagation of instrumental errors and optimal processing of observations in meteorology. *Mailing Add:* 3512 Beret Lane Silver Spring MD 20906. *Fax:* 301-871-1309; *E-Mail:* 71162.3305@compuserve.com

ACHESON, LOUIS KRUZAN, JR, SPACE SCIENCES, REMOTE SENSING. *Current Pos:* RETIRED. *Personal Data:* b Brazil, Ind, Apr 2, 26; m 58, Hyla A Cook; c Mari (Wood) & William. *Educ:* Case Inst Technol, BS, 46; Mass Inst Technol, PhD(physics), 50. *Prof Exp:* Systs analyst, tech staff, Hughes Aircraft Co, 50-58; mem tech staff ballistic missile defense, Inst Defense Analysts, 58-59; sr scientist space systs, Hughes Aircraft Co, 60-85, chief scientist Systs Design Lab, Space & Commun Group, 85-89. *Mem:* Am Phys Soc; Am Inst Aeronaut & Astronaut; Int Soc Syst Sci; Inst Elec & Electronics Engrs; AAAS. *Res:* Systems for defense against ballistic missiles; sensors and systems for meteorological, earth resources, solar terestrial and planetary exploration spacecraft; air traffic control systems; system analysis. *Mailing Add:* 17721 Marcello Pl Encino CA 91316-4328. *E-Mail:* lkacheson@aol.com

ACHESON, WILLARD PHILLIPS, PHYSICS, APPLIED MATHEMATICS. *Current Pos:* CONSULT, 85- *Personal Data:* b Cairo, Egypt, Nov 24, 27; US citizen; m 49, Patricia Marshall; c 3. *Educ:* Westminster Col, Pa, BS, 48; Pa State Univ, MS, 50; Univ Pittsburgh, PhD(appl math), 61. *Prof Exp:* Teacher sci & head dept, Assiut Col, Egypt, 50-53; fel struct clay prod, Mellon Inst, 53-60; asst prof physics, Muskingum Col, 60-62; sr res eng petrophys, Gulf Res & Develop Co, 62-75, res assoc energy resources, 75-81, dir, Alt Resource Recovery Sect, 81-83, sr res assoc, 83-85. *Mem:* Am Phys Soc; Soc Petrol Engrs; Soc Indust & Appl Math. *Res:* Plasticity; rheology; fluid flow; acoustics; petrophysics; enhanced recovery technology of petroleum and alternative fuels; fuel technology and petroleum engineering. *Mailing Add:* 128 N Craig St Pittsburgh PA 15213

ACHEY, FREDERICK AUGUSTUS, ANALYTICAL CHEMISTRY. *Current Pos:* RETIRED. *Personal Data:* b Lancaster, Pa, Sept 10, 29; m 58; c 3. *Educ:* Franklin & Marshall Col, BS, 51; Lehigh Univ, MS, 53, PhD, 56. *Prof Exp:* Asst, Lehigh Univ, 51-56; vpres, Serfass Corp, Pa, 56-60; supvr processes & temperature, Bethlehem Steel Corp, 60-73, asst sect mgr, 73-82, tech consult, 82-85. *Mem:* Am Chem Soc (treas, 63); Instrument Soc Am. *Res:* Analytical instrumentation; x-ray spectroscopy. *Mailing Add:* 3345 Linden St Bethlehem PA 18017

ACHEY, PHILLIP M, RADIATION BIOLOGY. *Current Pos:* asst prof biophys, 67-75, assoc prof, 75-80, PROF MICROBIOL, UNIV FLA, 80- *Personal Data:* b Lancaster, Pa, June 25, 39; c 4. *Educ:* Franklin & Marshall Col, AB, 61; Pa State Univ, MS, 64, PhD(biophys), 66. *Prof Exp:* Fel, M D Anderson Hosp & Tumor Inst Houston, 66-67. *Mem:* Biophys Soc; Am Soc Microbiol; Radiation Res Soc; Sigma Xi. *Res:* Biological and physical action of radiation on cells and DNA; repair of radiation damage. *Mailing Add:* Dept Microbiol Univ Fla PO Box 110330 Gainesville FL 32611-0330

ACHILLES, ROBERT F, SPEECH PATHOLOGY, AUDIOLOGY. *Current Pos:* RETIRED. *Personal Data:* b Inman, Kans, July 5, 24; m 46; c 2. *Educ:* McPherson Col, BS, 49; Wichita State Univ, MA, 55, PhD(logopedics), 68. *Prof Exp:* Speech pathologist, Inst Logopedics, 49-52; dir speech & hearing, Children's Rehab Ctr, Md, 52-53; clin supvr, Inst Logopedics, 53-58, dir clin serv, 58-60; assoc prof, Lamar Univ, 63-68, dir speech path, 63-, prof speech, 68- *Concurrent Pos:* Lectr logopedics, Wichita State Univ, 55-57, instr, 57-60. *Mem:* Am Speech & Hearing Asn. *Res:* Cerebral palsy and speech; voice science. *Mailing Add:* 17319 Sorrel Dr Excelsior Springs MO 64024

ACHOR, L(OUIS) JOSEPH MERLIN, SENSATION & PERCEPTION, HUMAN ELECTROPHYSIOLOGY. *Current Pos:* from asst prof to assoc prof, 78-91, dir, Undergrad Progs Neurosci & Psychol, 92-94, ASSOC PROF NEUROSCI & PSYCHOL, BAYLOR UNIV, 91- *Personal Data:* b Clarendon, Tex, Jan 2, 48; m 70, Sharon L Slack; c Shawn J & Amy C. *Educ:* Univ Calif, Los Angeles, BA, 71, MA, 72, Phd(psychobiol), 77. *Prof Exp:* Neurophysiologist, Univ Calif, Irvine, 77-78. *Mem:* Sigma Xi; Soc Neurosci; Int Brain Res Org; Am Psychol Soc. *Res:* Psychophysical and electrophysiological correlates of auditory, visual and intersensory perception. *Mailing Add:* PO Box 97334 Waco TX 76798-7334. *Fax:* 254-755-3033; *E-Mail:* l_joseph_achor@baylor.edu

ACHOR, WILLIAM THOMAS, PHYSICS EDUCATION, NOISE. *Current Pos:* dept chmn, 65-87, prof, 65-95, EMER PROF PHYSICS, WESTERN MD COL, 95- *Personal Data:* b Birmingham, Ala, June 18, 29; m 58, Dorothy Whipple; c Kathleen & Alison. *Educ:* Ala Polytech Inst, BS, 52; Vanderbilt Univ, MS, 54, PhD, 58. *Prof Exp:* Instr physics, Western Res Univ, 57-59; mem tech staff, Radio Corp Am Labs, 59-62; asst prof physics, Earlham Col, 63-65. *Concurrent Pos:* Consult, Carroll Co Bd Educ, 77-78; vis prof acoust res, Pa State Univ, 78-79; lectr, Hood Col, 82-83 & Loyola Col, 83-85; mem, Contemporary Physics Education Proj, Inc, 87- *Mem:* Am Solar Energy Soc. *Res:* Nuclear spectrometry; Auger effect; physical electronics; science education; noise; energy resources, uses and management. *Mailing Add:* 64 Ridge Rd Westminster MD 21157

ACHORN, FRANK P, CHEMICAL ENGINEERING. *Current Pos:* field engr, 60-63, engr-in-chg eng field servs, 63-66, HEAD PROCESS & PROD IMPROV SECT, NAT FERTILIZER DEVELOP CTR, TENN VALLEY AUTHORITY, 66-, SR SCIENTIST, 76- *Personal Data:* b Biloxi, Miss, Mar 23, 23; m 45; c 3. *Educ:* Univ Louisville, BChE, 47. *Prof Exp:* Process engr, Tenn Valley Authority, Wilson Dam, 47-50, process & prod engr, 52-57; asst plant mgr, Coastal Chem Corp, Miss, 57-60. *Concurrent Pos:* Consult, var US & foreign firms, 60- & C F Braun Co, Calif, 63-64. *Mem:* Hon mem Nat Fertilizer Solutions Asn; Am Chem Soc. *Res:* Fertilizer technology, especially distribution systems and technical service. *Mailing Add:* Box 176 Rte 6 Killen AL 35645-9625

ACKELL, EDMUND FERRIS, MEDICAL & EDUCATIONAL ADMINSTRATION, MAXILLOFACIAL SURGERY. *Current Pos:* pres, 78-90, EMER PRES, VA COMMONWEALTH UNIV, 90- *Personal Data:* b Danbury, Conn, Nov 29, 25; m 53; c 4. *Educ:* Col Holy Cross, BS, 49; Tufts Univ, DMD, 53; Western Reserve Univ, MD, 62; Am Bd Oral Surg, dipl. *Prof Exp:* From asst prof to assoc prof oral surg & chmn dept, Western Reserve Univ, 57-66, asst prof oral path, 62-66; dean col dent, Univ Fla, 66-69, vpres health affairs, J Hillis Miller Health Ctr, 69-74; vpres health affairs, Univ Southern Calif, 74-78. *Concurrent Pos:* Am Cancer Soc clin res fel, 55-56; mem rev comt, Health Prof Educ Act, 64-; HEW Comt Health Educ, 68; Health Planning, govt Yugoslavia, 73; mem, Nat Avd Coun, Educ Health Prof, 69. *Mem:* Am Dent Asn; AMA. *Res:* Dental education; education in the health professions. *Mailing Add:* Va Commonwealth Univ 600 W Franklin St Richmond VA 23233

ACKENHUSEN, JOHN GOODYEAR, ELECTRICAL ENGINEERING. *Current Pos:* MGR IMAGE PROCESSING LABS, ERIM ENVIRONMENTAL, 91- *Personal Data:* b South Charleston, WVa. *Educ:* Univ Mich, Ann Arbor, BS & BSE, 75, MS & MSE, 76, PhD(nuclear eng & exp plasma physics), 77. *Prof Exp:* Res assoc plasma physics, Laser Plasma Interaction Lab, Univ Mich, 76-77, interim lab dir, 77-78; mem tech staff elec eng, Bell Labs, 78-91. *Concurrent Pos:* Scholar, Laser Plasma Interaction Lab, Univ Mich, 77-78. *Mem:* Am Phys Soc; Optical Soc Am; Sigma Xi; sr mem Inst Elec & Electronics Engrs. *Res:* Implementation of man-machine communications, including information display and pattern recognition; optics and optical communications; experimental laser-plasma interaction. *Mailing Add:* 2724 Holyoke Ln Ann Arbor MI 48103

ACKER, ANDREW FRENCH, III, PARTIAL DIFFERENTIAL EQUATIONS, FREE BOUNDARY PROBLEMS. *Current Pos:* assoc prof, 87-91, PROF MATH, WICHITA STATE UNIV, 91- *Personal Data:* b New London, Conn, May 9, 43; m 91, Melissa Ann Stanton; c Michael J, Moncella I & Denise I. *Educ:* Union Col, Schenectady, NY, BS, 65; Boston Univ, PhD(math), 72; Univ Karlsruhe, Ger, Prof Dr, 81. *Prof Exp:* Asst prof math, Univ New Orleans, 72-73; asst, Univ Karlsruhe, 73-83; assoc prof, Iowa State Univ, 84-87. *Concurrent Pos:* Spec lectr, Boston Univ, 69-72; vis assoc prof, Iowa State Univ, 83-84. *Mem:* Am Math Soc. *Res:* Free-boundary problems in elliptic partial differential equations, with emphasis on uniqueness, the geometric form of the free boundary, especially convexity, and the successive approximation of the free boundary; multilayer fluid problem; plasma confinement in a magnetic field. *Mailing Add:* Dept Math & Statist Wichita State Univ Wichita KS 67260-0033

ACKER, DUANE CALVIN, ANIMAL NUTRITION. *Current Pos:* adminr, Int Coop & Develop, 90-91, ADMINR, FOREIGN AGR SERV, USDA, 91- *Personal Data:* b Atlantic, Iowa, Mar 13, 31; m 52; c 2. *Educ:* Iowa State Univ, BS, 52, MS, 53; Okla State Univ, PhD(animal nutrit), 57. *Prof Exp:* Asst animal nutrit, Iowa State Univ, 52-53; instr animal husb, Okla State Univ, 53-55; from instr to asst prof animal sci, Iowa State Univ, 55-58, assoc prof animal sci in-chg farm oper curriculum, 58-62; assoc dean agr & dir resident instr, Kans State Univ, 62-66, asst dir Agr Exp Sta, 65-66; dean agr & biol sci & dir agr exp sta, SDak State Univ, 66-74, dir coop exten serv, 71-74; vchancellor agr & natural resources, Univ Nebr-Lincoln, 74-75; pres, Kans State Univ, 75-86; dir & asst to adminr, US Agency Int Develop, 86-90. *Concurrent Pos:* exec comt, Great Plains Agr Coun, 66-67; US team for review of Marshall Plan Aid to WGer, 67; co-chmn, USDA, Exp Sta Task Force Qual of Environ, 67-68; dir, Northwest Nat Bank, Souix Falls, 70-74, Omaha, 74-75, Fed Reserve Bank Kans City, 82-86, KPL Gas Serv Co, 82-86. *Mem:* AAAS; Am Soc Animal Sci. *Res:* Meat quality as influenced by nutrients, hormones, drugs; protein and amino acid requirements and metabolism. *Mailing Add:* RFD 3 Rte 3 Box 61 Atlantic IA 50022

ACKER, FRANK EARL, ENGINEERING, ELECTRICAL ENGINEERING. *Current Pos:* ASSOC PROF, ROSE-HULMAN INST TECH, 85- *Personal Data:* b Pittsburgh, Pa, Mar 11, 37; m. *Educ:* Carnegie-Mellon Univ, BS, 59, MS, 61, PhD(elec eng), 67. *Prof Exp:* Electronics sect head, Naval Res Lab, 67-69; asst prof elec eng, Univ Pittsburgh, 69-74; sr res engr, US Steel Res Labs, 74-80; engr, res & develop ctr, Westinghouse Corp, 80-85. *Mem:* Sr mem Inst Elec & Electronics Engrs. *Res:* Industrial control systems; electrical engineering and robotics applied to industrial and mining equipment; mine power systems. *Mailing Add:* Rose-Hulman Inst Tech 5500 Wabash Ave Terre Haute IN 47803-3920

ACKERBERG, ROBERT C(YRIL), APPLIED MATHEMATICS, FLUID DYNAMICS. *Current Pos:* res assoc aerospace eng, Polytech Inst New York, 63, from asst prof to prof, 63-95, EMER PROF CHEM ENG, POLYTECH INST NEW YORK, 96- *Personal Data:* b Minneapolis, Minn, Sept 14, 34; c 2. *Educ:* Mass Inst Technol, BS, 56; Univ Mich, MSE, 57; Harvard Univ, MA, 60, PhD(appl math), 63. *Prof Exp:* Sr res scientist physics, Raytheon Corp, 62-63. *Concurrent Pos:* Fel, NSF, 56-59, grantee, 71-72 & 74-79, prin investr, 74-; res fel, Sci Res Coun of Gt Brit, 71-72; comnr, Water Authority Southeastern Nassau Co, 92- *Mem:* Am Inst Chem Engrs. *Res:* Boundary-layer theory; theory of boundary-layer separation; nonlinear theory of thin jets; potential flow; singular perturbations; matched asymptotic expansions; thermodynamics; heat transfer. *Mailing Add:* Dept Chem Eng Polytech Univ Long Island Ctr Rte 110 Farmingdale NY 11735. *E-Mail:* ackerber@rama.poly.edu

ACKERMAN, BRUCE DAVID, PEDIATRICS. *Current Pos:* ASSOC PROF PEDIAT, STATE UNIV NY AT BROOKLYN, 75- *Personal Data:* b New York, NY, Mar 12, 34; m 57; c 2. *Educ:* NY Univ, AB, 54; Univ Chicago, MD, 58. *Prof Exp:* Fel neonatology, Magee-Womens Hosp, Univ Pittsburgh, 63-65; from instr to assoc prof pediat, Univ Calif, Irvine, 65-72; assoc prof, State Univ NY Stony Brook, 72-74; assoc prof, Mt Sinai Sch Med, 74-75. *Mem:* Am Thoracic Soc; Soc Pediat Res; Am Acad Pediat; NY Pediat Soc. *Res:* Perinatal physiology; fetal, placental and neonatal blood flow; effect of narcotic drugs on the fetus and newborn; use of expressed breast milk for nutritional support of premature infants in less advaced societies. *Mailing Add:* Maimonides Med Ctr Brooklyn NY 11219

ACKERMAN, C(ARL) D(AVID), process design, synthetic fuels, for more information see previous edition

ACKERMAN, ERIC J, DNA REPAIR & REPLICATION, RNA METABOLISM. *Current Pos:* SR STAFF FEL MOLECULAR BIOL, NAT INST DIABETES & DIGESITIVE & KIDNEY DIS, NIH, 85-, SR SCIENTIST, PAC NORTHWEST NAT LAB. *Personal Data:* b Coral Gables, Fla, Feb 6, 54. *Educ:* Univ Fla, BSc, 75; Univ Chicago, PhD(biophys), 80. *Prof Exp:* Postdoctoral fel, Lab Molecular Biol, Med Res Coun, 81-85. *Concurrent Pos:* Fel, Anna Fuller Found, 81, Helen Hay Whitney Found, 82-84 & Deutsche Akademischeaustaush Dienst, 85. *Mem:* Fedn Am Socs Exp Biol. *Res:* Elucidating the molecular mechanisms used by toxins to kill cells; molecular biology of eukaryotic DNA repair and replication. *Mailing Add:* PAC NW Nat Lab P7-56 PO Box 999 Richland WA 99352-0999. *Fax:* 509-376-2149; *E-Mail:* ej_ackerman@pnl.gov

ACKERMAN, EUGENE, HEALTH & COMPUTER SCIENCES. *Current Pos:* assoc prof biophys, Mayo Grad Sch Med, 60-65, prof, 65-67, prof biomed comput & biomet, Col Med Sci, 67-69, dir, Div Health Comput Sci, 69-78, dir grad prog biophys sci, 79-88, PROF LAB MED & PATH, MED SCH, UNIV MINN, MINNEAPOLIS, 69- *Personal Data:* b Brooklyn, NY, July 8, 20; m 43; c 3. *Educ:* Swarthmore Col, BA, 41; Brown Univ, ScM, 43; Univ Wis, PhD(biophys), 49. *Prof Exp:* Asst, Brown Univ, 41-43; asst, Univ Wis, 46-47; res asst, Wis Alumni Res Found, 47-49; assoc biophys, Johnson Res Found, Univ Pa, 49-51; from asst prof to assoc prof physics, Pa State Univ, 51-58, prof biophys, 58-60. *Concurrent Pos:* Johnson Res Found fel, Univ Pa, 57-58; consult, Mayo Found, 60-67, dir comput facil, 63-65; mem var comts, NIH, 64-74; ed, Biophys J, 83-87. *Mem:* Asn Comput Mach; NY Acad Sci; Inst Elec & Electronics Engrs; Sigma Xi; Am Physiol Soc; Biophys Soc; fel Am Inst Med Info. *Res:* Health computer sciences; biomathematics; Monte Carlo models; biophysics; biomedical engineering. *Mailing Add:* Box 511 UMHC Univ Minn 420 Delaware St SE Minneapolis MN 55455

ACKERMAN, GUSTAVE ADOLPH, JR, ANATOMY, MEDICINE. *Current Pos:* from asst prof to assoc prof, 57-64, PROF ANAT, OHIO STATE UNIV, 64- *Personal Data:* b Columbus, Ohio; m 56; c 2. *Educ:* Ohio State Univ, BA, 48, MSc, 49, MD & PhD(anat), 54. *Honors & Awards:* Borden Award, 54. *Prof Exp:* Intern med, Salt Lake Co Hosp, 54-55. *Concurrent Pos:* Lederle Med Fac award, 61-63. *Mem:* Am Asn Anat; Histochem Soc; Am Soc Cell Biol. *Res:* Morphology and histochemistry of the cells of the blood and hemopoietic system; cellular differentiation and origin. *Mailing Add:* Dept Anat Ohio State Univ Col Med 370 W Ninth Ave Columbus OH 43210-1238

ACKERMAN, HERVEY WINFIELD, JR, ORGANIC CHEMISTRY. *Current Pos:* RETIRED. *Personal Data:* b Easton, Pa, Feb 28, 29; m 47, 64; c 6. *Educ:* Lafayette Col, BS, 49; Yale Univ, PhD(org chem), 53. *Prof Exp:* Res chemist, Film Dept, E I du Pont de Nemours & Co, 52-54; res chemist, Nat Aniline Div, Allied Chem Corp, 54-62; res chemist, Air Prod & Chem, Inc, 62-64; res chemist, M & T Chem, Inc, 64-68; opers res, Am Can Co, 68-70, adminr mgt sci, 70-72; assoc, ROI Controls Corp, 72-75; consult, Consolidated Edison Co NY, Inc, 75-77, control systs specialist, 77-91. *Mem:* Am Chem Soc. *Res:* Management sciences. *Mailing Add:* 13 Quail Run Circle Brevard NC 28712

ACKERMAN, JAMES HOWARD, MEDICINAL CHEMISTRY. *Current Pos:* RES INVESTR, STERLING RES GROUP, 58- *Personal Data:* b Detroit, Mich, Oct 4, 28; m 54, 76; c 2. *Educ:* Univ Mich, BS, 50; Univ Wis, PhD(org chem), 54. *Prof Exp:* Chemist, Mallinckrodt Chem Works, 54-58. *Mem:* Am Chem Soc. *Res:* Radiopaques; steroids. *Mailing Add:* 28 Marion Ave Albany NY 12203-1823

ACKERMAN, JAMES L, orthodontics, for more information see previous edition

ACKERMAN, JEROME LEONARD, MAGNETIC RESONANCE, BONE & BIOMATERIALS. *Current Pos:* asst prof radiol, 85-95, ASSOC PROF RADIOL, HARVARD MED SCH, 95-; ASST PHYSICS & DIR NUCLEAR MAGNETIC RESONANCE SPECTROS & CO-DIR, BIOMAT LAB, DEPT RADIOL, MASS GEN HOSP, 85- *Personal Data:* b New York, NY, Jan 4, 50; m 86; c 2. *Educ:* State Univ NY Stony Brook, BS, 71; Mass Inst Techol, PhD(phys chem), 76. *Prof Exp:* Res chemist, Dept Chem, Univ Calif, Berkeley, 76-77; assoc prof, Dept Chem, Univ Cincinnati, 77-85. *Concurrent Pos:* Scientist appointee, Argonne Nat Lab, 86-91; res affil, Mass Inst Technol, 90-; res assoc, Children's Hosp, Boston, 96- *Mem:* Am Chem Soc; AAAS; Int Soc Magnetic Resonance Med; Am Ceramic Soc; Mat Res Soc. *Res:* Nuclear magnetic resonance imaging techniques for biological and nonbiolgical systems; development of magnetic resonance imaging of solid materials; studies of bone and biomaterials. *Mailing Add:* NMR Ctr Mass Gen Hosp Rm 2301 149 13th St Charlestown MA 02129-2000. *Fax:* 617-726-7422; *E-Mail:* jerry@nmr.mgh.harvard.edu

ACKERMAN, JOSEPH JOHN HENRY, NUCLEAR MAGNETIC RESONANCE. *Current Pos:* from asst prof to assoc prof chem, 79-85, PROF CHEM, WASHINGTON UNIV, 85-, CHMN, 88-, PROF RADIOL, SCH MED, 95- *Personal Data:* b Tulsa, Okla, July 17, 49; div; c Joseph & Stephanie. *Educ:* Boston Univ, BA, 72; Colo State Univ, PhD(chem), 77. *Honors & Awards:* St Louis Award, Am Chem Soc, 87; William Simpson Award, Wayne State Univ, 89; Gold Medal Award, Soc Magnetic Resonance Med, 92- *Prof Exp:* Res assoc, Dept Chem, Colo State Univ, 77-78; NIH fel, Dept Biochem, Oxford Univ, 78-79; res asst prof chem med, Sch Med, Washington Univ, 80-86, res assoc prof, 86-92, res prof, 92- *Concurrent Pos:* Vpres, Dan Broida-Sigma-Aldrich Corp Scholar Fund, Inc, 84-89, pres, 89-; mem bd trustees, Soc Magnetic Resonance Med, 86-89; mem exec comt, Exp Nuclear Magnetic Resonance Conf, Inc, 88-91. *Mem:* AAAS; Am Chem Soc; Int Soc Magnetic Resonance Med; Am Phys Soc. *Res:* Nuclear magnetic resonanace imaging and spectroscopic studies of intact functioning biological systems including in vivo and perfused in vitro tissues. *Mailing Add:* Dept Chem Campus Box 1134 Washington Univ St Louis MO 63130-4899

ACKERMAN, LARRY JOSEPH, VETERINARY PATHOLOGY, ELECTRON MICROSCOPY. *Current Pos:* vet pathologist, Pharmakon Res Int, 76-78, dir path, 78-87, dir corp res, Exp Path Lab, Inc, 87-94, DIR PATH, PHARMAKON RES INT, 94- *Personal Data:* b Hanover, Pa, Jan 8, 39; m 63; c 3. *Educ:* Univ Pa, VMD, 63; Univ Mo, Columbia, 68, 70; Am Col Vet Pathologists, dipl. *Prof Exp:* Asst chief, Path Div & prin investr, US Army Med Res & Nutrit Lab, Denver, 64-66; teaching & res asst vet path & prin investr, Sch Vet Med, Univ Mo, Columbia, 66-68; asst chief, Path Div, US Army Med Res & Nutrit Lab, Denver, 68-71; chief, Path Div & prin investr, US Army Med Res Unit, Panama, 71-74; chief vet path, Biomed Lab Edgewood, Army Proving Ground, US Army, Md, 74-76. *Concurrent Pos:* Consult, Consumer Prod Safety Comn Studies, 74-76; lectr path, Exp Path Labs, Inc, 76- *Mem:* Soc Toxicol Pathologists; Int Acad Pathologists; Soc Comp Ophthal; Am Vet Med Asn. *Res:* Experimental pathology: viral, parasitic and nutritional diseases, safety and carcinogenic potential of various environmental, industrial and pharmaceutical compounds. *Mailing Add:* 16 Lakeside Dr Clarks Summit PA 18411

ACKERMAN, MICHAEL J, BIOMEDICAL ENGINEERING. *Current Pos:* ASST DIR, HIGH PERFORMANCE COMPUT & COMMUN, NIH, 94- *Personal Data:* b Brooklyn, NY, Apr 11, 46; m 67; c 2. *Educ:* Hofstra Univ, BA, 66; Clark Univ, MA, 69; Univ NC, Chapel Hill, PhD(biomed eng), 71. *Honors & Awards:* Serv Award, Am Inst Med & Biol Eng, 94; Spec Recognition Award, USPHS, 95. *Prof Exp:* Chief biomed eng, Naval Med Res Inst, 72-87; chief, Educ Technol Br, Nat Libr Med, 87-94. *Mem:* Am Inst Med & Biol Eng; Am Col Med Informatics. *Res:* Visible human project. *Mailing Add:* 8600 Rockville Pike Bethesda MD 20894. *Fax:* 301-402-4080; *E-Mail:* ackerman@nlm.nih.gov

ACKERMAN, NEIL, NEURO THERAPEUTICS DISCOVERY, DRUG DELIVERY SYSTEMS. *Current Pos:* VPRES RES & DEVELOP, CYGNUS THERAPEUT SYST, 94- *Personal Data:* b Baltimore, Md, May 1, 43. *Educ:* Univ Md, PhD(biol), 69. *Prof Exp:* Res scientist, Glycomed, Inc, 90-94. *Res:* Neurotherapeutics discovery; drug delivery systems. *Mailing Add:* Cygnus Therapeut Syst 400 Penobscot Rd Redwood City CA 94063

ACKERMAN, NORMAN BERNARD, surgery, cancer, for more information see previous edition

ACKERMAN, RALPH AUSTIN, ENVIRONMENTAL PHYSIOLOGY, REGULATORY PHYSIOLOGY. *Current Pos:* asst prof, 81-85, assoc prof, 85-90, PROF ZOOL, IOWA STATE UNIV, 90- *Personal Data:* b Mar 4, 45; m 73, 87, Adah Leshem; c Jessica, Alicia, Jonathan & Aaron. *Educ:* Univ Fla, PhD(zool), 75. *Prof Exp:* Asst res physiologist, Scripps Inst Oceanog, Univ Calif, 77-81. *Mem:* Am Physiol Soc; AAAS; Am Soc Zoologists. *Res:* Environmental physiology of embryonic and developing organisms. *Mailing Add:* Dept Zool & Genetics Iowa State Univ Ames IA 50011-3223. *Fax:* 515-294-8457; *E-Mail:* racker@iastate.edu

ACKERMAN, ROY ALAN, BIOENGINEERING. *Current Pos:* TECH DIR, ASTRE CORP GROUP, CHARLOTTESVILLE, VA, 76- *Personal Data:* b Brooklyn, NY, Sept 9, 51; m, Kathleen Smith; c Shanna, Shira & Daniel. *Educ:* Polytech Inst Brooklyn, BS, 72; Mass Inst Technol, SM, 75; Univ Va/ Univ Bev Hills, PhD, 86. *Prof Exp:* Asst mgr chem eng, Arlee, Inc, 67-72; process engr bioeng, Corning Glass Works, 73; chief ed med sci, Linguistics Systems, Inc, 74-75; chem engr, Tri-Flo Res Labs, Ltd, New York, 72-74; sr proj engr, Thetford Corp, 75. *Concurrent Pos:* Educ assoc, George Washington Univ, 76; consult, Indust Microgenics, Ltd, 81-, Bio Filtration Technologies, Inc, 81-84 & Bicarbolyte Corp, 84- *Mem:* Water Pollution Control Fedn; Am Inst Chem Engrs; Am Chem Soc; Am Soc Artificial Internal Organs; Am Soc Microbiol; Sigma Xi. *Res:* Development of biosupport apparatus drawing upon chemical engineering principles, hemodialysis, aerosol therapy, and membrane oxygenators; development of recycling systems for water and waste utilizing microbial and physicochemical techniques. *Mailing Add:* Astre PO Box 25766 Alexandria VA 22313-5766. *Fax:* 703-548-5737; *E-Mail:* ackerman@astrecg.com

ACKERMAN, STEVEN J, IMMUNOLOGY & BIOLOGY, MOLECULAR BIOL & MEDICINE. *Current Pos:* PROF BIOCHEM, MOLECULAR BIOL & MED, COL MED, UNIV ILL, 96- *Personal Data:* b New York, NY, Jan 13, 51. *Educ:* McGill Univ, PhD(path), 77. *Prof Exp:* Asst prof immunol, Mayo Clin, 78-83; prof med, Harvard Med Sch-Beth Israel Hosp, 84-96. *Mailing Add:* Dept Biochem & Molecular Biol MC 536 Col Med Univ Ill 1819 W Polk St Chicago IL 60612. *Fax:* 312-996-5623; *E-Mail:* sackerma@uic.edu

ACKERMANN, GUENTER ROLF, ORGANIC CHEMISTRY, PHARMACEUTICAL CHEMISTRY. *Current Pos:* RETIRED. *Personal Data:* b Fellbach, Ger, Mar 20, 24; US citizen; m 51, Isabelle A Barr; c Marjorie A, Janet E & Ruth A. *Educ:* Ursinus Col, BS, 51; Univ Md, MS, 54; Univ Mich, PhD(pharmaceut chem), 56. *Prof Exp:* Chemist, Synthetic Org Chem, Atlantic Refining Co, Pa, 56-62; sr res chemist, Rohm & Haas Co, Philadelphia, 62-78, mgr, Govt Regulatory Affairs, 78-89. *Mem:* AAAS; Am Chem Soc. *Res:* Polymer synthesis; synthesis, spinning and testing of synthetic fibers; synthesis of coagulants and flocculents; development of ion-exchange resins; development of desalination processes; pollution control research; removal of pollutants from waste streams. *Mailing Add:* 616 Andover Rd Newtown Square PA 19073-2398

ACKERMANN, HANS WOLFGANG, MEDICAL MICROBIOLOGY. *Current Pos:* from asst prof to assoc prof, 67-76, PROF, FAC MED, LAVAL UNIV, 76- *Personal Data:* b Berlin, Ger, June 16, 36; m 93, Jeanine Gauthier. *Educ:* Free Univ Berlin, MD, 62. *Prof Exp:* Asst gynec, Rudolf Virchow Hosp, Berlin, Ger, 61, asst surg & internal med, 62-63; sci asst, Inst Hyg & Med Microbiol, Free Univ Berlin, 63-67. *Concurrent Pos:* Airlift Mem Found res fel, Pasteur Inst, Paris, France, 61-62; Fr Govt spec training fel med microbiol, 63-64; chmn, Bact Virus Subcomt, Int Comt Taxon Viruses, 75-81 & 87-90, vpres, 84-90, vchmn, 90-; life mem, Int Comt Taxon Viruses. *Mem:* Can Soc Microbiol; Am Soc Microbiol; Can Soc Micros. *Res:* Bacteriophages, also their implications with bacterial and viral taxonomy; airborne fungi; human hepatitis viruses; baculoviruses. *Mailing Add:* Dept Microbiol Laval Univ Fac Med Quebec PQ G1K 7P4 Can. *Fax:* 418-656-7666

ACKERMANN, MARTIN NICHOLAS, INORGANIC CHEMISTRY. *Current Pos:* From asst prof to assoc prof, 66-78, PROF CHEM, OBERLIN COL, 78- *Personal Data:* b Philadelphia, Pa, Feb 19, 41; m 63; c 2. *Educ:* Carnegie-Mellon Univ, BS, 63; Univ Calif, Berkeley, PhD(chem), 66. *Honors & Awards:* Catalyst Award, Chem Mfr Asn, 96. *Concurrent Pos:* Res assoc, Univ Ga, 72-73; vis fel, Gen Elec Res & Develop Ctr, 79-80. *Mem:* Am Chem Soc. *Res:* Transition metal organometallic synthesis; complexes of N-coordinating ligands; chemistry of diazenes. *Mailing Add:* Dept Chem Oberlin Col Oberlin OH 44074

ACKERMANN, NORBERT JOSEPH, JR, NUCLEAR ENGINEERING, INSTRUMENTATION. *Current Pos:* SPEC INSTRUMENTS LAB INC, 88- *Personal Data:* b Chattanooga, Tenn, July 3, 42; div; c 4. *Educ:* Univ Tenn, Knoxville, BS, 65, MS, 67, PhD(nuclear eng), 71. *Prof Exp:* Res instr nuclear eng, Univ Tenn, Knoxville, 65-68; develop sect head, I&C Div, Oak Ridge Nat Lab, Union Carbide Corp, 68-76; pres, Technol Energy Corp, 75-88. *Concurrent Pos:* Fel, Atomic Energy Comn, 65-68; consult, Atomic Energy Comn-Nuclear Regulatory Comn, 68-76, Oak Ridge Nat Lab, 76-77 & Dept Energy, 76-78; adj prof nuclear eng, Univ Tenn, Knoxville, 70- *Mem:* Am Nuclear Soc; Inst Elec & Electronics Engrs; AAAS. *Res:* Measurement and control techniques and analysis methods for surveillance and diagnosis of power plant system's performance and operation. *Mailing Add:* 3110 Hinsen Rd Suite A1 Knoxville TN 37921

ACKERMANN, UWE, MAMMALIAN PHYSIOLOGY. *Current Pos:* from asst prof to assoc prof, 76-87, PROF PHYSIOL, FAC MED, UNIV TORONTO, 87- *Personal Data:* b Greifswald, Ger, Dec 24, 39. *Educ:* Univ Toronto, BASc, 66, MASc, 68, PhD(physiol), 73. *Prof Exp:* Asst prof physiol, Fac Med, Mem Univ, Nfld, 73-76. *Concurrent Pos:* Vis lectr biomed instrumentation, Univ Lagos, Nigeria, 79. *Mem:* Can Hypertension Soc. *Res:* Mechanisms of extracellular fluid volume regulation. *Mailing Add:* Dept of Physiol Fac of Med Univ of Toronto Toronto ON M5S 1A8 Can

ACKERS, GARY K, PHYSICAL BIOCHEMISTRY. *Current Pos:* RAYMOND H WITTCOFF PROF & HEAD, DEPT BIOCHEM & MOLECULAR BIOPHYS, WASHINGTON UNIV SCH MED, 89- *Personal Data:* b Dodge City, Kans, Oct 25, 39; m 83, Clarissa Cheney; c Lisa, Sandra & Keith. *Educ:* Harding Col, BS, 61; Johns Hopkins Univ, PhD(biochem), 64. *Honors & Awards:* Elisabeth S Cole Award, Biophys Soc, 94. *Prof Exp:* NIH fel physiol chem, Sch Med, Johns Hopkins, 64-65, instr, 65-66, prof biophys, 85-89, acting dir, Inst Biophys Res Macromolecular Assemblies, 87-89; from asst prof to assoc prof biochem, Univ Va, 66-77, chmn biophys prog, 73-76; prof biol, McCollum Draft Inst, 77-89. *Concurrent Pos:* Guggenheim fel, 72-73; chmn, Proteins Gordon Conf, 85; NIH Merit Award, 88- *Mem:* AAAS; Biophys Soc (pres, 85); Am Chem Soc; Am Soc Biochem & Molecular Biol. *Res:* Interacting systems of macromolecules proteins and nucleic acids; biophysical chemistry; regulatory mechanisms in gene control and allostenic proteins. *Mailing Add:* Dept Biochem & Molecular Biophys Wash Univ Sch Med 660 S Euclid St Louis MO 63110

ACKERSON, BRUCE J, CHEMICAL PHYSICS. *Current Pos:* From asst prof to assoc prof, 77-86, PROF PHYSICS, OKLA STATE UNIV, 86- *Personal Data:* b Omaha, Nebr, Feb 13, 48; m 69; c 2. *Educ:* Univ Nebr, BS, 70; Univ Colo, MS, 72, PhD(physics), 76. *Concurrent Pos:* Nat Bur Stand-Nat Res Coun grant, Cryog Div, Inst Basics Stand, Nat Bur Stand, Dept Com, 75-77. *Mem:* Am Phys Soc. *Res:* Complex fluids; scattering studies of structure and dynamics. *Mailing Add:* Dept Physics Okla State Univ Stillwater OK 74078. *Fax:* 405-744-6811

ACKLES, KENNETH NORMAN, PHYSIOLOGY. *Current Pos:* DEFENCE RES & DEVELOP LIAISON OFFICER, CAN DEFENCE LIAISON STAFF, 79-, DIR, HUMAN PROTECTION SYSTEMS DIV. *Personal Data:* b Hamilton, Ont, June 29, 35. *Educ:* Queen's Univ, Ont, BSc, 59, MSc, 61; Univ Alta, PhD(physiol), 66. *Prof Exp:* Sci officer hyperbaric physiol, 67-70, head pressure physiol group, Defence Res Estab, Toronto, 70-79. *Concurrent Pos:* Defence Res Bd Can fel aviation med, Royal Air Force, Eng, 66-67. *Mem:* Aerospace Med Asn; Undersea Med Soc. *Res:* Physiological measurement of inert gas narcosis in diving; bubble detection and hematological aspects of decompression sickness; physiological effects of exposure to hyperbaric environment; assessment of stress in operational environments; life support systems in high performance aircraft. *Mailing Add:* Defence Civil Inst Environ Med 1133 Sheppard Ave PO Box 2000 North York ON M3M 3B9 Can

ACKLEY, STEPHEN FRED, GEOPHYSICS, GLACIOLOGY. *Current Pos:* sci & eng asst ice physics, US Army Cold Regions Res & Eng Lab, 68-70, res physicist geophysics, 70-81, chief, Snow & Ice Br, 81-90, RES GEOPHYSICIST, US ARMY COLD REGIONS RES & ENG LAB, 91- *Personal Data:* b Nashua, NH, Jan 22, 44; m 65, Julia Sheehan; c Meghan, Matthew & Lorean. *Educ:* Cornell Univ, BS, 65. *Honors & Awards:* Antartic Serv Medal, NSF, 79. *Prof Exp:* Teacher physics & math, Manning's Sch, Jamaica, 65-67; physicist ocean acoust, Sanders Assocs, NH, 67-68. *Concurrent Pos:* Mem, Weather & Climate Working Group, NASA, 76-77; co-chmn glaciol, NSF Workshop on the Weddell Gyre, 77; mem comn, Polar Meteorol & Oceanog, Am Meteorol Soc, 81-85, Snow, Ice, Permafrost, Am Geophys Union, 85-; adj asst prof, 81-85, adj assoc prof eng, Dartmouth Col, 85-; vis prof, Arctic Marine Sci Chair, Naval Postgrad Sch, 85-86 & 92-93; Army Res & Study fel, 92. *Mem:* Am Geophys Union; Int Asn Hydrol Sci. *Res:* Geophysics of sea ice; sea ice climate and sea ice ocean interactions; ice physics; ice accretion and adhesion. *Mailing Add:* US Army Cold Regions Res & Eng Lab 72 Lyme Rd Hanover NH 03755. *E-Mail:* sackley@crrel.usace.urmg.mil

ACKLEY, WILLIAM BENTON, HORTICULTURE. *Current Pos:* RETIRED. *Personal Data:* b Portis, Kans, June 5, 18; m 41; c 2. *Educ:* Kans State Col, BS, 40, MS, 47; State Col Wash, PhD(hort), 53. *Prof Exp:* Tech asst, US Bur Census, Washington, DC, 40-43; asst, Kans State Col, 46-47; res asst, Wash State Univ, 47-48, horticulturist, 48-64, prof hort, 48-83, chmn dept, 64-74. *Concurrent Pos:* Consult, 84- *Mem:* Fel Am Soc Hort Sci; Int Soc Hort Sci. *Res:* Water relations of plants; physiological disorders of tree fruits; orchard pest control. *Mailing Add:* SE 740 Derby Rd Pullman WA 99163

ACKMAN, DOUGLAS FREDERICK, UROLOGY. *Current Pos:* ASST PROF SURG, MCGILL UNIV, 73- *Personal Data:* b Sept 15, 35; Can citizen; m 58; c 5. *Educ:* Mt Allison Univ, BSc, 56; McGill Univ, MDCM, 60; FRCS(C), 67; FACS, 69. *Concurrent Pos:* Surgeon, Montreal Gen Hosp, 67-; dir, Can Ski Patrol Syst, 68-; consult fertil, Fed Royal Comn, 77-78 & KLI Corp, Penn, 78- *Mem:* Royal Col Surgeons; Am Col Surgeons; Can Urol Asn; Am Urol Asn. *Res:* Computer systems for medical data management; artificial insemination techniques; fertility control techniques, especially male. *Mailing Add:* 4690 Westmont Ave Montreal PQ H3Y 1X1 Can

ACKMAN, ROBERT GEORGE, MARINE OILS & LIPIDS, ANALYSES OF FATTY ACIDS. *Current Pos:* PROF, TECH UNIV NOVA SCOTIA, HALIFAX, 79- *Personal Data:* b Dorchester, NB, Sept 27, 27; m 57; c 2. *Educ:* Univ Toronto, BA, 50; Dalhousie Univ, MS, 52; Univ London, PhD(org chem), 56; Imp Col, dipl(org chem), 56. *Honors & Awards:* H P Kaufman Mem Medal, Int Soc Fat Res, 80. *Prof Exp:* Asst scientist, Atlantic Fisheries Exp Sta, Halifax, NS, 52-53; assoc scientist, Halifax Lab, Fisheries Res Bd Can, 56-62, group leader marine lipids, 62-70, proj mgr, 70-72, head, Marine Oils Sect, Technol Br, 73-79. *Concurrent Pos:* Mem comt fats & oils, Nat Res Coun Can, 62-66, chmn, 67-84; mem, expert comt plant prod & expert comt fats & other lipids, Can Comt Food; mem tech comt ISO/TC 34/ SC II, subcomt animal & veg fats & oils, Can Adv Comt, Food & Agr Orgn/ UN Int Orgn Standardization; assoc referee fats & oils, Asn Off Analytical Chemists; assoc ed, Lipids. *Mem:* Fel Chem Inst Can; Am Oil Chemists Soc; Asn Off Analytical Chemists. *Res:* Analysis and utilization of marine lipids and oils; gas-liquid chromatography of fatty acids and derivatives. *Mailing Add:* 60 Sinlair St Dartmouth NS B2Y 1S3 Can

ACKRELL, BRIAN A C, RESPIRATORY FLAVO-ENZYMES, BIOENERGETICS. *Current Pos:* RES BIOCHEMIST, UNIV CALIF, SAN FRANCISCO, 72- *Educ:* Univ Bristol, UK, PhD(biochem), 61. *Mailing Add:* Div Molecular Biol Vet Admin Med Ctr 4150 Clement St San Francisco CA 94121-1598. *Fax:* 415-750-6959

ACOSTA, ALLAN JAMES, MECHANICAL ENGINEERING. *Current Pos:* Res engr, Calif Inst Technol, 46-48, sect chief, Hydrodyn Lab, 52-54, from asst prof to prof mech eng, 54-90, Richard L & Dorothy M Hayman prof, 90-91, EXEC OFFICER MECH ENG, CALIF INST TECHNOL, 88-, EMER RICHARD L & DOROTHY M HAYMAN PROF MECH ENG, 91- *Personal Data:* b Anaheim, Calif, Aug 10, 24; m 52; c 2. *Educ:* Calif Inst Technol, BS, 45, MS, 49, PhD(mech eng), 52. *Honors & Awards:* Fluids Eng Award, Am Soc Mech Engrs, 88. *Concurrent Pos:* NSF fel, 61-62; consult, Able Corp & Byron Jackson Pump Co. *Mem:* Nat Acad Eng; Int Asn Hydraul Res; Am Soc Mech Engrs; AAAS. *Res:* Fluid mechanics; hydrodynamics; turbomachines. *Mailing Add:* Dept Mech Eng Calif Inst Technol Mail Code 104-44 Pasadena CA 91125

ACOSTA, DANIEL, JR, PHARMACOLOGY. *Current Pos:* from asst prof to assoc prof, 74-83, PROF PHARMACOL, UNIV TEX, AUSTIN, 83- *Personal Data:* b El Paso, Tex, Mar 25, 45; m 73; c 3. *Educ:* Univ Tex, Austin, BS, 68; Univ Kans, PhD(pharmacol), 74. *Prof Exp:* Res asst pharmacol, Sch Pharm, Univ Kans, 70-74. *Concurrent Pos:* NSF trainee, 70-72; Ford Found fel, Nat Chicano Coun Higher Educ, 78-79; Eli Lilly-C R Sublet+Centennial fel, Univ Tex. *Mem:* Am Heart Asn, Basic Sci; AAAS; Tissue Cult Asn; Soc Toxicol; Am Soc Pharmacol & Exp Therapeut. *Res:* Cellular toxicology, particularly use of cell culture techniques to evaluate the effects of drugs and toxicants at the cellular and subcellular level; study of ischemic myocardial cell injury with cultured heart cells; in vitro approach to target organ toxicology. *Mailing Add:* Col Pharm Univ Tex Austin TX 78712-1074

ACOSTA, PHYLLIS BROWN, GENETICS. *Current Pos:* DIR, METAB DIS, ROSS PRODS DIV, ABBOTT LABS, 87- *Personal Data:* b Postell, NC, Dec 27, 33; wid; c Aissa, Clint & Mitzi. *Educ:* Andrews Univ, BA, 55; Univ Iowa, MS, 57; Univ Calif, Los Angeles, MPH, 65, DPH, 69. *Prof Exp:* Teaching dietitian & instr, White Mem Hosp, Loma Linda Univ, 57-59, asst prof & asst dir, Sch Dietetics, 59-62, assoc prof, Sch & dir dietary serv, White Mem Med Ctr, 62-64; prof nutrit, Sch Home Econ & Sch Med Sci, Univ Nev, Reno, 70-74; assoc prof foods & nutrit, Univ Ga, 74-75; assoc prof pediat, Sch Med, Univ NMex, 75-77; from assoc prof to prof allied health, Sch Med, Emory Univ, 77-81; prof & head, Dept Nutrit & Food Sci, Fla State Univ, 81-87. *Concurrent Pos:* Co-investr, NIH Grant Study Phenylketonuria, 61-64; nutrit consult, Child Develop Clin, Children's Hosp Soc, Los Angeles, 62-70, nutritionist, 65-83; consult nat collab study phenylketonuria, Maternal & Child Health Sect, Health Serv & Ment Health Admin, US Dept Health, Educ & Welfare; consult pediat, Div Med Genetics, Sch Med, Emory Univ, 75-81; mem adv comt, Nat Inst Child Health & Human Develop, Maternal PKU Study, 84- *Mem:* Am Inst Nutrit; Am Dietetic Asn; Soc Inherited Metab Dis; Soc Study Inborn Errors Metab. *Res:* Relationship of diet to mental retardation in phenyketonuria, galactosemia and other inborn errors of metabolism; nutrition and growth of infants, maternal nutrition. *Mailing Add:* Med Dept Ross Prods Div Abbott Labs 625 Cleveland Ave Columbus OH 43215-1724. *Fax:* 614-624-3453

ACREE, TERRY EDWARD, FOOD CHEMISTRY. *Current Pos:* From asst prof to assoc prof, 68-81, PROF BIOCHEM, NY STATE AGR EXP STA, CORNELL UNIV, 81- *Personal Data:* b West Hamlin, WVa, Aug 6, 40; m 66. *Educ:* Univ Calif, Berkeley, BA, 63; Cornell Univ, MS, 66, PhD(biochem), 68. *Concurrent Pos:* Fulbright-Hays res scholar, Portugal, 72-73. *Mem:* Am Chem Soc; Inst Food Technol; AAAS; Sigma Xi. *Res:* Chemistry and biochemistry of the flavor components of fruit and vegetable foods; chemistry of sensory perception. *Mailing Add:* Dept Food Sci-Tech NY State Agr Exp Sta Geneva NY 14451

ACRES, ROBERT BRUCE, CYTOKINE BIOLOGY, CANCER BIOLOGY. *Current Pos:* staff scientist, 88-91, GROUP LEADER, IMMUNOL, TRANSGENE SA, STRASBOURG, FRANCE, 91- *Personal Data:* b Kelowna, BC, June 14, 51; m 84; c 3. *Educ:* Univ BC, BSc, 74, MSc, 77; Univ Toronto, PhD(immunol), 82. *Prof Exp:* Fel immunol, Imp Cancer Res Fund, London, 82-84; asst staff scientist immunol, Immunex Corp, Seattle, 84-86, assoc staff scientist, 86-88. *Mem:* Brit Soc Immunol; Soc Francaise d'Immunol. *Res:* Immunobiology and tumour biology, particularly the regulation of the immune system by soluble mediators and the impact of this regulation on tumour development, rejection, therapy and possibly prevention by vaccination; animal models for vaccine research. *Mailing Add:* 11 rue de Molsheim Strasbourg 67082 France. *Fax:* 88-22-58-07

ACRIVOS, ANDREAS, SUSPENSION RHEOLOGY, TWO-PHASE FLOW. *Current Pos:* ALBERT EINSTEIN PROF SCI & ENG & DISTINGUISHED PROF CHEM ENG, CITY COL NEW YORK, 88- *Personal Data:* b Athens, Greece, June 13, 28; US citizen; m 56. *Educ:* Syracuse Univ, BChE, 50; Univ Minn, MS, 51, PhD(chem eng), 54. *Honors & Awards:* Colburn Award, Am Inst Chem Engrs, 63; Lewis Award, 84; Fluid Dynamics Prize, Am Phys Soc, 91; Bingham Medal, Soc Rheology, 94. *Prof Exp:* Asst, Univ Minn, 50-54; from instr to assoc prof chem eng, Univ Calif, Berkeley, 54-62; prof chem eng, Stanford Univ, 62-88. *Concurrent Pos:* Guggenheim Found fel, 60 & 77; mem, US Nat Comt Theoret & Appl Mech, 80-; ed, Am Inst Physics: Physics of Fluids A, 82-; S Fairchild distinguished scholar, Calif Inst Technol, 83-84; dir, Levich Inst PCH, City Col New York, 88- *Mem:* Nat Acad Sci; Nat Acad Eng; fel Am Inst Chem Engrs; Am Chem Soc; fel Am Phys Soc; fel Am Acad Arts & Sci. *Res:* Fundamental research, experimental and theoretical, on various aspects of viscous flow, including sedimentation, the rheology of suspensions and effective medium theories; fluid mechanics; heat and mass transfer; surface phenomena. *Mailing Add:* Levich Inst City Col New York Steinman Hall No 1-M New York NY 10031

ACRIVOS, JUANA LUISA VIVO, SOLID STATE PHYSICAL CHEMISTRY, QUANTUM CHEMISTRY. *Current Pos:* cac res grant, 62, from asst prof to assoc prof, 62-72, PROF PHYS CHEM, SAN JOSE STATE UNIV, 72- *Personal Data:* b June 24, 28; US citizen; m 56, Andreas. *Educ:* Univ Minn, PhD(phys chem, math), 56; Univ Havana, DSc(phys chem), 56. *Prof Exp:* Res assoc biophys, Hanasen Labs, Stanford Univ, 57-59; fel phys chem, Univ Calif, 59-62. *Concurrent Pos:* Res Corp grants, 64, 66 & 71; NSF res grants, 66-94; fel, San Jose State Univ, 74-75; vis fel, Trinity Col, Cambridge Univ, 83-84 & Lucy Cavendish Col, 90-91; NSF vis prof, Univ Calif, Berkeley, 87-88. *Mem:* Am Chem Soc; Am Phys Soc. *Res:* Molecular structure determinations of semiquinones, organic conductors, copper oxide superconductors and biologically active free radicals by synchrotron x-ray and electron spin resonance spectroscopy; alkali metal and alkali halide solutions in ammonia, amines and ethers; metal-insulator transitions in metal ammonia systems and in layer transition element dichalcogenides. *Mailing Add:* Dept Chem San Jose State Univ One Washington Sq San Jose CA 95192-0101

ACS, GEORGE, BIOCHEMISTRY. *Current Pos:* prof pediat, 74-86, PROF BIOCHEM, MT SINAI SCH MED, 75-, PROF NEOPLASTICS, 86- *Personal Data:* b Dunaszerdahely, Hungary, Aug 14, 23; m 48; c 1. *Educ:* Orvosegyetem, Budapest, MD, 50, PhD, 53. *Prof Exp:* Demonstr, Orvosivegytan, Szeged, 47-48; demonstr med chem, Orvosivegytan, Budapest, 48-50, from asst prof to assoc prof, 50-56; res assoc, Rockefeller Inst, 57-60; sr res chemist, NY Psychiat Inst, 60-61; asst prof, Columbia Univ, 61; mem, Inst Muscle Disease, 61-74. *Concurrent Pos:* Res fel, Mass Gen Hosp, 56-57. *Mem:* Am Soc Cell Biol; Fedn Am Soc Exp Biol; Am Cancer Soc. *Res:* Viral Replication. *Mailing Add:* Dept Biochem & Neoplastic Dis Mt Sinai Sch Med One Gustave L Levy Pl New York NY 10029

ACTON, DONALD FINDLAY, PEDOLOGY, GEOMORPHOLOGY. *Current Pos:* ASSOC PROF, DEPT SOIL SCI, UNIV SASK, 68- *Personal Data:* b Lemberg, Sask, June 16, 34; m 60; c 2. *Educ:* Univ Sask, BSA, 57, MSc, 61; Univ Ill, PhD(soil sci), 71. *Prof Exp:* Res officer, 57-68, head, Soil Surv, Agr Can, 68- *Mem:* Am Soc Agron; Agr Inst Can; Can Soc Soil Sci. *Res:* Soil survey; soil genesis; soil classification; mineralogy. *Mailing Add:* Dept Soil Surv Univ Sask Rm 5C 26 Agr Bldg Saskatoon SK S7N 5A8 Can

ACTON, EDWARD MCINTOSH, BIO-ORGANIC CHEMISTRY. *Current Pos:* CONSULT, 91- *Personal Data:* b Morgan Hill, Calif, May 30, 30. *Educ:* Stanford Univ, BS, 51; Mass Inst Technol, PhD(org chem), 57. *Prof Exp:* Chemist, Merck & Co, NJ, 51-53; from org chemist to sr org chemist, 57-75, prog mgr, SRI Int, 75-85; prof med chem, M D Anderson Hosp & Cancer Inst, Univ Tex, 86-87; expert, Nat Cancer Inst, 87-91. *Concurrent Pos:* Vis res sci, Dept Pharmacol, Yale Univ, 81; adj prof chem, Univ Houston, 86-87. *Mem:* Am Chem Soc; The Chem Soc; AAAS; Am Asn Cancer Res. *Res:* Synthetic organic chemistry for anticancer drug development; drug design based on biochemical mechanisms; anthracyclines, nucleosides, heterocycles, sugars; new artificial sweeteners. *Mailing Add:* 281 Arlington Way Menlo Park CA 94025

ACTON, JEAN D, VIROLOGY, IMMUNOLOGY. *Current Pos:* EMER PROF BIOL, JAMES MADISON UNIV, 92- *Personal Data:* b Charlottesville, Va, Feb 23, 30. *Res:* Virology; immunology. *Mailing Add:* Dept Biol James Madison Univ Harrisonburg VA 22801

ACTON, LOREN WILBER, SOLAR PHYSICS. *Current Pos:* RES PROF, MONT STATE UNIV, 93- *Personal Data:* b Lewistown, Mont, Mar 7, 36; m 57; c 2. *Educ:* Mont State Col, BS, 59; Univ Colo, PhD(astro-geophys), 65. *Hon Degrees:* DSc, Mont State Univ, 88. *Honors & Awards:* Spaceflight Achievement Award, Am Astronaut Soc, 86. *Prof Exp:* Jr scientist, Hanford Atomic Prod Oper, Gen Elec Co, 59; physicist, Cent Radio Propagation Lab, Nat Bur Standards, Colo, 60-61; physicist, US Naval Res Lab, DC, 62; res asst, High Altitude Observ, Colo, 62-64; assoc res scientist x-ray astron, Space Sci Lab, Lockheed Missiles & Space Co, 64-66, res scientist, 66-70, dir, Lockheed Solar Observ, 68-71, staff scientist & leader space astron group, 70-85, consult scientist, Space Sci Lab, 85-93. *Concurrent Pos:* Assoc astronomer, Inst Astron, Univ Hawaii, 68-69; vis scientist, Group Phys Space Res, WGer, 71-72; payload specialist, Spacelab 2, 78-86; chmn, solar physics spacelab team, NASA, 75-79, mem spacelab ad hoc working group, 76 & Space & Earth Sci Adv Comt, 87-; chmn, Sci Prog Eval Comt, High Altitude Observ, 84. *Mem:* AAAS; Am Astron Soc; Int Astron Union; Sigma Xi. *Res:* X-ray astronomy; solar physics. *Mailing Add:* 8490 Overlook Ln Bozeman MT 59715

ACTON, RONALD TERRY, MOLECULAR GENETICS, MEDICAL LABORATORY IMMUNOLOGY. *Current Pos:* asst prof, Univ Ala, 72-75, assoc prof microbiol, 75-78, co-dir, Diabetes OP Clin Lab Med, 79-85, dep dir, DRTC, 79-84, PROF MICROBIOL & EPIDEMIOL, UNIV ALA, BIRMINGHAM, 78-, PROF MED & DIR, IMMUNOGENETICS PROG, 82- *Personal Data:* b Birmingham, Ala, Oct 19, 41; m 62; c 2. *Educ:* Birmingham Southern Col, Ala, AB, 65; Univ Ala, Birmingham, PhD(microbiol), 70; Am Bd Med Lab Immunol, cert, 85. *Prof Exp:* Res fel microbiol, Div Clin Immunol-Rheumatology, Univ Ala, Birmingham, 69-70; res fel biol, Calif Inst Technol, Pasadena, 70-72; spec fel biochem, Univ Oxford, Eng, 72-73. *Concurrent Pos:* Consult, Separation Processes Br, George C Marshall Space Flight Ctr, NASA, 77-79; mem, Cancer Ctr Support Grant Rev Comt, NIH, 78-82, mem Ad Hoc Cancer Construct Rev Comt, 84-85; mem bd dirs, Creative Schs, Inc, 84; ed, Pediat Oncol Vols 1,2 & 3, 81-83 & Sports Med, 85- *Mem:* Sigma Xi; Am Asn Immunologists; Am Soc Biol Chemists; Am Soc Histocompatibility & Immunogenetics; Am Soc Human Genetics; Am Asn Clin Res; Am Soc Microbiol. *Res:* The role of genes within the major histocompatibility complex in predisposing individuals to autoimmune diseases; identifying and cloning genes. *Mailing Add:* Immunogenetic/DNA Diag Lab Univ Ala Birmingham Sta 1808 Seventh Ave S Rm 802 Birmingham AL 35294-0012. *Fax:* 205-934-4062

ACTOR, PAUL, ANTIMICROBIAL CHEMOTHERAPY. *Current Pos:* PRES, PAUL ACTOR ASSOC, 90- *Personal Data:* b New York, NY, 1933; m; c Carol, Jeff & Neil. *Educ:* Hunter Col, AB, 55; Rutgers Univ, MA, 58, PhD(zool), 59. *Prof Exp:* Asst zool, Rutgers Univ, 55-59; sr res scientist, Squibb Inst Med Res, 59-63; sr microbiologist, Smith Kline & French Labs, 63-66, group leader microbiol, 66-68, from asst dir to dir microbiol, 68-81, dir Dept Natural Prod Pharmacol, 81-84, dir strategic planning & technol eval, 84-86, dir compound & technol acquisition, 86-90. *Concurrent Pos:* Res prof microbiol & immunol, Med Sch, Temple Univ, Philadelphia, 81-; chmn, Antimicrobiol Chemother Sect, Am Soc Microbiol, 84-85, pres, EPa Br, 88-91; chair meetings bd, Am Soc Microbiol, 92-95. *Mem:* Fel Am Acad Microbiol; Am Soc Microbiol; Licensing Exec Soc; fel Infectious Dis Soc Am. *Res:* Chemotherapy and immunology of bacterial, fungal and parasitic infection. *Mailing Add:* 632 Pickering Lane Phoenixville PA 19460. *Fax:* 610-935-7490

ACUNA, MARIO HUMBERTO, SPACE SCIENCE, PHYSICS. *Current Pos:* design engr res & develop, 69-70, RES SCIENTIST, GODDARD SPACE FLIGHT CTR, NASA, 70-, PROJ SCIENTIST, PRIN INVESTR, NASA MISSIONS, 79- *Personal Data:* b Cordoba, Arg, Mar 21, 40; m 66; c 4. *Educ:* Nat Univ Tucuman, MS, 67; Cath Univ Am, PhD(space sci), 74. *Honors & Awards:* Sci Award, NASA, 69 & Group Achievement Award, 70, 74 & 75; Except Performance Award, Goddard Space Flight Ctr, NASA, 75; Moe Schneebaum Mem Award, 80; Except Sci Achievement Medal, NASA, 81, Except Serv Medal, 86. *Prof Exp:* Res asst ionospheric res, Nat Univ Tucuman, 63-67; sr engr electronics, Fairchild Hiller Corp, 67-69. *Concurrent Pos:* Distinguished lectr, Magnetics Soc, Inst Elec & Electronics Engrs, 85; pres, Nanotesla, Inc, 82- *Mem:* Am Geophys Union; Inst Elec & Electronics Engrs; Sigma Xi. *Res:* Magnetic fields and plasmas in space; planetary magnetospheres; geophysical and space research instrumentation. *Mailing Add:* NASA Goddard Space Flight Ctr Code 695 Greenbelt MD 20771

ACZEL, JANOS D, PURE AND APPLIED MATHEMATICS, FUNCTIONAL EQUATIONS. *Current Pos:* prof, 65-69, distinguished prof, 69-93, EMER PROF MATH, UNIV WATERLOO, 93- *Personal Data:* b Budapest, Hungary, Dec 26, 24; Can citizen; m 46, Susan Kende; c Catherine (Boivie) & Julie. *Educ:* Eotvos Lorand Univ, Budapest, PhD(math), 47; Hungarian Acad Sci, Habil, 52, DSc(functional equations), 57. *Hon Degrees:* DSc, Univ Karlsruhe, 90, Univ Graz, 95, Silesian Univ Katowice, 96. *Honors & Awards:* M Beke Award, 61; foreign fel Hungarian Acad Sci; Santiago Ramon Cajal Medal, Nat Coun Sci Res, Spain, 88. *Prof Exp:* Asst prof math, Univ Szeged, 48-50; assoc prof & dept head, Miskolc Inst Technol, 50-52; from assoc prof to prof & dept head, Debrecen Univ, 52-65. *Concurrent Pos:* Vis prof, Univ Fla, 63-64, 79, Stanford Univ, 64, Univ Cologne, 65, Univ Giessen, 66, 70, Fla Atlantic Univ, 68, Univ Bochum, 68, Nat Inst Math, Rome, 71, Monash Univ, 72, Ahmadu Bello Univ, Nigeria, 75-76, Univ Lecce, 76, Calif Inst Technol & Univ Ariz, 78, Graz Univ, 79, 86, 91, 93, Okayama Univ, Japan, 84, Univ Milan, 85, 91, Univ Hamburg, 85, Tech Univ Barcelona, 86, 92, Univ Karlsruhe, 92, Univ Bern, 86 & Univ Calif Irvine, 94; NSF grant, 63-64; ed in chief, J Aegratropes Math, 66-96, honed-in-chief, 96; Nat Res Coun Can grant, 66-; Naval Ocean Systs Ctr, San Diego, 79-81. *Mem:* Fel Royal Soc Can; Can Math Soc; Am Math Soc; Austrian Math Soc; NY Acad Sci. *Res:* Functional equations; inequalities; mean values; geometric objects; generalized groups; webs; rational decision making; allocation, taxation theory; production functions; analytic hierarchy processes; probability theory; statistical distributions; theory of measurement; theory of information; economic index numbers; applications to social and behavioral sciences; dimensional analysis. *Mailing Add:* Dept Math Univ Waterloo Waterloo ON N2L 3G1 Can. *Fax:* 519-725-0160

ADACHI, KAZUHIKO, ABNORMAL HEMAGLOBIN, SICKLE CELL DISEASE. *Current Pos:* ASSOC RES PROF, DEPT PEDIAT, UNIV PA, 84- *Educ:* Tokyo Med Univ, PhD(biochem), 72. *Mailing Add:* Pa Children's Hosp 34th St & Civic Ctr Blvd Philadelphia PA 19104

ADAIR, DENNIS WILTON, BIOPHARMACEUTICS. *Current Pos:* MGR VET FORMULATION RES, SCHERING PLOUGH CORP, KENILWORTH, NJ, 83- *Personal Data:* b San Jose, Calif, Dec 7, 39; m 66; c 1. *Educ:* Univ Calif, San Francisco, PharmD, 64, PhD(pharm chem), 76. *Prof Exp:* Sr scientist pharmaceut, Ciba-Geigy Pharmaceut Div, 74-79, asst dir pharmaceut, 79-81; res group chief pharmaceut res & develop, Hoffman-La Roche Pharmaceut, Nutley, NJ, 81-83. *Mem:* Sigma Xi; Am Pharmaceut Asn; Acad Pharmaceut Sci. *Res:* Gastrointestinal absorption of drugs; drug delivery system with in vivo-in vitro evaluation. *Mailing Add:* 4371 Edinburg Ct Suisun City CA 94585-1301

ADAIR, ELEANOR R, EXPERIMENTAL BIOLOGY. *Current Pos:* asst fel, 66-70, assoc fel, 70-86, FEL, JOHN B PIERCE FOUND, 86- *Personal Data:* b Arlington, Mass, Nov 28, 26. *Educ:* Mt Holyoke Col, BA, 48; Univ Wis, MA, 51, PhD(psychol & physics), 55. *Prof Exp:* Res assoc psychol, Mt Holyoke Col, 48-50; res asst, Univ Wis, 50-53; res asst, Yale Univ, 60-62, res assoc, 63-77. *Concurrent Pos:* Sr res assoc psychol, Yale Univ, 77-89, sr res scientist, 89-, lectr, 85-; consult, Bioelectromagnetics Res Lab, Dept Rehab Med, Sch Med, Univ Wash, Seattle, 83-85; Sigma Xi nat lectr, 85-88; secy, Comt Man & Radiation, Inst Elec & Electronics Engrs, 88-89. *Mem:* Fel AAAS; fel Am Psychol Asn; Sigma Xi; Am Physiol Soc; Am Soc Primatologists; Bioelectromagnetics Soc (secy-treas, 83-86); fel NY Acad Sci; sr mem Inst Elec & Electronics Engrs; Am Asn Lab Animal Sci; fel Am Psychol Soc. *Res:* Author or co-author of over 60 publications and 1 book. *Mailing Add:* John B Pierce Found Lab 290 Congress Ave New Haven CT 06519-1403. *Fax:* 203-624-4950

ADAIR, GERALD MICHAEL, SOMATIC CELL GENETICS, MOLECULAR GENETICS. *Current Pos:* asst biologist, 78-82, asst prof, 82-86, ASSOC PROF BIOL, SCI PARK RES DIV, UNIV TEX, M D ANDERSON CANCER CTR, 86-, ASSOC BIOLOGIST, 82- *Personal Data:* b St Louis, Mo, June 8, 49; m 72; c 1. *Educ:* Washington Univ, St Louis, BA, 72, PhD(biol), 75. *Prof Exp:* Res assoc, Lawrence Livermore Nat Lab, 75-78. *Concurrent Pos:* Mem grad fac, Univ Tex Grad Sch Biomed Sci, 83- *Mem:* Genetics Soc Am; Environ Mutagen Soc; Am Soc Microbiol; Am Soc Human Genetics. *Res:* DNA repair and mutagenesis in mammalian cells; molecular analysis of mutation in DNA repair-proficient versus deficient genetic backgrounds; targeted homologous recombination in mammalian cells; gene targeting. *Mailing Add:* Univ Tex M D Anderson Cancer Ctr Sci Park Res Div Smithville TX 78957

ADAIR, JAMES EDWIN, ELECTRICAL ENGINEERING. *Current Pos:* MEM STAFF, SPERRY GYROSCOPE, 80- *Personal Data:* b Farmington, Ky, Jan 18, 35; m 66; c 1. *Educ:* Univ Mich, BSE, 61, MSE, 63, PhD(elec eng), 68. *Prof Exp:* Asst, Univ Mich, 60-63, res assoc, 63-67; asst prof elec eng, Univ Mo-Rolla, 67-73; elec engr, Air Force Avionics Lab, Wright-Patterson AFB, 73-80. *Mem:* Inst Elec & Electronics Engrs; Sigma Xi. *Res:* Physical electronics-electron beams, traveling wave tubes, millimeter waves; guides waves-coupled transmission lines, microwave circuits and solid state devices. *Mailing Add:* 2254 Willowbrook Clearwater FL 34624

ADAIR, KENT THOMAS, FORESTRY, MANAGEMENT SCIENCES. *Current Pos:* DEAN, SCH FORESTRY, STEPHEN F AUSTIN STATE UNIV, 77- *Personal Data:* b Allegan, Mich, Jan 21, 33; m 55; c 3. *Educ:* Colo State Univ, BS, 58, PhD(forest econ), 68; Ore State Univ, MF, 61. *Prof Exp:* Forester, US Forest Serv, 58-59; forester & consult, Bigley & Feiss, Foresters, Inc, 60-61; res forester, Colo State Univ, 61-63; asst prof forest econ, Univ Mont, 63-66; prof forestry, Univ Mo-Columbia, 67-77. *Concurrent Pos:* Dir, Ctr Appl Studies, 77- *Mem:* Soc Am Foresters; Forest Prod Res Soc. *Mailing Add:* Box 6109 Forest Stephen F Austin State Univ 1936 N St Nacogdoches TX 75961-3940

ADAIR, ROBERT KEMP, ELEMENTARY PARTICLE PHYSICS, NUCLEAR PHYSICS. *Current Pos:* from assoc prof to prof, Yale Univ, 59-72, chmn dept, 67-70, dir, Div Phys Sci, 77-81, Eugene Higgins prof, 72-88, STERLING PROF PHYSICS, YALE UNIV, 88- *Personal Data:* b Ft Wayne, Ind, Aug 14, 24; m 52, Eleanor Reed; c 2. *Educ:* Univ Wis, PhD(physics), 51. *Hon Degrees:* DSc, Univ Wis, 94. *Prof Exp:* Instr physics, Univ Wis, 51-53; from assoc physicist to physicist, Brookhaven Nat Lab, 53 58. *Concurrent Pos:* Guggenheim fel, 53; Ford Found fel, Europ Orgn Nuclear Res, 62; assoc dir high energy & nuclear physics, Brookhaven Nat Lab, 87-88. *Mem:* Nat Acad Sci; fel Am Phys Soc. *Res:* Nuclear and particle physics. *Mailing Add:* Dept Physics Yale Univ PO Box 208121 New Haven CT 06520-8126. *Fax:* 203-432-6125; *E-Mail:* adair@hepmail.physics.yale.edu

ADAIR, SUZANNE FRANK, BIOPHARMACEUTICS. *Current Pos:* sr assoc, Ciba-Geigy Pharmaceut Corp, 77-78, asst dir clin pharmacol, 79-81, assoc dir human pharmacol, 81-83, ASSOC DIR CLIN RES, CIBA-GEIGY PHARMACEUT CORP, 83- *Personal Data:* b Milwaukee, Wis, Aug 17, 41; m 66; c 1. *Educ:* Univ Wis, BS, 63; Univ Calif, San Francisco, PhD(pharmaceut chem), 76. *Prof Exp:* Actg asst prof pharm, Univ Calif, San Francisco, 74; asst prof pharm, Rutgers Univ, Busch Campus, 74-77. *Mem:* Sigma Xi; NY Acad Sci; Acad Pharmaceut Sci; AAAS. *Res:* Clinical pharmacology; bioavailability and pharmacokinetics; clinical trials of anti-inflammatory and central nervous system agents. *Mailing Add:* 4371 Edinburg Ct Suisun City CA 94585-1301

ADAIR, THOMAS H, PHYSIOLOGY, CARDIOVASCULAR PHYSIOLOGY. *Current Pos:* PROF PHYSIOL & BIOPHYSIOL, UNIV MISS, MED CTR, 89- *Personal Data:* b Flint, Mich, Dec 25, 50. *Educ:* Univ Tex, PhD(physiol), 80. *Res:* Physiology; cardiovascular physiology. *Mailing Add:* Dept Physiol & Biophys Univ Miss Med Ctr 2500 N State St Jackson MS 39216-4505

ADAIR, THOMAS WEYMON, III, SOLID STATE PHYSICS, LOW TEMPERATURE PHYSICS. *Current Pos:* asst prof, Tex A&M Univ, 66-72, asst to pres, 72-75, assoc prof, 72-78, PROF PHYSICS, TEX A&M UNIV, 78- *Personal Data:* b Houston, Tex, Jan 23, 35; m 62. *Educ:* Tex A&M Univ, BS, 57, PhD(physics), 65; Rice Univ, MA, 60. *Prof Exp:* Res physicist, Prod Res Lab, Humble Oil & Refining Co, 59-62. *Concurrent Pos:* NSF fel, Kamerlingh Onnes Lab, Univ Leiden, 65-66. *Mem:* Am Phys Soc; Sigma Xi. *Res:* Magnetic properties of single crystals; magnetic properties of amorphous metal films. *Mailing Add:* 1018 Rose Circle College Station TX 77840-2309

ADAIR, WINSTON LEE, JR, BIOCHEMISTRY. *Current Pos:* Asst prof, 75-80, ASSOC PROF BIOCHEM, COL MED, UNIV SOUTH FLA, 80- *Personal Data:* b Chicago, Ill, May 27, 44; m 72; c 1. *Educ:* Brown Univ, ScB, 66; Georgetown Univ, PhD(biochem), 72. *Concurrent Pos:* NIH fel, Dept Hematol-Oncol, Sch Med, Wash Univ, 73-75. *Mem:* Sigma Xi; Am Chem Soc; Soc Complex Carbohydrates. *Res:* Cell surface glycoproteins; membrane biochemistry; biosynthesis of long chain polyisoprenoid alcohols; interactions of plant lectins with cell membranes. *Mailing Add:* Dept Biochem Univ SFla Col Med 12901 Bruce B Downs Blvd Tampa FL 33612-4742. *Fax:* 813-974-5798

ADAM, DAVID PETER, PALYNOLOGY, CLIMATOLOGY. *Current Pos:* res assoc palynology, 71-72, GEOLOGIST, US GEOL SURV, 71- *Personal Data:* b Berkeley, Calif, May 18, 41; m 67, Wansley Sharp; c John M, Theresa (Craven), Julia (Nunez), Anne (Roberts) & Margaret. *Educ:* Harvard Univ, BA, 62; Univ Ariz, MS, 65, PhD(geochronology), 70. *Prof Exp:* Res assoc palynology, Univ Ariz, 66-69, teaching asst, 70, res assoc dendrochronology, Lab Tree-ring Res, 70-71. *Concurrent Pos:* Pres, Long Terrestrial Records, Int Quaternary Asn, 87- *Mem:* Am Quaternary Asn; Ecol Soc Am; Brit Freshwater Biol Asn; Am Quaternary Asn; Sigma Xi; Am Geophys Union. *Res:* Theoretical palynology; causes of climatic change; computer applications in paleoecology; climatic history of California; Chrysophyte cysts. *Mailing Add:* 224 Edgehill Dr San Carlos CA 94070-4509. *E-Mail:* dadam@mojave.wr.usgs.gov

ADAM, JOHN ANTHONY, THEORY OF WAVE MOTION, MATHEMATICAL MODELS OF TUMOR GROWTH. *Current Pos:* PROF MATH & STATS, OLD DOMINION UNIV, 84- *Personal Data:* b Salisbury, Eng, Dec 18, 49; m 71; c 3. *Educ:* Univ London, BSc, 71, PhD(appl math & astrophysics), 75. *Prof Exp:* Res fel, Univ Sussex, Eng, 74-76; res asst, Univ St Andrews, Scotland, 76-78; lectr math, New Univ Ulster, Ireland, 78-83, sr lectr, 83-84. *Concurrent Pos:* Res fel theoret physics, Dublin Inst Advan Studies, 77-80; vis asst, prof & Fulbright Scholar, Univ Rochester, 83. *Mem:* Soc Math Biol; Inst Math & Applications UK. *Res:* Mathematical wave theory; astrophysical fluid dynamics; mathematical biology; models of tumor growth; differential operators arising in wave problems. *Mailing Add:* Dept Math & Stats Old Dominion Univ Norfolk VA 23529-0077

ADAM, KLAUS, ORGANIC CHEMISTRY. *Current Pos:* ASST PROF, GALVESTON COL, 88- *Personal Data:* b Merzig, WGer, Jan 8, 43; US citizen; m 72; c 2. *Educ:* St Edward's Univ, BS, 64; Tex A&M Univ, MS, 66, PhD(chem), 71. *Prof Exp:* Fel chem, Univ Saarland, 71-72 & Calif Inst Technol, 72-74; sr res chemist, Monsanto Co, 74-80; staff chemist, Exxon Chem Co, 80-83. *Mem:* Am Chem Soc. *Res:* Organic and biochemical synthesis; reaction mechanism; process improvement products development for agricultural application; water treatment application; lubrication and fire resistance application; refinery process aids. *Mailing Add:* 1706 Bowline Houston TX 77062-4536

ADAM, RANDALL EDWARD, physical chemistry, polymer physics, for more information see previous edition

ADAM, WALDEMAR, CHEMISTRY. *Current Pos:* PROF CHEM, UNIV WURZBURG, FED REPUB GER, 80- *Personal Data:* b Alexanderdorf, Russia, July 26, 37; m 58, Sonia Tirado; c Karin J, Heidi A, Adam W & Eva T. *Educ:* Univ Ill, BSc, 58; Mass Inst Technol, PhD, 61. *Hon Degrees:* Dr, Univ Sao Paulo, Brasil. *Honors & Awards:* Leonardo Igaravidez Award, 79; Brazilian Acad Sci Award, 80; Alexander von Humboldt J C Mutis Award, 81; Alexander von Humboldt Award, Japan Soc Pron Sci, 93. *Prof Exp:* Res assoc, Mass Inst Technol, Cambridge, 61 & Univ Karlsruhe, Fed Repub Ger, 62; from asst prof to prof, Univ PR, 61-80. *Concurrent Pos:* NSF postdoctoral fel, Univ Carlsruhe, 62 & 68-72; vis prof, Univ Zurich, Switz, 72-73, State Univ NY-Buffalo, 74, Univ Sao Paulo, Brazil, 74, Inter-Am Univ, Hato Rey, PR, 77, Univ Concepcion, Chile, 82, Univ Alta, Edmonton, 89, Univ Debreceu, Hungary, 91, Polytech Univ, Valencia, Spain, 92 & Univ Miami, Fla, 93; hon prof, Univ Marine Sci, Mayaguez, 75-80; career award, NIH, 75-80. *Res:* Contributed to over 450 science publications. *Mailing Add:* Lerchenhain 4 97074 Wurzburg Germany

ADAMANTIADES, ACHILLES G, REACTOR SAFETY. *Current Pos:* mem tech staff, 74-81, PROJ MGR, ELEC POWER RES INST, 81- *Personal Data:* b Volos, Greece, Apr 22, 34; m 63; c 3. *Educ:* Athens Tech Univ, dipl, 57; Mass Inst Technol, PhD(nuclear eng), 66. *Prof Exp:* Opers engr, Pub Power Corp Greece, 60; asst biol effect nuclear radiation, Mass Inst Technol, 61-62, asst reactor & nuclear physics, 62-63, asst neutron slowing down, 63-66; asst prof nuclear eng, Iowa State Univ, 66-71; vis prof, Univ Patras, 71-73; mem staff, Fed Power Comn, 73. *Concurrent Pos:* Consult, World Bank; assoc prof lectr, George Washington Univ, 74-79; consult prof, Stanford Univ, 82. *Mem:* Am Nuclear Soc; AAAS; Sigma Xi; Am Asn Univ Professors; Tech Chamber of Greece. *Res:* Pulsed neutron research; neutronics; nuclear reactor safety; power systems planning; power economics. *Mailing Add:* 5305 Moorland Lane Bethesda MD 20814

ADAMCIK, JOE ALFRED, ORGANIC CHEMISTRY. *Current Pos:* RETIRED. *Personal Data:* b Taylor, Tex, June 28, 30. *Educ:* Univ Tex, BS, 51, MA, 54; Univ Ill, PhD(chem), 58; Tex Tech Univ, JD, 91. *Prof Exp:* From asst prof to assoc prof chem, Tex Tech Univ, 57-88; atty at law, 91-95. *Mem:* AAAS; Am Chem Soc; Am Geophys Union; Royal Soc Chem. *Mailing Add:* 5223 42nd St Lubbock TX 79414. *E-Mail:* jadamcik@aol.com

ADAMEK, EDUARD GEORG, ENVIRONMENTAL MANAGEMENT, AIR POLLUTION. *Current Pos:* RETIRED. *Personal Data:* b Mistelbach, Austria, Apr 19, 25; Can citizen; m 54. *Educ:* Univ Vienna, BSc, 50; Innsbruck Univ, Drs, 52; McGill Univ, PhD(org chem), 59. *Prof Exp:* Res chemist, Starch & Chem Div, Ogilvie Flour Mills Co Ltd, 52-58; sr develop chemist, Textile Fibres Div, Du Pont Can, 59-60, from res chemist to sr res chemist, Cent Res Labs, 60-70; scientist, Air Mgt Br, Ont Dept Energy & Resources, 70-71; org lab supvr, Ont Ministry Environ, 71-89. *Mem:* AAAS; Am Chem Soc; Chem Inst Can; NY Acad Sci; Sigma Xi. *Res:* New organic products and processes; polymers; organic air and water pollutants research; waste product utilization; metallo-organic compounds; analytical methods development; carbohydrates, protein and amino acids. *Mailing Add:* 50 Quebec Ave Suite 1902 Toronto ON M6P 4B4 Can

ADAMKIEWICZ, VINCENT WITOLD, BIOMAGNETICS, DENTAL MICROBIOLOGY. *Current Pos:* assoc prof physiol, 56-67, PROF MICROBIOL & IMMUNOL, FAC MED, UNIV MONTREAL, 67- *Personal Data:* b Poland, Nov 27, 24; m 54, Lidia M Gowor; c Paul, Mark, Tom, Michael & Mathias. *Educ:* Bristol Univ, BSc, 48 & 49, MSc, 50; Univ Montreal, PhD(endocrinol), 53. *Prof Exp:* Agr engr, Poland, 44; res assoc, Sch Vet Med, Bristol Univ, 50. *Concurrent Pos:* Mem admin bd, Tech Col, Montreal, 93- *Mem:* Am Physiol Soc; Can Physiol Soc; Asn Fr Speaking Physiologists; Can Soc Immunol. *Res:* Dental pulp hypersensitivity reactions, including Arthus reaction and delayed hypersensitivity; modulation of the sorption of bacterial exopolysaccharides to surfaces by weak, static magnetic and geomagnetic fields and their effects on macrophage migration; bacterial identification in dental enamel carious lesions. *Mailing Add:* Dept Microbiol & Immunol Univ Montreal Fac Med CP6128A Succ Ctr Ville Montreal PQ H3C 3J7 Can. *Fax:* 514-343-5701

ADAMO, JOSEPH ALBERT, MICROBIOLOGY, NEMATOLOGY. *Current Pos:* coordr, Environ Ctr, 75-81, chmn, Sci Dept, 81-90, PROF MICROBIOL, OCEAN CO COL, 67- *Personal Data:* b Jersey City, NJ, Oct 22, 38; m 64, 78, Cornelia Everett; c Connie, Thomas, Jo-Anne & Samantha. *Educ:* Jersey City State Col, BA, 64; Fairleigh Dickinson Univ, MS, 67; Rutgers Univ, PhD(nematol), 75. *Prof Exp:* Instr bot, Fairleigh Dickinson Univ, 65-66; asst prof bot & zool, Jersey City State Col, 66-67. *Concurrent Pos:* Vis prof biol res, Rutgers Univ, 85-87 & 94 & Drexel Univ, 92 & 94; grad biol dept, Georgian Ct Col, 90, Monmouth Univ, 97. *Mem:* Soc Nematol; Am Phytopath Soc; Am Soc Microbiol; Nat Asn Biol Teachers. *Res:* Nematode behavior, physiology and bacterial gene (DNA) transfer via transformation; conjugation and transduction within nematode vector systems in the environment; mycology; virology. *Mailing Add:* Dept Biol Ocean Co Col Toms River NJ 08753. *Fax:* 732-255-0444; *E-Mail:* joadamo@aol.com

ADAMS, ALAYNE A(MERCIER), PHYSICAL CHEMISTRY, ELECTROCHEMISTRY. *Current Pos:* RES CHEMIST ELECTROCHEM, US ARMY MOBILITY EQUIP RES & DEVELOP COMMAND, 76- *Personal Data:* b Niagara Falls, NY, Jan 31, 38; m 61; c 2. *Educ:* Niagara Univ, BS, 59, MS, 61; Am Univ, PhD(chem), 71. *Honors & Awards:* Melvin Romanoff Award, North East Sect, Nat Asn Corrosion Engrs, 77. *Prof Exp:* Chem abstractor phys chem, Chem Abstracts Serv, 62-70; res asst electrochem, Am Univ, 68-71, asst res scientist phys chem, 72-74, assoc res scientist, 74-76. *Concurrent Pos:* Fel, US Army, 72-74; adj prof, Am Univ, 78-79. *Mem:* Electrochem Soc; Nat Asn Corrosion Engrs; Am Chem Soc; Sigma Xi. *Res:* Electrochemistry of fuel cell processes; use of fuel cells as energy conversion devices; corrosion processes occuring at metallic interfaces. *Mailing Add:* 8436 Rushing Creek Ct Springfield VA 22153-2531

ADAMS, ALBERT WHITTEN, ANIMAL NUTRITION. *Current Pos:* RETIRED. *Personal Data:* b Ft Scott, Kans, Oct 9, 27; m 54; c 4. *Educ:* Kans State Col, BS, 51, MS, 55; SDak State Univ, PhD(animal sci), 65. *Prof Exp:* Asst hatchery mgr, Swift & Co, 51-52, hatchery mgr, 52-54; asst poultry sci, Kans State Col, 54-55; from instr to asst prof, SDak State Univ, 55-60; mgr, Stants Turkey Farms, 60-62; asst prof dairy & poultry sci, 62-66, assoc scientist, Agr Exp Sta, 66-72, assoc prof, 66-75, prof animal sci & indust, Kans State Univ, 75-92, res poultry scientist, Agr Exp Sta, 73-92. *Mem:* Poultry Sci Asn; World Poultry Sci Asn. *Res:* Relationship between the effects of various nutritional and environmental factors on performance of cage layers. *Mailing Add:* 1816 Alabama Lane Kans State Univ Call Hall Manhattan KS 66502

ADAMS, ARLON TAYLOR, ANTENNAS, MICROWAVES. *Current Pos:* from asst prof to assoc prof, 63-74, PROF ELEC ENG, SYRACUSE UNIV, 74- *Personal Data:* b Bottineau, NDak, Apr 26, 31; m 58; c 4. *Educ:* Harvard Univ, BA, 53; Univ Mich, Ann Arbor, MS, 61, PhD(elec eng), 64. *Honors & Awards:* Achievement Award, Inst Elec & Electronic Engrs, 73. *Prof Exp:* Engr, Sperry Gyroscope Co, 57-59; res assoc, Univ Mich, 59-63. *Concurrent Pos:* Consult, Hughes Aircraft Corp, Int Bus Mach, USN, NCR & Syracuse Res Corp, 63-; assoc ed, Inst Elec & Electronic Engrs Electromagnet Compatibility Trans & Antennas Propagation Soc Newsletter, 75-88; vis scholar, Univ Calif, Berkeley, 76-77; Fulbright researcher, Univ Banja Luka, Yugoslavia, 84. *Mem:* Fel Inst Elec & Electronics Engrs; Inst Elec & Electronic Engrs Antennas & Propagation Soc. *Res:* Numerical methods for electromagnetics, especially with application to microstrip transmission lines, antennas, and waveguides. *Mailing Add:* 102 Kensington Rd Syracuse NY 13210

ADAMS, ARNOLD LUCIAN, SURFACE SCIENCE, SCIENTIFIC PROGRAMMING. *Current Pos:* PRES, ADAMS RES CORP, 85- *Personal Data:* b Aurora, Ill, Dec 24, 52; m 78; c 2. *Educ:* Univ Ill, Urbana, BS, 75; Univ Calif, Santa Barbara, PhD(physics), 80. *Prof Exp:* Res fel, Univ Calif, Santa Barbara, 80-82; staff, Santa Barbara Res, 82-85. *Concurrent Pos:* Sr analyst, Santa Barbara Focalplane. *Mem:* Am Phys Soc. *Res:* Electromagnetic interactions of molecules and atoms with various surfaces; surface properties of semiconductors; infrared camera development. *Mailing Add:* 811 Poinsettia Way Santa Barbara CA 93111

ADAMS, BRENT LARSEN, MECHANICAL BEHAVIOR OF SOLIDS. *Current Pos:* PROF MECH ENG, BRIGHAM YOUNG UNIV, 92- *Personal Data:* b Provo, Utah, Sept 26, 49; m 71; c 3. *Educ:* Univ Utah, BS, 74; Ohio State Univ, MS, 76, PhD(metall eng), 79. *Honors & Awards:* Henry Marion Howe Medal, Am Soc Metals Int, 87. *Prof Exp:* Sr res engr, Lynchburg Res Ctr, Babcock & Wilcox Co, 76-79; advan scientist, Hanford Eng & Develop Lab, US Dept Energy, 79-80; asst prof mat sci & eng, Univ Fla, 80-83; assoc prof mech eng, Brigham Young Univ, 83-88; assoc prof mech eng, Yale Univ, 88-92. *Concurrent Pos:* Consult, Aluminum Co Am, 82- *Mem:* Metall Soc, Am Inst Mining, Metall & Petrol Engrs; Am Soc Metals. *Res:* Mechanics and physics of flow and fracture in polycrystallic metals; texture and microstructural effects upon mechanical properties. *Mailing Add:* Mat Sci Eng Carnegie Mellon Univ 5000 Forbes Ave Pittsburgh PA 15213. *Fax:* 801-378-7575

ADAMS, C(HARLES) HOWARD, CHEMICAL ENGINEERING. *Current Pos:* RETIRED. *Personal Data:* b Bergen, NY, May 20, 17; m 41; c 3. *Educ:* Univ Ill, BS, 39, MS, 45. *Prof Exp:* Mem staff prod control & res, Am Plastics Corp, 40-41; asst chem eng res, Univ Ill, 41-45; sr group leader plastics res, Plastics Div, Monsanto Co, 45-56, mgr plastics prod develop, Res & Eng Div, 56-60, mgr, Prod Eng Plastics Div, 60-62, mgr, Mat Eng Cent Res Dept, 62-68, mgr systs eng dir, New Enterprise Div, 68-70, mgr prod eng, 70-72, sr res specialist, Rubber Chem Div, 72-73, com develop mgr, Plastics & Resins Co, 75-78, prin eng specialist, Corp Eng Dept, 78-82. *Concurrent Pos:* Chmn, US Plastics Comt, Int Orgn Stand, 56-58; res assoc, Ctr Fire Res, Nat Bur Stand, 73-82. *Mem:* Am Inst Chem Eng; hon mem Am Soc Test & Mat. *Res:* Theoretical and applied mechanics; physics and engineering mechanics of high polymers; polymeric materials engineering; plastics standards; plastics design processing and fabrication; acoustic emission engineering. *Mailing Add:* 710 Creekbriar Lane Kirkwood MO 63122

ADAMS, CHARLES HENRY, ANIMAL SCIENCE, MEAT SCIENCE. *Current Pos:* from asst prof to prof, Univ Nebr, 47-84, mem grad fac, 70-84, asst dean, Col Agr, 73-84, EMER PROF ANIMAL SCI, UNIV NEBR, LINCOLN, 84- *Personal Data:* b Burdick, Kans, Nov 7, 18; m 43, Eula M Peters. *Educ:* Kans State Univ, BS, 41, MS, 42; Mich State Univ, PhD, 64. *Honors & Awards:* R C Pollock Award, Am Meat Sci Asn, 92. *Prof Exp:* Asst instr animal husb, Kans State Univ, 46-47. *Mem:* AAAS; fel Am Soc Animal Sci; Am Meat Sci Asn; Inst Food Technol; Am Inst Biol Sci; Sigma Xi. *Res:* Meat and meat products; beef and pork carcass evaluation; packaging of frozen meat and meat products; tenderness of meat. *Mailing Add:* 7101 Colby St Lincoln NE 68505-1428

ADAMS, CHARLES REX, PETROLEUM CHEMISTRY. *Current Pos:* Res chemist, 54-64, on assignment to Shell Grundlagenforschung GmbH, Siegburg bei, Bonn, WGer, 64-66, res supvr, Petrol Chem Dept, 66-77, MGR, CHEM RES & APPLNS, SHELL DEVELOP CO, 77- *Personal Data:* b Mt Vernon, Tex, Aug 19, 30; m 51, 67; c 4. *Educ:* ETex State Teachers Col, BA, 50; Rice Inst, MA, 52, PhD(chem), 54. *Honors & Awards:* Ipatieff Prize, Am Chem Soc, 68. *Mem:* Am Chem Soc; fel Am Inst Chem; Catalysis Soc. *Res:* Mechanisms of heterogeneous catalysis; structure of solid catalysts; structure of the solid state. *Mailing Add:* 11918 Knippwood Houston TX 77024

ADAMS, CLARK EDWARD, MAMMALIAN ECOLOGY. *Current Pos:* WILDLIFE-FISHERIES, SCI, TEX A&M UNIV. *Personal Data:* b Algona, Iowa, Mar 18, 42; m 62; c 3. *Educ:* Concordia Teachers Col, BS, 64; Univ Ore, MS, 66; Univ Nebr, Lincoln, PhD(zool), 73. *Prof Exp:* Instr biol, St John's Acad & Jr Col, 64-65; assoc prof ecol, Concordia Teachers Col, 66-77, assoc prof biol, 77- *Mem:* Am Soc Mammalogists; Wildlife Soc; Sigma Xi; Nat Asn Biol Teachers. *Res:* Measuring territoriality in fox squirrels; Sciurus niger rufiventer pre and post weaning and pre and post mating. *Mailing Add:* Wildlife-Fisheries Sci Tex A&M Univ College Station TX 77843-0100

ADAMS, CLIFFORD LOWELL, physics; deceased, see previous edition for last biography

ADAMS, CURTIS H, entomology, zoology; deceased, see previous edition for last biography

ADAMS, DALE W, AGRICULTURAL ECONOMICS. *Current Pos:* prof 66-96, EMER PROF AGR ECON, OHIO STATE UNIV, 96- *Personal Data:* b Pleasant Grove, Utah, June 21, 34; m 60; c 3. *Educ:* Utah State Univ, BS, 56; Mich State Univ, MS, 61, PhD(agr econ), 64. *Prof Exp:* Asst prof agr econ, Univ Wis, 64-66. *Concurrent Pos:* Staff economist, AID, 68-69; vis prof, Stanford Univ, 74-75. *Mem:* Am Agr Econ Asn. *Res:* Rural savings and credit activities in low income countries. *Mailing Add:* 1997 Tommy Moe Place Park City UT 84098

ADAMS, DANIEL OTIS, CHEMISTRY, PAPER TECHNOLOGY & RESIN SATURATION OF PAPER. *Current Pos:* RETIRED. *Personal Data:* b Portland, Maine, Mar 14, 18; m 45, Elizabeth Greig; c Jane (Harwood), Susan (Howard), Ann (Moreno) & Nancy (Stelling). *Educ:* Oberlin Col, AB, 39; Lawrence Col, MS, 41, PhD(pulp & paper), 43. *Prof Exp:* Res chemist, WVa Pulp & Paper Co, 43-44, res proj leader, 44-48; res chemist, Bird & Son, Inc, 48-50, chief chemist, Res Div, 50-55; res dir, WVa Pulp & Paper Co, 55-59, supt tech serv, 59-64, mgr tech serv, 64-79, tech mgr, Kraft Div, Westvaco Corp, 79-86. *Mem:* Fel Tech Asn Pulp & Paper Indust. *Res:* Morphology of paper making fibers as related to their papermaking characteristics; air and water pollution abatement; resin solution saturation of paper; pulp and paper manufacture; manufacture of paperboard having structural strength. *Mailing Add:* 1446 Burningtree Rd Charleston SC 29412

ADAMS, DARIUS MAINARD, FOREST ECONOMICS. *Current Pos:* DEPT FOREST, UNIV MONT, 87- *Personal Data:* b Los Angeles, Calif, July 5, 44; m 66. *Educ:* Humboldt State Univ, BS, 66; Yale Univ, MFS, 68; Univ Calif, Berkeley, PhD(wildland resource sci), 73. *Prof Exp:* Asst prof forestry, Univ Wis-Madison, 71-74; asst prof, 75-77, assoc prof forest mgt, Ore State Univ, 77-87. *Mem:* Soc Am Foresters; Am Econ Asn. *Res:* Forest products, especially markets for public and private timber and logs; optimal management programs for uneven-aged stands and forests. *Mailing Add:* Univ Montana Sch Forest Missoula MT 59812-0001

ADAMS, DAVID B, PSYCHOSOMATIC & SOMATOFORM DISORDERS, CHRONIC PAIN. *Current Pos:* PVT PRACT CLIN PSYCHOL, ATLANTA MED & NEUROPSYCHOL, 83- *Personal Data:* b Cincinnati, Ohio, June 1, 45; m 84, Alice M; c Emily, Taylor & Payton. *Educ:* Univ Cincinnati, BA, 67; Xavier Univ, MA, 69; Univ Ala, FdS, 71 & PhD(psychol), 73. *Prof Exp:* Assoc prof behav med, Univ SC Sch Med, 75-83. *Concurrent Pos:* Fel psychol, Devereux Found, 75; mem bd dir, Bridge Counseling Ctr, 87-; vis prof behav sci, Oglethorpe Univ, 87-; consult, Ciba Vision Corp & Upjohn Labs, 88. *Mem:* Fel Acad Psychosomat Med; fel Am Orthopsychiat Asn; Am Psychol Asn; fel Acad Med Psychother; fel Acad Pain Mgt; Am Psychosomat Soc; fel Am Asn Sex Educrs Counselors & Therapist. *Res:* Adult children of mentally ill mothers; impact of psychopathology on work related injuries; psychological overlay to physical injury. *Mailing Add:* Suite 251 Med Quarters 5555 Peachtree-Dunwoody Rd NE Atlanta GA 30342-1710

ADAMS, DAVID LAWRENCE, SCIENCE EDUCATION. *Current Pos:* ASSOC PROF CHEM, BABSON COL, 89- *Personal Data:* b Brockton, Mass, Oct 10, 45; m 66, Lynne Connors; c 2. *Educ:* Univ Mass, BS, 67; Univ Conn, MS, 69, PhD(org chem), 71. *Prof Exp:* Instr org chem, Pa State Univ, 71-72; instr chem & chmn, Div Sci & Allied Health, 72-77, asst dean, 77-83, assoc dean fac, North Shore Community Col, 83-86; assoc prof chem, Bradford Col, 86-89. *Concurrent Pos:* Textbook consult, Wadsworth Publ Co, 73- & Prentice Hall Publ Co, 75-; consult ed, McGraw-Hill Publ Co, 76-80; vis lectr, Salem State Col, 85-88 & Harvard Univ, 90- *Mem:* Am Chem Soc; Sigma Xi; Nat Sci Teachers Asn; Nat Asn Sci Technol & Soc. *Res:* Determination and quantitative evaluation of environmental pollutants as influenced by various other environmental parameters; synthesis of bicyclic terpines and acid catalyzed rearrangements of same; science and chemical education for non-specialists and history of chemistry. *Mailing Add:* Chem Dept Babson Col Babson Park MA 02157-0310. *Fax:* 781-239-6465; *E-Mail:* adams@babson.edu

ADAMS, DAVID S, BIOLOGY, MOLECULAR BIOLOGY. *Current Pos:* asst prof, 84-90, ASSOC PROF, DEPT BIOL-BIOTECHNOL, WORCESTER POLYTECH INST, 90-; SCI ADV, NAR LABS, WESTBORO, 91- *Personal Data:* b June 10, 52; m 83, Sara Trillo. *Educ:* Okla State Univ, BS, 74; Univ Houston, MS, 76; Univ Tex, Austin, PhD(molecular biol), 79. *Prof Exp:* Teaching asst, Dept Biophys Sci, Univ Houston, 75, res asst, 76-77; res asst, Dept Zool, Univ Tex, Austin, 77-79, instr, 79; fel, Lab Cell Biol, Rockefeller Univ, 80-84. *Concurrent Pos:* Am Cancer Soc individual res fel, 81-82; NIH individual res fel, 82-84; consult, Transgenic Sci Inc, 88-92 & Neuromedica, Inc, Cambridge, MA, 91- *Mem:* Am Soc Cell Biol; AAAS; Sigma Xi. *Res:* Numerous publications; biology. *Mailing Add:* Dept Biol & Biotechnol Worcester Polytech Inst 100 Institute Rd Worcester MA 01609. *Fax:* 508-831-5753, 831-5483; *E-Mail:* dadams@wpi.wpi.edu

ADAMS, DENNIS JACK, GEOMICROBIOLOGY, ECOLOGY OF MICROORGANISMS & ENVIRONMENTAL BIOLOGY. *Current Pos:* RES PROF CIVIL & ENVIRON ENG, UNIV UTAH, 93-; DIR, CTR BIOREMEDIATION, WEBER STATE UNIV, 96-, RES PROF MICROBIOL, 96- *Personal Data:* b St George, Utah, July 11, 48; m 71, Kathleen. *Educ:* Univ Utah, BS, 74; Utah State Univ, MS, 78, PhD(microbiol), 81. *Prof Exp:* Dir, Aerobiol & Fermentation Progs, Dugway Proving Grounds, US Army, 79-84, prog mgr, Joint Oper Test & Info Directorate, 84-91; res supvr & dir, Biotechnol, US Bur Mines, 91-96. *Concurrent Pos:* Adj prof, Utah State Univ, 97- *Mem:* Am Soc Microbiol; Soc Indust Microbiol. *Res:* Development and enhancement of microorganisms and cell protein and enzyme components for applied bioremediation research; development of new bioprocesses and custom bio-components for pollution prevention, monitoring and remediation. *Mailing Add:* Ctr Bioremediation Weber State Univ Ogden UT 84408-2515. *Fax:* 801-626-7467; *E-Mail:* djadams@weber.edu

ADAMS, DENNIS RAY, EDUCATION ADMINISTRATION. *Current Pos:* dir, Div St Progs, 88-90, ASST DEAN INSTR, PELLISSIPPI STATE TECH COMMUNITY COL, KNOXVILLE, TENN, 90- *Personal Data:* b Celina, Ohio, Sept 13, 49; m 71; c 2. *Educ:* Bowling Green State Univ, BS, 71; Univ

Ala, Tuscaloosa, MA, 75, PhD(math educ), 77. *Prof Exp:* Teacher math, New Bremen Sch, Ohio, 71-72, Colegio Karl C Parrish, Barranquilla, Colombia, 72-73, Colegio Nueva Granada, Bogota, 73-75; asst, Univ Ala, 75-77; instr, State Tech Inst, Knoxville, 77-81, head dept math, 81-86, asst dean humanities & sci, 86-88. *Mem:* Nat Coun Teachers Math; Am Math Asn. *Mailing Add:* Dept Arts & Sci Pelissippi State Tech Community Col PO Box 22990 Knoxville TN 37933-0990

ADAMS, DOLPH OLIVER, PATHOLOGY, FORSENIC PATHOLOGY. *Current Pos:* from asst prof to assoc prof & dir autopsy serv, 72-81, chief, Div Autopsy Path, 81-93, PROF PATH, MED CTR, DUKE UNIV, 81- *Personal Data:* b Montezuma, Ga, Apr 12, 39; div. *Educ:* Duke Univ, AB, 60; Med Col Ga, MS & MD, 65; Univ NC, PhD(exp path), 72. *Honors & Awards:* Res Recognition Award, Noble Found, 85. *Prof Exp:* Chief path, US Army Joint Laser Safety Team, Frankford Arsenal, 70-72. *Concurrent Pos:* Dir, Lab Cell & Molecular Biol Leukocytes, Duke Univ, 83-, vchmn, 91-93, dir grad studies, Integrated Prog Toxicol, 86-89, prog dir, Host Resistance & Leukocyte Biol Prog, Duke Comprehensive Cancer Ctr, 92- *Mem:* Am Asn Pathologists & Bacteriologists; Am Soc Exp Path; Am Soc Cell Biol; Am Asn Immunologists; Am Asn Cancer Res; Soc Leukocyte Biol (pres, 90-91). *Res:* Role of macrophages in cellular immunology and tumor biology; host defense; regulation of macrophages by signal transduction and regulation of gene transcription; leukocyte biology; granulomas. *Mailing Add:* Dept Path Duke Univ Med Ctr Davidson Bldg Box 3712 Durham NC 27710-0001. *E-Mail:* adams025@mc.duke.edu

ADAMS, DON, CHEMICAL ENGINEERING. *Current Pos:* prof, Dept Mech Tech, Okla State Univ, 78-80, AT DEPT PETROL. *Personal Data:* b Oklahoma City, Okla, Apr 2, 40; m 59. *Educ:* Okla State Univ, BS, 62, MS, 64, PhD(chem eng), 68. *Prof Exp:* Chem engr, Phillips Petrol Co, 67-68; assoc prof chem eng, McNeese State Univ, 68-78. *Mem:* AAAS; Am Inst Chem Engrs; Am Chem Soc. *Res:* Heat transfer and pressure drop for flow of non-Newtonian fluids across ideal tube banks; heat transfer, fluid flow and analog/digital hybrid computer application. *Mailing Add:* Div Eng Technol Okla State Univ 294 Cordell S Stillwater OK 74078-8012

ADAMS, DONALD E, AEROSPACE GROUND TESTING, ENERGY ENGINEERING. *Current Pos:* sr engr, 69-78, PRIN ENGR, CALSPAN CORP, 78- *Personal Data:* b Burlington, Vt; m 65, Rosemarie Vara; c David E, Thomas J & Emily M. *Educ:* Univ Vt, BS, 60; Cornell Univ, MS, 63. *Prof Exp:* Jr engr, Texaco Res Ctr, 60; NSF res asst, Cornell Univ, 60-62; jr engr, Naval Ordnance Lab, 61; asst engr, Cornell Aeronaut Lab, 62-65, assoc engr, 65-69. *Mem:* Am Soc Mech Engrs; Sigma Xi. *Res:* Rocket stage separation testing; hypersonic wind tunnel testing; energy saving devices (safety and energy conservation potential); gas-fired appliances; railroad tank car safety; heat transfer; high temperature instrumentation; heating and erosion of ordnance. *Mailing Add:* PO Box 400 Buffalo NY 14225. *Fax:* 716-631-6815; *E-Mail:* adams@calspan

ADAMS, DONALD F, COMPOSITE MATERIALS, APPLIED MECHANICS. *Current Pos:* PROF MECH ENG, UNIV WYO, 72-; PRES, WYO TEST FIXTURES INC, 88- *Personal Data:* b Streator, Ill, Sept 25, 35; m 57; c 4. *Educ:* Univ Ill, BS, 57, PhD(appl mech), 63; Univ Southern Calif, MS, 60. *Honors & Awards:* Ralph Teetor Award, Soc Automotive Engrs, 78. *Prof Exp:* Engr, Northrop Corp, 57-60; instr appl mech, Univ Ill, 60-63; supvr, Ford Aerospace & Commun, 63-67; mem staff, Rand Corp, 67-72. *Concurrent Pos:* Consult & expert witness, indust groups, 72-; vis fac, NSF, 74; mem, Nat Res Coun, 79-81 & UN Independent Develop Orgn, 79- *Mem:* Am Soc Mech Engrs; Am Soc Composites; Am Soc Testing & Mats; Soc Aerospace Mat Engrs; Am Soc Eng Educ. *Res:* Composite materials research, both analytical and experimental for government and industry. *Mailing Add:* Dept Mech Eng Univ Wyo PO Box 3295 Laramie WY 82071-3295

ADAMS, DONALD ROBERT, RESPIRATORY MORPHOLOGY. *Current Pos:* from asst prof to assoc prof, 74-85, PROF ANAT, COL VET MED, IOWA STATE UNIV, 85- *Personal Data:* b Red Bluff, Calif, Aug 3, 37; m 74; c 3. *Educ:* Univ Calif, Davis, AB, 60, PhD(anat), 70; Chico State Col, Calif, MS, 67. *Prof Exp:* Govt secy educ officer, Tanganyika, 61-63; teacher biol, physiol & health sci, C K McClatchy Sr High Sch, Calif, 64-65; asst prof anat, Col Vet Med, Mich State Univ, 70-74. *Mem:* Am Asn Anatomists; Am Asn Vet Anatomists; World Asn Vet Anatomists. *Res:* Structure and function of the upper respiratory system with emphasis on secretory cells and blood vascular system of the mammalian nasal cavity. *Mailing Add:* Dept Vet Anat Col Vet Med Iowa State Univ Ames IA 50011

ADAMS, EARNEST DWIGHT, LOW TEMPERATURE PHYSICS. *Current Pos:* from asst prof to assoc prof, 62-70, PROF PHYSICS, UNIV FLA, 70- *Personal Data:* b Carrollton, Ga, Feb 16, 33; m 53, Joan Gordy; c Lowell, Darrell & Douglas. *Educ:* Berry Col, AB, 53; Emory Univ, MS, 54; Duke Univ, PhD, 60. *Honors & Awards:* Jesse W Beams Award, Am Phys Soc, 78. *Prof Exp:* Res assoc physics, Stanford Univ, 60-62. *Concurrent Pos:* Vis prof, Helsinki Univ Technol, 71. *Mem:* Fel Am Phys Soc. *Res:* Low temperature physics, especially properties of helium-3 and helium-4. *Mailing Add:* Dept Physics Univ Fla Gainesville FL 32611

ADAMS, EDWARD FRANKLIN, CERAMICS, CHEMICAL ENGINEERING. *Current Pos:* FINANCIAL REP, FIRST FINANCIAL GROUP, 83- *Personal Data:* b Washington, DC, Oct 15, 36; m 64. *Educ:* Univ Md, BS, 58; Rensselaer Polytech Inst, PhD(chem eng), 63. *Prof Exp:* Sr chem engr, Ceramic Res, Corning Glass Works, 62-65, res chem engr, 65-68, proj supvr, 68-71, plant eng mgr, 71-73, mgr, Corstar Prod, 73-77; dir res & develop, Anchor Hocking Corp, 77-79, vpres & engr, 77-83. *Mem:* Am Chem Soc; Am Ceramic Soc; Am Inst Chem Engrs. *Res:* Glass contact refractories; ceramic processing, including slip casting, isostatic pressing, ceramic coatings on metals; cellular structures for heat exchangers; crystal growth from melt; glass manufacturing technology; glass melting. *Mailing Add:* 1365 Escapade Ct Riva MD 21140-1308

ADAMS, EMORY TEMPLE, JR, BIOPHYSICAL CHEMISTRY. *Current Pos:* assoc prof, 70-76, PROF CHEM, TEX A&M UNIV, 76- *Personal Data:* b Tampico, Mex, Sept 5, 28; US citizen. *Educ:* Rice Univ, BA, 49; Baylor Col Med, MS, 52; Univ Wis-Madison, PhD(biochem), 62. *Prof Exp:* Res assoc chem, Univ Wis-Madison, 62-63; res chemist, Hercules Res Ctr, Del, 63-64; res assoc biol, Brookhaven Nat Lab, 64-65; staff fel, Nat Inst Arthritis & Metab Dis, 66; asst prof chem, Ill Inst Technol, 66-70. *Concurrent Pos:* Vis prof, Dept Med, Univ Chicago, 83-84. *Mem:* Am Chem Soc; Biophys Soc; Am Soc Biol Chemists. *Res:* Analysis of self-associating proteins and mixed associations of biopolymers by sedimentation equilibrium and osmometry; molecular weights and molecular-weight distributions from sedimentation equilibrium experiments; sedimentation equilibrium theory. *Mailing Add:* 3613 Oakridge Dr Bryan TX 77802

ADAMS, ERNEST CLARENCE, MEDICAL DIAGNOSTICS, IMMUNOCHEMISTRY. *Current Pos:* SR RES SCIENTIST, GENESIS LABS, 86- *Personal Data:* b Meridian, Miss, Mar 27, 25. *Educ:* Miss State Col, BS, 48; Northwestern Univ, PhD(biochem), 50. *Prof Exp:* Asst prof chem, Miss State Col, 50-51; res biochemist & group leader, Miles-Ames Res Lab, Miles Labs, 51-59, sr res biochemist & group leader, Ames Res Lab, 59-61, sect head, 61-70, adminr immunochem opers, 70-72, staff scientist, 72-76, prin investr, Ames Res Lab, 76-78 & Res Prod Div; dir res & develop, Chem-Elec, Inc, 83-86. *Mem:* AAAS; Am Chem Soc; NY Acad Sci; Asn Clin Scientists; Sigma Xi; Am Inst Chemists. *Res:* Immunochemistry; antisera production; protein isolation; immunogen preparation; medical diagnostics; clinical chemistry; solid state chemistry. *Mailing Add:* Genesis Labs Inc Minneapolis MN 55439-2904. *Fax:* 612-835-9406

ADAMS, EVELYN ELEANOR, OCCUPATIONAL MEDICINE. *Current Pos:* MED DIR, CTR HUMAN RADIO BIOL, ARGONNE NAT LAB, 78- *Personal Data:* b Georgetown, Ill, Feb 17, 25; m 51; c 2. *Educ:* Univ Chicago, BS, 46, MD, 49. *Prof Exp:* Intern med, Univ Chicago Hosp, 49-50; resident gen surg, Univ Iowa Hosp, 50-51; dir employee health, Univ Chicago Clin, 51-55; sr physician chest med, Suburban Cook Co Sanitarium, 60-68; assoc med dir employee health, Abbott Lab, 68-74; med dir, Johnson & Johnson, Chicago, 74-78. *Mem:* Am Occup Med Asn. *Res:* Effects of internally deposited radionuclides in humans. *Mailing Add:* 7255 Caldwell Ave Niles IL 60714-4501

ADAMS, FORREST HOOD, PEDIATRIC CARDIOLOGY. *Current Pos:* RETIRED. *Personal Data:* b Minneapolis, Minn, Sept 20, 19; m 43, 69; c 10. *Educ:* Univ Minn, BA, 41, MB, 43, MD, 44, MS, 46; Am Bd Pediat, dipl, 48, cert cardiol, 61. *Honors & Awards:* Theodore & Susan Cummings Humanitarian Award, 64, 65, 66, 67, 71 & 72; Distinguished Fel Award, Am Col Cardiol, 74. *Prof Exp:* Intern, Univ Minn Hosp, 43-44, from instr to asst prof pediat, 48-52; from assoc prof to prof, Sch Med, Univ Calif, Los Angeles, 52-78, actg chmn dept, 58-59 & 64-65, vchmn dept, 62-64; clin prof pediat, Sch Med, Univ Hawaii, 81-82. *Concurrent Pos:* Nat Res fel pediat, Univ Minn Hosp, 48-49; asst dir heart sect, Crippled Children's Prog, St Paul, 49-50; physician chg pediat, Sister Elizabeth Kenny Inst, 49-50; assoc physician chg pediat, Minneapolis Gen Hosp, 49-50, chief, 50-52; dir pediat heart clins, Univ Minn Hosp & Variety Club Heart Hosp, 51-52; med dir, Marion Davies Children's Clin, 52-55; mem staff, St John's Hosp & Harbor Gen Hosp, 52-78; consult, State Bd Pub Health, Calif, 63-78; pres, Sub-Specialty Bd Pediat Cardiol, 67, emer mem, 69-; mem adv bd, Inter-Soc Comn Heart Dis Resources, 68-, mem comt congenital heart dis, 68-71, mem exec comt, 68-71; consult, Off Surgeon Gen; Career Res Award, US Pub Health Serv, 62-67; chmn, Health Benefits Adv Coun, Calif Pub Employee's Retirement Syst, 89-91. *Mem:* Soc Pediat Res; Am Acad Pediat; Am Col Cardiol (vpres, 68-69, pres-elect, 70, pres, 71-72); Am Pediat Soc; Am Heart Asn. *Res:* Toxoplasmosis; congenital heart disease; rheumatic fever; hyaline membrane disease; pediatric cardiology; hypertension; exercize physiology. *Mailing Add:* 16767 Via Lago Azul PO Box 8066 Rancho Santa Fe CA 92067

ADAMS, FRANCIS L(EE), engineering, for more information see previous edition

ADAMS, FRANK WILLIAM, ANIMAL NUTRITION. *Current Pos:* Instr, 53-65, ASST PROF AGR CHEM, ORE STATE UNIV, 65- *Personal Data:* b Billings, Mont, Feb 17, 25; m 47; c 7. *Educ:* Mont State Col, BS, 48; Ore State Univ, MS, 50, PhD(zool, biochem), 65. *Mem:* AAAS; Am Chem Soc; Nutrit Today Soc; Sigma Xi. *Res:* Mammalian embryology; normal and nutritionally caused abnormalities in placentae; trace element relationships in animal nutrition; animal fluorosis. *Mailing Add:* 1153 NW 16th St Corvallis OR 97330-2608

ADAMS, FRED, SOIL SCIENCE. *Current Pos:* RETIRED. *Personal Data:* b Marion, La, Mar 1, 21; m 43; c 2. *Educ:* La State Univ, BS, 43, MS, 48; Univ Calif, PhD(soil sci), 51. *Prof Exp:* Prof soil sci, Am Univ, Beirut, 52-55; from assoc prof to prof soils, Auburn Univ, 55-77, prof agron & soils, 77-84, emer prof, 84- *Mem:* Fel Am Soc Agron; fel Soil Sci Soc Am. *Res:* Chemistry and fertility of soils. *Mailing Add:* 2568 E Glenn Ave Auburn AL 36830

ADAMS, GABRIELLE H M, CELL BIOLOGY. *Current Pos:* publ supvr res journals, 75-78, mgr res jour, 79-82, Div Biol Sci, Nat Res Coun Can, admin, 83-85, indust liaison, 85-86, head, Med Biosci Lab, 86-89, dir indust affairs, 89-91, acts dir gen, 91-93, DIR GEN INST BIOL SCI, NAT RES COUN CAN, 93- *Personal Data:* b Mateszalka, Hungary, Oct 29, 39; Can citizen; m 64, William A; c 2. *Educ:* McMaster Univ, BSc, 63; Carleton Univ, PhD(cell biol), 68. *Prof Exp:* Fel biochem, Nat Res Coun Can, 67-69; publ asst, Can J Bot, Nat Res Coun Can, 69-70; res assoc biochem, Nat Res Coun Can & Dept Biol, Carleton Univ, 70-75. *Mem:* Can Soc Cell Biol. *Res:* Chemistry and function of nuclear chromatin proteins. *Mailing Add:* Inst Biol Sci Nat Res Coun Can 1200 Montreal Rd Ottawa ON K1A 0R6 Can

ADAMS, GAIL DAYTON, radiological physics, for more information see previous edition

ADAMS, GAYLE E(LDREDGE), COMPUTER ENGINEERING. *Current Pos:* RETIRED. *Personal Data:* b Cherry Valley, Ill, Nov 24, 27; m 51, Lila M Johnson; c Jeffrey & Nancy (Haseman). *Educ:* Univ Wis, BS, 49, MS, 50, PhD(elec eng), 52. *Prof Exp:* Eng analyst, Gen Elec Co, NY, 52-59, opers analyst, Ariz, 59, consult comput engr, 60-63; prof eng, Ariz State Univ, 63-66; dir, Comput Eng & Develop Ctr, Univ Mo, Columbia, 66-73, prof elec eng, 66-90, prof comp eng, 73-90, dir grad studies, 88-90, emer prof elec & comp eng, 90- *Concurrent Pos:* Consult, Control Systs Assocs, 63-66, Integrated Circuits Eng Corp & Salt River Proj, 66, Gen Learning Corp, 67 & Health Serv & Ment Health Admin, 70; dir data eval & comput simulation proj, Mo Regional Med Prog, 67-73, Mede Quip Corp, 83; chief exec officer, Comput Syst Eng Inc, 74- *Mem:* Inst Elec & Electronics Engrs. *Res:* Digital systems and computers; health care systems engineering and design; systems engineering; electrical power engineering; FEM analysis of electrical machinery. *Mailing Add:* Dept Elec Eng-139 Ee Bldg Univ Mo Columbia MO 65211

ADAMS, GEORGE B(AKER), ELECTROCHEMICAL ENERGY CONVERSION, HYDROMETALLURGICAL CHEMISTRY. *Current Pos:* RETIRED. *Personal Data:* b Kentfield, Calif, Feb 23, 19. *Educ:* Univ Calif, BS(chem), 41, MS, 47; Ohio State Univ, PhD(phys chem), 51. *Prof Exp:* Asst chem, Univ Calif, 46-47; Res fel, Ohio State Univ, 48-51; res assoc, Univ Ore, 53-55, from instr to asst prof, 55-58; sr scientist, Lockheed Missiles & Space Co, Inc, 58-59, res scientist, 59-62, sr staff scientist, 62-69, sr mem res lab, 62- 88, consult scientist, 70-88. *Res:* Electrochemical energy conversion; chemical thermodynamics; environmental chemistry; hydrometallurgical chemistry; anodic oxide film formation kinetics; teaching physical and general chemistry; granted US patents. *Mailing Add:* 22069 McClellan Rd Cupertino CA 95014

ADAMS, GEORGE G, TRIBOLOGY, MOVING LOADS. *Current Pos:* from asst prof to assoc prof, Solid Mech & Design, 79-86, mech div head, 82-85, PROF SOLID MECH & DESIGN, NORTHEASTERN UNIV, 86- *Personal Data:* b Brooklyn, NY, Sept 12, 48; m 84, Janet Magenheim; c Juliana S & Daniel G. *Educ:* Cooper Union Col, BS, 69; Univ Calif, Berkeley, MS, 72, PhD(mech eng), 75. *Prof Exp:* Assoc engr vibrations, Curtiss-Wright Co, 69-70; asst prof solid mech & comput lang, Clarkson Univ, 75-79. *Concurrent Pos:* Prin investr, NSF, 76-78, 78-79, 96-, Ctr Dis Control, 82-83, IBM, 83-84, Seagate, 92-93; vis scientist res lab, IBM, Calif, 78-79; vis scholar, Univ Calif, Berkeley, 79; mem exec comt, Int Soc Phonetic Sci, Am Soc Mech Engrs. *Mem:* Am Acad Mech; fel Am Soc Mech Engrs; Am Soc Eng Educ; Soc Eng Sci; Soc Tribologists & Lubrication Engrs. *Res:* Deformation of thin-walled flexible bodies, and the response of systems to moving loads; tribology of magnetic storage systems; friction-induced vibrations; microelectromechanical systems (MEMS). *Mailing Add:* Dept Mech Eng Northeastern Univ Boston MA 02115. *Fax:* 617-373-2921; *E-Mail:* adams@neu.edu

ADAMS, HAROLD ELWOOD, POLYMER CHEMISTRY, PHYSICAL CHEMISTRY. *Current Pos:* RETIRED. *Personal Data:* b Altoona, Pa, Dec 10, 16; m 40, Caroline Goodyear; c Pendery B (Clark), Charles A, Lucinda J (Derwort), Harold E II & Scott R. *Educ:* Dickinson Col, BS, 38; Lafayette Col, MS, 39; Mass Inst Technol, PhD(phys chem), 42. *Prof Exp:* Res chemist, Armstrong Cork Co, 42-48; res chemist, Firestone Tire & Rubber Co, 48-70, div mgr chem, 70-73, sr res assoc, 73-79. *Mem:* Am Chem Soc. *Res:* Oxidation of drying oils; polymer characterization; polymerization; kinetics of polymerization. *Mailing Add:* 1930 12th St Cuyahoga Falls OH 44223-2404

ADAMS, HARRY, NUCLEAR PHYSICS. *Current Pos:* PROF PHYSICS, PAC LUTHERAN UNIV, 62- *Personal Data:* b Ft Riley, Kans, June 13, 24; m 53; c 4. *Educ:* Kans State Univ, BS, 45, MS, 47; Univ Minn, PhD(physics), 62. *Prof Exp:* Instr physics, Pac Lutheran Univ, 47-52; assoc scientist optical eng, Aeronaut Labs, Univ Minn, 53-55; res assoc & vis prof physics, Fla State Univ, 60-62. *Mem:* Am Phys Soc; Sigma Xi. *Res:* Nuclear reactions and structure. *Mailing Add:* 11613 67th Ave E Puyallup WA 98373

ADAMS, HELEN ELIZABETH, MATHEMATICS. *Current Pos:* ASST PROF MATH, SMITH COL, 73- *Personal Data:* b Cowra, Australia, Feb 21, 45; m 67. *Educ:* Univ New Eng, Australia, BS, 66; Monash Univ, Australia, PhD(math), 71. *Prof Exp:* Sr tutor math, Univ Melbourne, 66-68; fel, Mt Holyoke Col, 72-73. *Mem:* Am Math Soc; Math Asn Am. *Res:* Commutative algebra. *Mailing Add:* 3 Fisher Ave New South Vales 2016 Wahroonga NSW 2076 Australia

ADAMS, HENRY RICHARD, VETERINARY PHARMACOLOGY. *Current Pos:* asst prof, 72-75, ASSOC PROF PHARMACOL, SOUTHWESTERN MED SCH, UNIV TEX HEALTH SCI CTR DALLAS, 75-, PROF & CHMN, DEPT VET BIOMED SCI, UNIV MO. *Personal Data:* b Dallas, Tex, Apr 12, 42; m 65; c 2. *Educ:* Tex A&M Univ, BS, 65, DVM, 66; Univ Pittsburgh, PhD(pharmacol), 72. *Prof Exp:* Res vet, US Army, Ft Detrick, Md, 66-68; res assoc pharmacol, Univ Pittsburgh, 68-72. *Mem:* Am Vet Med Asn; Am Soc Pharmacol & Exp Therapeut; Am Soc Vet Physiol & Pharmacol. *Res:* Comparative cardiovascular pharmacology. *Mailing Add:* Dept Vet Biomed Sci Univ Mo Col Vet W116 Vet Med Bldg 1600 E Rollins Rd Columbia MO 65211

ADAMS, HERMAN RAY, CLINICAL CHEMISTRY. *Current Pos:* DIR, SPEC CHEM & TOXICOL LAB, SCOTT & WHITE CLIN, 72- *Personal Data:* b Abilene, Tex, Sept 15, 39; m 63; c 2. *Educ:* Tex A&M Univ, BS, 62, MS, 65; Univ Tex Southwestern Med Sch Dallas, PhD(pharmacol), 72; Am Bd Clin Chem, cert, 76. *Mem:* Am Acad Forensic Sci; Am Asn Clin Chemists; Am Chem Soc; Sigma Xi. *Mailing Add:* 4713 Ascot Pkwy Temple TX 76502

ADAMS, J MACK, COMPUTER SCIENCE. *Current Pos:* head dept, NMex State Univ, 65-73 & 75-80, prof, 65-93, assoc dean, Col Arts & Sci, 90-93, EMER PROF COMPUTER SCI, NMEX STATE UNIV, 93- *Personal Data:* b Marfa, Tex, Aug 14, 33; m 52; c 2. *Educ:* Tex Western Col, BS, 54; NMex State Univ, MS, 60, PhD(math), 63. *Honors & Awards:* US Govt Award, 64; Fulbright-Hays sr lectr, Cath Univ, Chile, 72. *Prof Exp:* Assoc scientist, Bettis Atomic Power Div, Westinghouse Elec Corp, 54-56; mathematician, Flight Simulation Lab, White Sands Missile Range, NMex, 56-58, supvr mathematician, 58-60, mathematician, 61-62, res mathematician, Electronics Res & Develop Activity, 63, supvry mathematician, 63-64; assoc prof math, Tex Western Col, 64-65; prog dir, NSF, 87-90. *Concurrent Pos:* Vis fel, Wolfson Col, Oxford Univ, 78. *Mem:* Math Asn Am; Asn Comput Mach; Sigma Xi. *Res:* Programming languages; theory of algorithms; computer science education; hyper media. *Mailing Add:* 905 Conway No 7 Las Cruces NM 88005. *E-Mail:* jma@nmsu.edu

ADAMS, JAMES ALAN, FLUID MECHANICS, COMPUTER GRAPHICS. *Current Pos:* assoc prof, 64-80, PROF ENG, US NAVAL ACAD, 80- *Personal Data:* b Fayetteville, Ark, Feb 11, 36; m 58; c 3. *Educ:* Univ Ark, BSME, 58; Purdue Univ, MSME, 63, PhD(mech eng), 65. *Prof Exp:* Instr mech eng, Purdue Univ, 63-64. *Mem:* Am Soc Eng Educ; Am Soc Mech Engrs. *Res:* Combined heat and mass transfer in boundary layer flow; density variations at a liquid-air interface; mathematics of computer graphics; computer aided design. *Mailing Add:* Dept Mech Eng US Naval Acad Annapolis MD 21402

ADAMS, JAMES HALL, JR, COSMIC RAY PHYSICS. *Current Pos:* res physicist, 74-92, SECT HEAD, COSMIC RAY PHYSICS, NAVAL RES LAB, 92- *Personal Data:* b Statesville, NC, Aug 7, 43; m 68, Rebekah Ellis; c Amanda & David. *Educ:* NC State Univ, BS, 66, MS, 68, PhD(physics), 72. *Prof Exp:* Res asst cosmic ray physics, Johnson Space Ctr, 69-72; res assoc, Nat Res Coun, 72-74. *Mem:* Am Phys Soc; AAAS; Am Geophys Union; Sigma Xi. *Res:* Measurements of cosmic ray, elemental composition and charge states; energy spectra; studies of heavy ion nuclear interactions; cosmic ray effects on microelectronics. *Mailing Add:* 7733 Wellington Rd Alexandria VA 22306

ADAMS, JAMES MILLER, ANALYTICAL CHEMISTRY, METHOD DEVELOPMENT. *Current Pos:* CONSULT, 86- *Personal Data:* b Cleveland, Ohio, Sept 9, 24; m 60, Lorraine G Waryold; c Pamela, Nancy, James, Carolyn, William, Claudia & Brian. *Educ:* Case Inst Technol, BS, 45; Va Polytech Inst, BS, 48, MS, 49, PhD(biochem), 54. *Honors & Awards:* Intergovt Rels Award, 72; Comnr Citation, US Customs Serv, 82. *Prof Exp:* Instr, Va Polytech Inst, 48-51; res chemist, Visking Corp, Ill, 54-55; chief chemist, Lab Vitamin Technol, 55-58; res chemist, Chemagro Corp, Mo, 58-63; res assoc drug residues & atherosclerosis, Merck Inst Therapeut Res, NJ, 63-67, sect leader phys & analytical res dept, Merck, Sharp & Dohme Res Labs, 67-69; regional dir lab div, US Customs Serv, 69-82, chief, Res Br, US Customs Serv Lab, NY, 82-86. *Concurrent Pos:* Instr, Univ Kansas City, 58-63 & Middlesex Co Col, 67-69; safety officer, US Customs, Region III, 69-75; charter mem, Mid Atlantic Asn Forensic Scientists, mem bd dirs, 73-74. *Mem:* Am Chem Soc; Am Soc Microbiol; Soc Appl Spectros; Asn Off Analytic Chemists. *Res:* Saran coatings; large cellulose casings; vitamin assays; radiation sterilization of meat; organophosphate insecticide assay; drug residue assay; bacterial metabolism; atherosclerosis; narcotics detection; forensic analysis; adulteration of fruit juices, vegetable oils and lime oil; aromatic components of petroleum products. *Mailing Add:* 307 Sheffield Ct Joppa MD 21085-4747

ADAMS, JAMES MILTON, BIOENGINEERING, BIOMEDICAL ENGINEERING. *Current Pos:* from asst prof to assoc prof, 78-92, PROF BIOMED ENG, UNIV VA, 92-, ASST DEAN GRAD PROGS, 96- *Personal Data:* b Roanoke, Va, Sept 22, 49; m 71; c 2. *Educ:* Va Polytech Inst & State Univ, BS, 71; Univ Va, PhD(biomed eng), 76. *Prof Exp:* Res assoc & instr physiol, Albany Med Col, 76-78. *Concurrent Pos:* Vis scientist, Dartmouth Med Sch, 84-85. *Mem:* Biomed Eng Soc; Am Physiol Soc; Am Inst Med & Biol Eng. *Res:* Pulmonary physiology; carbon dioxide transport. *Mailing Add:* Med Ctr Univ Va Box 377 Charlottesville VA 22908. *E-Mail:* jma@virginia.edu

ADAMS, JAMES RUSSELL, MICROELECTRONICS, RADIATION EFFECTS. *Current Pos:* VPRES ENG, TAEUS, 92- *Personal Data:* b North Platte, Nebr, Apr 10, 45; m 67; c 1. *Educ:* Univ Nebr, Lincoln, BS, 67, MS, 69, PhD(elec eng), 74. *Prof Exp:* Mem tech staff, Sandia Nat Labs, 69-79; mgr, Prod Tech Develop, Inmos Corp, 79-83, vpres, 83-85; vpres, Triad Semiconductors, 85-86; dir, Monolithic Memories Inc, 86-87; sr prin prog mgr, United Technol Microelectronics, 87-88, dir strategic planning, 88-92. *Mem:* Sr mem Inst Elec & Electronic Engrs; Electrochem Soc; Sigma Xi. *Res:* Optical properties of materials; radiation effects in microelectronics; mos vlsi wafer fabrication technology; strategic technology planning. *Mailing Add:* 1038 Oak Hills Dr Colorado Springs CO 80919

ADAMS, JAMES WILLIAM, INDUSTRIAL CHEMISTRY. *Current Pos:* CHEM SPECIALIST, J & B CONSULTS, 88- *Personal Data:* b Conover, Wis, Oct 29, 21; m 86, Barbara Backlund; c Judy & Neal. *Educ:* Univ Wis, BS, 43. *Prof Exp:* Control chemist, US Rubber Co, WVa, 43, res group leader, 43-47, chief chemist, Conn, 48-51; sr scientist, Marathon Corp, Am Can Co, 51-57, res assoc, Marathon Div, 57-63, sr res assoc, 63-71, res supvr II, 71-80; mgr process develop, Reed Lignin, 80-88. *Mem:* NY Acad Sci; Am Chem Soc. *Res:* Lignin chemicals; grafting vinyl polymers on cellulose. *Mailing Add:* 2008 Clarberth St Schofield WI 54476

ADAMS, JANE N, microbiology, genetics, for more information see previous edition

ADAMS, JASPER EMMETT, JR, MATHEMATICAL STATISTICS, MATHEMATICS. *Current Pos:* Instr math, 65-68, from asst prof to assoc prof, 71-78, PROF MATH STATIST, STEPHEN F AUSTIN STATE UNIV, 78- *Personal Data:* b Smith Co, Tex, Aug 27, 42; m 65; c 2. *Educ:* Stephen F Austin State Univ, BS, 64, MS, 65; Tex Tech Univ, PhD(math statist), 71. *Concurrent Pos:* NSF sci scholar fac fel, 70-71. *Mem:* Am Statist Asn; Am Soc Eng Educ; Nat Coun Teachers Math; Sigma Xi. *Res:* Bias reduction techniques and application of statistics. *Mailing Add:* Box 13040 Nacogdoches TX 75962

ADAMS, JEAN RUTH, INSECT PATHOLOGY, ELECTRON MICROSCOPY. *Current Pos:* res entomologist, 62-96, COLLABR, AGR RES CTR, USDA, 96- *Personal Data:* b Edgewater Park, NJ, Aug 17, 28. *Educ:* Rutgers Univ, BS, 50, PhD(entom), 62. *Honors & Awards:* Ed Bd, J Invert Path, 86-89. *Prof Exp:* Technician, Rohm & Haas Co, 51-57; res fel zool, Univ Pa, 61-62. *Concurrent Pos:* Ed, Atlas Invert Viruses, 91 & Insect Potpourri: Adventures Entomol, 92. *Mem:* Micros Soc Am; Entom Soc Am; Soc Invert Path (secy, 82-84); NY Acad Sci; Am Soc Microbiol; Sigma Xi. *Res:* Electron microscopic investigations on histopathology of pathogens of insects; virus invasion and replication of insect pathogens in insect tissues and in insect tissue culture cells. *Mailing Add:* USDA Insect Biocontrol Lab Agr Res Ctr-W Bldg 011A Rm 214 Beltsville MD 20705. *Fax:* 301-504-5104

ADAMS, JOHN ANDREW, REAL-TIME X-RAY SYSTEMS, FULLY AUTOMATED VISION SYSTEMS. *Current Pos:* CHIEF SCIENTIST, ATHENS, 94- *Personal Data:* b Cincinnati, Ohio, Feb 15, 46; m 69, Sally Howard; c John & Sarah. *Educ:* Univ San Diego, BS, 68; Ariz State Univ, PhD(physics), 78. *Honors & Awards:* IR-100 Award, 84. *Prof Exp:* Sr scientist, IRT Corp, 78-82, mgr, Geol Logging Servs, 82-84, mgr technol develop, 84-86; chief scientist, Four Pi Systs, 86-94. *Concurrent Pos:* Consult mach automation, Phase Matrics, 92, Athens Corp, 92- *Mem:* Int Elec Packaging Soc. *Res:* Automation of test equipment for factory floor, including vision systems, x-ray systems, tomography systems and chemical reprocessing equipment; granted five US patents. *Mailing Add:* 615 Valley Grove Lane Escondido CA 92025-7453

ADAMS, JOHN CLYDE, FORESTRY, SILVICULTURE. *Current Pos:* PROF FORESTRY, LA TECH UNIV, 76- *Personal Data:* b Angie, La, Dec 11, 47. *Educ:* La State Univ, BSF, 69, MS, 73, PhD(forestry), 76. *Mem:* Soc Am Foresters; Hardwood Res Coun; Int Union Forestry Res Orgn. *Res:* Forestry tree improvement, especially genetic improvement of water and willow oak for timber production and study of species diversity throughout the natural range; regeneration of hardwood stands to provide more usable high quality material. *Mailing Add:* Sch Forestry La Tech Univ PO Box 3168 Ruston LA 71272

ADAMS, JOHN COLLINS, MICROBIAL ECOLOGY, WATER POLLUTION. *Current Pos:* From asst prof to assoc prof, 69-86, PROF MICROBIOL, UNIV WYO, 86- *Personal Data:* b New Albany, Ind, Sept 18, 38; m 60; c 2. *Educ:* Purdue Univ, BS, 62; Iowa State Univ, MS, 64; Wash State Univ, PhD(bact), 69. *Mem:* Am Soc Microbiol; Water Pollution Control Fedn; AAAS; Am Water Works Asn; Int Ozone Asn. *Res:* Microbiology of process waters associated with oil shale; microbiology of coal strip mines in the western United States; microbiology of fresh waters and sediments; microbiology of game meat; fluorescent and denitrifying bacteria; causes of tastes and odors in drinking water; drinking water bacteriology; biofouled wells; direct viable count methodology. *Mailing Add:* Div Molecular Biol Univ Wyo Box 3944 Laramie WY 82071-3944

ADAMS, JOHN EDGAR, SOIL PHYSICS. *Current Pos:* SOIL SCIENTIST SOUTHERN REGION, OKLA-TEX AREA, SCI EDUC ADMIN, FED SERV, USDA, 55- *Personal Data:* b Curtis, Nebr, Jan 18, 18; m 42; c 3. *Educ:* Univ Nebr, BSc, 42, MSc, 49; Iowa State Univ, PhD(soil physics), 56. *Prof Exp:* Soil scientist sedimentation & hydrol, Qual Water Br, US Geol Surv, 48-50. *Mem:* Am Soc Agron; Soil Sci Soc Am; Soil Conserv Soc Am; Sigma Xi. *Res:* Water intake and erodibility of heavy clay soils; management factors affecting evaporation and water use efficiency of row crops in dryland areas. *Mailing Add:* 2213 49th St Temple TX 76504

ADAMS, JOHN EDWIN, NEUROSURGERY. *Current Pos:* Asst neuroanat, 47, from instr to assoc prof neurosurg, 48-65, res assoc med physics, 54-55, chmn div neurosurg, 57-65, prof neurol surg & chmn div, 65-68, GUGGENHEIM PROF NEUROL SURG, MED CTR, UNIV CALIF, SAN FRANCISCO, 68- *Personal Data:* b Berkeley, Calif, Apr 18, 14; m 35; c 3. *Educ:* Univ Calif, AB, 35; Harvard Univ, MD, 39; Am Bd Neurol Surg, dipl. *Concurrent Pos:* Attend neurosurgeon, Hosps, 50-; consult, Naval Hosp, 52- *Mem:* AAAS; Soc Univ Surg; Am Asn Neurol Surg; Am Col Surg; AMA. *Res:* Stereotactic surgery; cerebral metabolism and circulation; hypothermia. *Mailing Add:* Div Neurol Surg Univ Calif Med Ctr 533 Parnassus Ave San Francisco CA 94122-2722

ADAMS, JOHN EVI, psychiatry, for more information see previous edition

ADAMS, JOHN GEORGE, PHARMACOLOGY. *Current Pos:* RETIRED. *Personal Data:* b Pittsburgh, Pa, Jan 31, 21; m 53; c 2. *Educ:* Duquesne Univ, BS, 47; Univ Ill, MS, 52, PhD, 55. *Prof Exp:* Instr pharmacol & pharmacog, Sch Pharm, Duquesne Univ, 47-49, asst prof pharmacol, 52-55, prof & dean, 55-61; prof pharmacol, Univ Conn, 61-65; dir, Off Sci Activ, Pharmaceut Mfrs Asn, 65-68, vpres res, Off Sci & prof rels, 68-83. *Mem:* AAAS; Am Pharmaceut Asn; NY Acad Sci. *Res:* Relationship of molecular architecture to biological activity; biogenesis of neurohumoral agents in nerve impulse transmission and muscular contraction; drug enzymology; biochemical pharmacology. *Mailing Add:* 8107 Whites Ford Way Rockville MD 20854

ADAMS, JOHN KENDAL, GEOLOGY. *Current Pos:* ASSOC PROF GEOL, TEMPLE UNIV, 65- *Personal Data:* b Willimantic, Conn, June 14, 33; m 67. *Educ:* Univ Conn, BA, 55; Rutgers Univ, MS, 57, PhD(geol), 59. *Prof Exp:* Asst prof geol, Univ Del, 58-63; geologist, US Peace Corps, 63-65. *Mem:* Geol Soc Am; Soc Econ Paleont & Mineral; Sigma Xi. *Res:* Environmental stratigraphy; engineering soils mapping; diagenesis. *Mailing Add:* Dept of Geol Temple Univ Philadelphia PA 19122

ADAMS, JOHN PLETCH, ORTHOPEDIC SURGERY. *Current Pos:* DIR, CLIN LABS, MED COL GA, 79-, PROF PATH, 84- *Personal Data:* b Ashburn, Mo, Feb 2, 22; m 48; c 1. *Educ:* Univ Mo, BS, 43; Wash Univ, MD, 45; Harvard Univ, MPH, 78; Am Bd Orthop Surg, dipl, 51. *Prof Exp:* prof orthop surg, Sch Med, George Washington Univ, 53-, chmn dept, 69-, chief orthop serv, Univ Hosp, 53- *Concurrent Pos:* Consult orthop surg, Vet Hosp, Washington, DC, 53; dir clin labs, Franklin Sq Hosp, Baltimore, Md, 72-76; consult, Vet Admin Hosp, Augusta, Ga, 79-; consult, Vet Admin Hosp, WVa, Col Med, Howard Univ, Dept Child & Maternal Welfare, DC, Walter Reed Army Med Ctr, Hand Surg & Div Indian Health, USPHS & US Navy Med Ctr. *Mem:* Orthop Res Soc; AMA; Am Soc Surg of Hand; fel Am Col Surg; Am Acad Cerebral Palsy. *Res:* Children's orthopedics; office practice laboratories; vascular problems in the extremities. *Mailing Add:* 236 Second St Lewes DE 19958-1326

ADAMS, JOHN R, MEDICINE, PSYCHIATRY. *Current Pos:* PROF PSYCHIAT, MED SCH, NORTHWESTERN UNIV, CHICAGO, 54-, SR PSYCHIAT, INST PSYCHIAT, 75- *Personal Data:* b Eureka, Calif, Jan 6, 18; m 42; c 4. *Educ:* Northwestern Univ, 35-39; McGill Univ, MD & CM, 43. *Prof Exp:* Staff psychiatrist, Menninger Found, Kans, 49-54, dir admis, 52-54; chief psychiat, Passavant Mem Hosp, 54-72. *Concurrent Pos:* Consult, US Army Hosp, Ft Riley, Kans, 53-54, Vet Admin Res Hosp, Chicago, 54-61 & Ill State Psychiat Inst, 60- *Mem:* AMA; Am Psychiat Asn. *Res:* Psychiatry teaching; curriculum design; general hospital psychiatry. *Mailing Add:* Dept Psychiat Behav Sci 707 N Fairbanks Ct Chicago IL 60611

ADAMS, JOHN WAGSTAFF, economic geology; deceased, see previous edition for last biography

ADAMS, JOHN WILLIAM, MATHEMATICAL STATISTICS. *Current Pos:* ASSOC PROF INDUST ENG, LEHIGH UNIV, 65- *Personal Data:* b Hot Springs, SDak, Sept 24, 28. *Educ:* Univ Nebr, BS, 52; Univ NC, PhD(statist), 62. *Prof Exp:* Eng trainee, Dow Chem Co, 53-55; statist asst, Westinghouse Elec Co, 55-57; res assoc, Univ NC, Chapel Hill, 62-65. *Mem:* Inst Math Statist; Am Statist Asn. *Res:* Operations research; industrial applications; inventory control programming; queueing theory. *Mailing Add:* Dept Indust Eng Lehigh Univ 200 W Packer Ave Bethlehem PA 18015

ADAMS, JULIAN PHILIP, POPULATION GENETICS. *Current Pos:* asst prof bot, 70-75, assoc prof biol, 75-84, PROF BIOL, UNIV MICH, ANN ARBOR, 84-, CHAIR, BIOL DEPT, 97- *Personal Data:* b Windsor, Eng, Oct 30, 44. *Educ:* Univ Wales, BSc, 65; Univ Calif, Davis, PhD(genetics), 69. *Prof Exp:* Fel genetics, Dept Pomol, Univ Calif, Davis, 69-70. *Concurrent Pos:* Prof genetics, Fed Univ Rio de Janeiro, Brazil, 78-79; Alexander von Humboldt fel, WGer, 84; sr res fel, Inst Oswaldo Cruz, Rio de Janeiro, Brazil, 92. *Mem:* Genetics Soc Am; Am Soc Naturalists. *Res:* Population genetics of microorganisms; human population genetics and demography. *Mailing Add:* 4071c Nat Sci Biol Univ Mich Main Campus Ann Arbor MI 48109-1048

ADAMS, JUNIUS GREENE, III, HEMOGLOBINOPATHIES, THALASSEMIA. *Current Pos:* WITH NIH, NAT HEART, LUNG & BLOOD INST, 92- *Personal Data:* b Chicago, Ill, May 30, 43; m 76; c 2. *Educ:* Univ NC, Chapel Hill, AB, 66; Univ Mich, Ann Arbor, MS, 70, PhD(human genetics), 71. *Prof Exp:* Asst prof, Ctr Genetics, Col Med, Univ Ill, Chicago, 72-76, asst prof, Dept Med, 73-76; from asst prof to assoc prof genetics, dept prev med, Sch Med, Univ Miss, 83-92, assoc prof, dept med,

76-92, asst prof biochem, 80-92. *Concurrent Pos:* Chief, Hemoglobin Res Lab, Vet Admin Westside Hosp, Chicago, 72-76 & Vet Admin Ctr, Jackson, Miss, 76-; mem, Japan-USA Coop Hemogloblin Study Group, 74-76, CDC Task Force Abnormal Hemoglobins & Thalassemia, 76-78; chmn, Bd Dir, Davis Planetarium Found, 81- *Mem:* Am Soc Human Genetics; Am Soc Hemat; Sigma Xi; Am Fedn Clin Res; Undersea Med Soc; Fedn Am Socs Exp Biol; Am Soc Biol Chem. *Res:* Structure, function, synthesis and molecular biology of variant hemoglobins; hemoglobin variants which mimic the phenotype of thalassemia. *Mailing Add:* 6701 Rockledge Dr Bethesda MD 20892-7950

ADAMS, KENNETH ALLEN HARRY, ORGANIC CHEMISTRY. *Current Pos:* RETIRED. *Personal Data:* b Melville, Sask, Nov 16, 34; m 60; c 2. *Educ:* Univ Man, BSc, 55; McMaster Univ, MSc, 58; Univ Sask, PhD(chem), 61. *Prof Exp:* Res assoc chem, Ind Univ, 61-62; res & teaching fel, McMaster Univ, 62-63; asst prof, Mt Allison Univ, 63-68, assoc prof chem, 68-96. *Concurrent Pos:* Nat Res Coun Can grants, 63-65. *Mem:* Chem Inst Can; Royal Soc Chem. *Res:* Synthesis and chemistry of nitrogenous heterocyclic compounds, including natural products; chemistry and synthetic application of nitrene intermediates. *Mailing Add:* 1635 Cambridge St Halifax NS B3H 4A5 Can

ADAMS, KENNETH HOWARD, organic chemistry; deceased, see previous edition for last biography

ADAMS, LAURENCE J, ENGINEERING. *Current Pos:* RETIRED. *Prof Exp:* Independent consult. *Mem:* Nat Acad Eng. *Mailing Add:* 13401 Beall Creek Ct Potomac MD 20854

ADAMS, LEON MILTON, ORGANIC CHEMISTRY. *Current Pos:* RETIRED. *Personal Data:* b Waco, Tex, Mar 11, 13; wid; c 2. *Educ:* Agr & Mech Col Tex, BS, 33, MS, 34; Univ Nebr, PhD(phys chem), 37. *Prof Exp:* Res fel, Mellon Inst, 37-38; res chemist, Pittsburgh Plate Glass Co, 38-43; asst chief chemist, Taylor Ref Corp, Tex, 43-46; group leader, Am Oil Co, 46-60; mgr, Org & Polymers Sect, 60-78, inst scientist, Southwest Res Inst, 78-83. *Concurrent Pos:* Consult, 83- *Mem:* Am Chem Soc. *Res:* Encapsulation; polymers; organic synthesis; gelation; radiation grafting; reverse osmosis. *Mailing Add:* 2707 Gainesborough San Antonio TX 78230-4528

ADAMS, LEONARD C(ALDWELL), ELECTRICAL ENGINEERING. *Current Pos:* RETIRED. *Personal Data:* b Saluda, SC, Nov 7, 21; m 45; c 3. *Educ:* Clemson Univ, BSEE, 43; Okla State Univ, MS, 49; Univ Fla, PhD(elec eng, physics), 56. *Prof Exp:* From instr to prof elec eng, Clemson Univ, 46-58; nuclear reactor physicist, Savannah River Lab, E I du Pont de Nemours & Co, 58-59; dir, Eng Exp Sta, Clemson Univ, 59-61; prof elec eng & head dept, La State Univ, Baton Rouge, 61-84. *Concurrent Pos:* Asst, Okla State Univ, 49-50 & Univ Fla, 51-53. *Mem:* Am Soc Eng Educ; Inst Elec & Electronics Engrs. *Res:* Electron ballistics; travelling wave tubes; large heavy-water moderated nuclear reactor neutron economy research. *Mailing Add:* 12123 N Lakeview Dr Baton Rouge LA 70810

ADAMS, LESLIE GARRY, VETERINARY PATHOLOGY. *Current Pos:* From asst prof to assoc prof vet path & trop vet med, 68-78, PROF VET PATH, TEX A&M UNIV, 78- *Personal Data:* b Brownwood, Tex, Aug 17, 41; m 65; c 2. *Educ:* Tex A&M Univ, BS, 63, DVM, 64, PhD(vet path), 68; Am Col Vet Pathologists, dipl, 70. *Mem:* Am Col Vet Pathologists; Int Acad Path; AAAS; Am Vet Med Asn. *Res:* Veterinary pathology, immunopathology, intracellular parasitism, hepatic diseases and toxicology. *Mailing Add:* Dept of Vet Path Tex A&M Univ Col Vet Med College Station TX 77843

ADAMS, LOUIS W, JR, APPLIED MATHEMATICS. *Current Pos:* RES PHYSICIST, MILLIKEN RES CORP, 80- *Personal Data:* b Youngstown, Ohio, May 1, 51. *Educ:* Youngstown State Univ, BS, 73 NMex State Univ, MS, 75; La State, PhD(physics), 80. *Mem:* Am Phys Soc. *Res:* Computer aided design; low temperature plasmas; color science. *Mailing Add:* Milliken Res Corp PO Box 1927 M-420 Spartanburg SC 29304

ADAMS, LOWELL WILLIAM, URBAN WILDLIFE ECOLOGY & MANAGEMENT. *Current Pos:* biologist, Urban Wildlife Res Ctr, 76-80, res dir, 80-83, vpres res, 83-94, PRES, NAT INST URBAN WILDLIFE RESOURCE, 95- *Personal Data:* b Harrisonburg, Va, Aug 8, 46; m 70, Patricia A Ruhlman; c Christopher K. *Educ:* Va Polytech Inst & State Univ, BSc, 68; Ohio State Univ, MSc, 73, PhD(zool), 76. *Honors & Awards:* Chevron Coserv Award, 87; Daniel L Leedy Urban Wildlife Conserv Award, Nat Inst Urban Wildlife, 92. *Prof Exp:* Teaching assoc biol, ecol & mammal, Ohio State Univ, 72-73; res assoc, Ohio Coop Wildlife Res Unit, 73-76. *Concurrent Pos:* Chmn, Urban Wildlife Comt, Wildlife Soc, 84-86; Instr, Univ Md, 87-, Johns Hopkins Univ, 92- *Mem:* Sigma Xi; Wildlife Soc; Am Soc Mammalogists; Wilson Ornith Soc; Am Ornithologists Union. *Res:* Urban wildlife ecology and management; human-wildlife relationships in the urban environment; wildlife-habitat associations in disturbed environments; tritium kinetics in freshwater wetlands. *Mailing Add:* Urban Wildlife Resources 5130 W Running Brook Rd Columbia MD 21044

ADAMS, MARTHA LOVELL, ANALYTICAL CHEMISTRY. *Current Pos:* RETIRED. *Personal Data:* b Springfield, Ill, May 8, 25. *Educ:* Col William & Mary, BS, 46; Univ Md, MS, 52. *Prof Exp:* Instr inorg chem, St Helena Exten, Col William & Mary, 46-48; res chemist coating & chem lab, Aberdeen Proving Ground, 51-74; res chemist, US Army Mobility Equip Res & Develop Ccommand, Ft Belvoir, Va, 74-85. *Mem:* Am Chem Soc; Soc Appl Spectros. *Res:* Analytical methods for coating materials, especially the use of ultraviolet and infrared spectrophotometry. *Mailing Add:* 23438 Rocket Ave Port Charlotte FL 33954-3706

ADAMS, MAURICE WAYNE, PLANT BREEDING. *Current Pos:* assoc prof farm crops, 58-64, prof crop sci, 64-88, EMER PROF CROP SCI, MICH STATE UNIV, 88- *Personal Data:* b Rosedale, Ind, June 23, 18; m 45; c 5. *Educ:* Purdue Univ, BSA, 41; Univ Wis, PhD, 49. *Prof Exp:* Prof agron, SDak State Col, 47-58, agronomist, Exp Sta, 47-58. *Res:* Breeding behavior and genetics of legumes; genetic bases of yield structures and processes in edible dry beans. *Mailing Add:* 5607 Colby Rd Crystal MI 48818

ADAMS, MAX DAVID, PHARMACOLOGY, TOXICOLOGY. *Current Pos:* sr res pharmacologist, 77-81, res mgr, pharmacol & toxicol, 81-84, assoc dir, pharmaceut & device res & develop, 84-85, ASSOC DIR, PROD DEVELOP, MALLINCKRODT, INC, 85- *Personal Data:* b St Marys, WVa, July 25, 41; m 63; c 2. *Educ:* WVa Univ, BS, 65; Purdue Univ, MS, 68, PhD(pharmacol), 71; Am Bd Toxicol, dipl. *Prof Exp:* From instr to asst prof pharmacol, Med Col Va, 71-77. *Mem:* Am Soc Pharmacol & Exp Therapeut. *Res:* Cardiovascular pharmacology; hypertension and antihypertensive drugs; evaluation of x-ray contrast media and magnetic resonance contrast media; in vivo radiopharmaceuticals. *Mailing Add:* Mallinckrodt Med Inc PO Box 5840 675 McDonnell St Louis MO 63134-0840

ADAMS, MAX DWAIN, INORGANIC CHEMISTRY. *Current Pos:* RETIRED. *Personal Data:* b Red Oak, Iowa, May 23, 26; m 47; c 3. *Educ:* Tarkio Col, BA, 48; Okla State Univ, MS, 50; St Louis Univ, PhD(chem), 55. *Prof Exp:* Anal chemist, Mallinckrodt Chem Works, 50-52; res assoc, St Louis Univ, 52-55; chemist, Argonne Nat Lab, 55-73; proprietor, M D Adams Assocs, 73-90. *Mem:* Am Chem Soc; Sigma Xi; Am Inst Chemists; Am Nuclear Soc. *Res:* High temperature chemistry; nuclear materials and fission product elements; molten salt chemistry; microanalytical chemistry; particle identification; trace contamination detection methods. *Mailing Add:* M D Adams Assoc Naperville IL 60540

ADAMS, MICHAEL CURTIS, DEVELOPMENT OF ORGANIC TRACERS FOR GEOTHERMAL SYSTEMS, DEVELOPMENT OF HYDROGEOCHEMICAL MODELS OF GEOTHERMAL SYSTEMS. *Current Pos:* GEOCHEMIST, UNIV UTAH RES INST, 83- *Personal Data:* b Somerville, NJ, Nov 11, 53; m 86, Leslie Peterson; c Christopher M. *Educ:* Univ Utah, BS, 78, MS, 83. *Concurrent Pos:* Lectr, Ital Elec Comn, 89; expert consult, Int Atomic Energy Agency, 91, UN, 93; consult geochemist, Guatemalan Elec Utility, 91-93, Japanese Indust Develop Agency, 93- *Mem:* Am Geochem Soc; Geothermal Resources Coun; Int Geothermal Asn. *Res:* Developed organic compounds for use in liquid-, vapor- and two-phase geothermal systems; produced hydrogeochemical models of geothermal systems in the US, Canada, Guatemala and Ascension Island. *Mailing Add:* EGI Univ Utah 423 Wakara Way Salt Lake City UT 84108. *Fax:* 801-584-4453

ADAMS, MICHAEL STUDEBAKER, PLANT ECOLOGY. *Current Pos:* asst prof, 68-72, assoc prof, 72-78, PROF BOT, UNIV WIS-MADISON, 78- *Personal Data:* b Houston, Tex, Aug 26, 38; m 64. *Educ:* Univ Calif, Davis, BS, 62, MS, 64; Univ Calif, Riverside, PhD(biol), 68. *Prof Exp:* NASA trainee, Univ Calif, Riverside, 65-68. *Mem:* AAAS; Ecol Soc Am; Am Inst Biol Sci; Am Soc Limnol & Oceanog; Int Asn Theoret & Appl Limnol. *Res:* Physiological ecology of aquatic macrophytes; analysis of littoral ecosystems. *Mailing Add:* Dept Bot 132 Birge Hall Univ Wis 430 Lincoln Dr Madison WI 53706-1381

ADAMS, NANCY R, nursing, for more information see previous edition

ADAMS, OTTO EUGENE, JR, MECHANICAL ENGINEERING, APPLIED MECHANICS. *Current Pos:* assoc prof, 63-69, chmn dept, 67-74, prof, 69-, EMER PROF MECH ENG, OHIO UNIV, 69- *Personal Data:* b Baltimore, Md, Jan 2, 27; m 51; c 4. *Educ:* Cornell Univ, BME, 49; Univ Rochester, MS, 52; Lehigh Univ, PhD(mech eng), 57. *Prof Exp:* Engr, Delco Appliance Div, Gen Motors Corp, NY, 49-51; instr mech eng, Lehigh Univ, 53-57; res engr, Hanford Atomic Prod Oper, Gen Elec Co, Wash, 57-61; mem tech staff, Bell Tel Labs, Pa, 61-63. *Mem:* Am Soc Mech Engrs; Soc Exp Stress Anal; Am Soc Eng Educ. *Res:* Mechanical vibrations; stress analysis; machine design; nonlinear mechanics; dynamics. *Mailing Add:* Dept Mech Eng Russ Col Eng & Technol Stocker Ctr Ohio Univ Athens OH 45701-2979

ADAMS, P B, CERAMICS ENGINEERING, GLASS FRACTURE ANALYSIS. *Current Pos:* OWNER, PRECISION ANALYSIS, 88- *Personal Data:* b Elmira, NY, Sept 4, 29; m 61; c 2. *Educ:* Hobart Col, BS, 51. *Prof Exp:* From jr chemist to sr chemist, Corning Inc, 51-62, res chemist, 62-75, res supvr, Tech Staffs Div, 75-88. *Mem:* AAAS; Am Chem Soc; fel Am Ceramic Soc; Am Soc Testing & Mat; Risk Anal Soc; Sigma Xi; Human Factors Soc. *Res:* Silicate chemistry; degradation processes; product safety; surface chemistry and fractography; polarimethy. *Mailing Add:* Precision Analysis 300 S Madison Ave Watkins Glen NY 14891. *Fax:* 607-535-8956

ADAMS, PAUL ALLISON, PLANT PHYSIOLOGY. *Current Pos:* asst prof, 70-74, ASSOC PROF, UNIV MICH, FLINT, 74- *Personal Data:* b Davenport, Iowa, May 30, 40; m 65, Kathleen Hagan; c Nathan & Natalie. *Educ:* Calvin Col, BA, 62; Univ Mich, MA, 64, PhD(bot), 69. *Prof Exp:* Res assoc plant physiol, Mich State Univ/AEC Plant Res Lab, 68-70. *Mem:* AAAS; Am Soc Plant Physiologists; Sigma Xi; Am Sci Affil. *Res:* Physiology of plant development; mechanism of gibberellic acid-promoted growth; creation-evolution controversy. *Mailing Add:* Dept Biol Univ Mich Flint MI 48502. *Fax:* 810-762-3687; *E-Mail:* padams@umich.edu

ADAMS, PAUL LIEBER, PSYCHIATRY, SOCIOLOGY. *Current Pos:* PVT PRACTICE, 89- *Personal Data:* b Broken Bow, Okla, Jan 22, 24; m 46; c 3. *Educ:* Centre Col, AB, 43; Columbia Univ, MA, 48, MD, 55; Am Bd Psychiat & Neurol, dipl, 63, cert child psychiat, 64. *Prof Exp:* Instr soc sci, Bennett Col, 47-51; from asst to instr psychiat, Duke Univ, 56-60; from asst prof to prof psychiat & pediat, Col Med, Univ Fla, 60-74, dir, Children's Ment Health Unit, 66-72; prof psychiat & vchmn grad educ, Sch Med, Univ Louisville, 74-82; prof psychiat, Univ Tex, 82-89. *Concurrent Pos:* Fel child psychiat, Duke Univ Hosp & Durham Child Guid Clin, 58-60; vis prof, NC Col, 57-60; dir, Cumberland County Guid Ctr, 57-60; consult, Jacksonville Hosp Educ Prog, 60-; dir educ, Sch Med, Univ Miami, 72-74. *Mem:* Fel Am Psychiat Asn; fel Am Acad Child Psychiat; fel Am Col Psychiat; fel Am Orthopsychiat Asn; Acad Psychosom Med. *Res:* Child psychiatry. *Mailing Add:* 1169 Eastern Pkwy Ste 645 Louisville KY 40217

ADAMS, PAUL LOUIS, medical physics, for more information see previous edition

ADAMS, PETER D, CONDENSED MATTER PHYSICS, SCIENTIFIC EDITOR. *Current Pos:* ED, PHYS REV B, 69- *Personal Data:* b Cardiff, Wales, Nov 18, 37; m 60, June M Tatchell; c Joanne L & Lindsay S. *Educ:* Univ Wales, BS, 59; Univ London, PhD(physics), 64; Imp Col, DIC, 64. *Prof Exp:* Asst physicist, Brookhaven Nat Lab, 64-69; dep ed chief, Am Physics Soc, 80-89. *Mem:* AAAS; fel Am Phys Soc. *Res:* Condensed matter physics, materials physics, chemical and statistical physics. *Mailing Add:* Am Phys Soc One Research Rd PO Box 1000 Ridge NY 11961. *Fax:* 516-924-5294; *E-Mail:* prb@aps.org

ADAMS, PETER FREDERICK GORDON, CIVIL ENGINEERING, STRUCTURES. *Current Pos:* MEM STAFF, CAN INST PETROL INDUST DEVELOP, 92-, PRES, 92- *Personal Data:* b Halifax, NS, Feb 4, 36; m 57, Barbara; c David, Robert & Michael. *Educ:* NS Tech Col, BE, 58, ME, 61; Lehigh Univ, PhD(civil eng), 66. *Honors & Awards:* Sanderson Award, Can Soc Civil Eng, 86. *Prof Exp:* Design engr, Int Nickle Co Can, Ltd, 58-59; asst prof civil eng, Univ Alta, 60-63; res asst, Lehigh Univ, 63-66; from assoc prof to prof civil eng, Univ Alta, 66-84, dean eng, 76-84; pres, Ctr Frontier Eng, 84-88 & Tech Univ NS, 89-92. *Concurrent Pos:* Design engr, Dominion Bridge Co, 73-74. *Mem:* Am Soc Civil Engrs; fel Can Soc Civil Eng; fel Eng Inst Can; fel Can Acad Eng; hon mem Int Asn Bridge & Struct Eng. *Res:* Behavior of structural members and frames in the elastic and inelastic range; elastic and inelastic instability; behavior of structures subjected to blast and earthquake loadings. *Mailing Add:* Can Inst Petrol Indust Develop 100 Springwood Ct-4220 98 St Edmonton AB T6E 6A1 Can. *Fax:* 403-944-0772

ADAMS, PHILLIP, ORGANIC CHEMISTRY. *Current Pos:* asst dir res & develop, Berkeley Chem Co, 51-68, dir res & develop, Berkeley Chem Div & asst dir corp res & develop, Corp, 68-69, mem exec comt, 69-75, mem operating comt, 75-87, DIR ORG CHEM ONYX DIV, MILLMASTER ONYX CORP, 87- *Personal Data:* b Brooklyn, NY, June 2, 25; m 55; c 3. *Educ:* Univ Md, BS, 45; Cornell Univ, PhD(chem), 50. *Prof Exp:* Lab asst org chem, Cornell Univ, 45-50; res chemist, Am Cyanamid Co, NJ, 50-51. *Concurrent Pos:* Lectr, applied hydrogenation technol; pres, Applied Org Chem & consult practical org custom res, develop & mfg, 87- *Mem:* Am Chem Soc. *Res:* Custom synthesis in organic chemistry. *Mailing Add:* 27 Burlington Rd Murray Hill NJ 07974-2705

ADAMS, PHILLIP A, ENTOMOLOGY. *Current Pos:* from asst prof to prof, 63-91, EMER PROF ZOOL, CALIF STATE UNIV, FULLERTON, 91- *Personal Data:* b Los Angeles, Calif, Jan 13, 29. *Educ:* Univ Calif, BS, 51; Harvard Univ, AM & PhD(biol), 58. *Prof Exp:* From instr to asst prof zool, Univ Calif, Santa Barbara, 58-63. *Concurrent Pos:* Vis assoc prof biol & vis assoc cur insects, Yale Univ, 68-69. *Mem:* Am Entom Soc; World Asn Neuropterists (pres, 88-91). *Res:* Insect evolution; phylogeny and taxonomy of Neuroptera; Myrmeleontidae and Chrysopidae. *Mailing Add:* Dept Biol Calif State Univ Fullerton CA 92834

ADAMS, PRESTON, BOTANY. *Current Pos:* from asst prof to assoc prof, 61-73, PROF BOT, DEPAUW UNIV, 74- *Personal Data:* b Madison, Fla, Jan 12, 30; m 63. *Educ:* Univ Ga, BS, 54, MS, 56; Harvard Univ, PhD(biol), 59. *Prof Exp:* Asst bot, Univ Ga, 54-56 & Gray Herbarium, Harvard Univ, 56-57; res assoc bot, Fla State Univ, 59-61. *Mem:* Bot Soc Am; Am Soc Plant Taxon. *Res:* Evolution of vascular plants; monographic studies of flowering plants, especially the family Guttiferae. *Mailing Add:* 1215 East County Rd 350 S Greencastle IN 46135

ADAMS, RALPH M, BIOLOGY. *Current Pos:* from asst prof to assoc prof, 68-80, PROF ECOL, FLA ATLANTIC UNIV, 80- *Personal Data:* b New York, NY, Mar 31, 33; c 2. *Educ:* Univ Miami, BS, 55, MS, 59, PhD, 68. *Prof Exp:* Res instr marine physiol, Inst Marine Sci, Univ Miami, 59-60; res biologist microbiol, Seafood Res Lab, Univ Calif, San Francisco, 60-65. *Mem:* Ecol Soc Am; Soc Study Evolution. *Res:* Plant-animal interactions, particularly insect-orchid pollination and insect chemoreception also Caribbean orchid taxonomy, ecology and biogeography. *Mailing Add:* Dept Biol Sci Fla Atlantic Univ PO Box 3091 Boca Raton FL 33431-0991

ADAMS, RALPH MELVIN, nuclear medicine instrumentation, for more information see previous edition

ADAMS, RALPH NORMAN, ANALYTICAL CHEMISTRY, NEUROCHEMISTRY. *Current Pos:* from asst prof to assoc prof, 55-63, PROF CHEM, UNIV KANS, 63- *Personal Data:* b Atlantic City, NJ, Aug 26, 24; m 53; c 3. *Educ:* Rutgers Univ, BS, 50; Princeton Univ, PhD(analytic chem), 53. *Honors & Awards:* Fisher Award, Am Chem Soc, 82. *Prof Exp:* Instr analytic chem, Princeton Univ, 53-55. *Mem:* Am Chem Soc; Am Soc Neurosci. *Res:* Electroanalytical methods applied to neurochemistry, chemistry of the central nervous system. *Mailing Add:* Chem Dept Univ Kans Lawrence KS 60615-1500

ADAMS, RANDALL HENRY, ENTOMOLOGY, PLANT SCIENCE. *Current Pos:* ASST PROF ENTOM & PLANT SCI, SOUTHERN ARK UNIV, 74- *Personal Data:* b Milburn, Okla, Aug 24, 39; m 62; c 2. *Educ:* Okla State Univ, BS, 61, MS, 66, PhD(entom ecol), 72. *Prof Exp:* Res asst entom, Okla State Univ, 66-68; asst prof, NMex State Univ, 68-70, agron, 70-74. *Concurrent Pos:* Res consult entom & agron, Shell Chem Co, Dow Chem USA, PPG Chem Co, Thuron Industs & Cooper USA, 70- *Mem:* Sigma Xi; Entom Soc Am. *Res:* Evaluation of pesticides on animal and plant pests. *Mailing Add:* Dept Agr Southern Ark Univ, Box 1418 Magnolia AR 71753-5001

ADAMS, RAYMOND F, electrical engineering, electronics, for more information see previous edition

ADAMS, RAYMOND KENNETH, ELECTRICAL ENGINEERING, MEASUREMENTS & CONTROL ENGINEERING. *Current Pos:* RETIRED. *Personal Data:* b Denver, Colo, Apr 23, 28; m 50, Helen Louise O'Kare; c Paula (Hillard), Julia Anne & Roger K. *Educ:* Univ Colo, BS, 51; Univ Tenn, MS, 60. *Honors & Awards:* Donald P Eckman Award for Educ, Instrumentation Soc Am, 91. *Prof Exp:* Design engr instrumentation, Oak Ridge Gaseous Diffusion Plant, Union Carbide Corp, 51-53, development engr instrumentation & controls, Oak Ridge Nat Lab, 54-61, group leader, Instrumentation & Controls Div, 62-76, staff consult, 77-84; sr staff engr & group leader, Instrumentation & Controls Div, Oak Ridge Nat Lab, Martin Marietta Energy Systs Corp, 84-86; fac assoc, Elec & Comput Eng Dept, Univ Tenn, Knoxville, 86-94. *Concurrent Pos:* Gen chmn, Joint Automatic Control Conf, 60-61; mem steering comt, Am Automatic Control Coun, 60-62; expert witness & spec master, Embedded Microprocessor Intellectual Property Litigation, 84- *Mem:* Fel Instrument Soc Am. *Res:* Measurement and control devices and theory, development and application for energy RanD; pioneered mini-microcomputer acquisition and control systems application for scientific/engineering RanD; electric utility load control communications systems; modernizing the sophomore EE laboratory curriculum; student teams coached have won national alternate fuels automobile design and implementation contests since 1986- electronic/computer automotive engine controls. *Mailing Add:* 102 Wendover Circle Oak Ridge TN 37830

ADAMS, RICHARD A, IMMUNOLOGY & PATHOLOGY, GENETICS. *Current Pos:* res assoc, 74-84, sci dir toxicol, 84-86, CONSULT, BIO-RES CONSULT, INC, 86- *Personal Data:* b New York, NY. *Educ:* City Col New York, BA, 49; Boston Univ, AM, 51, PhD(biol), 56; Am Bd Toxicology, dipl, 82. *Prof Exp:* Res assoc, Children's Cancer Res Found, 56-74. *Concurrent Pos:* Res assoc, Children's Hosp, Boston, 59-74, & Med Sch, Harvard Univ, 60-74; ed, Hamster Info Serv, 79- *Mem:* Am Asn Cancer Res; Am Soc Exp Path; Am Col Toxicol; Sigma Xi; Hamster Soc; Soc of Toxicol. *Res:* Cancer research with principal interest in human tumor and leukemic hetero (xeno) transplantation and immunologic aspects; carcinogenesis, particularly in Syrian hamsters with emphasis on the use of this application for safety testing. *Mailing Add:* 10 Mount Pleasant St Rockport MA 01966-1723

ADAMS, RICHARD DARWIN, MOLECULAR STRUCTURE, CATALYSIS. *Current Pos:* prof chem, 84-95, WILLIAM S WILLIAMS PROF CHEM, UNIV SC, 95- *Personal Data:* b Reading, Pa, July 26, 47; m 72, Nancy Tuomala; c Todd & Amanda. *Educ:* Pa State Univ, BS, 69; Mass Inst Technol, PhD(inorg chem), 73. *Honors & Awards:* A P Sloan Fel, 79-83. *Prof Exp:* Asst prof chem, State Univ NY, Buffalo, 73-75; from asst prof to assoc prof, Yale Univ, 75-84. *Mem:* Am Chem Soc; Sigma Xi. *Res:* Chemistry of transition metal cluster compounds and x-ray crystallography. *Mailing Add:* Dept Chem Univ SC Columbia SC 29208. *Fax:* 803-777-6781

ADAMS, RICHARD E, AEROSPACE ENGINEERING. *Current Pos:* MGT CONSULT, 87- *Personal Data:* b Springfield, Ohio, Aug 14, 21; c 3. *Educ:* Purdue Univ, BS, 42. *Hon Degrees:* DSc, Purdue Univ, 77. *Honors & Awards:* Distinguished Engr Award, Univ Tex, 79; Outstanding Mech Engr, Purdue Univ, 91. *Prof Exp:* Vpres eng, Convair Div, San Diego, Gen Dynamics Corp, 70-71, vpres & gen mgr, Fort Worth Div, 71-74, corp vpres, 74-81, exec vpres aerospace, Gen Dynamics, 81-87. *Mem:* Nat Acad Eng. *Mailing Add:* 4200 S Hulen St Suite 319 Ft Worth TX 76109. *Fax:* 817-731-7353

ADAMS, RICHARD ERNEST, SCALE UP OF PHARMACEUTICAL INTERMEDIATES FOR IN-HOUSE USE. *Current Pos:* Res asst, R W Johnson Pharmaceut Res Inst, 69-71, asst scientist, 71-76, sr assoc scientist, 76-86, scientist, 87-93, SR SCIENTIST, R W JOHNSON PHARMACEUT RES INST, 94- *Personal Data:* b Ramsgate, Kent, Eng, Aug 21, 45; US citizen; m 67, Ethel Wilson; c Marc R. *Educ:* Grove City Col, BS, 67; John Carroll Univ, MS, 69. *Mem:* Am Chem Soc. *Res:* Preparation and scale up of pharmaceutical intermediates for internal use; synthesized compounds for drug discovery in numerous areas of interest. *Mailing Add:* R W Johnson Pharmaceut Res Inst PO Box 300 Raritan NJ 08869. *E-Mail:* adams@prius.jnj.com

ADAMS, RICHARD LINWOOD, POULTRY NUTRITION. *Current Pos:* POULTRY EXTEN SPECIALIST, PURDUE UNIV, WEST LAFAYETTE, 62-, ASSOC PROF ANIMAL SCI, 77- *Personal Data:* b Dixfield, Maine, Sept 17, 28; m 53, Beverly Forest; c Terry & Kimberly J. *Educ:* Univ Maine, BS, 52; Purdue Univ, MS, 59, PhD(poultry nutrit), 61. *Prof Exp:* Fieldman, Swift & Co, Ore, 52-53 & C M T Co, Maine, 53-55; 4-H Club agent, York Co Exten Serv, 55-57. *Mem:* Poultry Sci Asn. *Res:* Poultry nutrition. *Mailing Add:* 2825 Henderson St West Lafayette IN 47906

ADAMS, RICHARD MELVERNE, INORGANIC CHEMISTRY, REACTOR SAFETY. *Current Pos:* RETIRED. *Personal Data:* b Gary, Ind, Nov 1, 16; m 44, Marjorie Albright; c Victoria & Richard. *Educ:* Univ Chicago, BS, 39, MS, 48; Ill Inst Technol, PhD(chem), 53. *Prof Exp:* Chemist, Portland Cement Asn, 40-42; res assoc, Off Sci Res & Develop Proj, Univ Chicago, 42-43, jr chemist, Metall Lab, Manhattan Dist, 43-46; asst group leader, Los Alamos Sci Lab, 46; lectr chem, Ind Univ, 46-49; assoc chemist, Argonne Nat Lab, 49-59, sci asst to dir, 59-65, asst lab dir, 65-80, dep dir, Off Int Energy Develop Prog, 80-83. *Concurrent Pos:* Mem, Joint US-Korea Standing Comt on Energy Technol, 76-83. *Mem:* AAAS; Am Chem Soc; Sigma Xi; Am Nuclear Soc; Korean Nuclear Soc. *Res:* Etherates of boron trifluoride; radiochemistry; fission products; kinetics of exchange reactions; fluorine chemistry; reactor safety; science administration. *Mailing Add:* 3901 Grays Gables Rd Laramie WY 82070

ADAMS, RICHARD OWEN, SOLID STATE PHYSICS. *Current Pos:* Sr develop specialist, Storage Technol Corp, 63-67, sr res physicist, 67-68, res mgr, 68-75, sr res specialist, 75-87, assoc scientist, Rocky Flats Plant, Rockwell Int, 87-89, ADV ENG MGR, STORAGE TECHNOL CORP, 89- *Personal Data:* b Garden Home, Ore, Mar 5, 33; m 64. *Educ:* Willamette Univ, BA, 55; Wash State Univ, PhD(physics), 64. *Mem:* Am Vacuum Soc. *Res:* Surface science, particularly the structure and composition of surfaces, the interactions of gases with metal surfaces and the growth of films on metal substrates; acoustic emission, its sources and propagation through metals. *Mailing Add:* 2790 Regis Dr Boulder CO 80303

ADAMS, RICHARD SANFORD, ANIMAL NUTRITION, DAIRY HUSBANDRY. *Current Pos:* asst prof dairy sci, 54-57, from asst prof to prof, 58-92, EMER PROF DAIRY SCI, PA STATE UNIV, 92- *Personal Data:* b Lewiston, Maine, May 5, 28; m 51; c 4. *Educ:* Univ Maine, BS, 50; Univ Minn, PhD(dairy husb), 55. *Prof Exp:* Res assoc ruminant nutrit, Gen Mills, Inc, 57-58. *Concurrent Pos:* Consult, US Feed Grains Coun, SEurope, 69 & Univ Hawaii, 71. *Mem:* Am Dairy Sci Asn; Am Soc Animal Sci. *Res:* Dairy cattle nutrition; forage evaluation; extension teaching methods. *Mailing Add:* 445 Ridge Ave State College PA 16803

ADAMS, ROBERT D, MATHEMATICS. *Current Pos:* ASSOC PROF MATH, UNIV KANS, 60- *Personal Data:* b Grand Rapids, Mich, Dec 10, 26; m 56; c 2. *Educ:* Univ Minn, PhD(math), 60. *Mem:* Am Math Soc; Math Asn Am. *Res:* Application of functional analysis to partial differential equations. *Mailing Add:* Univ Kans 405 Snow Hall Lawrence KS 66045

ADAMS, ROBERT EDWARD, HAZARDOUS WASTE TECHNOLOGY. *Current Pos:* RETIRED. *Personal Data:* b Memphis, Tenn, Nov 4, 29; m 49, Betty Hickman; c Emily. *Educ:* Memphis State Univ, BS, 54; Univ Miss, MS, 56. *Prof Exp:* Res staff mem gas adsorption, Oak Ridge Nat Lab, 56-66, res group leader aerosol sci, 66-70; consult, Air-Tec, Inc, 70-75; proj leader aerosol sci, Oak Ridge Nat Lab, 75-86; prog mgr, Lockheed Martin Energy Systs, Oak Ridge, Tenn, 87-91, dep prog mgr, Demonstration Hazardous Waste Remediation Technol, 92-94. *Mem:* Am Chem Soc. *Res:* Management of technical projects to demonstrate remediation of hazardous wastes and/or waste sites. *Mailing Add:* 112 Amanda Dr Oak Ridge TN 37830

ADAMS, ROBERT JOHN, RADAR SYSTEMS & RADAR ANTENNAES. *Current Pos:* RETIRED. *Personal Data:* b Solon, Iowa, May 24, 15; m 41, Catherine Groshong; c John B & Robert N. *Educ:* Univ Iowa, BA, 36; Univ Wis, PhD(physics), 41. *Prof Exp:* Physicist, Corning Glass Works, NY, 40-42; head antenna sect, Naval Res Lab, 42-54, head search radar br, 54-76, consult, 76-90. *Concurrent Pos:* Assoc ed, Trans Antennas & Propagation, Inst Elec & Electronics Engrs. *Mem:* AAAS; Am Geophys Union; Am Phys Soc; Inst Elec & Electronics Engrs; Sigma Xi. *Res:* Radar antennas and systems; radio physics. *Mailing Add:* 3601 Keene Ave Baltimore MD 21214-2751

ADAMS, ROBERT JOHNSON, CARDIOVASCULAR PHARMACOLOGY, MEMBRANE BIOCHEMISTRY. *Current Pos:* DIV NEUROL RES, MEDICAL COL GA. *Personal Data:* b Charleston, SC, April 27, 50; m 74; c 2. *Educ:* Col Charleston, BS, 72; Univ Ark Med Sci, PhD(pharmacol), 78. *Prof Exp:* Lab technician res & develop, Med Univ SC, 72-73; grad asst pharmacol, Univ Ark Med Sci, 73-77; fel, Univ Cincinnati Med Ctr, 77-80, res asst prof, 80-81; asst prof anesthesiol, Med Col Ga, Augusta, 81- *Concurrent Pos:* Asst dir, Div Cardiovasc Res, Anesthesiol Med Col Ga, 82- *Mem:* Sigma Xi; Int Soc Oxygen Transp Tissue; Int Anesthesia Res Soc. *Res:* Cardiovascular physiology and biochemistry, mechanisms of cellular regulation of calcium transport, calcium utilization and muscle contractin; drug-receptor interactions and cellular mechanisms of drug action; pharmacology and membrane pathophysiology of the myocardium and vascular smooth muscle in myocardial ischemia, heart failure, hypertension. *Mailing Add:* Div Neurol Med Col Ga Sch Med Augusta GA 30901-3181

ADAMS, ROBERT MCCORMICK, ARCHEOLOGY, ANTHROPOLOGY. *Current Pos:* ADJ PROF, UNIV CALIF, SAN DIEGO, 93- *Personal Data:* b Chicago, Ill, July 23, 26; m 53, Ruth Salzman Skinner; c Megan. *Educ:* Univ Chicago, PhB, 47, MA, 52, PhD, 56. *Hon Degrees:* DSc, Univ Pittsburgh, 85, Dartmouth Col, 89; LHD, City Univ NY, 86, Col William & Mary, 89, Brandeis Univ, 92; LD, Harvard Univ, 92. *Honors & Awards:* Great Cross of Vasco Nunez de Balboa, Panama, 93; Distinguished Serv Award, Soc Am Archeol, 96. *Prof Exp:* Mem fac, Dept Anthrop, Oriental Inst, Univ Chicago, 55-84, assoc prof, 61-62, prof, 62-84, dir, 62-68 & 81-83, dean, Soc Sci Div, 70-74 & 79-80, provost, 82-84; res dir, Baghdal Sch, Am Schs Oriental Res, 68-69; Homewood prof, Dept Anthrop & New Eastern Studies, John Hopkins Univ, 84-94; fel, Inst Advan Study, Berlin, 95-96. *Concurrent Pos:* Archeol, Yucatan, Mex, 53, Iraq, Saudi Arabia & Iran, 56-77, Chiapas, Mex, 58-61; secy, Smithsonian Inst, 84-94, emer secy, 94-; chmn, Behav & Soc Sci, Nat Res Coun, 72-76 & 87-93; trustee, Nat Opinion Ctr, 70-94, Nat Humanities Ctr, 76-83, Russell Sage Found, 78-91, Santa Fe Inst, 84-, Am Univ Beruit, 89-94, Morehouse Col, 89-94, Ger Am Acad Coun, 93- *Mem:* Nat Acad Sci; fel AAAS; fel Am Anthrop Asn; fel Am Acad Arts & Sci; Mid East Studies Asn; Soc Am Archaeol; Ger Archaeol Inst; Am Philos Soc; Coun Foreign Rels; Sigma Xi. *Res:* Agricultural and urban history of the Middle East; history of technological and industrial innovation; institutions and policies for the support of research; author of 4 books and co-author of 3 books. *Mailing Add:* 4275 Frying Pan Rd PO Box ZZ Basalt CO 81621

ADAMS, ROBERT MONROE, OCCUPATIONAL SKIN DISEASE, CONTACT DERMATITIS & CONTACT ALLERGIC DERMATITIS. *Current Pos:* from instr to clin assoc prof, 66-82, CLIN PROF DERMAT, STANFORD UNIV, 83- *Personal Data:* b Pasadena, Calif, May 4, 26; m, Lorene Tassi; c Cynthia & Gregory. *Educ:* Stanford Univ, MD, 50. *Honors & Awards:* Jean Spencer Felton Award, Western Occup Med Asn, 83. *Concurrent Pos:* Dir, Contact Dermatitis Clin, Stanford Univ, 67-, pvt dermat pract, Menlo Park, 76-; dir, Am Acad Dermat, 89-93; ed-in-chief, Am J Contact Dermatitis, 89-92. *Mem:* Am Acad Dermat; Western Occup Med Asn (pres, 83-84); Am Contact Dermatitis Soc (pres, 89-91); hon mem Brit Asn Dermatologists; hon mem Mex Dermat Asn. *Res:* Contact dermatitis and occupational skin disease; published over 75 articles and authored 4 books. *Mailing Add:* 1300 University Dr No 8 Menlo Park CA 94025

ADAMS, ROBERT R(OYSTON), METALLURGICAL ENGINEERING. *Current Pos:* RETIRED. *Personal Data:* b McConnelsville, Ohio, May 26, 17; m 41; c 2. *Educ:* Antioch Col, BS, 39; Ohio State Univ, MS, 41. *Prof Exp:* Asst foundry metal, Battelle Mem Inst, 36-39, res engr, 39-42, admin asst, 42-81. *Concurrent Pos:* With AEC, Off Sci Res & Develop & Off Prod Res & Develop, 42-46; dir, Battelle Mem Inst Ger, 52-53; dir, Indust Inst Beirut, Lebanon, 56-58; with Advan Res Proj Agency, Field Off Beirut, Lebanon, 64-70. *Res:* Research administration. *Mailing Add:* 1812 Sandalwood Pl Columbus OH 43229-3649

ADAMS, ROBERT W, GEOLOGY. *Current Pos:* from asst prof to prof geol, 67-95, EMER PROF GEOL, STATE UNIV NY COL BROCKPORT, 95- *Personal Data:* b New York, NY, July 8, 34; m 57; c 3. *Educ:* Univ Rochester, BA, 56; Johns Hopkins Univ, PhD(geol), 64. *Prof Exp:* Explor geologist, Shell Oil Co, 64-67. *Mem:* Geol Soc Am; Soc Econ Paleontologists & Mineralogists; Am Asn Petrol Geologists; Sigma Xi. *Res:* Sedimentology and sedimentary petrology. *Mailing Add:* 11 Lancer Way Brockport NY 14420

ADAMS, ROGER JAMES, physical chemistry, for more information see previous edition

ADAMS, ROGER OMAR, IMMUNOGENETICS. *Current Pos:* RES ASSOC, FLA STATE UNIV, 81- *Personal Data:* b Willows, Calif, Apr 17, 33; m 61; c 3. *Educ:* Fla State Univ, Tallahassee, BS, 66, MS, 68, PhD(biol), 80. *Concurrent Pos:* Pres, Marisyst Res, Inc, Fla, 77- *Mem:* AAAS; Am Soc Zoologists. *Res:* Development, functional morphology, and genetics of Gorgonian Octocorals (anthozoa), with special interest in their self/not-self histocompatibility; symbiotic relationships of various animals with octocorals. *Mailing Add:* 200 Hickory Tree Lane Crestview FL 32539

ADAMS, ROY MELVILLE, CHEMISTRY. *Current Pos:* From instr to assoc prof, 46-58, chmn dept, 58-85, PROF CHEM, GENEVA COL, 58- *Personal Data:* b Cheung Chau, Hong Kong, Oct 19, 19; m 46, Madelyn Woods; c Melville, Renwick, Jonathan & Joel. *Educ:* Sterling Col, AB, 40; Univ Kans, AM, 42, PhD(chem), 49. *Concurrent Pos:* Chief dept chem, Callery Chem Co, 52-53, res coordr, 53-58; mem inorg nomenclature comn, Int Union Pure & Appl Chem, 68-78. *Mem:* Am Chem Soc; Am Sci Affil; Royal Soc Chemistry; Creation Res Soc; Sigma Xi; Am Inst Chem Engrs. *Res:* Boron; inorganic nomenclature. *Mailing Add:* Geneva Col Beaver Falls PA 15010-3599

ADAMS, RUSSELL S, JR, soil chemistry; deceased, see previous edition for last biography

ADAMS, S KEITH, INDUSTRIAL & HUMAN FACTORS ENGINEERING. *Current Pos:* ASSOC PROF INDUST ENG, IOWA STATE UNIV, 76- *Personal Data:* b Salisbury, Md, Mar 1, 38; m 66; c 2. *Educ:* Rensselaer Polytech Inst, BMgte, 60; Ariz State Univ, MSE, 62, PhD(indust eng), 66. *Prof Exp:* From asst prof to assoc prof indust eng, Okla State Univ, 65-76. *Concurrent Pos:* NSF res grant, 66-67. *Mem:* Am Inst Indust Engrs; Human Factors Soc; Am Soc Eng Educ; Sigma Xi. *Res:* Ergonomics in work system design and safety engineering; human factors in nuclear power plant operations and maintenance; human/computer interaction; human factors in maintainability; resource and energy recovery from municipal and industrial solid waste. *Mailing Add:* Indust Mfg Syst Eng Iowa State Univ Ames IA 50011-0001

ADAMS, SAM, SCIENCE EDUCATION. *Current Pos:* RETIRED. *Personal Data:* b Walthall, Miss, Mar 14, 16; m 44; c 1. *Educ:* Delta State Teachers Col, BS, 36; La State Univ, MA, 40, PhD(sci educ), 51. *Prof Exp:* Teacher high sch, Miss, 36-38; instr, Univ Ala, 40-42, Univ exten supvr, 42; civilian instr radio, US Air Force, SDak, 42-43; elec supply foreman, Tenn Eastman Corp, Oak Ridge, 43-44; physicist and spectroscopist, Carbide & Carbon Chem Co, 46-49; assoc prof physics, McNeese State Col, 51-54; assoc prof sci educ, La State Univ, Baton Rouge, 54-62, prof sci educ, 62-81, assoc dean acad affairs, 62-65. *Concurrent Pos:* Teacher high sch, Ala, 40-42. *Mem:* Nat Sci Teachers Asn. *Res:* Emission spectra of uranium isotopes; science education. *Mailing Add:* 2035 W Magna Carta Pl Baton Rouge LA 70815

ADAMS, SAMUEL S, MINERAL DEPOSIT. *Current Pos:* PRES, LOON MOUNTAIN RECREATION CORP, 91-; CONSULT, NEWMONT MINING, 92- *Personal Data:* b Lincoln, NH, July 26, 37. *Educ:* Harvard Univ, PhD(geol), 76. *Prof Exp:* Vpres, Anaconda Co, 67-77; consult, 77-86; prof & head, geol & geol eng, Colo Sch Mines, 86-92. *Mem:* Fel Geol Soc Am; Am Asn Petrol Geologists; Am Inst Petrol Geologists. *Mailing Add:* 10 Beechwood Acres Box 697 Lincoln NH 03251

ADAMS, SHEILA VALIANT, UNIVERSITY NURSING ADMINISTRATION, STRESS IN HOSPITALIZED CHILDREN. *Current Pos:* Prof, 73-91, dir, Baccalaureate Prog, 91-93, HEAD, DIV NURSING, MISS UNIV WOMEN, 93- *Personal Data:* b Saltville, Va, Apr 30, 47; m 74, Hudson E; c Taylor V & Seth M. *Educ:* Emory Univ, BSN, 71, MSN, 73, Miss State Univ, EdD, 80. *Concurrent Pos:* Vchair, Miss Asn Baccalaureate & Higher Degree Progs, 96-97; chair, Miss Coun Deans & Dirs, Sch Nursing, 97-98; consult, UAE, 97. *Mem:* Am Asn Cols Nursing; Am Nurses Asn; Nat League Nursing. *Res:* Teach nursing research and work with undergraduate and graduate research students; anxiety in hospitalized children and nursing students. *Mailing Add:* 650 Woodridge Pl Columbus MS 39702. *Fax:* 601-329-8555; *E-Mail:* sadams@muw.edu

ADAMS, TERRANCE STURGIS, INSECT PHYSIOLOGY. *Current Pos:* RES ENTOMOLOGIST, METAB LAB, AGR RES SERV, USDA, 66-, MEM STAFF, BIOSCI RES LAB. *Personal Data:* b Los Angeles, Calif, Dec 14, 38; div; c 2. *Educ:* Calif State Col Los Angeles, BA, 61; Univ Calif, Riverside, PhD(entom), 66. *Mem:* Entom Soc Am; Int Soc Insect Reproduction; Sigma Xi. *Res:* Factors affecting insect reproduction; endocrine control of reproduction in dipterous insects. *Mailing Add:* Metab & Radiation Lab Univ Sta Fargo ND 58105-5674

ADAMS, THOMAS, PHYSIOLOGY. *Current Pos:* PROF PHYSIOL, MICH STATE UNIV, 66- *Personal Data:* b Buffalo, NY, Oct 3, 30; m 53; c 2. *Educ:* Univ Md, BS, 52; Purdue Univ, MS, 55; Univ Wash, PhD(physiol), 63. *Prof Exp:* Chief thermal sect, Civil Aeromed Inst, Fed Aviation Agency, Okla, 63-66. *Mem:* AAAS; Am Physiol Soc; Soc Exp Biol & Med; Am Asn Univ Prof; Sigma Xi. *Res:* Body temperature regulation; neurophysiology of temperature regulation; mechanisms of thermal acclimatization; sweat gland physiology. *Mailing Add:* Dept Physiol Mich State Univ East Lansing MI 48824-1101

ADAMS, THOMAS C, FOREST ECONOMICS, INTERNATIONAL ECONOMICS. *Current Pos:* RETIRED. *Personal Data:* b San Francisco, Calif, Nov 4, 18; m 57, Laura M Kopp; c Anne (Abate) & Sally (Denning). *Educ:* Univ Calif, Berkeley, BS, 40, AB, 41; Univ Mich, MA, 51, PhD(forestry), 52. *Prof Exp:* Forest economist, Pac Northwest Res Sta, US Forest Serv, 52-55; asst prof forestry, Ore State Univ, 55-57; prin economist, Pac Northwest Res Sta, US Forest Serv, 57-84. *Concurrent Pos:* Consult, SRI Int, Ore, 55. *Mem:* Soc Am Foresters; Forest Prod Res Soc. *Res:* Marketing, market development and international trade of forest products; economic analysis of new logging systems, thinning operations and forest residue reduction; wood energy research and development. *Mailing Add:* 32200 SW French Prairie Apt B-102 Wilsonville OR 97070

ADAMS, THOMAS EDWARDS, BIOCHEMICAL ENDOCRINOLOGY, REPRODUCTIVE NEUROENDOCRINOLOGY. *Current Pos:* asst prof, 81-86, ASSOC PROF ANIMAL SCI, UNIV CALIF, DAVIS, 86- *Personal Data:* b Neenah, Wis, July 10, 47; m 75; c 2. *Educ:* Wash State Univ, BS, 72, MS, 75; Colo State Univ, PhD(endocrinol), 79. *Prof Exp:* Res asst physiol, Wash State Univ, 72-74, endocrinol, Colo State Univ, 74-79; NIH fel reprod endocrinol, Ore Regional Primate Res Ctr, 79-80. *Mem:* AAAS; Soc Study Reprod; Am Soc Animal Sci. *Res:* Temporal changes in gonadotropin releasing hormone receptor concentration in anterior pituitary tissue through the reproductive cycle of the normal female and in response to estradiol; the role of gonadotropin releasing hormone receptor dynamics in modulation of gonadotroph responsiveness and anterior pituitary function. *Mailing Add:* Dept Animal Sci Univ Calif Davis CA 95616-5200

ADAMS, WADE J, STRUCTURAL CHEMISTRY, CHEMICAL PHYSICS. *Current Pos:* MEM STAFF DRUG METAB RES, THE UPJOHN CO, 77- *Personal Data:* b Calhoun Co, Mich, Jan 9, 40; m 65; c 1. *Educ:* Western Mich Univ, BS, 65; Univ Mich, MS, 68, PhD(phys chem), 69. *Prof Exp:* Fel, Univ Mich, 71-72; asst prof chem, Macalester Col, 72-73; asst prof chem, Western Mich Univ, 73-77. *Mem:* Am Chem Soc. *Res:* Experimental studies of the structure and force field of molecules by gaseous electron diffraction; molecular mechanics calculations of physical and chemical properties. *Mailing Add:* Drug Metabolism 7256-300-113 Upjohn Co 7256-300-113 Kalamazoo MI 49007

ADAMS, WALTER C, ENDOCRINOLOGY, PHYSIOLOGY. *Current Pos:* from asst prof to assoc prof, 67-82, assoc dean, Grad Col, 87-92, PROF BIOL SCI, KENT STATE UNIV, 82-, DIR SCH BIOMED SCI, 79-, ASSOC DEAN RES & GRAD STUDIES, 92- *Personal Data:* b Newtown, Pa, Aug 22, 36; m 62, Nancy L Baier; c Christopher & Kenneth. *Educ:* Drew Univ, AB, 58; Rutgers Univ, MS, 62, PhD(endocrinol), 63. *Prof Exp:* Res scientist, NJ Bur Res Neurol & Psychiat, 63-67. *Mem:* AAAS; Am Physiol Soc; Soc Study Reproduction; Soc Exp Biol Med. *Res:* Control of gonadotrophin secretion and ovarian physiology with respect to abnormal ovarian responses; physiological influences on parturition; physiology of relaxin. *Mailing Add:* Dept Biol Sci Kent State Univ Main Campus PO Box 5190 Kent OH 44242-0001

ADAMS, WILLIAM ALFRED, GLACIOLOGY. *Current Pos:* PRES, ESTCO ENERGY INC, 95- *Personal Data:* b Toronto, Ont, June 15, 41; m 64; c 2. *Educ:* McMaster Univ, BSc, 63; Univ Ottawa, PhD(chem), 68. *Prof Exp:* Fel, Div Appl Chem, Nat Res Coun Can, 67-69; res scientist, Hydrol Sci Div, Inland Waters Br, Environ Can, 69-71, res scientist, Water Qual Br, 71-75, res scientist, Glaciol Div, Inland Waters Directorate, 75-77; defense scientist, Energy Conversion Div, Defense Res Estab Ottawa, Dept Nat Defense, 78-95. *Concurrent Pos:* Ed, Electrochem Soc, 75-78. *Mem:* Am Chem Soc; Chem Inst Can; Spectros Soc Can (pres, 75-76); Electrochem Soc. *Res:* Effects of pressure and temperature on the interactions of ions and polar molecules in solution using spectroscopic and electrochemical methods; high energy density battery; molten salt electrochemistry; impact of oil spills on Arctic aquatic ecosystems; deep well disposal. *Mailing Add:* 26 Foxmeadow Lane Nepean ON K2G 3W2 Can

ADAMS, WILLIAM EUGENE, MECHANICAL ENGINEERING. *Current Pos:* RETIRED. *Personal Data:* b Mt Vernon, Ohio, Oct 18, 30; m 53; c 2. *Educ:* Ohio State Univ, BME, 55. *Honors & Awards:* Horning Mem Award, Soc Automotive Engrs, 64. *Prof Exp:* Res engr, Ethyl Corp, 55-70, res adv, 70-74, dir auto res, 74-76, mgr Detroit Res Labs, 76-84, asst dir, Air Conserv Corp Staff, 84-86. *Mem:* Soc Automotive Engrs. *Res:* Fuel and engine research; fuel and lubricant additives. *Mailing Add:* County Rd 463 Mc Millan MI 49853

ADAMS, WILLIAM HENRY, THEORETICAL CHEMISTRY, QUANTUM CHEMISTRY. *Current Pos:* from asst prof to assoc prof, 66-75, PROF CHEM, RUTGERS UNIV, 75- *Personal Data:* b Baltimore, Md, Dec 21, 33; m 85, Sandra Sebastian; c 2. *Educ:* Johns Hopkins Univ, AB, 55; Univ Chicago, SM, 56, PhD(chem phys), 60. *Prof Exp:* NSF fel, Quantum Chem Group, Univ Uppsala, 60-62; asst prof chem, Pa State Univ, 62-66. *Concurrent Pos:* Vis prof, Tech Univ, Munich, 70-71. *Mem:* Am Phys Soc; Am Chem Soc. *Res:* Quantum theory, particularly interactions between many electron systems and the role played by the Pauli exclusion principle. *Mailing Add:* Dept Chem Rutgers State Univ PO Box 939 Piscataway NJ 08855-0939. *Fax:* 732-932-5312; *E-Mail:* adams@zodiac.rutgers.edu

ADAMS, WILLIAM JOHN, JR, MECHANICAL ENGINEERING, AGRICULTURAL ENGINEERING. *Current Pos:* asst gen mgr, Cent Eng Labs, Santa Clara, 53-71, dir planning & ventures, Advan Prod Div, 71-76, mgr new bus ventures, 76-80, MGR CONSULT, CENT ENG LABS, SANTA CLARA, 86-; REGENT, SANTA CLARA UNIV, 86- *Personal Data:* b Riverdale, Calif, Feb 9, 17; m 39, Marijane E Leishman; c W Michael & John P. *Educ:* Santa Clara Univ, BS, 37. *Prof Exp:* Regist prof mech engr & agr engr, Calif Design & Corp, San Jose, Calif, 46-49; proj engr, FMC Corp, San Jose, Calif, 46-47; chief engr, Bolens Div, Port Washington, Wis, 47-53. *Concurrent Pos:* Bd dirs, Santa Clara Co Coun Boy Scouts Am, 62-; Chmn, Santa Clara Indust Citizens Bd, 65-66, Santa Clara United Fund Dr, 67. *Mem:* Fel Am Soc Agr Engrs; Soc Automotive Engrs; Joint Coun Sci & Math Educ; Asn Soc Mech Engrs. *Res:* Mechanical engineering; granted 13 patents in the US, Canada and numerous foreign countries. *Mailing Add:* 7940 Caledonia Dr San Jose CA 95135-2113

ADAMS, WILLIAM LAWRESON, ELECTRICAL ENGINEERING. *Current Pos:* sr engr, 63-65, mgr electronic systs sect, New Prod Develop Dept, 65-66, mgr, Indust Systs Res & Develop Dept, 66-77, vpres eng, 77-80, sr vpres mfg & eng, 80-87, SR VPRES MEASUREMENT & ACTUATOR SYSTS, COMBUSTION ENG, INDUST NUCLEONICS CORP, 87- *Personal Data:* b Gay, Mich, July 9, 32; m 56; c 11. *Educ:* Mich Technol Univ, BS, 54; Mass Inst Technol, SM, 56; Purdue Univ, PhD, 62. *Prof Exp:* Instr elec eng, Mass Inst Technol, 54-56; proj engr, Gen Electronic Labs, Inc, Mass, 56-58; from instr to asst prof elec eng, Purdue Univ, 58-63. *Concurrent Pos:* Consult, Addressograph Multigraph, Ohio, 55-56 & Gen Electronic Labs, Inc, Mass, 58-63. *Mem:* Inst Elec & Electronics Engrs; sr mem Instrument Soc Am; Sigma Xi. *Res:* Electrical properties of materials; determination of moisture content in sheet materials; computerized process control systems; modeling and control of industrial processes. *Mailing Add:* 9600 Olentangy River Rd Powell OH 43065

ADAMS, WILLIAM MANSFIELD, GEOPHYSICS. *Current Pos:* OWNER, FINANCIAL FUTURE FORECASTING. *Personal Data:* b Kissimmee, Fla, Feb 19, 32; m 55, 76; c 5. *Educ:* Univ Chicago, BA, 51; Univ Calif, BA, 53; St Louis Univ, MS, 55, PhD, 57; Univ Santa Clara, MBA, 64. *Prof Exp:* Geophys trainee, Stanolind Oil & Gas Co, 53; computer, Western Geophys

Co, 54; seismologist, Geotech Corp, 57-58; physicist, Lawrence Radiation Lab, Univ Calif, 59-62; pres, Planetary Sci, Inc, 62-64; prof geophysics, Univ Hawaii, 65-90; res assoc, Western Wash Univ, 90-92. *Concurrent Pos:* Fulbright scholar, Italy, 56-57; dir tsunami res, Univ Hawaii, 67-72; vis fel, Coop Inst Trs Environ Sci, Univ Colo, 70-71; NATO grant, Geothermal Inst, Pisa, Italy, 73; vis prof geophys, Ind Univ, 75-76; sismol expert, Int Inst Seismol & Earthquake Eng, UNESCO, Tokyo, Japan, 71-72; oceanographer, Inst Physics Atmosphere, Nat Oceanic & Atmospheric Admin, Miami, Fla, 79-80; vis geophysicist, Desert Res Inst, Univ Nev, Las Vegas, 83; partic, Regional Crustal Stability & Natural Hazards, UNESCO, Beijing, China, 85 & Strong-motion Seismol, NATO, Ankara, Turkey, 85. *Mem:* Seismol Soc Am; Geol Soc Am; Soc Explor Geophys; Am Geophys Union; Tsunami Soc; Europ Asn Explor; Geophys Acoust Soc Am. *Res:* Direct exploration of the interior of the earth; indexing and retrieval of scientific literature; seismic holography; tsunamis; systems for alerting society to natural hazards; hydrogeophysics. *Mailing Add:* 3682 Prevost Way Ferndale WA 98248

ADAMS, WILLIAM S, METABOLISM. *Current Pos:* asst clin prof, 48-49, from asst prof to assoc prof, 49-59, vchmn dept, 67, PROF MED, SCH MED, UNIV CALIF, LOS ANGELES, 59- *Personal Data:* b Sodus, NY, May 28, 19; m 47; c 4. *Educ:* Univ Rochester, MD, 43. *Prof Exp:* Intern, Strong Mem Hosp, Rochester, NY, 44; asst resident med, Univ Rochester, 44-45, instr, 47-48; resident, Vet Admin Ctr Hosp, Los Angeles, 48-49, admin sect chief, asst resident & physician full grade, 49-50. *Concurrent Pos:* Res fel, Univ Rochester, 46-47; consult, Atomic Bomb Casualty Comn. *Mem:* Asn Am Physicians; Am Col Physicians; Sigma Xi. *Res:* Metabolic aspects of malignant disease. *Mailing Add:* 800 Westwood Plaza Univ Calif Ctr Health Sci Los Angeles CA 90024-1736

ADAMS, WILLIAM SANDERS, ELECTRICAL ENGINEERING, MATHEMATICS. *Current Pos:* RETIRED. *Personal Data:* b Williamsport, Pa, Jan 16, 34; m 60; c 3. *Educ:* Pa State Univ, BS, 56, MS, 58, PhD(elec eng), 63. *Prof Exp:* From instr to prof elec eng, Pa State Univ, 58-94, dir Eng Comput Lab, 70-94. *Mem:* Inst Elec & Electronics Engrs; Am Soc Eng Educ. *Res:* Computation, especially applied to biomedical simulation; non-linear analysis. *Mailing Add:* 112 Grandview Rd State College PA 16801

ADAMS, WILLIAM WELLS, DIOPHANTINE APPROXIMATIONS, COMPUTATIONAL NUMBER THEORY. *Current Pos:* assoc prof, 69-71, PROF MATH, UNIV MD, COLLEGE PARK, 71- *Personal Data:* b Redlands, Calif, July 23, 37; m 64, Elizabeth Shaw; c Ruth & Sarah. *Educ:* Univ Calif, Los Angeles, AB, 59; Columbia Univ, PhD(math), 64. *Prof Exp:* From instr to asst prof math, Univ Calif, Berkeley, 64-69. *Concurrent Pos:* NSF fel, Inst Advan Study, Princeton, NJ, 66-67; vis prof, Technion, Israel, 83-84, Imperial Col, London, 75; prog dir, NSF, 86-88; ed, Proc Am Math Soc, 88- *Mem:* Am Math Soc; Math Asn Am. *Res:* Asympotitic theory of diophantine approximations; primality testing; Groebner bases; computational commutative algebra. *Mailing Add:* Math Dept Univ Md College Park MD 20742-4015. *E-Mail:* wwa@math.umd.edu

ADAMSKI, ROBERT J, MEDICINAL CHEMISTRY. *Current Pos:* MGR OPHTHAL NEW PROD RES, ALCON LABS, INC, 68-, DIR RES, 80-, VPRES RES, 85- VPRES THERAPEUT RES, 91- *Personal Data:* b Newark, NJ, Mar 26, 35; m 56; c 3. *Educ:* Univ Wis-Madison, BS, 60; Univ Iowa, PhD(pharmaceut chem), 64. *Prof Exp:* Fel, Ciba Pharmaceut Co, NJ, 64-66; res assoc, Inst Microbiol, Rutgers Univ, 66-67; sr chemist, Carter-Wallace, Inc, 67-68. *Mem:* Am Chem Soc; Am Pharmaceut Asn; NY Acad Sci; Am Inst Chemists; Am Mgt Asn; Licensing Execs Soc. *Res:* Chemical modification of known and structural elucidation of unknown antimicrobial materials; design and synthesis of agents having potential medicinal value as antiglaucomics, anti-inflammatories, antibacterial, anticataract agents. *Mailing Add:* Alcon Labs Inc 6201 S Freeway M/S R2-33 Ft Worth TX 76134-2099. *Fax:* 817-551-4584

ADAMSON, ALBERT S, JR, perfumery, essential oils, for more information see previous edition

ADAMSON, ARTHUR WILSON, PHYSICAL CHEMISTRY. *Current Pos:* from asst prof to prof chem, 46-89, chmn dept, 72-75, EMER PROF CHEM, UNIV SOUTHERN CALIF, 89- *Personal Data:* b Shanghai, China, Aug 15, 19; m 42, Virginia Dillman; c Carol Ann, Janet Louise & Jean Elizabeth. *Educ:* Univ Calif, BS, 40; Univ Chicago, PhD(phys chem), 44. *Hon Degrees:* DSC, Univ Ferrara, Italy. *Honors & Awards:* Tolman Award, Am Chem Soc, 67, Kendall Award in Surface Chem, 79; Foster lectr, State Univ NY Buffalo, 70; Res Assocs Award, Univ Southern Calif, 71; Venable lectr, Univ NC, 75; Bikerman lectr, Case Western Univ, 82; Alexander von Humboldt Sr Scientist Award, 77; Bikerman lectr, Case Western Univ, 82; Distinguished Serv Award inorg chem, Am Chem Soc, 82; Chem Educ Award, Am Chem Soc, 84, Agne Ann Green Distinguished Service Award & Hary & Carol Mosher Award, 89, Arthur W Adamson Award, 92; Reilly lectr, Notre Dame Univ, 84; Gold Medal Award, Am Inst Chemists, 94. *Prof Exp:* Res asst, Metall Lab, Univ Chicago, 42-44; res assoc, Plutonium Proj, Tenn, 44-46. *Concurrent Pos:* NSF sr fel, 62-63; Unilever prof, Bristol Univ, 65-66; Australian Acad Sci sr fel, 69; vis prof, Univ Queensland, Australia, 80. *Mem:* Fel AAAS; fel Am Inst Chemists; Am Chem Soc; Sigma Xi. *Res:* Coordination chemistry; photochemistry of coordination compounds; surface chemistry. *Mailing Add:* Dept Chem Univ Southern Calif Los Angeles CA 90007

ADAMSON, DAN KLINGLESMITH, PETROLEUM ENGINEERING. *Current Pos:* asst dir, Soc Petrol Engrs, 64-67, ed jour, 67-71, gen mgr, 72-79, EXEC DIR, SOC PETROL ENGRS, 79- *Personal Data:* b Vernon, Tex, Oct 12, 39; m 62, Eva Diane Pope; c Larkin, Rebecca, Amy & Sarah. *Educ:* Southwestern Univ, Georgetown, Tex, BA, 62. *Mem:* Coun Eng Sci Soc Execs. *Mailing Add:* Soc Petrol Engrs 222 Palisades Creek Dr PO Box 833836 Richardson TX 75080

ADAMSON, IAN YOUNG RADCLIFFE, EXPERIMENTAL PATHOLOGY. *Current Pos:* From lectr to assoc prof path, 67-79, PROF PATH, UNIV MANITOBA, 79-, MEM SCI STAFF, HEALTH SCI CTR, 78- *Personal Data:* b Wishaw, Scotland, Mar 16, 41; m 67; c 2. *Educ:* Univ Glasgow, BSc, 63, PhD(chem), 66. *Honors & Awards:* Wild Leitz Jr Pathologist Award, 76. *Mem:* Am Asn Pathologists; Am Thoracic Soc. *Res:* Experimentally induced lung injury and repair, with emphasis on changes in ultrastructure, cell kinetics and the factors involved in producing pulmonary fibrosis; lung development. *Mailing Add:* Dept Path Univ Man D212-770 Bannatyne Ave Winnipeg MB R3E 0W3 Can

ADAMSON, JEROME EUGENE, PLASTIC & RECONSTRUCTIVE SURGERY. *Current Pos:* PROF PLASTIC SURG, HAND SURG, EASTERN VA MED SCH, 74- *Personal Data:* b Columbus, Ohio, Oct 2, 27; m 59; c 3. *Educ:* WVa Univ, BA, 50; Duke Univ, MD, 54. *Prof Exp:* Resident gen surg, Duke Univ Med Ctr, 54-57, plastic surg, 57-60; chief, Dept Plastic Surg, Med Ctr Hosps, 73-75. *Concurrent Pos:* Consult, Med Ctr Hosps, Naval Regional Med Ctr & Vet Admin Hosp; assoc ed, J Plastic & Reconstruct Surg, 80-85; pvt practice, Plastic Surg Specialists, Inc, 60- *Mem:* Am Soc Plastic & Reconstruct Surgeons (pres, 80-81); Am Col Surgeons; Am Asn Plastic Surgeons; Am Soc Surg Hand; Am Soc Maxillofacial Surgeons. *Res:* Peripheral nerve healing and clinical improvement of upper extremity rehabilitative methods. *Mailing Add:* Dept Plastic Surg 900 Wainwright Bldg 229 W Bute St Norfolk VA 23510-1405

ADAMSON, JOHN DOUGLAS, PSYCHIATRY, PSYCHOPHYSIOLOGY. *Current Pos:* lectr, 61-63, from asst prof to prof psychiat, 63-95, SR SCHOLAR, FAC MED, UNIV MAN, 95- *Personal Data:* b St Boniface, Man, Mar 1, 32; wid; c Barbara, Jan, Carol, James, Shelagh & Gavin. *Educ:* Univ Man, MD, 56; Royal Col Physicians & Surgeons Can, cert psychiat, 61. *Prof Exp:* Asst psychiat, Sch Med & Dent, Univ Rochester, 59-60, instr, 60-61. *Concurrent Pos:* Mem, Subcomt Rehab, Dept Nat Health & Welfare Can, 63-65 & Subcomt Ment Health Res, 65-68; coordr psychiat res, Dept Health & Social Develop, Govt Prov Man, 65-77; chmn prof & tech adv comt, Alcoholism Found Man, 65-75; dir, Psychiat Clin Invest, Health Sci Gen Ctr, 65-77; chmn, Man Ment Health Res Found, 74-84, vchmn & secy, 84-86, mem, Exec Comt, 86-88, hon mem, 88- *Mem:* Can Med Asn; Can Psychiat Asn. *Res:* Biology and psychopathology of schizophrenia; clinical and biological studies on alcoholism; psychophysiology of emotion; sleep. *Mailing Add:* Health Sci Ctr 820 Sherbrook St Winnipeg MB R3A 1R9 Can. *Fax:* 204-787-7480

ADAMSON, JOHN WILLIAM, HEMATOLOGY. *Current Pos:* PRES, NY BLOOD CTR, NEW YORK CITY, 89- *Personal Data:* b Oakland, Calif, Dec 28, 36; m 89, Christine Fenyvest; c Cairn E & Loch R. *Educ:* Univ Calif, Berkeley, BA, 58; Univ Calif, Los Angeles, MD, 62. *Prof Exp:* From intern to resident med, Univ Wash Med Ctr, Seattle, 62-64, clin & res fel hemat, 64-67; commanding officer, USPHS, 67-69; mem fac, Univ Wash Med Ctr, 69-90, prof hemat, 78-90, head, Div Hemat, 81-89; Josiah Macy Jr Found scholar & vis scientist, Nuffield Dept, Clin Med & Fac Med, Univ Oxford, Eng, 76-77. *Concurrent Pos:* Res Career Develop Award, NIH, 72-77, res grantee, 76- *Mem:* Fel AAAS; Am Soc Hemat; Asn Am Physicians; Am Soc Clin Invest. *Res:* Hematology; clinical medicine. *Mailing Add:* NY Blood Ctr 310 E 67th St New York NY 10021-6295. *Fax:* 212-570-3195

ADAMSON, LUCILE FRANCES, nutritional biochemistry, environmental sciences, for more information see previous edition

ADAMSON, MARTIN LEIF, PARASITOLOGY & NEMATOLOGY, SYSTEMATICS. *Current Pos:* asst prof, 85-90, ASSOC PROF, DEPT ZOOL, UNIV BC, 90- *Personal Data:* b Ottawa, Ont, June 22, 52; m, Lesley McLean; c Sidonie A & Aidan B. *Educ:* Univ Guelph, BSc, 75, PhD(zool), 81; Sch Practical Sci, Paris, dipl, 83. *Honors & Awards:* Henry Baldwin Ward Medal, Am Soc Parasitologists, 93. *Prof Exp:* Master asst, Zool Lab, Versicherung, Paris, 83-84. *Mem:* Am Soc Parasitologists; Can Soc Zoologists. *Res:* Evolutionary ecology of parasites, in particular parasitic nematodes. *Mailing Add:* Dept Zool Univ BC 6270 University Blvd Rm 2354 Vancouver BC V6T 1Z4 Can. *Fax:* 604-822-2416

ADAMSON, RICHARD H, TOXICOLOGY & PHARMACOLOGY, ONCOLOGY. *Current Pos:* VPRES SCI & TECH AFFAIRS, NAT SOFT DRINK ASN, 94- *Personal Data:* b Council Bluffs, Iowa, Aug 9, 37; m 63; c 2. *Educ:* Drake Univ, BA, 57; Univ Iowa, MS, 59, PhD(pharmacol), 61; George Washington Univ, MA, 68. *Honors & Awards:* Superior Serv Award, USPHS, 76 & 82; Lehmman Award, Soc Toxicol, 89; Presidential Meritorious Exec Rank Award, 89. *Prof Exp:* Asst, Col Med, Univ Iowa, 57-58; sr investr, Lab Chem Pharmacol, Nat Cancer Inst, 63-69, head, Pharmacol & Exp Therapeut Sect, 69-73, chief, Lab Chem Pharmacol, 73-81, dir, Div Cancer Cause & Prev, 80-83, dir, Div Cancer Etiol, 83-94. *Concurrent Pos:* Lectr, Col Med, George Washington Univ, 63-70; Fulbright vis scientist, Dept Biochem, St Mary's Hosp Med Sch, Univ London, 65-66; sr policy analyst, Off Sci & Technol Policy, Exec Off Pres, 79-80. *Mem:* AAAS; Am Asn Cancer Res; Am Soc Pharmacol & Exp Therapeut; NY Acad Sci; Soc Toxicol; hon mem

Japanese Cancer Asn; Toxicol Forum; Int Soc Beverage Tech. *Res:* Carcinogenesis, drug metabolism; cancer chemotherapy; antibiotics; toxicology; marine biology; comparative pharmacology; science and government. *Mailing Add:* Nat Soft Drink Asn 1101 16th St NW Washington DC 20036-4877

ADAMSON, S LEE, FETAL PHYSIOLOGY. *Current Pos:* asst prof, 85-92, ASSOC PROF OBSTET & GYNEC, PEDIAT & PHYSIOL, UNIV TORONTO, 92-; SCIENTIST, SAMUEL LUNENFELD RES INST, MT SINAI HOSP, TORONTO, 85- *Personal Data:* b Ajax, Ont, Mar 23, 54. *Educ:* Univ Guelph, BS, 77; Univ Western Ont, MS, 80, PhD(biophys), 84. *Prof Exp:* Fel, Med Res Coun, Univ Western Ont, London, 84-85. *Concurrent Pos:* Lab instr biophys, Univ Western Ont, 77-79, physics, 79-82; lectr physiol, Univ Toronto, 89-, path, 89-; res scholar, Heart & Stroke Found, Ont, 90- *Mem:* Soc Gynec Invest; Am Physiol Soc; Biophys Soc Can. *Mailing Add:* Res Inst Mt Sinai Hosp 600 University Ave Rm 138-P Toronto ON M5G 1X5 Can

ADAMSON, THOMAS C(HARLES), JR, AEROSPACE ENGINEERING. *Current Pos:* assoc res engr & lectr aeronaut eng, Res Inst, Univ Mich, 54-56, from asst prof to prof, 56-92, chmn, 83-91, EMER PROF AEROSPACE ENG, UNIV MICH, ANN ARBOR, 92- *Personal Data:* b Cicero, Ill, Mar 24, 24; m 49, Susan E Huncilman; c Thomas C III, William A & Laura E. *Educ:* Purdue Univ, BS, 49; Calif Inst Technol, MS, 50, PhD(aeronaut), 54. *Prof Exp:* Res engr, Guggenheim Aeronaut Lab, Calif Inst Technol, 49-50 & Jet Propulsion Lab, 52-54. *Concurrent Pos:* chmn, Francois Xavier Bagnoud Aerospace Prize Bd, 92. *Mem:* Fel Am Inst Aeronaut & Astronaut; Combustion Inst; Sigma Xi; Am Phys Soc. *Res:* Fluid Mechanics; combustion; gas dynamics. *Mailing Add:* Dept Aerospace Eng Univ Mich Ann Arbor MI 48109-2140. *Fax:* 313-763-0578; *E-Mail:* tcair@engin.umich.edu

ADAMSONS, KARLIS, JR, OBSTETRICS & GYNECOLOGY. *Current Pos:* PROF OBSTET & GYNEC & CHMN DEPT, BROWN UNIV, 75-; PROF & CHMN, DEPT OBSTET & GYNEC & DIR, UNIV HOSP, UNIV PR, 79- *Personal Data:* b Riga, Latvia, Oct 30, 26; US citizen; m 68; c 2. *Educ:* Univ Gottingen, MD, 52; Columbia Univ, PhD(pharmacol), 56. *Honors & Awards:* Outstanding Residency Prog Dir, Am Col Obstetricians & Gynecologists, 84. *Prof Exp:* Intern, St Vincents Hosp, NY, 52-53; asst resident obstet & gynec, Columbia-Presby Med Ctr, 56-58, from resident to chief resident, 59-61, asst prof, 61-65, assoc obstetrician & gynecologist, 65-69; from assoc prof to prof, Col Physicians & Surgeons, Columbia Univ, 65-70; prof obstet, gynec & pharmacol, Mt Sinai Sch Med, City Univ New York, 70-75; obstetrician & gynecologist-in-chief, Women & Infants Hosp RI, 75-79. *Concurrent Pos:* Macy fel, Nuffield Inst Med Res, Oxford Univ, Eng, 58-59; Wellcome sr res fel, 61-; vis scientist, NIH, 62, consult, Nat Inst Child Health & Human Develop, 66-71; vis prof obstet & gynec, Univ PR, 63; consult, Coun Drugs, AMA, 63; mem adv coun, Food & Drug Admin, 65-70; Fulbright prof, Univ Uruguay, 69; consult obstet & gynec, Beth Israel Hosp, NY, 80-86. *Mem:* Soc Pediat Res; Am Col Obstetricians & Gynecologists; Soc Gynec Invest. *Res:* Perinatal physiology; neurohypophyseal peptides; fetal oxygenation; acceleration of fetal maturation; causation of toxemia; tocolytic agents; biochemistry and physiology of neurohypophysical hormones. *Mailing Add:* Dept Obstet/Gynec Univ PR Med Sci Box 365067 San Juan PR 00936

ADASKAVEG, JAMES ELLIOTT, MYCOLOGY, TAXONOMY OF FUNGI. *Current Pos:* Researcher, Dept Plant Path, 87-90, lectr mycol, Dept Bot, 90-91, RES PLANT PATHOLOGIST, UNIV CALIF, DAVIS, 91- *Personal Data:* b Waterbury, Conn, Feb 27, 60; m 90, Peggy Mank. *Educ:* Univ Conn, BS, 82; Univ Ariz, MS, 84, PhD(plant path), 86. *Concurrent Pos:* Mem, Mycol Comt, Am Phytopath Soc, 89-92. *Mem:* Am Phytopath Soc; Brit Mycol Soc; Mycol Soc Am; Sigma Xi. *Res:* Biology, ecology, and taxonomy of plant pathogenic fungi of forest, fruit, and nut trees; identification, ultrastructure, and classical genetics of fungi; epidemiology of foliar diseases; degradation processes of wood. *Mailing Add:* Dept Plant Path Univ Calif Davis CA 95616

ADASKIN, ELEANOR JEAN, NURSING RESEARCH DEVELOPMENT, SOCIAL PSYCHOLOGY OF HEALTH. *Current Pos:* clin nursing head, 76-78, clin nurse specialist, 78-88, DIR NURSING RES, ST BONIFACE GEN HOSP, CAN, 88- *Personal Data:* b Manitoba, Can, July 27, 37; m 60; c 2. *Educ:* Univ Sask, BScN, 60, BA, 70; Univ Wash, MA, 76; Univ Tex, Austin, PhD(nursing), 87. *Honors & Awards:* Award Prof Nursing Res, Manitoba Asn Registered Nurses, 90. *Prof Exp:* Teacher psychiat nursing, 71-73, counr, Misericordia Sch Nursing, Can, 73-74; teaching asst, psycho-physiol nursing, Univ Wash, 74-75. *Concurrent Pos:* Mem, Task Force Educ Requirements, Can Nurses Asn, 78-79; asst prof psychiat, nursing, Univ Man, 78-79 & clin demonstrator family therap, 80-88; pvt pract counr, 79-; teaching asst, family therap, Univ Tex, Austin, 84-85; prin investr, Clin Nursing Res Prog, 86-; lectr, Univ Winnipeg, 88- *Mem:* Sigma Xi; Am Asn Marriage & Family Therap; Can Nurses Found; Can Nursing Res Group. *Res:* Family health; family strengths which may assist members to remain well under stress; psychosocial and physical aspects of stress-resistance. *Mailing Add:* 10-C-300 Roslyn Rd Winnipeg MB R2H 2A6 Can. *Fax:* 204-237-2606

ADAWI, IBRAHIM (HASAN), THEORETICAL SOLID STATE PHYSICS. *Current Pos:* PROF PHYSICS, UNIV MO ROLLA, 68- *Personal Data:* b Palestine, Apr 18, 30; US citizen; m 90, Suad Harb; c 4. *Educ:* Wash Univ, BS, 53; Cornell Univ, PhD(eng physics), 57. *Honors & Awards:* Fulbright lectr, Rabat, 82. *Prof Exp:* Teacher math & physics, Terra Santa Sch, Syria, 49-51; physicist, RCA Labs, 56-60; res consult, Battelle Mem Inst, 60-68. *Concurrent Pos:* Adj prof elec eng, Ohio State Univ, 65-68; vis prof, Univ Hamburg, 77-78; vis scientist & res leader, Int Ctr Theoret Physics, Trieste, Italy, 82, 83 & 85; vis prof, Sch Math & Physics, Univ East Anglia, Norwich, UK, 82. *Mem:* Am Phys Soc. *Res:* Penetration of charged particles and radiation in matter; transport theory; magnetic monopoles; solid state theory; hot electrons; interactions of lasers in matter; history of physics. *Mailing Add:* Dept Physics Univ Mo Rolla MO 65401. *Fax:* 573-341-4715; *E-Mail:* adawi@physics.umr.edu

ADCOCK, JAMES LUTHER, SYNTHETIC FLUORINE CHEMISTRY, AEROSOL DIRECT FLUORINATION. *Current Pos:* from asst prof to assoc prof, 74-93, PROF CHEM, UNIV TENN, KNOXVILLE, 93- *Personal Data:* b Crane, Tex, June 26, 43; m 67, Jane Barth; c Joel, James & Jayson. *Educ:* Univ Tex, Austin, BS, 66, PhD(chem), 71. *Prof Exp:* Res assoc fluorine chem, Mass Inst Technol, 71-74. *Concurrent Pos:* Chmn, div fluorine chem, Am Chem Soc, 89. *Mem:* Am Chem Soc; Sigma Xi. *Res:* Synthetic organofluorine and organometallic chemistry; elemental fluorine as a synthetic reagent; aerosol direct fluorination methodology; preparation of fluorinated monomers and polymers; physical-organic chemistry of elemental fluorine. *Mailing Add:* Dept Chem Univ Tenn Knoxville TN 37996-1600. *E-Mail:* jadcock@utk.edu

ADCOCK, LOUIS HENRY, ANALYTICAL CHEMISTRY. *Current Pos:* From asst prof to assoc prof phys sci & chem, 56-77, PROF CHEM, UNIV NC, WILMINGTON, 77- *Personal Data:* b Durham, NC, Mar 28, 29; m 60; c 3. *Educ:* Duke Univ, BS, 51, MA, 53; La State Univ, PhD, 70. *Concurrent Pos:* Pres, NC Inst Chemists. *Mem:* AAAS; Am Chem Soc; fel Am Inst Chemists. *Res:* Analysis of trace elements; pesticides in marine environment; lecture demonstration. *Mailing Add:* Dept Chem Univ NC Wilmington NC 28403

ADCOCK, WILLIS ALFRED, SEMICONDUCTORS, ELECTRONICS. *Current Pos:* RETIRED. *Personal Data:* b St Johns, Que, Nov 25, 22; nat US; m 43, Eleanor Goller; c William, Robert, Edward & Margaret. *Educ:* Hobart Col, BS, 43; Brown Univ, PhD(chem), 48. *Hon Degrees:* PhD, Hobart Col, 89. *Prof Exp:* Chemist, Stanolind Oil & Gas Co, 48-53; res group supvr, Tex Instruments, 53-55, dir device res, 55-58, mgr res & eng dept, 58-61, mgr qual assurance dept, 60-61, mgr integrated circuit dept, 61-64; tech dir, Sperry Semiconductor Div, Sperry Rand Corp, 64-65; mgr, Advan Planning Dept, Semiconductor Div, Texas Instruments Inc, 65-67, vpres tech develop, Components Group, 67-69, vpres strategic planning, Corp Develop, 69-72, asst vpres & tech dir consumer prod, 72-78, asst vpres corp res develop & eng, 78-82, vpres corp staff, 82-86, prin fel, 78-86; prof, Univ Tex, Austin, 87-93. *Mem:* Nat Acad Eng; Am Chem Soc; fel Inst Elec & Electronics Engrs; fel AAAS. *Mailing Add:* 3414 Mt Bonnell Dr Austin TX 78731

ADDA, LIONEL PAUL, SOLID STATE SCIENCE. *Current Pos:* RETIRED. *Personal Data:* b Allentown, Pa, Jan 17, 22. *Educ:* Lehigh Univ, BS, 49, MS, 50, PhD(physics), 62. *Prof Exp:* Engr fed tel telecommun labs, Int Tel & Tel Co, 50-54; distinguished mem tech staff, Bell Labs, 54-87. *Mem:* Electrochem Soc. *Res:* Measurement of electrical and infrared properties; crystalline perfection and impurities in semiconductors; role of imperfections on device behavior; insulator properties and metal-insulator-semiconductor systems; process development of very large scale integration circuits. *Mailing Add:* 5692 Burning Tree Lane Macungie PA 18062-8700

ADDAMIANO, ARRIGO, INORGANIC CHEMISTRY, PHYSICAL CHEMISTRY. *Current Pos:* RETIRED. *Personal Data:* b Molfetta, Italy, Feb 16, 23; US citizen; m 52; c 4. *Educ:* Univ Rome, PhD(chem), 44, PhD(physics), 46. *Prof Exp:* Asst prof gen & inorg chem, Univ Rome, 44-48; Ital Bd Educ scholar res x-ray crystallog, Res Assoc Dept X-ray, Oxford Univ, 48-50; asst prof gen & inorg chem, Univ Rome, 51-53; Fulbright fel & res assoc x-ray & crystal structure lab, Pa State Univ, 53-54; phys chemist, Gen Elec Co, 54-69; res chemist, US Naval Res Lab, 69-85. *Concurrent Pos:* Nat Res Coun fel, Rome, 51-53. *Mem:* Am Chem Soc; Am Crystallog Asn; Electrochem Soc. *Res:* Crystal structure determination; crystal physics; single crystal growth; inorganic syntheses; phosphors; semiconductors. *Mailing Add:* 4222 Robertson Blvd Alexandria VA 22309

ADDANKI, SOMASUNDARAM, CLINICAL CHEMISTRY, BIOCHEMISTRY. *Current Pos:* from instr to asst prof, 64-70, ASSOC PROF PEDIAT & PHYSIOL CHEM, OHIO STATE UNIV, 70-; CONSULT. *Personal Data:* b Lakkavaram, India, Mar 7, 32; m 54; c 3. *Educ:* Madras Univ, BVS, 57; Ohio State Univ, MSc, 62, PhD(nutrit biochem), 64; Am Bd Clin Chem, cert, 70. *Prof Exp:* dir labs, Clin Study Ctr, Columbus Children's Hosp, 66- *Concurrent Pos:* Consult, Pathologists, Inc, Licking Mem Hosp, Newark, Ohio, 73- *Mem:* Fel Am Asn Clin Chem; Am Fedn Clin Res; Brit Biochem Soc. *Res:* Metabolic pediatric chemistry; radio-immuno assays-ketotic hypoglycemia; catecholamine chemistry and metabolism; endocrinology. *Mailing Add:* 4856 Driffield Ct Columbus OH 43221-5802

ADDICOTT, FREDRICK TAYLOR, ABSCISSION, ABSCISIC ACID. *Current Pos:* prof agron, 61-72, prof, 72-77, EMER PROF BOT, UNIV CALIF, DAVIS, 77- *Personal Data:* b Oakland, Calif, Nov 16, 12; m 35, Alice Baldwin; c Donald J, Jean (McKinnon), John F & David B. *Educ:* Stanford Univ, AB, 34; Calif Inst Technol, PhD(plant physiol), 39. *Honors & Awards:* Charles Reid Barnes Life Mem Award, Am Soc Plant Physiol, 90. *Prof Exp:* Asst, Stanford Univ, 34-37; teaching fel, Calif Inst Technol, 37-39; from instr to asst prof bot, Santa Barbara State Col, 39-46; assoc physiologist, Spec Guayule Res Proj, USDA, Calif, 43-44; from asst prof to prof bot, Univ Calif, Los Angeles, 46-61. *Concurrent Pos:* Sigma Xi grant-in-aid, 40; Fulbright res scholar, Victoria Univ, Wellington, NZ, 57 & Royal Botanic Gardens, Kew,

UK, 76; vis prof, Univ Adelaide, 66 & Univ Natal, 70. *Mem:* Australian Soc Plant Physiol; Am Soc Plant Physiol; Bot Soc Am; Int Plant Growth Substances Asn; SAfrican Asn Bot; fel AAAS. *Res:* Physiology, ecology, cytology and morphology of abscission in plants; physiological and morphological responses to abscisic acid. *Mailing Add:* 1003 Pine Lane Davis CA 95616-1764

ADDICOTT, JOHN FREDRICK, ECOLOGY. *Current Pos:* from asst prof to assoc prof, 73-86, PROF ZOOL, UNIV ALTA, 86- *Personal Data:* b Santa Barbara, Calif, Dec 28, 44. *Educ:* Univ Calif, Davis, AB, 67; Univ Mich, MSc, 68, PhD(zool), 72. *Prof Exp:* Res asst prof biol, Univ Utah, 72-73. *Mem:* Ecol Soc Am; Soc Study Evolution. *Res:* Competition in patchy environments; effects of predation on prey community structure; mutualism; pollination-seed predation mutualism; applied ant mutualism. *Mailing Add:* Dept Zool Univ Alta Edmonton AB T6G 2M7 Can

ADDICOTT, WARREN O, STRATIGRAPHY. *Current Pos:* geologist, US Geol Surv, 62-70, res geologist, 70-82, supvry geologist, 82-86, RES GEOLOGIST, US GEOL SURV, 86- *Personal Data:* b Fresno, Calif, Feb 17, 30; m 55, 76, Suzanne Aubin; c Carol & Eric. *Educ:* Pomona Col, AB, 51; Stanford Univ, MA, 52; Univ Calif, PhD(paleont), 56. *Prof Exp:* Asst, Univ Calif, 52-54; geologist, Gen Petrol Corp, 54-62, explor coordr, 58-60, dist geologist, 60-62. *Concurrent Pos:* Consult prof, Stanford Univ, 71-82; dep chmn, Circum-Pac Map Proj, 79-82, gen chmn, 82-86, proj adv, 86-; dir, Cicum-Pac Coun Energy & Mineral Resources, 82-86; adj prof, S Ore State Col, 90- *Mem:* AAAS; Paleont Soc (secy, 71-77, pres, 80-81); Geol Soc Am; Am Asn Petrol Geol; Paleont Res Inst. *Res:* Cenozoic marine stratigraphy; molluscan zoogeography; paleoclimatology; molluscan taxonomy. *Mailing Add:* 2260 Old Siskiyou Hwy Ashland OR 97520

ADDINK, SYLVAN, AGRICULTURE, HORTICULTURE. *Current Pos:* INT CONSULT, 94- *Personal Data:* b Sheldon, Iowa, Dec 23, 41; m 62; c 2. *Educ:* Ore State Univ, BS, 69; NDak State Univ, MS, 72, PhD(agron), 73, Univ Iowa, JD, 94. *Prof Exp:* Plant sci rep, Eli Lilly & Co, 73-74, regional res rep, 74-78; owner, Addink Advisors, 78- *Mem:* Coun Agr Sci & Technol. *Res:* Control of pests that are harmful to crops, animals, mankind and his environment. *Mailing Add:* PO Box 1457 Iowa City IA 52244. *E-Mail:* sylvanag@aol.com

ADDIS, PAUL BRADLEY, NUTRITION. *Current Pos:* from asst prof to assoc prof food sci, 67-75, PROF FOOD SCI & NUTRIT, UNIV MINN, ST PAUL, 75- *Personal Data:* b Honolulu, Hawaii, Feb 13, 41; m 67; c 2. *Educ:* Wash State Univ, BS, 62; Purdue Univ, PhD(food sci), 67. *Prof Exp:* Fel, Max Planck Soc, Ger, 67. *Concurrent Pos:* Fulbright travel grant, 67; consult, Totino's Finer Foods, Inc & Brother Redi-Roast Prod, Inc, Minn, 70-72; researcher, Muscle Biol Lab, Univ Calif, Davis, 71; researcher Chem & Med Depts, Univ Calif, San Diego, 76; res, Biochem Dept, Univ Wash, Seattle, 79-80. *Mem:* AAAS; Am Chem Soc; Inst Food Technologists; Sigma Xi; Am Oil Chem Soc; Int Asn Milk, Food & Environ Sanitarians. *Res:* Lipid oxidation in foods; atherogenicity of cholesterol oxides and fatty acid hydroperoxides; human serum lipoproteins; omega 3 fatty acids in Lake Superior fishes; incorporation and stabilization of omega 3 fatty acids in foods. *Mailing Add:* Dept Food Sci & Nutrit Univ Minn 1334 Eckles Ave St Paul MN 55108-1040

ADDISON, ANTHONY WILLIAM, BIOINORGANIC CHEMISTRY. *Current Pos:* assoc prof, 78-91, FAC MEM BIOMED SCI & ENG INST, DREXEL UNIV, 90-, PROF CHEM, 91- *Personal Data:* b Sydney, NSW, June 24, 46; m 72, Barbara E Kocjan; c Nicholas & Alexander. *Educ:* Univ New South Wales, BSc, 68; Univ Kent, PhD(chem), 71. *Honors & Awards:* J von Geuns Fonds Lectr, Univ Amsterdam, 85; C & M Lindback Award, 87. *Prof Exp:* Res asst chem, Univ Kent, 68-70; res fel, Northwestern Univ, 70-72; asst prof chem, Univ BC, 72-78. *Concurrent Pos:* Adj assoc prof, Univ Med & Dent NJ - R W Johnson Mem Hosp, Camden, 91- *Mem:* Royal Soc Chem; Am Chem Soc; Chem Inst Can. *Res:* Chemistry of metalloproteins and of synthetic models for their properties particularly oxygen transport and redox chemistry. *Mailing Add:* Dept Chem Drexel Univ Philadelphia PA 19104. *Fax:* 215-895-1265; *E-Mail:* addisona@duvm.ocs.drexel.edu

ADDISON, JOHN WEST, JR, MATHEMATICAL LOGIC. *Current Pos:* assoc prof, 62-68, chmn group in logic & methodology of sci, 63-65 & 81-85, chmn dept, 68-77, PROF MATH, UNIV CALIF, BERKELEY, 68-, CHMN DEPT, 85- *Personal Data:* b Washington, DC, Apr 2, 30; m 55; c 4. *Educ:* Princeton Univ, AB, 51; Univ Wis, MS, 53, PhD(math), 55. *Prof Exp:* Instr math, Univ Mich, 54-56; asst prof math, Univ Mich, 57-62. *Concurrent Pos:* NSF fel, 56-57; mem, Inst Advan Study, Princeton, 56-57 & Math Inst, Polish Acad Sci, 57; vis lectr, Univ Calif, Berkeley, 59-60; vis scholar, Math Inst, Univ Oxford, 72-73 & vis fel, Wolfson Col, 79. *Mem:* Fel AAAS; Am Math Soc; Math Asn Am; Asn Symbolic Logic. *Res:* Theory of definability, including recursive function theory and descriptive set theory; foundations of mathematics; theory of models; axiomatic set theory. *Mailing Add:* Univ Calif Berkeley CA 94720

ADDISON, RICHARD FREDERICK, biochemistry, analytical chemistry, for more information see previous edition

ADDISS, RICHARD ROBERT, JR, SOLID STATE PHYSICS, SOLAR PHOTOVOLTAIC ENERGY SYSTEMS. *Current Pos:* RETIRED. *Personal Data:* b Jersey City, NJ, May 13, 29; m 52, Doris J Bolander; c Robert R. *Educ:* Rensselaer Polytech Inst, 51; Cornell Univ, MS, 56, PhD(physics), 58. *Prof Exp:* Asst mech, heat, sound, elec & magnetism, Cornell Univ, 51-56, asst oxidation metals, 56-58; mem tech staff evaporated films, Radio Corp Am Labs, 58-65; mem sci staff photoelectronic mat, Itek Corp, 65-75; mgr res & develop, Solar Power Corp, 75-77, tech dir, 78-84; consult, 84-89. *Concurrent Pos:* Mem steering comt, Int Conf Thin Films, Mass, 69; tech adv, US Nat Comt, Int Electrotech Comn, 84-96. *Mem:* Am Phys Soc; Inst Elec & Electronics Engrs; Sigma Xi. *Res:* Photoelectronic processes in crystals; properties of solids relating to defect structure; structure and properties of surfaces and thin film; photovoltaic devices. *Mailing Add:* 6 Dewey Rd Bedford MA 01730-1212

ADDOR, ROGER WILLIAMS, HETEROCYCLIC CHEMISTRY, ORGANO-SULFUR CHEMISTRY. *Current Pos:* RETIRED. *Personal Data:* b New Rochelle, NY, Apr 30, 26; m 50, Frances Jane; c Jane & Thomas. *Educ:* Univ Maine, BS, 49, MS, 50; Ohio State Univ, PhD(chem), 54. *Prof Exp:* Res chemist, Am Cyanamid Co, 54-61, sr res chemist, 61-68, group leader, 68-91. *Mem:* Sigma Xi; Am Chem Soc; AAAS; Soc Heterocyclic Chem. *Res:* Novel and better pesticides. *Mailing Add:* 28 Minuteman Dr Scarborough ME 04074

ADDUCI, JERRY M, ORGANIC CHEMISTRY, POLYMER CHEMISTRY. *Current Pos:* from asst prof to assoc prof, 66-84, PROF CHEM, ROCHESTER INST TECHNOL, 84- *Personal Data:* b Rochester, NY, June 5, 34; m 58; c 2. *Educ:* Univ Rochester, BS, 57; Univ Pa, PhD(org chem), 63. *Prof Exp:* Lab asst chem, Eastman Kodak Co, 52-53; instr math, Rochester Inst Technol, 58; lab technician, Strong Mem Hosp, Rochester, 58-59; res chemist, Fabrics & Finishes Dept, E I Du Pont de Nemours & Co, Del, 63-65; res assoc & fel, Univ Md, 65-66, instr chem, 66. *Concurrent Pos:* Guest prof, Inst Kemiindustri, Tech Univ Denmark, Lyngby, 79-80; consult res prof, Instituto Guido Donegani, Gruppo Montedison, Novara, Italy, 86-87. *Mem:* Am Chem Soc. *Res:* Reactions mechanisms; polymer synthesis; liquid crystalline polymers. *Mailing Add:* 89 Highland Pkwy Rochester Inst Tech Rochester NY 14620-2503

ADDY, ALVA LEROY, MECHANICAL ENGINEERING, FLUID DYNAMICS. *Current Pos:* from asst prof to assoc prof, 63-73, assoc head res & grad study, 80-86, PROF MECH ENG, UNIV ILL, URBANA-CHAMPAIGN, 73-, HEAD DEPT, MECH & INDUST ENG, 87- *Personal Data:* b Dallas, SDak, Mar 29, 36; m 58. *Educ:* SDak Sch Mines & Technol, BS, 58; Univ Cincinnati, MS, 60; Univ Ill, PhD(mech eng), 63. *Honors & Awards:* Educ Ralph Coates Roe Award, Am Soc Eng Educ, 90. *Prof Exp:* Engr, Gen Elec Co, 58-60. *Concurrent Pos:* Consult, Aerodyn Br, US Army Missile Command, 64- & var aerospace firms; vis res prof, US Army, 73. *Mem:* Assoc fel Am Inst Aeronaut & Astronaut; fel Am Soc Mech Engrs; Am Soc Eng Educ; Sigma Xi. *Res:* Aerodynamics and high velocity compressible flows, including base drag, turbulent mixing, ejector and propulsive nozzle design and performance problems; high energy lasers. *Mailing Add:* 1706 Golfview Dr Urbana IL 61801

ADDY, JOHN KEITH, PHYSICAL ORGANIC CHEMISTRY. *Current Pos:* from asst prof to assoc prof, 66-74, chmn, Chem Dept, 85-89, PROF CHEM, WAGNER COL, 74-, CHMN, PHYS SCI, 90- *Personal Data:* b Sheffield, Eng, June 30, 37; m 63; c 2. *Educ:* Univ London, BSc, 58; Univ Southampton, PhD(phys org chem), 62. *Prof Exp:* Res assoc phys chem, Univ Ore, 61-62; vis lectr chem, Northeast Essex Tech Col, Eng, 62-63; lectr phys chem, John Dalton Col, 63-66. *Mem:* The Chem Soc; fel Royal Soc Chem; Am Asn Univ Professors; Sigma Xi; Am Chem Soc. *Res:* Reaction kinetics, especially mechanisms of epoxide ring fission and allylic rearrangements; plasticization and structure of polymers, especially nylon. *Mailing Add:* 166 Chelsea St Wagner Col Staten Island NY 10307

ADDY, TRALANCE OBUAMA, INFECTION CONTROL TECHNOLOGY, MEDICAL INSTRUMENT STERILIZATION. *Current Pos:* vpres, 89-90, VPRES & GEN MGR, ASP DIV, JOHNSON & JOHNSON MED, 90- *Personal Data:* b Kumasi, Ghana, Aug 24, 44; US citizen; m 79; c 3. *Educ:* Swarthmore Col, BA & BS 69; Univ Mass, Amherst, MSME, 73, PhD(biomechanical eng), 74. *Prof Exp:* Teaching asst mech, Univ Mass, Amherst, 69-71, res asst food eng, 71-73; sr res engineer, Scott Paper Co, 73-76, res scientist, 76-79, prog leader, 79-80; dir appl res, Surgikos Inc, 80-85, dir technol ventures, 85-88; vpres res & gen mgr, Surgikos Inc, 88-89. *Mem:* ASME; AAAS; Sigma Xi. *Res:* Activities in the area of low temperature gas plasma and applications to surface modification and sterilization; also fibrous structures for use as microbial barriers; antimicrobial technology. *Mailing Add:* 8 Palomino Trabuco Canyon CA 92679

ADE, C WILLIAM, CHEMICAL ENGINEERING. *Current Pos:* RETIRED. *Personal Data:* b Moline, Ill, Feb 10, 27; m 69, C Sue McCauley; c Kristine S & Nancy E. *Educ:* Univ Mo, Columbia, BS, 48, MS, 49; Ill Inst Technol, MGT, 51; Wash Univ, PhD(chem eng), 69. *Prof Exp:* Chief engr, Miss River Transmission Corp, 55-64, mgr gas supply, 64-67, supvr special studies, 68-69, vpres supply & planning, 72-83; dir appl math, Northern Natural Gas Corp, 70-71, mgr gas control, 71-72; vpres, Kimball Resources Inc, 84-85. *Concurrent Pos:* From asst to vpres to asst to exec vpres, Miss River Fuel Corp, 55-64; pres, Gateway Resources, 86- *Mem:* AAAS; Am Chem Soc; Am Inst Chem Engrs. *Res:* Reversible rectification of low temperature natural gas streams and desalination of sea water via the propane hydrate process. *Mailing Add:* 1842 Newburyport Rd Chesterfield MO 63005

ADE, HARALD WERNER, X-RAY PHOTOEMISSION & ABSORPTION MICROSCOPY OF POLYMERIC SYSTEMS. *Current Pos:* ASST PROF PHYSICS, NC STATE UNIV, 92- *Personal Data:* b Altentriet, Ger, Sept 8, 60; m 87; c 1. *Educ:* Univ Tubingen, Ger, Vordiplom, 83; State Univ NY, Stony Brook, PhDD(physics), 90. *Honors & Awards:* Res & Develop 100 Award, Res & Develop Mag, 91. *Prof Exp:* Teaching fel, State Univ NY, Stony Brook, 90-92. *Concurrent Pos:* Consult, Exxon Res & Eng, 91-; asst prof physics, NC State Univ, 92- *Mem:* Am Phys Soc; Metaphys Soc Am; Optical Soc Am. *Res:* Development of new imaging techniques with chemical and orientational sensitivity; application to polymeric as well as electronic materials. *Mailing Add:* Dept Physics NC State Univ Raleigh NC 27695. *Fax:* 919-515-3031; *E-Mail:* harald-ade@ncsu.edu

ADEL, ARTHUR, astrophysics; deceased, see previous edition for last biography

ADELBERG, ARNOLD M, GEOMETRY, ALGEBRA. *Current Pos:* from instr to prof, Grinnell Col, 62-91, chmn, Dept Math, 69-71 & 77-79 & 85-87, chmn sci div, 71-73, chmn fac, 74-76, MYRA STEELE PROF MATH, GRINNELL COL, 91-, CHMN DEPT, 93- *Personal Data:* b Brooklyn, NY, Mar 17, 36; m 62, Harriet Diamond; c 2. *Educ:* Columbia Univ, BA, 56; Princeton Univ, MA, 62. *Prof Exp:* Instr math, Columbia Univ, 59-62. *Concurrent Pos:* Hon res fel, Harvard Univ, 68-69; vis scholar, Univ Chicago, 83-84, vis prof, 89-90. *Mem:* Am Math Soc; Math Asn Am; Am Asn Univ Prof. *Res:* Algebraic geometry, especially rationality questions of algebraic groups; Koszul resolutions; Bezout's theorem; elementary metric geometry; combinatoric identities; Bernoulli numbers and polynomials. *Mailing Add:* Grinnell Col Grinnell IA 50112-1640

ADELBERG, EDWARD ALLEN, MEMBRANE TRANSPORT SYSTEMS. *Current Pos:* prof microbiol, Yale Univ, 61-74, chmn dept, 61-64 & 70-72, dir biol sci, 64-69, prof human genetics, 74-91, DEP PROVOST BIOMED SCI, YALE UNIV, 83-, EMER PROF, GENETICS DEPT, 91- *Personal Data:* b Cedarhurst, NY, Dec 6, 20; m 42; c 3. *Educ:* Yale Univ, BS, 42, MS, 47, PhD(microbiol), 49. *Prof Exp:* From instr to prof bact, Univ Calif, Berkeley, 49-60, chmn dept, 57-61. *Concurrent Pos:* Guggenheim fels, Pasteur Inst, Paris, 56-57 & Nat Ctr Sci Res, 65-66; consult, Chem Res Div, Eli Lilly & Co, 59-67; ed, J Bact, 64-67; ed-in-chief, Bact Rev, 67-70; mem, Genetics Training Comt, Nat Inst Gen Med Sci, 70-73; consult, Genetics Br, NSF, 71-74; bd chmn, Med Sci Res Ctr, Brandeis Univ, 76-79. *Mem:* Nat Acad Sci; fel Am Acad Arts & Sci. *Res:* Genetics of cultured mammalian cells; membrane transport. *Mailing Add:* Dept Genetics Yale Univ PO Box 208005 New Haven CT 06520

ADELBERGER, ERIC GEORGE, EXPERIMENTAL NUCLEAR PHYSICS, EXPERIMENTAL GRAVITATIONAL PHYSICS. *Current Pos:* from asst prof to assoc prof, 71-75, PROF PHYSICS, UNIV WASH, 75- *Personal Data:* b Bryn Mawr, Pa, June 26, 38; m 61, Audra Browman; c 2. *Educ:* Calif Inst Technol, BS, 60, PhD(physics), 67. *Honors & Awards:* Tom W Bonner Prize, 85. *Prof Exp:* Res fel physics, Calif Inst Technol, 67-68; res assoc, Stanford Univ, 68-69; asst prof, Princeton Univ, 69-71. *Concurrent Pos:* Mem, Adv Panel Physics, NSF, 73-; fac adv nuclear physics, Max Planck Soc, Ger, 75-79; assoc ed, Phys Rev Lett, 78-81; mem, Adv Panel Physics, Argonne Univ Assoc, 79-; von Humboldt sr scientist award, 82; chmn, Div Nuclear Phys, Am Phys Soc, 87. *Mem:* Nat Acad Sci; Am Phys Soc. *Res:* Experimental studies of fundamental symmetries in nuclei and atoms; nuclear structure; experimental gravitation. *Mailing Add:* Nuclear Physics Box 354290 Univ Wash Seattle WA 98195. *Fax:* 206-685-4634

ADELBERGER, REXFORD E, NUCLEAR PHYSICS. *Current Pos:* ASSOC PROF PHYSICS, GUILFORD COL, 73- *Personal Data:* b Cleveland, Ohio, Mar 30, 40; m 66; c 2. *Educ:* Col William & Mary, BSc, 61; Univ Rochester, PhD(physics), 67. *Prof Exp:* Asst prof physics, State Univ NY Col Geneseo, 67-73. *Concurrent Pos:* Ed, J Undergraduate Research in Physics, 80- *Mem:* Am Asn Physics Teachers; Am Phys Soc. *Res:* Experimental study of the few nucleon problem at moderate energies; computer controlled machinery. *Mailing Add:* Dept of Physics Guilford Col Greensboro NC 27410

ADELI, HOJJAT, STRUCTURAL ENGINEERING, EARTHQUAKE ENGINEERING. *Current Pos:* assoc prof, 83-88, chmn struct fac, 88-91, PROF CIVIL ENG, OHIO STATE UNIV, 88-, DIR, KNOWLEDGE & ENG LAB, 93- *Personal Data:* b Langrood, Iran, June 3, 50; m 79, Nahid Dadmehr; c Anahita, Amir, Mona & Cyrus D. *Educ:* Univ Tehran, BS, 72, MS, 73; Stanford Univ, PhD(struct eng), 76. *Honors & Awards:* Distinguished Leadership Award, Am Biog Inst, 86 & Commemorative Medal of Honor, 87. *Prof Exp:* Res assoc appl mechs, Stanford Univ, 76; asst prof civil eng, Northwestern Univ, 77; from asst prof to assoc prof, Univ Tehran, 78-82; assoc prof, Univ Utah, 82-83. *Concurrent Pos:* Vis scientist, Wright Aeronaut Lab, USAF, 85; ed-in-chief & founder, Microcomput Civil Eng, 86-, Integrated Comput-Aided Eng, 93-; ed-in-chief, Heuristics-J Knowledge Eng, 91-93; assoc ed, Control Eng Pract, 93- *Mem:* Am Asn Artificial Intel; Asn Comput Mach; Inst Elec & Electronics Engrs Comput Soc; Earthquake Eng Res Inst; Am Soc Civil Engrs. *Res:* Authored or edited over 250 research and technical publications in the fields of computer-aided engineering, artificial intelligence, structural engineering, applied mechanics, mathematical optimization, earthquake engineering and numerical analysis. *Mailing Add:* Dept Civil Eng Ohio State Univ 470 Hitchcock Hall 2070 Neil Ave Columbus OH 43210

ADELMAN, ALBERT H, PHYSICAL CHEMISTRY. *Current Pos:* CONSULT, BURT ASSOCS, 89- *Personal Data:* b New York, NY, Dec 17, 30; m 52; c 2. *Educ:* Brooklyn Col, BS, 51; Polytech Inst Brooklyn, PhD(chem), 56. *Prof Exp:* Assoc res scientist, NY Univ, 56-60; sr scientist, 60-70, assoc chief, Chem Dept, 70-72, sect mgr org chem, 72-75, mgr, Chem Dept, 75-79, assoc dir, Columbus Div, Battelle Mem Inst, 79-85; pres, Oread Labs Inc, 86-87; dir, Nat Labs, Ensr, 88-89. *Concurrent Pos:* NSF fel, 56-58; instr, City Col New York, 59- *Mem:* AAAS; Am Phys Soc; Am Chem Soc. *Res:* Charge-transfer photochemistry; stepwise excitation of luminescence; solar energy utilization employing physical and biological systems. *Mailing Add:* 3 Landmark Dr Westford MA 01886

ADELMAN, BARNET REUBEN, JET PROPULSION & ORDINANCE, ROCKETS, MISSILES & EXPLOSIVES. *Current Pos:* PRES, ADELMAN ASSOC, 84- *Personal Data:* b Helena, Ark, Dec 17, 25; m 48; c 3. *Educ:* Columbia Univ, BS, 47, MS, 48. *Honors & Awards:* C N Hickman Award, Am Rocket Soc, 58; Propulsion Award, Am Inst Aeronaut & Astronaut. *Prof Exp:* Res engr, Picatinny Arsenal, NJ, 48-49; sr res engr, Jet Propulsion Lab, Calif Inst Technol, 49-51; tech dir, Rocket Fuels Div, Phillips Petrol Co, Tex, 51-55; dir, Vehicle Eng Lab, Ramo Wooldridge Corp, Calif, 55-59; exec vpres, United Technol Ctr, United Aircraft Corp, 59-62, div pres, 62-80, vpres, Power Group, United Technol Corp, 80-84, pres, Biother Systs, 84-86. *Concurrent Pos:* Adv & US deleg, Mutual Weapons Group, NATO, 55-56; pres, United Space Boosters, Inc, 74-80. *Mem:* NY Acad Sci; fel Am Inst Aeronaut & Astronaut; Am Defense Preparedness Asn; Am Inst Chem Engrs. *Mailing Add:* United Technol Corp 3301 El Camino Real #280 Atherton CA 94027-3803

ADELMAN, IRA ROBERT, FISHERIES SCIENCE. *Current Pos:* Res fel, Univ Minn, 69-70, res assoc, 70-74, from asst prof to assoc prof, 74-82, PROF FISHERIES & DEPT HEAD, UNIV MINN, ST PAUL, 83- *Personal Data:* b New York, NY, Nov 14, 41; m 66, Maureen Kelly; c Tanya. *Educ:* Univ Vt, BA, 63; Univ Minn, PhD(fisheries), 69. *Concurrent Pos:* Spec asst dir Fish & Wildlife, Minn Dept Natural Resources, 90. *Mem:* Am Fisheries Soc; AAAS; Sigma Xi; Am Inst Fisheries Res Biologists. *Res:* Effects of environmental variables and water quality on fish physiology; aquaculture; fisheries management. *Mailing Add:* Dept Fisheries & Wildlife Univ Minn St Paul MN 55108. *Fax:* 612-625-5299; *E-Mail:* ira@fw.umn.edu

ADELMAN, MARK ROBERT, MOLECULAR BIOLOGY, BIOPHYSICS. *Current Pos:* ASSOC PROF ANAT, MICROANAT, UNIFORMED SERV UNIV HEALTH SCI, 79- *Personal Data:* b Philadelphia, Pa, 1942; m 71; c 1. *Educ:* Princeton Univ, AB, 63; Univ Chicago, PhD(biophys), 69. *Prof Exp:* asst prof anat, Duke Univ, 71-79. *Mem:* Am Soc Cell Biol; Biophys Soc; Am Asn Anat; AAAS; NY Acad Sci. *Res:* Biochemistry of cytoskeletal proteins; dynamics of cytoskeletal changes during amoebaflagellate transformation in Physarum. *Mailing Add:* NHLBI NIH Bldg 10 Rm 8N-202 4301 MSC-1762 Bethesda MD 20892-1762. *Fax:* 301-295-1715

ADELMAN, RICHARD CHARLES, GERONTOLOGY, BIOCHEMISTRY. *Current Pos:* PROF BIOL CHEM & DIR, INST GERONT, UNIV MICH, 82- *Personal Data:* b Newark, NJ, Mar 10, 40; m 63, Lynn Richman; c Mindy R & Nicole A. *Educ:* Kenyon Col, AB, 62; Temple Univ, MA, 65, PhD(biochem), 67. *Honors & Awards:* Medalist Award, Intrasci Res Found, 77; Donald P Kent Award, Geront Soc Am, 90. *Prof Exp:* From asst prof to prof biochem Fels Res Inst, Med Sch, Temple Univ, 69-82, dir, Inst on Aging, 78-82; dir, Div Biomed Res, Philadelphia Geriat Ctr, 78-82. *Concurrent Pos:* Am Cancer Soc fel, Albert Einstein Col Med, 67-69; Am Can Soc res grant aging, Fels Res Inst, Med Sch, Temple Univ, 70-73; NIH res grants, 70-; mem Study Sect Pathobiol Chem, NIH, 75-78; estab investr, Am Heart Asn, 75-78; chmn, Gordon Res Conf Biol of Aging, 76; chmn, Vet Admin Nat Adv Comt, Geront & Geriat, 87- *Mem:* AAAS; fel Geront Soc (secy-treas 72-75, vpres, 75-76, pres, 87-88); Am Soc Biol Chemists; Am Chem Soc. *Res:* Biology of aging; hormonal regulation of enzyme activity; social construction of interdisciplinary science in gerontology. *Mailing Add:* Inst Geront Univ Mich 300 N Ingalls Ann Arbor MI 48109. *Fax:* 313-936-2116

ADELMAN, ROBERT LEONARD, ORGANIC CHEMISTRY. *Current Pos:* RETIRED. *Personal Data:* b Chicago, Ill, May 20, 19. *Educ:* Univ Chicago, BS, 41, PhD(org chem), 45. *Prof Exp:* Res chemist, Nat Defense Res Comt & Off Sci Res & Develop, Univ Chicago, 42-45; from res chemist to sr chemist, 45-61, staff scientist, 61-66, res assoc, Indust Chem Dept, 72-74, res assoc, Plastics Prod & Resins Dept, 74-79, res assoc, Polymer Prod Dept, E I du Pont De Nemours & Co, Inc, 79-84. *Mem:* Am Chem Soc; Sigma Xi. *Res:* Reaction mechanism; synthesis and characterization of monomers, polymers, adhesives, protective coatings, structural plastics, plated plastics, polymers in electroplating and electronics, synthetic elastomers and paper. *Mailing Add:* 2422 Riddle Ave Wilmington DE 19806-2127

ADELMAN, SAUL JOSEPH, ASTRONOMY, ASTROPHYSICS. *Current Pos:* from asst prof to assoc prof, 78-89, PROF PHYSICS, THE CITADEL, 89- *Personal Data:* b Atlantic City, NJ, Nov 18, 44; m 70, Carol J Sugarman; c Aaron, Barry & David. *Educ:* Univ Md, BS, 66; Calif Inst Technol, PhD(astron), 72. *Prof Exp:* Resident res assoc astron, Nat Acad Sci-Nat Res Coun, NASA Goddard Space Flight Ctr, 72-74; asst prof, Boston Univ, 74-78. *Concurrent Pos:* Guest investr, Hale Observ, 73-80; guest investr, Int Ultraviolet Satellite, 80, 82-87 & 89-96; guest observer, Dom Astrophys Observ, 84-97; res assoc, Goddard Space Flight Ctr, Nat Res Coun, NASA, 84-86; vis astronomer, Complejo Astronomio El Leoncito, 94-97. *Mem:* Int Astron Union; Am Astron Soc; Astron Soc Pac; Sigma Xi; Royal Astron Soc; Can Astron Soc. *Res:* Magnetic peculiar A stars; coude spectroscopy;

photoelectric spectrophotometry; abundance analyses; line identification techniques; atomic spectroscopy; mercury manganese stars; main sequence B, A and F stars; space astronomy; horizontal-branch stars. *Mailing Add:* 1434 Fairfield Ave Charleston SC 29407. *Fax:* 803-953-7084; *E-Mail:* adelmans@citadel.edu

ADELMAN, STEVEN A, NON-EQUILLIBRIUM STATISTICAL MECHANICS, THEORY OF CHEMICAL REACTION DYNAMICS IN CONDENSED PHASES. *Current Pos:* from asst prof to assoc prof, 75-82, PROF CHEM, PURDUE UNIV, 83- *Personal Data:* b Chicago, Ill, July 4, 45; m 74, Barbara Stolberg. *Educ:* Ill Inst Technol, BS, 67; Harvard Univ, PhD(chem physics), 72. *Prof Exp:* Fel, Mass Inst Technol, 72-74, Univ Chicago, 74-75. *Concurrent Pos:* Consult, Los Alamos Nat Lab, 84-87. *Mem:* Am Chem Soc; fel Am Phys Soc; AAAS; Sigma Xi; Am Statist Asn. *Res:* Statistical mechanics of solid surfaces, polymers and fluids; energy transfer and chemical reaction dynamics in liquids. *Mailing Add:* Dept Chemistry Purdue Univ West Lafayette IN 47907-1393. *Fax:* 765-494-0239; *E-Mail:* distill@vm.cc.purdue.edu

ADELMAN, STEVEN J, MEDICAL RESEARCH, HEART DISEASE. *Current Pos:* ASSOC DIR CARDIOVASC RES, WYETH-AYERST RES, 86- *Personal Data:* b Brooklyn, NY, 1954. *Educ:* State Univ NY, Buffalo, BS, 76, MS, 80; Med Col Pa, PhD(biochem), 84. *Prof Exp:* Fel, Bowman Gray Sch Med, 84-86. *Concurrent Pos:* Fel, Coun Arteriosclerosis, Am Heart Asn, 86- *Mem:* Am Heart Asn; NY Acad Sci. *Mailing Add:* Wyeth-Ayerst Res CN 8000 Princeton NJ 08543-8000

ADELMAN, WILLIAM JOSEPH, JR, PHYSIOLOGY, BIOPHYSICS. *Current Pos:* RETIRED. *Personal Data:* b Mt Vernon, NY, Jan 29, 28; m 51; c 3. *Educ:* Fordham Univ, BS, 50; Univ Vt, MS, 52; Univ Rochester, PhD(physiol), 55. *Honors & Awards:* Spec Recognition Award, Dept Health & Human Serv, USPHS, 85. *Prof Exp:* Asst physiol & biophys, Univ Vt, 50-52; aviation physiologist, US Air Force Sch Aviation Med, 55-56; from instr to asst prof physiol, Sch Med, Univ Buffalo, 56-59; physiologist, Biophys Lab, Nat Inst Neurol Dis & Blindness, 59-62; from assoc prof to prof physiol, Sch Med, Univ Md, Baltimore, 62-71; chief lab biophys, Nat Inst Neurol Commun Dis & Stroke, 71-91. *Concurrent Pos:* Nat Inst Neurol Dis & Stroke spec fel, Marine Biol Lab, Woods Hole, 69-70; adj prof physiol, Sch Med, Boston Univ, 75-91. *Mem:* AAAS; Am Physiol Soc; Biophys Soc; Soc Gen Physiol; Soc Neurosci. *Res:* Neurophysiology and electrobiology; role of ions in membrane phenomena in nerve; modeling of neural behavior; ultra structure of neurons and muscle. *Mailing Add:* 160 Locust St Falmouth MA 02540

ADELSON, BERNARD HENRY, MEDICINE, CHEMISTRY. *Current Pos:* Asst chem, Northwestern Univ, 42-44, res assoc, 44-46, instr, 46-47, lectr, 47, clin asst med, 54-57, from instr to asst prof med, 58-73, assoc prof, 73-81, PROF CLIN MED, NORTHWESTERN UNIV, CHICAGO, 81- *Personal Data:* b Tampa, Fla, Mar 16, 20; m 50; c 3. *Educ:* Northwestern Univ, BS, 41, PhD(chem), 46, BM, 50, MD, 51. *Concurrent Pos:* Resident, Evanston Hosp, Ill, 51-53, dir, Artificial Kidney Unit, chief nephrology & assoc chmn, Dept Med; resident, Cook County Hosp, 53-54; dir, Geriat Serv, Evanston Hosp, prog med ethics; clinician laureate, Ill Chap, Am Col Physicians. *Mem:* AAAS; AMA; Royal Soc Med; Am Soc Nephrology. *Res:* Organic chemistry; synthesis of 5-substituted quinolines; cardiac outputs in myocardial infarctions and medical shock; extracorporeal hemodialysis. *Mailing Add:* 595 Lincoln Ave Glencoe IL 60022-1467

ADELSON, HAROLD ELY, TECHNICAL MANAGEMENT. *Current Pos:* MUS STAFF SCIENTIST, INST ARCHAEOL, UNIV CALIF, LOS ANGELES, 94- *Personal Data:* b New York, NY, May 5, 31. *Educ:* City Col NY, BS, 53; Univ Calif, MA, 54, PhD(physics), 59. *Prof Exp:* Asst physics, Univ Calif, 53-55, asst nuclear physics, Radiation Lab, 55-59; sr res physicist, Convair Astronaut, 59-61, sr staff scientist, Gen Dynamics/Astronaut, 61-65; mgr, Environ Res Satellite Dept, TRW Systs Group, 65-67, from asst dir to dir, Res Appln Lab, 67-71, mgr viking lander biol & meteorol instruments prog, 71-75, mgr, Appl Technol Div, Design Rev Off, 75-80, mgr & sr tech staff, 80-92. *Mem:* Am Phys Soc; Am Geophys Union; Am Inst Aeronaut & Astronaut; Sigma Xi; Am Inst Archaeol. *Res:* Spacecraft technology; space instrumentation; prehistoric rock art. *Mailing Add:* 2170 Century Park E Apt 1902 Los Angeles CA 90067-2237

ADELSON, LESTER, FORENSIC PATHOLOGY. *Current Pos:* RETIRED. *Personal Data:* b Chelsea, Mass, Aug 20, 14; m 42, Luisa Menci; c 2. *Educ:* Harvard Univ, AB, 35; Tufts Univ, MD, 39. *Prof Exp:* Pathologist & chief dep coroner, Cuyahoga County, 50-87; from asst prof to assoc prof legal med, Sch Med, Case Western Reserve Univ, 53-69, emer prof forensic path, 69-84. *Concurrent Pos:* Res fel path & legal med, Harvard Med Sch, 49-50. *Mem:* AMA; Am Soc Clin Path; Sigma Xi. *Mailing Add:* 23005 Beachwood Blvd Beachwood OH 44122-1401

ADELSON, MARK DAVID, GYNECOLOGIC ONCOLOGY, GYNECOLOGY. *Current Pos:* PRES & DIR,COMPREHENSIVE GYNEC, PC, 93- *Personal Data:* b Cleveland, Ohio, Aug 14, 55; m 88, Katherine Rosenwinkel; c Leah M & Cara G. *Educ:* Med Col Ohio, MD, 79. *Honors & Awards:* Mead Johnson Serv Award, 79. *Prof Exp:* Resident obstet/gynec, Emory Univ Sch Med, 79-83; fel gynec, M D Anderson Cancer Ctr, 83-85; from asst prof to assoc prof, State Univ NY, 85-93, clin assoc prof, Dept Obstet & Gynec, 93-95. *Concurrent Pos:* Prin investr, Gynec Oncol Group, 86-93, investr, 95- *Mem:* Fel Am Col Obstetricians & Gynecologists; fel Am Col Surgeons; AAAS; AMA; Am Soc Clin Hypnosis; fel Am Qual Assurance & Rev Physicians. *Res:* Ultrasonic aspiration for the treatment of gynecologic cancer; tissue culture and enzyme chemistry of ovarian cancer; laproscopic surgery in gynecology and oncology. *Mailing Add:* 730 S Crouse Ave Suite 203 Syracuse NY 13210. *Fax:* 315-423-0305; *E-Mail:* madelson@mem.po.com

ADELSTEIN, PETER Z, PHYSICAL CHEMISTRY. *Current Pos:* SR RES ASSOC, IMAGE PERMANENCE INST, 86- *Personal Data:* b Montreal, Que, Sept 1, 24; nat US; m 47, Rose Magio; c David, Diane & Debra (Goldstein). *Educ:* McGill Univ, BE, 46, PhD(chem), 49. *Prof Exp:* Chemist, 49-63, unit dir, Eastman Kodak Co, 58-86. *Concurrent Pos:* Chmn, NAPM 1T9 Comt, Am Nat Stands Inst, 67-; chmn, WG-5 Int Stands Orgn, TC/42, 73-; chmn, rec preserv comt, NAS, 84-86. *Mem:* Am Chem Soc; Am Soc Testing & Mat; Nat Fire Protection Asn; Imaging Sci & Technol. *Res:* Behavior of high polymers in solution; physical properties of high polymer materials in solid states; physical behavior of photographic film; permanence of photographic materials. *Mailing Add:* 1629 Clover St Rochester NY 14618

ADELSTEIN, ROBERT SIMON, MEDICAL SCIENCE, MOLECULAR BIOLOGY. *Current Pos:* res assoc, Nat Heart Inst, NIH, 61-64, sr investr biochem, 66-72, sect head, 72-81, LAB CHIEF, NAT HEART LUNG & BLOOD INST, NIH, 81- *Personal Data:* b New York, NY, Jan 16, 34; m 61, Miriam Appleman; c Ben, Sandra & Mike. *Educ:* Princeton Univ, AB, 55, Harvard Med Sch, MD, 59. *Prof Exp:* Intern & resident med, Duke Med Ctr & Bellevue Hosp, 59-61, sr med researcher, 64-65. *Concurrent Pos:* Fel biochem, Univ Wash 65-66; chmn, Comt Concern Scientist, 77-79, Gordon Conf Muscle Protein, 81; mem molecular cytol, NIH, 81-85; sabbatical, Hebrew Univ Sch Med, Jerusalem, 83-84. *Mem:* Am Soc Biochem & Molecular Biol; Am Soc Cell Biol; AAAS; Biophys Soc; Am Soc Clin Invest. *Res:* Regulation of contractile activity invertebrate muscle and nonmuscle cell; regulation of the expression of contractile proteins in those cells; molecular genetics of vertebrate nonmuscle myosin. *Mailing Add:* NHBLI Bldg 10 Rm 8N-202 Bethesda MD 20892-1762. *Fax:* 301-402-1542; *E-Mail:* ra19t@nih.gov

ADELSTEIN, S JAMES, RADIATION BIOPHYSICS, NUCLEAR MEDICINE. *Current Pos:* assoc anat, 63-65, from asst prof to prof, 65-89, DEAN ACAD PROG, HARVARD MED SCH, 78-, PAUL C CABOT PROF MED BIOPHYSICS, 89- *Personal Data:* b New York, NY, Jan 24, 28; m 57, Mary Taylor; c Joseph B & Elizabeth (Donster). *Educ:* Mass Inst Technol, BS & MS, 49, PhD(biophys), 57; Harvard Univ, MD, 53. *Honors & Awards:* Aebersold Award, Soc Nuclear Med, Blumgart Award. *Prof Exp:* House officer, Peter Bent Brigham Hosp, Boston, 53-54, sr asst resident, 57-58, chief resident physician, 59-60. *Concurrent Pos:* Moseley traveling fel, Harvard Med Sch, 58-59, HA&C Christian fel, 59-60, Med Found fel, 60-63, P H Cook fel radiol, 60-68; USPHS career develop award, 65-68; assoc med & radiol, Peter Bent Brigham Hosp, 63-68, dir nuclear med, 68-93; vis fel, Johns Hopkins Med Inst, 68; chief nuclear med servs, Children's Hosp Med Ctr, Boston, 70-78; dir, Joint Prog Nuclear Med, Boston, 70-; mem, Am Bd Nuclear Med, 72-78. *Mem:* Biophys Soc; Radiation Res Soc; Soc Nuclear Med; Inst Med; fel AAAS. *Res:* Cellular and molecular radiation biology; experimental radionuclide therapy; microscopic dosimetry. *Mailing Add:* Off Exec Dean Acad Prog Harvard Med Sch 25 Shattuck St Boston MA 02115. *Fax:* 617-432-4043

ADEN, DAVID PAUL, IMMUNOBIOLOGY. *Current Pos:* DENTIST, MARILYN & ADEN, 90- *Personal Data:* b Quincy, Ill, Feb 23, 46; m 71. *Educ:* Quincy Col, BS, 68; Mont State Univ, MS, 70, PhD(microbiol), 73. *Prof Exp:* Res investr, 73-76; asst prof, Wistar Inst Anat & Biol, 76-90. *Concurrent Pos:* Nat Cancer Inst fel, 74-76. *Mem:* Am Asn Immunologists. *Res:* Cell surface antigens coded for by specific human chromosomes; genetic control of human serum proteins; chromosomes involved in tumorgenicity. *Mailing Add:* 2363 Oakwood Dr Prescott AZ 86301

ADENI, SAFIR M, HEATING & VENTILATION, AIR CONDITIONING. *Current Pos:* prod develop engr, 94-95, PROD ENGR RES & DEVELOP, YORK INT CORP, 95- *Personal Data:* b Bangalore, India, Apr 4, 67; m 91, Asra; c Samra & Hana. *Educ:* Jawaharlal Nehru Technol Univ, India, BS, 88; Southern Ill Univ, Carbondale, MSME, 93. *Honors & Awards:* Res Award, Am Soc Heating, Refrig & Air-Conditioning Engrs, 95. *Prof Exp:* Jr tech mgr, Rashtriya Ispat Nigam Ltd, India, 88-89; proj engr, Marcraft Inc, 91-94. *Concurrent Pos:* Tech adv heating vent & air conditioning, Harrisburg Area Community Col, 95-; mem, Int Stand Orgn Tech Comt 205, US, 95-, US deleg, Geneva, 96. *Mem:* Am Soc Mech Engrs; Am Soc Heating Refrig & Air Conditioning Engrs; Soc Mfg Engrs. *Res:* Design of energy efficient heating, ventilating and air conditioning systems for acceptable indoor air quality; airflow and minimum ventilation control; systems for bypass of gasphase filtration equipment; thermal conductivity of composite materials. *Mailing Add:* 315B Queensdale Dr York PA 17403. *Fax:* 717-771-7335; *E-Mail:* sadeni@aol.com

ADENT, WILLIAM A, OIL & GAS. *Current Pos:* CHIEF, DEVELOP UNIT, PAC OFFSHORE REGION, US GOVT, 78- *Personal Data:* b Chicago, Ill, May 27, 23. *Educ:* Stanford Univ, BA, 49. *Mem:* Am Asn Petrol Geologist; fel Geol Soc Am. *Mailing Add:* 5813 Washington Ave Whittier CA 90601

ADER, DEBORAH N, behavioral medicine, for more information see previous edition

ADER, ROBERT, PSYCHONEUROIMMUNOLOGY, PSYCHOSOMATICS. *Current Pos:* From instr to assoc prof, 57-68, PROF PSYCHIAT & PSYCHOL, DEPT PSYCHIAT, SCH MED & DENT, UNIV ROCHESTER, 68-, PROF MED & GEORGE L ENGEL PROF PSYCHOSOCIAL MED, 83-, DIR, DIV BEHAV & PSYCHOSOCIAL MED, 82-, DIR, CTR PSYCHONEUROIMMUNOL RES, 93- *Personal Data:* b New York, NY, Feb 20, 32; m 57, Gayle Simon; c Deborah N, Janet L, Norine L & Leslie A. *Educ:* Tulane Univ, BS, 53; Cornell Univ, PhD(exp psychol), 57. *Hon Degrees:* MD(hc), Univ Trondheim, Norway, 92. *Honors & Awards:* Res Scientist Award, USPHS, 69-94; Salmon lectr, NY Acad Med, 89. *Concurrent Pos:* Vis prof, Rudolf Magnus Inst Pharmacol, Univ Utrecht, Neth, 70-71; ed-in-chief, Brain, Behav & Immunity, 86-; fel, Ctr Advan Study Behav Sci, Stanford, Ca, 92-93. *Mem:* Am Psychosom Soc (pres, 79-80); Int Soc Develop Psychobiol (pres, 81-82); Acad Behav Med Res (pres, 84-85); Soc Behav Med; Am Asn Univ Prof; Psychoneuroimmunology Res Soc (pres, 93-94). *Res:* Brain, behavior and immune system interactions in health and disease. *Mailing Add:* Dept Psychiat Med Ctr Univ Rochester Rochester NY 14642. *Fax:* 716-271-1279

ADES, EDWIN W, BIOLOGY PRODUCTION. *Current Pos:* CHIEF, BIOL PROD BR, SRP, CID, CTR DIS CONTROL, ATLANTA, GA, 87- *Personal Data:* b Kew Gardens, NY, Mar 30, 49; m. *Educ:* Emory Univ, BS, 71, PhD(immunol-path), 77; Ga State Univ, MS, 73. *Prof Exp:* Res microbiologist, Ctr Dis Control, Atlanta, Ga, 74-76; postdoctoral res fel, Cellular Immunobiol Unit, Comprehensive Cancer Ctr, Univ Ala, Birmingham, 77-79; asst prof, Dept Basic & Clin Immunol & Microbiol, Med Univ SC, 79-81; sr scientist immunol, Eli Lilly & Co, 81-85; assoc prof & dir, Barton Immunomorphol Lab, Dept Path, Med Col Ga, 85-87. *Concurrent Pos:* Res assoc, Comprehensive Cancer Ctr, Univ Ala, Birmingham, 77-79; spec fel, Leukemia Soc Am, 78-80; chmn, Grad Fac Comt, Dept Basic & Clin Immunol & Microbiol, Med Univ SC, 79-81; adj asst prof, Med Univ SC, 81-86, Pasteur Inst, France, 81-86, Sch Med, Ind Univ, 82-85, Med Col Ga, 87-; mem ad hoc spec study sect, Nat Cancer Inst, 86; adj assoc prof, Sch Med, Emory Univ, 87-; mem adv comt, Clin invest, Immunol & Immunother, Am Cancer Soc, 89-90; lectr, Am Soc Microbiol, 90-91. *Mem:* AAAS; Sigma Xi; NY Acad Sci; Am Soc Microbiol; Am Asn Cancer Res; Am Asn Immunologists; Soc Exp Biol & Med; Am Asn Pathologists; Am Soc Clin Oncologists; Soc Biol Ther. *Res:* Cellular immunobiology; 3 patents. *Mailing Add:* Biol Prod Br OSS CID 3202 Ctr Dis Control 1600 Clifton Rd NE Atlanta GA 30329-4018

ADES, IBRAHIM Z, CELL BIOLOGY, BIOLOGY. *Current Pos:* asst prof, 82-87, actg chmn, Dept Microbiol, 92-95, ASSOC PROF ZOOL, UNIV MD, COLLEGE PARK, 87-, ASSOC PROF, MOLECULAR & CELL BIOL PROG, 89-, DIR, MOLECULAR & CELL BIOL PROG, 92-, CHMN DEPT MICROBIOL, 95- *Personal Data:* b Cairo, Egypt, May 24, 46; m 76, Jane Emrath; c Emily J. *Educ:* Univ Calif, Los Angeles, PhD(biol), 76. *Prof Exp:* Fel, Dept Biochem, Univ Tex Health Sci Ctr, Dallas, 76-79; asst prof, dept Biochem, Bowman Gray Sch Med, 79-82. *Concurrent Pos:* Am Cancer Soc fel, 77-78; cell biologist, Nat Cancer Inst, Bethesda, Md, 89-90. *Mem:* Am Soc Biol Chem & Molecular Biol; Am Soc Cell Biol. *Res:* Biosynthesis and processing of proteins and mechanisms of assembly of cell organelles; pathways of porphyrin production and regulation of biogenesis of their enzymes; signal transduction pathways toxic initiated by lymphokines. *Mailing Add:* Dept Microbiol Univ Md College Park MD 20742. *E-Mail:* aades@microb.umd.edu

ADESNIK, MILTON, CELL BIOLOGY. *Current Pos:* from asst prof to assoc prof, 72-86, PROF CELL BIOL, SCH MED, NY UNIV, 86- *Personal Data:* b May 28, 43; m 74, Judith Hauptman; c Ariel, Moshe & Hillel. *Educ:* City Col NY, BS, 64; Mass Inst Technol, PhD(biophys), 69. *Prof Exp:* fel biophys, Mass Inst Technol, 65-68; instr biol sci, Columbia Col, 68-70, res assoc, Dept Biol Sci, 70-72. *Concurrent Pos:* fel, Damon Runyon Fund Cancer Res, 70-72. *Mem:* Am Soc Microbiol; Am Soc Cell Biol; AAAS. *Res:* Regulation of expression of genes encoding liver microsomal cytochromes P450; mechanisms of insertion of proteins into membranes and for targetting these proteins to the specific membranes in the cell where they function; co-author of over 50 publications. *Mailing Add:* Dept Cell Biol Sch Med NY Univ 550 First Ave New York NY 10016-6402

ADEY, WALTER HAMILTON, SYNTHETIC ECOLOGY, MARICULTURE. *Current Pos:* RES SCIENTIST & CUR MARINE BIOL, ECOL & GEOL, SMITHSONIAN INST, 64-, DIR, MARINE SYSTS LAB, 75- *Personal Data:* b Stoneham, Mass, Apr 9, 34; m 85; c 2. *Educ:* Mass Inst Technol, BS, 55; Univ Mich, PhD(marine bot & geol), 63. *Concurrent Pos:* Res assoc, Colo Sch Mines, 63-64 & Hawaiian Inst Geophys, 71-75; adj prof, George Washington Univ, Georgetown Univ & Univ Md, 75-; prof, Univ Maine, 76- *Mem:* AAAS; Fedn Am Scientists. *Res:* Synthetic ecology; coral reef geology and ecology; theoretical marine biogeography; biology of coralline algae; simulation and modeling of marine ecosystems; mariculture; bioengineering. *Mailing Add:* 9478 Bay Meadows Rd Gloucester VA 23061

ADEY, WILLIAM ROSS, RESEARCH SERVICE. *Current Pos:* ASSOC CHIEF STAFF, RES & DEVELOP, PETTIS MEM VET HOSP, LOMA LINDA, CALIF. *Personal Data:* b Adelaide, Australia, Jan 31, 22; US Citizen; m 70; c 3. *Educ:* Univ Adelaide, BS & MB, 43, MD, 49. *Honors & Awards:* D'Arsonval Medal, Bioelectromagnetics Soc, 89; Sechenov Medal, Russ Acad Med Sci, 96. *Prof Exp:* Lectr, sr lect & reader anat, Univ Adelaide, Australia, 46-53, sr lectr, 55-56; asst prof anat, Univ Calif, Los Angeles, 54, prof anat & physiol, 57-77; distinguished prof neurol, Sch Med, Loma Linda Univ, Calif, 88- *Concurrent Pos:* Consult, NIH, NASA, Dept Energy, Vet Admin, WHO; Nuffield Found Dominion traveling fel med, Oxford, 50; fel, Royal Soc London & Nuffield Found, 56; dir, Space Biol Lab, Brain Res Inst, Univ Calif, Los Angeles, 61-74; prin investr, Long Duration Biosatellite Exp, NASA, 63-70; assoc, Neurosci Res Prog, Mass Inst Technol, 64-; mem, Space Sci Panel, Pres Sci Adv Comt, 69-71; mem, Telecommun Panel, Nat Acad Eng, 72-74; proj leader, Med Hazards Microwave Exposure, US/USSR Exchange Prog, 76-; mem, Assembly Life Sci, Nat Acad Sci, 76-, panel biosphere effects extremely low frequency radiation, 76; distinguished prof physiol, Sch Med, Loma Linda Univ, 87-, surg, 88- *Mem:* Fel Am Acad Arts & Sci; Am Physiol Soc; fel Am Asn Anatomists; fel Inst Elec & Electronics Engrs; Am EEG Soc; AAAS; Am Asn Neurol Surgeons; Biomed Eng Soc. *Res:* Behavioral neurophysiology; organization of cerebral systems and cerebral cellular mechanisms; computer applications in physiological data analysis and in models of brain systems; bioinstrumentation and bioengineering; aerospace medicine and physiology. *Mailing Add:* 31866 Third Ave Rte 1 Box 615 Redlands CA 92374-9759

ADHAV, RATNAKAR SHANKAR, CRYSTAL GROWTH FOR LASERS. *Current Pos:* FOUNDER & PRES, QUANTUM TECHNOL, INC, 69- *Personal Data:* b Sakri Bombay, India, Oct 30, 27; US citizen; m 53; c 3. *Educ:* Univ Poona, India, BSc, 49, MSc, 52; Gujarat Univ, Ahmedabad, PhD(physics), 58. *Prof Exp:* Lectr physics, Gujarat Col, 52-58; fel, Nat Res Coun, Can, 58-60; res physicist, Can govt, 60-63; dir res, EDO (Can) Ltd, 64-68. *Mem:* Optical Soc Am; Inst Elec Electronics Engrs. *Res:* Electro-optics; electronics engineering; engineering physics; electro-optics. *Mailing Add:* Quantum Technol Inc 108 Commerce St Lake Mary FL 32746

ADHIKARI, P K, internal medicine, for more information see previous edition

ADHOUT, SHAHLA MARVIZI, MATHEMATICS. *Current Pos:* PROF, LONG ISLAND UNIV, CW POST COL, 85- *Personal Data:* b Tehran, Iran, Apr 30, 54; m 82; c 1. *Educ:* Arya-Mehr Univ, BS, 79; Mass Inst Technol, PhD(math), 81. *Prof Exp:* Postdoctoral, Inst Adv Study, Princeton, 81-82; postdoctoral, Math Res Inst, Berkeley, 82-83; prof, Univ Calif, Berkeley, 83-85. *Mem:* Am Math Soc. *Res:* Geometry and analysis; symplictic geometry and inverse spectral problems. *Mailing Add:* Dept Math C W Post Ctr, Long Island Univ Greenvale NY 11548

ADHYA, SANKAR L, CONTROL OF GENE EXPRESSION, BACTERIOPHAGE BIOLOGY. *Current Pos:* CHIEF, DEVELOP GENETICS SECT, NAT CANCER INST, NIH, 80- *Personal Data:* b Calcutta, India, Oct 4, 37; m 70, Kathika Pal; c Sompa. *Educ:* Univ Calcutta, PhD(biochem), 63; Univ Wis, PhD(biochem), 66. *Concurrent Pos:* Adj prof, Dept Genetics, George Washington Univ, Washington, DC. *Mem:* Nat Acad Sci; Am Soc Microbiol; Am Soc Virol; Genetics Soc Am; Am Soc Biochem & Molecular Biol; Indian Nat Sci Acad. *Res:* Studies structure and function of regulatory proteins and DNA control elements in gene transcription; bacteriophage and bacteriophage therapy of infectious diseases. *Mailing Add:* Lab Molecular Biol Nat Cancer Inst NIH Bldg 37 Rm 2E16 Bethesda MD 20892. *E-Mail:* sadhya@helix.nih.gov

ADIARTE, ARTHUR LARDIZABAL, BIOPHYSICAL CHEMISTRY, ENERGY. *Current Pos:* INDUST ECONOMIST, MINN OFF TOURISM, MINN DEPT TRADE & ECON DEVELOP, 90- *Personal Data:* b San Nicolas, Philippines, Oct 27, 43; m 72; c 2. *Educ:* Univ Philippines, BS, 63; Univ Pittsburgh, PhD(biophys), 72. *Prof Exp:* Instr physics math, Univ Philippines, 63-66; teaching asst physics, Univ Pittsburgh, 66-67, res asst biophys, 67-72; fel, Univ Regensburg, 72-74 & Lab Biophys Chem, Dept Chem, Univ Minn, Minneapolis, 75-77; res scientist, Minn Energy Agency, 77-90. *Mem:* Biophys Soc; Sigma Xi; NY Acad Sci; AAAS. *Res:* Protein structure and function, thermodynamics and kinetics of biological processes; the role of water in protein systems and enthalpy-entropy compensation phenomena; energy and environment. *Mailing Add:* 767 Fairmont Ave St Paul MN 55105

ADIBI, SIAMAK A, CLINICAL NUTRITION, GASTROENTEROLOGY. *Current Pos:* PROF MED, UNIV PITTSBURGH SCH MED, 74-, PROF CLIN NUTRIT, 80-, HEAD, CLIN NUTRIT UNIT, MONTEFIORE UNIV HOSP, 80- *Personal Data:* b Tehran, Iran, Mar 17, 32; US citizen; m 63, Joan Foedisch; c 3. *Educ:* Johns Hopkins Univ, BA, 55; Jefferson Med Col, MD, 59; Mass Inst Technol, PhD(nutrit biochem), 67. *Concurrent Pos:* Mem various study sections, NIH, 75-; chmn, Gastroenterol Sect, Am Physiol Soc, 80-81. *Mem:* Asn Am Physicians; Am Inst Nutrit; Am Fedn Clin Res; Am Soc Clin Invest; Am Physiol Soc; Am Gastroenterol Asn. *Res:* Transport and metabolism of oligo peptides; metabolic and nutritional regulation of branched-chain amino acid metabolism; treatment of obesity. *Mailing Add:* Montefiore Univ Hosp Univ Pittsburgh Clin Nutrit Res Univ Univ Pittsburgh Med Ctr 200 Lothrop St Pittsburgh PA 15213-2582. *Fax:* 412-648-6316; *E-Mail:* scholar@vaxa.muh.upmc.edu

ADICKES, H WAYNE, SYNTHETIC ORGANIC CHEMISTRY, PACKAGING TECHNOLOGY. *Current Pos:* VPRES ENG & DEVELOP, PACKAGING CORP AM, 83- *Personal Data:* b Cuero, Tex, Sept 6, 40. *Educ:* Stephen F Austin State Univ, BS, 62; Tex Christian Univ, PhD(chem), 68. *Prof Exp:* Instr chem, Univ Tex , Arlington, 62-65; fel, La State Univ, 68-69 & Yale Univ, 69-70; res chemist, St Regis Corp, 70-71 & AM Int, 71-74; dir, St Regis Corp, 74-83. *Mem:* Tech Asn Pulp & Paper Indust; NY Acad Sci; Soc Plastics Engrs; Am Chem Soc; Sigma Xi. *Res:* Reactions of halothiophenes with metal amides; use of cyclopropanones in the synthesis of betta-lactoms; new synthetic routes to oldehydes; development of new organic photoconductors. *Mailing Add:* Chem Dept Univ Ariz Tucson AZ 85721-0002

ADICOFF, ARNOLD, SOLID ROCKET PROPELLANTS, SURFACE CHEMISTRY. *Current Pos:* RETIRED. *Personal Data:* b New York, NY, Oct 13, 23; m 50, Margaret C Farrer; c Keith D & Laurie C (Wodiske). *Educ:* Univ Calif, Los Angeles, BS, 49; Polytechnic Inst NY, Brooklyn, PhD(phys chem), 55. *Prof Exp:* Teaching fel chem, Polytechnic Inst NY, 49-50, res fel, 50-54; proj leader polymers & testing, Air Reduction Co, 54-56; res engr chem, Sci Lab, Ford Motor Co, Dearborn, Mich, 56-57; chemist polymers, Naval Weapons Ctr, China Lake, Calif, 57-68, head, Polymer Sci Br, 68-79, assoc head, Chem Div, 73-79, scientist chem, 82-83; assoc dir res, defense sci, Off Dep Under Secy Defense, 79-81; tech adv propulsion, Naval Sea Systs Command, Washington, DC, 81-82; sr scientist, Naval Weapons Ctr, China Lake, Calif, 82-83; staff scientist, TRW, Redondo Beach, Calif, 83-95. *Concurrent Pos:* Chmn, structures & mech behav, Joint Army-Navy-Air Force-NASA Subcomts, 68, 73, 75-78. *Mem:* Res Soc Am; AAAS; Am Chem Soc. *Res:* Research and development of solid rocket motor propellants; new polymeric materials; specialties, publications and patents include polymers, composite materials, adhesion, surface chemistry, combustion, electrostatic sensitivity effects and material mechanical properties; environmental effects of rocket motors. *Mailing Add:* 28251 Via Rueda San Juan Capistrano CA 92675

ADIN, ANTHONY, PHYSICAL INORGANIC CHEMISTRY. *Current Pos:* sr res chemist, 71-77, RES ASSOC, EASTMAN KODAK CO, 78- *Personal Data:* b Sheffield, Eng, Nov 11, 42; m 69; c 2. *Educ:* Leeds Univ, BSc, 64, PhD(chem), 67. *Prof Exp:* Fel, Brookhaven Nat Lab, 67-69 & Ames Lab, AEC, 69-71. *Res:* Application of inorganic and organometallic chemistry to unconventional photography; new technologies for silver-halide based photography. *Mailing Add:* 164 Belvista Dr Rochester NY 14625

ADINOFF, BERNARD, MATERIAL ENGINEERING, GENERAL COMPUTER SCIENCES. *Current Pos:* RETIRED. *Personal Data:* b Toronto, Ont, Mar 9, 19; US citizen; m 48, Madeline Shiller; c Allen, Bryon & Cheri. *Educ:* Univ Chicago, BS, 39, PhD(phys chem), 43. *Prof Exp:* Res asst, Univ Chicago, 43-44; chemist, Dayton Rubber Co, 44-59; chief chem engr, Fruehauf Trailer Co, 59-60; chief chem engr automotive opers, Rockwell Int, 60-82; lectr computer sci, Calif Lutheran Univ, 85-89. *Concurrent Pos:* Consult, 85- *Mem:* Am Chem Soc. *Res:* Lubrication; corrosion; plastics; adhesives; rubber; paints; latex foam; urethane foam; industrial fabrics. *Mailing Add:* 895 Tupelo Wood Ct Thousand Oaks CA 91320-3649

ADINOLFI, ANTHONY M, NEUROCYTOLOGY. *Current Pos:* Asst prof anat, Sch Med, Univ Calif, 69-74, asst prof anat & psychiat, 74-77, assoc prof anat & psychiat, 77-97, PROF PATH, SCH MED, UNIV CALIF, LOS ANGELES, 97- *Personal Data:* b New Haven, Conn, May 5, 39; m 63; c 2. *Educ:* Yale Univ, BA, 60; Columbia Univ, MA, 65, PhD(anat), 67. *Concurrent Pos:* Fel anat, Med Ctr, Univ Calif, Los Angeles, 67-69; chief, Neurocytol Res Lab, Vet Admin Hosp, 69-74. *Mem:* Am Asn Anat; Electron Micros Soc Am; Soc Neurosci. *Res:* Computer morphometric and electron microscopic analysis of neuronal organization in the central nervous system. *Mailing Add:* Dept Path Univ Calif Los Angeles Med Ctr 10833 LeConte Ave Los Angeles CA 90095

ADISESH, SETTY RAVANAPPA, PHYSICAL CHEMISTRY, INORGANIC CHEMISTRY. *Current Pos:* from asst prof to assoc prof, 65-72, PROF CHEM, ST LEO COL, 72- *Personal Data:* b Y N Hosakote, Mysore, India, June 17, 26; m 52, Prema Kumari; c Kausalya. *Educ:* Univ Mysore, BSc, 52, MSc, 56; Kent State Univ, PhD(chem), 65. *Prof Exp:* Lectr chem, Univ Mysore, 52-60. *Concurrent Pos:* Res assoc, Kent State Univ, 66; res appointment, Tex A&M Univ, 68 & Ga Inst Technol, 69; NSF res grant, 69. *Mem:* Am Chem Soc. *Res:* X-ray diffraction; voltometry; kinetic and reaction mechanisms. *Mailing Add:* PO Box 2134 St Leo Col St Leo FL 33574-2134

ADISMAN, I KENNETH, PROSTHODONTICS. *Current Pos:* PROF DEPT PROSTHODONT & CHMN DEPT REMOVABLE PROSTHODONT, UNIV NC SCH DENT, 78- *Personal Data:* b New York, NY, Aug 3, 19; m 57, Joan Sugarman; c Kathryn & Leslie. *Educ:* Univ Buffalo, DDS, 40; NY Univ, MS, 60. *Honors & Awards:* Ackerman Award, Am Acad Maxillofacial Prosthetics, 73; Carl O Boucher Distinguished Serv Award, Fedn Prosthodontics. *Prof Exp:* Prof maxillofacial prosthodont, NY Univ Dent Ctr, 71-78. *Concurrent Pos:* USPHS fel cancer control, NY Univ, 66-70; dir, Training Prog, Nat Cancer Inst, 74-76; consult, Vet Admin Hosp, 69-; sect ed, J Prosthetic Dent, 69-; consult, Clemson Univ, 72-; pres, Gtr NY Acad Prosthodont Res Found, 78-83; pres & dir, Int Circuit Courses, Am Prosthodontic Soc; chmn, Ed Coun J Prosthetic Dent, 87-; clin prof, Sch Dent, Univ NC. *Mem:* Fel Am Col Dent; fel Am Col Prosthodont; Int Asn Dent Res; fel Acad Prosthodontics (pres, 88-); Am Cleft Palate Asn; fel Int Col Dentists; fel Acad Maxillofacial Prosthetics. *Res:* Cleft palate prosthetics; maxillofacial prosthetics; bio-materials. *Mailing Add:* 133 Montrose Dr Durham NC 27707-3930

ADJEMIAN, HAROUTIOON, ELECTRICAL ENGINEERING. *Current Pos:* DIR, ADVAN DEVELOP GROUP & SALES & MKT, M/A-COM ADAMS RUSSELL, 86- *Personal Data:* b Sept 20, 48; US citizen; c 3. *Educ:* Worcester Polytechnic Inst, BSEE, 70; Univ Mich, MS, 72, MBA, 74. *Prof Exp:* Engr, Omnispectra, 75-80; dir mkt opers, Nat Micronetics, 80-86; opers mgr, NH Col, 88. *Mem:* Inst Elec & Electronic Engrs; Int Soc Hybrid Microelectronics; Am Optical Co; Armed Forces Commun & Electronics Asn. *Mailing Add:* 370 F W Hartford Dr Portsmouth NH 03801

ADKINS, DEAN AARON, AQUATIC ENTOMOLOGY. *Current Pos:* ASST PROF BIOL, MARSHALL UNIV, 72- *Personal Data:* b Wayne, WVa, April 3, 46; m 69; c 1. *Educ:* Marshall Univ, AB, 68, MS, 71; Univ Louisville, PhD(aquatic biol), 81. *Prof Exp:* Biol teacher, Wayne High Sch, 68-72. *Concurrent Pos:* Consult, Dept Health, Cabell-Huntington, 78-80. *Mem:* NAm Benthological Soc; Entom Soc Am; Nat Sci Teachers Asn. *Res:* Aquatic entomology with emphasis upon community interaction and life history data; effects of surface mining on aquatic communities. *Mailing Add:* 4383 Fifth St Rd Huntington WV 25701

ADKINS, JAMES SCOTT, PROTEIN QUALITY RESEARCH, NUTRIENT INTERACTION. *Current Pos:* PROF & CHMN DEPT HUMAN NUTRIT & FOOD, HOWARD UNIV, 76- *Educ:* Univ Wis, PhD(biochem & nutrit), 61. *Mailing Add:* Howard Univ Sch Human Ecol 2400 6th St NW Washington DC 20059-0001

ADKINS, JOHN EARL, JR, INDUSTRIAL HYGIENE MONITORING & ANALYSIS, ERGONOMICS. *Current Pos:* Res chemist, Plastics Dept, 63-68, div chemist, Tech Dept, 68-72, SR CHEMIST, PETROCHEM DEPT, E I DU PONT DE NEMOURS & CO, INC, 72- *Personal Data:* b Lynchburg, Va, June 20, 37; m 64, Martha Lenox; c Richard D & Karen E. *Educ:* Davidson Col, BS, 58; Univ Tenn, PhD(analytic chem), 63; Am Bd Indust Hyg, cert, 79. *Concurrent Pos:* Chmn, Analysis Chem Comt, Am Indust Hyg Asn, 87-88; off rep, Am Indust Hyg Asn to Am Chem Soc, 88-92; chmn, Gas & Vapor Detection Systs Comt, 93-94. *Mem:* Am Indust Hyg Asn; Am Chem Soc; fel Am Inst Chem. *Res:* Atomic absorption and infrared spectrophotometry; gas chromatography, ambient air quality monitoring and analysis; industrial hygiene monitoring and analytical method development and analysis; ergonomic workplace evaluations; heat stress monitoring. *Mailing Add:* E I du Pont & Co Box 1089 Orange TX 77631-1089. *Fax:* 409-886-6241

ADKINS, RONALD JAMES, NEUROPHYSIOLOGY. *Current Pos:* asst prof zool & physiol, 66-71, ASSOC PROF ZOOL & PHYSIOL, WASH STATE UNIV, 71- *Personal Data:* b Bremerton, Wash, June 28, 32; m 55; c 2. *Educ:* Univ Wash, BS, 54, MS, 57, PhD(physiol, psychol), 65. *Prof Exp:* Res asst neurophysiol, Univ Wash, 57-59; instr psychol & sociol, Lower Columbia Col, 59-61; behavioral trainee physiol & psychol, Univ Wash, 61-65; instr physiol, NY Med Col, 65-66. *Mem:* AAAS; assoc Am Physiol Soc. *Res:* Physiology of behavior; interaction among descending and ascending systems within the sensory apparatus, currently emphasizing the pyramidal tract and the dorsal column-medial lemniscal system in cats. *Mailing Add:* SE 400 Camino St Pullman WA 99163

ADKINS, THEODORE ROOSEVELT, JR, FORENSIC ENTOMOLOGY. *Current Pos:* LITIGATION CONSULT, 85- *Personal Data:* b San Antonio, Tex, Dec 26, 30; m 49; c 3. *Educ:* Auburn Univ, BS, 52, MS, 54, PhD(entom), 58. *Prof Exp:* Asst entom, Auburn Univ, 56-57; asst prof entom & zool & asst entomologist, Clemson Univ, 57-61, assoc prof entom & zool, 61-68, prof entom, 68-85. *Concurrent Pos:* Entom Soc Am travel grant, 13th Int Cong Entom, Moscow, 68; ed, J Agr Entom, 83- *Mem:* Entom Soc Am; Am Mosquito Control Asn; Sigma Xi. *Res:* Medical-veterinary entomology. *Mailing Add:* 1 Poplar Dr Clemson SC 29631

ADKINSON, NEWTON FRANKLIN, JR, CLINICAL IMMUNOLOGY, ALLERGY. *Current Pos:* from asst prof to assoc prof med allergy & clin immunol, 73-86, PROF MED, SCH MED, JOHNS HOPKINS UNIV, 87, CO DIR, DIV ALLERGY & CLIN IMMUNOL, 91- *Personal Data:* b Forest City, NC, May 18, 43; m 66, Judy H; c 2. *Educ:* Univ NC, Chapel Hill, BA, 65; Johns Hopkins Univ, MD, 69, MLA, 84. *Prof Exp:* Intern & resident med, Johns Hopkins Hosp & Univ, 69-71; clin assoc immunol, Lab Immunol, Nat Cancer Inst, Bethesda, Md, 71-73. *Concurrent Pos:* Mem, Immunol Sci Study Sect, NIH, 79-83; physician-in-chg, Asthma & Allergy Clins, Johns Hopkins Hosp, 84-; mem, Allergy & Immunol Rev Comt, NIH, 87-91. *Mem:* Am Asn Immunologists; Am Clin & Climat Asn; Am Thoracic Soc; Am Soc Clin Investr; Am Acad Allergy Immunol; Am Soc Clin Res. *Res:* Drug hypersensitivity states, especially penicillin allergy; immediate hypersensitivity reactions; IgE antibody; design and execution of clinical trials; childhood asthma allergen immunotherapy. *Mailing Add:* Prof Dept Med Johns Hopkins Asthma & Allergy Ctr 5501 Hopkins Bayview Circle Baltimore MD 21224-6801

ADKINS-REGAN, ELIZABETH KOCHER, BEHAVIORAL BIOLOGY. *Current Pos:* asst prof, 75-80, ASSOC PROF PSYCHOL, NEUROBIOL & BEHAV, CORNELL UNIV, 80- *Personal Data:* b Washington, DC, July 12, 45. *Educ:* Univ Md, BS, 67; Univ Pa, PhD(psychol), 71. *Honors & Awards:* Fulbright Res Scholar Award, 86. *Prof Exp:* Asst prof psychol, State Univ NY Col Cortland, 74-75. *Mem:* Fel AAAS; Animal Behav Soc; Am Ornithologists Union; Inst Soc Psychoneuroendocrinol; Soc Neuroscience; Sigma Xi. *Res:* Role of sex hormones in the development and maintenance of social behavior in vertebrates, especially reproductive behavior. *Mailing Add:* Uris Hall Ithaca NY 14853

ADKISON, CLAUDIA R, ANATOMY. *Current Pos:* asst prof, 71-80, ASSOC PROF ANAT, SCH MED, EMORY UNIV, 80- *Personal Data:* b Montgomery, Ala, Dec 9, 41. *Educ:* Huntingdon Col, BA, 64; Tulane Univ, PhD(anat), 69. *Prof Exp:* Instr myocardial biol, Baylor Col Med & anat, Sch Med, Tulane Univ, 70-71. *Concurrent Pos:* NIH training grant pharmacol, Baylor Col Med, 69-70. *Mem:* Am Soc Cell Biol; Electron Micros Soc Am; Am Heart Asn. *Res:* Pepsinogen secretion by chief cells; heart ultrastructure; heart organelle function; parietal cell function. *Mailing Add:* Emory Univ Sch Med Admin Bldg 412 Woodruff Health Sci Ctr Atlanta GA 30322-1100. *Fax:* 404-815-6555

ADKISON, DANIEL LEE, crustacean systematics, for more information see previous edition

ADKISON, HOLLIS LEON, SYSTEMS ANALYSIS, OPERATIONS RESEARCH. *Current Pos:* assoc prof, 74-80, DIR, SYSTS ANALYSIS PROG, TAYLOR UNIV, 74-, PROF SYSTS ANALYSIS, 80- *Personal Data:* b Dallas, Tex, Oct 28, 42; m 31, LaGatha Traylor; c John M & Christopher. *Educ:* Tex Christian Univ, BS, 64, MS, 68, PhD(physics), 70. *Prof Exp:* Asst prof info systs, Va Commonwealth Univ, 70-74. *Concurrent Pos:* Consult, Comput Ctr, Va Commonwealth Univ, 72-73, publ, Marion Chronicle Tribune, 77, Dept Nat Resources, State Ind, 77-80, Dept Higher Educ, 85-86, mgt consult, Ernest Whinney, 86-89, mkt info systs, Ameritech Bell Group, 90-91, Info Serv, Taylor Univ, 94. *Mem:* Asn Systs Mgt. *Res:* Knowledge-based intelligent systems implemented in decision support systems. *Mailing Add:* Dept Comput & Syst Sci Taylor Univ Upland IN 46989. *Fax:* 765-998-4940; *E-Mail:* inadkison@tayloru.edu

ADKISON, LINDA RUSSELL, GENE MAPPING, MUTATIONAL ANALYSES. *Current Pos:* asst prof, 89-93, ASSOC PROF GENETICS, MERCER UNIV SCH MED, 94-; ASSOC PROF OBSTET & GYNEC, MED CTR CENT GA, 95- *Personal Data:* b Columbia, SC, Apr 28, 51; m 78, Daniel L; c Emily K & Seth A R. *Educ:* Ga Southern Univ, BS, 73, MS, 77; Tex A&M Univ, PhD(genetics), 86. *Prof Exp:* Fel, Jackson Lab, 86-89; asst prof obstet & gynec, Med Ctr Cent GA, 91-95. *Mem:* AAAS; Am Women Sci; Am Soc Human Genetics; Southeastern Regional Genetics Group; Int Mammalian Genome Soc; Sigma Xi. *Res:* Gene mapping in mouse and fox; x-chromosome inactivation; mouse mutant analysis. *Mailing Add:* Mercer Univ Sch Med 1550 S College St Macon GA 31207-0001. *Fax:* 912-752-4038; *E-Mail:* adkison_lr@gain.mercer.edu

ADKISSON, CURTIS SAMUEL, ORNITHOLOGY. *Current Pos:* asst prof, 72-78, ASSOC PROF ZOOL, VA POLYTECH INST & STATE UNIV, 78- *Personal Data:* b Little Rock, Ark, Feb 25, 42; m 69; c 1. *Educ:* Oberlin Col, BA, 65; Miami Univ, MA, 67; Univ Mich, PhD(zool), 72. *Prof Exp:* Teaching fel zool, Univ Mich, 68-72. *Concurrent Pos:* Res fel Alexander von Humboldt Found, Bonn, WGer, 79-80. *Mem:* Am Ornith Union; AAAS. *Res:* Dialects in bird vocalizations; behavioral ecology of seed dispersal by birds; systematics and behavior of cardueline finches. *Mailing Add:* Dept Biol Va Polytech Inst & State Univ PO Box 0406 Blacksburg VA 24063-0001

ADKISSON, PERRY LEE, ECONOMIC ENTOMOLOGY. *Current Pos:* from assoc prof to prof, Tex A&M Univ, 58-79, head dept, 68-78, vpres agr & renewable resources, 78-80, distinguished prof, 79-96, dep chancellor agr, 80-83, dep chancellor, 83-86, chancellor, 86-96, EMER DISTINGUISHED PROF ENTOM & EMER CHANCELLOR, TEX A&M UNIV, 96- *Personal Data:* b Blytheville, Ark, Mar 11, 29; m 56; c 1. *Educ:* Univ Ark, BS, 50, MS, 54; Kans State Col, PhD(entom), 56. *Honors & Awards:* J Everett Bussart Award, Entom Soc Am, 67; Alexander von Humboldt Award, 80. *Prof Exp:* Asst prof entom, Univ Mo, 56-57. *Concurrent Pos:* Fel, Harvard Univ, 63-64; consult, Int Atomic Energy Agency, Vienna; chmn, Sci Adv Panel Agr Chem, Gov of Tex, 70-71; mem, Panel Experts Integrated Pest Control, Food & Agr Orgn, Rome, Italy, 70-74; consult, Hazardous Mat Adv Comt, US Environ Protection Agency, 71 & UC-USAID Pest Mgt Proj, 72-; mem, Exec Comt Study Prob Pest Mgt, Environ Sci Bd, Nat Acad Sci- Nat Acad 72-76; mem, Struct Pest Control Bd Tex, 72-78; chmn, Comt Biol Pest Species, Nat Res Coun, 73-; mem ed bd, Ann Rev Entom, 74-; mem, US Insect Control Deleg to People's Repub China, 75; mem UN-Food & Agr Orgn consult on pesticides in agr & pub health, Rome, Italy, 75; mem, US Directorate to UNESCO Man & Biosphere Prog, 75; mem, US Plant Protection Team to USSR, 76; mem, Nat Res Coun Study Comt world food & nutrition, 76; vchmn, Nat Acad Sci Comt use of sci & tech info in regulatory decision-making, 76-77; mem, Nat Sci Bd, 85- *Mem:* Nat Acad Sci; Entom Soc Am (pres, 74); Am Inst Biol Sci; Sigma Xi; Am Registry Prof Entomologists (pres, 77); Am Acad Arts & Sci. *Res:* Basic and applied research on cotton insects; insect photoperiodism. *Mailing Add:* Chancellor Tex A&M Univ Syst College Station TX 77843-2475

ADLDINGER, HANS KARL, virology, oncogenesis, for more information see previous edition

ADLEMAN, LEONARD M, COMPUTER VIRUSES. *Current Pos:* fac comput sci, 80-85, asst prof, 85, HENRY SALVATORI PROF COMPUT SCI, UNIV SOUTHERN CALIF. *Personal Data:* m 83, Lori Bruce; c 3. *Educ:* Univ Calif, Berkeley, BS, 68, PhD(comput sci), 76. *Prof Exp:* Assoc prof math, Mass Inst Technol, 76-80. *Concurrent Pos:* Asst prof math, RSA Data Security, 83- *Mem:* Nat Acad Eng. *Res:* Theoretical problems on the complexity of number, primality testing, public-key cryptography; computer viruses; DNA as a computer. *Mailing Add:* Comput Sci Dept Univ Southern Calif Los Angeles CA 90089. *Fax:* 213-740-7512

ADLER, ALAN DAVID, BIOPHYSICAL CHEMISTRY, MOLECULAR BIOLOGY. *Current Pos:* from assoc prof to prof, 74-92, EMER PROF CHEM, WESTERN CONN STATE COL, 92- *Personal Data:* b Nyack, NY, Oct 5, 31; m 54, Jean E Tremble; c Lucas S, Dana A & Chris P. *Educ:* Univ Rochester, BS, 53; Univ Pa, PhD(chem), 60. *Prof Exp:* Asst prof molecular biol, Univ Pa, 61-67; staff scientist & assoc prof chem sci & chmn div, New Eng Inst, 67-74. *Concurrent Pos:* Mem, Shroud of Turin Res Proj; consult. *Mem:* AAAS; Am Chem Soc; Am Phys Soc; Am Asn Clin Chemists; Sigma Xi; NY Acad Sci. *Res:* Physical, chemical and biological aspects of porphyrin materials; thermodynamics of electrolytic solutions; physical chemistry; history of science. *Mailing Add:* Dept Chem Western Conn State Univ Danbury CT 06810

ADLER, ALEXANDRA, NEUROLOGY, PSYCHIATRY. *Current Pos:* RETIRED. *Personal Data:* b Vienna, Austria, Sept 24, 01; nat US; m 59. *Educ:* Univ Vienna, MD, 26. *Honors & Awards:* Goldenes Ehrenzeichen der Stadt Wien, Austria, 77. *Prof Exp:* Intern, resident & vis physician, Univ Vienna Hosp, 26-34; res fel, asst & instr neurol, Harvard Univ, 35-44; clin prof psychiat, Duke Univ, 44-46; from asst to assoc clin prof neurol, Sch Med, NY Univ, 46-69, clin prof psychiat, 69- *Concurrent Pos:* Vis physician, Goldwater Mem Hosp, 46-56 & Bellevue & Univ Hosps, 46-; psychiatrist, Dept Correction, New York City, 48-72; med dir, Alfred Adler Ment Hyg Clin, 54- *Mem:* AMA; Am Psychiat Asn; Asn Res Nerv & Ment Dis; Am Acad Neurol; Int Asn Individual Psychol (past pres). *Res:* Psychotherapy; general psychiatry; organic mental syndromes; psycho-pharmacol-therapy. *Mailing Add:* 30 Park Ave Apt 12M New York NY 10016

ADLER, ALFRED, mathematics; deceased, see previous edition for last biography

ADLER, ALICE JOAN, BIOCHEMISTRY. *Current Pos:* assoc scientist, 76-84, SR SCIENTIST, SCHEPENS EYE RES INST, BOSTON, 85- *Personal Data:* b Jersey City, NJ, Dec 8, 35; wid; c Kyle, Andrew & Carrie. *Educ:* Barnard Col, AB, 56; Harvard Univ, PhD(phys chem), 61. *Prof Exp:* Fel biochem, Children's Cancer Res Found, Boston, 61-62; fel biol, Mass Inst Technol, 62-64; fel biochem, Oxford Univ, 64-65; sr res assoc biochem, Brandeis Univ, 65-76. *Mem:* AAAS; Am Chem Soc; Asn Res Vision & Ophthal; Int Soc Eye Res; Am Soc Biol Chem. *Res:* Biochemistry of retina and bordering tissues: retinoids and their binding proteins, biochemical studies of retinal adhesion and macular degeneration; physical studies of biological macromolecules and model compounds. *Mailing Add:* Schepens Eye Res Inst 20 Staniford St Boston MA 02114

ADLER, BEATRIZ C, biology, for more information see previous edition

ADLER, CARL GEORGE, EDUCATIONAL ADMINISTRATION. *Current Pos:* Assoc prof, 65-72, PROF PHYSICS, ECAROLINA UNIV, 72-, CHAIR, 85- *Personal Data:* b Buffalo, NY, Oct 3, 39; m 63; c 2. *Educ:* Univ Notre Dame, BS, 61, PhD(physics), 66. *Mem:* Am Asn Physics Teachers; Int Solar Energy Soc. *Res:* Solar energy; quantum mechanics; physics history; relativity. *Mailing Add:* 129 Forest Acres Dr Greenville NC 27834

ADLER, CHARLES H, NEUROLOGY, MOVEMENT DISORDERS. *Current Pos:* Asst prof, 92-97, ASSOC PROF NEUROL, MAYO CLIN, 97- *Personal Data:* b New York, NY, Mar 6, 58. *Educ:* Temple Univ, BA, 80; NY Univ, MS, 84, PhD(pharmacol), 86, MD, 86. *Concurrent Pos:* Consult neurol, Mayo Clin, 94- *Mem:* AMA; Am Acad Neurol; Movement Disorders Soc. *Res:* Clinical research in Parkinson's disease, dystonia, tremor and other movement disorders. *Mailing Add:* Dept Neurol Mayo Clin 13400 E Shea Blvd Scottsdale AZ 85259

ADLER, ERIC, SOLID STATE PHYSICS. *Current Pos:* SR ENGR, IBM CORP, 68- *Personal Data:* b Vienna, Austria, Oct 20, 37; US citizen; m 58; c 1. *Educ:* City Col New York, BS, 59; Columbia Univ, PhD(physics), 64. *Prof Exp:* Res asst physics, Watson Lab, Columbia Univ, 64-65; asst prof, City Col New York, 65-68. *Res:* Theoretical solid state physics; electron-phonon interaction; optical properties of semiconductors; semiconductor device and circuit design and reliability; FET integrated circuits. *Mailing Add:* 4 Cattle Creek Jericho VT 05465

ADLER, ERIC L, ELECTRICAL ENGINEERING, WAVE SCIENCES. *Current Pos:* instr elec eng, McGill Univ, 59-60, lectr, 60-61, from asst prof to assoc prof, 60-73, assoc dean, 77-85, PROF ELEC ENG, MCGILL UNIV, 73- *Personal Data:* b Alexandria, Egypt, Dec 10, 30; Can citizen; m 61. *Educ:* Univ London, BSc, 55; Univ Toronto, MASc, 59; McGill Univ, PhD(elec eng), 66. *Prof Exp:* Demonstr elec eng, Univ Toronto, 57-58. *Mem:* Fel Inst Elec & Electronics Engrs. *Res:* Acoustoelectric effects; thin film transducers; acoustic surface waves and waveguiding; surface wave devices for signal processing applications. *Mailing Add:* Dept Elec Eng McGill Univ 3480 University St Montreal PQ H3A 2A7 Can

ADLER, GEORGE, SOLID STATE & PHYSICAL ORGANIC CHEMISTRY, POLYMER CHEMISTRY. *Current Pos:* RETIRED. *Personal Data:* b Ger, Nov 25, 20; US citizen; m 49, Miriam Topaz; c Marc & Laurie. *Educ:* City Col NY, BS, 48; Brooklyn Col, MA, 52. *Prof Exp:* Asst lectr, Brooklyn Col, 49-51; rubber technologist, Mat Lab, NY Naval Shipyard, 50-56; chemist, Brookhaven Nat Lab, 56-79; adj res prof, State Univ NY, Stony Brook, 78-83. *Mem:* AAAS; Am Chem Soc. *Res:* Solid state polymerization; electron spin resonance; organic solid state chemistry; colloids and monolayers; gas-solid reactions; photo and radiation chemistry of organic solids; polymers. *Mailing Add:* 21 Harvard Rd Shoreham NY 11786

ADLER, HOWARD IRVING, BACTERIOLOGY. *Current Pos:* VPRES, RES & DEVELOP, OXYRASE INC, 93- *Personal Data:* b New York, NY, July 1, 31; m 53, Martha Vogeler; c David, Timothy & Elizabeth. *Educ:* Cornell Univ, BS, 53, MS, 55, PhD, 56. *Honors & Awards:* Indust Res-100 Award, 84. *Prof Exp:* Res assoc, Oak Ridge Nat Lab, 56-57, biologist, 57-69, dir, Biol Div, 69-75, sr staff mem, 75-88; dir microbiol, Med Div, ORAU, 88-93. *Concurrent Pos:* Adj prof, Univ Tenn, 69-; sr staff mem, Inst Energy Anal, Oak Ridge Assoc Univs, 75-76. *Mem:* Am Soc Microbiol; Radiation Res Soc; Sigma Xi; AAAS. *Res:* Mechanisms of radiation damage in microorganisms and control of cell division; anaerobic microbiology. *Mailing Add:* Oxyrase Inc 7327 Oak Ridge Hwy Knoxville TN 37931. *Fax:* 423-927-6540

ADLER, IRWIN L, FOOD BEVERAGE STABILITY, NEW PRODUCT DEVELOPMENT. *Current Pos:* PRES, FFI CORP CONSULTS, 72- *Personal Data:* b New York, NY, July 30, 28; m 54; c 3. *Educ:* Newark Col Eng, BS, 50; NY Univ, MS, 53, ScD, 61. *Prof Exp:* Res mgr, Gen Foods, 54-68; mgr technol ctrs, BeechNut, 68-72. *Mem:* Am Chem Soc; Am Inst Chem Engrs; Inst Food Technologists. *Res:* Coffee extraction, roasting and decaffeination; rheology of chocolate coating, puffed food products, stable beverage alcohol emulsion, shelf stable wine and juice beverages and plant by-products utilization. *Mailing Add:* 643 Primrose Lane River Vale NJ 07675-6511. *Fax:* 201-391-3293

ADLER, JOHN G, SOLID STATE PHYSICS. *Current Pos:* from asst prof to assoc prof, 65-72, EMER PROF PHYSICS, UNIV ALTA, 91- *Personal Data:* b Budapest, Hungary, Sept 29, 35; Can citizen; m 54, Merilyn Thorpe; c Richard, Wendy & Mark. *Educ:* Univ BC, BSc, 59; Univ Alta, MSc, 61, PhD(physics), 63. *Prof Exp:* Geophysicist, Imp Oil Ltd, 57-59; asst prof physics, Dalhousie Univ, 63-64; res fel, Case Western Res Univ, 64-65. *Concurrent Pos:* NSERC sr indust res fel, 85-86. *Mem:* Am Phys Soc. *Res:* Electron tunneling spectroscopy; superconductivity; low temperature physics; ion mobility in solids; scanning and tunneling microscopy. *Mailing Add:* 917 11th St Canmore AB T1W 1Z2 Can. *E-Mail:* jadler@banff.net

ADLER, JOHN HENRY, PLANT STEROID CHEMISTRY. *Current Pos:* assoc prof chem & head dept, 90-93, assoc prof biol sci, 84-94, PROF BIOL SCI, MICH TECH UNIV, 95-, HEAD, DEPT BIOL SCI, 95- *Personal Data:* b Brooklyn, NY, 48; div; c Michael C. *Educ:* Univ Md, College Park, BS, 70, MS, 73, PhD(plant physiol), 75. *Prof Exp:* Fel, 75-76, res assoc biochem, 76-77, asst prof biol sci, Drexel Univ, 77-84. *Mem:* Am Chem Soc; Am Soc Plant Physiologists; Am Oil Chemists Soc; Sigma Xi. *Res:* Examination of the role of sterols and steroids in the form and function of biological membranes; the ontogenetic and phylogenetic implications of different lipid structures; ecdysteroids in plants. *Mailing Add:* Dept Biol Sci Mich Tech Univ Houghton MI 49931. *Fax:* 906-487-3167; *E-Mail:* jhadler@mtu.edu

ADLER, JULIUS, BIOCHEMISTRY, GENETICS. *Current Pos:* from asst prof to prof, 60-95, EMER PROF, BIOCHEM & GENETICS, UNIV WIS-MADISON, 96- *Personal Data:* b Edelfingen, Ger, Apr 30, 30; nat US; m 63, Hildegard Wohl; c David & Jeane. *Educ:* Harvard Univ, AB, 52; Univ Wis, MS, 54, PhD(biochem), 57. *Hon Degrees:* DSc, Univ Tubingen, 87; DSc, Univ Regensburg, 95. *Honors & Awards:* Selman A Waksman Microbiol Award, Nat Acad Sci, 80; Otto-Warburg Medal, Ger Soc Biol Chem, 86; K H Wright Award, Simon Fraser Univ, 88; William C Rose Award, Am Soc Biochem & Molecular Biol, 96. *Prof Exp:* Fel microbiol, Wash Univ, 57-59; fel biochem, Stanford Univ, 59-60; from asst prof to prof biochem & genetics, Univ Wis-Madison, 60-66. *Concurrent Pos:* Edwin Bret Hart Prof, Univ Wis-Madison, 72-, Steenbock prof microbiol sci, 82- *Mem:* Nat Acad Sci; Am Acad Arts & Sci; Am Chem Soc; Am Soc Biol Chemists; fel AAAS; Am Philos Soc. *Res:* Biochemistry and genetics of behavior, especially in microorganisms. *Mailing Add:* Dept Biochem Univ Wis Madison WI 53706. *Fax:* 608-262-3453; *E-Mail:* adlerlab@macc.wisc.edu

ADLER, KENNETH B, CELL BIOLOGY. *Current Pos:* assoc prof, 87-90, PROF CELL BIOL, COL VET MED, NC STATE UNIV, 90- *Personal Data:* b New York, NY, Nov 21, 45; m 72; c 2. *Educ:* Queens Col, BA, 69; Adelphi Univ, MS, 75; Univ Vt, PhD(cell biol), 78. *Honors & Awards:* Award for Res Excellence, Smith Kline Beecham Corp, 91. *Prof Exp:* Biophysicist, Brooklyn Vet Admin Med Ctr, NY, 69-75; asst prof cell biol, Univ Vt, Burlington, 80-86. *Concurrent Pos:* Estab investr, Am Heart Asn, 87. *Mem:* Am Thoracic Soc; Am Soc Cell Biol; Am Asn Pathologists. *Res:* Study of the structure and function of airway epithelial cells in health and disease. *Mailing Add:* Sch Vet Med NC State Univ 4700 Hillsborough St Raleigh NC 27606-1428

ADLER, KRAIG (KERR), ANIMAL BEHAVIOR, EVOLUTION. *Current Pos:* assoc prof, 72-80, chmn neurobiol & behav, Div Biol Sci, 76-79 & 91-94, PROF BIOL, CORNELL UNIV, 80- *Personal Data:* b Lima Ohio, Dec 6, 40; m 67, Dolores R Pochocki; c Todd D. *Educ:* Ohio Wesleyan Univ, 62; Univ Mich, MS, 65, PhD(zool), 68. *Honors & Awards:* Baer Mem lectr, 77; Hefner lectr, 80; Anderson Mem lectr, 82. *Prof Exp:* Asst prof, Univ Notre Dame, 68-72. *Concurrent Pos:* Ed, Jour, Soc Study Amphibians & Reptiles, 58-63, miscellaneous publ, 61-; temporary cur, Mus Zool, Univ Mich, 65; co-ed, Int J Interdisciplinary Cycle Res, Neth, 70-78; assoc ed, Am Midland Nat, 77-82; vis prof zool, Ariz State Univ, 80; secy-gen World Cong Herpet, 82-89; distinguished scholar, China Prog, US Nat Acad, 84-85; vis fel, Pembroke Col, Univ Cambridge UK, 85; acad lectr, USSR Acad Sci, 86; assoc ed, Asian Herpet Res, 90- & Russ J Herpet, 94- *Mem:* Fel AAAS; Am Soc Ichthyologists & Herpetologists; Soc Study Evolution; Animal Behav Soc; Soc Study Amphibians & Reptiles (pres, 82). *Res:* Photoreception, orientation, navigation and circadian rhythms of vertebrates; evolution, systematics and zoogeography of amphibians and reptiles; paleo- and archeozoology. *Mailing Add:* Neurobiol & Behav Seeley G Mudd Hall Cornell Univ Ithaca NY 14853-2702. *Fax:* 607-254-4308; *E-Mail:* kka4@cornell.edu

ADLER, KURT ALFRED, PSYCHIATRY. *Current Pos:* DEAN & DIR, ALFRED ADLER INST, NEW YORK, 52-, PSYCHIAT CONSULT, ADVAN CTR PSYCHOTHER, 58- *Personal Data:* b Vienna, Austria, Feb 25, 05; US citizen; m, Tanya Drucker; c Margaret Adler-Gliedman. *Educ:* Univ Vienna, PhD(physics), 35; Long Island Col Med, MD, 41. *Honors & Awards:* Physicians Recognition Award, AMA, 70 & 78. *Prof Exp:* Chief psychiat serv, US Army, 42-46. *Concurrent Pos:* Consult psychiatrist, Youth-House, New York, 47-48; emer psychiatrist, Lenox Hill Hosp, New York, 47-; consult, Alfred Adler Inst Minn, 70-; dir, Bowie State Col, 75 & Alfred Adler Inst, Ottawa, Ont; dean, Advan Inst Analytic Psychother, 69- *Mem:* AMA; fel Am Psychiat Asn; Am Soc Adlerian Psychol; Int Asn Individual Psychol (pres, 63-70); fel Asn Advan Psychother. *Mailing Add:* 262 Central Park W New York NY 10024

ADLER, LASZLO, PHYSICAL ACOUSTICS. *Current Pos:* PROF WELDING ENG & ENG MECH, OHIO STATE UNIV, 80 - *Personal Data:* b Debrecen, Hungary, Dec 3, 32; US citizen; m 63; c 2. *Educ:* Mich State Univ, MS, 61; Univ Tenn, Knoxville, PhD(physics), 69. *Prof Exp:* Assoc prof physics, Gen Motors Inst, Univ Mich, 60-64; instr physics, Univ Tenn, Knoxville, 66-69, res assoc asst prof, 71-76, res asst prof, 76-80, assoc prof, 80. *Concurrent Pos:* Consult, Metal & Ceramic Div, Oak Ridge Nat Lab, Tenn, 69 -; vis prof, Univ Paris, 80. *Mem:* Fel Acoust Soc Am; Am Soc Nondestructive Testing. *Res:* Non-linear mechanisms of ultrasonic waves in liquids, especially harmonic and fractional harmonics generation and correlation to liquid structure; defects in metals by interference of a multifrequency pulse echo; physics of non-destructive testing. *Mailing Add:* 2850 Canterbury Rd Columbus OH 43221

ADLER, LAWRENCE, MINING ENGINEERING. *Current Pos:* RETIRED. *Personal Data:* b New York, NY, June 6, 23; m 57; c 3. *Educ:* NY Univ, AB, 46; Columbia Univ, BS, 49; Univ Utah, MS, 53; Univ Ill, PhD, 64. *Prof Exp:* Asst prof mining eng, Univ Mo, 55-56, Lehigh Univ, 56-58 & Mich Col Mining & Technol, 58-61; assoc prof mining eng, Va Polytech Inst & State Univ, 63-69, prof, 69-95; fac mem, Dept Mining, WVa Univ. *Concurrent Pos:* Gen consult. *Mem:* Am Inst Mining, Metall & Petrol Engrs; Am Soc Civil Engrs. *Res:* Design of underground openings; excavating and materials handling. *Mailing Add:* 1425 Dogwood Morgantown WV 26505

ADLER, LOUISE TALE, IMMUNOREGULATION, TRANSPLANTATION. *Current Pos:* RETIRED. *Personal Data:* b Brooklyn, NY, Nov 6, 25; m 49; c 2. *Educ:* Univ Miami, BS, 47; Univ Ky, Lexington, MS, 49; Wash Univ, St Louis, Mo, PhD(bact immunol), 53. *Prof Exp:* Teaching fel bact immunol, Harvard Med Sch, 52-54; adj asst prof microbiol, Adelphi Univ, 67-69; assoc immunol, Pub Health Res Inst, NY, 69-75; asst mem, St Jude Children's Res Hosp, Memphis, 75-77, assoc mem immunol, Memphis, 77-88; res prof, Dept Microbiol, Dartmouth Med Sch, Hanover, NH, 88. *Concurrent Pos:* Adj asst prof, Ctr Health Sci Microbiol, Univ Tenn, 77-78, assoc prof, 78-85; consult, Ad Hoc Biomed Sci Study Sect, NIH, 80-85, mem, 85- *Mem:* Am Asn Immunol. *Res:* Regulation of the immune system, using in vitro and in vivo tolerance, allotype suppression systems and genetically defined rabbits; immunocompetence in bone marrow transplantation using the rabbit model. *Mailing Add:* 201 Lakewood Dr Bradenton FL 34210-3005

ADLER, MARTIN W, NEUROPHARMACOLOGY, DRUGS OF ABUSE. *Current Pos:* From instr to assoc prof, 60-73, PROF PHARMACOL, SCH MED, TEMPLE UNIV, 73- *Personal Data:* b Philadelphia, Pa, Oct 30, 29; m 53, Toby Wisotsky; c Charles H & Eve R. *Educ:* NY Univ, BA, 49; Brooklyn Col Pharm, BS, 53; Columbia Univ, MS, 57; Albert Einstein Col Med, PhD(pharmacol), 60. *Honors & Awards:* Merit Award, Nat Inst Drug Abuse. *Concurrent Pos:* Prin investr, Nat Inst Drug Abuse, 70-, consult, 75-; chmn, Drug Abuse Biomed Res Review Comt, Nat Inst Drug Abuse, 80-82, 89-93 & Comt Substance Abuse, Am Soc Pharmacol & Exp Therapeut, 84-88; exec officer, Col Problems Drug Dependence, Inc, 86- *Mem:* Fel AAAS; fel Am Col Neuropsychopharmacol; Am Soc Pharmacol & Exp Therapeut; Am Pain Soc; Sigma Xi; fel Col Problems Drug Dependence. *Res:* Neuropharmacology; psychopharmacology; endogenous and exogenous opioid substances; narcotic receptors; interaction of drugs of abuse; thermo-regulation; neuropeptides; neuroimmunology; cytokines in brain. *Mailing Add:* 3247 W Bruce Dr Dresher PA 19025. *Fax:* 215-707-1904

ADLER, MICHAEL, PHARMACOLOGY, NEUROTOXICOLOGY. *Current Pos:* ADJ PROF, DEPT BIOL SCI, UNIV MD, BALTIMORE CO, 85-; PHARMACOLOGIST, NEUROTOXICOL BR, US ARMY MED RES INST CHEM DEFENSE, 82-, TEAM LEADER & SCI TECHNOL COORDR, 94- *Personal Data:* b Mezoladany, Hungary, Mar 3, 48; nat US; m 76, Suman Chona; c Karen A & Steven V. *Educ:* City Col NY, BS, 71; State Univ NY, Buffalo, PhD(pharmacol), 76. *Prof Exp:* Res assoc, Dept Pharmacol & Exp Therapeut, Sch Med, Univ Md, 76-77; staff fel, Lab Biochem Genetics, Nat Heart, Lung & Blood Inst, NIH, 78-80; sr staff fel, Lab Preclin Studies, Nat Inst Alcohol Abuse & Alcoholism, Alcohol, Drug Abuse & Ment Health Admin, 81-82; pharmacologist, Neurotoxicol Br, US Army Med Res Inst Chem Defense, 82- *Concurrent Pos:* Mem, Grant Rev Comt, Nat Inst Drug Abuse, 85-88, Chem Accident Response & Rescue Team, 86-92, US Army Med Res Inst Chem Defense & Atropine Equivalence Study Comt, 86-87. *Mem:* Inst Elec & Electronics Engrs, Eng Med & Biol Soc; Am Soc Pharmacol & Exp Therapeut; NY Acad Sci. *Res:* Synaptic transmission in smooth and skeletal muscle; excitation-secretion coupling in anterior pituitary cells; metabolic inhibitors on nerve and muscle fibers; neurotoxins on excitable tissues; botulinum toxin on transmitter release. *Mailing Add:* Neurotoxicol Br Bldg E3100 US Army Med Res Inst Chem Defense Aberdeen Proving Ground MD 21010. *Fax:* 410-671-1960; *E-Mail:* dr_michael_adler@ftdetrck_ccmail.army.mil

ADLER, MICHAEL STUART, POWER ELECTRONICS, SEMICONDUCTORS. *Current Pos:* Physicists, Gen Elec Co, 71-77, mgr, Advan Archival Memory, 77-79, Device Physics Unit, 79-81, Power Semiconductor Br, 81-84, Power Electric Lab, 84-91 & Elec Technol Lab, 91-93, MGR CONTROL SYSTS ELECTRONIC TECHNOL LABS, GEN ELEC CO, 93- *Personal Data:* b Detroit, Mich, Sept 13, 43; m 65; c Emily & Gerald. *Educ:* Mass Inst Technol, BS, 65, MS, 67, PhD(elec eng), 71.

Honors & Awards: Region I Award, Inst Elec & Electronics Engrs, 80, 82. *Mem:* Fel Inst Elec & Electronics Engrs. *Res:* Semiconductor device physics and design; high doping and high current effects; advanced device concepts; materials and process development; semiconductor packaging; computer aided design. *Mailing Add:* Gen Elec Co Mgr Control Syst & Elec Tech Lab Res & Develop Bldg KWC 1327 PO Box 8 Schenectady NY 12301. *E-Mail:* adler@crd.ge.com

ADLER, NANCY E, SOCIAL PSYCHOLOGY, HEALTH PSYCHOLOGY. *Current Pos:* Assoc prof, 77-84, PROF MED PSYCHOL, HEALTH PSYCHOL PROG, UNIV CALIF, SAN FRANCISCO, 84- *Personal Data:* b New York, NY, July 26, 46; m 75, Arnold Melstein; c Julia & Sarah. *Educ:* Wellesley Col, BA, 68; Harvard Univ, MA, 71, PhD(psychol), 73. *Prof Exp:* From asst prof to assoc prof, Univ Calif, Santa Cruz, 72-77. *Concurrent Pos:* Vchair, Dept Psychiat, Univ Calif, San Francisco; dir, MacArthur Found Res, Network. *Mem:* Inst Med-Nat Acad Sci; fel Am Psychol Asn; fel Am Psychol Soc; Acad Behav Med Res; Soc Exp Soc Psychol; Soc Behav Med. *Res:* Mechanisms by which socioeconomic status affects health; understanding health-risking behaviors, particularly in relation to reproductive health. *Mailing Add:* 1350 Seventh Ave San Francisco CA 94130. *Fax:* 415-476-7744; *E-Mail:* annadler@itsa.ucsf.edu

ADLER, NORMAN, ANALYTICAL CHEMISTRY, PHYSICAL CHEMISTRY. *Current Pos:* CONSULT, 79- *Personal Data:* b Brooklyn, NY, June 19, 28. *Educ:* Brooklyn Col, BS, 49; Polytech Inst Brooklyn, PhD(analytical chem), 54. *Prof Exp:* Res analyst, Control Div, Merck & Co, Inc, 53 & 55, chief instrumental analyst, 56-64; consult, Arthur D Little, Inc, 64-69; dir radiopharmaceut res & develop, New Eng Nuclear Corp, 70-71, div mgr, Radiopharm Div, 72-75; tech dir & vpres, Clin Assays, Inc, 75-76; vpres, RIA Projs Inc, 77-78. *Mem:* Am Chem Soc; Soc Nuclear Med. *Res:* Pharmaceutical and trace analysis; gas and liquid chromatography; isotope generators; diagnostic parenteral radiopharmaceuticals; in vitro radioactive clinical test kits. *Mailing Add:* 48 Bigelow Ave Watertown MA 02172

ADLER, PHILIP N(ATHAN), METALLURGY, MATERIALS SCIENCE. *Current Pos:* LAB HEAD, GRUMMAN AEROSPACE CORP, BETHPAGE, 69- *Personal Data:* b New York, NY, Feb 20, 35; m 56; c 3. *Educ:* City Col New York, BChE, 56; Stevens Inst Technol, MS, 59; NY Univ, DEngSc(phys metall), 64. *Prof Exp:* Asst res metallurgist, Gen Cable Corp, 56-59; res engr, Radio Corp Am, 59-61; res asst phys metall, NY Univ, 61-64; eng specialist, Gen Tel & Electronics Labs, Inc, 64-68. *Concurrent Pos:* Adj lectr, Polytech Inst Brooklyn, 66-67; adj assoc prof, NY Univ, 69-73. *Mem:* Am Inst Mining, Metall & Petrol Engrs; Am Soc Metals. *Res:* Physical metallurgy of nonferrous metals; high-pressure research; thermodynamics and kinetics of phase transformations; electronic materials; stress corrosion; strengthening mechanisms; hydrogen embrittlement. *Mailing Add:* 40 Flower Lane Roslyn Heights NY 11577

ADLER, RALPH PETER ISAAC, rapid solidification technology, manufacturing sciences, for more information see previous edition

ADLER, RICHARD, VIROLOGY. *Current Pos:* res assoc II, Ann Arbor, 75-77, asst prof biol, 77-83, ASSOC PROF BIOL & MICROBIOL, UNIV MICH, DEARBORN, 83- *Personal Data:* b Lebanon, Pa, Jan 7, 48; m 70; c 4. *Educ:* Pa State Univ, BS, 69, PhD(microbiol), 73. *Prof Exp:* Res fel, Roche Inst Molecular Biol, 73-75. *Concurrent Pos:* Vis assoc prof microbiol, Univ Western Ont, London, Ont, 84. *Mem:* Am Soc Microbiol. *Res:* Regulation of coronavirus replication. *Mailing Add:* Dept Natural Sci Univ Mich 4901 Evergreen Rd Dearborn MI 48128-2406

ADLER, RICHARD H, SURGERY. *Current Pos:* RETIRED. *Personal Data:* b Buffalo, NY, July 2, 22; m 70; c 5. *Educ:* Univ Buffalo, MD, 45; Univ Colo, MS, 55; Am Bd Surg, cert, 51; Am Bd Thoracic Surg, cert, 54. *Prof Exp:* Asst physiol, Sch Med, Univ Buffalo, 49; instr surg, Med Sch, Univ Mich, 50-52; hon registr, Brompton Hosp, London, Eng, 52-53; from asst prof to prof surg, Sch Med, State Univ NY, Buffalo, 55-90, dir thoracic surg, 75-88; dir thoracic surg & attend surgeon, Buffalo Gen Hosp, 57-90. *Concurrent Pos:* Markle scholar, 57-; attend thoracic surgeon, Vet Hosp, Buffalo, 55-; asst attend surgeon, Buffalo Children's Hosp, 56-; consult, Roswell Park Mem Inst, 57-; vis prof surg, Nat Defense Med Ctr, Taipei, Taiwan, 68-69; assoc consult, Erie Co Med Ctr; consult thoracic surg, Millard Fillmore, Brooks Mem & Tri-Co Hosps. *Mem:* AAAS; Am Col Surg; Am Asn Thoracic Surg; Am Heart Asn; Am Col Chest Physicians; Soc Univ Surgeons. *Res:* General and thoracic surgery. *Mailing Add:* 224 Barnstable Dr Wykoff NJ 07481

ADLER, RICHARD JOHN, INTENSE CHARGED PARTICLE BEAMS. *Current Pos:* PRES, NORTH STAR RES CORP, 88- *Personal Data:* b Port Alberno, BC, Feb 1, 55; m 73; c 2. *Educ:* Univ Alta, BSc, 76; Cornell Univ, PhD(elec eng), 80. *Prof Exp:* Res asst, Defence Res Estab Pac, 76, Dept Elec Eng, Cornell Univ, 77-80; tech staff mem, Mission Res Corp, 80-85; staff scientist, Pulse Sci, Inc, 86-87. *Mem:* Am Physiol Soc; Mat Res Soc. *Res:* Experimental physics of intense beams in vacuum, including magnetized beams, induction accelerators, electron and ion sources; collective acceleration theories of macroscopic beam behavior; plasma physics; high power electronics. *Mailing Add:* North Star Res Corp 4421 McLeod NE Suite A Albuquerque NM 87109

ADLER, ROBERT, ULTRASONICS, ELECTRONOPTICS. *Current Pos:* TECH CONSULT, 82- *Personal Data:* b Vienna, Austria, Dec 4, 13; nat US; wid. *Educ:* Univ Vienna, PhD(physics), 37. *Honors & Awards:* Edison Medal, Inst Elec & Electronics Engrs, 80. *Prof Exp:* Asst to patent atty, Vienna, Austria, 37-38; in charge lab, Sci Acoust, Ltd, London, 39-40 & Assoc Res, Inc, Chicago, 40-41; res engr, Zenith Radio Corp, 41-52, assoc dir res, 52-63, vpres res, 63-77; dir res, Extel Corp, 78-82. *Concurrent Pos:* Vis prof, Univ Ill, Urbana, 78; regent lectr, Univ Calif, Santa Barbara, 85. *Mem:* Nat Acad Eng; AAAS; fel Inst Elec & Electronics Engrs. *Res:* Electron beam parametric amplifiers; opto-acoustic interaction devices; surface wave touch systems; image display devices; ultrasonic devices. *Mailing Add:* 327 Latrobe Ave Northfield IL 60093. *Fax:* 708-450-8398

ADLER, ROBERT ALAN, INTERNAL MEDICINE, ENDOCRINOLOGY. *Current Pos:* assoc prof med endocrinol, 84-93, PROF INTERNAL MED, DIV ENDOCRINOL, MED COL, VA, 93- *Personal Data:* b Somerville, NJ, Jan 11, 45; m 72, Anne J Kruger; c Joel S & Andrew E. *Educ:* Johns Hopkins Univ, BA, 67, MD, 70. *Prof Exp:* Clin investr & asst chief endocrinol, Fitzsimons Army Med Ctr, 74-76; from asst prof to assoc prof med endocrinol, Dartmouth Med Sch, 76-84. *Concurrent Pos:* Clin & res fel, Mass Gen Hosp, 72-73 & Walter Reed Army Med Ctr, 73-74; clin instr med, Univ Colo Med Sch, 75-76; staff physician, Mary Hitchcock Mem Hosp, 76-84; consult endocrinol, Vet Admin Hosp, White River Jct, Vt, 78-84; chief endocrinol & metabol, McGuire Vet Admin Med Ctr, Richmond, Va, 84- *Mem:* Endocrine Soc; Am Soc Bone & Mineral Res; Am Fedn Clin Res; Pituitary Soc; fel Am Col Physicians; Southern Soc Clin Invest. *Res:* Pituitary physiology, pathology and biochemistry; hormonal and skeletal changes in aging men. *Mailing Add:* McGuire Vet Admin Med Ctr 1201 Broad Rock Blvd Richmond VA 23249. *Fax:* 804-675-5425; *E-Mail:* radler@gems.yco.edu

ADLER, ROBERT FREDERICK, METEOROLOGY. *Current Pos:* METEOROLOGIST, GODDARD SPACE FLIGHT CTR, NASA, 74- *Personal Data:* b West Reading, Pa, Jan 19, 44; m 72; c 2. *Educ:* Pa State Univ, BS, 65, MS, 67; Colo State Univ, PhD(atmospheric sci), 74. *Prof Exp:* Res meteorologist, Navy Weather Res Fac, Dept of Defense, 67-71. *Concurrent Pos:* Res assoc meteorol, Colo State Univ, 74. *Mem:* Am Meteorol Soc. *Res:* Dynamics and physics of intense atmospheric convection using satellite and aircraft remote sensing; application to detection of severe thunderstorms and to precipitation estimation from satellite observations. *Mailing Add:* 12532 Woodridge Lane Highland MD 20777

ADLER, ROBERT GARBER, ANALYTICAL CHEMISTRY. *Current Pos:* analytical chemist, Occup Safety & Health Admin, US Dept Labor, Utah, 72-74, dir, Div Qual Control, 74-86, METHODS DEVELOP CHEMIST, OCCUP SAFETY & HEALTH ADMIN, US DEPT LABOR, UTAH, 86- *Personal Data:* b Upland, Calif, July 11, 29; m 63, Marilyn Canfield; c Charles R, Paul D & Amelia M (Scott). *Educ:* Calif Inst Technol, BSc, 51; Univ Southern Calif, MSc, 55; Univ Calif, Riverside, PhD(inorg chem), 68; Am Bd Inst Hyg, Cert Chem Aspects of Indust Hyg. *Prof Exp:* Sr chemist, Whittier Res Lab, Am Potash & Chem Corp, 57-63; chemist, Sci Ctr, NAm Aviation, Inc, Calif, 63-64; asst prof chem, Bethel Col, Kans, 68-71. *Mem:* Am Chem Soc; Am Indust Hyg Asn; Am Conf Govt Indust Hygienists. *Res:* Boron hydrides, especially preparations and properties; improvement of analytical chemical techniques for industrial hygiene analyses. *Mailing Add:* 3947 S 3075 E Salt Lake City UT 84124-2015

ADLER, RONALD JOHN, THEORETICAL PHYSICS, GENERAL PHYSICS. *Current Pos:* PROF PHYSICS, SAN FRANCISCO STATE UNIV, 88- *Personal Data:* b Pittsburgh, Pa, Apr 17, 37. *Educ:* Carnegie Mellon Univ, BS, 59; Stanford Univ, PhD(physics), 65. *Prof Exp:* Res asst prof physics, Univ Wash, 64-66; res assoc, Univ Colo, 66-67; asst prof, Va Polytech Inst, 67-70; assoc prof, Am Univ, 70-73; prof physics, Fed Univ Pernambuco, Brazil, 74-77; sr scientist, Lockheed Palo Alto Lab, 79-93. *Concurrent Pos:* mem, Inst Adv Study, 73-74; vis scholar, Stanford Univ. *Mem:* Am Phys Soc; fel Brit Interplanetary Soc. *Res:* High energy theory; general relativity; mathematical physics. *Mailing Add:* 20 Athlone Ct Menlo Park CA 94026. *E-Mail:* adler@stars.sfsu.edu

ADLER, ROY LEE, MATHEMATICS. *Current Pos:* RES STAFF MEM MATH, INT BUS MACH CORP, 60- *Personal Data:* b Newark, NJ, Feb 22, 31; m 53; c 2. *Educ:* Yale Univ, BS, 52; Columbia Univ, AM, 54; Yale Univ, PhD(math), 61. *Prof Exp:* Jr engr, Nat Union Radio, 52 & Bendix Aviation Corp, 53-54. *Concurrent Pos:* Adj prof, Columbia Univ, 63-65 & Yeshiva Univ, 65-66; vis prof, Stanford Univ, 70- *Mem:* Am Math Soc; Math Asn Am; Sigma Xi. *Res:* Ergodic theory; classification and structure problems of dynamical systems. *Mailing Add:* 7 Killington St Chappaqua NY 10514-2307

ADLER, RUBEN, SURVIVAL & DIFFERENTIATION OF PHOTORECEPTORS. *Current Pos:* assoc prof neurosci & ophthal, 83-93, ARNALL PATZ DISTINGUISHED PROF OPHTHAL & PROF NEUROSCI, SCH MED, JOHNS HOPKINS UNIV, 93- *Personal Data:* b Los Toldos, Argentina, Nov 10, 40; m, Marta; c Gabriel, Pablo & Fernando. *Educ:* Univ Buenos Aires, MD, 63. *Prof Exp:* Asst res biologist, Univ Calif, San Diego, 78-83. *Mem:* Neurosci Soc; Am Soc Cell Biol; Asn Res Vision & Ophthal. *Mailing Add:* Dept Ophthal Johns Hopkins Univ Sch Med 600 N Wolfe St Maumenee 519 Baltimore MD 21287-9257. *Fax:* 410-955-0749; *E-Mail:* radler@ishtar.med.jhu.edu

ADLER, SANFORD CHARLES, OPERATIONS RESEARCH, SAFETY ENGINEERING. *Current Pos:* OPERS RES ANALYST, DEPT JUSTICE, 85- *Personal Data:* b Yonkers, NY, Jan 19, 40; m 64, Joan T; c 1. *Educ:* NY Univ, BS, 63, MS, 65, MS, 71. *Prof Exp:* Sci programmer comput appln physics, Nevis Cyclotron Labs, 63-64; res asst & asst res scientist ergonomics, Sch Eng & Sci, NY Univ, 64-66; systs engr comput systs, Int Bus Mach Corp, 66-68; prof mgt sci, Indust Col Armed Forces, 68-70; opers res analyst safety & data processing, Nat Bur Stand, 70-84. *Mem:* AAAS. *Res:* Health and safety; accessibility of buildings to the disabled; ergonomics; risk analysis. *Mailing Add:* 14238 Briarwood Terr Rockville MD 20853

ADLER, SEYMOUR JACOB, ANALYTICAL CHEMISTRY. *Current Pos:* RETIRED. *Personal Data:* b New York, NY, May 12, 18; m 47; c 3. *Educ:* Cooper Union, BChE, 41; Columbia Univ, MA, 50, PhD(chem), 54. *Prof Exp:* Analytical chemist, Columbia Mineral Beneficiation Lab, 53-56, Brookhaven Nat Lab, 56-57 & Radio Corp Am, NJ, 57-69; asst prof chem, Trenton State Col, 70-88. *Concurrent Pos:* Adj prof, Trenton State Col, 88- *Mem:* Am Chem Soc. *Res:* Trace analysis; spectrophotometry; radio-chemistry; emission spectrography; solvent extraction; ion exchange. *Mailing Add:* 287 Walnut Lane Princeton NJ 08540-3459

ADLER, SOLOMON STANLEY, HEMATOLOGY, ONCOLOGY. *Current Pos:* CHIEF, SPEC MORPHOL LAB, SECT HEMAT, PRESBY-ST LUKE'S MED CTR, 76- *Personal Data:* b New York, NY, May 26, 45; m 67; c 5. *Educ:* City Col New York, BS, 66; Albert Einstein Col Med, MD, 70. *Prof Exp:* Instr med, 73-75, chief, Spec Hemat Lab, 74-77, asst prof to assoc prof med, Rush Med Col, 73-95. *Concurrent Pos:* Adj attend physician, Presby-St Luke's Hosp, 74-75, asst attend physician, 75-78, assoc attend physician, 78-82; NIH res fel, Nat Cancer Inst, 74-77, sr attend physician, 82- *Mem:* Fel Am Col Physicians; Am Soc Clin Oncol; Am Fedn Clin Res; Am Soc Hematol. *Res:* Hemopoiesis in vitro and hemopoietic microenvironment; bone marrow transplantation. *Mailing Add:* Rush-Presby-St Lukes Med 1753 W Congress Chicago IL 60612

ADLER, STEPHEN FRED, INDUSTRIAL CHEMISTRY. *Current Pos:* dir, 87-90, SITE SERV DIR, DOBBS FERRY RES CTR, AKZO CHEMICALS INC, 90- *Personal Data:* b Berlin, Ger, Sept 27, 30; nat US; m 51, Judith; c Deborah & Barbara. *Educ:* Roosevelt Univ, BS, 51; Northwestern Univ, MS, 53, PhD(inorg chem), 54. *Prof Exp:* Res chemist, Am Cyanamid Co, 54-60, group leader, 60-69; sect mgr, Stauffer Chem Co, 68-70, mgr chem res dept, 70-76, asst dir, 76-79, dir, Eastern Res Ctr, 79-87. *Mem:* Am Chem Soc; Asn Res Dirs (pres, 91-92). *Res:* Information technology, information service. *Mailing Add:* 16 Grey Hollow Rd Norwalk CT 06850. *Fax:* 914-693-1059

ADLER, STEPHEN L, THEORETICAL HIGH ENERGY PHYSICS. *Current Pos:* mem, 66-69, prof theoret physics, 69-79, ALBERT EINSTEIN PROF, INST ADVAN STUDY, PRINCETON, NJ, 79- *Personal Data:* b New York, NY, Nov 30, 39; m 95, Sarah Catherine Brett-Smith; c Jessica Wendy, Victoria Stephanie & Anthony Curtis. *Educ:* Harvard Univ, AB, 61; Princeton Univ, PhD(physics), 64. *Honors & Awards:* JJ Sakurai Prize, Am Phys Soc, 88. *Prof Exp:* Jr fel, Soc Fel, Harvard Univ, 64-66. *Mem:* Nat Acad Sci; fel Am Phys Soc; fel Am Acad Arts & Sci; fel AAAS. *Res:* Theoretical research on problems in elementary particle physics and quantum field theory. *Mailing Add:* 287A Nassau St Princeton NJ 08540. *Fax:* 609-924-8399; *E-Mail:* adler@ias.edu

ADLER, WILLIAM, CLINICAL IMMUNOLOGY. *Current Pos:* CHIEF CLIN IMMUNOL, NIA, NIH, BALTIMORE, MD, 74- *Personal Data:* b Buffalo, NY, Sept 3, 39. *Educ:* Harvard Univ, AB, 61; State Univ NY, Buffalo, MD, 65. *Prof Exp:* Asst prof pediat & path, Univ Fla, 68-70; major MRO Corp, US Army, 70-72. *Concurrent Pos:* Assoc prof pediat, Sch Med, Johns Hopkins Univ. *Mem:* Am Asn Immunol; Soc Pediat Res; Geront Soc Am; Clin Immunol Soc. *Res:* Investigation of the immunodeficiencies associated with ageing and secondary to the HIV infection and the use of abused drugs. *Mailing Add:* Gerontol Res Ctr Nat Inst Aging NIH Baltimore MD 21224-2735. *Fax:* 410-558-8284

ADLER, WILLIAM FRED, PARTICULATE EROSION OF MATERIALS, ENGINEERING MECHANICS. *Current Pos:* mgr, Mat Sci Sect, 83-91, DIR, MAT SCI OPERS, GEN RES CORP, 91- *Personal Data:* b Chicago, Ill, Aug 19, 37; m 58; c 1. *Educ:* Ill Inst Technol, BS, 58, MS, 61; Columbia Univ, PhD(eng mech), 65. *Prof Exp:* Teaching asst, Ill Inst Technol, 58-61; sr res engr, Denver Div, Martin-Marietta Corp, 61-62; sr res scientist, Columbus Labs, Battelle Mem Inst, 65-71; prin res scientist, Bell Aerospace Co, 71-76; dir, Mat Sci Sect, Effects Technol, Inc, 76-79, assoc mgr, 79-81, mgr mat group, 81-82. *Concurrent Pos:* Chmn, Nat Mat Adv Bd Comt, Nat Acad Sci, 76-77; Int adv, Fifth Int Conf, 79, Sixth Int Conf, 83 & Seventh Int Conf, Erosion by Liquid & Solid Impact, Cambridge, UK, 87. *Mem:* Am Ceramic Soc; Am Soc Testing & Mat; Soc Eng Sci; Sigma Xi. *Res:* Application of continuum mechanical to problems in technology; theoretical and experimental studies in erosion of material surfaces by solid and fluid particles; fracture mechanics; development of testing procedures for evaluating the dynamic response of materials; non-destructive evaluation of materials and structures; structural analysis; microstructural analysis of materials. *Mailing Add:* GRC Int 5383 Hollister Ave Santa Barbara CA 93111

ADLERSTEIN, MICHAEL GENE, ELECTRONIC DEVICES. *Current Pos:* Sr scientist, 71-80, prin scientist, 80-87, CONSULT SCIENTIST, RES DIV, RAYTHEON CO, 87- *Personal Data:* b New York, NY. *Educ:* Polytech Inst, Brooklyn, BS, 66, MS, 66; Harvard Univ, SM, 71, PhD(appl physics), 71. *Concurrent Pos:* Assoc ed, Inst Elec & Electronics Engrs Electron Divices, 81-; Conf tech Comt, Cornell Univ. *Mem:* Am Phys Soc; sr mem Inst Elec & Electronics Engrs; Sigma Xi. *Res:* Microwave semiconductor devices; impact avalanche and transit time diodes and components for frequencies up to millimeter waves; gallium arsenide field effect transistors; millimeter wave monolithic integrated circuits; heterojunction bipolar transistors. *Mailing Add:* Raytheon Advan Device Ctr 362 Lowell St Andover MA 01810

ADLOF, RICHARD OTTO, LIPIDS. *Current Pos:* RES CHEMIST, NAT CTR AGR UTIL RES, AGR RES SERV, USDA, 69- *Personal Data:* b Vienna, Austria, Dec 14, 47; US citizen; m 76, Deborah L Ingram; c Jonathan R & Jessica L. *Educ:* Wabash Col, BS, 70; La State Univ, MS, 75. *Mem:* Am Chem Soc; Am Oil Chemists Soc; AAAS; Int Isotope Soc; Chem Heritage Found. *Res:* Synthesis of deuterium-labelled fats; utilization of deuterium-labelled fats to study the metabolism of fatty acids and fatty acid isomers in humans; lipid and lipoprotein fractionation and analysis. *Mailing Add:* USDA Nat Ctr Agr Util Res 1815 N University St Peoria IL 61604. *Fax:* 309-681-6679; *E-Mail:* adlofro@ncaur1.ncaur.gov

ADMAN, ELINOR THOMSON, BIOLOGICAL STRUCTURE. *Current Pos:* Sr fel crystallog, Univ Wash, 67-71, res assoc, 71-77, from res asst prof to res assoc prof, 77-90, RES PROF BIOL STRUCT, UNIV WASH, 90- *Personal Data:* b New York, NY, Jan 3, 41; c 2. *Educ:* Col Wooster, BA, 62; Brandeis Univ, MA, 64, PhD(phys chem), 67. *Concurrent Pos:* Mem, Metallobiochem Study Sect, NIH, 87-91 & US Nat Comt Crystallog, 90-95; adj res prof biochem, Univ Wash, 90- *Mem:* Fel AAAS; Am Crystallog Asn (pres, 94). *Res:* Determination and refinement of protein structures, iron-sulfur proteins, blue copper proteins; nitrite reductase. *Mailing Add:* Dept Biol Struct Box 357420 Univ Wash Seattle WA 98195-7420

ADNEY, JOSEPH ELLIOTT, JR, MATHEMATICS. *Current Pos:* assoc prof, 64-69, PROF MATH, MICH STATE UNIV, 69-, CHMN DEPT, 74- *Personal Data:* b DeLand, Fla, Aug 20, 23; m 52; c 2. *Educ:* Stetson Univ, BS, 44; Ohio State Univ, MA, 49, PhD(math), 54. *Prof Exp:* Assoc, Res Found, Ohio State Univ, 52-54, instr math, 54-55; asst prof, Purdue Univ, 55-64. *Concurrent Pos:* Consult, US Air Force, 57, 59. *Mem:* Am Math Soc. *Res:* Abstract algebra; ground theory. *Mailing Add:* 359 Marsh Pt Circle St Augustine FL 32084-5864

ADOLPH, ALAN ROBERT, NEUROPHYSIOLOGY. *Current Pos:* HEAD NEUROSCI LAB, EYE RES INST OF RETINA FOUND, 64- *Personal Data:* b New York, NY, Feb 5, 32; m 57; c 3. *Educ:* Rensselaer Polytech Inst, BEE, 53; Mass Inst Technol, SM, 57; Rockefeller Inst, PhD(biol sci), 63. *Prof Exp:* Sr scientist, Bolt, Beranek & Newman, Inc, 63-64. *Concurrent Pos:* Consult, Lockheed Missile & Space Co Labs, 58-59 & Stanford Res Inst, 62. *Mem:* Am Physiol Soc; Soc Neurosci; Asn Res Vision & Ophthal. *Res:* Neurophysiology and pharmacology of the retina; electrophysiology of sensory neurons; marine neurobiology; mathematical biophysics; visual behavior; psychophysiology of vision. *Mailing Add:* Schepens Eye Res Inst 20 Staniford St Boston MA 02114

ADOLPH, HORST GUENTER, ORGANIC CHEMISTRY. *Current Pos:* RES CHEMIST, US NAVAL SURFACE WARFARE CTR, 61- *Personal Data:* b Pforzheim, Ger, Nov 27, 32; m 60; c 2. *Educ:* Univ Tuebingen, Dr rer nat, 59. *Prof Exp:* Res asst, Inst Appl Chem & asst to ed, Houben-Weyl, Univ Tubingen, 61. *Mem:* Am Chem Soc. *Res:* Synthetic organic chemistry; reaction mechanisms; spectroscopy; chemistry of explosives; polymer chemistry. *Mailing Add:* 104 Brenda Ct Warrenton VA 20186

ADOLPH, KENNETH WILLIAM, GENE STRUCTURE & REGULATION, ELECTRON MICROSCOPY. *Current Pos:* asst prof, 78-84, ASSOC PROF, DEPT BIOCHEM, MED SCH, UNIV MINN, MINNEAPOLIS, 84- *Personal Data:* b Oldham, Eng, Dec 11, 44; US citizen. *Educ:* Univ Wis, Milwaukee, BS, 66, MS, 67; Univ Chicago, PhD(biophysics), 72. *Prof Exp:* Fel, Lab Molecular Biol, Med Res Coun, Eng, 73-74, Rosenstiel Basic Med Sci Res Ctr, Brandeis Univ, 75, & Dept Biochem Sci, Princeton Univ, 76-78. *Concurrent Pos:* Vis scientist, Dept Biochem, Univ Wash, Seattle, 93-94. *Mem:* Am Soc Biochem & Molecular Biol. *Res:* Gene structure and regulation; electron microscopy and image analysis of chromosome organization; role of non-histone proteins; biological assembly. *Mailing Add:* Dept Biochem Med Sch 4-225 Millard Hall Univ Minn 435 Delaware St SE Minneapolis MN 55455. *Fax:* 612-625-2163

ADOLPH, ROBERT J, INTERNAL MEDICINE. *Current Pos:* from asst prof to assoc prof, 62-70, PROF MED, COL MED, UNIV CINCINNATI, 70- *Personal Data:* b Chicago, Ill, Dec 12, 27; m 58; c 3. *Educ:* Univ Ill, MD, 52; Am Bd Internal Med, cert, 63; Am Bd Cardiovasc Dis, dipl. *Prof Exp:* Asst prof med, Univ Ill, 59-60. *Concurrent Pos:* Am Heart Asn res fel, Col Med, Univ Ill, 56-58; NIH res fel physiol & biophys, Sch Med, Univ Wash, 60-62; mem staff, Dept Internal Med, Cardiac Res Lab, Cincinnati Gen Hosp, 62-, dir lab, 70-; mem med adv bd, Sect on Circulation & Coun Clin Cardiol, Am Heart Asn. *Mem:* Am Fedn Clin Res; Am Col Cardiol. *Res:* Cardio-vascular physiology and investigation; myocardial contractility; effect of digitalis on myocardial electrolytes; high out-put states; cardiac pacing; biomedical engineering developments. *Mailing Add:* Cardiac Res Lab Rm 3407 Med Sci Bldg Univ Cincinati Col Med Cincinnati OH 45267

ADOMIAN, GEORGE, NONLINEAR STOCHASTIC DYNAMICAL SYSTEMS. *Current Pos:* CHIEF SCIENTIST, GEN ANALYTICS CORP, 90- *Personal Data:* b Buffalo, NY; m 56, Corinne Hodgson; c 4. *Educ:* Univ Mich, BS, MS; Univ Calif, Los Angeles, PhD(theoret physics), 63. *Honors & Awards:* Richard E Bellman Prize, 89. *Prof Exp:* Res engr, Gen Elec Co, 48-49; instr math, Wayne State Univ, 51-52; res assoc, Univ Mich, 52-53; sr scientist, Hughes Aircraft Co, 53-64; prof math & res prof eng, Pa State Univ, 64-66; distinguished prof math & dir, Ctr Appl Math, Univ Ga, 66-90. *Concurrent Pos:* Consult govt & indust. *Mem:* Fel AAAS; Am Phys Soc; Am Math Soc; sr mem Inst Elec & Electronics Engrs; Soc Indust & Appl Math. *Res:* Nonlinear stochastic partial differential equations and stochastic operator theory; theoretical physics and engineering applications. *Mailing Add:* Gen Analytics Corp 155 Clyde Rd Athens GA 30605-3813

ADOMIAN, GERALD E, CARDIAC TISSUE, NERVE TISSUE. *Current Pos:* ASSOC PROF MED & DIR FUNCTIONAL MORPHOLOGY, RES & EDUC INST, HARBOR-UCLA MED CTR, 75- *Educ:* Univ Calif, Los Angeles, PhD(biol), 80. *Mailing Add:* Med-Cardiovasc Harbor Univ Calif Los Angeles Med Ctr 1124 W Carson St Torrance CA 90502-2006

ADORANTE, JOSEPH S, MEMBRANE TRANSPORT, CELLULAR PHYSIOLOGY. *Current Pos:* SCIENTIST, DEPT BIOL SCI & MEMBRANE TRANSPORT, ALLERGAN PHARMACEUT, 90- *Personal Data:* b Bronx, NY, Mar 12, 49. *Educ:* NY Inst Technol, BS, 72; Univ San Francisco, MS, 75; Univ Calif, Berkeley, PhD(physiol), 82. *Prof Exp:* Fel, Univ Calif, Davis, 83-86 & Univ Calif, Berkeley, 86-90. *Mem:* Biophys Soc; Am Physiol Soc. *Mailing Add:* Dept Biol & Sci Allergan Pharmaceut 2525 Dupont Dr Irvine CA 92715

ADOVASIO, JAMES MICHAEL, GEOARCHAEOLOGY, LATE PLEISTOCENE HUMAN ADAPTATIONS. *Current Pos:* PROF ANTHROP, ARCHAEOL & GEOL, MERCYHURST COL, 90-; DIR, MERCYHURST ARCHAEOL INST, 90- *Personal Data:* b Youngstown, Ohio, Feb 17, 44; wid. *Educ:* Univ Ariz, BA, 65; Univ Utah, PhD(anthrop), 70. *Hon Degrees:* DSc, Washington & Jefferson Univ, 83. *Prof Exp:* Instr anthrop, Youngstown State Univ, 66-68, asst prof, 70-71; fel, Smithsonian Inst, 71-72; from asst prof to assoc prof anthrop, Univ Pittsburgh, 72-79, prof, 79-90; exec dir, Archaeol Res Prog, Southern Methodist Univ, 90-93. *Concurrent Pos:* Adj assoc prof anthrop, Youngstown State Univ, 76-78; dir cult resource mgt, Univ Pittsburgh, 76-89, prof Latin Am Studies, 79-90, chmn, Dept Anthrop, 80-89, prof geol & planetary sci, 85-90; prin investr, 70-; res assoc, Smithsonian Inst, 74-, Carnegie Mus, 78- *Mem:* Am Anthrop Asn; Am Quaternary Asn; Soc Am Anthrop; NY Acad Sci; Am Sch Orient Res; Sigma Xi. *Res:* Archaeological field and laboratory methodology, prehistoric technology (especially textiles, basketry and related products), ice-age adaptations and holocene adaptations to arid lands; geoarchaeology and the application of so-called hard science methods, techniques and analyses to archaeological problems. *Mailing Add:* 4676 White Pine Dr Erie PA 16506-1546. *Fax:* 814-824-2594

ADRAGNA, NORMA C, ION TRANSPORT. *Current Pos:* ASSOC PROF PHARMACOL, WRIGHT STATE UNIV, 85- *Personal Data:* b Cordoba, Arg. *Educ:* Nat Univ Cordoba, BCh, 69, PhD(biophys), 73. *Honors & Awards:* John Lawrence Mem Award, Am Heart Asn, 86. *Prof Exp:* Teaching asst, physico-chem, Nat Univ Cordoba, 66-69; res fel, Nat Res Coun Arg, 70-74; tech asst, biomed phys, Nat Univ Buenos Aires, Arg, 74-76; int res fel, NIH Fogarty Int Ctr, 77-79; res assoc biomed phys, Harvard Univ, 79-82; med res asst prof, Duke Univ, 82-85. *Concurrent Pos:* Lab asst, Nat Univ Cordoba, Arg, 69; res assoc, Nat Univ Buenos Aires, Arg, 74-76; vis prof, biomed phys, Ctr Nuclear Studies, Saclay, France, 76-77. *Mem:* Biophys Soc; Am Physiol Soc; Soc Gen Physiologists. *Res:* Studies of ion and water transport across artificial and biological membranes; red cells, cultured endothelial cells and frog bladder; the relationship between ion transport and exercise training and/or essential hypertension. *Mailing Add:* Dept Pharmacol/Toxicol Wright State Univ Dayton OH 45435-0002

ADRIAN, ALAN PATRICK, CHEMISTRY, MANAGEMENT OF PAPER SCIENCE & TECHNOLOGY APPLICATION. *Current Pos:* RETIRED. *Personal Data:* b Kaukauna, Wis, Feb 13, 16; m 42, Verna La Plante; c Patricia (Schmidtke) & Judith (Stadler). *Educ:* Lawrence Univ, AB, 38, MS, 40, PhD(paper chem & technol), 42. *Prof Exp:* Develop chemist, Detroit Sulphite Pulp & Paper Co, 42-45, tech dir, 45-50, oper mgr, 50-58; chief bond papers & allied prods, Res & Develop, Kimberly Clark Corp, 58-60, dir bus paper mfg, 60-62, prod mgr, Neenah Paper Div, 62-70, opers & develop mgr, 70-81. *Mem:* Am Chem Soc; Am Tech Asn Pulp & Paper Indust; Paper Indust Mgt Asn. *Res:* Chemistry and technology of pulp and paper; evaluating the optical constants of pigments in paper; resin application; specialty papers. *Mailing Add:* 1209 Nicolet Circle Appleton WI 54915

ADRIAN, ERLE KEYS, JR, ANATOMY. *Current Pos:* assoc prof, 69-74, actg chmn, Dept Anat, 80-81, PROF ANAT, HEALTH SCI CTR, UNIV TEX, SAN ANTONIO, 74-, DEPT CHMN, 81- *Personal Data:* b Temple, Tex, Apr 18, 36; m 62, Gwendolyn M Scharlach; c Sabrina L, E Paul & Don A. *Educ:* Rice Inst, BA, 58; Univ Tex, Galveston, MA, 61, PhD(anat), 67; Harvard Med Sch, MD, 63. *Prof Exp:* Res asst anat, Med Br, Univ Tex, 59-60, from instr to assoc prof, Galveston, 63-69. *Mem:* Am Asn Anat; Am Asn Clin Anat. *Res:* Neuropathology; gerontology. *Mailing Add:* Dept Cellular & Struct Biol Health Sci Ctr Univ Tex San Antonio TX 78284. *Fax:* 210-567-3803; *E-Mail:* adrian@uthscsa.edu

ADRIAN, FRANK JOHN, PHYSICAL CHEMISTRY, SOLID STATE PHYSICS. *Current Pos:* RETIRED. *Personal Data:* b Brooklyn, NY, Oct 7, 29; m 69; c 2. *Educ:* Cath Univ Am, AB, 51; Cornell Univ, PhD(phys chem), 55. *Honors & Awards:* Humboldt Sr Res Award, 94. *Prof Exp:* Prin prof staff chemist, Appl Physics Lab, Johns Hopkins Univ, 55-94; vis prof phys chem III, TH-Damstadt, Ger, 94-95. *Concurrent Pos:* Assoc ed, J Chem Physics, 75-78; adj prof, Chem Dept, Queen's Univ, Kingston, Can, 84-95. *Mem:* Fel Am Phys Soc. *Res:* Magnetic and nuclear quadrupole resonance; structure of molecules, free radicals and paramagnetic imperfections in solids; photochemistry; chemically induced magnetic polarization; surface enhanced Raman scattering; high-temperature superconductivity. *Mailing Add:* 17716 Queen Elizabeth Dr Olney MD 20832

ADRIAN, RONALD JOHN, TURBULENT FLOW, LASER VELOCIMETRY. *Current Pos:* from asst prof to assoc prof, 72-81, PROF THEORET & APPL MECH, UNIV ILL, URBANA-CHAMPAIGN, 81- *Personal Data:* b Minneapolis, Minn, June 16, 45; m 69; c 3. *Educ:* Univ Minn, BME, 67, MS, 69; Cambridge Univ, PhD(physics), 72. *Hon Degrees:* Dr, Inst Sup Teenieu, Lisbon, 96. *Honors & Awards:* A T Colwell Award, 90 & 91; D C Drucker Award, 89. *Prof Exp:* Engr, Boeing Co, Seattle, 67. *Mem:* Nat Acad Eng; Am Phys Soc; Am Optical Soc; Am Inst Aeronaut & Astronaut; Laser Inst Am; Am Soc Mech Engrs. *Res:* Experimental study of turbulent shear flows and turbulent thermal convection; scientific instruments for measurement of fluid velocity fields. *Mailing Add:* Dept Theoret & Appl Mech Univ Ill 216 Talbot Lab 104 S Wright St Urbana IL 61801

ADRIAN, THOMAS E, PHYSIOLOGY, BIOCHEMISTRY. *Current Pos:* PROF PHYSIOL & BIOCHEM, MED SCH, CREIGHTON UNIV, OMAHA, 88-, DIV HEAD PHYSIOL, DEPT BIOMED SCI, 91- *Personal Data:* b London, UK, Apr 26, 50; c 2. *Educ:* Inst Biol, MIBiol, 74; Brunel Univ, MSc, 76; Univ London, PhD(biochem), 80; MRCPath, 84. *Prof Exp:* Sr technician, Dept Chem Path, Devonport Lab, London, 71-73, chief technician, 73-74; res biochemist, Gastrointestinal Unit, Greenwich Dist Hosp, Eng, 74-75; res officer, Dept Med, Royal Postgrad Med Sch, Hammersmith Hosp, London, 75-80, sr res officer & lectr, 80-85; assoc res scientist surg, Sch Med, Yale Univ, 85-87, res scientist & assoc prof, 87-88. *Concurrent Pos:* Dir, Gastrointestinal Surg Res Lab, Vet Admin Med Ctr, West Haven, Conn, 85-88; prin investr, Am Inst Cancer Res, 89-91, NIH, 90-93 & 91-92, Nat Dairy Coun, 91-93 & Nat Livestock & Meat Bd, 91-92; mem, Rev Comt Gastrointestinal Core Ctr Grants, Nat Inst Diabetes & Digestive Kidney Dis, NIH, 90. *Mem:* Royal Col Pathologists; Asn Clin Chem; Endocrine Soc; Am Physiol Soc; Am Gastroenterol Soc; Brit Diabetic Asn; Am Pancreatic Asn; Int Asn Pancreatology. *Res:* Cholecystokinin effect on pancreatic growth and tumors; hormonal mechanism of potentiation of pancreatic cancer by polyunsaturated rather than saturated dietary fat; early diagnosis of pancreatic cancer; author of more than 450 technical publications. *Mailing Add:* Dept Physiol Med Sch Creighton Univ 2500 California Plaza Omaha NE 68178

ADRION, WILLIAM RICHARDS, TECHNOLOGY TRANSFER, SOFTWARE ENGINEERING. *Current Pos:* PROF COMPUT SCI, UNIV MASS, AMHERST, 86- *Personal Data:* b Alexandria, La, Nov 2, 43; m 71, Jacqueline Cotner; c Emily R & Carrie B. *Educ:* Cornell Univ, BS, 66, MEE, 67; Univ Tex, Austin, PhD(elec eng & comput sci), 71. *Honors & Awards:* Distinguished Serv Award, Am Comput Mach. *Prof Exp:* Sr res engr, 67-71, asst prof elec eng, Electronic Res Ctr, Univ Tex, Austin, 71-72; res engr, Electron Data Processing, Honeywell, Inc, 69-79; asst prof & group chmn, elec & comput engr, Ore State Univ, 72-78; prog dir theoret comput sci, NSF, 76-78; mgr, Software Eng Group, Nat Bur Stand, 78-80; prog dir spec proj comput sci, 80-82, coord exp res, 82-85, dep div dir comput res, 85-86; chief scientist, Comp Int Sci & Engr, NSF, 86. *Concurrent Pos:* Consult, Electron Data Processing Technol Ctr, Honeywell, Inc, 69-70, Tektronix, Inc, 73-74, Appl Theory Assocs, 73-78, Radio Free Europe & Radio Liberty, 81, Lawrence Livermore Labs, 85-87, Superconductivity Super Collider Lab, 90-91; chmn, Asn Comput Mach/SIGSoft, 85-91; chmn comput sci, Univ Mass, 86-95; dir, Comput Res Assoc, 87-; chair NSF adv panel for CISE/CDA, 89-91; chmn bd & proes ACSIOM, Inc ACSIOM, Lab, 89-; chair NSF adv panel for CISE/CDA, 89-91; vis prof, Univ Calif, 83-84 & Univ Paris Sud, 91-92; adj prof, Am Univ, 78-79, George Washington Univ, 79-80 & Georgetown Univ, 84-86. *Mem:* Fel AAAS; fel Asn Comput Mach; Inst Elec & Electronics Engrs; NY Acad Sci; Soc Indust & Appl Math; Sigma Xi. *Res:* Programming systems and software engineering with particular emphasis on programming environments and program analysis and testing; appropriate mechanisms for technology transfer and diffusion. *Mailing Add:* LGRC 307 Univ Mass Box 34610 Amherst MA 01003-4610. *Fax:* 413-545-3729; *E-Mail:* adrion@cs.umass.edu

ADROUNIE, V HARRY, PUBLIC & ENVIRONMENTAL HEALTH, EDUCATIONAL ADMINISTRATION. *Current Pos:* RETIRED. *Personal Data:* b Battle Creek, Mich, Apr 29, 15; m 43, 81, Agnes M Slone; c H Michael, V Patrick & Charles Ray. *Educ:* St Ambrose Univ, BS, 40, BA, 59; Am Bd Indust Hyg, dipl, 62; Am Acad Sanitarians, cert sanit, 67; Western States Univ Prof Studies, MS & PhD(environ health pub health), 84. *Honors & Awards:* Mangold Award, Nat Environ Health Asn, 63. *Prof Exp:* Chief labs & chief prev med, Med Serv Corps, USAF, 50-51, chief, Planning & Test Br, Field Test & Meteorol Div, 51-52, mem staff, Biol & Chem Spec Weapons Br & bioenviron specialist, Off Inspector Gen, 53-56, environ med officer, Off Surgeon Gen, 57-61, comdr, Detachment 10, 1st Aeromed Transport Group, 61-63; vis lectr environ health, Sch Pub Health, Am Univ Beirut, 63-64, vis assoc prof & actg chmn dept, 64-66; dep comdr, 1st Aeromed Evacuation Group, Pope AFB, 66-68; tech dir, ARA Environ Serv, 68-70; dir, Div Environ Protection, Chester Co Health Dept, Pa, 70-75 & Div Environ Health, Berrien Co Health Dept, Mich, 75-78; prof environ health, Sch Pub Health, Univ Hawaii, 78-80; dean & prof, Sch Pub Health, Western States

Univ, 80-83. *Concurrent Pos:* Assoc ed, J Environ Health, 58-70; USAF environ health rep, Nat Acad Sci, 59-61; mem, Nat Cong Environ Health, 59-60; USAF rep, US Interdept Comt Nutrit for Nat Defense, 59-61; mem, President's Coun Youth Fitness, 60; Nat Environ Health Asn deleg, Nat Health Coun, 61; consult, Health Mobilization Prog, USPHS, 61-62 & UN Relief, Works Agency Educ Div, 64-66 & Dist Health Dept, 81-; chmn, Bd Registr Sanitarians Pa, 70-77; mem bd dirs, Chester Co Pa Water Resources Auth, 70-76, chmn, 74-76; mem, Chester Co Bd Health, 75-78; adj prof environ health, Ferris State Col, 76-79; mem policy & sci adv bds, SW Mich Ground Water Surv & Monitoring Prog, 81-, chmn policy bd, 88-90; chmn, Solid Waste Planning Oversight Comt, Barry Co, 81-; bd dirs, World Safety Orgn, 84- & mem cert bd, 85-; mem, Environ issues comt, Bush for Pres Campaign, 88; vis prof environ & pub health, Am Univ, Armenia, 95; mem, UL Underwriters Adv Coun Environ Pub Health, 96- *Mem:* Emer mem Am Pub Health Asn (pres elect, 94-95, pres, 95-97); fel Royal Soc Health; Nat Coun Int Health; Asn Mil Surgeons US; Am Indust Hyg Asn; emer mem Int Health Soc US; Nat Environ Health Asn. *Res:* Environmental and public health through the media of research, teaching and direction; beneficial control of the environment for benefit of humanity; industrial hygiene; author of over 50 publications and journal articles in the preventive, occupational medicine and public health area. *Mailing Add:* 1905 N Broadway Hastings MI 49058-1056

ADROUNY, GEORGE ADOUR (KUYUMJIAN), BIOCHEMISTRY. *Current Pos:* RETIRED. *Personal Data:* b Kilis, Turkey, Apr 1, 16; US citizen; wid; c 3. *Educ:* Am Univ Beirut, BA, 34, PhC, 40; Emory Univ, PhD(biochem), 54. *Prof Exp:* Instr & res assoc biochem, Emory Univ, 54-57; from asst prof to assoc prof, Sch Med, Tulane Univ, 57-72, prof biochem, 72-81, emer prof, 81- *Mem:* AAAS; Am Chem Soc. *Res:* Isolation and characterization of fire ant venom; effects of nutritional and hormonal factors on the carbohydrate metabolism of cardiac and skeletal muscles; the glycogen storing effect of somatotrophin. *Mailing Add:* 103 Amberfield Lane Gaithersburg MD 20878

ADT, ROBERT (ROY), MECHANICAL & AUTOMOTIVE ENGINEERING, ACCIDENT INVESTIGATION. *Current Pos:* from asst prof to assoc prof, 67-95, EMER PROF MECH ENG, UNIV MIAMI, 95- *Personal Data:* b Brooklyn, NY, June 21, 40; m 63, Barbara Hopf; c James & Laura. *Educ:* Univ Miami, BSME, 62; Mass Inst Technol, SM, 65, DSc(mech eng), 67. *Honors & Awards:* Ralph R Teetor Award, Soc Automotive Engrs. *Prof Exp:* Res engr, Northern Res & Eng Corp, 62-65. *Concurrent Pos:* Consult & legal expert. *Mem:* Soc Automotive Engrs; Am Soc Mech Engrs; Sigma Xi. *Res:* Alternate fuels for automotive engines; automotive engineering; engineering analysis and forensics of accidents; heat transfer thermodynamics; product design analysis. *Mailing Add:* Mech Systs Analysis Assoc Inc 6391 SW 85th St Miami FL 33143-8046. *Fax:* 305-663-1470

ADUSS, HOWARD, ORTHODONTICS, CRANIOFACIAL ANOMALIES. *Current Pos:* PROF ORTHOD, DEPT PEDIAT, CTR CRANIOFACIAL ANOMALIES, UNIV ILL, 66-, DIR CTR, 84- *Personal Data:* b Brooklyn, NY, Mar 31, 32; m 53, Marcia K; c Kathy A (Fisher), Laura A (Rendlen), Robert W & Deborah A (Dushman). *Educ:* Purdue Univ, BS, 54; Northwestern Univ, DDS, 57; Univ Rochester, MS, 62, Eastman Dent Ctr, cert orthod, 62. *Concurrent Pos:* Prof orthod, Dept Surg, Div Plastic Surg, Med Sch, Rush Univ. *Mem:* Am Dent Asn; Am Asn Orthod; Am Cleft Palate Asn (pres, 75-76); fel Am Col Dent; Int Asn Dent Res. *Res:* Craniofacial malformations, particularly cleft lip and palate; craniofacial growth and development in syndromes. *Mailing Add:* Surg Rush Univ Med Col 600 S Paulina St Chicago IL 60612-3832

ADVANI, SUNDER, engineering, mechanical engineering; deceased, see previous edition for last biography

ADVANI, SURESH GOPALDAS, POLYMER & COMPOSITES PROCESSING, PROCESS MODELS FOR VARIOUS FLUIDS. *Current Pos:* asst prof, 87-92, ASSOC PROF MECH ENG, UNIV DEL, 92- *Personal Data:* b Pune, India, Aug 19, 59; m 87; c 1. *Educ:* Indian Inst Technol, Bombay, BTech, 82; Univ Ill, PhD(mech eng), 87. *Prof Exp:* Res asst turbo-expander, Indian Inst Technol, Bombay, 81-82; res asst polymer proc, Univ Ill, Urbana-Champaign, 83-87, teaching fel mech mach, 86-87. *Concurrent Pos:* Consult, Tex Instruments, Dallas, Tex, 88-90; ed, Am Soc Mech Engrs-Heat & Mass Transfer in Solidification Processing, 91; co-chmn, Int Conf Composite Mat, 92; chmn, Rheology in Composite Processing, 91 & Polymer Mat Div, Am Soc Mech Engrs, 91-93; vis prof, Imp Col, London, 93. *Mem:* Am Soc Mech Engrs; Polymer Processing Soc; Soc Rheology; Soc Plastic Engrs. *Res:* Rheology of short and continuous fiber reinforced polymer composites and incorporations of these concepts into process models to gain insight about the physical system; polymer and composites processing; transport phenomena in manufacturing processes; non-Newtonian fluid mechanics, rheology and heat transfer; porous media flows. *Mailing Add:* 274 Dallam Rd Newark DE 19711-3140

AEBERSOLD, RUEDI H, PROTEIN BIOCHEMISTRY. *Current Pos:* SR SCIENTIST BIOCHEM, BIOMED RES CTR, UNIV BC, 88-, ASST PROF, 89- *Personal Data:* b Switz, Sept 12, 54; m 81; c 3. *Educ:* Univ Basel, Switz, dipl, 79, PhD(cell biol), 83. *Prof Exp:* Postdoctoral protein chem, Calif Inst Technol, 84-86, sr res fel, 86-88. *Mem:* Protein Soc; Am Soc Biochem & Molecular Biol. *Res:* Development of improved technologies for protein primary structure analysis; investigation of signal transduction process induced by the activation of lymphocytes. *Mailing Add:* Dept Molecular Biotechnol Univ Wash FJ 20 Seattle WA 98195-3370

AEIN, JOSEPH MORRIS, COMMUNICATIONS, GUIDANCE & NAVIGATION. *Current Pos:* SR SCIENTIST, RAND CORP, 84- *Personal Data:* b Washington, DC, Jan 26, 36; div; c Michael M & Benjamin J. *Educ:* Mass Inst Technol, SB & SM, 58; Purdue Univ, PhD(elec eng), 62. *Prof Exp:* Instr elec eng, Purdue Univ, 58-61; mem tech staff, Sci & Technol Div, Inst Defense Anal, 62-84. *Concurrent Pos:* Vis lectr, Univ Calif, Berkeley, 65-66; prof lectr, George Washington Univ, 79- *Mem:* Fel Inst Elec & Electronics Engrs. *Res:* Communications satellites; signal processing; navigation sensors; communications theory. *Mailing Add:* 613 Northcliffe Dr Rockville MD 20853. *E-Mail:* joea@wash.rand.org

AELION, CLAIRE MARJORIE, BIOREMEDIATION OF ORGANIC CONTAMINATION IN GROUNDWATER, MICROBIAL METABOLISM. *Current Pos:* ASST PROF, DEPT ENVIRON & HEALTH SCI, UNIV SC, 91- *Personal Data:* b Paris, France, June 17, 56; US citizen. *Educ:* Univ Mass, Amherst, BS, 80; Mass Inst Technol, SMCE, 83; Univ NC, Chapel Hill, PhD(environ sci & eng), 88. *Prof Exp:* Hydrologist, US Geol Surv, 88-91. *Concurrent Pos:* NSF presidential fac fel, 93. *Mem:* Am Chem Soc; Am Soc Microbiol; Soc Women Engrs; Soc Environ Toxicol & Chem; Water Environ Fedn. *Res:* Remediation of groundwater contamination, primarily organic pollutants including petroleum hydrocarbons, using combined physical and biological treatment; bioremediation and microbial metabolism of organic compounds by native sediment microbial communities. *Mailing Add:* Dept Environ Health Sci Univ SC Columbia SC 29208

AEPPLI, ALFRED, MATHEMATICS. *Current Pos:* assoc prof, 62-66, PROF MATH, UNIV MINN, MINNEAPOLIS, 66- *Personal Data:* b Zurich, Switz, Nov 8, 28; nat US; m 55, Dorothee M Pfiffner; c Gabriel A & Andreas E. *Educ:* Swiss Fed Inst Technol, dipl, 51, Dr math, 56. *Prof Exp:* Asst math, Swiss Fed Inst Technol, 52-57; from instr to asst prof, Cornell Univ, 57-62. *Concurrent Pos:* Guest prof, Univ Heidelberg, 74-75; pres, Univ Minn Educ Asn, 76- *Mem:* Math Asn Am; Asn Women Math; Am Math Soc; Swiss Math Soc; Soc Indust & Appl Math. *Res:* Topology; differential geometry; complex variables. *Mailing Add:* Sch Math Univ Minn 127 Vincent Hall Minneapolis MN 55455-0487

AFANADOR, ARTHUR JOSEPH, OPTOMETRY, PHYSIOLOGICAL OPTICS. *Current Pos:* DEAN, SCH OPTOM, INTER-AM UNIV, PR, 81- *Personal Data:* b Tampa, Fla, Nov 2, 42; m 65; c 2. *Educ:* Southern Col Optom, BS & OD, 65; Univ Calif, Berkeley, PhD(physiol optics), 72. *Prof Exp:* From asst prof to assoc prof optom, Ind Univ, Bloomington, 72-81. *Mem:* Fel Am Acad Optom. *Res:* Neurophysiology of the retina; single cell recording of goldfish ganglion cells. *Mailing Add:* Inter-Am Univ Sch Optometry 118 Eleanor Roosevelt Hato Rey PR 00919. *Fax:* 787-767-3920

AFFELDT, JOHN E, MEDICAL ADMINISTRATION. *Current Pos:* RETIRED. *Personal Data:* b Lansing, Mich. *Prof Exp:* Resident internal med, White Mem Hosp, 46-49; chief resident, Commun Dis Serv, Los Angeles County Hosp, 49-50; res assoc physiol, Sch Pub Health, Harvard Univ, 50-52; chief, Phys Respiratory Ctr Poliomyeletis, Rancho Los Amigos Hosp, 52-56, med dir, 56-64; med dir, Los Angeles County Hosp, 64-72 & Dept Health Serv, Los Angeles County, 72-77; pres, Joint Comn Accreditation Hosp, 77-86. *Concurrent Pos:* Assoc prof med, Loma Linda Univ Sch Med, 62-66. *Mem:* Inst Med-Nat Acad Sci; AMA; fel Am Col Physicians; Am Cong Rehab Med. *Mailing Add:* 5140 Bareback Sq Box 8432 Rancho Santa Fe CA 92067

AFFENS, WILBUR ALLEN, CHEMISTRY. *Current Pos:* RETIRED. *Personal Data:* b New York, NY, Jan 9, 18; m 45, Ruth Davids; c Steven C & David W. *Educ:* City Col New York, BS, 37; Polytech Inst Brooklyn, MS, 46; Georgetown Univ, PhD(phys chem), 60. *Prof Exp:* Chemist, Rubatex Prod Inc, NY, 37-38; chemist, Maltbie Chem Co, NJ, 38-42; asst chemist, Corps Engrs, US War Dept, 42-45; assoc chemist, USDA, 45-53, phys chemist, Entom Res Br, Agr Res Serv, 53-56; res chemist, US Naval Res Lab, 56-83; Geo-Centers Inc, Washington DC, 84-87. *Mem:* Am Chem Soc; Combustion Inst; Am Soc Testing & Mat. *Res:* Hydrocarbon chemistry; combustion; ignition; flammability; petroleum; fuels. *Mailing Add:* 8302 26th Pl Adelphi MD 20783

AFFLECK, IAN KEITH, QUANTUM MANY BODY PHYSICS. *Current Pos:* PROF PHYSICS, UNIV BC, 87- *Personal Data:* b Vancouver, BC, July 2, 52; m 77, Glenda Harman; c Geoffrey & Kate. *Educ:* Trent Univ, BSc, 75; Harvard Univ, MA, 76, PhD(physics), 79. *Honors & Awards:* Steacie Prize, Nat Res Coun Can, 88; Hertzberg Medal, Can Asn Physicists, 90; Rutherford Medal, Royal Soc Can, 91. *Prof Exp:* Jr fel, Harvard Soc fels, 79-81; asst prof physics, Princeton Univ, 81-87. *Concurrent Pos:* Researcher, Div Phys Ther, Ctr Nuclear Studies, France, 84-85; fel, Can Inst Advan Res, 87- *Mem:* Royal Soc Can. *Res:* Application of quantum field theory techniques to condensed matter physics, renormalization group, low dimensional systems, quantum magnetism. *Mailing Add:* Physics Dept Univ BC Vancouver BC V6T 1Z1 Can

AFFLECK, STEPHEN BRUCE, SOIL PHYSICS & GROUND WATER HYDROLOGY, FLUID MECHANICS. *Current Pos:* assoc prof, 81-91, dept chair, 94-97, dir eng progs, 95-97, PROF ENG, BOISE STATE UNIV, 91- *Personal Data:* b Logan, Utah, Oct 6, 37; m 60, Carolyn Hall; c Erin, Adam, Jessica, Matthew, Jared, Anna, David & Sara. *Educ:* Univ Utah, BS, 60; Iowa State Univ, MS, 73, PhD(chem eng/water resources), 80. *Prof Exp:* Proj engr, Procter & Gamble Co, 60-68; res & teaching asst, Iowa State Univ, 68-72, res assoc, 72-76, proj leader, 76-78; asst prof civil eng, Univ Utah, 78-81. *Concurrent Pos:* Consult. *Mem:* Nat Soc Prof Engrs. *Res:* Groundwater hydrology; flow in porous media; general fluid flow; potential flow; treatment plant design; fluid mechanics in food processing. *Mailing Add:* 9108 Burnett Dr Boise ID 83709. *Fax:* 208-385-4800; *E-Mail:* safflec@bsu.idbsu.edu

AFFONSO, DYANNE D, CLINICAL PSYCHOLOGY, NURSING. *Current Pos:* DEAN & PROF, ATLANTA EMORY UNIV, 93- *Educ:* Univ Hawaii, BS, 67; Univ Ariz, MA, 80, PhD(clin psychol), 82. *Honors & Awards:* Nat Nurse of the Year, March of Dimes, 93; Maternal Child Nurse of the Year, Am Nurses Asn, 94. *Concurrent Pos:* Mem, Off Res Women's Health, NIH, 95. *Mem:* Inst Med-Nat Acad Sci. *Res:* Recruitment of women into biomedical careers; health issues for women from ethnically diverse backgrounds. *Mailing Add:* Nell Hodgson Woodruff Sch Nursing 531 Asbury Circle Atlanta GA 30322. *Fax:* 404-727-4645; *E-Mail:* daffonso@nurse. emory.eou

AFFRONTI, LEWIS FRANCIS, MICROBIOLOGY, IMMUNOLOGY. *Current Pos:* from asst prof to assoc prof, 62-72, PROF MICROBIOL, SCH MED, GEORGE WASHINGTON UNIV, 72-, CHMN DEPT, 73- *Personal Data:* b Rochester, NY, Aug 12, 28; m 56; c 4. *Educ:* Univ Buffalo, BA, 50, MA, 51; Duke Univ, PhD(microbiol), 58. *Honors & Awards:* Unione Cavalleresca Europa Award, Contribusion to Sci, 80. *Prof Exp:* Asst, Univ Buffalo, 50-51; res assoc, Vet Admin Hosp, 51-52; med entomologist, US Air Force, 52-54; res assoc, Roswell Park Mem Inst, 54; dir vaccine lab, Duke Univ Hosp, 56; res assoc tuberc, Henry Phipps Inst, Univ Pa, 57-58; from sr asst scientist to scientist, USPHS, 58-62. *Concurrent Pos:* Spec consult, Vet Admin Hosp, Wilmington, Del, 66-; consult, Vet Admin Ctr, Martinsburg, WVa; US rep, Int Meeting Stand & Uses of Tuberculins, WHO, Geneva, Switz, 66; USPHS spec res fel, Inst Superiore Sanita, Italy, 69-70; US-Japanese res in tuberc grant, 69-; WHO exchange of res workers fel, Univ Goteborg, 70; Nat Tuberc Asn travel fel, 71; mem med adv bd, Wilmington Vet Admin Hosp Ctr, 72-; Nat Acad Sci interacad exchange fel, Prague, 80. *Mem:* Fel Am Acad Microbiol; Asn Med Sch Microbiol (secy-treas, 76-87); Am Soc Microbiol; Am Asn Immunol; Protein Soc. *Res:* Antigens of mycobacteria; immunochemistry; bacterial physiology; isolation and characterization of bacterial tumor isolates; cellular mechanisms in delayed allergy. *Mailing Add:* Dept Microbiol & Immunol George Washington Univ Sch Med 2300 I St NW Washington DC 20037-2337. *Fax:* 202-223-3691

AFGHAN, BADERUDDIN KHAN, ANALYTICAL CHEMISTRY, ENVIRONMENTAL CHEMISTRY. *Current Pos:* res scientist environ analytical chem, Dept Environ, Can Centre Inland Waters, 72-75, res mgr analytical methods res, 75-77, head, Analytical Methods Res Sect, 77-83 & Analytical Chem Res Sect, 83-89, chief, Nat Water Res Lab, 85-89, sr scientist, Atomospheric Contaminant Impacts, 94-96, RES SCIENTIST, NAT WATER RES INST, CAN CENTRE INLAND WATERS, BURLINGTON, ONT, CAN, 89-, CHIEF, NAT WATER QUAL LAB, ENVIRON CAN, 89-, SR SCIENTIST, ECOL SYST HEALTH ASSESSMENT, 96- *Personal Data:* b Shikarpur, Pakistan, Dec 12, 40; Can citizen; m 69; c 3. *Educ:* Sind Univ, Pakistan, BSc, 62, Hons, 63; Univ London, DIC, 64, PhD(analytical chem), 66. *Prof Exp:* Fel, Dalhousie Univ, 66-68; res assoc, Univ Montreal, 68-69; res scientist analytical methods develop, Dept Energy Mines & Resources, Fed Govt, Ottawa, Ont, 69-72. *Mem:* Fel Chem Inst Can; Am Soc Testing & Mat; Int Stand Orgn; Chem Inst Can; Asn Chem Prof Ont. *Res:* Modern polarographic and related electroanalytical techniques; high speed liquid chromatography and high performance gas chromatography; atomic and molecular absorption as well as fluorescence spectroscopy; trace analysis; environmental analytical chemistry; pesticides and industrial chemicals analysis; trace and ultra trace organic analysis using high resolution gas chromatography. *Mailing Add:* Nat Water Res Inst PO Box 5050 867 Lakeshore Rd Burlington ON L7R 4A6 Can. *Fax:* 905-336-4972

AFNAN, IRAJ RUHI, NUCLEAR THEORY, SCATTERING THEORY. *Current Pos:* lectr, 70-73, sr lectr, 73-77, READER PHYSICS, FLINDERS UNIV, 77- *Personal Data:* b Beirut, Lebanon, May 27, 39; m 66; c 2. *Educ:* Am Univ, Beirut, BSc, 61; Mass Inst Technol, PhD(physics), 66. *Prof Exp:* Res assoc physics, Univ Minn, 66-68 & Univ Calif, Davis, 68-70; vis prof, Univ BC, 74-75. *Concurrent Pos:* Consult & collabr, Los Alamos Nat Lab, 79- *Mem:* Am Phys Soc. *Res:* Quantum theory of scattering with application to nuclear and particle physics. *Mailing Add:* Dept Physics Flinders Univ SAustralia Bedford Park SA 5042 Australia

AFONSO, ADRIANO, ORGANIC CHEMISTRY. *Current Pos:* res fel, Chem Res Div, 63-91, SR RES FEL, SCHERING-PLOUGH RES INST, 91- *Personal Data:* b Goa, India, Mar 5, 35; m 66, Beverly Schunk; c Suzanne & Eric. *Educ:* Univ Bombay, MS, 57; Univ Wis, PhD(pharmaceut chem), 61. *Honors & Awards:* Lunsford Richardson Award, 60. *Prof Exp:* Res assoc, dept chem, Ind Univ, Bloomington, 61-63. *Mem:* Am Chem Soc. *Res:* Synthetic organic chemistry; structural studies on veratrum alkaloids; syntheses of diterpene resin acids; chemical modifications of steroids for biological activity; peptide structure elucidations; peptide syntheses; chemical modifications of aminoglycoside antibiotics; syntheses of beta lactam antibacterials; syntheses of heterocycles. *Mailing Add:* Ten Woodmere Rd West Caldwell NJ 07006

AFREMOW, LEONARD CALVIN, ANALYTICAL CHEMISTRY, RESEARCH MANAGEMENT. *Current Pos:* VPRES RES & ADMIN, MIDLAND DIV, DEXTER CORP. *Personal Data:* b Chicago, Ill, July 11, 33; m 60; c 1. *Educ:* Univ Ill, BS, 59; Univ Wis, MS, 61; Univ Chicago, MBA, 72. *Prof Exp:* Analytical chemist, Universal Oil Prod, 61; analytical chemist, DeSoto Inc, 61-63, group leader, 63-65, sect leader, 65-66, mgr res serv, 66-69, tech dir, 69-70, mgr indust, 70-71, dir, 71-74, dir res, 74-80. *Concurrent Pos:* Instr chem, Roosevelt Univ, 68-71. *Mem:* Nat Paint & Coatings Asn; Fedn of Soc for Coatings Technol; Am Chem Soc; Paint Res Inst (vpres, 79). *Res:* Analytical instrumentation; chemical coatings; research management. *Mailing Add:* 337 Summerhill Lane Wheeling IL 60090

AFSAR, MOHAMMED NURUL, PHYSICS. *Current Pos:* PROF ELEC ENG & COMP SCI, TUFTS UNIV, 87- *Educ:* Univ Dacca, MS, 67; Univ London, MS, 72, PhD(physics), 78. *Honors & Awards:* Duddell Premium, Inst Elec Engrs, UK, 77. *Prof Exp:* Lectr Physics, Nizampur Col, Chittagong, 68-70; higher sci officer, Nat Phys Lab, Eng, 75-78; staff scientist & physicist, Mass Inst Technol, 78-87. *Concurrent Pos:* Guest scientist, Nat Phys Lab, UK, 72-75; res fel, Univ London, 78. *Mem:* Inst Elec & Electronics Engrs; Inst Elec Engrs UK; Inst Physics. *Res:* Millimeter and submillimeter wave techniques; high precision measurement techniques and measurements of millimeter, submillimeter and infrared materials; characterization of impurities in high purity gallium arsemide and related compounds; far infrared ziman spectroscopy. *Mailing Add:* Dept Elec Eng & Comput Sci Tufts Univ Halligan Hall Medford MA 02155. *Fax:* 617-627-3220

AFSHAR, SIROOS K, SOFTWARE ENGINEERING MANAGEMENT, COMPUTER COMMUNICATIONS. *Current Pos:* mem tech staff, AT&T Bell Labs, 82-87, supvr, 87-92, tech mgr, 93-95, DIST MGR, AT&T BELL LABS, 96- *Personal Data:* b Ghom, Iran, July 3, 49; US citizen; m 75, Simin Manii; c Pedram & Afsheen. *Educ:* Sharif Univ Technol, Tehran, BSEE, 72; Univ Mich, Ann Arbor, MSE, 76, PhD(elec & computer eng), 79. *Prof Exp:* Design engr, Nat Iranian Oil Co, 72-75; res asst computer eng, Univ Mich, 76-79; asst prof elec & computer eng, La State Univ, 79-82. *Concurrent Pos:* Vis prof, Monmouth Univ, 85. *Mem:* Inst Elec & Electronics Engrs; Asn Comput Mach; NY Acad Sci. *Res:* Leading a research and development group to understand the needs, to document the necessary features, to define standards, and to define and develop products for the management of voice and data networks, and for providing business features. *Mailing Add:* Ten Constitution Ct Englishtown NJ 07726. *E-Mail:* siroos@acm.org

AFT, HARVEY, ORGANIC CHEMISTRY. *Current Pos:* assoc prof, 69-72, chmn dept, 72-80, PROF CHEM, UNIV MAINE, FARMINGTON, 80- *Personal Data:* b Chicago, Ill, June 17, 29; m 53; c 4. *Educ:* Univ Southern Calif, AB, 50; Univ Puget Sound, MS, 52; Ore State Univ, PhD(chem), 62. *Prof Exp:* Res chemist, Forest Prod Res Lab, 57-61; asst prof forest prod chem, Forest Res Lab, Ore State Univ, 61-65; asst prof chem, Mich Technol Univ, 65-66; assoc prof, Ore State Univ, 66-69. *Mem:* AAAS; Am Chem Soc; Brit Chem Soc. *Res:* Chemistry of phenolic and oxygen containing heterocyclic compounds and natural products chemistry. *Mailing Add:* 9 Main St Farmington ME 04938-1809

AFTERGOOD, LILLA, BIOCHEMISTRY, NUTRITION. *Current Pos:* RETIRED. *Personal Data:* b Krakow, Poland, Jan 10, 25; nat US; m 49, Edgar; c David, Steven & Annette. *Educ:* Univ Paris, Sorbonne, Lic es Sc, 48; Univ Southern Calif, MS, 51, PhD(biochem), 56. *Honors & Awards:* Bond Award, Am Oil Chemists Soc, 74. *Prof Exp:* Asst biochem, Univ Southern Calif, 50-56, res assoc, 56-62; res biochemist, Sch Pub Health, Univ Calif, Los Angeles, 62-80. *Mem:* AAAS; Am Inst Nutrit; Sigma Xi. *Res:* Essential fatty acids; cholesterol, their metabolic interrelationship; effect of sex hormones on lipid metabolism; metabolic effects of oral contraceptives; vitamin E; nutrition and cancer, trans fatty acids. *Mailing Add:* 7050 Arizona Ave Los Angeles CA 90045-1317

AFTERGUT, SIEGFRIED, ORGANIC CHEMISTRY, POLYMER CHEMISTRY. *Current Pos:* INDEPENDENT CONSULT, 93- *Personal Data:* b Frankfurt am Main, Ger, Jan 7, 27; nat US; m 51; c 2. *Educ:* Syracuse Univ, BA, 50, MS, 54, PhD(org chem), 56. *Prof Exp:* Asst instr chem, Syracuse Univ, 51-56; proj engr, Advan Tech Labs, Gen Elec Co, 56-66, mgr photorecording mat, 66-73, mgr display mat, 73-76, mem staff, Res & Develop Ctr, 76-93. *Mem:* Am Chem Soc; Soc Info Display. *Res:* Mannich reaction; aromatic silanes and ethers; electrical properties of organic compounds; photoplastic recording; organic photoconductors; liquid crystals; dichroic dyes; color filters; electronic displays. *Mailing Add:* 1063 Nott St Schenectady NY 12308. *Fax:* 518-372-3796; *E-Mail:* saftergut@juno.com

AGABIAN, NINA, PHARMACOLOGY. *Current Pos:* actg sci dir, Naval Biosci Lab, 84-87, PROF BIOMED & ENVIRON HEALTH SCI, SCH PUB HEALTH, UNIV CALIF, BERKELEY, 84-, PROF PHARMACEUT CHEM, SAN FRANCISCO, 86-, DIR, MOLECULAR PARASITOL, INTERCAMPUS PROG, 87- *Educ:* Adelphi Univ, BA, 66, MS, 68; Albert Einstein Col Med, PhD(molecular biol), 71. *Prof Exp:* Teaching asst, Dept Biol, Adelphi Univ, 66-68; res fel, Dept Molecular Biol, Albert Einstein Col Med, 68-71; from asst prof to prof biochem, Sch Med, Univ Wash, Seattle, 73-84. *Concurrent Pos:* Res fel, NIH, 68-71 & 71-73; Guggenheim fel, 79-80; Burroughs Wellcome award molecular parasitol, 84-89; mem bd dirs, Drug & Vaccine Develop Corp, 86- *Mem:* Fel AAAS; Am Soc Biol Chemists. *Res:* Author or co-author of over 90 publications. *Mailing Add:* Box 0422 CSB C742 Univ Calif San Francisco Sch Dent 521 Parnassus St San Francisco CA 94143-0422

AGALLOCO, JAMES PAUL, PROCESS VALIDATION, SYSTEMS RELIABILITY. *Current Pos:* PRES, AGALLO CO & ASSOCS, 92- *Personal Data:* b Queens, NY, Apr 19, 48; m 74; c 3. *Educ:* Pratt Inst, Brooklyn, NY, BE, 68; Polytech Inst NY, Brooklyn, MS, 79; Fairleigh-Dickinson Univ, Teaneck, NJ, MBA, 83. *Prof Exp:* Chem eng, Merck & Co; mgr, Pfizer, Inc, 73-80; dir, Bristol-Myers Squibb, 80-92. *Concurrent Pos:* Co-founder, NJ Validation Discussion Group, 80; comt chmn, Int Soc Pharmaceut Eng, Tampa, Fla, 82. *Mem:* Parenteral Drug Asn, Philadelphia, Pa (pres, 88-89); Am Soc Qual Control; Parenteral Soc Gt Brit. *Res:* Process vilidation; process automation; pharmaceutical manufacturing; aseptic processing; sterilization processes. *Mailing Add:* 22 Carriage Trail Belle Mead NJ 08502

AGAMANOLIS, DIMITRIS, NEUROPATHOLOGY. *Current Pos:* DIR NEUROPATH, CHILDREN'S HOSP MED CTR. *Personal Data:* b Mytilene, Greece, Nov 3, 38. *Educ:* Univ Thesaloniki, Greece, MD, 62. *Mailing Add:* Children's Hosp Med Ctr One Perkins S8 Akron OH 44308-1062

AGAN, RAYMOND JOHN, AGRICULTURE, INTERNATIONAL DEVELOPMENT. *Current Pos:* PROF VOC EDUC & DIR INT EDUC PROGS, SAM HOUSTON STATE UNIV, 71- *Personal Data:* b Knoxville, Iowa, July 8, 19; m 39; c 2. *Educ:* Iowa State Univ, BS, 40, MS, 50; Univ Mo, EdD(agr), 55. *Honors & Awards:* Achievement Award, Ministry Agr, Indonesia. *Prof Exp:* Asst agr educ, Univ Mo, 54-55; from instr to asst prof, Ore State Univ, 55-58; from assoc prof to prof, Kans State Univ, 58-71. *Concurrent Pos:* Consult, Univ Costa Rica, 63-64, Indonesian & Malaysian ministries of agr; UNESCO consult, Colombian projs & ODECA/OCE PLAN, Cent Am, 65-70; pres, Agan Consultancy Int Agency. *Mem:* Asn Teachers Educators Agr (vpres, 63-64). *Res:* Agricultural occupations and training needs of Oregon Indian tribes; agricultural needs in Central and South America. *Mailing Add:* 2309 Ave S Huntsville TX 77340

AGAPITO, J F T, MINING ENGINEERING, MINE VENTILATION. *Current Pos:* pres, 78-94, CHMN BD, J F T AGAPITO ASSOC INC, GRAND JUNCTION, 94- *Educ:* Univ Mo, Rolla, MS; Colo Sch Mines, PhD(rock mech & mining eng). *Honors & Awards:* Rock Mech Award, Soc Mining, Metall & Explor, 92. *Prof Exp:* Miner & technician, Beralt Wolfram & Tin, Ltd, Port & S Crofty Ltd, Eng, 58-60; ventilation engr, White Pine Copper Co, 64-66, mine res engr, 66-68; instr, Colo Sch Mines, Golden, 68-72, sr rock mech engr, Atlantic Richfield Co, Grand Valley, Colo, 72-74; assoc, Golder Assoc, Inc, Grand Junction, Colo, 74-76; indust consult & mining engr, 76-78. *Mem:* Fel Inst Mining & Metall; Int Soc Rock Mech. *Res:* Mine Ventilation; mining engineering; rock mechanics; contributed articles to professional journals. *Mailing Add:* J F T Agapito & Assocs Inc 715 Horizon Dr Suite 340 Grand Junction CO 81506

AGAR, G(ORDON) E(DWARD), MINERAL PROCESSING. *Current Pos:* RETIRED. *Personal Data:* b Kindersley, Sask, Sept 17, 31; Can citizen; m 79, Kathleen Gerber; c Carl, Leslie & Roderick. *Educ:* Univ BC, BASc, 55; Mass Inst Technol, ScD(mineral eng), 61. *Prof Exp:* Metallurgist, Britannia Mining & Smelting, 55; asst, Mass Inst Technol, 55-56, from instr to asst prof, 57-62; metallurgist, Union Carbide Nuclear Corp, 56; mgr mineral res, Int Minerals & Chem Corp, 62-67; res engr, Duval Corp, 67-72; sect head mineral processing res, Inco Ltd, 72-92. *Concurrent Pos:* Adj prof, Univ Toronto, 77-, Univ BC, 90-93; distinguished lectr, Can Inst Mining & Metall. *Mem:* Can Inst Mining & Metall. *Res:* Mineral processing and extractive metallurgy, especially processes such as flotation, electrostatic separation and leaching; surface and colloid chemistry related to separation processes. *Mailing Add:* 129 Lakeshore Dr Toronto ON M8V 2A1 Can

AGARD, EUGENE THEODORE, MEDICAL PHYSICS, RADIOLOGICAL HEALTH. *Current Pos:* CONSULT, 93- *Personal Data:* b Christ Church, WI, Aug 15, 32; m 60; c 4. *Educ:* Univ WI, BSc, 56; Univ London, MSc, 58; Univ Toronto, PhD(physics), 70; Am Bd Radiol, cert radiol physics, 82. *Prof Exp:* Asst Physicist, Mass Gen Hosp, 59-63; lectr & asst prof physics, Univ WI, Trinidad, 63-72; dir, Med Physics, PR Nuclear Ctr, 72-76; radiation physicist, Kettering Med Ctr, 76-84; consult radiol physics, Radgard Inc, 84-90; assoc prof med physics, Med Col Ohio, 90-93. *Concurrent Pos:* Consult, Ministry Health, Trinidad & Tobago, 66-67, Vet Admin Med Ctr, PR, 73-76 & Dayton, Ohio, 78-90; rep, Comt n-44, Am Nat Standards Inst, 72-76; mem, Int Rels Comt, Am Asn Physicists Med, 74-77, Pub Educ Comt, 80-86; prof, Kettering Col Med Arts, 78-82; assoc clin prof, Dept Radiol Sci, Wright State Univ, 87-90. *Mem:* Am Asn Physicists Med; Health Physics Soc; Am Col RAdiol; Radiol Soc NAm. *Res:* Medical applications of radiation, especially in the practice of the radiological sciences; measurements of radiation doses and quality control of equipment used in radiation oncology, diagnostic radiology and nuclear medicine. *Mailing Add:* 8600 Hide-A-Way Lane Dayton OH 43560

AGARDY, FRANKLIN J, SANITARY ENGINEERING, ENVIRONMENTAL ENGINEERING. *Current Pos:* PRES, FORENSIC MGT ASSOCS INC, 88- *Personal Data:* b New York, NY, Mar 23, 33; m 79, Louise F Ehman; c Frederic & Harrison. *Educ:* City Col New York, BCE, 55; Univ Calif, Berkeley, MS, 57, PhD(sanit eng), 63. *Honors & Awards:* George A Elliot Mem Award, Am Water Works Asn, 73, Water Utility Educ Award, 74. *Prof Exp:* Prof civil eng, San Jose State Univ, 62-69; vpres, URS Res Co, 69-73, pres, 73-74, vpres, URS Corp, 74-80, sr vpres, 84-85, pres, 80-88, pres & chief operating officer, 85-88. *Concurrent Pos:* Consult radiation shielding, Off Civil Defense & US Govt, 61-69; forensic engr, 64-; consult indust pollution, US Environ Protection Agency, 72-73; hazardous & toxic waste investr, 80-; pres & chief exec officer, In-Process Technol Inc, 88-91, chmn bd, 90- *Mem:* Am Soc Civil Engrs; Water Pollution Control Fedn; Am Water Works Asn; Nat Fire Protection Asn; Forensic Soc Engrs & Scientists. *Res:* Pollution control, including biological treatment of industrial wastes; engineering principles of gamma radiation shielding; continency planning for water and waste water utilities. *Mailing Add:* Forensic Mgt Assocs Inc 400 S El Camino Real Suite 1460 San Mateo CA 94402. *Fax:* 418-347-1278

AGARWAL, ARUN KUMAR, PURE MATHEMATICS. *Current Pos:* assoc prof, 69-80, PROF MATH & COMPUTER SCI, GRAMBLING STATE UNIV, 80- *Personal Data:* b Lucknow, India, Mar 17, 44; m 67, Prabha; c Anju & Amit. *Educ:* Lucknow Univ, BSc, 60, MSc 63, PhD(math), 67. *Prof Exp:* Coun Sci Indust Res sr res fel, New Delhi, India, 67-68; fel, WVa Univ, 68-69. *Mem:* Am Math Soc; Math Asn Am; Asn Comput Mach. *Res:* Entire functions of a single and several complex variables; special functions; computer sciences, general. *Mailing Add:* Dept Math & Comput Sci Grambling State Univ Grambling LA 71245. *Fax:* 318-274-6091; *E-Mail:* agarwal@vax0.gram.edu

AGARWAL, GIRISH SARAN, PHYSICS. *Current Pos:* DIR, PHYS RES LAB, AHMEDABAD, INDIA, 95- *Personal Data:* b Bareilly, India, July 7, 46; m 70, Sneh Lata; c Anjali & Mranjali. *Educ:* Banaras Hindu Univ, MS, 66; Univ Rochester, PhD, 69. *Honors & Awards:* Shanti Swaroop Bhatnagar Award in Phys Sci, Govt India, 82; Max Born Award, Optical Soc Am, 88; Physics Prize, Third World Acad Sci, 94; Einstein Medal Optical & Quantum Electronics Soc, 94; Goyal Prize Physics, 94; G D Birla Sci Res Award, 95; R D Birla Award, Indian Physics Asn, 96; Humboldt Res Award, 97. *Prof Exp:* Res assoc, Univ Rochester, NY, 69-70, asst prof, 70-71; asst prof, Inst Theoret Physics, Univ Stuttgart, Ger, 71-73; vis fel, Tata Inst Fundamental Res, Bombay, 73-75; prof, Inst Sci, Bombay, 75-77 & Univ Hyderabad, India, 77-95. *Concurrent Pos:* Hon prof, J N Ctr Advan Sci Res, Bangalore, India. *Mem:* Nat Acad Sci India; Indian Acad Sci; fel Am Phys Soc; Third World Acad Sci; Indian Nat Sci Acad. *Res:* Theoretical research work in quantum optics, nonlinear optics and statistical physics; manipulation of atoms using laser fields; control of the nonlinear optical and quantum properties of various systems. *Mailing Add:* Phys Res Lab Dirs Bungalow Ahmedabad 380 009 India. *Fax:* 79-6420374; *E-Mail:* gsa@prl.ernet.in

AGARWAL, GYAN C, ELECTRICAL ENGINEERING, BIOENGINEERING. *Current Pos:* from asst prof to assoc prof systs eng, 65-73, from asst prof to assoc prof physiol, Med Ctr, 69-73, PROF ELEC ENG & COMPUT SCI, UNIV ILL CHICAGO & PROF PHYSIOL, MED CTR, 73-; DIR, GRAD STUDIES, ELEC ENG COMPUT SCI, 91- *Personal Data:* b Bhagwanpur, India, Apr 22, 40; m 65, Sadhna Garg; c Monika (Punjab) & Mudita (Bahadur). *Educ:* Agra Univ, BSc, 57; Univ Roorkee, BE, 60; Purdue Univ, MSEE, 62, PhD(elec), 65. *Prof Exp:* Instr elec eng, Purdue Univ, 62-65. *Concurrent Pos:* From asst to assoc biomed eng, Presby St Luke Hosp, Chicago, 65-73; vis prof physiol, Rush Med Col, Rush Univ, 76-; panel mem, Neurol Sect, Bur Med Devices, Food & Drug Admin, 81-; consult ed, J Motor Behav, 81-93; assoc ed, Trans on Biomed Eng, Inst Elec & Electronics Engrs, 88-, Electromyography & Kinesiology. *Mem:* Fel AAAS; fel Inst Elec & Electronics Engrs; Soc Neurosci; fel Am Inst Med & Biol Eng; Sigma Xi. *Res:* Application of control theory in physiological control systems; human motor control system; modeling and simulation; bio-instrumentation; control theory; optimization; man-machine systems. *Mailing Add:* Dept Elec Eng & Comput Sci MC-154 Univ Ill-Chicago, 851 S Morgan St 1120 SEO Chicago IL 60607-7053. *Fax:* 312-413-0024; *E-Mail:* agarwal@eecs.uic.edu

AGARWAL, JAGDISH CHANDRA, CERAMICS ENGINEERING, METALLURGICAL ENGINEERING. *Current Pos:* VPRES TECH ASSOCS, CHARLES RIVER ASSOC, 85- *Personal Data:* b Karachi, India, Sept 8, 26; US citizen; m 47; c 2. *Educ:* Benares Hindu Univ, BS, 45; Polytech Inst New York, MChE, 47, DChE, 51. *Honors & Awards:* fel Am Inst Chem Engrs; Henry Krumb Lectr, 86. *Prof Exp:* Res engr, Vulcan Copper & Supply Co, 48-49; process engr, Fleischmann Labs, Standard Brands, Inc, 49-51; sr process engr, Blaw-Knox Co, 51-54; res assoc, Appl Res Lab, US Steel Corp, 54-64, div chief process analysis, 64-69; asst dir develop, Ledgemont Lab, Kennecott Copper Corp, 69-73, dir develop, 73-79; vpres, 79-82; vpres tech, Amax Inc, 82-85. *Mem:* Am Inst Mining, Metall & Petrol Engrs; Am Inst Chem Engrs; Asn Iron & Steel Engrs; Am Chem Soc; Metal Soc. *Res:* Process plant design; process economic evaluation; methods of production of iron and steel; fluidization; heat transfer; blast furnaces; magnesium and other light metals; adv ceramics. *Mailing Add:* 125 Ford Rd Sudbury MA 01776-1213

AGARWAL, KAILASH C, BIOCHEMISTRY. *Current Pos:* res assoc bio-med, 68-71, instr, 71-74, ASSOC PROF BIO-MED, BROWN UNIV, 79- *Personal Data:* b Uttarpradesh, India; m 63; c 2. *Educ:* Allahabad Univ, India, MSc, 63; Agra Univ, India, PhD(sci), 67. *Prof Exp:* Lectr biochem, Kanpur Med Col, 66-68. *Mem:* Am Heart Asn; Am Soc Exp Pharmacol & Therapeut. *Res:* Blood platelet physiology and pharmacology. *Mailing Add:* Dept Molecular & Biochem Pharmacol Brown Univ Box G-B413 Providence RI 02912-0001. *Fax:* 401-863-1595

AGARWAL, KAN L, STRUCTURE OF NUCLEIC ACIDS, GENE EXPRESSION. *Current Pos:* PROF BIOCHEM & CHEM, UNIV CHICAGO, 75- *Educ:* Rajasthan Univ, India, PhD(org chem), 67. *Res:* Chemistry and molecular biology of nucleic acids. *Mailing Add:* Dept Biochem Univ Chicago 920 E 58th St Chicago IL 60637-1432. *Fax:* 773-702-0439

AGARWAL, RAM P, CANCER RESEARCH, ANTI-AIDS RESEARCH. *Current Pos:* ASSOC PROF MED ONCOL, UNIV MIAMI, 85- *Personal Data:* b India, June 2, 39; m 59, Prakash; c Reena, Arjun, Chitra, Bharti & Pavan. *Educ:* Lucknow Univ, India, BS, 56, MS, 59; Banaras Hindu Univ, PhD(biochem), 67. *Prof Exp:* Assoc prof biochem & pharmacol, Brown Univ, 67-77; assoc prof, Dept Pharmacol & Med, Boston Univ Med Sch, 77-85. *Mem:* Am Asn Cancer Res; Fedn Am Socs Exp Biol. *Res:* Mechanism of action of anticancer and anti-AIDS agents pharmacokinetics. *Mailing Add:* Comprehensive Cancer Ctr R71 PO Box 061960 Miami FL 33101-6960

AGARWAL, RAMESH CHANDRA, MATHEMATICAL SOFTWARE, VECTOR & PARALLEL ALGORITHMS. *Current Pos:* RES STAFF MEM, IBM, T J WATSON RES CTR, YORKTOWN HEIGHTS, NY, 82- *Personal Data:* b Gwalior, India, May 8, 46; m 81, Shashi Gupta; c Anit, Sumit & Vinit. *Educ:* Indian Inst Technol, B Tech, 68; Rice Univ, MS, 70, PhD(elec eng), 74. *Honors & Awards:* Sr Award, Inst Elec & Electronic Engrs, 74. *Prof Exp:* Fel, IBM, T J Watson Res Ctr, 74-76, res staff mem, 76-77; prin sci officer, Indian Inst Technol, 77-81. *Mem:* Fel Inst Elec & Electronics Engrs; Soc Indust & Appl Math; Asn Comput Mach. *Res:* Developing vector and parallel algorithms and software for supercomputers, that are used in most engineering and scientific computations. *Mailing Add:* IBM T J Watson Res Ctr PO Box 218 Yorktown Heights NY 10598. *Fax:* 914-945-3434; *E-Mail:* agarwal@watson.ibm.com

AGARWAL, RAMESH K, COMPUTATIONAL FLUID DYNAMICS, APPLIED MATHEMATICS. *Current Pos:* PROG DIR & MCDONNELL DOUGLAS FEL, AEROSPACE, MCDONNELL DOUGLAS, MO, 78- *Personal Data:* b India, Jan 4, 47; US citizen; m 76, Sugita Goel; c Vivek & Gautum. *Educ:* Indian Inst Technol, BTech, 68; Univ Minn, MS, 69; Stanford Univ, PhD(aeronaut sci), 75. *Honors & Awards:* St Louis Sect Tech Achievement Award, Am Inst Aeronaut & Astronaut. *Prof Exp:* Prin engr, Rao & Assocs, Calif, 75-76; Nat Res Coun assoc, Ames Res Ctr, NASA, Moffett Field, 76-78. *Concurrent Pos:* Consult, Joint Inst Aeronaut & Acoust, Stanford Univ, 75-76; affil prof mech eng, Wash Univ, St Lous, 86-; adj prof aerospace eng, Parks Col, St Lous Univ, 86-; mem, Tech Comt Fluid Dynamics, Am Inst Aeronaut & Astronaut, 86-89, Multidisciplinary Optimization Comt, 89- & Comput Fluid Dynamics, Papers Stand Task Force, 87-88; assoc ed, J Aircraft & J Fluids Eng, Am Soc Mech Engrs, 91-; adj prof elect eng, Univ Mo-Rolla, 90- *Mem:* Sigma Xi; Am Inst Aeronaut & Astronaut; Am Soc Mech Engrs; Am Helicopter Soc; fel Am Phys Soc; fel AAAS; sr mem Inst Elec & Electronics Engrs. *Res:* Computational fluid dynamics, supercomputing, parallel computing, fixed and rotary-wing aircraft aerodynamics, asymptotic methods in applied mathematics; computational electromagnetics, computational acoustics, optimization. *Mailing Add:* McDonnell Douglas Aerospace Co Dept 226/B 110MC1064126 PO Box 516 St Louis MO 63166-0516. *Fax:* 314-777-1328; *E-Mail:* agarwal@mdcgwy.mdc.com

AGARWAL, SHYAM S, MEDICAL GENETICS & CLINICAL IMMUNOLOGY, HAEMATOLOGICAL DISORDERS & BONE MARROW TRANSPLANTATION. *Current Pos:* PROF & HEAD, DEPT GENETICS & IMMUNOL, SANJAY GANDHI POSTGRAD INST MED SCI, LUCKNOW, 86-, DIR, 93- *Personal Data:* b Bareilly, India, July 5, 41; m 71, Pramila Das; c Rama & Rahul. *Educ:* Lucknow Univ, BSc, 58, MBBS(Hons), 63, MD(Hons), 66; FRCP(C), 76. *Hon Degrees:* FASc, Acad Sci, Bangalore; FAMS, Nat Acad Med Sci, New Delhi. *Honors & Awards:* Shanti Swarup Bhatnagar Prize, 86; Kamla Menon Res Award, 86; Glaxo Oration Award, 92. *Prof Exp:* Res physician genetics & oncol, Inst Cancer Res & Univ Pa, Philadelphia, 69-70; lectr med, K G Med Col, Lucknow, 70-73, reader, 73-86. *Concurrent Pos:* Vis scientist & res physician, Inst Cancer Res, Philadelphia, 74-77; vis res assoc, Mem Sloan Kettering Cancer Ctr, NY, 79-81; dean, SGPGI, 86-90. *Mem:* Fel Indian Col Physicians; Am Soc Human Genetics; Am Asn Immunologists; Indian Soc Human Genetics; Indian Immunol Soc; Indian Soc Hemat & Blood Transfusion. *Res:* Lymphocyte biology; DNA replication and repair; effect of elevated temperatures on lymphocyte function; immunomoonlakors; clinical genetics. *Mailing Add:* Dept Genetics & Immunol Sanjay Gandhi Postgrad Inst Med Sci PO Box 375 Lucknow 226001 India. *Fax:* 91-522-259973

AGARWAL, SOM PRAKASH, COSMIC RAY PHYSICS, NUCLEAR PHYSICS. *Current Pos:* asst prof, 65-66, ASSOC PROF PHYSICS, UNIV MINN, MORRIS, 66- *Personal Data:* b Aligarh, India, Apr 6, 30; US citizen; m 55; c 3. *Educ:* Agra Univ, BSc, 49; Aligarh Muslim Univ, MSc, 51; Temple Univ, PhD(physics), 62. *Prof Exp:* Lectr physics, MMH Col, India, 51-52; res scholar, Aligarh Muslim Univ, India, 52-56; res fel, Bartol Res Found, Franklin Inst, 56-62; assoc prof, Univ Tex, El Paso, 62-64; physicist, Braddock, Dunn & McDonald, Inc, 64-65. *Concurrent Pos:* Consult, Braddock, Dunn & McDonald, Inc, 63-64; adj assoc prof, Solid State Physics Lab, Univ Tex, El Paso, 78-79. *Mem:* Am Phys Soc; Am Geophys Union; Am Asn Physics Teachers; Nat Educ Asn. *Res:* Cosmic rays; interplanetary particles and fields; nuclear reactions; experimental solid state physics; thin film transport properties; elementary particles; radiation effects and electronic physics. *Mailing Add:* 8 N Court St Morris MN 56267

AGARWAL, SURESH KUMAR, RADIOLOGICAL PHYSICS. *Current Pos:* asst prof, 69-74, assoc prof, 74-80, PROF RADIOL PHYSICS, UNIV VA, 80- *Personal Data:* b Pilibhit, India, June 22, 32; m 50, Mithlesh Kumari; c Sushma, Sandhya, Poonam & Neelam. *Educ:* Agra Univ, BS, 50; Lucknow Univ, MS, 52, PhD(physics), 65; Am Bd Radiol, cert radiol physics, 72; Am Bd Med Physics, cert radiation oncol, 89. *Prof Exp:* Physicist, GM & Assoc Hosps, India, 52-58; lectr radiol physics, Lucknow Univ, 58-69. *Concurrent Pos:* Clin fel, Mem Cancer Hosp, New York, 57-58. *Mem:* Am Asn Physicists Med; fel Am Col Radiol; Health Physics Soc; Am Soc Therapeut Radiation Oncologists; Am Col Med Physics. *Res:* Radiation treatment planning of irregular fields and its computerization; radiation dosimetry; quality control in diagnostic radiology; role of hyperthermia in radiation oncology; radiation risk estimates; use of linear accelerators and gamma knife in treating small brain lesions (radio-surgery). *Mailing Add:* Radiol Univ Va Sch Med Hospital Dr Charlottesville VA 22908-0001. *Fax:* 804-982-3520; *E-Mail:* ska@virginia.edu

AGARWAL, VIJENDRA KUMAR, SOLAR ENERGY RESEARCH, APPLICATION THIN FILMS. *Current Pos:* assoc prof, 88-90, PROF, DEPT PHYSICS, MOORHEAD STATE UNIV, 90- *Personal Data:* b Kotah, India, Dec 15, 48; m 79; c 2. *Educ:* Agra Univ, BS, 66; Meerut Univ, MS, 68; Univ Roorkee, PhD(physics), 72. *Prof Exp:* Fel physics, Univ Parma, Italy, 73-74, Shizuoko Univ, Japan, 75-76; lectr, Kashmir Univ, India, 74-75; res assoc, Ecole Superieure d Electricite, France, 76-78; vis asst prof, Drexel Univ, 78-80, Stockton State Col, 81; from asst prof to assoc prof physics, Tex Tech Univ, 81-88. *Concurrent Pos:* Vis scientist, Int Ctr Theoret Physics, Italy, 74 & 77. *Mem:* Am Phys Soc; Inst Elec & Electronics Engrs; Indian Physics Asn; Am Asn Phys Teachers. *Res:* Experimental solid state physics; characterization and applied research on organic thin films; photothermal solar-energy conversion; solar cell encapsulation; solar energy; charge accumulation, electrical breakdown and aging of insulators under high voltage in space environment. *Mailing Add:* Dept Physics Moorhead State Moorhead MN 56560

AGARWAL, VINOD KUMAR, FAULT TOLERANT COMPUTING, BUILT-IN SELF-TEST. *Current Pos:* CHIEF EXEC OFFICER & PRES, LOGIC VISION, 95- *Personal Data:* b India, Apr 30, 52; m 78; c Anika & Atin. *Educ:* Birla Inst Tech & Sci, BEng, 73; Univ Pittsburgh, MEng, 74; Johns Hopkins Univ, PhD(elec eng), 77. *Prof Exp:* Asst prof, Wayne State Univ, 77-78; res asst elec eng, Johns Hopkins Univ, 78; from asst prof to prof elec eng, McGill Univ, 78-95, res chair, 87-95. *Concurrent Pos:* Prin investr, strategic res grant, Nat Sci & Eng Res Coun, 85-88; vis prof, Indian Inst Tech, Delhi, 86; indust res chair prof. *Mem:* Fel Inst Elec & Electronics Engrs; Sigma Xi; Asn Comput Mach. *Res:* Design and test integrated circuits and printed circuits boards; design for testability, built-in self test, and fault tolerant schemes. *Mailing Add:* Logic Vision 101 Metro Dr Santa Fe CA 95110. *Fax:* 514-398-4470

AGARWAL, VIPIN K, HIGH PERFORMANCE LIQUID, ANALYTICAL METHOD DEVELOPMENT CHROMATOGRAPHY. *Current Pos:* STAFF SCIENTIST, BAYER CORP, CONN, 93- *Personal Data:* b Badaun, India, Jan 22, 55; US citizen; m 82; c 2. *Educ:* Lucknow Univ, BSc, 73, MSc, 75, PhD(org chem), 80; Univ New Brunswick, PhD(org chem), 82; Rensselaer Polytech Int, MBA, 85. *Prof Exp:* Postdoctoral assoc analytical chem, Rensselaer Polytech Inst, 83-85; analytical chemist, Conn Agr Exp Sta, 85-92. *Mem:* Am Chem Soc. *Res:* Development of analytical methods for monitoring trace levels of residues in biological and nonbioloical matrices. *Mailing Add:* Miles Inc 400 Morgan Lane West Haven CT 06516-4134

AGARWALA, VINOD SHANKER, CORROSION, ELECTROCHEMISTRY. *Current Pos:* res metallurgist, 77-84, group leader, Surface Interactions Res, 84-94, CHIEF, MAT PROTECTION SR STAFF SCIENTIST, NAVAL AIR WARFARE CTR AIRCRAFT DIV, NAVAL AIR DEVELOP CTR, 95- *Personal Data:* b Sitapur, India, Aug 9, 39; US citizen; m 67, Asha Varma; c Veena & Vinay. *Educ:* Banaras Hindu Univ, India, MS, 61, PhD(corrosion), 68; Mass Inst Technol, MS, 66. *Honors & Awards:* Corrosion Specialist Award, Nat Asn Corrosion Engrs, 74; Captain Walter S Diehl Award, 86; Int Romanoff Award, Nat Acad Corrosion Engrs, 89. *Prof Exp:* Can Dept Energy Mines & Res fel corrosion, 67-69; metallurgist prod develop, Super Steel Ball Co, 70-71; res assoc corrosion, Univ Conn, 72-76; Sr Res Assoc, Air Force Mat Lab, Wright Patterson AFB, 76-77. *Concurrent Pos:* Tech consult, Corning Glass Works, 74, Crucible Steel Co, 74-75, Bethlehem Steel Corp, 74-75 & Allied Chem, 75; res grant atmospheric corrosion, Am Iron & Steel Inst, Washington DC, 74-75; adj asst prof, Wright State Univ, Ohio, 76-77; Nat Res Coun fel, Washington DC, 76-77; chmn, Comt Mil Corrosion, Nat Asn Corrosion Engrs Int, Tech Pract Comt, T-9, sect chmn, Am Soc Testing Mat, sub comt, G-105.02, chmn, Subcomt Sensors; mem, Develop Oper Div, Tri Serv Planning Comt Corrosion. *Mem:* Fel Nat Asn Corrosion Engrs Int; Am Chem Soc; Electrochem Soc; fel Am Soc Metals Int. *Res:* Corrosion of metals; electrochemistry; metallurgy; mechanism of corrosion and material failure; stress corrosion cracking; hydrogen embrittlement, corrosion fatigue in aircraft alloys; corrosion and corrosity sensors; aircraft materials protection and preservation. *Mailing Add:* 47259 Silver Slate Dr Lexington Park MD 20653. *Fax:* 215-441-1925

AGATHOKLIS, PANAJOTIS, DIGITAL SIGNAL PROCESSING. *Current Pos:* PROF ELEC ENG, UNIV VICTORIA, 83- *Personal Data:* m 82, Angelina Spyropoulos; c Genya & Smaragda. *Educ:* Swiss Fed Inst Technol, Zurich, Dipl el Ing, 75, Dr, 80. *Concurrent Pos:* Vis, Swiss Fed Inst Technol, Zurich, 82-84, 86 & 92; Nat Sci & Eng Res Coun Can univ res fel, 84-86; vis fel, Australian Nat Univ, Canberra, 87. *Mem:* Sr mem Inst Elec & Electronics Engrs; Greek Technol Chamber. *Res:* Design and implementation of digital signal processing algonthus for a variety of applications such as image processing, speech processing etc; design of various types of controllers. *Mailing Add:* Dept Elec & Comput Eng Univ Victoria PO Box 3055 Victoria BC V8W 3P6 Can. *E-Mail:* pan@ece.uvic.ca

AGATHOS, SPYRIDON NICHOLAS, BIOCHEMICAL ENGINEERING & BIOTECHNOLOGY. *Current Pos:* PROF BIOENG, CATH UNIV LOUVAIN, BELG, 93- *Personal Data:* b Zante, Greece, July 31, 50; Greek & US citizen; m 85, Helene Skikos; c Kallirroe I, Catherine P & Nicolas J. *Educ:* Nat Tech Univ Athens, dipl eng, 73; McGill Univ, MEng, 76; Mass Inst Technol, PhD(biochem eng), 83. *Prof Exp:* Res & teaching asst chem eng, Dept Chem Eng, McGill Univ, Montreal, Que, Can, 73-75; res asst appl biol, Naval Res Lab, Dept Hemat, Boston City Hosp, Mass, 75-77; teaching asst biochem eng, Dept Appl Biol Sci, Mass Inst Technol, Cambridge, 78-82; lectr chem & biochem eng, Univ Western Ont, London, Can, 82-83, asst prof, 83-85; asst prof chem & biochem eng, Rutgers State Univ NJ, New Brunswick, 85-93. *Concurrent Pos:* Prin investr, Natural Sci & Eng Res Coun, Ottawa, Can, 83-85 & NSF, Washington, DC, 87-, biotech grants, Europ Comn; external reviewer, Natural Sci & Eng Res Coun, Ottawa, Can, 83-90, Acad Press, Hanser Publ, 88-; organizer & chmn sci sessions ann meetings, Am Inst Chem Engrs, 84-; consult, Var Biotechnol Co, 84-; mem, Waksman Inst Microbiol, Rutgers Univ, 85- & Int Sci Bd Int Union Microbiol Socs 1994 World Cong Microbiol 89-; dir, Grad Cert Prog Biotechnol, Rutgers Univ, 86-; vis prof, Inst Molecular Biol & Biotechnol, Univ Crete, Iraklion, Greece, 87 & Univ Sao Carlos, Brazil, 92; panel mem & reviewer, NSF, Washington,

DC, 87. *Mem:* Am Inst Chem Engrs; Am Chem Soc; Soc Indust Microbiol; AAAS; NY Acad Sci; Am Soc Microbiol. *Res:* Biochemical engineering; applied microbiology; molecular cell biology; fungal immunosuppressants; insect cell cultivation scaleup; recombinant microbe dynamics; enzyme stability; toxic pollutant biodegradation; bioremediation. *Mailing Add:* Cath Univ Louvain Unit Bioeng Place Croix du Sud 2/19 Louvain-la-Neuve B-1348 Belgium. *Fax:* 32-10-473062; *E-Mail:* agathos@gebi.ucl.ac.be

AGATSTON, ROBERT STEPHEN, GEOLOGY. *Current Pos:* Div res geologist, Atlantic Refining Co, 48-67, DIR GEOL SCI, ATLANTIC RICHFIELD CO, 67- *Personal Data:* b New York, NY, Apr 20, 23; m 57. *Educ:* Ohio State Univ, BS, 43; Columbia Univ, MA, 47, PhD(geol), 52. *Mem:* Am Asn Petrol Geologists. *Res:* Pennsylvanian of Wyoming. *Mailing Add:* 11421 Cromwell Ct Dallas TX 75229

AGBABIAN, MIHRAN S, STRUCTURAL & EARTHQUAKE ENGINEERING. *Current Pos:* RETIRED. *Personal Data:* b Larnacca, Cyprus, Dec 9, 23; nat US; m 53; c 3. *Educ:* Am Univ, Beirut, Lebanon, BA, 44, BS, 47; Calif Inst Technol, MS, 48; Univ Calif, Berkeley, PhD(struct & fluid mech), 51. *Prof Exp:* Proj engr & tech dir, Ralph M Parsons Co, Los Angeles, Calif, 55-62; pres, Agbabian & Assoc, 63-91, mem bd dirs, 91-93. *Concurrent Pos:* Fred Champion prof civil eng & chmn dept, Univ Southern Calif, 84-93. *Mem:* Nat Acad Eng; Earthquake Eng Res Inst (pres, 83-85); fel Am Soc Civil Engrs; AAAS; fel Inst Advan Eng; NY Acad Sci; Am Soc Testing & Mat; Am Concrete Inst; Am Inst Aeronaut & Astronaut; Am Defense Preparedness Asn. *Mailing Add:* 968 Linda Flora Dr Los Angeles CA 90049

AGBETI, MICHAEL DOMINGO, LAKE EUTROPHICATION, LAKE RESTORATION. *Current Pos:* FEL, UNIV ALTA, 93- *Personal Data:* b Tegbi-Ghana, West Africa, Sept, 1954. *Educ:* Univ Ghana, BSc, 80; Brock Univ, MSc, 87; Queens Univ, PhD(biol), 93. *Mem:* NAm Lake Mgt Soc; Am Soc Limnol & Oceanog; Soc Int Limnologists. *Res:* Lake eutrophication, ecology, primary productivity, lake restoration using hypolimetic oxygenation and liming, paleolimnology. *Mailing Add:* Dept Zool Univ Alta Edmonton AB T6G 2E9 Can. *Fax:* 403-492-9234; *E-Mail:* magbeti@vm.usc.ualberta.ca

AGEE, CARL BERNARD, MINERALOGY-PETROLOGY, THERMODYNAMICS & MATERIAL PROPERTIES. *Current Pos:* asst prof, 90-94, ASSOC PROF, HARVARD UNIV, 94- *Personal Data:* b Belle Plaine, Iowa, Oct 19, 51; m 73, Hannah Ockers. *Educ:* Univ Calif, Berkeley, AB, 84; Columbia Univ, MA, 86, MPhil, 88, PhD(geol sci), 88. *Prof Exp:* Vis scientist, Univ Bayreuth, Ger, 88-90. *Mem:* Am Geophys Union; Meteorol Soc; Geochem Soc. *Res:* Investigations of the earth's interior through high-pressure experiments. *Mailing Add:* Dept Earth & Planetary Sci Harvard Univ 20 Oxford St Cambridge MA 02138. *Fax:* 617-495-8839; *E-Mail:* agee@eps.harvard.edu

AGEE, ERNEST M(ASON), DYNAMIC METEOROLOGY, FLUID MECHANICS. *Current Pos:* From asst prof to assoc prof, 68-78, PROF ATMOSPHERIC SCI, PURDUE UNIV, 78-, HEAD EARTH & ATMOSPHERIC SCI, 90- *Personal Data:* b Richmond, Ky, Oct 2, 42; m 63; c 2. *Educ:* Eastern Ky Univ, BS, 64; Univ Mo-Columbia, MS, 66, PhD(atmospheric sci), 68. *Concurrent Pos:* NSF res grant, 87-; contract, Dept Defense-Oceanic Nat Res, 86-, IBM, 89-; US rep, Int Asn Meteorol & Atmospheric Physics, 80-88. *Mem:* Fel Am Meteorol Soc; Meteorol Soc Japan; Sigma Xi. *Res:* Thunderstorms and tornadoes; mesoscale cellular convection; theoretical and laboratory study of convective patterns and vortex features; field study of convective clouds in the atmosphere; climate. *Mailing Add:* 8533 N 100 W West Lafayette IN 47906

AGEE, HERNDON ROYCE, INSECT PHYSIOLOGY. *Current Pos:* RETIRED. *Personal Data:* b Cottonburg, Ky, Dec 21, 33; m 53; c 2. *Educ:* Berea Col, BA, 58; Univ Minn, MS, 60; Tufts Univ, PhD, 68. *Prof Exp:* Asst entom, Univ Minn, 58-60; entomologist, Cotton Insect Br, Agr Res Serv, USDA, 60-75, prof entom, Univ Fla, 74-90, res entomologist insect attractants, Behav & Basic Biol Res Lab, 75-90. *Mem:* Entom Soc Am; Am Soc Zoologists; Am Soc Neurosci. *Res:* Electrophysiological and behavioral studies of the sensory systems of insects; visual and acoustic responses; quality control; neurobiology of central nervous system. *Mailing Add:* 401 NW 91st St Gainesville FL 32607

AGEE, JAMES KENT, FOREST ECOLOGY. *Current Pos:* res biologist, Forest Fire Mgt, Coop Park Studies Unit, 78-88, chair ecosyst sci, 88-93, PROF FOREST ECOL, NAT PARK SERV, UNIV WASH, 93- *Personal Data:* b Alameda Calif, July 7, 45; m 69; c 2. *Educ:* Univ Calif, Berkeley, BS, 67, MS, 68, PhD(wildland resource sci), 73. *Prof Exp:* Lectr, Univ Calif, Berkeley, 73, forest ecologist, Nat Park Serv, San Francisco, 74-78. *Mem:* Forest Hist Soc; Ecol Soc Am; Nat Areas Asn. *Res:* Role of fire in ecosystems; management of natural disturbances. *Mailing Add:* Col Forest Resources ARIO Univ Wash Seattle WA 98195. *Fax:* 206-543-3254; *E-Mail:* jagee@u.washington.edu

AGEE, MARVIN H, industrial engineering, materials handling; deceased, see previous edition for last biography

AGENBROAD, LARRY DELMAR, GEOLOGY, HYDROGEOLOGY. *Current Pos:* prof geol, 78-96, DIR, QUATERNARY STUDIES PROG, NORTHERN ARIZ UNIV, 78- *Personal Data:* b Nampa, Idaho, Apr 3, 33; m 55, Wanda Juanita Sommers; c Brett Matthew & Finn Thomas. *Educ:* Univ Ariz, BS, 59, MS, 62, PhD(geol), 67, MA, 70. *Honors & Awards:* Archaeol Geol Award, Geol Soc Am, 96. *Prof Exp:* Explor geophysicist, Pan Am Petrol Corp, 60-62; geologist AEC shoal event, Nev Bur Mines, 62-63; teaching asst geol, Univ Ariz, 63-65 , teaching asst geol & anthrop, 65-67; prof earth sci, Chadron State Col, 67-78. *Concurrent Pos:* Dir, Hudson-Meng Paleo-Indian Bison Kill, 70-75; asst dir, Lehner Ranch, 74-75; dir, Hot Springs Mammoth Site, 74-; consult, environ impact statement, cultural resource, hydrogeol, quaternary deposits, fauna & geochronology. *Mem:* Soc Am Archaeol; Am Quaternary Asn; Geol Soc Am; Am Geol Inst. *Res:* Quaternary geology and its relation to early man in the New World; present paleohydrology and ground water resources; archaeology; Pleistocene megafauna, particularly mammoth and paleoenvironment. *Mailing Add:* Dept Geol N Ariz Univ Box 4099 Flagstaff AZ 86011. *Fax:* 520-523-9220; *E-Mail:* ida@nauvax.ucc.nav.edu

AGER, DAVID JOHN, ORGANOSILICON CHEMISTRY, ASYMMETRIC SYNTHESIS. *Current Pos:* FEL, NSC TECHNOLOGIES, 95- *Personal Data:* b Northampton, Eng, Apr 10, 53; div; c Tracy, Stephen, Christopher & Paul. *Educ:* Univ London, BSc, 74; Imp Col, London, ARCS, 74; Univ Cambridge, PhD(org chem), 77. *Prof Exp:* Res fel org chem, Sci Res Coun, Univ Southampton, 77-79; sr demonstr org chem, Univ Liverpool, 79-82; asst prof, Univ Toledo, 82-86; res scientist, Nutrasweet, 86-88, from assoc fel to fel, 88-95. *Concurrent Pos:* Sci res coun Postdoc Award, 77-79. *Mem:* Am Chem Soc; Royal Soc Chem. *Res:* Asymmetric synthetic method development; new synthetic methods particularly those using alkylations, reductions and organosilicon chemistry. *Mailing Add:* NSC Technol 601 E Kensington Rd Mt Prospect IL 60056-1300. *Fax:* 847-506-2277; *E-Mail:* djager@ccmail.monsanto.com

AGER, JOHN WINFRID, CHEMISTRY. *Current Pos:* SR RES ASSOC, FMC CORP, 60- *Personal Data:* b Birmingham, Ala, Nov 2, 26; m 56, Sheila Wilcox; c John W & Catherine M. *Educ:* Harvard Univ, BA, 49; Univ NC, MA, 51; Oxford Univ, PhD(org chem), 55. *Prof Exp:* Res chemist, Olin Mathieson Chem Corp, NY, 56-60. *Mem:* Am Chem Soc. *Res:* Boron based high energy fuels; synthesis in the field of natural products; process development of commercial chemicals; agricultural chemicals. *Mailing Add:* FMC Corp Box 8 Princeton NJ 08540

AGER, THOMAS ALAN, GEOLOGY, PALEONTOLOGY. *Current Pos:* GEOLOGIST PALYNOLOGY, US GEOL SURV, 76- *Personal Data:* b Detroit, Mich, July 31, 46. *Educ:* Wayne State Univ, BS, 68; Univ Alaska, MS, 72; Ohio State Univ, PhD(geol), 75. *Prof Exp:* Res assoc geol, Inst Polar Studies, Ohio State Univ, 75-76. *Mem:* Am Quaternary Asn; Am Asn Stratig Palynologists; Ecol Soc Am. *Res:* Quaternary and Neogene palynology and paleo-ecology of Alaska and Eastern USA; paleoclimatology; biostratigraphy. *Mailing Add:* 31758 Quarter Horse Rd Evergreen CO 80439

AGERSBORG, HELMER PARELI KJERSCHOW, JR, PHYSIOLOGY, TOXICOLOGY. *Current Pos:* clin physiologist, Med Div, Wyeth Labs, Inc, 58-61, mgr toxicol & comp pharmacol, Res Div, 61-69, assoc dir, 69-76, vpres res & develop, 76-85, PRES, WYETH AYERST RES, 85- *Personal Data:* b Decatur, Ill, Dec 2, 28; m 52; c 3. *Educ:* Southern Ill Univ, AB, 54; Univ Tenn, PhD, 57. *Prof Exp:* Asst physiol, Univ Tenn, 54-57, instr clin physiol & obstet & gynec & dir obstet & gynec, 57-58. *Mem:* Am Soc Pharmacol & Exp Therap; Am Physiol Soc; Am Soc Zool; Soc Toxicol. *Res:* Metabolic disease; cardiovascular physiology; ion and fluid dynamics; drug safety evaluation. *Mailing Add:* Fieldcastle Inc 200 Eagle Rd Suite 200 Wayne PA 19087. *Fax:* 215-975-4428

AGGARWAL, BHARAT BHUSHAN, RECOMBINANT DNA TECHNOLOGY. *Current Pos:* PROF MED, BIOCHEM, M D ANDERSON CANCER CTR, UNIV TEX, 89- *Personal Data:* b Batala, India; m 82; c 2. *Educ:* Univ Delhi, BS, 70; Benaras Hindu Univ, India, MS, 72; Univ Calif, Berkeley, PhD(biochem), 77. *Prof Exp:* Fel hormone res, Univ Calif, San Francisco, 77-80; sr scientist protein biochem, Genentech Inc, S San Francisco, 80-89. *Mem:* Am Endocrine Soc; AAAS; Soc Biochem & Molecular Biol; Am Asn Immunologist. *Res:* Purification and physiochemical characterization of proteins derived from natural and recombinant DNA technology; relationship of the structure of a protein and carbohydrates to its function. *Mailing Add:* Dept Clinical Immunol & Biol Therapy Univ Texas M D Anderson Cancer Ctr 1515 Holcomb Blvd Houston TX 77030-4095

AGGARWAL, H(ANS) R(AJ), ENGINEERING MECHANICS, APPLIED MATHEMATICS. *Current Pos:* RETIRED. *Personal Data:* b Jullundur, India, Dec 12, 25; m 51; c 4. *Educ:* Panjab Univ, BA, 48, MA, 50; Cornell Univ, PhD(eng mech), 62. *Prof Exp:* Lectr math, Govt Col, Hoshiarpur, India, 50-57; teaching asst, Cornell Univ, 57-60; mem tech staff, Nat Eng Sci Co, Calif, 61-63; res mathematician, Stanford Res Inst, 63-70; sr res assoc appl mech, Ames Res Ctr, NASA, 71-73; sr res assoc, Univ Santa Clara, Calif, 73-80; sr res assoc, Ames Res Ctr, NASA, 80-95. *Mem:* Sigma Xi; Soc Indust & Appl Math. *Res:* Transonic flow; helicopter aerodynamics; aeroacoustics and helicopter noise; computational analysis; numerical solution of partial differential equations; planetology. *Mailing Add:* 3374 Tryna Dr Mountain View CA 94040-4548

AGGARWAL, ISHWAR D, MATERIALS SCIENCE, OPTICAL ENGINEERING. *Current Pos:* RESEARCHER, NAVAL RES LAB, 86- *Personal Data:* b Delhi, India, May 18, 45; US citizen; m 69, Shail Aggarwal; c 2. *Educ:* Indian Inst Technol, BS, 69; Cath Univ Am, MS, 71, PhD(mat sci), 74. *Prof Exp:* Sr mat scientist, Corning Glass Works, 74-75; mgr mat res, Galileo Electro Optic Corp, Sturbridge, Mass, 75-78; vpres res, Optical Commun, Valtec, 78-84; vpres eng, Lasertron Inc, Burlington, Mass, 84-86. *Concurrent Pos:* Prog co-chmn, Optical Fiber Conf, 84, gen co-chmn, 85. *Mem:* Optical Soc Am; Am Ceramic Soc; Nat Inst Ceramic Engrs. *Res:* Optical fiber communication; glass science; engineering management; optical engineering research; polymeric coating; laser and detector materials; quality engineering management; environmental sciences; optoelectronics; glass and ceramic engineering; published over 100 articles and awarded several patents; fiber optic chemical sensors; infrared materials; infrared optical fibers; optical fiber amplifiers. *Mailing Add:* Code 5606 Naval Res Lab Washington DC 20375-5338. *Fax:* 202-767-9311; *E-Mail:* ish.aggarwal@nrl.navy.mil

AGGARWAL, JAGDISHKUMAR KESHORAM, ELECTRICAL ENGINEERING, COMPUTER SCIENCE. *Current Pos:* from asst prof to assoc prof, 64-72, PROF ELEC ENG, UNIV TEX, AUSTIN, 72- *Personal Data:* b Amritsar, India, Nov 19, 36; m 65, Shanti Seth; c 2. *Educ:* Univ Bombay, BSc, 56; Univ Liverpool, BEng, 60; Univ Ill, MSc, 61, PhD(elec eng), 64. *Honors & Awards:* Sr Res Award, Am Soc Elec Engrs, 92. *Prof Exp:* Asst elec eng, Coord Sci Lab, Univ Ill, 61-64. *Concurrent Pos:* Vis assoc prof, Univ Calif, Berkeley, 69-70. *Mem:* Fel Inst Elec & Electronics Engrs; Pattern Recognition Soc; Asn Comput Mach; Am Asn Artificial Intel. *Res:* Digital filtering; image processing; computer vision. *Mailing Add:* Dept Comput & Vision Univ Tex Austin TX 78712. *Fax:* 512-471-5532; *E-Mail:* jka@emx.cc.utexas.edu

AGGARWAL, ROSHAN LAL, QUANTUM OPTICS, PHYSICS OF SEMICONDUCTORS. *Current Pos:* staff mem, Mass Inst Technol, 65-71, proj leader quantum optics, 71-74, group leader quantum optics & plasma physics, 74-76, group leader quantum optics, 76-84, assoc dir, 77-84, sr res scientist, Physics Dept, Francis Bitter Nat Magnet Lab, 75-90, group leader, Semiconductor Group, 84-86, STAFF MEM, MASS INST TECHNOL, LINCOLN LAB, 86-, SR LECTR, PHYSICS DEPT, 90- *Personal Data:* b Salala, India, Feb 15, 37; m 58, Pushap; c Rajesh & Achal. *Educ:* Punjab Univ, India, BSc, 57, MSc, 58; Purdue Univ, PhD(physics), 65. *Prof Exp:* Lectr, Punjab Univ, 58-60; res assoc physics, Purdue Univ, 65. *Mem:* Fel Am Phys Soc; Sigma Xi; Optical Soc Am. *Res:* Near and far infrared spectroscopy; modulation magnetospectroscopy; lasers and nonlinear optics; light scattering in solids; physics of semiconductors. *Mailing Add:* Mass Inst Technol Lincoln Lab PO Box 73 244 Wood St Lexington MA 02173. *Fax:* 781-276-6721; *E-Mail:* aggarwal@ll.mit.edu

AGGARWAL, SHANTI J, BIOMEDICAL ENGINEERING. *Current Pos:* res assoc zool, Univ Tex, Austin, 65-70, microbiol, 70-78, lectr, 74-78, SR RES SCIENTIST BIOMED ENG, UNIV TEX, AUSTIN, 83- *Personal Data:* b Balrampur, India, July 1, 33; m 65; c 2. *Educ:* Banaras Hindu Univ, India, BSc & MSc, 52; Univ Mich, Ann Arbor, MS, 58, PhD(microbiol), 62. *Prof Exp:* Res fel, Nat Res Coun Can, Ottawa, 62-63; res assoc microbiol, Univ Ill, Urbana, 63-64. *Concurrent Pos:* Res assoc, Space Sci Res Labs, Univ Calif, Berkeley, 69-70. *Mem:* Soc Cryobiol; AAAS; Microcirculatory Soc. *Res:* Cryopreservation of tissue for transplantation and tissue banking; cryopreservation of human pancreatic islets and human skin for tissue banking and subsequent transplantation in diabetic patients and grafting on burn sites, respectively; microcirculatory response after burn injury; computer vision analysis of biomedical scenes; 3-D reconstruction of biomedical images using light microscopy and stereo-microscopy; laser tissue interactions. *Mailing Add:* Biomed Eng Prog ENS 612 Univ Tex Austin TX 78712-1084

AGGARWAL, SUNDAR LAL, polymer chemistry; deceased, see previous edition for last biography

AGGARWAL, SURINDER K, TOXICOLOGY, TERATOLOGY. *Current Pos:* PROF ZOOL, MICH STATE UNIV, 67- *Personal Data:* b Panjab, India, June 3, 38; m 67; c 3. *Educ:* Panjab Univ, BSc, 57, MSc, 58, PhD(zool), 64. *Prof Exp:* Res assoc zool, Dept Biol Sci, Northwestern Univ, 64-67. *Concurrent Pos:* Fulbright exchange fel, 87-88. *Mem:* Histochem Soc Am; Electron Micros Soc Am; Cell Biol Soc Am; Cancer Res Asn Am. *Res:* Mechanism of action of various heavy metal coordination complexes as antitumor agents, using hitochemical and electron microscopical approach. *Mailing Add:* Dept Zool Mich State Univ 203 Natural Sci East Lansing MI 48824-1115

AGGARWALA, BHAGWAN D, APPLIED MATHEMATICS. *Current Pos:* assoc prof, 66-71, prof math, statist & comput sci, 71-95, EMER PROF DEPT MATH & STATIST, UNIV CALGARY, 95- *Personal Data:* b India, Mar 9, 31. *Educ:* Punjab Univ, India, BA, 50, MA, 52, PhD(math), 59. *Prof Exp:* Instr math, Indian Inst Technol, Kharagpur, 53-55; instr, Carnegie Inst Technol, 55-57; asst prof mech, Rensselaer Polytech Inst, 57-60; asst prof math, McGill Univ, 60-66. *Mem:* Can Cong Appl Math. *Res:* Stress analysis of elastic and viscoelastic materials; heat transfer; fluid mechnics, integral equations, partial differential equations. *Mailing Add:* Dept Math Statist Univ Calgary 2500 University Dr Calgary AB T2N 1N4 Can

AGGEN, GEORGE, METALLURGICAL ENGINEERING. *Current Pos:* Jr metallurgist Res & Develop, Allegheny Ludlum Industs Inc, 51-54, res metallurgist, 54-56, sr res metallurgist, 56-57, supv metallurgist, 57-62, proj supvr, 62-63, res assoc, 63-65, sr res specialist, 65-68, sr supv metallurgist, 68-70, sr supv metallurgist, 70-75, MGR RES, ALLEGHENY LUDLUM STEEL CORP, 75-, MGR STAINLESS RES, 75- *Personal Data:* b Rotterdam, NY, Sept 28, 24; m 52; c 5. *Educ:* Rensselaer Polytech Inst, BME, 51, DSc(metall eng), 63. *Mem:* Am Soc Metals; Am Inst Mining, Metall & Petrol Engrs; Am Soc Testing & Mat. *Res:* High temperature alloys; stainless steels, particularly precipitation-hardening types. *Mailing Add:* 245 Edgewood Dr Sarver PA 16055

AGHAJANIAN, GEORGE KEVORK, NEUROPHARMACOLOGY. *Current Pos:* resident, 59-63, from asst prof psychiat to assoc prof psychiat & pharmacol, 65-74, PROF PSYCHIAT & PHARMACOL, SCH MED, YALE UNIV, 74-, FOUND FUND PROF RES PSYCHIAT, 85- *Personal Data:* b Beirut, Lebanon, Apr 14, 32; m 59, Anne Hammond; c Michael, Andrew, Carol & Laura. *Educ:* Cornell Univ, AB, 54; Yale Univ, MD, 58. *Honors & Awards:* Efron Award, 75; Scheele Medal, 81; Res Prize, Found Fund, 81; Merit Award, NIMH, 90; Hillarp Award, 96. *Prof Exp:* Intern, Jackson Mem Hosp, 58-59. *Mem:* Am Soc Pharmacol & Exp Therapeut; fel Am Col Neuropsychopharmacol; Soc Neurosci; Int Brain Res Orgn. *Res:* Neurotransmitters and the mechanism of action of psychotropic drugs. *Mailing Add:* Dept Psychiat Yale Univ Sch Med 34 Park St New Haven CT 06508. *Fax:* 203-562-7079; *E-Mail:* george.aghajanian@yale.edu

AGHAJANIAN, JOHN GREGORY, MOLECULAR BIOLOGY, ELECTRON MICROSCOPY. *Current Pos:* DIR ELECTRON MICROSCOPY, WORCESTER FOUND EXP BIOL, 84- *Res:* Molecular biology; electron microscopy. *Mailing Add:* Worcester Found Exp Biol 222 Maple Ave Shrewsbury MA 01545-2795

AGIN, DANIEL PIERRE, NEUROPHYSIOLOGY, BIOPHYSICS. *Current Pos:* from instr to asst prof, 62-67, actg chmn dept, 68-69, ASSOC PROF PHYSIOL, UNIV CHICAGO, 67- *Personal Data:* b New York, NY, May 19, 30; m 56; c 2. *Educ:* City Col New York, BA, 53; Univ Rochester, PhD(psychol), 61. *Prof Exp:* NIH fel, 61-62. *Concurrent Pos:* Vis prof, Max Planck Inst Biophys, 69-70. *Res:* Membrane biophysics; biophysical pharmacology. *Mailing Add:* Dept Cell Biol & Genetics Univ Chicago Pritzker Sch Med 920 E 58th St Chicago IL 60637-1432

AGIN, GARY PAUL, NUCLEAR PHYSICS. *Current Pos:* Asst prof, 68-87, ASSOC PROF PHYSICS, MICH TECHNOL UNIV, 87- *Personal Data:* b Kansas City, Mo, Dec 22, 40. *Educ:* Univ Kans, BS, 63; Kans State Univ, MS, 67, PhD(physics), 68. *Concurrent Pos:* Zone 8 counr, Soc Physics Students, 81-88, coun pres, 89- *Mem:* AAAS; Am Asn Physics Teachers; Am Phys Soc. *Res:* Low energy nuclear physics; beta and gamma ray spectroscopy; computer applications. *Mailing Add:* Dept Physics Mich Technol Univ 1400 Townsend Dr Houghton MI 49931

AGINS, BARNETT ROBERT, MATHEMATICS. *Current Pos:* ADJ PROF, FLA ATLANTIC UNIV, 77- *Personal Data:* b New York, NY, May 19, 22; m 45, Esther Klein; c Ira & Harriet. *Educ:* NY Univ, BEE, 52, MEE, 56; Stanford Univ, MSc, 61. *Prof Exp:* USAF, 50-, commun off Air Defense Command, 50-54, proj engr electronic syst, 56-59, chief appl math div, Off Sci Res, 61-67; asst to dir, Courant Inst Math Sci, 67-69; prog dir appl math & statist, NSF, 69-77. *Concurrent Pos:* Prof lectr, Am Univ, 62-; assoc ed, J Optimization Theory & Applns, 67-; assoc ed, Comput & Math Appl, 74-87. *Mem:* Inst Elec & Electronic Engrs; Soc Indust & Appl Math. *Res:* Sophisticated electronic warfare techniques; mathematics with respect to ordinary differential equations, especially those of celestial mechanics. *Mailing Add:* Dept Math Fla Atlantic Univ Boca Raton FL 33431-7831

AGISHTEIN, MICHAEL ERNEST, DATA CLEANING, GRAPHIC INPUT SYSTEMS. *Current Pos:* math specialist, dir res & develop, 93-96, VPRES TECHNOL, HAMMOND INC, 96- *Personal Data:* b Moscow, Russia, July 8, 63; US citizen; m 84, Larisa Gefter; c Chany, Shlomo E, Abraham C, Judith M & Susan M. *Educ:* Moscow Inst Oil & Gas, BS, 85; Princeton Univ, PhD(appl math), 90. *Prof Exp:* Res staff mem, Princeton Univ, 90-93. *Concurrent Pos:* Consult, NEC, 92, DEC, 97- *Res:* Computational geometry in real life; processing and cleaning large geometrical databases. *Mailing Add:* 309 Squankum Rd Lakewood NJ 08701. *Fax:* 973-763-7658; *E-Mail:* misha@unx.dec.com

AGNELLO, ARTHUR MICHAEL, ECONOMIC ENTOMOLOGY, EXTENSION. *Current Pos:* asst prof, 86-92, ASSOC PROF ENTOM, CORNELL UNIV, 92- *Personal Data:* b Ithaca, NY, Sept 25, 52; m 81; c 1. *Educ:* Cornell Univ, BS, 74; Univ Fla, Gainesville, MS, 79; NC State Univ, PhD(entom), 85. *Prof Exp:* Aquatic weeds res officer, min agr, US Peace Corp, Repub Botswana, Africa, 74-76; surv entomologist, Ill Coop Ext Serv, Univ Ill, 80-81; res assoc, Dept Entom, NC State Univ, 85-86. *Mem:* Entom Soc Am; Sigma Xi. *Res:* Control of arthropod pests of fruit; monitoring and sampling strategies for fruit mites and insects; development of pest management recommendations and educational materials; pesticide application technology. *Mailing Add:* Dept Entom NY State Agr Exp Sta Geneva NY 14456. *Fax:* 315-787-2326; *E-Mail:* art_agnello@cornell.edu

AGNELLO, EUGENE JOSEPH, ORGANIC CHEMISTRY, MEDICINAL CHEMISTRY. *Current Pos:* from asst prof to prof, 64-90, chmn dept, 79-90, EMER PROF CHEM, HOFSTRA UNIV, 90- *Personal Data:* b Rochester, NY, Oct 3, 19; m 59, Dolores M Miller; c Paul, Marie, Jeanette, Lawrence & Margaret. *Educ:* State Univ NY Albany, AB, 41; Univ Rochester, PhD(chem), 50. *Prof Exp:* Teacher pub sch, NY, 41-46; asst, Univ Rochester, 46-50; fel, Univ Ill, 50-51; res chemist, Chas Pfizer & Co, Inc, 51-63; asst prof chem, Waynesburg Col, 63-64. *Concurrent Pos:* Teacher, Med Chem, Grad Elective Course, Div Continuing Educ, Univ Del, 91 & 94. *Mem:* Am Chem Soc. *Res:* Steroids; medicinal chemistry; natural products. *Mailing Add:* 10 Stirrup Run Stirrup Farms Newark DE 19711

AGNELLO, VINCENT, MEDICINE. *Current Pos:* DIR, CLIN IMMUNOL LAB, LAHEY CLIN MED CTR, 84- *Personal Data:* b Brooklyn, NY, Aug 1, 38. *Educ:* Rennsselaer Polytech Inst, BS, 60; Univ Rochester, MD, 64; Am Bd Internal Med, dipl, 74. *Prof Exp:* Intern, Vanderbilt Hosp, 64-65; from asst prof to assoc prof, Hosp Rockefeller Univ, 67-73; chief, Div Rheumat & Clin Immunol, New Eng Med Ctr, 73-81, dir, Clin Immunol Lab, 81-84; physician, Arthritus Geront Ctr, Edith Nourse Rogers Vet Hosp, 82-84. *Concurrent Pos:* Postdoctoral fel, Rockefeller Univ, 67-71, asst prof, 71-73; resident, NY Hosp, 72-73; assoc prof, Sch Med, Tufts Univ, 73-85; career develop award, NIH, 74-79; mem adv panel, Am Bd Med Lab Immunol, 78- *Mem:* Fel Am Col Physicians; fel Am Acad Microbiol; Sigma Xi; Am Asn Immunologists. *Res:* Author or co-author of over 60 publications. *Mailing Add:* Dept Lab Med Lahey Clin Med Ctr 41 Mall Rd PO Box 541 Burlington MA 01805

AGNEW, ALLEN FRANCIS, PUBLIC POLICY. *Current Pos:* COURTESY PROF, ORE STATE UNIV, 82- *Personal Data:* b Ogden, Ill, Aug 24, 18; m 46, Frances Keiffer; c Allen B, Larry P, Leslie (Seitz) & Heather (Moore). *Educ:* Univ Ill, AB, 40, MS, 42; Stanford Univ, PhD(geol), 49. *Honors & Awards:* Robert Peele Award, Am Inst Mining Engrs; Pub Serv Award, Am Inst Prof Geologists, Cert Merit. *Prof Exp:* Asst geologist, Ill State Geol Surv, 39-42; geologist, US Geol Surv, Wis, 42-47 & 49-55; asst prof geol, Univ Ala, 48-49; from assoc prof to prof, Univ SDak, 55-63, geologist, SDak Geol Surv, 55-57, dir & state geologist, 57-63; prof geol & dir water resources res ctr, Ind Univ, Bloomington, 63-69; prof geol & dir water res ctr, Wash State Univ, 69-73; sr specialist environ policy/mining, Cong Res Serv, Libr Cong, 74-81. *Mem:* Asn Eng Geol; Geol Soc Am; Soc Econ Geologists; Soc Environ Geochem Health; Soc Mining Engrs; Am Geophys Union; Am Inst Prof Geologists; Nat Water Well Asn; hon mem Asn Am State Geologists. *Res:* Hydrogeology; engineering geology. *Mailing Add:* 33125 White Oak Rd Corvallis OR 97333

AGNEW, HAROLD MELVIN, PHYSICS. *Current Pos:* RETIRED. *Personal Data:* b Denver, Colo, Mar 28, 21; m 42, Beverly Jackson; c John S & Nancy E (Owens). *Educ:* Univ Denver, AB, 42; Univ Chicago, MS, 48, PhD(physics), 49. *Hon Degrees:* Dr, Col Santa Fe, 81, Univ Denver, 92. *Honors & Awards:* Ernest Orlando Lawrence Award, Am Eng Coun, 66; Enrico Fermi Award, Dept Energy, 78. *Prof Exp:* Physicist, Manhattan Dist, Univ Calif, Los Alamos, NMex, 42-46; Nat Res fel, Physics Div, Los Alamos Sci Lab, 49-50, asst to tech assoc dir, 51-53 & Theoret Div, 54-56, leader, Alt Weapons Div, 56-61; sci adv, Supreme Allied Comdr, Europe, 61-64; leader, Weapons Div, Los Alamos Nat Lab, 64-70, dir, 70-79; pres, Gen Atomics Inc, San Diego, 79-85. *Concurrent Pos:* Mem, USAF Sci Adv Bd, 57-68; chmn, US Army Combat Develop Command Sci Adv Group, 65-66; mem, President's Sci Adv Comt, 65-73; mem, Defense Sci Bd, 66-70; chmn, US Army Sci Adv Panel, 66-70, mem, 70-74; mem, Aerospace Safety Adv Panel, NASA, 68-74, 85-87; mem, gen adv comt, US Arms Control & Disarmament Agency, 74-82, chmn, 74-78; mem, Coun Foreign Rels, 75-; mem bd dirs, Fedn Rocky Mtn States, Inc, 75-; mem, Army Sci Bd, 78-84; White House Sci Coun, 81-88; adj prof, Univ Calif, San Diego, 88-; dir, Charles Lee Powell Found, 92- *Mem:* Nat Acad Sci; Nat Acad Eng; fel AAAS; fel Am Phys Soc; Sigma Xi. *Res:* Neutron physics; light particle reactions; particle accelerators. *Mailing Add:* 322 Punta Baja Dr Solana Beach CA 92075. *Fax:* 619-481-8908

AGNEW, JEANNE LE CAINE, MATHEMATICS. *Current Pos:* from asst prof to prof, 56-84, EMER PROF MATH, OKLA STATE UNIV, 84- *Personal Data:* b Port Arthur, Ont, May 3, 17; US citizen; m 42, Thedore; c Lee, Sue, Hugh, Pete & Marion. *Educ:* Queen's Univ, Ont, BA, 37, MA, 38; Harvard Univ, PhD(math), 41. *Hon Degrees:* LLD Queen's Univ, Can, 88, Lakehead Univ, Thunder Bay, Ont, 90. *Prof Exp:* Instr math, Smith Col, 41-42; res physicist, Nat Res Coun Can, 42-45; instr math, Cambridge Jr Col, 46-47. *Concurrent Pos:* Vis assoc prof, Ga State Col, 66-67. *Mem:* Nat Coun Teachers & Maths; Math Asn Am. *Res:* Applications of undergraduate level mathematics to industrial problems; preparation of written material based on this research for use in high school and college. *Mailing Add:* 1216 N Lincoln St Stillwater OK 74075-2749

AGNEW, LEWIS EDGAR, JR, PHYSICS. *Current Pos:* staff mem, Lab, 59-69, GROUP LEADER, LAMPF ACCELERATOR PROJ, LOS ALAMOS NAT LAB, 70- *Personal Data:* b Glendale, Mo, June 20, 26; m 52; c 4. *Educ:* Univ Mo-Rolla, BS, 50; Univ Calif, Berkeley, MA, 56, PhD(physics), 60. *Prof Exp:* Res asst, Los Alamos Sci Lab, 50-53, staff mem, 53-54; res asst, Lawrence Radiation Lab, Univ Calif, 56-59. *Concurrent Pos:* Head physics sect, Div Res & Labs, Int Atomic Energy Agency, Vienna, Austria, 66-68. *Mem:* Fel AAAS; Am Phys Soc; Sigma Xi. *Res:* Medium energy physics; plasma spectroscopy. *Mailing Add:* 292 Cascabe St Los Alamos NM 87544-2517

AGNEW, ROBERT A, CORPORATE BUSINESS ANALYSIS. *Current Pos:* MGR, FMC BUSINESS ANALYSIS CORP, 76- *Personal Data:* b Ga, Jan 9, 42; m, Shashana Zagury; c Valerie. *Educ:* Cornell Univ, BME, 64, Northwestern Univ, PhD(appl math), 68; Univ Chicago, MBA, 85. *Prof Exp:* Asst prof opers res, USAF Inst Technol, 68-71; opers res proj mgr, Montgomery Ward, 72-76. *Mem:* Nat Asn Bus Economists; Am Statist Asn; Opers Res Soc Am; Inst Mgt Scis. *Mailing Add:* 2626 N Lakeview No 1503 Chicago IL 60614-1812. *Fax:* 312-861-6923

AGNEW, ROBERT MORSON, immunobiology of tumors, for more information see previous edition

AGNEW, STEPHEN FRANCIS, NUCLEAR WASTE SCIENCE, NUCLEAR PROCESSING SAFETY. *Current Pos:* postdoctoral assoc, 82-84, TECH STAFF MEM, LOS ALAMOS NAT LAB, 84- *Personal Data:* b Lewiston, Idaho, Oct 7, 52. *Educ:* Evergreen State Col, BA, 76; Wash State Univ, PhD(chem physics), 81. *Prof Exp:* Postdoctoral assoc, Max Planck Inst Beam Chem, 81-82. *Mem:* Am Chem Soc; Western Spectros Asn. *Res:* High level nuclear waste science related to storage, pretreatment, disposal and related safety issues; use of Raman and infrared vibrational spectroscopies for the study of waste and other chemical reactions at high pressure and temperature. *Mailing Add:* 531 Paul Pl Los Alamos NM 87544. *E-Mail:* sfagnew@lanl.gov

AGNEW, WILLIAM FINLEY, PHYSIOLOGY. *Current Pos:* lab and neurosurg res fel physiol, 55-63, SR INVESTR, INST MED RES, HUNTINGTON MEM HOSP, 63-, DIR NEUROL RES, HUNTINGTON MED RES INST, 76- *Personal Data:* b Greenville, SC, Aug 28, 25; m 58; c 2. *Educ:* Wheaton Col, AB, 49; Univ Ill, Urbana, MS, 54; Univ Southern Calif, PhD(physiol), 64. *Honors & Awards:* Commendation Medal, Functional elec Stimulation, Tohuku Med Soc, Japan, 95. *Prof Exp:* Res asst physiol, Baxter Labs, 52-53; res asst biol, Calif Inst Technol, 55. *Concurrent Pos:* Res asst, Univ Southern Calif, 57-60; NIH res grant, 61-63; Nat Inst Neurol Dis & Stroke fel, Univ Copenhagen, 65-66, res grant, 69-71; prin investr, NIH contract, 76-79, 80-82, 83-85, 86-88 & 87-90; NIH res grants, 77-80 & 81-84; ed, Neural Prostheses: Fundamental Studies, 90. *Mem:* Teratology Soc; Am Physiol Soc; Soc Exp Biol & Med; Soc Neurosci. *Res:* Cerebral circulation; blood-brain and cerebrospinal fluid barriers and development; testing of neuroprosthetic devices. *Mailing Add:* Huntington Med Res Insts 734 Fairmount Ave Pasadena CA 91105

AGNEW, WILLIAM G(EORGE), MECHANICAL ENGINEERING. *Current Pos:* CONSULT, 89- *Personal Data:* b Oak Park, Ill, Jan 12, 26; m 57; c 3. *Educ:* Purdue Univ, BSME, 48, MSME, 50, PhD(mech eng), 52. *Honors & Awards:* Horning Mem Award, Soc Automotive Engrs, 60, Medal of Honor, 92, Excellence Educ Award, 97. *Prof Exp:* Mem staff, Eng Proj Squid, US Navy, Purdue Univ, 48-50; sr res engr, Fuels & Lubricants Dept, Gen Motors Corp, 52-56, res assoc, 56-63, asst dept head, 63-67, head, 67-70, head, Emissions Res Dept, 70-71, tech dir, 71-87, dir prog & plans, Gen Motors Res Labs, 87-89. *Mem:* Nat Acad Eng; fel AAAS; fel Soc Automotive Engrs; Sigma Xi; Am Soc Mech Engrs; Am Soc Eng Educ. *Res:* The effects of atmospheric conditions on engine performance; radiant energy and radiation temperature measurement in gas turbine combustions; end-gas temperature measurement in spark-ignition engines; cool flames and pre-flame reactions; engine knock and antiknock mechanisms. *Mailing Add:* 3450 31 Mile Rd Washington MI 48095. *Fax:* 810-752-9192; *E-Mail:* agnew@misi.net

AGNEW-MARCELLI, G(LADYS) MARIE, BIOMEDICAL SCIENCES. *Current Pos:* RES FEL & COORDR, SCI ANALYTICAL SECT, JACOB, MEDINGER & FINNEGAN, 84- *Personal Data:* b Albany, NY, Mar 20, 27. *Educ:* Rensselaer Polytech Inst, BSCh, 48, MS, 52; Univ Sussex, PhD(biol sci & pub admin), 74. *Prof Exp:* Tech asst, Pharm Div, Sterling-Winthrop Res Inst, 48-51, res asst, Chem-Biol Coord Sect, 51-53, res assoc new drug develop, Off Dir Res, 54-57, sci liaison officer, Europ-Australian Tech Opers, Sterling Drug, Inc, 58-67, assoc mem new drug develop, 61-65, res chemist, 65-71, mem new prod develop comt, 70-71, dir spec projs, Prod Develop & Regulatory Affairs, 71; consult sci & med info, 72-83. *Concurrent Pos:* Curric adv comt, State Univ NY, Hudson Valley Community Col, 56-71; spec proj asst mild analgesics, Sterling Drug Res Bd, 67-70; sci consult, Ritual Object Sources & Authentication, Yeshiva Univ, Mus, 80 & mem, Mus Adv comt, 81-86; consult, Essex County, NY, 90-, NY State Archives & Records Admin, Regional Adv Comt, 91-96. *Mem:* Am Chem Soc; Am Soc Metals; Sigma Xi; Am Pub Health Asn; Biomet Soc; Soc Epidemiol Res. *Res:* Mild analgesics; barbiturates; toxicity of chemicals, occupational and environmental pollutants; epidemiology of chronic diseases; development of pharmaceuticals, toiletries and household products; scientific, medical and regulatory aspects of consumer product liability. *Mailing Add:* 61 Maple Ave Hastings-on-Hudson NY 10706

AGNISH, NARSINGH DEV, TOXICOLOGY. *Current Pos:* Sr scientist, 77-78, asst res group chief, 79-83, RES GROUP CHIEF, HOFFMAN-LA ROCHE, INC, 83- *Personal Data:* b Jullundur, India, Jan 3, 40; m 69; c 4. *Educ:* Panjab Univ, BSc, 59, MSc, 60; Univ Sask, PhD(anat & cancer res), 69; Am Bd Toxicol, dipl, 82. *Concurrent Pos:* Adj asst prof, Jefferson Med Col, 79- *Mem:* Teratol Soc; Am Asn Anatomists; Soc of Toxicol. *Res:* Preclinical testing of candidate drugs for effects on reproduction and developing fetus; normal and abnormal development of mammalian limbs. *Mailing Add:* Dept Toxicol Path Hoffman-La Roche Inc Bldg 100/3 340 Kingsland St Nutley NJ 07110-1199

AGOGINO, ALICE, COMPUTER SCIENCE. *Current Pos:* from asst prof to assoc prof, 84-92, PROF MECH ENG, UNIV CALIF, BERKELEY, 92-, ASSOC DEAN SPEC PROGS, COL ENG, 95- *Educ:* Univ NMex, BS, 75; Univ Calif, Berkeley, MS, 78; Stanford Univ, PhD, 84. *Honors & Awards:* Presidential Young Investr Award, NSF, 85; Ralph R Teetor Educr Award, Soc Automotive Engrs, 87. *Prof Exp:* Proj engr, Dow Chem, Tex, 72-73; mech engr, Gen Elec, San Jose & Sunnyvale, 75-78, com specialist, 78-79; dir, Women-in-Eng Prog, Univ Santa Clara, 80-81. *Concurrent Pos:* Chair, Santa Clara Valley Sect, Am Soc Mech Eng, 81-82, dir, 83-84. *Mem:* Nat Acad Eng; Am Soc Elec Engrs; Am Soc Mech Engrs; Inst Elec & Electronics Engrs; Am Asn Artificial Intel; Asn Comput Mach; fel AAAS. *Res:* Intelligent learning systems; multiobjective and strategic product design; nonlinear optimization; probabilistic modeling; intelligent control and manufacturing graphics, multimedia and computer aided design; design databases; artificial intelligence; decision and expert systems; author of numerous publications. *Mailing Add:* Univ Calif Eng Systs Res Ctr Synthesis Hq 3115 Etcheverry Hall Berkeley CA 94720. *Fax:* 510-642-6450; *E-Mail:* aagogino@euler.me.berkeley.edu

AGOSIN, MOISES, BIOCHEMISTRY, PARASITOLOGY. *Current Pos:* vis prof, 68-69, res prof, 69-92, EMER PROF ZOOL, UNIV GA, 92- *Personal Data:* b Marseille, France, Dec 1, 22; m 48, Frida Halpern; c Cynthia, Marjorie & Marid. *Educ:* Univ Chile, MD, 48. *Hon Degrees:* Dr, Peruvian Univ, Cayetano Heredia. *Honors & Awards:* Fel Chilean Acad Sci, 78; Bueding-von Brand Award, Am Soc Parasitol, 90. *Prof Exp:* From asst prof to assoc prof parasitol, Sch Med, Univ Chile, 48-57, prof biochem, 57-61 & chem, 61-68. *Concurrent Pos:* Rockefeller Found fel, NIH, 52-54, res assoc, 54-55, res grants, 58-90; Rockefeller Found res grant, 56; vis prof, Univ Calif, Berkeley, 61 & Univ London, 65. *Mem:* Fel Am Acad Microbiol; Am Chem Soc; Biochem Soc; fel Chilean Acad Sci. *Res:* Biochemistry of parasitic organisms; biochemistry of insecticide resistance. *Mailing Add:* Dept Cell Biol Univ Ga Athens GA 30602. *Fax:* 706-542-4271; *E-Mail:* agosin@zookeeper.zoo.uga.edu

AGOSTA, VITO, COMBUSTION OF ALTERNATIVE FUELS, PROPULSION. *Current Pos:* prof mech eng, 50-62, prof, 62-86, EMER PROF AEROSPACE ENG, POLYTECH INST NEW YORK, 86- *Personal Data:* b New York, NY, July 26, 23; m 52, Mary Frago; c John Mark, Diana Elizabeth & Charles Christopher. *Educ:* Polytech Inst Brooklyn, BS, 46; Univ Mich, MS, 49; Columbia Univ, PhD(mech eng), 59. *Prof Exp:* Thermodynamacist, DeLaval Steam Turbine Co, 46-47. *Concurrent Pos:* Consult, Gen Appl Sci Labs, Inc, 56-57, Appl Phys Lab, Johns Hopkins Univ, 56-79, Curtiss-Wright Corp, 62-63, Marquardt Corp, 64-67, Aerojet-Gen Corp, 64-67 & Jet Propulsion Labs, Calif Inst Technol, 64-68; Fulbright scholar, Univ London, 66-67; pres, Fuels Systs Design Corp, 76- *Mem:* Am Inst Aeronaut & Astronaut; Am Soc Mech Engrs; Combustion Inst. *Res:* Combustion; design of fuel services for the combustion of toxic and waste fuels in boilers and alternate fuels in engines; aerothermochemistry of subsonic and supersonic combustion systems in propulsion devices; air pollution. *Mailing Add:* 42 Cherry Ln Huntington NY 11743. *Fax:* 516-351-7190; *E-Mail:* 75020.3713@compuserve.com

AGOSTA, WILLIAM CARLETON, ORGANIC CHEMISTRY, PHOTOCHEMISTRY. *Current Pos:* from asst prof to assoc prof, 63-74, PROF CHEM, ROCKEFELLER UNIV, 74- *Personal Data:* b Dallas, Tex, Jan 1, 33; m 58, Karin Engstrom; c Jennifer Ellen & Christopher William. *Educ:* Rice Inst, BA, 54; Harvard Univ, AM, 55, PhD(chem), 57. *Prof Exp:* Nat Res Coun fel org chem, Dyson Perrins Lab, Oxford Univ, 57-58; Pfizer fel, Univ Ill, 58-59; asst prof chem, Univ Calif, 59-61; sci liaison officer, US Naval Forces Europe, 61-63. *Concurrent Pos:* Alfred P Sloan Found fel, 69-71; John Angus Erskine fel, Univ Canterbury, NZ, 81; vis prop, Univ Innsbruck, 95, Princeton Univ, 96. *Mem:* Inter-Am Photochem Soc; Am Chem Soc; The Chem Soc; Am Soc Photobiol; Europ Photochem Asn; fel AAAS. *Res:* Photochemistry; physical organic chemistry; pheromone chemistry. *Mailing Add:* Rockefeller Univ 1230 York Ave New York NY 10021-6399. *Fax:* 212-327-8263; *E-Mail:* agosta@rockvax.rockefeller.edu

AGOSTINI, ROMAIN CAMILLE, PERSONAL COMMUNICATIONS, USER INTERFACES & HI-SPEED NETS. *Current Pos:* COMPUT SCIENTIST RES & DEVELOP, STANFORD LINEAR ACCELERATOR CTR, 87- *Personal Data:* b Luxembourg, Mar 4, 59. *Educ:* Univ Karlsruhe, Ger, BS, 82, MS, 87; Stanford Univ, MS, 93. *Res:* Local area networks; data communications; software engineering; high-technology marketing; technology management; entrepreneurship; personal digital communications and information access. *Mailing Add:* Stanford Linear Accelerator Ctr PO Box 4349 Stanford CA 94309. *E-Mail:* ago@slac.stanford.edu

AGOSTON, MAX KARL, MATHEMATICS. *Current Pos:* asst prof, Dept Math & Comp Sci, 76-80, ASSOC PROF, SAN JOSE STATE UNIV, 80- *Personal Data:* b Stockerau, Austria, Mar 25, 41; US citizen. *Educ:* Reed Col, BA, 62; Yale Univ, MA, 64, PhD(math), 67; Stanford Univ, MS(CS), 78. *Prof Exp:* Lectr math, Wesleyan Univ, 66-67, asst prof, 67-75. *Concurrent Pos:* Vis prof math, Univ Heidelberg, 70-71; vis fel, Univ Auckland, 73-74. *Mem:* Am Math Soc; Asn Comp Mach; Inst Elect & Electronics Engr. *Res:* Geometric modeling; general software development; artificial intelligence. *Mailing Add:* Dept Math & Comp Sci San Jose State Univ San Jose CA 95192

AGRANOFF, BERNARD WILLIAM, BIOCHEMISTRY. *Current Pos:* assoc prof biochem, res biochemist & chief sect biochem, Univ Mich, Ann Arbor, 61-65, assoc dir, 77-83, dir, 83-95, PROF BIOCHEM, MENT HEALTH RES INST, UNIV MICH, ANN ARBOR, 65-, DIR, NEUROSCI LAB, 83- *Personal Data:* b Detroit, Mich, June 26, 26; m 57, Raquel Schwartz; c William & Adam. *Educ:* Wayne State Univ, MD, 50; Univ Mich, BS, 54. *Honors & Awards:* Fogarty Scholar-in-Residence Award, NIH, 1988. *Prof Exp:* Intern, Robert Packer Hosp, 50-51; res fel, Mass Inst Technol, 51-52; from asst officer chg to officer chg, Dept Chem, US Naval Med Sch, 52-54; biochemist, Nat Inst Neurol Dis & Blindness, NIH, 54-60. *Concurrent Pos:* Mem staff, Max Planck Inst Cell Chem, 58-59; adv ed, Advan in Lipid Res, 62-; fel comt biochem & nutrit, NIH, 64-67, mem study sect neurol A, 67-71 & neurol B, 75-79; mem adv comn fundamental res, Nat Multiple Sclerosis Soc, 70-73; chmn panel biochem, Nat Comn Multiple Sclerosis, 73; vis scientist, Med Res Coun, Mill Hill, 74-75; ed, J Biol Chem, J Neurochem & Brain Res; chmn, Int Soc Neurochem, 89-91. *Mem:* Inst Med-Nat Acad Sci; fel Am Psychol Soc; Soc Neurosci; Am Soc Neurochem (pres, 73-75); fel Am Col Neuropsychopharmacol; Int Soc Neurochem; fel NY Acad Sci. *Res:* Biochemistry of lipids; nerve regeneration; neurochemistry; biochemical correlates of behavior; non-invasive biochemical techniques (PET). *Mailing Add:* Univ Mich Neurosci Lab Bldg 1103 E Huron Ann Arbor MI 48104-1687

AGRAS, WILLIAM STEWART, MEDICINE, EXPERIMENTAL PSYCHIATRY. *Current Pos:* PROF PSYCHIAT, SCH MED, STANFORD UNIV, 73- *Personal Data:* b London, Eng, May 17, 29; Can citizen; m 55; c 2. *Educ:* Univ London, MB, BS, 55. *Prof Exp:* Demonstr psychiat, McGill Univ, 60-61; instr, Col Med, Univ Vt, 61-62, from asst prof to assoc prof, 62-69; prof & chmn dept, Med Ctr, Univ Miss, 69-73. *Concurrent Pos:* Ed, J Appl Behav Anal, 74-77; fel, Ctr Advan Study Behav Sci, 76-77, 90-91. *Mem:* Soc Behav Med (pres, 78); Psychiat Res Soc; Soc Exp Analysis Behav; Asn Advan Behav Ther (pres, 85). *Res:* Behavioral medicine, particularly applications of behavior change procedures to disease prevention; eating disorders, essential hypertension, stress prevention. *Mailing Add:* Psychiat Stanford Univ Sch Med Stanford Univ Stanford CA 94305-9991

AGRAWAL, ARUN KUMAR, MANUFACTURING AUTOMATION, MAN-MACHINE INTERFACE. *Current Pos:* ENG MGR, GEA CORP-INDUST SYSTS GROUP. *Personal Data:* b Agra, India, Nov 24, 45; m 74; c 1. *Educ:* Indian Inst Technol, Kanpur, BS, 67; Case Western Res Univ, MS, 68, PhD(comput sci), 74. *Prof Exp:* Electronic engr, Gould Inc, 69-71, sr engr, 74-76, group leader, 76-79, prog mgr, Gould Labs, 79- *Mem:* Inst Elec & Electronics Engrs Comput Soc; Robotics Int Soc Mech Engrs. *Res:* Robotic technology; speech recognition/synthesis; digital signal processing. *Mailing Add:* Motorola Inc 1295 E Algonquin Rd Schaumburg IL 60196

AGRAWAL, DHARMA PRAKASH, PARALLEL PROCESSING, COMPUTER ARCHITECTURE. *Current Pos:* PROF COMPUT ENG, DEPT ELEC ENG, NC STATE UNIV. *Personal Data:* b Balod, India, April 12, 45; m 71, Purnima Agrawal; c Sonali & Braj. *Educ:* Ravishankar Univ, India, BE, 66; Roorkee Univ, ME, 68; Fed Inst Technol, Switz, DScTech, 75. *Honors & Awards:* Cert Appreciation & Meritorious Serv Award, Inst Elec & Electronics Engrs Comput Soc. *Prof Exp:* Lectr elec eng, MNR Eng Col, India, 68-72 & Roorkee Univ, 72-73; asst mini & micro comput, Fed Inst Tech, Switz, 73-75; lectr elec eng, Univ Technol, Iraq, 76; instr comput sci, Southern Methodist Univ, Tex, 76-77; from asst prof to assoc prof comput eng, Wayne State Univ, 77-80. *Concurrent Pos:* Reviewer, NSF, 80-, Army Res Off, 82-; adv, Grad Reliability Eng. *Mem:* Asn Comput Mach; fel Inst Elec & Electronics Engrs. *Res:* VLSI; fault-tolerant computing; parallel processing; parallelism detection; scheduling techniques; multistage interconnection networks; hierarchical scalable networks; automatic teller machine networks; parallel and distributed systems reliability; high performance computer architecture. *Mailing Add:* Elec & Comput Eng 212 Daniel Hall NC State Univ Box 7911 Raleigh NC 27695. *Fax:* 919-515-5523; *E-Mail:* dpa@ncsu.edu

AGRAWAL, GOVIND P(RASAD), SEMICONDUCTOR LASERS, OPTICAL COMMUNICATIONS & NONLINEAR FIBER OPTICS. *Current Pos:* assoc prof, 89-92, PROF, UNIV ROCHESTER, 92- *Personal Data:* b Kashipur, India, July 24, 51; c 3. *Educ:* Univ Lucknow, BS, 69; Indian Inst Technol, MS, 71, PhD(physics), 74. *Honors & Awards:* Gold Medal, Univ Lucknow, 70. *Prof Exp:* Researcher polymers, Polytech Sch, France, 74-76; res assoc laser physics, City Univ New York, 77-80; staff scientist quantum electronics, Quantel, France, 80-81; mem tech staff semiconductor lasers, AT&T Bell Labs, 82-88. *Concurrent Pos:* Consult, AT&T Bell Labs, 81-82 & Quantel, France , 82. *Mem:* Am Phys Soc; fel Inst Elec & Electronics Engrs; fel Optical Soc Am; fel Optical Soc Am. *Res:* Optical communications; quantum electronics; nonlinear optics; semiconductor lasers; nonlinear fiber optics; fiber-optic communication systems; published 5 books and more than 230 research papers. *Mailing Add:* Inst Optics Univ Rochester Rochester NY 14627

AGRAWAL, HARISH C, MYELIN, OLIGODENDROGLIA. *Current Pos:* from res asst prof to assoc prof, 70-79, PROF PEDIAT & NEUROL, DEPT PEDIAT, SCH MED, WASH UNIV, ST LOUIS, MO, 79- *Personal Data:* b Allahabad, India, June 14, 39; US citizen; m 60; c 2. *Educ:* Allahabad Univ, India, BS, 57, MS, 59, PhD(biochem), 64. *Prof Exp:* Lectr res, Charing Cross Hosp, London, UK, 68-70. *Concurrent Pos:* RCDA, Nat Inst Neurol Dis & Stroke, NIH, 74-79; mem neurol B study sect, NIH, 79-82; vis prof, dept pediat, Univ Lussane, Switz, 82. *Mem:* Int Brain Res Orgn; Int Soc Neurochem; Am Soc Neurochem; Am Soc Biochem & Molecular Biol; Am Physiol Soc. *Res:* Isolation, characterization, localization, turnover and posttranslational modification(s) of myelin-glial cell specific proteins. *Mailing Add:* Dept Neurol 18 Chafford Woods St Louis MO 63144. *Fax:* 314-362-2826

AGRAWAL, KRISHNA CHANDRA, MEDICINAL CHEMISTRY, MOLECULAR BIOLOGY. *Current Pos:* assoc prof, 76-81, PROF PHARMACOL, SCH MED, TULANE UNIV, 81- *Personal Data:* b Calcutta, India, Mar 15, 37; nat US; m 60, Mani; c Sunil, Lina & Nira. *Educ:* Andhra Univ, India, BS, 59, MS, 60; Univ Fla, PhD(pharmaceut chem), 65. *Prof Exp:* Res assoc, Sch Med, Yale Univ, 66-69, from instr to assoc prof pharmacol, 69-76. *Concurrent Pos:* NIH fel grant, Univ Fla, 65-66; mem sci adv comt, Instnl Res Grants, Am Cancer Soc, 80-84 & 86-88; sci adv, Phase II Comt, SE Cancer Study Group, 83-86; mem, Study Sect AIDS Res, NIH, 88-94. *Mem:* Am Soc Pharmacol & Exp Therapeut; Am Asn Cancer Res; Am Chem Soc; Radiation Res Soc; Am Soc Hemat; Int Soc Antiviral Res. *Res:* Design and synthesis of chemical agents for chemotherapy of cancer and AIDS; development of radiosensitizing agents for use in combination with radiotherapy; studies of structure-activity relationship and biochemical mechanisms involved in cell death; study of hyperthermia and drug interactions. *Mailing Add:* Dept Pharmacol Tulane Univ Sch Med SL83 New Orleans LA 70112. *Fax:* 504-588-5283

AGRAWAL, PRADEEP KUMAR, ELECTROMAGNETISM. *Current Pos:* ASST PROF CHEM ENG, SCH CHEM ENGRS, GA INST TECHNOL, 80- *Personal Data:* b Meerut, India, Oct 26, 46; m 74; c 1. *Educ:* Agra Univ, India, BSc, 63; Indian Inst Technol, Kanpur, BTech, 68; Ohio State Univ, MSc, 69, PhD(elec eng), 72. *Honors & Awards:* NSG-1110, NASA Langley Res Ctr, 75. *Prof Exp:* Grad res assoc, Electro Sci Lab, Ohio State Univ, 68-72; asst prof, Ohio Inst Technol, 72-74; asst prof, Cleveland State Univ, 74-75; res scientist, Joint Inst Advan Flight Sci, NASA, 75-80. *Res:* Wire antennas; microstrip antennas; reflector antennas; computer simulation of antennas. *Mailing Add:* 2367 Doreen Ct NE Atlanta GA 30345

AGRAWAL, SUDHIR, CHEMISTRY, BIOCHEMISTRY. *Current Pos:* CHIEF SCI OFFICER & VPRES DISCOVERY, CHEM DEPT, HYBRIDON INC, 90- *Personal Data:* b Ollahabad, India, 1953. *Educ:* Univ Allahabad, BS, 73, MS, 75, PhD(chem), 80. *Prof Exp:* Found Scholar, Worcester Found Exp Biol, 87-90. *Mem:* Am Chemists Soc; NY Acad Sci. *Res:* Granted one patent on antisense approach. *Mailing Add:* Hybridon Inc 600 Memorial Dr Cambridge MA 02139

AGRAWAL, SUPHAL PRAKASH, TECHNICAL MANAGEMENT, SUPERPLASTIC FORMING. *Current Pos:* sr tech specialist & prog mgr, Aircraft Div, 80-89, DIR ADV TECH BUS DEVELOP, NORTHROP CORP AIRCRAFT DIV, 89- *Personal Data:* b Bareilly, India, Nov 10, 46; US citizen; m 76, Sushila Jain; c 3. *Educ:* Agra Univ, India, BSc, 63; Indian Inst Technol, Kanpur, BTech, 68; Univ Ky, Lexington, MS, 70, PhD(metal eng & mat sci), 73. *Prof Exp:* Scholar, Mat & Metall Eng, Univ Mich, 73-76; mem tech staff & prog mgr, NAm Aircraft Opers, Rockwell Int, 76-80. *Concurrent Pos:* Scholar, metall eng & mat sci, Univ Ky, 76; spec course lectr, dept mat sci, Univ Southern Calif, Los Angeles, 80; spec course lectr, Am Soc Metals Int, 90. *Mem:* Fel Am Soc Metals; Sigma Xi; Indian Inst Metals; Metall Soc. *Res:* Advanced materials and processes research and development; innovations fundamental to the development and implementation of superplastic forming process for fabricating titanium and aluminum structures; diffusion bonding; advanced materials and processes technologies; long-range planning for advanced technology thrusts. *Mailing Add:* Dept VH10/W7 Northrop Grumman Corp One Hornet Way El Segundo CA 90245-2804

AGRAWALA, ASHOK KUMAR, COMPUTER SCIENCE. *Current Pos:* ASST PROF COMPUT SCI, UNIV MD, COLLEGE PARK, 71- *Personal Data:* b Meerut, India, June 28, 43; m; c 2. *Educ:* Indian Inst Sci, Bangalore, BE, 63, ME, 65; Harvard Univ, AM, 70, PhD(appl math), 70. *Prof Exp:* Prin engr, Data Systs Div, Honeywell Inc, 70-71. *Concurrent Pos:* Chmn bd, AT&T Systs, 86- *Mem:* Fel Inst Elec & Electronics Engrs; Asn Comput Mach; AAAS; Sigma Xi. *Res:* Analysis, modelling, measurement and evaluation of computer systems, their design and architecture; distributed computing; real time systems; network protocols. *Mailing Add:* 18100 New Hampshire Ave Ashton MD 20861-9784

AGRE, COURTLAND LEVERNE, chemistry; deceased, see previous edition for last biography

AGRE, JAMES C, POST POLIO SYNDROME. *Current Pos:* from asst prof to assoc prof, 84-93, PROF REHAB MED, UNIV WIS MED SCH, 93-, CHMN DEPT, 93- *Personal Data:* Northfield, Minn, May 2, 50; m 82, Patti Soderberg. *Educ:* Augsburg Col, BA, 72; Univ Minn, MD, 76, PhD(phys med & rehab), 85. *Honors & Awards:* Licht Award, Am Acad Phys Med & Rehab, 88; New Investr Award, Am Col Sports Med, 91. *Prof Exp:* Instr phys med & rehab, Univ Minn, 79-84. *Mem:* AAAS; fel Am Acad Phys Med & Rehab; Am Cong Rehab Med; fel Am Col Sports Med; Asn Acad Physiatrists. *Res:* Effects of aging upon neuromuscular function in patients with post polio syndrome. *Mailing Add:* Univ Wis 600 Highland Ave Madison WI 53792-3256

AGRE, KARL, CLINICAL PHARMACOLOGY, PEDIATRICS. *Current Pos:* DIR MED AFFAIRS, TAP PHARMACEUT, ILL, 94- *Personal Data:* b Feb 24, 32; US citizen; m 55; c 3. *Educ:* Villanova Col, BS, 52; Hahnemann Med Col, MS, 54, PhD(pharmacol), 56; Duke Univ, MD, 59. *Prof Exp:* Instr pharmacol, Sch Med, Duke Univ, 56-59; intern-resident pediat, Bronx Munic Hosp Ctr, 59-62, clin instr, 64-66; dir clin pharmacol, Bristol Labs, Inc, 66-75; vpres med res, Pharmaceut Div, Searle Labs, 75-83; Smith Labs, Ill, 83-85; Syntex, Calif, 85-92. *Concurrent Pos:* Pvt med pract, NY, 64-66; clin instr, Upstate Med Ctr, State Univ NY, 66-75. *Mem:* Fel Am Acad Pediat. *Mailing Add:* 6410 Locust Lane Libertyville IL 60048

AGRESTA, JOSEPH, PHYSICS, APPLIED MATHEMATICS. *Current Pos:* physicist, Union Carbide Res Inst, 62-68, consult, 69-81, MGR OPERS RES, UNION CARBIDE CORP, 82- *Personal Data:* b Long Island City, NY, June 13, 29; m 53; c 7. *Educ:* Cooper Union, BEE, 50; NY Univ, MS, 52, PhD(physics), 58. *Prof Exp:* Asst physics, NY Univ, 50-53; physicist, Curtiss-Wright Corp, 53-56; res asst physics, NY Univ, 56-58; physicist, United Nuclear Corp, 58-62. *Concurrent Pos:* Lectr, City Col NY, 58-62; adj asst prof, NY Univ, 59-62. *Mem:* Sigma Xi. *Res:* Radiation transport; nuclear reactor theory; computing machine methods; hydrodynamics; operations research; systems analysis; simulation; computer science; computer graphics. *Mailing Add:* 23 Tanglewood Dr Danbury CT 06811-4220

AGRESTI, DAVID GEORGE, NUCLEAR SPECTROSCOPY, MATERIALS SCIENCE. *Current Pos:* asst prof, 69-74, chmn physics dept, 74-78, ASSOC PROF PHYSICS, UNIV ALA, BIRMINGHAM, 74- *Personal Data:* b Washington, DC, Aug 8, 38. *Educ:* Ohio State Univ, BSc, 59; Calif Inst Technol, MS, 62, PhD(physics), 67. *Prof Exp:* Asst prof physics, Calif State Col, Los Angeles, 67-69. *Mem:* Am Phys Soc. *Res:* Mossbauer spectroscopy; computer modeling of biomolecules. *Mailing Add:* Dept Physics Univ Ala 1300 University Blvd Birmingham AL 35294-1170

AGRESTI, WILLIAM W, COMPUTER SCIENCES. *Current Pos:* consult scientist, 88-96, DIR TECHNOL & QUAL, MITRETEK SYSTS, 96- *Personal Data:* b Erie, Pa, Oct 19, 46. *Educ:* Case Inst Technol, BS, 68; NY Univ, MS, 71, PhD(comput sci), 73. *Honors & Awards:* Group Achievement Award, NASA, 89. *Prof Exp:* Systs analyst oper res, Lord Corp, 68-69; from asst prof to assoc prof indust & systs eng, Univ Mich, Dearborn, 73-83; sr comput scientist, Comput Sci Corp, 83-88. *Concurrent Pos:* Dir comput & info sci, Univ Mich, Dearborn, 75-78; prog dir, NSF, 96- *Mem:* Asn Comput Mach; Inst Elec & Electronics Engrs Computer Soc. *Res:* Software engineering. *Mailing Add:* 4016 Shallow Brook Lane Olney MD 20832

AGRIOS, GEORGE NICHOLAS, PLANT PATHOLOGY, VIROLOGY. *Current Pos:* PROF & CHMN DEPT PLANT PATHOL, UNIV FLA, GAINESVILLE, 88- *Personal Data:* b Galarinos, Greece, Jan 16, 36; US citizen; m 62, Annette; c Nicholas, Anthony & Alexander. *Educ:* Univ Thessaloniki, BS, 57; Iowa State Univ, PhD(plant path & genetics), 60. *Prof Exp:* From asst prof to prof plant path, Univ Mass, Amherst, 63-88. *Concurrent Pos:* Ed-in-chief, Am Phytopath Soc Press. *Mem:* Fel Am Phytopath Soc (vpres, pres, 90-91); Can Phytopath Soc; AAAS. *Res:* Plant viruses, transmission and identification; physiological effects of viruses on host plants; methods for virus detection; behavior of viruses in tissue culture. *Mailing Add:* Dept Plant Path Univ Fla Gainesville FL 32611. *Fax:* 904-392-6532; *E-Mail:* gna@gnv.ifas.ufl.edu

AGRIS, PAUL F, BIOCHEMISTRY, MOLECULAR BIOPHYSICS. *Current Pos:* PROF & HEAD, DEPT BIOCHEM & SUPVR, BIOMACROMOLECULER NUCLEAR MAGNETIC RESONANCE FACIL, NC STATE UNIV, 88- *Personal Data:* b July 8, 44. *Educ:* Bucknell Univ, BS, 66; Mass Inst Technol, PhD(biochem), 71. *Prof Exp:* Postdoctoral fel, Dept Molecular Biophys & Biochem, Yale Univ, 71-73; from asst prof to prof biol sci, Univ Mo, Columbia, 73-87, chmn, Nuclear Magnetic Resonance Facil, 81-86, prof, Dept Med, 83-87, dir, Div Biol Sci Protein Sequencing Lab, 85-87. *Concurrent Pos:* Consult, New Eng Nuclear Corp, 71; assoc scientist & consult biochem, Cancer Res Ctr & Ellis Fischel State Cancer Hosp, 73-87; pres & bd mem, Am Found Aging Res, 79-; mem bd, Am Fedn Aging Res, 80-; vis scientist, Biochem Dept, Univ Oxford, Eng, 80-81 & Okla Med Res Found, 81-82; Fogarty sr int fel, Univ Oxford, 80-81; sr fel, Exeter Col, Oxford, 80-; Nat Res Serv spec fel, 81-82; mem, US-Japan Conf Werner's Syndrome, NSF, Japan, 82; res grants, NIH, 83-89 & 86-91, NSF, 88-91; exchange lectr & scientist, Nat Acad Sci & Polish Acad Sci, 84, spec vis scientist, 86 & 91. *Mem:* AAAS; Am Chem Soc; Am Soc Biochem & Molecular Biol; Am Soc Cell Biol; Tissue Cult Asn; Int Soc Magnetic Resonance. *Res:* Structure-function relationships for nucleic acids and proteins in biology and in medical problems. *Mailing Add:* Dept Biochem NC State Univ 128 Polk Hall PO Box 7622 Raleigh NC 27695-7622

AGRON, SAM LAZRUS, GEOLOGY. *Current Pos:* from asst prof to prof geol, 51-84, dir, NSF Earth Sci Inst, 64-67, EMER PROF GEOL, RUTGERS UNIV, NEWARK, 84- *Personal Data:* b Russia, Nov 27, 20; nat US; m 44; c 2. *Educ:* Northwestern Univ, BS, 41; Johns Hopkins Univ, PhD(geol), 49. *Prof Exp:* Instr geol, Brown Univ, 49-51. *Mem:* Geol Soc Am; Nat Asn Geol Teachers; Sigma Xi. *Res:* Structural, economic and environmental geology. *Mailing Add:* 12 Shawnee Trail Montville NJ 07045-9204

AGTERBERG, FREDERICK PIETER, MATHEMATICAL GEOLOGY, COMPUTERS IN GEOSCIENCE. *Current Pos:* res scientist, 62-81, SR RES SCIENTIST, GEOL SURV CAN, 81- *Personal Data:* b Utrecht, Holland, Nov 15, 36; Can citizen; m 65, Jacoba Berendina Felicia Zwaardemaker; c Daniel F, Timothy P, Franklin F & Marko J E. *Educ:* Utrecht Univ, BSc, 57, MSc, 59, PhD(geol), 61. *Honors & Awards:* William Krumbein Medal, Int Asn Math Geol, 78. *Prof Exp:* Postdoctoral fel, Univ Wis, 61-62. *Concurrent Pos:* Adj prof geol, Univ Ottawa, 68-, Syracuse Univ, 78-82; vis res scientist, Univ Kans, 69-70; proj leader, Int Geol Correlation Prog, 79-85; adj prof math, Carleton Univ, 86-94; hon prof, China Univ Geosci, 89-; chmn, Comt Quant Stratig, Int Comm Stratig, 94- *Mem:* Corresp mem Royal Dutch Acad Sci; Int Asn Math Geol; Can Inst Mining & Metall; Royal Dutch Geol & Mining Asn; fel Geol Asn Can. *Res:* Mathematical geology; nonrenewable resources; quantitative stratigraphy; multifractals; geographic information systems; numerical geological time-scales. *Mailing Add:* Geol Surv Can 601 Booth St Ottawa ON K1A 0E8 Can. *Fax:* 613-996-3726; *E-Mail:* agterberg@gsc.nrcan.gc.ca

AGUAYO, ALBERT J, MEDICINE. *Current Pos:* DIR, CTR RES NEUROSCI, MONTREAL GEN HOSP, 85- *Personal Data:* b Buenos Aires, Arg. *Educ:* Univ Cordoba, MD, 59. *Mem:* Inst Med-Nat Acad Sci; fel Royal Soc Can; Soc Neurosci; AAAS. *Mailing Add:* Ctr Res Neurosci Montreal Gen Hosp 1650 Cedar Ave Montreal PQ H3G 1A4 Can

AGUIAR, ADAM MARTIN, ORGANIC CHEMISTRY. *Current Pos:* CHAIR, CHEM DEPT, MONMOUTH COL, 93- *Personal Data:* b Newark, NJ, Aug 11, 29; m 80, Laura E Brand; c David L, Justine D, Adam A, Erick A, Aaron B & Evan J. *Educ:* Fairleigh Dickinson Univ, BS, 55; Columbia Univ, MA, 57, PhD(chem), 60. *Prof Exp:* Org chemist, Otto B May, 47-55; asst, Columbia Univ, 55-59; asst prof chem, Fairleigh Dickinson Univ, 59-63; from asst prof to prof, Tulane Univ, 63-72, chmn, Chem Dept, Newcomb Col, 70-72; dean grad progs & res, William Paterson Col, 72-73; prof, Fairleigh Dickinson Univ, 73-93, chmn dept, 84-89. *Concurrent Pos:* Fel, NIH, 59; sabbatical, Europe, 69-70 & Roche Inst Molecular Biol, 82; hon res prof, Birkbeck Col, Univ London, 70; res specialist, Rutgers Univ, Newark, 73-75; consult, 74-; pres, Sectox. *Mem:* AAAS; Am Chem Soc; NY Acad Sci; Sigma Xi. *Res:* Organo-phosphorus chemistry; medicinal chemistry; biochemistry and pharmacology. *Mailing Add:* 37 Wyncrest Lane Tinton Falls NJ 07753-7421

AGUILAR, RODOLFO J, CIVIL ENGINEERING. *Current Pos:* From asst prof to prof, 61-75, consult prof civil eng, 75-77, prof, 77-85, EMER PROF ARCHIT & FINANCE, 85- *Personal Data:* b San Jose, Costa Rica, Sept 28, 36; US citizen; m 56; c 4. *Educ:* La State Univ, BS, 58, MS, 60, BA, 61; NC State Univ, PhD(civil eng), 64; Tulane Univ, MBA, 89. *Concurrent Pos:* Consult, Iberia Parish Sch Bd, Perry Brown, Inc & C E Newman, La, 64, Gulf South Res Inst, La & Smith, Hinchman & Grylls, Mich, 67; struct examr, La State Bd Archit Exam, 65-66; consult systs eng & opers res; pres, A D H Systs, Inc, Planners, Archit, Engrs, 70-, Corp Develop Group Inc, 76-77 & Aguilar & Assocs, 77-; adj prof, Int & Free Enterprise Studies, 85-88; adj prof real estate, A B Freeman Sch Bus, Tulane Univ, 89- *Mem:* Am Soc Civil Engrs; Am Inst Architects; Am Planning Asn; Am Soc Appraisers. *Res:* Dynamic response of steel plate girder bridges with partially cracked lightweight concrete decks; stability of framed domes systems of concentrated loads; structural dynamics; real estate planning, finance and development; author of over 40 publications in architectural design. *Mailing Add:* 643 St Charles Baton Rouge LA 70802

AGUILO, ADOLFO, INDUSTRIAL CHEMISTRY. *Current Pos:* from res chemist to sr res chemist, Celanese Chem Co, 60-66, res assoc, 66-70, sect leader, 70-90, SR RES ASSOC, CELANESE CHEM CO, 90- *Personal Data:* b Buenos Aires, Arg, Sept 6, 28; m, Esther Zuccani; c Maria, Adolfo Jr, Juan J & Patricia. *Educ:* Univ Buenos Aires, MS, 53, PhD(chem), 55. *Honors & Awards:* Dr Lee Starr Award for Tech Excellence, Horchst Celanese Corp, 92. *Prof Exp:* group leader, Arg AEC, 53-60. *Concurrent Pos:* Lab supvr, Univ Buenos Aires, 55-58, assoc prof, 58-60. *Mem:* Am Chem Soc. *Res:* Organometallics; catalysts; coordination compounds in catalysis; liquid and vapor phase oxidation of parafins and olefins; petrochemicals from synthesis gas; hydroformylation; carbonylation. *Mailing Add:* 4606 Oxford Corpus Christi TX 78411-4817

AGULIAN, SAMUEL KEVORK, ION-SENSITIVE ELECTRODES, BIOSENSORS. *Current Pos:* res assoc physiol, 76-77, RES SCIENTIST, YALE UNIV, 90- *Personal Data:* b Beirut, Lebanon, Apr 9, 43; US citizen; m 76; c 3. *Educ:* Am Univ Beirut, BSc, 65, MSc, 73, PhD(med sci), 80. *Prof Exp:* Res asst physiol, Free Univ Berlin, 65-66; res asst, Am Univ Beirut, 66-76, res assoc, 77-80, asst prof, 80-85; proj dir, World Precision Instruments, 85-90. *Concurrent Pos:* Consult, Yale Univ, 85-90. *Res:* Developed first intracellular double-barreled electrodes to measure electro-chemical potentials of major intracellular ions; micro sensors, such as for carbon dioxide, oxygen and pH. *Mailing Add:* 47 Pearl Ave Hamden CT 06514

AGUS, ZALMAN S, PHYSIOLOGY, NEPHROLOGY. *Current Pos:* from asst prof to assoc prof med nephrol, 73-88, PROF MED, SCH MED, UNIV PA, 88- *Personal Data:* b Chicago, Ill, Apr 3, 41; m 63; c 3. *Educ:* Johns Hopkins Univ, BA, 61; Univ Md, MD, 65. *Hon Degrees:* MA, Univ Pa. *Prof Exp:* Intern, Sch Med, Univ Md, 65-66, resident, 66-68; res fel, Sch Med, Univ Pa, 68-71; attend physician, nephrology, USAF, Lackland AFB, Tex, 71-73. *Concurrent Pos:* NIH fel, 69-71; clin investigatorship, Vet Admin, 73-76; NIH res career develop award, 77; fel, Am Col Physicians, 77. *Mem:* Am Fedn Clin Res; AAAS; NY Acad Sci; Am Soc Nephrology; Int Soc Nephrology; Am Soc Clin Invest. *Res:* Renal and electrolyte physiology; calcium and phosphate metabolism. *Mailing Add:* Med Res 151 Vet Admin Med Ctr University & Woodland Aves Philadelphia PA 19104

AGYILIRAH, GEORGE AUGUSTUS, PHARMACEUTICS, DOSAGE FORM DESIGN & FORMULATION DEVELOPMENT. *Current Pos:* PHARM ASSOC, FMC CORP, 92- *Personal Data:* b Ghana, Sept 15, 47; m 80; c 3. *Educ:* Univ Sci & Technol, Ghana, BPharm, 75; Univ London, MSc, 78, PhD(pharmaceut), 81. *Prof Exp:* Postdoctoral fel, Purdue Univ, 82-85; res assoc indust pharm, Col Pharm, Univ Minn, 85-89, asst prof, Indust Pharm & Pharmaceut Calculations, 90-92. *Mem:* Am Asn Pharmaceut Scientists; Controlled Release Soc. *Res:* Design and formulation of pharmaceutical dosage forms and drug delivery systems including microencapsulations, tablets and tablet coatings, pellets and pelletization and various controlled release systems. *Mailing Add:* Pharm Biol Sci Div FMC Corp PO Box 8 Princeton NJ 08543. *Fax:* 609-951-3680

AH, HYONG-SUN, VETERINARY PARASITOLOGY, ACAROLOGY. *Current Pos:* Vet res assoc, Diag & Res Lab, Tifton, 69-71, ASST PROF PARASITOL, COL VET MED, UNIV GA, 71- *Personal Data:* b Suwon, Korea, May 27, 31; US citizen; m 58; c 3. *Educ:* Seoul Nat Univ, DVM, 55; Univ Ga, PhD(med entom), 68. *Mem:* Am Soc Parasitologists; Acarological Soc Am; Int Filariasis Asn; World Fedn Parasitologists. *Res:* Experimental filariasis in the areas of pathology, chemotherapy, immunology and host-parasite relationships. *Mailing Add:* 1475 Whit Davis Rd Athens GA 30605

AHARON, PAUL, SEDIMENTARY GEOCHEMISTRY, PALEOCLIMATES & PALEOENVIRONMENTS. *Current Pos:* PROF GEOL, LA STATE UNIV, 82- *Personal Data:* b Piatra-Neamtz, Romania, Mar 21, 45; US citizen; m 68, Sylvia Steiner; c Ariela & Abigail. *Educ:* Hebrew Univ, Jerusalem, BS, 70, MS, 73; Australian Nat Univ, PhD(environ geochem), 80. *Prof Exp:* Res geologist, Hebrew Univ, Jerusalem, 73-76; postdoctoral fel, Australian Nat Univ, 80-82. *Concurrent Pos:* Queen's fel award, Australian Sci & Technol Orgn, 80-82; res fel, Lamont-Doherty Earth Observ, 82-83; vis prof, Max-Planck Inst Chem, France, 89-90, Univ Bologna, Italy, 91-92; Forchheimer distinguished prof, Hebrew Univ, Jerusalem, 97- *Mem:* Geol Soc Am; Am Geophys Union; Int Asn Geochem; Soc Sedimentary Res. *Res:* Present and past reconstruction of atmosphere-biosphere-ocean interactions using geochemical tracers; investigate processes related to submarine seeps and vents and their association with chemosynthetic fauna. *Mailing Add:* Dept Geol & Geophys La State Univ Baton Rouge LA 70803. *Fax:* 504-388-2302; *E-Mail:* glahar@lsuvm.sncc.lsu.edu

AHARONI, SHAUL MOSHE, POLYMER CHEMISTRY. *Current Pos:* res assoc, Allied Chem Corp, 73-85, SR RES ASSOC, ALLIED-SIGNAL CORP, 85- *Personal Data:* b Tel Aviv, Israel, Dec 3, 33; US citizen; m 56; c 2. *Educ:* Univ Wis-Eau Claire, BS, 67; Case Western Res Univ, MS, 69, PhD(polymer sci), 72. *Prof Exp:* Asst chief chemist, Nat Presto Industs, Wis, 66-67, consult, 68-69; sr chemist, Gould Labs, Gould Inc, Ohio, 71-73. *Mem:* Am Chem Soc; Am Phys Soc. *Res:* Structure property relationships in polymers; rigid backbone polymers; organization of the amorphous state, packing density and free volume; condensation polymers; liquid crystalline polymers; polymer networks. *Mailing Add:* 36 Averell Dr Morris Plains NJ 07950

AHARONOV, YAKIR, PHYSICS, FOUNDATIONS OF QUANTUM THEORY. *Current Pos:* PROF, TEL AVIV UNIV, 67-; PROF, UNIV SC, 73- *Personal Data:* b Haifa, Israel, Aug 28, 32. *Educ:* Technion, Haifa, BS, 56; Bristol Univ, PhD, 60. *Hon Degrees:* Dr, Technion, Haifa, 92, DSc, Univ SC, 93. *Honors & Awards:* Weizmann Prize, 84; Rothschild Prize, 84; Nat Physics Prize, Israel, 89. *Prof Exp:* Res assoc, Brandeis Univ, 60-61; from asst prof to prof, Yeshiva Univ, 64-73; Miller prof, Univ Calif, Berkeley, 88-90. *Concurrent Pos:* Vis prof, Boston Univ, 91-92. *Mem:* Nat Acad Sci; fel Am Phys Soc; Nat Acad Sci Israel. *Mailing Add:* Physics Dept Rm 404 Univ SC Columbia SC 29208

AHARONY, DAVID, PHARMACOLOGY. *Current Pos:* res pharmacologist, Dept Pharmacol, Pulmonary Sect, ICI Pharmaceut Group, 82-86, sr res pharmacologist, 87-89, prin pharmacologist, 90, group leader, Dept Pharmacol, Pulmonary Sect, 90-93, TEAM LEADER, DEPT PHARMACOL, ZENECA PHARMACEUT, 93- *Personal Data:* m, Avivit; c 2. *Educ:* Bar-Ilan Univ, Israel, BS, 75; Tel-Aviv Univ, MS, 77; Thomas Jefferson Univ, PhD(pharmacol), 81. *Prof Exp:* Teaching asst, Dept Biochem, Tel-Aviv Univ, 75-77; res technician, Div Miles Labs, Miles-Yeda, Rehovot, Israel, 77-78; res asst, Cardeza Found Hemat Res, Thomas Jefferson Univ, 78-81. *Mem:* Am Soc Pharmacol & Exp Therapeut; AAAS; Sigma Xi; NY Acad Sci. *Res:* Molecular pharmacology of kinin receptors; author or co-author of over 50 publications. *Mailing Add:* Zeneca Pharmaceut Group Dept Pharmacol 1800 Concord Pike Wilmington DE 19897-0001. *Fax:* 302-886-8749

AHEARN, DONALD G, MYCOLOGY, MARINE MICROBIOLOGY. *Current Pos:* from asst prof to assoc prof microbiol, 67-72, dean, Grad Div, Sch Arts & Sci, 70-72, PROF MICROBIOL, GA STATE UNIV, 72-, ASST VPRES RES, 80- *Personal Data:* b Grove City, Pa, Feb 1, 34; m 59; c 3. *Educ:* Mt Union Col, BS, 57; Univ Miami, MS, 59, PhD(microbiol), 64. *Prof Exp:* Instr microbiol & marine biol, Univ Miami, 63-64, asst prof, Sch Med & Int Marine Sci, 64-66. *Concurrent Pos:* Mem, Int Oceanog Found. *Mem:* Am Soc Microbiol; Soc Indust Microbiol (pres-elect, 81); Mycol Soc Am; Int Soc Human & Animal Mycol; Am Acad Microbiol. *Res:* Ecology, physiology and systematics of fungi, chiefly yeasts, in aquatic habitats; contamination of industrial products, mascaras, SCP; epidemology of yeast-like fungi pathogenic to man. *Mailing Add:* Dept Biol Ga State Univ PO Box 4010 University Plaza Atlanta GA 30302-4010

AHEARN, GREGORY ALLEN, COMPARATIVE PHYSIOLOGY, CELL PHYSIOLOGY. *Current Pos:* asst prof, 76-79, ASSOC PROF ZOOL, UNIV HAWAII, 79- *Personal Data:* b Cambridge, Mass, Nov 28, 43; m 67. *Educ:* Univ Calif, Los Angeles, BA, 65; Univ Hawaii, MS, 67; Ariz State Univ, PhD(zool), 70. *Prof Exp:* Teaching asst gen zool, Ariz State Univ, 67-68, teaching assoc, 68-69; res fel, Zoophysiol Lab A, August Krogh Inst, Univ Copenhagen, 70-72; asst marine biologist, Hawaii Inst Marine Biol, 72-76. *Concurrent Pos:* Fel, Danish Res Coun, 70; NSF instnl grants, 75, 77 & 79; Nat Oceanic & Atmospheric Admin instnl sea grant, 76. *Mem:* Am Soc Zoologists; NY Acad Sci; Am Physiol Soc. *Res:* Membrane transport, epithelial biology, osmotic and ionic regulation, water balance, nutritional physiology, thermoregulation, environmental physiology. *Mailing Add:* Dept Zool Univ Hawaii 2538 The Mall Honolulu HI 96822. *Fax:* 808-956-9812

AHEARN, JAMES JOSEPH, JR, ANALYTICAL CHEMISTRY, PROCESS RESEARCH & DEVELOPMENT. *Current Pos:* res group leader analytical chem, 70-82, SR MGR CHEM DEVELOP LAB, POLAROID CORP, 82- *Personal Data:* b Beverly, Mass, May 21, 43. *Educ:* Boston Col, BS, 65, PhD(chem), 69. *Prof Exp:* Res chemist, Org Chem Dept, Res Div, E I du Pont de Nemours & Co, 69-70. *Mem:* Am Chem Soc. *Res:* Chromatographic procedures for dyes, dye intermediates and photographic chemicals; chemical process research and development. *Mailing Add:* 7 Ellsworth Ave Beverly MA 01915-1615

AHEARN, JOHN STEPHEN, materials science, for more information see previous edition

A'HEARN, MICHAEL FRANCIS, PLANETARY SCIENCE, COMETS & ASTEROIDS. *Current Pos:* From asst prof to assoc prof astron, Univ Md, 66-72, actg dir, Astron Prog, 85-87, acting chmn, Dept Astron, 91-93, PROF ASTRON, UNIV MD, 82- *Personal Data:* b Wilmington, Del, Nov 17, 40; m 63, Maxine Ramold; c Brian J, Kevin P & Patrick N. *Educ:* Boston Col, BS, 61; Univ Wis, PhD(astron), 66. *Honors & Awards:* Asteroid Named in Honor, Int Astron Union. *Concurrent Pos:* Adj astromr, Lowell Observ, 87-; chmn, Div Planetary Sci, Am Astron Soc, 93-94. *Mem:* Am Astron Soc; fel AAAS; Inst Navig; Int Astron Union (vpres, 90-93; pres, 94-97). *Res:* Small bodies of the solar system, primarily comets, to understand the origin and evolution of the solar system; observational but theoretical work. *Mailing Add:* Dept Astron Univ Md College Park MD 20742-2421. *Fax:* 301-314-9067

AHEARN, MICHAEL JOHN, CELL BIOLOGY. *Current Pos:* assoc biologist, 65-80, ASSOC PROF LAB MED, UNIV TEX M D ANDERSON HOSP & TUMOR INST, TEX MED CTR, 80-, LAB MED, SYST CANCER CTR. *Personal Data:* b Jacksonville, Tex, June 22, 36; m 64. *Educ:* Univ Tex, BA, 58, MA, 62, PhD(zool), 65. *Prof Exp:* Lectr zool, Univ Tex, 64-65. *Mem:* Int Soc Exp Hemat; Am Asn Cancer Res; Am Soc Cell Biol; Electron Micros Soc Am; Sigma Xi. *Res:* Hematology, especially cellular alterations induced by chemotherapeutic agents; electron microscopy; flow cytometry; cytological techniques. *Mailing Add:* 2200 Willowick Rd Houston TX 77027

AHEARNE, JOHN FRANCIS, NUCLEAR SAFETY. *Current Pos:* exec dir, 88-96, DIR, SIGMA XI, SCI RES SOC, 95- *Personal Data:* b New Britain, Conn, June 14, 34; m 56, Barbara H Drezek; c Tom, Paul, Mary A, Robert & Patricia. *Educ:* Cornell Univ, BEngPhys, 57, MS, 58; Princeton Univ, MA, 63, PhD(plasma phys), 66. *Prof Exp:* Analyst nuclear weapons effects, Weapons Lab, USAF, Kirtland AFB, NMex, 59-61; from instr to assoc prof physics, USAF Acad, 64-69; syst analyst, Off Asst Secy, Defense for Systs Anal, 69-70, dir tactical air prog, 70-72, dep asst secy defense, Off Asst Secy Defense Prog Anal & Eval, 72-74, prin dept asst secy defense, Off Asst Secy Defense for Manpower & Res Affairs, 75-76; syst analyst, White House Energy Off, 77; dep asst secy, Energy for Resource Appl, 78; comn, US Nuclear Regulatory comn, 78-83, chmn, 79-81; vpres & sr fel, Resources For Future, 84-89. *Concurrent Pos:* Consult, Comptroller Gen US, 83-84; mem, Nat Res Coun Comt, Nuclear Safety Res, 85-86, Yucca Mountain Stand, 93-, US comt, Int Inst Appl Systs Anal, mem, 89, vchair, 92-93, chair, 94-; chmn, Comt Risk Perception & Commun, Nat Res Coun, 87-90, chmn, Adv Comt Nuclear Facil Safety, Dept Energy, 88-91; chmn comt future nuclear power, Nat Res Coun, 90-93; adj scholar, Resources To Future, 92-; mem, President's Coun, Univ Calif Syst, 92-, Bd Radioactive Waste Mgt, Nat Res Coun, 94-; co-chmn, Comt Linking Sci & Tech Environ Goals, Nat Res Coun, 95-; lectr & adj prof civil & environ eng, Duke Univ, 96-; chmn, Environ Mgt Sci Prog, Nat Res Coun, 95-; vchmn, Comt Marine Risk & Mgt, NRS, 96- *Mem:* Nat Acad Eng; AAAS; Sigma Xi; Soc Risk Anal; Am Nuclear Soc; Am Phys Soc. *Res:* Resource allocation, particularly regarding energy supplies; science policy, especially the role of the federal government; safety of nuclear reactors; radiation hazards. *Mailing Add:* 105 Rose Lane Chapel Hill NC 27514-7820. *Fax:* 919-549-0090

AHERN, DAVID GEORGE, SYNTHESIS OF LABELLED COMPOUNDS. *Current Pos:* SR RES ASSOC, NEW LIFE SCI PROD, 95- *Personal Data:* b Winchester, Mass, May 21, 36; m 65, Jennie Gaom. *Educ:* Merrimack Col, BS, 58; Northeastern Univ, MS, 65; Boston Univ, PhD(biochem), 72. *Prof Exp:* Jr chemist, TracerLab Inc, 58-60; jr chemist, New Eng Nuclear Corp, 60-62, chemist, 62-66, sr chemist, 72-74, group leader, 74-78, sect leader, 78-86; area supvr, Dupont, New Eng Nuclear Prod, 87-95. *Mem:* Am Oil Chemists Soc; Int Isotope Soc; Am Chem Soc. *Res:* Chemistry and biochemistry of lipid metabolism synthesis of carbon 14 and tritium labelled lipids; synthesis of 3H labelled ligands for receptor site analysis. *Mailing Add:* 26 Dewey Rd Lexington MA 02173

AHERN, FRANCIS JOSEPH, APPLIED PHYSICS, REMOTE SENSING. *Current Pos:* RES SCIENTIST APPL PHYSICS, CAN CTR REMOTE SENSING, 75- *Personal Data:* b New York, NY, June 21, 44; m 70, Doyne Clark; c Erin Elizabeth & Catherine Margaret. *Educ:* Cornell Univ, AB, 66; Univ Md, PhD(astron), 72. *Honors & Awards:* Gold Medal, Can Remote Sensing Soc, 91. *Prof Exp:* Fel astrophys, Univ Toronto, 72-74. *Concurrent Pos:* Adj prof, Dept Geog, Univ Ottawa. *Mem:* Can Remote Sensing Soc. *Res:* Methods of remote sensing of the earth for environmental and resource management with emphasis on spectrometry in visual and near infrared regions; rador remote sensing of boreal and tropical forests; research into forestry applications of remotely sensed data; microwave backscattering research. *Mailing Add:* Can Ctr Remote Sensing 588 Booth St Ottawa ON K1A 0Y7 Can

AHERN, JUDSON LEWIS, GEOMECHANICS, SOLID EARTH GEOPHYSICS. *Current Pos:* asst prof, 79-85, ASSOC PROF GEOPHYS, SCH GEOL & GEOPHYS, UNIV OKLA, 85- *Personal Data:* b Canton, Ohio, Apr 11, 51; m 76, Carolyn Clark; c Patrick M & Kelly K. *Educ:* Ohio Wesleyan Univ, BA, 73; Ohio State Univ, MSc, 75; Cornell Univ, PhD(geophys), 80. *Prof Exp:* Geophysicist, Chevron Oil Co, New Orleans, La, 74. *Mem:* Sigma Xi; Am Geophys Union; Soc Explor Geophys. *Res:* Mechanical and thermal aspects of the solid earth, including problems such as convection in magma bodies, thermal and mechanical evolution of sedimentary basins, frictional heating along faults. *Mailing Add:* Geol Dept Univ Okla Main Campus 900 Asp Ave Norman OK 73019-4050. *Fax:* 405-325-3140

AHL, ALWYNELLE S, ZOOLOGY, MAMMALOGY. *Current Pos:* vet med officer, Animal & Plant Health Inspection Serv, USDA, 87-88, dep dir sci & prof educ & develop, 88-91, head, risk analysis systs, policy & prog develop, Animal & Plant Health Inspection Serv, 91-95, DIR OFFICE RISK ASSESSMENT & COST BENEFIT ANALYSIS OFF SECY AGR, USDA, 95- *Personal Data:* b Leesville, La, Mar 18, 41; m 63, James G Ahl; c Robert & Laura. *Educ:* Centenary Col, BS, 61; Univ Wyo, MS, 63, PhD(zool), 67; Mich State Univ, DVM, 87. *Prof Exp:* Res asst biochem, Univ Wyo, 65-67; from asst prof to prof natural sci, Mich State Univ, 67-87. *Concurrent Pos:* Supply asst prof biochem & human med, Univ Wyo, 76-77; adj assoc prof, Sch Vet Sci Univ Md, Col Park, 88- *Mem:* Am Vet Med Asn; Am Soc Mammalogists; Soc Trop Vet Med (secy); Asn Women Vets. *Res:* Applications of risk assessment, decision theory to problems in veterinary medicine; environmental epidemiology, particularly as concerns drug and pesticide residues in food animals; science policy in food safety, public health. *Mailing Add:* USDA 14th & Independence Ave SW Rm 5248 Washington DC 20250. *Fax:* 301-436-8229

AHLBERG, DAN LEANDER, PHYSICAL CHEMISTRY, PETROLEUM CHEMISTRY. *Current Pos:* CONSULT, 84- *Personal Data:* b Georgetown, Tex, Jan 6, 26; m 47, Nina L Barker; c Beverly J (McMillian) & Pamela K (Little). *Educ:* Southwestern Univ, BS(physics) & BS(chem), 51. *Prof Exp:* Chemist, E I du Pont de Nemours & Co, Inc, 51-54 & Eastern States Petrol Co, 54-60; anal mgr res, Signal Oil & Gas Co, 60-68; chief chemist labs, Charter Int Oil Co, 68-84, supt labs, 73-84, supt refinery environ serv, 81-84. *Concurrent Pos:* Legal consult, Injury & Prod. *Mem:* Am Soc Testing & Mat; Am Chem Soc. *Res:* Gas chromotography; mass spectroscopy; infrared spectroscopy, atomic absorption spectroscopy, general analytical chemistry and petroleum process chemistry. *Mailing Add:* 1126 Marshall Deer Park TX 77536-2796

AHLBERG, HENRY DAVID, MAMMALOGY,EVOLUTIONARY BIOLOGY. *Current Pos:* assoc prof, 76-85, PROF BIOL, AM INT COL, 85-, CHMN, DEPT BIOL, 89- *Personal Data:* b Boston, Mass, Oct 9, 39; m 62, Brenda Knight; c Geoffrey & Jessica. *Educ:* NPark Col, AB, 61; Boston Univ, PhD(biol), 69. *Prof Exp:* Asst prof biol, Northeastern Univ, 67-76. *Mem:* Wildlife Soc; Am Soc Zoologists; Am Soc Mammalogists; fel AAAS; Am Soc Microbiol; Soc Integrative & Comp Biol. *Res:* Geographic variation of North American porcupine; seasonal variation of genital systems in rodents; aging in natural populations of rodents; oxygen toxicity. *Mailing Add:* Dept Biol Am Int Col Springfield MA 01109

AHLBERG, JOHN HAROLD, APPLIED MATHEMATICS, NUMERICAL ANALYSIS. *Current Pos:* EMER PROF APPL MATH, BROWN UNIV, 68- *Personal Data:* b Middletown, Conn, Dec 10, 27. *Educ:* Yale Univ, BA, 50, MA, 54, PhD(math), 56; Wesleyan Univ, MA, 52. *Prof Exp:* Chief, Math Anal, United Aircraft Res Labs, 56-68. *Mem:* Am Math Soc; Math Asn Am; Soc Indust & Appl Math. *Res:* Application of splines to the numerical solution of boundary and initial value problems and their application to the representation of curves and surfaces. *Mailing Add:* 3 Northbrook Ct East Hartford CT 06018

AHLBORN, BOYE, PLASMA PHYSICS & CLASSICAL PHYSICS APPLIED TO TECHNICAL DEVICES & BIOLOGICAL SYSTEMS. *Current Pos:* instr, 64-65, from asst prof to prof, 65-95, EMER PROF PLASMA PHYSICS, UNIV BC, 95- *Personal Data:* b Kampen, Ger, July 16, 33; m 61; c 3. *Educ:* Univ Kiel, dipl physics, 60; Munich Tech Univ, Dr rer nat, 64. *Prof Exp:* Sci asst, Inst Plasma Physics, Garching, Ger, 62-64. *Res:* Plasma flow with heat sources--arcs physics of fluids; shock waves; gas dynamical and chemical lasers; thermal physics; physics of animals. *Mailing Add:* Dept Physics Univ BC 6224 Agriculture Rd Vancouver BC V6T 1Z1 Can

AHLBRANDT, CALVIN DALE, DIFFERENTIAL & DIFFERENCE EQUATIONS, NUMERICAL LINEAR ALGEBRA. *Current Pos:* From asst prof to assoc prof, 68-82, PROF MATH, UNIV MO, COLUMBIA, 82- *Personal Data:* b Scottsbluff, Nebr, Aug 13, 40; m 61, Evelyn Keller; c Robert, William & Michael. *Educ:* Univ Wyo, BS, 62; Univ Okla, MA, 65, PhD(math), 68. *Mem:* Am Math Soc; Soc Indust & Appl Math; Math Asn Am. *Res:* Behavior of solutions of linear difference equations and associated nonlinear (Riccati) equations, these equations arise in special functions and filtering and control. *Mailing Add:* Dept Math Univ Mo Columbia MO 65211. *E-Mail:* calvin@math.missouri.edu

AHLBRANDT, THOMAS STUART, PETROLEUM GEOLOGY, SEDIMENTOLOGY. *Current Pos:* res geologist, Oil & Gas Res Br, US Geol Surv, Denver, 74-78, assoc off chief, Ener Progs, Reston, Va, 88-91, br chief, petrol geol, Denver, 91-95, CHIEF SCIENTIST, ENER PROG, US GEOL SURV, DENVER, 95- *Personal Data:* b Torrington, Wyo, May 31, 48; m 86, Mary Jane Rutz; c Elizabeth & Wendy. *Educ:* Univ Wyo, BA, 69, PhD(geol), 73. *Prof Exp:* Sr res geologist, Esso Prod Res Co, Tex, 73-74; explor mgr, MRO & Assocs, 78-81; partner, Petrostrat Consults, 81-88. *Concurrent Pos:* NSF fel, 70, 71 & 72; chief, World Ener Proj, 95- *Mem:* Am Asn Petrol Geologists; AAAS. *Res:* Modern and ancient Eolian deposits; petroleum geology; Alaska; world energy; resource assessments; bypassed hydrocarbon reservoirs; elastics. *Mailing Add:* US Geol Sur Energy Team PO Box 25046 MS 939 Denver CO 80225. *Fax:* 303-236-8822; *E-Mail:* ahlbrandt@usgs.gov

AHLEN, STEVEN PAUL, ASTROPHYSICS, NUCLEAR PHYSICS. *Current Pos:* prof, Dept Physics, Ind Univ, Bloomington, 83-85, PROF DEPT PHYSICS, BOSTON UNIV, 85- *Personal Data:* b Oak Park, Ill, Dec 24, 49; m 78. *Educ:* Univ Ill, Chicago, BS, 70, MS, 71; Univ Calif, Berkeley, PhD, 76. *Honors & Awards:* Sloan Fel, 84. *Prof Exp:* Res physicist, Space Sci Lab, Univ Calif, Berkeley, 76-77, physicist, Lawrence Berkeley Lab, 77-78, asst res physicist, Space Sci Lab, 78-83. *Mem:* Am Phys Soc; Radiation Res Soc. *Res:* Experimental cosmic ray astrophysics; experimental and theoretical work related to charged particle penetration in matter; experimental high energy nuclear physics. *Mailing Add:* Dept Physics Boston Univ 590 Commonwealth Ave Boston MA 02215. *Fax:* 617-353-9393

AHLERS, GUENTER, PHYSICAL CHEMISTRY, SOLID STATE PHYSICS. *Current Pos:* PROF, DEPT PHYSICS, UNIV CALIF, SANTA BARBARA, 79- *Personal Data:* b Bremen, Ger, Mar 28, 34; US citizen; m. *Educ:* Univ Calif, Riverside, BA, 59; Univ Calif, Berkeley, PhD(phys chem), 63. *Honors & Awards:* Tenth Fritz London Mem Award in Low Temperature Physics, Am Phys Soc, 78; Morris Loeb Lectr, Harvard Univ, 79; Fritz-London Lectr, Duke Univ, 94; Otto von Guricke Sprecher Lectr, Univ Ger, 97. *Prof Exp:* Chemist silicate chem, Riverside Cement Co, 56-58; mem tech staff solid state physics, Bell Tel Labs, 63-80. *Concurrent Pos:* Mem, Condensed Matter Sci Oversight Rev Comt, NSF, 82, Mat Res Adv Comt, NSF, 85-88, External Adv Comt Ctr Nonlinear Studies, Los Alamos Nat Lab, 88-, Steering Comt, Soviet-US Conf Chaos, 90 & Sci Adv Group, Jet Propulsion Lab, NASA, 90-91; Erma & Jakob Michael vis prof, Rehovot, Israel, 85; presidential chair physics, Univ Calif, Santa Barbara, 89-94, fac res lectr, 89-90; Alexander von Humboldt sr US scientist award, 89-90; dir, Ctr Nonlinear Sci, Quantum Inst, 89-96; Guggenheim fel, 97- *Mem:* Nat Acad Sci; fel AAAS; fel Am Phys Soc. *Res:* Thermodynamic properties of solidified gases; hydrodynamic instabilities; heat capacities; critical phenomena; liquid helium; transport properties. *Mailing Add:* Dept Physics Univ Calif Santa Barbara CA 93106

AHLERT, ROBERT CHRISTIAN, ENVIRONMENTAL ENGINEERING. *Current Pos:* prof chem & biochem eng & exec dir eng res, 64-80, distinguished prof, 80-96, DISTINGUISHED EMER PROF CHEM & BIOCHEM ENG, RUTGERS UNIV, NEW BRUNSWICK, 96- *Personal Data:* b New York, NY, Jan 22, 32; m 54, Barbara Aldrich; c Christi, William & Michael. *Educ:* Polytech Inst Brooklyn, BChE, 52; Univ Calif, Los Angeles, MSEng, 58; Lehigh Univ, PhD(chem eng), 64. *Honors & Awards:* Cecil Award, Am Inst Chem Engrs, 88. *Prof Exp:* Res engr, Rocketdyne Div NAm Aviation, Inc, 54-56, sr res engr, 56-58, eng supvr, 58-62, propulsion specialist, 62-64, res group leader, 64. *Concurrent Pos:* Mem, Joint Army-Navy-Air Force Panel Liquid Propellant Test Methods, 58-64; consult, ad hoc panel liquid propellant test methods, US Dept Defense, 66-70; consult water qual, 71-; mem, Task Force Source Red, NJ Hazardous Waste Fac Siting Com, 84-; exec comt, Environ Div, Am Inst Chem Engrs, 88-94. *Mem:* Am Inst Chem Engrs; Nat Soc Prof Engrs; Nat Fire Protection Asn; Am Inst Chemists; Sigma Xi; Am Acad Environ Eng; Am Water Resources Asn. *Res:* Ignition and combustion phenomena; chemical and biochemical processes; thermodynamics; biochemical reactor analysis; water resources analysis and simulation; hazardous waste management. *Mailing Add:* PO Box 1982 Ormond Beach FL 32175. *Fax:* 904-673-9269

AHLFELD, CHARLES EDWARD, REACTOR PHYSICS. *Current Pos:* Res physicist, Savannah River Plant, 67-76, staff physicist, 76-78, asst chief supvr, reactor physics, 78-82, chief supvr, 82-84, asst dep supt, 84-85, res mgr, 85-86, prog mgr reactors, 87-89, NPR DEPT MGR, SAVANNAH RIVER SITE, WESTINGHOUSE SAVANNAH RIVER CO, 89- *Personal Data:* b Aug 9, 40; m 62; c 2. *Educ:* Univ Fla, BS, 62; Fla State Univ, MS, 64, PhD(physics), 68. *Mem:* Am Phys Soc; Am Nuclear Soc. *Res:* Experimental and theoretical studies of static and kinetic nuclear reactor behavior; cross sections and nuclear data pertinent to reactor design; application of computers to reactor experimentation; reactor core design; reactor operations; management of nuclear reactor operations. *Mailing Add:* 5720 Desert View Dr La Jolla CA 92037

AHLFORS, LARS VALERIAN, complex analysis, conformal mapping; deceased, see previous edition for last biography

AHLGREN, CLIFFORD ELMER, FORESTRY. *Current Pos:* RETIRED. *Personal Data:* b Toimi, Minn, Apr 22, 22; m 54; c 2. *Educ:* Univ Minn, BS, 48, MS, 53. *Hon Degrees:* DSc, Cornell Col, 76. *Prof Exp:* Forester, Iron Range Resources & Rehab, 48; res forester, Wilderness Res Found, 48-52, dir, Quetico-Super Wilderness Res Ctr, 52-63, dir res, Wilderness Res Found, 63-91. *Concurrent Pos:* Res assoc, Col Forestry, Univ Minn, St Paul, 63-91. *Mem:* Am Phytopath Asn; fel Soc Am Foresters; Am Forestry Asn; Ecol Soc Am; corresp mem Forestry Soc Finland. *Res:* Vegetational succession following natural disturbances in wilderness areas; field grafting and breeding of northern coniferous species; ecological effect of fire on northern coniferous forests. *Mailing Add:* 12734 W Copperstone Dr Sun City West AZ 85375

AHLGREN, GEORGE E, PLANT PHYSIOLOGY. *Current Pos:* Asst prof, 66-71, ASSOC PROF BIOL, UNIV MINN, DULUTH, 71- *Personal Data:* b Cloquet, Minn, Dec 20, 31; m 61; c 2. *Educ:* Univ Minn, BS, 59, MS, 62, PhD(agr, plant physiol), 66. *Mem:* Am Soc Plant Physiol. *Res:* Absorption and translocation of mineral ions and other substances by the plant. *Mailing Add:* 3540 Martin Rd Duluth MN 55803

AHLGREN, HENRY LAWRENCE, AGRONOMY. *Current Pos:* Asst agron & soils, Univ Wis-Madison, 29-35, from instr to prof agron, 35-74, chmn dept, 49-52, assoc dir agr exten, 52-67, asst chancellor, Univ Exten, 66-67, vchancellor, 67-69, chancellor, 69-74, dir coop exten serv, 69-70, EMER PROF AGRON & EMER CHANCELLOR UNIV EXTEN, UNIV WIS-MADISON, 74- *Personal Data:* b Wyoming, Minn, Oct 3, 08; m 36; c 2. *Educ:* Univ Wis, BS, 31, MS, 33, PhD(agron), 35. *Concurrent Pos:* Traveling fel, Europe, 36; dep undersecy rural develop, USDA, 70. *Mem:* Fel Am Soc Agron; fel Royal Swed Acad Agr & Forestry. *Res:* Pasture improvement, particularly the fertilization, management and ecological aspects; effect of various fertilizers, cutting treatments and irrigation on yield of forage and chemical composition of rhizomes of Kentucky bluegrass. *Mailing Add:* 5029 Sheboygan Ave Madison WI 53705

AHLGREN, MOLLY O, AQUATIC ECOLOGY, DETRITIVORY. *Current Pos:* ASST PROF AQUATIC RESOURCES, SHELDON JACKSON COL, 90- *Personal Data:* b Duluth, Minn, Nov 27, 57. *Educ:* Univ Idaho, BS, 80; Mich Tech Univ, MS, 84, PhD(aquatic ecol), 88. *Mem:* NAm Benthological Soc; Ecol Soc Am; Am Fisheries Soc; Sigma Xi. *Res:* Significance of detritus in the diet and nutrition of freshwater fish and role of marine invertebrates in processing organic matter in nearshore sediments. *Mailing Add:* Sci Div Sheldon Jackson Col 801 Lincoln St Sitka AK 99835. *Fax:* 907-747-5212; *E-Mail:* tsmoa@acad1.aiasca.edu

AHLQUIST, JON EDWARD, ECOLOGY. *Current Pos:* PROF, DEPT METEOROL, FLA STATE UNIV. *Honors & Awards:* Daniel Giruad Elliot Medal, Nat Acad Sci, 88. *Mailing Add:* Dept Meteorol Fla State Univ 600 W College Ave Tallahassee FL 32306-1096

AHLQUIST, PAUL G, MOLECULAR VIROLOGY. *Current Pos:* Asst scientist, Biophys Lab, 81-84, from asst prof to assoc prof, Biophys Lab & Plant Path Dept, 84-91, PROF, INST MOLECULAR VIROL & PLANT PATH DEPT, UNIV WIS-MADISON, 91-, CHMN, 96- *Educ:* Iowa State Univ, BS, 76; Univ Wis, PhD(biophys), 81. *Honors & Awards:* Allen Res Award, Am Phytopath Soc, 88. *Concurrent Pos:* Pres Young Investr Award, NSF, 85-90; mem, Exec Comt, Int Comn Taxon Viruses, 87-93; bd dir, Int Soc Plant Molecular Biol, 89-93; mem, Exec Coun, Am Soc Virol, 93-96; Van Arkel hon fac chair biochem, Leiden Univ, Neth, 95; Merit Award, NIH, 95- *Mem:* Nat Acad Sci; Am Soc Virol. *Res:* Mechanisms and regulation of RNA virus replication and gene expression; virus host interactions; genetics of viral recombination and sequence variability; mechanisms of viral infection spread. *Mailing Add:* Inst Molecular Virol Univ Wis 1525 Linden Dr Madison WI 53706-1596

AHLRICHS, JAMES LLOYD, SOIL CHEMISTRY & MINERALOGY. *Current Pos:* from instr to assoc prof, 57-68, PROF SOIL CHEM, PURDUE UNIV, WEST LAFAYETTE, 68- *Personal Data:* b Palmer, Iowa, Sept 13, 28; m 52, Kristina Jorgenson; c 4. *Educ:* Iowa State Univ, BS, 50, MS, 55; Purdue Univ, PhD(soil chem), 61. *Prof Exp:* Teacher, Pierson Pub Sch, 50-51. *Concurrent Pos:* Vis scientist, Macaulay Inst Soil Sci, Scotland, 66-67; sr Fulbright lectr, Coun Sci Invest & Autonomous Univ Madrid, 73-74; Agency Int Develop tech adv, Univ Tras-os-Montes e Alto Douro, Port, 81-83, Niger, 90 & Burkina Faso, 92. *Mem:* Am Chem Soc; Soil Sci Soc Am; Am Soc Agron; Clay Minerals Soc; Sigma Xi. *Res:* Aluminum toxicity in soils and tolerance of plant species and gersotypesto aluminum. *Mailing Add:* Dept Agron Purdue Univ West Lafayette IN 47901

AHLSCHWEDE, WILLIAM T, ANIMAL BREEDING, SWINE PRODUCTION. *Current Pos:* CONSULT, INDEPENDENT SWINE PROD, 94- *Personal Data:* b Lincoln, Nebr, Jan 31, 42; m 64; c 2. *Educ:* Univ Nebr, BS, 64; NC State Univ, MS, 67, PhD(animal sci), 70. *Prof Exp:* Instr animal sci, NC state Univ, 67-69; res assoc med genetics, Univ Wis, 69-70; asst prof, 70-75, assoc prof animal sci, Univ Nebr, 75-93; prof animal sci, Univ Tenn, 93-94. *Mem:* Am Soc Animal Sci. *Res:* Evaluation of crossbreeding systems in swine; development of specialized breeding systems. *Mailing Add:* 154 Glenwood Dr Martin NE 38237

AHLSTROM, HARLOW G(ARTH), AERONAUTICS, FLUID DYNAMICS. *Current Pos:* ASST DIR ENG TECHNOL, BOEING AEROSPACE CO, 85- *Personal Data:* b Yakima, Wash, Aug 20, 35; m 56; c 2. *Educ:* Univ Wash, BS, 57, MS, 59; Calif Inst Technol, PhD(aeronaut), 63. *Prof Exp:* Assoc res engr, Boeing Airplane Co, 57; aerodynamicist, Douglas Aircraft Co, 59; res fel magneto fluid dynamics, Calif Inst Technol, 62 & 63; from asst prof aeronaut & astronaut to prof, Univ Wash, 63-74; group leader, laser plasma interaction group, Lawrence Livermore Lab, Univ Calif, 74-75, assoc prog leader fusion exp, 75-81, asst dep assoc dir inertial fusion, 81-85. *Concurrent Pos:* Consult, Douglas Aircraft Co, 59-64, Boeing Co, 63-69, Math Sci Northwest, 69- & Nat Acad Sci, 69-; spec consult, NASA Hq, Washington, DC, 67; vis prof, Univ D'Aix-Marseille, France, 71. *Mem:* Am Inst Aeronaut & Astronaut; Am Phys Soc. *Res:* Magneto fluid dynamics; fluid dynamics; lasers; fusion. *Mailing Add:* Engr Inst Lab OPS Boeing Defense Space Group PO Box 3999 Seattle WA 98124-2499. *Fax:* 253-773-9308

AHLUWALIA, BALWANT SINGH, ENDOCRINOLOGY. *Current Pos:* from asst prof to assoc prof, 70-72, PROF OBSTET & GYNEC, COL MED, HOWARD UNIV, 72- *Personal Data:* b India, Mar 12, 32; m 62; c 2. *Educ:* Univ Minn, MS, 59, PhD(reproduction), 62. *Prof Exp:* Scientist, Worcester Found Exp Biol, 67-68; scientist, Nat Inst Arthritis & Metab Dis, 68-70. *Concurrent Pos:* Fel physiol, Hormel Inst, Univ Minn, 63-67. *Mem:* Am Vet Med Asn; Endocrine Soc; Am Inst Nutrit; Am Oil Chemists Soc; Am Androl Soc. *Res:* Lipid metabolism in the reproductive organs with respect to fertility and sterility in animals; substance abuse and reproduction. *Mailing Add:* 16409 Keats Terr Rockville MD 20855-1920

AHLUWALIA, DALJIT SINGH, APPLIED MATHEMATICS. *Current Pos:* PROF MATH & DIR, CTR APPL MATH & STATIST, NJ INST TECHNOL, 86- *Personal Data:* b Sialkot, India, Sept 5, 32; m 60, Devinder Kaur; c Gurpreet S, Jasjit S, Gurinder S & Muninder K. *Educ:* Punjab Univ, India, BA, 52, MA, 55; Ind Univ, Bloomington, MS, 65, PhD(appl math), 65. *Prof Exp:* Lectr math, R G Col, Phagwara, Punjab, 55-57, Khalsa Col, Bombay, 57-62 & Univ Bombay, 59-62; part time teaching assoc, Ind Univ, Bloomington, 62-65, asst prof, 65-66; vis mem & adj assoc prof, Courant Inst Math Sci, NY Univ, 66-68, from asst prof to prof, 68-87. *Concurrent Pos:* Prof math, Univ SFla, Tampa, 72-74; consult, Lamont Doherty Geol Observ, Columbia Univ, 77-, Inst Comput Appln Sci & Eng, 78-79 & Univ Miami, 79; vis prof, Northwestern Univ, 84 & Stanford Univ, 85 & 96; chmn, Dept Math & dir, Ctr Appl Math & Statist, NJ Inst Technol, 86-89; prog dir appl math, NSF, 93-95. *Mem:* Am Math Soc; Soc Indust & Appl Math; Tensor Soc; Acoustic Soc Am; Int Sci Radio Union. *Res:* Plastic flow and fracture in solids; uniform theories of diffraction for the edges and convex bodies; study of wave propagation in elastic media and acoustics; asymptotic methods in underwater acoustics and nonlinear wave propagation. *Mailing Add:* Dept Math NJ Inst Technol Newark NJ 07102. *Fax:* 973-596-6467; *E-Mail:* daahlu@m.njit.edu

AHLUWALIA, GURPREET S, PHARMACOLOGY. *Current Pos:* res scientist, 84-87, from res assoc to sr res assoc, 87-92, GROUP LEADER, GILLETTE RES INST, 92- *Personal Data:* b Oct 18, 55; m 83, Gail D Cruz. *Educ:* Delhi Univ, India, BS, 76; Howard Univ, MS, 78, PhD(biochem), 81. *Prof Exp:* Res assoc, Dept Biochem, Col Med, Howard Univ, 81-82; fel, Lab Med Chem & Pharmacol, Nat Cancer Inst, NIH, 82-84. *Mem:* Am Soc Pharmacol & Exp Therapeut; NY Acad Sci. *Res:* Clinical pharmacology and drug development; correlating drug disposition to its pharmacological effects; mechanism of action of compounds; formulations for effective drug delivery; author of 35 technical publications and three patents. *Mailing Add:* Gillette Res Inst 401 Professional Dr Gaithersburg MD 20879-3400

AHLUWALIA, HARJIT SINGH, COSMIC RAY PHYSICS, SOLAR & SPACE PHYSICS. *Current Pos:* assoc prof, 68-73, PROF PHYSICS, UNIV NMEX, 73- *Personal Data:* b Bombay, India, May 13, 34; m 64, Manjit K Pal; c Suvinder Singh & Davinder Singh. *Educ:* Panjab Univ, India, BSc Hons, 53, MSc, 54; Gujarat Univ, India, PhD(physics), 60. *Honors & Awards:* Distinguished Serv Award, Am Geophys Union, 88. *Prof Exp:* Sr res asst cosmic rays, Phys Res Lab, Ahmedabad, Gujarat, India, 54-62; tech asst expert, UNESCO, France, 62; res assoc cosmic rays & geomagnetism, Southwest Ctr Advan Studies, Tex, 63-64; vis prof physics, Int Atomic Energy Agency, Austria & sci dir, Lab Cosmic Physics, Univ La Paz, 65-67; vis prof physics, Pan Am Union, Washington, DC, 67. *Concurrent Pos:* NASA fel, 63-64; chmn, Bolivian Space Res Comt, 65-67; prin investr, US Air Force res proj, 65-68, NSF res proj, 68-81 & Sandia Corp res proj, Albuquerque, 69-71, NASA res proj, 72-77, 88-95; Bolivian nat rep, Comt Space Res & Int Union Pure & Appl Physics, 66-69; mem, Cosmic Ray Comn, Int Union Pure & Appl Physics, 66-69; gen secy high energy cosmic ray group, Int Coun Sci Unions, 76-85; sr vis scientist, NASA Hq, 87-88. *Mem:* AAAS; Am Geophys Union; sr mem Inst Elec & Electronics Engrs; Am Meteorol Soc; fel Am Phys Soc; Int Astron Union; Am Astron Soc; Sigma Xi. *Res:* Cosmic ray time variations; generation of energetic particles on sun; transport of very high energy charged particles (diffusion and drifts) in tangled magnetic fields permeating the heliospere; geomagnetism; nuclear electronics; space physics; plasma physics; astrophysics. *Mailing Add:* Dept Physics & Astron Univ NMex Albuquerque NM 87131-1156. *Fax:* 505-277-1520; *E-Mail:* hsa@unm.edu

AHMAD, FAZAL, LIPID SYNTHESIS, ENZYME REGULATION. *Current Pos:* PROF BIOCHEM, SCH MED, UNIV MIAMI, 72- *Educ:* Univ Edinburgh, Scotland, PhD(chem), 61. *Mailing Add:* Dept Biochem & Molecular Biol Univ Miami Sch Med 1600 NW Tenth Ave PO Box 016129 Miami FL 33101-9990. *Fax:* 305-547-3955

AHMAD, IBRAHIM A, NONPARAMETRIC STATISTICS. *Current Pos:* PROF, DIV STATIST, NORTHERN ILL UNIV, 87- *Personal Data:* b Egypt; m, Magda M Megahed, c Shereen, Mouneer, Ameer, Tarek & Mariam. *Educ:* Univ Cairo, BSc, 65; Fla State Univ, MS, 70, PhD(statist), 73. *Prof Exp:* Statist consult, Auditor Gen Off, State of Fla, 72-75; from asst to assoc prof, Dept Math & Statist, McMaster Univ, 75-80; assoc prof, Dept Math, Univ Md, 80-83; prof, Dept Math, Univ SFla, 83-87. *Concurrent Pos:* Vis asst prof, Mem Univ Nfld, 75-76; recipient res, indust & univ grants, 75-95; vis assoc prof, Univ Petrol & Minerals, Saudi Arabia, 80-81; statist prog coordr, Dept Math, Univ Md, 80-83, Univ SFla, 83-87; vis prof, King Saud Univ, Saudi Arabia, 85, 97 & 98; distinguished vis scholar, Dept Econ, Univ Western Ont, 87, 89; dir, Div Statist, Northern Ill Univ, 87-94; vis scientist, Armamant Lab, Eglin Air Force Base, 88; vis scholar, Dept Econ, London Sch Econ & Political Sci, 89; sr Fulbright res scholar, 94-95; vis scholar, Dept Math & Statist, Univ Brasilia, 96, 97. *Mem:* Int Statist Inst; Inst Math Statist; Am Statist Asn; Arabian Math Soc; hon mem Malysian Acad Sci; Statist Soc Can; Sigma Xi; Math Asn Am; fel Royal Statist Soc. *Res:* Nonparametric statistics; reliability and lifetesting; applied probability. *Mailing Add:* Div Statist Northern Ill Univ De Kalb IL 60115. *Fax:* 815-753-6798

AHMAD, IRSHAD, NUCLEAR CHEMISTRY, NUCLEAR PHYSICS. *Current Pos:* res assoc, 66-68, asst chemist, 68-70, CHEMIST, ARGONNE NAT LAB, 70- *Personal Data:* b Azamgarh, India, Nov 1, 39; m 69, Fauzia Mazhar; c 3. *Educ:* Univ Punjab, Pakistan, BSc, 58; Univ Peshawar, MSc, 62; Univ Pac, MS, 65; Univ Calif, Berkeley, PhD(chem), 66. *Prof Exp:* Demonstr chem, Edwardes Col, Peshawar, 58-60; res fel, Lawrence Radiation Lab, Univ Calif, Berkeley, 66. *Mem:* Am Phys Soc; Am Chem Soc; Sigma Xi. *Res:* Synthesis of new actinide isotopes; nuclear structure studies of transuranium nuclei by high-resolution alpha, beta and gamma spectroscopy and nuclear reactions; investigation of high spin states by heavy-ion reactions. *Mailing Add:* D-203-F-157 Argonne Nat Lab Argonne IL 60439

AHMAD, JAMEEL, CIVIL ENGINEERING, SOLID MECHANICS. *Current Pos:* assoc prof, 68-80, PROF & CHMN, DEPT CIVIL ENG, COOPER UNION, 80- *Personal Data:* b Lahore, Pakistan, May 22, 41; m 65; c 1. *Educ:* Univ Punjab, WPakistan, BSc, 61; Univ Hawaii, MS, 64; Univ Pa, PhD(civil eng), 67. *Prof Exp:* Asst engr, WAPDA, Pakistan, 61-62; asst prof eng, PMC Cols, 67-68. *Concurrent Pos:* Dir, PMA Corp, 78-; proj dir, Cooper Union Res Found, 80- *Mem:* Am Soc Civil Engrs; Am Concrete Inst; Am Soc Eng Educ. *Res:* Mechanics of materials and structural mechanics; environmental engineering; energy engineering. *Mailing Add:* Dept Civil Eng Cooper Union 30 Cooper Sq New York NY 10003-7136

AHMAD, MOGHISUDDIN, LIPID CHEMISTRY, ORGANIC SYNTHESIS OF FINE CHEMICALS. *Current Pos:* CHEMIST LIPIDS DEPT, SIGMA CHEM CO, 88- *Personal Data:* b Dhanbad, India, July 1, 50; m 85, Athar B Hussain; c Waseem. *Educ:* Aligarh Muslim Univ, India, BSc, 71, MSc, 73, MPhil, 75, PhD(org chem), 78. *Prof Exp:* Fel lipid chem, Aligarh Muslim Univ, India, 78-79; res assoc fatty acid chem, Tex A&M Univ, 79-81; res assoc food chem & toxicol, Ore State Univ, 81-88. *Mem:* Am Oil Chemists Soc; Am Chem Soc; Sigma Xi. *Res:* Organic synthesis; specialty chemicals, lipids product development and scale-up; process development; chromatographic and spectroscopic analysis; new fatty acids from vegetable oils; chemistry of nitrosamines; new product development. *Mailing Add:* Lipids Dept Sigma Chem Co PO Box 14508 St Louis MO 63178

AHMAD, MOID UDDIN, SURFACE HYDROLOGY, CONTAMINATION STUDY. *Current Pos:* assoc prof, 69-74, PROF HYDROL & GEOPHYS, OHIO UNIV, 74- *Personal Data:* b Agra, India, Aug 18, 27; m 45, Aulia; c Molz B & Kausar. *Educ:* Agra Univ, BSc, 44, LLB, 47; NMex Inst Mining & Technol, MS, 61; Univ London, PhD(geol, seismol), 66. *Prof Exp:* Asst seismologist, Geophys Inst Quetta, Pakistan, 49-58; head, Dept Physics, Battersea Grammar Sch, London, Eng, 61-67; geophysicist & hydrologist, Food & Agr Orgn, UN & consult to Govt of Kuwait, 67-69. *Concurrent Pos:* Spec consult, Libyan Govt Reclamation & Resettlement Dept; consult, Saudi Arabia, Syria, Sudan, Iraq & Pakistan. *Mem:* Am Geophys Union; Soc Explor Geophys; Europ Asn Explor Geophys; Am Water Resources Asn; Am Water Works Asn; Int Asn Hydrogeologists; Am Inst Hydrol; Soc Prof Well Log Analyst. *Res:* Exploration of groundwater in arid regions; acid mine drainage control, development of a hydrological approach to control acid discharge from strip and drift mines and techniques to map acid producing areas by thermal mapping; well field design; designed Sarir Well Field, consisting of 250 wells, one of the largest desert farms in Sahara; hazardous waste disposal; well head protection; pollution studies and remediation. *Mailing Add:* Dept Geol Ohio Univ Main Campus Athens OH 45701. *Fax:* 909-674-9262

AHMAD, NAZIR, HISTOLOGY, REPRODUCTIVE ENDOCRINOLOGY. *Current Pos:* ASSOC PROF HISTOL, SCH MED, UNIV SOUTHERN CALIF, 75- *Personal Data:* b Pakistan, Feb 22, 36; US citizen; m 55; c 2. *Educ:* San Francisco State Col, BA, 55; Univ Calif, Berkeley, MA, 59; Univ Calif, San Francisco, PhD(anat), 68. *Prof Exp:* Asst prof histol, Sch Med, Georgetown Univ, 68-69. *Mem:* AAAS; Soc Study Reproduction; Am Asn Anat; Endoctrine Soc. *Res:* Reproductive endocrinology, utilizing pituitary as well as ovarian hormones essential for the maintenance of gestation and lactation; maintenance of spermatogenesis; effects of toxic substances on male reproduction including developmental studies in human histology. *Mailing Add:* Dept Anat Univ Southern Calif Sch Med 711 W California Blvd Pasadena CA 91105

AHMAD, SARFRAZ, PROTEASES ENZYMOLOGY, MUSCLE PROTEIN DURING SEPSIS. *Current Pos:* NIH RES ASSOC, STRITCH SCH MED, LOYOLA UNIV, CHICAGO, 92- *Personal Data:* b Tanda, Faizabad, India, Apr 25, 61; m 94, Ghazala. *Educ:* Aligarh Muslim Univ, India, BSc Hons, 83, MSc, 85; Northeastern Hill Univ, MPhil, 86, PhD(biochem), 91. *Prof Exp:* Jr res fel biochem, Dept Environ, Govt India, New Delhi, 85-86, Univ Grants Comn, New Delhi, 86-88, Indian Coun Med Res, New Delhi, 88; sr res fel, Coun Sci & Indust Res, New Delhi, 88-90; sr res asst biochem, Indian Inst Technol, New Delhi, 90-92. *Mem:* AAAS; Soc Biol Chemists; US Shock Soc. *Res:* Assess the protein dynamics in the muscle of septic rats by simultaneous measurements of protein degradation and synthesis in vivo and in vitro; induction of proteases in physiological systems. *Mailing Add:* Dept Burn & Shock Unit Bldg 110 Rm 4208 Loyola Univ Med Ctr Maywood IL 60153. *Fax:* 708-216-6308

AHMAD, SHAIR, MATHEMATICS. *Current Pos:* CHMN, DEPT MATH & COMPUT SCI, UNIV MIAMI, 80- *Personal Data:* b Kabul, Afghanistan, June 19, 34; US citizen; m 58, 74; c 3. *Educ:* Univ Utah, BS, 60, MS, 62; Case Western Reserve Univ, PhD(math), 68. *Prof Exp:* Asst math, Univ Utah, 60-62; instr, SDak State Univ, 62-64; asst, Case Western Reserve Univ, 64-65, instr, 66-68; asst prof, Univ NDak, 65-66; from asst prof to prof math, Okla State Univ, 68-78, chmn dept, 78-80. *Mem:* Am Math Soc; Math Asn Am. *Res:* Dynamical systems; differential equations. *Mailing Add:* Dept Math Comput Sci Stat Univ Tex Sam Antonio 6900 N Loop 1604 W San Antonio TX 78249-0601

AHMAD, SHAMIM, elastomer technology, tire engineering, for more information see previous edition

AHMADI, GOODARZ, MULTIPHASE FLOWS & AEROSOLS, VIBRATION CONTROL. *Current Pos:* PROF MECH ENG DEPT, CLARKSON UNIV, 82-, CHAIR, 91- *Personal Data:* b Tehran, Iran, July 23, 43; US citizen; m 72, Behnoz Kafi; c Anahita A & Amir G. *Educ:* Tehran

Univ, BS, 65; Purdue Univ, MS, 68, PhD (mech eng), 70. *Prof Exp:* From asst prof to prof, Dept Mech Eng, Shiraz Univ, 70-81, dean 78-80. *Concurrent Pos:* Ed, Iranian J Sci & Technol, 73-74 & 78-80; acad visitor, Univ Sask, 74-75 & Mech Eng, Univ Calgary, 81. *Mem:* Am Soc Mech Engrs; Am Soc Eng Educ. *Res:* Multiphase flows; aerosol transport and deposition; granular flows; turbulence modeling; computational fluid mechanics; vibrations; random vibrations; vibration isolation and control; base isolation; continuum mechanics; stability of structures and fluids. *Mailing Add:* 14 Gilmore St Potsdam NY 13676. *Fax:* 315-268-6438; *E-Mail:* ahmadi@sun.soe.clarkson.edu

AHMADJIAN, VERNON, BOTANY. *Current Pos:* assoc dean grad sch, Clark Univ, 69-71, coordr res, 69-75, dean, Grad Sch, 71-75, PROF BOT, CLARK UNIV, 69- *Personal Data:* b Whitinsville, Mass, May 19, 30; m 56; c 3. *Educ:* Clark Univ, AB, 52, MA, 56; Harvard Univ, PhD, 60. *Honors & Awards:* Antarctic Medal. *Prof Exp:* From asst prof to prof bot, Clark Univ, 59-68; prof, Univ Mass, 68-69. *Concurrent Pos:* Vis prof, Univ Calif, Berkeley, 65-66 & Wellesley Col, 85-86. *Mem:* Fel AAAS; Bot Soc Am; Phycol Soc Am; Mycol Soc Am; Brit Lichen Soc. *Res:* Symbiosis; lichenology; molecular biology of lichens. *Mailing Add:* Biol Clark Univ 950 Main St Worcester MA 01610-1400

AHMANN, DONALD H(ENRY), MATERIALS SCIENCE, INORGANIC CHEMISTRY. *Current Pos:* RETIRED. *Personal Data:* b Struble, Iowa, Jan 9, 20; m 45; c 6. *Educ:* Iowa State Univ, BS, 41, PhD(phys & inorg chem), 48. *Prof Exp:* Jr chemist, Manhattan Proj, Iowa State Univ, 42-48; res chemist, Knolls Atomic Power Lab, Gen Elec Co, NY, 48-55, mgr chem & chem eng, 55-57, mgr chem, Vallecitos Nuclear Ctr, Calif, 57-60, mgr chem & chem eng, 60-66, mgr chem & metall, 66-67, mgr, Nuclear Mat & Propulsion Opers, Ohio, 67-68, mgr mat sci & technol, Nuclear Systs Progs, 68-69, mgr eng, Neutron Devices Dept, 69-85; consult, 88-90. *Mem:* Am Chem Soc; Am Nuclear Soc; Am Soc Metals; AAAS; Am Vacuum Soc. *Res:* Material science studies related to nuclear applications and vacuum components; chemistry of nuclear reactors and fuels; nuclear fuels reprocessing. *Mailing Add:* 1324 Golfview Dr Belleair FL 34616

AHMED, A RAZZAQUE, SKIN DISEASES. *Current Pos:* RES ASSOC, ORAL PATH, HARVARD SCH DENT MED, BOSTON, 85-, CONSULT, HARVARD HEALTH, 85- *Personal Data:* b Hyderabad, India, Oct 27, 48; US citizen. *Educ:* Nagpur Univ, India, BS, 66; All India Inst Med Sci, New Delhi, 72; Harvard Univ, DSc(oral biol), 88. *Honors & Awards:* Gold Award, Am Acad Dermat, 82. *Prof Exp:* Asst prof, dermat, Univ Calif Sch Med, Los Angeles, 78-85. *Mem:* Soc Invest Dermat; Am Asn Immunologists; Am Fedn Clin Res; Am Soc Clin Invest; Royal Soc Med. *Res:* Pathogenesis of actummune blistering skin disease. *Mailing Add:* Dept Dermatol Boston Univ Sch Med 80 E Concord St Boston MA 02118. *Fax:* 617-638-5515

AHMED, AHMED ELSAYED, ENVIRONMENTAL PATHOLOGY, TOXICOLOGY. *Current Pos:* PROF PATH, UNIV TEX MED BR, 85- *Personal Data:* b Cairo, Egypt, Aug 21, 42. *Res:* Environmental pathology; toxicology. *Mailing Add:* Dept Path Univ Tex Med Br 301 Rt F-09 3-152 Keiller Bldg Galveston TX 77555-0609

AHMED, ASAD, MOLECULAR GENETICS. *Current Pos:* from asst prof to assoc prof, 67-77, PROF GENETICS, UNIV ALTA, 77- *Personal Data:* b Saharanpur, India, Nov 7, 39; Can citizen; m 78, Samin. *Educ:* Aligarh Muslim Univ, India, BSc, 56, MSc, 58, PhD(plant path), 61; Yale Univ, PhD(biochem genetics), 64. *Prof Exp:* Fulbright scholar, Yale Univ, 60-64, univ fel, 61-62, Wadsworth fel, 62-63, Sterling fel, 63-64; res assoc, Inst Molecular Biol, Univ Ore, 64-65; res scientist biochem, Dept Nat Health & Welfare, Can, 66-67. *Mem:* AAAS. *Res:* Transposable genetic elements in Escherichia coli; recombinant DNA technology; cloning and sequencing vectors. *Mailing Add:* Dept Biol Scis Univ Alta Edmonton AB T6G 2E9 Can. *Fax:* 403-492-9234, 449-6059

AHMED, FAIZY, ANALYTICAL CHEMISTRY, HIGH PERFORMANCE LIQUID CROMOTOGRAPHY. *Current Pos:* TECH DIR, PHENOMENEX, INC, 90- *Personal Data:* b Udupi, India, Mar 28, 48. *Educ:* Univ Mysore, India, PhD(biochem), 77. *Res:* Analytical chemistry; high performance liquid cromotography. *Mailing Add:* Phenomenex Inc 2320 W 205th St Torrance CA 90501-1456

AHMED, ISMAIL YOUSEF, INORGANIC CHEMISTRY. *Current Pos:* asst prof, 69-73, ASSOC PROF CHEM, UNIV MISS, 73- *Personal Data:* b Silwad, Jordan, Sept 27, 39. *Educ:* Cairo Univ, BS, 60; Pa State Univ, MS, 65; Southern Ill Univ, Carbondale, PhD(chem), 68. *Prof Exp:* High sch teacher, Jordan, 60-64; lectr chem, Southern Ill Univ Carbondale, 68-69. *Mem:* Am Chem Soc. *Res:* Lewis acid-Lewis base interactions; interactions of metal halides with compounds containing N-S bond; characterization of solute species in nonaqueous solvents; solvation and rates of solvent exchange by nuclear magnetic resonance. *Mailing Add:* Dept Chem Univ Miss Gen Delivery University MS 38677-9999

AHMED, KHALIL, BIOCHEMISTRY. *Current Pos:* RES BIOCHEMIST & CHIEF, CELLULAR & MOLECULAR BIOCHEM LAB, DEPT VET AFFAIRS MED CTR, MINNEAPOLIS, 70-, RES CAREER SCIENTIST, 77- *Personal Data:* b Lahore, Pakistan, Nov 30, 34; US citizen; m 69; c 2. *Educ:* Univ Panjab, Pakistan, BSc, 54, MSc, 55; McGill Univ, PhD(biochem), 60. *Prof Exp:* Res chemist, WRegional Labs, Pakistan, 55-57; res asst biochem, Montreal Gen Hosp & Res Inst, McGill Univ, 57-60; res fel, Wistar Inst, Univ Pa, 60-61, res assoc, 61-63; asst prof metab res, Chicago Med Sch, 63-67; sr staff mem & res biochemist, Lab Pharmacol, Baltimore Cancer Res Ctr, Nat Cancer Inst, 67-72; assoc prof, 73-77, PROF LAB MED & PATH, UNIV MINN, MINNEAPOLIS, 77- *Concurrent Pos:* Vis lectr, Chicago Med Sch, 68-69; mem, Path B Study Sect, NIH, 78-81; mem, Pharmacol Study Sect, 88- *Mem:* AAAS; Am Soc Biochem & Molecular Biol; Am Soc Pharmacol & Exp Therapeut; Am Soc Cell Biol; Sigma Xi; Soc Gen Physiol. *Res:* Enzymic mechanism of drug action; biochemistry of ion transport; biochemistry of androgen action in male sex glands; neurochemistry; phosphoproteins; biochemistry of gene action; protein kinases and phosphatases. *Mailing Add:* Cellular & Molecular Biochem Lab 151 VA Med Ctr One Vet Dr Minneapolis MN 55417-2319. *Fax:* 612-725-2093

AHMED, MAHMOUD S, DRUG ABUSE DURING PREGNANCY, OPIOIDS & COCAINE. *Current Pos:* ASSOC PROF OBSTET/GYNEC, SCH MED, UNIV MO, KANSAS CITY, 86-, ASSOC PROF SCH NURSING & ASSOC PROF BIOCHEM, SCH BASIC LIFE SCI, 86- *Personal Data:* b Cairo, Egypt, Mar 17, 42; m 68; c 2. *Educ:* Cairo Univ, BSc, 64, MSc, 69; Univ Tenn, PhD(biochem), 74. *Prof Exp:* Fel biochem, Johns Hopkins Univ, 75-77; asst prof biochem, Univ Tenn, Sch Med, 77-86. *Concurrent Pos:* Vis scientist, Werner Klee Lab, NIH, 80. *Mem:* Sigma Xi; Am Soc Biol Chemists; Soc Perinatal Obstetricians. *Res:* Membrane structure function relationships; role of opiate peptides in analgesia during labor; mechanism of drug dependence and addiction. *Mailing Add:* Univ Kans Sch Med 39th & Rainbow Blvd Kansas City KS 66160-7417

AHMED, NAHED K, CANCER RESEARCH, EXPERIMENTAL THERAPEUTICS. *Current Pos:* DIR GLOBAL RES & DEVELOP PROJ CONT, MARION MERRELL DOW, 94- *Personal Data:* b Cairo, Egypt, Sept 29, 45; US citizen. *Educ:* Cairo Univ, Egypt, BS, 66, MS, 70; Univ Tenn, PhD(biochem), 75. *Prof Exp:* Vis fel res, Baltimore Cancer Res Ctr, Nat Can Inst, Md, 75-77; asst prof biochem, Ctr Health Sci, Univ Tenn, 82-84; res assoc, St Jude Children's Res Hosp, Memphis, Tenn, 77- 79, asst mem res & teaching, Dept Biochem & Clin Pharmacol, 79-89. *Concurrent Pos:* Prin investr, NSF grant, 81-84, Plough Found, 84-85 & Independent Tel Pioneer Asn, 85-88; Ad Hoc site visitor prog & proj, Nat Cancer Inst; reviewer grant proposals, NSF. *Mem:* Am Asn Cancer Res. *Res:* Study the mechanisms by which tumor cells develop resistance to drugs; study the use of inhibitors of key enzymes in the salvage pathway of pyrimidines in vivo and in vitro; study how cancer drugs are metabolized in cell culture and in vivo. *Mailing Add:* Hoechst Marion Roussel PO Box 9627 MS-F 3M 3332 Kansas City MO 64134-0627

AHMED, NASIR, SYSTEMS THEORY, INFORMATION SCIENCE. *Current Pos:* PROF ELEC ENG, DEPT ELEC & COMPUT ENG, UNIV NMEX. *Personal Data:* b Bangalore, India, Aug 11, 40; m 65; c 1. *Educ:* Col Eng, Bangalore, India, BS, 61; Univ NMex, MS, 63, PhD(elec eng), 66. *Prof Exp:* Prin res engr, Systs & Res Ctr, Honeywell, Inc, Minn, 66-68. *Mem:* Inst Elec & Electronics Engrs. *Res:* System and communication theory; information processing. *Mailing Add:* Dept Elec & Comput Eng Univ NMex Albuquerque NM 87131

AHMED, NASIR UDDIN, SYSTEMS & CONTROL THEORY. *Current Pos:* from asst prof to assoc prof, 68-75, PROF SYST OPTIMAL CONTROL, UNIV OTTAWA, 76- *Personal Data:* b Jan 1, 34; Can citizen; m 58; c 6. *Educ:* Univ Dhaka, BSc, 56; Univ Ottawa, MASc, 63, PhD(elec eng), 65. *Honors & Awards:* George Glinski Award for Excellence in Res, 92. *Prof Exp:* Asst engr, Power Syst Control Water & Power Develop Authority, Pakistan, 56-57; sr sci officer, Reactor Physics & nucleonics, Pakistan Atomic Energy Comn, 58-67; fel syst & control, Univ Alta, 67-68. *Concurrent Pos:* Vis prof, Univ Calif, Berkeley, 77-78, Univ NSW, Australia, 80; consult, Dept Nat Defence, Can, 84-87. *Mem:* Inst Elec & Electronics Engrs; Soc Indust & Appl Math; Am Math Soc; Asn Prof Engrs Ont; Can Asn Univ Teachers. *Res:* Systems and control theory for abstract evolution equations on Banach space with applications to ordinary, delay-differential, partial differential and stochastic differential equations and nonlinear filtering; mathematical modeling of spacecraft and space stations with flexible appendages. *Mailing Add:* Dept Elec Eng Univ Ottawa Ottawa ON K1N 6N5 Can. *Fax:* 613-564-6882; *E-Mail:* ahmed@trin.genie.uottawa.can

AHMED, S SULTAN, ADULT CARDIOLOGY, CARDIOVASCULAR RESEARCH. *Current Pos:* Asst in med & cardiol, Univ Med & Dent NJ, NJ Med Sch, 68-69, from instr to assoc prof med, 70-80, fel, 71-72, PROF MED & CARDIOL, UNIV MED & DENT NJ, NJ MED SCH, 80-, ATTEND PHYSICIAN, 72- *Personal Data:* b Delhi, India, Sept 13, 37; US citizen; m 67, Shaheen; c Salman & Sohaib. *Educ:* D J Science Col, Pakistan, BSc, 58; Dow Med Col, Pakistan, MB BS, 63. *Hon Degrees:* FRSM, Royal Soc Med, UK, 74, FACP, 73, FACP, 74, FACC, FACCP, FACA, 76, FAMS, Pakistan, 88, FECE, 90. *Concurrent Pos:* Educ coordr cardiol, St Joseph's Hosp, 74-76 & consult physician, 74-; consult physician, St Michael's Med Ctr, 75-93; vis prof, Dow Med Col, 84-, Post-Grad Inst Med & Air Force Inst Cardiol, 88- & Punjab Med Col, 90; mem affil res, Peer Rev Comt, Am Heart Asn, 85-86. *Mem:* Am Fedn Clin Res; Am Heart Asn; Am Col Cardiol; AAAS; Asn Pakistan Physicians. *Res:* Cardiovascular function and diseases, both in the basic research laboratory as well as part of patient care activities; diagnostic tests in the cardiac catherization lab and management as in a medical ward or intensive care unit; cardiac effects of cigarette smoking; alcohol and the heart; LV functional indices; systolic time intervals; diabetes and the heart; coronary artery disease and blood flow; hypertension; cardiac catherization and angiography. *Mailing Add:* UMDNJ-NJ Med Sch 100 Bergen St Rm I-534 Newark NJ 07103. *Fax:* 973-982-5041

AHMED, SAIYED I, MARINE MICROBIOLOGY, BIOCHEMICAL GENETICS. *Current Pos:* vis scientist, Sch Med, Univ Wash, 70-73, res assoc, 73-76, sr res assoc, 76-78, res assoc prof, 75-85, RES PROF, SCH OCEANOG, UNIV WASH, 85-, PROF, 90- *Personal Data:* b Desna, Pakistan, Jan 5, 41; m 64; c 2. *Educ:* Univ Karachi, BSc, 60; Univ Frankfurt, PhD(microbiol, biochem, bot), 63. *Honors & Awards:* Performance Award, Nat Oceanic & Atmospheric Admin. *Prof Exp:* Sr res off microbiol & fermentation res, Pakistan Coun Sci & Indust Res, 64; Nat Res Coun Can fel biochem genetics, Univ Man, 64-66; NIH sr fel, Yale Univ, 66-69, res assoc, 69-70. *Concurrent Pos:* Fel fac, Univ Wash, 85; assoc prog dir biotechnol, Nat Sea Grant, Nat Oceanic & Atmospheric Admin, 86-88. *Mem:* Am Soc Microbiol; Am Soc Plant Physiologists; Am Soc Limnol & Oceanog; NY Acad; AAAS. *Res:* Mutation genetics in serratia and E coli; control mechanisms and regulations; enzymology; mutagenicity; pollution and environmental studies; marine bacteria and marine phytoplankton metabolism; metabolic studies in anoxic marine environments; application of biotechnology in marine sciences. *Mailing Add:* Sch Oceanog W B-10 Univ Wash 3900 7th Ave NE Seattle WA 98195-0001. *Fax:* 206-685-3351

AHMED, SHABBIR, FUEL PROCESSING, MATHEMATICAL MODEL. *Current Pos:* Postdoctoral appointee, 88-90, SCIENTIFIC STAFF, ARGONNE NAT LAB, 90-, CHEM ENGR, 95- *Personal Data:* b Dhaka, Bangladesh, Aug 1, 58; m 85, Ismat Jahan; c Shayan H. *Educ:* Bangladesh Univ Eng & Technol, BSc, 82, MSc, 83; Univ Nebr, Lincoln, PhD(chem eng), 88. *Mem:* Am Inst Chem Engrs. *Res:* Low temperature catalytic reformers for transportation fuel cell systems; catalytic partial oxidation reaction that convert various fuels into hydrogen-rich gas; pyrolsis kinetics and modeling of chemical processes. *Mailing Add:* 9700 S Cass Ave Argonne IL 60439-4837

AHMED, SHAFFIQ UDDIN, METALLURGICAL ENGINEERING, MATERIALS SCIENCE. *Current Pos:* assoc prof, 60-69, chmn dept, 68-72, PROF METALL ENG, YOUNGSTOWN STATE UNIV, 69- *Personal Data:* b Howrah, India, Mar 1, 34; m 63; c 1. *Educ:* Univ Calcutta, BE, 54; Univ Ill, MS, 58; Case Inst Technol, PhD(metall eng), 65. *Honors & Awards:* Distinguished Serv Award, Am Soc Metals, 68, Prof Man of Year, 71; Western Electric Fund Award, Am Soc Eng Educ. *Prof Exp:* Res officer metall eng, Univ Ill, 55-60. *Concurrent Pos:* Pres, Dr S Ahmed & Assocs, Youngstown, 60- *Mem:* Fel AAAS; fel Am Inst Chemists; Am Soc Metals; Am Inst Mining, Metall & Petrol Engrs; Am Soc Eng Educ. *Res:* Alloys; x-rays; electron microscopy; phase transformation. *Mailing Add:* 1100 Boardman Canfield Rd No 83C Youngstown OH 44512-8051

AHMED, SUSAN WOLOFSKI, MULTIVARIATE ANALYSIS. *Current Pos:* DIR, DIV HAZARD ANAL, CONSUMER SAFETY COMMUN, 97- *Personal Data:* b Detroit, Mich, Apr 25, 46; m 72; c 2. *Educ:* Kalamazoo Col, BS, 68; Univ Mich, Ann Arbor, MPH, 70; Univ NC, Chapel Hill, PhD(biostatist), 75. *Prof Exp:* Res asst prof, Univ NC, Chapel Hill, 76-77; asst prof biostatist, Georgetown Univ, 77- *Mem:* Am Statist Asn; Biometric Soc; Sigma Xi. *Mailing Add:* Div Hazzard Anal Consumer Safety Commun Washington DC 20207

AHMED, SYED ASHRAFUDDIN, ENZYMOLOGY-ENZYME STRUCTURE & FUNCTION, PROTEIN STRUCTURE. *Current Pos:* vis fel/assoc, 83-87, SR STAFF FEL, NAT INST DIABETES & DIGESTIVE & KIDNEY DIS, NIH, 90- *Personal Data:* m, Jannatul Ferdouse; c S Rifat & Nasif S. *Educ:* Dhaka Univ, Bangladesh, BSc, 72, MSc, 74; Kyoto Univ, Japan, PhD(microbial biochem), 83. *Prof Exp:* Lectr biochem, Dhaka Univ, Bangladesh, 75-80; res instr & asst prof, Wake Forest Univ Med Sch, 87-90. *Mem:* Am Soc Biochem & Molecular Biol. *Mailing Add:* LBP/NIDDK/NIH Bldg 8 Rm 2A07 Bethesda MD 20892-0830. *Fax:* 301-402-0240; *E-Mail:* ahmed@helix.nih.gov

AHMED, SYED MAHMOOD, SURFACE CHEMISTRY. *Current Pos:* SR RES ENGR, RES CTR, HERCULES, INC, 79- *Personal Data:* b Hyderabad, India, Mar 30, 49; m 78; c 3. *Educ:* Osmania Univ, Hyderabad, India, BTech, 72; Lehigh Univ, MS, 76, PhD(polymer sci & eng), 79. *Prof Exp:* Res asst, Emulsion Polymers Inst, Lehigh Univ, 74-79. *Mem:* Am Chem Soc; Am Inst Chem Engrs. *Res:* Synthesis and applications of natural and synthetic water soluble polymers; emulsion polymers and emulsion polymerization; suspension polymerization; electrotheology. *Mailing Add:* PO Box 42503 Riyadh 11551 Saudi Arabia

AHMED, WASE U, MICROSCOPY, MATERIAL SCIENCE. *Current Pos:* MINERALOGIST, BUEHLER LTD, 62- *Personal Data:* b Moradabad, India, Sept 27, 31; m 62; c 4. *Educ:* Univ Sind, BS, 57; Univ Ill, 61. *Mem:* Int Metallog Soc; Geol Soc Am; Int Cement Micros Asn. *Res:* New product development to study structure of materials; new methods to prepare specimens for microstructure studies. *Mailing Add:* 720 Newport North Roselle IL 60172

AHMED-ANSARI, AFTAB, PATHOLOGY. *Current Pos:* PROF, DEPT PATH & LAB MED, WINSHIP CANCER CTR, EMORY UNIV, SCH MED, 85-, EXEC MEM, 85- *Personal Data:* b Karachi, Pakistan, Feb 18, 44; US citizen; m; c 2. *Educ:* Univ Karachi, Pakistan, MS, 63; Univ Calif, Los Angeles, MS, 67; Univ Ariz, PhD, 70. *Prof Exp:* Res assoc, NIH fel, Univ Ariz, 70-71; res assoc, Nat Res Coun, Naval Med Res Inst, Nat Naval Med Ctr, 71-73, head, Cellular Immunol Div, 73-74, chmn, res comt, 76-78, sci dir, Dept Immunol, 78-79; dir, Dept Immunol, Merck Inst Therapeut Res, 79-81; sci dir, Naval Med Res Unit No Three, Cairo, 81-84; sr res scientist, Rocky Mountain Lab, Nat Inst Allergy & Infectious Dis, NIH, 84-85. *Mem:* Am Asn Immunologists; Am Soc Microbiol; AAAS; Sigma Xi; Transplantation Soc; Int Soc Exp Hemat; Asn Clin Scientist. *Res:* Numerous publications; pathology. *Mailing Add:* Dept Path Emory Univ Sch Med 4100 WCC Bldg B Atlanta GA 30322. *Fax:* 404-248-5016

AHMED-ZAID, SAID, ELECTRIC POWER ENGINEERING, POWER ELECTRONICS. *Current Pos:* ASSOC PROF ELEC ENG, CLARKSON UNIV, POTSDAM, 89- *Personal Data:* b Algiers, Algeria, May 6, 56; m 83, Andrea Swengel. *Educ:* Univ Ill, Urbana-Champaign, BS, 79, MS, 81, PhD(elec eng), 84. *Prof Exp:* Prin res engr, Nat Elec & Gas Co, Algeria, 85-88. *Concurrent Pos:* Vis res assoc, Univ Ill, Urbana-Champaign, 84, vis asst prof, 89; consult, Gen Elec Co, Schenectady, 84; asst prof, Electronics Inst, Univ Blida, Algeria, 85-87; NSF presidential young investr award, 90. *Mem:* Inst Elec & Electronics Engrs; Inst Elec & Electronics Engrs Power Eng Soc; Am Soc Eng Educ. *Res:* Power system modeling and simulation; power system stability; computational methods; optimization; advanced control applications in power systems. *Mailing Add:* Clarkson Univ PO Box 5720 Potsdam NY 13699. *Fax:* 315-268-7600; *E-Mail:* azaid@sun.soe.clarkson.edu

AHN, HO-SAM, CARDIOVASCULAR PHARMACOLOGY, BIOCHEMICAL PHARMACOLOGY. *Current Pos:* sr scientist, 78-84, prin scientist, 84-90 SR PRIN SCIENTIST, SCHERING-PLOUGH RES, 90- *Personal Data:* b Seoul, South Korea, Feb 25, 40; US citizen; m 68; c 2. *Educ:* Seoul Nat Univ, BS, 63; Princeton Univ, MA, 67; Rutgers Univ, PhD(zool), 72. *Prof Exp:* Res assoc & fel, Einstein Col Med, 73-77, res asst prof, 77-78; adj assoc prof biochem, Fairley Dickinson Univ, 86-90. *Concurrent Pos:* Ed vpres, WeSearch Toastmaster Int, 87-88. *Mem:* Am Soc Pharmacol & Exp Therapeut; AAAS; NY Acad Sci; Sigma Xi. *Res:* Elucidation of biochemical and pharmacologic actions of PDE1; pharmacologic characterization of vascular thrombin receptors. *Mailing Add:* Dept CNS/CV Biol Schering-Plough Res Inst 2015 Galloping Hill Rd MS3600 Kenilworth NJ 07033. *E-Mail:* ho-sam.ahn@spcorp.com

AHN, K(IE) Y(EUNG), ELECTRICAL ENGINEERING. *Current Pos:* MEM RES STAFF, THOMAS J WATSON RES CTR, IBM CORP, 63- *Personal Data:* b Pyongnam, Korea, Apr 6, 30; m 61; c 3. *Educ:* Ore State Univ, BS, 58; Rensselaer Polytech Inst, MEE, 59, PhD(elec eng), 63. *Mem:* Inst Elec & Electronics Engrs. *Res:* Solid state electronics; applied research in magnetic-films applications and technology; VLSI technology. *Mailing Add:* IBM Thomas J Watson Res Ctr PO Box 218 Yorktown Heights NY 10598

AHN, KYUNGHYE, CHEMISTRY, ORGANIC CHEMISTRY. *Current Pos:* BIOCHEMIST RES BIOCHEM & ENZYMOL, WARNER-LAMBERT/PARKE-DAVIS, 90- *Personal Data:* b Seoul, SKorea, 1959. *Educ:* Yonsei Univ, SKorea, BS, 81; Ohio State Univ, PhD(org chem), 86. *Prof Exp:* Fel, Univ Calif, Berkeley, 87-88 & Stanford Univ, 88-90. *Concurrent Pos:* NIH fel, 88-90. *Mem:* Am Chem Soc; Am Soc Biochem & Molecular Biol. *Mailing Add:* Parke-Davis 2800 Plymouth Rd Ann Arbor MI 48105-2495

AHN, TAE IN, MEMBRANE BIOLOGY, SYMBIOSIS. *Current Pos:* from asst prof to assoc prof, 81-92, assoc dean acad affairs, Col Educ, 89-91, PROF CELL BIOL, SEOUL NAT UNIV, 92- *Personal Data:* b Kyungbuk, Korea, Jan 15, 47; m 77, Sang Sook Choi; c Dale & Jake. *Educ:* Seoul Nat Univ, BS, 74; Univ Tenn, MS, 77, PhD(zool), 81. *Prof Exp:* Teacher biol, Ohryu Girl's Jr High Sch, 74-75; res & teaching asst cell biol, Univ Tenn, 75-81. *Concurrent Pos:* Gen secy, Korean Zool Soc, 83-87; vis res prof cell biol, Univ Tenn, 87-88; chief ed, Korean J Genetics, 94-98. *Mem:* Am Soc Cell Biol; Korean Soc Zool (gen secy, 93-94); Korean Soc Genetics; Soc Protozool; Soc Endocytobiol. *Res:* Cellular and molecular biological studies on symbiotic amoeba; protein chemistry; actin cDNA cloning; GroEx cloning and characterization; phagolysosome; heat shock response. *Mailing Add:* Dept Biol Educ Seoul Nat Univ Seoul 151-742 South Korea. *E-Mail:* ahntaein@alliant.snu.ac.ky

AHO, PAUL E, PLANT PATHOLOGY. *Current Pos:* AT DEPT FOREST SCI, ORE STATE UNIV. *Personal Data:* b Worcester, Mass, June 29, 34; m 57; c 3. *Educ:* Univ Mass, BS, 56; Yale Univ, MF, 57; Ore State Univ, PhD(plant pathology), 76. *Prof Exp:* Plant pathologist, Forestry Sci Lab, Forest Serv, USDA, 57- *Mem:* Soc Am Foresters; Am Phytopath Soc. *Res:* Heart rots of western conifers; dwarf mistletoes; development of methods for estimating or predicting the extent of damage. *Mailing Add:* 223 NW 30th St Corvallis OR 97330

AHOKAS, ROBERT A, CARDIOVASCULAR PHYSIOLOGY, NUTRITION. *Current Pos:* ASSOC PROF PHYSIOL, UNIV TENN, 75- *Educ:* Univ NDak, PhD(biol), 73. *Res:* Perinatal physiology. *Mailing Add:* Dept Obstet & Gynec Univ Tenn 853 Jefferson Memphis TN 38103

AHR, WAYNE MERRILL, CARBONATE SEDIMENTOLOGY. *Current Pos:* asst prof, 70-83, PROF GEOL, TEX A&M UNIV, 83-, WILLIFORD PROF PETROL GEOL, 95- *Personal Data:* b San Antonio, Tex, Dec 11, 38; div; c Kelly L & Amanda C. *Educ:* Univ Tex, El Paso, BS, 60; Tex A&M Univ, MS, 65; Rice Univ, PhD(geol), 67. *Prof Exp:* Res geologist, Shell Develop Co Lab, 63-65; NASA fel geol, Rice Univ, 66-67; explor geologist, Shell Oil Co, 67-70. *Concurrent Pos:* Vis prof, La State Univ, 78; vis scholar, Leicester Univ, London, 84; consult, domestic & foreign petrol indust, 70-; Fulbright scholar, Belg, 88; vis prof, Univ Louvain La Neuve, Belgium, 88; Spanish govt study grant, Palma de Mallorca, 93. *Mem:* Am Asn Petrol Geologists; Soc

Econ Paleontologists & Mineralogists; Int Asn Sedimentologists; Fulbright Asn. *Res:* Geology of lower carboniferous reefs of Europe and North America; diagenesis of carbonate rocks and carbonate sedimentology; carbonate petroleum reservoirs. *Mailing Add:* 2711 Sandy Circle College Station TX 77845-5309. *Fax:* 409-845-6162; *E-Mail:* h501wa@tamvmi.edu

AHRENHOLZ, H(ERMAN) WILLIAM, MINING ENGINEERING. *Current Pos:* RETIRED. *Personal Data:* b New York, NY, Nov 1, 16; m 39, Gladys Telleen; c Glenn J. *Educ:* Lehigh Univ, BA & BS, 38, EM, 49. *Prof Exp:* Teaching fel, Mass Inst Technol, 38-39; mining engr, NJ Zinc Co, 39-49; assoc prof mining eng, WVa Univ, 49-54; mine supt, NJ Zinc Co, 54-57; prof, Univ Ala, 57-73, head, Sch Mines, 61-69, dir engr exten, 70-73; resident chief engr, Paul Weir Co, Zonguldak, Turkey, 73-75, vpres, Chicago, 75-82. *Concurrent Pos:* Consult, Ala Power Co, 57-65; consult & actg mine supt, Appalachian Sulphides Inc, 59; consult, Int Paper Co, 64, Ga Marble Co, 64-67, Mining Res Div, US Bur Mines, 65, Mineral Resources Div, 65- & NJ Zinc Co, 67-70. *Mem:* Am Soc Eng Educ; Am Inst Mining, Metall & Petrol Engrs; Am Mining Cong. *Res:* Blasting, ground control and mining methods. *Mailing Add:* 4313 Stonehill Lane Tuscaloosa AL 35405

AHRENKIEL, RICHARD K, SOLID STATE PHYSICS. *Current Pos:* AT SOLAR ENERGY RES INT; MEM STAFF, LOS ALAMOS NAT LAB, 77- *Personal Data:* b Springfield, Ill, Jan 7, 36; m 56; c 1. *Educ:* Univ Ill, BS, 59, PhD(physics), 64. *Prof Exp:* Res physicist, Eastman Kodak Co, 64-70, res assoc, Res Labs, 70-77. *Mem:* Am Phys Soc. *Res:* Transport phenomena in high impedance semiconductors, particularly the silver and alkali halides and studies of defect centers; optical properties of magnetic semiconductors. *Mailing Add:* Nat Renewable Energy Lab 1617 Cole Blvd 16/3 Rm 305 Golden CO 80401. *Fax:* 303-231-1381

AHRENS, EDWARD HAMBLIN, JR, METABOLISM. *Current Pos:* assoc, 52-58, from assoc prof to prof, 58-85, EMER PROF BIOCHEM & MED, ROCKEFELLER UNIV, 85- *Personal Data:* b Chicago, Ill, May 21, 15; m 40; c 3. *Educ:* Harvard Univ, BS, 37, MD, 41. *Hon Degrees:* MD, Lund, Swed, Univ Edinbourgh, Scotland. *Honors & Awards:* Heart & Vascular Res Award, Mitchell Found Int, 68; McCollum Award, Am Soc Clin Nutrit, 69; 25th Ann Res Award, Am Heart Asn, 78. *Prof Exp:* Intern, Babies Hosp, 42-43, chief resident, 51-52; asst, Rockefeller Inst, 46-49. *Concurrent Pos:* Nat Res Coun sr fel, 49-50; Nat Found Infantile Paralysis sr fel, 50-52; mem, Metab Study Sect, USPHS, 56-61, chmn, 59-61; NSF sr fel, 58-59; founder, J Lipid Res, 58, mem adv bd, 58-74; mem, Bd Sci Counsr, Nat Heart Inst, 63-67, chmn, Diet-Heart Rev Panel, 67-68; mem, Sci Adv Comt, New Eng Regional Primate Ctr, 63-69; mem, Tech Adv Comt, Inst Human Nutrit, Columbia Univ, 66-71; mem, Gen Clin Res Ctrs Comt, NIH, 70-74; master prof, Cornell Univ Med Col, 70-74; mem, Sci Adv Comt, Hirschi Trust, 72-74; mem bd dirs & exec comt, Regional Plan Asn, NY, 73-77 & 79-81; mem adv comt, Ernst Klenk Found, 75-85; mem, Assembly Life Sci, Nat Res Coun, 78-84; pres, Onteora Arboretum, 79-; mem bd dirs, NY Bot Garden, 81- *Mem:* Nat Acad Sci; Am Soc Clin Invest; Asn Am Physicians; Am Soc Biol Chem. *Res:* Biochemistry of lipids and clinical investigation in field of lipid metabolism. *Mailing Add:* Rockefeller Univ York Ave & 66th St New York NY 10021

AHRENS, FRANKLIN ALFRED, PHARMACOLOGY, TOXICOLOGY. *Current Pos:* Chmn dept, 82-90, from asst prof to assoc prof, 68-75, PROF PHARMACOL, IOWA STATE UNIV, 75- *Personal Data:* b Leigh, Nebr, Apr 27, 36; m 60, Kay Henning; c Jeffrey, Gregory, Matthew & Kristin. *Educ:* Kans State Univ, BS & DVM, 59; Cornell Univ, MS, 65, PhD(pharmacol), 68. *Mem:* NY Acad Sci; Sigma Xi; Acad Vet Pharmacol Therapeut; Asn Mil Surgeons US; Am Vet Med Asn. *Res:* Toxicity of chelating agents and lead; enteric disease and drug absorption; immune responses of isolated liver. *Mailing Add:* Dept Vet Physiol & Pharmacol Iowa State Univ Ames IA 50011. *Fax:* 515-294-2315

AHRENS, JOHN FREDERICK, WEED SCIENCE, WOODY & HERBACEOUS ORNAMENTAL PLANTS. *Current Pos:* From asst plant physiologist to assoc plant physiologist, 57-70, plant physiologist, 70-92, EMER SCIENTIST, VALLEY LAB, CONN AGR EXP STA, 92- *Personal Data:* b Bellmore, NY, Nov 21, 29; m 52, Phyllis Carle; c William H, John F Jr, Timothy M & Karl P. *Educ:* Univ Ga, BS, 54; Iowa State Univ, MS, 55, PhD(plant physiol), 57. *Honors & Awards:* Exten Award, Am Asn Nurserymen, 89. *Concurrent Pos:* Veg mgt consult, pvt, 70-, L I RR, 76-89. *Mem:* Fel Weed Sci Soc Am; Coun Agr Sci & Technol; dist mem Northeastern Weed Sci Soc (pres, 70); Weed Sci Soc Am (pres, 88). *Res:* Weed management and strategies in ornamental herbaceous woody plants, non-crop situations and small fruits; residual effects of herbicides in soils; plant growth; inactivation of herbicide residues in soil. *Mailing Add:* Valley Lab Conn Agr Exp Sta PO Box 248 Windsor CT 06095. *Fax:* 860-683-4887

AHRENS, RICHARD AUGUST, NUTRITION, PHYSIOLOGY. *Current Pos:* assoc prof, 66-75, coordr, Grad Prog Nutrit Sci, 89-92, PROF NUTRIT, UNIV MD, COLLEGE PARK, 75- *Personal Data:* b Manitowoc, Wis, Sept 18, 36; m 61, Joan E Morley; c Deborah J (Johnson), Jill L (Fronck) & David R. *Educ:* Univ Wis, BS, 58; Univ Calif, Davis, PhD(nutrit), 63. *Honors & Awards:* Fulbright lectr, Egerton Univ, Kenya, 87-88. *Prof Exp:* Res physiologist human nutrit, Agr Res Serv, USDA, 63-66. *Concurrent Pos:* Vis lectr nutrit, Univ London, UK, 73; chair, State Bd Dietetic Pract, 91- *Mem:* Am Inst Nutrit; Am Home Econ Asn; NY Acad Sci; Soc Nutrit Educ; Am Dietetic Asn. *Res:* Diet and atherosclerosis; enzymes and energy metabolism; dietary carbohydrate and the effects of physical activity on health; sucrose and high blood pressure; fermentation of weaning diets. *Mailing Add:* Dept Nutrit & Food Sci Univ Md College Park MD 20742-7521. *Fax:* 301-314-9327; *E-Mail:* ra7@umail.umd.edu

AHRENS, ROLLAND WILLIAM, PHYSICAL CHEMISTRY, MEASUREMENT QUALITY ASSURANCE. *Current Pos:* PRES, PHYSICOCHEM CONSULTS, INC, 94- *Personal Data:* b Clarkson, Nebr, Sept 28, 33; m 63, Rosalind Zucker; c Scott R & Todd M. *Educ:* Univ Nebr, BSc, 54, MS, 55; Univ Wis, PhD(phys chem), 59. *Prof Exp:* Chemist, Separations Div, Savannah River Lab, 59-64; chemist, Seaford Textile Fiber Plant, Dacron Qual Assurance, 65-67, anal res supvr, 67-77, sr res chemist, Spunbonded Res & Develop, 77-79, sr chemist, 80-86, sr res chemist, Fiber Surfaces Res, Kinston, NC, 87-93. *Concurrent Pos:* Traveling lectr, Oak Ridge Inst Nuclear Studies, 63-64. *Mem:* Am Chem Soc. *Res:* Radiation chemistry of aqueous solutions and liquid ammonia; recovery of transplutonium elements by solvent extraction; nylon carpet new products development; polyester spunbonded product development; measurement quality assurance. *Mailing Add:* 501 Bremerton Dr Greenville NC 27858. *Fax:* 919-355-0935; *E-Mail:* vhdk89a@prodigy.com

AHRENS, RUDOLF MARTIN (TINO), THEORETICAL PHYSICS. *Current Pos:* assoc prof, 57-66, prof theoret physics, 66-92, EMER PROF, GA INST TECHNOL, 92- *Personal Data:* b St Louis, Mo, Feb 6, 28; m; c 3. *Educ:* Wash Univ, PhD, 52. *Prof Exp:* Sr nuclear engr, Convair, 52-54; staff specialist, Lockheed Aircraft Corp, 54-56, dept mgr nuclear anal, 56-57. *Concurrent Pos:* Vis prof, Max-Planck Inst Physics & Astrophys, 59-60 & Univ SC, 67-68; consult & vpres, Advan Res Corp Ind, 62-71. *Res:* Elementary particles; symmetries; field theory. *Mailing Add:* 1455 Diamond Head Circle Decatur GA 30033

AHRENS, THOMAS J, GEOPHYSICS, HIGH-PRESSURE PHYSICS. *Current Pos:* assoc prof, 67-76, PROF GEOPHYS, CALIF INST TECHNOL, 76-, W M KECK PROF GEOPHYS, 96- *Personal Data:* b Wichita Falls, Tex, Apr 25, 36; m 58; c 3. *Educ:* Mass Inst Technol, BS, 57; Calif Inst Technol, MS, 58; Rensselaer Polytech Inst, 62. *Prof Exp:* Intermediate explor geophysicist, Pan Am Petrol Corp, 58-59; asst geophys, Rensselaer Polytech Inst, 62; geophysicist, Poulter Res Labs, Stanford Res Inst, 62-66, head, Geophys Group, Shock Wave Physics Div, 66-67. *Concurrent Pos:* Assoc ed, Rev Sci Instruments & J Geophys Res, 71-74; mem, Marth Sci Adv Panel, NSF, 72-75; ed, J Geophys Res, 79- *Mem:* Nat Acad Sci; Am Geophys Union; Soc Explor Geophys; Am Phys Soc; fel Royal Astron Soc; AAAS. *Res:* Shock and ultrasonic wave propagation in solids; exploration seismology; high-pressure physics of the earth's interior; impact effects on planetary surfaces; measurement of stress and tilt in the earth's crust. *Mailing Add:* Calif Inst Technol 1200 E California Blvd Pasadena CA 91125

AHRING, ROBERT M, AGRONOMY, SOILS. *Current Pos:* RES AGRONOMIST, FORAGE & RANGE, SOUTHERN REGION, SCI EDUC ADMIN, USDA, 57- *Personal Data:* b Lincoln, Kans, Oct 4, 28; m 51; c 4. *Educ:* Okla State Univ, BS, 52, MS, 58; Univ Nebr, PhD, 72. *Prof Exp:* Instr, 52-56, res asst, 56-57, asst prof, 57-75, ASSOC PROF AGRON, OKLA STATE UNIV, 75- *Mem:* Crop Sci Soc Am; Am Soc Agron; Am Soc Range Mgt; Int Herbage Seed Asn. *Res:* Seed production and technology; native and introduced grasses and legumes; crop physiology. *Mailing Add:* Rte 2 PO Box 1335 Perkins OK 74059

AHSANULLAH, MOHAMMAD, STATISTICAL INFERENCE, DISTRIBUTION THEORY. *Current Pos:* assoc prof statist, 84-87, PROF, RIDER COL, 87- *Personal Data:* b Tangra, India; Can citizen; c Nisar, Tabassum & Omar F. *Educ:* Calcutta Univ, BSc, 57, MSc, 59; NC State Univ, PhD(statist), 69. *Prof Exp:* Asst prof statist, NDak State Univ, 68-69; statistician, Nat Health & Welfare, 69-74 & 76-79; assoc prof, Univ Brasilia, 74-76 & 79-81; assoc prof, Temple Univ, 82-84. *Concurrent Pos:* Syst analyst, InterAm Inst Coop Agr, Orgn Am States, 74-76; vis prof statist, Univ Nat Autonoma, Mex, 81-82; ed, J Appl Statist Sci. *Mem:* Int Statist Inst; fel Royal Statist Soc; Inst Math Statist; Am Statist Asn. *Res:* Theory of inferences; record value theory; order statistics; characterizations of statistical distributions; time series and reliability theory; published over 150 scientific research papers; author of two books and co-author of three books. *Mailing Add:* Dept Mgt Sci Rider Col 2083 Lawrenceville Rd Lawrenceville NJ 08648-3099. *Fax:* 609-895-5304

AHSHAPANEK, DON COLESTO, PLANT ECOLOGY, MICROBIOLOGY. *Current Pos:* SERV OFFICER, TRIBAL GOVT, 94- *Personal Data:* b Milton, Del, Apr 29, 32; m 62, Carol Paddlety; c Darren, Don II & Brian. *Educ:* Cent State Univ, Okla, BS, 56; Univ Okla, MS, 59, PhD(bot), 62. *Prof Exp:* Asst prof biol, Kans State Teachers Col, 62-67, assoc prof, 67-71; instr, Haskell Am Indiana Jr Col, 71-73, chmn, Div Native Am Cult, 73-76, instr, 76-91; lease compliance officer, BIA/Anadarks Angency, 91-92; realty spec (A & D), 92-94. *Concurrent Pos:* Mem comt equal opportunities sci & technol, NSF. *Mem:* Am Indian Sci & Eng Soc; Nat Indian Educ Asn; Nat Cong Am Indians. *Res:* Ecological research in causes of plant succession in grasslands with studies in phenology, plant inhibition and the inter-relations between micro-organisms and plant roots in the rhizosphere and rhizoplane; studies on halophilic bacteria. *Mailing Add:* PO Box 309 Anadarko OK 73005. *Fax:* 406-247-9232

AHUJA, JAGAN N, BIOCHEMISTRY, CLINICAL CHEMISTRY. *Current Pos:* CHIEF CLIN CHEM, KAISER FOUND HOSP, 68- *Personal Data:* b Rawalpindi, WPakistan, Nov 12, 35; m 60; c 3. *Educ:* Agra Univ, BSc, 54, MSc, 56; Mich State Univ, PhD(biochem), 61. *Prof Exp:* NIH res asst, Mich State Univ, 58-61; instr biochem, Sch Med, Univ Miami, 61-64; reader, Maulana Azad Med Col, India, 66; NIH sr fel clin chem, Univ Hosp, Seattle, Wash, 66-68. *Mem:* AAAS; Am Asn Clin Chemists; Am Chem Soc. *Res:* Effects of cytotoxic alkylating agents on the metabolism of pyridine nucleotides in ascites tumor cells; techniques for the isolation and measurement of nucleotides; measurements of protein bound iodine and serum thyroxine. *Mailing Add:* 76 Moore Ct San Ramon CA 94583-2530

AHUJA, JAGDISH C, STATISTICS, MATHEMATICS. *Current Pos:* assoc prof, 66-69, PROF MATH, PORTLAND STATE UNIV, 69- *Personal Data:* b Rawalpindi, India; m 55; c 2. *Educ:* Banaras Hindu Univ, BA, 53, MA, 55; Univ BC, PhD(math), 63. *Prof Exp:* Teacher high sch, Nairobi, Kenya, 55-56; teacher math, Dept Educ, Tanganyika, 56-58; lab instr statist, Dept Econ, Univ BC, 59-61, lectr, 61-63; asst prof math, Univ Alta, 63-66. *Concurrent Pos:* Teaching fel, Univ BC, 61-63; Can Math Cong fel, Res Inst, 64-66. *Mem:* Inst Math Statist. *Res:* Distribution theory; regression analysis; estimation and statistical inference. *Mailing Add:* Dept Math Portland State Univ PO Box 751 Portland OR 97207. *Fax:* 503-725-3661

AHUJA, NARENDRA, COMPUTER VISION, ROBOTICS. *Current Pos:* from asst prof to assoc prof, 79-88, PROF ELEC & COMPUT ENG, UNIV ILL, URBANA-CHAMPAIGN, 88- *Personal Data:* b Achnera, India, Dec 8, 50; m 83, Pomila Chugh; c 2. *Educ:* Birla Inst Technol & Sci, BE, 72; Indian Inst Sci, ME, 74; Univ Md, PhD(comput sci), 79. *Honors & Awards:* Pres Young Investr Award, NSF, 84. *Prof Exp:* Sci officer software develop, Dept Elec, Govt India, New Delhi, 74-75. *Concurrent Pos:* Prin investr, NSF, 81-, Air Force Off Sci Res, 82-; prog chair, Inst Elec & Electronics Engrs, Workshop Comput Vision, 87, prog comt Conf Comput Vision & Pattern Recognition, 88, mem, Tech Comt Pattern Anal & Mach Intel, 84-, Tech Comt Robotics, 84- *Mem:* Fel Inst Elec & Electronics Engrs; fel Asn Comput Mach; fel Am Asn Artificial Intel; fel Int Soc Optical Eng; fel Int Asn Pattern Recognition. *Res:* Computational realization of visual perception: three dimensional sensing, object recognition, automatic inspection, visual monitoring and autonomous navigation; visual pattern recognition, image processing, robotic manipulation and computer architectures for vision. *Mailing Add:* Beckman Inst Univ Ill 405 N Mathews Ave Urbana IL 61801. *Fax:* 217-244-8371

AHUJA, SATINDER, CHROMATOGRAPHY. *Current Pos:* res assoc pharmaceut anal chem, Geigy Chem Corp, Ardsley, 66-69, group leader, 69-73, sr staff scientist, 73-90, SR RES FEL, CIBA-GEIGY CORP, 91- *Personal Data:* b Jehlum, Pakistan, Sept 11, 33; m 62; c 2. *Educ:* Banaras Univ, BPharm, 55, MPharm, 56; Philadelphia Col Pharm, PhD(pharmaceut anal chem), 64. *Prof Exp:* Asst prof pharmaceut chem & pharm, Univ Nagpur, 57-58; teaching asst pharmaceut analytical chem, Philadelphia Col Pharm, 58-64; assay develop chemist, Lederle Labs, NY, 64-66. *Mem:* Am Chem Soc. *Res:* Various modes of chromatography; kinetic studies; ultratrace methods; dosage variation and availability of drug products; automation and computerization; discovery of new compounds by chromatography; good manufacturing practice; good lab practice. *Mailing Add:* Ahuja Consult 27 Monsey Heights Rd Monsey NY 10952

AHUMADA, ALBERT JIL, JR, VISUAL PSYCHOPHYSICS. *Current Pos:* RES PSYCHOLOGIST, AERO-SPACE HUMAN FACTORS, NASA AMES RES CTR, 80- *Personal Data:* b Los Angeles, Calif, Jan 12, 40; m 60; c 3. *Educ:* Stanford Univ, BS, 61; Univ Calif, Los Angeles, PhD(psychol), 67. *Prof Exp:* Asst prof psychol, Sch Soc Sci, Univ Calif, Irvine, 67-75; sr res assoc psycho-acoustics, dept aeronaut & astronaut, Stanford Univ, 75-80. *Concurrent Pos:* Instr, San Jose State Univ, 80-82. *Mem:* Optical Soc Am; Asn Res Vision & Ophthal; Soc Info Display; Int Soc Optical Eng; Soc Math Psychol. *Res:* Mathematical and computer modelling of perceptual processes. *Mailing Add:* NASA Ames Res Ctr Mail Stop 262-2 Moffett Field CA 94035

AICHELE, DOUGLAS B, MATHEMATICS EDUCATION. *Current Pos:* REGENTS PROF MATH, OKLA STATE UNIV, 69- *Personal Data:* b Flushing, NY, Nov 2, 42; m 77, Kathryn Castle; c Adam & Clint. *Educ:* Univ Mo-Columbia, BA, 64, MA, 66, EdD(math), 69. *Mem:* Math Asn Am; Nat Coun Teachers Math. *Mailing Add:* 406 Math Sci Okla State Univ Stillwater OK 74078. *E-Mail:* aichele@math.okstate.edu

AICHELE, MURIT DEAN, DIAGNOSTICS, VARIETY EVALUATION. *Current Pos:* FRUIT TREE CONSULT, AICHELE CONSULTS, INC, 90- *Personal Data:* b Freewater, Ore, July 17, 28; m 52, 88; c 1. *Educ:* Wash State Col, BS, 52. *Honors & Awards:* Nat Serv Award, Nat Asn State Depts Agr, 87. *Prof Exp:* Plant pathologist, Wash State Dept Agr, 55-87; exec dir, Cent Wash Nursery Improvement Inst, 87-90. *Concurrent Pos:* Fruit tree consult, plant patents, Adjustment Serv. *Mem:* Am Phytopath Soc; Am Soc Hort Sci. *Res:* Horticulture; pomology; ornamental horticulture; fruit tree variety evaluation; fruit tree diseases; stone and pome fruit viruses. *Mailing Add:* 1420 S 25th Ave Yakima WA 98902

AICKIN, MIKEL G, BIOMETRICS, BIOSTATISTICS. *Current Pos:* ASST PROF STATIST, ARIZ STATE UNIV, 79-, DEPT MATH. *Personal Data:* b Seattle, Wash, Jan 17, 44; m 67; c 2. *Educ:* Univ Washington, BSc, 66, PhD(biomath), 76. *Prof Exp:* Asst prof statist, Ariz State Univ, 76-78, Univ Kans, 78-79. *Concurrent Pos:* Dir, Statist Consult Serv, 81- *Mem:* Inst Math Statist; Biomet Soc; Soc Clin Trials. *Res:* Statistical analysis, particularly for contingency tables, and simultaneous inference; adaptive design of clinical trials. *Mailing Add:* 333 E Glenhurst Dr Tucson AZ 85704

AIELLO, ANNETTE, TAXONOMIC BOTANY, EVOLUTIONARY ENTOMOLOGY. *Current Pos:* STAFF SCIENTIST, SMITHSONIAN TROP RES INST, 93- *Personal Data:* b Manhattan, NY, May 1, 41; m 81, Ricardo Cortez. *Educ:* Brooklyn Col, BA, 72; Harvard Univ, MA, 75, PhD(biol), 78. *Prof Exp:* Res assoc entom, Smithsonian Trop Res Inst, 78-92. *Concurrent Pos:* Res assoc entom, Mus Comparative Zool, Harvard Univ, 80-82. *Mem:* Lepidoptera Res Found; Lepidopterists' Soc; Sigma Xi. *Res:* Arthropod behavior, especially insect behavior; insect life histories and evolution. *Mailing Add:* Smithsonian Trop Res Inst PO Box 2072 Balboa Ancon Panama. *Fax:* 507-232-5978; *E-Mail:* stri.tivoli.aielloa@ic.si.edu

AIELLO, EDWARD LAWRENCE, PHARMACOLOGY. *Current Pos:* from assoc prof to prof, 65-94, chmn, 78-81, EMER PROF BIOL SCI, FORDHAM UNIV, 94- *Personal Data:* b Flushing, NY, June 12, 28; m 53; c 3. *Educ:* St Peters Col, BS, 53; Columbia Univ, MA, 54, PhD(zool), 60. *Prof Exp:* Instr anat & physiol, Flint Jr Col, 57-58; instr pharmacol, NY Med Col, 58-60, from asst prof to assoc prof, 60-65. *Mem:* Am Soc Zoologists. *Res:* Invertebrate neuropharmacology; ciliary movement; mucociliary transport. *Mailing Add:* Dept Biol Sci Fordham Univ Larkin Hall Rm 160 Bronx NY 10458

AIKAWA, JERRY KAZUO, CLINICAL MEDICINE. *Current Pos:* from asst prof to assoc prof med, Sch Med, 53-67, dir technol, 67-69, dir lab serv, 60-83, PROF MED, SCH MED, UNIV COLO MED CTR, DENVER, 67-, DIR ALLIED HEALTH PROG, 69-, ASSOC DEAN, 82- *Personal Data:* b Stockton, Calif, Aug 24, 21; m 44; c 1. *Educ:* Univ Calif, AB, 42; Wake Forest Col, MD, 45. *Prof Exp:* From intern to asst resident, NC Baptist Hosp, 45-57; instr med, Wake Forest Col, 51-53; Am Heart Asn estab investr, 53-58. *Concurrent Pos:* Nat Res Coun fel, Med Sch, Univ Calif, 48-49; Nat Res Coun & AEC fel, Duke Univ & Bowman Gray Sch Med, Wake Forest Col, 49-51, Am Heart Asn res fel, Wake Forest Col, 51-53. *Res:* Cell physiology; electrolyte metabolism; computer applications in medicine; allied health training programs. *Mailing Add:* 3233 Lake Albano Circle San Jose CA 95135

AIKAWA, MASAMICHI, PATHOLOGY, ELECTRON MICROSCOPY. *Current Pos:* from asst prof to assoc prof, 68-74, PROF PATH, CASE WESTERN RES UNIV, 74- *Personal Data:* b Japan, Sept 24, 31; m 68, Hiroko Ejiri; c Keiko & Taro. *Educ:* Kyoto Univ, MD, 58, DSc, 65; Georgetown Univ, MS, 63. *Hon Degrees:* PhD, T Kushima Univ, Japan, 90. *Honors & Awards:* Alexander von Humboldt Award, Ger, 85. *Prof Exp:* Assoc pathologist, Walter Reed Army Inst Res, 64-68. *Concurrent Pos:* Sr int fel, Fogarty Int Ctr, NIH, 75; consult, Mt Sinai Hosp & Vet Admin Hosp, Cleveland, 77-; vis prof, Kyoto Univ, Japan, 80, Nagasaki Univ, Japan, 90. *Mem:* Am Asn Pathologists; Am Soc Cell Biol; Am Soc Parasitol; Am Soc Trop Med Hyg; Royal Soc Med Hyg; Int Acad Pathologists. *Res:* Interaction between host cells and parasites. *Mailing Add:* Inst Med Sci Tokai Univ Isehara Kanagawa 259 Japan. *Fax:* 216-368-8649

AIKEN, JAMES G, ELECTRICAL ENGINEERING. *Current Pos:* PRES, IRVING CIRCUITBOARD CO, 84- *Personal Data:* b Midway, Pa, Jan 11, 40; m 65; c 2. *Educ:* Univ Cincinnati, BS, 63; Carnegie-Mellon Univ, MS, 64, PhD(elec eng), 67. *Prof Exp:* Mem tech staff semiconductors, Tex Instruments Inc, 66-84. *Res:* Effects of radiation on semiconductor devices and materials; electrical transport properties of semiconductors; ion implanted semiconductor devices; correlation between semiconductor processing and device parameters. *Mailing Add:* 5915 Bentwood Trail Dallas TX 75252

AIKEN, JAMES WAVELL, PHARMACOLOGY, PHYSIOLOGY. *Current Pos:* sr res scientist exp biol, 77-83, ASSOC DIR THERAPEUT, UPJOHN CO, 83- *Personal Data:* b Burlington, Vt, Jan 10, 43; m 65; c 2. *Educ:* Dartmouth Col, BA, 65; Univ Vt, PhD (pharmacol), 69. *Prof Exp:* Fel Am Thoracic Soc Pharmacol, Royal Col Surgeons Eng, 69-71; res scientist pharmacol, Eli Lilly & Co, 71-77. *Concurrent Pos:* Consult, Nat Heart, Lung & Blood Inst, 73-; adj asst prof med, Sch Med, Ind Univ, 75-77; adj prof pharmacol, Sch Med, Mich State Univ, 85-; bd trustees, Am Heart Asn, Mich. *Mem:* Am Soc Pharmacol & Exp Therapeut; Brit Pharmacol Soc; Am Heart Asn. *Res:* Physiological importance of neurohumoral substances in control of blood pressure, thrombosis, atherosclerosis, and neuro-endocrine function; manipulation of these systems with chemicals for therapeutic benefit. *Mailing Add:* Metabolic Dis Res Upjohn Co Kalamazoo MI 49001-0199

AIKEN, LINDA H, MEDICINE. *Current Pos:* assoc dir nursing affairs, 88-92, TRUSTEE PROF NURSING & SOCIOL, UNIV PA, 88-, DIR, CTR HEALTH SERV & POLICY RES, 92- *Personal Data:* b July 29, 43. *Educ:* Univ Fla, BSN, 64, MN, 66; Univ Tex, Austin, PhD(sociol & demog), 74. *Honors & Awards:* Jessie M Scott Award, Am Nurses' Asn, 84; Beverly Lectr, Asn Geront Higher Educ, 90. *Prof Exp:* Nurse, J Hillis Miller Health Ctr, 64-65; instr, Col Nursing, Univ Gainesville, 66-67; clin nurse spec cardiac surg, Med Ctr, Univ Mo, 67-70, instr, Sch Nursing, 68-70; lectr, Univ Wis, Madison, 73-74; prog officer, Robert Wood Johnson Found, 74-76, dir res, 76-79, asst vpres res, 79-81, vpres, 81-87. *Concurrent Pos:* Fel, NIH, Univ Fla, 65-66 & NIH Nurse Scientist, Univ Tex, 70-73; vis lectr, Sci Human Affairs Prog, Princeton Univ, 75-87 & Acad Sci Social Med, Hanover, Ger, 80; assoc ed, J Health & Social Behav, 78-81, Image, J Nursing Scholar, 80- & Tran/Soc, 85-ion/Soc, 85-; mem, Comt Sci, Eng & Pub Policy, Nat Acad Sci, 83-84; mem, Coun Nursing, Am Hosp Asn, 83-85; mem, Task Force Long-Term Health Care Policies, US Dept Health & Human Servs, 86-87, Secy Comm, Nursing, 88; mem panel, Nat Health Care Surv, Comt Nat Statist, Nat Res Coun-Nat Acad Sci, 90- *Mem:* Inst Med-Nat Acad Sci; fel Am Acad Nursing (pres, 79-80); Am Sociol Asn; Am Nurses Asn; AAAS; Am Pub Health Asn. *Res:* Health policy and evaluation research; health services for persons with AIDS; author of over 100 articles, journals and books. *Mailing Add:* Univ Pa 420 Guardian Dr Philadelphia PA 19104-6096

AIKEN, ROBERT MCCUTCHEN, CHEMICAL MANAGEMENT. *Current Pos:* MGT CONSULT SAFETY & ENVIRON LEADERSHIP, 91- *Personal Data:* b Washington, Pa, Nov 8, 30; m 57, Brenda Jean Ashton; c Jennifer Ann & Robert Ashton. *Educ:* Case Inst Technol, BS, 52. *Prof Exp:* Staff mem, E I duPont Co, 52-67, planning mgr, Plastics Dept, Wilmington, Del, 67-69, dist sales mgr, Atlanta, 69-70, asst plant mgr, Victoria, Tex, 70-71, mgr polymer intermediates opers, Cape Fear, NC, 71-74, dir, Caustic-Chlorine Div, Wilmington, 74-75, asst dir, Latin Am Div, 75-81, dir,

75-78, gen mgr, Int Dept, 78-81, vpres int, 81-83, group vpres petrochem, 83-91. *Concurrent Pos:* Mgt conserv safety & environ leadership, 91- *Mem:* World Affairs Coun. *Mailing Add:* 1225 S Birmingham Rd West Chester PA 19382-8201

AIKEN, ROBERT MCLEAN, COMPUTER SCIENCE. *Current Pos:* assoc prof, 84-87, PROF COMPUT SCI, TEMPLE UNIV, 87- *Personal Data:* b Springfield, Ill, May 24, 41; m 73; c 1. *Educ:* Northwestern Univ, BS, 63, MS, 65, PhD(indust eng), 68. *Honors & Awards:* Silver Core Award, Int Fedn Info Processing, 92; Outstanding Contribution Award, Asn Comput Mach/Spec Interest Group Comput Sci Educ, 95, 96. *Prof Exp:* From asst prof to assoc prof comput sci, Univ Tenn, Knoxville, 68-84. *Concurrent Pos:* Vis prof, Univ Info Ctr, Univ Geneva, Switz, 75-76; Fulbright prof, Nat Inst Statist & Appl Econ, Rabat, Morocco, 82-83; US deleg, Int Fedn Info Processing, Tech Comt Educ, 87-, vchmn, 91-; vis prof, Inst Informatics, Univ Zurich, Switz, 90-91; mem, Bd Dirs, Fedn Comput US, 91-, chair, 93. *Mem:* Inst Elec & Electronic Engrs Comput Soc; Asn Comput Mach; Int Asn Advan Comput Educ. *Res:* Intelligent tutoring systems; effective uses of computers as teaching tools. *Mailing Add:* Dept Comput Sci 038-24 Temple Univ Philadelphia PA 19122. *E-Mail:* aiken@cis.temple.edu

AIKENS, DAVID ANDREW, ELECTROANALYTICAL CHEMISTRY. *Current Pos:* from asst prof to assoc prof, 62-69, PROF CHEM, RENSSELAER POLYTECH INST, 69- *Personal Data:* b Boston, Mass, Apr 27, 32; m 58; c 6. *Educ:* Northeastern Univ, BS, 54; Mass Inst Technol, PhD, 60. *Prof Exp:* Fel, Univ NC, 60-62. *Mem:* Am Chem Soc. *Res:* Electrode reaction mechanisms; ion-selective electrodes; coordination chemistry. *Mailing Add:* 4 Deepkill Rd Troy NY 12180-3590

AIKENS, PATRICIA ANN, SURFACTANTS, RHEOLOGY. *Current Pos:* develop assoc, 93-96, APPLN SCI MGR, ICI AMERICAS, 96- *Personal Data:* b Boston, Mass, Mar 22, 60. *Educ:* Rensselaer Polytech Inst, BS, 82; Emory Univ, PhD(org chem), 90. *Prof Exp:* Chemist, FMC Corp, 82-85; postdoctoral assoc, Lehigh Univ, 90-91; res chemist, PPG Indust, 91-93. *Mem:* Am Chem Soc; Soc Cosmetic Chem; Am Oil Chemists Soc. *Res:* Physical properties and phase behavior of surfactants, emulsions, dispersions and solutions and their relationship to applications in the cosmetic, pharmaceutical, cleaning, agricultural, coatings, textiles and oil field chemical industries. *Mailing Add:* ICI Surfactants Wilmington DE 19850. *Fax:* 302-887-2454; *E-Mail:* pat_aikens@ici.com

AIKIN, ARTHUR COLDREN, ATMOSPHERIC PHYSICS, ASTRONOMY. *Current Pos:* ionospheric physicist, 61-70, head chemosphere br, 70-74, assigned US Senate staff, 75-76, SR SCIENTIST, GODDARD SPACE FLIGHT CTR, NASA, 76- *Personal Data:* b Gettysburg, Pa, Dec 21, 32; m 64; c 2. *Educ:* Gettysburg Col, AB, 54; Pa State Univ, MS, 56, PhD(physics), 60. *Prof Exp:* Physicist, Serv d'Aeronomie du Ctr Nat Res Sci, Meudon, France, 60-61. *Mem:* Sigma Xi; AAAS; Am Geophys Union. *Res:* Physics of the ionosphere, planetary atmospheres cometary structure, atmospheric chemistry. *Mailing Add:* 14301 Cantrell Rd Silver Spring MD 20905

AIKMAN, GEORGE CHRISTOPHER LAWRENCE, ASTROPHYSICS, ASTROMETRY. *Current Pos:* Res asst, 68-80, RES ASSOC ASTROPHYS, NAT RES COUN CAN, 80- *Personal Data:* b Ottawa, Ont, Nov 11, 43; m 83, 90, Hennie Marshall; c Donovan, Tabatha & Elysa. *Educ:* Bishop's Univ, BSc, 65; Univ Toronto, MSc, 68. *Concurrent Pos:* Pres, Seameadow Astronomics. *Mem:* Can Astron Soc (secy, 83-89); Astron Soc Pac; Royal Astron Soc Can; Spaceguard Found. *Res:* Asteroids and comets; stellar spectroscopy. *Mailing Add:* Herzberg Inst Nat Res Coun Can 5071 W Saanich Rd Victoria BC V8X 4M6 Can. *E-Mail:* aikman@dao.nrc.ca

AILION, DAVID CHARLES, SOLID STATE PHYSICS, NUCLEAR MAGNETIC RESONANCE. *Current Pos:* From asst prof to assoc prof, 64-78, PROF PHYSICS, UNIV UTAH, 78- *Personal Data:* b London, Eng, Mar 21, 37; US citizen; m 64, C Janie Kline; c Michael E & Jennifer L. *Educ:* Oberlin Col, AB, 56; Univ Ill, MS, 58, PhD(physics), 64. *Concurrent Pos:* Prin investr, NSF grants & NIH grants; vis assoc, Calif Inst Technol, 71-72; NIH spec fel, 71-72; David P Garder fel, 80; assoc mem, J Stefan Inst, Ljubljana, Slovenia, 87- *Mem:* Fel Am Phys Soc; Sigma Xi. *Res:* Biophysics; nuclear magnetic resonance imaging of lungs; nuclear magnetic resonance of incommensurate insulators and glasses. *Mailing Add:* Dept Physics Univ Utah Salt Lake City UT 84112. *Fax:* 801-581-4801

AINBINDER, ZARAH, ORGANIC CHEMISTRY. *Current Pos:* Res chemist, 63-69, sr res chemist, 69-80, RES ASSOC, E I DU PONT DE NEMOURS & CO, INC 81- *Personal Data:* b Brooklyn, NY, July 12, 37; m 62; c 2. *Educ:* Brooklyn Col, BS, 59; Univ Chicago, PhD(chem), 63. *Mem:* Am Chem Soc. *Res:* Polymer intermediates; catalysis; petro chemicals. *Mailing Add:* 1300 Grinnell Rd Green Acres Wilmington DE 19803-5106

AINES, PHILIP DEANE, NUTRITION. *Current Pos:* vpres res & eng, Pillsbury Co, 73-80. *Personal Data:* b Lancaster, Pa, Mar 29, 25; m 51; c 2. *Educ:* Rutgers Univ, BS, 49; Cornell Univ, MNS, 51, PhD(nutrit), 54. *Prof Exp:* Asst biochem, Cornell Univ, 53-54; res chemist, Procter & Gamble Co, 54-55; head, Prod Res Dept, Buckeye Cellulose Corp, 56-58, res chemist, Procter & Gamble Co, 59, Head basic develop, Food Prod Div, 60-65, from assoc dir to dir, Food Prod Develop Div, 65-73. *Mem:* AAAS; Am Chem Soc; Sigma Xi. *Res:* Protein nutrition and metabolism; food research and development; animal nutrition. *Mailing Add:* 63905 Quail Haven Dr W Bend OR 97701-8996

AINLEY, DAVID GEORGE, MARINE ECOLOGY, ORNITHOLOGY. *Current Pos:* BIOLOGIST MARINE ORNITH, POINT REYES BIRD OBSERV, BOLINAS, 71- *Personal Data:* b Bridgeport, Conn, Apr 3, 46. *Educ:* Dickinson Col, Pa, BS, 68; Johns Hopkins Univ, PhD(ecol), 71. *Prof Exp:* Res mem antarctic ecol, Johns Hopkins Univ, 68-70. *Concurrent Pos:* Polar Res Medal, US Antarctic Res Prog, 74-76. *Mem:* Am Ornithologists' Union; Cooper Ornith Soc; Wilson Ornith Soc. *Res:* Marine ecology of seabirds in California, the Gulf of California and Antarctica; trophic relationships of seabirds in marine communities. *Mailing Add:* Point Reyes Bird Observ 4990 Shoreline Hwy Stinson Beach CA 94970

AINSLIE, HARRY ROBERT, ANIMAL NUTRITION. *Current Pos:* RETIRED. *Personal Data:* b Hartwick, NY, Dec 2, 23; m 47; c 5. *Educ:* Kans State Univ, BS, 49, MS, 50, PhD(animal nutrit), 65. *Honors & Awards:* Delaval Exten Award, Am Dairy Sci Assoc, 79. *Prof Exp:* From asst prof to prof dairy husb, Cornell Univ, 50-83, exten leader, dept animal sci, 69-83. *Concurrent Pos:* Supt off testing, NY, 54-66; vis prof exten educ, Univ Philippines, 66-67; mem northeast subcomt, Nat Dairy Herd Improv Coord Group, 70. *Mem:* Am Diary Sci Asn. *Res:* Dairy husbandry extension; educational programs in dairy cattle nutrition; breeding, management and production testing; organization of inservice training programs for extension personnel. *Mailing Add:* 317 Savage Farm Dr Ithaca NY 14850-6503

AINSWORTH, AVERY JERALD, JR, NEUTROPHIL BIOLOGY, INFLAMMATORY RESPONSES. *Current Pos:* from asst prof to assoc prof, 80-94, PROF IMMUNOL, COL VET MED, MISS STATE UNIV, 94- *Personal Data:* b Jackson, Miss, Dec 21, 53; m 76; c 2. *Educ:* Delta State Univ, BS, 76; Univ Med Ctr, Jackson, Miss, MS, 77, PhD(immunol), 79. *Honors & Awards:* SmithKline Beecham Award Res Excellence, 90 & 92. *Prof Exp:* Postdoctoral fel, Univ Ala, Birmingham, 79-80. *Concurrent Pos:* NIH prin investr, Miss State Univ, 88-90, USDA prin investr, 93- *Mem:* Am Asn Immunol; Int Soc Develop & Comp Immunol. *Res:* Define and characterize the ontogeny of the channel catfish immune response; characterize the catfish neutrophil and develop more efficient and economical means to vaccinate catfish. *Mailing Add:* PO Box 9825 Mississippi State MS 39762. *Fax:* 601-325-1031; *E-Mail:* ainsworth@cvm.msstate.edu

AINSWORTH, CAMERON, ORGANIC CHEMISTRY, MEDICINE. *Personal Data:* b Alta, Can, Nov 13, 20; US citizen; m 48, Jeanette Freeborn; c John Victor. *Educ:* Univ Alta, BS, 45; Univ Rochester, PhD(chem), 49; Univ Cd Juarez, MD, 81; Univ Hawaii, MPH, 83. *Prof Exp:* Instr chem, Univ Colo, 49-51; sr org chemist, Eli Lilly & Co, 51-66; assoc prof chem, Colo State Univ, 66-71; prof chem, San Francisco State Univ, 72-83. *Mem:* AAAS; Am Chem Soc; Sigma Xi; AMA. *Res:* Synthetic organic compounds of nitrogen related to the natural products histamine and serotonin; primary health care in developing countries. *Mailing Add:* 3879 Vineyard Dr Redwood City CA 94061

AINSWORTH, LOUIS, reproductive endocrinology, for more information see previous edition

AINSWORTH, OSCAR RICHARD, MATHEMATICS. *Current Pos:* MATHEMATICIAN, REDSTONE ARSENAL, NASA, 53- *Personal Data:* b Vicksburg, Miss, July, 28, 22; m 47. *Educ:* Univ Miss, BA & MA, 46; Univ Calif, PhD(math), 51. *Prof Exp:* From asst prof to assoc prof, 50-60, prof math, Univ Ala, 60- *Mem:* Am Math Soc; Sigma Xi. *Res:* Special functions; elasticity; missile guidance systems. *Mailing Add:* 3102 30th St Northport AL 35476-3106

AINSWORTH, STERLING K, MEDICAL SCIENCE. *Current Pos:* ASSOC PROF PATH, MED UNIV SC, 72- *Personal Data:* b Meridian, Miss, Oct 23, 39. *Educ:* Univ Miss, PhD, 69. *Mailing Add:* Dept Path Med Univ SC 171 Ashley Ave Charleston SC 29425-0001

AIRD, STEVEN DOUGLAS, MOLECULAR BIOLOGY, BIOCHEMISTRY. *Current Pos:* ENTREPRENEUR. *Personal Data:* b Ann Arbor, Mich, June 12, 52; m 78; c 3. *Educ:* Mont State Univ, BS, 74; Northern Ariz Univ, MS, 77; La State Univ, PhD(zool), 84. *Prof Exp:* Teaching asst plant taxon, Northern Ariz Univ, 74-75 & cell physiol, 75-76; res asst & teaching asst biochem, Med Ctr, La State Univ, 76-77; teaching asst herpet & cell biol, Colo State Univ, 78-79; res assoc, Dept Biochem, Univ Wyo, 83-84, res assoc, Dept Molecular Biol, 85-88; res scientist, Natural Prod Sci, Inc, 88-91; sr scientist, Western Regional, 91-92. *Concurrent Pos:* Mem, Grants Herpet Comt, Soc Study Amphibians & Reptiles, 86- & Provisional Comt Toxin Nomenclature, Int Soc Toxinology, 90; lectr, Am Vet Med Asn, 87; tech consult, Colo Div Wildlife, 87; assoc researcher, Univ Catolica de Goias, Brazil; adj asst prof, Univ Utah State, 93- *Mem:* Int Soc Toxinol; Am Soc Biochem & Molecular Biol; Herpetologists' League; Soc Study Amphibians & Reptiles. *Res:* Isolation of toxins from spider, scorpion and snake venoms for bioassay and structural-functional studies; comparative biochemical studies of snake venoms; author of more than 50 technical publications. *Mailing Add:* 921 NE Capital Blvd Salt Lake City UT 84103

AIREE, SHAKTI KUMAR, PHYSICAL CHEMISTRY, BIOCHEMISTRY. *Current Pos:* From asst prof to assoc prof, 66-76, PROF CHEM & DIR, MUS/ARCHIVES, UNIV TENN, MARTIN, 76- *Personal Data:* b Hoshiarpur, India, Nov 12, 34; m 63; c 3. *Educ:* Panjab Univ, BSc, 56, MSc, 58; Okla State Univ, PhD(chem), 67. *Concurrent Pos:* Co-ed, KIMAT-Chemex. *Mem:* Sigma Xi; Am Chem Soc; Nat Sci Teachers Asn. *Res:* Glucose determinations; effects of vitamins C & E. *Mailing Add:* Dept Chem Univ Tenn Martin TN 38238-0001

AISEN, PHILIP, BIOCHEMISTRY, BIOPHYSICS MEDICINE. *Current Pos:* Assoc med, Albert Einstein Col Med, 60-63, from asst prof to assoc prof, 63-73, actg chmn dept biophys, 70-78, prof biophys & med, 73-81, PROF BIOPHYS PHYSIOL & MED, ALBERT EINSTEIN COL MED, 81- *Personal Data:* b New York, NY, Mar 28, 29; m 51; c 3. *Educ:* Columbia Univ, AB, 49, MD, 53. *Concurrent Pos:* Am Cancer Soc fel, 54-55; Nat Res Coun fel, 57-58; Guggenheim fel, Univ Gothenburg, 67-68; mem staff, Watson Lab, IBM Corp, 64-70; bioanalytical & metallobiochemistry study sect, NIH, 78-83, chmn, 82-83; Donders professorship, Univ Utrecht, Netherlands, 88. *Mem:* Am Soc Clin Invest; Asn Am Physicians; Am Soc Biol Chemists; NY Acad Sci; Am Fedn Clin Res. *Res:* Protein chemistry and function; physics of metal proteins; biophysics. *Mailing Add:* Dept Physiol & Biophys Albert Einstein Col Med Bronx NY 10461

AISENBERG, ALAN CLIFFORD, ONCOLOGY. *Current Pos:* Instr, Harvard Med Sch, 57-59, assoc, 59-62, asst prof, 62-69, assoc prof med, 69-84, PROF MED, HARVARD MED SCH, 84- *Personal Data:* b New York, NY, Dec 7, 26; m 52, Nadya Margulies; c James & Margaret. *Educ:* Harvard Univ, SB, 45, MD, 50; Univ Wis, PhD, 56. *Concurrent Pos:* Clin asst, Mass Gen Hosp, 57-61, asst physician, 61-69, assoc physician, 69-81, physician, 81- *Mem:* Am Col Physicians; Am Asn Immunol; Am Soc Clin Oncol. *Res:* Malignant lymphoma; cellular immunology. *Mailing Add:* Dept Med Mass Gen Hosp Boston MA 02114

AISENBERG, SOL, PHYSICS. *Current Pos:* sr scientist, Space Sci, Inc, 64-65, actg head physics dept, 65-69, vpres, 68-70, gen mgr, 69-70, GEN MGR, SPACE SCI DIV, WHITTAKER CORP, 70-, CHIEF RES ENGR, 74- *Personal Data:* b New York, NY, Aug 26, 28; m 56; c 3. *Educ:* Brooklyn Col, BS, 51; Mass Inst Technol, PhD(physics), 57. *Prof Exp:* Res staff mem, Res Div, Raytheon Co, 57-61, sr res scientist, 61-64. *Mem:* AAAS; Am Phys Soc; Am Vacuum Soc; Am Inst Aeronaut & Astronaut; Asn Adv Med Instrumentation; Sigma Xi. *Res:* Plasma diagnostics; gaseous discharges; thin films; lasers; energy conversion; electron emission; plasma accelerators; ultra high vacuum; physical electronics; atmospheric physics; electro-optics; solid state; medical instrumentation; diagnostic instrumentation. *Mailing Add:* Tech Dev Eval Prot Int Tech Group Natick MA 01760

AISNER, JOSEPH, ONCOLOGY. *Current Pos:* chief med oncol, Univ Md, Cancer Ctr, Baltimore 81-92, dep dir clin affairs, 82-88, prof oncol, 82, prof pharmacol, 85, prof clin pharmacol, 87, PROF MED, UNIV MD, 82-, PROF EPIDEMOL PREV MED, 93- *Personal Data:* b Munich, Jan 5, 44; m 69, Seena Feldman; c Dara L & Leon A. *Educ:* Wayne State Univ, BS, 65, MD, 70. *Prof Exp:* Intern, Sinai Hosp, Detroit, 70-71; resident, Georgetown Univ Hosp, Wash, 71-72; comndg med officer, USPHS, 72-81. *Concurrent Pos:* clin assoc, Nat Cancer Inst, Baltimore, 72-75, sr investr, 75-78, chief med oncology, 78-81; chmn, Breast Cancer Sect, Md Cancer Consortium, 92-93; bd dirs, Am Cancer Soc, 88-, Am Asn Cancer Educ, 90, Md Childrens Cancer Found, 91-; mem, Gov Coun Cancer Found, 91. *Mem:* Fel Am Fed Clin Res; Am Soc Clin Oncology; Am Asn Cancer Res; Am Radium Soc; fel Am Col Physicians. *Res:* Oncology; epidemiology preventive medicine; cancer; editor of 6 books. *Mailing Add:* Univ Med Cancer Ctr 22 S Greene St Baltimore MD 21201-1544

AISSEN, MICHAEL ISRAEL, MATHEMATICS. *Current Pos:* chmn dept, 70-76, prof, 70-89, EMER PROF MATH, NEWARK CAMPUS, RUTGERS UNIV, 89- *Personal Data:* b Istanbul, Turkey, Jan 16, 21; nat US; m 44, Mildred Davis; c Judith, Louis S & Claire (Deem). *Educ:* City Col New York, BS, 47; Stanford Univ, PhD(math), 51. *Prof Exp:* Instr & res assoc math, Univ Pa, 49-51; res scientist, Radiation Lab, Johns Hopkins Univ, 51-61; from assoc prof to prof, Fordham Univ, 61-70. *Mem:* Am Math Soc; Math Asn Am; Soc Indust & Appl Math; NY Acad Sci; Sigma Xi; Math Assoc Am. *Res:* Zeroes of polynomials; completion processes; combinatorics. *Mailing Add:* 5 Villanova Ct Seaside CA 93955-4505

AIST, JAMES ROBERT, PLANT PATHOLOGY, PLANT CYTOLOGY. *Current Pos:* asst prof, 72-78, ASSOC PROF PLANT PATH, CORNELL UNIV, 78- *Personal Data:* b Cheverly, Md, Feb 20, 45; m 67; c 3. *Educ:* Univ Ark, BS, 66, MS, 68; Univ Wis, PhD(plant path), 71. *Prof Exp:* NATO fel, Swiss Fed Inst Technol, 71-72. *Mem:* AAAS; Am Phytopath Soc; Am Soc Cell Biol. *Res:* Time course, experimental and cytochemical studies of a plant disease resistance response, wall apposition formation, during fungal attack; enzymatic degradation of plant cell walls; nuclear studies of plant pathogenic fungi. *Mailing Add:* Dept Plant Path Cornell Univ 334 Plant Sci Bldg Ithaca NY 14853-0001

AITA, CAROLYN RUBIN, THIN FILM GROWTH, SURFACE SCIENCE. *Current Pos:* from asst prof to assoc prof mat sci, 81-87, SCIENTIST, LAB SURFACE STUDIES, UNIV WIS, MILWAUKEE, 81- , PROF MAT SCI, 88- *Personal Data:* b Brooklyn, NY, Sept 7, 43; m 65; c Ann. *Educ:* Brooklyn Col, City Univ NY, BA, 66; Utica Col, Syracuse Univ, BS, 70; Queens Col, City Univ NY, MA, 74; Northwestern Univ, PhD(mat sci), 77. *Prof Exp:* Sr staff mem, US Gypsum Co, 77-78; sr scientist, Elec & Electronic Res, Gould Labs, Gould, Inc, 78-81. *Concurrent Pos:* Lectr, Queens Col, City Univ New York, 70-74. *Mem:* Am Vacuum Soc; Am Ceramic Soc; Mat Res Soc; Sigma Xi. *Res:* Growth of compound semiconductor and ceramic thin films by reactive sputter deposition; in situ discharge diagnostics by mass and optical spectrometry to obtain fundamental plasma-film growth relationships and for process monitoring and control; understanding film behavior in terms of microstructure, atomic order, chemistry and interfacial effects; film characterization by x-ray diffraction, electron spectroscopy, electron microscopy, spectrophotometry, and electrical measurements; optics; ceramic engineering; multilayed nanostructured materials. *Mailing Add:* 4067 N Farwell Ave Univ Wis Milwaukee WI 53211-2110. *Fax:* 414-229-6958; *E-Mail:* aita@csd4.csd.uwm.edu

AITA, JOHN ANDREW, NEUROLOGY, PSYCHIATRY. *Current Pos:* RETIRED. *Personal Data:* b Council Bluffs, Iowa, June 20, 14; m 37; c 2. *Educ:* Univ Iowa, MD, 37; Univ Minn, PhD(psychiat), 44. *Prof Exp:* Intern, US Marine Hosp, Calif, 37-38; asst instr, Sch Med, Yale Univ, 38-40; instr, Mayo Found, Univ Minn, 40-44; from assoc prof to prof neurol & psychiat, Col Med, Univ Nebr Med Ctr, Omaha, 46-89. *Concurrent Pos:* Res physician & ment hygienist, Yale Univ, 38-40; first asst, Mayo Clin, 43-44. *Mem:* Am Psychiat Asn; Am Acad Neurol. *Res:* Brain injury. *Mailing Add:* 2302 N 55th St Omaha NE 68104

AITKEN, ALFRED H, ELECTROMAGNETISM. *Current Pos:* PHYSICIST, CONSOLIDATED CONTROLS CORP, 85- *Personal Data:* b New York, NY, June 22, 25; m 50; c 1. *Educ:* Lehigh Univ, BS, 49; Ind Univ, MS, 50, PhD(physics), 55. *Prof Exp:* Physicist, US Naval Res Lab, 54-85. *Concurrent Pos:* Lectr, Univ Col, Univ Md, 55-67. *Mem:* Am Phys Soc. *Mailing Add:* 7604 Elba Rd Alexandria VA 22306

AITKEN, CAIRNS, REHABILITATION MEDICINE, AVIATION MEDICINE. *Current Pos:* hon consult psycholmed, Royal Infirmary & Royal Edinburgh Hosp, 66-74, from vdean to dean, Fac Med, 88-91, vprin planning & budgeting, 91-94, PROF REHAB STUDIES & HON CONSULT PHYSICIAN REHAB MED, PRINCESS MARGARET ROSE ORTHOP & ASTLEY AINSLIE HOSPS, UNIV EDINBURGH, 74-, DIR, DISABILITY MGT RES GROUP, 80-, CHMN, ROYAL INFIRMARY EDINBURGH, NHS TRUST, 93- *Personal Data:* b Dunoon, Argyllshire, Dec 20, 33; m 59, Audrey May Lunn; c 2. *Educ:* Univ Glasgow, MD & CHB, 57, MD, 65; FRCP(E), 71; FRC Psych, 74. *Hon Degrees:* DSc, Coun Nat Acad Awards. *Honors & Awards:* Officers Cross, Polish Repub, 94. *Concurrent Pos:* Ed, J Psychosom Res, 79-86; chmn, Napier Polytech Govs, 82-90; dir, Lothian Health Bd, 91-93; vis prof, Spain, US, Australia & Malaysia. *Mem:* Assoc mem Inst Med-Nat Acad Sci; hon fel Int Col Psychosom (pres, 85-87); Soc Res in Rehab (pres, 81-83). *Res:* Stress in aircrew and on their various symptoms; measurement of mood disturbance, such as in asthma, assessment of disability and rehabilitation, particularly in personal injury compensation and in breast cancer; published 130 articles. *Mailing Add:* 11 Succoth Pl Edinburgh EH12 6BJ England

AITKEN, DONALD W, JR, PHYSICS, ASTROPHYSICS. *Current Pos:* prof environ studies, San Jose State Univ, 70-91, SR ENERGY ANALYST, UNION CONCERNED SCIENTISTS, 91- *Personal Data:* b Hilo, Hawaii, Mar 14, 36; m 58; c 2. *Educ:* Dartmouth Col, AB, 58; Stanford Univ, MS, 61, PhD(physics), 63. *Prof Exp:* Res assoc physics, Stanford Univ, 63-70; US Dept Energy, 79-81. *Concurrent Pos:* Adj Prof, Frank Lloyd Wright Sch Arch, 76- *Mem:* AAAS. *Res:* X-ray astronomy; interaction mechanisms of x-rays in solids; nucleon structure from high energy electron scattering experiments. *Mailing Add:* Union Concerned Scientists 20100 Skyline Blvd Woodside CA 94062

AITKEN, G(EORGE) J(OHN) M(URRAY), DIGITAL & OPTICAL IMAGE PROCESSING, ADAPTIVE OPTICS. *Current Pos:* from asst prof to assoc prof elec eng, Queens Univ, Ont, 66-76, chmn, Appl Sci Div Grad Studies, 81-83, head dept, 86-95, PROF ELEC ENG, QUEEN'S UNIV, 76- *Personal Data:* b Orangeville, Ont, Sept 26, 36; m 61, Barbara Boyd; c Boyd, Frank & Murray. *Educ:* Queen's Univ, Ont, BSc, 59, MSc, 61, PhD(elec eng), 65. *Concurrent Pos:* NATO fel, 65-66; foreign investr radio astron, Observ Paris, France, 65-66 & 72-73; infrared interferometry, CERGA, Grasse, France, 79-80; France-Can exchange fel, 79-80. *Mem:* Inst Elec & Electronics Engrs; Optical Soc Am; Soc Photo-Optical Instrumentation Engrs; Can Asn Univ Teachers; Can Astron Soc. *Res:* High angular resolution imaging in astronomy; optical phase measurement and retrieval; neural networks applied to adaptive optics; image restoration. *Mailing Add:* Dept Elec Eng Queen's Univ Kingston ON K7L 3N6 Can. *Fax:* 613-545-6615; *E-Mail:* aitkeng@post.queensu.ca

AITKEN, JAMES HENRY, NUCLEAR PHYSICS. *Current Pos:* RETIRED. *Personal Data:* b Glasgow, Scotland, Mar, 25, 27; Can citizen; m 55; c 3. *Educ:* Univ Edinburgh, BSc, 52; Univ Toronto, PhD, 69. *Prof Exp:* Asst lectr physics, Univ Edinburgh, 53-56; physicist, Comput Devices Can, Ltd, 56-57; physicist res off, Nat Res Coun Can, 57-65; res assoc, Univ Toronto, 65-70; analyst, Ont Hydro, Ont Govt, 70-72, chief health physics, 72-88; adj prof, Univ Toronto, 75-93. *Mem:* Can Asn Physicists. *Res:* Methods of nuclear radiation detection and measurement; reactor physics; reactor safety; health physics. *Mailing Add:* 51 Broadview Dr Unit 31 Etobicoke ON M2N 2C6 Can

AITKEN, JOHN MALCOLM, SOLID STATE PHYSICS. *Current Pos:* RES STAFF MEM, T J WATSON RES CTR, IBM CORP, 74- *Personal Data:* b Staten Island, NY, Jan 1, 45; m 68; c 3. *Educ:* Fordham Univ, BS, 66; Rensselaer Polytech Inst, MS & PhD(physics), 73. *Prof Exp:* Assoc solid state physics, Rensselaer Polytech Inst, 73-74. *Mem:* Electrochemical Soc; Inst Elec & Electronics Engrs. *Res:* Metal-oxide-semiconductor device physics; electron and hole trapping in silicon dioxide; radiation damage in metal-oxide-semiconductor circuits and devices; hot-election effects in metal-oxide-semiconductor field-effect transistors; device measurements and characterization. *Mailing Add:* 17 Baycrest Dr South Burlington VT 05483

AITKEN, THOMAS HENRY GARDINER, MEDICAL ENTOMOLOGY, PARASITOLOGY. *Current Pos:* sr res scientist, 71-83, EMER SR RES SCIENTIST EPIDEMIOL, YALE ARBOVIRUS RES UNIT, SCH MED, YALE UNIV, 83- *Personal Data:* b Porterville, Calif, Aug 31, 12; m 48, Virginia Gale; c Bruce G & Brian T. *Educ:* Univ Calif, BS, 35, PhD(med entom), 40. *Honors & Awards:* Medal, USA Typhus Comn, 44; Gold Medal, Govt Sardinia, 51; Gilt Medal, Hort Soc Trinidad & Tobago, 74; Richard M Taylor Medal, Am Comt Arthropod-borne Viruses, 84; Harry Hoogstraal Medal, Am Comt Med Entom, 93. *Prof Exp:* Asst entom & parasitol, Univ Calif, 36-40; staff mem, Rockefeller Found, 46-74. *Concurrent Pos:* Consult, USPHS, Ctr Dis Control, Arbovirus Ecol Br, Ft Collins Co, 74, Gorgas Mem Lab, Panama, 76, Int Develop Res Ctr, Can, yellow fever Trinidad, 81-82. *Mem:* Am Soc Trop Med & Hyg; Am Mosquito Control Asn; Entom Soc Am. *Res:* Bloodsucking diptera, particularly mosquitoes; malaria and arthropod-borne viruses; experimental infection transmission. *Mailing Add:* 176 Mill Plain Rd Branford CT 06405

AIVAZIAN, GARABED HAGPOP, PSYCHIATRY. *Current Pos:* from asst prof to prof, Univ Tenn, 54-79, actg chmn to chmn dept, 63-74, dir residency training prog, 61-79, EMER PROF PSYCHIAT, COL MED, UNIV TENN, MEMPHIS, 79- *Personal Data:* b Turkey, Dec 11, 12; US citizen; m 39; c 2. *Educ:* Am Univ Beirut, MD, 35; Am Bd Psychiat & Neurol, cert psychiat, 59. *Prof Exp:* Intern internal med, Am Univ Beirut Hosp, 35-37; resident psychiat, Am Univ Beirut & Lebanon Hosp Ment & Nerv Dis, 38-41; clin asst, Am Univ Beirut, 41-52, clin asst prof, 52-54. *Concurrent Pos:* Consult, Am Univ Beirut Hosp, 41-54, John Gaston Hosp, Memphis, Tenn, 55-74, Gailor Ment Health Ctr, 56-75, Memphis Ment Health Inst, 62-75 & Methodist Hosp, 74-; Rockefeller Found fel psychiat, Col Med, Univ Tenn, Payne Whitney Clin & Med Col, Cornell Univ, 48; dir continuing psychiat educ, Univ Tenn Ctr Health Sci, 78-79. *Mem:* AMA; fel Am Psychiat Asn; Sigma Xi. *Res:* Medical education and psychopharmaco-therapy; clinical evaluation of psychotropic drugs. *Mailing Add:* 92 E Charlotte Circle Memphis TN 38117-2872

AIZENMAN, MICHAEL, STATISTICAL MECHANICS & QUANTUM FIELD THEORY, THEORY OF SCHRODINGER OPERATORS & DISORDER EFFECTS. *Current Pos:* fel, 75-77, asst prof physics, 77-82, PROF MATH & PHTSICS, PRINCETON UNIV, 90- *Personal Data:* b Aug 28, 45; m, Marta B Gershanik; c Nurith C & Ya'ir G. *Educ:* Hebrew Univ, Jerusalem, BS, 69; Yeshiva Univ, PhD, 75. *Honors & Awards:* Giudo Stampacchia Prize, Scuola Normale Superiore di Pisa, 82; Norbert Wiener Award, Am Math Soc & Soc Indust & Appl Math, 90. *Prof Exp:* Vis mem, Courand Inst Math Sci, NY Univ, 74-75, prof, Physics Dept, 87-90; from assoc prof to prof II math & physics, Rutgers Univ, 82-87. *Concurrent Pos:* Sloan fel, 81-84; Guggenheim fel, 84-85; vis prof, Inst des Hautes Etudes Sci, Bures-sur-Yvette Univ, Paris, 84-85, Inst Advan Study, 91; Fairchild scholar, Calif Inst Technol, 92. *Mem:* Nat Acad Sci. *Res:* Physics and mathematics with focus on mathematical analysis of issues arising in statistical mechanics, quantum field theory, theory of Schrodinger operators and disorder effects. *Mailing Add:* Princeton Univ Jadwin Hall PO Box 708 Princeton NJ 08544-0708. *E-Mail:* aizenman@princeton.edu

AIZLEY, PAUL, MATHEMATICS. *Current Pos:* from asst prof to assoc prof 68-80, admin asst to pres, 74-79, dir summer session & mini term, 76-79, PROF MATH, UNIV NEV, LAS VEGAS, 80- *Personal Data:* b Boston, Mass, Feb 16, 36; m 69; c 3. *Educ:* Harvard Univ, AB, 57; Univ Ariz, MS, 59; Ariz State Univ, PhD(math), 69. *Prof Exp:* Instr math, Tufts Univ, 59-61; vis asst prof, Ariz State Univ, 67-68. *Mem:* Am Math Soc; Math Asn Am. *Res:* Convolution algebras, number theory. *Mailing Add:* Univ Nev 4505 Maryland Pkwy Las Vegas NV 89154-1039

AJAMI, ALFRED MICHEL, STABLE ISOTOPE CHEMISTRY. *Current Pos:* AT MASS TRACE, WOBURN, MASS. *Personal Data:* b Caracas, Venezuela, May 18, 48; US citizen; m 79. *Educ:* Harvard Univ, AB, 70, AM, 72, PhD(biol), 73. *Prof Exp:* Vpres, KOR, Inc, 71-; at Tracer Technol Inc. *Concurrent Pos:* Dir res, KOR Isotopes; consult, Environ Protection Agency, 74-75 & NSF, 76. *Mem:* NY Acad Sci; Am Chem Soc; Am Asn Clin Chemists; AAAS; Sigma Xi. *Res:* Chemical and biochemical studies on pharmaceuticals and environmental chemical labeled with stable isotopes; non-radioactive, non-destructive, non-invasive isotopic tracer systems for the health care, chemical process and performance materials industries. *Mailing Add:* Mass Trace 3-G Gill St Woburn MA 01801

AJAX, ERNEST THEODORE, CLINICAL NEUROLOGY. *Current Pos:* Instr psychiat, Univ Utah, 58-65, from instr to assoc prof neurol, 59-71, instr med, 61-69, asst prof, 65-72, prof neurol, 71-87, ASSOC PROF PSYCHIAT, COL MED, UNIV UTAH, 72-, EMER PROF NEUROL, 87-; ASST NEUROLOGIST, UNIV HOSP, 65-; NEUROLOGIST, UNIV UTAH MED CTR, 65- *Personal Data:* b Salt Lake City, Utah, Oct 11, 26; m 50, Gwendolyn; c Ted J, Katherine, Wendy & Todd. *Educ:* Univ Utah, BS, 49, MD, 51. *Concurrent Pos:* Asst chief neurol serv, Vet Admin Hosp, Salt Lake City, 57-62, chief, 62-; assoc neurologist, Salt Lake Co Gen Hosp, 59-65. *Mem:* Am Acad Neurol; Am Electroencephalog Soc. *Res:* Electroencephalography; disorders of language. *Mailing Add:* Dept Neurol Univ Utah Salt Lake City UT 84112

AJELLO, LIBERO, MEDICAL MYCOLOGY. *Current Pos:* ADJ PROF, DEPT OPHTHAL, SCH MED, EMORY UNIV, 90- *Personal Data:* b New York, NY, Jan 19, 16; m 42, Gloria Wolfe; c Marc. *Educ:* Columbia Univ, AB, 38, MA, 40, PhD(mycol), 48. *Honors & Awards:* Distinguished Serv Medal, US Dept Health & Human Servs, 75; Lucille K Georg Award, Int Soc Human & Animal Mycol, 82; Arima Award, Int Union Microbiol Soc, 94. *Prof Exp:* Med mycologist, Off Sci Res & Develop, Ft Benning, Ga, 42-43 & Johns Hopkins Hosp, 43-46; scientist dir chg Med Mycol Div, Ctr Infectious Dis, Ctrs Dis Control, USPHS, 47-67, dir, Div Mycotic Dis, 67-90; prin invest head, WHO Col Ctr Mycol Dis, 79-90. *Concurrent Pos:* Burroughs-Wellcome vis prof microbiol, 85. *Mem:* AAAS; Am Soc Microbiol; Mycol Soc Am; Brit Mycol Soc; Int Soc Human & Animal Mycol. *Res:* Fungi pathogenic to humans; their taxonomy, identification, ecology and control. *Mailing Add:* Emory Univ Eye Ctr Ophthalmic Res Suite 2400 1327 Clifton Rd NE Atlanta GA 30322. *Fax:* 404-778-4143

AJERSCH, FRANK, METALLURGICAL ENGINEERING. *Current Pos:* res assoc chem metall, Ecole Polytechnique, 72-73, from assoc prof to prof, 73-89, chmn, Dept Metall Eng, 89-92, PROF METALL KINETICS, ECOLE POLYTECHNIQUE, MONTREAL, CAN, 89- *Personal Data:* b Poland, Feb 7, 41; Can citizen; m 69; c 2. *Educ:* McGill Univ, BE, 63; Univ Toronto, MASc, 68, PhD(metall eng), 71. *Prof Exp:* Res engr process metall, Noranda Res Ctr, 63-67; fel thermodyn, Univ Grenoble, France, 71-72. *Mem:* Metall Soc; Can Inst Mining & Metall; Am Inst Mining & Metall; Sigma Xi; Am Soc Metals. *Res:* Kinetics of metallurgical processes; transport phenomena; gaseous reduction of porous oxides; gas-solid and gas-liquid reactions applied to metallurgy; rheology of metal matrix composites. *Mailing Add:* Ecole Polytech CP 6079 Sta Centre-Ville Montreal PQ H3R 2A7 Can

AJL, SAMUEL JACOB, microbiology, for more information see previous edition

AJMONE-MARSAN, COSIMO, NEUROPHYSIOLOGY, NEUROSCIENCES. *Current Pos:* AT DEPT NEUROL, JACKSON MEM MED CTR, MIAMI, FLA, 79- *Personal Data:* b Cossato, Italy, Jan 2, 18; nat US; m 43, Rosetta Pesatori; c Barbara & Guido. *Educ:* Univ Turin, MD, 42. *Honors & Awards:* Lennox Award; H Jasper Award. *Prof Exp:* Asst neurol, Clin Nerv Dis, Italy, 41-47, chief EEG & neurophysiol, 48-49; Rockefeller fel, Montreal Neurol Inst, McGill Univ, 50-51, lectr, Inst, 52-53; chief neurosci br, Nat Inst Neurol Communicative Dis & Stroke, 54-79. *Concurrent Pos:* Clin instr, George Washington Univ, 55-58, assoc, 58-64, asst prof neurol, 65-73, assoc prof, 74-; chief ed, EEG J, 59-69; chief ed, J Clin Neurophysiol, 83-89. *Mem:* Am Epilepsy Soc (pres, 73); Am Acad Neurol; Am Physiol Soc; Int Brain Res Orgn; Am EEG Soc (pres, 62-63); Int Fedn Soc EEG Clin Neurophysiol (pres, 69-72). *Res:* Electroencephalography; physiology of cerebral cortex and thalamus; clinical electroencephalography; epilepsy; clinical neurophysiology. *Mailing Add:* Chief EEG Lab Univ Miami Sch Med 1611 NW 12th Ave Miami FL 33136. *Fax:* 305-545-7898

AJZENBERG-SELOVE, FAY, NUCLEAR PHYSICS. *Current Pos:* res prof, 70-73, assoc chair, 89-93, PROF PHYSICS, UNIV PA, 73- *Personal Data:* b Berlin, Ger, Feb 13, 26; m 55, Walter. *Educ:* Univ Mich, BSE, 46; Univ Wis, MS, 49, PhD(physics), 52. *Prof Exp:* From asst prof to assoc prof physics, Boston Univ, 52-57; from assoc prof to prof, Haverford Col, 57-70, actg chmn dept, 60-61 & 67-69, comnr, Comn Col Physics, 68-70. *Concurrent Pos:* Smith-Mundt fel, US Dept State, 55; vis asst prof, Columbia Univ, 55; vis prof, Nat Univ Mex, 55; vis assoc physicist, Brookhaven Nat Lab, 56; lectr, Univ Pa, 57; Guggenheim fel, Lawrence Radiation Lab, Univ Calif, 65-66; consult, Calif Inst Technol, 70-72, exec secy comt physics in cols, Am Inst Physics, 62-65, mem adv comt vis scientist prog, 63-65 & adv comt manpower, 64-68; mem exec comt, Div Nuclear Physics, Am Phys Soc, 70-75, chmn, 73-74; exec secy ad hoc panel nuclear data compilation, Nat Acad Sci-Nat Res Coun, 71-75; mem comn nuclear physics, Int Union Pure & Appl Physics, 72-81, chmn, 78-81; Sigma Xi Nat lectr, 74-75; mem, Nuclear Sci Adv Comt, Dept Energy, NSF, 77-80; mem, Comt Pub Educ & Info, Am Inst Physics, 80-83; mem phys sci panel, Associateship Progs, Nat Res Coun, 88-91. *Mem:* Fel AAAS; fel Am Phys Soc. *Res:* Neutron spectra; nuclear structure. *Mailing Add:* Dept Physics Univ Pa Philadelphia PA 19104-6396

AKAGI, JAMES MASUJI, MICROBIAL PHYSIOLOGY. *Current Pos:* from asst prof to assoc prof, 61-64, chmn dept, 76-85, PROF MICROBIOL, UNIV KANS, 67- *Personal Data:* b Seattle, Wash, Dec 23, 27; wid; c 2. *Educ:* Univ Ill, BS, 51; Univ Kans, MA, 55, PhD, 59. *Prof Exp:* Instr bact, Univ Kans, 58-59; fel microbiol, Sch Med, Western Reserve Univ, 59-61. *Concurrent Pos:* Res career develop award, 67-76. *Mem:* Am Soc Microbiol; Am Soc Biol Chemists; Am Acad Microbiol. *Res:* Biochemistry. *Mailing Add:* 1645 Oxford Rd Lawrence KS 66044

AKAMINE, ERNEST KISEI, POST HARVEST PHYSIOLOGY. *Current Pos:* Asst agr, 35-36, agron, 36-38, plant physiol, 38-42, assoc plant , 42-44, jr physiologist, 44-52, asst plant physiologist, 52-62, assoc pl ant physiologist & assoc prof plant, 62-68, plant physiologist & prof, 68-77, EMER PLANT PHYSIOLOGIST & EMER PROF PLANT PHYSIOL, UNIV HAWA II, 77- *Personal Data:* b Hilo, Hawaii, May 10, 12; m 38, Toki Nakasone; c Carol (Matsushita), Faye (McCoy) & Harry A. *Educ:* Univ Hawaii, BS, 35, MS, 41. *Concurrent Pos:* Mem sci invests, Ryukyu Islands Prog, Nat Res Coun, 52; cousult, Nat Lexicog Bd, Ltd, 53-; tech consult, New Wonder World Encycl, 57; vis consult, US Civil Admin Ryukyu Islands, US Dept Army, 62; vis scientist, Commonwealth Sci & Indust Res Orgn, Australia, 74-75. *Mem:* Fel AAAS; Am Soc Plant Physiol; Am Soc Hort Sci; Sigma Xi. *Res:* Commodity shipment studies; postharvest physiology. *Mailing Add:* 2255 Hulali Pl Honolulu HI 96819

AKASAKI, TAKEO, ALGEBRAIC TOPOLOGY. *Current Pos:* asst prof, 66-72, assoc prof, 72-94, EMER PROF MATH, UNIV CALIF, IRVINE, 94- *Personal Data:* b Long Beach, Calif, Dec 19, 36; m 73; c 2. *Educ:* Univ Calif, Los Angeles, BA, 58, MA, 61, PhD(math), 64. *Prof Exp:* Actg asst prof math & asst res mathematician, Air Force Off Sci Res grant, Univ Calif, Los Angeles, 64; asst prof math, Rutgers Univ, 64-66. *Mem:* Am Math Soc. *Res:* Integral group rings; projective modules/semi local rings. *Mailing Add:* Dept Math Univ Calif Irvine CA 92717

AKASOFU, SYUN-ICHI, SPACE PHYSICS. *Current Pos:* asst geophys, 58-61, res geophysicist, 61-62, from assoc prof to prof, 62-86, DIR, GEOPHYS INST, UNIV ALASKA, FAIRBANKS, 86- *Personal Data:* b Nagano-ken, Japan, Dec 4, 30; m 61, Emiko Endo; c Ken-Ichi & Keiko. *Educ:* Tohoku Univ, BS, 53, MS, 57; Univ Alaska, PhD(geophys), 61. *Honors & Awards:* Chapman Medal, Royal Astron Soc, Eng, 76; Japan Acad Award, 77; John Adam Fleming Medal, Am Geophys Union, 79; Spec lectr for Emperor Hirohito of Japan, 85. *Prof Exp:* Asst geophys, Nagasaki Univ, 53-55. *Concurrent Pos:* Assoc ed, J Geomagnetism & Geoelec, 72 & J Geophys Res, 72-74. *Mem:* Fel Am Geophys Union; Soc Terrestrial Magnetism & Elec Japan; Int Acad Aeronaut; fel Arctic Inst N Am. *Res:* Geomagnetic storms; aurora polaris; physics of the magnetosphere; solar-terrestrial relationships. *Mailing Add:* Geophys Inst Univ Alaska Fairbanks AK 99775-0800

AKAY, ADNAN, NOISE CONTROL, FRICTION. *Current Pos:* PROF & DEPT HEAD, MECH ENG CARNEGIE MELLON UNIV, 92- *Personal Data:* b Turkey. *Educ:* NC State Univ, BS, 71, MME, 72, PhD(mech eng), 76. *Prof Exp:* Res asst mech eng, NC State Univ, 72-75; res fel, Nat Inst Environ Sci, 76-78; from asst prof to assoc prof, WAYNE STATE UNIV, 78-86, prof mech eng, 86-92. *Concurrent Pos:* Prin investr, NSF grants, 80-; consult, Bendix Corp, 81- *Mem:* Am Soc Mech Engrs; Acoustical Soc Am; Soc Antom Eng; Am Soc Eng Educ; Sigma Xi. *Res:* Analytical and experimental investigation of sound radiation from mechanical systems; friction induced vibration and noise; impact mechanics and impact induced sound and vibration; dynamics of high-speed machinery. *Mailing Add:* Dept Mech Eng Carnegie Mellon Univ Pittsburgh PA 15213

AKAZAWA-EGUCHI, MIYUKI REI REAL, LANDSCAPE ARCHITECTURE. *Current Pos:* MANAGING PRIN & CREATIVE DIR, EGUCHI ASSOCS LANDSCAPE ARCHITECTS, 90-; DIR, DESIGN WITH NATURE INC, 90- *Personal Data:* b Toronto, Ont, Feb 2, 55; m, Barbara L Flanagan; c Jahra Jo Nami Typhina & Marlise Satori Alyssa. *Educ:* Ryerson Polytech Univ, BSLA, 83; Univ Guelph, MLA, 86; York Univ, BA, 87. *Honors & Awards:* Second Place Award, NAt Asn Japanese Canadians, 94; First Place Award, Am Soc Landscape Architects. *Prof Exp:* Designer & landscape architect, Toronto, 78-90. *Mem:* Can Soc Landscape Architects. *Mailing Add:* 39 Ferris Rd Toronto ON M4B 1G2 Can

AKBAR, HUZOOR, HEMATOLOGY, BIOCHEMISTRY. *Current Pos:* ASST PROF PHARMACOL, OHIO UNIV, 81- *Educ:* Australian Nat Univ, PhD(clin sci), 78. *Mailing Add:* Dept Zool & Biomed Sci Ohio Univ Col Osteop Med Irvine Hall No 416 Athens OH 45701-2979

AKCASU, AHMET ZIYAEDDIN, NUCLEAR ENGINEERING, STATISTICAL MECHANICS. *Current Pos:* from asst prof to assoc prof, 63-68, PROF NUCLEAR ENG, UNIV MICH, ANN ARBOR, 68- *Personal Data:* b Aydin, Turkey, Aug 26, 24; m 54, Melahat Turksal; c Nur, Feza & Aydin. *Educ:* Tech Univ Istanbul, MS, 48; Int Sch Nuclear Sci & Eng, Argonne Nat Lab, dipl, 57; Univ Mich, PhD(nuclear eng), 63. *Honors & Awards:* Class of 38E Distinguished Serv Award, Univ Mich, 65; Glenn Murphy Award, Am Soc Eng Educ, 86; Sci Award, Asn Turkish Am Scientists, 92. *Prof Exp:* Asst prof electronics, Tech Univ Istanbul, 48-53, assoc prof, 54-59; resident res assoc nuclear eng, Argonne Nat Lab, 59-61. *Concurrent Pos:* Vis res scientist, Brookhaven Nat Lab, Upton, NY, 65-69; vis prof, Nagoya Univ, Japan, 74, Argonne Nat Lab, Ill, 75, Inst Phys Sci & Technol, Univ Md, 77-78, Univ Konstanz, Ger, 86 & 93 & Polymer Res Ctr & Sch Eng, Bogazici Univ, Turkey, 91; physicist, Ctr Mat Res Polymer Sci & Stand Div, Nat Bur Stand, Washington, DC, 78-84, Nat Inst Stand & Technol, Gaithersburg, Md, 89; vis scientist, Univ Freiburg, Ger, 84, Univ Strasbourg, France & Nat Tsing-Hua Univ, Taiwan, 85; res scientist, Alcoa Labs, Pa, 87; guest prof, Physics Dept, Univ Konstanz, Ger, 90-92; Humboldt res award, sr US scientist, 91. *Mem:* Fel Am Phys Soc; fel Am Nuclear Soc; Turkish Phys Soc. *Res:* Nonlinear reactor dynamics; reactor noise analysis; correlation analysis in liquids and calculation of transport coefficients; kinetic theory of liquids and plasmas; polymer solution dynamics; interpretation of dynamic scattering from dense fluids and polymer solutions; stochastic differential equations. *Mailing Add:* 2820 Pebble Creek Dr Ann Arbor MI 48108-1728. *Fax:* 313-763-4540; *E-Mail:* ziya@engin.umich.edu

AKE, THOMAS BELLIS, III, ASTRONOMY. *Current Pos:* AT SPACE TELESCOPE SCI INST. *Personal Data:* b Woodbury, NJ, Mar 15, 49; m 69; c 3. *Educ:* Case Western Reserve Univ, BS, 71, MS, 74, PhD(astron), 77. *Prof Exp:* Res fel astron, Calif Inst Technol, 78-80; mem staff, Goddard Space Flight Ctr, NASA, 80- *Concurrent Pos:* Staff mem, Hale Observ, 78- *Mem:* Am Astron Soc. *Res:* Stellar spectroscopy. *Mailing Add:* 13311 Yarland Lane Bowie MD 20715

AKEEL, HADI A, MANUFACTURING ENGINEERING, ROBOTICS. *Current Pos:* SR VPRES & CHIEF ENGR, FANUC ROBOTICS NAMERICA INC, 82-, VCHMN, FANUC USA CORP, 92-, GEN MGR, FANUC BERKELEY LAB, 92-, TECH CONSULT, FANUC LTD, 92- *Personal Data:* b Apr 9, 38; m 63, Sofia; c Shereef & Nezar. *Educ:* Univ Cairo, BSc, 59; Univ Calif, Los Angeles, MSc, 63; Univ Calif, Berkeley, PhD(mech design), 66. *Honors & Awards:* Joseph F Engelberger Award, Robotics Indust Asn, 88. *Prof Exp:* Acting instr, Univ Calif, Berkeley, 63-66; specialist, Bendix Corp, 67-69; asst & assoc prof, Univ Ain Shams, Cairo, 70-74; dept head mfg staff, Gen Motors Corp, 74-82. *Concurrent Pos:* Chmn, Am Soc Mfg Engrs Conf, 88; mgt, Technol Prog, Univ Calif, Berkeley; chmn & mem, Bd Visitors, Opland Univ Sch Eng, 90-97. *Mem:* Nat Acad Eng; Fel Am Soc Mech Engrs; fel Soc Mfg Engrs; sr mem Robotics Int/Soc Mech Engrs; Inst Elec & Electronics Engrs. *Res:* Holder of over 50 patents in aerospace, machine tools, manufacturing and robotic devices. *Mailing Add:* Fanuc Robotics NAm Inc 3900 W Hamlin Rd Rochester Hills MI 48309-3253

AKELEY, DAVID FRANCIS, POLYMER CHEMISTRY. *Current Pos:* RETIRED. *Personal Data:* b Presque Isle, Maine, Apr 13, 28; m 56, Marcy McCullough; c Kurt & John. *Educ:* Univ Maine, BS, 49; Univ Wis, PhD(chem), 53. *Prof Exp:* Res chemist, Textile Fibers Dept, E I du Pont de Nemours & Co, Inc, 54-63, patent chemist, 63-89. *Res:* Patent law; textile fibers. *Mailing Add:* 1607 Shadybrook Rd Wilmington DE 19803

AKELEY, KURT B, COMPUTER GRAPHICS. *Current Pos:* VPRES & CHIEF ENG, SILICON GRAPHICS INC, 82- *Educ:* Univ Del, BS; Stanford Univ, MS. *Mem:* Fel Asn Comput Mach. *Res:* Granted eight patents. *Mailing Add:* Silicon Graphics Inc 2011 N Shoreline Blvd Mountainview CA 94039

AKELL, ROBERT B(ERRY), CHEMICAL ENGINEERING. *Current Pos:* CONSULT, 82- *Personal Data:* b Boston, Mass, May 14, 21; m 88, Dorothy Marshall; c Paul S, Sandra (Seidel) & June. *Educ:* Northeastern Univ, BS, 42; Univ Louisville, MChE, 46. *Prof Exp:* Asst, Polaroid Corp, 39-42; prod supvr, Joseph E Seagrams & Sons, Inc, 42-44, asst maintenance supt, 44-45, dir educ, 45-46; asst dir personnel, Calvert Distilling Co, 46-48, res & develop supvr, 48-50, chief chemist, 50-56; sr engr, E I Du Pont de Nemours, 56-62, consult, 62-68, sr consult, Dept Eng, 68-78, prin consult, 78-82. *Concurrent Pos:* Adj prof, Univ Del, 79-82. *Mem:* Fel Am Inst Chem Engrs. *Res:* Mass transfer; transport properties and phenomena; phase equilibria; liquid-liquid extraction; adsorption. *Mailing Add:* 1506 Fresno Rd Wilmington DE 19803-5124. *E-Mail:* rbakell@juno.com

AKELLA, JAGANNADHAM, GEOCHEMISTRY, MATERIALS SCIENCES. *Current Pos:* SR SCIENTIST EXP PETROL & HIGH PRESSURE PHYSICS, UNIV CALIF, LIVERMORE, 77- *Personal Data:* b Kakinada, Andhra, India, Sept 13, 37; US citizen; m 67, Lalita Vemparala; c Anita, Sadhana & Mamata. *Educ:* Andhra Univ, Waltair-India, BScHons, 57, MSc, 58; Indian Inst Technol, Kharagpur, PhD(geochem), 63. *Prof Exp:* Sr lectr petrol, Univ Rajastan, Udiapur, India, 62-63; res geophysicist high pressure geophys, Univ Calif, Los Angeles, 65-71; Carnegie res assoc exp petrol, Geophys Lab, Carnegie Inst, Washington, DC, 71-74; sr resident res assoc, Nat Res Coun & Nat Acad Sci, NASA Johnson Space Ctr, Houston, 74-77. *Concurrent Pos:* Fel, Ger acad exchange scholar, Univ Gottingen, WGer, 63-65; Adv UN Develop Proj, Geophys Res Inst , India. *Mem:* Am Geophys Union; fel Mineral Soc Am; fel Indian Mineral Soc; Asn Geoscientists for Int Develop. *Res:* High pressure and temperature phase equilibria properties of materials at elevated pressures and temperatures; equation of state studies; crystal growth, lunar and terrestrial mantle rock studies; high pressure and temperature work on trans-uranics. *Mailing Add:* Lawrence Livermore Nat Labs Univ Calif L-201 Livermore CA 94550. *Fax:* 510-423-1057

AKELLA, RAMA, natural killer cells as effectors to control tumor spreading, receptors & cell surface adhesion molecules, for more information see previous edition

AKER, FRANKLIN DAVID, NEUROANATOMY, ANATOMY. *Current Pos:* ASST PROF ANAT SCI, SCH DENT, TEMPLE UNIV, 70- *Personal Data:* b Norristown, Pa, Apr 26, 43; m 68; c 2. *Educ:* Gettysburg Col, BA, 65; Temple Univ, PhD(anat), 70. *Mem:* Am Asn Anat. *Res:* Peripheral and central nervous system in conjunction with fluorescence microscopy and ultra-freezing and drying techniques; development of hard tissues of head region. *Mailing Add:* Dept Anat Temple Univ Sch Dent 3400 N Broad St Philadelphia PA 19140

AKERA, TAI, CARDIOVASCULAR PHARMACOLOGY. *Current Pos:* VPRES, MSD RES LABS, JAPAN, 91- *Personal Data:* b Wakayama, Japan, July 13, 32; m 62, Chiseko Masuda; c Atsushi, Yukako & Chika. *Educ:* Keio Univ, Japan, MD, 58, PhD(pharmacol), 65. *Prof Exp:* Instr, Keio Univ Hosp, 64-66, asst prof, 66-71; assoc prof, Dept Pharmacol & Toxicol, Mich State Univ, 71-74, prof, 74-87; dir, Nat Children's Hosp Med Res Ctr, Japan, 87-91. *Concurrent Pos:* Fel, Dept Pharmacol, Univ Mich, 62-64; vis asst prof, Mich State Univ, 67-70; vis prof, Sch Med, Tokai Univ, 77, adj prof, 87-; adj prof, Sch Med, Keio Univ, 87- *Mem:* Am Soc Pharmacol & Exp Therapeut; Japanese Med Asn; Int Soc Heart Res. *Res:* Biochemical and biophysical studies on the pharmacological and toxic actions of the cardiac glycosides; studies on calcium movements in the cardiac muscle. *Mailing Add:* Banyu Pharmaceut Co Ltd 2-3 Nihonbashi-Honcho 2 Chome Tokyo Chuo-Ku Japan 103. *Fax:* 81-3-3582-0530

AKERLOF, CARL W, ELEMENTARY PARTICLE PHYSICS, ASTROPHYSICS. *Current Pos:* Res assoc, 66-68, asst prof, 68-72, assoc prof, 72-78, PROF PHYSICS, UNIV MICH, ANN ARBOR, 78- *Personal Data:* b New Haven, Conn, Mar 5, 38; m 65, Carol I Ruska; c Karen L & William G. *Educ:* Yale Univ, BA, 60; Cornell Univ, PhD(physics), 67. *Mem:* Fel Am Phys Soc; Am Astron Soc. *Res:* Strong and electromagnetic interactions of elementary particles; gamma-rays from compact stellar and extragalactic objects. *Mailing Add:* Dept Physics Univ Mich 500 E University Ave Ann Arbor MI 48109. *Fax:* 313-936-1817; *E-Mail:* akerlof@mich.physics.lsa.umich.edu

AKERS, ARTHUR, FLUID POWER, TRANSMISSION AND CONTROL. *Current Pos:* from asst prof mech engr, 75-80, assoc prof eng mech & sci dept eng sci & mech, 80-87, PROF AEROSPACE ENG & ENG MECH, IOWA STATE UNIV, 87- *Personal Data:* b Smethwick, UK, Mar 24, 27; m 78, Marcia Pratt; c Andrew & Judith. *Educ:* Univ London, UK, BSc, 53, PhD(mech eng), 69; Univ Cranfield, MSc, 55. *Honors & Awards:*

Achievement Award, Nat Fluid Power Asn, 92. *Prof Exp:* Sr lectr aeronaut & mech eng, Univ Bath, UK, 60-64; prin lectr mech engr, Lords of the Admiralty, Royal Naval Col, 65-68 & Her Britannic Majesty's Govt, Royal Mil Col Sci, 68-73 & 75-76. *Concurrent Pos:* Examr gen cert educ in eng sci, Univ London, UK, 71-75; vis prof, Dept Mech Eng, Univ Va, 73-74; consult, US Navy, Dahlgren, Va, 75-78, Fisher Controls, Marshalltown, Iowa, 78-82, Marshalltown Instruments, 78-85, Vector Corp, Marion, 82-83, 3M Corp, 82-83 & Sundstrand, Ames, 82-85, Pack Corp USA, Tampa, Iowa, 83, Midwest Carbide, Keokuk, Iowa, 84, Shivvers Inc, Corydon, Iowa, 86, Servus Rubber Louisville, Ky, 87, Eastern Iowa Hog Producers, Earlville, Iowa, 87; tech adv, Analytical Eng, Sunstrand Adv, Tech group, 87-88. *Mem:* Am Soc Mech Engrs; Fluid Power Soc; Soc Am Mil Engrs; fel Royal Aeronaut Soc UK; Sigma Xi. *Res:* Modelling of fluid power components and systems; optimally controlled fluid power systems. *Mailing Add:* 1519 Stone Brooke Rd Ames IA 50010-4100. *Fax:* 515-294-8584; *E-Mail:* aakers@iastate.edu

AKERS, CHARLES KENTON, SURFACE CHEMISTRY, ENVIRONMENTAL CHEMISTRY. *Current Pos:* PRES, AKERS ASSOCS, 90- *Personal Data:* b Eugene, Ore, May 11, 42; m 71; c 4. *Educ:* Willamette Univ, BA, 65; State Univ NY, Buffalo, PhD(biophys), 72. *Prof Exp:* Cancer scientist, Roswell Park Mem Inst, 67-72; engr, Town Amherst, 73-74; scientist, Calspan Corp, 74-85, prog dir, 85-90. *Concurrent Pos:* Chmn, Chem Opers Sect, Am Defense Preparedness Asn, 84- *Mem:* Fel Am Inst Chemists; Am Chem Soc; Am Defense Preparedness Asn. *Res:* Survivability in hazardous environment, chemical warfare, hazardous waste; surface chemistry for biomaterial development, biological- material interface; chemical detection technology; test methodology development for toxic materials. *Mailing Add:* 170 S Cayuga Rd Buffalo NY 14221-6731

AKERS, LAWRENCE KEITH, PHYSICS. *Current Pos:* RETIRED. *Personal Data:* b Ashburn, Ga, Apr 16, 19; m 46; c 4. *Educ:* Univ Ga, BS, 49, MS, 50; Vanderbilt Univ, PhD, 55. *Prof Exp:* Scientist, Oak Ridge Inst Nuclear Studies, 54-55, sr scientist, 55-58, res scientist & actg chmn univ rels div, 58-59; head training unit, Int Atomic Energy Agency, 59-60; prin scientist, Spec Training Div, Oak Ridge Inst Nuclear Studies, 61-64, asst chmn, 64-65, chmn spec training div, Oak Ridge Assoc Univs, 65-75; prog mgr, Dept Energy, 76-86; actg head physics dept, Univ Tenn, Chattanooga, 86-87, distinguished vis prof, 87, prof physics & astron, 88-90. *Concurrent Pos:* Consult, Cordoba Nat Univ; mem steering comt tech-physics proj, Am Inst Physics; dir res grad prog, Univ Tenn, 73-76. *Mem:* Am Phys Soc; Sigma Xi. *Res:* Infrared and Raman spectra of corrosive compounds; nuclear spectroscopy. *Mailing Add:* 401 Crewdson Ave Chattanooga TN 37405-4111

AKERS, LEX ALAN, ELECTRICAL ENGINEERING, SOLID STATE ELECTRONICS. *Current Pos:* ASSOC PROF, DEPT ELEC ENG, ARIZ STATE UNIV. *Personal Data:* b Washington, DC, May 7, 50; m 69; c 1. *Educ:* Tex Tech Univ, BSEE, 71, MSEE, 73, PhD(elec eng), 75. *Prof Exp:* Res asst integrated circuits, Dept of Elec Eng, Tex Tech Univ, 71-74, instr elec eng, 74-75; res engr digital design, Southwest Res Inst, 75-76; asst prof elec eng, Univ Nebr, 76- *Concurrent Pos:* Assoc ed elec devices, Soc Comput Simulation, 77- *Mem:* Inst Elec & Electronics Engrs; Soc Comput Simulation; Sigma Xi. *Res:* Small geometry and nonisothermal MOSFET models; simulation of semiconductor devices; microprocessor design and applications. *Mailing Add:* Dept Elec Eng Ariz State Univ Tempe AZ 85287

AKERS, MICHAEL JAMES, PHYSICAL PHARMACY, PARENTERAL TECHNOLOGY. *Current Pos:* res scientist, Eli Lilly & Co, 81-84, head, Dry Prod Develop, Lilly Res Lab, head, Parenteral & Liquid Ointment Prod Dev, 87-89, mgr, Parenteral Qual Control, 89-90, mgr, Corp Qual Assurance, 91-93, SR RES SCIENTIST, BIOPHARM PDT DEVELOP, ELI LILLY & CO, 94- *Personal Data:* b Beech Grove, Ind, Aug 24, 46; m 68, Mary; c Scott, Ryan & Allison. *Educ:* Wabash Col, BA, 68; Univ Iowa, PhD(pharm), 72. *Honors & Awards:* Res Award, Parenteral Drug Asn, 80. *Prof Exp:* Res investr pharm, Searle Labs, Inc, 72-74; sr scientist, Alcon Labs Inc, 74-77; assoc prof pharm, Univ Tenn, Memphis, 77-81. *Concurrent Pos:* Adj prof, Sch Pharm, Purdue Univ, 83- & Col Pharm, Univ Ill, 84- & Col Pharm, Univ Cincinnati, 93- *Mem:* Fel Am Asn Pharm Sci; Parenteral Drug Asn; Sigma Xi; AAAS. *Res:* Parenteral delivery systems; sterilizer validation; kinetics of drug degradation; parenteral quality control; formulation of polypeptides. *Mailing Add:* Biopharm Pdt Dev Drop Code 3842 Eli Lilly & Co Indianapolis IN 46285. *Fax:* 317-276-1856; *E-Mail:* mja@lilly.com

AKERS, SHELDON BUCKINGHAM, JR, computer science; deceased, see previous edition for last biography

AKERS, THOMAS GILBERT, VIROLOGY, MICROBIOLOGY. *Current Pos:* assoc dean, Sch Pub Health & Trop Med, 76-81, PROF ENVIRON HEALTH SCI, TULANE UNIV, 81- *Personal Data:* b Oakland, Calif, Jan 5, 28; m 54; c 3. *Educ:* Univ Calif, Berkeley, BS, 50, MPH, 56; Mich State Univ, PhD(virol), 63; Southern Ill Univ, Edwardsville, MBA, 73. *Prof Exp:* US Navy, 50-, pub health officer, Formosa, 51-54, res virologist, Naval Biomed Res Lab, Univ Calif, Berkeley, 54-56, res virologist, Cairo, Egypt, 56-60, res virologist, Naval Biomed Res Lab, Univ Calif, Berkeley, 63-76. *Mem:* Am Pub Health Asn; Soc Exp Biol & Med; Am Asn Immunol; Am Soc Trop Med & Hyg; NY Acad Sci; Sigma Xi. *Res:* Public health microbiology; biophysical properties of virus nucleic acids; epidemiology of respiratory and enteric virus; cytochemical techniques. *Mailing Add:* Dept Pub Health Tulane Univ Sch Pub Health 1430 Tulane Ave New Orleans LA 70112-2699

AKERS, THOMAS KENNY, COMPARATIVE PHYSIOLOGY, ENVIRONMENTAL PHYSIOLOGY. *Current Pos:* from asst prof to prof, 69-92, interim chair, 90-92, EMER PROF PHYSIOL, SCH MED, UNIV NDAK, 92- *Personal Data:* b Brooklyn, NY, Jan 16, 31; m 56; c 3. *Educ:* DePaul Univ, BS, 56; Loyola Univ Chicago, MS, 59, PhD(physiol), 61. *Honors & Awards:* Peck Fund Res Award, 62; B C Gamble Award, 87; Sigma Xi Medal, 90. *Prof Exp:* Instr physiol, Norweg Am Sch Nursing, 58-59; instr, St Anthony of Padua, 59-60; from instr to asst prof pharmacol, Stritch Sch Med, Loyola Univ Chicago, 61-65. *Concurrent Pos:* Res assoc, Inst Study Mind, Drug & Behav, 63-65, AMTE, Portsmouth, Eng, 80; dir, High Pressure Life Lab, 74-79, Olympic Peninsula Adult Learning Inst, 92-96. *Mem:* Am Physiol Soc; AAAS; Undersea Med Soc; Sigma Xi. *Res:* Hyperbaric studies; oxygen toxicity; adrenergic function; bioengineering. *Mailing Add:* 449 Guy Kelly Rd Port Angeles WA 98362

AKESON, ANN L, IMMUNOLOGY. *Current Pos:* DRUG RESEARCHER, MARION MERRELL DOW PHARMACEUT, 89- *Personal Data:* b Cedar Falls, Iowa, 1946. *Educ:* Iowa State Univ, BS, 69; Univ Calif, Los Angeles, MS, 75; Univ Cincinnati, PhD(biochem), 85. *Prof Exp:* Res fel biol studies, Childrens Hosp, 85-89. *Mem:* Am Soc Cell Biol. *Mailing Add:* Dept Immunol Sci Hoechst Marion Roussel Inc 2110 E Galbraith Rd Cincinnati OH 45215-6300

AKESON, WALTER ROY, BIOCHEMISTRY, AGRONOMY. *Current Pos:* SR PLANT PHYSIOLOGIST, MONO HY SUGAR BEET SEED, INC, 85- *Personal Data:* b Chappell, Nebr, Nov 2, 37; m 59; c 3. *Educ:* Univ Nebr, BS, 59, MS, 61; Univ Wis, PhD(biochem), 66. *Prof Exp:* Asst prof agron, Univ Nebr, Lincoln, 65-69; sr plant physiologist, Agr Res Ctr, Great Western Sugar Co, 69-85. *Mem:* AAAS; Am Soc Agron; Am Soc Plant Physiol; Am Soc Sugar Beet Technol; Sigma Xi. *Res:* Metabolism of aromatic compounds; extraction and evaluation of leaf protein concentrates; nature of biochemical resistance of plants to disease and insects; sugar beet storage losses; seed physiology; tissue culture. *Mailing Add:* 1815 Duchess Dr Longmont CO 80501-2033

AKESON, WAYNE HENRY, ORTHOPEDIC SURGERY. *Current Pos:* actg chmn, Dept Surg, 80-81, PROF ORTHOP & HEAD DIV, UNIV CALIF, SAN DIEGO, 70- *Personal Data:* b Sioux City, Iowa, May 5, 28; m 51, 69; c 4. *Educ:* Univ Chicago, MD, 53; Am Bd Orthop Surg, dipl. *Honors & Awards:* Nicholas Andry Award, 66; Sports Med Award, Am Ortho Soc, 83. *Prof Exp:* Instr orthop surg, Univ Chicago, 57-58; asst prof, Sch Med, Univ Wash, 61-70. *Concurrent Pos:* Consult, Vet Admin. *Mem:* Am Orthop Asn; Orthop Res Soc; Am Acad Orthop Surg; Orthop Res & Educ Found. *Res:* Collagen and mucopolysaccharides and their interaction; biochemical and biophysical basis of joint stiffness; metabolism of intercellular substances of articular cartilage and of arthroplastic surfaces. *Mailing Add:* Univ Calif Med Ctr 225 W Dickinson St San Clemente CA 92103-1910

AKESSON, NORMAN B(ERNDT), AGRICULTURAL ENGINEERING, PESTICIDE CHEMICAL SAFETY ENGINEERING. *Current Pos:* from instr to prof, 47-84, EMER PROF AGR ENG, AGR EXP STA, UNIV CALIF, DAVIS, 84- *Personal Data:* b Grandin, NDak, June 12, 14; m 46, Margaret Blasing; c Thomas R & Judith E. *Educ:* NDak Agr Col, BS, 40; Univ Idaho, MS, 42. *Prof Exp:* Asst res, Univ Idaho, 40-42; physicist bur ord, US Dept Navy, 42-47. *Concurrent Pos:* Fulbright fel, Eng & E Africa, 57-58; consult, WHO & Foreign Agr Orgn, Israel, 68, Japan, 72, China, 85, Can, 87; assoc ed, Am Soc Agr Eng, 83-93. *Mem:* Fel Am Soc Agr Engrs; Am Entom Soc; Brit Soc Res Agr Eng; Am Soc Testing & Mat; Weed Sci Soc Am; Am Mosquito Control Soc. *Res:* Machines for aerial and ground application of plant protection materials; spray atomization and distribution from air carrier and aircraft equipment; small particle analysis and behavior and air pollution meteorology as applied to particle drift and deposit; evaluation of pesticide application and reduction of potential damages to workers, crops and wildlife through safe application procedures; author or co-author of 350 publications including 3 manuals. *Mailing Add:* Dept Bio/Agr Eng Univ Calif Davis CA 95616-5294. *Fax:* 530-752-2640

AKGERMAN, AYDIN, SEPARATIONS, REACTION ENGINEERING. *Current Pos:* assoc prof, 80-86, PROF CHEM ENG & ASSOC DEPT HEAD, TEX A&M UNIV, 86- *Personal Data:* b Izmir, Turkey, July 12, 45; US citizen; m 69, Leyla Oner; c Cagla G & Bora A. *Educ:* Robert Col, Istanbul, Turkey, BS, 68; Univ Va, MS, 69, PhD(chem eng), 71. *Prof Exp:* Asst prof chem eng, Bogazici Univ, Istanbul, Turkey, 71-72; assoc prof, Ege Univ, Izmir, Turkey, 72-80. *Concurrent Pos:* Res & develop mgr, Cimentas Izmir Cement Plant, 76-80; fulbright scholar, Fulbright Comt France, 89; Halliburton prof, 89; consult various cos, 89- *Mem:* fel Am Inst Chem Engrs; Am Chem Soc. *Res:* Application of separations and reaction engineering fundamentals to environmental remediation/restoration problems. *Mailing Add:* 2608 Arbor Bryan TX 77802-2907. *Fax:* 409-845-6446

AKHTAR, MASYOOD, LOW TEMPERATURE SEALING GLASS, LOW TEMPERATURE SILVER-GLASS. *Current Pos:* SR SCIENTIST, JOHNSON MATTHEY, 88- *Personal Data:* b Bihar, India, July 12, 49; m 77, Masroora; c Shabana, Faisal & Maheen. *Educ:* Univ Mysore, BS, 72; Alfred Univ, MS, 81, PhD(ceramic eng), 84. *Prof Exp:* Res assoc, Univ Ill, 84-85; scientist, Int Inst Glass Res, 85-88. *Mem:* Am Ceramic Soc; Inst Ceramic Engrs; Int Soc Hybrid Microelectronics; Inst Elec & Electronics Engrs. *Res:* Ultra low temperature glass for use in electronic industry; monitoring procedure for silica polymer growth and shape analysis technique in liquid; microwave ion exchange implantation technology. *Mailing Add:* 17524 Ashburton Rd San Diego CA 92128. *Fax:* 619-566-1762

AKHTAR, MOHAMMAD HUMAYOUN, ORGANIC CHEMISTRY, ANALYTICAL CHEMISTRY. *Current Pos:* sr res scientist, 86, SR RES SCIENTIST CHEM & MYCOTOXINS, CTR FOOD & ANIMAL RES, AGR CAN, 75- *Personal Data:* b Patna, India, Jan 31, 43; Can citizen; m 74, Talat Ali; c Simar A & Saadia A. *Educ:* Univ Karachi, Pakistan, BSc Hons, 62; Univ Moncton, MSc, 66; Simon Fraser Univ, PhD(org chem), 70. *Prof Exp:* Demonstr & lectr chem, Haroon Col, Karachi, 62-64; res asst, Univ Moncton, 64-66 & Simon Fraser Univ, 66-70; fel org chem, Univ Alta, 70-75. *Mem:* Am Chem Soc; Chem Inst Can; NY Acad Sci; Soc Toxicol Can. *Res:* Assess the nature, extent and safety of agrichemicals in animal feedstuffs; determine the biochemical fate of these compounds in poultry and livestock; transmission of residues to animal derived products. *Mailing Add:* Ctr Food & Animal Res Neatby Bldg Rm 4008 Ottawa ON K1A 0C6 Can. *Fax:* 613-943-2353

AKHTAR, RASHID AHMAD, LIPID METABOLISM, MEMBRANE RECEPTORS. *Current Pos:* Assoc prof, 76-94, PROF CELLULAR & MOLECULAR BIOL & BIOCHEM, MED COL GA, 94- *Educ:* Univ London, PhD(biochem), 75. *Mailing Add:* Dept Biochem & Molecular Biol Med Col Ga 1120 15th St Augusta GA 30912-2100

AKI, KEIITI, SEISMOLOGY. *Current Pos:* W M KECK PROF GEOL SCI, UNIV SOUTHERN CALIF, 84- *Personal Data:* b Yokohama, Japan, Mar 3, 30; m 56; c 2. *Educ:* Univ Tokyo, BS, 52, PhD(geophys), 58. *Honors & Awards:* Medal, Seismol Soc Am, 87. *Prof Exp:* Fulbright res fel geophys, Calif Inst Technol, 58-60; res fel seismol, Earthquake Res Inst, Univ Tokyo, 60-62; vis assoc prof geophys, Calif Inst Technol, 62-63; assoc prof seismol, Earthquake Res Inst, Univ Tokyo, 63-65; prof geophys, Mass Inst Technol, 66-84. *Concurrent Pos:* Lectr, Int Inst Seismol & Earthquake Eng, UNESCO, 60-65; geophysicist, Nat Ctr Earthquake Res, US Geol Surv, 67-; vis prof, Univ Chile, 70 & 72, Univ Paris, 83; vis scientist, Royal Norweg Res Coun; consult, Sandia Labs & Los Alamos Sci Labs, 76-79; vis scholar, Japan Soc Prom Sci, 78; chmn, Comt Seismol, Nat Res Coun, 78-82; distinguished vis prof, Univ Alaska, 81; lectr, Int Asn Seismol & Earth's Interior, 81; consult, NSF, 81; ed-in-chief, Pure & Appl Geog, 83-87. *Mem:* Nat Acad Sci; Am Geophys Union; Seismol Soc Am (pres, 79-80); Soc Explor Geophys; fel Am Acad Arts & Sci; hon mem Europ Union Geosci. *Res:* Geophysical research directed toward predicting, preventing and controlling earthquake hazard; seismic wave propagation; earthquake statistics; structure of earth's crust and upper mantle; thermal processes in the earth; geothermal energy source exploration. *Mailing Add:* Dept Geol Sci Univ Southern Calif Los Angeles CA 90089

AKIL, HUDA, NEUROCHEMISTRY, NEUROSCIENCE. *Current Pos:* from asst prof to assoc prof neurochem, 78-91, PROF PSYCHIAT, MENT HEALTH RES INST, UNIV MICH, 91- *Personal Data:* b May 19, 45; US citizen; m 72; c 2. *Educ:* Am Univ Beirut, BA, 68; Univ Calif, Los Angeles, PhD(neurosci), 72. *Prof Exp:* Fel, Dept Psychiat, Stanford Univ, 74-77, res assoc, 77-78. *Concurrent Pos:* Fels, NIH, 74-77 & Alfred P Sloan 74-78; mem, Study Sect Preclin Psychopharmacol, NIH & adv bd, Ment Health Inst Med; chmn, Mode Action Opiates, Gordon Conf, 83; organizer, Decade of Brain. *Mem:* Inst Med-Nat Acad Sci; Int Asn Study Pain; Int Narcotic Res Conf; fel Am Col Neuropsychopharmacol; Neurosci Soc. *Res:* Endogenous opiate peptides, endorphins; pain control; neuroregulation and behavior; steroid receptors; stress; dopamine receptors; molecular neurobiology. *Mailing Add:* Dept Psych 84950 Univ Hosp Univ Mich Med Sch 1500 E Med Ctr Ann Arbor MI 48109

AKIN, CAVIT, BIOTECHNOLOGY, YEAST TECHNOLOGY. *Current Pos:* PRIN, AKIN BIOTECH, 85- *Personal Data:* b Nigde, Turkey, Feb 28, 31; m 78, Ingeborc K Tange; c Deniz, Suzan, Tulin & Aylin. *Educ:* Univ Ankara, MS, 54; Univ Ill, MS, 59, PhD(food technol), 61. *Prof Exp:* Asst chem technol, Univ Ankara, 54-55; res engr, Technol Lab, Sugar Corp, Turkey, 56; NIH res grant, Univ Mass, 61-62; sr bioengr, Dept Res & Develop, Falstaff Brewing Corp, 62-67; sr res engr, Am Oil Co, Whiting, Ind, 67-70; sr res engr, Corp Res, Stand Oil Co Ind, Naperville, 70-74, res supvr, Food & Yeast Sci, 74-77; mem staff, Amoco Foods Co, Naperville, Ill, 77-79; res assoc, Corp Res, Stand Oil Co, Inc, Ind, 79-85; res assoc, corp res, Amoco Corp, 85-87; assoc dir biotechnol res, Inst Gas Technol, 87-90, assoc inst scientist, 84-91. *Mem:* AAAS; Am Chem Soc; Am Soc Microbiol; Soc Indust Microbiol; Inst Food Technol. *Res:* Polymerization kinetics of acrylonitrile; batch and continuous propagation of yeasts; microbial food and fodder production; vapor phase sterilization; fermentation kinetics of beer; fermenter design; bioengineering and biotechnology; food from petroleum; torula yeast from ethanol; food applications of yeast; SCP texturization; functional proteins; textured meat alternates; genetic engineering plant tissue culture; biocatalysis, immobilized cells; environmental bioremediation; energy biotechnology; bio-activation of methane; coal and oil bio-desulfurization; biofuel cells, carbon dioxide mitigation. *Mailing Add:* 1462 Inverrary Dr Naperville IL 60563

AKIN, FRANK JERREL, PHARMACOLOGY, TOXICOLOGY. *Current Pos:* dir pharmacol & toxicol, Plough Div, 77-85, sr dir clin & toxicol res, consumer opers, SCHERING-PLOUGH CORP, INFANT DEVELOP LAB, RES & DEVELOP DEPT, KIMBERLY CLARK, ROSWELL, GA. *Personal Data:* b Carroll Co, Ga, Oct 8, 41; m 65; c 3. *Educ:* Univ Ga, BS, 64, MS, 69, PhD(pharmacol), 71; Am Bd Toxicol, cert. *Prof Exp:* Instr pharmacol, Univ Ga, 69-71; res pharmacologist, Richard B Russell Res Ctr, USDA, 71-77. *Concurrent Pos:* Adj asst prof, Sch Pharm, Univ Ga, 76-77; adj prof, Ctr Health Science, Univ Tenn, 82-85. *Mem:* Am Soc Pharmacol & Exp Therapeut; Fedn Am Soc Exp Biol; AAAS; Proprietary Asn; Cosmetic Toiletry & Fragrance Asn. *Res:* Pharmacology of analgesics, antifungals and topical steroids; sunscreen agents; toxicology of chemicals causing acute and subacute phototoxic and photoallergic reactions; toxicology of proprietary medications; natural toxicants. *Mailing Add:* Kimberly Clark Bldg 300/1 1400 Holcombe Bridge Rd Roswell GA 30076

AKIN, GWYNN COLLINS, pharmaceutical industry policy, health science policy, for more information see previous edition

AKIN, JIM HOWARD, MECHANICAL ENGINEERING. *Current Pos:* From asst prof to assoc prof mech eng, 63-77, PROF ENG SCI, UNIV ARK, FAYETTEVILLE, 77- *Personal Data:* b McAllen, Tex, Mar 8, 37; m 59; c 2. *Educ:* Univ Tex, Austin, BSME, 60, MSME, 61, PhD(mech eng), 67. *Mem:* Am Soc Mech Engrs; Am Soc Eng Educ; Nat Soc Prof Engrs; Sigma Xi. *Res:* Vibrational and systems analysis; machine design and analysis; structural dynamics. *Mailing Add:* Dept Mech Eng Univ Ark Fayetteville AR 72701

AKIN, LEE STANLEY, gear design analysis & research, tribology, for more information see previous edition

AKIN, WALLACE ELMUS, PHYSICAL GEOGRAPHY, HYDROLOGY RESOURCES. *Current Pos:* chmn dept, 53-83, prof, 53-93, EMER PROF GEOG & GEOL, DRAKE UNIV, 93- *Personal Data:* b Murphysboro, Ill, May 18, 23; m 48, Peggy J Holt; c Dianna & David. *Educ:* Southern Ill Univ, BA, 48; Ind Univ, MA, 49; Northwestern Univ, PhD(geog), 52. *Prof Exp:* Field team chief, Rural Land Classification Prog PR, Commonwealth Dept Agr & Com, 50-51; instr geog, Univ Ill, Chicago, 52-53. *Concurrent Pos:* Consult water resources, Iowa Natural Resources Coun, 54-61 & 75-82; Fulbright res grant, Univ Copenhagen, 61-62; ed, Iowa State Water Plan, 79-80; fac res grant, Study of Subsistence Agr, Solomon Islands, 80. *Mem:* Asn Am Geographers; Sigma Xi; AAAS; Soil Conserv Soc Am. *Res:* The role of physical geography in resource inventory and management; water resources; climate and climatic change in human affairs. *Mailing Add:* 5800 Pleasant Dr Des Moines IA 50312. *E-Mail:* wa8721R@acad.drake.edu

AKINS, RICHARD G(LENN), CHEMICAL ENGINEERING. *Current Pos:* asst prof, 63-77, assoc prof, 77-80, PROF CHEM ENG, KANS STATE UNIV, 80- *Personal Data:* b Harlan, Ky, Dec 14, 34; m 58; c 2. *Educ:* Univ Louisville, BS, 57, MS, 58; Northwestern Univ, PhD(chem eng), 62. *Prof Exp:* Res assoc, Chem Eng Div, Argonne Nat Lab, 62-63. *Concurrent Pos:* NSF res grant, 64-66; Off Saline Water res grant, 65-67. *Mem:* Am Inst Chem Engrs; Sigma Xi. *Res:* Laminar flow heat transfer in circular tubes; natural convection in liquid metals; Non-Newtonian flow. *Mailing Add:* 1832 Virginia Dr Manhattan KS 66502-2340

AKINS, VIRGINIA, biology; deceased, see previous edition for last biography

AKISKAL, HAGOP S, PSYCHIATRY, PSYCHOPHARMACOLOGY. *Current Pos:* dir med student educ psychiat, Univ Tenn, 74-78, assoc prof, 77-80, dir, Mood Clin & Affective Dis Prog, 75, DIR, CONTINUING MED EDUC PSYCHIAT, UNIV TENN, 79-, PROF PSYCHIAT & PHARMACOL, 80- *Personal Data:* b Beirut, Lebanon, Jan 16, 44; m. *Educ:* Am Univ Beirut, BSc, 65, MD, 69. *Honors & Awards:* Eli Roberts Lectr, Wash Univ, St Louis, 80; Clin Res Award, Am Acad Clin Psychiatrists, 81. *Prof Exp:* Res psychiatrist, Alcohol & Drug Dependence Clin, Memphis Ment Health Inst, 72-84. *Concurrent Pos:* Co-dir, Sleep Disorder Ctr, Baptist Hosp, 77-; mem Royal Col Physicians Can Speakers, Univ Toronto, 84; mem French Ministry External Rels Prog Invitation Am Scientists, Univ Paris, 84. *Mem:* AMA; Am Psychiat Asn; Soc Biol Psychiat; Sigma Xi; Am Psychopath Asn; Psychiat Res Soc; Am Col Psychiat. *Res:* Diagnosis, etiology and psychopharmacology of affective disorders; sleep disorders. *Mailing Add:* Dept Psychiat Univ Calif 9500 Gilman Dr La Jolla CA 92093-0603

AKIYAMA, STEVEN KEN, CELL BIOLOGY, CELL ATTACHMENT. *Current Pos:* ASST PROF ONCOLOGY, 85-, ASST PROF BIOCHEM, CANCER CTR, HOWARD UNIV, 87- *Educ:* Cornell Univ, PhD(phys chem), 81. *Mem:* AAAS; Am Cancer Soc; Am Soc Cell Biol. *Res:* Fibronectin. *Mailing Add:* NIH Bldg 30 Rm 414 Bethesda MD 20892-0001

AKKAPEDDI, MURALI KRISHNA, POLYMER CHEMISTRY. *Current Pos:* res chemist, 74-78, sr res chemist, 78-82, res assoc, corp res & develop, 82-85, MGR POLYMER RES, ENG PLASTICS RES & DEVELOP, ALLIED SIGNAL CORP, 85- *Personal Data:* b Vijayawada, India, Aug 31, 42; m 70; c 2. *Educ:* Osmania Univ, India, BSc, 60, MSc, 62; Univ Pa, PhD(org chem), 71. *Prof Exp:* Lectr chem, Osmania Univ, India, 62-67; sr chemist, Polysci Inc, Warrington, Pa, 71-74. *Mem:* Am Chem Soc. *Res:* Polymer synthesis and structure-property correlation; biomedical application of polymers; nylon reaction injection molding; barrier resins; high performance engineering plastics and polymer blends. *Mailing Add:* 7 Manor Dr Morristown NJ 07960-2600

AKKAPEDDI, PRASAD RAO, HIGH ENERGY LASERS, SPECTROSCOPY. *Current Pos:* DIR, HUGHES DANBURY OPTICAL SYSTEMS, 87- *Personal Data:* b Andhra Prudesh, India, Dec 23, 43; US citizen. *Educ:* Andhra Univ, Waltair, India, BSc, 61, MSc,63; Univ Southern Calif, MS, 70, PhD(elec eng), 73. *Prof Exp:* Res asst physics & elec eng, Univ Southern Calif, 66-73, asst elec eng, 73; tech staff physics, Comput Serv Corp, NASA, 73-76; mgr, adv tech high energy lasers, 76-81, group leader, lasers & devices, 81-83, assoc dir res, Perkin-Elmer Corp, Danbury, Conn, 83-87. *Concurrent Pos:* Adj prof elec eng, Univ Bridgeport, Cpnn, 78-80. *Mem:* Optical Soc Am; Laser Inst Am; Am Inst Physics. *Res:* Diode lasers; integrated and non-linear optics; thin films; surface sciences. *Mailing Add:* 7 Arrowhead Ct Norwalk CT 06851

AKKARA, JOSEPH A, BIOCATALYSIS, ENZYME-BASED POLYMER SYNTHESIS & MODIFICATION. *Current Pos:* RES CHEMIST, US ARMY NATICK RES DEVELOP & ENG CTR, 84-, PROJ OFFICER, 87-, GROUP LEADER, 90- *Personal Data:* b Trichur, Kerala, India, Feb 22, 38; US citizen; m 69, Mary A Maliackel; c Augustine V & Jeena T. *Educ:* Univ Kerala, India, BSc, 58; Univ Mo, PhD(biochem), 69. *Prof Exp:* Res assoc, Rockefeller Univ, 69-71; chief radioassay & res assoc, Brookdale Med Ctr, 71-80; supvr, Metpath Corning, 81-84. *Concurrent Pos:* Adv, Nat Res Coun Fel, 92-, Biotechnol Prog, Mass Commun Col, 93- *Mem:* Am Chem Soc; Mat Res Soc; Bio/Environmentally Degradable Polymer Soc; Sigma Xi; NY Acad Sci. *Res:* Synthesis, modification, derivatization and characterization of bioengineered materials for electro-optic and high performance applications; determination of biochemical pathways for the biotransformation of hazardous materials and waste products; enzymology; analytical biochemistry. *Mailing Add:* 18 Temi Rd Holliston MA 01746-1220

AKLONIS, JOHN JOSEPH, PHYSICAL CHEMISTRY, POLYMER CHEMISTRY. *Current Pos:* RETIRED. *Personal Data:* b Elizabeth, NJ, Sept 28, 40; m 66, 85. *Educ:* Rutgers Univ, BS, 62; Princeton Univ, MA, 64, PhD(phys chem), 65. *Honors & Awards:* Fel, Am Phys Soc. *Prof Exp:* Fel polymer physics, Princeton Univ, 65-66; from asst prof to assoc prof, Univ Southern Calif, 66-81, prof chem, Univ Southern Calif, 81-87. *Concurrent Pos:* Fulbright fel polymer chem, Cath Univ Louvain, 66-67; res assoc, Macromolecule Res Ctr, Strasbourg, France, 74-75; vis prof, Danish Tech Univ, 81-82. *Mem:* Am Chem Soc; Am Phys Soc. *Res:* Physics and physical chemistry of high polymeric systems. *Mailing Add:* PO Box 187 Univ Southern Calif San Pedro CA 90731

AKMAL, NAIM, INSTRUMENTATION, SENSORS & ANALYZERS. *Current Pos:* Res scientist, 92-93, SR SCIENTIST, TELEDYNE BROWN ENG ANALYTICAL INSTRUMENTS, 93- *Personal Data:* b Patna, India, July 25, 62; m 89, Rumana; c Sharukh M. *Educ:* Patna Univ, India, BS, Hons, 82, MS, 85; Wright State Univ, MS, 90; Univ Cincinnati, PhD(anal chem), 92. *Mem:* Am Chem Soc. *Res:* Synthetic polymer chemistry; rigid rod polymers; application of ethers in ion-selective electrodes; modified electrodes and its application in analysis of trace metals; toxic gas sensors based on liquid electrolytes; humidity and oxygen sensors important to PPb level. *Mailing Add:* 2401 S Hacienda Blvd Apt 327 Hacienda Heights CA 91745-6900. *Fax:* 626-961-2538

AKO, HARRY MU KWONG CHING, AQUACULTURE NUTRITION, FINE OILS. *Current Pos:* Asst prof, 75-82, ASSOC PROF BIOCHEM, UNIV HAWAII, 82- *Personal Data:* b Honolulu, Hawaii, Mar 16, 45; div; c 2. *Educ:* Univ Calif, Berkeley, AB, 67; Wash State Univ, PhD(biochem), 73. *Concurrent Pos:* Consult aquacult feeds develop, fine culinary & cosmetic oils. *Mem:* World Aquacult Soc. *Res:* Lawal, juvenile and growat feeds of marine shrimp and fish; ecotourism, kukui and macadamia nut oil. *Mailing Add:* Dept Environ Biochem Univ Hawaii Manoa Honolulu HI 96822-2270. *Fax:* 808-956-5037

AKOLKAR, PRADIP N, MOLECULAR MEDICINE, IMMUNOLOGY. *Current Pos:* RESEARCHER AUTOIMMUNE DIS, NORTH SHORE UNIV, 89- *Personal Data:* b Baroda, India, 1951. *Educ:* Univ Baroda, BS, 70, MS, 72, PhD(biochem), 78. *Prof Exp:* Researcher, Cancer Res Inst, Bombay, 78-83, Dept Microbiol, Columbia Univ 83-87 & Immunol Dept, Baroda Univ, 87-89. *Mem:* Am Asn Immunologists; Cell Biol Soc India. *Mailing Add:* Div Molecular Med North Shore Univ Hosp 350 Community Dr Manhasset NY 11030-3876

AKOVALI, YURDANUR A, NUCLEAR PHYSICS. *Current Pos:* MEM RES STAFF, PHYSICS DIV, OAK RIDGE NAT LAB, 67- *Personal Data:* b Ankara, Turkey; div; c Rosanna E Ellis & Gordan E Ellis. *Educ:* Univ Ankara, BS, 58; Univ Md, PhD(nuclear physics), 67. *Prof Exp:* Lab asst elec, Dept Physics, Sci Fac, Univ Ankara, 58-59; teaching asst physics, Univ Md, 59-61. *Concurrent Pos:* Consult & lectr, 78. *Mem:* Am Phys Soc; Sigma Xi. *Res:* Investigation of nuclear structure through alpha, beta and delayed-proton decays, in-beam reaction gammas and particle transfers. *Mailing Add:* Physics Div Oak Ridge Nat Lab PO Box 2008 Oak Ridge TN 37831-6371. *E-Mail:* akovali@orph01.phy.ornl.gov

AKPAN, EDWARD, power metallurgy, physical metallurgy & failure analysis, for more information see previous edition

AKRABAWI, SALIM S, MEDICINE. *Current Pos:* DIR, GEN MED, NUTRIT, MEAD JOHNSON CO, 80- *Personal Data:* b Amman, Jordan, Jan 20, 41; US citizen; m 67, Patricia L Jones; c Ronma F, Amira F & David M. *Educ:* Vanderbilt Univ, MD, 77; Univ Calif, Davis, PhD(nutrit), 68. *Prof Exp:* Asst prof nutrit, Am Univ, Lebanon, 71-74. *Mem:* Am Soc Parenteral & Enteral Nutrit; Sigma Xi; Am Soc Clin Nutrit. *Res:* Adult nutritional needs in trauma and illness. *Mailing Add:* Mead Johnson Nutrit Bristol-Myers VSPNG 2400 W Lloyd Expwy Evansville IN 47721-0001

AKRE, ROGER DAVID, entomology; deceased, see previous edition for last biography

AKRUK, SAMIR RIZK, REPRODUCTIVE BIOLOGY, ELECTRON MICROSCOPY. *Current Pos:* PRIMARY CARE INTERNAL MED, FRANCISCAN FAMILY CARE, 95- *Personal Data:* b Beirut, Lebanon, Feb 2, 43; m 77; c Ramsey & Viola. *Educ:* Am Univ Beirut, BS, 65, MS, 67; Univ Ga, PhD(zool), 77; Univ Auton Cd, Juarez, Mexico, MD, 83. *Honors & Awards:* 3M Award Res, 86. *Prof Exp:* Instr & coordr biol, Beirut Univ Col, 66-71; asst prof biol, Marietta Col, 78-80; internal med solo practice, 86-95. *Concurrent Pos:* Res assoc biochem, Univ Ga, 77-78; med dir, Attleboro Retirement Village, Langhorne, PA, 87-; assoc med dir, US Health Care, 93-96. *Mem:* Electron Micros Soc Am; Soc Study Reprod; Sigma Xi; AMA. *Res:* In vitro capacitation and fertilization in mammals; mammalian sperm acrosome reaction; scanning and transmission electron microscopy of gametes; ultrastructural localization of acrosomal enzymes. *Mailing Add:* 2205 Brookhaven Dr Yardley PA 19067. *Fax:* 215-321-3390

AKSAMIT, ROBERT ROSOOE, CHEMOTAXIS OF MAMMALIAN CELLS. *Current Pos:* RES CHEMIST, NIMH, 80- *Educ:* Okla State Univ, PhD(chem), 71. *Mailing Add:* 2209 Pinneburg Ave Rockville MD 20851

AKSELRAD, ALINE, EXPERIMENTAL SOLID STATE PHYSICS, MAGNETISM. *Current Pos:* MEM RES STAFF, AT&T ENG RES CTR, 77- *Personal Data:* b Wilno, Poland, Apr 14, 35; US citizen; m 62; c 1. *Educ:* McGill Univ, BSc, 57; Univ Toronto, MSc, 59, PhD(solid state spectros), 61. *Prof Exp:* Asst physics, Univ Toronto, 59-61; grant & mem tech staff, Weizmann Inst Sci, 61-62; mem tech staff, RCA Labs, 62-77. *Mem:* Am Phys Soc; AAAS; Sigma Xi. *Res:* Electronic structure and properties of solids; magnetic insulators and their properties; propagation and applications of acoustic waves; solar energy conversion; plasma deposition; semiconductor lasers; luminescence; semi-conductors, electronic and optical properties. *Mailing Add:* 960 Lawrenceville Rd Princeton NJ 08540-4320

AKST, GEOFFREY R, MATHEMATICAL STATISTICS. *Current Pos:* PROF MATH, BOROUGH MANHATTAN COMMUNITY COL, 66- *Personal Data:* b New York, NY, July 15, 43. *Educ:* Columbia Univ, EdD, 76. *Mem:* Am Math Asn Two Yr Col. *Mailing Add:* 220 Madison Ave Apt 14C New York NY 10016

AKTAS, YILDIRIN, FREE ELECTRON LASERS, WAVES IN PLASMAS. *Current Pos:* lectr, 89-92, ASST PROF PHYSIC, UNIV NC CHARLOTTE, 92- *Personal Data:* b Ankara, Turkey, Nov 24, 55;US citizen; m 86, Rebecca Wallace; c Chloe A. *Educ:* Middle East Tech Univ, Ankara, BS, Hons, 80; Univ Mo, Columbia, PhD(physics), 87. *Prof Exp:* Vis asst prof physics, Kans State Univ, 87-89. *Mem:* Am Phys Soc; Am Inst Physics. *Res:* Develop theories and conduct numerical investigations in free electron lasers with longitudal electric wiggler. *Mailing Add:* Dept Physics Univ NC Charlotte NC 28223. *Fax:* 704-547-4888; *E-Mail:* aktas@uncc.edu

AKTIK, CETIN, III-V COMPOUND SEMICONDUCTORS FABRICATION, VLSI CIRCUIT FABRICATION. *Current Pos:* Attach EO1 Recherche Microelectronics, 89-92, asst prof, 92-94, ASSOC PROF, UNIV SHERBROOKE, 94- *Personal Data:* b Erzincan, Turkey, Nov 14, 53; Can citizen; m 84. *Educ:* Inst Nat Sci Appl, Toulouse, France, BS, 77; Univ Paul Sabatier, Toulouse France, DEA, 78, DIng, 80. *Prof Exp:* Res assoc solid state physics, Ecole Polytechnique Montreal, 80-84; prof engr, Organometallic Vapor Phase Epitaxy Inc, Montreal, 85-88. *Concurrent Pos:* Vpres, Digiser Ltee, 88- *Mem:* Am Phys Soc. *Res:* Compound semiconductor technology and fabrication; solid state device physics; electronic transport properties of semiconductors; microelectronics; crystal growth by metal-organic chemical vapor deposition; deep level transient spectroscopy; infrared spectroscopy; very-large-scale integration circuit fabrication; ion implantation and vacuum techniques. *Mailing Add:* Dept Genie Elec Univ Sherbrooke Sherbrooke PQ J1K 2R1 Can. *Fax:* 819-821-7784

AKTIPIS, STELIOS, BIOCHEMISTRY, BIOPHYSICS. *Current Pos:* from asst prof to assoc prof, 66-74, PROF BIOCHEM, STRITCH SCH MED, LOYOLA UNIV CHICAGO, 74-, ASST CHMN DEPT, 70- *Personal Data:* b Athens, Greece, July 14, 35; US citizen; m 65; c 2. *Educ:* Nat Univ Athens, dipl, 59; Brown Univ, ScM, 62; Brandeis Univ, PhD(phys org chem), 65. *Prof Exp:* Res fel biochem, Harvard Med Sch, 65-66. *Mem:* AAAS; Am Soc Biol Chemists; Am Chem Soc. *Res:* Circular dichroism of macromolecules; interaction of nucleic acids with intercalating molecules; inhibition of RNA polymerase by template inactivators. *Mailing Add:* 134 Green Leaf Dr Hinsdale IL 60521

AL-AASM, IHSAN, CARBONATE GEOCHEMISTRY, LOW TEMPERATURE GEOCHEMISTRY & STABLE ISOTOPES. *Current Pos:* asst prof, 88-94, ASSOC PROF, DEPT EARTH SCI, UNIV WINDSOR, 94- *Personal Data:* b Baghdad, 1953; Can citizen; m 78, Loola; c Ali, Namir & Nadia. *Educ:* Univ Baghdad, BSc, 74, MSc, 77; Ottawa Univ,PhD(geol), 85. *Honors & Awards:* J H Remick Gold Award, Geol Asn Can, 95 & 96. *Prof Exp:* Lectr, Al-Mustanibyriah Univ, 77-78; geologist, Geol Surv Iraq, 78-80; postdoctoral fel, Univ Ottawa, 84-86, asst prof, 86-88. *Concurrent Pos:* Vis prof, Uppsala Univ, 92 & 94; assoc ed, Soc Sedimentary Geol, 96- *Mem:* Soc Sedimentary Geol; Am Asn Petrol Geologists; Geol Asn Can. *Res:* Diagenetic studies of carbonates and siliciclaptic sediments; chemical and environmental studies of lake water and sediments. *Mailing Add:* Dept Earth Sci Univ Windsor Windsor ON N9B 3P4 Can. *Fax:* 519-973-7081; *E-Mail:* alaasm@uwindsor.ca

ALADJEM, FREDERICK, IMMUNOCHEMISTRY, BIOPHYSICS. *Current Pos:* from instr to assoc prof, 56-65, PROF MOLECULAR MICROBIOL & IMMUNOL, SCH MED, UNIV SOUTHERN CALIF, 65- *Personal Data:* b Vienna, Austria, Feb 8, 21; nat US; m 57, Padma Ayengar; c David, Eva & Daniel. *Educ:* Univ Calif, AB, 44, PhD(biophys), 54. *Honors*

& *Awards:* Cancer Develop Awards, NIH. *Prof Exp:* Physicist, Radiation Lab, Univ Calif, 50-54; physicist, Nat Microbiol Inst, USPHS fel & res fel div chem, Calif Inst Technol, 54-57. *Concurrent Pos:* Consult path, Los Angeles Co Gen Hosp, 57-; fel Award, Nat Acad Sci. *Mem:* AAAS; Am Asn Immunol; Am Soc Microbiol; Biophys Soc. *Res:* Antigen-antibody reaction; immunochemistry of lipoproteins; chemical aspects of allergic reactions. *Mailing Add:* Molecular Microbiol & Immunol, EDM 100A Univ Southern Calif Sch Med 2025 Zonal Ave Los Angeles CA 90033

ALAGAR, VANGALUR S, THEORY, COMPUTER SCIENCE. *Current Pos:* from asst prof to assoc prof, 75-87, PROF COMPUT SCI, CONCORDIA UNIV, MONTREAL, 87- *Personal Data:* b Srivilliputtur, Tamil Nadu, India, Mar 15, 40; Can citizen; m 62; c 2. *Educ:* Madras Univ, BA, 59, MSc, 61; State Univ NY, Stony Brook, MA, 71; McGill Univ, PhD(comput sci), 75. *Prof Exp:* Lectr comput sci, McGill Univ, 74-75. *Concurrent Pos:* Lectr math, Vivekananda Col, Madras Univ, 62-70 & Annamalai Univ, India, 61-62; vis scientist, Vikram Sarabhai Space Ctr, Indian Space Res Orgn, Trivandrum, India, 86. *Mem:* Asn Comput Mach; Inst Elec & Electronic Engrs. *Res:* Investigation of formal models for the specification and proof of correctness for the functional behavior of real time distributed systems; formal specification methods for capturing geometric, physical and functional properties of objects to be manipulated in robotic and CAD systems; study on pure applicative real time language also useful for distributed computing. *Mailing Add:* Dept Comput Sci Concordia Univ 1455 DeMaisonneuve Blvd W Montreal PQ H3G 1M8 Can

ALAIMO, ROBERT J, ORGANIC CHEMISTRY. *Current Pos:* MGR, HEALTH SAFETY & ENVIRON QUAL, PROCTER & GAMBLE PHARMACEUT, 89- *Personal Data:* b Rochester, NY, Mar 2, 40; m 63; c 3. *Educ:* Univ Miami, BS, 61; Cornell Univ, PhD(org chem), 65. *Prof Exp:* Sr res chemist, Norwich Pharmacal Co, 65-79, unit leader, 79-83, mgr, tech opers, Norwich-Eaton Pharmaceut, 83-89. *Concurrent Pos:* Chmn, Div Chem Health & Safety, Am Chem Soc, 90, Am Chem Soc Comt, chem safety, 93- *Mem:* Am Chem Soc; Chem Soc; Nat Safety Coun. *Res:* Synthetic organic chemistry involving the synthesis of medicinal agents. *Mailing Add:* 29 Hillview Dr Norwich NY 13815-1006

AL-AISH, MATTI, diagnostic imaging research, for more information see previous edition

ALAM, ABU SHAFIUL, PHARMACEUTICS. *Current Pos:* SECT HEAD PROD DEVELOP, AM CRIT CARE, 81- *Personal Data:* b June 1, 45; US citizen. *Educ:* Philadelphia Col Pharm & Sci, BS, 67; Univ Iowa, MS, 69, PhD(pharm), 71. *Prof Exp:* Scientist pharm res develop, Rohm & Haas, 71-77; mgr pharm res & develop, Adria Labs Inc, 77-81. *Mem:* Acad Pharmaceut Sci; Am Pharmaceut Asn. *Res:* Develop pharmaceutical products which exhibit optimum stability and formula; process conditions and bioavailability; anti-cancer research, psychotropic; cardiovascular; analgesic and anti-inflammatory areas. *Mailing Add:* 1471 Littlefield Ct Lake Forest IL 60045

ALAM, BASSIMA SALEH, nutritional biochemistry; deceased, see previous edition for last biography

ALAM, JAWED, TRANSCRIPTIONAL REGULATION, INFLAMMATION & ACUTE PHASE RESPONSE. *Current Pos:* STAFF SCIENTIST MOLECULAR GENETICS, ALTON OCHSNER MED FOUND, 89- *Personal Data:* b Patna, India, Oct 16, 55; m 87. *Educ:* Clemson Univ, BS, 78; Purdue Univ, PhD(biochem), 83. *Prof Exp:* Postdoctoral fel genetics, NC State Univ, 84-86 & biochem & molecular biol, La State Univ Med Ctr, 87-89. *Concurrent Pos:* Adj asst prof, La State Univ Med Ctr, 90- *Mem:* Am Soc Biochem & Molecular Biol; Am Soc Microbiol; AAAS. *Res:* Role of hemopexin in heme transport to liver cells and iron conservation; heme-dependent regulation of gene transcription; regulation of the expression of acute phase proteins by inflammatory cytokines. *Mailing Add:* Dept Molecular Genetics Alton Ochsner Med Found 1516 Jefferson Hwy New Orleans LA 70121-2484

ALAM, M KHAIRUL, MATERIAL SYNTHESIS, MATERIAL PROCESSING & ENGINEERING. *Current Pos:* From asst prof to assoc prof, 83-93, PROF MECH ENG, OHIO UNIV, 93- *Personal Data:* US citizen. *Educ:* Indian Inst Technol, Kanpur, BTech, 78; Calif Inst Technol, MS, 79, PhD(mech eng), 84. *Honors & Awards:* Cert of Recog, NASA, 84. *Concurrent Pos:* Vis scientist, USAF. *Mem:* Am Soc Mech Engrs; Am Asn Aerosol Res; Am Asn Combustion Synthesis; Metall Soc. *Res:* Transport processes; materials processing; solidification processing; CVD and modified CVD processes; aerosol science and technology; combustion and air pollution; synthesis of powders and ceramics. *Mailing Add:* Ohio Univ 253 Stocker Ctr Athens OH 45701-2979

ALAM, MAKTOOB, MARINE NATURAL PRODUCTS, MARINE BIOLOGY. *Current Pos:* asst prof med chem, 77-82, ASSOC PROF CHEM, UNIV HOUSTON, 82- *Personal Data:* b Allahabad, India, Nov 15, 42; m 73. *Educ:* Govt Col, Pakistan, BSc, 62; Univ Karachi, Pakistan, MSc, 64; Univ NH, PhD(biochem), 72. *Prof Exp:* Asst Biochemist, Nat Health Labs, Islamabad, Pakistan, 64-66; lectr chem, Islamia Col, Karachi, Pakistan, 66-68. *Mem:* Am Soc Pharmacol; Am Asn Col Pharm; Roy Soc Chem; Am Soc Pharmacog. *Res:* Marine natural products with pharmacological activities and marine biotoxins. *Mailing Add:* Col Pharm Univ Houston Houston TX 77204-0001. *Fax:* 713-743-1229; *E-Mail:* malam@jetson.un.edu

ALAM, MANSOOR, SYNTHESIS PROCESSING & CHARACTERIZATION OF MATERIALS, PLASMA & LASER ASSISTED DEPOSITION OF THIN FILMS. *Current Pos:* asst prof, 89-93, ASSOC PROF MAT ENG, NMEX INST MINING & TECHNOL, 93- *Personal Data:* b Karachi, Pakistan, Mar 9, 53; m, Talat; c Amir & Raheel. *Educ:* Karachi Univ, BS, 78; Pa State Univ, MS, 88, PhD(metall), 86. *Honors & Awards:* Jerry Silver Mem Award, Iron & Steel Soc, 86. *Prof Exp:* Fel, Dept Mat Sci, Pa State Univ, 86, res assoc, Mat Res Lab, 87-89. *Mem:* Mat Res Soc. *Res:* Synthesis and evaluation of diamond coatings for high temperature and tribiological applications; kinetics of diamond-oxygen reaction; structural changes due to oxygen interaction; adhesion measurements; interfacial studies. *Mailing Add:* 1022 Rocky Rd Socorro NM 87801. *Fax:* 505-835-5626

ALAM, MOHAMMED ASHRAFUL, ANALYTICAL CHEMISTRY, PHYSICAL CHEMISTRY. *Current Pos:* assoc prof chem, 69-76, PROF PHYSICAL SCI & CHEM, ELIZABETH CITY STATE UNIV, 76- *Personal Data:* b Rajshahi, Bangladesh, Jan 1, 32; m 65; c 2. *Educ:* Rajshahi Govt Col, BSc, 51; Univ Dacca, MSc, 53; La State Univ, PhD(chem), 62. *Prof Exp:* Asst chemist, Jute Res Inst, Pakistan, 54-58; res assoc, Tulane Univ, 62; sr lectr phys chem, Univ Dacca, 64-65; assoc prof chem, Elizabeth City State Col, 65-68; reader phys chem, Islamabad Univ, 68-69. *Concurrent Pos:* NSF res fel, Univ Fla, 66 & 67. *Mem:* Am Chem Soc; Sigma Xi. *Res:* Physicochemical studies of proteins and enzymes; hydrogen bonding studies; metal ion interaction with nucleic acid and polynucleotides. *Mailing Add:* Elizabeth City State Univ Box 889 Elizabeth City NC 27909-4603

ALAM, MOHAMMED KHURSHID, WATER QUALITY & FISH HABITAT, LAKE RESTORATION & FISH POPULATION. *Current Pos:* BIOL SCIENTIST IV, FLA GAME & FRESHWATER FISH COMN, 93- *Personal Data:* b Lahore, Pakistan, Dec 3, 58; m 89, Karyn L Messner; c Zachary J. *Educ:* Govt Col, Lahore, BSc, 78; Univ Punjab, MSc, 80; Univ Wis-Madison, MS, 88; Univ Ariz, PhD(fisheries & wildlife sci), 91. *Prof Exp:* Lectr biol, Govt Col, Shakargarh, Pakistan, 82-85; sci officer, Pakistan Agr Res Coun, 85; res supvr, Food Agr Orgn, Islamabad, 90; res assoc, Univ Ariz, 91; resource mgr, Pyramid Lake Fisheries, Nev, 92-93. *Mem:* Am Fisheries Soc. *Res:* Effects of pollutants on water quality and aquatic resources and measures to restore quality aquatic habitat by the use of mathematical models and evolving lake restoration techniques. *Mailing Add:* Fla Game & Freshwater Fish Community 3900 Drane Field Rd Lakeland FL 33811-1299. *Fax:* 941-680-5594

ALAM, SYED QAMAR, LIPIDS BIOCHEMISTRY, DENTAL RESEARCH. *Current Pos:* from asst prof to assoc prof, 71-84, PROF BIOCHEM, LA STATE UNIV MED CTR, NEW ORLEANS, 84- *Personal Data:* b Jagrawan, India, June 22, 32; US citizen. *Educ:* Univ Punjab, WPakistan, BSc, 52; Univ Calif, Berkeley, MS, 61; Mass Inst Technol, PhD(nutrit biochem), 65. *Prof Exp:* Assoc prof nutrit, Fla A&M Univ, 65-67; res assoc nutrit & oral sci, Mass Inst Technol, 67-71. *Concurrent Pos:* Consult, UN Develop Prog, Pakistan, 81 & 96; dir salivary res group, Int Asn Dent Res & Am Asn Dent Res, 90-92. *Mem:* Int Asn Dent Res; Am Asn Dent Res; Am Oil Chemists Soc; Am Soc Biochem & Molecular Biol; NY Acad Sci; Am Soc Nutrit Sci. *Res:* Lipid biochemistry; nutrional effects on structure and function of oral tissues and fluids; membrane lipids and enzymes as influenced by nutritional modifications; carotenoids, retinoids and carcinogenesis; dietary lipids and eicosanoids. *Mailing Add:* Dept Biochem 1100 Florida Ave New Orleans LA 70119. *Fax:* 504-619-8775

ALAMPALLI, SREENIVAS, STRUCTURAL ENGINEERING, GEOTECHNICAL ENGINEERING. *Current Pos:* eng res specialist, 90-96, HEAD STRUCT RES, NY STATE DEPT TRANSP, 96- *Personal Data:* b Bangalore, India, May, 63; m 92, Sharada Devatha. *Educ:* SV Univ, India, BTech, 83; Indian Inst Technol, MTech, 85; Rensselaer Polytech Inst, PhD(civil eng), 90. *Prof Exp:* Asst exec engr, Irrig Dept, India, 86. *Concurrent Pos:* Consult, Alampalli Tech Servs, 90-, pres, 96-; adj prof, Union Col, NY, 95. *Mem:* Am Soc Civil Engrs; Am Soc Nondestructive Testing; Soc Exp Mech. *Res:* Bridge engineering, geotechnical engineering, dynamics, instrumentation and nondestructive testing; contributed more than 50 publications in technical journals, and national and international proceedings. *Mailing Add:* 1220 Washington Ave Bldg 7A Rm 600 Albany NY 12232-0869

ALARIE, YVES, PHYSIOLOGY. *Current Pos:* PROF TOXICOL, UNIV PITTSBURGH, 70- *Personal Data:* b Montreal, Que, Mar 18, 39; m 60; c 4. *Educ:* Univ Montreal, BS, 60, MS, 61, PhD(physiol), 63. *Honors & Awards:* F R Blood Award, 74 & 81. *Prof Exp:* Physiologist, Hazleton Labs, Inc, 63-70. *Concurrent Pos:* Nat Inst Environ Health Sci spec fel, 70. *Mem:* AAAS; Soc Toxicol; Am Bd Toxicol; Am Col Toxicol. *Res:* Respiratory physiology, effects of air pollutants on respiratory system; sensory irritation; chemoreceptors. *Mailing Add:* 1 Chestnut Rd Pittsburgh PA 15015

AL-ASKARI, SALAH, IMMUNOLOGY, UROLOGY. *Current Pos:* Instr, NY Univ, 58, univ fel transplantation immunol, 60, USPHS fel, 61, instr urol, 61-63, from asst prof to assoc prof, 63-70, PROF UROL, NY UNIV, 70- *Personal Data:* b Baghdad, Iraq, Nov 16, 27; m 56; c 2. *Educ:* Royal Col Med, Baghdad, MB, ChB, 51; NY Univ, MSc, 59. *Concurrent Pos:* Co-investr, res contract transplantation immunol, NY Health Res Coun, 61-64, career scientist award, 64- *Mem:* Harvey Soc; Soc Exp Biol & Med; Am Asn Immunol; Transplantation Soc; Am Urol Asn. *Res:* Ileal segments in genitourinary surgery; homograft rejection mechanism and transplantation antigens. *Mailing Add:* Dept Urol NY Univ Med Ctr 550 First Ave New York NY 10016

ALAUPOVIC, PETAR, BIOCHEMISTRY, ORGANIC CHEMISTRY. *Current Pos:* head, Lipoprotein Lab, 72-92, MEM CARDIOVASC SECT, OKLA MED RES FOUND, 60-, HEAD LIPOPROTEIN & ATHEROSCLEROSIS RES PROG, HEAD, LIPID & LIPOPROTEIN LAB, 92-; PROF RES BIOCHEM, SCH MED, UNIV OKLA, 60- *Personal Data:* b Prague, Czech, Aug 3, 23; m 47, Alexandra Vobanic; c Elizabeth. *Educ:* Univ Zagreb, ChemE, 48, PhD(chem), 56. *Hon Degrees:* DHC, Univ Lille, France, 87 & Univ Buenos Aires, Arg, 94. *Honors & Awards:* Spec Recognition Award, Am Heart Asn, 94. *Prof Exp:* Researcher, Pharmaceut Res Lab, Chem Corp, Prague, 48-49, Org lab, Inst Indust Res, Yugoslavia, 49-50; asst, Agr Fac, Univ Zagreb, 51-54 & Chem Inst Med Fac, 54-56; res biochemist, Univ Ill, 57-60. *Concurrent Pos:* NIH grants, 61-94; assoc ed, Lipids, 74-78; distinguished career scientist, Okla Med Res Found, 90. *Mem:* AAAS; Am Soc Biol Chemists; Am Chem Soc; Am Heart Asn; Am Oil Chem Soc; Arg Nat Acad Sci. *Res:* Chemistry of naturally occurring macromolecular lipid compounds such as serum and tissue lipoproteins and bacterial endotoxins; biochemistry of red cell membranes; isolation and characterization of tissue lipases. *Mailing Add:* Lipid & Lipoprotein Lab Okla Med Res Found Oklahoma City OK 73104. *Fax:* 405-271-8575; *E-Mail:* margo_french@omrf.uokhsc.edu

ALAVANJA, MICHAEL CHARLES ROBERT, EPIDEMIOLOGY, ENVIRONMENTAL HEALTH. *Current Pos:* SPEC ASST, NAT CANCER INST, 83-; ADJ PROF, EPIDEMIOL & BIOSTATIST, DEPT BIOL, GRAD SCH, HOOD COL, 90- *Personal Data:* b Brooklyn, NY, Sept 15, 48; m 70, Rosemarie Aspromonte; c Christian & Maria-Michelle. *Educ:* Brooklyn Col, BS, 70; Hunter Col, MS, 72; Columbia Univ, PhD(epidemiol), 77. *Honors & Awards:* Outstanding Serv Medal, USPHS, Commendation Medal. *Prof Exp:* From instr to assoc prof indust hyg & epidemiol, City Univ NY, 75-78; sr epidemiol, Nat Inst Occup Safety, 78-81; health sci admn, NIH, 81-83. *Concurrent Pos:* Mem, Comn Officers Asn, USPHS, Am Col Epidemiol. *Mem:* AAAS; Sigma Xi; Soc Epidemiol Res; Am Col Epidemiol. *Res:* Principal investigator environmental and occupational epidemiologic research projects concerning exposures to pesticides, industrial chemical and domestic radon. *Mailing Add:* Epidemiol & Biostat Prog Nat Cancer Inst Rm 418 6130 Exec Blvd Exec Plaza N Bethesda MD 20892. *E-Mail:* alavanjm@epndce.nci.nih.gov

ALAVI, MISBAHUDDIN ZAFAR, EXTRA CELLULAR MATRIX BIOLOGY, SCIENCE EDUCATION. *Current Pos:* asst prof pathobiol atherosclerosis, Dept Path, 85-91, ASSOC PROF PATHOBIOL OF ARTERIAL WALL & ATHEROSCLEROSIS, MCGILL UNIV, 91- *Personal Data:* b Hyderabad State, India, Feb 22, 46; Can citizen; m 77, Talat Alavi; c Kiran, Shahrukh & Farrukh. *Educ:* Univ Karachi, Pakistan, BSc, 67, BSc, 72, MSc, 73; Univ Heidelberg, Ger, dipl biol, 76 & Univ Ulm, ScD(human biol), 79; McGill Univ, dipl mgt appl, 95. *Honors & Awards:* Distinguished Leadership Award, Am Biog Inst, 93. *Prof Exp:* Sci asst, Dept Internal Med, Div Nutrit & Metab, Univ Med Clin, Ulm, Donau, Ger, 79-80; res fel, Ont Heart & Stroke Found, Dept Path, McMaster Univ, 80-82, asst prof arterial wall metab, 82-85. *Concurrent Pos:* Prin investr, Ont Heart & Stroke Found, 82-85; med res scholar, Can Heart Found, 85-90. *Mem:* Am Heart Asn; Am Asn Pathologists; Can Asn Univ Teachers; Can Atherosclerosis Soc; Europ Lipoprotein Club; Int Atherosclerosis Soc. *Res:* Exploration of factors like injury and dietary cholesterol which may act to bring about the changes in arterial wall leading to the clinical syndromes associated with atherosclerosis; interactions of matrix proteoglycan with plasma lipoproteins in health and disease; pathogenesis of atherosclerosis. *Mailing Add:* Dept Path McGill Univ Lyman Duff Med Sci Bldg 3775 University St Montreal PQ H3A 2B4 Can. *E-Mail:* alavi@pathology.lan.mcgill.ca

ALAVI, YOUSEF, MATHEMATICS. *Current Pos:* From asst prof to assoc prof, 58-68, PROF MATH, WESTERN MICH UNIV, 68- *Personal Data:* b 1929. *Educ:* Mich State Univ, BS, 53, MS, 55, PhD(math), 58. *Mem:* Am Math Soc; Sigma Xi; Math Asn Am. *Res:* Graph theory. *Mailing Add:* Dept Math & Statist Western Mich Univ Kalamazoo MI 49008-5152

AL-AWQATI, QAIS, PHYSIOLOGY, BIOPHYSICS. *Current Pos:* assoc prof, 77-84, PROF MED & PHYSIOL, COLUMBIA UNIV COL PHYSICIANS & SURGEONS, 84-, R F LOEB PROF, 88- *Personal Data:* b Baghdad, Iraq, Aug 18, 39. *Educ:* Univ Baghdad, Iraq, MB, ChB, 62; Am Bd Internal Med, cert, 72; Am Bd Nephrology, cert, 72. *Prof Exp:* Fel med, Johns Hopkins Med Sch, 67-70; fel med, Harvard Med Sch, Mass Gen Hosp, 70-71, instr, 71-73; asst prof med, Col Med, Univ Iowa, 73-77. *Concurrent Pos:* NIH res award, 76- *Mem:* Soc Gen Physiologists; Am Soc Clin Invest; Am Physiol Soc; Am Fedn Clin Res; Am Soc Nephrology; Am Asn Physicians. *Res:* Mechanisms of water and ion transport across biological membranes; particularly the energetics of active transport. *Mailing Add:* Dept Med Columbia Univ 630 W 168th St New York NY 10032-3702

ALAYASH, ABDU I, HEMOGLOBIN CHEMISTRY. *Current Pos:* SCIENTIST, CTR BIOLOGICS EVAL RES, FOOD & DRUG ADMIN, 89- *Personal Data:* b Baghdad, Iraq, 1948. *Educ:* Baghdad Univ, BS, 73; Essex Univ, UK, PhD(biochem), 78. *Prof Exp:* Scientist, Marine Biomed Ctr, Duke Univ, 87-89. *Mem:* Biophys Soc; Oxygen Soc. *Res:* Blood substitutes. *Mailing Add:* Cell Hemat 29-B10 Food & Drug Admin 8800 Rockville Pike Bethesda MD 20892

ALBACH, RICHARD ALLEN, CELL PHYSIOLOGY, MICROBIOLOGY. *Personal Data:* b Chicago, Ill, Mar 3, 31; m 53, Jane Boewe; c 7. *Educ:* Univ Ill, BS, 56, MS, 58; Northwestern Univ, PhD(microbiol), 63. *Honors & Awards:* Bd Trustees Res Award, Chicago Med Sch, 68. *Prof Exp:* Res assoc microbiol, Lutheran Gen Hosp, 63-67; assoc, Inst Med Res, Chicago Med Sch, 67-68, from asst prof to assoc prof, 68-73, vchmn dept, 74-82, actg chmn, 82-83, PROF MICROBIOL, CHICAGO MED SCH, 73- *Concurrent Pos:* Co-prin investr, Nat Inst Allergy & Infectious Dis grant, 65-68 & 68-73, prin investr, 74-78; vis prof, St Georges Univ Sch Med, Grenada, WI. *Mem:* Am Soc Microbiol; Soc Protozool; Soc Parasitologists; fel Am Acad Microbiol. *Res:* Aspects of DNA and RNA metabolism; nutritional requirements; metabolism of entamoeba histolytica. *Mailing Add:* Dept Microbiol/Immunol Univ Health Sci Chicago Med 3333 Green Bay Rd North Chicago IL 60064

ALBACH, ROGER FRED, ENVIRONMENTAL & FOOD CHEMISTRY. *Current Pos:* RES CHEMIST, SUBTROP AGR RES LAB, AGR RES SERV, USDA, 63- *Personal Data:* b Chicago, Ill, Mar 25, 32; m 57; c 3. *Educ:* Fresno State Col, BS, 57; Univ Calif, Davis, MS, 60, PhD(chem), 64. *Prof Exp:* Lab technician chem, Fresno State Col, 57. *Mem:* Am Chem Soc; AAAS; Sigma Xi; Am Soc Hort Sci; Phytochem Soc NAm; Int Soc Chem Ecol. *Res:* Phytochemistry; natural products; food chemistry; groundwater pollution. *Mailing Add:* 1105 Valley View Dr Weslaco TX 78596-5615

ALBANESE, ANTHONY AUGUST, biochemistry; deceased, see previous edition for last biography

ALBANO, ALFONSO M, NONLINEAR DYNAMICS CHAOS, STATISTICAL PHYSICS. *Current Pos:* lectr physics, 70-71, from asst prof to prof, 71-85, MARION REILLY PROF PHYSICS, BRYN MAWR COL, 85- *Personal Data:* b Laoag, Ilocos Norte, Philippines, Aug 2, 39; US citizen; m 67, Concepcion San Jose; c Mary T & Sarah E. *Educ:* Univ Philippines, BS, 59; Univ Iowa, MS, 64; State Univ NY, Stony Brook, PhD(physics), 69. *Prof Exp:* Asst instr physics, Univ Philippines, 60-62; instr physics, State Univ NY, Stony Brook, 69-70. *Concurrent Pos:* Vis physicist, Lorentz Inst, Univ Leiden, Neth, 74-75 & 78-79; Sloan vis fel, Dept Civil Eng, Princeton Univ, 85, 87, 88 & 89; consult, UN Develop Prog, 88; fac, Naval Air Develop Ctr, Navy-Am Soc Elec Eng prog, 89 & 90; mem, cognitive & functional neuroscience comt, NIMH, 91-95; Nat Reviewers Reserve, NIH, 95-99. *Mem:* Am Phys Soc; Am Asn Physics Teachers; Sigma Xi; Philippine-Am Acad Sci & Eng (pres, 88). *Res:* Nonlinear dynamics and chaos; nonlinear dynamical characterization of electrophysiological signals. *Mailing Add:* Dept Physics Bryn Mawr Col Bryn Mawr PA 19010. *E-Mail:* aalbano@brynmawr.edu

ALBANO, MARIANITA MADAMBA, MICROBIOLOGY. *Current Pos:* MEM FAC BIOL & MICROBIOL, UNIV MD, EASTERN SHORE, 73- *Personal Data:* b Dingras, Ilocos Norte, Philippines, Nov 15, 41. *Educ:* Univ Philippines, BSc, 64; Ohio State Univ, MSc, 69, PhD(med mycol), 77. *Prof Exp:* Cur asst, algal herbarium, Univ Philippines, 64-65, instr bot, 65-66. *Mem:* Sigma Xi; Am Soc Microbiologists; Med Mycol Soc. *Res:* Evaluation of antimicrobial properties of extracts from Ganyaulax monilata; effects of microwaves on aflatoxin production and growth of Aspergillus flavus on corn. *Mailing Add:* Dept Natural Sci Univ Md Eastern Shore Princess Anne MD 21853-1299

ALBATS, PAUL, COSMIC RAY PHYSICS. *Current Pos:* MEM STAFF, SCHLUMBERGER-DOLL RES CTR, 77- *Personal Data:* b Latvia, Dec 31, 41; US citizen; m 69; c 2. *Educ:* Univ Chicago, BS, 64; Cornell Univ, PhD(physics), 71. *Prof Exp:* From res assoc to sr res assoc physics, 69-73, asst prof physics, Case Western Reserve Univ, 74-76. *Mem:* Am Phys Soc; Sigma Xi. *Res:* Experimental high energy astrophysics gamma ray astronomy; experiments to measure atmospheric high energy neutron flux; experimental search for solar neutrons. *Mailing Add:* 141 Seth Low Mountain Rd Ridgefield CT 06877

ALBAUGH, A HENRY, MATHEMATICS, STATISTICS. *Current Pos:* CONSULT, 84- *Personal Data:* b Chicago, Ill, Aug 21, 22; m 50, Dora Cash; c Kathy, Laurie, Kevin, Kerry & Shena. *Educ:* Mich State Univ, BS, 48; Univ Mich, MA, 50. *Prof Exp:* Teacher high schs, Mich, 52-57; from asst prof to assoc prof math, Hillsdale Col, 57-84, head dept, 57-84. *Mem:* Nat Coun Teachers Math. *Res:* Educational games; thermocycling. *Mailing Add:* 26 N Norwood Hillsdale MI 49242-1511

ALBAUGH, FRED WILLIAM, NUCLEAR ENGINEERING, TECHNICAL MANAGEMENT. *Current Pos:* RETIRED. *Personal Data:* b Albia, Iowa, Apr 13, 17; m 50, Edrey Smith; c Jeffrey S, James F & Jean (McKnight). *Educ:* Univ Calif, Los Angeles, BA, 35; Univ Mich, MA, 38, PhD(chem), 42. *Prof Exp:* Res engr, Union Oil Co, Calif, 41-43 & 45-47, Manhattan Proj, Univ Chicago, 43-45; mgr res & develop, Gen Elec Co, 47-65; mgr res & develop & lab dir, Northwest Lab, Battelle Mem Inst, 65-71, corp tech dir, 71-76; chmn, Utility Adv Bd, Richland, Wash, 77-87; consult, 76-88. *Concurrent Pos:* Dir, Hanford Plutonium Recycle Prog, 56-66. *Mem:* Nat Acad Eng; Am Chem Soc; AAAS; fel Am Nuclear Soc; Sigma Xi. *Res:* Nuclear energy; nuclear chemistry; petroleum production research. *Mailing Add:* 1986 Greenbrook Blvd Richland WA 99352

AL-BAZZAZ, FAIQ J, MEDICINE, PHYSIOLOGY. *Current Pos:* from asst prof to assoc prof med, 71-86, PROF PHYSIOL & BIOPHYSICS, COL MED, UNIV ILL, 93-; CHIEF RESPIRATORY & CRITICAL CARE SECT, VET ADMIN W SIDE MED CTR, 77- *Personal Data:* b Baghdad, Iraq, July 1, 39; m 90, Thuraia Amily; c Alexandra N, Michael B, Brian S & Samara E. *Educ:* Univ Baghdad, MBChB, 62. *Prof Exp:* Resident med, Univ Miss Med Ctr, 66-68 & Univ Minn, 68-69; clin & res fel, Mass Gen Hosp,

Harvard Univ, 69-71. *Mem:* Fel Am Col Chest Physicians; fel Am Col Physicians; Am Thoracic Soc; Am Physiol Soc; AAAS. *Res:* Ion and water transport by airways epithelia, especially the distal bronchioles; regulation of ion transport in respiratory epithelia. *Mailing Add:* Med Serv MP 111 Vet Admin WSide Med Ctr 820 S Damen Ave Chicago IL 60612. *Fax:* 312-455-5886

ALBEE, ARDEN LEROY, GEOLOGY, PLANETARY SCIENCE. *Current Pos:* from vis asst prof to assoc prof, 59-66, PROF GEOL, CALIF INST TECHNOL, 66-, DEAN GRAD STUDIES, 84- *Personal Data:* b Port Huron, Mich, May 28, 28; m 53, 78, Charleen H Ettenheim; c 8. *Educ:* Harvard Univ, BA, 50, MA, 51, PhD(geol), 57. *Honors & Awards:* NASA Medal for Except Sci Achievement, 76. *Prof Exp:* Geologist, US Geol Surv, 50-59; chief scientist, Jet Propulsion Lab, NASA, 78-84. *Concurrent Pos:* Consult, Los Angeles Dept Water & Power, 64-70, Corral Canyon nuclear plant site & Pac DC Intertie, Converse, Davis & Assocs, 64-73 & Fugro, 74-78; assoc ed, Bull Geol Soc Am, 70-, Am Mineralogist, 72-76, Proc 5th Lunar Sci Conf, J Geophys Res, 77-82, Ann Rev Earth & Space Sciences, 78-; NASA serv: chmn, Lunar Sci Rev Panel, 72-77, Mars Sci Working Group, 77-78 & Mars Sci Steering Group, 77-, mem, Lunar Planning Comt, 73-75, Terrestrial Bodies Sci Working Group, 76-77, Phys Sci Comt, 76-77, Mars '84 Sci Working Group, 77 & Space Sci Adv Comt, 78-81, leader, Mars Prog, 78-79, Solar System Explor Comt, 80-83 & Mgt Coun, 83-88, proj sci, Mars Observer Mission, 84-93; mem, Task Force Planetary & Lunar Explor, Nat Acad Sci, 84-86; mem, Mars Rover Sample Return Sci Working Group, 87-; mem, US-USSR Joint Working Group Solar Syst Explor, 87-; proj scientist, Mars Gloval Survr, 93-; grad record exam bd mem, 95-; TOEFL bd, 95- *Mem:* Geol Soc Am; Microbeam Anal Soc; Mineral Soc Am; Geochem Soc; Am Geophys Union. *Res:* Planetary science; metamorphic petrology; electron microprobe; lunar rock investigations. *Mailing Add:* Div Geol & Planetary Sci Calif Inst Technol Pasadena CA 91125. *E-Mail:* aalbee@cco.caltech.edu

ALBEE, HOWARD F, ECONOMICS, COAL. *Current Pos:* RETIRED. *Personal Data:* b Fruitland, Idaho, Feb 1, 15. *Educ:* Idaho State Univ, BA, 50. *Prof Exp:* Dist geologist, Coal Explor, 50-84. *Mem:* Sr fel Geol Soc Am. *Mailing Add:* 3940 W Brambling Lane Grand Junction CO 81506-5240

ALBEN, JAMES O, BIOCHEMISTRY. *Current Pos:* from asst prof to assoc prof, 62-73, PROF PHYSIOL CHEM, OHIO STATE UNIV, 73- *Personal Data:* b Seattle, Wash, July 13, 30; m 54; c 3. *Educ:* Reed Col, BA, 51; Univ Ore, MS, 57, PhD(biochem), 59. *Prof Exp:* USPHS res fel physiol chem, Sch Med, Johns Hopkins Univ, 59-62. *Concurrent Pos:* NIH grant, 64- *Mem:* Am Chem Soc; NY Acad Sci; Coblentz Soc; Brit Chem Soc; Am Soc Biol Chemists. *Res:* Molecular spectroscopy and structure of heme proteins; Fourier transform infrared interferometry; hemoglobin structure and function; oxygen binding and transport; physical inorganic biochemistry of metal proteins; mechanisms of metal-enzyme catalysis. *Mailing Add:* Dept Physiol Chem Ohio State Univ 1645 Neil Ave 457 Hamilton Hall Columbus OH 43210

ALBEN, KATHERINE TURNER, DRINKING WATER CHEMISTRY & TREATMENT PROCESSES, ADSORPTION PROCESSES & SURFACE CHEMISTRY. *Current Pos:* from res scientist I to res scientist II, 77-87, RES SCIENTIST III, NY STATE DEPT HEALTH, 88-; ASST PROF ENVIRON HEALTH & TOXICOL, STATE UNIV NY, ALBANY, 90- *Personal Data:* b Bridgeport, Conn, Apr 28, 47; m 71, Richard S; c Jonah M, Elissa M & Silas D. *Educ:* Mt Holyoke Col, BA, 69; Yale Univ, MPhil, 71, PhD(phys chem), 76. *Prof Exp:* Chemist, Wash State Dept Health, 76 & Dept Eng & Appl Sci, Yale Univ, 77. *Concurrent Pos:* Prin investr, Am Water Works Asn Res Found, 85-87 & 88-90, Hudson River Found, 86-87; trustee, Res Div, Am Water Works Asn, 90-93, vchair, 94, chair, 95 & 96. *Mem:* Am Chem Soc; Sigma Xi; Am Water Works Asn; Int Adsorption Soc. *Res:* Sources of drinking water contamination and effectiveness of treatment processes for purification; adsorption-desorption processes for transfer of chemicals between water and surfaces (disinfection byproducts, pesticides, polycyclic aromatic hydrocarbons). *Mailing Add:* NY State Dept Health Empire State Plaza PO Box 509 Albany NY 12201. *Fax:* 518-473-2895; *E-Mail:* alben@wadworth.org

ALBEN, RICHARD SAMUEL, SOLID STATE PHYSICS, THERMODYNAMICS. *Current Pos:* MGR, BUS INTERFACE PLANNING, 93- *Personal Data:* b Brooklyn, NY, July 12, 44; m 71, Katherine Turner; c Jonah, Elissa & Silas. *Educ:* Harvard Col, AB, 64; Harvard Univ, AM, 65, PhD(physics), 67. *Prof Exp:* Res assoc physics, NSF fel, Univ Osaka, 67-68; from asst prof to assoc prof eng, Yale Univ, 68-77; tech staff, Gen Elec Res Ctr, 77-79, mgr technol eval, 79-82, consult technol eval, 83-89, mgr electronics planning, 89-93. *Concurrent Pos:* Consult, IBM Watson Res Ctr, 73; vis scholar, US-France Exchange Scientists Prog-Ctr Nat Res Sci, Grenoble, 74; chmn prog comt, Conf Magnetism & Magnetic Mat, 76; mem, Gas Res Inst Res Coord Coun, 83-86, Indust Planning Coun, Carnegie Mellon Univ Eng Res Ctr, 88- *Mem:* Am Phys Soc; AAAS. *Res:* Magnetism in insulators, amorphous semiconductors, disordered alloys, optical properties, thermodynamic cycles, solar energy systems, energy technology evaluation, utility economics, computer-aided design. *Mailing Add:* Gen Elec Res Ctr PO Box 8KWD 283 Schenectady NY 12301. *E-Mail:* alben@crd.ge.com

ALBERDA, WILLIS JOHN, MATHEMATICAL STATISTICS. *Current Pos:* PROF MATH, DORDT COL, 64- *Personal Data:* b Bozeman, Mont, Feb 7, 36; c 2. *Educ:* Calvin Col, AB, 59; Mont State Univ, MS, 63, Nat Defense Educ Act fel & PhD(math statist), 64. *Mem:* Am Math Soc; Am Statist Asn; Math Asn Am; Am Sci Affil. *Res:* Central limit theorems in probabilistic models; design and analysis of sampling procedures and population models. *Mailing Add:* Dordt Col Fourth Ave NE Sioux Center IA 51250-1697

ALBERGOTTI, J(ESSE) CLIFTON, EXPERIMENTAL NUCLEAR PHYSICS. *Current Pos:* from asst prof to assoc prof, 64-80, PROF PHYSICS, UNIV SAN FRANCISCO, 80-, CHMN DEPT, 68- *Personal Data:* b Columbia, SC, Jan 4, 37. *Educ:* Wheaton Col, BS, 58; Univ NC, PhD(physics), 63. *Prof Exp:* Asst prof physics, Davidson Col, 62-64. *Mem:* Am Phys Soc; Am Asn Physics Teachers. *Mailing Add:* Dept Physics Univ San Francisco San Francisco CA 94117. *E-Mail:* albergotti@usfea.edu

ALBERS, EDWIN WOLF, PHYSICAL CHEMISTRY. *Current Pos:* PRES, CMP INC, 88- *Personal Data:* b Schenectady, NY, July 29, 30; m 57; c 3. *Educ:* Clarkson Univ, BS, 52; Rensselaer Polytech Inst, PhD(phys chem), 62. *Prof Exp:* Chemist, Houston Refinery, Shell Oil Co, 52-55; asst chem, Rensselaer Polytech Inst, 55-57 & 58-60, instr, 60-61, from res asst to res assoc, 61-65; phys chemist, Inst Gas Technol, Ill Inst Technol Res Inst Ctr, 65-67; sr res scientist, Davison Chem, Div W R Grace & Co, 67-69, supvr catalytic prep, Davison Chem Div, 69-82; Consult, Albers Assoc, MD, 85-88. *Concurrent Pos:* Adj prof chem, Anne Arundel Community Col, 78-81. *Mem:* Am Chem Soc; Am Phys Soc. *Res:* Adsorption; gas solid systems; low temperature physics and chemistry; chemical kinetics related to the upper atmosphere; interstellar space research; zeolite and zeolitic promoted catalysts for petroleum and petrochemical applications. *Mailing Add:* 596 Severna Rd Severna Park MD 21226-3435

ALBERS, FRANCIS C, materials science engineering, metallurgy & physical metallurgical engineering; deceased, see previous edition for last biography

ALBERS, H ELLIOTT, NEUROENDOCRINOLOGY, CIRCADIAN RHYTHMS. *Current Pos:* ASSOC PROF BIOL & PSYCHOL, GA STATE UNIV, 86- *Personal Data:* b Ames, Iowa, 1953. *Educ:* Univ Nebr, BS, 74; Tulane Univ, MS, 78, PhD(psychol), 79. *Prof Exp:* Res fel, Harvard Med Sch, 79-82. *Mem:* Soc Neurosci; Endocrine Soc. *Mailing Add:* Lab Neuroendocrinol Dept Biol & Psychol Ga State Univ Atlanta GA 30303-4010

ALBERS, HENRY, ASTRONOMY. *Current Pos:* RETIRED. *Personal Data:* b Andover, Mass, Nov 17, 25; m 50; c 3. *Educ:* Harvard Univ, AB, 50; Univ Minn, MA, 52; Case Inst Technol, PhD(astron), 56. *Prof Exp:* Asst prof math & astron, Butler Univ, 56-58; from asst prof to assoc prof, Vassar Col, 58-77, prof & chmn dept, 77-91. *Concurrent Pos:* Vis lectr, Macalester Col, 54-55; NSF sci fac fel, 66. *Mem:* Am Astron Soc; Sigma Xi; AAAS. *Res:* Objective prism spectroscopy; galactic structure; Magellanic Clouds. *Mailing Add:* 62 Prospect St Falmouth MA 02540-2714

ALBERS, JAMES ARTHUR, aerospace engineering, for more information see previous edition

ALBERS, JAMES RAY, THEORETICAL PHYSICS. *Current Pos:* assoc prof, 71-74, vprovost instruct & planning, 74-83, PROF, HUXLEY COL ENVIRON STUDIES, WESTERN WASH UNIV, 74-, ASSOC VPRES ACAD AFFAIRS, 83- *Personal Data:* b Tacoma, Wash, Sept 4, 34; m 61; c 2. *Educ:* Wash State Univ, BS, 56; George Washington Univ, MS, 58; Univ Wash, PhD(physics), 62. *Prof Exp:* Physicist, Nat Bur Standards, 57-58; lectr physics, Seattle Univ, 63-66, from asst prof to assoc prof, 66-71. *Mem:* AAAS; Am Phys Soc; Soc Comput Simulation; Sigma Xi. *Res:* Field theory as it pertains to the elementary particle mass spectrum; neutrinos and weak interactions; alternate energy resources; computer modeling. *Mailing Add:* 120 Sea Pines Rd Bellingham WA 98226

ALBERS, JOHN J, MICROBIOLOGY, IMMUNOLOGY. *Current Pos:* from res asst prof to res assoc prof med, Univ Wash, 71-82, assoc dir, Northwest Lipid Res Ctr, Div Metab, Endocrin & Nutrit, 82-89, RES PROF MED, DIV METAB, ENDOCRIN & NUTRIT, UNIV WASH, 82- *Personal Data:* b Alton, Ill, Oct 5, 41. *Educ:* Univ Ill, PhD(microbiol & immunol), 69. *Honors & Awards:* Irvine H Page Res Award Young Invest, Council Aterioslcerosis, Am Heart Asn, 80. *Prof Exp:* Lab Dir, Northwest Lipid Res Clin, Div Metab, Endocrin & Nutrit, Seattle, Wash, 71-81. *Concurrent Pos:* Estab investr, Am Heart Asn, 79-84; adj res prof path, Univ Wash, 85-; dir NW Lipid Res Labs, Div Metab, Endocrin & Nutrit, Univ Wash, Seattle, 90- *Mem:* Am Asn Immunologists; Am Chem Soc; AAAS; Sigma Xi; Am Oil Chemist Soc; Am Asn Clin Chem. *Res:* Lipoprotein structure; metabolism; pathophysiology. *Mailing Add:* Northwest Lipid Res Lab 2121 N 35th St Seattle WA 98103

ALBERS, PETER HEINZ, ENVIRONMENTAL CONTAMINANTS, WILDLIFE BIOLOGY. *Current Pos:* WILDLIFE RES BIOLOGIST ENVIRON CONTAMINANTS, DEPT INTERIOR, PATUXENT WILDLIFE RES CTR, 76- *Personal Data:* b Staten Island, NY, May 4, 43; m 72; c 2. *Educ:* Univ Mont, BS, 65; Univ Guelph, MS, 66; Univ Mich, Ann Arbor, PhD(wildlife mgt), 75. *Prof Exp:* Instr wildlife mgt, Sch Forestry, Univ Maine, Orono, 75. *Mem:* Wildlife Soc; Ecol Soc Am; Sigma Xi; Soc Environ Toxicol & Chem. *Res:* Effects of environmental contaminants on animal populations and individual animal function; petroleum; metals; acid deposition; conservation tillage; agricultural drainwater; pesticides. *Mailing Add:* DOI/USGS/Patuxent Wildlife Res Ctr Stickel Lab ECR 12011 Beech Forest Rd Laurel MD 20708-4041. *Fax:* 301-493-5675; *E-Mail:* pete_albers@ubs.gov

ALBERS, ROBERT CHARLES, SOLID STATE PHYSICS. *Current Pos:* Fel, 77, MEM STAFF, THEORET PHYSICS DIV, LOS ALAMOS NAT LAB, 77- *Personal Data:* b San Jose, Calif, Feb 11, 49; m 78; c 2. *Educ:* Univ Santa Clara, BS, 71; Cornell Univ, MS, 74, PhD(physics), 77. *Mem:* Am Phys Soc; AAAS. *Res:* Electronic band structure of solids; x-ray absorption in solids; multiple-scattering theory. *Mailing Add:* Los Alamos Nat Lab Group T-11 M/S B262 PO Box 1663 Los Alamos NM 87545. *Fax:* 505-665-3003; *E-Mail:* rca@lanl.gov

ALBERS, ROBERT EDWARD, CHEMICAL ENGINEERING. *Current Pos:* Engr nuclear reactor testing, Savannah River Plant, E I Du Pont de Nemours & Co Inc 53-54, shift supvr, 54-55, hydraul supvr, 55, control room supvr, 55-57, res engr, pigments dept, Res Div, 57-58, develop engr, 59-60, res engr, 60-65, from res engr to sr res engr, Textile Fibers Dept, 65-80, sr engr, eng dept, 81-84, CONSULT, E I DU PONT DE NEMOURS & CO INC, 84- *Personal Data:* b Orange, NJ, Apr 19, 31; m 56; c 4. *Educ:* Lehigh Univ, BS, 53. *Res:* Nuclear reactor engineering and operation; refractory metal extractive and process metallurgy; titanium and columbium metals compounds and minerals; powder metallurgy; process planning and economic analyses; synthetic fiber processing, nonwovens; melt fiber spinning; ceramic fiber spinning; melt crystalization; gas permeation. *Mailing Add:* 2840 Kennedy Rd Wilmington DE 19810

ALBERS, ROBERT WAYNE, NEUROCHEMISTRY. *Current Pos:* Biochemist, Lab Neuroanat Sci, NIH,54-61, head sect enzymes, 61- 77, chief sect enzymes, 77-87, SECT CHIEF NEUROCHEM, LAB NEUROCHEM, NIH, 87- *Personal Data:* b Hebron, Nebr, Aug 5, 28. *Educ:* Univ Nebr, BS, 50; Wash Univ, PhD(pharmacol), 54. *Concurrent Pos:* Prof lectr, George Washington Univ, 64-65; lectr neurochem, Found Adv Educ Sci, 70-80. *Mem:* Am Soc Biol Chem; Am Soc Neurochem; Int Soc Neurochem; Fedn Am Socs Exp Biol. *Res:* Biochemistry of the nervous system; molecular biology of cell membranes and membrane transport systems. *Mailing Add:* Lab Neurochem NINDS Bldg 36 Rm 4D 20 Bethesda MD 20892

ALBERS, WALTER ANTHONY, JR, RESEARCH ADMINISTRATION, SOLID STATE PHYSICS. *Current Pos:* RETIRED. *Personal Data:* b McKeesport, Pa, July 19, 30; m 52, Betty MacKinley; c Patricia, Kevin, Jodie, Gaylen & Kurt. *Educ:* Wayne State Univ, BS, 52, MS, 54, PhD(physics), 59. *Prof Exp:* Mem tech staff, Bell Tel Labs, 54-55; physicist, Res Labs, Bendix Corp, 55-57, sr physicist, 59-62; supvry physicist Res Labs, Gen Motors Corp, 62-73, head, Societal Anal Dept, 73-87, head, Operating Sci Dept, 87-92. *Concurrent Pos:* Pres, Albers Systs, Inc, 92- *Mem:* AAAS; Am Phys Soc; Sigma Xi. *Res:* Surface and chemical physics; optics; quantitative social sciences; marketing sciences; manufacturing sciences; decision sciences; systems analyses. *Mailing Add:* 2068 S Hammond Lake Dr West Bloomfield MI 48324. *E-Mail:* nmks12a@prodigy.com

ALBERSHEIM, PETER, PLANT BIOCHEMISTRY, COMPLEX CARBOHYDRATES SCIENCE. *Current Pos:* RES PROF BIOCHEM & DIR COMPLEX CARBOHYDRATE RES CTR, UNIV GA, 85- *Personal Data:* b New York, NY, Mar 30, 34; m 58; c 3. *Educ:* Cornell Univ, BS, 56; Calif Inst Technol, PhD(biochem), 59. *Honors & Awards:* Charles A Shull Award, Am Soc Plant Physiologists, 73; Ruth & Tracey Storer life sci lectr, Univ Calif, Davis, 77; Robert L Stearns Award, 79; Kenneth A Spencer Award, Am Chem Soc, 84. *Prof Exp:* Fel biochem, Calif Inst Technol, 59; NSF fel, Swiss Fed Inst Technol, 59-60; from instr to asst prof biol, Harvard Univ, 60-64; from assoc prof to prof biochem, Univ Colo, 64-85, prof molecular biol, 70-85. *Concurrent Pos:* Fac fel, Univ Colo, 70-71 & 75-76, fac res lectr, 80. *Mem:* AAAS; Am Chem Soc; Am Soc Plant Physiol; Am Soc Biol Chem; Am Phytopath Soc; Soc Complex Carbohydrates; Int Soc Plant Molecular Biol; Am Soc Microbiol. *Res:* Structure and function of biologically active complex carbohydrates; function and nature of plant cell walls; mechanisms underlying disease resistance in plants and virulence in pathogens; development of new methods for the structural analysis of complex carbohydrates. *Mailing Add:* Complex Carbohydrates Res Ctr Univ Ga 220 Riverbend Rd Athens GA 30602-4712. *Fax:* 706-542-4412

ALBERS-SCHONBERG, GEORG, CHEMISTRY, NATURAL PRODUCT CHEMISTRY. *Current Pos:* RETIRED. *Personal Data:* b Berlin, Ger, 1929. *Educ:* Fed Inst Technol, Switz, dipl, 55; Univ Zurich, PhD(chem), 59. *Honors & Awards:* Discover's Award, Pharmaceut Mfg Asn, 92. *Prof Exp:* Fel, Mass Inst Technol, 62-65; exec dir natural prod chem, Merck, 65-93. *Mem:* Am Chem Soc; NY Acad Sci. *Mailing Add:* 43 Scribner Ct Princeton NJ 08540-6764

ALBERT, ANTHONY HAROLD, PHARMACEUTICAL CHEMISTRY. *Current Pos:* group leader chem process develop, 84-89, MGR PROCESS ENG & DEVELOP, MORTON INT/DYNACHEM, 89- *Personal Data:* b Los Angeles, Calif, Nov 24, 40; m 69. *Educ:* Occidental Col, BA, 63; San Diego State Univ, MS, 65; Ariz State Univ, PhD(org chem), 71. *Prof Exp:* Res assoc med chem, Nucleic Acid Res Inst, ICN Pharmaceut, 69-71, res chemist, 71-73, head process res, Prod Develop, 73-76; instr, Saddleback Col, 76-77; prin res chem RIA, Diag Oper, Beckman Instrument, 77-79; chemist, Fluorochem Inc, 79-80; dir org synthesis & scale up, Morton Thiokol/ Dynachem, 80-83; dir process develop, Newport Pharmaceut, 83-84. *Mem:* Am Chem Soc. *Res:* Direct development of processes for photoresist intermediate preparation; design equipment and processes for photoresist productions. *Mailing Add:* 18241 Montana Circle Villa Park CA 92667-4185

ALBERT, ARTHUR EDWARD, MATHEMATICAL STATISTICS, APPLIED MATHEMATICS. *Current Pos:* RETIRED. *Personal Data:* b New York, NY, Nov 6, 35; m 59; c 3. *Educ:* Mass Inst Technol, BS, 56; Stanford Univ, MS, 57, PhD(math statist), 59. *Prof Exp:* NSF fel math & statist, Inst Math Sci, Stockholm, 59-60; asst prof, Columbia Univ, 60-61; res assoc elec eng, Mass Inst Technol, 61-62; sr scientist, Arcon Corp, 62-70; prof math, Boston Univ, 70-84. *Mem:* Inst Math Statist; Soc Indust & Appl Math. *Res:* Statistical decision theory; stochastic processes; time series analysis; pattern recognition; statistical estimation procedures; design of experiments. *Mailing Add:* Ellsworth Hill Rd Campton NH 03223

ALBERT, CHARLES JOSEPH, VACUUM TECHNOLOGY, METALLURGY. *Current Pos:* LAB MGR, ACI ALLOYS, 84- *Educ:* Univ Calif, Berkeley, BA; Tex A&M Univ, PhD(physics), 91. *Concurrent Pos:* Atmospheric scientist, Radian Corp, 91-93; air qual coordr, Environ Dept, City Austin, 93-95; partner, Zytek Commun Corp, 95-; pvt consult comput appln, 96-; free-lance writer scientific articles. *Mem:* AAAS. *Res:* Application of theoretical physics to vacuum technology and metallurgy, to atmospheric chemistry and the dynamics of urban airsheds, and to communication technology. *Mailing Add:* 10473 Anderson Rd San Jose CA 95127. *E-Mail:* albert@zytek.com

ALBERT, EUGENE, MATHEMATICS. *Current Pos:* RETIRED. *Personal Data:* b New York, NY, Jan 9, 30; m 60; c 1. *Educ:* Brooklyn Col, BA, 50, MA, 51; Univ Va, PhD(math), 61. *Prof Exp:* Instr math, Brooklyn Col, 53-56; engr, Gen Elec Corp, NY, 56-57; asst prof math, Union Col, NY, 57-58; instr, Univ Va, 58-61; John Wesley Young res instr, Dartmouth Col, 61-63; asst prof, Univ Calif, Davis, 63-67; assoc prof math, Calif State Univ, Long Beach, 67-92. *Concurrent Pos:* Ed, "Ideal-Mate Rev", 83- *Mem:* Math Asn Am. *Res:* Probability theory; Markov chains; chess problems. *Mailing Add:* 1740 Interlachen Rd No 39G Seal Beach CA 90740

ALBERT, HAROLD MARCUS, CARDIOVASCULAR SURGERY. *Current Pos:* clin instr, 49-56, from asst prof to assoc prof, 56-73, prof, 73-80, EMER PROF SURG, SCH MED, LA STATE UNIV, NEW ORLEANS, 80- *Personal Data:* b Russellville, Ala, Mar 5, 19; m 47; c 2. *Educ:* Univ Chicago & Tulane Univ, BS, 40; Tulane Univ, MD, 44. *Prof Exp:* Intern, Touro Infirmary, 44-45, resident surg, 45-47; sr fel, Ochsner Found, 47-48; sr surgeon, Huey P Long Mem Hosp, 48-49. *Concurrent Pos:* Preceptorship, Huey P Long Mem Hosp, 49-51; La Heart Asn fel, Northwestern Univ, 51-52; mem staff, Charleston Naval Hosp & Portsmouth Naval Hosp, 54-56; mem cardiovasc surg coun, Am Heart Asn; sr vis surgeon, Charity Hosp La, New Orleans; sr assoc, Touro Infirmary; active staff mem, Hotel Dieu, New Orleans, Methodist Hosp & West Jefferson Hosp, Marrero. *Mem:* Am Col Surg; Soc Vascular Surg; Am Col Chest Physicians; Am Soc Artificial Internal Organs; Am Col Cardiol. *Res:* Congenital and acquired heart disease; shock. *Mailing Add:* 4475 Westbank Expressway No 1 Marrero LA 70072-3138

ALBERT, HARRISON BERNARD, CHEMICAL INSTRUMENTATION, COMPUTER SCIENCES. *Current Pos:* MEM STAFF, BALL AEROSPACE SYST, 80- *Personal Data:* b Oakland, Calif, Dec 12, 36; m 59; c 4. *Educ:* Univ Calif, Berkeley, BS, 59; Univ Colo, Boulder, PhD(phys chem), 69. *Prof Exp:* Mem res staff, Thomas J Watson Res Ctr, Int Bus Mach Corp, NY, 69-70; res assoc, Univ Colo, Boulder, 74-77, asst prof chem, 70-80, sr res assoc, 77-80. *Concurrent Pos:* NSF fel, 63-66. *Mem:* AAAS; Am Chem Soc; Sigma Xi. *Res:* Analytical chemistry instrumentation and computing science; gas and high pressure liquid chromatography and disc gel chromatography data acquisition hardware; algorithms for storage, compression, deconvolutions, displays and removing noise and drift; innovative microcalorimeter configurations and electronics. *Mailing Add:* 2380 Hillsdale Way Boulder CO 80303-5624

ALBERT, HENRICK HORST, SITE-SPECIFIC RECOMBINATION IN PLANT TRANSFORMATION, PLANT GENETIC ENGINEERING. *Current Pos:* PLANT PHYSIOLOGIST, AGR RES SERV, USDA, 91- *Personal Data:* b Coburg, Ger, Jan 7, 48; US citizen; m 90, Kathleen Houtchens. *Educ:* Univ Wis-Madison, BA, 71; Univ Hawaii, Manoa, MS, 88, PhD(bot sci), 91. *Concurrent Pos:* Assoc fac Dept Plant Molecular Physiol, Univ Hawaii. *Res:* Use of cre-lox system in directing site-specific integration of transgenes in plant transformation; control of transgene expression. *Mailing Add:* 1604 Ruth Pl Honolulu HI 96816. *Fax:* 808-486-5020; *E-Mail:* halbert@harc-hspa.com

ALBERT, JERRY DAVID, BIOCHEMISTRY & ANALYTICAL CHEMISTRY, HYDROLOGY & WATER RESOURCES. *Current Pos:* CHEMIST, CITY SAN DIEGO, 88- *Personal Data:* b Milwaukee, Wis, June 6, 37; m 61, Judith Brown; c Jill & Jennifer. *Educ:* Occidental Col, BA, 59; Iowa State Univ, PhD(biochem), 64. *Prof Exp:* Sr scientist appl res labs, Aeronutronic Div, Philco-Ford Corp, 64-67; fel prebiotic chem, Salk Inst Biol Studies, 67-68; staff res assoc IV, Univ Hosp, San Diego County, 68-73; res biochemist, Mercy Hosp & Med Ctr, 73-88. *Concurrent Pos:* Instr Chem, San Diego Mesa Col. *Mem:* Am Chem Soc. *Res:* Analysis of water; instrumentation; quality control. *Mailing Add:* 11223 Cascada Wy San Diego CA 92124-2878. *Fax:* 619-668-3250

ALBERT, JOHN PAUL, PARTIAL DIFFERENTIAL EQUATIONS, NONLINEAR WAVES. *Current Pos:* ASSOC PROF MATH, UNIV OKLA, 84- *Personal Data:* b Pittsburgh, Pa, Sept, 17, 57; m 93. *Educ:* Univ Santa Clara, BS, 78; Univ Chicago, MS, 79, PhD(math), 84. *Concurrent Pos:* Res fel, Inst Math & Appln, Minn, 88-89. *Mem:* Am Math Soc; Sigma Xi. *Res:* Analysis of model equations describing the propogation of nonlinear waves. *Mailing Add:* 6309 Oak Grove Dr Norman OK 73071. *E-Mail:* jalbert@ou. edu

ALBERT, LUKE SAMUEL, PLANT PHYSIOLOGY. *Current Pos:* from asst prof to prof, 60-90, EMER PROF BOT, UNIV RI, 90- *Personal Data:* b Palmyra, Pa, Feb 19, 27; m 50; c 2. *Educ:* Lebanon Valley Col, BS, 50; Rutgers Univ, MS, 52, PhD(plant physiol), 58. *Prof Exp:* Res plant physiologist, Biol Res Lab, Ft Detrick, Md, 53-55; plant physiologist, Am Cyanamid Co, 58-60. *Mem:* AAAS; Am Soc Plant Physiol; Bot Soc Am. *Res:* Physiological ecology; boron physiology; growth and development; leaf morphogenesis. *Mailing Add:* 127 Little Rest Rd Kingston RI 02881

ALBERT, MARY ROBERTS FORBES (DAY), CYTOLOGY, NEUROCHEMISTRY. *Current Pos:* DIR, BIOL LABS, BOSTON COL, 75- *Personal Data:* b Manchester, NH, Mar 2, 26; m 55; c Ross & Eric. *Educ:* Univ NH, BS, 48; Bryn Mawr Col, MA, 50; Brown Univ, PhD, 55. *Prof Exp:* Asst cytol, Brown Univ, 51-55; res fel med, Mass Gen Hosp, 55-61; instr, Northeastern Univ, 61-62 & Wellesley Col, 63-64; asst prof biol sci, Newton Col Sacred Heart, 64-75. *Res:* Irradiation effects on mitosis in the rat and mouse; effects of tetrahydrocannabinol on the reproductive organs of male and female rats; cytological studies of mouse brain tumors and hippocampi. *Mailing Add:* 56 Chapin Rd Newton MA 02159

ALBERT, PAUL A(NDRE), PHYSICAL METALLURGY. *Current Pos:* PRES, ALBERT CONSULT INC. *Personal Data:* b Van Buren, Maine, Apr 14, 26; m 55, Jeanne T Kachmar; c John P, Madeleine (Graf), Peter A, Charles J, Anthony J, Angeline (Turcan), David A & Lawrence L. *Educ:* Univ Maine, BS, 49; NY Univ, MS, 54, ScD(metall), 56. *Prof Exp:* Res asst, Res Div, NY Univ, 50-55; from engr to supvr engrs, Res & Develop Ctr, Westinghouse Elec Corp, 55-64; mgr electrochem, Thomas J Watson Res Ctr, Int Bus Mach Corp, 64-66, mgr plated films, 66-67, mgr advan device processing, Components Div, 67-71, res staff mem, Inorg Mat Dept, Res Div, 71-81; consult, Magnetic Recording & Mat, 81. *Mem:* Inst Elec & Electronics Engrs; Am Soc Metals. *Res:* Magnetism; metallurgy of magnetic materials; high density magnetic recording systems with film media and transducers. *Mailing Add:* 10473 Anderson Rd San Jose CA 95127. *Fax:* 408-729-0277; *E-Mail:* paalber@aol.com

ALBERT, PAUL JOSEPH, SENSORY PHYSIOLOGY. *Current Pos:* from asst prof to assoc prof, 73-92, PROF BIOL, CONCORDIA UNIV, 92- *Personal Data:* b Edmundston, Can, Nov 11, 46. *Educ:* Univ NB, BSc, 68, PhD(biol), 72. *Prof Exp:* Fel, Univ Sask, 72-73. *Mem:* Can Soc Zool; Entom Soc Can. *Res:* Structure and physiology of insect sense organs. *Mailing Add:* Dept Biol Concordia Univ 1455 DeMaisonneuve Blvd W Montreal PQ H3G 1M8 Can

ALBERT, RICHARD DAVID, NUCLEAR PHYSICS. *Current Pos:* ASSOC PROF PHYSICS, UNIV PAC, 81- *Personal Data:* b Elmira, NY, Aug 9, 22; m 46; c 4. *Educ:* Univ Mich, BA, 43; Columbia Univ, AM, 46, PhD(physics), 51. *Prof Exp:* Asst, Columbia Univ, 46-49; sr scientist, Westinghouse Elec Corp, 49-51; res assoc, Knolls Atomic Power Lab, 51-55; sr physicist, Lawrence Radiation Lab, Univ Calif, 55-65, res physicist, Space Sci Lab, Univ Calif, 66-70; physicist, Terradynamics, Inc, 70-71; pres, X-ray Systs, Inc, 71-; pres, Digiray Corp, 81- *Concurrent Pos:* Consult, Space Sci Lab, Univ Calif, 70-; NASA grant; consult x-ray field instrumentation, govt & indust, 73- *Mem:* AAAS; Am Phys Soc. *Res:* Low energy nuclear physics research and instrumentation; x-ray spectroscopy intrumentation; inventor of reverse geometry x-ray scanning system for low dosage digital radiography and industrial inspection; twenty-one US Patents. *Mailing Add:* 317 Hartford Rd Danville CA 94526. *Fax:* 510-838-1986

ALBERT, RICHARD K, MEDICINE. *Current Pos:* from instr to assoc prof, 76-88, PROF, DEPT MED, SCH MED, UNIV WASH, 88-, SECT HEAD, PULMONARY & CRITICAL CARE MED, MED CTR, 90- *Personal Data:* b Los Angeles, Calif, Sept 30, 45; m 67; c 2. *Concurrent Pos:* Asst chief, Pulmonary & Critical Care Sect, Vet Admin Med Ctr, Seattle, Wash, 76-90, dir, Med Intensive Care Unit, 76-90, actg chief, 85-86; vis res prof, Unit Res Physio-Path Respiratoire, Nat Inst Health & Med Res, France, 84-85; prin investr grant, Vet Admin Merit Rev, 88-, Nat Heart, Lung & Blood Inst, 89-; ad hoc mem, Respiratory & Appl Physiol Study Sect, NIH, 90. *Mem:* Fel Am Col Physicians; fel Am Col Chest Physicians; Am Thoracic Soc; Am Fedn Clin Res; Int Union Against Tuberculosis; Am Physiol Soc; Am Heart Asn; Am Soc Clin Invest. *Mailing Add:* Dept Med Univ Wash Med Ctr Rm-12 Seattle WA 98195-0001

ALBERT, ROBERT LEE, METALLURGY, MATERIAL SCIENCE. *Current Pos:* ADV ENGR PROCESS DEVELOP, BETTIS ATOMIC POWER LAB, WESTINGHOUSE ELEC CORP, 68- *Personal Data:* b Pittsburgh, Pa, June 4, 46; m 74; c 2. *Educ:* Carnegie-Mellon Univ, BS, 68, MS, 71. *Prof Exp:* Researcher metall, NSF, 65. *Concurrent Pos:* Abstractor, Int Am Soc Metals. *Mem:* Am Soc Metals; Am Powder Metall Inst. *Res:* Process development in metal and ceramic systems; physical metallurgy, powder metallurgy. *Mailing Add:* Bettis Atomic Power Lab PO Box 79 West Mifflin PA 15122

ALBERT, ROY ERNEST, ENVIRONMENTAL MEDICINE. *Current Pos:* PROF & CHMN, DEPT ENVIRON HEALTH, UNIV CINCINNATI MED CTR, 85- *Personal Data:* b New York, NY, Jan 11, 24; m 45; c 4. *Educ:* Columbia Univ, AB, 43; NY Univ, MD, 46. *Prof Exp:* Med officer, NY Opers Off, AEC, 52-54, chief med br, Div Biol & Med, 54-56; asst prof med, Sch Med, George Washington Univ, 56-59; from assoc prof to prof environ med, Med Ctr, NY Univ, 66-85. *Concurrent Pos:* USPHS fel, 49-51. *Mem:* Radiation Res Soc; Soc Epidemiol Res; Am Asn Cancer Res. *Res:* Radiation and chemical carcinogenesis; aerosol deposition and clearance; cancer and environmental toxicants epidemiology. *Mailing Add:* Environ Health Univ Cincinnati Col Med 231 Bethesda Ave Cincinnati OH 45267-0001

ALBERT, THOMAS F, WILDLIFE RESEARCH, BIOLOGY. *Current Pos:* SR SCIENTIST, DEPT WILDLIFE MGT, 81- *Personal Data:* b Westchester, Pa, 1937. *Educ:* Pa State Univ, BS, 59; Univ Pa, VMD, 62; Georgetown Univ, PhD(biol), 72. *Prof Exp:* Assoc prof, Dept Vet Sci, Univ Md, 67-81. *Mem:* Sigma Xi; Am Vet Med Asn. *Mailing Add:* Dept Wildlife Mgt Box 69 Slope Borough Barrow AK 99723-0069

ALBERTE, RANDALL SHELDON, PLANT PHYSIOLOGY, BIOCHEMISTRY. *Current Pos:* asst prof, 77-80, ASSOC PROF BIOL, UNIV CHICAGO, 81- *Personal Data:* b Newark, NJ, June 7, 47. *Educ:* Gettysburg Col, BA, 69; Duke Univ, PhD(bot), 74. *Prof Exp:* Res assoc, 73-75, NSF energy-related fel biochem, Univ Calif, Los Angeles, 75-76, NIH fel biochem, 76-77. *Concurrent Pos:* Consult, NSF grant oceanog, Univ Wash, 77-81 & Encycl Britannica, 80-81; Andrew Mellon Found fel, 79-80. *Mem:* Am Soc Plant Physiologists; Soc Exp Biol; Bot Soc Am; AAAS; Am Inst Biol Sci. *Res:* Photobiology and adaptive physiology of photosynthesis; chloroplast development; organization of chlorophyll in vivo; membrane biochemistry; biochemistry and physiology of water stress and of the control of development and differentiation. *Mailing Add:* Off Naval Res Code 341BST 800 N Quincy St Arlington VA 22217. *Fax:* 703-696-1212

ALBERTI, PETER W R M, OTOLARYNGOLOGY. *Current Pos:* clin teacher, Univ Toronto, 67-68, from asst prof to assoc prof, 68-77, assoc prof prev med & biostatist, 77-80, prof occup & environ med, 78-92, chmn otolaryngol, 82-92, PROF OTOLARYNGOL, UNIV TORONTO, 77- *Personal Data:* b Aug 23, 34; m 61, Elizabeth Smith; c 3. *Educ:* Univ Durham, MB, BS, 57; Washington Univ, PhD(anat), 63; FRCS, 65; FRCS(C), 68. *Honors & Awards:* Wilde Medalist, Irish Otolaryngol Soc, 86; Joshi Medalist, Asn Otolaryngologists, India, 88; Gold Award, Int Fed Otolaryngol Soc, 97. *Prof Exp:* Demonstr anat, Med Sch, Univ Durham, 58-59, first asst otolaryngol, 64-67; instr anat, Emory Univ, 60-61. *Concurrent Pos:* Gen secy, Int Fedn Otolaryngol Res Lab Socs, 91-; pres, Corlas. *Mem:* AAAS; Can Otolaryngol Soc; Royal Soc Med; Am Acad Otolaryngol; hon mem Brazilian Otolaryngol Soc; hon mem Irish Otolaryngol Soc; hon mem Indian Otolaryngol Soc; hon mem SAfrican Otolaryngol Soc. *Res:* Anatomy of middle ear; teaching techniques; hearing testing; industrial deafness. *Mailing Add:* 7-229 EN 200 Elizabeth St Toronto ON M5G 2C4 Can

ALBERTINE, KURT H, ANATOMY, PHYSIOLOGY. *Current Pos:* assoc prof pediat, med, neurobiol & anat, 93-96, PROF PEDIAT, UNIV UTAH, 96-, ADJ PROF MED, NEUROBIOL & ANAT, 97- *Personal Data:* b Newark, NJ, Nov 29, 52. *Educ:* Lawrence Univ, BA, 75; Loyola Univ, Chicago, PhD(anat), 79. *Prof Exp:* Adj asst prof anat, Univ Calif, San Francisco, 82-83; asst prof, Univ SFla, 84-86; res asst prof path, Univ Pa, 86-87; from asst prof to assoc prof med & physiol, Jefferson Med Col, 90-93. *Concurrent Pos:* Vis scientist, Univ Calif, San Francisco, 86 & 90. *Mem:* AAAS; Am Asn Anatomists; Am Physiol Soc; NY Acad Sci; Electron Micros Soc Am; Sigma Xi; Am Thoracic Soc. *Res:* Structure and function of the pulmonary circulation and lymphatic system; pathophysiology of pulmonary edema; neutrophil activation. *Mailing Add:* Dept Pediat Univ Utah Health Sci Ctr 50 N Medical Dr Salt Lake City UT 84132-1001. *E-Mail:* kurt.albertine@hsc.utah.edu

ALBERTINI, DAVID FRED, CELL BIOLOGY, REPRODUCTIVE BIOLOGY. *Current Pos:* ASSOC PROF ANAT, TUFTS MED SCH, 84- *Personal Data:* b Hudson, Mass, Mar 19, 49; m 72; c 2. *Educ:* Marquette Univ, BS, 70; Univ Mass, Ms, 72; Harvard Univ, PhD(anat & cell biol), 75. *Prof Exp:* Res assoc biophysics, Univ Conn Health Ctr, 75-77; asst prof anat, Harvard Med Sch, 77-83. *Concurrent Pos:* Ctr Environ Mgt, Tufts Univ. *Mem:* Am Soc Cell Biol; Am Asn Anatomists; Soc Study Reproduction; NY Acad Sci. *Res:* Female fertility/infertility; evaluation of gamete/embryo viability; role of hormones in reproduction of mammals; assisted reproductive technologies; environmental effects on reproduction. *Mailing Add:* Dept Anat & Cell Biol Tufts Med Sch 136 Harrison Ave Boston MA 02111

ALBERTINI, RICHARD JOSEPH, MUTAGENESIS, IMMUNOGENETICS. *Current Pos:* from asst prof to assoc prof, 72-79, PROF MED, COL MED, UNIV VT, 79-, ADJ PROF MICROBIOL & MOLECULAR GENETICS, 80- *Personal Data:* b Racine, Wis, Mar 15, 35; m 57; c 4. *Educ:* Univ Wis-Madison, BS, 60, MD, 63, PhD(med genetics), 72. *Honors & Awards:* Alexander Hollaender Award, Environ Mutagen Soc, 90; St George Medal, Am Cancer Soc, 90. *Prof Exp:* Instr med, Univ Wis-Madison, 70-72. *Concurrent Pos:* Sci dir, Vt-NH Red Cross Blood Ctr, 83-; dir, Vt Regional Cancer Ctr, Genetics Lab, Univ Vt, 84- & Genetics Unit, Dept Med, 88-; pres, Vt Div, Am Cancer Soc, 88-90; mem, Environ Health Sci Rev Comt, NIH, 88-; ed-in-chief, Environ & Molecular Mutagenesis, 88-; vis prof, Oncol & Pediat, Univ Wis-Madison, 90-91. *Mem:* Environ Mutagen Soc (pres, 84-85); Am Asn Cancer Res; Am Asn Clin Oncol; Am Soc Human Genetics. *Res:* Nature and consequences of somatic cell gene mutations that arise spontaneously or as a result of mutagen/carcinogen exposure in humans; mutations that involve immunocompetent lymphocytes and their effects in vivo. *Mailing Add:* Med Hema Given Bldg Univ Vt Col Med Burlington VT 05405-0001

ALBERTS, ALFRED W, BIOCHEMISTRY OF LIPIDS. *Current Pos:* SR SCIENTIST BIOCHEM, MERCK SHARP & DOHME RES LABS, 75- *Personal Data:* b New York, NY, May 16, 31. *Mailing Add:* PO Box 354 Wyckoff NJ 07481

ALBERTS, ALLISON CHRISTINE, CONSERVATION BIOLOGY. *Current Pos:* Res fel, 91-92, assoc physiologist, 93-94, COMP PHYSIOLOGIST, ZOOL SOC SAN DIEGO, 95- *Personal Data:* b San Francisco, Calif, Oct 13, 60; m 92, Michael B Worley; c Connor B Worley. *Educ:* Univ Calif, Berkeley, BA, 82, San Diego, PhD(biol), 89. *Prof Exp:* Fel, Tex A&M Univ, 89-91. *Concurrent Pos:* Sci consult, San Diego Mult Species Conserv Prog, 90-; co-coordr, Lizard Adv Group, Am Zoo & Aquarium Asn, 93-; adj asst prof, Dept Biol, San Diego State Univ, 94- *Mem:* Am Zoo & Aquarium Asn; Am Soc Ichthyologists & Herpetologists; Animal Behav Soc; Sigma Xi; Soc Conserv Biol. *Res:* Development of conservation strategies for recovery of depleted lizard populations; studies on the effects of social environment on reproduction in reptiles; investigations of communication and social dominance in lizards and tortoises. *Mailing Add:* CRES San Diego Zoo PO Box 551 San Diego CA 92112

ALBERTS, ARNOLD A, ORGANIC CHEMISTRY. *Current Pos:* RETIRED. *Personal Data:* b Davis, SDak, May 28, 06; m 31; c 2. *Educ:* Univ SDak, AB, 28; Univ Okla, MS, 30; Ohio State Univ, PhD(org chem), 34. *Prof Exp:* Asst gen & org chem, Univ Okla, 28-30; asst Ohio State Univ, 30-31, asst gen chem, 31-34, instr chem, 35-36, res asst metall eng exp sta, 35-37, investr indust probs, 36-37; asst prof org & phys chem, Otterbein Col, 37; from instr to asst prof chem, Washington & Jefferson Col, 37-42; from asst prof to assoc prof, Purdue Univ, 43-52; res chemist, Western Co, 52-56; prof chem & head dept, Hastings Col, 56-76; vis prof chem, Sterling Col, Kans, 78-79. *Concurrent Pos:* Admin asst, Res Found, Purdue Univ, 46-49, supvr chem, Exten Ctr, 47-52. *Mem:* Am Chem Soc. *Res:* Corrosion and corrosion inhibitors. *Mailing Add:* 1629 George Washington Way Apt 319 Richland WA 99352-5716

ALBERTS, BRUCE MICHAEL, MOLECULAR BIOLOGY, CELL BIOLOGY. *Current Pos:* PRES, NAT ACAD SCI, WASHINGTON, DC, 93- *Personal Data:* b Chicago, Ill, Apr 14, 38; m 60; c 3. *Educ:* Harvard Univ, AB, 60, PhD(biophys), 65. *Honors & Awards:* Eli Lilly Award, Am Chem Soc, 72; US Steel Award, Nat Acad Sci, 75; Lifetime Res Prof Award, Am Cancer Soc, 80; Baxter Award, Am Asn Med Col, 92. *Prof Exp:* NSF res fel, 65-66; asst prof chem, Princeton Univ, 66-71, from assoc prof to prof biochem sci, 73-76; prof biochem & chmn dept, Univ Calif, San Francisco, 76-81, Am Cancer Soc res prof, 81-85, chmn dept, 85-90, prof biochem & biophys, 85-93. *Concurrent Pos:* Mem, Adv Panel Human Cell Biol, NSF, 74-76, bd sci counr, Div Arthritis & Metab Dis, NIH, 74-78, bd sci adv, Jane Coffin Childs Mem Fund Med Res, 78-85, Adv Coun Dept Biochem Sci & Molecular Biol, Princeton Univ, 79085, Molecular Cytol Study Sect, NIH, 82-86 & chmn, 84-86; mem, Corp Vis Comt, Dept Biol, Mass Inst Technol, 78-, vis comt, Dept Embryol, Carnegie Inst Wash, 83, sci adv bd, Markey Found, 84, chmn, Vis Comt, Dept Biochem & Molecular Biol, Harvard Col, 83-86; assoc ed, Ann Reviews Cell Biol, 84-93; counr, Am Soc Biol Chemists, 84-; chmn, Comt Mapping & Sequencing Human Genome, Nat Res Coun, 86-88. *Mem:* Nat Acad Sci; Am Chem Soc; Am Soc Biol Chem; fel Am Acad Arts & Sci; Am Soc Microbiol; Am Soc Cell Biol; Genetics Soc Am. *Res:* Molecular genetics; DNA replication; eukaryotic gene control; author of approximately 100 publications on biochemistry. *Mailing Add:* Nat Acad Sci 2101 Constitution Ave NW Washington DC 20418

ALBERTS, GENE S, ANALYTICAL CHEMISTRY. *Current Pos:* Staff chemist, Systs Develop Div, Int Bus Mach Corp, 63-66, res staff mem, T J Watson Res Lab, 66-67, develop chemist, Component Div, IBM Corp, 67-69, sr eng, 69-72, sr engr, Systs Prod Div, 72-77, sr engr-mgr, Advan Monolithic Technol, 77-81, mgr lab staff, Burlington Gen Technol Div, 81-86, SR TECH STAFF MEM, IBM CORP, 87- *Personal Data:* b Brookings, SDak, Sept 20, 37; m 59. *Educ:* Wash State Univ, BS, 59; Univ Wis, PhD(chem), 63. *Mem:* Sigma Xi. *Res:* Electroanalytical and electrokinetic chemistry; magnetic film deposition; semi conductor process engineering. *Mailing Add:* General Delivery PO Box 41 Indianola WA 98342-9999

ALBERTS, JAMES JOSEPH, GEOCHEMISTRY. *Current Pos:* DIR & SR RES SCIENTIST, UNIV GA MARINE INST, 84- *Personal Data:* b Chicago, Ill, May 23, 43. *Educ:* Cornell Col, Iowa, AB, 65; Dartmouth Col, NH, MS, 67; Fla State Univ, PhD(chem oceanog), 70. *Honors & Awards:* Sr US Scientist Award, Alexander Von Humboldt Found, 89. *Prof Exp:* Res assoc, Kans State Geol Surv, 70; res assoc, Univ Ga, 70-72, asst res prof, 72-74; asst chemist, Argonne Nat Lab, 74-77; assoc res ecologist, Savannah River Ecol Lab, 77-84. *Mem:* Am Soc Limnol & Oceanog; Estuarine Res Fedn; Geochem Soc; Int Humic Substances Soc; Int Asn Water Qual; Societas Internationalis Limonolgiae Theoreticae & Applicatae. *Res:* Mechanisms and processes by which inorganic elements, organic compounds, and radioisotopes interact and cycle in aquatic environments. *Mailing Add:* Marine Inst Univ Ga Sapelo Island GA 31327. *Fax:* 912-485-2133; *E-Mail:* jalberts@uga.cc.uga.edu

ALBERTS, RUSSELL, engineering & biomechanics, for more information see previous edition

ALBERTS, WALTER WATSON, NEUROSCIENCES, RESEARCH ADMINISTRATION. *Current Pos:* RETIRED. *Personal Data:* b Los Angeles, Calif, Dec 31, 29; m 59; c 2. *Educ:* Univ Calif, AB, 51, PhD(biophys), 56. *Prof Exp:* Res physiologist, Univ Calif Med Ctr, San Francisco, 55-56; biophysicist, Mt Zion Hosp & Med Ctr, 56-72; spec asst to assoc dir, Nat Inst Neurol & Commun Dis & Stroke, NIH, 73-74, head, Res Contracts Sect, 74-75, asst dir contract res progs, 75-77; admin dir, Smith-Kettlewell Inst & Dept Visual Sci, Univ Pac, 77-78; dep dir, Div Fundamental Neurosci, Nat Inst Neurol & Commun Dis & Stroke, NIH, 79-89, actg dep dir, Nat Inst Neurol Dis & Stroke, 89-90, dep dir, Div Fundamental Neurosci, 90-94. *Concurrent Pos:* Consult, Donner Lab, Univ Calif, Berkeley, 59-64; res career prog award, Nat Inst Neurol Dis & Blindness, NIH, 63-68; lectr, Dept Physiol, Univ Calif Med Ctr, San Francisco, 69; grant assoc, NIH, 72-73; sr scientist, Inst Med Sci, San Francisco, 77-78. *Mem:* Am Physiol Soc; fel AAAS; Biophys Soc; Soc Neurosci. *Res:* Neurophysiology; biological and medical physics, particularly the central nervous system of man. *Mailing Add:* 865 Galvin Dr El Cerrito CA 94530

ALBERTSON, CLARENCE E, FRICTION MATERIALS, WEAR-RESISTANT MATERIALS. *Current Pos:* RETIRED. *Personal Data:* b Rockwell, Tenn, Oct 7, 22; m 47; c 3. *Educ:* Miami Univ, Ohio, AB, 43; Univ Cincinnati, MS, 48, PhD(chem), 49. *Prof Exp:* Teaching fel chem, Purdue Univ, 49-50; phys chemist, Robertshaw Fulton Controls Co, Pa, 50-51; phys chemist, Borg Warner Corp, Ill, 51-66, mgr phys chem, 66-78, sr scientist, 78-86. *Concurrent Pos:* Indust res assoc hard coatings, Argonne Nat Lab, Ill, 86-87. *Mem:* Am Soc Lubrication Engrs; Am Electroplaters Soc; Am Chem Soc; Soc Automotive Engrs; Soc Advan Mat & Process Eng; Am Ceramic Soc. *Res:* Development of wet and dry clutch linings for automobiles and light trucks and electroplated, porous metal surfaces to augment boiling heat transfer; measurement of friction and wear of materials for use in industrial equipment. *Mailing Add:* 240 S Monterey Villa Park IL 60181-2711

ALBERTSON, HAROLD D, ENGINEERING, ROBOTICS. *Current Pos:* instr, Richland Col, 73-77, chmn div, 77-78, dean instrnl serv, 78-83, prof, 83-95, ADJ PROF PHYSICS, RICHLAND COL, 95- *Personal Data:* b Parsons, Kans, Dec 28, 31; m 53, Margaret Bodden; c Anne. *Educ:* Univ Houston, BS, 53; Southern Methodist Univ, MS, 60; Univ Tex, Austin, PhD(elec eng), 68. *Prof Exp:* Design engr, Chance Vought Aircraft, Inc, 53-58; design engr, Tex Instruments, Inc, 58-60, prog mgr, 60-63, syst analyst, 63-65 & 68-73. *Concurrent Pos:* Mem, Simulation Coun; past chmn, Metroplex Alliance Eng Educ; Nat Comn Future Community Cols. *Mem:* Inst Elec & Electronics Eng; Fluid Power Soc; Robotics Int; Soc Mfg Engrs. *Res:* Study of the modal properties of linear dynamical systems and the construction of irreducible (minimum state) realizations of fixed and time varying systems; application to the practical simulation of transfer function matrices; robotics and automated systems. *Mailing Add:* Dept Math & Sci Richland Col 12800 Abrams Rd Dallas TX 75243-2199. *E-Mail:* hda8460@dcccd.edu

ALBERTSON, JOHN NEWMAN, JR, LABORATORY MANAGEMENT, BIOMEDICAL ENGINEERING. *Current Pos:* RETIRED. *Personal Data:* b New Haven, Conn, Jan 18, 33; m 55, Mary A Healey; c Laura, Kurt, Paul, Nina, Derek & Luke. *Educ:* Univ Conn, AB, 54; Hahnemann Med Col, MS, 64; Am Bd Microbiol, dipl. *Prof Exp:* Comndg officer med dispensary, US Army, Munich, Ger, 56-57, asst chief, Dept Immunol & Serol, Med Lab, Landstuhl, Ger, 57-59, chief clin path & bacteriologist, Valley Forge Gen Hosp, Phoenixville, Pa, 59-62, res assoc, Hahnemann Med Col, 62-64, chief, Bact & Virol Div, First Med Lab, Ft George C Meade, Md, 64-68, chief, Med & Biol Sci Br, Off Chief Res & Develop, Hq Dept Army, Washington, DC, 68-70, exec for res, 70-71, comndg officer, 9th Med Lab, Repub Vietnam, 71-72, exec officer, Walter Reed Army Inst Res, Washington, DC, 72-74, exec officer, Armed Forces Inst Path, 75-76, chief of staff, US Army Res & Develop Command, 76-79, dir, US Army Med Bioeng Res & Develop Lab, Fort Detrick, Md, 79-84. *Concurrent Pos:* Consult, Europ Command & partic coop study on Treponemal pallidum immobilization & other tests, WHO, Ger, 57-59; mem, Nat Res Resources Coun, Washington, DC, 80-84. *Mem:* Fel AAAS; Am Soc Microbiol; fel Am Acad Microbiol; Sigma Xi. *Res:* Bioengineering (teleradiography/telencephalography); chemotherapy and bacteriology of tuberculosis; research management; biomechanics; microbial mining and metal recovery; microbiology. *Mailing Add:* PO Box 100 Harpers Ferry WV 25425-0100. *E-Mail:* jackalb@intrepid.net

ALBERTSON, MICHAEL OWEN, COMBINATORIAL MATHEMATICS. *Current Pos:* from asst prof to assoc prof math, Smith Col, 73-84, chmn dept, 85-88, chmn computer sci dept, 87-88, PROF MATH, SMITH COL, 84- *Personal Data:* b Philadelphia, Pa, June 24, 46; div; c Matthew, Nicholas & Elizabeth. *Educ:* Mich State Univ, BS, 66; Univ Pa, PhD(math), 71. *Prof Exp:* Asst prof math, Swarthmore Col, 72-73. *Concurrent Pos:* Prin investr, Cottrell grant, Res Corp, 74; co-prin investr, NSF grant, 77-79, 80, prin investr, 84-88; vis scholar, Doshisha Univ, Kyoto, 89; prin investr, Nat Sect Agr, 93- *Mem:* Am Math Soc; Soc Indust & Appl Math. *Res:* Independent sets in graphs; chromatic graph theory; topological graph theory; perfect graphs; duality theory; graph homomorphisms; graph symmetries and symmetry breaking. *Mailing Add:* Dept Math Smith Col Northampton MA 01063

ALBERTSON, NOEL FREDERICK, MEDICINAL CHEMISTRY. *Current Pos:* RETIRED. *Personal Data:* b New Haven, Conn, Oct 29, 15; m 42, Dorothy Miller; c Wayne, Elaine & Vance. *Educ:* Polytech Inst Brooklyn, BS 36, MS, 38; Ohio State Univ, PhD, 41. *Prof Exp:* Jr chemist, Merck & Co, 38-39; asst, Ohio State Univ, 39-41, res assoc & fel, Univ Res Found, 41-43; group leader, Winthrop Chem Co, 43-46; group leader, Sterling-Winthrop Res Inst, 46-64, sect head, 64-66, asst dir, Chem Div, 66-77, res scientist, 77-80. *Mem:* Am Chem Soc. *Res:* Molecular addition compounds of sulphur dioxide; production of sulphur from natural gas; synthesis of amino acids, peptides, piperidines and benzomorphans; awarded patents and contributed to publications. *Mailing Add:* 155 Ida Red Ave Sparta MI 49345-1715

ALBERTSON, VERNON D(UANE), ELECTRICAL ENGINEERING. *Current Pos:* from asst prof to assoc prof, 63-70, PROF ELEC ENG, UNIV MINN, MINNEAPOLIS, 70- *Personal Data:* b Syre, Minn, Sept 28, 28; m 51; c 5. *Educ:* NDak State Univ, BSEE, 50; Univ Minn, Minneapolis, MSEE, 56; Univ Wis, PhD(elec eng), 62. *Prof Exp:* Test engr, Gen Elec Co, NY, 50-51, field engr, Minn, 51-52; from instr to asst prof elec eng, NDak State Univ, 56-58; syst planning engr, Otter Tail Power Co, Minn, 58-59; instr elec eng, Univ Wis, 59-60, asst prof, 62-63. *Mem:* Am Soc Eng Educ; Inst Elec & Electronics Engrs. *Res:* Electric power system analysis and transients; power system planning; environmental effects of electric and magnetic fields; effects of geomagnetically-induced currents in power systems. *Mailing Add:* 4-178-Elec Eng & Comp Sci, Elec Eng Bldg Univ Minn 200 Union St SE Minneapolis MN 55455-0150

ALBERTY, ROBERT ARNOLD, PHYSICAL CHEMISTRY, THERMODYNAMICS OF BIOCHEMICAL REACTIONS. *Current Pos:* dean sch sci, 67-82, prof, 67-91, EMER PROF CHEM, MASS INST TECHNOL, 91- *Personal Data:* b Winfield, Kans, June 21, 21; m 44, Lillian Wind; c Nancy, Steven & Catherine. *Educ:* Univ Nebr, BS, 43, MS, 44; Univ Wis, PhD(phys chem), 47. *Hon Degrees:* DSc, Lawrence Col, Univ Nebr. *Honors & Awards:* Eli Lilly Award, 56. *Prof Exp:* Asst, Univ Wis-Madison, 44-46, from instr to prof phys chem, 47-62, assoc dean letters & sci, 62-63, dean grad sch, 63-67. *Concurrent Pos:* Guggenheim fel, Calif Inst Technol, 50-51; chmn, Comn Human Resources, Nat Res Coun, 74-77; coun mem, Am Acad Arts & Sci, 91-94. *Mem:* Inst Med-Nat Acad Sci; Am Acad Arts & Sci; AAAS; Am Chem Soc. *Res:* Thermodynamics and kinetics of complex systems; fundamental theory of thermodynamics; legendre transforms; use of computers in thermodynamics; textbook in physical chemistry. *Mailing Add:* 7 Old Dee Rd Cambridge MA 02138-4633. *Fax:* 617-253-7030; *E-Mail:* alberty@mit.edu

ALBICKI, ALEXANDER, LARGE SCALE INTEGRATION DESIGNS, DESIGN FOR TESTABILITY. *Current Pos:* from asst prof to assoc prof, 83-96, PROF ELEC ENG, UNIV ROCHESTER, 96- *Personal Data:* b Warsaw, Poland, May 24, 41; m 70; c 2. *Educ:* Tech Univ Warsaw, BS/MS, 64, PhD(telecommun), 73, Habilitation(elec), 80. *Prof Exp:* Design engr, Tech Univ Warsaw, 64-73, asst prof telecommun, 73-80. *Concurrent Pos:* Prin Investr, Ministry Telecommun, Poland, 73-80, Semiconductor Res Corp, 85-88 & NY State Sci & Technol Found, 86-87, NSF, 93-, Rochester Gas & Elec, 91-94; lectr, Nat Higher Sch Telecommun, Paris, 78; vis prof, Univ Rochester, 81-83. *Mem:* Sr men Inst Elec & Electronics Engrs. *Res:* Design for testability with emphasis on built-in-self-test; very-large scale integrated designs; developing protocols for computers communication. *Mailing Add:* Dept Elec Eng Univ Rochester Rochester NY 14627. *Fax:* 716-275-2073; *E-Mail:* albicki@ee.rochester.edu

ALBIN, ROBERT CUSTER, ANIMAL NUTRITION. *Current Pos:* From asst prof animal husb to prof animal sci, 64-80, PROF ANIMAL SCI & DEAN, COL AGR SCI, TEX TECH UNIV, 80- *Personal Data:* b Beaver City, Okla, May 19, 39; m 60; c 2. *Educ:* Tex Technol Col, BS, 61, MS, 62; Univ Nebr, PhD(animal nutrit), 65. *Mem:* Am Soc Animal Sci; Sigma Xi. *Res:* Ruminant nutrition; beef cattle nutrition and management. *Mailing Add:* 1803 Bangor Lubbock TX 79416-5518

ALBIN, SUSAN LEE, QUALITY ENGINEERING, STOCHASTIC MODELING. *Current Pos:* from asst prof to assoc prof, 81-94, PROF INDUST ENG & GRAD DIR RUTGERS NJ STATE UNIV, 94- *Personal Data:* b New York, NY, Sept 25, 50; m 79, Michael Juliar; c Anna & Noah. *Educ:* NY Univ, BS, 71, MS, 73; Columbia Univ, DSc(opers res), 81. *Prof Exp:* Res asst community health, Albert Einstein Col Med, 71-74, res assoc neurosci, 74-77; mem tech staff, Bell Labs, 77-81. *Concurrent Pos:* Prin investr, NSF, 82-84 & 91-92, Coun Solid Waste Solutions, 90-91; chair, Int Conf Queueing Networks, 87; assoc ed, Mgt Sci, 88-, IIE Trans, 92-; panel mem, NSF, 89, 90, 92, 95 & 96; vis prof, Tel Aviv Univ, 90; consult, Gen Cable Co, 90-91; Exxon Educ Found award, 93-94; coun mem, Opers Res Soc Am, 93- *Mem:* Inst Oper Res & Mgt Sci (secy, 96-97); Inst Indust Engrs; Am Soc Qual Control. *Res:* Quality engineering; stochastic modeling; semiconductor manufacturing; plastics recycling; aviation; telecommunications systems; public health and epidemiology. *Mailing Add:* Dept Indust Eng Rutgers Univ PO Box 909 Piscataway NJ 08855-0909. *Fax:* 732-932-5467; *E-Mail:* salbin@rci.rutgers.edu

ALBINAK, MARVIN JOSEPH, ENVIRONMENTAL SCIENCES. *Current Pos:* prof & chmn div sci & math, 68-77, dir spec projs, 77-79, PROF CHEM, ESSEX COMMUNITY COL, 79-, HEAD DEPT, 85- *Personal Data:* b Detroit, Mich, June 21, 28; m 61, Gloria Galamb; c Stephen, Anne & Alexandra. *Educ:* Univ Detroit, AB, 49, MS, 52; Wayne State Univ, PhD(inorg chem), 59. *Prof Exp:* Chemist explor res, Ethyl Corp, 52-54; from instr to asst prof chem, Univ Detroit, 54-61; sr res scientist, Elec Autolite, 61-62; res chemist, Owens-Ill Glass Co, 62-65; from asst prof to assoc prof chem, Wheeling Col, 65-68. *Mem:* Sigma Xi; Am Chem Soc. *Res:* Inorganic chemistry of glass; synthesis and resolution of coordination compounds; absorption and fluorescence of inorganics; science for the layman; science and public policy. *Mailing Add:* 819 Providence Rd Baltimore MD 21286

ALBINI, FRANK ADDISON, MECHANICAL ENGINEERING, APPLIED PHYSICS. *Current Pos:* adj prof, 93-96, RES PROF, MONT STATE UNIV, 96- *Personal Data:* b Madera, Calif, May 15, 36; m 58; c 3. *Educ:* Calif Inst Technol, BS, 58, MS, 59, PhD(mech eng philos), 62. *Prof Exp:* Consult, Cosmodyne Corp, Calif, 59-60; mem tech staff aerodyn, Hughes Aircraft Co, 60-63; mem tech staff, Defense Res Corp, 66-70, dir, Defensive Systs Dept, Gen Res Corp, 70-71; mech engr, Intermountain Forest & Range Exp Sta, US Forest Serv, USDA, 73-85; sr mem tech staff systs anal, Res & Eng Support Div, Inst Defense Anal, 63-66, mem res staff, 71-73 & 85-86; consult, 86-91; sr analyst, Sci Appln Int Corp, 91-93. *Concurrent Pos:* Lectr, Univ Southern Calif, 60-62. *Mem:* NY Acad Sci; Combustion Inst; Sigma Xi; Soc Am Foresters; Am Soc Mech Engrs. *Res:* Electromagnetic theory; statistical and fluid mechanics; combustion; plasma physics; applied mechanics; weapon systems analysis; wildland fire behavior and effects. *Mailing Add:* 114 Arrowhead Trail Bozeman MT 59718

ALBISSER, ANTHONY MICHAEL, biomedical engineering, for more information see previous edition

ALBO, DOMINIC, JR, SURGERY. *Current Pos:* from instr to prof, 68-95, PROF SURG, COL MED, UNIV UTAH, 95- *Personal Data:* b Helper, Utah, Dec 26, 34; m 60; c 7. *Educ:* Carbon Col, AS, 55; Univ Utah, BS, 65; St Louis Univ, MD, 60, Am Bd Surg, dipl, 69. *Hon Degrees:* DHH, Col Eastern Utah. *Prof Exp:* Intern, NC Mem Hosp, Chapel Hill, 61; resident, Univ Utah Affil Hosps, Salt Lake City, 61-62, 64-68; US Army post physician, Ft Douglas, 62-64. *Concurrent Pos:* Grants, Resnick Award, prin investr, 68-69, NSF, co-prin investr, 71- & Nat Inst Gen Med Sci, co-investr, Univ Utah, 78-81; coordr gen surg, Holy Cross Hosp, Salt Lake City, 68-,; consult staff, Vet Admin Hosp, Salt Lake City, 68-; instr postgrad med, Col Med, Univ Utah, 69-73; chief peripheral vascular serv, Col Med, Univ Utah & Vet Admin Hosp, 72-78; dir med educ, Holy Cross Hosp. *Mem:* AMA; Asn Academic Surg; Am Col Surgeons; Int Cardiovasc Soc. *Res:* Polymer implant materials. *Mailing Add:* 50 N Med Dr Univ Utah Salt Lake City UT 84132. *Fax:* 801-350-4323

ALBOHN, ARTHUR R(AYMOND), CHEMICAL ENGINEERING. *Current Pos:* ASSEMBLYMAN, STATE NJ, 80- *Personal Data:* b New York, NY, Dec 27, 21; m 44; c 3. *Educ:* Columbia Univ, AB, 42, BS, 43. *Prof Exp:* Chem engr, Res & Develop Depts, Goodyear Tire & Rubber Co, 43-50; sr chem engr, Summit Res Labs, Celanese Corp Am, 50-56; supvr film sect, Eastern Res Div, Rayonier, Inc, 56-59, supvr fiber sect, 59-60, asst res mgr, 60-66; group leader spinning res, Celanese Res Co, NJ, 66-69, staff assoc mat sci res, 69-70; mgr tech serv, Komline-Sanderson Eng Corp, 71-90. *Concurrent Pos:* Mem, NJ Comn Sci & Technol, 85- *Mem:* Am Chem Soc; Am Inst Chem Eng. *Res:* Cellulose and synthetic polymer processing, especially in the fields of films and fibres; pollution control; solids/liquid separations. *Mailing Add:* 29 Hilltop Circle Whippany NJ 07981-2017

ALBRECHT, ANDREAS CHRISTOPHER, QUANTUM CHEMISTRY, SOLID STATE CHEMISTRY. *Current Pos:* from instr to assoc prof, 56-65, PROF CHEM, CORNELL UNIV, 65- *Personal Data:* b Berkeley, Calif, June 3, 27; m 51; c 4. *Educ:* Univ Calif, BS, 50; Univ Wash, PhD(chem), 54. *Honors & Awards:* Photochem Award, Polychrom Corp, 86; Ellis R Lippincott Medal, 88; Earle K Plyler Prize, Am Physical Soc, 90. *Prof Exp:* Res assoc, Mass Inst Technol, 54-56. *Concurrent Pos:* Consult, Eastman Kodak, 66-93; partic, US-USSR Cult Exchange, 63-64 & US-USSR Acad Sci Exchange Prog, 74 & 83; NSF sci fac fel, 70-71; mem adv comt on USSR & Eastern Europe, Nat Acad Sci, 70-73; vis prof, Univ Calif, Santa Cruz, 71, SUNY Col at Purchase, 79-80, Rockefeller Univ, 79-80; mem rev comt, Dept Chem, State Univ NY Stony Brook, 85, Bd Chem, Univ Calif, Santa Cruz, 87, Rev Comt, Chem Div, Argonne Nat Lab, Univ Chicago, 86-89. *Mem:* Fedn Am Scientists; fel Am Physical Soc; AAAS; fel Am Acad Arts & Scis. *Res:* Theoretical and experimental molecular spectroscopy-laser based nonlinear spectroscopies in particular; ultrashort time photophysics, ionization and transient spectroscopies; author of over 210 papers. *Mailing Add:* Baker Lab Chem Cornell Univ Ithaca NY 14853-1301. *Fax:* 607-255-4137

ALBRECHT, BOHUMIL, ENGINEERING MECHANICS. *Current Pos:* PROF MECH ENG, UNIV NMEX, 65- *Personal Data:* b Teplicka, Czech, May 6, 21; nat US; m 51. *Educ:* Slovak Inst Technol, CE, 44; Columbia Univ, MS, 49, PhD(eng), 56. *Prof Exp:* Instr bridge eng, Slovak Inst Technol, 44-47; asst eng mat, Columbia Univ, 48-51, res assoc, 51-56, from asst prof to assoc prof civil eng, 56-65. *Mem:* Soc Rheol; Soc Exp Stress Anal. *Res:* Mechanical properties of engineering materials. *Mailing Add:* Dept Mech Eng 7016 Veranda Rd NE Albuquerque NM 87110-2749

ALBRECHT, BRUCE ALLEN, ATMOSPHERIC SCIENCE. *Current Pos:* ASSOC PROF METEOROL, PA STATE UNIV, 77- *Personal Data:* b Aug 14, 48; m 70; c 2. *Educ:* Ill State Univ, BS, 72; Colo State Univ, MS, 74, PhD(atmospheric sci), 77. *Concurrent Pos:* Vis scientist, Nat Ctr Atmospheric Res, 80 & 82; mem, Am Meteorol Soc Comt, atmospheric radiation, 84-90; ed, Monthly Weather Rev, 85-90; lead scientist, First Int Satellite Cloud Climat Proj Regional Exp Sci Exp, 86-90, Atlantic Stratocumulus Exp, Intensive Observations, 89- *Mem:* Am Meteorol Soc; Sigma Xi; Am Geophys Union. *Res:* Theoretical and observational studies of clouds; cloud-climate interactions. *Mailing Add:* RSMA-MPO Univ Miami 4600 Rickenbacker Causeway Miami FL 33149

ALBRECHT, EDWARD DANIEL, MICROSTRUCTURAL ANALYSIS & ADVICE TO ENTREPRENEURS, CORPORATE MANAGEMENT CONSULTANT. *Current Pos:* vpres & gen mgr, 71-76, pres & chief exec officer, 76-90, chmn, 76-91, CHMN EMER, BUEHLER INT INC, LAKE BLUFF, ILL, 91-; CHMN, ADV CERAMICS RES INC, TUCSON, AZ, 97- *Personal Data:* b Kewanee, Ill, Feb 11, 37; m 88, Martha Litman; c Deborah J. *Educ:* Univ Ariz, Tucson, BSMetE, 59, MS, 61, PhD(metall & solid state physics), 64. *Honors & Awards:* Pres Award, Int Metallog Soc, 81, Henry Clifton Sorby Award, 90. *Prof Exp:* Sr physicist, Lawrence Livermore Labs, 64-71; pres, Metall Innovations Inc, Pleasanton, Calif, 69-72. *Concurrent Pos:*

Mem, Nat Adv Bd, Heard Mus Anthrop, Phoenix, Ariz, 80-, chmn, 90-; mem bd trustees, Millicent Rogers Mus, Taos, NMex, 82-91, hon life trustee, 93, vpres, 95-97, pres, 97. *Mem:* Int Metallog Soc (pres & vpres, 70-81 & 93-97); fel Am Soc Mat; Mat Soc; fel Royal Micros Soc UK; Am Ceramics Soc. *Res:* Design and development of equipment, supplies and technological procedures for preparation, examination and interpretation of the microstructure of solid materials including metals, minerals, coal, ceramics, refractories, glasses, composites and non-metallics; author of various publications. *Mailing Add:* 5219 N Casa Blanca Dr No 55 Paradise Valley AZ 85253

ALBRECHT, FELIX ROBERT, MATHEMATICS. *Current Pos:* prof, 68-92, EMER PROF MATH, UNIV ILL, URBANA, 92- *Personal Data:* b Cernauti, Bucovina, Romania, Apr 19, 26; US citizen; m 47, Isidora Wiegler. *Educ:* Dipl math, Univ Bucharest, Romania, 51. *Prof Exp:* From res fel to sr res fel, res math, Inst Math of Romanian Acad, 51-63; from assoc prof math to prof, Wesleyan Univ, Middletown, Conn, 64-68. *Mem:* Am Math Soc; Math Asn Am. *Res:* Geometric control theory; dynamical systems; singularity theory. *Mailing Add:* Dept Math Univ Ill 1409 W Green St Urbana IL 61801

ALBRECHT, FREDERICK XAVIER, PHYSICAL ORGANIC CHEMISTRY. *Current Pos:* RES CHEMIST, EASTMAN KODAK CO, 74- *Personal Data:* b New York, NY, Oct 25, 43. *Educ:* State Univ NY Albany, BS, 67; State Univ NY Buffalo, PhD(chem), 72. *Prof Exp:* Asst prof chem, State Univ NY Col Canton, 69-70; fel chem, Univ Wis-Madison, 72-74. *Mem:* Am Chem Soc; Sigma Xi. *Res:* Mechanistic study of organic photoconductive materials for use in electrophotography. *Mailing Add:* 50 Straub Rd Rochester NY 14626

ALBRECHT, G(EORGE) H(ENRY), CHEMICAL ENGINEERING. *Current Pos:* GEN ENGR, ELECTRONICS RES & DEVELOP COMMAND, US ARMY, ADELPHI, MD, 78- *Personal Data:* b Rochester, NY, Feb 14, 32. *Educ:* Univ Cincinnati, ChE, 54; Rensselaer Polytech Inst, MS, 55. *Prof Exp:* Tech writer, Sperry Gyroscope Co, Inc, NY, 55-56 & Burson-Marsteller Assocs, Inc, 56; chem engr, Appl Physics Lab, 59-65, Airtronics, Inc, 65-67, Booz-Allen Appl Res, Inc, 67-70 & Va Res, Inc, Arlington, 70-78. CONSULT, 78- *Mem:* Am Chem Soc; Am Inst Aeronaut & Astronaut; Am Defense Prep Asn. *Res:* Cost schedule control systems criteria; contractor performance measurement; value engineering; engineering analysis; technical writing; design to cost. *Mailing Add:* 4701 Willard Ave Apt 1711 Chevy Chase MD 20815-4633

ALBRECHT, KENNETH ADRIAN, TROPICAL GRASSES & LEGUMES. *Current Pos:* ASST PROF AGRON, UNIV FLA, 85- *Personal Data:* b Sheboygan, Wis, Feb 23, 53. *Educ:* Univ Wis-Oshkosh, BS, 76; Univ Minn, MS, 78; Iowa State Univ, PhD(agron), 83. *Mem:* Am Soc Agron; Crop Sci Soc Am; Am Forage & Grassland Coun. *Res:* Identify and investigate specific physiological processes that limit the productivity and nutritive value of tropical and temperate forage crops in the subtropics; water relations; photosynthesis. *Mailing Add:* Dept Agron 373 Moore Hall Univ Wis 1575 Linden Dr Madison WI 53706-1597

ALBRECHT, MARY LEWNES, FLORICULTURE, GREENHOUSE MANAGEMENT. *Current Pos:* PROF HEAD, DEPT ORNAMENTAL HORT & LANDSCAPE DESIGN, UNIV TENN, 96- *Personal Data:* b New York, NY, 1953; m, WC Albrecht III; c WC IV. *Educ:* Rutgers Univ, BS, 75; Ohio State Univ, MS, 77, PhD(hort), 80. *Prof Exp:* From asst prof to assoc prof, 80-92, PROF HORT & UNDERGRAD PROG COORDR, KANS STATE UNIV, 92-96. *Concurrent Pos:* Teacher fel, Nat Asn Cols & Teachers Agr, 88; vpres, educ div, Am Soc Hort Sci, 95-96. *Mem:* Sigma Xi; Am Soc Hort Sci; Asn Women Sci. *Res:* Floral induction and development in herbaceous perennials; adaptation of native plant material for use in commercial horticulture. *Mailing Add:* Dept Ornamental Hort Landscape Design, Univ Tenn 2431 Center Dr Rm 252 Knoxville TN 37996-4500. *Fax:* 423-974-1947; *E-Mail:* mlalbrecht@utk.edu

ALBRECHT, PAUL, virology, tissue culture, for more information see previous edition

ALBRECHT, ROBERT WILLIAM, NUCLEAR ENGINEERING. *Current Pos:* PROF NUCLEAR ENG, UNIV WASH, 61- *Personal Data:* b Cleveland, Ohio, Mar 31, 35; m 57; c 2. *Educ:* Purdue Univ, BSEE, 57; Univ Mich, MS, 58, PhD(nuclear eng), 61. *Honors & Awards:* Mark Mills Award, Am Nuclear Soc, 61. *Concurrent Pos:* Researcher, Inst Fur Neutronenphysik und Reaktortechnik, Kernforschungs Zentrum, Karlsruhe, Ger, 67-68. *Mem:* Am Nuclear Soc; Am Soc Eng Educ. *Res:* Nuclear reactor dynamics; stochastic processes in nuclear reactors. *Mailing Add:* Dept Elec Eng Univ Wash Ft-10 Seattle WA 98195

ALBRECHT, RONALD FRANK, ANESTHESIOLOGY. *Current Pos:* CHMN & ATTEND PHYSICIAN, DEPT ANESTHESIOL, MICHAEL REESE MED CTR, 71- *Personal Data:* b Chicago, Ill, Apr 17, 37; m 62; c 3. *Educ:* Univ Ill, Urbana, BA, 58, BS, 59, MD, 61. *Prof Exp:* Intern, Univ Cincinnati Hosp, 61-62; resident anesthesiol, Univ Ill Res & Educ Hosp, 62-64; clin assoc, NIH, Bethesda, 64-66; asst prof anesthesiol, Univ Ill Col Med, 66-69, clin assoc prof, 69-73; prof, 73-76, clin prof anesthesiol, Pritzker Sch Med, Univ Chicago, 76- *Mem:* Am Soc Anesthesiologists; Am Physiol Soc; Int Anesthesia Res Soc. *Res:* Effect of anesthetics upon the brain, especifically blood flow, intracranial pressure and brain metabolism; effect of anesthetics on cardiovascular system. *Mailing Add:* Dept Anesthesiol Univ Ill Chicago 1740 W Taylor St 3200 W MC515 Chicago IL 60612

ALBRECHT, STEPHAN LAROWE, SOIL MICROBIAL ECOLOGY, PLANT-MICROBE INTERACTIONS. *Current Pos:* plant physiologist, 78-90, SOIL MICROBIOLOGIST, USDA, 92- *Personal Data:* b Apr 14, 43. *Educ:* Univ NMex, BS & BA, 68, MS, 71; Kings Col, Univ London, PhD(plant physiol), 74. *Prof Exp:* Res asst, Biochem Dept, Univ Wis, 74-77 & Lab Nitrogen Fixation Res, Ore State Univ, 77-78; assoc res scientist, Univ Fla, 90-92. *Mem:* Am Soc Microbiol; Crop Sci Soc Am; Soil Sci Soc Am; Am Soc Agron; Sigma Xi. *Res:* Carbon and nitrogen transformations in the soil; microbial ecology; physiology of roots; bioenergetics of the rhizosphere. *Mailing Add:* PO Box 100177-1329 Univ Fla Gainesville FL 32610. *Fax:* 541-278-4188

ALBRECHT, THOMAS BLAIR, VIROLOGY, CELL CYCLE REGULATION. *Current Pos:* from asst prof to assoc prof, 76-86, PROF MICROBIOL, MED BR, UNIV TEX, GALVESTON, 86- *Personal Data:* b Philadelphia, Pa, July 31, 43; m 67; c Christine D, Thomas E & Alan W. *Educ:* Brigham Young Univ, BS, 67, MS, 69; Pa State Univ, PhD(microbiol & biochem), 73. *Prof Exp:* Res fel virol, Harvard Univ, 74-75. *Concurrent Pos:* Prin investr, Nat Inst Allergy & Infectious Dis, NIH & US Environ Protection Agency, 81; mem, Sci Rev Panel, US Environ Protection Agency, 81 - *Mem:* Am Soc Microbiol; Am Soc Cell Biol; Soc Exp Biol & Med; Sigma Xi; NY Acad Sci; Soc Gen Microbiol; Environ Mutagen Soc. *Res:* Cellular responses to human herpesvirus infections; regulation of cytomegalovirus replication and expression; antiviral drugs; interaction of herpesvirus and genotoxic chemicals in initiation and progression of cancers. *Mailing Add:* Dept Microbiol Med Br Univ Tex Galveston TX 77555-1019. *Fax:* 409-772-5065; *E-Mail:* thomas.albrecht@utmb.edu

ALBRECHT, WILLIAM LLOYD, PHYSICAL CHEMISTRY. *Current Pos:* Sr res chemist, 60-66, group leader, 66-69, mgr water treat chem res, 69-70, tech dir, 70-71, mgr technol & mkt, 71-75, mgr res, Pulp & Paper Chem, 75-76, corp qual assurance mgr, 76-82, MGR PURCHASES, NALCO CHEM CO, 82- *Personal Data:* b Aurora, Ill, May 9, 33; m 56; c 4. *Educ:* Oberlin Col, AB, 55; Univ Wis, PhD(phys chem), 60. *Mem:* Am Chem Soc. *Res:* Radiochemistry and tracer techniques; colloid chemistry; paper process chemicals. *Mailing Add:* 1009 Anne Rd Naperville IL 60540

ALBRECHT, WILLIAM MELVIN, PHYSICAL CHEMISTRY, MATERIALS ENGINEERING. *Current Pos:* CONSULT, 86- *Personal Data:* b Hungerford, Pa, Feb 18, 26; m 48, Kathleen Eyster; c Gary, Jeffery, Robert, Phillip, Cheryl, Keith, Karen & Marsha. *Educ:* Lebanon Valley Col, BS, 48; Univ Cincinnati, MS, 50. *Prof Exp:* Prin chemist physics div, Battelle Mem Inst, 50-57, asst div chief ferrous metall div, 57-60; staff chemist, IBM Corp, 60-62, adv chemist, 60-66, develop engr & mgr advan technol, 66-73, sr engr & mgr, 73-86. *Mem:* Fel Am Inst Chem; Sigma Xi. *Res:* Analysis, diffusion, kinetics, thermodynamics and sorption in gas metal systems; electrochemistry; surface chemistry; research and development of new materials for electronic packaging. *Mailing Add:* 414 Corey Ave Endicott NY 13760

ALBRECHT-BUEHLER, GUENTER WILHELM, CELL BIOLOGY. *Current Pos:* staff investr cell biol, 74-82, HEAD, CELL BIOL DEPT, COLD SPRING HARBOR LAB, MED SCH, NORTHWESTERN UNIV, 82- *Personal Data:* b Berlin, WGer, Mar 8, 42; m 67; c 3. *Educ:* Univ Munich, BSc, 63, dipl physics, 67, PhD(physics), 71. *Prof Exp:* Investr elec physiol, Ger Radiol Soc, 67-70; fel cell biol, Friedrich Miescher Inst, Basel, Switz, 70-73; fel, Univ Fla, 73-74. *Concurrent Pos:* Training fel, Int Agency Res Cancer, Lyon, France, 73-74. *Mem:* Fel Inst Advan Studies. *Res:* Control of animal cell movement as expression of cell intelligence. *Mailing Add:* Dept Cell Bio/Anat Northwestern Univ Med Sch 303 E Chicago Ave Chicago IL 60611. *Fax:* 312-503-7912; *E-Mail:* g-buehler@nwu.edu

ALBRECHTSEN, RULON S, GENETICS, PLANT BREEDING. *Current Pos:* PROF AGRON, UTAH STATE UNIV, 69- *Personal Data:* b Emery, Utah, Mar 12, 33; m 59; c 6. *Educ:* Utah State Univ, BS, 56, MS, 57; Purdue Univ, PhD(genetics), 65. *Prof Exp:* Res agronomist, Agr Res Serv, USDA, 57-59; res asst agron, Purdue Univ, 59-63; from asst prof to assoc prof, SDak State Univ, 63-69. *Mem:* Am Soc Agron. *Res:* Genetics and breeding of barley, safflower, birdsfoot trefoil, oats, flax, rye, and wheat. *Mailing Add:* Plant & Earth Sci Utah State Univ Logan UT 84322-0001

ALBREGTS, EARL EUGENE, SOIL CHEMISTRY. *Current Pos:* Asst prof, 67-73, assoc prof, 73-80, PROF SOIL CHEM, UNIV FLA, 80- *Personal Data:* b Earl Park, Ind, May 30, 29; m 49; c 3. *Educ:* Purdue Univ, BS, 64, PhD(soils), 68. *Mem:* Am Soc Agron; Am Soc Hort Sci. *Res:* Soil fertility; plant nutrition. *Mailing Add:* 603 Valle Vista Dr Brandon FL 33511

ALBRETHSEN, A(DRIAN) E(DYSEL), METALLURGY, MINERAL ENGINEERING. *Current Pos:* CONSULT, 92- *Personal Data:* b Carey, Idaho, June 20, 29; m 61, Joan Phelan; c Thomas C, Eric R & Carl F. *Educ:* Univ Idaho, BS, 52, MS, 58; Mass Inst Technol, PhD(mineral eng), 63. *Prof Exp:* Chemist, Bunker Hill Co, Idaho, 54-55 & 57; asst mining engr, Anaconda Co, Mont, 55-57; sr engr res & develop, Hanford Labs, Gen Elec Co, 63-65; sr res engr, Pac Northwest Labs, Battelle Mem Inst, 65-66 & Centr Res Dept, Asarco, Inc, 66-86; consult, 86-89; plant metallurgist, Nord Ilmenite Corp, Jackson, NJ, 89-92. *Mem:* Am Inst Mining, Metall & Petrol Eng; Am Soc Metals; Electrochem Soc. *Res:* Surface chemistry; extractive metallurgy; hydrometallurgy; electrometallurgy; mineral processing. *Mailing Add:* 485 Vicki Dr Bridgewater NJ 08807-1941

ALBRIDGE, ROYAL, NUCLEAR PHYSICS, ATOMIC PHYSICS. *Current Pos:* From asst prof to assoc prof, 61-73, PROF PHYSICS, VANDERBILT UNIV, 73- *Personal Data:* b Lima, Ohio, Jan 20, 33; m 57; c 2. *Educ:* Ohio State Univ, BS, 55; Univ Calif, Berkeley, PhD(nuclear physics), 60. *Concurrent Pos:* Res officer, US Air Force, 58-60; sabbatical leave, Univ Uppsala, Sweden, 66-67 & 72-73. *Mem:* AAAS; Am Asn Physics Teachers; Am Phys Soc; NY Acad Sci. *Res:* Photoelectron, beta and gamma ray spectroscopy. *Mailing Add:* Dept Physics Box 1815 Sta B Vanderbilt Univ Nashville TN 37235

ALBRIGHT, BRUCE CALVIN, NEUROSCIENCES. *Current Pos:* From asst prof to assoc prof, 74-90, PROF & CHMN, PHYS THER, ECAROLINA UNIV, 90- *Personal Data:* b Kansas City, Mo, July 30, 46; m 69; c 2. *Educ:* Univ Md, BS, 69; Med Col Va, Va Commonwealth Univ, MS, 72, PhD(anat), 74. *Mem:* Am Asn Anatomists; Sigma Xi. *Res:* Comparative prosimian neuroanatomy. *Mailing Add:* Dept Physical Ther ECarolina Univ 1000 W 5th St Greenville NC 27834-3006

ALBRIGHT, CARL HOWARD, PARTICLE PHYSICS. *Current Pos:* assoc prof, 68-71, PROF PHYSICS, NORTHERN ILL UNIV, 71-, DISTINGUISHED RES PROF, 86- *Personal Data:* b Allentown, Pa, June 1, 33; m 70, Cynthia A. *Educ:* Lehigh Univ, BS, 55; Princeton Univ, PhD(physics), 60. *Prof Exp:* Instr physics, Princeton Univ, 59-61; res assoc, Northwestern Univ, 61-62, asst prof, 62-68. *Concurrent Pos:* NSF grants, 65-68 & 74-94. *Mem:* Am Phys Soc; NY Acad Sci. *Res:* Theoretical particle physics; quark and lepton masses and mixings. *Mailing Add:* Dept Physics Northern Ill Univ DeKalb IL 60115. *E-Mail:* albright@fnal.gov

ALBRIGHT, DARRYL LOUIS, METALLURGICAL ENGINEERING. *Current Pos:* DIR, MKTG & DEVELOP THE AMERICAS, HYDRO MAGNEZIUM, 89- *Personal Data:* b Chicago, Ill, Oct 8, 37; m 60; c 2. *Educ:* Univ Ill, Urbana, BS, 59; Rensselaer Polytech Inst, MS, 62; Lehigh Univ, PhD(metall eng), 65. *Prof Exp:* Res engr, Mat Sect, Res Labs, United Aircraft Corp, 59-62; instr & res asst metall eng, Lehigh Univ, 62-65; res assoc eng res, Int Harvester Co, 65-68; assoc prof metall eng, Ill Inst Technol, 68-79. *Concurrent Pos:* Gen indust consult, 68- *Mem:* Am Soc Metals; Am Inst Mining, Metall & Petrol Engrs; Am Soc Eng Educ; Sigma Xi. *Res:* Structural evaluation of materials by x-ray diffraction; controlled solidification processes. *Mailing Add:* Hydro Magnezium 21644 Melrose Ave Southfield MI 48075

ALBRIGHT, FRED RONALD, MICROBIOLOGY, NUTRITION. *Current Pos:* asst tech dir, 72-76, vpres & tech dir, 76-84, vpres & lab dir, 84-87, SR VPRES & DIR, HEALTH SCI DIV, LANCASTER LABS, INC, 87- *Personal Data:* b Talmage, Pa, Feb 16, 44; m 66; c 1. *Educ:* Muhlenberg Col, BS, 66; Univ Ill, PhD(biochem), 70. *Prof Exp:* Fel, Johns Hopkins Univ, 70-72. *Concurrent Pos:* Damon Runyon Mem Fund Cancer Res fel, 70-71; Am Cancer Soc fel, 71-72. *Mem:* Am Asn Cereal Chemists; Am Oil Chemists Soc; Inst Food Technologists. *Res:* Analytical method development for detection of trace elements, pesticides, nutrients, and toxins in agricultural products and our environment; effect of these materials on plant and animal life. *Mailing Add:* 230 N Mary St Lancaster PA 17603

ALBRIGHT, JACK LAWRENCE, ANIMAL PHYSIOLOGY. *Personal Data:* b San Francisco, Calif, Mar 14, 30; m 57, Lorraine Hughes; c Maryann (Williams) & Amy (Warner). *Educ:* Calif Polytech State Univ, BS, 52; Wash State Univ, MS, 54, PhD(animal sci), 57; Mich State Univ, cert(animal behav), 64. *Honors & Awards:* Dairy Mgt Res Award, 86; Animal Mgt Res Award, 88. *Prof Exp:* Actg instr dairy sci, Wash State Univ, 54; from instr to asst prof dairy husb, Calif Polytech State Univ, 55-59; asst prof dairy sci, Univ Ill, 59-63; assoc prof, Purdue Univ, West Lafayette, 63-66, prof animal sci, 66-96, emer prof animal mgt & behav, Sch Vet Med, 74-96. *Concurrent Pos:* Partic, Int Dairy Cong, Copenhagen, 62, Munich, 66, Sydney, 70 & Paris, 78; Fulbright sr res fel, Ruakura Animal Res Sta, Hamilton, NZ, 70-71; vis prof zool, Univ Reading, UK, 77-78; secy-treas, Comn Farm Animal Care, 81-; vis prof animal behav, Univ Ill, 88-89; vis prof animal behav, Univ Ariz & NMex State Univ. *Mem:* Fel AAAS; Animal Behav Soc; Soc Vet Ethology; Am Dairy Sci Asn; Am Soc Animal Sci; Int Soc Appl Ethology. *Res:* Analysis and measurement of management; life cycle management, housing and behavior; improving large dairy herd management practices; animal behavior; bovine physiology; dairy herd health; animal welfare; animal care and well-being. *Mailing Add:* Dept Animal Sci Purdue Univ West Lafayette IN 47907. *Fax:* 765-494-9347; *E-Mail:* jalbrigh@ansc.purdue.edu, gla@juno.com

ALBRIGHT, JAMES CURTICE, OIL WELL LOGGING. *Current Pos:* RETIRED. *Personal Data:* b Madison, Wis, Sept 8, 29; m 51, Velma Pliley; c James P, Kristine, Tamera & Jennifer. *Educ:* Univ Wichita, BA, 50; Univ Okla, MS, 52, PhD(physics), 56. *Prof Exp:* Res engr, Conoco, Inc, 55-57, sr res engr, 57-61, res group leader, 61-64, res assoc, 64-70; tech data div coordr, Oasis Oil Co, 70-74; res assoc, 74-82, sr res assoc, Conoco, Inc, 82-93. *Mem:* Soc Petrol Eng; Soc Prof Well Log Anal. *Res:* Oil well logging; computer systems; physics. *Mailing Add:* RR 3 Box 121 Stillwater OK 74075. *Fax:* 405-624-9993; *E-Mail:* 102451.3065@compuserve.com

ALBRIGHT, JAY DONALD, ORGANIC, MEDICINAL, HETEROCYCLIC CHEMISTRY & MEDICINAL CHEMISTRY. *Current Pos:* PRIN RES SCIENTIST, WYETH-AYERST RES, 97- *Personal Data:* b Lancaster Co, Pa, Apr 28, 33; m 54, Thelma I Reagan; c Douglas E, Brian J & Andrew M. *Educ:* Elizabethtown Col, BS, 55; Univ Ill, PhD(chem), 58. *Prof Exp:* Asst org chem, Univ Ill, 55-57; from res chemist to sr res chemist, Lederle Labs, Am Cyanamid Co, 58-74, group leader, 74-96. *Mem:* Am Chem Soc; Int Soc Heterocyclic Chem. *Res:* Synthetic organic and medicinal chemistry; heterocycles; hypotensive and anxiolytic agents; synthesis of protease inhibitors; receptor antagonists. *Mailing Add:* Five Clifford Ct Nanuet NY 10954

ALBRIGHT, JOHN GROVER, LIQUID STATE DIFFUSION, OPTICAL INTERFEROMETERS. *Current Pos:* PROF CHEM, TEX CHRISTIAN UNIV, 66- *Personal Data:* b Winfield, Kans, June 29, 34; m 60, Sharon Rudd; c Mary (Schneider) & David L. *Educ:* Wichita Univ, BA, 56; Univ Wis, PhD(chem), 62. *Concurrent Pos:* Vis prof, Lawrence Livermore Nat Lab, 68, 71, 74, 77-81 & 85-88, Australian Nat Univ, 81 & Univ Naples, 88 & 91. *Mem:* Am Chem Soc; Sigma Xi. *Res:* Transport processes in liquid systems. *Mailing Add:* Dept Chem Tex Christian Univ Ft Worth TX 76129

ALBRIGHT, JOHN RUPP, PHYSICS, PHYSICAL MATHEMATICS. *Current Pos:* From asst prof to prof, 63-95, assoc chmn, 80-85, EMER PROF PHYSICS, FLA STATE UNIV, 95-; PROF PHYSICS & HEAD CHEM & PHYSICS, PURDUE UNIV, 95- *Personal Data:* b Wilkes-Barre, Pa, June 10, 37; m 60, 84, 91, Carol Rausch; c Helen (Heminway), Catherine (Pottorff), John R III, Andrea T & Benjamin. *Educ:* Susquehanna Univ, AB, 59; Univ Wis, MS, 61, PhD, 64. *Concurrent Pos:* Consult, Fermi Nat Accelerator Lab, 75-; sr res fel, Cavendish Lab, Cambridge, Eng, 76; vis scholar, Chicago Ctr Relig & Sci, 90-95; assoc, Chicago Ctr Religion & Sci, 95-; dir, Southern Region John Templeton Course Prog, 96- *Mem:* Am Phys Soc; Am Asn Physics Teachers; Inst Relig Age Sci; Ctr Advan Studies Relig & Sci. *Res:* Elementary particles; digital computer programming; theoretical and elementary particle physics; science and religion. *Mailing Add:* Dept Chem & Physics Purdue Univ Hammond IN 46323-2094. *Fax:* 219-989-2130; *E-Mail:* albright@calumet.purdue.edu

ALBRIGHT, JOSEPH FINLEY, ZOOLOGY. *Current Pos:* CHIEF, BASIC IMMUNOL BR, NIAID, NIH, 84- *Personal Data:* b New Tazewell, Tenn, Mar 9, 27; m 51, 73; c 2. *Educ:* Southwestern Univ, Tex, BS, 49; Ind Univ, PhD(zool), 56. *Prof Exp:* Res assoc biol, Oak Ridge Nat Lab, 56-57; NIH fel, Nat Cancer Inst, 57-58; asst prof surg, Med Col Va, 58-61; biologist, Oak Ridge Nat Lab, 61-70; sr immunologist, Smith, Kline & French Labs, 70-71; prof life sci, Ind State Univ, Terre Haute, 71-84, prof microbiol, Terre Haute Ctr Med Educ, 73-84. *Concurrent Pos:* Sr fel, Carnegie Inst Wash, 75-76; consult, Div Biol Med, Argonne Nat Lab, 77-79; adj prof, Dept Microbiol and Immunol, George Washington Univ Med Sch, 84- *Mem:* AAAS; Am Asn Immunologists. *Res:* Immunology; immunoparasitology; interactions of parasites and the immune system of their hosts (mechanisms of immune reactions, immunodepression, lymphocyte activation); age-associated decline of immunological competence and aberrations of the immune system. *Mailing Add:* Div Allergy Immunol & Transplantation NIAID NIH Solar Bldg Rm 4A25 Bethesda MD 20892-0001

ALBRIGHT, JULIA W, MICROBIOLOGY. *Current Pos:* assoc prof, 80-81, PROF, DEPT MICROBIOL, MED CTR, GEORGE WASHINGTON UNIV, 85- *Personal Data:* m. *Educ:* E Tenn State Univ, BS; Univ Akron, MS; Ind State Univ, PhD(microbiol-immunol), 78. *Honors & Awards:* Outstanding Res Award, Geront Soc Am, 76. *Prof Exp:* Res asst, Dept Biochem, Mem Res Ctr, Univ Tenn, 63-65; res biologist, Biol Div, Radiation Immunol, Oak Ridge Nat Lab, 65-68; res asst, Infectious Dis-Immunol Unit, Sch Med, Univ Rochester, 68-70; microbiologist, Lab Cellular & Comp Biol, Nat Inst Aging, NIH, 72-76; teaching fel, Dept Life Sci, Ind State Univ, 76-78, asst prof, 78-80, assoc prof, 81-84, dir, Immunol & Cellular Studies Aging, 81-85, prof, 84-85. *Concurrent Pos:* Adj prof, Dept Life Sci, Ind State Univ, 85-; grants, NSF, 88-91 & 91, NIH, 90- *Mem:* Sigma Xi; Tissue Cult Asn; Geront Soc Am; Am Asn Immunologists; Am Soc Microbiol; AAAS. *Res:* Age-related changes in competence for immune responses; all aspects of the interactions between parasites and the immune system of their hosts; biotechnology, hybridoma production and molecular genetics. *Mailing Add:* Dept Microbiol George Washington Univ Med Ctr 2300 Eye St NW Washington DC 20037-2803

ALBRIGHT, LAWRENCE JOHN, FISH DISEASES & FISH IMMUNOLOGY, TOXIC-HARMFUL PHYTOPLANKTON. *Current Pos:* from asst prof to assoc prof, 67-82, PROF SALMONID CULT & DIS, SIMON FRASER UNIV, 82- *Personal Data:* b Hepworth, Ont, July 22, 41; m 70, Giselle Wittneben; c Christopher J, Jennifer A & Ashlee M. *Educ:* McGill Univ, BSc, 63; Ore State Univ, MS, 65, PhD(marine microbiol), 67. *Prof Exp:* Res asst, Ore State Univ, 63-67. *Concurrent Pos:* Grants, Nat Sci & Eng Res Coun Can, 67- & Sci Coun BC; dir, Master Aquacult Prog, Simon Fraser Univ 91-94, Inst Aquacult Res, 91-94. *Mem:* Can Soc Microbiologists; Am Soc Microbiol; Aquacult Asn Can; Am Fisheries Soc; Asian Fisheries Soc. *Res:* Bacterial disease control in salmonids; use of immuno-stimulants to control mollusc, crustacean and finfish diseases; mode of action of toxic/harmful phytoplankton on finfish. *Mailing Add:* Dept Biol Sci Simon Fraser Univ Burnaby BC V5A 1S6 Can. *Fax:* 604-291-3490; *E-Mail:* albright@sfu.ca

ALBRIGHT, LYLE F(REDERICK), CHEMICAL ENGINEERING. *Current Pos:* assoc prof, 55-58, PROF CHEM ENG, PURDUE UNIV, 58- *Personal Data:* b Bay City, Mich, May 3, 21; m 50; c 2. *Educ:* Univ Mich, BS, 43, MS, 44, PhD(chem eng), 50. *Honors & Awards:* Potter Award, 88; Shreve Prize, 60, 70 & 88. *Prof Exp:* Lab technician, Dow Chem Co, 39-41; chem engr, Manhattan Proj, E I du Pont de Nemours & Co, Inc, 44-46; res assoc, Univ Mich, 48-49; res chem engr, Colgate-Palmolive Co, 50-51; from asst prof to assoc prof chem eng, Univ Okla, 51-55. *Concurrent Pos:* Vis prof, Univ Tex, 52 & Tex A&M Univ, 85; indust consult, 56-; ed chem processing & eng ser, Marcel Dekker, Inc, 72-97. *Mem:* Fel Am Inst Chem Eng; Am Chem Soc. *Res:* Chemical processes and kinetics of alkylation, pyrolysis, partial oxidation, hydrogenation and chlorination; thermodynamics; fuel cells. *Mailing Add:* Sch Chem Eng Purdue Univ Lafayette IN 47907. *Fax:* 765-494-0805

ALBRIGHT, MELVIN A, chemical engineering, for more information see previous edition

ALBRIGHT, PENROSE CARBALLO, MILITARY SYSTEMS ANALYSES, INFRARAD PHENOMENOLOGY. *Current Pos:* RES STAFF MEM, INST DEFENSE ANALYSIS, 86- *Educ:* George Washington Univ, BS, 79; Univ Md, MS, 83, PhD(physics), 85. *Prof Exp:* Postdoctoral fel, Nat Inst Sci & Technol, 85-86. *Mem:* Soc Indust & Appl Math. *Res:* Ballistic and cruise missile defense systems, as well as various advanced surveillance systems; laser weapon system effectiveness, target discrimination, hyperspectral surveillance concepts; air defense issues associated with combat identification and air picture maintenance. *Mailing Add:* 1801 N Beauregard St Alexandria VA 22311

ALBRIGHT, ROBERT JAMES, ELECTRICAL ENGINEERING & ENGINEERING EDUCATION, POWER & CONTROL SYSTEMS. *Current Pos:* From asst prof to assoc prof elec eng, 70-81, CHAIR, MULTNOMAH SCH ENG, UNIV PORTLAND, 71-, PROF, 81- *Personal Data:* b Silverton, Ore, Mar 6, 41; m 79, Elizabeth J Gerber; c Mary A & Anna M. *Educ:* Ore State Univ, BS, 63, MS, 65; Univ Wash, PhD(elec eng), 71. *Concurrent Pos:* Actg dean eng, Univ Portland, 76-77; elec engr, US Army Engrs, Portland, 78-80, US Dept Energy, Vancouver, Wash, 91-92. *Mem:* Inst Elec & Electronics Engrs; Am Soc Eng Educ. *Res:* Signal processing and modeling in biomedical engineering and electric power systems; engineering education. *Mailing Add:* Univ Portland 5000 N Willamette Blvd Portland OR 97203

ALBRIGHT, ROBERT LEE, ORGANIC & POLYMER CHEMISTRY. *Current Pos:* OWNER, ALBRIGHT CONSULT, 94- *Personal Data:* b Leola, Pa, Jan 28, 32; m 59, Wanda C Sprow; c Rhonda & Colleen. *Educ:* Elizabethtown Col, BS, 54; Univ Ill, PhD(org chem), 58. *Honors & Awards:* John C Vaaler Award. *Prof Exp:* Asst, Univ Ill, 54-56; res chemist, Rohm & Haas Co, 58-70, sr chemist & consult, 70-78, sr scientist & group leader, 78-82, res fel, 82-91, sr res fel, 91-93. *Concurrent Pos:* Instr, Elizabethtown Col, 59; lectr, Holy Family Col, 63; instr, Ion Exchange & Theory & Pract, Am Inst Chem Eng. *Mem:* Am Chem Soc; Int Absorption Soc. *Res:* Reaction mechanisms; anchimerically assisted reactions; polymerization, especially mechanism of formation of macrostructure and microstructure; polymer morphology; mechanism of reactions of polymers; synthesis and properties of ion exchange polymers; catalysis by porous polymers; polymeric adsorbents; design of polymers for molecular recognition separation phenomina by polymeric materials; bio-catalysts. *Mailing Add:* 36 Autumn Rd Southampton PA 18966-1011. *Fax:* 215-396-9014

ALBRIGHT, THOMAS D, BIOLOGY. *Current Pos:* PROF, SALK INST BIOL STUDIES. *Honors & Awards:* Initiatives Award in Res, Nat Acad Sci, 95. *Mailing Add:* Salk Inst Biol Studies PO Box 85800 San Diego CA 92186-5800

ALBRIGHTSON, CHRISTINE R, RESEARCH COLLABORATIONS, TECHNOLOGY ALLIANCES. *Current Pos:* investr, 86-90, sr investr, 90-97, ALLIANCE MGR, SMITHKLINE BEECHAM PHARMACEUT, 97- *Educ:* Ohio State Univ, BS, 74, PhD(pharmacol), 83. *Prof Exp:* Postdoctoral fel, Wash Univ Sch Med, 83-86. *Mem:* Am Soc Neurochem; Fedn Am Socs Exp Biol. *Res:* Investigation of progression of renal failure; manage research collaborations between corporate alliance partners; manage technology development with alliance partners. *Mailing Add:* Smith Kline Beecham Pharmaceut UW2214 PO Box 1539 King of Prussia PA 19406-0939

ALBRIGO, LEO GENE, HORTICULTURE, PLANT PHYSIOLOGY. *Current Pos:* asst horticulturist, 68-74, assoc horticulturist, 74-79, HORTICULTURIST, CITRUS RES & EDUC CTR, UNIV FLA, 79- *Personal Data:* b Palmdale, Calif, Aug 24, 40; m 59; c 3. *Educ:* Univ Calif, Davis, BS, 62, MS, 64; Rutgers Univ, PhD(hort), 68. *Prof Exp:* From res asst to res assoc pomol, Rutgers Univ, 64-68. *Concurrent Pos:* Consult, Food & Agr Orgn. *Mem:* Am Hort Soc; Int Soc Citricult; Am Soc Plant Physiol; Int Soc Hort Sci (pres, 96-). *Res:* Fresh fruit quality; environmental influences on fruit development; stress physiology. *Mailing Add:* Citrus Exp Sta 700 Exp Sta Rd Lake Alfred FL 33850

ALBRINK, MARGARET JORALEMON, INTERNAL MEDICINE, ENDOCRINOLOGY. *Current Pos:* from assoc prof to prof, 61-90, EMER PROF MED, SCH MED, WVA UNIV, 90- *Personal Data:* b Bisbee, Ariz, Jan 6, 20; wid; c Frederick H, Jonathan W & Peter V. *Educ:* Radcliffe Col, BA, 41; Yale Univ, MD, 46, MPH, 51. *Honors & Awards:* McCollum Award, Am Soc Clin Nutrit, 78; Spec Recognition Award, Arteriosclerosis Coun, Am Heart Asn, 94. *Prof Exp:* Asst med, Yale Univ, 46-47, from instr internal med to asst prof med, 51-61. *Concurrent Pos:* Intern, New Haven Hosp, 46-47; estab investr, Am Heart Asn, 58-63; Res Career Award, NIH, 63-90. *Mem:* Am Soc Clin Invest; Am Fedn Clin Res; Am Soc Clin Nutrit; fel Am Col Physicians; fel Am Col Nutrit. *Res:* Serum lipids in metabolic diseases; lipid metabolism in atherosclerosis, diabetes, mellitus, and obesity; nutrition and serum lipids. *Mailing Add:* Dept Med Health Sci Ctr WVa Univ PO Box 9159 Morgantown WV 26506-9159

ALBRITTON, DANIEL L, DIATOMIC MOLECULAR STRUCTURE. *Current Pos:* DIR, AERONOMY LAB, ENVIRON RES LABS, NAT OCEANIC & ATMOSPHERIC ADMIN. *Personal Data:* b Camden, Ala, June 8, 36. *Educ:* Ga Inst Technol, BS, 59, MS, 63, PhD(physics), 67. *Honors & Awards:* Sci Freedom & Responsibility Award, AAAS, 93; Sci Assessments Award, Am Meteorol Asn. *Concurrent Pos:* Leader, Atmospheric Chem Proj, Climate & Global Change Prog, Nat Oceanic & Atmospheric Admin; vpres, comn Atmospheric Chem & Global Pollution; co-chmn, Sci Assessments Stratospheric Ozone, UN Environ Prog. *Mem:* Fel Am Phys Soc; fel Am Geophys Union. *Res:* Laboratory investigation of atmospheric ion-molecule reactions and theoretical studies of diatomic molecular structure; investigation of atmospheric trace-gas photochemistry. *Mailing Add:* NOAA/ERL/Aeronomy Lab Rm 24-2204 R/E/AL 325 Broadway Boulder CO 80303-3328. *Fax:* 303-497-5373

ALBRITTON, JAMES R, PLASMA PHYSICS. *Current Pos:* PHYSICIST, REGIONAL ATMOSPHERIC SCI DIV, LAWRENCE LIVERMORE NAT LAB, 91-, SCIENTIST, 79- *Educ:* Ga Inst Technol, BS, 67; Yale Univ, PhD(eng appl sci), 73. *Prof Exp:* Res assoc, Univ Rochester, 73-76, group leader, plasma theory, 77-79; consult, Lawrence Livermore Lab, 75; physicist, plasma theory, X Div, 79-86, proj leader xray, 86-91. *Concurrent Pos:* Mem, Sch Natural Sci, Inst Advan Study, 75-76; vis scientist, Univ Calif, 76- *Mem:* Fel Am Physical Soc, 86. *Mailing Add:* Lawrence Livermore Nat Lab L262 Livermore CA 94550

ALBRITTON, WILLIAM LEONARD, microbiology & pediatrics, for more information see previous edition

ALBRO, PHILLIP WILLIAM, BIOCHEMISTRY. *Current Pos:* BIOCHEMIST, NAT INST ENVIRON HEALTH SCI, 68- *Personal Data:* b Geneva, NY, Aug 24, 39; m 65; c 4. *Educ:* Univ Rochester, BA, 61; St Louis Univ, PhD(biochem), 68. *Prof Exp:* Chemist, US Army Biol Labs, Md, 64-65. *Concurrent Pos:* Adj asst prof, Duke Univ, 75-; adj assoc prof, Univ NC, 80- *Mem:* AAAS; Am Chem Soc; NY Acad Sci. *Res:* Analytical biochemistry; intermediary metabolism of xenobiotics, especially environmental pollutants. *Mailing Add:* 808 Griffis St Cary NC 27511-3757

ALBU, EVELYN D, MEDICAL EDUCATION. *Current Pos:* VPRES & GEN MGR, GARDNER-CALDWELL SYNERMMED, 95- *Personal Data:* b Mt Vernon, NY, Sept 25, 38. *Educ:* Ohio Univ, BS, 60; Georgetown Univ Med & Dent Sch, PhD(microbiol), 73. *Prof Exp:* Microbiol biochemist res, Squibb Inst Med Res, 60-64, med writer, 64-65; clin res assoc int clin res, Schering Corp, 65-69; teaching asst microbiol, Georgetown Univ, 69-73; dir prof commun, Schering Corp, 73-79, assoc dir prof serv, 79-82, dir prof serv, 82-95. *Mem:* Am Soc Microbiol. *Res:* Clinical use of antibiotics, resistance development, epidemiology. *Mailing Add:* Gardner-Caldwell Synermmed PO Box 458 Califon NJ 07830

ALBUQUERQUE, EDSON XAVIER, MOLECULAR PHARMACOLOGY, NEUROBIOLOGY. *Current Pos:* PROF PHARM & CHMN DEPT, UNIV MD SCH MED, BALTIMORE, 74- *Personal Data:* b Recife, Brazil, Jan 22, 36; US citizen; wid; c 2. *Educ:* Salesiano Col, Brazil, BS, 53; Univ Recife, MD, 59; Univ Sao Paulo, PhD(physiol & pharmacol), 62. *Prof Exp:* Asst prof anat & physiol, Fac Med Sci, Recife, 57-59; instr pharmacol, Univ Ill Col Med, 64-65; asst prof Int Brain Res Orgn, UNESCO fel, Univ Lund, 65-67; from asst prof to prof, State Univ NY Buffalo, 68-73, actg chmn dept, 73-74. *Concurrent Pos:* Trainee fel, Rockefeller Found, Univ Ill, 63-65; asst prof, UNESCO fel, Royal Vet Col, Stockholm, 65-67; res asst prof, State Univ NY Buffalo, 67-68; fel, Paulista Sch of Sao Paulo, 69-72. *Mem:* AAAS; Soc Neurosci; Am Physiol Soc; Am Soc Pharmacol & Exp Therapeut; Latin Am Soc Physiol Sci. *Res:* Neurophysiology; electrophysiology; biophysics of excitable membranes. *Mailing Add:* Dept Pharmacol & Exp Therapeut Univ Md Sch Med 655 W Baltimore St Baltimore MD 21201-1559

ALBURGER, DAVID ELMER, BETA RAY & GAMMA RAY SPECTROSCOPY. *Current Pos:* RETIRED. *Personal Data:* b Philadelphia, Pa, Oct 6, 20; m 45, Mary Mickle; c David R, Mary J, Eve A & Andrew R. *Educ:* Swarthmore Col, BA, 42; Yale Univ, MS, 46, PhD(physics), 48. *Prof Exp:* Proj engr, Naval Res Lab, 42-45; lab asst physics, Yale Univ, 45-47; sr physicist, Brookhaven Nat Lab, 48-90. *Concurrent Pos:* NSF fel, Nobel Inst Physics, Sweden, 52-53. *Mem:* Fel Am Phys Soc. *Res:* Radioactivity and Van de Graaff accelerator research on nuclear energy levels; gamma-ray pair spectrometer design; new isotopes from heavy-ion reactions. *Mailing Add:* Brookhaven Nat Lab Upton NY 11973

ALBUS, JAMES S, INTELLIGENT SYSTEMS, INDUSTRIAL & MANUFACTURING ENGINEERING. *Current Pos:* prof mgr, sensors & comput control technol, 73-79, group leader, programmable automation, 79-80, CHIEF, ROBOT SYSTS DIV, NAT BUR STANDARDS, 80- *Personal Data:* b Louisville, Ky, May 4, 35. *Educ:* Wheaton Col, BS, 57; Ohio State Univ, MS, 58; Univ Md, PhD(elec eng), 72. *Honors & Awards:* IR-100 Award, 76. *Prof Exp:* Sect chief, cybernet & subsysts develop, Goddard Space Flight Ctr, NASA, 58-73. *Mailing Add:* 9520 W Stanhope Rd Kensington MD 20895

ALCALA, JOSE RAMON, ANATOMY, BIOCHEMISTRY. *Current Pos:* PROF ANAT & CELL BIOL & OPHTHAL, SCH MED, WAYNE STATE UNIV, 72- *Personal Data:* b Ponce, PR, May 1, 40; m 64; c 1. *Educ:* Univ Mo-Columbia, BA, 64, MA, 66; Univ Ill Med Ctr, PhD(anat), 72. *Concurrent Pos:* Consult, subcomt cataract res, Nat Adv Eye Council, Dept Health & Human Serv, NIH, 80- *Mem:* NY Acad Sci; Am Asn Clin Anatomists; Asn Res Vision & Ophthal; Int Soc Eye Res; Am Asn Anatomists. *Res:* Biochemistry and immunochemistry of lens plasma membranes. *Mailing Add:* Dept Anat Ponce Sch Med PO Box 7004 Ponce PR 00732-7004

ALCAMO, I EDWARD, MICROBIOLOGY, BIOLOGY. *Current Pos:* PROF BIOL, STATE UNIV NY AGR & TECH COL, FARMINGDALE, 65- *Personal Data:* b New York, NY, Oct 16, 41; m 64; c 3. *Educ:* Iona Col, BS, 63; St John's Univ, NY, MS, 65, PhD(microbiol), 71. *Prof Exp:* Teaching fel, St John's Univ, NY, 63-65. *Concurrent Pos:* NSF res grant, 66; assoc prof biol, C W Post Col, Long Island Univ, 71-75 & City Univ New York, 73-75; prof microbiol, NY Chiropractic Col, 74-; assoc prof microbiol, Adelphi Univ, 75; Whitmire Res Corp res grant, 75-78. *Mem:* Sigma Xi; Am Soc Microbiol; Nat Asn Biol Teachers; Asn Col & Univ Biologists. *Res:* Arthropod vectors of disease; effects of ultrasonic vibrations on bacterial spores; lysosomes and hyaluronidase of trichomonads. *Mailing Add:* Dept Biol State Univ NY Tech Col Farmingdale Hale Hall Rm 123 Rte 110 Farmingdale NY 11735-1021

ALCANTARA, EMERITA N, NUTRITIONAL SCIENCES. *Current Pos:* dir mfr rels, 90-92, VPRES, SCI & REGULATORY AFFAIRS, DAIRY COUN WIS, 92- *Personal Data:* b Philippines, Jan 16, 43. *Educ:* Univ Philippines, BS, 61; Univ Wis-Madison, MS, 67, PhD(nutrit sci), 70. *Prof Exp:* Intern dietetics, Yale New Haven Hosp, Conn, 62-63; therapeut dietitian, Univ Wis Hosp, Madison, 63-64; res asst human metab studies, Univ Wis-Madison, 64-69; res asst, Nat Dairy Coun, 70-74, asst dir, Nutrit Res Div, 75-85, dir, Nutrit Policy Issues, 85, vpres, Nutrit Res, 85-90. *Mem:* Am Dietetic Asn; Inst Food Technologists; Sigma Xi; Am Inst Nutrit; AAAS. *Res:* Protein and mineral metabolism; amino acid requirements; nutrition research and public policy development. *Mailing Add:* Dairy Coun Wis 999 Oakmount Plaza Dr Westmont IL 60559. *Fax:* 630-655-8995

ALCANTARA, VICTOR FRANCO, SANITARY ENGINEERING, ENGINEERING SURVEYS. *Current Pos:* ADJ LECTR, CAPITAL COMMUNITY TECH COLL, 92- *Personal Data:* b Davao City, Philippines, Nov 4, 25; US citizen; m 62, Shirley Tang; c Victor J & Shila-Vi. *Educ:* Mapua Inst Technol, Phillipines, BS, 51; Miss State Univ, MS, 69. *Prof Exp:* Civil engr & survr, Alcantara & Assocs, Philippines, 51-57; dean, Col Eng, Cent Mindanao Univ, Philippines, 57-70; assoc prof civil eng technol, Hartford State Tech Col, 70-75, chmn, 75-85, prof, 85-92. *Concurrent Pos:* Mem vis fac, Yale Univ, 79-80; civil engr, Arlombardi Assocs, 85-86, Hayden-Wegman, 87-89; WMC Consult Eng, 89- *Mem:* Nat Soc Prof Engrs; Am Soc Civil Engrs; Am Soc Eng Educ; Am Inst Steel Consruct; Soc Hist Technol. *Res:* Construction. *Mailing Add:* 6 Cadwell St West Hartford CT 06107

ALCARAZ, ERNEST CHARLES, LASER, ATMOSPHERIC CHEMISTRY & PHYSICS. *Current Pos:* SR PROG CONSULT, WJ SCHAFER ASSOC, 85- *Personal Data:* b Coronado, Calif, Dec 4, 35; m 91, Gail Scribner; c Deborah L. *Educ:* San Diego State Col, BA, 58, MS, 60; Wayne Univ, PhD(physics), 68. *Prof Exp:* Instr physics, San Diego State Col, 60-62; from teaching asst to instr, Wayne State Univ, 62-68; res physicist, Signature & Propagation Lab, US Army Ballistic Res Labs, 68-75; scientist, Sci Appln, Inc, 75-78; div mgr, Jaycor, 78-82; sr prog consult, Berkeley Res Assoc, 82-85. *Mem:* Optical Soc Am; Sigma Xi; Am Inst Aeronaut & Astronaut; Inst Elec & Electronics Engrs. *Res:* Properties of liquid helium; coherent light propagation through the near earth atmosphere; micrometeorological structure of the near earth atmosphere; field test evaluation of laser/eo systems; survivability of space and ground systems; natural and nuclear radiation hardening of systems, BMC4I. *Mailing Add:* 10209 Westford Dr Vienna VA 22182-1534. *Fax:* 703-525-2691; *E-Mail:* ealcaraz@wjsa.com

ALCOCK, ALFRED JOHN, ADVANCED SOLID STATE LASERS & APPLICATIONS, HIGH POWER GAS LASERS. *Current Pos:* Fel, Nat Res Coun Can, 65-66, from asst res officer to sr res officer, 66-85, head, Laser & Plasma Physics Sect, 74-90, mgr, Advan Laser Technol & Appln, Sci Affairs Off, 91-92, PRIN RES OFFICER, NAT RES COUN CAN, 85-, MGR ADVAN LASER TECHNOL & APPLNS, INST MICROSTRUCT SCI, 92- *Personal Data:* b Glasgow, Scotland, Feb 3, 38; Can citizen. *Educ:* Univ Toronto, BASc, 59; Oxford Univ, DPhil(eng sci), 65. *Honors & Awards:* Herzberg Medal, Can Asn Physicists, 75. *Concurrent Pos:* Mem, Comn Quantum Elec, Int Union, Pure & Appl Physics, 78-84. *Mem:* Fel Royal Soc Can; Can Asn Physicists; Optical Soc Am; fel Inst Elec & Electronics Engrs; Am Phys Soc. *Res:* High power gas lasers, including large aperture and multi-atmosphere transverse discharge carbon dioxide lasers and excimer lasers; the excimer laser contribution included studies of x-ray preionization, injection locking, short pulse generation and vibrational relaxation processes. *Mailing Add:* Inst Microstruct Sci Nat Res Coun Can Montreal Rd Bldg M23A Ottawa ON K1A 0R6 Can

ALCORN, STANLEY MARCUS, PHYTOPATHOLOGY. *Current Pos:* from assoc prof to prof, 63-89, EMER PROF PLANT PATH, UNIV ARIZ, 89- *Personal Data:* b Modesto, Calif, June 18, 26; m 49, Esther Eastvold; c Steven, Joseph, Eric & Mark. *Educ:* Univ Calif, BSc, 48, PhD(plant path), 54. *Prof Exp:* Res asst plant path, Univ Calif, 49-53, Merck & Co fel, 54-55; plant pathologist, USDA, 55-63. *Mem:* Fel AAAS; Am Soc Microbiol; Am Phytopath Soc; Am Soc Hort Sci; Guayule Rubber Soc (past pres); Sigma Xi. *Res:* Verticillium dahliae; cactus-rotting Erwinia; Macrophomina phaseolina; cacti; guayule; jojoba; diseases of new crops and native plants. *Mailing Add:* Dept Plant Path Univ Ariz Tucson AZ 85721

ALCORN, WILLIAM R(OBERT), CATALYSIS. *Current Pos:* CONSULT, 94- *Personal Data:* b Chicago, Ill, Nov 11, 35; m 88, Susan Probasco; c 2. *Educ:* Mass Inst Technol, SB, 57, SM, 60, ScD(chem eng), 65. *Prof Exp:* Indust engr, Tousey Varnish Co, Ill, 57-58; asst prof chem eng, Mass Inst Technol, 61-62; proj chem engr, Northern Res & Eng Corp, Mass, 64-66; res group leader, Leesona Moos Labs, NY, 66-69; res assoc, Catalyst Div, Harshaw Chem Co, 71-73, prog mgr synthetic fuels, 74-76, mgr catalyst res, 77-81, tech dir, Catalyst Dept, 82-83; consult, 84-85; mgr res & develop, Camet Co, 86-93. *Mem:* Am Chem Soc; Am Inst Chem Engrs; Soc Automotive Engrs. *Res:* Applied chemical kinetics and heterogeneous catalysis; heat and mass transport; fuel cells and batteries; research and development management. *Mailing Add:* 289 Orchard St Chagrin Falls OH 44022

ALDAG, ARTHUR WILLIAM, JR, CHEMICAL ENGINEERING, PHYSICAL CHEMISTRY. *Current Pos:* ENGR ASSOC, PHILLIPS PETROL, 80- *Personal Data:* b Chicago, Ill, Oct 13, 41; m 61; c 3. *Educ:* Univ Ill, Urbana, BS, 63; Stanford Univ, MS, 65, PhD(chem eng), 68. *Prof Exp:* Res scientist, Universal Oil Prod Co, Ill, 67; actg asst prof & fel chem eng, Univ Minn, 67-69; asst prof chem eng & mat sci, Univ Okla, 69-76, assoc prof, 76-80. *Concurrent Pos:* Adj prof chem eng & mat sci, Univ Okla, 80- *Mem:* AAAS; Am Inst Chem Engrs; Am Chem Soc; Am Soc Eng Educ; Sigma Xi. *Res:* Heterogeneous catalysis; coupled heat and mass transfer in reacting systems; clean surface chemistry; enzyme catalysis; enzyme reactor technology. *Mailing Add:* 1705 N Desert Palm Ave Broken Arrow OK 74012-1202

ALDEN, RAYMOND W, III, MARINE POLLUTION ECOLOGY. *Current Pos:* from asst prof to assoc prof biol, 76-88, PROF BIOL, OLD DOMINION UNIV, 88- *Personal Data:* b Daytona, Fla, Dec 29, 49; m 71; c 3. *Educ:* Stetson Univ, BS, 71; Univ Fla, PhD(marine biol), 76. *Prof Exp:* Grad res asst, Univ Fla, 71-73, marine biologist II, 74-75. *Concurrent Pos:* Dir appl marine res lab, Old Dominion Univ, 82- *Mem:* Estuarine Res Fed; Am Chem Soc; Soc Environ Toxicol & Analytical Chem; Limnology & Oceanog; Sigma Xi. *Res:* Marine pollution ecology; effect of contaminants on marines and estuarine communities; marine toxicology. *Mailing Add:* Appl Marine Res Lab Old Dominion Univ Norfolk VA 23529

ALDEN, ROLAND HERRICK, ANATOMY. *Current Pos:* mem fac, Div Anat, 49-51, chief, 51-61, assoc dean grad sch med sci, 60-68, chancellor pro tem, 70, dean col basic med sci, 61-79, dean grad sch med sci, 68-79, EMER DEAN & EMER PROF, CTR HEALTH SCI, UNIV TENN, MEMPHIS, 79- *Personal Data:* b Champaign, Ill, Feb 4, 14; m 37, Aimee Neff; c 3. *Educ:* Stanford Univ, AB, 36; Yale Univ, PhD(zool), 41. *Prof Exp:* Instr zool, Yale Univ, 41-42. *Concurrent Pos:* Mem, Anat Comt, Nat Bd Med Examrs, 59-62; spec consult, Anat Sci Training Comt, USPHS, 60-64; secy-treas, Tenn Bd Basic Sci Examrs, 63-75. *Mem:* Am Asn Anat (pres, 69-70); Am Physiol Soc; Soc Exp Biol & Med; Am Soc Zoologists. *Res:* Mammalian reproduction; experimental embryology; implantation. *Mailing Add:* 6081 Golden Ctr Ct No 206 Placerville CA 95667-6262

ALDEN, THOMAS H(YDE), PHYSICAL METALLURGY. *Current Pos:* CONSULT, 91- *Personal Data:* b Philadelphia, Pa, Oct 20, 33; m 57; c 4. *Educ:* Amherst Col, AB, 55; Mass Inst Technol, MS, 57, PhD(phys metall), 60. *Honors & Awards:* Grossman Award, Am Soc Metals, 69; Hofmann Prize, 74; Mathewson Gold Medal, TMS-AIME, 90. *Prof Exp:* Mem res staff metall, Gen Elec Res Lab, 60-67; from assoc prof to prof Metall, Univ BC, 67-91. *Res:* Fatigue fracture; strain hardening; theory of creep; superplasticity. *Mailing Add:* 2660 Balaclava St Vancouver BC V6K 4E2 Can

ALDER, BERNI JULIAN, CHEMICAL PHYSICS, STATISTICAL MECHANICS. *Current Pos:* Instr chem, Univ Calif, Berkeley, 51-54, theoret physicist, Lawrence Livermore Lab, 55-93, prof, 87-93, EMER PROF, DEPT APPL SCI, UNIV CALIF, DAVIS, 93- *Personal Data:* b Duisburg, Ger, Sept 9, 25; nat US; m 56, Esther R Berger; c Kenneth, Daniel & Janet. *Educ:* Univ Calif, BS, 47, MS, 48; Calif Inst Technol, PhD(chem), 51. *Honors & Awards:* Hildebrand Award, Am Chem Soc, 85; G N Lewis lectr, Univ Calif, Berkeley, 85; G Kistiakowski Lectr, Harvard Univ, 90; Royal Soc Lectr, 91. *Concurrent Pos:* Guggenheim fel, 54-55; NSF fel, 63-64; ed, J Computational Physics, 66-91; Van der Waals prof, Univ Amsterdam, 70-71, Hinshelwood prof, Oxford, 86, Lorentz prof, Leiden, 90; lectr, Japanese Prom Sci, 89. *Mem:* Nat Acad Sci; Am Chem Soc; Am Phys Soc. *Res:* Computational classical and quantum mechanical statistical mechanics. *Mailing Add:* 1245 Contra Costa Dr El Cerrito CA 94530. *Fax:* 510-423-4371; *E-Mail:* alderl@eene.gov

ALDER, EDWIN FRANCIS, PESTICIDES. *Current Pos:* RETIRED. *Personal Data:* b Hugo, Okla, Sept 1, 27; m 51; c 4. *Educ:* Univ Okla, BS, 51, PhD(plant sci), 56; Univ Chicago, MS, 52. *Prof Exp:* Instr sci, Ark State Col, 53; from asst to instr plant sci, Univ Okla, 54-55; instr bot, Univ Ark, 55-57; sr plant physiologist, Eli Lilly & Co, 57-59, asst head agr res, 59-61, head plant sci res, 61-65, dir, plant sci res, 65-66 & agr res, 66-69, vpres agr res & develop, 69-73, vpres, Lilly Res Lab Div, 73-86. *Concurrent Pos:* Mem bd dirs, Eli Lilly & Co, 78-86. *Res:* Pesticide research and development. *Mailing Add:* 10140 E Troy Ave Indianapolis IN 46239

ALDER, HENRY LUDWIG, MATHEMATICS, STATISTICS. *Current Pos:* from instr to assoc prof, 48-65, chmn, Dept Math, 92-94, PROF MATH, UNIV CALIF, DAVIS, 65- *Personal Data:* b Duisburg, Ger, Mar 26, 22; nat US; m 63, Benne B Daniel; c Lawrence J. *Educ:* Univ Calif, Berkeley, AB, 42, PhD(math), 47. *Honors & Awards:* Lester R Ford Award, Math Asn Am, 70, Award for Distinguished Serv to Math, 80; Cert of Merit, Nat Coun Teachers Math, 75. *Prof Exp:* Asst math, Univ Calif, Berkeley, 42-43, assoc & jr instr meteorol, 43-44. instr math, 47-48. *Concurrent Pos:* Chmn, Coun Sci Soc Pres, 80; mem, Calif State Bd Educ, 82-85. *Mem:* Am Math Soc; Math Asn Am (secy, 60-74, pres-elect, 76, pres, 77-78). *Res:* Number theory; existence and nonexistence of certain identities in the theory of partitions and compositions. *Mailing Add:* Dept Math Univ Calif Davis CA 95616. *Fax:* 530-752-6722; *E-Mail:* hlalder@ucdavis.edu

ALDERDICE, MARC TAYLOR, NEUROPHARMACOLOGY, NEUROPHYSIOLOGY. *Current Pos:* DIR CLIN RES, SIGMA-TAU PHARMACEUT INC, 89- *Personal Data:* b Crane, Tex, May 26, 48; m 75; c 2. *Educ:* Univ Tex, Arlington, BS, 70; Univ Tex Health Sci Ctr Dallas, PhD(pharmacol), 75. *Prof Exp:* Asst prof pharmacol, La State Univ Med Ctr, New Orleans, 77-82; asst dir clin studies, Bristol-Meyers US Pharmaceut Group, 82-89. *Concurrent Pos:* NIH fel, Nat Inst Neurol & Commun Dis & Stroke, Univ Conn Health Ctr Farmington, 75-77. *Mem:* Am Soc Pharmacol & Exp Therapeut; Soc Neurosci; AAAS. *Res:* Clinical studies involving buspirone (anxiolytic) and trazodone (antidepressant); investigation of synaptic mechanisms electrophysiological and pharmacokinetictechniques. *Mailing Add:* BRI Inst 1300 N 17th St Suite 300 Arlington VA 22209-3801

ALDERFER, JAMES LANDES, NUCLEAR MAGNETIC RESONANCE SPECTROSCOPY. *Current Pos:* ASSOC CANCER RES SCIENTIST, ROSWELL PARK MEM INST, 77- *Educ:* Univ Ky, PhD(org chem), 70. *Res:* Structure and confirmation of biological molecules; nucleic acids. *Mailing Add:* Dept Biophys Roswell Park Cancer Inst Elm St & Carlton Buffalo NY 14263

ALDERFER, RONALD GODSHALL, environmental sciences, for more information see previous edition

ALDERFER, RUSSELL BRUNNER, SOIL & PLANT WATER RELATIONS. *Current Pos:* prof & chmn dept, 54-62, res prof soils, 62-75, EMER PROF SOILS, RUTGERS UNIV, NEW BRUNSWICK, 75- *Personal Data:* b Lansdale, Pa, Sept 27, 13; m 41, Dorothy M Pearce; c Catharine (Tokash) & Margaret (Moore). *Educ:* Pa State Col, BS, 36, MS, 40, PhD(soil technol), 47. *Prof Exp:* Soil technologist, Soil Conserv Serv, USDA, 36-43; instr soil technol & coop agent, Pa State Univ, 43-47, from asst prof to prof soil technol, 47-54. *Mem:* Fel AAAS; Soil Sci Soc Am; Am Soc Agron; Soil Conserv Soc Am; Int Soc Soil Sci. *Res:* Soil physics; soil, water and waste management. *Mailing Add:* 390 Independence Blvd North Brunswick NJ 08902

ALDERMAN, EDWARD M, IMMUNOCHEMISTRY & IMMUNOBIOLOGY. *Current Pos:* RES SCIENTIST IMMUNOL-BIOL, GENETICS INST, 86- *Personal Data:* b Greensboro, NC, 1948. *Educ:* NC State Univ, BS, 73, MS, 77; Med Univ SC, PhD(microbiol immunol), 79. *Prof Exp:* Fac fel, Harvard Med Sch, 79-86. *Mem:* AAAS; Am Asn Immunol. *Mailing Add:* 20 Cahill Park Dr Framingham MA 01701-6135

ALDERMAN, MICHAEL HARRIS, PUBLIC HEALTH, INTERNAL MEDICINE. *Current Pos:* from asst prof to assoc prof med & pub health, 70-79, PROF PUB HEALTH, MED SCH, CORNELL UNIV, 79- *Personal Data:* b New Haven, Conn, Mar 26, 36; m 68; c 4. *Educ:* Harvard Col, BA, 58; Yale Univ, MD, 62. *Prof Exp:* Fel human genetics, New York Hosp, 67-68; chief renal serv, Lincoln Hosp, 68-70. *Concurrent Pos:* Coordr pub health, Rural Health Proj, Jamaica, WI, 71-; mem comt mother & child health, Jamaican Govt, 71-; mem NY comt, US Civil Rights Comn, 72-76; WHO traveling fel, 73 & 76; assoc ed, Milbank Mem Quart Health & Soc, 73-77; contrib ed, Sci Yearbk, 73-; mem bd dirs, Int Med & Res Found, 74-, chmn bd dirs, 81-; chmn commun progs, NY Heart Asn, 75-79; physician to outpatients, New York Hosp, 75-; chmn adv comt hypertension, New York City Health Dept, 75-77; sr asst ed, Cardiovasc Rev & Reports, 80- *Mem:* Fel Am Col Physicians; Am Heart Asn; fel Am Soc Clin Nutrit; Am Soc Nephrol; Am Soc Trop Med & Hyg. *Res:* Developing and establishing methods of health care delivery; malnutrition in Jamaica and detection and treatment of hypertension in the United States. *Mailing Add:* Dept Epidemiol Pub Health Albert Einstein Col Med 13th Floor 1300 Morris Park New York NY 10461-1924

ALDERS, C DEAN, STATISTICS. *Current Pos:* RETIRED. *Personal Data:* b Nebr, 24. *Educ:* Peru State Univ, BA, 49; Iowa State Univ, MA, 50 & 74, Phd (statist), 76. *Prof Exp:* Instr statist & undergrad math, Mankato State Univ, 56- *Mem:* Math Asn Am; Am Statist Asn. *Mailing Add:* 1503 N Broad St Mankato MN 56001-3224

ALDERSON, NORRIS EUGENE, ANIMAL NUTRITION, RESEARCH ADMINISTRATION. *Current Pos:* animal husbandman, Bur Vet Med, 71-80, dep dir, 80-83, dir, Div Vet Med Res, 83-88, DIR, OFF SCI, FOOD & DRUG ADMIN, 88- *Personal Data:* b Columbia, Tenn, Aug 13, 43; m 68, Susan E Moore; c Brian & Bethany. *Educ:* Univ Tenn, BS, 65; Univ Ky, MS, 68, PhD(animal nutrit), 70. *Prof Exp:* Res assoc animal sci, Univ Ky, 70-71. *Mem:* Am Soc Animal Sci; Am Dairy Sci Asn. *Res:* Directs intramural and extramural research programs which provide support to regulatory issues in the Center for Veterinary Medicine. *Mailing Add:* 10217 Scaggsville Rd Laurel MD 20723. *Fax:* 301-594-2298

ALDERSON, THOMAS, ORGANIC CHEMISTRY,TEXTILE TECHNOLOGY. *Current Pos:* RETIRED. *Personal Data:* b New York, NY, Aug 18, 17; m 42; c 3. *Educ:* Ripon Col, BA, 39; Ohio State Univ, MS, 41, PhD(org chem), 47. *Prof Exp:* Asst chem, Ohio State Univ, 39-40 & 46-47; res chemist, Exp Sta, 47-61, res assoc, textile fibers dept, E I Du Pont de Nemours & Co, Inc, 61-82. *Concurrent Pos:* Consult, textile technol, 82- *Mem:* Am Chem Soc. *Res:* Fine chemicals; petroleum; natural gas; organic fluorine compounds; organic synthesis; preparation of trifluoracetic acid and a study of ethyltrifluoro acetate; preparation and evaluation of addition and condensation polymers; catalytic chemistry; synthetic fibers; textile technology. *Mailing Add:* 1748 Brentwood Dr Clearwater FL 34616-4607

ALDO-BENSON, MARLENE ANN, IMMUNOLOGY TOLERANCE SYSTEMIC, LUPUS FRYTHEMATOSUS. *Current Pos:* PROF, MICROBIOL & IMMUNOL, 86- *Personal Data:* b Bridgeport, Conn, July 31, 39; m 65; c 4. *Educ:* Univ Vt, MD, 65. *Prof Exp:* PROF MED, SCH MED, IND UNIV, 84- *Mem:* Am Rheumatism Asn (pres cent region, 83-84); Am Asn of Immunologists; Cent Soc Clin Res; Fel Am Col Soc; Sigma Xi. *Res:* Research interest is regulation of antibody production by B lymphocytes, in health and disease; this includes mechanism of self tolerance and autoimmunity and suppression of B cells by toxins such as alcohol. *Mailing Add:* Arthritis Care Ctr 1801 N Senate Blvd Indianapolis IN 46202-1206

ALDON, EARL F, FORESTRY, RESEARCH ADMINISTRATION. *Current Pos:* Forester, 53-56, RES FORESTER, ROCKY MOUNTAIN FOREST & RANGE EXP STA, US FOREST SERV, 56- *Personal Data:* b Chicago, Ill, Mar 5, 30; wid; c 2. *Educ:* Univ Mich, BSF, 52, MS, 53. *Mem:* AAAS; Soc Am Foresters; Am Geophys Union; Am Soc Surface Mining & Reclamation; AAAS. *Res:* Watershed rehabiliation; stabilizing mine spoils in the Southwest. *Mailing Add:* 2937 Santa Cruz SE Albuquerque NM 87106

ALDOUS, DAVID J, PROBABILITY THEORY, STATISTICS. *Current Pos:* from asst prof to assoc prof, 79-86, PROF STATIST, UNIV CALIF, BERKELEY, 86- *Educ:* Univ Cambridge Eng, BA, 73, PhD(statist), 77. *Honors & Awards:* Rollo Davidson Prize, 80; Wald lectr, Inst Math Statist, 93; Loeve Prize, 93. *Prof Exp:* Res fel, St John's Col, Univ Cambridge, 77-79. *Concurrent Pos:* Henry fel, Yale Univ, 73-74; assoc ed, Annals of Probability 82-87, J Math Anal, 86-91, J Theoret Probability, 88-, Annals Appl Probability, 89- *Mem:* Fel Inst Math Statist; Am Math Soc. *Mailing Add:* Dept Statist Univ Calif Berkeley CA 94720-3860

ALDOUS, DUANE LEO, ORGANIC CHEMISTRY, PHARMACY. *Current Pos:* DIR, NUSKIN LABS, 90- *Personal Data:* b Albuquerque, NMex, Nov 2, 30; m 55; c 5. *Educ:* Univ NMex, BS, 53, PhD(chem), 61. *Prof Exp:* res chemist, E I du Pont de Nemours & Co, NC, 62-68; res chemist, E I du Pont de Nemours & Co, NC, 62-68; from asst prof to assoc prof, 68-80, dir, Res Pharm & Dean, Col Pharm, 74-79, Res Assoc, Nat Ctr for Health Serv Res, 79-80; prof pharmaceut chem, Xavier Univ La, 80-90. *Concurrent Pos:* Fel, Univ NMex, 61-62; Consult, 80-; Res assoc, Nat Ctr for Health Serv Res, 79-80. *Mem:* Am Chem Soc; Sigma Xi. *Res:* Synthetic organic and heterocyclic chemistry; synthesis of potential antitumor compounds; formulation of cosmetics. *Mailing Add:* NuSkin Int Inc 370 E 1130 S Provo UT 84606

ALDRED, ANTHONY T, MATERIALS SCIENCE, SOLID STATE PHYSICS. *Current Pos:* resident res assoc, 60-62, asst metallurgist, 62-67, assoc metallurgist, 68-72, METALLURGIST, ARGONNE NAT LAB, 72- *Personal Data:* b Rainhill, Eng, Feb 5, 35; m 64; c 2. *Educ:* Univ Birmingham, BSc, 56, PhD(phys metall), 59. *Prof Exp:* Fel phys metall, Univ Birmingham, 59-60. *Concurrent Pos:* Res assoc, Atomic Energy Res Estab, Harwell, Eng, 68-69. *Mem:* Am Inst Mining, Metall & Petrol Engrs. *Res:* Electronic structure and magnetic properties of actinide compounds and transition metal alloys; conduction processes in high-temperature oxides; structures and physical properties of complex oxides. *Mailing Add:* 1615 Briarcliffe Blvd Wheaton IL 60187

ALDRETE, JORGE ANTONIO, anesthesiology, for more information see previous edition

ALDRICH, C KNIGHT, PSYCHOTHERAPY. *Current Pos:* RETIRED. *Personal Data:* b Chicago, Ill, Apr 12, 14; m 42, Julie Murphy; c Carol (Barkin), Michael, Thomas & Robert. *Educ:* Wesleyan Univ, BA, 35; Northwestern Univ, MD, 40. *Prof Exp:* Staff mem, USPHS, 40-46; asst prof neuropsychiat, Univ Wis, 46-47; from asst prof to assoc prof psychiat, Sch Med, Univ Minn, 47-55; prof, Sch Med, Univ Chicago, 55-69, chmn dept, 55-64; prof & chmn dept, NJ Col Med & Dent, 69-73; prof psychiat & family pract, Sch Med, Univ Va, 73-84. *Concurrent Pos:* Vis prof, Univ Edinburgh, 63-64; Erskine fel, Univ Canterbury, 71; dir, Blue Ridge Community Ment Health Ctr, 73-76, mem, Ctr Advan Studies, 81-84; Mayne fel, Univ Queensland, 86. *Mem:* Am Psychiat Asn; Am Orthopsychiat Asn; Am Col Psychiatrists. *Res:* Psychiatric and family practice education; community mental health; relocation of the elderly. *Mailing Add:* 905 Cottage Lane Charlottesville VA 22903

ALDRICH, DAVID VIRGIL, MARINE ECOLOGY, AQUACULTURE. *Current Pos:* RETIRED. *Personal Data:* b Jamestown, NY, Oct 22, 28; m, Anita Sievers. *Educ:* Kenyon Col, AB, 50; Rice Inst, MA, 52, PhD(parasitol), 54. *Honors & Awards:* Piper Found Achievement Award, 77. *Prof Exp:* Physiologist, US Fish & Wildlife Serv, 56-66; assoc prof biol, TexA&M Univ, Galveston, 66-78, assoc prof wildlife & fishery sci, 70-92, head, Dept Marine Biol, 78-79, prof marine biol, 78-92. *Mem:* AAAS; Am Soc Limnol & Oceanog; Ecol Soc Am; Animal Behav Soc; Marine Biol Asn UK; World Mariculture Soc. *Res:* Ecology and behavior of penaeid shrimp, dinoflagellates and parasites; mariculture. *Mailing Add:* Box 817-89 Galveston TX 77554-9802

ALDRICH, FRANKLIN DALTON, TOXICOLOGY. *Current Pos:* corp med toxicologist, 76-81, mgr health effects res, 81-93, CONSULT, IBM CORP, 93- *Personal Data:* b Detroit, Mich, Jan 25, 29; m 52, 84, Gertrude Melsom; c Allison (Cobb), Janet & George P. *Educ:* Mich State Univ, BS, 50; Ore State Univ, MA, 53, PhD(plant physiol), 54; Western Res Univ, MD, 62. *Prof Exp:* Plant physiologist, US Dept Agr, Denver, Colo, 56-58; intern, State Univ

Iowa Hosps, 62-63; resident, Vet Admin Hosp, Denver, 63-64; staff physician, Upjohn Co, Mich, 64-65; prin investr, Colo Community Study Pesticides, Colo Dept Health, Greeley, 66-69; from resident to chief resident med, Lemuel Shattuck Hosp, Boston, 69-71; asst med dir, Med Dept & physician-in-chg, Environ Med Serv, Mass Inst Technol, 71-76. *Concurrent Pos:* Res fel, Sch Med, Western Res Univ, 58-62; fel med, Univ Colo, Denver, 65-66; Mead Johnson scholar med, 70-71; assoc, clin prof med, Univ Colo Health Sic Ctr, Denver, Colo. *Mem:* Fel Am Acad Clin Toxicol (pres, 80-82); fel Am Col Physicians; Am Col Occup Med. *Res:* Environmental and clinical toxicology; chemical human ecology. *Mailing Add:* 1094 Quince Ave Boulder CO 80304

ALDRICH, HARL P, JR, ENGINEERING. *Current Pos:* RETIRED. *Personal Data:* b 1923. *Educ:* Mass Inst Technol, BS, 47, DSc, 51. *Prof Exp:* Teaching asst, Mass Inst Technol, 47-49, instr soil mech, 49-51, asst prof, 51-57; chmn, Haley & Arldrich Inc, 57-93. *Concurrent Pos:* Vis lectr, Harvard Univ, 55-56, Mass Inst Technol, 72. *Mem:* Nat Acad Eng; Asn Soil & Found Engr; Am Soc Testing & Mat; Sigma Xi; Am Soc Civil Engrs. *Res:* Published numerous articles in various journals. *Mailing Add:* Haley & Aldrich Inc 58 Charles St Cambridge MA 02141

ALDRICH, HAVEN SCOTT, PHYSICAL CHEMISTRY, THEORETICAL CHEMISTRY. *Current Pos:* staff chemist, 80-83, SR STAFF CHEMIST, PROD RES DIV, EXXON RES & ENG CO, 83- *Personal Data:* b Middletown, Conn, Dec 4, 43; m 69; c 3. *Educ:* Millsaps Col, BS, 67; Tulane Univ, PhD(phys chem), 72. *Prof Exp:* Instr chem, Mass Col Pharm, 72-73; res assoc, Northeastern Univ, 72-73; asst prof chem, St Mary's Dominican Col, 73-77, assoc prof, 77-80. *Concurrent Pos:* NIH Nat Inst Neurol Dis & Stroke res grant, 75-77; researcher, Am Heart Asn La Inc, 77-78; acad consult, Exxon Prod Res Co, Houston, 77. *Mem:* Sigma Xi; Am Chem Soc; Soc Automotive Eng; Soc Tribologists & Lubricant Engrs. *Res:* Semiempirical molecular orbital studies of small and large molecules including heavier elements, and compounds of biological or pharmacological interest; research and development of aviation lubricants; antioxidants; thermal and thermal oxidation chemistry. *Mailing Add:* Exxon Res & Eng 10 Dartmouth Rd Annandale NJ 08801-3304

ALDRICH, HENRY CARL, MICROBIOLOGY, MYCOLOGY. *Current Pos:* Asst prof, 66-71, assoc prof bot, 71-77, PROF MICROBIOL, UNIV FLA, 77- *Personal Data:* b Beaumont, Tex, Feb 17, 41; m 78, Sylvia E Coleman; c John C & Clay C. *Educ:* Univ Tex, BA, 63, PhD(bot), 66. *Mem:* Mycol Soc Am (pres, 85); Bot Soc Am; Am Soc Cell Biol; Am Soc Microbiol. *Res:* Ultrastructure of myxomycetes, algae, fungi; bacteria. *Mailing Add:* Microbiol & Cell Sci Univ Fla Box 110700 Gainesville FL 32611-0700. *Fax:* 352-392-5922; *E-Mail:* haldrich@micro.ifas.ufl.edu

ALDRICH, JEFFREY RICHARD, PHEROMONAL HUSBANDRY, CHEMOTAXONOMY. *Current Pos:* RES ASSOC ENTOM, AGR RES STA, INSECT & NEMATODE HORMONE LAB, USDA, 80- *Personal Data:* b Columbus, Ohio, June 14, 49; m 80; c 1. *Educ:* Univ Mo, BS, 71, MS, 74; Univ Ga, PhD(entom), 77. *Prof Exp:* Post doctoral fel entom, Univ Ga, 77-78, NY State Agr Exp Sta, Cornell Univ, 78-80. *Concurrent Pos:* Prog chmn, Entom Soc Wash, 82-85. *Mem:* Entom Soc Am; Sigma Xi; Int Soc Chem Ecol; Am Soc Zoology. *Res:* Chemical communication of hemiptera and other insects; hormonal regulation of pheromone production and the mode of action of hormone inhibitors; chemotaxonomy of beneficial insects. *Mailing Add:* USDA Bldg 007 Rm 301 Barc W Beltsville MD 20705

ALDRICH, LYMAN THOMAS, GEOPHYSICS. *Current Pos:* from asst dir to assoc dir, 65-74, actg dir, 74-75, mem staff, 50-84, EMER MEM, CARNEGIE INST DEPT TERRESTRIAL MAGNETISM, 84- *Personal Data:* b Hopkins, Minn, June 28. 17; m 41, Margaret Glockler; c Carol (Pfeiffer) & Peggy (Kidwell). *Educ:* Univ Minn, PhD(physics), 48. *Prof Exp:* Asst physicist, Naval Ord Lab, 40-45, assoc physicist, 45; asst & res assoc, Univ Minn, 45-48; asst prof physics, Univ Mo, 48-50. *Concurrent Pos:* Vis prof, Kyoto Univ, 62. *Mem:* AAAS; Seismol Soc Am; Am Phys Soc; Am Geophys Union (gen secy, 74-80). *Res:* Properties of earth's crust and upper mantle from electrical conductivity measurements and use of controlled and natural seismic sources in South American Andes. *Mailing Add:* Carnegie Inst 5241 Broad Branch Rd NW Washington DC 20015

ALDRICH, MICHELE L, HISTORY OF SCIENCE. *Current Pos:* VIS FEL, SCI & TECHNOL STUDIES, CORNELL UNIV, 96- *Personal Data:* b Seattle, Wash, Oct 6, 42; m 65, Mark Aldrich. *Educ:* Univ Calif, Berkeley, AB, 64; Univ Tex, Austin, PhD(hist sci), 74. *Honors & Awards:* Hist Geol Div Award, Geol Soc Am, 92. *Prof Exp:* Lectr hist of sci, Smith Col, 69-70; staff women's studies, Valley Women's Ctr, 70-73; asst ed hist of sci, Joseph Henry Papers, Smithsonian Inst, 74-75; fieldworker women's studies, Women's Hist Sources Surv, Univ Minn, 76-77; proj dir, Women in Sci, 77-84, mgr comput serv & archivist, 85-90, dir info servs, 91-95. *Concurrent Pos:* Consult, Aaron Burr Papers, NY Hist Soc, 75-76; Biomed Res Opportunities Women, NIH, 78-79; deleg, Mass Govs Conf Libr, 78-; chmn, Hist Geol Div, Geol Soc Am, 79-80, secy-treas, 85-; res assoc, Herpet Dept, Calif Acad Sci, 80-; vchmn, Women's Comt, Hist Sci Soc, 84-86; US Nat Comt Hist Geol, Nat Acad Sci, 85-90. *Mem:* Hist Sci Soc; fel Geol Soc Am; fel AAAS. *Res:* Nineteenth century American geologists and geological surveys; women in American science. *Mailing Add:* 24 Elm St Hatfield MA 01038. *E-Mail:* 73061.2420@compuserve.com

ALDRICH, PAUL E, ORGANIC CHEMISTRY. *Current Pos:* res org chemist, 58-78, RES ASSOC, E I DU PONT DE NEMOURS & CO, 78- *Personal Data:* b Springfield, Ohio, June 29, 28; m 63; c 2. *Educ:* Mass Inst Technol, BS, 52; Univ Wis, PhD(chem), 58. *Prof Exp:* Res org chemist, Merck & Co, 52-54. *Mem:* Am Chem Soc. *Res:* Fluorocarbons. *Mailing Add:* 306 Spalding Rd Sharpley Wilmington DE 19803-2422

ALDRICH, RALPH EDWARD, ACTIVE & ADAPTIVE OPTICS. *Current Pos:* mgr device technol, 83-89, asst dir, 89-90, DIR RES, LITTON-ITEK OPTICAL SYSTS, 90- *Personal Data:* b Worcester, Mass, Jan 29, 40; m 68. *Educ:* Amherst Col, AB, 61; Univ Nebr, MS, 63; Tufts Univ, PhD(physics), 67. *Prof Exp:* Sr mem tech staff, Cent Res Labs, Itek Corp, 67-73, mgr mat sci, 73-75, mgr device technol, Itek Optical Systs, 75-83. *Concurrent Pos:* Vis prof, Electro-Optics Technol Ctr, Tufts Univ, 88- *Mem:* Am Phys Soc. *Res:* Active and adaptive optics. *Mailing Add:* 23 Birch Ridge Rd Afton MA 01720

ALDRICH, RICHARD JOHN, AGRONOMY, WEED SCIENCE. *Current Pos:* prof agron, Univ Mo, Columbia, 79-87, res agronomist, Agr Res Serv, 81-87, res leader, Crops Res Unit, 86-87, EMER PROF AGRON, UNIV MO, COLUMBIA, 88- *Personal Data:* b Fairgrove, Mich, Apr 16, 25; m 43, June E Ellison; c Judith A (Allman), Sharon D (Channer) & Jeffrey. *Educ:* Mich State Col, BS, 48; Ohio State Univ, PhD(agron), 50. *Prof Exp:* Agronomist & coordr weed control res, Northeastern Region, USDA, 50-57, asst dir, Mich Agr Exp Sta, 57-64; assoc dir agr exp sta, Univ Mo, Columbia, 64-67, assoc dean col agr, 67-76; adminr, Coop State Res Serv, USDA, Washington, DC, 76-77, actg dep dir, Coop Res, Sci & Educ Admin, 78. *Concurrent Pos:* Mem gov bd, Agr Res Inst, Nat Res Coun-Nat Acad Sci, 64-67 & 67-70, pres elect, 74, pres, 74-75; chmn, North Cent Agr Exp State Dir Asn, 70-71, Nat Soybean Res Coord Comt, 72-76 & Div Agr, Nat Asn State Univs & Land Grant Cols, 74-75; mem, Int Sci & Educ Coun, 76-78, US/USSR Joint Comt, Coop Field Agr, 77-78 & Joint Coun Food & Agr Sci, 78; interim chair, Agron Dept, Univ Mo, Columba, 79-80; ed, Weed Sci, 89-94. *Mem:* Fel AAAS; Weed Sci Soc Am. *Res:* Weed crop ecology: influence of changes in crop production practices on composition of weed community; relationship between production practices and weed emergence and competitiveness; reducing the number of viable weed propagules in soil. *Mailing Add:* 701 Wildwood Dr Columbia MO 65203

ALDRICH, ROBERT A(DAMS), AGRICULTURAL ENGINEERING. *Current Pos:* head, 79-88, prof, 88-90, EMER PROF AGR ENG, UNIV CONN, 90-, EMER PROF NATURAL RESOURCE ENG. *Personal Data:* b Horseheads, NY, Apr 25, 24; m 46, Roberta A Bowlby; c Susan C, Gail J, Kathleen L & Margaret L. *Educ:* Wash State Univ, BS, 50, MS, 52; Mich State Univ, PhD(eng), 58. *Prof Exp:* Instr & jr agr engr, Wash State Univ, 51-54, asst prof & asst agr engr, 54-56; asst, Mich State Univ, 56-58; assoc prof agr eng, Univ Ky, 58-59, Mich State Univ, 59-62 & Pa State Univ, 62-79. *Concurrent Pos:* Consult, agr bldg indust. *Mem:* Am Soc Agr Engrs; Nat Soc Prof Engrs. *Res:* Structural research; teaching in agricultural engineering; agricultural structures and environment; greenhouse engineering. *Mailing Add:* 295 Wormwood Hill Rd Mansfield Center CT 06250

ALDRICH, ROBERT ANDERSON, PEDIATRICS. *Current Pos:* CLIN PROF PEDIAT, UNIV WASH, 80- *Personal Data:* b Evanston, Ill, Dec 13, 17; m 40; c 3. *Educ:* Amherst Col, BA, 39; Northwestern Univ, MD, 44. *Prof Exp:* Instr pediat, Grad Sch, Univ Minn, 50; asst prof, Sch Med, Univ Ore, 51-53, assoc prof pediat & res assoc biochem, 53-56; prof & exec officer pediat, Sch Med, Univ Wash, 56-62; dir, Nat Inst Child Health & Human Develop, 62-64; prof pediat, Sch Med, Univ Wash, 64-70; vpres health affairs, 70-74, prof pediat & prev med, Univ Colo, Denver, 70-81. *Concurrent Pos:* Mem training comt, NIH, 59; vchmn, President's Comt Ment Retardation, 66-71; chief pediat, King County Hosp, Seattle; pediatrician-in-chief, Univ Wash Hosp; assoc chief med serv, Children's Orthop Hosp, 57-62. *Mem:* AAAS; fel Am Psychiat Asn; Soc Pediat Res; Am Pediat Soc. *Res:* Biochemistry of porphyrins; chemistry of bilirubin; mechanisms of heme synthesis; inborn errors of metabolism; health services research. *Mailing Add:* Dept Pediat RD-20 Univ Wash Seattle WA 98195

ALDRICH, SAMUEL ROY, AGRONOMY. *Current Pos:* prof soils exten agron, 57-73, asst dir, Ill Agr Exp Sta, 73-80, EMER PROF AGRON, UNIV ILL, URBANA-CHAMPAIGN, 80- *Personal Data:* b Fairgrove, Mich, June 12, 17; m 40; c 1. *Educ:* Mich State Col, BS, 38; Ohio State Univ, PhD(agron), 42. *Honors & Awards:* Agron Educ Award, Am Soc Agron, 65. *Prof Exp:* Asst agron, Ohio State Univ, 38-42, instr, 42; from asst prof to assoc prof, Exten, Cornell Univ, 42-52, prof field crops, 52-57. *Concurrent Pos:* Mem, Ill Pollution Control Bd, 70-71. *Mem:* AAAS; fel Am Soc Agron; Soil Sci Soc Am. *Res:* Corn maturity; culture of corn and small grains, land use, rotations; soil fertility; environmental problems. *Mailing Add:* V3 Country Club Village Lake Wales FL 33853-5235

ALDRICH, THOMAS K, RESPIRATORY PHYSIOLOGY, MUSCLE PHYSIOLOGY. *Current Pos:* asst prof med, 82-87, ASSOC PROF MED, ALBERT EINSTEIN COL MED, 87- *Personal Data:* b Minneapolis, Minn, Sept 11, 50; m 72; c 2. *Educ:* Swarthmore Col, BA, 72, Univ Minn, MD, 75. *Honors & Awards:* J Burns Amberson Award, NY Lung Asn, 83; Edward Livingston Trudeau Award, Am Lung Asn, 86. *Prof Exp:* Intern & resident intern med, Univ Calif, Irvine, 75-78; fel pulmonary & allergy, Univ Va, 78-80; post doctoral respiratory physiol, Univ Pa, 80-82. *Concurrent Pos:* Asst attend pulmonary med, 82-87, adj attend pulmonary med, Montefiore Med Ctr, 87- *Mem:* Am Thoracic Soc; Am Col Chest Physicians; Am Physiol Soc; Am Fedn Clin Res. *Res:* Studies of respiratory muscle function and fatigue. *Mailing Add:* Pulmonary Med Div Albert Einstein Col Med Montefiore Hosp 111 E 210th St Bronx NY 10467-2490

ALDRIDGE, DAVID WILLIAM, PHYSIOLOGICAL ECOLOGY OF FRESHWATER MOLLUSCS. *Current Pos:* Asst prof, 82-87, ASSOC PROF BIOL, NC A&T STATE UNIV, 87- *Personal Data:* b Honolulu, Hawaii, July 26, 52; m 82, Linda R Myers; c 3. *Educ:* Univ Tex, Arlington, BS, 74, MA, 76; Syracuse Univ, PhD(biol), 80. *Concurrent Pos:* Prin investr, NSF, 83-86 & 89-92; consult, Army Corp Engrs, 83. *Mem:* Am Soc Zoologists; Am Malacol Union; Malacological Soc London. *Res:* Physiological ecology of freshwater molluscs; control of pest species. *Mailing Add:* Dept Biol NC A&T State Univ Greensboro NC 27411. *Fax:* 910-334-7105

ALDRIDGE, EDWARD C, JR, AEROSPACE TRANSPORTATION, AERONAUTICAL ENGINEERING. *Current Pos:* PRES/CHIEF EXEC OFFICER, AEROSPACE CORP, EL SEGUNDO, CALIF, 92- *Personal Data:* b Houston, Tex, Aug 18, 38. *Educ:* Tex A&M Univ, BS, 60; Ga Inst Tech, MS, 62. *Honors & Awards:* George M Low Space Transp Award, Am Inst Aeronaut & Astronaut. *Prof Exp:* Mgr, Missile & Space Div, Douglas Aircraft Co, Santa Monica, Calif & Wash, 62-67; dir, Strategic Defense Div, Dept Defense, 67-72, dep asst secy strategic progs, 74-76; sr mgr, LTV Aerospace Corp, Dallas, 72-73; sr mgt assoc, Off Mgt & Budget, Wash, 73-74; dir, Planning & Eval Off, Secy Defense, 76-77; vpres, Strategic Systs Group, Syst Planning Corp, Arlington, Va, 77-81; under secy, Dept Air Force, 81-86; secy, Air Force, 86-88; pres, McDonnell Douglas Electronic Systs Co, McLean, Va, 88-92. *Concurrent Pos:* Adv, Strategic Arms Limitation Talks, Helsinki & Vienna. *Res:* Aerospace transportation; aeronautical engineering. *Mailing Add:* Aerospace Corp PO Box 92957 MI/001 Los Angeles CA 90009

ALDRIDGE, JACK PAXTON, III, EXPERT SYSTEM DEVELOPMENT. *Current Pos:* SECY/TREAS, ADVANTEX, INC, 93- *Personal Data:* b Greenwood, Miss, Sept 6, 38; m 65; c Mary & Elizabeth. *Educ:* Rice Univ, BA, 60, MA, 62, PhD(physics), 65. *Prof Exp:* Res assoc nuclear physics, Fla State Univ, 65-68, asst prof physics, 69-72; staff-group leader, Los Alamos Nat Lab, 72-86; tech mgr, A I McDonnell Astronaut Co, 86-91; vpres, Technol Systs Div, TOGAI Infralogic Inc, 91-93. *Concurrent Pos:* Consult, Advan Technol Assocs, 82-86. *Mem:* Am Asn Artificial Intel; Laser Inst Am (pres, 82); Instrument Soc Am; Inst Elec & Electronics Eng Comput Soc. *Res:* Design of expert systems; rule-systems; natural language interfaces; handling constraints. *Mailing Add:* 810 Baronridge Seabrook TX 77586. *E-Mail:* 73521.2260@compuserve.com

ALDRIDGE, MARY HENNEN, organic chemistry, biochemistry; deceased, see previous edition for last biography

ALDRIDGE, MELVIN D(AYNE), ELECTRICAL ENGINEERING. *Current Pos:* assoc dean, Res & Dir Eng, 84-89, PROF ELEC ENG, EXP STA, COL ENG, AUBURN UNIV, 84-, ASSOC DEAN CD PROG & DIR TW CTR TECHNOL MGT, 89- *Personal Data:* b Crab Orchard, WVa, July 20, 41; m 63; c 2. *Educ:* WVa Univ, BS, 63; Univ Va, MEE, 65, DSc(elec eng), 68. *Prof Exp:* Aerospace technologist, Langley Res Ctr, NASA, 63-68; from asst prof to prof elec eng, WVa Univ, 68-84, actg dir, 78-79, dir, Energy Res Ctr, 79-84. *Concurrent Pos:* Mem, Secy of Interior's Adv Comt Coal Mine Safety Res, 76-77; mem, Eng Accreditation Comn, Accreditation Bd Eng & Technol, 91- *Mem:* Indust Appln Soc; fel Inst Elec & Electronics Engrs; Am Soc Eng Educ. *Res:* Quantum effects in communication systems; photon statistics for signal plus noise; phase noise in traveling wave tube power amplifiers; electronic monitoring and communications in coal mines; technology management; professional engineering practice research. *Mailing Add:* Tiger Dr Rm 104 Auburn Univ Auburn AL 36849

ALDRIDGE, ROBERT DAVID, REPTILIAN REPRODUCTION. *Current Pos:* From asst prof to assoc prof biol, 73-85, chmn dept, 81-89, PROF BIOL, ST LOUIS UNIV, 85- *Personal Data:* b St Louis, Mo, July 15, 44. *Educ:* Univ Mo, BS, 66, MA, 69; Univ N Mex, PhD(biol), 73. *Concurrent Pos:* Publ secy, Soc Amphibians & Reptiles, 88- *Mem:* Am Soc Ichthyologists & Herpetologists; Herpetologists League; Soc Study of Amphibians & Reptiles. *Res:* Environmental and hormonal control of reptilian reproduction. *Mailing Add:* Dept Biol St Louis Univ 221 N Grand St Louis MO 63103

ALDRIDGE, WILLIAM GORDON, ANATOMY. *Current Pos:* From instr to asst prof, 63-71, ASSOC PROF ANAT & RADIATION BIOL & DIR MULTIDISCIPLINE LABS, UNIV ROCHESTER, 71-, ASSOC PROF BIOPHYSICS, MED EDUC & COMMUN & ASST DIR AUXILIARY SERV, ENERGY CONSERV OFF, MED CTR, 76- *Personal Data:* b Gladstone, NJ, Apr 28, 34; m 55; c 5. *Educ:* Rutgers Univ, AB, 60; Univ Rochester, NIH fel, 60-62, PhD(anat), 62. *Mem:* Sigma Xi; Asn Multidiscipline Educ Health Sci; Histochem Soc; Am Soc Cell Biologists; Am Asn Anatomists. *Res:* Human anatomy; biology of nucleic acids and correlation of biochemical and electron morphological observations; evaluation of medical education programs; educational facility design and operation. *Mailing Add:* Sch Med Dent Univ Rochester 601 Elmwood Ave Rochester NY 14642

ALDRIN, BUZZ, ASTRONAUTICS. *Current Pos:* RETIRED. *Personal Data:* b Montclair, NJ, Jan 20, 30; m 88, Lois Driggs; c James Michael, Janice Ross & Andrew John. *Educ:* US Mil Acad, BS, 51; Mass Inst Technol, ScD(astronaut), 63. *Hon Degrees:* ScD, Gustavus Adolphus Col, 67, Clark Univ, 69, Univ Portland, 70, St Peter's Col, 70; DLitt, Montclair State Col, 69; HHD, Seton Hall Univ, 70. *Honors & Awards:* Presidential Medal of Freedom, 69. *Prof Exp:* Cmndg oficer, USAF, 51, Col, 53, pilot, Gemini XII, 66, lunar module pilot, Apollo, XI, comdr, Aerospace Res Pilots Sch, Edwards AFB, 71-72. *Concurrent Pos:* Founder, Starcraft Enterprises, 88; staff, Ctr Aerospace Sci, Univ NDak, 89; consult, Beverly Hills Oil Co, Inforex Comput Co, Laser Video Corp & Mutual of Omaha Ins. *Mem:* Fel Am Inst Aeronaut & Astronaut; Nat Space Soc; Soc Exp Test Pilots; hon mem Royal Aeronaut Soc; Int Acad Astronaut; Sigma Xi. *Res:* Author of 2 books; established record over 7 hours and 52 minutes outside spacecraft in extravechicular activity. *Mailing Add:* 233 Emerald Bay Laguna Beach CA 92651-1210

ALEEM, M I HUSSAIN, MICROBIAL BIOCHEMISTRY. *Current Pos:* assoc prof, 66-69, PROF MICROBIOL, UNIV KY, 69- *Personal Data:* b Lyallpur, WPakistan, Jan 2, 24; m 64; c 1. *Educ:* Univ Panjab, WPakistan, BSc, 45, MSc, 50; State Univ Groningen, dipl, 53; Cornell Univ, PhD(microbiol), 59. *Honors & Awards:* Distinguished Res Award, Univ Ky Res Found, 74. *Prof Exp:* Asst bacteriologist, Punjab Govt, Pakistan, 51-52; res assoc biochem, Johns Hopkins Univ, 58-61; asst prof microbiol, Univ Man, 61-64; biochemist, Res Inst Advan Studies, 64-66. *Concurrent Pos:* Brit Coun vis prof, Oxford & Bristol Univs, 63; chief sci officer & guest prof, Lab Microbiol, Free Univ Amsterdam, 75-76; Fulbright prof agr biochem, Univ Adelaide, 76; consult, UN Develop Prog, Pakistan, 81; Brit Coun Award, 63, Fulbright Award, 54, UNESCO-Neth Govt Award, 52, Fulbright Sr Award, 76. *Mem:* Am Soc Microbiol; Am Soc Biochem & Molecular Biol. *Res:* Energy conversions in autotrophic bacteria. *Mailing Add:* Dept Biol Sci Univ Ky 500 S Limestone St Lexington KY 40506-0001

ALEINIKOFF, JOHN NICHOLAS, GEOLOGY. *Current Pos:* GEOLOGIST GEOCHRONOLOGY, US GEOL SURV, 78- *Personal Data:* b Washington, DC, Apr 11, 50; m 80; c 2. *Educ:* Beloit Col, BA, 72; Dartmouth Col, AM, 75, PhD(geol), 78. *Prof Exp:* Geol field asst econ geol, Bear Creek Mining Co, 69-71, 75. *Mem:* Geol Soc Am. *Res:* U-Th-Pb geochronology; Pb/Pb isotope tracer geochemistry; tectonics. *Mailing Add:* 1760 Locust St Denver CO 80220

ALEKMAN, STANLEY L, PHYSICAL ORGANIC CHEMISTRY. *Current Pos:* AT NUODEX. *Personal Data:* b New York, NY, Mar 21, 38; m 61; c 3. *Educ:* City Col New York, BA, 62; Univ Del, PhD(phys org chem), 68. *Prof Exp:* Res chemist, US Army Ballistics Res Lab, 63-64 & Atlas Chem Co, Inc, 65; res chemist, E I du Pont de Nemours & Co, Inc, 68-80; mem staff, Air Products Chem Inc, 80- *Mem:* AAAS; Sigma Xi; Am Chem Soc; Royal Soc Chem; NY Acad Sci. *Res:* Kinetics of chromic acid oxidation; carbonium ion structure; kinetics of polycondensation reactions; kinetics of fast reactions. *Mailing Add:* One MacIntosh Ct East Brunswick NJ 08816

ALEKSANDROV, GEORGIJ NIKOLAEVICH, HIGH VOLTAGE TECHNIQUES. *Current Pos:* Asst prof high voltage tech, Leningrad Polytech Inst, 53-58, sci worker, 58-62, lectr, 62-70, prof, 71-74, prorector sci activ, 77-82, SCI DIR LAB, ST PETERSBURG POLYTECH INST, 60-, DIR, ELEC APPARATUS DEPT, 74- *Personal Data:* b Leningrad, USSR, Jan 7, 30; m 54, Alexandzova Galina Kizpicheva; c Andzej, Maria & Pavel. *Educ:* Leningrad Polytech Inst, Cand Dr Tech Sci, 57; All Union Electrotech Inst, Moscow, Dr Tech Sci, 67. *Concurrent Pos:* Pres, Energetic State Comt Sci & High Educ Russian Repub, 69-; mem sci coun, All Union Electrotech Inst, 80-; vis prof, Chong Qing Tech Univ, China & Wuhan Inst Hydraul & Elec Eng, 88-, Xian Tech Univ & Tsinghua Univ, Beijing, 89- *Mem:* Fel Inst Elec & Electronics Engrs; corresp mem Russ Acad Sci. *Res:* Dielectric behavior of large air insulating configurations; ultra high voltage transmission lines design and compact lines with increased transmission capacity. *Mailing Add:* St Petersburg Tech Univ 195251 St Petersburg Polytechnicheskaya St 29 St Petersburg Russia. *Fax:* 7812-2472088

ALEKSOFF, CARL CHRIS, OPTICS, ELECTRICAL ENGINEERING. *Current Pos:* RES ENGR, ENVIRON RES INST MICH, 72- *Personal Data:* b Flint, Mich, Apr 3, 40; m 71; c 2. *Educ:* Univ Mich, BSE, 62, MSE, 63, PhD(lasers & holography), 69. *Prof Exp:* Res asst mod optics, Radar & Optics Lab, Univ Mich, 64-67, res assoc coherent optics, 67-69, Inst Sci & Technol fel, 69-70, res engr lasers & holography, 69-71. *Mem:* Inst Elec & Electronics Engrs; Optical Soc Am. *Res:* Modern coherent optics; holography; lasers; coherence; electro-optics; optical processing; signal processing. *Mailing Add:* Environ Res Inst Mich PO Box 134001 Ann Arbor MI 48113. *Fax:* 313-994-5704; *E-Mail:* aleksoff@erim.org

ALEO, JOSEPH JOHN, pathology, for more information see previous edition

ALERS, GEORGE A, MATERIALS SCIENCE ENGINEERING, ULTRASONICS. *Current Pos:* SUPVR & PHYSICIST, NAT INST STAND & TECHNOL, 92- *Personal Data:* b Bisbee, Ariz, Nov 22, 28; m 56, Stella Kush; c Brian, Ron & Glenn. *Educ:* Rice Univ, BA, 50; State Univ Iowa, MS, 52, PhD(physics), 54. *Honors & Awards:* Achievement Award, Am Soc Nondestructive Testing. *Prof Exp:* Res engr metallurgy, Westinghouse Res Labs, 54-56; res engr physics, Ford Motor Co Sci Labs, 56-68; mem tech staff, mat sci, Rockwell Int Sci Ctr, 68-79; res prof physics, Univ NMex, 79-81; pres & chief exec officer, Magnasonics Inc, NMex, 81-92. *Concurrent Pos:* Nat lectr, Sonics & Ultrasonics Group, Inst Elec & Electronics Engrs, 83-84, tech chmn, Sonics & Ultrasonics Group Symp, 76, 79 & 95, pres, 80-82; chmn, Physics Metals Comt, Metall Soc, 66-68. *Mem:* Am Soc Nondestructive Testing; Inst Elec & Electronics Engrs; fel Am Phys Soc. *Res:* Commercial application of non-contact, electromagnetic transducers; development of novel ultrasonic nondestructive testing techniques; effects of temperature and pressure on elastic properties of materials; origins of mechanical strength of metals. *Mailing Add:* Nat Inst Stand & Technol MS 853 325 Broadway Boulder CO 80303. *Fax:* 303-497-5030; *E-Mail:* alers@bldr.nist.gov

ALERS, PERRY BALDWIN, PHYSICS, GEOPHYSICS. *Current Pos:* RETIRED. *Personal Data:* b Bisbee, Ariz, Mar 24, 26; m 55, Flora A Campbell; c Perry C, Ellen V & Paul E. *Educ:* Rice Univ, BA, 48, MA, 50; Univ Md, PhD(physics), 55. *Prof Exp:* Res physicist low temperature physics, Marine Systs, Naval Res Lab, 50-59, high pressure physics, 59-66, head, Crystal Physics Br Admin, 66-71, physics consult geophys, 71-75, physics systs analyst, 75-83; mgr adv progs, Eastport Int, Inc, 83-88. *Concurrent Pos:* Sabbatical, Brigham Young Univ, 64-65 & Univ Calif, San Diego, 71-72; Res & develop plans officer, Off Chief Naval Opers, 78-79. *Mem:* Fel Am Phys Soc; Am Geophys Union; Sigma Xi. *Res:* Superconductivity; magnetic properties of metals and insulators at low temperatures; luminescence at high pressures; geomagnetism of ocean floor; geomagnetic noise; ocean instrumentation; ocean vehicles. *Mailing Add:* 9405 Caldran Dr Clinton MD 20735

ALEX, JACK FRANKLIN, PLANT TAXONOMY, ECOLOGY. *Current Pos:* from assoc prof to prof, 68-93, actg chair dept, 89-90, EMER PROF TAXON, UNIV GUELPH, 93- *Personal Data:* b Rutland, Sask, Aug 20, 28; m 57, Gwen Sproat; c 3. *Educ:* Univ Sask, BSA, 50, MSc, 52; Wash State Univ, PhD(bot), 59. *Honors & Awards:* T R Hilliard Distinguished Agr Exten Award. *Prof Exp:* Asst plant ecol, Univ Sask, 50-52; field asst, Div Bot, Can Dept Agr, 52; asst bot, State Col Wash, 52-54; lectr agr bot, Univ Ceylon, 54-56; res assoc, Univ Sask, 57-58; weed ecologist, Plant Res Inst, Can Dept Agr, 58-62, ecologist, Regina Res Sta, 62-68. *Concurrent Pos:* Weed biol, Sri Lanka, Indonesia & Thailand. *Mem:* Ont Inst Agrol; Weed Sci Soc Am; Agr Inst Can; Can Bot Asn; Int Weed Sci Soc. *Res:* Ecological investigations on weeds and native vegetation; taxonomy and ecology of weedy species; biological control of weeds. *Mailing Add:* Dept Environ Biol Univ Guelph 50 Stone Rd E Guelph ON N1G 2W1 Can. *Fax:* 519-837-0442

ALEX, LEO JAMES, EXPONENTIAL DIOPHANTINE EQUATIONS. *Current Pos:* From asst prof to assoc prof, 70-78, PROF MATH, STATE UNIV COL, ONEONTA, 78-, DEPT CHMN, 88- *Personal Data:* b Rochester, Minn, Dec 3, 42; m 67; c 3. *Educ:* Univ Minn, BA, 64, PhD(math), 70. *Concurrent Pos:* Vis asst prof, Univ Va, 74. *Mem:* Am Math Soc; Math Asn Am. *Res:* Finite group representation theory; solving exponential diophantine equations. *Mailing Add:* State Univ NY Col Oneonta Oneonta NY 13820

ALEXANDER, A ALLAN, VERTEBRATE ANATOMY, TAXONOMY. *Current Pos:* from instr to assoc prof, 61-78, chmn dept, 71-78, 71-78, PROF BIOL, CANISIUS COL, 76- *Personal Data:* b Hudson, Mass, July 19, 28; m 52; c 1. *Educ:* Univ Mass, BS, 50; Springfield Col, MS, 47; State Univ NY, Buffalo, PhD(biol), 66. *Prof Exp:* Asst biol, Springfield Col, 54-55, asst physiol, 55-57; asst biol, State Univ NY, Buffalo, 58-60. *Mem:* Am Soc Zoologists; Soc Study Evolution; Am Soc Ichthyologists & Herpetologists; Asn Study Animal Behav. *Res:* Herpetological taxonomy and comparative herpetological morphology and development. *Mailing Add:* Dept Biol Canisius Col 2001 Main St Buffalo NY 14208-1035

ALEXANDER, AARON D, MEDICAL MICROBIOLOGY. *Current Pos:* prof, 74-86, EMER PROF MICROBIOL, CHICAGO COL OSTEOP MED, 86- *Personal Data:* b New York, NY, Jan 14, 17; m 41, Rosalind Steinberg; c Judith, Joshua & Zachary. *Educ:* City Col NY, BS, 38; George Washington Univ, MS, 53, PhD(microbiol), 61; Am Bd Microbiol, dipl, 65. *Prof Exp:* Bacteriologist antibiotics, Food & Drug Admin, 46-49; res bacteriologist, Div Vet Med, Walter Reed Army Inst Res, 49-53, chief, Res Sect, Dept Vet Bact, 53-60, from asst chief to chief, Dept Vet Microbiol, 60-74. *Concurrent Pos:* Mem, Expert Comt Leptospirosis, WHO-Food Agr Argn, Orgn, 57-73; Leptospira Subcomt, Int Comt Bact Nomenclature & Taxon, 58-; chief, Leptospirosis Ref Lab, 60-74. *Mem:* Am Soc Microbiol; Am Asn Immunol; AAAS; Sigma Xi. *Res:* Microbial zoonoses; leptospirosis, melioidosis. *Mailing Add:* 1001 City Ave Apt ED-829 Wynnewood PA 19096-3914

ALEXANDER, ALLEN LEANDER, CHEMISTRY. *Current Pos:* RETIRED. *Personal Data:* b Statesville, NC, Feb 12, 10; m 41; c 2. *Educ:* Univ NC, BS, 31, MS, 32, PhD(chem), 36. *Prof Exp:* Teaching fel chem, Univ NC, 31-32 & 33-36; res chemist, Sherwin-Williams Co, Ohio, 36-38; chemist, US Naval Res Lab, 38-40, head org chem br, 40-72. *Mem:* Am Chem Soc; Nat Asn Corrosion Engrs; Fedn Socs Paint Technol. *Res:* Paints, varnishes, lacquers; fungicides; antifouling and temperature indicating paints; chemical compounds obtained from destructive distillation of tobacco; wood preservation; corrosion and biodegradation in tropical environments. *Mailing Add:* 4216 Sleepy Hollow Rd Annandale VA 22003-2046

ALEXANDER, ARCHIBALD FERGUSON, VETERINARY PATHOLOGY. *Current Pos:* from instr to assoc prof, 56-65, head, Dept Path, 66-81, PROF VET PATH, COLO STATE UNIV, 65-, DIR, DIAG LABS, 81- *Personal Data:* b Minneapolis, Minn, Oct 13, 28; m 53; c 4. *Educ:* Univ Minn, BS & DVM, 51; Colo State Univ, MS, 58, PhD(animal path), 62. *Prof Exp:* Chief animal supply, Dugway Proving Ground, Utah, 51-56. *Concurrent Pos:* Nat Heart Inst spec fel, Glasgow, 63-64. *Mem:* AAAS; Am Vet Med Asn; Am Col Vet Path; Int Acad Path; Sigma Xi. *Res:* Experimental veterinary medicine; cardiovascular-pulmonary pathology in relation to high altitude acclimatization. *Mailing Add:* 922 S Summit View Dr Ft Collins CO 80524

ALEXANDER, BENJAMIN H, BIOCHEMISTRY, ENVIRONMENTAL CHEMISTRY. *Current Pos:* PRES, DREW DAWN ENTERPRISES, INC, 83- *Personal Data:* b Roberta, Ga, Oct 18, 21; m 48; c 2. *Educ:* Univ Cincinnati, BA, 43; Bradley Univ, MS, 50; Georgetown Univ, PhD(chem), 57. *Hon Degrees:* LLD, Bradley Univ, 79. *Honors & Awards:* Cert Achievement, Am Chem Soc. *Prof Exp:* Technician, Cincinnati Chem Works, 44-45; chemist, Agr Res Serv, USDA, Ill, 45-54, res chem, Md, 54-62, Walter Reed Army Inst Res, 62-67; health scientist admin, NIH, 67-68, spec asst to dir for disadvantaged, Nat Ctr Health Serv Res & Develop, Health Serv & Ment Health Admin, USPHS, 68-69, adminr, New Health Career Projs & Dep Equal Employ Off, 69-70, prog officer, Health Care Orgn & Resources Div, 70-74; pres, Chicago State Univ, 74-82, Univ DC, 82-83; dep asst secy, Dept Educ, Interim, 84. *Concurrent Pos:* Adj prof, Am Univ, 58-74; lectr, Grad Sch, USDA, 60-68; mem, comt women higher educ, Am Coun Educ, 75-77; comnr, NCent Comn Inst Higher Educ, 75-78; consult, Nat Ctr Health Serv Res & NSF, 77-81; distinguished vis prof, Nat Grad Univ, Arlington, Va, 83-; res prof, Am Univ, Washington, DC; vpres, Wash Acad Sci, 85-86; chmn, Joint Bd on Sci & Eng Educ, 85-86; mem, Acad Joint Bd Sci & Eng Educ. *Mem:* Am Chem Soc; fel Acad Scis. *Res:* Syntheses of organophosphorus compounds for medicinal purposes; syntheses of pesticide chemicals including insect attractants and repellents, dextrans and glucuronic acids; preparation of useful compounds from agricultural wastes. *Mailing Add:* PO Box 41126 Washington DC 20018-0526

ALEXANDER, CAROLINE M, CELL BIOLOGY, BIOCHEMISTRY. *Current Pos:* INSTR, HARVARD MED SCH, 96- *Personal Data:* b Hong Kong, 1960; m, John A T Young; c Logan. *Educ:* Univ Aberdeen, UK, BSc, 81; Univ Kent, UK, PhD(biochem), 86. *Prof Exp:* Fel cell biol, Imp Cancer Res Fund, 86-88; cell biologist, Lab Radialbiol & Environ Health, Univ Calif, San Francisco, 88-96. *Mem:* Am Soc Cell Biol. *Mailing Add:* Dept Newborn Med Enders 950 Children's Hosp 320 Longwood Ave Boston MA 02115. *Fax:* 617-355-7677

ALEXANDER, CHARLES EDWARD, JR, MEDICINE, PUBLIC HEALTH. *Current Pos:* DEP DIR HEALTH SERVS, TEX DEPT CRIMINAL JUSTICE-INSTNL DIV, 88- *Personal Data:* b Port Washington, NY, Nov 25, 30; m 60; c 3. *Educ:* Yale Univ, BA, 51; Univ Pa, MD, 55; Johns Hopkins Univ, MPH, 59; DrPH(chronic dis), 64; Am Bd Prev Med, dipl, 64. *Prof Exp:* Intern med, Geisinger Hosp, Danville, Pa, 55-56; Med Corps, US Navy, 56-, med officer, 56-57, clinician, Naval Air Sta, Alameda, Calif, 57-58, resident pub health, Johns Hopkins Univ, 58-60, asst officer in chg, Prev Med Unit 6, 60-62, head venereal dis & tuberc control sects, Bur Med & Surg, 62-64, head commun dis br, 63-65, officer in chg, Prev Med Univ 7, 65-67, officer in chg, Navy Prev Med Unit, Danang, Vietnam, 67-68, prev med officer, US Mil Assistance Command, Thailand, 68-71, dep surgeon, 68-71, dir prev med div, Bur Med & Surg, 71-75, dir occup & prev med div, Bur Med & Surg, Navy Dept, 75-76; chief bur tuberc serv, 76-81, chief, bur commun dis serv, 81-84, chief, bur epidemiol, 84-87, chief, bur AIDS/STD Control, Tex Dept Health, 87-88. *Mem:* Am Asn Pub Health Physicians; fel Am Col Prev Med; Soc Med Consult Armed Forces. *Res:* Communicable diseases; venereal disease; tuberculosis; military preventive medicine; public health administration; epidemiology. *Mailing Add:* Tex Dept Criminal Justice Instnl Div Box 99 Huntsville TX 77342-0099

ALEXANDER, CHARLES WILLIAM, AGRONOMY. *Current Pos:* RETIRED. *Personal Data:* b Olathe, Kans, June 2, 31; m 53, Irene Owens; c John A & Leigh Ann (Bailey). *Educ:* Kans State Col, BS, 53, MS, 54; NC State Col, PhD(agron), 57. *Prof Exp:* Res agronomist, Humid Pasture Mgt, 57-62, agr res admin, 62- 75, area dir, Agr Res Serv, USDA, Columbia, MO, 75-88. *Mem:* Crop Sci Soc Am; Am Soc Agron; Am Soc Pub Admin; Sigma Xi. *Res:* Plant physiology; forage crop ecology; agricultural research administration; public administration. *Mailing Add:* 1610 Stoney Brook Pl Columbia MO 65201

ALEXANDER, CHESTER, JR, PHYSICS. *Current Pos:* from asst prof to assoc prof, 68-78, asst pres, 90-97, PROF PHYSICS, UNIV ALA, 79- *Personal Data:* b Tarboro, NC, Nov 6, 37; m 61; c 2. *Educ:* Davidson Col, BS, 60; Emory Univ, MS, 62; Duke Univ, PhD(physics), 68. *Prof Exp:* Instr physics, Emory Univ, 61-62; physicist, Feltman Labs, Picatinny Arsenal, 62-64. *Concurrent Pos:* Vis researcher, Univ Oslo, 75-76. *Mem:* Am Phys Soc; Inst Elec & Electronics Engrs. *Res:* Electron spin resonance; microwave spectroscopy. *Mailing Add:* Off Acad Affairs Univ Ala Box 870114 Tuscaloosa AL 35487. *E-Mail:* calexand@rosie.ua.edu

ALEXANDER, CLAUDE GORDON, ZOOLOGY. *Current Pos:* RETIRED. *Personal Data:* b San Diego, Calif, Sept 15, 24; m 54; c 3. *Educ:* Ore State Col, BS, 48, MS, 50; Univ Calif, Los Angeles, PhD, 55. *Prof Exp:* From asst prof to prof biol, San Francisco State Univ, 55-87. *Mem:* Am Soc Parasitol; Am Soc Zoologists; Sigma Xi. *Res:* Helminth parasites comparative physiology of Elasmobranch fishes. *Mailing Add:* San Francisco Univ 1330 Univ Dr Menlo Park CA 94025-4241

ALEXANDER, DAVID MICHAEL, OTHER MEDICAL & HEALTH SCIENCES. *Current Pos:* COMPUT SPECIALIST, VET ADMIN MED CTR, BIRMINGHAM, ALA, 86- *Personal Data:* b Cleveland, Ohio, Nov 4, 41; m 66. *Educ:* Case Inst Technol, BS, 63, MS, 65, PhD(biomed eng), 68. *Prof Exp:* Asst prof elec eng, Christian Bros Col, Tenn, 68-71; res engr, Pulmonary Lab, Baptist Mem Hosp, 71-83; Comput Specialist, Vet Admin Med Ctr, Memphis, Tenn, 83-86. *Concurrent Pos:* Res assoc clin physiol, Med Units, Tenn, 68-69. *Mem:* AAAS; Inst Elec & Electronics Engrs; Am Soc Mech Eng Educ; Sigma Xi. *Res:* Mathematical modeling of physiological systems; statistical and time series analysis of biological variables. *Mailing Add:* Vet Admin Med Ctr 600 Beacon Pkwy W Suite 201 Birmingham AL 35209

ALEXANDER, DENTON EUGENE, PLANT BREEDING, AGRONOMY. *Current Pos:* fel bot, 50-51, from instr & asst prof to assoc prof, 51-63, PROF PLANT BREEDING, UNIV ILL, URBANA-CHAMPAIGN, 63- *Personal Data:* b Potomac, Ill, Dec 18, 17; m 43, Elizabeth Bowman. *Educ:* Univ Ill, BS, 41, PhD(agron), 50. *Honors & Awards:* Crop Sci Award, Am Soc Agron, 70. *Prof Exp:* Instr aircraft engine mechs, Army Air Force, 41-44; prod supvr Manhattan proj, Oak Ridge Nat Lab, 44-47. *Concurrent Pos:* Hybrid maize expert, Food & Agr Orgn, Yugoslavia, 57; Ford Found consult, Latin Am, 65-67; mem bd dir, Funk Bros Seed Co, 69-74; consult, Dept Agr, Repub SAfrica, 76. *Mem:* Am Soc Agron; Soviet Acad Agr Sci; hon mem Asn Genetic Soc Yugoslavia. *Res:* Breeding and genetics of oil and protein in maize. *Mailing Add:* 701 W Pennsylvania Ave Urbana IL 61801

ALEXANDER, DREW W, MEDICINE. *Current Pos:* AT DEPT PEDIAT, UNIV TEX HEALTH SCI CTR. *Personal Data:* b Peoria, Ill, Dec 21, 48. *Educ:* Earlham Col, BA, 70; Med Col Ohio, MD, 73; Albert Einstein Col Med, cert pediat, 76. *Prof Exp:* Asst prof, Univ Tex Health Sci Ctr, Dallas, 77-, health team physician, West Dallas Youth Clinic, Children & Youth Proj, 77-; partner, Adolescent Health Assocs, 81- *Concurrent Pos:* Fel adolescent med, Univ Tex Health Sci Ctr Dallas, 76-77; consult, multidisciplinary adolescent health training proj, 77- *Mem:* Soc Adolescent Med; Am Acad Pediat; AMA. *Res:* Adolescent growth and development; adolescent health care delivery; adolescents as parents; adolescent medicine. *Mailing Add:* Dept Pediat Univ Tex Southwestern Med Sch 5323 Harry Hines Blvd Dallas TX 75235-7200

ALEXANDER, DUANE FREDERICK, PEDIATRICS, DEVELOPMENT DISABILITIES. *Current Pos:* asst sci dir, Nat Inst Child Health & Human Develop, 71-74, asst to dir, 78-82, dep dir, 82-86, DIR, NAT INST CHILD HEALTH & HUMAN DEVELOP, 86- *Personal Data:* b Baltimore, MD, Aug 11, 40; m 63, Mariane Ellis; c Keith & Kristin. *Educ:* Pa State Univ, BS, 62. *Honors & Awards:* Commendation Medal, Pub Health Serv, 70, Meritorious Serv Medal, 85, Spec Recognition Award, 85; Surgeon General's Exemplary Serv Medal, 90; Distinguished Pub Serv Award, Am Acad Phys Med & Rehab, 93. *Prof Exp:* Med officer, Nat Comn Protection Human Subjects Res, HEW, 74-78. *Mem:* Am Acad Pediat; Soc Develop Pediat; Asn Retarded Citizens; Am Pediat Soc. *Mailing Add:* Nat Inst Child Health & Human Develop NIH Bldg 31 Rm 2A03 Bethesda MD 20892. *Fax:* 301-402-1104

ALEXANDER, EARL L(OGAN), JR, CHEMICAL ENGINEERING. *Current Pos:* RETIRED. *Personal Data:* b Flint, Mich, May 22, 20; wid; c 3. *Educ:* Purdue Univ, BS, 42, MS, 48, PhD(chem eng), 52. *Prof Exp:* Plant operator, Joseph E Seagram & Sons, 42-43; chem engr, Streptomycin Pilot Plant, Parke Davis, 46-47; asst chem engr, Purdue Univ, 49-51; chem engr, Distillation Design & Textile Polymers, Exp Sta, E I du Pont de Nemours & Co, 52-59; prin scientist, Advan Concepts Composite Mat, Res Div, Rocketdyne, 59-71; mem tech staff composites, mat & processes, Los Angeles Div, 71-81, systs analyst, Solar Power, Shale Oil Processing, Energy Technol Eng Ctr, North AM Rockwell, 81-86. *Mem:* Am Chem Soc; Am Inst Chem Engrs. *Res:* Advanced solid propellants; filament reinforced composite structures anisotropic solid propellant combustion; high temperature polymers; heat and mass transfer; chemical process computer simulating. *Mailing Add:* 19380 Halsted St Northridge CA 91324

ALEXANDER, EDWARD CLEVE, ORGANIC CHEMISTRY, PHOTOCHEMISTRY. *Current Pos:* asst prof, 89-94, PROF, DEPT CHEM, SAN DIEGO MESA COL, 94-, CHAIR, 95- *Personal Data:* b Knoxville, Tenn, Nov 20, 43; m 72, Edwina Carr; c Everett, Erika & Efrem. *Educ:* City Col New York, BS, 65; State Univ NY, Buffalo, PhD(org chem), 69. *Prof Exp:* Fel, Iowa State Univ, 69-70; asst prof chem, Univ Calif, San Diego, 70-78; lectr chem, Calif State Univ, Los Angeles, 78-82; supvr, Dept Math & Sci, San Diego Community Col Dist, Boost Prog, Naval Training Ctr, 82-89. *Concurrent Pos:* Consult, IBM, San Jose, 76. *Mem:* Am Chem Soc; NY Acad Sci. *Res:* Organic photochemistry; highly strained ring systems; small ring heterocyclic chemistry; organic synthesis. *Mailing Add:* Dept Chem San Diego Mesa Col 7250 Mesa College Dr San Diego CA 92111-4998

ALEXANDER, ELAINE E, mathematics, for more information see previous edition

ALEXANDER, EMMIT CALVIN, JR, GEOCHRONOLOGY. *Current Pos:* from asst prof to assoc prof, 73-87, PROF UNIV MINN, MINNEAPOLIS, 87- *Personal Data:* b Lawton, Okla, July 4, 43; m 66; c 3. *Educ:* Okla State Univ, BS, 66; Univ Mo-Rolla, PhD(chem), 70. *Prof Exp:* Asst res chemist, Univ Calif, Berkeley, 70-73. *Concurrent Pos:* Prin investr & co-investr, Lunar Sample Analysis Prog, NASA, 70-80. *Mem:* Am Geophys Union; AAAS; Geochem Soc; Sigma Xi; Geol Soc Am; Meteoritical Soc; Nat Speleological Soc; Nat Water Well Asn. *Res:* Geohydrology; isotope geochemistry; ground water pollution and environmental geology; karst hydrology and geomorphology; geochronology; cosmochronology; rare-gas isotope studies. *Mailing Add:* Dept of Geol & Geophys Univ of Minn Minneapolis MN 55455-0219

ALEXANDER, FORREST DOYLE, MATHEMATICS. *Current Pos:* instr, Stephen F Austin State Univ, 56-59, from asst prof to assoc prof math, 61-67, admin asst, 68-79, PROF MATH, STEPHEN F AUSTIN STATE UNIV, 67-, ASST CHMN, 79- *Personal Data:* b Trenton, Tenn, Oct 27, 27; m 51, Bettye Patton; c James, Stephen & Linda. *Educ:* Union Univ, Tenn, BS, 50; George Peabody Col, MA, 55, PhD(math), 61. *Prof Exp:* Teacher high schs, Tenn, 51-56. *Concurrent Pos:* NSF grant, 61-62, lectr, NSF Coop Col-Sch Sci Prog, Stephen F Austin State Univ, 70-71; consult math staff, ETex Baptist Col & Nacogdoches County Pub Schs, 63-64. *Mem:* Math Asn Am; Nat Coun Teachers Math. *Res:* Elementary modern mathematics; abstract algebra; geometry; analysis. *Mailing Add:* Box 13040 Stephen F Austin State Univ Nacogdoches TX 75962

ALEXANDER, FRANK CREIGHTON, JR, PHYSICS, ELECTRONICS ENGINEERING. *Current Pos:* RETIRED. *Personal Data:* b Aspinwall, Pa, Nov 30, 18; m 42; c 3. *Educ:* Carnegie Inst Technol, 42. *Prof Exp:* Physicist, Gulf Res & Develop Co, 47-56; head, Electronic Lab, Res & Develop Div, Am Viscose Corp, 56-58, instrumentation group, FMC Corp, 58-62, head appl physics & instrumentation, Res & Develop Lab, 62-78; consult, Tech Physics Co, 78. *Concurrent Pos:* Instr, Carnegie Inst Technol, 50-51; instr physics & math, Friends Cent Sch, 78-79; instr antenna instrumentation, Rois Mfg Co, Inc, 79-81. *Mem:* Am Phys Soc; Inst Elec & Electronics Engrs. *Res:* Design and development of electronic instrumentation; electrical properties of organic materials; digital computer application. *Mailing Add:* Riddle Village 310 Lexington Mida PA 19063-6021

ALEXANDER, FRED, INTERNAL MEDICINE. *Current Pos:* ASST PROF MED, UNIV PA, 52-, DIR CLIN LAB, SMITH KLINE & FRENCH LABS, 62- *Personal Data:* b NJ, Sept 17, 17; m 50; c 4. *Educ:* St John's Col, Md, AB, 37; Univ Md, MD, 41. *Prof Exp:* Intern med, Univ Pittsburgh Hosps, 42-43; asst resident pediat, Children's Hosp, Philadelphia, 43-45; resident med, Jefferson Hosp, 45-46; resident cardiol, Mass Gen Hosp, 46-50; sr scientist med, Los Alamos Sci Lab, 50-52. *Concurrent Pos:* Consult, Pa Mutual Ins Co, 50-51. *Mem:* Am Col Physicians; Sigma Xi; AMA; Am Col Cardiol. *Res:* Initial human pharmacological trials of potential therapeutic agents; cardiovascular diseases, hypertension and renal pathology; chemotherapy; metabolism; psychopharmacological entities and diseases of nervous system. *Mailing Add:* Presbyterian Med Ctr Univ Pa 51 N 39th St Philadelphia PA 19104-2640

ALEXANDER, GEORGE JAY, neurotoxicology, for more information see previous edition

ALEXANDER, GERALD CORWIN, ELECTRICAL & ELECTRONICS ENGINEERING. *Current Pos:* asst prof elec eng, 55-63, ASSOC PROF ELEC ENG, ORE STATE UNIV, 64- *Personal Data:* b Corvallis, Ore, Mar 8, 30; m 53. *Educ:* Ore State Col, BS, 51; Mass Inst Technol, ScM, 60; Univ Calif, Berkeley, PhD, 73. *Prof Exp:* Eng trainee, Allis-Chalmers Mfg Co, Inc, 54-55. *Concurrent Pos:* Power systs anal, Bohn Power Admin; econ generator selection CHZM. *Mem:* Inst Elec & Electronics Engrs; Nat Soc Prof Engrs; Am Soc Eng Educ. *Res:* Power systems; electric machines; power electronics; on-line data acquisition and processing. *Mailing Add:* Dept Elec & Comput Eng Ore State Univ Corvallis OR 97331

ALEXANDER, GUY B, CHEMISTRY, METALS. *Current Pos:* RETIRED. *Personal Data:* b Ogden, Utah, May 31, 18; m 41; c 2. *Educ:* Univ Utah, BS, 41, MS, 42; Univ Wis, PhD(inorg chem), 47. *Prof Exp:* Res chemist, Manhattan Proj, Monsanto Chem Co, Ohio, 44-45; instr chem, Univ Utah, 46-47; res chemist, E I du Pont de Nemours & Co, 47-50, res supvr, 50-68; mgr chem res, Fansteel Inc, Md, 68-69, dir res, Vr-Wesson Div, Ill, 69-70 & San Fernando Labs, 70-73, dir res & lab mgr, Fansteel Res Ctr, 73-79; dir, Energy Dept, Univ Utah Res Inst, 80-83; pres, Tech Res Assocd Inc, 83-91. *Concurrent Pos:* Mem adv bd, Chem Mag, 72-75; adj prof, Univ Utah, 73- *Mem:* Am Chem Soc. *Res:* Colloid chemistry; sintered carbides; arc reactions; hot pressing; carbide powder processes; cermets; metals for high temperatures. *Mailing Add:* 4381 S Fortuna Way Salt Lake City UT 84124

ALEXANDER, HAROLD, BIOENGINEERING, ORTHOPEDIC RESEARCH. *Current Pos:* PRES & DIR, DEPT BIOENG, HOSP JOINT DIS ORTHOP INST, NEW YORK CITY, 86-; PROF ORTHOP SURG, SCH MED, NY STATE UNIV, 87-, ASST PROF OCCUP HEALTH & SAFETY, 87- *Personal Data:* b New York City, NY, Nov 12, 40; m 64, Shiela M Eisner; c Robin & Andrea. *Educ:* NY State Univ, BS, 62, MS, 63, PhD, 67. *Prof Exp:* Scientist, NY Univ, Bronx, 66-67, assoc res scientist, 67-68; asst prof, Stevens Inst Technol, Hoboken, NJ, 68-71, assoc prof, 71-77, co dir, Med Eng Lab, 73-77; assoc prof, Dept Surg & dir, G L Schultz Labs Orthop Res NJ Med Sch, Newark, 77-81, prof, 81-86. *Concurrent Pos:* Head, Lab Balloon Technol & adv fabrication on balloons, USAF, 68-74; vpres, CAS Inc, 74-78, pres, 78-83, sr adv CAS Med Syst, 84; lectr pediat, Mt Sinai Sch Med, New York City, 75-77; vis prof, Col Eng, Rutgers Univ, 75-76; consult, Johnson & Johnson Res Labs, New Brunswick, NJ, 75-76; dir, Orthomatrix Inc, 84-86; ed, J Biomed Mat Res, 87-89, J Appl Biomat, 90- *Mem:* Orthop Res Soc; Soc Biomat; Am Soc Mech Engrs; Am Soc Testing & Mats. *Res:* Development of new system for orthopedic implant use; bioengineering. *Mailing Add:* Orthogen Corp 530 Morris Ave Suite 204 Springfield NJ 07081-1033

ALEXANDER, HENRY R(ICHARD), ELECTRICAL ENGINEERING. *Current Pos:* systs prog mgr, 61-80, TECH STAFF, EQUIP DIV, RAYTHEON CO, 80- *Personal Data:* b Scranton, Pa, June 13, 25; m 52; c 5. *Educ:* Rutgers Univ, BSEE, 45, MSEE, 47; Princeton Univ, PhD(elec eng), 52. *Prof Exp:* Instr elec eng, Rutgers Univ, 45; asst, Princeton Univ, 48-50, res assoc, 50-51; physicist, Off Naval Res, 51-54, sci staff, Naval Attache, London, 55-56; mem tech staff, Inst Defense Analysis, DC, 56-59; mgr systs design, Gen Dynamics Electronics, NY, 59-61. *Concurrent Pos:* Consult, Mitre Corp, Mass, 60. *Mem:* Inst Elec & Electronics Engrs. *Res:* Circuit analysis; wave propagation; information processing; underwater sound systems; reconnaissance systems; radar. *Mailing Add:* Raytheon Co Hotwell Rd Bedford MA 01730

ALEXANDER, HERMAN DAVIS, NUTRITION, BIOCHEMISTRY. *Current Pos:* Asst nutrit & biochem, Auburn Univ, 50-55, asst prof nutrit, 55-60, from asst prof to assoc prof physiol, 60-66, assoc prof pharmacol, 66-76, ASSOC PROF ZOOL & ENTOM, AUBURN UNIV, 76- *Personal Data:* b Sweetwater, Tex, Dec 19, 19; m 46; c 2. *Educ:* Auburn Univ, BS, 50, MS, 52, PhD(nutrit, biochem), 55. *Mem:* Am Chem Soc. *Res:* Nutrition, effects of various nutritional deficiencies. *Mailing Add:* 498 Cary Dr Auburn AL 36830

ALEXANDER, IRA H(ENRIS), GEODESY, CIVIL ENGINEERING. *Current Pos:* CONSULT GEOD, 78- *Personal Data:* b Ft Leavenworth, Kans, July 9, 20; m 49; c 2. *Educ:* Univ Calif, BS, 42. *Honors & Awards:* Surv & Mapping Award, Am Soc Civil Engrs, 80. *Prof Exp:* Hwy engr, US Pub Roads Admin, 42-43 & 46; from civil engr asst to sr civil engr asst, Dept County Engr, County of Los Angeles, 47-53, civil engr assoc & asst geod sect chief, 53-56, assoc civil engr & geod sect chief, 56-60, civil engr, 60-63, asst div engr, Surv Div, 63-65, div engr, Mapping Div, 65-71, asst chief dep county engr, 71-78. *Concurrent Pos:* Lectr, Univ Calif, los Angeles, 51-91, Calif State Polytech, Pomona, 85-87, Calif State, Fresno, 89-; vpres, Metrex Systs Corp, 84-89; consult, Geodetic & Cadastral, 89-; mem, Eng Accreditation Comn, Accreditation Bd Eng & Technol, 85-90. *Mem:* Fel Am Soc Civil Engrs; Am Cong Surv & Mapping (pres-elect, 81, pres, 82); Am Geophys Union. *Res:* Application of geodetic techniques to subsidence problems; analysis of triangulation networks with time and movement parameters; criteria for intensification of mapping control. *Mailing Add:* 3812 Shannon Rd Los Angeles CA 90027

ALEXANDER, JAMES CRAIG, BIOCHEMISTRY, TOXICOLOGY. *Current Pos:* assoc prof biochem, 66-69, actg chmn, dept nutrit, 71-72 & 80-81, PROF BIOCHEM, UNIV GUELPH, 69- *Personal Data:* b Ont, Feb 12, 26; m 53; c 3. *Educ:* Univ Toronto, BSA, 49, MSA, 51; Univ Wis, PhD(biochem), 54. *Prof Exp:* Res biochemist, Procter & Gamble Co, 54-66. *Concurrent Pos:* Indust consult, 68-91. *Mem:* Fel AAAS; Am Inst Nutrit; Am Oil Chemists' Soc; Sigma Xi; Can Inst Food Sci & Technol; Can Soc Nutrit Sci. *Res:* Nutritional, biochemical and physiological studies on the effect of lipids on biological systems; nutritional value of germinated cereals. *Mailing Add:* Dept Nutrit Sci Univ Guelph Guelph ON N1G 2W1 Can

ALEXANDER, JAMES CREW, MATHEMATICS. *Current Pos:* res assoc, 69-70, asst prof, 70-73, assoc prof, 73-79, PROF MATH, UNIV MD, COLLEGE PARK, 79- *Personal Data:* b Zanesville, Ohio, Mar 22, 42; m; c 2. *Educ:* Johns Hopkins Univ, BA, 64, PhD(math), 68. *Prof Exp:* Instr math, Johns Hopkins Univ, 67-69. *Mem:* Am Math Soc; Soc Indust Appl Math. *Res:* Topological and functional methods applied to differential equations and dynamic systems of physical interest; mathematical modelling and simulation of systems in biology and engineering. *Mailing Add:* Univ Md College Park MD 20742-4015

ALEXANDER, JAMES KERMOTT, CARDIOLOGY. *Current Pos:* from asst prof to assoc prof med, Baylor Col Med, Houston, 54-60, chief, Cardiac Sect & dir, Cardiopulmonary Lab, 60-70, head, Cardiac Sect, Dept Med, 63-72, dir cardiovasc teaching, 82-87, PROF MED, BAYLOR COL MED, HOUSTON, TEX, 65- *Personal Data:* b Evanston, Ill, Dec 25, 20; m 45, 77, Carolyn Barr; c 3. *Educ:* Amherst Col, AB, 42; Harvard Univ, MD, 46; Am Bd Internal Med, dipl, 55. *Prof Exp:* Intern, First Med Div, Bellevue Hosp, NY, 46-47; chief, Radiol Sect, US Army Hosp, Guam, 47-49; resident internal med, Bellevue Hosp, 50-51; asst med, Columbia Univ, 53-54. *Concurrent Pos:* Res fel, Cardiopulmonary Lab, Bellevue Hosp, NY, 49-50; Am Heart Asn res fels, Dept Physiol, Harvard Med Sch, 51-52 & Cardiopulmonary Lab, Presby Hosp, 52-53; asst attend physician, Presby Hosp, 53-54; dir, Cardiac Lab, Ben Taub Gen Hosp, 54-; assoc internal med, Methodist Hosp, 55; chief cardiol, Ben Taub Gen Hosp, 70-82, Houston Vet Admin Ctr, 84-91; actg chief cardiol, Vet Admin Hosp, Houston, 84-94; sr physician, Methodist Hosp, 93. *Mem:* Asn Univ Cardiologists; Am Heart Asn; Am Fedn Clin Res; Am Physiol Soc; Am Soc Clin Invest. *Res:* Cardiopulmonary function in a variety of chronic lung and circulatory diseases, including obesity; cardiopulmonary function at high altitude. *Mailing Add:* Houston Vet Admin Med Ctr Sect 111B 2002 Holcombe Blvd Houston TX 77030. *Fax:* 713-794-7492

ALEXANDER, JAMES KING, microbiology, biochemistry, for more information see previous edition

ALEXANDER, JAMES WESLEY, SURGERY & TRANSPLANTATION, IMMUNOLOGY. *Current Pos:* from asst prof to assoc prof surg, 66-75, actg dir, Blood Ctr, 72-79, PROF SURG, MED CTR, UNIV CINCINNATI, 75-, DIR, TRANSPLANTATION DIV, 67- *Personal Data:* b El Dorado, Kans, May 23, 34; m 84, Maureen L Foertsch; c Judith, Joseph, Lori, Moley, Elizabeth, Randolph & John Charles. *Educ:* Univ Tex, MD, 57; Univ Cincinnati, ScD(surg), 64; Am Bd Surg & Bd Thoracic Surg, cert, 65. *Honors & Awards:* Altemeier Lectr, Surg Infection Soc, 85; Cuthbertson lectr, Europ Soc Parenteral & Enteral Nutrit, 89; Strauss Lectr, Univ Wash, 90; Harvey Stuart Allen Distinguished Serv Award, Am Burn Asn, 94. *Prof Exp:* Chief, Trauma Study Br, Surg Res Unit, Ft Sam Houston, Tex, 65-66; dir res, Shriners Burn Inst, Cincinnati Unit, 79-90. *Concurrent Pos:* Ad hoc consult, NIH, 67-; mem, NIH Study Sect Surg, Anesthesiol & Trauma, 83-93, chmn, 90-93; pres & med dir, Ohio Valley Life Ctr. *Mem:* Fel Am Col Surg; Am Asn Surg Trauma; Am Soc Transplant Surgeons (pres, 87-88); Int Soc Surg; Transplantation Soc; Am Burn Asn (pres, 84-85); Surg Infection Soc (pres, 86-87); Am Asn Immunol; Asn Acad Surg; Int Soc Burn Injuries; Am Surg Asn. *Res:* Infections; host defense mechanisms; transplantation; burn injury; nutrition; immunomodulation; immunonutrient; transplantation tolerance. *Mailing Add:* Dept Surg Univ Cincinnati Med Ctr Cincinnati OH 45267-0558. *Fax:* 513-558-3580; *E-Mail:* alexanjw@healthall.com

ALEXANDER, JOHN BRADFIELD, NON-LETHAL WEAPONS DEVELOPMENT, PHENOMENOLOGY. *Current Pos:* PRES, APOLLINAIRE GROUP, 94-; CONSULT, IR DEFENSE RES & ENG, OFF SECY DEFENSE, PENTAGON, 96- *Personal Data:* b New York, NY, Nov 21, 37; m, Victoria Lacas; c Marc B & Joshua J. *Educ:* Univ Nebr, BGS, 71; Pepperdine Univ, MA, 75; Walden Univ, PhD(educ), 80. *Honors & Awards:* Nat Award for Volunteerism, Pres Reagan, 87; Weapons Prog Recognition of Excellence, 94. *Prof Exp:* Chief, Human Resources Div, US Army, Ft McPherson, 77-79, inspector gen, 80-82, chief, Human Tech Army Intel Command, 82-83, mgr tech integration, Army Material Command, 83-85, dir advan concepts, US Army Lab Command, 85-88; mgr nonlethal weapons defense technol, Los Alamos Nat Lab, 88-95, mgr anti-material tech, Defense Initiatives Off, 88-91, prog mgr contingency missions tech, Conventional Defense Technol, 91-92, prog mgr nonlethal defense, Spec Technol Group, Nonproliferation & Int Security Div, 92-95. *Concurrent Pos:* Adj prof, Grad Sch, Union Inst, Ohio, 92-97; mem, Non-Lethal Warfare Study Group, Coun Foreign Rels, NY & Washington, 93; US deleg, NATO Adv Group Aerospace Res & Develop, 94-; distinguished guest lectr, USAF Command & Staff Col, Air Univ, Maxwell AFB, 94- *Mem:* Soc Sci Explor. *Res:* Contributed numerous articles to professional journals. *Mailing Add:* 9521 Grand Canal Las Vegas NV 89117

ALEXANDER, JOHN J, INORGANIC CHEMISTRY, ORGANOMETALLIC CHEMISTRY. *Current Pos:* from asst prof to assoc prof, 70-79, PROF CHEM, UNIV CINCINNATI, 79- *Personal Data:* b Indianapolis, Ind, Apr 13, 40. *Educ:* Columbia Col, AB, 62; Columbia Univ, MA, 63, NSF fel & PhD(chem), 67. *Prof Exp:* Res assoc chem, Ohio State Univ, 67-69, fel, 67-68. *Concurrent Pos:* Vis prof, Ohio State Univ, 85-86 & 94. *Mem:* Am Chem Soc; Sigma Xi. *Res:* Electronic structures of transition metal complexes; synthetic organometallic chemistry. *Mailing Add:* Dept Chem Univ Cincinnati Cincinnati OH 45221-0172. *Fax:* 513-556-9239; *E-Mail:* john.j.alexander@uc.edu

ALEXANDER, JOHN MACMILLAN, JR, PHYSICAL CHEMISTRY, NUCLEAR SCIENCE & CHEMISTRY. *Current Pos:* assoc prof, 63-68, chmn dept, 70-72, PROF CHEM, STATE UNIV NY STONY BROOK, 68- *Personal Data:* b Columbia, Mo, Aug 17, 31; m 53, Betty Jo Linton; c Mary Jo, John M III, Frank L & James H. *Educ:* Davidson Col, BS, 53; Mass Inst Technol, PhD(phys chem), 56. *Honors & Awards:* Nuclear Chem Award, Am Chem Soc, 91. *Prof Exp:* Res assoc chem, Mass Inst Technol, 56-57; chemist, Lawrence Radiation Lab, Univ Calif, Berkeley, 57-63. *Concurrent Pos:* Researcher, AEC-ERDA, Dept Energy, res collabr, Brookhaven Nat Lab, 64-; Sloan fel, 64-66; chmn, Gordon Res Conf Nuclear Chem, 66; assoc ed, Am Chem Soc Monographs, 68-69; Guggenheim fel, 69-70; vis scientist, Nuclear Study Ctr, Bordeaux, France, 69-70; mem exec comt, Berkeley Superhilac Accelerator, 75-78; prog adv comt, Van de Graaff Accelerator, Brookhaven Nat Lab, 77-81, Holifield Heavy Ion Res Facil, Oak Ridge Nat Lab, 86-89, Systême Accélérateur Rhône-Alpes, Inst des Sci Nuclérires de Grenoble, Grenoble, France, 88-89; vis prof, Nuclear Study Ctr, Bordeaux-Gradignan & Inst Nuclear Physics, Orsay, France, 78-79; chmn, Div Nuclear Chem Technol, Am Chem Soc. *Mem:* Am Chem Soc; fel Am Phys Soc. *Res:* Nuclear chemistry and reactions; high-energy nuclear reactions, especially fission, spallation, and fragmentation; heavy ion reaction dynamics; elastic scattering, complete and incomplete fusion, energy and spin dissipation, evaporative deexcitation, lifetimes of hot nuclei. *Mailing Add:* Dept Chem State Univ NY Stony Brook NY 11794-3400. *Fax:* 516-632-7987

ALEXANDER, JONATHAN, CARDIOLOGY. *Current Pos:* fel, Dept Cardiol, Sch Med, Yale Univ, New Haven, 76-78, asst clin prof, 78-83, assoc clin prof, Sch Med, 83-94, CLIN PROF MED, YALE UNIV, 95-; DIR, CARDIAC REHAB UNIT & NUCLEAR CARDIOL, DANBURY HOSP, CONN, 78- *Personal Data:* b New York City, NY, Nov 29, 47; m 71, Karen D Einhorn; c Jessica B, Daniel L & Benjamin J. *Educ:* Harvard Univ, BA, 68; Albert Einstein Col Med, MD, 73. *Honors & Awards:* Revlon Award, Cong Chemother, 83. *Prof Exp:* Intern resident, Yale New Haven Hosp, 73-76. *Concurrent Pos:* Attend physician, Danbury Hosp, Conn, 80, West Haven, Vets Hosp, 78-, New Milford Hosp, 80; counr, Clin Cardiol, Am Heart Asn; gov, Am Coll Cardiol, Conn, 93-96; pres, Conn Chap, Am Coll Cardiol, 94-96. *Mem:* Am Col Cardiol; Am Col Chest Physicians; Am Heart Asn; Soc Nuclear Med; fel Am Col Physicians. *Res:* Cardiology; consulting. *Mailing Add:* Danbury Hosp Danbury CT 06810

ALEXANDER, JOSEPH KUNKLE, SPACE PHYSICS, RADIO ASTRONOMY. *Current Pos:* DEP ASST ADMIN RES & DEVELOP, ENVIRON PROTECTION AGENCY, 94- *Personal Data:* b Staunton, Va, Jan 9, 40; m 62, Diana Titolo; c Kathryn C, Stephen A & David A. *Educ:* Col William & Mary, BS, 60, MA, 62. *Honors & Awards:* Sci Achievement Medal, NASA, 81. *Prof Exp:* Physicist, NASA Hq, 62-70, sect head, 70-76, br head, Goddard Space Flight Ctr, 76-83, sr policy analyst, White House Sci Off, 84-85, assoc lab chief, Goddard Space Flight Ctr, 85, dep chief scientist, 85-87, asst assoc admin, Sci & Appln, 87-93, assoc dir, space sci, Goddard Space Flight Ctr, 93-94. *Concurrent Pos:* Vis scientist, Univ Colo, 73-74; mem space sci adv comt, NASA, 80-82, space & earth sci adv comt, 82-84, proj scientist, Origins Plasmas Earth's Neighborhood Proj, 81-83 & Int Solar-Terrestrial Physics Proj, 83-85, acting dir, Life Sci, 92-93. *Mem:* Am Geophys Union; Int Astron Union; Am Astron Soc; Soc Environ Toxicol & Chem. *Res:* Planetary magnetospheres and solar-planetary relationships, especially in the area of radio-wave and plasma-wave phenomena and their relation to the interactions of charged particles and fields in space. *Mailing Add:* 6410 Forest Mill Lane Laurel MD 20707-2700. *Fax:* 202-260-9500; *E-Mail:* alexander.joseph@epamail.epa.gov

ALEXANDER, JOSEPH WALKER, VETERINARY MEDICINE & ADMINISTRATION, MARINE MAMMAL MEDICINE. *Current Pos:* PROF VET SURG & DEAN COL VET MED, OKLA STATE UNIV, 85- *Personal Data:* b Washington, DC, Jan 22, 47; m 70; c 2. *Educ:* Univ Ariz, BS, 69; Colo State Univ, DVM, 73; Univ Tenn, MS, 81; Am Col Vet Surgeons, dipl, 79. *Prof Exp:* Staff vet, Cheshire Vet Clin, 76-77; from asst prof to assoc prof vet surg, Univ Tenn, 77-81; prof vet surg, Va Tech, 81-85, chmn div agr & urban pract, 82-85, dir Vet Med Teaching Hosp, 83-85. *Concurrent Pos:* Consult, Marine Animal Prod, 86- *Mem:* Asn Am Vet Med Col (pres, 90-91); Comn Vet Med; Asn Aquatic Animal Med (pres-elect, 91-92). *Res:* Veterinary orthopedics and veterinary orthopedic diseases; author of three books and over 60 publications. *Mailing Add:* 6310 Coventry Stillwater OK 74074

ALEXANDER, KENNETH ROSS, VISION. *Current Pos:* RES ASSOC PHYSIOL OPTICS, ILL EYE & EAR INFIRMARY, 81- *Personal Data:* b Seattle, Wash, Feb 23, 45; m 81. *Educ:* Univ Wash, BA & BS, 67, MS, 68, PhD(psychol), 72. *Prof Exp:* Fel vision, Univ Rochester, 72-73; asst assoc prof physiol optics, Ill Col Optom, 73-81. *Concurrent Pos:* Instr, Sch Art Inst Chicago, 80-81. *Mem:* AAAS; Asn Res Vision & Ophthal; Optical Soc Am. *Res:* Psychophysical investigation of visual characteristics and underlying mechanisms of various types of inherited retinal disorders, such as retinitis pigmentosa and cone dystrophy, with an emphasis on rod and cone mechanisms. *Mailing Add:* Dept Ophthal & Vision Sci Univ Ill 1855 W Taylor St Chicago IL 60612

ALEXANDER, LESLIE LUTHER, MEDICINE, RADIOLOGY. *Current Pos:* PROF RADIOL, HEALTH SCI CTR, STATE UNIV NY STONY BROOK & DIR RADIOL, LONG ISLAND JEWISH-HILLSIDE MED CTR AFFIL, QUEENS HOSP CTR, 77- *Personal Data:* b Kingston, Jamaica, Oct 10, 17; US citizen; m 51; c 5. *Educ:* NY Univ, AB, 47, AM, 48; Howard Univ, MD, 52. *Prof Exp:* From instr to prof radiol, Col Med, State Univ NY Downstate Med Ctr, 56-77. *Concurrent Pos:* Nat Med Fels, Inc fel, 54-56; consult, Brooklyn Vet Hosp, 62-71, Cath Med Ctr Brooklyn & Queens, 67- & Bur Health Prof Educ & Manpower Training, NIH, 70-74; asst ed, J Nat Med Asn, 64-; dir radiation ther, North Shore Hosp, Manhasset, NY, 70-77; consult, Bur Med Devices, Food & Drug Admin, HEW, 75- & med adv comt, Bur Radiol Health, State NY, 77-81; mem, Bd Chancellors, Am Col Radiol, Chicago, 80- *Mem:* AMA; Asn Univ Radiologists; fel Am Col Radiol; Am Soc Therapeut Radiologist; fel NY Acad Med. *Res:* Radiology, including radiation therapy, nuclear medicine, radiobiology and cancer research. *Mailing Add:* Queens Hosp Ctr 82-68 164th St Jamaica NY 11432-1140

ALEXANDER, LLOYD EPHRAIM, embryology; deceased, see previous edition for last biography

ALEXANDER, MARTIN, SOIL MICROBIOLOGY, MICROBIAL ECOLOGY. *Current Pos:* From asst prof to assoc prof, 55-64, PROF SOIL MICROBIOL, CORNELL UNIV, 64-, LIBERTY HYDE BAILEY PROF, 77- *Personal Data:* b Newark, NJ, Feb 4, 30; m 51; c 2. *Educ:* Rutgers Univ, BS, 51; Univ Wis, MS, 53, PhD(bact), 55. *Honors & Awards:* Fisher Award. *Concurrent Pos:* Consult to var pvt industs, int & nat agencies. *Mem:* Fel AAAS; fel Am Soc Agron; fel Am Acad Microbiol; Am Soc Microbiol. *Res:* Biodegradation; bioremediation; environmental fate; pesticide decomposition; biochemical ecology; environmental pollution. *Mailing Add:* 708 Bradfield Hall Cornell Univ Ithaca NY 14853

ALEXANDER, MARTIN DALE, INORGANIC CHEMISTRY. *Current Pos:* From asst prof to assoc prof, 64-74, PROF CHEM, NMEX STATE UNIV, 74- *Personal Data:* b Grants, NMex, Nov 27, 38; m 68; c 1. *Educ:* NMex State Univ, BSc, 60; Ohio State Univ, PhD(inorg chem), 64. *Mem:* Am Chem Soc; fel Brit Chem Soc. *Res:* Mechanisms of reactions of coordination compounds of transition metals; synthesis of transition metal coordination compounds. *Mailing Add:* Dept Chem NMex State Univ Box 30001 Dept 3C Las Cruces NM 88003

ALEXANDER, MARY LOUISE, genetics, for more information see previous edition

ALEXANDER, MAURICE MYRON, VERTEBRATE ECOLOGY, WETLAND ECOLOGY. *Current Pos:* teaching fel, 47-49, from instr to prof, 49-83, chmn dept, 65-77, EMER PROF FOREST ZOOL, STATE UNIV NY COL ENVIRON SCI & FORESTRY, 83- *Personal Data:* b South Onondaga, NY, Dec 18, 17; m 43, Annette R Blain; c Ralph J, Richard M & Robert A. *Educ:* NY State Col Forestry, BS, 40, PhD(wildlife mgt), 50; Univ Conn, MS, 42. *Prof Exp:* Res asst, State Bd Fisheries & Game, Conn, 45-46; instr forestry & wildlife mgt, Univ Conn, 46-47. *Concurrent Pos:* Dir, Roosevelt Wildlife Forest Exp Sta, 65-83. *Mem:* Wildlife Soc; Am Soc Mammalogists; Ecol Soc Am; Soc Study Amphibians & Reptiles. *Res:* Animal ecology; aging techniques; furbearer management; wetland ecology. *Mailing Add:* 4039 Tanner Rd RD 2 Syracuse NY 13215-9728

ALEXANDER, MICHAEL NORMAN, SOLID STATE PHYSICS & MATERIALS SCIENCE FOR ELECTRONICS & PHOTONICS. *Current Pos:* br chief, 88-89, DIV CHIEF, ROME LAB, HANSCOM, MASS, 89-, ROME LAB, 91- *Personal Data:* b Washington, DC, Mar 27, 41; m 64, Judith Deutsch; c Daniel & Shana. *Educ:* Harvard Univ, AB, 62; Cornell Univ, PhD(physics), 67. *Prof Exp:* Res asst physics, Cornell Univ, 64-67; res physicist, Mat Sci Div, Army Mat & Mech Res Ctr, Watertown, Mass, 67-79; sr mem of tech staff, GTE Labs, Inc, 79-86; prin scientist, Res & Develop & New Bus Ctr, Thermo Electron Corp, Waltham, Mass, 86-88. *Concurrent Pos:* Mem adv comt on wetlands, Planning Bd, Lexington, Mass, 75-76; exec comt, New Eng Sect Am Phys Soc, 84-86; co-chmn, High Sch Guidance Adv Comt, 84-87; mem, Adv Comt, Okla State Univ Ctr Laser & Photonics Res, 96- *Mem:* AAAS; Sigma Xi; Am Phys Soc; Inst Elec & Electronics Engrs; Mat Res Soc. *Res:* Electronic structure of metals, alloys and semiconductors; optical properties of crystalline insulators, glasses and semiconductors; III-V semiconductor materials fabrication and properties; research and development management and policy. *Mailing Add:* 66 Baskin Rd Lexington MA 02173. *E-Mail:* alexande@maxwell.rl.plh.af.mil

ALEXANDER, MILLARD HENRY, THEORETICAL CHEMISTRY. *Current Pos:* asst prof molecular physics, 71-73, from asst prof to assoc prof chem, 73-79, PROF CHEM, UNIV MD, COLLEGE PARK, 79- *Personal Data:* b Boston, Mass, Feb 17, 43; m 91, Veryla Lee; c Stephanie, William Halker & Alyssa Henry. *Educ:* Harvard Col, BA, 64; Univ Paris, PhD(chem), 67. *Honors & Awards:* Alexander von Humboldt Sr Scientist Prize, 89. *Prof Exp:* Res fel chem, Harvard Univ, 67-71. *Mem:* Am Chem Soc; fel Am Phys Soc. *Res:* Theoretical study of rotationally and electronically inelastic collisions between atoms and molecules; chemical reactions of electronically excited atoms and molecules; photofragmentation of small molecules. *Mailing Add:* Dept Chem Univ Md College Park MD 20742. *Fax:* 301-314-9121; *E-Mail:* millard_h_alexander@nmail.umd.edu

ALEXANDER, NANCY J, REPRODUCTIVE PHYSIOLOGY, IMMUNOLOGY. *Current Pos:* CHIEF, CONTRACEPTIVE DEVELOP PROG, NAT INST CHILD HEALTH & HUMAN DEVELOP, 90- *Personal Data:* b Cleveland, Ohio, Dec 1, 39; m 70; c 2. *Educ:* Miami Univ, BS, 60, MA, 61; Univ Wis, PhD(entom), 65. *Prof Exp:* Asst prof zool, Miami Univ, 66-67; fel electron micros, Ore Health Sci Univ, 67-69, from asst scientist to assoc scientist, 69-78, scientist reproductive biol & behav, Ore Regional Primate Ctr, 78-86, dir andrology infertility serv, 75-86, prof anat & cell biol & obstet & gynec & urol, 80-86, prof microbiol & immunol, 84-86; prof obstet & gynec, Eastern Va Med Sch, 86-90, dir appl & basic res, Contraceptive Res & Develop Prog, 86-90. *Concurrent Pos:* Mem animal resources adv comt, NIH, 73-77, sci adv comt, Prog Applied Res Fertility Regulation, 76-83, Nat Adv Res Resources Coun, NIH, 80-84. *Mem:* Am Soc Cell Biol; Am Fertility Soc; Am Soc Andrology (treas, 75-77, vpres, 78, pres, 79); Soc Study Reproduction; AAAS. *Res:* Semen banking, infertility and immunoreproduction; immunological effects of vasectomy. *Mailing Add:* 10 Loganwood Ct Rockville MD 20852

ALEXANDER, NANCY J, GENETICS. *Current Pos:* MICROBIOLOGIST, AGR RES SERV, USDA, PEORIA, 80- *Personal Data:* b Ithaca, NY, Jan 14, 47; m 90, Verle Davison. *Educ:* State Univ NY, Oswego, BS, 68; Duke Univ, MA, 71, PhD(genetics), 77. *Prof Exp:* Res & teaching asst, Dept Bot, Duke Univ, 68-70, Dept Bot & Genetics, 70-73 & Dept Zool, 73-77; res assoc, Dept Genetics, Ohio State Univ, 77-80. *Mem:* Sigma Xi; Genetics Soc Am. *Res:* Molecular and physiological studies of yeast; fermentations; biomass conversion; xylose conversion to ethanol; molecular characterization of mycotoxin biosynthetic pathways. *Mailing Add:* Northern Regional Res Lab USDA 1815 N University St Peoria IL 61604. *E-Mail:* alexannj@ncaurl.ncaur.gov

ALEXANDER, NATALIE, NEURAL CONTROL CIRCULATION, HYPERTENSION. *Current Pos:* From instr to asst prof physiol, 50-58, res assoc med physiol, 58-70, from asst prof med to assoc prof med, 70-82, PROF MED, SCH MED, UNIV SOUTHERN CALIF, 82- *Personal Data:* b Los Angeles, Calif, Aug 31, 26; m 50; c 2. *Educ:* Univ Southern Calif, MS, 48, PhD(med physiol), 52. *Concurrent Pos:* USPHS career develop grant, 60-; mem staff, Los Angeles County Hosp, 55; mem nat adv comt, Nat Heart & Lung Inst, 73-75, 79, 81-84, CV & Renal Study Sect, 76-80. *Mem:* AAAS; Am Physiol Soc; Am Heart Asn; Soc Exp Biol Med; Sigma Xi. *Res:* Circulatory physiology and hypertension. *Mailing Add:* Dept Med Hoffman Res Bldg 801 Univ Southern Calif 2011 Zonal Ave Los Angeles CA 90033

ALEXANDER, NICHOLAS MICHAEL, BIOCHEMISTRY. *Current Pos:* assoc adj prof, 70-74, PROF PATH, UNIV CALIF, SAN DIEGO, 74-, DIR CLIN CHEM, UNIV HOSP, 85- *Personal Data:* b Boise, Idaho, June 30, 25; m 53; c 3. *Educ:* Univ Calif, AB, 50, PhD(biochem), 55. *Honors & Awards:* Van Meter Award, Am Thyroid Asn, 60. *Prof Exp:* Lectr biochem, Yale Univ, 56-64, from asst prof to assoc prof, Sch Med, 64-70. *Concurrent Pos:* Prin scientist biochem & assoc dir radioisotope serv, Vet Admin Hosp, 55-63. *Mem:* Am Chem Soc; Am Thyroid Asn; Am Soc Biol Chem; Endocrine Soc; Acad Clin Lab Physicians & Scientists; Am Asn Clin Chem. *Res:* Iodine and amino acid metabolism; thyroid hormone biosynthesis; fatty acid and protein metabolism; clinical chemistry, thyroid hormones and liver regeneration. *Mailing Add:* Univ Calif San Diego Sch Med 8390 Cliffridge Ln La Jolla CA 92037

ALEXANDER, PAUL MARION, PLANT PATHOLOGY, HORTICULTURE. *Current Pos:* PRES, GRASS ROOTS, INC, 81- *Personal Data:* b Akron, Ohio, Aug 21, 27; wid; c Geoffrey, James & Richard. *Educ:* Calif State Polytech Col, BS, 53; Ohio State Univ, MSc, 55, PhD(bot, plant path), 58. *Prof Exp:* Asst plant pathologist, Clemson Univ, 58-66, from asst prof to assoc prof hort, 66-69; agronomist, Green Sect, US Golf Asn, 69-70; dir educ, Golf Course Supt Asn Am, 70-73; staff vpres agron, Sea Pines Co, 73-74; chief agronomist & turf mgr, Goltra, Inc, Winston-Salem, NC, 75-77; staff agronomist, Porter Bros, Inc, 77-79; vpres, Golf Operations, Sea Pines Co, 79-81; lectr, Horry-Georgetown Tech Col, 87-92, instr, 87-93. *Concurrent Pos:* Proj leader, SC Turfgrass Res Proj, 58-69; pres, PM's Corp, Clemson, 81-83; nat training dir & agronomist, Chemlawn Serv Corp, 82-87.

Mem: Am Phytopath Soc; Soc Nematologists; Golf Course Supt Asn Am. *Res:* Diseases of turf grasses and ornamental plants; phytonematology; turf fungicides; weed control; soil amendments; irrigation practices; turf insects. *Mailing Add:* Grass Roots Inc 105 Dogwood Circle Conway SC 29526

ALEXANDER, RALPH WILLIAM, MEDICINE. *Current Pos:* RETIRED. *Personal Data:* b Schley, Ohio, Mar 14, 11; m 37, Gladys Robin; c Ralph Jr, Judith A (Goodloe), Anne A (Koehler), Nancy & David. *Educ:* Marietta Col, AB, 32; Univ Rochester, MD, 36. *Honors & Awards:* Ruth Boynton Award, Am Col Health Asn, 70, Edward Hitchcock Award, 73. *Prof Exp:* Rotating intern, Jefferson Hosp, Philadelphia, Pa, 36-38; resident, William Pepper Lab Clin Med, Hosp Univ Pa, 38-39, student health serv, 39-40, staff physician, 40-46; from asst prof to assoc prof clin & prev med, Cornell Univ, 46-61, attend physician clin & infirmary, 53-61, dep dir & attend physician, Gannett Clin & Sage Infirm, 61-69, actg dir, Dept Univ Health Serv, 69-71, prof clin med, Dept Univ Health Serv, 61-77, dep dir dept, 71-77. *Concurrent Pos:* Ed, Student Med, 52-62 & J Am Col Health Asn, 62-73; mem, Am Bd Internal Med. *Mem:* AMA; Am Col Physicians; fel Am Col Health Asn. *Res:* Internal medicine; university students health. *Mailing Add:* Bldg 5 Apt 7 Quail's Run Blvd Englewood FL 34223

ALEXANDER, RALPH WILLIAM, JR, SOLID STATE PHYSICS, SPECTROSCOPY. *Current Pos:* fel, Univ Mo, Rolla, 70, from asst prof to assoc prof, 70-80, chmn, 84-92, PROF PHYSICS, UNIV MO, ROLLA, 80- *Personal Data:* b Philadelphia, Pa, May 17, 41; m 65, Janet Bradley; c Ralph & Margaret. *Educ:* Wesleyan Univ, BA, 63; Cornell Univ, PhD(physics), 68. *Prof Exp:* Ger Res Asn fel, Univ Freiburg, 68-69. *Mem:* Am Phys Soc; Am Asn Physics Teachers. *Res:* Spectroscopy of solid surfaces; millimeter and submillimeter spectroscopy. *Mailing Add:* Physics Dept Univ Mo Rolla MO 65401. *Fax:* 573-341-4715; *E-Mail:* alexande@physics.umr.edu

ALEXANDER, RENEE R, MOLECULAR BIOLOGY, BIOCHEMISTRY. *Current Pos:* RETIRED. *Personal Data:* b Leipzig, Ger, Jan 23, 32; US citizen; m 51; c 2. *Educ:* Univ Wis, BS, 54, MS, 55; Cornell Univ, PhD(microbiol), 58. *Prof Exp:* Asst bact, Univ Wis, 54-55; asst bact, Cornell Univ, 55-58, res assoc microbiol, 58, phys biol, 62-65 & biochem & molecular biol, 65-70, lectr, 71-81, sr lectr biochem, 81-95; asst prof genetics, State Univ NY Col Cortland, 70-71. *Concurrent Pos:* Vis scientist, Soils Crops Atmospheric Sci, Cornell Univ. *Mem:* Am Soc Microbiol; Sigma Xi. *Res:* Development of ussay procedures to follow fate of toxic chemicals in soil. *Mailing Add:* 301 Winthrop Dr Ithaca NY 14850

ALEXANDER, RICHARD DALE, ZOOLOGY. *Current Pos:* from instr to assoc prof, 57-69, CUR INSECTS, MUS ZOOL, UNIV MICH, ANN ARBOR, 57-, PROF ZOOL, 69-, HUBBELL DISTINGUISHED UNIV PROF EVOLUTIONARY BIOL, 90- *Personal Data:* b White Heath, Ill, Nov 18, 29; m 50; c 2. *Educ:* Ill State Univ, BSc, 50; Ohio State Univ, MSc, 51, PhD(entom), 56. *Hon Degrees:* LHD, Ill State Univ. *Honors & Awards:* Daniel Giraud Elliot Medal, 71; Newcomb Cleveland Prize, AAAS, 61. *Prof Exp:* Res assoc, Rockefeller Found, 56-57. *Concurrent Pos:* J S Guggenheim fel, 68-69. *Mem:* Nat Acad Sci; Am Soc Naturalists; fel AAAS; Animal Behav Soc. *Res:* Acoustical communication in insects; systematics of Orthoptera and Cicadidae; evolution and human behavior; evolution of insect and social behavior. *Mailing Add:* Mus Zool Univ Mich 1109 Geddes Ann Arbor MI 48109-1079

ALEXANDER, RICHARD RAYMOND, PALEOECOLOGY. *Current Pos:* assoc prof, 81-86, PROF GEOL, RIDER COL, 86-, DEPT CHMN, 83- *Personal Data:* b Covington, Ky, Feb 2, 46; m 72. *Educ:* Univ Cincinnati, BS, 68; Ind Univ, MA, 70, PhD(geol), 72. *Prof Exp:* From asst prof to assoc prof geol, Utah State Univ, 72-81. *Concurrent Pos:* Chmn, Northeast Sect, Paleont Soc, 88. *Mem:* Soc Econ Paleont & Mineral; Paleont Soc; Paleont Asn; Sigma Xi; Int Paleont Union. *Res:* Paleoautecology of brachiopods and bivalves, particularly demographic and morphologic adaptations to sedimentologic influences and intraspecific-interspecific competition, and secondly, the relationship of functional morphology to generic longevity. *Mailing Add:* Geol & Marine Sci Rider Col 2083 Lawrenceville Rd Lawrenceville NJ 08648

ALEXANDER, ROBERT L, CIVIL ENGINEERING. *Current Pos:* RETIRED. *Personal Data:* b London, Eng, Feb 9, 23; US citizen; m 57; c 2. *Educ:* Rensselaer Polytech Inst, BArch, 49; Harvard Univ, MSc, 56; Univ Calif, DEng(transp), 64. *Prof Exp:* Architect, Stephenson & Turner, Australia, 49-51; archit engr, Western Elec Co, NY, 51-53; struct engr, Skidmore, Owings & Merrill, Okinawa, 53-54; found engr, Koppers Co, Pa, 56-57; asst prof civil eng, Univ Conn, 57-60; from assoc prof to prof, Calif State Univ, Long Beach, 64-90, emer prof civil eng, 90- *Concurrent Pos:* Assoc mem, Hwy Res Bd, Nat Acad Sci-Nat Res Coun, 64- *Mem:* Am Soc Civil Engrs. *Res:* Architectural sciences; transportation engineering; phenomenological viscoelasticity. *Mailing Add:* Dept Civil Eng Calif State Univ 1250 Bellflower Blvd Long Beach CA 90840

ALEXANDER, ROBERT SPENCE, PHYSIOLOGY. *Current Pos:* chmn dept, 55-73, prof physiol, 55-79, EMER PROF PHYSIOL, ALBANY MED COL, 79-, EMER PROF PHYSIOL. *Personal Data:* b Melrose, Mass, June 14, 17; m 42, Eleanor Paddock; c Joan (Fordham), Helen (Adams), Carolyn (Perez), Beverly (Pill) & Bruce E. *Educ:* Amherst Col, AB, 38, MA, 40; Princeton Univ, PhD(gen physiol), 42. *Hon Degrees:* DSc, Albany Med Col, 82. *Prof Exp:* Asst physiol, Princeton Univ, 40-42; instr, Med Col, Cornell Univ, 42-45; sr instr, Sch Med, Western Reserve Univ, 45-47, from asst prof to assoc prof, 47-53; assoc prof, Med Col, Univ Ga, 53-55. *Concurrent Pos:* Res consult, Vet Admin Hosp, 48-52 & Off Naval Res, 65-81. *Mem:* AAAS; Am Physiol Soc; Harvey Soc. *Res:* Dynamics of arterial pulses; regulation of venous system; smooth muscle tone. *Mailing Add:* 69 Murray Ave Delmar NY 12054

ALEXANDER, ROGER KEITH, NUMERICAL ANALYSIS, NONLINEAR ANALYSIS. *Current Pos:* ASSOC PROF MATH SCI, IOWA STATE UNIV. *Personal Data:* b Wichita, Kans, Dec 17, 46; m 68; c 2. *Educ:* Univ Kans, BA, 68; Univ Calif, Berkeley, MA, 74, PhD(math), 75. *Prof Exp:* Asst prof math, Univ Colo, Boulder, 75-77; asst prof math sci, Rennselaer Polytech Inst, 77- *Mem:* Math Asn Am; Am Math Soc; Soc Indust & Appl Math. *Res:* Analysis of methods and development of numerical software for stiff differential equations; analysis of nonlinear differential equations, especially nonlinear eigenvalve problems and free boundary problems. *Mailing Add:* Iowa State Univ Ames IA 50011-0001

ALEXANDER, SAMUEL CRAIGHEAD, JR, ANESTHESIOLOGY, PHARMACOLOGY. *Current Pos:* chmn dept, 72-77, PROF ANESTHESIOL, MED SCH, UNIV WIS-MADISON, 72- *Personal Data:* b Upper Darby, Pa, May 3, 30; m 51; c 3. *Educ:* Davidson Col, BS, 51; Univ Pa, MD, 55. *Prof Exp:* Intern, Philadelphia Gen Hosp, 55-56; sr asst surgeon, USPHS, 56-58; instr pharmacol, Univ Pa, 58-60, instr anesthesiol, 60-63, assoc, 63-65, asst prof, 65-70; prof & head dept, Univ Conn, 70-72. *Concurrent Pos:* Pharmaceut Mfrs fel clin pharmacol, 57-58; USPHS career develop award, 65-70; consult, Philadelphia Vet Admin Hosp, 64-68 & Madison Vet Admin Hosp, 72-; vis scientist clin physiol, Bispebjerg Hosp, Copenhagen, Denmark, 68-69. *Mem:* Am Soc Pharmacol & Exp Therapeut; Am Soc Anesthesiol; Asn Univ Anesthetists; Sigma Xi. *Res:* Respiratory control; effects of anesthetics on brain metabolism. *Mailing Add:* Allegheny Univ Health Sci Sch Med Broad & Vine Sts Philadelphia PA 19102-1192. *Fax:* 215-762-7301

ALEXANDER, STEPHEN, INTERCELLULAR INTERACTIONS, REGULATION OF DEVELOPMENTAL TIMING. *Current Pos:* ASSOC PROF, DIV BIOL SCI, UNIV MO, COLUMBIA, 88- *Personal Data:* b Chicago, Ill, Sept 28, 48; m 76; c 3. *Educ:* Univ Ill, Urbana, BS, 71; Brandeis Univ, PhD(biol), 76. *Prof Exp:* Res fel biochem, Dana-Farber Cancer Inst, Harvard Med Sch, 76-80; res assoc develop biol, Dept Immunol, 80-83, asst mem develop biol, Dept Molecular Biol, Res Inst Scripps Clin, La Jolla Calif, 83-87. *Concurrent Pos:* NIH Cell Biol Study Sect, 88-92. *Mem:* Am Soc Microbiol; Soc Develop Biol. *Res:* Molecular and genetic basis of developmentally regulated gene expression; intercellular interactions during multicellular morphogenesis; control of developmental timing. *Mailing Add:* Div Biol Sci 105 Tucker Hall Univ Mo Columbia Columbia MO 65211-0001

ALEXANDER, STEVEN ALBERT, many body theory, computational physics, for more information see previous edition

ALEXANDER, STUART DAVID, PULP & PAPER TECHNOLOGY, PROCESS CONTROL. *Current Pos:* RETIRED. *Personal Data:* b Brooklyn, NY, Nov 18, 38; m 62; c 2. *Educ:* Cornell Univ, BChE, 60; State Univ NY Col Environ Sci & Forestry, PhD(pulp & paper technol), 66. *Honors & Awards:* Res & Develop Div Leadership & Serv, Tech Asn Pulp & Paper Indust, 86. *Prof Exp:* Tech serv engr, Papermill, Westvaco Corp, NY, 60-62; sr develop engr, St Regis Paper Co, 66-74, staff specialist-papermaking field serv, Tech Ctr, 74-77; res sect head, Scott Paper Co, 77-83, res & develop mgr, 83-95. *Mem:* Tech Asn Pulp & Paper Indust; Am Chem Soc. *Res:* Paper grade development based on paper and fiber rheology and chemistry; paper making process control; papermaking chemistry. *Mailing Add:* Scott Paper Co Scott Plaza Philadelphia PA 19113

ALEXANDER, TAYLOR RICHARD, BOTANY. *Current Pos:* RETIRED. *Personal Data:* b Hope, Ark, May 27, 15; m 40; c 2. *Educ:* Ouachita Col, AB, 36; Univ Chicago, MS, 38, PhD(physiol), 41. *Prof Exp:* From instr to assoc prof, Univ Miami, 40-46, chmn dept, 47-65, prof bot, 47-77. *Mem:* Am Inst Biol Sci. *Res:* Plant nutrition in subtropical conditions; minor element deficiencies and subtropical ecology. *Mailing Add:* 6900 SW 73rd Ct Miami FL 33143

ALEXANDER, THOMAS GOODWIN, PHARMACEUTICAL CHEMISTRY. *Current Pos:* RETIRED. *Personal Data:* b Washington, DC, Sept 6, 28; m 91, Amy Turner; c Lyle S, Helen R (Nelson) & Carol A (Fredericks). *Educ:* Univ Md, BS, 50; George Washington Univ, MS, 57. *Prof Exp:* Chem analyst, NY State Dept Agr, Cornell Univ, 50; analytical chemist dairy prod lab, USDA, DC, 52-56; res analysis chemist, Div Pharmaceut Chem, Food & Drug Admin, 56-67, supvry chemist, Div Pharmaceut Sci, 67-70, supvry chemist, Nat Ctr Antibiotic Analysis, 70-82, supvry chemist, Div Drug Biol, 82-89. *Concurrent Pos:* Res chemist, Food & Drug Admin, 90-93. *Mem:* fel Asn Off Analytical Chem Int (secy-treas, 86-88). *Res:* Elemental analysis milk and milk products; analysis of ergot alkaloids; chromatographic methods; development of nuclear magnetic resonance methods for pharmaceuticals; analysis of particulate matter in parenterals; interfacing computers and analytical instruments. *Mailing Add:* 16716 Huron St Accokeek MD 20607-9710

ALEXANDER, THOMAS KENNEDY, NUCLEAR PHYSICS. *Current Pos:* RETIRED. *Personal Data:* b Vancouver, BC, Mar 6, 31; m 55, Loretta O Dick; c Michael, Stuart & Stephen. *Educ:* Univ BC, BA, 53, MSc, 55; Univ Alta, PhD(physics), 64. *Prof Exp:* Res officer reactor physics, Atomic Energy Can Ltd, 55-56, electronics, 56-61, res officer nuclear physics, 64-91. *Concurrent Pos:* Vis prof, Queen's Univ, 86-87. *Mem:* Can Asn Physicists; fel Am Phys Soc. *Res:* Nuclear spectroscopy; measurements of lifetimes, moments and reactions with heavy ions. *Mailing Add:* PO Box 1634 Deep River ON K0J 1P0 Can

ALEXANDER, VERA, AQUATIC ECOLOGY. *Current Pos:* sr res asst, Univ Alaska, Fairbanks, 63-65, from asst prof to assoc prof, 65-74, actg dean, Col Environ Sci, 77-79, dir, Inst Marine Sci, 80-93, PROF MARINE SCI, UNIV ALASKA, FAIRBANKS, 74-, DEAN, SCH FISHERIES & OCEAN SCI, 79- *Personal Data:* b Budapest, Hungary, Oct 26, 32; m 53, 67; c Graham & Elizabeth. *Educ:* Univ Wis, BA, 55, MS, 62; Univ Alaska, PhD(marine sci), 65. *Concurrent Pos:* Mem, Oceanog Panel, NSF, 75-76; chmn, Alpha Helix Rev Comt, Univ Nat Oceanog Lab Syst, 75-78; mem, Ocean Sci Bd, Nat Res Coun, 76-79, Polar Res Bd & Comt Geophys & Environ, 93-; adv comt, Ocean Sci, NSF, 80-84, chair, 83-84, vchmn, Arctic Ocean Sci Bd, 87-88; actg dean, Sch Fisheries & Ocean Sci, Univ Alaska, Fairbanks, 87-89; US Deleg, NPac Marine Sci Orgn, 92-; comnr, Marine Mammal Comn, 95- *Mem:* AAAS; Sigma Xi; Am Soc Limnol & Oceanog; Explorers Club; Am Inst Naut Archaeol; Am Geophys Union; Arctic Inst NAm. *Res:* Primary production and nitrogen cycle processes in marine and freshwater systems, with special application to ice-covered seas and artic lakes. *Mailing Add:* Sch Fisheries & Ocean Sci Univ Alaska PO Box 757200 Fairbanks AK 99775-7220. *Fax:* 907-474-7386; *E-Mail:* vera@ims.alaska.edu

ALEXANDER, WILLIAM CARTER, CARDIOVASCULAR CONTROL SYSTEMS, RESEARCH & DEVELOPMENT MANAGEMENT. *Current Pos:* PRES, ALEXANDER & SONS, 93- *Personal Data:* b Wichita Falls, Tex, June 19, 37; m 76, Heather Owens; c Craig, Curt & Clifton. *Educ:* NTex State Col, Denton, BA, 60; NTex State Univ, Denton, MA, 62; Bowman Gray Sch Med, Winston-Salem, NC, PhD(physiol), 69. *Honors & Awards:* Hitchcook Excellence in Aerospace Physiol, 85. *Prof Exp:* Aerospace technologist physiol, NASA Johnson Space Ctr, Tex, 62-79, Kennedy Space Ctr, Fla, 79-82; dir crew technol physiol, USAF Sch Aerospace Med, 82-91; dir plans & prog physiol, H G Armstrong Lab, 91-93. *Concurrent Pos:* Adj prof, Univ Tex San Antonio, 83-; exec coun, Aerospace Med Asn, 87-90; distinguished vis prof, USAF Acad, Colo, 90-91; prof physiol, Sch Aerospace Measure, USAF; consult, 93- *Mem:* Fel Aerospace Med Asn (vpres 90-91); Am Physiol Soc; Aerospace Physiol Soc (pres, 89-90). *Res:* Integration of man into weapon system or civilian spacecraft; cardiovascular control of fluid and electrolyte balance in hypo and hypergravic environments; development of manual and/or physiologic countermeasures for crew protection. *Mailing Add:* 612 Hospital Blvd Floresville TX 78114

ALEXANDER, WILLIAM DAVIDSON, III, CIVIL ENGINEERING. *Current Pos:* CONSULT, 79- *Personal Data:* b Charlotte, NC, June 20, 11; m 36; c 1. *Educ:* Va Mil Inst, BS, 34; NC State Univ, CE, 53. *Prof Exp:* Engr, High Point, NC, 34-40; partner, Eng Serv, Idaho, 45-46; proj mgr, Urbahn-Roberts-Seeyle-Moran, NY, 62-63; from vpres to vchmn bd dir, Seelye Stevenson Value & Knecht, NY, 63-65; asst gen mgr transit syst develop, Metrop Atlanta Regional Transit Authority, 75-79. *Concurrent Pos:* Mem, Eng Found, NY, 63-75, chmn, 66-75. *Mem:* Nat Acad Eng; fel Am Soc Civil Engrs. *Mailing Add:* PO Box 770 Pawleys Island SC 29585

ALEXANDER, WILLIAM NEBEL, oral medicine, oral pathology, for more information see previous edition

ALEXANDERSON, GERALD LEE, MATHEMATICS. *Current Pos:* From instr to prof math, 58-79, mem, bd trustees, 79-86, dir, div math & natural sci, 81-90, vchmn, 84-86, CHAIR, MATH, SANTA CLARA UNIV, 67-, MICHAEL & ELIZABETH VALERIOTE PROF MATH, 79- *Personal Data:* b Caldwell, Idaho, Nov 13, 33. *Educ:* Univ Ore, BA, 55; Stanford Univ, MS, 58. *Concurrent Pos:* Assoc dir, William Lowell Putman Math Competition, 75-; assoc ed, Col Math J, 79-84 & Am Math Monthly, 83-86; ed, Math Mag, 86-90. *Mem:* Am Math Soc; Math Asn Am (vpres, 84-86, secy, 90-96, pres, 97-). *Res:* Combinatorial geometry; theory of partitions. *Mailing Add:* Dept Math Santa Clara Univ Santa Clara CA 95053-0290. *Fax:* 408-554-2370; *E-Mail:* galexanderso@scuacc.scu.edu

ALEXANDRATOS, SPIRO, ORGANIC CHEMISTRY, POLYMER CHEMISTRY. *Current Pos:* from asst prof to assoc prof chem, 81-93, PROF CHEM, UNIV TENN, KNOXVILLE, 93- *Personal Data:* b New York, NY, Dec 11, 51. *Educ:* Manhattan Col, BS, 73; Univ Calif, Berkeley, PhD(chem), 77. *Honors & Awards:* R&D 100 Award, Res & Develop, 94. *Prof Exp:* Sr chemist, Rohm & Haas Co, 77-81. *Concurrent Pos:* Consult, Oak Ridge Nat Lab, 82-, Argonne Nat Lab, 84-; chmn, Separations Sci Subdiv, Am Chem Soc, 91, Indust & Eng Chem Div, 94. *Mem:* Sigma Xi; Am Chem Soc. *Res:* Polymers; ion-exchange resins; polymeric catalysts; novel uses of membranes, physical organic chemistry; quantum chemistry. *Mailing Add:* Chem Dept Univ Tenn Knoxville TN 37996-1600

ALEXANDRIDIS, ALEXANDER A, VEHICLE DYNAMICS & CONTROL THEORY. *Current Pos:* SR STAFF RES ENGR, GEN MOTORS RES LABS, 76- *Personal Data:* b Patras, Greece, Jan 17, 49; m 77; c 2. *Educ:* Princeton Univ, BSE, 71, MA, 74, PhD(aerospace & mech eng), 77. *Prof Exp:* Tech consult, Aereon Corp, 70-76; res & teaching asst math & internal combustion eng, Princeton Univ, 72-76. *Concurrent Pos:* Tech consult, Dynalysis Princeton, 74-76. *Mem:* Soc Automotive Engrs; Inst Elec & Electronics Engrs. *Res:* Vehicle dynamics, stability and control; powertrain dynamics and control; control systems design and optimization; active vehicle vibration isolation (active suspensions design); computer-aided design of optimal control systems; human factors. *Mailing Add:* Gen Motors Res labs 3500 Mound Rd Gen Motors Res Labs Warren MI 48090-9055

ALEXANIAN, VAZKEN ARSEN, ORGANIC CHEMISTRY, PATENT LAW. *Current Pos:* res chemist synthesis & process develop, Am Cyanamid Co, 78-80, sr res chemist, 78-88, PATENT SCIENTIST, CYTEC INDUST, 88-; CONSULT, PATENT LAW, 88- *Personal Data:* b Aleppo, Syria, Nov 6, 43; US citizen. *Educ:* Am Univ Beirut, BS, 68, MS, 70; Univ Ala, PhD(chem), 74. *Prof Exp:* Res assoc organic chem, Univ Colo, 74-75 & State Univ NY, Binghamton, 75-78. *Mem:* Am Chem Soc. *Res:* Intermolecular and intramolecular reactions of sulfonyl carbenes, pyridinium ylides, azirines, heterocyclic chemistry of sulfur, nitrogen and phosphorus, plastics additives, urethane chemistry and coatings; polymer chemistry; chemistry of crosslinking; process chemistry. *Mailing Add:* Cytec Indust 1937 W Main St Stamford CT 06904-0060

ALEXEFF, IGOR, PLASMA PHYSICS. *Current Pos:* prof, 67-95, EMER PROF ELEC ENG, UNIV TENN, KNOXVILLE, 95- *Personal Data:* b Pittsburgh, Pa, Jan 5, 31; m 54; c 2. *Educ:* Harvard Univ, BA, 52; Univ Wis, MS, 55, PhD(physics), 59. *Honors & Awards:* Centennial Medal, Inst Elec & Electronics Engrs, 84; R&D 100 Award, 89 & 91. *Prof Exp:* Res engr nuclear physics, Westinghouse Res Labs, 52-53; NSF fel, Univ Zurich, 59-60; group leader turbulent heating, basic physics & levitated multipole, Oak Ridge Nat Lab, 60-71. *Concurrent Pos:* Consult, Oak Ridge Nat Lab & Space Inst, Tenn; chmn, Gordon Res Conf, 74; organizer, First Int Inst Elec & Electronics Engrs Conf Plasma Sci, Tenn, 74; vis prof, Physics Dept, Univ Fluminense, Rio de Janeiro, Phys Res Lab, Ahmedabad, India, Inst Plasma Physics, Nagoya Univ, Japan & Univ Natal, Durban, SAfrica; chmn, Plasma Div, Nuclear & Plasma Sci; Chancellor's Res Scholar, 84- *Mem:* Fel Inst Elec & Electronics Engrs; fel Am Phys Soc. *Res:* Experimental plasma physics; controlled thermonuclear fusion; low energy nuclear physics; ultra-high vacuum techniques; ultra-high frequency microwave production; author of over 100 publications and one book. *Mailing Add:* Dept Elec Eng Univ Tenn Knoxville TN 37996-2100

ALEXIOU, ARTHUR GEORGE, OCEAN CLIMATE, MARINE SCIENCE. *Current Pos:* ASST SECY, WORLD CLIMATE RES PROGS, INT OCEANOG COMN, UNESCO, 85- *Personal Data:* b Manchester, NH, Feb 26, 30; div; c Gregory & Philip. *Educ:* Univ NH, BS, 51, MS, 64. *Honors & Awards:* Silver Medal, Dept Com, 73; Meritorious Serv Award, Marine Technol Soc, 78. *Prof Exp:* Meteorologist, USAF, 51-53; dep dir instrumentation, US Naval Oceanog Off, 53-65, proj mgr spacecraft oceanog, Joint USN-Nat Aeronaut & Space Admin Proj, 65-67; dir inst progs, NSF, 67-70; assoc dir progs, Off Sea Grant, Nat Oceanic & Atmospheric Admin, 70-85. *Concurrent Pos:* Res assoc, Scripps Inst Oceanog, Univ Calif, 77-78. *Mem:* Am Geophys Union. *Res:* Ocean climate research , ocean engineering, including instrumentation, remote sensing, and coastal processes. *Mailing Add:* UNESCO 106 Seven PL Frontenoy 75700 Paris France. *Fax:* 33-1-4056-9316; *E-Mail:* Omnet: a.alexiou

ALFANO, MICHAEL CHARLES, PERIODONTICS, DENTAL PRODUCT DEVELOPMENT. *Current Pos:* vpres dent res, 82-85, pres prof dent prod, 85-88, SR VPRES RES TECHNOL & CORP OFF, BLOCK DRUG CO, INC, 87- *Personal Data:* b Newark, NJ, Aug 8, 47; m 69; c 2. *Educ:* Univ Med & Dent NJ, DMD, 71; Mass Inst Technol, PhD(nutrit), 75. *Prof Exp:* From asst prof to prof periodont, Sch Dent, Fairleigh Dickinson Univ, 74-82, dir, Oral Health Res Ctr, 77-82, asst dean res & grad affairs, 81-82. *Concurrent Pos:* Consult dent, Inst Nutrit Cent Am & Panama, 72, Nat Inst Dent Res, NIH, 76-82, Am Dent Asn, 79-82, Int Life Sci Inst, 80-82 & numerous food & pharmaceut co; instr, Sch Dent Med, Tufts Univ, 73-74; Nat Inst Dent Res Indust & Found grants, Fairleigh Dickinson Univ, 74-; prin investr numerous grants, NIH & indust, 74-82; vis prof, Nat Dairy Coun, 81; mem, Sci Adv Coun, State of NJ, 81-84; chmn, prog comt, Found Univ Med & Dent NJ, 90. *Mem:* Am Dent Asn; Int Asn Dent Res; Am Acad Periodont; Am Inst Nutrit; fel Am Col Dentists; Am Asn Dent Res; Am Col Prosthodontics; Am Asn Oral Biologists. *Res:* Nutritional and chemotherapeutic aspects of periodontal disease; pathogenesis of dental caries and periodontal disease; nutritional and pharmacologic modulation of epithelial permeability; development of new dental restorative materials and devices. *Mailing Add:* Block Drug Co Inc 257 Cornelison Ave Jersey City NJ 07302. *Fax:* 201-434-0842

ALFANO, ROBERT R, BIOMEDICAL OPTICS, MEDI PHOTONICS. *Current Pos:* DISTINGUISHED PROF SCI & ENG, CITY COL NY, 72- *Personal Data:* b New York, NY, May 5, 41. *Educ:* Fairleigh Dickinson Univ, BS, 63, MS, 64; NY Univ, PhD(physics), 72. *Prof Exp:* Physicist lasers, Gen Tel & Electronics, 64-72. *Concurrent Pos:* Sloan fel, 75. *Mem:* Fel Am Phys Soc; Optical Soc Am; Inst Elec & Electronics Engrs. *Res:* Femtoselond and Picosecond laser spectroscopy, in solids, liquids and biological materials, medical materials; optical imaging in turbid and random media; optical mammography and tomography; laser development. *Mailing Add:* 3777 Independence Ave Bronx NY 10463. *Fax:* 212-650-5330

ALFARO, RENE IVAN, ASSESSMENT OF IMPACTS OF PESTS ON FOREST DEVELOPMENT, ENTOMOLOGY. *Current Pos:* RES SCIENTIST, CAN FOREST SERV, 80- *Personal Data:* m 72, Hilda; c Claudio & Javier. *Educ:* Simon Fraser Univ, MSc, 75, PhD(entom), 80. *Concurrent Pos:* Guest lectr, Simon Fraser Univ, 80-; adj prof, Univ BC, 86-; dir, Entom Soc, BC, 86; sect Leader, Entomol Sect, Int Union Forestry Res Orgn. *Mem:* Entom Soc Can. *Res:* Forest insects on forest development. *Mailing Add:* Pac Forestry Ctr Can Forest Serv 506 W Burnside Victoria BC V8Z 1M5 Can. *Fax:* 250-363-0775; *E-Mail:* ralfaro@a1.pfc.forestry.ca

ALFELD, PETER, MATHEMATICS. *Current Pos:* Instr Math, 77-79, from asst prof assoc prof 79-87, PROF MATH, UNIV UTAH, SALT LAKE CITY, 87. *Personal Data:* b Feb 20, 50; m; c 3. *Educ:* Univ Hamburg, WGer, Vordiplom, 74; Univ Dundee, Scotland, MS, 75, PhD, 77. *Concurrent Pos:* Vis assoc prof, math, Math Res Ctr, Univ Wis-Madison, 83-84. *Mem:* Am Math Soc; Asn Comput Mach; AAAS. *Mailing Add:* Univ Utah Salt Lake City UT 84112-1107

ALFERT, MAX, CYTOCHEMISTRY. *Current Pos:* From instr to prof, 50-90, EMER PROF ZOOL, UNIV CALIF, BERKELEY, 90- *Personal Data:* b Vienna, Austria, Apr 23, 21; nat US; m 45, Elizabeth Muller; c Peter. *Educ:* Wagner Col, BS, 47; Columbia Univ, MA, 48, PhD(zool), 51. *Concurrent Pos:* Guggenheim fel, 56. *Mem:* Int Soc Cell Biol; Am Soc Cell Biol; Europ Acad Sci, Art & Letters. *Res:* Quantitative cytochemical studies of nuclear composition; development of cytochemical techniques. *Mailing Add:* Dept Integrative Biol Univ Calif Berkeley CA 94720

ALFIERI, CHARLES C, ORGANIC CHEMISTRY, INORGANIC CHEMISTRY. *Current Pos:* RETIRED. *Personal Data:* b Groton, Conn, July 19, 22; m 53, Rosalie T Giordano; c Charles R & James P. *Educ:* Brown Univ, ScB, 44; Purdue Univ, MS, 48, PhD(org chem), 50. *Prof Exp:* Jr chemist, Shell Oil Co, 43-44; asst chemist, Ansco Div, Gen Aniline & Film Corp, 44, 46-47; sr res chemist, Cent Res Labs, US Rubber Co, 50-52, group leader explosives & agr chem res, Naugatuck Chem Div, 52-58; head chem res sect, Elkton Div, Thiokol Chem Corp, 58-71; counr, Tech Serv Div, Univ Del, 71-80. *Concurrent Pos:* Consult chem, 81- *Mem:* Am Chem Soc. *Res:* Use of high energy chemicals for solid rocket propellants and high explosives; synthesis and application of new liquid polymers. *Mailing Add:* 24 Chestnut Hill Sq Groton CT 06340

ALFIN-SLATER, ROSLYN BERNIECE, BIOCHEMISTRY. *Current Pos:* assoc prof nutrit, Univ Calif, Los Angeles, 59-65, head, Div Environ & Nutrit Sci, 69-77, prof nutrit, Sch Pub Health, prof biol chem, 71-87, asst dean, acad affairs, 83-87, EMER PROF, UNIV CALIF LOS ANGELES, 87- *Personal Data:* b New York, NY, July 28, 16; m 48. *Educ:* Brooklyn Col, AB, 36; Columbia Univ, AM, 42, PhD(biochem), 46. *Honors & Awards:* Osborne Mendel Award, Am Inst Nutrit, 70, Borden Award, 81; Bond Award, Am Oil Chemists' Soc, 74. *Prof Exp:* Lectr asst, Chem Dept, Brooklyn Col, 38-43, tutor, 43; asst instr, Columbia Univ, 43-45; res chemist enzymes, Takamine Labs, 46-47; res fel cancer, Sloan-Kettering Inst, 47-48; res assoc, Dept Biochem & Nutrit, Med Sch, Univ Southern Calif, 48-52, vis asst prof, 52-56, vis assoc prof, 56-59. *Concurrent Pos:* Mem US nat comt, Int Union Nutrit Sci, Nat Res Coun, 74-80, vchmn, 75-78, chmn comt biol eval of fat, 78-; mem expert panel food safety & nutrit, Inst Food Technol, 80-83; mem, Coun Arteriosclerosis, Am Heart Asn. *Mem:* Fel AAAS; Am Pub Health Asn; Am Soc Biol Chemists; fel Am Inst Nutrit (treas, 77-80). *Res:* Biochemical and nutritional aspects of lipid metabolism; cholesterol and essential fatty acids; saturated and unsaturated fats; carbohydrate-lipid interrelationships; essential fatty acids and vitamin E; experimental atherosclerosis; studies with aflatoxin; nutrition and aging. *Mailing Add:* Dept Community Health Sci Univ Calif Sch Public Health Los Angeles CA 90024

ALFONSO, AIXA, GENETICS OF NEUROSECRETION, GENETICS OF NEURONAL CELL FATE SPECIFICATION. *Current Pos:* ASST PROF, UNIV ILL, CHICAGO, 96- *Personal Data:* b Santurce, PR, Nov 10, 57; US citizen. *Educ:* Univ PR, BS, 78; Univ Wis, PhD(oncol), 86. *Prof Exp:* Postdoctoral fel, Ford Found, Univ Wis, 87-88; NIH postdoctoral fel, Univ Wis, 88-89; res scientist, Okla Med Res Found, Oklahoma City, 90-92; asst prof, Univ Iowa, 92-96. *Mem:* Soc Neurosci; Genetics Soc Am; Soc Develop Biol; AAAS. *Res:* Taking a genetic approach to the identification and analysis of gene products involved in regulated neurosecretion and synaptic vesicle encocytosis in the soil nematode Caenorhabditis elegans. *Mailing Add:* Dept Biol Sci MC 066 Univ Ill Chicago IL 60607

ALFORD, BETTY BOHON, NUTRITION. *Current Pos:* instr foods & nutrit, Tex Woman's Univ, 58-63, res assoc nutrit, 63-66, from asst prof to assoc prof nutrit, 66-78, chmn nutrit & food sci, 75-77, dean, Col Nutrit, Textile & Human Develop, 78-88, PROF NUTRIT, TEX WOMAN'S UNIV, 78- *Personal Data:* b St Louis, Mo, June 9, 32; m 58; c 2. *Educ:* Tex Woman's Univ, BS, 54, MA, 56, PhD(nutrit), 65. *Prof Exp:* Instr nutrit & home econ, Baylor Univ, 56-57. *Concurrent Pos:* Consumer adv, Cotton Bd, 85-; extramural assoc, Nat Inst Health, 88; vis prof, Div Nutrit Res Coord, NIH, 89. *Mem:* Am Dietetic Asn; Am Inst Nutrit; Am Soc Clin Nutrit. *Res:* Nutrition of elderly, assessment and requirement; cottonseed and plant protein for human needs; effectiveness of nutrition education for low income families; nutrition during the life cycle; obesity. *Mailing Add:* PO Box 425888 Tex Woman's Univ Denton TX 76204

ALFORD, BOBBY R, OTOLARYNGOLOGY, HEAD & NECK SURGERY. *Current Pos:* From asst prof to assoc prof, 62-66, dean, Acad & Clin Affairs, 84-88, PROF OTOLARYNGOL, BAYLOR COL MED, 66-, CHMN DEPT, 67-, DISTINGUISHED SERV PROF, 85-, EXEC VPRES & DEAN MED, 88- *Personal Data:* b Dallas, Tex, May 30, 32; m 53, Othelia Dorn; c Bradley K, Raye L & Alan S. *Educ:* Baylor Col Med, MD, 56. *Honors & Awards:* Herman Johnson Award, Baylor Col Med, 56. *Concurrent Pos:* NIH fel, Sch Med, Johns Hopkins Univ, 61-62; consult to Surgeon Gen, US Army, 64-70 & USPHS, 65-68 & 70-; chief ed, Arch Otolaryngol, AMA, 70-80; mem, Nat Adv Neurol & Commun Disorders & Stroke Coun, NIH, 77-80; mem adv coun, Nat Inst Deafness & Other Commun Dis, NIH, 91-95 & Aerospace Med, NASA, 92-94; mem, Life & Microgravity Sci & Appln, NASA, 93-95, Adv Comt Redesign Space Sta, 93, Adv Comt, 92-95. *Mem:* Inst Med-Nat Acad Sci; Am Laryngol, Rhinol & Otol Soc; Soc Univ Otolaryngol (secy, 65-69); Am Col Surg; Am Acad Otolaryngol-Head & Neck Surg (pres, 81); Am Otol Soc. *Res:* Otology; otophysiology; otopathology. *Mailing Add:* Exec Vpres & Dean Med Baylor Col Med One Baylor Plaza Houston TX 77030

ALFORD, CECIL ORIE, ELECTRICAL ENGINEERING, COMPUTER SCIENCE. *Current Pos:* assoc prof, 68-77, PROF ELEC ENG, GA INST TECHNOL, 77- *Personal Data:* b Gay, Ga, Sept 28, 33; m 59; c 3. *Educ:* Ga Inst Technol, BEE, 56, MSEE, 57; Miss State Univ, PhD(elec eng), 66. *Prof Exp:* Tech asst, Western Elec Co, 52-56; engr, Radiation, Inc, 57-59, res engr, Res Div, 60-61; sr engr, Martin Co, 61-63; asst prof elec eng, Miss State Univ, 63-66; assoc prof, Tenn Technol Univ, 66-68. *Concurrent Pos:* Res engr, Res Sta, Ga Inst Technol, 56, Aerospace Corp, Patrick Air Force Base, Fla, 64, Boeing Co, Ala, 65, ARO, Inc, Tenn, 66, Oak Ridge Assoc Univs, 67 & Western Elec, Atlanta, 69. *Mem:* Inst Elec & Electronics Engrs. *Res:* Computer architecture and organization; microprogramming; real-time computer control; robotics. *Mailing Add:* Sch Elec Eng Ga Inst Technol 400 Tenth St CRB 373 Atlanta GA 30332

ALFORD, CHARLES AARON, JR, VIROLOGY. *Current Pos:* from asst prof to assoc prof pediat, 65-67, MEYER PROF PEDIAT, SCH MED, UNIV ALA, BIRMINGHAM, 67-, ASSOC PROF CLIN PATH, 69-, PROF MICROBIOL & SR SCIENTIST CANCER RES TRAINING PROG, 73- *Personal Data:* b Birmingham, Ala, Dec 8, 28; m 62; c 2. *Educ:* Univ Ala, BS, 51; Med Col Ala, MD, 55. *Honors & Awards:* P R Edwards Award, Am Soc Microbiol, 77. *Prof Exp:* From intern to chief resident pediat, Med Col Ala, 55-58; pediatrician in chief, Sta Naval Hosp, Sasebo, Japan, 58-60; instr pediat, Med Col Ala, 60-62; Nat Inst Allergy & Infectious Dis spec fel virol, Dept Trop Pub Health, Sch Pub Health, Harvard Univ & res fel med, Children's Hosp Med Ctr, Boston, 62-65. *Concurrent Pos:* Mem basic res adv comt, March of Dimes Birth Found, 76- & Nat Adv Child Health & Human Develop Coun, NIH, 79-83. *Mem:* Soc Pediat Res; Am Fedn Clin Res; Infectious Dis Soc Am; Am Pediat Soc; Am Asn Immunologist; Am Acad Microbiol. *Res:* Pediatric virology and immunology in the study of congenital infections. *Mailing Add:* Dept Pediat Univ Ala Sch Med 1717 Seventh Ave S Birmingham AL 35294-0001

ALFORD, DONALD KAY, PLANT PHYSIOLOGY, HORTICULTURE. *Current Pos:* PROF BIOL, METROP STATE COL, 70- *Personal Data:* b Long Beach, Calif, Dec 30, 36; m 67; c 2. *Educ:* Whittier Col, BA, 58, MS, 61; Univ Wis-Madison, PhD(bot & hort), 70. *Honors & Awards:* Fulbright-Hays Lectr, Philippines, 80. *Prof Exp:* Instr biol defense, US Army Chem Corps, 61-63; res scientist microbiol, Space Gen Corp, 64-65; res engr space res, NAm Rockwell Corp, 65-67; mem staff circadian rhythms, Univ Calif, Los Angeles, 70. *Concurrent Pos:* Consult, Oshkosh Paving Co, 75 & Controlled Environ Life Support Syst Prog, NASA, 80; dir, Summer Sci Inst, 85. *Mem:* Am Soc Plant Physiologists; Am Inst Biol Sci; AAAS. *Res:* Circadian rhythms of bean plants under controlled environmental conditions; tissue culture studies. *Mailing Add:* Dept Biol Metrop State Col PO Box 173362 Denver CO 80217-3362

ALFORD, GEARY SIMMONS, EXPERIMENTAL CLINICAL PSYCHOLOGY. *Current Pos:* assoc prof psych & psychiat, 80-87, PROF PSYCH & PSYCHIAT, UNIV MISS MED CTR, 87- *Personal Data:* b McComb, Miss, April 11, 45; m 76; c 2. *Educ:* Millsaps Col, BA, 68; Univ Ariz, MA, 71, PhD (clin psych), 72. *Prof Exp:* Psych resident, Dept Psych, Univ Miss Med Ctr, 71-72, asst prof psych & psychiat, 73-75; fel, Nat Inst Drug Abuse & Nat Inst Alcoholism & Alcohol Abuse, 75-77. *Concurrent Pos:* Assoc prof, Dept Pharmacol & Toxicol, Univ Miss Med Ctr, 77-; Nat Adv Bd, Am Coun Alcoholism, 86-; psychol consult, Miss Bur Narcotics, 72-75 & 78- *Mem:* Fel Am Psychol Asn; Asn Adv Behav Ther; Behav Ther & Res Soc. *Res:* Behavior therapy, application of experimental psychology to clinical psychopathology; psychopharmacology and chemical substance misuse and addiction. *Mailing Add:* Dept Psychiat Univ Miss Sch Med 2500 N State St Jackson MS 39216-4505

ALFORD, HARVEY EDWIN, ORGANIC CHEMISTRY. *Current Pos:* RETIRED. *Personal Data:* b Ashtabula, Ohio, Aug 30, 24; m 47; c 2. *Educ:* Hiram Col, BA, 47; Western Reserve Univ, MS, 52. *Prof Exp:* Res assoc, Standard Oil Co Ohio, 47-75, sr res assoc, 75-83. *Mem:* Am Chem Soc. *Res:* Petroleum processing; coke production; activated carbon production and use; waste treatment; microballoons; resid upgrading. *Mailing Add:* 177 Orchard Hill Amherst OH 44001-1763

ALFORD, WILLIAM LUMPKIN, NUCLEAR PHYSICS. *Current Pos:* PROF, 64-91, assoc dean, Sch Arts & Sci, 80-86, col sci & math & dir, Nuclear Sci Ctr, 86-91, EMER PROF PHYSICS, AUBURN UNIV, 91- *Personal Data:* b Albertville, Ala, Oct 6, 24; m 48, Ruth Wiggs; c Linda (Yeager), Charles, Lois (Molony), John & Barbara (Hogan). *Educ:* Vanderbilt Univ, AB, 48; Calif Inst Technol, MS, 49, PhD(physics), 53. *Honors & Awards:* Pegran Award, Am Phys Soc, 83; Algernon Sydney Sullivan Award, 85. *Prof Exp:* From asst prof to assoc prof physics, Auburn Univ, 53-58; nuclear physicist, US Army Missile Command, 58-64. *Mem:* Fel Am Phys Soc. *Res:* Nuclear reactions induced by neutrons in the zero to twenty MeV energy range; measurement of reaction cross sections and investigation of the gamma activities of reaction product nuclei. *Mailing Add:* Dept Physics Auburn Univ Auburn AL 36849-5311

ALFORD, WILLIAM PARKER, NUCLEAR PHYSICS. *Current Pos:* chmn dept, 73-84, prof, 73-92, EMER PROF PHYSICS, UNIV WESTERN ONT, 92- *Personal Data:* b London, Ont, Mar 22, 27; m 49, Jeannette Wadland; c 3. *Educ:* Univ Western Ont, BSc, 49; Princeton Univ, PhD(physics), 54. *Honors & Awards:* Lyle Fel, Univ Melbourne, 88. *Prof Exp:* Instr physics, Princeton Univ, 54-55; from instr to prof, Univ Rochester, 55-73. *Concurrent Pos:* Vis prof, Univ Munich, 70-71, Univ Colo, 78-79 & Univ BC, 84-85. *Mem:* Fel Am Phys Soc; Can Asn Physicists. *Res:* Nuclear reactions and spectroscopy. *Mailing Add:* 2050 Beach Dr Comox BC V9M 1T8 Can. *E-Mail:* alford@erich.triumf.ca

ALFORS, JOHN THEODORE, GEOLOGY. *Current Pos:* RETIRED. *Personal Data:* b Reedley, Calif, Nov 24, 30; m 69, Patricia L; c Barbara E & Michael J. *Educ:* Univ Calif, Berkeley, BA, 52, MA, 56, PhD(geol), 59. *Prof Exp:* Geologist, Calif Dept Mines-Geol, 60-93. *Mem:* Geol Soc Am; Mineral Soc Am. *Res:* Mineralogy and petrology of glaucophane schists; geology and mineralogy of the barium silicate deposits of Fresno County, California; geochemical study of the Rocky Hill granodiorite, Tulare County, California; urban geology master plan for California; geology of Tiburon Peninsula, Marin County, California. *Mailing Add:* 4337 Vista Way Davis CA 95616-4334

ALFRED, LOUIS CHARLES ROLAND, SOLID STATE PHYSICS, PHYSICAL METALLURGY. *Current Pos:* PROF PHYSICS, TRENT UNIV, 70- *Personal Data:* b Mauritius, June 2, 29; m 64; c 3. *Educ:* Univ Bombay, BSc, 52, MSc, 54; Univ Sheffield, PhD(theoret physics), 57. *Prof Exp:* Res assoc phys chem, Brandeis Univ, 57-59; res fel physics, Brookhaven Nat Lab, 59-61 & Atomic Energy Res Estab, Eng, 61-65; assoc physicist, Argonne Nat Lab, 65-70. *Res:* Defect properties and structure of solids; electron states in solids; magnetic resonance; atomic structure and surface physics; mathematical methods. *Mailing Add:* Dept Physics Trent Univ Peterborough ON K9J 7B8 Can

ALFREY, CLARENCE P, JR, HEMATOLOGY, BIOENGINEERING. *Current Pos:* AT HEMATOL SOC, METHODIST HOSP, TEX MED CTR. *Personal Data:* b Brownwood, Tex, May 25, 30; m 55; c 4. *Educ:* Baylor Univ, MD, 55; Univ Minn, PhD(med), 66. *Prof Exp:* From instr to assoc prof, 61-71, prof med, Baylor Col Med, 71-, co-dir hemat res, 66- *Concurrent Pos:* Chief radioisotope & hemat serv, Vet Admin Hosp, Houston, 61-66, assoc chief of staff res & educ, 62-66; adj assoc prof bioeng, Rice Univ, 67-71, adj prof, 71- *Mem:* Am Soc Hemat; Am Fedn Clin Res; AMA; Sigma Xi. *Res:* Medical uses of radioisotopes; iron metabolism in man; effects of physical forces on red blood cells; ultrasound in medical diagnosis. *Mailing Add:* 275 Pine Hollow Lane Houston TX 77056-1501

ALFVEN, HANNES OLOF GOSTA, geophysics, plasma physics; deceased, see previous edition for last biography

ALGER, NELDA ELIZABETH, ZOOLOGY. *Current Pos:* asst prof, 64-70, ASSOC PROF ZOOL, UNIV ILL, URBANA-CHAMPAIGN, 70- *Personal Data:* b Ithaca, NY, Dec 14, 23. *Educ:* Univ Mich, BS, 45, MS, 47; NY Univ, PhD(zool), 62. *Prof Exp:* Instr zool, Highland Park Jr Col, 47-48; instr zool, Hunter Col, 49-50; lab instr parasitol, Columbia Univ, 50-51; from instr to asst prof prev med, NY Univ, 52-64. *Mem:* Am Soc Parasitol; Am Soc Trop Med & Hyg; Am Soc Invert Path; Soc Protozool; Tissue Cult Asn; Sigma Xi. *Res:* Malaria; trypanosomiasis; parasitic immunology. *Mailing Add:* 2206 Sothmoor Dr Champaign IL 61821

ALGERMISSEN, SYLVESTER THEODORE, PROBABILISTIC EARTHQUAKE HAZARD & RISK STUDIES. *Current Pos:* chief, Seismicity & Risk Analysis Br, US Geol Surv, 73-75, res geophysicist, 75-79, supvry geophysicist, 80-93, DEP CHIEF, GEOL HAZARD & RISK ASSESSMENT, OFF INT GEOL, US GEOL SURV, 93- *Personal Data:* b St Louis, Mo, May 9, 32; m 68; c 1. *Educ:* Mo Sch Mines, BS, 53; Wash Univ, AM, 55, PhD(geophys), 57. *Honors & Awards:* Meritorious Serv Award, US Dept Interior, 85. *Prof Exp:* Proj engr, Sinclair Res Labs, Inc, 57-59; asst prof geophys, Univ Utah, 59-63; chief data analysis & res br, Coast & Geod Surv, Environ Sci Serv Admin, 63-65, chief geophys res group, 65-71; dir seismol res group, Environ Res Labs, Nat Oceanic & Atmospheric Admin, 71-73. *Concurrent Pos:* Mem sci & eng task force, Fed Reconstruct & Develop Comn for Alaska, 64; mem comt Alaska earthquake, Nat Acad Sci-Nat Res Coun, 64-; vis prof, Univ Chile, 70; mem US deleg, UNESCO Intergovt Conf Mitigation of Seismic Risk, 76; dir, Seismol Soc Am, 73-75 & Earthquake Eng Res Inst, 77-79. *Mem:* Fel AAAS; Soc Explor Geophys; Seismol Soc Am; Am Geophys Union. *Res:* Earthquake and risk (loss) assessment; seismicity; engineering seismology; interpretation of geophysical data; structure of the earth. *Mailing Add:* Geo Risk Inc PO Box 26 Golden CO 80401

ALGUIRE, MARY SLANINA (HIRSCH), STATISTICAL-COMPUTER DATA ANALYSIS. *Current Pos:* Res assoc statist, Dept Math Sci, 77-79, Agr Statist Lab, 79-82, STATISTICIAN & SYSTS ANALYST, BUR BUS & ECON RES, UNIV ARK, 82- *Personal Data:* b Garrett, Ind, Feb 14, 43; m 65, 88, Robert T; c Matthew & Gwynne. *Educ:* Marquette Univ, BS, 65; Univ Ark, MS, 77. *Concurrent Pos:* Lectr statist, Dept Agron, Univ Ark, 79-82, instr statist & programming, Comput Info Systs/Quant Anal Dept, 82-; mem, Transp Res Bd. *Mem:* Sigma Xi; Am Statist Asn. *Res:* Analytical techniques in international marketing; transportation/planning and accident rates; time series analysis of water quality and filter field systems; computer access to commercial and government databases. *Mailing Add:* CISQ-BBER Univ Ark Fayetteville AR 72701. *E-Mail:* ma24265@uafsysb.uark.edu

ALHADEFF, JACK ABRAHAM, GLYCOCONJUGATES, ENZYMOLOGY. *Current Pos:* PROF BIOCHEM, LEHIGH UNIV, 82- *Personal Data:* b Vallejo, Calif, May 9, 43; m 81, Janice Moon; c Amber & Samuel. *Educ:* Univ Chicago, BA, 65; Univ Ore Med Sch, PhD(biochem), 72. *Prof Exp:* Fel, Univ Calif, San Diego, 72-74, asst res neuroscientist, 74-75, from asst prof to assoc prof, 75-82. *Concurrent Pos:* Res Career Develop Award, NIH, 78. *Mem:* Sigma Xi; AAAS; Am Chem Soc; Biochem Soc. *Res:* Biochemical studies on glycoconjugate metabolism in normal and pathological (cancer, diabetes, cystic fibrosis) human tissues. *Mailing Add:* Dept Chem Lehigh Univ Bethlehem PA 18015. *Fax:* 215-758-5851

AL-HASHIMI, AHMAD, ENVIRONMENTAL IMPACT OF MINING, NUCLEAR CHEMICAL ENGINEERING. *Current Pos:* SR LECTR, UNIV TORONTO, 90- *Personal Data:* m 82, Faaka; c Aminah, Yasir & Afnan. *Educ:* Baghdad Univ, BSc, 76; Columbia Univ, MSc, 81, PhD(chem eng), 83. *Prof Exp:* Res assoc, Columbia Univ, 83-84; process engr, Atomic Energy Orgn Iran, 84-90. *Concurrent Pos:* Adj prof nuclear eng, eng math & eng thermodyn, Tehran Univ, 87-90; consult, E I Robinsky Assocs Ltd, 91- *Mem:* Am Inst Chem Engrs; Union Iraqi Engrs. *Res:* Solid waste characterization; leachability of hazardous elements from selected wastes; compatability of underlying soils with leachate; developed geopolymers that are able to substantially suppress advective transport; suitability of general transport models for specific applications. *Mailing Add:* 122-220 College St Toronto ON M5S 1A4 Can. *Fax:* 905-770-5696, 416-978-8605

ALHOSSAINY, EFFAT M, BIOCHEMISTRY. *Current Pos:* CHEMIST, TEX DEPT HEALTH, 82- *Personal Data:* b Mosul, Iraq, Sept 15, 22; m. *Educ:* Univ Tex, Austin, MED, 63, MA, 70. *Prof Exp:* Res asst microbiol, Univ Tex, 78-81. *Mem:* Sigma Xi; Am Asn Chem; Am Soc Biol. *Mailing Add:* 7302 Sevilla Dr Austin TX 78752-2030

ALI, M KERAMAT, CHAOS IN MACROSCOPIC & MICROSCOPIC DYNAMICAL SYSTEMS, QUANTIZATION OF DYNAMICAL SYSTEMS. *Current Pos:* from asst prof to assoc prof, 81-90, PROF & CHAIR, DEPT PHYSICS, UNIV LETHBRIDGE, CAN, 90- *Personal Data:* b Benipur, Bangladesh, Jan, 1938; Can citizen; m 67, Ahida Parvin; c Seema, Shahina, Saqib, Karim & Rahim. *Educ:* Peshawar Univ, Pakistan, BSc Hons, 64, MSc, 65; Mem Univ Nfld, MSc, 69; Univ Western Ont, PhD(physics), 75. *Prof Exp:* Res physicist spectros, Pakistan Coun Sci & Indust Res, 65-67; fel intermolecular forces, Univ Western Ont, 75-77; res assoc soliton solutions, Nat Res Coun Can, 77-81. *Mem:* Can Asn Physicists; Am Inst Physicists. *Res:* Chaos in classical and quantum dynamical systems. *Mailing Add:* Dept Physics Univ Lethbridge Lethbridge AB T1K 3M4 Can. *Fax:* 403-329-2057

ALI, MAHAMED ASGAR, PHYSICAL CHEMISTRY, QUANTUM CHEMISTRY. *Current Pos:* PROF CHEM, HOWARD UNIV, 69- *Personal Data:* b Burdwan, India, Nov 1, 34; m 68; c 2. *Educ:* Presidency Col, Calcutta, India, BSc, 54; Univ Col Sci, Calcutta, MSc, 56; Oxford Univ, DPhil(theoret chem), 60. *Prof Exp:* Fel, Quantum Chem Group, Royal Univ Uppsala, 60-61; Imp Chem Indust res fel, Univ Keele, 61-62; prof chem, Presidency Col, Calcutta, 62-65; lectr, Univ Sheffield, 65-66 & Univ York, 66-68; res fel, Battelle Mem Inst, 68-69; vis assoc prof, Vanderbilt Univ, 69; res fel metals & ceramics, Oak Ridge Nat Lab, 69. *Mem:* Am Phys Soc; fel Brit Inst Physics & Phys Soc; Am Chem Soc; fel Inst Physics. *Res:* Study of atomic structure and spectra by quantum mechanical methods; theoretical study of molecular electronic structure; potential scattering involving atoms and molecules; theoretical molecular spectroscopy. *Mailing Add:* 2108 Dayton St Silver Spring MD 20902-4222

ALI, MIR KURSHEED, MATHEMATICS. *Current Pos:* Mem fac, 68-92, prof, 75-92, EMER PROF MATH, CALIF STATE UNIV, 92- *Personal Data:* b Hyderabad, India, Apr 16, 26; Nat US; m 52, Mohammadi Begum; c 2. *Educ:* Osmania Univ, Hyderabad, BS, 47, MA, 49; Mont State Univ, MS, 64; Wash State Univ, PhD, 68. *Prof Exp:* Lectr math, City Col Hyderabad, 49-52; lectr, Sci Col, Saifabad, India, 52-58, head dept, 58-61; instr, Wash State Univ, 64-66. *Concurrent Pos:* NSF fel, 65; Edwin W Rice fel, 66; vis prof, Abadan Inst Technol, Iran, 76-77. *Mem:* Am Math Soc; Math Asn Am; Am Asn Univ Prof; Soc Muslim Scientists. *Mailing Add:* Dept Math Calif State Univ Fresno CA 93740-0108

ALI, MIR MASOOM, MATHEMATICAL STATISTICS. *Current Pos:* from asst prof to assoc prof math, 61-66, PROF MATH, UNIV WESTERN ONT, 66- *Personal Data:* b Patuakhali, Bangladesh, Mar 1, 29; Can citizen; m 62; c 5. *Educ:* Univ Dacca, Pakistan, BSc, 48, MSc, 50; Univ Mich, MS, 58; Univ Toronto, PhD, 61. *Prof Exp:* Lectr statist, Univ Dacca, Pakistan, 51-52; mem actuarial dept, Norwich Union Ins Soc, Eng, 52-56; group actuarial dept, Can Life Assurance Co, 56-57. *Mem:* Inst Math Statist; Can Math Cong; fel Royal Statist Soc; Am Statist Asn; Statist Sci Asn Can. *Res:* Theory of estimation; statistical inference; foundation of probability theory; multivariate statistics. *Mailing Add:* Dept Math Sci Ball State Univ Muncie IN 47306

ALI, MOHAMED ATHER, ZOOLOGY. *Current Pos:* from asst prof to assoc prof, 61-64, PROF BIOL, UNIV MONTREAL, 68- *Personal Data:* b Bangalore, India, July 16, 32; nat Can. *Educ:* Presidency Col, Madras, India, BSc, 52; Univ Madras, MSc, 54, DSc(physiol), 69; Univ BC, PhD(zool), 58; Dr es Sc Nat, Sorbonne, 71. *Honors & Awards:* Mem Int Comt Photobiol Res Award, Arctic Inst NAm, 58, 59; Albert Monaco Medal, 86. *Prof Exp:* Demonstr invert embryol, Madras, 52-54; demonstr comp anat, Univ BC, 54-56, demonstr physiol, 56-58; asst prof physiol & histol, McGill Univ, 58-59; asst prof biol, Mem Univ, 59-61. *Concurrent Pos:* Res fel, Queen's Univ, Ont, 59; Alexander von Humboldt sr fel, Max-Planck Inst Physiol

Behav, Ger, 64-65; NATO investr, Mus Nat, Paris, 65; Brit Coun vis prof, UK, 65; chief scientist, Te Vega Exped 15, Stanford Univ, 67; vis investr, Harvard Univ, 68, 78 & Carnegie-Mellon Univ, 69; vis prof, Univ Sao Paulo, Univ Rio de Janeiro & Rio Grande do Sul, Brazil, 71-74, Harvard Univ, 78, Iceland, 78-, Japan, 78, 85, & 90, Norway, 80, 82, Austria, 87-88 & Repub China, 90; dir, NATO-Advan Study Inst, 74, 77, 79, 82, 86 & 91; ed, Revue Can de Biologie, 78-83 & Mikroskopie, 82 & 86; ed-in-chief, Exp Biol, 84-89. *Mem:* Fel AAAS; Am Soc Ichthyologists & Herpetologists; Sigma Xi. *Res:* Sensory physiology; behavior; neurophysiology; histology; embryology; experimental biology and ecology. *Mailing Add:* Dept Biol Stn C-V Univ Montreal CP 6128 Montreal PQ H3C 3J7 Can. *Fax:* 514-343-2293; *E-Mail:* alima@ere.umontreal.ca

ALI, MONICA MCCARTHY, CHEMISTRY. *Current Pos:* ASST PROF GEN & ORG CHEM, OXFORD COL, EMORY UNIV, 75- *Personal Data:* b Boston, Mass, Nov 22, 41; c 2. *Educ:* Emmanuel Col, AB, 63; Georgetown Univ, MS, 66, PhD(org anal chem), 71; Univ Ga, BS, 91. *Prof Exp:* Teacher chem, biol & gen sci, Gate of Heaven High Sch, South Boston, Mass, 63-64; org chemist drug synthesis, Arthur D Little, Inc, Mass, 66-67; teacher chem, Georgetown Visitation Prep Sch, Washington, DC, 71-72; lectr gen & org chem, George Mason Univ, 72-75. *Concurrent Pos:* Lectr org chem, Northern Va Community Col, 74-75. *Mem:* Am Chem Soc. *Res:* Formation of aziridinium ion intermediates in the reactions of beta chloro amines. *Mailing Add:* 5206 Ashford Ct SW Lilburn GA 30247

ALI, MOONIS, FAULT MONITORING, ROCKET & JET ENGINE DIAGNOSITICS. *Current Pos:* PROF & CHMN COMPUTER SCI, SOUTHWEST TEX STATE UNIV, 91- *Personal Data:* b Gunnaur, India, Sept 21, 44; US citizen; m 75; c 1. *Educ:* Aligarh Univ, India, BSc, 64, MSc, 66, PhD, 69. *Prof Exp:* Sr programmer & lectr, Aligarh Univ, 68-74; Fulbright postdoctoral fel, Univ Tex, Austin, 74-75, fac mem & res engr, 75-77; sr researcher, Al-Hazen Res Inst, 77-78; prof computer sci, Mosul Univ, 79-80; assoc prof, Dept Computer Sci, Old Dom Univ, 80-83; prof computer sci & chmn dept, Univ Tenn Space Inst, 83-91. *Concurrent Pos:* NASA-Am Soc Eng Educ fel, Langley Res Ctr, 83; numerous res grants, NASA, Intel Corp & Arnold Eng Develop Ctr, 85-; ed-in-chief, Int J Appl Intel; prog chmn, Int Conf Indust & Eng Applications Artificial Intel & Expert Systs, 88, gen chmn, 89, 90, 91 & 92. *Mem:* Sr mem Inst Elec & Electronic Engrs; Asn Comput Mach; Inst Elec & Electronic Engrs Computer Soc; Am Asn Artificial Intel; Sigma Xi. *Res:* Development of expert systems to perform automatic data analysis to identify anomalous events in complex physical mechanisms where faults develop rapidly and early detection and diagnosis is critically important; architecture of these expert systems integrates design-based reasoning with mechanism behavior analysis and automatic learning approaches; intelligent robotics; diagnosing systems; author of numerous publications. *Mailing Add:* Computer Sci Southwest Tex State Univ San Marcos TX 78666-4602

ALI, NAUSHAD, HIGH-TECHNETIUM SUPERCONDUCTIVITY, MAGNETISM. *Current Pos:* asst prof, 86-90, ASSOC PROF PHYSICS, SOUTHERN ILL UNIV, 90- *Personal Data:* b Dubra, India, Mar 10, 53; m 83; c 2. *Educ:* Aligarh Univ, India, BSc Hons, 73, MSc, 75; Mem Univ, Can, MS, 78; Univ Alta, Can, PhD(physics), 84. *Prof Exp:* Postdoctoral fel physics, McMaster Univ, Can, 85-86. *Concurrent Pos:* Prin investr, Ill Dept Energy & Natural Resources, 88- *Mem:* Am Phys Soc. *Res:* High temperature superconductivity; magnetism of rare earths and rare earth alloys to investigate the magnetic structures. *Mailing Add:* Physics Dept Southern Illinois Univ Carbondale IL 62901. *Fax:* 618-453-3000

ALI, RIDA A, CLINICAL NUTRITION, FOOD SCIENCE AND TECHNOLOGY. *Current Pos:* VPRES BUS & TECH DIV, MEAD JOHNSON INT, 89- *Personal Data:* b Cairo, Egypt, Dec 22, 38; US citizen; m 61; c 3. *Educ:* Cairo Univ, BSc, 59; Univ Calif, Davis, MSc, 63; Rutgers Univ, PhD(nutrit), 66. *Prof Exp:* From asst prof to assoc prof nutrit, Cairo Univ, 67-71; res assoc clin res, Pharmacia Inc, US, 71-72, dept head, 72-73, res mgr clin & biol res, US & Sweden, 73-76; corp res mgr nutrit & health sci, Tech Ctr, Gen Foods Corp, 76-81; dir, Bristol-Myers Int, 81-83, vpres nutrit & res develop, 83-89. *Concurrent Pos:* Fullbright fel, 62-64; fel & res assoc, Rutgers Univ, 66-67 & 70-71; consult clin nutrit, Pharmacia Can Ltd, 73-76; vchmn, Food & Nutrit Coun, Am Health Found, 82- *Mem:* Am Inst Nutrit; Inst Food Technologists; Am Soc Clin Path; Am Mgt Asn; Am Chem Soc; fel Am Col Nutrit; Am Soc Parenteral & Enteral Nutrit. *Res:* Clinical and experimental nutrition in infants and adults; biochemical and nutritional factors affecting body composition, energy metabolism, aging and development; physiology of the gastrointestinal tract. *Mailing Add:* Nutrit Develop Int 6 Abbotts Hill Rd PO Box 3402 Newton CT 06470-3402

ALI, SHAHIDA PARVIN, QUANTUM CHEMISTRY. *Current Pos:* FEL PHYSICIST, UNIV LETHBRIDGE, 82- *Personal Data:* b Peshawar, Pakistan, Oct 10, 42; Can citizen; m 67; c 5. *Educ:* Univ Peshawar, Pakistan, BSc, 65, MSc, 65; Mem Univ Newfoundland, MSc, 71; Univ Western Ont, PhD(physics), 76. *Prof Exp:* Fel physics, Univ Ottawa, 78-80, res assoc, 80-82. *Res:* Charge exchange total cross-section measurements of singly and doubly charged ions with inert gas targets at intermediate energy range. *Mailing Add:* 330 Laval Blvd Lethbridge AB T1K 3W5 Can

ALI, SYED AFAQ, FORMATION DAMAGE CONTROL, SANDSTONE ACIDIZING. *Current Pos:* supvr, Eng Lab, 84-94, TECH ADV, CHEVRON USA PROD CO, 94- *Personal Data:* b Gawalior, India, Dec 11, 40; nat US; m 76, Joanne Suda; c David Suda. *Educ:* Univ Karachi, Pakistan, BS, 62, MS, 63; Ohio State Univ, MS, 67; Rensselaer Polytech Inst, PhD(geol), 74. *Prof Exp:* Postdoctoral scholar, Woods Hole Oceanog Inst, 74-75; proj geologist, Gulf Res & Develop Co, 76-78, sr proj geologist, 78-79; sedimentologist, Sohio Petrol Co, 79; sr res geologist, Gulf Sci & Technol Co, 80-81; sr staff geologist, Gulf Oil Explor & Prod Co, 81-84. *Concurrent Pos:* Mem, Prod Effluent Task Force & Produced Water Oil & Grease Work Group, Am Petrol Inst. *Mem:* Soc Petrol Engrs; Am Asn Petrol Geologists. *Res:* Rock-fluid interaction, sandstone acidizing, formation damage control, fluids chemistry, horizontal completion, frac-packing, high-rate water packing and formation mineralogy; formation damage control and sandstone acidizing. *Mailing Add:* 935 Gravier St New Orleans LA 70112. *Fax:* 504-592-7059; *E-Mail:* syed@chevron.com

ALI, SYED S, ARTIFICIAL INTELLIGENCE. *Current Pos:* ASST PROF, DEPT COMPUT SCI, SW MO STATE UNIV, 93- *Educ:* Univ Alta, Edmonton, BS, 83; Univ Southern Calif, Los Angeles, MS, 85; State Univ NY, Buffalo, PhD(comput sci), 94. *Prof Exp:* Teaching asst, dept comut sci, State Univ NY, Buffalo, 86-87, 90-93, res asst, 87-89. *Concurrent Pos:* lectr, Millard Fillmore Col, Buffalo, 88-93; SW Mo State Univ Fac Res Grant, 94. *Mem:* Asn Comput Ling; Asn Comput Mach; Am Asn Artificial Intel; Can Soc Comput Studies Intel. *Res:* Artificial intelligence, natural language processing, knowledge representation and reasoning, computational linguistics; programming languages, theory and design of languages, data and control abstraction mechanisms, language semantics; contributed numerous articles to professional journals. *Mailing Add:* Dept Comput Sci SW Mo State Univ 901 S National Springfield MO 65804-0027. *Fax:* 417-836-6659; *E-Mail:* ssa231r@cncs.smsu.edu

ALI, YUSUF, OPHTHALMIC DRUG DEVELOPMENT, OPHTHALMIC DRUG DELIVERY. *Current Pos:* Assoc drug delivery, Alcon Labs, Inc, 84-85, sr scientist prod develop, 85-89, mgr prod develop, 90-93, assoc dir prod & process develop, 93-, DIR PROD & PROCESS DEVELOP, ALCON LABS INC. *Personal Data:* b Dohad, Gujarat, India, Dec 9, 53; US citizen; m 85. *Educ:* MS Univ, India, BS, 76; Polytech Inst NY, MS, 78; Univ Fla, PhD(chem eng), 84. *Mem:* Am Asn Pharmaceut Scientists; Am Chem Soc; Am Inst Chem Engrs. *Res:* Pharmaceutical product development of various ophthalmic drugs; identification of ophthalmic drug delivery systems; enhancement of stability of drugs in aqueous media; improvement of bioavailability of ophthalmic drugs using appropriate excipients; opthalmic process development; granted two US patents. *Mailing Add:* 6904 Wicks Trail Ft Worth TX 76133

ALIC, JOHN A, INTERNATIONAL COMPETITIVENESS. *Current Pos:* LECTR, JOHNS HOPKINS SCH ADV INT STUDY, 95- *Personal Data:* b Oak Park, Ill, Nov 24, 41. *Educ:* Cornell Univ, BME, 64; Stanford Univ, MS, 65; Univ Md, PhD(mat eng), 72. *Honors & Awards:* Wright Bros Medal, Soc Automotive Engrs, 75. *Prof Exp:* Case writer, Stanford Univ, 65-66; instr mech eng, Univ Md, 66-72; from asst prof to assoc prof, Wichita State Univ, 72-79; proj dir, Off Technol Assessment, 79-95. *Concurrent Pos:* Sr res fel, John F Kennedy Sch Govt, Harvard Univ, 88-89. *Mem:* AAAS; Am Soc Metals; Soc Automotive Engrs; Am Soc Eng Educ. *Res:* Technology assessment, particularly international competitiveness of United States industries, services as well as manufacturing. *Mailing Add:* 1425 Fourth St SW Washington DC 20024. *Fax:* 202-228-6344; *E-Mail:* jalic@ota.gov

ALICATA, JOSEPH EVERETT, microbiology research, parasitology; deceased, see previous edition for last biography

ALICH, AGNES AMELIA, ORGANOMETALLIC CHEMISTRY. *Current Pos:* PROF CHEM & CHAIRPERSON DEPT, COL ST SCHOLASTICA, 67- *Personal Data:* b International Falls, Minn, June 10, 32. *Educ:* Marquette Univ, BS, 60, MS, 61; Northwestern Univ, Evanston, PhD(inorg chem), 72. *Honors & Awards:* Burlington Northern Res Award. *Prof Exp:* Instr chem, Col St Scholastica, 61-64; instr, Gerard High Sch, Phoenix, 64-67. *Mem:* Am Chem Soc; Sigma Xi; The Chem Soc; Int Union Pure & Appl Chem. *Res:* Synthesis of low- and zero-valent compounds of transition metals, mainly organometallic carbonyls; trace metal drug interactions; transition metal complexes of phytic acid. *Mailing Add:* Nat Sci Col St Scholastica 1200 Kenwood Ave Duluth MN 55811-4199. *Fax:* 218-723-6472

ALICINO, NICHOLAS J, ANIMAL SCIENCE. *Current Pos:* PRES & TECH CONSULT, ALICINO & ASSOCS, INC, 83- *Personal Data:* b New York, NY, Apr 29, 21; m 44; c 8. *Educ:* Fordham Univ, BS, 42. *Prof Exp:* Anal chemist, Calco Div, Am Cyanamid Co, 42-44; anal chem, Nopco Chem Co, 46-50, chief analyst, 50-58, dir anal chem, 58-70; mgr res fire chem div, Diamond Shamrock Chem Co, NJ, 70, mgr res & develop, Nutrit & Animal Health Div, 70-82, consult, tech & regulatory, Ohio, 82-83. *Concurrent Pos:* President's pvt sector survey, Grace Comn, 82-83. *Mem:* Am Chem Soc; Am Microchem Soc. *Res:* Analytical research; chemical method by means of functional groups; new drug research for animal diseases and growth promotion. *Mailing Add:* 79 Carriage Stone Dr Chagrin Falls OH 44022

ALIG, ROGER CASANOVA, SOLID STATE PHYSICS, ELECTRON OPTICS. *Current Pos:* MEM TECH STAFF PHYSICS, DAVID SARNOFF RES CTR, SARNOFF RES INT, 67- *Personal Data:* b Indianapolis, Ind, Nov 7, 41; m 63, Marcia Pritchard; c Paul, Graham & Heidi. *Educ:* Wabash Col, BA, 63; Purdue Univ, MS, 65, PhD(physics), 67. *Honors & Awards:* Sarnoff Medal, RCA, 83. *Concurrent Pos:* Vis prof, Sao Carlos Sch Eng, Brazil, 70-71; adj prof, Rider Col, 90-92. *Mem:* Am Phys Soc; Soc Info Display. *Res:* Electron optics in television picture tubes; electron scattering in semiconductors. *Mailing Add:* 17 Landing Ln Princeton Junction NJ 08550. *E-Mail:* ralig@sarnoff.com

ALIKHAN, MUHAMMAD AKHTAR, ANIMAL PHYSIOLOGY, BIOCHEMISTRY & ECOTOXICOLOGY. *Current Pos:* from asst prof to assoc prof, 67-73, PROF BIOL, LAURENTIAN UNIV, 73- *Personal Data:* b Lyallpur, Pakistan, Apr 1, 32; Eng citizen; m 61, Rena nee' Bienko; c Camilla, Hassan & Margaret. *Educ:* Univ Panjab, Pakistan, BSc, 52; Univ Leeds, Eng, MSC, 58; Marie Curie-Sklodowska Univ, Poland, PhD(physiol), 61. *Prof Exp:* Lectr zool, Agr Col, Lyallpur, 52-57; assoc prof, WPakistan Agr Univ, 61-64; asst prof biol, Univ Calgary, 64-65 & Lethbridge Univ, 65-67. *Concurrent Pos:* Polish Acad Sci res fel, 64, 68 & 69; Nat Res Coun fel physiol & travel grant, 66 & res grant, 66-; vis scientist, Czechoslovak Acad Sci, Prague, 72, 73, 80, Univ Lodz, Poland, 76 & UN Develop Prog, Pakistan, 81; vis prof, State Univ Gent, Belg, 73, Univ Agr, Lyallpur, Pakistan Univ Mosul, Iraq, 74, Univ Tech Sci, Montpellier, France, 78, Univ Garyounis, Beida, Libya, 81, Warsaw Agr Univ, Poland, 83, Univ Agr, Faisalabad, Pakistan, 88, Ger Sci Soc, 88 & Can Univ, France, 95-96. *Mem:* Fel Royal Entom Soc; Zool Soc Can; Soc Environ Toxicol & Chem; Can Asn Water Qual; Int Asn Water Pollution Res & Control; Crustacean Soc; Int Asn Astacology. *Res:* Biochemical adaptations in crustacea to their environments; environmental toxicology; biomonitoring metal ions in aquatic environment and their effect on crustacean species diversity. *Mailing Add:* Dept Biol Laurentian Univ Ramsey Lake Rd Sudbury ON P3E 2C6 Can

ALIN, JOHN SUEMPER, ALGEBRA. *Current Pos:* assoc prof, 72-81, PROF MATH, LINFIELD COL, 81- *Personal Data:* b LaMoure, NDak, Aug 14, 40; m 77; c 5. *Educ:* Concordia Col, BA, 63; Univ Nebr, MA, 65, PhD(math), 67. *Prof Exp:* Vis asst prof math, Univ Southern Calif, 67-68; asst prof, Univ Utah, 68-72. *Concurrent Pos:* Consult, India Prog, NSF, 70; adj prof math, Portland State Univ, 72-; adj prof, C S Ore Grad Ctr, 86- *Mem:* Am Math Soc; Math Asn Am; Am Comput Mach. *Mailing Add:* Linfield Col McMinnville OR 97128-6894

ALINCE, BOHUMIL, COLLOID CHEMISTRY IN PAPERMAKING PROCESS. *Current Pos:* RETIRED. *Personal Data:* b Bratislava, Czech, Feb 22, 30; Can citizen; m 65, Vesna Zabkayova; c Petra & Karin. *Educ:* Tech Univ, Bratislava, Dipl Ing, 54; Acad Sci, Bratislava, PhD(chem), 65. *Prof Exp:* Scientist, Water Res Inst, Bratislava, 54-59, Acad Sci, Bratislava, 59-69; sr scientist, Paper Chem, Pulp & Paper Res Inst Can, 69-95. *Concurrent Pos:* Adj prof chem eng, McGill Univ, Montreal, Can. *Mem:* Fel Tech Asn Pulp & Paper Indust; Can Pulp & Paper Asn; Am Chem Soc; Can Chem Soc. *Res:* Colloid and surface phenomena in papermaking; applications and performance of pigments, their optical and rheological properties; interaction of pigments and cellulosic fibers; modification of cellulosic fibers by polyelectrolytes. *Mailing Add:* 3420 University St Montreal PQ H3A 2A7 Can. *Fax:* 514-398-8254

ALIPRANTIS, CHARALAMBOS DIONISIOS, MATHEMATICAL ANALYSIS, MATHEMATICAL ECONOMICS. *Current Pos:* from asst to assoc prof, Ind Univ-Purdue Univ, Indianapolis, 75-81, prof math, 81-83, actg chmn, Dept Math & Comput Sci, 88-89, actg chmn, Dept Math, 93-94, PROF MATH & ECONS, IND UNIV-PURDUE UNIV, INDIANAPOLIS, 84- *Personal Data:* b Cephalonia, Greece, May 12, 46; US citizen; m 74; c 2. *Educ:* Univ Athens, dipl math, 68; Calif Inst Technol, MS, 71, PhD(math), 73. *Prof Exp:* Lectr math, Occidental Col, 73-74, asst prof, 74-75. *Concurrent Pos:* Res scientist, STD Res Corp, 73-74; grantee, NSF, 81-86 & NATO, 95-97; vis prof, Calif Inst Technol, 82, 89-91 & 96, Calif Inst Technol & Univ Ariz, 91 & Cornell Univ, 96. *Mem:* Am Math Soc; Soc Advan Econ Theory. *Res:* Functional analysis; operator theory; mathematical economics; author of numerous publications. *Mailing Add:* Dept Math Sci Ind Univ-Purdue Univ 402 N Blackford St Indianapolis IN 46202-3216

ALIRE, RICHARD MARVIN, CHEMISTRY, MANAGEMENT OF RESEARCH IN CHEMISTRY. *Current Pos:* div leader, Lawrence Livermore Lab, 76-83, dept head, 83-86, assoc div leader, 86-88, PROG MGR, LAWRENCE LIVERMORE LAB, 88- *Personal Data:* b Mogote, Colo, July 5, 32; m 57; c 2. *Educ:* York Col, Nebr, BA, 54; Univ Nebr, Lincoln, MS, 56; Univ NMex, PhD(chem), 62. *Prof Exp:* Staff mem chem res, Los Alamos Sci Lab, 61-69, sect leader, 69-76. *Mem:* Am Chem Soc; fel Am Inst Chemists; AAAS. *Res:* Molecular spectroscopy of rare earth chelates; kinetics of gas-solid reactions; application of microbalance techniques to studying gas-solid interactions; materials for controlled thermonuclear reactors; supervising research on tritium technology; plutonium processing; energetic materials. *Mailing Add:* 716 Club Circle Lewisville CO 80027

ALIVISATOS, A PAUL, MATERIALS SCIENCE. *Current Pos:* asst prof, 88-92, ASSOC PROF CHEM, UNIV CALIF, BERKELEY, 92- *Personal Data:* b Chicago, Ill, Nov 12, 59. *Educ:* Univ Chicago, BA, 81; Univ Calif, Berkeley, PhD(chem), 86. *Honors & Awards:* Exxon Solid State Chem Award, Am Chem Soc, 91; Coblenty Award, 94. *Prof Exp:* Mem tech staff, AT&T Bell Labs, 86-88. *Concurrent Pos:* NSF presidential young investr, 90; Alfred P Sloan fel, 91. *Mem:* Mat Res Soc; Am Chem Soc; Am Phys Soc; AAAS. *Res:* Preparation and properties of very small crystals of semiconductors, comprised of a few hundred to tens of thousands of atoms. *Mailing Add:* Dept Chem Univ Calif Berkeley CA 94720. *Fax:* 510-642-6911; *E-Mail:* alivis@garnet.berkeley.edu

AL-JURF, ADEL SAADA, SURGICAL ONCOLOGY. *Current Pos:* AT UNIV IOWA HOSP & CLINS, DEPT SURG, 77- *Personal Data:* US citizen. *Educ:* Cairo Univ Col Med, MB, ChB(med), 66. *Prof Exp:* Intern, Cairo Univ Col Med, 66-67, St Vincent Charity Hosp, 72-73; resident fel Cleveland Clin Found, 73-77. *Mem:* Fel Am Col Surgeons; Asn Acad Surg; Soc Surg Alimentary Tract; Am Soc Parenteral & Enteral Nutrit; Am Soc Clin Oncol. *Mailing Add:* Dept Surg Univ Iowa Hosp & Clins Iowa City IA 52242-0001

ALKADHI, KARIM A, GANGLIONIC TRANSMISSION, BRAIN RESEARCH. *Current Pos:* asst prof, 81-87, ASSOC PROF PHARMACOL, COL PHARM, UNIV HOUSTON, 87- *Personal Data:* b Baghdad, Iraq, July 29, 38; US citizen; m 67, Ann Bragdon; c Salwa, Isam & Rheim. *Educ:* Univ Baghdad, BSc, 60; Univ Conn, MSc, 67; State Univ NY Buffalo, PhD(pharmacol), 72. *Prof Exp:* Pharmacist, Repub Hosp, Baghdad, Iraq, 60-65; res asst pharmacol, Sch Med, Yale Univ, 67-68; teaching fel pharmacol, Sch Med, State Univ NY Buffalo, 72-73; asst prof pharmacol, Sch Med, Univ Benghazi, 73-75; from asst prof to assoc prof pharmacol, Sch Med, Mustansiria Univ, 75-80. *Concurrent Pos:* Vis prof, dept pharmacol, Sch Med, Univ Conn, Farmington, 76-81. *Mem:* Brit Pharmacol Soc; Am Soc Pharmacol Exp Therapeut; Soc Exp Biol & Med; Soc Neurosci; Int Brain Res Orgn. *Res:* Pharmacology of synaptic transmission; electrophysiology of the hippocampus; investigation of the possible role of natural neurotransmitters (for example serotonin) in the control of excessive (epileptic) activity in the limbic system. *Mailing Add:* Dept Pharmacol Univ Houston Houston TX 77204-5515. *Fax:* 713-743-1229; *E-Mail:* kalkadhi@uh.edu

ALKANA, RONALD L, NEURO-PHARMACOLOGY, ALCOHOL & BRAIN RESEARCH. *Current Pos:* PROF MOLECULAR-PHARMACOL, SCH PHARMACOL, UNIV SOUTHERN CALIF, 76- *Personal Data:* b Los Angeles, Calif, Oct 17, 45. *Educ:* Univ Southern Calif, DPharm, 70; Univ Calif, Irvine, PhD(pharmacol), 75. *Mem:* Soc Neurosci; Res Soc Alcoholism; Am Soc Pharmacol & Exp Therapeut. *Mailing Add:* Dept Molecular-Pharmacol & Toxicol Univ So Calif 1985 Zonal Ave Los Angeles CA 90033-1086

ALKEZWEENY, ABDUL JABBAR, CLOUD PHYSICS, AIR POLLUTION. *Current Pos:* RES PROF, GEOPHYS INST, UNIV ALASKA. *Personal Data:* b Amarah, Iraq, Sept 1, 35. *Educ:* Univ Baghdad, BS, 58; Univ Calif, Santa Barbara, MA, 63; Univ Wash, PhD(atmospheric sci), 68. *Prof Exp:* Scientist, Meteorol Res Inc, 68-71; sr res scientist, Battelle-Pac Northwest Lab, 71-86; cert, 86-89; res prof, Univ NDak, 89- *Mem:* Am Meteorol Soc; Sigma Xi. *Res:* Physical and chemical transformations of pollutants in clear and cloudy atmosphere using airborne and ground instrumentation. *Mailing Add:* 150 Allegheny Way Fairbanks AK 99709

AL-KHAFAJI, AMIR WADI NASIF, ORGANIC SOILS. *Current Pos:* PROF CIVIL ENG & CHMN DEPT, BRADLEY UNIV, 86- *Personal Data:* b Baghdad, Iraq, Aug 14, 49; m 81, Wilma J; c Ali, Laith & Elise. *Educ:* Wayne State Univ, BSCE, 73, MSCE, 74; Mich State Univ, MS, 76, PhD(civil eng), 79. *Honors & Awards:* Rothberg Prof Excellence Award, 91. *Prof Exp:* Sr engr, Mich Testing, 79-81; asst prof civil eng, Univ Detroit, 80-82; assoc prof & chmn dept, Univ Evansville, 82-86. *Concurrent Pos:* Vis prof, Mich State Univ, 79-80; vpres, Corbin Drilling & Testing, 81-82; consult, Gerling Law Off, 82-84, Morley & Assocs, 82- & Nat Labs, 82- *Mem:* Am Soc Civil Engrs; Am Concrete Inst. *Res:* Numerical method; computer programming; geotechnical engineering programs; organic soils; author of 9 textbooks in engineering. *Mailing Add:* 5411 N Big Hollow Rd Peoria IL 61625

ALKIRE, RICHARD COLLIN, CHEMICAL ENGINEERING. *Current Pos:* from asst prof to assoc prof, 69-77, head, Dept Chem Eng, 86-94, PRIN INVESTR, MAT RES LAB, UNIV ILL, URBANA, 76-, PROF CHEM ENG, 77-, DEAN, VCHANCELLOR, RES, 94- *Personal Data:* b Easton, Pa, Apr 19, 41; wid; c 2. *Educ:* Lafayette Col, BS, 63; Univ Calif, Berkeley, MS, 65, PhD(chem eng), 68. *Honors & Awards:* Res Award, Electrochem Soc, 83, Carl Wagner Mem Award, 85, EG Acheson Medal, 96; Prof Progress Award, Am Inst Chem Engrs, 85; McGabe lectr, NC State Univ, 85; Lindsey lectr, Tex A&M, 86; Berkeley lectr, Univ Calif, 87; Eltech lectr, Case Western Res Univ, 87; Tech Achievement Award, Nat Asn Corrosion Engrs, 90; Lacey lectr in Chem Eng, Calif Inst Technol, 90; E V Murphree Award in Indust & Eng Chem, Am Chem Soc, 91. *Prof Exp:* Fel, Max Planck Inst Phys Chem, 68-69. *Concurrent Pos:* Chmn, Indust Electrolytic Div, Electrochem Soc, 78-80, Long Range Planning Comt, 86-88, ed, J Electrochem Soc, 73-90; chmn, Heat Transfer & Energy Conversion Div, Am Inst Chem Engr, 82-83, tech prog, 85, Nat Heat Transfer Conf, Pittsburgh, 87, coord conf, San Francisco, 86, electrochem fundamentals, Nat Prog Comt Area, 74, consult ed, Am Inst Chem Engr J, Awards Comt, 86-, dir coun, 88-; keynote lectr, Int Soc Electrochem, 84; plenary lect, Conf Corrosion Chem, 84 & Int Soc Electrochem, 89; mem, Comt Surv Chem Eng, Panel Surface & Interfacial Engr, Nat Res Coun, 85, Nat Mat Adv Bd, 85-88, chmn, Comt Fuel Cell Mats Technol Vehicular Propulsion, Nat Mat Adv Bd, 83 & Comt New Horizons Electrochem Sci & Technol, 86. *Mem:* Nat Acad Eng; hon mem, fel Electrochem Soc (vpres, 82-83, pres, 85-86); Am Inst Chem Engrs; fel AAAS; Am Chem Soc; Mat Asn Corrosion Engrs. *Res:* Electrochemical reaction engineering; localized corrosion and etching; plasma reactor design; author over 135 publications. *Mailing Add:* Dept Chem Eng Univ Ill 600 S Matthews Ave Urbana IL 61801

ALKJAERSIG, NORMA KIRSTINE (MRS A P FLETCHER), BIOCHEMISTRY. *Current Pos:* res asst prof, 58-69, RES ASSOC PROF MED, SCH MED, WASHINGTON UNIV, 69- *Personal Data:* b Ikast, Denmark, Dec 25, 21; nat US; m 61. *Educ:* Tech Univ Denmark, 49; Univ Copenhagen, PhD, 65. *Prof Exp:* Res assoc, Biol Inst, Carlsberg Found, 49-51 & Col Med, Wayne State Univ, 51-55; res asst, Jewish Hosp, 55-58. *Mem:* Am Physiol Soc; Cent Soc Clin Res; Am Fedn Clin Res; Int Soc Hematol. *Res:* Fibrinolytic enzymes; blood clotting. *Mailing Add:* 30 Oak Bend Ct St Louis MO 63124

ALKS, VITAUTS, MEDICINAL CHEMISTRY. *Current Pos:* fel, 73-74, cancer res scientist I, 74-79, CANCER RES SCIENTIST II, ROSWELL PARK MEM INST, 79- *Personal Data:* b Bauska, Latvia, Sept 28, 38; US citizen; m 67. *Educ:* Univ Buffalo, BS, 61; State Univ NY, Buffalo, MS, 64, PhD(med chem), 74. *Prof Exp:* Res chemist, Starks Assoc Inc, 63-65. *Mem:* Am Chem Soc; AAAS; Royal Soc Chem; NY Acad Sci. *Res:* Chemical problems of biological and medicinal interest; design and synthesis of enzyme inhibitors; synthesis of steroid analogs; design of active site alkylating agents; studies of metabolic pathways; synthesis of polynuclear aromatic hydrocarbon derivatives; chemotherapeutic agents; amino acid analogues; especially methionine analogues; photosensitizers. *Mailing Add:* 73 Woodward Ave Buffalo NY 14214

ALLABEN, WILLIAM THOMAS, BIOCHEMISTRY, NUTRITION. *Current Pos:* fel, Food & Drug Admin, 76-77, res toxicologist, 77-84, dep dir comp toxicol, 84-87, ASSOC DIR SCI COORD, NAT CTR TOXICOL RES & LIASON TO NAT TOXICOL PROG, FOOD & DRUG ADMIN, 87- *Personal Data:* b Chicago, Ill, Nov 23, 39; m 69, Anita K Gray; c Heather L & Timothy R. *Educ:* Southern Ill Univ, BA, 66, MS, 68, PhD(physiol), 75. *Prof Exp:* Actg dir res, Endocrinol-Pharmacol Res Lab, 67-68; scientist, Mead Johnson & Co Pharmaceut, 68-72; res asst, Southern Ill Univ, 72-74, instr, Dept Physiol & actg dir, Endocrinol-Pharmacol Res Lab, 75. *Concurrent Pos:* Chem mgr, Nat Toxicol Prog, 80-; dir, Nat Toxicol Prog Study, Nat Ctr Toxicol Res, 84-; adj asst prof, Dept Pharmacol & Toxicol, Univ Ark Med Sci & Dept Med Chem, Univ Tenn Med Ctr, 82-88, adj assoc prof, 88-96; adj prof, Dept Pharmacol & Toxicol, Univ Ark MEd Sci, 96-; bd dirs, Toxicol Forum, vpres progs. *Mem:* AAAS; Am Col Toxicol; Sigma Xi; Am Asn Cancer Res; Soc Toxicol; Am Chem Soc. *Res:* Effect of caloric restriction on the expression of non-neoplastic and neoplastic disease and studies to determine the mechanism(s) by which caloric restrictions prevents the expression of toxic endpoints; determining specific genetic or epigenetic events critical for the expression of neoplastic disease; whole body toxicology studies to determine risks associated with exposure to chemicals, food addititives, drugs, and pesticides; other chemicals of interest to government regulatory agencies; risk assessment. *Mailing Add:* Food & Drug Admin Nat Ctr Toxicol Res 3900 NCTR Rd Jefferson AR 72079-9502. *Fax:* 870-543-7136; *E-Mail:* wallaben@nctr.fda.gov

ALLAIRE, FRANCIS RAYMOND, DAIRY SCIENCE. *Current Pos:* From fel to assoc prof, 65-82, PROF DAIRY SCI, OHIO STATE UNIV, 82- *Personal Data:* b Fall River, Mass, Nov 18, 37; m 61; c 4. *Educ:* Univ Mass, BVA, 59, MS, 63; Cornell Univ, PhD(animal breeding), 65. *Concurrent Pos:* Fulbright res scholar, Ireland, 78. *Mem:* Am Soc Animal Sci; Am Dairy Sci Asn; Biomet Soc; AAAS. *Res:* Selection and breeding methods for the economic improvement of dairy cattle populations; studies include theoretical and empirical analyses of alternative multiple trait selection procedures among cows and bulls; developing breeding goals within an economic framework. *Mailing Add:* Dept Poultry Sci Oh State Univ 674 W Lane Ave Columbus OH 43210-1098

ALLAIRE, PAUL A, TECHNICAL MANAGEMENT. *Current Pos:* Financial analyst, Xerox, 66-69, Rank Xerox Ltd London, 69-80, managing dir, 80-83, sr vpres & chief staff officer, Xerox, 83, pres 86, MEM BD, XEROX, 86- CHIEF EXEC OFFICER, 90-, CHMN, 91- *Personal Data:* b Worcester, Mass, July 21, 38; c 2. *Educ:* Worcester Polytech Inst, BS, 60; Carnegie-Mellon Univ, MS, 66. *Concurrent Pos:* Chmn, Coucil Competitiveness; mem bd, coun Foreign Relations; trustee, Worcester Polytech Inst & Carnegie-Mellon Univ. *Mem:* Nat Acad Eng. *Mailing Add:* Xerox Corp 800 Long Ridge Rd Stanford CT 06904

ALLAIRE, PAUL EUGENE, MECHANICAL ENGINEERING, BIOMEDICAL ENGINEERING. *Current Pos:* asst prof, 72-77, assoc prof mech eng, 77, DIR ROTATING MACH & CONTROLS INDUST RES PROG, UNIV VA, 81- *Personal Data:* b Bristol, Conn, Sept 23, 41; m 71; c 1. *Educ:* Yale Univ, BE, 63, ME, 64; Northwestern Univ, PhD(mech eng), 72. *Prof Exp:* Asst prof mech eng, Mem Univ Nfld, 71-72. *Concurrent Pos:* Chmn bearing educ, Am Soc Lubrication Engrs, 78. *Mem:* Am Soc Mech Engrs; Sigma Xi; Am Soc Eng Educ; Am Soc Lubrication Engrs. *Res:* Turbomachinery flows; dynamics of rotating machinery; finite element analysis; lubrication. *Mailing Add:* Dept Mech & Aerosp Eng Univ Va Thornton Hall Charlottesville VA 22093

ALLAIS, MAURICE-FELIX, PHYSICS. *Current Pos:* DIR, ECON ANALYSIS CTR, PARIS, 44- *Personal Data:* b Paris, France, May 31, 11; m 60, Jacqueline Bouteloup; c Christine. *Hon Degrees:* DEng, Fac Sci, Paris, 49; Dr, Univ Groningen, Neth, 64, Univ Mons, Belg, 92, Am Univ, Paris, 92 & Univ Lisbonne, Portugal, 93; dipl, Univ Paris, 93. *Prof Exp:* Engr, Dept Mines & Quarries, 37-43; prof econ analysis, Nat Higher Sch Mines, Paris, 44-88; prof econ theory, Inst Statist, Univ Paris, 47-58; prof, Grad Inst Int Studies, Geneva, 67-70. *Concurrent Pos:* Dir, Bur Documentation & Statist, 43-48, Econ & Social Res Group, Paris, 44-70, res, Nat Ctr Sci Res, Paris, 54-79 & Ctr Clement Juglar Monetary Analysis, Univ Paris, 70-85. *Res:* Theoretical and experimental physics; authored numerous publications. *Mailing Add:* 15 rue Des Gate-Ceps St Cloud 92210 France

ALLAMANDOLA, LOUIS JOHN, INTERSTELLAR SPECTROSCOPY, INTERSTELLAR CHEMISTRY. *Current Pos:* ASTROCHEM LAB GROUP LEADER, SPACE SCI, NASA-AMES RES CTR, 83- *Personal Data:* b New York, NY, Aug 28, 46; m 68; c Monica, Patrick, Kees & Anthony. *Educ:* St Peter's Col, BS, 68; Univ Calif, Berkeley, PhD(phys chem), 74. *Honors & Awards:* H Julian Allen Award, NASA, 86. *Prof Exp:* Fel energy transfer low temperature solids, Ore State Univ, 74-75, NSF fel, 75-76, instr molecular spectros, 76; from asst to assoc prof low temperature spectros, Lab Astrophysics Group, Univ Leiden, 76-83, instr molecular physics, optics, 78-82. *Mem:* Am Chem Soc; Sigma Xi; Am Astron Soc. *Res:* Spectroscopy of low temperature (IOK) solid analogs of celestial materials and the chemical reactions possible at this temperature in vacuum; ultra-violet irradiated samples; infra-red astronomy; interstellar molecule formation; presence and properties of large aromatic molecules in space; astrophysics; published over 140 articles. *Mailing Add:* Ames Res Ctr NASA M/S 245-6 Moffett Field CA 94035-1000. *Fax:* 650-604-6779

AL-LAMI, FADHIL, ANATOMY, PHYSIOLOGY. *Current Pos:* PROF, MONTEVALLO UNIV, 80- *Personal Data:* b Baghdad, Iraq, Sept 6, 32; m 75; c 2. *Educ:* Univ Baghdad, BSc, 55; Ind Univ, MSc, 59, PhD(anat), 64. *Prof Exp:* Res assoc electron micros, Ind Univ, 66-67; researcher, Putnam Hosp, 67-71; asst prof, Ind Univ, 74-77 & Baghdad Univ, 78-79. *Concurrent Pos:* Sabbatical leave, Case Western Reserve Univ, 79. *Mem:* Am Asn Anatomists; Sigma Xi. *Res:* Ultrastructure of the carotid body of normal anoxic mammals as well as the study of the effects of some cholenergic drugs on this organ. *Mailing Add:* 5106 Spring Creek Rd Montevallo AL 35115

ALLAN, A J GORDON, chemical engineering, surface chemistry; deceased, see previous edition for last biography

ALLAN, BARRY DAVID, PHYSICAL CHEMISTRY, LASERS. *Current Pos:* CONSULT, ALLAN CONSULT, 96- *Personal Data:* b Steubenville, Ohio, Jan 20, 35; m 61, Inge Bergeler; c Barbara & Stephen. *Educ:* Ariz State Univ, BS, 56; Univ Ala, MS, 64, PhD(chem), 68. *Honors & Awards:* Army Res & Develop Award, Dept Army,62. *Prof Exp:* Proj officer propellants, Army Rocket & Guided Missile Agency, Army Missile Command, 56-58, from chemist to res chemist, 58-70, res staff, Chem Laser Br, 70-75, chief high energy laser directorate, Device-Components Br, 75-78, mem staff high energy laser syst proj off, 78-80, mem staff advan technol function, Propulsion Directorate, 80-95. *Concurrent Pos:* Mem, Army Explosives & Propellant Res & Develop Liaison Group, 58-62; mem panel on liquid test methods, Chem Propellant Info Agency, 62-; mem Army Ad Hoc Comt Sensitivity of New Mat, 62-; reviewer, NSF, 74- *Mem:* Am Chem Soc. *Res:* Combustion and oscillatory combustion; physico-chemical properties of high energy compounds; sensitivity and desensitization of high energy compounds; theoretical propellant performance analysis; physico-chemical and rheological analysis of thixotropic gels. *Mailing Add:* 7803 Michael Circle Huntsville AL 35802

ALLAN, DAVID, CHEMISTRY, POLYMER CHEMISTRY. *Current Pos:* RESEARCHER CHEM RES, DOW CHEM CO, 92- *Personal Data:* b Berwyn Pa, 1961. *Educ:* Case Western Res Univ, BS, 83, MS 85; Univ Mich, PhD(macro- molecular sci), 89. *Prof Exp:* Researcher nonlinear optics, Northwestern Univ, 90-92. *Mem:* Am Chem Soc; Am Inst Chemists. *Mailing Add:* Dow Chem Co 1603 Bldg Dow Chem Co Midland MI 48674

ALLAN, DAVID WAYNE, PHYSICS, MATHEMATICS. *Current Pos:* RETIRED. *Personal Data:* b Mapleton, Utah, Sept 25, 36; m 59; c 7. *Educ:* Brigham Young Univ, BS, 60; Univ Colo, MS, 65. *Honors & Awards:* Silver Medal Award & Sustained Super Performance Award, Dept Commerce, 68; IR-100 Award, 76. *Prof Exp:* Physicist, 60-68, asst sect chief, Time & Frequency Div, 68-77, chief, Time & Frequency Coord Group, 79-88, sr scientist, Time & Frequency Div, Nat Inst Standards & Technol, Dept Com, 88-92; consult, 67-92. *Concurrent Pos:* Ital Govt vis prof grant, 69; consult, UN Develop Prog, New Delhi, India, 81; guest scientist, Peoples Repub of China, 82; vis scientist, Int Astron Union Symp, Leningrad, USSR, 85; assoc ed, Frequency & Time, Inst Elec & Electronic Engrs, 85; lectr & consult to dir, Nat Phys Lab, Israel, 87; group leader, Nat Inst Standards & Technol. *Mem:* Sci Res Soc Am; Inst Elec & Electronic Engrs; Sigma Xi; Int Radio Consultative Comt; Int Astron Union. *Res:* Atomic time scale; classification of the statistical characteristics of atomic and molecular frequency standards; international time and frequency metrology; Air Force invention award and patent. *Mailing Add:* PO Box 66 Fountain Green UT 84632

ALLAN, FRANK DUANE, ANATOMY, EMBRYOLOGY. *Current Pos:* from asst prof to prof, George Washington Univ, 54-90, dir, AV Serv, 62-90, dir, AV Educ, 73-90, EMER PROF ANAT, SCH MED, GEORGE WASHINGTON UNIV, 90- *Personal Data:* b Salt Lake City, Utah, May 19, 25; m 46; c 7. *Educ:* Univ Utah, BS, 47, MS, 49; La State Univ, PhD(anat), 54. *Prof Exp:* Asst anat, Univ Utah, 48-49. *Concurrent Pos:* Vis scientist, Carnegie Inst Washington, 62-64, mem, Int Anat Nomenclature Subcomt Embryol. *Mem:* Am Asn Anatomists; Asn Biomed Commun Dirs (pres, 81-82); Health Sci Commun Asn. *Res:* Early human embryology; cardiovascular physiology; electrophysiological studies on the development of tolerance to alcohol; anomalous arteries; innervation of the ducts arteriosus; anatomy of the fetus and newborn; audiovisual technology in medical education; gross and microscopic anatomy; neuroanatomy. *Mailing Add:* Blue Run Farm Rte 1 Box 116W Stanardsville VA 22973

ALLAN, GEORGE B, COMPUTER SCIENCE. *Current Pos:* RETIRED. *Personal Data:* b London, Ont, May 8, 35; m 62; c 2. *Educ:* McGill Univ, BS, 59; Bowdoin Col, MA, 67. *Prof Exp:* Prof math, Lambton Col, 67-, acad vpres, 75-81, pres, 81-84. *Mem:* Math Asn Am. *Mailing Add:* 445 Lake Shore Rd Sarnia ON N7V 2S4 Can

ALLAN, GEORGE GRAHAM, ORGANIC CHEMISTRY, POLYMER & FIBER SCIENCE. *Current Pos:* PROF FIBER SCI & POLYMER CHEM, DEPT CHEM ENG & COL FOREST RESOURCES, UNIV WASH, 66- *Personal Data:* b Glasgow, Scotland, Nov 21, 30; m 55, Margaret M Allingham; c Frederick James, Lesley Allingham, George Graham, Robert Gordon, Ian Malcolm & Catherine Holly. *Educ:* Royal Col Sci & Technol, Scotland, dipl, 51, assoc, 52; Glasgow Univ, BSc, 52, PhD(org chem), 55; Univ Strathclyde, DSc(fiber & polymer sci), 70; FRSC. *Prof Exp:* Asst to Prof F S Spring, Royal Col Sci & Technol, Scotland, 55-56; res chemist electrochem, E I du Pont de Nemours, 56-62; sr scientist, Pioneering Res Dept, Weyerhaeuser Co, 62-66. *Concurrent Pos:* Head sci leather technologists, David Dale Tech Col, Glasgow & lectr, Paisley Tech Col, Scotland, 52-56. *Mem:* Am Chem Soc; Am Inst Chem Engrs; Tech Asn Pulp & Paper Indust; Controlled Release Soc. *Res:* Lignin and forest products chemistry; polymers; biologically active organic heterocycles; epoxidation; nonwovens; fiber surface modification; adhesion; controlled release pesticides; pollution control; marine polymers. *Mailing Add:* Univ Wash PO Box 352100 Seattle WA 98195-2100. *Fax:* 425-486-3348, 543-3254; *E-Mail:* create@u.washington.edu

ALLAN, J DAVID, ECOLOGY. *Current Pos:* PROF CONSERV, SCH NATURAL RESOURCES & ENVIRON, UNIV MICH, 90- *Personal Data:* b London, Ont, Feb 5, 45; m 68. *Educ:* Univ BC, BSc, 66; Univ Mich, MS, 68, PhD(zool), 71. *Prof Exp:* Fel biol, Univ Chicago, 71-72; from asst prof to assoc prof zool, Univ Md, College Park, 72-90. *Mem:* AAAS; Ecol Soc Am; Int Soc Theoret & Appl Limnol; Am Soc Naturalists; Soc Study Evolution. *Res:* Ecology and aquatic biology; population dynamics and life histories; competition and predation; distributional patterns. *Mailing Add:* Sch Natural Resources Dana Bldg Univ Mich Main Campus 430 E Univ Ave Ann Arbor MI 48109-1115

ALLAN, JOHN R, PLANT PHYSIOLOGY. *Current Pos:* RETIRED. *Personal Data:* b Detroit, Mich, Feb 6, 37; m 63; c 4. *Educ:* Univ Mich, BS, 59; Ind Univ, MA, 62; Univ Sask, PhD(biol, plant physiol), 67. *Prof Exp:* Teaching asst aquatic plants, Mich Biol Sta, 59; res asst plant physiol, Argonne Nat Lab, 61; teaching asst, Ind Univ, 61-62; res asst, Univ Sask, 62-64; res scientist plant physiol, Agr Can Res Sta, 66-93. *Mem:* Phytochem Soc NAm; Weed Sci Soc Am; Aquatic Plant Mgt Soc NAm. *Res:* Aquatic plant physiology; limnology; aquatic plant taxonomy and ecology; management of aquatic vegetation to provide maximum water efficiency with minimum ecological damage; integrated Aquatic Vegetation Management Program using chemical, biological, mechanical and nutrient limitation techniques to maintain aquatic plant populations at non-nuisance levels. *Mailing Add:* 1313 Huron Pl Lethbridge AB T1K 3L1 Can

ALLAN, ROBERT EMERSON, AGRONOMY. *Current Pos:* RETIRED. *Personal Data:* b Morris, Ill, Jan 12, 31; c 4. *Educ:* Iowa State Univ, BS, 52; Kans State Univ, MS, 56, PhD(agron), 58. *Prof Exp:* Res asst, Kans State Col, 54-57; agronomist, USDA, 57-59, geneticist & res leader wheat breeding & prod, agr res serv, 59-; prof agron, Wash State Univ, 59- *Concurrent Pos:* Adj prof agron, Univ Idaho, 79- *Mem:* Genetics Soc Am; fel Am Soc Agron; Am Genetic Asn; Am Phytopath. *Res:* Genetics and cytogenetics of wheat and its relatives; genetics of host, parasite relationships; nuclear and cytoplasmic interactions in Triticum species. *Mailing Add:* USDA Agr Res Serv 209 Johnson Hall Dept Agron Wash State Univ Pullman WA 99164

ALLAN, ROBERT K, BIOCHEMISTRY. *Current Pos:* Asst prof, 66-70, ASSOC PROF CHEM, YORK UNIV, 70-, ASSOC DEAN, FAC SCI, 72- *Personal Data:* b Hamilton Ont, Jan 25, 40; m 62; c 3. *Educ:* McMaster Univ, BSc, 62, PhD(biochem), 67. *Mem:* Inst Can. *Res:* Biochemistry of microorganisms; chloroplast mutagenesis; mechanism of action of chemical mutagens. *Mailing Add:* Dept Chem Rm 456 Bldg CCB York Univ 4700 Keele St Downsview ON M3J 1P3 Can

ALLANSMITH, MATHEA R, immunology, allergies, for more information see previous edition

ALLARA, DAVID LAWRENCE, SURFACE CHEMISTRY. *Current Pos:* PROF CHEM & MAT SCI, PA STATE UNIV, 87- *Personal Data:* b Vallejo, Calif, Nov 3, 37; m 68; c 2. *Educ:* Univ Calif, Berkeley, BS, 59; Univ Calif, Los Angeles, PhD(chem), 64. *Prof Exp:* NSF fel Oxford Univ, 64-65; fel, Stanford Res Inst, 65-66, org chemist, 66-67; assoc prof chem. San Francisco State Col, 67-69; mem tech staff, Bell Tel Labs, 69-84, res mgr, Bell Commun Res, Inc, 84-87. *Mem:* AAAS; Am Chem Soc; Am Phys Soc; Mat Res Soc. *Res:* Interfacial chemistry; surface spectroscopy. *Mailing Add:* Mat Sci Dept 185 MRI Bldg 230 Innovation Blvd University Park PA 16802

ALLARD, GILLES OLIVIER, GEOLOGY, ECONOMIC GEOLOGY. *Current Pos:* assoc prof, Univ Ga, 65-69, actg head dept, 69-70, prof, 70-91, EMER PROF GEOL, UNIV GA, 91- *Personal Data:* b Rougemont, Que, Dec 12, 27; m 52, Bernadette Martiruaudu; c Claude, Martine & Mitch. *Educ:* Univ Montreal, BA, 48, BS, 51; Queen's Univ, Ont, MA, 53; Johns Hopkins Univ, PhD(geol), 56. *Honors & Awards:* Duncan Derry Medal, Geol Asn Can; Grand Prix Mente Geoscientifique, Asn Geologists & Geophysicists Quebec. *Prof Exp:* Consult, Que Dept Natural Resources, 52-55; field mgr, Chibougamau Mining & Smelting, Que, 55-58; asst prof geol, Univ Va, 58-59; prof, Ctr Res & Develop Petrol-Petrobras, Salvador, Brazil, 59-64; vis lectr, Univ Calif, Riverside, 64-65. *Concurrent Pos:* Consult, Que Dept Energy & Resources, 66-; Sandy Beaver Prof, 78-82; Can Inst Mining Distinguished lectr, 84-85; pres, Southeastern Sect Geol Soc Am, 85-86. *Mem:* Fel Geol Soc Am; fel Mineral Soc Am; Can Inst; Soc Econ Geologists. *Res:* Structural and economic geology of Chibougamau, Quebec; discovery of Henderson Copper Mine, Chibougamau; Dore Lake layered complex; Propria geosyncline, Brazil; geologic link Brazil-Gabon and continental drift; volcanic ore deposits; metamorphism and ores. *Mailing Add:* Dept Geol Univ Ga Athens GA 30602. *Fax:* 706-542-2425; *E-Mail:* goallar@uga.cc.uga.edu

ALLARD, JOHANE, MEDICINE. *Current Pos:* res fel nutrit, 87-89, ASST PROF, DEPT MED, UNIV TORONTO, 89- , STAFF PHYSICIAN, DIV GASTROENTEROL, TORONTO GEN HOSP, 89- *Personal Data:* b Montreal, Sept 29, 56; m; c 2. *Educ:* Ahuntsic Col, DEC, 75; Univ Montreal, MD, 81; Am Bd Internal Med, cert, 85; FRCP(C). *Prof Exp:* Resident I & I internal med, Maisonneuve-Rosemont Hosp, 81-83; resident III, Hotel-Dieu de Montreal Hosp, 83-84; resident IV, McGill Univ, 84-86. *Concurrent Pos:* Chief resident, Maisonneuve-Rosemont Hosp, 82-83; mem training comt, McGill Univ, 85-86; mem nutrit comt, Toronto Gen Hosp, 89- *Mem:* Am Gastroenterol Asn; Can Asn Gastroenterol; Am Soc Enteral & Parenteral Nutrit; Int Soc Burn Injuries; Am Soc Clin Nutrit. *Mailing Add:* Dept Med Toronto Gen Hosp 200 Elizabeth St 7th Floor Bell Wing Rm 637 Toronto ON M5G 2C4 Can

ALLARD, NONA MARY, MATHEMATICS. *Current Pos:* instr, 60-61, from instr to asst prof, 65-73, ASSOC PROF MATH, ROSARY COL, 74- *Personal Data:* b Minneapolis, Minn, Dec 23, 28. *Educ:* Col St Catherine, BA, 50; Cath Univ Am, MA. 60, PhD(math), 67. *Prof Exp:* Teacher, Cromwell High Sch, Minn, 50-52, Alexander Ramsey High Sch, 53-54 & Visitation High Sch, Ill, 56-58. *Mem:* Math Asn Am. *Res:* Functional analysis; convex topological algebras and other generalizations of Banach algebras. *Mailing Add:* 7900 W Division St River Forest IL 60305

ALLARD, ROBERT WAYNE, GENETICS & PLANT BREEDING, AGRONOMY. *Current Pos:* From asst prof to prof genetics, Univ Calif, Davis, 46-86, chmn, Dept Genetics, 67-75, chmn, Acad Senate, 74-76, EMER PROF GENETICS, UNIV CALIF, DAVIS, 86- *Personal Data:* b Los Angeles, Calif, Sept 3, 19; m 44, Ann Wilson; c Susan, Thomas, Jane, Gillian & Stacy. *Educ:* Univ Calif, BS, 41; Univ Wis, PhD, 46. *Hon Degrees:* ScD, Univ Helinki, Finland, 95, Univ Leon, Spain, 97. *Honors & Awards:* Crop Sci Award, Am Soc Agron, 64; Nilsson Ehle lectr, Mendelian Soc, Sweden, 80; De Kalb-Phizer Distinguished Career Award, Crop Sci Soc, 83; Wilhelmine Key lectr, Am Genetics Asn, 87. *Concurrent Pos:* Guggenheim fel, 54-55 & 60-61; Fulbright sr res fel, 55; centennial prof, Am Univ, Beirut, 67; Nat Res Coun comt Managing Global Plant Genetics Resources, chair, 86-89; fac res lectr, Univ Calif, 74. *Mem:* Nat Acad Sci; Genetics Soc Am (pres, 84); Am Genetic Asn (pres, 88); Am Soc Naturalists (pres, 75); fel Crop Sci Soc Am; Am Acad Arts & Sci; fel AAAS; fel Am Soc Agron. *Res:* Population, ecological, and evolutionary genetics; genetic resource conservation; genetics of host-pathogen interactions; plant breeding. *Mailing Add:* PO Box 185 Bodega Bay CA 95616

ALLARD, WILLIAM KENNETH, PURE MATHEMATICS. *Current Pos:* chmn dept, 85-86, PROF MATH, DUKE UNIV, 76- *Personal Data:* b Lowell, Mass, Oct 29, 41; m 68; c 2. *Educ:* Villanova Univ, ScB, 63; Brown Univ, PhD(math), 68. *Prof Exp:* Asst prof to math, Princeton Univ, 68-78. *Concurrent Pos:* Sloan Found fel, 70-72; man ed, Duke Math J, 83-85. *Mem:* Am Math Soc. *Res:* Application of geometric measure theoretic techniques to the study of elliptic variational problems. *Mailing Add:* Duke Univ Durham NC 27707

ALLARDT, ERIK ANDERS, SOCIOLOGY, POLITICAL SOCIOLOGY. *Current Pos:* RETIRED. *Personal Data:* b Helsingfors, Finland, Aug 9, 25; m, Sagi E Nylander; c Jorn, Monica & Barbro. *Educ:* Univ Helsinki, MA, 47, PhD, 52. *Hon Degrees:* PhD, Univ Stockholm, 78, Abo Acad, Finland, 78, Univ Uppsala, Sweden, 84, Univ Bergen, 96. *Honors & Awards:* Finland Prize, Swedish Acad, 86; Hon Prize, Finish Academy Sci, 93. *Prof Exp:* Instr sociol, Univ Helsinki, 48-53, prof, 58-70 & 80-85; res asst, Bur Appl Social Res Columbia Univ, 54; res dir, Helsinki Sch Social Sci, 55-57; res prof, Acad Finland, 70-80, pres, 86-91; chancellor, Abo Acad Univ, 92-94. *Concurrent Pos:* Vis prof, Univ Calif, Berkely, 62-63, Univ Ill, Urbana, 66-67, Univ Wis-Madison, 70, Univ Mannheim, Ger, 85; chmn, Finnish Sect, Amnesty Int, 77-78, Tampere Inst Peace & Conflict Res, Finland, 77-78 & Com Develop Future Studies, 88-89; vis scholar, Wilson Ctr, Washington, 78-79. *Mem:* Foreign mem Norweg Acad Sci & Lett; hon mem Finnish Soc Sci & Lett; foreign mem Royal Swed Acad Lett Hist & Antiq; Europ Sci Found (vpres, 90-92); hon mem Polish Sociol Asn. *Res:* Sociology, Political Science and Economics related to social policy; studies of the history of the Social Sciences. *Mailing Add:* Unionsgatan 45 B 40 Helsinki FIN 00014 Finland. *Fax:* 358-135-2926

ALLCOCK, HARRY R(EX), INORGANIC CHEMISTRY, POLYMER CHEMISTRY. *Current Pos:* from assoc prof to prof, 66-85, EVAN PUGH PROF CHEM, PA STATE UNIV, 85- *Personal Data:* b Loughborough, Eng, Apr 8, 32; nat US citizen; m 59. *Educ:* Univ London, BSc, 53, PhD(chem), 56. *Honors & Awards:* Nat Award in Polymer Chem, Am Chem Soc, 84, Nat Award Mat Chem, 92, Herman Mark Award Polymer Chem, 94; Pioneer Award, Am Inst Chemists, 89. *Prof Exp:* Fel org chem, Purdue Univ, 56-57; res fel phys-org chem, Nat Res Coun Can, 58-60; res chemist, Stamford Res Labs, Am Cyanamid Co, 61-65, sr res chemist, 65-66. *Concurrent Pos:* Guggenheim fel, 86-87. *Mem:* Am Chem Soc; Chem Soc; Royal Soc Chem. *Res:* Inorganic-organic polymer chemistry; solid state chemistry; biomedical polymers; synthesis; reaction mechanisms; molecular structure studies; phosphorus-nitrogen, organosilicon and transition metal organometallic systems. *Mailing Add:* Dept Chem Pa State Univ University Park PA 16802

ALLDAY, CHRISTOPHER J, ALGEBRAIC TOPOLOGY. *Current Pos:* PROF MATH, UNIV HAWAII, 70- *Personal Data:* b Sutton Coldfield, Eng, Sept 5, 43. *Educ:* Cambridge Univ, Eng, BA, 65, MA, 69; Univ Calif, PhD(math), 70. *Mem:* Am Math Soc. *Mailing Add:* Univ Hawaii Honolulu HI 96822-2273

ALLDREDGE, ALICE LOUISE, BIOLOGICAL OCEANOGRAPHY, MARINE ECOLOGY. *Current Pos:* from asst prof to assoc prof biol, 76-86, PROF, UNIV CALIF, SANTA BARBARA, 86- *Personal Data:* b Denver, Colo, Feb 1, 49; m 78, James M King; c Matthew. *Educ:* Carleton Col, BA, 71; Univ Calif, Davis, PhD(ecol), 75. *Honors & Awards:* Henry Bryant Bigelow Medal, Oceanog, 92. *Prof Exp:* NATO fel marine ecol, Australian Inst Marine Sci, 75-76. *Concurrent Pos:* Prin investr, NSF grant biol oceanog, 77-, Org Nat Res grant biol oceanog, 86- *Mem:* AAAS; Am Asn Limnol & Oceanog; Sigma Xi. *Res:* Ecology of gelatinous marine zooplankton; macroscopic aggregates and the particle size distribution of particulate organic matter in the sea; behavior and ecology of demersal reef zooplankton. *Mailing Add:* Dept Biol Sci Univ Calif 7295 Almeda Ave Gol Santa Barbara CA 93106. *E-Mail:* alldredg@lifesci.lscf.ucsb.edu

ALLDREDGE, GERALD PALMER, SURFACE PHYSICS, SURFACE CHEMISTRY. *Current Pos:* PRIN STAFF MEM, BDM INT, 86- *Personal Data:* b Hereford, Tex, Oct 20, 35. *Educ:* Tex Technol Col, BA, 58, MS, 60; Mich State Univ, PhD(physics), 66. *Prof Exp:* From instr to asst prof physics, Southern Ill Univ, 64-68; res scientist & lectr physics, Univ Tex, Austin, 68-75; sr res investr, Grad Ctr Mat Res, Univ Mo, Rolla, 75-77, assoc prof physics, Rolla, 76-79 & Columbia, 79-85; prof physics, Northeast Mo State Univ, 85-86. *Concurrent Pos:* Partic, Prof Activ Continuing Educ Prog, Argonne Nat Lab, resident res assoc, 65 & 66; consult, Columbia Sci Res Inst, Tex, 69-75; vis scholar, Univ Tex, Austin, 75-83; guest prof, Tech Univ of Denmark, 83-84; vis res scientist, UK AERE-Harwell, 84; vis prof, Univ Calif, Irvine, 84; vis scholar, Univ Mo, Columbia, 85. *Mem:* AAAS; Am Phys Soc; Am Asn Physics Teachers; Am Chem Soc; Sigma Xi; Mat Res Soc; Am Vacuum Soc; Asn Comput Mach; Inst Elec & Electronics Engrs; Comput Soc; Soc Indust & Appl Math. *Res:* Theory of condensed matter; physics and chemistry of surfaces and interfaces; chemical physics; statistical mechanics; computational physics; mathematical physics; materials science, quantum chemistry. *Mailing Add:* MS-C-23 BDM Int Inc 1801 Randolph Rd SE Albuquerque NM 87106

ALLDREDGE, LEROY ROMNEY, GEOPHYSICS. *Current Pos:* RETIRED. *Personal Data:* b Mesa, Ariz, Feb 6, 17; m 40; c 7. *Educ:* Univ Ariz, MS, 40; Harvard Univ, ME, 52; Univ Md, PhD, 55. *Prof Exp:* Instr physics, Univ Ariz, 40-41; radio inspector, Fed Commun Comn, 41-44; radio engr, Dept Terrestrial Magnetism, Carnegie Inst Washington, 44-45; physicist & div chief, Res Dept, Naval Ord Lab, 45-55; analyst, Opers Res Off, Johns Hopkins Univ, 55-59; geophysicist, Coast & Geodetic Surv, US Dept Com, 59-65; from actg dir to dir, Inst Earth Sci, Environ Sci Serv Admin, 65-70, dir, Earth Sci Labs, Nat Oceanic & Atmospheric Admin Environ Res Labs, 70-73; res geophysicist, US Geol Surv, Dept Interior, Denver, 73-88. *Mem:* Am Geophys Union; Int Asn Geomag & Aeronomy. *Res:* Electricity and magnetism. *Mailing Add:* 4475 Chippewa Dr Boulder CO 80303-3616

ALLEE, MARSHALL CRAIG, ENTOMOLOGY, ZOOLOGY. *Current Pos:* AT DEPT BIOL, FLOYD JR COL, CHMN DIR NAT SCI, SHORTER COL, GA, 67- *Personal Data:* b Rome, Ga, July 18, 41; m 60; c 3. *Educ:* Shorter Col, Ga, BA, 63; Clemson Univ, MS, 65, PhD(entom), 68. *Prof Exp:* Instr biol, Clemson Univ, 66-67; assoc prof biol, Shorter Col, Ga, 68-, dean, Div Student Serv, 72- *Mem:* Entom Soc Am. *Res:* Response of the face fly, Musca autumnalis DeGeer, to various concentrations of aphotate and tepa; potential of Aleochara tristis Gravenhorst as a means of controlling the face fly. *Mailing Add:* 109 Keown Rd SE Rome GA 30161

ALLEGRE, CHARLES FREDERICK, BIOLOGY. *Current Pos:* from asst prof to prof, 50-80, EMER PROF BIOL, UNIV NORTHERN IOWA, 80- *Personal Data:* b Osage City, Kans, Oct 6, 11; m 38. *Educ:* Kans State Teachers Col, BS, 36; Univ Iowa, MS, 41, PhD(zool), 47. *Prof Exp:* Assoc prof biol & actg head dept, Gustavus Adolphus Col, 47-50. *Mem:* AAAS; assoc Am Soc Zool; Am Micros Soc. *Res:* Protozoology; fresh water and parasitic taxonomy; microbiology; life history of a gregarine parasite in grasshoppers. *Mailing Add:* 1403 W Seventh St Cedar Falls IA 50613

ALLEGRETTI, JOHN E, CHEMICAL ENGINEERING. *Current Pos:* RETIRED. *Personal Data:* b Weehawken, NJ, Aug 23, 26; m 51, Mildred DeConto; c Joel A & Amy. *Educ:* NY Univ, BChE, 51. *Prof Exp:* Supvr pilot plant, Merck Sharp & Dohme Res Labs, 51-53, assoc chemist process develop, 53-55, res assoc eng develop, 55-57, group leader, 57-59, sr res engr, 59-61, res assoc, Electronic Chem Div, Merck & Co, Inc, 61-63, mgr process res, 63-64, sect mgr, Merck Sharp & Dohme Res Labs, Rahway, NJ, 64-66, mgr & chem engr res & develop, 66-69, dir pharmaceut develop, West Point, Pa, 69-75, sr dir pharmaceut res & develop, 75-90. *Mem:* Am Inst Chem Engrs; NY Acad Sci; AAAS. *Res:* Materials science; epitaxial growth of single crystal silicon layers on silicon substrates for producing unique electronic device structures; optical isomer separation; automation of pharmaceutical processes; development of pharmaceutical dosage forms. *Mailing Add:* 31 Hamlin Rd East Brunswick NJ 08816

ALLEMAND, CHARLY D, APPLIED PHYSICS. *Current Pos:* AT INSPEX CORP, 78- *Personal Data:* b Soengeiliat, Banka, Sept 2, 24; m, Paulette Honsberger; c 1. *Educ:* Swiss Fed Inst Technol, dipl, 49; Univ Neuchatel, PhD(semiconductors), 54. *Honors & Awards:* Meggers Award, Soc Appl Spectros, 71. *Prof Exp:* Asst solid state physics, Univ Neuchatel, 51-52, chief adv, 52-54; scientist, Fabrique Suisse de Ressorts d'Horlogerie, SA, 54-58, tech mgr metall, 58-60, gen mgr method, time & motion orgn prog, 60-61; mgr eng res, Jarrell-Ash Co, Switz, 62-66, staff scientist, Jarrell-Ash Div, Fisher Sci Co, 66-69, Fisher Res Labs, 69-73, sr staff scientist, Jarrell-Ash Div, 73-78. *Concurrent Pos:* Self employed, 78- *Mem:* Optical Soc Am; Int Soc Optical Eng; Int Soc Optical Eng. *Res:* Underwater telephony; electronic conduction in dielectric crystals; high tensile strength alloys; excitation sources for spectroscopy; geometrical and physical optics; ICP spectroscopy; atomic fluorescence spectroscopy; raman spectroscopy; inspection instrumentation for silicon wafers. *Mailing Add:* 3 Wamasquid Pl Nantucket MA 02554. *Fax:* 508-325-5676

ALLEN, ALEXANDER CHARLES, PEDIATRICS, NEONATOLOGY. *Current Pos:* assoc prof pediat & asst prof obstet & gynec, 75-88, PROF PEDIAT & PROF OBSTET & GYNEC, FAC MED, DALHOUSIE UNIV, 88-; HEAD NEONATAL PEDIAT DEPT, GRACE MATERNITY HOSP, 76- *Personal Data:* b Morristown, NJ, Dec 27, 33; m 60, Vivian; c Laura, Victoria & Andrew. *Educ:* Haverford Col, BS, 55; McGill Univ, MD, CM, 59; FRCP(C); Am Pediat, dipl, 70. *Prof Exp:* Intern med, Royal Victoria Hosp, Montreal, Que, 59-60; jr asst resident pediat, Montreal Children's Hosp, 60-61; jr asst resident internal med, Royal Victoria Hosp, 61-62; sr asst resident pediat, Montreal Children's Hosp, 62-63; res assoc neonatology, McGill Univ & Royal Victoria Hosp, Montreal, 63-66; asst prof pediat, obstet & gynec, Sch Med, Univ Pittsburgh, 69-75. *Concurrent Pos:* Dir, Infant Referral Ctr, Magee-Women's Hosp, 73-75. *Mem:* Fel Am Acad Pediat; Can Pediat Soc; Soc Pediat Res. *Res:* Idiopathic respiratory distress syndrome of prematurity; asphyxia neonatorum; pulmonary blood flow and pulmonary water changes during neonatal adaptation to extra-uterine life; intraventricular hemorrhage in neonates; tracheal suction at birth and meconium aspiration; retinopathy of prematurity. *Mailing Add:* Dept Neonatal Pediat Grace Maternity Hosp 5980 University Ave Halifax NS B3J 3G9 Can. *Fax:* 902-420-6469; *E-Mail:* newborn@ac.dal.ca

ALLEN, ANNEKE S, PHYSICAL CHEMISTRY. *Current Pos:* asst prof, 64-71, assoc dean lab, 77-81, ASSOC PROF CHEM, WICHITA STATE UNIV, 71- *Personal Data:* b Dronrijp, Netherlands, Sept 14, 30; US citizen; m 57; c 3. *Educ:* Tulane Univ, PhD(phys chem), 55. *Prof Exp:* Instr chem, Tulane Univ, 54-55; chemist, Cent Labs, Dow Chem Co, Tex, 55-58; pres, Alchem, Fla, 59-63. *Concurrent Pos:* Asst prof, Orlando Jr Col, 62-63. *Mem:* AAAS; Am Chem Soc; Sigma Xi. *Res:* Inorganic reactions in solution; electrochemistry of organometallic compounds. *Mailing Add:* 8118 Levitt Wichita KS 67207

ALLEN, ANTON MARKERT, VETERINARY PATHOLOGY. *Current Pos:* asst chief, 59-61, CHIEF COMP PATH SECT, VET RESOURCES BR, NIH, 61- *Personal Data:* b Augusta, Ga, Feb 9, 31; m 51; c 4. *Educ:* Univ Ga, DVM, 55; Univ Wis, PhD(path), 61. *Prof Exp:* Asst vet officer, Comp Path Sect, Nat Cancer Inst, 55-57; vet officer, Comp Path & Cytol, Sch Med, Univ Wis, 57-59. *Mem:* AAAS; Int Primatol Soc; Am Vet Med Asn; Am Asn Path & Bact. *Res:* Pathology of primate diseases; mitosis and binucleation of mast cells; pathogenesis of naturally occurring diseases of laboratory animals. *Mailing Add:* Dir Vet Med Microbiol Assocs Inc 9900 Blackwell Rd Rockville MD 20850-3349

ALLEN, ARCHIE C, ZOOLOGY, GENETICS. *Current Pos:* RETIRED. *Personal Data:* b Ash, NC, Dec 23, 29; m 59; c 2. *Educ:* Univ NC, BS, 55, MA, 58; Univ Pittsburgh, PhD(zool), 61. *Prof Exp:* NIH fel genetics, Univ Tex, 61-63; asst prof biol, 63-67, assoc prof, Tex Tech Univ, 67- *Mem:* AAAS; Genetics Soc Am. *Res:* Recombination, population and lethal studies of Drosophila melanogaster. *Mailing Add:* 3413 23rd St Lubbock TX 79410

ALLEN, ARNOLD ORAL, MATHEMATICS. *Current Pos:* WITH HEWLETT-PACKARD, 86- *Personal Data:* b Malcolm, Nebr, Aug 2, 29; m 61; c 1. *Educ:* Univ Nebr, BA, 50; Univ Calif, Los Angeles, MA, 59, PhD(math), 62. *Prof Exp:* Asst physics, Univ Nebr, 50; comput programmer, IBM Corp, 56-58; asst math, Univ Calif, Los Angeles, 58-59; systs engr, IBM Corp, 62-64, mathematician, 64-68, PhD col rels rep, 68-71, sr staff mem, Systs Sci Inst, 71-84. *Concurrent Pos:* Lectr, Univ Calif, Los Angeles, 65-71. *Mem:* Math Asn Am; Sigma Xi. *Res:* Applications of probability, statistics and queueing theory to analysis of computer systems. *Mailing Add:* 1420 Wabash Way Roseville CA 95678-2085

ALLEN, ARTHUR, BIOCHEMISTRY. *Current Pos:* from asst prof to assoc prof biochem, 58-83, PROF BIOCHEM & MOLECULAR PHARMACOL, JEFFERSON MED COL, 83- *Personal Data:* b Philadelphia, Pa, Nov 20, 28; m 56, Dolores Benson; c Brian & Amy. *Educ:* Temple Univ, BA, 50, MA, 53, PhD(chem), 56. *Prof Exp:* Chief, Div Chem & Toxicol, First US Army Med Lab, NY, 56-58. *Concurrent Pos:* Lectr chem, Temple Univ, 60-67, adj assoc prof, 67-69. *Mem:* AAAS; Am Chem Soc; Sigma Xi. *Res:* Intermediary metabolism of carbohydrates and lipids. *Mailing Add:* Dept Biochem & Molecular Pharmacol Jefferson Med Col Philadelphia PA 19107. *Fax:* 215-923-9162

ALLEN, ARTHUR (SILSBY), PLANT PATHOLOGY, MYCOLOGY. *Current Pos:* assoc prof phytopath, 68-74, PROF BOT & FORESTRY, NORTHWESTERN STATE UNIV, 74- *Personal Data:* b Brewer, Maine, Mar 5, 34; m 58; c 2. *Educ:* Univ Maine, BS, 56, MS, 60; Mich State Univ, PhD(phytopath), 68. *Prof Exp:* Asst prof bot, Univ Maine, 58-60; asst phytopath, Mich State Univ, 60-63, res assoc & asst instr, 65-68; asst prof bot, Humboldt State Col, 63-65. *Concurrent Pos:* NSF fel. *Mem:* Am Phytopath

Soc; Sigma Xi; Am Soc Soil Conserv; Am Forestry Asn. *Res:* Host-pathogen relations; epidemiology and control of pecan diseases; biocontrol aquatic plants; forest restoration; post lignite mining operations. *Mailing Add:* Dept Life Sci Northwestern State Univ La 209 Bienvenue Hall Natchitoches LA 71497-0003

ALLEN, ARTHUR LEE, SOIL CHEMISTRY, PLANT PHYSIOLOGY. *Current Pos:* res agronomist & assoc prof, 76-78, ASST DEAN DIV AGR & TECHNOL, 78-, DIR COOP RES PROG & COOP EXTEN SERV, UNIV ARK, PINE BLUFF, 78- *Personal Data:* b Los Angeles, Calif, June 7, 44; c 2. *Educ:* Univ Ark, Pine Bluff, BS, 66; Okla State Univ, MS, 68; Univ Ill, PhD(soil chem), 71. *Prof Exp:* Lab technician soil & water testing, Okla State Univ, 64-67, asst clay minerol, 66-71; assoc prof chem, Langston Univ, Okla, 71-75. *Concurrent Pos:* Reviewer proposals minority div, Environ Protection Agency, 75-76; asst dir Sci & Educ Admin-Coop Res Prog & asst state coordr 1890 inst, Coop Exten Serv, Univ Ark, Pine Bluff, 78- *Mem:* Am Soc Agron; Soil Sci Soc Am; Crop Sci Soc Am. *Res:* Nitrate in soil and water; aluminum-hydroxide polymers in soil clays; chemical distribution and residual fertilizer derived nitrogen in soil; nitrogen forms under feedlots; slow release fertilizers; irrigation studies with soybeans; foliar fertilization; nitrogen uptake in nutrients solution cultures. *Mailing Add:* 7929 Claremont Dr North Little Rock AR 72116

ALLEN, AUGUSTINE OLIVER, physical chemistry, radiation chemistry; deceased, see previous edition for last biography

ALLEN, BONNIE L, SOIL GENESIS, SOIL MINERALOGY. *Current Pos:* assoc prof, 59-72, PROF SOILS, TEX TECH UNIV, 72- *Personal Data:* b Hillsboro, Tex, Aug 11, 24. *Educ:* Tex Tech Univ, BS, 48; Mich State Univ, MS, 51, PhD(soil sci), 60. *Prof Exp:* Asst prof agron, Eastern NMex Univ, 52-57, assoc prof soils & geol, 57-59. *Mem:* Fel Am Soc Agron; fel Soil Sci Soc Am; Am Chem Soc; Clay Minerals Soc; Int Soc Soil Sci; Int Soc Study Clays. *Res:* Mineralogical transformations and micromorphological changes with soil development; soil-native vegetation relationships. *Mailing Add:* Plant/Soil Sci Dept Tex Tech Univ Lubbock TX 79409

ALLEN, BRUCE, COSMOLOGY, THE EARLY UNIVERSE. *Current Pos:* asst prof, 89-92, ASSOC PROF PHYSICS, UNIV WIS-MILWAUKEE, 92- *Personal Data:* b Boston, Mass, May 11, 59. *Educ:* Mass Inst Technol, BS, 80; Cambridge Univ, PhD(gravitation & cosmology), 84. *Honors & Awards:* First Prize, Gravity Res Found, 90. *Prof Exp:* Fel, Univ Calif, Santa Barbara, 83-85, Tufts Univ, 85-86; res assoc, Paris Obsev, 86-87; res asst prof, Tufts Univ, 87-89. *Concurrent Pos:* Marshall Scholar, Brit Parliament/Cambridge Univ, 80-83; prin investr, NSF res grants, 87-; vis fel, Isaac Newton Math Inst, UK, 94; vis assoc, Calif Inst Technol, 95 &96. *Mem:* Am Phys Soc. *Res:* Focuses on the very early universe, cosmology, curved space quantum field theory; gravitational wave detection. *Mailing Add:* Dept Physics Univ Wis PO Box 413 Milwaukee WI 53211. *Fax:* 414-229-5589; *E-Mail:* ballen@dirac.phys.uwm.edu

ALLEN, CHARLES A, electronics engineering, for more information see previous edition

ALLEN, CHARLES C(ORLETTA), MICROWAVE ANTENNA SYSTEMS, COMMUNICATIONS. *Current Pos:* CONSULT ENGR, ALLEN CONSULT, 87- *Personal Data:* b New York, NY, Mar 1, 21; m 44, 73, Evelyn Aultfather; c Bruce, Gilbert, James & Catherine. *Educ:* Worcester Polytech Inst, BS, 49, MS, 50. *Honors & Awards:* Technol Innovation Awards, NASA, 74. *Prof Exp:* Develop engr, Corp Res & Develop Ctr, Gen Elec Co, Schenectady, NY, 50-55, microwave engr, 55-59, mgr microwave eng, 59-61, microwave engr, 61-75, tech staff engr, GE Space Systs Div, Valley Forge Space Ctr, Pa, 75-87. *Concurrent Pos:* Asst prof elec eng, Union Col, NY, 67-68, vis assoc prof, 68-69, adj assoc prof, 69-70; mem, Antenna Stand Comt, Inst Elec & Electronics Engrs, 59- *Mem:* Fel Inst Elec & Electronics Engrs; Sigma Xi. *Res:* Ultra high frequency current measurement; microwave antenna systems analysis and development; computer-aided antenna pattern and noise temperature calculations; microwave microelectronic circuits; satellite antenna systems communications; system performance evaluation; space based radar. *Mailing Add:* 604 Hickory Lane Berwyn PA 19312-1437

ALLEN, CHARLES EUGENE, AGRICULTURAL RESEARCH. *Current Pos:* from asst prof to prof animal sci, Food Sci & Nutrit, Univ Minn, 67-84, dean, Col Agr & assoc dir, Minn Agr Exp Sta, 84-88, actg vpres, Inst Agr, Forestry & Home Econ & actg dir, Minn Agr Exp Sta, 88-90, vpres, Inst Agr, Forestry & Home Econ, 90-95, PROVOST PROF STUDIES & DIR, MINN AGR EXP STA, UNIV MINN, 95- *Personal Data:* b Burley, Idaho, Jan 25, 39. *Educ:* Univ Idaho, Moscow, BS, 61; Univ Wis, MS, 63, PhD(meat & animal sci), 65. *Honors & Awards:* Meats Res Award, Am Soc Animal Sci, 77, 80; Signal Serv Award, Am Meat Sci Asn, 85. *Prof Exp:* Res asst, Univ Wis, 61-65; NSF fel, Div Food Res, Commonwealth Sci & Indust Res Orgn, Sidney, Australia, 66-67. *Concurrent Pos:* Vis prof animal sci, Pa State Univ, 78. *Mem:* Fel Inst Food Technol; Am Soc Animal Sci; AAAS. *Res:* Animal growth biology and the functional and nutritional characterists of animal food products. *Mailing Add:* Univ Minn Coffey Hall 1420 Eckles Ave St Paul MN 55108. *Fax:* 612-625-0286

ALLEN, CHARLES FREEMAN, ORGANIC CHEMISTRY, BIOCHEMISTRY. *Current Pos:* from asst prof to assoc prof chem, 54-66, PROF CHEM, POMONA COL, 66- *Personal Data:* b Berkeley, Calif, Feb 16, 28; m 50; c 3. *Educ:* Univ Calif, BS, 48; Univ Wis, PhD(org chem), 52. *Prof Exp:* Res chemist, Univ Calif, 52-54, instr, 53-54. *Concurrent Pos:* NSF fac fel, Univ Cologne, 61-62, Kettering Res Lab, Ohio & Scripps Inst Oceanog, 68-69 & Nat Bur Standards, 81-82. *Mem:* Am Chem Soc; AAAS. *Res:* Air pollution chemistry; lipid biochemistry. *Mailing Add:* 394 Blaisdell Dr Claremont CA 91711

ALLEN, CHARLES MARSHALL, JR, BIOCHEMISTRY. *Current Pos:* from asst prof to assoc prof, 67-79, PROF BIOCHEM, UNIV FLA, 79- *Personal Data:* b Cortland, NY, Sept 13, 38; m 63; c 2. *Educ:* Syracuse Univ, BS, 60; Brandeis Univ, PhD(biochem), 64. *Prof Exp:* USPHS fel chem, Harvard Univ, 64-67. *Mem:* Am Chem Soc; Am Soc Biol Chemists. *Res:* Biosynthesis and function of polyprenyl phosphates in bacterial and mammalian cells; mechanism of action of prenyltransferases. *Mailing Add:* Dept Biochem & Molecular Biol Box 100245 Gainesville FL 32601-0245. *Fax:* 352-392-2953; *E-Mail:* cmal@icbr.ifas.ufl.edu

ALLEN, CHARLES MARVIN, CYTOLOGY, INVERTEBRATE ZOOLOGY. *Current Pos:* From instr to assoc prof, 41-62, PROF BIOL, WAKE FOREST UNIV, 62-, DIR CONCERTS & LECTS, 74- *Personal Data:* b Mt Gilead, NC, July 31, 18; m 43. *Educ:* Wake Forest Col, BS, 39, MA, 41; Duke Univ, PhD, 55. *Mem:* AAAS; Sigma Xi. *Res:* Chromosome morphology and germ cell cycles; morphology and cytology of marine annelids. *Mailing Add:* Dept Biol 2108 Faculty Dr Winston-Salem NC 27106

ALLEN, CHARLES MICHAEL, MEDICAL IMAGING, PROCESS CONTROL. *Current Pos:* PROF COMPUTER ENG, UNIV NC, CHARLOTTE, 74- *Personal Data:* b New Castle, Pa, Sept 1, 42; m 87, Bonnie Heberlig; c Chuck, Jim, Tracy & Julie. *Educ:* Carnegie Mellon Univ, 64, MS, 65; State Univ NY, Buffalo, PhD(systs eng), 68. *Prof Exp:* Asst prof elec eng, State Univ NY, Buffalo, 68-74; dir res & develop, DataSpan, Inc, 82-85, pres, 85-87. *Concurrent Pos:* Consult eng design, Int Bus Mach, Kodak, AT&T, Sylvania & numerous eng firms, 65-; sect chmn, Inst Elec & Electronics Engrs, 81. *Mem:* Inst Elec & Electronics Engrs; Asn Comput Mach; Am Soc Eng Educr. *Res:* Embedded micro-computer control of processors; medical imaging; process control; parallel computing. *Mailing Add:* 3816 Smokerise Hill Dr Charlotte NC 28277. *E-Mail:* cma@uncc.edu

ALLEN, CHARLES W(ILLARD), PHYSICAL METALLURGY. *Current Pos:* from asst prof to prof, 59-86, EMER PROF METALL ENG, UNIV NOTRE DAME, 86-; MAT SCIENTIST, ARGONNE NAT LAB, 86- *Personal Data:* b Akron, Ind, Jan 7, 32; m 59, Teresa C Law; c Sean, Jamina, Thane & Joslyn. *Educ:* Univ Notre Dame, BS, 54, MS, 56, PhD(metall), 58. *Prof Exp:* Air Force Off Sci Res fel phys metall, 58, Off Naval Res fel, 58-59. *Concurrent Pos:* Fulbright res fel, SCK-Ctr Study Nuclear Energy, Mol, Belg, 70-71; fac leave for res at Argonne, 82-83; assoc ed, Appl Physics Lett, 89. *Mem:* Am Soc Metals Int; Am Phys Soc; Electron Miscros Soc Am; Mat Res Soc. *Res:* Dislocations and ferromagnetism; phase transformations, radiation effects; control of dislocation substructure; defects in intermediate alloy phases. *Mailing Add:* Argonne Nat Lab 9700 S Cass Ave MSD/212 Argonne IL 60439-4838

ALLEN, CHARLES WILLIAM, MECHANICAL ENGINEERING, TRIBOLOGY. *Current Pos:* RETIRED. *Personal Data:* b Newbury, Eng, July 24, 32; US citizen; m 57, Rita J Pembroke; c Malcolm & Verity. *Educ:* Univ London, BS, 57; Case Inst Technol, MS, 62; Univ Calif, Davis, PhD(mech eng), 66. *Prof Exp:* Design engr, Lear Siegler Inc, Ohio, 57-62; group leader bearing develop, Aerojet Gen Corp, 62-63; assoc eng, Univ Calif, Davis, 63-66; from assoc prof to emer prof mech eng, Calif State Univ, Chico, 66-95, head, Dept Mech Eng, 76-79 & 82-84. *Concurrent Pos:* Fac fel, Stanford Univ, 67; res fel, Lewis Res Lab, NASA, 68 & 69; vis fel, Univ Leicester, 74; vis prof, Univ Guadalajara, Mex, 86. *Mem:* Am Soc Mech Engrs. *Res:* Traction and film thickness in elastohydrodynamic lubrication, squeeze film lubrication, melt lubrication, extending life of mechanical devices; electric and hybrid vehicles. *Mailing Add:* 1601 Filbert Ave Chico CA 95929

ALLEN, CHERYL, BIOCHEMISTRY, MEDICAL ETHICS. *Current Pos:* congregational adminr, 84-89, VPRES, SISTERS ST JOSEPH, 89- *Personal Data:* b Detroit, Mich, Jan 30, 39. *Educ:* Nazareth Col, BS, 69; Univ Ill Med Ctr, PhD(biochem), 74. *Prof Exp:* Sec teacher math & sci, Detroit Parochial Sch Syst, 59-68; teaching asst, Univ Ill Med Ctr, 69-73; asst prof biochem, Nazareth Col, 74-84; bioethics consult, 84-89. *Mem:* Inst Soc, Ethics & Life Sci; Am Soc Law & Med. *Res:* The role of serum proteins, especially the alpha-2 macro-globulins, in immunity and host defense; ethical aspects of issues of life sciences. *Mailing Add:* Sisters St Joseph 3427 Gull Rd Nazareth MI 49074

ALLEN, CHRISTOPHER WHITNEY, INORGANIC CHEMISTRY, POLYMER CHEMISTRY. *Current Pos:* From asst prof to assoc prof, 67-76, PROF CHEM, UNIV VT, 76- *Personal Data:* b Waterbury, Conn, Oct 19, 42; m 65, Elizabeth Fleming; c Stephen & Mark. *Educ:* Univ Conn, BA, 64; Univ Ill, MS, 66, PhD(inorg chem), 67. *Mem:* The Chem Soc; Am Chem Soc. *Res:* Synthesis, structure and spectroscopic properties of non-metal and organometallic compounds; inorganic polymers. *Mailing Add:* 11 Hanley Lane Essex Junction VT 05452. *Fax:* 802-656-8705

ALLEN, CLARENCE RODERIC, GEOLOGY, SEISMOLOGY. *Current Pos:* from asst prof to assoc prof geol, Calif Inst Technol, 55-64, interim dir, Seismol Lab, 65-67, actg chmn, Div Geol Sci, 67-68, chmn fac, 70-71, prof, 64-90, EMER PROF GEOL & GEOPHYS, CALIF INST TECHNOL, 90- *Personal Data:* b Palo Alto, Calif, Feb 15, 25. *Educ:* Reed Col, BA, 49; Calif Inst Technol, MS, 51, PhD(geol), 54. *Honors & Awards:* G K Gilbert Award in Seismic Geol, 60; Medal Seismol Soc Am, 97. *Prof Exp:* Asst prof geol, Univ Minn, 54-55. *Concurrent Pos:* Consult, Calif Dept Water Resources, US Geol Surv & UNESCO; mem adv panel earth sci, NSF, 65-68, chmn, 67-68, mem adv panel environ sci, 70-; mem, Calif State Mining & Geol Bd, 65-75, chmn, 75; mem task force earthquake hazard reduction, Off Sci & Technol, Exec Off President, 70; chmn, Panel Earthquake Prediction, Nat Acad Sci, 73-76, Nat Earthquake Prediction Eval Coun, 79-84 & Am Plate Tectonics Deleg People's Repub China, 79; vchmn, Am Seismol Deleg People's Repub China, 74; consult, Bur Reclamation, Metrop Water Dist, Yellow River Conservancy Comn, China & Nat Eng Serv, Pakistan. *Mem:* Nat Acad Sci; Nat Acad Eng; fel Geol Soc Am(pres, 73-74); Seismol Soc Am(pres, 75-76); fel Am Acad Arts & Sci; fel Am Geophys Union. *Res:* Mechanics of faulting; San Andreas fault system; relation of seismicity to geologic structure; geophysical exploration of glaciers; tectonics of Southern California and Baja California; Circum-Pacific earthquakes and faulting; micro-earthquakes; geologic hazards; nuclear waste management; seismic hazard assessment; nuclear waste disposal. *Mailing Add:* Seismol Lab 252-21 Calif Inst Technol Pasadena CA 91125. *Fax:* 626-564-0715; *E-Mail:* allen@gps.caltech.edu

ALLEN, CLIFFORD MARSDEN, VOLCANOLOGY, METAMORPHISM. *Current Pos:* RETIRED. *Personal Data:* b Winnipeg, Man, Dec 14, 27; m 60; c 3. *Educ:* Univ Man, BSc, 49, MSc, 51. *Prof Exp:* From asst prof to prof geol, Mt Allison Univ, 54-93, head dept, 87-93. *Mem:* Geol Soc Am; Nat Asn Geol Teachers; fel Geol Asn Can. *Res:* Igneous and metamorphic petrology; volcanic geology of the Maritime Provinces of Canada. *Mailing Add:* 5 Estabrook PO Box 291 Sackville NB E0A 3C0 Can

ALLEN, DAVID MITCHELL, STATISTICS. *Current Pos:* Asst prof, 67-72, ASSOC PROF STATIST, UNIV KY, 72- *Personal Data:* b Sebree, Ky, July 15, 38; m 64; c 3. *Educ:* Univ Ky, BS, 61; NC State Univ, MES, 66, PhD(statist), 68. *Concurrent Pos:* Consult, Mead Johnson & Co, 68-; vis assoc prof, Cornell Univ, 74-75; assoc ed, Biometrics, 75- & Commun Statist, Algorithms Sect, 78- *Mem:* Biomet Soc; Inst Math Statist; Am Statist Asn. *Res:* Statistical computation; linear models; prediction. *Mailing Add:* Dept Statist Patterson Off Tower Univ Ky Lexington KY 40506-0027

ALLEN, DAVID THOMAS, ENERGY & ENVIRONMENT. *Current Pos:* ASSOC PROF CHEM ENG, UNIV CALIF, LOS ANGELES, 83- *Personal Data:* b Pittsburgh, Pa, Jan 23, 58; m 86; c 2. *Educ:* Cornell Univ, BS, 79; Calif Inst Technol, MS, 81, PhD(chem eng), 83. *Concurrent Pos:* NSF presidential young investr, 87; Mem, Am Inst Pollution Prev, Environ Protection Agency, 90-92 & Nat Adv Comt Environ Policy & Technol, 90-93. *Mem:* Am Inst Chem Engrs; Am Asn Aerosol Res; Am Chem Soc. *Res:* Energy and the environment; characterization of hazardous chemical mixtures; thermodynamic and kinetic modeling of heavy fuels; development of a catalytic hydrodechlorination process for recycling chlorinated organics; establishing new methods for characterizing atmospheric aerosols. *Mailing Add:* 5531 Boelter Hall Univ Calif Los Angeles CA 90024

ALLEN, DAVID WEST, RED CELL MEMBRANES, RED CELL ENZYMES. *Current Pos:* PROF MED, UNIV MINN, 74- *Educ:* Harvard Univ, MD, 54. *Mailing Add:* Hemacol-Oncol Dept Univ Minn Med Sch Vet Admin Hosp Minneapolis MN 55417-2300

ALLEN, DELL K, COMPUTER INTEGRATED MANUFACTURING. *Current Pos:* RETIRED. *Personal Data:* b Cove, Utah, Dec 1, 31; m; c 8. *Educ:* Utah State Univ, BS, 54; Brigham Young Univ, MS, 60; Utah State Univ, EdD(industr educ), 73. *Honors & Awards:* Ray J Spies Award, CAM-I Inc, Cannes, 80; Carl G Mazer Res Award, 88. *Prof Exp:* Process engr, EIMCO Corp, 59-60; prof mfr eng technol, Brigham Young Univ, 60-94. *Concurrent Pos:* Mech engr, Lawrence Livermore Lab, 75; res engr, Boeing Com Airplane Co, 76. *Mem:* Fel Nat Acad Eng. *Res:* Integrated manufacturing; published numerous articles in various journals. *Mailing Add:* 610 E 2330 N North Logan UT 84321

ALLEN, DELMAS JAMES, HUMAN ANATOMY, NEUROANATOMY. *Current Pos:* VPRES ACAD AFFAIRS, NGA COL, 88- *Personal Data:* b Hartsville, SC, Aug 13, 37; m 58; c 3. *Educ:* Am Univ Beirut, BSc, 65, MSc, 67; Univ NDak, PhD(anat), 74. *Honors & Awards:* Acad Med Award, Brazilian Acad Med, 80; Res Award, Electron Micros Soc, 80; Res Award, Sigma Xi, 74. *Prof Exp:* Asst prof biol & chmn dept, Clarke Col, Iowa, 68-72; asst prof anat, Univ SAla, 74-75; prof anat, Med Col Ohio, 75-86; prof & assoc dean acad affairs & res, Ga State Univ, Atlanta, 86-88. *Concurrent Pos:* Dir, NSF Res Grant, 70-72; grant-in-aid, Ala Heart Asn, 74-75 & Am Heart Asn, 76-78; Am Cancer Soc res grant, 77-79; NSF fel; NSF grant, 81; vis prof, Col Med, Riyad Univ, Kingdom of Saudi Arabia, 81. *Mem:* AAAS; Sigma Xi; Electron Micros Soc Am; Am Asn Anatomists; British Brain Res Asn. *Res:* Cranial meninges; ventricular system of the brain, choroid plexus; electron microscopy of dura mater cardiac valves recovered at surgery; pineal gland; smooth muscle in the ovary; scanning electron microscopy; transmission electron microscopy; x-ray microanalysis; cat scan and mri interpretation. *Mailing Add:* Price Mem Hall NGa Col Dahlonega GA 30597. *Fax:* 302-451-2281

ALLEN, DELORAN MATTHEW, ANIMAL SCIENCE, MEAT SCIENCE. *Current Pos:* VPRES QUAL & TRAINING, EXCEL CORP, 88- *Personal Data:* b Cherryvale, Kans, Feb 28, 39; m 65. *Educ:* Kans State Univ, BSAgr, 61; Univ Idaho, MSAgr, 63; Mich State Univ, PhD(meat sci), 66. *Prof Exp:* Asst prof animal sci, Kans State Univ, 66-70, assoc prof animal sci & indust & assoc animal scientist, 70-80, prof animal sci & indust, 80-88. *Concurrent Pos:* Consult, ITAL, Campinas, Sao Paulo, Brazil, 78 & Chicago Mercantile Exchange, 80-81. *Mem:* Am Soc Animal Sci; Am Meat Sci Asn. *Res:* Beef carcass composition and cutability. *Mailing Add:* Excel Corp PO Box 2519 Wichita KS 67201-2519

ALLEN, DON LEE, PERIODONTICS. *Current Pos:* dean, dent br, 82-92, FINNEGAN PROF DENT SCI, UNIV TEX, 85- *Personal Data:* b Burlington, NC, Mar 13, 34; m 58, Martha Winifred Roore; c Don Jr, Michael & Susan (Bossley). *Educ:* Univ NC, DDS, 59; Univ Mich, MS, 64. *Prof Exp:* From instr to prof periodont, Univ NC, 59-70, assoc dean admin, 69-70; assoc dean, Col Dent, Univ Fla, 70-73, dean, 73-82. *Concurrent Pos:* Consult, USPHS, 60-62, Philip Morris Co, 68-69 & Dent Educ, Am Dent Asn, 70-78; mem nat adv comt, Dept Health & Human Servs, 78-82; mem coun dent educ, Am Dent Asn, 78-86, chmn, 84-86; chmn, Comn Dent Accredidation, 78-86; chair, Fla Sect, Am Col Dentists, 80-81; mem coun dent educ, Int Dent Fedn, 81-87 & 89-, chmn, 84-86, chair, 90-91; pres, Southern Conf Dent Deans & Examiners, 83-84. *Mem:* Int Col Dentists (pres, 81-82); Am Asn Dent Sch (pres, 82-83); Am Dent Asn; Am Col Dentists; Int Dent Fedn. *Res:* Bone development, peridontal surgery, preventive dentistry and dental education. *Mailing Add:* Univ Eval Admin Univ Tex Health Sci Ctr PO Box 20036 Houston TX 77225. *Fax:* 713-500-4372; *E-Mail:* dallen@admin4.hsc.uth.tmc.edu

ALLEN, DONALD ORRIE, PHARMACOLOGY, LIPOLYSIS CONTROL. *Current Pos:* PROF & CHMN PHARMACOL, SCH MED, UNIV SC, 75- *Personal Data:* b Belding, Mich, Jan 11, 39; m 61; c 4. *Educ:* Ferris State Col, BS, 62; Marquette Univ, PhD(pharmacol), 67. *Prof Exp:* Res assoc pharmacol, Sch Med, Ind Univ, Indianapolis, 67-68, from asst prof to assoc prof, 68-75. *Mem:* Am Soc Pharmacol & Exp Therapeut. *Res:* Autonomic pharmacology and drug interaction; metabolic pharmacology; cyclic nucleotides. *Mailing Add:* Dept Pharmacol Univ SC Sch Med Columbia SC 29208

ALLEN, DONALD STEWART, CHEMISTRY. *Current Pos:* prof chem & dir div sci & math, 68-77, EMER PROF CHEM, EISENHOWER COL, 78- *Personal Data:* b Saugus, Mass, Sept 9, 11; m 42, Catharine Cochrane; c Patricia A (Kisha) & Barbara. *Educ:* Dartmouth Col, AB, 32, AM, 34; Yale Univ, PhD(chem), 43. *Hon Degrees:* DSc, NY Chiropractic Col, 94. *Prof Exp:* Instr chem, Dartmouth Col, 32-34; master sci & math, Tex Country Day Sch, 34-40; from asst instr to instr chem, Yale Univ, 41-43; asst prof chem, Bates Col, 43-45; prof chem & chmn div natural sci, State Teachers Col, New Paltz, 45-59; prof chem, State Univ NY Albany, 59-68, chmn dept, 59-63. *Concurrent Pos:* Res scientist, Oak Ridge Inst Nuclear Studies, 59; consult, State Univ NY Ford Found Proj, Indonesia, 63-65; vis scholar hist & philos sci, Cambridge Univ, 74-75; vis fel, SEAP, Cornell Univ, 79-84; Paul Harris fel, Rotary, 85; Fulbright fel, Indonesia, 81. *Mem:* Am Chem Soc; fel Am Inst Chemists; Hist Sci Soc; Sigma Xi. *Res:* Friedel-Crafts reaction; latex research; standard electrode potentials. *Mailing Add:* 2976 Cayuga Blvd Rte 89 Seneca Falls NY 13148

ALLEN, DOUGLAS CHARLES, INSECT ECOLOGY, FOREST ENTOMOLOGY. *Current Pos:* Assoc prof, 73-80, PROF FOREST ENTOM, STATE UNIV NY COL ENVIRON SCI & FORESTRY, 80- *Personal Data:* b Brattleboro, Vt, Mar 8, 40; m 65, Barbara Fowles; c Matthew & Mark. *Educ:* Univ Maine, BS, 62, MS, 65; Univ Mich, PhD(forest entom), 68. *Mem:* Entom Soc Am; fel Soc Am Foresters; Entom Soc Can; Sigma Xi. *Res:* Population dynamics and bionomics of forest insects. *Mailing Add:* State Univ NY Col Environ Sci & Forestry Rm 146 Illick Hall 1 Forestry Dr Syracuse NY 13211

ALLEN, DUFF SHEDERIC, JR, ORGANIC CHEMISTRY. *Current Pos:* RETIRED. *Personal Data:* b St Louis, Mo, Dec 8, 28; m 60; c 3. *Educ:* Princeton Univ, BA, 49; Univ Wis, PhD(org chem), 60. *Prof Exp:* Res chemist, Monsanto Chem Co, 52-53; asst org chem, Univ Wis, 54-58, res assoc, 58-60; res chemist, Org Chem Div, Am Cyanamid Co, 60-62, group leader, Lederle Labs, 63-65, head dept org chem process res, process & prep res sect, Lederle Labs, 65-91. *Mem:* Am Chem Soc; AAAS; NY Acad Sci. *Res:* Organic synthesis of steroids; heterocycles; natural products; medicinal chemicals. *Mailing Add:* 25 Upland Ave Falmouth MA 02540

ALLEN, DURWARD LEON, VERTEBRATE ECOLOGY. *Current Pos:* assoc prof wildlife mgt, 54-57, prof wildlife ecol, 57-76, EMER PROF WILDLIFE ECOL, PURDUE UNIV, 76- *Personal Data:* b Uniondale, Ind, Oct 11, 10; m 35; c 3. *Educ:* Univ Mich, AB, 32; Mich State Univ, PhD(zool), 37. *Hon Degrees:* LHD, Northern Mich Univ, 71; DAgr, Purdue Univ, 85. *Honors & Awards:* Leopold Mem Medal, 69; Audubon Medal, 90. *Prof Exp:* Res biologist, Game Div, Mich State Dept Conserv, 35-46; biologist in charge wildlife invest on agr lands, US Fish & Wildlife Serv, Washington, DC, 46-50, asst chief, Br Wildlife Res, 51-53, actg chief, Br Wildlife, 53-54. *Concurrent Pos:* Asst secy gen, Inter-Am Conf Renewable Natural Resources, 48; mem, comt conserv, Nat Coun, Boy Scouts Am, 48-72; counr wildlife mgr, Nat Merit Badge, 52-64; mem, bd trustees, Nat Parks Asn, 64-75; mem & ed comt, wildlife & land-use relationships, Nat Acad Sci, 65-76; mem, Nat Park Syst Adv Bd, 66-72, chmn, 72-, coun of the bd, 72-84; mem bd dir, Nat Audubon Soc, 73-84; mem bd, Am Forestry Asn, 83-89. *Mem:* Wildlife Soc (pres, 56-57); Ecol Soc Am; Am Soc Mammalogists; Sigma Xi; fel AAAS; Am Inst

Biol Sci; Am Forestry Asn; George Wright Soc. *Res:* Ecological and management studies on fox squirrel, skunk, rabbit, pheasant, moose and wolf; management of renewable natural resources; ecology of the wolf and its prey in Isle Royale Nat Park. *Mailing Add:* 2627 Calvin Ct West Lafayette IN 47906

ALLEN, EDWARD DAVID, CRYOBIOLOGY, DEVELOPMENTAL BIOLOGY. *Current Pos:* RES BIOLOGIST CRYOBIOL, VET ADMIN HOSP, 72- *Personal Data:* b Madison, Wis, Apr 3, 42; m 67; c 2. *Educ:* Univ Wis, BS, 64, MS, 67; Univ Mich, PhD(bot), 72. *Prof Exp:* Consult electron micros, 70-72, RES SCIENTIST DEVELOP BIOL, UNIV MICH, 74- *Mem:* Am Soc Cell Biologists; Soc Cryobiol. *Res:* Freeze preservation of blood components; developmental systems in fungi. *Mailing Add:* Dept Internal Med Univ Mich 5240 MSRB III Ann Arbor MI 48109-0640

ALLEN, EDWARD FRANKLIN, PHYSICS. *Current Pos:* Instr math & physics, 28-45, head Dept Math & Phys Sci, 52-69, prof math, 45-78, prof philos & chmn dept, 69-78, EMER PROF, ACAD NEW CHURCH, 78- *Personal Data:* b Denver, Colo, Aug 28, 07; wid; c Natalie & Edward. *Educ:* Acad New Church, BS, 28; Univ Pa, MA, 32. *Honors & Awards:* Naval Ord Develop Award, 45; Glencairn Award, 58. *Concurrent Pos:* Res physicist, Franklin Inst, 42-45; ed, New Philos, 61-70. *Mem:* Am Asn Physics Teachers. *Res:* History and philosophy of science; instrumentation; specialization in the philosophy of Swedenborg. *Mailing Add:* 9870 E Jenan Dr Scottsdale AZ 85260

ALLEN, EDWARD PATRICK, PERIODONTICS. *Current Pos:* assoc prof, 76-88, PROF PERIODONT, COL DENT, BAYLOR UNIV, 88- *Personal Data:* b Dallas, Tex, Sept 20, 43; m 65, Karen Callaway; c 5. *Educ:* Baylor Univ, DDS, 69, PhD(physiol), 72. *Prof Exp:* Res fel physiol, Grad Sch, Baylor Univ, 69-72; asst prof periodont, Med Col Va, 72-76. *Concurrent Pos:* Consult, Div Oral Surg, Southwestern Med Sch, 78-, J Periodont, 80- & Eurp J Esthetic Dent, 96- *Mem:* Am Acad Periodont; Am Dent Asn; fel Int Col Dentists; Am Acad Restor Dent; Am Acad Esthetic Dent; Am Col Dentists. *Res:* Development of periodontal plastic surgery procedures including use of guided tissue regeneration methods for treatment of gingival recession. *Mailing Add:* 8335 Walnut Hill Lane Suite 210 Dallas TX 75231. *Fax:* 214-691-8174

ALLEN, ELIZABETH MOREI, GENETICS, IMMUNOLOGY. *Current Pos:* SR RES SCIENTIST, RHONE POULENC RORER PHARMACEUT, 92- *Educ:* Univ Tenn, MA, 72. *Prof Exp:* Res assoc, Med Col Wis & Vet Admin Med Ctr, 75-87, res scientist instr, Dept Dermatol, Med Col Wis, 90-92. *Mailing Add:* 302 Carmen Dr Collegeville PA 19426

ALLEN, EMORY RAWORTH, ANATOMY, CELL BIOLOGY. *Current Pos:* adj assoc prof anat, Dept Occup Ther, 86, ASSOC PROF ANAT, LA STATE UNIV MED CTR, NEW ORLEANS, 71- *Personal Data:* b Augusta, Ga, Jan 21, 35; m 59; c 4. *Educ:* Univ Md, BS, 59; Univ Pa, PhD(develop anat), 64. *Prof Exp:* Asst instr anat, Univ Pa, 62-65; from instr to asst prof anat & cell biol, Sch Med, Univ Pittsburgh, 65-71. *Concurrent Pos:* Fel anat, Univ Pa, 64-65. *Mem:* Sigma Xi; Int Acad Path; Am Asn Anatomists; Electron Micros Soc Am. *Res:* Ultrastructure of developing muscle; myosin synthesis. *Mailing Add:* Dept Anat La State Univ Med Ctr 1542 Tulane Ave New Orleans LA 70112

ALLEN, ERIC RAYMOND, ATMOSPHERIC & AIR POLLUTION CHEMISTRY. *Current Pos:* PROF ENVIRON ENG SCI, UNIV FLA, 81- *Personal Data:* b Teneriffe, Canary Isles, Apr 12, 32; m 61; c Geoffrey & David. *Educ:* Univ Liverpool, BSc, 56, PhD(phys chem), 59. *Prof Exp:* Fel photochem, Nat Res Coun, Can, 59-61; asst chemist, Gas Kinetics, Univ Calif, Riverside, 61-63; sr staff scientist, Nat Ctr Atmospheric Res, 63-68, prog scientist, 68-74; sr res assoc, Atmospheric Sci Res Ctr, State Univ NY Albany, 74-81. *Concurrent Pos:* Vis assoc prof dept civil eng, Univ Tex, Austin, 71; mem, panel on carbon monoxide, Div Med Sci, Nat Acad Sci-Nat Res Coun, lectr, Environ Studies Prog, State Univ NY Albany, 74-77 & adj assoc prof innovative & interdisciplinary studies, 74-75; adj prof chem, State Univ NY Albany, 77-81. *Mem:* Air Pollution Control Asn; Am Chem Soc; Soc Appl Spectros; Sigma Xi; fel Am Inst Chemists; Am Asn Environ Eng Prof. *Res:* Gas phase kinetics; atomic and free radical reactions; photochemistry; atmospheric and air pollution chemistry; water chemistry; solar energy storage systems; combustion and oxidations of hydrocarbons; source and ambient-air sampling and analysis, air toxics and odors, fluoride pollution, indoor air pollution; biofiltration, acid rain, "greenhouse" gas emissions and climate change. *Mailing Add:* 406 Black Hall Gainesville FL 32611. *Fax:* 352-392-3076

ALLEN, ERNEST E, MATHEMATICS EDUCATION. *Current Pos:* assoc prof, 63-74, PROF MATH, UNIV SOUTHERN COLO, 74-, DEAN, SCH OF SCI & MATH, 79- *Personal Data:* b Detroit, Mich, Sept 7, 33; m 57; c 3. *Educ:* Wayne State Univ, BA, 55; Mich State Univ, BA, 57, MA, 59; Univ Detroit, MATM, 63; Univ Northern Colo, EdD(math educ), 70. *Prof Exp:* Pub sch teacher, 58-60; asst prof math educ, Eastern Mich Univ, 60-63. *Concurrent Pos:* Dir, Colo Coun Teachers Math, 68-70, ed, 70-, pres, 72. *Res:* Selected characteristics of junior high level mathematics teachers; methods of teaching mathematics. *Mailing Add:* Dept Math Univ Southern Colo 2200 Bonforte Blvd Pueblo CO 81001-4901

ALLEN, ERNEST MASON, PUBLIC HEALTH ADMINISTRATION. *Current Pos:* RETIRED. *Personal Data:* b Terrell, Tex, Dec 1, 04; m 28, Virginia Williamson; c 3. *Educ:* Emory Univ, PhB, 26, MA, 39, DSc, 56. *Hon Degrees:* LLD, Clemson Univ, 68; DSc, Emory Univ, 56. *Honors & Awards:* Dirs Award, NIH, 77. *Prof Exp:* Instr French, Jr Col Augusta, 26-41; proj mgr, Nat Youth Admin, 41-43; sr pub health rep, Div Venereal Dis, USPHS, 43-46; asst chief div res grants, NIH, 46-51, chief div res grant, 51-60, assoc dir, Insts, 60-63; grants policy officer, USPHS, 63-68, dir off extramural prog, Off Asst Secy Health & Sci Affairs, 68-69, dir div grants admin policy, 69-70, dep asst secy grant admin policy, 70-73, assoc dir nat libr med, 73-82. *Mem:* AAAS; Biol Sci Info Exchange; Nat Health Forum. *Mailing Add:* 1010 Hickman Rd No B6 Augusta GA 30904-6312

ALLEN, EUGENE (MURRAY), COLOR SCIENCE. *Current Pos:* prof chem, 67-82, EMER PROF CHEM, LEHIGH UNIV, 82- *Personal Data:* b Newark, NJ, Nov 7, 16; m 37, Beatrice Hyman; c Marlene & Julian. *Educ:* Columbia Univ, BA, 38; Stevens Inst Technol, MS, 44; Rutgers Univ, PhD(chem), 52. *Honors & Awards:* Armin J Bruning Award, Fedn Socs Coatings Technol, 82; Godlove Award, Intersoc Color Coun, 83. *Prof Exp:* Res chemist, Utility Color Co, 38-39, United Color & Pigment Co, 39-41 & E R Squibb & Sons, 41-42; anal res chemist, Picatinny Arsenal, 42-45; anal res chemist, Am Cyanamid Co, NJ, 45-56, group leader, 56-61, sr res scientist, 61-63, res assoc, 63-66, res fel, 66-67,. *Concurrent Pos:* Consult, Int Comn Illum, 67-; mem US nat comt, Int Comn on Illumination, 67. *Mem:* Am Chem Soc; fel Optical Soc Am; Am Asn Textile Chem & Colorists; Sigma Xi. *Res:* Measurement and specification of color; colorimetry of fluorescent substances; color matching by digital computer; radiative transfer theory. *Mailing Add:* 2100 Main St Bethlehem PA 18017-3752

ALLEN, FRANCES ELIZABETH, COMPUTER SCIENCE. *Current Pos:* FEL & SR MGR, IBM, YORKTOWN HEIGHTS, 57- *Personal Data:* b Peru, NY, Aug 4, 32; m 72. *Educ:* State Univ NY, Albany, BA, 54; Univ Mich, MA, 57. *Hon Degrees:* DSc, Univ Alta, 91. *Concurrent Pos:* Indust sabbatical fel, Courant Inst Math Sci, 69-70, adj assoc prof comput sci, NY Univ, 70-71 & 72-73; nat lectr, Asn Comput Mach, 72-73, chmn, Software Syst Award Comt, 83, gen chmn, Conf Principles Prog Lang, 90, mem, Comt Women & Minorities, 90-; mem comput sci adv bd, NSF, 72-75, consult, 75; instr, Peking Inst Comput Sci, 77; consult prof, Stanford Univ, 77-78; assoc ed, Trans Prog Lang & Systs J, 79-90, J Comput Lang, 81-; IBM fel, 89; distinguished lectr, Comput Sci Dept, Mass Inst Technol, 91. *Mem:* Nat Acad Eng; fel Asn Comput Mach; fel Inst Elec & Electronics Engrs; AAAS. *Res:* Optimizing compilers; software for parallel systems; numerous publications. *Mailing Add:* T J Watson Res Ctr IBM PO Box 704 Yorktown Heights NY 10598. *Fax:* 914-784-7879; *E-Mail:* allen@watson.ibm.com

ALLEN, FRANK B, MATHEMATICS, PHYSICS. *Current Pos:* RETIRED. *Personal Data:* b Mt Vernon, Ill, Oct 21, 09; m 43; c 3. *Educ:* Southern Ill Univ, BEd, 29; Univ Iowa, MS, 34. *Prof Exp:* High sch teacher, Ill, 29-41; teacher math, Lyons Twp High Sch & Jr Col, 41-42, 46-56, chmn dept, 56-68; from assoc prof to prof math, Elmhurst Col, 68-76, chmn dept, 70-74, adj prof, 76-79. *Mem:* Math Asn Am. *Res:* Application of elementary logic to the improvement of exposition in school mathematics. *Mailing Add:* 567 Berkley Ave Elmhurst IL 60126-3756

ALLEN, FRED ERNEST, veterinary medicine; deceased, see previous edition for last biography

ALLEN, FREDDIE LEWIS, AGRONOMY. *Current Pos:* From asst prof to assoc prof, 75-90, PROF PLANT & SOIL SCI, UNIV TENN, 90- *Personal Data:* b Jellico, Tenn, Dec 6, 47; m 69; c 2. *Educ:* Tenn Technol Univ, BS, 70; Va Polytech Inst & State Univ, MS, 72; Univ Minn, PhD(plant breeding), 75. *Concurrent Pos:* Consult to EPA on acid precipation on soybeans, 85; consult, Nat Biol Impact Assessment Prog-Soybeans, 89; vis prof, Henan & Shandong Acad Agr Scis, Narying Agr Univ, People's Repub China, 90. *Mem:* Am Soc Agron; Crop Sci Soc Am; Am Soybean Asn; Sigma Xi. *Res:* Soybean breeding and genetics with emphasis on improved efficiency of breeding and selection methodology; effects of biotic and abiotic stresses on yield. *Mailing Add:* Dept Plant & Soil Sci Univ Tenn PO Box 1071 Knoxville TN 37901

ALLEN, FREDERICK GRAHAM, ELECTRICAL ENGINEERING. *Current Pos:* chmn dept, 69-76, 85-87, PROF ELEC SCI & ENG, UNIV CALIF, LOS ANGELES, 69- *Personal Data:* b Boston, Mass, Feb 2, 23; m 49; c 3. *Educ:* Cornell Univ, BME, 44; Harvard Univ, PhD(appl physics), 56. *Prof Exp:* Mem tech staff, Bell Tel Res Labs, NJ, 55-65; dept head manned space flight exp prog, Bellcomm, Inc, Washington, DC, 67-69. *Mem:* Fel Am Phys Soc; Inst Elec & Electronics Engrs. *Res:* Physics of semiconductor and metal surfaces; photoemission; molecular beam epitaxy of silicon. *Mailing Add:* 823 Westholme Ave Los Angeles CA 90024. *Fax:* 310-446-1509

ALLEN, GARLAND EDWARD, III, HISTORY OF SCIENCE, HISTORY OF BIOLOGY. *Current Pos:* from asst prof to assoc prof, 67-79, PROF BIOL, WASHINGTON UNIV, 79- *Personal Data:* b Louisville, Ky, Feb 13, 36; m 66; c Tania L & Carin T. *Educ:* Univ Louisville, AB, 57; Harvard Univ, AMT, 58, AM, 64, PhD(hist sci), 66. *Prof Exp:* Allston-Burr sr tutor & instr hist sci, Harvard Univ, 65-67. *Concurrent Pos:* Comnr, Comn Undergrad Educ Biol Sci, 65-68; consult, Educ Res Coun, Ohio, 67; mem div soc sci, NSF Panel, 68-70; Charles Warren fel, Harvard Univ, 81-82; trustee, Marine Biol Lab, Woods Hole, Mass, 85-93; vis prof hist sci, Harvard Univ, 89-91; NIH panel, Ethical, Legal & Social Implications Human Genome Proj; coun mem & chair, Comt Meetings & Prog Hist Sci Soc, 94-96. *Mem:* AAAS; Hist

Sci Soc; Am Asn Hist Med; Brit Soc Hist Sci. *Res:* History of late 19th and early 20th century biology, especially genetics and evolution; history of eugenics in the 20th century; dialectical materialism in Darwin and Marx. *Mailing Add:* Dept Biol Wash Univ St Louis MO 63130

ALLEN, GARY CURTISS, GEOCHEMISTRY, PETROLOGY & ENVIRONMENTAL SCIENCE. *Current Pos:* assoc prof, 72-78, dir, Environ Training Prog, 93-94, PROF GEOL, UNIV NEW ORLEANS, 78- *Personal Data:* b Stockton, Calif, July 18, 39; m 65, Ruth L Mayeux; c Adrienne & Christopher. *Educ:* Stanford Univ, BS, 61; Rice Univ, MA, 63; Univ NC, PhD(geochem), 68. *Prof Exp:* Geologist, Va Div Mineral Resources, 66-68; asst prof earth sci, La State Univ, New Orleans, 68-72. *Concurrent Pos:* Consult indust firms & sch systs, 71; consult mineral, Med Sch, Tulane Univ, 72-80; pres, Sunbelt Assocs, Inc, 78-; dir, Amguy Mining Ltd, 83-85, Placer Explor Ltd, 85-, Holocene Res Inst, 90-; coordr radiation safety, La State Univ Syst, 90- *Mem:* Geol Soc Am; Sigma Xi. *Res:* Petrogenic geochemistry; mineralogy; analytical chemistry of major and trace elements in rocks and minerals; medical mineralogy of silica and asbestos; archeological geochemistry. *Mailing Add:* Dept Geol & Geophys Univ New Orleans New Orleans LA 70148. *Fax:* 504-286-7396

ALLEN, GARY WILLIAM, PHYSICAL ORGANIC & PHOTOGRAPHIC CHEMISTRY. *Current Pos:* SR RES CHEMIST, EASTMAN KODAK CO, 75- *Personal Data:* b Washington, DC, Mar 3, 44; m 73; c 1. *Educ:* Univ Wash, BA, 67; Wesleyan Univ, PhD(chem), 71. *Prof Exp:* NIH res fel chem, Harvard Univ, 71-73; asst prof, Ariz State Univ, 73-75. *Mem:* AAAS; Am Chem Soc; The Chem Soc; Sigma Xi. *Res:* Physical organic chemistry of the photographic process. *Mailing Add:* 129 Buckland Ave Rochester NY 14618

ALLEN, GEORGE HERBERT, WASTEWATER AQUACULTURE. *Current Pos:* RETIRED. *Personal Data:* b Zurich, Switz, Aug 16, 23; m 55; c 3. *Educ:* Univ Wyo, BS, 50; Univ Wash, PhD(fisheries), 56. *Prof Exp:* From asst prof to prof fisheries, Humboldt State Univ, 56-82, prog leader, 67-75, chmn, 78-82, emer prof fisheries, 82- *Concurrent Pos:* Aquacult prog dir, City Arcata, Calif, 77-87, consult, 87- *Mem:* AAAS; Am Inst Biol Sci; Am Inst Fish Res Biol. *Res:* Development of public salmon culture system using treated wastewater. *Mailing Add:* Col Fisheries Humboldt State Univ Arcata CA 95521-8299

ALLEN, GEORGE PERRY, VIROLOGY. *Current Pos:* from asst prof to assoc prof, 78-85, PROF VET SCI, UNIV KY, 86- *Personal Data:* b Frankfort, Ky, Dec 16, 41; m 72; c 2. *Educ:* Georgetown Col, BS, 63; Univ Ky, PhD(microbiol), 75. *Prof Exp:* Lab technician microbiol, Ky State Dept Health, 64-66; lab technician, Univ Cincinnati, 66-68 & Univ Ky, 68-70; Am Cancer Soc fel, Univ Miss Med Ctr, 75-77, res asst microbiol, 75-78. *Concurrent Pos:* Mem, Conf Res Workers Animal Dis; postdoctoral training, Med Ctr, Univ Miss, 75-78. *Mem:* Am Soc Microbiol; Sigma Xi; Am Soc Virol. *Res:* Pathogenesis, epidemiology, and control of equine herpes virus disease; molecular characterization of antigens of equine herpes virus. *Mailing Add:* Gluck Equine Ctr Vet Sci Dept Rm 108 Univ Ky Lexington KY 40356

ALLEN, GEORGE RODGER, JR, MEDICINAL CHEMISTRY. *Current Pos:* RETIRED. *Personal Data:* b Port Arthur, Tex, Nov 8, 29; m 55; c 2. *Educ:* Univ Tex, BS, 49, AM, 51, PhD(chem), 53. *Prof Exp:* Instr, Lamar Col, 51-52; assoc, Univ Tex, 52-53; res chemist, Calco Div, Am Cyanamid Co, 53-54, Lederle Labs, 55-58; res chemist, Mead Johnson & Co, 58-60; res chemist, Lederle Labs, 60-65, group leader, 65-74, dept head, 74-75, assoc dir new prod acquisitions, 75-76, dir pharmaceut & mech res & develop, Lederle Labs, 76-82; mgr, Info Systs, Admin/Planning, Am Cyanamid Co, 82-90, dir planning, Med Res Div, 90-94. *Mem:* Am Chem Soc; Am Asn Pharmaceut Sci. *Res:* Inositols; steroids; antibiotics and related compounds; synthetic antibacterials and heterocyclic compounds. *Mailing Add:* 16 Moeser Pl Old Tappan NJ 07675

ALLEN, GORDON AINSLIE, ENVIRONMENTAL MANAGEMENT, PULPING & BLEACHING OF WOODPULP. *Current Pos:* RETIRED. *Personal Data:* b London, Ont, May 24, 22; m 54, Jean M Weatherup; c Margaret, Susan & John. *Educ:* Univ Western Ont, BA, 43; Univ Rochester, PhD(chem), 49. *Prof Exp:* Demonstr chem, Univ Toronto, 43-44; develop chemist, L-Air Liquide Soc, Montreal, 44-46; res asst chem, Univ Rochester, 46-49; fel, Nat Res Coun Can, 49-50; chemist, Pulp & Paper Res Inst Can, 50-53; asst dir res, Fraser Co, Ltd, 53-58, spec asst admin dept, 58-62, coordr com develop, 62-65; dir res & develop, Great Lakes Paper Co, 65-74, dir environ serv, Great Lakes Forest Prod, Ltd, 74-87; consult, 87-89. *Mem:* Am Chem Soc; Am Tech Asn Pulp & Paper Industs; Can Pulp & Paper Asn; Chem Inst Can. *Res:* Pulp and paper. *Mailing Add:* 622 Rosewood Crescent Thunder Bay ON P7E 2R7 Can

ALLEN, HAROLD DON, CURRICULUM DEVELOPMENT, TEACHER EDUCATION. *Current Pos:* TEACHER EDUC, EASTERN ARCTIC TEACHER EDUC PROG, IQUALUITE & CORAL HARBOUR, NT, 93- *Personal Data:* b Montreal, Que, July 2, 31; m 55, Frances Mary Marven; c Nigel D, Laura M, Elizabeth K & Rosalie E. *Educ:* McGill Univ, BSc, 52; Univ Santa Clara, MSTM, 67; Rutgers Univ, EdM, 68, EdD(math educ), 77. *Honors & Awards:* Metric Serv Award, Govt Can, 83; Damon Award, Am Cryptogram Asn, 90. *Prof Exp:* Teacher math, Protestant Sch Bd Greater Montreal, 53-63; teaching prin, Chibougamau Protestant Sch Bd, 63-65; supv prin, Saguenay Valley Sch Bd, 65-68; teaching asst math, Rutgers Univ, 68-69; from assoc prof to prof math & sci, NS Teachers Col, 69-87; teacher & coordr math, St George's Sch Montreal, 87-93. *Concurrent Pos:* Lectr, Prince Edward Island Teacher Educ, 60, Protestant Sch Bd Teacher Educ, 60-63, Govt Que Prog Teachers, 68 & Col Cape Breton Educ, 77-79; comt mem, Task Force Metric Usage Textbooks, Govt Can, 74-77; counr, Can Col Teachers, 79-81; consult math curric, NS, Adult Educ Prog, 80-81; demonstration teacher, McGill Univ Gifted-Talent Summer Schs, 83-91, adj prof, Fac Educ, 91- *Mem:* Math Asn Am; Nat Coun Teachers Math; Sch Sci & Math Asn. *Res:* Heuristics; problem solving; mathematical recreations; recreational cryptography; mathematics and its applications for non-technical audiences. *Mailing Add:* 6150 Ave Bienville Brossard PQ J4Z 1W8 Can

ALLEN, HARRY CLAY, JR, CHEMICAL PHYSICS, SPECTROSCOPY. *Current Pos:* chmn, chem dept, Clark Univ, 69-78 & 84-85, dean, Grad Sch & coodr res, 78-80, actg provost, 80-81, assoc provost & dean res, 81-83, prof chem, 69-86, EMER PROF, CLARK UNIV, 86- *Personal Data:* b Saugus, Mass, Nov 26, 20; m 48, Carolyn A Bliss; c Carol B & Paul T. *Educ:* Northeastern Univ, BS, 48; Brown Univ, MS, 49; Univ Wash, PhD(phys chem), 51. *Honors & Awards:* Stratton Award, 65. *Prof Exp:* AEC fel, Harvard, Univ, 51-53; asst prof physics, Mich State Col, 53-54; physicist, Radiometry Sect, Atomic & Radiation Physics Div, Nat Bur Stands, 54-61, chief, Analytical & Inorg Chem Div, 61-63, chief, Inorg Mat Div, 63-65, dep dir, Inst Mat Res, 65-66; asst dir minerals res, Bur Mines, US Dept Interior, 66-69. *Concurrent Pos:* Vis prof, Univ Wash, 58 & Univ NC, Chapel Hill, 78; res fel theoret chem, Cambridge Univ, 59-60; vis lectr, Univ Md, 64. *Mem:* Am Chem Soc; fel Am Phys Soc; fel Am Inst Chemists; Sigma Xi. *Res:* Solid state; molecular spectroscopy. *Mailing Add:* Box 1092 Seven Lakes West End NC 27376

ALLEN, HARRY PRINCE, MATHEMATICS. *Current Pos:* ASSOC PROF MATH, OHIO STATE UNIV, 70- *Personal Data:* b New York, NY, July 31, 38; m 62; c 2. *Educ:* Brooklyn Col, BS, 60; Yale Univ, MA, 62, PhD(math), 65. *Prof Exp:* Actg instr math, Yale Univ, 64-65; instr, Mass Inst Technol, 65-67; NATO res fel, Math Inst, State Univ Utrecht, 67-68; asst prof, Rutgers Univ, 68-70. *Mem:* Am Math Soc. *Res:* Nonassociative and lie algebras. *Mailing Add:* Ohio State Univ 231 W 18th Ave 640 Math Tower Columbus OH 43210-1101. *Fax:* 614-292-1479

ALLEN, HENRY L, VETERINARY PATHOLOGY. *Current Pos:* res fel path, 75-77, sr res fel path, 77-79, dir, 79-85, SR INVESTR, TOXICOL & PATH, MERCK SHARP & DOHME RES LABS, 85- *Personal Data:* b Philadelphia, Pa, Apr 26, 45; div; c 1. *Educ:* Pa State Univ, BA, 67; Univ Pa, VMD, 71. *Prof Exp:* From resident to instr vet path, Sch Vet Med, Univ Pa, 71-75. *Concurrent Pos:* Consult & vet surg pathologist. *Mem:* Am Vet Med Asn. *Res:* Naturally occurring and drug-induced diseases in laboratory and domestic animals; comparative aspects. *Mailing Add:* Merck Sharp & Dohme Res Labs 45-207 West Point PA 19486

ALLEN, HERBERT CLIFTON, JR, INTERNAL MEDICINE, NUCLEAR MEDICINE. *Current Pos:* RETIRED. *Personal Data:* b Richmond, Va, Jan 7, 17; m 49; c 6. *Educ:* Univ Richmond, BSc, 37; Med Col Va, MD, 41. *Prof Exp:* Intern, Philadelphia Gen Hosp, 41-42; resident path, Pa Hosp, 46-47; resident med, Med Col Va, 47-48; asst chief, Radioisotope Sect, Dept Med & Surg, Vet Admin, Washington, DC, 48-49; chief metab serv & asst dir, Birmingham Vet Admin Hosp, Van Nuys, Calif, 49-50; asst dir, Radioisotope Univ, Wadsworth Vet Admin Hosp, Los Angeles, 50-51; asst prof med, Baylor Col Med, 51-77; pres, Nuclear Med Labs Tex, 77-95. *Concurrent Pos:* Dir, Radioisotope Univ, Vet Admin Hosp, Houston, 51-55, actg dir, 55-57; dir, Dept Nuclear Med, Methodist Hosp, 52-, Hermann Hosp, 56- & Mem Baptist Hosp, 65-; mem, Radiation Adv Bd; secy, Tex State Dept Health, 61-65; pres, Atomic Energy Indust Labs Southwest, Inc & Atomic Food Processing Corp Am. *Mem:* AMA; Am Thyroid Asn; NY Acad Sci. *Res:* Diagnostic and therapeutic atomic medicine; diseases of thyroid; development of diagnostic instrumentation for nuclear medicine, particularly thyroid, brain and renal scanning. *Mailing Add:* 9261 Kirby Dr Houston TX 77054-2514

ALLEN, HERBERT E, FATE OF POLLUTANTS, ENVIRONMENTAL STANDARDS. *Current Pos:* PROF ENVIRON ENG, UNIV DEL, 89- *Personal Data:* b Sharon, Pa, July 19, 39; m 63, 84, 94, Ronnie Magil; c 4. *Educ:* Univ Mich, BS, 62, PhD(environ chem), 74; Wayne State Univ, MS, 67. *Prof Exp:* Chemist, US Bur Com Fisheries, 62-70; lectr environ chem, Sch Pub Health, Univ Mich, 70-74; from asst prof to prof, Dept Environ Eng, Ill Inst Technol, 74-83; prof chem & dir, Environ Studies Inst, Drexel Univ, 83-89. *Concurrent Pos:* Fac assoc, Argonne Nat Lab, 78-79; vis prof, Water Res Ctr, Eng, 80-81 & Nankai Univ, China, 93; consult, Environ Protection Agency. *Mem:* Am Chem Soc; Water Environ Fedn; Soc Environ Toxicol & Chem; Int Asn Water Qual; Asn Environ Eng Profs; Am Agron Soc. *Res:* Fate of metals and organic contaminants in water, sediment and soil systems; development of criteria useful for prevention of pollution and to set adequate remediation targets; methods of remediation of metals, chemical warfare agents and explosives. *Mailing Add:* Dept Civil & Environ Eng Univ Del Newark DE 19716. *E-Mail:* allen@ce.udel.edu

ALLEN, HOWARD JOSEPH, PSYCHOSOCIAL GENETICS, CANCER GENETICS. *Current Pos:* CANCER RES SCIENTIST, ROSWELL PARK, BUFFALO, 72-; ASST PROF, STATE UNIV NY, BUFFALO, 74-; RES PROF, NIAGRA UNIV, 76- *Personal Data:* b Gloversville, NY, Mar 11, 41; m 96, Carol Pease; c Tina M, Theresa A, Howard J III, Scott T & Craig R. *Educ:* State Univ NY, Albany, BS, 65; State Univ NY, Buffalo, PhD(biol), 70, MSW, 95. *Prof Exp:* Teaching fel, Fla State Univ, 70-72. *Concurrent Pos:* Hon prof, Biol Dept, Canisius Col, Buffalo; coun, private practice. *Mem:* Am Chem Soc; Am Asn Biol Chemists; Am Asn Cancer Res; Nat Asn Social Workers; Am Soc Cell Biol; Nat Soc Genetic Counrs. *Res:* Psychosocial issues of cancer genetics; genetic counseling. *Mailing Add:* Roswell Park Cancer Inst Buffalo NY 14263

ALLEN, J FRANCES, ECOLOGY. *Current Pos:* RETIRED. *Personal Data:* b Arkville, NY, Apr 14, 16. *Educ:* Radford Col, BS, 38; Univ Md, MS, 48, PhD(zool), 52. *Hon Degrees:* Bronze Medal, Environ Protection Agency. *Prof Exp:* Teacher various high schs, 38-47; asst zool, Univ Md, 47-48, instr, 48-55, asst prof, 55-58; prof asst, Syst Biol Prog, NSF, 58-61, assoc prog dir, 61-67; chief br water qual requirements, Fed Water Pollution Control Admin, US Dept Interior, 67-68, asst dir biol sci, Div Water Qual Res, 68-70; chief biol sci br, Div Water Qual Res, Environ Protection Agency, 70-71, chief ecol effects, Processes & Effects Div, 71-73, staff scientist-ecologist, sci adv bd, 73-82. *Concurrent Pos:* Biol Exam, NY State Dept Educ, 47. *Mem:* Fel AAAS; Am Fisheries Soc; Am Inst Biol Sci. *Res:* Fisheries biology; shellfish; gastropod ecology and distribution; taxonomy of the gastropods; aquatic biology; pollution; biology; ecological effects. *Mailing Add:* RR 1, Box 9 Roxbury NY 12474-9779

ALLEN, JACK C, JR, GEOLOGY. *Current Pos:* from asst prof to assoc prof, 63-74, chmn coun univ courses, 76-80, PROF GEOL, BUCKNELL UNIV, 74-, CHMN DEPT, 82- *Personal Data:* b Dallas, Tex, Sept 17, 35; m 61; c 2. *Educ:* Southern Methodist Univ, BS, 58; Princeton Univ, MA, 60, PhD(geol), 61. *Prof Exp:* Asst prof geol, Wesleyan Univ, 61-63. *Mem:* AAAS; Geol Soc Am; fel Mineral Soc Am. *Res:* Structure and petrology of granitic rocks; stability of amphibole in andesite and basalt. *Mailing Add:* 26 S Third St Lewisburg PA 17837

ALLEN, JAMES DURWOOD, ORGANIC POLYMER CHEMISTRY. *Current Pos:* mgr res & develop, 75-81, TECH DIR, ADVAN COMPOSITE DIV, FIBERITE CORP, 81- *Personal Data:* b Commerce, Tex, Nov 22, 35; m 58; c 3. *Educ:* ETex State Col, BA, 58; Rice Univ, PhD(chem), 62. *Prof Exp:* Res chemist, Shell Oil Co, 62-63; NIH fel chem, Northwestern Univ, 63-64; res chemist, Phillips Petrol Co, 64-69; mem tech staff, NAm Rockwell Corp, 69-75. *Mem:* Am Chem Soc; Soc Aerospace Mat & Process Engrs; Sigma Xi. *Res:* Polymer chemistry as applied to graphite fiber reinforced advanced composites. *Mailing Add:* 3926 E Lavender Ln Phoenix AZ 85044-4586

ALLEN, JAMES FREDERICK, ARTIFICIAL INTELLIGENCE, COMPUTATIONAL LINGUISTICS. *Current Pos:* From asst prof to prof, 79-92, chmn, 87-90, JOHN H DESSAUER PROF COMPUT SCI, UNIV ROCHESTER, 92- *Personal Data:* b London, Eng, Mar 25, 50; Can citizen; m 86, Judith Hook. *Educ:* Univ Toronto, BSc, 73, MSc, 75, PhD(comput sci), 79. *Concurrent Pos:* Prin investr, NSF, 80-, Off Naval Res, 82-, Rome Air Develop Ctr, 84- & Advan Res Projs Agency, 90-; ed-in-chief, Computational Ling, 83-93; auth, Natural Language Understanding, Benjamin-Cummings Pub Co, 88 & Reasoning About Plans, Morgan Kaufman, 91; Pres Young Investr Award, NSF, 84-89. *Mem:* Asn Computational Ling; fel Am Asn Artificial Intel; Asn Comput Mach. *Res:* Artificial intelligence, especially in the areas of natural language understanding (dialogue understanding) and the representations of knowledge (time, action and planning). *Mailing Add:* Dept Comput Sci Univ Rochester 601 Elmwood Ave Rochester NY 14627. *Fax:* 716-461-2018; *E-Mail:* james@cs.rochester.edu

ALLEN, JAMES LAMAR, MICROWAVE TECHNIQUES, COMPUTER APPLICATIONS. *Current Pos:* chief engr & vpres, 83-91, PRES, KAMAN SCI CORP, 91- *Personal Data:* b Graceville, Fla, Sept 25, 36; m 59; c 2. *Educ:* Ga Inst Technol, BEE, 59, MSEE, 61, PhD(elec eng), 66. *Prof Exp:* Sr engr, Sperry Microwave Electronics, 61-63; instr elec eng, Ga Inst Technol, 63-66; res staff consult, Sperry Microwave Electronics, 66-68; assoc prof elec eng, Univ SFla, 68-70, Colo State Univ, 70-72; from assoc prof to prof, Univ SFla, 72-81; pres, Lamar Allen Enterprises, Inc, 81-83. *Concurrent Pos:* Chief ed, Transactions Microwave Theory & Techniques, Inst Elec & Electronics Engrs, 77-79. *Mem:* Fel Inst Elec & Electronics Engrs. *Res:* Electromagnetic interference; microprocessor applications; microwave theory and techniques; high power microwave weapon systems. *Mailing Add:* Kaman Sci Corp PO Box 7463 Colorado Springs CO 80933

ALLEN, JAMES R, JR, pathology, for more information see previous edition

ALLEN, JAMES RALSTON, CROP PHYSIOLOGY, PLANT PHYSIOLOGY. *Current Pos:* DIR AGR EXP STA, COL LIFE SCI, UNIV DC, 89- *Personal Data:* b Jamaica, WI, Oct 4, 38; US citizen; m 63; c 2. *Educ:* Tuskegee Inst, BS, 68; Pa State Univ, MS, 70, PhD(crop physiol), 74. *Prof Exp:* Head plant & soil sci dept, Tenn State Univ, 73-76; asst prof plant & soil sci, Tuskegee Inst, 76-89. *Mem:* Am Soc Agron; Sigma Xi. *Res:* Nitrogen fixation, micronutrients in agronomic crop plant physiology. *Mailing Add:* Col Life Sci Agr Exp Sta Univ DC 4250 Rm 561 Connecticut Ave Washington DC 20008

ALLEN, JAMES ROY, theoretical physics, for more information see previous edition

ALLEN, JAMES WARD, SOLID STATE PHYSICS. *Current Pos:* PROF PHYSICS, UNIV MICH, 87-, GRAD CHAIR PHYSICS DEPT, 91- *Personal Data:* b Livingston, Mont, May 4, 41; m 62; c 2. *Educ:* Stanford Univ, BS, 63, MS, 65, PhD(elec eng), 68. *Honors & Awards:* Sr US Scientist Award, Alexander von Homboldt Found, Ger, 89. *Prof Exp:* Staff mem, Lincoln Lab, Mass Inst Technol, 68-73; staff mem, 73-85, sr staff mem, Xerox Palo Alto Res Ctr, 85-87. *Concurrent Pos:* Acad guest, Swiss Fed Inst Technol, Zurich, 78, Max Planck Inst Solid State Physics, Stuttgart, 89-90. *Mem:* Fel Am Phys Soc. *Res:* Optical properties of transition metal and rare earth compounds; magnetic anisotropy and magnetoelastic effects; insulator-to-metal transition materials; synchrotron radiation and electron spectroscopy of narrow band and other materials. *Mailing Add:* 595 Riverview Dr Ann Arbor MI 48104. *Fax:* 313-763-9694

ALLEN, JOE FRANK, INORGANIC CHEMISTRY, SCIENCE EDUCATION. *Current Pos:* from asst prof to assoc prof inorg chem, 64-78, PROF CHEM, CLEMSON UNIV, 78-, ASSOC HEAD, 89- *Personal Data:* b Hogansville, Ga, June 3, 34; m 55; c 2. *Educ:* Berry Col, AB, 55; Univ Miss, MS, 59; Ga Inst Technol, PhD(inorg chem), 63. *Prof Exp:* Instr chem, Ga Inst Technol, 57-61; radiochemist, Oak Ridge Nat Lab, 62-64. *Concurrent Pos:* Consult, mobile lab prog, Oak Ridge Assoc Univs, 66-72; Am Soc Eng Educ fac fel, NASA, Houston, 69-70; consult develop learning mat, Humbolt State Univ, Utah State Univ, Charles County Community Col, Ulster County Community Col & Environ Protection Agency, 72-82; consult, nuclear chem & lab skills workshops, Westinghouse SRS, 80-, Duke Power Co, 81-83 & Ga Power Co, 82- *Mem:* Am Chem Soc. *Res:* Chemistry of complex compounds; application of radioisotopes; chemical separations using ion exchange and solvent extraction; development of individualized instructional systems for science and technical training. *Mailing Add:* 214 Brook St Clemson SC 29631-1605

ALLEN, JOE HASKELL, SOLAR-TERRESTRIAL PHYSICS, GEOMAGNETISM. *Current Pos:* VISITING SCIENTIST, 94-; SCI SECY, SCI COMT SOLAR TERRESTRIAL PHYSICS, 94- *Personal Data:* b Oklahoma City, Okla, June 6, 39; m 61, Charlotte A Moody; c Melissa, Susan & Melinda. *Educ:* Univ Okla, BS, 61; Univ Calif, Berkeley, MS, 66. *Prof Exp:* Teacher math, Casady Sch, 61-63; geophysicist, geomagnetism, US Dept Com, 63-71, chief data studies div, 73-81, chief, Solar-Terrestrial Physics Div & Dir World Data Ctr-A Solar Terrestrial Physics, US Dept Com, 81-94. *Concurrent Pos:* Head, Int Magnetospheric Study Cent Info Exchange Off, 76-80; mem-at-large, Int Coun Sci Unions Panel World Data Ctrs, 94- *Mem:* Am Geophys Union; Soc Terrestrial Magnetism & Elec Japan; Int Asn Geomagnetism & Aeronomy; Int Coun Sci Unions. *Res:* Measurement and classification of geomagnetic variations associated with natural and man-caused phenomena; promotion of international cooperation in science; direct national and international data exchange for solar, interplanetary, ionospheric and geomagnetic data; solar activity affecting technology on earth and in space. *Mailing Add:* Sci Comt Solar Terrestrial Physics Nat Oceanic & Atmospheric Admin Nat Geophys Data Ctr 325 Broadway Boulder CO 80303. *Fax:* 303-497-6513; *E-Mail:* jallen@ngdc.noaa.gov

ALLEN, JOHN BURTON, ELECTRICAL ENGINEERING. *Current Pos:* SR MEM TECH STAFF ELEC ENG, TEX INSTRUMENTS INC, 71- *Personal Data:* b Detroit, Mich, Mar 21, 40; m 66; c 1. *Educ:* Univ Mich, BSE & MS, 63; Ga Inst Technol, MS, 69, PhD(elec eng), 73. *Prof Exp:* Res eng, NAm Aviation Co, 64-65; assoc scientist, Lockheed-Ga Co, 65-71. *Mem:* Sigma Xi. *Res:* Coherent optics; holography; laser communication systems; image processing; optical missile guidance systems; thermal imaging systems; statistical estimation and decision theory. *Mailing Add:* PO Box 869305 MS 8490 Plano TX 75086

ALLEN, JOHN CHRISTOPHER, VOLCANOLOGY, EXPERIMENTAL PETROLOGY. *Current Pos:* from asst prof to assoc prof, 63-74, chmn dept, 82-94, PROF GEOL, BUCKNELL UNIV, 74-, CHMN DEPT, 82- *Personal Data:* b Dallas, Tex, Sept 17, 35; m 61, Joan Stout; c Julia Lee & John Christopher. *Educ:* Southern Methodist Univ, BS, 58; Princeton Univ, MA, 60, PhD(geol), 61. *Prof Exp:* Instr geol, Wesleyan Univ, 61, asst prof, 61-63. *Concurrent Pos:* Vis prof, Univ Tex, 82-84. *Mem:* Fel Mineral Soc Am; Geol Soc Am. *Res:* Stability of amphiboles in andesite and basalt at high pressures and temperatures. *Mailing Add:* Dept Geol Bucknell Univ Lewisburg PA 17837-2005. *E-Mail:* allen@bucknell.edu

ALLEN, JOHN ED, MATHEMATICS. *Current Pos:* Asst prof, 63-72, ASSOC PROF MATH, NORTH TEX STATE UNIV, 72-, CHMN DEPT, 76- *Personal Data:* b Danville, La, Nov 18, 37; m 60; c 3. *Educ:* La Polytech Inst, BS, 58; Okla State Univ, MS, 60, PhD(math), 63. *Concurrent Pos:* NSF sci fac fel, Purdue Univ, 71-72. *Mem:* Soc Indust & Appl Math; Math Asn Am; Am Math Soc. *Res:* Convexity; numerical analysis. *Mailing Add:* Univ Tex PO Box 5116 Denton TX 76203-5116

ALLEN, JOHN EDWARD, JR, PHOTODISSOCIATION & MOLECULAR DYNAMICS, THERMODYNAMICS & SPECTROSCOPY. *Current Pos:* space scientist, Atmospheric Physics Br, 78-84, ASTROPHYSICIST, ASTROCHEM BR, GODDARD SPACE FLIGHT CTR, NASA, 84- *Personal Data:* b Lakeland, Fla, Apr 12, 45; m 62, 90, Patricia J Webb; c John E III & Michael L. *Educ:* Univ Fla, BS, 67, MS, 70, PhD(appl physics), 76. *Prof Exp:* Res asst aeronomy, Ctr Aeronomy & Atmospheric Sci, Dept Physics, Univ Fla, 69-70, res asst appl physics, Dept Eng Sci & Appl Math, 70-73, res assoc, 73-76; res assoc, Nat Acad Sci-Nat Res Coun, Chem Physics Br, US Army Ballistic Res Lab, Aberdeen Proving Ground, 76-78. *Mem:* Am Phys Soc; Optical Soc Am; Am Geophys Union; Am Astron Soc. *Res:* Application of lasers, electro optical and nonlinear optical techniques to chemical physics; chemical kinetics, laser-matter interactions, light scattering, isotope separation; application of chemical physics to astrophysical and atmospheric systems; comets, upper atmosphere, circumstellar shells, planetary atmospheres, interstellar matter; thermodynamics; spectroscopy. *Mailing Add:* Code 691 NASA Goddard Space Flight Ctr Greenbelt MD 20771. *E-Mail:* john.e.allen@gsfc.nasa.gov

ALLEN, JOHN ELIOT, GEOLOGY. *Current Pos:* prof & head, Dept Earth Sci, 56-74, EMER PROF GEOL, PORTLAND STATE UNIV, 74- *Personal Data:* b Seattle, Wash, Aug 12, 08; m 33, Margaret Moss; c 1. *Educ:* Univ Ore, BA, 31, MA, 32; Univ Calif, Berkeley, PhD(geol), 44. *Honors & Awards:* Niel Miner Award, Nat Asn Geol Teachers, 75. *Prof Exp:* Field geologist, Rustless Iron & Steel Co, Md, 35-38; field geologist, Ore Dept Geol & Mineral Indust, 38-39, chief geologist-in-chg field invests & assoc ed publ, 39-47; head, Dept

Geol, NMex Inst Mining & Technol, 49-51; chief, Navaho Mineral Surv, 51-54; econ geologist, Bur Mines, NMex, 54-56. *Concurrent Pos:* SEATO prof & chmn dept, Univ Peshawar, 63-64; prof geol, Whitman Col, 75; res geologist, Nev Bur Mines & Geol, 75-76, NMex Bur Mines, 76-77; columnist, Oregonian, 83-87. *Mem:* Fel Geol Soc Am; Nat Asn Geol Teachers; Sigma Xi. *Res:* Structural relations of chromite deposits; Oregon economic geology and areal geology of the Coos Bay and Wallowa Mountains; geology of San Juan Bautista Quadrangle, California and Northern Sacramento Mountains, New Mexico; glaciation in Northwest; volcanoes of Cascade Range; geology of Columbia River gorge. *Mailing Add:* Geol Dept Portland State Univ Portland OR 97207-0751

ALLEN, JOHN JEFFERY BECK, PSYCHOPHYSIOLOGY, CLINICAL PSYCHOLOGY. *Current Pos:* ASST PROF PSYCHOL, COGNITIVE SCI & NEUROSCI, UNIV ARIZ, 92- *Personal Data:* b Northhampton, Mass, Aug 10, 61; m, Connie Beck; c Gabrielle Allenbeck. *Educ:* Univ Wis, BS, 86; Univ Minn, MA, 91, PhD(clin psychol), 92. *Prof Exp:* Instr psychol, Univ Minn, 88-92; intern, Vet Admin Med Ctr, Minneapolis, 91-92. *Concurrent Pos:* Consult, NIH, 93. *Mem:* Am Psychol Asn; Am Psychol Soc; Soc Psychophysiol Res; Int Neuropsychol Soc. *Res:* Relationship between brain function and behavior, especially emotion, emotional disorders, memory and memory disorders; identifying psychophysiological indicators of risk for mood disorders; acupuncture in the treatment of depression. *Mailing Add:* Dept Psychol Univ Ariz Tucson AZ 85721

ALLEN, JOHN KAY, POLYMER CHEMISTRY. *Current Pos:* RETIRED. *Personal Data:* b Rochdale, Eng, Mar 14, 36; m 67; c 2. *Educ:* Univ Birmingham, BS, 57, PhD(chem), 60. *Prof Exp:* Res asst chem, Univ Louisville, 60-62; res chemist, Shell Chem Co, Eng, 62-65; proj chemist, Amoco Chem Corp, 65-68, sr proj chemist, 68-70, res chemist, 70-78, staff res chemist, 78-88, sr res scientist, 88-92; res assoc, ITW Tech Ctr, 92-94. *Mem:* Am Chem Soc. *Res:* Use of radioactive tracers in polymer chemistry; properties of ion-exchange resins; chemistry of polyether polyols and polyurethanes; preparation of fire resistant cellular plastics; plasticizer alcohols synthesis and aromatic acids synthesis; chemical waste disposal; pyrolysis of aromatic acids; waste water treatment; unsaturated polyesters and polyurethanes used in reinforced plastics. *Mailing Add:* 50 Stirling Circle Apt No 201 Wheaton IL 60187-2114

ALLEN, JOHN L(OYD), ELECTRONICS. *Current Pos:* RETIRED. *Personal Data:* b Estherville, Iowa, June 13, 31; m 52; c 4. *Educ:* Pa State Univ, BS, 58; Mass Inst Technol, SM, 62, PhD(commun biophys), 68. *Prof Exp:* Jr engr, H R B Singer, Inc, 54-58; staff mem, Lincoln Lab, Mass Inst Technol, 58-60, assoc group leader spec radars, 60-62, group leaders array radars, 62-65, group leader, Radar Div, 65-68 & tactical radars, 68-69, assoc head, Radar Measurements Div, 69-71; assoc dir res electronics, Naval Res Lab, 71-74; dep dir, Defense Res & Eng, 74-77; vpres, Gen Res Corp, 77-78, pres, 78-81; pvt consult, 81-96. *Concurrent Pos:* Vpres, Flow Gen, Inc, 77-81; mem, Air Force Studies Bd, Nat Res Coun, 83-85, sci adv bd, USAF 85-89, bd dirs, Sparta, Inc & Jamieson Sci & Eng. *Mem:* Fel Inst Elec & Electronics Engrs. *Res:* Antennas; radar system design; optics of invertebrates; aerospace systems. *Mailing Add:* 9B2 President Pt Dr Annapolis MD 21403

ALLEN, JOHN P, ALCOHOLISM. *Current Pos:* CHIEF, TREATMENT RES BR, NAT INST ALCOHOL AUBSE & ALCOHOLISM, NIH, 87- *Personal Data:* b Minneapolis, Minn, Mar 16, 47. *Educ:* St Meinrad Col, BA, 69; Univ St Louis, MS, 71, PhD(clin psychol), 74; Univ Puget Sound, MPA, 79. *Res:* Measurement of treatment outcome; effective assignment of patients to alternative treatments. *Mailing Add:* Treat Res Br Willco Bldg Suite 505 6000 Executive Blvd MSC 7003 Bethesda MD 20892-7003

ALLEN, JOHN POLK, GLOBAL ECOLOGY, EXPERIMENTAL BIOSPHERICS. *Current Pos:* CHMN & DIR RES, BIOSPHERES, LLC, 94- *Personal Data:* b Carnegie, Okla, May 6, 29. *Educ:* Colo Sch Mines, BS, 57; Harvard Univ, MBA, 62. *Prof Exp:* Spec metals res metallurgist, Allegheny Ludlum Steel Corp, 57-59; head teaching & crushing, Ur-Van Plant, Union Carbide Nuclear, 59-60; asst vpres regional develop, Develop & Resources Corp, New York, 61-63; total systs ecol consult, Inst Ecotech, UK, 65-69, dir total systs ecol, 69-84; inventor, founder, dir res & develop, Biosphere 2, 84-94. *Concurrent Pos:* Consult ecosysts, Ecofrontiers, 78-; chmn, Planetary Coral Reef Found, 90- *Mem:* AAAS; fel Royal Geog Soc; fel Linnean Soc. *Res:* Global ecology and biospherics theoretical and experimental; invention and design of test module and Biosphere Two; next generation of closed life systems; coral reef structure. *Mailing Add:* 30238 Caminito Quieto Bonsall CA 92003. *E-Mail:* biospheres@compuserve.com

ALLEN, JOHN RYBOLT, CHEMISTRY, BIOCHEMISTRY. *Personal Data:* b Indianapolis, Ind, Sept 14, 26; m 53. *Educ:* Ball State Teachers Col, AB, 49; Univ Ill, Urbana, PhD(biochem), 54. *Prof Exp:* Res assoc biochem, Northwestern Univ, 53-56; asst prof, Col Med, Baylor Univ, 56-59; sr scientist, Warner-Lambert Pharm Co, NJ, 59-60; res assoc dent sch, Wash Univ, 60-62; prof chem & head dept, Union Col, Ky, 62-64; clin assoc clin chem, Univ Hosp, Case Western Reserve Univ, 64-65; asst prof path & radiol, Col Med, Ohio State Univ, 65-68; clin chemist, St John's Mercy Hosp, St Louis, Mo, 68-69, Decatur Mem Hosp, Ill, 69-70, San Diego Inst Path, 70 & San Bernardino County Hosp, 70-75; instr chem, Phoenix Col, 75-80. *Mem:* Fel AAAS; fel Am Asn Clin Chem; Am Chem Soc; Acad Clin Lab Physicians & Scientists; fel Am Inst Chem. *Res:* Quality control and methods; creatine phosphokinase; vitamin E deficiency, lipid metabolism and structure. *Mailing Add:* 9627 N 32 St Phoenix AZ 85028-4832

ALLEN, JON CHARLES, ENTOMOLOGY, MATHEMATICAL MODELING. *Current Pos:* Asst prof, 73-80, ASSOC PROF ENTOM, UNIV FLA, 80- *Personal Data:* b Ventura, Calif, Nov 24, 40; m 64; c 2. *Educ:* Univ Calif, Santa Barbara, BA, 66, MA, 67; Univ Calif, Riverside, PhD(pop biol), 73. *Mem:* Entom Soc Am; Int Soc Citricult. *Res:* Mathematical modeling of plant-pest interactions; simulation of plant growth and development; modeling micrometeorological dynamics and population effects; biological system dynamics, chaos. *Mailing Add:* Dept Entomol Univ Fla Gainesville FL 32611-2002

ALLEN, JONATHAN, ELECTRICAL ENGINEERING. *Current Pos:* asst prof elec eng, 68-76, ASSOC PROF ELEC ENG & ASSOC DIR RES LAB ELECTRONICS, MASS INST TECHNOL, 76- *Personal Data:* b Hanover, NH, June 4, 34; m 60; c 2. *Educ:* Dartmouth Col, AB, 56, MS, 57; Mass Inst Technol, PhD(elec eng), 68. *Prof Exp:* Supvr human factors eng, Bell Tel Labs, 61-67. *Concurrent Pos:* Consult, Lincoln Lab & Sperry Rand Res Corp, 68- *Mem:* Inst Elec & Electronics Engrs; Sigma Xi. *Res:* Computation; linguistic analysis; speech analysis and synthesis. *Mailing Add:* Mass Inst Technol Cambridge MA 02139

ALLEN, JONATHAN, PHYSICS, ENVIRONMENTAL SCIENCE & RF ENGINEERING. *Current Pos:* CONSULT, R&D INSTRUMENTATION, 93-; STAFF SCIENTIST, RF POWER PROF INC, VOORHEES, NJ, 95- *Personal Data:* b Fall River, Mass, Dec 29, 42; m 71; c 1. *Educ:* Colby Col, AB, 64; Southeastern Mass Univ, MS, 71; Washington Univ, PhD(physics), 77. *Prof Exp:* Engr res & develop, Trans-Sonics, Inc, 64-65, advan develop, Hamilton Stand Div, United Aircraft, 65-68; physicist consult, High Energy Processing Corp, 68-71; res scientist physics, Aerochem Res Labs, Inc. 78-83; sr scientist process develop, Chronar Corp, 83-90; dir RF & process electronics, Advan Photovoltaic Systs, Inc 90-93. *Concurrent Pos:* Lectr physics, Harris-Stowe Col, 73-74; contrib ed, NJ Hazardous Waste News, 81- *Mem:* Am Phys Soc; Fedn Am Scientists; Optical Soc Am; NY Acad Sci; Sigma Xi; Inst Elec & Electronic Engrs. *Res:* Process research and development for manufacture of amorphous photovotaic panels including radio frequency systems, controls, instrumentation and electrical measurements. *Mailing Add:* Three Creek Rim Dr Titusville NJ 08560. *Fax:* 609-627-1311; *E-Mail:* jon-a@ix.netcom.com

ALLEN, JOSEPH HUNTER, RADIOLOGY. *Current Pos:* From asst prof to prof, 58-93, EMER PROF RADIOL, VANDERBILT UNIV, 93- *Personal Data:* b St Joseph, Mo, Aug 31, 25; m 56; c 1. *Educ:* Westminster Col, 42-43; Washington Univ, MD, 48. *Mem:* AMA; Am Soc Neuroradiol; fel Am Col Radiol; Asn Univ Radiol. *Res:* Neuroradiology. *Mailing Add:* Dept Radiol Vanderbilt Univ 403 Sunnyside Dr Nashville TN 37205

ALLEN, JULIA NATALIA, VETERINARY MEDICINE & PARASITOLOGY, TERRESTRIAL ECOLOGY. *Current Pos:* DOCTOR VET MED, INTERBAY ANIMAL HOSP, 85- *Personal Data:* b Seattle, Wash. *Educ:* Mich State Univ, BS, 70; Wash State Univ, PhD(zool), 78, DVM, 86. *Prof Exp:* Tech specialist plant tissue cult, Wash State Univ, 78-80; tech specialist virol, USDA, 80; field biologist, US Army Corps Engrs, 80-81; tech specialist, Fruit & Trees, USDA, 81-82. *Mem:* Sigma Xi; Am Vet Med Asn. *Res:* Ecology and behavior of long billed curlews; plant tissue culture; prey base study and habitat analysis in Columbia Basin; frost tolerance of fruit tree buds; pea seed borne mosaic virus; veterinary parasitology. *Mailing Add:* Interbay Animal Hosp 3040 16th Ave W Seattle WA 98119

ALLEN, JULIUS CADDEN, CELL PHYSIOLOGY, VASCULAR CELL BIOLOGY. *Current Pos:* Asst prof pharmacol, 70-72, asst prof cell biophys, 72-73, ASSOC PROF CELL BIOPHYS, BAYLOR COL MED, 73-, ASSOC PROF & ASSOC HEAD, SECT CARDIOVASC SCI, DEPT MED, 76-, PROF MED & PHYSIOL, 83. *Personal Data:* b New London, Conn, Oct 18, 38; m 61; c 2. *Educ:* Amherst Col, BA, 60; Univ Mass, MA, 62; Univ Alta, PhD(pharmacol), 67. *Concurrent Pos:* Fel, Baylor Col Med, 67-69, Nat Heart & Lung Inst fel pharmacol, 69-70, Nat Heart & Lung Inst grants, 74-77 & 80-; Am Heart Asn grant, 70-73; mem, Int Study Group Res Cardiac Metab, 72-; estab investr, Am Heart Asn, 74-79; prin investr, Nat Heart Lung Inst Training grant, 77 -; ed, J Molecular & Cellular Cardiol, 77-80; assoc prof physiol, Baylor Col Med, 79-; dir, Grad Prog Cardiovasc Sci, NIH. *Mem:* Am Heart Asn; Am Soc Pharmacol & Exp Therapeut; Biophys Soc; Am Physiol Soc. *Res:* Biology of smooth muscle membrane systems; molecular basis of smooth muscle contractile heterogeneity; biochemistry and biophysics of ion transport; Napump function in smooth muscle; molecular control of contraction & cell growth. *Mailing Add:* Dept Med Baylor Col Med Houston TX 77030. *Fax:* 713-790-0681; *E-Mail:* juliusa@bcm.tmc.edu

ALLEN, KENNETH G D, TRACE METAL BIOCHEMISTRY. *Current Pos:* From asst prof to assoc prof, 78-87, PROF, NUTRIT, COLO STATE UNIV, 87-, PROF, DEPT PHYSIOL, 93- *Personal Data:* b Colwyn Bay, Wales, UK, July 30, 43; m 84, Glenda Taton; c Charles, Gillian & Hillary. *Educ:* Univ London, BS, 65; Mont State Univ, PhD(biochem), 73. *Concurrent Pos:* Res biochem, USDA Human Nutrit Lab, NDak, 75-78; sabbatical leave, Rowett Res Inst, Aberdeenn, Scotland, 85-86, Grad Fac, Sch Med, Univ Colo Health Sci Ctr. *Mem:* Am Inst Nutrit; Nutrit Soc (UK); Sigma Xi; Oxygen Soc. *Res:* Trace metal biochemistry and nutrition with particular emphasis on copper; lipid metabolism; eicosanoids and oxy radical metabolism. *Mailing Add:* Dept Food Sci & Human Nutrit Colo State Univ Ft Collins CO 80523-0001. *Fax:* 970-491-7252; *E-Mail:* allen@condor.cahs.colostate.edu

ALLEN, KENNETH WILLIAM, ZOOLOGY. *Current Pos:* RETIRED. *Personal Data:* b St Stephens, NB, June 20, 30; nat US; m 52; c 4. *Educ:* Wheaton Col, BS, 52; Univ Maine, MS, 56; Rice Univ, PhD, 59. *Prof Exp:* Fel biol, Rice Univ, 59-60; asst prof zool, Univ Calif, Los Angeles, 60-63; prof zool & oceanog & head dept, Univ Maine, Orono, 63-77, actg dean, Col Arts & Sci, 74-76, actg pres, Univ Maine, Augusta, 76-77 & Univ Southern Maine, 77-78, prof zool, Univ Maine Orono, 77-78, actg pres, 79-80; prof zool, Husson Col, Bangor, Maine, 80-91, vpres acad affairs, 91-93. *Mem:* Am Soc Zoologists; Am Soc Parasitol. *Res:* Comparative biochemistry and parasitology. *Mailing Add:* 174 Forest Ave Orono ME 04473

ALLEN, LARRY MILTON, ONCOLOGY, DERMATOLOGY. *Current Pos:* PRES MED PROD, ELANTEC INC, 89- *Personal Data:* b Los Angeles, Calif, Nov 22, 42; m 66, Rose M Allen; c Russell S. *Educ:* Univ Pac, BS, 66, MS, 67; Univ Ore, PhD(chem), 71; Univ Colo, MBA, 87. *Prof Exp:* Res pharmacologist, NCI/Vet Admin Med Oncol, 70-75; sr scientist cancer pharmacol, Roswell Park Mem Cancer Inst, 75-77; assoc prof cancer pharmacol, Sch Med, Univ Miami, 77-82; from assoc dir res to vpres corp develop & sci affil, Chemex Pharmaceut, 82-89; actg vpres prod develop, Magnetically Delivered Ther, 92- *Concurrent Pos:* Travel grant, Fedn Am Soc Exp Biol & Am Soc Pharmacol & Exp Therapeut, 73; mem comt, Phase II Clin Res Grants-NIH, 84 & SBIR-NIH, 87; consult, Regulatory Affairs/Formulations, Patents, Book Rev & Biopharmacol. *Mem:* Am Col Clin Pharmacol; Am Asn Cancer Res; Am Soc Pharmacol & Exp Therapeut; Soc Exp Dermat. *Res:* Biotherapy (immunology) of cancer; drug delivery system design and development; topical-parenteral formulations; drug development. *Mailing Add:* Elantec Med Inc 85 S Union Blvd Suite G-160 Lakewood CO 80228-2207. *Fax:* 303-278-4968

ALLEN, LAWRENCE HARVEY, PHYSICAL CHEMISTRY, COLLOID CHEMISTRY. *Current Pos:* Res scientist colloid chem, 72-80, DIR, PROCESS CHEM DIV & DIR RES CHEM SCI, PULP & PAPER INST CAN, 90- *Personal Data:* b Ottawa, Ont, Mar 27, 43; Can citizen; m 68; c 4. *Educ:* Carleton Univ, BSc, 65; Clarkson Univ, PhD(phys chem), 70. *Concurrent Pos:* Nat Res Coun Can fel, Inland Waters Directorate, Environ Can, 71-72; postdoctoral assoc, Clarkson Univ, 69-71. *Mem:* Am Chem Soc; fel Chem Inst Can; Can Pulp & Paper Asn; fel Tech Asn Pulp & Paper Indust. *Res:* Chemistry of pulping and papermaking processes; colloid and surface chemistry; chemistry of wood resins; pitch control; foam control; retention and drainage on paper machines; research management. *Mailing Add:* 107 Seigniory Ave Pointe Claire PQ H9R 1J6 Can

ALLEN, LELAND CULLEN, CHEMISTRY. *Current Pos:* from asst prof to assoc prof, 60-65, PROF CHEM, PRINCETON UNIV, 65- *Personal Data:* b Cincinnati, Ohio, Dec 3, 26; m 60; c 3. *Educ:* Univ Cincinnati, BS, 49, EE, 55; Mass Inst Technol, PhD(theoret physics), 57. *Prof Exp:* Fel, Mass Inst Technol, 57-59; NSF fel physics, Univ Calif, Berkeley, 59-60. *Concurrent Pos:* NSF sr fel, Centre Mecanique Ondulatoire Appliquee, Paris, 67; Guggenheim fel, Math Inst, Oxford Univ, 67; NIH spec fel biochem sci, Princeton Univ, 72. *Mem:* AAAS; Am Phys Soc; Am Chem Soc. *Res:* Electronic structure theory, applications to inorganic, organic and biochemistry. *Mailing Add:* Dept Chem Frick Lab Princeton Univ Princeton NJ 08544-1009

ALLEN, LEROY RICHARD, RESEARCH ADMINISTRATION, PUBLIC HEALTH. *Current Pos:* RETIRED. *Personal Data:* b Garden Grove, Calif, Sept 14, 13; m 38; c 3. *Educ:* Univ Redlands, AB, 36; Univ Southern Calif, MD, 41; Univ Mich, MPH, 48; Am Bd Prev Med & Pub Health, dipl, 49. *Prof Exp:* Tuberc control officer, State Dept Pub Health, Md, 45-48; tuberc consult, Regional Off San Francisco, USPHS, 49-50; med dir, US Tech Coop Mission to Burma, 50-53, prof prev & social med, Vellore Med Col, South India, 54-56; med educ & pub health rep, Rockefeller Found, New Delhi, India & Quezon City, Philippines, 57-72; from dep dir to dir, Atomic Bomb Casualty Comn, Nat Acad Sci, 72-75, vchmn, Radiation Effects Res Found, Japan, 75-78. *Concurrent Pos:* Consult, Indian Pub Health Asn, USPHS, 44-53; vis prof community med, Med Col, Univ Philippines, 68-71; on leave, consult, Atomic Bomb Casualty Comn, US Nat Acad Sci-Japanese Nat Inst Health, 71-72; mem bd dirs, Hospice Monterey Peninsula, 79-, vpres, 81-82 & 85-89; consult health sci, Rockefeller Found, 79. *Mem:* Am Thoracic Soc; Am Pub Health Asn; hon mem Indian Pub Health Asn. *Res:* Medical education and care; problems related to population control. *Mailing Add:* 3765 Raymond Way Carmel CA 93923

ALLEN, LEW, JR, PHYSICS. *Current Pos:* CHMN, CHARLES STARK DRAPER LAB, 91- *Personal Data:* b Miami, Fla, Sept 30, 25; m 49; c 5. *Educ:* US Mil Acad, BS, 46; Univ Ill, MS, 52, PhD(physics), 54. *Honors & Awards:* Thomas White Award, Nat Geog Soc; George Goddard Award, Int Soc Opt Eng; Von Karman Lect, Am Inst Astronaut & Aeronaut; Distinguished Serv Award, NASA. *Prof Exp:* Mem staff, Los Alamos Sci Lab, 54-57; sci adv, Air Force Spec Weapons Ctr, 57-61, mem staff defense dir res & eng, 61-65, dep dir spec projs, Off of Secy of Air Force, 65-68, dir space systs, 68-70, dir spec projs, 71-73; dir, Nat Security Agency, 73-77; comdr, Air Force Systs Command, USAF, 77-78, chief staff, 78-82; dir, Jet Propulsion Lab & vpres, Calif Inst Technol, 82-91. *Mem:* Nat Acad Eng; fel Am Phys Soc; Am Geophys Union. *Mailing Add:* Charles Stark Draper Lab 1040 S Arroyo Blvd Pasadena CA 91105

ALLEN, LEWIS EDWIN, ORGANIC CHEMISTRY, ENVIRONMENTAL CHEMISTRY. *Current Pos:* MENTOR, EMPIRE STATE COL, STATE UNIV NY, 93- *Personal Data:* b Monroe, La, Aug 9, 37; m 64; c 3. *Educ:* Queens Col, BS, 58; Syracuse Univ, PhD(org chem), 70. *Prof Exp:* Assoc prof chem, Fla A&M Univ, 63-70; sr chemist, Eastman Kodak Co, 70-74, coordr environ serv, 74-82, unit dir, Environ Anal Serv, 82-92. *Concurrent Pos:* Adj assoc prof, Monroe Community Col, Rochester, NY, 92- *Mem:* Am Chem Soc; Nat Orgn Prof Advan Black Chemists & Chem Engrs. *Res:* Physical organic chemistry; stereochemistry; organometallic compounds; photographic science; disposal of photographic waste solutions. *Mailing Add:* 34 Circle Wood Rd Rochester NY 14625. *E-Mail:* lallen@sescva.esc.edu

ALLEN, LINDSAY HELEN, NUTRITION. *Current Pos:* from asst prof to assoc prof, 74-84, PROF NUTRIT, UNIV CONN, 84- *Personal Data:* b Chippenham, Eng, July 24, 46; m 89; c 1. *Educ:* Univ Nottingham, BSc, 67; Univ Calif, PhD(nutrit), 73. *Prof Exp:* Res asst nutrit, Med Res Coun, Cambridge Univ, 67-69, Univ Calif Davis, 69-73; fel nutrit, Univ Calif, Berkeley, 73-74. *Concurrent Pos:* Vis prof, Nat Inst Nutrit, Mexico City. *Mem:* Brit Nutrit Soc; Am Inst Nutrit; AAAS; Am Dietetic Asn; Am Soc Clin Nutrit; Am Anthrop Asn. *Res:* Calcium and trace mineral metabolism; assessment of nutritional status; nutrition and development; nutrition and function; international nutrition. *Mailing Add:* Dept Nutrit Sci Univ Calif Meyer Hall Davis CA 95616-8669

ALLEN, LINUS SCOTT, APPLIED PHYSICS. *Current Pos:* RETIRED. *Personal Data:* b Dallas, Tex, Dec 9, 35; m 54; c 2. *Educ:* Southern Methodist Univ, BS, 59, MS, 61, PhD(physics), 71. *Prof Exp:* Scientist reactor physics, Jet Propulsion Lab, Calif Inst Technol, 61-62; scientist, Mobil Res & Develop Corp, 62- *Mem:* Am Nuclear Soc; Soc Prof Well Log Analysts; Sigma Xi. *Res:* Development of new or improved methods for locating and assessing petroleum and mineral occurances. *Mailing Add:* 15118 Leafy Lane Dallas TX 75248

ALLEN, LISA PARECHANIAN, THIN FILM TECHNOLOGY & CRYSTAL GROWTH & CHARACTERIZATION, SILICON ON INSULATOR MATERIAL DEVELOPMENT. *Current Pos:* SR SCIENTIST, IBIS TECHNOL CORP, 90-, TECHNOL PROG MGR. *Personal Data:* b Bridgeport, Conn, May 10, 59; m 87, Scott M. *Educ:* Mass Inst Technol, SB & MS, 82; Univ Calif, Berkeley, PhD(mat eng), 87. *Prof Exp:* Staff scientist, Kopin Corp, 87-90. *Concurrent Pos:* Lectr, Dept Aeroeng, Univ Wash, 87, Dept Elec Eng, Univ Mass, 91, Dept Mat Sci & Eng, Univ Fla, 92, Mass Inst Technol, 93; consult, Epion Corp, 92-, Krytek Corp, 93-, Southern Cross Corp, 93- *Mem:* Minerals Metals & Mat Soc; Inst Elec & Electronics Engrs; Armed Forces Commun & Electronics Asn. *Res:* Growth and characterization of semiconductor thin films; program management of ion implantation processes and development of ion implanted material; granted four US patents; small business innovative research grant programs. *Mailing Add:* 3 Eagle Lane Beverly MA 01915. *Fax:* 978-777-6570; *E-Mail:* lisa_allen@ibis.com

ALLEN, LOIS BRENDA, VIROLOGY, CHEMOTHERAPY. *Current Pos:* MGR, INFECTIOUS DIS GROUP, SOUTHERN RES INST, 89- *Personal Data:* b Martin, Ky, July 4, 39. *Educ:* Georgetown Col, Ky, BS, 61; Mich State Univ, MS, 63; Univ Mich, Ann Arbor, PhD(epidemiol), 71. *Prof Exp:* From virologist to sr virologist, ICN Nucleic Acid Res Inst, 71-75, head dept virol, 75-76; asst prof microbiol & dir Virus Lab, Univ Tex Health Sci Ctr, 76-89. *Mem:* AAAS; Am Asn Immunol; Am Soc Microbiol. *Res:* Susceptibility and resistance factors of disease with emphasis on development of new antiviral drugs; development of Virazole and ara-HxMP. *Mailing Add:* Southern Res Inst PO Box 55305 Birmingham AL 35255. *Fax:* 205-581-2877; *E-Mail:* allen@ori.org

ALLEN, MALWINA I, NUCLEAR MAGNETIC RESONANCE SPECTROSCOPY. *Current Pos:* PROF CHEM, FRAMINGHAM STATE COL, 68- *Personal Data:* US citizen; c 2. *Educ:* Mass Inst Technol, SB, 52, SM, 53, PhD(chem), 60. *Prof Exp:* Res chemist, Moleculon Res Corp, 61-63; consult, Riverside Res Lab, 66-68. *Concurrent Pos:* Vis assoc, Calif Inst Technol, 76-77; vis scientist, Weizman Inst Sci, Israel, 86. *Mem:* Am Chem Soc. *Res:* Application of nuclear magnetic resonance investigation to the investigation of dynamic processes such as hydrogen bonding, segmental motion and host guest complexation; guest dynamics in solid inclusion compounds. *Mailing Add:* Framingham State Col HA 325 Framingham Center MA 01701-2471

ALLEN, MARCIA KATZMAN, MICROBIAL GENETICS. *Current Pos:* CONSULT, 86- *Personal Data:* b New York, NY, Jan 10, 35; m 57; c 3. *Educ:* Bryn Mawr Col, BA, 56; Stanford Univ, PhD(biol), 62. *Prof Exp:* NIH res fel, Mass Inst Technol, 63-65; instr molecular biol, Syntex Corp, 65-67; sr lectr biol sci, Stanford Univ, 67-82; clin studies coordr, Syva Co, 82-84; tech publ coordr, Nellcor Co, 84-85; bionet sci consult, Intelligenetics Inc, 85-86. *Res:* Biochemical genetics; biochemistry; gene action. *Mailing Add:* 325 Chatham Way Mountain View CA 94040

ALLEN, MARSHALL B, JR, NEUROSURGERY. *Current Pos:* PROF NEUROSURG & CHIEF DIV, MED COL GA, 65- *Personal Data:* b Long Beach, Miss, Oct 19, 27; m 57, Dorothy Horron; c Lori Lynn (Athey), Marshall B III & George Michael. *Educ:* Univ Miss, BA, 49; Harvard Med Sch, MD, 53. *Prof Exp:* Intern, Jefferson Med Col, 53-54; asst thoracic surg, Miss State Sanitorium, 54-55; gen pract med, Houston Hosp Inc, Miss, 55-56; resident gen surg, Sch Med, Univ Miss, 56-57, resident neurosurg, 57-61; chief serv neurosurg, Vet Admin Hosp, Jackson, Miss, 62-64. *Concurrent Pos:* Nat Inst Neurol Dis & Blindness fel neurophysiol, Hosp Henri-Rouselle, Paris, France, 61-62; consult, Vet Admin Hosp, Augusta & Ga State Penitentiary, 65- & Milledgeville State Hosp, 66- *Mem:* Am Med Asn; Cong Neurol Surgeons; Am Asn Neurol Surgeons; Soc Neurol Surgeons; Am Col Surgeons. *Res:* Neurophysiology; clinical neurosurgery. *Mailing Add:* Dept Surg Med Col Ga Augusta GA 30912. *Fax:* 706-721-8084; *E-Mail:* mballen@mail.mcg.edu

ALLEN, MARTIN, PHYSICAL CHEMISTRY. *Current Pos:* from assoc prof to prof, Univ St Thomas, 56-84, chmn dept, 75-84, dir sci & math div, 77-82, EMER PROF CHEM, UNIV ST THOMAS, 84- *Personal Data:* b New York, NY, Mar 26, 18; m 42, Sophie; c Susan, Scott, Barbara & Robert. *Educ:* Brooklyn Col, AB, 38; Univ Minn, MS, 41, PhD(phys chem), 44. *Prof Exp:* Asst, Univ Minn, 40-43, instr phys chem, 43-45; res assoc, Allegany Ballistics Lab, Md, 45; sr technician, B F Goodrich Chem Co, Ohio, 45-47; assoc prof chem, Butler Univ, 47-56. *Concurrent Pos:* Abstractor, Chem Abstr Serv, 57-77; vis prof, Univ Minn, 81-82, adj prof chem eng, 82-83, sr res assoc, 84-86; assoc dir interfacial eng, Univ Minn, 89-90; educ consult, Ctr Int Eng, 94- *Mem:* AAAS; Am Chem Soc; Fedn Am Scientists. *Res:* Thermodynamics; solutions of electrolytes; properties of high polymers; solubility of silver acetate in mixed solvents containing other electrolytes; surfactants. *Mailing Add:* 4620 Bassett Creek Ln Golden Valley MN 55422. *Fax:* 612-626-9563; *E-Mail:* allen046@gold.tc.umn.edu

ALLEN, MARVIN CARROL, ANALYTICAL CHEMISTRY. *Current Pos:* Res scientist, 69-93, CHIEF CHEM, CONOCO, 93- *Personal Data:* b Searcy, Ark, Nov 30, 39; m 65; c 2. *Educ:* Ark State Univ, BS, 61; Univ Ark, MS, 64, PhD(phys chem), 67. *Mem:* Am Chem Soc; Sigma Xi. *Res:* Separation and quantitation of organic compounds by thin layer chromatography and high performance liquid chromatography; characterization of polynuclear aromatic compounds in petroleum fractions by fluorescence spectrophotometry and/or chromatography. *Mailing Add:* 13841 Silverton Dr Broomfield CO 80020-6030

ALLEN, MARY A MENNES, MICROBIOLOGY. *Current Pos:* from instr to assoc prof, 68-80, William R Kenan Jr prof, 82-90, PROF BIOL SCI, WELLESLEY COL, 80-, JEAN GLASSCOCK PROF, 89- *Personal Data:* b Owatonna, Minn, Apr 26, 38; m 61. *Educ:* Univ Wis-Madison, BS, 60, MS, 61; Univ Calif, Berkeley, PhD(microbiol), 66. *Prof Exp:* USPHS trainee, Univ Calif, Berkeley, 62-63. *Concurrent Pos:* Res assoc dept biol sci, Tufts Univ, 68; Brown-Hazen res grant, Res Corp, 69; NSF res grants, 71-; Cottrel Col sci grants, Res Corp, 73 & 80; NIH res grant, 90-93; chair, Biol Coun, Coun Undergrad Res, 89-91. *Mem:* Fel AAAS; Phycol Soc Am; Am Soc Cell Biol; Am Soc Microbiol; Coun Undergrad Res. *Res:* Biochemistry and physiology of cyanobacteria; growth and cell division of unicellular blue-green algae; nitrogen chlorosis and heterotrophy in cyanobacteria; effect of changes in environment on cyanobacteria. *Mailing Add:* Dept Biol Sci Wellesley Col 106 Central St Wellesley MA 02181

ALLEN, MATTHEW ARNOLD, PHYSICS. *Current Pos:* mem tech staff & head dept, 65-90, ASSOC LAB DIR, STANFORD LINEAR ACCELERATOR CTR, STANFORD UNIV, 90- *Personal Data:* b Edinburgh, Scotland, Apr 27, 30; US citizen; m 57, Marcia Katzman; c Bruce W, Peter J & David M. *Educ:* Univ Edinburgh, BSc, 51; Stanford Univ, PhD(physics), 59. *Prof Exp:* Res assoc microwave physics, Hansen Labs, Stanford Univ, 55-61; mgr, Res Tube Div, Microwave Assocs, Inc, Mass, 61-65. *Mem:* Fel Am Phys Soc; fel Inst Elec & Electronics Engrs. *Res:* Microwave electronics; accelerator and plasma physics; high energy electron-positron storage ring research. *Mailing Add:* Stanford Linear Accelerator Ctr Stanford Univ PO Box 4349 Stanford CA 94309

ALLEN, MAX SCOTT, INTERNAL MEDICINE. *Current Pos:* From assoc prof to oprof, 50-81, EMER PROF MED, UNIV KANS MED CTR, KANSAS CITY, 81- *Personal Data:* b Chanute, Kans, Jan 13, 11; m 37; c 3. *Educ:* Univ Wichita, AB, 33, Univ Kans, MD, 37. *Mem:* AMA; fel Am Col Physicians; Am Asn Hist Med. *Res:* Clinical research in internal medicine. *Mailing Add:* 8101 Mission Rd Shawnee Mission KS 66208

ALLEN, MERRILL JAMES, VISION & HIGHWAY SAFETY, TRANSPORTATION RESEARCH. *Current Pos:* from asst prof to prof, 53-87, EMER PROF OPTOM, IND UNIV, BLOOMINGTON, 87- *Personal Data:* b San Antonio, Tex, Aug 2, 18; m 42, Mary J Gower; c Marjorie J & Merrill J Jr. *Educ:* Ohio State Univ, BSc, 41, MSc, 42, PhD(physiol optics), 49. *Honors & Awards:* Res Medal, Brit Optical Asn, 70; Apollo Award, Am Optom Asn, 71, Cert of Commendation, 73; Mike Drain Mem Award, Mid Am Vision Conf, 89. *Prof Exp:* Grad asst, Ohio State Univ, 41-43, asst prof, 49-53; physicist, Frankfort Arsenal, Pa, 43-44. *Concurrent Pos:* Visual consult to attys, 52-; mem adv panel automotive safety, US Gen Serv Admin, 66-69; consult, Potters Indust, Inc, 79-87 & Gen Motors Tech Ctr, 85-87; guest speaker, Kikuchi Optical Co, Nagoya, Japan, 80; transp res ctr assoc, Ind Univ, 90; chmn, Int Colour Blind Comt, 93- *Mem:* Am Optom Asn; AAAS; Sigma Xi; Physicians Automotive Safety; Am Asn Automotive Med; Am Asn Univ Profs; Am Acad Optom. *Res:* Vision related problems in drivers and in the design of vehicles, highways and railroads; attorney subsidized research; visual training, electrical stimulation and nutritional therapy of vision; published 235 articles and granted several patents. *Mailing Add:* Ind Univ Sch Optom Bloomington IN 47405. *Fax:* 812-855-7045

ALLEN, MICHAEL THOMAS, psychophysiology, for more information see previous edition

ALLEN, MYRON BARTLETT, III, NUMERICAL ANALYSIS, PARTIAL DIFFERENTIAL EQUATIONS. *Current Pos:* from asst prof to assoc prof, 83-92, PROF & HEAD MATH, UNIV WYO, 92- *Personal Data:* b Winder, Ga, Aug 2, 54; m 89. *Educ:* Dartmouth Col, AB, 76; Princeton Univ, MA, 78, PhD(math eng), 83. *Prof Exp:* Scientist, Eng Resource Co Inc, 78-80. *Concurrent Pos:* Vis assoc prof eng, Univ Vt, 91-92. *Mem:* Soc Indust & Appl Math; Math Asn Am; Am Geophys Union; Soc Petrol Engrs. *Res:* Numerical analysis of porous-media flows. *Mailing Add:* Dept Math Univ Wyo Laramie WY 82071. *Fax:* 307-766-6838; *E-Mail:* allen@uwyo.edu

ALLEN, NEIL KEITH, POULTRY NUTRITION & ANIMAL NUTRITION, ANIMAL PHYSIOLOGY, SWING NUTRITION. *Current Pos:* NUTRITIONIST, GOLDSBORO MILLING CO, NC, 85- *Personal Data:* b Elburn, Ill, July 24, 44; m 79, Sandra Aakhus. *Educ:* Univ Ill, Urbana, BS, 67, MS, 68, PhD(animal sci), 71. *Prof Exp:* Res asst animal nutrit, Univ Ill, Urbana, 67-71; res assoc poultry nutrit, Cornell Univ, 71-73; formulation mgr, Dawe's Lab, Inc, 73-75; asst prof animal sci, Univ Minn, St Paul, 75-82. *Mem:* Poultry Sci Asn; Am Animal Sci Asn. *Res:* Protein and amino acid requirements of turkeys as a function of age and production; effects of fusariummycotoxins on poultry; nutrition of swine. *Mailing Add:* Goldsboro Milling Co PO Box 10009 Goldsboro NC 27532. *Fax:* 919-778-8111

ALLEN, NINA STROMGREN, LIGHT MICROSCOPY & VIDEO IMAGES, PLANT CELL BIOLOGY. *Current Pos:* assoc prof, 84-93, PROF BIOL, WAKE FOREST UNIV, 93- *Personal Data:* b Copenhagen, Denmark, Sept 17, 35; wid; c Erik R, Harriet D (Hopf), Barbara S, Elizabeth H & Wayne E. *Educ:* Univ Wis, BS, 57; Univ Md, Col Park, MS, 70, PhD(plant physiol), 73. *Prof Exp:* Teaching asst bot, Univ Wis-Madison, 57-58; teaching asst, Univ Md, College Park, 64-67, res asst, 67-70; res asst biol, State Univ NY, Albany, 70-73, res assoc, 73-75; vis asst prof biol, Dartmouth Col, 75-76, asst prof, 76-83. *Concurrent Pos:* NIH fel, 67-70; Trustee exec comt, Corp Marine Biol Lab, Woods Hole, Mass, 79-82; chmn, Women in Cell Biol, Am Soc Cell Biol, 84-85; series ed, Plant Biol, Alan R Liss, Inc, 85-; mem Biomed Res Technol Rev Comt, NIH, 88, 89; NSF vis prof women, Stanford Univ, 90-91. *Mem:* Am Soc Plant Physiologists; fel AAAS; Sigma Xi; Am Soc Cell Biol; Phycological Soc Am; Am Soc Gravitational & Space Biol; Electron Micros Soc Am. *Res:* Cell biology and cell motility; study of movements in and of plant (especially algae) and animal cells with a particular interest in the cytoskeleton and the endoplasmic reticulum and its relation to cytoplasmic streaming and intracellular particle motions, signal transduction; high resolution video-enhanced light microscopy, electron microscopy and vibrating probe analysis; gliding motility of bacteria. *Mailing Add:* Dept Bot NC State Univ PO Box 7612 Raleigh NC 27695-7612. *Fax:* 910-759-6008; *E-Mail:* allen@wfunet.wfu.edu

ALLEN, NORRIS ELLIOTT, MICROBIOLOGY. *Current Pos:* sr microbiologist, 71-78, res scientist, 79-87, SR RES SCIENTIST, LILLY RES LABS, ELI LILLY & CO, 87- *Personal Data:* b Baltimore, Md, Sept 15, 39; m 64, Carole Medley; c Carrie. *Educ:* Univ Md, BS, 64, MS, 66, PhD(microbiol), 69. *Prof Exp:* Res assoc biol, Univ Pa, 69-71. *Mem:* Am Soc Microbiol; Soc Indust Microbiol; AAAS. *Res:* Mechanisms of antibiotic action and resistance; screening and evaluation of new antimicrobial agents. *Mailing Add:* 1481 E 77th Indianapolis IN 46240. *Fax:* 317-277-0778; *E-Mail:* nea@lilly.com

ALLEN, PETER MARTIN, HYDROLOGY, GEOLOGY. *Current Pos:* lectr, 78-79, ASST PROF GEOL, BAYLOR UNIV, 79- *Personal Data:* b Chicago, Ill, Sept 18, 47; m 79; c 1. *Educ:* Denison Univ, BA, 70; Baylor Univ, MS, 72; Southern Methodist Univ, PhD(geol), 77. *Prof Exp:* Geologist & planner, Dept Planning, City Dallas, 72-78. *Concurrent Pos:* Consult, Dept Urban Planning, Dallas, 78-82. *Mem:* Asn Eng Geologists; Asn Prof Geol Scientists; Am Planning Asn. *Res:* Analysis of geological information for land use planning, urban geology and geomorphology: stream chanel enlargement due to urbanization, hillslope ordinances, shrink-swell soils, archaeology and flood plain use, bed load transport and gravel mining. *Mailing Add:* Dept Geol Baylor Univ PO Box 97354 Waco TX 76706-9989

ALLEN, PETER ZACHARY, immunology, immunochemistry, for more information see previous edition

ALLEN, PHILIP B, ELECTRONIC STRUCTURE THEORY, TRANSPORT THEORY. *Current Pos:* from asst prof to assoc prof, 71-81, PROF PHYSICS, STATE UNIV NY, STONY BROOK, 81- *Personal Data:* b Boston, Mass, Sept 22, 42; m 64, Ellen M Sweetser; c Elizabeth, Katherine, Emily & Benjamin. *Educ:* Amherst Col, BA, 64; Univ Calif, Berkeley, PhD(physics), 69. *Honors & Awards:* US Sr Scientist Award, Alexander von Humboldt Found, 84. *Prof Exp:* Mem tech staff res, Bell Tel Labs, 70-71. *Concurrent Pos:* Vis researcher, Cavendish Lab, Cambridge, Eng, 73-74; vis assoc prof, Univ Calif, Berkeley, 76-77; vis scientist, Max-Planck Inst Solid State Res, 79-80 & 84, Naval Res Lab, 87; B Mathias vis scholar, Los Alamos Nat Lab, 90; vis scholar, IRRMA, Lausanne, Switzerland, 94-95. *Mem:* Fel Am Phys Soc; Am Asn Physics Teachers; AAAS; Mat Res Soc. *Res:* Theory of solids; electronic structure and electron-phonon interactions; transport properties; superconducting transition temperature; vibrations and heat transport in glasses. *Mailing Add:* Dept Physics State Univ NY Stony Brook NY 11794-3800. *E-Mail:* philip.allen@sunysb.edu

ALLEN, PHILIP G, ANATOMIC BIOLOGY. *Current Pos:* POSTDOCTORAL RES FEL, DEPT MOLECULAR MED, BRIGHAM & WOMEN'S HOSP, 91- *Educ:* Colby Col, AB, 83; Harvard Univ, PhD(cell & develop biol), 89. *Prof Exp:* Postdoctoral res fel, Dept Anat & Cellular Biol, LHRRB, Harvard Med Sch, 90-91. *Mem:* Am Soc Cell Biol; AAAS. *Mailing Add:* Div Exptl Med LMRC301 Brigham & Women's Hosp 221 Longwood Ave Boston MA 02115-5701

ALLEN, RALPH ORVILLE, JR, HAZARDOUS WASTE MANAGEMENT, FORENSIC ANALYSIS. *Current Pos:* From asst prof to assoc prof, 70-85, PROF CHEM, UNIV VA, 85-, DIR ENVIRON HEALTH & SAFETY, 81-, PROF ENVIRON SCI, 90- *Personal Data:* b Nashville, Tenn, Aug 3, 43; m 65, Karen Kubly; c Krister, Karakahl & Katriel. *Educ:* Cornell Col, BA, 65; Univ Wis-Madison, PhD(chem), 70. *Honors & Awards:*

Erickson Award, Nat Acad-Fed Bur Invest, 84. *Concurrent Pos:* Vis scientist, Chem Div, Argonne Nat Lab, 70-76 & Norweg Inst Atomic Energy, 77-78; res fel, Norweg Marshall Fund, Univ Trondheim, 85. *Mem:* Am Chem Soc; Sigma Xi. *Res:* Development of analytical techniques for monitoring air pollutants; application of nuclear techniques to study trace element geochemistry and archaeological materials; forensic analysis. *Mailing Add:* 80 Apple Lane Charlottesville VA 22903. *Fax:* 804-982-4921; *E-Mail:* roa2s@virginia.edu

ALLEN, RANDY DALE, PLANT GENE EXPRESSION, PLANT STRESS. *Current Pos:* asst prof, 89-94, ASSOC PROF BIOL, DEPT BIOL SCI, TEX TECH UNIV, 94- *Personal Data:* b Lincoln, Nebr, Mar 11, 56; m 78, Kathryn J Flyger; c Eric & Sarah. *Educ:* Southwestern Adventist Col, BS, 78; Univ Tex, Arlington, MA, 82; Tex A&M Univ, PhD(biol), 86. *Prof Exp:* Res assoc, Dept Biol, Washington Univ, St Louis, 86-89. *Mem:* Am Soc Plant Physiologists; Int Soc Plant Molecular Biol. *Res:* Analysis of the protective properties of anti-oxidant enzymes in the protection of plants from environmental stress; molecular genetic manipulation of superoxide dismutase catalase and ascorbate peroxidase expression in transgenic plants and physiological analysis to determine the protective effects of modifications. *Mailing Add:* Dept Biol Sci Tex Tech Univ Lubbock TX 79409-0001. *Fax:* 806-742-2963; *E-Mail:* brrda@ttacsi.ttu.edu

ALLEN, RAYMOND A, PATHOLOGY. *Current Pos:* PROF PATH, UNIV CALIF, IRVINE, 76-, PROF OPHTHAL, 77- *Personal Data:* b Lyman, Utah, Nov 7, 21; m 60; c 2. *Educ:* Univ Utah, BS, 46; Univ Louisville, MD; Univ Minn, MS, 54. *Prof Exp:* Asst path & microbiol, Rockefeller Inst, 54-56; from asst prof to prof path, Univ Calif, Los Angeles, 56-68, assoc dir, Jules Stein Eye Inst, 66-68; pathologist, Good Samaritan Hosp, Phoenix, Ariz, 68-70; chief path & dir labs, St Dominic-Jackson Mem Hosp, 70-75; pathologist, Centinela Hosp, Inglewood, 75-76. *Concurrent Pos:* Attend physician, Los Angeles County Harbor Gen Hosp, 55-67; consult, Vet Admin Ctr, Los Angeles, Calif, 54-67; staff physician, Long Beach Veterans Admin Hosp, 76- *Mem:* AAAS; Am Soc Clin Path; Col Am Path; Int Acad Path. *Res:* Clinical pathology; pathology of eye disease. *Mailing Add:* 1272 Via Landeta Palos Verdes Peninsula CA 90274-1969

ALLEN, RICHARD CHARLES, MEDICINAL CHEMISTRY. *Current Pos:* res assoc, Chem Res Dept, Hoechst-Roussel Pharmaceut, Inc, NJ, 70-72, res group supvr, 73-74, dir chem res, 74-89, group dir, 89-91, VPRES & GEN MGR NEUROSCI, HOECHST-ROUSSEL PHARMACEUT, INC, NJ, 91- *Personal Data:* b Nov 22, 42; m 66; c 5. *Educ:* Med Col Va, BS, 65, PhD(med chem), 68. *Prof Exp:* Res fel, Univ NC, Chapel Hill, 68-69, instr med chem, Sch Pharm, 69-70. *Mem:* Sigma Xi; Am Chem Soc; Int Soc Heterocyclic Chem; Asn Res Vision & Ophthal; NY Acad Sci; Am Chem Soc. *Mailing Add:* 155 Hillcrest Rd Flemington NJ 08822

ALLEN, RICHARD CRENSHAW, JR, APPLIED MATHEMATICS. *Current Pos:* ASST PROF MATH, UNIV NMEX, 68- *Personal Data:* b Detroit, Mich, July 17, 33; m 56; c 2. *Educ:* Murray State Univ, BS, 59; Univ Mo-Columbia, MA, 60; Univ Colo, 64-66; Univ NMex, PhD(math), 68. *Prof Exp:* Mathematician, Martin-Marietta Corp, Colo, 60-64. *Mem:* Am Math Soc; Soc Indust & Appl Math. *Res:* Transport theory; analytical and numerical studies of partial differential integral equations arising from transport theory; numerical solution of two-point boundary value problems, linear and nonlinear; integral equations and ordinary differential equations. *Mailing Add:* Sandia Nat Labs Dir Org 1422 PO Box 5800 Albuquerque NM 87185-1110

ALLEN, RICHARD DEAN, MEMBRANE BIOLOGY, ELECTRONMICROSCOPY. *Current Pos:* assoc prof, 69-75, PROF MICROBIOL, PAC BIOMED RES CTR, UNIV HAWAII, MANOA, 75-, DIR, BIOL EM FACIL, 85- *Personal Data:* b Dallas Center, Iowa, Sept 20, 35; wid; c Lorna, Steven & William. *Educ:* Greenville Col, BA, 57; Univ Ill, MS, 60; Iowa State Univ, PhD(cell biol), 64. *Honors & Awards:* Seymour H Hutner Prize, Soc Protozoologists, 78. *Prof Exp:* Teacher sci & math, Niagara Christian Col, Ont, 57-59; instr biol & bot, Greenville Col, 60-61; asst prof biol, Messiah Col, 65-68; lectr biol & res assoc electron micros, Biol Labs, Harvard Univ, 68-69. *Concurrent Pos:* NIH res fel cell biol, Biol Labs, Harvard Univ, 64-65; prin investr, NIH grants, 72-79 & 80-82; vis prof, Univ Colo, Boulder, 75-76; bd reviewers, J Protozool, 75-79 & 81-86, J Histochem & Cytochem,; Am Heart Asn grant, 76-78; mem grad fac, trop med, Univ Hawaii, 77-, cellular, molecular & neurosci, 88-; NSF grants, 79-82, 81-84, 82-85, 83-84, 84-87, 84-85, 85-88, 88-90, 88-91, 89-92, 89-91, 91-93, 92-95 & 95-98; co-ed, Europ J Cell Biol, 79-84; ed, Protoplasma, 90- *Mem:* Fel AAAS; Soc Protozool (pres, 81-82); Am Soc Cell Biologists; Sigma Xi. *Res:* Fine structure, function and morphogenesis of cell organelles and organelle systems with emphasis on ciliated protozoans; studies on intracellular digestion; membrane reutilization and contractile vacuole function. *Mailing Add:* Dept Microbiol 2538 The Mall Univ Hawaii Honolulu HI 96822. *Fax:* 808-956-5339; *E-Mail:* allen@pbrc.hawaii.edu

ALLEN, RICHARD GLEN, EVAPOTRANSPIRATION, IRRIGATION MANAGEMENT. *Current Pos:* asst prof, 86-90, ASSOC PROF IRRIG ENG, UTAH STATE UNIV, 91- *Personal Data:* b Sioux City, Iowa, Mar 8, 52; m 79; c 3. *Educ:* Iowa State Univ, Ames, BS, 74; Univ Idaho, Moscow, MS, 77, PhD(civil eng), 84. *Prof Exp:* Res assoc water resources, Univ Idaho, 77-83; asst prof civil eng, Iowa State Univ, 84-85. *Concurrent Pos:* Consult, US Agency Int Develop, 88-90, UN Food & Agr Org, 88-91, UN Develop Prog, 90-91; chmn, Irrig Water Req Comm, Am Soc Civil Eng, 88-91, Int Symp Lysimeters Eng, Honolulu, HI, 88-91; expert panel, Crop Water Req, UN Food & Agr Org, Rome, Italy, 90-91; co-ed, Am Soc Civil Eng Manual Evapotranspiration, 90. *Mem:* Am Soc Civil Eng; Am Soc Agr Eng; Am Geophys Union; Am Water Resources Asn; Int Comn Irrig & Drainage. *Res:* Evapotranspiration measurement and equation development; irrigation water requirements; water management; computer modeling; soil moisture movement; finite element; sprinkler design; climate change. *Mailing Add:* Dept Agr Eng Utah State Univ Logan UT 84322-4105

ALLEN, ROBERT B, COMPUTER SCIENCE. *Current Pos:* SR SCIENTIST, BELLCORE. *Personal Data:* b Pittsburgh, Pa, Sept 16, 51; c Dianne K. *Educ:* Reed Col, BA, 73; Univ Calif, San Diego, PhD(exp psychol), 79. *Prof Exp:* Mem tech staff, Bell Labs, 78-85; mem tech staff, Bell Commun Res, 85- *Concurrent Pos:* Ed-in-chief, Asn Comput Mach Trans & Info Systs, 84- *Mem:* Asn Comput Mach; sr mem Inst Elec & Electronics Engrs. *Mailing Add:* Bellcore IA 352R 445 South St Morristown NJ 07960

ALLEN, ROBERT CARTER, PATHOLOGY, MOLECULAR BIOLOGY. *Current Pos:* assoc prof path, 73-76, prof & chmn, 76-85, PROF PATH, DEPT LAB ANIMAL MED, MED UNIV SC, 81- *Personal Data:* b Natick, Mass, Feb 5, 30; m 56; c 2. *Educ:* Univ Vt, BS, 52, MS, 55; Va Polytech Inst, PhD(bact), 59. *Honors & Awards:* Electrophoresis Soc Award, 92. *Prof Exp:* Asst prof vet path, Va Polytech Inst, 55-60; NIH training grant, Jackson Mem Lab, 60-62; sr scientist radiation path, Oak Ridge Nat Lab, 62-68; sr scientist life sci, Ortec Inc, 68-73. *Concurrent Pos:* Consult, Biol Div, Oak Ridge Nat Lab, 68-69; guest prof, Univ Heidelberg, 71-72, 74 & 82; consult, Vet Admin Hosp, Charleston, 76-85; vis scientist, Nat Inst Stand & Technol, 89-90; guest scientist, NIMH, 96. *Mem:* AAAS; Am Soc Biochem & Molecular Biol; Am Soc Clin Path; Electrophoresis Soc. *Res:* Chronic obstructive lung disease; isozymes, proteinases and antiproteinases; molecular pathology; electrophoretic methodology. *Mailing Add:* Dept Path Med Univ SC Charleston SC 29425-2645. *Fax:* 803-792-4157

ALLEN, ROBERT CHARLES, INFLAMMATION, CHEMILUMINESCENCE. *Current Pos:* MED DIR, SMITHKLINE BEECHAM CLIN LABS, SAN ANTONIO, TEX, 93-; DIR CLIN RES SERV, TEX HEADACHE INST & FACIAL PAIN CTR, SAN ANTONIO, 97- *Personal Data:* b Pueblo, Colo, Aug 12, 45; m 76; c Robert L, Christina M & John C. *Educ:* Southeastern La Univ, BS, 67; Tulane Univ, PhD(biochem), 73, MD, 77; Am Bd Path, dipl, 85. *Prof Exp:* Res assoc biochem, Tulane Univ, New Orleans, La, 73-76; intern med, Brooke Army Med Ctr, Ft Sam Houston, Tex, 77-78, resident clin path 83-85; med officer infectious dis, US Army Inst Surg Res, Ft Sam Houston, 78-83, med officer infectious dis & path, 85-87; sci dir, Exoxemis, Inc, San Antonio, Tex, 87-96. *Concurrent Pos:* Consult ed, J Leukocyte Biol, 84-85; ed, Wiley-Intersci Press, 86- & J Bioluminescence Chemiluminescence. *Mem:* Am Asn Immunologists; Am Soc Biol Chemists; fel Am Soc Clin Pathologists; Am Soc Microbiol; Am Soc Invest Path; Am Soc Biochem & Molecular Biol; fel Col Am Pathologists; Soc Leukocyte Biol. *Res:* Chemistry of oxygen and biological redox reactions; oxygenation reactions yielding excited products and chemiluminescence; granulocytic leukocyte and macrophage microbicidial action; humoral immune mechanisms; haloperoxidase-based therapeutics; basic and clinical research in broad areas of inflammation. *Mailing Add:* 601 N Frio St San Antonio TX 78207. *Fax:* 210-822-0948; *E-Mail:* 73372.612@compuserve.com

ALLEN, ROBERT ERWIN, MEDICAL PHYSIOLOGY, RESEARCH ADMINISTRATION. *Current Pos:* spec asst to dir, Med Res Serv, 78-87, dep dir, Aids Prog Off, 88-90, SPEC ASST, ENVIRON MED & PUB HEALTH OFF, VET ADMIN, WASHINGTON, DC, 90- *Personal Data:* b Lufkin, Tex, Oct 9, 41; m 69, Roma L Trobaugh; c Jennifer K & David W. *Educ:* Stephen F Austin State Col, BA, 63; Vanderbilt Univ, PhD(med physiol), 68. *Prof Exp:* Mem staff human factors eng, NASA, 68-72, sect chief biomet sect, 72-74, br chief biotechnol br, 74-76; spec asst to vpres, Univ Ala Med Sch, Birmingham, 76; fel NIH, Bethesda, Md, 76-78. *Res:* Exercise and aerospace physiology, transfer RNA and protein synthesis. *Mailing Add:* Dept Vet Affairs 116 810 Vermont Ave NW Washington DC 20420-0001. *Fax:* 202-535-7572

ALLEN, ROBERT H, HEMATOLOGY. *Current Pos:* PROF MED & DIR, DIV HEMAT, HEALTH SCI CTR, UNIV COLO, DENVER, 77-, PROF BIOCHEM, BIOPHYS & GENETICS, 80- *Personal Data:* b Detroit, Mich, Apr 15, 38; m; c 2. *Educ:* Amherst Col, BA, 60; Wash Univ, St Louis, MD, 66; Am Bd Internal Med, cert, 74, cert hemat, 76. *Prof Exp:* Intern med, Parkland Mem Hosp, Dallas, 66-67; staff assoc, Nat Inst Arthritis, Metab & Digestive Dis, 67-69; sr resident med, Barnes Hosp, St Louis, 69-70; fel hemat-oncol, Sch Med, Wash Univ, St Louis, 70-72, from asst prof to assoc prof med, 72-77. *Concurrent Pos:* Am Cancer Soc fac res award, 74-78; mem, Vet Admin Hemat Study Sect, 75-77, chmn, 77; mem, Task Force Vitamin B12 Assay, Nat Comt Clin Lab Standards, 79-82. *Mem:* Sigma Xi; Asn Am Physicians; Am Soc Clin Invest; Am Soc Hemat; Am Soc Biol Chemists; Am Fedn Clin Res. *Res:* Cobalamin metabolism and the cellular uptake of macromolecules; author of more than 80 technical publications. *Mailing Add:* Div Hemat Campus Box B170 Univ Colo Health Sci Ctr 4200 E Ninth Ave Denver CO 80262-0001

ALLEN, ROBERT HARRY, expert systems, tactile sensing, for more information see previous edition

ALLEN, ROBERT MAX, FORESTRY. *Current Pos:* RETIRED. *Personal Data:* b Ill, June 5, 21; m 46; c 3. *Educ:* Iowa State Univ, BS, 47, MS, 51; Duke Univ, PhD(tree physiol), 58. *Prof Exp:* Forester, Southern Forest Exp Sta, US Forest Serv, 48-57, plant physiologist, 57-66; Belle W Baruch prof forestry, Clemson Univ, 66-70, head dept, 70-82, prof, 70-92. *Mem:* Fel Soc Am Foresters. *Res:* Tree physiology and genetics; growth of southern pine. *Mailing Add:* 1562 Ft Hill Dr Seneca SC 29678

ALLEN, ROBERT PAUL, HYDROCARBON RESINS. *Current Pos:* From chemist to sr chemist, 70-90, DEVELOP ASSOC, TEX EASTMAN CO, 91- *Personal Data:* b Milwaukee, Wis, Jan 13, 41; m 63; c 3. *Educ:* Univ Wis-Milwaukee, BS, 65; Univ NDak, PhD(org chem), 70. *Res:* Resin chemistry; vapor-phase processes; heterogeneous catalysis; mass spectrometry. *Mailing Add:* 4 Wildwood Ct Longview TX 75604

ALLEN, ROBERT THOMAS, systematic entomology, for more information see previous edition

ALLEN, ROBERT WADE, MOLECULAR IMMUNOLOGY, IMMUNOGENETICS. *Current Pos:* DIR HUMAN IDENTIFICATION, H A CHAPMAN INST MED GENETICS, 92- *Personal Data:* b 1950; c 2. *Educ:* Univ Tulsa, BS, 72; Purdue Univ, PhD(cell biol), 77. *Prof Exp:* Fel molecular immunol, Scripps Clin & Res Found, 77-80; asst sci dir, Am Red Cross, 81-85; asst prof, Sch Med, St Louis Univ, 81-91. *Concurrent Pos:* Am Red Cross res grant awardee; sci dir, Am Red Cross, 85-91. *Mem:* AAAS; NY Acad Sci; Am Soc Hemat; Am Soc Cell & Molecular Biol. *Res:* Isolation/characterization of DNA probes detecting polymorphisms in the human genome and their use in paternity testing & forensics eg: "DNA Fingerprinting". *Mailing Add:* H A Chapman Inst Med Genetics 5300 E Skelly Dr Tulsa OK 74135

ALLEN, ROBIN LESLIE, fisheries, statistics, for more information see previous edition

ALLEN, ROGER BAKER, PHYSICAL CHEMISTRY, OPERATION RESEARCH. *Current Pos:* RETIRED. *Personal Data:* b Portland, Maine, Mar 26, 29; m 54; c 3. *Educ:* Univ Idaho, BS, 51; Univ NH, MS, 57, PhD(chem), 59. *Prof Exp:* Res chemist, Electrochem Syst, US Naval Ord Lab, Md, 59-61; Res chemist, S D Warren Co Div, Scott Paper Co, 61-92. *Mem:* Am Chem Soc; Tech Asn Pulp & Paper Indust. *Res:* Kinetic studies of electrochemical systems for ordnance hardware; specialty coatings for paper, pressure sensitive adhesive systems, grease resistance, lithographic and electrophotographic. *Mailing Add:* 23 Mitchell Rd South Portland ME 04106-4822

ALLEN, ROGER W, JR, MATHEMATICS. *Current Pos:* PROF & CHMN MATH, FRANCIS MARION COL, 71- *Personal Data:* b Montgomery, Ala, Sept 25, 41; m; c 3. *Educ:* Auburn Univ, BS, 63; Univ Va, MA, 66, PhD(math), 68. *Mem:* Am Math Soc; Math Asn Am; Nat Coun Teachers Math. *Mailing Add:* Dept Math & Comput Sci Francis Marion Univ Florence SC 29501-0547

ALLEN, ROLAND EMERY, THEORETICAL PHYSICS. *Current Pos:* from asst prof to assoc prof 70-83, PROF PHYSICS, TEX A&M UNIV, 83- *Personal Data:* b Houston, Tex, Sept 3, 41; m 83, Susan Milliken; c Ethan. *Educ:* Rice Univ, BA, 63; Univ Tex, Austin, PhD(physics), 68. *Prof Exp:* Resident assoc, Argonne Nat Lab, 69; res assoc physics, Univ Tex, Austin, 69-70. *Concurrent Pos:* Scientist, Solar Energy Res Inst, Golden, Colo, 79-80, vis assoc prof physics, Univ Ill-Urbana, 80-81. *Mem:* AAAS; Am Phys Soc; fel Am Vacuum Soc. *Res:* Theoretical physics. *Mailing Add:* Dept Physics Tex A&M Univ College Station TX 77843. *Fax:* 409-845-2590; *E-Mail:* allen@tamu.edu

ALLEN, RYNE C, cold plasma research, anodic arc-cathodic arc coating techniques, for more information see previous edition

ALLEN, S JAMES, JR, PHYSICS. *Current Pos:* PROF PHYSICS & DIR, CTR FREE-ELECTRON LASER STUDIES, UNIV CALIF, SANTA BARBARA, 91-, DIR, QUANTUM WST, 92- *Educ:* Mass Inst Tech, BS, 60, MS, 61, PhD(elec eng), 65. *Honors & Awards:* Humboldt Sr Sci Award, 95 *Prof Exp:* Mem staff, Bell Labs, Murray Hill, 65-83, distinguished mem tech staff, 83; dist res mgr solid state physics res, Bellcore, 83-91. *Concurrent Pos:* Metall & Mat Sci, Imp Col, 74-75; adj prof, Princeton, 88, Northeastern Univ, 89-90; mem, Solid State Sci Comt, Nat Res Coun, 94- *Mem:* Fel Am Phys Soc. *Res:* Hot-electron dynamics, high temperature superconductivity; granted three patents; transport in semiconductor nano-structures; submillimeter wave transport in semiconductor nanostructures; magnetism, superionic conductors, metal physics and clothrate inclusion compounds; author and co-author of over 140 publications. *Mailing Add:* Quantum Inst Univ Calif Santa Barbara CA 93106

ALLEN, SALLY LYMAN, GENETICS. *Current Pos:* res asst, 53-54, res assoc zool, 55-73, from assoc prof to prof bot, 67-75, prof zool, 73-75, chairperson cell & molecular biol dept, Div Biol Sci,75-76, PROF BIOL SCI & BIOL, UNIV MICH, 75-, PROF BIOL, 75-, ASSOC DEAN, 88- *Personal Data:* b New York, NY, Aug 3, 26; c 1. *Educ:* Vassar Col, AB, 46; Univ Chicago, PhD(zool), 54. *Prof Exp:* Asst, R B Jackson Mem Lab, Bar Harbor, 46-48. *Concurrent Pos:* Assoc prof bot, Univ Mich, 67-70; vis prof genetics, Ind Univ, 67; assoc ed, Genetics, 73-; mem, Coun Am Soc Cell Biol, 73-75; consult, Am Type Cult Collection, 76-; assoc ed, Developmental Genetics, 90- *Mem:* Genetics Soc Am; Am Soc Cell Biol; Am Soc Zool; Soc Protozool; Sigma Xi; fel AAAS. *Res:* Genetics of tumor transplantation; bacteriophage and protozoan genetics; isozymes of protozoa; phenotypic drift; genomic exclusion; DNA hybridization between species of Tetrahymena; comparison of DNA sequences of micronucleus and macronucleus of Tetrahymena thermophila. *Mailing Add:* Biol Dept Univ Mich 830 N University Ann Arbor MI 48109-1048. *Fax:* 313-747-0884

ALLEN, SAMUEL MILLER, PHASE TRANSFORMATIONS. *Current Pos:* res assoc, 77-79, asst prof, 79-83, ASSOC PROF METALL, MASS INST TECHNOL, 83- *Personal Data:* b Washington, DC, July 1, 48; m 73; c 2. *Educ:* Stevens Inst Technol, BE, 70; Mass Inst Technol, SM, 71, PhD(metall), 75. *Prof Exp:* Instr metall, Mass Inst Technol, 74-75, res assoc, 75-76; res engr, Univ Calif, Berkeley, 76. *Concurrent Pos:* Vis lectr, Univ Calif, Berkeley, 76. *Mem:* Am Soc Metals; Am Inst Mech Engrs Metall Soc; Electron Micros Soc Am; Sigma Xi; Mat Res Soc. *Res:* Physical metallurgy; the theory of phase transformations, the structure and behavior of interfaces in materials and the experimental study of these phenomena using electron microscopy. *Mailing Add:* Mass Inst Technol Rm 13-5018 Cambridge MA 02139

ALLEN, SANDRA LEE, PHYSICAL CHEMISTRY, COLLOID CHEMISTRY. *Current Pos:* EDUC PRESENTATIONS, 87- *Personal Data:* b Kingston, Ont, Jan 18, 48; m 68; c 4. *Educ:* Univ Western Ont, BSc, 68; Clarkson Col Technol, MS, 71, PhD(phys chem), 72. *Prof Exp:* Res assoc phys chem, Pulp & Paper Res Inst Can, McGill Univ, 72-74; proj leader nonwoven fabrics & air filters, Johnson & Johnson, Can, Ltd, 74-77. *Res:* Colloidal stability; defoamers; adsorption from solution; fibrous structures. *Mailing Add:* 107 Seigniory Ave Pointe Claire PQ H9R 1J6 Can

ALLEN, STEPHEN IVES, MATHEMATICS. *Current Pos:* RETIRED. *Personal Data:* b Holyoke, Mass, Dec 13, 14; m 43; c 2. *Educ:* Amherst Col, BA, 37; Harvard Univ, MA, 46; Univ Pittsburgh, PhD(math, analytical), 63. *Prof Exp:* Instr math & physics, Ruston Acad, Havana, Cuba, 38-39 & Wilbraham Acad, 39-40; instr & prin, Grahmam-Eckes Sch, Fla, 40-41 & 46-48; from instr to asst prof, Univ Mass, Amherst, 48-67, assoc prof math, 67-, assoc dean, Col Arts & Sci, 73-76. *Mem:* Math Asn Am; Am Math Soc. *Res:* Algebraic functions; algebra. *Mailing Add:* 17 Fairfield St Amherst MA 01002-1303

ALLEN, STEVEN, UNDERSEA APPLICATIONS, MAN IN THE SEA. *Current Pos:* CONSULT, 89- *Personal Data:* b Vienna, Austria, Apr 28, 27; US citizen; m 51; c 2. *Educ:* NY Univ, BME, 50; Mass Inst Technol, SM, 51, ScD, 59. *Prof Exp:* Res asst metall, Mass Inst Technol, 51-59; sr scientist staff mat res, ManLabs Inc, 59-62; prin eng staff, C S Draper Lab Inc, 62-75, mem staff, Ocean & Sci Syst, 75-89. *Concurrent Pos:* Lectr, Mass Inst Technol, 71-90. *Mem:* Am Soc Metals; Marine Technol Soc; Soc Advan Mat & Process Eng; Am Soc Composites. *Res:* Underwater vehicles, underwater research and diving; autonomous underwater vehicles; materials engineering for state of the art high reliability, mechanical applications; advanced composites fabrication. *Mailing Add:* 7 Country Corners Rd Wayland MA 01778-3605

ALLEN, SUSAN DAVIS, CHEMICAL PHYSICS, OPTICS. *Current Pos:* VPRES RES, FLA STATE UNIV, 96- *Personal Data:* b Jacksonville, Fla, Sept 13, 43; m 62; c 2. *Educ:* Colo Col, BS, 66; Univ Southern Calif, PhD(chem physics), 71. *Prof Exp:* Res assoc chem physics, Univ Southern Calif, 71-73; mem tech staff, Hughes Res Lab, 73-77; from res scientist to sr res scientist chem physics, Ctr Laser Studies, Univ Southern Calif, 77-87; mem fac, Univ Iowa, 87-92 & Tulane Univ, 93-96. *Concurrent Pos:* Consult, Hughes Res Labs, 77-78, Xerox Corp, 79- & TRW, 79- *Mem:* Am Phys Soc; Am Chem Soc; Am Vacuum Soc; AAAS; Optical Soc Am; Sigma Xi. *Res:* Laser/interface interactions including laser chemical vapor deposition, laser induced desorption and laser induced interfacial mixing in semiconductors; surface and bulk optical properties of solids. *Mailing Add:* Fla State Univ 217 W Cott Bldg Tallahassee FL 32306-1330

ALLEN, SYDNEY HENRY GEORGE, BIOCHEMISTRY. *Current Pos:* from asst prof to prof, 63-96, EMER PROF BIOCHEM, ALBANY MED COL, 96- *Personal Data:* b Cambridge, Mass, Aug 26, 29; m 52; c 2. *Educ:* Tufts Univ, BS, 51; Univ Mass, MS, 53; Purdue Univ, PhD, 57. *Prof Exp:* Instr bact, Univ Conn, 57-60. *Concurrent Pos:* Fel biochem, Sch Med, Western Reserve Univ, 60-63; Lederle med fac award, 65-68. *Mem:* AAAS; Am Soc Microbiol; Am Soc Biol Chemists. *Res:* Subunit structure and function of biotin containing enzymes especially propionyl coenzyme A carboxylase; metabolic pathways involving biotin and vitamin B12; lactate and malate dehydrogenases as well as other enzymes in clinical chemistry; relationship between vitamin and enzyme activity; fermentation pathways; membrane-bound enzymes and intestinal lipid absorption. *Mailing Add:* Dept Biochem Albany Med Col 47 New Scotland Ave Albany NY 12208. *Fax:* 518-262-5689

ALLEN, TED TIPTON, VERTEBRATE ZOOLOGY, ORNITHOLOGY. *Current Pos:* From instr to assoc prof biol, 61-74, head dept, 63-75, PROF BIOL, JACKSONVILLE UNIV, 74- *Personal Data:* b McKenzie, Tenn, Mar 22, 32; m 58, Suzan M O'Brien; c Jeffrey (deceased) & David C. *Educ:* Murray State Col, BA, 54; Univ Wis, MS, 58; Univ Fla, PhD(zool), 62. *Honors & Awards:* Adams Environ Award, 79. *Concurrent Pos:* Vert biol surv, Ariz, 78-80. *Mem:* Colonial Waterbirds Soc. *Res:* Ornithology; ecology and myology of birds. *Mailing Add:* Dept Biol Div Sci & Math Jacksonville Univ 2800 Univ Blvd N Jacksonville FL 32211. *Fax:* 904-744-0101

ALLEN, TERENCE DAVID, CELL BIOLOGY. *Current Pos:* Postdoctoral fel, Paterson Inst/Christie Hosp, Manchester, 70-73, group leader, Emergency Med Unit, 73-75, dept head, Ultrastructure, 75-89, dept head structural cell biol, 90-97, DIV HEAD CELL & TISSUE DEVELOP, PATERSON INST/CHRISTIE HOSP, MANCHESTER, 97- *Personal Data:* b Manchestter, UK, Dec 1, 44; m 69, Gabrielle Anne Ogden; c Neil James & Deborah Jane. *Educ:* Univ Manchester, BSc, 67, PhD, 70, DSc, 84. *Concurrent Pos:* Counsr & sci tutor, Open Univ, 72-85; ed, Chromosome Res

J, 92-97. *Mem:* Fel Micros Soc Am; Royal Micros Soc UK; Biochem Soc; Brit Soc Cell Biol; hon SAfrican Soc Pathologists. *Res:* Pioneering of field emission scanning electron microscopy in biology; contributed over 150 articles to professional journals. *Mailing Add:* Dept Struct Cell Biol Paterson Inst Manchester M209BX England. *Fax:* 44-161-446-3109; *E-Mail:* ulttda@picr.cr.man.ac.uk

ALLEN, THERESA O, neuroendocrinology, for more information see previous edition

ALLEN, THOMAS, ANALYSIS. *Current Pos:* COMDR, AIR FORCE STUDIES & ANALYSIS AGENCY, USAF. *Mailing Add:* 1570 Air Force Pentagon Washington DC 20330

ALLEN, THOMAS CORT, JR, PLANT PATHOLOGY. *Current Pos:* from asst prof to prof plant path, 62-92, ARTIST IN RESIDENCE, COL AGR SCI, ORE STATE UNIV, 92- *Personal Data:* b Madison, Wis, Oct 28, 31; m 53; c 1. *Educ:* Univ Wis, BS, 53; Univ Calif, PhD(plant path), 56. *Prof Exp:* Plant pathologist, Biol Warfare Labs, Ft Detrick, Md, 56-58; head plant path sect, Agr Res & Develop Labs, Stauffer Chem Co, Calif, 58-62. *Concurrent Pos:* NSF fel, 64; NATO sr fel sci, 70. *Mem:* Am Phytopath Soc; Sigma Xi; Am Inst Biol Sci; Electron Micros Soc Am; fel Royal Hort Soc. *Res:* Ultrastructural events in virus-infected plant cells; virus diagnosis; tissue culture manipulations to control viruses of vegetatively propagated plants. *Mailing Add:* Dept Bot & Plant Path Cordley 1048 Ore State Univ Corvallis OR 97331-2902

ALLEN, THOMAS HUNTER, AEROSPACE PHYSIOLOGY, BLOOD VOLUME OXIDATED ENZYMES. *Current Pos:* RETIRED. *Personal Data:* b Sept 24, 14. *Educ:* Univ Iowa, PhD(zool), 41. *Prof Exp:* Chief, Physiol Div, Sch Aerospace Med, Brooks AFB, Tex, 61-71, sci adv, 71-74. *Mailing Add:* 633 Balfour Dr San Antonio TX 78239-2526

ALLEN, THOMAS JOHN, DESIGN ENGINEERING, MANAGEMENT. *Current Pos:* res assoc, Mass Inst Technol, 63-66, from asst prof to assoc prof, 66-79, assoc fac chmn, 83-85, prof orgn psychol & mgt, Sloan Sch Mgt, 74-85, Billard Fund prof mgt, 85-93, HOWARD W JOHNSON PROF MGT, MASS INST TECHNOL, 93-; MACVILAR FAC FEL, 93-, SR ASSOC DEAN, 94- *Personal Data:* b Newark, NJ, Aug 20, 31; m 61, Joan M Gilmartin; c Thomas J Jr, Susan M (Golden) & Mairin C. *Educ:* Upsala Col, BS, 54; Mass Inst Technol, SM, 63, PhD(mgt), 66. *Hon Degrees:* Dr Mgt honoris causa, Rijksuniversiteit, Gent, Belgium, 90; ScD, Chalmers Univ Technol, Sweden, 92. *Prof Exp:* Design engr, Tung-Sol Elec Co, Bloomfield, 56-57; res engr, Boeing Co, Seattle, Wash & Lexington, Mass, 57-65. *Concurrent Pos:* Vis sr lectr, Manchester Bus Sch, Univ Manchester, Eng, 69, hon sr res fel, 70-; hon mem fac, Chalmers Univ Technol, 92-; distinguished vis prof, Univ Col, Dublin, Ireland, 93. *Mem:* Fel AAAS; Inst Elec & Electronics Engrs; Am Psychol Asn; Sigma Xi. *Res:* Communication pattern among engineers and scientist; organizational structure for research and development organizations; architecture of research and development laboratories and its impact on communication; nature of engineering design; author of numerous books, articles and reviews in scientific publications. *Mailing Add:* Sloan Sch Mgt Mass Inst Technol Cambridge MA 02139

ALLEN, THOMAS LOFTON, THEORETICAL CHEMISTRY. *Current Pos:* from asst prof to prof, 52-92, EMER PROF CHEM, UNIV CALIF, DAVIS, 93- *Personal Data:* b San Jose, Calif, Jan 20, 24; m 44, Patricia Powers; c Kathleen, Timothy, Jacquelyn & Keith. *Educ:* Univ Calif, BS, 44; Calif Inst Technol, PhD(chem), 49. *Prof Exp:* Asst chem, Calif Inst Technol, 46-47; asst prof chem, Univ Idaho, 48-49; lectr chem, Univ Calif, Davis, 49-51; res chemist, Calif Res Corp, 51-52. *Concurrent Pos:* Vis res scholar, Ind Univ, 59-60, vis prof, 70-71; vis prof, Univ Nottingham, 71; vis scholar, Univ Calif, Berkeley, 79 & 85-86. *Mem:* Am Chem Soc; Sigma Xi; Am Phys Soc; AAAS. *Res:* Chemical bonding; molecular quantum mechanics. *Mailing Add:* Dept Chem Univ Calif Davis CA 95616. *Fax:* 530-752-8995; *E-Mail:* tlallen@ucdavis.edu

ALLEN, TIMOTHY THORPE, STABLE ISOTOPE GEOCHEMISTRY, GROUND WATER & VADOSE ZONE HYDROLOGY. *Current Pos:* ASSOC PROF GEOL & ENVIRON STUDIES, KEENE STATE COL, 92- *Personal Data:* b New London, NH, June 18, 62; m 93, Wendy. *Educ:* Harvard Univ, BA, 84; Dartmouth Col, MS, 90, PhD(geol), 92. *Mem:* Geol Soc Am; Am Geophys Union; Asn Groundwater Scientists & Engrs. *Res:* Dynamics of hydrolic cycle; groundwater recharge using stable isotopes and geochemistry as well as hydrologic measurements. *Mailing Add:* Keene State Col MS 2001 Keene NH 03431-2001. *E-Mail:* tallen@keene.edu

ALLEN, VERNON R, PHYSICAL CHEMISTRY, POLYMER CHEMISTRY. *Current Pos:* asst prof phys chem, 63-69, assoc prof chem, 69-74, PROF CHEM, TENN TECHNOL UNIV, 74- *Personal Data:* b Nashville, Tenn, Mar 25, 28; m 51; c 4. *Educ:* Tenn Polytech Inst, BS, 52; Univ Akron, MS, 57, PhD(polymer chem), 60. *Prof Exp:* Analyst, Carbide & Carbon Chem Co, 53-54; instr gen chem, Univ Wis, Milwaukee Exten, 54-55; res fel polymer physics, Mellon Inst, 60-63. *Mem:* Am Chem Soc. *Res:* Rheology of polymeric system; physical properties of rubbery materials. *Mailing Add:* 261 Farley Rd Cookeville TN 38506

ALLEN, VIVIEN GORE, MINERAL INTERRELATIONSHIPS IN GRAZING LANDS, FORAGE LIVESTOCK SYSTEMS. *Current Pos:* from asst prof to assoc prof, Agron Dept, 80-93, PROF, DEPT CROP & SOIL ENVIRON SCI, VA POLYTECH INST & STATE UNIV, 93- *Personal Data:* b Nashville, Tenn, Mar 31, 40; m 62, Harry E Jr; c Harry E III, Warren L & Stephen H. *Educ:* Univ Tenn, BS, 62; La State Univ, MS, 73, PhD(agron/animal sci), 79. *Honors & Awards:* Merit Award, Am Forage & Grassland Coun, 89. *Prof Exp:* Researcher, Agron Dept, La State Univ, 79-80. *Concurrent Pos:* Consult, Gabon, Africa & Sri Lanka. *Mem:* Sigma Xi; Am Soc Agron; Am Soc Animal Sci; Soc Range Mgt; Crop Sci Soc Am; AAAS; Am Forage & Grassland Coun (pres, 92-93). *Res:* Forage management and forage systems, soil plant-animal interrelationships; mineral interrelationships in forage-livestock grazing systems, related to magnesium, sulphur and aluminum; integration of grazing animals into sustainable whole-farm systems. *Mailing Add:* Dept Plant & Soil Sci Texas Tech Univ MS2122 Lubbock TX 79409-2122

ALLEN, WAYNE ROBERT, PLANT PATHOLOGY. *Current Pos:* RES SCIENTIST, AGR CAN, 61-, HEAD PLANT PATH, 66-, ORNAMENTALS PROG, 89- *Personal Data:* b New Castle, Pa, Feb 28, 34; m 63, Shirley J Wilson; c Scott W, Shawn W & Todd M. *Educ:* Hiram Col, BA, 56; Cornell Univ, PhD(plant path), 62. *Mem:* Am Phytopath Soc; Can Phytopath Soc. *Res:* Chemical and physical properties of plant viruses; epidemiology of nematode (and insect) transmitted plant viruses; serological and biochemical assessment of insect predator-prey interactions; virus-free plant production. *Mailing Add:* Res Sta Agr Can PO Box 6000 Vineland Station ON L0R 2E0 Can. *Fax:* 905-562-4335; *E-Mail:* allenw@em.agr.ca

ALLEN, WENDALL E, MICROBIOLOGY, MICROBIAL GENETICS. *Current Pos:* PROF BIOL & UNIV COORDR MOLECULAR BIOL & BIOTECHNOL, ECAROLINA UNIV. *Personal Data:* b Elizabethtown, Ky, Nov 16, 36; m 96, Joan Schmidt; c Stephen. *Educ:* Vanderbilt Univ, BA, 58, MA, 61; Univ Ky, PhD(microbiol), 68. *Prof Exp:* Instr microbiol, Ala Col, 61-63; res assoc bact genetics, Univ Ky, 65-67. *Concurrent Pos:* Assoc dean, Gen Col, 70-81. *Mem:* Am Soc Microbiol; AAAS; Sigma Xi. *Res:* Genetics of staphylococci and their bacteriophage; effects of lysogeny and conversion on extracellular products of staphylococci; phage and plasmid relationships among the species of staphylococci. *Mailing Add:* Dept Biol ECarolina Univ Greenville NC 27858-4353. *Fax:* 919-328-4178

ALLEN, WILLARD M, OBSTETRICS & GYNECOLOGY, ENDOCRINOLOGY. *Current Pos:* PROF OBSTET & GYNEC, SCH MED, UNIV MD, BALTIMORE CITY, 71- *Personal Data:* b Macedon, NY, Nov 5, 04; m 27, 46; c 1. *Educ:* Hobart Col, BS, 26; Univ Rochester, MS, 29, MD, 32. *Hon Degrees:* ScD, Hobart Col, 40 & Univ Rochester, 57. *Honors & Awards:* Eli Lilly Award in Biochem, 35. *Prof Exp:* From instr to asst prof obstet & gynec, Sch Med & Dent, Univ Rochester, 36-40; prof & chmn dept, 40-71, EMER PROF OBSTET & GYNEC, SCH MED, WASH UNIV, 71- *Mem:* AMA; Am Gynec Soc; Am Asn Obstet & Gynec; Endocrine Soc; Am Physiol Soc. *Res:* Female sex hormones and endocrinology. *Mailing Add:* Univ Md Hosp Obstet/Gynec Baltimore MD 21201

ALLEN, WILLIAM CORWIN, ORTHOPEDIC SURGERY, BIOMEDICAL ENGINEERING. *Current Pos:* PROF & CHIEF ORTHOP, UNIV MO, 77- *Personal Data:* b Geneva, Ohio, Sept 30, 34; m 57, Kathryn Engelhard; c Elizabeth, Matthew & Benjamin. *Educ:* Hiram Col, BA, 56; Univ Chicago, MD, 60. *Prof Exp:* From asst prof to prof orthop, Univ Fla, 65-77. *Concurrent Pos:* Spec fel, Case Western Reserve Univ, 67-68. *Mem:* Am Acad Orthop Surgeons; Am Orthop Asn; Int Soc Orthop & Traumatic Surg; AMA; Int Soc Knee; Am Orthop Soc Sports Med. *Res:* Biomechanics and sports medicine. *Mailing Add:* Dept Orthop Surg Univ Mo Med Ctr Columbia MO 65212

ALLEN, WILLIAM F, JR, SCIENCE ADMINISTRATION. *Current Pos:* RETIRED. *Personal Data:* b North Kingstown, RI, June 22, 19. *Educ:* Brown Univ, ScB, 41; Harvard Univ, MS, 47. *Hon Degrees:* DTech, Wentworth Inst Technol, 83, DEng, Northeastern Univ, 90. *Prof Exp:* Instr, Brown Univ, 41-44; teaching fel, mech eng, Harvard Univ, 48; vpres & dir eng, Stone & Webster, Inc, 68-71, sr vpres eng, construct & qual assurance, 71, pres, 72 & 86-87, chief exec officer, 73-94, chmn bd, 88-94. *Concurrent Pos:* Trustee, Northwestern Univ, Thayer Acad, 75-84, chmn, 80-82; mem adv comt, Jr Achievement Eastern Mass, dir nat bd; dir, US Coun Energy Awareness; dir & chair, Blue Cross & Blue Shield, Mass; mem, Res Comt on Properties Steam, Am Soc Mech Engrs, 54-62, finance comt, 72-77, chmn, 76-77. *Mem:* Nat Acad Eng; AAAS; fel Am Soc Mech Engrs; Nat Soc Prof Engrs; Sigma Xi. *Res:* Author and co-author of 12 articles. *Mailing Add:* Stone & Webster Inc One Penn Plaza 250 W 34th St New York NY 10119

ALLEN, WILLIAM MERLE, ORGANIC REACTION KINETICS & MECHANISMS. *Current Pos:* DIR, CTR LIFELONG LEARNING, LA SIERRA UNIV, RIVERSIDE, 88-; WORLD MUS NATURAL HIST, 88- *Personal Data:* b San Luis Obispo, Calif, Oct 9, 39; m 63, Laurentine; c Barbara & Gregory. *Educ:* Loma Linda Univ, BA, 61; Univ Md, College Park, PhD(org chem), 67. *Prof Exp:* Asst prof chem, Andrews Univ, 66-68; from asst prof to prof chem, Loma Linda Univ, La Sierra Campus, 68-84, chmn dept, 71-77, dir, Div Natural Sci & Math, 78-81, dean grad sch, Dir Sponsored Res, 87-88; vpres acad admin, Southern Col Seventh-Day Adventists, Tenn, 84-87. *Mem:* Am Asn Higher Educ. *Res:* Synthetic and mechanistic studies of organic compounds; synthesis of organo-cadmium reagents as intermediates in organic synthesis. *Mailing Add:* 11760 Valiant St Riverside CA 92505. *Fax:* 909-785-2901; *E-Mail:* ballen@lasierra.edu

ALLEN, WILLIAM PETER, MEDICAL MICROBIOLOGY. *Current Pos:* CONSULT, 90- *Personal Data:* b Buffalo, NY, Jan 15, 27; m 51, 89, Judith A Davis; c 3. *Educ:* Univ Buffalo, BA, 49, MA, 51; Univ Mich, PhD(med bact), 56. *Honors & Awards:* Res Award, Sci Res Soc Am, 62. *Prof Exp:* Res asst immunol, Univ Mich, 54-55; microbiologist, US Army Biol Labs, 55-68; supvry microbiologist, US Dept Army, 68-71; res scientist, Delta Primate Ctr, Tulane Univ, 71-75; health scientist, adminr, Nat Inst Allergy & Infectious Dis, NIH, 75-89. *Concurrent Pos:* Prog officer, Viral Dis Panel, US-Japan Coop Med Sci Prog; exec secy, Nat Inst AID Task Force on Virol; adj assoc prof microbiol & immunol, Tulane Univ, 73-75; consult, viral res admin, 89-91. *Mem:* AAAS; Am Soc Microbiol; Sigma Xi; Am Soc Virol. *Res:* Natural and acquired immunity to microbial diseases; administrator of grants on viral diseases. *Mailing Add:* 7101 Ridge Crest Dr Frederick MD 21702. *Fax:* 301-371-5356; *E-Mail:* 102025.2101@compuserve.com

ALLEN, WILLIAM RICHARD, SURFACE ANALYSIS. *Current Pos:* TECH STAFF MEM, MARTIN MARIETTA ENERGY SYSTS, 86- *Personal Data:* b Albingdon, Va, Oct 18, 57; m 90, Jenny A McNew. *Educ:* Emory & Henry Col, BS, 80; Univ NC, Chapel Hill, PhD(physics), 86. *Concurrent Pos:* Fel, Oak Ridge Nat Lab, 86-88; res prof, Univ Tenn, 88-92; consult, Martin Marietta Energy Systs, 92-94. *Mem:* Am Phys Soc; Mat Res Soc; Am Soc Metals. *Res:* Microanalysis of surfaces. *Mailing Add:* 142 Highpoint Lane Oak Ridge TN 37830

ALLEN, WILLIAM WESTHEAD, AGRICULTURAL ENTOMOLOGY, PEST MANAGEMENT. *Current Pos:* From asst entomologist to entomologist, 52-85, assoc dean res, 85-90, EMER DEAN RES, COL NATURAL RESOURCES, DEPT ENVIRON SCI, POLICY & MGT, UNIV CALIF, BERKELEY, 90- *Personal Data:* b Santa Cruz, Calif, Oct 13, 21; m 54, Adele Zimmerman; c Joan K (Husted), Mary E (Knott). *Educ:* Univ Calif, BS, 43, PhD(entom), 52. *Mem:* Entom Soc Am; Sigma Xi; AAAS. *Res:* Insect pest management of agricultural crops with emphasis on economic injury levels and the use of selective pesticides. *Mailing Add:* 11 Edgewood Rd Orinda CA 94563

ALLENBACH, CHARLES ROBERT, INORGANIC CHEMISTRY, PHYSICAL CHEMISTRY. *Current Pos:* sect mgr, Chem Eng Process Develop Div, Tech Dept, Metals Div, Union Carbide Corp, 52-63, sr develop chemist, Develop Dept, Consumer Prod Div, 63-66, sect mgr res & develop, Mining & Metals Div, 66-70, staff Engr environ control, Eng Dept, Ferroalloys Div, 70-75, mgr, environ health & prod safety affairs, Metals Div, 75-87, DIR, ENVIRON, HEALTH & PROD SAFETY AFFAIRS, ELKEM METALS CO, 87- *Personal Data:* b Buffalo, NY, Aug 3, 28; m 55; c 2. *Educ:* Univ Buffalo, BA, 49, PhD(chem), 52. *Prof Exp:* Instr chem, Univ Buffalo, 51-52. *Concurrent Pos:* Corp specialist, Elkem Metals, Norway. *Mem:* Am Chem Soc; Am Inst Mining, Metall & Petrol Eng; Am Soc Test Mat; Chem Mfg Asn. *Res:* Environmental control activities; new product development; powder technology; aerosol technology; metal chemicals and compounds and reactive metals. *Mailing Add:* 88 Cherrywood Dr Williamsville NY 14221-1607

ALLENBY, RICHARD JOHN, JR, GEOPHYSICS, TECTONOPHYSICS. *Current Pos:* staff scientist, Off Space Sci, NASA, 62-63, chief planetology, 63-64, dep dir, Manned Space Sci Div, 64-68, asst dir lunar sci, 68-75, RES GEOPHYSICIST, GODDARD SPACE FLIGHT CTR, 75- *Personal Data:* b Chicago, Ill, July 4, 23; m 46; c 3. *Educ:* Dartmouth Col, AB, 43, MA, 48; Univ Toronto, PhD(geophys), 52. *Honors & Awards:* Apollo 8 Letter of Commendation; Apollo Achievement Award; NASA Medal Exceptional Sci Achievement, 71. *Prof Exp:* Instr physics, Dartmouth Col, 46-48; demonstr, Univ Toronto, 49-52; res seismologist, Calif Res Corp, Standard Oil Co, Calif, 52-55, lead geophysicist, 59-62; chief geophysicist, Richmond Petrol Co, 55-59. *Mem:* AAAS; Am Geophys Union; Seismol Soc Am. *Res:* Geophysics and geology of earth moon and planets; spacecraft scientific instrumentation; explorational petroleum geophysics and geology. *Mailing Add:* Goddard Space Flight Ctr Code 9201 Greenbelt Rd Greenbelt MD 20771

ALLENDE, JORGE EDUARDO, BIOCHEMISTRY, MOLECULAR BIOLOGY. *Current Pos:* asst prof biochem, 63-68, assoc prof, 68-71, PROF BIOCHEM & MOLECULAR BIOL, UNIV CHILE, 72- *Personal Data:* b Catargo, Costa Rica, Nov 11, 34; m 61, Catherine C Connelly; c 4. *Honors & Awards:* Fogarty Scholar-In-Residence, NIH. *Prof Exp:* Res assoc, Rockefeller Univ, 61-62. *Concurrent Pos:* Regional coordr, Latin Am Network Biol Sci, 75-; pres, Pam Am Asn Biochem Socs, 76; mem exec comt, Int Cell Res Orgn, 76-, Int Union Biochem, 82-91; mem exec bd, Int Coun Sci Unions, 86-90; foreign assoc Inst Med, Nat Acad Sci. *Mem:* Foreign assoc Inst Med-Nat Acad Sci; fel Third World Acad Sci; Chilean Acad Sci (pres, 91-); hon mem Chilean Acad Med. *Res:* Contributed various articles to professional journals. *Mailing Add:* Academia Chilena de Ciencias Clasificador 1349 Santiago Correo Central Chile

ALLENDER, DAVID WILLIAM, THEORETICAL SOLID STATE PHYSICS. *Current Pos:* ASST PROF PHYSICS, KENT STATE UNIV, 75-, MEM STAFF DIV PHYSICS & ASTRON, LIQUID CRYSTAL INST, 77- *Personal Data:* b Mt Pleasant, Iowa, Nov 20, 47; m 70; c 2. *Educ:* Univ Iowa, BA, 70; Univ Ill, MS, 71, PhD(physics), 75. *Prof Exp:* Res assoc physics, Brown Univ, 74-75. *Mem:* Am Phys Soc. *Res:* Liquid crystal; phase transitions; superconductivity. *Mailing Add:* Dept Physics Kent State Univ Kent OH 44242. *Fax:* 330-672-2792

ALLENDER, ERIC WARREN, COMPLEXITY THEORY. *Current Pos:* asst prof, 85-91, ASSOC PROF COMPUT SCI, RUTGERS UNIV, DEPT COMPUT SCI, 91- *Personal Data:* b Mt Pleasant, Iowa, Nov 19, 56; m 85, Claire Todd. *Educ:* Univ Iowa, BA, 79; Ga Inst Technol, PhD(comput sci), 85. *Concurrent Pos:* Prin investr, var NSF grants, 88-; vis prof, Univ Wurzburg, 89; vis scientist, Princeton Univ, 92-93. *Mem:* Asn Comput Mach; Soc Indust & Appl Math; Asn Symbolic Logic; AAAS; Europ Asn Theoret Comput Sci. *Res:* Circuit complexity, complexity classes, intractability. *Mailing Add:* Dept Comput Sci Rutgers Univ New Brunswick NJ 08903. *Fax:* 732-932-0537; *E-Mail:* allender@cs.rutgers.edu

ALLENDORF, FREDERICK WILLIAM, POPULATION GENETICS. *Current Pos:* from asst prof to assoc prof, 76-84, PROF ZOOL, UNIV MONT, 84- *Personal Data:* b Philadelphia, Pa, Apr 29, 47; m; c 2. *Educ:* Pa State Univ, BS, 71; Univ Wash, MS, 73, PhD(fisheries, genetics), 75. *Prof Exp:* Lectr, Genetics Inst, Aarhus Univ, Denmark, 75-76. *Concurrent Pos:* NATO fel, Genetics Dept, Univ Nottingham, Eng, 78-79; vis scientist, Univ Calif, Davis, 83-84; prog dir, NSF, 89-90. *Mem:* Genetics Soc Am; Soc Study Evolution; Am Genetic Asn; Am Soc Naturalists; fel AAAS; Soc Conserv Biol. *Res:* Evolutionary genetics; application of population genetics to the management of fish species; conservation of genetic resources. *Mailing Add:* Div Biol Sci Univ Mont Missoula MT 59812-0001

ALLENSON, DOUGLAS ROGERS, ANALYTICAL CHEMISTRY, PHYSICAL CHEMISTRY. *Current Pos:* CHIEF CHEMIST, HERROH TESTING LABS, 71- *Personal Data:* b Oak Park, Ill, Sept 23, 26; m 48; c 5. *Educ:* Oberlin Col, AB, 48; Ore State Univ, MS, 51; Duke Univ, PhD(phys chem), 63. *Prof Exp:* Asst prof chem, La State Univ, 54-55; res chemist electrochem, Union Carbide Corp, 55-68; assoc prof chem, Heidelberg Col, 68-69; chief labs, Dept Utilities, Cleveland, 69-71. *Concurrent Pos:* Mem Cuyohoga River Basin Water Facil Comt, 75- *Mem:* Am Chem Soc; Am Indust Hyg Asn; Sigma Xi. *Res:* Instrumental analytical chemistry; electrochemistry of metal oxide cathodes and of alkaline and solid electrolytes; water pollution analysis; methods of industrial hygiene. *Mailing Add:* 4160 E Sprague Rd Broadview Heights Cleveland OH 44147-1409

ALLENSPACH, ALLAN LEROY, DEVELOPMENTAL BIOLOGY. *Current Pos:* ASSOC PROF ZOOL & PHYSIOL, MIAMI UNIV, 66- *Personal Data:* b Campbell, Minn, Sept 23, 35; m 57; c 3. *Educ:* Sioux Falls Col, BS, 57; Iowa State Univ, MS, 59, PhD(embryol, bot), 61; Marine Biol Lab, cert, 61. *Prof Exp:* Asst prof biol, Albright Col, 61-66. *Concurrent Pos:* Res consult, Bernville Biol Labs, 64; USPHS fel, 65. *Mem:* AAAS; Am Soc Zoologists; Am Soc Cell Biol; Soc Develop Biol; Am Inst Biol Sci. *Res:* Normal and experimental studies on organogenesis in the chick embryo. *Mailing Add:* Dept Zool Miami Univ 500 E High St Oxford OH 45056-1618

ALLENSTEIN, RICHARD VAN, ANALYTICAL CHEMISTRY. *Current Pos:* from asst prof to assoc prof, 69-80, PROF CHEM, NORTHERN MICH UNIV, 80- *Personal Data:* b Lamont, Iowa, Aug 28, 30; m 55; c 3. *Educ:* Univ Minn, BS, 52, MA, 57; Wash Univ, EdD, 61. *Prof Exp:* Dir NSF acad yr inst, Wash Univ, 62-66; asst prof chem, Univ Wis, Waukesha, 66-69. *Mem:* Fel AAAS; Am Chem Soc; Nat Sci Teachers Asn. *Res:* Measuring the effectiveness of science teaching and determining its correlates; energy education; aerospace education. *Mailing Add:* 61 Elder Dr Marquette MI 49855

ALLENTOFF, NORMAN, PHOTOGRAPHIC CHEMISTRY. *Current Pos:* RETIRED. *Personal Data:* b New York, NY, Nov 16, 23; wid; c Michael, Alban, Aaron & Theresa. *Educ:* Univ Toronto, BA, 50, MA, 51, PhD(org chem), 56. *Prof Exp:* Res chemist, Chem Div, Can Dept Agr, 51-53, 55-58; sr chemist, Photog Chem Res Labs, Eastman Kodak Co, 58-63, res assoc, 64-65, sr tech assoc, Film Emulsion Div, 65-80, sr res assoc, Kodak Res Labs, 80-86; patent consult, 86-92. *Mem:* Am Chem Soc. *Res:* Plant biochemistry; stereochemistry of the Grignard reaction; chemistry; photographic emulsion chemistry-patent liaison. *Mailing Add:* 17 Stuyvesant Rd Pittsford NY 14534

ALLENTUCH, ARNOLD, solid mechanics; deceased, see previous edition for last biography

ALLER, HAROLD ERNEST, ENTOMOLOGY. *Current Pos:* SR ENTOMOLOGIST, ROHM & HAAS CO, 67- *Personal Data:* b New York, NY, May 13, 34; m 57; c 3. *Educ:* City Col New York, BS, 55; Cornell Univ, PhD(entom), 62. *Prof Exp:* Res entomologist, Niagara Chem Div, FMC Corp, 62-67. *Mem:* Entom Soc Am; Am Mosquito Control Asn. *Res:* Chemical control; pesticides; toxicology; acaricides. *Mailing Add:* 3036 Arrowhead Lane Norristown PA 19401

ALLER, JAMES CURWOOD, ELECTRICAL ENGINEERING, COMPUTER SCIENCE. *Current Pos:* CONSULT, BD REGENTS, LA, 86- *Personal Data:* b Yakima, Wash, Aug 19, 21; m 43, Mary Bramble; c Charles C, James D, Robert C, Mary S (Williams) & Cynthia J (Kelly). *Educ:* US Naval Acad, BS, 42; Harvard Univ, MA, 49, MES, 54; George Washington Univ, DSc(biomed), 68. *Prof Exp:* Mem prof staff, Ctr Naval Analysis, 63-66, sect head command & control, 66-67; prof phys sci, Naval War Col, RI, 68-70; assoc prof clin eng, Sch Med, George Washington Univ, 70-73; sr assoc, Ketron Inc, 73-75; var prog off assignments, NSF, 75-85; prog dir, Eng Res Ctr, 85-86. *Concurrent Pos:* Res assoc prof clin eng, Sch Med, George Washington Univ, 73-74, adj prof, Sch Eng & Appl Sci, 74-75; mem comt, Environ Quality, Inst Elec & Electronics Eng, 74-75 & Career & Prof Develop, Am Soc Eng Educ; mem, Vis Comt, EE Dept, Univ Wis. *Mem:* Fel

AAAS; sr mem Inst Elec & Electronics Engrs; NY Acad Sci. *Res:* Computer-based systems particularly for use in measurement control; instrumentation particularly as applied in clinical medicine; technology for aiding the physically disabled; biosaline research. *Mailing Add:* 250 Pantops Mountain Rd No 2 Charlottesville VA 22911

ALLER, LAWRENCE HUGH, SPECTROSCOPY OF STARS & NEBULAE. *Current Pos:* prof, 62-84, EMER PROF ASTRON & RES ASTRONR, UNIV CALIF, LOS ANGELES, 84- *Personal Data:* b Tacoma, Wash, Sept 24, 13; m 41, Rosalind D Hall; c Hugh D, Raymond D & Gwendolyn J. *Educ:* Univ Calif, AB, 36; Harvard Univ, AM, 38, PhD(astron), 43. *Honors & Awards:* Henry Norris Russell Prize, Am Astron Soc, 92. *Prof Exp:* Lectr astron, Tufts Col, 40; instr physics, Harvard Univ, 42-43, res assoc, Observ, 42-43, 47; physicist, Univ Calif, 43-45; asst prof astron, Ind Univ & res assoc, W J McDonald Observ, 45-48; from assoc prof to prof, Univ Mich, 48-62. *Concurrent Pos:* Pres, Stellar Spectros Comn, Int Astron Union, 58-64; vis prof, Australian Nat Univ, 60-61 & Univ Toronto, 61-62; NSF sr fel, Australia, 60-61 & 68-69; vis prof, Univ Sydney & Univ Tasmania, 68-69; res assoc, Commonwealth Sci & Indust Res Orgn, Australia, 68, 69 & 71; vis prof, Univ Queensland, 77-78 & Raman Res Inst, Bangalore, India, 78; vis res prof, Observ Astrophys Arcetri, Florence, Italy & Univ Florence, 81. *Mem:* Fel Nat Acad Sci; fel AAAS; fel Am Acad Arts & Sci; Am Astron Soc; Royal Astron Soc Gt Brit; Int Astron Union. *Res:* Spectroscopic and theoretical studies of the gaseous nebulae and stellar atmospheres; transition probabilities for spectral lines; cosmic abundances of elements. *Mailing Add:* 18118 W Kingsport Malibu CA 90265. *Fax:* 310-206-2096; *E-Mail:* aller@bonnie.astro.ucla.edu

ALLER, MARGO FRIEDEL, ASTRONOMY. *Current Pos:* teaching fel, Univ Mich, 62-66, res asst, 66-68, teaching fel, 69, res assoc astron, 70-76, assoc res scientist, 76-85, RES SCIENTIST, UNIV MICH, 85- *Personal Data:* b Springfield, Ill, Aug 27, 38; m 64, Hugh; c Monique. *Educ:* Vassar Col, BA, 60; Univ Mich, MS, 64, PhD(astron), 69. *Prof Exp:* Mathematician programmer astron, Smithsonian Astrophys Observ, 60-62. *Mem:* Sigma Xi; Am Astron Soc; Int Astron Union. *Res:* Microwave extragalactic astronomy to study active extragalactic sources. *Mailing Add:* Dept Astron David Dennison Bldg Univ Mich Ann Arbor MI 48109-1090. *Fax:* 313-763-6317; *E-Mail:* margo@astro.lsa.umich.edu

ALLER, ROBERT CURWOOD, LOW TEMPERATURE GEOCHEMISTRY. *Current Pos:* PROF GEOCHEM, STATE UNIV NY, STONY BROOK, 86- *Personal Data:* b Chelsea, Mass, May 17, 50; m 86, Josephine J Yudkin; c Edward L & Deborah M. *Educ:* Univ Rochester, BS, 72, BA, 72; Yale Univ, MS, 74, PhD(geol), 77. *Prof Exp:* From asst prof to assoc prof, Univ Chicago, 77-85, prof geophys sci & geochem, 85-86. *Concurrent Pos:* Alfred P Sloan Found fel, 78-80; assoc ed, Geochimica et Cosmochimica Acta; teacher scholar grant chem, Dreyfus Found, 82-87. *Mem:* Am Soc Limnol & Oceanog; Geochem Soc; Sigma Xi; Am Geophys Union; Estuarine Res Fedn. *Res:* Early chemical diagenesis of marine sediments; animal-sediment interactions and controls on sediment water exchange of dissolved material; elemental cycling in estuarine and shelf environments. *Mailing Add:* 31 Main St Stony Brook NY 11790-1901. *Fax:* 516-632-8820; *E-Mail:* raller@ccmail.sunysb.edu

ALLERHAND, ADAM, PHYSICAL CHEMISTRY, BIOPHYSICAL CHEMISTRY. *Current Pos:* from asst prof to assoc prof, 67-72, chmn dept, 78-81, PROF CHEM, IND UNIV, BLOOMINGTON, 72- *Personal Data:* b Krakow, Poland, May 23, 37; c 2. *Educ:* State Tech Univ, Chile, BS, 58; Princeton Univ, PhD(chem), 62. *Prof Exp:* Res assoc chem, Univ Ill, 62-63, instr phys chem, 63-64, res assoc, 64-65; asst prof chem, Johns Hopkins Univ, 65-67. *Mem:* Am Chem Soc; Am Soc Biol Chemists. *Res:* Nuclear magnetic resonance. *Mailing Add:* Dept Chem Ind Univ Bloomington IN 47405

ALLERTON, JOSEPH, FOOD ENGINEERING, RESEARCH ADMINISTRATION. *Current Pos:* RETIRED. *Personal Data:* b New York, NY, Mar 17, 19; m 44, Muriel Jobst; c Peter, Steven, Paul & Martha. *Educ:* NY Univ, BChE, 41, MChE, 44; Univ Mich, PhD(chem eng), 48. *Prof Exp:* Asst, Off Sci Res & Develop, Columbia Univ, 41-42; instr chem eng, Cooper Union, 42-44; chem engr, Manhattan Proj, Kellex Corp, NY, 44-45; chem engr, Nat Dairy Res Labs Inc, 48-51; sect head, Res Ctr, Gen Foods Corp, 52-63; mgr tech servs-Fulton, Nestle Co Inc, 63-72, mgr technol develop, 72-84. *Concurrent Pos:* Consult, 84- *Mem:* Am Chem Soc; Am Inst Chem Engrs; Inst Food Technol; Sigma Xi. *Res:* Engineering aspects of food processing; research administration; chocolate research and development; environmental sciences. *Mailing Add:* 827 Forest Ave Fulton NY 13069-3337. *E-Mail:* jallert@swega.oswego.edu

ALLERTON, SAMUEL E, BIOPHYSICAL CHEMISTRY, MEDICAL SCIENCE. *Current Pos:* asst prof biophys, Sch Dent, Univ Southern Calif, 65-67, asst prof biochem, 77-84, ASSOC PROF BIOCHEM, SCH DENT, UNIV SOUTHERN CALIF, 69- *Personal Data:* b Three Rivers, Mich, Aug 21, 33; m 66, Theresa Pawlak; c Adam & Eve. *Educ:* Kalamazoo Col, BA, 55; Harvard Univ, PhD(biochem), 62. *Prof Exp:* Res assoc biochem, Rockefeller Inst, 61-64. *Concurrent Pos:* Consult med devices & nutrit. *Mem:* Fel Am Col Nutrit; Sigma Xi; NY Acad Sci. *Res:* Isolation and characterization of proteins; ultracentrifugation and electrophoresis; biochemical pathology; acidic glycosaminoglycans in tumors; pediatric oncology; nutrition. *Mailing Add:* 9572 Smokey Circle Huntington Beach CA 92646-5362

ALLESSIE, MAURITS, REENTRANT CARDIAC ARRHYTHMIAS, FLUTTER FIBRILLATION. *Current Pos:* From asst prof to assoc prof, 70-84, PROF PHYSIOL, DEPT PHYSIOL, UNIV LIMBURG, 84- *Personal Data:* b Gemert, Neth, Aug 14, 45; m 68; c 3. *Educ:* Univ Amsterdam, MD, 71; Univ Limburg, PhD(cardiac arrhythmias), 77. *Concurrent Pos:* Vis prof, Columbia Univ, NY, 80; mem bd, Working Group Arrhythmias & Intracardiac Electrophysiol, Europ Soc Cardiol, 87-, Dutch Sci Res Orgn, NWO, 88-; div head, Cardiovasc Res Inst, Maastricht, 88-; sci coun, ICIN, 88-; consult, Medtronic, 89-; chmn, Working Group Heart Function, NWO, 89- *Mem:* Am Physiol Soc; Dutch Soc Physiol. *Res:* Electrophysiological mechanisms of cardiac arrhythmias; development of animal models of reentrant mechanisms underlying atrial flutter-fibrillation and ventricular tachycardia-fibrillation; high resolution mapping, 256 points, of reentrant impulse propagation in the heart. *Mailing Add:* Dept Physiol Univ Limburg PO Box 616 Maastricht 6200 MD Netherlands. *Fax:* 31-43-671028

ALLEVA, FREDERIC REMO, IMMUNOTOXICOLOGY, PERINATAL TOXICOLOGY. *Current Pos:* RETIRED. *Personal Data:* b Norristown, Pa, Oct 16, 33; m 62. *Educ:* Gettysburg Col, AB, 56; George Washington Univ, MPhil, 70, PhD(zool), 71. *Prof Exp:* Neuropharmacologist & toxicologist, Merck Sharp & Dohme, 59-66; pharmacologist, Food & Drug Admin, 66-96. *Mem:* Sigma Xi; Endocrine Soc; Soc Toxicol. *Res:* Determine the effects of perinatally administered pediatric drugs on various parameters of development in animals. *Mailing Add:* 353 Butternut Ct Millersville MD 21108

ALLEVA, JOHN J, REPRODUCTIVE ENDOCRINOLOGY, BIOLOGICAL RHYTHMS. *Current Pos:* RETIRED. *Personal Data:* b Norristown, Pa, Apr 17, 28; m 60; c Brian, David, Lynn & Diane. *Educ:* Univ Pa, AB, 50; Univ Mo, MS, 52; Harvard Univ, PhD(biol), 59. *Prof Exp:* Sr scientist biochem, Smith Kline & Fr Labs, 59-62; instr physiol, Albany Med Col, 62-63; res biologist & pharmacologist, Div Res & Testing, Food & Drug Admin, 63-96. *Mem:* AAAS; Soc Res Biol Rhythms; Int Soc Chronobiol. *Res:* The biological clock, pineal gland and other central mechanisms; controlling fertility and biorhythms in hamsters. *Mailing Add:* 9511 Spode Ct Fairfax VA 22032-1264

ALLEWELL, NORMA MARY, PHYSICAL BIOCHEMISTRY, PROTEIN CHEMISTRY. *Current Pos:* from asst prof to prof biol, 73-84, chmn, molecular biol & biochem, 84-87, PROF MOLECULAR BIOL & BIOCHEM, WESLEYAN UNIV, 84- *Personal Data:* b Hamilton, Ont; m 70; c 1. *Educ:* McMaster Univ, BSc, 65; Yale Univ, PhD, 69. *Prof Exp:* Fel, Nat Inst Arthritis & Metab Dis, 69-70; asst prof biochem, Polytech Inst Brooklyn, 70-73. *Concurrent Pos:* Instr, Marine Biol Labs, Woods Hole, Mass, 81-83. *Mem:* Am Chem Soc; Biophys Soc; fel AAAS; Am Soc Cell Biol; Am Soc Biol Chemists; Sigma Xi. *Res:* Energetics of macromolecular interactions; biomolecular regulatory mechanisms. *Mailing Add:* Dept Biochem Univ Minn 1479 Gortner Ave St Paul MN 55108

ALLEY, EARL GIFFORD, PESTICIDE CHEMISTRY, PHOTOCHEMISTRY. *Current Pos:* DIR, RES DIV, MISS STATE CHEM LAB, 70- *Personal Data:* b Corsica, SDak, Dec 10, 35; m 62; c 2. *Educ:* Miss State Univ, BS, 59, MS, 61; Univ Ill, Urbana, PhD(org chem), 68. *Prof Exp:* Chemist, Dow Chem Co, 67-69. *Concurrent Pos:* Prof chem, Chem Dept, Miss State Univ; consult. *Mem:* Am Chem Soc; AAAS; Sigma Xi. *Res:* Photochemistry and degradation of agricultural chemicals; involvement of charge transfer and adsorption in these processes; analyses of trace metals and organic materials. *Mailing Add:* Miss State Chem Lab Box CR Mississippi State MS 39762-5622

ALLEY, FORREST C, ENVIRONMENTAL ENGINEERING. *Current Pos:* from asst prof to assoc prof, 58-69, PROF CHEM ENG, CLEMSON UNIV, 69- *Personal Data:* b Tuskegee, Ala, Aug 14, 29; m 52; c 3. *Educ:* Auburn Univ, BS, 51, MS, 55; Univ NC, PhD(environ eng), 62. *Prof Exp:* Eng technologist, Shell Oil Co, La, 55-58. *Mem:* Am Inst Chem Engrs; Air Pollution Control Asn. *Res:* Process development; industrial pollution control; atmospheric chemistry. *Mailing Add:* 500 Shorecrest Dr Clemson SC 29631

ALLEY, KEITH EDWARD, NEUROMUSCULAR PLASTICITY. *Current Pos:* asst dean, 91-94, PROF ORAL BIOL & CHMN DEPT, OHIO STATE UNIV, 85-, PROF CELL BIOL, NEUROL & ANAT, 85-, ASSOC DEAN, 94- *Personal Data:* b Palm Springs, Calif, June 27, 43; m 66, Jill Doyle; c Colin D. *Educ:* Univ Ill, DDS, 68, PhD(anat), 72. *Prof Exp:* Fel anat, Univ Ill, 68-72; asst prof oral biol, Univ Iowa, 72-74; asst prof anat, Case Western Reserve Univ, 74-80, assoc prof oral biol, 80-85, asst dean res, 84-85. *Concurrent Pos:* Fel neurobiol, Univ Iowa, 72-74; mem, Oral Biol & Med Study Sect, NIH, 88-92. *Mem:* Soc Neurosci; Am Asn Anatomists; Int Asn Dent Res; AAAS. *Res:* Molecular and physiologic aspects of neuromuscular development; metamorphic transformation of cranial systems; developmental mechanisms and evolutionary biology. *Mailing Add:* Ohio State Univ 305 W 12th Ave Columbus OH 43210-1239. *Fax:* 614-292-7619; *E-Mail:* kalley@magnus.acs.ohio.state.edu

ALLEY, MARCUS M, AGRONOMY. *Current Pos:* asst prof, 77-83, asoc prof, 83-89, PROF SOIL & CROP MGT, VA POLYTECH INST & STATE UNIV, 89- *Educ:* Berea Col, BS, 69, Va Polytech Inst & State Univ, MS, 71, PhD(agron), 75. *Honors & Awards:* Werner L Nelson Award, Fluid Fertil Found, 86; Agron Achievement Award, 88; Robert E Wagner Award, Potash & Phosphate Inst, Am Soc Agron, 90. *Prof Exp:* Res rep, Ohio & Ky Divs, Ciba-Geigy Corp, 75-77. *Concurrent Pos:* Agronomist, Park Forest Farms

Inc, Baskerville, Va, 75; adv to exec bd, Va Agr Chem & Soil Fertil Asn, 89-; mem proj comt, Best Mgt Pract Manual Wheat Growers, 93- *Mem:* Am Soc Agron; Soil Sci Soc Am. *Res:* Development of restoration strategies for prime farmlands disturbed by mineral sands mining in the coastal plain of the Eastern US; research in tissue and soil testing for increasing the efficiency of nitrogen utilization by wheat; efficient placement of N and P fertilizer for corn production; increasing nitrogen use efficiency in barley production; program for increasing barley yields and quality. *Mailing Add:* Va Tech Dept Corp & Environ Blacksburg VA 24061-0404

ALLEY, MICHAEL C, CANCER PHARMACOLOGY. *Current Pos:* PHARMACOLOGIST, DEVELOP THERAPEUT PROG, FCRDC, NAT CANCER INST, 89- *Res:* Cancer pharmacology. *Mailing Add:* Nat Cancer Inst-FCRDC Develop Therapeut Prog Fairview Bldg Rm 205 1003 W 7th St Frederick MD 21701-8527

ALLEY, PHILLIP WAYNE, SOLID STATE PHYSICS. *Current Pos:* PROF PHYSICS, STATE UNIV NY COL GENESEO, 64- *Personal Data:* b Chicago, Ill, Mar 11, 32; m 58; c 4. *Educ:* Lawrence Col, BS, 53; Rutgers Univ, PhD(physics), 58. *Prof Exp:* Asst physics, Rutgers Univ, 53-56, instr, 56-58; asst prof, Franklin & Marshall Col, 58-64. *Mem:* Am Phys Soc; Am Asn Physics Teachers; Sigma Xi. *Res:* Electrical conductivity in dilute metal alloys; teaching physics at undergraduate and graduate level. *Mailing Add:* Dept Phys State Univ NY Geneseo NY 14454

ALLEY, REUBEN EDWARD, JR, PHYSICS. *Current Pos:* PROF ELEC ENG, US NAVAL ACAD, 65- *Personal Data:* b Petersburg, Va, July 16, 18; m 49; c 1. *Educ:* Univ Richmond, BA, 38; Princeton Univ, EE, 40, PhD(elec eng), 49. *Prof Exp:* Instr physics, Univ Richmond, 40-42; staff mem, radiation lab, Mass Inst Technol, 42-43; instr elec eng, Princeton Univ, 43-44; assoc prof physics & chmn dept, Univ Richmond, 49-51; mem tech staff, Bell Tel Labs, 51-53; assoc prof physics & chmn dept, Univ Richmond, 53-55; assoc prof physics, Washington & Lee Univ, 55-57; mem tech staff, Bell Tel Labs, 57-59; sr proj engr, semiconductor-components div, Tex Instruments, Inc, 59-60; prof physics, Vassar Col, 60-62, chmn dept, 61-62; prof elec eng, Univ SC, 62-65. *Concurrent Pos:* Bd of Gov, Am Inst Physics, 75-78. *Mem:* Am Phys Soc; Am Asn Physics Teachers; Sigma Xi. *Res:* Direct current controlled reactors; electrical analogy networks for solution of nonlinear differential equations; magnetic materials and high frequency magnetic properties; nuclear radiation effects. *Mailing Add:* 299 Halsey Rd Annapolis MD 21401-3216

ALLEY, RICHARD BLAINE, GLACIER DYNAMICS, ICE-CORE PALEOCLIMATES. *Current Pos:* asst prof, 88-96, PROF GEOSCI, DEPT GEOSCI & EARTH SYST SCI CTR, PA STATE UNIV, 96- *Personal Data:* b Columbus, Ohio, Aug 18, 57; m 80; c 2. *Educ:* Ohio State Univ, BSc, 80, MSc, 83; Univ Wis-Madison, PhD(geol), 87. *Prof Exp:* Asst scientist, Geophys & Polar Res Ctr, Univ Wis-Madison, 87-88. *Concurrent Pos:* NSF presidential young investr, 90. *Mem:* Int Glaciol Soc; Am Geophys Union. *Res:* Flow, stability and deposits of ice sheets and glaciers; paleoclimatic records in ice cores. *Mailing Add:* Dept Geosci 306 Deike Bldg Pa State Univ University Park PA 16802-2711

ALLEY, STARLING KESSLER, PETROLEUM CHEMISTRY. *Current Pos:* sr res chemist, 61-69, res assoc, 70-73, supvr catalyst res, 73-78, mgr refining res, 78-81, VPRES, REFINING & PROD RES, UNOCAL CORP, 81- *Personal Data:* b Crab Orchard, Tenn, Sept 20, 30; m 52; c 2. *Educ:* Berea Col, AB, 52; Univ Calif, Los Angeles, PhD(phys chem), 61. *Prof Exp:* Res chemist. Olin Mathieson Chem Corp, NY, 52-55, res chemist, high energy fuels div, Calif, 55-57; asst chem, Univ Calif, Los Angeles, 57-61. *Mem:* Am Chem Soc; Am Petrol Inst; Soc Automotive Engrs; Indust Res Inst. *Res:* High energy fuels; boron chemistry; thermodynamics of nonelectrolytes; nuclear magnetic resonance; hydrogen bonding; heterogeneous catalysis. *Mailing Add:* 15717 W Huron Dr Sun City West AZ 85375

ALLEY, THOMAS ROBERTSON, PERCEPTION & RECOGNITION OF FACES, PSYCHOLOGY OF EATING & FOOD PREFERENCES. *Current Pos:* from asst prof to assoc prof, 84-92, PROF PSYCHOL, CLEMSON UNIV, 92- *Personal Data:* b Bryn Mawr, Pa, Oct 21, 53; c Becky & Jennifer. *Educ:* Pa State Univ, BS & BA, 75; Univ Conn, MA, 79, PhD(exp psychol), 81. *Prof Exp:* Fel, Univ Conn Health Ctr, 81-84. *Concurrent Pos:* Vis scholar, Emory Univ, 91-92; consult ed, Ecol Psychol, 91- *Mem:* Psychonomic Soc; Int Soc Ecol Psychol; Int Soc Human Ethology; Am Psychol Soc. *Res:* Perception and recognition of human faces and other psychosocial aspects of physical appearance, especially the determinants and consequences of physical attractiveness; human food preferences and food neophobia. *Mailing Add:* Dept Psychol Clemson Univ Clemson SC 29634-1511. *Fax:* 864-656-0358; *E-Mail:* alley@clemson.edu

ALLFREY, VINCENT GEORGE, CELL BIOLOGY, GENETICS. *Current Pos:* assoc prof, 57-63, PROF, ROCKEFELLER UNIV, 63- *Personal Data:* b June 28, 21; m 43; c 2. *Educ:* Col City New York, BS, 43; Columbia Univ, MS, 48, PhD(chem), 49. *Prof Exp:* Res asst, Rockefeller Inst Med Res, 49-52, res assoc, 52-57. *Concurrent Pos:* Vis prof cell biol, Yale Univ, 64-65; mem, Adv Comts, Am Cancer Soc, 66-88 & Nat Cancer Inst, NIH, 71-89, coun, Am Cancer Soc, 69-72 & Molecular Cytol Study Sect, NIH, 82; chmn, Coun Res, Am Cancer Soc, 71-74 & Gordon Res Conf Nuclear Proteins, Chromatin Struct & Gene Regulation, 74; adj prof cell biol & genetics, Grad Sch Med Sci, Cornell Univ, 73- *Mem:* Am Soc Biochem & Molecular Biol; Am Soc Cell Biol; Am Soc Microbiol; Am Asn Cancer Res; AAAS; Biochem Soc. *Res:* DNA-binding proteins and their post-synthetic modifications in controlling chromosome structure and RNA synthesis; separation of transcriptionally active and inactive DNA sequences of oncogenes and anti-oncogenes; differences in carcinogen-induced DNA damage and repair in active and inactive genes. *Mailing Add:* Rockefeller Univ 1230 York Ave Box 281 New York NY 10021-6399

ALLGAIER, DARRELL EMORY, NONLINEAR WAVES, ASYMPTOTICS. *Current Pos:* ASSOC PROF MATH, ILL COL, 92-, CHAIR, DEPT MATH, 93- *Personal Data:* b Belleville, Ill, Mar 30, 49; m 77, Lyla Riepma; c John, Jennifer, Sarah, Diana, Susan & David. *Educ:* Univ Cent Fla, BS, 75, MS, 79; Southern Methodist Univ, PhD(appl math), 86. *Prof Exp:* Commun electronics officer, USAF, 75-80, sci analyst, 90-92; asst prof math, USAF Acad, 80-90. *Res:* Published numerous articles; wave number shocks for solitary waves; large scale logistics problems. *Mailing Add:* 1320 W Lafayette Jacksonville IL 62650

ALLGAIER, ROBERT STEPHEN, MAGNETOTRANSPORT PROPERTIES, IV-VI SEMICONDUCTORS. *Current Pos:* RETIRED. *Personal Data:* b Union City, NJ, Nov 29, 25; m 54, Athanasia Lalos; c Stephanie I & Eric L. *Educ:* Columbia Univ, AB, 50, AM, 52; Univ Md, PhD(physics), 58. *Prof Exp:* Asst physics, Columbia Univ, 50-51; physicist, Naval Ord Lab, 51-73, chief, Solid State Div, 73-74; adminr mat technol prog, Off Chief Naval Develop, 74-75 & 76; sr scientist, Solid State Br, Naval Surface Weapons Ctr, Silver Spring, 75-81; consult, Solid State Br, Naval Surface Warfare Ctr, 81-90, consult, Sci & technol prog off, 90-96. *Concurrent Pos:* Vis scientist, Cavendish Lab, Cambridge Univ, 65-66; mem tech rev comt, Joint Serv Electronics Prog, Dept Defense, 72-81; lectr physics, Univ Md, 75-79; prog officer, Off Naval Res, 83; vis prof, Linz Univ, Austria, 87; tech ed, Nat Acad Sci, 89. *Mem:* Fel Am Phys Soc. *Res:* Transport properties of semiconductors and metals in liquid, solid, amorphous and crystalline forms; electronic properties of IV-VI semiconductors; science and technology history writer. *Mailing Add:* 11034 Seven Hill Lane Potomac MD 20854-3244. *Fax:* 301-299-3154

ALLGOOD, JOSEPH PATRICK, PHYSIOLOGY. *Current Pos:* Instr, 62-63, ASST PROF PHYSIOL, DENT SCH, NORTHWESTERN UNIV, CHICAGO, 63- *Personal Data:* b Calvert, Ala, June 27, 27. *Educ:* Univ Ala, BS, 49; Northwestern Univ, DDS, 53, MS, 60, PhD(physiol), 63. *Mem:* AAAS; Int Asn Dent Res; Sigma Xi. *Res:* Masticatory efficiency; electromyography; temporomandibular joint disturbances; intro-oral force measurements. *Mailing Add:* 201 E Chestnut St 17-D Chicago IL 60611-2358

ALLGOWER, EUGENE L, MATHEMATICS. *Current Pos:* assoc prof, 67-74, PROF MATH, COLO STATE UNIV, 67- *Personal Data:* b Chicago, Ill, Aug 11, 35; m 58; c 1. *Educ:* Ill Inst Technol, BS, 57, MS, 59, PhD(math), 64. *Prof Exp:* Instr math, Ill Inst Technol, 60-62 & Univ Ariz, 62-64; asst prof, Sacramento State Col, 64-65; assoc prof, Univ Tex, El Paso, 65-67. *Concurrent Pos:* Marathon Oil Co Indust fel, 65; vis prof, Swiss Fed Inst Technol, Zurich, 72 & Univ Bonn, 77-78 & 81; Richard Merton prof, Univ Stuttgart, 78; vis prof, Univ Hamburg, 83, Ore State Univ, 87; Sr Alexander von Humboldt fel, WGer, 88-89. *Mem:* Am Math Soc; Soc Indust & Appl Math. *Res:* Analysis; numerical analysis; approximation of fixed points; differential equations; continuation methods. *Mailing Add:* Dept Math Colo State Univ Ft Collins CO 80521. *Fax:* 970-491-2161

ALLIEGRO, MARK C, CELLULAR & DEVELOPMENTAL BIOLOGY. *Current Pos:* ASST PROF ANAT, LA STATE UNIV MED CTR, 93- *Personal Data:* b Brooklyn, NY, Jan 14, 57. *Educ:* Fairleigh Dickinson Univ, BS, 78; Univ Md, MS, 81; State Univ NY, Buffalo, PhD(anat & cell biol), 86. *Prof Exp:* Sr scientist cell & develop biol, Retina Ctr, St Joseph's Hosp, Baltimore, 89-93. *Mem:* Am Soc Cell Biol; Soc Develop Biol. *Mailing Add:* Dept Anat La State Univ Med Ctr 1901 Perdido St New Orleans LA 70112

ALLIEGRO, RICHARD ALAN, CERAMICS ENGINEERING. *Current Pos:* develop engr, 57-59, supvr process eng, 59-61, tech develop, 61-63, mgt eng, 63-66, chief armor res & develop, 66-67, asst dir res & develop, 67-71, mgr res & develop, Indust Ceramics Div, 71-73, dir res & new bus develop, 73-78, dir mkt & sales, 78-82, vpres & gen mgr, Indust Ceramics Div, 82-84, VPRES, HIGH PERFORMANCE CERAMICS, NORTON CO, 84- *Personal Data:* b New York, NY, Mar 20, 30; m 52; c 6. *Educ:* Alfred Univ, BS, 51, MS, 52. *Honors & Awards:* Ceramist of the Year, Amer Ceramic Soc, 82. *Prof Exp:* Res assoc ceramics, Alfred Univ, 52-54. *Concurrent Pos:* Trustee, Alfred Univ. *Mem:* Fel Am Ceramic Soc; Nat Inst Ceramic Engrs (pres, 75-76); US Advan Ceramics Asn (pres, 87-88). *Res:* Development of high temperature materials, usually fabrication by way of hot pressing; development of monolithic boron carbide ballistic armor for use on helicopter crewmen in Vietnam; patented furnace components for silicon diffusion processing. *Mailing Add:* 26 Woodstone Rd Northborough MA 01532

ALLIET, DAVID F, LASER DIFFRACTION. *Current Pos:* Chemist, 65-70, sr chemist, 70-73, PROJ LEADER, XEROX CORP, 73- *Personal Data:* b Rochester, NY, May 9, 38; m 60; c 3. *Educ:* Rochester Inst Technol, BS, 67. *Concurrent Pos:* Adj assoc prof chem, Monroe Community Col, 81- *Mem:* Am Chem Soc; fel Am Inst Chemists. *Res:* Investigating methods for measuring very fine particles; laser diffraction; laser velocimetry; quasi elastic light scattering methods. *Mailing Add:* Six Cypress Circle Fairport NY 14450

ALLIN, EDGAR FRANCIS, ANATOMY. *Current Pos:* assoc prof, 78-84, PROF ANAT, CHICAGO COL OSTEOPATH MED, 84- *Personal Data:* b Edmonton, Alta, Jan 31, 39; m 67. *Educ:* Univ Alta, MD, 63, BSc, 66. *Prof Exp:* Instr anat, Univ Alta, 61-62; intern, Vancouver Gen Hosp, 63-64; jr asst resident surg, Univ Hosp, Edmonton, Alta, 64-65; from proj specialist & teaching asst to asst prof anat, Sch Med, Univ Wis-Madison, 67-75; asst prof, Univ Ill Med Ctr, Chicago, 75-78. *Concurrent Pos:* Hon res assoc geol, Field Mus Natural Hist, 79- *Mem:* AAAS; Am Asn Anat; Soc Vert Paleontol. *Res:* Evolution of the middle ear and feeding apparatus of mammal-like reptiles and early mammals; skeletal muscle fiber type histochemistry. *Mailing Add:* Dept Anat Midwestern Univ 555 31st Downers Grove IL 60515-1235

ALLING, DAVID WHEELOCK, MATHEMATICAL STATISTICS, MEDICINE. *Current Pos:* med officer statist, Nat Cancer Inst, 59-60, med officer statist, 60-64, res math statistician, Nat Inst Allergy & Infectious Dis, 64-95, RES MATH STATISTICIAN, CLIN CTR, NIH, 95- *Personal Data:* b Rochester, NY, July 5, 18; wid; c Susan A (Trettel). *Educ:* Univ Rochester, BA, 40, MD, 48; Cornell Univ, PhD(statist), 59. *Prof Exp:* Intern med, Arnot-Ogden Hosp, 48-49; resident, Hermann M Biggs Mem Hosp, 49-56. *Mem:* Inst Math Statist; Am Statist Asn; Biomet Soc. *Res:* Partition of chi-squared variables; sequential tests of hypotheses; stochastic models of chronic diseases. *Mailing Add:* NIH Bldg 10 Rm 4A21 Bethesda MD 20892

ALLING, NORMAN LARRABEE, MATHEMATICS. *Current Pos:* from assoc prof to prof, 65-93, EMER PROF MATH, UNIV ROCHESTER, 93- *Personal Data:* b Rochester, NY, Feb 8, 30; m 57; c 2. *Educ:* Bard Col, BA, 52; Columbia Univ, MA, 54, PhD(math), 58. *Prof Exp:* Lectr math, Columbia Univ, 55-57; from asst prof to assoc prof, Purdue Univ, 57-65. *Concurrent Pos:* NSF fel, Harvard Univ, 61-62; lectr, Mass Inst Technol, 62-64, NSF fel, 64-65; vis prof, math inst, Univ Wurzburg, 71. *Mem:* Am Math Soc. *Res:* Topological modle theory. *Mailing Add:* 215 Saudringham Rd Rochester NY 14610-3450. *E-Mail:* nalg@troi.cc.rochester.edu

ALLINGER, NORMAN LOUIS, COMPUTATIONAL CHEMISTRY. *Current Pos:* PROF CHEM, UNIV GA, 69- *Personal Data:* b Alameda, Calif, Apr 6, 28; m 92, Irene Saez; c Alan, James, Ilene (Candreva), Maritza (Quinn), Aida (Quinones) & Vilma (Velez). *Educ:* Univ Calif, BS, 51; Univ Calif, Los Angeles, PhD, 54. *Hon Degrees:* Dr, Russian Acad Sci, 93. *Honors & Awards:* Herty Medal, Am Chem Soc, Atlanta, 82, Arthur C Cope, 88, James Flack Norris, 89. *Prof Exp:* Fel, Univ Calif, Los Angeles, 54-55, NSF fel, 55-56; from asst prof to prof chem, Wayne State Univ, 56-69. *Mem:* Nat Acad Sci; Am Chem Soc. *Res:* Conformational analysis; organic quantum chemistry; physical properties of organic compounds; macro-rings; computational chemistry. *Mailing Add:* Dept Chem Univ Ga Athens GA 30602-2556. *E-Mail:* allinger@sunchem.chem.uga.edu

ALLINGTON, ROBERT W, ELECTRICAL ENGINEERING, CHEMICAL INSTRUMENTATION. *Current Pos:* Pres, 61-95, CHMN BD, ISCO INC, 59-, CHIEF EXEC OFFICER, 61- *Personal Data:* b Madison, Wis, Sept 18, 35; m 76, Mary L Kaylor; c 5. *Educ:* Univ Nebr, BS, 59, MS, 61. *Hon Degrees:* DSc, Univ Nebr, 85. *Honors & Awards:* Indust Res 100 Award, Res & Develop Mag, 78 & 85. *Concurrent Pos:* Chmn, Nebr EPSCOR Comt, 91-; bd mem, Lincoln Chem Indust Adv Bd, Univ Nebr, 88- *Mem:* Inst Elec & Electronics Engrs; Instrument Soc Am; Am Chem Soc; fel Am Inst Chem; Nat Soc Prof Engrs; AAAS. *Res:* Instrumentation and measurement methods in the fields of liquid chromatography, electrophoresis, supercritical fluids and spectrophotometry; data processing and handling; laboratory automation; analytical chemistry; granted 83 patents. *Mailing Add:* Isco Inc 4700 Superior Lincoln NE 68504-1398

ALLINSON, MORRIS JONATHAN CARL, RADIOLOGY. *Current Pos:* RETIRED. *Personal Data:* b New Haven, Conn, Feb 20, 12; m 48, Roz Rappaport; c Arthur, Robert, Nancy & Jeffrey. *Educ:* Yale Univ, BS, 32; Boston Univ, PhD(biochem), 38; Univ Ark, MD, 45; Am Bd Radiol, dipl, 54. *Prof Exp:* Res biochemist, Res Lab, Sharp & Dohme, 34-35; instr biochem, Sch Med, La State Univ, 39-40; instr physiol & pharmacol, Sch Med, Univ Ark, 40-45; intern, Grace-New Haven Hosp, 45-46; resident radiol, Hosp St Raphael's New Haven, 50-52 & Bridgeport Hosp, 52; resident radiation ther, Hosp, Joint Dis, 53, staff therapist, 53-57; practicing radiologist, 53-57; radiologist, Franklin Hosp, 57-76. *Concurrent Pos:* Radiologist, A G Holley State Hosp, Lantana, Fla. *Res:* Metabolism and colorimetric methods of analysis of creatine and creatinine; action of bacterial enzymes on creatine and nicotinic acid analysis of inositol and penicillin; relation of cyanamid to cancer therapy; use of zymomonas bacteria in producing alchohol from sugar and oranges. *Mailing Add:* 550 S Ocean Blvd Apt 306 Boca Raton FL 33432

ALLIS, C DAVID, CELL BIOLOGY, GENE EXPRESSION. *Current Pos:* PROF CELL & MOLECULAR BIOL, SYRACUSE UNIV, 89- *Personal Data:* b Cincinnati, Ohio, Mar 22, 51. *Res:* Molecular and cellular biology; gene expression. *Mailing Add:* Dept Biol 326A Hutchinson Hall Univ Rochester Rochester NY 14627

ALLIS, JOHN W, MECHANISMS IN TOXICOLOGY, CYTOCHROME P-FOUR FIFTY. *Current Pos:* supvry res chemist, 76-89, RES CHEMIST, ENVIRON PROTECTION AGENCY, 71-76 & 90- *Personal Data:* b Buffalo, NY, Apr 24, 39; m 65, Marilyn R Etzelmueller; c Richard J & Robert C. *Educ:* Syracuse Univ, BS, 60; Univ Wis, PhD(phys chem), 65. *Honors & Awards:* Bronze Medal, Environ Protection Agency, 85. *Prof Exp:* Res assoc protein chem, Georgetown Univ, 67-69; res chemist, USPHS, 70-71. *Concurrent Pos:* In US Army, 65-67. *Mem:* Am Chem Soc; Bioelectromagnet Soc (secy-treas, 86-89); Int Soc Study Xenobiotics; Biophys Soc. *Res:* Role of cytochromes P450 in toxicity of organic compounds; interaction of compoynds administered sequentially or simultaneously to enhance or decrease toxic response; mechanism of action of cytochromes P450 2E1 and 2B1. *Mailing Add:* Health Effects Res Lab MD-7 Environ Protection Agency Research Triangle Park NC 27711-2055. *Fax:* 919-541-5394

ALLIS, WILLAM PHELPS, PLASMA PHYSICS, ELECTRON PHYSICS. *Current Pos:* Res assoc plasma physics, 25-29, from instr to prof, 31-67, sr lectr, 67-77, EMER PROF PLASMA PHYSICS, MASS INST TECHNOL, 67- *Personal Data:* b Menton, France, Nov 15, 01; US citizen; m 35, Nancy Morison; c Nancy (Bella), Edward A (deceased) & John C. *Educ:* Mass Inst Technol, BS, 23, MS, 24; Univ Nancy, DSc(high frequency resonance), 25. *Hon Degrees:* MA, Oxford Univ, 68; Dr, Univ Paris, 79. *Honors & Awards:* Legion of Honor, France, 68. *Concurrent Pos:* Vis prof, Harvard Univ, 58, Univ Tex, 60, St Catherine's Col, Oxford Univ, 68, Univ Paris, Sud, 69-83, Mid East Tech Univ, Ankara, 70 & Univ SFla, 71; chmn, Gaseous Electronics Conf, 49-62, hon chmn, 66-; consult, Los Alamos Sci Lab, 52-; asst secy gen sci affairs, NATO, France, 62-64; Fulbright sr lectr, Univ Innsbruck, 74-75; consult, Lawrence Livermore Lab, Univ Calif, 78; vis fel, Joint Inst Lab Astrophys, Boulder, Colo, 79-80. *Mem:* Fel Am Phys Soc; Am Acad Arts & Sci (vpres, 61-62); fel Brit Inst Physics; Royal Soc Arts; fel AAAS. *Res:* Free electrons in gases; ionized gases; electron distributions and processes in lasers; plasma physics; ionized gases in general. *Mailing Add:* 33 Reservoir St Cambridge MA 02138-3335

ALLISON, ANTHONY CLIFFORD, IMMUNOLOGY, PATHOLOGY. *Current Pos:* VPRES RES, SYNTEX RES, PALO ALTO, CALIF, 81- *Personal Data:* b East London, SAfrica; UK citizen. *Educ:* Oxford Univ, DPhil(biol), 50, BM & BCh, 52; FRCPath, 70. *Honors & Awards:* Murgatroyd Prize, Royal Col Physicians, 70; Heberden Medal, Heberden Soc, 73. *Prof Exp:* Mem sci staff virol, Nat Inst Med Res, Mill Hill, London, 57-67; head div path, Clin Res Ctr, Harrow, Eng, 67-77; dir parasitol, Int Lab Res Animal Dis, Nairobi, Kenya, 77-80. *Mem:* Europ Molecular Biol Orgn; Am Asn Immunologists. *Res:* Development of an adjuvant formulation to elicit cell-mediated immunity against antigens produced by recombinant DNA technology and peptide synthesis; development of novel immunosuppressive drugs for prevention of allograft rejection; treatment of patients with autoimmune disease. *Mailing Add:* 2513 Hastings Dr Belmont CA 94002-3321

ALLISON, DAVID B, OBESITY, QUANTITATIVE GENETICS. *Current Pos:* NIH res fel, Dept Med & Obesity Res Ctr, 91-94, ASSOC RES SCIENTIST, NY OBESITY RES CTR, ST LUKE'S/ROOSEVELT HOSP CTR, 94-; ASST PROF CLIN PSYCHOL, COL PHYSICIANS & SURGEONS, COLUMBIA UNIV, 94- *Educ:* Vassar Col, BA, 85; Hofstra Univ, MA, 87, PhD(clin & sch psychol), 90. *Honors & Awards:* Neal Miller Early Career Award, Acad Behav Med, 96. *Prof Exp:* Behav therapist, Physicians Weight Loss Ctr, 85-86; psychiat asst, St Francis Hosp, 86-87; ment health asst, Mercy Hosp Commun Residence, 87-88; appl behav specialist, Plus Group Homes, 88-90; res fel, Dept Pediat & Behav Psychol, Sch Med & Kennedy Inst, Johns Hopkins Univ, 90-91. *Concurrent Pos:* Child care worker, Blueberry Treatment Ctr, 85-86; intern psychologist, Farmingdale Sch Dist, 87-88, Astor Child Guidance Ctr, 88-89; adj fac, St Johns Univ, Nassau Commun Col & Hofstra Univ, 90; prin investr, NSF, 91, Original Mkt, Inc & Int Resource Ctr Down Syndrome, 93-94, NIH-Obesity Res Ctr, Col Physicians & Surgeons, Columbia Univ, 93 & 94-95, Henry A Murray Res Ctr, Radcliff Col, 93-94 & 96, Am Diabetes Asn, 94-96, Nat Inst Diabetes, Digestive & Kidney Dis, 94-, Int Life Sci Inst & NIH, 95-96, Millennium Pharmaceut, Inc & Pfizer, Inc, 96, Ctr Dis Control & Prev, 96-97; adj asst prof, St Johns Univ, 92-; consult, NIH, Hofstra Univ, Columbia Univ, Johns Hopkins Univ & Albert Einstein Col Med; co-investr, NIH, NATO, Am Psychol Asn, Fogarty Int Res Collab & Nat Inst Aging. *Mem:* AAAS; NY Acad Sci; Am Psychol Asn; Am Psychol Soc; Am Asn Appl Prevent Psychol; Soc Behav Med; Nam Asn Study Obesity; Inst Math Statist; Soc Study Ingestive Behav; Behav Genetic Asn; Asn Advan Behav Ther; Am Statist Asn; Math Asn Am; Classification Soc NAm; Asn Measurement & Eval Coun & Develop; Am Diabetes Asn; Am Asn Human Genetics; Human Genome Orgn. *Res:* Etiology, effects and treatment of human obesity; methodology and statistical analysis; author of over 58 publications. *Mailing Add:* 1090 Amsterdam Ave 14th Floor New York NY 10025. *Fax:* 212-523-3571; *E-Mail:* dba8@columbia.edu

ALLISON, DAVID C, PLANT GENETICS, CYTOLOGY. *Current Pos:* from asst prof to assoc prof, 62-73, PROF BIOL, MONMOUTH COL, ILL, 73- *Personal Data:* b Monmouth, Ill, Feb 25, 31; m 54; c 3. *Educ:* Univ Ill, BS, 56, MS, 57; Pa State Univ, PhD(genetics, breeding), 60. *Prof Exp:* Asst plant breeder, Univ Ariz, 61-62. *Mem:* Am Soc Agron; Crop Sci Soc Am; Am Inst Biol Sci. *Res:* Taxonomy and cytotaxonomy of the Gramineae; plant breeding. *Mailing Add:* Dept Biol Monmouth Col 700 E Broadway Monmouth IL 61462-1963

ALLISON, DAVID COULTER, CANCER BIOLOGY, MEDICINE. *Current Pos:* ASST CHIEF, VET ADMIN MED CTR, 78-; CHMN SURG, MED COL, 92- *Personal Data:* b Detroit, Mich, June 2, 42; c 3. *Educ:* Univ Mich, MD, 67; Univ Chicago, PhD(microbiol), 76. *Prof Exp:* Intern, Univ Chicago, 67-68; med officer, US Army, 68-70; resident, Univ Chicago, 74-77, assoc instr & chief resident, 77-78; asst prof surg, Univ NMex, 78-92. *Mem:* Cell Kinetics Soc; Histochem Soc; Soc Anal Cytol; Asn Vet Admin Surgeons. *Res:* Tumor cell biology and cytometry. *Mailing Add:* Med Coll Univ Ohio PO Box 10008 Toledo OH 43699-0008

ALLISON, FRED, JR, MEDICINE. *Current Pos:* prof, 87-96, EMER PROF MED, VANDERBILT UNIV, 96- *Personal Data:* b Abingdon, Va, Sept 8, 22; m 49, Clara Knox; c Rebecca A (Pasley), Martha A (Brown), Fred III & Robert G. *Educ:* Ala Polytech Inst, BS, 44; Vanderbilt Univ, MD, 46. *Prof Exp:* Instr microbiol, Sch Med, La State Univ, 50-51, instr med, 51-52; fel, Div Infectious Dis, Univ Wash, 52-53, instr med, 53-54, from instr to asst prof prev med, 54-55; from asst prof to prof med, Univ Miss, 55-68, chief div infectious dis, 55-68, assoc prof microbiol, 64-68; prof med & head dept, Med Ctr, La State Univ, New Orleans, 68-87. *Concurrent Pos:* Consult infectious dis, Jackson Vet Hosp, 55-67; vis investr, Rockefeller Univ, 66-67; consult med, New Orleans Vet Hosp, 77-87. *Mem:* AAAS; Asn Am Physicians; Am Soc Clin Invest; Am Col Physicians; Am Clin & Climatol Asn. *Res:* Mechanisms relating to acute inflammatory reaction; clinical aspects of infectious diseases. *Mailing Add:* 418 Fairfax Ave Nashville TN 37212

ALLISON, JAMES PATRICK, IMMUNOLOGY. *Current Pos:* interim head, Div Immunol, Dept Molecular & Cell Biol, 87-89, PROF IMMUNOL, DEPT MICROBIOL & IMMUNOL, UNIV CALIF, BERKELEY & DIR CANCER RES LAB, 85-, HEAD, DIV IMMUNOL, 89- *Personal Data:* b Alice, Tex, Aug 7, 48; m, Malinda Bell; c Robert. *Educ:* Univ Tex, Austin, BS, 69, PhD(biol sci), 73. *Prof Exp:* Fel, Dept Molecular Immunol, Scripps Clinic & Res Found, 74-77; asst biochemist & asst prof biochem, Univ Tex Syst Cancer Ctr, 77-83, assoc biochemist & assoc prof biochem, 83-84. *Concurrent Pos:* adj asst prof zool, Univ Tex, Austin, 79-84; spec assoc mem grad fac, 80-84; asst prof biochem, Grad Sch Biomed Sci, 81-84; vis scholar, Dept Path, Stanford Univ Sch Med, 83-84; mem & chmn, ASC Eleanor Roosevelt Fel Comt, Int Union Against Cancer, 85-; Reviewing ed, Sci, 85-87; chmn, Exp Immunol Study Sect, Nat Cancer Inst, NIH, 87-90; assoc ed, J Immunol, 87- *Mem:* Nat Acad Sci; Am Asn Immunologists; Am Asn Cancer Res; AAAS. *Res:* Structure-function relationships of cell surface antigens; molecular immunology of plasma membrane of normal and malignant cells; molecular immunology of the T-cell antigen receptor; co-stimulation in t-cell activation. *Mailing Add:* Cancer Res Labs 401LSA Univ Calif Berkeley CA 94720-3200

ALLISON, JERRY DAVID, RADIATION PHYSICS, HEALTH PHYSICS. *Current Pos:* ASST PROF RADIOL, MED COL GA, 78- *Personal Data:* b Brevard, NC, June 18, 48; m 69; c 2. *Educ:* NC State Univ, BS, 70; Old Dominion Univ, MS, 74; Univ Fla, PhD, 78. *Prof Exp:* Radiol control engr health physics, Newport News Shipbuilding, 70-75; grad asst radiol, Univ Fla, 75-78. *Mem:* Health Physics Soc; Am Asn Physicists Med; Sigma Xi. *Res:* Nuclear medicine instrumentation. *Mailing Add:* Radiol Med Col Ga Med Sch 1120 15th St Augusta GA 30901-3181

ALLISON, JOHN, ANALYTICAL & PHYSICAL CHEMISTRY. *Current Pos:* asst prof, Mich State Univ, 79-84, assoc prof, 84-89, assoc chairperson, Chem Grad Prog, 90-94, PROF ANALYTICAL CHEM, MICH STATE UNIV, 89- *Personal Data:* b Philadelphia, Pa, Nov 14, 51. *Educ:* Widener Col, BS, 73; Univ Del, PhD(chem), 77. *Prof Exp:* Res fel chem, Univ Del, 73-77; NSF fel chem, Stanford Univ, 77-79. *Mem:* Am Chem Soc; Am Soc Mass Spectrometry. *Res:* Ion cyclotron resonance spectroscopy; organometallic chemistry in the gas phase; ion-molecule reactions; laser-induced fluorescence as a probe of chemical processes; electron impact dissociative excitation; mass spectrometry; peptide analysis; spectroscopy of ions; desorption ionization of molecules; laser spectroscopy. *Mailing Add:* Dept Chem Mich State Univ East Lansing MI 48824. *Fax:* 517-355-9715; *E-Mail:* allison@cemvax.ccm.msu.edu

ALLISON, JOHN EVERETT, anatomy; deceased, see previous edition for last biography

ALLISON, JOHN P, ORGANIC CHEMISTRY, POLYMER CHEMISTRY. *Current Pos:* RES CHEMIST, KIMBERLY-CLARK CORP, 70- *Personal Data:* b Beckenham, Kent, Eng, Feb 17, 36; US citizen; m 66; c 2. *Educ:* Univ Birmingham, BSc, 58, PhD(chem), 61. *Prof Exp:* Fel chem, Univ Ariz, 61-63; sr res chemist, polymer dept, res labs, Gen Motors Tech Ctr, 63-66; staff mem, polymer chem, res div, Raychem Corp, 66-70. *Mem:* Am Chem Soc; Royal Soc Chem. *Res:* Synthetic polymer chemistry; fiber bonding; chemistry of natural polymers and polymer reactions; flexible foams. *Mailing Add:* 2584 N Arbor Trail Marietta GA 30066-2254

ALLISON, MERLE LEE, DIPLOG INTERPRETATION, VARIOUS CRUSTAL STRUCTURES. *Current Pos:* DIR & STATE GEOLOGIST, UTAH GEOL SURV, SALT LAKE CITY, 89- *Personal Data:* b Philadelphia, Pa, Jan 15, 48. *Educ:* Univ Calif, Riverside, BS, 70; San Diego State Univ, MS, 74; Univ Mass, PhD, 86. *Prof Exp:* Gas engr, Calif Div Oil & Gas, Inglewood, 71-72; press secy & mgr, Caprio for Congress, San Diego, 72, 74; geologist, Chevron Corp, San Francisco, 74-79, Sohio Petrol-BP, Dallas & Houston, 84-87; consult geologist, Amherst, Mass, 80-84; sr geologist, Univ Utah Res Inst, Salt Lake City, 87-89. *Concurrent Pos:* Scientist II, Jet Propulsion Lab-NASA, Pasadena, 81; pres, Western Earth Sci Tech, Inc, Casper, Wyo, 88-93; energy adv, Clifford for Cong, Houston, 90; chair, Utah Geog Info Coun, Salt Lake City, 92-93. *Mem:* Am Asn Petrol Geologists; Geol Soc Am; Soc Prof Well Log Analysts; Am Geophys Union; Asn for Geoscientists. *Res:* Geology of Ganymede; diplog interpretation; various of in-situ crustal structures; numerous articles in professional journals. *Mailing Add:* Utah Geol Surv 1594 W North Temple #3410 Salt Lake City UT 84114-6100

ALLISON, MILTON JAMES, MICROBIOLOGY. *Current Pos:* bacteriologist, Dairy Cattle Res Br, Agr Res Serv, 57-62, RES MICROBIOLOGIST, NAT ANIMAL DIS CTR, USDA, 62- *Personal Data:* b South Shore, SDak, May 10, 31; m 53; c 3. *Educ:* SDak State Col, BS, 53, MS, 54; Univ Md, PhD, 61. *Prof Exp:* Instr bact, SDak State Col, 54-55. *Mem:* Am Soc Microbiol; Sigma Xi; Am Soc Animal Sci; AAAS; Am Acad Microbiol. *Res:* Ecology of microorganisms; bacterial physiology and nutrition; biosynthesis of microbial amino acids and lipids; anaerobic bacteria of the mammalian digestive system and their interactions with toxic substances. *Mailing Add:* 1434 Linden Dr Ames IA 50010-5532

ALLISON, RICHARD C, invertebrate paleontology, biostratigraphy, for more information see previous edition

ALLISON, RICHARD GALL, NUTRITIONAL BIOCHEMISTRY. *Current Pos:* EXEC OFFICER & SCI OFFICER, AM SOC NUTRIT SCI, 84- *Personal Data:* b Hanover, Pa, Jan 28, 43; m 92, Insun Kim; c Dina N, Stephen C & Sara K. *Educ:* Pa State Univ, BS, 64; Univ Calif, Davis, PhD(nutrit), 68. *Honors & Awards:* Commissioner's Spec Award, Food & Drug Admin. *Prof Exp:* Res biochemist, Dept Food Sci & Technol, Univ Calif, Davis, 69; biochemist, Walter Reed Army Inst Res, Walter Reed Army Med Ctr, 69-73; res assoc, Life Sci Res Off, Fedn Am Socs Exp Biol, 74-78, sr staff scientist, 78-84; sci officer, Am Soc Clin Nutrit, 84-86. *Mem:* AAAS; Am Soc Nutrit Sci; Am Soc Clin Nutrit. *Res:* Biomedical research evaluation; nutrition; food ingredients; water. *Mailing Add:* Am Soc Nutrit Sci 9650 Rockville Pike Bethesda MD 20814-3990. *Fax:* 301-571-1892; *E-Mail:* rallison@asns.faseb.org

ALLISON, ROBERT DEAN, CLINICAL PHARMACOLOGY, BIOENGINEERING. *Current Pos:* PRES, DYNAMIC RES ENTERPRISES INC, 73- *Personal Data:* b Farmersville Station, NY, Feb 29, 32; m 81; c 3. *Educ:* Hartwick Col, BA, 54; Wayne State Univ, MS, 60, Col Med, PhD(physiol & pharmacol), 62. *Prof Exp:* Instr, Anesthesiol Dept, Grace Hosp, Mich, 61-62; staff physiologist & assoc, Dept Physiol, Lovelace Found Med Educ & Res, NMex, 62-66; asst prof, Dept Biol, Univ NMex, 65-66; ASSOC PROF & SPEC LECTR, LA STATE UNIV MED SCH, 70- *Concurrent Pos:* Chief, Sect Cardiovascular Physiol & dir, Cardiovasc Labs, Scott & White Clin, Tex, 66-73; consult clin res, Santa Fe Hosp, Tex & Vet Admin Med Ctr, Tex, 66-73; res physiologist, Vet Med Ctr, Tex, 73-75; consult, Clin Path Lab, Grand Prairie Community Hosp, Tex, 78-80; adj assoc prof physiol, Tex Health Sci Ctr, Southwestern Med Sch, 76-; adj assoc prof bioeng, Univ Tex, Arlington, 76-; assoc prof biol, Tex Wesleyan Col, 76- & Brookhaven Col, 82-; assoc prof & div chmn basic sci & res, Parker Col, 83- *Mem:* Fel Am Geriat Soc; Am Physiol Soc; fel Int Col Angiol; Sigma Xi; Int Soc Nephrology. *Res:* Development of non-invasive (no needle or catheter) techniques for measuring cardiovascular and pulmonary function in human subjects, the systems utilize ultrasound, plethysmographs and other parameters that do not require skin puncture. *Mailing Add:* 3600 N 29th St Waco TX 76708

ALLISON, RONALD C, PULMONARY MEDICINE. *Current Pos:* Asst Prof, 80-85, ASSOC PROF MED & PHYSIOL, COL MED, UNIV S ALA, 85- *Personal Data:* b San Angelo, Tex, Jan 11, 45. *Educ:* Univ Tex, San Antonio, MD, 71. *Mem:* Am Col Physicians; Am Col Chest Physicians; Am Thoracic Soc; Am Physiol Soc. *Mailing Add:* Col Med & Physiol Univ S Ala 2451 Fillingim St Mobile AL 36617-2238

ALLISON, STEPHEN WILLIAM, FIBEROPTIC SENSORS, THERMOMETRY. *Current Pos:* DEVELOP STAFF PHYSICIST, OAK RIDGE GAS DIFFUSION PLANT, LOCKHEED MARTIN ENERGY SYSTS, 78- *Personal Data:* b Pocahontas, Ark, Nov 3, 50; m 75; c 2. *Educ:* Harding Univ, BS, 72; Memphis State Univ, MS, 74; Univ Va, PhD(eng physics), 79. *Prof Exp:* Develop staff physicist, Union Carbide Nuclear Div, 78-84. *Concurrent Pos:* Adj prof elec eng, Univ Tenn, 87-; vis assoc res prof, Dept Nuclear Eng & Eng Physics, Univ Va, 89-90. *Mem:* Optical Soc Am; Laser Inst Am; Soc Photo-Optical Instrumentation Engrs. *Res:* Diagnostic and remote measurement techniques with lasers, fiberoptics, and electro-optics; spectroscopy; rotational systems; nonlinear optics; thermometry; received three patent awards related to thermometry and fiber sensors. *Mailing Add:* Lockheed Martin Energy Res PO Box 2009 MS 7280 Oak Ridge TN 37831

ALLISON, WILLIAM EARL, ENTOMOLOGY. *Current Pos:* RETIRED. *Personal Data:* b Claremore, Okla, Oct 2, 32; m 56; c 2. *Educ:* Okla A&M Col, BS, 57; Okla State Univ, MS, 58; Tex A&M Univ, PhD(biochem), 63. *Prof Exp:* Res entomologist, Dow Chem Co, Seal Beach, Calif, 63-67, group leader entom, Midland, Mich, 67-71, group leader entom & nematol, Walnut Creek, 71-73, sr res entomologist, Dow Chem Co Japan Ltd, 74 & Dow Chem Co Pac Ltd, Malaysia, 75, res mgr, Insecticides Discovery Group, Dow Chem Co, Walnut Creek, 83-92, mgr, Western Tech Serv & Develop, Dow Elanco, 90-92. *Concurrent Pos:* Sr develop specialist entom, Plant Path & Plant Nutrit, Dow Chem Co, Walnut Creek, 75-, regional mgr tech serv & develop, Agr Prod Dept, 78- *Mem:* Entom Soc Am; AAAS. *Res:* Structure versus activity to search for new insecticides. *Mailing Add:* 9499 Bush Plymouth CA 95669-0596

ALLISON, WILLIAM HUGH, mycology; deceased, see previous edition for last biography

ALLISON, WILLIAM S, PROTEIN CHEMISTRY, EMZYMOLOGY. *Current Pos:* from asst to assoc prof, 73-80, PROF CHEM, UNIV CALIF, SAN DIEGO, 80- *Personal Data:* b North Adams, Mass, June 16, 35; m 64, Irene F Carrigan; c Carl & Catherine. *Educ:* Dartmouth Col, AB, 57, MA, 59; Brandeis Univ, PhD(biochem), 63. *Honors & Awards:* Career Develop Award, NIH, 67-69. *Prof Exp:* USPHS fel, Lab Molecular Biol, Cambridge Univ, 64-65; res assoc, Brandeis Univ, 65-66, asst prof biochem, 66-69. *Mem:* Am Soc Biochem & Molecular Biol; Biophys Soc; Am Chem Soc; Protein Soc. *Res:* Enzymology; comparative biochemistry; functional groups of enzymes; mechanism of enzyme action. *Mailing Add:* Dept Chem Univ Calif San Diego M-0601 La Jolla CA 92093-0601

ALLISTON, CHARLES WALTER, ENVIRONMENTAL PHYSIOLOGY, REPRODUCTIVE PHYSIOLOGY. *Current Pos:* assoc prof, 67-75, PROF ANIMAL SCI, PURDUE UNIV, 75- *Personal Data:* b Florence, Miss, May 27, 30; m 53; c 2. *Educ:* Miss State Col, BS, 51, MS, 57; NC State Col, PhD(physiol), 60. *Honors & Awards:* Sigma Xi Res Award, 66. *Prof Exp:* Res asst, Miss State Col, 55-56, res technician, 56-57; res asst, NC State Col, 57-60, from asst prof to assoc prof zool, 60-67. *Concurrent Pos:* NIH res grant, 62-; David Ross res grant, 67-69 & 77-79; NSF grant, 74- *Res:* Environmental and reproductive physiology, particularly influence of the physical environment upon reproductive efficiency of the mammalian female. *Mailing Add:* 263 Blueberry Lane West Lafayette IN 47906

ALLMAN, JOHN MORGAN, NEUROPHYSIOLOGY, PRIMATOLOGY. *Current Pos:* assoc prof, 74-84, PROF BIOL, CALIF INST TECHNOL, 84-, HIXON PROF PSYCHOBIOL, 89- *Personal Data:* b Columbus, Ohio, May 17, 43. *Educ:* Univ Va, BA, 65; Univ Chicago, PhD(anthrop), 71. *Honors & Awards:* Golden Brain Award, Minerva Found. *Prof Exp:* Fel neurophysiol, Univ Wis, 70-73; res asst prof psychol, Vanderbilt Univ, 73-74. *Concurrent Pos:* Sloan fel, 74; USPHS career develop, 76-81. *Mem:* Soc Neurosci; Asn Res Vision & Ophthal; Int Brain Res Orgn; Am Soc Primatologists. *Res:* Functional organization of the visual system in primates; evolution of brain and behavior in primates; brain and lifespan. *Mailing Add:* Div Biol 156-29 Calif Inst Technol 1201 E California Pasadena CA 91125-0001

ALLMANN, DAVID WILLIAM, BIOCHEMISTRY. *Current Pos:* assoc prof biochem, 70-80, assoc prof, Dent Sch, 73-80, PROF BIOCHEM, SCH MED & PROF DENT SCH, IND UNIV-PURDUE UNIV, INDIANAPOLIS, 80- *Personal Data:* b Peru, Ind, May 20, 35; m 56; c 2. *Educ:* Ind Univ, BS, 58, PhD(biochem), 64. *Prof Exp:* Res asst bact, Ind Univ, 57, res asst biochem, 58-60; asst prof, Univ Wis-Madison, 66-70. *Concurrent Pos:* NIH fel biochem, Univ Wis-Madison, 64-66; res biochemist, Vet Admin Hosp, 70-72; consult, Am Dent Asn Accreditation Comt & mem, Study Sect, Nat Inst Dent Res, 80; rev, J Dent Res & Arch Oral Biol, 80-; pres, Pharmacol, Toxicol Therapeut Sect, Int Asn Dent Res, 85-86. *Mem:* Am Inst Nutrit; Int Asn Dent Res; Am Soc Biol Chemists; fel Am Inst Chemists; Am Soc Cell Biologists; Europ Orgn Caries Res. *Res:* Effect of F-ions on adenylate cyclase and glucose metabolism in vivo. *Mailing Add:* Dept Biochem Ind Univ Sch Med 635 Barnhill Dr Indianapolis IN 46202-5122

ALLMARAS, RAYMOND RICHARD, SOIL SCIENCE. *Current Pos:* SR SOIL SCIENTIST, AGR RES SERV, USDA, UNIV MINN. *Personal Data:* b New Rockford, NDak, Sept 11, 26; m 52; c 6. *Educ:* NDak State Univ, BS, 52; Univ Nebr, MS, 56; Iowa State Univ, PhD(soil sci), 60. *Prof Exp:* Soil scientist, Agr Res Serv, USDA, Nebr, 52-56; asst, Iowa State Univ, 57-60; soil scientist, Columbia Plateau Conserv Res Ctr, Agr Res Serv, USDA, 60-72, res leader & tech adv, 72-80, res & location leader, 80-; Dept Soil Sci, Ore State Univ. *Mem:* Am Soc Agron; Soil Sci Soc Am; Biomet Soc; Am Statist Asn; AAAS. *Res:* Tillage, soil structure, plant rooting, soil and plant environment and plant-water relations. *Mailing Add:* Agr Res Serv USDA Univ Minn 439 Borlaug Hall St Paul MN 55108

ALLMENDINGER, E EUGENE, NAVAL ARCHITECTURE, MECHANICAL ENGINEERING. *Current Pos:* RETIRED. *Personal Data:* b Dearborn, Mich, July 4, 17; m 49, Ann Waldron; c Nancy A (Walker), Richard W & Eugene S. *Educ:* Univ Mich, BSE, 41; Univ NH, MS, 50. *Hon Degrees:* Dr, Univ NH, 92. *Prof Exp:* Asst prof naval eng, US Naval Acad, 50-53; asst prof naval archit, Mass Inst Technol, 53-58; assoc prof mech eng, Univ NH, 58-73, assoc prof naval archit, 73-83. *Concurrent Pos:* Prof, Univ Sao Paulo, 59-61; Gulf Oil Corp grant, 63; vis assoc prof, Univ Hawaii, 68-69 & Univ Trondheim, Norway, 76; chmn, NH Oceanog Found; vis prof, Chalmers Inst Technol, Gothenburg, Sweden, 80, 81. *Mem:* Fel Soc Naval Archit & Marine Eng; Marine Technol Soc; Am Soc Eng Educ; Sigma Xi. *Res:* Submarine and submersible vehicle systems design, both manned and unmanned systems. *Mailing Add:* 46 Oyster River Rd Durham NH 03824

ALLNATT, ALAN RICHARD, STATISTICAL MECHANICS, SOLID STATE. *Current Pos:* PROF CHEM, UNIV WESTERN ONT, 69- *Personal Data:* b Portsmouth, Eng, July 18, 33; m 73. *Educ:* Univ London, BSc, 56, PhD(phys chem), 59. *Prof Exp:* NATO fel chem, Univ Chicago, 59-61; lectr, Univ Manchester, 61-69. *Concurrent Pos:* Fel, Chem Inst Can, 74. *Mem:* Royal Soc Chem; fel Can Inst Chem. *Res:* Statistical mechanics of matter transport and thermodynamic properties of imperfect solids and simple liquids. *Mailing Add:* Dept Chem Univ Western Ont London ON N6A 5B7 Can

ALLNUTT, F C THOMAS, DEVELOPMENT OF PRODUCTS FROM MICROALGAE, MANIPULATION OF MICROALGAE & BACTERIAL STRAINS. *Current Pos:* MICROBIOL GROUP LEADER, MARTEK BIOSCI CORP, 89- *Personal Data:* b Frederick, Md, June 27, 54; m 87, Virginia Pierce; c B Dawson, Annie L & Mary Alice. *Educ:* Va Polytech Inst & State Univ, BS, 76, MS, 79; Univ Pa, PhD(biol), 85. *Prof Exp:* Assoc, Purdue Univ, 85-87, Rutgers Univ, 87-89. *Mem:* Am Soc Microbiol; Am Soc Plant Physiologists; Soc Indust Microbiologists; Sigma Xi. *Res:* Production of useful products from microalgae either directly using standard separation and biochemical approaches or indirectly using microalgae as the starting material. *Mailing Add:* Martek Biosci Corp 6480 Dobbin Rd Columbia MD 21045. *Fax:* 410-740-2985; *E-Mail:* 74242.2565@compuserve.com

ALLRED, ALBERT LOUIS, INORGANIC CHEMISTRY. *Current Pos:* Instr chem, Northwestern Univ, 56-58, from asst prof to assoc prof, 58-69, assoc dean arts & sci, 70-74, chmn dept, 80-86, interim dean, Col Arts & Sci, 87-88, prof chem, 69-91, actg vpres res & dean, Grad Sch, 92, ACTG PROVOST, NORTHWESTERN UNIV, 95. *Personal Data:* b Mt Airy, NC, Sept 19, 31; m 58, Nancy Willis; c Kevin S, Gregg W & Sarah E. *Educ:* Univ NC, BS, 53; Harvard Univ, AM, 55, PhD(chem), 56. *Concurrent Pos:* Alfred P Sloan res fel, 63-65; hon res assoc, Univ Col London, 65; fel, Univ Rome, 67; consult, World Book Encycl, 77-92, organometallic chem, UNESCO, Columbia, 79; vis scholar, Cambridge Univ, 87. *Mem:* Am Chem Soc; Royal Soc Chem; Sigma Xi; fel AAAS. *Res:* Synthetic inorganic and organometallic chemistry; electronegativity; electrochemistry. *Mailing Add:* Dept Chem Northwestern Univ Evanston IL 60208-3113

ALLRED, DAVID D, THIN FILMS, THERMOELECTRIC MATERIALS. *Current Pos:* assoc prof, 87-93, PROF PHYSICS & ASTRON, BRIGHAM YOUNG UNIV, 93- *Personal Data:* b Salt Lake City, Utah, June 22, 47; m 69, Janice Merrill; c 9. *Educ:* Brigham Young Univ, BS, 71; Princeton Univ, MA, 73, PhD(physics & phys chem), 77. *Prof Exp:* NSF fel, Oak Ridge Nat Lab, 77-78; res assoc, Optical Sci Ctr, Univ Ariz, 78-79, res asst prof, 80; group leader solar thermal res, Energy Conversion Devices, Inc, 80-82, group leader thermoelec res, 82-87. *Concurrent Pos:* Scientist & bd mem, Moytek, Inc, 87-94. *Mem:* Int Thermoelec Soc (secy, 88-91); Am Vacuum Soc; Mat Res Soc; Am Optical Soc. *Res:* Thin film phenomena-deposition and characterization of optical applications soft x-ray optics; thermoelectric materials; amorphous semiconductors; nanostructures; raman spectroscopy and photoluminescences applications of heavy element semiconductors and dielectrics for scintillators, detectors and thermoelectricity; chemical vapor deposition; multilayers; solar energy materials. *Mailing Add:* 221 W 3700 N Provo UT 84604. *Fax:* 801-378-2265; *E-Mail:* allred@xray.byu.edu

ALLRED, DAVID R, PARASITOLOGY, IMMUNOLOGY. *Current Pos:* asst res sci, 86-90, asst prof, 90-95, ASSOC PROF, UNIV FLA, 95- *Educ:* Univ Calif, Riverside, PhD(cell biol), 82. *Honors & Awards:* C E Cornelius Young Investr Award, 95. *Prof Exp:* Res assoc, Univ Colo, 83-86. *Mem:* Am Soc Cell Biol; Am Soc Parasitol; AAAS. *Res:* Molecular biology of host-parasite interactions involving blood-borne rickettsial and protozoan parasites. *Mailing Add:* Dept Patholbiol Univ Fla Col Vet Med PO Box 110880 Gainesville FL 32611-0880. *E-Mail:* allred.vetmed3@mail.health.ufl.edu

ALLRED, DORALD MERVIN, ENTOMOLOGY, ECOLOGY. *Current Pos:* from asst prof to assoc prof, 56-66, PROF ZOOL, BRIGHAM YOUNG UNIV, 66- *Personal Data:* b Lehi, Utah, July 11, 23; m 52; c 5. *Educ:* Brigham Young Univ, AB, 50, MA, 51; Univ Utah, PhD(entom), 54. *Prof Exp:* Field entomologist, State Exten Serv, Utah, 48-50; ranger-naturalist, US Nat Park Serv, 50-51; res fel entom, Brigham Young Univ, 51-53; instr biol, St Mary-of-the-Wasatch Acad, 53; instr biol, Univ Utah, 53-54, assoc ecologist & chief entom & arachnid sect, ecol res, 54-56. *Res:* Parasitic acarology; parasitology; medical entomology and ecology. *Mailing Add:* 2797 N 700 East Provo UT 84604

ALLRED, E(VAN) R(ICH), CIVIL & AGRICULTURAL ENGINEERING. *Current Pos:* from asst prof to assoc prof, 45-57, PROF AGR ENG, UNIV MINN, ST PAUL, 57- *Personal Data:* b St Charles, Idaho, May 6, 16; m 39; c 3. *Educ:* Utah State Univ, BS, 39; Univ Minn, MS, 41. *Prof Exp:* Civil engr, US Bur Reclamation, 41-43 & US Engrs Off, 43-45. *Mem:* Am Soc Civil Engrs; Am Soc Agr Engrs. *Res:* Water supply; irrigation, agricultural drainage and hydrology. *Mailing Add:* 1426 Raymond Ave St Paul MN 55108

ALLRED, EVAN LEIGH, ORGANIC CHEMISTRY, STRUCTURAL CHEMISTRY. *Current Pos:* from asst prof to assoc prof, 63-70, PROF CHEM, UNIV UTAH, 70- *Personal Data:* b Deseret, Utah, May 22, 29; m 55; c 4. *Educ:* Brigham Young Univ, BS, 51, MS, 56; Univ Calif, Los Angeles, PhD(chem), 59. *Prof Exp:* Res chemist, Phillips Petrol Co, 51-54; asst org chem, Brigham Young Univ, 54-55 & Univ Calif, Los Angeles, 55-59; instr chem, Univ Wash, 60-61; sr res chemist, Rohm and Haas Co, 61-63. *Concurrent Pos:* NSF fel, Univ Colo, 59-60; David P Gardner fac fel, Univ Utah, 76. *Mem:* Am Chem Soc. *Res:* Physical-organic chemistry; factors affecting the reactivity of molecules; synthesis and reactivity of structures of theoretical interest; reaction mechanisms. *Mailing Add:* 4195 S 2700 E Salt Lake City UT 84124

ALLRED, JOHN B, BIOCHEMISTRY, NUTRITION. *Current Pos:* dir, Inst Nutrit, 68-71, assoc prof food sci & nutrit, 71-74, PROF FOOD SCI & TECHNOL, OHIO STATE UNIV, 74- *Personal Data:* b Oklahoma City, Okla, June 17, 34; m 79; c 4. *Educ:* Okla State Univ, BS, 55; Wash State Univ, MS, 57; Univ Calif, Davis, PhD(biochem), 62. *Prof Exp:* Asst nutrit, Wash State Univ, 55-57; asst nutrit & biochem, Univ Calif, Davis, 58-60; from asst prof to assoc prof chem, Okla City Univ, 61-68, chmn dept, 62-63. *Mem:* Am Soc Biochem & Molecular Biol; Am Inst Nutrit; Brit Biochem Soc. *Res:* Intermediary metabolism; metabolic control mechanisms; enzymology; nutritional interest in lipid metabolism. *Mailing Add:* Dept Food Sci & Technol Ohio State Univ 2121 Fyffe Rd Columbus OH 43210-1097

ALLRED, JOHN C(ALDWELL), ACOUSTICS. *Current Pos:* PUBL & PRES, EXCEPT BOOKS LTD, 87- *Personal Data:* b Breckenridge, Tex, Apr 24, 26; m 50; c Susan E, Katherine A & John R. *Educ:* Tex Christian Univ, BA, 44; Univ Tex, MA, 48, PhD(physics), 50. *Prof Exp:* Asst, Los Alamos Sci Lab, 48-49, mem staff, 49-55; res scientist, Convair, 55-56; from assoc prof to prof physics & biophys sci, Univ Houston, 56-79, assoc dean, Col Arts & Sci, 59-61, asst to pres, 61-62, vpres & dean faculties, 62-68; consult, Los Alamos Nat Lab, 79-93. *Mem:* Fel Am Phys Soc; Am Nuclear Soc; Acoust Soc Am; Sigma Xi. *Res:* Light particle scattering and interactions; neutron scattering and spectra; fluid dynamics; reactor design; architectural acoustics. *Mailing Add:* 798 47th St Los Alamos NM 87544. *E-Mail:* 77076.730@compuserve.com

ALLRED, KEITH REID, crop production, plant biochemistry, for more information see previous edition

ALLRED, KELLY WAYNE, PLANT TAXONOMY. *Current Pos:* ASST PROF RANGE SCI, NMEX STATE UNIV, 79- *Personal Data:* b Sacramento, Calif, April 23, 49; m 72; c 3. *Educ:* Brigham Young Univ, BS, 74, MS, 75; Tex A&M Univ, PhD(range sci), 79. *Prof Exp:* Instr bot, State Univ NY, Geneseo, 78-79. *Mem:* Am Soc Plant Taxonomists; Int Asn Plant Taxonomists; Soc Range Mgt; Sigma Xi. *Res:* Plant taxonomy, particularly of new world grasses with emphasis in the tribe Andropogoneae and genus Bothriochloa; floristics of the southwestern United States with emphasis on New Mexico. *Mailing Add:* Dept Animal Sci NMex State Univ PO Box 30003 Las Cruces NM 88003-8003

ALLRED, LAWRENCE ERVIN (JOE), CELL BIOLOGY. *Current Pos:* SR RES ASSOC, EXPLOR RES & NEW TECHNOL DEPT, S C JOHNSON & SON, INC, 80- *Personal Data:* b Matewan, WVa, June 9, 46; div; c Aaron W & Brenna K. *Educ:* Univ Houston, BS, 68; Univ Tex, MS, 70, PhD(cellular biophys), 73. *Prof Exp:* Fel, dept molecular cell develop biol, Univ Colo, 73-77; asst prof, Dept Pharmacol, Ohio State Univ, 78-80, clin asst prof, 80-82. *Concurrent Pos:* Adj assoc prof, Univ Wis-Parkside, 81-87; assoc clin prof, Dept Med, Med Col Wis, 84-87. *Mem:* Entomo Soc Am. *Res:* urban pest entomology. *Mailing Add:* S C Johnson & Son Inc 1525 Howe St Racine WI 53403

ALLRED, V(ICTOR) DEAN, FUEL ENGINEERING. *Current Pos:* RETIRED. *Personal Data:* b Delta, Utah, Sept 13, 22; m 44, Alice Jackson; c David D, Thomas J, Margaret A (Wilkins), Wendell K, Marilyn A (Riddle) & Kevin L. *Educ:* Univ Utah, BChE, 48, PhD(fuel technol), 51. *Prof Exp:* Res engr, Catalytic Construct Co, 53-54; res chemist, Union Carbide Nuclear Co, Oak Ridge Nat Lab, 54-56; sr res engr, Denver Res Ctr, Ohio Oil Co, 56-62, mgr, Anal Dept, Marathon Oil Co, 62-66, res assoc, Denver Res Ctr, Marathon Oil Co, 66-86. *Concurrent Pos:* Adj prof fuels eng, Univ Utah, 85-88. *Mem:* Emer mem Am Chem Soc. *Res:* Catalytic chemistry; synthetic fuels and lubricants; petroleum production; oil shale and bituminous sand processing; petroleum coke production and processing; author of one book. *Mailing Add:* 1925 E Otero Lane Littleton CO 80122. *E-Mail:* 73651.2533@compuserve.com

ALLUKIAN, MYRON, ECOLOGICAL DENTISTRY. *Current Pos:* ASST DEP COMNR & DIR BUR COMMUNITY DENT PROGS, DEPT HEALTH & HOSP, BOSTON, 71-, ASST DEP COMNR & DIR, PERSONNEL HEALTH SERVS, 91- *Personal Data:* b Cambridge, Mass. *Educ:* Tufts Univ, BS, 60; Univ Pa, DDS, 64; Harvard Univ, MPH, 67; Inst de Nutrit de Centro Am, Guatemala, cert, 67; Am Bd Dent Pub Health, dipl, 73. *Honors & Awards:* Cert Commendation, Am Dent Asn, 78; Spec Merit Award, Am Asn Pub Health Dent, 87. *Prof Exp:* Clin dir, prosthetics officer, US Naval Dent Corps, 64-66; dent consult, Curric Comt, Training Ctr Comprehensive Care, Lemuel Shattuck Hosp, 67-69; asst oral surg, Mass Gen Hosp, 69-70, chief, Dent Health Serv, 70-77, clin assoc, 71-87; assoc, Dept Ecol Dent, Harvard Sch Dent Med, 69-70, instr, 70-71, asst clin prof, 71-77; instr, Dept Social Dent, Tufts Univ, 70-72, clin instr, Oral Health Serv, 72-78. *Concurrent Pos:* Lectr, Forsyth Sch Dent Hygenists, 70-; assoc vis dentist, Boston City Hosp, 70-; regional dent consult, Job Corps, US Dept Labor, 73-; assoc clin prof, Dent Care Admin, Harvard Sch Dent Med, 77-; mem numerous comts, asns & orgns; dent clin dir, New Eng AIDS Educ Training Ctr; Exemplary Serv Award, Chief Dent Offier, US Surgeon Gen's Off, 97. *Mem:* Inst Med-Nat Acad Sci; hon fel Royal Soc Health Gt Brit; fel Int Col Dentists; Am Pub Health Asn. *Res:* Policy, vulnerable populations, prevention, education and delivery systems; has over 90 professional publications. *Mailing Add:* Bur Community Dent Prog Dept Health & Hosp 1010 Massachusetts Ave Boston MA 02118

ALLUM, FRANK RAYMOND, COSMIC RAY PHYSICS, SPACE PHYSICS. *Current Pos:* vis res assoc cosmic rays, Univ Tex, Dallas, 66, res assoc, 66-69, asst prof, 69-71, res scientist, 71-76, mem cosmic ray group, 76-80. *Personal Data:* b Melbourne, Australia, Jan 31, 36; m 68. *Educ:* Univ Melbourne, BS, 55, MS, 58, PhD(nuclear physics), 63. *Prof Exp:* Sr demonstr, Dept Physics, Univ Melbourne, 61-63; res assoc auroral physics, Space Sci Dept, Rice Univ, 64-66. *Mem:* Am Geophys Union; Am Phys Soc. *Res:* Propagation characteristics of low energy solar cosmic rays in the interplanetary medium using temporal, spectral and anisotropic data from the satellites, Explorers 34 and 41; solar-terrestrial relationships. *Mailing Add:* 633 Timberlake Circle Richardson TX 75080

ALLY, MOONIS RAZA, INSTRUMENTATION IN CHEMICAL ANALYSIS, DEVELOPMENT OF IONIC LATTICE MODELS. *Current Pos:* Leader indust chem heat pump technol, Energy Div, Oak Ridge Nat Lab, 85-90, group leader, 87-95, strategic planning group, Chem Technol Div, 95-96, leader, Emphasis Area, 96-97, SR RES STAFF, OAK RIDGE NAT LAB, 95- *Personal Data:* b Karachi, Pakistan, June 6, 52; US citizen; c 4. *Educ:* Nat Col Sci & Technol, Karachi, Pakistan, BSc, 75; Ill Inst Technol, MS, 77; Univ Pittsburgh, PhD(chem eng), 81. *Honors & Awards:* Lockheed-Martin Energy Res Technol Transfer Award, 96; Silver Acorn, Martin Marietta Energy Systs Inc, 96. *Concurrent Pos:* Prin investr, Off Indust Techol, US Dept Energy, 85-90, mem, Traveling Lectr Prog, 94-; mem, Comt T-7N, Nat Asn Conrosion Engrs, 93, Seed Money Comt, Oak Ridge Nat Lab, 95-97; adj prof, Univ Tenn, 95-97. *Mem:* Am Chem Soc. *Res:* Understanding the structure and properties of aqueous electrolytes from dilute solutions to essentially molten salts; constructing mathematical models that explain the behavior and properties of concentrated solutions; applications are in food science and technology, biology, agriculture, soil solutions, commercial heating and refrigeration, and in aquatic chemistry; thermodynamics and kinetics of chemical reactions; hardware development and testing; data acquisition and statistical analysis. *Mailing Add:* Oak Ridge Nat Lab Bldg 3017 PO Box 2008 Oak Ridge TN 37831-6044. *Fax:* 423-576-4195; *E-Mail:* allymr@ornl.gov

ALM, ALVIN ARTHUR, FORESTRY. *Current Pos:* res asst forestry, Univ Minn, 63-65, res fel forestry, 66-71, from asst prof to assoc prof, 71-80, PROF FORESTRY, UNIV MINN, 80- *Personal Data:* b Albert Lea, Minn, July 30, 35; m 60; c 2. *Educ:* Univ Minn, BS, 61, MS, 65, PhD(forestry), 71. *Prof Exp:* Assoc forester, Forestry Consult Serv, Inc, 61-62; appraiser real estate, Bur Pub Rds, 65-66. *Mem:* Soc Am Foresters; Sigma Xi. *Res:* Forest regeneration; vegetative successional changes; silvicultural practices such as site preparation, thinnings and harvesting; Christmas tree management; moisture and tree growth relationships. *Mailing Add:* 402 Dalewood Ave Cloquet MN 55720-1206

ALM, ROBERT M, ORGANIC CHEMISTRY. *Current Pos:* RETIRED. *Personal Data:* b Princeton, Ill, Sept 19, 21; m 43; c 3. *Educ:* Monmouth Col, BS, 43; Ohio State Univ, PhD(chem), 48. *Prof Exp:* Chemist, Standard Oil Co (Ind), 48-53, group leader, 53-63, res assoc, 63-69, dir anal res, Naperville, 70-74, sr consult chemist, 74-76, sr res assoc, 76-79. *Mem:* Am Chem Soc. *Res:* Shale oil; synthetic fuels. *Mailing Add:* PO Box 247 Union WV 24983-0247

ALMASAN, ALEXANDRU, MOLECULAR BIOLOGY. *Current Pos:* STAFF SCI, CLEVELAND CLIN, OHIO, 95- *Personal Data:* b St Petersburg, Russia, Mar 15, 54; m 78, Carmen C Pricajan. *Educ:* Univ Brasov, BS, 77, MS, 79; Univ SC, PhD(biol), 84. *Prof Exp:* Res teaching asst, Univ SC, 84-89, fel, 89; res assoc, Salk Inst Biol Studies, 89-95. *Concurrent Pos:* Nat res serv award fel, NIH, 91-93. *Mem:* Genetics Soc Am; Am Soc Human Genetics; Sigma Xi. *Res:* Disruption of cell cycle control and genetic stability in mammalian cells; homologous recombination and DNA repair in human cells; novel methods of mapping human genes. *Mailing Add:* 10358 Hanford Lane Twinsburg OH 44087. *Fax:* 619-457-2762; *E-Mail:* almasan@salk.sc2.salk.edu

ALMASAN, CARMEN CRISTINA, SUPERCONDUCTIVITY, MAGNETISM. *Current Pos:* res physicist, 90-92, asst proj scientist, 93-94, ASST PROF, UNIV CALIF, SAN DIEGO, 95- *Personal Data:* b Cluj-Napoca, Romania, Dec 9, 54; US citizen; m 79. *Educ:* Univ Bucharest, Romania, BS, 77, MS, 79; Univ SC, PhD(physics), 89. *Prof Exp:* Res assoc, Inst Physics & Technol of Mat, 79-83; teaching asst res, Univ SC, Columbia, 84-88, Amelia Earhart fel res, 87-89, Link fel, 88-89, postdoctoral res, 89. *Concurrent Pos:* Vis res scientist, Matsushita Int Res & Develop Ctr, Japan, 89. *Mem:* Am Phys Soc; AAAS. *Res:* Normal and superconducting properties of the high transition temperature cuprates; dynamic and steady-state magnetic behaviors; electric and magnetic critical fluctuations; coexistence of superconductivity and magnetism; high pressure physics. *Mailing Add:* Dept Physics Kent State Univ Kent OH 44242. *Fax:* 619-534-1241; *E-Mail:* ccambm@sdphv1.ucsd.edu

ALMASI, GEORGE STANLEY, ELECTRICAL ENGINEERING. *Current Pos:* MEM RES STAFF, EXPLOR MAGNETICS, THOMAS J WATSON RES CTR, IBM CORP, 66-, MGR, ADVAN VERY LARGE SCALE INTEGRATION DESIGN, 80- *Personal Data:* b Budapest, Hungary, Oct 8, 38; US citizen; m 65; c 2. *Educ:* Syracuse Univ, BSc, 61; Mass Inst Technol, MSc, 62, PhD(elec eng), 66. *Mem:* Sr mem Inst Elec & Electronics Engrs. *Res:* Photovoltaic effects in semiconductors; mercury telluride-cadmium telluride heterostructures; memory design and sensing; low-temperature behavior of magnetic films; magnetic bubble-domain devices; very large scale integration design. *Mailing Add:* Thomas J Watson Res Ctr IBM Corp PO Box 218 Yorktown Heights NY 10598

ALMEIDA, SILVERIO P, ELECTROOPTICS, BIOPHYSICS. *Current Pos:* PROF PHYSICS & CHMN, UNIV NC, CHARLOTTE, 89- *Personal Data:* b Hudson, Mass, July 27, 33; m 71, Christine S Renaud; c Alicia C & Christopher J. *Educ:* Clark Univ, BA, 57; Mass Inst Technol, MS, 59; Cambridge Univ, PhD(physics), 64. *Prof Exp:* Res asst physicist, Lawrence Radiation Lab, Univ Calif, Berkeley, 60-62; res asst physicist, Europ Orgn Nuclear Res, Geneva, Switz, 62-63, fel, 63-64; sr res assoc elem particle physics, Cavendish Lab, Cambridge Univ, 64-66; sr scientist, Aeronutronic-Philco Ford, Calif, 66-67; from asst prof to prof physics, Va Polytech Inst, 68-89. *Mem:* Am Optical Soc. *Res:* Coherent optics; holography; pattern recognition; image analysis; light scattering; biophysics. *Mailing Add:* Dept Physics Univ NC Charlotte Charlotte NC 28223. *Fax:* 704-547-3160; *E-Mail:* almeida@uncc.edu; fph00spa@unccvm.uncc.edu

ALMENAS, KAZYS KESTUTIS, NUCLEAR ENGINEERING. *Current Pos:* from asst prof to assoc prof, 68-89, PROF NUCLEAR ENG, UNIV MD, 90- *Personal Data:* b Lithuania, Apr 11, 35; US citizen; m 68; c 3. *Educ:* Univ Nebr, Lincoln, BS, 57; Univ Warsaw, PhD(nuclear eng), 68. *Prof Exp:* Res engr, Argonne Nat Lab, 59-65. *Concurrent Pos:* Consult, Argonne Nat Lab, 72 & Bechtel Power Corp, 76, Nuclear Regulatory Comn, 77-85, Elec Power Res Indust, Brookhaven Nat Lab, Los Alamos Lab, 88, Gen Physics, 90. *Mem:* Am Nuclear Soc; Am Soc Mech Engrs. *Res:* Light water reactor safety; containment analysis; evaluation of fluid mass and energy transfer between large, complex geometry volumes; analysis of condensing and convective heat transfer. *Mailing Add:* Dept Mat & Nuclear Eng Univ Md Bldg 090 Rm 2135 College Park MD 20742-2115. *E-Mail:* almenas@eng.umd.edu

ALMERS, WOLFHARD, BIOPHYSICS, PHYSIOLOGY. *Current Pos:* from asst prof to assoc prof, 74-82, PROF PHYSIOL, UNIV WASH, 82- *Personal Data:* b Helmstedt, WGer, May 29, 43. *Educ:* Univ Rochester, PhD(physiol), 71. *Honors & Awards:* Alexander von Humboldt Sr Scientist Award, 84; Cole Award, Biophys Soc, 91. *Prof Exp:* Res assoc physiol, Duke Univ, 67-69; res worker, Cambridge Univ, 71-74. *Concurrent Pos:* Fel Muscular Dystrophy Asn, 71-74; tutor, Churchill Col, Cambridge Univ, 72-73; Guggenheim fel, 84. *Mem:* Biophys Soc; Soc Neurosci; Physiol Soc Gt Brit; Soc Gen Physiologists; Am Soc Cell Biol. *Res:* Electrical properties of and ion transport by biological membranes; mechanism of secretion. *Mailing Add:* Max Planck Inst Med Res Jahnstr 29 69120 Heidelberg Germany

ALMETER, FRANK M(URRAY), PHYSICAL METALLURGY, MATERIALS ENGINEERING. *Current Pos:* RETIRED. *Personal Data:* b Rochester, Minn, Mar 23, 29; m 61; c 1. *Educ:* Mo Sch Mines, BS, 53; Univ London, DIC, 56, MS, 58, PhD(phys metall), 59. *Prof Exp:* Consult metallurgist, London, Eng, 55-59; process engr, Gen Dynamics/Convair, 59-60; assoc res scientist, Lockheed Missiles & Space Co, 60-61; res metallurgist, Res Lab, Int Nickel Co, 61-63; staff scientist, Aerospace Res Ctr, Gen Precision Inc, 63-65; group leader mat res & res specialist, Airplane Div, Boeing Co, 65-68; chief metallurgist, Burndy Corp, 68-71; metallurgist, Off Saline Water, US Dept Interior, 71-74; mat engr, US Nuclear Regulatory Comn, 74-80; gen engr, US Dept Energy, 80-92. *Concurrent Pos:* Mem, Corrosion Adv Comt, Elec Power Res Inst, 77- *Mem:* Am Inst Mining, Metall & Petrol Engrs; Am Soc Metals; Am Mgt Asn; Brit Inst Metals; Nat Asn Corrosion Engrs. *Res:* Corrosion of metals and alloys; surface science of electrical contact surfaces; structure and properties of magnetic oxides; microplasticity and piezoresistivity of materials; fracture and surface damage; fatigue and stress corrosion cracking. *Mailing Add:* 12004 Settle Ct Fairfax VA 22033

ALMGREN, FREDERICK JUSTIN, JR, mathematics; deceased, see previous edition for last biography

ALMLOF, JAN ERIK, structural & theoretical chemistry; deceased, see previous edition for last biography

ALMOG, RAMI, BIOPHYSICS. *Current Pos:* RES SCIENTIST, WADSWORTH CTR LABS & RES, NY STATE DEPT HEALTH, ALBANY, 79- *Personal Data:* b Israel; Israeli & US citizen; m; c 1. *Educ:* Univ Calif, Los Angeles, BS, 59; Calif State Univ, MS, 74; State Univ NY, PhD, 76. *Prof Exp:* Chemist, Res Org & Inorg Chem Corp, 70-72; postdoctoral res assoc, State Univ NY, Binghamton, 78-79; asst prof, Sch Pub Health, State Univ NY, Albany, 89- *Mem:* Am Chem Soc. *Res:* Structure and function of cell membranes and their role in cellular action and pathological conditions. *Mailing Add:* Wadsworth Ctr Labs & Res PO Box 509 Albany NY 12201-0001

ALMON, RICHARD REILING, BIOCHEMISTRY, PHARMACOLOGY. *Current Pos:* ASST PROF CELL & MOLECULAR BIOL, STATE UNIV NY, BUFFALO, 77- *Personal Data:* b San Bernardino, Calif, Aug 24, 46; m 85, Debra DuBois; c 3. *Educ:* Univ Ill, Urbana-Champaign, BS, 68, MS, 70, PhD(physiol & biochem), 72. *Prof Exp:* Teaching asst, Dept Physiol, Univ Ill, Urbana-Champaign, 68-70; fel med biochem, Duke Univ, 71-75; asst res prof biol, Univ Calif, San Diego, 75-77. *Concurrent Pos:* Adj assoc prof pharmaceut, State Univ NY, Buffalo. *Mem:* Soc Neurosci; Am Physiol Soc; Am Soc Pharmacol & Exp Therapeut. *Res:* Neurochemistry; membrane biochemistry; muscle biochemistry; endocrinology; biological information processes; pharmacodynamics. *Mailing Add:* Dept Biol Sci State Univ NY 107 Hochstetter Hall Buffalo NY 14260. *Fax:* 716-645-2975; *E-Mail:* almon@acsu.buffalo.edu

ALMOND, HAROLD RUSSELL, JR, COMPUTATIONAL CHEMISTRY. *Current Pos:* Sr res chemist, Janssen Res Found, Johnson & Johnson, 60-63, group leader anal chem, 64-76, res fel, McNeil Pharmaceut Div, 76-86, res fel, 87-89, RES FEL, R W JOHNSON PHARMACEUT RES INST, 90- *Personal Data:* b Oakland, Calif, Dec 21, 34; m 56, Ruth Douglas; c Russell & Robert. *Educ:* Calif Inst Technol, BS, 56, PhD(org chem), 61. *Mem:* AAAS; assoc mem Sigma Xi; Am Chem Soc; NY Acad Sci. *Res:* Computer aided drug design using molecular modeling with computers; quantitative structure-activity relationship analysis. *Mailing Add:* 1330 Hanover Place Maple Glen PA 19002-3225

ALMOND, HY, INORGANIC CHEMISTRY. *Current Pos:* RETIRED. *Personal Data:* b Chattanooga, Tenn, June 11, 14; m 49; c 2. *Educ:* Univ Chicago, BS, 38. *Prof Exp:* Explosives supvr, Army Ord, 42-43; chemist, US Geol Surv, 46-57; process control supvr, Autonetics Group, Rockwell Int Corp, 57-81. *Mem:* Am Chem Soc; Geochem Soc. *Res:* Printed circuitry; geochemistry; analytical chemistry; general electroplating; thin films; thick films. *Mailing Add:* 5021 Hamer Lane Placentia CA 92670-3648

ALMOND, PETER R, MEDICAL PHYSICS. *Current Pos:* VCHMN & PROF RES, DEPT RADIATION ONCOL, UNIV LOUISVILLE, 85- *Personal Data:* b Downton Wiltshire, Eng, Sept 10, 37; m 60; c 2. *Educ:* Nottingham Univ, BSc, 58; Rice Univ, MA, 62, PhD(med physics), 65, Am Bd Radiol, Cert, 90. *Prof Exp:* Dep head physics, M D Anderson Hosp & Tumor Inst, Univ Tex, 72-74, physicist, 72-85, prof biophys, 72-85, head radiation physics, 72-85, dir physics, 80-85. *Concurrent Pos:* Mem, Nat Coun Radiation Protection & Measurements, 84-; comt mem, Radiation Study Sect, NIH, 86-, chmn, 88-; study sect mem, Construct Grant Study Sect, Nat Cancer Inst, 86-; consult & task group mem, Int Comn Radiation Units & Measurements, 67-84; vchmn, Int Soc Coun Radiation Oncol, 82-; consult, Nuclear Regulatory Comn, 78-; chmn, Am Col Med Physics, 86. *Mem:* Am Soc Therapeut Radiol & Oncol; Am Phys Soc; Am Asn Physicists Med (pres, 70-71); Sigma Xi; Am Col Med Physics; Am Bd Med Physics; Am Bd Radiol. *Res:* Application of imaging techniques to radiation oncology treatment planning using computers; two-dimensional treatment planning is done using a computed tomography scanner as input; plan to use magnetic resonance imaging input for three-dimensional planning; basic measurements of radiation; applications to radiation therapy and radiobiology. *Mailing Add:* Radiation Oncol Univ Louisville 529 S Jackson St Louisville KY 40202. *Fax:* 502-852-7725

ALMQUIST, DONALD JOHN, ELECTRONICS. *Current Pos:* RETIRED. *Personal Data:* b Elwood, Ind, Aug 30, 33; m 55, Charline G Mull; c Gregory J & Tracy G. *Educ:* Gen Motors Inst, BIE, 55. *Prof Exp:* Supvr, Delco Remy Div, Gen Motors Co, Anderson, Ind, 56-64, plant supt, 64-69, planning mgr, 69-72, asst dir personnel, 72-74, mgr mfg, 74-78, gen mgr mfg, 78-82, gen mgr, 82-84, gen mgr, Delco Electronics Div, Gen Motors Corp, Kokomo, Ind, 84-86, vpres & gen mgr, 86-89, pres & chief exec officer, 89-93. *Concurrent Pos:* Mem bd dirs, St Johns Med Ctr, 82-84, Ind Voc Tech Col, Kokomo, 84-86, St Joseph Hosp, Kokomo, 84-86; mem bd mgrs, Rose Hulman Inst Technol, Terre Haute, 84-; mem bd dirs, Ind Corp Sci & Technol, Indianapolis; mem, Ind Telecommun Network Comn, 85-89; exec vpres, GM Hughes Electronics, 89-93. *Res:* Industrial engineering. *Mailing Add:* 7249 Lands End Circle Noblesville IN 46060

ALMS, GREGORY RUSSELL, POLYMER CHEMISTRY, CHEMICAL PHYSICS. *Current Pos:* SR RES SUPVR, POLYMER PROD DEPT, WASHINGTON WORKS, E I DU PONT DE NEMOURS & CO, INC, 78- *Personal Data:* b Sycamore, Ill, July 8, 47; m 69; c 4. *Educ:* Monmouth Col, BA, 69; Stanford Univ, PhD(chem), 73. *Prof Exp:* Fel chem, Univ Ill, 73-75; asst prof chem, Fordham Univ, 75-78. *Mem:* Am Phys Soc. *Res:* Laser light scattering spectroscopy studies on polymer systems; emulsion polymerization studies; fluoropolymers; engineering plastics. *Mailing Add:* One Ashleaf Ct Hockessin DE 19707. *Fax:* 302-695-1513

ALMY, CHARLES C, JR, GEOPHYSICS, HYDROGEOLOGY OF GROUNDWATER. *Current Pos:* PROF GEOL, GUILFORD COL, 72- *Personal Data:* b 1935; m 34, Aurora Pagin; c Julia Irene, Jessica E, Charles Edward & Teresa Ellis. *Educ:* Rice Univ, MA, 60, PhD(geol), 65. *Prof Exp:* Explor geologist, Chevron Oil Co, New Orleans. *Mem:* Geol Soc Am; Am Asn Petrol Geologists; Soc Explor Geophysicists; Sigma Xi. *Res:* Image processing and geographic information systems to complement seismic and stratigraphic studies in Puerto Rico; teaching of science using these techniques in secondary education; geologic images of North Carolina. *Mailing Add:* Dept Geol Guilford Col 5800 W Friendly Ave Greensboro NC 27410. *Fax:* 910-316-2951; *E-Mail:* almycc@rascal.guilford.edu

ALMY, THOMAS PATTISON, INTERNAL MEDICINE. *Current Pos:* Nathan Smith prof & chmn dept, Dartmouth Med Sch, 68-74, third century prof med, 74-86, prof community & family med, 81-86, EMER PROF MED & COMMUNITY & FAMILY MED, DARTMOUTH MED SCH, 86- *Personal Data:* b New York, NY, Jan 10, 15; m 43; c 3. *Educ:* Cornell Univ, AB, 35, MD, 39. *Hon Degrees:* MA, Dartmouth Col, 70. *Honors & Awards:* Friedenwald Medal, Am Gastroenterol Asn, 76. *Prof Exp:* Asst med, Med Col, Cornell Univ, 40-42, from instr to asst prof, 42-48, assoc prof neoplastic dis, 48-54, from assoc prof to prof med, 54-68. *Concurrent Pos:* Asst attend physician, Mem Hosp, 48-68 & James Ewing Hosp, 50-68; vis physician & dir, 2nd Med Div, Bellevue Hosp, 54-68; consult med, Vet Admin Hosp, NY, 54-68 & Vet Admin Ctr, White River Junction, Vt, 68-; dir med, Dartmouth-Hitchcock Affil Hosps, 68-74; distinguished physician, Vet Admin, 82-85. *Mem:* Inst Med-Nat Acad Sci; Asn Am Physicians; Am Gastroenterol Asn (pres, 64); Am Physiol Soc; master Am Col Physicians. *Res:* Psychosomatic medicine; physiology of human gastrointestinal tract; methods of medical teaching. *Mailing Add:* Dept Med-Community & Family Med Dartmouth Med Sch Hanover NH 03756

ALO, RICHARD ANTHONY, COMPUTER SCIENCES. *Current Pos:* PROF, DEPT APPL MATH SCI, UNIV HOUSTON, DOWNTOWN, 82- *Personal Data:* b Erie, Pa; c 4. *Educ:* Gannon Col, BA, 60; Pa State Univ, MA, 65, PhD(math), 65. *Prof Exp:* Systs test retrofit engr, Defense Projs Div, Western Elec Co, 60-61; teaching asst math, Pa State Univ, 61-63, res asst, 63-64, instr, 65-66; from asst prof to assoc prof, Carnegie-Mellon Univ, 66-76; prof math & head dept, Lamar Univ, 76-82. *Concurrent Pos:* Kanpur Indo-Am Prog math sci adv, Indian Inst Technol, 69-70; Nat Res Coun Italy vis fel, 74; vis prof math, Univ Parma, 75; Nat Acad Sci vis fel, 75; consult appl math, Math Asn Am, 79- *Mem:* Am Math Soc; Math Asn Am; Ital Math Union; Soc Indust & Appl Math; Sigma Xi. *Res:* General topology; analysis and functional analysis; biomathematics; non-linear analysis; software systems; operations research; computer science theory. *Mailing Add:* Dept Math Sci Univ Houston Downtown One Main St Rm 570 Houston TX 77002

ALOIA, ROLAND C, CELL BIOLOGY, IMMUNOLOGY. *Current Pos:* RES CHEMIST, ANESTHESIA SERV, PETTIS MEM VET HOSP, 79-; CHMN & PRES, LOMA LINDA VET ASN RES & EDUC, 88-; PROF, DEPT ANESTHESIOL & BIOCHEM, SCH MED, LOMA LINDA UNIV, 89- *Personal Data:* b Newark, NJ, Dec 21, 43. *Educ:* St Mary's Col, BS, 65; Univ Calif, Riverside, PhD(cell biol), 71. *Prof Exp:* Res biologist, Univ Calif, Riverside, 75-76; from asst prof to assoc prof, Sch Med, Loma Linda Univ, 76-89. *Concurrent Pos:* Fel, Calif Heart Asn, 71-74, bd dirs, 73-80, pres, Riverside Chap, 79-80 & 84-86, vpres, 84-86. *Mem:* Am Oil Chem Soc; NY Acad Sci; Sigma Xi; AAAS. *Res:* Structure-function relationships of biological membranes as it relates to the adaptation of membranes to low temperatures during hybernation and as is involved in cellular form; relationship of lipids in lymphocytes and the human immunodeficiency virus to the processes of human immunodeficiency infection and syneytia formatin. *Mailing Add:* Dept Anesthesiol Sch Med Loma Linda Univ Loma Linda CA 92350. *Fax:* 909-422-3149

ALOIMONOS, YIANNIS JOHN, COMPUTER SCIENCES. *Current Pos:* ASST PROF, DEPT COMPUT SCI, UNIV MD, 86-, HEAD, COMPUT VISION LAB, CTR AUTOMATION RES, 90- *Personal Data:* b Sparta, Laconia, Greece, Aug 17, 57. *Educ:* Rochester Univ, PhD, 86. *Honors & Awards:* Presidential Young Investr Award, White House/NSF, 90. *Concurrent Pos:* Grantee, Defense Advan Res Projs Agency, US Army Eng. *Res:* Integration of visual modules. *Mailing Add:* Comput Vision Lab Ctr Automation Res A V Williams Bldg 115 Univ Md College Park MD 20742-3275

ALONSO, CAROL TRAVIS, PHYSICS. *Current Pos:* dep A-div leader, Lawrence Livermore Nat Lab, 85-89, asst dep dir, 89-95, PROG MGR RES, 75-, ASST ASSOC DIR NAT SECURITY, LAWRENCE LIVERMORE NAT LAB, 95- *Personal Data:* b Montreal, Que, Dec 5, 41; US citizen; m 69, Jose Alonso; c Laura & Christopher. *Educ:* Allegheny Col, BS, 63; Bryn Mawr Col, MS, 65; Mass Inst Technol, PhD(nuclear physics), 70. *Prof Exp:* Mem res staff heavy ion physics, Yale Univ, 70-72; staff physicist heavy ion physics, Lawrence Berkeley Lab, 72-75. *Concurrent Pos:* Vis comt physics, Mass Inst Technol, 81-86. *Mem:* Am Phys Soc. *Res:* Hydrodynamics; thermonuclear fusion; particle transport; plasma physics; computer modelling of liquid drop and heavy nucleus collisions. *Mailing Add:* Lawrence Livermore Nat Lab L-20 PO Box 808 Livermore CA 94551. *Fax:* 510-424-3858; *E-Mail:* alonsoct@llnl.gov

ALONSO, JOSE RAMON, ACCELERATOR PHYSICS, HEAVY ION PHYSICS. *Current Pos:* SR SCIENTIST, LAWRENCE BERKELEY NAT LAB, 85- *Personal Data:* b San Francisco, Calif, July 26, 41; m 69, Carol Travis; c Laura & Chris. *Educ:* Mass Inst Technol, SB, 62, PhD(physics), 67. *Honors & Awards:* R & D 100 Award, 87. *Prof Exp:* Instr physics, Mass Inst Technol, 67-68; res physicist, Yale Univ, 68-72; res physicist, Lawrence Berkeley Lab, 72-82, Bevalac opers mgr, 82-89, asst div dir, Accelerator & Fusion Res Div, 89-92. *Mem:* Am Phys Soc. *Res:* Accelerator physics; nuclear, biomedical and atomic physics aspects of heavy ion physics; medical physics. *Mailing Add:* Lawrence Berkeley Nat Lab Mail Stop 71-259 Berkeley CA 94720. *Fax:* 510-486-5788; *E-Mail:* jralonso@lbl.gov

ALONSO, KENNETH B, PATHOLOGY, NUCLEAR MEDICINE. *Current Pos:* DIR, INST ADVAN STUDY MED, ATLANTA, 92- *Personal Data:* b Tampa, Fla, Nov 26, 42; m 67. *Educ:* Princeton Univ, AB, 64; Univ Fla, MD, 68. *Prof Exp:* Intern surg, Riverside Hosp, Newport News, Va, 68-69; resident, Univ Fla, 69, resident path, 69-70 & Fitzsimons Gen Hosp, Denver, 71-73, chief resident path, 73, actg comdr, US Army Regional Med Lab, Atlanta, 74-75; pathologist, Clayton Gen Hosp, Riverdale, Ga, 75-76; dir, Lab Procedures South, Upjohn Co, Atlanta, 76-79; chief staff, Physicians & Surgeons Commun Hosp, 78-79; chief staff, Henry Gen Hosp, Stockbridge, Ga, 81-82, pathologist, 79-84; dir, Lab Atlanta, Riverdale, Ga, 84-92. *Concurrent Pos:* Clin assoc prof chem, Auburn Univ, 77-79; clin assoc prof path, Morehouse Col, 77-83, prof, 84-; chief med examr, Dept Orgn & Field Serv, GBI, Decatur, Ga, 85-88. *Mem:* Am Col Physicians; Am Soc Clin Path; Col Am Pathologists; Soc Nuclear Med; Am Col Nuclear Physicians; Nat Asn Med Examrs; Am Soc Clin Oncol. *Res:* Immunologic disorders, especially receptors, cytokines, membrane transport, human tumor stem cell assay & monoclonal antibodies; oncology; hyperthermia. *Mailing Add:* 679 Juniper St NE Atlanta GA 30308

ALONSO, MARCELO, NUCLEAR PHYSICS, QUANTUM THEORY. *Current Pos:* exec dir res & eng, 80-88, PRIN RES SCIENTIST, FLA INST TECHNOL, 88- *Personal Data:* b Havana, Cuba, Feb 6, 21; US citizen; m 43; c 4. *Educ:* Univ Havana, PhD(physics), 43. *Prof Exp:* Fel physics, Yale Univ, 43-44; prof physics, Univ Havana, 44-60, chmn dept, 56-60; lectr physics, Georgetown Univ, 61-71; dep dir, Orgn Am States, 60-73, dir sci & technol, 73-80. *Concurrent Pos:* Dir, Nuclear Energy Comn, Cuba, 55-60; tech dir, Nat Bank Econ Develop, Cuba, 58-60; hon prof, Univ Guadalajara, Mex, 71. *Mem:* Hon mem, Guatemala Acad Sci; Am Phys Soc; Am Asn Physics Teachers; AAAS; Am Nuclear Soc. *Res:* Energy policy & planning; science education. *Mailing Add:* 509 Third Ave Melbourne Beach FL 32951. *Fax:* 407-984-8461

ALONSO, WILLIAM R, PROTEIN CHEMISTRY. *Current Pos:* RES SCIENTIST PROD DEVELOP, MILES INC, 92- *Personal Data:* b Goldsboro, NC, June 22, 57. *Educ:* Emory Univ, BA, 79; Univ Houston, PhD(biochem), 86. *Prof Exp:* Res assoc plant biochem, Wash State Univ, 86-92. *Mem:* Sigma Xi; Am Soc Biochem & Molecular Biol. *Mailing Add:* Dept PMT Bayer Hwy 70 E PO Box 507 Clayton NC 27520-0507

ALONSO-CAPLEN, FIRELLI V, PROTEIN EXPRESSION SYSTEMS, PROTEIN PURIFICATION. *Current Pos:* ASSOC SCIENTIST, SALK INST, 91- *Personal Data:* b Cebu City, Philippines, Oct 19, 56; US citizen; m 82, Howard S; c Samuel D & Daniel J. *Educ:* Univ Ala, Birmingham, PhD(microbiol), 84. *Prof Exp:* Res assoc, US Army Med Res Inst, 84-85; res fel, Mem Sloan Kettering Cancer Inst, 85-90; asst res prof, Rutgers Univ, 90-91. *Mem:* Am Soc Virol; Am Soc Microbiol; Am Soc Cell Biol; Sigma Xi. *Res:* Heterologous protein production in various systems of expression including bacterial, insect and mammalian systems; developing methods in chromatographic separation of recombinant proteins. *Mailing Add:* Salk Inst PO Box 250 Swiftwater PA 18370. *Fax:* 717-839-0922

ALOUSI, ADAWIA A, MOLECULAR CARDIOLOGY. *Current Pos:* res biologist, 71-74, sr res biologist, 74-78, sect head, 79-84, INST FEL PHARMACOL, STERLING-WINTHROP RES INST, 84- *Personal Data:* b Baghdad, Iraq; US citizen. *Educ:* Univ Baghdad, BS, 55; Univ Mich, MS, 59; State Univ NY, PhD(pharmacol), 64. *Prof Exp:* Fel pharmacol, Med Sch, Harvard Univ, 64-66; asst prof, Univ Baghdad, 66-67 & State Univ NY Upstate Med Ctr, 67-68; res scientist, Geigy Pharmaceut, 68-70. *Concurrent Pos:* vis scholar, Univ Calif, San Diego, 89- *Mem:* Am Soc Pharmacol & Exp Therapeut; Am Soc Cell Biol; NY Acad Sci; Am Heart Asn; Int Soc Heart Res. *Res:* Cardiovascular pharmacology and biochemistry, with special emphasis on congestive heart failure; new cardiotonic agents; etiology of congestive heart failure and new approaches to its management; signal transduction; G-proteins. *Mailing Add:* Hopkins Marine Sta Oceanview Blvd Pacific Grove CA 93950

ALPEN, EDWARD LEWIS, PHYSIOLOGY, RADIOBIOLOGY. *Current Pos:* Donner Lab, 75-85, PROF BIOPHYS, UNIV CALIF, BERKELEY, 75-, PROF RADIOL, SAN FRANCISCO, 75- *Personal Data:* b San Francisco, Calif, May 14, 22; m 45, Wynella; c Angela & Jeannette. *Educ:* Univ Calif, BS, 46, PhD(pharmaceut chem), 50. *Honors & Awards:* Mem Award, Asn Mil Surg US, 61; Sci Medal, US Secy Navy, 62; Distinguished Civilian Serv Medal, US Dept Defense, 63. *Prof Exp:* Asst prof pharmacol, Sch Med, George Washington Univ, 50-51; investr & head thermal injury br, Biol & Med Sci Div, US Naval Radiol Defense Lab, San Francisco, 53-55, head biophys br, 55-58, head div, 58-69; assoc lab dir, 69-73, lab dir, Pac Northwest Labs, Battelle Mem Inst, 73-75; dir, Donner Lab, Univ Calif Berkeley, 75-85; assoc dir, Lawrence Berkeley Lab, 75-86. *Concurrent Pos:* NSF fel, Oxford Univ, 58-59; Guggenheim fel, Univ Paris, 65-66; dir, Univ Calif Study Ctr, London, 88-90; Sigma Xi Nat lectr, 95-96. *Mem:* Radiation Res Soc; Biophys Soc; Bioelectromagnetics Soc (pres, 78-); Soc Exp Biol & Med; Royal Soc Med. *Res:* Radiation biology and biophysics; cellular kinetics; erythropoetic mechanisms; regulation of erythropoesis; environmental science. *Mailing Add:* 1182 Miller Ave Berkeley CA 94708. *Fax:* 510-849-9670

ALPER, ALLEN MYRON, MATERIALS SCIENCE ENGINEERING. *Current Pos:* mgr chem & electronic mat, GTE Sylvania Inc, 69-70, mgr res & develop, 70-71, chief engr, 71-72, dir res & eng, Chem & Metall Div, GTE Sylvania Inc, 72-80, PRES, GTE WALMET, 80-, VPRES & GEN MGR, GTE PROD CORP. *Personal Data:* b New York, NY, Oct 23, 32; m 59; c 2. *Educ:* Brooklyn Col, BS, 54; Columbia Univ, PhD(petrol, mineral), 57. *Prof Exp:* Instr phys geol, Brooklyn Col, 56-57; sr mineralogist, Ceramic Res Lab, Corning Glass Works, 57-59, res mineralogist, 59-62, res mgr, 62-69. *Concurrent Pos:* Kemp Mem res grant, 54; lectr, St John's Seminary, NY, 58 & Elmira Col, 59-60. *Mem:* Explorers Club; fel Am Ceramic Soc; Am Chem Soc; Am Inst Mining, Metall & Petrol Eng; fel Geol Soc Am. *Res:* Superalloys; rhenium; tungsten; molybdenum; powder metallurgy; rare-earth oxides and metals; iodides; metallurgical extraction; photochemical machining technology; phosphors; crystal growth; ceramics; phase studies; crystal chemistry; silicon nitride; metallurgy and physical metallurgical engineering. *Mailing Add:* Osram Sylvania Inc VPres & Gen Mgr Hawes St Towanda PA 18848

ALPER, ANNE ELIZABETH, MANAGEMENT, CHEMISTRY. *Current Pos:* mgr, 81-86, EXEC DIR PUBLS, CHEM INST CAN, OTTAWA, ONT, 86- *Personal Data:* b Montreal, Que, Nov 7, 42; m 66, Howard; c Ruth & Lara. *Educ:* Marianopolis Col, BS, 62; McGill Univ, Montreal, PhD(org chem), 66. *Res:* Organic chemistry. *Mailing Add:* Chem Inst Can 130 Slater St Suite 550 Ottawa ON K1P 6E2 Can

ALPER, CARL, CLINICAL BIOCHEMISTRY. *Current Pos:* CONSULT, 85- *Personal Data:* b Hoboken, NJ, May 28, 20; m 49; c 4. *Educ:* Drew Univ, BA, 41; Tulane Univ, MS, 43, PhD(chem), 47. *Prof Exp:* Instr chem, Tulane Univ, 43-46; res assoc nutrit, E R Squibb & Sons, 47-48, res assoc immunochem develop, 48-49; from asst prof to assoc prof biochem, Hahnemann Med Col, 49-66, biochemist, Hahnemann Hosp, 62-66; assoc prof biochem & dir dept clin biochem, Temple Univ, 66-70; dir, Philadelphia Br, Bio-Sci Labs, 70-85. *Concurrent Pos:* Adj assoc prof, Temple Univ, 70-73. *Mem:* Am Chem Soc; Am Soc Clin Path; Am Asn Clin Chem; Am Inst Nutrit; Soc Acad Clin Lab Physicians & Scientists. *Res:* Biochemistry of disease; protein nutrition and metabolism; body composition; enzymology; immunochemistry. *Mailing Add:* 1126 S Park Ave Haddon Heights NJ 08035-1494

ALPER, CHESTER ALLAN, SERUM PROTEIN GENETICS. *Current Pos:* SCI DIR, CTR BLOOD RES, 72- *Personal Data:* b New York, NY, May 21, 31; m 61; c 1. *Educ:* Harvard Col, AB, 52; Harvard Med Sch, MD, 56. *Prof Exp:* Res fel med, 62-64, res assoc, 64-66, assoc, 66-69, assoc prof, 69-75, PROF PEDIAT, HARVARD MED SCH, 75- *Concurrent Pos:* Sr assoc med, Children's Hosp Med Ctr, 74-; consult med, Brigham & Women's Hosp, 75-; mem Microbiol & Immunol Study Comt, Am Heart Asn, 79-82; consult & panel mem vitro diagnosis, Food & Drug Admin, Health & Human Serv,

74-80; assoc ed, J Immunol, 77-81. *Mem:* Am Soc Clin Invest; Asn Am Physicians; Am Asn Immunologists; Am Asn Clin Chemists; Am Fedn Clin Res. *Res:* Control of metabolism of complement proteins. *Mailing Add:* Dept Pediat Sci Dir Blood Res Harvard Med Sch 800 Huntington Ave Boston MA 02115-6303

ALPER, HOWARD, ORGANIC CHEMISTRY, ORGANOMETALLIC CHEMISTRY. *Current Pos:* assoc prof, Univ Ottawa, 75-78, chmn dept, 82-85 & 88-94, asst vpres, 95-96, assoc vpres res, 96, PROF CHEM, UNIV OTTAWA 78- *Personal Data:* b Montreal, Que, Oct 17, 41; m 66, Anne Fairhurst; c 2. *Educ:* Sir George Williams Univ, BSc, 63; McGill Univ, PhD(chem), 67. *Honors & Awards:* E W R Steacie Award, Natural Sci & Eng Res Coun, Can; Alcan Award, Chem Inst Can, Catalysis Award, 84; Alfred Bader Award Org Chem, 90; W R Steacle Award, Am Soc Chem, 93; Urgel-Archambaul Prize, Asn Can-Fr Advan Sci. *Prof Exp:* NATO fel, Princeton Univ, 67-68; from asst prof to assoc prof chem, State Univ NY Binghamton, 68-74. *Concurrent Pos:* J S Guggenheim fel. *Mem:* Am Chem Soc; Chem Inst Can; Royal Soc Chem; fel Royal Soc Can. *Res:* Metal complexes as catalysts and reagents in organic chemistry; mechanistic organometallic chemistry; phase transfer catalysis; polymer chemistry; clays; asymmetric synthesis. *Mailing Add:* Dept Chem Univ Ottawa Ottawa ON K1N 6N5 Can. *Fax:* 613-562-5871; *E-Mail:* halper@oreo.uottawa.ca

ALPER, JOSEPH SETH, THEORETICAL CHEMISTRY. *Current Pos:* ASSOC PROF CHEM, UNIV MASS, DORCHESTER, 69- *Personal Data:* b Brooklyn, NY, Aug 2, 42; m 68. *Educ:* Harvard Univ, AB, 63; Yale Univ, PhD(chem), 68. *Prof Exp:* Fel chem, Mass Inst Technol, 68-69. *Concurrent Pos:* Petrol Res Fund-Am Chem Soc type G grant, 70-73. *Mem:* Am Phys Soc. *Res:* Applications of group theory to problems in atomic and molecular structure and spectra. *Mailing Add:* Dept Chem Univ Mass 100 Morrisey Blvd Boston MA 02125-3393

ALPER, MARSHALL EDWARD, SYSTEMS DESIGN. *Current Pos:* RETIRED. *Personal Data:* b New York, NY, Feb 9, 30; m 56, Marcia Edith Uflund; c Ian, Robin, Julia & Sharon. *Educ:* Mass Inst Technol, SB, 51, ScD(civil eng), 62. *Honors & Awards:* Except Serv Medal, NASA, Douglas Michel Nastram Achievement Award & Outstanding Leadership Award. *Prof Exp:* Res asst civil eng, Mass Inst Technol, 51-55; develop engr, Calif Inst Technol, 55-60, group supvr structures & dynamics res, 60-64, chief, Appl Mech Sect, 64-71, mgr, Civil Systs Proj Off, 71-72, environ syst prog, 72-74, energy systs prog develop, 74-75, mgr, Solar Energy Prog, 75-85, Energy Environ & Health Prog, 85-88, mgr, Instnl Comput & Info Serv Off, Jet Propulsion Lab, 88-95, spec asst to assoc dir, 95-96. *Concurrent Pos:* Mem res adv comt missile & spacecraft structures, NASA, 59-62; mem, Apollo Systs Support Group, 62-63. *Mem:* Am Inst Aeronaut & Astronaut; AAAS; Asn Comput Mach. *Res:* Systems engineering; mission studies leading to definition of future programs and required supporting research and advanced development; development and applications of solar energy. *Mailing Add:* 2286 Lambert Dr Pasadena CA 91107

ALPER, RICHARD H, CARDIOVASCULAR PHYSIOLOGY, NEUROENDOCRINOLOGY. *Current Pos:* asst prof, 86-92, ASSOC PROF PHARMACOL, TOXICOL & THERAPEUT, UNIV KANS MED CTR, 92- *Personal Data:* b Suffern, NY, Sept 27, 53. *Educ:* State Univ NY, Stony Brook, BS, 75; Mich State Univ, PhD(pharmacol & toxicol), 81. *Prof Exp:* fel physiol, Univ Calif, San Francisco, 81-84; res assoc pharmacol, Univ Iowa, 84-86. *Mem:* Soc Neurosci; Am Soc Pharmacol & Exp Therapeut; Am Heart Asn; Am Physiol Soc; AAAS. *Res:* Central neurotransmitters in the integrated cardiovascular and endocrine responses to pharmacologic and physiologic stimuli. *Mailing Add:* Dept Pharmacol Univ Kans Med Ctr 3901 Rainbow Blvd Kansas City KS 66160-7417. *Fax:* 913-588-7501; *E-Mail:* alper@ukanvm.bit

ALPER, ROBERT, CONNECTIVE TISSUE BIOCHEMISTRY. *Current Pos:* RETIRED. *Personal Data:* b New York, NY, Sept 8, 33; m 70; c 4. *Educ:* Utica Col, BA, 59; State Univ NY Upstate Med Ctr, PhD(biochem), 69. *Prof Exp:* Res asst biochem, Vet Admin Hosp, Syracuse, NY, 60-64; res assoc, State Univ NY, Buffalo, 68-69 & Fla State Univ, 69-71; res assoc med, Univ Pa Div, Philadelphia Gen Hosp, 71-72, asst prof biochem, Sch Dent Med, 72-77; asst dir, Connective Tissue Res Inst, Univ City Sci Ctr, 77-91; consult, 91- *Concurrent Pos:* Consult, Advan Technol Ctr, Southeastern Pa, 83-89. *Mem:* AAAS; Am Chem Soc; Asn Res Vision & Ophthal. *Res:* Involvement of glycoproteins and mucopolysaccharides in atherosclerosis; corneal structural glycoproteins; identification and characterization of cell surface glycoproteins in neoplastic cells; biochemistry of basement membrane; collagen biochemistry; connective tissue and skin diseases; cell biology of the cardiovascular system. *Mailing Add:* 27 Morningside Dr Yardley PA 19067

ALPER, SETH L, MOLECULAR MEDICINE, NEPHROLOGY. *Current Pos:* Asst prof, 89-95, ASSOC PROF, HARVARD MED SCH, 95- *Personal Data:* b Philadelphia, Pa, Jan 31, 52. *Educ:* Haverford Col, BS, 73; Yale Univ, PhD(pharmacol), 79, MD, 80. *Concurrent Pos:* Researcher, Molecular Med Unit, Beth Israel Hosp, 90-; estab investr, Am Heart Asn. *Mem:* Am Soc Nephrol; Nat Kidney Fund; Am Heart Asn; Am Physiol Soc; Soc Gen Physiol; Am Soc Cell Biol. *Mailing Add:* Beth Israel Deaconess Med Ctr Molecular Med Unit 330 Brookline Ave Boston MA 02215

ALPERIN, HARVEY ALBERT, MATERIALS SCIENCE, NEUTRON SCATTERING & PHYSICS EDUCATION. *Current Pos:* PHYSICS TEACHER, BLAIR HIGH SCH, 90- *Personal Data:* b New York, NY, Mar 13, 29; m 56, Irma Levine; c Michael & Sharon. *Educ:* Rensselaer Polytech Inst, BS, 49; Univ Mich, MS, 50; Univ Conn, PhD(physics), 60. *Prof Exp:* Res assoc physics, Willow Run Res Ctr, Univ Mich, 50-53; physicist, Underwater Sound Lab, USN, 53-57, US Naval Surface Weapons Ctr, 57-88; physicist, Vela Assocs, 89-90. *Concurrent Pos:* Guest scientist, Brookhaven Nat Lab, 60-68; vis scientist, Weizmann Inst Sci, 70-71; guest scientist, Nat Bur Standards, 68-84. *Mem:* AAAS; Am Phys Soc; Am Asn Physics Teachers; Sigma Xi. *Res:* Neutron scattering; magnetic materials; computer applications; hydrogen in metals; amorphous metals; very-large-scale integration; parallel processing. *Mailing Add:* 317 Westlawn Dr Ashton MD 20861. *E-Mail:* cknw04a@prodigy.com

ALPERIN, JACK BERNARD, VITAMIN K, ANTICOAGULATION. *Current Pos:* fel hematol, 63-65, FAC HEMAT & MED, UNIV TEX MED BR, 65- *Personal Data:* b Memphis, Tenn, June 19, 32; m 60; c 1. *Educ:* Univ Tenn, MD, 57. *Prof Exp:* Intern med, Michael Reese Hosp, 57-58, resident, 58-61, fel hematol, 61-62; instr fac med, Chicago Med Sch, 62-63. *Concurrent Pos:* Prof internal med, human biochem & genetics, Univ Tex Med Br, Galveston, Tex, 65- *Mem:* Am Soc Hemat; Am Soc Clin Nutrit; Nutrit Soc Am; Am Med Asn; Am Asn Blood Banks; Southern Soc Clin Invest. *Res:* Traditional hematology including nutritional anemias, coagulathids and inherited blood diseases; hemoglobin. *Mailing Add:* Dept Internal Med Univ Tex Med Br Galveston TX 77555-0565

ALPERIN, JONATHAN L, MATHEMATICS. *Current Pos:* asst prof, 63-73, PROF MATH, UNIV CHICAGO, 73- *Personal Data:* b Boston, Mass, June 2, 37. *Educ:* Harvard Univ, AB, 59; Princeton Univ, MA, 60, PhD(math), 61. *Prof Exp:* Inst math, Mass Inst Technol, 62-63. *Mem:* Am Math Soc; Math Asn Am. *Mailing Add:* Univ Chicago 5734 University Ave Chicago IL 60637-1514

ALPERIN, RICHARD JUNIUS, CYTOCHEMISTRY, DEVELOPMENTAL BIOLOGY. *Current Pos:* from asst prof to assoc prof, 75-81, PROF BIOL, COMMUN COL PHILADELPHIA, 87- *Personal Data:* b Philadelphia, Pa, Dec 16, 41. *Honors & Awards:* Bronze Medalha Pro Mundi Beneficio, Academia Brasilera de Ciencias Humanas, 75; Int Order Merit, Int Biographical Ctr, 90; Grande Medaglia d'Argento, per Ricerche e Meriti Scientifici, Accademia Internazionale di Pontzen, 90, Gran Collare Accademico d'oro, Accademia Internazionale di Pontzen di Lettere, Scienze ed Arti, 96. *Prof Exp:* Teaching fel, Univ Pa, 63-69. *Concurrent Pos:* Fel, Prof I Gersh's Lab, Dept Animal Biol, Univ Pa, 69-74; consult, Bahamas mariculture activ, 90, Maritek Corp; guest lectr electron micros, Sch Vet Med, Univ Pa, 71-74; chmn fac sen, Community Col Philadelphia, 74 & 75; mem health delivery planning bd, AFL-CIO Cent Comt, Philadelphia, 76-89; lectr, McCrone Res Inst, 80. *Mem:* Am Micros Soc; Am Soc Zool; Pattern Recognition Soc; Am Soc Testing & Mat. *Res:* Assay of biomaterials as mutagens; materials science; methods of in vitro testing of biomaterials in blood and blood simulating fluids during preclinical trials; role of hypoblast in avian embryos; author of 3 books. *Mailing Add:* 842 Lombard St Philadelphia PA 19147-1317

ALPERN, HERBERT P, PSYCHOPHARMACOLOGY, NEUROSCIENCES. *Current Pos:* Nat Inst Gen Med Sci grant, 69-71, from asst to assoc prof, 68-79, PROF PSYCHOL, UNIV COLO, BOULDER, 79-, FAC FEL, INST BEHAV GENETICS, 69- *Personal Data:* b New York, NY, Oct 3, 40. *Educ:* City Col New York, BS, 63; Univ Ore, MA, 65; Univ Calif, Irvine, PhD(psychobiol), 68. *Concurrent Pos:* NIMH grant, 71-74; mem, Coun Tobacco res grant, 76-79. *Mem:* AAAS; Soc Neurosci; Int Brain Res Orgn. *Res:* Behavioral pharmacogenetics, emphasizing drugs that facilitate and disrupt memory processes; animal models of behavior pathology, especially convulsive disorders, hyperkinesis and drug tolerance and dependence. *Mailing Add:* Dept Psychol Univ Colo Boulder Box 345 Boulder CO 80309-0345

ALPERN, MATHEW, visual physiology; deceased, see previous edition for last biography

ALPERN, MILTON, CIVIL & STRUCTURAL ENGINEERING. *Current Pos:* MGR, SPEC PROJ DIV, SHAH ASSOCS, 92- *Personal Data:* b June 25, 25; US citizen; m 46, Beverly Katzman; c Warren & Barbara (Foran). *Educ:* Cooper Union, BCE, 45; Columbia Univ, MSCE, 50. *Honors & Awards:* Lincoln Arc Welding Award, 61. *Prof Exp:* From instr to asst prof civil eng, Cooper Union, 48-59; consult engr, 59-70; prin, Alpern & Soifer, Consult Engrs, 70-92. *Concurrent Pos:* Consult, Alexander Crosett, 50-52, Ammann & Whitney, 52-53, Edwards & Hjorth, 53, NY State Bldg Code Comn, 54 & Norden-Ketay Corp, 54-56; adj prof struct, NY Inst Technol, 77-79; mem, NY State Bd Engrs & Land Surv, 78-87, chmn, 84-86; vis prof, Pratt Inst, 86-92 & Polytechnic Univ, 93 & 94. *Mem:* Fel Am Soc Civil Engrs; Am Concrete Inst; Nat Soc Prof Engrs; Am Soc Testing & Mat; fel Nat acad Forensic Engrs; Am Inst Steel Construct. *Res:* Collate information on structural parameters of burst protection; structural engineering; engineering education. *Mailing Add:* 153 Biltmore Blvd Massapequa NY 11758. *Fax:* 516-783-8375

ALPERS, DAVID HERSHEL, CELL BIOLOGY, NUTRITION. *Current Pos:* from asst to assoc prof, 69-73, PROF MED, WASH UNIV MED CTR, 73-, CHIEF, DIV GASTROENTEROL, 69- *Personal Data:* b Philadelphia, Pa, May 9, 35; m 77, Melanie Goldman; c Ann, Ruth & Barbara. *Educ:* Harvard Univ, BA, 56, MD, 60. *Prof Exp:* From intern to asst prof med, Harvard Med Sch, 64-69. *Concurrent Pos:* Prin investr grants, Nat Inst Diabetes & Digestive & Kidney Dis, 69-, mem, 75-81; assoc ed, J Clin Invest, 77-82; ed, Am J Physiol, 91- *Mem:* Asn Am Physicians; Am Gastroenterol

Asn, (pres, 90-91); Am Soc Biochem & Molecular Biol; Am Soc Cell Biol; Am Soc Clin Nutrit. *Res:* Physiology of cobalamin absorption, structure and cell biology of cobalamin binding proteins, secretion of intestinal proteins. *Mailing Add:* Dept Med Box 8124 Wash Univ Med Sch 660 S Euclid Ave St Louis MO 63110-1093. *Fax:* 314-362-8959; *E-Mail:* alpers@telesphere.wustl.edu

ALPERS, JOSEPH BENJAMIN, BIOLOGICAL CHEMISTRY, METABOLISM. *Current Pos:* RETIRED. *Personal Data:* b Salem, Mass, Aug 24, 25; m 56; c 2. *Educ:* Yale Univ, AB, 49; Columbia Univ, MD, 53; NY Univ, PhD(biochem), 62. *Prof Exp:* Res fel med, Sloan-Kettering Inst, NY, 53-55; from intern to asst resident med, NY Hosp, 55-57; res fel biochem, New York City Pub Health Res Inst, 57-60, asst biochem, 60-61; assoc, Harvard Med Sch, 61-65, assoc prof biochem, 61-91. *Concurrent Pos:* Dir clin labs, Children's Hosp, 71-91. *Mem:* Am Soc Biol Chemists. *Res:* Intermediary metabolism; enzymology of carbohydrates. *Mailing Add:* 67 Lakeshore Rd Natick MA 02115

ALPERT, DANIEL, COMPUTER-BASED SYSTEMS, SCIENCE POLICY. *Current Pos:* dir,Co-ordinated Sci Lab, 59-65, dean, Grad Col, 65-72, dir, Ctr Advan Study & assoc dir, Comput-Based Educ Res Lab, 72-87, PROF PHYSICS, UNIV ILL, URBANA-CHAMPAIGN, 57-, DIR PROG SCI, TECHNOL & SOC, 86- *Personal Data:* b Hartford, Conn, Apr 10, 17; m 42; c 2. *Educ:* Trinity Col, Conn, BS, 37; Stanford Univ, PhD(physics), 42. *Hon Degrees:* DSc, Trinity Col, Conn, 57. *Honors & Awards:* Newcomb Cleveland Award, AAAS, 54; Gaede-Longmuir Award, Am Vacuum Soc, 80. *Prof Exp:* Res physicist, Westinghouse Res Labs, 42-50, mgr, Physics Dept, 50-55, assoc dir, 55-57. *Concurrent Pos:* Civilian with AEC, 44; mem, Defense Sci Bd, 63-72; ed, J Vacuum Sci & Technol, 64-66; charter trustee, Trinity Col, Conn, 64- *Mem:* Fel AAAS; fel Am Phys Soc; Am Vacuum Soc; Sigma Xi. *Res:* Ultrahigh vacuum technology; surface physics; computer-based education; study of higher education. *Mailing Add:* Ctr Advan Study Univ Ill Urbana-Champaign 912 W Ill St Urbana IL 61801. *Fax:* 217-244-3396

ALPERT, ELLIOT, MEDICINE. *Current Pos:* PHYSICIAN-IN-CHIEF, SIR MORTIMER B DAVIS JEWISH GEN HOSP, MONTREAL, 90- *Personal Data:* b New York, NY, July 8, 36. *Educ:* City Univ NY, BS, 57; State Univ NY, MD, 61. *Prof Exp:* Intern, II & IV, Harvard Med Serv, Boston City Hosp, 61-62, asst resident, 62-63; preceptor med, Dept Med, Albany Med Col, 63-65; teaching fel, Harvard Med Sch, 65-66, instr, 69-71; asst med, Mass Gen Hosp, 70-74, asst physician, 75-81; attend physician, Methodist Hosp, Houston, Tex, 81-90, head, Gastroenterol Serv, 81-90. *Concurrent Pos:* Epidemiologist, WHO Med Exped Easter Island, 64-65; res fel med, Harvard Med Sch, 66-67, 67-69 & 69-71, assoc prof, 76-81; lectr physiol chem, Mass Inst Technol, 73-81; mem, Comt Cancer, Am Gastroenterol Asn, 74-78; mem, Res Comt, Am Asn Study Liver Dis, 75-78; prof med & chief, Gastroenterol Sect, Baylor Col Med, 81-89, dir, NIH, Inst Res Training Grant, 83-89, prof cell biol, 89; consult staff, St Luke's Episcopal Hosp, Houston, Tex, 82-90; assoc ed, Tumor Biol, 84-; mem, Res Comt, Am Col Gastroenterol, 87-90; consult staff, M D Anderson Hosp & Tumor Inst, Houston, Tex, 87-90. *Mem:* Am Fedn Clin Res; AAAS; Am Asn Study Liver Dis; Am Gastroenterol Asn; NY Acad Sci; Am Asn Immunol; Am Asn Cancer Res; Am Soc Clin Invest; Int Asn Study Liver; Int Soc Oncodevelop Biol (vpres, 83-). *Res:* Author or co-author of over 140 publications. *Mailing Add:* Dept Med M B Davis Jewish Gen Hosp 3755 St Catherine Rd Montreal PQ H3T 1E2 Can

ALPERT, JOEL JACOBS, PEDIATRICS. *Current Pos:* chmn, 72-93, PROF, DEPT PEDIAT, BOSTON UNIV SCH MED, 72- *Personal Data:* b New Haven, Conn, May 9, 30; m 57, Barbara Wasserstrom; c Norman, Mark & Deborah. *Educ:* Yale Univ, AB, 52; Harvard Med Sch, MD, 56; Am Bd Pediat, dipl, 61. *Honors & Awards:* Colin Stewart Lectr, Dartmouth Med Sch, 86; George Armstrong Award, Ambulatory Pediat Asn, 89; job lewis smith award, am acad pediats. *Prof Exp:* Intern med, Children's Hosp Med Ctr, Boston, Mass, 56-57, jr asst resident, 57-58, chief resident ambulatory serv & fel, 61-62, asst dir, Family Health Care Prog, 62-64, asst med, 63-64, assoc, 64-66, chief, Family & Child Health Div, 64-72, sr assoc med, 66-73; res fel pediat, Sch Pub Health, Harvard Med Sch, 62-63, asst dir, Family Health Care Prog, 62-64, instr pediat, 63-66, assoc, 64-68, med dir, Family Health Care Prog, 64-72, from asst prof to assoc prof, 68-72, lectr pediat, 72-92. *Concurrent Pos:* Exchange registrar, St Mary's Hosp Med Sch, London, Eng, 58-59, vis consult pediatrician, 71-72; lectr med, Simmons Col, Boston, 64-72; assoc med, Beth Israel Hosp, Boston, 64-72; exec secy, Boston Poison Control Info Ctr, 64-71, chmn exec comt, 76-78; assoc pediatrician, Boston Hosp for Women, 66-76; mem, Sect Child Develop, Am Acad Pediat, 66-, consult oper head start, 66-72, mem, Community Pediat, 69-, Adolescent Med, 79-, chmn, Subcomt Accidental Poisoning, 68-71, mem, Comt Community Health Serv, 86-; mem, Health Serv Res Study Sect, HEW, 68-73; hon res fel, Univ London, Bedford Col, 71-72; dir, Pediat Serv, Boston City Hosp, 72-93; consult child & family med, Children's Hosp Med Ctr, 72-, consult pediat, Franciscan Children's Hosp & Rehab Ctr, 72-92, Carney Hosp, 72-80, Ctr Health Serv Res & Develop, Dept Health & Human Serv, 72-, Pub Health Serv, Health Resources Admin, Div Med, Bur Health Professions, 76-; pediatrician-in-chief, Univ Hosp, 72-93; vis res assoc, Dept Econ, Northeastern Univ, 75-80; prof, Dept Socio-Med Sci, Boston Univ Sch Med, 76-85, Dept Community Med, 76-80, adj prof pub health law, Sch Pub Health, 80-85, prof socio-med sci & community med, 85-; vis lectr health serv, Harvard Sch Pub Health, 76-79; Dozer vis prof, Ben Gurion Sch Med, Beer Sheva, Israel, 79; Raine Found vis scholar, Dept Child Health, Univ Western Australia & Princess Margaret Hosp, 83; Leonard Erlich vis prof, North Shore Children's Hosp, Manhasset, NY, 84; assoc ed, Pediat Rev & Commun, 85-; Stacey White vis prof, Emory Med Sch, Atlanta, Ga, 86; vis prof pediat, Columbia Col Physicians & Surgeons, New York, 89, NY Univ Sch Med, 89; Jane & John Davis prestige vis, Univ Otug E Dunedin, Christchurch, Wellington, NZ, 95. *Mem:* Inst Med-Nat Acad Sci; Ambulatory Pediat Asn (pres, 69); Am Acad Pediat; Am Pub Health Asn; AAAS; emer mem Soc Pediat Res; Am Pediat Soc; AMA. *Res:* Pediatric education; substance use during pregnancy; utilization; career outcomes. *Mailing Add:* Boston Univ Sch Med 818 Harrison Ave Boston MA 02118

ALPERT, LEO, ENVIRONMENTAL SCIENCES, METEOROLOGY. *Current Pos:* PRES, WEATHER-ENVIRON SURVEYS, INC, 81- *Personal Data:* b Boston, Mass, Oct 31, 15; m 43; c 2. *Educ:* Mass State Col, BS, 37; Clark Univ, MA, 39, PhD(climat), 46. *Prof Exp:* Staff weather officer, USAF, Panama, 41-43; res weather officer, Hqs Air Weather Serv, DC, 44-46; environ specialist, Engr Intel Div, Corps Engrs, 50-51; chief climat lab, Geophys Directorate, Air Force Cambridge Res Labs, 52; geogr, Engr Strategic Intel Div, Corps Engrs, US Army, 53-60, trop environ scientist, Environ Sci Div, Army Res Off, DC, 61-62, chief scientist, Tropic Test Ctr, Panama, CZ, 63-65, meteorologist, Environ Sci Div, Army Res Off, Washington, DC, 65-71, chief atmospheric sci bd, Army Res Off, Res Triangle Park, 71-78, dir, Geosci Div, 78-81. *Concurrent Pos:* Consult climatologist, US, SAm & Cent Am, 52-; deleg, Pan Am Inst Geog & Hist, DC, 52, Mex, 55; Nat Res Coun deleg, Int Geog Cong, Brazil, 56; chief engr, Field Party, Mex, 57; deleg, Comn Climat, DC, 57; Geophys Union deleg, Int Union Geod & Geophys, Finland, 60; deleg, Int Geog Cong, Sweden, 60; Nat Res Coun deleg, Pac Sci Cong, Hawaii, 61; Int Geog Union deleg, Comn Agr Climat, Can, 62; deleg, Int Union Conserv Nature & Natural Resources, Galapagos Island Symp, Ecuador, 64; cert consult meteorologist, 81- *Mem:* Am Meteorol Soc. *Res:* Environmental research and testing of material; tropical environment forest; applied meteorology; climate of the Galapagos Islands and eastern Tropical Pacific Ocean Area; weather related accidents and storm damage. *Mailing Add:* 4122 Cobblestone Pl Durham NC 27707

ALPERT, NELSON LEIGH, MEDICAL TECHNOLOGY, SPECTROSCOPY INSTRUMENTATION. *Current Pos:* INDEPENDENT CONSULT, 68- *Personal Data:* b New Haven, Conn, June 14, 25; m 50, Ruth Sachs; c Stephen H & Nancy J (Halpert). *Educ:* Yale Univ, BS, 45; Mass Inst Technol, PhD(physics), 48. *Honors & Awards:* Seligson-Golden Award, Am Asn Clin Chem, 88. *Prof Exp:* Asst prof physics, Rutgers Univ, 48-52; physicist, White Develop Corp, 52-58; group leader, Perkin-Elmer Corp, 58-61, chief engr, Spectros Prod Develop, 61-67; dir instrument develop, Becton Dickinson & Co, 67-68. *Concurrent Pos:* Ed, Clin Instrument Systs, 80- *Mem:* AAAS; Am Asn Clin Chem. *Res:* Analytical and clinical instruments, particularly spectroscopic, ultraviolet, visible, infrared atomic absorbtion and emission, flame, fluoresence. *Mailing Add:* 447 Glenbrook Rd Stamford CT 06906. *Fax:* 203-327-3462

ALPERT, NORMAN ROLAND, PHYSIOLOGY. *Current Pos:* PROF PHYSIOL & CHMN DEPT, COL MED, UNIV VT, 66- *Personal Data:* b Stamford, Conn, July 28, 22; m 52. *Educ:* Wesleyan Univ, AB, 43; Columbia Univ, PhD(physiol), 51. *Prof Exp:* From asst to instr physiol, Columbia Univ, 38-53; from asst prof to prof, Col Med, Univ Ill, 53-66. *Mem:* Am Physiol Soc; Biophys Soc; Harvey Soc; Am Soc Gen Physiol; Am Soc Exp Biol & Med. *Res:* Anaerobiosis in vivo; metabolism, respiration and circulation; thermodynamics, chemistry and mechanics of skeletal and cardiac muscle contraction. *Mailing Add:* Dept Physiol Univ Vt Given Med Bldg Burlington VT 05405-0001

ALPERT, PETER, CLONAL PLANT BIOLOGY, INTEGRATED CONSERVATION & DEVELOPMENT. *Current Pos:* asst prof, 84-92, ASSOC PROF, DEPT BIOL, UNIV MASS, 92- *Educ:* Oxford Univ, BA, 74; Harvard Univ, MA, 78, PhD(biol), 82. *Prof Exp:* Vis scholar & NSF fel, Stanford Univ, 82-84. *Concurrent Pos:* Mass media fel, AAAS, 83, diplomacy fel, 90-92; vis asst prof, Earlham Col, 83; vis prof, Ctr Nat Res Sci, 88-89; prog assoc, Sustainable Biosphere Proj, 93-94; vis assoc prof, Ore State Univ, 93-94; vis researcher, V.C. Bodega Marine Lab, 96- *Mem:* Bot Soc Am; Ecol Soc Am. *Res:* Integration of ecological processes across levels of organization within natural systems, using clonal growth and resource landscapes as a model system and on the application of basic ecology to natural resources management. *Mailing Add:* Dept Biol Univ Mass Amherst MA 01003-5810. *Fax:* 413-545-3243; *E-Mail:* palpert@bio.umass.edu

ALPERT, PINHAS, MESOSCALE METEOROLOGY, CLIMATE CHANGE. *Current Pos:* sr lectr, 87-93, assoc prof dynamic meteorol, 93-97, PROF ATMOSPHERIC SCI, TEL-AVIV UNIV, 97- *Personal Data:* b Jerusalem, Israel, Sept 28, 49; m 71, Rachel Malca Safari; c Limor, Yuval, Ehud, Aaron, Michal, Yael, Eitan & Shimon. *Educ:* Hebrew Univ, Jerusalem, BSc, 70, MSc, 72, PhD(meteorol), 80. *Prof Exp:* Postdoctoral fel, Harvard Univ, 80-82, Coop Inst Mesoscale Metereol Studies, Univ Okla, 83; vis scientist, NASA/Goddard, 86-87, Reading Univ, 87. *Concurrent Pos:* Res forcaster, Israel Defense Forces, 72, maj, 90-; referee, US-Israel Binat Sci Found, 85-, Ministry Found, 85-, Ger Israeli Found, 85-, Israel Ministry Environ, 85-; coun mem, Israel Meteorol Soc, 91-; vis prof, Pa State Univ, 92; mem, Mintz Organizing Comt, 92; vchmn, World Meteorol Orgn, 93-; sr assoc, Nat Res Coun, 95-96. *Mem:* Am Meteorol Soc; Israel Meteorol Soc; Europ Geophys Soc; Royal Meteorol Soc. *Res:* Dynamics of cyclone, cyclogenesis; mechanisms of regional and mesoscale climate changes; rainfall changes in semi-arid zone; dust and weather; numerical weather prediction; orographic rainfall and winds; storms. *Mailing Add:* Dept Geophysics Tel-Aviv Univ Tel-Aviv 69978 Israel. *Fax:* 972-3-6409282; *E-Mail:* pinhas@cyclone.tau.ac.il

ALPERT, RONALD L, HEAT TRANSFER, FIRE DYNAMICS. *Current Pos:* sr res scientist basic fire res, Factory Mutual Res Corp, 69-74, asst mgr basic res, 74-86, mgr, 86-90, mgr fire & explosion res, 91-96, ASST MGR, RES DIV, FACTORY MUTUAL RES CORP, 96- *Personal Data:* b Rochester, NY, Apr 27, 41; m 69, Judith Reinherz; c 2. *Educ:* Mass Inst Technol, SB & SM, 65, ScD(mech engr), 70. *Prof Exp:* Res asst mech eng, Mass Inst Technol, 64-69. *Concurrent Pos:* Mem, Comt Heat Transfer in Fires & Combustion Systs, Heat Transfer Div, Am Soc Mech Engrs; mem, Tech Comt, Halon Alternatives Res Corp, 77- *Mem:* Combustion Inst; Am Soc Mech Engrs; Nat Fire Protection Asn. *Res:* Fire detection, growth, suppression, modeling; heat transfer in two phase and buoyant flows; spray dynamics. *Mailing Add:* Factory Mutual Res Corp PO Box 9102 Norwood MA 02062

ALPERT, SEYMOUR, MEDICINE, ANESTHESIOLOGY. *Current Pos:* from instr to prof, George Washington Univ, 48-83, from asst dir to assoc dir, 61-69, vpres develop, 69-83, EMER PROF ANESTHESIOL, SCH MED, GEORGE WASHINGTON UNIV, 83-, EMER VPRES DEVELOP, 88- *Personal Data:* b New York, NY, Apr 20, 18; m 41, Cecile B Cohen. *Educ:* Columbia Univ, AB, 39; Health Sci Ctr Brooklyn, MD, 43; Am Bd Anesthesiol, dipl, 49. *Prof Exp:* Intern, Beth Israel Hosp, 43-44; med officer anesthesiol, Army US, 44-46; chief med officer anesthesiol, Gallinger Munic Hosp, 46-47. *Concurrent Pos:* Univ fel anesthesiol, Sch Med, George Washington Univ, 48; consult, Walter Reed Army Hosp, 48-83, DC Gen Hosp, 48-69 & Mt Alto Vet Hosp, 59-69. *Mem:* Am Soc Anesthesiologists; AMA; fel Am Col Anesthesiologists; Pan-Am Med Asn. *Res:* Clinical anesthesiology in operating and delivery rooms; teaching medical students and residents. *Mailing Add:* 2660 S Ocean Blvd No 502N Palm Beach FL 33480

ALPERT, SEYMOUR SAMUEL, PHYSICS. *Current Pos:* from asst prof to assoc prof, 66-74, PROF PHYSICS, UNIV NMEX, 74- *Personal Data:* b Amsterdam, NY, Dec 21, 30; div; c 3. *Educ:* Univ Calif, Berkeley, AB, 53, PhD(physics), 62. *Prof Exp:* Physicist, Lawrence Radiation Lab, 61-62; mem tech staff, Bell Tel Labs, Inc, 62-64; res assoc laser scattering, Columbia Univ, 64-66. *Mem:* Am Phys Soc; Am Asn Physics Teachers. *Res:* Laser light scattering; energetic modelling of human body; optical spectroscopy of liquids; critical opalescence. *Mailing Add:* 4115 Marble Ave NE Albuquerque NM 87110

ALPHA, ANDREW G, TECTONICS, GROUND WATER. *Current Pos:* RETIRED. *Personal Data:* b Leth Bridge Alberta, Can, May 1, 12. *Educ:* Univ NDak, MA, 35. *Prof Exp:* Mgr exploration, Mobil Oil Corp, 43-77; independent consult, 77- *Mem:* Fel Geol Soc Am; Geol Soc Am; Am Asn Petrol Geologists. *Mailing Add:* 3455 S Corona St Englewood CO 80110

ALPHER, RALPH ASHER, ASTROPHYSICS, COSMOLOGY. *Current Pos:* ADMINR & DISTINGUISHED SR SCIENTIST, DUDLEY OBSERV, 87-; DISTINGUISHED RES PROF PHYSICS, UNION COL, 87- *Personal Data:* b Washington, DC, Feb 3, 21; m 42, Louise E Simons; c Harriet R (Lebetkin) & Victor S. *Educ:* George Wash Univ, BS, 43, PhD(physics), 48. *Hon Degrees:* DSc, Union Col, 92 & Renssalaer Polytech Inst, 93. *Honors & Awards:* Magellanic Premium, Am Philos Soc, 75; Prix Georges Vanderlinden, Royal Acad Sci, Lett & Fine Arts, Belg, 75; John Price Wetherill Medal, Franklin Inst, 80; Physics & Math Sci Award, NY Acad Sci, 81; Henry Draper Medal, Nat Acad Sci, 93. *Prof Exp:* Physicist, Appl Physics Lab, Johns Hopkins Univ, 44-55; physicist, Gen Elec Co, 55-86. *Concurrent Pos:* Adj prof, Rensselaer Polytech Inst, 60-64 & 87-93; assoc ed, Physics Fluids, 60-62; Am Inst Physics Comt Manpower, 77-82; Am Phys Soc Panel Pub Affairs, 78-82, Comt Opportunities Physics, 78-82; coun mem, Am Phys Soc, 78-82; mem steering comt, Sect B (Physics), AAAS, 82-86. *Mem:* Fel Am Phys Soc; fel AAAS; Sigma Xi; fel Franklin Inst; Am Astron Soc; fel Am Acad Arts & Sci; Int Astron Union. *Res:* Cosmology; astrophysics. *Mailing Add:* Dept Physics Union Col Schenectady NY 12308. *Fax:* 518-388-6947

ALPHIN, REEVIS STANCIL, PHARMACOLOGY, BIOCHEMISTRY. *Current Pos:* pharmacologist, 60-64, head sect gastroenterol, 64-73, ASSOC DIR PHARMACOL, A H ROBINS CO, INC, 73- *Personal Data:* b Mt Olive, NC, Apr 21, 29; m 55; c 2. *Educ:* Univ NC, BA, 51; Duke Univ, MA, 56; Med Col Va, PhD(pharmacol), 66. *Prof Exp:* Res asst physiol, Duke Univ, 53-56; pharmacologist, Lilly Res Labs, Eli Lilly & Co, 56-60. *Mem:* AAAS; assoc Am Gastroenterol Asn; Am Physiol Soc; NY Acad Sci; Am Soc Pharmacol & Exp Therapeut. *Res:* Gastrointestinal tract; peptic ulcer; anorectic agents. *Mailing Add:* 8525 Gilliam Rd Sanford NC 27330-9333

ALRUTZ, ROBERT WILLARD, ECOLOGY. *Current Pos:* from asst prof to assoc prof, 52-64, PROF BIOL, DENISON UNIV, 64- DIR BIOL RES, 69- *Personal Data:* b Pittsburgh, Pa, Aug 20, 21; m 46; c 1. *Educ:* Univ Pittsburgh, BS, 43; Univ Ill, MS, 47, PhD, 51. *Prof Exp:* Instr biol, Univ Minn, 51-52. *Concurrent Pos:* Chmn dept biol, Denison Univ, 64-65, chmn biol reserve, 65-89. *Mem:* AAAS; Ecol Soc Am; Am Inst Biol Sci; Nat Asn Biol Teachers; Conserv Educ Asn. *Res:* Biology of wild populations of peromyscus. *Mailing Add:* One Sunset Dr Granville OH 43023

AL-SAADI, ABDUL A, CELL BIOLOGY, MICROSCOPIC ANATOMY & CLINICAL GENETICS. *Current Pos:* CHIEF CYTOGENETICS & ASSOC DIR RES, DEPT ANAT PATH, WILLIAM BEAUMONT HOSP, 70-, DIR, SCH HISTOTECHNOL, 77- *Personal Data:* b Baqubah, Iraq, Oct 20, 35; US citizen; m 61, 87, Cassandra Z Rodger; c 4. *Educ:* Univ Baghdad, BA, 55; Univ Kans, MA, 59; Univ Mich, PhD(zool), 63; Am Bd Med Genetics, cert, 83. *Prof Exp:* Res asst radiation effects, Sch Med, Univ Mich, 62-66, asst prof cellular biol, 66-70. *Concurrent Pos:* NIH grant, 62-67; Univ Mich Cancer Inst grants, 67, 68-69; Am Cancer Soc grant; asst clin prof, Health Ctr, Oakland Univ, 77-; clin prof, Med Col Ohio, 92-; mem, Genetics Adv Bd, State Mich, 80-; clin prof, Health Allied Sci, Oakland Univ, 77-; fel Am Col Med Genetics, 93. *Mem:* AAAS; Am Soc Human Genetics; Am Thyroid Asn; Am Asn Cancer Res; Int Soc Prenatal Diag; Am Soc Cell Biol; Tissue Cult Asn. *Res:* Cytogenetics in cancer research; clinical cytogenetics; ultrastructure changes in carcinogenesis; thyroid physiology in health and disease; radiation biology; relationship between chromosomal abnormalities and development of cancer; cytogenetic studies of human brain tumors; clinical genetic studies on the role of chromosomal abnormalities in fetal malformation and birth defects. *Mailing Add:* Dept Anat Path William Beaumont Hosp 3601 W 13 Mile Rd Royal Oak MI 48073-6769. *Fax:* 248-551-1257; *E-Mail:* alsaadi@beaumont.edu

AL-SAADOON, FALEH T, RESERVOIR ENGINEERING, PETROLEUM PRODUCTION ENGINEERING. *Current Pos:* prof chem & natural gas eng & chmn dept, 82-87, interim dir, Off Sponsored Res, 87-89, PROF NATURAL GAS ENG, TEX A&M UNIV, 89- *Personal Data:* b Baghdad, Iraq, Jan 11, 43; US citizen; m 72; c 3. *Educ:* WVa Univ, BS, 65, MS, 66; Univ Pittsburgh, PhD(chem eng), 70. *Prof Exp:* Head, Dept Petrol Eng, Baghdad Univ, 70-75; asst prof petrol eng, Al-Fateh Univ, Libya, 75-78; assoc prof, WVa Univ, 78-82. *Mem:* Soc Petrol Engrs; Am Inst Chem Engrs; Soc Prof Well Log Analysts. *Res:* Unconventional gas resources; thermal recovery of heavy crude oils and tar sands; enhanced oil recovery. *Mailing Add:* Chem & Natural Gas Eng Dept Tex A&M Univ Kingsville Campus PO Box 193 Kingsville TX 78363

AL-SALAMEH, DANIEL YOUSEF, PHYSICS. *Current Pos:* mem tech staff, 84-90, DISTINGUISHED MEM TECH STAFF, AT&T BELL LABS, 90- *Personal Data:* b Ajloun, Jordan, Nov 26, 49; m 82, Christina Y Adidjaja; c Josef D, John D & Julius D. *Educ:* Univ Jordan, BS, 71; Polytech Univ, NY, PhD(physics), 82. *Prof Exp:* Instr physics, Ajloun Community Col, 71-77; teaching fel, Polytech Univ, NY, 78-82; res scientist, Fusion Energy Corp, Princeton, NJ, 82-84. *Res:* Research in fusion; soft x-ray laser; network operation and restoration; patents in the field. *Mailing Add:* AT&T Bell Labs Crawfords Corner Rd Holmdel NJ 07733

AL-SARRAF, MUHYI, ONCOLOGY. *Current Pos:* PROF MED, SCH MED, WAYNE STATE UNIV, 81-; MED DIR, PROVIDENCE CANCER CTR, 94- *Personal Data:* b Baghdad, Iraq, Sept 15, 38; US citizen; m 76, Ellen Conners; c Renee & Ramsey. *Educ:* Univ Baghdad, MD, 61; Royal Col Physicians Can, cert internal med, 69; Am Bd Int Med, Cert, 71. *Concurrent Pos:* Chief head & neck cancer, Harper Grace Hosp, 76-94; Mem, SW Oncol Group, Radiation Ther Oncol Group. *Mem:* Am Soc Clin Oncol; Am Asn Cancer Res; Am Asn Cancer Educ; Am Soc Prev Oncol; Am Soc Hon Surgeon. *Res:* Chemotherapy; clinical trial research; combined mobility therapy; head and neck cancer; esophagul cancer. *Mailing Add:* Providence Cancer Ctr Med Oncol Div 22301 Foster Winter Dr Southfield MI 48075. *Fax:* 248-424-2919; *E-Mail:* muhyia@mail.ic.net

ALSBERG, HENRY, POLYMER CHEMISTRY, INDUSTRIAL CHEMISTRY. *Current Pos:* MGR RES & DEVELOP, RICHARDSON CO, 64- *Personal Data:* b Ger, Oct 6, 21; US citizen; m 49; c 2. *Educ:* Univ Toronto, BASc, 47; Purdue Univ, MS, 49. *Prof Exp:* Group leader polymers, Koppers Co, 51-64. *Mem:* Am Chem Soc; Soc Plastics Engrs; Am Soc Testing & Mat. *Res:* Development of specialty suspension and emulsion polymers; pilot plant operations; plant process development. *Mailing Add:* 1847 Tanglewood Dr Apt 2A Glenview IL 60025-1628

ALSCHER, RUTH, PLANT PHYSIOLOGY. *Current Pos:* ASSOC PROF, DEPT PLANT PATH PHYSIOL & WEED SCI, VA POLYTECH INST & STATE UNIV, 88- *Personal Data:* b Chicago, Ill, July 17, 43; c Lucy & Nicholas. *Educ:* Trinity Col, BA, 65; Washington Univ, MA, 68; Univ Calif, Davis, PhD(plant physiol), 72. *Prof Exp:* Fel, Dept Biochem, Univ Calif, Davis, 73; Nat Res Serv Awards, Lab Chem Biodynamics, Sect Genetics Develop & Physiol, Cornell Univ, 74-75 & 75-77; res assoc, NY State Agr Exp Sta, 77-79; res assoc, Boyce Thompson Inst, Cornell Univ, 79-88, adj asst prof Plant Biol, 85-88. *Concurrent Pos:* NIH postdoctoral fel, 73-74 & 75-77; NSF Career Advan award, 92-94. *Mem:* Am Soc Plant Physiologists; Am Chem Soc; Sigma Xi. *Res:* Effects of air pollutants on photosynthesis; mechanisms of plant resistance to air pollutants; effects of herbicides on photosynthesis; molecular biology of antioxidant responses to stress. *Mailing Add:* Dept Plant Path Physiol & Weed Sci Va Polytech Inst & State Univ Blacksburg VA 24061-0330. *Fax:* 540-231-5753; *E-Mail:* ralscher@vt.edu

AL-SHAIEB, ZUHAIR FOUAD, DIAGENESIS OF CLASTIC ROCKS. *Current Pos:* asst prof, 72-76, assoc prof, 76-81, prof geol & dept head, 81-, BROWN, MONNETT & REGENTS PROF & HEAD, OKLA STATE UNIV. *Personal Data:* b Damascus, Syria, Sept 23, 40; US citizen; m 70; c 1. *Educ:* Univ Damascus, BS, 63; Univ Mo, Rolla, MS, 67, PhD(geol), 72. *Prof Exp:* Instr phys sci, Shaiwk Col, Kuwait, 65-66. *Concurrent Pos:* Consult, Erico, Inc, Tulsa, 70-, Mid-Am Pipeline Co, 77-80 & Shell Develop Co, Houston & Amereda Hess Corp, Tulsa, 80-81; prin investr, AEC, Dept Engery, 75-80 & Environ Protection Agency, 81- *Mem:* Soc Econ Paleontologists & Mineralogists; Am Inst Mineral Petrol & Metall Engrs; Sigma Xi. *Res:* Energy (hydrocarbon and uranium); relationship between hydrocarbon migration and generation of secondary porosity in sandstone reservoir which has application in hydrocarbon exploration. *Mailing Add:* Sch Geol Okla State Univ Stillwater OK 74078

ALSMEYER, RICHARD HARVEY, MEAT SCIENCE, BIOCHEMISTRY. *Current Pos:* pres, Alsmeyer Consult, 84-88, PRES, ALSMEYER FOOD CONSULT, 89-; EXEC DIR, NAT SEASONING MFRS ASN, 97- *Personal Data:* b Sebring, Fla, Feb 4, 29; m 53; c Dartlin & Angus. *Educ:* Univ Fla, BSA, 52, MSA, 56, PhD(animal sci & nutrit), 60. *Prof Exp:* Res technician meat sci, Agr Exp Sta, Univ Fla, 56-57; res animal husbandman, Meat Qual Lab, Agr Res Serv, USDA, 60-67, head standards group, Tech Serv Div, 67-71, sr staff officer, Prod Standards, Sci & Tech Serv, 71-75, dir prog eval & spec reports, Coop Res Sci & Educ Admin, 75-79, nat res prog leader, Animal Prod Processing & Mkt, 79-83. *Concurrent Pos:* Res fel, Brit Meat Res Inst, Cambridge Univ, Eng, 66; mem adv bd marine safety & ecol, Int Mariners, Inc; Am Meat Sci Asn rep, Nat Res Coun-Nat Acad Sci, 72-75; food sci consult, 83-84; consult, Webb Tech Group, Webb Foodlab Inc. *Mem:* Am Meat Sci Asn; Inst Food Sci & Technol; Am Soc Animal Sci; Am Soc Agr Consults; assoc mem Am Meat Inst. *Res:* Meat and poultry products, seafood, and other protein foods of plant and animal origin; specialties are: meat and poultry products, seafood, and other protein foods of plant and animal origin; food science. *Mailing Add:* 8905 Maxwell Dr Potomac MD 20854-3125. *Fax:* 301-299-7523

ALSMILLER, RUFARD G, JR, PHYSICS, MATHEMATICS. *Current Pos:* assoc dir div, 69-73, GROUP LEADER HIGH & MEDIUM ENERGY SHIELDING, ENG PHYSICS DIV, OAK RIDGE NAT LAB, 57- *Personal Data:* b Louisville, Ky, Nov 16, 27; m 52. *Educ:* Univ Louisville, BS, 49; Purdue Univ, MS, 52; Univ Kans, PhD(physics), 57. *Prof Exp:* Fire control systs analyst, Naval Ord Plant, Ind, 52-53; physicist, Allison Div, Gen Motors Corp, 56. *Mem:* Am Phys Soc; fel Am Nuclear Soc. *Mailing Add:* Eng Physics Div Oak Ridge Nat Lab MS 6364 PO Box 2008 Oak Ridge TN 37831. *Fax:* 423-574-9619; *E-Mail:* tut@ornl.gov

ALSON, ELI, BEHAVIORAL MEDICINE, APPLIED PSYCHOPHYSIOLOGY. *Current Pos:* DIR BEHAV MED SERV, LIFE PERFORMANCE CTR, DENVILLE, NJ, 92- *Personal Data:* b New York, NY, Aug 1, 29; m 56, Annette Shiffman; c 2. *Educ:* Brooklyn Col, BA, 52; Univ Buffalo, PhD(psychol), 59. *Prof Exp:* Clin psychologist, Vet Admin Med Ctr, Lyons, NJ, 69-75, dir psychol training, 75-84, dir behav med clin, 82-86; dir stress & pain mgt ctr, St Clares-Riverside Med Ctr, Denville, NJ, 87-92. *Concurrent Pos:* Dir, Biofeedback Clin, Bernardsville, 80-87; consult, NJ Dept Vet Servs, 85-86; med advisor, Off Hearings & Appeals, Social Security Admin, 86- *Mem:* Am Psychol Asn; Asn Appl Psychophysiol & Biofeedback. *Res:* Biofeedback; psychophysiology; interpersonal perception; post-traumatic stress disorder. *Mailing Add:* 25 Kitchell Rd Denville NJ 07834. *Fax:* 973-625-7325

ALSOP, DAVID W, CYTOLOGY, MORPHOLOGY. *Current Pos:* ASSOC PROF BIOL, QUEENS COL, NY, 70- *Personal Data:* b Lindsay, Ont, Nov 15, 39. *Educ:* Cornell Univ, BS, 64, PhD(biol), 70. *Mem:* Entom Soc Am; Sigma Xi. *Res:* Comparative studies on cockroaches. *Mailing Add:* Dept Biol City Univ NY Queens Col 6530 Kissena Blvd Flushing NY 11367-1575

ALSOP, FREDERICK JOSEPH, III, ORNITHOLOGY, VERTEBRATE ECOLOGY. *Current Pos:* from asst prof to assoc prof, 72-83, chmn biol sci, 83-91, PROF BIOL, ETENN STATE UNIV, 83- *Personal Data:* b Owensboro, Ky, Jan 9, 42; div. *Educ:* Austin Peay State Univ, BS, 64; Univ Tenn, Knoxville, MS, 68, PhD(zool), 72. *Prof Exp:* Sec sch teacher sci & fine arts, Ft Campbell Dependent Sch Syst, 64-66; asst zool, Univ Tenn, 66-72. *Concurrent Pos:* Primary investr, environ impact statement-vertebrates, Tenn Valley Authority, 75-76 & grant, Tenn endangered & threatened bird species, Tenn Wildlife Resources Agency, 78-79; consult environ res & technol, 81- & US Army Engrs, 81; nat lectr, Sigma Xi, 84-91. *Mem:* Am Ornithologists Union; Wilson Soc; Soc Field Ornithologists. *Res:* Life history, distribution population dynamics of birds, primarily of Tennessee; avian photography; tropical ornithology; neotropical migratory breeding birds; author of 2 books. *Mailing Add:* Dept Biol Sci ETenn State Univ PO Box 10001 Johnson City TN 37614-0002

ALSOP, JOHN HENRY, III, ANALYTICAL CHEMISTRY. *Current Pos:* PROJ CHEMIST, PORT ARTHUR RES LABS, TEXACO INC, 76- *Personal Data:* b Okmulgee, Okla, Oct 4, 24; m 51; c 2. *Educ:* Okla State Univ, BS, 50; Univ Tex, PhD(anal chem), 57. *Prof Exp:* Chemist, Eagle-Picher Co, Okla, 50-51, Am Window Glass Co, 51-52 & Stanolind Oil & Gas Co, 56-58; sr chemist, Pan Am Petrol Corp, 58-59, Chemstrand Corp, Ala, 59-60 & Chemstrand Res Ctr, NC, 60-62; res chemist, Richmond Res Labs, Texaco Inc, 62-76. *Mem:* Am Chem Soc; Nat Asn Corrosion Engrs; Soc Appl Spectros; Sigma Xi. *Res:* Analytical methods development in air and water conservation. *Mailing Add:* 8150 Kahilan Boerne TX 78015

ALSOP, LEONARD E, GEOPHYSICS. *Current Pos:* CONSULT, AT&T BELL LABS, 88- *Personal Data:* b Oroville, Calif, Apr 10, 30; m 55; c 3. *Educ:* Columbia Univ, AB, 51, AM, 56, PhD(physics), 61. *Prof Exp:* Res scientist, Lamont-Doherty Geol Observ, Columbia Univ, 59-65, adj assoc prof geol, 65-73, mem acad staff, 73-82. *Concurrent Pos:* Mem staff, IBM Corp, 65-73. *Mem:* Am Geophys Union; Am Seismol Soc; Royal Astron Soc. *Res:* Free oscillations of the earth; use of a laser as a transducer for seismograph; tides of the solid earth. *Mailing Add:* 42 Kristin Pl Westwood NJ 07675

ALSPACH, BRIAN ROGER, GRAPH THEORY. *Current Pos:* from asst prof to assoc prof, 66-80, PROF MATH, SIMON FRASER UNIV, 80- *Personal Data:* b Minot, NDak, May 29, 38; m 61, 80, Katherine A Heinrich; c Alina R (Mars) & Mark C. *Educ:* Univ Wash, BA, 61; Univ Calif, Santa Barbara, MA, 64, PhD(math), 66. *Prof Exp:* Teacher math, Cordell Hull Jr High Sch, 61-62. *Concurrent Pos:* Ed, Discrete Math, 81-, Ars Combin, 84-, J Graph Theory, 93-, Can Math Bull, 95-, Can J Math, 95- *Mem:* Am Math Soc; Math Asn Am; Can Math Soc; Combinatorial Math Soc Australia; Can Appl Math Soc. *Res:* Graph theory with emphasis on automorphism groups of graphs, graph decompositions and tournaments. *Mailing Add:* Dept Math Simon Fraser Univ Burnaby BC V5A 1S6 Can. *Fax:* 604-291-4947; *E-Mail:* alspach@cs.sfu.ca

ALSPACH, DANIEL LEE, CONTROL THEORY, STOCHASTIC SYSTEMS. *Current Pos:* vpres & tech dir, 73-80, PRES, ORINCON CORP, 80- *Personal Data:* b Wenatchee, Wash, July 4, 40; m 65; c 2. *Educ:* Univ Wash, BS, 62, MS, 66; Univ Calif, San Diego, PhD(eng sci), 70. *Prof Exp:* Design engr, Honeywell, Inc, 63-66; staff assoc, Gen Atomic Div, Gen Dynamics Corp, 66-67; assoc prof elec eng, Colo State Univ, 70-73; vis fac mem, Dept Appl Mech & Eng Sci, Univ Calif, San Diego, 73-74. *Mem:* Inst Elec & Electronics Engrs; Sigma Xi. *Res:* Signal processing; surveillance systems; stochastic control; estimation theory; digital systems; system modeling and simulation. *Mailing Add:* Orincon Corp 9363 Town Ctr Dr San Diego CA 92121

ALSPAUGH, DALE W(ILLIAM), AERONAUTICAL ENGINEERING. *Current Pos:* instr, Purdue Univ, 57-58 & 59-64, from asst prof to assoc prof eng sci, 64-81, prof aeronaut & astronaut, 81, CHANCELLOR, PURDUE UNIV N CENT, 82- *Personal Data:* b Dayton, Ohio, May 25, 32; m 55, Marlowe Anne Beckley; c Susan (Briggs), Michael, Patricia & Barbara (Flosi). *Educ:* Univ Cincinnati, ME, 55; Purdue Univ, MS, 58, PhD(eng sci), 65. *Prof Exp:* Jr proj engr, Frigidaire Div, Gen Motors Corp, 55-56. *Concurrent Pos:* Consult, Midwest Appl Sci Corp, 64-70, Los Alamos Lab, 77- & US Army Missile Res & Develop Command, 78- *Res:* Dynamics; optimization of engineering systems; shell theory; applied mathematics. *Mailing Add:* Chancellor Purdue Univ N Central Campus Westville IN 46391-9528. *Fax:* 219-785-5355; *E-Mail:* dwa@purduenc.edu

ALSTADT, DON MARTIN, PHYSICS. *Current Pos:* Develop engr, Lord Corp, 47-50, chief physicist, 50-52, head basic res, 52-56, mgr cent res, 56-61, vpres & gen mgr, 64-66, exec vpres & mem bd dirs, 66-68, VPRES, LORD MFG CO, 61-, GEN MGR, HUGHSON CHEM CO DIV, 58-, PRES, LORD CORP, 68-, VCHMN, 75- *Personal Data:* b Erie, Pa, July 29, 21; c 1. *Educ:* Univ Pittsburgh, BS, 47. *Honors & Awards:* Behrend Medallion, Pa State Univ; Francis Wright Davis Distinguished Lectr, Acad Appl Sci, 83. *Concurrent Pos:* Consult, Carborundum Co, 47-48, Sci Specialties Corp, 51-52 & Transistor Prod Corp, 52-56; metrop chmn, Nat Alliance Businessmen, 69-; mem bd dirs, Lord Corp, Kiethley Instruments, Inc; Schs Mgt, Univ Pittsburgh, Case Western Reserve Univ & Univ Denver, 69-; mem bd adv, Case Inst Technol, Sch Eng, Tulane Univ & Mellon Inst, 70-; mem bd trustees, Polytech Univ NY, Mercyhurst Col; mem corp, Conf Bd, NY; vchmn, Res & Develop Div, Nat Asn Mfrs; mem adv coun, Kolff Found; guest lectr, Int Inst Mgt Sci Ctr, Berlin, 79 & Swed Royal Acad Eng Sci, 84; mem sci & technol adv bd & hardwoods working comt, Pa Gov Casey's Economic Develop Partnership. *Mem:* Am Chem Soc; Am Phys Soc; Electrochem Soc; fel Am Inst Chemists; Inst Mgt Sci. *Res:* Adhesives and adhesion; dielectrics and rheology of materials; physics and chemistry of surfaces; frictional phenomena; bioengineering. *Mailing Add:* c/o Lord Corp 110 Corning Rd 100 II Cary NC 27511-9229

ALSTON, JIMMY ALBERT, PLANT BREEDING. *Current Pos:* plant breeder, 70-79, DIR RES, GEORGE W PARK SEED CO, INC, 79- *Personal Data:* b Temple, Tex, Mar 23, 42; m 67; c 2. *Educ:* Tex A&M Univ, BS, 64, MS, 67, PhD(plant breeding), 68. *Prof Exp:* Res asst, Tex A&M Univ, 64-68; supvr plant breeding dept, Seed Prod Div, Baker Castor Oil Co, Tex, 68-70. *Mem:* Am Soc Agron; Crop Sci Soc Am. *Res:* Cyclic gametic selection as a breeding method in corn; inheritance of female characters in Ricinus communis; development of new floricultural varieties by selective breeding methods; devising more efficient methods of seed production. *Mailing Add:* George W Park Seed Co Hwy 254 N Greenwood SC 29647

ALSTON, PETER VAN, PHYSICAL ORGANIC CHEMISTRY, ANALYTICAL CHEMISTRY. *Current Pos:* Res chemist, 74-80, sr res chemist, 81-90, RES ASSOC, E I DU PONT DE NEMOURS & CO, INC, 91- *Personal Data:* b Windsor, NC, Apr 27, 46; m 68; c 3. *Educ:* Univ NC, BS, 68; Va Commonwealth Univ, PhD(chem), 74. *Concurrent Pos:* Adj fac, J Sargeant Reynolds Community Col, 74-77. *Mem:* Am Chem Soc. *Res:* Mechanism of cycloaddition reactions; perturbation molecular orbital theory in organic chemistry; open-end-spinning of polyester fibers. *Mailing Add:* 305 Plantation Circle Kinston NC 28501

ALSTON, THEODORE A, ANESTHESIOLOGY, ENZYMOLOGY. *Current Pos:* ASST PROF ANESTHESIA, HARVARD MED SCH, 90- *Personal Data:* b Philadelphia, Pa, May 10, 54. *Educ:* Univ Pa, BA, 76, MD & PhD(biochem), 81. *Prof Exp:* Intern surg, Yale-New Haven Hosp, 81-82; res fel, Brandeis Univ, 85-87; resident anesthesia, Mass Gen Hosp, 87-90, Cardiac anesthesia fel, 90. *Concurrent Pos:* res assoc, Brandeis Univ, 90-; Parker Frances investr, Found Anesthesia Educ & Res, 91-93. *Mem:* Am Soc Anesthesiol; Int Anesthesia Res Soc; Am Soc Biochem & Molecular Biol. *Res:* Mechanisms of enzyme action and enzyme inhibition. *Mailing Add:* Dept Anesthesia Mass Gen Hosp Boston MA 02114. *Fax:* 617-726-5985; *E-Mail:* alston@etherdome.mgh.harvard.edu

ALSTON-GARNJOST, MARGARET, HIGH ENERGY PHYSICS. *Current Pos:* physicist, 59-72, SR STAFF SCIENTIST, LAWRENCE BERKELEY LAB, UNIV CALIF, 72- *Personal Data:* b Ashtead, Eng, Jan 23, 29; m 66. *Educ:* Univ Liverpool, BSc, 51, Hons, 52, PhD(physics), 55. *Prof Exp:* Demonstr physics, Univ Liverpool, 54-56, Imp Chem Industs res fel, 56-58. *Mem:* Am Phys Soc. *Res:* High energy particle physics; experimental high energy physics. *Mailing Add:* 41505 Little Nestucca River Rd Cloverdale OR 97112

ALSUM, DONALD JAMES, REPRODUCTIVE PHYSIOLOGY, NEURO-RECEPTOR PHYSIOLOGY. *Current Pos:* asst prof, 74-76, assoc prof biol, 76-85, chmn dept, 80-85, PROF BIOL, ST MARY'S COL, 83- *Personal Data:* b Randolph, Wis, June 27, 37; m 61; c 2. *Educ:* Calvin Col, BA, 61; Purdue Univ, MS, 66; Univ Minn, PhD(animal physiol), 74. *Prof Exp:* Jr high sch teacher sci, Western Suburbs Sch, Ill, 61-63; sec sci teacher, Timothy Christian High Sch, Ill, 63-70; res asst physiol, Univ Minn, Minneapolis, 70-74. *Concurrent Pos:* Physiol consult, Mcmillan Publ Co & Charles E Merrill; vis scientist neuro physiol, Mayo Found, 84-85. *Mem:* Am Soc Allied Health Prof; Am Inst Biol Sci. *Res:* Testicular functions with particular interests in spermatozial maturation and levels of acid and alkaline phosphatases in certain regions of the male reproductive tracts of specific mammals. *Mailing Add:* Dept Biol St Mary's Univ Minn 700 Terrace Heights Winona MN 55987-1321

ALT, DAVID D, GEOLOGY, GEOCHEMISTRY. *Current Pos:* from asst prof to assoc prof, 65-73, PROF GEOL, UNIV MONT, 73- *Personal Data:* b St Louis, Mo, Sept 17, 33. *Educ:* Washington Univ, St Louis, AB, 55; Univ Minn, MS, 58; Univ Tex, PhD(geol), 61. *Prof Exp:* Sr res assoc chem, Univ Leeds, 61-62; asst prof geol, Univ Fla, 62-65. *Mem:* Geol Soc Am; Soc Econ Paleont & Mineral; Nat Asn Geol Teachers. *Res:* Emergent shorelines and coastal plain geomorphology; karst landscapes. *Mailing Add:* Dept Geol Univ Mont Missoula MT 59812-0001

ALT, FRANZ L, MATHEMATICS, COMPUTER SCIENCE. *Current Pos:* RETIRED. *Personal Data:* b Vienna, Austria, Nov 30, 10; m 38, 85, Annice Mills; c Theresa F & James E. *Educ:* Univ Vienna, Austria, PhD(math), 32. *Prof Exp:* Dep dir, Div Appl Math, Nat Bur Standards, 48-67 & Info Div, Am Inst Physics, 67-73. *Mem:* Fel Asn Comput Mach; Am Math Soc. *Mailing Add:* 250 Cabrini Apt 9H New York NY 10033

ALT, FREDERICK W, MICROBIOLOGY. *Current Pos:* PROF GENETICS & PEDIAT, HARVARD MED SCH, 91-, INVESTR, HOWARD HUGHES MED INST, CHILDRENS HOSP, 91-, SR INVESTR, CTR BLOOD RES, 91-, CHARLES A JANEWAY PROF GENETICS & PEDIAT, 93- *Educ:* Brandeis Univ, BS, 71; Stanford Univ, PhD(biol sci), 77. *Honors & Awards:* Stephen J Fox Mem Award, Stanford Univ, 73; Irma T Hirschl Career Scientist Award, 83; Searle Scholars Award, 83; Mallinckrodt Scholar, 84. *Prof Exp:* Res fel, Mass Inst Technol, 77-82; from asst prof to prof biochem, Columbia Univ, 82-91, prof microbiol, 86-91. *Concurrent Pos:* Investr, Howard Hughes Med Inst, 87-91. *Mem:* Nat Acad Sci (pres, 94); Am Acad Microbiol (pres, 94); AAAS (pres, 94). *Res:* Contributed numerous articles to publications. *Mailing Add:* Howard Hughes Med Inst Childrens Hosp 300 Longwood Ave Boston MA 02115

ALT, GERHARD HORST, ORGANIC CHEMISTRY. *Current Pos:* AT AGR RES DEPT, MONSANTO CHEM CO. *Personal Data:* b Berlin, Ger, Jan 24, 25; m 59; c 2. *Educ:* Univ London, BSc, 49, PhD(org chem), 54. *Prof Exp:* Res fel, Wayne State Univ, 54-56; res chemist, Monsanto Co, 56-64, res specialist, Agr Div, 64-67, sr res specialist, Monsanto Agr Prod Co, 67- *Mem:* Am Chem Soc; The Chem Soc. *Res:* Enamine chemistry; steroids; conformational analysis; reaction mechanisms; heterocycles. *Mailing Add:* PO Box 345 Clarksville MO 63336-0345

ALTAN, TAYLAN, METAL FORMING PROCESSES & MACHINES, COMPUTER AIDED DESIGN & MANUFACTURING. *Current Pos:* PROF MECH ENG, OHIO STATE UNIV, 86- *Personal Data:* b Trabzon, Turkey, Feb 12, 38; US citizen; m 64, Susan Borah; c Peri & Aylin. *Educ:* Tech Univ Hannover, dipl eng, 62; Univ Calif, Berkeley, MS, 64, PhD(mech eng), 66. *Honors & Awards:* Gold Medal, Soc Mfg Eng. *Prof Exp:* Res scientist, Dupont Co, 66-68; sr res scientist, Batelle Columbus Labs, 68-78, from res leader to sr res leader, 78-86. *Concurrent Pos:* Prof indust & mech eng, Ohio State Univ, 86. *Mem:* Fel Am Soc Mech Engrs; fel Am Soc Metals Int; Am Mgt Asn; fel Soc Mfg Engrs. *Res:* Manufacturing process development; cold forming; sheet metal forming; die casting; injection and gas injection molding; die design and manufacturing, including EDM, ECM and machining. *Mailing Add:* 1380 Sherbrooke Pl Columbus OH 43209

ALTAR, CHARLES ANTHONY, NERVE GROWTH FACTORS, NEURONAL PLASTICITY & NEUROPHARMACOLOGY. *Current Pos:* SR STAFF SCIENTIST, REGENERON PHARMACEUT, 91- *Personal Data:* b Pittsburgh, Pa, July 1, 51; m 83, Kristin Iverson; c Melanie E & David A. *Educ:* Univ Calif, Los Angeles, BS, 73; Univ Calif, Santa Barbara, PhD(psychol), 81. *Prof Exp:* Scientist, Univ Calif, Irvine, 81-84, Genentech, Inc, 88-91; from scientist to sr scientist, CIBA - Geigy Corp, 84-88. *Concurrent Pos:* Lectr introductory psychobiol & adj fac, Univ Calif, Irvine, 82-84; adj assoc prof, NY Med Col, 92-96. *Mem:* Soc Neurosci; Int Soc Neurochem; Can Col Neuropsychopharmacol; Am Asn Pharmacol & Exp Therapeut. *Res:* Basic and applied research of neuronal plasticity of the central nervous system, particularly regarding neuronal pathways affected in neurodegenerative disease; developing therapeutic strategies based on pharmacological and endogenous growth factor agents that regulate these systems; neuropharmacology of psychiatric diseases. *Mailing Add:* Regeneron Pharmaceut 777 Old Saw Mill River Rd Tarrytown NY 10591. *Fax:* 914-345-7739; *E-Mail:* tony.altar@regpha.com

ALTEMEIER, WILLIAM ARTHUR, III, PEDIATRICS, NEONATOLOGY. *Current Pos:* PROF PEDIAT, VANDERBILT UNIV, 72-; VCHMN DEPT, 83-; CHAIR PEDIAT, UNIV MO, SCH MED, COLUMBIA, 90- *Personal Data:* b Detroit, Mich, Oct 3, 36; m 61; c 3. *Educ:* Univ Cincinnati, BA, 58; Vanderbilt Univ, MD, 62. *Prof Exp:* Fel infectious dis, Univ Fla, 64-66, asst prof pediat, 69-72; res assoc immunol, Walter Reed Res Inst, 66-68. *Mem:* Soc Pediat Res; Am Asn Immunologists. *Res:* Causes and prevention of child abuse. *Mailing Add:* 2245 Bluff Blvd Columbia MO 65201

ALTEMOSE, VINCENT O, PHYSICS, MATERIALS SCIENCE. *Current Pos:* RES SCIENTIST PHYSICS, CORNING GLASS WORKS, 56- *Personal Data:* b Nazareth, Pa, Aug 8, 28; m 50; c 4. *Educ:* Lafayette Col, BS, 52; Lehigh Univ, MS, 55. *Prof Exp:* Instr, Lafayette Col, 53-56. *Concurrent Pos:* Mem comt, Int Comn Glass, 77-83. *Mem:* Am Ceramic Soc; Am Vacuum Soc; Am Soc Mass Spectrometry; Sigma Xi. *Res:* Gases in glass and ceramics; gas diffusion and out gassing of glassy material by various forms of energy; high temperature vaporization studies. *Mailing Add:* Cross St Campbell NY 14821

ALTENAU, ALAN GILES, ANALYTICAL CHEMISTRY. *Current Pos:* DIR, INT TECH CTR, ROME, ITALY, 90- *Personal Data:* b Cincinnati, Ohio, May 16, 38; m 74, Janet Riley; c Jennifer, Jeffrey & Lindsay. *Educ:* Univ Cincinnati, BS, 59; Purdue Univ, MS, 61, PhD(anal chem), 64. *Prof Exp:* Group leader, Anal Div, Firestone Tire & Rubber Co, 66-69, mgr, 69-74, asst dir, Cent Res, 74-79, dir, 79-90. *Mem:* Am Chem Soc. *Res:* Research and development of tires. *Mailing Add:* 6763 St James Circle Hudson OH 44236

ALTENBURG, LEWIS CONRAD, CYTOGENETICS. *Personal Data:* b Houston, Tex, May 12, 42; m 65; c 1. *Educ:* Rice Univ, BA, 65; Univ Tex Grad Sch Biomed Sci, MS, 68, PhD(biochem), 70. *Prof Exp:* Asst prof med genetics, Univ Tex Grad Sch Biomed Sci, Houston, 73-77. *Concurrent Pos:* Fel, Max Planck Inst Exp Med, Gottingen, WGer, 70-71; fel, Univ Tex Grad Sch Biomed Sci, 71-72; NIH fel, Dept Biol, Univ Tex M D Anderson Hosp & Tumor Inst, 71-73; res assoc med genetics, Univ Tex Grad Sch Biomed Sci, Houston, 73. *Mem:* Am Chem Soc; Am Soc Microbiol; Am Soc Cell Biol; Am Soc Human Genetics; Genetics Soc Am. *Res:* Molecular cytogenetics of human chromosomes. *Mailing Add:* 5800 Lost Forest Dr Houston TX 77092

ALTENKIRCH, ROBERT AMES, COMBUSTION, THERMAL SCIENCES. *Current Pos:* DEAN, COL ENG & ARCH, WASH STATE UNIV, 95- *Personal Data:* b St Louis, Mo, May 13, 48; m 70; c 2. *Educ:* Purdue Univ, BSME, 70, PhD(mech eng), 75; Univ Calif, Berkeley, MS, 71. *Honors & Awards:* Teetor Award, Soc Automotive Eng, 79; Gustus L Larson Award, Am Soc Mech Engrs, 84. *Prof Exp:* From asst prof to prof mech eng, Univ Ky, 75-88, chmn dept, 85-88; dean, Col Eng, Miss State Univ, 88-95. *Concurrent Pos:* Prin investr, NSF, 76-78, NASA, 82-; co-prin investr, NASA, 76-81 & NSF, 77-79 & 80-82. *Mem:* Combustion Inst; fel Am Soc Mech Engrs. *Res:* Pollutant formation during coal combustion; buoyancy effects on flames; flame spreading; two phase flow; continuous flow combustion. *Mailing Add:* Col Eng & Arch Wash State Univ 146 Dana Hall Pullman WA 99164

ALTER, AMOS JOSEPH, SANITARY ENGINEERING, PUBLIC HEALTH. *Current Pos:* RETIRED. *Personal Data:* b Rensselaer, Ind, Aug 4, 16; m 40; c 4. *Educ:* Purdue Univ, BS, 38, CE, 49; MPH, Univ Mich, 48. *Honors & Awards:* Arthur Sidney Bedell Award, Water Pollution Control Fedn, 70; Pub Works, Man-of-the-year-Am Pub Works Asn, 67; Hon mem, Am Soc Civil Engrs, 90. *Prof Exp:* Sanit engr, Ind State Bd Health, 38-42; comn officer sanit engr, USPHS, 42-44; chief engr, Alaska Dept Health, 44-67; environ res engr, State of Alaska, 67-75; environ eng consult, 75-85. *Concurrent Pos:* Fel, WHO, Scandinavia, 50-51; mem sanit eng & environ comt, Nat Res Coun, 50-66; mem, Conf State Sanit Engrs; vis lectr, Univ Alaska, 70-75. *Mem:* Arctic Inst NAm; Am Soc Civil Engrs; Am Pub Health Asn; Am Water Works Asn; Am Acad Environ Engrs; Nat Soc Prof Engrs. *Res:* Civil engineering; cold weather design and construction problems. *Mailing Add:* PO Box 20304 Juneau AK 99802-0304

ALTER, GERALD M, PHYSICAL BIOCHEMISTRY, ENZYMOLOGY. *Current Pos:* ASSOC PROF BIOL CHEM, WRIGHT STATE UNIV, 77- *Educ:* Wash State Univ, PhD(biol chem), 75. *Res:* Confirmational properties of proteins and enzymes; in vivo enzymology. *Mailing Add:* Dept Biol Chem Wright State Univ Dayton OH 45435

ALTER, HARVEY, PHYSICAL CHEMISTRY, ENVIRONMENTAL CHEMISTRY. *Current Pos:* MGR, RESOURCES POLICY DEPT, US CHAMBER COMMERCE, 79- *Personal Data:* b New York, NY, Sept 4, 32; m 57, Cora Wolff; c Julie & Lisa. *Educ:* City Univ New York, BS, 52; Univ Cincinnati, MS, 54, PhD(phys chem), 57. *Honors & Awards:* Award of Merit, Am Soc Testing & Mat, 80. *Prof Exp:* Physicist plastics dept, Union Carbide Corp, 57-59; sr chemist, Harris Res Labs, Gillette Co Res Inst, 59-63, group leader, 64-65, assoc dir res, Toni Div, 65-66, tech dir res, 66-68, mgr,68-72, vpres, 72; dir res progs, Nat Ctr for Resource Recovery, Inc, 72-79. *Concurrent Pos:* Lectr, City Col New York, 58-59; prof lectr, Am Univ, 70-74, adj prof, 74-87; mem US Air Force PBI Technol Rev Comt, 70, ad hoc adhesion Adv Comt, 71, Environ Res Guid Comt Md, 77-79; chmn, Gordon Res Conf Sci Adhesion, 72, Am Soc Test & Mat Comt E-38 Resource Recovery, 73-78, Outside Evaluation Panel Recycled Mat, Nat Bureau Stand, 79-82; ed, Resources Conserv, 72-87, Resources Conserv & Recycling, 88-95; Gov's Task Force Solid Waste Mgt, Md, 87-, bd dir, WTE, Bedford, Mass, 82-; chrm Gov adv coun recycling, 89, adv panel Assessment of Mat Technol,

90; adj prop, Univ Col Univ Grad Sch Mgt & Technol. *Mem:* Fel Am Soc Testing & Mat; Am Chem Soc. *Res:* Materials and energy recovery from wastes; science and public policy; chemistry of non-metallic materials; recovery of materials and energy from municipal solid waste, environmental policy. *Mailing Add:* 10 Watchwater Way 1615 H St NW Rockville MD 20850. *Fax:* 202-887-3445; *E-Mail:* halter@uschimber.com

ALTER, HARVEY JAMES, INTERNAL MEDICINE, HEMATOLOGY. *Current Pos:* chief immunol sect, Blood Bank, 78-92, SR INVESTR, NIH, 69-, FAC, FOUND ADVAN EDUC SCI, 76-, CHIEF, INFECTIOUS DIS SECT, DEPT TRANSFUSION MED. *Personal Data:* b New York, NY, Sept 12, 35; m 65; c 2. *Educ:* Univ Rochester, BA, 56, MD, 60; Am Bd Path, cert, 78. *Honors & Awards:* Superior Serv Award, Dept Health, Educ & Welfare, 74 & Distinguished Serv Medal, 77; Landsteiner Award, Am Asn Blood Banks, 92; Lean Schiff Lectr, Am Asn Study Liver Dis. *Prof Exp:* From intern to resident med, Strong Mem Hosp, Univ Rochester, 60-61; clin assoc blood bank, NIH, 61-64; resident med, Seattle Univ Hosp, 64-65; from instr to asst prof med, Georgetown Univ Hosp, 66-69. *Concurrent Pos:* Univ fel hemat, Georgetown Univ Hosp, 65-66, clin assoc prof, 69-86, clin prof, 87- *Mem:* Fedn Clin Res; Am Soc Hemat; Am Asn Blood Banks; Int Soc Hemat; Am Asn Study Liver Dis; Asn Am Physicians. *Res:* Studies relating to nature and significance of the hepatitis B virus and its associated antigens to the hepatitus C virus and to other transfusion-transmitted agents; discoveries of hepatitis B, C and G viruses. *Mailing Add:* NIH Dept Transfuslon Med Bldg 10 Rm 1C-711 Bethesda MD 20892

ALTER, HENRY WARD, PHYSICAL CHEMISTRY. *Current Pos:* RETIRED. *Personal Data:* b Taxila, Punjab, India, Dec 26, 23; US citizen; m 44, 79; c 3. *Educ:* Univ Calif, AB, 43, PhD(chem), 48. *Prof Exp:* Asst chem, Univ Calif, 42-44, 46-47, chemist, Manhattan Proj, 44-48; mgr separations chem & res assoc, Knolls Atomic Power Lab, Gen Elec Co, 48-57; tech specialist & mgr nuclear & inorg chem, Vallecitos Atomic Lab, 57-68; mgr nucleonics lab, Gen Elec Co, 68-71, mgr nuclear technol & appln oper, 71-74; pres, Terradex Corp, 74-86; consult, Tech-Ops Laudauer, 86-88. *Mem:* Am Chem Soc; fel Am Nuclear Soc; Sigma Xi. *Res:* Nuclear energy; nuclear fuels; plutonium technology; nuclear chemistry; fuel reprocessing; uranium exploration; environmental monitoring; radon. *Mailing Add:* 110 Haslemere Ct Lafayette CA 94549

ALTER, JOSEPH DINSMORE, GERIATRICS, COMMUNITY MEDICINE. *Current Pos:* clin prof & actg chmn dept, 67-77, PROF COMMUNITY MED & CHMN DEPT, SCH MED, WRIGHT STATE UNIV, 77-, CHMN, CTR AGING RES EDUC & SERV, 80- *Personal Data:* b Lawrence, Kans, Apr 19, 23; m 46, 81; c 3. *Educ:* Hahnemann Med Col, MD, 50; Univ Calif, Berkeley, MPH, 61; Am Bd Prev Med, cert, 68. *Prof Exp:* Med staff, Group Health Coop, Seattle, 51-60; lectr, Sch Pub Health, Univ Calif, Berkeley, 61-62; from lectr to asst prof, Sch Hygiene & Pub Health, Johns Hopkins Univ, 62-68; assoc & field prof community med, Col Med, Univ Ky Med Ctr, 68-70; med dir, Pilot City Health Serv, Cincinnati, Ohio, 70-73; med dir, Health Care Louisville Inc, Ky, 73-75; chief domiciliary med serv, Vet Admin Ctr, Dayton, Ohio, 75-77. *Concurrent Pos:* Clin assoc prof community med, Col Med, Univ Ky Med Ctr, 70-73; field dir, rural health res projs, Narangwal, India, Johns Hopkins Univ, 62-67; clin prof family pract, Sch Med, Univ Louisville, 73-75. *Mem:* Am Acad Family Physicians; Am Col Prev Med; fel Am Pub Health Asn; Am Geriat Soc; Geront Soc. *Res:* Consumer health education; geriatrics; self-care and health promotion for older persons. *Mailing Add:* 551 Crestgrove Ave Vandalia OH 45377-2527

ALTER, MILTON, NEUROLOGY, EPIDEMIOLOGY. *Current Pos:* CLIN PROF NEUROL, ALLEGHENY UNIV, 95- *Personal Data:* b Buffalo, NY, Nov 11, 29; m 52, Reina Rolnick; c David S, Daniel M, Michael A, Naomi T & Joel S. *Educ:* State Univ NY, Buffalo, BA, 51, MD, 55; Univ Minn, PhD, 64. *Prof Exp:* Mem staff, Epidemiol Br, Nat Inst Neurol Dis & Blindness, 56-62; consult neurol, Vet Hosp, St Cloud & Ancker Hosp, St Paul, 64-65; consult neurologist, Vet Admin Hosp, Fargo, NDak & Faribault State Hosp, Minn, 65-67; chief neurol serv, Minneapolis Vet Admin Hosp, Minneapolis, 67-76; from assoc prof to prof, Med Sch, Univ Minn, Minneapolis, 71-76; chmn dept, Temple Univ Hosp, 76-87, prof, 76-89; prof, Med Col Pa, 89-94. *Concurrent Pos:* USPHS fel, 62-64; Minn Asn Retarded Children grant, 63-64; Off Int Res grant, NIH, 63-66; consult, Honeywell, Inc, 63-72; USPHS grant, 65-68; Multiple Sclerosis Soc grants, 68, 71, 73 & 78; mem, Task Force Epidemiol Epilepsy, NIH, 70-73; ed, Neurol, 73-78 & J Neurol, 73-; mem adj comt, Nat Multiple Sclerosis Soc; assoc ed, Neuroepidemiol, 83-89 emer lectr, 97-; grant neuroepidemiol, Safety Monitoring Comt, NIH, 85-; adj prof epidemiol, Univ Pittsburgh, 89- & Univ Pa, 94-; clin prof neurol, Allegheny Univ, 95- *Mem:* Am Acad Neurol; AMA; Soc Epidemiol Res; fel Am Neurol Asn; World Fedn Neurol; Am Heart Asn. *Res:* Epidemiology and genetics of neurological disorders, especially multiple sclerosis, myasthenia gravis and congenital malformations of the nervous system; dermatoglyphics of mental retardation; dementia, especially transmissable types and stroke; effect of controlling risk factors for stroke recurrence on mortality and second stroke. *Mailing Add:* Med Col Pa 3300 Henry Ave Philadelphia PA 19129-1121. *Fax:* 610-668-8236

ALTER, RALPH, computer communications, distributed computer systems, for more information see previous edition

ALTER, RONALD, MATHEMATICS, COMPUTER SCIENCE. *Current Pos:* RETIRED. *Personal Data:* b New York, NY, Mar 27, 39; m 63; c 3. *Educ:* City Col New York, BS, 60; Univ Pa, MA, 62, PhD(math), 65. *Prof Exp:* Asst prof math, Univ Calif, Los Angeles, 64-67; res fel, Syst Develop Corp, 67-68, assoc res scientist, Res & Technol Div, 68-69; asst prof math & computer sci, Univ Ky, 69-70, assoc prof computer sci, 70-83. *Concurrent Pos:* Math analyst, Litton Systs, Inc, 66; fac res fel, Oak Ridge Nat Lab, 75. *Mem:* Am Math Soc; Asn Comput Mach; Math Asn Am. *Res:* Analytic, algebraic and elementary number theory; combinatorial mathematics; graph theory; algebraic coding theory; computer applications to mathematics. *Mailing Add:* 521 N Broadway Lexington KY 40508-1328

ALTER, THEODORE ROBERTS, PUBLIC FINANCE, RURAL DEVELOPMENT. *Current Pos:* from asst prof to assoc prof, 76-89, regional dir Southeast, Pa State Coop Ext, 89-94, PROF, PA STATE UNIV, 89-, HEAD, DEPT AGR ECON & RURAL SOCIOL, 94-, INTERIM DEAN, COL AGR SCI, 96- *Personal Data:* b Toledo, Ohio, Sept 16, 46; m 68; c 2. *Educ:* Univ Rochester, BA, 68; Mich State Univ, MS, 73, PhD(resource econ), 76. *Honors & Awards:* Distinguished Exten Prog Award, Am Agr Econ Asn, 85. *Concurrent Pos:* Chmn, Exten Comt Orgn & Policy Task Force on Local Govt Educ, 82-85; consult, Orgn Econ Coop & Develop, 87-89. *Mem:* Am Agr Econ Asn; Asn Evolutionary Econ; Community Develop Soc. *Res:* The economics of community issues in agricultural and rural areas; comparative analysis of rural development policy. *Mailing Add:* 103 Armsby Pa State Univ University Park PA 16802

ALTER, WILLIAM A, III, cardiovascular physiology, for more information see previous edition

ALTERA, KENNETH P, VETERINARY PATHOLOGY. *Current Pos:* PATHOLOGIST, SYNTEX CORP, 73- *Personal Data:* b Chicago, Ill, June 30, 36; m 63; c 2. *Educ:* Univ Ill, BS, 58, DVM, 60; Univ Calif, PhD(comp path), 65. *Prof Exp:* Asst pathologist, Univ Calif, 64-65; asst prof vet path, 65-71, assoc prof vet path & vet pathologist, Colo State Univ, 71-72; pathologist, United Med Labs, 72-73. *Mem:* Am Col Vet Path; Sigma Xi. *Res:* Comparative and experimental oncology; drug safety evaluation. *Mailing Add:* 736 Casa Bonita Ct Los Altos CA 94024

ALTES, RICHARD ALAN, MATHEMATICAL MODELS OF ANIMAL SENSORY SYSTEMS, NEURAL NETWORKS. *Current Pos:* PRES, CHIRP CORP, 86- *Personal Data:* b New York, NY, Aug 23, 41; m 94, Lynn Jubelirer; c David & Lauren. *Educ:* Cornell Univ, BEE, 64, MEE, 65; Univ Rochester, MS, 66, PhD (elec eng), 71. *Prof Exp:* Res engr, Raytheon Res Div, 66-67; eng specialist, Electromagnetic Systs Lab, Inc, 70-76; sr scientist, Sci Applications Int Corp, 76-78; sr prin engr, Orincon Corp, 78-86. *Concurrent Pos:* Res assoc neurobiol, Scripps Inst Oceanog, Univ Calif, San Diego, 78-86, res engr, Ctr Res Lang, 86-88; res assoc, Hubbs-Sea World Res Inst, 80-86; adj prof, San Diego State Univ, 87- *Mem:* Inst Elec & Electronics Engrs; Acoust Soc Am; Int Neural Network Soc. *Res:* Radar/sonar signal processing and signal design; acoustic analysis; sensor fusion; pattern recognition; multidimensional signal processing; speech recognition; biomedical data processing (brain waves, medical ultrasound, tomography); models of animal sensory systems from a statistical viewpoint; applications and innovations with respect to neural networks; granted 4 patents. *Mailing Add:* 8248 Sugarman Dr La Jolla CA 92037

ALTEVEER, ROBERT JAN GEORGE, PHYSIOLOGY, BIOPHYSICS. *Current Pos:* asst prof, 67-72, ASSOC PROF PHYSIOL, HAHNEMANN UNIV SCH MED, 72- *Personal Data:* b Rheden, Neth, June 5, 35; US citizen; m 74; c 4. *Educ:* Acad Phys Educ, Amsterdam, BPE, 57; Springfield Col, MS, 58; Univ Minn, PhD(educ, physiol), 65. *Honors & Awards:* Lindback Award. *Prof Exp:* Instr physiol hyg, Univ Minn, 62-65; lectr physiol, Ind Univ, Bloomington, 65, asst prof physiol & med, 65-67. *Concurrent Pos:* Adj asst prof, Univ Nev, Las Vegas, 66-67; vis prof bioeng, Rose Polytech Inst; dir, Trauma Res & Educ, Dept Surg, Hahnemann Univ, 87-90. *Mem:* AAAS; Am Asn Univ Professors; Am Col Sports Med; Sigma Xi; Shock Soc. *Res:* Physiology of circulatory shock; environmental stress; biophysics of respiration and circulation; exercise physiology. *Mailing Add:* Med Col Penn Hahnemann Univ Sch Med 2900 Queen Lane Philadelphia PA 19102

ALTEVOGT, RAYMOND FRED, ECONOMIC BOTANY, GENETICS. *Current Pos:* CONSULT, 81- *Personal Data:* b St Louis, Mo, Oct, 9, 40; m 69; c 2. *Educ:* Wash Univ, AB, 63, PhD(bot), 70. *Prof Exp:* Asst prof biol, bot & math, Southern Ill Univ, Edwardsville, 70-71 & Lewis & Clark Community Col, 71-73; consult agr & germ plasm, Iranian Dept Environ, 74-75; lead analyst agr, World Food & Nutrit Study, Nat Acad Sci, 76; mem staff bot, Off Endangered Species, US Dept Interior, 76-77; asst dir & head, Agr Sect, Nat Food Processors Asn, 77-81. *Mem:* Soc Econ Bot. *Res:* Germ plasm conservation; crop evolution; agricultural research policy and pesticide regulation. *Mailing Add:* 7049 Eastern Ave Silver Spring MD 20912

ALTGELT, KLAUS H, PHYSICAL CHEMISTRY, PETROLEUM CHEMISTRY. *Current Pos:* CONSULT, 86- *Personal Data:* b Ger, Jan 30, 27; m 51, Sigrid M Adolph; c Tom & Claudia. *Educ:* Univ Mainz, BS, 52, MS, 55, PhD(phys chem), 58. *Prof Exp:* Instr phys chem, Inst Phys Chem, Univ Mainz, 54-59; res assoc phys chem, Mass Inst Technol, 59-61; res chemist, Chevron Res Co, 61-65, sr res chemist, 65-68, sr res assoc, 68-86. *Concurrent Pos:* Fel, Univ Mainz, 58-59; pres, Ger Sch San Francisco, 68-71. *Mem:* Am Chem Soc. *Res:* Polymeric fuel and oil additives in petroleum chemistry; chemical composition of asphalt, heavy petroleum fractions, and coal; compatibility in and between asphalts; thermodynamics of wax in fuels; mechanism and suppression of oil misting; mechanism of detergent action in combustion engines; stability of coal slurries; oxidation stability of lubricants in engines; deoiling industrial wastes; nuclear magnetic resonance analysis of complex mixtures; author of 28 papers and 3 books; granted 2 patents. *Mailing Add:* 555 Appleberry Dr San Rafael CA 94903

ALTHAUS, RALPH ELWOOD, PLANT PATHOLOGY. *Current Pos:* AGR BUS CONSULT, 85- *Personal Data:* b Bluffton, Ohio, May 27, 25; m 49; c 3. *Educ:* Bluffton Col, BS, 49; Ohio State Univ, MS, 51. *Prof Exp:* Asst, Boyce-Thompson Inst, 51-53; prod develop rep, B F Goodrich Chem Co, 53-57 & Merck & Co, Inc, 57-60; prod develop rep, 60-68, mgr prod develop dept, Agr Prod, 68-80, tech dir, Peoples Repub China, Monsanto Co, 80-85. *Mem:* Weed Sci Soc Am. *Res:* Herbicides for agricultural and industrial vegetation control. *Mailing Add:* 11107 Oak Lake Ct St Louis MO 63146

ALTHOEN, STEVEN CLARK, FINITE-DIMENSIONAL REAL DIVISION ALGEBRAS. *Current Pos:* PROF MATH, UNIV MICH, FLINT, 75- *Personal Data:* b Dayton, Ohio, Mar 3, 46; m 66, Marcia A Warrick; c Michael D & Tosca A. *Educ:* Kenyon Col, BA, 69; City Univ New York, PhD(math), 73. *Prof Exp:* Prof math, Hofstra Univ, 73-75. *Mem:* Am Math Soc; Math Asn Am; Nat Coun Teachers Math. *Res:* Classification of non-associative, finite-dimensional real division algebras. *Mailing Add:* Dept Math Univ Mich Flint MI 48502-2186. *E-Mail:* althoen_s@msb.flint.umich.edu

ALTHUIS, THOMAS HENRY, ORGANIC & GENERAL CHEMISTRY, MEDICAL SCIENCE. *Current Pos:* From res scientist to sr res scientist, Med Chem Res Dept, 68-78, MGR SCI AFFAIRS & DIR SCI POLICY AFFAIRS, PUB AFFAIRS DIV, PFIZER, INC, 80- *Personal Data:* b Kalamazoo, Mich, June 21, 41; c 3. *Educ:* Western Mich Univ, BS, 63, MA, 65; Mich State Univ, PhD(org chem), 68. *Concurrent Pos:* Am Chem Soc Cong Fel, Sci & Technol Comt, US House Rep, 78-79; mem, Comt Chem & Pub Affairs, Am Chem Soc, 84-90, Technol Task Force, Coun Competitiveness, 87-88; bd dirs, Am Inst Chemists, 90-91, Conn United Res Excellence, 93, Am Med Progress, 97- *Mem:* Am Chem Soc; AAAS; NY Acad Sci; fel Am Inst Chemists; Soc Indust Chem. *Res:* Synthesis of nitrogen heterocycles; natural product synthesis; asymmetric synthesis; drugs for the treatment of allergies and pain; science and technology policy issues affecting research, development, approval and marketing of drugs; drugs for rare diseases; science education; US industrial competitiveness. *Mailing Add:* Pfizer Inc Eastern Point Rd Groton CT 06340

ALTICK, PHILIP LEWIS, ATOMIC PHYSICS. *Current Pos:* RETIRED. *Personal Data:* b Los Angeles, Calif, June 27, 33; m 55; c 4. *Educ:* Stanford Univ, BS, 55; Univ Calif, Berkeley, MA, 60, PhD(atomic physics), 63. *Prof Exp:* Res physicist, Lawrence Radiation Lab, Univ Calif, Berkeley, 63; from asst prof to prof physics, Univ Nev, Reno, 63-95, chmn dept, 76-79 & 85-86. *Concurrent Pos:* Consult, Lockheed Missile & Space Co, 63-; res assoc, Univ Chicago, 67-68; vis prof, Univ Trier-Kaiserslautern, 72-73; sr vis fel, Daresbury Lab & Univ Col, London, 81-82; prin investr, NASA G471 & NSF, 84- *Mem:* Fel Am Phys Soc. *Res:* Theoretical study of atomic processes, especially electron impact ionization. *Mailing Add:* Physics Dept 220 Univ Nev Reno NV 89557. *Fax:* 702-784-1398

ALTIERI, A(NGELO) M(ICHAEL), CHEMICAL ENGINEERING. *Current Pos:* RETIRED. *Personal Data:* b Watertown, Mass, Oct 11, 07; m 34; c 2. *Educ:* Mass Inst Technol, SB, 29. *Prof Exp:* Res chemist, Dennison Mfg Co, 29-31; foreman, US Rubber Co, 31-32; from chem engr to asst res dir, Fitchburg Paper Co, 33-46; chief chemist & tech dir, Tileston & Hollingsworth Co, Diamond-Int, 46-70; engr, Fay, Spofford & Thorndike, 70-73. *Mem:* Tech Asn Pulp & Paper Indust; Am Inst Chemists. *Res:* Papermaking; de-inking and waterproofing processes; paper coating; printing; laminating; resins and adhesives; gelatin foils; latex thread; emulsions; design and operation of chemical processing equipment; water purification; waste water treatment. *Mailing Add:* 67 Copeland St Watertown MA 02172

ALTIERI, DARIO CARLO, CLINICAL HEMATOLOGY. *Current Pos:* res fel, 87-89, ASST MEM, SCRIPPS CLIN, LA JOLLA, CALIF, 89- *Personal Data:* b Milan, Italy, July 20, 58. *Educ:* Univ Milan, MD, 82. *Prof Exp:* Resident clin hemat, ABB Hemophilia & Thrombosis Ctr, Milan, 83-86. *Concurrent Pos:* Adj prof hemat, Univ Milan Sch Med, 90- *Mem:* Am Asn Pathologists; Am Asn Immunologists; AAAS. *Res:* Adhesion receptors in the immune system; role of proteases and protease receptors in the modulation of the immune response. *Mailing Add:* Boyer Ctr Molecular Med Rm 436 Yale Univ Sch Med 295 Congress Ave New Haven CT 06536

ALTIERO, NICHOLAS JAMES, JR, THEORETICAL MECHANICS, APPLIED MECHANICS. *Current Pos:* from asst prof to assoc prof, 75-86, PROF MECH, MICH STATE UNIV, 86-, ASSOC DEAN ENG, 90- *Personal Data:* b Youngstown, Ohio, Sept 22, 47; m 78, Amy Johnson; c Elizabeth. *Educ:* Univ Notre Dame, BS, 69; Univ Mich, MSE, 70, AM, 71, PhD(aerospace eng), 74. *Prof Exp:* Scholar aerospace eng, Univ Mich, 74-75. *Concurrent Pos:* Consult mech engr, US Bur Mines; Fulbright scholar; Alexander von Humboldt fel. *Mem:* Am Soc Mech Engrs; Soc Eng Sci; Int Soc Comput Methods Eng; Am Acad Mech; Am Soc Eng Educ; Int Soc Boundary Elements. *Res:* Numerical methods in mechanics; fracture mechanics; composite materials. *Mailing Add:* Col Eng Mich State Univ East Lansing MI 48824. *Fax:* 517-353-7782; *E-Mail:* altiero@egr.msu.edu

ALTLAND, HENRY WOLF, ORGANIC CHEMISTRY, EXPERIMENTAL DESIGN. *Current Pos:* sr res chemist, 73-81, RES ASSOC EASTMAN KODAK RES LABS, 81- *Personal Data:* b Takoma Park, Md, Feb 26, 45; m 68; c 1. *Educ:* Gettysburg Col, AB, 67; Princeton Univ, PhD(org chem), 71, Rochester Inst Tech, MS, 87. *Prof Exp:* NIH fel, Univ Va, 71-73. *Concurrent Pos:* Asst instr eve exten, Univ Rochester, 77-80. *Mem:* Am Chem Soc; Am Soc Qual Control. *Res:* Synthesis and reactions of heterocyclic compounds, heterocyclic rearrangements; application of organometallic reactions to organic synthesis; application of experimental designs, (mixture taguchi central composite, etc) to chemical problems; emulsion addenda. *Mailing Add:* 547 Pinegrove Ave Rochester NY 14617

ALTLAND, PAUL DANIEL, ZOOLOGY, PHYSIOLOGY. *Current Pos:* from asst physiologist to physiologist, 44-50, sr physiologist, 50-57, physiologist, 57-62, chief, Physiol Sect, Lab Phys Biol & Lab Chem Physics, 62-81, EMER SCIENTIST, NIH, USPHS, 81- *Personal Data:* b York, Pa, Apr 1, 13; m 44; c 3. *Educ:* Gettysburg Col, BS, 34; Duke Univ, AM, 36, PhD(cytol), 37. *Prof Exp:* Asst zool, Duke Univ, 34-36; from instr to asst prof biol, Gettysburg Col, 37-44. *Mem:* Am Soc Zool; Soc Exp Biol & Med; Am Physiol Soc; Am Inst Biol Sci; Int Soc Biometeorol; Sigma Xi. *Res:* Physiology, pathology, and tolerance of animals exposed to simulated altitude, exercise and cold; reptile physiology; experimental endocarditis in animals; cigarette smoke, carbon monoxide, nicotine and restraint effects in rats. *Mailing Add:* Nat Lutheran Home 9701 Veirs Dr Rockville MD 20850-3462

ALTMAN, ALBERT, THEORETICAL NUCLEAR PHYSICS, SOLID STATE PHYSICS. *Current Pos:* PROF PHYSICS, LOWELL TECHNOL INST, 66- *Personal Data:* b New York, NY, Dec 11, 32; c 2. *Educ:* Brooklyn Col, BS, 54; Univ Md, MS, 58, PhD(nuclear physics), 62. *Prof Exp:* Sr physicist, Gen Dynamics Convair, 60-61; asst prof nuclear theory, Univ Va, 62 & Univ Md, 63-64; physicist, Naval Ord Lab, 64-66. *Mem:* Sigma Xi. *Res:* Nuclear reactions and nuclear structure; quantum mechanics and scattering theory; molecular physics. *Mailing Add:* 124 Bellingham Rd Chestnut Hill MA 02167

ALTMAN, ALLEN BURCHARD, ALGEBRAIC GEOMETRY. *Current Pos:* PROF MATH, SIMON'S ROCK COL, 86- *Personal Data:* b Berkeley, Calif, Nov 16, 42; m 64, Karin M Olive. *Educ:* Columbia Univ, PhD(math), 68. *Prof Exp:* Actg asst prof math, Univ Calif, San Diego, 68-69, asst prof, 69-75; prof math, Univ Simon Bolivar, 75-86. *Concurrent Pos:* Fulbright fel, 71-72; res assoc, Mass Inst Technol, 81-82; vis prof, Univ Nacional de Pernambuco, 85, Northern Ariz Univ, 93. *Mem:* AAAS; Am Math Soc; Math Asn Am. *Res:* Algebraic geometry. *Mailing Add:* Dept Math Simon's Rock Col Great Barrington MA 01230-1559. *Fax:* 413-528-7365; *E-Mail:* altman@simons_rock.edu

ALTMAN, DAVID, CHEMISTRY. *Current Pos:* RETIRED. *Personal Data:* b Paterson, NJ, Feb 13, 20; m 47, Beverly Adlis; c Jody, Jan & Rick. *Educ:* Cornell Univ, AB, 40; Univ Calif, PhD(chem), 43. *Honors & Awards:* Propulsion Award, Am Inst Aeronaut & Astronaut, 64; Apollo Achievement Award, NASA, 68, Pub Serv Award, 81 & 88. *Prof Exp:* Teaching asst chem, Univ Calif, 40-43; res assoc, Radiation Lab, Manhattan Proj, 43-45; chief chemist, Jet Propulsion Lab, 45-56; mgr vehicle technol, Aeronutronic Systs, Inc, 56-59; sr vpres, Chem Systs Div, United Technol Corp, 59-81, aerospace consult, 81-95. *Concurrent Pos:* Consult, Dept Defense, USAF & NASA; consult prof, Stanford Univ, 87-92. *Mem:* Am Chem Soc; fel Am Inst Aeronaut & Astronaut; Aerospace Indust Asn Am; Sigma Xi. *Res:* High temperature; equilibrium and kinetics; thermodynamics; aerochemistry; surface chemistry; propulsion; missile systems. *Mailing Add:* 1670 Oak Ave Menlo Park CA 94025. *Fax:* 650-329-8255

ALTMAN, JACK, PLANT PATHOLOGY, SOIL MICROBIOLOGY. *Current Pos:* From asst prof & asst plant pathologist to assoc prof & assoc plant pathologist, 57-70, PROF BOT & PLANT PATH & PLANT PATHOLOGIST, EXP STA, COLO STATE UNIV, 70- *Personal Data:* b Antwerp, Belg, Feb 17, 23; nat US. *Educ:* Rutgers Univ, BSc, 54, PhD(plant path), 57. *Concurrent Pos:* Tech rep, Regional Res Proj W-56, 58-; mem Colo Gov Comt Air Pollution, 63-; Colo State Rep, Fed Mold Metabolites, 64-; NSF awards, 63-65; Indust Res grants, 64-68; HEW Air Pollution Proj res award, 67-69; pest control adv & plant pathologist, Khuzestan Water & Power Authority, Iran, 70-72; Sr Scientist Award, Alexander von Humboldt Found, 77-78; partic, Distinguished Scholar Exchange Prog, People's Repub China, Nat Acad Sci, 81; mem, Comt Int Coop, Am Phytopath Soc, 92- *Mem:* Am Phytopath Soc; Soc Nematologists; Sigma Xi; Int Soc Plant Pathologists. *Res:* Associated nematode complex of root rot diseases of plants; use of antibiotics to control plant diseases; side effects of chlorinated hydrocarbons on nitrogenous transformations in soil; use of chemicals for Rhizoctonia control; pesticide interactions in crop production-beneficial and deleterious effects; published one book. *Mailing Add:* Bioagriculture Sci & Pest Mgt Colo State Univ Ft Collins CO 80523. *Fax:* 970-491-5261

ALTMAN, JOSEPH, NEUROPSYCHOLOGY. *Current Pos:* prof psychol sci, 74-80, prof, 68-96, EMER PROF, DEPT BIOL SCI, PURDUE UNIV, 96- *Personal Data:* b Budapest, Hungary, Oct 7, 25; m 50; c 1. *Educ:* NY Univ, PhD(physiol psychol), 59. *Prof Exp:* Asst neurophysiol, Mt Sinai Hosp, NY, 57-59; res fel neuroanat, Col Physicians & Surg, Columbia Univ, 59-60; res assoc physiol psychol, Sch Med, NY Univ, 60-61; res assoc, Psychophysiol Lab, Mass Inst Technol, 61-62, assoc prof psychol, 62-68. *Mem:* Soc Neurosci; Int Soc Develop Psychobiol. *Res:* Development of the nervous system and behavior under normal and experimental conditions. *Mailing Add:* 7715 W 88th St Indianapolis IN 46278-1164. *Fax:* 317-733-0237

ALTMAN, JOSEPH HENRY, PHYSICS. *Current Pos:* RETIRED. *Personal Data:* b Cambridge, Mass, Oct 11, 21; m 48, Miriam Block; c Karen A & William D. *Educ:* Mass Inst Technol, BS, 42. *Honors & Awards:* Jour Award, Soc Motion Picture & TV Eng, 68. *Prof Exp:* Physicist, Res Labs, Eastman Kodak Co, 46-59, res assoc, 59-70, lab head, 70-75, sr lab head, 75-78, sr res assoc, 78-85. *Concurrent Pos:* Part-time lectr, Univ Rochester, 68-; adj fac, Rochester Inst Technol, 85- *Mem:* Fel Optical Soc Am; fel Soc Photog Sci & Eng. *Res:* Structures of optical and photographic images; microphotography; microminiaturization; properties of photographic materials; photographic sensitometry. *Mailing Add:* 2856 Elmwood Ave Rochester NY 14618

ALTMAN, KURT ISON, BIOCHEMISTRY, RADIOBIOLOGY. *Current Pos:* res assoc radiation biol, Univ Rochester, 47-65, head, Div Radiation Chem, Atomic Energy Proj, 61-65, assoc prof radiation biol & biophysiol, 63-92, from asst prof to assoc prof biochem, 65-85, emer prof biophys, 92-95, EMER PROF BIOCHEM & BIOPHYS, UNIV ROCHESTER, 95- *Personal Data:* b Breslau, Ger, Oct 13, 19; US citizen; m 45, Babette S; c Carl, Ted & Peter. *Educ:* Univ Chicago, BS, 41, MS, 42; Univ Rochester, PhD(biochem), 63. *Prof Exp:* From res assoc to instr biochem, Univ Chicago, 44-47. *Concurrent Pos:* Vis sr scientist, Ctr Study Nuclear Energy, Europ AEC, Mol & Geel, Belg, 64-65; vis prof physiol chem, Fac Med, Univ Dusseldorf, 73; mem adv bd, Advan in Radiation Biol; consult-in-residence, Sandoz Res Inst, Vienna, Austria, 79, consult, Univ Waterloo, Prog Aging, Waterloo, Can, 83-85; assoc ed, Radiation Res, 79-82; vis scientist, Res Ctr Julich Inst Med, 86-94. *Mem:* AAAS; Radiation Res Soc Am; Am Soc Biol Chemists; NY Acad Sci. *Res:* Enzymology; intermediary metabolism; isotope technology; biosynthesis of porphyrins and bile pigments; biochemical effects of ionizing radiations; physiological and radiological aging; connective tissue metabolism; bio-organic aspects of organic chemistry; erythrocyte metabolism; splenic function in hemolysis; antimycotic agents; radiation effects on bone marrow; suppressor genes in human brain tumors. *Mailing Add:* Univ Rochester Sch Med & Dent Dept Biophys 601 Elmwood Ave Rochester NY 14642. *Fax:* 716-275-6007

ALTMAN, LANDY B, JR, AGRICULTURAL ENGINEERING. *Current Pos:* ENERGY RES COORDR, AGR RES SERV CTR, USDA, 77- *Personal Data:* b Georgetown, SC, Mar 26, 19; m 49; c 1. *Educ:* Univ NC, BS, 40; Univ Ga, MS, 47; Iowa State Univ, PhD(eng), 60. *Prof Exp:* Engr, Rural Electrification Admin, USDA, 40-48, res engr curing tobacco, Agr Res Serv, 48-50, res engr elec demand, 50-67; asst chief, Farm Electrification Res Br, 66-68, chief, 68-77. *Mem:* Am Soc Agr Engrs; Inst Elec & Electronics Engrs. *Res:* Prediction of electrical demands of farms for sizing distribution transformers, services, and farm wiring circuits. *Mailing Add:* 11904 Renick Lane Silver Spring MD 20904

ALTMAN, LAWRENCE JAY, ORGANIC CHEMISTRY. *Current Pos:* GROUP LEADER, MOBIL TECHNOL CO, 80- *Personal Data:* b Chicago, Ill, Nov 12, 41; m 65; c 2. *Educ:* Calif Inst Technol, BS, 62; Columbia Univ, PhD(org chem), 65. *Prof Exp:* Air Force Off Sci Res fel photochem, Calif Inst Technol, 65-66; asst prof org chem, Stanford Univ, 66-72; from assoc prof to prof chem, State Univ NY, Stony Brook, 72-80. *Concurrent Pos:* Grants, Res Corp, 66-67 & 70-71, Am Chem Soc, 66-71, Lilly Res Found, 67-69 & NIH, 72-80; A P Sloan Found fel, 71-75; NSF fel, 75-80. *Mem:* Am Chem Soc. *Res:* Process analysis; near infrared spectroscopy; petroleum process and chemistry; analytical chemistry. *Mailing Add:* 16 Lavenham Ct Cherry Hill NJ 08003-2598. *Fax:* 609-224-3633; *E-Mail:* ljaltman@pau.mobil.com

ALTMAN, LAWRENCE KIMBALL, MEDICAL JOURNALISM. *Current Pos:* MED CORRESP, NY TIMES, 69- *Personal Data:* b Quincy, Mass, June 19, 37. *Educ:* Harvard Univ, BA, 58; Tufts Univ, MD, 62; Am Vet Epidemiol Soc, dipl. *Honors & Awards:* George Polk Award, 86; Claude Bernard Award, Nat Soc Med Res, 71, 74; Howard Blekeslee Award, Am Heart Asn, 82-83. *Prof Exp:* Intern, Mt Zion Hosp, San Francisco, 62-63, Epidemic Intel Serv Off, USPHS, 63-66, consult, US Aid, Dept State, Pub Health Serv, Measles Immunization Prog, WAfrica & resident internal med, Univ Wash Affil Hosps, 66-68, sr fel, Dept Med & Med Genetics, 68-69. *Concurrent Pos:* Sr asst med, Univ Wash, Seattle, 66-69; attend physician & clin assoc prof med, Bellevue Med Ctr, NY Univ, 70-; vis scientist, Univ Wash, 71; vis physician, Serafimer Hosp, Karolinska Inst, 73; mem, Bd Dir, Josiah Macy Jr Found, NY, 84. *Mem:* Inst Med-Nat Acad Sci; fel NY Acad Sci; fel Am Col Epidemiol; fel Am Col Physicians; Am Soc Trop Med & Hyg. *Mailing Add:* 140 W End Ave Apt 18-G New York NY 10023

ALTMAN, LEONARD CHARLES, IMMUNOLOGY, ALLERGY. *Current Pos:* asst prof, 75-78, assoc prof med, Dept Med, Div Allergy & Infectious Dis, 78-88, affil assoc prof oral biol, 85-88, CLIN PROF MED & AFFIL PROF ORAL BIOL & ENVIRON HEALTH, UNIV WASH, 88- *Personal Data:* b Fresno, Calif, Sept 1, 44; m 70, Gaylene M Bouska; c Jonathan D, Matthew C & Katherine A. *Educ:* Univ Pa, BA, 65; Harvard Med Sch, MD, 69. *Prof Exp:* From intern to resident med, Univ Wash Affil Hosps, 69-71, chief resident, Harborview Med Ctr, 74-75. *Concurrent Pos:* From res assoc to sr res assoc, Lab Microbiol & Immunol, Nat Inst Dent Health, NIH, 71-74. *Mem:* Am Asn Immunologists; fel Am Acad Allergy; fel Am Bd Internal Med; Am Fedn Clin Res. *Res:* Host defense mechanisms with emphasis on white cell function, leukocyte chemotaxis; leukocyte function in allergic and infectious diseases; inflammatory aspects of allergic diseases. *Mailing Add:* Div Allergy & Infectious Dis Dept Med Univ Wash RM-13 Box 356523 Seattle WA 98195

ALTMAN, PHILIP LAWRENCE, SCIENCE COMMMUNICATIONS, ZOOLOGY. *Current Pos:* RETIRED. *Personal Data:* b Kansas City, Mo, Jan 6, 24; m 46, Lillian Berlinsky; c Paul A & Ann (Preston). *Educ:* Univ Southern Calif, AB, 48; Western Reserve Univ, MS, 49. *Honors & Awards:* Cert of Appreciation, Coun Biol Ed, 84, Meritorious Award, 91. *Prof Exp:* Technician histopath, Univ Kans Med Ctr, 51; biologist mycol, Kansas City Field Sta, USPHS, 52-54; biologist virol, NIH, 55-56; res analyst, Nat Acad Sci, 57-59; dir off biol handbks, Fedn Am Socs Exp Biol, 59-79, sr staff scientist, Life Sci Res Off, 79-86, exec ed, Biol Data Book Ser, 83-86, exec dir, Coun Biol Ed, 81-90. *Concurrent Pos:* Int Union Biol Sci del, Comt on Data for Sci & Technol, 70-78, chmn adv panel biosci, 73-78, chmn task group presentation biol data primary lit, 75-78. *Mem:* Coun Biol Ed. *Res:* Comparative vertebrate anatomy; histoplasmosis; virus crystallization; analysis, editing and compilation of data in biological and medical sciences; information retrieval in life sciences. *Mailing Add:* 9206 Ewing Dr Bethesda MD 20817-3314

ALTMAN, ROBERT LEON, CERAMICS ENGINEERING. *Current Pos:* RES SCIENTIST, NASA AMES RES CTR, 66- *Personal Data:* b Brooklyn, NY, Apr 27, 31; m 58; c 1. *Educ:* NY Univ, BA, 52; Univ Southern Calif, PhD(phys chem), 59. *Prof Exp:* Sr res engr, Rocketdyne Div, NAM Aviation, Inc, 56-59; fel phys chem, Univ Calif, Berkeley, 59-60, chemist, Lawrence Radiation Lab, 60-62; asst prof, Calif State Univ, Hayward, 62-66. *Concurrent Pos:* Vis asst prof, Univ Calif, Berkeley, 64. *Mem:* Am Chem Soc; Combustion Inst. *Res:* Protein chemistry; calculation of thermodynamic properties; high temperature chemistry; improvement of fire extinguishment by use of dry chemical powders; polymer research for development of anti-misting kerosene to reduce incidence of post-crash fires; fuel technology and petroleum engineering; development of emissive coatings stable in high temperature airflow. *Mailing Add:* 16 Gravatt Dr Berkeley CA 94705-1527. *Fax:* 650-604-0487

ALTMAN, SAMUEL PINOVER, SPACE SCIENCE, CONTROL SYSTEMS. *Current Pos:* PRES, OPTILOGIC INC, OTTAWA, ONT, 86- *Personal Data:* b Atlantic City, NJ, Apr 15, 21; m 43, Francine Danish; c Ellen B & Sharon A. *Educ:* City Col New York, BME, 42. *Prof Exp:* Mech engr ord prod, Rochester Ord Dist, NY, 42; ord shop officer ord maintenance, 206th Ord Co, Ft Leonard Wood, Mo, 42-43; design & develop officer aircraft avionics, Eng Div, Army Air Corps, Wright Field, Dayton, Ohio, 43-46; develop engr tractors, Wilkes-Barre Carriage Co, Philadelphia, Pa, 46; mech engr aircraft flight control systs, Eng Div, Wright Air Develop Ctr, Wright-Patterson AFB, Ohio, 46-50, electronic scientist mil aircraft testing & eval, All-Weather Flying Div, 50-51, design & develop officer, 51-53; sr proj engr aircraft flight control systs, Eng Div, Lear Inc, Grand Rapids, Mich, 53-54; res specialist missile systs, Res & Develop Div, Lockheed Missile Systs, Van Nuys, Calif, 54; sr engr Ramjet engines, Tech Div, Marquardt Aircraft Co, Van Nuys, Calif, 54-55; sr systs anal missile systs, Missile Sect, Bendix Prod, Mishawaka, Ind, 55-56; sr scientist aerospace systs, Elec Eng Res Div, Armour Res Found, Chicago, Ill, 56-57; sr systs engr ICBM defense systs, Tech Develop Sect, Bendix Prod, South Bend, Ind, 57-58; prin engr missile systs, Martin Co, Waterton, Colo, 58-61; supvr space systs & sci, United Aircraft Corp Systs Ctr, Farmington, Conn, 61-63; consult engr spacecraft systs, Missile & Space Div, Gen Elec, King of Prussia, Pa, 63-69; chief systs scientist aerospace systs seismol, State-Space Systs Co, Norristown, Pa, 69; sr staff engr mil aerospace systs, Syst Develop Corp, Santa Monica, Calif, 69-72; dir space mech, Commun Res Ctr, Can Fed Govt, Ottawa, Ont, 72-85; vpres eng, Adv Beam Control Inc, Woodbridge, Ont & Dir Govt Rels, Proj Res Group Ltd, Woodbridge, Ont, 85-86; mkt dir, Dynacon Enterprises Ltd, Downsview, Ont, 88-91. *Mem:* Am Astronaut Soc; Am Inst Aeronaut & Astronaut; Can Aeronaut & Space Inst; Inst Elec & Electronics Engrs. *Res:* Aircraft, missile and space research and development with specializations in astrodynamics; spacecraft control and stabilization; missile guidance and control; aircraft avionics; aircraft flight dynamics; missile and aircraft intercept dynamics. *Mailing Add:* 465 Richmond Rd No 2107 Ottawa ON K2A 1Z1 Can. *Fax:* 613-722-8204

ALTMAN, SIDNEY, MOLECULAR BIOLOGY. *Current Pos:* from asst prof to prof, Yale Univ, 71-96, chmn dept, 83-85, dean, 85-89, STERLING PROF BIOL, YALE UNIV, 90- *Personal Data:* b Montreal, Que, May 7, 39. *Educ:* Mass Inst Technol, BS, 60; Univ Colo, PhD(biophys), 67. *Hon Degrees:* DSc, Univ Montreal, 90, York Univ (Toronto), 90, Conn Col, 90, McGill Univ, 91, Univ Colo, 91, Univ BC, 91. *Honors & Awards:* Nobel Prize in Chem, 89; Rosentiel Award for Basic Biomed Res, 89. *Prof Exp:* Teaching asst, Columbia Univ, 60-62; Damon Runyon Mem Fund cancer res fel molecular biol, Harvard Univ, 67-69; Anna Fuller Fund fel, Lab Molecular Biol, Med Res Coun, 69-70, med res coun fel, 69-71. *Concurrent Pos:* Tutor biol, Radcliffe Col, 68-69; dean, Yale Col, 85-89, William Clyde DeVane prof, 91; merit award, NIH, 89; Fairchild fel, Calif Inst Technol, 89-90; Montgomery fel, Dartmouth Col, 92. *Mem:* Nat Acad Sci; Am Soc Biol Chemists; Genetics Soc Am; fel AAAS; Am Philos Soc; Am Acad Arts & Sci. *Res:* Effects of acridines on T4 DNA replication; mutants; precursors of tRNA; RNA processing by catalytic RNA and ribonuclease function. *Mailing Add:* Dept Biol PO Box 208103 Yale Univ 219 Prospect St New Haven CT 06520-8103. *Fax:* 203-432-5713

ALTMANN, JEANNE, ONTOGENY, DEMOGRAPHY. *Current Pos:* res assoc, Dept Biol, 70-85, assoc prof, 85-89, PROF, DEPT ECOL & EVOLUTION, UNIV CHICAGO, 89- *Personal Data:* b New York, NY, Mar 18, 40; m 59, Stuart A; c Michael & Rachel. *Educ:* Univ Alta, BA, 62; Emory Univ, MAT, 69; Univ Chicago, PhD(behav sci), 79. *Prof Exp:* Res assoc & co-investr primate field studies, Dept Zool, Univ Alta, 63-65, Yerkes Regional Primate Res Ctr, Atlanta, Ga, 65-67 & 69-70. *Concurrent Pos:* Ed, Animal Behav, 78-82; res cur & assoc cur primates, Chicago Zool Soc, 85-; hon lectr, Dept Zool, Univ Nairobi, 89-90; chair, Comt Evolutionary Biol, Univ Chicago, 91- *Mem:* Animal Behav Soc; Int Primatological Soc; fel Am Asn Zool Parks & Aquariums. *Res:* Ecology and evolution of family relationships and of behavioral development; primate demography and life histories; parent-offspring relationships; infancy and the ontogeny of behavior and social relationships; conservation education and behavioral aspects of conservation. *Mailing Add:* Ecol & Evolution Univ Chicago 940 E 57th St Chicago IL 60637-1455. *Fax:* 773-702-0988; *E-Mail:* altj@midway.uchicago.edu

ALTMANN, STUART ALLEN, BEHAVIORAL ECOLOGY. *Current Pos:* prof anat, 70-80, PROF BIOL, DEPT ECOL & EVOLUTION, UNIV CHICAGO, 70- *Personal Data:* b St Louis, Mo, June 8, 30; m 59, Jeanne Glaser; c Michael & Rachel. *Educ:* Univ Calif, Los Angeles, BA, 53, MA, 54; Harvard Univ, PhD(biol), 60. *Prof Exp:* Biologist, NIH, 56-58; from asst prof to assoc prof zool, Univ Alta, 60-65; sociobiologist, Yerkes Regional Primate Res Ctr, 65-70. *Concurrent Pos:* Res grants, Nat Res Coun Can, 61-63, NIMH, 62-64 & 70-82 & NSF, 63-65 & 69-; mem, Comt Evolutionary Biol,

Univ Chicago, 70- *Mem:* Fel AAAS; Am Soc Primatology; fel Animal Behav Soc; Int Primatology Soc; Am Soc Naturalists. *Res:* Behavioral ecology of animals; field studies of primate behavior; foraging behavior and nutrition. *Mailing Add:* 940 E 57th St Univ Chicago Chicago IL 60637. *Fax:* 773-702-0988; *E-Mail:* alts@midway.uchicago.edu

ALTMILLER, DALE HENRY, CLINICAL CHEMISTRY, MEDICAL GENETICS. *Current Pos:* asst prof path, 75-79, ASSOC PROF PATH, COL MED, UNIV OKLA, 79-; DIR, GENETICS & METABOLIC CHEM SERV LAB, CHILDREN'S HOSP OKLA, 82- *Personal Data:* b Shattuck, Okla, Sept 11, 40; m 64, Carolyn J Duke; c 2. *Educ:* WTex State Univ, BS, 63; Univ Tex, PhD(genetics), 69; Am Bd Clin Chem, cert, 79. *Prof Exp:* Asst prof human genetics, Univ Tex Med Br, 69-75; dir, clin endocrinol & toxicol serv lab, 75-82,. *Concurrent Pos:* Res grants, NSF, 70-72 & Robert A Welch Found, 71-74. *Mem:* Am Asn Clin Chem; Am Soc Human Genetics; Sigma Xi; AAAS. *Res:* Development of new molecular diagnostic; molecular basis of inherited disorders; human gene characterization and mapping; genetic factors in cancer. *Mailing Add:* Childrens Hosp PO Box 26307 Oklahoma City OK 73126-0307

ALTMILLER, HENRY, PHYSICAL CHEMISTRY, PHOTO CHEMISTRY. *Current Pos:* from asst prof to assoc prof, St Edward's Univ, 69-82, exec vpres, 78-82, acad dean, 74-82, PROF CHEM, ST EDWARD'S UNIV, 82- *Personal Data:* b Ft Smith, Ark, July 13, 41; m, Eileen Sullivan; c Henry B & Kathleen M. *Educ:* Univ Notre Dame, BS, 64, PhD(chem), 69. *Prof Exp:* Teacher, Holy Cross High Sch, Tex, 64-65. *Mem:* Am Chem Soc; Sigma Xi. *Res:* Energy transfer; production of excited species in photo and radiation chemistry. *Mailing Add:* Dept Chem St Edward's Univ Austin TX 78704

ALTNER, PETER CHRISTIAN, ORTHOPAEDIC SURGERY. *Current Pos:* PROF & CHIEF, DIV ORTHOP SURG, CHICAGO MED SCH, UNIV HEALTH SCI, 73-, VET ADMIN MED CTR, NORTH CHICAGO, 74- *Personal Data:* b Starnberg, Ger, April 19, 32; m 59; c 3. *Educ:* Univ Wurzburg, Ger, Physicum, 54; Univ Kiel, Ger, MD, 57. *Prof Exp:* Intern, Univ Kiel, Ger, 57-58 & Muhlenberg Hosp, NJ, 58-59; resident, Evangelic Luthern Diakonissenanstalt, 60-61, Borgess Hosp, Mich, 61-62 & Univ Chicago Hosps & Clins, 62-66. *Concurrent Pos:* Prof orthop surg, Cook County Grad Sch Med, Chicago, 67-; lectr, Dept Orthop Surg, Northwestern Univ, 68-; clin prof, Ill Col Podiatric Med, 79- *Mem:* Am Acad Orthopaed Surgeons; Am Col Surgeons; Int Col Surgeons; Am Med Asn. *Res:* Clinical appraisal of amputees, prosthetics and rehabilitation; author or coauthor of numerous publications. *Mailing Add:* Dept Orhtopaedic Surg Vet Admin Med Ctr No 112A Middleville Rd Northport NY 11768

ALTON, ALVIN JOHN, FOOD SCIENCE. *Current Pos:* RETIRED. *Personal Data:* b Linden, Wis, Mar 31, 13; m 40; c 1. *Educ:* Univ Wis, BS, 36. *Prof Exp:* Asst dairy indust, Univ Wis, 36-37; food chemist, Beatrice Creamery Co, Chicago, 36-48; dir prod res, Taylor Freezer, Wis, 48-49; dir prod res, Beatrice Foods Co, 49-65, gen mgr, 65-76, group mgr, 76-78. *Mem:* Am Dairy Sci Asn; Inst Food Technol. *Res:* Dairy and allied food products. *Mailing Add:* 18219 Gardenview Dr Sun City West AZ 85375

ALTON, DONALD ALVIN, PARALLEL GRAPH PROCESSING, DESIGN ANALYSIS ALGORITHMS. *Current Pos:* Asst prof math, 70-71, from asst prof to assoc prof, 71-81, PROF COMPUT SCI, UNIV IOWA, 81- *Personal Data:* b Chicago, Ill, Sept 28, 43; m 86, Joan Bealer; c Jay, Andrew, Sharon, Sarah, Sheri, Thomas & Carol Wendler. *Educ:* Rice Univ, BA, 65; Cornell Univ, PhD(math), 70. *Concurrent Pos:* Fulbright-Hays lectureship, Novosibirsk State Univ, USSR, 79; fac scholar, Univ Iowa, 80-83. *Mem:* Asn Comput Mach. *Res:* Computational complexity; recursion-theoretic computational complexity in the spirit of work of Manuel Blum and others; recursion theory; object-oriented databases. *Mailing Add:* Dept Comput Sci 15 Maclean Hall Univ Iowa Iowa City IA 52242. *E-Mail:* alton@cs.uiowa.edu

ALTON, EARL ROBERT, INORGANIC CHEMISTRY, GENERAL CHEMISTRY. *Current Pos:* From asst prof to assoc prof, Augsburg Col, 60-69, chmn, Nat Sci Div, 72-83, actg assoc dean, 81 & 85, PROF CHEM, AUGSBURG COL, 69-, DIR GEN EDUC, 89-, ASSOC ACAD DEAN, 94- *Personal Data:* b Oelwein, Iowa, Oct 28, 33; m 78, Sharon L Ecker; c John, Sharon & Stephanie. *Educ:* St Olaf Col, BA, 55; Univ Mich, MS, 58, PhD(chem), 61. *Concurrent Pos:* NSF sci fac fel, 67-68; vis instr, 3M Co, 69-71, 77-78, 84-85 & 87-94. *Mem:* Fel AAAS; Am Chem Soc; Sigma Xi. *Res:* Chemistry of phosphorus trifluoride, especially reactions with group II and III halides and with transition metal halides; inorganic complexes; kinetics and bonding; chemistry of coordination compounds and of hydrides. *Mailing Add:* Acad Affairs Augsburg Col Minneapolis MN 55454

ALTON, ELAINE VIVIAN, MATHEMATICS EDUCATION. *Current Pos:* asst prof, 64-71, assoc prof, 71-77, PROF MATH EDUC, IND UNIV-PURDUE UNIV, INDIANAPOLIS, 77- *Personal Data:* b Watertown, NY, Aug 30, 25. *Educ:* State Univ NY Albany, BA, 42; St Lawrence Univ, MEd, 51; Univ Mich, MA, 58; Mich State Univ, PhD(math educ), 65. *Prof Exp:* Teacher math, Cobleskill High Sch & Fultonville High Sch, 46-48; assoc prof math, Ferris State Col, 48-62; asst instr, Mich State Univ, 62-64. *Concurrent Pos:* Mem, Adv Comt Math, State Ind, 68-; NSF proposal panelist, Coop Col-Sch Proj, 71. *Mem:* Nat Coun Teachers Math; Math Asn Am; Asn Teacher Educrs; Am Math Asn Two Yr Cols. *Res:* Methods and materials for teaching the metric system; commercial and teacher made materials for teaching concepts and computational skills to a wide range of abilities; changing teacher attitudes towards mathematics; remedial algebra; reasons for failure in college calculus. *Mailing Add:* Math Dept Ind Univ-Purdue Univ 402 N Blackford St Indianapolis IN 46202

ALTON, EVERETT DONALD, ELECTRICAL ENGINEERING. *Current Pos:* RETIRED. *Personal Data:* b Frederika, Iowa, Jan 8, 15; m 41; c 2. *Educ:* Iowa State Teachers Col, BA, 39; Univ Iowa, MSEE, 55. *Prof Exp:* Teacher pub sch, Iowa, 47-54; from instr to assoc prof elec eng, Univ Iowa, 55-68, assoc chmn dept, 68-81, supvr, Hybrid Comput Lab, 71-81. *Concurrent Pos:* Mem, Simulations Coun & rev comt, Electronics & Commun in US, Inst Elec & Electronics Eng & NSF, 64-; Univ Iowa rep, Am Power Conf, annually. *Mem:* Inst Elec & Electronics Engrs; Am Soc Eng Educ. *Res:* Nuclear reactor control; phototransistors at the temperature of liquid nitrogen; analog computer simulation and computation. *Mailing Add:* 1029 Gun River Dr N Plainwell MI 49080

ALTON, GERALD DODD, EXPERIMENTAL ATOMIC PHYSICS, THEORETICAL ATOMIC PHYSICS. *Current Pos:* Develop physicist atomic physics, Isotopes Div, 60-72, RES STAFF PHYSICIST EXP & THEORET ATOMIC PHYSICS, PHYSICS DIV, OAK RIDGE NAT LAB, 73- *Personal Data:* b Murray, Ky. *Educ:* Murray State Univ, Ky, BS, 60; Univ Tenn, Knoxville, MS, 67, PhD(physics), 72. *Concurrent Pos:* Consult, GCA Corp, Sunnyvale, Calif, 74- *Res:* Negative and multiply charged positive ion source research and development; accelerating systems and theoretical and experimental atomic physics. *Mailing Add:* Rte 2 Box 233E Kingston TN 37763

ALTOSE, MURRAY D, PULMONARY DISEASES. *Current Pos:* CHIEF STAFF, CLEVELAND VET ADMIN MED CTR, 88- *Personal Data:* b Winnipeg, Can, Oct 1, 41; US citizen; m 73; c 3. *Educ:* Univ Man, BSc & MD, 65; FRCP(C), 72; Am Bd Internal Med, cert internal med, 74, cert pulmonary dis, 76. *Prof Exp:* Fel pulmonary, Univ Pa, 71-73, asst prof med, 73-77; assoc prof, 77-84, PROF MED, CASE WESTERN RESERVE UNIV, 84- *Concurrent Pos:* Chief, Cleveland Metro Gen Hosp, 77-88; assoc dean, Case Western Reserve Univ, 88-; chmn, Sect Respiratory Neurobiol & Sleep, Am Thoracic Soc, 89. *Mem:* Am Fedn Clin Res; Am Physiol Soc; Cent Soc Clin Res; Am Thoracic Soc; Am Col Chest Physicians. *Res:* Effects of aging, lung disease and neuromuscular diseases on the reflex and behavioral control of breathing. *Mailing Add:* Vet Admin Med Ctr 10701 East Blvd Cleveland OH 44106

ALTPETER, LAWRENCE L, TECHNICAL MANAGEMENT, CHEMISTRY. *Current Pos:* proj mgr, 81-84, sr proj mgr, 84-86, PROG MGR SAFETY INSTRUMENTATION, GAS RES INST, 86- *Personal Data:* b New York, NY, Nov 4, 32. *Educ:* Manhattan Univ, BS, 54; Iowa State Univ, MS, 59; Tex A&M Univ, PhD(phys chem), 67. *Prof Exp:* Sr chemist, Honeywell Corp Res Ctr, 67-71 & N Star Res & Develop Inst, 71-76; prin chemist, Midwest Res Inst, 76-78; analysis lab mgr, Environ Sci & Eng Co, 78-81. *Concurrent Pos:* Welch fel, 63-65. *Mem:* Am Chem Soc. *Res:* Development of trace analytical instrumentation. *Mailing Add:* 503 W Brittany Dr Arlington Heights IL 60004-2017

ALTROCK, RICHARD CHARLES, SOLAR PHYSICS, SPACE PHYSICS. *Current Pos:* ASTROPHYSICIST, AIR FORCE MAT COMMAND PHILLIPS LAB, NAT SOLAR OBSERV, SUNSPOT, NMEX, 67- *Personal Data:* b Omaha, Nebr, Dec 20, 40; m 79, Sally Kosky; c Craig, Christopher, Kristin & Krystal. *Educ:* Univ Nebr, BSc, 62; Univ Colo, PhD(astro-geophys), 68. *Prof Exp:* Res asst, High Altitude Observ, Nat Ctr Atmospheric Res, Boulder, Colo, 63-67. *Concurrent Pos:* Vis res fel, Dept Appl Math, Univ Sydney, 71-72; proj mgr, Coronal Synoptic Prog, 76-; guest investr, NASA Solar Maximum Mission Cornagraph/Polarimeter, 84-86; res adv, Res Assoc Prog, Nat Res Coun, 80-; co-investr, Orbiting Solar Lab, 81-94; proj mgr, Solar Mass Ejection Imager, 86-91, co-investr, 91- *Mem:* Fel AAAS; Am Astron Soc; Int Astron Union; Am Geophys Union. *Res:* Global variations in solar physical conditions; solar effects on the geomagnetic field; solar corona. *Mailing Add:* Nat Solar Observ Sunspot NM 88349-0062. *Fax:* 505-434-7029; *E-Mail:* altrock@sunspot.noao.edu

ALTSCHER, SIEGFRIED, POLYMER CHEMISTRY, ORGANIC CHEMISTRY. *Current Pos:* mgr, Polymer & Anal Dept, 66-79, asst dir, Eastern Res Ctr, 79-84, DIR, RES ADMIN, STAUFFER CHEM CO, 84- *Personal Data:* b Berlin, Germany, July 18, 22; US citizen; m 46; c 3. *Educ:* Brooklyn Col, BA, 42; Polytech Inst Brooklyn, MS, 50, PhD(chem), 65. *Prof Exp:* Prod supvr fine chem, Wallace & Tiernan Prod Inc, 46-54; group leader res & develop, Nopco Chem Co, 54-66. *Mem:* Am Chem Soc; Fedn Socs Paint Technol; Soc Plastics Engrs. *Res:* Development of commercial specialty and surfactant chemicals; basic studies of polymer and plastic properties to develop new compositions which satisfy newer commercial requirements of improved performance. *Mailing Add:* 81 Ludvigh Rd Bardonia NY 10954-2013

ALTSCHUL, AARON MAYER, nutrition, for more information see previous edition

ALTSCHUL, ROLF, PHYSICAL ORGANIC CHEMISTRY. *Current Pos:* CHMN DEPT CHEM, SARAH LAWRENCE COL, 45- *Personal Data:* b Duesseldorf, Ger, Jan 24, 18; nat US; m 55; c 2. *Educ:* Harvard Univ, AM, 39, PhD(chem), 41. *Prof Exp:* Fel, Harvard Univ, 41, Pittsburgh Plate Glass fel, 41-44; lectr, Bryn Mawr Col, 44-45. *Concurrent Pos:* Res assoc, Brandeis Univ, 54- *Mem:* Am Chem Soc. *Res:* Kinetics and mechanisms of liquid phase reactions. *Mailing Add:* 405 E 56th St Apt 6D New York NY 10022-2466

ALTSCHUL, STEPHEN FRANK, BIOMATHEMATICS. *Current Pos:* MATHEMATICIAN, NAT CTR BIOTECHNOL INFO, 89- *Personal Data:* b New York, NY, Feb 28, 57; m 94, Caroline James; c James Wagner. *Educ:* Harvard Univ, AB, 79; Mass Inst Technol, PhD(math), 87. *Prof Exp:* Fel, Nat Inst Diabetes & Digestive & Kidney Dis, 87-89. *Res:* Measures, algorithms and statistics for the analysis and comparison of nucleic acid and protein sequence data. *Mailing Add:* Nat Ctr Biotechnol Info Nat Libr Med 8600 Rockville Pike Bethesda MD 20894. *Fax:* 301-480-9241; *E-Mail:* altschul@nih.gov

ALTSCHULER, HELMUT MARTIN, ELECTROPHYSICS. *Current Pos:* RETIRED. *Personal Data:* b Mannheim, Ger, Feb 13, 22; US citizen; m 42; c 3. *Educ:* Polytech Inst Brooklyn, BEE, 47, MEE, 49, PhD(electrophys), 63. *Prof Exp:* Res asst, Microwave Res Inst, Polytech Inst Brooklyn, 48-51, jr res assoc, 51-52, sr res assoc, Electrophys Dept, 52-63, res assoc prof, 63-64; chief radio standards eng div, Nat Bur Standards, 64-69, sr res scientist, Electromagnetics Div, 69-77, sr standards specialist, Off Domestic & Int Measurement Standards, 77-82; consult, 82-87. *Concurrent Pos:* Mem US nat comt, Int Union Radio Sci, chmn comn A. *Mem:* Fel Inst Elec & Electronics Engrs. *Res:* Impedance measurement techniques; equivalent network representations; strip transmission lines; electromagnetic and transmission line and modal theory; dielectric constant measurement techniques; microwave bridge measurement methods; nonreciprocal and active two-ports; electromagnetic standards; measurements, standards and laboratories. *Mailing Add:* 2250 Bluebell Ave Boulder CO 80302

ALTSCHULER, MARTIN DAVID, RADIOLOGY, RADIATION THERAPY. *Current Pos:* ASSOC PROF, DEPT RADIATION THER, HOSP UNIV PA, 80- *Personal Data:* b Brooklyn, NY, Feb 25, 40; m 62, Susan Gamm; c Steven, Daniel & Rachel. *Educ:* Polytech Inst Brooklyn, BS, 60; Yale Univ, MS, 61, PhD(astron), 64. *Prof Exp:* Instr astron, Yale Univ, 64-65; solar physicist, High Altitude Observ, Nat Ctr Atmospheric Res, 65-76; res assoc prof, Dept Comput Sci, State Univ NY, Buffalo, 76-80. *Concurrent Pos:* Adj assoc prof astrogeophys, Univ Colo, 74-76; mem comts 10 & 12, Int Astron Union. *Mem:* Am Phys Soc; Inst Elec & Electronics Engrs; Am Asn Physicists in Med; Sigma Xi; Am Astron Soc. *Res:* Solar magnetic fields; structure and dynamics of solar corona; medical image reconstruction; computer tomography; surface imaging; 3-D radiation therapy treatment planning, medical decisions; anthropometry. *Mailing Add:* 3400 Spruce St 2 Donner Dept Radiation Oncol HUP Philadelphia PA 19104-4283. *Fax:* 215-349-5978

ALTSHULER, BERNARD, BIOMATHEMATICS, ENVIRONMENTAL HEALTH. *Current Pos:* Asst math, NY Univ Med Ctr, 49-51, from instr to assoc prof, 51-69, assoc dir, Inst Environ Med, 75-86, PROF ENVIRON MED, NY UNIV MED CTR, 69- *Personal Data:* b Newark, NJ, June 22, 19; m 44, Lillian Schulsinger; c Jean & Miriam. *Educ:* Lehigh Univ, BS, 40; NY Univ, PhD(math), 53. *Mem:* Am Math Soc; Am Phys Soc; Soc Risk Anal; Soc Indust & Appl Math. *Res:* Environmental health; pulmonary handling of aerosols; quantitative aspects of carcinogenesis. *Mailing Add:* 431 E 20th St New York NY 10010

ALTSHULER, CHARLES HASKELL, pathology; deceased, see previous edition for last biography

ALTSHULER, EDWARD E, PHYSICS, ELECTRONICS. *Current Pos:* chief, Microwave Propogation Sect, Rome Air Develop Ctr, 76-82, PHYSICIST, ROME LAB, 82- *Personal Data:* b Boston, Mass, Jan 10, 31; m 78, Ruth M Liberfarb; c Robin, Michael, David & Robert. *Educ:* Northeastern Univ, BS, 53; Tufts Univ, MS, 54; Harvard Univ, PhD(appl physics), 60. *Prof Exp:* Antenna engr, Sylvania Elec Prod Inc, 54-57; electronic scientist, Air Force Cambridge Res Labs, 60-61; dir eng antennas, Gabriel Electronics Div, Gabriel Co, 61-63; chief, Transmission Br, Air Force Cambridge Res Labs, 63-69, chief, Millimeter Wave Br, 69-76. *Concurrent Pos:* Lectr, Grad Sch, Northeastern, 64-91. *Mem:* Fel Inst Elec & Electronics Engrs; Sigma Xi; Union Radio Sci Int. *Res:* Applied physics; antennas; propagation; electromagnetics; microwaves; genetic algorithms. *Mailing Add:* 55 Montrose St Newton MA 02158. *E-Mail:* ed@crimson.rl.plh.af.mil

ALTSTETTER, CARL J, PHYSICAL METALLURGY. *Current Pos:* From asst prof to assoc prof, Univ Ill, Urbana, 59-70, prof phys metall, 70-90, assoc dean acad affairs, 90-93, PROF, PHYS METALL, UNIV ILL, URBANA, 93- *Personal Data:* b Lima, Ohio, Oct 26, 30; m 54; c 2. *Educ:* Univ Cincinnati, MetE, 53; Ill Inst Technol, MS, 54; Mass Inst Technol, ScD(metall), 58. *Concurrent Pos:* Asst dean eng & dir, Int Prog Eng, Univ Ill. *Mem:* Am Inst Mining, Metall & Petrol Engrs; Am Soc Metals; Mat Res Soc. *Res:* Phase transformations; thermodynamics of gas-metal systems; fatigue and hydrogen embrittlement of steel; hydrogen in metals. *Mailing Add:* Dept Mat Sci & Eng Univ Ill 1304 W Green St Urbana IL 61801. *E-Mail:* caltstet@uiuc.edu

ALTSZULER, NORMAN, pharmacology, endocrinology; deceased, see previous edition for last biography

ALTURA, BELLA T, PHYSIOLOGY, PHARMACOLOGY. *Current Pos:* asst prof, 74-81, ASSOC PROF PHYSIOL, STATE UNIV NY MED CTR, 81- *Personal Data:* b Solingen, Ger, US citizen; m 61, Burton M; c Rachel A. *Educ:* Hunter Col, BA, 53, MA, 64; City Univ NY, PhD(physiol), 68. *Honors & Awards:* Gold-Silver Medal, Fr Nat Acad Med, Paris, 84. *Prof Exp:* Clin biochemist, Mem Hosp-Sloan Kettering Cancer Inst, 57-64; NASA fel, 64-67; from res assoc to instr anesthesiol, Albert Einstein Col Med, 69-74. *Concurrent Pos:* Vis prof, Beijing Col Traditional Chinese Med & Jianxi Med Col, Jianxi, China, 88, Humboldt Univ, Charite Hosp, Berlin, 95 & Univ Birmingham, UK, 96. *Mem:* Am Physiol Soc; Am Soc Magnesium Res; Am Soc Pharmacol Exp Therapeut. *Res:* Physiology, pharmacology and biochemistry of blood vessels; excitation-contraction coupling mechanisms of vascular smooth muscles; drug abuse and the cardiovascular system; first measurements of ionized magnesium in blood of humans. *Mailing Add:* Dept Physiol State Univ NY Health Sci Ctr Brooklyn NY 11203. *Fax:* 718-270-3103

ALTURA, BURTON MYRON, PHYSIOLOGY, PHARMACOLOGY. *Current Pos:* PROF PHYSIOL, STATE UNIV NY DOWNSTATE MED CTR, 74-, PROF MED, 92- *Personal Data:* b New York, NY, Apr 9, 36; m 61; c 1. *Educ:* Hofstra Univ, BA, 57; NY Univ, MS, 61, PhD(physiol), 64. *Honors & Awards:* Medaille Vermeil (Gold-Silver), French Nat Acad Med, 84. *Prof Exp:* Res asst physiol, Sch Med, NY Univ, 61-62, instr exp anesthesiol, 64-65, asst prof anesthesiol, 65-66; from asst prof to assoc prof anesthesiol & physiol, Albert Einstein Col Med, 70-74. *Concurrent Pos:* Res fel, Bronx Munic Hosp Ctr, 67-; NIH travel fel, Gothenburg, Sweden, 68; USPHS res career develop award, 68-72; prin investr, NIH grant, 68-, Nat Inst Alcohol Abuse & Alcoholism grant, 90-; mem, Coun Stroke, Circulation & Basic Sci, Am Heart Asn, 73-; vis prof anesthesiol & physiol, Albert Einstein Col Med, 74-78; mem spec study sect, Nat Inst Environ Health Sci, 77-; consult, NSF, NIH, NIMH, Alcohol Drug Abuse & Ment Health Admin, Nat Inst Alcohol Abuse & Alcoholism, City Univ NY & Upjohn Co; ed, var med jour; ed-in-chief & founder, Microcirculation & Magnesium, 81-; vis prof, Max-Planck Inst Molecular Physiol, Ger, 92 & 94, Yamaguchi Univ Med Sch, Japan, 88 & 93, Tokyo Univ, 93 & 96, Humboldt Univ, Charity Hosp, Berlin, Ger, 95, Kagoshima Univ, Japan, 95 & Self Defense Med Col, Totokozawki, Japan, 96. *Mem:* Fel Am Physiol Soc; Am Soc Pharmacol & Exp Therapeut; Am Asn Pathologists; Am Inst Nutrit; fel Am Heart Asn; fel Am Col Nutrit; Soc Exp Biol & Med; Microcirc Soc; fel Am Col Angiol; fel Am Inst Chemists; fel AAAS. *Res:* Local regulation of blood flow; physiology and therapeutics in experimental shock; cardiovascular actions of drugs of abuse; cardiovascular biology; magnesium, its physiology, biology and chemistry; pioneered relationship of magnesium to cardiovascular biology and disease; pioneered quantitative approaches to studying pharmacology of microcirculation in health and disease. *Mailing Add:* 450 Clarkson Ave Brooklyn NY 11203-2098. *Fax:* 718-270-3103

ALTWICKER, ELMAR ROBERT, AIR POLLUTION RESEARCH. *Current Pos:* assoc prof chem, Bio-Environ Div, 68-75, prof chem & environ eng, 75-86, PROF, DEPT CHEM ENG, RENSSELAER POLYTECH INST, 86- *Personal Data:* b Wolfen-Bitterfeld, Ger, Apr 4, 30; US citizen; m 58; c 3. *Educ:* Univ Dayton, BS, 52; Ohio State Univ, PhD(org chem), 57. *Prof Exp:* Asst, Ohio State Univ, 52-57; res chemist, Am Cyanamid Co, NJ, 57-62; res assoc, Univ Vt, 62-63; res chemist, Princeton Chem Res, Inc, 63-65, group leader, UOP Chem Div, 65-68. *Concurrent Pos:* Guest scientist, Dechema Inst, Frankfurt, 74-75; vis scholar, LSGC-ENSIC, Nancy, France, 89-90; Fulbright travel grant, 89-90. *Mem:* Am Chem Soc; Air Pollution Control Asn; Sigma Xi. *Res:* Air pollution; atmospheric chemistry; combustion/incineration; formation of combustion by products; acid rain. *Mailing Add:* Dept Chem Eng Rensselaer Polytech Inst Troy NY 12180. *Fax:* 518-276-4030

AL-UBAIDI, MUAYYAD R, RETINAL MOLECULAR BIOLOGY, BIOCHEMISTRY. *Current Pos:* RESEARCHER, DEPT OPHTHAL & VISUAL SCI, UNIV ILL, 92- *Personal Data:* b Baghdad, Iraq, May 1, 52. *Educ:* Univ Baghdad, BS, 74, MS, 77; Baylor Col Med, PhD(biochem), 86. *Prof Exp:* Researcher biochem, Cullen Eye Inst, Baylor Col Med, 88-92. *Mem:* Int Soc Eye Res; Am Soc Cell Biol. *Mailing Add:* 8850 W 98th Pl Palos Hills IL 60465

ALVAGER, TORSTEN KARL ERIK, BIOPHYSICS, NUCLEAR PHYSICS. *Current Pos:* PROF PHYSICS, IND STATE UNIV, TERRE HAUTE, 68- *Personal Data:* b Halsberg, Sweden, Aug 22, 31; US citizen; m 58; c 2. *Educ:* Univ Stockholm, PhD(physics), 60. *Prof Exp:* Asst prof physics, Univ Stockholm, 60-66; vis prof, Princeton Univ, 66-68. *Mem:* Am Phys Soc, AAAS; Sigma Xi. *Res:* Relativity. *Mailing Add:* Dept Physics Ind State Univ Main Campus 217 N 6th St Terre Haute IN 47809-0001

ALVARADO, RONALD HERBERT, ZOOLOGY. *Current Pos:* chmn dept, 74-81, PROF ZOOL, ARIZ STATE UNIV, 74- *Personal Data:* b San Bernardino, Calif, Dec 26, 33; m 55; c 3. *Educ:* Univ Calif, Riverside, BA, 56; Wash State Univ, MS, 59, PhD(zool physiol), 62. *Prof Exp:* Res fel physiol, Wash State Univ, 62; from asst prof to prof zool, Ore State Univ, 62-74. *Mem:* AAAS; Am Physiol Soc; Soc Gen Physiologists; Am Soc Zoologists. *Res:* Osmotic and ionic regulation in amphibians; mechanism of ion transport. *Mailing Add:* 1984 E Hermosa Dr Tempe AZ 85282

ALVARES, ALVITO PETER, PHARMACOLOGY, TOXICOLOGY. *Current Pos:* assoc prof, 77-78, PROF, DEPT PHARMACOL, UNIFORMED SERV UNIV, 78- *Personal Data:* b Bombay, India, Dec 25, 35; US citizen; m 69, Joy A Schmidt; c Christopher & Kevin. *Educ:* Univ Bombay, BSc, 55, BSc, 57; Univ Detroit, MS, 61; Univ Chicago, PhD(pharmacol), 66. *Prof Exp:* USPHS grant, Univ Minn, 65-67; sr res biochemist, Burroughs Wellcome & Co, 67-70; res assoc biochem pharmacol, 70-71, asst prof, 71-74; assoc prof, Rockefeller Univ, 74-77; adj assoc prof pharmacol, Med Col, Cornell Univ, 75-77. *Concurrent Pos:* Hirschl career scientist award, 74-78; NIH career develop award, 75-78. *Mem:* Am Soc Biochem & Molecular Biol; Am Soc Clin Pharmacol & Therapeut; NY Acad

Sci; Soc Toxicol; Am Soc Pharmacol & Exp Therapeut. *Res:* Effects of drugs, carcinogens and environmental chemicals on hepatic microsomal enzymes and heme biosynthetic pathway; cytochrome P-450 and mechanisms of enzyme induction; clinical pharmacology. *Mailing Add:* Dept Pharmacol Uniformed Serv Univ 4301 Jones Bridge Rd Bethesda MD 20814-4799. *Fax:* 301-295-3220; *E-Mail:* alvares@usuhsb.usuhsb.mil

ALVARES, NORMAN J, MECHANICAL ENGINEERING, FIRE SCIENCE. *Current Pos:* INDEPENDENT CONSULT, 88- *Personal Data:* b Oakland, Calif, Mar 13, 33; m 60; c 3. *Educ:* San Francisco State Univ, AB, 56; Univ Minn, MS, 69. *Prof Exp:* Thermal physicist, US Naval Radiol Defense Lab, 56-69; mech engr, Stanford Res Inst, 69-75; sr mech engr, Lawrence Livermore Lab, 75-78, fire sci group leader, 78-88. *Concurrent Pos:* US Navy fel, Univ Minn, 67-69; consult, Fire Protection Eng Group, 75-76, Failier Anal Asn, 78, Nuclear Regulatory Comn, 78-, Univ San Francisco, 78- & Fed Emergency Mgt Agency, 78-; adv, Fusion-Laser Safety Coord Comt, Dept Energy, 76-88; NAm ed, J Fire & Mat. *Mem:* Sigma Xi; Combustion Inst; Soc Fire Protection Engrs; Am Soc Testing & Mat; Int Asn Fire Safety Sci. *Res:* Ignition and thermal balance in fires; experimental modeling of fires; parametric analysis of fire hazards in industrial size enclosures; physics and chemistry of extinguishants; fire accident analysis. *Mailing Add:* 3628 Oak Knoll Dr Redwood City CA 94062

ALVAREZ, JOSE O, PUBLIC HEALTH, NUTRITION. *Current Pos:* PROF & CHMN, DEPT INT HEALTH, UNIV ALA, 69- *Personal Data:* b Havana, Cuba, Jan 16, 27. *Educ:* Mass Inst Technol, BS, 50, MS, 51, PhD(food sci & food nutrit), 65. *Honors & Awards:* Hatton Award, Int Asn Dent Res, 92. *Prof Exp:* Assoc prof nutrit, Mass Inst Technol, 61-68. *Mem:* Am Inst Nutrit; Int Asn Dent Res. *Mailing Add:* Dept Int Health Univ Ala Tidwell Hall Rm 106 Birmingham AL 35294-0008

ALVAREZ, LAURENCE RICHARDS, MATHEMATICS. *Current Pos:* coordr prog planning & budgeting, 72-88, FROM INSTR TO PROF MATH, UNIV OF THE SOUTH, 64-, ASSOC PROVOST, 88- *Personal Data:* b Jacksonville, Fla, Sept 27, 37; m 60; c 3. *Educ:* Univ of the South, BS, 59; Yale Univ, MA, 62, PhD(graph theory), 64. *Prof Exp:* Instr math, Trinity Col, Conn, 63-64. *Concurrent Pos:* Am Coun Educ acad admin intern, Pomona Col; Pugh fel, Univ Ky, 91; bd dirs HEDS, 94-97; bd trustees & treas, Educom, 95-98. *Mem:* Math Asn Am; Sigma Xi. *Res:* Graph theory. *Mailing Add:* 160 S Carolina Ave Sewanee TN 37375

ALVAREZ, ORLANDO, PHYSICS. *Current Pos:* from asst prof to assoc prof, 82-89, PROF PHYSICS, UNIV CALIF, BERKELEY, 89-; FAC SR SCIENTIST, LAWRENCE BERKELEY LAB, 86- *Personal Data:* b Havana, Cuba, Apr 10, 53; US citizen. *Educ:* Princeton Univ, AB, 74; Harvard Univ, AM, 75, PhD, 79. *Honors & Awards:* Kusaka Mem Prize Physics, Princeton Univ, 73 & 74. *Prof Exp:* Res assoc, Newman Lab Nuclear studies, Cornell Univ, 79-82; assoc fac, Lawrence Berkeley Lab, 82-86. *Concurrent Pos:* NSF fel, 74-77; Alfred P Sloan found fel, 83-87; Dep group leader, Lawrence Berkeley Lab, Univ Calif, Berkeley, 87-89, group leader, 91-93; dir res CNRS, Lab physics theory & high energies, Univ Pierce & Marie Curie, 89-90. *Mailing Add:* Dept Physics Univ Calif Berkeley CA 94720

ALVAREZ, RAYMOND ANGELO, JR, PHYSICS, PARTICLE ACCELERATORS. *Current Pos:* RETIRED. *Personal Data:* b Mobile, Ala, May 15, 34; m 61; c 2. *Educ:* La State Univ, BS, 55; Stanford Univ, PhD(physics), 64. *Prof Exp:* Res assoc physics, Stanford Univ, 60-61; from instr to asst prof, Mass Inst Technol, 61-68; Physicist, Lawrence Livermore Lab, 68-93. *Mem:* Am Phys Soc. *Res:* Microwave propagation; high-frequency electric discharges. *Mailing Add:* 547 Grizzly Peak Blvd Berkeley CA 94708

ALVAREZ, RONALD JULIAN, CIVIL & STRUCTURAL ENGINEERING. *Current Pos:* from asst prof too assoc prof eng sci, 62-74, dir eng sci & mech progs, 68-78, PROF ENG, HOFSTRA UNIV, 74-, DIR CONTINUING ENG EDUC, 70- *Personal Data:* b Brooklyn, NY, Feb 17, 35; m 56; c Judith, Nancy & Daniel. *Educ:* Manhattan Col, BCE, 57; Univ Wash, MS, 60; NY Univ, PhD(eng), 67. *Prof Exp:* Jr engr, Boeing Co, 57-58, assoc engr, 58-60, eng designer, 60-61; sr res engr, Repub Aviation Corp, 61-62. *Concurrent Pos:* Consult engr, 67-; dir, Appl Systs, Inc, 68-71; consult, City of Glen Cove; consult solid waste mgt, NY State Dept Environ Conserv, 71-74. *Mem:* Am Soc Civil Engrs; Nat Soc Prof Engrs. *Res:* Behavior of multistory, multibay plane rigid frames subjected to static in-plane loadings; solid waste disposal; solid waste management. *Mailing Add:* Nine Duke Pl Glen Cove NY 11542. *Fax:* 516-463-4939

ALVAREZ, VERNON LEON, BIOCHEMISTRY. *Current Pos:* prin res scientist, 83-85, group leader biochem, 85-88, DIR CHEM RES, CYTOGEN CORP, 88- *Personal Data:* b Dec 19, 46. *Educ:* Univ Colo, BA, 69; Univ Utah, PhD(phys chem), 72. *Prof Exp:* Prof chem, Northwest Nazarene Col, 73-75; from instr to asst res prof, Dept Path, Col Med, Univ Utah, 75-77; mem, Basel Inst Immunol, Switz, 79-81; expert, Protein Chem Sect, Lab Biochem, Nat Cancer Inst, NIH, 81-83. *Concurrent Pos:* Vis lectr chem, Col Idaho, 74; NIH postdoctoral fel, 75-77; vis scientist, Lab Cell Biol, Nat Cancer Inst, NIH, 78-79. *Mem:* Soc Nuclear Med; AAAS; Am Asn Immunologists. *Res:* Biotechnology; conjugates of monoclonal antibodies for in vivo human clinical applications; membrane receptors; immunology; protein chemistry; molecular recognition units; peptides; author of 24 technical publications. *Mailing Add:* Res & Develop Dept Cytogen Corp 201 College Rd E Princeton NJ 08540-5309. *Fax:* 609-987-8245

ALVAREZ, VINCENT EDWARD, INORGANIC CHEMISTRY. *Current Pos:* PROJ LEADER, CLOROX CO, 76- *Personal Data:* b Shanghai, China, Aug 15, 46; US citizen; m 72. *Educ:* Calif State Univ, Hayward, BS, 69; Univ Calif, Santa Barbara, MA, 72, PhD(chem), 74. *Prof Exp:* Res chemist, E I du Pont de Nemours & Co, Inc, 74-76. *Concurrent Pos:* Asst prof chem, Del Tech & Community Col, 74-, Chabot Community Col, 77. *Mem:* Am Chem Soc. *Res:* Reactions at metal oxide surfaces; reactions of singlet oxygen; oxidation chemistry; surfactants. *Mailing Add:* Clorox Tech Ctr 7200 Johnson Dr Pleasanton CA 94566-3208

ALVAREZ, WALTER, STRATIGRAPHIC & STRUCTURAL GEOLOGY. *Current Pos:* from asst prof to assoc prof, 77-81, PROF, DEPT GEOL & GEOPHYS, UNIV CALIF, BERKELEY, 81- *Personal Data:* b Berkeley, Calif, Oct 3, 40; m 65. *Educ:* Carleton Col, BA, 62; Princeton Univ, PhD(geol), 67. *Prof Exp:* Geologist, Am Overseas Petrol, Ltd, Neth, 67-68, sr geologist, Libya, 68-70; NATO fel, Brit Sch Archaeol, Rome 70-71; res scientist, Lamont-Doherty Geol Observ, 71-73, res assoc, 73-77. *Concurrent Pos:* Lectr geol, Columbia Univ, 73-74; vis sr res assoc, Lamont-Doherty Geol Observ, 77- *Mem:* Nat Acad Sci; Geol Soc Am; Am Geophys Union; AAAS; Ital Geol Soc. *Res:* Plate tectonics and mountain belt structure; causes of mass extinctions; paleomagnetism; Alpine-Mediterranean region. *Mailing Add:* Dept Geol & Geophys Univ Calif Berkeley CA 94720

ALVAREZ-GONZALEZ, RAFAEL, ENZYMOLOGY, PROTEIN CHEMISTRY. *Current Pos:* ASST PROF, DEPT MICROBIOL & IMMUNOL, TEXAS COL OSTEOP MED, 89- *Personal Data:* b Michoacan, Mex, Nov 25, 58; m 77; c 2. *Educ:* Michoacan Univ, BS, 79; N Tex State Univ, MS, 82, PhD(biochem), 85. *Prof Exp:* Post-doctoral fel biochem & pharmacol, Inst Biochem & Pharmacol, Univ Zurich, Switz, 85-86; post-doctoral fel biochem, Biomed Div, Samuel Roberts Nobel Found, Inc, 87-88. *Mem:* Am Soc Biochem & Molecular Biol; Am Asn Cancer Res; NY Acad Sci; AAAS; Am Chem Soc; Am Soc Microbiol. *Res:* Biological role of enzyme catalyzed post-translational covalent modification of eukaryotic proteins with residues of ADP-ribose in modulating chromatin structure and function; membrane-receptor mediated signal transduction mechanisms. *Mailing Add:* Dept Microbiol & Immunol Univ N Tex Health Sci Ctr 3500 Camp Bowie Blvd Ft Worth TX 76107-2699

ALVERSON, DAVID ROY, INSECT PEST MANAGEMENT. *Current Pos:* ASST PROF ENTOM, CLEMSON UNIV, 78- *Personal Data:* b Spartanburg, SC, Dec 25, 46; m 67; c 1. *Educ:* Clemson Univ, BS, 68, MS, 76; Univ Ga, PhD(entom), 79. *Mem:* Sigma Xi; Entom Soc Am. *Res:* Economic entomology: insect pests of pecans, forage and field crops, small grains, ornamental plants; apiculture; insect vectors of plant and animal diseases. *Mailing Add:* Dept Entom Clemson Univ Clemson SC 29632-0001

ALVERSON, DAYTON L, MARINE BIOLOGY. *Current Pos:* PRES, NATURAL RESOURCES CONSULT, 81- *Personal Data:* b San Diego, Calif, Oct 7, 24; m 51; c 2. *Educ:* Univ Wash, BS, 50, PhD, 67. *Honors & Awards:* Distinguished Serv Award, Dept Interior, 66; Nat Oceanic & Atmospheric Admin Award; Gold Medal Award Distinguished Serv, Dept of Com, 76. *Prof Exp:* Specialist method & equip, US Fish & Wildlife Serv, 50-53; biologist, Wash State Dept Fisheries, 53-58; chief, Explor Fishing & Gear Res Unit, US Fish & Wildlife Serv, 58-60, dir res base, Seattle, 60-67, Bur Com Fisheries, 67-69, assoc dir fisheries, Washington, DC, 69-70; assoc regional dir resource progs, Nat Oceanic & Atmospheric Admin, 70, dir Northwest Fisheries Ctr, Seattle, 71-80; at Dept Marine Studies, Univ Wash. *Concurrent Pos:* Affil prof, Inst Marine Studies, Univ Wash; mem, Marine Bd, Nat Res Coun; chmn, Adv Comt Marine Resources Res, Food & Agr Orgn, UN; chief of staff, US/Can Salmon Interceptions Negotiations, US State Dept; comnr, US Sect Int N Pacific Fisheries Comn; deleg, US Law of the Sea Conf. *Mem:* Am Inst Fisheries Res Biologists; Sigma Xi. *Res:* Author of 130 papers, books and articles covering fisheries, management, population diagnosis, resource distribution and behavior. *Mailing Add:* 17916 Brittany Dr SW Seattle WA 98166

ALVES, LEO MANUEL, PLANT PHYSIOLOGY, PLANT PATHOLOGY. *Current Pos:* asst prof biol, Lab Plant Morphogenesis, Manhattan Col, 78-84, assoc prof & chmn biol dept, Col Mt St Vincent, 84-88, ASSOC PROF, BIOL DEPT, LAB PLANT MORPHOGENESIS, MANHATTAN COL, 88- *Personal Data:* b Philadelphia, Pa, May 21, 45. *Educ:* St Norbert Col, BS, 68; Univ Chicago, PhD(biol), 75. *Prof Exp:* Asst prof biol, Lincoln Univ, Pa, 75-76; Nat Res Coun res assoc & res plant pathologist, ERegional Res Ctr, Agr Res Serv, USDA, Pa, 76-78. *Concurrent Pos:* Sigma Xi res grant-in-aid, 74-75, 80-81; USDA Specific Coop Agreement, 80-83; Scopas Technol Sponsored Proj, 84-89; vis assoc prof, Rockefeller Univ, New York, 88-89. *Mem:* Am Phytopath Soc; Am Soc Plant Physiologists; Japanese Soc Plant Physiologists; Sigma Xi. *Res:* Investigations of physiology and biochemistry of phytoalexin biosynthesis in white potato tuber; role phytoalexins play in expression of resistance to various pathogens; role played by cyclic nucleotides in regulating cell division in oncogenetically-transformed tissue. *Mailing Add:* 7 Overhill Rd Peekskill NY 10566-9753

ALVES, RONALD V, QUANTUM ELECTRONICS, LASERS IN MEDICINE. *Current Pos:* MGR, LASERS RES & DEVELOP, HEWLETT-PACKARD, SANTA CLARA DIV, SANTA CLARA, CALIF, 89- *Personal Data:* b Oakland, Calif, Apr 11, 35; m 80; c 4. *Educ:* Univ San Francisco, BS, 58; Univ Calif, Berkeley, PhD(physics), 68; Stanford Univ, MSEE, 73. *Prof Exp:* Physicist, US Navy Radiol Defense Lab, 57-60; res scientist, Lockheed Missiles & Space Co, Lockheed Aircraft Corp, 68-74; mem staff, Coherent Radiation, Palo Alto, Calif, 74-76; develop mgr & head, Lab Res, Develop & Applications, Uthe Technol, Inc, Sunnyvale, Calif,

76-77; chief scientist, Quantex Corp, Sunnyvale, Calif, 77; cofounder & vpres Technol, Luxtron Corp, Mountain View, Calif, 78-83; mgr, Advanced Develop Coherent Med Group, Palo Alto, Calif, 83-88. *Concurrent Pos:* Consult in lasers, optics, physics. *Mem:* Am Phys Soc; Optical Soc Am; Soc Photo-Optical Instrumentation Eng; Am Soc Lasers Med & Surg. *Res:* Solid state laser materials and rare earth activated luminescent materials; lasers in medicine. *Mailing Add:* 475 Marion Ave Palo Alto CA 94301

ALVEY, DAVID DALE, PLANT BREEDING & GENETICS. *Current Pos:* PLANT BREEDING CONSULT, 94- *Personal Data:* b Harrisburg, Ill, Jan 2, 32; m 55, Emma L Patty; c Edward D, Raymond L & Paula J. *Educ:* Univ Ill, BS, 57, MS, 58; Purdue Univ, PhD(genetics), 62. *Prof Exp:* Asst agron, Purdue Univ, 58-62, instr, 62; res agronomist, DeKalb Agr Asn, Inc, 62-70; corn res dir, Farmers Forage Res, 70-94. *Mem:* Am Soc Agron; Am Genetic Asn; Sigma Xi. *Res:* Genetics and plant breeding; coordinating corn breeding programs; developing commercial corn varieties; data handling specialists. *Mailing Add:* 237 Myrtle Dr West Lafayette IN 47906

ALVI, ZAHOOR M, RADIATION PHYSICS, RADIOLOGY. *Current Pos:* DIR MED PHYSICS, RADIOLOGICAL SYSTS, INC, 72- *Personal Data:* b Sept 11, 32; US citizen; div; c Feroz, Rebekah, Mehar, Faizan & Fawad. *Educ:* Carnegie-Mellon Univ, BS, 56; Univ Calif, Los Angeles, MS, 66, PhD(med physics, nuclear eng), 68; Am Bd Health Physics, dipl, 65, recert, 90; Am Bd Radiol, dipl & cert radiol physics, 71. *Prof Exp:* Radiol physicist, Radiation Ther & Nuclear Med, Cedars Lebanon Hosp, Los Angeles, 58-64 & Dept Radiother, Kaiser-Permanente Med Ctr, Hollywood, 64-72. *Concurrent Pos:* Mem eng exten fac, Univ Calif, Los Angeles, 71-80; laser physicist, Northrop Corp, Hawthorne, Calif; vis med physicist, Martin Luther King, Jr, Gen Hosp, 74-; res affil, Jet Propulsion Lab, Calif Inst Technol, 74- *Mem:* Am Asn Physicists Med; Health Physics Soc; Int Radiation Protection Asn; Biomed Eng Soc. *Res:* Mathematical modeling of human physiological systems; mathematical model of non-equilibrium kinetics of four major electrolytes in the human body; catheter probe system for gastrointestinal motility automatic monitoring; in-vivo neutron activation analysis using microgram Californium-252 sealed ug sources; enhanced visualization through digital radiography; neutron dosimetry techniques; optimization of hyperthermia in conjunction with radiation therapy; designing compact magnetic resonance systems; Excimer laser systems. *Mailing Add:* 25291 Barents Laguna Hills CA 92653

ALVING, CARL RICHARD, PHOSPHOLIPIDS, GLYCOLIPIDS. *Current Pos:* res investr immunol, 70-78, CHIEF, DEPT MEMBRANE BIOCHEM, WALTER REED ARMY INST RES, 78- *Personal Data:* b Chicago, Ill, July 10, 39; m 70, Barbara M Nelson; c 1. *Educ:* Haverford Col, BS, 61; Univ Miami, MD, 66. *Honors & Awards:* Alec D Bangham Lifetime Achievement Award. *Prof Exp:* Intern med, Barnes Hosp, Wash Univ Sch Med, 66-67, resident, 67-68 & fel pharmacol, 68-70. *Mem:* Am Soc Biochem & Molecular Biol; Am Asn Immunologists; Int Soc Vaccines; fel AAAS; Int Endotoxin Soc. *Res:* Vaccines; adjuvants; drug carriers; antigen, antibody and complement interactions at the surface of liposomes; receptor properties of lipids; use of liposomes as carriers of drugs or antigens. *Mailing Add:* Dept Membrane Biochem Walter Reed Army Inst Res Washington DC 20307-5100. *Fax:* 202-782-0721; *E-Mail:* alvinec@wrair-emhl.army.mil

ALVINO, WILLIAM MICHAEL, POLYMER CHEMISTRY, PLASTICS IN ELECTRONICS APPLICATIONS. *Current Pos:* from res chemist to sr res chemist, 66-82, FEL SCIENTIST, WESTINGHOUSE ELEC CORP, 82- *Personal Data:* b New York, NY, Jan 12, 39; m 60, Barbara Martin; c Dona & Terilynn. *Educ:* Iona Col, BS, 60; Seton Hall Univ, MS, 66. *Prof Exp:* Sr tech aide polymers, Bell Tel Labs, 60-66, assoc mem tech staff, 66. *Mem:* Am Chem Soc. *Res:* Thermal and ultraviolet stability of polymers; development and formulation of polymers as coating, films, adhesives and laminating resins for electrical insulation; synthesis and modification of polymers for high temperature applications; electophoretic deposition of polymers from non-aqueous systems; composites; printed wiring boards; radiation curing of polymers; applications of plastics in electrical and electronics industries, battery industries; environmental remediation. *Mailing Add:* 729 Heathergate Dr Pittsburgh PA 15238. *Fax:* 412-256-1222

ALVIR, JOSE MA J, RESEARCH DESIGN, DATA ANALYSIS. *Current Pos:* ASSOC DIR, BIOSTATIST, HILLSIDE HOSP-LONG ISLAND JEWISH MED CTR, 85- *Personal Data:* b Manila, Philippines, Nov 19, 51; m 80, Gloria Sotelo; c Marie T. *Educ:* Univ Philipines, BA, 74; Columbia Univ, MPH, 81, PhD(epidemiol), 85. *Prof Exp:* Dep proj dir, Dept Sociol, Univ Philipines, 74; res asst fel, Columbia Univ Sch Pub Health, 81; res scientist, NY State Res Found, 82-84. *Concurrent Pos:* Assoc prof psychiat, Albert Einstein Col Med, 91- *Mem:* Am Statist Asn; Soc Epidemiol Res; Soc Clin Trials. *Res:* Psychiatry, specifically schizophrenia research; correlates and outcome of first episode schizophrenia, as well as the side effects of anti-psychotic medications. *Mailing Add:* Hillside Hosp PO Box 38 Glen Oaks NY 11004. *E-Mail:* alvir@aecom.yu.edu

ALVORD, DONALD C, economic geology, chemistry; deceased, see previous edition for last biography

ALVORD, ELLSWORTH CHAPMAN, JR, NEUROPATHOLOGY. *Current Pos:* assoc prof, 60-62, PROF PATH, SCH MED, UNIV WASH, 62-, ADJ PROF NEUROL SURG, 88- *Personal Data:* b Washington, DC, May 9, 23; m 43, Nancy Delaney; c Ellsworth C III, Katharyn A (Gerlich), Jean A (Rhodes) & Richard W. *Educ:* Haverford Col, BS, 44; Cornell Univ, MD, 46. *Prof Exp:* Asst path, Med Col, Cornell Univ, 47-48; instr neurol, Sch Med, Georgetown Univ, 50-55; assoc prof neurol & path, Col Med, Baylor Univ, 55-60. *Concurrent Pos:* Prof lectr, Sch Med, George Washington Univ, 50-51; neurologist, Neurophysiol Sect, Army Med Serv Grad Sch, 51-53; instr, Wash Sch Psychiat, 52-55; chief, Clin Neuropath Sect, Nat Inst Neurol Dis & Blindness, NIH, 53-55; consult, Seattle hosps. *Mem:* AAAS; Am Asn Neuropath (pres, 64-65); Am Soc Exp Biol & Med; Asn Res Nervous & Ment Dis; assoc Am Neurol Asn. *Res:* Allergic encephalomyelitis; Multiple Sclerosis; growth of gliomas. *Mailing Add:* Dept Neuropathal Univ Wash Med Ctr 1959 NE Pacific St Box 356480 RR 840 Seattle WA 98195-6480

ALWAN, ABDUL-MEHSIN, ENGINEERING MECHANICS. *Current Pos:* assoc prof, 63-77, PROF ENG MECH, US NAVAL ACAD, 77- *Personal Data:* b Baghdad, Iraq, Nov 22, 27; m 59; c 2. *Educ:* Bournemouth Munic Col, Eng, BS, 51; Univ Wis, MS, 56, PhD(eng mech), 63. *Prof Exp:* Supvr, Port Directorate of Basra, Iraq, 52-53; engr, Kellogg Int Corp, 53-54; struct designer, Erik Floor & Assoc, Ill, 57-58; instr eng mech, Univ Wis, 58-63. *Mem:* Am Soc Eng Educ. *Res:* Elasticity; theory of plates and shells; rigid body mechanics. *Mailing Add:* 223 Cardamon Dr Edgewater MD 21037

ALWARD, RON E, SOLAR THERMAL SYSTEMS, BIOMASS ENERGY SYSTEMS. *Current Pos:* ASST DIR, BRACE RES INST, 79- *Personal Data:* b St Thomas, Can, July 9, 41; m 69; c 2. *Educ:* Univ Western Ont, BEngSc, 63, MEngSc, 68. *Prof Exp:* Res assoc solar wind energy, Brace Res Inst, 68-76; appropriate technol specialist, Bu-Ali Sina Univ, Iran, 76-77; solar engr III, Nat Ctr Appropriate Technol, Mont, 78-79. *Concurrent Pos:* Consult, various nat & int govt agencies, 69-, Lab Solar Energy, Univ Algiers, 81; mem, Memphremagog Community Technol Group, 79-; mem, UN Univ, 84- *Mem:* Solar Energy Soc Can; Int Solar Energy Soc. *Res:* Solar distillation; solar agricultural dryers; solar and fuel conserving cookers; air to air heat exchangers, passive solar houses, greenhouses. *Mailing Add:* RR 4 Mansonville PQ J0E 1X0 Can

ALWAY, STEPHEN EDWARD, MUSCLE BIOLOGY. *Current Pos:* asst prof, 90-93, ASSOC PROF EXERCISE PHYSIOL, OHIO STATE UNIV, 93- *Personal Data:* b St Thomas, Ont, Jan 26, 56; m 82; c 3. *Educ:* Univ Waterloo, BS, 78; McMaster Univ, MS, 81, PhD(neurosci), 85. *Prof Exp:* Grad teaching assoc, McMaster Univ, 78-81, grad res assoc, 81-83, instr human gross anat, 83-84; res fel, Univ Waterloo, 84-86; instr, Univ Tex Southwestern Med Ctr, 86-89; asst prof, Oral Roberts Univ Sch Med, 89-90. *Mem:* Sigma Xi; fel Am Col Sports Med; Am Physiol Soc; AAAS. *Res:* Gene expression and control of protein expression in aging skeletal muscle and aging myocardium in response to overload. *Mailing Add:* 8470 Seabright Dr Powell OH 43065. *Fax:* 614-292-7240; *E-Mail:* salway@magnus.acs.ohio_state.edu

ALWITT, ROBERT S(AMUEL), ELECTROCHEMISTRY, OXIDE FILMS. *Current Pos:* PRES, BOUNDARY TECHNOL INC, BUFFALO GROVE, ILL, 84- *Personal Data:* b New York, NY, Nov 4, 33; m 60; c 2. *Educ:* Cooper Union, BChE, 54; Rensselaer Polytech Inst, MChE, 58, PhD(chem eng), 63. *Prof Exp:* Jr engr electrochem processing, Eng Labs, Sprague Elec Co, 54-58, dept head, 58-61, mgr electrochem res & develop, 63-73; mgr res & develop, United Chemi-Con, Inc, Northbrook, Ill, 74-84. *Concurrent Pos:* Sr vis fel, Sci Res Coun, UK, 72-73; div ed, J Electrochem Soc, 72-90; mem, Honors & Awards Comt, Electrochem Soc, 85-89 & Finance Comt, 90-94, tech affairs comt, 95- *Mem:* AAAS; Am Chem Soc; Electrochem Soc; Am Electroplaters & Surf Finish Soc; Mat Res Soc. *Res:* Properties of metal and oxide surfaces; growth and properties of anodic oxide films; electrochemical processes; aluminum surface treatment; electrolytic capacitor technology. *Mailing Add:* 1136 Jeffrey Ct Northbrook IL 60062

ALWORTH, WILLIAM LEE, BIO-ORGANIC CHEMISTRY. *Current Pos:* asst prof org chem, 65-71, assoc prof chem, 71-78, PROF CHEM, TULANE UNIV, 78- *Personal Data:* b Twin Falls, Idaho, Jan 3, 39; m 59; c 2. *Educ:* Harvard Univ, AB, 60; Univ Calif, Berkeley, PhD(org chem), 64. *Prof Exp:* NIH fel, Harvard Univ, 64-65. *Concurrent Pos:* NIH career develop award, 72; adj assoc prof biochem, Tulane Univ, 75- *Mem:* Am Chem Soc; Am Soc Biol Chemists; Sigma Xi. *Res:* Biosynthesis of vitamins; chemical carcinogenesis; enzyme mechanisms. *Mailing Add:* Dept Chem Tulane Univ New Orleans LA 70118-5645

ALY, ABDEL FATTAH, CHEMICAL ENGINEERING. *Current Pos:* CONSULT, 93- *Personal Data:* b Mallawi, Egypt, Nov 28, 42; US citizen. *Educ:* Cairo Univ, BS, 64, MS, 67; Columbia Univ, ScD(chem eng), 70. *Prof Exp:* Res engr, Mobil Oil Corp, 69-72, sr res engr, 72-76, assoc tech serv, 76-78, supv engr tech serv, 78-80, sr refinery tech adv, 80-84, adv tech serv engr, 84-91, eng consult, 91-93. *Mem:* Am Inst Chem Engrs. *Res:* Kinetics; fluidization; dynamics; catalysis; scale-up; simulation and modeling; petroleum refinery operations. *Mailing Add:* 4201 N Ocean Blvd No C-804 Boca Raton FL 33431. *E-Mail:* afaly@prodigy.com

ALY, ADEL AHMED, INDUSTRIAL ENGINEERING, OPERATIONS RESEARCH. *Current Pos:* AT AM UNIV CAIRO, 89- *Personal Data:* b Fayoum, Egypt, Oct 30, 44; US citizen. *Educ:* Univ Cairo, BSc, 66; NC State Univ, MS, 72; Va Polytech Inst & State Univ, PhD(indust eng), 74. *Honors & Awards:* Halliburton lectr, Halliburton Found Inc, 82. *Prof Exp:* Jr consult mgt sci, Mgt Consult Ctr, 66-67; instr prod eng, Univ Cairo, 67-69; From asst prof to prof Indust Eng, Univ Okla, 75-89. *Mem:* Am Inst Indust Eng; Soc Mfg Engrs; Nat Soc Prof Engrs; Inst Mgt Sci; Am Soc Opers Res. *Res:* Mathematical programming; facility design and location analysis; distribution systems; application of operations research in the public sector. *Mailing Add:* 651 Danbury Ct Newtown PA 18940 Cairo

ALY, HADI H, HIGH ENERGY PHYSICS. *Current Pos:* PROF PHYSICS, SOUTHERN ILL UNIV, EDWARDSVILLE, 69- *Personal Data:* b Baghdad, Iraq, Aug 8, 30; US citizen; m 67; c 2. *Educ:* Univ Calif, Berkeley, BS, 52, MS, 53; Univ Bristol, Eng, PhD(physics), 60. *Prof Exp:* Instr, Univ Baghdad, Iraq, 53-56; res fel, Nat Res Coun, Can, 61-62; res assoc, Univ Rochester, NY, 62-64; res fel, Max Planck Inst, Munich, 64-65; assoc prof, Am Univ Beirut, Lebanon, 65-69. *Res:* Quantum theory of scattering. *Mailing Add:* 805 Linden Ave Boulder CO 80304

ALY, RAZA, SKIN MICROBIOLOGY, DERMATOMYCOLOGY. *Current Pos:* Asst res microbiologist, 69-72, from asst prof to assoc prof, 73-83, PROF MICROBIOL & DERMTOMYCOL, UNIV CALIF, SAN FRANCISCO, 83- *Personal Data:* b Quetta, Pakistan, June 3, 35; US citizen; c 2. *Educ:* Punjab Univ, BSc, 58; Univ Mich, MS, 62, MPH, 65; Univ Okla, PhD(microbiol), 69. *Concurrent Pos:* Vis prof, Harvard Univ, 87- *Mem:* Fel Pakistan Acad Med Sci; Am Soc Microbiol; Soc Invest Dermat; Int Soc Human & Animal Mycol; Am Acad Microbiol; Am Fedn Clin Res. *Res:* Pathogenesis of skin infections with emphasis on ecological mechanisms of microbial colonization; bacterial interference, microbial adherence and antimicrobial properties of skin lipids; product testing of topical antibiotics, surgical soaps and acne preparation. *Mailing Add:* Dept Dermat Univ Calif San Francisco Med Sch 513 Parnassus Ave San Francisco CA 94122-2722

ALYEA, ETHAN DAVIDSON, JR, PHYSICS. *Current Pos:* From asst prof to assoc prof, 62-71, prof, 71-95, EMER PROF PHYSICS, IND UNIV, BLOOMINGTON, 96- *Personal Data:* b Orange, NJ, Mar 7, 31; m 57; c 4. *Educ:* Princeton Univ, AB, 53; Calif Inst Technol, PhD(physics), 62. *Mem:* Am Asn Physics Teachers; Am Phys Soc; Sigma Xi. *Res:* Experimental high energy physics; astrophysics underground neutrino detector, Gran Sasso Lab. *Mailing Add:* Dept Physics Ind Univ Bloomington IN 47401

ALYEA, FRED NELSON, DYNAMIC METEOROLOGY. *Current Pos:* PRIN RES SCIENTIST, GA INST TECHNOL, 79- *Personal Data:* b Harlingen, Tex, Oct 26, 38; m 62; c 2. *Educ:* Univ Wis-Madison, BS, 64; Colo State Univ, PhD(atmospheric sci), 72. *Prof Exp:* Res assoc meteorol, Mass Inst Technol, 72-79. *Concurrent Pos:* Consult, Mfg Chemists Asn, 75- *Mem:* Am Meteorol Soc; Am Geophys Union; Sigma Xi. *Res:* Stratospheric modeling and climatology; large-scale dynamic processes in the atmosphere; numerical weather prediction methods; atmospheric predictability; paleoclimatology; climatological effects of anthropogenic pollution sources. *Mailing Add:* 4170 Chestnut Ridge Dr Dunwoody GA 30338-4678

ALYEA, HUBERT NEWCOMBE, physical chemistry, public lectures; deceased, see previous edition for last biography

ALZERRECA, ARNALDO, ORGANIC CHEMISTRY. *Current Pos:* PROF ORG CHEM, INTERAM UNIV PR, 76-, DEAN, DIV SCI & TECHNOL, DIR, OFF SPONSORED BIOMED RES. *Personal Data:* b La Paz, Bolivia, Mar 5, 43; m 69, Aline Frambes; c Javier. *Educ:* Univ Karlsruhe, WGer, dipl chem, 70; Univ Marburg, WGer, Dr rer nat, 74; Univ PR Rio Piedras, PhD, 75. *Prof Exp:* Teaching asst, Univ Marburg, WGer, 71-74. *Concurrent Pos:* prin investr, Minority Biomed Res Support Prog, Nat Inst Gen Med Sci, NIH, 80-; Res assoc, Univ Giessen, WGer, 83-84; investr, NSF, 94-96. *Mem:* Am Chem Soc; AAAS; Sigma Xi. *Res:* Natural products; steroid alkaloids; synthesis of small ring compounds; synthesis of spiroannelated oxa-aza ring systems; SAR-studies of biologically active glycoalkaloids; development of molluscicides; synthesis of exocyclic vinyl ethers. *Mailing Add:* PO Box 191293 Rio Piedras PR 00919-1293. *Fax:* 787-250-8736; *E-Mail:* aalzerre@interam.univ.pr

ALZHEIMER, WILLIAM EDMUND, STRUCTURAL MECHANICS, ENGINEERING MANAGEMENT. *Current Pos:* Mem tech staff, Sandia Nat Labs, 66-69, supvr, 69-76, mgr 76-86, DIR ADVAN MFG, SANDIA NAT LABS, 86- *Personal Data:* b Conrad, Mont, May 15, 40; m 59, Rebecca D Wilson; c Christine. *Educ:* Mont State Univ, BS, 63, MS, 64; Va Polytech Inst, PhD(eng mech), 66. *Mem:* Fel Am Soc Mech Engrs; Sigma Xi. *Res:* Research and development in engineering analysis, component design and management of technical programs; program development in advanced manufacturing technology for electronic and electromechanical subsystems. *Mailing Add:* 184 Bighorn Ridge NE Albuquerque NM 87122

AL-ZUBAIDI, AMER AZIZ, NUCLEAR PHYSICS. *Current Pos:* grad teaching asst, 76-82, RES SCI NUCLEAR PHYSICS, VA POLYTECH INST & STATE UNIV, 82-; OWNER, AL'S INT. *Personal Data:* b Najaf, Iraq, June 10, 45; m 72, Haifa M; c Samer & Akrum. *Educ:* Univ Baghdad, BS, 66; Pa State Univ, MS, 76. *Prof Exp:* High sch teacher, Inst Teachers, Riyadh, Saudi Arabia, 66-68, Saudi Ministry Educ, 66-68, Agr Voc Sch, Iraqi Ministry Educ, Baghdad, 68-74. *Concurrent Pos:* Chmn & bd dirs, Kufa Ctr Islamic Knowledge. *Mem:* Union Concerned Scientists; Sigma Xi. *Mailing Add:* 2319 Tenth St NW Roanoke VA 24012-3929

AMACHER, DAVID E, CELLULAR TOXICOLOGY, BIOCHEMICAL TOXICOLOGY. *Current Pos:* genetic toxicologist, 76-83, CELLULAR BIOCHEM TOXICOLOGIST DRUG SAFETY EVAL, PFIZER CENT RES, 84- *Educ:* Kent State Univ, MS, 71, BA, 87, PhD(mammalian physiol), 73; Univ N Haven, MBA, 81, Am Bd Toxicol, dipl. *Prof Exp:* Grad asst biol, Kent State Univ, 67-72; res assoc, Dept Pharmacol, Univ Sch Med, 73-74; NCI postdoctoral fel, Nat Inst Environ Health Sci, 74-76. *Concurrent Pos:* Consult, NCI carcinogenesis prog, Nat Coun prog, Nat Inst Health; adj assoc prof dept zool, 82-88, asst res prof, sch pharm, Univ Conn, 88. *Mem:* Am Asn Cancer Res; Soc Toxicol; Soc Biochem & Molecular Biol; Sigma Xi. *Mailing Add:* Drug Safety Dept Pfizer Cent Res Ctr Groton CT 06340-5196

AMACHER, PETER, INFORMATION SCIENCE. *Current Pos:* RETIRED. *Personal Data:* b Portland, Ore, Jan 29, 32; m 73; c 2. *Educ:* Amherst Col, BA, 54; Univ Wash, PhD(hist sci), 62. *Prof Exp:* Fel hist neurol, Brain Res Inst, Univ Calif, Los Angeles Ctr Health Sci, 62-64, asst & assoc prof hist med, Ctr Health Sci, 64-71, asst to dir, Brain Info Serv, 64-69, dir, 69-71; prin, Amacher & Assocs Info Serv, 71-72; dir, Conf Prog, Kroc Found Advan Med Sci, 72-81; consult, Med Commun, 82-87. *Mailing Add:* 375 Hillside Santa Fe NM 87501

AMADO, RALPH, THEORETICAL PHYSICS. *Current Pos:* Res assoc, 57-59, from asst prof to assoc prof, 59-65, PROF PHYSICS, UNIV PA, 65- *Personal Data:* b Los Angeles, Calif, Nov 23, 32; m 61, Carol Stein; c Richard L & David P. *Educ:* Stanford Univ, BS, 54; Oxford Univ, PhD(physics), 57. *Mem:* Fel Am Phys Soc; fel AAAS. *Res:* Theoretical nuclear physics; many-body problem; particle physics; scattering theory; three-body problem. *Mailing Add:* Dept Physics Univ Pa Philadelphia PA 19104

AMADOR, ELIAS, MEDICINE, PATHOLOGY. *Current Pos:* PROF UNIV SOUTHERN CALIF, 72-, CHIEF PATH, MARTIN LUTHER KING JR GEN HOSP, 72-; PROF PATH & CHMN DEPT, CHARLES R DREW POSTGRAD MED SCH, 72- *Personal Data:* b Mexico City, Mex, June 8, 32; m 61; c 3. *Educ:* Cent Univ Mex, BS, 59; Nat Univ Mex, MD, 56; Am Bd Path, dipl, 63. *Prof Exp:* Resident, Univ Hosps, Boston Univ, 59-60; assoc path, Peter Bent Brigham Hosp, 64-66; assoc prof, Inst Path, Case Western Reserve Univ, 66-72. *Concurrent Pos:* Teaching fel, Harvard Med Sch, 57-58 & Sch Med, Boston Univ, 59-60; Dazian Found fel, 60-61; fel med, Peter Bent Brigham Hosp & Biophysics Res Lab, 60-64; Med Found, Inc fel, 61-64. *Mem:* Am Chem Soc; Am Asn Path & Bact; Am Soc Exp Path; Am Asn Clin Chem; Sigma Xi. *Res:* Development of accurate and sensitive methods for diagnosis and detection of disease. *Mailing Add:* Dept Path Martin Luther King Jr Gen Hosp 12021 S Wilmington Ave Los Angeles CA 90059

AMADOR, JOSE MANUEL, PLANT PATHOLOGY, RESEARCH ADMINISTRATION. *Current Pos:* Exten plant pathologist, 65-91, DIR, AGR RES & EXTEN CTR, TEX A&M UNIV, 91- *Personal Data:* b Calimete, Matanzas, Cuba, Mar 3, 38; m 65, Silvia G Garcia; c Silvia G, Amador B, Marian L & Daniel J. *Educ:* Univ Havana, BS, 60; La State Univ, MS, 62, PhD(plant path & biochem), 65. *Honors & Awards:* Excellence in Exten Award, Int Soc Plant Path, 90. *Concurrent Pos:* Chmn, Int Coop Comt, Int Soc Plant Path, 80-89, counr, Carib Div, 80-89, rep, 89, chmn, Trop Plant Path Comt, 89; mem, Exten Futures Task Force, Tex A&M Univ Exten, 88, Int Task Force Agr Complex, 89; consult, Rio Grande Sugar Growers Inc, USAID, Univ Fla-El Salvador, Int Planning Servs Inc, Citrus Develop Corp, Chiqueta Brands Int & Xafra Inc. *Mem:* Am Phytopath Soc; Int Soc Plant Path. *Res:* Plant pathology; contributed articles to professional and scientific publications. *Mailing Add:* Agr Res & Exten Ctr Tex A&M Univ 2415 E Hwy 83 Weslaco TX 78596

AMAI, ROBERT LIN SUNG, ORGANIC CHEMISTRY. *Current Pos:* Res assoc, NMex Highlands Univ, 60-62, from asst prof to assoc prof, 62-74, chmn dept, 70-74, PROF CHEM, NMEX HIGHLANDS UNIV, 74- *Personal Data:* b Hilo, Hawaii, Oct 19, 32; m 59; c 1. *Educ:* Univ Hawaii, BA, 54, MS, 56; Iowa State Univ, PhD(org chem), 62. *Mem:* AAAS; Sigma Xi; Am Chem Soc. *Res:* Natural products; medicinal chemistry; correlation of structure with activity; psychopharmacology. *Mailing Add:* 731 Dalbey Dr Las Vegas NM 87701-4907

AMANN, CHARLES A(LBERT), MECHANICAL & AERONAUTICAL ENGINEERING. *Current Pos:* PRIN ENGR, KAB ENG, 91- *Personal Data:* b Thief River Falls, Minn, Apr 21, 26; m 50, Marilynn Reis; c Richard, Barbara, Nancy & Julie. *Educ:* Univ Minn, BS, 46, MSME, 48. *Honors & Awards:* Colwell Merit Award, Soc Automotive Engrs, 72 & 84; James Clayton Fund Prize, Brit Inst Mech Engrs, 75; Richard T Woodbury Award, Am Soc Mech Engrs, 89, Soichiro Honda lectr, 92. *Prof Exp:* Instr, Univ Minn, 46-49; res engr, Gen Motors Res Lab, 49-54, supvry res engr, 54-71, asst head, Gas Turbine Res Dept, 71-73, head, Engine Res Dept, 73-89, res fel, 89-91. *Concurrent Pos:* Spec instr, Wayne State Univ, 52-55; vis prof, Univ Ariz, 83; guest lectr, Mich State Univ, 83- *Mem:* Nat Acad Eng; Am Soc Mech Engrs; Sigma Xi; Combustion Inst; fel Soc Automotive Engrs. *Res:* Engines; automotive emissions; thermodynamics; fluid mechanics; turbomachinery; alternative fuels. *Mailing Add:* 984 Satterlee Rd Bloomfield Hills MI 48304

AMANN, JAMES FRANCIS, INTERMEDIATE ENERGY, NUCLEAR PHYSICS. *Current Pos:* MEM STAFF, LOS ALAMOS NAT LAB, 77- *Personal Data:* b Buffalo, NY, Jan 8, 45. *Educ:* Fordham Univ, BS, 66; State Univ NY Stony Brook, MS, 68, PhD(physics), 72. *Prof Exp:* Res assoc, Carnegie-Mellon Univ, 72-77. *Res:* Medium energy physics; nuclear structure using proton and pions as probes. *Mailing Add:* 1171 San Idlefonso Rd Los Alamos NM 87544

AMANN, RUPERT PREYNOESSL, REPRODUCTIVE PHYSIOLOGY. *Current Pos:* VPRES, RES BIOPORE INC, 89- *Personal Data:* b Boston, Mass, Dec 27, 31; m 63; c 2. *Educ:* Univ Maine, BS, 53; Pa State Univ, MS, 57, PhD(dairy sci), 61. *Honors & Awards:* Physiol & Endocrinol Award, Am Soc Animal Sci, 79; Res Award, Nat Asn Animal Breeders, 82; Physiol Award, Am Dairy Sci Asn, 84; Distinguished Anerologist, Am Soc Anerology, 95. *Prof Exp:* Asst reprod physiol, Pa State Univ, 55-61, res assoc, 61-62; NIH res fel, Royal Vet & Agr Col, Denmark, 62-63; from asst prof to prof dairy physiol, Pa State Univ, 63-79; prof physiol, Colo State Univ, 79-95, head dept, 89-95. *Concurrent Pos:* Vis prof, Dept Physiol Biophys, Colo State

Univ, 75-76; vis prof, Dept Biochem, Wash State Univ, 90. *Mem:* Am Soc Reprod Med; Am Soc Animal Sci; Soc Study Reprod (dir, 67-69); Brit Soc Study Fertil; Am Soc Andrology (dir, 77-80, secy, 83-86, pres, 89-90). *Res:* Male reproductive physiology; testicular and epididymal physiology; spermatogenesis; spermatozoan maturation; semen physiology; reproductive capacity and sexual behavior of the male. *Mailing Add:* BioPore Inc PO Box 10074 State College PA 16805-0074

AMARA, ROY C, SYSTEMS SCIENCE, POLICY RESEARCH. *Current Pos:* exec vpres, 70-71, pres, RES FEL, INST FOR FUTURE, 90- *Personal Data:* b Boston, Mass, Apr 7, 25; m 49; c 3. *Educ:* Mass Inst Technol, SB, 48; Harvard Univ, AM, 49; Stanford Univ, PhD(elec eng), 58. *Prof Exp:* Jr res engr control systs, Stanford Res Inst, 52-53, res engr digital comput, 53-55, sr res engr systs eng, 55-61, mgr systs eng, 61-64, asst to pres, 63, exec dir systs sci, 64-68, vpres inst progs, 68-69. *Concurrent Pos:* US deleg, First Int Fedn Automatic Control, Moscow. *Mem:* AAAS; Inst Elec & Electronics Engrs; Inst Mgt Sci; Opers Res Soc Am. *Res:* Information systems; communication networks; technology assessment; methodologies for long range planning; decision analysis; private-public sector interfaces; future of the city; corporate planning. *Mailing Add:* 491 La Mesa Dr Porto Valley CA 94028

AMARANATH, L, ANESTHESIOLOGY. *Current Pos:* STAFF, DEPT GEN ANESTHESIOL, CLEVELAND CLIN FOUND, OHIO, 78- , DEPT ANESTHESIOL, CLEVELAND CLIN FLA, FT LAUDERDALE, 88- *Personal Data:* b Mysore, India, July 27, 39; US citizen; c 2. *Educ:* Mysore Univ, BS & MB, 63; Christian Med Col, India, DA, 67; Am Bd Anesthesiol, dipl, 72. *Prof Exp:* Intern, K R Hosp, Mysore, India, 64-65; resident, CMC Hosp, Vellore, India, 66-67, Parkland Hosp, Dallas, Tex, 67-69, Univ Hosp, Cleveland, Ohio, 69-70, fel, 70-71; researcher, Sch Med, Case Western Reserve Univ, Cleveland, Ohio, 71-72, from instr to asst prof, 72-78. *Concurrent Pos:* Lectr, Bellary Med Col, Karnataka St, India, 65-66; prin investr or co-investr grants, NIMH, 74-77, Nat Inst Gen Med Sci, 75-78, Hoffman-LaRoche Co, 80-81, Cleveland Clin Found, 84-86 & 88-89; sect head, pain ther, Cleveland Clin Found, 81-82, orthop anesthesia, 85-88. *Mem:* Fel Am Col Anesthesiologists; Am Acad Pain Mgt; AMA; Am Soc Anesthesiologists; Am Soc Clin Pharmacol & Therapeut; Am Soc Pharmacol & Exp Therapeut; Int Asn Study Pain. *Res:* Non-surgical control of musculoskeletal cancer pain; anesthesia for patients with multiple neurofibromatosis; postoperative pain management with epidural morphine in pediatric patients; atracurium and phenochromocytoma. *Mailing Add:* Dept Anesthesiol Cleveland Clin Fla 3000 W Cypress Creek Rd Ft Lauderdale FL 33309-1743

AMAREL, S(AUL), COMPUTER SCIENCE. *Current Pos:* chair, Dept Comput Sci, Rutgers Univ, 69-84, dir, Res Resource Comput Biomed, 71-83, dir info sci & technol off, Defense Advan Res Proj Agency, 85-87, ALAN M TURING PROF COMPUT SCI, RUTGERS UNIV, 87-, DIR, HYPERCOMPUT & DESIGN (HPCD) PROJ, 93- *Personal Data:* b Saloniki, Greece, Feb 16, 28; nat US; m 53, 90; c 2. *Educ:* Israel Inst Technol, BS, 48, IngEE, 49; Columbia Univ, MS, 53, DEngSc, 55. *Prof Exp:* Res engr, Sci Dept, Israeli Ministry of Defense, 48-52 & 55-57; res engr, Electronics Res Labs, Columbia Univ, 53-55; head comput theory res, RCA Labs, 57-69. *Concurrent Pos:* Comt mem, Int Joint Artificial Intel Conf, 81-89, gen chmn, 83; trustee, Ramapo Col NJ, 69-73; mem chem/bio info handling rev comt, Nat Inst Health, 71-75, mem exec & adv comt, SUMEX-AIM, 74-; dir, Rutgers Res Resource Comput in Biomed, 71-83; vis scholar, Stanford Univ, 79, vis sr res scientist, Carnegie Mellon Univ, 85, vis res fel, SRI Intern, 83. *Mem:* Fel AAAS; Asn Comput Mach; Soc Indust & Appl Math; Sigma Xi; fel Inst Elec & Electronics Engrs; founding fel Am Asn Artificial Intel. *Res:* Artificial intelligence; applications of artificial intelligence to engineering, science and medicine. *Mailing Add:* Dept Comput Sci Busch Campus Rutgers Univ New Brunswick NJ 08903

AMAROSE, ANTHONY PHILIP, GENETICS, BIOETHICS. *Current Pos:* from asst prof to assoc prof, 67-90, dir, Cytogenetics Lab, 77-90, EMER ASSOC PROF, BIOL SCI DIV & BIOL SCI COL DIV, UNIV CHICAGO, 94- *Personal Data:* b Oneonta, NY, Mar 17, 32. *Educ:* Fordham Univ, BS, 53, MS, 57, PhD(cytol), 59. *Prof Exp:* Asst biol, Fordham Univ, 56-57; instr, Marymount Col, NY, 57-59; resident res assoc, Argonne Nat Lab, 59-61; res assoc radiobiol, Cancer Res Inst, New Eng Deaconess Hosp, Boston, 61-62; asst prof cytogenetics & lectr path, Albany Med Col, 63-66, res assoc prof, 66-67; assoc prof obstet & gynec, Chicago Lying-In Hosp, 71-90. *Concurrent Pos:* Fel gen path, Harvard Med Sch, 61; personal consult to Shields Warren, MD, Cancer Res Inst, Mass, 62-67; abstractor, Excerpta Medica Found, 63-88, mem int ed bd, 73-88; consult, Albany Med Ctr Hosp, 63-67 & Inst Defense Anal, Arlington, Va, 65-67; hon trustee Charles A Berger Scholar Fund, Fordham Univ, 66-; mem int ed bd, Excerpta Medica Found, 73-; pres, Genetics Task Force, Ill, 89-90. *Mem:* AAAS; Am Soc Cell Biol; Am Inst Biol Sci; Environ Mutagen Soc; Am Soc Human Genetics; Sigma Xi. *Res:* Pharmacogenetics, radiation cytology; prediction of fetal sex; chromosomology; human bone marrow; contemporary issues in biomedical ethics. *Mailing Add:* Biol Sci Div & Biol Sci Col Div HM-49 Univ Chicago 1116 E 59th St Chicago IL 60637

AMASINO, RICHARD M, PLANT HORMONES, FLOWERING. *Current Pos:* asst prof, 85-90, assoc prof, 90-95, PROF BIOCHEM, UNIV WIS-MADISON, 95- *Personal Data:* b May 11, 56; US citizen. *Educ:* Pa State Univ, BS, 77; Ind Univ, PhD(biol & biochem), 82. *Prof Exp:* Postdoctoral, Univ Wash, 82-85. *Concurrent Pos:* NSF presidential young investr award, 88. *Res:* Plant development; regulation of cell division and differentiation by cytokinins and the control of flowering. *Mailing Add:* Dept Biochem Univ Wis 420 Henry Hall Madison WI 53706-1569

AMASSIAN, VAHE EUGENE, NEUROPHYSIOLOGY. *Current Pos:* PROF PHYSIOL & CHMN DEPT, STATE UNIV NY DOWNSTATE MED CTR, 72- *Personal Data:* b Paris, France, Nov 11, 24; nat US; m 56; c 1. *Educ:* Cambridge Univ, BA, 46, MB, 48. *Prof Exp:* House physician, Middlesex Hosp, London, 48-49; from instr to assoc prof physiol, Sch Med, Univ Wash, 49-55; prof, Albert Einstein Col Med, 57-72. *Concurrent Pos:* Markle Found scholar, 52-59; mem postgrad training comt, USPHS, 59-63. *Mem:* Am Physiol Soc. *Res:* Neurophysiology of cerebral cortex; brainstem and sensory systems. *Mailing Add:* Dept Physiol SUNY Health Sci Ctr 450 Clarkson Ave Brooklyn NY 11203-2098

AMATA, CHARLES DAVID, PHYSICAL CHEMISTRY, PLASTICS ENGINEERING. *Current Pos:* PRES & CHIEF EXEC OFFICER, C P TECHNOLOGIES, INC, 92- *Personal Data:* b Sagata, Italy, Feb 11, 41; US citizen; m 61; c Charles Jr, Richard & Timothy. *Educ:* John Carroll Univ, BS, 64; Univ Notre Dame, PhD(chem), 68. *Prof Exp:* Res asst chem, Parma Tech Ctr, Union Carbide Corp, 60-64, res scientist, Carbon Prod Div, 67-71; sr res scientist, Addressograph-Multigraph Corp, 71-74; mgr res, Conwed Plastics Corp, 74-80, tech dir, Plastics Div, 80-83, vpres, 83-92. *Mem:* Am Chem Soc; Soc Plastics Engrs; Sigma Xi. *Res:* Molecular luminescence and energy transfer; thermal degradation of polymeric systems; organic photoconductors; high temperature inorganic fibers; composites; specialty plastics. *Mailing Add:* CD Technol Inc 3155 Lamb Ave Columbus OH 43219. *Fax:* 614-475-9399; *E-Mail:* cptech@sprynet.com

AMATO, IVAN ABEL, CHEMISTRY, MATERIALS SCIENCE. *Current Pos:* TECH COMMERCIALIZATION SPECIALIST, NAT INST STUDIES & TECHNOL, 93- *Personal Data:* b East Orange, NJ, May 12, 61; m 89, Mary Koepke; c Maxwell Key & Simon Abraham. *Educ:* Rutgers Univ, BA, 83; Ind Univ, MA, 86. *Honors & Awards:* James T Grady-James H Stack Award for Sci Writing, Am Chem Soc, 95. *Prof Exp:* Staff writer news serv, Am Chem Soc, 87-88, asst ed analytical chem, 88; ed chem & mat sci, Sci News, 88-91; staff writer, Sci, 91-93. *Concurrent Pos:* Freelance writer, 86-; sci writer fel, Marine Biol Lab, Woods Hole, Mass, 88; lectr, Ind State Univ, 92. *Mem:* Mat Res Soc. *Res:* Contributed numerous articles to professional journals. *Mailing Add:* 9213 Bradford Rd Silver Spring MD 20901

AMATO, JOSEPH CONO, SUPERCONDUCTIVITY, LOW TEMPERATURE PHYSICS. *Current Pos:* vis asst prof, 77-81, asst prof, 84-86, ASSOC PROF PHYSICS, COLGATE UNIV, 86- *Personal Data:* b Hartford, Conn, Jan 21, 45; m 66; c 2. *Educ:* Univ Conn, BA, 66; Stevens Inst Technol, MS, 68; Rutgers State Univ NJ, PhD(physics), 75. *Prof Exp:* Mem tech staff grad study, Bell Labs, 66-70; res assoc physics, McGill Univ, 75-77; res assoc physics, Cornell Univ, 81-84. *Concurrent Pos:* Vis asst prof, Cornell Univ, 85, vis assoc prof, 86-, vis scientist, 87-88; mem nat adv bd, Continuous Electron Beam Accelerator Facil, Newport News, Va, 86-88, consult, 87-89. *Mem:* Am Phys Soc. *Res:* Basic studies and applications of superconductivity; microwave response of thin films; applications to particle accelerators; low temperature condensed matter physics. *Mailing Add:* Dept Physics & Astron Colgate Univ Hamilton NY 13346. *Fax:* 315-824-7187

AMATO, R STEPHEN, HUMAN GENETICS, PEDIATRICS. *Current Pos:* CHMN PEDIAT, GREATER BALTIMORE MED CTR, 86-, CLIN PROF PEDIAT, UNIV MD, 86- *Personal Data:* b Brooklyn, NY, July 11, 36; m 83; c 3. *Educ:* Manhattan Col, BS, 58; Columbia Univ, MA, 59; NY Univ, PhD(genetics), 68; Univ Nebr, MD, 73. *Prof Exp:* Instr basic sci, St Johns Riverside Hosp, Yonkers, NY, 60-63; asst prof biol, State Univ NY Westchester, 63-65; fel genetics, NY Univ & Beth Israel Med Ctr, 65-67; cytogeneticist, Div Labs, Beth Israel Med Ctr, 68; asst prof human genetics, Univ Nebr Med Ctr, Omaha, 68-72, instr pediat & anat, 72-76, dir lab med & molecular genetics, 70-76, med geneticist, Muscular Dystrophy Clin, 74-76; from assoc prof to prof pediat, Med Ctr, WVA Univ, 76-86, dir med genetics, 76-86. *Concurrent Pos:* Lectr pediat, Johns Hopkins Univ, 86- *Mem:* Am Soc Human Genetics; Am Soc Cell Biol; Am Genetics Soc; Pub Health Asn. *Res:* Chromosome structure and function; cell cycle and nucleic acid synthesis; slow virus infections and the central nervous system; genetic counseling and delivery of genetics and pediatrics services. *Mailing Add:* Greater Baltimore Medical Ctr 6701 N Charles St Baltimore MD 21204-6892. *Fax:* 410-828-2303

AMATO, VINCENT ALFRED, PLANT PATHOLOGY, HORTICULTURE. *Current Pos:* RETIRED. *Personal Data:* b New York, NY, July 20, 15; m 43. *Educ:* Mich State Univ, BS, 54, MS, 55; Tex A&M Univ, PhD(plant path), 64. *Prof Exp:* Res instr hort, Mich State Univ, 54-56; asst exten horticulturist, WVa Univ, 56-57; instr floricult, Tex A&M Univ, 59-60 & plant path, 60-64, res asst plant physiol & microtech, 64; from asst prof to prof hort, Sam Houston State Univ, 64-85. *Mem:* Am Phytopath Soc; Am Soc Hort Sci. *Res:* Horticultural crops; microtechniques; pathological and physiological plant parasitism. *Mailing Add:* 3353 Winter Way Huntsville TX 77340

AMATUCCI, EDWARD G, ENGINEERING MECHANICS. *Current Pos:* MECH ENGR, NAT INST STAND & TECHNOL, 82- *Personal Data:* b Silver Spring, Md, June, 64. *Educ:* Johns Hopkins Univ, MA, 93, MA, 97. *Honors & Awards:* Design Award, Soc Automotive Engrs. *Mem:* Soc Automotive Engrs; Am Soc Mech Engrs. *Res:* Machine design and robotics. *Mailing Add:* Nat Inst Stand & Technol Bldg 220 Rm B124 Rte 270 Gaithersburg MD 20899. *E-Mail:* anatucci@cme.nist.gov

AMAZEEN, PAUL GERARD, ELECTRICAL ENGINEERING. *Current Pos:* PRES, FRANTZ IMAGING, INC, 85- *Personal Data:* b Portsmouth, NH, Mar 24, 39; m 61; c 1. *Educ:* Univ NH, BS, 61; Worcester Polytech Inst, MS, 64, PhD(elec eng), 71. *Prof Exp:* Res assoc physics, Univ NH, 61-62; instr elec eng, Worcester Polytech Inst, 64-70; chief engr, Vitacomp, Inc, 70-72; prog mgr, Raytheon Med Electronics, 72-74; opers mgr, Rohe Sci Corp, 74-76; eng mgr, Folsom Oper, Gen Elec Co, 76-85. *Concurrent Pos:* Partner, United Eng Consult, 67- *Mem:* Inst Elec & Electronics Engrs; Am Inst Ultrasound Med; Sigma Xi; Am Soc Echocardiography. *Res:* Communication-information theory; signal processing, especially in biomedical situations such as processing of ultrasound echo signals. *Mailing Add:* 33 Cape Rd New Castle NH 03854

AMBADY, NALINI, PSYCHOLOGY. *Current Pos:* ASST PROF, HARVARD UNIV, 94- *Personal Data:* b Calcutta, India; US citizen; m 88. *Educ:* Harvard Univ, PhD(social psychol), 91. *Honors & Awards:* Behav Sci Prize, AAAS, 93. *Prof Exp:* Asst prof, Holy Cross Col, 93-94. *Res:* Accuracy of social and perceptual judgments. *Mailing Add:* 12 Rebecca Rd Newton MA 02165. *E-Mail:* na@wjh.harvard.edu

AMBEGAOKAR, VINAY, SOLID STATE PHYSICS, THEORETICAL PHYSICS. *Current Pos:* from asst prof to assoc prof, 62-68, PROF PHYSICS, CORNELL UNIV, 68- *Personal Data:* b Nagpur, India, Jan, 16, 34; m 56, Saga M; c Maia & Liisa. *Educ:* Mass Inst Technol, MS & SB, 56; Carnegie Inst Technol, PhD(physics), 60. *Prof Exp:* Res assoc physics, Niels Bohr Inst, Copenhagen, 60-62. *Concurrent Pos:* Dir, Inst Theoret Physics, Univ Helsinki, Finland, 69-71; vis scientist, IBM Watson Res Lab, 76-77; Guggenheim fel, Univ Calif, Santa Barbara, 83-84; US sr scientist, Humboldt Found, Univ Karlsruke, Ger, 90. *Mem:* Fel Am Phys Soc. *Res:* Theory of condensed matter physics; superconducting tunnel junctions; equilibrium and transport properties of superconductors; superfluid helium 3 and superfluid helium 4 films; properties of semiconductors and disordered systems. *Mailing Add:* Clark Hall Cornell Univ Ithaca NY 14853

AMBELANG, JOSEPH CARLYLE, ORGANIC CHEMISTRY, RUBBER CHEMISTRY. *Current Pos:* CONSULT, 84- *Personal Data:* b Bellevue, Ohio, Nov 7, 14; m 48; c 2. *Educ:* Univ Akron, BS, 35; Yale Univ, PhD(chem), 38. *Honors & Awards:* Dinsmore Award, 61. *Prof Exp:* Asst chem, Yale Univ, 38-40; instr, D'Youville Col, 40-42; res chemist, Firestone Tire & Rubber Co, 42-56; sr compounder, Goodyear Tire & Rubber Co, 56-61, prin compounder, 61-83, res & develop assoc, 83-84. *Mem:* Am Chem Soc; Am Soc Testing Mat. *Res:* Pyrimidines; synthesis and catalytic hydrogenation; rubber chemistry; softeners; tackifiers; age-resistors; textile treating; antiozonants; curing agents; vulcanization; heat flow; analysis of test data. *Mailing Add:* 366 Dorchester Rd Akron OH 44320-1352

AMBERG, HERMAN R(OBERT), SANITARY & CHEMICAL ENGINEERING. *Current Pos:* RETIRED. *Personal Data:* b Ger, Feb 10, 20; nat US; m 47, Martha Taylor; c Carl, Karen (Pike) & David. *Educ:* Syracuse Univ, BS, 43; Rutgers Univ, MS, 49, PhD(sanit eng), 51. *Honors & Awards:* Individual Achievement Award, Pollution Control Asn, 71; Environ Award, Tech Asn Pulp & Paper Indust, 74. *Prof Exp:* Res engr, Johns-Manville Res Ctr, 46-48 & Eng Exp Sta, Ore State Col, 51-56; proj leader Cent Res Dept, Crown Zellerbach Corp, 56-61, mgr chem & biol res, 61-71, dir environ serv, Cent Res Div, 71-85. *Concurrent Pos:* Consult environ eng, 85- *Mem:* AAAS; Am Chem Soc; Am Tech Asn Pulp & Paper Indust; Water Pollution Control Fedn; fel Tech Asn Pulp Paper Indust. *Res:* Chemical and sanitary engineering research on industrial wastes from pulp and paper industry. *Mailing Add:* 2713 SE Balboa Dr Vancouver WA 98684-9182

AMBLER, ERNEST, CRYOGENICS, SCIENCE ADMINISTRATION. *Current Pos:* RETIRED. *Personal Data:* b Bradford, Eng, Nov 20, 23; nat US; m 55; c 2. *Educ:* Oxford Univ, BA, 44, MA & PhD(physics), 53. *Honors & Awards:* Arthur S Flemming Award, 60; John Price Wetherill Medal, Franklin Inst, 62; Samuel Wesley Stratton Award, 64; William A Wildhack Award, 76; President's Award for Distinguished Fed Civilian Serv, 77. *Prof Exp:* Physicist, Metall Lab, Armstrong Siddeley Motors, Ltd, Eng, 44-48; physicist, Cryogenic Physics Sect, 53-65, head div inorg mat, 65-58, dir, Inst Basic Stand, 68-73, dep dir, 73-75, actg dir, 75-78, dir, Nat Bur Standards, 78-88, Under Sec Comm, 88-89. *Concurrent Pos:* Guggenheim fel, 63; US Rep to Int Comt Weights & Measures, 72; chmn, Consult Comt Ionizing Radiation, 74; exofficio pres, Nat Conf Weights & Measures, 78; Dept Com mem bd gov, Israel/US Bi-Nat Indust Res & Develop Found, 81. *Mem:* Am Phys Soc; fel AAAS. *Mailing Add:* 4 Oyster Rake Ct Hilton Head Island SC 29926

AMBLER, JOHN EDWARD, PLANT NUTRITION. *Current Pos:* RETIRED. *Personal Data:* b Bidwell, Ohio, Apr 5, 17; m 62; c 1. *Educ:* Marshall Univ, BS, 52, MS, 53; Univ Md, PhD(plant physiol), 69. *Prof Exp:* Plant physicologist, Stress Lab, USDA, 56-78. *Mem:* Soc Am Plant Physiologists; Am Soc Agron. *Res:* Effect of stress-nutrition, temperature, water, ultraviolet B light, on growth and development of food and fiber crops. *Mailing Add:* 28 Manteo Ave Hampton VA 23661-3443

AMBLER, MICHAEL RAY, POLYMER CHEMISTRY. *Current Pos:* Develop engr, Goodyear Tire & Rubber Co, 68-75, proj leader, 75-77, sect mgr, 77-87, DEPT MGR, GOODYEAR TIRE & RUBBER CO, 87- *Personal Data:* b Wichita, Kans, Feb 20, 47; m 68, Maryann Horner; c David. *Educ:* Wichita State Univ, BS, 68; Akron Univ, MS, 71, PhD(polymer sci), 75. *Mem:* Am Chem Soc. *Res:* Polymer characterization; polymer rheology; physical chemistry of colloidal and macromolecular species; analytical chemistry; spectroscopy; emulsion polymerization, structure property relationships; process engineering. *Mailing Add:* Corp Res Goodyear Tire & Rubber Co Akron OH 44305

AMBORSKI, LEONARD EDWARD, ENVIRONMENTAL HEALTH, TOXICOLOGY. *Current Pos:* RES ASSOC, TOXICOL RES CTR, STATE UNIV NY, BUFFALO, 91- *Personal Data:* b Buffalo, NY, Aug 23, 21; m 44, Irene Kazmierczak; c Donna & David. *Educ:* Canisius Col, BS, 43; State Univ NY Buffalo, AM, 49, PhD(chem), 52; Am Bd Indust Hyg, cert. *Prof Exp:* Civilian instr physics, USAAF, Canisius Col & civilian res physicist magnetism, Carnegie Inst, 44-45; res chemist polymer chem, E I DuPont de Nemours & Co, Inc, 45-59, staff scientist, 59-62, group mgr, bldg mat div, 62-68, staff scientist, Specialty Mkt Div, Film Dept, 68-90, environ coordr, 72-90, occup health coordr, 77-90. *Concurrent Pos:* Lectr occup health & environ, Canisius Col & State Univ NY, Buffalo; consult environ health, Toxicol Res Ctr, State Univ NY, Buffalo. *Mem:* Am Chem Soc; Am Indust Hyg Asn; Am Soc Testing & Mat; Air Pollution Control Asn; Water Pollution Control Fedn; Am Acad Indust Hyg; Am Lung Asn; Sigma Xi; Am Soc Safety Engrs. *Res:* Chemistry of high polymers; physical and chemical properties of synthetic fibers; properties of polymeric films; electrical properties of polymers; structure-property relationship of polymers; rubber chemistry; mechanism of reinforcement plastic building materials; environmental health. *Mailing Add:* 62 Wedgewood Dr Buffalo NY 14221. *Fax:* 716-829-2806

AMBRE, JOHN JOSEPH, CLINICAL PHARMACOLOGY, TOXICOLOGY. *Current Pos:* DIR, DEPT TOXICOL & DRUG ABUSE, AMA, 90- *Personal Data:* b Aurora, Ill, Sept 14, 37; m 62; c 4. *Educ:* Notre Dame Univ, BS, 59; Loyola Univ, Chicago, MD, 63; Univ Iowa, PhD(pharmacol), 72. *Prof Exp:* Clin fel internal med, Mayo Clin, 66-68; fel clin pharmacol, Univ Iowa, 68-72, from asst prof to assoc prof med & pharmacol, 72-78; dir, Clin Bio-Tox Labs, Inc, 78-80; assoc prof med, Med Sch, Northwestern Univ, 80-90. *Concurrent Pos:* Clin investr, Vet Admin, 73; consult, Met Path Inc, 80- *Mem:* Am Soc Clin Pharmacol & Therapeut; Am Fedn Clin Res; Am Soc Pharmacol & Exp Therapeut; Am Acad Clin Toxicol; AAAS; NY Acad Sci. *Res:* Drug metabolism in man; toxicology; pharmacology of cocaine. *Mailing Add:* AMA 1210 Walden Ln Deerfield IL 60015-3128

AMBROMOVAGE, ANNE MARIE, PHYSIOLOGY. *Current Pos:* Res instr, 64-66, 68-69, res asst prof, 69-70, ASST PROF HUMAN PHYSIOL, HAHNEMANN MED COL, 70-, RES ASSOC, 63- *Personal Data:* b Gilberton, Pa, Aug 27, 36. *Educ:* Susquehanna Univ, BA, 58; Jefferson Med Col, MS, 61, PhD(physiol), 68. *Concurrent Pos:* Merck Found fac develop grant, 70. *Mem:* AAAS; NY Acad Sci. *Res:* Gastrointestinal physiology; water of electrolyte absorption; pancreatic enzymes; mesenteric blood flow; physiology of shock and vasoactive substances. *Mailing Add:* 100 Lombard St Philadelphia PA 19147-1602

AMBRON, RICHARD THOMAS, NEUROBIOLOGY, NEUROCHEMISTRY. *Current Pos:* instr, 74-76, ASST PROF ANAT & CELL BIOL, COL PHYSICIANS & SURGEONS, COLUMBIA UNIV, 76- *Personal Data:* b New York, NY, June 15, 43; m 66; c 2. *Educ:* Villanova Univ, BS, 65; Med Sch, Temple Univ, PhD(biochem), 71. *Prof Exp:* Fel neurobiol, Sch Med, NY Univ, 71-74. *Concurrent Pos:* Mem, Div Neurobiol & Behav, Columbia Univ, 74-; career develop award, NIH, 79. *Mem:* Soc Neurosci; NY Acad Sci; Sigma Xi. *Res:* Synthesis, assembly and distribution of membrane components in single identified neurons of the marine mollusc aphysia californica, to elucidate the mechanisms underlying the sorting and movement of organelles in neurons, to maritan neurons in the differentiated state. *Mailing Add:* Dept Anat & Cell Biol Columbia Univ Col Physicians & Surgeons 630 W 168 St New York NY 10032-3702

AMBROSE, CHARLES T, IMMUNOLOGY. *Current Pos:* prof cell biol, 73-76, PROF MICROBIOL & IMMUNOL, SCH MED, UNIV KY, 76- *Personal Data:* b Indianapolis, Ind, Nov 29, 29. *Educ:* Ind Univ, AB, 51; Johns Hopkins Univ, MD, 55. *Prof Exp:* Intern med, New Eng Med Ctr, Boston, 55-56; asst resident infectious dis, Mass Mem Hosp, 56-57; resident, New Eng Med Ctr, 57-59; from instr to assoc prof bacteriol & immunol, Harvard Med Sch, 62-72; assoc prof, Col de France, Paris, 72-73. *Concurrent Pos:* NSF fel, 59-60; res fel bacteriol & immunol, Harvard Med Sch, 59-62; dir res, Nat Inst Health & Med Res. *Mem:* Am Asn Immunologists; Brit Soc Immunol; Soc Fr Immunol; Reticuloendothelial Soc; Soc Exp Biol & Med; Sigma Xi. *Res:* Regulation of antibody synthesis in vitro; organ cultures; antigenic competition; antimetabolites; salicylates; insecticides; corticosteroids. *Mailing Add:* 163 N Arcadia Park Lexington KY 40503-1354

AMBROSE, ERNEST R, DENTISTRY. *Current Pos:* dean, 77-85, PROF RESTORATIVE DENT, COL DENT, UNIV SASK, 77- *Personal Data:* b Montreal, Que, May 12, 26; m 49; c 7. *Educ:* McGill Univ, DDS, 50; FRCD(C). *Prof Exp:* From instr to assoc prof oper dent, McGill Univ, 50-77, chmn dept, 58-70, dean fac dent, 70-77. *Concurrent Pos:* Consult, Montreal Gen Hosp, 58-77. *Mem:* Fel Am Col Dent; Can Acad Restorative Dent; fel Int Col Dent. *Res:* Restorative dentistry; clinical use of dental materials; assessing and maintaining the pulp potential of human teeth. *Mailing Add:* Col Dent Univ Sask 105 Wiggins Rd Saskatoon SK S7N 5E5 Can

AMBROSE, HARRISON WILLIAM, III, ECOLOGY, ANIMAL BEHAVIOR, AIDS. *Current Pos:* EXEC DIR, AIDS PREVENTION EDUCATION COALITION, 94- *Personal Data:* b Winter Haven, Fla, Feb 26, 38; m 93, Katherine Peckham; c Harrison, Joel, Douglas Emlen &

Katherine Emlen. *Educ:* Univ Fla, BS, 60; Univ Ky, MS, 62; Cornell Univ, PhD(ecol), 67. *Prof Exp:* From instr to asst prof biol, Cornell Univ, 66-73; asst prof, Univ Ill, Urbana, 73-76; assoc prof, Univ Tenn, 76-80. *Res:* Behavioral animal ecology; social and orientation behavior; population regulation; predator-prey interactions; human behavior modification/AIDS prevention. *Mailing Add:* 6507 Bull Run Knoxville TN 37938. *Fax:* 423-974-2617

AMBROSE, JOHN DANIEL, RESTORATION ECOLOGY, CONSERVATION BIOLOGY. *Current Pos:* CUR BOT, METRO TORONTO ZOO, 91- *Personal Data:* b Detroit, Mich, June 20, 43; m 71, Cherry Booth; c Robin. *Educ:* Univ Mich, BS, 65, MS, 66; Cornell Univ, PhD(bot), 75. *Honors & Awards:* Conserv Award, Can Wildflower Soc. *Prof Exp:* Asst hydrographic officer, US Navy, 67-68; cur arboretum, Univ Guelph, 74-91, grad fac, 89- *Concurrent Pos:* Sci adv, Nature Conservancy Can, 91-; adv, Can Bot Conserv Network, 96- *Mem:* Am Asn Bot Gardens & Arboreta; Soc Conserv Biol; Sigma Xi; Soc Ecol Restoration. *Res:* Restoration ecology of forests, wetlands and meadows in a landscape and community context; conservation biology of the rare woody plants of Ontario; conservation roles of botanical gardens. *Mailing Add:* Metro Toronto Zoo 361A Old Finch Ave Scarborough ON M1B 5K7 Can. *Fax:* 416-392-4979; *E-Mail:* lvcjda@250.metrotor.on.ca

AMBROSE, JOHN RUSSELL, PHYSICAL CHEMISTRY, MATERIALS SCIENCE. *Current Pos:* ASSOC PROF, UNIV FLA, 78- *Personal Data:* b Orange, NJ, Feb 25, 40; m 62; c 2. *Educ:* Washington & Lee Univ, BSc, 61; Univ Md, College Park, PhD(phys chem), 72. *Honors & Awards:* Romanoff Award, Nat Asn Corrosion Engrs, 74. *Prof Exp:* High sch teacher chem, Va Beach City Sch Bd, 62-64; res chemist, Newport News Shipbuilding & Dry Dock Co, 64-66; res chemist, Nat Bur Standards, 66-78. *Mem:* Electrochem Soc; Nat Asn Corrosion Engr; Am Soc Testing & Mat. *Res:* Relationships between susceptibility to localized corrosion attack and interfacial properties; repassivation kinetics and electrochemistry of solutions. *Mailing Add:* Dept Mat Sci Univ Fla 153A Rhines Hall Gainesville FL 32611-2002

AMBROSE, JONATHAN PAUL, CONSERVATION BIOLOGY, COMMUNITY ECOLOGY. *Current Pos:* Ecologist, 86-94, ASST PROG MGR, GA NAT HERITAGE PROG, GA DEPT NAT RESOURCES, 94- *Personal Data:* b Knoxville, Tenn, Feb 28, 56; m 78, Dana Lee McCallister; c Stephanie Elyse & Elliot Timothy. *Educ:* Univ Tenn, Knoxville, BA, 78, MS, 81; Univ Ga, PhD(ecol), 86. *Res:* Rare species and natural communities of the southeast; conservation planning at local, regional and national scales; protection and restoration of natural communities and rare species populations. *Mailing Add:* 1440 Brittain Estates Dr Watkinsville GA 30677

AMBROSE, RICHARD JOSEPH, POLYMER SCIENCE. *Current Pos:* mgr mat & process res & develop, Lord Corp, 79-85, assoc dir res, 85-92, dir chem res, 92-93, DIR CHEM TECHNOL, LORD CORP, 93- *Personal Data:* b Youngstown, Ohio, July 4, 42; m 65, Marsha Powers; c Paul, Jason & Alex. *Educ:* Bowling Green State Univ, BS, 64; Univ Akron, PhD(polymer sci), 68. *Prof Exp:* Res scientist, Plastics Div, Firestone Tire & Rubber Co, 68-73, group leader, 73-79. *Concurrent Pos:* Chmn, NC Polymer Group, 88; bd dirs, Phys & Math Sci Found, NC State Univ, 89- *Mem:* Am Chem Soc. *Res:* Chemical reactions of polymers; hydrolysis of acrylate and methacrylate polymers; structure physical property relationships of block copolymers; thermosetting resins; polar-nonpolar block polymers; cationic and anionic polymerization; polymer processing; composites; morphology of multiphase systems; surface chemistry of organic-metal systems; adhesives and coatings. *Mailing Add:* 405 Gregson Dr Thomas Lord Res Ctr Cary NC 27511

AMBROSE, ROBERT T, ANALYTICAL CHEMISTRY, CLINICAL CHEMISTRY. *Current Pos:* RETIRED. *Personal Data:* b Palmdale, Calif, Sept 21, 33. *Educ:* Univ Calif, Riverside, BA, 60; Northwestern Univ, PhD(anal chem), 65. *Prof Exp:* Res assoc, Eastman Kodak Co Res Labs, 64-91. *Concurrent Pos:* Instr, Rochester Inst Technol, 72-74. *Mem:* Am Chem Soc; Sigma Xi. *Res:* Analytical approaches to reference methods in clinical chemistry; application of chromatographic procedures to the analysis of diverse analytes in human serum. *Mailing Add:* 3280 S Avenida Oconor Green Valley AZ 85614-4673

AMBROSE, WILLIAM PATRICK, SCANNING PROBE MICROSCOPY, SINGLE MOLECULE DETECTION. *Current Pos:* postdoctoral fel, 91-93, TECH STAFF MEM, LOS ALAMOS NAT LAB, 93- *Personal Data:* b Santa Monica, Calif, Oct 23, 59; m, Carol Cohenour; c Anne, Mary & William. *Educ:* Calif State Univ, Northridge, BS, 82; Cornell Univ, MS, 86, PhD(physics), 89. *Prof Exp:* Vis scientist, IBM Almaden Res Ctr, 89-91. *Res:* Ultra sensitive optical detection including single molecule detection in solids, liquids and on interfaces; developing scanning probe microscopies; novel laser spectroscopies and high resolution interferometry of solids at liquid helium temperatures; phonon generation and detection. *Mailing Add:* 1895 Camino Mora Los Alamos NM 87544

AMBROSIANI, VINCENT F, PHYSICAL CHEMISTRY. *Current Pos:* OWNER, AC PRODUCTS, 92- *Personal Data:* b Oneida, NY, Aug 4, 29; m 52; c 8. *Educ:* Le Moyne Col, NY, BS, 52; Syracuse Univ, MS, 57, PhD(phys chem), 64. *Prof Exp:* Res chemist, Exp Sta, E I du Pont de Nemours & Co, Inc, 59-63 & Textile Res Lab, 63-66; tech dir fiber & fabric develop, Blue Ridge-Winkler Textiles, Pa, 66-68; dir res & develop, Vanity Fair Mills, Inc, 68-70, dir res & develop, V F Corp, Reading, 70-82; sr scientist, Burlington Indust, 84, res mgr res & develop, 85-87; owner, Ambrosiana Consults, Textile Prod Develop, 87-92. *Mem:* Am Chem Soc; Am Asn Textile Chem & Colorists. *Res:* Fibers, yarns and fabrics in new and improved fabrics for apparel and industrial applications. *Mailing Add:* 4628 Lake Geanette Rd Greensboro NC 27455

AMBRUS, CLARA MARIA, HEMATOLOGY. *Current Pos:* Pharmacol Grad Sch, 65, RES PROF PEDIAT, SCH MED, STATE UNIV NY BUFFALO, 69-, OBSTET/GYNEC, 83- *Personal Data:* b Rome, Italy, Dec 28, 24; nat US; m 45, Julian L; c Madeline (Lillie), Peter, Julian L Jr, Linda (Broenniman), Steven, Katherine (Cheney) & Charles. *Educ:* Univ Zurich, MD, 49; Jefferson Med Col, PhD, 55; Am Bd Clin Chem, dipl. *Prof Exp:* Asst histol, Budapest Med Sch, 43-46, demonstr pharmacol, 46-47; asst, Med Sch, Univ Zurich, 47-49; asst therapeut chem & virol, Pasteur Inst, Univ Paris, 49; asst pharmacol, Philadelphia Col Pharm, 50-51, from asst prof to assoc prof, 51-55; asst prof pharmacol & assoc med, Sch Med, State Univ NY Buffalo, 55-65, asst res prof pediat, 65-69, assoc res prof pediat, 69-77; assoc cancer res scientist, Roswell Park Mem Inst, 55-69, assoc res prof pharmacol, 66-69, prin cancer res scientist, 69-83, prof pharmacol, Roswell Park Mem Inst, 70- *Concurrent Pos:* Staff mem, Buffalo Gen Hosp, Dept Med. *Mem:* Am Asn Cancer Res; Am Physiol Soc; Am Soc Pharmacol & Exp Therapeut; Am Soc Exp Biol; fel Am Col Physicians; Am Soc Hematol. *Res:* Pediatric hematology and oncology; hyaline membrane disease of infants; biochemistry and pathology of the blood coagulation and fibrinolysin systems; immobilized enzymes; transplantation and regeneration of hemic tissue; environmental health; experimental and clinical pharmacology; clinical detoxification; detoxification using immobilized antidotes, delivery of enzymatic activity with immobilized enzymes. *Mailing Add:* Buffalo Gen Hosp 100 High St Buffalo NY 14203-1154. *Fax:* 716-884-3035

AMBRUS, JULIAN LAWRENCE, HEMATOLOGY, ONCOLOGY. *Current Pos:* RETIRED. *Personal Data:* b Budapest, Hungary, Nov 29, 24; nat US; m 45, Clara M Bayer; c Madeline A (Lillie), Peter S, Julian L, Linda C (Broenniman), Steven G, Kathrine A (Cheney), & Charles Y. *Educ:* Univ Zurich, MD, 49; Jefferson Med Col, PhD(med sci), 54; Am Bd Clin Chem, dipl, 54. *Hon Degrees:* ScD, Niagara Univ, 84. *Honors & Awards:* Nelson Hacket Gold Medal, 72; Cheplow Award Med, Milard Filmore Hosp, 84; Foreign Mem, Nat Acad Sci, Hungary, 91. *Prof Exp:* Asst histol, Med Sch, Univ Budapest, 43-46, demonstr pharmacol, 46-47; asst, Med Sch, Univ Zurich, 47-49; asst therapeut chem & tropical med virol, Pasteur Inst, Paris, 49; from asst prof to prof pharmacol, Philadelphia Col Pharm, 50-55; from prin cancer res scientist to dir, Cancer Res (Pathoaphysiol), State Dept Health, NY, 55-89; assoc prof pharmacol, Grad Sch & from asst prof to prof internal med, Sch Med, 55-; prof & chmn, Exp Path & Internal Med, Sch Med & Grad Sch, State Univ NY, Buffalo, 65-92. *Concurrent Pos:* Consult adv comt coagulation components, Comn Plasma Fractionation & Related Processes; consult, Bur Drugs, Food & Drug Admin; mem coun drugs, AMA; ed-in-chief, J Med & Hematol Rev; mem comt thrombolytic agents, Nat Heart Inst; fel, Am Col Physicians, Coun Clin Cardiol & Am Heart Asn; mem, Dept Med, Roswell Park Mem Inst, 55-92, head, Dept Pathophysiol, 75-89. *Mem:* Fel AAAS; Am Soc Pharmacol & Exp Therapeut; Am Fedn Clin Res; Asn Am Med Cols; fel NY Acad Sci; fel Am Col Physicans. *Res:* Hemorrhagic and thromboembolic diseases; blood coagulation, platelet and fibrinolysin systems; physiology of the leukocytes; leukemias; radiation sickness; biochemistry and chemotherapy of neoplastic diseases; experimental and clinical pharmacology; resistance to drugs; pathophysiology of AIDS; effects of oral contraceptive agents; carcino-genesis (environmental, industrial); metabolic diseases diabetes and obesity. *Mailing Add:* 143 Windsor Ave Buffalo NY 14209-1020. *Fax:* 716-859-1491

AMBS, LAWRENCE LACY, MECHANICAL ENGINEERING. *Current Pos:* from asst prof to assoc prof, 68-93, PROF MECH ENG, UNIV MASS, AMHERST, 93- *Personal Data:* b St Paul, Minn, Aug 14, 37; m 57; c 3. *Educ:* Univ Minn, BSME, 60, MSME, 64, PhD(mech eng), 68. *Honors & Awards:* Ralph Teetor Award, Soc Automotive Engrs, 67. *Prof Exp:* Teaching assoc mech eng, Univ Minn, 66-67. *Mem:* Am Soc Mech Engrs; Combustion Inst: Am Soc Eng Educ. *Res:* Combustion research involving gases and solids; combustion in propulsion applications; reduction of exhaust emissions in combustion devices; solar energy; ocean thermal energy conversion; energy conservation. *Mailing Add:* Dept Mech Eng Univ Mass Amherst Campus Amherst MA 01003-0014

AMBS, WILLIAM JOSEPH, SURFACE CHEMISTRY, PHYSICS. *Current Pos:* SCI SYSTS ENGR CONSULT, MARTIN MARIETTA, 93- *Personal Data:* b Philadelphia, Pa, Dec 3, 29; m 57; c 1. *Educ:* Villanova Univ, BS, 52; Stevens Inst Technol, MS, 54; Cath Univ Am, PhD(phys chem), 61. *Prof Exp:* Asst chem, Stevens Inst Technol, 52-54 & Cath Univ Am, 54-56; phys chemist, Nat Bur Standards, 56-63; phys chemist, Air Prod & Chem, Inc, 63-71, sr prin res chemist, 71-84; sci software analyst, Gen Elec, Inc, 85-88, sci systs engr, 88-93. *Mem:* Am Chem Soc; Catalysis Soc; Sigma Xi. *Res:* Catalysis; chemical kinetics; surface chemistry of solids; field emission microscopy; thin film optics; x-ray diffraction; scientific software design and programming. *Mailing Add:* 505 E Lancaster Ave Apt 419 St Davids PA 19087-5136

AMBUDKAR, INDU S, PATIENT CARE. *Current Pos:* vis assoc, 85-88, SR STAFF FEL, CIPCB, NAT INST DENT RES, NIH, 88- *Personal Data:* b Madras, India, Feb 17, 54. *Educ:* Isabella Thoburn Col, India, BS, 73; Lucknow Univ, MS, 75; Madurai-Kamaraj Univ, PhD(biochem), 79. *Prof Exp:* Jr res asst, Res Doc, Indust Toxicol Res Ctr, Lucknow, India, 75; jr res fel, Dept Biochem, Madurai-Kamaraj Univ, Madurai, India, 76-77, sr res fel, 77-79; res assoc, Dept Biol Chem, Sch Med, Univ Md, 80-83, res asst prof, Dept Path, 84-85. *Concurrent Pos:* Res supvr, Madurai-Kamaraj Univ, Madurai, India, 77-79; teaching asst, grad level biochem, Univ Madurai, India, 77-79, biochem tutorials & conf, Univ Md, 81-83 & biochem course grad students, Dept Path, 84-85; postdoctoral fel award, Am Heart Asn, 81-82. *Mem:* Am Soc Biochem & Molecular Biol; Biophys Soc; Soc Gen Physiologists; AAAS. *Res:* Author or co-author of over 40 publications. *Mailing Add:* Clin Invest & Patient Care Br Nat Inst Dent Res NIH Bldg 10 Rm 1N113 Bethesda MD 20892-0001

AMBUEL, JOHN PHILIP, pediatrics; deceased, see previous edition for last biography

AMBUR, DAMODAR REDDY, EXPERIMENTAL & ANALYTICAL STRUCTURAL MECHANICS RESEARCH. *Current Pos:* sr engr, 89-96, ASST BR HEAD, STRUCT MECH BR, LANGLEY RES CTR, NASA, 96- *Personal Data:* m 73, Manjula Yaramakala; c Sumanth & Vishnu V. *Educ:* Sree Venkateswara Univ, BE, 68; Indian Inst Technol, MTech, 72; Ga Inst Technol, PhD(aerospace eng), 80. *Prof Exp:* Sr engr, Indian Space Res Orgn, 72-77; res assoc prof, Ga Inst Technol, 80-85; eng specialist, Lockheed Aeronaut Systs Co, 85-87 & 89; dep gen mgr, Hindustan Aeronaut Ltd, India, 88. *Mem:* Assoc fel Am Inst Aeronaut & Astronaut; Indian Soc Advan Mat & Processes; Inst Cert Prof Mgrs. *Res:* Advanced aerospace structures technologies by performing research in the areas of structural concepts, optimization, buckling/postbuckling, nonlinear response, damage tolerance, impact and penetration dynamics, and experimental methods for structures subjected to combined thermal and mechanical loading conditions. *Mailing Add:* 108 Flag Creek Rd Yorktown VA 23693

AMBURGEY, JUDITH CHARLAYNE, PHOSPHOLIPID-PROTEIN INTERACTIONS. *Current Pos:* ASST PROF ORG CHEM, COL WOOSTER, 96- *Personal Data:* b Kingsport, Tenn, Oct 19, 66. *Educ:* Georgetown Col, Ky, BS, 88; Univ NC, Chapel Hill, PhD(org chem), 93. *Prof Exp:* Postdoctoral fel, Univ Md, Baltimore, 93-95; res assoc, Pharmacol Toxicol Res Lab, 95-96. *Mem:* Am Chem Soc; AAAS. *Res:* Model system to study protein-membrane interactions; metal ion-mediated interactions of proteins and membranes. *Mailing Add:* Dept Chem Col Wooster Wooster OH 44691. *Fax:* 330-263-2386; *E-Mail:* jamburgey@acs.wooster.edu

AMBURGEY, TERRY L, WOOD BIODETERIORATION, WOOD PRESERVATION. *Current Pos:* ASSOC PROF, MISS STATE UNIV, 79- *Personal Data:* b Trenton, NJ, Dec 11, 40; m 61; c 2. *Educ:* State Univ Col Forestry, Syracuse Univ, BS, 63, MS, 65; NC State Univ, PhD(plant path), 69. *Prof Exp:* Res plant pathologist, Southern Forest Exp Sta, 69-79. *Concurrent Pos:* Mem, Int Res Group Wood Preserv. *Mem:* Asn Preserv Technol; Am Wood Preservers Asn; Forest Prod Res Soc. *Res:* Prevention and control of wood decay in structures; interactions between wood-inhabiting fungi and termites. *Mailing Add:* Forest Prod Miss State Univ Mississippi Station MS 39762-9999

AMDAHL, GENE M, COMPUTER SCIENCE. *Current Pos:* CHMN, COMMERCIAL DATA SERRERS, 94- *Personal Data:* b Flandreau, SDak, Nov 16, 22; m 46; c 3. *Educ:* SDak State Univ, BSEP, 48; Univ Wis, MS & PhD(theoret physics), 52. *Hon Degrees:* DEng, SDak State Univ, 74; DSc, Univ Wis-Madison, 79, Luther Col, Iowa, 80, Augustana Col, SDak, 84. *Honors & Awards:* W Wallace McDowell Award, Inst Elec & Electronics Engrs Comput Soc, 76; Comput Sci Man Of The Year Award, Data Processing Mgt Asn, 76; Michelson-Morley Award, Western Res Univ, 77; Harry Goode Mem Award, Am Fedn Info Processing Soc, 83; Legend Award, Comp & Commun Ind Asn, 95. *Prof Exp:* Wis Alumni Res Found res assoc comput develop, Univ Wis, 51-52; sr engr, IBM Corp, NY, 52-55; mem tech staff comput res & develop, Ramo-Wooldridge, Calif, 56; lab mgr, Aeronutronic, Inc, 56-60; dir, Comput Res & Develop Lab, IBM Corp, 60-71; pres, Amdahl Corp, 70-74, chmn bd, 70-79; chmn bd, Trilogy/Elxsi Corp, 80-94. *Concurrent Pos:* Vis asst prof, Stanford Univ, 65-67; IBM fel, 65-71; lectr, NATO Sch, 69 & 76; chmn, pres & chief exec officer, Andor Int Inc, 87-94. *Mem:* Nat Acad Eng; Am Phys Soc; fel Inst Elec & Electronics Engrs; fel Brit Comput Soc; Marconi Soc Italy. *Res:* Internal machine and system organization of high performance computing systems suited to office-like environments. *Mailing Add:* Andor Int Inc 383 Moffett 10131 Bubb Rd Cupertino CA 95014

AMDE, AMDE M, ENGINEERING MECHANICS. *Current Pos:* assoc prof, 83-88, chmn, Struct Tech Group, Dept Civil Eng, 85-90, DIR GRAD STUDIES, DEPT CIVIL ENG, UNIV MD, COLLEGE PARK, 83-, PROF CIVIL ENG, 88- *Personal Data:* b Ethiopia, Apr 9, 47; m 84, Marta Zekiros; c Kaleb, Lulade, Shashi, Lishan & Chiban. *Educ:* Johns Hopkins Univ, BES, 70; Univ Calif, Berkeley, MS, 71; State Univ NY, Buffalo, PhD(civil eng), 76. *Honors & Awards:* Innovation in Civil Eng Award of Merit, Am Soc Civil Engrs, 91. *Prof Exp:* Vis asst prof civil eng & eng mech, McMaster Univ, Hamilton, Ont, 76-77; from asst prof to assoc prof civil eng, Iowa State Univ, 77-83. *Concurrent Pos:* Consult, Doefer Eng Consults, Designers & Fabricators, 80, Johnson Machine Works, Inc, 80, WTA Eng, Inc, 84-, Occup Safety & Health Admin, US Dept Labor, 84-85, UN Develop Prog, 86-87 & 88- 89; proj engr, Anal Nuclear Reactor Containment Vessels, Nuclear Regulatory Comn, US Dept Energy, 80-81, Anal Barriers Turbine Missiles Nuclear Reactor Power Plants, 81-83; dir, Ethiopian Sci Soc NAm; vol, Vols Tech Assistance; assoc ed, J Struct Eng, Am Soc Civil Engrs, 93- *Mem:* Am Soc Civil Engrs; Nat Soc Prof Engrs; Int Standards Orgn; Masonry Soc; Int Asn Shell & Spatial Structures. *Res:* Non-linear analysis and stability of large space enclosures; soil structure interactions in bridges; behavior of integral and jointless bridge structures; rehabilitation and retrofitting of bridges; limit analysis of nuclear reactor containment vessels; analysis of turbine missile impact in nuclear power plants; masonry structures. *Mailing Add:* Dept Civil Eng Univ Md College Park MD 20742. *Fax:* 301-405-2585; *E-Mail:* aw29@umail.umd.edu

AMDUR, MARY OCHSENHIRT, PULMONARY TOXICOLOGY. *Current Pos:* RES PROF ENVIRON MED, NY UNIV, 88- *Personal Data:* b Pittsburgh, Pa, Feb 18, 21; m 44; c David. *Educ:* Univ Pittsburgh, BS, 43; Cornell Univ, PhD(biochem), 46. *Honors & Awards:* Donald E Cummings Mem Award, Am Indust Hyg Asn, 74; Henry F Smyth Award, Am Acad Indust Hyg, 84; Herbert E Stokinger Award, Am Conf Govt Indust Hyg, 89. *Prof Exp:* Asst ophthal res, Howe Lab, Med Sch, Harvard, 47-48; res biochemist, Vet Admin Hosp, 48-49; res assoc, Harvard Univ, 49-57, asst prof physiol, Sch Pub Health, 57-63, assoc prof toxicol, 63-91; lectr nutrit & food sci, Mass Inst Technol, 76-88, sr res scientist, Energy Lab, 80-88. *Mem:* AAAS; Am Chem Soc; Am Indust Hyg Asn; Am Conf Govt Indust Hygienists; Soc Toxicol; Sigma Xi. *Res:* Bone formation in the rat; effect of manganese and choline on liver fat in the rat; effect of inhalation of sulfur dioxide and sulfuric acid mist on guinea pigs and humans; interaction of irritant gases and aerosols; analyses for lead in air and urine; physiologic response to respiratory irritants. *Mailing Add:* 89 Rock Meadow Rd Westwood MA 02090

AMEER, GEORGE ALBERT, OPTICAL PHYSICS. *Current Pos:* SR SCIENTIST, ITEK CORP, 93-; BOEING NAM, KIRKLAND AFB, ALBUQUERQUE, NMEX. *Personal Data:* b Norwalk, Conn, July 26, 31; m 72; c 6. *Educ:* Univ Maine, BS, 53; Univ Pittsburgh, PhD(physics), 61. *Prof Exp:* Sr physicist, J W Fecker Div, Am Optical Co, Pa, 61-64; asst prof physics, Am Univ Beirut, 64-67; tech specialist optics, Autonetics Div, NAm Rockwell Corp, Anaheim, 67-73, supvr, Advan Sensor Technol Autonetics Group, 73-78; vpres, Optical Sci Co, 78-93. *Mem:* Am Phys Soc; Optical Soc Am. *Res:* Molecular spectroscopy; optical instrumentation; physical optics. *Mailing Add:* 6012 Tierra NE Albuquerque NM 87111-7020

AMEIN, MICHAEL, CIVIL ENGINEERING, HYDRODYNAMICS. *Current Pos:* from asst prof to assoc prof, 60-70, PROF CIVIL ENG, NC STATE UNIV, 70- *Personal Data:* b Kabul, Afghanistan, Jan 15, 26; US citizen; m 55; c 3. *Educ:* Stanford Univ, BS, 52; Cornell Univ, MS, 54, PhD(civil eng), 55. *Prof Exp:* Design engr, Corbett-Tinghir & Co, NY, 55-56 & F L Ehasz, NY 56-57; hydraul engr, Anderson-Nichols & Co, Mass, 57-60. *Concurrent Pos:* Prin res investr, US Bur Yards & Docks, 63-64, Off Water Res, 65-69, US Weather Bur, 70-73, Sea Grant, 70-75, Environ Protection Agency, 76-78 & State NC, 79-80; consult, Parana River develop, Arg, 80-81. *Mem:* Am Soc Civil Engrs; Am Geophys Union; Int Asn Hydraul Res. *Res:* Flow in open channels; numerical analysis; computer applications to hydrodynamical problems; long period waves; water quality modeling; flood movements; ocean outfall dispersion. *Mailing Add:* 1301 Kershaw Dr Raleigh NC 27609

AMELIN, CHARLES FRANCIS, MATHEMATICAL ANALYSIS. *Current Pos:* From asst prof to assoc prof, 69-80, PROF MATH, CALIF STATE POLYTECH UNIV, POMONA, 80- *Personal Data:* b Worcester, Mass. *Educ:* Col of the Holy Cross, AB, 64; Univ Calif, Berkeley, PhD(math), 72. *Concurrent Pos:* Vis asst prof math, Univ Md, College Park, 72-73 & Ariz State Univ, 73-74. *Mem:* Am Math Soc. *Res:* Operator theory; functional analysis. *Mailing Add:* PO Box 208 Claremont CA 91711

AMELIO, GILBERT FRANK, SOLID STATE ELECTRONICS. *Current Pos:* PRES, CHMN & CHIEF EXEC OFFICER, NAT SEMICONDUCTOR, 91. *Personal Data:* b New York, NY, Mar 1, 43; m 63; c 3. *Educ:* Ga Inst Technol, BS, 65, MS, 67, PhD(physics), 69. *Prof Exp:* Mem tech staff device physics, Bell Tel Labs, Inc, 68-71; mgr charge coupled devices, Faidchild Camera & Instrument Corp, 71-; pres, Semiconductor Prod Div, Rockwell Int, 83-91. *Mem:* Am Phys Soc; Inst Elec & Electronics Engrs; Sigma Xi. *Res:* Semiconductor surfaces with Auger spectroscopy; hot electron transport theory; silicon diode array camera tube; theory and experiment of charge coupled devices; management of design and manufacture of charge coupled devices. *Mailing Add:* Apple Comput 1 Infinite Loop Santa Clara CA 95014

AMELL, ALEXANDER RENTON, PHYSICAL CHEMISTRY. *Current Pos:* asst prof, 55-60, chmn dept 60-77, prof chem, Univ NH, 60-88, interim dean, Col Eng & Phys Sci, 80-88, EMER PROF, 88- *Personal Data:* b North Adams, Mass, Mar 3, 23; m 45; c 4. *Educ:* Univ Mass, BS, 47; Univ Wis, PhD(chem), 50. *Prof Exp:* Instr phys chem, Hunter Col, 50-52; asst prof chem, Lebanon Valley Col, 52-55; asst prof, 55-60, chmn dept 60-77, emer prof chem, Univ NH, 60-88, interim dean, Col Eng & Phys Sci, 80-88. *Concurrent Pos:* Fulbright lectr, San Marcos Univ, Lima, 63. *Mem:* Am Chem Soc. *Res:* Radiation chemistry; kinetics. *Mailing Add:* 4 Chesley Dr Durham NH 03824

AMELUNXEN, REMI EDWARD, MICROBIOLOGY. *Current Pos:* RETIRED. *Personal Data:* b Kansas City, Mo, Jan 27, 28. *Educ:* Rockhurst Col, BS, 49; Univ Kans, MA, 57, PhD(microbiol), 59. *Prof Exp:* USPHS fel biochem, Univ Kans, 59-62, instr, 62-64, asst prof microbiol & biochem, 64-66, assoc prof microbiol, 66-71, prof microbiol, Sch Med, 71- *Concurrent Pos:* Res grant, USPHS; NIH grant, 64-69. *Mem:* Am Soc Microbiol; Sigma Xi. *Res:* Physico-chemical characterization of thermophilic enzymes and studies on the genetic bases of thermophily. *Mailing Add:* Dept Microbiol Univ Kans Med Ctr 39th & Rainbow Blvd Kansas City KS 66160

AMEMIYA, FRANCES (LOUISE) CAMPBELL, mathematics, for more information see previous edition

AMEMIYA, KEI, GENE REGULATION, RNA POLYMERASE. *Current Pos:* INSTR MOLECULAR BIOL, ALBERT EINSTEIN COL MED, YESHIVA UNIV, 84- *Educ:* Rutgers Univ, PhD(microbiol), 73. *Res:* Transcription. *Mailing Add:* NIH Bldg 10 Rm 4N248 10 Ctr Dr MSC 1382 Bethesda MD 20892-1382

AMEMIYA, KENJIE, REPRODUCTIVE TOXICOLOGY. *Current Pos:* RES LEADER, HOFFMAN LAROCHE, NUTLEY, NJ, 96- *Educ:* Univ Calif, Davis, BS, 82, PhD(nutrit pharmacol & physiol chem), 87. *Prof Exp:* Res asst, Calif Primate Res Ctr, Univ Calif, Davis, 83-85, teaching asst, 83-87; sr scientist, Ciba-Geigy Corp, 87-89, res scientist III, Div Toxicol & Path, Reproductive Toxicol Dept, Novartis, 89-96. *Mem:* Teratology Soc; Behav Teratology Soc; Am Inst Nutrit. *Mailing Add:* Toxicol & Pathol Dept Hoffman-LaRoche 340 Kingsland St Nutley NJ 07110-1199

AMEMIYA, MINORU, SOIL MANAGEMENT & CONSERVATION, AGRONOMY. *Current Pos:* res soil scientist, Iowa State Univ, 60-68, from assoc prof agron to prof agron, 68-88, exten agronomist, 68-88, PROF EMER AGRON, IOWA STATE UNIV, 88- *Personal Data:* b San Francisco, Calif, Mar 17, 22; m 47, Grace Obata; c Michael & Robert. *Educ:* Univ Calif, Berkeley, BS, 42; Ohio State Univ, MS, 48, PhD(agron), 50. *Prof Exp:* Lab technician, Carpenter Bros, Inc, Wis, 43-44; res asst, Ohio Agr Exp Sta, 48-50; soil scientist, Agr Res Serv, USDA, Colo, 50-58 & Tex, 58-60. *Concurrent Pos:* Assoc agronomist, Colo Agr Exp Sta, 50-58; mem, Coun Agr Sci & Tech. *Mem:* Fel Soil Sci Soc Am; fel Am Soc Agron; fel Soil Conserv Soc Am; fel AAAS; Int Soc Soil Sci. *Res:* Reclamation of saline and alkali soils; soil, water and crop management; soil and water conservation; soil-water-plant relationships; soil tilth and tillage. *Mailing Add:* 304 Hilltop Rd Ames IA 50014-7525

AMEN, RALPH DUWAYNE, PHILOSOPHY OF BIOLOGY & MEDICINE, BIOMEDICAL ETHICS. *Current Pos:* asst prof plant physiol, Wake Forest Univ, 62-67, chmn dept, 67-72, assoc prof, 67-80, prof biol, 80-93, EMER PROF BIOL, WAKE FOREST UNIV, 93- *Personal Data:* b Cheyenne, Wyo, Feb 26, 28; m 52; c 4. *Educ:* Univ Northern Colo, AB, 52, AM, 54; Univ Colo, MBS, 59, PhD(bot), 62. *Honors & Awards:* ISI citation classic, current contents Sept 15, 80. *Prof Exp:* Instr high sch, Colo, 55-58; instr biol, Univ Colo, 59-60, teaching assoc, 61-62. *Concurrent Pos:* Sigma Xi res grant, 61-62; NC Bd Sci & Technol grant, 68-69; assoc ed, Ecology, 71-72. *Mem:* Ecol Soc; Sigma Xi. *Res:* Seed germination and dormancy; biomedical philosophy. *Mailing Add:* Dept Biol Wake Forest Univ Reynolds Sta Winston-Salem NC 27101-3818

AMEN, RONALD JOSEPH, food science, nutrition, for more information see previous edition

AMEND, DONALD FORD, FISH PATHOLOGY. *Current Pos:* GEN MGR, SOUTHERN SOUTHEAST REGIONAL AQUACULT ASN, 83- *Personal Data:* b Portland, Ore, Jan 8, 39; m 62; c 3. *Educ:* Ore State Univ, BS, 60, MS, 65; Univ Wash, PhD(fish path), 73. *Prof Exp:* Aquatic biologist, Ore Fish Comn, 60-63; res asst food toxicol, Ore State Univ, 63-65; proj leader virol, US Fish & Wildlife Serv, 66-73, sect leader microbiol, 74-76; dir res, Tavolek, Inc, Redmond, 76-81; assoc prof, Univ Calif, Davis, 81-83. *Concurrent Pos:* Affil asst prof, Univ Wash, 74-78. *Mem:* Am Fisheries Soc; Sigma Xi; Am Soc Microbiol; AAAS. *Res:* Controlling infectious diseases of fish including chemotherapy, immunization, environmental and biological control. *Mailing Add:* 11091 Coburn Rd ND Ketchikan AK 99901

AMEND, JAMES FREDERICK, CARDIOVASCULAR PHYSIOLOGY, AUTONOMIC PHARMACOLOGY. *Current Pos:* PROF PHYSIOL, ATLANTIC VET COL, 85- *Personal Data:* b Mount Vernon, Wash, Jan 6, 43; m 64; c 2. *Educ:* Pac Lutheran Univ, BS, 65; Baylor Col Med, PhD(physiol), 69; Wash State Univ, DVM, 77. *Prof Exp:* Asst prof physiol, Baylor Col Med, 70-71; asst prof zool & physiol, Univ Idaho, 72-74; res assoc physiol, Wash State Univ, 74-76; asst prof vet med, Univ Mo, Columbia, 76-78; assoc prof vet sci, Univ Nebr, Lincoln, 78-85. *Mem:* Am Physiol Soc; Sigma Xi; NY Acad Sci; Am Acad Vet Pharmacol & Therapeut; Am Soc Vet Physiologists & Pharmacologists. *Res:* Role of pulmonary fluid transport disturbances in the susceptibility of bovine lung to respiratory disease. *Mailing Add:* Dept Anat & Physiol Univ Prince Edward Island Atlantic Vet Col Charlottetown PE C1A 4P3 Can

AMEND, JOHN ROBERT, ANALYTICAL CHEMISTRY. *Current Pos:* PROF CHEM, MONT STATE UNIV, 67- *Personal Data:* b Yakima, Wash, July 20, 38; m 66; c 2. *Educ:* Pac Lutheran Univ, BA, 60; Mont State Univ, MS, 64; Univ Tex, Austin, PhD(sci educ), 67. *Prof Exp:* Dept head physics & chem, Curtis Sr High, Tacoma, Wash, 60- 65; res assoc chem, Univ Tex Austin, 66-67. *Concurrent Pos:* Vis scientist, Oak Ridge Assoc Univs, 70 & 73; assoc dept head, Mont State Univ, 88- *Mem:* Am Chem Soc. *Res:* Instrument design for analytical chemistry; author of various publications. *Mailing Add:* Dept Chem Mont State Univ Bozeman MT 59715

AMENDE, LYNN MERIDITH, CELL BIOLOGY, MEMBRANE STRUCTURE & FUNCTION. *Current Pos:* Sr staff fel, 83-87, prog officer, Fogarty Int, 87-89, EXEC SECY, NAT HEART LUNG BLOOD INST, NIH, 89- *Personal Data:* b June 24, 50; m. *Educ:* Col William & Mary, BS, 72; Univ Md, MS, 76, PhD(zool), 79. *Prof Exp:* Fel, Lab Neurochem, Nat Inst Neurol & Commun Dis & Stooke, 79-81; NIH/Nat Res Coun fel, Biochem Dept, Armed Forces Radiobiol Res Inst, 81-83. *Concurrent Pos:* Sr staff fel, Lab Cell & Develop Biol, Nat Inst Diabetes & Digestive & Kidney Dis, 83-87; Health Servs Admin trainee, NIH, 87-89. *Mem:* AAAS; Am Soc Cell Biol; Am Soc Zool; Biophys Soc; Sigma Xi; Am Soc Zoologists. *Res:* Cell membranes: structure function, lipid asymmetry, signal transduction, ion transport; calcium transport. *Mailing Add:* NIH 45 Ctr Dr Blvd 45 Rm 3AN12 MSC 6300 Bethesda MD 20892-6300

AMENOMIYA, YOSHIMITSU, CATALYSIS. *Current Pos:* HON VIS PROF, UNIV OTTAWA, 87- *Personal Data:* b Tokyo, Japan, May 13, 24; Can citizen; m 48. *Educ:* Tokyo Inst Technol, BEng, 47; Hokkaido Univ, DSc, 59. *Honors & Awards:* Catalysis Award, Chem Inst Can, 77. *Prof Exp:* Asst, Tokyo Inst Technol, 51-61; assoc res officer, 61-67, sr res officer, Nat Res Coun Can, 68-87. *Concurrent Pos:* Nat Res Coun Can fel, 59-61; chmn, Catalysis Div, Chem Inst Can, 78-79; dir, Can Catalysis Found, 90- *Mem:* Chem Inst Can; Am Chem Soc; Chem Soc Japan; Catalysis Soc Am; Catalysis Soc Japan. *Res:* Heterogeneous catalysis; chemisorption. *Mailing Add:* 1852 Beattie Ave Ottawa ON K1H 5R8 Can

AMENT, ALISON STONE, INVERTEBRATE ZOOLOGY. *Current Pos:* BIOL TEACHER, FALMOUTH ACAD, FALMOUTH, MASS, 87- *Personal Data:* b Danbury, Conn, Dec 7, 48; c 2. *Educ:* Conn Col, AB, 70; Univ Pa, PhD(biol), 78. *Prof Exp:* Res asst virol, Ctr Oral Health Res, Univ Pa, 70-71; investr biol, Woods Hole Oceanog Inst, 78-80; educ intern, Green Briar Sci Ctr, Sandwich, Mass, 86. *Concurrent Pos:* Sci writer, 80-81; guest investr, Woods Hole Oceanog Inst, 84-85. *Res:* Forest ecology; population genetics; evolution; physiology of adaptation; larval biology and ecology of marine invertebrates. *Mailing Add:* 23 Two Ponds Rd Falmouth MA 02540

AMENT, MARVIN EARL, PEDIATRICS, GASTROENTEROLOGY. *Current Pos:* asst prof pediat & med, 73-80, PROF PEDIAT & GASTROENTEROL, CTR HEALTH SCI, UNIV CALIF, LOS ANGELES, 80- *Personal Data:* b Dec 5, 38. *Educ:* Ill Inst Technol, BS, 59; Univ Minn, Minneapolis, MD, 63. *Prof Exp:* Resident pediat, Hosps, Univ Wash, 64-65; sr resident, Sch Med, Univ Calif, Los Angeles, 65-66; instr gastroenterol, Dept Med, Univ Wash, 70-71, actg asst prof med, 71-73. *Concurrent Pos:* NIH fel, Univ Wash, 68-70; mem attend staff, Children's Orthop Hosp, Seattle, 69-70, head gastroenterol clin, 71; mem attend staff gastroenterol, Olive View Med Ctr, 73- *Mem:* Am Fedn Clin Res; Am Gastroenterol Asn; Soc Pediat Res. *Res:* Intractable diarrhea in neonates; development of gastric secretion in infancy; peptic ulcer disease in childhood; inflammatory bowel disease in childhood; endoscopy in children; parenteral nutrition. *Mailing Add:* 10833 Leconte Ave UCLA Med Ctr MDCC 22-340 Los Angeles CA 90024-1300

AMENTA, PETER SEBASTIAN, ANATOMY. *Current Pos:* from instr to assoc prof, Hahnemann Med Col, 58-71, actg chmn dept, 73-75, dir electron micros lab, 70-80, PROF ANAT, HAHNEMANN MED COL, 71-, CHMN DEPT, 75- *Personal Data:* b Cromwell, Conn, Mar 26, 27; m 53, Rose P Russo; c Mary V & Rosemarie. *Educ:* Fairfield Univ, BS, 52; Marquette Univ, MS, 54; Univ Chicago, PhD(anat), 58. *Honors & Awards:* Cert Distinction, Am Cancer Soc; Centenial Medal, Am Asn Anatomists. *Prof Exp:* Asst biol, Fairfield Univ, 49-52; asst zool, Marquette Univ, 52-54; asst anat, Univ Chicago, 55-58. *Concurrent Pos:* Instr, Marine Biol Lab, Woods Hole Oceanog Inst, 56; consult, Franklin Inst, NSF; dir, Raymond C Truex Mus, 81-; assoc ed, J Histol & Histopath. *Mem:* Fel AAAS; Tissue Cult Asn; NY Acad Sci; Am Soc Photobiol; Am Asn Anat; Sigma Xi; Asn Anat Chairmen. *Res:* Culture; histology; cytology; hematology; nucleocytoplasmic relationships; effects of microbeams of ultraviolet and infrared light on parts of cells; nucleolar activity; edited and published several books on histology. *Mailing Add:* One RWJ Pl Med Educ Bldg New Brunswick NJ 08019

AMER, MOHAMED SAMIR, PHARMACOLOGY, BIOCHEMISTRY. *Current Pos:* PRES, AMER & CO, 83- *Personal Data:* b Tanta, Egypt, Sept 2, 35; m 58, 87, C Marguerite Smith; c Amre, Nancy, Mona & Suzanne. *Educ:* Univ Alexandria, BS, 56, dipl hosp pharm, 57; Univ Ill, MS, 60, PhD(pharmacol), 62; Columbia Univ, MS, 80. *Prof Exp:* Assoc prof pharmacol, Univ Alexandria, 62-66; sr res pharmacologist & proj coordr, Wilson Labs Div, Wilson Pharmaceut & Chem Corp, Ling-Temco-Vought, Inc, 66-69; prin investr pharmacol, Mead Johnson Res Ctr, Bristol-Myers Labs, Inc, 69, dir, Biol Res Labs, 75-80; dir biol res, Int Div, Bristol Myers Co, 80-83. *Concurrent Pos:* Chmn & CEO, Amstell Inc, 85-89. *Mem:* Am Fedn Clin Res; Acad Pharmaceut Sci; Soc Exp Biol & Med; Am Soc Pharmacol & Exp Therapeut; Am Soc Biol Chemists. *Res:* Biochemical pharmacology of the gastrointestinal tract; mechanisms of hormonal regulation; schistosomiasis. *Mailing Add:* Sam Amer & Co Inc PO Box 50840 Montecito CA 93150-0840. *Fax:* 805-684-0344

AMER, NABIL MAHMOUD, CONDENSED MATTER PHYSICS. *Current Pos:* mgr interface physics, 87-91, sr mgr mat physics, 91-93, SR MGR NANOSCOPIC PHYSICS, PHYS SCI DEPT, IBM WATSON RES CTR, 93- *Personal Data:* b Alexandria, Egypt, May 1, 42; m 67; c 2. *Educ:* Univ Alexandria, BS, 57; Univ Calif, Berkeley, PhD(biophys), 65. *Prof Exp:* Res assoc, Lawrence Berkeley Lab, Univ Calif, 66-68, staff scientist, 68-83, sr staff physicist, 83-86. *Concurrent Pos:* Lectr physics, Univ Calif, Berkeley, 70-76. *Mem:* Fel Am Phys Soc; AAAS; Sigma Xi; Am Optical Soc. *Res:* Nanoscopic and mesoscopic physics. *Mailing Add:* IBM Almaden Res Ctr 650 Harry Rd San Jose CA 95120. *Fax:* 914-945-4001; *E-Mail:* nabil@yktvmv

AMER, PAUL DAVID, HIGH PERFORMANCE NETWORKS, FORMAL DESCRIPTION TECHNIQUES. *Current Pos:* asst prof, 79-83, assoc prof, 83-91, PROF COMPUT SCI, UNIV DEL, 91- *Personal Data:* b New York, NY, Dec 25, 53; m; c 2. *Educ:* State Univ NY, Albany, BS, 74; Ohio State Univ, MS, 76, PhD(comput sci), 79. *Prof Exp:* Data Processor statist, Comput Ctr, State Univ NY, 71-74; teaching/res assoc, Ohio State Univ, 78-79. *Concurrent Pos:* Comput scientist, Nat Bur Stand, 78-85; assoc ed, Simulation, 81-90; assoc ed, Comput Networks & ISDN Systs, 83-; vis scientist, Agence de l'Informatique, Paris, France, 85-86; dir res, Lab Automatique Anal Syst, Tuolouse, France, 92-93. *Mem:* Asn Comput Mach; Inst Elec & Electronics Engrs. *Res:* Protocol specification, testing and verification; transport protocols for multimedia. *Mailing Add:* 25 Nightingale Circle Newark DE 19711. *Fax:* 302-831-8458; *E-Mail:* amer@cis.udel.edu

AMERINE, MAYNARD ANDREW, PSYCHO-PHYSICS OF SENSORY RESPONSE, ENOLOGY. *Current Pos:* From jr enologist to prof, 36-73, EMER PROF ENOL, UNIV CALIF, DAVIS, 73- *Personal Data:* b San Jose, Calif, Oct 30, 11. *Educ:* Univ Calif, BS, 32, PhD(plant physiol), 36. *Concurrent Pos:* Guggenheim fel, 54; consult, Wine Inst, San Francisco, 73-85. *Mem:* Am Chem Soc; Sigma Xi; Inst Food Technol; Am Soc Enol & Viticulture; AAAS. *Res:* Wine making, including grape varieties, fermentation, finishing and sensory evaluation of foods and wines. *Mailing Add:* PO Box 208 St Helena CA 94574-0208

AMERMAN, CARROLL R(ICHARD), AGRICULTURAL ENGINEERING. *Current Pos:* Res hydraul engr, Agr Res Serv, USDA, 58-77, res leader, 77-85, nat prog leader, Nat Prog Staff, 85-87, assoc dir, Midwest Region, 87-89, EXEC SECY, WATER GROUP, USDA, 89- *Personal Data:* b Danville, Ill, July 25, 30; m 56; c 5. *Educ:* Purdue Univ, BS, 57, MS, 58, PhD, 69. *Mem:* Am Soc Agr Engrs; Am Geophys Union; Soil Conserv Soc Am; Sigma Xi. *Res:* Hydrology of agricultural lands, both surface and subsurface. *Mailing Add:* 1348 Windmill Lane Silver Spring MD 20905

AMERO, BERNARD ALAN, PROCESS CONTROL, PROCESS SIMULATION. *Current Pos:* SCIENTIST, CHAMPION INT CORP, 76- *Personal Data:* b Malden, Mass, Feb 29, 48. *Educ:* Providence Col, BS, 70; Ohio State Univ, PhD(chem), 76. *Mem:* Am Chem Soc; Tech Asn Pulp & Paper Indust. *Mailing Add:* 15 Normandy Village Apt 2 Nanuet NY 10954-2823. *E-Mail:* bernie_amero@champint.com

AMERO, R(OBERT) C, FUEL TECHNOLOGY, IN-TRANSIT CRUDE OIL LOSS. *Current Pos:* CONSULT 82- *Personal Data:* b Rochester, NY, Oct 25, 17; m 42, Grace Kunselman; c Robert S & Sally A. *Educ:* Univ Rochester, BS, 39. *Prof Exp:* Asst, Floridin Co, 39-41, asst tech dir, 41-46, tech dir, vpres & mem bd dirs, 46-48; sr res engr, Res Ctr, Johns-Manville, 48-51; group leader, Gulf Res & Develop Co, 51-57, sec head, 57-60, fuels engr, 60-66, staff engr, 66-82. *Concurrent Pos:* Local sect chmn, Am Chem Soc, 48; chmn, Fuels Div, Am Soc Mech Engrs, 74-75. *Mem:* Am Inst Chem Engrs; Am Soc Mech Engrs; Int Gas Turbine Inst. *Res:* Adsorbents; granular desiccants; diatomaceous earth; synthetic silicates; colloidal clays; properties and combustion of petroleum fuels and coal-derived liquid fuels; in-transit crude oil loss; cogeneration unit design. *Mailing Add:* 801 DeHaven Ct Glenshaw PA 15116

AMERO, SALLY ANN, CHROMATIN STRUCTURE, GENE REGULATION. *Personal Data:* b Pittsburgh, Pa, Feb 24, 52. *Educ:* Ind Univ Pa, BS, 74; WVa Univ, PhD(molecular genetics), 79. *Prof Exp:* Res assoc, Dept Chem, Univ Va, 79-80, res assoc, Dept Biol, 80-84; res assoc, Dept Biol, Wash Univ, 84-87, res asst prof, Dept Microbiol, 87-91, asst prof, Dept Molecular, Cellular & Biochem, 91-97. *Mem:* AAAS; Am Soc Biol Chemists; Am Soc Microbiol; Genetics Soc Am; Am Soc Cell Biol; RNA Soc. *Res:* Mechanisms involved in pre-MRNA synthesis, processing and transport; chromosome structure and nuclear architecture; mechanisms of gene regulation during development; protein/nucleic acid interactions. *Mailing Add:* Loyola Univ Chicago, Stritch Sch Med Dept Molecular Cellular Biochem 2160 S First St Maywood IL 60153. *Fax:* 708-216-8523

AMERSON, GRADY MALCOLM, ENTOMOLOGY, INVERTEBRATE ZOOLOGY. *Current Pos:* Asst prof biol, 68-69, asst dean of col, 69-70, DEAN OF COL, OGLETHORPE UNIV, 70- *Personal Data:* b Gordon, Ga, Feb 20, 39; m 62; c 2. *Educ:* Berry Col, BS; Clemson Univ, MS, 66, PhD(entom), 68. *Mem:* Entom Soc Am. *Res:* Chemical sterilants. *Mailing Add:* 1350 Hampton Hall Dr NE Atlanta GA 30319

AMES, ADELBERT, III, NEUROPHYSIOLOGY, NEUROCHEMISTRY. *Current Pos:* res assoc, Harvard Med Sch, 55-69, prof physiol, Dept Surg, 69-83, Charles Anthony Pappas prof, 83-91, EMER PROF NEUROSCI, HARVARD MED SCH, 91-; NEUROPHYSIOLOGIST NEUROSURG, MASS GEN HOSP, 69- *Personal Data:* b Boston, Mass, Feb 25, 21; m 48, 75, Mary F Williams; c Mark A, Judith Q & David H. *Educ:* Harvard Univ, MD, 43. *Prof Exp:* Intern & sr resident internal med, Presby Hosp, 45-52. *Concurrent Pos:* Res fel biochem, Harvard Med Sch, 52-55; NIMH res scientist award, 68- *Mem:* Am Physiol Soc; Am Soc Neurochem; Soc Neurosci; Int Soc Neurochem. *Res:* Brain function; correlation of electrophysiology with metabolism of electrolytes, proteins and neurotransmitters in an in vitro preparation of retina; formation of cerebrospinal fluid; cerebral ischemia. *Mailing Add:* Dept Surg 414 Edwards Bldg Mass Gen Hosp Boston MA 02114

AMES, BRUCE NATHAN, CANCER RESEARCH, MOLECULAR BIOLOGY. *Current Pos:* chmn dept, 84-89, PROF BIOCHEM & MOLECULAR BIOL, UNIV CALIF, BERKELEY, 68-, DIR, NAT INST ENVIRON HEALTH SCI CTR, 79. *Personal Data:* b New York, NY, Dec 16, 28; m 60; c 2. *Educ:* Cornell Univ, BA, 50; Calif Inst Technol, PhD(biochem), 53. *Honors & Awards:* John Scott Medal, 79; Bolton L Corson Medal, 80; Wadsworth Award, 81; Mott Prize, Gen Motors Cancer Res Found, 83; Gairdner Award, Can, 83; Tyler Prize, 85; Spencer Award, 86; Roger J Williams Award, 89; Gold Medal Award, Am Chem Soc, 91; Glenn Found Award, Geront Soc Am, 92; Lovelace Award, 95; Messel Medal, Brit Soc Chem Indust, 96; Honda Prize, 96; Japan Prize, 97; Kehoe Award, Am Col Occup & Environ Med, 97. *Prof Exp:* USPHS fel, NIH, 53-54, biochemist, Nat Inst Arthritis & Metab Dis, 54-67. *Mem:* Nat Acad Sci; Am Soc Biol Chemists; Am Acad Arts & Sci; Am Chem Soc; Genetics Soc Am; Soc Toxicol; Am Soc Microbiol; Am Asn Cancer Res; Environ Mutagen Soc. *Res:* Identifying agents damaging human DNA and the consequences for aging and cancer; endogenous oxidants and defenses against them; mutagenesis and carcinogenesis. *Mailing Add:* Univ Calif 401 Barker Hall Berkeley CA 94720

AMES, DONALD PAUL, SPECTROSCOPY & SPECTROMETRY, ATOMIC & MOLECULAR PHYSICS. *Current Pos:* PRES, TREAS & OWNER/DIR, FLUOTECH INC, 91- *Personal Data:* b Brandon, Man, Sept 13, 22; m 49, Doris E Ubbelhode; c Elizabeth C (Herbert) & Barbara L (Jones). *Educ:* Univ Wis, BS, 44, PhD, 49. *Hon Degrees:* DL, Univ Mo, St Louis, 78. *Prof Exp:* AEC postdoctoral fel, 49; staff chemist, Los Alamos Sci Lab, 50-52; asst prof, Univ Ky, 52-54; res chemist, E I du Pont de Nemours & Co, 54-56; res chemist, Monsanto Chem Co, 56-59, scientist & fel, 59-61; sr scientist, McDonnell Aircraft Corp, 61-68, dep dir res, McDonnell Res Labs, 68-70, dir res, 70-76, staff vpres, 76-86, gen mgr, staff vpres, MDC distinguished fel, McDonnell Douglas Res Labs, 86-89. *Concurrent Pos:* Adv, Air Force Off Sci Res, 71-76; mem, Am Inst Physics Comt on Corp Assocs, 77-80, 82-85; adv, Univ Mo Res Reactor, 82-89, St Louis Inst molecular electronics, 85- *Mem:* Am Chem Soc; Am Phys Soc; Sigma Xi; Soc Eng Sci; Combustion Inst. *Res:* Radiochemistry; exchange kinetics; diffusion; complex ions; microwave masers; electron and nuclear resonance spectroscopy; nuclear chemistry; actinide elements chemistry; beta and gamma ray spectroscopy; chemical and molecular lasers; polymers; fluorescence; positron annihilation spectroscopy of polymers; fluorescence spectroscopy of polymers; electron paramagnetic resonance spectrometry. *Mailing Add:* 914 Black Twig Lane Kirkwood MO 63122-2212. *Fax:* 314-984-8045

AMES, EDWARD R, MEDICAL EDUCATION, SCIENCE EDUCATION SPECIALTIES. *Current Pos:* dir continuing educ, 73-80, staff consult continuing educ, 80-87, DIR, DIV SCI ACTIV & VET COL ACCREDITATION, AM VET MED ASN, 87- *Personal Data:* b Denver, Colo, Apr 10, 35; m 57, Janice Painter; c Denise, Marjorie & Susan. *Educ:* Colo State Univ, BS, 57, DVM, 59, PhD(vet parasitol), 68. *Prof Exp:* Field sta mgr, eval vet therapeut, Merck Sharp & Dohme Res Labs, 60-68; from asst prof to assoc prof vet parasitol, Col Vet Med, Univ Mo-Columbia, 68-73. *Mem:* Am Vet Med Asn; Am Soc Vet Parasitol; Asn Am Vet Med Cols; Asn Teachers Vet Pub Health & Prev Med. *Res:* Human motivity and applied principles of adult learning; self-assessment evaluation; definition and measurement of competencies for veterinarians; outcomes assessment for veterinary education. *Mailing Add:* 600 N Taylor Oak Park IL 60302

AMES, GIOVANNA FERRO-LUZZI, BACTERIAL GENETICS, MEMBRANE FUNCTION. *Current Pos:* res biochemist, 68-78, adj prof, 78-80, PROF BIOCHEM, UNIV CALIF, BERKELEY, 80- *Personal Data:* b Rome, Italy, Jan 20, 36; US citizen; m 60; c 2. *Educ:* Univ Rome, Italy, DrBiol, 58. *Honors & Awards:* Agnes Fay Morgan Award, 75. *Prof Exp:* Res biochemist, NIH, 62-68. *Concurrent Pos:* Prin investr, NIH grant, 68- & NSF grant, 83-88; ed, Microbiological Reviews, 79-81, J Sci Molecular Structure, 79-88. *Mem:* Am Soc Biol Chemists; Am Soc Microbiol; Genetics Soc Am. *Res:* Studies on active transport of amino acids in bacteria; studies on the structure and function of bacterial membrane; studies on cellular regulation; studies on bacterial chromosome structure. *Mailing Add:* Dept Molecular & Cell Biol Univ Calif Berkeley CA 94720-3202. *Fax:* 510-643-7935

AMES, IRA HAROLD, CELL BIOLOGY. *Current Pos:* from asst prof to assoc prof anat, 68-89, PROF ANAT, HEALTH SCI CTR, STATE UNIV NY, SYRACUSE, 89- *Personal Data:* b Brooklyn, NY, Apr 27, 37; m 58; c 2. *Educ:* Brooklyn Col, AB, 59; NY Univ, MS, 62, PhD(biol), 66. *Prof Exp:* Instr biol, Brooklyn Col, 60-63, lectr, 63-64. *Concurrent Pos:* Fel, Brookhaven Nat Lab, 66-68; NSF grant, 72-76. *Mem:* AAAS; Am Soc Cell Biol; Am Asn Anat; Sigma Xi. *Res:* Role of natural killer and lymphokine-activated killer cells in tumor surveillance; experimental oncology. *Mailing Add:* Dept Anat & Cell Biol Health Sci Ctr State Univ NY 776 Irving Ave Syracuse NY 13210-1605. *Fax:* 315-464-8535; *E-Mail:* amesi@vax.cs.hscsyr.edu

AMES, IRVING, PHYSICS. *Current Pos:* ASSOC ED, IBM JOUR RES DEVELOP, 83- *Personal Data:* b New York, NY, June 15, 29; m 52; c 2. *Educ:* Syracuse Univ, BS, 51; Cornell Univ, PhD(physics), 55. *Honors & Awards:* Cledo Brunetti Award, Inst Elec & Electronics Engrs, 88. *Prof Exp:* Teaching & res asst physcis, Brown Univ, 51 & Cornell Univ, 51-55; res staff mem, IBM Res Div, T J Watson Res Ctr, 55-83. *Mem:* Am Phys Soc; Inst Elec & Electronics Engrs. *Res:* Surface phenomena; superconducting thin film devices and circuits; electromigration in aluminium thin films. *Mailing Add:* 500 High Point Dr Apt 401 Hartsdale NY 10530

AMES, JOHN WENDELL, COMMUNICATION, RADAR. *Current Pos:* res engr, 70-82, STAFF SCIENTIST, STANFORD RES INST, 82- *Personal Data:* b Lincoln, Nebr, Aug 13, 36; m 57; c 2. *Educ:* Stanford Univ, BS, 59, MS, 60, PhD(elec eng), 64. *Prof Exp:* Res engr, Granger Assocs, 64-70. *Mem:* Inst Elec & Electronics Engrs; Am Geophys Union; Armed Forces Commun & Electronics Asn. *Res:* High frequency ionospheric radio propagation; radio fading and multipath studies; ionospheric radar; radio communication system design. *Mailing Add:* 320 Canyon Dr Portola Valley CA 94028-7811

AMES, LAWRENCE LOWELL, ELECTRO-OPTICS, SENSORS. *Current Pos:* STAFF ENGR, LOCKHEED MARTIN, 83- *Personal Data:* b Washington, DC, Sept 10, 51; m 77; c 3. *Educ:* Univ Ariz, BS, 72; Univ Wis, MS, 74, PhD(physics), 79. *Prof Exp:* Sr physicist, Measurex, 79-80 & Envirotech Measurement Systs, 80-81; sr physicist, Tracor X-Ray, 81-83. *Mem:* Am Phys Soc; Sigma Xi. *Res:* Electro-optical sensor design; data analysis; computer algorithms. *Mailing Add:* Dept H1-52 Bldg 201 Lockheed Martin 3251 Hanover St Palo Alto CA 94304. *E-Mail:* lawrence.ames@lmco.com

AMES, LLOYD L, MINERALOGY, INORGANIC CHEMISTRY. *Current Pos:* RETIRED. *Personal Data:* b Norwich, Conn, Aug 23, 27; m 53; c Marc, Sue, Jan & Vanna. *Educ:* Univ NMex, BA, 52; Univ Utah, MS, 55, PhD(mineral), 56. *Prof Exp:* Res fel, Univ Utah, 56-57; sr scientist, Gen Elec Co, 57-65; sr res scientist, Ecol Sci Dept, Pac NW Labs, Battelle Mem Inst, 65-81, staff scientist, Water & Waste Mgt Dept, 81-92. *Mem:* Mineral Soc Am. *Res:* Mineralogy and geochemistry applied to removal of radioisotopes from radioactive wastes; inorganic ion exchangers; migration of radionuclides in the natural environment. *Mailing Add:* 43703 E Austin Ct West Richland WA 99353

AMES, LYNFORD LENHART, PHYSICAL CHEMISTRY. *Current Pos:* from asst prof to assoc prof, NMex State Univ, 66-78, from asst head to head dept, 76-87, assoc dean, 88-92, interim dean grad sch, 92-93, PROF CHEM, NMEX STATE UNIV, 78-, ASSOC DEAN, 93- *Personal Data:* b Fresno, Ohio, May 20, 38; m 63, Judith Kilbourne; c Graham G & Constance E. *Educ:* Muskingum Col, BS, 60; Ohio State Univ, PhD(phys chem), 65. *Prof Exp:* NSF fel, 65-66. *Mem:* AAAS; Am Chem Soc; Sigma Xi. *Res:* High temperature chemistry; matrix isolation; infrared spectroscopy; mass spectroscopy; electronic band spectroscopy. *Mailing Add:* Dept Chem NMex State Univ Box 3C Las Cruces NM 88001. *Fax:* 505-646-6166

AMES, MATTHEW MARTIN, DRUG METABOLISM, CANCER CHEMOTHERAPY. *Current Pos:* instr, 78-79, asst prof, 79-81, ASSOC PROF PHARMACOL, MAYO MED & GRADSCH, 81-, CHMN, DIV DEVELOP ONCOL RES, DEPT ONCOL, 87- *Personal Data:* b Richland, Wash, Dec 17, 47; m 77. *Educ:* Whitman Col, BA, 70; Univ Calif, San Francisco, PhD(pharmaceut chem), 76. *Prof Exp:* Res asst, Pomona Col, 70-71; res fel, NIH, 75-77. *Concurrent Pos:* Res assoc pharmacol, Div Develop Oncol Res, Dept Oncol, Mayo Clin, 77-78, assoc consult, 78-80, consult, 80- *Mem:* Am Chem Soc; Am Asn Cancer Res; Am Soc Pharmacol & Exp Therapeut; Am Soc Mass Spectrometry; Am Soc Clin Pharmacol Therapeut. *Res:* Disposition and metabolism of anticancer agents, particularly the role of metabolism in the antitumor activity and/or toxicity; clinical pharmacokinetics of anticancer agents. *Mailing Add:* Dept Oncol Mayo Clin 200 1st St SW Rm 132-C Guggenheim Bldg Rochester MN 55905

AMES, PETER L, ENVIRONMENTAL SCIENCES. *Current Pos:* head, Terrestrial Biol Sect, 87-90, HEAD, ENVIRON SCI SECT, HARZA ENG CO, 73-, ASST HEAD, ENVIRON SCI DEPT, 91- *Personal Data:* b St Paul, Minn, May 2, 31; m 58; c 2. *Educ:* Harvard Col, BA, 58; Yale Univ, MS, 62, PhD(biol), 65. *Prof Exp:* Res asst, Smith, Kline & French Labs, 58-59; asst prof zool & asst cur birds, Mus Vert Zool, Univ Calif, Berkeley, 65-68; assoc ed life sci, Encycl Britannica, 68-72. *Concurrent Pos:* Res assoc, Field Mus of Natural Hist, Chicago, 87- *Mem:* Am Ornith Union; Brit Ornith Union; Cooper Ornith Soc; Wilson Ornith Soc. *Res:* Avian anatomy; ecology of raptorial birds; environmental management. *Mailing Add:* Harza Eng Co 233 S Wacker Dr Sears Tower Chicago IL 60606-4288

AMES, ROGER LYMAN, GEOCHEMISTRY. *Current Pos:* RETIRED. *Personal Data:* b Northampton, Mass, Nov 6, 33; m 57, Suzanne Manwell; c 4. *Educ:* Williams Col, BA, 55; Yale Univ, MS, 59, PhD(econ geol), 63. *Prof Exp:* Sr res assoc, Amoco Prod Co Res Ctr, 62- *Mem:* AAAS; Geol Soc Am; Am Geochem Soc; Am Asn Petrol Geologists. *Res:* Application of stable isotope studies to exploration for petroleum and metallic deposits; geochemistry in petroleum exploration and exploitation. *Mailing Add:* 3726 S Darlington Tulsa OK 74135. *Fax:* 918-660-4163

AMES, STANLEY RICHARD, COMPUTER SCIENCE, NUTRITIONAL BIOCHEMISTRY. *Current Pos:* NUTRIT CONSULT, 83- *Personal Data:* b Madison, Wis, Dec 18, 18; m 43, Edwina Powers; c Edwina M, Stanley R Jr, Suzanne C & Judith A. *Educ:* Univ Mont, BA, 40; Columbia Univ, AM, 42, PhD(chem), 44. *Prof Exp:* Asst chem, Univ Mont, 37-40; asst, Columbia Univ, 40-41, statutory asst, 41-42, asst, 42-43; Rockefeller fel biochem, Univ Wis, 43-46; sr res chemist, Distillation Prod Industs, Eastman Kodak Co, 46-53, res assoc, 53-63, head biochem res dept, 63-65, dir, Biochem Res Labs, 65-69, sr res assoc, Tenn Eastman Res Labs, 69- 80, head, Biochem Res Labs, Health & Nutrit Res Div, Eastman Chem Div, 69-82, res fel, 80-82, consult, Kodak Res Labs, 82-83. *Concurrent Pos:* Mem adv bd, Off Biochem Nomenclature, Nat Acad Sci-Nat Res Coun, 65-68; mem comt nomenclature, Int Union Nutrit Sci, 67-86, actg chmn, 69, 75, chmn, 76-86, mem comn I, nomenclature, procedures & stand, 76-86; actg chmn adv comt, NIH Guide to Nutrit Terminol, 68-69; mem, Interdiv Comt on Nomenclature & Symbols, Int Union Pure & Appl Chem, 76-86. *Mem:* Fel AAAS; Am Chem Soc; Am Soc Biol Chem; fel Am Inst Nutrit; Nutrit Soc. *Res:* Vitamins A and E; biochemistry of monoglycerides; acetylated monoglycerides; bioassay; nutrition; lipid metabolism; enzymes; organic and biological oxidations; feed preservatives; ruminant nutrition. *Mailing Add:* 61 Biltmore Dr Rochester NY 14617

AMEY, RALPH LEONARD, PHYSICAL CHEMISTRY. *Current Pos:* asst prof, 65-74, ASSOC PROF CHEM, OCCIDENTAL COL, 74- *Personal Data:* b Huntington Park, Calif, June 5, 37; m 64. *Educ:* Pomona Col, AB, 59; Brown Univ, PhD(phys chem), 64. *Prof Exp:* Instr chem, Barrington Col, 62-63; mat res & develop specialist missile & space systs div, Douglas Aircraft Co, Inc, 63-65. *Mem:* Am Chem Soc. *Res:* Properties of the condensed state; intermolecular forces and local liquid structure; dielectric behavior of materials; thermal analysis of solids and solutions. *Mailing Add:* Dept of Chem Occidental Col 1600 Campus Rd Los Angeles CA 90041-3397

AMEY, WILLIAM G(REENVILLE), ELECTRICAL ENGINEERING, MEASUREMENT TECHNOLOGY. *Current Pos:* RETIRED. *Personal Data:* b Baltimore, Md, Feb 24, 18; m 41, 65, Julie Valkusky; c Kathryn (Graebner), Michael B & Margaret M (Thatcher). *Educ:* Johns Hopkins Univ, BEE, 38, DEE, 47. *Prof Exp:* Instr math, Johns Hopkins Univ, 39-41, res assoc elec eng, 46-47; instr elec eng, US Naval Acad, 41-43; asst sect head measure & components, Naval Res Lab, Washington, DC, 43-46; engr, Res Div, Leeds & Northrup Co, 47-49, supvry res engr, 49-54, asst sect head elec res, 54-55, nucleonics develop, 55-56, sect head elec res, 56-57, mgr res div, 57-68, assoc dir corp res, Res & Develop Ctr, 68, assoc dir res planning, Corp Res Dept, 68-72; asst chief control systs eng, Bechtel Assoc Prof Corp, Control Systs Eng Sect, Ann Arbor, Mich, 72-74, chief, 74-83. *Concurrent Pos:* Consult. *Mem:* Fel Instrument Soc Am; fel Inst Elec & Electronics Engrs; Sigma Xi. *Res:* Electrical and electronic measurements associated with precision potentiometers and bridges; spectroscopy; electro-chemistry and control of complex systems. *Mailing Add:* 2036 SW Stratford Way Palm City FL 34990

AMICK, JAMES ALBERT, SOLID STATE ELECTRONICS, SEMICONDUCTORS & SOLAR CELLS. *Current Pos:* RETIRED. *Personal Data:* b Lawrence, Mass, Feb 18, 28; m 61, Nancy J Scott; c D'Maris A. *Educ:* Princeton Univ, AB, 49, AM, 51, PhD(phys chem), 52. *Honors & Awards:* David Sarnoff Outstanding Achievement Award, 65. *Prof Exp:* Res assoc electron micros, Princeton Univ, 52-53; res engr, Radio Corp Am Labs, 53-56, res engr, Zurich Labs, 56-57, res phys chemist, 57-68, head process res, RCA Labs, 68-71, mgr mat & processes, Solid State Div, RCA, 71-76; res assoc, Exxon Res & Eng, 76-79, sr res assoc, 79-85, group head, coatings & composites, 85-87; sect head, Cell Processing Res & Develop, Mobil Solar Energy Corp, 87-93. *Concurrent Pos:* Ethyl Corp Fel, 51-52; secy, Dielectrics & Insulation Div, Am Chem Soc, 80-81, vchmn, 81-82, chmn, 82-83, 83-84. *Mem:* Electrochem Soc (secy, 85-90, vpres, 91-); Am Chem Soc (actg secy-treas, 53); fel Am Inst Chemists; Sigma Xi; AAAS. *Res:* Infrared absorption intensities; electron microscopy of aerosols; mass spectrometry of hydrocarbons; x-ray diffraction; electrophotographic processes; surface chemistry of semiconductors; epitaxial growth of semiconductors; processes for electronic components; processing and modeling silicon for solar cells; thin film strain gauges. *Mailing Add:* 76 Leabrook Lane Princeton NJ 08540-3659

AMICK, JAMES L(EWIS), AERODYNAMICS, VEHICLE DESIGN. *Current Pos:* CONSULT, 88- *Personal Data:* b Detroit, Mich, May 18, 25; m 47, Jean E Tracy; c James R, Richard N, Marilyn J (Ackeson), Douglas J & Ronald N. *Educ:* Univ Mich, BSE, 45; Univ Va, MA, 52. *Prof Exp:* Aeronaut res scientist, Langley Aeronaut Labs, Nat Adv Comt Aeronaut, 46-51; res assoc, Univ Mich, 51-57, assoc res engr, 57-59, res engr, 59-70, consult aerodyn, 70-; prod develop engr, Photon Sources, Inc, 82-86. *Concurrent Pos:* Mem, Bumblebee Aerodyn Panel, 60-63 & rocket nozzles & jet effects panel, Adv Comt Aeroballistics, Bur Weapons, 60-69; consult, Ammann & Whitney, Inc, 66-67, US Army Missile Command, Redstone Arsenal, 66-69, US Naval Weapons Ctr, 69, Camcheck, Inc, 65-82 & KMS Fusion, Inc, 78. *Mem:* Int Human-Powered Vehicle Asn. *Res:* Interaction of side jets with supersonic streams; supersonic flow past wings and bodies; flow thru nozzles; sailboat performance; wind-tunnel testing; windmobiles; fast-flow lasers; automotive cam design and evaluation. *Mailing Add:* 1464 Cedar Bend Dr Ann Arbor MI 48105-2305

AMIDON, ROGER WELTON, CHEMISTRY. *Current Pos:* RETIRED. *Personal Data:* b Rockford, Ill, Nov 29, 14; m 38, Frances McCrary; c 3. *Educ:* Univ Minn, BChem, 36, MS, 40, PhD(org chem), 49. *Prof Exp:* Petrol chemist, Midcontinent Petrol corp, 36-39; org res chemist, Dow Chem Co, 40-41; chemist, Gen Labs, US Rubber Co, 49-54 & Naugatuck Chem Div, 54-68; sr info scientist, Chem Div, Uniroyal Inc, 68-79. *Mem:* Am Chem Soc; Sigma Xi. *Res:* New rubbers and elastomers; plastics and resins; rubber chemicals; polyester resins; special organic chemicals. *Mailing Add:* 227 Ponce de Leon Spartanburg SC 29302-2765

AMIDON, THOMAS EDWARD, SILVICULTURE, QUANTITATIVE GENETICS. *Current Pos:* res assoc, 77-79, sr res assoc, 79-80, res analyst Forest Sci, 80-94, FAC MGR, INT PAPER CO, 94- *Personal Data:* b Seneca Falls, NY, Sept 30, 46; m 68; c 2. *Educ:* State Univ NY, BS, 68, MS, 72, PhD(silvicult), 75. *Prof Exp:* Res asst paper sci, Empire State Paper Res Inst, 75-77. *Mem:* Tech Asn Pulp & Paper Indust; Soc Am Foresters. *Res:* Silviculture; genetics; asexual propagation; plant growth regulation; physiology; regeneration; computer modeling of biological processes; research evaluation. *Mailing Add:* CRC Long Meadow Rd Tuxedo NY 10987

AMIN, OMAR M, PARASITOLOGY. *Current Pos:* DIR, INST PARASITIC DIS, TEMPE, ARIZ, 93-; ADJ PROF PARASITOL, ARIZ STATE UNIV, TEMPE, 94- *Personal Data:* b Minya El Kamh, Egypt, Jan 23, 39; nat US; c Sharif & Karim. *Educ:* Cairo Univ, Egypt, BSc, 59, MSc, 63; Ariz State Univ, PhD(zool-parasitol), 68. *Prof Exp:* Res asst med zool, US Naval Med Res Unit, Cairo, 60-64; assoc agr & zool, Ariz State Univ, 66-67; res assoc & instr biol, Old Dom Univ, 67-69; vis fel virol, Ctr Dis Control, Ga, 69-70; from asst prof to prof biol, Univ Wis-Parkside, 71-92; dir, Inst Parasitic Dis, Racine, Wis, 92-93. *Concurrent Pos:* Grantee, US Army, 68, Sigma Xi, 69, Univ Wis, 72, Am Motors Qual Prog, 76 & NIH, 76, 77 & 84; Fulbright scholar, 86-87; foreign sr exchange scholar, 89; biol fac, Northern Ariz Univ, Flagstaff & Maricopa Co Col, Phoenix & Frank L Wright Found, Scottsdale. *Mem:* Entom Soc Am; Am Soc Parasitologists; Acarology Soc Am; Am Micros Soc; Brit Soc Parasitol. *Res:* Helminth parasites of vertebrates, particularly Acanthocephalans of fishes; bio ecology and host relationships of arthropod ectoparasites, of vertebrates; taxonomy, ecology and host-parasite relationships of acanthocephalans, trematodes, cestodes, nematodes, leeches and crustacea; human clinical parasitology. *Mailing Add:* Dir Inst Parasitic Dis PO Box 28372 Tempe AZ 85285-8372. *Fax:* 602-955-4102

AMIN, SANJAY INDUBHAI, CHEMICAL ENGINEERING, INDUSTRIAL CHEMISTRY. *Current Pos:* from res scientist to sr res scientist, Chem Process Res Develop, Upjohn Co, 75-83, dir, Specialty Chem Prod, 75-89, dir chem prod, 90-96, GROUP MGR, FINE CHEM PROD, UPJOHN CO, 75-; VPRES OPERS, PHARMACIA & UPJOHN INC, 96- *Personal Data:* b Baroda, India, Mar 4, 48; m 72, Kalpana; c Taner & Weerja. *Educ:* Univ Baroda, BE, 70; Mass Inst Technol, SM, 71, ScD(chem eng), 75. *Honors & Awards:* Cert of Merit, All India Stud Asn, 70. *Prof Exp:* Asst dir chem eng, Mass Inst Technol, Prac Sch, Oak Ridge Nat Lab, 71-72, teaching asst, 72-73, res asst, 73-75. *Mem:* Am Inst Chem Engrs; Sigma Xi; Am Chem Soc; Int Soc Pharmaceut Engrs; Pharmaceut Mfrs Asn. *Res:* Applied chemical engineering; industrial production of fine and speciality chemicals; industrial production of bulk pharmaceutical chemicals and related chemicals. *Mailing Add:* Pharm UpJohn Inc Upjohn Co 1300-87-2 Kalamazoo MI 49008

AMINOFF, DAVID, BIOCHEMISTRY, IMMUNOGENETICS. *Current Pos:* res assoc, Rackham Arthritis Res Unit, 60-62, res assoc, Simpson Mem Inst, 62-66, asst prof, 66-70, assoc prof, 70-80, PROF BIOL CHEM, DEPT INTERNAL MED, SIMPSON MEM INST, UNIV MICH, ANN ARBOR, 80- *Personal Data:* b Kokand, Russia, Jan 16, 26; US citizen; m 56; c 3. *Educ:* Univ London, BSc, 45, PhD(biochem), 49, DSc(biochem), 74. *Prof Exp:* Res asst biochem, Lister Inst Prev Med, 49-50; res assoc, Israeli Inst Biol Res, 50-55, 56-57; res assoc, Pub Health Res Inst, NY, 57-60. *Concurrent Pos:* Consult, Marcus Inst, Israeli Red Cross, 53-57; exchange scientist, Col Physicians & Surgeons, Columbia Univ, 55-56. *Mem:* Am Fedn Clin Res; Am Soc Hemat; Am Chem Soc; Am Soc Biol Chem; Brit Biochem Soc. *Res:* Immunochemistry and biosynthesis of the blood group substances; glycoprotein chemistry and metabolism; erythrocyte viability in circulation and role of glycoconjugates in health and disease. *Mailing Add:* Biochem 5416 Med Sci I Univ Mich Med Sch 1301 Catherine Rd Ann Arbor MI 48109-0606

AMIRAIAN, KENNETH, BIOCHEMISTRY, IMMUNOCHEMISTRY. *Current Pos:* ASST DIR LAB DIAG IMMUNOL, NY STATE DEPT HEALTH, 85- *Personal Data:* b Richmond Hill, NY, Sept 29, 26; m 51; c 2. *Educ:* Brooklyn Col, BS, 49; Columbia Univ, MA, 50, PhD, 59. *Prof Exp:* Asst biochem, Sloan-Kettering Inst, 50-53; asst, Columbia Univ, 53-55; asst immunochem, Rutgers Univ, 55-57; from res scientist to assoc res scientist biochem, NY State Dept Health, 57-85; from lectr to asst prof, 60-84, adj prof microbiol, Albany Med Col, 84- *Mem:* AAAS; Am Asn Immunol; Am Soc Microbiol. *Res:* Immunochemistry research on immune hemolytic reaction and gamma globulins; human immunodeficiency virus; correlation of western blot densitometric analysis with clinical status. *Mailing Add:* Div Labs & Res NY State Dept Health Empire State Plaza PO Box 509 Albany NY 12201

AMIRKHANIAN, JOHN DAVID, NEONATAL LUNG RESEARCH, LUNG SURFACTANT DEVELOPMENT. *Current Pos:* RES SCIENTIST, DIV NEONATOLOGY, UNIV CALIF, DAVIS, 93- *Personal Data:* b Julfa-Esfahan, Iran, Nov 10, 27; US citizen; m 57, Roma; c Varoujan, Areg & Aspet. *Educ:* Univ Tehran, BSc, 73; Univ London, PhD(fungal genetics), 77. *Prof Exp:* WHO sr res fel, Mainz Univ, WGer, 76; asst prof, Univ Tehran, Iran, 77-79; sr res assoc fac, Dept Pediat, King-Drew Med Ctr, Sch Med, Univ Calif, Los Angeles, 81-92. *Concurrent Pos:* Vis prof molecular biol & classic genetics, Univ Southern Calif, 79-81; res fel, Mus Natural Hist, Calif, 79- *Mem:* Genetic Asn Am; AAAS; NY Acad Sci; fel Royal Micros Soc; fel Oxygen Soc. *Res:* Neonatal lung research: synthetic and semi-synthetic lung surfactant replacement models; mechanisms of lung surfactant inactivation by reactive oxygen species or toxins; antioxidant defence mechanisms aging; fungal genetics: the use of diploid strains of Coprinus for screening mutagens; mosquito genetics: genetic manipulation of insect pests for eradication purposes. *Mailing Add:* 3310 Sparr Blvd Glendale CA 91208. *E-Mail:* jamirkhani@aol.com

AMIRKHANIAN, VAROUJ DAVID, OPTICA & OPTO-MECHANICAL ENGINEERING, HARDWARE SYSTEMS ENGINEERING. *Current Pos:* SR RES & DEVELOP OPTICAL SYSTS ENGR, BECKMAN INST/BOC DIV, 92- *Personal Data:* b Teheran, Iran, Mar 28, 58; US citizen; m, Ielen Sarkisian. *Educ:* Houghton Col, BA, 81; ITT Tech Inst, BS, 88. *Prof Exp:* Mus guide, Griffith Observ, 81-83; laser engr, Hi-Tech Med Lasers, 83-86; staff res & develop optical engr, Baxter-Edwards Div, 86-89; sr fiber optics laser engr, Pfizer, 89-91, Premier Laser Systs, 91-92. *Concurrent Pos:* Consult optical fiber optics, Trimedyne Laser Inc, 90, Baxter-Edwards Div, 91 & Camino Labs, 93. *Mem:* Optical Soc Am; Soc Photo-Optical Engrs. *Res:* Design of optical, fiber optical, laser systems for medical therapeutic, bio-industrial and diagnostic applications. *Mailing Add:* 735 W California No 103 Glendale CA 91203. *Fax:* 714-773-8426

AMIR-MOEZ, ALI R, MATHEMATICS. *Current Pos:* RETIRED. *Personal Data:* b Tehran, Iran, Apr 7, 19; US citizen. *Educ:* Univ Tehran, BA, 43; Univ Calif, Los Angeles, MA, 51, PhD(math), 55. *Prof Exp:* Instr math, Tehran Technol Col, 43-47; asst prof, Univ Idaho, 55-56, Queens Col, NY, 56-60, Purdue Univ, 60- 61 & Univ Fla, 61-63; res & writing, 63-64; prof math, Clarkson Col Technol, 64-65; prof math, Tex Tech Univ, 65-88. *Mem:* Am Math Soc; Math Asn Am; Sigma Xi; NY Acad Sci. *Res:* Singular values of linear transformations and matrices. *Mailing Add:* Tex Tech Univ Lubbock TX 79409-1042

AMIRO, BRIAN DOUGLAS, MICROMETEOROLOGY, RADIOECOLOGY. *Current Pos:* RES SCIENTIST, ATOMIC ENERGY CAN LTD, 83- *Personal Data:* b Toronto, Ont, Apr 6, 55; m 92, Leslie Olchowy. *Educ:* Laurentian Univ, BSc (Hons), 77, MSc, 79; Univ Guelph, PhD(land resource sci), 83. *Concurrent Pos:* Asst prof agr meteorol & analysis turbulence data, Univ Hawaii, 91; adj fac, Univ Man, 93- *Mem:* Can Soc Agrometeorol (pres, 93-94); Am Geophys Union; Can Geophys Union; Can Meteorol & Oceanog Soc. *Res:* Environmental assessment of contaminants; experimental studies of mass and energy transport between surfaces and the atmosphere; studies of contaminant transport through the biosphere; radiation ecology. *Mailing Add:* AECL Whiteshell Labs Pinawa MB R0E 1L0 Can. *Fax:* 204-753-2455; *E-Mail:* amirob@wl.aecl.ca

AMIRTHARAJAH, APPIAH, WATER TREATMENT PROCESSES, HYDRAULICS & DESIGN. *Current Pos:* PROF ENVIRON ENG, GA INST TECHNOL, 86- *Personal Data:* b Colombo, Sri Lanka, Apr 4, 40; US citizen; m 68; c 2. *Educ:* Univ Ceylon, Colombo, BSc, 63; Iowa State Univ, Ames, MS, 70; PhD(environ eng), 71. *Honors & Awards:* Rudolph Hering Medal, Am Soc Civil Engrs, 85; G W Fuller Award, Am Water Works Asn, 86. *Prof Exp:* Engr, Dept Water Supply & Drainage, Sri Lanka, 63-67, sr engr, 67-68, chief training officer, 73-74; chief engr, Nat Water Supply & Drainage Bd, Sri Lanka, 75-76; from assoc prof to prof environ engr, Mont State Univ, 77-86, coordr, Environ Eng Progs, 79-86. *Concurrent Pos:* Vis prof, Univs Sri Lanka, Peradeniya & Katubedde, 72-76, Johns Hopkins Univ, 84-85 & Univ Sao Paulo, Brazil, 89; prin investr, US Environ Protection Agency, NSF, Am Water Works Res Found, 80-; mem, Coagulation Comn & Student Act Comn, Am Water Works Asn, 80- & Res Adv Coun, 88-91; environ sci & eng fel, AAAS, Environ Protection Agency, 85; ed, J Environ Eng, 86-88; res fel, Univ Col, London, 89. *Mem:* Am Soc Civil Engrs; Am Water Works Asn; Asn Environ Eng Professors; Int Asn Water Pollution Res & Control; Am Filtration Soc. *Res:* Environmental engineering with special reference to the physiochemical processes of coagulation, mixing, flocculation, filtration and backwash of filters; drinking water regulations; design of water treatment plants. *Mailing Add:* Sch Civil Eng Ga Inst Technol Atlanta GA 30332-0001

AMIS, ERIC J, LIGHT SCATTERING, POLYMER VISCOELASTICITY. *Current Pos:* asst prof, 84-90, ASSOC PROF, DEPT CHEM, UNIV SOUTHERN CALIF, 90- *Personal Data:* b Topeka, Kans, March 2, 54; m 76, Marilyn Johnston; c Jennifer. *Educ:* Willamette Univ, Salem Ore, BS, 76; Univ Wis-Madison, PhD(chem), 81. *Prof Exp:* Nat Res Coun res assoc, Nat Bur Standards, 81-82; res assoc, Dept Chem, Univ Wis, 82-84. *Concurrent Pos:* Ed, J Polymer Sci, Polymer Phys, 92- *Mem:* Am Chem Soc; fel Am Phys Soc; AAAS; Sigma Xi; Soc Rheology; Mat Res Soc. *Res:* Physical chemistry of polymer solutions by quasielastic and elastic light scattering and neutron scattering; synthetic as well as biological polymers; light scattering characterization of biomembranes; dilute solution dynamic viscoelasticity; forced Rayleigh scattering. *Mailing Add:* 224 B210 Polymers Div NIST Rte 270 & Quince Orchard Rd Gaithersburg MD 20899. *Fax:* 213-740-4118; *E-Mail:* amis@ramoth.usc.edu

AMITAY, NOACH, PERSONAL COMMUNICATIONS SYSTEMS, ELECTROMAGNETICS. *Current Pos:* mem tech staff, 62-84, CONSULT, LUCENT TECHNOL, 84- *Personal Data:* b Tel-Aviv, Israel, Apr 30, 30; US citizen; m 60; c 4. *Educ:* Technion, Israel Inst Technol, BSc, 53, dipl Ing, 54; Carnegie Inst Technol, MSc, 58, PhD(elec eng), 60. *Prof Exp:* Head, Elec Measurement Dept, Signal Corps, Defense Army Israel, 54-56; asst prof elec eng, Carnegie Inst Technol, 60-62. *Concurrent Pos:* Consult, Electronic Inst Magnetics Inc, 57-58 & 60-61 & New Prod Lab, Westinghouse Elec Corp, 60-62. *Mem:* Fel Inst Elec & Electronics Engrs; Int Union Radio Sci. *Res:* Microcellular mobile and personal radio and microwave communications; urban propagation measurements and modeling; system concepts and architecture; single mode optical fiber up-tapers and hardware; fiber based local communications systems and networks; electromagnetic theory; numerical methods; antenna and phased arrays design; computer-aided design; author of 50 publications and co-author of one book; holder of 10 patents. *Mailing Add:* 17 High Point Rd Holmdel NJ 07733

AMITH, AVRAHAM, MATERIALS SCIENCE, OPTOELECTRONICS. *Current Pos:* PRES, AMTECH ENG CORP, MD, 95- *Personal Data:* b Przemysl, Poland, Mar 16, 29; US citizen; m 52, Marcia Rabinowitz; c Jonathan D & Adina N. *Educ:* Univ Mich, BS, 51; Harvard Univ, MA, 53, PhD(chem phys), 61. *Honors & Awards:* RCA Outstand Achievement Award, 66. *Prof Exp:* Mem tech staff, RCA Labs, 56-70; prof physics, City Univ New York, 71-72; sr engr & leader, RCA Thermoelec Opers, 72-74; sr scientist & prog mgr, Inst Energy Conversion, Univ Del, 74-76; vis lectr & sr res scientist, Princeton Univ, 76-78; mgr mat & devices lab III-V, ITT-Electro-Optical Div, Va, 78-82, mgr, Opto-electronics Dept, 82-87, fel, 87-89, sr sci fel & actg chief scientist, 89-94. *Concurrent Pos:* Adj prof, City Univ New York, 72-74; adj prof, Va Polytech Inst & State Univ, 91-; assoc ed, Nanostructured Mat. *Mem:* Am Phys Soc; Inst Elec & Electronics Engrs; Mat Res Soc; Int Soc Optical Eng. *Res:* Molecular quantum mechanics; photoeffects, lifetimes and transport in semiconductors; electrical properties of thin films and surface layers; thermoelectric properties of semiconductors; galvanomagnetic and thermomagnetic properties of semiconductors and semimetals; magnetism and thin films; surface properties of gallium arsenide; LED's and junction lasers; photodetectors; photoemission; image intensifiers; optical properties of galium arsenide; ferroelectricity. *Mailing Add:* 5602 Enderly Rd Baltimore MD 21212-2939. *Fax:* 540-231-8919; *E-Mail:* aamith@worldnet.att.net

AMJAD, ZAHID, KINETICS OF CRYSTAL GROWTH, CHEMICAL TREATMENT. *Current Pos:* from res & develop assoc to sr res & develop assoc, 82-89, RES & DEVELOP FEL, B F GOODRICH CO, 89- *Personal Data:* b Lahore, Pakistan, Aug 10, 46; nat US; m 78; c 1. *Educ:* Panjab Univ, Lahore, Pakistan, BSc, 66, MS, 67; Western Mich Univ, MA, 72; Glasgow Univ, PhD (physical chem), 76. *Prof Exp:* Lectr chem, Panjab Univ, 67-69; teaching asst chem, Western Mich Univ, 70-72; demonstr chem, Glascow Univ, Scotland, 73-75; asst res prof chem, State Univ NY, Buffalo, 76-79;

group leader, Prod Develop, Calgon Corp, Pittsburgh, 79-82. *Concurrent Pos:* Res & develop fel & supvr, Polymers & Chem Div, Brecksville Res Ctr, 82- *Mem:* Nat Assoc Corrosion Engr; Cooling Tower Inst; NY Acad Sci; Soc Cosmetic Scientists. *Res:* Surface and colloid chemistry of hydrophilic polymers-sparingly soluble salt systems; performance evaluation and definition of the role of hydrophilic polymers in water treatment cosmetics and personal care; new raw materials development; product formulation. *Mailing Add:* BF Goodrich 9921 Brecksville Rd Brecksville OH 44141

AMKRAUT, ALFRED A, IMMUNOLOGY, IMMUNOCHEMISTRY. *Current Pos:* RETIRED. *Personal Data:* b Saarbruecken, Ger, Sept 21, 26; US citizen; m 55; c 2. *Educ:* Univ Calif, Berkeley, BA, 49; NY Univ, MS, 55; Stanford Univ, PhD(med microbiol), 63. *Prof Exp:* Res asst immunohemat, Med Sch, Stanford Univ, 55-62; vis scientist, Ore Regional Primate Res Ctr, 64-67; asst prof immunol, Med Sch, Univ Ore, 65-67; asst prof med microbiol, Sch Med, Stanford Univ, 67-74; dir biol sci, Alza Res, 87-93, head microbiol, 74-95, prin scientist, 87-95. *Concurrent Pos:* Res fel immunochem, Calif Inst Technol, 62-64; Nat Acad Sci-Nat Res Coun fel, 63-64; NIH fel, 64- *Mem:* Fel AAAS; Am Asn Immunol; Am Chem Soc; Am Soc Microbiol; Sigma Xi; Soc Investigative Dermat; Soc Clin Immunol. *Res:* Antigen-antibody interactions and their biological manifestations; mechanism of antibody formation; central nervous system and the immune response; contact sensitivity. *Mailing Add:* 3358 Kenneth Dr Palo Alto CA 94303

AMLANER, CHARLES JOSEPH, JR, SLEEP PHYSIOLOGY, BIOTELEMETRY & RADIO TRACKING. *Current Pos:* DIR, ANIMAL SLEEP RES GROUP, 81- *Personal Data:* b Philadelphia, Pa, Nov 26, 51; m 73; c 2. *Educ:* Andrews Univ, Mich, BS, 74, MA, 76; Oxford Univ, UK, DPhil(zool), 82. *Prof Exp:* Asst prof behav physiol, Dept Biol Sci, Walla Walla Col, 80-85; chmn, Dept Zool, 86-90, assoc prof behav sci, Dept Zool, Univ Ark, Fayetteville, 86-, prog chmn, Dept Biol Sci, 90- *Concurrent Pos:* Adj assoc prof biomed eng, Dept Eng, Walla Walla Col, 81-85 & Univ Ark, Fayetteville, 86-; prin investr, NIMH, 82-89 & US Dept Interior, 87-; comnr, Ark Game & Fish Comn, 86-91; mem, Fish & Wildlife Res Comt, Nat Asn State Univs & Land Grant Cols, 87- *Mem:* Int Soc Biotelemetry (pres, 72-); Animal Behav Soc; Asn Prof Sleep Socs; Sigma Xi; Sleep Res Soc; Int Asn Fish & Wildlife Agencies. *Res:* Biotelemetry and use in evaluating temporal and spatial patterns of behavior and physiology in unrestrained animals; sleep physiology of birds and mammals; simulation modeling of behavior; animal population dynamics. *Mailing Add:* Dept Life Scis Indiana State Univ Terre Haute IN 47809-0001

AMLING, HARRY JAMES, HORTICULTURE. *Current Pos:* INT CONSULT, PECAN GROWING, 87- *Personal Data:* b Baltimore, Md, Jan 22, 31; 53, 78; c 5. *Educ:* Rutgers Univ, BS, 52; Univ Del, MS, 54; Mich State Univ, PhD(hort), 58. *Honors & Awards:* Gold Pecan Award, Nat Pecan Shellers & Processors Asn, 64. *Prof Exp:* Asst, Univ Del, 52-54; res asst, Mich State Univ, 56-58; from asst prof to assoc prof, 58-68, prof hort, Auburn Univ, 68-87. *Concurrent Pos:* Consult, pecan grower. *Mem:* Am Soc Hort Sci. *Res:* Practical and fundamental aspects of use of herbicides and growth regulators on pecans; growth and development; mineral nutrition of pecans; high density pecan culture; tissue culture. *Mailing Add:* 1004 Lee Rd 157 Opelika AL 36804

AMMA, ELMER LOUIS, BIOINORGANIC CHEMISTRY, BIOPHYSICAL CHEMISTRY. *Current Pos:* assoc prof, 65-70, PROF CHEM, UNIV SC, 70- *Personal Data:* b Cleveland, Ohio, Feb 13, 29. *Educ:* Case Inst, BS, 52; Iowa State Univ, PhD(chem), 57. *Honors & Awards:* Russell Award in Res, 70; Stone Award, Am Chem Soc, 80. *Prof Exp:* Asst chem, Iowa State Univ, 52-54; asst, Ames Lab, AEC, 54-57; res assoc, Radiation Lab, Univ Pittsburgh, 57-58, lectr & res assoc, Radiation Lab & Physics Dept, 58-59, asst prof chem, 59-65. *Concurrent Pos:* Consult, Exxon Res, 65-70. *Mem:* AAAS; Am Inst Chem; Am Chem Soc; Am Crystallog Asn; Am Phys Soc. *Res:* Protein crystallography, structure of model enzymes and proteins; structure of carriers of molecular oxygen and nitrogen; structure of molecules of importance to homogeneous catalysis, structure and metal nuclear magnetic resonance. *Mailing Add:* Rt 1 Box 141 Swansea SC 29160

AMMAN, GENE DOYLE, FOREST ENTOMOLOGY. *Current Pos:* RETIRED. *Personal Data:* b Greeley, Colo, Feb 26, 31; m 54; c 5. *Educ:* Colo State Univ, BS, 56, MS, 58; Univ Mich, PhD(forest insect ecol), 66. *Honors & Awards:* Gov Medal, State Utah, 91; Founders Award, Western Forest Insect World Conf, 94. *Prof Exp:* Assoc entomologist, Southeastern Forest Exp Sta, US Forest Serv, USDA, 58-66, prin entomologist, 66-83, proj leader, Intermountain Forest & Range Exp Sta, 84-93. *Mem:* AAAS; Int Union Forestry Res Orgn; Entom Soc Am; Entom Soc Can; Sigma Xi; Am Registry Prof Entomologists. *Res:* Population ecology; natural and cultural control of forest insects. *Mailing Add:* 3175 N Mountain View Dr North Ogden UT 84414. *E-Mail:* buggdr@aol.com

AMMANN, E(UGENE) O(TTO), LASERS, NONLINEAR OPTICS. *Current Pos:* adv develop engr, 63-64, eng specialist, 64-75, SR MEM TECH STAFF, SYLVANIA ELECTRONIC SYSTS, GEN TEL & ELECTRONICS CORP, 75- *Personal Data:* b Portland, Ore, June 26, 35; m 70. *Educ:* Univ Portland, BS, 57; Stanford Univ, MS, 59, PhD(elec eng), 63. *Prof Exp:* Res assoc elec eng, Stanford Univ, 63. *Mem:* Inst Elec & Electronics Engrs; Am Phys Soc; Optical Soc Am. *Res:* Microwave masers; optical birefringent filters; modulation and demodulation of light; lasers; nonlinear optics; optical parametric oscillators; stimulated Raman scattering. *Mailing Add:* 585 Los Altos Ave Los Altos CA 94022

AMMANN, HARRIET MARIA, ZOOLOGY, ENVIRONMENTAL HEALTH ASSESSMENT. *Current Pos:* LEAD TOXICOLOGIST, OFF TOXIC SUBSTANCES, WASH STATE DEPT HEALTH, 90- *Personal Data:* b Munich, Germany, Feb 2, 39; US citizen. *Educ:* Univ Dayton, BS, 61; NMex Highlands Univ, MS, 65; NC State Univ, PhD(zool), 78. *Prof Exp:* Asst prof gen med sci, Bowman Gray Sch Med, 70-73; assoc prof biol & physiol, NC Cent Univ, 76-82; vis prof physiol, NC State Univ, 82-84; biologist, Environ Criteria & Assessment Off, US Environ Protection Agency, 84-90. *Mem:* AAAS; Sigma Xi. *Res:* Write health assessments for hazardous air pollutants, hydrogen sulfide, styrene, woodsmoke and indoor air pollution. *Mailing Add:* 333 Sherman St NW Olympia WA 98502

AMMAR, RAYMOND GEORGE, EXPERIMENTAL ELEMENTARY PARTICLE PHYSICS. *Current Pos:* PROF PHYSICS, UNIV KANS, 69-, CHMN, DEPT PHYSICS & ASTRON, 89- *Personal Data:* b Kingston, Jamaica, July 15, 32; US citizen; m 61, Carroll Ikerd; c Elizabeth, Robert (deceased) & David. *Educ:* Harvard Univ, AB, 53; Univ Chicago, SM, 55, PhD(physics), 59. *Prof Exp:* Res assoc, Enrico Fermi Inst, Univ Chicago, 59-60; from asst prof to assoc prof physics, Northwestern Univ, 60-69. *Concurrent Pos:* Prin investr NSF grant, Res High Energy Physics, 62-; consult, High Energy Physics Div, Argonne Nat Lab, 65-69, vis scientist, 71-72; vis scientist, FermiLab, Batavia, Ill, 76-81, Deutsches Elektronen Synchrotron, Hamburg, Ger, 82-88 & Lab Nuclear Studies, Cornell Univ, 89- *Mem:* Fel Am Phys Soc. *Res:* Study of particles produced in electron-position annihilations at a center-of-mass energy of approximately 10 GeV. *Mailing Add:* Dept Physics & Astron Univ Kans Lawrence KS 66045-2151

AMME, ROBERT CLYDE, EXPERIMENTAL ATOMIC PHYSICS, ATMOSPHERIC PHYSICS. *Current Pos:* res physicist, Denver Res Inst, Univ Denver, 59-68, from asst prof to assoc prof, 61-68, actg dean arts & sci, 75-76, dir acad res, 77-81, dean, Grad Sch, 78-81, chmn dept, 81-85, PROF PHYSICS, UNIV DENVER, 68- *Personal Data:* b Ames, Iowa, May 15, 30; m 51; c David & Dianne. *Educ:* Iowa State Univ, BS, 53, MS, 55, PhD(physics), 58. *Prof Exp:* Res physicist, Humble Oil & Refining Co, 58-59. *Concurrent Pos:* Sr res physicist, Denver Res Inst, 68-77. *Mem:* Fel Am Phys Soc; Sigma Xi; Mat Res Soc; Am Asn Physics Teachers; Acoust Soc Am. *Res:* Atomic and molecular physics; collision phenomena; energy and charge transfer; ionization; gaseous transport properties; acoustics; stratospheric composition; applied mechanics. *Mailing Add:* Dept Physics Univ Denver Denver CO 80208. *Fax:* 303-871-4405; *E-Mail:* ramme@du.edu

AMMERMAN, CLARENCE BAILEY, ANIMAL NUTRITION. *Current Pos:* from asst prof to assoc prof, 58-70, PROF ANIMAL SCI & ANIMAL NUTRITIONIST, UNIV FLA, 70- *Personal Data:* b Cynthiana, Ky, May 21, 29; m 50, Beatrice M Charles; c David K, Douglas E & Annette L. *Educ:* Univ Ky, BS, 51, MS, 52; Univ Ill, PhD(animal sci), 56. *Honors & Awards:* Gustav Bohstedt Award, Am Soc Animal Sci, 73; Am Feed Mfrs Asn Nutrit Res Award, 77; Morrison Award, Am Soc Animal Sci, 89. *Prof Exp:* Asst animal nutrit, Univ Ky, 51-52; asst animal sci, Univ Ill, 54-56; Med Serv Corps, US Army Med Res & Nutrit Lab, Fitzsimons Gen Hosp, Denver, 56-58. *Concurrent Pos:* Moorman travel fel, Animal Nutrit Res, Nat Feed Ingredients Asn, 69. *Mem:* AAAS; Am Soc Animal Sci; Am Inst Nutrit; Am Dairy Sci Asn; Soc Exp Biol & Med; Sigma Xi. *Res:* Animal nutrition mineral elements; forage utilization by ruminants. *Mailing Add:* 3756 SW Fifth Pl Gainesville FL 32607. *Fax:* 352-392-7652; *E-Mail:* ammerman@animal.ufl.edu

AMMERMAN, GALE RICHARD, NEW FOOD PRODUCT DEVELOPMENT, FOOD CANNING & FREEZING. *Current Pos:* prof, 67-85, head, Dept Food Sci, 85-88, EMER PROF, MISS STATE UNIV, 85- *Personal Data:* b Sullivan, Ind, Mar 6, 23; m 43, Jane Burxe; c Kathleen, John, Joe, Mark & Chris. *Educ:* Purdue Univ, BS, 50, MS, 53, PhD(food sci), 57. *Honors & Awards:* Res Award, Inst Food Technologists, 77; Calvert L Willey Award, 96. *Prof Exp:* Prof food sci, Purdue Univ, 54-57, actg head dept, 57-58; assoc dir res, Libby McNeill & Libby Co, 58-67. *Concurrent Pos:* Pres, Coun Agr Sci & Tech, 86-87. *Mem:* Inst Food Technologists. *Res:* Packaging, processing and preservation of the nutritional quality of mainly channel catfish but also southern fruits and vegetables. *Mailing Add:* 210 Quail Trail Aliceville AL 35442

AMMIRATI, JOSEPH FRANK, JR, MYCOLOGY, FUNGAL SYSTEMATICS & ECOLOGY. *Current Pos:* from asst prof to assoc prof, 79-86, PROF BOT, UNIV WASH, 86- *Personal Data:* b Dunsmuir, Calif, Jan 10, 42; m 86; c 4. *Educ:* San Francisco State Univ, BA, 65, MA, 67; Univ Mich, PhD(bot), 72. *Prof Exp:* Res mycologist, USDA, 73-74; asst prof biol & bot, Univ Toronto, 74-79. *Concurrent Pos:* Adj prof bot, Univ Toronto, 79-80; assoc prof forest resources, Univ Wash, 81-86, prof, 86- *Mem:* Mycological Soc Am; NAm Mycological Asn; Am Inst Biol Sci. *Res:* Classification, distribution and ecology of higher fungi, especially agaricales; montane, boreal, arctic and alpine fungi; poisionous mushrooms; ectomycorrhizal fungi; fungus diversity, especially old-growth forest species. *Mailing Add:* Dept Bot KB-15 Univ Wash 3900 7th Ave NE Seattle WA 98195-0001

AMMIRATO, PHILIP VINCENT, PLANT PHYSIOLOGY. *Current Pos:* ASST PROF BIOL SCI, BARNARD COL, COLUMBIA UNIV, 74- *Personal Data:* b New York, NY, Nov 22, 43. *Educ:* City Col New York, BS, 64; Cornell Univ, PhD(plant physiol), 69. *Prof Exp:* NY State Col teaching fel, Cornell Univ, 64-65; asst prof bot, Rutgers Univ, 69-74. *Concurrent Pos:* Assoc ed, Torreya, 78- *Mem:* Tissue Cult Asn; Torrey Bot Club; Bot Soc Am; Am Soc Plant Physiol; Sigma Xi. *Res:* Plant growth and development; tissue culture; economic botany; morphogenesis; embryogenesis. *Mailing Add:* Biol Dept Barnard Col 3009 Broadway New York NY 10027

AMMLUNG, RICHARD LEE, INORGANIC CHEMISTRY. *Current Pos:* SR SCIENTIST, UNIV RES FOUND, 94- *Personal Data:* b Havre de Grace, Md, May 7, 52; m 77. *Educ:* Univ Del, BS, 74; Northwestern Univ, MS, 76, PhD(chem), 79. *Prof Exp:* Sr res chemist, Monsanto Co, 78-81, res specialist, 81-85, sr res specialist chem, 85-93. *Mem:* Am Chem Soc. *Res:* Solid fast ion conductors; new processes for the production of electronic grade silicon. *Mailing Add:* 1901 Cross Trails Rd Baltimore MD 21244-1268

AMMON, HERMAN L, ORGANIC CHEMISTRY. *Current Pos:* from asst prof to assoc prof, 69-76, PROF CHEM, UNIV MD, COLLEGE PARK, 76- *Personal Data:* b Passaic, NJ, Nov 24, 36; m 58; c 2. *Educ:* Brown Univ, ScB, 58; Univ Wash, PhD(chem), 63. *Prof Exp:* NIH fel, 63-64; res instr x-ray crystallog, Univ Wash, 64-65; asst prof chem, Univ Calif, Santa Cruz, 65-69. *Mem:* Am Chem Soc; Am Crystallog Asn. *Res:* Organic compound and macromolecular structure; computer programming; x-ray crystallography; conformational analysis. *Mailing Add:* Dept Chem Univ Md College Park MD 20742-0001

AMMON, VERNON DALE, PLANT PATHOLOGY. *Current Pos:* asst prof, 73-78, ASSOC PROF PLANT PATH, MISS STATE UNIV, 78- *Personal Data:* b Mendon, Mo, May 15, 41; m 62; c 1. *Educ:* Univ Mo, BS, 64, MS, 65, PhD(plant path), 72. *Prof Exp:* Res assoc plant path, Univ Ky, 72-73. *Mem:* Am Phytopath Soc. *Res:* Disease physiology, ultrastructure of diseased plants. *Mailing Add:* Entom Miss State Univ Box EM Mississippi State MS 39762-9999

AMMONS, VERNON GIBBS, POLYURETHANE & POLYCARBONATE CHEMISTRY. *Current Pos:* RETIRED. *Personal Data:* b Kenmore, Ohio, Sept 3, 17; m 43, Mary Gormley; c Thomas, Annloud & Doris (Hardesty). *Educ:* Univ Cincinnati, BS, 49; Carnegie-Mellon Univ, MS, 69, PhD(org chem), 71- *Prof Exp:* Paint chemist, Interchem, 49-52 & Gilhert Spruance Co, 52-55; res assoc & staff scientist, PPG Industs, 55-82. *Concurrent Pos:* Consult, 82- *Mem:* Am Chem Soc; Sigma Xi. *Res:* Synthesizing polyurethanes intended for use as interlayers for automotive and aircraft windshields; devising an all aliphatic carbonate urethane copolymer with potential for aircraft transparencies, eye glasses, etc; granted 15 US & Canadian patents. *Mailing Add:* 3924 Green Valley Dr Glenshaw PA 15116

AMOLS, HOWARD IRA, radiological physics, medical physics, for more information see previous edition

AMON, MAX, OPTICS, ENGINEERING. *Current Pos:* OPTICAL DESIGNER, MARTIN MARIETTA CORP, 73- *Personal Data:* b New York, NY, Feb 28, 39; c 3. *Educ:* Hofstra Univ, BS, 63. *Honors & Awards:* Improved Ritchey Chretien Telescope Award, NASA, 72. *Prof Exp:* Optical designer, Goerz Am Optical Co, 63-65, Kollsman Instrument Corp, 65-72, Photronics Corp, 72-73 & Opcom Assocs, 73. *Concurrent Pos:* consult various industs. *Mem:* Optical Soc Am; Soc Photo-Optical Instrumentation Engrs; Inst Elec & Electronics Engrs. *Res:* Color corrected and coma corrected Mangin Mirror; large objective for night observation; extending the field of the Ritchey Chretien Telescope; guidance beam assembly, command optics, zoom projection optics, TIR window; Tactical Air Defense Systems/ Pilot Night Vision System boresight module, telescope stabilization, laser television, infrared optics; compact optical ware length discriminator. *Mailing Add:* 1727 Lake Waumpi Dr Maitland FL 32751

AMON PARISI, CRISTINA HORTENSIA, COMPUTATION FLUID MECHANICS, THERMAL-FLUID SCIENCES. *Current Pos:* from asst prof to assoc prof, 88-97, PROF MECH ENG, CARNEGIE MELLON UNIV, 97- *Personal Data:* m, Carmelo; c Andreina & Gabriel. *Educ:* Univ Simon Bolivar, Caracas, Venezuela, Mech Eng, 81; Mass Inst Technol, MSME, 85, PhD, 88. *Hon Degrees:* DSc, Mass Inst Technol, 88. *Honors & Awards:* Res Initiation Award, NSF, 89; Teetor Educ Award, Soc Automotive Engrs, 94. *Prof Exp:* Instr, Univ Simon Bolivar, 81-83; researcher & teaching asst, Mass Inst Technol, 84-88. *Mem:* Am Soc Mech Engrs; Am Inst Aeronaut & Astronaut; Inst Elect & Electronics Engrs; Am Soc Eng Educ; Soc Women Engrs; Soc Automotive Engrs. *Res:* Computational fluid dynamics and heat transfer; stability and transition to turbulence; numerical algorithms; cooling electronic equipment and thermal phenomenon in manufacturing processes; artificial organs and biomedical devices. *Mailing Add:* Dept Mech Eng Carnegie Mellon Univ Pittsburgh PA 15213-3890. *Fax:* 412-268-3348; *E-Mail:* camon@cmu.edu

AMOORE, JOHN ERNEST, OLFACTORY PHYSIOLOGY, ENVIRONMENTAL CHEMISTRY. *Current Pos:* PARTNER, OLFACTO-LABS, 79- *Personal Data:* b Derbyshire, Eng, Apr 28, 30; US citizen; m 59, Annie Bodjayian; c Ronald & Marie. *Educ:* Oxford Univ, BA, 52, MA & PhD(biochem), 58. *Prof Exp:* Sci officer microanal, John Innes Hort Inst, Eng, 58-59; Nuffield Found res fel plant biochem, Univ Edinburgh, 59-62; Jane Coffin Childs Mem Fund res fel zool, Univ Calif, Berkeley, 62-63; res chemist, Western Regional Res Lab, USDA, Berkeley, Calif, 63-78. *Concurrent Pos:* Mem, sci adv comt acid deposition, State Calif, 83-; regist environ assessor, State Calif, 89- *Mem:* Asn Chemoreception Sci; Air & Waste Mgt Asn; Am Water Works Asn; Am Soc Testing Mat. *Res:* Stereochemical theory of olfaction; smell-blindness; primary odors; hyperosnia air and water pollution. *Mailing Add:* Olfacto-Labs 7701 Potrero Ave El Cerrito CA 94530. *Fax:* 510-235-1635

AMORY, DAVID WILLIAM, CARDIAC ANESTHESIOLOGY, CLINICAL PHARMACOLOGY. *Current Pos:* PROF, CHIEF CARDIAC ANESTHESIA & DIR RES, DEPT ANESTHESIOL, ROBERT WOOD JOHNSON MED SCH, 88- *Personal Data:* b Newark, NJ, Jan 27, 28; m 60, Margaret Lynch; c David & John. *Educ:* St John's Univ, NY, BS, 52, MS, 55; Univ Wash, PhD(pharmacol), 61; Univ BC, MD, 67. *Honors & Awards:* Walter Stewart Baird Mem Prize, Sch Med, Univ BC, 67; Residents' Res Prize, Am Soc Anesthesiologists, 70; Res Prize in Anesthesiol, Mt Sinai Sch Med, 70. *Prof Exp:* Pharmacologist toxicol, Ciba Pharmaceut Co, Inc, 55-57; res asst pharmacol, Univ Wash, 57-61; USPHS fel neuropharmacol, Univ Calif, San Francisco, 61-62; intern med, Virginia Mason Hosp, Seattle, 67-68; USPHS scholar, Cardiovasc Res Inst, Univ Calif, San Francisco, 68-69; resident anesthesiol, Sch Med, Univ Wash, 69-71, assoc prof anesthesiol & pharmacol, 75-82, prof, 82-88. *Concurrent Pos:* Nat Heart & Lung Inst res grants, 72-75 & 79-86; mem, Comt Res, Am Soc Anesthesiologist, 82-85, Comt Exp Circulation, 94; Cardiovasc Inst res grant, 88-91. *Mem:* Am Soc Anesthesiologists; Sigma Xi; Soc Cardiovasc Anesthesiologists; Int Anesthesia Res Soc; Asn Univ Anesthesiologists; World Asn Cardiac Thoracic & Vascular Anesthesia. *Res:* Near infrared spectroscopy for assessing cerebral and myocardial oxygen metabolism; excitatory amino acids and spinal cord ischemia; cardioplegia and right ventricular function; iontophoretic transdermal delivery of drugs. *Mailing Add:* Dept Anesthesiol Robert Wood Johnson Med Sch New Brunswick NJ 08903-0019. *Fax:* 732-235-6131

AMOS, DENNIS BERNARD, IMMUNOGENETICS. *Current Pos:* James B Duke prof, 61-93, chief, Div Immunol, 62-88, EMER JAMES B DUKE PROF IMMUNOL & EXP SURG, MED CTR, DUKE UNIV, 93- *Personal Data:* b Bromley, Kent, Eng, Apr 16, 23; m 49; c 5. *Educ:* Univ London, MB, BS, 51, MD, 63. *Hon Degrees:* Dr, Univ Curitiba, Brazil, 88. *Honors & Awards:* Rose Payne Award, 88. *Prof Exp:* Intern, Guy's Hosp, London, 51; from assoc cancer res scientist to prin cancer res scientist, Roswell Park Mem Inst, 56-62. *Concurrent Pos:* Res fel, Guy's Hosp, London, 52-55; sr res fel, Roswell Park Mem Inst, 55-56; chmn, Human Lymphocyte-Antigen Stand Comt, Am Asn Clin Histocompatibility Testing & NIH Nat Inst Allergy & Infectious Dis & Nomenclature Comt Leukocyte Antigens, WHO, Int Union Immunol Socs. *Mem:* Nat Acad Sci; Am Asn Immunologists; Am Asn Cancer Res; Transplantation Soc; Am Asn Clin Histocompatability Test; AAAS; Inst Med. *Res:* Tissue and tumor transplantation genetics; immunology; mouse genetics; antigen differentiation; human lymphocyte-antigen and disease. *Mailing Add:* Med Ctr Duke Univ Box 3010 Durham NC 27710

AMOS, DEWEY HAROLD, PETROLOGY. *Current Pos:* PROF GEOL, EASTERN ILL UNIV, 65- *Personal Data:* b Harrisville, WVa, Feb 27, 25; m 48; c 3. *Educ:* Marietta Col, BS, 49; Univ Ill, MA, 50, PhD(geol), 58. *Prof Exp:* Asst geol, Univ Ill, 49-51; geologist, US Geol Surv, 52-55; asst prof geol, Southern Ill Univ, 55-65. *Concurrent Pos:* Consult, US Geol Surv & Defense Minerals Explor Admin, 55-64; consult geologist, US Geol Surv, 64- *Mem:* Fel Geol Soc Am; Soc Econ Geologists. *Res:* Structural geology; geology of base metals and nonmetallic deposits. *Mailing Add:* 2003 University Dr Charleston IL 61920

AMOS, DONALD E, MATHEMATICS, CHEMICAL ENGINEERING. *Current Pos:* RETIRED. *Personal Data:* b Lafayette, Ind, Feb 28, 29; m 52, Rosie A Carter; c 2. *Educ:* Purdue Univ, BS, 51; Ore State Univ, MS, 56, PhD(math), 60. *Prof Exp:* Chem engr, Gen Elec Co, 51-53; staff mem appl math, Sandia Corp, 60-64; assoc prof math, Univ Mo-Columbia, 64-66; mathematician, Sandia Labs, 66, staff mem, 66-93. *Concurrent Pos:* Ed, Communications in Statist, 72-81. *Mem:* Asn Comput Mach; Soc Indust & Appl Math. *Res:* Special functions; numerical analysis and solution of ordinary and partial differential equations. *Mailing Add:* 7704 Pickard Ave NE Albuquerque NM 87110-1562

AMOS, HAROLD, BACTERIOLOGY. *Current Pos:* assoc, 54-59, from asst prof to assoc prof, 59-70, PROF MICROBIOL & MOLECULAR GENETICS, HARVARD MED SCH, 70-, CHMN, DEPT MICROBIOL, 79- *Personal Data:* b Pennsauken, NJ, Sept 7, 19. *Educ:* Springfield Col, BS, 41; Harvard Univ, PhD(bact), 52. *Prof Exp:* Instr bact, Springfield Col, 48-49. *Concurrent Pos:* Fulbright res fel, Pasteur Inst, France, 51-52; res fel, Harvard Med Sch, 52-54; USPHS fel, 52-54, sr res fel, 58; mem, Nat Cancer Adv Bd, 72-; trustee, Josiah Macy Found, 73- *Mem:* Inst Med-Nat Acad Sci; Am Soc Biol Chemists; Tissue Cult Asn; Am Soc Microbiol. *Res:* Hexose metabolism in mammalian cells; surface changes and hormonal influences. *Mailing Add:* Dept Microbiol & Molecular Genetics Harvard Med Sch 25 Shattuck St Boston MA 02115

AMOS, HENRY ESTILL, RUMINANT NUTRITION, AGRICULTURE. *Current Pos:* PROF ANIMAL NUTRIT, UNIV GA, 90- *Personal Data:* b Bowling Green, Ky, Aug 20, 41; m 69, Wanda Barlow; c Stephen & Dawn. *Educ:* Western Ky Univ, BS, 62; Univ Ky, MS, 64, PhD(ruminant nutrit), 69. *Prof Exp:* Instr animal nutrit, Western Ky Univ, 64-67; res assoc, Univ Ky, 69-71; res physiologist animal nutrit, Agr Res, USDA, 71-90. *Concurrent Pos:* Res fel, Univ Ky, 69-71. *Mem:* Am Soc Animal Sci; Am Dairy Sci Asn; Am Registry Cert Animal Scientists. *Res:* Primary emphasis on intraruminal protein transformations; microbial protein syntesis, digestion and utilization and rumen protein by-pass in dairy cattle. *Mailing Add:* Dept Animal & Dairy Sci Univ Ga Athens GA 30602. *Fax:* 706-542-1852; *E-Mail:* hamos@uga.cc.uga.edu

AMOSCATO, ANDREW ANTHONY, CELL-SURFACE ENZYMES OF THE IMMUNE SYSTEM, LYMPHOCYTE ENZYMES. *Current Pos:* INSTR, PITTSBURGH CANCER INST, UNIV PITTSBURGH, SCH MED, 89- *Personal Data:* b New York, NY, May 22, 56. *Educ:* Univ Tex Health Sci Ctr, PhD(biochem), 84. *Prof Exp:* Res assoc, Dept Surg, Univ Cincinnati, 84-89. *Mem:* AAAS; Am Asn Immunologists. *Res:* Role of cell surface enzymes in immune function; mechanism of NK cytolytic function; psychoneuro immunology and the regulation of immune function by enkephalins and endorphins. *Mailing Add:* Dept Pathol Univ Pittsburgh 300 Technol Dr Biotech Ctr Pittsburgh PA 15219

AMOSS, MAX ST CLAIR, ENDOCRINOLOGY, ONCOLOGY. *Current Pos:* from asst prof to assoc prof, 75-85, PROF VET PHYSIOL, TEX A&M UNIV, 85- *Personal Data:* b Baltimore, Md, May 9, 37; m 87; c 3. *Educ:* Pa State Univ, BS, 62; Tex A&M Univ, MS, 65; Baylor Col Med, PhD(physiol), 69. *Prof Exp:* Fel, Baylor Col Med, 69, asst prof endocrinol, 69-70; asst res prof neuroendocrinol, Salk Inst, 70-75. *Concurrent Pos:* Instr, San Diego Eve Col, 72-75. *Mem:* Endocrine Soc; Am Physiol Soc; Soc Study Reproduction; Int Soc Neuroendocrinol; Soc Neurosci; Am Asn Cancer Res. *Res:* Hypothalamic control of hypophyseal function with special emphasis on reproduction; development of radioimmunoassay procedures for use in veterinary medicine; melanoma in swine as model of human disease. *Mailing Add:* Dept Vet Physiol & Pharmacol Tex A&M Univ Col Vet Med Admin Bldg Rm 326D College Station TX 77843-4466. *Fax:* 409-845-6544

AMPLATZ, KURT, RADIOLOGY. *Current Pos:* From instr to assoc prof, 58-70, PROF RADIOL, SCH MED, UNIV MINN, MINNEAPOLIS, 70- *Personal Data:* b Weistrach, Austria, Feb 25, 24; US citizen; m 56; c 3. *Educ:* Univ Innsbruck, MD, 50. *Res:* Detection of cardiac shunts with radioactive and nonradioactive gases; blood flow measurements by radiographic technics; radiographic evaluation of renovascular hypertension; pneumotomography; development of see-through film changers; magnification coronary angiography; development of angiographic injection; nonthrombogenic catheter; development of angiographic equipment and endovrologic technics. *Mailing Add:* Dept Radiol Box 292 Univ Minn Hosp & Clin 420 Delaware St SE Minneapolis MN 55455-0374

AMPULSKI, ROBERT STANLEY, CELLULOSE CHEMISTRY, MASS SPECTROMETRY. *Current Pos:* group leader mass spectrometry, Miami Valley Labs, 72-78, group leader catalysis pulp process develop, Pager Div, 80-95, RES FEL, PROCTER & GAMBLE CO, 95- *Personal Data:* b Grand Rapids, Mich, Sept 22, 42; m 65; c 3. *Educ:* Aquinas Col, BS, 64; Marquette Univ, MS, 69; Fla State Univ, PhD(phys chem), 72. *Prof Exp:* Res chemist, Milwaukee Blood Ctr Inc, 67-68. *Mem:* AAAS; Am Soc Mass Spectrometry; Sigma Xi. *Res:* Stable isotopes; gas phase kinetics; ion molecule reactions; catalysis, cellulose chemistry and wood pulping; chemical bonding; surface science; molecular design. *Mailing Add:* 5674 Red Oak Dr Fairfield OH 45014

AMPY, FRANKLIN, MUTAGENESIS, BIOSTATISTICS. *Current Pos:* actg chmn, 73-75, 84-86 & 90-92, assoc prof zool, 71-89, VCHMN, HOWARD UNIV, 81-, PROF BIOL, 90- *Personal Data:* b Dinwiddie, Va, June 22, 36. *Educ:* Va State Col, BS, 58; Ore State Univ, MS, 60, PhD(genetics), 62. *Prof Exp:* Asst prof genetics, Am Univ Beirut, Lebanon, 62-68; fel, Univ Calif, Davis, 68-70. *Concurrent Pos:* Assoc dean educ opportunity prog, Univ Calif, Davis, 70-71; NASA-AMES fac res fel, 76; prin investr, Minority Biomed Prog, Howard Univ, NIH, 78-; NIH consult, Site Visit Fla Int Univ, 81 & 83; reviewer, Va Sci Talent Search, Va Jr Acad Sci, 81- *Mem:* Environ Mutagenesis Soc; Genetics Soc Am; Am Genetics Asn; Am Soc Cell Biol. *Res:* Environmental mutagenesis, specifically in the hormonal regulation of environmental mutagens. *Mailing Add:* Dept Biol Howard Univ 415 Col St NW Washington DC 20059-0001

AMR, SANIA, HORMONE ACTION, PROTEIN CHEMISTRY. *Current Pos:* VIS ASSOC, DEPT HEALTH & HUMAN SERVS, NIH, 83- *Educ:* Univ Toulouse, France, MD, 77. *Mailing Add:* 209 Churchwardens Rd Baltimore MD 21212-2937

AMRANI, DAVID L, HEMATOLOGY, CARDIOVASCULAR PROBLEMS. *Current Pos:* From asst prof to assoc prof hemat, Dept Med, 81-88, PROF CLIN LAB SCI, DEPT HEALTH SCI, UNIV WIS-MILWAUKEE, 88- *Personal Data:* b Brooklyn, NY, Apr 13, 48. *Educ:* City Univ NY, BA, 70, MA, 73; St Johns Univ, PhD(biol & biochem), 80. *Concurrent Pos:* Investr, NIH, 83-86. *Mem:* Am Soc Biochem & Molecular Biol; Int Soc Thrombosis & Haemostasis. *Mailing Add:* Dept Health Sci Univ Wis Milwaukee Milwaukee WI 53201

AMREIN, YOST URSUS LUCIUS, ANIMAL PARASITOLOGY. *Current Pos:* from instr to assoc prof, Pomona Col, 51-59, chmn dept, 59-68, prof, 59-81, EMER PROF ZOOL, POMONA COL, 81- *Personal Data:* b Arosa, Switz, Jan 3, 18; nat US; m 48, Brown; c Lucius. *Educ:* Univ Calif, Los Angeles, BA, 47, MA, 48, PhD(parasitol), 51. *Prof Exp:* Teaching asst zool, Univ Calif, Los Angeles, 47-51. *Concurrent Pos:* USPHS fel, Nat Inst Med Res, London, 57-58; NIH res grantee, 59-64 & 66-74; res fel, Swiss Trop Inst, 64-65; lectr, Calif State Polytech Univ, Pomona, 81-84. *Mem:* AAAS; Am Soc Parasitol; fel Royal Soc Trop Med & Hyg. *Res:* Physiology of hemoflagellates; ecology of parasites in arid areas. *Mailing Add:* Dept Biol Seaver Lab Pomona Col Claremont CA 91711-6339

AMROMIN, GEORGE DAVID, neuropathology; deceased, see previous edition for last biography

AMRON, IRVING, BATTERY DESIGN, COMPUTER MODELING & COST ANALYSIS. *Current Pos:* CONSULT, 87- *Personal Data:* b Bayonne, NJ, Jan 18, 21; wid; c Arlene J(deceased) & Steven C(deceased). *Educ:* NY Univ, BA, 41, MS, 44, PhD(phys chem), 49; Am Bd Forensic Examrs, dipl. *Prof Exp:* Sr chemist, SAM Labs, Manhattan Dist, NY, 44-46; instr qual analysis chem, NY Univ, 46-47; res assoc textile chem, Textile Found, 47-49; res assoc combustion, NY Univ, 49-50 & Gen Elec Co Inc, 50-52; sr engr cathode coatings, Sylvania Elec Prod Inc, 52-54; mem tech staff electronic mat, processes, devices, batteries & systs eng, AT&T Bell Labs, 54-87. *Concurrent Pos:* Consult, batteries & process econometrics. *Mem:* Sigma Xi; Am Chem Soc; Electrochem Soc; Asn Comput Mach; fel Am Inst Chemists; AAAS. *Res:* Gas phase kinetics; heterogeneous equilibria; econometrics; electrochemical energy sources; nickel-cadmium batteries; plumbum acid. *Mailing Add:* 19 Lexington Dr Livingston NJ 07039-4303. *Fax:* 973-992-0533

AMSBURY, DAVID LEONARD, GEOLOGY. *Current Pos:* GEOLOGIST, JOHNSON SPACE CTR, NASA, 67- *Personal Data:* b Topeka, Kans, Dec 30, 32; m 54, Ann Long; c Linda (Land) & Steven. *Educ:* Sul Ross State Col, BS, 52; Univ Tex, Austin, PhD(geol), 57. *Prof Exp:* Geologist, Shell Develop Co, 56-64, res geologist, 64-66. *Concurrent Pos:* Lectr, Univ Houston, 70- *Mem:* Soc Econ Paleont & Mineral; Geol Soc Am; Sigma Xi. *Res:* Physical stratigraphy; remote sensing in environmental geology. *Mailing Add:* 1422 Brookwood Ct Seabrook TX 77586

AMSDEN, THOMAS WILLIAM, INVERTEBRATE PALEONTOLOGY. *Current Pos:* geologist, 55-85, EMER GEOLOGIST, OKLA GEOL SURV, 85- *Personal Data:* b Wichita, Kans, Jan 31, 15; m 40; c 2. *Educ:* Univ Wichita, AB, 39; Univ Iowa, MA, 41; Yale Univ, PhD(geol), 47. *Honors & Awards:* Levorsen Award, Am Asn Petrol Geologists, 73. *Prof Exp:* Geologist, US Geol Surv, 43-45; asst geol, Yale Univ, 42-43 & 45-46, Nat Res fel, 46-47; geologist, Md State Geol Surv, 47; from instr to assoc prof geol, Johns Hopkins Univ, 47-55. *Concurrent Pos:* NSF grants, Wales, Sweden & Czech, 64-66, Russia, 68, Poland, 71. *Mem:* Paleont Soc; Geol Soc Am; Am Asn Petrol Geologists; Soc Econ Paleontologists & Mineralogists; Brit Palaeont Asn. *Res:* Late Ordovician, Silurian and early Devonian stratigraphy and paleontology; brachiopods; middle Paleozoic analysis of petroliferous deep sedimentary basins. *Mailing Add:* 1222 Westlawn Dr Norman OK 73069

AMSEL, LEWIS PAUL, PHARMACEUTICAL CHEMISTRY. *Current Pos:* mgr, 74-81, DIR PHARMACEUT DEVELOP, PHARMACEUT DIV, PENNWALT CORP, 81- *Personal Data:* b New York, NY, Mar 23, 42; m 64; c 2. *Educ:* Columbia Univ, BSc, 63; State Univ NY Buffalo, PhD(pharm), 69. *Prof Exp:* Assoc res pharmacist, Sterling-Winthrop Res Inst, 69-74. *Mem:* AAAS; Am Pharmaceut Asn; Acad Pharmaceut Sci. *Res:* Biopharmaceutics and pharmacokinetics; drug dosage design and evaluation. *Mailing Add:* Searle 700 E Business Center Dr Mt Prospect IL 60056-2176

AMSTER, ADOLPH BERNARD, PHYSICAL CHEMISTRY. *Current Pos:* head, Chem Div, 78-85, SR SCIENTIST, NAVAL WEAPONS CTR, CHINA LAKE, CALIF, 85-, CONSULT. *Personal Data:* b New York, NY, Nov 22, 24; m 53, Ruth Mittelman; c Kenneth. *Educ:* City Col New York, BS, 43; Columbia Univ, AM, 47; Ohio State Univ, PhD(phys chem), 51. *Prof Exp:* Chemist, US Bur Stands, 51-54; res assoc, Naval Ord Lab, 54-57, supv chemist, 57-60; mgr phys chem, Stanford Res Inst, 61-65, chmn, Phys & Inorg Chem Div, 65-68; chief, Explosives & Pyrotech Br, Naval Sea Systs Command, 68-78. *Mem:* AAAS; Sigma Xi; Am Phys Soc; Combustion Inst. *Res:* Experimental physical chemistry; thermochemistry; explosives and propellant sensitivity; detonations; pollution abatement; hazard analysis; chemiluminescence; accident investigation; energy conservation. *Mailing Add:* PO Box 1106 Ridgecrest CA 93555-1106. *E-Mail:* 73557.2273@compuserve.com

AMSTER, HARVEY JEROME, THEORETICAL PHYSICS, APPLIED MATHEMATICS. *Current Pos:* RETIRED. *Personal Data:* b Cleveland, Ohio, Sept 30, 28; m 81, Kathy Krohn; c Heidi & Irene. *Educ:* Calif Inst Technol, BS, 50; Mass Inst Technol, PhD, 54. *Prof Exp:* Adv scientist, Westinghouse Bettis Plant, 54-61; from assoc prof to prof eng, Univ Calif, Berkeley, 61-79; vis prof, Western Res Univ & Univ Wis, 79- *Concurrent Pos:* Researcher, Lawrence Livermore Lab, Argonne Nat Lab, Inst Defense Anal, Univ London & Northrop Space Labs. *Mem:* AAAS. *Res:* Nuclear physics; reactor theory; environmental effects, especially of nuclear technology. *Mailing Add:* 4208 Ridgemont Ct Oakland CA 94619-3727

AMSTERDAM, ABRAHAM, CANCER RESEARCH, MOLECULAR ENDOCRINOLOGY. *Current Pos:* sr scientist, 75-78, ASSOC PROF HORMONE RES, WEIZMANN INST SCI, 79- *Personal Data:* b Haifa, Israel, Apr 28, 39; m 69; c 4. *Educ:* Hebrew Univ, BSc, 64, MSc, 66, PhD(biochem), 71. *Honors & Awards:* Pfizer Lectr, Clin Res Inst, Montreal, 83. *Prof Exp:* Res asst biochem, Hebrew Univ, Jerusalem, 65-68, instr, 69- 70; res assoc cell biol, Rockefeller Univ, 71-72. *Concurrent Pos:* Vis scientist, NIH, Bethesda, 79-81; vis prof, Johns Hopkins Univ, Baltimore, 86-87, Univ Basel, 89-90, Max-Planck Inst, Munich, 91- *Mem:* Am Soc Cell Biol; Am Soc Endocrinol; Israel Soc Electron Micros; Israel Biochem Soc; Israel Endocrine Soc; Fedn Am Socs Exp Biol. *Res:* Structure and function of exocrine and endocrine cells; role of peptide and steroid hormones and growth factors in ovarian physiology; effect of oncogene expression on ovarian cell differentiation; ovarian cancer; induction of steroidogenesis. *Mailing Add:* Dept Hormone Res Weizmann Inst Sci Box 26 Rehovot 76100 Israel

AMSTERDAM, DANIEL, MICROBIOLOGY, CLINICAL MICROBIOLOGY. *Current Pos:* PROF MICROBIOL & PATH & ASSOC PROF MED, SCHS MED & DENT, STATE UNIV NY, BUFFALO, 80-; DIR, DEPT LAB MED, ERIE CO MED CTR, BUFFALO, 93- *Educ:* City Col NY, BS, 55; Brooklyn Col, MA, 57; NY Univ, PhD, 65; Am Bd Microbiol, dipl, 81. *Honors & Awards:* NSF-NATO Award Cell Biol, Stresa, Italy, 70, Moore Award Neuropath, 80. *Prof Exp:* Bacteriologist, Mt Sinai Hosp, NY, 55-57, res asst, Dept Microbiol, 58-60; sr microbiologist, Kingsbrook Jewish Med Ctr, Brooklyn, NY, 60-61, chief microbiol, Isaac Albert Res Inst, 61-80; dir clin microbiol & immunol, Erie County Lab, Erie County Med Ctr, Buffalo, NY, 80- *Concurrent Pos:* Assoc, Dept Microbiol, Mt Sinai Sch Med, City Univ NY, 69-80; head, Human Cell Biol Prog, Neurosci Ctr, Kingsbrook Jewish Med Ctr & Downstate Med Ctr, 71-80; adj prof, Dept Biol, Long Island Univ, Brooklyn, NY, 72-80; consult, microbiol, Prof Exam Serv, New York, NY, 77-80; dir, postdoctoral training prog, Med & Pub Health Lab Microbiol, Buffalo, NY, 81- *Mem:* Fel Am Acad Microbiol; fel AAAS; Am Asn Pathologists; Am Soc Cell Biol; Am Soc Microbiol; fel Infectious Dis Soc Am; Tissue Cult Asn. *Res:* Author or co-author of over 120 publications in the areas of clinical and molecular microbiology, antimicrobial activity and opportunistic infections. *Mailing Add:* Dept Microbiol & Immunol Erie Co Med Ctr & State Univ NY 462 Grider St Buffalo NY 14215-3098. *Fax:* 716-898-3090

AMSTERDAM, JAY D, PSYCHIATRY. *Current Pos:* from asst prof to assoc prof, 80-92, PROF PSYCHIAT, UNIV PA, PHILADELPHIA, 92-; DIR, DEPRESSION RES UNIT, UNIV PA MED CTR, 80- *Personal Data:* b Philadelphia, Pa, Feb 10, 49. *Educ:* Syracuse Univ, BA, 70; Jefferson Med Col, MD, 74; Am Bd Psychiat & Neurol, dipl. *Honors & Awards:* Marie H Eldredge Award, Am Psychiat Asn, 86; Curt P Richter Prize, Int Soc Psychoneuroendocrinol. *Prof Exp:* Intern obstet-gynec, Upstate Med Ctr, Syracuse, 74; resident psychiat, Thomas Jefferson Univ Hosp, Philadelphia, 74-77, chief resident, 76-77; sr resident, Depression Res Unit, Vet Admin Med Ctr, Philadelphia, 77-78; NIMH fel neuropsychopharmacol, Vet Admin Med Ctr/Univ Pa Hosp, 78-79. *Concurrent Pos:* Grantee, NIMH, 80-85 & 89-, Jack Warsaw Fund, 84- & NIH, 89-90; asst prof psychiat, Thomas Jefferson Univ, Philadelphia, 78-83, adj assoc prof, 83-88; assoc ed, J Affective Dis, 86-; asst ed, Psychosomatics, 87-; adj assoc prof, Wistar Inst Anat, 88- *Mem:* Fel Am Psychiat Asn; fel Am Bd Med Psychotherapists; Am Fedn Clin Res; Am Asn Hist Med; Int Soc Psychoneuroendocrinol; Int Soc Invest Stress; Soc Biol Psychiat. *Res:* Depression and mood disorders; psychoneuroendocrinology; contributed over 125 articles to medical and scientific journals; psychopharmacology; refractory depression; brain imaging; psychoimmunovirology; clinical pharmacokinetics. *Mailing Add:* Depression Res Unit Univ Pa 3600 Market St 8th Flr Philadelphia PA 19104-2649. *Fax:* 215-662-6443

AMSTUTZ, HARLAN CABOT, ORTHOPAEDICS, JOINT REPLACEMENT. *Current Pos:* prof & chief orthop, Div Orthop, 70-91, EMER PROF ORTHOP, SCH MED, UNIV CALIF, LOS ANGELES, 91-; MED DIR, JOINT REPLACEMENT INST, 91- *Personal Data:* b Santa Monica, Calif, July 17, 31; c 3. *Educ:* Univ Calif, Los Angeles, BA, 53, MD, 56. *Honors & Awards:* Charnley Award, 77, 84, 90 & 94; Aufranc Award, 79; Nicolas Audry Award, 87. *Prof Exp:* Intern, Los Angeles Co Gen Hosp, 56-57; resident surg, Med Ctr Hosp, Univ Calif, Los Angeles, 57-58; resident orthop, Hosp Spec Surg, 58-61; res asst, Inst Orthop, London, 63-64. *Concurrent Pos:* Hon registr, Royal Nat Orthop Hosp, London, 63-64; lectr, Polytech Inst Brooklyn; chief prosthetics & orthotics, dir bioeng, assoc scientist & asst attend, Hosp Spec Surg; asst prof, Cornell Med Col; Am-Brit-Can traveling fel, 70; mem, Comt Skeletal Systs & Mem Subcomt Bioeng, Nat Acad Sci-Nat Res Coun; mem, Subcomt Prosthetic & Orthotics Educ, Nat Acad Sci; mem, Comt Interplay Eng Biol & Med, Nat Mat Adv Bd; chief orthop surg, Vet Admin Ctr, Los Angeles. *Mem:* Am Orthop Asn; Orthop Res Soc; NY Acad Sci; Am Soc Testing & Mat; Am Col Surgeons; fel Int Asn Med & Biol Environ. *Res:* Biomechanics, biomaterials and tribology of hip, knee, shoulder replacement; biological consequences of "wear"; total and surface replacements of the hip and shoulder replacements. *Mailing Add:* Joint Replacement Inst 2400 S Flower St Los Angeles CA 90007. *Fax:* 213-744-1175

AMSTUTZ, HAROLD EMERSON, VETERINARY MEDICINE. *Current Pos:* prof vet sci & head dept large animal clins, 61-89, EMER PROF, PURDUE UNIV, WEST LAFAYETTE, 89- *Personal Data:* b Barrs Mill, Ohio, June 21, 19; m 49, Mabelle J Bower; c Suzanne M, Cynthia L, Patricia L & David B. *Educ:* Ohio State Univ, BS, 42, DVM, 45. *Honors & Awards:* Borden Award, Am Vet Med Asn, 78; Amstutz Williams Award, Am Asn Bovine Pratitioners, 86; Gustav Rosenberger Mem Award, Dutch Vet Asn, 92; Twelfth Int Vet Cong Prize, Am Vet Med Asn, 95. *Prof Exp:* From instr to prof vet med, Ohio State Univ, 47-61, actg chmn dept, 55-56, chmn, 56-61. *Concurrent Pos:* Organizer, VI Int Conf Cattle Dis, US, 70, XVII Int Conf Cattle Dis, 92. *Mem:* Am Asn Vet Clinicians (pres, 62-64); World Asn Buiatrics (pres, 72-82); Asn Bovine Practitioners (exec vpres, 89-93); Am Col Internal Med (pres, 73); Am Vet Med Asn. *Res:* Cattle respiratory diseases; cattle lameness; stray voltage. *Mailing Add:* Lynn Hall Purdue Univ West Lafayette IN 47907. *Fax:* 765-494-8560; *E-Mail:* gus@vet.purdue.edu

AMSTUTZ, LARRY IHRIG, SOLID STATE PHYSICS. *Current Pos:* Physicist, Electrotech Lab, 69-76, PHYSICIST, ELEC EQUIP DIV, US ARMY MOBILITY EQUIP RES & DEVELOP COMMAND, 76- *Personal Data:* b Wooster, Ohio, July 11, 41. *Educ:* Col Wooster, BA, 63; Duke Univ, PhD(physics), 69. *Mem:* Am Phys Soc; Sigma Xi. *Res:* Magnetic resonance; solid hydrogen; thermal and electrical conductivity in alloys; magnetic behavior of rare-earth alloys; applied superconductivity; numerical methods; high energy laser power supplies. *Mailing Add:* 8054 N Geyers Chapel Rd Smithville OH 44677

AMUNDRUD, DONALD LORNE, SAFEGUARDS, REACTOR PHYSICS. *Current Pos:* SAFEGUARDS OFFICER & INSPECTOR, IAEA, TOKYO, JAPAN, 91- *Personal Data:* b Calgary, Alta, May 22, 43; m 69; c 2. *Educ:* Univ Sask, Regina, BA Hons, 66; Purdue Univ, MS, 69. *Prof Exp:* Nuclear design engr, Ont Hydro, 69-72; reactor physicist, Atomic Energy Can Ltd Whiteshell Nuclear Res Estab, 72-77, safeguards analyst reactor physics, 77-79; reactor & start up & licensing engr, New Brunswick Elec Power Comn, 79-85; safeguards officer & inspector, IAEA, Vienna, Austria, 85-91. *Mem:* Can Asn Physicists; Chem Inst Can. *Res:* Safeguards methods and techniques on all aspects of the nuclear fuel cycle; start up planning, licensing engineering and emergency planning at point lepreau; tests of point lepreau; 600 mw candu; safeguards equipment, performance monitoring analysis of safeguards equipment. *Mailing Add:* c/o Mrs H Amundrud 14 Dunning Cres Regina SK S4S 3W1 Can

AMUNDSEN, CLIFFORD C, PHYSIOLOGICAL ECOLOGY, APPLIED ECOLOGY. *Current Pos:* res assoc, 67-69, asst prof, 69-74, ASSOC PROF BOT, UNIV TENN, KNOXVILLE, 74- *Personal Data:* b Norwalk, Conn, Dec 21, 33; m 56, Margie Roth; c 2. *Educ:* Idaho State Col, BS, 61; Univ Colo, Boulder, PhD(bot, physiol ecol), 67. *Prof Exp:* Res ecologist, Inst Arctic & Alpine Res, Univ Colo, Boulder, 65-67. *Concurrent Pos:* Consult, Battelle Mem Inst, US Forest Serv; prin investr Aleutian res, US Dept Energy, 68-; consult, Nat Park Serv, 75- & TVA, 92- *Mem:* Ecol Soc Am; Am Polar Soc. *Res:* Arctic-alpine and subarctic-subalpine physiological plant ecology and remote sensing; reservoir ecology disturbance ecology. *Mailing Add:* Dept Ecol & Evolutionary Biol Univ Tenn Knoxville TN 37996-1610. *Fax:* 423-974-3067

AMUNDSEN, LAWRENCE HARDIN, ORGANIC CHEMISTRY. *Current Pos:* from instr to prof, 36-73, actg head dept, 45-46, EMER PROF CHEM, UNIV CONN, 73- *Personal Data:* b Pine River, Wis, Sept 23, 09; wid; c Albert L, Ralph F (deceased), Franklin H & Bruce L. *Educ:* Col Ozarks, BS, 31; Univ Fla, PhD(org chem), 35. *Prof Exp:* Asst org chem, Univ Fla, 31-35; instr chem, Adelphi Col, 35-36. *Concurrent Pos:* Nat Defense Res Comt fel, Purdue Univ, 42-43; chemist, Venereal Dis Res Lab, USPHS, Staten Island, NY, 43-44. *Mem:* AAAS; Am Chem Soc. *Res:* Preparation and properties of aliphatic diamines; preparation of sulfonamides; allylic rearrangements in amination reactions. *Mailing Add:* 10-A Sycamore Dr Storrs CT 06268

AMUNDSON, CLYDE HOWARD, FOOD SCIENCE, AQUACULTURE. *Current Pos:* from instr to assoc prof, 56-70, from assoc chmn to chmn dept, 64-85, DIR FOOD ENG, UNIV WIS-MADISON, 70-, DIR AQUACULT RES CTR, 81- *Personal Data:* b Nekoosa, Wis, Aug 15, 27; m 52; c 2. *Educ:* Univ Wis-Madison, BS, 55, MS, 56, PhD(food sci, biochem), 60. *Honors & Awards:* Am Dairy Sci Asn Res Award, 71; Pfizer Res Award, 86. *Prof Exp:* Chemist, Sherwin-Williams Co, 50-52. *Concurrent Pos:* Consult, Bur Com Fisheries, Wash; prof food sci, 70-, prof agr eng, 82-, prof oceanog & limnol, Univ Wis-Madison, 80- *Mem:* Fel AAAS; fel NY Acad Sci; fel Am Inst Chem; Inst Food Technol; Am Chem Soc; World Aquacult Soc. *Res:* Flavor chemistry of food and food products; dehydration of foods and biological materials; fermentation chemistry of foods and food products; fat and oil chemistry and food enzymes. *Mailing Add:* 96 E Deer Run Park Rd Edgerton WI 53534

AMUNDSON, KARL RAYMOND, BLOCK COPOLYMERS, LIQUID CRYSTAL POLYMERS. *Current Pos:* RES SCIENTIST, AT&T BELL LABS, 89- *Personal Data:* b Minneapolis, Minn, Mar 11, 61; m 83. *Educ:* Univ Minn, BS(chem eng) & BS(physics), 83; Univ Calif, Berkeley, PhD(chem eng), 89. *Mem:* Am Phys Soc; AAAS. *Res:* Morphologies in thermotropic liquid crystalline polymers by means of nuclear magnetic resonance spectroscopy; effect of shear flow on polymer morphology by means of nuclear magnetic resonance spectroscopy; effect of electric fields on block copolymer morphology. *Mailing Add:* 34 Hill St Morristown NJ 07960-5362

AMUNDSON, MARY JANE, PSYCHIATRIC NURSING. *Current Pos:* ASSOC PROF NURSING, UNIV HAWAII, 75- *Personal Data:* b Keokuk, Iowa, Jan 23, 36; m 58; c 1. *Educ:* Univ Iowa, BS, 57; Univ Calif, Los Angeles, MS, 66, PhD(spec educ), 74. *Prof Exp:* Head nurse, Mendocino State Hosp, Talmage, Calif, 58-60; staff nursing, Langley Porter Inst, San Francisco, 60-61; clinical specialist & lectr nursing, Univ Calif, Los Angeles, Neuropsychiat Inst, 61-74; asst prof, Univ Ore, 74-75. *Mem:* Asn Women Sci; Am Asn Univ Prof. *Res:* Network for Pacific Island Mental Health Workers. *Mailing Add:* 1380 Saint Louis Dr Honolulu HI 96816

AMUNDSON, MERLE E, ANALYTICAL & PHARMACEUTICAL CHEMISTRY, CLINICAL SCIENCE. *Current Pos:* Sr analytical chemist, Eli Lilly & Co, 61-67, res scientist, 67-68, head agr prod develop dept, 68-71, head agr biochem, 71-75, dir analytical chem & agr biochem, 75-78, dir toxicol div, 78-83, EXEC DIR, LILLY RES LABS, DIV ELI LILLY & CO, 84- *Personal Data:* b Sioux Falls, SDak, Aug 21, 36; m 58; c 3. *Educ:* SDak State Univ, BS, 58; Mass Col Pharm, MS, 59, PhD(pharm), 61. *Mem:* Am Chem Soc; Soc Environ Toxicol & Chem; NY Acad Sci. *Res:* Degradation of pesticides in soil and plants; analytical methodology for determination of residues in soil, plant tissue, and animal tissue; toxicology of chemicals; clinical trials. *Mailing Add:* 1414 Sherwood Dr Greenfield IN 46140-1142

AMUNDSON, NEAL R, CHEMICAL ENGINEERING. *Current Pos:* vpres, 87-89, CULLEN PROF CHEM ENG, UNIV HOUSTON, 77- *Personal Data:* b St Paul, Minn, Jan 10, 16. *Educ:* Univ Minn, BCE, 37, MS, 41, PhD(math), 45. *Hon Degrees:* ScD, Univ Minn, 85, EngD, Univ Notre Dame,

86. *Honors & Awards:* Indust & Eng Chem Award, Am Chem Soc, 60; William H Walker Award, Am Inst Chem Engrs, 61, Warren K Lewis Award, 71, Richard H Wilhelm Award, 73; Vincent Bendix Award, Am Soc Eng Educ, 70. *Prof Exp:* Process engr, Stand Oil Co, NJ, 37-39; from teaching asst to asst prof, Dept Math, Univ Minn, 39-47, from assoc prof to prof, Dept Chem Eng, 47-67, Regents' prof, 67-77, head, 49-77. *Concurrent Pos:* Fulbright scholar, Cambridge Univ, Eng, 54-55, Guggenheim fel, 55; Guggenheim fel, NATO sr fel, 75. *Mem:* Nat Acad Sci; Am Acad Eng; Am Inst Chem; Am Math Soc; fel Am Inst Chem Engrs; Am Chem Soc. *Res:* Author 5 books and 300 journal publications. *Mailing Add:* Dept Chem Eng 4800 Calhoun 5222D Univ Houston Houston TX 77204-4792

AMUNDSON, ROBERT GALE, PLANT GAS EXCHANGE, AIR POLLUTION. *Current Pos:* CONSULT, 93- *Personal Data:* b Sunnyside, Wash, Oct 20, 46; m 80. *Educ:* Whitman Col, BA, 69; Univ Wash, MS, 73, PhD(bot), 78. *Prof Exp:* Fel, Boyce Thompson Inst Plant Res, Cornell Univ, 78-80, res assoc, 80-83, from asst scientist to assoc scientist, 83-93. *Mem:* Am Soc Plant Physiologists; Sigma Xi; Air Pollution Control Asn; AAAS; Am Forestry Asn. *Res:* Effects of air pollution on the net photosynthesis, transpiration and pollutant uptake of plants and how these effects are manifested in plant growth and yield. *Mailing Add:* 1616 SW Harbor Way No 403 Portland OR 97201-5165

AMY, JONATHAN WEEKS, CHEMISTRY, CHEMICAL INSTRUMENTATION. *Current Pos:* Res assoc chem, 54-60, from assoc prof to prof chem, 63-88, dir instrumentation 75-88, ASSOC DIR LABS, PURDUE UNIV, 60-, EMER PROF CHEM, 88- *Personal Data:* b Delaware, Ohio, Mar 3, 23; m 47; c 3. *Educ:* Ohio Wesleyan Univ, BA, 48; Purdue Univ, MS, 50, PhD(molecular spectros), 55. *Honors & Awards:* Instrumentation Award, Am Chem Soc, 81. *Concurrent Pos:* Consult chem instrumentation, Asn Am Univs Adv Panel, 80 & AAAS Adv Panel, 81; dir res, Finnigan MAT, 83-84. *Mem:* Am Chem Soc; Sigma Xi; AAAS. *Res:* Molecular and mass spectroscopy; gas chromatography; chemical instrumentation; surface chemistry. *Mailing Add:* 357 Overlook Dr West Lafayette IN 47906

AMY, NANCY KLEIN, BIOCHEMISTRY, ENZYMOLOGY. *Current Pos:* asst prof biochem, 81-88, ASSOC PROF NUTRIT, UNIV CALIF, BERKELEY, 88- *Personal Data:* b Philadelphia, Pa, June 23, 47; m 71, Christopher; c Alex & Robert. *Educ:* Gwynedd Mercy Col, AB, 69; Univ Va, PhD(enzym), 73. *Prof Exp:* Fel membrane biochem, Med Ctr, Univ Va, 73-74, res assoc enzym, Dept Biol, 74-77; res assoc biochem, Duke Univ Med Ctr, 77-81. *Mem:* Am Soc Microbiol; Am Soc Biochem & Molecular Biol; Am Soc Nutrit Sci. *Res:* Role of metals in enzyme function; molybdenum cofactor and incorporation into nitrate reductase; molybdenum carrier protein. *Mailing Add:* Dept Nutrit Sci Univ Calif Berkeley CA 94720. *E-Mail:* nkamy@nature.berkeley.edu

AMY, ROBERT LEWIS, ZOOLOGY. *Current Pos:* RETIRED. *Personal Data:* b Jamestown, Pa, July 18, 19; m 44; c 3. *Educ:* Thiel Col, BS, 41; Univ Pittsburgh, MS, 49; Univ Va, PhD(biol), 55. *Prof Exp:* From asst prof to assoc prof, Susquehanna Univ, 49-58; assoc prof, Southwestern Univ, Memphis, 58-61, prof biol, 61-86, chmn dept, 68-86. *Concurrent Pos:* Res partic, Oak Ridge Nat Lab, 55 & 56; USPHS fel, Nat Blood Transfusion Ctr, France, 64-65; coinvestr, Habrobracon proj, NASA Biosatellite Prog, 66-69; USPHS fel, Inst Cellular Path, France, 71-72. *Mem:* AAAS; Radiation Res Soc; Am Soc Zool; Soc Develop Biol. *Res:* Effects of radiation on development in insects. *Mailing Add:* 816 Charles Pl Memphis TN 38112

AMZEL, L MARIO, X-RAY DIFFRACTION ANALYSIS, PROTEIN CONFORMATION. *Current Pos:* teaching fel, 69-70, instr, 70-73, from asst prof to assoc prof, 73-83, PROF BIOPHYS, MED SCH, JOHNS HOPKINS UNIV, 84- *Personal Data:* b Buenos Aires, Arg, Oct 25, 42; US citizen; c 2. *Educ:* Univ Buenos Aires, lic, 65, PhD(phys chem), 68. *Prof Exp:* Grad teaching asst, Univ Buenos Aires, 65-66; instr phys chem, Univ Cent Venezuela, 67-69. *Mem:* Am Crystallog Asn; Biophys Soc; AAAS; Soc Latin Am Biophysicists. *Res:* Structure and conformation of proteins, immunoglobulins and proteins involved in ATP synthesis; modeling of the conformation of the combining site of immunoglobulins. *Mailing Add:* Dept Biophys Johns Hopkins Med Sch 725 N Wolfe St Baltimore MD 21205-2185

ANACKER, ROBERT LEROY, RICKETTSIAE ANTIGENS. *Current Pos:* RES MICROBIOLOGIST, NAT INST ALLERGY & INFECTIOUS DIS, NIH, ROCKY MOUNTAIN LAB, HAMILTON, MT, 60- *Educ:* Univ Wash, Seattle, PhD(microbiol), 56. *Mailing Add:* 223 Hilltop Dr Hamilton MT 59840

ANAGNOSTAKIS, SANDRA LEE, MYCOLOGY, GENETICS. *Current Pos:* PLANT PATHOLOGIST & GENETICIST FUNGAL PLANT PATHOGENS, CONN AGR EXP STA, 66- *Personal Data:* b Coffeyville, Kans, May 14, 39; m 69, Christopher; c Kathryn. *Educ:* Univ Calif, Riverside, BA, 61; Univ Tex, Austin, MA, 66; Justus Liebig Univ, Giessen, PhD, 85. *Mem:* Mycol Soc Am; Ecol Soc Am. *Res:* Genetic studies of fungal plant pathogens, including maize smut, chestnut blight and Dutch elm disease; techniques for production of haploids of higher plants. *Mailing Add:* Conn Agr Exp Sta PO Box 1106 New Haven CT 06504. *Fax:* 203-789-7232; *E-Mail:* slanagno@caes.state.ct.us

ANAGNOSTOPOULOS, CONSTANTINE E, ORGANIC CHEMISTRY, POLYMER CHEMISTRY. *Current Pos:* MANAGING GEN PARTNER, GATEWAY VENTURE PARTNERS, 86- *Personal Data:* b Greece, Nov 1, 22; nat US; m 49; c 1. *Educ:* Brown Univ, ScB, 49; Harvard Univ, MA, 50, PhD(chem), 52. *Prof Exp:* Res chemist, Monsanto Co, 52-57, scientist, 57-61, from asst dir to dir res, 61-68, dir res, Org Chem Div, 68-69, Rubber Chem, 69-70 & Tire Textiles Div, 70-71, gen mgr, New Enterprise Div, 71-75, gen mgr, Rubber Chem Div, 75-80, vpres & managing dir, Europe-Africa & chmn, Monsanto Europe, 81-82, corp vpres, Corp Develop, Monsanto Co, St Louis, 82-86. *Concurrent Pos:* Mem, Nat Inventors Coun, 64-72; mem, Presidential Panel Prizes for Innovation; US-USSR Trade & Econ Coun, 80-82; chmn bd, St Louis Technol Ctr, Mo, 85-89. *Mem:* Am Chem Soc; Sigma Xi (vpres, 59); Soc Chem Indust; Com Develop Asn. *Res:* Synthesis of steroids, derivatives, amino acids and analogs; plasticization of vinyl polymers; polymer-diluent interactions; photocatalyzed oxidation of polyalkylenes. *Mailing Add:* 8000 Maryland Suite 1190 Clayton MO 63105-3752

ANAGNOSTOPOULOS, CONSTANTINE N, MICROELECTRONICS. *Current Pos:* Res physicist, Eastman Kodak Co, 75-79, sr res physicist, 79-82, group leader, CMOS/BICMOS Tech Group, 85-89, RES ASSOC & MEM SR STAFF, EASTMAN KODAK CO, 82-, GROUP LEADER ASIC DESIGN GROUP, 89- *Personal Data:* b Patras, Greece, July 4, 44; US citizen; m 69; c Effie & Athena. *Educ:* Merrimack Col, BS, 67; Brown Univ, ScM, 71; Univ RI, PhD(elec eng), 75. *Honors & Awards:* Centennial Medal, Inst Elec & Electronics Engrs. *Concurrent Pos:* Founder, Custom Integrated Circuits Conf, 79, tech prog chmn, 79, 80, conf chmn, 81, gen chmn, 82, mem tech prog & steering comts, 79-91; guest ed, J Solid State Circuits Spec Issues Technol Custom Integrated Circuits, 84, 86 & 87; assoc ed, J Solid Circuits, Inst Elec & Electronics Engrs, 90- *Mem:* Inst Elec & Electronics Engrs. *Res:* Solid state image sensors, custom integrated circuits, ASIC's and imaging systems. *Mailing Add:* Eastman Kodak Co Digital & Appl Imaging Div Rochester NY 14650. *E-Mail:* cna@kodak.com

ANAND, AMARJIT SINGH, REPRODUCTIVE PHYSIOLOGY, BIOCHEMISTRY & VETERINARY MEDICINE. *Current Pos:* from asst prof to assoc prof physiol, Univ Wis-Oshkosh, 67-73, assoc prof biol, 73-78, univ vet, 77-85, PROF BIOL, UNIV WIS-OSHKOSH, 79- *Personal Data:* b New Delhi, India, June 1, 40; US citizen; m 88, Antonia; c Michael & Stephen. *Educ:* Univ Panjab, India, DVM, 62; Univ Wis-Madison, MS, 65, PhD(physiol), 67. *Prof Exp:* Vet, Vet Med Sch, Univ Panjab, India, 58-62; res asst physiol & biochem, Univ Wis-Madison, 62-67. *Concurrent Pos:* Co-recipient, Wis State Univ Bd Regents res grant, 68-69; NSF instnl res grant & Ford Found fel, 70-71. *Mem:* Am Vet Med Asn. *Res:* Veterinary medicine. *Mailing Add:* Dept Biol Univ Wis 800 Algoma Blvd Oshkosh WI 54901. *Fax:* 920-424-1101; *E-Mail:* anand@uwash.edu

ANAND, DAVINDER K, SYSTEMS ANALYSIS & ENERGY, DESIGN PROTOTYPING. *Current Pos:* from asst prof to prof mech eng, 65-89, prof mech eng & systs res, 89-92, PROF & CHMN MECH ENG, UNIV MD, 91- *Personal Data:* b Lahore, India, Apr 4, 39; US citizen; m 61, Asha; c Dilip & Anita. *Educ:* George Washington Univ, BS, 59, MS, 61, DSc(mech eng), 65. *Honors & Awards:* Superior Performance Award & Outstanding Accomplishment Award, NSF, 81. *Prof Exp:* Engr, Carrier Corp, 59-63; asst prof mech eng, George Washington Univ, 64-65. *Concurrent Pos:* Consult, Tracor Corp, 75-78; prin investr, Dept Energy, 75-81, NSF, NASA, Nat Inst Stand & Technol & pvt industs, 81-88; pres, TPI, Inc, 78-89; prof engr, State of Md, 84- *Mem:* Fel Am Soc Mech Engrs. *Res:* Satellite thermal and attitude control; solar and photovoltaic energy systems, energy analysis, magnetic bearings and manufacturing automation; published 150 papers and 3 books; patented heatpipe control. *Mailing Add:* Dept Mech Eng Univ Md College Park MD 20742-3035. *Fax:* 301-314-9477; *E-Mail:* dkanand@eng.umd.edu

ANAND, RAJEN S(INGH), FETAL PHYSIOLOGY. *Current Pos:* prof physiol & biol, Calif State Univ, 70-85, chmn, Dept Anat & Physiol, 85-89, chair, Commun Dis Dept, 90-92, PROF PHYSIOL, CALIF STATE UNIV, LONG BEACH, 92-; DIR, CTR NUTRIT POLICY & PROM, USDA, 95- *Personal Data:* b Kohat, India, June 8, 37; US citizen; m 69, Angela Bawa; c Sunjay & Shabeen. *Educ:* Agra Univ, BSc, 56; Marathwada Agr Univ, Parbhani, DVM, 60; Univ Calif, Davis, PhD(physiol), 69. *Honors & Awards:* Hertzendorf Mem Physiol Award, 69. *Prof Exp:* Instr biol chem, Col Vet Sci & Res Inst, Mhow, India, 60-63; res asst physiol chem, Univ Calif, Davis, 63-69, res physiologist, 69-70. *Concurrent Pos:* New fac res grant, Calif State Univ, Long Beach, 70-71; fel endocrinol, Sch Med, Univ Calif, Los Angeles, 77-78; mem exec bd, Calif Dem Party, 88-; deleg, Dem Nat Conv, 88, 92; chair, Indo-Am Polit Asn, 89-, Asian & Pac Islander Caucus, 91-93, vchair, 89-91. *Mem:* Am Physiol Soc; AAAS; Sigma Xi; Am Heart Asn; Am Inst Biol Sci. *Res:* Energy metabolism in the fetus in utero; placental transfer of glucose; glucose metabolism in the fetal sheep. *Mailing Add:* USDA Ctr Nutrit Policy & Prom 1120 20th St NW Suite 200 N Lobby Washington DC 20036. *Fax:* 202-208-2322

ANAND, SATISH CHANDRA, PLANT BREEDING, PLANT GENETICS. *Current Pos:* assoc prof, 80-84, PROF, UNIV MO, COLUMBIA, 85- *Personal Data:* b India, Aug 9, 30; US citizen; m 58, Sushma Ahuja; c Ajay, Alka & Sanjay. *Educ:* Univ Delhi, BS, 51; NC State Univ, MAgr, 59; Univ Wis, PhD(agron), 62. *Honors & Awards:* Prod Res Award, Am Soybean Asn, 93. *Prof Exp:* Res assoc, Univ Ill, Urbana, 62-63; wheat breeder, Punjab Agr Univ, India, 64-71, sr geneticist, 72-73; soybean breeder, McNair Seed Co, 73-79. *Concurrent Pos:* Mem cereals & pulses subcomt, Indian Stand Inst, 64-72; zonal coordr wheat, Indian Coun Agr Res, 68-72; mem, Nat Soybean Variety Rev Bd, Am Soc Agron, 90-93. *Mem:* Am Soc Agron; fel Indian Soc Genetics & Plant Breeding; Crop Sci Soc Am; Soc Nematologists. *Res:* Breeding and development of high yielding soybean varieties resistant to diseases and nematodes; develop soybeans with lower saturated fatty acids and higher levels of protein inseed. *Mailing Add:* Univ Mo Columbia PO Box 160 Portageville MO 63873. *Fax:* 573-379-5875; *E-Mail:* agrosam@showme.missouri.edu

ANAND, SUBHASH CHANDRA, CIVIL ENGINEERING, ENGINEERING MECHANICS. *Current Pos:* assoc prof, 72-76, PROF CIVIL ENG, CLEMSON UNIV, 76- *Personal Data:* b Lyallpur, India, July 27, 33; m 65, Vera Barata; c Mina L & Indu S. *Educ:* Banaras Univ, BS, 55; Northwestern Univ, MS, 65, PhD(struct eng), 68. *Honors & Awards:* Fac Achievement Award, Col Eng, Clemson Univ, 79; Fulbright lectr, Univ Uruguay, 80. *Prof Exp:* Asst engr, Pub Works Dept, India, 56 & Indian Iron & Steel Co, 56-58; engr-in-training, Hein, Lehmann & Co, WGer, 58-59; struct designer, Kloeckner-Humboldt-Deutz Co, 60-64; teaching asst, Northwestern Univ, 65-68; asst prof, Calif State Univ, Sacramento, 68-70; assoc prof, Ill Inst Technol, 70-72. *Concurrent Pos:* Educ grant, NSF, 72, res grants, 73, 78, 81, 85, 88, 91 & 93; Off Water Resources & Technol grant, 80. *Mem:* Am Acad Mech; fel Am Soc Civil Engrs; Am Soc Eng Educ; Int Asn Comp Mech. *Res:* Mathematical and finite element modelling of masonry; shear strength of masonry; creep and moisture strains in masonry; prestressed masonry wall panels. *Mailing Add:* 116 Valley View Dr Clemson SC 29631-0911. *Fax:* 864-656-2670; *E-Mail:* anandsub@eng.clemson.edu

ANANDALINGAM, G, SYSTEMS SCIENCE. *Current Pos:* from asst prof to assoc prof, 87-96, dir, Exec Eng Prog, 90-95, PROF SYSTS ENG, UNIV PA, 96-, DEPT CHAIR, 97- *Personal Data:* b Cambridge, Eng, Oct 27, 53; US citizen; m 87, Deepa Ollapally; c Kavitha & Siddharth. *Educ:* Univ Cambridge, Eng, BA & MA, 75; Harvard Univ, SM, 77, PhD(opers res & econ), 81. *Prof Exp:* Engr & economist, Brookhaven Nat Lab, 81-84; asst prof systs eng, Univ Va, 84-87. *Mem:* Fel AAAS; fel Inst Elec & Electronics Engrs; Opers Res Soc; Inst Mgt Sci. *Res:* Optimization and design of networks with application to telecommunications, computer, and electric power networks; multi-agent multi-attribute decision problems; games on networks; technology policy. *Mailing Add:* Dept Systs Univ Pa Philadelphia PA 19104-6315. *Fax:* 215-573-2065; *E-Mail:* anand@seas.upenn.edu

ANANDAN, JEEVA S, FOUNDATIONS QUANTUM MECHANISMS, GENERAL RELATIVITY & GAUGE THEORIES. *Current Pos:* assoc prof, 86-90, PROF PHYSICS, UNIV SC, 90- *Personal Data:* b Jaffna, Sri Lanka, June 10, 48; US citizen. *Educ:* Univ Colombo, BSd(Hons), 70; Univ Pittsburgh, MS, 73, PhD(physics), 78. *Honors & Awards:* First Prize, Gravity Res Found, 83; Russell Res Award Sci & Eng, 92. *Prof Exp:* Asst lectr math, Univ Colombo, 70-72; postdoctoral fel, Univ Md, 78-80, Univ Calif, Berkeley, 80-82, Max-Planck-Inst, Munich, 82-85. *Concurrent Pos:* Nat Ctr Sci Res fel, France, 85; vis prof physics, NY Univ, 87-88, Univ Oxford, 95; Alexander von Humboldt fel physics & astrophys, Max-Planck-Inst, Munich, 89-90. *Mem:* Fel Am Phys Soc. *Res:* Foundations of physics, especially foundations of quantum theory, gravitation and gauge fields and their effects on quantum systems, geometry of quantum theory, quantum gravity. *Mailing Add:* Dept Physics Univ SC Columbia SC 29208. *Fax:* 803-777-3065; *E-Mail:* jeeva@sc.edu

ANANDAN, MUNISAMY, PLASMA DISPLAYS, LIQUID CRYSTAL DISPLAYS. *Current Pos:* RES SCIENTIST PLASMA, BACKLIGHT DEVICE FOR FULL COLOR, LIQUID CRYSTAL DISPLAY, THOMAS ELECTRONICS INC, WAYNE, NJ, 88- *Personal Data:* b India, July 1, 39; m 68; c 2. *Educ:* Voorhees Col, Vellore, India, BS, 60; Annamali Univ, India, MS, 64; Indian Inst Technol, Bombay, MTech, 67; Indian Inst Sci, Bangalore, PhD(plasma display), 80. *Honors & Awards:* First Prize in Res & Develop Excellence, Electronics Industs Asn India, 85. *Prof Exp:* Sci officer electronics, Atomic Energy Estab, Bombay, 63-64; develop engr electron devices, Bharat Electronics Ltd Bangalore, 67-72, dept mgr display devices, 72-82, mgr res & develop, liquid crystal display, 82-87; vis scientist plasma displays, Bell Commun Res, Red Bank, NJ, 87-88. *Concurrent Pos:* Mat adv, Randl Tube Inc & Dept Health & Human Serv, Fla Int Univ, 90- *Mem:* Am Phys Soc; Inst Elec & Electronics Engrs; Soc Info Display; Illumination Eng Soc. *Res:* Plasma display; electric field pattern study of coplanar DC plasma display; new self-aligned process for color plasma display; liquid crystal display; novel three terminal true analogue liquid crystal display with new electrode structure-detailed investigation; backlighting devices; plasma row backlight device development for ferro electric column shutter liquid crystal display; novel flat fluorescent backlight device development for full color LCD; author of many publications; 6 patents. *Mailing Add:* 509 Somerset Ct Fishkill NY 12524

ANAND-SRIVASTAVA, MADHU BALA, BIOCHEMICAL PHARMACOLOGY. *Current Pos:* ASST PROF, UNIV MONTREAL, 81- *Educ:* Delhi Univ, India, MSc, 72; Univ Man, Can, PhD(physiol), 78. *Prof Exp:* Res assoc, Vanderbilt Univ, 78-80. *Concurrent Pos:* Sr investr, Clin Res Inst, Montreal, 81-90; scholar, Can Heart Found, 82-88; scientist, Med Res Coun, 90- *Mem:* Int Soc Heart Res; Can Biochem Soc; Am Soc Pharmacol & Exp Therapeut; Am Soc Biochem & Molecular Biol; Can Hypertension Soc. *Res:* Hormonal regulation of adenylate cyclase in cardiovascular system in health and disease; G-binding proteins and gene expression; atrial natriuretic factor and second messengers. *Mailing Add:* Dept Physiol Univ Montreal PO Box 6128 Succursale Centre Ville Montreal PQ H3C 3J7 Can

ANANTHA, NARASIPUR GUNDAPPA, SOLID STATE PHYSICS. *Current Pos:* staff engr, Components Div, 67-69, develop eng, Systs Prods Div, 69-74, sr engr mgr devices, Gen Tech Div, 74-82, consult, semiconductor technol, CHQ, 82-86, SR TECH STAFF, IMD, IBM, 86- *Personal Data:* b Hassan, Mysore, India, Feb 4, 34; US citizen; m 64, Lavanya Vundavalli; c Ramesh & Ravi. *Educ:* Mysore Univ, India, BScHons, 54; Indian Inst Sci, DIISc, 58; Mass Inst Technol, SM, 60; Harvard Univ, PhD(appl physics), 65. *Honors & Awards:* Gold Medal Physics, Mysore Univ, India. *Prof Exp:* Design engr semiconductor devices, Gen Elec Co, 65-67. *Mem:* Sr mem Inst Elec & Electronics Engrs. *Res:* Study of semiconductor device physics and operation with emphasis on silicon high speed switching devices for very large scale integrated circuits applications; study of physical limits, process limits of microelectronics. *Mailing Add:* 3 Darci Dr Hopewell Junction NY 12533. *Fax:* 914-892-6083; *E-Mail:* nanantha@vnet.ibm.com

ANANTHA NARAYANAN, VENKATARAMAN, PHYSICS, SPECTROSCOPY. *Current Pos:* PROF PHYSICS & THEORET VIBRATIONAL SPECTRAL STUDIES, SAVANNAH STATE COL, 65- *Personal Data:* b Madras City, India, Oct 22, 36; m 67, Jayalakshmi; c Radha. *Educ:* Annamalai Univ, Madras, MA, 57, MSc, 58; Indian Inst Sci, Bangalore, PhD(physics, spectros), 62. *Prof Exp:* Vis fel, Mellon Inst, 63-64; Robert A Welch Found fel chem, Tex A&M Univ, 64-65. *Concurrent Pos:* Hon Chem Abstractor, Am Chem Soc, 69-; coop res partic, Oak Ridge Nat Lab, 70, 88, 89-93, 94 & 96; summer res, Bruceton Lab, 85, 86 & 88- *Mem:* Optical Soc Am; Am Asn Physics Teachers; fel Brit Inst Physics; Am Asn Univ Prof; Indian Inst Sci Alumni Asn; Soc Appl Spectroscopists. *Res:* Vibrational spectra of crystals and hydrogen bonded systems; far infrared and Raman techniques; use of spectral data for evaluation of force constants and other chemical bond properties; vibrational spectra; molecular constants; crystal fields; computer oriented physics teaching; innovative general physics curriculum materials; laser spectroscopic diagnostics. *Mailing Add:* Dept Math & Physics PO Box 20473 Savannah State Col Savannah GA 31404. *Fax:* 912-927-9330; *E-Mail:* ananthv@mb.ssc.peachnet.edu

ANANTHANARAYANAN, VETTAIKKORU S, BIOPHYSICAL CHEMISTRY, PROTEIN PHYSICAL CHEMISTRY. *Current Pos:* PROF BIOCHEM, MCMASTER UNIV, ONT. *Personal Data:* b Madras, India, Nov 29, 38; m 64; c 2. *Educ:* Madras Univ, BSc, 58, MSc, 60, PhD(phys chem), 65. *Prof Exp:* Teaching fel biochem, Univ Western Ont, 66-68; teaching fel chem, Cornell Univ, 68-71; asst prof molecular biophys, Indian Inst Sci, Bangalore, 72-78; assoc prof, 79-82, prof biochem, Mem Univ Nfld, 82- *Concurrent Pos:* Vis asst prof, Cornell Univ, 72; Can commonwealth res fel & vis asst prof, Mem Univ Nfld, 76-77; prin investr grants, Med Res Coun Can, 79-, NIH, 80-82 & Can Heart Found, 80-; vis scientist, Med Res Coun Can, 85-86; mem, Biochem Grants Comt, Med Res Coun Can, 87-90. *Mem:* Can Biochem Soc; Am Soc Biol Chemists; NY Acad Sci; AAAS; Can Biophys Soc. *Res:* Biomolecular spectroscopy; conformation of peptides, polypeptides and proteins; conformational transitions; structure-function relationship in proteins; structural aspects of collagen biosynthesis; structure-function studies on antifreeze proteins; structure of hormones and drugs. *Mailing Add:* Dept Biochem McMaster Univ Health Sci Ctr 1200 Main St W Hamilton ON L8N 3Z5 Can

ANANTHARAMAN, TANJORE RAMACHANDRA, structural metallurgy, rapid solidification technology, for more information see previous edition

ANASTASIO, SALVATORE, MATHEMATICS, COMPUTER SCIENCE. *Current Pos:* assoc prof, 70-72, PROF MATH, STATE UNIV NY COL NEW PALTZ, 72- *Personal Data:* b Brooklyn, NY, Mar 12, 32; m 57; c 2. *Educ:* Cathedral Col, AB, 54; NY Univ, MS, 61, PhD(math), 64. *Prof Exp:* Instr math, Iona Col, 59-61; asst prof, Fordham Univ, 64-70. *Mem:* Am Math Soc; Math Asn Am; Hist Sci Soc. *Res:* History of mathematics; von Neumann algebras; history and philosophy of science. *Mailing Add:* State Univ NY Col New Paltz NY 12561-2499

ANASTASSIOU, DIMITRIS, SIGNAL PROCESSING, COMMUNICATIONS. *Current Pos:* PROF ELEC ENG, COLUMBIA UNIV. *Personal Data:* b Athens, Greece, Mar 31, 52; m 78. *Educ:* Nat Tech Univ Athens, Grad dipl, 74; Univ Calif, Berkeley, MS, 75, PhD(elec eng), 79. *Prof Exp:* Res asst, Electron Res Lab, Univ Calif, Berkeley, 74-75 & 76-78; mem res staff, TJ Watson Res Ctr, IBM Corp, 78- *Concurrent Pos:* Teaching asst, Dept Elec Eng & Comput Sci, Univ Calif, Berkeley, 76; mem staff, LK Comput Systs Consults Ltd, Nicosia, Cyprus. *Mem:* Sigma Xi; Inst Elec & Electronics Engrs. *Res:* Signal processing and communications; development and implementation of algorithms for image processing and data compression for teleconferencing systems. *Mailing Add:* Dept Elec Eng Columbia Univ Main Div New York NY 10027

ANBAR, MICHAEL, MASS SPECTROMETRY, INFRARED IMAGING. *Current Pos:* prof biophys sci & chmn dept, 77-90, FAC PROF, SCH MED, STATE UNIV NY, BUFFALO, 90- *Personal Data:* b Danzig, June 29, 27; m 53, Ada Komet; c Ran D & Ariel D. *Educ:* Hebrew Univ, Jerusalem, MSc, 50, PhD(phys org chem), 53. *Honors & Awards:* Zondek Award, Israel Med Asn, 62; Pres Award, Am Acad Thermology, 90. *Prof Exp:* Instr chem, Univ Chicago, 53-55; sr scientist, Weizmann Inst Sci, 55-60, prof, Frienberg Grad Sch, 60-67; sr res assoc exobiol, Ames Res Ctr, 67-68; dir phys sci, SRI Int, 68-72, dir mass spectrometry, Res Ctr, 72-77. *Concurrent Pos:* Dir, Radioisotope Training Ctr, Weizmann Inst Sci, 56-59 & Radiation Res Dept, AEC Soreq Nuclear Res Ctr, Israel, 59-66; head chem div, Israel AEC Res Lab, 62-66; sr res assoc, Argonne Nat Lab, 63-64; prof inorg chem, Univ Tel Aviv, 66-67; assoc dean appl res & dir, Health Care Instrument & Device Inst, 83-85; dir, Interdept Clin Biophys Group, 90- *Mem:* Am Chem Soc; Royal Chem Soc; Am Soc Mass Spectrom; NY Acad Sci; Biophys Soc; Inst Elec & Electronics Engrs; Clin Chem Soc; Am Acad Thermology; Am Asn Clin Chem; Am Phys Soc; Soc Photo-Optical Instrumentation Engrs. *Res:* Mechanisms of organic and inorganic reactions; isotope methodology in biology and medicine; radiation chemistry and molecular radiobiology;

hydrated electron chemistry; mass spectrometry, field ionization mass spectrometry in particular; molten salt electrochemistry; ultrasonics and sonochemistry; hard tissue biochemistry; evolvement of life; computer assisted learning; clinical thermography. *Mailing Add:* 145 Deer Run Rd Amherst NY 14221-1823. *E-Mail:* manbar@ubmedf.buffalo.edu

ANCEL, FREDRIC D, TOPOLOGY. *Current Pos:* ASSOC PROF MATH, UNIV WIS, MILWAUKEE, 86- *Personal Data:* b Chicago, Ill, Aug 2, 43. *Educ:* Amherst Col, BA, 65; Univ Wis-Madison, PhD(math), 76. *Mem:* Am Math Soc. *Mailing Add:* Dept Math Univ Wis Milwaukee WI 53201

ANCHEL, MARJORIE WOLFF, BIOCHEMISTRY. *Current Pos:* sr chemist & adminr lab, 72-77, EMER SR SCIENTIST, NY BOT GARDEN, 77- *Personal Data:* b New York, NY, May 6, 10; m 42. *Educ:* Columbia Univ, BA, 31, MA, 33, PhD(biol chem), 39. *Prof Exp:* Fel, Col Physicians & Surg, Columbia Univ, 37; asst chem, Queens Col, NY, 39-41 & Columbia Univ, 41-43; res assoc, Squibb Inst Med Res, 43-46. *Mem:* Fel AAAS; Am Chem Soc; Mycol Soc Am; fel NY Acad Sci; Am Soc Biol Chemists. *Res:* Antibiotics; natural polyacetylenes; chemistry and biogenesis of fungal products. *Mailing Add:* 147-01 Third Ave Whitestone NY 11357

ANCKER, CLINTON J(AMES), JR, APPLIED MATHEMATICS, MILITARY OPERATIONS RESEARCH. *Current Pos:* prof indust & systs eng & chmn dept, 68-84, EMER PROF, UNIV SOUTHERN CALIF, 84- *Personal Data:* b Cedar Falls, Iowa, June 21, 19; m 47, Margaret Rees; c Clinton J III, Evan R, Megan L & Scott R. *Educ:* Purdue Univ, BSME, 40; Univ Calif, Berkeley, MS, 49, ME, 50; Stanford Univ, PhD(eng mech), 55. *Prof Exp:* Cadet engr, Detroit Edison Co, 40-41, jr engr, 46; instr eng mech, Purdue Univ, 46-47; asst prof eng design, Univ Calif, Berkeley, 47-55; opers analyst, Opers Res Off, Md, 55-56; sr engr, Booz-Allen Appl Res, Inc, Ill, 56-58; mgr, Analco Serv Co, Ill, 58-59; head math & opers res staff, Syst Develop Corp, 59-67; dir, Nat Hwy Safety Inst, US Dept Transp, 67-68. *Concurrent Pos:* Consult, Opers Res Off, 56-57; mem exec comt, Mil Opers Res Symp, 61-65; mem nat coun, Opers Res Soc, 70-73. *Mem:* Opers Res Soc Am. *Res:* Theory of elasticity; theory of queues; stochastic models of combat; traffic flow theory. *Mailing Add:* 23908 Malibu Knolls Rd Malibu CA 90265-4823

ANCKER-JOHNSON, BETSY, ENVIRONMENTAL SCIENCE POLICY. *Current Pos:* RETIRED. *Personal Data:* b St Louis, Mo, Apr 27, 29; m 58; c 4. *Educ:* Wellesley Col, BA, 49; Tubingen Univ, PhD(physics), 53. *Hon Degrees:* DSc, NY Polytech Inst, 79, Univ Southern Calif, 84; LLD, Bates Col, 80. *Prof Exp:* Jr res physicist & lectr physics, Univ Calif, Berkeley, 53-54; mem staff, Inter-Varsity Christian Fel, 54-56; sr res physicist, Microwave Physics Lab, Sylvania Elec Prods, Inc, 56-58; mem tech staff, David Sarnoff Res Ctr, Radio Corp Am, 58-61; res specialist, Electronic Sci Lab, Boeing Sci Res Labs, Boeing Aerospace Co, 61-70, supvr solid state & plasma electronics, 70-71, mgr advan energy syst, 71-73; asst secy com for sci & technol, US Dept Com, 73-77; assoc lab dir phys res, Argonne Nat Lab, 77-79; vpres, Environ Activ Staff, GM Tech Ctr, Gen Motors Corp, 79-92. *Concurrent Pos:* Mem, US-USSR Comn Sci Technol, 73-77, Comn Energy, 75-77; mem bd dirs, Soc Automotive Engrs, 79-82, Motor Vehicle Mfrs Asn, 82-; chair, Eng Policy Comt, Motor Vehicle Mfrs Asn, 81-84; mem, US Safety Rev Panel Antarctica, NSF, 87-88; regents lectr, Dept Elec Eng & Computer Sci, Univ Calif, Berkeley, 88-89; chair bd dirs, World Environ Ctr, 88-; mem, Relative Risk Reduction Strategies Comt, US Environ Protection Agency, 89-, Sci Adv Bd & Int Environ Technol Transfer Adv Bd, 89- *Mem:* Nat Acad Eng; fel AAAS; fel Am Phys Soc; fel Inst Elec & Electronics Engrs; Soc Automotive Engrs; Sigma Xi. *Res:* Solid state physics; plasma in solids; microwaves and molecular electronics; ferromagnetism and nonreciprocal effects; x-ray studies of imperfections in nearly perfect crystals; author of more than 70 scientific papers and holds several patents in the field of solid state physics, microwave and semiconductor electronics. *Mailing Add:* 222 Harbour Dr Apt 311 Naples FL 34103

ANCSIN, JOHN, PHYSICS. *Current Pos:* RES OFFICER PHYSICS, NAT RES COUN CAN, 66- *Personal Data:* b Hungary, May 1, 33; Can citizen. *Educ:* Univ Ottawa, BSc, 59, MSc, 60, PhD(physics), 65. *Res:* Low temperature fixed points of the temperature scale. *Mailing Add:* Nat Res Coun Can 1500 Montreal Rd Bldg M-36 Ottawa ON K1A 0R6 Can

ANCTIL, MICHEL, NEUROTRANSMITTERS, BIOLUMINESCENCE. *Current Pos:* Asst prof physiol, 76-82, assoc prof comp physiol, 82-88, PROF COMP PHYSIOL, UNIV MONTREAL, 88- *Personal Data:* b Warwick, Que, June 18, 45; m 74, Susan Strnad; c Eric & Tristan. *Educ:* Univ Montreal, BSc, 67, MSc, 69; Univ Calif, Santa Barbara, PhD(neurobiol), 76. *Mem:* AAAS; Asn Physiologists; Soc Neurosci. *Res:* Comparative neurobiology of bioluminescent animals; evolution of nervous systems; neurotransmitters of primitive nervous systems. *Mailing Add:* Dept Biol Sci Univ Montreal CP 6128 Montreal PQ H3C 3J7 Can. *Fax:* 514-343-2293; *E-Mail:* anctilmgere@umontreal.ca

ANDALAFTE, EDWARD ZIEGLER, ORTHOGONALITY. *Current Pos:* assoc prof, 64-85, chmn dept, 65-67, 68-69 & 90-91, PROF MATH, UNIV MO, ST LOUIS, 85- *Personal Data:* b Springfield, Mo, Aug 7, 35. *Educ:* Southwest Mo State Col, BS, 56; Univ Mo-Columbia, AM, 59, PhD(math), 61. *Prof Exp:* Assoc prof math, Southwest Mo State Col, 61-64. *Concurrent Pos:* NSF fac fel, 70-71; vis assoc prof, Math Res Ctr, Univ Wis-Madison, 70-71 & Univ Tex San Antonio, 78-79. *Mem:* Am Math Soc; Math Asn Am; Am Asn Univ Professors; Sigma Xi. *Res:* Geometry of metric spaces and their generalizations; metric characterizations of Banach and Euclidean spaces; orthogonality in normed linear spaces. *Mailing Add:* Dept Math Univ Mo St Louis MO 63121-4499

ANDEEN, RICHARD E, TECHNICAL MANAGEMENT. *Current Pos:* RETIRED. *Personal Data:* b Chicago, Ill, Oct 14, 27; m 62, Anne Waterman; c Eric, Evan & Ellen. *Educ:* Northwestern Univ, BS, 49, MS, 51, PhD(elec eng), 58. *Prof Exp:* Engr, Sperry Gyroscope Co, Sperry Corp, 51-56 & 58-80, eng dir, Sperry Flight Systs Div & gen mgr, Sperry Space Systs, 81-87; vpres, Cent Tech Opers, Honeywell Inc, 88-91, vpres opers, 91-92. *Mem:* Am Inst Aeronaut & Astronaut. *Res:* Automatic flight control systems; computers; sampled data systems. *Mailing Add:* 5936 N Hummingbird Lane Paradise Valley AZ 85253

ANDELMAN, JULIAN BARRY, WATER CHEMISTRY, ENVIRONMENTAL CHEMISTRY. *Current Pos:* from asst prof to assoc prof water chem, 63-73, PROF WATER CHEM, GRAD SCH PUB HEALTH, UNIV PITTSBURGH, 73- *Personal Data:* b Boston, Mass, Sept 23, 31; m 53; c 3. *Educ:* Harvard Univ, AB, 52; Polytech Inst Brooklyn, PhD(chem), 60. *Prof Exp:* Res fel chem, NY Univ, 59-61; mem tech staff, Bell Tel Labs, Inc, 61-63. *Concurrent Pos:* Consult, WHO, 69, 71 & 74 & Nat Res Coun-Nat Acad Sci, 71-85; vis lectr, Univ Col, London, 70-71. *Mem:* AAAS; Am Water Works Asn; Am Chem Soc; Int Asn Water Pollution Res; Air & Waste Mgt Asn; Soc Risk Analysis. *Res:* Chemistry of trace constituents in natural and treated waters. *Mailing Add:* Grad Sch Pub Health Univ Pittsburgh Pittsburgh PA 15261

ANDELSON, JONATHAN GARY, PHYSICAL ANTHROPOLOGY, ETHNOLOGY. *Current Pos:* Asst prof, 74-80, ASSOC PROF ANTHROP, GRINNELL COL, 80- *Personal Data:* b Chicago, Ill, Feb 10, 49. *Educ:* Grinnell Col, BA, 70; Univ Mich, Ann Arbor, MA, 73, PhD(anthrop), 74. *Mem:* Am Anthrop Asn; Soc Med Anthrop. *Res:* Small scale communal societies of the nineteenth and twentieth centuries. *Mailing Add:* Dept Anthrop Grinnell Col Box 805 Grinnell IA 50112-0805

ANDEREGG, DOYLE EDWARD, LICHENOLOGY. *Current Pos:* head dept biol sci, 67-75, asst grad dean, 69-70, fiscal & personnel asst to dean col lett & sci, 78-82, PROF BIOL SCI, UNIV IDAHO, 67-, ASSOC DEAN COL LETT & SCI, 82- *Personal Data:* b Uhrichsville, Ohio, Jan 19, 30; m 57; c 2. *Educ:* Ohio State Univ, BSc, 52, MSc, 57, PhD(bot, plant path), 59. *Prof Exp:* Asst bot, Ohio State Univ, 55-59; from instr bot & microbiol to assoc prof, Univ Okla, 59-67, chmn dept, 63-67. *Mem:* AAAS; Mycol Soc Am; Int Soc Plant Taxonomists; Am Bryol & Lichenological Soc. *Res:* Biogeography, taxonomy and ecology of lichens. *Mailing Add:* 1022 E Eighth St Moscow ID 83843-3717

ANDEREGG, JOHN WILLIAM, BIOPHYSICS. *Current Pos:* Asst physics, 46-52, fel & instr, 53-56, proj assoc oncol, 56-57, asst prof zool & physics, 57-62, assoc prof physics, 62-69, PROF PHYSICS & BIOPHYS, UNIV WIS-MADISON, 69- *Personal Data:* b White Lake, Wis, Nov 12, 23. *Educ:* Univ Wis, BS, 47, MS, 49, PhD(physics), 52. *Concurrent Pos:* Fulbright scholar, Royal Inst, London, 52-53. *Mem:* Am Phys Soc; Biophys Soc; Am Crystallog Asn. *Res:* Virus structure; neutralization of viruses; x-ray scattering. *Mailing Add:* 5706 Lake Mendota Dr Madison WI 53705

ANDEREGG, ROBERT JAMES, MASS SPECTROMETRY, CHROMATOGRAPHY. *Current Pos:* SR RES INVESTR, GLAXO, INC, RESEARCH TRIANGLE PARK, 90- *Personal Data:* b Antigo, Wis, May 25, 51. *Educ:* Univ Wis-Madison, BS, 73; Mass Inst Technol, PhD(anal chem), 77. *Prof Exp:* Res assoc, Mass Inst Technol, 77-79; from asst prof to prof chem, Univ Maine, Orono, 79-89. *Concurrent Pos:* Coop asst prof, 80-83, coop assoc prof, Univ Maine, Orono, 83-; vis assoc prof chem, Addis Abada Univ, Ethiopia, 84-85; vis consult, Smith Kline & French Res Labs, Philadelphia, 86-87. *Mem:* Am Chem Soc; Am Soc Mass Spectrometry; Sigma Xi. *Res:* Biomedical and biochemical applications of chromatography and mass spectrometry; mass spectrometric peptide and protein sequencing; computer techniques for the selective reduction of mass spectrometric data. *Mailing Add:* Glaxo Res Labs 5 Moore Dr Research Triangle Park NC 27701-4613

ANDERMANN, GEORGE, SPECTROSCOPY. *Current Pos:* from asst prof to assoc prof, 65-74, PROF CHEM, UNIV HAWAII, MANOA, 74- *Personal Data:* b Szarvas, Hungary, Oct 14, 24; US citizen; m 50; c 1. *Educ:* Univ Calif, Los Angeles, BS, 49; Univ Southern Calif, MS, 61, PhD(chem), 65. *Prof Exp:* Chemist, Southern Pac Co, 49-51; spectroscopist, Appl Res Labs, 51-53, lab supvr, 53-60, sr physicist, 60-61; sr chemist, Austin Robinson Lab, 61-62; instrument consult mat testing div, Magnaflux Corp, 62-63; res asst chem, Univ Southern Calif, 63-65, res assoc mat sci, 65. *Concurrent Pos:* Assoc chemist, Hawaii Inst Geophys; NSF grant, 66-71. *Mem:* Am Chem Soc; Soc Appl Spectros. *Res:* Optical properties of solids; x-ray emission spectroscopy, fundamental and analytical; infrared spectroscopy; lattice dynamics, particularly electrical anharmonicity. *Mailing Add:* Dept Chem Univ Hawaii Manoa Honolulu HI 96822-1888

ANDERS, EDWARD, COSMOCHEMISTRY, METEORITES. *Current Pos:* from asst prof to prof, 55-73, Horace B Horton prof, 73-91, HORACE B HORTON EMER PROF CHEM, UNIV CHICAGO, 91- *Personal Data:* b Latvia, June 21, 26; nat US; m 55, Joan Fleming; c George & Nanci. *Educ:* Columbia Univ, AM, 51, PhD(chem), 54. *Honors & Awards:* Newcomb Cleveland Prize, AAAS, 59; Univ Medal for Excellence, Columbia Univ, 66; J Lawrence Smith Medal, Nat Acad Sci, 71; Medal Exceptional Sci Achievement, NASA, 73; Leonard Medal, Meteoritical Soc, 74; USCD Found lectr, Univ Calif, San Diego, 75; Priestley lectr, Pa State Univ, 79; Philips Fund lectr, Haverford Col, 79; Marple-Schweitzer lectr, Northwestern Univ, 81; Storer lectr, Univ Calif Davis, 89; Goldschmidt Medal, Geochem

Soc, 90; Kuiper Prize Am Astron Soc, 91; Hess Medal, Am Geophys Union, 95. *Prof Exp:* Instr chem, Univ Ill, 54-55. *Concurrent Pos:* Vis prof, Calif Inst Technol, 60; Nat Acad Sci resident res assoc, Goddard Space Flight Ctr, 61; consult, NASA, 61-69 & 73; NSF sr fel & vis prof, Univ Berne, 63-64, vis prof, 70, 78, 80, 83, 87 & 89; res assoc, Field Mus Natural Hist, 69-; chmn comt meteorites, Int Astron Union, 70-73, pres, Comn on Moon, 76-79; Guggenheim fel, 73-74; distinguished vis lectr, Univ Rochester, 76; chmn div planetary sci, Am Astron Soc, 71-72; assoc ed, Icarus, 70-, Earth, Moon & Planets, 74-; chmn, Div Planetary Sci, Am Astron Soc, 71-72; dist lectr, Nat Sci Coun, Taiwan, 91; Fairchild Scholar, Calif Inst Tech, 92-93. *Mem:* Nat Acad Sci; fel Am Acad Arts & Sci; fel Am Geophys Union; fel AAAS; fel Meteoritical Soc (vpres, 68-72, 89-90, pres, 91-92); Am Chem Soc; Am Astron Soc; assoc Royal Astron Soc; hon mem Geochem Soc (vpres, 88-89). *Res:* Origin and age of meteorites; interstellar grains, mass extinctions caused by meteorite impact. *Mailing Add:* Hint Engehaldenstr 12 Bern 3004 Switzerland. *E-Mail:* anders@phim.unibe.ch

ANDERS, EDWARD B, MATHEMATICAL ANALYSIS. *Current Pos:* RETIRED. *Personal Data:* b Chatham, La, Jan 7, 30; m 63; c 2. *Educ:* La Polytech Univ, BS, 50; Pa State Univ, BS, 54; Northwestern State Univ, MS & ME, 58; Auburn Univ, PhD(math), 65. *Prof Exp:* High sch teacher, La, 50; instr, Northeastern La State Col, 58-60, from asst prof to prof math, 63-86; assoc prof & chmn div math & physics, Ark State Univ, 66-67. *Mem:* Nat Acad Sci; Am Math Soc; Math Asn Am; Asn Comput Mach. *Res:* Numerical and error analysis; numerical filter theory; least squares curve fitting and numerical integration theory. *Mailing Add:* 300 E Seventh St Natchitoches LA 71457

ANDERS, MARION WALTER, TOXICOLOGY. *Current Pos:* AT DEPT PHARMACOL & TOXICOL, UNIV ROCHESTER. *Personal Data:* b Alden, Iowa, May 10, 36; m 58; c 3. *Educ:* Iowa State Univ, DVM, 60; Univ Minn, PhD(pharmacol), 64. *Prof Exp:* Instr pharmacol, Univ Minn, 64-65; from asst prof to assoc prof, Cornell Univ, 65-69; assoc prof, Univ Minn, Minneapolis, 69-75, prof pharmacol, 75- *Concurrent Pos:* Mem ad hoc sci adv comt, Food & Drug Admin, 70-71; mem toxicol study sect, NIH, 73-77; USP comt of revision, 75-; mem, Environ Health Sci Rev Comt, 81- *Mem:* AAAS; Soc Toxicol; Am Soc Biol Chem; Am Soc Pharmacol & Exp Therapeut. *Res:* Relationship of metabolism to toxicity; analytical chemistry. *Mailing Add:* Pharmacol Dept Sch Med & Dent Univ Rochester 601 Elmwood Ave Box 711 Rochester NY 14642-8711

ANDERS, OSWALD ULRICH, COLLOID CHEMISTRY, RADIOCHEMISTRY. *Current Pos:* RETIRED. *Personal Data:* b Karlsruhe, Ger, Nov 10, 28; nat US; m 53, Edith Leyerer; c Peter, Carl & Edgar. *Educ:* Georgetown Univ, BS, 52; Univ Mich, MS, 54, PhD(chem), 57. *Prof Exp:* Asst, Univ Mich, 54-57; radiochemist, Dow Chem Co, 57-63, assoc scientist, radiochem res lab, 63-78, res scientist, anal lab & reactor supvr, Triga Reactor, 67-80, res scientist, Designed Latexes & Resins Lab, Mich Div Appl Sci & Technol Dept, 80-88; assoc, Mich Molecular Inst, 88-91. *Concurrent Pos:* Mem, adv comt anal chem, Nat Res Coun, 65-67, exec comt int conf activation anal, 72-75 & atomic scattering factor subcomt nuclear & radiochem, 78-81; prin investr, develop technol complete decontamination Dreden-1 Nuclear Plan, 72-84; consult, Oztech Res & Consult. *Mem:* fel Am Nuclear Soc; Am Chem Soc. *Res:* Activation analysis; particle accelerators; nuclear reactor; nuclear instrumentation; nuclear reactions; ion exchange separations; tracer chemistry, radioactive waste solidification; decontamination of nuclear power plants. *Mailing Add:* 801 Linwood Dr Midland MI 48640. *E-Mail:* ozofoztec@aol.com

ANDERS, WILLIAM A, ASTRONAUTICS. *Current Pos:* CHMN, APOGEE GROUP LTD. *Personal Data:* b Hong Kong, Oct 17, 33; m, Valerie E Hoard; c 6. *Educ:* US Naval Acad, BS, 55; USAF Inst Technol, MS, 62. *Honors & Awards:* Distinguished Serv Medals, USAF, NASA & Nuclear Regulatory Comn; Hubbard Medal for Explor, Nat Geog Soc; Flight Achievement Award, Am Astronaut Soc; Collier, Harmon, Goddard & White Flight Trophies. *Prof Exp:* Astronaut, Apollo Space Prog, NASA, 63-69; exec secy, Nat Aeronaut & Space Coun, 69-73; comnr, AEC, 73-75, chmn, Nuclear Regulatory Comn, 75-76; vpres & gen mgr, Nuclear Energy Prods Div, Gen Elec Co, 77-80, vpres & gen mgr, Aircraft Equip Div, 80-84; exec vpres aerospace, Textron Inc, 84-86, sr exec vpres opers, 86-89; vchmn, Gen Dynamics Corp, 90-91, chief exec officer, 91-93, chmn, 91-94. *Concurrent Pos:* US Ambassador, Norway, 76-77. *Mem:* Nat Acad Eng; Soc Exp Test Pilots. *Res:* Crew member astronaut on Apollo 8 and backup pilot for Apollo 11. *Mailing Add:* Apogee Group Ltd PO Box 184 Deer Harbor WA 98243. *Fax:* 360-376-5137

ANDERSEN, ARNOLD E, PSYCHIATRY, DEVELOPMENTAL NEUROBIOLOGY. *Current Pos:* PROF PSYCHIAT, UNIV IA, 91- *Personal Data:* b Brooklyn, NY, June 12, 43; c 3. *Educ:* Cornell Univ, BA, 64, MD, 68. *Prof Exp:* Res assoc develop neurobiol, Lab Biomed Sci, Nat Inst Child Health & Develop, 70-74; clin assoc drug abuse & anorexia nervosa, Adult Psychiat Br, NIH, 74-75, staff psychiatrist, 75-76; fel psychiat, 75-76, from instr to asst prof, 76-84, assoc prof psychiat, Johns Hopkins Sch Med, 84-91. *Concurrent Pos:* Attend physician, Henry Phipps Psychiat Clin, Johns Hopkins Hosp, 77-, dir, Eating & Weight Disorder Clin & Clin Clerkship Psychait. *Mem:* AAAS; Am Psychiat Asn; Am Psychopath Asn. *Res:* Anorexia nervosa; Bulimia nervosa; psychopharmacology; psychological tests. *Mailing Add:* 2887 JPP Univ Iowa Col Med 200 Hawkins Dr Iowa City IA 52242

ANDERSEN, AXEL LANGVAD, PLANT PATHOLOGY, PLANT BREEDING. *Current Pos:* assoc prof, Dept Bot & Plant Path, Mich State Univ, ELansing, 51-64, prof, 64-77, proj leader, Exten Plant Path, 68-74, exten specialist, Dept Bot & Plant Path & asst to dir, Agr Exp Sta, 71-77, EMER PROF, DEPT BOT & PLANT PATH, MICH STATE UNIV, 77- *Personal Data:* b Askov, Minn, Sept 24, 14; m 42, Maude M Woodcock; c Nancy M & Linda K (White). *Educ:* Univ Minn, BS, 37; Mich State Univ, MS, 41, PhD(plant path), 47. *Honors & Awards:* Meritorious Serv Award, Int Bean Improv Coop, 89. *Prof Exp:* Plant pathologist, Dept Defense, Ft Detrick, Md, 46-48; res plant pathologist, US Dept Agr, Mich State Univ, ELansing, 48-65; res coordr, Res Prog Develop & Eval Staff, Off Secy, USDA, Washington, DC, 65-68. *Concurrent Pos:* Mem, Nat Steering Comt Plant Dis Mgt, USDA 74-77; consult plant health probs, 77-86; collabr, Plant Health Inspection Serv, USDA, 78-80. *Mem:* Am Phytopath Soc; Sigma Xi. *Res:* Plant diseases; bean disease and breeding investigations; turfgrass diseases; disease management, detection, development, loss appraisal and control strategies; epidemiology, air pollution injury, remote sensing. *Mailing Add:* 902 Whitman Dr East Lansing MI 48823-2473

ANDERSEN, BLAINE WRIGHT, MECHANICAL ENGINEERING. *Current Pos:* RETIRED. *Personal Data:* b Salt Lake City, Utah, Dec 29, 25; m 52; c 5. *Educ:* Univ Utah, BS, 49; Univ Ill, Urbana, MS, 51, PhD(eng mech), 53. *Prof Exp:* Instr eng mech, Univ Ill, Urbana, 52-53; sr res engr, Stress & Vibrations Anal, NAm Aviation, Calif, 53-55; asst prof mech eng, Brigham Young Univ, 55-57; sr eng specialist pneumatic systs analysis, AiResearch Mfg Co, Ariz, 57-66, supvr dynamic systs analysis, 66-70; prof mech eng, Brigham Young Univ, 70-90. *Concurrent Pos:* Consult, AiResearch Mfg Co, Ariz, 56-57 & 70-; fac assoc, Ariz State Univ, 60-66. *Mem:* Fluid Power Soc. *Res:* Pneumatic systems dynamics; analytical techniques for predicting the performance of pneumatic systems. *Mailing Add:* 3014 Comanche Lane Provo UT 84604

ANDERSEN, BURTON, INTERNAL MEDICINE, IMMUNOLOGY. *Current Pos:* Assoc prof, 70-76, PROF MED & MICROBIOL, COL MED, UNIV ILL, 76-; CHIEF, SECT INFECTIOUS DIS, UNIV ILL, 86- *Personal Data:* b Chicago, Ill, Aug 27, 32; m 86, Susan M Mills; c Ellen, Julia & Brian. *Educ:* Univ Ill, BS, 55, MD & MS, 57. *Prof Exp:* Rotating intern, Minneapolis Gen Hosp, 57-58; resident internal med, Univ Hosps, Univ Ill, 58-60; asst prof med, Univ Rochester, 64-67; asst prof microbiol, NWestern Univ, 67-70. *Concurrent Pos:* Fel infectious dis, Univ Ill, 59-61; Nat Inst Allergy & Infectious Dis fel, 61-64; fel, Med Ctr, Univ Rochester, 64-67. *Mem:* Am Asn Immunol; Am Fedn Clin Res; Am Soc Microbiol; Infectious Dis Soc Am; Am Soc Clin Ivest. *Res:* Infectious diseases; mechanism of phagocytic cell fuction; worked to develop drug delivery systems for the treatment of tuberculosis. *Mailing Add:* Sect Infectious Dis Univ Ill Col Med 808 S Wood St Chicago IL 60612

ANDERSEN, CARL MARIUS, THEORETICAL PHYSICS. *Current Pos:* asst prof theoret physics, 67-72, SR RES ASSOC MATH & COMPUT SCI, COL WILLIAM & MARY, 72-, PROF MATH. *Personal Data:* b Detroit, Mich, Mar 10, 36; m 59; c 3. *Educ:* Univ Mich, BS, 58, MS, 59; Univ Pa, PhD(physics), 64. *Prof Exp:* Res assoc theoret physics, Purdue Univ, 64-65, asst prof, 65-67. *Mem:* Am Phys Soc; Asn Comput Mach; Soc Indust & Appl Math. *Res:* Applied mathematics; algebraic computation by computer; structural mechanics computations; nonlinear mechanics; theory of group representations. *Mailing Add:* Dept Math Col William & Mary Williamsburg VA 23187-8795

ANDERSEN, DEAN MARTIN, MEDICAL ENTOMOLOGY, ENVIRONMENTAL BIOLOGY. *Current Pos:* RETIRED. *Personal Data:* b Monroe, Utah, Dec 14, 31; m 61; c 5. *Educ:* Univ Utah, BS, 60, MS, 62, PhD(entom), 66. *Prof Exp:* Inspector entomologist, Salt Lake City Mosquito Abatement, 58-62; dir field res, Inst Environ Res, Univ Utah, 63-66; from assoc prof to prof biol, Brigham Young Univ, Hawaii Campus, 66-97. *Concurrent Pos:* Vis prof, Brigham Young Univ, 73-74. *Mem:* Am Mosquito Control Asn. *Res:* Ecological control of mosquitoes through water management; host preferences of mosquitoes; audio-tutorial systems of teaching biological sciences and individualized approaches to learning for both science and nonscience majors. *Mailing Add:* 55697 Wahinepee St Laie HI 96762

ANDERSEN, DEWEY RICHARD, SANITARY ENGINEERING, NUCLEAR SCIENCE. *Current Pos:* RETIRED. *Personal Data:* b Harlan, Iowa, Oct 15, 27; m 54; c 4. *Educ:* Univ Iowa, BS, 58, MS, 59; Iowa State Univ, PhD(civil eng), 67. *Honors & Awards:* Fuller Award, Am Water Works Asn. *Prof Exp:* Pub health engr, Iowa State Dept Health, 59-68; from asst prof to prof civil eng, Univ Nebr, Lincoln, 68-94. *Mem:* Am Water Works Asn; Water Pollution Control Fedn; Am Soc Civil Eng. *Res:* Industrial and municipal wastewater treatment; water treatment; radiological health. *Mailing Add:* 335 Dale Dr Lincoln NE 68510

ANDERSEN, DONALD EDWARD, PHYSICAL CHEMISTRY, RESEARCH ADMINISTRATION. *Current Pos:* PRES, MYTHOS CONSULTS, 85- *Personal Data:* b New Haven, Conn, June 3, 23; m 47; c 1. *Educ:* Brown Univ, ScB, 48, PhD(phys chem), 52; Stanford Univ, MS, 49. *Prof Exp:* Res chemist, E I Du Pont de Nemours & Co, Inc, 52-56, res supvr, 56-60, supt develop, 60-61, gen supt res & develop, 61-63, asst plant mgr, 63-65, plant mgr, 65-70, lab dir & mgr elastomers res & develop, 70-81, consult mgt resources, 82-85. *Mem:* AAAS; Am Chem Soc. *Mailing Add:* 1608 N Rodney St Wilmington DE 19806-3020

ANDERSEN, FERRON LEE, PARASITOLOGY. *Current Pos:* assoc prof, 67-72, PROF ZOOL, BRIGHAM YOUNG UNIV, 72- *Personal Data:* b Howell, Utah, July 10, 31; m 58, Stenna Turley; c 6. *Educ:* Utah State Univ, BS, 57, MS, 60, PhD(zool), 63; Univ Ill, MS, 62. *Prof Exp:* Asst prof vet med sci & assoc staff mem, Zoonoses Res Ctr, Univ Ill, 63-67. *Mem:* Am Soc Parasitol. *Res:* Coccidiosis; micrometeorology and ecology of parasites; hydatid disease. *Mailing Add:* Dept Zool Brigham Young Univ 575 WIBD Provo UT 84602-1049. *Fax:* 801-378-7499

ANDERSEN, FRANK ALAN, BIOLOGICAL SCIENCES. *Current Pos:* Chief, Genetics Studies Sect, Exp Studies Br, Food & Drug Admin, 71-76, chief, Standards Support Staff, 76-79, assoc dir biol effects, Bur Radiol Health, 79-81, dir standards, Bur Med Devices, 81-83, dep dir, Standards & Regulations, 83-85, dir, Off Sci & Technol, Ctr Devices & Radiol Health, 85-90, dir, Off Sci & Technol, 90-93, actg dir, Off Develop Eval, 92-93, DIR, COSMETIC INGREDIENT REV, FOOD & DRUG ADMIN, 93- *Personal Data:* b Lewiston, Maine, May 20, 44; m 75; c 5. *Educ:* Muhlenberg Col, BS, 66; Pa State Univ, MS, 69, PhD(biophys), 72. *Honors & Awards:* Super Serv Award, USPHS, 89. *Concurrent Pos:* Chmn, Standards Mgt Comt, Nat Comt Clin Lab Standards, 84-88 & Med Device Standards Bd, Am Nat Standards Inst, 85-86; mem bd dir, Nat Comt Clin Lab Standards, 87-, secy, 90- *Mem:* Am Soc Photobiol; Sigma Xi. *Res:* Biological effects of radiation, including acoustic energy with special reference to emissions from electronic products; development of criteria in support of performance standards to assure product safety and effectiveness and safety assessments of cosmetic ingredients. *Mailing Add:* Cosmetic Ingredient Rev 1101 17th St NW Suite 310 Washington DC 20036

ANDERSEN, GLEN ROBERT, GEOTECHNICAL ENGINEERING, EXPERIMENTAL SOIL MECHANICS. *Current Pos:* ASST PROF CIVIL ENG, TEX A&M UNIV, 95- *Personal Data:* b Glendale, Calif, Aug 15, 60; m 83, Suzanne Bertch; c Eric, Caitlin, Jacob & Mikaela. *Educ:* Brigham Young Univ, BS, 85; Mass Inst Technol, MSc, 87, DSc(biotech eng), 91. *Prof Exp:* Res civil engr, Chevron Oil Field Res Co, 91-92; asst prof civil eng, Tulane Univ, 92-95. *Concurrent Pos:* Prin investr, US Army Corps Engrs, 92-, NSF, 93-97, Naval Res Lab, 93- *Mem:* Am Soc Civil Engrs. *Res:* Experimental investigation of soil/structure interaction; fundamental aspects of soil behavior; decision analysis for aging civil infrastructure systems. *Mailing Add:* 2812 Rayado Ct College Station TX 77845. *Fax:* 409-845-6554; *E-Mail:* glen-andersen@tamu.edu

ANDERSEN, HANS CHRISTIAN, PHYSICAL CHEMISTRY, STATISTICAL MECHANICS. *Current Pos:* from asst to assoc prof chem, 68-80, PROF CHEM, STANFORD UNIV, 80-, ASSOC DEAN NAT SCIS, SCH HUMANITIES & SCIS, 96- *Personal Data:* b Brooklyn, NY, Sept 25, 41; m 67, June Jenny; c Hans C & Albert W. *Educ:* Mass Inst Technol, BS, 62, PhD(phys chem), 66. *Honors & Awards:* Joel Henry Hildebrand Award, Am Chem Soc, 88. *Prof Exp:* Jr fel, soc fels, Harvard Univ, 65-68. *Concurrent Pos:* Vis prof chem, Columbia Univ, 81-82; co-dir, Ctr Mat Res, Stanford Univ, 88-89, dep dir, 89-95, actg dir, 94-95. *Mem:* Nat Acad Sci; AAAS; Am Chem Soc; Am Phys Soc. *Res:* Statistical mechanics; structure and properties of amorphous materials; structure of fluids; computer simulation methods; energy transfer in condensed phases. *Mailing Add:* Dept Chem Stanford Univ Stanford CA 94305. *Fax:* 650-723-3235; *E-Mail:* fb.hca@forsythe.stanford.edu

ANDERSEN, HOWARD ARNE, MEDICINE, THORACIC DISEASES. *Current Pos:* From assoc prof to prof med, 69-73, prof, 73-81, EMER PROF MED, MAYO MED SCH, UNIV MINN, 81- *Personal Data:* b Minneapolis, Minn, June 10, 16; m 42, Adella Louise Nichols; c Patricia L, Richard D & Robert B. *Educ:* Univ Minn, BS, 40, BM, 42, MD, 43, MSc, 50. *Honors & Awards:* Honore lectr, World Cong Bronchology, 86; Laureate Award, Am Col Physicians. *Concurrent Pos:* Consult internal med, Thoracic Dis & Bronco-Esophagology, Mayo Clin, 50-85; pres, World Cong Bronchology, 82. *Mem:* Am Thoracic Soc; AMA; fel Am Col Physicians; fel Am Col Chest Physicians; Sigma Xi; Am Broncho-Esophalogical Asn (pres, 74-75). *Res:* Pulmonary and esophageal diseases. *Mailing Add:* Mayo Clin Rochester MN 55905

ANDERSEN, JON ALAN, microbiology, biochemistry, for more information see previous edition

ANDERSEN, JONNY, ELECTRICAL ENGINEERING, BIOENGINEERING. *Current Pos:* from asst prof to assoc prof, 67-78, PROF ELEC ENG, UNIV WASH, 78- *Personal Data:* b Oslo, Norway, Aug 13, 35; m 58; c 3. *Educ:* Univ Colo, BS, 60; Mass Inst Technol, SM, 62, PhD(elec eng), 65. *Honors & Awards:* TV Shares Mgt, Mass Inst Technol, 63; Baker Award, Inst Elec & Electronics Eng, 67. *Prof Exp:* Asst prof elec eng, Mass Inst Technol, 65-67. *Concurrent Pos:* Ford fel, 65-67; consult, Sylvania Appl Res Lab, 66, Boeing Aerospace Co, 69-76 & Boeing Com Airplane Co, 78- *Mem:* AAAS; Inst Elec & Electronics Eng. *Res:* CAD/CAM; nonlinear device modeling; circuits and systems design; large scale systems simulation; broadband matching. *Mailing Add:* Univ Wash Seattle WA 98195

ANDERSEN, KENNETH F, FOURIER ANALYSIS, MATHEMATICS. *Current Pos:* PROF MATH, UNIV ALBERTA, 71- *Personal Data:* b Innisfail, Alta Apr 5, 45. *Educ:* Univ BC, BS, 67; Univ Toronto, MS, 68, PhD(math), 70. *Mem:* Am Math Soc; Can Math Soc; Math Asn Am. *Mailing Add:* Dept Math Univ Alta Edmonton AB T6G 2G1 Can

ANDERSEN, KENNETH J, RESEARCH MANAGEMENT. *Current Pos:* PRES, ANDERSEN LABS INC, 83- *Personal Data:* b Brooklyn, NY, Dec 24, 36; m 62, Judith G; c David & Mark. *Educ:* Davis & Elkins Col, BS, 59; Syracuse Univ, MS, 62, PhD(microbiol), 65. *Honors & Awards:* Outstanding Scientist, Life Scis, Battelle Mem Inst, 66. *Prof Exp:* Bacteriologist, Syracuse Univ Res Corp, 60-62, asst microbiol, Syracuse Univ, 62-65; res microbiologist, Battelle Mem Inst, 65-67, sr microbiologist, 67-70, assoc chief microbiol & environ biol div, 70-72; assoc dir diag serv, Johnson & Johnson Int, 72-73; dir chemother, 73-75, dir biol res, Norwich-Eaton Pharmaceut, Inc, 75-82. *Mem:* Fel AAAS; Am Soc Microbiol; Am Inst Biol Sci. *Res:* Microbiology; virology; bacteriology; immunology; anti-infectious and cardiovascular drugs; microbial genetics and physiology; new drugs for human diseases; drug metabolism, pathology and toxicology; pharmaceutical and health care products. *Mailing Add:* RD 2 Box 165A South New Berlin NY 13843

ANDERSEN, KENNETH K, ORGANIC CHEMISTRY. *Current Pos:* from asst prof to assoc prof, 60-70, PROF CHEM, UNIV NH, 70- *Personal Data:* b Perth Amboy, NJ, May 13, 34; m 57, Barbara Fowler; c David K, Peter C & Joyce K. *Educ:* Rutgers Univ, BS, 55; Univ Minn, PhD(chem), 59. *Prof Exp:* USPHS fel, 59-60. *Concurrent Pos:* NSF sci fac fel, Univ EAnglia, 66-67; Fulbright lectr, Tech Univ Denmark, 71; vis lectr, Polish Acad Sci, 73; vis prof, Colo State Univ, 79; guest prof, Tech Univ, Denmark, 88. *Mem:* Am Chem Soc; fel AAAS. *Res:* Chemistry of organosulfur compounds with emphasis on stereochemistry. *Mailing Add:* 16 Garden Lane Durham NH 03824-3041. *Fax:* 603-862-4278; *E-Mail:* k_andersen@unh.edu

ANDERSEN, KENNETH W, CONSTRUCTION MANAGEMENT, CONSTRUCTION SAFETY. *Current Pos:* ASST PROF CONSTRUCT MGT, COL ENG & ARCHIT, DEPT CIVIL ENG & CONSTRUCT, NDAK STATE UNIV, 91- *Personal Data:* b Fingal, NDak, Oct 9, 44; m, Norma Jean; c Benjamin & Mathew. *Educ:* NDak State Univ, BS, 66; Mont State Univ, BS, 70; Northern Mont Col, MS, 72; Colo State Univ, PhD(human resource develop), 89. *Prof Exp:* Owner & mgr, Andersen Construct Inc & Casper, Wyoming Com & Indust Construct, 72-86; consult, Ft Collins, Colo, 89-91. *Concurrent Pos:* Fulbright grantee, Sierra Leone, WAfrica, 96-97. *Mem:* Am Soc Eng Educ; Am Tech Educ Asn; Am Inst Contructors (secy, 97-98). *Res:* Applying recent statistical and methodological advances to research problems in human resource development; educational evaluation; small business; cost benefit analysis; training and development; apprenticeship construction safety and construction management. *Mailing Add:* 3657 21st St S 58104 ND 58104. *Fax:* 701-231-7431; *E-Mail:* kanderse@plains.nodak.edu

ANDERSEN, L(AIRD) BRYCE, CHEMICAL ENGINEERING. *Current Pos:* DEAN, COL ENG, SOUTHEASTERN MASS UNIV, 80- *Personal Data:* b Madison, SDak, Sept 16, 28; m 61; c 2. *Educ:* Univ Minn, BS, 50, MS, 51; Univ Ill, PhD(chem eng), 54. *Prof Exp:* Asst prof chem eng, Lehigh Univ, 54-59; assoc prof, Rice Univ, 59-60 & Univ Nebr, 61-63; prof chem eng, NJ Inst Technol, 63-80, from assoc dean to dean eng, Newark Col Eng, 63-75. *Mem:* Am Inst Chem Engrs; Am Soc Eng Educ; Sigma Xi. *Res:* Transport phenomena; applied statistics. *Mailing Add:* 28 Holly Lane Mattapoisett MA 02739-2110

ANDERSEN, MELVIN ERNEST, PHARMACOKINETIC MODELING, HEALTH RISK ASSESSMENTS FOR ENVIRONMENTAL CHEMICALS. *Current Pos:* VPRES, KS CRUMP DIV, ICF KAISER ENGRS INC, 94- *Personal Data:* b Providence, RI, Dec 13, 45; m 68, Christine A Jaeger; c Kathryn L, Heidi L & Rebecca A. *Educ:* Brown Univ, SBSc 67; Cornell Univ, PhD(biochem & molecular biol), 71; Am Bd Toxicol, dipl, Am Bd Indust Hygiene, dipl. *Honors & Awards:* Frank R Blood Award, Soc Toxicol, 82, Achievement Award, 84; Herbert Stokinger Award, Am Conf Govt Indust Hygienists, 88; Kenneth Morgareidge Award, Int Life Sci Inst, 89; George H Scott Award, Toxicol Forum, 93. *Prof Exp:* Res toxicologist, Navy Toxicol Detachment, Wright-Patterson AFB, 71-78; res pharmacologist, Toxic Hazards Div, Armstrong Aerospace Med Res Lab, 78-82, br chief, 82-86, actg div dir, 87, sr scientist, 87-89; sr scientist & dept head, Chem Indust Inst Toxicol, 89-92; sr res toxicologist, St-006, Health Effects Res Lab, US Environ Protection Agency, 92-94. *Concurrent Pos:* Mem, Threshold Limit Value-Airborne Contaminants Comt, Am Conf Govt Indust Hygienists, 81-84; assoc ed, Toxicol & Pharmacol, 82-84; assoc clin prof, Wright State Univ, 82-90; mem, Safe Drinking Water Comt, Nat Acad Sci, 85-87; adj assoc prof curric toxicol, Univ NC, 93-; adj prof med, Duke Univ, 93- *Mem:* Soc Toxicol; Soc Risk Anal; Am Conf Govt Indust Hygienists; Am Acad Indust Hygiene; AAAS. *Res:* Develop computer simulation models of the absorption, tissue interactions and toxicity of pollutants; devise methods to assess or calculate constants necessary for these models; apply these models in human health risk assessments. *Mailing Add:* ICF Kaiser Engrs Inc PO Box 14348 Research Triangle Park NC 27709. *Fax:* 919-547-1710; *E-Mail:* andersenme@.aol.com

ANDERSEN, NEIL RICHARD, CHEMICAL OCEANOGRAPHY. *Current Pos:* PROF, HORN POINT ENVIRON LAB, UNIV MD, 95- *Personal Data:* b Lynn, Mass, Sept 22, 35; m 56; c 2. *Educ:* Clark Univ, AB, 60; Mass Inst Technol, PhD(anal chem), 65. *Prof Exp:* Res asst oceanog, Woods Hole Oceanog Inst, 60-65; prin investr, US Naval Oceanog Off, 65-67, br head, 67-70; chief appl chem oceanog br, Off Res & Develop, US Coast Guard, 70-72; chem oceanogr, Off Naval Res, 72-73, prog dir, Chem Oceanog Prog, 73-75; head marine pollution, Intergovt Oceano Comn, UNESCO, Paris, 81-83; prog dir, NSF 75-79, 80-81, prof dir, Chem Oceanog Prog, 83-95. *Concurrent Pos:* Fel, Woods Hole Oceanog Inst, 62-65; assoc prof, George Washington Univ, 68-78, prof, 78-80; dep US deleg, Global Invest Pollution in Marine Environ Comt Intergovt Oceanog Comn, UNESCO,

74-76, head US deleg, 76-81, chmn, Group Experts on Methods, Stand & Intercalibration, 76-81 & US Nat coordr, 76-81; vis scholar, Scripps Inst Oceanog, 79-81; vis scholar, Scripps Inst Oceanog, La Jolla, 80-81; chmn, Sci Comt, Global Invest Pollution in Marine Environ, 84- *Mem:* AAAS; Oceanog Soc; Am Geophys Union. *Res:* Trace metal and radioisotope distributions in the oceans; chemical, geological and biological mechanisms causing variations such that measured distributions can aid in solving oceanographic problems and in identifying and regulating marine pollution. *Mailing Add:* 7959 Bozman Neavitt Rd Bozman MD 21612

ANDERSEN, NIELS HJORTH, BIOCHEMISTRY & BIOPHYSICS, PROTEINS & PEPTIDES. *Current Pos:* from asst prof to assoc prof, 68-76, PROF CHEM, UNIV WASH, 76- *Personal Data:* b Copenhagen, Denmark, Oct 9, 43; US citizen; m 87, Susan Howell; c Marin C & Beth (Arkady). *Educ:* Univ Minn, Minneapolis, BA, 63; Northwestern Univ, PhD(org chem), 67. *Prof Exp:* NIH res fel chem, Harvard Univ, 66-68. *Concurrent Pos:* Consult, Worchester Found Exp Biol, 68-69 & Alza Corp, 70-75; prin scientist, Alza Corp, Calif, 70-75; Alfred P Sloan res fel, 72-74; Dreyfus Found scholar, 74-79; NIH career develop award, 75-80; consult, Genetic Systs, Seattle, 84-86, Squibb Inst Res, NJ, 84-90, Bristol Myer Squibb, 90-95 & Amylin Pharmaceut, 92- *Mem:* Am Chem Soc; Chem Soc; AAAS; Protein Soc; Am Peptide Soc. *Res:* Nuclear magnetic resonance and CD of peptides and proteins, protein folding, helix/coil transition theory, conformation analysis peptides. *Mailing Add:* Dept Chem Univ Wash Seattle WA 98195. *E-Mail:* andersen@chem.washington.edu

ANDERSEN, OLAF SPARRE, ION PERMEABLE CHANNELS. *Current Pos:* from asst prof to assoc prof, 73-82, PROF PHYSIOL, CORNELL UNIV MED COL, 82- *Personal Data:* b Hellerup, Denmark, Sept 10, 45; m 73, Johanne J Jorgensen; c Jesper & Martin. *Educ:* Univ Copenhagen, MD, 71. *Prof Exp:* Fel biophys, Univ Copenhagen, 71-72, Rockefeller Univ, 72-73. *Concurrent Pos:* Assoc ed, J Gen Physiol, 84-95, ed 95-; mem NIH Physiol Study Sect, 82-86; mem res coun, NY Heart Asn, 80-89, chmn, 84-89; NY city affil, Am Heart Asn, 85-, pres, 92-93. *Mem:* Biophys Soc; Soc Gen Physiologists (pres, 96-97); Am Physiol Soc; Soc Neurosci; foreign mem, Royal Danish Acad Sci & Lett. *Res:* Structure function studies in ion selective channels using single amino acid replacements; physical chemistry of ion movement through channels; control of membrane protein function by the material properties of the host lipid bilayer. *Mailing Add:* Dept Physiol & Biophys Cornell Univ Med Col 1300 York Ave New York NY 10021. *Fax:* 212-746-8690

ANDERSEN, RICHARD NICOLAJ, REPRODUCTIVE ENDOCRINOLOGY. *Current Pos:* assoc prof, 70-77, PROF BIOCHEM, OBSTET & GYNEC, UNIV TENN, MEMPHIS, 77-, DIR REPRODUCTIVE ENDOCRINOL LAB, 76- *Personal Data:* b Oakland, Calif, Mar 11, 30; m 58; c 3. *Educ:* Abilene Christian Col, BS, 56; Baylor Univ, PhD(biochem), 60. *Prof Exp:* Asst res prof surg, Med Col Va, 63; res assco biochem, Mayo Found, 63-66; asst prof pharmacol, Univ NC, Chapel Hill, 66, asst prof obstet & gynec, 67-69. *Concurrent Pos:* USPHS fels, Univ Calif, Berkeley, 60-61 & Med Col Va, 61-63. *Mem:* AAAS; Soc Study Reproduction; Endocrine Soc; Clin Ligand Assay Soc; Am Soc Clin Chem. *Res:* Control of gonadal function; steroid radioimmunoassay; control of adrenal androgen secretion; role of C-19 steroids in insulin resistance. *Mailing Add:* Div Reproductive Endocrinol Univ Tenn 956 Court Rm D-322 Memphis TN 38163

ANDERSEN, ROBERT ARTHUR, ALGAL SYSTEMATICS BASED UPON ULTRASTRUCTURE, MOLECULAR BIOLOGY & CLADISTICS. *Current Pos:* DIR, PROVASOLI-GUILLARD NAT CTR CULT MARINE PHYTOPLANKTON, 89- *Personal Data:* b Jamestown, NDak, Sept 26, 48; m, Theresa A Kump; c Michael S, Jennifer L & Eric P. *Educ:* NDak State Univ, BS, 70; St Cloud State Col, MS, 72; Univ Ark, PhD(bot), 81. *Prof Exp:* From asst prof to assoc prof biol, DePaul Univ, 80-89. *Mem:* Phycol Soc Am; Int Phycol Soc; AAAS; Bot Soc Am; Am Soc Limnol & Oceanog. *Res:* Systematics and evolutionary relationships of algae, especially chrysophytes (golden algae); algal cytoskeletons, expecially flagellar apparatus; 18SrRNA sequence comparisons for chromophyte algae; algal culturing. *Mailing Add:* Bigelow Lab Ocean Sci West Boothbay Harbor ME 04575. *Fax:* 207-633-9641; *E-Mail:* potter@maine.maine.edu

ANDERSEN, ROBERT NEILS, PLANT PHYSIOLOGY. *Current Pos:* RETIRED. *Personal Data:* b Steele City, Nebr, June 8, 28; m 52; c 2. *Educ:* Univ Nebr, BS, 51, MS, 53; Univ Minn, PhD, 60. *Prof Exp:* Asst agronomist, Weed Invest Sect, Field Crops Res Br, Agr Res Serv, USDA, Agr Exp Sta, NDak, 53-57; res agronomist, USDA & Univ Minn, 57-61, plant physiologist, Agr Res Serv, 61- *Mem:* Weed Sci Soc Am. *Res:* Weed control. *Mailing Add:* 1771 City Heights Dr Maplewood MN 55117

ANDERSEN, ROGER ALLEN, BIOCHEMISTRY, ONCOLOGY. *Current Pos:* asst prof, 65-71, ASSOC PROF AGRON, UNIV KY, 71-; RES CHEMIST, AGR RES SERV, USDA, 65- *Personal Data:* b Milwaukee, Wis, June 24, 30; m 63; c 3. *Educ:* Univ Wis, BS, 53, PhD(oncol), 63; Marquette Univ, MS, 58. *Prof Exp:* Analytical chemist, Allis-Chalmers Mfg Co, Wis, 53-58; res asst oncol, McArdle Mem Labs, Univ Wis, 58-63; USPHS fel biochem, Roswell Park Mem Inst, NY, 63-65. *Mem:* Am Chem Soc; Am Asn Cancer Res. *Res:* Biochemistry of chemical carcinogens, plant volatiles, plant alkaloids, plant secondary metabolites. *Mailing Add:* 119 Greenbriar Lane Lexington KY 40503-2631

ANDERSEN, RONALD, SCIENCE ADMINISTRATION. *Current Pos:* PROF HEALTH SERV, UNIV CALIF, LOS ANGELES, 90- *Personal Data:* b Omaha, Nebr, June 15, 39; c 1. *Educ:* Univ Santa Clara, BS, 60; Purdue Univ, MS, 62, PhD(sociol), 68. *Prof Exp:* Res assoc, Farm Cardiac Proj, Purdue Univ, 62-63; res assoc, Ctr Health Admin Studies, Univ Chicago, 63-77, assoc prof, 74-77, assoc dir, 77-80, prof sociol, Grad Sch Bus, 77-91, dir, Grad Prog Health Admin, Ctr Health Admin Studies, 80-90. *Mem:* Inst Med-Nat Acad Sci; Am Sociol Asn; Am Pub Health Soc; Asn Health Serv Res; Asn Progs Health Admin. *Mailing Add:* Sch Pub Health Univ Calif 10833 LeConte Ave Los Angeles CA 90024-1772

ANDERSEN, ROY STUART, ELECTRON SPIN RESONANCE, BIOPHYSICS. *Current Pos:* chmn dept, Clark Univ, 60-70, 71-73 & 77-78, prof, 60-92, dean, Grad Sch, 70-71, EMER PROF PHYSICS, CLARK UNIV, 92- *Personal Data:* b Springfield, Mass, Oct 16, 21; m 44, Barbara A Norris; c 3. *Educ:* Clark Univ, BA, 43; Dartmouth Col, AM, 48; Duke Univ, PhD(physics), 51. *Prof Exp:* Res engr, Stanford Res Inst, Calif, 51-52; from asst prof to assoc prof physics, Univ Md, 52-60. *Concurrent Pos:* Res assoc, Duke Univ, 51, 53 & 54, Univ Calif, Berkeley, 58-59, Woods Hole Oceanog Inst, 60, Biophysics Inst, Univ Oslo, Norway, 73; consult, United Aircraft Corp; sr sci fel, NATO, 73. *Mem:* Fel Am Phys Soc; Am Asn Physics Teachers; Hist Sci Soc. *Res:* Microwave and radio spectroscopy; electron spin resonance; radiation damage in single crystals. *Mailing Add:* Dept Physics Clark Univ Worcester MA 01610. *Fax:* 508-793-8861

ANDERSEN, TERRELL NEILS, PHYSICAL CHEMISTRY. *Current Pos:* PRIN CHEMIST, KERR-MCGEE TECH CTR, 85- *Personal Data:* b Central, Idaho, Apr 22, 37; m 57, Virginia Lee; c Bill, Susan & John. *Educ:* Univ Utah, BS, 58, PhD(phys chem), 62. *Prof Exp:* Fel & res assoc electrochem, Univ Utah, 62 & Univ Pa, 62-63; res assoc, Univ Utah, 63-64, asst res prof chem & metall, 64-69; sr scientist, process technol, Kennecott Copper Co, 69-85. *Concurrent Pos:* NSF fel, 58-60; adj prof metall, Univ Utah, 75-85. *Mem:* Am Chem Soc; Sigma Xi; Electrochem Soc; Int Battery Mat Asn. *Res:* Electrochemical kinetics and double layer; electrowinning; electrorefining; corrosion; batteries; industrial electrochemical processes; photocatalysis. *Mailing Add:* 500 Concord Lane Edmond OK 73034-2614. *Fax:* 405-775-5632

ANDERSEN, THORKILD WAINO, anesthesiology, for more information see previous edition

ANDERSEN, WILFORD HOYT, PHYSICAL CHEMISTRY, FLUID DYNAMICS. *Current Pos:* CONSULT, 94- *Personal Data:* b Central, Idaho, Dec 15, 24; m 56, Jeanette Dick; c Laura & Sally. *Educ:* Univ Utah, BS, 49, PhD(chem), 52. *Prof Exp:* Res assoc chem, Univ Utah, 52-53 & Brown Univ, 53-55; tech specialist ord, Aerojet-Gen Corp, 55-64; prin res scientist, Heliodyne Corp, 64-65; prin scientist, Shock Hydrodynamics Div, Whittaker Corp, 65-77, chief scientist, 77-82; sr staff engr, Ballistic Missiles Div, TRW, 82-94. *Mem:* NY Acad Sci; AAAS; Combustion Inst; Planetary Soc. *Res:* Fundamental and applied research in shock, detonation, combustion and related ordnance phenomena; physical chemistry; fluid dynamics; molecular theory of biological processes; nuclear weapons effects; ballistic missiles. *Mailing Add:* 1165 E Comstock Ave Glendora CA 91741-2911

ANDERSEN, WILLIAM RALPH, BIOCHEMICAL GENETICS. *Current Pos:* PROF BOT, BOT & RANGE SCI DEPT, BRIGHAM YOUNG UNIV, 66- *Personal Data:* b Rexburg, Idaho, Dec 11, 30; m 54; c 5. *Educ:* Utah State Univ, BS, 56, MS, 58; Univ Calif, Davis, PhD(genetics), 63. *Prof Exp:* Asst prof hort & genetics, Univ Minn, 63-66. *Concurrent Pos:* Fel & grants, Univ Calif, 67-69. *Mem:* Am Soc Plant Physiol; Genetics Soc Am; Sigma Xi. *Res:* Genetics of photosynthesis. *Mailing Add:* Dept Bot Brigham Young Univ 401 WIDB Provo UT 84602-1049

ANDERSLAND, MARK STEVEN, DECENTRALIZED CONTROL, COORDINATION THEORY. *Current Pos:* asst prof, 89-95, ASSOC PROF ELEC & COMPUT ENG, UNIV IOWA, 95- *Personal Data:* b Lansing, Mich, June 9, 61; m 95, Mary Pruzinsky. *Educ:* Univ Mich, BSE, 83, MSE, 84, PhD(elec eng systs), 89. *Mem:* Inst Elec & Electronics Engrs; Soc Indust & Appl Math. *Res:* Decentralized control, coordination theory and distributed information processing; estimation resource allocation in broadband communication networks; event trace recovery in intrusively monitored parallel and distributed computing systems. *Mailing Add:* Dept Elec & Computer Eng 4408 Eng Bldg Univ Iowa Iowa City IA 52242

ANDERSLAND, ORLANDO BALDWIN, CIVIL ENGINEERING, GEOTECHNICAL ENGINEERING. *Current Pos:* from asst prof to prof, 60-94, EMER PROF CIVIL ENG, MICH STATE UNIV, 94- *Personal Data:* b Albert Lea, Minn, Aug 15, 29; m 58, Phyllis Burgess; c Mark S, John M & Ruth M. *Educ:* Univ Minn, BCE, 52; Purdue Univ, MSCE, 56, PhD(civil eng), 60. *Honors & Awards:* Soc Res Merit Award, Sigma Xi, 60. *Prof Exp:* Officer, US Army Corps Engrs, US & Korea, 52-55; staff engr, Nat Acad Sci-Am Asn State Hwy Off Rd Test, Ottawa, Ill, 56-57; res engr, Purdue Univ, 57-59. *Concurrent Pos:* NSF res grants, 63-66, 67-70, 76-78, 80-82 & 84-86; Royal Norweg Coun Sci & Indust Res fel, Norweg Geotech Inst, Oslo, 66; Nat Coun Paper Indust Air & Stream Improv res grant, 69-71; Environ Protection Agency res grant, 71-73; ed geotech eng, Cold Regions, 78. *Mem:* Fel Am Soc Civil Engrs; Am Soc Test & Mat; Am Soc Eng Educ; Int Soc Soil Mech & Found Engr. *Res:* Soil mechanics; mechanical properties of frozen ground and organic soils; ground freezing for construction; co-author of over 80 technical publications; frozen ground engineering. *Mailing Add:* Dept Civil & Environ Eng Mich State Univ East Lansing MI 48824-1212. *Fax:* 517-432-1827

ANDERSON, A EUGENE, ELECTRICAL ENGINEERING. *Current Pos:* RETIRED. *Personal Data:* b Lima, Ohio, Apr 22, 16; m 42; c 5. *Educ:* Ohio State Univ, BS & MS, 39. *Prof Exp:* Engr, Bell Tel Labs, NJ, 39-49, supvr electronic apparatus develop, 49-53, head subdept, 53-55, head dept & dir develop, Pa, 55-57; supt mfg eng, Western Elec Co, 57-59, works engr mgr, 59-68, dir eng, 68-75. *Concurrent Pos:* Mem, Signal Corps Radar Lab, US Dept Defense, 42-47, adv panel electronics, 54-60. *Mem:* Fel AAAS; fel Inst Elec & Electronics Engrs. *Res:* Electron tube and semiconductor development and manufacture. *Mailing Add:* 1621 E Sawmill Rd Quakertown PA 18951-5703

ANDERSON, ALBERT EDWARD, COMPUTER & MEDICAL SCIENCES. *Current Pos:* RETIRED. *Personal Data:* b Jamestown, NY, July 4, 28; m 50; c 1. *Educ:* Allegheny Col, BS, 50; Univ Rochester, PhD(org chem), 53. *Prof Exp:* res chemist, Eastman Kodak Co, 53-59, sr res chemist, 59-65, res assoc, 65-77, tech assoc, Info Serv, 77-88. *Mem:* Am Chem Soc; Sigma Xi. *Res:* Synthetic organic chemistry; photographic chemistry; film emulsion making. *Mailing Add:* 15 Powdermill Dr Pittsford NY 14534

ANDERSON, ALBERT GORDON, ORGANIC CHEMISTRY. *Current Pos:* RES CHEMIST PHOTOCHEM, CATALYSIS, INTEGRATED OPTICS, ANTIBIOTICS, PAINTS & POLYMERS, E I DUPONT DE NEMOURS & CO INC, 77- *Personal Data:* b Evanston, Ill, Nov 21, 45; m 73, Christine R Minton; c Robert W & Barbara R. *Educ:* Calif State Univ, Sacramento, BA, 67; Univ Utah, PhD(chem), 77. *Mem:* Am Chem Soc; Optical Soc Am. *Res:* Physical organic chemistry, organic synthesis; elucidation of physical relations between chemical structure and physical properties such as heat of fusion, melting point, stability and refractive index; catalysis; antibiotics. *Mailing Add:* 2410 St Francis St Wilmington DE 19808-4050

ANDERSON, ALFRED TITUS, JR, PETROLOGY, VOLCANOLOGY. *Current Pos:* from asst prof to assoc prof, 68-82, PROF GEOL, UNIV CHICAGO, 82- *Personal Data:* b Port Jefferson, NY, Aug 3, 37; m; c 2. *Educ:* Northwestern Univ, BA, 59; Princeton Univ, PhD(geol), 63. *Prof Exp:* NSF res fel, Univ Chicago, 63-66; geologist, US Geol Surv, 66-68. *Mem:* Am Geophys Union. *Res:* Physical-chemical conditions of crystallization of igneous rocks as revealed by field and mineralogical studies; role of gases in volcanism; igneous sources of excess volatiles. *Mailing Add:* Dept Geophys Sci Univ Chicago 5734 Ellis Ave Chicago IL 60637-1434

ANDERSON, AMOS ROBERT, ORGANIC CHEMISTRY. *Current Pos:* PRES, OCEANA MINERALS LTD, 90- *Personal Data:* b Delavan, Wis, Feb 11, 20; m 45; c 2. *Educ:* Adrian Col, BS, 42, PhD, 65. *Hon Degrees:* DSc, Adrian Col, 65. *Prof Exp:* Res chemist, 46; res chemist Gas Process Div, Girdler Corp, 43; chief chemist, Houdaille Hershey Corp, Manhattan Proj, 44-45; pres, Anderson Chem Co, 46-58, vpres & gen mgr, Anderson Chem Div, Stauffer Chem Co, 58-65, vpres & gen mgr, Silicone Div, 64-66; pres, Anderson Develop Co, 66-90. *Concurrent Pos:* Pres & gen mgr, Tex Alkyls, Inc, 60-65; pres, Indust Accessories, Inc, 64-66; pres, Valjo Corp, 66-; vpres, AvTec Co, 67-69; vpres, Aquaphase Labs, 67-; dir, Am Dynamics Int, 68-72, pres, 72; vpres, Fabridyne Corp & Kemerica Inc, 73-75; pres, Interamerican Zinc, Inc, 74- *Mem:* NY Acad Sci; Am Chem Soc; Armed Forces Chem Asn. *Res:* Organometallics; silicones; organic chemicals; pharmaceutical intermediates; activated carbon. *Mailing Add:* 11 Lakeridge Rt 6 Adrian MI 49221-9226

ANDERSON, AMY ELIN, symbiosis, marine bacterial-invertebrate, for more information see previous edition

ANDERSON, ANNE JOYCE, MOLECULAR BIOLOGY, MICROBIOLOGY. *Current Pos:* From asst to assoc prof biol, 79-88, PROF BIOL, UTAH STATE UNIV, 88- *Personal Data:* b Eng, Aug 3, 46. *Educ:* Univ London, BSc, 67, PhD(biochem), 70. *Mem:* Am Plant Physiol Soc; Am Phytopath Soc. *Res:* Plant-microbe interaction; the molecular basis of colonization is being studied to promote plant interaction with beneficial organisms and deter plant pathogen growth. *Mailing Add:* Dept Biol Utah State Univ Logan UT 84322-0001

ANDERSON, ANSEL COCHRAN, LOW TEMPERATURE PHYSICS. *Current Pos:* RETIRED. *Personal Data:* b Warren, Pa, Sept 17, 33; m 55, Janet Belles; c Gail & Alan. *Educ:* Allegheny Col, BS, 55; Wesleyan Univ, MA, 57; Univ Ill, PhD(physics), 61. *Prof Exp:* Res assoc, Univ Ill, Urbana, 61-62, from asst prof to prof physics, 62-92, dept head, 86-92. *Concurrent Pos:* Guggenheim fel, 66; Fulbright-Hays res grant, 66; assoc, Ctr Advan Studies, 71-72. *Mem:* Fel Am Phys Soc. *Res:* Acoustics of quartz plates; properties of materials at temperatures below 1 Kelvin; ultralow temperature refrigeration and instrumentation. *Mailing Add:* Dept Physics Univ Ill 1110 W Green St Urbana IL 61801

ANDERSON, ANTHONY, MOLECULAR SPECTROSCOPY, SOLID STATE PHYSICS. *Current Pos:* from asst prof to assoc prof, 66-77, PROF INFRARED & RAMAN SPECTROS, UNIV WATERLOO, 77- *Personal Data:* b London, Eng, June 8, 35; Can citizen; m 61, Sigrid M Meinecke; c Mark C & Christine M. *Educ:* Oxford Univ, BA, 56, MA & PhD(low temperature physics), 60. *Prof Exp:* Sci officer far infrared spectros, Nat Phys Lab, Eng, 60-63; res assoc infrared & Raman spectros, Princeton Univ, 63-65; vis asst prof, Kans State Univ, 65-66. *Concurrent Pos:* Consult, Parsons & Co, Ltd, Eng, 63-65; vis prof, Univ Grenoble, 72-73, Univ Utah, 79-80, Ariz State Univ, 86, Univ Canterbury, New Zealand, 87. *Mem:* Can Asn Physicists; Spectros Soc Can. *Res:* Infrared and Raman spectroscopic studies of molecular crystals, especially lattice vibrations and crystal field splittings; electric field induced absorption; lattice dynamics; collision-induced absorption; spectroscopy at high pressures. *Mailing Add:* Dept Physics Univ Waterloo Waterloo ON N2L 3G1 Can

ANDERSON, ARNOLD LYNN, FIRE RETARDANT POLYMERS, ORGANIC FLUORINE CHEMISTRY. *Current Pos:* CONSULT & OWNER, A LYNN ANDERSON & ASSOCS, 78- *Personal Data:* b Ft Dodge, Iowa, Aug 26, 40; m 68; c 2. *Educ:* Luther Col, Decorah, Iowa, BA, 62; Univ Iowa, MS, 67, PhD(chem), 71. *Prof Exp:* Chemist, Sinclair Res, Inc, 62-64; sr res chemist, Mich Chem Corp, 70-75; group leader, Stepan Chem Co, 75-78. *Concurrent Pos:* Cong Sci Coun, Am Chem Soc, 79-81; consult, David W Young & Assocs, Inc, 81-82. *Mem:* Am Chem Soc; Am Inst Chemists; AAAS. *Res:* New products and processes; organic halogen chemistry; fire retardant polymers; organic synthesis. *Mailing Add:* 501 Longview Antioch IL 60002

ANDERSON, ARTHUR G, JR, ORGANIC CHEMISTRY. *Current Pos:* from instr to prof chem, 46-88, assoc chmn dept, 78-88, EMER PROF CHEM, UNIV WASH, 88- *Personal Data:* b Sioux City, Iowa, July 1, 18; m 44, Sue Rinker; c Lynn, Joyce & Beth. *Educ:* Univ Ill, AB, 40; Univ Mich, MS, 42, PhD(chem), 44. *Prof Exp:* From jr to sr chemist, Tenn Eastman Corp, Oak Ridge, 44-45; spec asst, Univ Ill, 46. *Concurrent Pos:* NSF sr fel, 60-61; vis prof, Heidelberg Univ, 60-61 & Australian Nat Univ, 66; Am Chem Soc int study award, 66. *Mem:* Am Chem Soc; The Chem Soc; fel NY Acad Sci; fel Am Inst Chem. *Res:* Nonclassical aromatic compounds; novel heterocyclic systems; polynuclear alicyclic compounds; new synthetic reactions. *Mailing Add:* Dept Chem Box 35-1700 Univ Wash Seattle WA 98195. *Fax:* 206-685-8665

ANDERSON, ARTHUR GEORGE, PHYSICS. *Current Pos:* RETIRED. *Personal Data:* b Evanston, Ill, Nov 22, 26; m 47; c 6. *Educ:* Univ San Francisco, BS, 49; Northwestern Univ, MS, 51; NY Univ, PhD(physics), 58. *Hon Degrees:* DSc, Univ Nev, Reno, 85. *Honors & Awards:* Pake Award, Am Phys Soc, 84. *Prof Exp:* Tech engr, IBM Corp, 51-53, comput & physics res, Watson Lab, 53-58, physicist, 58-59, res physicist, 59-61, dir, San Jose Res Lab, 61-63, asst dir res, 63-65, staff dir, Corp Tech Comt, 65-67, dir res, 67-70, vpres, 69-72, vpres & pres, Gen Prod Div, 72-79, vpres & group exec, DP Prod Group, 79-81, vpres & group exec, Info Syst & Technol Group, IBM Corp,51-84. *Concurrent Pos:* Vis fel, Ctr Study Democratic Insts, 70-71; consult, R & D Mgt, 84-; dir, Compression Labs Inc, 84, bd dirs, 84- *Mem:* Nat Acad Eng; fel Am Phys Soc; fel Inst Elec & Electronics Engrs; AAAS. *Res:* Nuclear magnetic resonance in solids; computer engineering. *Mailing Add:* PO Box 1032 Prescott AZ 86302

ANDERSON, ARTHUR O, RESPIRATORY MUCOSAL IMMUNITY, IMMUNOPATHOLOGY. *Current Pos:* prin investr immunol, 74-80, chief, Dept Respiratory & Mucosal Immunol, 83-95, CHIEF, DEPT CLIN PATHOL, US ARMY MED RES INST INFECTIOUS DIS, FT DETRICK, 95- *Personal Data:* b Staten Island, NY, Mar 12, 45; m 69, Julane Pynn; c Phoebe M. *Educ:* Wagner Col, BS, 66; Univ Md, MD, 70. *Prof Exp:* Intern path, Johns Hopkins Hosp, 70-71, resident, 71-73, fel, Johns Hopkins Univ, 70-74, instr arts appl med, 73-74; asst prof path & biol, Sch Med, Univ Pa, 80-83. *Concurrent Pos:* Lectr, Johns Hopkins Immunol Coun, 70-83 & Found Advan Educ Sci, NIH, 79-; vis fel, Geront Res Ctr, NIH, 72-74; res ethicist, 92- *Mem:* Am Asn Immunologists; Am Soc Invest Path; Int Acad Path; NY Acad Sci; AAAS; Soc Mucosal Immunol; Appl Res Ethics Nat Asn. *Res:* Physiological mechanisms that regulate in vivo immune responses; lymph node microvasculature; angiogenesis; lymphocyte-endothelial interactions; lymphocyte recirculation, motility and chemotaxis; cellular and molecular mechanisms that regulate mucosal immune responses, especially with regard to the respiratory tract; development of vaccine carrier proteins based on Cholera Toxin B subunit for simultaneous induction of mucosal and systemic immunity; discovered the fibroblastic reticular cell conduit system that is essential to normal function of lymphatic tissues. *Mailing Add:* 122 W Third St Frederick MD 21701. *Fax:* 301-619-2492; *E-Mail:* art_anderson@detrick.army.mil

ANDERSON, ARTHUR R(OLAND), engineering; deceased, see previous edition for last biography

ANDERSON, ARTHUR W, BACTERIOLOGY. *Current Pos:* assoc prof food microbiol, 53-77, prof, 77-80, EMER PROF MICROBIOL, ORE STATE UNIV, 80- *Personal Data:* b Lisbon, NDak, Dec 2, 14; m 48; c 3. *Educ:* NDak State Col, BS, 43; Univ Wis, MS, 47; Ore State Col, PhD, 52. *Prof Exp:* Asst prof bact, Univ Calif, Berkeley, 52-53. *Mem:* Inst Food Technol; Am Soc Microbiol. *Res:* Food borne pathogens and irradiation microbiology. *Mailing Add:* 892 Normandy Ave S Salem OR 97302

ANDERSON, AUBREY LEE, ACOUSTICS, OCEANOGRAPHY. *Current Pos:* PROF, DEPT OCEANOG, TEX A&M UNIV, COL STATION, 84- *Personal Data:* b Ft Worth, Tex, Apr 24, 40; m 60, Linda G Armstrong; c Michelle & David. *Educ:* Baylor Univ, BS, 62; Univ Tex, Austin, PhD(eng acoust), 74. *Prof Exp:* Physicist, Naval Ord Lab, Corona, Calif, 62-63 & Navy Electronics Lab, San Diego, 63-64; res scientist underwater sound, Appl Res Labs, Univ Tex, Austin, 65-77; physicist, Off Naval Res, Naval Ocean Res & Develop Activ, 77-81, dep dir, Environ Sci Directorate, 81-83. *Mem:* Acoust Soc Am; Sigma Xi; Am Inst Physics; Marine Technol Soc; Am Geophy Union; Oceanog Soc. *Res:* Underwater acoustics; mathematical modeling of ocean sound and noise fields and of oceanographic variables; use of acoustics as a tool in geophysics and oceanography; marine sediment studies; physical and geological oceanography. *Mailing Add:* Route 3 Box L264 Franklin TX 77856. *E-Mail:* aanderson@ocean.tamu.edu

ANDERSON, BERNARD A, SPEECH PATHOLOGY, AUDIOLOGY. *Current Pos:* prof, 58-74, PROF EMER SPEECH PATH & DIR SPEECH & HEARING CLIN, UNIV NEV, RENO, 74- *Personal Data:* b Thornton, Wash, Aug 23, 09; m 42; c 8. *Educ:* Univ Wash, BA, 33, dipl, 37; Univ Wis, PhD(speech path), 50. *Prof Exp:* Actg dir speech & hearing, Univ Okla, 39-40; instr speech path, Ind Univ, 46-48; assoc prof, Univ Utah, 49-57. *Concurrent Pos:* Consult, Easter Seal Soc, 51-71, Shriner's Hosp Crippled Children, 55-57. *Mem:* Fel Am Speech & Hearing Asn. *Res:* Photography of the human larynx; disorders of speech and hearing. *Mailing Add:* 220 Brownstone Reno NV 89512

ANDERSON, BERNARD JEFFREY, SPACE VEHICLE, ENVIRONMENT INTERACTIONS. *Current Pos:* AEROSPACE ENGR, GEORGE C MARSHALL SPACE FLIGHT CTR, NASA, 75- *Personal Data:* b Waco, Tex, Feb 23, 44; m 71; c 8. *Educ:* Univ Nev, Reno, BS, 66, MS, 68, PhD(physics), 74. *Prof Exp:* Res assoc cloud physics, Desert Res Inst, Lab Atmospheric Physics, Univ Nev, 74-75. *Concurrent Pos:* Interagency Nuclear Safety Rev Panel. *Mem:* Am Meteorol Soc. *Res:* Space environment definition for space station; hydrogen ignition hazards in space vehicle launch and test environment; environment effects from solid rocket launch and test; meteorological impacts on space vehicle operations. *Mailing Add:* EL 23 G C Marshall Space Flight Ctr Systs Anal & Integration Labs Marshall Space Flight Ctr AL 35812

ANDERSON, BERTIN W, ZOOLOGY. *Current Pos:* assoc prof, 73-86, ADJ PROF ZOOL, ARIZ STATE UNIV, 86-; PRES, REVEGETATION & WILDLIFE MGT CTR, 86- *Personal Data:* b Luverne, Minn, Dec 15, 39; m 69; c 1. *Educ:* Mankato State Col, BS, 62; Univ Minn, MS, 66; Univ SDak, PhD(zool), 69. *Prof Exp:* Asst prof biol, Northwestern State Col, Okla, 69-72; vis prof zool, Eastern Mich Univ, 72-73. *Mem:* Am Ornith Union; Cooper Ornith Soc; Ecol Soc; Wildlife Soc; Soc Study Evolution. *Res:* Ornithology; evolutionary and systematic biology; community ecology. *Mailing Add:* 201 S Palm Dr Blythe CA 92225

ANDERSON, BEVERLY, BIOMEDICAL RESEARCH. *Current Pos:* RETIRED. *Personal Data:* b Milwaukee, Wis, Mar 6, 33. *Educ:* Univ Ore, PhD(biol), 71. *Prof Exp:* Sr biologist, biosci res lab, 3M Co, 81-87. *Mem:* Am Soc Cell Biol. *Mailing Add:* 5616 Mount Normandale Dr Bloomington MN 55437-1016

ANDERSON, BRADLEY DALE, PHARMACEUTICAL CHEMISTRY, PHYSICAL CHEMISTRY. *Current Pos:* RES SCIENTIST PHARM, UPJOHN CO, 77- *Personal Data:* b Columbus, Nebr, Nov 23, 48; m 72. *Educ:* Univ Kans, BA, 71, MS, 77, PhD(pharmaceut chem), 78. *Prof Exp:* Qual control chemist pharmaceut, Haver-Lockhart Labs, 71-74. *Mem:* Am Pharmaceut Asn. *Res:* Design of physicochemical properties of drugs through molecular modification; solution thermodynamics. *Mailing Add:* Dept Pharmaceut & Pharmceut Chem Univ Utah 421 Wakara Way Res Park Salt Lake City UT 84108-1210

ANDERSON, BRUCE MARTIN, TITANIUM DIOXIDE PIGMENT TECHNOLOGY. *Current Pos:* qual control mgr, Kemira, Inc, 85-88, asst tech dir, 88-90, tech dir, 90-91, vpres res & develop, 91-93, RES DIR, KEMIRA, INC, 93- *Personal Data:* b Charleston, WVa, Aug 11, 42; m 69, Lora Matheny; c Brian & Michelle. *Educ:* Morris Harvey Col, Charleston, BS, 64; WVa Univ, PhD(inorg chem), 69. *Prof Exp:* Process chemist, Am Cyanamid Co, 69-81, process develop mgr, 81-85. *Concurrent Pos:* Chmn, Coastal Empire Sect, Am Chem Soc, 74; rep to Chem Mfr Asn, Kemira, Inc. *Mem:* Am Chem Soc. *Res:* Titanium dioxide pigment technology; chemistry of various titanium compounds; environmental control process relating to manufacture of titanium dioxide. *Mailing Add:* 139 Grays Creek Dr Savannah GA 31410

ANDERSON, BRUCE MURRAY, BIOCHEMISTRY. *Current Pos:* head dept, 70-82, PROF BIOCHEM, VA POLYTECH INST & STATE UNIV, 70- *Personal Data:* b Detroit, Mich, July 14, 29; m 50, Constance Derr; c David B, Marcia A & Nancy L. *Educ:* Ursinus Col, BS, 53; Purdue Univ, MS, 54; Johns Hopkins Univ, PhD(biochem), 58. *Prof Exp:* NIH fel biochem, Brandeis Univ, 58-60; asst prof, Univ Louisville, 60-63; from assoc prof to prof, Univ Tenn, 63-70. *Concurrent Pos:* NSF res grants, 60-; NIH res grants, 64-69. *Mem:* AAAS; Am Chem Soc; Am Soc Biol Chem. *Res:* Mechanism of enzyme action; function of pyridine nucleotide coenzymes. *Mailing Add:* Dept Biochem Va Polytech Inst & State Univ 306 Engel Hall Blacksburg VA 24061-0308

ANDERSON, BRYON DON, NUCLEAR PHYSICS, NUCLEAR ASTROPHYSICS. *Current Pos:* from asst prof to assoc prof, 75-86, PROF PHYSICS, KENT STATE UNIV, 86- *Personal Data:* b Ft Riley, Kans, Dec 23, 44; m 69, Joan Briggs; c James E & Jennie L. *Educ:* Univ Idaho, BS, 66; Case Western Res Univ, PhD(physics), 72. *Prof Exp:* Res asst nuclear physics, Idaho Nuclear Corp, 66-67; res assoc, Calif Inst Technol, 71-73; sr res assoc, Case Western Res Univ, Los Alamos Nat Lab, 73-75. *Concurrent Pos:* Planetarium dir, 79-96. *Mem:* Am Phys Soc. *Res:* Neutron and charged-particle spectrometry at intermediate energies, nuclear structure and reaction mechanisms; few-body systems and nucleon form factors. *Mailing Add:* Dept Physics Kent State Univ Kent OH 44242. *Fax:* 330-672-2959; *E-Mail:* anderson@rsuvxd.kent.edu

ANDERSON, BYRON, BIOCHEMISTRY, IMMUNOLOGY. *Current Pos:* From asst prof to assoc prof, 71-84, PROF BIOCHEM, MED & DENT SCHS, NORTHWESTERN UNIV, 84- *Personal Data:* b Hammond, Ind, Dec 30, 41; m 64. *Educ:* Kalamazoo Col, BA, 63; Univ Mich, PhD(biochem), 68. *Concurrent Pos:* Helen Hay Whitney & Nat Cystic Fibrosis Res Found fel, Col Physicians & Surgeons, Columbia Univ, 68-71; NIH career develop award, 74-79; sr investr, Arthritis Found, 73-74; consult, Abbott Labs, 74- *Mem:* AAAS; Am Rheumatism Asn; Am Chem Soc; Am Soc Biol Chem; Am Asn Immunologists. *Res:* Autoimmune diseases, especially rheumatoid arthritis; cancer research and membrane glycoprotein antigens. *Mailing Add:* Dept Molecular Biol Northwestern Univ Med 303 E Chicago Chicago IL 60611-3072

ANDERSON, CARL EINAR, PHYSICS. *Current Pos:* RETIRED. *Personal Data:* b Brooklyn, NY, Sept 15, 23; m 57. *Educ:* Rensselaer Polytech Inst, BS, 49; Yale Univ, MS, 50, PhD(physics), 53. *Prof Exp:* Res assoc electron physics res lab, Gen Elec Co, 52-54; res assoc nuclear physics, Yale Univ, 54-61; sr scientist appl physics lab, Johns Hopkins Univ, 61; mgr, Radiation & Space Physics Re-Entry Systs Dept, Gen Elec Co, 61-65, mgr appl physics, Space Sci Lab, 65-81, mgr electro-optics & sensors, 81-83, consult physicist, Space Div, 83-92. *Concurrent Pos:* Consult, Wallingford Steel Co, 56-59. *Mem:* Am Phys Soc; Soc Photo-Optical Instrumentation Engrs; Am Inst Aeronaut & Astronaut; Sigma Xi. *Res:* Nuclear, reentry and space physics; lasers. *Mailing Add:* 695 Knox Rd Wayne PA 19087-2015

ANDERSON, CARL FREDERICK, NUTRITIONAL ASSESSMENT, NUTRITION & RENAL DISEASE. *Current Pos:* PROF MED, MAYO MED SCH, 83- *Educ:* State Univ Iowa, MD, 59. *Res:* Chronic renal failure. *Mailing Add:* Mayo Med Sch Mayo Clin Rochester MN 55901

ANDERSON, CARL WILLIAM, MOLECULAR BIOLOGY, ANIMAL VIROLOGY. *Current Pos:* asst geneticist, 75-76, assoc geneticist, 76-79, GENETICIST, BROOKHAVEN NAT LAB, 79- *Personal Data:* b Washington, DC, May 19, 44; m 68, Mary E Daniell; c Carl E & Christine E. *Educ:* Harvard Col, BA, 66; Wash Univ, PhD(microbiol), 70. *Prof Exp:* Fel, DNA cancer viruses, Cold Spring Harbor Lab, 70-73, mem staff, 73-75. *Concurrent Pos:* NIH fel, 70-72; consult, NSF, 75-79; adj asst prof, Dept Microbiol, State Univ NY, Stony Brook, 76-79, adj assoc prof, 79-90, adj prof, 90- *Mem:* Am Soc Microbiol; AAAS; Am Soc Virol; Protein Soc; Am Soc Biochem & Molecular Biol. *Res:* Control of gene expression in mammalian cells; protein kinases. *Mailing Add:* Dept Biol Brookhaven Nat Lab Bldg 463 Upton NY 11973-5000. *Fax:* 516-282-3407; *E-Mail:* anderson@bnloxl.bnl.gov

ANDERSON, CARL WILLIAM (BILL), ANALYTICAL CHEMISTRY, BIOCHEMISTRY. *Current Pos:* ASST PROF ANALYTICAL CHEM, DUKE UNIV, 78- *Personal Data:* b Schenectady, NY, Apr 7, 50. *Educ:* Univ Mass, BS, 72; Univ Cincinnati, MS, 75, PhD(analytical chem) & PhD (Biochem), 78. *Prof Exp:* Res assoc phys chem, Amherst Col, 72-73. *Mem:* Am Chem Soc. *Res:* Applications of electrochemistry to biochemical problems with respect to quantitative, mechanistic and thermodynamic behavior of biochemically significant compounds. *Mailing Add:* Chem Dept Hampden Sydney Col Hampden Sydney VA 23943

ANDERSON, CAROL PATRICIA, ENVIRONMENTAL ANALYSIS, PATTERN RECOGNITION TECHNIQUES. *Current Pos:* Fel, 73-75, asst prof, 75-80, ASSOC PROF CHEM, UNIV CONN, AVERY POINT, 80- *Personal Data:* b Bluefield, WVa, May 19, 46; m 78. *Educ:* Concord Col, BS, 68; Univ Tenn, PhD(chem), 73. *Mem:* Am Chem Soc; Nat Sci Teachers Asn. *Res:* Detecting and quantifying spilled hazardous chemicals; pattern recognition techniques for spilled oils; permeation of protective clothing material; more effective methods of presenting chemistry to the general public. *Mailing Add:* Univ Conn Avery Point 1084 Shennecossett Rd Groton CT 06340-6094

ANDERSON, CHARLES DEAN, BIO-ORGANIC CHEMISTRY. *Current Pos:* assoc prof org chem, Pac Lutheran Univ, 59-62, chmn, Dept Chem, 61-66, 78-80 & 86, prof chem, 62-91, dean, Col Arts & Sci, 66-70, Regency professorship, 74-75, EMER PROF CHEM, PAC LUTHERAN UNIV, 92- *Personal Data:* b Redwood Falls, Minn, Mar 8, 30; m 53, Margaret Ann Tufte; c Kristen (Kalbrener), Mark S T & Peter C O. *Educ:* St Olaf Col, BA, 52; Harvard Univ, MA, 54, PhD(org chem), 59. *Prof Exp:* Org chemist, Stanford Res Inst, Calif, 56-59. *Concurrent Pos:* NSF fac fel, Univ Minn, 64-65; Northwest Col & Univ Asn Sci vis fac appointment, Pac Northwest Labs, Battelle Mem Inst, 70-71; vis scholar, Col Forest Resources, Univ Wash, 81 & 88-89; co-dir, Chengdu Exchange Prog, 86-89; vis fac appointment, Chengdu Univ of Sci & Technol, China, 87. *Mem:* Am Chem Soc; Royal Soc Chem; Am Asn Univ Professors. *Res:* Synthetic methods; natural products and analogs; lignin chemistry. *Mailing Add:* Dept Chem Pac Lutheran Univ Tacoma WA 98447

ANDERSON, CHARLES E, JR, COMPUTATIONAL MODELING, COMPUTATIONAL MECHANICS. *Current Pos:* sr res physicist, 80-84, mgr, 84-93, DIR, SOUTHWEST RES INST, 94- *Personal Data:* b Baltimore, Md, Mar 7, 46; m 74, Gail J Schubert; c Marcia L & Tricia G. *Educ:* Va Polytech Inst, BS, 68; Rensselaer Polytech Inst, MS & PhD(physics), 72. *Prof Exp:* Res physicist, Ballistic Res Lab, US Army, 72-80. *Concurrent Pos:* Lectr, Univ Tex, San Antonio, 83-89; bd dir, Hypervelocity Impact Soc, 89-94 & 96-, publ chmn, 93- *Mem:* Hypervelocity Impact Soc (pres, 89-92); AAAS; Sigma Xi; Am Phys Soc. *Res:* Physical sciences: dynamic modeling of fire spread, intumescent paint, warhead mechanics, penetration mechanics, shock mechanics; dynamic material response, hypervelocity impact. *Mailing Add:* Southwest Res Inst 6220 Culebra Rd PO Drawer 28510 San Antonio TX 78228-0510. *Fax:* 210-522-3042; *E-Mail:* canderson@swri.edu

ANDERSON, CHARLES EDWARD, PHYSICAL METEOROLOGY. *Current Pos:* prof space sci & eng, 67-69, PROF METEOROL & CHMN CONTEMP TRENDS COURSE, UNIV WIS-MADISON, 66-, PROF AFRO-AM STUDIES & CHMN DEPT, 70-, ASSOC DEAN, 78- *Personal Data:* b St Louis, Mo, Aug 13, 19; m 43; c 3. *Educ:* Lincoln Univ, Mo, BS, 41; Univ Chicago, cert meteorol, 43; Polytech Inst Brooklyn, MS, 48; Mass Inst Technol, PhD(meteorol), 60. *Prof Exp:* Chief, Cloud Physics Br, Air Force Cambridge Res Ctr, Mass, 48-61 & Atmospheric Sci Br, Douglas Aircraft Co, Calif, 61-65; dir, Off Fed Coord Meteorol, Environ Sic Serv Admin, US Dept Com, Washington, DC, 65-66. *Concurrent Pos:* Prin investr, NSF grant, 69-; consult, Sci Ctr, NAm Rockwell Corp, Calif, 67- & Rand Corp, 68-; chmn, Aviation Adv Panel, Nat Ctr Atmospheric Res, Colo, 63- *Mem:* AAAS; Sigma Xi. *Res:* Cloud and aerosol physics; high polymer chemistry; space and planetary science; meteorology of other planets; science and society; science, technology and race. *Mailing Add:* 6301 Westgate Madison WI 53716

ANDERSON, CHARLES EUGENE, MORPHOLOGY. *Current Pos:* from asst prof to assoc prof, 69-78, PROF BOT, NC STATE UNIV, 78- *Personal Data:* b Winfield, Kans, Dec 3, 34; m 54; c 3. *Educ:* Purdue Univ, BSA, 56, MS, 61, PhD(biol sci), 63. *Prof Exp:* Asst prof bot, Univ Okla, 63-66. *Mem:* AAAS; Bot Soc Am. *Res:* Developmental morphology of salt marsh and dune plants; environmental factors influencing cell and tissue differentiation. *Mailing Add:* Dept Bot NC State Univ Box 7612 Raleigh NC 27695-0001

ANDERSON, CHARLES HAMMOND, NEUROSCIENCE. *Current Pos:* RES PROF NEUROBIOL, SCH MED, WASHINGTON UNIV, 92- *Personal Data:* b Mineola, NY, May 31, 35; m 60; c 3. *Educ:* Calif Inst Technol, BS, 57; Harvard Univ, PhD(molecular physics), 62. *Prof Exp:* Res assoc, Harvard Univ, 61-62, instr physics, 62-63; mem tech staff, RCA Lab9, 63-77, fel staff, 77-78, group head appl math & phys sci, 78-82, fel staff, 82-87; mem tech staff, Jet Propulsion Lab, 87-90. *Concurrent Pos:* NSF fel, 62-63; RCA fel, Clarendon Lab, Oxford, Eng, 71-72; res assoc, Calif Inst Tech, 84, vis assoc, Biol Div, 88- *Mem:* Fel Am Phys Soc; AAAS. *Res:* Ion physics in solids; liquid helium; acoustics; low temperature physics; flat television displays; electron optics; mathematical models of human vision-pattern recognition; general applied math. *Mailing Add:* Sch Med Campus Box 8108 Washington Univ 660 S Euclid Ave St Louis MO 63110-1093

ANDERSON, CHARLES THOMAS, PHYSICAL INORGANIC CHEMISTRY. *Current Pos:* from asst prof to prof, 55-86, EMER PROF CHEM, EASTERN MICH UNIV, 86- *Personal Data:* b Fairmont, WVa, Feb 26, 21; m 50; c 2. *Educ:* Fairmont State Col, AB, 42; Ohio State Univ, PhD(chem), 55. *Prof Exp:* Teaching asst chem, Ohio State Univ, 43-46; instr, Ohio Univ, 46-51. *Mem:* Am Chem Soc; Sigma Xi. *Res:* Coordination compounds; equilibrium constants. *Mailing Add:* 720 Kewanee Ave Ypsilanti MI 48197-1741

ANDERSON, CHARLES V, AUDIOLOGY. *Current Pos:* asst prof, 66-68, ASSOC PROF AUDIOL, UNIV IOWA, 68- *Personal Data:* b Little Sioux, Iowa, Aug 18, 33; m 66; c 1. *Educ:* Univ Nebr, BS, 55, MA, 57; Univ Pittsburgh, PhD(psychoacoust), 62. *Prof Exp:* Instr hearing ther, Univ Nebr, 56-58; asst prof audiol, Purdue Univ, 62-66. *Mem:* AAAS; fel Am Speech-Lang-Hearing Asn; Acoust Soc Am; Sigma Xi. *Res:* Hearing loss and aging; auditory phenomena and noise. *Mailing Add:* Speech Path & Audiol Univ Iowa 119 Speech & Hearing Iowa City IA 52242-1000

ANDERSON, CHARLES W, COMPUTER SCIENCE. *Current Pos:* asst prof, 91-97, ASSOC PROF COMPUT SCI DEPT, COLO STATE UNIV, 97- *Educ:* Univ Nebr, BS, 78; Univ Mass, MS, 82, PhD(comput & info sci), 86. *Prof Exp:* Systs analyst, Agnet, Univ Nebr, 77-79; sr mem tech staff, GTE Labs, Mass, 86-90. *Concurrent Pos:* Teaching asst, Univ Mass, 79, comput graphics consult, 84-86; instr, Granby Libr, 83; NSF grantee, 92- *Mem:* Inst Elec & Electronics Engrs; Asn Comput Mach; Int Neural Network Soc; Am Asn Artificial Intel. *Res:* Neural network learning algorithms with applications to control and signal processing problems; efficient learning in hidden units; reinforcement learning; parallel implementation of neural networks; recognition of EEG patterns; control of heating, ventilation and air conditioning systems; control of alternative fuel engines. *Mailing Add:* Dept Comput Sci Colo State Univ Ft Collins CO 80523. *E-Mail:* anderson@cs.colostate.edu

ANDERSON, CHRISTIAN DONALD, EXPLORATION GEOPHYSICS, GEOPHYSICAL ENGINEERING. *Current Pos:* OWNER, CDA ENTERPRISES, 87- *Personal Data:* b Ft Dodge, Iowa, Apr 10, 31; m 57, Barbara Schweiger; c Kris, Tim, Hank, Marge, Rose, Ben & Michael. *Educ:* Univ Minn, Duluth, BA, 57; Univ NMex, MS, 61; Univ Utah, PhD(geophys), 66. *Prof Exp:* Physicist, Los Alamos Sci Lab, 58-61; geophysicist, Newmont Mining Corp, 66-67; assoc prof geophys, Univ Man, 67-87. *Concurrent Pos:* Consult explor geophys, 67- *Mem:* Can Inst Mining & Metal; Sigma Xi. *Res:* Development of geophysical methods and exploration strategies to improve discovery probabilities in mineral exploration. *Mailing Add:* 826 Dorchester Winnepeg MB R3M 0R7 Can

ANDERSON, CHRISTINE MARLENE, SOFTWARE ENGINEERING. *Current Pos:* comput res, Avionics Lab, Dayton, Ohio, 71-74, chief comput tech, Wright Lab/Armament Directorate, Ft Walton Beach, Fla, 81-82, DIR SPACE SOFTWARE RES CTR, PHILLIPS LAB, USAF, ALBUQUERQUE, 92- *Personal Data:* b Washington, DC, Nov 19, 47. *Educ:* Univ Md, BS, 69. *Honors & Awards:* Aerospace Software Eng Award, Am Inst Aeronaut & Astronaut, 91. *Prof Exp:* Mathematician, Naval Oceanog Off, Suitland, Md, 69-71; sr analyst, Syst Develop Corp, Colorado Springs, Colo, 74-76. *Concurrent Pos:* Chair software systs tech comt, Am Inst Aeronaut & Astronaut, 87-89; co-chmn Ad compt prog lang, Am Nat Stand Inst, 89- *Mem:* Fel Am Inst Aeronaut & Astronaut. *Res:* Co-author of one book; contributed articles to professional journals. *Mailing Add:* Air Force Phillips Lab PL/VTES Kirtland AFB NM 87117

ANDERSON, CHRISTOPHER MARLOWE, ASTRONOMY. *Current Pos:* Asst prof, 68-74, assoc prof, 74-80, PROF ASTRON, UNIV WIS-MADISON, 80- *Personal Data:* b Las Cruces, NMex, Feb 21, 41; m 70. *Educ:* Univ Ariz, BS, 63; Calif Inst Technol, PhD(astron), 68. *Mem:* Am Astron Soc; Int Astron Union. *Res:* Photoelectric spectrophotometry; interstellar extinction; stellar rotation and chromospheric activity; spectrum variability. *Mailing Add:* Dept Astron Univ Wis 475 N Charter St Madison WI 53706-1582

ANDERSON, CLYDE LEE, CHEMISTRY. *Current Pos:* assoc prof, 57-81, PROF CHEM, SAN BERNARDINO VALLEY COL, 81-, CHMN DEPT, 68- *Personal Data:* b El Paso, Tex, Sept 17, 26; m 50; c 3. *Educ:* Univ Utah, BS, 52, MS, 53; PhD(org chem), 67. *Prof Exp:* Head chem dept, Dixie Jr Col, 53-57. *Concurrent Pos:* Lectr, Westminster Col, 65-66; NSF sci fac fel, 65-66; col, US Army Reserve, 51-86. *Mem:* Soc Appl Spectros; Am Chem Soc; Sigma Xi. *Res:* Organic thesis; natural products. *Mailing Add:* Dept Chem San Barnardino Valley Col 701 S Mount Vernon Ave San Bernardino CA 92410

ANDERSON, CURTIS BENJAMIN, ORGANIC CHEMISTRY. *Current Pos:* Lectr, Univ Calif, Santa Barbara, 62, assoc, 62-63, lectr, 63-64, actg asst prof, 64-65, asst prof, 65-69, ASSOC PROF CHEM, UNIV CALIF, SANTA BARBARA, 69- *Personal Data:* b Fargo, NDak, Feb 19, 32; m 93, Hana Grimova; c Olivia E. *Educ:* Univ Minn, BS, 56; Univ Calif, Los Angeles, PhD(org chem), 63. *Mem:* Am Chem Soc. *Res:* Physical organic chemistry; conformational analysis of heterocyclic compounds; reactions of olefins complexes of metal salts; neighboring group participation. *Mailing Add:* Dept Chem Univ Calif Santa Barbara CA 93106

ANDERSON, DALE ARDEN, AEROSPACE & ELECTRICAL ENGINEERING. *Current Pos:* PROF AEROSPACE ENG, UNIV TEX, ARLINGTON, 84-; PRES, MDA ENG, INC, 87- *Personal Data:* b Alta, Iowa, Aug 11, 36; m 58; c 2. *Educ:* St Louis Univ, BS, 57; Iowa State Univ, MS, 59, PhD(aerospace & elec eng), 64. *Prof Exp:* From instr to asst prof aerospace eng, Iowa State Univ, 57-64; mem tech staff, Aerospace Corp, Calif, 64-65; from assoc prof to prof aerospace eng, Iowa State Univ, 65-84, dir, CompFluid Dynamics Inst, 80-84,. *Concurrent Pos:* Consult, Lockheed Corp. *Mem:* Assoc fel Am Inst Aeronaut & Astronaut. *Res:* Unsteady aerodynamics; nonequilibrium gas dynamics; finite difference methods in fluid mechanics; hypersonic flow. *Mailing Add:* Dept Mech & Aerospace Eng Univ Tex UTA Box 19018 Arlington TX 76019-0018

ANDERSON, DANA ZACHARY, NEURAL NETWORKS, SELF-ORGANIZING SYSTEMS. *Current Pos:* asst prof, 84-89, ASSOC PROF PHYSICS, UNIV COLO, 89-, FEL, JOINT INST LAB ASTROPHYS, 85- *Personal Data:* b Chicago, Ill, Apr 10, 53; m 93, Sandy Marcione; c Christopher. *Educ:* Cornell Univ BSEE, 75; Univ Ariz, PhD(physics), 81. *Honors & Awards:* Pres Young Investr, 85; RW Wood Prize, Optical Soc Am, 94. *Prof Exp:* Res fel, Calif Inst Technol, 81-84. *Concurrent Pos:* Lectr physics, Calif Inst Technol, 83-84; Alfred P Sloan res fel, 86; bd ed, J Neural Networks. *Mem:* Fel Optical Soc Am; Am Phys Soc. *Res:* Development of self-organizing nonlinear optical systems for communications and information processing. *Mailing Add:* Joint Inst Lab Astrophys Univ Colo CB440 Boulder CO 80309-0440. *Fax:* 303-492-5504; *E-Mail:* dana@jila.colorado.educ

ANDERSON, DANIEL D, COMMUTATIVE ALGEBRA, LATTICE THEORY. *Current Pos:* From asst prof to assoc prof, 74-83, PROF MATH, UNIV IOWA, 83- *Personal Data:* b Ft Dodge, Iowa, Dec 20, 48; m 70, Kathleen R Whalen; c Caitlin A. *Educ:* Univ Iowa, BA, 71; Univ Chicago, MS, 71, PhD(math), 74. *Concurrent Pos:* Asst prof math, Va Polytech Inst, 75-76 & Univ Mo, Columbia, 76-77. *Mem:* Am Math Soc; Math Asn Am. *Res:* Divisibility theory (Euclidean, factorial and Krull domains, class groups); multiplicative ideal theory; rings with zerodivisors; lattice-theoretic questions. *Mailing Add:* Dept Math Univ Iowa Iowa City IA 52242. *Fax:* 319-335-0627; *E-Mail:* dan-anderson@uiowa.edu

ANDERSON, DANIEL WILLIAM, WILDLIFE ECOLOGY, POLLUTION BIOLOGY. *Current Pos:* AVIAN ECOLOGIST & PROF, UNIV CALIF, DAVIS, 76- *Personal Data:* b Underwood, NDak, Feb 5, 39; m 71; c 3. *Educ:* NDak State Univ, BS, 61; Univ Wis-Madison, MS, 67, PhD(wildlife ecol, zool), 70. *Prof Exp:* Res biologist, US Fish & Wildlife Serv, 70-75. *Concurrent Pos:* Regional rep/exec coun, Pac Seabird Group, 73-75 & 85-86, chmn, 78 & 85; mem bd dirs, Bodega Bay Inst Pollution Ecol, 71-; bd mem, Cooper Ornith Soc, 85-87. *Mem:* Wildlife Soc; AAAS; fel Am Ornithologists Union; Soc Environ Toxicol & Chem; Ecol Soc Am; Soc Conserv Biol. *Res:* Effects of environmental pollution on wildlife populations and individuals; ecological and physiological effects of pollutants; study of avian ecology, with emphasis on marine birds. *Mailing Add:* Dept Wildlife/Fisheries Biol Univ Calif-Davis Davis CA 95616-5200

ANDERSON, DARWIN WAYNE, SOIL SCIENCE. *Current Pos:* res scientist soil surv, 72-79 & 81-90, PROF SOIL & HEAD, DEPT SOIL SCI, UNIV SASK, 90- *Personal Data:* b Winnipeg, Man, Dec 12, 40; m 67; c 3. *Educ:* Univ Man, BSA, 63, MSc, 66; Univ Sask, PhD(soil sci), 72. *Prof Exp:* Soil survr, Univ Man, 63-66; soil scientist, Ore State Univ, 66-68; vis scientist, Colo State Univ, 79-80. *Concurrent Pos:* Tech adv, Comt on Reclamation, Sask Power Corp, 76-77; assoc ed, Can J Soil Sci, 80- *Mem:* Agr Inst Can; Can Soc Soil Sci; Can Land Reclamation Asn; Soil Conserv Soc Am. *Res:* Soil organic matter; humus transformations and clay-humus interactions; nutrient cycling in forest ecosystems. *Mailing Add:* 2237 Lansdowne Saskatoon SK S7J 1G7 Can

ANDERSON, DAVID BENNETT, ANIMAL SCIENCE & NUTRITION, FOOD SCIENCE & TECHNOLOGY. *Current Pos:* sr scientist, 79-83, res scientist, 83-88, SR RES SCIENTIST, LILLY RES LABS, ELI LILLY & CO, 88- *Personal Data:* b Hutchinson, Minn, Nov, 21, 44. *Educ:* SDak State Univ, BS, 66; Univ Wis, MS, 68, PhD(animal sci), 71. *Prof Exp:* Asst prof animal sci, Univ Ill, 75-79. *Concurrent Pos:* Adj prof animal sci, Purdue Univ, W Lafayette, 88- *Mem:* Am Meat Sci Asn; Am Soc Animal Sci; Am Inst Nutrit; AAAS; Sigma Xi. *Res:* Growth and development of domestic animials for growth, efficiency and leanness enhancers through the study of muscle, adipose tissue metabolism and development. *Mailing Add:* Lilly Res Lab PO Box 708 Greenfield IN 46140-0708

ANDERSON, DAVID EUGENE, CANCER GENETICS. *Current Pos:* Assoc biologist & assoc prof biol, 58-65, actg head, Dept Biol, 75-80, GENETICIST & ASHBEL SMITH PROF GENETICS, UNIV TEX M D ANDERSON CANCER CTR, HOUSTON, 65- *Personal Data:* b Ashby, Mass, May 16, 26; m 46; c 2. *Educ:* Univ Mass, BS, 50; Univ Conn, MS, 52; Iowa State Univ, PhD(animal breeding & genetics), 54. *Concurrent Pos:* Nat Cancer Inst fel, Okla State Univ, 54-57 & spec fel human genetics, Univ Mich, 63-65. *Mem:* AAAS; Genetics Soc Am; Am Soc Human Genetics. *Res:* Human genetics as it relates to cancer and allied diseases. *Mailing Add:* HMB Box 209 M D Anderson Cancer Ctr Houston TX 77030

ANDERSON, DAVID EVERETT, BEHAVIORAL MEDICINE. *Current Pos:* CHIEF, BEHAV MED SECT, NAT INST AGING, 87- *Personal Data:* b Bloomington, Ill, Oct 17, 39; m 64; c Michele (Hulst), Evelyn (Engel) & Robert. *Educ:* Columbia Univ, BA, 61; Univ Ore, MA, 64, PhD(psychol), 66. *Honors & Awards:* Pavlovian Award, Pavlovian Soc N Am. *Prof Exp:* Asst prof psychiat, Johns Hopkins Univ Sch Med, 70-81; assoc prof psychiat, Univ SFla Col Med, 81-86, prof psychiat & behav med, 86-88. *Concurrent Pos:* Prin investr, Nat Heart, Lung & Blood Inst, 75-87; mem res comt, Am Heart Assoc, 83-86; chmn, Task Force Restrained Animals, NIH, 84. *Mem:* Fel Soc Behav Med; fel Acad Behav Med Res; Pavlovian Soc NAM; Am Psychosomatic Soc. *Res:* Behavioral influences in cardiovascular regulation; developed a model of experimental hypertension in genetically normotensive animals resulting from interaction of task performances and high sodium intake. *Mailing Add:* Lab Cardio Scis Nat Inst Aging Gerontol Res Ctr 4940 Eastern Ave Baltimore MD 21224

ANDERSON, DAVID G, obstetrics & gynecology, for more information see previous edition

ANDERSON, DAVID J, NEUROPHYSIOLOGY, BIOENGINEERING. *Current Pos:* PROF OTORHINOLARYNGOL, KRESGE HEARING RES INST, UNIV MICH, ANN ARBOR, 81-, PROF ELEC ENG & COMPUT SCI, 81- *Personal Data:* b Rochester, NY, Apr 16, 39; m 67, Sandra Nordim; c Christine & Neil. *Educ:* Rensselaer Polytech Inst, BSEE, 61; Univ Wis, MS, 63, PhD(elec eng), 67. *Prof Exp:* Trainee, Lab Neurophysiol, Univ Wis-Madison, 67-69. *Concurrent Pos:* Fel life sci, NASA-Johnson Space Ctr, 75-76. *Mem:* Soc Neurosci; Acoust Soc Am; Inst Elec & Electronics Engr; Asn Res Otolaryngol. *Res:* Neurophysiology of auditory and vestibular systems; application of digital computers and digital signal processing to medicine and biomedical research; implantable devices for stimulation and recording in the nervous system. *Mailing Add:* Dept Comput Sci & Elec Eng EECS Bldg Univ Mich Ann Arbor MI 48109-2122. *Fax:* 313-763-8041; *E-Mail:* dja@umich.edu

ANDERSON, DAVID JOHN, DRUG METABOLISM, TECHNICAL MANAGEMENT. *Current Pos:* Pharmacologist, 69-71, group leader, 71-73, MGR, DEPT 46W ABBOTT LABS, 73- *Personal Data:* b Baraboo, Wis, Jan 7, 42; m 66; c 2. *Educ:* Univ Wis, Superior, BS, 65; Univ Wis, Madison, MS, 67, PhD(pharmacol), 71; Lake Forest Sch Mgt, MBA, 86. *Mem:* Sigma Xi. *Res:* Metabolism methods development; identification of metabolic profiles and metabolities; pharmacokinetic analysis. *Mailing Add:* D-46W Abbott Labs 100 Abbott Park Rd Bldg AP9 Abbott Park IL 60064

ANDERSON, DAVID LEONARD, physics; deceased, see previous edition for last biography

ANDERSON, DAVID LESLIE, NEUTRON ACTIVATION ANALYSIS. *Current Pos:* CHEMIST, US FOOD & DRUG ADMIN, 87- *Personal Data:* b Jamestown, NY, Jan 24, 49. *Educ:* Allegheny Col, BS, 71; Clark Univ, MS, 73, PhD(nuclear chem), 77. *Prof Exp:* Res assoc, Univ Md, College Park, 76-82, asst res scientist, 82-87. *Mem:* Am Chem Soc; Asn Off Analytical Chemists; Am Soc Testing & Mat. *Res:* Neutron activation analysis, prompt gamma-ray activation analysis, x-ray fluorescence spectrometry, quality assurance, and method development for foods, housewares, ceramics and other food-related materials. *Mailing Add:* Nat Inst Stand & Technol Bldg 235 B125 Gaithersburg MD 20899-0001. *Fax:* 301-921-9847; *E-Mail:* dave@rrdvaxb.nist.gov

ANDERSON, DAVID MARTIN, ENVIRONMENTAL HEALTH. *Current Pos:* RETIRED. *Personal Data:* b Boston, Mass, July 19, 30; m 58; c 4. *Educ:* Northeastern Univ, BS, 53; Harvard Univ, SM, 55, PhD(indust hyg), 58. *Prof Exp:* Pub health engr, USPHS, 58-60; indust health engr, Bethlehem Steel Corp, 60-67, asst mgr, 67-71, mgr environ qual control, 71-94. *Concurrent Pos:* Chmn coun tech adv, Pa Dept Health, 64- *Mem:* AAAS; Am Chem Soc; Am Inst Chem Eng; Indust Hyg Asn; Air Pollution Control Asn; Sigma Xi. *Res:* Air cleaning methods and devices; air pollution studies; control of industrial airborne contaminants. *Mailing Add:* 1037 West Gate Circle Bethlehem PA 18107

ANDERSON, DAVID PREWITT, VETERINARY MICROBIOLOGY. *Current Pos:* RETIRED. *Personal Data:* b Twin Falls, Idaho, Sept 14, 34; m 62; c 2. *Educ:* Wash State Univ, BS, 59, DVM, 61; Univ Wis, MS, 64, PhD(vet sci, med microbiol), 65. *Prof Exp:* Asst prof vet sci & asst dir biotron, Univ Wis, 65-69; prof med microbiol & dir, Poultry Dis Res Ctr, Univ Ga, 69-70, chmn, Dept Avian Med, 70-71, assoc dean res & grad affairs, 71-73, prof avian med, 73-75, dean, Col Vet Med, 75-96. *Concurrent Pos:* Ed, J Avian Dis, 73-93. *Mem:* Vet Med Asn; Am Asn Avian Path; Am Col Vet Microbiol; Am Col Poultry Veterinarians. *Res:* Avian diseases, particularly those caused by mycoplasmas. *Mailing Add:* 190 Harris St Winterville GA 30683

ANDERSON, DAVID R, WILDLIFE SCIENCE, QUANTITATIVE ECOLOGY. *Current Pos:* UNIT LEADER & PROF, COOP FISH & WILDLIFE RES UNIT, COLO STATE UNIV, 85- *Personal Data:* b Norton, Kans, Dec 13, 42; m 88; c 2. *Educ:* Colo State Univ, BS, 65, MS, 67; Univ Md, PhD(theoret ecol), 74. *Honors & Awards:* Outstanding Performance Award, Bur Sport Fisheries & Wildlife, 68 & US Fish & Wildlife Serv, 72. *Prof Exp:* Res biologist migratory birds, US Fish & Wildlife Serv, 67-75; res biologist, Utah State Univ, 75-80, prof wildlife sci & leader, Coop Wildlife Res Unit, 80-85. *Concurrent Pos:* Consult, Nat Marine Fisheries Serv, 76-78. *Mem:* Wildlife Soc; Ecol Soc Am. *Res:* Theoretical ecology; biometrics; estimation theory; optimization theory; migratory bird research; population ecology; sampling theory; statistics. *Mailing Add:* Colo Coop Fish Wildlife Res Unit Col State Univ Rm 201 Wagar Bldg Ft Collins CO 80523

ANDERSON, DAVID ROBERT, ZOOLOGY, PARASITOLOGY. *Current Pos:* asst prof, 67-80, ASSOC PROF ZOOL, PA STATE UNIV, FAYETTE, 80- *Personal Data:* b Cuba, NY, Feb 10, 40; m 63. *Educ:* Lycoming Col, BA, 62; Pa State Univ, MS, 64; Colo State Univ, PhD(parasitol, zool), 67. *Concurrent Pos:* NSF inst grant, 68-69. *Mem:* Am Soc Parasitol; Soc Protozool; Wildlife Dis Asn; Wildlife Soc; Am Inst Biol Sci. *Res:* Ecology of helminths in relation to host's environment; all phases of research on coccidia, especially ecology, immunity and life cycle. *Mailing Add:* Dept Biol Pa State Fayette Campus Univ Box 519 Uniontown PA 15401-0519

ANDERSON, DAVID VINCENT, plasma physics, for more information see previous edition

ANDERSON, DAVID WALTER, NUCLEAR PHYSICS, HEALTH PHYSICS. *Current Pos:* PROF & DIR RADIOL PHYSICS, TULSA REGIONAL MED CTR, COL MED, OKLA STATE UNIV, 88- *Personal Data:* b Heron Lake, Minn, June 18, 37; m 60, Jane L Friedlund; c 2. *Educ:* Hamline Univ, BS, 59; Iowa State Univ, PhD(physics), 65; Am Bd Radiol, cert radiol physics, 75. *Prof Exp:* AEC fel physics, Iowa State Univ, 65-66; prof radiol sci, Health Sci Ctr, Univ Okla, 76-82, prof physics, 78-82; prof & dir radiol physics, Med Sch, Oral Roberts Univ, 82-88. *Mem:* Am Asn Physicists Med; Am Phys Soc; fel Am Col Radiol; Am Sci Affil; Soc Nuclear Med. *Res:* Radiation dosimetry; photonuclear reactions; radiation spectroscopy. *Mailing Add:* Tulsa Regional Med Ctr Radiol Dept Tulsa OK 74127

ANDERSON, DEAN MAURITZ, ETHIOLOGY OF FREE-RANGING ANIMALS UNDER MIXED SPECIES MANAGEMENT. *Current Pos:* RES ANIMAL SCIENTIST, AGR RES SERV, USDA, 77- *Personal Data:* b Pueblo, Colo, Feb 14, 47. *Educ:* Univ S Colo, BS, 70; Colo State Univ, MS, 72; Tex A&M Univ, PhD(range sci), 77. *Mem:* Soc Range Mgt; Sigma Xi. *Res:* Range animal nutrition and ethology research directed toward developing mixed species grazing management systems for arid rangeland with special emphasis on group grazing behavior. *Mailing Add:* US Dept Agr-Agr Res Serv Jornada Exp Range Box 30003 MSC JER NMexico State Univ Las Cruces NM 88003-8003. *Fax:* 505-646-5889; *E-Mail:* deanders@nmsu.edu

ANDERSON, DEBORAH JEAN, REPRODUCTIVE IMMUNOLOGY. *Current Pos:* From instr to asst prof, path & obstet gynec, 81-86, ASSOC PROF, HARVARD MED SCH, 86- *Personal Data:* b Ft Belvoir, Va, Dec 28, 49; m 90; c 1. *Educ:* Univ Tex, Houston, PhD(immunol), 76. *Mem:* Am Asn Immunologists; Am Asn Pathologists. *Res:* Interactions between the immune system, reproductive processes and sexually transmitted diseases. *Mailing Add:* Brigham & Women's Hosp 250 Longwood Ave Rm 204 Boston MA 02115-5719

ANDERSON, DEBRA F, FETAL PHYSIOLOGY. *Current Pos:* ASST PROF ANESTHESIOL, ORE HEALTH SCI UNIV, 81- *Educ:* Univ Wis, PhD(physiol), 79. *Mailing Add:* Dept Physiol L334 Ore Health Sci Univ 3181 SW Sam Jackson Pkwy Portland OR 97201-3098

ANDERSON, DENNIS, INFORMATION SCIENCE & SYSTEMS. *Current Pos:* CHAIR/FAC, COMPUT INFO SYSTS DEPT, ST FRANCIS COL, 94- *Educ:* Fordham Univ, BA, 91; NY Univ, MS, 93; Columbia Univ, Edmn, 95. *Concurrent Pos:* Pres/consult, Anderson Consult, 89-96; textbook writer, Houghton Mifflin, 95, 96. *Mem:* Asn Info Systs; Asn Comput Mach; Inst Elec & Electronics Engrs Comput Soc; Nat Coun Teachers Math. *Res:* History of computing and formation technology; computer information systems; computer science and education. *Mailing Add:* 220 E 26th St 4H New York NY 10010. *E-Mail:* andersnd@cs.nyu.edu

ANDERSON, DENNIS ELMO, plant taxonomy, for more information see previous edition

ANDERSON, DON LYNN, GEOPHYSICS, SEISMOLOGY. *Current Pos:* res fel, Calif Inst Technol, 62-63, from asst prof to prof geophys, 63-89, dir seismol lab, 67-89, ELEANOR & JOHN R MCMILLAN PROF GEOPHYS, CALIF INST TECHNOL, 89- *Personal Data:* b Frederick, Md, Mar 5, 33; m 56; c 2. *Educ:* Rensselaer Polytech Inst, BS, 55; Calif Inst Technol, MS, 59, PhD(geophys, math), 62. *Honors & Awards:* Arthur L Day Medal, Am Geol Soc, 87; Gold Medal, Royal Astron Soc, 88; Bowie Medal, Am Geophys Union, 90; John C Lindsay Mem Lectr, Goddard Space Flight Ctr, 92. *Prof Exp:* Geophysicist, Air Force Cambridge Res Ctr, Bedford, Mass, 56-58 & Arctic Inst NAm, Boston, Mass, 58-60. *Concurrent Pos:* Consult, var NASA, Nat Acad Sci & NSF comts; consult, Chevron Oil Co, 71-78; Fulbright-Hayes Found sr scholar, 75; H Burr Steinbach vis scholar, Woods Hole Oceanog Inst, 95. *Mem:* Fel Nat Acad Sci; fel Am Geophys Union (pres, 88-90); fel Am Acad Arts & Sci; fel Sigma Xi; fel AAAS; Geol Soc Am; fel Royal Astron Soc; hon foreign fel Europ Union Geasci; Am Philos Soc. *Res:* Structure and composition of the Earth and planets. *Mailing Add:* Seismol Lab 252-21 Calif Inst Technol Pasadena CA 91125

ANDERSON, DONALD E, AGRICULTURAL POLICY, AGRICULTURAL MARKETING. *Current Pos:* Grad asst, 55-57, from instr to prof agr econ, 57-79, DIR RES, NDAK STATE UNIV, 79- *Personal Data:* b Fullerton, NDak, Sept 22, 31; m 55; c 5. *Educ:* NDak State Univ, BS, 53, MS, 57; Univ Minn, PhD(agr econ), 68. *Res:* Agricultural and related disciplines. *Mailing Add:* 2664 W 89th Ct Northfield MN 55057-4767

ANDERSON, DONALD GORDON MARCUS, APPLIED MATHEMATICS. *Current Pos:* Lectr & res fel, 63-65, asst prof, 65-69, PROF APPL MATH, HARVARD UNIV, 69- *Personal Data:* b Sarnia, Ont, Jan 4, 37. *Educ:* Univ Western Ont, BSc, 59; Harvard Univ, AM, 60, PhD(appl math), 63. *Mem:* AAAS; Soc Indust & Appl Math. *Res:* Numerical mathematics and scientific computation; applications of mathematics and computing in the physical sciences and engineering. *Mailing Add:* Aiken Comput Lab 240 Harvard Univ Cambridge MA 02138

ANDERSON, DONALD HERVIN, ANALYTICAL CHEMISTRY. *Current Pos:* RETIRED. *Personal Data:* b Seattle, Wash, July 5, 16; m 40; c 2. *Educ:* Univ Wash, BS, 38, PhD(chem), 43. *Prof Exp:* Instr physics, Univ Wash, 43; from instr to asst prof chem, Univ Idaho, 44-47; mem staff, Eastman Kodak Co, 47-56, dir indust lab, 56-77. *Mem:* Am Chem Soc. *Res:* Absorption and emission spectroscopy; instrumental methods of analysis; analytical chemical research; corrosion and surface treatment of metals; oceanographic chemistry; absorption phenomena. *Mailing Add:* 2142 Cays Rd Sequim WA 98382

ANDERSON, DONALD K(EITH), CHEMICAL ENGINEERING. *Current Pos:* From asst prof to assoc prof chem eng, 60-69, PROF CHEM ENG & PHYSIOL, MICH STATE UNIV, 69-, CHMN CHEM ENG DEPT, 78- *Personal Data:* b Iron Mountain, Mich, July 15, 31; m 57, Gina Garrett; c Shannon E & Amanda J. *Educ:* Univ Ill, BS, 56; Univ Wash, MS, 58, PhD(chem eng), 60. *Concurrent Pos:* Mem bd dirs, Accreditation Bd Eng & Technol, 92- *Mem:* Am Inst Chem Engrs; Am Chem Soc; Am Soc Eng Educ; Sigma Xi. *Res:* Mass transfer in chemical processes and in biological systems. *Mailing Add:* Dept Chem Eng A202 Eng Bldg East Lansing MI 48824-1226. *Fax:* 517-336-1105; *E-Mail:* anderson@che.msu.edu

ANDERSON, DONALD LINDSAY, ANIMAL NUTRITION. *Current Pos:* RETIRED. *Personal Data:* b Cambridge, Mass, July 2, 25; m 48; c 3. *Educ:* Univ Mass, BS, 50, Univ Conn, MS, 52; Cornell Univ, PhD, 55. *Prof Exp:* Asst nutrit, Univ Conn, 50-52; asst, Cornell Univ, 52-54, res assoc, 54-55; from asst prof to prof nutrit, Univ Mass, 55-87. *Mem:* AAAS; Am Inst Nutrit; Poultry Sci Asn; Nutrit Today Soc; Sigma Xi. *Res:* Poultry nutrition; physiology; animal biochemistry; relationships between environmental stress and nutritional physiology. *Mailing Add:* Laurel Lane PO Box 175 Elkins NH 03233-0175

ANDERSON, DONALD MORGAN, SYSTEMATIC ENTOMOLOGY. *Current Pos:* res entomologist, 60-90, RES ASSOC, AGR RES SERV, USDA, 90- *Personal Data:* b Washington, DC, Dec 27, 30. *Educ:* Miami Univ, BA, 53; Cornell Univ, PhD(entom), 58. *Prof Exp:* Res asst entom, Ohio Agr Exp Sta, 53; asst prof biol, State Univ NY Col Buffalo, 59-60. *Concurrent Pos:* Res assoc, Buffalo Mus Sci, 72-, Dept Entom, Smithsonian Inst, 78- *Mem:* Coleopterists Soc; Entom Soc Am; Am Inst Biol Sci; Sigma Xi. *Res:* Taxonomy of immature Coleoptera in general, and of adult and immature Curculionidae. *Mailing Add:* Syst Entom Lab USDA c/o Nat Mus Natural Hist NHB Stop 168 Washington DC 20560

ANDERSON, DONALD OLIVER, EPIDEMIOLOGY, MEDICAL CARE ADMINISTRATION. *Current Pos:* RETIRED. *Personal Data:* b Vancouver, BC, May 22, 30; m 56; c 4. *Educ:* Univ BC, BA, 50, MD, 54; FRCP(C), 59; Harvard Univ, SM, 61. *Prof Exp:* Asst prof prev med & med, Univ BC, 61-64, assoc prof, 64-68, head dept, 68-70, prof health care & epidemiol, Fac Med, 68-, dir, Div Health Serv Res & Develop, Health Sci Ctr, 72-79. *Concurrent Pos:* Mead Johnson residency scholar med, 57-58; McLaughlin traveling fel, 60-61; Can Coun fel, 64; mem task force on cost of health serv, Dept Nat Health & Welfare, Can, 69; mem, Health Serv Res Study Sect, Nat Ctr Health Serv Res & Develop, Dept Health, Educ & Welfare, 67-71; chmn, Specialty Comt Pub Health, Royal Col Physicians & Surgeons Can, 70-; fac mem, London Sch Hyg & Trop Med, 70-71; chmn, Health Serv Demonstration Comt, Nat Health Grant, Can, 71-74; BC rep, Fed-Provincial Health Manpower Comt, 72-; consult epidemiol & statist, BC Med Ctr, 73-; mem exec comt, Int Epidemiol Asn; consult & secy health manpower planning, Province of BC; mem, Expert Adv Panel on Air Pollution, WHO, 68-, temp adv, Div Strengthening Health Servs, Columbia, 71-, Geneva, 75; mem study of int migration of health workers, Geneva, 75; mem, Steering Comt Children's Dent Health Res Study for Minister of Health, BC, 74-76. *Mem:* Am Col Physicians; Am Pub Health Asn; Asn Teachers Prev Med; Can Med Asn. *Res:* Epidemiology of non-infectious disease, especially non-tuberculous respiratory diseases; health manpower studies; health sciences education; medical school selection practices; hospital utilization; health resources planning; international studies of medical care utilization; internal medicine. *Mailing Add:* 8739 Crest Burnaby BC V3N 4A1 Can

ANDERSON, DONALD T, economic geology, for more information see previous edition

ANDERSON, DONALD WERNER, MATHEMATICS. *Current Pos:* chmn dept, 73-77, PROF MATH, UNIV CALIF, SAN DIEGO, 71-, DIR ACAD COMPUT, 85- *Personal Data:* b Atlantic, Iowa, Apr 16, 38; m 86; c 2. *Educ:* Calif Inst Technol, BS, 60; Univ Calif, Berkeley, PhD(math), 64. *Prof Exp:* Nat Acad Sci-Nat Res Coun fel, Oxford Univ, 64-65; from asst prof to assoc prof math, Mass Inst Technol, 65-71. *Concurrent Pos:* Sloan fel, 67-68. *Mem:* Am Math Soc; Asn Comput Mach. *Res:* Computer graphics. *Mailing Add:* Dept Math B-028 Univ Calif La Jolla CA 92093

ANDERSON, DOUGLAS I, CIVIL ENGINEERING, MATERIALS SCIENCE ENGINEERING. *Current Pos:* Res engr, 71-78, res coordr, 78-83, RES & DEVELOP ENGR, UTAH DEPT TRANSP, 83- *Personal Data:* b Salt Lake City, Utah, Sept 22, 47; m 75; c 3. *Educ:* Univ Utah, BS, 71, MS, 73. *Concurrent Pos:* Comt mem, Pavement Mgt Task Force, Utah Dept Transp, 82-, chmn, Res Adv Comt, 83-, adv, Motor Vehicle Carrier Adv Comt, 83-; Utah state rep, Transp Res Bd, 83-, Comt Pavement Design, 85- *Res:* Material science, pavement management, transportation economics, viscoelastic materials. *Mailing Add:* 4501 S 2700 W Salt Lake City UT 84119-5998

ANDERSON, DOUGLAS K, CENTRAL NERVOUS SYSTEM TRAUMA, PATHOPHYSIOLOGY. *Current Pos:* DEPT NEUROSCI, UNIV FLA, 93- *Educ:* Mich State Univ, PhD(physiol), 72. *Prof Exp:* Res physiologist, Vet Admin Med Ctr, Cincinnati, 78-93. *Concurrent Pos:* Assoc prof neurol & physiol, Col Med, Univ Cincinnati, 81- *Res:* Spinal cord injuries. *Mailing Add:* Dept Neurosci Col Med Univ Fla PO Box 10024 Gainesville FL 32610-0244

ANDERSON, DOUGLAS POOLE, IMMUNOLOGY, MARINE MICROBIOLOGY & FISH DISEASES. *Current Pos:* IMMUNOLOGIST, US FISH & WILDLIFE SERV, 65- *Personal Data:* b Portland, Ore, Jul 11, 39. *Educ:* Willamette Univ, BS, 61; Indiana Univ, MA, 63; Univ Maryland, PhD(immunol), 79. *Honors & Awards:* Fisheries Scientist, Am Fisheries Soc, 79; S F Snieszko Distinguished Scientist Award, 89. *Prof Exp:* Biologist, Ore State Game Comn, 64. *Concurrent Pos:* Auxillary fac, Univ Wash, 68-72; guest scientist, Univ Miyazaki, Japan, 86; consult, Kuwait Inst Sci Res, 88; adj fac mem, Shephard Col, 93- *Mem:* Am Fisheries Soc, Fish Health Sect (pres, 88); Am Soc Zool; Am Asn Immunologist; NY Acad Sci; fel Am Inst Fishery Res Biologist. *Res:* The immune response and protection against disease in salmonids and other fish; fish immunology; serodiagnostic identification of fish disease agents; fish immunotoxicology. *Mailing Add:* Salmon Bay Biol 2805 NW Golden Dr Seattle WA 98117. *Fax:* 304-728-6203

ANDERSON, DOUGLAS RICHARD, OPHTHALMOLOGY, GLAUCOMA. *Current Pos:* from asst prof to assoc prof, 69-82, PROF OPHTHAL, SCH MED, UNIV MIAMI, 82- *Personal Data:* b Memphis, Tenn, Apr 7, 38; m 64, Anne R Wirtley; c John D, Wendy A & Michelle A (Scott). *Educ:* Univ Miami, AB, 58; Wash Univ, MD, 62. *Prof Exp:* Rotating intern, Univ Hosps, Western Res Univ, 62-63; staff assoc, Nat Cancer Inst, 63-65; resident ophthal, Med Ctr, Univ Calif, San Francisco, 65-68. *Concurrent Pos:* Res fel, Howe Lab Ophthal, Mass Eye & Ear Infirmary, Boston, 68-69; Nat Eye Inst res grants, 69-91 & 93-; Res to Prevent Blindness, Inc prof, 69-74, William & Mary Greve int scholar, 78; Visual Sci A Study Sect, NIH, 72-76, chmn, 75-76; assoc ed, Am J Ophthal, 73-90; glaucoma sect ed, Investigative Ophthal, 78-82; bd gov, Anne Bates Leach Eye Hosp, 87-93; dir, Am Bd Opthal, 88-; mem, Int Glaucoma Comt. *Mem:* Am Acad Ophthal; Int Perimetric Soc; Pan-Am Glaucoma Soc (secy-treas, 79-85); Asn Res Vision & Ophthal (pres, 87); Am Ophthal Soc; Am Glaucoma Soc (pres, 90-92). *Res:* Electron microscopy of cartilage, viruses, mycoplasma, leukemia, eye; blood flow and pathophysiology of optic nerve; papilledema, optic atrophy and glaucom, using electron microscopy, pharmacologic and physiologic techniques. *Mailing Add:* Bascom Palmer Eye Inst Univ Miami Sch Med PO Box 016880 Miami FL 33101-6880. *Fax:* 305-326-6306; *E-Mail:* dander@mednet.med.miami.edu

ANDERSON, DUWAYNE MARLO, EARTH SCIENCES, SOIL PHYSICS. *Current Pos:* DEAN, FAC NATURAL SCI & MATH, STATE UNIV NY BUFFALO, 79- *Personal Data:* b Lehi, Utah, Sept 9, 27; m 53; c 3. *Educ:* Brigham Young Univ, BS, 54; Purdue Univ, PhD(soil chem), 58. *Honors & Awards:* Dept of Army Commendation for Res Achievement, US Army Cold Regions Res & Eng Lab, 64, 65 & 68, Sci Achievement Award, 68. *Prof Exp:* From asst prof to prof soil physics, Univ Ariz, 58-63; geologist, US Army Cold Regions Res & Eng Lab, 63-67, chief earth sci br, 67-76; chief scientist, Div Polar Progs, NSF, 76-79. *Concurrent Pos:* Soil physicist, Ariz Agr Exp Sta, 61-63; vis prof, Dartmouth Col, 65, adj prof earth sci, 75-76; guest researcher, Royal Inst Technol, Sweden & vis prof, Univ Stockholm, 67; vis scientist, Soil Sci Soc Am, 68-71; mem molecular analysis team, Viking Sci Team, 69-77; distinguished vis prof, Univ Wash, 70, vis prof, 71, Sloan Found distinguished vis lectr, 75; mem, US Deleg 2nd Int Conf on Permafrost, Yakutsk, USSR, 73; mem comt on permafrost, Nat Acad Sci, 73; NSF consult, 79-80. *Mem:* AAAS; fel Soil Sci Soc Am; Am Geophys Union; Int Clay Minerals Soc; Antarctican Soc. *Res:* Physical chemistry of soils; thermodynamics of soil processes; surface phenomena in soils; phase relationships in permafrost and frozen ground; physicochemical processes in cold environments; physics and chemistry of planetary surface materials. *Mailing Add:* Dept Geol Col Geosci Tex A&M Univ College Station TX 77843-0100

ANDERSON, DWIGHT LYMAN, MICROBIOLOGY. *Current Pos:* Asst bact, 57-60, from instr microbiol to asst prof microbiol & dent, 61-66, assoc prof, 66-74, PROF MICROBIOL & DENT, UNIV MINN, MINNEAPOLIS, 74- *Personal Data:* b Cokato, Minn, Oct 28, 35; m 60; c 3. *Educ:* Univ Minn, BA, 57, MS, 59, PhD(microbiol), 61. *Concurrent Pos:* USPHS career develop awardee, 66-73; ed, J Virol, 74-83. *Mem:* Am Soc Microbiol; Electron Micros Soc Am; Am Soc Virol; AAAS. *Res:* Viral morphogenesis. *Mailing Add:* Moos Tower Rm 18-246 Univ Minn 515 Delaware St SE Minneapolis MN 55455. *Fax:* 612-626-2651; *E-Mail:* dlander@epx.cis.umn.edu

ANDERSON, EDMUND GEORGE, PHARMACOLOGY. *Current Pos:* RETIRED. *Personal Data:* b Seattle, Wash, Sept 1, 28; m 60; c 4. *Educ:* Univ Wash, BS, 50, MS, 55, PhD(pharmacol), 57. *Prof Exp:* Asst pharmacol, Univ Wash, 53-54; instr, Seton Hall Col Med, 57-60; from asst prof to prof pharmacol, Univ Ill Col Med, 60-94, head dept, 76-94. *Mem:* AAAS; Am Soc Pharmacol & Exp Therapeut; Am Soc Neurosci. *Res:* Neuropharmacology; central synaptic transmission and biogenic amines. *Mailing Add:* 550 East End Dr Holland MI 49423

ANDERSON, EDMUND HUGHES, fermats last theorem; deceased, see previous edition for last biography

ANDERSON, EDWARD EVERETT, FOOD SCIENCE, NUTRITION. *Current Pos:* RETIRED. *Personal Data:* b Peabody, Mass, Dec 20, 19; m 48; c 5. *Educ:* Mass State Col, BS, 41, MS, 42; Univ Mass, PhD, 49. *Prof Exp:* Fed food inspector, War Food Admin, USDA, 42-44; from asst res prof to assoc res prof food technol, Univ Mass, 48-56; food technologist, A D Little, Inc, 56-63; chief, Plant Prod Br, Food Div, US Army Natick Labs, 63-69, spec asst, Dept of Defense Food Prog, US Army Natick Res & Develop Command, 69-80; dir, Anderson Assoc, 80-86. *Mem:* Fel AAAS; fel Inst Food Technol; fel Pub Health Asn; Soc Nutrit Educ; Sigma Xi. *Res:* Administration and evaluation of food research and development programs; design and development of new food and ration components and processing methods; sensory and objective methods of quality evaluation and improvement of existing canned or frozen foods; technological factors associated with flavor and packaging problems in foods. *Mailing Add:* 61 Arnold Rd Amherst MA 01002

ANDERSON, EDWARD EVERETT, ENERGY. *Current Pos:* PROF MECH ENG, TEX TECH UNIV, 86- *Personal Data:* b Algona, Iowa, Jan 9, 41; c 3. *Educ:* Iowa State Univ, BS, 64, MS, 66; Purdue Univ, PhD(mech eng), 72. *Prof Exp:* Asst prof mech eng, Univ Southwestern La, 72-74 & SDak Sch Mines & Technol, 74-76; from assoc prof to prof mech eng, Univ Nebr, 76-86. *Concurrent Pos:* Asst dean, Univ Nebr, 80-86; chmn, Tex Tech Univ, 86- & K-6 Tech Comt, Am Soc Mech Engrs. *Mem:* Am Soc Mech Engrs; Am Inst Astronaut & Aeronaut; Am Soc Eng Educators. *Res:* Radioactive heat transfer; energy conversion; solar energy. *Mailing Add:* Dept Mech Eng Tex Tech Univ Lubbock TX 79409-1021

ANDERSON, EDWARD FREDERICK, BOTANY, PLANT TAXONOMY. *Current Pos:* SR RES BOTANIST, DESERT BOT GARDEN, PHOENIX, 92- *Personal Data:* b Covina, Calif, June 17, 32; m 56; c 7. *Educ:* Pomona Col, BA, 54; Claremont Grad Sch, MA, 59, PhD(bot), 61. *Prof Exp:* Instr bot, Pomona Col, 61-62; from asst prof to prof biol, Whitman Col, 62-92. *Concurrent Pos:* Fulbright lectr, Ecuador, 65-67 & Malaysia, 69-70. *Mem:* Soc Econ Bot; Int Orgn Succulent Plant Study. *Res:* Taxonomy of Cactaceae; ethnobotany of hill tribes of northern Thailand. *Mailing Add:* Desert Bot Garden 1201 S Galvin Pkwy Phoenix AZ 85008

ANDERSON, EDWARD G, III, AERONAUTICAL ENGINEERING. *Current Pos:* US Army, 61-, Battery B, First Battalion, 19th Field Artil, Fifth Infantry Div, Ft Carson, Colo, cmdr battery D, Sixth Battalion, 80th Field Artil, 7th Infantry Div, Korea, asst S-3 & battery comdr, Second Battalion, 12th Field Artil, asst group S-3, 23rd Field Artil Group, Vietnam, battalion S-1 & S-3, First Battalion, 18th Field Artil, Augsburg, Ger, 82-84, comdr, 17th Field Artil Brigade, Augsburg, Ger, 87-88, Off Dep Chief Staff, Res, Develop & Acquisition, Pentagon, dir firepower, Off Dep Chief Staff Combat Develop, Hq, Training & Doctrine command, Va, dir combat develop, Ft Sill, Okla, 89-91, asst div comdr, First Armored Div & Comdr, Banberg, 91-92, asst div comdr, Third Infantry Div, dep comndg gen combat develop combined arms command, Ft Leavenworth, Kans, 92-94, asst dep chief staff opers & plans force develop, Hq, 94-96, COMDR, SPACE & STRATEGIC DEFENSE COMMAND, US ARMY, ARLINGTON, VA, 96- *Personal Data:* b San Diego, Calif; m, Ann; c Ed IV, Lisa & Scott. *Educ:* US Military Acad, BS, 66; Ga Inst Technol, MS; Naval War Col, MA. *Res:* National security and strategic studies. *Mailing Add:* US Army Space & Strategic Defense Command PO Box 15280 Arlington VA 22215-0280

ANDERSON, EDWIN J, STRATIGRAPHY, PALEOECOLOGY & SEDIMENTOLOGY. *Current Pos:* asst prof, 67-75, assoc prof, 75-84, PROF GEOL, TEMPLE UNIV, 84- *Personal Data:* b Concord, Mass, Mar 16, 39; m 79; c 3. *Educ:* Cornell Univ, AB, 61; Brown Univ, ScM, 64, PhD(geol), 67. *Prof Exp:* Instr geol, Univ NH, 65-66. *Concurrent Pos:* Res Corp Grant, 67; Leverhulm fel, 74-75; NSF Grants, 81-83, 84-87, NSF US-UK Grant, 84-85. *Mem:* Int Asn Sedimentologists; Soc Econ Paleontologists & Mineralogists; Int Paleont Union. *Res:* Paleoecology and paleoenvironments of Paleozoic skeletal limestones for the purpose of providing a base for community analysis and evaluation of speciation within selected invertebrate groups; punctuated aggradational cycles; a technique for environmental and stratigraphic analysis of sedimentary sequences; coauthor of the hypothesis of punctuated aggradational cycles a general model of strategraphic accumulation; a new method for stratigraphic correlation and paleoenvironmental and paleogeographic analysis. *Mailing Add:* Dept Geol Temple Univ 1701 N Broad St Philadelphia PA 19122-2504

ANDERSON, EDWIN MYRON, ELECTRICAL ENGINEERING. *Current Pos:* RETIRED. *Personal Data:* b St Paul, Minn, Nov 14, 20; m 42; c 4. *Educ:* Univ Denver, BS, 48, MS, 49. *Hon Degrees:* DSc, NDak State Univ, 85. *Prof Exp:* From instr to prof elec eng, NDak State Univ, 49-82, actg chmn dept, 54-55 & 57-58, chmn, 58-78, actg chmn, Physics Dept, 62-63, emer prof elec eng, 82-86. *Concurrent Pos:* NSF fel, Purdue Univ, 59-60. *Mem:* Inst Elec & Electronics Engrs; Am Soc Eng Educ. *Res:* Advanced mathematical concepts in electrical engineering. *Mailing Add:* 1415 S Ellsworth Rd No 2071 Mesa AZ 85208

ANDERSON, ELMER EBERT, MAGNETISM, OPTICS. *Current Pos:* prof physics & vpres acad affairs, 79-85, univ prof, 85-92, EMER UNIV PROF, UNIV ALA, HUNTSVILLE, 92- *Personal Data:* b Ottawa, Ill, June 28, 22; m 43, 76, Diane Cayey; c Kenneth, Mark, Scott, Ruth, Carl, Sven & Kurt. *Educ:* Occidental Col, AB, 50; Univ Ill, MS, 56; Univ Md, PhD(physics), 64. *Prof Exp:* Chief electromagnets div, US Naval Ordnance Lab, 57-65; prof & chmn dept physics, dean arts & sci, Clarkson Univ, 65-77; dean arts & sci & prof physics, Purdue Univ, 77-79. *Concurrent Pos:* Sr Fulbright-Hays fel, 72-73; provost, Univ Ala, Huntsville, 89-90. *Mem:* Fel Am Phys Soc; Sigma Xi. *Res:* Solid state physics; area of magnetism; crystal growth; superconductivity. *Mailing Add:* 3220 Monarch Dr Huntsville AL 35801. *Fax:* 205-895-6873

ANDERSON, ERNEST R, GEOLOGY. *Current Pos:* SUPVRY RES GEOLOGIST, US GEOL SURV, 61- *Personal Data:* b Mt Kisco, NY, Dec 25, 32. *Educ:* Wash Univ, PhD(geol), 61. *Mem:* Fel Geol Soc Am. *Res:* Geology. *Mailing Add:* US Geol Surv Mail Stop 966 Box 25046 Fed Ctr Denver CO 80225

ANDERSON, ETHEL IRENE, BIOCHEMISTRY. *Current Pos:* RES ASSOC, DEPT OPHTHAL, COLUMBIA UNIV, 62- *Personal Data:* b Brooklyn, NY, June 20, 24. *Educ:* Ursinus Col, BS, 45; Univ Del, MS, 47, PhD(bio-org chem), 50. *Prof Exp:* Res fel biochem, Inst Cancer Res, Philadelphia, 50-52, res assoc, 52-58; sr res biochemist, Colgate Palmolive Co, 58-62. *Concurrent Pos:* NIH res grant, Nat Eye Inst, 71-76. *Mem:* Am Soc Biol Chemists; AAAS; Am Chem Soc; Asn Res Vision & Ophthal; Sigma Xi. *Res:* Effects of the limiting cell layers on corneal function; the metabolic basis of transendothelial fluid transport and the nature and influence of epithelial proteolytic enzymes in pathophysiologies. *Mailing Add:* 16 Harrison Ave Red Bank NJ 07701-2334

ANDERSON, FLETCHER N, CHEMICAL ENGINEERING. *Current Pos:* CONSULT, 91- *Personal Data:* b Kansas City, Mo, Nov 5, 30; m 56, Marilyn Henke; c Karl, Keith & Susan. *Educ:* Univ Mo, BS, 51; Washington Univ, MS, 56. *Prof Exp:* Proj engr, Uranium Div, Mallinckrodt Inc, 51-53, sect supvr, 53-58, proj eng supvr, 58-60, maintenance supt, 60-62, maintenance mgr, 62-63, mgr eng & maintenance, 63-64, opers, 64-66, plant serv, 66-68, paper & plastics, 68-70, gen mgr, Calsicat Div, 70-72, Catalysts & Spec Projs, 72-73, vpres & gen mgr, Drug & Cosmetic Chem Div, 73-75, group vpres, food, drug & chem group, 75-76, chem group, 76-78, sr vpres chem group, 78-81, dir, 79-81; pres & dir, Chomerics Inc, 82-85; pres, chief exec officer & dir, Chem Tech Industs Inc, 86-89 & Brulin Corp, 90; exec vpres, chief operating officer & dir, F & C Int, 92-93, pres & chief exec officer, 93. *Concurrent Pos:* Dir, Cytogen Corp, 87-95; dir, Med Mat Corp, 90-92, chmn, 92-93; dir, Sepralor, 94-96. *Mem:* Am Inst Chem Engrs. *Res:* Uranium refining and specialty chemical business management. *Mailing Add:* 752 Fairfield Lake Dr Chesterfield MO 63017-5928. *E-Mail:* marand@earthlink.net

ANDERSON, FLOYD EDMOND, organic chemistry; deceased, see previous edition for last biography

ANDERSON, FRANCES JEAN, PHYSICS. *Current Pos:* INSTR PHYSICS & CHEM, ABBOTT-NORTHWESTERN HOSP, MINN, 74-; SR SCIENTIST, LIGHTNING & TRANSIENTS RES INST, ST PAUL, MINN, 85-; ASST PROF, UNIV ST THOMAS, ST PAUL, MINN, 87- *Personal Data:* b Watertown, SDak, Apr 23, 37; m 59. *Educ:* SDak State Univ, BS, 59; Univ Minn, MS, 63, PhD(physics), 68. *Prof Exp:* Res assoc, Univ Minn, 68-77. *Mem:* Am Geophys Union; Am Asn Physics Teachers. *Res:* Anesthesia into quantitative physical terms; cloud physics; atmospheric-electricity; initiation of lightning discharges. *Mailing Add:* 1755 Maple Ct Falcon Heights MN 55113-2453

ANDERSON, FRANCIS DAVID, STRUCTURAL & ECONOMIC GEOLOGY. *Current Pos:* CONSULT, 86- *Personal Data:* b Cabano, Que, May 12, 25; m 48, Robina Tillier; c Bruce, Robert & Janet. *Educ:* Univ NB, BSc, 48; McGill Univ, MSc, 51, PhD(geol), 56. *Prof Exp:* Geologist, Geol Surv Can, 52-86, asst dir, Econ Geol Div, 72-82. *Concurrent Pos:* Coordr, Fed-Prov Mineral Agreement, New Brunswick, 82-86; prog coordr, Fed Geosci Asbestos Proj, Que, 84-86. *Mem:* Fel Geol Soc Am; fel Geol Asn Can. *Res:* General problems of field geology, particularly structural and economic geology. *Mailing Add:* RR 2 Clayton ON K0A 1P0 Can. *Fax:* 613-256-2073

ANDERSON, FRANK A(BEL), CHEMICAL ENGINEERING. *Current Pos:* from actg chmn to chmn dept chem and dept chem eng & prof, 47-55, chmn dept chem eng, 55-63 & 65-78, prof chem eng, 55-79, assoc dean, Sch Eng, 63-79, EMER ASSOC DEAN, UNIV MISS, 79- *Personal Data:* b Bridgeport, Conn, June 22, 14; m 42, Mary Courtney; c Frank & Phyllis A. *Educ:* Univ Southern Calif, BS, 36; Univ Maine, MS, 40; La State Univ, PhD(chem eng), 47. *Prof Exp:* Jr technologist, Shell Oil Co, Calif, 36-38; asst prof chem, Univ Miss, 40-45; res assoc, Gaylord Container Corp, La, 45-47. *Concurrent Pos:* Res assoc, La State Univ, 45-47. *Mem:* Am Chem Soc; Am Soc Eng Educ; Am Inst Chem Engrs. *Res:* Tall oil; fluid mechanics; heat transfer; solar energy. *Mailing Add:* 410 S 11th St Oxford MS 38655

ANDERSON, FRANK DAVID, ANATOMY. *Current Pos:* chmn dept, 67-83, prof, 67-90, EMER PROF ANAT, MED COL WIS, 90- *Personal Data:* b Duncan, Okla, May 24, 27; m 54; c 3. *Educ:* Westminster Col, Mo, BA, 48; Cornell Univ, MS, 50, PhD, 52. *Prof Exp:* Instr anat, Med Col, Cornell Univ, 52-56; from asst prof to assoc prof, Seton Hall Col Med & Dent, 56-67. *Concurrent Pos:* Consult, Med Ctr, Univ Ala, 59 & Inst Crippled & Disabled, Med Ctr, NY Univ, 63-64. *Mem:* Am Acad Neurol; Am Asn Anat; Soc Neurosci. *Res:* Neuroanatomy; anatomy of ductus arteriosus in newborn; central pathways of vagus nerve and of trigeminal nerve; experimental degeneration studies of spinal cord and brain stem; segmental anatomy of the spinal cord; ascending fiber systems in the spinal cord and brain stem. *Mailing Add:* Dept Anat Med Col Wis 8701 Watertown Plank Rd Milwaukee WI 53226

ANDERSON, FRANK WALLACE, PHYSICAL CHEMISTRY, ELECTRON MICROSCOPY. *Current Pos:* SR CHEMIST, IBM CORP, E FISHKILL, 68- *Personal Data:* b Milwaukee, Wis, Feb 12, 21; m 49; c 2. *Educ:* Univ Ariz, BS, 51, MS, 52. *Prof Exp:* Res chemist, Martinez Res Lab, Shell Oil Co, 52-61, Shell Develop Co, Calif, 61-62; sr res chemist, Sprague Elec Co, Mass, 62-68. *Mem:* Am Chem Soc; Sigma Xi. *Res:* Secondary ion mass spectrometry; ion scattering spectrometry; gas chromatography-mass spectrometry; transmission and scanning electron microscopy; analytical methods development; organic separations; electrophoresis in non-aqueous solvents, colloids and surfaces; ion cyclotron resonance mass spectrometry; gas chromatography fourier transform infrared spectroscopy. *Mailing Add:* PO Box 133 Hopewell Junction NY 12533-0133

ANDERSON, FRANK WYLIE, MATHEMATICS. *Current Pos:* from asst prof to assoc prof, 57-69, PROF MATH, UNIV ORE, 69- *Personal Data:* b Omaha, Nebr, Feb 5, 28. *Educ:* Univ Iowa, BA, 51, MS, 52, PhD, 54. *Prof Exp:* From instr to asst prof math, Univ Nebr, 54-57. *Mem:* Am Math Soc; Math Asn Am. *Res:* Algebra; topological algebra. *Mailing Add:* Univ Ore Eugene OR 97403-1226

ANDERSON, FRANZ ELMER, OCEANOGRAPHY, ESTUARINE SEDIMENTATION. *Current Pos:* assoc prof oceanog, 67-83, actg dir, Seagrant, 79, PROF OCEANOG, UNIV NH, 83- *Personal Data:* b Cleveland, Ohio, July 23, 38; m 63; c 3. *Educ:* Ohio Wesleyan Univ, BA, 60; Northwestern Univ, MS, 62; Univ Wash, PhD(oceanog), 67. *Prof Exp:* Res asst oceanog, Univ Wash, 62-67, lectr, 66; interim dir, Jackson Estuarine Lab, 79-80, dir, 87-89; dir, Romberg-Tiburon Ctrs, 89-90. *Concurrent Pos:* NSF res grants, 66-68, 78-79 & 84-85; Cottrell res grant, 70-72; Off Naval Res grant, 72-74; Fulbright grant, Turkey, 73-74; Nat Ocean & Atmospheric Admin grant, 79-82, 84-85 & 86-89; fel, Nat Environ Res, Stirling, Scotland, 80-81. *Mem:* Fel Geol Soc Am; Soc Econ Paleontologists & Mineralogists; Estuarine Res Fedn; Int Asn Sedimentologist; Marine Educ Asn. *Res:* Distribution of particulate matter in estuarine and marine environments; effects of small amplitude waves on estuarine erosion; effects of Mya arenaria and Arenicola marina digging on estuarine sediment transportation; effects of rainfall on estuarine sediment transport; measurement of estuarine currents as a low cost solution. *Mailing Add:* Dept Earth Sci James Hall Univ NH Durham NH 03824

ANDERSON, G HARVEY, NUTRITION, FOOD INTAKE & HEALTH. *Current Pos:* from asst prof to assoc prof, Univ Toronto, 70-78, chmn, 81-91, actg dean fac med, 92, PROF, NUTRIT SCI DEPT, UNIV TORONTO, 78-, PROF, PHYSIOL & INST MED SCI, 82-, DIR, PROG FOOD SAFETY, 91- *Personal Data:* b Provost, Alta, 1941; m 64, Ethel E MacKenzie. *Educ:* Univ Alta, BS, 64, MS, 66; Univ Ill, PhD(nutrit sci), 69. *Honors & Awards:* Borden Award, Can Soc Nutrit Sci, McHenry Award. *Prof Exp:* Res fel, Mass Inst Technol, 69-70. *Concurrent Pos:* Bd mem, Int Life Sci Inst, 83-; chmn bd, Nat Inst Nutrit, 84-89; vis prof, Dept Clin Nutrit, Sun Yat Sen Univ Med Sci, Guanzhou, People's Repub China, 86. *Mem:* Soc Neurosci; Am Inst Nutrit; Am Soc Clin Nutrit; Can Soc Nutrit Sci; NAm Asn Obesity Study. *Res:* Amino acid nutrition; diet and brain function; infant nutrition; control of feeding behavior; food safety and public health; international nutrition (China). *Mailing Add:* Dept Nutrit Sci Fac Med Univ Toronto Fitzgerald Bldg Toronto ON M5S 1A8 Can. *Fax:* 416-978-5882

ANDERSON, G(EORGE) M(ULLEN), ELECTRICAL ENGINEERING. *Current Pos:* DEPT HEAD, AT&T INFO SYSTS. *Personal Data:* b Rochester, Pa, May 7, 21; m 47; c 3. *Educ:* Carnegie Inst Technol, BS, 42, DSc(elec eng), 48. *Prof Exp:* Asst prof elec eng, Carnegie Inst Technol, 48-51; sr scientist, Atomic Power Div, Westinghouse Elec Corp, 51-53; head, Eng Dept, Res Lab, McGraw-Edison Co, 53-60, pres, 60-64; Dept Head Systs Anal, Bellcomm, Inc, 64-76; mem staff, Bell Tel Labs, Holmdel, NJ, 76- *Mem:* Sr mem Inst Elec & Electronics Engrs. *Res:* Circuit theory; control systems; electricity and magnetism. *Mailing Add:* 17 Oakes Rd Rumson NJ 07760

ANDERSON, GARY, PHYSIOLOGICAL ECOLOGY, AQUACULTURE. *Current Pos:* from asst prof to assoc prof, 75-84, PROF BIOL SCI, UNIV SOUTHERN MISS, 84- *Personal Data:* b Norristown, Pa, Oct 5, 48; m 70; c 2. *Educ:* Univ RI, BS, 70; Univ SC, MS, 72, PhD(marine sci), 74. *Prof Exp:* Asst prof zool, Univ Maine, Orono, 74-75. *Concurrent Pos:* US Army Engr, Waterways Exp Sta. *Mem:* Am Inst Biol Sci; Crustacean Soc; Am Soc Zoologists; Sigma Xi; World Aquacult Soc. *Res:* Ecology of host-symbiont interrelationships, host finding behavior, energy flow in host-parasite systems, bopyrid isopods and anostracans shrimp aquaculture. *Mailing Add:* Dept Biol Sci Univ Southern Miss Box 5018 Southern Sta Hattiesburg MS 39406-0002

ANDERSON, GARY BRUCE, ANIMAL SCIENCE. *Current Pos:* Asst prof, 74-78, ASSOC PROF ANIMAL SCI & PHYSIOL, UNIV CALIF, DAVIS, 78- *Personal Data:* b Kent City, Mich, Apr 21, 47; m 77; c 1. *Educ:* Mich State Univ, BS, 69; Cornell Univ, PhD(vert physiol), 73. *Mem:* Soc Study Reprod; Am Soc Animal Sci; Int Embryo Transfer Soc. *Res:* Increase of reproductive performance and efficiency in farm animals; development, culture and transfer of preimplantatis-mammalian embryos. *Mailing Add:* Dept Animal Sci Univ Calif Davis CA 95616-5200

ANDERSON, GARY DON, ORGANIC CHEMISTRY, X-RAY CRYSTALLOGRAPHY. *Current Pos:* AT DEPT CHEM, MARSHALL UNIV. *Personal Data:* b Purcell, Okla, Sept 23, 43. *Educ:* Univ Okla, BS, 64, MS, 65; Fla State Univ, PhD(org chem), 72. *Prof Exp:* Res assoc org chem, Fla State Univ, 72-73; res assoc, Stanford Univ, 73-74, NIH fel, 74-75; asst prof org chem, Univ Mo-Kansas City, 75- *Mem:* Am Chem Soc; Sigma Xi. *Res:* Chemistry of plant natural products; terpene synthesis; x-ray crystal structures. *Mailing Add:* Dept Chem Marshall Univ Huntington WV 25701

ANDERSON, GARY LEE, MICRO-CIRCULATION, HYPERTENSION. *Current Pos:* Instr, 82-86, ASST PROF PHYSIOL & BIOPHYS, UNIV LOUISVILLE, 86- *Educ:* Univ Ariz, PhD(physiol), 80. *Mailing Add:* Dept Physiol Univ Louisville Health Sci Ctr Louisville KY 40292

ANDERSON, GEOFFREY ROBERT, HUMAN DIAGNOSTIC PRODUCT DEVELOPMENT. *Current Pos:* res prog mgr, 87-95, MGR PROCESS DEVELOP, HYCOR BIOMED INC, 95- *Personal Data:* b Eckville, Alta, July 30, 46; US citizen; m 71, Lee Steele; c Scott J & Matthew J. *Educ:* Calif State Univ, Long Beach, BS, 68; Univ Calif, Los Angeles, MS, 69. *Prof Exp:* Res technician, City of Hope, 70-72 & Univ Southern Calif, 72-73; biol instr, Mt St Mary's Col, 73-77; res assoc, Harbor Univ Calif Los Angeles Med Ctr, 78-80; scientist, Diag Prods Inc, 80-81; sr scientist, Beckman Instruments Inc, 81-86. *Concurrent Pos:* Lectr, Santa Monica Community Col, 73, Pasadena Community Col, 74, Los Angeles SW Col, 74, Ventura Community Col, 77-78. *Mem:* Am Asn Clin Chem; Am Chem Soc; Clin Ligard Assay Soc. *Res:* In vitro product design and validation, stability assessment, immunoassay and clinical chemistry manufacturing. *Mailing Add:* 19912 Corby Ave Lakewood CA 90715

ANDERSON, GEORGE ALBERT, MATHEMATICS. *Current Pos:* assoc prof, 71-80, PROF MATH, RI COL, 80- *Personal Data:* b New Britain, Conn, May 3, 37. *Educ:* Trinity Col, BS, 59; Yale Univ, MA, 61, PhD(math), 64. *Prof Exp:* Actg instr, Yale Univ, 63-64; from instr to asst prof math, Trinity Col, Conn, 64-71. *Concurrent Pos:* Consult res div, United Aircraft Corp, 61-64. *Mem:* Math Asn Am; Inst Math Statist. *Res:* Mathematics of sound theory in an inhomogeneous media; mathematical statistics; multivariate analysis; asymptotic distributions for latent roots of Wishart matrices. *Mailing Add:* 49 Eric Dr Coventry CT 06238-1326

ANDERSON, GEORGE CAMERON, BIOLOGY & BIOLOGICAL OCEANOGRAPHY, ECOLOGY. *Current Pos:* teaching fel, res asst & actg instr, Univ Wash, 50-54, res assoc, 54-58, from res asst prof to res prof, 58-70, actg asst chmn res, 70-71, res prof zool, 72-77, assoc chmn res, 77-81, prof, 77-83, dir, Sch Oceanog, 81-83, EMER PROF OCEANOG, UNIV WASH, 83- *Personal Data:* b Vancouver, BC, Oct 8, 26; m 57, Harriett Batie. *Educ:* Univ BC, BA, 47, MA, 49; Univ Wash, PhD(zool, bot), 54. *Prof Exp:* Teaching asst zool, Univ BC, 47-49; marine biologist, AEC, 71-72. *Concurrent Pos:* Consult, US Bur Reclamation, 55, Seattle, Wash, 59 & State Fisheries Dept, Wash, 63-83; mem, Ship Opers Panel, NSF, 70-72, Ocean Sci

Panel, 73; mem & admin judge, Atomic Safety & Licensing Bd Panel, US Nuclear Regulatory Comn, 73-; chief scientist, Deep Ocean Mining Environ Study, Nat Oceanic & Atmospheric Admin, 75-78. *Mem:* Am Soc Limnol & Oceanog. *Res:* Biological oceanography and limnology; phytoplankton ecology; marine primary productivity. *Mailing Add:* 7719 Ridge Dr NE Seattle WA 98115. *E-Mail:* gca@u.washington.edu

ANDERSON, GEORGE ROBERT, PHYSICAL CHEMISTRY, MICROWAVE HEATING TECHNOLOGY. *Current Pos:* SR RES SCIENTIST, PILLSBURY RES & DEVELOP LAB, 76- *Personal Data:* b Burlington, Iowa, Jan 10, 34; m 58; c 2. *Educ:* Augustana Col, Ill, BA, 56; Univ Iowa, PhD(phys chem), 61. *Prof Exp:* Res chemist, E I du Pont de Nemours & Co, until 68; collabr, Univ Groningen, Neth, 68-69; res fel chem, Wesleyan Univ, 69-70; instr, Bowdoin Col, 70-71, asst prof, 71-76. *Concurrent Pos:* Vis lectr, Swarthmore Col, 65-66; vis prof, Univ Minn, 74-75. *Mem:* Am Chem Soc; Int Microwave Power Inst. *Res:* Molecular structure and spectroscopy; electronic, infrared and Raman spectroscopy; hydrogen bonding, studies of vibrational states; physical chemistry of food products; microwave heating technology; microwave dielectrics. *Mailing Add:* 1100 W 53 St Minneapolis MN 55419-1103

ANDERSON, GEORGE WILLIAM, ELECTRICAL ENGINEERING. *Current Pos:* mgr electronic systs, Mobile Mid-Range Ballistic Missile, 62, dir, Guid & Command Systs, 62-64, dir, Guid & Command Systs, Minuteman, 64-65, assoc group dir, Advan Weapon Systs, 65-66, group dir, WS 120A Integration & Airborne Systs, 66-68, assoc gen mgr, Missile Systs Div, 68-70 & Defense Systs Div, 70-71, assoc gen mgr, Advan Systs Div, 71-72 & Develop Planning Div, 72-76, prin dir develop, Advan Prog Div, 76-79, PRIN DIR, LONGBOW OFF, AEROSPACE CORP, LOS ANGELES, 79- *Personal Data:* b Chicago, Ill, Jan 17, 24; m 47; c 1. *Educ:* Northwestern Univ, BSEE, 48. *Prof Exp:* Sect chief, Aerial Measurements Lab, Northwestern Univ, 47-55; proj mgr, J B Rea Co, 55-56; dept mgr, Aeronutronic Div, Ford Motor Co, 56-62. *Mem:* Inst Elec & Electronics Engrs; Sigma Xi. *Res:* Engineering management; automatic control systems. *Mailing Add:* 18792 Silver Maple Way Santa Ana CA 92705-2254

ANDERSON, GERALD M, SYSTEMS THEORY, OPERATIONS RESEARCH. *Current Pos:* sr prin engr, 77-78, prog mgr tracking, navig, guid & control, 78-87, TECH DIR, HAWAII OPERS, ORINCON CO, 87- *Personal Data:* b Shanghai, China, Oct 14, 35; US citizen; m 59, Edith C Feiss; c 2. *Educ:* US Naval Acad, BS, 57; Mass Inst Technol, MS, 61; Univ Mich, PhD(aerospace eng), 66. *Prof Exp:* USAF, 57-78, planning study officer command & control, Electronic Systs Div, Air Force Systs Command, 61-64, from asst prof to prof mech, USAF Inst Technol, 66-77. *Mem:* Am Inst Aeronaut & Astronaut; Inst Elec & Electronics Engrs. *Res:* Optimal control; differential games; estimation theory; guidance and control; personnel systems and economics systems. *Mailing Add:* PO Box 167 Maunaloa HI 96770-0167. *Fax:* 808-254-5622

ANDERSON, GERALD S, SOLID STATE PHYSICS. *Current Pos:* RES MGR, MINN MINING & MFG CO, 69- *Personal Data:* b Montevideo, Minn, July 28, 30; m 57; c 2. *Educ:* Luther Col, Iowa, BA, 52; Iowa State Univ, PhD(physics), 57. *Prof Exp:* Res assoc, Iowa State Univ, 57-58; prin scientist, Electronics Div, Gen Mills, Inc, 58-63; tech specialist, Appl Sci Div, Litton Industs, Minn, 63-69. *Mem:* Am Phys Soc; Am Vacuum Soc. *Res:* Thin film physics; sputtering. *Mailing Add:* 2453 Cohansey St St Paul MN 55113

ANDERSON, GERALDINE LOUISE, CLINICAL RESEARCH IN MEDICAL INVITRO DIAGNOSTICS & PHARMACEUTICALS. *Current Pos:* CLIN RES MONITOR, ELI LILLY RES LABS, 95-, CLIN RES ASSOC, CLIN DESIGN GROUP, 97- *Personal Data:* b Minneapolis, Minn, July 7, 41; m 66, Henry; c Bruce & Julie. *Educ:* Univ Minn, BS, 60. *Prof Exp:* Clin res assoc, United Children's Hosp, 75-88; sr lab analyst, Cascade Med, 88-89; tech support scientist, Incstar Corp, 90-94; prod analyst coordr, Medtronic Inc, 95. *Concurrent Pos:* Dir, Am Soc Med Technol, 81-85; pres & dir, Grad Women Sci, Inc, 94 & 96- *Mem:* Am Soc Med Technol; Am Med Writers' Asn. *Res:* Medical and scientific writing for invitro diagnostics, flow cytometry, medical devices and pharmaceuticals. *Mailing Add:* 8400 33rd Pl N Minneapolis MN 55427. *E-Mail:* ander367@maroon.tc.umn.edu

ANDERSON, GLEN DOUGLAS, ANALYSIS & FUNCTIONAL ANALYSIS. *Current Pos:* asst prof, 65-70, assoc prof, 70-78, PROF MATH, MICH STATE UNIV, 78- *Personal Data:* b Madison, SDak, Oct 18, 30; m 53; c 5. *Educ:* Drury Col, AB, 58; Univ Mich, AM, 59, PhD(math), 65. *Honors & Awards:* Fulbright grant, Univ Helsinki, 72-73. *Prof Exp:* From asst prof to assoc prof math, Eastern Mich Univ, 60-65. *Concurrent Pos:* Fulbright grant, Univ Helsinki, 72-73; vis prof, Univ Mich, 79-80, Stanford, 80, Univ Auckland, 86-87, ITM/MUCIA Coop Program Malaysia, Indiana Univ, 88-90. *Mem:* Am Math Soc; Math Asn Am; New Zealand Math Soc; Finnish Math Soc. *Res:* Complex variables; quasiconformal mappings; special functions. *Mailing Add:* Dept Math Mich State Univ A336 Wells Hall East Lansing MI 48824-1027. *Fax:* 517-432-1562; *E-Mail:* anderson@math.msu.edu

ANDERSON, GLENN ARTHUR, zoology, for more information see previous edition

ANDERSON, GLORIA LONG, ORGANIC CHEMISTRY. *Current Pos:* assoc prof, Morris Brown Col, 68-73, chairperson, Chem Dept, 68-89, dean acad affairs, 84-89, interim pres, 92-93, FULLER E CALLAWAY PROF CHEM, MORRIS BROWN COL, 73-, DEAN SCI & TECHNOL FAC, 95- *Personal Data:* b Altheimer, Ark, Nov 5, 38; m 60; c 1. *Educ:* Agr, Mech & Norm Col, Ark, BS, 58; Atlanta Univ, MS, 61; Univ Chicago, PhD(org chem), 68. *Prof Exp:* Instr chem, SC State Col, 61-62 & Morehouse Col, 62-64; teaching & res asst, Univ Chicago, 64-68. *Concurrent Pos:* Res fel, NSF, Ga Inst Technol, 69-, NSF, Lockheed Ga Corp, 81-; res consult, Lockheed Ga Corp, 82-, Biospecs, Neth, 90-; SCEEE fac res fel, Air Force Rocket Propulsion Lab, Edwards AFB, 84-; contract reviewer, Nat Inst Drug Abuse, 90-91; mem, Ford Found Fel Prog, Nat Res Coun, 94, Associateship Prog, 96, Instrumentation & Lab Improvement Prog, NSF, 96, 97, Grand Res Fel Prog, Oak Ridge Assoc Univs, 97. *Mem:* AAAS; Am Chem Soc; Nat Sci Teachers Asn; Nat Inst Sci; Sigma Xi; fel Am Inst Chemists; NY Acad Sci; Am Asn Univ Women. *Res:* Synthetic organic fluorine chemistry; fluorine-19 nuclear magnetic resonance spectroscopy; mechanism of transmission of substituent effects, synthetic organic chemistry. *Mailing Add:* 560 Lynn Valley Rd SW Atlanta GA 30311. *Fax:* 404-220-0058; *E-Mail:* ganderso@morrisbrown.edu

ANDERSON, GORDON FREDERICK, AUTONOMIC NERVOUS SYSTEM, SMOOTH MUSCLE & NEUROTRANSMISSION. *Current Pos:* Instr physiol & pharmacol, 61-64, from asst prof to assoc prof, 64-75, PROF PHARMACOL, WAYNE STATE UNIV, 75- *Personal Data:* b Grand Rapids, Mich, Oct 16, 34; m 57; c 2. *Educ:* Ferris State Col, BS, 56; Wayne State Univ, MS, 58, PhD(physiol & pharmacol), 61. *Concurrent Pos:* Prin investr, NIH grants, 78-88. *Mem:* Pharmacol Soc Can; Am Physiol Soc. *Res:* Physiology and pharmacology of the urinary bladder and its autonomic control. *Mailing Add:* Dept Pharmacol Sch Med Wayne State Univ 540 E Canfield Detroit MI 48201. *Fax:* 313-577-6739; *E-Mail:* ganders@med.wayne.edu

ANDERSON, GORDON MACKENZIE, PETROLEUM SERVICE CONTRACTING. *Current Pos:* exec vpres, 74-80, pres & chief exec officer, 80-87, EXEC VPRES, SANTA FE INT CORP, 87-; PRES, SANTA FE DRILLING CO, ALHAMBRA, CALIF, 87- *Personal Data:* b Los Angeles, Calif, Mar 25, 32; m 59, Elizabeth A Pugh; c Michael J, Greg M & Jeffrey S. *Educ:* Univ Southern Calif, BSME, 54. *Prof Exp:* Mgr, Santa Fe Drilling Co, Chile, 60-63, Libya, 63-67, mgr contracts admin, Calif, 67-70, pres, Alhambra, Calif, 70-80. *Concurrent Pos:* Mem bd dirs, St Jude Hosp, Fullerton, Calif. *Mem:* Int Asn Oilwell Drilling Contractors. *Res:* Petroleum engineering. *Mailing Add:* Santa Fe Int 5420 Lyndon B Johnson Fwy No 1100 Dallas TX 75240-2648

ANDERSON, GORDON WOOD, SOLID STATE DEVICES, PHOTODETECTORS FOR OPTICAL PROCESSING. *Current Pos:* RES PHYSICIST, NAVAL RES LAB, 71- *Personal Data:* b Evanston, Ill, Mar 8, 36; m 69, Gillian Anne Bunshaft. *Educ:* Cornell Univ, BEE, 59; Univ Ill, Urbana-Champaign, MS, 61, PhD(physics), 69. *Prof Exp:* Res asst & teaching asst physics, Univ Ill, Urbana-Champaign, 59-69; instr physics, Tougaloo Col, Miss, 65; res assoc solid state physics, Nat Res Coun, 69-70, adv, Planning of Human Systs, 78-79. *Concurrent Pos:* Ford Found fel, Univ Ill, Urbana-Champaign, 59-61; NSF grant, 63; consult, Planning Human Systs, Inc, 78-79; Naval Res Lab awards, 75, 76, 80, 83, 85, 86, 88-93; adv, Off Naval Res, 91- *Mem:* Inst Elec & Electronics Engrs; Am Phys Soc; AAAS; Found Sci & Disability; Sigma Xi. *Res:* Solid state optical detectors for optical processing and communications; acousto-optical and opto-electronic devices; metal-insulator-semiconductor device design-fabrication for high-speed, infrared radiation and interface problems; signal processing; metallic, semiconducting, insulating thin-films, materials; fabrication and optical, electrical, magnetic, and strength properties, thin films, materials, devices; technical research program management and supervision; contract management; safety management; equal employment opportunity management. *Mailing Add:* Naval Res Lab Code 6813 Washington DC 20375-5347. *E-Mail:* anderson1@estd.nil.navy.mil

ANDERSON, GREGOR MUNRO, GEOCHEMISTRY. *Current Pos:* from asst prof to assoc prof, 65-72, PROF GEOL, UNIV TORONTO, 72- *Personal Data:* b Montreal, Que, Aug 18, 32; m 57; c 2. *Educ:* McGill Univ, BEng, 54; Univ Toronto, MASc, 56, PhD(geol), 61. *Prof Exp:* Geologist, Ventures, Ltd, 56-57; res assoc, Pa State Univ, 61-64, asst prof geol, 64-65. *Concurrent Pos:* Nuffield fel, 73; assoc ed, Can Mineralogist. *Mem:* Mineral Asn Can; Int Asn Biochem & Cosmochem (secy); Geochem Soc; Soc Econ Geologists; Geol Asn Can. *Res:* Chemistry of solutions and melts at high temperatures and pressures. *Mailing Add:* Dept Geol Univ Toronto 22 Russell St Toronto ON M5S 3B1 Can. *Fax:* 416-978-3938

ANDERSON, GREGORY JOSEPH, BIOSYSTEMATICS, POLLINATION BIOLOGY. *Current Pos:* from asst to assoc prof, 73-82, PROF BIOL SCI, UNIV CONN, 82-, DEPT HEAD, 90- *Personal Data:* b Chicago, Ill, Nov 26, 44; m 66; c 2. *Educ:* St Cloud State Univ, BS, 66; Ind Univ, Bloomington, MA, 68, PhD(bot), 71. *Honors & Awards:* George R Cooley Award, Am Soc Plant Taxonomists, 81. *Prof Exp:* Asst prof bot, Univ Nebr, Lincoln, 71-73. *Concurrent Pos:* Secy, Orgn Trop Studies, NSF, 83-86 & Bot Soc Am, 89-91. *Mem:* Ecol Soc Am; Soc Econ Bot (secy, 81-84, vpres, 85-86, pres, 85-86); Soc Study Evolution; Bot Soc Am (secy, 89-91, pres elect, 91, pres, 92); Am Soc Plant Taxon. *Res:* Systematics and evolution of vascular plants; reproductive biology; evolution of domesticated plants. *Mailing Add:* Univ Conn U-42 75 N Eagleville Storrs CT 06269-0002

ANDERSON, HARLAN U(RIE), CERAMICS ENGINEERING. *Current Pos:* assoc prof, 70-76, PROF CERAMIC ENG, UNIV MO, ROLLA, 76- *Personal Data:* b Cedar City, Utah, July 15, 35; m 57; c 2. *Educ:* Univ Utah, BS, 57; Univ Calif, Berkeley, PhD(eng sci), 62. *Prof Exp:* Engr ceramics, Lawrence Radiation Lab, Univ Calif, Berkeley, 61-62; sr chemist, Sprague Elec Co, 62-69; assoc prof ceramics, Ore Grad Ctr, 69-70. *Mem:* Fel Am Ceramic Soc. *Res:* Kinetics of gas-solid reactions; sintering of oxides; thermodynamics of high temperature reactions; high melting inorganic solids; ferroelectric oxides; vapor pressure determination; electronic materials. *Mailing Add:* 11926 Springhouse Lane Rolla MO 65401

ANDERSON, HAROLD DEAN, INORGANIC CHEMISTRY, PHYSICS. *Current Pos:* PROF CHEM & PHYSICS, STEPHENS COL, 70- *Personal Data:* b Holdrege, Nebr, May 23, 40; m 62; c 2. *Educ:* Augustana Col, Ill, BA, 62; Univ Northern Iowa, MA, 66; Univ Iowa, PhD(sci ed), 70. *Prof Exp:* Sci instr chem & physics, Cent Col Iowa, 66-68. *Mem:* Am Chem Soc; Am Asn Physics Teachers. *Res:* Neutron activation analysis applied to medically related problems; x-ray crystallography of clays. *Mailing Add:* 2900 Northland Dr Columbia MO 65202

ANDERSON, HAROLD J, PHYSICAL CHEMISTRY, RESEARCH ADMINISTRATION. *Current Pos:* CONSULT, 91- *Personal Data:* b Green Bay, Wis, Sept 4, 28; m 50, Patricia M Basten; c Mark J, Therese L, Debra J, Tricia A, John J & Christopher P. *Educ:* St Norbert Col, BS, 52. *Prof Exp:* Scientist, Marathon Div, James River Corp, 52-58, sr scientist, 58-62, group leader, 62-66, supvr, 66-72, mgr prod develop & improv, 72-75, mgr maj proj consumer prod, 75-79, assoc dir, paperboard process develop, Am Can Co, 79-83, dir paperboard develop, 83-91. *Mem:* Tech Asn Pulp & Paper Indust. *Res:* Decorative and functional coatings for paper and paperboard; air laid, nonwoven technology; paperboard process technology. *Mailing Add:* 2608 Kunzer Beach Lane Little Suamico WI 54141-9343

ANDERSON, HARRISON CLARKE, PATHOLOGY. *Current Pos:* prof path & chmn dept, 78-90, HARRINGTON PROF ORTHOP RES, UNIV KANS MED CTR, KANSAS CITY, 90- *Personal Data:* b Louisville, Ky, Sept 2, 32; m 61, Nina L; c Mary K, H Clarke Jr, Zachary L & Heather W. *Educ:* Univ Louisville, BA, 54, MD, 58. *Honors & Awards:* Elizabeth Winston Lanier Award, Kappa Delta, 82; Biol Mineralization Res Award, Int Asn Dent Res, 85. *Prof Exp:* Intern path, Mass Gen Hosp, Boston, 58-59; Nat Cancer Inst path trainee, Univ Louisville, 59-60; fel Mem Hosp, New York, 60-61, chief resident, 61-62; res fel, Sloan-Kettering Inst, 62-63; from asst prof to prof path, State Univ NY Downtown Med Ctr, 63-78. *Concurrent Pos:* Grants, Nat Inst Cancer Res, Nat Inst Arthritis, Metabolism & Digestive Dis, Nat Inst Dent Res, NIH, Air Force Off Sci Res & Kyocera Corp, 67-68; fel, Nat Inst Arthritis, Metab & Digestive Dis, NIH, 71-72; mem study sect, Nat Inst Dent Res, NIH, 78-82; jour ed, J Bone & Joint Surg, 81-86, J Exp Pathol, 82-, Am J Pathol, 82-94, J Orthop Res, 82-93, Bone, 81-94. *Mem:* Am Soc Cell Biol; Am Soc Invest Path; Royal Soc Med; Am Soc Bone & Mineral Res; Int Acad Pathol; Orthop Res Soc. *Res:* Experimental bone induction; calcium metabolism; fine structure of cartilage and bone; mechanism of biological and pathological calcification; development and differentiation of skeletal tissues. *Mailing Add:* Dept Path Univ Kans Med Ctr Rainbow Blvd at 39th St Kansas City KS 66160. *Fax:* 913-588-7073; *E-Mail:* handerso@kumc.edu

ANDERSON, HARVEY L(AWRENCE), chemical engineering; deceased, see previous edition for last biography

ANDERSON, HENRY WALTER, HYDROLOGY, WATERSHED MANAGEMENT. *Current Pos:* RETIRED. *Personal Data:* b Des Moines, Iowa, Dec 27, 11; m 40; c 3. *Educ:* Univ Calif, BS, 43, MS, 47. *Honors & Awards:* Hydrol Award, Am Geophys Union, 46; US Forest Serv Award, 58. *Prof Exp:* Res forester, Univ Calif, 43-46; hydrologist, Soil Conserv, US Forest Serv, 46-51, soil scientist, 51-55, snow res leader, 55-62, water source hydrol proj leader, 63-71, chief res hydrologist, 71-76. *Concurrent Pos:* Mem nat comt, Int Asn Sci Hydrol, 72-76; consult, Calif State Bd Forest. *Mem:* Fel Am Geophys Union; Soc Am Foresters; Int Water Resources Asn, Sigma Xi. *Res:* Forest effects on floods; sedimentation and water yield; snow accumulation; snow melt. *Mailing Add:* 900 N Mountain St Carson City NV 89703

ANDERSON, HERBERT GODWIN, JR, BIOLOGICAL SCIENCES. *Current Pos:* assoc prof, 64-74, PROF BIOL SCI, CENT CONN STATE COL, 74- *Personal Data:* b Roanoke, Ala, Dec 29, 31. *Educ:* Auburn Univ, BS, 58, MS, 60; Univ Miami, PhD(marine sci), 64. *Prof Exp:* Fishery biologist, Sandy Hook Marine Lab, US Bur Sport Fisheries, 62-64. *Mem:* Am Soc Parasitol; Sigma Xi. *Res:* Animal parasites; invertebrate taxonomy. *Mailing Add:* 650 Flotella Dr 212 Holmes Beach FL 34217

ANDERSON, HERBERT HALE, inorganic chemistry, for more information see previous edition

ANDERSON, HOWARD BENJAMIN, APPLIED MATHEMATICS, GEOMETRY. *Current Pos:* from assoc prof to prof, 46-81, EMER PROF MATH, MICH TECHNOL UNIV, 81- *Personal Data:* b Escanaba, Mich, Dec 13, 14; m 46, Selma W Holquist; c William H & Olivia S. *Educ:* Northern Mich Univ, AB, 38; Univ Mich, MA, 39; Mich Technol Univ, BS, 54. *Prof Exp:* Teacher pub sch, Mich, 39-42 & 45-46. *Concurrent Pos:* Chmn calculus distinguished teacher, Mich Technol Univ. *Mem:* Math Asn Am; Am Astron Soc. *Res:* Mathematics education; astronomy; author text "Analytical Geometry with Vectors". *Mailing Add:* 1034 Second St Hancock MI 49930

ANDERSON, HOWARD W(AYNE), CHEMICAL ENGINEERING. *Current Pos:* RETIRED. *Personal Data:* b Cincinnati, Ohio, Feb 18, 34; m 58; c 2. *Educ:* Univ Del, BChE, 56; Univ Calif, Berkeley, MS, 58. *Prof Exp:* Chem engr, E I Du Pont de Nemours & Co, 58-67, sr engr, Petrochem Dept, 67-97, div suptr, 75-97, res mgr, 80-87, prin consult process eng, 87-97. *Mem:* Am Inst Chem Engrs; Sigma Xi. *Res:* Research and development of processes for manufacture and/or use of olefin high polymers and nylon intermediates. *Mailing Add:* 809 Grande Lane Hockessin DE 19707

ANDERSON, HUGH JOHN, HISTORY OF CHEMISTRY & CHEMICAL TECHNOLOGY. *Current Pos:* from assoc prof to prof, 53-91, EMER PROF CHEM, MEM UNIV NFLD, 91- *Personal Data:* b Winnipeg, Man, Mar 17, 26. *Educ:* Univ Man, BSc, 47, MSc, 49; Northwestern Univ, PhD(chem), 52. *Honors & Awards:* Union Carbide Award for Chem Educ, Chem Inst Can, 81. *Prof Exp:* Lectr chem, Univ Man, 47-49; Nat Res Coun Can fel & Corday-Morgan Commonwealth fel, Oxford Univ, 52-53. *Mem:* Chem Inst Can; Chem Soc; Am Chem Soc. *Res:* History of chemistry; chemical technology. *Mailing Add:* Dept Chem Mem Univ Nfld St John's NF A1B 3X7 Can. *Fax:* 709-737-3702; *E-Mail:* handerso@morgan.ucs.mun.ca

ANDERSON, HUGH RIDDELL, SPACE PHYSICS. *Current Pos:* SR RES SCIENTIST, SCI APPLN INT CORP, 81- *Personal Data:* b Iowa City, Iowa, June 16, 32; m 56. *Educ:* Univ Iowa, BA, 54, MS, 58; Calif Inst Technol, PhD(physics), 61. *Prof Exp:* Sr scientist, Jet Propulsion Lab, Calif Inst Technol, 62-65; from asst prof to prof space sci, Rice Univ, 65-81. *Mem:* Am Phys Soc; Am Geophys Union. *Res:* Primary cosmic radiation variations in space and time caused by solar modulation; ionizing radiation in space; auroral and ionospheric physics. *Mailing Add:* Sci Appln Int Corp 13400B Northup Way No 36 Bellevue WA 98005

ANDERSON, HUGH VERITY, ORGANIC CHEMISTRY. *Current Pos:* res chemist, Mich, Upjohn Co, 50-58, sect head, 58-65, mgr chem process res & develop, 65-69, gen mgr, Lab Procedures Div, King of Prussia, 69-73, dir corp purchasing, 73-84, EXEC DIR CORP PURCHASING, UPJOHN CO, 84- *Personal Data:* b Chicago, Ill, Aug 25, 21; m 46; c 1. *Educ:* Kalamazoo Col, AB, 46; Univ Ill, PhD(org chem), 49. *Prof Exp:* Fel, Ohio State Univ, 49-50. *Concurrent Pos:* VChmn, Kalamozoo Col Bd Trustees. *Mem:* Am Chem Soc; Am Asn Clin Chem. *Res:* Steroids; pharmaceutical chemistry; clinical chemistry. *Mailing Add:* 9820 West H Ave Kalamazoo MI 49009-8559

ANDERSON, INGRID, NUTRITION. *Current Pos:* from asst prof to assoc prof nutrit & physiol, 65-77, PROF NUTRIT, COL ST BENEDICT, MINN, 77- *Personal Data:* b Sioux Falls, SDak, Oct 7, 30. *Educ:* Col St Benedict, Minn, BS, 53; Univ Minn, MS, 55, PhD(nutrit), 67. *Prof Exp:* Instr, St Benedicts High Sch, Minn, 53-54; instr home econ, Col St Benedict, Minn, 53-54, instr home econ & biol, 55-60; res asst nutrit, Univ Minn, 63-65. *Concurrent Pos:* Vis assoc prof, Univ Minn, 74-75. *Mem:* AAAS; Am Pub Health Asn; Am Home Econ Asn; Am Dietetic Asn; Soc Nutrit Educ; Sigma Xi. *Res:* Congenital abnormalities in folic acid deficiency; growth factors; nutrition education; competency-based dietetic education. *Mailing Add:* Nutrit Col St Benedict 37 College Ave S St Joseph MN 56374-2001

ANDERSON, IRVIN CHARLES, PLANT PHYSIOLOGY. *Current Pos:* from asst prof to assoc prof agron, 58-72, PROF AGRON & BOT, IOWA STATE UNIV, 72- *Personal Data:* b Iowa, Apr 4, 28; m 56; c 2. *Educ:* Iowa State Univ, BS, 51; NC State Col Agr & Eng, MS, 54, PhD, 56. *Prof Exp:* Fel biol, Brookhaven Nat Lab, 56-58. *Mem:* Am Soc Plant Physiol; Am Soc Agron. *Res:* Biochemical aspects of genetic mutants; plant growth regulatory chemicals and nodulation. *Mailing Add:* Dept Agron Iowa State Univ Ames IA 50011-2010

ANDERSON, J(OHN E(RLING), CHEMICAL ENGINEERING. *Current Pos:* Res engr, Union Carbide Corp, 54-57, res group leader, 57-59, res supvr, 59-63, asst mgr res, 63-64, sr res assoc, 64-65, sect mgr develop, 65-69, develop fel, 69-82, SR DEVELOP FEL, LINDE DIV, UNION CARBIDE CORP, 82-; SR DEVELOP FEL, PRAXAIR, INC, 92- *Personal Data:* b Quincy, Mass, Mar 12, 29; m 51, Karin Thornberg; c Mark, Lynn, Kristin & Claire. *Educ:* Mass Inst Technol, BS, 50, DSc(chem eng), 55; Ill Inst Technol, MS, 51. *Mem:* Nat Acad Eng; Am Inst Chem Engrs; Am Chem Soc; Combustion Inst. *Res:* Arc technology; high temperature chemistry; welding; combustion; solid waste disposal. *Mailing Add:* Praxair Inc 777 Old Saw Mill River Rd Tarrytown NY 10591-6714. *Fax:* 914-345-6405; *E-Mail:* john_e_anderson@praxair.com

ANDERSON, J ROBERT, PHYSICS. *Current Pos:* Asst prof, 64-72, assoc prof physics, 72-80, PROF PHYSICS & ASTRON, UNIV MD, COLLEGE PARK, 80- *Personal Data:* b Ames, Iowa, Sept 29, 34. *Educ:* Iowa State Univ, BS, 55, PhD(physics), 62. *Concurrent Pos:* NSF fel, Cambridge Univ, 63-64; AEC fel, Iowa State Univ, 64. *Mem:* Am Phys Soc. *Res:* Fermi surface studies; de Haas-van Alphen effect. *Mailing Add:* Dept Physics & Astron Univ Md College Park MD 20742

ANDERSON, JAMES B, PHYSICAL CHEMISTRY, CHEMICAL ENGINEERING. *Current Pos:* EVAN PUGH PROF CHEM, PA STATE UNIV, 74- *Personal Data:* b Cleveland, Ohio, Nov 26, 35; m 58; c 3. *Educ:* Pa State Univ, BS, 57; Univ Ill, MS, 58; Princeton Univ, MA, 62, PhD(chem eng), 63. *Honors & Awards:* Evan Pugh Medal; Humboldt Res Award. *Prof Exp:* Process engr, Shell Chem Co, 58-60; res assoc chem eng, Princeton Univ, 62-64, asst prof, 64-68; assoc prof eng & appl sci, Yale Univ, 68-74. *Concurrent Pos:* Vis lectr, Rutgers Univ, 64; vis prof, Cambridge Univ, 86;

grad fel, NSF. *Mem:* AAAS; Am Chem Soc; Am Inst Chem Engrs; Am Phys Soc; Sigma Xi. *Res:* Chemical kinetics; molecular dynamics; molecular beams; rarefied gas dynamics; quantum chemistry; theoretical physics. *Mailing Add:* 152 Davey Lab Pa State Univ University Park PA 16802

ANDERSON, JAMES E, PHYSICAL CHEMISTRY. *Current Pos:* staff scientist, Sci Lab, 65-94, ADV, COOP TECH PROG, FORD MOTOR CO, 94- *Personal Data:* b Hartford, Conn, July 31, 38; m 62; c 4. *Educ:* Union Col, NY, BS, 60; Princeton Univ, PhD(chem), 63. *Prof Exp:* Appointee, Bell Tel Labs, Inc, 63-65. *Concurrent Pos:* Vis scientist biophys, Max-Planck Inst, 75-76; vis scientist phys chem, Univ Mainz, Ger, 75-76; adj res assoc nuclear eng, Univ Mich, 77-, adj res prof chem, 79- *Mem:* Am Chem Soc; AAAS; Am Phys Soc. *Res:* Dielectric and nuclear relaxation in solids and liquids; high polymer physics; stochastic processes; reverse osmosis; membrane transport. *Mailing Add:* 2967 Devonshire Rd Ann Arbor MI 48104

ANDERSON, JAMES EDWARD, psychiatry, physical anthropology, for more information see previous edition

ANDERSON, JAMES GERARD, SOLID STATE PHYSICS, ELECTRONICS. *Current Pos:* assoc prof, 66-74, PROF PHYSICS, UNIV WIS-EAU CLAIRE, 74- *Personal Data:* b Ceylon, Minn, July 27, 24; m 70, Dolores Van Risseghem; c Ann M. *Educ:* Univ Minn, BS, 45; St Mary's Col, Minn, BA, 51; Univ Colo, MS, 59, PhD(physics), 63. *Prof Exp:* Res elec engr, Univ Minn, 45-46; aircraft electronic engr, Northwest Orient Airlines, Minn, 46-48; instr physics, St John's Univ, Minn, 53-58; asst prof, Wis State Univ, Oshkosh, 63-64; asst prof, Colo State Univ, 64-66. *Mem:* Sigma Xi; Am Asn Physics Teachers. *Res:* De-Haas-Van Alphen effect in metals measured in high pulsed magnetic fields. *Mailing Add:* 1717 Oaklawn Dr Eau Claire WI 54703-1681

ANDERSON, JAMES GILBERT, CHEMISTRY. *Current Pos:* prof, 78-82, PHILIP S WELD PROF ATMOSPHERIC CHEM, HARVARD UNIV, 82- *Educ:* Univ Wash, Seattle, BS, Univ Colo, Boulder, PhD(physics & astrogeophys), 70. *Honors & Awards:* Gustavus John Esseleen Award, Am Chem Soc, 93; Arthur L Day Prize & Lectr, Nat Acad Sci, 96. *Mem:* Nat Acad Sci. *Res:* Stratospheric physics and chemistry central to the understanding of atmospheric ozone and the ozone hole above the Antartic. *Mailing Add:* Dept Chem & Chem Biol Harvard Univ 12 Oxford St Cambridge MA 02138

ANDERSON, JAMES HENRY, agricultural & engineering, for more information see previous edition

ANDERSON, JAMES HOWARD, PHYSIOLOGY, RADIOLOGY. *Current Pos:* ASSOC PROF, DEPT RADIOL & RADIOL SCI, JOHNS HOPKINS MED SCH, JOHNS HOPKINS HOSP. *Personal Data:* b Joliet, Ill, Nov 17, 44; m 70. *Educ:* Ill Wesleyan Univ, BA, 66; Univ Ill, MS, 68, PhD(physiol), 71. *Prof Exp:* Asst prof radiol, M D Anderson Hosp & Tumor Inst, Univ Tex Syst Cancer Ctr, 71-, head sect exp diag radiol, biol sci div, 74-, asst prof physiol, Univ Tex Med Sch Houston, 72-, asst prof radiol, 74- *Mem:* Am Physiol Soc. *Res:* Experimental diagnostic radiology; gastrointestinal physiology; scanning electron microscopy. *Mailing Add:* Dept Radiol Johns Hopkins Univ Med Sch Johns Hopkins Hosp Baltimore MD 21205

ANDERSON, JAMES JAY, FISH DIVERSION & RESOURCE MODELS, RISK ANALYSIS. *Current Pos:* Oceanogr, Univ Wash, 69-81, res assoc, 81-82, from res asst prof to res assoc prof, 82-91, ASSOC PROF, UNIV WASH, 91- *Personal Data:* b Seattle, Wash, July 29, 46. *Educ:* Univ Wash, BS, 69, cert, 75, PhD(oceanog), 77. *Concurrent Pos:* Vis prof, Nat Oceanog Lab, Indonesia, 80-81; consult, Exxon, Nat Oceanic & Atmospheric Admin, Tech Arts, Chelan Pub Utility, Bonneville Power Admin, Mont Dept Fish Wildife & Parks & Army Engrs; res fac fel, Col Ocen & Fishery Scis, 85 & 89. *Mem:* Sigma Xi; Am Soc Limnol & Oceanog; Animal Behav Soc; Am Fisheries Soc; Resource Modeling Asn. *Res:* Stochastic models in fisheries and ecology; risk analysis; animal and human decision processes; fish toxicology; decision support software for fisheries management. *Mailing Add:* Columbia Basin Res Fisheries Res Inst Univ Wash Box 358218 Seattle WA 98195. *Fax:* 206-616-7452; *E-Mail:* jim@fish.washington.edu

ANDERSON, JAMES LEROY, THEORETICAL PHYSICS. *Current Pos:* assoc prof, 56-66, PROF PHYSICS, STEVENS INST TECHNOL, 66- *Personal Data:* b Chicago, Ill, Apr 16, 26; m 50; c 2. *Educ:* Univ Chicago, BS, 46, MS, 49; Syracuse Univ, PhD(physics), 52. *Prof Exp:* Asst instr physics, Ill Inst Technol, 47-49; instr, Rutgers Univ, 52-53; res assoc, Univ Md, 53-56. *Concurrent Pos:* Guggenheim fel, 60-61; res fel, Woods Hole Oceanog Inst, 66 & 69; vis res scientist, Cambridge Univ, 68-69; consult, Ramo-Wooldridge, 57, Combustion Engr, 57-58 & Sci Teaching Ctr, Mass Inst Technol, 66 & 67; Fulbright fel, 76; res scientist, Inst of Theoret Physics, Univ Amsterdam. *Mem:* NY Acad Sci. *Res:* General relativity; relativistic astrophysics. *Mailing Add:* Dept Physics Stevens Inst Technol Hoboken NJ 07030

ANDERSON, JAMES LEROY, ELECTROANALYTICAL CHEMISTRY, SPECTROELECTROCHEMISTRY. *Current Pos:* from asst prof to assoc prof, 79-93, PROF CHEM, UNIV GA, 93- *Personal Data:* b Detroit, Mich, Jan 21, 46; m 68, Lauren Binda; c Byron. *Educ:* Kalamazoo Col, BA, 67; Univ Wis, Madison, PhD(analytical chem), 74. *Prof Exp:* Lectr chem, Ohio State Univ, 74-75; asst prof, NDak State Univ, 75-79. *Concurrent Pos:* Postdoctoral assoc chem, Ohio State Univ, 74-75; panelist, US Environ Protection Agency, Chem, Physics Water Res, 81-83; comt mem, Am Chem Soc Exam Comt, Grad Analytical Chem, 82-; div ed, J Electrochem Soc, 86-90, juror Am Chem Soc Analytical Div Awards Comt, 87-90. *Mem:* Am Chem Soc; Electrochem Soc; Sigma Xi; Soc Electroanalytical Chemists; Int Soc Electrochem. *Res:* Development and fundamental characterization and modeling of sensitive and selective electrochemical methods including microelectrode array flow sensors and spectroelectrochemistry; electrochemistry and analytical chemistry; environmental redox chemistry. *Mailing Add:* Dept Chem Univ Ga Athens GA 30602-2556. *Fax:* 706-542-9454; *E-Mail:* jlanders@uga.cl.uga.edu

ANDERSON, JAMES MORLEY, RESEARCH & DEVELOPMENT OF POLYMERS FOR MEDICAL APPLICATIONS, PATHOGENESIS OF PROSTHETIC VALVE ENDOCARDITIS. *Current Pos:* sr res assoc, Case Western Res Univ, 70-76, from asst prof to assoc prof macromolecular sci, 76-84, from asst prof to assoc prof path, 76-84, assoc prof biomed eng, 82-84, PROF PATH, MACROMOLECULAR SCI & BIOMED ENG, CASE WESTERN RES UNIV, 84-; PATHOLOGIST, INST PATH, UNIV HOSPS CLEVELAND, 79- *Personal Data:* b Eau Claire, Wis, Sept 14, 40; m 92, Mary L Loriando; c Michael, Matthew & John. *Educ:* Wis State Univ, Eau Claire, BS, 63; Ore State Univ, Corvallis, PhD(org chem), 67; Case Western Res Univ, Cleveland, MD, 76. *Honors & Awards:* Pennwalt Award, Controlled Release Soc, 86. *Concurrent Pos:* Prof pharmaceut, Univ Utah, 84-; ed-in-chief, J Biomed Mat Res, 88-; mem cardiol adv comt, NIH, Nat Heart Lung & Blood Inst, 92-, merit award, 93-; co-chair, Am Chem Soc workshop, 92, Future Perspectives Biomed Polymers Symps 92. *Mem:* Fel Am Inst Med & Biol Eng; fel Biomat Sci & Eng; Soc Biomat (pres, 84-85); Am Soc Clin Pathologists; Can Soc Biomat; Am Soc Artificial Internal Organs; Am Chem Soc; Sigma Xi; AAAS; Int Soc Artificial Organs; Am Heart Asn; Soc Advan Contraception; Am Acad Exp Surg. *Res:* Research activities have focused on the question, what is biocompatibility; a better and more fundamental understanding of the chemical, physical and biological properties controlling biological responses in biocompatibility is the overall goal. *Mailing Add:* Dept Path Case Western Res Univ 2085 Adelbert Rd Cleveland OH 44106-2622. *Fax:* 216-844-8004

ANDERSON, JAMES WINGO, ENDOCRINOLOGY, NUTRITION. *Current Pos:* PROF MED, 78- *Personal Data:* b Hinton, WVa, Aug 6, 36; m 57; c 2. *Educ:* WVa Univ, BA, 58; Northwestern Univ, MD, 61; Mayo Grad Sch, MS, 65. *Prof Exp:* Asst prof med, Univ Calif Med Sch, San Francisco, 68-73; assoc prof med, Univ Ky, 73-78; chief med serv, Vet Admin Med Ctr, Lexington, Ky, 80-83; vis scientist, Mass Inst Technol, 83-84; cheif, metab endocrine sect, Vet Admin Med Ctr, Univ Ky, 73- *Concurrent Pos:* Prin investr, Diabetes Res Fund, 74-, Nat Inst Arthritis, Metab & Digestive Dis, 77-80, VA Med Ctr, 85-88, NIH HL 37902 Prog Proj, 86-89. *Mem:* Fel Am Col Nutrit; fel Am Col Physicians; Am Diabetes Asn; Am Fedn Clin Res; Am Inst Nutrit; Am Soc Clin Nutrit. *Res:* Applied clinical research applying high-fiber diets to individuals with diabetes, obesity and high blood fat levels. *Mailing Add:* Dept Vet Affairs Med Ctr Lexington KY 40511

ANDERSON, JAY ENNIS, PLANT ECOLOGY. *Current Pos:* from asst prof to assoc prof, 75-85, PROF ECOL, DEPT BIOL SCI, IDAHO STATE UNIV, 85- *Personal Data:* b Logan, Utah, Oct 18, 37; m 59; c 1. *Educ:* Mont State Univ, BS, 59; Syracuse Univ, MS, 67, PhD(bot), 71. *Prof Exp:* Teacher biol, Powell Co High Sch, Deer Lodge, Mont, 63-68; consult ecol, Biol Sci Curric Study, 71-74; res assoc, Dept Chem Eng, Univ Colo, 74-75. *Concurrent Pos:* Asst attend prof, Dept EPO Biol, Univ Colo, 71-75, res assoc, Inst Arctic & Alpine Res, 74-75; vis scientist, Res Sch Biol Sci, Australian Nat Univ, 92. *Mem:* AAAS; Ecol Soc Am; Sigma Xi; Soc Range Mgt; Am Inst Biol Sci; Australian Soc Plant Physiol. *Res:* Factors affecting transpiration, photosynthesis, and water status of terrestrial plants; vegetation dynamics in cold-desert ecosystems; water use and water use efficiency of cold-desert species. *Mailing Add:* 3566 Stockman Rd Pocatello ID 83204. *E-Mail:* andejay@ucs.isu.edu

ANDERSON, JAY LAMAR, POMOLOGY, WEED SCIENCE. *Current Pos:* From asst prof to assoc prof, 61-75, PROF HORT, UTAH STATE UNIV, 75- *Personal Data:* b Madison, Wis, Apr 22, 31; m 55; c 4. *Educ:* Utah State Univ, BS, 55; Univ Wis, PhD(plant path), 61. *Mem:* Weed Sci Soc Am; fel Am Soc Hort Sci. *Res:* Pomology; fruit growth and development; physiology of herbicides and plant growth regulators; weed control in fruit crops; orchard floor management; cherry rootstocks; modeling of fruit trees and weed species. *Mailing Add:* Plant & Earth Sci Utah State Univ Logan UT 84322-0001

ANDERSON, JAY MARTIN, COMPUTER SCIENCE, PHYSICAL CHEMISTRY. *Current Pos:* PROF COMPUT SCI, FRANKLIN & MARSHALL COL, 88- *Personal Data:* b Paterson, NJ, Oct 16, 39; m 92, Patricia Jones; c Carl Christopher. *Educ:* Swarthmore Col, BA, 60; Harvard Univ, AM, 61, PhD(chem), 64. *Prof Exp:* From asst prof to prof chem, Bryn Mawr Col, 63-86, dir comput sci, 75-86. *Concurrent Pos:* Alfred P Sloan res fel, 67-70; secy-treas, Exp Nuclear Magnetic Resonance Conf, 67-71; Kettering vis lectr, Univ Ill, 68-69; vis assoc prof, Sloan Sch Mgt, Mass Inst Technol, 71-72. *Mem:* Asn Comput Mach. *Res:* Computer science; nuclear magnetic resonance; computing machinery; environmental systems simulation. *Mailing Add:* Dept Math Franklin & Marshall Col PO Box 3003 Lancaster PA 17604-3003. *Fax:* 717-399-4507; *E-Mail:* j_anderson@acad.fandm.edu

ANDERSON, JAY OSCAR, POULTRY NUTRITION. *Current Pos:* PROF, ANDERSON ANIMAL CLIN, 84- *Personal Data:* b Brigham, Utah, Dec 5, 21; m 44; c 6. *Educ:* Utah State Univ, BS, 43; Univ Md, MS, 48, PhD(poultry nutrit), 50. *Prof Exp:* Chemist, Merck & Co, 50-51; prof animal sci, Utah State Univ, 51-84. *Concurrent Pos:* Secy-treas, Utah Feed Mfrs & Dealers Asn, 66-; assoc ed, Poultry Sci. *Mem:* Poultry Sci Asn. *Res:* Amino acid and protein requirements of chickens and turkeys; amino acid content of feedstuffs. *Mailing Add:* 1550 N Stapley Dr No 132 Mesa AZ 85203

ANDERSON, JEFFREY JOHN, AGRICULTURAL & FOOD CHEMISTRY. *Current Pos:* RES CHEMIST, BIOCHEM DEPT, E I DU PONT DE NEMOURS & CO INC, 80- *Personal Data:* b Chicago, Ill, Dec 30, 53; m 77; c 1. *Educ:* Ill State Univ, BS, 75; Univ Minn, PhD(biochem), 80. *Mem:* Am Chem Soc. *Res:* Elucidation of metabolic pathways for aromatic compounds in truchosporm cutoneum; determining the environmental fate of experimental pesticides. *Mailing Add:* 1300 Tulane Rd Wilmington DE 19803-5140

ANDERSON, JOHN ANSEL, cereal chemistry, for more information see previous edition

ANDERSON, JOHN ARTHUR, BIOCHEMISTRY. *Current Pos:* from asst prof to prof, 66-93, EMER PROF CHEM, TEX TECH UNIV, 93- *Personal Data:* b Chicago, Ill, Mar 6, 32; m 56; c 2. *Educ:* Colo State Univ, BS, 52, MS, 54; Ore State Univ, PhD(biochem), 62. *Prof Exp:* Asst prof chem, Univ Tex, Arlington, 54-55. *Mem:* AAAS; Am Chem Soc; Am Soc Biochem & Molecular Biol. *Res:* Enzyme mechanisms; biosynthesis of mycotoxins. *Mailing Add:* 5017 15th St Lubbock TX 79416

ANDERSON, JOHN B, MARINE GEOLOGY. *Current Pos:* asst prof, 75-80, ASSOC PROF GEOL, RICE UNIV, 80- *Personal Data:* b Mobile, Ala, Sept 5, 44; m 65; c 2. *Educ:* Univ SAla, BS, 68; Univ NMex, MS, 70; Fla State Univ, PhD(geol), 72. *Prof Exp:* Asst prof geol, Hope Col, 72-75. *Mem:* Sigma Xi; Geol Soc Am. *Res:* Glacio-marine geology of antarctic regions; environmental geology of coastal waters. *Mailing Add:* Dept Geol Rice Univ 6100 Main St Houston TX 77005-1827

ANDERSON, JOHN BAILEY, ELECTRICAL ENGINEERING, INFORMATION SCIENCE & SYSTEMS. *Current Pos:* from assoc prof to PROF ELEC, COMPUT & SYSTS ENG, RENSSELAER POLYTECH INST, 81- *Personal Data:* b Canandaigua, NY, May 30, 45; m 68, Janet Smith; c Katherine E & Alix C. *Educ:* Cornell Univ, BSEE, 67, MS, 69, PhD, 72. *Honors & Awards:* Humboldt Sr Scientist Award, 91. *Prof Exp:* From asst prof to assoc prof elec eng, McMaster Univ, Hamilton, 72-80. *Concurrent Pos:* Vis assoc prof elec, comput & systs eng, Univ Calif, Berkeley, 78-79; guest researcher, Info Theory Dept, Chalmers Tech Univ, Gotenburg, Sweden, 87; vis prof elec eng, Queens Univ, Kingston, 87; vis scientist, Inst Commun Eng, Ger Aerospace Res, Munich, 91-92. *Mem:* Fel Inst Elec & Electronics Engrs; Inst Elec & Electronics Engrs Info Theory Soc (vpres, 83-84, pres, 85); Sigma Xi. *Res:* Communication theory; error-correcting codes; coded modulation; mobile radio communication; communication algorithms. *Mailing Add:* 120 Greenleaf Dr Latham NY 12110-5115

ANDERSON, JOHN D, NUCLEAR PHYSICS. *Current Pos:* Sr staff physicist, Lawrence Livermore Lab, Univ Calif, 56-70, dep div leader, 70-73, div leader, 73-76, dept head, 76-78, asst to assoc dir physics, 78-91, LAB ASSOC, LAWRENCE LIVERMORE LAB, UNIV CALIF, 91- *Personal Data:* b Jamestown, NY, Dec 10, 30; m 55, Leona; c David A, Carol-Gay & Eric K. *Educ:* San Diego State Col, BA, 51; Univ Calif, Berkeley, MA, 53, PhD(physics), 56. *Honors & Awards:* Tom W Bonner Prize, 72. *Mem:* Fel Am Phys Soc; Sigma Xi. *Res:* Fast neutron physics; polarization phenomena; nuclear reactions. *Mailing Add:* 4909 Dawes St San Diego CA 92109-2008

ANDERSON, JOHN DENTON, PRIMITIVE MOBILE SYSTEMS. *Current Pos:* RETIRED. *Personal Data:* b July 15, 1912; m 43, Jane Collier; c 4. *Educ:* Stanford Univ, PhD(biol), 49. *Prof Exp:* Assoc dean, Med Sch, Basic Sci, Univ Ill, Urbana, 72-77. *Mailing Add:* 1305 W Clark St Champaign IL 61821-3155

ANDERSON, JOHN DONALD, medical microbiology, for more information see previous edition

ANDERSON, JOHN EDWARD, TRANSPORTATION. *Current Pos:* PRES & CHIEF EXEC OFFICER, TAXI 2000 CORP, 94- *Personal Data:* b Chicago, Ill, May 15, 27; m 75, Cynthia Howard; c Candice, James & Stanley. *Educ:* Iowa State Univ, BSME, 49; Univ Minn, MSME, 55; Mass Inst Technol, PhD(aeronaut & astronaut), 62. *Prof Exp:* Aeronaut res scientist, Nat Adv Comt Aeronaut, 49-51; develop engr, Aero Div, Honeywell, Inc, 51-53, proj engr, 53-54, sr res engr aero res, 54-55, res proj engr, 55-56, prin res engr, 56-57, staff engr, 57-58, adv to dir, Mil Prod Res, 62-63, proj mgr, Systs & Res Div, 63; lectr, Univ Minn, Minneapolis, 62-63, assoc prof thermodyn, 63-71, prof mech eng, 71-86, dir, Indust Eng Div, 78-86; prof aerospace & mech eng, Boston Univ, 86-94. *Concurrent Pos:* Consult, Systs & Res Div, Honeywell, Inc, 63-67, Colo Regional Transp Dist, 74-75, Raytheon Co, 75-76, State Ind, 79-81, Dary McKee Corp, 84-85; Space Sci Ctr grant, 65-67; Nat Acad Sci exchange prof, Soviet Union, 67-68; coordr, Task Force New Concepts in Urban Transp, 68-78, Colo Regional Transp Dist, 74-75, The Raytheon Co, 75-76, Mannesmann Demag, 77-78, Indianapolis Transit Comn, 78-81 & Arthur D Little, Inc, 81-82; founder, Anderson MacDonald, Inc, 80- & Davy McKee Corp, 84-85. *Mem:* AAAS; Am Soc Mech Engrs. *Res:* New concepts in urban transportation; transportation systems analysis; innovative interdisciplinary education on environmental problems; science and engineering policy in government; transit system theory; wind energy; research on determination of optimum characteristics of public transportation through study of economic, social, environmental and technical characteristics. *Mailing Add:* 5164 Rainer Pass NE Fridley MN 55421-1338

ANDERSON, JOHN FRANCIS, ANIMAL PHYSIOLOGY. *Current Pos:* Asst prof, 69-74, ASSOC PROF ZOOL, UNIV FLA, 74- *Personal Data:* b Hartford, Conn, July 25, 36; m 63, Marjorie Barrett; c Gretchen & Alicia. *Educ:* Cent Conn State Col, BS, 62; Univ Fla, MS, 65, PhD(zool), 68. *Mem:* Am Soc Zool; Sigma Xi; Am Arachnological Soc. *Res:* Arthropod physiology; energetics in arachnids. *Mailing Add:* Dept Zool Univ Fla 223 Bartram Hall Gainesville FL 32611-2009. *Fax:* 904-392-3704

ANDERSON, JOHN FREDRIC, ENTOMOLOGY. *Current Pos:* from asst entomologist to assoc entomologist, 64-69, head dept entom, 69-87, DIR, CONN AGR EXP STA, 87- *Personal Data:* b Fargo, NDak, Feb 25, 36; m 58; c Linda, John Jr & Kristin. *Educ:* NDak State Univ, BS, 57, MS, 59; Univ Ill, PhD(entom), 63. *Honors & Awards:* Author's Citation Award, Int Soc Arboriculture. *Prof Exp:* NSF fel, 63-64. *Concurrent Pos:* Res affil, Dept Epidemiol, Yale Univ. *Mem:* Entom Soc Am; Soc Invert Path; Am Mosquito Control Asn; Am Soc Parasitol; Am Soc Microbiol; Am Soc Trop Med Hyg. *Res:* Medical entomology; insect pathology; forest entomology. *Mailing Add:* Conn Agr Exp Sta Box 1106 New Haven CT 06504. *Fax:* 203-789-7232

ANDERSON, JOHN G(ASTON), HIGH VOLTAGE ENGINEERING, LIGHTNING & POWER SYSTEMS. *Current Pos:* PVT CONSULT ENGR, 92- *Personal Data:* b Dante, Va, Aug 21, 22; m 94, Avery Holmes; c David J. *Educ:* Va Polytech Inst, BS, 43. *Honors & Awards:* Centennial Medal, Inst Elec & Electronics Engrs, Herman Halperin Award, 91, Medal Eng Excellence, 97. *Prof Exp:* Engr, High Voltage Lab, Gen Elec Co, Pittsfield, 47-53, develop engr, 53-57, res engr systs insulation, 57-63, tech dir, Proj Extra-High Voltage, 64-67, mgr, 67-70, mgr, Proj Ultra-High Voltage, Pittsfield, 70-72, mgr, AC Transmission Studies, Schenectady, 72-75, mgr, High Voltage Lab, 75-80, consult engr elec power transmission systs, Schenectady, 80-84; sr consult, Power Technologies, Inc, 84-92. *Concurrent Pos:* Dir, Elec & Mech Res; consult eng, 84-88. *Mem:* Nat Acad Eng; fel Inst Elec & Electronics Engrs; Int Conf Large Elec High Tension Systs. *Res:* Dielectric strength of liquid and solid insulations; lightning; extra-high voltage transmission; ultra-high voltage transmission; electric power transmission; electrical energy systems. *Mailing Add:* 525 Old Windsor Rd Dalton MA 01226

ANDERSON, JOHN GREGG, STRONG MOTION SEISMOLOGY, EARTHQUAKE HAZARD ANALYSIS & GEOPHYSICS. *Current Pos:* assoc prof, 88-92, PROF GEOPHYS, UNIV NEV, RENO, 92- *Personal Data:* b Niagara Falls, NY, Aug 31, 48; m 74, Gisela M Wagner; c Kristina J & Peter J. *Educ:* Mich State Univ, BS, 70; Columbia Univ, PhD(geophysics), 76. *Prof Exp:* Res fel, Calif Inst Technol, 76-77; res assoc, Univ Southern Calif, 77-80; asst to assoc res seismologist, Univ Calif, San Diego, 80-88. *Concurrent Pos:* Mem, Comt Probabilistic Seismic Hazard Assessment, Nat Acad Sci, 85-88, Comt Seismic Base Isolation, 89-93; mem, Nev Earthquake Safety Coun, 92-, chair, 93- *Mem:* Seismol Soc Am; Royal Astron Soc; Am Geophys Union; Earthquake Eng Res Inst. *Res:* Strong ground shaking caused by earthquakes; recording systems; physical understanding; numerical modeling; average properties; probability of occurence; relationship of earthquakes and earthquake occurence rates to geological processes. *Mailing Add:* Seismol Lab Univ Nevada Reno Reno NV 89557. *Fax:* 702-784-1833; *E-Mail:* jga@seismo.unr.edu

ANDERSON, JOHN HOWARD, CHEMICAL PHYSICS. *Current Pos:* RETIRED. *Personal Data:* b Northfork, WVa, Jan 26, 24; m 46; c 3. *Educ:* Univ NC, BS, 44, MS, 47; Univ Chicago, PhD(chem), 55. *Prof Exp:* Asst prof physics & chem, Talladega Col, 46-49; fel glass sci, Mellon Inst, 54-58; from assoc prof to prof physics, Univ Pittsburgh, 58-86. *Concurrent Pos:* Fulbright-Hays fel, Coun Int Exchange Scholars, 70. *Mem:* Am Phys Soc; Am Asn Physics Teachers; AAAS. *Res:* Electron spin resonance; color centers; energy conversion; energy utilization. *Mailing Add:* 231 Woodside Rd Pittsburgh PA 15221

ANDERSON, JOHN JEROME, geology, for more information see previous edition

ANDERSON, JOHN JOSEPH BAXTER, PHYSIOLOGY, NUTRITION. *Current Pos:* assoc prof, 72-77, dept chmn, 84-87, PROF NUTRIT, SCH PUB HEALTH, UNIV NC, CHAPEL HILL 77- *Personal Data:* b Cleveland, Ohio, June 12, 34; m 57; c 3. *Educ:* Williams Col, BA, 56; Harvard Univ, MAT, 58; Boston Univ, MA, 62; Cornell Univ, PhD(phys biol), 66. *Prof Exp:* Teacher high sch, Maine, 58-59; instr biol, Bradford Jr Col, 59-62; asst prof vet physiol & pharmacol, Col Vet Med, Univ Ill, Urbana, 66-71. *Concurrent Pos:* NIH fel phys biol, Cornell Univ, 66; vis scientist, USDA, Beltsville, 80, Univ Copenhagan, Glostrup Hosp, 85 & Karolinska Hosp & Inst, Stockholm, 90. *Mem:* AAAS; Am Inst Nutrit; Am Pub Health Asn; Brit Nutrit Soc; Am Soc Clin Nutrit; Am Col Nutrit; Am Physiol Soc. *Res:* Metabolism of calcium and phosphorus, especially bone, intestine, kidneys and endocrines; nutrition and body composition; diet and bone health; nutrition and cancer; determinants of bone health in pre and post menopausal women, especially dietary, lifestyle and activity variables. *Mailing Add:* 15 Rogerson Dr Chapel Hill NC 27514-4036

ANDERSON, JOHN LEONARD, BIOENGINEERING, BIOPHYSICS. *Current Pos:* assoc prof chem eng, Carnegie-Mellon Univ, 76-79, dir biomed eng, 80-85, dept head, 83-94, PROF CHEM ENG, CARNEGIE-MELLON UNIV, 79-, UNIV PROF, 94-, DEAN, COL ENG, 96- *Personal Data:* b Wilmington, Del, Sept 29, 45; m 68; c 2. *Educ:* Univ Del, BChE, 67; Univ Ill, Urbana, MS, 69, PhD(chem eng), 71. *Honors & Awards:* Prof Progress Award, Am Inst Chem Engrs, 89; Holtz lectr, Johns Hopkins Univ, 90. *Prof Exp:* Asst prof, Cornell Univ, 71-76. *Concurrent Pos:* Vis prof chem eng, Mass Inst Technol, 82-83; Guggenheim fel, 82-83; Fifth Berkeley lectr, Univ Calif, 89; NSF commemorative lectr, 89. *Mem:* Nat Acad Eng; Am Inst Chem Engrs; Am Chem Soc; Sigma Xi; Coun Chem Res; AAAS; Am Phys Soc. *Res:* Theory of transport through porous membranes, emphasizing the role of solute-pore interactions; transport phenomena in colloidal suspensions; transport of polymers in micropores and near surfaces; electrokinetics, electrophoresis. *Mailing Add:* CIT Dean's Off Carnegie-Mellon Univ Pittsburgh PA 15213-3890. *Fax:* 412-268-6421; *E-Mail:* johna@cmu.edu

ANDERSON, JOHN M(ELVIN), ELECTRICAL ENGINEERING, PLASMA PHYSICS. *Current Pos:* RETIRED. *Personal Data:* b Kansas City, Mo, Oct 9, 24; m 50, Lois Koester; c Charles M, James M, Ruth C & Julie C. *Educ:* Univ Ill, BSEE, 47, MSEE, 48, PhD(elec eng), 55. *Prof Exp:* Physicist gaseous electronics, Res Lab, Gen Elec Co, 55-87. *Mem:* Fel Am Phys Soc; fel Inst Elec & Electronics Engrs. *Res:* Gaseous electronics; microwave electronics; electro-magnetic and plasma interaction; lamp research and development. *Mailing Add:* 17 Cedar Lane Scotia NY 12302

ANDERSON, JOHN MURRAY, AQUACULTURE. *Current Pos:* PRES, ANDERSON CONSULTS, INC, 79- *Personal Data:* b Toronto, Ont, Sept 3, 26; m 51, 86, Sylvia Richard; c Nancy, Susan, Peter, Katherine, Tanya & Traci. *Educ:* Univ Toronto, BScF, 51, PhD(physiol), 58. *Hon Degrees:* LLD, St Thomas Univ, 74, Univ Maine, 76, Dalhouse Univ, 79. *Prof Exp:* Res assoc, Univ Toronto, 58; asst prof biol, Univ NB, 58-63; assoc prof animal physiol, Carleton Univ, 63-67; dir biol sta, Fisheries Res Bd Can, 67-72; dir gen, Fisheries Res & Develop, Can Dept Environ, 72-73; pres, Univ NB, Fredericton, 73-79. *Concurrent Pos:* Treas & mem bd dirs, Huntsman Marine Lab, NB, 69-72, pres & chmn bd dir, 74-77 & 96; mem comt on Canada's Energy Opportunities, Sci Coun Can, 73-74; mem bd gov, Inst Can Bankers, 74-79; mem exec comt, St John Mus, 74-; vpres, Biol Coun Can, 77-79; trustee, MacKenzie King Scholar Trust, 77-, chmn bd trustees, 86-; mem bd dirs, Bradfield Educ Fund, Noranda Mines, 78-84; vpres opers, Atlantic Salmon Fedn, 84-96; mem bd dirs, NB Nature Trust, 87-91; mem, Sci Coun Can, 88-93; pres, Atlantic Aquacult Fair, 93-94; chmn, McCain Fouds Schoar Comt, 96- *Mem:* AAAS; Am Fisheries Soc; Can Soc Zool (vpres, 71, pres, 73-74); Aquacult Asn Can (pres, 83-85). *Res:* Marine biology; physiological and behavioural effects of sub-lethal pollutants on aquatic organisms; salmonid aquaculture; sub-lethal effects of chlorinated hydrocarbon insectides on salmonid physiology and behavior. *Mailing Add:* PO Box 547 St Andrews NB E0G 2X0 Can. *Fax:* 506-529-4438; *E-Mail:* atlsal@abnet.nb.ca

ANDERSON, JOHN NICHOLAS, MOLECULAR BIOLOGY, ENDOCRINOLOGY. *Current Pos:* ASST PROF MOLECULAR BIOL, PURDUE UNIV, 76- *Personal Data:* b Pittsburgh, Pa, Sept 25, 46; m 69; c 1. *Educ:* Slippery Rock State Col, BA, 69; Purdue Univ, PhD(molecular biol), 73. *Prof Exp:* Res assoc, Stanford Univ, 73-76. *Concurrent Pos:* Am Cancer Soc fel, 73-76 & grant, 76-78. *Mem:* Endocrine Soc. *Res:* Mechanisms of gene expression in higher organisms. *Mailing Add:* Dept Biol Sci Purdue Univ West Lafayette IN 47907-1968

ANDERSON, JOHN NORTON, polymer chemistry, for more information see previous edition

ANDERSON, JOHN P, ENGINEERING MECHANICS. *Current Pos:* VPRES, ADMIN & PLANNING, WAKE FOREST UNIV, 84- *Personal Data:* b New Orleans, La, Mar 27, 39; m 62; c 5. *Educ:* Ga Inst Technol, BS, 61, MS, 63 & 64, PhD(eng mech), 66; Univ Ala, Birmingham, MBA, 75. *Prof Exp:* Asst prof eng mech, Ga Inst Technol, 65-68; asst to vpres for Univ Col, Univ Ala Birmingham, 71-73, asst to vpres fiscal affairs, 73-74, dir financial planning, 73-75, asst to vpres for finance, 74-75, dir, Div Spec Studies, 74-78, assoc prof math, 69-, prof eng, 73-, asst to pres & dir, long-range planning, 77-, dean, spec studies, 78-84. *Concurrent Pos:* Instr, USAF Acad, 66-68; consult, Kaman Nuclear Co, 66- & Rust Eng Co, 68-71. *Res:* Elastic stability theory; shell theory; applied mathematics. *Mailing Add:* Wake Forest Univ PO Box 7249 Reynolda Sta Winston Salem NC 27109

ANDERSON, JOHN R, MATHEMATICS EDUCATION. *Current Pos:* CONSULT, 92- *Personal Data:* b Stromsburg, Nebr, Aug 1, 28; m 50, Bertha M Nore; c Eric J & Mary L. *Educ:* Univ Nebr, BA & MA, 51; Purdue Univ, PhD(math), 70. *Prof Exp:* High sch math teacher, 51-52; prog engr, Allison Div Gen Motors, 54-60; prof math, DePauw Univ, 60-92, asst dean univ, 72-76, dir grad studies, 72-86, chmn dept, 86-90. *Concurrent Pos:* NSF Grant, 65; Danforth teacher fel, 64. *Mem:* Math Asn Am; Nat Coun Teachers Math. *Res:* Mathematics education; teaching calculus. *Mailing Add:* 1560 Bloomington St Greencastle IN 46135

ANDERSON, JOHN RICHARD, MEDICAL & VETERINARY ENTOMOLOGY, PARASITOLOGY. *Current Pos:* from asst prof to assoc prof, 61-71, chm div, 70-71, PROF ENTOM, UNIV CALIF, BERKELEY, 71- *Personal Data:* b Fargo, NDak, May 5, 31; m 55, Shereen V Erickson; c Scott F, Lisa K & Steven F. *Educ:* Utah State Univ, BS, 57; Univ Wis, MS, 58, PhD(med entom, vet sci), 60. *Honors & Awards:* Woodworth Award, Entom Soc Am, 88. *Prof Exp:* Biol aide, USPHS, 55; proj assoc arbo viruses, Dept Vet Sci, Univ Wis, 60-61. *Concurrent Pos:* Trustee & past chmn, Mosquito Abatement Dist, Alamedo Co, Calif, 61-73 & 79-94; assoc dean res, Col Nat Resources, 78-85; prin investr, NIH & other grants; gov bd, Entomol Soc Am, 87-90. *Mem:* Fel AAAS; Entom Soc Am; Can Entom Soc; Am Mosquito Control Asn; Soc Vector Ecol; fel Royal Entomol Soc. *Res:* Ecology and behavior of Diptera of medical and veterinary importance; host-vector-parasite interrelationships of Hematozoa; anthropod parasites of deer. *Mailing Add:* 1283 NW Trenton Bend OR 97701

ANDERSON, JOHN SEYMOUR, BIOCHEMISTRY. *Current Pos:* asst prof biochem, 67-73, assoc prof 73-86, PROF BIOCHEM, UNIV MINN-ST PAUL, 86- *Personal Data:* b Kearney, Nebr, Oct 27, 36; m 76; c 1. *Educ:* Nebr State Teachers Col, AB, 58; Univ Nebr, Lincoln, MS, 60, PhD(chem), 63. *Prof Exp:* NSF res fels, Sch Med, Washington Univ, 63-64 & Sch Med, Univ Wis-Madison, 64-65; USPHS fel, Med Res Coun Lab Molecular Biol, Cambridge, Eng, 65-67. *Concurrent Pos:* Hon vis assoc prof, Dept Chem, Univ BC, 83. *Mem:* Am Chem Soc; Am Soc Microbiol; Am Soc Bichem & Molecular Biol. *Res:* Biosynthesis and structure of bacterial cell walls and membranes; biosynthesis of polysaccharides; intermediary metabolism of monosaccharides. *Mailing Add:* Dept Biochem Univ Minn 1479 Gortner Ave St Paul MN 55108-1041

ANDERSON, JOHN THOMAS, LOW TEMPERATURE PHYSICS. *Current Pos:* AT HEWLETT PACKARD LABS, PALO ALTO, CALIF. *Personal Data:* b Paterson, NJ, Apr 7, 45; m 68. *Educ:* Case Inst Technol, BS, 67; Univ Minn, PhD(physics), 71. *Prof Exp:* From teaching asst physics to res asst, Dept Physics, Univ Minn, 67-71; res assoc, Hansen Lab Physics, Stanford Univ, 71-74, res physicist, 74- *Mem:* Am Phys Soc; Sigma Xi. *Res:* Application of superconducting quantum interference device magnetometry to measurement of very small angles, specifically in a gyroscope with a London moment readout, or to precise angle measurement; noise characteristics of superconducting quantum interference devices. *Mailing Add:* Hewlett Packard Labs Bldg 26M Palo Alto CA 94303-0867

ANDERSON, JOHN TRUMAN, FISHERIES OCEANOGRAPHY & RESOURCE ASSESSMENT. *Current Pos:* res scientist & biologist, 79-90, SECT HEAD FISHERIES ECOL, DEPT FISHERIES & OCEANS, ST JOHN'S, NFLD, 91- *Personal Data:* b Hamilton, Ont, Sept 8, 50; m 76, Margaret Stewart; c Jessica & Ryan. *Educ:* Univ Guelph, BSc, 73, MSc, 78; Univ BC, PhD(fisheries ecol), 92. *Prof Exp:* Aquatic ecologists, EAG Ltd, 78-79. *Mem:* Am Soc Limnol & Oceanog; Can Soc Zoologists. *Res:* Growth and survival mechanisms in marine fish, larval and juvenile stages. *Mailing Add:* Dept Fisheries & Oceans PO Box 5667 St John's NF A1C 5X1 Can. *Fax:* 709-772-4188; *E-Mail:* anderson@granite.nwafc.nf.ca

ANDERSON, JOHN WALBERG, ANATOMY, HISTOLOGY. *Current Pos:* DEAN PROGS, PENDLE HILL, WALLINGFORD, PA, 90- *Personal Data:* b New York, NY, Dec 3, 27; m 64; c 3. *Educ:* Swarthmore Col, BA, 50; Univ NH, MS, 52; Cornell Univ, PhD(histol), 56. *Prof Exp:* From instr to prof anat, Univ Wis-Madison, 56-90. *Mem:* Am Soc Cell Biol; Am Asn Anat; Soc Study Reproduction. *Res:* Histophysiology, especially of reproduction; materno-fetal transfer of immunity. *Mailing Add:* 801 Yale Ave 919 Swarthmore PA 19081

ANDERSON, JOSEPH EUGENE, II, FUEL MANAGEMENT, PLASMA ENERGY. *Current Pos:* DIR RES & DEVELOP, METRO MOTORSPORTS, 96-, VPRES, 97- *Personal Data:* b July 12, 53; m 53, Linda; c Joseph III, Michael, Rachael & Stephanie. *Educ:* LaSalle Univ, BSME, 93. *Honors & Awards:* Outstanding Achievement Award, US Dept Energy, 94; R&D 100 Award, Res & Develop Mag, 95. *Prof Exp:* Dir opers, Power Shop, 90-91; dir ignition, Enox Technol, 91-96. *Concurrent Pos:* Prof ignition, Gulf S Res Coun, Pipeline Res Coun, Univ Va & Univ Houston, 92-96. *Mem:* Soc Automotive Engrs; Instrument Soc Am; Nat Hot Rod Asn; Am Gas Inst. *Res:* Air flow and fuel management in internal combustion engine; plasma energy as an ignition source in internal combustion engines; plasma energy to disassociate nitrous oxide as an after combustion process. *Mailing Add:* 9359 Sharp Antler Columbia MD 21045. *Fax:* 301-937-6782; *E-Mail:* enox.joe@aol.com

ANDERSON, JULIUS HORNE, JR, pharmacology, biochemistry, for more information see previous edition

ANDERSON, KARL E, GASTROENTEROLOGY. *Current Pos:* assoc dir, Div Human Nutrit, 87-90, PROF, DEPTS PREV MED & COMMUNITY HEALTH, INTERNAL MED & PHARMACOL, UNIV TEX MED BR, GALVESTON, 87-, DIR, 90-, ASSOC PROG DIR, GEN CLIN RES CTR, 93- *Personal Data:* b Buffalo, NY, May 16, 40; m 83; c 3. *Educ:* John Hopkins Univ, MD, 65. *Prof Exp:* Assoc prof & physician, Rockefeller Univ, 79-85; prof, Dept Med & Pharmacol & dir, Clin Res Ctr, NY Med Col, Valhalla, 85-87. *Concurrent Pos:* Mem, Gastroenterol & Clin Nutrit Rev Group, NIH, 80-82, Scientific Adv Bd, Am Porphyria Found, Montgomery, Ala, 82-, chmn, 82-87, Gastroenterol Adv Panel, US Pharmacopeial Convention, Inc, 91- *Mem:* Fel Am Col Physicians; Am Asn Study Liver Dis; Am Gastroenterol Asn; Am Soc Clin Pharmacol & Therapeut; Am Soc Pharmacol & Exp Therapeut; Am Soc Nutrit Sci. *Res:* Nutritional pharmacology; drug-nutrient intereactions; effects of diet on cytochrome P450 and drug metabolism; porphyrias and other disorders of heme metabolism. *Mailing Add:* Univ Texas Med Br 700 Harborside Dr Galveston TX 77555-1109

ANDERSON, KEITH PHILLIPS, PHYSICAL CHEMISTRY. *Current Pos:* chmn dept chem, 58-60, PROF CHEM, BRIGHAM YOUNG UNIV, 53- *Personal Data:* b Morgan, Utah, Oct 6, 19; m 42; c 3. *Educ:* Brigham Young Univ, AB, 46; Cornell Univ, PhD, 50. *Honors & Awards:* Fulbright lectr, Valencia & Barcelona, Spain, 60-61, Columbia, SAm, 66. *Prof Exp:* Mem staff, Univ Calif at Los Alamos, NMex, 50-51; instr, exten div, Univ NMex, 51; chief radiol warfare div, Dugway Proving Ground, Utah, 51-52; assoc res prof physics & develop dir radiol res, Univ Utah, 52-53. *Mem:* AAAS; Am Chem Soc; Sigma Xi; AAAS. *Res:* Tracer chemistry; calorimetry; amino acid chelates; equilibria in slightly soluble salt solutions in aqueous-nonaqueous media. *Mailing Add:* 3758 Foothill Dr Provo UT 84604-5345

ANDERSON, KELBY JOHN, ELEMENTARY PARTICLE PHYSICS. *Current Pos:* SR RES ASSOC, ENRICO FERMI INST, UNIV CHICAGO, 72- *Personal Data:* b Ogden, Utah, Feb 15, 44. *Educ:* Idaho State Univ, BS, 66; Univ Colo, PhD(physics), 71. *Res:* Experimental elementary particle physics, counter experiments. *Mailing Add:* Enrico Fermi Inst Univ Chicago 5630 S Ellis Ave Chicago IL 60637

ANDERSON, KENNETH ELLSWORTH, bacteriology; deceased, see previous edition for last biography

ANDERSON, KENNETH VERLE, NEUROPSYCHOLOGY, NEUROANATOMY. *Current Pos:* AREA MGR, BORG-WARNER PROTECTIVE SERVS, 92- *Personal Data:* b La Crosse, Wis, Sept 14, 38; m 67. *Educ:* Carleton Col, AB, 60; Brown Univ, MSc, 62, PhD(exp psychol), 64. *Prof Exp:* Res psychologist, US Naval Electronics Lab, Calif, 62; lab instr neuroanat, Yale Univ, 65-66; from instr to assoc prof neurol, Emory Univ, 66-77, prof anat, 77-80; mem fac, Dept Anat, Univ Miss Med Ctr, 80-84; dir res & bus mgr, Riverview Phys Ther & Rehab Ctr, 84-88; dir biol & comput sci, Brandon Acad, 88-92. *Concurrent Pos:* USPHS fel neurophysiol & neuroanat, Yale Univ, 64-66; NIMH res scientist develop award, 68-72, Nat Inst Neurol Dis & Blindness res grant, 69-71; grants, NIMH, 73-74, Nat Inst Dent Res, 75-78 & 79-82 & Nat Eye Inst, 77-79. *Mem:* AAAS; Am Psychol Asn; Am Asn Anat; Soc Neurosci; Int Asn Study Pain. *Res:* Analysis of neuroanatomical correlates of perception and learning, including microelectrode assessment of sensory codes and rigorous analysis of behavior concomitant with changes in sensory transmission; visual system and the somatosensory system. *Mailing Add:* 115 Hillview Dr Brandon MS 39042

ANDERSON, KENNING M, ENDOCRINOLOGY, ONCOLOGY. *Current Pos:* ASSOC PROF BIOCHEM, RUSH MED COL, CHICAGO & RUSH-PRESBY ST LUKE'S MED CTR, 76- *Personal Data:* b Oak Park, Ill, July 17, 33; m 64, Muir; c Kirsten, Colin & Christopher. *Educ:* Northwestern Univ, Evanston, BS, 54; Northwestern Univ, Chicago, MD, 58, MSc, 65; Univ Chicago, PhD(biochem), 69; FRCP(C), 76. *Prof Exp:* Intern med, Northwestern Univ, 58-59, resident, 59-62; capt, US Army, 62-64; fel, Univ Chicago, 64-68; from asst to assoc prof clin biochem, Univ Toronto, Ont, 69-76. *Mem:* Am Soc Biol Chem; Am Asn Cancer Res; Am Soc Cell Biol; Biophys Soc. *Res:* Endocrinology; medical oncology; mechanisms of hormone action. *Mailing Add:* Sect Med Oncol Rush Med Col 1753 W Congress Pkwy Chicago IL 60612. *Fax:* 312-942-3192

ANDERSON, KINSEY AMOR, SOLAR PHYSICS, SPACE PHYSICS. *Current Pos:* from asst prof to assoc prof, Univ Calif, Berkeley, 60-66, assoc dir, Space Sci Lab, 68-70, dir, 70-79, PROF PHYSICS, UNIV CALIF, BERKELEY, 66- *Personal Data:* b Preston, Minn, Sept 18, 26; m 54; c 2. *Educ:* Carleton Col, BA, 49; Univ Minn, Minneapolis, PhD(physics), 55. *Hon Degrees:* Dr, Univ Paul Sabatier, 89. *Honors & Awards:* Space Sci Award, Am Inst Aeronaut & Astronaut, 68; Except Sci Achievement Medal, NASA, 72; Alexander von Humboldt Award, 78. *Prof Exp:* Res assoc, Univ Minn, Minneapolis, 55; res assoc, Univ Iowa, 55-58, asst prof physics, 58-60. *Concurrent Pos:* Guggenheim fel, Royal Inst Technol, Stockholm, Sweden & Nat Observ, Athens, Greece, 59-60; mem, Lunar Sci Rev Panel, NASA, 76, Solar Syst Explor Comt, Off Space Sci, 80-84, Class Mem Comt, Nat Acad Sci, 85 & NASA Ctr Sci Assessment Team, 87; Fulbright lectr & res award, France, 81; chmn, Res Assoc Prog, Nat Res Coun, 84 & Ad Hoc Comt Rev Inst Geophys & Planetary Physics, 89. *Mem:* Nat Acad Sci; fel Am Phys Soc; fel Am Geophys Union; Am Astron Soc; Int Astron Union; fel AAAS; Int Union Radio Sci; Am Asn Physics Teachers; Sigma Xi. *Res:* Solar cosmic rays; auroral zone phenomena; radiation zone studies using high altitude balloons and satellites; tensiometer for measurements on biaxially stressed films; published numerous articles in various journals; awarded one patent; numerous technical publications. *Mailing Add:* Space Sci Lab Univ Calif Mail Code 7450 Berkeley CA 94720

ANDERSON, LARRY A, NUMERICAL ANALYSIS. *Current Pos:* PROF MATH & COMPUT SCI, LE TOURNEAU UNIV, 74- *Personal Data:* b Ames, Iowa, Nov 2, 45; m 72, Barbara Krohn; c Ginger & Jonathan. *Educ:* Wheaton Col, BS, 67; Purdue Univ, MS, 69, PhD(math), 74. *Mem:* Math Asn Am; Asn Comput Mach. *Mailing Add:* Le Tourneau Univ PO Box 7001 Longview TX 75607

ANDERSON, LARRY BERNARD, ANALYTICAL CHEMISTRY, ELECTROCHEMISTRY. *Current Pos:* asst prof, 66-72, acad vchmn dept, 68-72, 78-80, ASSOC PROF CHEM, OHIO STATE UNIV, 72- *Personal Data:* b Cottonwood, Idaho, July 18, 37; m 62, Ruth Janeiro; c Gary, Kevin & Alan. *Educ:* Univ Wash, Seattle, BSc, 59; Syracuse Univ, PhD(chem), 64. *Prof Exp:* Res assoc chem, Univ NC, 64-66. *Concurrent Pos:* Consult, Allyn Corp, Gen Elec, DuPont & Yellow Springs Inst. *Mem:* Am Chem Soc; Electrochem Soc. *Res:* Electroanalytical chemistry; electrode kinetics; electrochemistry of organic and inorganic materials in non-aqueous system; photovoltaic solar energy conversion; semiconductor electrolyte interfaces; filar microlelectrodes for analysis. *Mailing Add:* 100 W 18th Ave Ohio State Univ Columbus OH 43210-1106. *Fax:* 614-292-1685

ANDERSON, LARRY DOUGLAS, ENDOCRINOLOGY, MOLECULAR BIOLOGY. *Current Pos:* NIH fel res-reproduction endocrinol, Dept Physiol, Univ Md, 76-78, asst prof, 78-83, dir, In Vitro Fertilization Unit, 87, ASSOC PROF, DEPT ANAT, SCH MED, UNIV MD, 83- *Personal Data:* b Traverse City, Mich, Sept 15, 47; m 71; c 2. *Educ:* Oakland Univ, BS, 70; Wayne State Univ, MS, 73, PhD(physiol), 76. *Concurrent Pos:* Vis prof, Dept Physiol, Univ Goteborg, Sweden, 81 & Mich State Univ, 81. *Mem:* Endocrine Soc; Soc Study Reproduction; AAAS. *Res:* Basic mechanisms by which cells differentiate and the regulation by hormones and their control of steroid and protein synthesis and secretion in ovary, pituitary gland and mammary gland. *Mailing Add:* Dept Anat Sch Med Univ Md 655 W Baltimore Baltimore MD 21201-1559

ANDERSON, LARRY ERNEST, NEUROCHEMISTRY, RESEARCH ADMINISTRATION. *Current Pos:* res assoc, 77-78, sr scientist, 78-85, STAFF SCIENTIST, BATTELLE NW, 85-, PROG DIR, BIOELECTROMAGNETICS, 85- *Personal Data:* b Corvallis, Ore, Jan 30, 43; m 67, Sally A; c Nicol, Todd, Kevin, Trevor, Jared, Mark, Brittney, Bradley & Tyrelle. *Educ:* Brigham Young Univ, BSc, 68; Univ Ill, PhD(biochem), 73. *Prof Exp:* NIH sr fel biochem, Univ Wash, 73-77. *Concurrent Pos:* Mem, Comt on Non-Ionizing Radiation, WHO, 85; deleg, US/USSR Coop Prog on Biol Effects of Phys Factors in Environ, 85-91; bd dirs, Bioelectromagnetics Soc, 86-88; mem, Int Union Radio Sci Comn K 92-, comt on elec & magnetic fields, Nat Acad Sci/Nat Res Coun, 93-; coun mem, Nat Coun Radiation Protection, 94- *Mem:* Bioelectromagnetics Soc (vpres, 88-89, pres, 89-90); Soc Neurosci. *Res:* Axoplasmic transport; proteases-isolation and mechanism of action; growth regulation-neural cells; neurotoxicity; biological effects of electric and magnetic fields; biological rhythms and pineal gland function. *Mailing Add:* Environ & Health Sci MSK4-28 Battelle Northwest Richland WA 99352. *Fax:* 509-375-3764; *E-Mail:* le_anderson@pnl.gov

ANDERSON, LARRY GENE, PHYSICAL CHEMISTRY, ATMOSPHERIC CHEMISTRY. *Current Pos:* ASSOC PROF, DEPT CHEM, UNIV COLO, DENVER, 82- *Personal Data:* b Terre Haute, Ind, Nov 23, 46; div; c Neil & Kyle. *Educ:* Rose Polytech Inst, BS, 68; Ind Univ, Bloomington, PhD(phys chem), 72. *Prof Exp:* Fel, Advan Study Prog, Nat Ctr Atmospheric Res, 72-73; assoc sr res scientist, Gen Motors Res Lab, 73-82, staff res scientist, environ sci dept & group leader, atmospheric chen, 82. *Concurrent Pos:* Vis scientist, Jet Propulsion Labs, 90-91. *Mem:* Am Chem Soc; Inter-Am Photochem Soc; Air & Waste Mgt Asn; Sigma Xi. *Res:* Investigation of the kinetics and mechanisms of chemical reactions of atmospheric importance; measurements of atmospheric pollutants to develop a more complete understanding of the chemistry of the atmosphere. *Mailing Add:* Dept Chem Univ Colo PO Box 173364 Denver CO 80217-3364. *Fax:* 303-556-4292; *E-Mail:* lganderson@cudnur.denver.colorado.edu

ANDERSON, LARS WILLIAM JAMES, PLANT PHYSIOLOGY & WEED SCIENCE, AQUATIC PLANT MANAGEMENT. *Current Pos:* RES LEADER, AQUATIC WEED RES LAB, AGR RES SERV, UNIV CALIF, USDA, 76- *Personal Data:* b Pasadena, Calif, Apr 22, 45; c Lisa, Ryan & Kristin. *Educ:* Univ Calif, Irvine, BA, 67; Calif State Univ, San Diego, MA, 70; Univ Calif, Santa Barbara, PhD(biol), 74. *Prof Exp:* Consult-marine biologist, Oceanog Serv Inc, 72-73; aquatic plant physiologist herbicides, Environ Protection Agency, 74-76. *Mem:* AAAS; Aquatic Plant Mgt Soc; Weed Sci Soc Am; Am Soc Plant Physiologists; Sigma Xi. *Res:* Phytoplankton physiology pertaining to vertical distribution; intracellular ion regulation in relation to cell buoyancy; control of aquatic weeds; function of plant growth regulators in aquatic macrophytes; uptake and translocation of herbicides in aquatic macrophytes; methods for assessing toxicity of pesticides to aquatic microorganisms; biological control of aquatic plants; development of methods to alter aquatic plant canopy structure. *Mailing Add:* Aquatic Weed Res Lab Agr Res Serv Plant Biol Univ Calif USDA Davis CA 95616. *Fax:* 530-752-5410; *E-Mail:* lwanderson@ucdavis.edu

ANDERSON, LAURENS, CARBOHYDRATE CHEMISTRY. *Current Pos:* from asst prof to assoc prof, Univ Wis-Madison, 51-61, prof biochem, 61-86, Steenbock prof biomolecular struct, 81-86, EMER PROF BIOCHEM, UNIV WIS-MADISON, 86- *Personal Data:* b Belle Fourche, SDak, May 19, 20; m 45, Doris E Young; c Eric E, Karl A & Kristine E. *Educ:* Univ Wyo, BS, 42; Univ Wis, MS, 48, PhD(biochem), 50. *Honors & Awards:* Claude S Hudson Award, Carbohydrate Chem, Am Chem Soc, 84. *Prof Exp:* Merck fel natural sci, Swiss Fed Inst Technol, 50-51. *Concurrent Pos:* NIH sr fel, Ind Univ, 71-72; assoc ed, Carbohydrate Res, 84-94. *Mem:* Am Chem Soc; Am Soc Biochem & Molecular Biol; Int Endotoxin Soc; Int Carbohydrate Orgn; Sigma Xi. *Res:* Organic chemistry of carbohydrates; chemical synthesis of oligosaccharides; mutarotation of sugars. *Mailing Add:* Dept Biochem Univ Wis 420 Henry Mall Madison WI 53706-1569. *Fax:* 608-262-3453; *E-Mail:* anders2@facstaff.wisc.edu

ANDERSON, LAURIE CLAIRE, MOLLUSCAN PALEONTOLOGY, PALEOECOLOGY. *Current Pos:* Asst prof, 91-97, ASSOC PROF GEOL, LA STATE UNIV, 97- *Personal Data:* b Appleton, Minn, Mar 14, 62; M, John M Kruger. *Educ:* Univ Minn, Morris, BA, 85; Bowling Green State Univ, MS, 87; Univ Wis-Madison, PhD(geol), 91. *Concurrent Pos:* Res assoc, Va Mus Natural Hist, 94- *Mem:* Geol Soc Am; Paleont Soc; Soc Sedimentary Geol; Paleont Res Inst; Am Malacol Union. *Res:* Integrate morphometric, phylogenetic and paleoecologic data to reconstruct and interpret causes of species-level evolution; rich fossil record of marine mollusks from tropical America. *Mailing Add:* Dept Geol & Geophysics La State Univ Baton Rouge LA 70803. *E-Mail:* glande@unix1.sncc.lsu.edu

ANDERSON, LAWRENCE SVEN, ASTRONOMY. *Current Pos:* ASST PROF ASTRON & PLANETARIUM DIR, UNIV TOLEDO, 78-, AT RITTER OBSERV. *Personal Data:* b Boston, Mass, Mar 4, 44; m 72; c 1. *Educ:* Calif Inst Technol, BS, 66; Univ Calif, Berkeley, MA, 74, PhD(astron), 77. *Prof Exp:* Instr astron, Chabot Col, Hayward, Calif, 74-75; res astron, Univ Calif, Berkeley, 77-78. *Concurrent Pos:* Ritter Observ. *Mem:* Am Astron Soc; AAAS. *Res:* Theory of the structure and appearance of contact binary stars; reflection effect in close binary stars; convection in stellar photospheres. *Mailing Add:* Dept Physics/Astron Univ Toledo 2801 W Bancroft Toledo OH 43606-3390

ANDERSON, LEIGH, ORAL BIOLOGY. *Current Pos:* ASSOC PROF ORAL BIOL, EMORY UNIV, ATLANTA, GA. *Personal Data:* b Minneapolis, Minn, Aug 23, 49. *Educ:* Univ Minn, PhD(oral biol), 79. *Mailing Add:* Dept Oral Biol Univ Wash B-224 Health Sci MS SB22 Seattle WA 98195

ANDERSON, LEONARD MAHLON, ELEMENTARY PHYSICS, APPLIED PHYSICS. *Current Pos:* PRIN PHYSICIST, MEASUREX CORP, 81- *Personal Data:* b Palo Alto, July 11, 44; m 83. *Educ:* Univ Calif, Berkeley, BS, 66, PhD(physics), 78. *Prof Exp:* Postdoctoral res, Ecole Polytech, 78-81. *Mem:* Am Phys Soc. *Res:* On-line measurement of paper moisture, coating weight and strength. *Mailing Add:* 1355 Stockbridge Dr San Jose CA 95130

ANDERSON, LEWIS L, PHYSICAL BIOCHEMISTRY. *Current Pos:* RES CHEMIST, E I DU PONT DE NEMOURS & CO, 61- *Personal Data:* b Deadwood, SDak, Jan 22, 35; m 56; c 2. *Educ:* SDak Sch Mines & Technol, BS, 56; Univ NMex, PhD(chem), 61. *Mem:* Sigma Xi. *Res:* Isotopic exchange; absorption spectroscopy; ultracentrifugation applied to biochemical systems; isolation of proteins; physical characterization and study of biological systems. *Mailing Add:* 223 S Summit Ave Quarryville PA 17566-1120

ANDERSON, LLOYD JAMES, RADIOPHYSICS. *Current Pos:* RETIRED. *Personal Data:* b Salt Lake City, Utah, Dec 18, 17; m 41; c 3. *Educ:* Univ Calif, Los Angeles, AB, 39; Univ Calif, MA, 42. *Prof Exp:* Asst physicist, USN Electronics Lab, 42-44, head radio-meteorol sect, 50-53, head, Environ Studies Br, 53-55; supvry physicist, Smyth Res Assocs, 55-61; prin physicist, Calspan Corp, 61-82. *Mem:* Sigma Xi; AAAS. *Res:* Effects of weather and terrain on tropospheric radio propagation; atmospheric effects on refraction of tracking radar beams; radar/optical analysis of satellites. *Mailing Add:* 7948 Represa Circle Carlsbad CA 92009

ANDERSON, LLOYD L, ANIMAL SCIENCE, PHYSIOLOGY. *Current Pos:* Asst animal reprod, Iowa State Univ, 57-58, res assoc, 58-61, from asst prof to assoc prof, 61-65, PROF ANIMAL SCI, IOWA STATE UNIV, 71-, CHARLES F CURTISS DISTINGUISHED PROF AGR, 92- *Personal Data:* b Nevada, Iowa, Nov 18, 33; m 70, JaNelle R Hall; c Marc C & James R. *Educ:* Iowa State Univ, BS, 57, PhD(animal sci), 61. *Honors & Awards:* Animal Physiol & Endocrinol Award, Am Soc Animal Sci, 88; Innovation Award Basic Res, Nat Pork Producers Coun, 93. *Concurrent Pos:* NIH res fel, 61-62; Lalor Found res fel, Nat Inst Agron Res, France, 63-64; counr, Soc Exp Biol & Med, 80-83; sect ed endocrinol & physiol, J Animal Sci, 83-86; mem, Reproductive Biol Study Sect, NIH, 84-88; mem peer review panel, animal health spec res grants beef & dairy cattle reproductive dis, USDA, 86-88; mem NIH Reviewers, 88-92; hon lectr, Iowa State Univ, Mid-Am State Univs Asn, 89-90; mem agr panel USDA, Agr Res Svc, 93, Janice Peterson Anderson Excellence Award, Col Design, Iowa State Univ. *Mem:* Hon fel Am Soc Animal Sci; Am Asn Anat; Am Physiol Soc; Endocrine Soc; Soc Exp Biol & Med; Soc Study Reproduction; Soc Study Fertil; Sigma Xi; hon fel AAAS; Soc Neurosci. *Res:* Central nervous system, pituitary, ovarian, uterine relationships primarily in farm animals, especially endocrine and neural influences in rhythmic regulation of reproduction cycle, hypothalamic regulation of prolactin, luteinizing hormone and growth hormone secretion in beef cattle and pigs, cytoplasmic localization and physiology of porcine relaxin, physiology of relaxin on parturition in cattle, maternal nutrition on fetal development in farm animals, neuroendocrine regulation of puberty in beef calves and pigs. *Mailing Add:* 11 Kildee Hall Dept Animal Sci Iowa State Univ Ames IA 50011-3150. *Fax:* 515-294-4471; *E-Mail:* llanders@iastate.edu

ANDERSON, LORAN C, BOTANY. *Current Pos:* assoc prof, 74-85, PROF BIOL SCI & CUR HERBARIUM, FLA STATE UNIV, 85- *Personal Data:* b Idaho Falls, Idaho, Feb 7, 36; m 57, Renee Roueche; c Cindy & Perry. *Educ:* Utah State Univ, BS, 58, MS, 59; Claremont Grad Sch, PhD(bot), 62. *Prof Exp:* Asst prof bot, Mich State Univ, 62-63 & Kans State Univ, 63-74. *Concurrent Pos:* Assoc prog dir, NSF, 70-71. *Mem:* Am Soc Plant Taxonomists (treas, 74-); Am Inst Biol Sci; Int Asn Wood Anatomists. *Res:* Comparative anatomy of Chrysothamnus and related genera of tribe Astereae of Compositae; forensic work with Cannabis; flora of Florida. *Mailing Add:* Dept Biol Sci Fla State Univ Tallahassee FL 32306-1096. *Fax:* 850-644-0481; *E-Mail:* anderson@bio.fsu.edu

ANDERSON, LOUIS WILMER, ATOMIC PHYSICS. *Current Pos:* From asst prof to assoc prof, 60-68, PROF PHYSICS, UNIV WIS-MADISON, 68-, JULIAN E MACK PROF PHYSICS, 94- *Personal Data:* b Houston, Tex, Dec 24, 33; m 62, Rita Gilespie; c Margaret Mary, Louis Charles & Elizabeth (Brockett). *Educ:* Rice Inst, BA, 56; Harvard Univ, AM, 57, PhD(physics), 60. *Honors & Awards:* Particle Accelerator Conf Award, Inst Elec & Electronics Engrs, 93. *Mem:* Fel Am Phys Soc; Optical Soc Am. *Res:* Radio frequency spectroscopy; atomic hyperfine structure; atomic structure; nuclear magnetic resonance in solids; atomic collisions; atom ion charge changing collisions; production of negative ions; magnetism; lasers; optical pumping; polarized ion sources; electron excitation collisions; ultra sensitive absorption spectroscopy. *Mailing Add:* Dept Physics Univ Wis Madison WI 53706. *Fax:* 608-265-2334; *E-Mail:* lwanders@facstaff.wisc.edu

ANDERSON, LOUISE ELEANOR, BIOCHEMISTRY. *Current Pos:* from asst prof to assoc prof, 68-75, PROF BIOL SCI, UNIV ILL, CHICAGO, 75- *Personal Data:* b Cleveland, Ohio, May 18, 34. *Educ:* Augustana Col, AB, 56; Cornell Univ, PhD(biochem), 61. *Prof Exp:* Res assoc bot, Wash Univ, 60-62; res assoc microbiol, Dartmouth Med Sch, 62-64, 66-67; Kettering Int fel, Food Preservation Div, Plant Physiol Unit, Commonwealth Sci Indust & Res Orgn, Australia, 64-65; res asst prof, Oak Ridge Biomed Grad Sch, Univ Tenn, 67-68. *Concurrent Pos:* Katzir-Katchalsky fel, Weizmann Inst Sci, Israel, 74-75; Fogarty Sensor Int fel, Univ Lund, Sweden, 81-82. *Mem:* AAAS; Am Soc Biol Chemists & Molecular Biol; Am Soc Plant Physiol. *Res:* Carbohydrate metabolism; metabolic control in plants and photosynthetic bacteria; enzymology. *Mailing Add:* Dept Biol Sci M/C 066 Univ Ill 845 N Taylor Chicago Chicago IL 60607-7060. *Fax:* 312-413-2435; *E-Mail:* u25317@uicvm.uic.edu

ANDERSON, LOWELL LEONARD, BIOPHYSICS. *Current Pos:* AT MED PHYSICS DEPT, MEM HOSP, NEW YORK. *Personal Data:* b Spokane, Wash, Sept 3, 30; m 55; c 2. *Educ:* Whitworth Col, Spokane, Wash, BS, 53; Univ Rochester, PhD(biophys), 58. *Prof Exp:* From asst biophysicist to assoc biophysicist, Argonne Nat Lab, 58-69; assoc attend physicist, Mem Sloan-Kettering Cancer Ctr, Med Col, Cornell Univ, 69-77, asst prof physics in radiol, 70-77; asst prof psychiat, Sch Med, NY Univ, 77- *Mem:* AAAS; Health Physics Soc; Am Phys Soc; Sigma Xi; Am Asn Physicists in Med. *Res:* Neutron measurement methods for health physics; nuclear accident dosimetry; intermediate-energy neutron calibration source; medical radiation dosimetry. *Mailing Add:* 345 East 68th St Apt 14 New York NY 10021

ANDERSON, LOWELL RAY, ORGANIC CHEMISTRY. *Current Pos:* RES SCIENTIST, ISP CORP, 79- *Personal Data:* b Burnt Prairie, Ill, Nov 4, 34; m 60, Janet Slater. *Educ:* Southern Ill Univ, BA, 56; Ohio State Univ, PhD(chem), 64. *Prof Exp:* Res chemist, Allied Chem Corp, 64-66, sr res chemist, 66-68, tech supvr, 68-69, res group leader, 69-79. *Mem:* Am Chem Soc. *Res:* Synthesis of fluorinated compounds, particularly fluorinated hypohalites, peroxides and ethers; catalysis; acetylenic compounds and derivatives; pyrrolidones, vinyl ethers and other vinyl compounds. *Mailing Add:* 27 Sunderland Dr Morristown NJ 07960

ANDERSON, LUCY MACDONALD, CANCER, ETIOLOGY. *Current Pos:* spec expert, 83-89, res biologist, 89-90, SECT CHIEF, NAT CANCER INST, 90- *Personal Data:* b Huntington, WVa, Oct 10, 42; m 64, Robert S; c Robert S & Donald P. *Educ:* Bryn Mawr Col, AB, 64; Univ Pa, PhD(biol), 68. *Prof Exp:* Res assoc biol, Univ Pa, 68-70; asst prof biol, Carleton Col, 71; asst prof biol, Macalester Col, 73; asst mem carcinogenesis, Sloan-Kettering Inst Cancer Res, 73-82. *Concurrent Pos:* NIH training grant biochem, Univ Minn, Minneapolis, 70-72; lectr, Bryn Mawr Col, 68-69; NIH Altox study sect, 94- *Mem:* Am Asn Cancer Res; Soc Toxicol; Fedn Am Soc Exp Biol. *Res:* Insect egg follicle development; metabolism of environmental carcinogens; mechanistic factors in transplacental carcinogenesis; promotion of lung tumors. *Mailing Add:* Natl Cancer Inst Bldg 538 Ft Detrick Frederick MD 21702

ANDERSON, MARGARET, DEVELOPMENTAL BIOLOGY. *Current Pos:* from asst prof to assoc prof, 73-85, PROF BIOL, SMITH COL, NORTHAMPTON, MASS, 85- *Personal Data:* b Omaha, Nebr, June 17, 41; m 71. *Educ:* Augustana Col, BA, 63; Stanford Univ, PhD(biol), 67. *Prof Exp:* Fel biol, Harvard Univ, Cambridge, Mass, 68-70; res assoc neurobiol, Lab Neurobiol, Univ PR, 70-71; affil asst prof biol, Clark Univ, Worcester, Mass, 72; instr biol, Bennington Col, Bennington, Vt, 73. *Concurrent Pos:* Prin investr, NIH grants, 75-85; mem, Bingham Selection Comt, Excellence Teaching, Transylvania Univ, Lexington, Ky, 87-94; assoc ed, Advances Physiol Educ, Am Physiol Soc, 88-92; co-prin investr, NSF grant, 89-90; dean sr class, Smith Col, 93-96. *Mem:* Am Physiol Soc; Soc Gen Physiologists; Biophys Soc; Soc Neurosci. *Res:* Polarity in the unfertilized cockroach egg using electrophysiological techniques and scanning and transmission electron microscopy. *Mailing Add:* Dept Biol Sci Smith Col Northampton MA 01063-0010

ANDERSON, MARILYN P, BONE PATHOLOGY, REPTILIAN & AVIAN PATHOLOGY. *Current Pos:* PATHOLOGIST, ZOOL SOC SAN DIEGO, 77- *Educ:* Ohio State Univ, PhD(comp biol), 76. *Mailing Add:* 10956 Parkdale Ave San Diego CA 92126

ANDERSON, MARION C, SURGERY. *Current Pos:* prof & chmn dept surg, 77-88, exec assoc dean, 88-96, SR ASSOC DEAN, COL MED, MED UNIV SC, 96- *Personal Data:* b Concordia, Kans, Oct 9, 26; m 49, Sonia B Bennett; c 4. *Educ:* Northwestern Univ, BM, 50, MD, 53, MS, 62. *Prof Exp:* Resident surg, Passavant Mem Hosp, Chicago, 54-55; resident, Vet Admin Res Hosp,

55-56 & Passavant Mem Hosp, 56-57; assoc, Cook County Hosp, 57-58; clin asst, Sch Med, Northwestern Univ, 58-59, instr, 59-60, assoc, 60-61, from asst prof to assoc prof, 61-69; chmn, Dept Med, Med Col Ohio, 69-72, prof surg, 69-77, pres, Col, 72-77. *Concurrent Pos:* Kemper res scholar, Am Col Surgeons, 61-64; assoc dean, grad med educ & continuing educ, Med Univ SC. *Mem:* AMA: Am Asn Surg of Trauma; Soc Univ Surg; Am Surg Asn; Soc Surg Alimentary Tract. *Res:* Biliary and pancreatic diseases. *Mailing Add:* Dean's Off Med Univ SC Charleston SC 29425

ANDERSON, MARJORIE ELIZABETH, NEUROPHYSIOLOGY, MOTOR CONTROL. *Current Pos:* PROF PHYSIOL & BIOPHYSIOL, UNIV WASH, 71- *Educ:* Univ Wash, PhD(physiol), 69. *Res:* Basalganglia function. *Mailing Add:* Rehab Med Univ Wash Box 356490 Seattle WA 98195-0001

ANDERSON, MARLIN DEAN, ANIMAL NUTRITION, ANIMAL PHYSIOLOGY. *Current Pos:* DIR, FEED ADDITIVE DEVELOP, FERMENTA ANIMAL HEALTH CO, 84- *Personal Data:* b Stanton, Iowa, Nov 30, 34; m 68; c 1. *Educ:* Iowa State Univ, BS, 59, MS, 62, PhD(animal nutrit), 64. *Prof Exp:* Animal nutritionist, Hess & Clark Div, Rohdia, Inc, 65-76; mgr antibiotic prod develop, SDS Biotech Corp, 77-83. *Mem:* AAAS; Am Soc Animal Sci; Am Soc Prof Animal Scientists; Am Asn Swine Practr. *Res:* Animal health and nutrition; drug efficacy; safety. *Mailing Add:* 1575 State Rte 511 Ashland OH 44805

ANDERSON, MARVIN DAVID, INTERNAL MEDICINE. *Current Pos:* fel med, 71-72, SR STAFF PHYSICIAN, HENRY FORD HOSP, 73- *Personal Data:* b Detroit, Mich, Apr 30, 38; m 79; c 2. *Educ:* Univ Notre Dame, BS, 60; Georgetown Univ, MD, 64. *Prof Exp:* Intern rotating, Harper Hosp, Detroit, 64-65, resident med, 65-66; res assoc cancer, NIH, Bethesda, Md, 66-68; sr resident med, Harlem Hosp Ctr, Col Physicians & Surgeons, Columbia Univ, 68-70, res assoc microbiol, 70-71. *Concurrent Pos:* Asst clin prof med, Sch Med, Univ Mich, Ann Arbor, 74- *Mem:* Am Col Physicians. *Res:* Nutrition. *Mailing Add:* Henry Ford Hosp Second Med Div Detroit MI 48202

ANDERSON, MARY BITNER, REPRODUCTIVE TOXICOLOGY, REPRODUCTIVE ENDOCRINOLOGY. *Current Pos:* from asst prof to assoc prof, 78-94, PROF ANAT, TULANE UNIV, 94- *Personal Data:* b Kansas City, Kans, Feb 16, 40; c 1. *Educ:* Univ Kans, AB, 62; Univ Calif, San Francisco, MA, 68, PhD(endocrinol), 73. *Prof Exp:* Res fel antifertil agents, Pop Res Inst, Oak Ridge Assoc Univs, 72-75; res assoc reproduction, Vanderbilt Univ, 75-77, instr, 77-78. *Concurrent Pos:* Med Histol Course Dir. *Mem:* Soc Study Reproduction; Endocrine Soc; Am Asn Anatomists. *Res:* Effects of metals and hydrocarbons on reproductive function. *Mailing Add:* Dept Anat Tulane Univ Med Sch 1430 Tulane Ave New Orleans LA 70112-2699

ANDERSON, MARY ELIZABETH, BIOCHEMISTRY. *Current Pos:* Postdoctoral fel, 83-87, instr, 87-89, ASST PROF, DEPT BIOCHEM, MED COL, CORNELL UNIV, 89- *Personal Data:* b San Antonio, Tex, Jan 2, 56. *Educ:* Hollins Col, BA, 77; Cornell Univ, PhD(biochem), 83. *Concurrent Pos:* Postdoctoral fel training grant, NIH, 83-86. *Mem:* Am Chem Soc; Sigma Xi; Am Soc Biochem & Molecular Biol. *Mailing Add:* Cornell Univ Med Col 1300 York Ave New York NY 10021-4896

ANDERSON, MARY PIKUL, HYDROGEOLOGY. *Current Pos:* from asst prof to assoc prof, 75-97, PROF HYDROGEOL, UNIV WIS-MADISON, 97-;. *Personal Data:* b Buffalo, NY, Sept 30, 48; m 73, Charles. *Educ:* State Univ NY Buffalo, BA, 70; Stanford Univ, MS, 71, PhD(hydrogeol), 73. *Honors & Awards:* M K Hubbert Award, 92. *Prof Exp:* Adj asst prof stratig & hydrogeol, Southampton Col, Long Island Univ, 73-75. *Concurrent Pos:* Assoc ed, EOS, Am Geophys Union, 82-84; mem, Water Sci & Technol Bd, Nat Acad Sci, 85-87; pres, Hydrology Sect, Am Geophys Union, 96- *Mem:* Am Geophys Union; Asn Groundwater Scientists & Engrs. *Res:* Analysis of mathematical models of subsurface flow systems; groundwater-surface water interaction; contaminant transport. *Mailing Add:* Geol 225 Weeks Hall Univ Wis 1215 W Dayton St Madison WI 53706-1612. *E-Mail:* andy@geology.wisc.edu

ANDERSON, MAURITZ GUNNAR, FOOD SCIENCE & TECHNOLOGY, INDUSTRIAL MICROSCOPY. *Current Pos:* from instr to prof, 63-88, EMER PROF BIOL, TOWSON STATE UNIV, 88- *Personal Data:* b Chicago, Ill, Aug 11, 18; m 42, Jeannette S; c William S & John G. *Educ:* Univ Mich, AB, 42; Ind Univ, MS, 62; Va Polytech Inst & State Univ, PhD, 76. *Prof Exp:* Supvr, Histol & Micros Div, Swift & Co, 49-57; chief histologist, Norwich Pharmacal Co, 57; res histologist & microscopist, Swift & Co, 58-63. *Concurrent Pos:* Mem, Deleg Appl Microbiologists to China, 84. *Mem:* Bot Soc Am; Mycol Soc Am; Am Asn Feed Micros; Int Asn Aerobiol; Inst Food Technol; Sigma Xi. *Res:* Application of microscopy and microchemistry to biology, pollution and food technology; mycology; granted 2 patents. *Mailing Add:* 18 Maryland Ave Towson MD 21286

ANDERSON, MELVIN JOSEPH, ANIMAL NUTRITION. *Current Pos:* dairy husbandman, Agr Res Serv, 61-82, RES ASSOC PROF, UTAH STATE UNIV, 86- *Personal Data:* b Heber City, Utah, Feb 14, 27; m 55; c 5. *Educ:* Utah State Univ, BS, 50; Cornell Univ, MS, 57, PhD(animal nutrit), 59. *Prof Exp:* Asst animal nutrit, Cornell Univ, 55-58; asst prof animal sci, Univ Maine, 58-61; res animal sci, Off Int Coop & Develop, Dept Agr, Riyadh, Saudi Arabi, 82-85. *Concurrent Pos:* Assoc prof, Utah State Univ, 71. *Mem:* Am Dairy Sci Asn; Am Soc Animal Sci. *Res:* Dairy nutrition; nutritional evaluation of forages, hay cubes and level of concentrates for livestock; utilization of liquid whey for feeding dairy animals; effect of exercising pregnant dairy cows; feeding whole cottonseed to dairy animals; testing infrared spectroscopy to evaluate forages and feeds; effect of bovine somatotropin on lactating cows. *Mailing Add:* 1235 E 1700 N Logan UT 84341

ANDERSON, MELVIN LEE, INORGANIC CHEMISTRY. *Current Pos:* from asst prof to assoc prof, 69-85, PROF CHEM, LAKE SUPERIOR STATE UNIV, 85- *Personal Data:* b Perkins, Mich, Jan 19, 28; m 55; c 2. *Educ:* Mich Technol Univ, BS, 53, MS, 55; Mich State Univ, PhD(inorg chem), 65. *Prof Exp:* Resident assoc actinide ion solution chem, Argonne Nat Lab, 53-54, jr chemist, 54-55; chemist, Dow Chem Co, Midland, 56-61, res chemist, 63-65, Rocky Flats Div, Colo, 65-69. *Concurrent Pos:* vis assoc prof, Gustavus Adolphus Col, St Peter, Minn, 80-81. *Mem:* Am Chem Soc; Sigma Xi. *Res:* Actinides and lanthanides; coordination complexes; separation and purification; nonaqueous solvents; chemical education; organometallics; nitrogen-fluorine oxidizers. *Mailing Add:* 16 Erin Pl Kincheloe MI 49788-1327

ANDERSON, MELVIN W(ILLIAM), WATER RESOURCES. *Current Pos:* assoc prof water resources, 69-72, chmn, dept civil eng & mech, 79-89, PROF WATER RESOURCES ENG, UNIV SFLA, 72-, ASSOC DEAN ACAD AFFAIRS, 89- *Personal Data:* b Baltimore, Md, Jan 9, 37; m 60; c 2. *Educ:* Va Mil Inst, BS, 59; Carnegie-Mellon Univ, MS, 63, PhD(water resources), 67. *Prof Exp:* From asst prof to assoc prof civil eng, La State Univ, 63-69. *Mem:* Am Soc Civil Engrs; Am Soc Eng Educ; Am Water Resources Asn; Nat Soc Prof Engrs. *Res:* Multidisciplinary studies involved in sustaining and managing the quality and quantity of water available for human activities. *Mailing Add:* Col Engr 118 Univ SFla 4202 Fowler Ave Tampa FL 33620. *Fax:* 813-974-5094; *E-Mail:* anderson@sunburn.ec.usf.edu

ANDERSON, MILES EDWARD, ACOUSTICS, ELECTROMAGNETISM. *Current Pos:* RETIRED. *Personal Data:* b Ft Worth, Tex, Dec 13, 26; m 48; c 3. *Educ:* NTex State Univ, BS, 49, MS, 50; Stanford Univ, PhD(physics), 63. *Prof Exp:* Instr physics, NTex State Univ, 50-52; asst, Willow Run Res Ctr, Univ Mich, 52-54; asst prof, Univ NTex, 54-56, assoc vpres acad affairs, 69-75, vpres acad affairs, 75-79, prof physics, 60-91, vpres acad affairs, 75-91. *Concurrent Pos:* Lectr, Washington Univ, 62-63. *Mem:* Am Phys Soc; Am Asn Physics Teachers; Acoust Soc Am. *Mailing Add:* 529 Mimosa Dr Denton TX 76201

ANDERSON, MILO VERNETTE, MICROWAVE PHYSICS, MEDICAL PHYSICS. *Current Pos:* INDEPENDENT CONSULT, MED PHYSICS, 87- *Personal Data:* b Wolsey, SDak, Dec 24, 24; m 43, Marjorie H Osborn; c Terry, Arthur, Karen & Carol. *Educ:* Union Col, Nebr, BA, 49; Univ Nebr, MA, 55; Univ Colo, Boulder, PhD(elec eng), 71. *Prof Exp:* From instr to asst prof physics, Union Col, Nebr, 49-57, chmn dept, 57-59; physicist, Nat Bur Stand, 59-64; from assoc prof to prof physics, Pac Union Col, 64-86, chmn dept, 73-81. *Concurrent Pos:* High sch teacher sci & math, Platte Valley Acad, Shelton, Nebr, 49-52; res physicist, IBM, San Jose, Calif, 81; vis prof, Andrews Univ, Berrien Springs, Mich, 89. *Mem:* Am Asn Physics Teachers; Am Asn Physicists Med; Sigma Xi. *Res:* Applications of microwave resonant structures. *Mailing Add:* PO Box 417 Angwin CA 94508-0417

ANDERSON, MILTON MERRILL, ELECTRONICS ENGINEERING. *Current Pos:* DIST MGR, BELL COMMUN RES, 84- *Personal Data:* b Litchfield, Minn, Dec, 5, 43; m 69; c 3. *Educ:* Univ Minn, BS, 65, MS, 67. *Prof Exp:* Mem tech staff, Bell Tel Labs, 67-73, supvr, 73-82; supvr, Am Bell, 82-84. *Mem:* Inst Elec & Electronics Engrs. *Res:* Compressed digital video and image coding; audio coding; speech processing; telecommunications network applications of digital signal coding and processing. *Mailing Add:* Bellcore 445 South St Morristown NJ 07962

ANDERSON, NEIL ALBERT, PLANT PATHOLOGY, MYCOLOGY. *Current Pos:* From instr to assoc prof, 59-70, PROF MYCOL & PLANT PATHOGEN GENTICS, UNIV MINN, ST PAUL, 70- *Personal Data:* b Minneapolis, Minn, Oct 21, 28; m 60; c 2. *Educ:* Univ Minn, BS, 51, MS, 57, PhD(plant path), 60. *Concurrent Pos:* Vis prof, Waite Inst, Univ Adelaide, 70-71. *Mem:* Am Phytopath Soc; Mycol Soc Am; Sigma Xi; Potato Asn Am; AAAS. *Res:* Genetic studies on the plant pathogen, Rhizoctonia solani; plant pathology studies on Hypoxylon mammosum and Verticillium on potato. *Mailing Add:* Univ Minn 206 Plant Path St Paul MN 55108

ANDERSON, NEIL OWEN, CELL PHYSIOLOGY. *Current Pos:* PROF BIOL, EAST STROUDSBURG STATE COL, 70- *Personal Data:* b Chicago, Ill, Oct 10, 35; m 57; c 2. *Educ:* Ripon Col, BA, 57; Drake Univ, MS, 64; Univ Ill, PhD(physiol), 70. *Mem:* AAAS; Sigma Xi (secy). *Res:* Examination of the nuclear proteins and their role in the cell. *Mailing Add:* 14 Spangenburg Ave East Stroudsburg PA 18301-2724

ANDERSON, NEIL R, OCEANOGRAPHY. *Honors & Awards:* Ocean Sci Award, Am Geophys Union, 94. *Mailing Add:* Univ Md Horn Point Environ Lab 2020 Horn Point Rd Cambridge MD 21613

ANDERSON, NELS CARL, JR, ENDOCRINOLOGY, BIOPHYSICS. *Current Pos:* ASST PROF OBSTET, GYNEC, PHYSIOL & PHARMACOL, MED CTR, DUKE UNIV, 66- *Personal Data:* b Detroit Lakes, Minn, June 15, 36; m 63; c 2. *Educ:* Concordia Col, Moorhead, Minn, BA, 58; Kans State Univ, MS, 60; Purdue Univ, PhD(endocrinol), 64. *Prof Exp:* NIH fel, 64-66. *Mem:* Soc Gen Physiol; Am Physiol Soc; Sigma Xi. *Res:* Hormonal control of myometrial structure and function, particularly the hormonal and ionic basis of excitation in uterine smooth muscle. *Mailing Add:* Dept Cell Biol Duke Univ Med Ctr Durham NC 27710

ANDERSON, NORMAN GULACK, PHYSIOLOGY. *Current Pos:* CHMN & CHIEF SCIENTIST, LARGE SCALE BIOL CORP, 84- *Personal Data:* b Davenport, Wash, Apr 21, 19; m 43; c 2. *Educ:* Duke Univ, BA, 47, MA, 49, PhD(physiol), 52. *Prof Exp:* Biologist, Oak Ridge Nat Lab, 52-66, coordr joint NIH-AEC Zonal Centrifuge Develop Prog, Biol Div, 66-69, dir joint NIH-AEC Molecular Anat Prog, 69-74; mem fac, Dept Basic & Clin Immunol & Microbiol, Med Univ SC, 74-77; head, Molecular Anat Prog, Argonne Nat Lab, 77-84. *Mem:* Am Physiol Soc; Am Soc Zool; Biophys Soc. *Res:* Cellular physiology; biochemistry; isolation of cell components; effects of ionizing radiations; embryonic antigens in cancer; development of zonal centrifuges; rotating fast chemical analyzers; isopyenometric serology; early cancer detection. *Mailing Add:* 10916 Wickshire Way Rockville MD 20852

ANDERSON, NORMAN HERBERT, AQUATIC ECOLOGY, ENTOMOLOGY. *Current Pos:* from asst prof to assoc prof, 62-75, PROF ENTOM, ORE STATE UNIV, 75- *Personal Data:* b Edam, Sask, Mar 17, 33; m 56; c 4. *Educ:* Univ BC, BSA, 55; Ore State Col, MS, 58; Imp Col, Univ London, dipl, 61; Univ London, PhD(entom), 61. *Prof Exp:* Res officer entom, Can Dept Agr, 55-62. *Concurrent Pos:* NSF, US Dept Interior & Agr Res Serv, US Dept Agr grants. *Mem:* Ecol Soc Am; Entom Soc Am; Entom Soc Can; Brit Freshwater Biol Asn; NAm Benthological Soc. *Res:* Aquatic entomology; insect and animal ecology; ecology and taxonomy of aquatic insects. *Mailing Add:* Dept Entom Cordley Hall Ore State Univ Cordley Hall 2046 Corvallis OR 97331-2907

ANDERSON, NORMAN LEIGH, MOLECULAR BIOLOGY. *Current Pos:* vpres res, 85-92, PRES LARGE SCALE BIOL CORP, 92- *Personal Data:* b Durham, NC, Aug 3, 49; m 84. *Educ:* Yale Univ, BA, 71; Cambridge Univ, PhD(molecular biol), 75. *Honors & Awards:* Young Investr Award, Am Asn Clin Chem. *Prof Exp:* Fel, Med Univ SC, 75-76; fel, Argonne Nat Lab, 76-78, asst biophysicist molecular anat, 78-85; vpres res, Proteus Technol, 85-88. *Mem:* Am Soc Cell Biol; Electrophoresis Soc; Am Asn Clin Chem; Soc Toxicol. *Res:* Molecular anatomy; gene product mapping; cataloging all human protein gene products; molecular toxicology. *Mailing Add:* Large Scale Biol Corp 9620 Medical Center Dr Rockville MD 20850

ANDERSON, NORMAN RODERICK, GEOLOGY & GEOMORPHOLOGY, ELEMENTARY SCIENCE EDUCATION. *Current Pos:* from instr to prof, 46-84, chmn dept, 57-84, EMER PROF GEOL, UNIV PUGET SOUND, 84- *Personal Data:* b Tacoma, Wash, Oct 12, 21; m 49; c 2. *Educ:* Univ Puget Sound, BS, 46; Univ Wash, MS, 54; Univ Utah, PhD(geol), 65. *Prof Exp:* Geologist, US Army Engrs, 47-48. *Concurrent Pos:* Dir, NSF Prog, Elementary Sci Teachers, 85-, NSF grant, TPE 8855548. *Mem:* Fel Geol Soc Am; Soc Econ Paleont & Mineral; Nat Asn Geol Teachers; Sigma Xi. *Res:* Pleistocene geology; glacial geology of Western Washington; geology of the Snake River Plain, Southwestern Idaho. *Mailing Add:* 1914 N Union Ave Tacoma WA 98406

ANDERSON, O(RVIL) ROGER, CELL BIOLOGY, MARINE BIOLOGY. *Current Pos:* From asst prof to assoc prof, 64-70, PROF NATURAL SCI, TEACHERS COL, COLUMBIA UNIV, 70- *Personal Data:* b East St Louis, Ill, Aug 4, 37. *Educ:* Washington Univ, AB, 59, MAEd, 61, EdD(bot), 64. *Honors & Awards:* Diatom species named in honor, Cocconeis andersonii. *Concurrent Pos:* From res scientist to sr res scientist, Lamont-Doherty Geol Observ, 66-; biol consult, Bd Higher Educ, State NJ, 68; ed, J Res in Sci Teaching; vis res prof cellular micropaleont, Tubingen Univ, 79, 84 & 87; assoc ed, J Protozool, 88-; pres, Columbia Univ Chap, Sigma Xi, 95. *Mem:* AAAS; Sigma Xi; NY Acad Sci; Am Inst Biol Sci; Nat Asn Res Sci Teaching (pres, 76); Soc Protozoologists (pres,94). *Res:* Ultrastructure and physiological ecology of marine microplankton; author of textbooks on protozoology. *Mailing Add:* 525 W 120th St New York NY 10027. *Fax:* 914-365-8150; *E-Mail:* ora@ldeo.columbia.edu

ANDERSON, OREN P, INORGANIC CHEMISTRY. *Current Pos:* from asst prof to assoc prof, 74-86, PROF CHEM, COLO STATE UNIV, 86-, CHMN, DEPT CHEM, 89- *Personal Data:* b Iowa City, Iowa, June 19, 42; m 67, Jennifer E Bates; c 2. *Educ:* Carleton Col, Northfield, Minn, BA, 64; Northwestern Univ, Evanston, Ill, PhD(chem), 68. *Prof Exp:* Res fel chem, Univ Bergen, Norway, 68-70; Univ res fel chem, Univ Leicester, Eng, 70-72; asst prof chem, Univ Mich, Ann Arbor, 72-74. *Concurrent Pos:* Vis prof, Univ Minn, 89. *Mem:* Am Chem Soc; Royal Soc Chem; Am Crystallog Asn. *Res:* Structural and synthetic studies on transition metal complexes, especially those of biological interest. *Mailing Add:* Dept Chem Colo State Univ Ft Collins CO 80523-0002

ANDERSON, ORSON LAMAR, GEOPHYSICS, MINERAL PHYSICS. *Current Pos:* prof geophys, Inst Geophys & Planetary Physics & Dept Geophys & Space Physics, 66-74, DIR, SYSTEMWIDE INST GEOPHYS & PLANETARY PHYSICS, UNIV CALIF, LOS ANGELES, 78- *Personal Data:* b Price, Utah, Dec 23, 24; m 76; c 2. *Educ:* Univ Utah, BS, 48, MS, 49, PhD(physics), 51. *Honors & Awards:* Meyer Award, Am Ceramic Soc, 54. *Prof Exp:* Instr mech eng, Univ Utah, 50-51, asst res prof physics, 51; mem tech staff, Bell Tel Labs, 51-60; mgr mat dept, Res Div, Am Standard Co, 60-63; res assoc geophys, Lamont Geol Observ, Columbia Univ, 63-64, adj prof, 64-65, prof mineral, Dept Geol & Lamont Geol Observ, 66-71. *Concurrent Pos:* Ed-in-chief, J Geophys Res, 67-73. *Mem:* Am Ceramic Soc; Am Phys Soc; Am Geophys Union. *Res:* Mechanical properties of solids; equations of state; high pressure physics; acoustics; physics of the earth's interior. *Mailing Add:* Dept Earth Space Sci Univ Calif 405 Hilgard Ave Los Angeles CA 90024-1301

ANDERSON, OSCAR EMMETT, AGRONOMY, SOIL FERTILITY. *Current Pos:* head soil sect, 55-67, head dept, 71-81, PROF & SOIL SCIENTIST, DEPT AGRON, GA EXP STA, UNIV GA, 65- *Personal Data:* b Englewood, Fla, Nov 4, 16; m 46; c 2. *Educ:* Univ Fla, BS, 41, Rutgers Univ, PhD(soils), 55. *Honors & Awards:* Carter-Jones Soil Sci Award, 77. *Prof Exp:* Asst soil scientist, Ga Exp Sta & Ga Br Exp Sta, 55-58, assoc soil scientist, 58-65. *Concurrent Pos:* Consult soil problems, Nigeria, 76, 80, 81 & 83. *Mem:* Sigma Xi; Am Soc Agron; Am Soc Crop Sci; Am Soc Soil Sci; Int Soc Soil Sci. *Res:* Soil-plant relationships, particularly trace elements in soils and their availability to plants; microelements. *Mailing Add:* 627 Windy Hill Rd Griffin GA 30223-5330

ANDERSON, OWEN THOMAS, PHYSICS. *Current Pos:* RETIRED. *Personal Data:* b Adams, Minn, May 11, 31; m 56, Judith Ehlg; c Owen, Margaret, Douglas, Ellen & Steven. *Educ:* St Olaf Col, BA, 53; Univ Wis, MS, 55, PhD(physics), 60. *Prof Exp:* Assoc engr, Adv Systs Develop Div, Int Bus Mach Corp, 58-60, adv engr, 60-61; from asst prof to prof physics, Bucknell Univ, 61-93. *Mem:* Am Phys Soc; Am Asn Physics Teachers. *Res:* Low temperature physics; properties of the liquid helium II film; atmospheric optical effects. *Mailing Add:* Box 214 Rd No 2 Lewisburg PA 17837

ANDERSON, PAUL DEAN, ANALYTICAL CHEMISTRY, COMPUTER APPLICATIONS. *Current Pos:* Res chemist, Phillips Petrol Co, 66-68, sr res chemist, 68-78, supvr, 78-82, SR RES ASSOC, PHILLIPS PETROL CO, 82- *Personal Data:* b Grand Junction, Colo, Oct 28, 40; m 62; c 2. *Educ:* Univ Calif, Berkeley, BS, 62; Mass Inst Technol, PhD(analytical chem), 66. *Mem:* Am Chem Soc; Sigma Xi. *Res:* Computer applications to analytical chemistry; laboratory automation; data acquistion and process control; computer applications to research. *Mailing Add:* 2301 Avalon Rd Bartlesville OK 74006-6302

ANDERSON, PAUL J, NEUROPATHOLOGY, NEUROLOGY. *Current Pos:* assoc prof path, 65-66, assoc prof neurol, 66-68, PROF NEUROPATH, MT SINAI SCH MED, 67-, PROF NEUROL, 87- *Personal Data:* b Akron, Ohio, Oct 11, 25. *Educ:* Ohio Univ, BS, 49; Univ Chicago, MD, 53; Am Bd Psychiat & Neurol, dipl, 59; Am Bd Path, dipl, 60. *Prof Exp:* Clin instr neurol, NY Univ, 60-61; asst prof neuropath, Col Physicians & Surgeons, Columbia Univ, 61-67. *Concurrent Pos:* Nat Inst Neurol Dis & Blindness spec fel, 57-59; asst attend pathologist, Mt Sinai Hosp, New York, 58-61, from asst attend neurologist to assoc attend neurologist, 59-68, assoc attend pathologist in charge, Div Neuropath, 61-74, attend pathologist in charge, Div Neuropath, 74-; ed, J Neuropath & Exp Neurol, 61-81; consult neuropathologist, City Hosp Elmhurst, 64-; ed-in-chief, J Histochem & Cytochem, 73- *Mem:* Fel Am Acad Neurol; Am Asn Neuropath; Am Asn Path & Bact; Asn Res Nerv & Ment Dis; Am Neurol Asn. *Res:* Electron microscopy and electron histochemistry of neuromuscular diseases. *Mailing Add:* 133 E 73rd St New York NY 10021

ANDERSON, PAUL JOSEPH, RHEUMATOLOGY. *Current Pos:* asst prof, 90-93, ASSOC PROF MED, HARVARD MED SCH, 94-; ASSOC PROF MED, DANA-FARBER CANCER INST, 86- *Personal Data:* b Syracuse, NY, Nov 25, 56. *Educ:* State Univ NY, Stony Brook, BS, 78; NY Univ Sch Med, PhD(microbiol), 83, MD, 84. *Prof Exp:* Resident internal med, Brigham & Women's Hosp, 84-86, rheumatology fel, 86-89. *Mem:* Am Asn Immunologists; Fedn Am Socs Exp Biol; fel Am Col Rheumatology. *Res:* Mechanisms of actions of cytotoxic lymphocytes; study the surface receptors and intracellular effector molecules involved in cell-mediated cytotoxicity. *Mailing Add:* Div Tumor Immunol Dana-Farber Cancer Inst 44 Binney St Boston MA 02115-6084

ANDERSON, PAUL KNIGHT, VERTEBRATE ECOLOGY. *Current Pos:* from assoc prof to prof, 68-84, EMER PROF ZOOL, UNIV CALGARY, 84- *Personal Data:* b Ludlow, Mass, Aug 6, 27; m 57, 68, Donna R Lynch; c Erik S & Kristin J (Belair). *Educ:* Cornell Univ, AB, 49; Tulane Univ, MS, 51; Univ Calif, PhD(zool), 58. *Prof Exp:* Assoc zool, Univ Calif, 58, instr, 58-59; res assoc, Columbia Univ, 59-61; asst prof, Univ Alta, 61-65, assoc prof zool & asst dean arts & sci, 65-67; sr res fel, Nat Res Coun Can, 67-68; vis assoc prof zool, Stanford Univ, 67-68. *Concurrent Pos:* Exchange scientist, USSR-Can, 67; hon res fel, James Cook Univ, 74-75 & Univ Western Australia, 81-82 & 87-89. *Mem:* Am Soc Mammalogists; Am Soc Ichthyologists & Herpetologists; Soc Marine Mammal. *Res:* Population structure, dynamics and evolution in vertebrate populations, particularly rodents; behavior and ecology of sirenians. *Mailing Add:* Dept Biol Sci Univ Calgary Calgary AB T2N 1N4 Can. *Fax:* 403-289-9311; *E-Mail:* pkanders@acs.ucalgary.ca

ANDERSON, PAUL LEROY, organic chemistry, for more information see previous edition

ANDERSON, PAUL M, BIOCHEMISTRY. *Current Pos:* assoc prof, 71-76, head dept, 71-85, PROF BIOCHEM, UNIV MINN-DULUTH, 76- *Personal Data:* b Jackson, Minn, May 1, 38; m 59; c 3. *Educ:* Univ Minn, BS, 59, PhD(biochem), 64. *Prof Exp:* NSF res fel biochem, Sch Med, Tufts Univ, 64-65, NIH res fel, 65-66; from asst prof to assoc prof, Southern Ill Univ, 66-70; res biochemist, Molecular Biol Dept, Miles Labs, Inc, 70-71. *Concurrent Pos:* Vis assoc prof, Univ Wash, 77-78; vis prof, Univ Wash, 87-88. *Mem:* AAAS; Am Chem Soc; Am Soc Biol Chemists; Sigma Xi; Protein Soc. *Res:* Purification, mechanisms of catalytic action and regulation of enzymes of the cyanase operon and of enzymes related to nucleotide and urea biosynthesis; nitrogen and energy metabolism in fish (the urea cycle and associated enzymes). *Mailing Add:* Biochem Dept Univ Minn 252 Sch Med 10 University Dr Duluth MN 55812-2487

ANDERSON, PAUL MAURICE, ELECTRIC POWER SYSTEM DYNAMICS & RELIABILITY. *Current Pos:* PRES, POWER MATH ASSOC, 78- *Personal Data:* b Des Moines, Iowa, Jan 22, 26; m 50, Virginia Worsnick; c William, Mark, James & Thomas. *Educ:* Iowa State Univ, BS, 49, MS, 58, PhD (elec eng), 61. *Prof Exp:* Elec engr, Iowa Pub Serv Co, 49-55; from instr to prof elec eng, Iowa State Univ, 55-75; prog mgr, Elec Power Res Inst, 75-78. *Concurrent Pos:* Consult, NSF Summer Inst, Kharagpur, India & Ford Found, Univ Philippines, 69 & Pac Gas & Elec Co, 71-72; chmn, Syst Dynamic Performance Subcomt, Inst Elec & Electronics Engrs, 73-; mem, Task Force, Dept Energy Nat Power Grid Study, 78-79; consult ed, Encycl Sci & Technol, 79-; mem, Int Conf des Grands Re Electriques; prof elec eng, Ariz State Univ, 80-84; ed, Press Series in Power, Inst Elec & Electronics Engrs, 94-; vis prof elec eng, Wash State Univ, Pullman, 96-97. *Mem:* Fel Inst Elec & Electronics Engrs; Am Soc Mech Engrs. *Res:* Analytical methods for large power systems; author of technical books in power systems. *Mailing Add:* Power Math Assocs Inc 13335 Roxton Circle San Diego CA 92130. *E-Mail:* p.anderson@ieee.org

ANDERSON, PAUL MILTON, AGRICULTURAL ENGINEERING. *Current Pos:* RETIRED. *Personal Data:* b Penna, Ind, June 27, 27; m 51; c 3. *Educ:* Pa State Univ, BS, 50, MS, 57. *Prof Exp:* Farm mgr, Woodville State Hosp, Pa, 50-51; from instr to assoc prof agr eng, Pa State Univ, 51-92. *Mem:* Am Soc Agr Engrs; Am Soc Eng Educ. *Res:* Electric power for production and processing of agricultural products; equipment for harvesting forage crops and for the application of feed additives, including anhydrous ammonia, to improve feed quality and reduce storage losses. *Mailing Add:* 298 Pine Grove Rd State College PA 16801

ANDERSON, PAUL NATHANIEL, INTERNAL MEDICINE, ONCOLOGY. *Current Pos:* PHYSICIAN, ROCKY MOUNTAIN CANCER CTR, 95- *Personal Data:* b Omaha, Nebr, May 30, 37; m 65; c 2. *Educ:* Univ Colo, BA, 59, MD, 63; Am Bd Internal Med, dipl, 73, dipl oncol, 75. *Prof Exp:* Intern internal med, Johns Hopkins Hosp, 63-64, resident, 64; res assoc embryol, Sect Exp Embryol, Lab Neuroanat Sci, Nat Inst Neurol Dis & Blindness, 65-67, staff assoc, Carcinogenesis Sect, Lab Biol, Nat Cancer Inst, 67-70; staff assoc, Div Oncol, Dept Med, Johns Hopkins Hosp, 70-76; asst prof med & oncol, Johns Hopkins Univ, 72-76; dir med oncol, Penrose Cancer Hosp, Colorado Springs, 76-86, dir, 79-86; dir, Cancer Ctr Colorado Springs, 86-95. *Concurrent Pos:* Fel internal med, Johns Hopkins Hosp, 63-64; asst physician, Johns Hopkins Hosp; attend physician, Baltimore City Hosps; consult, Mem Hosp & St Francis Hosp, Colorado Springs, 76-; lectr cancer treat & rehab, Belo Horizonte, Brazil, sponsored by Partners Am, 78; med dir, Southern Colo Cancer Prog, 80-; mem, Colo Cancer Control & Res Panel, 80-, mem, Nat Cancer Inst Ad Hoc Comt Eval Community Hosp Oncol Progs, 82-83, mem bd dirs, Med Mgt Inc, 84-86, Health Care Stand Comt, Colo Found Med Care, 85-, Steering Comt Mammograph Screening Proj, Colo Dept Health, 87-; consult oncol, USAF Acad Hosp, 80-, Ft Carson Army Hosp, 84-, Ont Cancer Found, 87-; prin investr, Colo Cancer Commun Network & Cancer Info Serv, 81-87, Colo Community Clin Oncol Prog, 83-84; mem, Colo Govs Panel, Rocky Flats Employee Health Assessment Group, 83-84, bd adv, Colo Tumor Registry, Colo State Dept Health, 83-; bd mem, Share Health Plan Colo, Inc, 85-; founding mem, bd trustees, Southern Colo AIDS Proj, 86-, founding dir, Timberline Med Asssoc, 86-87; pres, Preferred Physicians Inc, 86-, asst med dir, Pikes Peak Hospice, 86-; ed bd, J Cancer Prog Mgt, 87-, ed bd, Health Care Mgt Rev, 88-; mem, Nat bd med dir, Fox Chase Ltd Fox Chase Comprehensive Cancer Ctr, Philadelphia, Pa, 87- *Mem:* AAAS; AMA; Am Soc Clin Oncol; Am Asn Cancer Res; NY Acad Sci; Am Asn Prof Consult; Am Mgt Asn; Am Hospice Asn; Int Platform Asn; Am Soc Int Med; Coalition Cancer Res; Am Asn Med Dirs. *Res:* Cancer chemotherapy; clinical investigation in cancer treatment; immunotherapy of cancer; combined modality cancer therapies; tumor immunology; anti-leukemia cellular immunity; efficacy of granulocyte transfusions during therapy-induced aplasia; cancer control res methodology; gall bladder infections in convalescent cholera patients; optimal antibiotic therapy in cholera; plasma cell tumor induction in BALB/c mice; cancer patient symptoms and disease management. *Mailing Add:* Rocky Mountain Cancer Ctr 110 E Monroe Suite 200 Colorado Springs CO 80933

ANDERSON, PAUL S, PHARMACEUTICALS. *Current Pos:* RES CHEMIST, DUPONT MERCK PHARMACEUT CO. *Honors & Awards:* E B Herschberg Award, Am Chem Soc, 95. *Mailing Add:* DuPont Merck Pharmaceut Co PO Box 80025 Wilmington DE 19880-0025

ANDERSON, PETER ALEXANDER VALLANCE, CNIDARIAN NEUROBIOLOGY, PHYSIOLOGY OF CNIDOCYTES. *Current Pos:* assoc prof, 85-90, PROF PHYSIOL, UNIV FLA, 90-, INTERIM DIR, WHITNEY LAB, 96- *Personal Data:* b Labuan, North Borneo, July 28, 51; Brit citizen; m 76; c 1. *Educ:* Univ St Andrews, Scotland, BSc, 73; Univ Calif, Santa Barbara, MA & PhD(biol), 76. *Prof Exp:* Lectr zool, St Andrews Univ, 77-79; asst specialist neurobiol, Univ Calif, Irvine, 79-81, from asst prof to assoc prof physiol, 81-90. *Concurrent Pos:* Vis prof, Univ Sao Paolo, 85; summer investr, Marine Biol Lab, 81-84; Alexander von Humboldt fel, 90. *Mem:* Soc Neurosci; Soc Exp Biol. *Res:* The physiology, pharmacology and structure of simple nervous systems with particular reference to evolution of lower nervous systems. *Mailing Add:* Whitney Lab 9505 Ocean Shore Blvd St Augustine FL 32086-8623

ANDERSON, PETER GLENNIE, CARDIAC HYPERTROPHY, ISCHEMIC INJURY. *Current Pos:* Fel comp path, 81-84, fel hypertension, 84-86, asst prof, Dept Comp Med, 86-92, ASST PROF, DEPT PATH, UNIV ALA, BIRMINGHAM, 92- *Personal Data:* b Oxford, NY, Dec 28, 54; m 88, Cherre; c Robert & Matthew. *Educ:* Univ Wash, BA, 77; Wash State Univ, DVM, 81; Univ Ala-Birmingham, PhD(path), 86. *Concurrent Pos:* Vis scientist, Univ Health Ctr, Univ Ariz, 88-89; mem Basic Sci Coun, Am Heart Asn. *Mem:* Am Vet Med Asn; Soc Cardiovasc Path; Sigma Xi; Am Asn Pathologists; Int Soc Heart Res; Am Heart Asn. *Res:* The changes that occur during cardiac hypertrophy and how these changes make the hypertrophied heart more susceptable to ischemic injury; use morphologic techniques to correlate structural changes with physiologic changes in normal and hypertrophied hearts; Vascular biology. *Mailing Add:* Dept Path Univ Ala Birmingham G046 VH Birmingham AL 35294-0019. *E-Mail:* peter@vhth.uab.edu

ANDERSON, PETER GORDON, NEURAL NETWORKS. *Current Pos:* PROF COMPUT SCI, ROCHESTER INST TECHNOL, 80- *Personal Data:* b Bay City, Mich, Jan 3, 40; m 62; c 2. *Educ:* Mass Inst Technol, SB, 62, PhD(math), 64. *Prof Exp:* Assoc prof computer sci, NJ Inst Technol, 71-78; prof, Seton Hall Univ, 78-80. *Concurrent Pos:* Prof, Shanghai Univ Technol & Zhejiang Univ, 86. *Mem:* Inst Elec & Electronics Engrs; Asn Comput Mach; Mat Asn Am; Int Neural Network Soc. *Res:* Neural networks and application to image processing and image understanding; developing reliable Monte Carlo methods. *Mailing Add:* Comput Sci Dept Rochester Inst Technol Rochester NY 14623

ANDERSON, PHILIP CARR, DERMATOLOGY. *Current Pos:* asst prof, 63-68, dir res training, 65-68, ASSOC PROF DERMAT & ASST DEAN FOR PLANNING, SCH MED, UNIV MO-COLUMBIA, 68-, CHMN DEPT, 70-, MEM BD DIRS, 75- *Personal Data:* b Grand Rapids, Mich, Dec 25, 30; m 62; c 3. *Educ:* Univ Mich, AB, 51, MD, 55; Am Bd Dermat, dipl, 62. *Prof Exp:* From jr clin instr to sr clin instr dermat, Med Ctr, Univ Mich, 60-63. *Concurrent Pos:* NIH res fel, 61-63; Markle scholar, 66-; spec asst to dir, NIH, 67-68; mem bd dirs, Nat Prog Dermat, 70- *Mem:* Fel Am Acad Dermat; Am Dermat Asn; Soc Invest Dermat; Tissue Cult Asn; Am Asn Prof Dermat. *Res:* Tissue culture; education; management; cholesterol in cell walls. *Mailing Add:* Dept Dermat Univ Mo Health Sci Ctr Columbia MO 65212

ANDERSON, PHILIP O, PHARMACY. *Current Pos:* staff pharmacist, Dept Pharm, Univ Calif Med Ctr, San Diego, 75-78, clin pharmacist, Burn Serv, 77-81 & Burn/Trauma Serv, 82-84, dir, Home Health Drug Info Serv, 84-87, DIR, DRUG INFO SERV, UNIV CALIF MED CTR, SAN DIEGO, 78-, PHARMACIST SPECIALIST, 81-; VPRES, HEALTHWARE INC, SAN DIEGO, 86- *Educ:* Univ Calif, San Francisco, DPharm, 71. *Honors & Awards:* Achievement Award, Am Soc Hosp Pharmacists Res & Educ Found, 89. *Prof Exp:* Chief pharmacist, Pub Health Serv Indian Hosp, Okla, USPHS, 71-73; asst ed, Am Hosp Formulary Serv, Am Soc Hosp Pharmacists, Md, 73-74. *Concurrent Pos:* Vol clin fac mem, Univ Calif Sch Pharm, San Francisco, 75-78, clin instr pharm, 79-81, from asst clin prof to assoc clin prof, 84-91, clin prof, 92-; consult, Med Ctr Pharm & Therapeut Comt, Univ Calif, San Diego, 78-82, Lactation Clin, 79-85, San Diego Pediat Nutrit Group, 80-85, Wellstart/San Diego Lactation Prog, 83- & Oceania Comput Systs, 90-; J William Fulbright scholar, Univ Chile, 94; ed, Discourse, 79- & Med Ctr Formulary, Dept Pharm, Univ Calif, 80. *Mem:* Fel Am Soc Hosp Pharmacists. *Res:* Clinical pharmacy education; development of a clinical pharmacokinetics service; breast feeding, drugs and medication. *Mailing Add:* Drug Info Serv Sch Med Dept Pharm Univ Calif San Diego La Jolla CA 92093

ANDERSON, PHILIP WARREN, THEORETICAL PHYSICS. *Current Pos:* PROF PHYSICS, PRINCETON UNIV, 75- *Personal Data:* b Indianapolis, Ind, Dec 13, 23; m 47, Joyce Gothwaite; c Susan. *Educ:* Harvard Univ, BS, 43, MA, 47, PhD, 49; Cambridge Univ, MA, 78. *Hon Degrees:* ScD, Univ Ill, 80, Rutgers Univ, 90, Ecole Normal Superieur, 95, Gustavus Adolphus Col, 95, Univ Sheffield, 96. *Honors & Awards:* O F Buckley Prize, Am Phys Soc, 64; Dannie Heinemann Prize, Ger Acad Sci, 75; Nobel Prize in Physics, 77; Guthrie Medal, Inst Physics, 78; Nat Medal Sci, 82. *Prof Exp:* Mem tech staff, Bell Tel Labs, 49-84; prof theoret physics, Cambridge Univ, 67-75. *Concurrent Pos:* Overseas fel, Churchill Col Cambridge, 61-62; eastern prof, Balliol Col, Oxford, 93-94. *Mem:* Nat Acad Sci; fel Am Phys Soc; AAAS; Royal Soc London; Am Philos Soc; Japan Acad. *Res:* Quantum theory; theoretical physics of solids; spectral line broadening; magnetism; superconductivity. *Mailing Add:* Dept Physics Princeton Univ Princeton NJ 08544

ANDERSON, R F V, MATHEMATICS, DIFFERENTIAL EQUATIONS & TIME DELAY PROBLEMS. *Current Pos:* asst prof, 69-74, ASSOC PROF MATH, UNIV BC, 74- *Personal Data:* b Montreal, Que, Dec 23, 43; m 71. *Educ:* McGill Univ, BSc, 64; Princeton Univ, MA, 66, PhD(math), 67. *Prof Exp:* Instr math, Mass Inst Technol, 67-69. *Mem:* Am Math Soc; Can Math Soc. *Res:* Spectral theory of non-commuting operators; stability of systems with time delays. *Mailing Add:* Dept Math Univ BC Rm 121 1984 Mathematics Rd Vancouver BC V6T 1Z5 Can

ANDERSON, R(ICHARD) L(OUIS), SOLID STATE ELECTRONICS, LOW TEMPERATURE ELECTRONICS. *Current Pos:* dir, prog mat sci, 81-91, PROF ELEC ENG & MAT SCI, UNIV VT, 78- *Personal Data:* b Minneapolis, Minn, Feb 4, 27; m 50, Claire Petersen; c Gretchen, Betty L & Karl. *Educ:* Univ Minn, BEE, 50, MS, 52; Syracuse Univ, PhD, 60. *Hon Degrees:* Dr, Univ Sao Paulo, 70. *Honors & Awards:* Brazilian Prize for Microelectronics, 80. *Prof Exp:* Asst, Univ Minn, 51-52; assoc physicist, res ctr, Int Bus Mach Corp, 52-60; from assoc prof to prof elec eng, Syracuse Univ, 61-78; consult, Int Telecommun Union, 75-80, Orgn Am States, 86-93, UN Develop Prog, 90. *Concurrent Pos:* Adj prof, Syracuse Univ, 57-60; Fulbright vis prof, Univ Madrid, 60-61; vis prof, Univ Sao Paulo, 67-69 & Univ Vt, 78-79. *Mem:* Fel Inst Elec & Electronics Engrs; Am Phys Soc. *Res:* Investigation of physical electronics of semiconductor devices; field effect transistors at low cryogenic temperatures with applications to integrated circuits; heterojunction bipolar transistors. *Mailing Add:* Dept Elec Eng Univ Vt Burlington VT 05405. *Fax:* 802-656-0696; *E-Mail:* anderson@emba.uvm.edu

ANDERSON, R(OBERT) M(ORRIS), JR, ELECTRICAL ENGINEERING, SOLID STATE PHYSICS. *Current Pos:* VPROVOST EXTEN, IOWA STATE UNIV, 90- *Personal Data:* b Crookston, Minn, Feb 15, 39; m 60; c 2. *Educ:* Univ Mich, BSEng, 61, MSEng, 63, MS, 65, PhD(elec eng), 67. *Prof Exp:* Asst res engr, Dept Elec Eng, Univ Mich, 64-67; lectr integrated circuits, Purdue Univ, 68, from asst prof to assoc prof elec eng, 70-76, eng coordr continuing educ, 73-79, Ball Bros prof eng, 76-79; mgr tech educ oper, Gen Elec Co, 79-90. *Concurrent Pos:* Lectr, Western Elec Co, Ind, 69-71. *Mem:* Inst Elec & Electronics Engrs; Am Soc Eng Educ; Am Vacuum Soc; AAAS; Am Soc Training & Develop. *Res:* Electrical and optical properties of amorphous, binary, non-stoichiometric, semiconducting thin films; professionalism in engineering; engineering ethics; continuing engineering education. *Mailing Add:* Iowa State Univ 303 Coover Hall Ames IA 50011

ANDERSON, RALPH ROBERT, DAIRY SCIENCE. *Current Pos:* RETIRED. *Personal Data:* b Fords, NJ, Nov 1, 32; m 61; c 2. *Educ:* Rutgers Univ, BS, 53, MS, 58; Univ Mo, PhD(endocrinol), 61. *Prof Exp:* Instr endocrinol, Univ Mo, 61-62; asst prof reproductive physiol, Iowa State Univ, 62-64; trainee endocrinol, Univ Wis, Madison, 64-65; from asst prof to assoc prof, Univ Mo, Columbia, 65-76, prof dairy sci, 76- *Concurrent Pos:* Sr Fulbright scholar, Ruakura, NZ, 73-74. *Mem:* Am Dairy Sci Asn; Am Soc Animal Sci; Soc Exp Biol & Med; Endocrine Soc; Soc Study Reproduction; Am Physiol Soc. *Res:* Endocrine control of mammary gland growth and lactation. *Mailing Add:* 2517 Shepard Blvd Columbia MO 65201

ANDERSON, RAYMOND KENNETH, WILDLIFE ECOLOGY. *Current Pos:* conserv, 58-61, PROF WILDLIFE, UNIV WIS-STEVENS POINT, 66- *Personal Data:* b White Lake, Wis, May 2, 28; m 53; c 4. *Educ:* Wis State Univ, Stevens Point, BS, 54; Univ Mich, MA, 58; Univ Wis, PhD(wildlife ecol), 69. *Prof Exp:* High sch instr, Wis, 54-58. *Mem:* Am Inst Biol Sci; Wilson Ornith Soc; Wildlife Soc. *Res:* Behavior and management of wild animals associated with grasslands; anuran inventory methods; habitat use, movements via radio-telemetry and behavior of wild mammals, birds, and amphibians; hunter behavior. *Mailing Add:* Dept Natural Resources Univ Wis Stevens Point WI 54481

ANDERSON, REBECCA JANE, neuropharmacology, neurotoxicology, for more information see previous edition

ANDERSON, RICHARD ALAN, ATOMIC & MOLECULAR PHYSICS. *Current Pos:* From asst prof to assoc prof, 58-69, PROF PHYSICS, UNIV MO, ROLLA, 69- *Personal Data:* b Rock Rapids, Iowa, Aug 9, 30; m 57; c 1. *Educ:* Augustana Col, BA, 52; Kans State Univ, MS, 54, PhD(physics), 59. *Mem:* Am Phys Soc; Am Asn Physics Teachers; Optical Soc Am; Soc Photo-Optical Instrumentation Engrs; Am Asn Univ Professors. *Res:* Lasers and optoelectronics; optical propagation of coherent and incoherent radiation; radiative transfer problems. *Mailing Add:* 403 S Adrian Rolla MO 65401

ANDERSON, RICHARD ALLEN, CHROMIUM & HUMAN HEALTH, NUTRITIONAL ROLE OF TRACE ELEMENTS. *Current Pos:* LEAD SCIENTIST, BELTSVILLE HUMAN NUTRIT RES CTR, USDA, 75-; ADJ VIS SCIENTIST, NAVAL MED RES INST, 89- *Personal Data:* b Middle River, Minn, May 28, 46; m 66, Sylvia Griffin; c Brent & Deborah. *Educ:* Concordia Col, BA, 68; Iowa State Univ, PhD(biochem), 73. *Honors & Awards:* Merit Awards, USDA, 83, 91 & 92; Labcatral Award, 91. *Prof Exp:* Res assoc biochem, Harvard Med Sch, 73-75. *Mem:* Am Inst Nutrit; Nat Audobon Soc; Int Soc Trace Element & Human Health; Am Col Nurtrit; Soc Int Nutrit Res; Am Soc Clin Nutrit. *Res:* Nutritional role of chromium in diabetes and cardiovascular diseases; role of chromium and other trace elements in controlling stress; role of trace element in exercise. *Mailing Add:* USDA Bldg 307 Rm 224 Human Nutrit Inst Beltsville MD 20705. *Fax:* 301-504-9062

ANDERSON, RICHARD CHARLES, GLACIAL GEOLOGY. *Current Pos:* prof geol, 65-96, chmn dept, 69-87, EMER PROF GEOL, AUGUSTANA COL, ILL, 96- *Personal Data:* b Moline, Ill, Apr 22, 30; m 53; c 3. *Educ:* Augustana Col, AB, 52; Univ Chicago, MS, 53, PhD(geol), 55. *Honors & Awards:* Neil Minor Award, Nat Asn Geol Teachers. *Prof Exp:* Geologist, Geophoto Servs, Colo, 55-57; from asst prof to assoc prof geol & geog, 57-65. *Concurrent Pos:* Res affil, Ill Geol Surv, 59-; asst dir, Earth Sci Summer Inst, Iowa State Univ, 66-71. *Mem:* Geol Soc Am; Am Geophys Union; Int Union Quaternary Res; Am Quaternary Asn; Am Meteorol Soc. *Res:* Glacial geology; geomorphology; Tertiary and Quaternary geomorphic history. *Mailing Add:* Dept Geol Augustana Col Rock Island IL 61201

ANDERSON, RICHARD DAVIS, MATHEMATICS. *Current Pos:* prof, 56-59, BOYD PROF MATH, LA STATE UNIV, BATON ROUGE, 59- *Personal Data:* b Hamden, Conn, Feb 17, 22; m 43; c 5. *Educ:* Univ Minn, BA, 41; Univ Tex, PhD(math), 48. *Prof Exp:* Instr math, Univ Tex, 41-42 & 45-48; from instr to assoc prof, Univ Pa, 48-56. *Concurrent Pos:* Inst Advan Study, 51-52 & 55-56; Alfred P Sloan res fel, 60-63; colleague, Mathematisch Centrum, Amsterdam, 62-63; panel mem, Sch Math Study Group & mem comt undergrad prog in math, chmn, 66-68. *Mem:* AAAS; Am Math Soc; Math Asn Am. *Res:* Topology; point set theory; collections of continua; dimension theory; transformation groups. *Mailing Add:* 2954 Fritchie Baton Rouge LA 70809-1501

ANDERSON, RICHARD ERNEST, INTEGRATED CIRCUIT FAILURE ANALYSIS. *Current Pos:* Mem tech staff, 74-81, supvr, 81-92, MGR, MICRO ELECTRONICS FAILURE ANALYSIS, SANDIA NAT LABS, 92- *Personal Data:* b Princeton, Ind, Mar 7, 45; m 67, Carolyn A Brock-Jones; c David R, James B & Sarah L. *Educ:* Univ Ill, Urbana, BS, 67, MS, 70, PhD(elec eng), 74. *Res:* Development of advanced failure analysis techniques for integrated circuits and other semiconductor components. *Mailing Add:* Sandia Nat Labs PO Box 5800 Albuquerque NM 87185-1081

ANDERSON, RICHARD GILPIN WOOD, CELL BIOLOGY. *Current Pos:* from asst prof to assoc prof, 73-81, PROF CELL BIOL, UNIV TEX HEALTH SCI CTR, DALLAS, 81- *Personal Data:* b Bryn Mawr, Pa, Mar 25, 40; m 64; c 2. *Educ:* Ore State Univ, BS, 65; Univ Ore Sch Med, PhD(anat), 70. *Prof Exp:* Res assoc reprod physiol, Ore Regional Primate Res Ctr, 70-73, asst scientist, 73. *Mem:* Am Asn Cell Biol; Am Asn Anat. *Res:* Receptor mediated endocytosis; structure and function of clathrin coated membrane; structure function of careulae; potocytosil and cell signaling. *Mailing Add:* Dept Cell Biol Univ Tex Southwestern Med Ctr 5323 Harry Hines Blvd Dallas TX 75235-9039. *Fax:* 214-648-7577

ANDERSON, RICHARD JOHN, ATOMIC PHYSICS. *Current Pos:* PROG MGR, EXP PROG STIMULATE COMPETITIVE RES, NSF, 89- *Personal Data:* b Chicago, Ill, June 11, 38; m 60; c 2. *Educ:* Coe Col, BA, 59; DePaul Univ, MS, 62; Univ Okla, PhD(physics), 66. *Prof Exp:* Appl physicist, Eastman Kodak Co, 61-62; from asst prof to prof physics, Univ Ark, Fayetteville, 66-89. *Concurrent Pos:* Dir hons studies, Univ Ark, Fayetteville, 82- *Mem:* Am Phys Soc; Am Asn Physics Teachers; Sigma Xi. *Res:* Spectroscopic investigation of electronic and atomic collision processes. *Mailing Add:* 2730 Franklin Ct Alexandria VA 22302-3019

ANDERSON, RICHARD L, EXPERIMENTAL STATISTICS. *Current Pos:* VPRES, CLIN TRIALS, INC, LEXINGTON. *Personal Data:* b North Liberty, Ind, Apr 20, 15; m 46, Mary Turner; c Kathryn & William. *Educ:* DePauw Univ, AB, 36; Iowa State Col, MS, 38, PhD(math statist), 41. *Prof Exp:* Asst math, Iowa State Col, 36-41; from instr to prof statist, Inst Statist, NC Univ, 41-66; res mathematician, Princeton Univ, 44-45; vis res prof statist, Univ Ga, 66-67; prof statist, Univ Ky, 67-80, chmn dept, 67-79, asst to dean, Col Agr, 80-85. *Concurrent Pos:* Consult, Off Sci Res & Develop, US Army & US Navy, 44-45; prof, Purdue Univ, 50-51 & London Sch Econ, 58; consult, Pan-Am World Airways Guided Missile Range Div, 63-67; partic, NSF-Japan Soc Promotion Sci Seminar Sampling of Bulk Mat, Tokyo, 65; pres, NE Am Region, Biomet Soc, 66; Inaugural Conf for Sci Comput Ctr, Univ Cairo, 69; mem adv bd, Int Math & Statist Libr, 71-; mem census adv comt, Am Statist Asn, 72-77; consult, Merrill Labs, 73-81, Health Sci Comput Ctr, Univ Calif, Los Angeles, 73-81; chmn, Sect U, AAAS, 79. *Mem:* Fel AAAS; fel Inst Math Statist; fel Am Statist Asn (pres-elect, 82, pres, 83); Int Statist Inst; Biomet Soc (pres, NE Am Region, 66); Int Asn Statist Comput. *Res:* Experimental designs and estimating procedures for variance components; time series analysis, including serial correlation; econometrics; regression analysis, selection of predictors, prior information, intersecting straight lines; linear-plateau models. *Mailing Add:* Clin Trials Inc Lexington 2365 Harrodsburg Rd Suite A290 Lexington KY 40504-3399. *Fax:* 606-224-2430

ANDERSON, RICHARD LEE, OPHTHALMOLOGICAL SURGERY. *Current Pos:* from asst prof to assoc prof ophthal plastic surg, Dept Ophthal, 76-84, PROF & CHIEF, DIV OPHTHAL, UNIV UTAH, 84- *Personal Data:* b Grinnell, Iowa, Feb 24, 45; m 65; c 2. *Educ:* Grinnell Col, BA, 67; Univ Iowa, MD, 71. *Prof Exp:* Resident ophthal, Univ Iowa, 72-75; fel plastic surg, Albany Med Ctr, 75 & Univ Calif Med Ctr, San Francisco, 76; Head fel, Head Ophthalmic Found, 76. *Concurrent Pos:* NSF grants, 65 & 66. *Mem:* Am Med Asn; fel Am Col Surgeons; fel Int Col Surgeons. *Res:* Acquired Ptosis, levator aponeurosis defects and their repair; nasolacrimal duct obstructions; anatomy of the levator muscle; blepharospasm eyelid and orbital tumors. *Mailing Add:* Univ Utah Hosp - Ophthal 1002 E South Temple No 308 Salt Lake City UT 84102-1525

ANDERSON, RICHARD LEE, CARBOHYDRATE METABOLISM, ENZYMOLOGY. *Current Pos:* NIH fel, 59-61, from asst prof to assoc prof, 61-70, PROF BIOCHEM, MICH STATE UNIV, 70- *Personal Data:* b Astoria, Ore, June 14, 33. *Educ:* Univ Wash, BS, 54, PhD(microbiol), 59. *Prof Exp:* Asst, Univ Wash, 54-59. *Concurrent Pos:* Ed, J Bact, 70-75. *Mem:* Am Chem Soc; Am Soc Microbiol; Am Soc Biochem & Molecular Biol; Soc Glycobiol. *Res:* Enzymology and metabolism of plants, animals and microorganisms; pathways, mechanisms and control of carbohydrate metabolism; carbohydrate binding proteins; expression of nuclear lectins in cultured fibroblasts. *Mailing Add:* Dept Biochem Mich State Univ East Lansing MI 48824-1319

ANDERSON, RICHARD LOUIS, METROLOGY, PHYSICAL CHEMISTRY. *Current Pos:* HEAD METEROL, RES & DEVELOP LAB, OAK RIDGE NAT LAB, 74-, GROUP LEADER MEASUREMENT RES, INSTRUMENTATION & CONTROLS DIV, 79-, CHIEF SCIENTIST. *Personal Data:* b Hale Center, Tex, Nov 27, 35; m 60; c 2. *Educ:* Mass Inst Technol, BS, 58; Rice Univ, PhD(chem), 66. *Honors & Awards:* IR-100 Award, 82, 87. *Prof Exp:* Res chemist, Heat Div, Nat Bur Standards, 63-71; scientist, Nat Phys-Tech Inst, Bur Standards, Brunswick, Germany, 71-74. *Concurrent Pos:* Res prof, Univ Tenn. *Mem:* Am Vacuum Soc; Sigma Xi; Inst Elec & Electronics Engrs; fel Am Phys Soc; Soc Photo-Optical Instrumentation Engrs; fel Instrument Soc Am. *Res:* Low temperature calorimetry and thermometry; gas thermometry; high temperature resistance thermometry; vacuum devices; pressure measurement; thermocouple thermometry; automated, precision measurements; microcomputers; computer graphics, ultrasonics. *Mailing Add:* 149 Whippoorwill Lane Oak Ridge TN 37830-8646

ANDERSON, RICHARD ORR, AQUATIC ECOLOGY. *Current Pos:* RETIRED. *Personal Data:* b Evanston, Ill, Oct 23, 29; m 51; c 2. *Educ:* Univ Wis, BS, 51; Univ Mich, MS, 53, PhD(fisheries), 59. *Honors & Awards:* Gulf Conservation Award, 84. *Prof Exp:* Fishery biologist, Mich Inst Fisheries Res, 52-58; instr, Dept Fisheries, Univ Mich, 58-59; biologist-in-charge, Wolf Lake Fish Hatchery, 59-63; leader, Mo Coop Fishery Res Unit, 63-85; dir, Nat Fish Hatchery & Technol Ctr, San Marcos, Tex, 85-89, sr scientist, 89-92. *Concurrent Pos:* Prof, Sch Forestry, Fisheries & Wildlife, Univ Mo, 63-85; vis grad fac, Tex A&M Univ, 87-92. *Mem:* Am Fisheries Soc. *Res:* Aquatic and fishery biology and ecology; fish production and growth; aquaculture. *Mailing Add:* 3618 Elms Ct Missouri City TX 77459

ANDERSON, RICHARD VERNON, ECOLOGY. *Current Pos:* from asst prof to assoc prof, 79-87, PROF, WESTERN ILL UNIV, MACOMB, 87-, DIR, KIBBE LIFE SCI FIELD STA, 87- *Personal Data:* b Julesburg, Colo, Sept 9, 46; m 71, Arline J Rosentreter; c Rustle R, Michael C & Theodore F. *Educ:* Northern Ill Univ, BS, 74, MS, 75; Colo State Univ, PhD, 78. *Prof Exp:* Fel, Nat Resource Ecol Lab, Colo State Univ, 78-79. *Concurrent Pos:* Grantee, NSF, Western Ill Univ, Upper Miss River Basin, Abbott Labs, Ill Dept Transp, Cent Ill Light Co, Nat Fish & Wildlife Serv/Ill Dept Conserv, Environ Consults & Planners, Booker Assocs, Ill Natural Hist Surv, Wetlands Res Inc & USDA, 72-92; environ consult, Aquatic Sect, Environ Consults & Planners, DeKalb, 74; vis asst prof, Inst Environ Studies, Water Resources Ctr, Univ Ill, 80; mem, Ecol Comt, Soc Nematologists, 81-82, Syst Resources Comt, 81-82; mem assoc fac, Argonne Nat Lab, 85-; assoc supportive scientist, Ill Natural Hist Surv, 85- *Mem:* Entom Soc Am; NAm Benthological Soc; Ecol Soc; Soc Nematologists; Int Cong Ecologists; Sigma Xi. *Res:* Invertebrate ecology; aquatic ecology with an emphasis on large river ecosystems, aquatic invertebrates and freeliving nematodes; effects of invertebrates on nutrient cycling; author of over 225 scientific publications. *Mailing Add:* Dept Biol Sci Western Ill Univ Macomb IL 61455. *Fax:* 309-298-2270; *E-Mail:* randerson@ccmail.wiu.edu

ANDERSON, ROBBIN COLYER, PHYSICAL CHEMISTRY. *Current Pos:* prof, 67-81, DEAN & EMER PROF CHEM, UNIV ARK, FAYETTEVILLE, 81- *Personal Data:* b DeRidder, La, June 8, 14; m 46, Marg Ball; c 3. *Educ:* La State Univ, BS, 34, MS, 36; Univ Wis, PhD(phys chem), 39. *Prof Exp:* From instr to prof chem, Univ Tex, Austin, 39-67, assoc dean grad sch, 66-67; dean, Col Arts & Sci, 67-79. *Concurrent Pos:* Mem adv coun col chem, AAAS, 63-66. *Mem:* AAAS; Am Chem Soc; Nat Sci Teachers Asn. *Res:* Complex ions; mechanism of flame propagation and carbon formation. *Mailing Add:* 1923 E Joyce C104 Fayetteville AR 72701

ANDERSON, ROBERT, ENVIRONMENTAL HEALTH & SAFETY. *Current Pos:* corp med dir, Manville Corp, 82-87, vpres health, safety & environ, 87-89, vpres sci & technol, 89-90, SR VPRES SCI & TECHNOL, SCHULLER INT INC, DENVER, 80- *Personal Data:* b Ft Sill, Okla, May 22, 44. *Educ:* George Washington Univ, MD, 70; Univ Tex, MPH, 74. *Prof Exp:* chief med servs, TWA, Kansas City, Kans, 76-81; med dir, Air Can, Montreal, 81-82. *Concurrent Pos:* Mem bd dirs, Rocky Mountain Mult Sclerosis Ctr, Denver, 91- *Mem:* AMA; Am Occup Health Asn; Am Col Prev Med; Aerospace Med Asn. *Res:* Health, safety and environment. *Mailing Add:* Schuller Int Inc PO Box 625005 Littleton CO 80162-5005

ANDERSON, ROBERT ALAN, DIELECTRIC BREAKDOWN, HYDROGEN IN SILICON. *Current Pos:* sr mem tech staff, 71-95, DISTINGUISHED MEM TECH STAFF, SANDIA NAT LABS, 95- *Personal Data:* b Princeton, Ind, Sept 14, 42; m 65, Constance White; c Angela & Michael. *Educ:* Univ Ill, Urbana, BS, 65, MS, 66, PhD(physics), 71. *Prof Exp:* Res asst & fel low-temperature physics, Univ Ill, Urbana, 67-71. *Mem:* Am Phys Soc. *Res:* Electrical breakdown, including insulator surface flashover in vacuum, breakdown of solid dielectrics, and high-field conduction mechanisms; piezoelectricity and pyroelectricity in polymers; kinetics of hydrogen in silicon; electrorheological fluids. *Mailing Add:* MS 0333 Sandia Nat Labs PO Box 5800 Albuquerque NM 87185-0333

ANDERSON, ROBERT AUTHUR, preventive medicine, health promotion, for more information see previous edition

ANDERSON, ROBERT CHRISTIAN, organic chemistry, for more information see previous edition

ANDERSON, ROBERT CLARK, METALLURGICAL ENGINEERING. *Current Pos:* RETIRED. *Personal Data:* b Galesburg, Ill, July 18, 26; m; c 2. *Educ:* Univ Ill, BS, 51. *Prof Exp:* Trainee, Sheffield Steel Div, Armco Steel Corp, 51-52; chief metallurgist, WKM Co Div, ACF Industs, 52-57; pres, Anderson & Assocs, Inc, 57-79. *Concurrent Pos:* Consult, NASA Manned Spacecraft Ctr, 68- *Mem:* Nat Soc Prof Engrs; fel Am Soc Metals; Am Inst Mining, Metall & Petrol Engrs; Nat Asn Corrosion Engrs; Int Metallog Soc. *Res:* Analyzing metal failures; application of scientific analysis to resolution of legal problems. *Mailing Add:* PO Box 1107 Pearland TX 77588-1107

ANDERSON, ROBERT CLARKE, TOXICOLOGY. *Current Pos:* RETIRED. *Personal Data:* b Salem, Ind, Feb 19, 11; m 34; c 3. *Educ:* Purdue Univ, BS, 31, DSc, 53. *Prof Exp:* Lab asst, Eli Lilly & Co, 31-34, pharmacologist, 34-36, head dept toxicol, 46-61, dir toxicol div, 61-66, dir res biol, 66-70, dir res toxicol, 70-72. *Mem:* AAAS; Am Pharmaceut Asn (secy-treas, 58-64); Am Soc Toxicol; Am Soc Pharmacol & Therapeut. *Res:* Toxicology of antibiotics, analgesics, steroids and pesticides. *Mailing Add:* 2028 Titleist Way Indianapolis IN 46229-4319

ANDERSON, ROBERT CURTIS, ENTOMOLOGY. *Current Pos:* from asst prof to assoc prof, 69-82, chmn dept, 74-82, PROF BIOL, IDAHO STATE UNIV, 82 - *Personal Data:* b Columbus, Ohio, May 10, 41; m 67, Marianne; c Arah & April. *Educ:* Calif State Col, Long Beach, BS, 63; Purdue Univ, MS, 66, PhD(entom), 68. *Prof Exp:* Instr entom, Purdue Univ, 68-69. *Concurrent Pos:* Sr Fulbright scholar, Egypt, 83-84; adv coun, Environ Health Sci, NIH, 85-90. *Mem:* AAAS; Sigma Xi; Entom Soc Am. *Res:* Biology and ecology of insect parasites, Scorpionida, Acarina; biological control; medical entomology; applied ecology; invertebrate zoology; parasitology. *Mailing Add:* Dept Biol Idaho State Univ 921 S 8th Ave Pocatello ID 83209-0001. *Fax:* 208-236-4570

ANDERSON, ROBERT E(DWIN), electrical engineering, education; deceased, see previous edition for last biography

ANDERSON, ROBERT E, SOLID STATE PHYSICS. *Current Pos:* chmn dept, 66-77, PROF PHYSICS, SOUTHWEST TEX STATE UNIV, 66- *Personal Data:* b Carrizo Springs, Tex, Aug 26, 26; m 47; c 3. *Educ:* Tex Col Arts & Indust, BS, 47, MS, 49; Univ Tex, PhD(physics), 55. *Prof Exp:* Teacher math & physics, San Antonio Jr Col, 49-52; asst physics, Univ Tex, 52-55; res engr, Tex Instruments, Inc, 55-57; co res fel low temperature physics, Univ Tex, 57-58; prof physics, Tex Col Arts & Indust, 58-66. *Concurrent Pos:* Res asst, Defense Res Lab, Tex, 54-55; consult, Tex Instruments, Inc, 60- *Mem:* Am Asn Physics Teachers. *Res:* Semiconductor physics; electronics; vacuum techniques; acoustics; transistor design. *Mailing Add:* Rte 1 Box 596-B Cedar Creek TX 78612

ANDERSON, ROBERT E, biochemistry, ophthalmology, for more information see previous edition

ANDERSON, ROBERT EDWIN, PATHOLOGY. *Current Pos:* asst prof, 64-69, PROF PATH, SCH MED, UNIV NMEX, 69-, CHMN DEPT, 68- *Personal Data:* b Los Angeles, Calif, Aug 20, 31; m 53; c 3. *Educ:* Col Wooster, BA, 53; Western Reserve Univ, MD, 57. *Prof Exp:* Intern med, Strong-Mem-Rochester Munic Hosps, NY, 57-58; resident path, Univ Hosps, Cleveland, Ohio, 58-59; resident, Med Ctr, Univ Calif, Los Angeles, 59-62, from instr to asst prof, 60-64, consult, Clin Labs, 60-62. *Concurrent Pos:* Consult, Community Blood & Plasma Inc, 61-62 & Bernalillo County Indian Hosp, NMex, 64- *Mem:* AAAS; Am Asn Pathologists; Am Soc Exp Path; Am Asn Path & Bact (secy-treas, 74-); Asn Path Chmn (pres, 75). *Res:* Hematologic pathology; radiation in the immune response. *Mailing Add:* Dept Path Univ Minn Health Ctr Box 609 420 Delaware St SE Minneapolis MN 55455-0385

ANDERSON, ROBERT EMRA, WATER CHEMISTRY, ION EXCHANGE. *Current Pos:* group leader ion exchange, 68-78, SR RES SCIENTIST, DIAMOND SHAMROCK CHEM CO, 78- *Personal Data:* b Mentone, Ind, Jan 6, 24; m 45; c 2. *Educ:* Ind Univ, BS, 49, MA, 51. *Prof Exp:* Chemist, Dow Chem Co, 50-54, proj leader ion exchange, 54-56, group leader, 56-68. *Concurrent Pos:* Chmn, Gordon Res Conf Ion Exchange, AAAS, 71. *Mem:* Am Chem Soc; Sigma Xi. *Res:* Study of ion exchange and ion-exchange resins, particularly as applied to water treatment and industrial processing. *Mailing Add:* 1617 Wright Ave Sunnyvale CA 94087-5251

ANDERSON, ROBERT GLENN, plant genetics, plant breeding, for more information see previous edition

ANDERSON, ROBERT HUNT, COMPUTER SCIENCE, CHEMISTRY. *Current Pos:* RETIRED. *Personal Data:* b Kansas City, Kans, Oct 20, 24; m 50, Yoko M Omura; c Tomio, Dale W, Lynda, Joseph H, Kimiko & Robert O. *Educ:* Baker Univ, AB, 46; Columbia Univ, MA, 48, PhD(chem), 54. *Prof Exp:* Instr chem, Bloomfield Col, 51-56; asst res specialist, Rutgers Univ, 56-57; from asst prof to prof chem, Western Mich Univ, 57-89. *Mem:* AAAS; Am Chem Soc; NY Acad Sci. *Res:* Neutron spectroscopy in chemical analysis; phase rule; corrosion inhibitors; computers in chemistry. *Mailing Add:* Dept Chem Western Mich Univ Kalamazoo MI 49008-3804. *Fax:* 616-387-2909

ANDERSON, ROBERT L, biochemistry, nutrition, for more information see previous edition

ANDERSON, ROBERT LESTER, PHYSICS INSTRUMENTATION. *Current Pos:* AT DEPT PHYSICS, UNIV GA. *Personal Data:* b Parkersburg, WVa, Dec 30, 33; m 56; c 4. *Educ:* Marietta Col, AB, 55; Pa State Univ, MS, 59, PhD(physics), 61. *Prof Exp:* From asst prof to assoc prof physics, Marietta Col, 61-71, head dept, 66-77, prof, 71- *Mem:* AAAS; Am Phys Soc; Am Asn Physics Teachers. *Res:* Viscosity and density of pure hydrocarbon liquids at moderately elevated pressures; electrical and thermal transport properties of metals and semiconductors. *Mailing Add:* Dept Physics Univ Ga Physics Bldg Athens GA 30602

ANDERSON, ROBERT LEWIS, BIOCHEMISTRY, PROTEIN CHEMISTRY. *Current Pos:* BIOCHEMIST, NAT CTR AGR UTILIZATION RES, USDA, 57- *Personal Data:* b Springfield, Ill, Sept 30, 33; m 55; c 3. *Educ:* Bradley Univ, BS, 55, MS, 67; Univ Nebr, PhD, 86. *Concurrent Pos:* Res asst, Univ Nebr, 67-70. *Mem:* Am Chem Soc; Am Asn Cereal Chem; Inst Food Technol; Sigma Xi. *Res:* Soybean proteins; electrophoresis. *Mailing Add:* 400 S Mississippi Ave Morton IL 61550

ANDERSON, ROBERT NEIL, CHEMICAL ENGINEERING, METALLURGICAL ENGINEERING. *Current Pos:* assoc prof metall, 75-78, chmn dept mat eng, 84-86, PROF METALL, SAN JOSE STATE UNIV, 78- *Personal Data:* b San Jose, Calif, Nov 8, 33; m 65; c 2. *Educ:* Univ San Francisco, BS, 56; Univ Calif, Berkeley, BS, 58, MS, 59; Stanford Univ, PhD(metall), 69. *Prof Exp:* Res engr, US Naval Radiol Defense Lab, 59-66, opers res analyst, 66-69; res metallurgist, Stanford Univ, 69-73. *Concurrent Pos:* Consult, 69-; actg assoc prof, Stanford Univ, 73-76. *Mem:* Am Chem Soc; Am Inst Chem Engrs; Am Soc Metals; Am Inst Mining, Metall & Petrol Engrs; Am Nuclear Soc. *Res:* Physical metallurgy; chemical metallurgy; high temperature chemistry; chemical thermodynamics and kinetics; forensic engineering. *Mailing Add:* 27820 Saddle Ct Los Altos Hills CA 94022-1810

ANDERSON, ROBERT PHILIP, GENETICS. *Current Pos:* from asst prof to assoc prof, 81-92, PROF GENETICS, UNIV WIS-MADISON, 92- *Personal Data:* b Norwood, Mass, Aug 28, 50; m 72; c 2. *Educ:* Johns Hopkins Univ, BA, 72; Univ Calif, Berkeley, PhD(molecular biol), 77. *Prof Exp:* Fel, Lab Molecular Biol, Med Res Coun, Cambridge, Eng, 78-81. *Mailing Add:* Dept Genetics Univ Wis 445 Henry Mall Madison WI 53706

ANDERSON, ROBERT SIMPERS, IMMUNOTOXICOLOGY, COMPARATIVE IMMUNOLOGY. *Current Pos:* PROF IMMUNOTOXICOL, CHESAPEAKE BIOL LAB, UNIV MD, 86- *Personal Data:* b Bryn Mawr, Pa, Jan 4, 39; m 64, Lucy A MacDonald; c Robert S Jr & Donald P. *Educ:* Drexel Univ, Philadelphia, Pa, BS, 61; Hahnemann Med Univ, MS, 68; Univ Del, Newark, Del, PhD(immunol), 71. *Honors & Awards:* Except Performance Award, US Army, 84, 86, Outstanding In-House Lab Independent Res Award, 86. *Prof Exp:* Fel comp immunol, dept path, Univ Minn, 70-73; asst mem, Sloan-Kettering Inst Cancer Res, 73-82; asst prof, Cornell Univ Grad Sch Med Sci, 75-82; immunologist immunotoxicol, US Army Chem Res & Develop Ctr, Aberdeen Proving Ground, 82-86. *Concurrent Pos:* Mem, Comt Animal Models & Genetic Stocks, Nat Res Coun, Nat Acad Sci, 77-79; actg ed-in-chief, J Develop & Comp Immunol, 77-83 & 93-, J Invert Path, 86-87, Reviews in Aquatic, 86-92, Rev Fisheries Sci, 93-; mem, Trop Med & Parasitol Study Sect, (AHR), NIH, 85-91. *Mem:* Am Asn Immunologists; Int Soc Develop & Comp Immunol; Soc Invert Path (secy, 89-91, trustee, 92-96); Sigma Xi; Soc Toxicol; Soc Leuboryte Biol. *Res:* Immunotoxicology; effects of xenobiotics on the immune response of aquatic invertebrates and fish; bacterial and parasitici diseases of aquatic species; use of immunostimulants and vaccines in disease prevention during aquaculture procedures. *Mailing Add:* Chesapeake Biol Lab Univ Md Box 38 Solomons MD 20688-0038. *E-Mail:* anderson@cbl.umd.edu

ANDERSON, ROGER, INTERNET COMMERCE, DATABASE CONSTRUCTION. *Current Pos:* PRES & CHIEF EXEC OFFICER, ANDERSON UNICOM GROUP INC, 96- *Personal Data:* b Nyack, NY, May 9, 60; m 84; c 2. *Educ:* Univ Calif, San Diego, BA, 87; Calif Inst Technol, PhD(biol), 96. *Prof Exp:* consult, Ciphergen Biosysts Inc, 95. *Res:* web based order placement systems with a detailed product database for lifescience and biotech researchers. *Mailing Add:* 18200 Yorba Linda Blvd Suite 101 Yorba Linda CA 92886

ANDERSON, ROGER ARTHUR, botany, biology; deceased, see previous edition for last biography

ANDERSON, ROGER CLARK, BOTANY, ECOLOGY. *Current Pos:* assoc prof, 76-80, PROF BIOL, ILL STATE UNIV, 80-, DISTINGUISHED PROF BIOL, 94- *Personal Data:* b Wausau, Wis, Oct 30, 41; m 67, Mary R Blocher; c John A & Nancy L. *Educ:* Wis State Univ, La Crosse, BS, 63; Univ Wis-Madison, MS, 65, PhD(bot), 68. *Prof Exp:* Asst prof bot, Southern Ill Univ, Carbondale, 68-70; asst prof bot & managing dir arboretum, Univ Wis-Madison, 70-73, assoc prof, 73; assoc prof biol, Cent State Univ, Okla, 73-76. *Concurrent Pos:* Vis assoc prof, Univ Okla Biol Sta, 74, 75 & 79, Univ Mich Biol Sta, 80; consult, Metrop Sanitary Dist Great Chicago, 77-81, Kerr McGee Corp, 85; mem, Environ Adv Comt, Fermi Nat Accelerator Lab; Ill Nature Preserve Comnr, 85-90. *Mem:* Ecol Soc Am; Sigma Xi; Bot Soc Am; Soc Ecol Restoration; Natural Areas Asn; AAAS. *Res:* Plant community ecology including studies of prairie plants and their associated mycorrhizal fungi; role of fire in prairies and savannas, restoration of native plant communities. *Mailing Add:* Dept Biol Campus Box 4120 Ill State Univ Normal IL 61790-4120. *Fax:* 309-438-3722

ANDERSON, ROGER E, PHYSICAL CHEMISTRY, COMPUTER SCIENCES. *Current Pos:* CHEMIST, LAWRENCE RADIATION LAB, UNIV CALIF, LIVERMORE, 59-, AT LAWRENCE LIVERMORE NAT LAB. *Personal Data:* b Donovan, Ill, May 14, 30; m 59; c 2. *Educ:* Univ Ill, BS, 51; Wash State Univ, PhD(phys chem), 61. *Mem:* Inst Elec & Electronics Eng; Asn Comput Mach; Sigma Xi. *Res:* Instrumentation; laboratory automation; on-line computer utilization; data processing techniques; minicomputer systems analysis. *Mailing Add:* 4354 Guilford Ave Livermore CA 94550

ANDERSON, ROGER FABIAN, FOREST ENTOMOLOGY. *Current Pos:* assoc prof, 50-59, prof, 59-80, EMER PROF FOREST ENTOM, DUKE UNIV, 80- *Personal Data:* b St Paul, Minn, Sept 14, 14; m 50; c 2. *Educ:* Univ Minn, PhD(entom), 45. *Honors & Awards:* A D Hopkins Award, 83. *Prof Exp:* Entomologist, USDA, 40-48; asst prof entom, Univ Ga, 49-50. *Mem:* Entom Soc Am. *Res:* Ecology of forest insects; biology, behavior, and physiological relation between boring insects and host trees; pollution damage to trees by acid rain and other toxins. *Mailing Add:* 2528 Perkins Rd Durham NC 27706

ANDERSON, ROGER HARRIS, LOW TEMPERATURE PHYSICS, MANY-FERMION PROBLEM. *Current Pos:* PROF PHYSICS, DEPT PHYSICS, SEATTLE PAC UNIV, 61- *Personal Data:* b Seattle, Wash, Feb 3, 30; wid; c John K & Linda K. *Educ:* Univ Wash, BSc, 51, PhD(physics), 61. *Prof Exp:* Asst, Univ Wash, 52-58; res scientist, Boeing Co, 58-61. *Concurrent Pos:* NSF sci fac fel, Univ Ill, 68-69; sr scientist, Gulf Res, 78. *Mem:* Am Phys Soc; Am Asn Physics Teachers. *Res:* Electron self-energies in solids; calculation of thermal properties of monomolecular layers of liquid helium-3; transport phenomena in Landau theory of Fermi liquids; spin-polarized Fermi systems; 2-Dim Helium-3 systems. *Mailing Add:* Dept Physics Seattle Pac Univ Seattle WA 98119. *Fax:* 206-281-2882; *E-Mail:* rha@spu.edu

ANDERSON, ROGER W(HITING), PHYSICAL CHEMISTRY, CHEMICAL ENGINEERING. *Current Pos:* Develop staff mem II, 48-50, res & develop group leader enrichment technol, 50-69, CONSULT TO PLANT DIV, MAT & SYSTS DEVELOP DEPT, GASEOUS DIFFUSION PLANT, NUCLEAR DIV, UNION CARBIDE CORP, 69-; CONSULT, MARTIN MARIETTA ENERGY SYSTS, 92- *Personal Data:* b Minneapolis, Minn, July 2, 24; m 50, Mary E Throgmorton; c Melissa J. *Educ:* Univ Minn, BChEng, 48; Univ Tenn, PhD(phys chem), 63. *Honors & Awards:* R&D 100 Award, 91. *Concurrent Pos:* Res & develop scientist, Martin Marietta Energy Systs, Oak Ridge, Tenn; pres, Knoxville Chap, United Scleroderma Found. *Mem:* Am Chem Soc; Sigma Xi; AAAS. *Res:* Colloid, surface, and electrochemistry; isotope exchange; gas-solid reactions; ion exchange; water treatment; adsorption; Waste treatment electroless nickel and copper bath recycling; corrosion inhibition. *Mailing Add:* 304 Boundary Lane Knoxville TN 37922-3810

ANDERSON, ROGER W, PHYSICAL CHEMISTRY. *Current Pos:* from asst prof to assoc prof, 69-91, PROF CHEM, UNIV CALIF, SANTA CRUZ, 91- *Personal Data:* b Fargo, NDak, Jan 9, 43; m 82, Myrna; c Kirsten & Lenore. *Educ:* Carleton Col, BA, 64; Harvard Univ, MA, 65, PhD(chem), 68. *Mem:* AAAS; Am Phys Soc; Sigma Xi; Am Chem Soc. *Res:* Photo-activated CVD; simulation of sputtering deposition; nucleation and cluster growth; point-of-use synthesis of hazardous compounds; fractal structure of molecules; discrete bases in quantum mechanics. *Mailing Add:* 311 Dickens Way Univ Calif Santa Cruz CA 95064-1065. *Fax:* 408-459-2935; *E-Mail:* anderso@cats.ucsc.edu

ANDERSON, ROGER YATES, GEOLOGY. *Current Pos:* from instr to assoc prof, 56-74, PROF GEOL, UNIV NMEX, 74- *Personal Data:* b Oak Park, Ill, Oct 4, 27; m 48; c 4. *Educ:* Univ Ariz, BS, 54, MS, 55; Stanford Univ, PhD, 60. *Prof Exp:* Asst biochem, Univ Ariz, 55-56. *Concurrent Pos:* NSF prin investr varve res. *Res:* Paleoecology; palynology; varves. *Mailing Add:* Dept Geol Univ NMex Main Campus 1 University Campus Albuquerque NM 87131-0001

ANDERSON, ROLAND CARL, optical systems, interferometry, for more information see previous edition

ANDERSON, RON JOE, HEALTHCARE ADMINISTRATION. *Current Pos:* asst prof internal med, 76-81, asst dean clin affairs, 79-82, PROF INTERNAL MED, UNIV TEX HEALTH SCI CTR, 81-; CHIEF EXEC OFFICER, PARKLAND HEALTH & HOSP SYST, 82- *Personal Data:* b Chickasha, Okla, Sept 6, 46; m 75, Sue A Blakely; c Sarah E, Daniel J & John C. *Educ:* SW Univ Okla, BS, 69; Univ Okla, MD, 73; Am Bd Internal Med, dipl; Am Bd Geriat, dipl. *Honors & Awards:* James E Peavy Mem Award, Tex Pub Health Asn, 88; Safety Net Award, Nat Asn Pub Hosps, 90. *Prof Exp:* Intern, Univ Tex Southwestern Med Sch, Parkland Mem Hosp & Vet Admin Hosp, Dallas, 73-74, resident & chief resident internal med, 74-76; med dir ambulatory-emergency servs, Dallas Co Hosp Dist, 79-82, actg med dir, 81-82. *Concurrent Pos:* Consult high blood pressure, Am Heart Asn, 81-83; mem, Dallas Coun Alcoholism & Drug Abuse, 82; mem, Task Force Teaching Hosps, Tex Hosp Asn, 82-, Task Force Indigent Health Care, 83-86; mem, Tex Bd Health, 83-, chmn, 83-87 & 91-; mem, Tex Gov's Task Force Indigent Health Care, 83-86; mem, Tex Cancer Coun, 85-87; mem, Ment Health Comn Community Care of Mentally Ill, Hogg Found, 87- *Mem:* Inst Med-Nat Acad Sci; fel Am Col Physicians; AMA; Nat Pub Health & Hosp Inst; Am Soc Internal Med; Soc Gen Internal Med. *Mailing Add:* Dallas Co Hosp Dist Parkland Mem Hosp 5201 Harry Hines Blvd Dallas TX 75235-7708

ANDERSON, RONALD E, COMPUTER SCIENCE, COMPUTER APPLICATIONS. *Current Pos:* PROF SOCIOL, UNIV MINN, 68- *Personal Data:* b Sikeston, Mo, June 14, 41; m 90, Nancy Kehmeier; c Gina M & Evan E. *Educ:* Stanford Univ, PhD(sociol), 70. *Honors & Awards:* Outstanding Contrib Microcomput, Am Sociol Asn, 92. *Concurrent Pos:* Mem coun & chair, Spec Interest Group Comput & Soc, Asn Comput Mach, 87-93 & chair, Task Force Rev Code Ethics, 90-93. *Mem:* Asn Comput Mach; Am Sociol Asn; Am Educ Res Asn; Am Pub Opinion Res Asn; Am Statist Asn. *Res:* International and national studies of computer use in education, computer literacy performance assessment, and equity in access to information technology. *Mailing Add:* Dept Sociol 909 Sociol Sci Bldg Univ Minn 267 19th Ave S Minneapolis MN 55455. *Fax:* 612-624-4586; *E-Mail:* rea@vx.cis.umn.edu

ANDERSON, RONALD EUGENE, GENETICS, PLANT BREEDING. *Current Pos:* from asst prof to assoc prof, 54-88, EMER PROF PLANT BREEDING & BIOMET, CORNELL UNIV, 88- *Personal Data:* b Sioux City, Iowa, Sept 15, 20; m 48, Jean Burr; c Susan, Scott, Carol & Burr. *Educ:* Univ Nebr, BS, 48; Univ Wis, MS, 49, PhD(genetics), 52. *Prof Exp:* Asst prof agron, Univ Ky, 52-54. *Res:* Cytology; breeding of forage crops species; effects of radiation on forage species. *Mailing Add:* 252 Emerson Hall Plant Breed Cornell Univ Main Campus Ithaca NY 14853-0001

ANDERSON, RONALD KEITH, NUCLEAR PHYSICS, ACOUSTICS. *Current Pos:* instr, 65-68, asst prof, 71-73, ASSOC PROF PHYSICS & CHMN DEPT, BEMIDJI STATE UNIV, 73- *Personal Data:* b Duluth, Minn, Sept 12, 41; m 66; c 2. *Educ:* Augustana Col, SDak, BA, 63; SDak Sch Mines & Technol, MS, 65; Univ Kans, PhD(nuclear physics), 71. *Prof Exp:* Inst physics, SDak Sch Mines & Technol, 63-65. *Mem:* Am Phys Soc; Audio Eng Soc; Am Asn Physics Teachers; Sigma Xi. *Res:* Theoretical low-energy nuclear structure; isobaric spin; acoustics-vibrations and its engineering applications. *Mailing Add:* Dept Physics Bemidji State Univ 1500 Birchmont Dr NE Bemidji MN 56601-2699

ANDERSON, RONALD M, HYDROLOGY & WATER RESOURCES. *Current Pos:* PROF & CHMN MATH DEPT, TEX TECH UNIV, 65- *Personal Data:* b Mower County, Minn, Nov 14, 35. *Educ:* Luther Col, BA, 57; Iowa State Univ, MS, 59, PhD(math), 62. *Prof Exp:* Collins Radio Co, 62-65. *Mem:* Am Math Soc; Soc Indust & Appl Math; Math Asn Am. *Res:* Porous media, with application to water uptake in plants; solar power. *Mailing Add:* 3104 76th St Lubbock TX 79423-1311

ANDERSON, ROSALIND COOGAN, COMBUSTION TOXICOLOGY, INHALATION TOXICOLOGY. *Current Pos:* PRES, ANDERSON LABS INC, 88- *Personal Data:* b Cleveland, Ohio; m 63; c 3. *Educ:* Mt Holyoke Col, BA, 59; Yale Univ, MA, 64, PhD(physiol), 65. *Prof Exp:* Res assoc endocrinol, Sch Med, Yale Univ, 65-68; assoc prof physiol, Duquesne Univ, 70-75; res assoc toxicol, Grad Sch Pub Health, Univ Pittsburgh, 76-79; head toxicol unit, Arthur D Little Inc, 79-87. *Concurrent Pos:* Nat Acad Sci Comt Fire Toxicol. *Mem:* Am Soc Testing & Mat; Nat Fire Protection Asn; Soc Toxicol. *Res:* Developing methods for the evaluation of the effects of inhalation exposure to products of thermal decomposition; application of combustion toxicology to building codes; health effects of indoor air pollution. *Mailing Add:* Anderson Labs Inc Box 323 West Hartford VT 05084

ANDERSON, ROY CLAYTON, PARASITOLOGY. *Current Pos:* chmn dept, 79-89, prof, 65-92, EMER PROF ZOOL, UNIV GUELPH, 92- *Personal Data:* b Camrose, Alta, Apr 26, 26; m 48, Phyllis; c 2. *Educ:* Univ Alta, BSc, 50; Univ Toronto, MA, 52, PhD(parasitol), 56; Sch Advan Studies, Paris, dipl helminth, 58. *Honors & Awards:* Henry Baldwin Ward Medal, Am Soc Parasitol, 68; Distinguished Serv Award, Wildlife Dis Asn, 78; Wardle Medal, Can Soc Zoologists, 88; Dirs Award, Friends of Algonquin Park, 92. *Prof Exp:* Sr res scientist parasitol, Ont Res Found, 54-65. *Concurrent Pos:* Fel Rothmansted Exp Sta, London Sch Hyg & Trop Med, 56-57; med fac, Univ Paris, 57-58. *Mem:* Am Soc Parasitol; Wildlife Dis Asn; Sigma Xi; Wildlife Soc; Royal Soc Trop Med & Hyg; Can Soc Zoologist; hon mem Helminthological Soc. *Res:* Nematode parasites, their systematics, development, transmission and pathology with special reference to those on vertebrate animals. *Mailing Add:* Dept Zool Univ Guelph Guelph ON N1G 2W1 Can

ANDERSON, ROY E, EXPERIMENTAL DEMONSTRATION OF CONCEPTS FEASIBILITY, TECHNICAL & REGULATORY STANDARDS. *Current Pos:* RETIRED. *Personal Data:* b Batavia, Ill, Oct 30, 18; m 43, Gladys Nelson; c Paul, David, Barbara & Dorothy. *Educ:* Augustana Col, Ill, BA, 43; Union Col, MSEE, 52. *Prof Exp:* Physics instr, Augustana Col, 43-44 & 46-47; consult engr, Corp Res & Develop, Gen Elec Co, 47-83; co-founder & vpres, Mobile Satellite Corp, 83-88; owner & pres, Anderson & Assocs, 88-91. *Concurrent Pos:* Coolidge fel, Gen Elec Co, 70; pres, Rega Assocs Inc, 93- *Mem:* Fel Inst Elec & Electronics Engrs; fel AAAS; Am Inst Aeronaut & Astronaut; Soc Satellite Prof Int; Inst Navig. *Res:* Development of concepts and systems engineering of mobile satellite communications and position fixing systems for land, aeronautical and maritime users. *Mailing Add:* PO Box 2531 Glenville NY 12325-2531. *Fax:* 518-384-1211

ANDERSON, RUSSELL D, ENTOMOLOGY, INVERTEBRATE ZOOLOGY. *Current Pos:* RETIRED. *Personal Data:* b Salt Lake City, Utah, Dec 27, 27; m 58; c 3. *Educ:* Univ Utah, BS, 54, MS, 56, PhD(entom), 61. *Prof Exp:* Entomologist, South Salt Lake County Mosquito Abatement Dist, 55-58; from instr to assoc prof zool, Church Col, Hawaii, 58-64, head, Dept Biol Sci, 59-64; from asst prof to prof zool, Southern Utah State Col, 64-, head, Dept Life Sci, 81- *Concurrent Pos:* Consult environ impact statements. *Mem:* AAAS; Entom Soc Am. *Res:* Taxonomy of the Dytiscidae; revisionary study of the genus Hygrotus. *Mailing Add:* 449 Circle Way Dr Cedar City UT 84720

ANDERSON, RUSSELL K, ANIMAL NUTRITION, PHYSIOLOGY. *Current Pos:* from asst prof to prof, 55-91, EMER PROF ANIMAL SCI, CALIF POLYTECH STATE UNIV, SAN LUIS OBISPO, 91- *Personal Data:* b LeRoy, Minn, Mar 13, 24; m 48, Judy Potter; c Linda L & David K. *Educ:* Univ Minn, BS, 48; Iowa State Univ, MS, 50, PhD(animal nutrit), 56. *Prof Exp:* Instr animal sci, Iowa State Univ, 48-55. *Mem:* Am Soc Animal Sci; Sigma Xi. *Res:* Ruminant nutrition; mineral requirement for rumen microorganisms and sources of phosphorus. *Mailing Add:* 520 Cuesta Dr San Luis Obispo CA 93405

ANDERSON, RUTH MAPES, nursing, for more information see previous edition

ANDERSON, SABRA SULLIVAN, MATHEMATICS, EDUCATION ADMINISTRATION. *Current Pos:* PROF MATH, UNIV MICH, 82-, ASSOC DEAN, COL SCI & ENG, 87- *Personal Data:* b Philadephia, Pa, June 10, 39; m 65; c 2. *Educ:* Smith Col, AB, 61; Univ Mich, MA, 63. *Prof Exp:* Fulbright fel, Univ Manchester, Eng, 61-62; res fel math, Inst Social Res, Univ Mich, 65-66; asst prof, Eastern Mich Univ, 66-69. *Concurrent Pos:* Vis scholar math, Western Mich Univ, 79 & Stanford Univ, 80; assoc ed, Math Asn Am, 83-86. *Mem:* Am Math Soc; Math Asn Am; Asn Women Am; Asn Women Sci; Sigma Xi. *Res:* Discrete math specifically finite graph theory; combinatorial and algebraic problems. *Mailing Add:* Col Sci & Eng Univ Minn Duluth 140 Eng Duluth MN 55812

ANDERSON, SAMUEL, ANALYTICAL CHEMISTRY, INORGANIC CHEMISTRY. *Current Pos:* PROF CHEM, NORFOLK STATE COL, 63- *Personal Data:* b Clarksdale, Miss, Aug 26, 34; m 65; c 2. *Educ:* Univ Mo, Kansas City, BS, 57; Iowa State Univ, MS, 60, PhD(analytical chem), 62. *Prof Exp:* Asst prof chem, Tenn State Univ, 62-63. *Concurrent Pos:* Res partic, NSF, 64-65. *Mem:* Am Chem Soc; Sigma Xi. *Res:* Preparation, physical and chemical properties of vanadium B-diketone complexes; evaluation of an immobilized chelate for extraction of metal ions from solutions. *Mailing Add:* Dept Chem Norfolk State Col 2401 Coppnew Ave Norfolk VA 23504-3989

ANDERSON, SCOTT, ELECTROLUMINESCENCE. *Current Pos:* PHYSICS CONSULT, APL, INC, 83- *Personal Data:* b Johnsonville, Ill, June 26, 13; m 41; c 5. *Educ:* Ill Wesleyan Univ, BS, 35; Univ Ill, MS, 36, PhD(physics), 40. *Hon Degrees:* Ill Wesleyan Univ, DSc,60. *Prof Exp:* Asst prof physics, Carleton Col, 43-44; physicist, Aluminum Res Labs, 40-43; sub-consult, Univ Chicago Metall Lab, 44-45; owner & dir, Anderson Physics Labs, 44-83. *Mem:* Fel Am Phys Soc; Am Ceramic Soc; Optical Soc Am; AAAS. *Res:* Purification of salts; other problems relating to metal halide lamps; author of journal publications. *Mailing Add:* 1116 W Church St Champaign IL 61821

ANDERSON, SONIA R, BIOCHEMISTRY, BIOPHYSICS. *Current Pos:* from asst prof to assoc prof, 68-81, PROF, ORE STATE UNIV, 81- *Personal Data:* b Omaha, Nebr, Mar 14, 39. *Educ:* Univ Nebr, BS, 61; Univ Ill, PhD(biochem), 64. *Prof Exp:* Postdoctoral, Univ Ill, 64-67, Univ Rome, Italy, 67-68. *Concurrent Pos:* Vis asst prof, Univ Ill, 68; res grant, USPHS, 70-, res career develop award, 70-75; mem, bd sci counselors, Nat Heart, Lung & Blood Inst, NIH, 91- *Mem:* Am Soc Biol Chemists; Protein Soc; AAAS; Sigma Xi. *Res:* Biophysical characterization of physiologically relevant protein-protein interactions; fluorescence spectroscopy; associations of glycolytic enzymes with contractile proteins; calcium-dependent protein kinases; calmodulin; polypeptide hormones and neurotransmitters; venom peptides; author or co-author of over 50 publications. *Mailing Add:* Dept Biochem & Biophys Ore State Univ Corvallis OR 97331-6503

ANDERSON, STANLEY H, ECOLOGY, ENVIRONMENTAL SCIENCES. *Current Pos:* MAT SCIENTIST & PROG MGR, SRI INT, 78-; LEADER, WYO COOP, FISH & WILDLIFE UNIT, LARAMIE, 80- *Personal Data:* b San Francisco, Calif, Aug 6, 39; m 65; c 2. *Educ:* Univ Redlands, BSc, 61; Ore State Univ, MA, 68, DrPhil(ecol), 70. *Prof Exp:* Asst prof biol, Kenyon Col, 70-75; ecologist, Oak Ridge Assoc Univs, 75-76. *Concurrent Pos:* Regist prof metall engr, Calif. *Mem:* AAAS; Am Inst Biol Sci; Am Ornith Union; Am Defense Preparedness Asn; Ecol Soc Am. *Res:* Community interaction of avifauna; determination of effects of habitat alteration on vertebrate populations. *Mailing Add:* 1062 Arapaho Dr Laramie WY 82070. *Fax:* 307-766-5400; *E-Mail:* anderson@uwyo.edu

ANDERSON, STANLEY ROBERT, AGRONOMY. *Current Pos:* RETIRED. *Personal Data:* b Rudyard, Mich, Mar 11, 20; m 46; c 3. *Educ:* Mich State Col, BS, 46, MS, 49; Iowa State Col, PhD, 54. *Prof Exp:* Field rep, Mich Crop Improv Asn, Mich State Col, 46-49; instr pub schs, Mich, 49-50; instr agron, Iowa State Col, 50-54; from asst prof to prof, Ohio State Univ, 54-67; dean agr, Tex A&I Univ, 67-75; pres, Abraham Baldwin Agr Col, 75-85. *Concurrent Pos:* Chmn, Am Asn Univ Agr Adminr, 75. *Mem:* Am Soc Agron; Crop Sci Soc Am. *Res:* Crop production; management and utilization of pasture and forage establishment. *Mailing Add:* 1815 Columbine Pl Ruskin FL 33573-5053

ANDERSON, STEVEN CLEMENT, SYSTEMATICS, ECOLOGY. *Current Pos:* from asst prof to assoc prof, 70-80, PROF BIOL & ENVIRON SCI, UNIV PACIFIC, 80- *Personal Data:* b Grand Canyon Nat Park, Ariz, Sept 7, 36; m 60, Kay Bratsch; c Malcolm. *Educ:* Univ Calif, Riverside, BA, 57; San Francisco State Col, MA, 62; Stanford Univ, PhD(biol), 66. *Prof Exp:* Lab technician entom, Univ Calif, Riverside, 60; res asst herpet, Calif Acad Sci, 63-64, from asst cur to assoc cur, 64-70. *Concurrent Pos:* Vis res assoc, Iran Dept Environ, 75-79; res assoc, Calif Acad Sci, 77-; consult ed, Encycl Iranica, 77- *Mem:* Am Soc Ichthyol & Herpetol; Soc Study Amphibians & Reptiles; fel Herpetologists League; AAAS; Sigma Xi. *Res:* Systematics, ecology, zoogeography of amphibians and reptiles of Southwest Asia. *Mailing Add:* Dept Biol Sci Univ Pacific Stockton CA 95211. *E-Mail:* sanderson@vms1.cc.uop.edu

ANDERSON, STEVEN WILLIAM, PHOTOCHEMISTRY, POLYMER CHEMISTRY. *Current Pos:* asst prof, 87-92, dept chair, 93-96, ASSOC PROF CHEM, UNIV WIS, WHITEWATER, 92- *Personal Data:* b Evanston, Ill, Apr 3, 56. *Educ:* Carthage Col, BA, 78; Marquette Univ, MS, 81; Northern Ill Univ, PhD(chem), 85. *Prof Exp:* Lab technician, Universal Oil Prod, 77, res chemist, 78; postdoctoral res fel gen & org chem, Univ Toronto, 84-87, lectr, 86-87. *Concurrent Pos:* Coun Undergrad Res. *Mem:* Sigma Xi; Am Chem Soc; Inter-Am Photochem Soc. *Res:* Thermal solvolytic reactions; cationic and anionic photoinitiators for polymerizations; solvent nucleophilicity in the excited state. *Mailing Add:* Dept Chem Univ Wis-Whitewater 800 W Main St Whitewater WI 53190-1790. *E-Mail:* andersos@uwwvax.uww.edu

ANDERSON, SUE ANN DEBES, NUTRITION, FOOD SAFETY. *Current Pos:* SR STAFF SCIENTIST, LIFE SCI RES OFF, FEDN AM SOCS EXP BIOL, 78- *Personal Data:* b Harrisburg, Ill, Jan 8, 47; m 78; c 2. *Educ:* Univ Ill, BS, 69; Auburn Univ, MS, 72; Purdue Univ, PhD(nutrit), 74. *Prof Exp:* Res home economist sensory eval, Armour Food Res Labs, 69-70; asst prof nutrit, Sch Home Econ, Auburn Univ, 75-78. *Concurrent Pos:* Adj prof, Va Polytech Inst & State Univ, 87. *Mem:* Am Inst Nutrit; Am Dietetic Asn. *Res:* Nutrition and public health; food safety issues. *Mailing Add:* Off Spec Nutritionals Food & Drug Admin 200 St SW Washington DC 20204-0001

ANDERSON, SYDNEY, VERTEBRATE ZOOLOGY. *Current Pos:* from asst cur to cur, 60-92, EMER CUR, AM MUS NATURAL HIST, 92- *Personal Data:* b Topeka, Kans, Jan 11, 27; m 51, R Justine Klusmire; c Evelyn L, Charles S & Laura L. *Educ:* Univ Kans, AB, 50, MA, 52, PhD, 59. *Honors & Awards:* Jackson Award, Am Soc Mammal, 85. *Prof Exp:* NSF fel, 52-54; asst cur mammals, Mus Natural Hist, Kans, 54-59. *Concurrent Pos:* Instr, Univ Kans, 54-59; consult, Bk Div, Time, Inc & C S Hammond Co. *Mem:* Fel AAAS; hon mem Am Soc Mammal; Am Ornith Union; Am Inst Biol sci. *Res:* Distribution, variation and relationships of mammals; instrumentation and methodology; bibliography and information retrieval. *Mailing Add:* Am Mus Natural Hist Central Park W 79th St New York NY 10024. *E-Mail:* syd@2mnh.org

ANDERSON, TED L, CELL BIOLOGY, GENE EXPRESSION. *Current Pos:* GYNEC RESIDENT, MED CTR, VANDERBILT UNIV, 93- *Educ:* Univ Southern Miss, BS, 76, MS, 78; Vanderbilt Med Sch, PhD, 85. *Prof Exp:* Res assoc, Baylor Col Med, 85-86; instr, Eastern Va Med Sch, 86-88, asst prof reproductive biol, 88-89. *Mem:* Am Soc Cell Biol. *Res:* Hormone action in the uterus. *Mailing Add:* R-1214 Med Ctr N Vanderbilt Univ Nashville TN 37232-2521

ANDERSON, TERA LOUGENIA, DATABASE MANAGEMENT SYSTEMS. *Current Pos:* DIR, ENTERPRISES SOLUTIONS, 93- *Personal Data:* b Dothan, Ala, Nov 26, 49; m 79; c 1. *Educ:* Univ Wash, BS (physics) & BS(math), 73, MS, 77, PhD(comput sci), 81. *Prof Exp:* Mgr info mgt res, Austin Res Ctr, Burroughs Corp, 80-85; prin scientist, Tektronix, Inc, 85-91; prog mgr object tech, Sequent Comput Systs Inc, 91-93. *Concurrent Pos:* Adj fac mem, Ore Grad Ctr. *Mem:* Asn Comput Mach. *Res:* Data models and data semantics for database management systems; object-oriented database management; representation of time in information systems; description of user interfaces for database management systems; CAO/CAM databases. *Mailing Add:* Sequent Comput Systs Inc 15450 SW Koll Pkwy Beaverton OR 97006

ANDERSON, TERRY LEE, THEORETICAL PHYSICS, COMPUTER SCIENCE. *Current Pos:* mem tech staff, AT&T Bell Labs, 86-96, DISTINGUISHED MEM TECH STAFF, LUCENT TECHNOL BELL LABS, 96- *Personal Data:* b Lincoln, Nebr, Sept 11, 47; m 71, Janice Hanson; c Katherine. *Educ:* Pac Union Col, BS, 69, MA, 69; Univ Neb, Lincoln, MS, 72, PhD(physics), 75. *Prof Exp:* Asst instr physics, Univ Nebr, Lincoln, 69-72; from instr to assoc prof, Walla Walla Col, 72-81, prof physics & comput sci, 81-86, chmn, Dept Comput Sci, 79-86. *Mem:* Am Asn Physics Teachers; Am Phys Soc; Asn Comput Mach; Soc Computer Simulation. *Res:* Computer languages; instructional computer software; theoretical relativistic astrophysics; properties of ice nucleation; learning theory applied to science instruction and application of computers to science instruction. *Mailing Add:* 24 Hill St Bernardsville NJ 07924. *Fax:* 908-582-7988; *E-Mail:* tla@bell_labs.com

ANDERSON, TERRY ROSS, SOIL BORNE DISEASE, BIOLOGICAL CONTROL. *Current Pos:* RES SCIENTIST, AGR CAN, 78- *Personal Data:* b Newmarket, Ont, April 8, 44; m 68, Candace Bassett; c Emily & Laura. *Educ:* Univ Guelph, BSA, 69; Univ Hawaii, MSc, 75; Univ Toronto, PhD(plant path), 79. *Mem:* Am Phytopath Soc; Can Phytopath Soc. *Res:* Mycophagous amoeboid organisms in soil; control of phytophtora rot phytophthora rot, sclerotinia stem decay and seed mould of soybean. *Mailing Add:* Agr & Agr Food Can Res Sta Harrow ON N0R 1G0 Can

ANDERSON, THEODORE E, CHEMISTRY & ORGANIC CHEMISTRY, MICROBIOLOGY. *Current Pos:* RETIRED. *Personal Data:* b Dallas, Tex, 1929. *Educ:* Univ Mich, BS, 53; Mich State Univ, MS, 58, PhD(microbiol), 63. *Prof Exp:* Chemist qual control, Miles Lab, 69-79, Diversey Corp, Mich, 79-81. *Mem:* Am Chem Soc; Am Soc Qual Control. *Mailing Add:* 8534 Manchester Rd Grosse Ile MI 48138-1850

ANDERSON, THEODORE WILBUR, MATHEMATICAL STATISTICS, ECONOMETRICS. *Current Pos:* prof, 67-88, EMER PROF STATIST & ECON, STANFORD UNIV, 88- *Personal Data:* b Minneapolis, Minn, June 5, 18; m 50, Dorothy Fisher; c Robert L, Janet L & Jeanne E. *Educ:* Northwestern Univ, BS, 39; Princeton Univ, MA, 42, PhD(math), 45. *Hon Degrees:* DL, N Park Col & Theol Sem, 88; DSc, Northwestern Univ, 89. *Honors & Awards:* R A Fisher Award, 85; S S Wilks Medal, 88. *Prof Exp:* Asst math, Northwestern Univ, 39-40; instr, Princeton Univ, 41-43; res assoc, Appl Math Panel Contract, Nat Defense Res Comt, 43-45 & Cowles Comn, Chicago, Ill, 45-46; from instr to prof math statist, Columbia Univ, 46-67. *Concurrent Pos:* Consult, Cowles Found, 46-60, Bur Appl Social Res, New York, 47 & Rand Corp, 49-66; Guggenheim fel, Univ Stockholm & Cambridge Univ, 47-48; ed, Ann Math Statist, 50-52; vis assoc prof, Stanford Univ, 54; mem, Nat Acad Sci-Nat Res Coun Comt Basic Res, adv to Off Ord Res, 55-58; fel, Ctr Advan Study Behav Sci, 57-58; actg exec officer, Columbia Univ, 50-51 & 63, chmn, dept math statist, 56-60 & 64-65; mem, comt statist, Nat Res Coun, 60-63, chmn, 61-63, comt pres statist soc, 62-64; mem, Nat Acad Sci-Nat Res Coun Panel Appl Math, adv to Nat Bur Stand, 64-65; mem, comt support res math sci, Nat Acad Sci, 65-68; acad vis, Imp Col, Univ London, & vis prof, Univs Moscow & Paris, 67-68; vis scholar, Ctr Advan Study Behav Sci, 72-73 & 80; sci dir, Advan Study Inst Discriminant Analysis & Its Appln, NATO, Kifissia, Greece, 72; acad vis, London Sch Econ & Polit Sci, 74-75; Wesley C Mitchell vis prof econ, Columbia Univ & NY Univ, 83-84; IBM Systems Res Inst, 84; Sherman Fairchild distinguished scholar, Calif Inst Technol, 80; res assoc, Naval Postgrad Sch, 86-87. *Mem:* Nat Acad Sci; Inst Math Statist (pres, 63); Am Math Soc; fel Am Statist Asn (vpres, 71-73); fel Economet Soc; Am Acad Arts Sci; Psycmet Soc; AAAS; Norweg Acad Sci & Lett. *Res:* Multivariate statistical analysis; time series analysis; theory of statistical inference; econometric methodology. *Mailing Add:* Dept Statist Stanford Univ Stanford CA 94305-4065. *Fax:* 650-725-8977; *E-Mail:* twa@stat.stanf.edu

ANDERSON, THOMAS ALEXANDER, BIOCHEMISTRY, NUTRITION. *Current Pos:* RETIRED. *Personal Data:* b Elkhart, Ind, Feb 23, 28; m 52; c 2. *Educ:* Univ Wash, BA, 50; Calif State Polytech Col, BS, 56; Univ Ariz, MS, 61, PhD(agr biochem & nutrit), 62. *Prof Exp:* Sr scientist, Sci Info Dept, Smith, Kline & French Labs, Pa, 62-63; asst prof biochem, Univ SDak, 63-65; chief nutrit res lab, H J Heinz Co, 65-70; from assoc prof to prof pediat, Col Med, Univ Iowa, 70-85. *Concurrent Pos:* Partic, White House Conf Food, Nutrit & Health, 69. *Mem:* AAAS; Am Chem Soc; Am Soc Clin Nutrit; Brit Nutrit Soc; Am Soc Animal Sci. *Res:* Pediatric nutrition,especially influence of the pattern of food intake on body composition and digestibility of complex carbohydrates by the human infant. *Mailing Add:* 10921 W Roundelay Circle Sun City AZ 85351

ANDERSON, THOMAS EDWARD, NEUROSCIENCE, NEUROPHYSIOLOGY. *Current Pos:* from asst sr res scientist to staff res scientist, 79-86, SR STAFF RES SCIENTIST & SECT MGR NEUROL SYST, BIOMED SCI DEPT, GEN MOTORS RES LABS, WARREN, 86-, MGR TECHNOL TRANSFER & COMMERCIALIZATION. *Personal Data:* b Evergreen Park, Ill, Dec 9, 47; m 71, Nita Gociehtly; c 3. *Educ:* Hamline Univ, BA, 68; Univ Tex, Austin, MA, 71; Univ Mich, Ann Arbor, PhD(neurosci), 77. *Prof Exp:* Fel neurobiol, Dept Zool, Univ Tex, Austin, 77-79. *Concurrent Pos:* Vis asst prof, Col Eng, Wayne State Univ, 80-84, adj prof bioeng, 84- *Mem:* Soc Neurosci; Sigma Xi; AAAS; Am Asn Automotive Med; Bioelectromagnetic Soc; Neurotrauma Soc (pres, 91-92). *Res:* Study of mechanisms for progressive pathology and dysfunction following brain or spinal cord traumatic injury; neurotoxic effects and mechanisms; biomedical effects of non-ionizing electromagnetic radiation. *Mailing Add:* Technol Bus Develop Gen Motors Res & Develop Ctr 30500 Mound Rd Warren MI 48090. *Fax:* 810-986-0294; *E-Mail:* tanderso@cmsa.gmr.com

ANDERSON, THOMAS ERNEST, PESTICIDE DEVELOPMENT, PEST MANAGEMENT. *Current Pos:* INSECTICIDE GROUP LEADER, BASF CORP, 85- *Personal Data:* b Chicago, Ill, Jan 28, 52; m 77, Susan Eckenbeck; c Gwynneth & Kirsten. *Educ:* Univ Ill, Urbana, BS, 74, MS, 77; NC State Univ, PhD(entom), 81. *Prof Exp:* Teaching asst, Dept Entom, Univ Ill, 74-77; res asst, NC Agr Exp Sta, 77-81; asst entomologist, Boyce Thompson Inst Plant Res, 81-85. *Concurrent Pos:* Pres, NC Entom Soc, 91; mem, Insecticide Resistance Action Comt. *Mem:* Entom Soc Am; Sigma Xi; AAAS; Soc Invert Path. *Res:* Discovery and development of new insecticides and nematicides; bioassays of microbial insecticides; investigations of entomopathogen-pesticide interactions in pest management systems. *Mailing Add:* BASF Corp PO Box 13528 Research Triangle Park NC 27709-3528

ANDERSON, THOMAS FRANK, GEOCHEMISTRY. *Current Pos:* asst prof, 67-73, assoc prof, Geol, 73-82, assoc dean, Col Lib Arts & Sci, 87-90, PROF GEOL, UNIV ILL, URBANA, 82- *Personal Data:* b Chicago, Ill, Dec 7, 39; m 63. *Educ:* DePauw Univ, BA, 61; Columbia Univ, PhD(geochem), 67. *Prof Exp:* Res assoc geochem, Enrico Fermi Inst, Univ Chicago, 67-68. *Concurrent Pos:* Exchange scientist, NSF and Nat Ctr Sci Res, France, 75-76; vis res lectr, Univ Leicester (UK), 84; vis prof, Chengdu Col Geol, 86. *Mem:* AAAS; Am Geophys Union; Geochem Soc; Geol Soc Am; Sigma Xi. *Res:* Stable isotope geochemistry; geochemistry of sediments and natural waters. *Mailing Add:* 2116 Burlison Dr Urbana IL 61801

ANDERSON, THOMAS PATRICK, MECHANICAL ENGINEERING. *Current Pos:* PROF ENG & DEAN, SCH SCI & ENG, SOUTHERN ILL UNIV, EDWARDSVILLE, 78- *Personal Data:* b Chicago, Ill, Oct 22, 34; m 60; c 2. *Educ:* Northwestern Univ, BSME, 56, MS, 58, PhD(mech eng), 61. *Prof Exp:* Assoc prof mech eng & astron sci, Northwestern Univ, 58-66; prof mech eng, Univ Iowa, 66-75, chmn dept, 66-70; dir indust prog, NSF, 74-78. *Concurrent Pos:* Assoc dir interdept energy study, US Off Sci & Technol, 63-65. *Mem:* AAAS; Am Inst Aeronaut & Astronaut; Am Phys Soc; Am Soc Mech Engrs; Sigma Xi. *Res:* Gas dynamics; thermodynamics; magnetohydrodynamics; energy. *Mailing Add:* Sch Sci & Eng Southern Ill Univ Edwardsville IL 62026-1805

ANDERSON, TIMOTHY J, MATERIAL SCIENCE. *Current Pos:* PROF & CHMN, DEPT CHEM ENG, UNIV FLA. *Honors & Awards:* Charles M A Stine Award, Am Inst Chem Engrs, 94. *Mailing Add:* Chem Eng Dept Univ Fla Gainesville FL 32611

ANDERSON, TODD ALAN, ENVIRONMENTAL TOXICOLOGY, ENVIRONMENTAL FATE. *Current Pos:* ASST PROF, TIWET, CLEMSON UNIV, 96- *Personal Data:* b Alma, Nebr, Nov 4, 63; m 93, Brenda F Pawling. *Educ:* Peru State Col, BS, 86; Univ Tenn, Knoxville, MS, 88, PhD(environ toxicol), 91. *Prof Exp:* US Dept Energy fel, Oak Ridge Nat Lab, 89-91; fel, Iowa State Univ, 92-93, res assoc, Pesticide Toxicol Lab, 93-96. *Mem:* Soc Environ Toxicol & Chem; Am Soc Microbiol; AAAS. *Res:* Fate and effects of organic contaminants in terrestrial systems. *Mailing Add:* One Tiwet Dr Clemson Univ Pendleton SC 29670. *E-Mail:* etox@iastate.edu

ANDERSON, VICTOR CHARLES, UNDERWATER ACOUSTICS. *Current Pos:* RETIRED. *Personal Data:* b Shanghai, China, Mar 31, 22; m 43, Anne Dowden; c Mary, Victor Jr & Judith. *Educ:* Univ Redlands, AB, 43; Univ Calif, Los Angeles, MA, 50, PhD(physics), 53. *Honors & Awards:* Adm Charles D Martell Tech Excellence Award, Inst Elec & Electronics Engrs, 86, Oceanic Eng Soc Distinguished Tech Achievement Award, 89; Silver Medal Underwater Acoust & Eng Acoust, Acoust Soc Am, 92. *Prof Exp:* Tech asst, Radiation Lab, Univ Calif, 43-45; asst, Los Alamos, NMex, 45-46 & Univ Calif, Los Angeles, 46-47; from asst res physicist to res physicist, Scripps Inst, Univ Calif, San Diego, 47-68, actg dir, Marine Physical Lab, 64, 68 & 74, prof appl physics & assoc dir Marine Physical Lab, 68-90. *Concurrent Pos:* Res fel, Harvard Univ, 54-55. *Mem:* Fel Acoust Soc Am; Inst Elec & Electronics Engrs. *Res:* Acoustics; experimental and theoretical work in field of underwater sound and electronics; methods and instrumentation for digital signal processing; remotely controlled sea floor work systems. *Mailing Add:* 1562 Viejas Creek Trail Rd Alpine CA 91901-2351

ANDERSON, VICTOR ELVING, HUMAN GENETICS, BEHAVIORAL GENETICS. *Current Pos:* asst scientist, Univ Minn, 49-54, asst dir, Dight Inst Human Genetics, 54-78, actg dir, 78-84, assoc prof zool, 61-65, assoc prof genetics, 65-66, PROF GENETICS, UNIV MINN, MINNEAPOLIS, 66- *Personal Data:* b Stromsburg, Nebr, Sept 6, 21; m 46; c 4. *Educ:* Univ Minn, BA, 45, MS, 49, PhD(zool), 53. *Prof Exp:* From instr to prof biol, Bethel Col, Minn, 46-60, chmn dept, 52-60; vis scientist, NIH, 60-61. *Concurrent Pos:* Regent, Bethel Col & Seminary, St Paul, 69-74 & 82-87; mem, Develop Behav Sci Study Sect, NIH, 72-75, chmn, 74-75. *Mem:* Fel AAAS; Am Sci Affil (pres, 63-65); Am Soc Human Genetics; Behav Genetics Asn (secy, 72-74, pres 79-80); Sigma Xi (pres, 82-83). *Res:* Genetic factors in epilepsy, mental retardation, psychotic disorders, and other human behavioral problems. *Mailing Add:* Box 197 Univ Minn Health Ctr 1-210 Moos Tower 420 Delaware St SE Minneapolis MN 55455-0381

ANDERSON, VIRGIL LEE, MATHEMATICS, STATISTICS. *Current Pos:* From asst prof to assoc prof statist, 51-60, dir statist lab, 56-66, PROF STATIST, PURDUE UNIV, WEST LAFAYETTE, 60- *Personal Data:* b North Liberty, Ind, May 2, 22; m 43; c 3. *Educ:* Iowa State Univ, BS, 47, PhD(statist), 53. *Concurrent Pos:* Statist consult to var govt, mil & pvt orgn, 58- *Mem:* Fel Am Statist Asn; Biomet Soc. *Res:* Quantitative genetics; design of experiments; transportation; environmental effects of cadmium. *Mailing Add:* Dept Statist 1399 Math Sci Bldg Purdue Univ West Lafayette IN 47907-1399

ANDERSON, W FRENCH, BIOCHEMISTRY & MEDICINE, GENETICS. *Current Pos:* DIR GENE THER LABS, SCH MED, UNIV SOUTHERN CALIF, 92-, PROF BIOCHEM & PEDIAT, 92- *Personal Data:* b Tulsa, Okla, Dec 31, 36; m 61. *Educ:* Harvard Univ, AB, 58, MD, 63; Cambridge Univ, MA, 60. *Hon Degrees:* LHD, Univ Okla, 92. *Honors & Awards:* Sci Achievement Biol Sci Award, Wash Acad Sci, 71; Thomas B Cooley Award Sci Achievement, Cooley's Anemia Blood & Res Found Children, 77; Mary Ann Liebert Biotherapeut Award, 91; President's Award lectr, Am Thoracic Soc, 91; Maude L Menten, Univ Pittsburgh; Mider Lectr, NIH, 92; Myron Karon Mem Lectr, Children's Hosp Los Angeles, 92; Martin Mem Lectr, 79th Annual Cong Am Col Surgeons, 93; Dr Murray Thelin Award, Nat Hemophilia Found, 93; King Faisal Int Prize Med, 94. *Prof Exp:* Intern pediat med, Childrens Hosp Med Ctr, Boston, 63-64; res assoc, Lab Biochem Genetics, Nat Heart, Lung & Blood Inst, 65-67, res med officer, 67-68, head, Sect Human Biochem, 68-71 & Sect Molecular Hemat, 71-73, chief, Molecular Hemat Br, 73-92 chief, Lab Molecular Hemat, 77-92; Full Mem, Norris Comprehensive Cancer Ctr, 92-; Mem, Inst Genetic Med, 92- *Concurrent Pos:* Am Cancer Soc res fel bact & immunol, Harvard Med Sch, 64-65; vol asst, Childrens Hosp Med Ctr, 64-65; prof lectr, Sch Med, George Washington Univ, 67-75; mem fac, Dept Genetics, NIH Grad Prog, 67-, fac, Dept Med & Physiol, 81- & chmn, 84-; mem heart fel bd, Nat Heart & Lung Inst, 68-70; mem task force hemoglobinopathies, Nat Heart, Lung & Blood Inst, NIH, 72, Nat Task Group on Cooley's Anemia, 77-78, pres, Assembly Scientists, 82; chmn, Inter-Inst Coord Comt on Cooley's Anemia, NIH, 72-77; mem hemoglobin subcomt, Am Soc Hemat, 72-74; mem Med Resources Coun, Cooley's Anemia Blood & Res Found for Children, 74-77; chmn, Inter-Agency Coord Comt on Cooley's Anemia, HEW, 75-77; med adv bd, Cooley's Anemia Found, Inc, 77-; mem, Coun Acad Socs, Asn Am Med Col, 77-80, Ad Hoc Adv Group, Inst Med, Nat Acad Sci, 84, Exec Comt Bd Dirs, Found Adv Ed in Sci, Inc, NIH, 84-, Working Group Human Gene Ther, Recombinant DNA Adv Comt, 84-87 & Working Group on Viruses, 85, Sci Adv Comt, Children's Hosp Res Found, Cincinnati, Ohio, 85-89; sr exec sci serv, Dept Health & Human Serv, 80-; consult, Pres Comn Study Ethical Probs Med & Biomed Behav Res, 81-82, Human Gene Ther Ctr for Bioehtics, Kennedy Inst Ethics, Washington, DC, 82-; hemat prog dir, Lab Molecular Hemat, Nat Heart, Lung & Blood Inst, NIH-George Washington Univ-Vet Med Ctr, 85; chmn, Sci Adv Bd, Genetic Ther Inc, Gaithersburg, Md, 86-87; sci adv bd, S/L Health Care Ventures, NY, 86-88; mem, NIH Coord Comt Human Genome, 88-92; consult Human Gene Therapy: St Jude Childrens Res Hosp, Memphis Tenn, 90-92 & Univ Pittsburgh, Pittsburgh, 90-92; chmn, Res Adv Coun, Children's Nat Med Ctr, Washington, DC, 90-92; Outstanding Performance Award, Huguenot Historical Soc, 82, 84-90; mem, Comt Social & Ethical Imact Biomed Soc, Nat Acad Sci, 90; consult, Genetic Ther, Inc, Gaithersburg, Md, 92- *Mem:* Asn Am Physicians; Am Soc Clin Invest; Am Soc Hemat; Am Soc Human Genetics; Am Soc Biol Chem; Am Fedn Clin Res; fel AAAS. *Res:* Human biochemical genetics; hematology; regulation of RNA and protein synthesis; hemoglobin biosynthesis; thalassemia and hemoglobinopathies; gene expression in mammalian cells; genetic engineering of mammalian cells; human gene therapy; first HGT protocol for ADA. *Mailing Add:* Univ Southern Calif Gene Ther Labs Norris Cancer Ctr 1441 Eastlake Ave Rm 612 Los Angeles CA 90033. *Fax:* 213-342-3618

ANDERSON, W(ENDELL) L, CHEMICAL ENGINEERING. *Current Pos:* RETIRED. *Personal Data:* b Altoona, Pa, Sept 8, 22; m 45, Shirley Smith; c Larry & Wendell. *Educ:* Pa State Univ, BS, 44. *Honors & Awards:* Kratel Award, Ger, 70; Mark Hollingsworth Award, Tech Asn Pulp & Paper, 95. *Prof Exp:* Sect head aerosols, Naval Res Lab, 44-71; dept head & assoc tech dir, Naval Surface Weapons Ctr, 71-83. *Concurrent Pos:* Indust consult; vis lectr. *Mem:* Am Chem Soc; Am Asn Contamination Control; Sci Res Soc Am; Am Filtration Soc. *Res:* Aerosols, filters, microfibers, chemical biological warfare, light scattering; air pollution contamination control; ion effects; naval weapons; technical management. *Mailing Add:* 9254 Mimosa Dr La Plata MD 20646

ANDERSON, W ROBERT, PULMONARY PATHOLOGY, RENAL PATHOLOGY. *Current Pos:* chmn, Dept Path, 84-95, STAFF PATHOLOGIST, HENNIPEN CO MED CTR, 95-; PROF PATH, UNIV MINN, 67- *Personal Data:* c 6. *Educ:* Univ Pa, MD, 58. *Mem:* Col Am Pathologists; Int Acad Path; Am Asn Path; Sigma Xi. *Res:* Electron-microscopy; surgical pathology. *Mailing Add:* Dept Path Hennipen Co Med Ctr 701 Park Ave Minneapolis MN 55415-1623. *Fax:* 612-347-3125

ANDERSON, WALLACE ERVIN, PHYSICS. *Current Pos:* RETIRED. *Personal Data:* b Florence County, SC, Oct 28, 13; m 39; c 2. *Educ:* The Citadel, BS, 34; Univ Ky, MS, 36; Univ Mich, PhD(physics), 49. *Hon Degrees:* DSc, The Citadel, 81. *Honors & Awards:* Legion of Merit, 46. *Prof Exp:* From asst prof to prof physics, The Citadel, 36-66, head dept, 53-66, acad dean, 66-70, vpres acad affairs, 70-79, interim pres, 78-79. *Mem:* Am Phys Soc; Am Asn Physics Teachers; Am Soc Eng Educ. *Res:* Infrared and microwave spectroscopy; determination of molecular structure; optics. *Mailing Add:* 11 Country Club Dr Charleston SC 29412

ANDERSON, WALLACE L(EE), ELECTRICAL ENGINEERING, PHYSICS. *Current Pos:* chmn dept, 72-77, PROF ELEC ENG, UNIV HOUSTON, 69- *Personal Data:* b Adams, NDak, Sept 2, 22; m 56, 73, Claire Corley; c Julie R & Cristina A. *Educ:* Univ NDak, BS, 48; Rice Univ, MA, 57; Univ NMex, ScD(elec eng), 61. *Prof Exp:* Seismog operator, McCollum Explor Co, Tex, 48-50, seismog party mgr, 50-51, res engr, 54-55; res assoc elec eng, Univ NMex, 57-60, lectr, 60-61; assoc prof, NY Univ, 61-64; sr res engr, Southwest Res Inst, 64-68, staff scientist, 68-69. *Mem:* Am Phys Soc; Inst Elec & Electronics Engrs; Optical Soc Am. *Res:* Coherent optics; optical information processing; biomedical engineering; electromagnetic and acoustic wave propagation; holographic particle velocimetry; optical matched filtering; signal processing. *Mailing Add:* Dept Elec Eng Univ Houston 4800 Calhoun Houston TX 77204-4793. *Fax:* 713-743-4444; *E-Mail:* wanderson@uh.edu

ANDERSON, WALTER L(EONARD), ELECTRONICS, TECHNICAL MANAGEMENT. *Current Pos:* CONSULT, 90- *Personal Data:* b St Paul, Minn, Aug 6, 22; 46, Catherine; c David, Douglas, Dale & Donald. *Educ:* Univ Minn, BEE, 44, MS, 48. *Honors & Awards:* Chester Morrill Mem Award, Am Systs Mgt, 80; Supreme Achievement Award, Interagency Comt ADP, 82; Centennial Award, Inst Elect & Electronics Engrs, 84. *Prof Exp:* Asst, Univ Minn, 43-44; staff elec engr, Eng Res Assoc Div, Remington Rand, Inc, 46-55; vpres opers, Gen Kinetics, Inc, 55-63, exec vpres & chmn bd dirs, 63-65, pres, 65-74; from assoc dir to sr assoc dir, US Gen Acct Off, 74-85, sr adv, 85-90. *Concurrent Pos:* Dir, Comput Test Corp, 62-66, Tape Serv Co, 63-67, Ocean Space Systs, 64-68, Allo Precision Metals Eng, Inc, 65-67, Food Technol Corp, 66-74 & Nat Instrument Labs, Inc, 68-72; data processing consult, Fairfax Hosp, 64-65; dir, Am Fedn Info Processing Socs, 62-66, mem exec comt, 64-66, chmn admissions comt, 66-68, mem financial comt, 68-71, vpres, 71-72, pres, 73-74; mem, Info Systs Coun, Am Mgt Asn, 75-87; Europ community fel, German Marshall Fund, 79. *Mem:* Inst Elec & Electronics Engrs; Asn Comput Mach. *Res:* Electronic digital computers and communication systems; digital test systems. *Mailing Add:* 2427 Lexington Rd Falls Church VA 22043. *Fax:* 703-237-3216

ANDERSON, WALTER T(HEODORE), ELECTRICAL ENGINEERING. *Current Pos:* RETIRED. *Personal Data:* b Iron River, Mich, Mar 30, 23; m 45; c 8. *Educ:* Mich Technol Univ, BS, 43, MS, 50. *Honors & Awards:* Distinguished Serv Award, Nat Coun Eng Examrs, 78. *Prof Exp:* Test engr, Gen Elec Co, 43-44; process engr, Tenn Eastman Co, 44-45; instr physics, Mich Technol Univ, 45-46, from instr to asst prof elec eng, 50-51; proj engr, Union Carbide Nuclear Co, Tenn, 52-54; from asst prof to prof elec eng, Mich Technol Univ, 54-88, admin asst dept, 70-81, asst dept head, 81-88, emer prof elec eng, 88- *Concurrent Pos:* Dir, Appelt, Criner & Wedeven, Consult Engrs, Grand Rapids, 75-; consult engr; mem, Mich Bd Registr Prof Engrs, Mich Bd Registr Land Surveyors & Nat Coun Eng Examrs, 65-81. *Mem:* Sr mem Inst Elec & Electronics Engrs; Am Soc Eng Educ; Nat Soc Prof Engrs; Illum Eng Soc NAm. *Res:* Electrical power and machinery; electrical power distribution systems and illumination engineering. *Mailing Add:* Woodland Rd RR 1 Box 14 Houghton MI 49931

ANDERSON, WARREN BOYD, SOIL CHEMISTRY & FERTILITY. *Current Pos:* asst prof, 64-71, ASSOC PROF SOIL & CROP SCI, TEXAS A&M UNIV, 71- *Personal Data:* b Oak City, Utah, Nov 1, 29; m 53; c 6. *Educ:* Brigham Young Univ, BS, 58; Colo State Univ, MS, 62, PhD(soil sci), 64. *Prof Exp:* Phys sci technician, Agr Res Serv, USDA, 60; res assoc soil fertil, Colo Agr Exp Sta, 60-64. *Mem:* Am Soc Agron; Int Soc Soil Sci; Soil Sci Soc Am; Sigma Xi. *Res:* Soil fertility and plant nutrition; micronutrient nutrition of crops. *Mailing Add:* 1315 Timm Dr College Station TX 77840

ANDERSON, WARREN R(ONALD), ELECTRICAL ENGINEERING. *Current Pos:* Prof elec eng, 46-79, head dept electronic & elec eng, 76-79, EMER PROF ELEC ENG, CALIF POLYTECH STATE UNIV, SAN LUIS OBISPO, 79- *Personal Data:* b Houston, Minn, July 31, 14; m 45; c Richard G, John W & Deborah A. *Educ:* Univ Minn, BS, 39; La State Univ, BS, 44. *Prof Exp:* Team chief, Plant Eng Agency, US Army Signal Corps. *Concurrent Pos:* Design engr, Automatic Elec Co, 46 & Gen Elec Co, 51; res analyst, Northrup Aircraft Co, 52; consult, Western Gear Corp, 55 & Gen Elec Co, 56. *Mem:* Inst Elec & Electronics Engrs; Am Soc Eng Educ. *Res:* Engineering problem analysis; creative development part of engineering. *Mailing Add:* Dept Elec & Electronic Eng Calif Polytech State Univ San Luis Obispo CA 93407

ANDERSON, WAYNE ARTHUR, SEMICONDUCTORS, THIN-FILMS. *Current Pos:* assoc chair, EGE Dept, State Univ NY, Buffalo, 85-89, dir, Ctr Electronics & Electro-Optic Mat, 86-97, dept chmn, 89-95, ASSOC & PROF ELECTRONICS, STATE UNIV NY, BUFFALO, 78-, ASSOC CHAIR, EGE DEPT, 95-, ASSOC DIR, CTR ADVAN PHOTONIC & ELECTRONIC MAT, 97- *Personal Data:* b Jamestown, NY, May 20, 38; m 62, Marilyn; c Wayne P & Leslie M. *Educ:* Univ Buffalo, BS, 61; State Univ NY, MS, 65, PhD(elec eng), 70. *Prof Exp:* Proj supvr, Great Lakes Carbon Corp, 61-65; instr electronics, Univ Buffalo, 65-70; asst prof electronics, Rutgers Univ, 70-78. *Mem:* Inst Elec & Electronics Engrs; Am Inst Physics; Mat Res Soc. *Res:* III-V semiconductor surfaces, Schottky barriers and defects; silicon photovoltaic devices and MOS interfaces; thin-film superconductors, resistors and capacitors. *Mailing Add:* 39 Sleepy Hollow Lane Orchard Park NY 14127. *Fax:* 716-645-5964

ANDERSON, WAYNE I, GEOLOGY. *Current Pos:* Assoc prof, 63-73, PROF EARTH SCI, UNIV NORTHERN IOWA, 73-, HEAD DEPT, 63- *Personal Data:* b Montrose, Iowa, Sept 14, 35; m 58; c 4. *Educ:* Univ Iowa, BA, 58, MS, 61, PhD(geol), 64. *Mem:* Geol Soc Am; Soc Econ Paleontologists & Mineralogists; AAAS; Nat Asn Geol Teachers; Sigma Xi. *Res:* Paleozoic stratigraphy and paleontology; geology of Iowa; history of geology. *Mailing Add:* Dept Earth Sci Univ Northern Iowa Cedar Falls IA 50614-0001

ANDERSON, WAYNE KEITH, MEDICINAL CHEMISTRY & ORGANIC CHEMISTRY, SYNTHETIC ORGANIC & NATURAL PRODUCTS CHEMISTRY. *Current Pos:* from asst prof to assoc prof, 68-81, PROF MED CHEM, STATE UNIV NY, BUFFALO, 81-, PROF CHEM, 93-, DEAN, SCH PHARM, 95- *Personal Data:* b Pine Falls, Man, Apr 4, 41; m 62; c 3. *Educ:* Univ Man, BSc, 62, MSc, 65; Univ Wis-Madison, PhD(med chem), 68. *Prof Exp:* Instr med chem, Univ Wis, 67 & 68. *Mem:* Am Chem Soc; Chem Soc London; Am Pharmaceut Asn; Am Asn Cancer Res. *Res:* Synthetic approaches to and structural modifications of naturally occurring antitumor compounds; design and synthesis of new classes of antitumor agents; synthetic heterocyclic chemistry; synthesis and structure of tumor inhibitory metal coordination compounds; the design of new anti-cancer drugs using computer graphics. *Mailing Add:* Sch Pharm Univ Buffalo 126 Cooke Hall Buffalo NY 14260. *Fax:* 716-645-3688; *E-Mail:* wka@acsu.buffalo.edu

ANDERSON, WAYNE PHILPOTT, COMPUTATIONAL CHEMISTRY. *Current Pos:* from asst prof to assoc prof, Bloomsburg State Col, 75-84, PROF CHEM, BLOOMSBURG UNIV, PA, 84- *Personal Data:* b Jamestown, NY, Apr 1, 42; m 72. *Educ:* Harpur Col, BA, 64; Univ Ill, MS, 66, PhD(chem), 68. *Prof Exp:* Asst prof chem, Univ Del, 68-75. *Mem:* Am Chem Soc. *Res:* Determination of the electronic structure of transition metal complexes; applications of molecular mechanics and quantum mechanics to chemical systems; electronic structure of solids. *Mailing Add:* Dept Chem Bloomsburg Univ Bloomsburg PA 17815. *E-Mail:* wpa@bloomu.edu

ANDERSON, WESTON ARTHUR, PHYSICS, MAGNETIC RESONANCE INSTRUMENTATION. *Current Pos:* res physicist, Varian Assocs, 55-63, dir res, Analytic Instrument Div, 63-72, dir systs lab, 72-87, PRIN SCIENTIST, VARIAN ASSOCS, 87-, FEL, 88- *Personal Data:* b Kingsburg, Calif, Mar 28, 28; m 52, Jeanette Arndt; c Joel & Lucy (Jacob). *Educ:* Stanford Univ, BS, 50, MS, 53, PhD(physics), 55. *Prof Exp:* Res physicist, Europ Coun Nuclear Res, 54-55. *Mem:* Inst Elec & Electronics Engrs; Am Asn Physics Teachers; Am Phys Soc. *Res:* Magnetic resonance; biomedical engineering; vacuum microelectronics; x-rays; granted 42 US patents. *Mailing Add:* 763 La Para Ave Palo Alto CA 94306

ANDERSON, WILLARD EUGENE, APPLIED PHYSICS. *Current Pos:* res scientist, Aeronaut Div, Res Dept, Honeywell, Inc, 59-64, sr res scientist, Mil Prod Group, Res Dept, 64-65, prin res scientist, 65-74, prin systs engr, Aerospace & Defense Group, Systs & Res Ctr, 74-76, prin develop engr, Energy Resources Ctr, Advan Power Systs, 74-79, PRIN DEVELOP ENGR, TECHNOL STRATEGY CTR, BLDG & INDUST SYST, HONEYWELL INC, 79- *Personal Data:* b Vilas, SDak, Aug 27, 33; m 59. *Educ:* Huron Col, SDak, BS, 55. *Prof Exp:* Res asst & tech asst, Corp Res Ctr, Honeywell Inc, 55-56; teaching asst math, SDak State Univ, 56-59. *Concurrent Pos:* Consult gen physics, 59-; consult, Manned Orbiting Lab, Controls Subcontract, Aerospace Div, Honeywell Inc, 66-69, prin investr, Technol Strategy Ctr, 79-80. *Mem:* AAAS. *Res:* Heat transfer and radiant thermometry; gyroscopes, precision spheres, rotor spin-up, pickoffs, voltage breakdown; density, atmosphere, ocean; trace gas sensing, chemistry, ionic mobility; optics, laser Doppler, opdar, correlators, spatial filtering, scattering; space physics; atmospheric physics; guidance and control, missile simulations; solar energy systems, photovoltaic solar cell modules; combined cycle and cogeneration. *Mailing Add:* 2418 Lone St St Paul MN 55108

ANDERSON, WILLARD WOODBURY, MECHANICAL ENGINEERING, AEROSPACE SYSTEMS. *Current Pos:* asst head, 66-72, head, Stability & Control Br, 72-76, asst chief, 76-79, CHIEF, FLIGHT DYNAMICS & CONTROL DIV, LANGLEY RES CTR, NASA, 79- *Personal Data:* b Boston, Mass, July 22, 39; m 57; c 5. *Educ:* Northeastern Univ, BS, 62; Mass Inst Technol, MS, 64, ScD(mech eng), 67. *Prof Exp:* Engr, Dynatech Corp, 60-62; res asst fiber & polymer res, Mass Inst Technol, 62-65; sr engr & partner, Cohoon & Heasley, Inc, 64-66. *Res:* Attitude control of large manned spacecraft utilizing momentum storage systems; automated air traffic control systems research; flight dynamics and control of aircraft and spacecraft. *Mailing Add:* NASA Langley Res Ctr NASA Mail Stop 479 Hampton VA 23681-0001

ANDERSON, WILLIAM ALAN, MOLECULAR BIOLOGY, P FOUR FIFTY. *Current Pos:* from asst prof to assoc prof, 71-83, PROF BIOL, LAVAL UNIV, 83- *Personal Data:* b St Peter's Bay, PEI, Can, Jan 5, 41; m 63; c Avis, Robin & Kerri. *Educ:* Queen's Univ, Ont, BSc, 62; Mass Inst Technol, PhD(microbiol), 69. *Prof Exp:* Fel molecular biol, Univ Geneva, 69-70. *Concurrent Pos:* Sabbatical fel, CNRS, Gif-sur-Yvette, 77-78; mem, Laval Univ Cancer Res Ctr, Hotel-Dieu Quebec, 80. *Mem:* Can Biochem Soc; Genetics Soc Can; Am Soc Microbiol. *Res:* Diversity, function and expression of mammalian cytochrome P450 genes; promutagen activation by P450 synthesized in mammalian cells transfected by P450 expression vectors. *Mailing Add:* Centre de Recherche De l'Hote de Dieu 1 Rue de L'Arsenal Quebec PQ G1R 2J6 Can. *Fax:* 418-691-5439

ANDERSON, WILLIAM AVERETTE, ENVIRONMENTAL HAZARDS. *Current Pos:* prog dir, 76-90, HEAD, HAZARD MITIGATION SECT, NSF, 90- *Personal Data:* b Akron, Ohio, May 28, 37; m 68, Norma Doneghy; c Candice. *Educ:* Univ Akron, BA, 60; Kent State Univ, MA, 61; Ohio State Univ, PhD(sociol), 66. *Prof Exp:* Res assoc, Disaster Res Ctr, Ohio State Univ, 66-69; from assoc prof to prof sociol, Ariz State Univ, 69-76. *Concurrent Pos:* Dir, Minority Fel Prog, Am Sociol Asn, 74-75. *Mem:* Am Sociol Asn. *Res:* Investigated the socioeconomic impacts of natural disasters; support interdisciplinary research including seismology; engineering and social science on natural hazards. *Mailing Add:* 13725 Creekside Dr Silver Spring MD 20904

ANDERSON, WILLIAM B, PSYCHIATRY. *Current Pos:* ASST PROF PSYCHIAT, MED CTR, DUKE UNIV, 65- *Personal Data:* b Montevideo, Minn, Nov 8, 23; m 59; c 3. *Educ:* Univ Minn, BS, 45, MD, 48. *Prof Exp:* Instr pediat & asst dir pediat clin, Univ Pa, 54-56; asst prof pediat, asst dir state serv crippled children & dir pediat clin, State Univ Iowa, 56-61. *Concurrent Pos:* Fel pediat, Tulane Univ, 49-50; fel child psychiat, Med Ctr, Duke Univ, 63-65. *Res:* Adult and child psychiatry. *Mailing Add:* Box 3313 Univ Med Ctr Duke Univ Hosp Durham NC 27702-3313

ANDERSON, WILLIAM CARL, ENVIRONMENTAL ENGINEERING. *Current Pos:* trustee, 82-85, EXEC DIR, AM ACAD ENVIRON ENGRS, 85-; PARTNER, PICKARD & ANDERSON, 73-, EXEC DIR, COUN ENG SPECIAL BDS. *Personal Data:* b Vinton, Iowa, Sept 24, 43; m 66, Elizabeth A Dingman; c William C III & Erica D. *Educ:* Iowa State Univ, BSCE, 67. *Honors & Awards:* Philip F Morgan Medal, Water Pollution Control Fedn, 73; Outstanding Serv Award, Am Soc Civil Engrs, 81 & 86. *Prof Exp:* Dir environ health, Cayuga Co Health Dept, Auburn, NY, 69-73. *Concurrent Pos:* Mem health & safety comt, Cayuga Co Coun Boy Scouts Am, 69-83; ed, Diplomate, 85-; mem, Nat Water Policy Coun, Am Soc Civil Engrs, 86-87. *Mem:* Fel Am Soc Civil Engrs; Am Water Works Asn; Air & Waste Mgt Asn; Asn Environ Eng Profs; Water Environ Fedn. *Res:* Water pollution control; solid waste management; hazardous waste management. *Mailing Add:* Am Acad Environ Engrs 130 Holiday Ct Suite 100 Annapolis MD 21401-7032

ANDERSON, WILLIAM J, MECHANICAL ENGINEERING, MATHEMATICS. *Current Pos:* RETIRED. *Personal Data:* b Brooklyn, NY, Oct 7, 22; m 51; c 2. *Educ:* Mass Inst Technol, SB, 50; Case Inst Technol, MS, 56. *Honors & Awards:* Hunt Mem Award, Am Soc Lubrication Engrs, 62. *Prof Exp:* Res engr lubrication, Nat Adv Comt Aeronaut, 50-53, head, Bearings Sect, 53-57; chief mech, Technologies Br, Lewis Res Ctr, NASA, 57-81, consult engr, 81- *Concurrent Pos:* Lectr, Univ Calif, Los Angeles, 63-80, Case Inst Technol, 66, Univ Tenn, Va Polytech Inst & State Univ, Carnegie-Mellon Univ & Univ Pittsburg; vis prof, Univ Akron, 81. *Mem:* Fel Am Soc Mech Engrs; fel Am Soc Lubrication Engrs. *Res:* Lubrication; friction and wear; bearing dynamics. *Mailing Add:* 5031 Devon Dr North Olmsted OH 44070

ANDERSON, WILLIAM JOHN, NEUROANATOMY, NEUROCHEMISTRY. *Current Pos:* asst prof neuroanat, 75-82, assoc prof anat, Ind Univ Sch Med, Terre Haute Ctr Med Educ, 82-84, PROF ANAT, IND STATE UNIV, 84- *Personal Data:* b Boston, Mass, Dec 9, 38; m 68. *Educ:* Univ Miami, BA, 62; Purdue Univ, MS, 73, PhD(anat), 75. *Prof Exp:* Res assoc psychol, Mass Inst Technol, 62-68; fac instr neurobiol, Purdue Univ, 68-71, grad instr anat, Sch Vet Med, 71-75. *Concurrent Pos:* Mem, Neurol A Study Sect, NIH, 84-94. *Mem:* Int Soc Develop Psychobiol; Am Asn Anatomists; Soc Neurosci; Am Asn Vet Anatomists; Sigma Xi; World Asn Vet Anatomists. *Res:* Morphological analysis of brain development and brain abnormalities due to toxic elements, with special reference to postnatal development; spinal cord motoneuron organization, development and pathological excitotoxicity. *Mailing Add:* Ind State Univ 135 Homestead Hall Terre Haute IN 47809. *Fax:* 812-237-7646; *E-Mail:* memit@thcme.indstate.edu

ANDERSON, WILLIAM LENO, WILDLIFE BIOLOGY. *Current Pos:* conserv resource prog mgr, 77-89, CONSERV RESOURCE ADMIN, ILL DEPT CONSERV, 89- *Personal Data:* b Carney, Okla, Mar 13, 35; m 62; c 2. *Educ:* Okla State Univ, BS, 58; Southern Ill Univ, MA, 64. *Prof Exp:* Field asst pop ecol, 58-62, res asst, 62-63, res assoc ecol & physiol, 63-68, assoc wildlife specialist, Ill Natural Hist Surv, 68-77. *Mem:* Wildlife Soc; Wilson Ornith Soc. *Res:* Population dynamics; behavioral and physiological responses of birds and mammals to pesticides, lead, trace elements, heated water, power plants and power lines; hunter activity and opinion surveys. *Mailing Add:* 2 Floral Park Ct Savoy IL 61870

ANDERSON, WILLIAM LOYD, IMMUNOLOGY. *Current Pos:* ASST PROF CELL BIOL, UNIV NMEX, 81- *Personal Data:* b Minneapolis, Minn, Aug 8, 47; m 70; c 2. *Educ:* Univ Minn, BA, 69, PhD(biochem), 74. *Prof Exp:* Teaching asst biochem, Univ Minn, 69-74, res assoc, 74-75; fel, Dept Immunol, Mayo Clinic, 75-78, assoc consult, 78-81. *Mem:* Am Chem Soc; Sigma Xi; AAAS. *Res:* Role of soluble factors in the regulation of immunological responses; effect of aging on the immune system. *Mailing Add:* Dept Cellular Biol Univ NMex Sch Med 900 Camino de Salud NE Albuquerque NM 87131-5226

ANDERSON, WILLIAM MCDOWELL, PULMONARY MEDICINE, CRITICAL CARE MEDICINE. *Current Pos:* DIR MED INTENSIVE CARE UNIT, VET ADMIN MED CTR, 85-, SECT CHIEF PULMONARY & CRITICAL CARE MED, 88- *Personal Data:* b Richmond, Va, Sept 13, 51; m 81; c 2. *Educ:* Univ Va, BA, 73; Old Dominion Univ, MS, 75; Eastern Va Med Sch, MD, 78. *Prof Exp:* Med intern & resident, Univ Hosp, Jacksonville, Fla, 78-81, chief resident internal med, 81-82, fel critical care med, 82-83; fel pulmonary med, Univ Fla, 83-85. *Concurrent Pos:* Asst prof med, La State Univ Sch Med, Shreveport, 85-, asst prof physiol & biophys, 88- *Res:* Investigation of the mechanisms involved in respiratory muscle fatigue; investigation of the roles of sleep fragmentation versus hypoxemia in symptoms related to obstructive sleep apnea. *Mailing Add:* James A Haley Vet Admin Hosp 1300 Bruce B Downs Blvd Tampa FL 33612

ANDERSON, WILLIAM NILES, JR, BIOMETRICS-BIOSTATISTICS. *Current Pos:* MGR BIOSTATIST, BAXTER HEALTHCARE, 94- *Personal Data:* b Pittsburgh, Pa, Nov 27, 39; m 69, Marion Waldron; c Nicholas & Susan. *Educ:* Carnegie-Mellon Univ, BS, 60, MS, 67, PhD(math), 68. *Prof Exp:* Res assoc math, Rockefeller Univ, 68-70; asst prof, Univ Md, 70-75; assoc prof math & comput sci, WVa Univ, 75-79; prof & chmn, East Tenn State Univ, 79-84 & Fairleigh Dickinson Univ, 84-94. *Mem:* Soc Indust & Appl Math; Asn Comput Mach; Inst Elec & Electronics Engrs; Sigma Xi; Am Statist Asn; Inst Math Statist. *Res:* Survival analysis for medical devices. *Mailing Add:* 21672 Montbury Dr Lake Forest CA 92630

ANDERSON, WILLIAM RAYMOND, PHYSICS. *Current Pos:* from instr to assoc prof, 47-79, EMER PROF PHYSICS, UNIV ILL, CHICAGO CIRCLE, 79- *Personal Data:* b St Charles, Ill, Mar 12, 11; wid. *Educ:* Univ Ill, BS, 33; DePaul Univ, MS, 47. *Prof Exp:* Pvt & pub acct, 34-42; pub sch teacher, Ill, 43-47. *Mem:* Am Asn Physics Teachers. *Res:* Spectroscopy; molecular physics. *Mailing Add:* 4215 N Kedvale Ave No 1L Chicago IL 60641

ANDERSON, WILLIAM RUSSELL, SYSTEMATIC BOTANY. *Current Pos:* PROF, CUR & DIR, UNIV MICH HERBARIUM, 86- *Personal Data:* b Tucson, Ariz, Sept 25, 42; m 67; c 2. *Educ:* Duke Univ, BS, 64; Univ Mich, MS, 66, PhD(bot), 71. *Honors & Awards:* Greenman Award, Mo Bot Garden, 73; Cooley Award, Am Soc Plant Taxonomists, 75. *Prof Exp:* Assoc cur, New York Bot Garden, 71-74; assoc cur & asst prof, Univ Mich, 74-80, assoc prof bot, 80-86. *Concurrent Pos:* Gen ed, Flora Novo-Galiciana. *Mem:* Am Soc Plant Taxonomists; Int Asn Plant Taxon; Sigma Xi. *Res:* Systematics and evolution of flowering plants, especially the family Malpighiaceae; Mexican floristics. *Mailing Add:* Univ Mich Herbarium North Univ Bldg Ann Arbor MI 48109-1057. *E-Mail:* wra@umich.edu

ANDERSON, WILLIAM W, ELECTRICAL ENGINEERING, SOLID STATE ELECTRONICS & PHOTONICS. *Current Pos:* CONSULT ENGR ELECTRO-OPTICS, LOCKHEED MARTIN ADVAN TECHNOL CTR, 75- *Personal Data:* b Tacoma, Wash, Feb 26, 33; m 54, Anne La Pointe; c David, Carolyn & Kevin. *Educ:* Mass Inst Technol, BS & MS, 56; Stanford Univ, PhD(elec eng), 59. *Prof Exp:* Instr elec eng, Stanford Univ, 57-58; mem tech staff solid state electronics, Bell Tel Labs, 58-60; asst prof elec eng, Stanford Univ, 60-65; prof, Ohio State Univ, 65-75. *Concurrent Pos:* Consult to Watkins-Johnson, Battelle Mem Inst, Corning, Varina Assoc. *Mem:* Inst Elec & Electronics Engrs. *Res:* Solid state electronic devices; electro-optic devices, photonic technology applications. *Mailing Add:* Lockheed Martin Advan Technol Ctr 0-H154 Bldg 202 3251 Hanover St Palo Alto CA 94304-1187. *Fax:* 650-354-5400; *E-Mail:* willy.anderson@lmco.com

ANDERSON, WYATT W, POPULATION GENETICS, MOLECULAR EVOLUTION. *Current Pos:* assoc prof, Univ Ga, 72-75, prof zool, 75-80, prof & head genetics, 80-87, ALUMNI FOUND DISTINUISHED PROF GENETICS, UNIV GA, 87-, DEAN, FRANKLIN COL ARTS & SCIS, 92- *Personal Data:* b New Orleans, La, Mar 27, 39; m 62, Margaret Ann Shugart; c James, Elizabeth & Karen. *Educ:* Univ Ga, BS, 60, MS, 62; Rockefeller Univ, PhD(life sci), 67. *Prof Exp:* From lectr to assoc prof biol, Yale Univ, 66-72. *Concurrent Pos:* Vis lectr, Inst Genetics & Ecol, Univ Aarhus, Denmark, 79; vis res, Dept Genetics, Univ Calif, Davis, 82-83; distinguished prof, Dept Zool, Ariz State Univ, 87. *Mem:* Nat Acad Sci; Genetics Soc Am; Am Soc Naturalists; Ecol Soc Am; Am Soc Human Genetics; Soc Study Evolution; Soc molecular biol & evolution. *Res:* Science education; selection in natural and experimental populations; relationships between genetical and ecological aspects of populations; molecular evolution. *Mailing Add:* Dept Genetics Univ Ga Life Sci Bldg Athens GA 30602-7223

ANDERSON-COOK, CHRISTINE MICHAELA, INDUSTRIAL STATISTICS, DESIGN OF EXPERIMENTS. *Current Pos:* ASST PROF, VA INST TECHNOL, 96- *Personal Data:* b Manhattan, Kans, Mar 15, 66; US & Can citizen; m 95, G Stanley. *Educ:* Univ Waterloo, BM, 89, PhD(statist), 94; Univ Western Ont, BEd, 89; Univ Toronto, MSc, 90. *Prof Exp:* Asst prof, Univ Western Ont, 94-96. *Concurrent Pos:* Lectr statist, Univ Waterloo, 92-; Gertrude Cox scholar, Am Statist Asn, 91. *Mem:* Am Statist Asn; Statist Soc Can; Caucus Women Sci. *Res:* Design of experiment and analysis issues arising from the study of circular data; location, dispersion and graphical methods for investigating caused relationships between factors and an angular response, cylindrical data analysis. *Mailing Add:* Dept Statist Va Inst Technol Blacksburg VA 24061-0439. *Fax:* 540-231-3863; *E-Mail:* candcook@vt.edu

ANDERSON-MAUSER, LINDA MARIE, MOLECULAR BIOLOGY. *Current Pos:* SR RES SCIENTIST, MILES LAB, 87- *Personal Data:* b South Bend, Ind, Apr 27, 54; m. *Educ:* Ind Univ, BA, 77; Univ NC, PhD(genetics), 84. *Mem:* Am Soc Microbiol. *Res:* Molecular biology and genetics of procaryotes, with special emphasis on bacteriophage; fermentation products research immuno assay development. *Mailing Add:* PO Box 70 Elkhart IN 46515

ANDERSON-ROWLAND, MARY RUTH, INDUSTRIAL ENGINEERING, STATISTICS. *Current Pos:* lectr math, 66-72, Ariz State Univ, asst to dean, Col Lib Arts, 72-79, asst prof eng, 74-78, ASSOC PROF ENG, FAC INDUST ENG, ARIZ STATE UNIV, 79-, DIR, GRAD REENTRY PROG, 81-, ASSOC CHAIRPERSON & GRAD STUDENT COORDR, 83- *Personal Data:* b Bellingham, Wash, Feb 3, 39; m 66; c 2. *Educ:* Hope Col, BA, 61; Univ Iowa, MS, 63, PhD(math & statist), 66. *Prof Exp:* Teaching asst math, Univ Iowa, 63-66. *Concurrent Pos:* Consult, US Indian Health Serv, 73-74, Ariz Solar Energy Comn, 80-, Rogers Corp, 81-, NIH, 82, Digital Equip Corp, 82, Sperry Flight Systs, 83, Motorola, 84 & Dept Transp, 85-; chairperson, Women Academia Comt, Soc Women Engrs, 84-86. *Mem:* Am Inst Indust Engrs; Soc Women Engrs; Asn Women Math; Am Soc Eng Educ. *Res:* Exponential class characterizations; applied statistics in engineering, nursing and transportation; economic analysis of solar water heating; reentry programs for women and men in engineering; women in engineering. *Mailing Add:* Dept Eng Ariz State Univ PO Box 875506 Tempe AZ 85287-5506

ANDERSON-SHAW, HELEN LESTER, AMINO ACIDS, ZINC. *Current Pos:* PROF & CHAIR, DEPT FOOD NUTRIT & FOOD SERV MGT, UNIV NC, GREENSBORO, 89- *Personal Data:* b Lexington, Ky, Oct 18, 36; m 88. *Educ:* Univ Ky, BS, 58; Univ Wis, MS, 65, PhD(nutrit sci), 69; Am Bd Nutrit dipl. *Prof Exp:* Dietitian, Roanoke Mem Hosp, Va, 59-60; Santa Barbara Cottage Hosp, 60-61; unit mgr, De La Guerra Commons, Univ Calif, Santa Barbara, 61-63; from asst prof to prof nutrit, Univ Mo, Columbia, 69-88, assoc dean res & grad studies home econ, 77-83. *Concurrent Pos:* Dietetic internship, Univ Mich Hosps, 58-89. *Mem:* Am Inst Nutrit; Am Soc Clin Nutrit; Am Dietetic Asn; Am Home Econ Asn; Soc Nutrit Educ. *Res:* Amino acid nutrition in humans and small animals; zinc bioavailability in humans. *Mailing Add:* 235 Stone Bldg Univ NC Greensboro NC 27412-5001

ANDERSON-STOUT, ZOE ESTELLE, NUTRITION. *Current Pos:* assoc prof, 65-78, EMER PROF FOODS & NUTRIT, SAN DIEGO STATE UNIV, 78- *Personal Data:* b Glenview, Ill, Jan 20, 13; m 76. *Educ:* Ill Inst Technol, BSAS, 39; Univ Ill, MS, 47, PhD(animal nutrit), 50. *Prof Exp:* Mgr plant cafeteria, Hydrox Ice Cream Co, 35-39; fac mem cafeteria mgt & home econ, Frankfort Community High Sch, 39-42; dietician sch food serv, J Sterling Morton High Sch, 42-43; asst dept nutrit res, Nat Dairy Coun, 49-51, dir, 51-60; asst prof home econ & chmn dept, Wayne State Univ, 60-62; assoc prof nutrit, Dept Internal Med, Col Med, Iowa State Univ, 62-64. *Mem:* Am

Dietetic Asn; Am Inst Nutrit; Am Home Econ Asn; Soc Nutrit Educ. *Res:* Nutrition in health and disease; effects of diet on voluntary activity; bone ash; growth; tissues; blood and urinary values. *Mailing Add:* 5183 Roxbury Rd San Diego CA 92116

ANDERTON, LAURA GADDES, EXPERIMENTAL EMBRYOLOGY, HUMAN CYTOGENETICS. *Current Pos:* instr biol & counsr, Univ NC, Greensboro, 48-55, instr biol, 56-58, from asst prof biol & embryol to assoc prof biol, 58-68, DIR CYTOGENETICS LAB, UNIV NC, GREENSBORO, 65-, PROF BIOL, 68- *Personal Data:* b Providence, RI, Sept 6, 18. *Educ:* Wellesley Col, BA, 40; Brown Univ, MS, 48; Univ NC, PhD, 59. *Prof Exp:* Instr biol & chem, Howard Sem, 41-43. *Concurrent Pos:* NIH grant, 68-71; consult, Moses H Cone Mem Hosp, 69- *Mem:* AAAS; Am Inst Biol Sci; Am Soc Human Genetics; Am Soc Zoologists; Int Union Against Cancer; Sigma Xi. *Res:* Cell renewal system in the colon mucosa; familial polyposis; tissue culture of adenomas of the colon. *Mailing Add:* 600 HS Chapman St Greensboro NC 27403-0592

ANDES, CHARLES LOVETT, MUSEUMOLOGY, TECHNOLOGY. *Current Pos:* chmn & chief exec officer, 85-91, CHAIR, FRANKLIN INST, PHILADELPHIA, 91-; PRES & CHIEF EXEC OFFICER, TECH COUN GREATER PHILADELPHIA, 91- *Personal Data:* b Philadelphia, Pa, Sept 23, 30; m 61, Dorothea R Abbott; c Elizabeth, Susan, Karen & Page. *Educ:* Syracuse Univ, BA, 52. *Prof Exp:* Pres, Adtech Industs, Philadelphia, 54-68; exec vpres & dir, Franklin Mint Corp, Franklin Ctr, Pa, 69-73, pres, 72-73, chmn bd & chief exec officer, 73-85. *Concurrent Pos:* Mem bd dirs, O'Brien Environ Energy Systs, Clin Nutrit Found. *Mem:* Inst Biotech & Advan Molecular Med (pres). *Res:* Museum and technology administration. *Mailing Add:* McClurp Group 1325 Morris Dr, Ste 100 Chesterbrook Wayne PA 19087

ANDES, W(ILLARD) ABE, HEMATOLOGY. *Current Pos:* PROF INTERNAL MED, HEMAT, ONCOL CANCER CTR, WAKE FOREST UNIV, 92- *Personal Data:* b Miami, Fla, Feb 19, 42; m 72; c 2. *Educ:* Univ NC, BA, 64; Tulane Univ Sch Med, MD, 68. *Prof Exp:* From instr to assoc prof, Tulane Univ Sch Med, 75-85, prof med, 85-92. *Mem:* NY Acad Sci; Am Fedn Clin Res; Am Soc Clin Oncol; Am Soc Hemat. *Mailing Add:* Cancer Ctr Wake Forest Univ Med Ctr Blvd Winston-Salem NC 27157

ANDO, WATARU, CHEMISTRY. *Current Pos:* DEAN, COL ENG, UNIV TSUKUBA, JAPAN. *Honors & Awards:* Frederic Stanley Kipping Award, Am Chem Soc, 95. *Mailing Add:* Univ Tsukuba 1-1-1 Tennodai Tsukuba-Ibaraki 305 Japan

ANDON, MARK B, MINERAL NUTRITION. *Current Pos:* SCIENTIST NUTRIT RES & DEVELOP, PROCTER & GAMBLE CO, 87- *Personal Data:* b Riverside, Calif, Jan 17, 58. *Educ:* Calif State Univ, Long Beach, BA, 81; Univ Md, PhD(nutrit sci), 87. *Mem:* Am Inst Nutrit; Am Soc Chem Nutrit. *Mailing Add:* Procter & Gamble Co Miami Valley Labs PO Box 45253-8700 Cincinnati OH 45253-8700

ANDONIAN, ARSAVIR TAKFOR, ENGINEERING MECHANICS. *Current Pos:* sr res scientist, 84-93, RES & DEVELOPMENT ASSOC, GOODYEAR, AKRON, OH, 93- *Personal Data:* b Istanbul, Turkey, July 26, 50; m 76; c 2. *Educ:* Bogazici Univ, BS; Va Polytech Inst & State Univ, MS, 75, PhD(eng mech), 78. *Prof Exp:* Instr mech mat, Dept Eng Sci & Mech, Va Polytech Inst & State Univ, 77-78; asst prof exp solid mech, Dept Math Eng, Univ Ill, Chicago Circle, 79-84. *Mem:* Soc Exp Stress Analysis. *Res:* Experimental applications of moire, three dimensional photoelasticity, birefrigent coating, brittle coating and holography in fracture mechanics and biomechanics; predicting cracking patterns in reinforced concrete; tire mechanics, cord/rubber composites and material characterization. *Mailing Add:* 5859 Bradford Way Hudson OH 44236

ANDOSE, JOSEPH D, SCIENTIFIC PROGRAMMING. *Current Pos:* systs analyst comput-assisted molecular modeling, 74-75, systs assoc comput-assisted org synthesis, 75-77, proj mgr sci systs, 77-80, MGR SCI PROG, MERCK & CO, INC, 80- *Personal Data:* b Philadelphia, Pa, July 26, 44. *Educ:* Temple Univ, BA, 66; Princeton Univ, MA, 68, PhD(org chem), 71. *Prof Exp:* Res assoc phys org chem, Princeton Univ, 71-74. *Mem:* Am Chem Soc; AAAS; Asn Comput Mach. *Res:* Computer-assisted molecular modeling; computer-assisted organic synthesis. *Mailing Add:* Merck & Co Inc Bldg 84-26 PO Box 2000 Rahway NJ 07065-4687

ANDOW, DAVID A, INSECT ECOLOGY, AGRICULTURAL ECOLOGY. *Current Pos:* asst prof insect ecol, 84-90, ASSOC PROF INSECT ECOL, UNIV MINN, 91- *Personal Data:* b Cleveland, Ohio. *Educ:* Brown Univ, ScB, 77; Cornell Univ, PhD(ecol), 83. *Prof Exp:* Assoc, Ecosysts Res Ctr, Cornell Univ, 82-84. *Concurrent Pos:* Vis scientist, Nat Inst Agr Sci, Japan, 82-83 & Nat Inst Agroenviron Sci, Japan, 83-86. *Mem:* Ecol Soc Am; Entom Soc Am; AAAS; Sigma Xi. *Res:* Ecological interactions agricultural systems; development of resource-conserving, sustainable, thought-intensive food production technologies. *Mailing Add:* Dept Entom 219 Hodson Hall Univ Minn 1980 Folwell Ave St Paul MN 55108

ANDRADE, JOHN ROBERT, PHARMACEUTICS. *Current Pos:* sect head, 94-95, ASSOC DIR IMAGING & PARTICLE CHARACTERIZATION & THERMAL ANALYSIS, WYETH-AYERST, DIV AM HOME PRODS, 95- *Personal Data:* b Providence, RI, Aug 23, 44; m 69, Paula Moynihan; c 6. *Educ:* Col Holy Cross, BS, 66, MS, 67; Brown Univ, PhD(org chem), 79. *Prof Exp:* Instr chem, US Naval Acad, 71-72 & Brown Univ, 77; res chemist, Med Res Div, Am Cyanamid Co, 77-83, group leader, 83-90, mgr process develop & analysis serv, 90-91, mgr chem process develop, 91-93, mgr spectros support & protein analysis, 93-94. *Mem:* Am Chem Soc; Sigma Xi; Am Asn Pharmaceut Scientists. *Res:* Synthesis of bulk chemicals for preclinical and clinical evaluation; development processes for the scale-up and manufacture of new drugs; improvement of processes for the manufacture of existing drugs; pharmaceutical process development management; spectroscopic analysis of pharmaceuticals; protein analysis; imaging and particle characterization; thermal analysis. *Mailing Add:* 107 Rivervale Rd Park Ridge NJ 07656-2310. *Fax:* 914-732-5693; *E-Mail:* andradj@war.wyeth.com

ANDRADE, JOSEPH D, BIOENGINEERING, MATERIALS SCIENCE. *Current Pos:* Dean Col Eng, 83-87, PROF BIOENG, MAT SCI, ENG & PHARM, UNIV UTAH, 69-, CHMN DEPT, 78-80 & 88- *Personal Data:* b Hayward, Calif, July 13, 41; m 66; c 2. *Educ:* San Jose State Col, BS, 65; Univ Denver, PhD(metall, mat), 69. *Honors & Awards:* Ebert Prize, Acad Pharmaceut Soc, 78; Clemson Award, Soc Biomat, 85. *Mem:* AAAS; NY Acad Sci; Am Chem Soc; Am Soc Higher Educ; Biomed Eng Soc. *Res:* Interface between non-living materials and living systems; bloodmaterials interface; biosensors; polymer surface chemistry; adsorption from solution; biomaterials; science education. *Mailing Add:* Col Eng Univ Utah 2480 Merrill Eng Bldg Salt Lake City UT 84112

ANDRADE, MANUEL, METAL CORROSION. *Current Pos:* RES ASSOC, WARNER-LAMBERT CO, 70- *Personal Data:* b Fall River, Mass, Mar 14, 39; m 69; c 4. *Educ:* RI Sch Design, BS, 60; Southern Conn State Univ, MS, 85. *Prof Exp:* Exp engr, United Technol Corp, 62-69. *Mem:* Am Chem Soc; fel Am Inst Chemists; Nat Asn Corrosion Engrs; Am Soc Testing & Mat; NY Acad Sci. *Res:* Electrochemical aspects of metal corrosion; infrared spectroscopy; quantitative determination of surface cleanliness; metal cleaning; metal surface treatment; polymeric and metallic thin film adhesion and deposition. *Mailing Add:* Warner-Lambert Co Ten Webster Rd Milford CT 06460

ANDRADY, ANTHONY LAKSHMAN, CROSSLINKED ELASTOMERS, PERMEABILITY OF POLYMERS. *Current Pos:* sr res scientist, 85-89, DIR, DEPT POLYMER SCI, RES TRIANGLE INST, NC, 89- *Personal Data:* b Sri Lanka; m 73, Lalitha C; c Anthony I & Gerald C. *Educ:* Univ Ceylon, BSc, 72; Univ Akron, Ohio, MS, 75; Univ NLondon, Eng, PhD(polymer sci), 78. *Prof Exp:* Res assoc, Univ Cincinnati, 78-80; sr res chemist, Monsanto Co, Mo, 80-82; res scientist, contract consult, Kuwait Inst Sci Res, 82-84. *Concurrent Pos:* Consult, numerous co. *Mem:* Fel Nat Col Rubber Technol Eng; fel Royal Inst Chem; Am Chem Soc. *Res:* Investigation of structure-property relationships in crosslinked polymers; transport phenomena in polymers; weathering and stabilization of polymers; plastics environment; plastic solid waste management; biodegradation of polymers and paper substrates; low voc coatings development. *Mailing Add:* PO Box 12194 Research Triangle Park NC 27709. *Fax:* 919-541-8868; *E-Mail:* andrady@rcc.rti.org

ANDRAKO, JOHN, MEDICINAL CHEMISTRY. *Current Pos:* assoc prof, Va Commonwealth Univ, 56-62, asst dean, Sch Pharm, 65-73, asst vpres health sci, 73-75, asst provost, 75-78, asst vpres health sci, 78-82, assoc vpres health sci, 82-91, interim vpres health sci, 88-91, PROF MED CHEM, MED COL VA, VA COMMONWEALTH UNIV, 62-, EMER PROF, 91- *Personal Data:* b Perth Amboy, NJ, Jan 19, 24; m 78, Wanda J Schutt; c John David, Diane A (Shasky) & Susan A (Heiligman). *Educ:* Rutgers Univ, BS, 47, MS, 49; Univ NC, PhD(pharmaceut chem), 53. *Prof Exp:* Instr pharmaceut chem, Univ NC, 49-50, instr pharm, 50-53, from asst prof to assoc prof pharmaceut chem, 53-56. *Concurrent Pos:* Chmn, US Adopted Names Coun; sr admin assoc dir, Inst Struct Biol & Drug Discovery, Va Biotechnol Park, Va Commonwealth Univ. *Mem:* Am Chem Soc; Am Pharmaceut Asn. *Res:* Synthesis of derivatives of various heterocyclic systems as antihypertensives and psychotropic agents. *Mailing Add:* 1970 Albion Rd Midlothian VA 23113-4147. *E-Mail:* andrako@gems.vcu.edu

ANDRE, MICHAEL PAUL, ULTRASOUND, MEDICAL IMAGING & X-RAY DETECTORS. *Current Pos:* ASSOC PROF RADIOL, UNIV CALIF, SAN DIEGO, 81-, CHIEF, PHYSICS & ENG DIV, SCH MED, 93-; PHYSICIST RADIOL, VET ADMIN MED CTR, 81- *Personal Data:* b Des Moines, Iowa, April 25, 51; m 88, Janice Hanecak. *Educ:* Cent Univ Iowa, BA, 72; Univ Calif, Los Angeles, MS, 75, PhD(med physics), 80. *Honors & Awards:* Silverman Award, Health Physics Soc, 79. *Prof Exp:* Prog consult comput sci, Univ Comput Ctr, Cent Univ Iowa, 69-72; tech staff aerospace eng, N Island Naval Air Sta, San Diego, 70-71; res assoc atmospheric physics, Inst Atmospheric Physics, Univ Ariz, 72-73; tech staff systs eng, Hughes Aircraft Co, 73-74; teaching researcher physics, Univ Calif, Los Angeles, 74-77; physicist radiol safety officer radiol physics, Los Angeles County Med Ctr, 77-81; sr physicist radiol, Cedars-Sinai Med Ctr, 79-85. *Concurrent Pos:* Physicist, Wadsworth Vet Admin Med Ctr, Los Angeles, 77-81; lectr, Sch Pharm, Univ Southern Calif, 79-81; consult, Centinela Hosp Med Ctr, Inglewood, 79-85, Univ Calif, Los Angeles-Los Angeles County Med Ctr, 81- & Children's Hosp & Health Ctr, San Diego, 84-; prin investr, Vet Admin Res Serv, 89-, Univ Calif, San Diego Found, 88-; ed, J Investigative Radiol; bd dirs, San Diego Radiol Res & Educ Found, 93- *Mem:* Am Asn Physicists Med; Soc Photo-Optical Instrumentation Engrs; Inst Elec & Electronics Engrs; Am Inst Physics; Am Inst Ultrasound Med; Am Coll Radiol. *Res:* Medical imaging systems including x-ray, computed tomography, ultrasound and nuclear magnetic resonance; biological effects and dosimetry of ultrasound; assessment of skeletal strength by non-invasive methods; ultrasound inverse scattering; direct digital x-ray sensors; digital mammography. *Mailing Add:* Dept Radiol V-114 Vet Admin Med Ctr 3350 La Jolla Village Dr San Diego CA 92161. *E-Mail:* mandre@ucsd.edu

ANDRE, PAMELA Q J, AGRONOMY. *Current Pos:* DIR, NAT AGR LIBR. *Personal Data:* b Lewiston, Maine, Sept 29, 42. *Educ:* Univ NH, BS, 64; Univ Md, MLS, 69. *Mailing Add:* Nat Agr Libr 10301 Baltimore Ave Beltsville MD 20705-2351

ANDRE, PETER P, ALGEBRA. *Current Pos:* PROF MATH, US NAVAL ACAD, 74- *Personal Data:* b Glenridge, NJ May 8, 41. *Educ:* Develis Col, BA, 63; Yale Col, MS, 65, PhD(math), 70. *Mem:* Am Math Soc; Am Med Asn. *Res:* Algebra. *Mailing Add:* Dept Math US Naval Acad 572 Holloway Rd Annapolis MD 21402-5002

ANDREA, STEPHEN ALFRED, MATHEMATICS. *Current Pos:* PROF, SIMON BOLIVAR UNIV, VENEZUELA, 71- *Personal Data:* b Cuba, NY, July 10, 38. *Educ:* Oberlin Col, BA, 60; Calif Inst Technol, PhD(math), 64. *Prof Exp:* Instr math, Harvard Univ, 64-67; asst prof, Univ Calif, San Diego, 67-71. *Mem:* Am Math Soc. *Res:* Differential topology; topological dynamics. *Mailing Add:* Apartado Postal 80-184 Zona Postal 1080-A Caracas Venezuela

ANDREADIS, THEODORE GEORGE, ENTOMOLOGY, INSECT PATHOLOGY. *Current Pos:* from asst res entomologist to res entomologist, 78-92, HEAD, DEPT SOIL & WATER, CONN AGR EXP STA, 92- *Personal Data:* b Chelsea, Mass, Mar 22, 50; m 76; c 2. *Educ:* Univ Mass, BS, 72, MS, 75; Univ Fla, PhD(entom), 78. *Prof Exp:* Res asst entom, Univ Mass, 73-74; instr biol & field naturalist, Cape Cod Mus Natural Hist, 75; res & teaching asst entom, Univ Fla, 75-78. *Concurrent Pos:* Mem, Conn State Salt Marsh Mgt Comt, 85-, Conn State Mosquito Control Adv Bd, 86-; chmn, Div Microsporida, Soc Invertebrate Path, 86-88; Lectr epidemiol & pub health, Sch Med, Yale Univ, 87-; bd reviewers, Jour Protozool, 90- *Mem:* Entom Soc Am; Sigma Xi; Soc Invertebrate Path; Am Mosquito Control Asn; Soc Protozoologists. *Res:* Development of microbial agents for control of insects of public health importance; mosquitoes; biology of Microsporida; electron microscopy. *Mailing Add:* Dept Soil & Water Conn Agr Exp Sta 123 Huntington St PO Box 1106 New Haven CT 06504-2016. *Fax:* 203-789-7232

ANDREADIS, TIM DIMITRI, SURFACE SCIENCE. *Current Pos:* RES PHYSICIST, NAVAL RES LAB, 87- *Personal Data:* b Suez, Egypt, Oct 3, 51; US citizen. *Educ:* Univ Md, College Park, BS, 74, MS, 77, PhD(nuclear eng), 81. *Prof Exp:* Spacecraft analyst, Comput Sci Technicolor Assocs, 74-77; res asst, Dept Nuclear Eng, Univ Md, 77-81; nuclear engr, Nat Bur Standards, 81-82; res assoc & lectr dept chem & nuclear eng, Univ Md, College Park, 82-87. *Mem:* Am Nuclear Soc; Am Vacuum Soc. *Res:* Near surface phenomena brought about by ion bombardment (implantation, diffusion, sputtering, and composition changes); investigations using Monte Carlo computer simulation of near surface interactions and with surface science techniques such as x-ray and Auger spectroscopy and quartz resonator microbalance. *Mailing Add:* Naval Res Lab Code 6653 4555 Overlook Ave Washington DC 20375-5345

ANDREAE, MEINRAT OTTO, MARINE CHEMISTRY, BIOGEOCHEMISTRY. *Current Pos:* DIR, MAX PLANCK INST, WGER. *Personal Data:* b Augsburg, Ger. *Educ:* Univ Karlsruhe, BSc, 70; Univ Gottingen, MSc, 74; Univ Calif, San Diego, PhD(oceanog), 78. *Honors & Awards:* Gerbier/Mumm Prize, World Meteorol Orgn, 90. *Prof Exp:* Res asst geochem, Univ Gottingen, 71-74 & marine chem, Scripps Inst Oceanog, Univ Calif, San Diego, 74-78; from asst prof to prof oceanog, Fla State Univ, 82. *Mem:* Sigma Xi; AAAS; Am Chem Soc; Am Geophys Union; Europ Geophys Soc. *Res:* Chemistry of trace elements in the marine environment and the atmosphere; biosynthesis of trace compounds by marine plankton; atmospheric sulfur and nitrogen cycles; biomass burning. *Mailing Add:* Max Planck Inst Post Fach 3060 55128 Mainz Germany

ANDREAS, BARBARA KLOHA, BIOSYSTEMATICS. *Current Pos:* ASSOC PROF BIOL, CUYAHOGA COMMUNITY COL, 74- *Personal Data:* b Dundee, Ohio, Sept 21, 46; m 66; c 2. *Educ:* Kent State Univ, BA, 68, MA, 70, PhD(plant taxon), 80. *Prof Exp:* Instr bot, Kent State Univ, 70-71. *Concurrent Pos:* Field botanist, Div Natural Areas & Preserves, ODNR, 80-; NSF grant award bot, 81-; botanist, US Fish & Wildlife, 85. *Mem:* Am Inst Biol Sci; Am Soc Plant Taxonomists; Sigma Xi. *Res:* Biosystematics of angiosperms, especially Asclepiadaceae and Gentianaceae; Midwest floristics; bog and fen floristics and ecology. *Mailing Add:* Health Sci Cuyahoga Community Col Eastern 4250 Richmond Rd Cleveland OH 44122-6104

ANDREAS, JOHN M(OORE), PHOTOGRAPHIC CHEMISTRY. *Current Pos:* CONSULT CHEM ENG, 70- *Personal Data:* b New York, NY, June 17, 12; c 2. *Educ:* Princeton Univ, BS, 35; Mass Inst Technol, SM, 37, ScD(chem eng), 38. *Prof Exp:* Sr res engr, res & develop div, Technicolor Corp Am, 38-69, chem engr, systs res div, 69-70. *Mem:* AAAS; Am Chem Soc; Soc Motion Picture & TV Eng; Am Inst Chem Engrs; Am Defense Preparedness Asn; Am Inst Chem; Am Asn Textile Chem & Colorists; Sigma Xi. *Res:* Friction for air flow; boundary tension by pendant drops; color motion picture photography; color measurements; dyestuffs; photographic processes and processing; interfacial tension by pendant drops; inks; dye transfer; azo dyes. *Mailing Add:* 890 Hillcrest Pl Pasadena CA 91106-4505

ANDREASEN, ARTHUR ALBINUS, INDUSTRIAL MICROBIOLOGY. *Current Pos:* RETIRED. *Personal Data:* b Springfield, Ill, Dec 18, 17; m 44, Mary Ellen; c 2. *Educ:* Univ Ill, BS, 40, MS, 42; Ind Univ, PhD(cytophysiol), 53. *Prof Exp:* From bacteriologist to chief chemist & head fermentation res, Joseph E Seagram & Sons, Inc, 41-61, dir res, 61-81. *Concurrent Pos:* In chg fermentation, Exp Wood Hydrolysis Distillery, Vulcan Copper & Supply Co, Ore, 46-47. *Mem:* Am Chem Soc; Am Soc Brewing Chem. *Res:* Anaerobic growth and nutrition of yeast; yeast and mold fermentations; enzyme production. *Mailing Add:* 508 Hill Ridge Rd Louisville KY 40214-3545

ANDREASEN, NANCY COOVER, PSYCHIATRY. *Current Pos:* asst prof eng, 63-66, from asst prof to assoc prof psychiat, 77-81, PROF PSYCHIAT, UNIV IOWA, 81-, ANDREW H WOODS PROF, 92- *Personal Data:* b Lincoln, Nebr, Nov 11, 38; c 2. *Educ:* Univ Nebr, BA, 58 & PhD(eng), 63; Radcliffe Col, MA, 59; Univ Iowa, MD, 70. *Honors & Awards:* Menninger Award Psychiat Res, Menninger Found, 73; Hibbs Award, Am Psychiat Asn; Nelson Urban Res Award; Found Fund Prize & Dean Award, Am Col Psychiatrists. *Prof Exp:* Instr Eng, Nebr Wesleyan Univ, 60-61 & Univ Nebr, 62-63. *Concurrent Pos:* Prin investr, NIMH Collab Study Depression, 73-; mem, Am Psychiat Asn Task Force Diag & Statist Manual, 74-; mem, Nat Merit Rev Bd Behav Sci, 78-; consult, training grant study sect, NIMH, 78-79. *Mem:* Inst Med-Nat Acad Sci; Am Col Psychiatrists; Psychiat Res Soc; Am Psychiat Asn; Am Psychopath Asn (vpres); Neurosci Soc. *Res:* Brain imaging in the major psychoses and schizophrenia; study of depression; speech, language, thought and communication in mania, depression and schizophrenia; family history and psychiatric symptoms in creative individuals; psychiatric aspects of facial deformity; study of depression. *Mailing Add:* Dept Psychiat MHRC 2911 JPP Univ Iowa 200 Hawkins Dr Iowa City IA 52242. *Fax:* 319-353-8300

ANDREEN, BRIAN H, ANALYTICAL CHEMISTRY. *Current Pos:* midwest rep, Res Corp, 64-69, regional dir, 69-87, grants prog coordr, 87-89, dir, Sci Advan Progs, 90-92, VPRES RES CORP, 92- *Personal Data:* b Superior, Wis, Aug 15, 34; m 56; c 4. *Educ:* Wis State Univ, Superior, BS, 56; Fla State Univ, MS, 59. *Prof Exp:* Assoc chemist, Inst Gas Technol, 59-60, res chemist, 60-62, supvr chem res, 62-64. *Mem:* AAAS; Am Chem Soc; Coun Undergrad Res. *Res:* Gas chromatographic analysis; detection of air pollutants; nurture of undergraduate research. *Mailing Add:* Res Corp 101 N Wilmont Suite 250 Tucson AZ 85710

ANDREGG, CHARLES HAROLD, surveying & mapping, physical science administration; deceased, see previous edition for last biography

ANDREIS, HENRY JEROME, SOIL FERTILITY. *Current Pos:* Soil technologist res, 55-69, FIRST ASST TO DIR & VPRES RES DEPT, US SUGAR CORP, 69- *Personal Data:* b Milwaukee, Wis, Sept 1, 31; m 54; c 5. *Educ:* Univ Wis, BS, 54, MS, 55. *Mem:* Am Soc Agron; Int Soc Sugarcane Technologists; Am Soc Sugarcane Technologists; Am Soc Agron. *Res:* Sugarcane and pasture fertility studies, silage research, seed cane germination studies; water table and irrigation studies and citrus nursery. *Mailing Add:* 1012 Palmetto St Clewiston FL 33440

ANDREJ, LADISLAV, NEURAL NETWORKS, DYNAMICAL SYSTEMS THEORY & CHAODYNAMICS. *Current Pos:* SR SCIENTIST, ACAD SCI, CZECH REPUB, 89- *Personal Data:* b Wlaca, Slovakia, July 15, 48; Czech & Slovak citizen; m 77, Helena Broulik; c Margaret & Helena. *Educ:* Charles Univ, Prague, RNDr, 75, CSc(biol), 87. *Prof Exp:* Asst prof biophysics, Univ PJF, 74-78; Monbusho fel, Kyoto Univ, Japan, 78-80; pvt docent res phys biol, Unit Fundamental, 87-89. *Concurrent Pos:* Prin investr, Grant Agency, Czech, 91-98; comt mem, Neurosci Soc, 92-98. *Mem:* NY Acad Sci; Am Math Soc; Japan Phys Soc; Europ Phys Soc; Neurosci Soc; Union Math & Phys. *Res:* Study of qualitatively new neural networks endowed with a novel dynamics of lambda-theta mechanism and potentiality of chaotic behavior in such nets; neural nets with attention; deterministic chaos in other biological systems-an origin of some leukemias. *Mailing Add:* Klicanska 1 18200 Prague 8 Czech Republic. *E-Mail:* andreetuivt.cas.cz

ANDREOLI, ANTHONY JOSEPH, BACTERIOLOGY, BIOCHEMISTRY. *Current Pos:* from asst prof to assoc prof chem & microbiol, 55-64, PROF CHEM, CALIF STATE UNIV, LOS ANGELES, 64- *Personal Data:* b New York, NY, Sept 13, 26; m 52. *Educ:* Univ Southern Calif, AB, 50, PhD(bact), 55. *Prof Exp:* Asst bact, Univ Southern Calif, 50-52, clin lab technician, 52-53, lectr, 54-55. *Mem:* Am Soc Microbiol; Am Soc Biol Chemists. *Res:* Bacterial metabolism and physiology; NAD metabolism; bacterial sporulation. *Mailing Add:* Dept Chem Calif State Univ 5151 State Univ Dr Los Angeles CA 90032-4221

ANDREOLI, KATHLEEN GAINOR, NURSING ADMINISTRATION. *Current Pos:* VPRES NURSING AFFAIRS & DEAN, COL NURSING, RUSH-PRESBY ST LUKE'S MED CTR, CHICAGO, 87- *Personal Data:* b Albany, NY, Sept 22, 35; div; c Paula, Thomas & Karen. *Educ:* Georgetown Univ, BSN, 57; Vanderbilt Univ, MSN, 59; Univ Ala, DSN, 79. *Prof Exp:* Instr, St Thomas Hosp Sch Nursing, Nashville, 58-59, Georgetown Univ Sch Nursing, 59-60, Duke Univ Sch Nursing, 60-61 & Bon Secours Hosp Sch Nursing, Baltimore, 62-64; clin assoc prof cardiovasc nursing, Sch Nursing, Univ Ala Med Ctr, Birmingham, 70, educ dir & physician asst prof, Dept Med, 70-75, asst prof nursing, 71-72, assoc prof, Sch Pub & Allied Health, 73, assoc dir, Family Nurse Practitioner Prog, Sch Nursing, 76-77, assoc prof, Community Health Nursing Grad Prog, 77, assoc prof, Dept Pub Health, 78, prof, Sch Nursing, 79; spec asst to pres educ affairs, Univ Tex Health Sci Serv Ctr, Houston, 79, actg dean, Sch Allied Health Sci, 80-81, spec asst to pres & dir acad affairs, 81, exec dir acad affairs, 81-84, vpres educ servs, Interprof Educ & Int Progs, assoc dir, Ctr Health Prom Res & Develop, 84-87. *Concurrent Pos:* Consult, 66-; ed, Heart & Lung, J Total Care, St Louis, 71; mem comt educ health prof, Int Med-Nat Acad Sci, 73, mem study comt effectiveness of Community Ment Health Ctrs, 74-75, mem comt, 74-77; mem clin assoc prog, Univ Ky, 74; mem physician's asst prog, Western Mich Univ, 75, Long Island Univ & Brooklyn-Cumberland Med Ctr, 76; mem cancer prevention & control adv comt, Univ Tex Syst Cancer Ctr, 81; mem, Coun Cardiovasc Nursing, Am Heart Asn; bd mem, Houston Acad Med, Tex Med Ctr, Inc, Libr, 82-; mem bd trustees, Found Mus Med Sci, Houston, 82-87; mem, Nat Adv Comt, Robert Wood Johnson Clin Scholars Prog, 88-; mem, Nat Nursing Adv Coun, Vol Hosps Am, 91-; mem gov coun, Am Hosp Asn, Inst Hosp Clin Nursing Educ. *Mem:* Inst Med-Nat Acad Sci; fel Am Acad Nursing; Am Nurses Asn; Nat League Nursing; Am Asn Critical Care Nurses; Am Heart Asn; Am Orgn Nurse Execs. *Res:* Co-author or author of numerous publications. *Mailing Add:* Rush Presby St Luke's Med Ctr 1653 W Congress Pkwy Chicago IL 60612. *Fax:* 312-942-3043

ANDREOLI, THOMAS E, INTERNAL MEDICINE. *Current Pos:* PROF & CHMN, DEPT INTERNAL MED & PROF PHYSIOL & BIOPHYS, COL MED, UNIV ARK, LITTLE ROCK, 88-, NOLAN CHAIR INTERNAL MED, 91- *Personal Data:* b Bronx, NY, Jan 9, 35. *Educ:* St Vincent Col, BA, 56; Georgetown Univ, MD, 60; Am Bd Internal Med, dipl, nephrology, dipl. *Hon Degrees:* ScD, St Vincent Col, 87. *Prof Exp:* From intern to jr asst resident med, Duke Hosp, 60-61; mem, Lab Intermediary Metab, Geront Sect, NIH, Baltimore City Hosps, 61-64; assoc med & physiol, Duke Univ, 65-66, asst prof med & assoc physiol, 66-67, asst prof med & physiol, 67-69, assoc prof med & asst prof physiol, 69-70; dir, Nephrology Res & Training Ctr, prof med & dir, Div Nephrology, Sch Med, Univ Ala, 70-79; prof & chmn, Dept Internal Med, Med Sch, Univ Tex, Houston, 79-86, Edward Randall, III prof, 86-88, chmn, 86-87. *Concurrent Pos:* Jr asst resident med, Duke Hosp, 64; chief resident & instr med, Duke Univ & Durham Vet Admin Hosp, 65; res career develop award, Nat Inst Gen Med Sci, NIH, 67 & 70; from assoc prof to prof physiol & biophys, Sch Med, Univ Ala, 70-79; ed, Am J Physiol, 76-83; assoc ed, Am J Med, 79-86; prof physiol & cell biol, Med Sch, Univ Tex, Houston, 79-88; co-chmn, External Monitoring Comt, Modification of Diet Renal Dis Study, Nat Inst Diabetes, Digestive & Kidney Dis, NIH, 89-, mem, Gen Clin Res Ctrs Comt, Div Res Resources, 89- *Mem:* Fel Am Col Physicians; Am Fedn Clin Res; Am Physiol Soc; Am Soc Clin Invest (secy-treas, 77-80); Am Soc Nephrology; Asn Am Physicians; Asn Prof Med; Biophys Soc; Int Soc Nephrology; Soc Gen Physiologists. *Mailing Add:* Dept Internal Med Col Med Univ Ark 4301 W Markham Slot 640 Little Rock AR 72205-7199. *Fax:* 501-686-8188

ANDRES, GIUSEPPE A, CLINICAL IMMUNOLOGY. *Current Pos:* prof microbiol, 70-74, PROF MED, STATE UNIV NY, BUFFALO, 74- *Personal Data:* b Torino, Italy, Mar 11, 24; m 64; c 2. *Educ:* Univ Pisa, Italy, MD, 49; Univ Roma, PhD(med), 65. *Prof Exp:* Asst prof med, Univ Pisa, 54-55; fel, Dept Med, Col Physicians & Surgeons, Columbia Univ, 55-56, res fel, Univ, 58-59, res fel microbiol, Col Physicians & Surgeons, 60-61, vis prof, 64-70. *Concurrent Pos:* Asst prof med, Univ Roma, 56-70; Fogarty Sr Int fel, NIH, 77-78; mem, Path Study Sect, NIH, 77-81. *Mem:* Harvey Soc; Am Soc Cell Biol; Am Asn Immunologists; Transplantation Soc. *Res:* Human and experimental immunopathology with special interest in diseases of the kidney and the lung; biology and immunopathology of organ transplantation, especially kidney and liver. *Mailing Add:* Div Surg Sci Columbia Univ Col Physicians & Surgeons 630 W 168th St 17th Floor New York NY 10032

ANDRES, JOHN MILTON, MICROWAVE ELECTRONICS. *Current Pos:* RETIRED. *Personal Data:* b Santa Ana, Calif, Feb 4, 27; m 56, Anne MacLeod; c Jamie, Paul, David & Phillip. *Educ:* Calif Inst Technol, BS, 49, MS, 50; Mass Inst Technol, PhD(physics), 53. *Prof Exp:* Mem tech staff, Calif Res Corp, 53-54; mem tech staff, Space Technol Labs, Thompson-Ramo-Wooldridge, Inc, 54-60, sect head, TRW Systs Group, 60-63, mgr quantum electronics dept, 62-70, mem sr staff, Electronic Systs Div, 70-87. *Mem:* Am Phys Soc; Sigma Xi; Inst Elec & Electronics Engrs. *Res:* Field effect transistor amplifiers; oscillators; laser communications. *Mailing Add:* 1340 via Margarita Palos Verdes Estates CA 90278-2027

ANDRES, KLAUS, SUPERCONDUCTIVITY, MAGNETISM. *Current Pos:* PROF, TECH UNIV MUNICH, GER, 80- *Personal Data:* b Zurich, Switz, Mar 1, 34; m 70, Maria Stauffacher; c Philip, Dieter & Karin. *Educ:* Swiss Fed Inst Technol, PhD(physics), 63. *Prof Exp:* Mem tech staff physics, Bell Tel Labs, 63-80. *Concurrent Pos:* Acad guest, Swiss Fed Inst Technol, 68-69; guest prof, Tech Univ Munich, 73. *Mem:* Fel Am Phys Soc; Swiss Phys Soc; Ger Phys Soc. *Res:* Superconductivity; magnetism; rare earth compounds; nuclear magnetism at very low temperatures; organic conductors. *Mailing Add:* Walter Meissner Inst Fuer Tieftemperatureforschung Walter Meissner Str 8 85748 Garching Germany

ANDRES, LLOYD A, ENTOMOLOGY, WEED SCIENCE. *Current Pos:* RETIRED. *Personal Data:* b Santa Ana, Calif, May 17, 28; m 56; c 3. *Educ:* Univ Calif, Berkeley, PhD(entom), 57. *Prof Exp:* Res entomologist, Univ Calif, Riverside, 56-58; res entomologist, USDA, 58-64, leader biol control weeds invests, 64-72, res leader & nat tech adv biol control weeds, Sci & Educ Admin-Agr Res, 72-82, proj leader, Biol Control Unit, 82-88. *Mem:* AAAS; Entom Soc Am; Am Inst Biol Sci; Weed Sci Soc Am. *Res:* Biological control of weeds. *Mailing Add:* 1324 Arch Berkeley CA 94708

ANDRES, REUBIN, MEDICINE, GERONTOLOGY. *Current Pos:* fel med, Johns Hopkins Univ, 50-55, from instr to asst prof, 55-63, assoc prof, 63-76, PROF MED, JOHNS HOPKINS UNIV, 76-; CHIEF CLIN PHYSIOL BR, NAT INST ON AGING, 62-, CLIN DIR, 75- *Personal Data:* b Dallas, Tex, June 13, 23; m 48; c 4. *Educ:* Southwestern Med Col, MD, 44; Am Bd Internal Med, dipl. *Honors & Awards:* Kleemeier Award, Geront Soc Am, 74; Edward Henderson Award, Am Geriat Soc, 85; Allied Signal Achievement Award in Aging, 86; Enrico Greppi Geront Prize, Italy, 87; Clin Res Award, Am Aging Asn, 89; Freeman Award, Geront Soc Am 93. *Prof Exp:* Intern, Gallinger Munic Hosp, Washington, DC, 45; resident med, Vet Admin Hosp, McKinney, Tex, 47-50. *Concurrent Pos:* Asst physician, Outpatient Dept, Johns Hopkins Hosp, 50-58; instr, Sch Hyg & Pub Health, Johns Hopkins Univ, 53-55, asst prof, 55-60, lectr, 60-61; vis physician, Baltimore City Hosps, 55-57, asst chief med, 58-62; asst prof, Univ Md, 58-62. *Mem:* Am Physiol Soc; Am Soc Clin Invest; Geront Soc Am; Am Diabetes Asn; Endocrine Soc; Asn Am Physicians. *Res:* Carbohydrate and lipid metabolism; physiology of aging; epidemiology of obesity and fat distribution pattern. *Mailing Add:* Clin Dir Gerontol Res Ctr NIA NIH Box 24 4940 Eastern Ave Baltimore MD 21224-2780

ANDRES, RONALD PAUL, CHEMICAL ENGINEERING. *Current Pos:* prof & head chem eng, 81-88, PROF ENG RES, PURDUE UNIV, 88- *Personal Data:* b Chicago, Ill, Jan 9, 38; m 61, Jean Elwood; c Douglas, Jennifer & Mark. *Educ:* Northwestern Univ, BS, 59; Princeton Univ, PhD(chem eng), 63. *Prof Exp:* From asst prof to prof chem, Princeton Univ, 62-81. *Concurrent Pos:* Vis prof, Indian Inst Technol, Kanpur, 70; distinguished prof, Univ Eindhoven, 74. *Mem:* Am Inst Chem Engrs; Am Chem Soc; AAAS; Sigma Xi; Mat Res Soc; Am Asn Aerosol Res. *Res:* Aerosol physics; physics and chemistry of molecular clusters; nanostructured materials; chemical kinetics and catalysis. *Mailing Add:* Sch Chem Eng Purdue Univ West Lafayette IN 47907-1283. *Fax:* 765-494-0805; *E-Mail:* ronald@ecn.purdue.edu

ANDRES, SCOTT FITZGERALD, PROGRAM ADMINISTRATOR, PLACENTAL RESEARCH PROGRAM. *Current Pos:* sci rev adminr, 86-91, HEALTH SCIENTIST ADMINR & PROG ADMINR, NIH, 91- *Personal Data:* b Ann Arbor, Mich, July 23, 45; m 92, Doris Lorraine Manspeaker; c Kristin E & Kerry L. *Educ:* Mich State Univ, BS, 67; Wayne State Univ, PhD(biochem), 72. *Prof Exp:* Res assoc, Wayne Co Gen Hosp, 72-77; chemist, US Food & Drug Admin, 77-78, consumer safety officer, 78-82, chemist, 82-86. *Concurrent Pos:* Prin investr, Wayne Co Gen Hosp, 76-77. *Mem:* AAAS; Int Fed Placenta Asn; Europ Placental Group. *Res:* Investigation of the roles of specific amino acid residues in the conformation and immunochemistry of sperm whale myoglobin; active site characterization of parathyroid hormone; radioimmunoassay. *Mailing Add:* NIH-NICHD-CRMC Pregnancy & Perinatology Br Bldg 61E Rm 4B03C 6100 Exec Blvd Rockville MD 20892-7510. *Fax:* 301-496-3790; *E-Mail:* andress@hd01.nichd.nih.gov

ANDRE-SCHWARTZ, JANINE, electron microscopy, immunology; deceased, see previous edition for last biography

ANDRESEN, BRIAN DEAN, MASS SPECTROMETRY, ORGANIC CHEMISTRY. *Current Pos:* mem fac pharmacol, 80-83, CTR MGR, FORENSIC SCI CTR, OHIO STATE UNIV, 83- *Personal Data:* b Reed City, Mich, Jan 20, 47. *Educ:* Fla State Univ, BS, 69; Mass Inst Technol, SM, 71, PhD(chem), 74; Woods Hole Oceanog Inst, SM, 72. *Prof Exp:* Asst prof pharmaceut chem, Col Pharm, Univ Fla, 74-80. *Concurrent Pos:* Dir, Forensic Sci Ctr. *Mem:* Am Chem Soc; Int Oceanog Found; Am Col Forensic Examiners; Am Acad Forensic Scientists. *Res:* Application of gas chromatography, mass spectrometry and computer analysis for the identification of biologically active compounds; application of synthetic organic chemistry for the preparation of useful pharmaceuticals; clinical chemistry and toxicology. *Mailing Add:* Lawrence Livermore Lab L-371 PO Box 808 Livermore CA 94551

ANDRESEN, MICHAEL CHRISTIAN, NEURAL CONTROL OF CIRCULATION, HYPERTENSION. *Current Pos:* ASSOC PROF, ORE HEALTH SCIS UNIV, 92- *Personal Data:* b Lynwood, Calif, Dec 1, 49; m 74; c 2. *Educ:* Univ Calif, Irvine, BS, 71; San Diego State Univ, MS, 73; Univ Tex Med Br, PhD(physiol), 78. *Prof Exp:* Teaching asst biol, San Diego Univ, 72-73; teaching & res asst physiol, Med Br, Univ Tex, 75-77, res assoc, 77-78, NIH fel, 78-79, res scientist, 79-80; vis scientist, Baker Med Res Inst, 80-81; from asst prof to assoc prof physiol, Med Br, Univ Tex, Galveston, 81-92. *Concurrent Pos:* Prin investr, NIH res grants, 82-; Am Heart Asn res grants, 81-; ad hoc mem Heart Lung & Blood Comt A, NIH, 89, Heart Lung & Blood Cardiovasc & Pulmonary Study Sect 89, Vet Admin Merit Review, 90 & 94; Welcome Trust, 95-; Coun High Blood Pressure, Am Heart Asn. *Mem:* Biophys Soc; AAAS; Am Physiol Soc; Soc Neurosci. *Res:* Nature of mechanotransduction by arterial baroreceptors and cardiopulmonary mechanoreceptors; the role of receptor properties in the reflex regulation of cardiovascular system; synaptic transmission and medullary neurons in the solitary tract nucleus and cardiovascular integration. *Mailing Add:* Dept Physiol & Pharmacol Mail Code L334 Ore Health Scis Univ 3181 SW Sam Portland OR 97201-3098. *Fax:* 503-494-4352; *E-Mail:* andresen@ohsu.edu

ANDRESEN, NORMAN A, ALGAL TAXONOMY, ALGAL ECOLOGY. *Current Pos:* RES ASSOC, UNIV MICH, 89- *Personal Data:* b Chicago, Ill, Aug 12, 43; m 66; c 1. *Educ:* Taylor Univ, AB, 65; Mich State Univ, MS, 68; Univ Mich, PhD(bot), 76. *Prof Exp:* Asst prof biol, Ball State Univ, 76-77; vis lectr bot, Eastern Mich Univ, 77-79, 90; chief aquatic biologist, Bionetics Corp, 81-88. *Mem:* AAAS; Phycol Soc Am; Brit Phycol Soc; Int Soc Diatom Res; Int Phycol Soc. *Res:* Taxonomy and ecology of diatoms paleoecological reconstructions of environments from sediment cores and biological fossils; population dynamics in Great Lakes phytoplankton assemblages. *Mailing Add:* 5742 Princeton Pl Ypsilanti MI 48197. *Fax:* 313-647-2748; *E-Mail:* andresen@umich.edu

ANDRESEN, PETER LOUIS, STRESS CORROSION CRACKING, CORROSION. *Current Pos:* SR SCIENTIST, RES & DEVELOP CTR, GE CORP, 78- *Personal Data:* b Oakland, Calif, Apr 16, 50; m, Myra Jane Brugger; c Matthew A & Elise L. *Educ:* Rensselaer Polytech Inst, BS, 72, MS, 74, PhD(mat sci), 79. *Honors & Awards:* Speller Award, Nat Asn Corrosion Engrs, 96. *Concurrent Pos:* Consult, Dept Energy, 89-97. *Mem:* Nat Asn Corrosion Engrs; fel Am Soc Metals. *Res:* Localized corrosion and environmental effects on mechanical properties and integrity of materials. *Mailing Add:* 1204 Rugbyu Rd Schenectady NY 12308-2518

ANDREW, BRYAN HAYDN, radio astronomy, for more information see previous edition

ANDREW, DAVID ROBERT, MATHEMATICS. *Current Pos:* RETIRED. *Personal Data:* b Wink, Tex, Nov 10, 35; m 58, Catherine A Vige; c Robert C, Lisa L & David H. *Educ:* Univ Southwestern La, BS, 58; Iowa State Univ, MS, 59; Univ Pittsburgh, PhD(math), 61. *Prof Exp:* From asst prof to assoc prof, Univ Southwestern La, 61-66, head dept, 69-75, prof math, 66-87 & 90-, dean Col Sci, 75-86. *Concurrent Pos:* Consult, Minn Sch Math & Sci Teaching Proj, 64-66; mem, Coun Cols Arts & Sci, 79. *Mem:* Math Asn Am. *Res:* Point set topology. *Mailing Add:* 412 Kim Dr Lafayette LA 70503

ANDREW, EDWARD RAYMOND, NUCLEAR MAGNETIC RESONANCE, MAGNETIC RESONANCE IN MEDICINE. *Current Pos:* PROF PHYSICS, UNIV FLA, 83- *Personal Data:* b Boston, Lincolnshire, Eng, June 27, 21; m 72, Eunice Tinning; c Charmian & Patricia. *Educ:* Cambridge Univ, Eng, BA, 42, MA, 46, PhD(physics), 48, ScD, 64. *Hon Degrees:* DSc, Univ Turku, Finland, 80, Univ Poznan, Poland, 89 & Univ Leipzig, Ger, 90. *Honors & Awards:* Distinguished Serv Medal, Soc Magnetic Resonance Med, 91; Wellcome Medal, Royal Soc, London, 84. *Prof Exp:* Sci officer, Royal Radar Estab, Eng, 42-45; commonwealth fund fel, Harvard Univ, 48-49; lectr physics, Univ St Andrews, Scotland, 49-54; prof physics, Univ Wales, Bangor, 54-64; Lancashire-Spencer prof physics, Nottingham Univ, 64-83, dean, sci, 75-78. *Concurrent Pos:* Pres, Groupement Ampere, 74-80, Int Soc Magnetic Resonance, 84-87; fel, Christs Col, Cambridge, 89 & Clare Col, Cambridge, 96. *Mem:* Fel Royal Soc London; fel Royal Soc Edinburgh; fel Am Phys Soc; European Phys Soc; fel Inst Physics UK; Soc Magnetic Resonance Med. *Res:* Nuclear magnetic resonance in physics; applied physics; chemical physics; biophysics and medicine. *Mailing Add:* Dept Physics Univ Fla Gainesville FL 32611. *Fax:* 904-392-8863; *E-Mail:* andrew@phys.ufl.edu

ANDREW, JAMES F, experimental solid state physics, for more information see previous edition

ANDREW, KENNETH L, ATOMIC EMISSION SPECTROSCOPY, FOURIER SPECTROSCOPY. *Current Pos:* from assoc prof to prof, 57-89, EMER PROF PHYSICS, PURDUE UNIV, WEST LAFAYETTE, 89- *Personal Data:* b Wichita, Kans, June 14, 19; m 40, Lois Ranner; c Ralph K, Dale E & Nancy (Lee). *Educ:* Friends Univ, AB, 40; Johns Hopkins Univ, MA, 42; Purdue Univ, PhD(physics), 51. *Prof Exp:* Head, Dept Physics, Friends Univ, 42-56; chmn dept physics, Dickinson Univ, 56-57. *Concurrent Pos:* Prin investr, NSF Res Grants Atomic Emission Spectroscopy, 58-83, mem comt line spectra of elements, Nat Res Coun, 61-73, chmn, 66-68; consult, Int Astron Union, 64-71, Los Alamos Nat Lab, 65-72 & 77-; mem, Comn 14, Int Astron Union, 71-; prof d'Exchange Labs Aime Cotton, Orsay, France, 68-69; guest scientist, Nat Bur Standards, 86, 88 & 91. *Mem:* Am Phys Soc; fel Optical Soc Am; Am Asn Physics Teachers; Europ Group Atomic Spectroscopists. *Res:* Atomic emission spectroscopy; interferometric measurements; analysis of atomic spectra; atomic energy levels; standard wavelengths; comparison of atomic theory with experiments. *Mailing Add:* 1637 May No 1002 Wichita KS 67213

ANDREW, ROBERT HARRY, AGRONOMY. *Current Pos:* From asst prof to prof, 46-58, EMER PROF AGRON, UNIV WIS-MADISON, 84- *Personal Data:* b Platteville, Wis, Aug 2, 16; m 44, Nancy Wright; c Stephen, Elizabeth, Sarah, Martha & Charles. *Educ:* Univ Wis, BA, 38, PhD(agron-genetics), 42. *Honors & Awards:* Fel Am Soc Agron; fel Crop Sci Soc Am; fel AAAS. *Concurrent Pos:* Vis lectr, Wageningen, Neth, 53-54; vis prof, Portoalegre, Rio Grande Do Sul, Brazil, 68; consult, Padang, W Sumatra, Indonesia, 86, Medan, N Sumatra, 87, Kharkov, Ukraine & Krasnodar, Russia, USSR, 87. *Mem:* Fel Am Soc Agron; Ecol Soc Am; Am Genetics Asn; fel Crop Sci Soc Am; fel AAAS. *Res:* Corn production; sweet corn breeding, genetics; plant ecology. *Mailing Add:* Dept Agron Univ Wis Madison WI 53706

ANDREW, WILLIAM TRELEAVEN, vegetable crops, for more information see previous edition

ANDREWES, ARTHUR GEORGE, ORGANIC CHEMISTRY, BIOCHEMISTRY. *Current Pos:* asst prof, 76-80, ASSOC PROF CHEM & CHMN DEPT, SAGINAW VALLEY STATE UNIV, 80- *Personal Data:* b Springfield, Mass, Sept 21, 39; m 72; c 3. *Educ:* Am Int Col, BA, 60; Univ Md, MS, 63; NMex State Univ, PhD (chem), 70. *Prof Exp:* Analytical chemist, Food & Drug Admin, 63-66; res assoc chem, Univ Calif, 74-76. *Concurrent Pos:* Res asst, Univ Wis-Madison, 69-71; fel, Univ Trondheim, Norway, 71-74. *Mem:* Am Chem Soc; Sigma Xi. *Res:* Structures; stereochemistry; total synthesis and biosynthesis of naturally occuring polyene compounds, particularly carotenoids. *Mailing Add:* Dept Chem Saginaw Valley State Univ University Center MI 48710

ANDREWS, AUSTIN MICHAEL, II, electrical engineering, solid state electronics, for more information see previous edition

ANDREWS, BETHLEHEM KOTTES, CHEMISTRY, MATHEMATICS. *Current Pos:* Res chemist durable press, 57-75, res chemist, spec prod res, 76-84, LEAD SCIENTIST, TEXTILE FINISHING CHEM RES, SOUTHERN REGIONAL RES CTR, USDA, 85- *Personal Data:* b New Orleans, La, Sept 18, 36; m 59; c 2. *Educ:* Tulane Univ, BA, 57. *Concurrent Pos:* Am Heart Asn res grant, 57; vis woman scientist, NSF, 78; US deleg, Int Sci Orgn. *Mem:* Am Chem Soc; Am Asn Textile Chemists & Colorists; Fiber Soc; Sigma Xi; Int Sci Orgn. *Res:* Chemical modification and finishing of cotton and cellulose derivatives; finishing systems for knitted cotton; chemistry and catalysis of crosslinking finishes for cellulose; chemistry of formaldehyde release in crosslinked cellulose. *Mailing Add:* 5844 Sylvia Dr New Orleans LA 70124-1132

ANDREWS, BILLY FRANKLIN, PEDIATRICS & NUTRITION, METABOLISM. *Current Pos:* from asst prof to assoc prof pediat, Sch Med, Univ Louisville, 64-68, dir, Newborn Serv, 64-75, co-dir, Genetic Coun Unit, 65-68, chmn, 69-93, chief-of-staff, 69-93, PROF PEDIAT, KOSAIR CHILDREN'S HOSP SCH MED, UNIV LOUISVILLE, 68-, DIR COMPREHENSIVE HEALTH CARE CTR FOR HIGH RISK INFANTS & CHILDREN, 68-, EMER CHMN DEPT PEDIAT, 93-, EMER CHIEF-OF-STAFF, KOSAIR CHILDREN'S HOSP, 93-, DIR, INBORN ERRORS OF METAB CLIN, 95- *Personal Data:* b Graham, NC, Sept 22, 32; m 53, Faye Rich; c Ann E (Feigenbaum), Billy Franklin Jr & David Ashley. *Educ:* Wake Forest Col, BS, 53; Duke Univ, MD, 57; Am Bd Pediat, dipl, 63. *Honors & Awards:* Helen B Fraser Award, 78; Selma Collin Perinatal Lectr, Med Sch Ohio, 79; Joseph E Coleman Lectr, 81; Munster Pediat Lectr, Cork, Ireland, 84; Serv Award, Am Col Osteop Pediatricians, 84. *Prof Exp:* Intern, US Army Hosp, Ft Benning, Ga, 57-58; resident pediat, Walter Reed Gen Hosp, Washington, DC, 58-60 & Walter Reed Army Inst Res, 60-61; chief pediat serv, Rodriguez US Army Hosp, Ft Brooke, PR, 61-63; chief pediat, US Army Trop Res Med Lab, Ft Brooke, PR, 63-64. *Concurrent Pos:* Consult div maternal & child health, Ky State Dept Health, 66-; civilian consult, US Army, 69-; lectr, J Pediat Found, 72; dir, Community training in pediat, Sch Med, Univ Louisville, 75-77, Pilot Proj in Community Pediat, 76-77; Phi Rho Sigma lectureship, Sch Med, Ind Univ; lectr, Lubbock Pediat Soc, 86; distinguished lectr, Louisville Pediat Soc, 86; vis scholar, Green Col, Oxford, Eng, 93. *Mem:* Fel Am Acad Pediat; fel Am Col Physicians; Am Pediat Soc; Soc Pediat Res; fel Royal Soc Med; Am Soc Law & Med; Am Osler Soc (pres elect, 94); NY Acad Sci; AAAS; AMA. *Res:* Low birth weight infants; respiratory distress in infants; amniotic fluid studies; infant nutrition; author or coauthor of over 200 publications and abstracts and six books. *Mailing Add:* Kosain Charities Pediat Ctr 571 S Floyd St Suite 449 Louisville KY 40202

ANDREWS, BRIAN S, MEDICAL RESEARCH. *Current Pos:* PROF, DEPT RHEUMATOLOGY, & IMMUNOL, UNIV CALIF, COL MED, IRVINE, 80- *Personal Data:* b Sydney, Australia, Sept 2, 44. *Educ:* Univ Sydney, Australia, BS, 69, MD, 69; Univ NSW, PhD(immunol), 78. *Mem:* Fel Am Col Physicians; fel Royal Australian Col Physicians. *Res:* Immunology. *Mailing Add:* Col Med Dept Rheumatology & Immunol Univ Calif Irvine CA 92717-0001

ANDREWS, CECIL HUNTER, AGRONOMY. *Current Pos:* Asst prof agron & asst agronomist, 58-70, PROF AGRON, MISS STATE UNIV & AGRONOMIST, MISS AGR & FORESTRY EXP STA, 70- *Personal Data:* b Starkville, Miss, July 26, 32; m 60; c 3. *Educ:* Miss State Univ, BS, 54, MS, 58, PhD(agron), 66. *Concurrent Pos:* Asst agronomist, Chile & Taiwan, 59 & 60; chief of party, Miss State Univ-AID Brazil Contract, 67-68 & Seed Develop Progs in Ecuador, Colombia, Nicaragua, Honduras, Costa Rica, Thailand, Upper Volta, Ghana, Botswana, Sri Lanka, Indonesia & Burma, Senegal, Gambia, 69-88, Burundi, 88-90. *Mem:* Am Soc Agron; Sigma Xi. *Res:* Biochemical and physiological research in seeds of field crops. *Mailing Add:* Dept Agron Miss State Univ PO Box 9655 Mississippi State MS 39762-9555

ANDREWS, CHARLES EDWARD, INTERNAL MEDICINE. *Current Pos:* CHIEF MED OFFICER, STATE NEBR, 97- *Personal Data:* b Stratford, Okla, Jan 22, 25; m 46; c 2. *Educ:* Boston Univ, MD, 49. *Prof Exp:* Instr med, Univ Minn, 55-56; assoc, Med Sch, Univ Kans, 56-57, from asst prof to assoc prof, 57-60; from assoc prof to prof med, WVa Sch Med, 61-63, provost health sci, 61-83; chancellor, Univ Nebr Med Ctr, 83-91. *Concurrent Pos:* Chief med serv, Vet Admin Hosp, Kansas City, Mo, 56-61; lectr, Sch Dent, Univ Kans, 58- *Mem:* Am Thoracic Soc; AMA; Fedn Clin Res; Am Col Physicians. *Res:* Pulmonary disease and function. *Mailing Add:* Dept Health & Human Serv State Nebr PO Box 95007 Lincoln NE 68509-5007

ANDREWS, CHARLES LAWRENCE, wildlife ecology, parasitology, for more information see previous edition

ANDREWS, DANIEL KELLER, POULTRY SCIENCE. *Current Pos:* RETIRED. *Personal Data:* b Rockland, Maine, Sept 5, 24; m 50, 77; c 6. *Educ:* Univ Maine, BS, 49; Kans State Univ, MS, 51; Univ Wis, PhD(poultry sci), 63. *Prof Exp:* Supvr, Swift & Co, Pa, 51-52; inspector, US Dept Agr, Iowa, 52-53; asst prof poultry teaching & admin, State Univ NY Agr & Tech Inst Delhi, 53-56; exten poultry specialist, Univ Conn, 56-60; res asst poultry nutrit, Univ Wis, 60-63; exten poultry scientist, Western Wash Res & Exten Ctr, Wash State Univ, 63-90. *Concurrent Pos:* Assoc ed, World Poultry Sci Asn, 82-88; sabbatical leave, Yemen, 80 & 85, NC State Univ, 84, voca Cairo, Egypt, 95. *Mem:* Poultry Sci Asn. *Res:* Effects of arsanilic acid on egg production; extension education for poultrymen and youth; poultry management; fan ventilation for light restricted houses; ahemeral light cycles; molting layers; primary wing feather molt; egg quality; energy efficient light sources for broilers. *Mailing Add:* 11203 92nd Ave E Puyallup WA 98373-3882

ANDREWS, DAVID F, STATISTICS. *Current Pos:* asst prof, 71-77, PROF STATIST, UNIV TORONTO, 77- *Personal Data:* b Indianapolis, Ind, Apr 3, 43; Can citizen; m 65; c 3. *Educ:* Univ Toronto, BSc, 65, MSc, 66, PhD(statist), 68. *Prof Exp:* Lectr statist, Imp Col, Univ London, 68-69; lectr, Princeton Univ, 69-71. *Concurrent Pos:* Consult, Bell Lab, 69-77; vis asst prof, Univ Chicago, 73; assoc ed, Am Statist Asn, 73-75. *Mem:* Int Statist Inst; Am Statist Asn; Statist Soc Can (pres, 85). *Res:* Robust statistical procedures; graphical methods for data display. *Mailing Add:* Dept Statist Univ Toronto 100 St George St Toronto ON M5S 1A1 Can

ANDREWS, DAVID WILLIAM, BIOTECHNOLOGY, CELL BIOLOGY. *Current Pos:* asst prof, 88-93, ASSOC PROF BIOCHEM, MCMASTER UNIV, 93- *Personal Data:* b Windsor, Ont, July 14, 57; m, Alison Cowie; c Tallulah. *Educ:* Univ Ottawa, BSc, 79; Univ Toronto, PhD(med biophys), 85. *Prof Exp:* Fel, Univ Calif, 85-88. *Mem:* Can Micros Soc; Can Biochem Soc; Am Soc Cell Biol. *Res:* How different classes of proteins recognize the ER membrane as the correct subcellular destination; examine the interactions of signal recognition particle, the signal recognition particle receptor and the nascent polypeptide during targeting to the ER membrane. *Mailing Add:* Dept Biochem McMaster Univ 1200 Main St W Hamilton ON L8N 3Z5 Can. *Fax:* 905-522-9033; *E-Mail:* andrewsd@fhs.csu.mcmaster.ca

ANDREWS, DOUGLAS GUY, CHEMICAL ENGINEERING, MECHANICAL ENGINEERING. *Current Pos:* from assoc prof to prof, 57-84, EMER PROF NUCLEAR ENG, UNIV TORONTO, 84- *Personal Data:* b Boston, Eng, Oct 17, 17; Can citizen; m 42, Robina Dobbins; c Glenys W, Douglas G & Randall K (deceased). *Educ:* Univ Cambridge, BA, 39, MA, 43, ScD, 92. *Honors & Awards:* Pro Mundi Beneficio Medal, Brazilian Acad Humane Sci, 76. *Prof Exp:* Exp asst & officer underwater weapons res, Royal Naval Sci Serv, UK, 39-49; engr nuclear reactor & plant design, UK Atomic Energy Authority, 49-57. *Concurrent Pos:* Dir, Chem Eng Res Consults Inc, 63-84; pres, Youth Sci Found, Can, 71-73; vpres, Int Coord Comt Presentation Sci, 72-73. *Mem:* Am Nuclear Soc; Can Nuclear Soc; Brit Nuclear Energy Soc; fel Brit Inst Mech Eng. *Res:* Nuclear radiation shielding; nuclear reactor heat transfer; nuclear reactor safety; radioactive waste management. *Mailing Add:* 2185 Marine Dr No 703 Oakville ON L6L 5L6 Can

ANDREWS, EDWIN JOSEPH, VETERINARY MEDICINE. *Current Pos:* DEAN & PROF VET MED, UNIV PA SCH VET MED, 87- *Personal Data:* b Boston, Mass, Feb 27, 41; m 88; c 3. *Educ:* Pa State Univ, BS, 64; Univ Pa, VMD, 67, PhD(path), 71. *Prof Exp:* NIH res fel path, Univ Pa Sch Vet Med, 67-71; asst prof comp med, Col Med, Pa State Univ, 71-74; assoc prof vet path, NY State Col Vet Med, 74-77; vpres res & develop, Hancock Labs, Johnson & Johnson, 77-82, mkt dir, Extracorporeal Inc, 82-84, vpres res & develop, Johnson & Johnson Cardiovasc Inc, 84-87. *Concurrent Pos:* Res assoc, Inst Cancer Res, 68-71. *Mem:* Am Vet Med Asn; Am Asn Cancer Res; Am Soc Exp Path; Int Acad Path; Am Col Vet Pathologists; Am Col Lab Animal Med. *Res:* Animal models of human disease, chemical carcinogenesis & tumor immunology. *Mailing Add:* Mallinckrodt Vet Inc 421 Hawley St Mundelein IL 60060

ANDREWS, EUGENE RAYMOND, ORGANIC CHEMISTRY. *Current Pos:* RETIRED. *Personal Data:* b Rockford, Ill, Apr 29, 18; m 48; c 2. *Educ:* Cent YMCA Col, BS, 41. *Prof Exp:* Chief chemist, US Indust Chem Co, 42-57; res chemist, Allied Mills Inc, 58-66, mgr res lab, 66-82. *Mem:* AAAS; Am Chem Soc; Asn Off Anal Chemists. *Res:* Scientific feeding of farm animals, effect of drugs and hormones on such animals. *Mailing Add:* 5810 Nicolet Ave Chicago IL 60631-2429

ANDREWS, FRANCES E, NUTRITION. *Current Pos:* CHMN, DEPT HOME ECON, UNIV MONTEVALLO, 92- *Personal Data:* b Birmingham, Ala. *Educ:* Univ Ala, BS, 67, MS, 68; Ohio State Univ, PhD(nutrit), 74. *Prof Exp:* Assoc dean, Col Human Ecol, Univ Tenn, Knoxville, 80-92. *Concurrent Pos:* Am Home Econ Asn leader, 88. *Mem:* Am Inst Nutrit; Am Dietic Asn. *Mailing Add:* 408 Granada Dr Birmingham AL 35216-1518

ANDREWS, FRANK CLINTON, CHEMICAL PHYSICS. *Current Pos:* assoc prof phys chem, 67-74, PROF CHEM, UNIV CALIF, SANTA CRUZ, 74- *Personal Data:* b Manhattan, Kans, May 29, 32; m 64; c 2. *Educ:* Kans State Univ, BS, 54; Harvard Univ, AM, 59, PhD(chem physics), 60. *Prof Exp:* NIH fel chem physics, Univ Calif, Berkeley, 60-61; asst prof phys chem, Univ Wis, 61-67, on leave, Theoret Physics Dept, Oxford Univ, 66-67. *Concurrent Pos:* Fulbright scholar, Univ Hull, Eng, 54-55; Sloan fel, 63-67; Danforth assoc, 76-86; vis prof chem, Dartmouth Col, 79-80. *Mem:* Sigma Xi; Asn Humanistic Psychol. *Res:* Statistical mechanics and thermodynamics; general problem-solving; psychological unblocking; role of values in living. *Mailing Add:* Chem Dept Univ Calif Santa Cruz CA 95064. *Fax:* 408-459-2935; *E-Mail:* andrews@chemistry.ucsc.edu

ANDREWS, FRED CHARLES, MATHEMATICAL STATISTICS. *Current Pos:* dir statist lab & comput ctr, Univ Ore, 60-69, assoc prof, 57-66, head dept, 73-80, prof, 66-90, EMER PROF MATH, UNIV ORE, 90- *Personal Data:* b Aylesbury, Sask, July 13, 24; nat US; m 44, Joyce D Andrews; c Linda (Dunn), David & Gail Crandell. *Educ:* Univ Wash, BS, 46, MS, 48; Univ Calif, PhD(statist), 53. *Hon Degrees:* PhD, Univ Tampere, Finland, 85. *Prof Exp:* Lectr math, Univ Calif, 51-52; res assoc statist, Stanford Univ, 52-54; asst prof math & assoc statistician, Univ Nebr, 54-57. *Concurrent Pos:* Fulbright-Hays sr lectr, Univ Tampere, Finland, 69-70, Univ Col, Cork, Ireland, 76-77 & Univ Jordan, 83-84. *Mem:* Fel AAAS. *Res:* Statistical theory, including non-parametric inference; statistical computations. *Mailing Add:* 2705 Emerald St Eugene OR 97403. *E-Mail:* fandrews@darkwing.uoregon.edu

ANDREWS, FRED GORDON, SYSTEMATIC ENTOMOLOGY. *Current Pos:* SYST ENTOMOLOGIST, CALIF DEPT FOOD & AGR, 70- *Personal Data:* b Los Angeles, Calif, Nov 15, 33; m 60; c 2. *Educ:* Los Angeles State Univ, BA, 61; Univ Calif, Riverside, PhD(entom), 72. *Concurrent Pos:* Grants, Off Endangered Species, Dept Interior, 75-76 & Bur Land Mgt, 77-78 & 78-79. *Mem:* Pan-Pacific Entom Soc (pres, 75); Coleopterist Soc; Entom Soc Am; Soc Syst Zool; Sigma Xi. *Res:* Systematics and ecology of Lathridiidae; coleoptera of sand dunes; coleoptera associated with fungi. *Mailing Add:* Dept Agr Entomol Calif Food & Agr Sacramento CA 95814-5621

ANDREWS, FREDERICK NEWCOMB, ANIMAL PHYSIOLOGY, RESEARCH ADMINISTRATION. *Current Pos:* RETIRED. *Personal Data:* b Boston, Mass, Feb 5, 14; m 38; c 2. *Educ:* Univ Mass, BS, 35, MS, 36; Univ Mo, PhD(physiol reprod), 39. *Hon Degrees:* ScD, Univ Mass, 62; Dr Agr, Purdue Univ, 83. *Honors & Awards:* Morrison Award, 61. *Prof Exp:* From asst prof to assoc prof, Purdue Univ, 40-49, head dairy dept, 60-62, head animal sci dept, 62-63, prof animal sci, 49-80, dean grad sch & vpres res, 63-80, vpres & gen mgr, Purdue Res Found, 64-80. *Concurrent Pos:* Agr consult, Rockefeller Found, 61-66; mem bd dirs, Indianapolis Ctr for Advan Res, 70-, vpres, 73-80, chmn bd dir, 81-82; consult, Nat Inst Health, 81-83. *Mem:* Fel AAAS; Am Asn Anat; fel Am Soc Animal Sci; Am Soc Zool; Am Dairy Sci Asn; Nat Acad Univ Res Admin. *Res:* Physiology of reproduction; endocrinology; nutrition; environmental physiology; growth and development. *Mailing Add:* 691 Sugar Hill Dr Purdue Univ West Lafayette IN 47906

ANDREWS, FREDERICK T, JR, TELECOMMUNICATIONS. *Current Pos:* INDEPENDENT CONSULT, 90- *Personal Data:* b Palmerton, Pa, Oct 6, 26; c 3. *Educ:* Pa State Univ, BSEE, 48. *Honors & Awards:* Inst Elec & Electronics Engrs Award, 85; Nat Acad Eng Award, 88; Telephony Ray Blain, Telephony, 91. *Prof Exp:* Switching res, AT&T Bell Lab, 48-55, supvr, Transmission Systs Develop, 55-58, dept head, 58-62, dir, Transmission Systs Eng, 62-66, dir, Mil Commun Systs Eng, 66-68, dir, Loop Systs Eng, 68-79, exec dir, Switching Systs Eng, 79-83, exec dir, 79-83, exec dir, Technol Systs Planning, 83-84; vpres, Technol Systs, Bellcore, 84-90. *Mem:* Nat Acad Eng; fel Inst Elec & Electronics Engrs; Inst Elec & Electronics Engrs Commun Soc (vpres, 82-83 & 84-85). *Res:* Systems engineering and management in the field of telecommunications with emphasis on network evolution and international standardization; author of 14 articles. *Mailing Add:* PO Box 249 Colts Neck NJ 07722. *Fax:* 732-946-8694

ANDREWS, GEORGE EYRE, MATHEMATICS. *Current Pos:* From asst prof to prof, 64-81, EVAN PUGH PROF MATH, PA STATE UNIV, 81- *Personal Data:* b Salem, Ore, Dec 4, 38; m 60, Joy M Brown; c Amy B, Katherine Y & Derek G. *Educ:* Ore State Univ, BS & MA, 60; Univ Pa, PhD(math), 64. *Honors & Awards:* Hendrick lectr, Math Asn Am, 80; Distinguished Teaching Award, Allegheny Region, Math Asn Am, 93. *Concurrent Pos:* Vis prof math, Univ Wis, 75-76 & Univ NSW, 78-79; vis lectr, NZ Math Soc, 79; Guggenheim fel, 82-83; adj prof, Univ Waterloo, 82-92; vis fel, Australian Nat Univ, 83; vis prof, Univ Strasbourg, 83; prin lectr, NSF-Conf Bd Math Sci Regional Conf, Tempe, 85; vis Ordway prof, Univ Minn, 88; vis scientist, T J Watson Res Ctr, IBM, 90-91. *Mem:* Am Math Soc; Edinburgh Math Soc; Math Asn Am; Soc Indust & Appl Math; Australian Math Soc; NZ Math Soc. *Res:* Basic hypergeometric series; partitions; number theory; combinatorics; special functions. *Mailing Add:* Dept Math McAllister Bldg Pa State Univ University Park PA 16802. *Fax:* 814-865-3735; *E-Mail:* andrews@math.psu.edu

ANDREWS, GEORGE HAROLD, MATHEMATICS & NUMERICAL ANALYSIS, ACTUARIAL SCIENCE & STATISTICS. *Current Pos:* From asst prof to prof math, 62-94, ANDREW & PAULINE PROF MATH, OBERLIN COL, 94- *Personal Data:* b Syracuse, NY, July 31, 32; m 55, Marlene Erickson; c Erik, Geoffrey, Elise & Christopher. *Educ:* Oberlin Col, AB, 54; Univ Mich, AM, 55, PhD(math), 63. *Concurrent Pos:* NSF fac fel, 68-69; consult numerical anal, Am Soc Actuaries, 74-; vis prof, Univ Mich, 75-76; vis scholar, Univ Mich, 82-83 & MacQuarrie Univ, 90-91. *Mem:* Math Asn Am; Soc Indust & Appl Math; Am Soc Actuaries; Sigma Xi; Am Math Soc. *Res:* Mathematical statistics; foundations of mathematics; actuarial mathematics; numerical solution of differential equations. *Mailing Add:* Dept Math Oberlin Col Oberlin OH 44074. *Fax:* 440-775-8124; *E-Mail:* gha@cs.oberlin.edu

ANDREWS, GEORGE WILLIAM, GEOLOGY, DIATOMS. *Current Pos:* CONSULT, 89- *Personal Data:* b Eau Claire, Wis, Oct 15, 29; m 56; c 3. *Educ:* Univ Wis-Madison, BA, 51, MA, 53, PhD(geol), 55. *Prof Exp:* Geologist, Tech Serv Div, Shell Oil Co, 55-58 & E&P Res Div, Shell Develop Co, 58-59; geologist, US Geol Surv, 59-89. *Concurrent Pos:* Assoc ed, J Bacillaria, 78-84. *Mem:* Int Soc Diatom Res. *Res:* Marine and nonmarine diatoms; paleontology, stratigraphy and paleoecology of Cenozoic strata; petroleum geology. *Mailing Add:* 20 Ridgewood Dr Akron PA 17501

ANDREWS, GLENN COLTON, PROTEIN BIOCHEMISTRY. *Current Pos:* res scientist, 75-77, sr res scientist org synthesis, 77-81, RES ADV, PFIZER CENT RES, 81- *Personal Data:* b Alhambra, Calif, Feb 7, 48; m 72. *Educ:* Univ Calif, Los Angeles, BSc, 70, PhD(org chem), 74. *Prof Exp:* Res scientist org synthesis, Stanford Univ, 74-75. *Res:* Total synthesis directed toward vitamins and other commercially important natural products. *Mailing Add:* Pfizer Cent Res Eastern Point Rd Groton CT 06340. *E-Mail:* glenn_andrews_@groton.pfizer.com

ANDREWS, GORDON LOUIS, AGRICULTURE. *Current Pos:* Dept Entom, Miss State Univ, 82-86, assoc entomologist, Delta Br, 86-89, area crop model specialist, 89-95, ENTOM SPECIALIST, MISS STATE UNIV, 95- *Personal Data:* b New Orleans, La, Sept 22, 45; m 74; c 3. *Educ:* Southeastern La Col, BS, 67; La State Univ, MS, 69; Miss State Univ, PhD(entom), 72. *Prof Exp:* Res assoc entom, Miss State Univ, 72-76; area pest mgt specialist, Miss Coop Exten Serv, 76-82. *Res:* Cotton insects; field evaluation and modeling of Heliothis species; optimum pest management trial. *Mailing Add:* Delta Br Exp Sta Box 69 Stoneville MS 38776

ANDREWS, GREGORY RICHARD, COMPUTER SCIENCE. *Current Pos:* assoc prof, 79-87, PROF COMPUTER SCI, UNIV ARIZ, 87- *Personal Data:* b Olympia, Wash, Mar 9, 47; m 67; c 2. *Educ:* Stanford Univ, BS, 69; Univ Wash, PhD(comput sci), 74. *Prof Exp:* Assoc engr comput sci, Boeing Co, 69-70; asst prof comput sci, Cornell Univ, 74-79. *Concurrent Pos:* Co-investr grant, NSF, 74-77, prin investr grants, 77-80, 82 & 84-; consult, US Army Electronics Command, 75-; co-prin investr grant, US Army, 80-82, Air Force Off Sci Res, 84-89, NSF, 87-90; vis prof comput sci, Univ Wash, 83-84. *Mem:* Asn Comput Mach. *Res:* Operating systems; concurrent programming languages; protection and security; distributed computing. *Mailing Add:* Dept Comput Sci Univ Ariz Gould Simpson Bldg Rm 721 1040 E 4th St Tucson AZ 85721-0721

ANDREWS, HENRY NATHANIEL, JR, PALEOBOTANY. *Current Pos:* prof, 64-75, chmn dept, 64-70, EMER PROF BIOL, UNIV CONN, 75- *Personal Data:* b Melrose, Mass, June 15, 10; m 39; c 3. *Educ:* Mass Inst Technol, BS, 34; Washington Univ, MS, 37, PhD, 39. *Honors & Awards:* Cert of Merit, Bot Soc Am, 66. *Prof Exp:* From instr to prof bot, Washington Univ, 38-64, dean sch, 47-64. *Concurrent Pos:* Paleobotanist, Mo Bot Garden, St Louis, 41-64; botanist, US Geol Surv, 50-54, 59-; Guggenheim Mem Found fel, 50-51, 58-59; Fulbright teaching fel, Univ Poona, 60-61; NSF sr fel, Sweden, 64. *Mem:* Nat Acad Sci; Bot Soc Am. *Res:* Carboniferous and Devonian plants; Arctic paleobotany; history of paleobotany. *Mailing Add:* 560 Old Range Rd Box 146 Laconia NH 03246

ANDREWS, HOWARD LUCIUS, BIOPHYSICS. *Current Pos:* RETIRED. *Personal Data:* b Davisville, RI, Oct 27, 06; m 31; c 3. *Educ:* Brown Univ, BS, 27, MS, 28, PhD(physics), 31. *Prof Exp:* Instr physics, Brown Univ, 29-34, res assoc psychol, 34-37; assoc physicist, US Pub Health Serv, 37-41, physicist, 41-48, chief nuclear radiation biol sect, Nat Insts Health, 48-61, dept radiation safety, 62-65; asst dir health & safety, PR Nuclear Ctr, 65-67; prof radiation biol & biophysics, Univ Rochester, 67-71. *Concurrent Pos:* Exec secy biol effects of atomic radiation comt, Nat Acad Sci-Nat Res Coun, 59-64; consult, Radiation Safety, 71- *Mem:* Fel Am Phys Soc; Radiation Res Soc; Health Physics Soc (pres, 64-65). *Res:* Biological effects of high energy radiations; radiation health protection. *Mailing Add:* 303 Valley Rd No 308 Middletown RI 02842-5282

ANDREWS, HUGH ROBERT, EXPERIMENTAL NUCLEAR PHYSICS, ACCELERATOR MASS SPECTROMETRY & APPLICATIONS OF NUCLEAR TECHNIQUES. *Current Pos:* SR SCIENTIST, BUBBLE TECHNOL INDUSTS, 97- *Personal Data:* b Fredericton, NB, Apr 29, 40; m 71, Josephine D Kennedy; c J Matthew, E Louise & Anthony C. *Educ:* Univ NB, BSc, 62; Harvard Univ, AM, 63, PhD(physics), 71. *Prof Exp:* Res officer nuclear physics, Atomic Energy Can Ltd, 71-82, sr res scientist, 83-97. *Concurrent Pos:* Chmn, Div Nuclear Physics, Can Asn Physicists, 89-90. *Mem:* Sigma Xi; Can Asn Physicists; Can Nuclear Soc; Am Phys Soc. *Res:* Hyperfine interactions and perturbed angular correlations; in-beam gamma ray spectroscopy applied to measurement of short lifetimes and the nature of high spin states in nuclei; atomic physics-heavy ion stopping powers; radioisotope dating using accelerator techniques; public affairs aspects of nuclear energy; applications of nuclear techniques. *Mailing Add:* Bubble Technol Industs Sta 49 Chalk River ON K0J 1J0 Can. *Fax:* 613-589-2763; *E-Mail:* bubble@intranet.ca

ANDREWS, JAMES EINAR, GEOLOGICAL OCEANOGRAPHY, NAVAL OCEANOGRAPHY. *Current Pos:* sci dir, Off Naval Res, London, UK, 87-91, spec asst ocean sci, 91-95, DIR, OFF NAVAL RES, 96-, DIR SCI & TECH REQ, OFF CHIEF NAVAL OPER, 96- *Personal Data:* b Minneapolis, Minn, Oct 31, 42; m 65, 81; c 1. *Educ:* Amherst Col, BA, 63; Univ Miami, PhD(oceanog), 67. *Honors & Awards:* Humboldt Award, Fed Repub Ger. *Prof Exp:* Asst prof, Univ Hawaii, 67-74, chmn dept, 73-76, from assoc prof to prog oceanog, 74-81; tech dir, Naval Ocean Res & Develop Activ, Miss, 81-87. *Concurrent Pos:* Chmn, Hawaii Marine Res, Inc, 75-80; vis prof, Technische Hochschule Aachen, WGer, 76; vis scientist, Ctr Nat Exploitation Oceans, France, 80. *Mem:* Fel Geol Soc Am; AAAS; Europ Geophys Soc; Oceanog Soc. *Res:* Deep sea sediments; sea floor structure and topography; manganese nodules; seafloor mining; ocean resources. *Mailing Add:* Chief Naval Oper CNO-N911C Navy Pentagon Washington DC 20350-2000

ANDREWS, JAY DONALD, ZOOLOGY, MARINE ECOLOGY. *Current Pos:* prof, 60-83, EMER PROF MARINE SCI, COL WILLIAM & MARY, 83-; EMER FAC MARINE SCI. *Personal Data:* b Bloom, Kans, Sept 9, 16; m 48, Mary S Hornsby; c Donna & Jay S. *Educ:* Kans State Col, BS, 38; Univ Wis, MS, 40, PhD(zool), 47. *Prof Exp:* From asst biologist to sr biologist, Va Inst Marine Sci, 46-83. *Concurrent Pos:* Ed, Proc, Nat Shellfisheries Asn, 57-58; assoc prof marine sci, Univ Va, 60-83. *Mem:* Hon mem Atlantic Estuarine Res Soc; Am Soc Limnol & Oceanog; Soc Syst Zool; hon mem Nat Shellfisheries Asn (secy-treas, 60-62, vpres, 62-64, pres, 64-66); Am Inst Fishery Res Biologists. *Res:* Marine biology; biological oceanography; ecology of marine invertebrates; shellfish ecology, epizootiology of molluscan diseases; oyster pathogens. *Mailing Add:* Va Inst Marine Sci PO Box 1346 Gloucester Point VA 23062

ANDREWS, JOHN EDWIN, GENETICS, PLANT BREEDING. *Current Pos:* RETIRED. *Personal Data:* b Selkirk, Man, Mar 15, 22; m 48; c 4. *Educ:* Univ Man, BSA, 49; Univ Minn, MS, 50, PhD(genetics), 53. *Honors & Awards:* Merit Award, Pub Serv Can, 76. *Prof Exp:* Cerealist, Rust Res Lab, Univ Man, 47-51; sr cerealist, Res Sta, Alta, 51-60, res dir, Res Br, Man, 60-65; res dir, Res Br, Sask, 65-69, dir res sta, Res Br, Agr Can, Alta, 69-81, dir, Gen Western Res Group, 81-83, sr adv foreign agr, Res Br, Agr Can, 83-86. *Concurrent Pos:* Dir Indo-Canadian Res Proj on Dryland Agr, India, 70-79. *Mem:* Fel Agr Inst Can; Can Soc Agron. *Res:* Physiology of cold hardiness; winter wheat breeding. *Mailing Add:* 27 Elm Crescent Lethbridge AB T1K 4W8 Can

ANDREWS, JOHN FRANK, ENVIRONMENTAL & CIVIL ENGINEERING. *Current Pos:* PROF ENVIRON SCI & ENG, RICE UNIV, 81- *Personal Data:* b Cave City, Ark, July 10, 30; m 52; c 3. *Educ:* Univ Ark, BS, 51, MS, 53; Univ Calif, Berkeley, PhD(sanit eng), 64; Am Acad Environ Engrs, dipl. *Honors & Awards:* Harrison Prescot Eddy Medal, Water Pollution Control Fedn, 75. *Prof Exp:* From instr to assoc prof civil eng, Univ Ark, 53-60; proj engr, Univ Calif, Berkeley, 60-63; from assoc prof to prof environ eng, Clemson Univ, 63-74, head dept, 68-74; prof civil eng, Univ Houston, 75-81. *Concurrent Pos:* Consult, City of Greenwood, SC, 64, Eng Sci, Arcadia, Calif, 67-72, Union Carbide, 69, Bacardi Distilleries, 69, United Aircraft, 70, Pan Am Health Orgn, 70, Int Bus Mach, 71, US Army Environ Hyg Agency, 75-77, Metrop Waste Comn, Minneapolis, 76-78, Shell Develop Co, 78-80, Greeley & Hansen Engrs, 78-80, Weyerhaeuser Co, 80-81, Reynolds, Smith & Hills, 82, Woodlands Develop Corp, 82-83, Gulf Coast Waste Disposal Authority, 84 & Metrop San Dist Greater Chicago, 85-; US ed, Water Res, 74-84; prof eng, Ark, SC, & Tex. *Mem:* Asn Environ Eng Prof (pres, 85); Int Asn Water Pollution Res; Am Water Works Asn; Am Soc Civil Eng; Am Chem Soc; Water Pollution Control Fedn; Am Inst Chem Engrs; AAAS. *Res:* Biological processes for waste treatment; dynamics and control of wastewater treatment plants. *Mailing Add:* Rice Univ 1719 Rayview Fayetteville AR 72701

ANDREWS, JOHN HERRICK, PLANT PATHOLOGY, AQUATIC BIOLOGY. *Current Pos:* from asst prof to assoc prof, 76-86, PROF PLANT PATH, UNIV WIS-MADISON, 86- *Personal Data:* b Montreal, Que, May 16, 46; m 76; c 3. *Educ:* McGill Univ, BSc, 67; Univ Maine, MS, 69; Univ Calif, Davis, PhD(plant path), 73. *Prof Exp:* Fel plant path, Cambridge Univ, 74-75; fel bot, Univ BC, 75-76. *Concurrent Pos:* Leopold Schepp Found fel, 74-75; Nat Res Coun Can fel, 75-76. *Mem:* Am Phytopath Soc; Can Phytopath Soc; AAAS; Am Soc Naturalists. *Res:* Integrated control; aquatic pathology; microbial ecology; biological control. *Mailing Add:* Dept Plant Path 284 Russell Lab Univ Wis 1630 Linden Dr Madison WI 53706-1520

ANDREWS, JOHN PARRAY, PHARMACOKINETICS, DRUG METABOLISM. *Current Pos:* RES SCIENTIST V BIOANALYTIC CHEM & DRUG METABOLISM, NORWICH-EATON PHARMACEUT, 81- *Personal Data:* b Cambridge, Mass, June 29, 49; m 80. *Educ:* Ohio State Univ, BS, 70, PhD(biochem), 74. *Prof Exp:* Fel neurochem, Cornell Univ, 74-77; res assoc chem carcinogenesis, Fox Chase Cancer Ctr, Inst Cancer Res, 77-79; staff scientist drug metabolism, Hazleton Labs Am, 79-81. *Mem:* Am Col Toxicol; AAAS; Am Chem Soc; Sigma Xi. *Res:* Biochemical pharmacology; pharmacokinetics; analytical biochemistry; drug metabolism; chemical carcinogenesis; protein chemistry; enzymology. *Mailing Add:* Bradley Hill Rd Oxford NY 13830

ANDREWS, JOHN STEVENS, JR, BIOCHEMISTRY. *Current Pos:* asst prof, 68-70, ASSOC PROF OPHTHAL, VANDERBILT UNIV, 70- *Personal Data:* b Lawrence, Mass, July 12, 27; m 55; c 4. *Educ:* Univ NH, BS, 51, MS, 52; NC State Col, PhD(animal nutrit), 55. *Prof Exp:* Asst res physiol chemist, Univ Calif, Los Angeles, 55-58; instr ophthal res, Harvard Univ, 59-66, assoc, 66-68. *Mem:* Am Chem Soc; Am Soc Biol Chemists. *Res:* Abnormal tissue lipid deposition and metabolism; lipid-protein interrelationships; cataractogenesis. *Mailing Add:* Dept Ophthal Vanderbilt Univ Sch Med 5920 Robert E Lee Dr Nashville TN 37215-5224

ANDREWS, JOHN THOMAS, GEOMORPHOLOGY, QUATERNARY GEOLOGY. *Current Pos:* asst prof geol, 68-74, PROF GEOL SCI, UNIV COLO, 74- *Personal Data:* b Millom, Eng, Nov 8, 37; m 61; c 1. *Educ:* Univ Nottingham, BSc, 59, PhD(geomorphol), 65, DSc(geol), 78; McGill Univ, MSc, 61. *Honors & Awards:* Kirk Bryan Award, Geol Soc Am, 73. *Prof Exp:* Res scientist, Can Govt, 61-67. *Mem:* Geol Soc; Asn Am Geog. *Res:* Glacial chronology and glacioisostatic uplift. *Mailing Add:* Geol Sci Univ Colo Campus Box 250 Boulder CO 80309-0250

ANDREWS, JOHN W, BUILDING SCIENCE. *Current Pos:* assoc scientist, 77-81, head, Solar-technol div, Brookhaven Nat Lab, 81-83, SCIENTIST & HEAD, ENERGY EFFICIENCY & CONSERV DIV, 83- *Personal Data:* b Dec 30, 41. *Educ:* Mass Inst Tech, SB, 63; Univ Notre Dame, PhD(physics), 67. *Prof Exp:* Res staff physicist, Yale Univ, New Haven, Conn, 67-69; assoc prof, Natural Sci Div, Southampton Col Long Island Univ, 69-77. *Concurrent Pos:* Granted continuing appointment, Brookhaven Nat Lab, 81. *Mem:* Am Phys Soc; Am Soc Heating, Refrigerating & Air Conditioning Engrs. *Res:* Theoretical and field studies of energy use in buildings; solar energy; combustion space heating; thermal distribution; systems analysis. *Mailing Add:* Bldg 526 Brookhaven Nat Lab Upton NY 11973-5000. *E-Mail:* jwandrews@bnl.gov

ANDREWS, KEN J, HOT SPRINGS MICROBIOLOGY, BIOMASS CONVERSION. *Current Pos:* instr, 77, asst prof biol, 78-85, ASSOC PROF BIOL, COLO COL, 86- *Personal Data:* b Sandusky, Ohio, Aug 1, 47; m 79; c 4. *Educ:* Purdue Univ, BS, 69; Univ Calif, Berkeley, MA, 71, PhD(microbiol), 74. *Prof Exp:* Fel med micro, Harvard Med Sch, 74-77. *Concurrent Pos:* Consult biosci, 81- *Mem:* Am Soc Microbiol; Am Inst Biol Sci; Soc Indust Microbiol; Sigma Xi. *Res:* Analysing selected alkaline hot springs (chemically and biologically) with the intent of determining the applicability of using thermophilic organisms in biomass conversion to neutral fuels. *Mailing Add:* Biol Dept Colo Col 14 E Cache La Poudre Colorado Springs CO 80903-3243

ANDREWS, LAWRENCE JAMES, CHEMISTRY. *Current Pos:* from instr to prof, 45-87, chmn dept, 59-62, actg dean, Col Lett & Sci, 62-63, dean, 64-85, fac res lectr, 65, EMER PROF CHEM, UNIV CALIF, DAVIS, 88- *Personal Data:* b San Diego, Calif, Sept 27, 20; m 44; c 2. *Educ:* Univ Calif, Berkeley, BS, 40; Univ Calif, Los Angeles, AM, 41, PhD(chem), 43. *Prof Exp:* Asst chem, Univ Calif, 40-43, Sharp & Dohme fel & lectr, 43-44; chemist, Tenn Eastman Corp, Oak Ridge, 44-45. *Concurrent Pos:* Advan Educ Fund fel, 53-54; consult, Kasetsart Univ, Bangkok, 66-68; Fulbright res scholar, Univ Hull, 67-68; chmn, Comn Arts & Sci, Nat Asn State Univs & Land Grant Cols, 73-74. *Mem:* Am Chem Soc; Sigma Xi. *Res:* Mechanisms organic reactions in solution; coordination compounds; molecular complex formation; electrophilic aromatic substitution processes. *Mailing Add:* Dept Chem Univ Calif Davis CA 95616-5224

ANDREWS, LUTHER DAVID, management, environment, for more information see previous edition

ANDREWS, MARGARET M, TRANSCULTURAL CROSS-CULTURAL & INTERNATIONAL HEALTH CARE, PEDIATRIC HEALTH CARE. *Current Pos:* CHAIRPERSON & PROF, DEPT NURSING, NAZARETH COL, 89- *Personal Data:* b Cleveland, Ohio, Mar 25, 50. *Educ:* St John Col, BSN, 72; Case Western Res Univ, MSN, 74; Univ Utah, PhD(nursing), 85. *Honors & Awards:* Leininger Award, Transcult Nursing Soc, 94. *Prof Exp:* Prog dir, Cath Relief Servs/USAID, 85; chairperson & prof, Dept Nursing, St Francis Col, 86-89. *Mem:* Transcult Nursing Soc (pres, 93-95). *Res:* Native American elders and their health beliefs and practices; international consultation in health care/nursing; co-author of textbook on transcultural nursing and journal articles on transcultural health and nursing topics. *Mailing Add:* 4245 East Ave Rochester NY 14618-3790. *Fax:* 716-586-2452; *E-Mail:* mmandrew@naz.edu

ANDREWS, MARK ALLEN, ORGANOMETALLIC CHEMISTRY, HOMOGENEOUS CATALYSIS. *Current Pos:* asst chemist, 79-81, assoc chemist, 81-83, chemist, 83-84, CHEMIST, DEPT CHEM, BROOKHAVEN NAT LAB, 86- *Personal Data:* b Scranton, Pa, Oct 24, 51; m 74; c 2. *Educ:* New Col, BA, 73; Univ Calif, Los Angeles, PhD(chem), 77. *Prof Exp:* Res assoc, Dept Chem, Univ Wis-Madison, 77-79. *Mem:* Am Chem Soc. *Res:* Synthetic and mechanistic transition metal organometallic chemistry; homogeneous catalysis; metal-mediated reactions of carbohydrates and carbohydrate model compounds; metal-catalyzed biomass conversion. *Mailing Add:* 1211 Grinnell Rd Wilmington DE 19803. *Fax:* 516-282-5815; *E-Mail:* maa@bnl.gov

ANDREWS, MARK PAUL, OPTICAL MATERIALS, NANOCOMPOSITES & SUPRAMOLECULAR STRUCTURES. *Current Pos:* ASSOC PROF CHEM, MCGILL UNIV, 90- *Personal Data:* b Halifax, NS, Jan 13, 51. *Educ:* Univ Toronto, PhD(chem), 85. *Prof Exp:* Mem tech staff, AT&T Bell Labs, 84-90. *Mem:* Am Chem Soc; Can Soc Chem; Int Soc Optical Eng. *Res:* Integrated optics spectroscopy; spectroscopy of thin films and interfaces; chemical reactions at interfaces; molecular self assembly; new polymerization catalysts; sol-gel chemistry; chemistry of photonic materials and devices; nonlinear optics; polymer relaxation phenomema. *Mailing Add:* Dept Chem McGill Univ 801 Sherbrooke St W Montreal PQ H3A 2K6 Can. *E-Mail:* andrews@omc.lan.mcgill.ca

ANDREWS, MATTHEW TUCKER, EUKARYOTIC GENE EXPRESSION, MECHANISMS OF RNA SYNTHESIS. *Current Pos:* asst prof, 87-93, ASSOC PROF GENETICS, NC STATE UNIV, 93- *Personal Data:* b Grand Rapids, Mich, Sept 4, 57; m 84, Katherine E Goodrow. *Educ:* Univ Mich, BS, 79; Cent Mich Univ, MS, 81; Wayne State Univ, PhD(biochem), 84. *Prof Exp:* Fel, Carnegie Inst Wash, 84-87. *Concurrent Pos:* Damon Runyon-Walter Winchell Cancer Fund fel, 84-86; nat res serv award, NIH, 86-87. *Mem:* Am Soc Cell Biol; Soc Develop Biol. *Res:* Mechanisms controlling eukaryotic gene expression during early animal development; protein-DNA interactions responsible for maintaining differential gene activity in embryos. *Mailing Add:* Dept Genetics NC State Univ PO Box 7614 Raleigh NC 27695-7614. *Fax:* 919-515-3355; *E-Mail:* andrews@ncsu.edu

ANDREWS, MERRILL LEROY, plasma laser media; deceased, see previous edition for last biography

ANDREWS, MICHAEL, PARALLEL COMPUTER ARCHITECTURES. *Current Pos:* CHIEF SCIENTIST, SPACE TECH CORP, 84- *Personal Data:* b Passaic, NJ, Apr 19, 40; m 65, Sandra Hines; c Jennifer, Chris, Ginger & Rebecca. *Educ:* Rutgers Univ, BS, 62, BA, 63; Univ Ariz, MS, 70, PhD(elec eng), 72. *Prof Exp:* Prof, Colo State Univ, 74-82. *Res:* Design of parallel computer architectures for complex seismic signal and medical imaging. *Mailing Add:* Space Tech Corp 2324 Manchester Ct Ft Collins CO 80526

ANDREWS, MYRON FLOYD, veterinary parasitology, for more information see previous edition

ANDREWS, NEIL CORBLY, THORACIC SURGERY. *Current Pos:* chmn, Div Community & Postgrad Med, 71-79, chmn, Dept Postgrad Med, 73-81, prof surg, 70-86, EMER PROF SURG, SCH MED, UNIV CALIF DAVIS, 86- *Personal Data:* b Spokane, Wash, Mar 31, 16; m 43, 70; c 2. *Educ:* Univ Ore, BA, 40, MD, 43; Ohio State Univ, MSc, 50. *Prof Exp:* Intern surg, Union Mem Hosp, Baltimore, Md, 43, asst resident, 44; resident, Jefferson Hosp, Roanoke, Va, 44-45; from asst resident to resident, Col Med, Ohio State Univ, 47-50, from instr to prof thoracic surg, 47-70. *Concurrent Pos:* Chief surg, Ohio Tuberc Hosp, 50-68; consult, Vet Admin Hosp, Chillicothe, 53-70 & Dayton, 54-70; area consult, Vet Admin, 60-70; coordr, Ohio State Regional Med Prog, 66-70 & Area II, Calif Regional Med Prog, 70-73; mem attend staff, Univ Calif, Davis, Med Ctr, 70-89. *Mem:* AAAS; fel Am Col Surg; fel Am Col Chest Physicians; Am Heart Asn; AMA; Sigma Xi; Am Cancer Soc. *Res:* Cancer chemotherapy. *Mailing Add:* Dept Surg PO Box 3007 El Macero CA 95618

ANDREWS, OLIVER AUGUSTUS, CHEMISTRY, SCIENCE EDUCATION. *Current Pos:* RETIRED. *Personal Data:* b Plymouth, Wis, Dec 15, 31; m 51; c 5. *Educ:* Univ Wis-Stevens Point, BS, 53; Univ Wis-Madison, MS, 57. *Prof Exp:* Teacher high schs, Wis, 53-59; traveling sci teacher, Mich State Univ & NSF, 59-60; from instr to assoc prof chem, Univ Wis-Stevens Point, 60-89. *Mem:* Nat Educ Asn; Nat Sci Teachers Asn. *Res:* Investigation of learner initiated cues. *Mailing Add:* 409 Weir Dr Stevens Point WI 54481

ANDREWS, PETER BRUCE, AUTOMATED THEOREM PROVING, TYPE THEORY. *Current Pos:* From asst prof to assoc prof, 63-79, PROF MATH, CARNEGIE-MELLON UNIV, 79- *Personal Data:* b New York, NY, Nov 1, 37; m 85, Catherine Clair; c Lyle & Bruce. *Educ:* Dartmouth Col, AB, 59; Princeton Univ, PhD(math), 64. *Mem:* AAAS; Asn Symbolic Logic; Asn Comput Mach; Am Asn Artificial Intel; Asn Automated Reasoning. *Res:* Symbolic logic, especially type theory and theorem proving by computer; formalization of mathematics; developer of the TPS automated theorem proving system. *Mailing Add:* Dept Math Sci Carnegie-Mellon Univ Pittsburgh PA 15213-3890. *E-Mail:* peter.andrews@cmu.edu

ANDREWS, PETER WALTER, DEVELOPMENTAL BIOLOGY, CELL BIOLOGY. *Current Pos:* res investr, Wistar Inst, 78-80, res assoc, 80-83, asst prof, 83-90, assoc prof develop biol, 91-92, ARTHUR JACKSON PROF BIOMED SCI, WISTAR INST ANAT & BIOL, 92-, CHMN, DEPT BIOMED SCI, 95- *Personal Data:* b London, Eng, June 5, 50; m 81; c 3. *Educ:* Univ Leeds, BSc, 71; Oxford Univ, DPhil(genetics), 75; Univ Pa, MBA, 89. *Prof Exp:* Res fel develop biol, Pasteur Inst, Paris, 74-75; res fel immunobiol, Sloan-Kettering Inst Cancer Res, 76-78. *Mem:* Soc Develop Biol; Gt Brit Soc Develop Biol. *Res:* Regulation of cell differentiation in teratocarcinomas and early mammalian embryos; changes in surface antigen expression; control gene activity during cell differentiation; changes in susceptibility to early mammalian development; viral replication. *Mailing Add:* Dept Biomed Sci Univ Sheffield Sheffield S102 TN England. *E-Mail:* p.w.andrews@sheffield.ac.uk

ANDREWS, RICHARD D, zoology, for more information see previous edition

ANDREWS, RICHARD MARK, POWDER METALLURGY, METAL MATRIX COMPOSITES. *Current Pos:* RES ASSOC, NORTON SUPERABRASIVES, 93- *Personal Data:* m 88, Sandra G Swammy; c Fiona L & Geoffrey M. *Educ:* Southampton Univ, BSc, 81; Univ Nebr, MS, 85; Mass Inst Technol, ScD, 91. *Prof Exp:* Design engr, Marconi Space & Defense Systs, 79-82; design engr, Brunswick Defense, 85-87; consult engr, TEMAU, Venice, Italy, 91-92. *Mem:* Am Soc Metals; Am Powder Metall Inst; Mining, Minerals & Mat Soc. *Res:* Processing and properties of metal matrix composites. *Mailing Add:* 56 Upton Rd Westborough MA 01581. *Fax:* 508-795-5455; *E-Mail:* richard.m.andrews@sgc.infonet.com

ANDREWS, RICHARD NIGEL LYON, ENVIRONMENTAL POLICY. *Current Pos:* dir, Inst Environ Studies, 81-91, chmn, Environ Mgt & Policy Prog, 90-93, PROF ENVIRON POLICY, UNIV NC, CHAPEL HILL, 81- *Personal Data:* b Newport, RI, Dec 6, 44; m 69, Hannah Page Wheeler; c Sarah & Christopher. *Educ:* Yale Univ, AB, 66; Univ NC, Chapel Hill, MRP, 70, PhD(environ planning), 72. *Prof Exp:* Budget analyst, US Off Mgt & Budget, 70-72; from asst prof to assoc prof natural resources policy, Sch Natural Resources, Univ Mich, 72-81, chmn, Resource Policy & Mgt Prog, 78-81. *Concurrent Pos:* Rockefeller fel, 77-78; vis scholar, US Dept State, 81; chief staff mem, Natural Resources Panel, Gov's Comn Future NC, 82-84; consult, NSF, 83-85 & Conserv Found, 84; mem, Bd Environ Studies & Toxicol, Nat Acad Sci, 86-88; chair, Pub Affairs & Policy Comt, NC Acad Sci, 87-89; chair, Sect X Social Impacts Sci & Eng, AAAS, 89-90 & 96-97; Fulbright fel, Vienna Univ Econ, 90; fac, Salzburg Sem, 90; consult US aid, Czech Repub, 91-95; mem, Exec Comt Fac Coun, 94-97; mem, AAAS Comt Sci Eng & Rib Policy, AAAS, 97- *Mem:* Fel AAAS; Sigma Xi; Asn Pub Policy Analysis & Mgt; fel Nat Acad Pub Admin. *Res:* United States and comparative environmental policy; environmental policy analysis; science and values in public policy decisions. *Mailing Add:* 298 Azalea Dr Chapel Hill NC 27514. *Fax:* 919-966-7911; *E-Mail:* pete_andrews@unc.edu

ANDREWS, RICHARD VINCENT, PHYSIOLOGY. *Current Pos:* VIS INVESTR, AUSTRALIAN ANTARCTIC RES DIV, 93- *Personal Data:* b Arapahoe, Nebr, Jan 9, 32; wid; c Thomas, William, Robert, Catherine, James & John. *Educ:* Creighton Univ, BS, 58, MS, 59; Univ Iowa, PhD(physiol), 63. *Prof Exp:* Instr biol, Creighton Univ, 58-60; instr physiol, Univ Iowa, 60-63; from instr to prof biol, Creighton Univ, 63-70, prof physiol & asst dean med,

70-75, grad dean, 75-85. *Concurrent Pos:* NSF sci fac fel, Univ Iowa, 61-63; Arctic Inst NAm vis investr, Naval Arctic Res Lab, 63-72; vis prof zool, Univ BC, Can, 85-86; vis investr, Australian Antarctic Res Div, 93-94; emer prof & dean, Creighton Univ, 97- *Mem:* Endocrine Soc; Am Physiol Soc; Am Soc Mammologists; Ecol Soc Am; Soc Exp Biol & Med; fel Explorer's Club; Int Soc Biometeorol. *Res:* Regulatory and environmental physiology; neuroendocrine mechanisms related to adaptation and fitness traits of small mammals in natural environments. *Mailing Add:* Creighton Univ 2500 California Omaha NE 68178. *Fax:* 402-280-2690

ANDREWS, ROBERT SANBORN, GEOPHYSICS, SCIENCE ADMINISTRATION. *Current Pos:* SR STAFF OFFICER, BD RADIOACTIVE WASTE MGT, NAT ACAD SCI, 90- *Personal Data:* b Minneapolis, Minn, Sept 20, 35; m 60, Lois Christensen; c Kara & Kristen. *Educ:* Univ Minn, Minneapolis, BGE, 58; Univ Wash, MS, 65; Tex A&M Univ, PhD(oceanog), 70. *Prof Exp:* Assoc prof oceanog, Naval Postgrad Sch, 68-80; sr staff officer, Continental Sci Drilling Comt, Nat Acad Sci, 80-85; sr opers officer, Deep Observ & Sampling Earth's Continental Crust, Inc, 85-89. *Concurrent Pos:* Actg dir, Earth Physics Prog, Off Naval Res, 77-80. *Mem:* Am Geophys Union; Geol Soc Am; Sigma Xi. *Res:* Marine seismic exploration; theoretical seismograms; sedimentary petrology; acoustic and physical properties of marine sediments; hydrographic surveying; crustal tectonics; optical oceanography; antisubmarine warfare; scientific drilling; environmental remediation. *Mailing Add:* 6837 Lemon Rd McLean VA 22101-5422. *Fax:* 202-334-3077; *E-Mail:* randrews@nzs.edu

ANDREWS, ROBIN M, PHYSIOLOGICAL ECOLOGY. *Current Pos:* from asst prof to assoc prof, 76-95, PROF, VA POLYTECH INST & STATE UNIV, 95- *Educ:* Univ Minn, BS, 64; Harvard Univ, MA, 67; Univ Kans, PhD(zool), 71. *Prof Exp:* Fel, Smithsonian Trop Res Inst, 71-72, Int Biol Prog, Grassland Biomed, 73-75; vis asst prof biol, Washington Univ, 75-76. *Mem:* Soc Integrated & Comp Biol; Soc Study Amphibians & Reptiles; Am Soc Naturalists. *Res:* Evolutionary ecology of reptiles; physiological ecology of reptiles. *Mailing Add:* Dept Biol Va Polytech Inst PO Box 0406 Blacksburg VA 24063-0406. *E-Mail:* randrews@vt.edu

ANDREWS, RONALD ALLEN, XEROGRAPHY, INTELLIGENT SYSTEMS. *Current Pos:* STAFF VPRES & DIR, ADVAN TECHNOL LABS, RCA/GE AEROSPACE, 83- *Personal Data:* b Pontiac, Mich, Mar 1, 40; m 67; c 1. *Educ:* Wayne State Univ, BS, 62, PhD(physics), 66; Mass Inst Technol, MS, 76. *Prof Exp:* Fel solid state physics, Wayne State Univ, 66-67; res physicist quantum optics, Naval Res Lab, 67-71, head, Optical Physics Br, 71-72, head, Interaction Physics Br, 72-76; Mgr, Forward Develop Area, Wilson Ctr Technol, Xerox Corp, 77-79, mgr, Foward Prod Syst Eng, 79-83. *Concurrent Pos:* Sloan fel, Mass Inst Technol, 75-76. *Mem:* Fel Am Phys Soc; fel Am Optical Soc; sr mem Inst Elec & Electronics Engrs; Sigma Xi. *Res:* Nonlinear optics and parametric phenomenon; product development and engineering; optical waveguides and devices; lasers physics; x-ray lasers; systems engineering; laser-matter interactions; technical program management; xerography; artificial intelligence; digital signal processing; advanced computing architectures; distributed real time processing; intelligent processing systems. *Mailing Add:* Lockheed Martin 1 Federal St Camden NJ 08102

ANDREWS, RUSSELL J, NEUROSURGERY, NEUROSCIENCE. *Current Pos:* neurosurg residency, 81-86, ASST PROF NEUROSURG, VET ADMIN MED CTR, STANFORD UNIV, 92- *Personal Data:* b Pittsburgh, Pa, Apr 6, 47. *Educ:* Dartmouth Col, BA, 67, MD, 78; Harvard Univ, DEd, 74. *Honors & Awards:* G Milton Shy Award, Am Acad Neurol, 75. *Prof Exp:* Surg internship, Walter Reed Army Med Ctr, 78-79; asst prof neurosurg, Vet Admin Med Ctr, Univ Calif, Davis, 86-91. *Concurrent Pos:* Prin investr, Vet Admin Merit Rev Grant, 87-90. *Mem:* Cong Neurol Surgeons; fel Am Heart Asn; Am Asn Neurol Surgeons; AAAS; NY Acad Sci. *Res:* Cerebral ischemia; cerebral aneurysms; cerebral organization and fuctional brain mapping; published numerous articles. *Mailing Add:* 8092 Squirrel Lane Manlius NY 13104-9794

ANDREWS, RUSSELL S, JR, PULP CHEMISTRY. *Current Pos:* mgr primary processing develop, Int Paper Co, 77-79, mgr Chem & Energy Recovery, Corp Res Ctr, 79-83, supt Process Eng, Natchez Mill, 83-84, mgr Energy Conserv, NY Off, 84-85, sr coordr, 85-90, STAFF ENGR, PROCESS TECHNOL, INT PAPER CO, MOBILE, 91- *Personal Data:* b Mobile Ala, July 22, 42; m 68, Mary Ruth Armfield; c Russell III, Neal, Joel & Camille. *Educ:* Univ Ala, BSch, 64, PhD(org chem), 69. *Prof Exp:* Teaching asst, Univ Ala, 64-68; res assoc, Erling Riis Res Lab, Int Paper Co, Mobile, Ala, 69-76, pulp sect leader, 76-77. *Mem:* Tech Asn Pulp & Paper Indust; Am Chem Soc; Sigma Xi. *Res:* Organic photochemistry; cellulose and lignin chemistry; pulping, bleaching and chemical recovery technology; environmental technology. *Mailing Add:* 6013 Cumberland Rd S Mobile AL 36608

ANDREWS, STEPHEN BRIAN, CELL BIOLOGY, BIOPHYSICAL CHEMISTRY. *Current Pos:* res scientist, Spec Expert, Lab Neurobiol, 83-90, CHIEF, ANALYTICAL CELL BIOL, LAB NEUROBIOL, NAT INST NEUROL DIS & STROKE/NIH, 90- *Personal Data:* b McKeesport, Pa, Apr 13, 44; m 69, Sheryl Biesemeier; c Ethan & Mark. *Educ:* Providence Col, BS, 66; Mass Inst Technol, PhD(inorganic chem), 71. *Prof Exp:* Asst prof, 73-79, sr res assoc, physiol & cell biol, Sch Med, Yale Univ, 73-83. *Concurrent Pos:* USPHS fel, Sch Med, Yale Univ, 71-73; Consult, NIH; lectr, Marine Biol Lab. *Mem:* Am Chem Soc; Am Soc Cell Biol; Microbeam Anal Soc. *Res:* Physiology and cell biology of neuron and glia; structure and function of synapses; direct freezing and microanalysis of tissues; analytical electron microscopy. *Mailing Add:* NIH Bldg 36 Rm 2A21 Bethesda MD 20892. *Fax:* 301-480-1485; *E-Mail:* sba@nelix.nih.gov

ANDREWS, THEODORE FRANCIS, ECOLOGY. *Current Pos:* actg vpres acad affairs, 76-78, dean, Col Environ & Appl Sci, 69-80, prof, 80-82, EMER PROF BIOL, GOVERNORS STATE UNIV, 82- *Personal Data:* b Atchison, Kans, Aug 17, 17; m 36, 70; c 4. *Educ:* Emporia State Univ, BS, 40; Univ Iowa, MS, 42; Ohio State Univ, PhD(zool), 48. *Prof Exp:* From asst prof to prof biol, Emporia State Univ, 48-56, prof & head dept, 57-66; dir sci, Educ Res Coun Am, Ohio, 66-69. *Concurrent Pos:* Consult, Biol Sci Curriculum Study, 64-65 & Harvard Univ Nigerian Proj, 65; assoc dir comn undergrad educ biol sci, George Washington Univ, 65-66. *Mem:* AAAS; Nat Asn Biol Teachers (pres, 64); Am Inst Biol Sci; Nat Sci Teachers Asn; Ecol Soc Am. *Res:* Electrophysiology; biological assay of industrial wastes; freshwater biology; limnological trends in artificially impounded waters in Kansas; comparative limnology of Kansas streams; ecology of blue heron Ardea herodias in Kansas; science curriculum development; interdisciplinary science program; environmental science curriculum. *Mailing Add:* 34 Cambre Cr Hot Springs Village AR 71909-3419

ANDREWS, WALLACE HENRY, MICROBIOLOGY, ENTERIC BACTERIOLOGY. *Current Pos:* Res microbiologist, Shellfish Sanit Br, Div Food Technol, 69-71, RES MICROBIOLOGIST, FOOD MICROBIOL BR, DIV MICROBIOL STUDIES, FOOD & DRUG ADMIN, 71- *Personal Data:* b Biloxi, Miss, Oct 6, 43. *Educ:* Univ Miss, BA, 65, MS, 67, PhD(microbiol), 69. *Honors & Awards:* Harvey W Wiley Award, Asn Off Anal Chemists, 95. *Concurrent Pos:* Adv, Nat Shellfish Sanit Prog, 73-77; agency expert Salmonella methodoly, 77-; consult, UN Food & Agr Orgn, 83-; gen referee food microbiol, Asn Off Anal Chemists Int, 83-; Asn Off Anal Chemists Int rep, Int Dairy Fedn, Int Asn Cereal Chemists, 85-; consult, Pan Am Health Orgn, 89- *Mem:* Am Soc Microbiol; fel Asn Off Anal Chemists Int; Int Asn Milk Food & Environ Sanitarians Inc. *Res:* Development of sensitive methods for detecting Salmonella and other foodborne enterics; bacteriological standards for foods; recovery of stressed or damaged bacteria. *Mailing Add:* 2121 Jamieson Ave Apt 1701 Alexandria VA 22314. *Fax:* 202-401-7740; *E-Mail:* wha@fdacf.ssw.dhhs.gov

ANDREWS, WILLIAM ALLEN, CIVIL ENGINEERING. *Current Pos:* prof civil eng, 65-88, EMER PROF CIVIL ENG, UNIV MO-ROLLA, 88- *Personal Data:* b St Louis, Mo, Oct 12, 22; m 55; c 2. *Educ:* Wash Univ, BS, 43, MS, 48, ScD(civil eng), 54. *Prof Exp:* Jr engr, Curtiss Wright Corp, 43 & US Engrs, 44-46; lectr math, St Louis Univ, 46; instr civil eng, Wash Univ, 47-54; asst prof, NC State Col, 54-55; assoc prof, Wash Univ, 55-65. *Concurrent Pos:* Struct engr, R L Eason & Assocs, 46-50; consult, Steel Joist Inst, 55-65. *Mem:* Am Soc Civil Engrs. *Res:* Structural engineering. *Mailing Add:* Dept Civil Eng Rm 111 Univ Mo Rolla MO 65409-0030

ANDREWS, WILLIAM LESTER SELF, PHYSICAL CHEMISTRY, SPECTROSCOPY. *Current Pos:* Asst prof, 66-70, assoc prof, 70-76, PROF PHYS CHEM, UNIV VA, 76- *Personal Data:* b Lincolnton, NC, Jan 31, 42; m 65, Marjorie Hare; c Scott H & Ross L. *Educ:* Miss State Univ, BS, 63; Univ Calif, Berkeley, PhD(phys chem), 66. *Honors & Awards:* Coblentz Award. *Concurrent Pos:* Univ Va Ctr Advan Studies sub-grant, 66-68; NSF grants, 68-95; A P Sloan fel, 73-75; Petrol Res Fund grants, 75-78, 79-81 & 82-85; Sci Res Coun & Fulbright Res fels, 82-83; Martin Marietta Energy Systs grants, 89-93; Fulbright Res fel, 93-94; grant, Off Sci Res, Air Force, 93- *Mem:* Am Chem Soc; fel Am Phys Soc; Sigma Xi. *Res:* Infrared matrix spectroscopic studies of complexes, chemical intermediates and molecular ions produced by reactions of laser-ablated metal atoms with suitable molecules. *Mailing Add:* Dept Chem Univ Va Charlottesville VA 22901

ANDRIACCHI, THOMAS PETER, BIOMECHANICS, MECHANICAL ENGINEERING. *Current Pos:* Asst prof, 74-78, ASSOC PROF & DIR BIOMECH RES, RUSH-PRESBY-ST LUKE'S MED CTR, 78- *Personal Data:* b Chicago, Ill, May 30, 47. *Educ:* Univ Ill, Chicago Circle, BS, 69, MS, 71, PhD(mech eng), 74. *Concurrent Pos:* Adj asst prof, Univ Ill, Chicago Circle, 74-; NIH res fel, 75-78 & res career develop award, 78-82, prin investr, 78-82; prin investr, Orthop Res Educ Found, 78-79. *Mem:* Orthop Res Soc; Am Soc Mech Engrs; Am Soc Biomech. *Res:* Biomechanics of the musculoskeletal system and the mechanics of walking; application of biomechanics to the development of internal joint replacement and the treatment of cerebral palsy. *Mailing Add:* Dept Biomech Rush Presbyterian St Luke Med Ctr 1653 W Congress Pkwy 1471 Jelk Chicago IL 60612

ANDRICHUK, JOHN MICHAEL, PETROLEUM GEOLOGY, SEDIMENTOLOGY. *Current Pos:* CONSULT GEOLOGIST, ANDRICHUK & EDIE, 56- *Personal Data:* b Downing, Alta, July 4, 26; m 55, Olga J Solodky; c Carol (Sykes), Janet (Armstrong) & Craig. *Educ:* Univ Alta, BSc, 46, MSc, 49; Northwestern Univ, PhD(geol), 51. *Honors & Awards:* Pres Award, Am Asn Petrol Geologists, 59; Medal of Merit, Can Soc Petrol Geologists, 59. *Prof Exp:* Res geologist, Gulf Oil Corp, 51-54; consult geologist, Alex McCoy Assocs, 54-56. *Mem:* Geol Soc Am; Soc Econ Paleontologists & Mineralogists; Am Asn Petrol Geologists; Can Geol Asn; hon mem Can Soc Petrol Geologists; Asn Prof Engrs. *Res:* Developing new geological methods to locate commercial oil and natural gas accumulations. *Mailing Add:* Andrichuk & Edie Third Floor 205 Ninth Ave SE Calgary AB T2G 0R3 Can

ANDRINGA, KEIMPE, LASERS. *Current Pos:* RES ASSOC LASERS, E I DU PONT DE NEMOURS & CO, INC, 81- *Personal Data:* b Salatiga, Indonesia, Oct 25, 35; US citizen. *Educ:* Delft Univ Technol, MSc, 61. *Prof Exp:* Engr lasers, Laser Advan Develop Ctr, Raytheon Co, 63-66, sr scientist electro-optics, Res Div, 66-74; sr scientist lasers, Exxon Nuclear Corp, 74-81. *Mem:* Inst Elec & Electronics Engrs. *Res:* High-power laser development; electro-optics; non-linear optics. *Mailing Add:* 205 Northwood Dr Aiken SC 29803

ANDRIOLE, VINCENT T, INTERNAL MEDICINE, INFECTIOUS DISEASES. *Current Pos:* from asst prof to assoc prof, 63-74, PROF INTERNAL MED, SCH MED, YALE UNIV, 74- *Personal Data:* b Scranton, Pa, Aug 3, 31; m 56; c 3. *Educ:* Col of Holy Cross, BS, 53; Yale Univ, MD, 57. *Prof Exp:* Intern med, NC Mem Hosp, 57-58, asst resident, 58-59; clin assoc infectious dis, NIH, 59-61. *Concurrent Pos:* USPHS res fel, Sch Med, Yale Univ, 61-63; clin investr, Vet Admin Hosp, West Haven, Conn, 63-66; estab investr, Am Heart Asn, 66-71. *Mem:* Am Soc Clin Invest; Am Soc Nephrology; Infectious Dis Soc Am; Am Col Physicians; Am Soc Microbiol. *Res:* Host defense mechanisms in the pathogenesis of infectious diseases. *Mailing Add:* Yale Univ Sch Med New Haven CT 06510

ANDRIST, ANSON HARRY, PHYSICAL ORGANIC CHEMISTRY. *Current Pos:* from asst prof to assoc prof, 73-80, PROF CHEM, CLEVELAND STATE UNIV, 80- *Personal Data:* b Omaha, Nebr, Sept 28, 43; m 68; c 3. *Educ:* Calif State Univ, San Diego, BS, 66; Univ Ill, Urbana, PhD(chem), 70. *Prof Exp:* Assoc chem, Univ Ore, 70-71; res worker, Univ Sheffield, 71; vis lectr, Univ Colo, Boulder, 72-73. *Mem:* Am Chem Soc. *Res:* Mechanistic complexities, including reaction stereochemistry of thermal as well as photochemical molecular rearrangements are being probed through structural, kinetic and isotopic labeling studies. *Mailing Add:* Dept Chem Cleveland State Univ Cleveland OH 44115-2440

ANDRLE, ROBERT FRANCIS, BIOGEOGRAPHY, ORNITHOLOGY. *Current Pos:* Asst preparator exhibs, Buffalo Mus Sci, 56-59, cur div biogeog, 59-65, asst dir, 65-72, assoc dir, 72-76, cur, Div Vertebrate Zool, 76-84, RES ASSOC, BUFFALO MUS SCI, 84-; ENVIRON CONSULT, 82- *Personal Data:* b Buffalo, NY, Oct 28, 27; m 53; c 4. *Educ:* Canisius Col, BA, 48; Univ Buffalo, MA, 60; La State Univ, PhD(geog), 64. *Concurrent Pos:* Res grants, Frank M Chapman Mem Fund, Am Mus Natural Hist, 65, Buffalo Soc Natural Sci & Am Philos Soc, 67 & Int Coun Bird Preserv, 73, ed, The Atlas of Breeding Birds of New York State, 88. *Mem:* Am Inst Biol Sci; Am Ornithologists' Union; Birdlife Int. *Res:* Niagara frontier region ornithology; rare and endangered bird species in Mexico, Guatemala, and West Indies. *Mailing Add:* 3188 Mill Rd Eden NY 14057

ANDRULIS, MARILYN ANN, ACOUSTICS. *Current Pos:* PRES, ANDRULIS RES CORP, 72- *Personal Data:* b Ft Monmouth, NJ, Sept 6, 40; c 2. *Educ:* Univ Mich, BS, 62; Univ Ill, MS, 64; Univ Tex, PhD(mech eng), 68. *Prof Exp:* Consult, Underwater Syst, Inc, 67-68, B-K Dynamics, 69-71 & Tracor Inc, 71-72; res assoc & dir, Ocean Acoust Course, Cath Univ Am, 72-73. *Concurrent Pos:* Vpres, Mid-Atlantic Res Inst, 73-77; mem bd dirs, Mil Opers Res, 75-79. *Mem:* Acoust Soc Am; Nat Security Indust Asn; Nat Asn Women Fed Contractors. *Res:* Application of underwater acoustics to detection and classification of underwater systems; mathematical modelling. *Mailing Add:* 9220 Armat Dr Bethesda MD 20817

ANDRULIS, PETER JOSEPH, JR, PHARMACEUTICAL DEVELOPMENT. *Current Pos:* dir, Chem & Biol Sci Group, 72-82, dir bus develop & vpres lab opers, Andrulis Res Corp, 82-91, PRES & CHIEF EXEC OFFICER, ANDRULIS PHARMACEUT CORP, 91- *Personal Data:* b New York, NY, Apr 16, 40; m 64; c 2. *Educ:* Canisius Col, BS, 61, MS, 64; Univ Tex, Austin, PhD(phys org chem), 67. *Prof Exp:* Res asst chem, Canisius Col, 62-64 & Univ Tex, Austin, 64-67; res chemist, US Army Mobility Equip Res & Develop Ctr, 67-69; asst prof chem, Am Univ, 69-71 & Trinity Col, DC, 71-75. *Concurrent Pos:* Lectr, NSF High Sch Teachers Inst, Am Univ, 68-69; exec dir, Mid-Atlantic Res Inst, 74-89. *Mem:* Am Chem Soc; Chem Soc; Am Asn Cancer Res. *Res:* Pharmaceutical design development and clinical trials of anticancer agents and tumor necrosis factor agents; tumor necrosis factor inhibitors against inflammatory and autoimmune diseases. *Mailing Add:* Andrulis Pharmaceut Corp 11800 Baltimore Ave No 113 Beltsville MD 20705-1561

ANDRUS, CHARLES HIRAM, SURGICAL ENDOSCOPY, MINIMALLY INVASIVE SURGERY. *Current Pos:* Pediat resident, St Louis Univ Sch Med, 79-81, gen surg resident, 81-86, instr gen surg, Dept Surg, 86, instr surg, 87, asst prof, 88-92, ASSOC PROF SURG, DEPT SURG, ST LOUIS UNIV, 92- *Personal Data:* m 85, Pamela Bergkamp; c Charles, Patrick & Thomas. *Educ:* Univ Calif, San Francisco, BS, 75; St Louis Univ, MD, 79. *Concurrent Pos:* Fel surg endoscopy, Mt Sinai Hosp, Case Western Res Univ, 87; chief, Unit II Surg, St Louis Vet Admin Med Ctr, 90-; prin investr, Vet Admin, 92- *Mem:* Am Chem Soc; Am Col Surgeons; Soc Am Gastrointestinal Endoscopic Surgeons; Soc Surgeons Alimentary Tract; Am Gastroenterol Asn; Asn Acad Surg. *Res:* Evaluation of the hemodynamic and ventilatory effects of laparoscopic pneumoperitoneum; evaluation of new methods of proximal gastric vagotomy; development of new laparoscopic urologic techniques. *Mailing Add:* Dept Surg St Louis Univ 3635 Vista PO Box 15250 St Louis MO 63110-0250. *Fax:* 573-771-1945

ANDRUS, JAN FREDERICK, NUMERICAL ANALYSIS, THEORY OF TIME. *Current Pos:* assoc prof math, 73-79, PROF MATH, UNIV NEW ORLEANS, 79- *Personal Data:* b Washington, DC, Sept 17, 32; m 61, Nancy Swing; c Lynn & Leslie. *Educ:* Col Charleston, BS, 54; Emory Univ, MA, 55; Univ Fla, PhD(math), 58. *Prof Exp:* Sr mathematician, Ga Div, Lockheed Aircraft Corp, 58-61, math specialist, 61-62; consult mathematician, Huntsville Oper, Comput Dept, Gen Elec Co, 62-63, sub-oper mgr, 63-64, consult mathematician, 64-66; mem tech staff, Northrop-Huntsville, Northrop Corp, 66-68, gen supvr, 68-69, mem sr tech staff, 69-73. *Mem:* Am Math Soc; Soc Indust & Appl Math. *Res:* Optimization; numerical analysis; numerical integration of systems of ordinary differential equations separated into subsystems; numerical solution of two-point boundary-value problems; nonlinear programming; optimal control theory; the theory of time. *Mailing Add:* 237 Dorrington Blvd Metairie LA 70005-3813

ANDRUS, MILTON HENRY, JR, ORGANIC POLYMER CHEMISTRY, ORGANIC CHEMISTRY. *Current Pos:* SR CHEM SPECIALIST, 3M CO, 67- *Personal Data:* b Omaha, Nebr, Sept 2, 38; m 64; c 2. *Educ:* Augustana Col, SDak, BS, 61; Univ Wash, PhD(chem), 67. *Mem:* Am Chem Soc. *Res:* Reaction rates and mechanisms of solvolysis of allylic compounds; light sensitive and polymer materials used in printing; synthesis of acrylic monomers and polymers and other organic compounds and polymers. *Mailing Add:* 3M Co 3M Ctr 236-3B-01 St Paul MN 55144-0001

ANDRUS, PAUL GRIER, FIBER OPTICS MICROFABRICATION, ELECTROPHOTOGRAPHY. *Current Pos:* res engr, Battelle Mem Inst, 47-51, prin physicist, 51-57, asst chief appl physics div, 57-73, sr researcher, 73-76, SR RES PHYSICIST, BATTELLE MEM INST, 76- *Personal Data:* b Due West, SC, Dec 23, 25; m 48, Alyce Casper. *Educ:* Univ Wis, PhB, 46. *Prof Exp:* Asst physics, Univ Wis, 46-47. *Mem:* Soc Imaging Sci & Technol. *Res:* Fiber optics sensors and couplers; electrostatics; graphic arts; xerography; low reflectivity surfaces. *Mailing Add:* 9518 Olentangy River Rd Powell OH 43065

ANDRUS, RICHARD EDWARD, BRYOLOGY, ECOLOGY. *Current Pos:* asst prof environ studies, 73-76, asst prof, 76-80, ASSOC PROF ENVIRON STUDIES & BIOL SCI, STATE UNIV NY, BINGHAMTON, 80- *Personal Data:* b Fulton, NY, Apr 18, 41; m 85; c 3. *Educ:* Rensselaer Polytech Inst, BS, 63; State Univ NY, Syracuse, PhD(plant ecol), 74. *Prof Exp:* Policy analyst environ, NY State Dept Environ Conserv, 70-72. *Concurrent Pos:* Co-prin investr, NSF grant, 78-81. *Mem:* Am Bryological & Lichenological Soc; Soc Conserv Biol; Soc Wetland Scientists; Torrey Botanical Club. *Res:* Taxonomy, phytogeography and ecology of Sphagnum. *Mailing Add:* Dept Biol Sci State Univ NY Binghamton PO Box 6000 Binghamton NY 13902-6000

ANDRUS, WILLIAM DEWITT, JR, ZOOLOGY, CELL PHYSIOLOGY. *Current Pos:* From instr to assoc prof, 60-74, chmn dept, 70-73, PROF ZOOL, POMONA COL, 74- *Personal Data:* b Cincinnati, Ohio, Sept 24, 28; m 56; c 3. *Educ:* Oberlin Col, AB, 52; Stanford Univ, PhD(biol), 62. *Mem:* AAAS; Soc Cryobiol; Tissue Cult Asn; Sigma Xi. *Res:* Brine algae and protozoa; cryobiology; mammalian hibernation; tissue culture applications. *Mailing Add:* 231 W Tenth St Claremont CA 91711-6339

ANDRUSHKIW, ROMAN IHOR, NUMERICAL ANALYSIS. *Current Pos:* from asst prof to assoc prof, 78-84, PROF MATH, NJ INST TECHNOL, 84- *Personal Data:* b L'viv, Ukraine, May 3, 37; US citizen; m 75, Svitlana M Lutzky; c Pavlo M. *Educ:* Stevens Inst Technol, BE, 59, PhD(math), 73; Newark Col Eng, MSEE, 64; Univ Chicago, MS, 67. *Honors & Awards:* NSF Award, 66. *Prof Exp:* From elec engr to sr elec engr, Weston Instruments & Electronics Co, Schlumberger Inc, 59-64; instr math, Newark Col Eng, 64-66; res asst, Univ Chicago, 66-68; instr, Newark Col Eng, 68-70. *Concurrent Pos:* Union Carbide Corp Scholar, 55-59; consult, Bendix Corp; Nat Res Coun award, Coop Appl Sci & Technol Prog, 93-94; grant, Nat Res Coun, Coop Appl Sci & Technol Prog, 93-94 & NAFSA, 93-95. *Mem:* Soc Indust & Appl Math; Int Asn Math & Comput Simulation; Shevchenko Sci Soc; Int Fedn Nonlinear Analysts. *Res:* Spectral theory of non-selfadjoint unbounded operators; finite element analysis with application to parabolic partial differential equations; iterative methods for the solution of linear and nonlinear eigenvalue problems; free boundary problems of the stefan type; integrable nonlinear dynamical systems. *Mailing Add:* Dept Math NJ Inst Technol 323 King Blvd Newark NJ 07102. *Fax:* 973-596-6467; *E-Mail:* roandr@m.njit.edu

ANDRYCHUK, DMETRO, SPECTROSCOPY. *Current Pos:* RETIRED. *Personal Data:* b Fisher Branch, Man, Dec 10, 18; nat US; m 44; c 3. *Educ:* Univ Man, BS, 41, MA, 42; Univ Toronto, PhD(spectros), 49. *Prof Exp:* Jr res officer spectros, Nat Res Coun, Ottawa, Ont, 49-51; spectroscopist, Diamond Alkali Co, Ohio, 51-57; res scientist, Leeds & Northrup Co, Pa, 57-58; mem tech staff res, Tex Instruments Inc, 58-84. *Mem:* Am Chem Soc; Can Physics Soc. *Res:* Emission, raman, infrared and x-ray spectroscopy; infrared studies of semiconductors; analytical instruments; application of laser and infrared technology to reconnaisance. *Mailing Add:* 422 Terrace Dr Richardson TX 75224

ANDRYKOVITCH, GEORGE, MICROBIAL PHYSIOLOGY. *Current Pos:* Asst prof, 68-77, ASSOC PROF BIOL, GEORGE MASON UNIV, UNIV VA, 77- *Personal Data:* b St Michael, Pa, Jan 1, 41. *Educ:* Univ Pittsburgh, BS, 62, MS, 65; Univ Md, PhD(microbiol), 68. *Mem:* AAAS; Am Inst Biol Sci; Sigma Xi; Am Soc Microbiol. *Res:* Regulation and control of the biosynthesis of extracellular polysaccharides of yeasts and bacteria; mechanisms of action of bacteriolytic enzymes elaborated by soil microorganisms. *Mailing Add:* Biol George Mason Univ 4400 Univ Dr Fairfax VA 22030-4443

ANDY, ORLANDO JOSEPH, NEUROSURGERY. *Current Pos:* chmn dept, 60-80, PROF NEUROSURG, SCH MED, UNIV MISS, 55- *Personal Data:* b New Britain, Conn, Jan 21, 20. *Educ:* Ohio Univ, BS, 43; Univ Rochester, MD, 45. *Prof Exp:* Instr neurol surg, Univ & neurol surgeon, Hosp, Johns Hopkins Univ, 52-55. *Concurrent Pos:* USPHS fel, Johns Hopkins Univ, 52-55. *Mem:* Neurosurg Soc Am; Am Asn Neurol Surgeons; AMA; Am Fedn Clin Res; Cong Neurol Surgeons; Sigma Xi. *Res:* Epilepsy. *Mailing Add:* Dept Neurosurg Univ Miss Med Ctr Jackson MS 39216

ANEJA, VINEY P, ATMOSPHERIC SCIENCE, ENVIRONMENTAL ENGINEERING & AIR QUALITY. *Current Pos:* vis assoc prof, 87-90, res assoc prof, 90-95, RES PROF, ATMOSPHERIC SCI, NC STATE UNIV, RALEIGH, 95- *Personal Data:* b Jullunder, India, Nov 21, 48; m 81, Poonam; c Sonia & Saurarm. *Educ:* Indian Inst Technol, Kanpur, BTech, 71; NC State Univ, Raleigh, MS, 75, PhD(chem eng), 77; Union Col, MBA, 86. *Honors & Awards:* Distinguished Serv Award, Air Pollution Control Asn, 84. *Prof Exp:* Mem sci staff, Brookhaven Nat Lab, 73-75; proj scientist, Northrop Serv, Inc, 76-80; staff chem engr, Gen Elec Co, 80-87. *Concurrent Pos:* Vis prof, Univ Uppsala, Sweden, 79, Jawahar Lal Nehru Univ, India, 80; consult, UN Environ Prog & US Govt; indust reviewer proposals, NSF, US Environ Protection Agency & NASA; tech prog chmn, Int Specialty Conf Environ Impact Natural Emissions, 84; vis scientist, Arrhenius Lab, Sweden, 85; prin investr, US Environ Protection Agency, 87, 88, 89, 90 & 91, USDA Forest Serv, 90-91, Ga Inst Technol, 90-91; mem, comt Global Environ Mgt, Air & Waste Mgt Asn, 89- *Mem:* Am Inst Chem Engrs; Am Chem Soc; Air & Waste Mgt Asn; Am Meteorol Soc; Am Geophys Union. *Res:* Atmospheric chemistry; natural emissions; gas exchange; atmospheric monitoring of trace gases; biospheric-atmospheric interactions; cloud chemistry and physics; photochemical oxidants; transformation and transport of pollutants; climate change; awarded six US patents; author of one book and numerous publications on atmospheric chemistry. *Mailing Add:* Dept Marine Earth & Atmospheric Sci NC State Univ Raleigh NC 27695-8208. *Fax:* 919-515-7802; *E-Mail:* viney_aneja@ncsu.edu

ANELLO, CHARLES, BIOSTATISTICS, EPIDEMIOLOGY & PUBLIC HEALTH. *Current Pos:* DEP DIR OFF EPIDEMIOL & BIOSTATISTICS, CTR DRUG EVAL & RES, FDA, 69- *Personal Data:* b Philadelphia, Pa, Dec 20, 35; m 58; c 2. *Educ:* Towson State Col, BS, 58; Johns Hopkins Univ, ScM, 62, ScD(biostatist), 64. *Honors & Awards:* Merit Award, Food & Drug Admin, 85; Super Serv Award, Pub Health Serv, 87; Distinguished Serv Award, Dept Health & Human Serv, 89. *Prof Exp:* Consult statist, Booz-Allen Appl Res, Md, 64-65; prin investr, Res Anal Corp, Va, 65-67; asst prof biostatist & epidemiol, Sch Hyg & Pub Health, Johns Hopkins Univ, 67-69. *Concurrent Pos:* Teacher, George Wash Univ. *Mem:* Biomet Soc; Am Statist Soc; Soc Epidemiol Res. *Res:* Competing risk models; application of stochastic processes to medical problems; clinical trial design and analysis; post marketing surveillance. *Mailing Add:* 23 Valerian Ct Rockville MD 20852

ANET, FRANK ADRIEN LOUIS, ORGANIC CHEMISTRY, NATURAL MAGNETIC REMANENCE. *Current Pos:* PROF CHEM, UNIV CALIF, LOS ANGELES, 64- *Personal Data:* b Doulcon/Meuse, France, Oct 24, 26; US citizen; m 55. *Educ:* Univ Sydney, BSc, 49, MSc, 50; Oxford Univ, DPhil(chem), 52. *Prof Exp:* Fel, Nat Res Coun Can, 53-54; from asst prof to prof chem, Univ Ottawa, Can, 54-64. *Mem:* Am Chem Soc; Royal Soc Chem; Sigma Xi; fel AAAS. *Res:* Stereochemistry; nuclear magnetic resonance. *Mailing Add:* Dept Chem Univ Calif Los Angeles CA 90095-1569

ANEX, BASIL GIDEON, SINGLE-CRYSTAL SPECTROSCOPY, ELECTRONIC-STRUCTURE OF MOLECULES. *Current Pos:* PROF CHEM, UNIV NEW ORLEANS, 71- *Personal Data:* b Seattle, Wash, May 4, 31; m 59, Gretchen Fleming; c Deon, Liese & Robin. *Educ:* Wesleyan Univ, BA, 53; Univ Wash, PhD(chem), 59. *Prof Exp:* Res assoc quantum chem, Ind Univ, 59-60; from instr to asst prof chem, Yale Univ, 60-67; prof & head dept, NMex State Univ, 67-71. *Concurrent Pos:* Vis assoc, Comt prof training, Am Chem Soc. *Mem:* Am Chem Soc; fel Am Inst Chem; Sigma Xi. *Res:* Visible, ultraviolet and reflection spectroscopy; electronic properties of highly absorbing crystals; electronic structure of organic molecules, inorganic complexes and charge-transfer complexes; quantum chemistry. *Mailing Add:* 9602 42nd Ave NE Seattle WA 98115-2524. *Fax:* 504-286-6860

ANFINSEN, CHRISTIAN BOEHMER, protein chemistry; deceased, see previous edition for last biography

ANG, ALFREDO H(UA)-S(ING), CIVIL ENGINEERING. *Current Pos:* UNIV CALIF, IRVINE, 88- *Personal Data:* b Davao City, Philippines, July 4, 30; m 54, Myrtle Mae; c Evelyn, Irene & James. *Educ:* Univ Ill, MS, 57, PhD(struct mech), 59. *Honors & Awards:* Walter L Huber Prize, Am Soc Civil Engrs, 68, State-of-the-Art Award, 73, Ernest Howard Award, 96; Freudenthal Medal, 82; Sr Res Award, Am Soc Eng Educ, 83; Newmark Medal, 88; Res Prize, Int Asn Struct Safety & Reliability, 93. *Prof Exp:* Struct designer, Mulvaney-McMillan Co, 54-55; asst civil eng, Univ Ill, Urbana, 55-57, res assoc, 57-59, from asst prof to assoc prof, 59-65, assoc mem, Ctr Advan Study, 64-65, prof civil eng, 65-88. *Concurrent Pos:* Consult, 62-; NSF res grant, 63- *Mem:* Nat Acad Eng; hon mem Am Soc Civil Engrs; fel Am Inst Aeronaut & Astronaut; fel Am Soc Mech Engrs; Seismol Soc Am; Earthquake Eng Res Inst; Int Asn Struct Safety & Reliability (pres); Am Soc Eng Educ; Int Asn Struct Mech Reactor Technol; Soc Naval Architects & Marine Engrs. *Res:* Continuum dynamics; non-linear behavioral theories of solid continuant and the development of general mathematical approaches to non-linear solids; probability theory in structural mechanics; structural safety and reliability; earthquake engineering; structural control. *Mailing Add:* Dept Civil Eng Univ Calif Irvine CA 92697. *Fax:* 714-856-5051; *E-Mail:* aang@ang3.eng.uci.edu

ANG, TJOAN-LIEM, POLYMER SCIENCE. *Current Pos:* sr res chemist polymer appln & prod develop, 76-78, RES ASSOC, POLYMER RES & DEVELOP, AVERY INT CORP, 78- *Personal Data:* b Bogor, Indonesia, Jan 7, 33; m 62; c 2. *Educ:* Inst Technol Bandung, Indonesia, Drs, 62; Univ Akron, MSc, 65, PhD(polymer sci), 75. *Prof Exp:* Lectr org chem, Inst Technol Bandung, 63-71; sr chemist polymer res, Swedlow, Inc, 74-75; sr res chemist, Swedcast Corp, 75-76. *Mem:* Am Chem Soc. *Res:* Impact modification of glassy polymers; activatable pressure sensitive adhesives; release and anti blocking agents; surfactants; bulk and emulsion polymerization; thermal and radiation curing. *Mailing Add:* 1704 Alhambra Rd South Pasadena CA 91030-4621

ANGEL, AUBIE, METABOLIC DISEASE, LIPOPROTEIN METABOLISM. *Current Pos:* PROF & HEAD, DEPT MED, UNIV MAN, 91- *Personal Data:* b Winnipeg, Man, Can, Aug 28, 35; Can citizen; m 61; c 3. *Educ:* Univ Man, BSc, 59, MD, 59; McGill Univ, MSc, 63, FRCP(C), 64. *Prof Exp:* Asst prof, McGill Univ, 65-68; assoc prof, Univ Toronto, 72-81, prof med, 81-90; staff endocrinol, Toronto Gen Hosp, 68-90. *Concurrent Pos:* Staff physician, endocrinol, Royal Victoria Hosp, Montreal, 65-68; scholar med, Med Res Coun, Can, 65-70; proj dir, CIDA grant with INCENSA Costa Rice, 87- *Mem:* Can Soc Clin Invest; Am Soc Clin Invest; Endocrine Soc; Can Soc Endocrinol & Metab; Am Soc Study Obesity; Am Diabetes Asn. *Res:* Regulation of cholesterol storage in adipose tissue and the characterization of lipoprotein-cell interactions; hormonal and nutritional control of lipoprotein binding and metabolism in animals and man. *Mailing Add:* Int Med Univ Manitaba Health Sci Ctr Rm GC430 820 Sherbrook St Winnipeg MB R3A 1R9 Can

ANGEL, CHARLES, BIOCHEMISTRY. *Current Pos:* RETIRED. *Personal Data:* b Lockney, Tex, June 10, 23; m 45; c 3. *Educ:* Tex Tech Col, BS, 48, MS, 49; Univ Tex, PhD(biochem), 54. *Prof Exp:* Lab asst org chem, Tex Tech Col, 47-48, fel chem, 48-49; teaching & asst, Med Br, Univ Tex, 49-53; from asst prof to assoc prof physiol chem, Sch Med, Univ Miss, 53-57; chief res lab, Vet Admin Ctr, Gulfport Div, 57-72; res chemist, Vet Admin Hosp, Little Rock, 78-83; prof biochem, Univ Ark Med Ctr, 72-83, emer prof, 87-93. *Concurrent Pos:* Lectr biochem & psychiat, Sch Med, Tulane Univ, 57-73; clin assoc prof anat, La State Univ Med Ctr, 70-73. *Mem:* Fel AAAS; Am Chem Soc; fel Am Inst Chem; Soc Biol Psychiat; Pavlovian Soc Am; Sigma Xi. *Res:* Biochemical studies in mental diseases; studies relating behavior to physiological and biochemical variables; effects of stress and adrenal hormones on brain protein synthesis and permeability function in the central nervous system. *Mailing Add:* 2524 Queenview Dr Gulfport MS 39507-2200

ANGEL, HENRY SEYMOUR, ORGANIC CHEMISTRY. *Current Pos:* RETIRED. *Personal Data:* b London, Eng, Jan 20, 19; nat US; m 41, Martha T Brainerd; c Elizabeth J, Carol A & David J. *Educ:* Yale Univ, BS, 40; Univ Pa, MS, 47, PhD(org chem), 48. *Prof Exp:* Res chemist, Socony-Vacuum Oil Co, NJ, 40-45; asst instr org chem, Univ Pa, 45-47; sr chemist, Sherwin-Williams Co, 48-52; res chemist, Quaker Oats Co, 53 & Am Cyanamid Co, 53-60; sr scientist, Engelhard Minerals & Chem Corp, 60-83. *Mem:* AAAS; Am Chem Soc. *Res:* Synthesis of organic compounds; synthesis of precious metal-organic compounds. *Mailing Add:* 3503 E Creek Club Dr Missouri City TX 77459

ANGEL, JAMES ROGER PRIOR, WHITE DWARF STARS, ASTRONOMICAL INSTRUMENTS. *Current Pos:* MEM FAC, UNIV ARIZ, TUCSON, 74-, PROF ASTRON, 75-, PROF ASTRON & OPTICAL SCI, 84-, REGENTS PROF, 90- *Personal Data:* b St Helens, Eng, Feb 7, 41; m 65, Ellinor M Goonan; c Jennifer & James. *Educ:* Oxford Univ, Eng, BA, 63, DPhil, 67; Calif Inst Technol, MS, 66. *Honors & Awards:* Pierce Prize, Am Astron Soc, 76; MacArthur Fel, John D & Catherine T MacArthur Found, 96. *Prof Exp:* From res assoc to assoc prof physics, Columbia Univ, 67-74. *Concurrent Pos:* Sloan fel, 70-74; vis assoc prof astron, Univ Tex, Austin, 74. *Mem:* Fel Royal Soc; fel Royal Astron Soc; Am Astron Soc (vpres, 87-90). *Res:* White dwarf stars, quasars, astronomical instruments, telescopes and adaptive optics. *Mailing Add:* Univ Ariz Steward Observ Tucson AZ 85721. *E-Mail:* rangel@as.arizona.edu

ANGEL, JOSEPH FRANCIS, NUTRITION, BIOCHEMISTRY. *Current Pos:* assoc prof, 75-83, PROF BIOCHEM & HEAD DEPT, UNIV SASK, 83- *Personal Data:* b Nablus, Palestine, Aug 31, 40; Can citizen; m 66, Sumayya Ghannam; c Steven & Christopher. *Educ:* Ain Shams Univ, Cairo, BSc, 63; Am Univ Beirut, MSc, 65; Univ Toronto, PhD(nutrit), 71. *Prof Exp:* Res asst biochem, Dept Pediat, Augusta Victoria Hosp, Jerusalem, 65-66; asst prof human nutrit, Univ BC, 69-75. *Mem:* Can Soc Nutrit Sci; Can Biochem Soc. *Res:* Energy utilization in pyridoxine deficiency; lipogenesis in meal-fed animals; evolutionary aspects of nutrition; nutrition and metabolic development in mammalia. *Mailing Add:* Dept Biochem Col Med Univ Sask Saskatoon SK S7N 5E5 Can. *E-Mail:* angel@sask.usask.ca

ANGELAKOS, DIOGENES JAMES, ELECTRICAL ENGINEERING, APPLIED PHYSICS. *Current Pos:* from asst prof to assoc prof, 51-61, dir electronics res lab, 64-85, PROF ELEC ENG, UNIV CALIF, BERKELEY, 61- *Personal Data:* b Chicago, Ill, July 3, 19. *Educ:* Univ Notre Dame, BS, 42; Harvard Univ, MS, 46, PhD(eng sci), 50. *Honors & Awards:* Axion Award, Hellenic Am Prof Soc, 78. *Prof Exp:* Engr microwaves, Westinghouse Elec, 42-43; instr electronics, Univ Notre Dame, 43-46; teaching fel & res asst eng sci, Harvard Univ, 47-50; asst prof elec eng, Univ Notre Dame, 50-51. *Concurrent Pos:* Guggenheim Found fel, 57-58; liaison scientist electronics, Off Naval Res, US Embassy, London, Eng, 61-62; mem eval panel, EM Div, Nat Bur Standards, 72-76 & Associateship Prog, Nat Res Coun, 75-; mem, bd dirs, Mod Greek Studies Found, San Francisco State Univ, 85- *Mem:* Sigma Xi; fel Inst Elec & Electronics Engrs. *Res:* Microwave scattering; snow pack measurements; electronics; antennas; microwave communications. *Mailing Add:* Cory Hall Univ Calif Berkeley CA 94720

ANGELAKOS, EVANGELOS THEODOROU, PHYSIOLOGY. *Current Pos:* chmn dept, 68-83, PROF PHYSIOL & BIOPHYS, GRAD SCH, HAHNEMANN UNIV, 68-, DEAN, 83- *Personal Data:* b Tripolis, Greece, July 15, 29; nat US; c 1. *Educ:* Nat Univ Athens, BS, 48; Boston Univ, MA, 53, PhD(physiol), 55; Harvard Univ, MD, 59. *Prof Exp:* Asst physiol, Sch Med, Boston Univ, 52-53, from instr to prof, 55-68. *Concurrent Pos:* Med Found fel, 59-60; USPHS res career develop award, 60-68; res assoc biomath, Mass Inst Technol, 59-61; res assoc cardiol Maine Med Ctr, Portland, 59-68; vis scientist, Karolinska Inst, Sweden, 62-63; consult, US Army Natick Labs Environ Med, 63-70; consult, Merck Inst Therapeut Res, 68-73; dir, Biomed Res Inst, Univ Maine, Portland, 72-79. *Mem:* AAAS; fel Am Col Cardiol; fel Am Col Angiol; Microcirc Soc; Am Physiol Soc. *Res:* Physiology and pharmacology of the heart and circulation and autonomic nervous system; electrophysiology of the heart; hypothermia; catecholamines; physiology of emotion and stress; primate physiology; hypertension. *Mailing Add:* Allegheny Univ Health Sci Broad & Vine MS 344 Philadelphia PA 19102-1192

ANGELETTI, RUTH HOGUE, EXPERIMENTAL BIOLOGY. *Current Pos:* PROF & DIR, LAB MACROMOLECULAR ANALYSIS, DEPT DEVELOP BIOL & CANCER, ALBERT EINSTEIN COL MED, 88- *Personal Data:* b May 26, 43. *Educ:* Wash Univ, BA, 65, PhD, 69. *Prof Exp:* Res guest, Istituto Superiore di Sanita, Rome, 69-70; postdoctoral fel, Wash Univ, 70-71, res assoc, 73-74; res consult, Lab Cellular Biol, Rome, 71-73; res assoc, Inst Cancer Res, Philadelphia, 74-75; from asst prof to prof, Dept Path & Lab Med, Div Neuropath, Med Sch, Univ Pa, 75-88, dir, Protein Chem Lab, 82-88. *Concurrent Pos:* Res career develop award, NIH, 77-81, mem, Biochem Study Sect, 81-85; lectr peptide synthesis, Albert Einstein Col Med; lectr neurochem-neuropharmacol & develop neurobiol, Univ Pa. *Mem:* NY Acad Sci; AAAS; Am Soc Neurochem; Am Soc Biochem & Molecular Biol; Am Chem Soc; Protein Soc. *Res:* Biochemistry; macromolecular analysis; neurobiology. *Mailing Add:* Biochem Albert Einstein Col Med 1300 Morris Park Ave Bronx NY 10461-1926

ANGELICI, ROBERT JOE, INORGANIC CHEMISTRY, ORGANOMETALLIC CHEMISTRY. *Current Pos:* from instr to prof, 63-87, chmn dept, 77-81, DISTINGUISHED PROF CHEM, IOWA STATE UNIV, 87- *Personal Data:* b Rochester, Minn, July 29, 37; m 60; c 2. *Educ:* St Olaf Col, BA, 59; Northwestern Univ, PhD(inorg chem), 62. *Prof Exp:* NSF fel, 62-63. *Concurrent Pos:* Alfred P Sloan Found fel, 70-72; fel, Royal Soc Guest Res, 87. *Mem:* Am Chem Soc; Royal Soc Chem London. *Res:* Organometallic chemistry of the transition metals; synthesis, characterization, mechanistic studies and catalysts; catalysis. *Mailing Add:* Dept Chem Iowa State Univ Ames IA 50010-0061

ANGELIDES, KIMON JERRY, NEUROSCIENCE, CELL BIOLOGY. *Current Pos:* from assoc prof to prof molecular physiol & biophys, neurosci, biochem, 91-92, PROF CELL BIOL & NEUROSCI, BAYLOR COL MED, 92- *Personal Data:* b Sacramento, Calif, Aug 8, 51; m 91, Karauiti Lefkothea; c Alexei, Nicholas, Philip & Eleni. *Educ:* Lawrence Univ, BA, 73; Univ Calif, Santa Cruz, PhD(chem), 77. *Prof Exp:* NIH fel, Dept Chem, Cornell Univ, 77-79; asst prof biochem, McGill Univ, 79-81; from asst prof to assoc prof biochem, molecular biol & neurosci, Col Med, Univ Fla, 81-86. *Concurrent Pos:* Basil O'Connor scholar, March of Dimes, 79-81; Nat Res Coun award, First World Cong, Int Brain Res Orgn, Lausanne, Switz, 82 & 8th Int Biophys Cong, Bristol, UK, 84; vis prof, Nat Ctr Sci Res, Lab Biochem, Univ d'Aix-Marseille, 84 & Nat Inst Physiol Sci, Japan, 84-85; NIH res career develop award, 87-92, res grants, 90-95; mem, Biol Sci Study Sect, NIH, 87-90 & Neurosci & Behav, 92-; mem, Res Adv Comt, Nat Mult Sclerosis Soc, 93- *Mem:* Am Soc Cell Biol; Soc Neurosci; Am Chem Soc; Int Soc Toxicol. *Res:* Molecular and cellular basis for signalling in the nervous system and organization of the neuronal membrane and those intra- and extra-cellular elements that are important in its organization during development; development and organization of the cortex; author of numerous technical publications. *Mailing Add:* Dept Cell Biol Baylor Col Med One Baylor Plaza Houston TX 77030-3411. *Fax:* 713-798-8005

ANGELINI, ARNALDO M, ENVIRONMENT, MATHEMATICS & ELECTRICAL ENGINEERING. *Current Pos:* RETIRED. *Personal Data:* b Force, Italy, Feb 2, 09; m 37; c 3. *Educ:* Univ Rome, Libero Docente(elec eng), 36. *Honors & Awards:* Simon Ramo Gold Medal, Inst Elec & Electronic Engrs, 86, Eng Leadership Recognition, 89. *Prof Exp:* Prof elec eng, Univ Rome, 49-73, prof nuclear eng, 57-69. *Concurrent Pos:* Cent mgr, Power Sector, Soc Indust Elec, 44-49, gen mgr, 49-63; gen mgr, Ital Nat Elec Bd, 63-73, chmn, 73-79, hon chmn, 79-; vpres, World Energy Conf, 68-71; hon prof, Polytech Inst NY, 75. *Mem:* Foreign mem Nat Acad Eng; fel Am Nuclear Soc; fel Inst Elec & Electronic Engrs. *Res:* Energy in general; electric power and nuclear energy; transmission of electric power; application of systems science and engineering; complete reconstruction and large development of the electric power system in central Italy destroyed during the second World War. *Mailing Add:* Enel, Via G B Martini 3 Rome 00198 Italy

ANGELINI, CORRADO ITALO, neurology, for more information see previous edition

ANGELINI, PIO, FOOD CHEMISTRY. *Current Pos:* CONSULT, 91- *Personal Data:* b Ipswich, Mass, May 2, 32; m 62; c 8. *Educ:* Univ Mass, BS, 54; Mich State Univ, MS, 56, PhD(food sci), 63. *Prof Exp:* Analytical chemist, US Army Natick Labs, 62-91. *Mem:* Inst Food Tech; Am Chem Soc; Sigma Xi. *Res:* Analysis of food flavors using gas chromatographic and mass spectrometric techniques. *Mailing Add:* 117 Winter St Ashland MA 01721-1116

ANGELINO, NORMAN J, ORGANIC CHEMISTRY. *Current Pos:* SCIENTIST, NY STATE DEPT HEALTH, ROSWELL PARK MEM INST, 67- *Personal Data:* b Buffalo, NY, May 21, 43; m 83; c 3. *Educ:* State Univ NY, Buffalo, BA, 67. *Mem:* Am Chem Soc; AAAS. *Res:* Synthesis of cell-surface related carbohydrate analogs as potential anti-tumor agents; modification of oligonucleotides as anti-sense agents. *Mailing Add:* 666 Elm St Buffalo NY 14263

ANGELL, C A, PHYSICAL CHEMISTRY. *Current Pos:* PROF CHEM, ARIZ STATE UNIV, 89- *Personal Data:* b Canberra, Australia, Dec 14, 33; c 5. *Educ:* Univ Melbourne, BSc, 54, MSc, 56; Univ London, PhD(chem), 61. *Honors & Awards:* Sigma Xi Fac Res Award, Purdue Univ, 78, McCoy Fac Res Award, 86; Murey Award, Am Ceramic Soc, 90; Mott Award, J Non-Crystalline Solids, 92. *Prof Exp:* Lectr chem metall, Univ Melbourne, 62-64; res assoc & fel chem, Argonne Nat Lab, 64-66; from asst prof to prof chem, Purdue Univ, 66-88. *Concurrent Pos:* Mem ad hoc comt infra-red transmitting mat, Nat Res Coun, 67-68; mem ed adv bd, J Phys Chem, 74-78, J Chem Phys, 87- *Mem:* Am Chem Soc; Sigma Xi. *Res:* Mass transport properties of ionic liquids; nature of supercooled liquids and glass transition; spectroscopic studies of coordination states in, and vibrational dynamics of, ionic liquids; geochemical liquids; protein dynamics; solid electrolytes. *Mailing Add:* Dept Chem Ariz State Univ Tempe AZ 85287-0002

ANGELL, CHARLES LESLIE, PHYSICAL CHEMISTRY. *Current Pos:* RETIRED. *Personal Data:* b July 4, 26; US citizen; m 58; c 2. *Educ:* Univ Sydney, BSc, 49, MSc, 50; Cambridge Univ, PhD(chem), 55. *Prof Exp:* Res officer, NSW Univ Technol, 51-53; fel & res assoc spectros, Univ Mich, 56 & Purdue Univ, 57-58; res scientist, Tarrytown Tech Ctr, Union Carbide Corp, 58-69, group leader spectros, 70-78, scientist, 78-92. *Mem:* Am Chem Soc; Soc Appl Spectros; Coblentz soc (pres 69-71); Royal Soc Chem; Am Soc Testing Mat. *Res:* Structural investigations of molecules by infrared and Raman spectroscopy; adsorbed molecules and catalysis; molecular and bond moments; tautomeric systems; infrared absorption band intensities; solvent effects. *Mailing Add:* 49 Academy St Pleasantville NY 10570

ANGELL, FREDERICK FRANKLYN, PLANT BREEDING, GENETICS. *Current Pos:* PROJ LEADER, ASGROW SEED CO, 85-, STA MGR, PAC COAST BREEDING STA, 87- *Personal Data:* b Alto Pass, Ill, July 25, 37; m 64; c 4. *Educ:* Southern Ill Univ, BS, 60, MS, 61; Univ Wis, PhD(hort, plant path), 65. *Prof Exp:* From asst prof to assoc prof hort, Univ Md, College Park, 70-74; dir res, A L Castle, Inc, 74-85. *Mem:* Tomato Genetics Coop; Cucurbit Genetics Coop; Am Soc Hort Sci; Int Hort Soc. *Res:* Vegetable breeding; development of processor tomato, varieties; genetics of tomatoes; especially mutants, gene location and inheritance of disease resistance; direct variety development and evaluation program. *Mailing Add:* 7281 Miller Ave Gilroy CA 95020

ANGELL, JAMES BROWNE, ELECTRICAL ENGINEERING. *Current Pos:* assoc prof, 60-62, PROF ELEC ENG, STANFORD UNIV, 62-, ASSOC CHMN DEPT, 69- *Personal Data:* b Staten Island, NY, Dec 25, 24; m 50; c 2. *Educ:* Mass Inst Technol, SB & SM, 46, ScD(elec eng), 52. *Prof Exp:* Asst electronics, Mass Inst Technol, 46-52; proj engr, Res Div, Philco Corp, 52-56, mgr solid state circuit res, 56-60. *Concurrent Pos:* Consult, Philco Corp, 60-62 & Fairchild Semiconductor Div, 63-74; chmn Int Solid-State Circuits Conf, 64-65; mem electronics adv group, US Electronics Command, 64-74 & US Army Sci Adv Panel, 68-75. *Mem:* Fel Inst Elec & Electronics Engrs; Sigma Xi. *Res:* Principles, design and application of solid state devices and integrated circuits; application of integrated circuit technology to bio-medical instrumentation and transducers. *Mailing Add:* 1400 Geary Blvd Apt 2309 San Francisco CA 94109

ANGELL, ROBERT WALKER, PROTOZOOLOGY, CYTOLOGY. *Current Pos:* ASSOC PROF ZOOL, UNIV DENVER, 67- *Personal Data:* b Milwaukee, Wis, Apr 24, 29; m 58. *Educ:* Beloit Col, BS, 58; Univ Chicago, PhD(paleozool), 65. *Prof Exp:* USPHS traineeship, 66; asst prof zool, Univ NC, 66-67. *Mem:* Soc Protozool. *Res:* Biological mineralization, especially calcification in invertebrates; biology of Foraminifera. *Mailing Add:* 702 S Corona St Denver CO 80209

ANGELL, THOMAS STRONG, MATHEMATICS. *Current Pos:* From asst prof to assoc prof, 69-83, PROF MATH, UNIV DEL, 83- *Personal Data:* b Bakersfield, Calif, Jan 8, 42; m 67; c 4. *Educ:* Harvard Univ, AB, 63; Univ Mich, MA, 62, PhD(math), 69. *Concurrent Pos:* Vis assoc prof, Ga Inst Technol, 76-77; vis prof, Univ Gottingen, 80-81, Univ NMex, 84-85. *Mem:* Am Math Soc; Soc Indust & Appl Math; Math Asn Am. *Res:* Mathematical theory of optimal control; calculus of variations; ordinary and functional differential equations; scattering theory. *Mailing Add:* Dept Math Sci Univ Delaware Newark DE 19716

ANGELLO, STEPHEN JAMES, PHYSICS, SEMICONDUCTORS. *Current Pos:* RETIRED. *Personal Data:* b Haddonfield, NJ, Mar 2, 18; m 44; c 3. *Educ:* Univ Pa, BS, 39, MS, 40, PhD(physics), 42. *Prof Exp:* Res engr, Westinghouse Elec Co, 42-46; asst prof elec eng, Univ Pa, 46-47, head spec proj, Res Inst, 46-47; res engr, Westinghouse Elec Corp, 47-52, sect mgr, 52-54, eng mgr, Semiconductor Dept, 54-57, consult engr, 57-59, mgr thermoelec proj, 59-60, mgr molecular electronics, 60-62, mgr solid state res & develop, 62-64; prof elec eng, Univ Calif, Santa Barbara, 64-66; consult, Res & Develop Ctr, Westinghouse Elec Corp, 66-82. *Concurrent Pos:* Spec lectr, Duquesne Univ, 47-48. *Mem:* Fel Inst Elec & Electronics Engrs; Am Phys Soc. *Res:* Electrical properties of metal-semiconductor contacts; oxide coated cathodes; Hall effect in semiconductors; low-loss, low-noise crystal rectifier for 3 cm microwave mixers; Hall effect and conductivity of cuprous oxide; silicon rectifier development and thermoelectricity; microelectronics. *Mailing Add:* 112 Woodgate Rd Pittsburgh PA 15235

ANGELO, RUDOLPH J, POLYMER CHEMISTRY. *Current Pos:* CONSULT, 83- *Personal Data:* b Ellwood City, Pa, June 16, 30; m 57, Shirley Nuckles; c Anthony. *Educ:* Geneva Col, BS, 51; Univ Fla, MS, 53, PhD(chem), 55. *Prof Exp:* Technician analysis, Callery Chem Co, 51; instr, Univ Fla, 51-52, asst, AEC, 52-55; res chemist, Exp Sta, 55-58, Iowa, 58-59, res chemist, Exp Sta, 59-73, res assoc, Exp Sta, E I Du Pont de Nemours & Co, Inc, 73-83. *Mem:* Am Chem Soc; Am Inst Chemists; NY Acad Sci. *Res:* Syntheses of vinyl and condensation polymers; cyclic polymerization mechanism of non-conjugated diolefins; film and plastic technology. *Mailing Add:* 934 Glackens Lane Wilmington DE 19808

ANGELONE, LUIS, PHYSIOLOGY. *Current Pos:* exec secy hemat study sect, NIH, 65-67, dep chief, Pac Off, 67-68, asst chief spec progs, Res Grants Review Br, Div Res Grants, 68-71, asst chief referral, 71-74, chief referral, 74-78, CHIEF, REV UNIT, EXTRAMURAL ACTIV PROG, NAT INST ARTHRITIS, DIABETES & DIGESTIVE & KIDNEY DIS, NIH, 78- *Personal Data:* b Alliance, Ohio, Oct 3, 19; m 46; c 3. *Educ:* Ohio State Univ, BA, 47, MA, 49, PhD(physiol), 52. *Honors & Awards:* Dirs Award, NIH, 78. *Prof Exp:* Asst physiol, Ohio State Univ, 49-52, asst instr, 52; res physiologist, Army Chem Ctr, Md, 52-53; from instr to prof physiol, Wash Univ, 53-65. *Concurrent Pos:* Expert adv, Aberdeen Proving Ground, Md, 53-54; consult, Army Chem Ctr, 53-59; Nat Bd Dent Exam, 62-67. *Mem:* AAAS; Am Physiol Soc. *Res:* Hematology; cardiovascular physiology; neurophysiology. *Mailing Add:* 5806 Madawaska Rd Bethesda MD 20816

ANGELONI, FRANCIS M, ANALYTICAL CHEMISTRY. *Current Pos:* RETIRED. *Personal Data:* b Butler, Pa, Apr 26, 28; m 52; c 2. *Educ:* Pa State Univ, BS, 52, MS, 59, PhD(analytical chem), 65. *Prof Exp:* Res asst, Petrol Ref Lab, Pa State Univ, 52-61; chief chemist, Appl Sci Lab, Inc, Pa, 61-65; sr scientist, Koopers Co, 65-66, group leader physics & phys chem group, 66-69, mgr analysis & res serv sect, Res Dept, 69-78, mgr, res & develop, 78-82, chem prods & process res, 82-83, vpres & dir chem res, 83-88, vpres technol assessment, 88-89. *Mem:* AAAS; Indust Res Inst. *Res:* Thermal methods of analysis; x-ray analysis; petroleum chemistry; instrumental analysis; polymer characterization; organic synthesis; coal tar products; high performance insulating materials; chemical process development. *Mailing Add:* 2359 Harrison City Rd Export PA 15632

ANGELOPOULOS, EDITH W, PARASITOLOGY, ENTOMOLOGY. *Current Pos:* Asst prof, 67-71, ASSOC PROF BIOL, DALHOUSIE UNIV, 71- *Personal Data:* b Vienna, Austria, Jan 31, 36; US citizen; m 67. *Educ:* Univ Minn, Minneapolis, BA & BS, 61, MS, 64, PhD(zool), 67. *Res:* Structural and functional aspects of parasitic flagellates; physiology and ultrastructure of Trypanosomatidae and Trichomonas tenax; microtubules in Trypanosomatidae; scanning and transmission microscopy; freeze etching and histochemical studies of Trichomonas tenax; relation of house dust mites to disease transmission; symbiotic bacteria of Hirudinea; relation of hormones to feline mammary cancer. *Mailing Add:* Dept Biol Sci Dalhousie Univ Halifax NS B3H 4H6 Can

ANGER, CLIFFORD D, SPACE SCIENCE, IMAGE PROCESSING. *Current Pos:* From asst prof to assoc prof, 62-74, prof physics, 74-89, EMER PROF PHYSICS & ASTRON, UNIV CALGARY, 92-; PRES, ITRES RES LTD CALGARY, 84- *Personal Data:* b Long Beach, Calif, Nov 15, 34; m 67, Patricia Anne Ryckman; c John & Susan. *Educ:* Univ Calif, Berkeley, BA, 56, MA, 59, PhD(physics), 63. *Honors & Awards:* Group Achievement Award, NASA, 91 & 96. *Concurrent Pos:* Mem, Galileo Mission Imaging Sci Team, NASA; prin investr, Satellite Auroral Imaging Instruments; adj prof, Ctr Res Exp Space Sci, York Univ, Toronto, Ont, Can, 88- *Mem:* Am Soc Photogram & Remote Sensing. *Res:* Upper atmosphere physics; satellite, balloon and ground level studies of auroral phenomena. *Mailing Add:* ITRES Res Ltd 155-2635 37th Ave NE Calgary AB T1Y 5Z6 Can. *Fax:* 403-250-9916

ANGER, HAL OSCAR, INSTRUMENTATION, NUCLEAR MEDICINE. *Current Pos:* CONSULT, 81- *Personal Data:* b Denver, Colo, May 24, 20. *Educ:* Univ Calif, Berkeley, BS, 43. *Hon Degrees:* DSc, Ohio State Univ, 72. *Honors & Awards:* John Scott Award, 64; Nuclear Med Pioneer Citation, Soc Nuclear Med, 74; Centennial Award, Inst Elec & Electronics Engrs, 84, Benedict Cassen Prize, 94. *Prof Exp:* Res assoc, Harvard Univ, 43-46; biophysicist, Lawrence Radiation Lab & Donner Lab, Univ Calif, Berkeley, 46-81. *Concurrent Pos:* Guggenheim fel, 66-67. *Mem:* Inst Elec & Electronics Engrs; Soc Nuclear Med. *Res:* Instruments for detecting and measuring radioactive isotopes and for mapping their distribution in patients; invention of the first clinically successful radioisotope camera and other instruments. *Mailing Add:* 2236 Channing Way Berkeley CA 94704-2163

ANGERER, J(OHN) DAVID, ORGANIC CHEMISTRY, POLYMER CHEMISTRY. *Current Pos:* Res chemist, 68-74, develop supvr, 78-81, RES SUPVR, HERCULES INC, 74-, RES ASSOC, 81-, DIR TECHNOL. *Personal Data:* b Columbus, Ohio, Mar 9, 42; m 63; c 3. *Educ:* Ohio State Univ, BSc, 63; Univ Ill, Urbana, MSc, 65, PhD(org chem), 68. *Mem:* Sigma Xi; Am Chem Soc. *Res:* Monomer and polymer synthesis; process development of organic reaction mechanisms; chemistry and rheology of polysaccharides. *Mailing Add:* 11 Slashpine Circle Southwood Hockessin DE 19707-9206

ANGERER, LYNNE MUSGRAVE, MOLECULAR GENETICS. *Current Pos:* SR RES ASSOC, UNIV ROCHESTER, 78- *Personal Data:* b Ft Sill, Okla, Dec 7, 44; m 66; c 2. *Educ:* Ohio State Univ, BSc, 66, MSc, 67; Johns Hopkins Univ, PhD(cell & develop biol), 73. *Prof Exp:* Fel molecular genetics, Calif Inst Technol, 73-78. *Concurrent Pos:* Damon Runyan-Walter Winchell fel cancer res, 73-75; NIH fel, 76. *Mem:* Sigma Xi; Am Soc Cell Biol. *Res:* Study of gene expression in the developing sea urchin embryo. *Mailing Add:* 27 Chelmsford Rd Rochester NY 14618

ANGERER, ROBERT CLIFFORD, DEVELOPMENTAL BIOLOGY, GENE REGULATION. *Current Pos:* from asst prof to assoc prof, 78-89, PROF BIOL & PEDIAT, UNIV ROCHESTER, 89- *Personal Data:* b Columbus, Ohio, Nov 4, 44; m 66, Lynne Musgrave; c Jennifer & Mark. *Educ:* Ohio State Univ, BSc, 66; Johns Hopkins Univ, PhD(cell & develop biol), 73. *Prof Exp:* Res fel molecular biol, Calif Inst Technol, 73-78. *Concurrent Pos:* Am Cancer Soc fel, 73-78; res career develop award, NIH, 84-89, molecular biol study sect, 91-94. *Mem:* Am Soc Cell Biol; Soc Develop Biol; Sigma Xi; Am Soc Marine Molecular Biol & Biotechnol. *Res:* Early animal development; cell fate specification studied primarily by molecular genetic approaches. *Mailing Add:* Dept Biol Univ Rochester Rochester NY 14627. *E-Mail:* rangerer@rca.biology.rochester.edu

ANGERS, DENIS ARTHUR, SOIL CONSERVATION, SOIL PHYSICS. *Current Pos:* RES SCIENTIST, AGR CAN RES STA, 88- *Personal Data:* b Quebec, Que, Dec 12, 59; m 83, Anne Grenier; c Mathieu & Anne-Marie. *Educ:* Laval Univ, BScA, 83; Univ Guelph, MSc, 85; McGill Univ, PhD(soil sci), 88. *Concurrent Pos:* Adj prof, Laval Univ, 89; assoc grad fac, Univ Guelph, 91. *Mem:* Soil Sci Soc Am; Can Soc Soil Sci. *Res:* Evaluating the impacts of current and novatine farming practices on soil quality. *Mailing Add:* Agr Can Res Sta 2560 Hochelaga Blvd Ste Foy PQ G1V 2J3 Can

ANGERS, ROCH, METALLURGY, CERAMICS. *Current Pos:* from asst prof to assoc prof, 69-74, PROF MAT, LAVAL UNIV, 74- *Personal Data:* b Jonquiere, Que, Nov 16, 34; m 64, Josee; c Nathalie & Stephan. *Educ:* Laval Univ, BASc, 59, DSc(metall), 68. *Prof Exp:* Engr, Bell Tel Co Can, 59-62; fel, Univ BC, 68-69. *Concurrent Pos:* Consult many industs. *Mem:* Am Ceramic Soc; Can Ceramic Soc; Am Powder Metall Inst; Am Soc Metals; Can Inst Metall. *Res:* Mechanical properties of ceramics; applied research on powder metallurgy. *Mailing Add:* Dept Metall Laval Univ Quebec PQ G1K 7P4 Can. *Fax:* 418-656-5343, 656-5385; *E-Mail:* roch.angers@gmn.ulaval.ca

ANGEVINE, JAY BERNARD, JR, NEUROANATOMY. *Current Pos:* assoc prof, 67-70, PROF ANAT, COL MED, UNIV ARIZ, 70-, ASSOC HEAD ANAT, 80- *Personal Data:* b Boston, Mass, June 29, 28; m; c 3. *Educ:* Williams Col, BA, 49; Cornell Univ, MA, 52, PhD, 56. *Prof Exp:* Asst histol & embryol, Cornell Univ, 49-51, neuroanat, 52-54, embryol, 54, instr zool, 55-56; asst neuropath, Harvard Med Sch, 56-57, instr, 57-60, assoc anat, 59-64, asst prof, 64-67. *Concurrent Pos:* USPHS career develop award, 64; mem, Neurol B Study Sect, Nat Inst Neurol Dis & Stroke, 72-74, chmn, 74-76; mem clin teaching fac, Dept Neurol Surg, St Joseph's Hosp & Med Ctr, Phoenix, 74- *Mem:* Sigma Xi; Am Asn Anat; Am Neurol Asn. *Res:* Human and comparative neuroanatomy and neuroembryology. *Mailing Add:* Dept Anat Univ Arizona Col Med Tucson AZ 85724

ANGEVINE, OLIVER LAWRENCE, ACOUSTICS. *Current Pos:* PRES, ANGEVINE ACOUST CONSULT, INC, 64- *Personal Data:* b Rochester, NY, Apr 28, 14; m 40, Helene R Berman; c 3. *Educ:* Mass Inst Technol, BS, 36; Univ Buffalo, MS, 69. *Prof Exp:* Engr, Stromberg Carlson Co, 36-46, chief sound equip engr, 46-51; chief engr, Caledonia Electronics & Transformer Co, 51-60 & Progress Webster Corp, 61-62; mgr new prod, Espey Mfg Co, 62-64. *Concurrent Pos:* Instr, Dept Archit, Univ Buffalo, 78-84. *Mem:* Fel Acoust Soc Am; Am Soc Testing & Mat; Nat Coun Acoust Consult (secy, 70-77); Inst Noise Control Eng; Inst Elec & Electronics Engrs. *Res:* Active noise cancellation, especially of the hum of transformers for electric power. *Mailing Add:* Angevine Acoust Consults Inc Box 725 East Aurora NY 14052. *Fax:* 716-652-3442

ANGHAIE, SAMIM, NUCLEAR REACTOR DESIGN, THERMAL HYDRAULICS. *Current Pos:* vis asst prof, 82-84, assoc prof nuclear eng, 86-91, ASSOC DIR SPACE POWER, INNOVATIVE NUCLEAR SPACE POWER & PROPULSION INST, UNIV FLA, 87-, PROF, NUCLEAR ENG, 91- *Personal Data:* b Mallayer, Iran, Sept 18, 49; US citizen; m 76; c Amir-Ali-Reza & Amir-Hamid-Reza. *Educ:* Shiraz Pahlavi Univ, Iran, BS, 72, MS, 74; Pa State Univ, PhD(nuclear eng), 82. *Prof Exp:* Asst prof nuclear eng, Ore State Univ, 84-86. *Concurrent Pos:* Sr res engr & consult, Fla Nuclear Assocs, 82-88; consult, RS&H United Technologies, United Space Boosters, 84 & Exxon Nuclear Co, Licensing & Safety, 85-86; mem, Nuclear Heat Exchanger Comt, Am Soc Mech Engrs, 85-; Norcus appointment, Battelle Pac Northwest Lab, Physics, 86-87; chmn, Am Soc Mech Engrs, Emerging Technol Comt, 88-; mem, Tech Comt, Space Nuclear Power Conf; consult, Rockwell Int, Rocketdyne, 90-92, United Technol, Pratt & Whitney, 90- *Mem:* Am Soc Mech Engrs; Am Inst Aeronaut & Astronaut; Am Nuclear Soc. *Res:* Advanced reactor design; nuclear propulsion; high temperature energy conversion; high temperature materials; thermal hydraulics; single-and-multi-phase flow and heat transfer; applied particle transport; high temperature nuclear fuel materials. *Mailing Add:* Nuclear Eng Sci Univ Fla Gainesville FL 32611-0001

ANGIER, ROBERT BRUCE, ORGANIC CHEMISTRY. *Current Pos:* RETIRED. *Personal Data:* b Litchfield, Minn, Mar 24, 17; m 45; c 2. *Educ:* Hamline Univ, BS, 40; Univ Nebr, MS, 42, PhD(org chem), 44. *Prof Exp:* Res chemist, 44-56, res assoc, 56-62, group leader, Lederle Labs Div, Am Cyanamid Co, 62-82. *Mem:* Am Chem Soc. *Res:* Synthetic organic chemistry; folic acid; synthesis of pteroylglutamic acid; pteridine, pyrimidine and purine chemistry; antineoplastic, antifungal and antiviral compounds. *Mailing Add:* 38 Boston Ct Whiting NJ 08759-1707

ANGINO, ERNEST EDWARD, GEOCHEMISTRY, ENVIONMENTAL SCIENCES. *Current Pos:* assoc prof civil eng, Univ Kans, 67-71, chmn, Dept Geol, 72-86, PROF CIVIL ENG, UNIV KANS, 71-, PROF GEOL, 72-; DIR, WATER RESOURCES CTR, 90- *Personal Data:* b Winsted, Conn, Feb 16, 32; m 54, Margaret Lachat; c Cheryl A & Kimberly A. *Educ:* Lehigh Univ, BS, 54; Univ Kans, MS, 58, PhD(geochem), 61. *Honors & Awards:* Geog feature named in honor, Angino Buttress, Antartica, 67; Dept Defense Medal for Res, 69. *Prof Exp:* Instr, Univ Kans, 61-62; asst prof oceanog, Tex A&M Univ, 62-65; res assoc & head div geochem, Kans State Geol Surv, 65-70, assoc dir, 70-72. *Concurrent Pos:* Mem, US Nat Comt Geochem, Nat Acad Sci-Nat Res Coun, 71-76; assoc ed, Soc Econ Paleontologists & Mineralogists, 73-84; vchmn tech adv comt, Comt Res & Develop, Fed Power Comn, 75-78; mem, NAS-NRC Hydrocarbon res drilling, 86-87; mem, Irrig Induced Water Quality Prob, 85-90; NAS-NRC hazardous waste disposal; consult, 62- *Mem:* Geochem Soc (secy, 70-76); Soc Environ Geochem & Health (pres, 78-79); Int Asn Geochem & Cosmochem (treas, 80-95). *Res:* Trace element complexing in natural waters, sediment-water interactions; origin natural hydrogen gas; interactions hazardous wastes & natural materials; water chemistry (quality); environmental geochemistry and geology. *Mailing Add:* Dept Geol Univ Kans Lindley 120 Lawrence KS 66045. *Fax:* 785-864-5276

ANGLEMIER, ALLEN FRANCIS, FOOD SCIENCE. *Current Pos:* RETIRED. *Personal Data:* b Tiffin, Ohio, Sept 10, 26; m 52; c 4. *Educ:* Fresno State Col, BS, 53; Ore State Univ, MS, 55, PhD(animal nutrit, physiol), 57. *Prof Exp:* Instr food technol, Ore State Univ, 56-58, from asst prof to prof food sci, 58-89. *Concurrent Pos:* Res grants, NIH, 62-69 & Bur Com Fisheries, 69-71. *Mem:* AAAS; Inst Food Technol; Am Meat Sci Asn. *Res:* Chemistry and physiology of muscle; food protein systems. *Mailing Add:* 1555 NW Hillcrest Corvallis OR 97330

ANGLETON, GEORGE M, RADIATION BIOLOGY, BIOMETRICS. *Current Pos:* from asst prof to assoc prof, 62-77, PROF BIOSTATIST & RADIATION BIOL, COLO STATE UNIV, 78-, HEAD BIOMETRY & RADIATION BIOPHYS, COLLAB RADIOL HEALTH LAB, 62-, HEAD COMPUT CTR, VET HOSP, 78- *Personal Data:* b Pontiac, Mich, May 25, 27; m 55; c 5. *Educ:* Mich State Univ, BS, 49; Univ Rochester, MS, 52; Med Col Va, PhD(biophys, biomet), 61. *Prof Exp:* Asst health physics, Los Alamos Sci Lab, 50-55, staff mem, 55-57; instr biophys, Med Col Va, 61. *Concurrent Pos:* Fel biomath, NC State Col, 61-62; prin investr radiation recovery studies & thermoluminescent dosimetry studies, US Air Force Contracts, 65-69 & 74; consult, Martin Co, 61-62, Los Alamos Sci Lab, 64-65, Datametrics, 67-69, US Air Force Acad, 70-74 & Univ Utah, 76-80. *Mem:* Am Statist Asn; Biomet Soc; Health Physics Soc; Radiation Res Soc. *Res:* Theoretical radiation biology; mathematical biology; computer applications. *Mailing Add:* 521 Cornell Ave Ft Collins CO 80525

ANGLIN, J HILL, JR, organic biochemistry, for more information see previous edition

ANGLIN, JEANNE MARIE, AEROSPACE MATERIALS & PROCESSES, AIRCRAFT STRUCTURE. *Current Pos:* Engr com struct eng, Boeing Co, 73-84, mgr, 84-94, corp auditor, 94, mgr mfg res & develop, Defense & Space Group, 94-95, SR MGR MFG RES & DEVELOP, DEFENSE & SPACE GROUP, BOEING CO, 95- *Personal Data:* b Seattle, Wash, July 26, 45; m 70, Don Allen; c Matthew Allen & Mark Dare. *Educ:* Univ Wash, BS, 69; Pac Lutheran Univ, MS, 76. *Mem:* Soc Women Engrs. *Res:* Materials and processes utilized in the design and fabrication of aircraft structures and interiors; carbon fiber reinforced plastics (advanced composites). *Mailing Add:* 27725 156th Ave SE Kent WA 98042. *Fax:* 425-393-5848; *E-Mail:* jeanne.m.anglin@boeing.com

ANGONA, FRANK ANTHONY, GEOPHYSICS, ACOUSTICS. *Current Pos:* technologist seismic explor, Socony Mobile Oil Co, 52-53, sr res technologist, 53-70, RES ASSOC, MOBIL RES & DEVELOP CORP, 70- *Personal Data:* b Los Angeles, Calif, Apr 15, 20; m 44; c 4. *Educ:* Univ Calif, Los Angeles, BA, 42, MA, 50, PhD(physics), 52. *Prof Exp:* Res asst, Univ Calif, Los Angeles, 50-52. *Mem:* Acoustical Soc Am; Soc Explor Geophys; Sigma Xi (pres, Sci Res Soc Am, 58). *Res:* Transmission of sound in rarified gases; propagation of seismic waves in the earth with seismic and Loggina applications. *Mailing Add:* 1607 Nob Hill Rd Dallas TX 75208

ANGOTTI, RODNEY, MATHEMATICS. *Current Pos:* asst head dept math, 69-71, asst dean, Col Liberal Arts & Sci, 71-83, ASSOC PROF MATH, NORTHERN ILL UNIV, 67- *Personal Data:* b Ellsworth, Pa, Apr 14, 37; m 59; c 2. *Educ:* Univ Pittsburgh, BS, 59, PhD(math), 63. *Prof Exp:* Asst prof math, Univ Akron, 63-64 & State Univ NY Buffalo, 64-67. *Mem:* Am Math Soc; Math Asn Am; Ital Math Union. *Res:* Geometric invariant theory; algebraic and topological foundations of geometry. *Mailing Add:* Dept Comput Sci Northern Ill Univ De Kalb IL 60115

ANGRIST, STANLEY W, RESEARCH ADMINISTRATION. *Current Pos:* STAFF REPORTER, WALL STREET JOUR, 89- *Personal Data:* b Dallas, Tex, June 3, 33; m 55; c 3. *Educ:* Tex A&M Univ, BSc, 55; Ohio State Univ, MSc, 58, PhD(mech eng), 61. *Prof Exp:* Instr mech eng, Ohio State Univ, 57-62; from asst prof to assoc prof, Carnegie-Mellon Univ, 62-71. prof mech eng, 71-82; columnist, Forbes Magazine, 76-88. *Concurrent Pos:* US Air Force res grant, 62-; NSF lab grant, 63-; Western Elec Fund award, 66-67. *Mailing Add:* 152 Maple Heights Rd Pittsburgh PA 15232

ANGSTADT, CAROL NEWBORG, BIOCHEMISTRY, COMPUTER ASSISTED INSTRUCTION SOFTWEAR. *Current Pos:* ASST PROF BIOCHEM, MED COL & GRAD SCH, HAHNEMANN MED COL, PA, 62-, ASSOC PROF, COL ALLIED HEALTH PROF, 76-, ASST DEAN ADMIS, GRAD SCH. *Personal Data:* b Gladwyne, Pa, Oct 23, 35; m 58; c 2. *Educ:* Juniata Col, BS, 57; Purdue Univ, West Lafayette, PhD(biochem), 62. *Concurrent Pos:* Consult, Thomas Jefferson Univ, 76. *Mem:* Chromat Lab Automatic Software; Am Asn Univ Prof; Am Asn Univ Women. *Res:* Radio immunoassay of VIP and substance P; development of CAI programs. *Mailing Add:* Dept Biochem Hahnemann Univ Broad & Vine Sts Philadelphia PA 19102-1178

ANGSTADT, ROBERT B, ANIMAL BEHAVIOR, ANIMAL PHYSIOLOGY. *Current Pos:* PROF BIOL, LYCOMING COL, 87- *Personal Data:* b Kutztown, Pa, Mar 13, 37; m 62; c 2. *Educ:* Ursinus Col, BS, 59; Cornell Univ, MS, 61, PhD(ethology), 69. *Mem:* Animal Behav Soc. *Res:* Behavior of vertebrates; neural control of behavior. *Mailing Add:* Lycoming Col 700 College Pl Lycoming Col Williamsport PA 17701-5157

ANGUS, JOHN COTTON, MATERIALS SCIENCE ENGINEERING, CHEMICAL ENGINEERING. *Current Pos:* from asst prof to assoc prof, 63-70, PROF ENG, CASE WESTERN RESERVE UNIV, 70- *Personal Data:* b Grand Haven, Mich, Feb 22, 34; m 60; c 2. *Educ:* Univ Mich, BS, 56, MS, 58, PhD(chem eng), 60. *Honors & Awards:* Pioneer Award, Electrochem Soc, 93. *Prof Exp:* Res engr thermoelec mat res, Minn Mining & Mfg Co, 60-63. *Concurrent Pos:* Vis lectr, Univ Edinburgh, 72-73; vis prof, Northwestern Univ, 80-81. *Mem:* Nat Acad Eng; fel Am Inst Chem Engrs; Electrochem Soc; Mat Res Soc; Am Chem Soc. *Res:* Crystal growth and etching; electrochemistry; diamond growth. *Mailing Add:* Dept Chem Eng Case Western Reserve Univ Cleveland OH 44106

ANGUS, THOMAS ANDERSON, INSECT PATHOLOGY. *Current Pos:* RETIRED. *Personal Data:* b Toronto, Ont, Sept 19, 15; m 50; c 2. *Educ:* Univ Toronto, BSA, 49, MSA, 50; McGill Univ, PhD, 55. *Hon Degrees:* DSc, Laurentian Univ, Sudbury, Ont, 92. *Prof Exp:* Res scientist, Can Dept Environ, Can Forestry Serv, 49-70, assoc dir, 70-75, dir, Insect Path Res Inst, 75-78, dep dir, Forest Pest Mgt Inst, 78-80. *Mem:* Soc Invert Path; fel Entom Soc Can. *Res:* Bacterial diseases of insects; emphasis on mode of action of B thoringiensis. *Mailing Add:* 24 McCrea St Sault Ste Marie ON P6A 4A1 Can

ANHALT, GRANT JAMES, MEDICINE, IMMUNOLOGY. *Current Pos:* from asst prof to assoc prof, 82-93, PROF DERMAT, JOHNS HOPKINS UNIV SCH MED, 93- *Personal Data:* b Shaunavon, Sask, Dec 14, 52; Can citizen; m 80; c Branden & Brian. *Educ:* Univ Manitoba, Winnipeg, MD, 75; Am Bd Dermat, 80; FRCP(C), 80. *Prof Exp:* Resident, internal med, Health Sci Ctr, Winnipeg, 75-77; resident dermat, Univ Mich, 77-79, chief resident, 79-80, fel immunol, 80-81, instr dermat, 81-82. *Concurrent Pos:* Prin investr, Va res assoc, 81-82; prin investr, NIH, 83-, consult, Ad Hoc Study Sect, 87- *Mem:* Am Fedn Clin Res; fel Soc Investigative Dermat; fel Royal Col Physicians & Surgeons Can; fel Am Acad Dermat; Dermat Found; Am Soc Clin Invest. *Res:* Immunology in dermatology; autoimmune skin disease and immunologically; mediated mucosal disease; pemphigus; remphigold, lichen pianus; benign mucous membrane; pemphigold; empidermoysis bullosa; lupus. *Mailing Add:* Dept Dermat Johns Hopkins Univ Sch Med 720 Rutland Ave Baltimore MD 21205-2109. *Fax:* 410-955-0520

ANJARD, RONALD P, SR, MICROELECTRONICS, HI TECH ELECTRONICS SEMICONDUCTOR EDUCATION. *Current Pos:* PRES, ANJARD INT CONSULT, 83- *Personal Data:* b Chicago, Ill, July 31, 35; m 57, Marie B Sampler; c Ronald P Jr, Michael P, Michele M & John R. *Educ:* Carnegie-Mellon Univ, BS, 57; Purdue Univ, MS, 68; Univ State of NY, BS, 78; Univ Wis, PhD, 79; T A Edison Col, BA, 79; Columbia Pac Univ, Calif, PhD(educ), 81, PhD(metal eng), 82; Webster Univ, M-CRM, 92. *Hon Degrees:* DHH, London Inst Appl Res, 76. *Prof Exp:* Metall trainee, US Steel, 56-57; metall engr, Crucible Steel, 57-58; process engr, Raytheon Mfg, 58-59; sr engr, Delco Electronics, Gen Motors Co, 59-81; div qual mgr metals, Johnson Matthey/AVX Electronic Metals, 81-83. *Concurrent Pos:* Adj fac, Kokomo Indust Apprentice Prog, 73-81 & Ind Voc Tech Col, 79-81; lectr, Ball State Univ & Chapman Col, 83, Nat Univ, 83, Ala A&M, 84, San Diego Community Col, 84-89 & Univ Southern Calif, 85; Univ La Verne, 82, Univ Cal San Diego, 86, La Jolla Univ, 86-, Union Inst, 87-, Sierra Univ, 87-, Coleman Col, 83-86; corp qual dir, Kaypro Comput, 83-86; bd mem, Deming Users group; rev ed & rev comt, Am Soc Qual Control; chmn, Inst Elec & Electronics Engrs; qual mgr, Circuits Processing Tech, 86-89; int consult, Int Acad Ceramics, 86-; pres, Acad Screen Printing Technol, 86-; coordr & internal tech consult, Gen Dynamics Electronics & Convair, 89-94. *Mem:* Fel Int Soc Hybrid Microelectronics; Sigma Xi; Int Electronics Packaging Soc; Am Soc Testing & Mat; Am Ceramic Soc; Inst Elec & Electronics Engrs; Am Soc Qual Control. *Res:* Total quality management, SPC, QFD, Dept of Energy; thick film materials and testing; solder paste materials and testing; nondestructive testing; computer hardware testing; specialized materials evaluations and tests; manufacture and history of bricks; ancient metallurgy in the Americas and the world; varied leak detection techniques; computer resource management; ancient astronomy & sciences in India and the Americas; author or coauthor of over 1000 international technology, business, management, quality, presentations and publications in 16 countries. *Mailing Add:* Box 420950 San Diego CA 92142. *Fax:* 619-277-5044; *E-Mail:* dranjard@aol.com

ANKEL, HELMUT K, BIOCHEMISTRY, IMMUNOLOGY. *Current Pos:* from asst prof to assoc prof, 65-75, PROF BIOCHEM, MED COL WIS, 75- *Personal Data:* b Saarbrucken, Germany, Apr 9, 33. *Educ:* Univ Marburg, diplom chemiker, 57, PhD(biochem), 60. *Honors & Awards:* NIH res career award, 71-76. *Prof Exp:* Nat Res Coun Can fel biochem, 60-61; res assoc, Univ Marburg, 62; NASA fel, Univ Pittsburgh, 63-65. *Concurrent Pos:* Vis scientist, Inst Nat de la Sante et de la Recherche Med, Paris, France, 72-75; adj prof biol, Marquette Univ, Milwaukee, 80-; vis scientist, Ger Cancer Res Ctr, Heidelburg, 83-84 & 86. *Mem:* Am Soc Biol Chem; Soc Complex Carbohydrates; Am Chem Soc; German Chemists Soc; Am Asn Immunol. *Res:* Cell membrane glycoproteins; sugar nucleotides; enzymology; interferon; NK cell action. *Mailing Add:* 2400 E Bradford Ave Milwaukee WI 53211

ANKEL-SIMONS, FRIDERUN ANNURSEL, PRIMATOLOGY, COMPARATIVE ANATOMY. *Current Pos:* vis scholar anthrop, 80-82, curratorial assoc, Primate Ctr, 93-96, RES ASSOC ANAT, DUKE UNIV, DURHAM, NC, 82-, RES ASSOC, 96- *Personal Data:* b Krofdorf, WGer, Oct 23, 33; m 72, Elwyn L; c Cornelia & Verne. *Educ:* Univ Giessen, Dr rer nat(marine biol), 60; Univ Zurich, Habil(phys anthrop), 68. *Honors & Awards:* Rolex Enterprise Award. *Prof Exp:* Res grant primatol, Ger Res Team, Max Planck Inst Brain Res, Univ Giessen, 60-63; res asst & lectr, Inst Anthrop, Univ Zurich, 63-69; instr human anat, Univ Kiel Med Sch, 70-71; assoc cur, Peabody Mus, Yale Univ, 71-78; vis assoc prof anthrop, Univ NC, Chapel Hill, 78-79. *Concurrent Pos:* Res asst paleont, Univ Giessen, 60; Wenner-Gren Found res award, 70; Boise Fund res travel grant, Oxford Univ, 72; lectr human anat, Brown Univ, 72 & Yale Univ, 73-74; Leakey Found res grant, 73-75. *Mem:* Int Primatol Soc; Soc Vert Paleont. *Res:* Locomotor behavior and comparative anatomy of living and fossil primates and man; investigations of the anatomy of vertebrae, of hands and feet and of the limbs in various extinct primates. *Mailing Add:* 2518 Lanier Pl Durham NC 27705. *Fax:* 919-490-5394; *E-Mail:* friderun@aolcom, friderun@ucpub.duke.edu

ANKENBRANDT, CHARLES MARTIN, ACCELERATOR PHYSICS, EXPERIMENTAL HIGH ENERGY PHYSICS. *Current Pos:* PHYSICIST HIGH ENERGY & ACCELERATOR PHYSICS, FERMI NAT ACCELERATOR LAB, 73- *Personal Data:* b Cleveland, Ohio, Aug 20, 39; m 83; c 5. *Educ:* St Louis Univ, BS, 61; Univ Calif, Berkeley, PhD(physics), 67. *Prof Exp:* Fel high energy physics, Lawrence Radiation Lab, Univ Calif, Berkeley, 67-68; fel, Brookhaven Nat Lab, 68-70; asst prof physics, Ind Univ, 70-73. *Mem:* Am Phys Soc. *Res:* Experiment and theory for the design and improvement of high-energy particle accelerators and colliding-beam facilities, supervision of such activities. *Mailing Add:* Nat Accelerator Lab PO Box 500 Batavia IL 60510

ANKENEY, JAY LLOYD, MEDICINE. *Current Pos:* RETIRED. *Personal Data:* b Cleveland, Ohio, June 7, 21; m 46; c 3. *Educ:* Ohio Wesleyan Univ, BA, 43; Western Reserve Univ, MD, 45. *Prof Exp:* Dir Div Cardiothoracic Surg, Univ Hosp Cleveland, 74-86; from instr to assoc prof thoracic surg, 55-69, chmn Div Cardiothoracic Surg, 74, Actg Dir, Dept Surg, 77-80, prof surg, Sch Med, Case Western Univ, 69-86. *Mem:* Am Asn Thoracic Surg; fel Am Col Surgeons; Am Surg Asn; Soc Thoracic Surgeons; Soc Vascular Surg. *Res:* Physiological aspects of cardiovascular and thoracic surgery. *Mailing Add:* Univ Hosps Cardiothoracic Surg 2074 Abington Rd Cleveland OH 44106-5011

ANKLEY, GERALD THOMAS, TEST METHOD DEVELOPMENT, RISK ASSESSMENT. *Current Pos:* RES TOXICOLOGIST, US ENVIRON PROTECTION AGENCY, 88- *Personal Data:* b Lapeer, Mich, May 24, 59; m 82; c Scott & Anthony. *Educ:* Mich State Univ, BS, 82; Univ Ga, MS, 84, PhD(aquatic toxicol), 87. *Prof Exp:* Res assoc, Mich State Univ, 87-88. *Concurrent Pos:* Adj prof, Mich Technol Univ, 93-; res adv, Nat Res Coun, 93- *Mem:* Soc Environ Toxicol & Chem; Sigma Xi. *Res:* Development and validation of methods for assessing the ecological risk of contaminants in aquatic systems; published over 60 articles. *Mailing Add:* RR 1 Two Harbors MN 55616. *Fax:* 218-720-5539

ANKNEY, C(LAUDE) DAVISON, PROXIMATE & ULTIMATE FACTORS DETERMINING CLUTCH-SIZE IN BIRDS, INTERSPECIFIC HYBRIDIZATION & COMPETITION IN MALLARDS & AMERICAN BLACK DUCKS. *Current Pos:* From asst prof to assoc prof, 74-86, PROF ZOOL, UNIV WESTERN ONT, 86- *Personal Data:* b Cleveland, Ohio, Sept 20, 46; US & Can citizen; m 76, Sandra L Johnson. *Educ:* Mich State Univ, BS, 68; Univ Western Ont, PhD(zool-animal ecol), 74. *Concurrent Pos:* Dir, Can Wildlife Fedn, 90-; sci adv, Inst Wetlands & Waterfowl Res, 90-, Long Point World Biosphere Comt, 90- *Mem:* AAAS; fel Am Ornithologists Union; Wildlife Soc; Can Soc Zoologists; Human Behav & Evolution Soc; Soc Can Ornithologists. *Res:* Ecology, bioenergetics, behavior and genetics of waterfowl. *Mailing Add:* Dept Zool Collf Bldg Univ Western Ont London ON N6A 5B7 Can. *Fax:* 519-661-3412

ANKRUM, PAUL DENZEL, ELECTRICAL ENGINEERING. *Current Pos:* from instr to prof elec eng, 42-82, EMER PROF ELEC ENG, CORNELL UNIV, 82- *Personal Data:* b Hamlin, Kans, Aug 14, 15; m 40; c 2. *Educ:* Ind Inst Technol, BS, 35; Ashland Col, AB, 39; Cornell Univ, MS, 44. *Prof Exp:* Asst instr eng drawing, Ashland Col, 35-36; instr elec theory, Ind Inst Technol, 36-38, instr in charge commun eng, 38-42; engr, Magnavox Co, 42. *Concurrent Pos:* Mem tech staff, Hughes Aircraft Co, 57-58; elec engr, Electronics Lab, Gen Elec Co, 66; consult engr, Semiconductor Prod Div, Gen Elec Co, 73 & Borg Warner Electronics, 79. *Mem:* Sr mem Inst Elec & Electronics Engrs; Am Soc Eng Educ. *Res:* Electronics; physics; basic electronics; electron devices; semiconductor electronics. *Mailing Add:* Cornell Univ Phillips Hall Ithaca NY 14853

ANLAGE, STEVEN MARK, ELECTRODYNAMIC PROPERTIES & APPLICATIONS OF SUPERCONDUCTORS, NEAR-FIELD MICROWAVE MICROSCOPY. *Current Pos:* asst prof, 91-96, ASSOC PROF, PHYSICS DEPT, UNIV MD, 96- *Personal Data:* b NJ. *Educ:* Rensselaer Polytech Inst, BS, 82; Calif Inst Technol, MS, 84, PhD(appl physics), 87. *Honors & Awards:* NSF New Young Investr, 92. *Prof Exp:* Postdoctoral researcher, Stanford Univ, 88-91. *Mem:* Am Phys Soc; Mat Res Soc; Inst Elec & Electronics Engrs. *Res:* High frequency superconductivity; near field microwave microscopy; experimental chaos. *Mailing Add:* Physics Dept CSR Univ Md College Park MD 20742-4111. *Fax:* 301-405-3779; *E-Mail:* anlage@squid.umd.edu

ANLAUF, KURT GUENTHER, ACID-RAIN, ATMOSPHERIC OXIDANTS. *Current Pos:* RES SCIENTIST, ATMOSPHERIC ENVIRON SERV, 73- *Personal Data:* b WGer, 42; Can citizen. *Educ:* Univ Toronto, BSc, 64, PhD(chem), 69. *Prof Exp:* Fel, Univ Wis, 69-71; res assoc, Univ Laval, 71-72, res prof, 72-73. *Res:* Measurement of atmospheric pollutants, reaction and transport of atmospheric pollutants, development of new techniques for measurements of these species, specifically acid-rain and photochemical smog related chemistry and processes. *Mailing Add:* 29 Four Winds Dr No 5 Downsview ON M3J 1K7 Can

ANLYAN, WILLIAM GEORGE, SURGERY. *Current Pos:* Intern & resident, Gen & Thoracic Surg, Duke Univ, 49-55, instr surg, 50-51, assoc, 51-53, from asst prof to assoc prof, 53-61, assoc dean, Sch Med, 63-64, dean, 64-69, assoc provost, 69, vpres health affairs, 69-83, chancellor health affairs, 83-87, univ chancellor, 88-90, exec vpres, 87-88, PROF SURG, SCH MED, DUKE UNIV, 61-, EMER CHANCELLOR, 90- *Personal Data:* b Alexandria, Egypt, Oct 14, 25; US citizen; c William G Jr, John P & Louise. *Educ:* Yale Univ, BS, 45, MD, 49; Am Bd Surg, cert, 55, Am Bd Thoracic Surg, cert, 56. *Hon Degrees:* DSc, Rush Med Col, 73. *Honors & Awards:* Abraham Flexner Award, Asn Am Med Col, 80. *Concurrent Pos:* Markle scholar med sci, Duke Univ, 53-58; consult, numerous orgn, 55- & mem numerous bd dirs & nat comts, 63-; mem, bd dirs, G D Searle & Co, 74-85; mem, bd trustees, NC Sch Sci & Math, 78-85, vchmn, 81-84. *Mem:* Inst Med-Nat Acad Sci; Soc Univ Surg; Soc Vascular Surg; fel Am Col Surg; AMA; Int Cardiovasc Soc; Soc Clin Surg; Am Heart Asn; Soc Med Adminr (pres, 83-85); Am Surg Asn; AAAS; Sigma Xi. *Res:* Pancreatic physiology; abnormalities in blood clotting; serotonin metabolism and thromboembolic disease; author of numerous articles and publications. *Mailing Add:* Duke Med Ctr 109 Seeley G Mudd Bldg Durham NC 27710

ANNAN, MURVEL EUGENE, GENETICS. *Current Pos:* from asst prof to prof, 54-81, EMER PROF BIOL, WAGNER COL, 81- *Personal Data:* b Coin, Iowa, July 11, 20; m 45. *Educ:* Univ Nebr, PhD(zool), 54. *Prof Exp:* Instr zool, Univ Nebr, 50-51. *Mem:* Soc Study Evolution; Genetics Soc Am; Sigma Xi. *Res:* Genetics of Drosophilas. *Mailing Add:* 300 N Second St Bridgewater VA 22812-1706

ANNAS, GEORGE J, HEALTH LAW. *Current Pos:* Dir, Ctr Law & Health Sci, 72-77, assoc prof health law, 77-82, PROF & CHAIR, DEPT HEALTH LAW, BOSTON UNIV, 82-, DIR, LAW, MED & ETHICS PROG, 88- *Personal Data:* b St Cloud, Minn, July 13, 45; m 69, Mary F Roche; c Katie & David. *Educ:* Harvard Univ, BA, 67, JD, 70, MPH, 72. *Hon Degrees:* LHD, Salem State Col, 94. *Honors & Awards:* Lifetime Award, Am Soc Law Med & Ethics, 90; Milton Greenblatt Award, Mass Psychiat Soc, 96. *Concurrent Pos:* Chair, Mass Task Force Organ Transplant, 83-84; emer ed-in-chief, Law Med & Health Care; chmn, Comt Legal Probs Med Sci, Am Bar Asn. *Mem:* Inst Med-Nat Acad Sci; Am Pub Health Asn. *Mailing Add:* Boston Univ Sch Med 80 E Concord St Boston MA 02118-2307

ANNAU, ZOLTAN, BEHAVIORAL TOXICOLOGY. *Current Pos:* ENVIRON HEALTH SCIENTIST, DEPT STATE, US GOVT, 92- *Personal Data:* b Szeged, Hungary, May 20, 36; US citizen; m 60; c 1. *Educ:* Carleton Univ, Ont, BA, 58; McMaster Univ, MA, 60, PhD(psychol), 64. *Prof Exp:* Res assoc & lectr psychol, Univ Mich, 64-65; fel environ med, Johns Hopkins Univ, 65-66, lectr med psychol, 66-68, from asst prof to assoc prof environ med, 68-73, from asst prof to assoc prof, 73-80, prof environ health sci, 80-92. *Mem:* Soc Neurosci; fel AAAS; Soc Toxicol; Int Brain Res Orgn. *Res:* Neurobehavioral effects of exposure to toxic environmental agents. *Mailing Add:* 2202 Clove Terr Baltimore MD 21209

ANNE, ANTHARVEDI, BIOMEDICAL ENGINEERING. *Current Pos:* PROF BIOMED ENG, UNIV VA, 68- *Personal Data:* b India, Feb 20, 33. *Educ:* Univ Madras, BS, 52; Univ Pa, MS, 60, PhD(elec eng), 63. *Prof Exp:* Prof elec eng, Washington Univ, St Louis, 66-68. *Mem:* Biomed Eng Soc. *Mailing Add:* Dept Biomed Eng Univ Va PO Box 377 Charlottesville VA 22908

ANNEAR, PAUL RICHARD, ASTRONOMY. *Current Pos:* RETIRED. *Personal Data:* b Cedar Rapids, Iowa, Jan 19, 15; m 39, Elizabeth Barkley; c Sanora S (Thompson), Marcia L (Beery) & Craig B. *Educ:* Drake Univ, BA, 36; Case Western Reserve Univ, MS, 38; Univ Mich, PhD, 49. *Prof Exp:* Tutor physics & astron, Hunter Col, 40-41; from instr to prof & dir, Burrell Mem Observ, Baldwin-Wallace Col, 41-80, emer prof math & astron, 80-84. *Mem:* Am Astron Soc; Math Asn Am. *Res:* Astronomical photometry; galactic structure in the constellation of Cygnus; artificial satellite tracking and orbit computation. *Mailing Add:* 66 Barberry Dr Berea OH 44017-1202

ANNELLI, JOSEPH, VETERINARY MEDICINE. *Current Pos:* CHIEF, EMERGENCY PROG STAFF, USDA, 96- *Personal Data:* b Brooklyn, NY, Jan 27, 56. *Educ:* St Francis Col, BS, 77; Long Island Univ, MS, 81; Araneta Univ, DVM, 84; Univ Minn, MSc, 91. *Mailing Add:* Vet Serv/USDA 4700 River Rd Unit 43 Riverdale MD 20737

ANNESTRAND, STIG A, TRANSMISSION ENGINEERING. *Current Pos:* CONSULT, 93- *Personal Data:* b Husby, Sweden, Sept 18, 33. *Educ:* Royal Inst Technol, Sweden, MS, 58. *Honors & Awards:* Order Big Thunder, Sweden, 67; Recognition Award, Nat Working Group, 73. *Prof Exp:* Sr transmission engr, Sceco-East, Dammam, Saudi Arabia, 88-93. *Mem:* Nat Acad Eng; fel Inst Elec & Electronics Engrs. *Mailing Add:* 32461 SW Lake Dr Wilsonville OR 97070

ANNETT, ROBERT GORDON, BIOCHEMISTRY. *Current Pos:* Asst prof, 68-75, ASSOC PROF BIOCHEM, TRENT UNIV, 75- *Personal Data:* b Windsor, Ont, Feb 24, 41; m 64, Harlene Allchin; c Mark R & Christine L. *Educ:* Univ Windsor, BSc, 64, PhD(biochem), 68. *Concurrent Pos:* Fel, Univ Calif, Davis, Univ Windsor & Wayne State Univ, 81-82; master, Otonabee Col, 94- *Mem:* Am Chem Soc; Chem Inst Can; Can Cystic Fibrosis Found. *Res:* Enzymology of oxalacetic acid tautomerization, fatty acid a-oxidation, furanocoumarin biosynthesis, localization studies and clinical biochemistry; immunochemical determination of lactate dehydrogenase isozyme-1; radioimmunoassay of serum estriol; immuno-assisted determination of prostatic acid phosphatase; ketone and bilirubin interference in creatinine analyses; serum b-endorphin levels in chiropractic manipulation; synthesis and enzymology of b-carboxy aspartic acid, spectrophotometric determination of hemoglobin derivatives; effect of sugars on milk protein heat denaturation; rem-sleep deprivation and brain acetycholine enzymology. *Mailing Add:* Dept Chem Trent Univ Peterborough ON K9J 7B8 Can. *Fax:* 705-748-1335; *E-Mail:* bannett@trentu.ca

ANNINO, RAYMOND, ANALYTICAL CHEMISTRY, PHYSICAL CHEMISTRY. *Current Pos:* PRIN RES SCIENTIST, FOXBORO CO, MASS, 81- *Personal Data:* b NY, Sept 5, 27; m 50; c 5. *Educ:* Columbia Univ, BA, 50; Okla State Univ, PhD, 56. *Honors & Awards:* Jacob Schoelkopf Medal, Am Chem Soc, 83. *Prof Exp:* Asst scientist, Nat Dairy Res Labs, Inc, 50-53; supvr anal res, Westvaco Chlor-Alkali Div, 55-57; assoc prof chem, Northeastern La State Col, 57-60 & Canisius Col, 60-67; sr res scientist, Foxboro Co, Mass, 67-72; prof chem, Canisius Col, 72-81, chmn dept, 77-81. *Concurrent Pos:* Sci adv, Food & Drug Admin, Buffalo Dist, 73-81. *Mem:* Am Chem Soc; Soc Appl Spectros; Instrument Soc Am. *Res:* Application of signal enhancement techniques to various instrumental methods; design of new chromatographic techniques and instruments; electrochemical methods of analysis. *Mailing Add:* 9 Winchester Rd North Smithfield RI 02896-6831

ANNIS, BRIAN KITFIELD, CHEMICAL PHYSICS. *Current Pos:* RES STAFF MEM CHEM, OAK RIDGE NAT LAB, 68- *Personal Data:* b Arlington, Mass, Aug 25, 40; m 66; c 2. *Educ:* Brown Univ, ScB, 62; Univ Md, PhD(chem physics), 67. *Mem:* Am Phys Soc; Sigma Xi. *Res:* Experimental atomic and molecular collision dynamics, gas phase transport properties. *Mailing Add:* 869-A West Outer Dr Oak Ridge TN 37830-8315

ANNIS, JASON CARL, AIR POLLUTION, PARTICULATE TECHNOLOGY. *Current Pos:* ENG CONSULT, 78- *Personal Data:* b Minneapolis, Minn, July 11, 30; m 61; c 2. *Educ:* Univ Minn, Minneapolis, BS, 53; Mich Technol Univ, MS, 56; Kans State Univ, PhD(mech eng), 69. *Prof Exp:* Instr mining eng, Mich Technol Univ, 53-55; res fel mech eng, Univ Minn, Minneapolis, 55-59; from instr to assoc prof, Kans State Univ, 59-78. *Concurrent Pos:* Mem, Maj Appliance Consumer Action Panel, 72-88, chmn, 80-84; mem adv comn, US Patent Off, 77-78. *Mem:* Air Pollution Control Asn; Am Indust Hyg Asn; Am Chem Soc; Am Soc Heating, Refrig & Air Conditioning Engrs. *Res:* Atmospheric aerosol measurement; air cleaning device evaluation; fine particle size analysis; air filtration theory; air pollution through process alteration in the grain processing industry. *Mailing Add:* 1325 Hudson Ave Manhattan KS 66503

ANNO, JAMES NELSON, PHYSICS, NUCLEAR ENGINEERING. *Current Pos:* prof, 70-89, EMER PROF NUCLEAR ENG, UNIV CINCINNATI, 89- *Personal Data:* b Niles, Ohio, Feb 6, 34; m 55, 92, Angela Labmeier; c James D, Sara J (Butler) & Jefferson N. *Educ:* Ohio State Univ, BS, 55, MS, 61, PhD(physics), 65. *Prof Exp:* Physicist, Battelle Mem Inst, 55-70. *Concurrent Pos:* Consult, Battelle Mem Inst, 70-85; pres, Res Dynamics Inc, 77- *Res:* Industrial applications of atomic energy, nuclear fusion, heat transfer and fluid flow; lubrication mechanics; radiation effects. *Mailing Add:* Univ Cincinnati Mail Location 163 Cincinnati OH 45221

ANNULIS, JOHN T, MATHEMATICS. *Current Pos:* from asst prof to assoc prof, 72-80, head dept, 79-93, PROF MATH, UNIV ARK, MONTICELLO, 81-, DEAN, COL GEN STUDIES, 93-, ASSOC VCHANCELLOR ACAD AFFAIRS, 94- *Personal Data:* b Cincinnati, Ohio, Nov 13, 45; m 69, Elizabeth Bruce; c Laura & Leah. *Educ:* Grand Valley State Col, BA, 66; Univ NMex, MA, 68, PhD(math), 71. *Prof Exp:* Asst prof math, Univ Wis-Whitewater, 71-72. *Mem:* Math Asn Am. *Res:* Applications of decompositions of the indentity to problems in vector lattices. *Mailing Add:* Sch Sci & Math Univ Ark Monticello AR 71656. *Fax:* 870-460-1933; *E-Mail:* annulisj@uamont.edu

ANOUCHI, ABRAHAM Y, ELECTRONIC INSTRUMENTATION, GAS DETECTING SENSORS. *Current Pos:* PRES & CHIEF EXEC OFFICER, AYA INSTRUMENTS, 90- *Personal Data:* b Tel-Aviv, Israel, Oct 3, 30; US citizen; m 58; c 1. *Educ:* Ind Inst Technol, BS, 54; Harvard Univ, MS, 56. *Prof Exp:* Chief engr & partner, Flow Corp, 64-70; chief engr, Environ Equip Div, EG&G, 70-76; vpres res & eng, Instruments Div, United Technologies, 76-86; pres, Elpaz Instruments Inc, 86-90. *Concurrent Pos:* Consult. *Mem:* Sr mem Instrument Soc Am; Inst Elec & Electronics Engrs; Int Soc Photoelectronic Engrs. *Res:* Instrumentation technologies using state-of-the-art techniques. *Mailing Add:* 1537 S Negley Ave Pittsburgh PA 15217

ANSARI, AFTAB A, RESEARCH ADMINISTRATION, IMMUNOLOGY. *Current Pos:* HEALTH SCI ADMINR, NIH, 92- *Personal Data:* b Allahabad, India, 1950. *Educ:* Gorakhpur Univ, BS, 56; Aligarh Muslim Univ, MS, 68, PhD(biochem), 71. *Prof Exp:* Assoc prof med, Johns Hopkins Univ, 85-91. *Mem:* Am Asn Immunologists; AAAS; Sigma Xi. *Mailing Add:* NIH 9000 Rockville Pike Bldg 45 5AS25S Bethesda MD 20892

ANSARI, ALI, CLINICAL CHEMISTRY, LIPID CHEMISTRY. *Current Pos:* Res assoc lipid biochem dermat, Sch Med, Univ Southern Calif, 66-71, asst prof path, 71-80, asst clin biochemist, Med Ctr, 70-71, ASSOC PROF PATH, CHAS R DREW POSTGRAD MED SCH, UNIV SOUTHERN CALIF, 72-; CLIN CHEMIST, LOS ANGELES COUNTY KING/DREW MED CTR, 71- *Personal Data:* b Hyderabad, India, Dec 29, 34; US citizen; m 67; c 2. *Educ:* Osmania Univ, India, BSc, 57; Kans State Univ, MS, 63; Tex A&M Univ, PhD(biochem), 66. *Concurrent Pos:* Mem fac, Univ Calif, Los Angeles, 80- *Mem:* Am Chem Soc; Am Asn Clin Chem; AAAS; Am Oil Chem Soc. *Res:* Analytical and clinical chemistry and biochemistry of enzymes, lipids and lipoproteins, and their diagnostic and prognostic application in disease. *Mailing Add:* 15511 Grovehill Lane La Mirada CA 90638

ANSARI, AZAM U, CRITICAL CARE MEDICINE, CARDIOLOGY & GASTROENTEROLOGY. *Current Pos:* SOLO CONSULTATIVE PRACT, CARDIOL, GASTROENTEROL & CRITICAL CARE MED, 88- *Personal Data:* b Hyderbad, India, Sept 28, 40; US citizen. *Educ:* Osmania Univ, Hyderabad, India, MB & BS, 63. *Prof Exp:* Instr, Dept Internal Med, Tulane Med Sch, 66-68, St Lukes Hosp, St Paul, 68-70; staff physician, Metrop Mt Sinai Med Ctr, Minneapolis, 72-88. *Concurrent Pos:* Asst vis physician, Tulane Med Serv, Charity Hosp, New Orleans, 67-68; consult internal med, Lallie Kemp Charity Hosp, Independence, La, 67-68; tutor, Vet Admin Hosp, Minneapolis, 70; med & cardiol consult, Minn Armed Forces Ctr, 73-; staff physician, N Mem Med Ctr, Robbinsdale, Minn & Fairview-Southdale Hosp, Edina, Minn, 73-, Abbott-Northwestern Hosp, Minneapolis, Minn, 75-, Fairfield Ridges Hosp, Burnsville, Minn, 85- *Mem:* AMA; fel Coun Clin Cardiol; fel Am Col Cardiol; fel Am Col Physicians; fel Am Col Gastroenterol. *Res:* Improvement by research in the diagnosis and management of critical cardiovascular, nutritional and gastrointestinal diseases. *Mailing Add:* Metrop Med Off Bldg 825 S Eighth St Suite 812 Minneapolis MN 55404. *Fax:* 612-321-0331

ANSARI, GUHLAM AHMAD SHAKEEL, ORGANIC CHEMISTRY & BIOCHEMISTRY, TOXICOLOGY. *Current Pos:* fel, Univ Tex Med Br, 76-77, res assoc biochem, 78-79, from asst prof to assoc prof, 79-90, PROF BIOCHEM & PATH, UNIV TEX MED BR, GALVESTON, 90- *Personal Data:* b Barabanki, India, Oct 4, 47; m 74, Naseem Hasan; c Faheem A. *Educ:* Aligarh Muslim Univ, India, BS, 66, MS, 69, MPhil, 70, PhD(chem), 73. *Prof Exp:* Asst prof chem, Aligarh Muslim Univ, India, 73-74; fel, Univ Idaho, 74-76. *Concurrent Pos:* Assoc ed, Bull Environ Contamination & Toxicol. *Mem:* Am Chem Soc; Soc Toxicol; Am Soc Biochem and Molecular Biol. *Res:* Chemistry and biochemistry lipids; lipid conjugates of xenobiotics; biomarkers of chemical exposure. *Mailing Add:* Dept Path Univ Tex Med Br Keiller Bldg Rm 3108 301 University Blvd Galveston TX 77555-0609

ANSBACHER, RUDI, OBSTETRICS & GYNECOLOGY, REPRODUCTIVE BIOLOGY. *Current Pos:* PROF OBSTET & GYNEC, UNIV MICH MED CTR, ANN ARBOR, 80- *Personal Data:* b Sidney, NY, Oct 11, 34; m 65, Elisabeth C Valinga; c Rudi T & Jeffrey N. *Educ:* Va Mil Inst, BA, 55; Univ Va, MD, 59; Univ Mich, MS, 70. *Honors & Awards:* Chmn Award for Clin Res, Armed Forces Dist, Am Col Obstet & Gynec, 70. *Prof Exp:* Intern, Univ Va Hosp, 59-60; Physician, Richmond Mem Hosp, US Army, 60-62, surg resident, Womack Army Hosp, Ft Bragg, NC, 62-63, resident obstet-gynec, Letterman Gen Hosp, San Francisco, Calif, 63-66, mem staff, US Army Hosp, Ryukyu Islands, Okinawa, 66-68, researcher mil med & allied sci, Walter Reed Army Inst Res, Washington, DC, 68-69; teaching assoc, Dept Obstet & Gynec, Med Ctr, Univ Mich, 69-71, chief family planning & consult serv, Dept Obstet & Gynec & chief clin invest serv, 71-74; asst chief, Dept Obstet & Gynec & chief, Obstet Serv, Brooke Army Med Ctr, Ft Sam Houston, 74-77, chief, Dept Obstet & Gynec, Letterman Army Med Ctr, 77-80. *Concurrent Pos:* clin instr, Dept Obstet & Gynec, Univ Hawaii, 67-68; fel, Ctr Res Reprod Biol, Univ Mich, 69-71, asst chmn, Dept Obstet & Gynec, 81-84 & 85-88, actg chmn, 84-85, interim chmn, 91-93. *Mem:* AMA; Asn Mil Surg US; fel Am Col Obstet & Gynec; Int Fedn Gynec & Obstet; Am Fertil Soc; Am Soc Andrology. *Res:* Reproductive biology, keying on the clinical aspects, using immunologic techniques, especially in the fields of infertility and conception control. *Mailing Add:* Dept Obstet & Gynec MPB Rm D-2206 Univ Mich Med Ctr Ann Arbor MI 48109-0718. *Fax:* 313-763-5992

ANSBACHER, STEFAN, biomedicine; deceased, see previous edition for last biography

ANSCOMBE, FRANCIS JOHN, STATISTICS. *Current Pos:* prof, 63-88, EMER PROF STATIST, YALE UNIV, 88- *Personal Data:* b Elstree, Eng, May 13, 18; m 54; c 4. *Educ:* Cambridge Univ, BA, 39, MA, 43. *Honors & Awards:* R A Fisher lectr, Joint Statist Meetings, Cincinnati, 82. *Prof Exp:* With Brit Ministry Supply, 40-45 & Rothamsted Exp Sta, Eng, 45-47; lectr math, Cambridge Univ, 48-56; res assoc, Princeton Univ, 53-54, from assoc prof to prof, 56-63. *Concurrent Pos:* Corresp consult, Higher Coun Sci Invests, Madrid, 53; vis assoc prof, Univ Chicago, 59-60. *Mem:* Int Stat Inst; fel Inst Math Statist; fel Am Statist Asn; Asn Comput Mach; Royal Statist Soc; Sigma Xi. *Res:* Theory and practice of statistical method; statistical computing. *Mailing Add:* 23 Edgehill Rd New Haven CT 06511-1327

ANSEL, HOWARD CARL, PHARMACY. *Current Pos:* from asst prof to assoc prof, 62-70, head dept, 68-77, PROF PHARM, UNIV GA, 70-, DEAN, COL PHARM, 77- *Personal Data:* b Cleveland, Ohio, Oct 18, 33; m 60; c 3. *Educ:* Univ Toledo, BS, 55; Univ Fla, MS, 57, PhD(pharmaceut sci & chem), 59. *Prof Exp:* Asst prof pharm, Univ Toledo, 59-62. *Mem:* Am Pharmaceut Asn; Am Asn Col Pharm. *Res:* Pharmaceutical sciences; hemolytic effect of various chemical agents; binding of antibacterial preservatives by macromolecules; relationship between bacteriolysis, hemolysis and chemical structure. *Mailing Add:* 145 Mansfield Ct Athens GA 30606

ANSELL, GEORGE S(TEPHEN), PHYSICAL METALLURGY. *Current Pos:* from asst prof to prof, 60-67, dean, 74-84, ROBERT W HUNT PROF METALL ENG, RENSSELAER POLYTECH INST, 67-, CHMN MAT DIV, 69-; PRES, COLO SCH MINES, 84- *Personal Data:* b Akron, Ohio, Apr 1, 34; m 60; c 3. *Educ:* Rensselaer Polytech Inst, BMetE, 54, MMetE, 55, PhD(phys metall), 60. *Honors & Awards:* Hardy Gold Medal, Am Inst Mining, Metall & Petrol Engrs, 60; Alfred H Geisler Award, Am Soc Metals, 64, Bradley Stoughton Award, 68; Curtis W McGraw Res Award, Am Soc Eng Educ. *Prof Exp:* Metallurgist, US Naval Res Lab, 57-58. *Concurrent Pos:* Vis scientist, Ford Sci Lab, 61 & Allegheny Ludlum Steel Corp, 59- *Mem:* Am Inst Mining, Metall & Petrol Engrs; fel Am Soc Metals; fel Metall Soc; Nat Soc Proj Eng. *Res:* Powder metallurgy; mechanical properties of crystals; electron microscopy; dispersion strengthening; diffusion in metals; irradiation damage; magnetic properties. *Mailing Add:* Colo Sch Mines Golden CO 80401

ANSELL, JULIAN S, UROLOGY. *Current Pos:* from asst prof to assoc prof, 59-65, prof & chmn dept, 65-87, PROF, DEPT UROL, UNIV WASH, 59- *Personal Data:* b Portland, Maine, June 30, 22; m 51; c 5. *Educ:* Bowdoin Col, BA, 47; Tufts Univ, MD, 51; Univ Minn, Minneapolis, PhD(urol), 59. *Prof Exp:* Instr urol, Med Col & mem staff, Univ Hosp, Univ Minn, Minneapolis, 56-59. *Concurrent Pos:* Chief urol, Vet Admin Hosp, Minneapolis, 56-59; urologist in chief, King Co Hosp & chief consult, Vet Admin Hosp, Seattle, 59- *Mem:* AAAS; AMA; Am Col Surg; Am Urol Asn. *Res:* Physiology of urinary apparatus; pediatric urology. *Mailing Add:* Dept Urol RL-10 Univ Wash Sch Med Seattle WA 98195

ANSELME, JEAN-PIERRE L M, ORGANIC CHEMISTRY. *Current Pos:* from asst prof to assoc prof, 65-70, PROF ORG CHEM, UNIV MASS, BOSTON, 70- *Personal Data:* b Port-au-Prince, Haiti, Sept 22, 36; US citizen; m 60, Marie-Celine Carrie; c Fabiene (Madsen), Veronika (Testa) & Vanessa. *Educ:* St Martial Col, Haiti, BA, 55; Fordham Univ, BS, 59; Polytech Inst Brooklyn, PhD(org chem), 63. *Prof Exp:* Res fel org chem, Polytech Inst Brooklyn, 60-63, res assoc, 63, sr instr, 65; NSF fel, Inst Org Chem, Univ Munich, 64-65. *Concurrent Pos:* Founder & ed, Org Prep & Procedures, 67-70; A P Sloan Found fel, 69-71; founder & ed, Org Prep & Procedures Int, 71-; vis prof, Kyushu Univ, Japan, 72 & Univ Miami, 79. *Mem:* Am Chem Soc; Royal Soc Chem; fel Japan Soc Prom Sci; Sigma Xi. *Res:* Synthetic organic chemistry; reaction mechanisms; meso-ionic systems; N-nitrenes; diazoalkanes; azides; thionylhydrazines; 3-pyrazolidinones; hydrazinium salts; N-nitrosamines; sulfinyl and sulfenylhydratines; N-nitrosamines; pyrazoles and imidazoles; author of numerous publications. *Mailing Add:* Dept Chem Univ Mass Harbor Campus Boston MA 02125. *Fax:* 617-287-7173

ANSELMO, VINCENT C, TRACE ANALYSIS. *Current Pos:* CHIEF, INORG ANALYSIS LAB, TEX AIR CONTROL BD, 83- *Personal Data:* b New York, NY, July 29, 30; m 54; c 5. *Educ:* Fordham Univ, BS, 51, MS, 59; Univ Kans, PhD(chem), 61. *Prof Exp:* Instr pharm, Fordham Univ, 53-57; asst prof chem, John Carroll Univ, 61-64; from asst prof to prof chem, NMex Highlands Univ, 64-77, chmn dept chem, 74-77. *Mem:* Fel AAAS; Am Chem Soc. *Res:* Trace analysis of inorganic air pollutants using x-ray fluorescence, ion chromatography or inductively coupled plasma. *Mailing Add:* 2622 W 49 1/2 St Austin TX 78731

ANSELONE, PHILIP MARSHALL, mathematical analysis, for more information see previous edition

ANSEVIN, ALLEN THORNBURG, UNUSUAL DNA STRUCTURES, CHROMATIN. *Current Pos:* asst physics, Univ Tex, 64-70, from asst prof to assoc prof, Grad Sch Biomed Sci, 65-80, assoc physicist, M D Anderson Hosp & Tumor Inst, 70-86, prof biophys, Grad Sch Biomed Sci, 80-86, ADJ PROF, GRAD SCH BIOMED SCI, UNIV TEX, 86- *Personal Data:* b Springfield, Ohio, Nov 22, 28; m 61, Krystyna; c 2. *Educ:* Earlham Col, AB, 51; Univ Pittsburgh, MS, 58, PhD(biophys), 61. *Prof Exp:* Res asst pharmacol, Christ Hosp Int Med Res, 53-56; res assoc biochem, Rockefeller Univ, 61-64. *Mem:* AAAS; Biophys Soc. *Res:* Virus structure; protein-protein associations; ultracentrifuge methods; nucleoprotein structure; radiation biology; DNA thermal denaturation; sequence-specific protein-DNA complexes; left-handed DNA, molecular modeling. *Mailing Add:* 2127 McArthur Dr Houston TX 77030

ANSHEL, MICHAEL, MATHEMATICS, COMPUTER SCIENCE. *Current Pos:* from asst prof to assoc prof, 68-78, PROF COMPUT SCI, CITY COL NY, 79- *Personal Data:* b New York, NY, Nov 2, 41; m 65, Zwa Goven; c Iris & Daphne. *Educ:* Adelphi Univ, BA, 63, MS, 65, PhD(math), 67. *Prof Exp:* Asst prof math, Polytech Inst Brooklyn, 66-67 & Univ Ariz, 67-68; systs analyst, Lambda Corp, 68. *Concurrent Pos:* Consult, Princeton-Bethesda, 68 & Mt Sinai Sch Med, 75-80; reviewer, Math Rev, Am Math Soc, 75-; doctoral fac, Grad Ctr, City Univ NY, 73-; NASA-Am Soc Eng Edu fac fel, Goddard Space Flight Ctr, 82 & 83; Delphi assoc, 83; AT&T Bell Labs, 86-88. *Mem:* Am Math Soc; Math Asn Am; Ann Symbolic Logic; Sigma Xi; Asn Comput Mach; Inst Elec & Electronics Engrs Comput Soc; AAAS; Soc Indust Appl Math. *Res:* Group-theoretic decision-problems and their relation to the theory of computation; applications of algebra and logic in the computer sciences and combinatorial mathematics; cryptology and computer security. *Mailing Add:* 1140 Fifth Ave Apt 3C New York NY 10128-0806. *Fax:* 212-650-8184; *E-Mail:* mikeat1140@aol.com

ANSHER, SHERRY SINGER, BIOCHEMISTRY, PHARMACOLOGY. *Current Pos:* COORDR, RES & DEVELOP AGREEMENTS, CANCER THER EVAL PROG, NAT CANCER INST. *Personal Data:* b Washington, DC, Mar 3, 57; m 80; c 1. *Educ:* Univ Md, College Park, BS, 78; Johns Hopkins Univ, Md, PhD(biochem & pharmacol), 82. *Prof Exp:* Staff fel, Nat Inst Arthritis, Diabetes & Digestive & Kidney Dis, NIH, 82-85, sr staff fel Biochem, Enzymes & Cellular Metab Sect, 85-87; sr staff fel, Lab Bact Toxins, Fed Drug Admin. *Mem:* AAAS; Am Chem Soc; Am Soc Metals; Am Soc Biochem & Molecular Biol. *Res:* Investigation and purification of enzymes responsible for detoxication of xenobiotics and carcinogens; mechanism by which compounds inhibiting carcinogenesis in animals through alteration of metabolism may work; role of endogenous methylation inhibitor in gene regulation; adverse reactions to vaccines and cytokines. *Mailing Add:* 9116 Willow Gate Lane Bethesda MD 20817

ANSON, FRED (COLVIG), ELECTROANALYTICAL CHEMISTRY. *Current Pos:* From instr to assoc prof, 57-68, chmn div chem & eng, 84-94, PROF CHEM, CALIF INST TECHNOL, 68-,. *Personal Data:* b Los Angeles, Calif, Feb 17, 33; m 59, Roxana; c 2. *Educ:* Calif Inst Technol, BS, 54; Harvard Univ, AM, 55, PhD(chem), 57. *Hon Degrees:* Docteur Honoris Causa, Univ Paris, 93. *Honors & Awards:* David C Grahame Award, Electrochem Soc, Inc, 83; Alexander von Humboldt Award, Fritz-Haber Inst, Berlin, 84; C N Reilley Award, Soc Electroanalytical Chem, 86; Elizabeth W Gilloon Prof Chem, 95, ACS Award in Anal Chem, 89; Am Chem Soc Div Anal Chem Award in Electrochem, 94. *Concurrent Pos:* Guggenheim fel, 64; Alfred P Sloan res fel, 65-69; Fulbright scholar, 72; chmn, Gordon Res Conf Electrochem, 70. *Mem:* Nat Acad Sci; fel AAAS; Am Electrochem Soc; Int Soc Electrochem; Am Chem Soc; Soc Electroanalytical Chem; fel Electrochem Soc. *Res:* Kinetics of electrode reactions; mechanisms of electrode processes; chemical education. *Mailing Add:* Div Chem & Eng Calif Inst Technol Pasadena CA 91125. *Fax:* 626-405-0454; *E-Mail:* fanson@cco.caltech.edu

ANSPAUGH, LYNN RICHARD, ENVIRONMENTAL SCIENCES, HEALTH PHYSICS. *Current Pos:* RES PROF, RADIOBIOL DIV, UNIV UTAH, 97- *Personal Data:* b Rawlins, Wyo, May 25, 37; m 93, Larisa F Movchan; c 3. *Educ:* Nebr Wesleyan Univ, BA, 59; Univ Calif, Berkeley, MBioradiol, 61, PhD(biophys), 63. *Prof Exp:* Biophysicist, Lawrence Livermore Nat Lab, 63-82, div leader, 82-92, dir, Risk Sci Ctr, 92-95, dir, Dose Reconstruct Prog, 95-96. *Concurrent Pos:* Teacher, Univ Exten, Univ Calif, Berkeley, 66-69; lectr, San Jose State Univ, 75; fac affil, Colo State Univ, 75; sci dir, Nev Test Site Off-Site Radiation Exposure Rev Proj, 79-, Nev Appl Ecol Group, 83-86 & Basic Environ Compliance & Monitoring Proj, 86-92; consult, sci adv bd, Environ Protection Agency, 84-85 & Int Atomic Energy Agency, 88-; mem, US deleg to UN Sci Comt Effects of Atomic Radiation, 87- & Nat Coun Radiation Protection, 89-; vis lectr, Univ Calif, Los Angeles & Davis, 92- *Mem:* AAAS; fel Health Physics Soc; Soc Risk Analysis; Sigma Xi; Radiation Res Soc. *Res:* Study of the environmental effects of utilizing geothermal energy resources; experimental study of the resuspension of pollutant aerosols with emphasis on plutonium; calculation of radiation doses from nuclear tests and nuclear reactors. *Mailing Add:* Radiobiol Div Univ Utah Salt Lake City UT 84112. *E-Mail:* lanspaugh@aol.com

ANSPON, HARRY DAVIS, ORGANIC CHEMISTRY, POLYMER CHEMISTRY. *Current Pos:* CONSULT PLASTICS & CHEM, 78-, PATENT AGT, 79- *Personal Data:* b Washington, DC, Sept 25, 17; m 56, Nannette Green; c Catherine (Davis) & Ellen (Graham). *Educ:* Univ Md, BS, 39, PhD(org chem), 42. *Prof Exp:* Asst, Univ Md, 42-46; res chemist, US Rubber Co, NJ, 46-48; res chemist, Cent Res Labs, Gen Aniline & Film Corp, 48-56, res fel, 56-58; plant chemist, Acetylene Chem Plant, Ky, 58-59; sect leader, Gulf Res & Develop, Res Ctr, Spencer Chem Co, 59-68; mgr prod-process develop, Plastics Dept, USS Chem Div, United States Steel Corp, 68-69, tech dir, 69-76, asst mgr, New Polymer Planning, 76-78. *Concurrent Pos:* With Nat Defense Res Coun. *Mem:* Am Chem Soc; Soc Plastics Eng. *Res:* Hydrogenation and dehydrogenation of pyrethrosin; organic polymers; organic synthesis; plastics; manufacture of plastics. *Mailing Add:* 29 Beaver Sewickley PA 15143-1244

ANSTEY, THOMAS HERBERT, GENETICS, PLANT BREEDING. *Current Pos:* SR VPRES AGR, INT DEVELOP ASSOCS CAN, INC, 86- *Personal Data:* b Victoria, BC, Dec 27, 17; m 45, L Winnifred Ferguson; c Kevin T, Robyn L & Marilyn P. *Educ:* Univ BC, BSA, 41, MSA, 43; Univ Minn, PhD(plant breeding), 49. *Prof Exp:* Horticulturist, Exp Farm, Agassiz, BC, 46-49, sr horticulturist, 49-53, supt exp sta, Summerland, 53-59, dir res sta, Lethbridge, 59-69, asst dir gen western res br, 69-78, sr adv, Int Res &

Develop, Res Br, Cent Exp Farm, Can Dept Agr, Ottawa, 78-82. *Mem:* Can Soc Hort Sci; fel Agr Inst Can (pres, 70-71); Ont Ins Agr. *Res:* Genetics and breeding for strawberries and broccoli. *Mailing Add:* 12 Warbonnet Dr Ottawa ON K2E 5M2 Can

ANSUL, GERALD R, ORGANIC CHEMISTRY. *Current Pos:* RETIRED. *Personal Data:* b Philadelphia, Pa, July 17, 25; m 58, Harriet Polikoff; c Susan, Stephen & Michael. *Educ:* Temple Univ, AB, 50; Pa State Univ, PhD(org chem), 54. *Prof Exp:* Res chemist, Marshall Lab, Fabrics & Finishes Dept, E I du Pont de Nemours & Co, Inc, 54-58, chem assoc, 58-60, mkt specialist, 60-62, proj supvr, Indust Sales Div, 62-64, tech coord, Wynnewood Automotive & Indust Sales Div, 64-65, Lincolnwood Automotive & Indust Prod, 65-68, mgr insulation sales, Fabrics & Finishes Dept, 68-69, mgr new prod develop & elec sales, Indust Prod Div, 70-71, mgr new prod, 72-76, prod mgr, Corian Bldg Prod, 76-80, prod mgr, Appl Technol Div, Fabrics & Finishes Dept, 80-85; pres, Brandywine Mkt Servs, Inc, Wilimington, Del, 85-96. *Mem:* AAAS; Am Chem Soc; Am Telemarketing Asn; Nat Safety Coun. *Res:* Organosilicon chemistry; urethane chemistry; chemistry of the vinyl dioxolanes; automotive finishes; diallyl phthalate pre-pregs and laminates; wood furniture finishes; adhesives; sealants and paper coatings; polyimide resins; wire enamels; epoxy pre-pregs; rigid and flexible printed circuitry; filled acrylic polymers; industrial hygiene noise and air monitoring instruments. *Mailing Add:* 17 Stonecrop Rd Northminster Wilmington DE 19810

ANTAKLY, TONY, HORMONE ACTION & STEROID PHARMACOLOGY, CELL SPECIFIC GENE REGULATION. *Current Pos:* ASSOC PROF PATH, UNIV MONTREAL, 91- *Personal Data:* b Nov 9, 51; m 85; c 1. *Educ:* Am Univ, Beirut, BSc, 72; Univ Paris, PhD(cell biol), 78; Univ Paris, Sorbonne, DSc, 83. *Prof Exp:* Asst prof anat, McGill Univ, 83-90. *Mem:* Endocrine Soc; Am Asn Anatomists; Am Soc Cell Biol; Am Soc Microbiol. *Res:* Molecular mechanisms of steroid hormone action including carcinogenesis, hormone resistance, leukemias; neuroendocrine regulation of pituitary and endocrine cell function. *Mailing Add:* Dept Biochem Univ Montreal 2900 Ed Montpetit Montreal PQ H3C 3J7 Can

ANTAL, JOHN JOSEPH, NUCLEAR RADIATION PHYSICS, MATERIALS SCIENCE. *Current Pos:* RETIRED. *Personal Data:* b Taylor, Pa, Apr 23, 26; m 55, Berniece Baumann; c Anita & Christopher. *Educ:* Univ Scranton, BS, 48; St Louis Univ, MS, 49, PhD(physics), 52. *Prof Exp:* Res physicist, Watertown Arsenal Lab, US Army, 52-53, ord mat res off, 53-62, mat res agency, 62-67, res physicist, Mat & Mech Res Ctr, 67-81, leader, Characterization Res Group, 81-89, res physicist, US Army Mat Lab, 89-93. *Concurrent Pos:* Guest assoc physicist, Brookhaven Nat Lab, 53-65; secy Army Res & Study fel, CNRN, ISPRA, Italy, 61-62. *Mem:* Am Phys Soc; AAAS; Mat Res Soc. *Res:* Thermal neutron spectroscopy; neutron and x-ray characterization of materials; digital instrumentation. *Mailing Add:* 116 Lake Rd Framingham MA 01701-4244. *Fax:* 508-877-0571; *E-Mail:* 73524.1325@compuserve.com

ANTAL, MICHAEL JERRY, JR, CARBOHYDRATE THERMOCHEMISTRY. *Current Pos:* CORAL INDUST DISTINGUISHED PROF RENEWABLE ENERGY RESOURCES, HAWAII NATURAL ENERGY INST & DEPT MECH ENG, UNIV HAWAII, 82- *Personal Data:* b Monroe, Mich, May 18, 47; m 72, Ann G Slaughter; c Dickinson J & Rachel C. *Educ:* Dartmouth Col, AB, 69; Harvard Univ, MS, 70, PhD(appl math), 73. *Prof Exp:* Res staff, Thermonuclear Weapons Physics Group, Los Alamos Nat Lab, 73-75; asst prof energy sci & appl math, Dept Mech Aerospace Eng, Princeton Univ, 75-81. *Concurrent Pos:* Consult, President's Coun Environ Qual, 77-78, Off Technol Assessment, US Cong, 78-79, Exxon Corp, 79, Solar Eng Group, 79-81, Aerospace Corp, 80, Sao Paulo Elec Ctr, Brazil, 85-; pres, Hawaii Sect, Am Chem Soc, 89; consult, Nat Energy Admin Sweden, 91 & World Bank, 91-92. *Mem:* Am Chem Soc; Am Phys Soc; Am Inst Chem Eng. *Res:* Biomass pyrolysis and gasification, emphasizing mechanisms and kinetics; chemical reactor design; chemical reaction engineering and catalysis in supercritical fluids. *Mailing Add:* Dept Mech Eng Univ Hawaii 2540 Dole St Honolulu HI 96822. *Fax:* 808-956-2336; *E-Mail:* antal@wiliki.eng.hawaii.edu

ANTAR, ALI A, ATOMIC & MOLECULAR PHYSICS, OPTICS. *Current Pos:* PROF PHYSICS, CENT CONN STATE UNIV, 80- *Personal Data:* b Egypt, Sept 20, 40. *Educ:* Air Shams Univ, BA, 60, Univ Conn, MA, 72, PhD(nuclear physics), 77. *Prof Exp:* Fel, Univ Conn, 77-78, syst prof physics, 78-80. *Mem:* AAAS; Am Asn Physics Teachers; Am Phys Soc; Sigma Xi. *Res:* A research project involving experimental atomic and molecular physics. *Mailing Add:* Phys Dept Cent Conn State Univ New Britain CT 06050

ANTAR, MOHAMED ABDELCHANY, RADIATION BIOLOGY, NUCLEAR CARDIOLOGY. *Current Pos:* PROF MED & CHIEF NUCLEAR MED, CONN VET ADMIN MED CTR, 74- *Educ:* Univ Iowa, MD & PhD(metab radiation biol), 64. *Mailing Add:* StateUniv NY Stony Brook Vet Admin Med Ctr 79 Middleville Rd Northport NY 11768-2290

ANTCZAK, DOUGLAS, ANIMAL HEALTH, IMMUNOLOGY. *Current Pos:* PROF IMMUNOL, CORNELL UNIV VET MED CTR, 92- *Res:* Animal health; immunology. *Mailing Add:* James A Baker Inst Animal Health Cornell Univ NY Col Vet Med Ithaca NY 14853-0001

ANTEL, JACK PERRY, NEUROLOGY, NEUROIMMUNOLOGY. *Current Pos:* PROF NEUROL, MCGILL UNIV, 86-, CHMN NEUROL & NEUROSURG, 89- *Personal Data:* b Winnipeg, Man, Oct 25, 45; m 69, Avis Bay; c 3. *Educ:* Univ Man, BSc & MD, 69; FRCP(c), 74; Am Bd Psychiat & Neurol, cert neurol, 76. *Prof Exp:* From asst prof to prof neurol, Univ Chicago, 76-86. *Concurrent Pos:* Neurologist-in-chief, Montreal Neurol Hosp & Royal Victoria Hosp, 86-; assoc mem microbiol & immunol, McGill Univ, 87- *Mem:* Am Acad Neurol; Am Neurol Asn; Soc Neurosci; Am Asn Immunologists. *Res:* Neuroimmunology; mechanisms whereby immune mediators can induce tissue injury within brain and whereby immune and nervous system constituents can modulate the activity of each other. *Mailing Add:* Montreal Neurol Inst 3801 University St Montreal PQ H3A 2B4 Can. *Fax:* 514-486-7170

ANTES, HARRY W, FASTENER ENGINEERING, TEACHING. *Current Pos:* dir, res & develop, 79-86, VPRES, SPS TECHNOL, 86- *Personal Data:* b Philadelphia, Pa, June 20, 30; m 53; c 4. *Educ:* Drexel Inst Tech, BS, 53; Univ Pa, MS, 63; Drexel Univ, PhD, 79. *Prof Exp:* Metallurgist, Frankford Arsenal, 50-68; prof, Drexel Univ, 60-87. *Concurrent Pos:* Adv, Adv Tech Ctr Southeast Pa, 80- *Mem:* Am Mgt Asn. *Res:* Mechanical metallurgy; metalworking; materials processing; powder metallurgy; fastener technology; magnetics. *Mailing Add:* 3896 Jeffrey Rd Huntingdon Valley PA 19006

ANTHES, JOHN ALLEN, ORGANIC CHEMISTRY, CHEMICAL ENGINEERING. *Current Pos:* RETIRED. *Personal Data:* b Janesville, Wis, Aug 18, 13; m 38; c Jeanne, Janet & John Jr. *Educ:* Univ Minn, BChE, 34, PhD(org chem), 39. *Prof Exp:* Asst, Univ Minn, 35-38; res chemist, Union Oil Co, Calif, 39-40; contracting off rep, Ord Dept, US Army, 41-42, asst chief spec Mat Sect, Manhattan Dist, 43-45; res chemist, Am Cyanamid Co, Conn, 46-48, asst chief chemist, Pa, 48-50, chief chemist, 50-53; proj engr, Dravo Corp, 53-58, asst dir res & develop, 58-65, mgr res, 65-71, sr consult, 71-78; consult engr, 78-80. *Mem:* AAAS; Am Chem Soc; Am Inst Chem Eng; Am Inst Mining, Metall & Petrol Engrs; NY Acad Sci. *Res:* Ore agglomeration processes; compounds related to perinaphthenone; synthesis of lubricating oil additives and of ion exchange resins; esterification of high boiling alcohols; dehydration of maleic acid; process metallurgy; continuous coking of coal; purification of coke oven gas. *Mailing Add:* 21603 141st Dr Sun City West AZ 85375-9712

ANTHES, RICHARD ALLEN, METEOROLOGY. *Current Pos:* PRES, UNIV CORP ATMOSPHERIC RES, 88- *Personal Data:* b St Louis, Mo, Mar 9, 44; m 66, Susan Hill; c David & Katy. *Educ:* Univ Wis, BS, 66, MS, 67, PhD(meteorol), 70. *Honors & Awards:* Meisinger Award, Am Meteorol Soc, 80, Charney Award, 87. *Prof Exp:* Res meteorologist, Nat Hurricane Res Lab, Nat Oceanic & Atmospheric Admin, 68-71; from asst prof to prof meteorol, Pa State Univ, 71-81; dir, Atmospheric Anal & Prediction Div, 81-86, dir, 86-88. *Concurrent Pos:* Consult, Atmospheric Sci Lab, White Sands Missile Range, 73-76 & Nat Weather Serv, 73-81; mem storm fury panel, Bd Atmospheric Sci & Climate, Nat Res Coun, 75-81, chair, Panel Mesoscale Res, 84-86, chair, 87-89; mem, Nat Weather Serv Modernization Comt, 92- *Mem:* Am Meteorol Soc; Sigma Xi. *Res:* Numerical modeling of atmospheric phenomena, especially on the mesoscale; hurricane modeling and parameterization of physical processes in models. *Mailing Add:* 1631 Gillespie St Boulder CO 80303-7028. *Fax:* 303-497-1654; *E-Mail:* anthes@mcar.ucar.edu

ANTHOLINE, WILLIAM E, PHYSICAL BIOCHEMISTRY, BIOPHYSICS. *Current Pos:* NIH fel & instr phys biochem, Radiation Biol & Biophys Div, Nat Cancer Inst, 75-80, asst prof, 80-86, assoc prof, Dept Radiol & Mem, Biophys Group Grad Prog, 86-92, ASSOC PROF BIOPHYS, MED COL WIS, 92- *Personal Data:* b Milwaukee, Wis, July 1, 43; m 65; c 3. *Educ:* Univ Wis-Madison, BS, 65; Iowa State Univ, PhD(phys chem), 71. *Prof Exp:* Fel phys biochem, Radiation Biol & Biophys Div, Med Col Wis, 72-74. *Concurrent Pos:* Fac res specialist, Biochem Sect, Univ Wis-Milwaukee, 75-; lectr, Gordon Res Conf Magnetic Resonance Biol & Med, 74, 85 & 87. *Mem:* Am Chem Soc; Biophys Soc. *Res:* Applying physical chemical principles in order to better understand the origin and interaction of paramagnetic metal compounds found in tissues, especially tumor tissue, and in enzymes and proteins containig copper. *Mailing Add:* Nat Biomed ESR Ctr Biophys Res Inst Med Col Wis 8701 W Watertown Plank Rd Milwaukee WI 53226

ANTHONISEN, NICHOLAS R, RESPIRATORY PHYSIOLOGY. *Current Pos:* PROF MED, DEPT MED, UNIV MAN, 75- *Personal Data:* b Boston, Mass, Oct 12, 33; m 57; c 3. *Educ:* Dartmouth Col, AB, 55; Harvard Univ, MD, 58; McGill Univ, PhD(exp med), 69. *Prof Exp:* Intern med, NC Mem Hosp, 58-59, jr asst resident, 59-60; sr asst resident, Respiratory Dept, Royal Victoria Hosp, 63-64; demonstr med, McGill Univ, 64-66, asst prof exp med, 69-70, assoc prof exp med, 70-73, prof exp med, 73-75. *Concurrent Pos:* Med Res Coun Can scholar, 69-71. *Mem:* Can Soc Clin Invest; Am Physiol Soc; Can Thoracic Soc; Am Soc Clin Invest; Am Thoracic Soc. *Res:* Chest disease; pulmonary physiology; physiologic aspects of respiratory disease. *Mailing Add:* Med Univ Manitoba 753 McDermot Ave Winnipeg MB R3E 0W3 Can

ANTHONY, ADAM, PHYSIOLOGY. *Current Pos:* from asst prof to assoc prof zool, 52-61, chmn comt physiol, Col Sci, 69-73, PROF ZOOL, PA STATE UNIV, UNIVERSITY PARK, 61- *Personal Data:* b Buffalo, NY, Oct 19, 23; div; c 2. *Educ:* Univ Buffalo, BA, 43; Marquette Univ, MS, 48; Univ Chicago, PhD(zool), 52. *Prof Exp:* Lab asst comp anat & bact, Univ Buffalo, 43; asst gen zool, parasitol & histol, Marquette Univ, 46-48 & med parasitol, biol sci, endocrinol & vert embryol, Univ Chicago, 49-52. *Concurrent Pos:* Darbaker Award, 66, 68 & 69. *Mem:* Am Physiol Soc; Soc Exp Biol & Med; AAAS. *Res:* Cytochemical aspects of toxication; vascular and neural cytochemistry; cytodiagnosis of neoplasms; scanning microspectrophotometry and interferometry. *Mailing Add:* 418 Mueller Bldg Pa State Univ University Park PA 16802-0001

ANTHONY, DONALD BARRETT, RESEARCH ADMINISTRATION & TECHNICAL MANAGEMENT. *Current Pos:* PRES, BAILEY CONTROLS CO, 96- *Personal Data:* b Kansas City, Kans, Jan 28, 48; m 72, Darla S Donovan; c Jennifer & Danielle S. *Educ:* Univ Toledo, BS, 70; Mass Inst Technol, SM, 71, DSc, 74. *Prof Exp:* Asst prof chem eng, Mass Inst Technol, 74-75; supvr coal res, Stand Oil Prod Co, 76-78, mgr, Marine Opers Anal & Control, 78-80, Synfuels Develop, 80-82, vpres & gen mgr, Pfander, 82-85, vpres res develop, 85-87, vpres technol serv & res, 88-90; vpres technol, Bechtel, 90-94, vpres oper, 95-96. *Concurrent Pos:* Dir, Sch Chem Eng Pract, Mass Inst Technol, 74-75. *Mem:* Am Chem Soc; Am Inst Chem Engrs; Sigma Xi; AAAS. *Res:* Synthetic fuels research; systems analysis. *Mailing Add:* 6336 Canterbury Dr Hudson OH 44236

ANTHONY, DONALD JOSEPH, FISSION & FUSION, ENERGY SYSTEMS. *Current Pos:* RETIRED. *Personal Data:* b Troy, NY, May 30, 22; m 45; c 5. *Educ:* Siena Col, BS, 47; Univ Notre Dame, PhD(physics), 53. *Prof Exp:* Instr chem & math, Siena Col, Univ Notre Dame, 46-47 & physics, 47-52; res assoc, Knolls Atomic Power Lab, 52-56, mgr exp physics, 56-59, reactor physics, 59-68 & operating nuclear plants, 68-74; mem staff, Energy Systs & Technol Div, Gen Elec Co, 74-76, mgr power technol, 76-77, mgr advan energy systs, Energy Systs Progs Dept, 77-80, mgr GE Advan Energy Systs, 80-84, mgr servs mkt develop, GE Nuclear Energy, 84-87; mkt develop & mgt consult, 87. *Concurrent Pos:* Indust consult, Dept Energy Fusion Power Coord Com, 77-; mem, Oak Ridge Nat Lab Fusion Adv Com, 78-81; mem Univ Chicago Rev Comt Components Technol Div, Argonne Nat Lab, 83-86, Rochester Inst Technol, Dept Physics Planning Coun, 83, Atomic Indust Forum Fusion Comt, 82-84. *Mem:* Am Nuclear Soc; Sigma Xi; Fusion Power Asn. *Res:* Reactor, nuclear physics and energy systems. *Mailing Add:* Three Schuyler Rd Loudonville NY 12211

ANTHONY, EDWARD JOHN, FLUIDIZED BED COMBUSTION, SOLIDS CHEMISTRY. *Current Pos:* SR RES SCIENTIST, NATURAL RESOURCES CAN, 79- *Personal Data:* b Regensburg, Ger, Oct 17, 48; US citizen; m 86, Louise F Green; c Michael, Ross & William-Blaise. *Educ:* Univ Wales, UK, BSc, 71, PhD(chem), 75; Open Univ, UK, BA, 79. *Honors & Awards:* Merit Award, Govt Can, 93 & 96. *Prof Exp:* Higher sci officer, Dept Environ, UK, 73-79. *Mem:* Fel Royal Soc Chem; Sigma Xi; Inst Energy; Am Inst Chem. *Res:* Agglomeration and fouling in CFBC boilers; ash disposal and utilization from high temperature processes with limestone addition; chemical probe for supressing radical processes in fluidized bed combustions to study gas-phase reactions. *Mailing Add:* 1 Hannel Dr Nepean ON K1A 1M1 Can. *Fax:* 613-992-9335; *E-Mail:* ben.anthony@nrcan.gr.ca

ANTHONY, ELIZABETH YOUNGBLOOD, PETROLOGY, GEOCHEMISTRY. *Current Pos:* PROF GEOL SCI, UNIV TEX, 88- *Personal Data:* b Springfield, Ill, Jan 25, 53; wid. *Educ:* Carleton Col, BA, 75; Univ Ariz, MS, 79, PhD(geol), 86. *Prof Exp:* res assoc, Univ Ariz, 77-88. *Concurrent Pos:* Post-doctoral fel, Univ Oslo, Norway, 86, Univ Col, Wales, 87. *Mem:* Geol Soc Am; Mineral Soc Am; Geochem Soc; Am Asn Univ Prof; Am Geophys Union. *Res:* Igneous petrology and geochemistry of mineralized granites; petrogenesis of rift-related volcanic rock in the Rio Grande rift and the Kenya rift. *Mailing Add:* Dept Geol Sci Univ Tex El Paso TX 79968. *E-Mail:* anthony@geo.utep.edu

ANTHONY, HARRY D, veterinary medicine; deceased, see previous edition for last biography

ANTHONY, LEE SAUNDERS, PHYSICS. *Current Pos:* CONSULT, 79- *Personal Data:* b Roanoke, Va, Sept 11, 32; m 53; c 2. *Educ:* Roanoke Col, BS, 53; Va Polytech Inst, MS, 58, PhD(physics), 62; Am Bd Health Physics, cert, 80; Am Bd Radiol, cert, 82. *Prof Exp:* Asst prof, Roanoke Col, 62-65, actg dean, 63-65, chmn, Dept Physics, 62-77, prof physics, 65-79. *Concurrent Pos:* Consult physicist, Roanoke Mem Hosp, 64-80, Physics Asn, 63- *Mem:* Am Phys Soc; Health Physics Soc; Sigma Xi; Am Col Radiol. *Res:* Nuclear, reactor and radiological physics. *Mailing Add:* 3779 Carvins Cove Rd Salem VA 24153-2511

ANTHONY, LINDA JEAN, CHROMATOGRAPHY & INSTRUMENT ANALYSIS. *Current Pos:* MEM TECH STAFF, ANALYTICAL CHEM RES DEPT, AT&T BELL LABS, 80- *Personal Data:* b Boston, Mass, Feb 1, 51; m 82, Harold R Clark; c Alexander & Andrew. *Educ:* Mt Holyoke Col, AB, 73; Mass Inst Technol, SM, 76, PhD(anal chem), 80. *Mem:* Am Chem Soc; Soc Appl Spectros; Sigma Xi. *Res:* Capillary chromatography and electrophoreses; miniaturizahm and sensors; process analytical chemistry; trace chemical analysis for electronics/semiconductor manufacturing. *Mailing Add:* Lucent Tech Bell Labs Rm IC-259 600 Mountain Ave Murray Hill NJ 07974-0636. *E-Mail:* lja@clockwise.att.com

ANTHONY, MARGERY STUART, BOTANY. *Current Pos:* RETIRED. *Personal Data:* b New York, NY, Feb 23, 24. *Educ:* Univ Mich, BS, 45, MS, 46, PhD(bot), 50. *Prof Exp:* Asst bot, Univ Mich, 44-49; from asst prof to assoc prof biol & bot, Calif State Univ, Chico, 49-62, prof biol, 62-83. *Concurrent Pos:* Lectr, NSF Inst, Univ Wyo, 58-62. *Mem:* Ecol Soc Am. *Mailing Add:* PO Box 1469 Gualala CA 95445. *E-Mail:* msanth@aol.com

ANTHONY, PHILIP JOHN, SEMICONDUCTOR MATERIALS TECHNOLOGY. *Current Pos:* mem staff, 78-82, supvr, 82-87, DEPT HEAD, AT&T BELL LABS, 87- *Personal Data:* b New Bremen, Ohio, May 6, 52; m 74; c 2. *Educ:* Univ Dayton, BS, 74; Univ Ill, MS, 75, PhD(physics), 78. *Mem:* Am Phys Soc; Inst Elec & Electronics Engrs; Sigma Xi. *Res:* Low temperature properties of glasses and crystals; electrical and optical properties of semiconductor lasers; photonic switching. *Mailing Add:* 267 White Oak Ridge Rd Bridgewater NJ 08807

ANTHONY, RAYFORD GAINES, CHEMICAL ENGINEERING. *Current Pos:* From asst prof to assoc prof, 66-74, PROF CHEM ENG, TEX A&M UNIV, 74-, C D HOLLAND PROF, 93- *Personal Data:* b Abilene, Tex, Dec 26, 35; m 59; c 2. *Educ:* Tex A&M Univ, BS, 58, MS, 62; Univ Tex, PhD(chem eng), 66. *Mem:* Am Chem Soc; Am Inst Chem Engrs. *Res:* Catalytic and reaction engineering; synthesis of new catalytic materials for removal of toxic waste. *Mailing Add:* Dept Chem Eng Tex A&M Univ College Station TX 77843-3122

ANTHONY, RONALD LEWIS, parasitology, tropical diseases, for more information see previous edition

ANTHONY, THOMAS RICHARD, MATERIALS SCIENCE ENGINEERING, INORGANIC CHEMISTRY. *Current Pos:* APPL PHYSICIST, GEN ELEC RES CTR, NY, 67- *Personal Data:* b Pittsburgh, Pa, June 27, 41; m 66, Angela U Klugert; c Jason W & Wendy C. *Educ:* Univ Fla, BS, 62; Harvard Univ, MS, 64, PhD(appl physics), 67. *Honors & Awards:* I R 100 Award, Indust Res Mag, 77 & Nat Acad Eng, 90; Gold Medal, US Patent & Com Asn, 90; John A Thornton Mem Award, Am Vacuum Soc, 92; David Turnbull Lectr Award, Mat Res Soc, 92. *Prof Exp:* Staff metallurgist, Mellon Inst, 62-63; physicist, Lawrence Radiation Lab, 64. *Concurrent Pos:* Woodrow Wilson fel, 63; NSF fel, 63-67; Coolidge fel, Gen Elec, 78. *Res:* Solid state and gaseous diffusion; grain boundaries; segregation in solids; ultracentrifuges; diamond synthesis; artificial intelligence; chemical vapor deposition; laser drilling; diamond crystals are fabricated by a CVD process utilizing hydrogen and hydrocarbons; 170 publications and 153 patents. *Mailing Add:* 2142 Lynnwood Dr Niskayuna NY 12309-2514. *Fax:* 518-387-7563; *E-Mail:* anthony@crd.ge.com

ANTHONY, W BRADY, RUMINANT NUTRITION. *Current Pos:* EMER PROF ANIMAL NUTRIT, AUBURN UNIV, 53- *Personal Data:* b McLinna Co, Tex, Nov 2, 16. *Educ:* Cornell Univ, PhD(nutrit), 52. *Concurrent Pos:* Consult nutrit, 80- *Mailing Add:* 8173 W Lake Rd Riesel TX 76682-3507

ANTHONY-TWAROG, BARBARA JEAN, ASTRONOMY. *Current Pos:* from asst prof to assoc prof, 82-92, PROF ASTRON, UNIV KANS, 92- *Personal Data:* b 1953; m 77, Bruce A; c Nathaniel R & Anthony A. *Educ:* Univ Notre Dame, BS, 75; Yale Univ, MS, 77, PhD(astron), 81. *Prof Exp:* Instr astron, Univ Tex, Austin, 80-82. *Mem:* Am Astron Soc; Int Astron Union; Sigma Xi. *Res:* Stellar photometry in open and globular clusters; white dwarf progenitors; digital image processing. *Mailing Add:* Dept Physics & Astron Univ Kans Lawrence KS 66045-2151. *Fax:* 785-864-5262; *E-Mail:* anthony@kuphsx.phsx.ukans.edu

ANTIPA, GREGORY ALEXIS, PROTOZOOLOGY, CELL BIOLOGY. *Current Pos:* from asst prof to assoc prof 78-86, actg dir res, 86-89, PROF BIOL, SAN FRANCISCO STATE UNIV, 86- *Personal Data:* b San Francisco, Calif, Aug 9, 41; wid; c Alexander Thoma & Christopher Alexis. *Educ:* Univ Calif, Berkeley, AB, 63; San Francisco State Univ, MA, 66; Univ Ill, Urbana-Champaign, PhD(zool), 70. *Prof Exp:* NIH fel cell biol, Univ Chicago, 70-71; AEC fel, Argonne Nat Lab, 71-74; asst prof biol, Wayne State Univ, 74-78. *Concurrent Pos:* NSF grant, San Francisco State Univ, 78-; vis scientist, Zool Sta, Ville Franche-sur-Mer, France, 97- *Mem:* Soc Integrative & Comp Biol; Am Soc Cell Biol; Am Soc Zoologists; Micros Soc Am; Soc Protozoologists; AAAS. *Res:* Temporal events and control of eukaryotic and circadian cell cycles; fine structure; development and phylogeny of ciliates; ciliated protozoa as indicators of water quality and role in activated sludge process. *Mailing Add:* Dept Biol San Francisco State Univ 1600 Holloway Ave San Francisco CA 94132

ANTKIW, STEPHEN, NUCLEAR PHYSICS. *Current Pos:* RETIRED. *Personal Data:* b Passaic, NJ, Sept 27, 22. *Educ:* Marietta Col, BS, 47; Univ Del, MS, 53. *Prof Exp:* Physicist x-rays, Atomic & Nuclear Physics Div, Nat Bur Standards, 47-49, physicist nuclear, 49-50, physicist mass spectrometry, 51-53; res physicist nuclear & mass spectrometry, Nucleonics Group, US Geol Surv, 53-54; res physicist, 56-61, sr res physicist nuclear, Schlumberger-Doll Res Ctr, 61-86; consult, 89-97. *Mem:* Am Phys Soc; Sigma Xi. *Res:* Experimental nuclear physics; gamma ray spectroscopy; nuclear radiation detectors; scintillation counters; neutron induced reactions; neutron transport; coincidence techniques; x-ray shielding and dosimetry; mass spectrometry; nuclear well logging. *Mailing Add:* 104 Blackman Rd Ridgefield CT 06877

ANTLE, CHARLES EDWARD, MATHEMATICAL STATISTICS, BIOSTATISTICS. *Current Pos:* assoc prof, 62-64, EMER PROF STATIST, PA STATE UNIV, 64- *Personal Data:* b East View, Ky, Nov 11, 30; m 53; c 3. *Educ:* Eastern Ky State Col, BS, 54, MA, 55; Okla State Univ, PhD(math), 62. *Prof Exp:* Aerophysics engr, Gen Dynamics/Convair, 55-57; from instr to asst prof math, Univ Mo, Rolla, 57-60. *Concurrent Pos:* Adj prof, Sch Pub Health, Univ Pittsburgh. *Mem:* Am Statist Asn; Inst Math Statist; Royal Statist Soc; Biomet Soc. *Res:* Biostatistics; reliability; Bayesian decision rules; the Weibull Model; stopping rules for clinical trials. *Mailing Add:* Dept Statist Pa State Univ 326 Thomas Bldg University Park PA 16802-6106

ANTLER, MORTON, TRIBOLOGY, ELECTRICAL CONTACTS. *Current Pos:* PRES & PRIN CONSULT, CONTACT CONSULTS, INC, 89- *Personal Data:* b New York, NY, Apr 27, 28; m 50, Esther Baron; c 3. *Educ:* NY Univ, BA, 48; Cornell Univ, PhD(inorg chem), 53. *Honors & Awards:* Sci Achievement & Precious Metal Plating Awards, Am Electroplaters & Surface Finishers Soc, 68, 71 & 87; Capt Alfred E Hunt Mem Award, Soc Tribologists

& Lubrication Engrs, 71; Spec Recognition Award, Int Inst Connector & Interconnection Technol, Inc, 75; Ralph Armington & Ragnar Holm Sci Achievement Awards, Inst Elec & Electronics Engrs, 80, 89 & 90; Award of Merit, Am Soc Testing & Mat, 88. *Prof Exp:* Res chemist, Ethyl Corp, 53-58; supvr phys chem, Borg-Warner Res Ctr, 58-59; adv chemist, Eng Lab, Int Bus Mach Corp, 59-63; dep dir res, Burndy Corp, 63-70; distinguished mem tech staff, Bell Labs, 70-89. *Concurrent Pos:* Mem steering comt, Holm Conf Elec Contacts, Inst Elec & Electronics Engrs; chmn & USA rep, Adv Group, Int Conf Elec Contacts, 76-92; mem, Tech Comt Elec Contacts, Inst Elec & Electronic Engrs; instr, Elec Contacts & Connectors, Inst Elec & Electronics Engrs. *Mem:* Am Chem Soc; fel Inst Elec & Electronics Engrs; fel Am Electroplaters & Surface Finishers Soc; fel Am Soc Testing & Mat; Sigma Xi. *Res:* Inorganic and surface chemistry; friction, wear and lubrication; electric contacts; seminars and training in connector contact engineering. *Mailing Add:* 821 Strawberry Hill Rd E Columbus OH 43213. *Fax:* 614-861-2670

ANTMAN, STUART S, APPLIED MATHEMATICS, SOLID MECHANICS. *Current Pos:* PROF MATH, UNIV MD, COLLEGE PARK, 72- *Personal Data:* b Brooklyn, NY, June 2, 39; m 68, Wilma Richlin; c Rachel & Melissa. *Educ:* Rensselaer Polytech Inst, BS, 61; Univ Minn, MS, 63, PhD(mech), 65. *Honors & Awards:* Lester R Ford Award, Math Asn Am, 87. *Prof Exp:* Vis mem, Courant Inst Math Sci, NY Univ, 65-67, from asst prof to assoc prof math, 67-72. *Concurrent Pos:* Sci Res Coun Brit sr vis fel, Oxford Univ, 69-70; co-ed, Springer Tracts in Natural Philos, 72-80; prin investr, NSF grants, 72-; Soc Indust & Appl Math lectr, 73-75; vis prof, Univ de Paris-Sud, 75, Heriot-Watt Univ, Edinburgh, 77, Brown Univ, 78-79, Ecole Polytech, Palaiseau, France, 79, Univ Aut Mex, 81, Univ P&M Curie, Paris, 83 & 92, Math Sci Res Inst, Berkeley, 83, Math Res Ctr, Univ Wis, 84, Inst Math Appln, Univ Minn, 85, Univ Bonn, 87 & Univ Leipzig, 95; Guggenheim fel, 78-79; consult, Div Appl Math & Comput Sci, NSF, 80-81; mem, US Nat Comt Theoret & Appl Mech, 80-88; assoc ed, Notices of Am Math Soc, 85-87; ed-in-chief, Arch Rational Mech & Anal, 90- *Mem:* Am Math Soc; Soc Natural Philos; Soc Indust & Appl Math; Math Asn Am; Soc Interaction Mech & Math. *Res:* Nonlinear equations of solid mechanics; bifurcation and stability theory; theories of rods and shells; nonlinear differential equations. *Mailing Add:* Dept Math Univ Md College Park MD 20742. *E-Mail:* ssa@math.umd.edu

ANTOINE, JOHN EUGENE, RADIATION ONCOLOGY, CLINICAL RESEARCH. *Current Pos:* PROF RADIATION MED, LOMA LINDA MED CTR, 91-, ASSOC DIR CLIN RES, CANCER INST, 91- *Personal Data:* b Sheboygan, Wis, May 28, 37; m 87, Florence S Schwarz; c Marc & Mimi. *Educ:* Beloit Col, BS, 59; Univ Chicago, MD, 63. *Prof Exp:* Dir, Radiation Res Prog, Nat Cancer Inst, NIH, 85-91. *Concurrent Pos:* Bd dirs, Calif Div, Am Cancer Soc. *Mem:* Fel Am Col Radiol; Am Soc Therapeut Radiation & Oncol; Radiol Soc NAm; Am Soc Clin Oncol; Asn Am Med Asn; Am Col Radiation Oncol. *Res:* Radiation oncology related to proton beam therapy; multimodality clinical cancer research. *Mailing Add:* Dept Radiation Med Loma Linda Med Ctr 11234 Anderson St Loma Linda CA 92354. *Fax:* 909-799-6020; *E-Mail:* jantoine@lluci.llu.edu

ANTOLAK, ARLYN JOE, COMPUTATIONAL PHYSICS, NUMERICAL METHODS. *Current Pos:* MEM TECH STAFF, SANDIA NAT LAB, 83- *Personal Data:* b Ladysmith, Wis, Nov 11, 53; m 86. *Educ:* Univ Wis, BS, 76; Northwestern Univ, MS, 80 & PhD(appl math), 83. *Res:* Charged particle transport theory; numerical modeling; law energy particle physics. *Mailing Add:* 515 Amberina Dr Patterson CA 95363

ANTOLOVICH, STEPHEN D, MATERIALS SCIENCE, ENGINEERING. *Current Pos:* DIR, DEPT MECH & MAT ENG, WASH STATE UNIV, 94- *Personal Data:* b Milwaukee, Wis, Dec 29, 39; m 61; c 3. *Educ:* Univ Wis, Madison, BS, 62, MS, 63; Univ Calif, Berkeley, PhD(mat sci), 66. *Prof Exp:* Lectr, Univ Calif, Berkeley, 66-67; res metallurgist, Lawrence Radiation Lab, Calif, 67-68; from assoc prof to prof mat sci, Univ Cincinnati, 68-83; prof & head, Dept Metall & dir, Fracture & Fatigue Res Lab, Ga Inst Technol 83-94. *Concurrent Pos:* Grants, Air Force Off Sci Res, 74-, Nat Aeronaut & Space Admin, 76- & NATO, 78-; pres, Metall Res Consult Inc. *Mem:* Am Soc Metals; Am Soc Mech Engr; Am Soc Testing & Mat; assoc Inst Mining Engrs. *Res:* Fatigue and fracture of metallic materials; mathematical models of fatigue crack propagation and low cycle fatigue; electron microscopy; high temperature low cycle fatigue; composite materials. *Mailing Add:* Dept Mech & Mat Eng Wash State Univ Pullman WA 99164-2920

ANTON, AARON HAROLD, PHARMACOLOGY. *Current Pos:* EMER PROF ANESTHESIOL & PHARMACOL, SCH MED, CASE WESTERN RES UNIV, 92- *Personal Data:* b Hartford, Conn, Sept 4, 21; m 47, Marie V (Kohout); c 2. *Educ:* Univ Conn, BS, 44; Trinity Col, Conn, BS, 52; Yale Univ, PhD(pharmacol), 56. *Prof Exp:* Instr pharmacol, Col Med, Univ Fla, 56-59, asst prof psychiat, 59-65, from assoc prof to prof anesthesiol & pharmacol, Div Anesthesiol, 65-69. *Mem:* Am Soc Pharmacol; Sigma Xi; AAAS; NY Acad Sci; Am Soc Anesthesiologists. *Res:* Biochemical changes in hypertension and mental disease; pharmacological significance of protein binding. *Mailing Add:* Dept Anesthesiol Sch Med Case Western Res Univ Cleveland OH 44106. *Fax:* 216-844-3781; *E-Mail:* ahan@po.cwru.edu

ANTON, DAVID L, ENZYMOLOGY, BIOCATALYSIS. *Current Pos:* prin investr enzymol, E I Du Pont de Nemours, 83-88, proj leader, 88-92, res supvr, 92-94, RES MGR, E I DUPONT DE NEMOURS, 94- *Personal Data:* b Seattle, Wash, Mar 20, 53; m 75; c 2. *Educ:* Univ Calif, Berkeley, AB, 75; Univ Minn, PhD(biochem), 80. *Prof Exp:* Fel biochem, Brandeis Univ, 80-82; res assoc, Harvard Med Sch, 82-83. *Concurrent Pos:* Technol leader biocatalysis, E I du Pont de Nemours, 88. *Mem:* Am Soc Biochem & Molecular Biol; Am Chem Soc. *Res:* Development of fermentation and enzymatic processes for the industrial production of chemicals and intermediate; metabolic pathway engineering; enzyme mechanism and inhibitors for pharmaceutical and agricultural applications. *Mailing Add:* Cent Res Exp Sta 328/248 E I du Pont de Nemours Wilmington DE 19880-0328. *Fax:* 302-695-9861; *E-Mail:* antondl@a1.esvax.umc.dupont.com

ANTON, HOWARD, MATHEMATICS. *Current Pos:* PRES, ANTON TEXTBOOKS, INC, 83- *Personal Data:* b Philadelphia, Pa, July 27, 39; m 65; c 3. *Educ:* Lehigh Univ, BA, 60; Univ Ill, MA, 63; Polytech Inst Brooklyn, PhD(math), 68. *Prof Exp:* Mathematician, Burroughs Corp, 60-61; lectr math, Hunter Col, City Univ New York, 64-66; assoc prof math, Drexel Univ, 68-83. *Mem:* Am Math Soc; Sigma Xi; Math Asn Am. *Res:* Functional analysis; Banach algebras; distribution theory; approximation theory; linear algebra; calculus; finite mathematics; computer software for linear algebra. *Mailing Add:* Anton Text Books Inc 2301 Evesham Rd Suite 506 Voorhees NJ 08043-4506

ANTONACCIO, MICHAEL JOHN, PHARMACOLOGY. *Current Pos:* VPRES, CV RES & DEVELOP, BRISTOL-MYERS SQUIBB CO, 83- *Personal Data:* b Yonkers, NY, Mar 6, 43; m 78; c 1. *Educ:* Duquesne Univ, BS, 66; Univ Mich, PhD(pharmacol), 70. *Honors & Awards:* Goldblatt Award, 81. *Prof Exp:* From sr scientist I, Geigy Pharmaceut to sr scientist II, 70-73, sr staff scientist, 73-75, mgr CV pharmacol, 75-77; dir pharmacol, Squibb Inst Med Res, 77-81; vpres, new drug discovery, Schering-Plough Corp, 81-83. *Mem:* Am Soc Exp Ther & Pharmacol; Soc Neurosci; Int Soc Hypertension. *Res:* Central regulation of blood pressure; resin-angiotensin system in the control of blood pressure. *Mailing Add:* Human Genome Sci Inc 9410 Key West Ave Rockville MD 20850-3338

ANTONELLI, PETER LOUIS, TOPOLOGY, GEOMETRY. *Current Pos:* assoc prof, 70-79, PROF MATH, UNIV ALTA, 79- *Personal Data:* b Syracuse, NY, Mar 5, 41; div; c 2. *Educ:* Syracuse Univ, BS, 63, MA, 65, PhD(math), 67. *Prof Exp:* Asst prof math, Univ Tenn, Knoxville, 67-68; fel, Inst Advan Study, Princeton, 68-70. *Concurrent Pos:* Fel biol, Univ Sussex, Eng, 72-73. *Mem:* Am Math Soc; Can Math Cong; Can Appl Math Soc. *Res:* Mathematical genetics and ecology; geometric diffusion and theoretical developmental biology and non-linear growth mechanics. *Mailing Add:* Dept Math Univ Alta Edmonton AB T6G 2M7 Can

ANTONIADES, HARRY NICHOLAS, biochemistry; deceased, see previous edition for last biography

ANTONIAK, CHARLES EDWARD, BAYESIAN STATISTICAL ANALYSIS, ACOUSTO-OPTIC ELECTRONICS. *Current Pos:* PRIN STAFF ENGR, LOCKHEED-ONT, 83- *Personal Data:* b Norfolk, Va, Apr 11, 40; m 64, Jeanette M Leavenworth; c Catherine & Michael. *Educ:* Calif Inst Technol, BS, 60; Calif State Univ, San Diego, MS, 63; Univ Calif, Los Angeles, PhD(math), 69. *Prof Exp:* Res physicist, US Navy Electronics Lab, San Diego, 60-61, opers analyst, 63-65, res math, 65-70; asst prof statist, Univ Calif, Berkeley, 70-76; mem Tech Staff, Bell Tel Labs, 76-83. *Concurrent Pos:* Off Naval Res grant, Univ Calif, Berkeley, 71-77; consult, Lawrence-Berkeley Lab, 74-75; expert witness, Alameda County, Fed Appeals Court, 73. *Mem:* Am Math Soc; Math Asn Am; Inst Elec & Electronics Eng; Inst Math Statist; Am Statist Asn; fel Inst Adv Eng; Am Soc Qual Control. *Res:* Bayesian, distribution free and sequential applied statistics especially signal detection and data compression; RF spectral analysis using acousto-optic technology; multidisciplinary problem solving; granted 2 patents for signal processing innovations. *Mailing Add:* 98 Carson Upland CA 91786. *Fax:* 909-395-6500

ANTONIEWICZ, PETER R, THEORETICAL SOLID STATE PHYSICS, SURFACE PHYSICS. *Current Pos:* Asst prof, 65-70, ASSOC PROF PHYSICS, UNIV TEX, AUSTIN, 70- *Personal Data:* b Tarnow, Poland, Feb 5, 36; US citizen; m 61; c 3. *Educ:* NC State Univ, BS, 59; Purdue Univ, MS, 64, PhD, 65. *Mem:* AAAS; Am Phys Soc; Am Asn Physics Teachers. *Mailing Add:* 3009 Carlisle Dr Austin TX 78757

ANTONIOU, A(NDREAS), ELECTRICAL ENGINEERING. *Current Pos:* chmn dept, 83-90, PROF ELEC & COMPUT ENG, UNIV VICTORIA, 83- *Personal Data:* b Cyprus, Mar 3, 38; Can Citizen; wid, Rosemary; c Anthony, David, Dino & Helen. *Educ:* Univ London, BSc, 63, PhD, 66. *Honors & Awards:* Christopher Columbus Premium, Post Off Res Dept UK, 68; Ambrose Fleming Premium, Inst Elec Engrs, 69. *Prof Exp:* Mem sci staff, GEC Ltd, Eng, 66; sr sci officer, Post Off Res Dept, Eng, 66-69; mem sci staff, Northern Elec Co, Ltd, 69-70; from asst prof to prof elec eng, Concordia Univ, 70-83 & chmn dept, 77-83. *Concurrent Pos:* Assoc ed, Inst Elec & Electronics Engrs Trans Circuits & Systs, 83-85, ed, 85-87; counr, Asn Prof Engrs & Geoscientists BC, 88-90. *Mem:* Fel Inst Elec Engrs UK; fel Inst Elec & Electronics Engrs. *Res:* Passive and active networks; active and digital filters; digital signal processing; optimization methods. *Mailing Add:* Dept Elec & Comput Eng Univ Victoria PO Box 3055 Victoria BC V8W 3P6 Can. *Fax:* 250-721-6052; *E-Mail:* andreas@ece/.uvic.ca

ANTONOFF, MARVIN M, THEORETICAL PHYSICS, SOLID STATE PHYSICS. *Current Pos:* from asst prof to assoc prof, 65-78, PROF PHYSICS, UNIV MASS, BOSTON, 78- CHMN DEPT, 68- *Personal Data:* b New York, NY, Nov 29, 30; m 53; c 3. *Educ:* NY Univ, BS, 52, MA, 53; Cornell Univ, PhD(solid state physics), 62. *Prof Exp:* Staff mem, Gen Elec Co, NY,

55-59; asst physics, Cornell Univ, 59-61; staff mem, Lincoln Lab, Mass Inst Technol, 61-62 & Sperry Rand Res Ctr, 62-65. *Concurrent Pos:* Guest scientist, Nat Magnet Lab, Mass Inst Technol, 70-; fel, UK Atomic Energy Res Establishment, Harwell, 71-72; consult, Kennecott Copper Corp, 74-75; vis prof, Tufts Univ, 80- *Mem:* Am Phys Soc; Inst Elec & Electronics Eng. *Res:* Theory of cooperative phenomena in solid state physics, especially ferromagnetism and superconductivity; theory of semiconductor devices; computer-based data acquisition and laboratory automation systems. *Mailing Add:* Dept Physics Univ Mass Boston MA 02125. *Fax:* 617-265-7173

ANTONSEN, DONALD HANS, industrial chemistry, for more information see previous edition

ANTONSSON, ERIK KARL, COMPUTER-AIDED ENGINEERING DESIGN, MEMS DESIGN. *Current Pos:* from asst prof to assoc prof, 84-96, PROF MECH ENG, CALIF INST TECHNOL, 97- *Personal Data:* b Milwaukee, Wis, Aug 7, 54; m 85; c 3. *Educ:* Cornell Univ, BS, 76; Mass Inst Technol, MS, 78, PhD(mech eng), 82. *Honors & Awards:* Richard P Feyman Prize, 95. *Prof Exp:* Asst prof mech eng, Univ Utah, 83; asst prof orthop biomech, Harvard Univ, 84. *Concurrent Pos:* Presidential Young Investr, NSF, 85; assoc ed, Am Soc Mech Engrs J Mech Design, 89- *Mem:* Am Soc Mech Engrs; Soc Mfg Engrs; Inst Elec & Electronics Engrs. *Res:* Engineering design; computer aided design and computer aided engineering; representing and manipulating imprecision in preliminary engineering design; structured design of micro-electrical-mechanical systems. *Mailing Add:* Eng & Appl Sci 104-44 Calif Inst Technol Pasadena CA 91125-0002

ANTONUCCI, FRANK RALPH, ORGANIC CHEMISTRY, ENVIRONMENTAL ANALYSIS. *Current Pos:* mgr analytical serv, 84-91, DEPT LEADER ENVIRON TECHNOL, CHAMPION INT CORP, 91- *Personal Data:* b Auburn, NY, Sept 8, 46; m 68, Mary E Bellew; c Donald & Philip. *Educ:* St Michaels Col, BA, 68; Col of Holy Cross, MS, 69; Rensselaer Polytech Inst, PhD(org chem), 73. *Prof Exp:* Sr res chemist, Addressograph-Multigraph Corp, 75-77; group leader, St Regis Paper Co, 77-84. *Mem:* Am Chem Soc; Tech Asn Pulp & Paper Indust; Am Soc Testing Mats. *Res:* spectroscopy and chromatography; environmental analysis; ultratrace organic analysis. *Mailing Add:* 3 North Dr Washingtonville NY 10992-1903. *Fax:* 914-578-7272

ANTONUCCI, TAMMY, CLINICAL RESEARCH. *Current Pos:* CLIN SCIENTIST, PARKE-DAVIS PHARMACEUT, 90- *Personal Data:* b San Francisco, Calif, May 2, 58. *Educ:* Univ Calif, Berkeley, BS, 80; Univ Mich, MS, 82, PhD(human genetics), 85. *Prof Exp:* Res fac virol, Univ Mich, 85-86, Univ Calif, San Francisco, 86-90. *Mem:* AAAS; Am Soc Microbiol. *Res:* Clinical research. *Mailing Add:* Parke-Davis Pharmaceut Res Div Warner-Lambert Co 2800 Plymouth Rd Ann Arbor MI 48105-2430

ANTOSIEWICZ, HENRY ALBERT, MATHEMATICAL ANALYSIS, ORDINARY DIFFERENTIAL EQUATIONS. *Current Pos:* vis assoc prof, Univ Southern Calif, 58-59, assoc prof, 59-61, chmn math dept, 68-77, UNIV PROF MATH, UNIV SOUTHERN CALIF, 61- *Personal Data:* b Wollersdorf, Austria, May 14, 25; US citizen; m 58, 70, 80; c 1. *Educ:* Univ Vienna, PhD(math, theoret physics), 47. *Prof Exp:* Assoc prof math, Mont State Col, 48-52; assoc prof, Am Univ, 52-55, adj prof, 55-57; assoc ed, Math Rev, 57-58. *Concurrent Pos:* Mathematician, Nat Bur Stand, 52-57; consult, Space Technol Labs, Thompson-Ramo-Wooldridge, Inc, 59-70; consult var financial insts, 74-; mem bd trustees, Math Sci Res Inst, Berkeley, 81-; dir, Beaumont & Co, Newport Beach, 84-88. *Res:* Qualitative theory of ordinary differential equations; applications to finance. *Mailing Add:* Dept Math Univ Southern Calif Los Angeles CA 90089-1113

ANTROBUS, JOHN SIMMONS, SPEECH PERCEPTION, COGNITIVE PSYCHOLOGY. *Current Pos:* PROF PSYCHOL, CITY COL NY, 70- *Personal Data:* b Peace River, Alta, Aug 8, 32; US & Can citizen; m 88, Suzanne Salzinger; c Natalia & Nadia. *Educ:* Columbia Univ, PhD(psychol), 63. *Mem:* Am Psychol Asn; Am Psychol Soc; Int Neural Network Soc; AAAS. *Res:* Neural network simulation of speech perception with emphasis on serial and parallel filtering of speech by auditory pathway nuclei and cortical regions; cognition in sleep versus wake states. *Mailing Add:* Dept Psychol City Col NY New York NY 10031. *Fax:* 212-650-5673; *E-Mail:* psyja@ccnyvme.bitnet

ANTZELEVITCH, CHARLES, CARDIAC ELECTROPHYSIOLOGY, CARDIAC ARRHYTHMIAS. *Current Pos:* res scientist, 80-83, sr res scientist, 84, EXEC DIR & DIR RES, MASONIC MED RES LAB, 84-; PROF PHARMACOL, STATE UNIV NY HEALTH SCI CTR, SYRACUSE, 87- *Personal Data:* b Ramat-Gan, Israel, Mar 25, 51; US citizen; m 73, Brena Reisner; c Daniel & Lisa. *Educ:* City Univ New York, Queens, BA, 73; State Univ New York, Syracuse, PhD(pharmacol), 78. *Honors & Awards:* Van Horne Award, 82; Distinguished Serv Award, RAM Med Res Found, 96; Charles Henry Johnson Medal, Grand Lodge F & Am, 96. *Prof Exp:* Fel cardiol, Masonic Med Res Lab, 77-80; asst prof pharmacol, Upstate Med Ctr, 80-83; assoc prof pharmacol, State Univ NY Health Sci Ctr, Syracuse, 83-87. *Concurrent Pos:* Teaching fel, NIH, 73-80, prog dir, minority high sch student res apprentice prog, 84-85, consult, ad hoc study sect, 85, prog dir, training grant, 85-89; prin investr & co-prin, Am Heart Asn & NIH grant, 80-; consult, res peer rev comm, Am Heart Asn, 82-85, mem basic sci coun, 82-; fel, cardiovasc sect, Am Physiol Soc, 84; res comt, Am Heart Asn, 87-90; Gordon K Moe Scholar; mem bd dirs, Clin Med Network, 89-, Cent NY Heart Asn, 89-, RAM Med Res Found, 89-; mem instnl rev bd, Faxton Hosp, 90- *Mem:* Am Heart Asn; AAAS; Am Physiol Soc; Cardiac Electrophysiol Soc; NY Acad Sci; Int Soc Heart Res; fel Am Col Cardiol; Int Cardiac Electrophysiol Soc (pres, 96). *Res:* Electrophysiologic basis of cardiac arrhythmias and mechanisms of action of antiarrhythmic drugs. *Mailing Add:* Masonic Med Res Lab 2150 Bleeker St Utica NY 13501-1787. *Fax:* 315-735-5648; *E-Mail:* ca@mmrl.edu

ANUCHA, THEOPHILUS CHIBUZO, CONTROLLED RELEASE DRUG PRODUCTS, BUSINESS DEVELOPMENT & STRATEGY. *Current Pos:* RES & DEVELOP SCIENTIST, BIOVAIL CORP INT, 95- *Personal Data:* b Aba, Nigeria, Feb 2, 50; m 84, Uzoamaka Cliche; c Adanna, Jaachi, Chizara & Alfred. *Educ:* Univ Benin, Nigeria, BPharm, 76; Univ London, UK, PhD(pharmaceut chem), 82. *Prof Exp:* Prof pharmaceut chem, Univ Benin, Nigeria, 82-92; dir pharmaceut serv, General Arabian Med Co, Saudi Arabia, 92-95. *Concurrent Pos:* Wellcome res fel, Wellcome Nigeria Ltd, 87; fel, Inst Pharm Mgt Int, UK, 83; consult, Roche Ltd, 83-85, Gama, Saudi Arabia, 92-95. *Mem:* Am Asn Pharmaceut Scientists; Pharmaceut Sci Group Can. *Res:* Pharmaceutical research and development. *Mailing Add:* 2488 Dunwin Dr Mississauga ON L5L 1J9 Can. *Fax:* 416-285-6499; *E-Mail:* anucha@cpol.com

ANURAS, SINN, INTERNAL MEDICINE, GASTROENTEROLOGY. *Current Pos:* PROF MED, TEX TECH UNIV, 85- *Personal Data:* b Bangkok, Thailand, Apr 6, 41; m 69; c 2. *Educ:* Mahidol Univ, Thailand, dipl sci, 62; Chulalongkorn Univ, Bangkok, MD, 66. *Prof Exp:* Assoc, Univ Iowa, 74-75, from asst prof to assoc prof med, 75-85. *Concurrent Pos:* Fel hepatology, Vet Admin Hosp, Boston, 70-72; fel gastroenterol, Univ Iowa, 72-74. *Mem:* Fel Am Col Physicians; Am Fedn Clin Res; Am Gastroenterol Asn; Am Asn For Study Liver Dis. *Res:* Gastrointestinal motility; clinical liver disease; control mechanisms of portal blood flow. *Mailing Add:* Dept Internal Med Tex Tech Univ Health Sci Ctr Lubbock TX 79430

ANUSAVICE, KENNETH JOHN, PORCELAINS, CERAMICS. *Current Pos:* PROF & CHMN DEPT DENT BIOMAT, COL DENT, UNIV FLA, GAINESVILLE, 83- *Personal Data:* b Worcester, Mass, Aug 6, 40. *Educ:* Worcester Polytechnic Inst, BS, 62; Med Col Ga, DMD, 77; Univ Fla, PhD(metall mat eng),77. *Prof Exp:* From asst prof to assoc prof, Dept Restorative Dent, Div Dental Mat, Med Col Ga, 73-83. *Concurrent Pos:* Mem, NIH oral biol & med study sect, 86-90; mem, Am Dent Asn Mat, Instruments & Equip, 90- *Mem:* Am Asn Dent Res; Am Asn Dent Sch; Int Asn Dent Res; Acad Dent Mat; Am Dent Asn. *Res:* Metal-ceramic adherence; thermal stress; thermal compatibility; solidification stress; brazing of nickel-chromium alloys; clinical dental research; optimal design of dental restorations; strengthening of ceramics; ceramic fractology. *Mailing Add:* 1000 NW 112th Terr Gainesville FL 32606

ANVERSA, PIERO, EXPERIMENTAL PATHOLOGY, CELL BIOLOGY. *Current Pos:* vis asst prof, 72-74, res assoc prof, 76-80, assoc prof, 80-82, PROF PATH, NY MED COL, 82- *Personal Data:* b Parma, Italy, Sept 11, 38; m 68; c 1. *Educ:* Univ Parma, Italy, MD, 65. *Prof Exp:* Asst prof path, Univ Parma, Italy, 66-78. *Concurrent Pos:* Fel, North Atlantic Treaty Orgn, 71-72. *Mem:* Int Study Group Res Cardiac Metab; Int Soc Stereology; Am Heart Asn. *Res:* Quantitative structure and function of the heart and kidney; light and electron microscopic morphometry. *Mailing Add:* Dept Path NY Med Col Vosburgh Pavillion Rm 303 Valhalla NY 10595-1690

ANWAR, RASHID AHMAD, BIOCHEMISTRY. *Current Pos:* from res assoc to assoc prof, 63-74, PROF BIOCHEM, UNIV TORONTO, 74- *Personal Data:* b Nakodar, India, Oct 15, 30; m 63. *Educ:* Univ Panjab, WPakistan, BSc, 51, MSc, 52; Mich State Univ, PhD(chem), 57. *Prof Exp:* Lectr pharmaceut chem, Univ Panjab, WPakistan, 52-54; asst biochem, Mich State Univ, 55-57, res instr, 57-60. *Concurrent Pos:* Nat Res Coun Can fel, 60-62. *Mem:* AAAS; Am Chem Soc; Am Soc Biol Chem; Can Biochem Soc. *Res:* Proteolytic enzymes; structure of proteins; bacterial cell wall biosynthesis. *Mailing Add:* Dept Biochem Univ Toronto MSB Toronto ON M5S 1A8 Can

ANWAY, ALLEN R, PHYSICS, ELECTRONICS. *Current Pos:* CONSULT, 88-; PARTNER, A2D2 ELECTRONICS, 88- *Personal Data:* b Cloquet, Minn, Mar 19, 41; m 64, Dorothy Comstock; c Carol (Wiese), Karen & Ruth. *Educ:* Univ Minn, Duluth, BA, 63; Univ Chicago, MS, 65, PhD(physics), 68. *Prof Exp:* Asst prof physics, Chicago State Col, 68-69; asst prof, Univ Wis-Superior, 69-72, lectr, 74-76 & 78-79, electronics consult, 83-88. *Concurrent Pos:* Chmn new prod div, Duluth Sci, 73-74; consult, Plaunt & Anderson & Tech Systs, Inc, 74-79. *Mem:* Am Phys Soc; Am Asn Physics Teachers; Sigma Xi. *Res:* Electronic detector of leaks in water mains. *Mailing Add:* 1219 N 21st St Superior WI 54880

ANWER, M SAWKAT, LIVER RESEARCH IN ANIMALS, VETERINARY MEDICINE. *Current Pos:* ASSOC DEAN RES, TUFTS UNIV, SCH VET MED, 84- *Personal Data:* b India. *Res:* Liver research in animals; veterinary medicine; pharmacology. *Mailing Add:* Dept Pharmacol & Med Tufts Univ Sch Vet Med 200 Westboro Rd North Grafton MA 01536-1895

ANYSAS, JURGIS ARVYDAS, CHEMICAL PHYSICS. *Current Pos:* asst prof, De Paul Univ, 66-77, chmn dept, 77-86, assoc prof, 77-, EMER PROF CHEM, DEPAUL UNIV. *Personal Data:* b Hamburg, Ger, Sept 5, 34; Can citizen; m 69, Dalia Stake. *Educ:* Univ Toronto, BASc, 56; Ill Inst Technol, PhD(chem), 66. *Prof Exp:* Geophysicist, Imp Oil Ltd, Can, 56-60. *Concurrent Pos:* Fel, Ill Inst Technol, 66-67. *Mem:* AAAS; Am Chem Soc. *Res:* Quantum chemistry; environmental chemistry; molecular spectroscopy. *Mailing Add:* Dept Chem DePaul Univ Chicago IL 60614. *Fax:* 312-362-6636

ANZALONE, LOUIS, JR, PHYTOPATHOLOGY. *Current Pos:* RETIRED. *Personal Data:* b Independence, La, Oct 7, 31; m 53; c 4. *Educ:* Southeastern La Col, BS, 54; La State Univ, MS, 56, PhD(plant path), 58. *Prof Exp:* asst bot bact & plant path, La Agr Exp Sta, La State Univ, Baton Rouge, 54-58, from asst prof to prof bot & plant path, 58-68, prof plant path & supt, Burden Res Ctr Br, 68-77, proj leader dis wheat & grain sorghum, 77-81. *Concurrent Pos:* Mem, Burden Res Found, Sugarcane Variety Comt, Rural Life Mus Comt & Centennial Comt, Exp Sta, La State Univ; Sugarcane Variety Comt; LA State Univ Exp Sta Centennial Comt; Rural Lite Mus Comt. *Mem:* Am Phytopath Soc; Sigma Xi. *Res:* Fungus diseases of ornamental plants; sugar cane breeding and pathology; virus diseases of sugar cane; diseases of winter wheat and grain sorghum. *Mailing Add:* PO Box 404 Coloma CA 95613-0404

AOKI, MASANAO, ECONOMICS, SYSTEM SCIENCE TIME SERIES. *Current Pos:* prof syst sci, 60-81, PROF COMPUT SCI, UNIV CALIF, LOS ANGELES, 84- *Personal Data:* b Hiroshima City, Japan, May 14, 31; m 62; c 1. *Educ:* Univ Calif, Los Angeles, PhD(eng), 60. *Hon Degrees:* DSc, Tokyo Inst Technol, 66. *Honors & Awards:* Fel, Control Systs Soc, Inst Elec & Electronic Engrs; fel, Economet Soc. *Prof Exp:* Prof econ, Inst Social & Econ Res, 81-84. *Concurrent Pos:* Prof econ, Univ Ill, 71-73. *Mem:* Inst Elec & Electronic Engrs; Am Econ Asn; Economet Soc; Soc Econ Dynamics & Control. *Res:* Economics; decision analysis. *Mailing Add:* Dept Econ Univ Calif Los Angeles CA 90095

AOKI, TADAO, VIROLOGY, INTERNAL MEDICINE & BIOLOGY. *Current Pos:* DIR, MED SCI LAB, AJINOMOTO CO INC, 88- *Personal Data:* b Niigata City, Japan; m 40, Junko Kitamura; c Manato & Tomoo. *Educ:* Niigata Univ Sch Med, MD, 30, PhD(internal med), 36. *Prof Exp:* Clin assoc internal med, Nigate Sch Med, 36-62; sect head tumor immunol, NY, 62-70; head immunol, NIH, 70-77; chief, Internal Med & Res Div, Shinrakuen Hosp, 77-88. *Concurrent Pos:* Sci consult, Furirebio Inc, 77-92. *Mem:* Int Asn Immunopharmacol; Am Asn Cancer Res; Am Asn Immunologists. *Res:* Action mechanism of antiviral agents; low known killer syndrome as amino deficiency. *Mailing Add:* Ajinomoto Co Bio Tech Res Labs 3 Taft Ct Rockville MD 20850-5315

AOYAMA, HIROYUKI, STRUCTURAL ENGINEERING. *Current Pos:* lectr, 60-64, assoc prof, 64-78, PROF, UNIV TOKYO, 93- *Personal Data:* b Tokyo, Japan, July 14, 32; m 60, Kikko Sugiura; c Masaka & Nobuyuki. *Educ:* Univ Tokyo, BA, 55, MA, 57, DEng, 60. *Honors & Awards:* Alfred E Lindau Award, Am Concrete Inst, 95. *Prof Exp:* Emer prof, Nihon Univ, 78-93, prof, 93-96. *Concurrent Pos:* Vis researcher, Univ Ill, 61-63, vis prof, 71-72; vis prof, Univ Canterbury, 80-81; grantee, Univ Tex, Austin, 89. *Mem:* Foreign assoc Nat Acad Eng; NZ Nat Soc Earthquake Eng; Am Soc Civil Engrs; Japan Concrete Inst; Japan Soc Civil Engrs. *Mailing Add:* 4-2-13 Takadanobaba Shinjuku-Ku Tokyo 169 Japan

AOYAMA, ISAO, WATER QUALITY ENGINEERING, ENVIRONMENTAL POLLUTION & CONTROL. *Current Pos:* assoc prof, 77-90, PROF, RES INST BIORESOURCES, OKAYAMA UNIV, 90-, DIR, 94- *Personal Data:* b Kyoto, Japan, Nov 1, 42; m 76, Naoko Mikuriya; c Chihiro & Tomotsugu. *Educ:* Kyoto Univ, BS, 66, MS, 68, PhD(eng), 76. *Prof Exp:* Res assoc, Kyoto Univ, 71-77. *Concurrent Pos:* Counr, Kobayashi Found Stud Abroad, 82-; ed, Int J Environ Toxicol & Water Qual, 84-; chmn, Environ Pollution Protectional Coun Okayama, 89; dir, Soc Res Seto Inlandsea, 92- *Mem:* Int Asn Water Qual. *Res:* Many kinds of hazardous chemicals are released to an aquatic environment through human activities; investigate the fate and effects of chemicals in an aquatic ecosystem. *Mailing Add:* 2-20-1 Chuo Kurashiki 710 Japan. *Fax:* 81-86-434-1233

APAI, GUSTAV RICHARD, II, SURFACE CHEMISTRY,. *Current Pos:* res chemist, 77-80, SR RES CHEMIST, EASTMAN KODAK CO, NY, 80- *Personal Data:* b Elyria, Ohio, May 27, 46; m 80. *Educ:* Univ Col, BA, 68; Univ Calif, Berkeley, MS, 70, PhD(chem), 77. *Prof Exp:* Commun & electronics officer, US Air Force, 70-74. *Mem:* Am Phys Soc; Sigma Xi. *Res:* Electronic structure of small metallic clusters and surfaces of bulk materials; surface chemistry studies in heterogeneous catalysis. *Mailing Add:* 110 Bay Knoll Rd Rochester NY 14622-3032

APEL, CHARLES TURNER, EMISSION SPECTROSCOPY, ANALYTICAL CHEMISTRY. *Current Pos:* RETIRED. *Personal Data:* b Kearney, Nebr, Apr 28, 31; m 58, Rita Martinez; c Charles A, Bernadette (Miller), David, Peter & Valerie. *Educ:* Morehead State Univ, BS, 52; Iowa State Univ, MS, 56. *Prof Exp:* Teaching asst chem, Iowa State Univ, 53-54; res asst phys chem, Ames Lab, Dept Energy, 54-56; analytical chemist, Los Alamos Nat Lab, 56-67, emission spectrochemist analytical chem, 67-79, spectrochem sect leader, 79-86, spectrochemist, 86-89, environ spectrochemist, 89-93. *Mem:* Am Chem Soc; Soc Appl Spectros. *Res:* Emission spectrochemistry with emphasis on the inductively coupled plasma source and the computerization and automation of analytical techniques; special interest in nebulizers; development of fritted disk nebulizer; lasers in analytical chemistry; computer programming and interfacing. *Mailing Add:* 1331 Sage Loop Los Alamos NM 87544-2963

APEL, JOHN RALPH, WAVES AND INSTABILITIES, REMOTE SENSING. *Current Pos:* asst dir, 82-84, CHIEF SCIENTIST, MILTON EISENHOWER RES CTR, APPL PHYSICS LAB, JOHNS HOPKINS UNIV, 84- *Personal Data:* b Absecon, NJ, June 14, 30; m 56, Martha E Davis; c Denise A (Jay) & Jacqueline J. *Educ:* Univ Md, BS, 57, MS, 61; Johns Hopkins Univ, PhD(plasma physics), 70. *Honors & Awards:* Gold Medal, US Dept Com, 74. *Prof Exp:* Assoc mathematician, Appl Physics Lab, Johns Hopkins Univ, 57-61, sr physicist, 61-70, asst supvr plasma dynamics, 66-70; supvry physicist & dir, Ocean Remote Sensing Lab, Atlantic Oceanog & Meteorol Labs, Nat Oceanic & Atmospheric Admin, Fla, 70-76, Pac Marine Environ Lab, Nat Oceanic & Atmospheric Admin, Wash, 76-81. *Concurrent Pos:* Adj prof physics, Univ Miami, 71-76; consult, NASA, 72-, Dept Defense, 73-, UNESCO/Intergovt Oceanog Comn, 75-80, Int Coun Explor Sea, 78-81; mem comn F, Int Union Radio Sci, 73-, Int Union Comn on Radio Meterol, 75-80 & Sci Comt Oceanic Res, 81-85; expert witness, US House Rep & US Senate, 74; chmn ocean dynamics subcomt, Space Appl Comn, NASA, 73-76; affil prof oceanog & atmospheric sci, Univ Wash, 76-81; sr fel, Joint Inst for Study of Atmosphere & Ocean & Joint Inst for Marine & Atmospheric Res, 77-82; mem, US Nat Comt, Int Union Geod & Geophys, 82-87, Comt Ocean Sci from Shuttle, Off Naval Res, 84-88, adv comt, Inst Naval Oceanog, Univ Corp Atmospheric Res, 88- & Comt Earth Sci, Nat Acad Sci, 88-; lectr, Johns Hopkins Univ, 85-; ed-in-chief, Johns Hopkins APL Tech Digest, 87-89; ed, Rev Geophys, 88-90; interim dir, Inst Naval Oceanog, 92. *Mem:* Am Phys Soc; Am Geophys Union; Sigma Xi; NY Acad Sci; Explorers Club; Norweg Acad Tech Sci. *Res:* Fluid and plasma instabilities; waves in fluids; physical oceanography; ocean remote sensing; electromagnetic interactions with ocean surface. *Mailing Add:* 14605 Carrolton Rd Rockville MD 20853. *Fax:* 301-460-7018

APELIAN, DIRAN, MATERIALS SCIENCE. *Current Pos:* from asst prof to assoc prof, 76-90, HOWMUTH PROF ENG, DREXEL UNIV, 90-; EXEC DIR, METAL PROCESSING INST, WORCHESTER POLYTECH INST, 96- *Personal Data:* b Oct 28, 45; m 76; c 2. *Educ:* Drexel Univ, BS, 68; Mass Inst Technol, ScD, 72. *Prof Exp:* Teaching asst, Mass Inst Technol, 69-72; sr res engr metall, Bethlehem Steel Corp, 72-75. *Concurrent Pos:* Consult, var corp, 79-; vis prof, Katholieke Univ, Belg, 81; provost vpres acad affairs, Worcester Polytech Inst, 90-96. *Mem:* AAAS; Am Inst Minerals Metall & Petrol Eng; Am Soc Metals; Am Inst Chem Eng; Am Powder Metall Inst. *Res:* Field of solidification processing; liquid metal filtration; development of rapid cycle casting technologies such as diffusion solidification; rheocasting; low pressure plasma processing; injection of secondary phases and dissolution kinetics. *Mailing Add:* Exec Dir Metal Processing Inst Worchester Polytech Inst 100 Institute Rd Worchester MA 01609-2280

APFEL, JOSEPH H, OPTICAL THIN FILM PHYSICS. *Current Pos:* staff mem, Optical Coating Lab Inc, 61, dir corp res, vpres & chief tech officer, STAFF MEM, OPTICAL COATING LAB INC, 61- *Personal Data:* m 54, Phyllis Murray. *Educ:* Univ Calif, Berkeley, AB, 54, MA, 56, PhD(physics), 59. *Honors & Awards:* Joseph Fraunhofer Award, Optical Soc Am, 95, Robert M Burley Prize, 95. *Mem:* Fel Optical Soc Am. *Res:* Contributed numerous articles to science journals. *Mailing Add:* 1501 Park St Santa Rosa CA 95404-3642. *E-Mail:* joe_apfel@compuserve.com

APFEL, ROBERT EDMUND, ACOUSTICS, FLUID PHYSICS. *Current Pos:* from asst prof to assoc prof, Yale Univ, 71-81, prof eng & appl sci & chmn, Dept Mech, 81-82, chmn, Coun Eng, 88-90, CHMN, DEPT MECH ENG, YALE UNIV, 82-86 & 91- *Personal Data:* b New York, NY, Mar 16, 43; m 68; c Darren & Alison. *Educ:* Tufts Univ, BA, 64; Harvard Univ, MA, 67, PhD(appl physics), 70. *Honors & Awards:* A B Wood Medal & Prize, Inst Physics, Gt Brit, 71; Biennial Award, Acoust Soc Am, 76. *Prof Exp:* Res fel acoust, Harvard Univ, 70-71. *Concurrent Pos:* Independent consult acoust, 74-; pres, Apfel Enterprises, Inc, New Haven, Conn, 87- *Mem:* Fel Acoust Soc Am (vpres, 91-92); Am Phys Soc; Am Asn Physics Teachers; Am Soc Mech Engrs. *Res:* Study of superheated, supercooled, supersaturated and/or tensilely stressed liquids, possibly irradiated, with emphasis on acoustical techniques for producing phase changes or probing properties of liquids and biological materials; neutron detection with superheated drops; safety of diagnostic ultrasound; cavitation phenomena. *Mailing Add:* 92 Anita St New Haven CT 06511

APGAR, BARBARA JEAN, NUTRITION. *Current Pos:* RETIRED. *Personal Data:* b Tyler, Tex, Mar 4, 36. *Educ:* Tex Woman's Univ, BA, 57; Cornell Univ, MS, 59, PhD(biochem), 64. *Prof Exp:* Res chemist, Soil & Nutrit Lab, US Plant, 59-97. *Mem:* Am Soc Animal Sci; Am Inst Nutrit. *Res:* Effect of zinc deficiency on reproduction in the female. *Mailing Add:* US Plant Plant Soil & Nutrit Lab Ithaca NY 14853. *Fax:* 607-255-2459

APIRION, DAVID, nucleic acids, microbial genetics, for more information see previous edition

APLAN, FRANK F(ULTON), METALLURGY, MINERAL ENGINEERING. *Current Pos:* prof mineral prep & head dept, Pa State Univ, 68-71, prof, 68-90, chmn, Mineral Processing Sect, 71-77, chmn, Metall Sect, 73-75, DISTINGUISHED PROF METALL & MINERAL PROCESSING, PA STATE UNIV, 90- *Personal Data:* b Boulder, Colo, Aug 11, 23; m 55, Clare M Donaghue; c Susan, Peter & Lucy. *Educ:* SDak Sch Mines & Technol, BS, 48; Mont Sch Mines, MS, 50; Mass Inst Technol, ScD(metall), 57. *Hon Degrees:* Minl, Engr Mont Col Mineral Sci & Technol, 68. *Honors & Awards:* Richards Award, Am Inst Mining, Metall & Petrol Engrs, 78; Taggart Award, 85; Eng Found Award, Nat Acad Eng, 89; Gaudin Award, 92; Award for Educ, Am Inst Mech Engrs, 92. *Prof Exp:* Mill engr, Climax Molybdenum Co, 50-51; asst prof metall, Univ Wash, 51-53; sr scientist, Kennecott Copper Corp, 57; res & develop group mgr, Mineral Eng, Mining & Metals Div, Union Carbide Corp, 57-67. *Concurrent Pos:* Chmn, Minerals & Metall Processing Div, Soc Mining Engrs, 72-73, mem bd dirs, 73-76; mem bd dirs, Engr Found, 77-90, chmn, 85-87. *Mem:* Nat Acad Eng; Am Chem Soc; Am Inst Chem Engrs; Am Soc Metals; Sigma Xi; Am Filtration Soc; hon mem Am Inst Mining Metal & Petrol Engrs; Archaeol Inst Am; Soc Mining Engrs; Metall Soc; Am Inst Mech Engrs. *Res:* Mineral process engineering;

ore and coal preparation; flotation; flocculation and dispersion; applied surface chemistry; particulate matter systems; hydrometallurgy; pollution control. *Mailing Add:* Mineral Processing Sect Pa State Univ University Park PA 16802. *Fax:* 814-865-3248

APLEY, MARTYN LINN, INVERTEBRATE ZOOLOGY, AQUATIC ECOLOGY. *Current Pos:* ASSOC PROF BIOL, WESTERN STATE COL, COLO, 78- *Personal Data:* b Fairbury, Nebr, May 27, 38. *Educ:* Kans State Univ, BS, 60; Syracuse Univ, MS, 63, PhD(zool), 67. *Prof Exp:* Fel, Woods Hole Oceanog Inst, 68; fel, Freshwater Biol Lab, Copenhagen Univ, 69; asst prof biol, Brooklyn Col, 69-72, fac res award, 70-71; asst prof biol, Merrimack Col, 75-78. *Mem:* AAAS. *Res:* Physiological ecology of mollusks, biorhythms and reproductive periodicites neurosecretion and hormonal control mechanisms in invertebrates; limnology, study of high altitude lakes. *Mailing Add:* Dept Sci Western State Col 600 N Adams St Gunnison CO 81231-0001

APOSHIAN, HURAIR VASKEN, CELL BIOLOGY, PHARMACOLOGY. *Current Pos:* PROF CELL & DEVELOP BIOL & CHMN DEPT, COL LIB ARTS & PROF PHARMACOL, COL MED, UNIV ARIZ, 75- *Personal Data:* b Providence, RI, Jan 28, 26; m 48; c 3. *Educ:* Brown Univ, BS, 48; Univ Rochester, MS, 51, PhD(physiol), 54. *Honors & Awards:* Res Award, Am Col Adv Med, 87; Am Soc Toxicol. *Prof Exp:* Asst, Univ Rochester, 48-49; from instr to asst prof pharmacol, Sch Med, Vanderbilt Univ, 54-59; USPHS fel biochem, Stanford Univ, 59-62; assoc prof microbiol, Sch Med, Tufts Univ, 62-67; head dept, 67-72, prof cell biol & pharmacol, Sch Med, Univ Md, Baltimore City, 67-75. *Concurrent Pos:* Vis prof biol, Mass Inst Technol, 83. *Mem:* AAAS; Am Soc Microbiol; Am Soc Biol Chem. *Res:* Development of gene therapy; enzymology of DNA and its precursors; biochemistry of bacterial and animal virus infection; biological chelation; toxicology. *Mailing Add:* Life Sci S Rm 444 Univ Ariz PO Box 210106 Tucson AZ 85721-0106

APOSTOL, TOM M, MATHEMATICS. *Current Pos:* from asst prof to prof, 50-92, EMER PROF MATH, CALIF INST TECHNOL, 92- *Personal Data:* b Helper, Utah, Aug 20, 23; m 59. *Educ:* Univ Wash, BS, 44, MS, 46; Univ Calif, Berkeley, PhD(math), 48. *Prof Exp:* Lectr math, Univ Calif, Berkeley, 48-49; C L E Moore instr, Mass Inst Technol, 49-50. *Concurrent Pos:* Dir, Proj Math, 87- *Mem:* Am Math Soc; Math Asn Am; Nat Coun Teachers Math. *Res:* Theory of numbers. *Mailing Add:* Calif Tech 253-37 Pasadena CA 91125-0001. *E-Mail:* apostol@caltech.edu

APP, ALVA A, SOILS & PLANT SCIENCE. *Current Pos:* RETIRED. *Personal Data:* b Bridgeton, NJ, Feb 19, 32; m 86, Shirley Powers; c Jeffrey, Linda & Marylou. *Educ:* Cornell Univ, BS, 53; Rutgers Univ, MS, 55, PhD(soils), 56. *Prof Exp:* Tech adv, Valley Green Mushroom Farms, Pa, 59-61; res assoc, McCollum Pratt Inst, Johns Hopkins Univ, 61-64; assoc seed physiologist, Boyce Thompson Inst, Cornell Univ, 64-69, prog dir cell physiol & virol, 69-76, prog dir nitrogen & crop yields, 77-81; dep dir, Int Ctr Insect Physiol & Ecol, Nairobi, Kenya, 81-83; dir agr sci, Rockefeller Found, 83-87; sr sci adv, UN Develop Prog, 87-93. *Concurrent Pos:* Adj prof biochem, City Univ NY, 73-76; consult, Biochem Prog, US Army Med Res & Develop Command, 75-76 & UN Develop Progs, 76-81; vis scientist, Int Rice Res Inst, Los Banos, Philippines, 76-81; adj prof soil sci, Agron Dept, Cornell Univ, 81-83; bd dirs, Campbell Soup Co, Camden, NJ, 86- *Mem:* Fel AAAS; Am Soc Plant Physiol; Sr mem Am Chem Soc; Am Soc Agron; Tissue Cult Asn; Sigma Xi. *Res:* Soil and plant chemistry. *Mailing Add:* 95 Turtlepoint Rd Pinehurst NC 28374

APPANNA, VASU DHANANDA, STRESS BIOCHEMISTRY, CELLULAR METAL HOMEOSTASIS. *Current Pos:* asst prof, 89-92, ASSOC PROF BIOCHEM, LAURENTIAN UNIV, 93- *Personal Data:* b Poudre D'Or Hamlet, Mauritius, Sept 13, 55; Can citizen. *Prof Exp:* Fel, McGill Univ, 85-86; res assoc, Montreal Neurol Inst, 87-88. *Res:* Biochemical mechanisms mediating cellular adaptation to metals (aluminum, zinc, iron, gallium, calcium) are delineated and how living systems sense these metals and the strategies involved in attaining metal homeostases. *Mailing Add:* Dept Chem & Biochem Laurentian Univ 935 Ramsey Lake Rd Sudbury ON P3E 2C6 Can. *Fax:* 705-675-4844; *E-Mail:* vappanna@nickel.laurentian.ca

APPEL, ANDREW WILSON, COMPILERS, PROGRAMMING LANGUAGES. *Current Pos:* Asst prof, 86-92, ASSOC PROF COMPUT SCI, PRINCETON UNIV, 92- *Personal Data:* b Princeton, NJ, June 30, 60; m 85, Maia Ginsburg; c Avi & Joseph. *Educ:* Princeton Univ, AB, 81; Carnegie-Mellon Univ, PhD(comput sci) 85. *Concurrent Pos:* Consult, AT&T Bell Labs, 84-; prin investr, NSF, 86-; assoc ed, Trans Programming Lang & Systs, Asn Comput Mach, 90-92, ed-in-chief, 93- *Mem:* Asn Comput Mach. *Res:* Implementation of functional programming languages; optimizing compilers, runtime systems, garbage collection, continuation-passing style, programming environments. *Mailing Add:* 43 Philip Dr Princeton NJ 08540-2087. *E-Mail:* appel@princeton.edu

APPEL, ARTHUR GARY, URBAN ENTOMOLOGY, ENVIRONMENTAL PHYSIOLOGY. *Current Pos:* asst prof, 85-90, ASSOC PROF ENTOM, AUBURN UNIV, ALA, 90- *Personal Data:* b Inglewood, Calif, Feb 10, 58; m 87, Kim McRae; c 2. *Educ:* Univ Calif, Los Angeles, BA, 80, Riverside, MS, 82, PhD(entom), 85. *Honors & Awards:* Recog Award in Urban Entom, Entom Soc Am, 93 & 96. *Concurrent Pos:* Prin invest, Dept Entom, Auburn Univ; consult, Am Cyanamid Co, 84-, Rainbow Mfg, 85-, Bell S Serv, 86- *Mem:* Entom Soc Am; AAAS; Sigma Xi; Am Soc Zoologists; Animal Behav Soc. *Res:* Cockroach biology, behavior and physiology; urban pest biology and control; distribution and ecology of nonpest cockroaches; environmental physiology of both invertebrates and vertebrates. *Mailing Add:* Dept Entom Auburn Univ Auburn AL 36849-5413. *Fax:* 334-844-5005; *E-Mail:* aappel@acesag.auburn.edu

APPEL, DAVID W(OODHULL), HYDRAULICS. *Current Pos:* RETIRED. *Personal Data:* b Washington, DC, July 23, 24; m 49, Julia Stimson; c George D, Jane W (Snyder) & Raymond W. *Educ:* Lehigh Univ, BS, 47; Univ Iowa, MS, 49, PhD(hydraul), 53. *Honors & Awards:* Ernst Mahler Award, Kimberly-Clark Corp. *Prof Exp:* Test engr, Gen Elec Co, 47-48; asst prof, Col Eng, Univ Iowa, 49-56; from assoc prof to prof eng mech, Univ Kans, 56-64; fluid mech engr, Kimberly-Clark Corp, 64-66, sr res scientist, 66-67, sr res assoc res & eng, 67-79. *Concurrent Pos:* Res assoc hydraul, Iowa Inst Hydraul Res, 56-60; consult, 59-64; NSF fel, Univ Mich, 62-63. *Res:* Papermaking and dry forming processes; turbulence and secondary flows. *Mailing Add:* N 8594 Cranberry Rd Box 163 Wittenberg WI 54499-8332

APPEL, JAMES B, BEHAVIORAL PHARMACOLOGY. *Current Pos:* prof dept psychol, 72-86, Carolina res prof, 86-94, CAROLINA DISTINGUISHED PROF PSYCHOL, UNIV SC, 95- *Personal Data:* b New York, NY, Feb 18, 34; wid. *Educ:* Columbia Univ, AB, 55; Ind Univ, PhD(psychol), 60. *Honors & Awards:* Merit Award, Nat Ist Drug Abuse, NIH, 89. *Prof Exp:* Asst prof psychol, Dept Psychiat, Sch Med, Yale Univ, 61-66; assoc prof, Dept Psychiat, Univ Chicago, 66-72. *Concurrent Pos:* USPHS res scientist develop award, 69-72; consult, NSF, 70-71; vis prof, Med Res Coun Unit, Neural Mechanisms of Behav, Univ Col, London, UK, 78, NIMH, 81-85, Addiction Res Ctr, NIDA, 86; Educ Found Res Award, Univ SC, 89. *Mem:* Fel Am Col Neuropsychopharmacol; fel AAAS; fel Am Psychol Asn; Sigma Xi; Soc Neurosci; Soc Stimulus Properties Drugs (pres, 81-82); Behav Pharmacol Soc. *Res:* Behavioral and neurochemical effects of drugs; learning and conditioning; history and logic of psychology. *Mailing Add:* Dept Psychol Univ SC Columbia SC 29208. *Fax:* 803-777-9558; *E-Mail:* appel@sc.edu

APPEL, JEFFREY ALAN, ELEMENTARY PARTICLE PHYSICS. *Current Pos:* PHYSICIST, FERMI NAT ACCELERATOR LAB, 75- *Personal Data:* b Cleveland, Ohio, Aug 11, 42; m 65, Marjorie Bearman; c Deborah (Harris) & Hilary. *Educ:* Williams Col, AB, 64; Harvard Univ, MA, 65, PhD(physics), 69. *Prof Exp:* From res assoc to sr res assoc physics, Nevis Labs, Columbia Univ, 68-75, asst prof, 70-74. *Mem:* Fel Am Phys Soc. *Res:* Discrete symmetries, resonance phenomena and weak and electromagnetic phenomena; heavy flavor quark production and decay. *Mailing Add:* Fermi Lab PO Box 500 Batavia IL 60510. *Fax:* 630-840-3867; *E-Mail:* appel@fnal.fnal.gov

APPEL, KENNETH I, MATHEMATICS. *Current Pos:* PROF & CHAIR MATH, UNIV NH, 93. *Personal Data:* b Brooklyn, NY, Oct 8, 32; m 59, Carole Stein; c Andrew, Laurel & Peter. *Educ:* Queens Col, NY, BS, 53; Univ Mich, MA, 56, PhD(math), 59. *Honors & Awards:* Fulkerson Prize, 79. *Prof Exp:* Mathematician, Inst Defense Anal, 59-61; from asst prof to prof math, Univ Ill, Urbana-Champaign, 61-93. *Mem:* Am Math Soc; Math Asn Am; Asn Symbolic Logic. *Res:* co-solver four color problem; small cancellation theory. *Mailing Add:* Dept Math Univ NH Kingsbury Hall Durham NH 03824. *E-Mail:* kia@oregano.unh.edu

APPEL, MAX J, VETERINARY MICROBIOLOGY. *Current Pos:* res asst vet virol, Vet Virus Res Inst, 64-67, from asst prof to assoc prof, 67-76, PROF VET VIROL, NY STATE COL VET MED, CORNELL UNIV, 76- *Personal Data:* b Giessen, Ger, Dec 13, 29; m 61, Barbara Hoeke; c Barbara, Christine, Monika & Klaus. *Educ:* Vet Col, Hannover, DVM, 56; Cornell Univ, PhD(vet virol), 67. *Prof Exp:* Res asst vet med, Univ Munich, 57-59; fel, Univ Sask, 59-60; res off, Animal Dis Res Inst, Hull, Que, 61-64. *Mem:* Am Vet Med Asn; Am Soc Virol; Am Asn Vet Immunol; US Animal Health Asn. *Res:* Infectious diseases of domestic animals. *Mailing Add:* NY State Col Vet Med Cornell Univ Ithaca NY 14853. *Fax:* 607-256-5608; *E-Mail:* mja13@cornell.edu

APPEL, MICHAEL CLAYTON, ENDOCRINOLOGY. *Current Pos:* Fel, Univ Mass, 76-78, asst prof anat, 78-81, asst prof path, 79-88, ASSOC PROF PATH, UNIV MASS, MED SCH, 88-, VIS PROF BIOCHEM. *Personal Data:* b Milwaukee, Wis, Nov 19, 47; m 68; c 3. *Educ:* Western Mich Univ, BS, 70, MA, 73; Univ Minn, PhD(anat), 76. *Concurrent Pos:* Consult, Bio-Hybrid Technologies & T-cell Scis Inc. *Mem:* Am Diabetes Asn; Europ Asn Study Diabetes; Endocrine Soc. *Res:* Etiology of diabetes mellitus; identify and characterize laboratory animal models of human diabetes; immunology of diabetes. *Mailing Add:* COBE Labe 1185 Oak St Lakewood CO 80215

APPEL, STANLEY HERSH, NEUROLOGY. *Current Pos:* PROF NEUROL & CHMN DEPT, BAYLOR COL MED, 77-, CHMN PROG NEUROSCI, 77-, DIR, JERRY LEWIS NEUROMUSCULAR DIS RES CTR, 77- *Personal Data:* b Boston, Mass, May 8, 33; m 56; c 2. *Educ:* Harvard Univ, AB, 54; Columbia Univ, MD, 60; Am Bd Psychiat & Neurol, dipl, 68. *Prof Exp:* Intern med, Mass Gen Hosp, 60-61; resident neurol, Mt Sinai Hosp, 61-62; res assoc, Lab Molecular Biol, NIH, 62-64; chief res assoc, Sch Med, Univ Pa, 65-66, asst prof, 66-67; assoc neurol, Med Ctr, Duke Univ, 64-65, from assoc prof to prof neurol, 67-77, assoc prof biochem, 68-77, chief div neurol, 69-77. *Concurrent Pos:* USPHS res career develop award, 65-70. *Mem:* Am Acad Neurol; Am Soc Biol Chem; Am Soc Clin Invest; Am Neurol Asn. *Res:* Molecular neurobiology; neurochemistry; synapse function; muscle membranes and disease. *Mailing Add:* Dept Neurol Baylor Col Med Tex Med Ctr 6501 Fannin NB 302 Houston TX 77030-2703

APPEL, WARREN CURTIS, PHARMACOLOGY & PHARMACOEPIDEMIOLOGY, REGULATORY AFFAIRS. *Current Pos:* SCI ADV, BUR DRUGS, HEALTH & WELFARE CAN, 73-; CHIEF, ADVERSE DRUG REACTION MONITORING DIV, BUR PHARM SURVEILLANCE. *Personal Data:* b Cheyenne, Wyo, Oct 19, 44; m 69; c 1. *Educ:* Univ Wyo, BSc, 67; Univ Wash, MSc, 70, PhD(pharmacol), 71. *Prof Exp:* Lectr pharmacol, Univ Man, 72-73. *Concurrent Pos:* Actg chief, Div Gastroenterol & Miscellaneous Drugs, Bur Drugs, 85; WHO Travel Fel, Japan, China, 88; bd dirs, Int Soc Pharmacoepidemiol. *Mem:* Can Soc Clin Pharmacol; Drug Info Asn; Int Soc Pharmacoepidemiol; Can Asn Pop Therapeut (pres-elect). *Res:* Mechanisms of drug dependence. *Mailing Add:* Kusuri Can Corp PO Box 8304 Station T Ottawa ON K1E 3H7 Can. *Fax:* 613-523-5993; *E-Mail:* wcappel@cyberus.ca

APPELBAUM, ELIZABETH BERMAN, MATHEMATICS. *Current Pos:* WRITER, 96- *Personal Data:* m 57, Bradley E; c James & Sharon (Hoffman). *Educ:* Univ Minn, BA, 58, MA, 59; Univ Mo, Kansas City, PhD(math), 70. *Prof Exp:* Asst prof math, Rockhurst Col, 70-75, head math dept, 73-74; lectr, Univ Mo, Kansas City, 76-80; programmer & analyst, AT&T, 81-85; assoc prof math, Baker Univ, 85-86; adj fac comput sci & math, Johnson Co Community Col, 88; adj fac math, Longview Community Col, 89-90; adj fac econ, Avila Col, 90-94; adj fac, Park Col, 94-95, asst prof, 95-96. *Concurrent Pos:* Consult, NSF Progs, 74 & 75. *Mem:* Math Asn Am; Nat Coun Teachers Math; Asn Women Math. *Res:* Textbooks in basic algebra for college and high school; non-commutative rings. *Mailing Add:* 8275 W 116th Terr Shawnee Mission KS 66210. *E-Mail:* bappelba@aol.com

APPELBAUM, JOEL A, SOLID STATE PHYSICS. *Current Pos:* EXEC VPRES & GEN MGR, MICROPOLIS CORP. *Personal Data:* b Brooklyn, NY, Dec 30, 41; m 63; c 1. *Educ:* City Col New York, BS, 63; Univ Chicago, MS, 64, PhD(physics), 66. *Prof Exp:* Teaching asst physics, Univ Chicago, 63-64; mem tech staff, Bell Labs, NJ, 67; asst prof, Univ Calif, Berkeley, 67-68; mem tech staff, Bell Labs, 68- *Mem:* Am Phys Soc. *Res:* Solid state physics, particularly electron tunneling, surface physics and magnetism. *Mailing Add:* 100 Leotar Ct Los Gatos CA 95032

APPELLA, ETTORE, IMMUNOLOGY. *Current Pos:* vis scientist, Lab Molecular Biol, Nat Inst Arthritis & Metab Dis, 63-64, MED OFFICER IMMUNOL, LAB BIOL, NAT CANCER INST, 67- *Personal Data:* b Castronuovo, Italy, Aug 5, 33; US citizen. *Educ:* Univ Rome, MD, 59. *Prof Exp:* Res asst biol, Johns Hopkins Univ, 60-63. *Concurrent Pos:* Am Cancer Soc fel, Nat Inst Arthritis & Metab Dis, 64-66. *Mem:* Am Asn Biol Chemist; Am Cancer Soc. *Res:* Biochemistry; protein chemistry. *Mailing Add:* NCI NIH Bldg 37 Rm 1B04 Bethesda MD 20892

APPELMAN, EVAN HUGH, INORGANIC FLOURINE CHEMISTRY, INORGANIC REACTION MECHANISMS. *Current Pos:* RETIRED. *Personal Data:* b Chicago, Ill, June 6, 35; m 60, Mary Goold; c Harold & Hilary. *Educ:* Univ Chicago, AB, 53, MS, 55; Univ Calif, Berkeley, PhD(chem), 60. *Honors & Awards:* E O Lawrence Award, US Energy Res & Develop Admin, 76. *Prof Exp:* from asst chemist to assoc chemist, Argonne Nat Lab, 60-76, sr chemist 76-95. *Concurrent Pos:* Guggenheim Mem fel, 73-74; vis sr res fel, Brit Sci Res Coun & Univ Oxford, 83-84; Kipping vis, Univ Nottingham, 84; fel, Alexander von Humboldt Found, 89. *Mem:* Fedn Am Scientists; fel AAAS; Am Chem Soc. *Res:* Inorganic reaction kinetics and equilibria in aqueous solution, particularly kinetics of oxidation-reduction reactions; chemistry of the less familiar elements; inorganic fluorine chemistry; chemistry of powerful inorganic oxidants and fluorinating agents. *Mailing Add:* Argonne Nat Lab Bldg 200 9700 S Cass Ave Argonne IL 60439

APPELQUIST, THOMAS, THEORETICAL PHYSICS. *Current Pos:* PROF THEORET PHYSICS, YALE UNIV, 75-, CHMN, PHYSICS DEPT, 83- *Personal Data:* b Emmetsburg, Iowa, Nov 1, 41; m 65; c 2. *Educ:* Ill Benedictine Col, BS, 63; Cornell Univ, PhD(theoret physics), 68. *Prof Exp:* Res assoc theoret physics, Stanford Linear Accelerator Ctr, 68-70; from asst prof to assoc prof, Harvard Univ, 70-75. *Concurrent Pos:* AP Sloan Found fel, 74-76; US Sr Scientist Award, Alexander von Humboldt Found, 86- *Mem:* Fedn Am Sci; Am Phys Soc; AAAS. *Res:* Applications of quantum field theory to the interactions of elementary particles. *Mailing Add:* Dept Physics Yale Univ New Haven CT 06520. *Fax:* 203-432-6175

APPELT, GLENN DAVID, ETHNOPHARMACOLOGY. *Current Pos:* assoc prof, 67-79, asst dean student affairs, 77-82, PROF PHARMACOL, SCH PHARM, UNIV COLO, BOULDER, 79- *Personal Data:* b Yoakum, Tex, Aug 24, 35; m 83; c 1. *Educ:* Univ Tex, BS, 57, MS, 59; Univ Colo, PhD(pharm), 63. *Prof Exp:* Asst prof pharmacol, Univ Tex, Austin, 63-67. *Concurrent Pos:* Consult, Pharm Corp Am, Boulder, Colo & Smithkline Beecham Consumer Brands, Clifton, NJ; regist pharmacist; consult pharmacol, Legal & Ins Co. *Mem:* Am Pharm Asn; Am Asn Cols Pharmacy; Sigma Xi; Herb Res Found; Am Soc Pharmacog; fel Am Col Apothecaries. *Res:* Biochemical pharmacology; weight control products; toxicology of natural products; herbal medicines; auth pharmacol textbook. *Mailing Add:* 3120 Ponce de Leon Ct Gulf Shores AL 36542

APPENZELLER, OTTO, NEUROLOGY, MEDICINE. *Current Pos:* PRES, NMEX HEALTH ENHANCEMENT & MARATHON CLIN RES FOUND, 92- *Personal Data:* b Czernowitz, Romania, Dec 11, 27; m 56, Judith Bryce; c Timothy, Martin & Peter. *Educ:* Univ Sydney, MB & BS, 57, MD, 66; Univ London, PhD, 63. *Prof Exp:* Jr resident, Royal Prince Alfred Hosp, Sydney, Australia, 57-58, sr resident, 58-59, med registr, 59-60; clin asst, Nat Hosp Nerv Dis, London, Eng, 61-62; asst prof neurol, Col Med, Univ Cincinnati, 65-67; assoc prof med, Sch Med, Univ NMex, 67-70, prof neurol & med, 70-90; vis scientist, Lovelace, Med Found, 90-92. *Concurrent Pos:* Mass Gen Hosp & Harvard Med Sch fel, 63-64; Harvard Med Sch fel, 64-65; Boston Med Found fel, 65; chief neurol sect, Vet Admin Hosp, Cincinnati, Ohio, 65-67; consult neurologist, Vet Admin Hosp, Albuquerque, NMex, 68; mem res comt sports & phys educ, UNESCO; vis prof neurol, McGill Univ, 77; hon fel, Dept Anat, Univ Col, London, 83; Fogarty Int exchange scientist, 93. *Mem:* AAAS; fel Am Acad Neurol; Brit Med Asn; Royal Australasian Col Physicians; Am Col Physicians. *Res:* Clinical neurology; experimental neuropathology; physiology and pathology of autonomic and peripheral nervous systems; neuropathology; biochemistry of peripheral nerves; headache and its mechanism; immunology as applied to the nervous system; sports medicine; sports neurology. *Mailing Add:* NMex Health Enhancement & Marathon Clin Res Found 1559 Eagle Ridge Rd NE Albuquerque NM 87122. *Fax:* 505-266-4524

APPERSON, CHARLES HAMILTON, CHEMICAL ENGINEERING, PRODUCT & PROCESS DEVELOPMENT TECHNOLOGY. *Current Pos:* PROF ENGR, WVA, 80-; CHEM ENGR CONSULT, 90- *Personal Data:* b Fairfield, Ala, Feb 19, 25; m 51; c 3. *Educ:* Auburn Univ, BS, 49; WVa COES, MS, 80. *Prof Exp:* Sales engr, Fulbright Labs Div, 49-50; metall engr, US Steel Corp, 50-52; res engr, Chemstrand Res Ctr, Monsanto Co, 52-58, res group leader, 58-63, develop proj supvr, 63-66; res group leader, Union Carbide Tech Ctr, 66-81, res group leader & technol mgr, Union Carbide, Res Triangle Park, 81-87; res group leader, Rhone Poulenc Agr Co, Woodbine, Ga & RTP, NC, 87-90. *Concurrent Pos:* Vchmn local chapt, Am Inst Chem Engrs, 56-57. *Mem:* Am Inst Chem Engrs; Fiber Soc. *Res:* Product/process development and formulations on agricultural chemicals (insecticides and herbicides), polymers and fibers; process design, construction, start-up, technology support for operation and technical writing. *Mailing Add:* 995 Jones Wynd Wake Forest NC 27587

APPERT, HUBERT ERNEST, PANCREATIC PHYSIOLOGY, GLYCOCONJUGATES. *Current Pos:* ASSOC PROF GASTROINTESTINAL PHYSIOL, MED COL OHIO, TOLEDO, 73- *Educ:* Jefferson Med Col, Toledo, PhD(physiol), 60. *Mailing Add:* 5444 Morrow Rd Toledo OH 43615

APPL, FRANKLIN JOHN, THEORETICAL & APPLIED MECHANICS. *Current Pos:* PRES, APPL ENG CO, 78- *Personal Data:* b Great Bend, Kans, Dec 23, 37; m 59, Velma C Finkenbinder; c Patricia J, Virginia A & Kathryn L. *Educ:* Kans State Univ, BS, 60; Univ Ill, MS, 62, PhD(theoret & appl mech), 64. *Honors & Awards:* Ralph R Teetor Award, Soc Automotive Engrs, 68. *Prof Exp:* From asst prof to prof, Sch Aerospace & Mech Eng, Univ Okla, 64-78, asst dir, 71-78, adj prof, 78-91. *Concurrent Pos:* Res resident, Caterpillar Tractor Co, 66-67. *Mem:* Am Soc Mech Engrs; Soc Exp Mech; Am Soc Testing & Mat; Soc Automotive Engrs; Am Acad Mech; Am Soc Agr Engrs. *Res:* Solid mechanics; design, design analysis and testing. *Mailing Add:* Appl Eng Co 3503 Charleston Rd Norman OK 73069

APPL, FREDRIC CARL, MECHANICAL ENGINEERING, APPLIED MATHEMATICS. *Current Pos:* from assoc prof to prof, 60-67, JENNINGS PROF MECH ENG, KANS STATE UNIV, 67- *Personal Data:* b Great Bend, Kans, Nov 17, 32; m 54; c 3. *Educ:* Carnegie Mellon Univ, BS, 54, MS, 56, PhD(mech eng), 58. *Prof Exp:* Instr mech eng, Carnegie Inst Technol, 57-58, asst prof, 58; res engr drilling, Jersey Prod Res Co, 58-60. *Concurrent Pos:* Consult, Mine Safety Appliances, 57-58, Jersey Prod Res Co, 60-65 & Christensen Diamond Prod Co, 65- *Mem:* Am Soc Mech Engrs; Soc Petrol Engrs. *Res:* Vibration; mechanics; rock mechanics. *Mailing Add:* 1916 Indiana Lane Manhattan KS 66502

APPLE, DAVID JOSEPH, OPHTHALMOLOGY. *Current Pos:* PROF, DEPT OPHTHAL, STORM EYE INST, MED UNIV SC, CHARLESTON, 88-, CHMN DEPT, 88-; DIR, CTR INTRAOCULAR LENS RES, 88- *Personal Data:* b Alton, Ill, Sept 14, 41. *Educ:* Northwestern Univ, BS, 62; Univ Ill, MD, 66. *Honors & Awards:* Temoignage d'Honneur, Can Implant Soc, 86; Ridley Medal, 88; Choyce Medal; Binkhorst Lectr & Medal, Am Acad Ophthal, 88; Walter Wright lectr, Toronto, 93. *Prof Exp:* Intern & resident path, Charity Hosp La, La State Univ, New Orleans, 66-71; assoc prof ophthal & path, Univ Ill Eye & Ear Infirmary, 74-76; ophthal resident, Univ Iowa, Iowa City, 77-80; prof ophthal & path, O'Brien Lab Ocular Path, Tulane Univ Sch Med, 80-81, Univ Utah Health Sci Ctr, Salt Lake City, 81-88, dir, Ctr Intraocular Lens Res, Sch Med, 84-88. *Concurrent Pos:* Vis res prof, Univ Tuebingen, 75-77, Univ Bonn, 81, Univ Munich, 81 & Fed Repub Ger; lectr, UK Intraocular Soc, Scotland, 89; consult, McGraw Hill Pub Co & WHO Prev Blindness Prog. *Mem:* Am Acad Ophthal; Int Acad Path; Am Asn Ophthal Pathologists; Int Soc Eye Res. *Res:* Pathology of the eye; ocular pathology; intraocular lenses. *Mailing Add:* Dept Ophthal Storm Eye Inst Med Univ SC 171 Ashley Ave Charleston SC 29425-2236

APPLE, JASON KINCHLOE, MEAT SCIENCE & TECHNOLOGY, MUSCLE BIOLOGY. *Current Pos:* ASST PROF MEAT SCI & MUSCLE BIOL, UNIV ARK, 95- *Personal Data:* b Lawton, Okla, June 4, 65; m 90, Allison Amis; c Hanna & Augusta. *Educ:* Okla State Univ, BS, 87; Kans State Univ, MS, 89, PhD(animal sci), 94. *Prof Exp:* Lectr animal sci, Univ Mass, Amherst, 93. *Mem:* Am Meat Sci Asn; Am Soc Animal Scientists; Sigma Xi. *Res:* Study of the factors that affect postmortem metabolism, muscle quality and palatability of cooked beef and pork; determining the yield and value of livestock produced in Arkansas, especially called breeding stock. *Mailing Add:* Animal Sci Dept E202A ANSC Bldg Univ Ark Fayetteville AR 72701. *Fax:* 501-575-7294; *E-Mail:* japple@comp.uark.edu

APPLE, JAY LAWRENCE, GENETICS. *Current Pos:* From res instr to assoc prof, NC State Univ, 49-63, dir inst biol sci, 67-71, asst dir acad affairs & res for biol sci, 71-77, assoc dir res & coordr int prog, 77-81, dir, Int Prog, 81-91, EMER PROF PLANT PATH & GENETICS, NC STATE UNIV, 91- *Personal Data:* b Guilford Co, NC, Jan 8, 26; m 45, Ella Holt. *Educ:* NC State Col, BS, 49, MS, 53, PhD(plant path), 55. *Concurrent Pos:* Plant path adv, NC State Univ-US AID Mission, Peru, 63-65, chief-of-party, 65-67; consult int develop, Univ Calif, Berkeley, 72-80; consult pest mgt, Environ Protection Agency, 73-74, Off Tech Assessment, 78-79 & FAO, 81-90; secy gen, Int Plant Protection Cong, 91- *Mem:* Fel AAAS; fel Am Phytopath Soc; Sigma Xi. *Res:* Genetics of disease resistance in plants; integrated pest management; research administration; international agricultural development. *Mailing Add:* 1208 Bancroft Dr Raleigh NC 27612. *Fax:* 919-515-6835; *E-Mail:* j_apple@ncsu.edu

APPLE, MARTIN ALLEN, MOLECULAR PHARMACOLOGY, GENETIC ENGINEERING. *Current Pos:* EXPERT, NSF, 91-, EXPERT, DEPT EDUC, 96- *Personal Data:* b Duluth, Minn, Sept 17, 39; c 4. *Educ:* Univ Minn, AB, 59, MSc, 62; Univ Calif, PhD(biochem), 67. *Honors & Awards:* Am Cancer Soc Award, 69. *Prof Exp:* Asst microbiol, Med Sch, Univ Minn, 60-62; asst res biochemist, Sch Med, Univ Calif, San Francisco, 66-68 & Cancer Res Inst, 68-75, lectr biochem, 68-70, asst prof pharmacol & exp therapeut in residence, 70-75, asst prof pharmaceut chem in residence, Sch Pharm, 71-75, assoc res biochemist, Cancer Res Inst, 75-78; pres, Int Plant Res Inst, 78-82; pres, Adytum Int, 82-89; scholar in residence, Nat Humanities Ctr, 90; nat proj mgr, Nat Sci Teacher Asn, 91-92. *Concurrent Pos:* Consult enzyme, Vet Admin Hosps, 63-69 & Nat Cancer Inst, 73-74; mem bd of regents, Am Col Clin Pharmacol; bd trustees, East-West Ctr, 83-88; chief exec offier, LEADERS, 90-; exec dir, Coun Sci Soc Pres, 93-; exec officer, Sci Watch Inc, 95-96. *Mem:* Am Soc Microbiol; Am Fedn Clin Res; fel Am Inst Chem; fel Am Col Clin Pharmacol; Am Soc Pharmacol & Exp Therapeut; Inst Elec & Electronics Engrs; Inst Elec & Electronics Engrs; Am Asn Cancer Res; Sigma Xi. *Res:* Biochemical and clinical pharmacology; computer aided chemical structure design; biochemical oncology; new drug designs; genetic engineering; agriculture; computer aided chemical structure design; science education-new models; federal and national science policy; granted several patents; author of 36 publications. *Mailing Add:* Coun Sci Soc pres 1155 16th St NW Washington DC 94126. *E-Mail:* cssp@acs.org

APPLE, SPENCER BUTLER, JR, HORTICULTURE. *Current Pos:* assoc prof, Ore State Univ, 50-55, horticulturist & head, Dept Hort, 55-73, prof, 73-75, EMER PROF HORT, ORE STATE UNIV, 75- *Personal Data:* b Kansas City, Mo, June 11, 12; m 40; c 3. *Educ:* Agr & Mech Col Tex, BS, 33, MS, 36; Wash State Univ, PhD(hort), 53. *Prof Exp:* From instr to asst prof hort, Agr & Mech Col Tex, 35-41; res asst & exten specialist, Mich State Col, 41-46; exten specialist, Agr & Mech Col Tex, 47-48, assoc prof, 49-50. *Concurrent Pos:* Gen Educ Bd fel, 48-49. *Mem:* Fel AAAS; Am Soc Hort Sci. *Res:* Plant nutrition; physiological problems in vegetable crop production. *Mailing Add:* 5209 Davidson St SE Albany OR 97321

APPLE, TOM MARK, NUCLEAR MAGNETIC RESONANCE, HETEROGENEOUS CATALYSIS. *Current Pos:* CHMN, CHEM DEPT, RENSSELAER POLYTECH INST, 97- *Personal Data:* b Bethlehem, Pa, Nov 2, 54; m 79, Anne Juagk. *Educ:* Pa State Univ, BS, 76; Univ Del, PhD(chem), 81. *Prof Exp:* From asst prof to assoc prof chem, Univ Nebr, 83-91. *Mem:* Am Chem Soc; Soc Appl Spectros. *Mailing Add:* Chem Dept Rensselaer Polytech Inst Troy NY 12180-3590

APPLEBAUM, CHARLES H, MATHEMATICAL LOGIC. *Current Pos:* asst prof, 69-74, ASSOC PROF MATH, BOWLING GREEN STATE UNIV, 74- *Personal Data:* b Newark, NJ, Nov 26, 42; m 64, Barbara Glasberg; c Robin & Laura. *Educ:* Case Inst Technol, BS, 64; Rutgers Univ, MS, 66, PhD(math), 69. *Prof Exp:* Asst math, Rutgers Univ, 64-69. *Concurrent Pos:* Consult & tech staff mem, Mass Inst Technol Res Estab Corp, 81-88. *Mem:* Math Asn Am; Am Math Soc; Asn Symbolic Logic. *Res:* Theory of recursive equivalence types and recursive functions and their application to various areas of algebra; verification and specification theory in the field of computer science. *Mailing Add:* Dept Math & Statist Bowling Green State Univ Bowling Green OH 43403. *E-Mail:* applebau@math.bgsu.edu

APPLEBAUM, GARY E, GERIATRICS. *Current Pos:* ATTEND PHYSICIAN, JOHNS HOPKINS BAYVIEW MED CTR & ST AGNES HOSP, 89-; MED DIR, CHARLESTOWN CARE CTR, 89-; ASST PROF, SCH MED JOHNS HOPKINS UNIV, 91- *Personal Data:* b Philadelphia, Pa, Feb 11, 59; m 82, Julie Ellen Levitt; c Michael Louis & Philip Ross. *Educ:* Univ Pa, BA, 81, MD, 85; Am Bd Internal Med, dipl. *Prof Exp:* Intern & resident gen internal med, Francis Scott Key Med Ctr, 85-88; fel geriat med, Sch Med, Johns Hopkins Univ, 88-89, instr med, 89-90. *Concurrent Pos:* Consult, US Hosp Reps Select Comt Aging, Subcomt Long Term Care, 90-92. *Mem:* Am Col Physicians; Am Geriat Soc; Am Med Dirs Asn. *Res:* Contributed numerous articles to professional journals. *Mailing Add:* 42 Latimore Way Owings Mills MD 21117-6000

APPLEBURY, MEREDITHE L, VISION, RETINAL GENETICS. *Current Pos:* PROF, DEPT OPHTHAL & VISION SCI, UNIV CHICAGO, 88- *Personal Data:* b Hamilton, Mont, Feb 7, 42; m 76. *Educ:* Univ Wash, BS, 64; Yale Univ, PhD(biochem), 68. *Prof Exp:* Mem tech staff biophys, Bell Labs, Murray Hill, NJ, 70-72; res fel biochem, Max Planck Inst, Gottingen, WGer, 72-75; asst prof biochem, Princeton Univ, 75-82; assoc prof, Dept Biol Sci, Lily, Purdue Univ, 75-82. *Concurrent Pos:* Fel biochem, Yale Univ, 68-70, res assoc, 68-72; prin investr, Nat Eye Inst, Bethesda, Nat Found March Dimes, 78- *Mem:* Am Chem Soc; AAAS. *Res:* Primary processes of vision; photoreception and transduction; biochemistry of the retina; molecular genetics of retina. *Mailing Add:* Mass Eye & Ear Infirmary Harvard Med Sch 243 Charles St Rm 550 Boston MA 02114

APPLEBY, ALAN, RADIATION CHEMISTRY. *Current Pos:* asst prof, 67-71, assoc prof, 71-77, PROF RADIATION SCI, RUTGERS UNIV, 77- *Personal Data:* b Newcastle, Eng, Apr 25, 37; m 60, Kathleen A Shippen; c Sarah K & Emily J. *Educ:* Univ Durham, BSc, 58, PhD(radiation chem), 63. *Prof Exp:* Res assoc radiation chem, Univ Durham, 61-63 & Brookhaven Nat Lab, 63-65; sr sci officer, Radiochem Ctr, UK Atomic Energy Authority, Eng, 65-67. *Concurrent Pos:* Adj prof radiol, Univ Med & Dent, NJ. *Mem:* Sigma Xi. *Res:* Radiation chemistry of water and aqueous systems; radiation dosimetry by magnetic resonance. *Mailing Add:* 240 Beechwood Ave Middlesex NJ 08846

APPLEBY, ARNOLD PIERCE, WEED SCIENCE. *Current Pos:* Instr agron, Ore State Univ, 59-62, asst prof, Pendleton Br Exp Sta, 62-63 & Univ, 63-67, from assoc prof to prof, 72-92, EMER PROF AGRON, ORE STATE UNIV, 92- *Personal Data:* b Formoso, Kans, Oct 24, 35; m 56, Geraldine A Smith; c Brian D & Brent D. *Educ:* Kans State Univ, BS, 57, MS, 58; Ore State Univ, PhD(herbicide physiol), 62. *Mem:* Fel Am Soc Agron; fel Crop Sci Soc Am; fel Weed Sci Soc Am; fel Western Soc Weed Sci. *Res:* Agronomic and physiological aspects of herbicides. *Mailing Add:* Dept Crop Sci Ore State Univ Corvallis OR 97331. *Fax:* 541-737-3407; *E-Mail:* applybya@css.orst.edu

APPLEBY, JAMES E, ENTOMOLOGY. *Current Pos:* From asst prof to assoc prof, 64-75, PROF ENTOM, ILL NATURAL HIST SURV, 75-, PROF SCI. *Personal Data:* b Canton, Ohio, Aug 6, 36. *Educ:* Ohio State Univ, BS, 59, MS, 60, PhD(entom), 64. *Res:* Life histories and control of insects and mites injurious to trees, shrubs and garden flowers. *Mailing Add:* Nat Resources & Exp Sci Univ Ill 172 S-517 Turner Hall Urbana IL 61801

APPLEBY, JOHN FREDERICK, planetary atmospheres, for more information see previous edition

APPLEBY, ROBERT H, LOCAL AREA NETWORK COMMUNICATIONS, FIBER OPTIC COMMUNICATIONS. *Current Pos:* VPRES, BAJA SYSTS INC, 92- *Personal Data:* b Visalia, Calif, Dec 16, 31; m 56; c 4. *Educ:* Washington Col, BS, 54; Va Polytech Inst, MS, 60. *Prof Exp:* Sr eng assoc, E I du Pont de Nemours & Co Inc, 60-90. *Concurrent Pos:* US Naval Pilot. *Mem:* Instrument Soc Am; World Futures Soc. *Res:* High speed, high density electronic interconnections; low cost local area networks. *Mailing Add:* 207 Watts St Durham NC 27701-2036. *Fax:* 919-688-2710

APPLEGARTH, ADRIENNE P, ADULT PSYCHIATRY & PSYCHOANALYSIS. *Current Pos:* asst prof physiol, 53-61, CLIN PROF PSYCHIAT, UNIV CALIF MED SCH, 67- *Personal Data:* b San Francisco, Calif, May 2, 26; m 83, Bud T. *Educ:* Harvard Med Sch, MD, 50; Univ Calif, Berkeley, PhD(physiol), 54. *Concurrent Pos:* Dean Stud, Univ Calif, San Francisco. 58-61; training & supvr analyst, San Francisco Psychoanalytic Inst, 80- *Mem:* Am Physiol Asn; Am Psychoanalytic Asn. *Res:* Factors controlling the activity of the Isles of Langerhans in the pancreas. *Mailing Add:* 1610 Scott St San Francisco CA 94115

APPLEGARTH, DEREK A, GENETICS. *Current Pos:* dir, 69-96, ASSOC DIR, BIOCHEM DIS LAB, CHILDREN'S HOSP, VANCOUVER, 96- *Personal Data:* b London, Eng, July 5, 37; Can citizen; m 84; c 3. *Educ:* Univ Durham, BSc, 58, PhD, 62. *Prof Exp:* Fel, Univ BC, 62-63; asst clin chemist, Vancouver Gen Hosp, 63-66; from asst prof to assoc prof pediat, Univ BC, 71-78, prof pediat, 78- *Concurrent Pos:* Clin instr, Univ BC, 63-66. *Mem:* Am Soc Human Genetics; fel Can Col Med Genetics; Soc Pediat Path. *Res:* Biochemical diseases of children. *Mailing Add:* Biochem Dis Lab Dept Path Childrens Hosp 4480 Oak St Rm F22 Vancouver BC V6H 3V4 Can

APPLEGATE, HOWARD GEORGE, ENVIRONMENTAL SCIENCES. *Current Pos:* PRES, APPL ENVIRON SERVS, EL PASO, TEX, 85- *Personal Data:* b Philadelphia, Pa, Mar 9, 22. *Educ:* Colo State Univ, BS, 50, MS, 52; Mich State Univ, PhD(physiol), 56. *Prof Exp:* Asst prof floricult, Univ Conn, 56-58; asst biochemist, State Col Wash, 58-60; asst prof plant physiol, Southern Ill Univ, 60-61; assoc prof, Ariz State Univ, 61-62 & Tex A&M Univ, 62-69; assoc prof plant physiol, Univ Tex, El Paso, 69-81, prof environ sci, 81-87. *Mem:* Air Pollution Control Asn; Am Chem Soc; US-Mex Border Health Asn. *Res:* Air pollution. *Mailing Add:* PO Box N Canutillo TX 79835

APPLEGATE, JAMES DAVID ROBERT, GEOSCIENCE POLICY. *Current Pos:* DIR GOVT AFFAIRS, AM GEOL INST, 95- *Personal Data:* b Chambersburg, Pa, Sept 24, 67; m 95, Heidi Stoltzgus. *Educ:* Yale Univ, BS, 89; Mass Inst Technol, PhD(geol), 94. *Prof Exp:* Cong sci fel, Am Geophys Union, 94-95. *Concurrent Pos:* Prof staff mem, US Senate Comt Energy & Natural Resources, 95. *Mem:* Geol Soc Am; Am Geophys Union; Am Asn Petrol Geologists. *Res:* Application of structural geology, geochronology and metamorphic petrology to tectonic problems. *Mailing Add:* Am Geol Inst 4220 King St Alexandria VA 22302. *Fax:* 703-379-7563; *E-Mail:* applegate@agineb.org

APPLEGATE, JAMES EDWARD, WILDLIFE BIOLOGY. *Current Pos:* asst prof, 71-76, ASSOC PROF WILDLIFE BIOL, RUTGERS UNIV, 76- *Personal Data:* b South Amboy, NJ, Aug 28, 42; m 65; c 2. *Educ:* Rutgers Univ, BS, 64; Pa State Univ, MS, 66, PhD(zool), 68. *Prof Exp:* NIH trainee arbovirus ecol, Pa State Univ, 64-66, teaching asst zool, 66-67, USPHS fel parasitol, 67-68; res parasitologist, Naval Med Res Inst, 68-71. *Concurrent Pos:* Assoc ed, J Wildlife Mgt. *Mem:* Wildlife Dis Asn; Wildlife Soc; Am Inst Biol Sci. *Res:* Ecology of malaria; social aspects of wildlife management. *Mailing Add:* Environ Res Rutgers Univ New Brunswick NJ 08903

APPLEGATE, JAMES KEITH, exploration geophysics, geotechnical engineering, for more information see previous edition

APPLEGATE, LYNN E, MEMBRANE SEPARATIONS. *Current Pos:* Sr tech rep, 67-81, tech consult, 81-86, SR TECH CONSULT, E I DU PONT DE NEMOURS & CO, INC, 86- *Personal Data:* b Dayton, Ohio, Apr 3, 41; m 61; c 3. *Educ:* Univ Dayton, BS, 63; Ind Univ, PhD(chem), 67. *Honors & Awards:* Outstanding Serv Award, Am Soc Testing & Mat. *Mem:* Am Soc Testing & Mat; Am Chem Soc; Am Inst Chemists; Int Desalination Asn; Water Qual Asn. *Res:* Separations with membranes; purification and or concentration using ultrafiltration and reverse osmosis; water purification; polymer chemistry. *Mailing Add:* 5115 New Kent Rd Wilmington DE 19808-2705

APPLEGATE, RICHARD LEE, ENTOMOLOGY, ZOOLOGY. *Current Pos:* RETIRED. *Personal Data:* b Mt Carmel, Ill, Jan 15, 36; m 57; c 2. *Educ:* Univ Southern Ill, BA, 59, MA, 61; SDak State Univ, PhD, 74. *Prof Exp:* Fishery biologist, Va Comn Game & Inland Fisheries, 61-63; fishery res biologist, Bur Sport Fisheries & Wildlife, Scent Reservoir Invests, 63-67; fishery res biologist & unit leader aquatic biol & fisheries, Bur Sport Fisheries & Wildlife, SDak Coop Fishery Unit, SDak State Univ, 67-84; US Fish & Wildlife Serv, 84-87; coordr, Nat Fish Hatchery & Technol Ctr, 87-93. *Concurrent Pos:* Mem, Task Force Team 4 Conserv Aquatic Ecosyst, Int Biol Prog, Nat Acad Sci-Nat Res Coun, 67- *Mem:* Am Fisheries Soc; Am Soc Limnol & Oceanog. *Res:* Aquatic biology and ecology; limnology; fisheries. *Mailing Add:* 4050 Marjean Ct Pensacola FL 32504

APPLEMAN, GABRIEL, chemical engineering, project management, for more information see previous edition

APPLEMAN, JAMES R, BIOCHEMISTRY. *Current Pos:* res assoc, 85-88, ASST MEM, DEPT BIOCHEM & CLIN PHARMACOL, ST JUDE CHILDREN'S RES HOSP, MEMPHIS, TENN, 88- *Personal Data:* b Woodward, Okla, Sept 21, 56; c 2. *Educ:* Okla State Univ, BS, 78, PhD(biochem), 83. *Prof Exp:* Res assoc, Dept Biochem, Dartmouth Med Sch, Hanover, NH, 83-85. *Concurrent Pos:* Guest lectr protein eng, Dept Biochem, Univ Tenn, Knoxville, 91; grant, Nat Inst Gen Med Sci, NIH, 91- *Mem:* AAAS; Am Soc Biochem & Molecular Biol; NY Acad Sci; Sigma Xi; Protein Soc. *Res:* Relationship between the structure of enzymes and their functions utilizing biochemical and biophysical techniques; binding and other interactions of substrates and inhibitors with enzymes and subsequent conformational changes in enzyme-ligand complexes. *Mailing Add:* 13850 Bruyere Ct San Diego CA 92129

APPLEMAN, M MICHAEL, BIOCHEMISTRY, SCIENCE EDUCATION. *Current Pos:* from asst prof to assoc prof, 66-76, chmn, dept biol sci, 81-85, PROF BIOCHEM, UNIV SOUTHERN CALIF, 76- *Personal Data:* b Los Angeles, Calif, June 13, 33; m 58; c 3. *Educ:* Univ Calif, Berkeley, BA, 57; Univ Wash, Seattle, PhD(biochem), 62. *Prof Exp:* Technician, Berkeley Lab, Nat Canners Asn, 57-58; NSF res fel metab, Inst Biochem Res, Argentina, 63-65; actg asst prof biochem, Univ Wash, Seattle, 65-66. *Mem:* AAAS; Am Soc Biochem & Molecular Biol. *Res:* enzymology; biological education. *Mailing Add:* Dept Molecular Biol Univ Southern Calif MC1340 Los Angeles CA 90089-1340

APPLEQUIST, DOUGLAS EINAR, ORGANIC CHEMISTRY. *Current Pos:* From instr to prof, 55-86, EMER PROF ORG CHEM, UNIV ILL, URBANA-CHAMPAIGN, 86- *Personal Data:* b Salt Lake City, Utah, Oct 29, 30; m 66, Linda Donlon; c Wendy & Jenny. *Educ:* Univ Calif, Berkeley, BS, 52; Calif Inst Technol, PhD(chem), 55. *Mem:* Am Chem Soc. *Res:* Small-ring compounds; photochemical reactions; bridgehead displacements and eliminations; free-radical reactions. *Mailing Add:* 204 Pell Circle Urbana IL 61801-6637

APPLEQUIST, JON BARR, BIOPHYSICS, PHYSICAL CHEMISTRY. *Current Pos:* assoc prof, 65-68, PROF BIOPHYS, IOWA STATE UNIV, 68- *Personal Data:* b Salt Lake City, Utah, Mar 19, 32; m 60, Nancy Bruce; c Karen, Reid, Jennifer, Scott & George. *Educ:* Univ Calif, BS, 54; Harvard Univ, PhD(chem), 59. *Prof Exp:* Asst prof chem, Univ Calif, Berkeley, 58-60 & Columbia Univ, 61-65. *Concurrent Pos:* Prin investr, Sponsored Res, NIH, 60-96, biophys & biophys chem study sect, NIH, 69-73,; secy-treas, Ames Sect, Am Chem Soc, 75, chmn, 76; prof chem courtesy appointment, Iowa State Univ, 86-89. *Res:* Molecular conformations; molecular optical properties; molecular interactions. *Mailing Add:* Dept Biochem & Biophys Iowa State Univ Ames IA 50011

APPLETON, B R, SOLID STATE PHYSICS. *Current Pos:* sect head, 74-86, div dir, 86-87, ASSOC DIR PHYS RES, OAK RIDGE NAT LAB, 87- *Personal Data:* b Pampa, Tex, Nov 24, 37; m 59; c 3. *Educ:* Univ Mo, BS, 60; Rutgers Univ, MS, 64, PhD(physics), 66. *Prof Exp:* Mem res staff, Radio Corp Am, 61-63 & Bell Tel Labs Inc, 66-67. *Mem:* Fel Am Phys Soc; fel AAAS; Bohmische Phys Soc; Mat Res Soc. *Res:* Basic ion-solid interactions; alteration of materials properties by ion bombardment and ion implantation techniques. *Mailing Add:* Box 2008 Oak Ridge Nat Lab Oak Ridge TN 37831

APPLETON, JOHN P(ATRICK), FLUID MECHANICS, APPLIED THERMODYNAMICS. *Current Pos:* from assoc prof to prof, 67-74, SR LECTR MECH ENG, MASS INST TECHNOL, 74-; VPRES RES & DEVELOP, THERMO ELECTRON CORP, 74- *Personal Data:* b Wolverton, Eng, Dec 17, 34; m 59; c 3. *Educ:* Univ Southampton, BSc, 58, PhD(aeronaut eng), 61. *Prof Exp:* Eng apprentice, Aeronaut Engine Div, Rolls Royce Ltd, Eng, 51-55; res asst aeronaut eng, Univ Southampton, 57-61, lectr, 61-64; sr staff scientist, AC-Electronics Defense Res Labs, Calif, 64-67. *Mem:* Am Phys Soc; Combustion Inst; Am Soc Metals; Tech Asn Pulp & Paper Indust. *Mailing Add:* 38 Sagamore Dr Andover MA 01810

APPLETON, JOSEPH HAYNE, CIVIL & STRUCTURAL ENGINEERING. *Current Pos:* chmn, Div Eng, 67-71, dean eng, 71-78, PROF CIVIL ENG, UNIV ALA, BIRMINGHAM, 59- *Personal Data:* b Collinsville, Ala, Aug 5, 27; m 54; c 6. *Educ:* Auburn Univ, BCE, 47; Univ Ill, MS, 49, PhD(civil eng), 59. *Prof Exp:* Res engr, US Bur Pub Roads, 49-50; instr civil eng, NC State Col, 50-51; res assoc, Univ Ill, 51-54; struct engr, Ala Cement Tile Co, 54-59. *Mem:* Am Soc Civil Engrs; Am Concrete Inst: Am Soc Eng Educ; Nat Soc Prof Engrs; Sigma Xi. *Res:* Reinforced and prestressed concrete; structural analysis and design; nature and properties of concrete and dental cements. *Mailing Add:* 4237 Antietam Dr Birmingham AL 35213

APPLETON, MARTIN DAVID, BIOCHEMISTRY. *Current Pos:* from instr to prof, 55-88, CHMN DEPT, 75-, EMER PROF CHEM, UNIV SCRANTON, 88- *Personal Data:* b Bangor, Pa, Feb 11, 17; m 85, Marina; c 2. *Educ:* Univ Scranton, BS, 39; Pa State Univ, MS, 41, PhD, 61. *Honors & Awards:* Rosemary Dybwad Int Award, Nat Asn Retarded Children, 70; Spec Citation, Pa Asn Retarded Children, 70. *Prof Exp:* Group leader & sr res chemist, Nuodex Prod Co, NJ, 41-42; tech dir & partner, Com & Indust Prod Co, 45-55. *Concurrent Pos:* Consult indust chem & biochem; tech dir, Scicon, Inc. *Mem:* Fel AAAS; Am Chem Soc; fel Am Inst Chem; Sigma Xi. *Res:* Organic synthesis; clinical biochemistry; biochemistry of mental retardation; mechanism of cholera toxin. *Mailing Add:* 1605 Coventry Lane Glen Mills PA 19342

APPLEWHITE, THOMAS H, ORGANIC CHEMISTRY. *Current Pos:* CONSULT FATS & OILS, 87- *Personal Data:* b Imperial, Calif, Dec 30, 24; m 45, Harriet M Kaplan; c Pamela E (Burke) & Thomas T. *Educ:* Calif Inst Technol, BS, 53, PhD(chem, plant physiol), 57. *Honors & Awards:* A E Bailey Medal, Am Oil Chemists Soc. *Prof Exp:* Res chemist, Dow Chem Co, 56-59; org chemist, Western Utilization Res & Develop Div, Agr Res Serv, USDA, 59-63, head oilseed invest, 63-67; res dir, Pac Veg Oil Corp, 67-69; mgr, Edible Oil Prod Lab, Kraft, Inc, 69-78, dir res serv, Res & Develop, 78-87. *Concurrent Pos:* Ed, J Am Oil Chemists' Soc, 85-91 & INFORM, 90-93. *Mem:* Am Chem Soc; Am Oil Chemists Soc (pres, 77-78); Sigma Xi; Inst Food Technologists. *Res:* Enzyme-catalyzed reactions and the chemistry of amino acids; physical chemistry of water-soluble high polymers; chemistry and biochemistry of fats and fatty acids; mechanisms of organic reactions; analytical chemistry; health and nutrition. *Mailing Add:* 1032 Verbena Dr Austin TX 78750

APPLEYARD, EDWARD CLAIR, GEOLOGY. *Current Pos:* asst prof, 65-68, actg chmn dept, 69-70, ASSOC PROF EARTH SCI, UNIV WATERLOO, 68- *Personal Data:* b Strathroy, Ont, June 22, 34; m 62; c 2. *Educ:* Univ Western Ont, BSc, 56; Queen's Univ, Ont, MSc, 60; Cambridge Univ, PhD(petrol), 62. *Prof Exp:* Asst lectr geol, Bedford Col, Univ London, 62-65. *Concurrent Pos:* Vis res scientist, Commonwealth Sci & Indust Res Orgn, Australia, 79-80, vis scientist, Geothermal Inst, Univ Auckland, NZ, 86-87. *Mem:* Fel Geol Asn Can; Mineral Asn Can. *Res:* Geochemistry of altered rocks; wall rock alteration; metasomatism; metamorphism of evaporatic deposits; Precambrian geology. *Mailing Add:* Dept Earth Sci Univ Waterloo Waterloo ON N2L 3G1 Can

APPLING, WILLIAM DAVID LOVE, MATHEMATICS. *Current Pos:* from asst prof to assoc prof, 63-69, PROF MATH, NTEX STATE UNIV, 69- *Personal Data:* b Chicago, Ill, Sept 13, 34; m 64; c 2. *Educ:* Univ Tex, BA, 55, PhD(math), 58. *Prof Exp:* Instr math, Duke Univ, 60-63. *Mem:* Am Math Soc. *Res:* Real analysis; integral theory; absolute continuity. *Mailing Add:* Univ NTex Denton TX 76203-6737

APPS, MICHAEL JOHN, environmental sciences, for more information see previous edition

APRAHAMIAN, ANI, NUCLEAR MODELS, NUCLEAR STRUCTURE. *Current Pos:* asst prof, 89-94, ASSOC PROF PHYSICS, UNIV NOTRE DAME, 94- *Personal Data:* b Beirut, Lebanon, Aug 15, 58; US citizen. *Educ:* Clark Univ, BA, 80, PhD(nuclear chem), 86. *Prof Exp:* Postdoctoral nuclear chem, Lawrence Livermore Nat Lab, 85-88. *Mem:* Sigma Xi; Am Phys Soc; Am Chem Soc; AAAS. *Res:* Experimental and theoretical nuclear structure research. *Mailing Add:* Physics Dept Univ Notre Dame Notre Dame IN 46556. *Fax:* 219-631-5952; *E-Mail:* aprahamian.1@nd.edu

APRIL, ERNEST W, HUMAN ANATOMY, MUSCLE PHYSIOLOGY. *Current Pos:* ASSOC PROF ANAT & CELL BIOL, COL PHYSICIANS & SURGEONS, COLUMBIA UNIV, 69- *Personal Data:* b Salem, Mass, Nov 6, 39; m 77; c 2. *Educ:* Tufts Univ, BS, 61; Columbia Univ, PhD(anat), 69. *Concurrent Pos:* Vis asst prof, Sch Med, Univ Miami, 70-71; USPHS grant, 71-; vis assoc prof, Albert Einstein Col Med, 76-78. *Mem:* Sigma Xi; Am Asn Anat; Am Soc Cell Biol; Biophys Soc Am. *Res:* Investigation, using electron microscopic, x-ray diffraction and physiological methods, of the biophysical aspects of muscle contraction in single fibers by correlation of morphological ultrastructure, physiological processes and physical-chemical phenomena; investigations of anatomical bases of muscular dysfunction, particularly in the upper and lower limbs; author of three books. *Mailing Add:* Col Physicians & Surgeons Columbia Univ New York NY 10032. *E-Mail:* ewa1@columbia.edu

APRIL, GARY CHARLES, CHEMICAL ENGINEERING. *Current Pos:* from asst prof to prof, 69-82, asst dean res & grad studies, 83-89, UNIV RES PROF, UNIV ALA, 82-, DEPT HEAD, 96- *Personal Data:* b New Orleans, La, Jan 5, 40; m 62, Lynne Slocovich; c Andrew G, Brian R & Elizabeth L. *Educ:* La State Univ, BS, 62, MS, 68, PhD(chem eng), 69. *Honors & Awards:* Nat Serv Soc Award, Am Inst Chem Engrs, 91. *Prof Exp:* Engr, Sabine River Works, E I du Pont de Nemours & Co, 62-66; grad asst chem eng, La State Univ, 66-69. *Concurrent Pos:* Consult chem process indust; res scholar, Univ Ala, 80, res fel, 84-86; expert witness & prin investr res grants; state dir, Exp Prog Stimulate Competitive Res, Ala Dept Energy, 91- *Mem:* Am Inst Chem Engrs; Am Soc Eng Educ; Tech Asn Pulp & Paper Indust. *Res:* Chemicals from woody biomass; modeling natural and reacting systems; transport processes; mathematical modeling; kinetics. *Mailing Add:* Dept Chem Eng Univ Ala PO Box 870203 Tuscaloosa AL 35487-0203. *Fax:* 205-348-7558; *E-Mail:* gcapril@coe.eng.ua.edu

APRIL, ROBERT WAYNE, ECOLOGICAL ASSESSMENT, WATER QUALITY CRITERIA. *Current Pos:* chemist, US Environ Protection Agency, 78-81, environ scientist, 81-86, chief, Capacity & Storage Sect, 86-89, CHIEF, ECOL RISK ASSESSMENT BR, US ENVIRON PROTECTION AGENCY, 89- *Personal Data:* b Chicago, Ill, Nov 15, 46; div. *Educ:* Univ Chicago, SB, 68; Mass Inst Technol, PhD(analytical chem), 72. *Prof Exp:* Asst prof chem, Univ Colo, Denver, 72-74; vis asst prof chem, Colo Sch Mines, 74-77. *Mem:* Soc Environ Toxicol & Chem. *Res:* Developing tools for ecological quality assessment including water quality criteria, sediment criteria, wildlife criteria, biological criteria, and ecological risk assessment methodologies. *Mailing Add:* 12106 Rockridge Rd Greenbelt MD 20770

APRILLE, THOMAS JOSEPH, JR, TRANSMISSION SYSTEMS ENGINEERING, SONET SDH & ARCHITECTURE. *Current Pos:* MGR, LUCENT TECHNOLOGIES-BELL LABS, NORTH ANDOVER, 72- *Personal Data:* b Boston, Mass, Sept 26, 43. *Educ:* Northeastern Univ, BS, 67; Univ Ill, Urbana, MS, 68, PhD(elec eng), 72. *Honors & Awards:* Guillemin-Cauer Award, Inst Elec & Electronics Engrs, Circuits & Systs Soc, 76. *Prof Exp:* Elec engr, Magnavox Co, Urbana, 68-70. *Concurrent Pos:* Tech assoc ed, Inst Elec & Electronics Engrs Commun Mag, 80-84; assoc ed, Inst Elec & Electronics Engrs Trans Commun, 81-84; mem, Hist Comt, Inst Elec & Electronics Engrs, 82-92, chmn, 90-91; prog evaluator, Accreditation Bd Eng & Technol, 89-93. *Mem:* Fel Inst Elec & Electronics Engrs. *Res:* Computer analysis of autonomous circuits; development of novel amplifier and equalizer circuits; architecture definition of synchronous and ATM telecommunication systems; awarded 5 patents. *Mailing Add:* Lucent Technologies-Bell Labs PO Box 369 Andover MA 01810. *E-Mail:* aprille@bell-labs.com

APRISON, BARRY STEVEN, PRODUCTION OF SCIENCE EXHIBITS, CREATE EDUCATIONAL PROGRAMS. *Current Pos:* asst dir sci, 88, proj dir & sr scientist, 92-95, SR SCIENTIST, MUS SCI & INDUST, 89-, DIR SCI & RES, 96- *Personal Data:* b Galesburg, Ill, July 3, 53; m 85, Erin Zucker; c Margaret & Nathan. *Educ:* Ind Univ, AB, 75, MS, 78; Brandeis Univ, PhD(biol), 84. *Prof Exp:* NIH fel biol, Ind Univ, 84-87, res assoc, 87. *Concurrent Pos:* Vis asst prof biol, Ind Univ, 87-88; prin investr, NIH & Great Lakes Regional Genetics Group, 90, Chicago Community Trust, 90, Ctrs for Dis Control, 91-93, NSF, 91-93 & 97-99, Howard Hughes Med Inst, 92-97. *Mem:* Genetics Soc Am; Soc Develop Biol; Am Soc Cell Biol; Am Asn Mus; AAAS; Nat Asn Mus Exhib. *Res:* Development and production of major new science exhibits. *Mailing Add:* Mus Sci & Indust 57th St & Lake Shore Dr Chicago IL 60637

APRISON, MORRIS HERMAN, NEUROCHEMISTRY, NEUROBIOLOGY. *Current Pos:* from asst prof to assoc prof, Dept Biochem & Psychiat, Ind Univ, Indianapolis, 56-64, chief Sect Neurobiol, Inst Psychiat Res, 69-74, prof biochem, Dept Biochem & Psychiat, Med Ctr, 64-78, exec adminr, 73-74, dir, Inst Psychiat Res, 74-78, distinguished prof, 78-93, chief, Sect Appl & Theoret Neurobiol, 78-93, EMER DISTINGUISHED PROF NEUROBIOL & BIOCHEM, SCH MED, IND UNIV, 93- *Personal Data:* b Milwaukee, Wis, Oct 6, 23; m 49, Shirley Reder; c Barry S & Robert B. *Educ:* Univ Wis, BS, 45, cert, 47, MS, 49, PhD(biochem), 52. *Honors & Awards:* Gold Metal Award Distinguished Res, Soc Biol Psychiat, 75. *Prof Exp:* Teaching asst physics, Univ Wis, 47-49; tech asst, Inst Paper Chem, Lawrence Col, 49-50; asst path, Univ Wis, 50-51, asst biochem, 51-52; head biophys sect, Galesburg State Res Hosp, Ill, 52-56. *Concurrent Pos:* Mem, study sect neuropsychol, NIMH, 70-74 & adv panel, Molecular & Cellular Neurobiol Prog, NSF, 84-86; co-ed, Advances Neurochem, 73-92; mem bd overseers, St Meinrad, 74-77; adv ed, J Biol Psychiat, 68-83, J Develop Neuropharmacol, 69-93, J Neurochem, 75-79, J Comparative & Gen Pharmacol, 74-75, J Develop Psychobiol, 74-77, J Gen Pharmacol, 75-93; co-chmn, Am Soc Neurochem, 70 & 71, chmn, Sci Prog Comt, 72, coun, 71-73 & 75-79; dep chief ed, J Neurochem, 80-83; mem, Comt Recommendation US Army Sci Res, Bd Physics & Astron, Nat Res Coun, 87-89; mem bd govs, Inst Advan Studies, Ind Univ, 89-93. *Mem:* Biophys Soc; Soc Biol Psychiat; Int Soc Neurochem (secy, 75-79, chmn 79-81); Am Soc Neurochem; Soc Neurosci; Sigma Xi. *Res:* Neurochemical correlates of behavior; molecular modeling of neurotransmitter-receptor interactions with computers; applied and theoretical neurobiology; development of animal models for studying depression and psychosomatic disease. *Mailing Add:* 9268 Spring Forest Dr Indianapolis IN 46260. *Fax:* 317-274-1365

APRUZESE, JOHN PATRICK, PLASMA RADIATION SOURCES, SPECTROSCOPY. *Current Pos:* SUPV RES PHYSICIST & HEAD RADIATION DYNAMICS SECT, NAVAL RES LAB, 82- *Personal Data:* b Hartford, Conn, Nov 2, 48; m 78, Janice Hadler; c Laura & Stephanie. *Educ:* Yale Univ, BS, 70; Univ Wis-Madison, PhD, 74. *Prof Exp:* Lectr & Planetarium dir astron, Univ Wyo, 74-75; post doc res fel, Naval Res Lab, 75-76; physicist, Sci Appln Int Corp, 76-82. *Mem:* Am Phys Soc; Am Astron Soc. *Res:* Plasma radiation sources; radiation transport and hydrodynamics in plasmas; numerical modeling of atomic kinetics and radiation transport; laser propagation and interaction with plasma; plasma processing. *Mailing Add:* Naval Res Lab Radiation Hydrodynamics Br Code 6721 Washington DC 20375-5346

APSIMON, JOHN W, ORGANIC CHEMISTRY. *Current Pos:* from asst prof to assoc prof, 62-70, dean grad studies & res, 90-96, assoc vpres res, 93-96, vpres acad, 96-97, PROF ORG CHEM, CARLETON UNIV, ONT, 70-, ASSOC DEAN & DIR RES, 81-, VPRES EXTERNAL & RES, 97- *Personal Data:* b Liverpool, Eng, Aug 5, 35; m 61, 80, Karen Bergenstein; c Joanne, Paul, Michele, Megan & Noah. *Educ:* Univ Liverpool, BSc, 56, PhD(org chem), 59. *Honors & Awards:* Merck Sharpe & Dohme lectr, 74. *Prof Exp:* Demonstr org chem, Univ Liverpool, 59-60; fel, Nat Res Coun Can, 60-62. *Concurrent Pos:* Sr ed, Can J Chem, 78-83; co-ed in chief, Natural Toxins, 91- *Mem:* Am Chem Soc; Chem Inst Can; Royal Soc Chem; AAAS; Am Soc Pharmacog. *Res:* Synthesis, structure and function of natural products, especially mycotoxins; organic synthesis. *Mailing Add:* 601 Robertson Hall Carleton Univ 1125 Colonel By Drive Ottawa ON K1S 5B6 Can

APT, KENNETH ELLIS, NUCLEAR CHEMISTRY. *Current Pos:* asst assoc dir chem, Earth & Life Sci, 80-84, assoc chem div leader, 84-88, arms control analyst, Ctr Nat Security Studies, 88-91, PROG MGR, ARMS REDUCTION VERIFICATION, LOS ALAMOS NAT LAB, 91- *Personal Data:* b Bellingham, Wash, Apr 27, 45; c 2. *Educ:* Western Wash Univ, BA, 67; Mass Inst Technol, PhD(nuclear chem), 71. *Prof Exp:* Res asst, Mass Inst Technol, 67-71; fel, Chem & Nuclear Chem Group, Los Alamos Sci Lab, 71-73, staff mem, Environ Studies Group, 73-76, staff mem, Chem & Nuclear Chem Group, 76-78; int nuclear safeguards officer, Int Atomic Energy Agency, Vienna, 78-80. *Concurrent Pos:* Mem, Tech Comn Natural Fission Reactors, Int Atomic Energy Agency, 77-78. *Mem:* AAAS; Am Chem Soc. *Res:* Low-energy nuclear physics, analytical chemistry, isotope geochemistry, nuclear waste disposal, solid-state radiation dosimetry and atmospheric monitoring; international nuclear safeguards, non-destructive assay, policy analysis; arms control verification. *Mailing Add:* Los Alamos Nat Lab MS E550 Los Alamos NM 87545

APTE, CHIDANAND, KNOWLEDGE BASED SYSTEMS, BUSINESS APPLICATIONS. *Current Pos:* RES STAFF MEM, INT BUS MACH T J WATSON RES CTR, 84- *Personal Data:* b Miraj, India. *Educ:* Indian Inst Technol, India, BTech, 76; Rutgers Univ, PhD(computer sci), 84. *Prof Exp:* Programmer, Indian Inst Technol Bombay Computer Ctr, 76-78; mem tech staff, RCA Astro-Electronics, 80-82. *Concurrent Pos:* Adj lectr, Polytech Univ, 85; assoc ed, Expert Mag, Inst Elec & Electronics Engrs, Computer Soc, 89- *Mem:* Sr mem Inst Elec & Electronics Engrs; Asn Comput Mach; Am Asn Artificial Intel. *Res:* Knowledge base organizations for intelligent problem solving applications, with an emphasis on knowledge representation and qualitative modeling; exploring use of large-scale knowledge bases in business and marketing applications. *Mailing Add:* Int Bus Mach Corp Thomas J Watson Res Ctr PO Box 218 Yorktown Heights NY 10598

APTER, NATHANIEL STANLEY, PSYCHIATRY. *Current Pos:* RETIRED. *Personal Data:* b New York, NY, May 10, 13; m 41, 80, Valerie Wane; c Marion (Quinn), Terri (Newbery) & Jessie (Cooley). *Educ:* Cornell Univ, AB, 33; Univ Buffalo, MD, 38; Chicago Inst Psychoanal, grad, 58. *Prof Exp:* Rotating intern, Beth Israel Hosp, NY, 38-39; psychiat intern, Bellevue Hosp, 39-40; resident neurol, Kings Co Hosp, 40-42; asst psychiat, Johns Hopkins Univ, 42-44, house officer, Johns Hopkins Hosp, 42-44; from asst prof to assoc prof & head dept, Univ Chicago, 46-55, prof lectr psychiat, 55-84; resident adj prof oceanog, Nova Univ, 84-95. *Concurrent Pos:* Chief investr res proj schizophrenia, Manteno State Hosp, 51-69, chief psychiat consult, 69-; attend psychiat, Michael Reese Hosp, 54-73, sr attend & res psychiat, 73-; psychiat consult, State Dept Ment Health, 54-; chief consult, McLean Co Ment Health Clin, Bloomington, Ill, 57-68; sr psychiat consult, Ill State Psychiat Inst, 59-71, distinguished consult, 71-78; chief psychiat consult, Tinley Park Ment Health Clin, 70-74, 75-81. *Mem:* Fel AAAS; fel Am Psychiat Asn. *Res:* Schizophrenia; shell development in marine gastropods. *Mailing Add:* 55 Country Club Lane PO Box 407 New London NH 03257

APUZZIO, J J, MATERNAL-FETAL MEDICINE. *Current Pos:* DIR, HUMAN GENETICS & INFECTIOUS DIS, UNIV HOSP, NEWARK, 83- *Educ:* Rutgers Univ, BA, 69; Col Med & Dent, MD, 73. *Prof Exp:* Clin instr, Col Med & Dent NJ, 74-76, from instr to asst prof obstet & gynecol, 76-83; assoc prof obstret & gynecol, Univ Med & Dent NJ, 83-86, prof radiol, dir maternal-fetal med. *Concurrent Pos:* Consult, obstet & gynecol, Vet Admin Hosp, East Orange, NJ, 79-88; attending, Univ Hosp, 79-; consult maternal fetal med, St Michaels Hosp, Newark, 80-88, St Elizabeths Hosp, Elizabeth, NJ, 76-88. *Mem:* Fel Am Col Surgeons; Am Fertility Soc; Am Col Obstetricians & Gynecologists. *Mailing Add:* Dept Obstet & Gynecol Univ Med & Dent NJ Med Sch 185 S Orange Ave Newark NJ 07103-2757

AQUALINO, ALAN, RADIATION THERAPY. *Current Pos:* res assoc physics, Univ Va, 81-82, fel biomed eng, 83-85, radiol physics specialist, Med Ctrs, 85-90, ASST PROF RADIOL PHYSICS, UNIV VA MED CTR, 90- *Personal Data:* b Glen Cove, NY, Sept 15, 51; m 82, Sandra Bryant. *Educ:* Univ Va, BA, 74, PhD(physics), 82; Am Bd Radiol, dipl, 90. *Mem:* Sigma Xi; Am Asn Physicists Med; Am Asn Physics Teachers. *Res:* Development of treatment modalities in radiation therapy; computer applications in medicine; integration of multimedia into medical apprenticeship programs. *Mailing Add:* Creek Bend Sunset Ave Charlottesville VA 22903. *E-Mail:* aa2h@virginia.edu

AQUINO, DOLORES CATHERINE, CHEMISTRY. *Current Pos:* INSTR, SAN JACINTO COL, PASADENA TEX, 93- *Personal Data:* b Chicago, Ill, Oct 12, 49. *Educ:* Ill Inst Technol, BS, 70; Ohio State Univ, PhD(inorg chem), 77. *Prof Exp:* Res chemist, Exxon Res & Eng Co, 77-80, sr chemist, 80-82, coordr technician training, 81-82; instr, Lee Col, Baytown, Tex, 82-92. *Concurrent Pos:* Lectr, Univ Houston, Clear Lake City, 81. *Mem:* Am Chem Soc. *Res:* Synthetic fuels, particularly the chemistry of coal gasification processes; inorganic chemistry, particularly synthesis and characterization of organosilanes and homogeneous catalysis by transition metals. *Mailing Add:* PO Box 56744 Houston TX 77256-6744

ARABYAN, ARA, PARALLEL COMPUTATIONAL METHODS. *Current Pos:* asst prof, 86-92, ASSOC PROF MECH ENG, UNIV ARIZ, 92- *Personal Data:* b Istanbul, Turkey, Mar 11, 53; US citizen; m 85, Colette Djeredjian; c Sanahin. *Educ:* Tex A&M Univ, BSc, 80; Univ Southern Calif, MSc, 82, PhD(mech eng), 86. *Prof Exp:* Grad asst, Univ Southern Calif, 81-86; mem tech staff, Allied-Signal Garrett Corp, 86. *Concurrent Pos:* Consult, Adelberg Labs, 81-85, Phys Educ Dept, Univ Southern Calif, 85-86 & accident invests var law firms, 88-; prin investr, NSF, 86-89 & 88-89, NASA Space Eng Ctr grant & Honeywell, Inc, 90-; panelist, NSF, 89 & 94; NSF presidential young investr, 90; vis prof, Am Univ Armenia, 93; Boeing A D Weilliver fel, 97. *Mem:* Am Soc Mech Engrs. *Res:* Parallel computational methods for simulation and control of complex mechanical systems; distributed control of articulated multijoint biosystems and mechanical linkages. *Mailing Add:* Univ Ariz AME Dept Tucson AZ 85721. *Fax:* 520-621-8191; *E-Mail:* arabyan@arshak.ame.arizona.edu

ARAGAKI, MINORU, PLANT PATHOLOGY. *Current Pos:* RETIRED. *Personal Data:* b Honolulu, Hawaii, June 26, 26; m 52; c 3. *Educ:* Univ Hawaii, BS, 50, MS, 54, PhD(bot), 63. *Prof Exp:* Lab technician, Univ Hawaii, 46-54, jr plant pathologist, 54-61, from asst prof to prof, 61-93. *Mem:* Am Phytopath Soc; Mycol Soc Am. *Res:* Light induced fungal sporulation including inhibitory effects of light; biology of Phytophthora; anatomical changes following invasion by fungal pathogen, particularly host barrier formation. *Mailing Add:* Dept Plant Path Rm 304C St Johns Bldg Univ Hawaii Manoa Honolulu HI 96822

ARAGON, SERGIO RAMIRO, CHEMISTRY. *Current Pos:* assoc prof, 85-91, PROF CHEM, SAN FRANCISCO STATE UNIV, 91- *Personal Data:* b Guatemala City, Guatemala, Mar 6, 49; c 2. *Educ:* Rice Univ, BA, 71; Stanford Univ, MS, 76, PhD(phys chem), 76. *Prof Exp:* Teaching asst, Stanford Univ, 71-75, res asst, 72-76, fel, 76; prof & chmn, Dept Chem, Univ del Valle Guatemala, 77-85. *Concurrent Pos:* Vis scholar chem, Stanford Univ, 80-83. *Mem:* Am Phys Soc; Am Chem Soc. *Res:* Chemistry; published over 24 articles. *Mailing Add:* Dept Chem & Biochem San Francisco State Univ 1600 Holloway Ave San Francisco CA 94132. *E-Mail:* aragons@esmeralda.sfsu.edu

ARAI, HISAO PHILIP, PARASITOLOGY. *Current Pos:* assoc prof, 65-77, PROF ZOOL, UNIV CALGARY, 77- *Personal Data:* b Los Angeles, Calif, Oct 8, 26; m 58. *Educ:* Univ Calif, Los Angeles, AB, 54, PhD(zool), 60. *Prof Exp:* USPHS fel zool, Univ BC, 60-61; assoc prof biol, Ill State Univ, 61-63; asst prof, Univ Alta, 63-65. *Concurrent Pos:* Assoc mem ctr for zoonoses res, Univ Ill, 62. *Mem:* Am Soc Parasitol; Soc Syst Zool; Can Soc Zool; Sigma Xi. *Res:* Physiological ecology; taxonomy; ecology and physiology of animal parasites. *Mailing Add:* Dept Biol Univ Calgary 2500 University Dr NW Calgary AB T2N 1N4 Can

ARAI, KEN-ICHI, DNA REPLICATION, LYMPHOKINES. *Current Pos:* PROF, UNIV TOKYO, 89- *Personal Data:* b Sapporo, Japan, Oct 18, 42; m 71, Naoko; c 1. *Educ:* Univ Tokyo, MD, 67, PhD, 74. *Prof Exp:* Prin sci, DNAX Res Inst, 81-83, dir, 83-89. *Concurrent Pos:* Consult prof, Stanford Univ, 87- *Mem:* Am Asn Biochem & Molecular Biol; Am Asn Immunologists; Japan Molecular Biol Soc. *Res:* T-cell activation and molecular biology of lymphokines; DNA replication. *Mailing Add:* Dept Molecular & Develop Biol Univ Tokyo Inst Med Sci 4-6-1 Shirokanedai Minato-Ku 108 Japan. *Fax:* 813-5449-5429; *E-Mail:* ken-ichi@ims.u-tokyo.ac.jp

ARAKAWA, EDWARD TAKASHI, SOLID STATE PHYSICS, OPTICS. *Current Pos:* CONSULT. *Personal Data:* b Honolulu, Hawaii, Apr 8, 29; m 55, Harue Yamashiro; c Sandra Kay, David Ken, Paul Edward & Carolyn Ann. *Educ:* Howard Col, BS, 51; La State Univ, MS, 53; Univ Tenn, PhD(physics), 57. *Honors & Awards:* IR-100 Award, 81 & 86. *Prof Exp:* Res assoc med physics, Inst Nuclear Studies, Oak Ridge Nat Lab, 53-56, sr res staff mem, 57-93, group leader, 65-93. *Concurrent Pos:* Consult, Radiation Effects Res Found, 58-60; guest scientist, Europ Sci Res Orgn, 70. *Mem:* Fel Optical Soc Am; fel Am Phys Soc. *Res:* Dosimetry of nuclear radiation; electron physics; vacuum ultraviolet spectroscopy; soft x-ray spectroscopy; thin film physics; resonance ionization mass spectroscopy; ellipsometry. *Mailing Add:* Oak Ridge Nat Lab PO Box 2008 4500 S H-160 Oak Ridge TN 37831-6123. *Fax:* 423-574-6210; *E-Mail:* arakawae@ornl.gov

ARAKAWA, TSUTOMU, BIOCHEMISTRY, BIOPHYSICS. *Current Pos:* RES CHEMIST, AMGEN INC, 84- *Personal Data:* b Japan, May 8, 48. *Educ:* Osaka Presecture, BS, 71, MS, 74, PhD(biochem), 77. *Prof Exp:* Res chemist, Washington Univ, St Louis, 83-84. *Mem:* Biophys Soc; Am Soc Biochem & Molecular Biol. *Mailing Add:* 4217 Minnecota Dr Thousand Oaks CA 91360

ARAKI, GEORGE SHOICHI, BIOLOGY. *Current Pos:* From asst prof to assoc prof, 62-74, PROF BIOL, SAN FRANCISCO STATE UNIV, 74-; DIR, CTR INTERDISCIPLINARY SCI, 74- *Personal Data:* b Oakland, Calif, Jan 11, 32; m 58; c 3. *Educ:* San Francisco State Col, AB, 57; Stanford Univ, PhD(biol), 64. *Mem:* AAAS; Sigma Xi. *Res:* Comparative invertebrate physiology; cellular physiology; physiology of feeding and digestion in asteroids; human healing and health processes; biofeedback; autogenic training; intracellular digestive processes in asteroids and slime molds. *Mailing Add:* Dept Biol San Francisco State Univ 1600 Holloway Ave San Francisco CA 94132

ARAKI, MASASUKE, DEVELOPMENTAL NEUROBIOLOGY, STRUCTURE OF THE RETINA. *Current Pos:* Res assoc anat, 78-88, LECTR ANAT, JICHI MED SCH, 88-; SR RESEARCHER, BIOHIST RES HALL, 93-; PROF, DEPT BIOL, KYOTO PREFECTURAL UNIV MED, 94- *Personal Data:* b Kyoto, Japan, Mar 13, 50. *Educ:* Kyoto Univ, BSc, 74, MSc, 76, PhD(develop biol), 79; Jichi Med Sch, DMed, 89. *Concurrent Pos:* Res fel, Univ BC, 83-84; vis lectr, Shiga Univ Med Sci, 85-86 & Kyoto Prefectural Univ Med, 93-94. *Res:* Cellular and molecular mechanism for the development of nervous systems, particularly the neural retina and pineal. *Mailing Add:* Dept Biol Kyoto Prefectural Univ Med Taishogun Kita-Ku Kyoto 603 Japan. *Fax:* 81-75-465-7651; *E-Mail:* araki@koto.kpu__m.ac.jp

ARAKI, MINORU S, AERONAUTICS. *Current Pos:* RETIRED. *Educ:* Stanford Univ, BS, 54, MS, 55. *Prof Exp:* Res asst, Stanford Univ, 54-55; sr res engr, NAm Rocketdyne Div, 55-58; sr scientist, Lockheed Missiles & Space Syst Co Inc, 58-67, chief systems engr, 67-75, asst chief engr, 75-76, dir, Systs Eng, 76-78, dir, Advan Systs, 78-81, vpres, Advan Prog & Develop, 81-83, vpres & prog mgr, Milstar Prog, 83-85, vpres & gen mgr, Space Systs Div, 85-87, exec vpres, 88-95, pres, 95-96. *Mem:* Nat Acad Eng; fel Am Astronaut Soc; Am Inst Aeronaut & Astronaut; Inst Elec & Electronics Engrs; Nat Mgt Asn. *Mailing Add:* 19519 Montevina Rd Los Gatos CA 95030

ARAL, SEVGI O, SOCIOLOGY. *Current Pos:* res sociol, Div Venereal Dis Control, Ctr Prev Servs, Ctrs Dis Control, 78-89, sect chief, Behav Studies sect, 89-91, asst Behav & Epidemiol Interventions, Off Dir, 91-93, ASSOC DIR SCI, DIV SEXUALLY TRANSMITTED DIS, NAT CTR PREV SERVS, CTRS DIS CONTROL, 93- *Personal Data:* b Istanbul, Turkey, May 14, 46. *Educ:* Middle E Tech Univ, BS, 67; Univ Pa, MA, 68; Emory Univ, MA, 70, PhD(sociol), 72. *Prof Exp:* From asst prof to assoc prof sociol, Middle E Tech Univ, Andara, Turkey, 72-79, chairperson, Dept Soc Sci, 77-79. *Concurrent Pos:* Vis assoc prof sociol, Sch Soc Sci, Ga Inst Technol, 81-83; clin prof, Div Health Servs Res, Univ Wash Sch Public Health, 92-; mem, Int Soc Sexually Transmitted Dis Res Bd. *Res:* Author of numerous publications. *Mailing Add:* Div Std Prev Ctr Dis Control & Prev 1600 Clifton Rd NE Atlanta GA 30333

ARALA-CHAVES, MARIO PASSALAQUA, immunobiology, for more information see previous edition

ARAMINI, JAN MARIE, health psychology, for more information see previous edition

ARAMS, F(RANK) R(OBERT), TELECOMMUNICATIONS. *Current Pos:* V PRES, LNR COMMUN, INC, 71- *Personal Data:* b Danzig, Ger; nat US; m, Edith Knoll; c Mark & Ronald. *Educ:* Univ Mich, BSE, 47; Harvard Univ, ScM, 48; Stevens Inst Technol, MS, 53; Polytech Inst Brooklyn, PhD(electrophysics), 61. *Prof Exp:* Group leader, RCA Corp, 48-56; consult advan tech develop, AIL Div, Eaton Corp, 56-59, head, Infrared & Electrooptics Dept, 65-71. *Mem:* Fel Inst Elec & Electronics Engrs; Optical Soc Am. *Res:* Satellite communications; low-noise receivers; lasers and coherent optical and infrared systems. *Mailing Add:* LNR Commun Inc 180 Marcus Blvd Hauppauge NY 11788. *E-Mail:* farams@lnr.com

ARANDA, JACOB VELASCO, PEDIATRICS, NEONATOLOGY. *Current Pos:* from asst prof to assoc prof pediat & pharmacol, 74-84, PROF PEDIAT & PHARMACOL, FAC MED, MCGILL UNIV, 84-; DIR, PERINATAL RES CTR, LADY DAVIS INST. *Personal Data:* b Isabela, Philippines, Dec 29, 42; Can citizen; m 74; c Kenneth F & Christopher J. *Educ:* Manila Cent Univ, MD, 65; McGill Univ, PhD(pharmacol), 75; FRCP(C), 85. *Honors & Awards:* Queen Elizabeth II Res Scientist Award, Queen Elizabeth II Res Found, 76. *Prof Exp:* Intern med, US Naval Hosp, 64-65, Wash Hosp Ctr, 65-66; resident pediat, State Univ NY Hosp Ctr, 66-68; fel neonatology, Case Western Res Univ, Cleveland Metrop Gen Hosp, 68-69; res fel, McGill Univ, Montreal Children's Hosp, 69-71; res fel pharmacol, Med Res Coun Can, 71-74. *Concurrent Pos:* Neonatologist & pediatrician, Royal Victoria Hosp, Jewish Gen Hosp, St Mary's Hosp & Montreal Children's Hosp, 74-; dir develop pharmacol & perinatal res, Apnea-Sudden Infant Death Syndrome Treat & Res Ctr, Montreal Children's Hosp, 78-94; ed-in-chief develop pharmacol & therapeut, Int J Perinatal-Pediat Drug Ther, Karger, Switz, 79-94. *Mem:* Am Acad Pediat; Am Soc Pharmacol & Exp Therapeut; Am Soc Clin Pharmacol & Therapeut; Can Soc Clin Invest; NY Acad Sci; Soc Pediat Res. *Res:* Pharmacology of the fetus and newborn; effects of drugs on control breathing; regulation and drug effect on cerebral blood flow of the newborn; adverse drug effects and utilization in the perinatal period; epidemiology. *Mailing Add:* McGill Univ Lady Davis Inst 3755 Cote St Catherine Rd Montreal PQ H3T 1E2 Can. *Fax:* 514-340-7565

ARANEO, BARBARA ANN, IMMUNOBIOLOGY OF RECOMBINANT VACCINES. *Current Pos:* ASST PROF IMMUNOL, UNIV UTAH, 82- *Personal Data:* c 2. *Educ:* Univ Rochester, PhD(microbiol), 76. *Mem:* Am Asn Immunologists; Am Asn Pathologists. *Res:* Immunobiology of T-cell ion responsiveness to antigen and new strategies for the development of effective anti-viral vaccines. *Mailing Add:* Paradigm Biosci Inc 2401 Foothill Dr Salt Lake City UT 84109

ARANOW, RUTH LEE HORWITZ, PHYSICAL CHEMISTRY. *Current Pos:* NIH spec fel, 69-71, res scientist, 69-74, FEL CHEM, JOHNS HOPKINS UNIV, 74-, LECTR, 76-, SR ACAD ADV. *Personal Data:* b Brooklyn, NY, Aug 25, 29; m 50, George Jr; c 3. *Educ:* Brooklyn Col, BS, 51; Johns Hopkins Univ, MA, 52, PhD(chem), 57. *Prof Exp:* Jr instr chem, Johns Hopkins Univ, 51-53,; asst, 53-54, inst, McCoy Col, 54-57, staff scientist, Res Inst Advan Studies, Martin-Marietta Co, 57-69. *Res:* Statistical mechanics; effect of noise on neural membranes; effects of chemicals on behavior. *Mailing Add:* Off Acad Advising 235 Mergenthaler Hall Johns Hopkins Univ 34th & Charles Sts Baltimore MD 21218

ARASTOOPOUR, HAMID, MULTIPHASE FLOW, PARTICLE TECHNOLOGY & FLUIDIZATION. *Current Pos:* assoc prof chem eng & dir, Energy Ctr, 85-89, prof & chmn, 89-95, CHMN CHEM & ENVIRON ENG, ILL INST TECHNOL, 95- *Personal Data:* b Sept 1, 51; m, Sheila; c Golnaz & Nassim. *Educ:* Abadan Inst Technol, BS, 73; Ill Inst Technol, MS, 75, PhD(gas eng), 78. *Prof Exp:* Adj asst prof & supvr, Inst Gas Technol, 78-83, adj assoc prof & mgr, 83-85. *Concurrent Pos:* Am Chem Soc rep, Steering Comt, Intersociety Energy Conversion Eng Conf, 79-93; chmn fluidization & particle, Am Inst Chem Engrs, 94- *Mem:* Am Inst Chem Engrs; Am Chem Soc; Soc Petrol Eng; Sigma Xi; Am Soc Eng Educ. *Res:* Multiphase flow and powder technologies application in energy conversion, material processing and environmental processes; use of kinetic theory in gas/particle flow; theory of agglomeration and attrition; pulverization of polymeric materials; biodegradable materials processing; flow through porous media. *Mailing Add:* Dept Chem Eng Ill Inst Technol 3300 S Federal St Chicago IL 60616-3732. *Fax:* 312-567-8874

ARATA, DOROTHY, NUTRITION. *Current Pos:* from asst prof to prof foods & nutrit, 57-69, assoc dir, Honors Col, 69-71, PROF HUMAN DEVELOP, COL HUMAN MED, MICH STATE UNIV, 69-, ACTG DIR, HONORS COL, 75-, ASST PROVOST, 71- *Personal Data:* b New York, NY, Mar 8, 28. *Educ:* Pratt Inst, BS, 48; Cornell Univ, MS, 50; Univ Wis, PhD(biochem), 56. *Prof Exp:* Asst dept foods & nutrit, Cornell Univ, 48-50, technician dept biochem, Med Sch, 50-52, fel, 56-57; asst biochem, Univ Wis, 53-56. *Concurrent Pos:* Acad admin intern, Am Coun Educ, 68, mem comn educ credit, 74-77; mem, Mich Comt Selection of Rhodes Scholars, 77 & 78; mem, Col Level Exam Prog, Am Coun Educ, 78-; mem, Mich State Planning Comt Concerning Nat Identification Women in Higher Educ, 78- *Mem:* AAAS; Am Chem Soc; Am Inst Nutrit; Am Inst Chem; Am Asn Higher Educ. *Res:* Biochemical disorders associated with nutritional deficiencies; cellular disruptions in fatty livers induced by threonine deficiency. *Mailing Add:* 5670 Chapman Ave Memphis TN 38119

ARAUJO, FAUSTO G, MEDICAL RESEARCH. *Current Pos:* RESEARCHER IMMUNOL TOXOPLASMOSIS, RES INST PALO ALTO MED FOUND, 78- *Personal Data:* b Brazil, Dec 3, 35. *Educ:* Arnaldo Col, Brazil, BS, 55; Fed Univ Miras Gerais, DVM, 59; Tulane Univ, MPH, 64; Stanford Univ, PhD(microbiol), 78. *Mem:* Am Soc Microbiol; Am Soc Trop Med. *Mailing Add:* Res Inst Palo Alto Med Found 860 Bryant St Palo Alto CA 94301-2799

ARAUJO, OSCAR EDUARDO, PHARMACY. *Current Pos:* from asst prof to assoc prof, 62-74, PROF PHARM, UNIV FLA, 74- *Personal Data:* b Brazil, June 2, 27; nat US; m 50; c 2. *Educ:* Purdue Univ, BS, 54, MS, 55, PhD(pharm), 57. *Prof Exp:* Asst pharm, Purdue Univ, 54-55; asst prof, Ohio Northern Univ, 57-62. *Mem:* Am Pharmaceut Asn; Am Asn Cols Pharm; Acad Pharmaceut Sci. *Res:* Dermatology and clinical pharmacy. *Mailing Add:* Dept Pharm Univ Fla PO Box 100484 Gainesville FL 32610-0484

ARAUJO, ROGER JEROME, PHYSICAL CHEMISTRY. *Current Pos:* RES FEL, CORNING INC, 61- *Personal Data:* b Fall River, Mass, Mar 13, 34; m 54; c 4. *Educ:* Bradford Durfee Tech Inst, BS, 56; Brown Univ, PhD(phys chem), 62. *Mem:* Am Chem Soc; fel Am Ceramic Soc; Mat Res Soc. *Res:* Hydrogen aging of optical fibers; radiation damage in optical fibers. *Mailing Add:* 5 Seneca Dr Horseheads NY 14845-1082

ARAVE, CLIVE W, ANIMAL BREEDING. *Current Pos:* from asst prof to assoc prof, 65-93, PROF ANIMAL DAIRY VET SCI, UTAH STATE UNIV, 93- *Personal Data:* b Idaho Falls, Idaho, May 12, 31; m 50, Carley McMurtrey; c Wendy, Stephanie, Joe, Christine, Lorraine & James. *Educ:* Utah State Univ, BS, 56, MS, 57; Univ Calif, Davis, PhD(genetics), 63. *Prof Exp:* Asst mgr, Lavacre Farms, Calif, 57-59; lab technician genetics, Univ Calif, 59-60; asst prof dairy husb, Chico State Col, 63-65. *Concurrent Pos:* NSF res grant, New Zealand, 80-81; mem, Animal Care Comt, Am Dairy Sci Asn, 87-, regional proj NC-119, 83-, secy, 86-87 & 88-89, chmn, 87-88 & 90-91, regional proj NCR-131, 84-; consult, Livestock Conserv Inst, 92-95 & Off Int Coop & Develop, 93. *Mem:* Am Dairy Sci Asn; Am Soc Animal Sci. *Res:* Dairy cattle production genetics and management; animal breeding; animal behavior of domesticated species. *Mailing Add:* Animal Sci Utah State Univ Logan UT 84322-0001. *Fax:* 435-750-2118; *E-Mail:* carave@cc.usu.edu

ARBEENY, CYNTHIA M, LIPOPROTEIN METABOLISM. *Current Pos:* ASST PROF MED, ALBERT EINSTEIN COL MED, 82- *Educ:* Rutgers Univ, PhD(physiol), 77. *Mailing Add:* Dept Clin Pharmacol Sepracor Pharmaceut 33 Locke Dr Marlborough MA 01752-1183

ARBENZ, JOHANN KASPAR, GEOLOGY. *Current Pos:* CONSULT GEOLOGISTS, 83- *Personal Data:* b Berne, Switz, Aug 27, 18; nat US; m 45; c 3. *Educ:* Univ Berne, PhD(geol), 45. *Prof Exp:* Asst geologist, R Helbling Surv Off, 46-47 & Swiss Geol Surv, 47; from asst prof to assoc prof geol, Univ Okla, 48-55; geologist, Shell Oil Co, 55-75, sr staff geologist, 75-83. *Mem:* Geol Soc Am; Am Asn Petrol Geologists; Swiss Geol Soc. *Res:* Structural and petroleum geology. *Mailing Add:* 3964 Wonderland Hill Ave Boulder CO 80304

ARBER, WERNER, MOLECULAR GENETICS. *Current Pos:* prof, 71-96, rector, 86-88, EMER PROF MICROBIOL, UNIV BASEL, 96- *Personal Data:* b Granichen, Switz, June 3, 29; m 66; c 2. *Hon Degrees:* Dr, Univ Southern Calif, 86, Univ Louis Pasteur, Strasbourg, 88. *Honors & Awards:* Nobel Prize in Med, 78. *Prof Exp:* Asst, Lab Biophys, Univ Geneva, 53-58; res assoc , Dept Microbiol, Univ Southern Calif, 58-59; prof molecular genetics, Univ Geneva, 62-70; vis investr, Dept Molecular Biol, Univ Calif, Berkeley, 70-71. *Mem:* Foreign mem Nat Acad Sci; hon foreign mem Am Acad Arts & Sci. *Res:* Biological evolution; genetic basis of microbial evolution; DNA rearrangements; transposition; horizontal gene transfer; restriction-modification systems; microbial genetics; bacteriophage development. *Mailing Add:* Biozentrum Universitat Basel 70 Klingelbergstr CH-4056 Basel Switzerland

ARBIB, MICHAEL A, COMPUTER SCIENCES. *Current Pos:* chmn dept comput & info sci, 70-75, PROF COMPUT & INFO SCI & ADJ PROF PSYCHOL, UNIV MASS, AMHERST, 70-, DIR, CTR SYSTS NEUROSCI, 74- *Personal Data:* b Eastbourne, Eng, May 28, 40; m 65; c 2. *Educ:* Univ Sydney, BSc, 61; Mass Inst Technol, PhD(math), 63. *Prof Exp:* Assoc prof elec eng, Stanford Univ, 69-70. *Res:* Brain modelling; information processing in complex systems, in automata and system theory and in neurophysiology and psychology; social implications of computer science. *Mailing Add:* Dept Comput Sci Univ Southern Calif 3614 Wattway HNB-03 Los Angeles CA 90089

ARBITER, NATHANIEL, MINERAL PROCESSING, HYDROMETALLURGY. *Current Pos:* res asst eng, 36-43, from assoc prof to prof, 51-69, EMER PROF MINERAL ENG, COLUMBIA UNIV, 77-; ADJ PROF METALL, UTAH, SALT LAKE CITY, 84- *Personal Data:* b Yonkers, NY, Jan 2, 11; m 34, 60; c 6. *Educ:* Columbia Univ, BA, 32. *Prof Exp:* Res metallurgist, Battelle Mem Inst, 43-44 & Phelps Dodge Corp, 44-51; dir res & chief metall, Anaconda Co, Tucson, Ariz, 51-77. *Concurrent Pos:* Consult, 51-68, 77- *Mem:* Nat Acad Eng; hon mem Am Inst Mining Engrs; Soc Mining Eng. *Res:* Author of 70 publications in mineral processing; extract metal. *Mailing Add:* 6300 S High Valley Rd Vail AZ 85641. *Fax:* 520-647-3845

ARBOGAST, RICHARD TERRANCE, insect pests stored products, ecology, for more information see previous edition

ARBUCKLE, GEORGIA ANN, CONDUCTING POLYMERS-SYNTHETIC METAL, ELECTROCHEMISTRY. *Current Pos:* ASST PROF CHEM, RUTGERS STATE UNIV, NJ, 89- *Personal Data:* b Philadelphia, Pa, Sept, 1961. *Educ:* Rutgers Univ, BA, 83; Univ Penn, PhD(chem), 87. *Prof Exp:* Researcher, Princeton Univ, 87-89. *Concurrent Pos:* Henry Rutgers res fel, Rutgers Univ, 89-91; prin investr, Res Corp grant, 90-91, 92-94, petroleum res, Am Chem Soc, 90-92 & 93-; Young Investr Award, NSF, 92-; Rutgers innovative res award, Hoechst Celanese, 93-94. *Mem:* Am Chem Soc; AAAS; Asn Women Sci; Electrochem Soc. *Res:* Research involving synthesis and characterization of conducting polymers is carried out to understand the factors influencing high conductivity, both chemically and electrochemically prepared polymers are studied with the quartz crystal microbalance and various spectroscopic methods. *Mailing Add:* Dept Chem Rutgers Univ Camden NJ 08102. *Fax:* 609-225-6506

ARBULU, AGUSTIN, SURGERY, THORACIC SURGERY. *Current Pos:* from instr to assoc prof, 62-72, PROF SURG, SCH MED, WAYNE STATE UNIV, 72- *Personal Data:* b Lima, Peru, Sept 15, 28; US citizen; c 3. *Educ:* San Marcos Univ, Lima, MB, 54, MD, 55. *Honors & Awards:* Frederick A Coller Award, Am Col Surgeons, 68 & 72; Cecile Lehman Mayer Res Award, Am Col Chest Physicians, 68, 69 & 70, Regents Award, 72. *Prof Exp:* Asst chief surg, Wichita Vet Admin Hosp, Kans, 61-62. *Concurrent Pos:* Asst chief surg, Vet Admin Hosp, Allen Park, Mich, 62-66, actg chief surg, 66-67, consult, 67-; fel res coun, Am Heart Asn, 78; assoc, Hutzel & Harper Hosps, Detroit; attend surg, Detroit Gen Hosp; consult chest surg, Grace Hosp, Providence Hosp & Oakwood Hosp; cardiac surgeon, St Joseph Mercy Hosp, Pontiac & St John Hosp, Detroit; gov, Am Col Chest Physicians, 83-88, chmn, Int Comt, 89- *Mem:* Am Thoracic Soc; Am Col Chest Physicians; Soc Thoracic Surg; Peruvian Am Med Soc (pres, 73-74); Am Asn Thoracic Surg; Europ Asn Thoracic Surg. *Mailing Add:* Midwest Surg Assn 829 Harper Prof Bldg 4160 John R St Detroit MI 48201-2021

ARCADI, JOHN ALBERT, UROLOGICAL ONCOLOGY, UROLOGIC RESEARCH. *Current Pos:* res assoc, 57-70, RES PROF BIOL, WHITTIER COL, 70- *Personal Data:* b Whittier, Calif, Oct 23, 24; m 51, Doris Bohanan; c 7. *Educ:* Univ Notre Dame, BS, 47; Johns Hopkins Univ, MD, 50. *Prof Exp:*

Nat Cancer Inst fel urol, Brady Urol Inst, Johns Hopkins Hosp, 51-52, 53-55; asst prof, Univ Southern Calif Sch Med, 55-60. *Concurrent Pos:* Attend urologist, Presby Community Hosp, Whittier, Calif, 59-; coordr prostate cancer res, Huntington Med Res Inst. *Mem:* Am Asn Anatomists; Endocrine Soc; Am Soc Cell Biol; Am Col Surgeons; Am Urol Asn; fel AAAS. *Res:* Factors associated with the growth and atrophy of the prostate gland; role of the extracellular matrix components including mast cells in prostate growth particularly its role in the production of benign prostatic hyperplasia. *Mailing Add:* PO Box 9220 Whittier CA 90608. *Fax:* 562-693-5936

ARCAND, GEORGE MYRON, ANALYTICAL CHEMISTRY, INORGANIC CHEMISTRY. *Current Pos:* RETIRED. *Personal Data:* b Ocean Falls, BC, Feb 9, 24; nat US; m 52. *Educ:* Calif Inst Technol, BS, 50, PhD(chem), 55. *Prof Exp:* Asst prof chem, Univ Mo, 55-58 & Mont State Col, 58-62; sr scientist, Jet Propulsion Lab, Calif Inst Technol, 62-65, scientist specialist, 65; from assoc prof to prof chem, Idaho State Univ, 65-90, dept chmn, 87-90. *Mem:* Am Chem Soc; Sigma Xi. *Res:* Electro-analytical methods; mechanisms of liquid-liquid extraction processes and their use in the study of aqueous systems; inorganic complex ions in aqueous solutions; electrochemistry of batteries; environmental trace analysis. *Mailing Add:* 425 S 19th St Pocatello ID 83201-3463

ARCE, A ANTHONY, PSYCHIATRY. *Current Pos:* PROF PSYCHIAT, MED COL, HAHNEMANN UNIV, 76-, CHMN DEPT, 85- *Personal Data:* b San Juan, Puerto Rico, June 13, 23; m 71; c 3. *Educ:* Washington & Jefferson Col, BS, 42; Med Sch, Temple Univ, MD, 46. *Honors & Awards:* Warren Williams Award, Am Psychiat Asn, 84. *Prof Exp:* Assoc dir psychiat, Grasslands Hosp, 62-67; dir aftercare, NY State Dept Ment Hyg, 68-71; assoc clin prof, Col Physicians & Surgeons, Columbia Univ, 71-76. *Concurrent Pos:* Vis prof, Univ Mex Res Ctr, 69 & Staff Col, Nat Inst Ment Health, 79-81; dir, Meyer-Manhattan Psychiat Ctr, 71-76 & Hahnemann Community Ment Health Ctr, 76-84. *Mem:* Fel Am Psychiat Asn; fel Am Col Ment Health; fel Am Orthopsychiat Asn. *Res:* Mental health services minorities; administration (planning and development) programs; cross-cultural issues on mental health services and training; homeless mentally ill. *Mailing Add:* Dept Mental Health Sci Hahnemann Med Col Broad & Vine Sts Philadelphia PA 19102

ARCE, GINA, BIOLOGY. *Current Pos:* assoc prof, 58-69, PROF BOT, CALIF STATE UNIV, FRESNO, 69- *Personal Data:* b Cuba, Aug 28, 29; nat US. *Educ:* George Peabody Col, BA, 48, MA, 49; Vanderbilt Univ, PhD(biol), 56. *Prof Exp:* Teacher high sch, 49-51; instr bot, Vanderbilt Univ, 56-57. *Mem:* Bot Soc Am; Phycol Soc Am. *Res:* Taxonomy of green algae. *Mailing Add:* Dept Biol Calif State Univ 2555 E San Ramon Fresno CA 93740-8034

ARCE, JOSE EDGAR, geophysics, geology, for more information see previous edition

ARCENEAUX, JOSEPH LINCOLN, MICROBIOLOGY, BACTERIAL PHYSIOLOGY. *Current Pos:* asst prof, 70-75, asst dean student affairs, 78-92, ASSOC PROF MICROBIOL, MED CTR, UNIV MISS, 75-, ASSOC DEAN STUDENT AFFAIRS, SCH MED, 92- *Personal Data:* b Lafayette, La, Aug 13, 41; m 70, Jean E LeBlanc; c Jacques L. *Educ:* Univ Southwestern La, BS, 63; Univ Tex, Austin, PhD(microbiol), 68. *Prof Exp:* NIH fel, Princeton Univ, 67-70. *Mem:* Am Soc Microbiol. *Res:* Chromosome replication and genetic studies in Bacillus subtilis. *Mailing Add:* Dept Microbiol Univ Miss Sch Med 2500 N State St Jackson MS 39216-4505

ARCESE, PAUL SALVATORE, MEDICAL RESEARCH. *Current Pos:* from res assoc to asst dir clin res, 65-74, sr assoc dir clin res, 74-78, DIR CLIN RES, SANDOZ PHARMACEUT, 78- *Personal Data:* b West New York, NJ, Mar 14, 30; m 53; c 2. *Educ:* NY Univ, BA, 51, MS, 58, PhD(endocrinol), 64. *Prof Exp:* Lab technician biochem & endocrinol, Merck Inst Therapeut Res, 54-60, from res asst to res assoc, 60-65. *Mem:* Acad Psychosom Med; Am Asn Study Headache. *Res:* Adrenal steroid metabolism; hormonal effects on erythropoiesis in the hypophysectomized rat. *Mailing Add:* 48 Valleyview Rd Warren NJ 07059

ARCESI, JOSEPH A, ORGANIC CHEMISTRY, POLYMER CHEMISTRY. *Current Pos:* Sr polymer chemist, Eastman Kodak Co, 67-81, asst supt, Synthetic Chem Div, 81-84, div dir, Chem Develop Div, 84-90, DIV MGR, SYNTHETIC CHEM, EASTMAN KODAK CO, 90- *Personal Data:* b Sayre, Pa, Sept 1, 38; m 78; c 3. *Educ:* Gettysburg Col, BA, 60; Univ Del, PhD(org polymer chem), 64. *Res:* Polymer preparation and evaluation; photo-polymers; photo-resist. *Mailing Add:* Eastman Kodak Co 2400 Mt Reed Blvd Rochester NY 14650-3033

ARCH, STEPHEN WILLIAM, NEUROBIOLOGY. *Current Pos:* from asst prof to assoc prof, 72-82, PROF BIOL, REED COL, 82-, L N RUBEN PROF BIOL, 96- *Personal Data:* b Los Angeles, Calif, May 15, 42; m 64, Elizabeth Clark; c Alexandra & Victoria. *Educ:* Stanford Univ, AB, 64; Univ Chicago, PhD(biol), 70. *Prof Exp:* Res fel neurobiol, Calif Inst Technol, 70-72. *Concurrent Pos:* Alfred P Sloan Found res fel neurobiol, 73-75; prin investr grants, Med Res Found Ore, NSF & NIH; mem neurol B study sect, NIH, 82-86; adj prof cell biol, Ore Health Sci Univ, 92-; consult, cell & molecular biol, GRE, Ore Health Sci Found; vis sr scientist, Ore Health Sci Univ, 93-94. *Mem:* Soc Gen Physiol; Sigma Xi; Soc for Neuroscience. *Res:* Analysis of biochemical and molecular regulation at the cellular level in identified neuroendocrine cells. *Mailing Add:* Dept Biol Reed Col Portland OR 97202-8199. *Fax:* 503-777-7773; *E-Mail:* sarch@reed.edu

ARCHAMBAULT, DENIS, VIROLOGY, VACCINE DEVELOPMENT. *Current Pos:* RES SCHOLAR & PROF, UNIV QUE, MONTREAL, 90- *Personal Data:* b St Thomas D'Aquin, Que, May 14, 53; m 85, Guylaine Morin; c Marie-Helene & Pierre-Philippe. *Educ:* Univ Montreal, DVM, 76, MSc, 83, PhD(microbiol & immunol), 86. *Prof Exp:* Res fel, Nat Cancer Inst, NIH, Bethesda, 86-88, Nat Lab Immunol, Ottawa, 89-90. *Concurrent Pos:* Med Res Coun Can fel, 86-88 & 89-90; res scientist, Agr Can, 88-89; res scholar, Found Res Health Que, 90- *Mem:* Am Soc Microbiol; AAAS. *Res:* Research program in animal virology and immunology and comparative medicine is associated to the determination of the mechanisms of pathogenesis; the modulation of immune cell activity by viral agents and the development of diagnosis assays and vaccines. *Mailing Add:* Dept Biol Sci Univ Que Sta Centre-Ville PO Box 8888 Montreal PQ H3C 3P8 Can. *Fax:* 514-987-4647

ARCHAMBEAU, CHARLES BRUCE, PHYSICS, GEOPHYSICS. *Current Pos:* prof geol sci, 75-92, PROF PHYSICS, UNIV COLO, BOULDER, 92- *Personal Data:* b Chisholm, Minn, Sept 1, 33; div; c Richard, Annette & Jane. *Educ:* Univ Minn, BS, 55; Calif Inst Technol, PhD, 65. *Honors & Awards:* Pub Serv Award, Fedn Am Scientists, 86. *Prof Exp:* Seismologist, United Electrodynamics, 62-64, Teledyne Industs Inc, 64-66; assoc prof geophys, Calif Inst Technol, Pasadena, 66-69, prof, 69-74. *Concurrent Pos:* Consult, Systs, Sci & Software-Maxwell Indust, La Jolla, Calif & Reston, Va, 70-92, Amoco Prod Res Lab, Tulsa, 86-89, Sci Applns Int, Dept Energy, Las Vegas, 90-91; sr vis fel, Coop Inst Res in Environ Sci, Univ Colo/Nat Ocean Agency Hq, 74-75, mem, 76-82, res assoc, 82-92; mem bd dirs, Tech & Resource Assessment Corp, Boulder; adv arms control affairs, Parliamentarians for Global Action, 84-88, Nat Resources Defense Coun, 85-87; MacArthur Found fel, 88. *Mem:* AAAS; Am Geophys Union; Seismol Soc Am; Fedn Am Scientists; NY Acad Sci. *Res:* Seismology; geophysics. *Mailing Add:* Univ Colo Campus Box 553 Boulder CO 80309

ARCHAMBEAU, JOHN ORIN, RADIATION ONCOLOGY. *Current Pos:* DIR RADIATION BIOL, LOMA LINDA UNIV MED CTR, 84- *Personal Data:* b Maine, Aug 5, 25; c 8. *Educ:* Stanford Univ, AB, 50, MD, 55. *Prof Exp:* Resident path, Univ Chicago, 54-58; fel oncol, Swedish Hosp, 58-60; Fulbright scholar & fel oncol, Curie Found, 60-61; assoc scientist med, Brookhaven Nat Lab, 61-66; dir radiation oncol, Nassau Co Med Ctr, 66-77; chmn radiation oncol, City Hope, 77-82, dir, Dept Radiation Biol Res, 82-84. *Concurrent Pos:* Res collabr, Brookhaven Nat Lab, 66-; prof radiol, State Univ NY Stony Brook, 70-77. *Mem:* Radiation Res Soc; fel Am Col Radiol; Am Soc Therapeut Radiol. *Res:* Cell kinetics; radiation therapy; cell kinetics of irradiated tissues. *Mailing Add:* Loma Linda Univ Med Ctr 11234 Anderson St Loma Linda CA 92354

ARCHANGELSKY, SERGIO, PALEOBOTANY, PALYNOLOGY. *Current Pos:* RES FEL, BUENOS AIRES NATURAL HIST MUS, ARG, 82- *Personal Data:* b Casablanca, Morocco, Mar 27, 31; m 58, Josefa Ballester; c Ana & Miguel. *Educ:* Univ Buenos Aires, Lic en cie, 55, Dr(geol), 57. *Honors & Awards:* Arg Paleontol Asn Award, 78 & 92; Arg Geol Soc Award, 87; Arg Acad Exact Phys & Natural Sci Award, 90; Canon-Konex Award, 93. *Prof Exp:* Prof paleont, Inst Miguel Lillo, Nat Univ Tucuman, 56-61; prof paleobot, La Plata Univ, 61-78; head, Paleobot-Palynol Res Unit, Cirgeo, 75-82. *Concurrent Pos:* Arg Nat Res Coun res fel, 61-; consult, Yacimientos Petroliferos Fiscales, 75-82; distinguished vis prof, Ohio State Univ, Columbus, 84. *Mem:* Arg Paleont Asn (vpres, 61-63 & 74-75, pres, 63-65 & 67-69); Latin Am Paleobot & Palynol Asn (pres, 74-78); Int Paleontol Asn (vpres, 76-85); corresp mem Bot Soc Am; fel Nat Acad Sci Arg; fel Paleobot Soc India. *Res:* Paleobotany and palynology of the Cretaceous in Argentina; palynology of the Lower Tertiary in Argentina; paleobotany and palynology of Carboniferous and Permian periods in Argentina. *Mailing Add:* Urquiza 1132 Vicente Lopez 1638 Buenos Aires Argentina. *Fax:* 54-1-982-5243

ARCHARD, HOWELL OSBORNE, ORAL PATHOLOGY. *Current Pos:* PROF ORAL PATH, SCH DENT MED, STATE UNIV NY, STONY BROOK, 87- *Personal Data:* b Yonkers, NY, Mar 25, 29; m 61; c 1. *Educ:* Rutgers Univ, BSci, 51; Columbia Univ, DDS, 55; Am Bd Oral Path, dipl, 64. *Prof Exp:* Sr asst dent surg, Alaska Native Health Serv, 55-57; dent intern, Columbia-Presby Med Ctr, NY, 57-58; clin assoc stomatology, Sch Dent & Oral Surg, Columbia Univ, 58-60; resident oral path, Nat Inst Dent Res, USPHS, 60-62; asst pathologist, Armed Forces Inst Path, Walter Reed Army Med Ctr, 62-64; chief diag path, Lab Exp Path, Nat Inst Dent Res, 64-79. *Concurrent Pos:* Guest lectr, Armed Forces Inst Path, Nat Naval Med Ctr, Smithsonian Inst, Univ Ala, Stanford Univ & Georgetown Univ, 64-; consult, Advan Training Oral Path, Am Acad Oral Path, 69; asst ed, J Oral Path, 72-; vis scientist, Inst Dent Res, Univ Ala, 72-78. *Mem:* Am Dent Asn; fel Am Acad Oral Path; Int Asn Dent Res; Am Asn Dent Res; Int Asn Oral Pathologists. *Res:* Clinico-pathologic studies of human oral mucosal diseases; inherited and acquired metabolic diseases affecting the dentition. *Mailing Add:* State Univ NY Health Sci Col Med 100 Nicolls Rd Stony Brook NY 11794-0001

ARCHBOLD, NORBERT L, GEOLOGY. *Current Pos:* PROF GEOL, WESTERN ILL UNIV, 68- *Personal Data:* b Ft Wayne, Ind, Apr 7, 30; m 51; c 2. *Educ:* Western Reserve Univ, BS, 52; Univ Mich, MS, 56, PhD(geol), 62. *Prof Exp:* Geologist, US Geol Surv, 53-58, Homestake Mining Co, 61-64 & Nev Bur Mines, 64-68. *Concurrent Pos:* Consult to various mining companies. *Mem:* Geol Soc Am; Am Inst Mining, Metall & Petrol Engrs; Soc Econ Geologists. *Res:* Diabase dikes in Canadian shield; mineral deposit exploration; ore deposits of Nevada. *Mailing Add:* 298 Jana Rd Macomb IL 61455

ARCHBOLD, THOMAS FRANK, METALLURGICAL ENGINEERING, PHYSICAL METALLURGY. *Current Pos:* From asst prof to assoc prof 61-77, PROF METALL ENG, UNIV WASH, 77- *Personal Data:* b Ft Wayne, Ind, Aug 24, 33; m 60; c 3. *Educ:* Purdue Univ, BS, 55, MS, 57, PhD(metall), 61. *Concurrent Pos:* Metall consult, 61- *Mem:* Am Soc Metals; Nat Asn Corrosion Eng; Sigma Xi. *Res:* Diffusion processes; electron microscopy; diffraction; oxidation kinetics; solid state reaction kinetics; metallography; nuclear materials; failure analysis; corrosion. *Mailing Add:* 15863 37th Ave NE Seattle WA 98155

ARCHER, CASS L, MATHEMATICS EDUCATION. *Current Pos:* RETIRED. *Personal Data:* b Spearman, Tex, June 1, 24; m 53; c 3. *Educ:* Univ Tex, Austin, BS, 50, MEd, 54, MA, 59, PhD(math educ), 67. *Prof Exp:* Teacher pub schs, Tex, 50-58; prof math & head dept, Angelo State Univ, 59-84. *Concurrent Pos:* Math consult, Tex Educ Agency, 62-64. *Mem:* Am Math Soc; Math Asn Am. *Res:* Mathematics programs of institutions changing from a two-year to a four-year college. *Mailing Add:* 2810 Vista Delarroyo Dr San Angelo TX 76904

ARCHER, DAVID HORACE, PROCESS DEVELOPMENT, PLANT DESIGN. *Current Pos:* from asst prof to assoc prof, 53-61, ADJ PROF, CARNEGIE-MELLON UNIV, 91- *Personal Data:* b Pittsburgh, Pa, Jan 20, 28; m 50, 76, Alice A Parsons; c Catherine, Miriam, Amy & Marsi. *Educ:* Carnegie Mellon Univ, BS, 48; Univ Del, PhD(chem eng), 53. *Prof Exp:* Instr chem eng, Univ Del, 51-53; mgr, Fuel Cells Systs Technol & Chem Eng, Westinghouse Res Labs, Westinghouse Energy Systs, 61-83, mgr process eng & consult engr, 83-90. *Concurrent Pos:* Mem, Comt on Nitrogen Oxide, Nat Acad Sci, 76-78. *Mem:* Nat Acad Eng; Am Chem Soc; Combustion Inst; Am Asn Cost Engrs; Sigma Xi; Am Inst Chem Engrs. *Res:* Development of fossil and nuclear fuel processes related to power generation, particularly coal gasification, pyrolysis, fluidized bed combustion, hot gas cleaning, gas turbine corrosion-erosion-deposition; plant design and evaluation; optimum operations; power plant operations, control. *Mailing Add:* 114 Kentzel Rd Pittsburgh PA 15237

ARCHER, DOUGLAS HARLEY, PHYSICS. *Current Pos:* RETIRED. *Personal Data:* b Saskatoon, Sask, May 20, 25; m 59; c 2. *Educ:* Univ BC, BA, 47, MA, 48; Harvard Univ, PhD(physics), 53. *Prof Exp:* Staff mem radiowave propagation, Lincoln Lab, Mass Inst Technol, 53-58; staff mem radiowave & auroral physics, Hughes Aircraft Co, 58; staff mem atmospheric physics, Gen Elec Co, 58-71; staff mem atmospheric physics, Mission Res Corp, 71-90. *Mem:* Am Geophys Union. *Res:* Atomic and molecular physics; radiowave propagation; atmospheric physics and chemistry with emphasis on ionization/deionization and the optical and infrared radiation from perturbed regions, including the aurora. *Mailing Add:* 877 Cieneguitas Rd Santa Barbara CA 93110

ARCHER, JUANITA ALMETTA, INTERNAL MEDICINE. *Current Pos:* instr, Dept Med, 73-75, asst prof med, 75-77, dir, Endocrine/Metabolic Labs, 77-86, ASSOC PROF MED, HOWARD UNIV HOSP, 77- *Personal Data:* b Washington, DC, Nov 3, 34; m 58, Frederick I; c Frederick I II. *Educ:* Howard Univ, BS, 56, MS, 58, MD, 65. *Honors & Awards:* Nat Podiatric Asn Award, 86; Moses Wharton Young Res Award, 87. *Prof Exp:* Intern, Freedmens Hosp, 65-66, resident internal med, 66-69, fel endocrinol, 69-70; with NIH, 70-73. *Concurrent Pos:* Josiah Macy fac fel, Dept Internal Med, Howard Univ, 74-, Coordr internal med educ, Col Dent. *Mem:* Endocrine Soc; Am Fedn Clin Res. *Res:* Physiological significance of insulin receptors in man. *Mailing Add:* Howard Univ Hosp 2041 Georgia Ave NW Washington DC 20060

ARCHER, ROBERT ALLEN, ORGANIC CHEMISTRY. *Current Pos:* Sr org chemist, Chem Res Div, Lilly Res Labs, 64-73, res scientist, 73-78, RES ASSOC, CHEM & CANCER RES DIV, ELI LILLY & CO, 78-, SR RES SCIENTIST, CHEM CANCER & VIROL RES, 84- *Personal Data:* b Reading, Pa, Apr 3, 36; m 63; c 3. *Educ:* Harvard Univ, AB, 58; Univ Del, MS, 60; Stanford Univ, PhD(chem), 63. *Mem:* AAAS; Am Chem Soc; Sigma Xi. *Res:* Immunology; connective tissue; rheumatoid and osteoarthritis; medicinal chemistry. *Mailing Add:* 5563 N Pennsylvania Indianapolis IN 46220

ARCHER, ROBERT JAMES, solid state physics, for more information see previous edition

ARCHER, ROBERT RAYMOND, APPLIED MATHEMATICS, ENGINEERING MECHANICS. *Current Pos:* PROF CIVIL ENG, UNIV MASS, AMHERST, 66- *Personal Data:* b Omaha, Nebr, Sept 8, 28; m 50; c 5. *Educ:* Mass Inst Technol, SB, 52, PhD(math), 56. *Prof Exp:* Asst prof mech eng, Mass Inst Technol, 56-59; from asst prof to assoc prof, Univ Mass, 59-61; assoc prof eng, Case Western Reserve Univ, 61-66. *Concurrent Pos:* Fulbright lectr, Indian Inst Technol, Kanpur, India, 74-75. *Mem:* Sigma Xi; Am Soc Mech Eng. *Res:* Mathematical elasticity; anisotropic stress analysis; continuum mechanical models for study of tree growth stresses and reaction wood mechanics. *Mailing Add:* Dept Civil Eng Univ Mass Amherst MA 01002

ARCHER, RONALD DEAN, COORDINATION CHEMISTRY, METAL-CONTAINING POLYMERS. *Current Pos:* assoc prof, 66-70, head dept, 77-83, PROF CHEM, UNIV MASS, 70- *Personal Data:* b Rochelle, Ill, July 22, 32; m 54, Joyce Carlson; c Paul, Lynn, Sharon & Julie. *Educ:* Ill State Univ, BS, 53, MS, 54; Univ Ill, PhD(chem), 59. *Prof Exp:* Asst prof chem, Univ Calif, 59-63; from asst prof to assoc prof, Tulane Univ, 63-66. *Concurrent Pos:* Vis prof, Tech Univ Denmark, 72; consult, Alden Res Found, 73-; vis scientist, Naval Res Lab, Washington, DC, 80; consult, Ventron, 84-85, Monsanto, 85-86; chief chem reader, Educ Testing Serv Advan Placement Prog, 85-88; chair, Am Chem Soc Comn Educ, 87-89; vis prof, Univ Vienna, 87. *Mem:* Fel AAAS; Am Chem Soc; Royal Soc Chem; Sigma Xi. *Res:* Coordination compounds; synthesis; properties; kinetics; biometallic studies; photochemistry; spectroscopy; inorganic polymers. *Mailing Add:* Dept Chem Univ Mass Amherst MA 01003-4510. *E-Mail:* archer@chemistry.umass.edu

ARCHER, STANLEY J, IMMUNOLOGY, ALLERGY. *Current Pos:* DIR RES & DEVELOP, IATRIC CORP, 80- *Personal Data:* b Stephenville, Tex, Aug 13, 44; m 66; c 2. *Educ:* Abilene Christian Col, BS, 66, MS, 68; Univ Tenn, Knoxville, PhD(microbiol), 72. *Prof Exp:* Instr microbiol, Univ Tex, Austin, 72-74; asst prof microbiol, Ariz State Univ, 74-80. *Mem:* Am Soc Microbiol; AAAS; NY Acad Sci. *Res:* Cellular and molecular events involved in the initiation of an immune response. *Mailing Add:* 21420 S Lindsay Rd Chandler AZ 85249

ARCHER, SYDNEY, MEDICINAL CHEMISTRY. *Current Pos:* dean, Sch Sci, 80-85, RES PROF MED CHEM, RENSSELAER POLYTECH INST, 73- *Personal Data:* b New York, NY, Jan 23, 17; m 46, Therese Neiman; c Eve, David & Daniel. *Educ:* Univ Wis, AB, 37; Pa State Col, MS, 38, PhD(org chem), 40. *Honors & Awards:* Award, Am Chem Soc, 68. *Prof Exp:* Procter & Gamble fel, Northwestern Univ, 40-41; Lilly fel, Univ Chicago, 41-42; res chemist, Sun Oil Co, 42-43; res chemist, Sterling-Winthrop Res Inst, 43-60, asst dir chem res, 60-64, dir chem res & develop, 64-68, assoc dir res, 68-73. *Concurrent Pos:* Consult, Spec Action Off Drug Abuse Prev, 73 & Nat Inst Drug Abuse, 74-75; chmn, Med Chem Study Sect, NIH, 76-78; mem, Nat Inst Drug Abuse Study Sect, 79-83 & Schistosomasis Working Group, WHO, 82-85. *Mem:* Am Chem Soc; Am Soc Pharmacol & Exp Therapeut. *Mailing Add:* Res Prof Med Chem 52 Wisconsin Ave Delmar NY 12054-4118. *Fax:* 518-276-4045

ARCHER, VERNON SHELBY, ANALYTICAL CHEMISTRY. *Current Pos:* Asst prof, 64-74, ASSOC PROF CHEM, UNIV WYO, 74- *Personal Data:* b Ada, Okla, Dec 5, 39; m 67. *Educ:* Univ Okla, BS, 61, PhD(anal chem), 64. *Mem:* Am Chem Soc. *Res:* Electrochemistry; fluoride chemistry. *Mailing Add:* 362 N Seventh St Laramie WY 82070-3218

ARCHER, VICTOR EUGENE, RADIOLOGICAL HEALTH, EPIDEMIOLOGY OF CANCER & LOW LEVEL RADIATION. *Current Pos:* CLIN PROF, MED SCH, UNIV UTAH, 79- *Personal Data:* b Teigen, Mont, May 21, 22; m 49, Violet L Ommodt; c Steven M & Keith E. *Educ:* Northwestern Univ, BS, 45, MB, 48, MD, 49; Am Bd Prev Med, dipl. *Prof Exp:* Instr physics, Mont State Univ, 43-44; intern clin med, USPHS Hosp, 48-49, instr radiol health, Environ Health Ctr, USPHS, 50-51; radiation safety officer, NIH, 51-55, field investr, Nat Cancer Inst, 56-59; chief, Coffman Res Lab, 59-61; chief epidemiol serv, Occup Health Field Sta, USPHS, 61-72, med dir & epidemiologist, western area lab for occup safety & health, Nat Inst Occup Safety & Health, 72-79. *Concurrent Pos:* Clin lectr, Med Sch, Univ Utah, 58-70. *Mem:* Health Physics Soc; Am Pub Health Asn. *Res:* Radiobiology; environmental causes of lung disease and cancer; low level radiation exposures. *Mailing Add:* 4370 Spruce Circle Salt Lake City UT 84124

ARCHIBALD, FREDERICK S, LIGNIN BIODEGRADATION BIOCHEMISTRY, TRACE METAL METABOLISM & TRANSPORT. *Current Pos:* SR SCIENTIST, PULP & PAPER RES INST CAN, 86- *Personal Data:* b Cambridge, Mass, Dec 9, 46; m 72, Helen Murray; c Andrew & Margaret. *Educ:* Acadia Univ, BSc, 69; Dalhousie Univ, MS, 75; McGill Univ, PhD(microbiol), 79. *Prof Exp:* Res assoc, Dept Biochem, Duke Univ, 79-81; asst prof, Dept Microbiol, McGill Univ, 81-86. *Concurrent Pos:* Assoc prof, Dept Nat Res Sci, McGill Univ, 86- *Mem:* Am Soc Microbiol; Can Soc Microbiologists; AAAS; Tech Asn Pulp & Paper Indust. *Res:* Biochemistry, physiology and genetics of Trametes versicolor to elucidate the mechanisms of biological lignin degradation; biological activities of iron and manganese and the environmental fate of chloroorganic compounds. *Mailing Add:* Pulp & Paper Res Inst Can 570 Boulevard St Jean Pointe Claire PQ H9R 3J9 Can. *Fax:* 514-630-4134

ARCHIBALD, JAMES, VETERINARY MEDICINE. *Current Pos:* From asst prof to prof, 49-93, EMER UNIV PROF MED VET, ONT VET COL, UNIV GUELPH, 93- *Personal Data:* b Bellshill, Scotland, Jan 4, 19; Can citizen; m 48, Hilda Corless; c 3. *Educ:* Ont Vet Col, DVM, 49; Univ Toronto, MVSc, 51; Univ Giessen, Dr med vet, 58; FRCVS; Am Col Vet Surgeons, dipl. *Honors & Awards:* Order of Ontario, 90. *Concurrent Pos:* Consult, Defense Res Med Labs, Can, 58; chmn, Dept Clin Studies, Univ Guelph, 63-80. *Mem:* Can Vet Med Asn (pres, 63); Am Col Vet Surgeons (pres, 77-78); Commonwealth Vet Asn (secy-treas, 84-91). *Res:* Experimental surgery; liver and tissue transplantation. *Mailing Add:* Dept Clin Studies Ont Vet Col Univ Guelph Guelph ON N1G 2W1 Can

ARCHIBALD, JAMES DAVID, BIOLOGY, PALEONTOLOGY. *Current Pos:* from assoc prof to PROF, DEPT BIOL, SAN DIEGO STATE UNIV, 83- *Personal Data:* b Lawrence, Kans, Mar 23, 50. *Educ:* Kent State Univ, BS, 72; Univ Calif, Berkeley, PhD(paleont), 77. *Prof Exp:* Gibbs instr, Dept Geol, Yale Univ, 77-79, from asst prof to assoc prof, Dept Biol, 79-83. *Concurrent Pos:* Exten field expeds, Mont, Colo, NMex & Pakistan, 73-; cur mammals, Peabody Mus Natural Hist, New Haven, 79-83; trustee, San Diego Natural

Hist Mus; grantee, Sigma Xi, Nat Geog Soc, NSF, Petrol Res Found & San Diego State Univ. *Mem:* Soc Vert Paleont; Geol Soc Am; Paleont Soc; Soc Syst Zoologists; Am Soc Mammalogists. *Res:* Study of mammalia and geology across the Cretaceous-Tertiary boundary; author of one book and contributed articles to professional journals. *Mailing Add:* Dept Biol San Diego State Univ San Diego CA 92182-4614

ARCHIBALD, JULIUS A, JR, SIMULATION & MODELING. *Current Pos:* assoc prof to prof, comput sci, Col Arts & Sci, 70-74, AT STATE UNIV NY, PLATTSBURGH. *Personal Data:* b New York, NY, May 9, 31; m 54; c 3. *Educ:* NY Univ, BA, 52, MS, 53. *Prof Exp:* Mathematician, Wright Air Develop Ctr, USAF, 53-55, comput scientist, Knolls Atomic Power Lab, Ben Elec Co, 55-68, sys specialist, Gen Elec Co, 68-70. *Concurrent Pos:* Chair, comput sci, Col Arts & Sci, State Univ NY, Plattsburgh, 74-; vis chair, comput sci accreditation comn, 85-87 & 88-89; actg chair math, State Univ NY, Plattsburgh, 88-90. *Mem:* Inst Elec & Electronics Engrs Computer Soc; Asn Comput Mach; Sigma Xi; Am Math Soc; Math Asn Am; Soc Indust & Appl Math. *Mailing Add:* State Univ NY Col Arts & Sci Plattsburgh NY 12901

ARCHIBALD, KENNETH C, PHYSICAL MEDICINE. *Current Pos:* RETIRED. *Personal Data:* b White Plains, NY, Aug 1, 27. *Educ:* Cornell Univ, MD, 53; St Lawrence Univ, BS, 53. *Prof Exp:* Sr instr phys med, Sch Med, Western Res Univ & assoc dir, Dept Phys Med & Rehab, Univ Hosps Cleveland, 57-58; asst prof phys med, Med Col, Cornell Univ & dir, Phys Med & Rehab & asst attend physician, NY Hosp-Cornell Med Ctr, 58-66; from assoc prof to prof phys med & rehab, Sch Med, Temple Univ & dir dept, Episcopal Hosp, 66-69; dir phys med & rehab, Jerd Sullivan Rehab Ctr, Garden Hosp & Presby Hosp of Pac Med Ctr, San Francisco, 69-78; dir phys med & rehab, Children'S Hosp, 74-95. *Concurrent Pos:* Consult, Muscle Dis Clin, Univ Hosps Cleveland, 58-69; assoc clin prof orthop surg, Med Ctr, Univ Calif, San Francisco, 70- *Mem:* Am Cong Rehab Med; Am Acad Phys Med & Rehab; Am Asn Electromyography & Electrodiag. *Res:* Physical medicine and rehabilitation; neuromuscular disorders. *Mailing Add:* 2360 Clay St San Francisco CA 94115-1932

ARCHIBALD, PATRICIA ANN, ALGOLOGY, PHYCOLOGY. *Current Pos:* from asst prof to assoc prof, 69-80, PROF BIOL, SLIPPERY ROCK UNIV, 80- *Personal Data:* b Olney, Ill, July 18, 34. *Educ:* Ball State Univ, BS & MA, 61; Univ Tex, Austin, PhD(bot), 69. *Honors & Awards:* Fulbright lectr, Harrow Technol Col, Eng, 62-63. *Prof Exp:* Teacher high sch, Ind, 59-64; instr biol, Palm Beach Jr Col, 64-66 & Cuyahoga Community Col, 66-67. *Concurrent Pos:* Mem, NSF US-Japan Phycol Sem, 75; Int Res & Exchanges Bd exchangee, Czech Acad Sci, 77; Nat Acad Sci exchangee, USSR Acad Sci, 78; coordr, US-Mex phycol sem, 80; assoc sci rev adminr, comp grants prog, Environ Protection Agency, 81-82; Proj-Flora partic, Brazilian Amazon Collection Exped, NY Bot Garden, 84; US-China Exchange Leader, Freshwater Biologist, 88. *Mem:* Phycol Soc Am; Sigma Xi; Int Phycol Soc. *Res:* Phycology, systematics morphology and physiology of zoosporic Chlorococcales and Chlorosarcinales; edaphic algae, distribution, morphology, physiology; culturing of algae. *Mailing Add:* PO Box 429 Grove City PA 16803-1376

ARCHIBALD, REGINALD MACGREGOR, PEDIATRIC ENDOCRINOLOGY. *Current Pos:* mem staff, 48-59, prof, 59-80, EMER PROF MED, ROCKEFELLER UNIV, 80-, SR PHYSICIAN EMER, ROCKEFELLER UNIV HOSP, 88- *Personal Data:* b Syracuse, NY, Mar 2, 10; m 48; c 2. *Educ:* Univ BC, BA, 30, MA, 32; Univ Toronto, PhD(path chem), 34, MD, 39. *Prof Exp:* Asst, Univ BC, 30-32; asst, Univ Toronto, 32-33; intern, Hosp for Sick Children, Toronto, 37-38; intern, Toronto Gen Hosp, 39-40; asst resident, Rockefeller Inst Hosp, 41-46; prof biochem & head dept, Johns Hopkins Univ, 46-48. *Concurrent Pos:* Nat Res Coun fel, 40-42; vis investr, Rockefeller Univ, 40-43, spec investr, 43-45, assoc, 46, physician, Univ Hosp, 48-59, sr physician, 59-80; vpres, Am Bd Clin Chem, 57-63; mem adv bd, Analytical Chem, 57-60. *Mem:* AAAS; Am Chem Soc; Am Soc Biol Chemists; Soc Res Child Develop; Soc Adolescent Med; Lawson Wilkins Pediat Endocrin Soc. *Res:* Non-fermentable carbohydrates of urines; fractionation of urinary steroids; physiological roles of glutamine and other amino acids; measurement of enzymes; use of enzymes in analysis; influences of hormones on enzymes; problems of growth and development of children; skeletal anomalies in children. *Mailing Add:* Rockefeller Univ Hosp 1230 York Ave New York NY 10021-6399

ARCHIBALD, WILLIAM JAMES, PHYSICS. *Current Pos:* RETIRED. *Personal Data:* b Sydney, NS, Oct 30, 12; m 36; c 3. *Educ:* Dalhousie Univ, BA, 33, MA, 36; Univ Va, PhD, 38. *Hon Degrees:* DSc, Univ NB, 61. *Prof Exp:* Sterling fel, Yale Univ, 38-39; res scientist, Nat Res Coun, 39-42; from assoc prof to prof, 42-73, dean arts & sci, 55-60, Dr A C Fales Prof theoret physics & dean freshmen, Dalhousie Univ, 73-78. *Concurrent Pos:* Fel, Univ Va, 51-52; mem, Defense Res Bd, Can, 56-59. *Mem:* Fel Royal Soc Can. *Res:* Ultra centrifuge; theory of molecular weight determination; theoretical physics; nuclear magnetism; field theory. *Mailing Add:* Park Victoria Apt 1120 Park Lane Halifax NS B3J 2K9 Can

ARCHIE, CHARLES NEILL, QUANTUM FLUIDS & SOLIDS, MACROSCOPIC QUANTUM TUNNELING. *Current Pos:* PROF, DEPT PHYSICS, STATE UNIV NY, STONY BROOK, 79- *Personal Data:* b Coranado, Calif, Feb 22, 48; m 78; c 1. *Educ:* Univ Calif, Davis, BS, 70; Cornell Univ, PhD(physics), 78. *Prof Exp:* Engr, Comn Atomic Energy, Solid Physics & Magnetic Resonance, Ctr Nuclear Studies, Saclay, France, 78-79. *Mem:* Am Phys Soc. *Res:* Very low temperature physics experiments; the production of a new quantum liquid, spin polarized helium 3; the development of devices which exhibit purely quantum properties on a macroscopic scale. *Mailing Add:* 34 Raemont Rd Granite Springs NY 10527

ARCHIE, JOSEPH PATRICK, JR, VASCULAR SURGERY, BIOFLUID MECHANICS. *Current Pos:* VASCULAR SURGEON, WAKE MED CTR, RALEIGH, 81-; CLIN PROF SURG, UNIV NC, 84- *Personal Data:* b Nashville, Tenn, July 14, 38; m 60, Sarah E White; c Sarah (Grainger), Joseph P III & Thomas J. *Educ:* NC State Univ, BS, 60, MS, 62, PhD(eng mech), 68; Univ NC, MD, 68. *Honors & Awards:* Resident Res Award, AMA, 69; Young Investr Award, Am Col Cardiol, 74. *Prof Exp:* Resident surg, Univ Ala Med Ctr, 68-74, asst prof surg, 76-77; fel, Univ Calif, San Francisco, 70-71; asst chief vascular surg, Wilford Hall, USAF Med Ctr, 74-76; dir surg residency, Carraway Methodist Med Ctr, 77-81. *Concurrent Pos:* Adj prof eng, NC State Univ, 85-; fel, Stroke Coun, Am Heart Asn. *Mem:* Soc Vascular Surg; fel Am Col Surgeons; Int Soc Cardiovasc Surg; Am Heart Asn; Biomed Eng Soc; Asn Acad Surg. *Res:* Clinical vascular surgery, method of improving outcome and safety of operative procedures; mathematical modeling of the vascular system for atherosclerosis; published 125 articles. *Mailing Add:* 2309 Woodrow Dr Raleigh NC 27609

ARCHIE, WILLIAM C, JR, PHYSICAL ORGANIC CHEMISTRY. *Current Pos:* SR RES CHEMIST, EASTMAN KODAK CO, 72- *Personal Data:* b Brownsville, Tex, Mar 1, 44; m 70; c 2. *Educ:* Duke Univ, BS, 66; Stanford Univ, PhD(chem), 70. *Prof Exp:* Fel chem, Harvard Univ, 70-72. *Mem:* Am Chem Soc. *Res:* Photographic science; use of physical organic chemical methods to elucidate reaction mechanisms in film; stability of photographic color images. *Mailing Add:* 46 Greylock Ridge Pittsford NY 14534-2334

ARCOS, JOSEPH (CHARLES), TOXICOLOGY, ONCOLOGY. *Current Pos:* from assoc prof to prof, 60-80, EMER PROF MED & BIOCHEM, SCH MED, TULANE UNIV, 87-; SR SCI ADV, OFF TOXIC SUBSTANCES, US ENVIRON PROTECTION AGENCY, 80- *Personal Data:* b Hungary, Aug 22, 21; US citizen. *Educ:* Univ Cluj, LChem, 47; Conserv Nat Arts et Metiers, France, ChE, 50; Univ Paris, DSc, 51. *Honors & Awards:* Fac Res Award, Am Cancer Soc, 72; Creative Advan Environ Sci & Technol Award, Am Chem Soc, 87. *Prof Exp:* Res engr surface chem, Tech Ctr Graphic Indust, 52; asst tech dir develop & prod, Jouan Co, Paris, France, 52-53; res assoc cancer res, McArdle Lab, Univ Wis, 53-57; asst res prof, Cancer Res Lab, Univ Fla, 57-60. *Concurrent Pos:* Sci ed; ecosystem concept rev. *Mem:* Am Soc Biol Chemists; Biophys Soc; Am Asn Cancer Res; Soc Exp Biol & Med; Am Soc Pharmacol & Exp Therapeut; Am Col Toxicol; Europ Asn Cancer Res; fel Am Col Toxicol, 85. *Res:* Structure-activity relationships and molecular geometry of chemical carcinogens; chemical risk assessment; combination carcinogenic effects with complex mixtures; system concept and network analysis of ecocrisis interactions; ecology. *Mailing Add:* US Environ Protection Agency Mail Code 7403 401 M St SW Washington DC 20460. *Fax:* 202-260-1283

ARD, WILLIAM BRYANT, JR, PHYSICS. *Current Pos:* RETIRED. *Personal Data:* b Jackson, Tenn, Oct 8, 27; m 50; c 8. *Educ:* Auburn Univ, BS, 50, MS, 51; Duke Univ, PhD(physics), 55. *Prof Exp:* From asst prof to assoc prof, Univ Ala, 55-59; assoc prof, Univ Fla, 59-62; physicist, Oak Ridge Nat Lab, 62-73; sr res scientist, United Technol Res Ctr, 73-78; staff dir MDC Fel, McDonnell Douglas Missile Systs Co, 78-92. *Mem:* Fel Am Phys Soc. *Res:* Plasma physics and controlled thermonuclear fusion research; particle beam physics. *Mailing Add:* 5609 SE Horseshoe Point Rd Stuart FL 34997

ARDELL, ALAN JAY, METALLURGY, MATERIALS SCIENCE. *Current Pos:* from actg assoc prof to assoc prof, 68-74, PROF MAT, DEPT MAT SCI ENG, UNIV CALIF, LOS ANGELES, 74- *Personal Data:* b Brooklyn, NY, Mar 24, 39; m 60, 87; c 3. *Educ:* Mass Inst Technol, BS, 60; Stanford Univ, MS, 62, PhD(mat sci), 64. *Prof Exp:* Nat Sci Found fel, Cambridge Univ, 64-66; asst prof mat sci, Calif Inst Technol, 66-68. *Concurrent Pos:* Fulbright-Hays Res fel, Comn Atomic Energy-Ctr Nuclear Studies, Saclay, France, 74-75. *Mem:* Am Inst Mining, Metall & Petrol Engrs; Electron Micros Soc Am; fel Am Soc Metals; Mat Res Soc. *Res:* Coarsening of precipitates; transmission electron microscopy; mechanical behavior of solids, including aluminum alloys, ion irradiated ordered intermetallic alloys, and creep of metals and alloys. *Mailing Add:* 381 Dalkeith Ave Los Angeles CA 90049

ARDELL, JEFFREY LAURENCE, CARDIOVASCULAR PHYSIOLOGY. *Current Pos:* ASST PROF PHYSIOL, SCH MED, UNIV S ALA, 84- *Educ:* Univ Wash, PhD(physiol & biophys), 80. *Mailing Add:* Sch Med Dept Physiol Univ S Ala MSB 3024 Mobile AL 36688-0001

ARDELT, WOJCIECH JOSEPH, PROTEIN CHEMISTRY, ENZYMOLOGY. *Current Pos:* chief chemist protein chem, 87-96, DIR BIOCHEM, ALFACELL CORP, BLOOMFIELD, NJ, 97- *Personal Data:* m 62, Barbara Broniszewska; c Agnieszka & Magdalena. *Educ:* Warsaw Univ, Poland, BS, 62, Dr Habilitus, 75; Polish Acad Sci, PhD(biochem), 68. *Prof Exp:* Grad res asst biochem, Inst Rheumatol, Warsaw, Poland, 62-68, fel biochem, 69-70 & biochem/enzymol, 70-71, from asst prof to assoc prof, 71-78; vis prof protein chem, Dept Chem, Purdue Univ, Lafayette, Ind, 79-80, sr res assoc, 81-86. *Mem:* Sigma Xi; Am Soc Biochem & Molecular Biol; Protein Soc. *Res:* Structure and function of ribonucleases, proteinases and protein proteinase inhibitors. *Mailing Add:* Alfacell Corp 225 Belleville Ave Bloomfield NJ 07003. *Fax:* 973-748-1355

ARDEMA, MARK D, OPTIMAL CONTROL & DIFFERENTIAL GAMES, SINGULAR PERTURBATIONS & ASYMPTOTIC ANALYSIS. *Current Pos:* PROF & CHMN, DEPT MECH ENG, SANTA CLARA UNIV, 86- *Personal Data:* b Minneapolis, Minn, Dec 2, 40; m 63, Lynda Olinger; c Aubrey & Matthew. *Educ:* Univ Calif, Berkeley, BS, 63, MS, 64, PhD(mech eng), 74. *Honors & Awards:* Boeing Lectr, Wichita State Univ, 88. *Prof Exp:* Res scientist, NASA Ames Res Ctr, 65-80 & 82-86, res asst to dir, 80-82. *Concurrent Pos:* Lectr, Univ Calif, Berkeley, 78, vis prof, 84; vis scholar, Twente Univ Technol, Neth, 82; consult, NASA Ames Res Ctr, 86-; short course instr, Am Inst Aeronaut & Astronaut, 89; assoc ed, J Dynamics & Control, 90-; vchair, Math Control Comt, Int Fedn Automatic Control, 90-93, chair, Mech Eng Dept Heads, 92-95. *Mem:* Assoc fel Am Inst Aeronaut & Astronaut. *Res:* Optimal control; differential games; singular perturbations; asymptotic analysis; trajectory optimization; aircraft flight dynamics; structural analysis; aircraft conceptual design; performance analysis; author of over 120 publications. *Mailing Add:* Dept Mech Eng Santa Clara Univ Santa Clara CA 95035. *Fax:* 408-554-5474

ARDEN, BRUCE WESLEY, COMPUTER SCIENCE, ELECTRICAL ENGINEERING. *Current Pos:* prof elec eng & comput sci & dean eng & appl sci, Univ Rochester, 86-95, vprovost comput, 92-95, William F May prof eng, 93-95, EMER WILLIAM F MAY PROF & EMER DEAN APPL SCI, UNIV ROCHESTER, 95- *Personal Data:* b Minneapolis, Minn, May 29, 27; m 51, Patricia A Joy; c Wayne W & Michelle J. *Educ:* Purdue Univ, BS, 49; Univ Mich, MA, 55, PhD, 65. *Prof Exp:* Detail engr, Allison Div, Gen Motors Corp, 50-51; from res asst to assoc dir, Comput Facil, Univ Mich, Ann Arbor, 51-73, from asst prof to prof, Dept Comput & Commun Sci, 65-73, chmn dept, 71-73; prof & chmn, Dept Elec Eng & Comput Sci, Princeton Univ, 73-85, Arthur Le Grand Doty prof eng, 81-86. *Concurrent Pos:* Chmn, Comt Anti-Ballistic Missile Data Processing, Nat Acad Sci, 66-71; vis prof, Univ Grenoble, France, 71-72; consult, Gen Motors Corp, Ford Corp, Westinghouse Co, RCA, Xerox Data Systs & IBM; mem sci coun, Inst Comput Applns Sci & Eng, Univs Space Res Asn, 73-79 & 82-88, mem bd dirs, 82-88, mem sci coun, Inst Advan Comput Sci, 82-88; panel mem, Inst Comput Sci & Technol, 82-88; guest prof, Siemens Res, Munich, Ger, 83; mem study sect, NIH, 85-88. *Mem:* Fel AAAS; sr mem, Inst Elec & Electronics Engrs; Asn Comput Mach; Univs Space Res Asn; Sigma Xi. *Res:* Digital computing; origins and applications of numerical algorithms. *Mailing Add:* 101 N Main St Apt 906 Ann Arbor MI 48104-1475

ARDEN, DANIEL DOUGLAS, EXPLORATION GEOLOGY. *Current Pos:* RETIRED. *Personal Data:* b Bainbridge, Ga, Sept 24, 22; m 43; c 4. *Educ:* Emory Univ, AB, 48, MS, 49; Univ Calif, Berkeley, PhD(paleont), 61. *Prof Exp:* Asst prof geol, Birmingham-Southern Col, 49-51; geologist petrol geol, Standard Oil Co Calif, 54-56; staff geologist, Standard Oil Co Ohio, 56-65; explor adv, Signal Oil & Gas Co, 65-70; prof geol, Ga Southwestern Col, 70-82. *Concurrent Pos:* Chief geol consult, Geophys Serv Inc, 71-; mem, Int Comn Hist Geol, 75- *Mem:* Geol Soc Am; Am Geophys Union; Am Inst Prof Geologists. *Res:* Geobotanical relationships; stratigraphy of Ocala and Tivola limestones in Georgia. *Mailing Add:* 428 Merlin Way Tallahassee FL 32301

ARDIS, COLBY V, JR, engineering management, for more information see previous edition

ARDITTI, JOSEPH, ORCHIDS. *Current Pos:* from asst prof to assoc prof, 66-77, PROF BIOL, UNIV CALIF, IRVINE, 77- *Personal Data:* b Sofia, Bulgaria, May 1, 32; US citizen; div; c Jonathan Omar. *Educ:* Univ Calif, Los Angeles, BS, 59; Univ Southern Calif, PhD(biol, plant physiol), 65. *Honors & Awards:* Gold Medal, Orchid Soc SE Asia. *Prof Exp:* Teaching asst biol, Univ Southern Calif, 60-65, lectr, 65-66. *Mem:* AAAS; Am Soc Plant Physiol; Bot Soc Am; Am Orchid Soc; Linnean Soc London. *Res:* Orchid biology. *Mailing Add:* Dept Develop & Cell Biol Univ Calif Irvine CA 92657-2300. *Fax:* 714-824-4709; *E-Mail:* jarditti@uci.edu

ARECCHI, F TITO, PHYSICS. *Current Pos:* PROF PHYSICS, UNIV FLORENCE, ITALY. *Honors & Awards:* Max Born Award, Optical Soc Am, 95. *Prof Exp:* Dir, Nat Inst Ottica, Florence. *Mem:* Optical Soc Am. *Mailing Add:* Nat Inst Ottica Largo Enrico Fermi 6 Arcetri-Firenze 50125 Italy

AREF, HASSAN, FLUID MECHANICS, COMPUTATIONAL SCIENCE. *Current Pos:* PROF & HEAD, DEPT THEORET & APPL MECHS, UNIV ILL, URBANA-CHAMPAIGN, 92- *Personal Data:* b Alexandria, Egypt, Sept 28, 50; Can citizen; m 74, Susanne Eriksen; c Michael & Thomas. *Educ:* Univ Copenhagen, Denmark, Cand Sci, 75; Cornell Univ, PhD(physics), 80. *Honors & Awards:* Presidential Young Invest Award, NSF, 85; Corrsin lectr, Johns Hopkins Univ, 88; Westinghouse lectr, Univ Mich, 91. *Prof Exp:* Asst prof eng, Brown Univ, 80-85; from assoc prof to prof fluid mech, Univ Calif, San Diego, 85-92. *Concurrent Pos:* Collabr, Los Alamos Nat Lab, 84-92; assoc ed, J Fluid Mech, 84-94; guest prof, Tech Univ Denmark, 86; chief scientist, San Diego Supercomputer Ctr, 89-92; lectr, Midwest Mechs, 91. *Mem:* Fel Am Phys Soc; Soc Indust & Appl Math. *Res:* Theoretical and computational fluid mechanics; particular emphasis on problems in vortex dynamics and applications of nonlinear dynamics to flow problems. *Mailing Add:* Dept Theoret & Appl Mech Univ Ill Urbana IL 61801. *E-Mail:* h-aref@uiuc.edu

AREM, JOEL EDWARD, GEMOLOGY. *Current Pos:* PRES, JOEL E AREM, INC, 74- *Personal Data:* b Brooklyn, NY, Dec 28, 43; m 79, Deborah; c Benjamin & Jocelyn. *Educ:* Brooklyn Col, BS, 64; Harvard Univ, MA, 67, PhD(mineral), 70. *Hon Degrees:* FCGmA, Can Gemmological Asn, 84. *Honors & Awards:* Tully Mem Medal, Gemmological Asn, Gt Brit, 76; Spectrum Award, Am Gem Trade Asn, 85. *Prof Exp:* Teaching fel econ geol & mineral, Geol Dept, Harvard Univ, 66-69, res asst, 69-70; crystallogr, Dept Mineral Sci, Smithsonian Inst, 70-73, founder-cur, Nat Synthetics Collection, 71-73. *Concurrent Pos:* Instr, Smithsonian Docent Prog, 70-73; consult gems & minerals, Nat Geog Soc, 71-, Encycl Britannica Educ Corp, 75-76; consult gems & minerals photog, Eastman Kodak Co, 71-75, tech writing, US Atomic Energy Comn, 73-74, gemstones, US Dept Com, 75-76; pres, Gemstones, Accredited Gemologists Asn, 77-79. *Mem:* Mineral Soc Am; Am Asn Crystal Growth; fel Gemmological Asn Gt Brit; fel Can Gemmological Asn; Sigma Xi. *Res:* Public education in science and the relationship of gemstones to global economics, as well as the characterization and identification of gemstones; author of many publications. *Mailing Add:* PO Box 5056 Laytonsville MD 20882. *Fax:* 301-869-5898; *E-Mail:* jarem@idsonline.com

ARENA, JAY M, pediatrics; deceased, see previous edition for last biography

ARENA, JOSEPH P, BIOCHEMICAL PARASITOLOGY. *Current Pos:* SR RES BIOLOGIST, BASIC ANIMAL SCI RES, MERCK SHARP & DOHME RES LABS, RAHWAY, NJ, 89- *Personal Data:* b Jersey City, NJ, Oct 2, 54; c 1. *Educ:* St Johns Univ, BS, 77; Univ Med & Dent, PhD(pharmacol), 86. *Prof Exp:* Mem staff & supv pharmacist, Univ Hosp, Univ Med & Dent, Newark, NJ, 78-81; postdoctoral fel, Dept Physiol, Univ Rochester, NY, 86-89. *Concurrent Pos:* Adj asst prof pharmacol & toxicol, Univ Med & Dent, Newark, NJ, 91- *Mem:* AAAS; Biophys Soc; Am Soc Pharmacol & Exp Therapeut. *Res:* Electrophysiology and pharmacology of excitable tissues; neurotransmitter receptors and voltage-gated channels of invertebrates. *Mailing Add:* Dept Cell Biochem & Physiol Merck Sharp & Dohme Res Lab Box 2000 Rm RY80T-126 Rahway NJ 07065-0900

ARENAZ, PABLO, CARCINOGENESIS-DNA REPAIR, ENZYMOLOGY OF DNA REPAIR. *Current Pos:* asst prof, 84-90, ASSOC PROF GENETICS & MOLECULAR BIOL, UNIV TEX, EL PASO, 90- *Personal Data:* b Reno, Nev, Sept 9, 50; m 87; c 1. *Educ:* Univ Nev, BS, 72, MS, 76; Wash State Univ, PhD(genetics & cell biol), 81. *Prof Exp:* Fel, Fels Res Inst, Temple Univ Sch Med, 81-84. *Concurrent Pos:* Adj asst prof, Tex Tech Univ Sch Med, 87- *Mem:* Am Asn Cancer Res; Am Soc Cell Biol; AAAS; Environ Mutagen Soc. *Res:* Enzymology and molecular biology of DNA repair in eukaryotes; the relationship between aberrant control of DNA repair and carcinogenesis. *Mailing Add:* Col Sci Univ Tex El Paso TX 79968-0509

ARENBERG, DAVID (LEE), COGNITIVE PSYCHOLOGY, GERONTOLOGY. *Current Pos:* WRITER/CONSULT, 89- *Personal Data:* b Baltimore, Md, Nov 14, 27; m 89, Muriel Groubert; c Mark W & Josh L. *Educ:* Johns Hopkins Univ, AB, 51; Duke Univ, PhD(psychol), 60. *Prof Exp:* Personnel technician, Civil Serv Comm, City of Baltimore, 52-53; res psychologist & chief, Cognition Sect, NIH, 60-89. *Concurrent Pos:* Assoc ed, J Geront, 70-72. *Mem:* Fel Am Psychol Asn. *Res:* Experimental studies of human learning, memory and problem solving with special emphasis on aging and adult development. *Mailing Add:* 13665A Via Aurora Delray Beach FL 33484-1607

AREND, WILLIAM PHELPS, RHEUMATOLOGY, IMMUNOLOGY. *Current Pos:* PROF MED & HEAD, RHEUMATOL DIV, MED SCH, UNIV COLO, 83-, PROF MICRO & IMMUNOL, 88-, SCOVILLE PROF RHEUMATOL, 93- *Personal Data:* b Utica, NY, Aug 24, 37; m 64; c Thomas, Christopher & Jeffrey. *Educ:* Williams Col, BA, 59; Columbia Univ, MD, 64. *Prof Exp:* Intern, Sch Med, Univ Wash, 64-65, resident, 65-66 & 68-69, fel rheumatol, 69-71, from asst prof to assoc prof med, 71-81; prof med & dir, rheumatol, div, Med Sch, Univ Tex, Houston, 81-82. *Concurrent Pos:* Prin investr res grants, NIH, 71-; chief, arthritis sect, Vet Admin Hosp, Seattle, 71-80; vis scholar, Strangeways Res Lab & Corpus Christi Col, Cambridge, Eng, 80-81; Guggenheim Found fel, 80-81; attend physician, Hermann Hosp, Houston, 81-82 & Univ & Vet Admin Hosp, Denver, 83-; consult, Fitzsimons Army Med Ctr, Denver, 83- *Mem:* Am Soc Clin Invest; Am Asn Immunologists; Am Rheumatism Asn; fel Am Col Physicians; Asn Am Physicians. *Res:* Immunopathology of human autoimmune diseases and the role of monocytes and macrophages, particularly the expression of Fc receptors, production of interleukin-1 and of an interleukin-1 receptor antagonist. *Mailing Add:* Univ Colo Health Sci Ctr Box 115 4200 E Ninth Ave Denver CO 80262-0001. *Fax:* 303-270-5540

ARENDALE, WILLIAM FRANK, CHEMICAL PHYSICS. *Current Pos:* prof chem & asst dir res inst, Univ Ala, Huntsville, 64-66, dir div natural sci & math, 66-70, PROF CHEM, 70- *Personal Data:* b South Pittsburg, Tenn, Nov 11, 21; m 45; c 3. *Educ:* Mid Tenn State Univ, BS, 42; Univ Tenn, MS, 48, PhD(chem & phys), 53. *Prof Exp:* Chemist, Ala Ord Works, 42-44, Tenn Eastman Co, 44-46 & Carbide & Carbon Co, 48-50; chief res, Alpha Div, Thiokol Chem Corp, 51-56, dir res, 56-59, tech dir & asst to gen mgr, 59-64. *Mem:* Fel AAAS; Am Chem Soc; Am Phys Soc; Am Inst Aeronaut & Astronaut; Optical Soc Am. *Res:* Infrared spectroscopy; organometallic compounds; materials properties; organo-selenium chemistry; environmental chemistry; interaction of electromagnetic energy with matter. *Mailing Add:* Univ Ala Ctr Robotics & Automation Huntsville AL 35899

ARENDS, CHARLES BRADFORD, PLASTICS CHEMISTRY, PLASTIC MECHANICS. *Current Pos:* RETIRED. *Personal Data:* b Chicago, Ill, June 10, 31; m 55; c 4. *Educ:* Ill Inst Technol, BS, 52; Univ Wash, PhD(phys chem), 55. *Prof Exp:* From chemist to sr res chemist, Dow Chem Co, 55-74, from res specialist to sr res specialist, 74-84, assoc scientist, 84-93. *Res:* Micromechanics of composite plastics; reinforcement of thermoplastics and thermosets; rheology of thermoplastic melts. *Mailing Add:* 1913 Plymouth St Midland MI 48642

ARENDSEN, DAVID LLOYD, MEDICINAL CHEMISTRY. *Current Pos:* Jr res chemist, 69-79, sr res chemist, 79-92, RES INVESTR, ABBOTT LABS, 92- *Personal Data:* b Grand Rapids, Mich, Nov 22, 42; m 66, Ruth Neuman; c Peter J & John M. *Educ:* NCent Col, Ill, BA, 65; Northern Ill Univ, MS, 68. *Mem:* Am Chem Soc; Sigma Xi. *Mailing Add:* Dept 4MJ Abbott Labs (AP-10) Abbott Park IL 60064. *Fax:* 847-938-1674

ARENDSHORST, WILLIAM JOHN, RENAL PHYSIOLOGY, RENAL PATHOPHYSIOLOGY. *Current Pos:* res fel, 71-74, from asst prof to assoc prof, 74-86, PROF PHYSIOL, UNIV NC, CHAPEL HILL, 87- *Personal Data:* b Bloomington, Ind, Aug 25, 44; m 74; c 1. *Educ:* De Pauw Univ, BA, 66; Ind Univ, PhD(physiol), 70. *Prof Exp:* Res fel physiol, Ind Univ, 70-71. *Concurrent Pos:* NIH res career develop grant, 80-85; mem, sect adv comt & chmn, renal sect, Am Physiol Soc, 87-; mem, Cardiorenal Study Comt, Am Heart Asn, 87- *Mem:* Am Physiol Soc; Am Heart Asn; Am Soc Nephrol; Int Soc Nephrol. *Res:* Mechanisms that control renal hemodynamics and single nephron function in the mammalian kidney; role of the kidney in the pathogenesis of hypertension. *Mailing Add:* Dept Physiol Univ NC Sch Med CB 7545 Med Sci Res Bldg Chapel Hill NC 27599-7545

ARENDT, KENNETH ALBERT, PHYSIOLOGY. *Current Pos:* from instr to assoc prof, 57-70, PROF PHYSIOL, SCH MED, LOMA LINDA UNIV, 70- *Personal Data:* b New Britain, Conn, July 24, 25; m 49; c 2. *Educ:* Union Col, AB, 49; Boston Univ, AM, 52, PhD(biol), 55. *Prof Exp:* Res assoc, Biol Res Labs, Boston Univ, 53-57. *Mem:* Am Physiol Soc; Microcirculatory Soc; Sigma Xi. *Res:* Microcirculatory physiology. *Mailing Add:* Dept Physiol Loma Linda Univ Sch Med Loma Linda CA 92350-0001

ARENDT, RONALD H, PHYSICAL CHEMISTRY, MATERIALS CHEMISTRY. *Current Pos:* MEM RES STAFF, GEN ELEC RES & DEVELOP CTR, 68- *Personal Data:* b Chicago, Ill, Apr 20, 41; m 64; c 2. *Educ:* Univ Chicago, BS, 62, MS, 65, PhD(phys chem), 68. *Mem:* Am Chem Soc; Electrochem Soc. *Res:* Molten salts; inorganic synthesis; thermodynamics. *Mailing Add:* 1910 Pawtucket Ave 1 River Rd Schenectady NY 12309-4020

ARENDT, VOLKER DIETRICH, POLYMER CHEMISTRY, RUBBER CHEMISTRY. *Current Pos:* res chemist, 64-73, SR RES SCIENTIST, AM CYANAMID CO, 73- *Personal Data:* b Berlin, Ger, Sept 18, 34; US citizen; m 66; c 4. *Educ:* NC State Col, BS, 60; Princeton Univ, MA, 62, PhD(org chem), 64. *Prof Exp:* Textile tech supvr, Duncan Fox Co, Peru, 55-57 & W R Grace Co, Peru, 57. *Mem:* Am Chem Soc. *Res:* Cellulose and carbohydrate chemistry; chemical structure determinations; new analytical methods; synthetic organic and polymer chemistry; structure property relationships; research in elastomers; specialty polyacrylates; polyurethanes; controlled drug release formulations; herbicide and pesticide formulations. *Mailing Add:* 8 Monroe Ct RD 4 Princeton NJ 08540-9515

ARENS, JOHN FREDERIC, INFRARED ASTRONOMY. *Current Pos:* AT UNIV CALIF, SPACE SCI LAB. *Personal Data:* b New York, NY, July 30, 39. *Educ:* Mass Inst Technol, BS, 61; Univ Calif, Berkeley, PhD(physics), 66. *Prof Exp:* Astrophysicist, Goddard Space Flight Ctr, NASA, 66- *Concurrent Pos:* Assoc, Nat Acad Sci, 66-69. *Mem:* Am Phys Soc. *Res:* Experimental high energy physics; measurements of cross-sections and polarizations of hadrons; satellite measurements of electrons and protons in the radiation belts and interplanetary space; cosmic ray element and isotope measurements; infrared astronomy photodetectors. *Mailing Add:* Space Sci Lab Univ Calif Berkeley CA 94720

ARENS, MAX QUIRIN, VIROLOGY. *Current Pos:* ASST RES PROF, DEPT PEDIAT, WASHINGTON UNIV SCH MED, 88- *Personal Data:* b South Bend, Ind, July 22, 45; m 67; c 2. *Educ:* Purdue Univ, BSA, 67; Va Polytech Inst & State Univ, PhD(microbiol), 71. *Prof Exp:* Res assoc, 71-75, instr, 75-76, asst res prof, Inst Molecular Virol, Med Sch, St Louis Univ, 75-80,; assoc res prof, Dept Pediat, St Louis Univ Sch Med, 80-88. *Mem:* Sigma Xi. *Res:* Mechanism and enzymology of adenovirus DNA replication; specific functions of various enzymes involved in DNA replication. *Mailing Add:* 514 Pointe Essex Ct St Louis MO 63122-3644

ARENS, RICHARD FRIEDERICH, MATHEMATICS. *Current Pos:* from asst prof to prof math, 47-89, EMER PROF MATH, UNIV CALIF, LOS ANGELES, 57- *Personal Data:* b Iserlohn, Ger, Apr 24, 19; nat US; m 43; c Philip. *Educ:* Univ Calif, Los Angeles, AB, 41; Harvard Univ, AM, 42, PhD(math), 45. *Prof Exp:* Tutor math, Harvard Univ, 42-45, staff asst, Inst Advan Study, 45-47. *Concurrent Pos:* Mem, Inst Advan Study, 53-54; ed, Pac J Math, 64-; Fulbright fel, India, 83. *Mem:* Am Math Soc; Sigma Xi; fel AAAS. *Res:* Analysis of function spaces; topological algebra; dynamics; theoretical physics. *Mailing Add:* 12436 Deerbrook Lane Los Angeles CA 90049-1912

ARENS, YIGAL, INTEGRATION OF HETEROGENEOUS INFORMATION SOURCES, HUMAN-COMPUTER INTERFACES. *Current Pos:* Asst prof computer sci, 83-89, PROJ LEADER, INFO SCI INST, UNIV SOUTHERN CALIF, 87- *Personal Data:* b New York, NY, Sept 18, 51; m 74; c 1. *Educ:* Hebrew Univ, Israel, BA, 74; Univ Calif, Berkeley, MA, 77, PhD(math), 86. *Mem:* Am Asn Artificial Intel; Cognitive Sci Soc; Asn Comput Mach. *Res:* Intelligent integration of multiple heterogeneous information sources; intelligent interfaces to computer systems; multimedia interfaces; natural language understanding and generation; representation of information in memory. *Mailing Add:* Info Sci Inst Univ Southern Calif Suite 1001 4676 Admiralty Way Marina Del Rey CA 90292. *E-Mail:* arens@isi.edu

ARENSON, DONALD L, APPLIED MATHEMATICS. *Current Pos:* PRES, ASSOC CONSULT INT CORP, 76- *Personal Data:* b Chicago, Ill, June 15, 26; m 48, Marcia Terman; c Gregory, Michael & Steven. *Educ:* Ill Inst Technol, BS, 47, MA, 50. *Prof Exp:* Asst gen mgr, Mech Res, AMF, 58-62; pres, Basys Inc, 62-72; managing dir, Mitsubishi Chase Manhattan Consult, 72-76. *Mem:* Inst Mgt Consult; Am Math Asn; assoc fel Am Inst Aeronaut & Astronaut; Nat Soc Prof Engs. *Res:* Engineering mechanics. *Mailing Add:* 7544 N Karlov Ave Skokie IL 60076-3863. *Fax:* 847-933-9102

ARENSTORF, RICHARD F, MATHEMATICS. *Current Pos:* PROF MATH, VANDERBILT UNIV, 69- *Personal Data:* b Hamburg, Ger, Nov 7, 29; US citizen; m 56; c 3. *Educ:* Univ Gottingen, BS, 52, MS, 54; Univ Mainz, Dr rer nat(math), 56. *Honors & Awards:* Medal for Except Sci Achievement, NASA, 66. *Prof Exp:* Develop engr, Telefonaktiebelaget L M Ericsson, Ger, 55-56; physicist, Army Ballistic Missile Agency, Redstone Arsenal, Ala, 57-60; staff scientist, Marshall Space Flight Ctr, NASA, 60-69. *Concurrent Pos:* Asst prof, Univ Ala, 58-59, from assoc prof to prof, 60-69; consult, Math Res Ctr, US Naval Res Lab, Washington, DC, 70-75. *Mem:* Am Math Soc; Soc Indust & Appl Math. *Res:* Analytic number theory; nonlinear differential equations; celestial mechanics. *Mailing Add:* 4633 Benton Smith Rd Nashville TN 37215-4301

ARENTS, JOHN (STEPHEN), PHYSICAL CHEMISTRY. *Current Pos:* lectr, 56-57, from instr to assoc prof, 57-79, prof, 79-91, EMER PROF CHEM, CITY COL, NY, 91- *Personal Data:* b Brooklyn, NY, Dec 11, 26; m 65, Gabriele Schatz. *Educ:* Columbia Univ, AB, 50, AM, 51, PhD(chem), 57. *Prof Exp:* Asst chem, Columbia Univ, 50-56. *Mem:* AAAS; Am Chem Soc; Am Phys Soc. *Res:* Quantum chemistry. *Mailing Add:* 53 Southfield Rd Mt Vernon NY 10552-1337

ARENZ, ROBERT JAMES, POLYMER MECHANICS, COMPOSITE MATERIALS. *Current Pos:* PROF MECH ENG, GONZAGA UNIV, SPOKANE, 85- *Personal Data:* b Primghar, Iowa, Aug 20, 24. *Educ:* Ore State Univ, BS, 45; St Louis Univ, PhL, 56, MS, 57; Calif Inst Technol, PhD(aeronaut), 64; Alma Col, Calif, STL, 66; Univ Santa Clara, MST, 66. *Prof Exp:* Eng asst, Douglas Aircraft Co, 45-46, mathematician, 46-47, aerodynamicist, 47-50; instr eng mech, Loyola Univ, Los Angeles, 57-58; res asst, Calif Inst Technol, 59-62, res fel, 63-66; vis res scientist, Ernst-Mach-Inst, 66-67; from asst prof to assoc prof mech eng, Loyola Univ, Los Angeles, 67-78, chmn dept, 77-78; prof aerospace eng & dean fac, Parks Aeronaut Col, St Louis Univ, 78-80; prof eng & dean arts & sci, Gonzaga Univ, Spokane, 80-83; Cong fel, Off Technol Assessment, US Cong, Washington, DC, 83-85. *Concurrent Pos:* Consult, Lockheed Missiles & Space Co, 64-66; vis sr scientist, NASA Jet Propulsion Lab, 69-78; Nat Sci Found grant, Va Polytech Inst, 70. *Mem:* Assoc fel Am Inst Aeronaut & Astronaut; Am Soc Mech Engrs; Soc Exp Mech; Am Acad Mech. *Res:* Solid mechanics, especially experimental and theoretical research in wave propagation in viscoelastic media; structural mechanics; spacecraft meteoroid impact effects; multiaxial mechanical testing of polymeric materials; finite deformation behavior of elastomers. *Mailing Add:* LMU Jesuit Community PO Box 45041 Los Angeles CA 90045

ARFIN, STUART MICHAEL, BIOCHEMISTRY. *Current Pos:* ASSOC PROF BIOL CHEM, SCH MED, UNIV CALIF, IRVINE, 71- *Personal Data:* b New York, NY, Sept 4, 36; m 64; c 2. *Educ:* City Col New York, BS, 58; Albert Einstein Col Med, PhD(biochem), 66. *Prof Exp:* Res assoc biol, Purdue Univ, 66-69; asst prof biochem, Sch Med, Univ Pittsburgh, 69-71. *Mem:* Am Soc Microbiol; Am Soc Biol Chemists; AAAS. *Res:* Biochemical control mechanisms; enzymology. *Mailing Add:* Dept Biol Chem Univ Calif Col Med Irvine CA 92717-0001

ARGABRIGHT, LOREN N, MATHEMATICS. *Current Pos:* PROF MATH & HEAD DEPT, DREXEL UNIV, 74- *Personal Data:* b Nemaha, Nebr, Jan 29, 33; m 61. *Educ:* Nebr State Teachers Col, Peru, BS, 54; Univ Kans, MA, 58; Univ Wash, PhD(math), 63. *Prof Exp:* Instr math, Univ Calif, Berkeley, 63-65; asst prof, Univ Minn, 65-70; assoc prof & chmn dept, Univ Nebr, Lincoln, 70-74. *Mem:* Am Math Soc; Math Asn Am. *Res:* Functional analysis; harmonic analysis; group representations. *Mailing Add:* Drexel Univ Philadelphia PA 19104-2875

ARGABRIGHT, PERRY A, CHEMISTRY. *Current Pos:* RETIRED. *Personal Data:* b Pueblo, Colo, June 6, 29; m 51; c 4. *Educ:* Univ Denver, BS, 51; Univ Colo, PhD (org chem), 56. *Honors & Awards:* Gold Medallion, Am Chem Soc, 72. *Prof Exp:* Res chemist, Shell Develop Co, 51-52; res chemist, Esso Res & Eng Co, NJ, 56-58, group leader, 58-59, sr chemist, 59-62; sr res scientist org synthesis, Marathon Oil Co, 62-68, res assoc, 68-82, mgr, 82-86, assoc dir, 86-90. *Mem:* AAAS; Sigma Xi (vpres, Sci Res Soc Am, 63); Am Chem Soc; NY Acad Sci; fel Am Inst Chemists. *Res:* Synthesis and characterization of organic compounds containing N-F bonds; influence of polar-aprotic solvents on rate and course of organic reactions; synthesis of nitrogen heterocycles; preparation and study of polyelectrolytes; chemicals for oil recovery. *Mailing Add:* 5020 S Perry Park Rd Sedalia CO 80135-8209

ARGANBRIGHT, DONALD G, FORESTRY. *Current Pos:* DIR WOOD PROCESSING, FOREST PROD LAB, UNIV CALIF, 81-; CHAIR, SCH FORESTRY, NORTHERN ARIZ UNIV, 95- *Personal Data:* b North Platte, Nebr, Dec 27, 39; m 86; c 2. *Educ:* Iowa State Univ, BS, 62, MS, 64; Univ Calif, Berkeley, PhD(wood sci), 71. *Prof Exp:* Asst specialist, Forest Prod Lab, Univ Calif, 64-70; from asst prof to prof wood sci, Univ Calif, Berkeley, 70-80. *Concurrent Pos:* Prin investr, Agr Exp Sta, Univ Calif, 70-; consult, Centre Technique du Bois, France, 75-76. *Mem:* AAAS; Int Acad Wood Sci

& Technol; Forest Prod Res Soc; Soc Wood Sci & Technol; Int Res Group Wood Preservation; Am Soc Testing Mats; Int Union Forestry Res Org; Soc Am Forestry. *Res:* Physical properties and processing of forest products with emphasis on heat and mass transfer; drying and preservative impregnation. *Mailing Add:* Sch Forestry Northern Ariz Univ PO Box 15018 Flagstaff AZ 86011-5018

ARGANBRIGHT, ROBERT PHILIP, ORGANIC CHEMISTRY, HETEROGENEOUS CATALYSIS. *Current Pos:* SR SCIENTIST, CHEM RES & LICENSING CORP, 88- *Personal Data:* b Ft Leavenworth, Kans, Nov 7, 23; m 57; c 2. *Educ:* Univ Kans, BS, 50; Univ Colo, PhD(chem), 56. *Prof Exp:* Chemist, Continental Oil Co, 50-52; chemist, Monsanto Chem Co, 56-60, res specialist, 60-67; res assoc, Petro-Tex Chem Corp, 67-74, res mgr, 74-76; res supvr, M W Kellog Co, 76-82, consult, 83-87. *Mem:* Catalysis Soc; Am Chem Soc. *Res:* Heterogeneous catalysis; process development. *Mailing Add:* 814 Devonport Seabrook TX 77586-4203. *Fax:* 713-474-0660

ARGAST, SCOTT FREDERICK, CHEMISTRY & MINERALOGY OF SEDIMENTARY ROCKS, CLAY MINERALOGY. *Current Pos:* From instr to asst prof, 85-92, ASSOC PROF GEOL, IND-PURDUE UNIV, FT WAYNE, 92-, CHMN, DEPT GEOSCI, 93- *Personal Data:* b Long Branch, NJ, Sept 19, 56; m 91, Deborah K Hanson; c David F. *Educ:* Univ Rochester, BS, 78; State Univ NY, Binghamton, MA, 82, PhD(geol), 86. *Mem:* Sigma Xi; Mineral Soc Am; Clay Minerals Soc; Geol Soc Am. *Res:* Mineralogy and chemistry of sedimentary rocks; the effect of elastic processes on sediment composition; diagenesis and metamorphism of sediments; chemistry and structure of clay minerals; Web resources for teaching and research. *Mailing Add:* Dept Geosci Ind-Purdue Univ Ft Wayne IN 46805-1499

ARGAUER, ROBERT JOHN, ANALYTICAL CHEMISTRY. *Current Pos:* RES CHEMIST, USDA, 65- *Personal Data:* b Buffalo, NY, Feb 23, 37; m 64; c 5. *Educ:* Canisius Col, BS, 58; Univ Md, PhD(inorg chem), 63. *Prof Exp:* Res chemist, Mobil Oil Co, 63-65. *Mem:* Am Chem Soc; Entom Soc Am; Sigma Xi. *Res:* Application of light and flame absorption and emission spectro-fluorometry and spectrophotometry, gas chromatography, infrared, mass spectroscopy and radiochemical methods to chemical problems, especially pesticide analysis. *Mailing Add:* 4208 Everett St Kensington MD 20895

ARGENAL-ARAUZ, ROGER, GEOMAGNETISM, SEISMOLOGY. *Current Pos:* PROF PHYSICS, UNIV NICARAGUA, 60-; DIR, INST SEISMIC RES, 81- *Personal Data:* b Leon, Nicaragua, Feb 18, 37; m 65; c 4. *Educ:* Monterrey Inst Technol, Mex, BS, 60; Univ Tex, Austin, MS, 68, PhD(physics), 75. *Concurrent Pos:* Sci adv geophys, Inst Seismic Res, 75-80. *Mem:* Soc Centroamericana de Fisica; Soc Nicaraguense de Fisica (pres, 76); Am Geophys Union; Soc Explor Geophysicists. *Res:* Crustal structure in the Nicaraguan region; studies being made through the regional magnetic field anomalies and the seismic characteristics shown by the Seismic Net of Nicaragua formed by sixteen stations; acceleration, attenuation curves for Nicaragua; assessment of seismic risk in Nicaragua. *Mailing Add:* 16 Sandarac Way NW Calgary AB T3K 2Y7 Can

ARGENZIO, ROBERT ALAN, PHYSIOLOGY, GASTROENTEROLOGY. *Current Pos:* PROF, DEPT ANAT SCH VET MED, NC STATE UNIV. *Personal Data:* b Denver, Colo, Apr 27, 41. *Educ:* Colo State Univ, BS, 66, MS, 68; Cornell Univ, PhD(nutrit), 71. *Prof Exp:* Res assoc physiol, Dept Vet Physiol, Cornell Univ, 71-76; physiologist, Nat Animal Dis Ctr, 76- *Concurrent Pos:* Assoc prof, Dept Vet Physiol, Iowa State Univ, 78- *Mem:* Am Gastroenterol Asn; Am Physiol Soc; Comp Gastroenterol Asn. *Res:* Intestinal absorption; pathophysiology of diarrheal diseases. *Mailing Add:* Dept Anat Sch Vet Med NC State Univ 4700 Hillsborough Raleigh NC 27606-1428

ARGO, HAROLD VIRGIL, ASTRONOMY. *Current Pos:* RETIRED. *Personal Data:* b Walla Walla, Wash, Jan 20, 18; m 42; c 4. *Educ:* Whitman Col, AB, 39; George Washington Univ, MA, 41; Univ Chicago, PhD, 48. *Prof Exp:* Jr physicist, Naval Ord Lab, Washington, DC, 42-44; physicist, Los Alamos Nat Lab, 44- *Mem:* AAAS; Am Geophys Union; Am Phys Soc; Am Astron Soc. *Res:* Experimental nuclear physics; space physics; satellites and probes; solar physics. *Mailing Add:* 301 Potrillo Dr Los Alamos NM 87544

ARGO, PAUL EMMETT, IONOSPHERIC PHYSICS, RADIO PROPAGATIONS. *Current Pos:* STAFF SCIENTIST, LOS ALAMOS NAT LAB, 82- *Personal Data:* b Los Alamos, NMex, Nov 25, 48; m 83; c 2. *Educ:* Pomona Col, BA, 70; Univ Calif San Diego, MS, 78, PhD(appl physics), 80. *Prof Exp:* Scientist, Naval Ocean Systs Ctr, 71-81; engr, Linkabit, 81-82. *Mem:* Am Geophys Union; Union Radio Sci Int. *Res:* Radio propagation through ionosphere; effects of ionospheric perturbations on both the propagation channel and communication systems using the channel. *Mailing Add:* 1300 20th St Los Alamos NM 87544

ARGON, ALI SUPHI, MATERIALS SCIENCE, MECHANICAL & POLYMER ENGINEERING. *Current Pos:* asst prof mat, 60-65, from assoc prof to prof, 65-82, QUENTIN BERG PROF MECH ENG, MASS INST TECHNOL, 82- *Personal Data:* b Istanbul, Turkey, Dec 19, 30; m 53, Xenia Lacher; c 2. *Educ:* Purdue Univ, BS, 52; Mass Inst Technol, SM, 53, ScD(mat), 56. *Honors & Awards:* C R Richards Award, Am Soc Mech Engrs, 76; Hon Fel, Int Cong Fracture, 83; Alexander Von Humboldt US Sr Scientist Award, Ger, 92. *Prof Exp:* Proj engr, High Voltage Eng Corp, 56-58; instr, Middle East Tech Univ, Ankara, 59-60. *Concurrent Pos:* Vis prof polymer physics, Univ Leeds, UK, 71-72; Humbolt fel, Univ Gottingen; vis scholar mat sci, Stanford Univ, 92. *Mem:* Nat Acad Eng; fel Am Phys Soc; Am Inst Mining, Metall & Petrol Engrs; fel Am Phys Soc; Am Soc Metals; Mat Res Soc. *Res:* Mechanical behavior of materials; physical mechanisms of deformation and fracture of materials. *Mailing Add:* Mass Inst Technol Rm 1-306 Cambridge MA 02139

ARGOS, PATRICK, BIOCOMPUTING. *Current Pos:* SR RES GROUP LEADER, EUROP MOLECULAR BIOL LAB, 84- *Personal Data:* b Carbondale, Ill, Nov 24, 42. *Educ:* St Louis Univ, BS, 64, MS, 66, PhD(physics), 68. *Prof Exp:* USPHS fel protein crystallog, Sch Med, Washington Univ, 69-71; asst prof physics, Pomona Col, 71-73; res assoc, Purdue Univ, 73-74; assoc prof biophys, Southern Ill Univ, 74-78; assoc prof biol, Purdue Univ, 78-84. *Concurrent Pos:* Woodrow Wilson fel; career fel, Nat Cancer Soc. *Mem:* Am Soc Biol Chemists. *Res:* Theoretical studies of proteins involving sequence companson, structural modelling and biological database information handling. *Mailing Add:* Europ Molecular Biol Lab Postfach 102209 Meyerhofstr 1 69012 Heidelberg Germany

ARGOT, JEANNE, MICROBIOLOGY. *Current Pos:* PROF BIOL & DIR MED, LAB TECHNOL, IND WESLEYAN UNIV, 79- *Personal Data:* b Pocono Lake, Pa, Mar 12, 36. *Educ:* Moravian Col, BS, 65; Lehigh Univ, MS, 67, PhD(biol), 69. *Prof Exp:* Biologist, Pharmachem Corp, Pa, 62-66; Asst prof biol, Lebanon Valley Col, 69-79. *Mem:* Am Soc Med Technol; Am Soc Microbiol; Sigma Xi; Am Sci Affil. *Mailing Add:* Ind Wesleyan Univ 4201 S Washington St Marion IN 46953. *Fax:* 765-677-2284; *E-Mail:* jargot@inwes.edu

ARGOUDELIS, CHRIS J, ORGANIC CHEMISTRY, BIOCHEMISTRY. *Current Pos:* Res asst food technol, 60-61, asst prof, 61-77, ASSOC PROF FOOD SCI, UNIV ILL, URBANA-CHAMPAIGN, 77- *Personal Data:* b Piraeus, Greece, July 30, 29; nat US. *Educ:* Nat Univ Athens, BS, 56; Univ Ill, PhD(food technol), 61. *Concurrent Pos:* NIH res grant, 64-71. *Mem:* AAAS; Am Chem Soc; Sigma Xi. *Res:* Chemistry and metabolism of vitamin B6. *Mailing Add:* 260 Bevier Hall Food Sci & Human Nutrit Univ Ill 905 S Goodwin Urbana IL 61801

ARGRAVES, W SCOTT, BIOCHEMISTRY. *Current Pos:* RES ASST PROF, DEPT ORAL PATH, UNIV MD, 89- *Personal Data:* b Jan 30, 56. *Educ:* Univ Conn, BS, 78, PhD(cellular & develop biol), 85. *Prof Exp:* Res asst, Dept Biol Sci & Dept Animal Genetics, Univ Conn, 79-84; postdoctoral fel, La Jolla Cancer Res Found, Calif, 85-87, res assoc, 87-88; staff scientist I, 88-91, staff scientist II, Am Red Cross, Rockville, MD, 91- *Concurrent Pos:* Postdoctoral fel, Am Chem Soc, 86-88. *Mem:* Soc Develop Biol; Sigma Xi; Am Soc Cell Biol. *Mailing Add:* Dept Cell Biol & Anat Univ SC 171 Ashley Ave Charleston SC 29425-2743

ARGUS, GEORGE WILLIAM, SYSTEMATIC BOTANY. *Current Pos:* assoc cur to cur, 72-95, EMER CUR VASC PLANTS, NAT MUS NATURAL SCI, 95-; TAXON ED, FLORA N AM, 86- *Personal Data:* b Brooklyn, NY, Apr 14, 29; m 55; c Michael (deceased), Eric, John, Martin & Rebecca. *Educ:* Univ Alaska, BS, 52; Univ Wyo, MS; Harvard Univ, PhD(biol), 61. *Honors & Awards:* Conserv Award, Fedn Ont Naturalists; Lawson Medal, Can Bot Asn. *Prof Exp:* Nat Res Coun Can fel plant taxon, Univ Sask, 61-63, asst prof plant ecol & lectr biol, 63-67, cur, W P Fraser Herbarium, 63-69, actg dir, Inst North Studies, 65-66, assoc prof, 67-69; cur herbarium, Mus Natural Hist, Univ Ore, 69-70; res scientist, Can Forest Serv, 70-72. *Concurrent Pos:* Mem, Nat Res Coun Can, 73-77, chmn, Plant Biol Grant Selection Comt, 75-76; sci authority plants, Int Conv Trade in Endangered Species, 75- *Mem:* Am Soc Plant Taxon; Int Asn Plant Taxon; Can Bot Asn. *Res:* Taxonomy and evolution of Salix in North America; rare plants of Canada. *Mailing Add:* RR 3-310 Haskins Rd Merrickville ON K0G 1N0 Can

ARGUS, MARY FRANCES, ONCOLOGY, TOXICOLOGY. *Current Pos:* SR SCI ADV, OFF TOXIC SUBSTANCES, US ENVIRON PROTECTION AGENCY, 80- *Personal Data:* b Ironton, Ohio, July 16, 24. *Educ:* Col Mt St Joseph, BS, 45; Univ Cincinnati, MS, 47; Univ Fla, PhD(biochem), 52. *Honors & Awards:* Joseph Seifter Award, 83. *Prof Exp:* Instr chem, Marygrove Col, 47-49; from asst prof to assoc prof cancer res, Univ Fla, 52-60; from assoc prof to prof biochem & med, Sch Med, Tulane Univ, 60-80. *Mem:* Am Soc Biol Chem; Am Asn Cancer Res; Am Soc Pharmacol & Exp Therapeut; Am Col Toxicol; Soc Toxicol. *Res:* Chemical carcinogenesis; drug metabolism; conformational changes in macromolecules during carcinogenesis; alterations in oxidative metabolism in cardiac hypertrophy; chemical risk assessment. *Mailing Add:* US Environ Protection Agency MC 7403 401 M St SW Washington DC 20460-0001

ARGY, DIMITRI, MATERIALS SCIENCE, METALLURGY. *Current Pos:* chmn dept mech eng, 67-76, PROF MECH ENG, SOUTHEASTERN MASS UNIV, 67- *Personal Data:* b Athens, Greece, Mar 13, 21; US citizen; m 56; c 2. *Educ:* Athens Tech Univ, dipl, 46; Aachen Tech Univ, Dr Ing, 55. *Prof Exp:* Res metall engr, Carnegie Inst Technol, 56-58 & E I du Pont de Nemours & Co Inc, 58-60; sr res metallurgist, Foote Mineral Co, 60-61; chief metallurgist, Hoeganaes Corp, 61-63 & Starlite Indust Inc, 63-65; sect head, Metals & Controls Inc, 65-67. *Mem:* Am Inst Mining, Metall & Petrol Engrs; Am Soc Metals; Nat Soc Prof Engrs; Am Soc Eng Educ; Brit Inst Metals; Sigma Xi. *Res:* Composite materials, properties and evaluation; direct rolling of powders; compaction and sintering mechanism; production of powders by the atomizing process and reduction; alloy development; high temperature oxidation protective coatings; conductivity of molten salts; constitution of the liquid state. *Mailing Add:* Shore Acres Rd South Dartmouth MA 02748

ARGYRES, PETROS, THEORETICAL PHYSICS OF CONDENSED MATTER. *Current Pos:* PROF PHYSICS, NORTHEASTERN UNIV, 67- *Personal Data:* b Lefkas, Greece, Mar 9, 27; nat US; m 58; c 3. *Educ:* Univ Calif, AB, 50, MA, 52, PhD(physics), 54. *Prof Exp:* Res physicist, Westinghouse Res Lab, 54-58 & Lincoln Lab, Mass Inst Technol, 58-67. *Concurrent Pos:* Lectr, Univ Pittsburgh, 55-57; vis assoc prof, Mass Inst Technol, 65-66; vis prof, Ecole Normale Superieure, Univ Paris, 69-70; vis prof, Tech Univ Greece, Athens, 82-83. *Mem:* Fel Am Phys Soc; corresp mem Acad Arts & Sci Greece; AAAS. *Res:* Solid state physics; irreversible phenomena; transport processes; statistical mechanics; spin resonance; many-body theories; equilibrium and transport properties of disordered systems with consideration of electron-electron and electron-phonon interactions and use of formal projection operator techniques. *Mailing Add:* Dept Physics Northeastern Univ Boston MA 02115

ARGYRIS, BERTIE, IMMUNOLOGY. *Current Pos:* assoc prof urol, 68-71, prof microbiol, 71-85, EMER PROF MICROBIOL, STATE UNIV NY UPSTATE MED CTR, 85- *Personal Data:* b Holland, June 27, 30; nat US; m 55, Thomas S. *Educ:* Columbia Univ, BA, 51; Brown Univ, MS, 53; Syracuse Univ, PhD, 58. *Prof Exp:* Res assoc exp morphol, Syracuse Univ, 58-62 & immunobiol, 62-68. *Mem:* Am Soc Zool; Soc Study Develop Biol; Am Inst Biol Sci; Am Asn Immunol; Transplantation Soc; fel Am Soc Exp Biol. *Res:* Endocrinology-insulin resistance; experimental morphology-tissue interaction; effects of tumors on mammary glands; transplantation immunity; acquired homograft tolerance; tumor immunology; immunosuppression; cellular interactions during immune response; immunological maturation; neonatal suppressor cells; macrophage immunology; author computer based tutorials in immunol. *Mailing Add:* 24 Applecrest Rd Weston MA 02193

ARGYRIS, THOMAS STEPHEN, EXPERIMENTAL PATHOLOGY. *Current Pos:* prof, 72-84, EMER PROF PATH, STATE UNIV NY, UPSTATE MED CTR, 84- *Personal Data:* b Newark, NJ, July 16, 23; m 55, Bertie F Frankenhuis. *Educ:* Rutgers Univ, BS, 48; Brown Univ, PhD, 53. *Prof Exp:* Instr & fel, Harvard Univ, 53-55; from asst prof to prof zool, Syracuse Univ, 55-72. *Concurrent Pos:* NSF sr fel embryol, Carnegie Inst, 61-62; NIH spec res fel zool, Univ Col, Univ London, 65-66. *Mem:* Fel AAAS; Am Asn Cancer Res; Am Asn Pathologists; Soc Invest Dermat. *Res:* Wound healing; carcinogenesis; tumor promotion. *Mailing Add:* 24 Applecrest Rd Weston MA 02193-1102

ARGYROPOULOS, STAVROS ANDREAS, REALTIME SYSTEMS, PROCESS CONTROL. *Current Pos:* asst prof, 86-89, ASSOC PROF METALL, UNIV TORONTO, 89- *Personal Data:* b Pireocus, Greece, Dec 15, 45; Can citizen; m 78; c 1. *Educ:* Nat Tech Univ Athens, dipl eng, 69; Grad Sch Indust Studies, dipl statist, 73; McGill Univ, MEng, 77, PhD(metall), 81. *Honors & Awards:* C W Briggs Award, Iron & Steel Soc US, 84, 85 & 89, R W Hunt Award, 90. *Prof Exp:* Univ res fel metall, 81-86. *Concurrent Pos:* Chmn, Comput Appln Comt, Metall Soc, Can Inst Mining & Metall, 90- *Mem:* Iron & Steel Soc US; Metall Soc, Can Inst Mining & Metall; Am Soc Qual Control; Instrument Soc Am. *Res:* Transport phenomena in materials processing; mass transfer of ferroalloys in liquid steel; convection in liquid metals. *Mailing Add:* Dept Metal & Mat Sci Univ Tonoto 184 College Toronto ON M5S 1A1 Can

ARGYROS, IOANNIS KONSTANTINOS, MATHEMATICS. *Current Pos:* PROF MATH, CAMERON UNIV, 90- *Personal Data:* b Greece, Feb 20, 56. *Educ:* Univ Ga, PhD(math), 84. *Prof Exp:* Prof math, Univ Iowa, 84-86, NMex State Univ, 86-90. *Concurrent Pos:* Founder & ed-in-chief, SW J Pure & Appl Math. *Mem:* Am Math Soc. *Res:* Author of three graduate textbooks and over 200 peer reviewed scientific manuscripts. *Mailing Add:* Dept Math Cameron Univ 2800 Gore Blvd Lawton OK 73505-6320. *Fax:* 580-581-2616; *E-Mail:* ioannisa@cua.cameron.edu

ARHELGER, ROGER BOYD, MEDICINE, PATHOLOGY. *Current Pos:* PATHOLOGIST, MISS BAPTIST MED CTR, 77-; ASSOC CLIN PROF, MED CTR, UNIV MISS, 77- *Personal Data:* b Green Bay, Wis, May 23, 32; m 53; c 3. *Educ:* Hamline Univ, BS, 54; Univ Minn, MD, 58. *Prof Exp:* Intern, USPHS Hosp, Boston, Mass, 58-59; resident, Med Ctr, Univ Miss, 59-62, from instr to asst prof path, 62-66; assoc prof path, Univ Tex Med Sch San Antonio, 66-68; assoc prof, Med Ctr, Univ Miss, 68-72; chief surg path & cytol, Fresno Community Hosp, 72-75; chmn dept path, Kern Med Ctr, 75-77. *Concurrent Pos:* USPHS res career develop award, 63- *Mem:* Electron Micros Soc Am; Am Soc Exp Path; Am Asn Path & Bact; Int Acad Path; AMA; Sigma Xi. *Res:* Experimental pathology; electron microscopy. *Mailing Add:* Baptist Mem Hosp Path 111 Dallas St San Antonio TX 78205-1201

ARIANO, MARJORIE ANN, NEUROCHEMISTRY. *Current Pos:* PROF, NEUROSCI DEPT, CHICAGO MED SCH, 92- *Personal Data:* b Tokyo, Japan, Feb 13, 51; US citizen. *Educ:* Univ Calif, Los Angeles, BS, 72, PhD(anat), 77. *Prof Exp:* Asst molecular biol, Univ Southern Calif, 77-80; asst prof anat & neurobiol, Univ Vt, 80-86, mem cell biol prog, 82-88, assoc prof anat & neurobiol, 86-92. *Concurrent Pos:* Mem bd dirs, Am Heart Asn, 83-87; mem, adv panel, Cell & Molecular Neurobiol, NSF, 85-87; mem, Neurol Sci Study Sect, NIH, 87-91; Res Career Develop Award, Nat Inst Neurol Dis & Stroke, 84-89. *Mem:* Soc Neurosci. *Res:* Elucidation of the specific cellular site of second messenger production in response to dopamine neurotransmitter receptor activation in basal ganglia and sympathetic nervous system in mammals. *Mailing Add:* 11 Hampton Bin North Chicago IL 60064-3095

ARIAS, IRWIN MONROE, MEDICINE, GASTROENTEROLOGY. *Current Pos:* CHMN DEPT PHYSIOL, TUFTS UNIV. *Personal Data:* b New York, NY, Sept 4, 26; m 53; c 4. *Educ:* Harvard Univ, SB, 46; Long Island Col Med, MD, 52; Am Bd Internal Med, dipl. *Honors & Awards:* Suiter Mem Lectr, 59; Hon Achievement Award, Am Gastroenterol Asn, 69; Citation in Sci, Univ Recife, 70. *Prof Exp:* From intern to resident med, Boston City Hosp, 52-54; resident, Boston Vet Admin Hosp, 54-55; assoc, Albert Einstein Col Med, 56-64, assoc prof, 64-67, prof med, 67- *Concurrent Pos:* Res fel, Boston City Hosp, 55-56; NY Heart Asn fel, 56-; instr, NY Heart Asn, 56-; Suiter Mem lectr, 59; attend physician, Albert Einstein Col Med Hosp, 67-; assoc vis prof, Bronx Munic Hosp Ctr; consult, New Rochelle Hosp, Mt Vernon Hosp, USPHS, Pan Am Union & Kellogg Found. *Mem:* AAAS; Am Soc Gastrointestinal Endoscopy; Am Gastroenterol Asn; Am Physiol Soc; Am Asn Study Liver Dis. *Res:* Academic gastroenterology; mechanisms of hepatic excretory function. *Mailing Add:* Dept Physiol Tufts Univ Sch Med 136 Harrison M & V 701 Boston MA 02111-1800

ARIAS, JOSE MANUEL, SEMICONDUCTOR EPITAXIAL GROWTH, ADVANCED INFRARED, MATERIALS & DEVICES. *Current Pos:* MEM TECH STAFF ADVAN MAT, SCI CTR, ROCKWELL INT, 85- *Personal Data:* b Los Angeles, Calif, June 22, 54; m 79; c 4. *Educ:* ITESO, Guadalajara, Mex, BS, 78; Univ Calif, Santa Barbara, PhD(phys chem), 84. *Prof Exp:* Teaching asst chem, Univ Calif, Santa Barbara, 79-81, res asst phys chem, 82-84. *Res:* Surface science and solid state physics; research and development of the molecular beam epitaxy growth technology of II-VI semiconductor materials for opto-electronic device applications; author or co-author of 50 scientific papers. *Mailing Add:* PO Box 1085 Thousand Oaks CA 91350

ARIEFF, ALLEN I, MEDICINE. *Current Pos:* asst prof med & dir hemodialysis, Vet Admin Med Ctr, Univ Calif, 75-76, assoc prof & dir nephrology sect, 76-83, chief, clin nephrology, 83-86, PROF MED, VET ADMIN MED CTR, UNIV CALIF, 83-, DIR RES & EDUC, GERIAT, 86- *Educ:* Univ Ill, BS, 60; Northwestern Univ, MS & MD, 64; Am Bd Internal Med, cert, 72, cert nephrology, 76. *Prof Exp:* Rotating intern, Philadelphia Gen Hosp, Univ Pa Serv, 64-65; res med & chief resident, Downstate Med Ctr, State Univ NY, Brooklyn, 67-68; renal fel, Univ Colo, Denver, 68-69; res & educ assoc & clin investr, Wadsworth Vet Admin Med Ctr, Los Angeles, Calif, 70-74; asst prof med & res scientist, Cedar-Sinai Med Ctr, Univ Calif, Los Angeles, 71-74. *Concurrent Pos:* Res career develop award, Vet Admin, 70-76; sci adv coun, Nat Kidney Found; numerous invited lectrs, 73-91; consult, Food & Drug Admin, 77 & 89, Mobil Oil Co, Dallas, Tex, 85, Abbott Labs, Ill, 87, Vet Admin Coop Studies Sect, 90 & others. *Mem:* Am Soc Nephrology; Int Soc Nephrology; Am Fedn Clin Res; Am Diabetes Asn; Am Physiol Soc; fel Am Col Physicians; Am Soc Neurochem; Am Soc Clin Invest; Am Soc Bone & Mineral Res. *Mailing Add:* Geriat Res Vet Admin Med Ctr Univ Calif 4150 Clement St San Francisco CA 94121. *Fax:* 415-750-6904

ARIET, MARIO, SYSTEMS & CHEMICAL ENGINEERING. *Current Pos:* ASSOC PROF INDUST & SYSTS ENG, UNIV FLA, 67-, PROF COMMUNITY HEALTH 78-, PROF MED & DIR COMPUT SCI DIV, 82- *Personal Data:* b Havana, Cuba, July 9, 39; m 60; c 5. *Educ:* Univ Fla, BChE, 60, MSE, 62, PhD(chem eng, math), 65. *Prof Exp:* Sr engr, Humble Oil & Refining Co, Tex, 65-67. *Mem:* Am Inst Chem Engrs; Asn Comput Mach. *Res:* Computerized analysis of electrocardiagrams; computer simulation of physiochemical systems; computerized closed-loop control of chemical and biological systems; automation of health care delivery systems; management of clinical data base. *Mailing Add:* Comput Sci Univ Fla Col Med Box 100372 Gainesville FL 32610. *Fax:* 352-392-7337; *E-Mail:* mario_cme@shands.ufl.edu

ARIF, BASIL MUMTAZ, VIROLOGY, NUCLEIC ACIDS. *Current Pos:* res scientist, 72-84, SR RES SCIENTIST VIROL, FOREST PEST MGT INST, 85- *Personal Data:* b Baghdad, Iraq, April 12, 40; Can citizen; m 75. *Educ:* Queen's Univ, Belfast, UK, BSc, 67; Queen's Univ, Kingston, Ont, MSc, 69, PhD(virol), 71. *Prof Exp:* Sr demonstr microbiol, Queen's Univ, Kingston, Ont, 68-71. *Concurrent Pos:* Vis prof, Lake Superior State Col, 78; prof, Algoma Campus, Laurentian Univ, 79; vis scientist, Univ Cologne, WGer, 81-83. *Mem:* Am Soc Microbiol; Am Soc Virol; Soc Invert Path. *Res:* Molecular biology of baculoviruses including molecular cloning, mapping and DNA sequencing to elucidate the nature, mode of action and specificity and to examine the potential of improving these viruses as forest pest control agents. *Mailing Add:* Forest Pest Mgt Inst PO Box 490 Sault Ste Marie ON P6A 5M7 Can

ARIF, SHOAIB, RESEARCH & DEVELOPMENT PERSONAL CARE HOUSE-HOLD OR I & I PRODUCTS. *Current Pos:* APPLN SPECIALIST, OLIN CORP, CHESHIRE, CONN, 89- *Personal Data:* b Karachi, Pakistan, May 28, 50; US citizen; m 79; c 5. *Educ:* Univ Karachi, Pakistan, BS, 69, MS, 71. *Prof Exp:* Chemist, Kohimoor Chem Co, Karachi, Pakistan, 71-77, Pvt Formulations, Edison, NJ, 77-78, Dept Water Resources, New York, 78-80; chief chemist, Cameo Inc, Toledo, Ohio, 80-83; assoc dir res & develop, GO-JO Industs, Akron, Ohio, 83-85; chemist res & develop, Sani-Fresh Inc, San Antonio, Tex, 85-87; dir res & develop, Jeri Jacobs Labs, Carrollton, Tex, 87-89. *Mem:* Am Soc Testing & Mat; Soc Cosmetic Chemists; Chem Specialties Mfrs Asn; Cosmetic Toiletry & Fragrance Asn. *Res:* Developed numerous new consumer products in personal care (cosmetics), house-hold and I and I areas; granted 1 US patent. *Mailing Add:* 155 Alexander Dr Cheshire CT 06410. *Fax:* 203-271-4351

ARIMA, AKITO, NUCLEAR PHYSICS. *Current Pos:* Dir, Comput Ctr, Univ Tokyo, 81-85, dean sci fac, 85-87, vpres, 87-89, PRES, UNIV TOKYO, 89- *Personal Data:* b Osaka, Japan, Sept 13, 30; m 57, Hiroko Aota; c Yoshihito & Akiko. *Educ:* Univ Tokyo, BS, 53, DSc, 58. *Hon Degrees:* DSc, Glasgow Univ, 84, Drexel Univ, 92. *Honors & Awards:* Tom W Bonner Prize, Am Phys Soc, 93. *Mem:* Phys Soc Japan (pres, 81-82). *Res:* Author and contributor of articles to professional journals. *Mailing Add:* Sangenjaya 2-23-6 Setagaya-ku 154 Japan

ARIMOTO, SUGURU, ROBOTICS, INFORMATION THEORY. *Current Pos:* res asst appl physics, 62-67, lectr control theory, 67-68, PROF INFO THEORY & ROBOTICS, UNIV TOKYO, 88- *Personal Data:* b Hiroshima, Japan, Aug 3, 36; m 65; c 2. *Educ:* Kyoto Univ, BS, 59; Univ Tokyo, DEng, 67. *Prof Exp:* Engr, Oki Elec Indust Co Ltd, 59-62; assoc prof control eng, Osaka Univ, 68-73, prof robotics, 73-90. *Concurrent Pos:* Vis prof, Tokyo Inst Technol, 88- *Mem:* Fel Inst Elec & Electronics Engrs. *Res:* Theory of learning for skill refinement; information theory; machine intelligence. *Mailing Add:* Fac Eng Univ Tokyo Bunkyo-Ku Tokyo 113 Japan

ARIMURA, AKIRA, NEUROENDOCRINOLOGY, PHYSIOLOGY. *Current Pos:* from asst to instr med, 58-61, from asst prof to assoc prof, 65-73, PROF MED, SCH MED, TULANE UNIV, 73- *Personal Data:* b Kobe, Japan, Dec 26, 23; m 57, Katsuko Yamashita; c Jerome, Mark & Margaret. *Educ:* Nagoya Univ, BS, 43, MD, 51, PhD(physiol), 57. *Prof Exp:* Instr & res assoc physiol, Sch Med, Hokkaido Univ, 61-65. *Concurrent Pos:* Fulbright Comn Exchange Scholar, 56; J H Brown fel, Sch Med, Yale Univ, 56-58; USPHS res grants, Sch Med, Hokkaido Univ, 63-64 & Sch Med, Tulane Univ, 65-; res physician, Vet Admin Hosp, New Orleans, 65-81; dir, Clin Res Inst Am, 80-87. *Mem:* AAAS; Endocrine Soc; Am Physiol Soc; Soc Exp Biol & Med; hon men Hungarian Endocrinol Soc; hon mem Japan Endocrin Soc; NY Acad Sci. *Res:* Experimental and clinical neuroendocrinology. *Mailing Add:* Dir US-Japan Biomed Res Labs Herbert Ctr 3705 Main St Bldg 30 Belle Chasse LA 70037

ARING, CHARLES DAIR, NEUROLOGY. *Current Pos:* prof neurol, 47-74, dir neurol serv, 47-76, EMER PROF NEUROL, COL MED, UNIV CINCINNATI, 74- *Personal Data:* b Dent, Ohio, June 21, 04; m 31, Mary Shroder; c Dair (Rausch) & Charles Shroder. *Educ:* Univ Cincinnati, BS & MD, 29. *Hon Degrees:* LHD, Univ Cincinnati, 90. *Prof Exp:* Rotating intern, Cincinnati Gen Hosp, 29-30, resident physician, 30-31; resident, Longview State Hosp, Cincinnati, 31; house officer neurol, Boston City Hosp, 32, resident, 33-34; house officer, Children's Hosp, Boston, 33; from instr to assoc prof, Col Med, Univ Cincinnati, 36-46; prof, Col Med, Univ Calif, 46-47, dir neurol serv, 46-47. *Concurrent Pos:* Fel neuro-physiol, Yale Univ, 34-35; Rockefeller fel neurol, Madrid, Breslau & Nat Hosp, London, 35-36; attend neurologist, Cincinnati Gen Hosp, 36-45; mem comn neurotropic virus dis, Bd Invest Control Influenza & Other Epidemic Dis. *Mem:* AMA; Am Neurol Asn (pres, 63); Am Psychiat Asn; Asn Res Nerv & Ment Dis (vpres, 47-52). *Res:* Psychiatry; medical administration; medical philosophy. *Mailing Add:* 2444 Madison Rd Cincinnati OH 45208

ARION, DOUGLAS, RADIATION EFFECTS ON ELECTRONICS & STRUCTURES, INSTRUMENTATION DEVELOPMENT. *Current Pos:* sr scientist, 84-88, div mgr & asst vpres, 89-94, CONSULT & ASST VPRES, SCI APPLN INT CORP, ALBUQUERQUE, NM, 94-; HEDBERG PROF ENTREPRENEURIAL STUDIES & PROF PHYSICS, CARTHAGE COL, 94- *Personal Data:* b New York, NY, Jan 27, 57; m 90, Teresa Sandoval. *Educ:* Dartmouth Col, AB, 78, Univ Md, MS, 80, PhD(physics), 84. *Prof Exp:* Grad res fel, Goddard Space Flight Ctr, NASA, 82-84. *Mem:* Am Phys Soc; AAAS. *Res:* Effects of ionizing radiation of electronics, optics and structures; development of instruments for hazardous (shock, heat, radiation) environments. *Mailing Add:* 9010 Lakeshore Dr Kenosha WI 53143. *Fax:* 414-551-6208; *E-Mail:* ariond1@carthage.edu

ARION, WILLIAM JOSEPH, BIOCHEMISTRY. *Current Pos:* from asst prof to prof biochem, 68-80, PROF BIOCHEM, DIV NUTRIT SCI & SECT BIOCHEM MOLECULAR CELL BIOL, CORNELL UNIV, 80- *Personal Data:* b Cando, NDak, May 31, 40; m 85; c 3. *Educ:* Jamestown Col, BS, 62; Univ ND, 62-65, MS, 64, PhD(biochem), 66. *Prof Exp:* NIH fel biochem, Cornell Univ, 66-68. *Concurrent Pos:* Vis prof biochem, Univ Stockholm, 76-77. *Mem:* Am Inst Nutrit; NY Acad Sci; Am Soc Biochem & Molecular Biol; Sigma Xi. *Res:* Mechanisms of glucose homeostasis; membrane structure-function; bioenergetics and energy balance. *Mailing Add:* Div Nutrit Sci Cornell Univ 227 Savage Hall Ithaca NY 14853-6301

ARIS, RUTHERFORD, APPLIED MATHEMATICS, CHEMICAL ENGINEERING. *Current Pos:* from asst prof to prof, 58-78, regents prof, 78-96, EMER PROF CHEM ENG, UNIV MINN, MINNEAPOLIS, 96- *Personal Data:* b Bournemouth, Eng, Sept 15, 29; US citizen; m 58, Claire M Holman. *Educ:* Univ London, BSc, 48, PhD(math, chem eng), 60, DSc, 64. *Hon Degrees:* DSc, Univ Exeter, 84 & Clarkson Univ, 85; DEng, Notre Dame Univ, 90. *Honors & Awards:* E Harris Harbison Award, Distinguished Teaching, Danforth Found, 69; Alpha Chi Sigma Award, Res Chem Eng, Am Inst Chem Engrs, 69 & Wilhelm Award, 75; Lewis Award, 81; Damkohler Medal, Deutsche Vereinigung fur chemie und Verfahrensteknik, 91. *Prof Exp:* Tech officer, Imp Chem Industs, 50-55; res fel chem eng, Univ Minn, 55-56; lectr tech math, Univ Edinburgh, 56-58. *Concurrent Pos:* Consult, Am Oil Co, Ind, 62-87, Gen Elec Co, 62-64 & Gen Motors, 77-85; Nat Sci Found sr fel, Cambridge Univ, 64-65, Guggenheim fel, 71-72; Lacey lectr, Calif Inst Technol, 70; Hougen Prof, Univ Wis, 79; Fairchild scholar, Calif Inst Tech, 80. *Mem:* Nat Acad Eng; Soc Natural Philos; Soc Indust & Appl Math; Soc Scribes & Illum; Mediaeval Acad Am; Am Acad Arts & Sci; fel Inst Math & Appln; Am Inst Chem Engrs. *Res:* Stability and control of chemical reactors; mathematics of chemical kinetics and of diffusion and reaction; mathematical modeling; intellectual history 12th century Anglo-Norman script. *Mailing Add:* 9600 Portland Ave No 306 Bloomington MN 55420

ARIYAN, STEPHAN, PLASTIC SURGERY, GENERAL SURGERY. *Current Pos:* From asst prof to prof surg, 76-91, chmn plastic surg, 79-91, CLIN PROF SURG, PLASTIC SURG & OTOLARYNGOL, SCH MED, YALE UNIV, 91- *Personal Data:* b Cairo, Egypt, July 30, 41; m 67, Sandy; c 3. *Educ:* Long Island Univ, BS, 62; New York Med Col, MD, 66; Yale Univ, MA, 81; Univ New Haven, MBA, 93. *Hon Degrees:* MA, Yale Univ, 81. *Honors & Awards:* Distinguished Serv Award, Soc Head & Neck Surgeons; Presidential Award, Am Soc Head Head & Neck Surgeons; President's Award, Repub Armenia CIS. *Concurrent Pos:* Vis prof, Univ Calif, San Diego, 76, Univ Calif, Irvine, 79, Brown Univ, 80, Roswell Park Mem Inst, 80, Nat Naval Med Ctr, 81, Harvard Univ, 84, Brown Univ, 89, Dartmouth, 93, Johns Hopkins, 94. *Mem:* Plastic Surg Res Coun; Soc Head & Neck Surgeons (pres); Am Surg Asn; Asn Acad Chmn Plastic Surg (pres); Sigma Xi. *Res:* Cancer immunology, with particular reference to malignant melanoma and head and neck cancer; wound healing; effects of ionizing radiation and chemotherapy; reconstruction following head and neck surgery. *Mailing Add:* 16 Yowago Ave Branford CT 06405

ARIYAN, ZAVEN S, ORGANIC CHEMISTRY. *Current Pos:* DIR RES, FAIRMOUNT CHEM CO, INC, 79- *Personal Data:* b Cairo, Egypt, Oct 10, 33; m 66. *Educ:* Univ London, BSc, 57, PhD(org chem), 64. *Prof Exp:* Lectr chem, Medway Col Technol, Eng, 57-59; demonstr org chem, Royal Mil Col Sci, Eng, 60-64; fel, Univ Southern Calif, 64-65; sr res chemist, Uniroyal, Inc, 65-69, coord pharmaceut prog, 69-71, sr group leader pharmaceut chem res, 71-75; mgr, T R Evans Res Ctr, Pharmaceut Diamond Shamrock Corp, 75-79. *Concurrent Pos:* Grants, Gulbenkian Found, 56-57 & Stauffer Chem Co, 64-65. *Mem:* Am Chem Soc; Brit Chem Soc. *Res:* Chemistry of sulfur compounds. *Mailing Add:* 47 Gallinson Dr Murray Hill NJ 07974-2721

ARKANI-HAMED, JAFAR, DYNAMICS OF THE PLANETARY INTERIORS, MAGNETIC PROPERTIES OF THE EARTHS LITHOSPHERE. *Current Pos:* PROF PLANETARY SCI, MCGILL UNIV, 88- *Personal Data:* b Tabriz, Iran, Feb 2, 40; Can citizen; m 71, Hamideh Alasti; c Nima & Sanaz. *Educ:* Univ Tehran, Iran, BS, 62; Mass Inst Technol, PhD(geophys), 69. *Hon Degrees:* Hon dipl, Int Space Univ, 86. *Prof Exp:* From asst prof to prof physics, Arya-Mehr Univ Technol, Iran, 69-82; prof geol, Univ Toronto, 82-86; prof geophys, Univ BC, 86-87; assoc prof geophys, Brock Univ, Can, 87-88. *Concurrent Pos:* MAGSAT sci invest, 83; Sci adv, Atlantic Geosci Ctr, Can, 92-96. *Mem:* Am Geophys Union; Geophys Soc Am; Can Geophys Union. *Res:* Thermal evolution and internal dynamics of terrestrial planets; dynamics of the Earth's lithosphere and sedimentary basins; analysis and interpretation of satellite gravity and magnetic data; magnetic properties of the Earth's lithosphere; tectonics of Earth and Venus. *Mailing Add:* 1801 Delaney Dr Mississauga ON L5J 3L2 Can. *Fax:* 514-398-4680; *E-Mail:* jafar@planet.eps.mcgill.ca

ARKELL, ALFRED, ORGANIC CHEMISTRY. *Current Pos:* RETIRED. *Personal Data:* b Chicago, Ill, Feb 16, 24; m 43; c 3. *Educ:* Kalamazoo Col, AB, 54; Ohio State Univ, PhD(chem), 58. *Honors & Awards:* Upjohn Prize, 54; Clark MacKenzie Prize, 54; Texaco Res Award, Am Chem Soc, 68. *Prof Exp:* Asst gen & org chem, Ohio State Univ, 54-55; sr res chemist, Texaco Res Ctr, Texaco Inc, Beacon, NY, 58-82. *Mem:* Am Chem Soc; fel Am Inst Chem. *Res:* Synthesis of highly-branched aliphatic compounds; derivatives of acetylene; low temperature infrared spectroscopy; matrix isolation technique; isolation and identification of radicals and unstable compounds. *Mailing Add:* 28 McFarland Rd Wappingers Falls NY 12590

ARKILIC, GALIP MEHMET, APPLIED MECHANICS. *Current Pos:* assoc prof, 58-63, chmn dept eng mech, 66-69, asst dean, Sch Eng & Appl Sci, 69-74, PROF APPL SCI, GEORGE WASHINGTON UNIV, 63- *Personal Data:* b Sivas, Turkey, Mar 10, 20; US citizen; m 56; c 4. *Educ:* Cornell Univ, BME, 46; Ill Inst Technol, MS, 48; Northwestern Univ, PhD(mech), 54. *Prof Exp.* Develop engr, Miehle Printing Press & Mfg Co, 48-49; res & develop engr, Mech & Chem Indust, Turkey, 49-52; analyst, Miehle Printing Press & Mfg Co, 54-56; asst prof, Pa State Univ, 56-58. *Concurrent Pos:* Consult, Beers Co, 62-63, Page Commun Co, 63-64, Bechtel Power Co, 73-75 & Wigman & Cohen Co, 76-77; prin investr, Air Force Off Sci Res, 63-70. *Mem:* Sigma Xi; Am Soc Mech Engrs; Soc Eng Sci; Am Acad Mech. *Res:* Elasticity; plates and shells; mechanics of composite materials. *Mailing Add:* 8403 Camden St Alexandria VA 22308-2111

ARKIN, GERALD FRANKLIN, AGRICULTURAL ENGINEERING. *Current Pos:* AT CENT TEX RES, BLACKLAND RES CTR. *Personal Data:* b Washington, DC, Sept 16, 42; m 66; c 2. *Educ:* Cornell Univ, BS, 66; Univ GA, MS, 68; Univ Ill, PhD(agr eng), 72. *Prof Exp:* Res asst agr eng, Univ Ga, 67-68 & Univ Ill, 68-72; assoc prof, 72-81, prof agr eng, Tex agr exp sta, Tex A&M Univ, 81- *Concurrent Pos:* Consult comt climate & weather fluctuations & agr prod, Nat Acad Sci, 75-76; prin investr, Statist Reporting Serv, US Dept Agr & Bur Reclamation, US Dept Interior, 81- *Mem:* Am Soc Agr Engrs; Am Soc Agron; Soil Sci Soc Am; Sigma Xi. *Res:* Crop growth simulation modeling to optimize yield and water efficiency. *Mailing Add:* 117 Tamerlane Peachtree City GA 30269-2700

ARKIN, JOSEPH, MATHEMATICS. *Current Pos:* PROF & SR LECTR, DEPT MATH, US MIL ACAD, WEST POINT, NY. *Personal Data:* b Brooklyn, NY, May 25, 23; m 54, Judith Lubel; c Helen, Aviva, Jessica & Sarah. *Educ:* PhD. *Hon Degrees:* PhD Brantridge School, Eng, 67. *Mem:* NY Acad Sci; AAAS; Asn Am Math. *Mailing Add:* 197 Old Nyack Turnpike Spring Valley NY 10977-5304

ARKING, ALBERT, PHYSICS. *Current Pos:* physicist astrophys & atmospheric physics, Goddard Inst Space Studies, New York, 59-74, PHYSICIST, GODDARD SPACE FLIGHT CTR, NASA, GREENBELT, MD, 74- *Personal Data:* b Brooklyn, NY, Nov 5, 32. *Educ:* Columbia Univ, AB, 53; Cornell Univ, PhD(physics), 59. *Prof Exp:* Physicist, Artificial Intel, Hughes Aircraft Co, 59. *Concurrent Pos:* Instr, City Col New York, 61-62; from adj asst prof to adj assoc prof, NY Univ, 62-70; vis res assoc, Univ Calif, Los Angeles, 70-71. *Mem:* AAAS; Am Phys Soc; Am Astron Soc; Am Geophys Union; Am Meteorol Soc. *Res:* Atmospheric and nuclear physics; radiative transfer; astrophysics. *Mailing Add:* 11810 Gainsborough Rd Potomac MD 20854

ARKING, ROBERT, GENETICS OF AGING, BIOGERONTOLOGY. *Current Pos:* from asst prof to assoc prof, 75-94, PROF BIOL, WAYNE STATE UNIV, 94- *Personal Data:* b New York, NY, July 1, 36; m 59, Lucille M Musser; c Henry D & Jonathan J. *Educ:* Dickinson Col, BS, 58; Temple Univ, PhD(develop biol), 67. *Prof Exp:* Postdoctoral fel NIH, Univ Va, 67-68; asst prof zool, T H Morgan Sch Biol, Univ Ky, 68-70; res assoc, Develop Biol Labs, Univ Calif, Irvine, 70-75. *Concurrent Pos:* Coordr, Molecular Biotechnol Prog, Biol Sci, Wayne State Univ, 90- *Mem:* Soc Develop Biol; Sigma Xi; AAAS; fel Geront Soc Am; Genetics Soc Am. *Res:* Genetic and molecular analysis of delayed senescence and aging mechanisms in Drosophila; antioxidant gene expression, oxidant damage and onset of senescence. *Mailing Add:* Dept Biol Sci Wayne State Univ Detroit MI 48202. *Fax:* 313-577-6891; *E-Mail:* rarking@biology.biosci.wayne.edu

ARKINS, JOHN A, INTERNAL MEDICINE. *Current Pos:* RETIRED. *Personal Data:* b Milwaukee, Wis, Sept 13, 26; m 48; c 3. *Educ:* Univ Wis, BS, 50, MD, 52. *Prof Exp:* Prof med, Med Col Wis, 70-87, coordr, Clin Student Affairs, 73-87. *Concurrent Pos:* Consult, Vet Admin Hosp, Wood, Wis & Milwaukee Children's Hosp, 65- *Mem:* Am Acad Allergy; Am Thoracic Soc; Am Asn Med Cols; Am Fedn Clin Res; NY Acad Sci. *Res:* Clinical sensitivity to animal danders; induction of homocytotropic antibody in canine models. *Mailing Add:* 10421 E Champagne Dr Chandler AZ 85248

ARKLE, THOMAS, JR, GEOLOGY. *Current Pos:* SUPVR COAL RESOURCES STUDY, WVA GEOL ECON SURV, 73- *Personal Data:* b Colerain, Ohio, Sept 10, 18; m 45; c 2. *Educ:* Marietta Col, AB, 40; Ohio State Univ, MS, 50. *Prof Exp:* Teacher high schs, WVa, 40-42 & Ohio, 46-47; asst geol, Ohio State Univ, 48-50; asst geologist, 50-51, asst to dir, 52-58, econ geologist, State Geol Surv, WVa, 58-73. *Mem:* Am Geol Soc; Geol Soc Am; Am Inst Mining Metall Engrs; Am Inst Prof Geol; Sigma Xi. *Res:* Stratigraphy, especially coal bearing strata; economic geology, especially of coal and sandstone; to collect, interpret and collate data for use in the determination of the physical and chemical characteristics of the remainder of coal seams and the associated rocks in West Virginia. *Mailing Add:* 94179 Hulahe Waipahu HI 96797

ARKLES, BARRY CHARLES, POLYMER CHEMISTRY, MATERIALS SCIENCE. *Current Pos:* PRES, GEIST INC, 91- *Personal Data:* b Philadelphia, Pa, Feb 1, 49; m 67, Janine Black; c Elise, Amanda & Jeffrey. *Educ:* Temple Univ, BS, 69, PhD(chem), 75. *Honors & Awards:* Leo Friend Award, Am Chem Soc, 83; I R 100, Award 84. *Prof Exp:* Mgr tech develop, LNP Corp, Beatrice Foods, 69-77; pres, Petrarch Systs Inc, 77-87; vpres, Huls Am, 87-91. *Mem:* Am Chem Soc; Mat Res Soc; Soc Plastics Engrs; Soc Mfg Engrs. *Res:* Thermoplastic composites; wear and lubrication; silicon chemistry; immobilized biomaterials; microelectronic materials. *Mailing Add:* 428 Bluebird Lane Dresher PA 19025-1921

ARKO, ALOYSIUS JOHN, SOLID STATE PHYSICS, ELECTRONIC STRUCTURE. *Current Pos:* PHYSICIST, LOS ALAMOS NAT LAB, 87- *Personal Data:* b Loski Potok, Slovenia, Feb 6, 40; US citizen; m 64, Christine Kosir; c Alenka, Michael & Maria. *Educ:* Ill Inst Technol, BS, 62; Northwestern Univ, PhD(physics), 67. *Prof Exp:* Res assoc solid state physics, Northwestern Univ, 67-68; asst physicist, 68-73, physicist, Argonne Nat Lab, 73-87. *Mem:* Fel Am Phys Soc. *Res:* Angle-resolved photoemission in bulk and surface studies. *Mailing Add:* Los Alamos Nat Lab MS-K764 Los Alamos NM 87545. *Fax:* 505-665-7652; *E-Mail:* arko@lanl.gov

ARKOWITZ, MARTIN ARTHUR, TOPOLOGY. *Current Pos:* from asst prof to assoc prof, 64-71, chmn dept, 81-84, PROF MATH, DARTMOUTH COL, 71- *Personal Data:* b Brooklyn, NY, Apr 17, 35; m 57, Eleanor Silver; c David, Robert & Steven. *Educ:* Columbia Univ, BA, 56, MA, 57; Cornell Univ, PhD(math), 60. *Hon Degrees:* MA, Dartmouth Col, 71. *Prof Exp:* Teaching asst, Cornell Univ, 57-60; Off Naval Res assoc, Johns Hopkins Univ, 60-61; instr math, Princeton Univ, 61-63, lectr, 63-64. *Concurrent Pos:* Dartmouth fac fel, Math Inst, Oxford Univ, 67-68; vis prof, Math Inst, Aarhus Univ, Denmark, 72-73; vis prof, Univ Ariz, 79-80, Max Planck Inst, Bonn, Germany, 85; vis scholar, Univ Penn, 86. *Mem:* Am Math Soc; Math Asn Am. *Res:* Topology. *Mailing Add:* Dept Math Dartmouth Col 6188 Bradley Hall Hanover NH 03755-3551. *E-Mail:* martin.arkowitz@dartmouth.edu

ARKY, RONALD ALFRED, MEDICINE. *Current Pos:* CHARLES S DAVIDSON PROF MED, HARVARD UNIV MED SCH, 84- *Personal Data:* b New Brunswick, NJ, June 26, 29; m 63, Marie Mahoney. *Educ:* Cornell Univ, AB, 51, MD, 55. *Prof Exp:* Intern, Bellevue Hosp, NY, 55-56; resident, NY Vet Admin Hosp, 58-60; fel, Thorndike Mem Lab, Boston City Hosp, 61-63, dir, Diabetes Clin, 66-71; chmn, Dept Med, Mt Auburn Hosp, 71-93. *Concurrent Pos:* Pres, Assocs Prog Dirs Internal Med, 90-91. *Mem:* Fel AAAS; master Am Col Physicians; Am Diabetes Asn (pres, 79-80); Am Soc Clin Invest. *Mailing Add:* Francis W Peabody Soc Harvard Med Sch 260 Longwood Ave Boston MA 02115-5701

ARLIAN, LARRY GEORGE, PHYSIOLOGY, MEDICAL ENTOMOLOGY. *Current Pos:* from asst to assoc prof biol, 72-82, assoc prof physiol, Sch Med, 80-82, PROF BIOL, PHYSIOL, & BIOPHYS, WRIGHT STATE UNIV, 82- *Personal Data:* b Aspen, Colo, Aug 5, 44; m 66; c 2. *Educ:* Colo State Univ, BS, 66, MS, 68; Ohio State Univ, PhD(entom), 72. *Prof Exp:* Asst chemist, Great Western Sugar Co, 68-69. *Concurrent Pos:* NIH grant, 76-79, 81-84 & 85-; res fel, Wright State Univ, 77-79. *Mem:* Sigma Xi; Entom Soc Am; Acarological Soc Am; Am Soc Parasitologists. *Res:* House dust mite allergies; water balance in insects, mites and mammals; scabies biology, culture and host specificity. *Mailing Add:* Dept Biol Sci Wright State Univ 3640 Colonel Glenn Dayton OH 45435-0001

ARLINGHAUS, HEINRICH FRANZ, LASER SPECTROSCOPY, DNA SEQUENCING. *Current Pos:* from scientist to sr scientist, 88-93, DIR, SURFACE & DEPTH CHARACTERIZATION, ATOM SCI INC, 93- *Personal Data:* b Damme, Ger, Mar 11, 58; m 82, Claudia; c Henrik, Franziska & Nicolas. *Educ:* Westfalische Wilhems Univ, dipl, 82, PhD(physics), 86. *Prof Exp:* Undergrad res asst, West falische Wilhems Univ, Munster, Ger, 81, undergrad teaching asst physics, 81-82, grad res asst physics, 82-84, res scientist, 86; res scientist, Ger Res Asn, 84-86; fel, Argonne Nat Lab, Lawrence Livermore Nat Lab, 86-88. *Concurrent Pos:* Prin investr, Small Bus Innovation Res Prog, Phase I, 89-, Phase II, 90-, Defense Advan Res Projs Agency, Phase I, 91-, NIH, Phase I, 91- *Mem:* Am Vacuum Soc; AAAS; Mat Res Soc. *Res:* Emission process of sputtered particles from various ion- bombarded and laser-irradiated materials; laser spectroscopy; optical damage mechanism; ultra-trace element analysis and imaging; depth profile analysis; DNA sequences; 51 publications and 50 (13 invited) conference presentations. *Mailing Add:* 106 Davis Lane Oak Ridge TN 37830. *Fax:* 423-483-3316; *E-Mail:* 72124.2400@compuserve.com

ARLINGHAUS, RALPH B, BIOCHEMISTRY. *Current Pos:* PROF & CHMN, DEPT MOLECULAR PATH, UNIV TEX M D ANDERSON CANCER CTR, HOUSTON, 86- *Personal Data:* b Newport, Ky, Aug 16, 35; m 57, 68; c 4. *Educ:* Univ Cincinnati, BS, 57, MS, 59, PhD(biochem), 61. *Prof Exp:* NIH fel protein synthesis, Univ Ky, 61-63, Am Cancer Soc fel, 63-65; res chemist, Plum Island Animal Dis Lab, USDA, NY, 65-69; from asst prof to prof biol, Univ Tex M D Anderson Hosp & Tumor Inst, 69-83, chief, sect environ biol, 69-77, chief, sect tumor virol, 77-80, actg head, dept tumor virol, 80-83; dir vaccine develop, Johnson & Johnson Biotechnol Ctr, La Jolla, Calif, 83-86. *Concurrent Pos:* Vis scientist & mem, Scripps Clin & Res Found, La Jolla, Calif, 83-86. *Mem:* AAAS; Am Chem Soc; Am Soc Microbiol; Am Asn Biol Chem; Am Soc Virol. *Res:* Protein biosynthesis and nucleic acid synthesis; animal virus replication at the molecular level; RNA-containing viruses such as Picornaviruses and Murine leukemia viruses; molecular biology of retroviruses and oncogenes. *Mailing Add:* Dept Molecular Pathol Univ Tex MD Anderson Cancer Ctr 1515 Holcombe Blvd 89 Houston TX 77030

ARLINGHAUS, SANDRA JUDITH LACH, MATHEMATICAL GEOGRAPHY, LOCATION THEORY. *Current Pos:* DIR, INST MATH GEOG, 84-; ADJ PROF MATH GEOG & POP ENVIRON DYNAMICS, SCH NAT RES & ENVIRON, UNIV MICH, ANN ARBOR, 94- *Personal Data:* b Elmira, NY, April 18, 43; m 66, William C; c William E. *Educ:* Vassar Col, BA, 64; Wayne State Univ, MA, 76; Univ Mich, PhD(geography), 77. *Honors & Awards:* 20th Century Award for Achievement, Int Biog Ctr, 93. *Prof Exp:* From lectr to asst prof math, Loyola Univ, 79-82. *Concurrent Pos:* Vis asst prof geog, Ohio State Univ, 77-78; lectr math, Ohio State Univ, 78-79, Loyola Univ, 79-81; lectr math & geog, Univ Mich, 82-83, consult, 84 & 85, 92, invited lectr, 90; mem bd trustees Community Systs Fdn, Ann Arbor, 95-, dir, mapping spatial anal & fel training divs, 96-; planning comnr, Cty Ann Arbor, 95- *Mem:* NY Acad Sci; Assoc Am Geographers; Am Math Soc; fel Am Geog Soc; AAAS; Math Asn Am. *Res:* Geographic location theory; geographic modeling; mathematical modeling; applications of geometry, graph theory, topology in geography; cartographic analysis; environmental analysis of public transportations systems; fractals and central places; network analysis-algorithms; mapping; urban systems. *Mailing Add:* 1964 Boulder Dr Ann Arbor MI 48104. *E-Mail:* sarhaus@umich.edu

ARLINGHAUS, WILLIAM CHARLES, ALGEBRAIC GRAPH THEORY. *Current Pos:* from asst prof to prof math, 85-89, PROF & CHMN, DEPT MATH & COMPUT SCI, LAWRENCE TECHNOL UNIV, 89- *Personal Data:* b Detroit, Mich, July 17, 44; m 66, Sandra Lach; c William E. *Educ:* Univ Detroit, BS, 64; Wayne State Univ, PhD(math), 79. *Prof Exp:* Mathematician, Gen Motors Tech Ctr, 68-72; asst prof math, Loyola Univ, Chicago, 79-82; from asst prof to prof math, Lawrence Technol Univ, 85-89, prof & chmn, Dept Math & Comput Sci, 90-95. *Concurrent Pos:* NSF fel, 64 & 70. *Mem:* Am Math Soc; Math Asn Am. *Res:* Using group theory as a tool to explore symmetric structure in graphs; algebraic-graph theory in those dealing with transport networks. *Mailing Add:* Dept Math & Comput Sci Lawrence Technol Univ 21000 W Ten Mile Rd Southfield MI 48075-1058. *E-Mail:* arlinghaus@ltuvax

ARMACOST, DAVID LEE, MATHEMATICS. *Current Pos:* Asst prof, 69-74, assoc prof, 74-81, PROF MATH, AMHERST COL, 81- *Personal Data:* b Santa Monica, Calif, Mar 9, 44. *Educ:* Pomona Col, BA, 65; Stanford Univ, MS, 66, PhD(math), 69. *Mem:* Am Math Soc; Sigma Xi. *Res:* Topological groups; infinite Abelian groups; locally compact Abelian groups. *Mailing Add:* Dept Math Amherst Col Box 2239 Amherst MA 01002-5000

ARMACOST, WILLIAM L, MATHEMATICS. *Current Pos:* Asst prof, 68-72, assoc prof, 72-77, PROF MATH, CALIF STATE COL, DOMINGUEZ HILLS, 77- *Personal Data:* b Santa Monica, Calif, Oct 6, 41; c 2. *Educ:* Pomona Col, BA, 63; Univ Calif, Los Angeles, MA, 65, PhD(math), 68. *Mem:* Am Math Soc; Sigma Xi; Math Asn Am. *Res:* Group representation theory and functional analysis; Frobenius reciprocity theorem. *Mailing Add:* 902 Stanford St Santa Monica CA 90403-2224

ARMALY, BASSEM FARID, MECHANICAL ENGINEERING, HEAT TRANSFER. *Current Pos:* From asst prof to assoc prof, 69-76, PROF MECH ENG, 76-, CHMN, MECH & AEROSPACE EXP DEPT, UNIV MO, ROLLA, 85- *Personal Data:* b Israel, Dec 5, 37; US citizen; m 62, Gery C Hazard; c Nicole T & Samir B. *Educ:* Univ Iowa, BS, 63, MS, 64; Univ Calif, Berkeley, PhD(mech eng), 69. *Concurrent Pos:* Prin investr, NSF grants, 72-73, 75-82, 78-88, 88-92 & 93- & Off Water Res & Technol grant, 74-76; fel, Langley Res Ctr, NASA, 78; Fulbright sr res investr, 79-80. *Mem:* Fel Am Soc Mech Eng; Am Soc Eng Educ; Am Inst Aeronaut & Astronaut. *Res:* Heat and mass transfer; thermophysical properties; solar energy; mixed convection separated flow. *Mailing Add:* Dept Mech Eng Univ Mo Rolla MO 65401. *Fax:* 573-341-4607

ARMALY, MANSOUR F, OPHTHALMOLOGY, GLAUCOMA. *Current Pos:* PROF OPHTHAL, 66-, CHMN DEPT, GEORGE WASHINGTON UNIV MED CTR, 70- *Personal Data:* b Shefa Amer, Palestine, Feb 25, 27. *Educ:* Univ Iowa, MS, 57. *Mem:* Am Acad Ophthal & Otolaryngol; Am Asn Ophthal; Am Col Surgeons; AMA; Am Interocular Lens Implant Soc. *Mailing Add:* Dept Ophthal George Washington Univ Med Ctr 2150 Pennsylvania Ave NW Washington DC 20037

ARMAMENTO, EDUARDO T, industrial waste management, general chemistry & nuclear engineering, for more information see previous edition

ARMAN, ARA, CIVIL ENGINEERING. *Current Pos:* from asst prof to assoc prof civil eng, La State Univ, 63-70, asst dir, Div Eng Res, 65-77, chmn dept, 77-80, assoc dean, Col Eng, 80-87, dir, La Transp Res Ctr, 87-90, PROF CIVIL ENG, LA STATE UNIV, 70-; VPRES, WOODWARD CLYDE CONSULT, BATON ROUGE, LA, 90- *Personal Data:* b Istanbul, Turkey, Sept 12, 30; US citizen; m 63; c 2. *Educ:* Robert Col, Istanbul, BS, 55; Univ Tex, MS, 56. *Prof Exp:* Asst lab engr, La Dept Hwy, 56-58, head lab engr, 58-61, soil design engr, 61-63. *Concurrent Pos:* Mem maintenance bituminous pavement comt, Hwy Res Bd, Nat Res Coun, Nat Acad Sci, 65, chmn soil-cement stabilization comt, 66; chmn, comt placement of soils, Am Soc Civil Engrs, 76-83; secy, Comt on Geotextiles, Int Soc Soil Mech & Found Eng, 86-90. *Mem:* Am Road Builders Asn (vpres, 70-71, pres, 72-73); Am Soc Eng Educ; Am Soc Testing & Mat; fel Am Soc Civil Engrs. *Res:* Soil mechanics in soil stabilization; organic soils; sampling; pavement design; placement of soils; geotextiles; geomembranes. *Mailing Add:* 1148 Verdun Dr Baton Rouge LA 70810

ARMANINI, LOUIS ANTHONY, PHYSICAL CHEMISTRY. *Current Pos:* RETIRED. *Personal Data:* b New York, NY, Feb 11, 30; m 58; c 4. *Educ:* Manhattan Col, BS, 57. *Prof Exp:* Res chemist, Curtiss-Wright Corp, Pa, 57-59; res chemist, Francis Earle Labs, Mearl Corp, 59-67, group leader interference films, 67-75, asst dir res, 76-90, vpres, 89-, dir res, 90- *Mem:* Am Chem Soc; AAAS; Soc Cosmetic Chemists. *Res:* Optical interference pigments made by thin film deposition or controlled crystal growth and the instrumental measurement and optical properties of such films. *Mailing Add:* 343 Washington Ave Pleasantville NY 10570

ARMANIOS, ERIAN A, COMPOSITE STRUCTURES, FRACTURE MECHANICS. *Current Pos:* res engr, 85-86, from asst prof to assoc prof, 86-97, PROF AEROSPACE ENG, GA INST TECHNOL, 97- *Personal Data:* b Cairo, Egypt, July 6, 50; US citizen; m 80, Mahera S Philobos; c Daniel & Laura. *Educ:* Univ Cairo, BS, 74, MS, 79; Ga Inst Technol, PhD(aerospace eng), 85. *Honors & Awards:* Jr Fac Award, Sigma Xi, 91. *Prof Exp:* Asst lectr aeronaut eng, Col Eng, Univ Cairo, 79-80. *Concurrent Pos:* Consult, Rolls Royce, Inc, 89-95, Allison Engine Co, 95-96; dir, Ga Space Grant Consortium, 91- *Mem:* Assoc fel Am Inst Aeronaut & Astronaut; Am Soc Testing & Mat; Am Helicopter Soc; Am Soc Composites. *Res:* Structural analysis, design and damage tolerance of advanced composites; modeling, stress analysis testing and failure prediction of elastically tailored composites; energy dissipation concepts in composites; use of active materials for flow control. *Mailing Add:* Sch Aerospace Eng Ga Inst Technol Atlanta GA 30332-0150. *Fax:* 404-894-2760; *E-Mail:* erian.armanios@al.gatech.edu

ARMANT, D RANDALL, DEVELOPMENTAL BIOLOGY, CELL-CELL INTERACTIONS. *Current Pos:* ASSOC PROF OBSTET, GYNEC & ANAT CELL BIOL, WAYNE STATE UNIV SCH MED, 88- *Personal Data:* b Plainfield, NJ, Nov 13, 51; m 88, Rachel A Sterman. *Educ:* Va Polytech Inst & State Univ, BS, 74, PhD(develop biol), 80. *Prof Exp:* Res assoc, Worcester Found Exp Biol, 80-82; fel, Dept Biol Chem, Johns Hopkins Univ Sch Med, 82-83 & Dept Biochem & Molecular Biol, Anderson Tumor Inst, Houston, Tex, 83-85; asst prof obstet, gynec & reproductive biol, Beth Israel Hosp, Harvard Med Sch, 85-88. *Concurrent Pos:* Nat Res Serv Award, NIH, 82, New Investr Award, 85. *Mem:* Am Soc Cell Biol; Soc Study Reproduction; Am Fertil Soc; Soc Develop Biol; Soc Cryobiol. *Res:* Biochemistry of early mammalian development; cell adhesion and glycoprotein biosynthesis in mouse embryos; in vitro fertilization and oocyte/embryo cryopreservation; biochemistry of development in the cellular slime mold; role of discoidin and alkaline phosphatase; pattern formation. *Mailing Add:* Dept OB/GYN Mott Ctr Wayne State Univ 275 E Hancock Detroit MI 48201-1415

ARMANTROUT, GUY ALAN, ELECTRONICS ENGINEERING. *Current Pos:* Sr res engr, 68-72, ENG GROUP LEADER RES, LAWRENCE LIVERMORE LAB, 72-, PROJ ENGR & SECT LEADER, UNIV CALIF, 83- *Personal Data:* b Salt Lake City, Utah, May 9, 40; m 62; c 9. *Educ:* Ore State Univ, BS, 62, MS, 64; Purdue Univ, PhD(elec eng), 69. *Concurrent Pos:* Adj prof elec eng, Univ Calif Sch Med, San Francisco, 74-; asst prof appl sci, Univ Calif, Davis, 76- *Mem:* Inst Elec & Electronics Engrs. *Res:* Semiconductor device research and development including gamma radiation detector development and applications and terrestrial photovoltaics basic research and cell development. *Mailing Add:* Lawrence Livermore Nat Lab L-036 7000 East Ave Livermore CA 94550

ARMATO, UBALDO, TUMOR BIOLOGY & GROWTH REGULATION, ARTIFICIAL TISSUES. *Current Pos:* PROF HISTOL & EMBRYOL, UNIV VERONA, ITALY, 86-, PROF EXP ONCOL, SCH MED DERMAT, 94- *Personal Data:* b Trieste, Italy; wid; c Anorea & Federico. *Educ:* Univ Padua, Med, 67, Hemat, 69, Internal Med, 75. *Honors & Awards:* Premio Tito Livio Colonnello, Ital Anat Soc, 75. *Prof Exp:* From jr to sr lectr human anat, Univ Padva, Italy, 69-80, assoc prof, 80-86. *Concurrent Pos:* Consult hemat, Civic Hosp, Este, Italy, 78-87; consult, Rejione Veueto Ctr Treatment Prev Burn Injuries, 89-; mem, Atheneitm's Linguistic Ctr Directorate, 94-, Tech Comt, 95- *Mem:* Tissue Cult Asn; Am Soc Cell Biol; Fedn Am Soc Exp Biol; Europ Tissue Cult Asn. *Res:* Regulation of normal and abnormal growth of fetal neonatal and adult rat and human hepatocytes and adult human keratynocytes and adrenocytes in primary tissue cultures; studies into artificial givez and stein models. *Mailing Add:* Inst Anat & Histol Strada Le Grazie 8 Verona I-37134 Italy. *Fax:* 39-45-8098159

ARMBRECHT, FRANK MAURICE, JR, CHEMISTRY. *Current Pos:* CONSULT, 96- *Personal Data:* b Norfolk, Va, Jan 29, 42; m 65; c 2. *Educ:* Duke Univ, BS, 63; Mass Inst Technol, PhD(chem), 68. *Prof Exp:* Res chemist elastomers chem, E I Du Pont de Nemours & Co Inc, 68-77, process supvr, 77-78, supt res & develop, 78-81, res mgr, 80-82, tech mgr ethylene polymers, 82-87, lab mgr, 84-87, strategic planning consult, 87-90, technol mgr, 91-92; pres, Systech, 92-94; dir technol, Allied Signal, 94-96. *Mem:* Am Chem Soc. *Res:* Organometallic chemistry; homogeneous catalysis; elastomers. *Mailing Add:* 158 Peaceable Ridge Ridgefield CT 06877

ARMBRECHT, HARVEY JAMES, GERONTOLOGY. *Current Pos:* RES CHEMIST, VET ADMIN HOSP, ST LOUIS, 77- *Personal Data:* b Philadelphia, Pa, March 7, 47; m 71; c 2. *Educ:* Drexel Univ, BS, 70; Univ Rochester, PhD(biophysics), 74. *Prof Exp:* Fel, Cornell Univ, 74-77; asst prof, 81-85, Assoc Prof Biochem 85- & Prof Med, Med Sch, St Louis Univ, 90- *Mem:* AAAS; Biophys Soc; Gerontol Soc; Am Aging Asn; Am Soc Bone & Mineral Metab; Am Soc Biochem & Molecular Biol. *Res:* Mechanisms of steroid and peptide hormone action; hormonal regulation of calcium metabolism by parathyroid hormone and vitamin B in the elderly and diabetic. *Mailing Add:* Geriatric Ctr 111G-JB St Louis Vet Admin Hosp St Louis MO 63125

ARMBRUSTER, BARBARA L, BOTANY, ELECTRON MICROSCOPY. *Current Pos:* SR BIOL APPLN SPECIALIST, GATON INC, 94- *Personal Data:* b Oceanside, NY, May 27, 52. *Educ:* Hamilton Kirkland Col, BA, 75; Duke Univ, PhD(bot), 80. *Prof Exp:* Researcher electron micros, Monsanto Corp Anal Sci Ctr, 85-94. *Concurrent Pos:* Indust fel scanning probe micros, Univ Minn, 93- *Mem:* AAAS; Electron Micros Soc. *Mailing Add:* Gatan Inc 6678 Owens Dr Pleasanton CA 94588

ARMBRUSTER, CHARLES WILLIAM, ORGANIC CHEMISTRY. *Current Pos:* From instr to asst prof, Univ Mo, 62-66, div sci, 63-67, chmn chem dept, 67-75, ASSOC PROF CHEM, UNIV MO-ST LOUIS, 66- *Personal Data:* b St Louis, Mo, Mar 24, 37. *Educ:* Univ Notre Dame, BS, 58; Wash Univ, PhD(org chem), 66. *Mem:* Am Chem Soc; AAAS. *Res:* Physical organic chemistry; biochemical mechanisms. *Mailing Add:* Dept Chem Univ Mo St Louis MO 63121

ARMBRUSTER, DAVID CHARLES, INDUSTRIAL CHEMISTRY, ORGANIC POLYMER CHEMISTRY. *Current Pos:* PRES, CHEM CONSULT & SPECIALTY PROD, ARMBRUSTER ASSOC, 82- *Personal Data:* b Cincinnati, Ohio, Feb 21, 39; div; c Michael, Thomas & Cathy. *Educ:* Xavier Univ, Ohio, BS, 61; Univ Cincinnati, PhD(org chem), 65. *Prof Exp:* Sr res chemist, Rohm and Haas Co, 65-66, res & develop mgr, 66-76; mkt/tech develop mgr, Celanese Chem Co, 76-81; commercial develop mgr, CPS Chem Co, 81-82. *Concurrent Pos:* Chmn, NJ group small chem bus. *Mem:* Asn Consult Chemists & Chem Engrs; Am Chem Soc; Commercial Develop Asn; Fedn Soc Coatings Technol; Licensing Execs Soc; Soc Cosmetic Chemists; Soc Plastics Engrs. *Res:* Organic chemistry; heterocycles; polymers; plastics; monomers; emulsion polymerization; radiation curing/photopolymerization; coatings; adhesives; acrylics; epoxies; urethanes; specialty chemicals; water treatment chemicals; applications; marketing; market research; commercial development; technology assessment; technological forecasting; hydrophilic polymers; new products. *Mailing Add:* 43 Stockton Rd Summit NJ 07901

ARMBRUSTER, FREDERICK CARL, FERMENTATION, ENZYMOLOGY. *Current Pos:* CONSULT, INDUST ENZYMES, 90- *Personal Data:* b Aurora, Ill, Apr 14, 31; m 54; c 3. *Educ:* Purdue Univ, BS, 53, MS, 55. *Prof Exp:* res chemist, CPC Int, Inc, 57-61, sect head fermentation res, 61-83, sr sect leader, 83-86; mgr indust enzyme res & develop, Enzyme Biosysts Ltd, 86-90. *Mem:* Am Soc Microbiol; Am Chem Soc. *Res:* Fermentation processes; industrial production, purification, and use of enzymes; industrial microbiol enzymes, including strain selection and improved fermentation development and scale-up, through enzyme recovery and application. *Mailing Add:* 5969 Howard Ave La Grange IL 60525-3711

ARMBRUSTER, GERTRUDE D, FOOD SCIENCE. *Current Pos:* asst prof, 52-58, ASSOC PROF FOOD & NUTRIT, CORNELL UNIV, 59-61 & 65- *Personal Data:* b Alta, Nov 29, 25; US citizen. *Educ:* Univ Alta, BS, 47; Wash State Univ, MS, 50, PhD(food sci), 65. *Prof Exp:* Co agent exten home econ, Wash State Univ, 50-52. *Mem:* Am Home Econ Asn; Inst Food Technologists; Am Soc Hort Sci; Am Dietetic Asn. *Res:* Interrelationship of plant tissue properties and product quality; plant texture; microwave applications. *Mailing Add:* Natural Sci 124 Savage Hall Cornell Univ Main Campus Ithaca NY 14853-6301

ARMBRUSTMACHER, THEODORE J, MINEROLOGY-PETROLOGY. *Current Pos:* GEOLOGIST, US GEOL SURV, 65- *Personal Data:* b Owosso, Mich, Jan 11, 38; c 2. *Educ:* Univ Iowa, PhD(geol), 65. *Mem:* Fel Geol Soc Am; Soc Econ Geologists. *Res:* Nd-Ta-Th commodities; alkaline rock complexes. *Mailing Add:* 29721 Fairway Dr Evergreen CO 80439

ARMELAGOS, GEORGE JOHN, BIOLOGICAL ANTHROPOLOGY. *Current Pos:* PROF ANTHROP, EMORY UNIV, 93- *Personal Data:* b Lincoln Park, Mich, May 22, 36; m 91. *Educ:* Univ Mich, BA, 58; Univ Colo, MA, 64, PhD(anthrop), 68. *Prof Exp:* Res assoc, Univ Colo Nubian Exped, 63; instr, Univ Utah, 65-66, asst prof, 67-69; from asst prof to assoc prof, Univ Mass, Amherst, 69-78, dir univ honors, 74-78, prof anthrop, 78-89; prof & chmn, Dept Anthrop, Univ Fla, Gainesville, 89-93. *Concurrent Pos:* NIH co-prin investr, 67-69; mem, Adv Comt Behav & Neural Sci, NSF Anthropol Panel, 76-78; NSF co-prin investr; pres, Biol Unit, Am Anthrop Asn, 84-87. *Mem:* Am Asn Phys Anthrop; AAAS; Human Biol Coun; Am Anthrop Asn; Sigma Xi; Am Asn Phys Anthrop (pres, 87-89). *Res:* Bone growth and development in archaeological populations, especially nutritional stress; paleopathology; hominid evolution; nutrition; skeletal biology and demography of archaeological populations; paleopathology human evolution; race; history of physical anthropology. *Mailing Add:* Dept Anthrop Emory Univ Geo Sci Bldg Suite 207 Atlanta GA 30322

ARMEN, HARRY, JR, APPLIED MECHANICS. *Current Pos:* dir corp res, 93-94, DIR, RES & DEVELOP, NORTHROP GRUMMAN CORP, 94- *Personal Data:* b New York, NY, Feb 4, 40; m 63, Mary P DiMasso; c Christopher, Renee & Joseph. *Educ:* Cooper Union, BCE, 61; NY Univ, MCE, 62, ScD, 64. *Honors & Awards:* Achievement Award, NASA; Applied Mech Award, Am Soc Mech Engrs. *Prof Exp:* Head, Appl Mech Br, Grumman Aircraft Eng Corp, 64-70, head, Appl Mech Br, Gruman Aerospace Corp, 70-79, tech specialist, 80-82, head, Struct Mech, 82-86, prin engr, 86-88, tech adv, 88-90; Cong fel, US Senate, 91-92. *Concurrent Pos:* Adj prof civil eng & appl mech, Cooper Union, 65-73 & Hofstra Univ, 73-79; Cong fel, Am Soc Mech Engrs, 91. *Mem:* Am Inst Aeronaut & Astronaut; Am Soc Mech Engrs (vpres, 94-); Sigma Xi. *Res:* Development of methods for the static and dynamic nonlinear analysis of structures; fracture mechanics; crashworthiness evaluation techniques; large displacement and stability analysis of structures; advanced materials development. *Mailing Add:* 27 Jefferson St Glen Cove NY 11542. *E-Mail:* h_armen@atdc.northqrum.com

ARMENAKAS, ANTHONY EMANUEL, STRUCTURAL ANALYSIS & DESIGN. *Current Pos:* PROF AEROSPACE ENG, POLYTECH UNIV NY, 67- *Personal Data:* b Mytilene, Greece, Aug 23, 24; US citizen; wid; c Alexandra Daphne, Noel Anthony & Melina Cybele. *Educ:* Ga Inst Technol, BS, 50; Ill Inst Technol, MS, 52; Columbia Univ, PhD(appl mech), 59. *Honors & Awards:* Fulbright lectr to Greece, 72-74. *Prof Exp:* Instr, Ill Inst Technol, 50-52; sr struct engr, Edwards, Kelcy & Beck, 52-54; lectr, City Col New York, 54-57; assoc prof, civil eng & appl mech, Cooper Union, 58-64; vis assoc prof, Div Eng, Brown Univ, 64-65; prof eng sci, Univ Fla, 65-67. *Concurrent Pos:* Consult vector eng, Springfield, NJ, 54-59; res assoc, Columbia Univ, 58-62; res consult, Northwestern Univ, 62-65 & Polytech Inst Brooklyn, 62-67; pres, Stress Optics Inc, 70-72; prof & dir, Inst Struct Anal, Nat Tech Univ Athens, 77-84. *Mem:* NY Acad Sci; fel Am Soc Civil Engrs; Am Soc Eng Educ; fel Am Soc Mech Engrs; Am Inst Aeronaut & Astronautics. *Res:* Solid mechanics; vibrations; fracture; shells and structures; author of four books. *Mailing Add:* Dept Mech & Aerospace Eng 333 Jay St Brooklyn NY 11201

ARMENAKAS, NOEL ANTHONY, GENITOURINARY TRAUMA & RECONSTRUCTIVE SURGERY. *Current Pos:* clin instr, Dept Surg & Urol, 92-94, CLIN ASST PROF, DEPT UROL, CORNELL UNIV MED COL, NY, 94-; PHYSICIAN-IN-CHARGE, OUTPATIENT UROL CLINS, LENOX HILL HOSP, NY, 92- *Personal Data:* b Orange, NJ, Sept 29, 58; m 96, Macrene R Alexiades. *Educ:* Univ Athens, Greece, MD, 85; Am Bd Urol, dipl, 94. *Prof Exp:* Intern surg, Lenox Hill Hosp, NY, 85-86; resident, Monmouth Med Ctr, NJ, 86-87, urol, Lenox Hill Hosp, NY, 87-91; fel trauma & reconstructive surg, Univ Calif, San Francisco, 91-92, clin instr, Dept Urol, 91-92. *Concurrent Pos:* Attending staff, San Francisco Gen Hosp, 91-92, NY Hosp, 92- *Mem:* Am Asn Clin Urologists; Am Col Surgeons; AMA; Am Urol Asn; Soc Urol & Eng; Soc Genitourinary Reconstructive Surgeons; Hellenic Med Asn. *Res:* Genitourinary trauma and reconstruction of the genitourinary tract. *Mailing Add:* 880 Fifth Ave New York NY 10021. *Fax:* 212-861-7964

ARMENDAREZ, PETER X, PHYSICAL CHEMISTRY. *Current Pos:* asst prof physics & phys chem, 65-68, chmn, Div Natural Sci & Math, 74-78, PROF PHYSICS & CHMN DEPT, 68-, CHMN CHEM DEPT, BRESCIA COL, KY, 85- *Personal Data:* b San Pedro, Calif, Sept 7, 30; m 54; c 8. *Educ:* Loyola Univ Los Angeles, BS, 52; Wash Univ, MS, 54; Univ Ariz, PhD(phys chem), 64. *Prof Exp:* Instr chem, Odessa Col, 58-59; asst prof, Univ Tenn, Martin, 63-65. *Concurrent Pos:* Res chemist, US Navy Weapons Support Group, Crane, Ind, 83-84. *Mem:* Am Crystallog Asn; Am Chem Soc; fel Am Inst Chemists. *Res:* Molecular spectra and structure of inorganic complexes; low temperature emission and absorption spectra of chromium complexes; infrared studies and normal coordinate analyses of metal chelate compounds; air-sensitive organometallic complexes: synthesis and IR characterization. *Mailing Add:* 1224 W Parrish Ave Owensboro KY 42301

ARMENDARIZ, EFRAIM PACILLAS, ALGEBRA. *Current Pos:* assoc prof, 72-81, PROF MATH, UNIV TEX, AUSTIN, 81- *Personal Data:* b Brownsville, Tex, July 9, 38; m 61; c 2. *Educ:* Agr & Mech Col, Tex, BA, 60, MS, 62; Univ Nebr, PhD(math), 66. *Prof Exp:* Instr math, Agr & Mech Col, Tex, 62-63 & Univ Nebr, 64-66; asst prof, Univ Tex, 66-67, Univ Southern Calif, 67-68 & Univ Tex, Austin, 68-71; assoc prof, Univ Southwestern La, 71-72. *Mem:* Am Math Soc. *Res:* Ring theory; mathematics. *Mailing Add:* 4717 Timberline Dr Austin TX 78746

ARMENIADES, CONSTANTINE D, POLYMER CHEMISTRY. *Current Pos:* Asst prof, 69-73, assoc prof, 73-78, PROF CHEM ENG, RICE UNIV, 78- *Personal Data:* b Thessaloniki, Greece, May 29, 36; US citizen; m 59; c 2. *Educ:* Northeastern Univ, BS, 61; Case Inst Technol, MS, 67, PhD(polymer sci), 69. *Concurrent Pos:* Master, Will Rice Col, Rice Univ, 76-82; consult polymer properties, E I du Pont de Nemours & Co, 76-78, Southwestern Bell, 74-79; vis sr lectr, Edinburgh Univ, Scotland, 80-81. *Mem:* Am Inst Chem Engrs; Soc Plastics Engrs; Asn Res Vision & Ophthal; Soc Biomat. *Res:* Structure-property relations in synthetic polymers; formulation of polymer composites for application as structural materials; synthesis of fire retardant and thermally stable polymers; biocompatibility of synthetic polymers. *Mailing Add:* Rice Univ 6100 S Main St Houston TX 77005

ARMENTANO, LOUIS ERNST, RUMINANT NUTRITION. *Current Pos:* From asst prof to assoc prof, 83-95, PROF ANIMAL NUTRIT, UNIV WIS, 95-, CHAIR, 96- *Personal Data:* b Brooklyn, NY, Dec 24, 54; m, Sue Shoener; c Vincent. *Educ:* Cornell Univ, BS, 75; NC State Univ, MS, 77; Iowa State Univ, PhD(nutrit physiol), 82. *Mem:* Am Inst Nutrit; Am Dairy Sci Asn; Am Soc Animal Sci. *Res:* Use of by-product feeds; hepatic metabolism; ruminants. *Mailing Add:* Dairy Sci 266 Animal Sci Univ Wis 1675 Observatory Rd Madison WI 53706. *E-Mail:* armentan@calshp.cals.wisc.edu

ARMENTI, ANGELO, JR, THEORETICAL PHYSICS. *Current Pos:* PRES, CALIF UNIV PA, 94- *Personal Data:* b Bridgeport, Pa, Feb 13, 40. *Educ:* Villanova Univ, BS, 63; Temple Univ, MA, 65, PhD(physics), 70. *Prof Exp:* Asst prof physics, Temple Univ, 70-72; from asst prof to assoc prof, Villanova Univ, 72-79, prof physics, 79-, dean, Univ Col, 81- *Mem:* Am Phys Soc; Int Soc Gen Relativity & Gravitation. *Res:* Exact solutions of Einstein's field equations, in particular geodesic motion in the field of compact masses and black holes. *Mailing Add:* Off Pres 250 University Ave California PA 15419

ARMENTROUT, DARYL RALPH, NUCLEAR QUALITY ASSURANCE, AIR QUALITY. *Current Pos:* civil engr, Tenn Valley Authority, 68-74, staff chief, 74-77, asst mgr eng & construct, 77-85, qual assurance mgr, 86-95, MGR BUS SERV, ENG LAB, TENN VALLEY AUTHORITY, 95- *Personal Data:* b Greeneville, Tenn, Apr 6, 42; m 69, Mary Rose Carmichael; c Rose & Michael. *Educ:* Univ Tenn, Knoxville, BS, 65, PhD(civil eng), 81; Va Polytech Inst, Blacksburg, MS, 68. *Prof Exp:* Prod engr, Humble Oil & Refining Co, 65-66. *Concurrent Pos:* Dir, activ under US-China Protocol Hydroelec, Tenn Valley Authority, 80-85. *Mem:* Am Soc Civil Engrs; Nat Soc Prof Engrs; Am Arbit Asn. *Res:* Finite element predictions of the behavior of post tensioned reinforced concrete containment vessels specifically the load- deflection behavior of the steel liner and contract interaction; integration of all resources in the planning and development of hydroelectric resources in China; air quality; environmental science, structural engineering. *Mailing Add:* Tenn Valley Authority 129 Pine Rd Norris TN 37828

ARMENTROUT, DAVID NOEL, ANALYTICAL CHEMISTRY. *Current Pos:* Sr res chemist, 66-80, RES ASSOC ANALYTICAL CHEM, DOW CHEM CO, 80- *Personal Data:* b San Francisco, Calif, Dec 7, 38; m 63; c 3. *Educ:* Univ Kans, BS, 61; Cornell Univ, PhD(anal chem), 65. *Honors & Awards:* IR-100 Award, 85. *Prof Exp:* Fel anal chem, NIH, 65-66. *Mem:* Am Chem Soc; Sigma Xi. *Res:* Analytical characterization of polymers. *Mailing Add:* 3707 McKeith Midland MI 48642

ARMENTROUT, PETER BRUCE, ION-MOLECULE REACTIONS, MASS SPECTROMETRY. *Current Pos:* assoc prof, 87-89, PROF CHEM, UNIV UTAH, 89- *Personal Data:* b Dayton, Ohio, Mar 13, 53; m 83, Mary Ann White; c Matthew M, Patricia C & Erin I. *Educ:* Case Western Res Univ, BS, 75; Calif Inst Technol, PhD(chem), 80. *Honors & Awards:* Buck-Whitney Award, Am Chem Soc, 93; Mack Mem Award Lectr, Ohio State Dept Chem, 97. *Prof Exp:* Postdoctoral mem tech staff, Bell Labs, Murray Hill, NJ, 80-81; asst prof chem, Univ Calif, Berkeley, 81-87. *Concurrent Pos:* Prin investr, Camille & Henry Dreyfus Found, 81; Presidential Young Investr Award, NSF, 84-89; Alfred P Sloan res fel, 86-90; mem, Air Force Off Sci Res Rev Panel, 88-92; vis prof, Univ Paris, 94. *Mem:* Am Chem Soc; Am Soc Mass Spectrometry; fel Am Phys Soc; fel AAAS. *Res:* Detailed understanding of the thermochemistry, kinetics and dynamics of simple and complex chemical reactions. *Mailing Add:* Dept Chem Univ Utah 315 S 1400 E Rm Dock Salt Lake City UT 84112. *Fax:* 801-581-8433; *E-Mail:* armentrout@chemistry.utah.edu

ARMENTROUT, STEVE, TOPOLOGY. *Current Pos:* PROF MATH, PA STATE UNIV, 70- *Personal Data:* b Eldorado, Tex, June 19, 30; m 62; c 3. *Educ:* Univ Tex, BA, 51, PhD(math), 56. *Prof Exp:* Teaching asst math, Univ Tex, 52-55; from instr to prof, Univ Iowa, 56-70. *Concurrent Pos:* Res fel, Univ Iowa, 62; vis prof, Univ Wis, 66-67. *Mem:* Am Math Soc; Math Asn Am. *Res:* Topology of manifolds; upper semicontinuous decompositions of manifolds. *Mailing Add:* Pa State Univ 207 McAllister Bldg University Park PA 16802-6401

ARMETT-KIBEL, CHRISTINE, BIOLOGY. *Current Pos:* from asst prof to assoc prof, 68-85, PROF, DEPT BIOL, 85-, DEAN FAC SCI, COL ARTS SCI, UNIV MASS, BOSTON, 91- *Personal Data:* b Dec 16, 35. *Educ:* Univ Col, London, BSc, 57; PhD(physiol), 61. *Prof Exp:* Lectr physiol, Regent St Polytech, London; fel, Dept Pharmacol, Albert Einstein Col Med; res assoc, Dept Psychol, Wesleyan Univ, Middletown, Conn, 62-63; instr, Dept Pharmacol, Yale Univ Sch Med, 63-65. *Concurrent Pos:* Fel, NIH, 59-62, Radcliffe Inst, 74-75; prin investr, NSF, 77-79, 81 & 87, NIH, 82, 85, 90 & 92; chair, Dept Biol, Univ Mass, 85-89, assoc Provost, 90-91. *Mem:* Brit Physiol Soc; Am Physiol Soc; AAAS. *Res:* The transmission of information in the sensory nervous system, in particular the neuroanatomy and neurophysiology of the insect visual system, using techniques of electronmicroscopy, tissue culture and electrophysiology; author of 16 publications. *Mailing Add:* Col Arts & Sci Wheatley Hall Univ Mass 100 Morrissey Blvd Boston MA 02125-3393

ARMIJO, JOSEPH SAM, NUCLEAR ENGINEERING, TECHNICAL MANAGEMENT. *Current Pos:* mgr plant mat develop, Breeder Reactor Develop Opers, Gen Elec Co, 69-73, mgr fuel chem, 73-75, mgr fuel, mat & mech, 75-76, mgr core mat eng, 76-82, mgr domestic fuel projs, 82-84, mgr nuclear systs technol oper, nuclear energy bus oper, 84-88, PROG GEN MGR SPACE POWDER, ASTRO SPACE DIV, GEN ELEC CO, 88- *Personal Data:* b El Paso, Tex, Dec 20, 38; m 58; c 3. *Educ:* Univ Tex, El Paso, BS, 59; Univ Ariz, MS, 62; Stanford Univ, PhD(mat sci), 69. *Honors & Awards:* Indust Res-100 Award, 83; Steinmentz Award, Gen Elec Co, 83. *Prof Exp:* Qual control engr, Gen Elec Co, Ill, 60; res asst, Los Alamos Sci Lab, NMex, 61; res asst, Univ Ariz, 61-62; res scientist, Vallecitos Nuclear Ctr, Gen Elec Co, Calif, 62-69. *Mem:* Am Inst Mining, Metall & Petrol Engrs; Sigma Xi; fel Am Nuclear Soc. *Res:* Metallurgical research on stress corrosion of stainless steels in oxidizing media; radiation damage to stainless steels by fast neutrons and fission fragments; light water reactor nuclear fuel and cladding, corrosion and stress corrosion; advanced nuclear reactor design and development. *Mailing Add:* 1548 Radian Rd Wilmington NC 28405

ARMINGTON, ALTON, PHYSICAL CHEMISTRY, FUEL TECHNOLOGY. *Current Pos:* from chief chemist to sr chief chemist, 57-81, CHIEF SECT ACOUST & OPTICAL MAT, SOLID STATE CHEM LAB, DEPT AIR FORCE, 81-; ADJ PROF OKLA STATE UNIV, 89- *Personal Data:* b Everett, Mass, Sept 20, 27; m 52, Faith; c 2. *Educ:* Boston Univ, BA, 50; Tufts Univ, MS, 51; Pa State Univ, PhD(fuel technol), 61. *Prof Exp:* Chemist develop, Congoleum-Nairn, 52; phys res, Naval Res Labs, 52-54; asst fuel technol, Pa State Univ, 54-57; chief, Electromagnetic Mat Div, Solid State Sci Lab, Rome Air Develop Command, 87-89. *Concurrent Pos:* Consult, 89- *Mem:* Am Chem Soc; Am Asn Crystal Growth. *Res:* Preparation and properties of ultra-pure chemical elements and intermetallic compounds; surface properties; graphite surfaces; crystal preparation. *Mailing Add:* 525 Marrett Rd Lexington Boston MA 02173-7608

ARMINGTON, RALPH ELMER, ELECTRICAL ENGINEERING. *Current Pos:* CONSULT ELEC ENG, 84- *Personal Data:* b Medford, Mass, June 24, 18; m 44, Mary Kurtanich; c 4. *Educ:* Tufts Univ, BS, 40; NY Univ, MS, 42; Pa State Univ, EE, 53; Univ Pittsburgh, PhD(elec eng), 57. *Prof Exp:* Design engr, Transformer Div, Westinghouse Elec Corp, 41-46; asst prof eng res, Pa State Univ, 46-47, from asst prof to assoc prof, 47-61; prof & head dept, Univ Maine, 61-66; lectr, Ill Inst Technol, 66-69, prof elec eng, 69-84. *Mem:* Inst Elec & Electronics Engrs; Sigma Xi. *Res:* Education in electrical engineering, especially circuit analysis; electric power systems, electrical contacts and electrical precipitation; educational administration. *Mailing Add:* 6927 Kenton Lincolnwood IL 60646

ARMISTEAD, WILLIS WILLIAM, VETERINARY MEDICINE, MEDICAL EDUCATION. *Current Pos:* RETIRED. *Personal Data:* b Detroit, Mich, Oct 28, 16; m 38, 67, Mary W Kirk; c Willis W Jr, Jack M & Sidney M. *Educ:* Agr & Mech Col, Tex, DVM, 38; Ohio State Univ, MSc, 50; Univ Minn, PhD(vet med), 55; Am Col Vet Surgeons, dipl, 75. *Honors & Awards:* Award, Am Vet Med Asn, 77. *Prof Exp:* Gen vet practitioner, 38-40; from instr to prof vet med & surg, Agr & Mech Col, Tex, 40-53, dean col vet med, 53-57; dean col vet med, Mich State Univ, 57-74; dean, Col Vet Med, 74-79, vpres agr, Univ Tenn, Knoxville, 79-87. *Concurrent Pos:* Ed, NAm Vet, 50-56 & J Vet Med Educ, 74-80; consult, Southern Regional Educ Bd, 53-56, Surgeon Gen, US Air Force, 60-62 & Tenn Higher Educ Comn, 73-74; collabr, Animal Dis & Parasite Res Div, Agr Res Serv, USDA, 54-65; mem adv bd, Inst Lab Animal Resources, Nat Res Coun, 62-66; mem vet med resident investr selection comt, US Vet Admin, 67-70; mem vet med rev comt, Bur Health Professions Educ & Manpower Training, US Dept Health, Educ & Welfare, 67-71. *Mem:* Nat Inst Med-Nat Acad Sci; Fedn Asns Schs Health Professions (pres, 74-75); Am Vet Med Asn (pres, 57-58); Asn Am Vet Med Col (pres, 64-65, 73-74); NY Acad Sci; hon mem Animal Hosp Asn. *Res:* General surgery; tissue transplantation; wound healing. *Mailing Add:* 1101 Cherokee Blvd Knoxville TN 37919

ARMITAGE, IAN MACLEOD, BIOPHYSICAL CHEMISTRY-NMR, BIOCHEMISTRY. *Current Pos:* asst prof phys sci, Yale Univ, 74-77, asst prof, 77-80, assoc prof biophys & biochem, 80-83, ADJ PROF RES BIOPHYS, BIOCHEM & RADIOL, YALE UNIV, 83- *Personal Data:* b Sherbrooke, Que, Nov 15, 47; Can citizen; div; c 2. *Educ:* Bishop's Univ, BSc, 68; Univ BC, PhD(phys chem), 72. *Prof Exp:* Fel biophys chem, Calif Inst Technol, 73-74. *Concurrent Pos:* Prin investr, NIH & NSF grants, 77-; consult med res div, Am Cyanamid Co, 79-, E I du Pont de Nemours & Co, 85-89; mem, NIH Spec Study Sect, 81-83, NSF Comt Biol Instrumentation, 80-83; consult med res div, Am Cyanamid Co, 79-, NSF Biol Facil Centers, 87-90, NIH metallobiochemical Study Sect, 90-94, Nat Adv Comt, NMR Facil, Madison, 86-, Yale Univ, Sch Med, Admis Comt, 89-; consult, Merck & Co Inc, 86-88. *Mem:* Am Chem Soc; Int Soc Magnetic Resonance; Biophys Soc; NY Acad Sci; AAAS; Soc Magnetic Res Med. *Res:* Application of multinuclear magnetic resonance techniques to the elucidation of macromolecular structure and dynamics; role of metal ions in biology. *Mailing Add:* Univ Minnesota 435 Delaware St SE Minneapolis MN 55455-0347

ARMITAGE, JOHN BRIAN, ORGANIC POLYMER CHEMISTRY. *Current Pos:* res chemist, Exp Sta, 55-60, res supvr, 60-61, sr res supvr, Dupont Tex, 61-66, sr res supvr, Plastics Dept, 67-71, res assoc, Plastic Prod & Resins Dept, 71-76, REGULATORY AFFAIRS CONSULT, E I DUPONT DE NEMOURS & CO, 76- *Personal Data:* b Ripon, Eng, Oct 28, 27; m 54; c 2. *Educ:* Univ Manchester, BSc, 48, PhD(chem), 51. *Prof Exp:* Fel, Ohio State Univ, 51-52; sr res fel, Cambridge Univ, 52-55. *Concurrent Pos:* Sr studentship of 1851 Royal Exhib, 52-54; consult, Chester Water Co, Eng, 54-55. *Mem:* Am Chem Soc; Soc Plastics Eng; fel Royal Soc Chem. *Res:* Synthesis of polyacetylenes; structure of vitamin B12; potato root eel worm chemistry; polymer chemistry; polyolefins; polyamides; fire retardance and toxicity of thermoplastics. *Mailing Add:* 621 Haverhill Rd Wilmington DE 19803

ARMITAGE, KENNETH BARCLAY, BEHAVIOR, PHYSIOLOGY. *Current Pos:* from asst prof to prof zool, Univ Kans, 56-75, chmn, Dept Biol, 68-75, chmn dept, 81-88, PROF SYST & ECOL, UNIV KANS, 75- *Personal Data:* b Steubenville, Ohio, Apr 18, 25; m 53; c 3. *Educ:* Bethany Col, WVa, BS, 49; Univ Wis, MS, 51, PhD, 54. *Honors & Awards:* Antarctic Medal, 68; Baumgartner Distinguished Prof, 87. *Prof Exp:* Asst zool, Univ Wis, 49-52, proj asst bot, 53, instr bot & zool, 54-56. *Concurrent Pos:* Trustee, Rocky Mountain Biol Lab, 70-86 & pres, 85-86; pres, Orgn Biol Field Stas, 88-89. *Mem:* Fel AAAS; Am Soc Naturalists (treas, 84-86); Ecol Soc Am; Soc Study Evolution; Am Soc Zool. *Res:* Behavioral and physiological ecology; social ecology of marmots. *Mailing Add:* 5050 Ohio St Lawrence KS 66044

ARMOR, JOHN N, HETEROGENEOUS CATALYSIS ADSORBENTS CERAMICS. *Current Pos:* PRIN RES ASSOC, AIR PROD & CHEM INC, 89- *Personal Data:* b Philadelphia, Pa, Sept 14, 44; m 66; c 3. *Educ:* Pa State Univ, BS, 66; Stanford Univ, PhD(chem), 70. *Honors & Awards:* Houdry Award, 97. *Prof Exp:* Asst prof inorg chem, Boston Univ, 70-74; sr res chemist, Allied Corps, 74-77, res assoc, Cent Res Ctr, 77-81, sr res assoc, 81-85. *Concurrent Pos:* Am ed, J Appl Catalysis, 87-96; bd dir, NAm Catalysis Soc. *Mem:* Am Chem Soc; Int Zealite Asn; NAm Catalysis Soc (treas); Catalysis Soc. *Res:* Homo and heterogeneous catalysis using inorganic and organometallic compounds; material synthesis; novel inorganic materials; adsorbents; catalytic process chemistry. *Mailing Add:* Air Prod & Chem Inc Corp Sci & Tech Ctr 7201 Hamilton Blvd Allentown PA 18195. *Fax:* 610-481-2989; *E-Mail:* armorjn@apci.com

ARMOUDIAN, GARABED, ELECTRODYNAMICS, THEORETICAL PHYSICS. *Current Pos:* ASSOC PROF PHYSICS, SOUTHWESTERN OKLA STATE UNIV, 68- *Personal Data:* b Houch-Hala, Lebanon, Aug 1, 38; m 62; c 2. *Educ:* Am Univ Beirut, BS, 62; La State Univ, PhD(physics), 66. *Prof Exp:* Instr physics, La State Univ, 65-66; AEC res fel, Columbia Univ, 66-68. *Mem:* Am Phys Soc; Am Asn Physics Teachers. *Res:* Quantum electrodynamics; theoretical studies on the structure of proton and other elementary particles. *Mailing Add:* 1200 N Illinois St Weatherford OK 73096

ARMOUR, EUGENE ARTHUR, ORGANIC CHEMISTRY, PHOTOGRAPHIC CHEMISTRY. *Current Pos:* Sr res chemist org chem, 73-80, res assoc, 80-82, LAB MGR, EASTMAN KODAK CO, 80- *Personal Data:* b Mercer, Pa, Sept 21, 46; m 68, Janis A Thielke; c Paul, Aaron, Julie & Jenny. *Educ:* Purdue Univ, BS, 68; Ohio State Univ, PhD(org chem), 73. *Mem:* Soc Photog Scientists & Engrs; Am Chem Soc. *Res:* Materials research and development. *Mailing Add:* 15 Hidden Spring Circle Rochester NY 14616-1922

ARMOUR, JOHN ANDREW, PHYSIOLOGY, ANATOMY. *Current Pos:* asst prof, 78-84, PROF PHYSIOL & BIOPHYS, FAC MED, DALHOUSIE UNIV, 84- *Personal Data:* b Montreal, Can, May 22, 37; m 82, Carolle A Lacroix; c Iain K & Kevin M. *Educ:* McGill Univ, BSc, 58; Univ Western Ont, MD, 63; Loyola Univ, Chicago, PhD(physiol), 73. *Prof Exp:* Teaching fel physiol, Loyola Univ, 67-73. *Mem:* Am Physiol Soc; Can Physiol Soc; Soc Neurosci; Can Med Asn; Soc Exp Biol & Med; Am Heart Asn. *Res:* Neural control of the heart as it relates to the thoracic autonomic nervous system; neurocardiology. *Mailing Add:* Dept Physiol & Biophys Fac Med Dalhousie Univ Halifax NS B3H 4A7 Can. *Fax:* 902-494-1685

ARMSON, KENNETH AVERY, SILVICULTURE, SOIL SCIENCE. *Current Pos:* FORESTRY CONSULT, 89- *Personal Data:* b Newton Brook, Ont, Feb 19, 27; m 52; c 1. *Educ:* Univ Toronto, BScF, 51; Oxford Univ, dipl forestry, 55. *Hon Degrees:* DSc, Lakehead Univ, 91. *Honors & Awards:* Gold Medal, Can Inst Forestry, 78; Ont Forestry Award, Ont Forestry Asn, 90. *Prof Exp:* Forester, Soils Surv, Res Div, Ont Dept Lands & Forests, 51-52; lectr, Univ Toronto, 52-57, from asst prof to prof forestry, 57-78; spec adv, Ont Ministry Natural Resources,78-80, chief forester, 80-83, exec coordr forest resources, 83-86, prov forester, 86-89. *Mem:* Soc Am Foresters; Soil Sci Soc Am; Can Inst Forestry. *Res:* Forest soils; effect of fertility on tree growth. *Mailing Add:* 446 Heath St E Toronto ON M4G 1B5 Can

ARMSTEAD, ROBERT LOUIS, THEORETICAL PHYSICS. *Current Pos:* ASSOC PROF PHYSICS, NAVAL POSTGRAD SCH, 64- *Personal Data:* b Blair, Nebr, Nov 5, 36; m 61; c 2. *Educ:* Univ Rochester, BS, 58; Univ Calif, Berkeley, PhD(theoret physics), 65. *Mem:* Am Phys Soc; Sigma Xi; Am Asn Physics Teachers. *Res:* Theoretical atomic scattering; laser light propagation. *Mailing Add:* Dept Physics Code Ph Naval Postgrad Sch Monterey CA 93943

ARMSTEAD, WILLIAM M, PHYSIOLOGY, PHARMACOLOGY. *Current Pos:* ASST PROF, DEPT ANESTHESIA & PHARMACOL, UNIV PA, 92- *Personal Data:* b Meriden, Conn, May 13, 57. *Educ:* Univ Pa, BA, 79; Tulane Univ, MS, 83, PhD(pharmacol), 85. *Prof Exp:* Fel & instr pharmacol, Tulane Univ, 85-86; fel, Univ Tenn, Memphis, 86-88, instr, 88-90, asst prof, Dept Physiol & Biophys, 90-92. *Concurrent Pos:* Guest lectr, Pharmacol Dept, NY Med Col, NJ Med Sch, Northeastern Univ, Albany Med Sch, Tex A&M Med Sch, Univ Iowa, Mich State Univ, Neurobiol Dept, Cornell Med Sch, Anat Dept, Univ Ark Med Sch; mem, Stroke Coun, Basic Sci Coun & Circulation Coun, Am Heart Asn; training grant, NIH, 86-87, First award, 89-94. *Mem:* Am Physiol Soc; Sigma Xi; Am Soc Pharm & Exp Therapeut; Int Soc Cerebial Blood Flow & Metab. *Res:* Control of newborn cerebiol circulation; role of opioids, prostanoids, vasopressin, and nitric oxide in cerebrohemodynamic control; brain injury. *Mailing Add:* Dept Anesthesia & Critical Care Children's Hosp Philadelphia 34th & Civic Ctr Blvd Philadelphia PA 19104-4399. *Fax:* 215-222-2861

ARMSTRONG, ALFRED RINGGOLD, ANALYTICAL CHEMISTRY. *Current Pos:* RETIRED. *Personal Data:* b Washington, DC, July 6, 11; m 34; c 2. *Educ:* Col William & Mary, BS, 32, AM, 34; Univ Va, PhD(chem), 45. *Honors & Awards:* Thomas Jefferson Award, Col William & Mary, 75. *Prof Exp:* Instr, Col William & Mary, 33-35, asst prof chem, 36-42; asst to Dr J. H. Yoe, Nat Defense Res Comt & investigator, Chem Warfare Serv, Univ Va, 44-45; from assoc prof to prof chem Col William & Mary, 45-76. *Mem:* Am Chem Soc. *Res:* Chemistry of sea water; organic analytical reagents. *Mailing Add:* 512 Newport Ave Williamsburg VA 23185-4013

ARMSTRONG, ANDREW THURMAN, PHYSICAL CHEMISTRY. *Current Pos:* PRES, ARMSTRONG FORENSIC LAB INC, 80- *Personal Data:* b Haslet, Tex, May 26, 35; m 58; c 3. *Educ:* North Tex State Univ, BS, 58, MS, 59; La State Univ, PhD(chem), 67. *Honors & Awards:* W T Doherty Award, Am Chem Soc, 82. *Prof Exp:* Instr chem, West Tex State Univ, 59-61 & La State Univ, 63-66, vis asst prof, 67-68; from asst prof to assoc prof chem, Univ Tex, Arlington, 74-84. *Concurrent Pos:* Chief chemist, Arlington Fire Dept, 78-; dipl, Am Bd Criminalistics. *Mem:* Am Chem Soc; fel Am Inst Chemists; Am Indust Hyg Asn; fel Am Acad Forensic Sci; Int Asn Arson Investr. *Res:* Trace analytical techniques for environmental and forensic applications; numerous papers and publications. *Mailing Add:* 903 Oakview Ct Arlington TX 76012-2922

ARMSTRONG, BAXTER HARDIN, GEOPHYSICAL APPLICATIONS OF ACOUSTIC EMISSION, MICROSEISMIC ACTIVITY. *Current Pos:* GEOPHYSICIST VOL, US GEOL SURV, MENLO PARK, CALIF, 92- *Personal Data:* b Portland, Ore, Jan 27, 29; m 54, Helen Himes; c 4. *Educ:* Univ Calif, Berkeley, AB, 51, MA, 53, PhD(physics), 56. *Prof Exp:* From assoc res scientist to res scientist, Lockheed Missiles & Space Co, 56-62, staff scientist, 62-63, sr staff scientist & sr mem res lab, 63-64; mem staff, Sci Ctr, IBM Corp, 64-68, sci staff mgr, 69-73, dir, Centro Cientifico de Am Latina, IBM de Mex, 73, sci staff mgr, IBM Sci Ctr, 74-78; vis scholar, Stanford Univ, 78-79, consult prof aeronaut & astronaut, 79-83; mgr eng res, IBM Corp, 83-85; affil prof mat sci & eng, Univ Wash, 85-86; mgr numerically intensive comput applns, Palo Alto Sci Ctr, IBM Corp, 87-92. *Concurrent Pos:* Asst prof, San Jose State Col, 58-60; guest staff mem, Queen's Univ Belfast, 60-61; vis scholar, Stanford Univ, 78-79, consult prof aeronaut & astronaut, 79-83; assoc ed, J Quant Spectros & Radiative Transfer, 66-86; consult, Syst, Sci & Software Co, 69, Lockheed Missiles & Space Co, 88-89 & Foster-Miller, Inc, 94. *Mem:* Am Phys Soc; Am Asn Physics Teachers; Sigma Xi; Am Geophys Union; Acoustic Emission Working Group. *Res:* Theoretical atomic physics; interaction of atoms with radiation fields; atmospheric radiative transfer; thermal conductivity of dielectric crystals; acoustic attenuation theory; geophysical applications of acoustic emission. *Mailing Add:* 4339 Miranda Ave Palo Alto CA 94306-3742

ARMSTRONG, CARTER MICHAEL, PLASMA PHYSICS. *Current Pos:* DIR ADVAN TUBE RES DEVELOP & ENG, NORTHROP GRUMMAN, 94- *Personal Data:* b Jersey City, NJ, Nov 17, 50; m 72; c 1. *Educ:* Rutgers Univ, AB, 72; Univ MD, PhD(plasma physics), 76. *Prof Exp:* Nat Res Coun assoc laser fusion, Nat Acad Sci, Naval Res Lab, 76-77; asst prof plasma physics, NC State Univ, 77-85; head, Fast Wave Devices Sect, Naval Res Lab, 85-94. *Mem:* Am Phys Soc. *Res:* Intense relativistic electron and ion beams; laser fusion. *Mailing Add:* 23174 N Providence Dr Kildeer IL 60047

ARMSTRONG, CLAY M, PHYSIOLOGY, BIOPHYSICS. *Current Pos:* PROF PHYSIOL, SCH MED, UNIV PA, 76- *Personal Data:* b Chicago, Ill, Sept 26, 34; m 63; c 3. *Educ:* Rice Univ, BA, 56; Wash Univ, MD, 60. *Honors & Awards:* K S Cole Award, Biophys Soc, 75; Bowditch Lectr, Am Physiol Soc, 75. *Prof Exp:* Res assoc biophys, Lab Biophys, NIH, 61-64; hon res asst physiol, Univ Col, Univ London, 64-66; asst prof, Duke Univ, 66-69; assoc prof, Univ Rochester, 69-75, prof, 74-75. *Concurrent Pos:* Mult Sclerosis Soc fel, Neurol Dept, Sch Med, Wash Univ, St Louis, 61; distinguished lectr, Soc Gen Physiologists, 86. *Mem:* Nat Acad Sci; Inst Med-Nat Acad Sci; Soc Gen Physiologists (pres, 85-86); Fedn Am Socs Exp Biol; Biophys Soc. *Res:* Permeability mechanisms in excitable membranes; excitation-contraction coupling; author of numerous technical publications. *Mailing Add:* Dept Physiol Univ Pa Philadelphia PA 19104-6085

ARMSTRONG, DALE DEAN, NUCLEAR PHYSICS, ACCELERATOR PHYSICS. *Current Pos:* RETIRED. *Personal Data:* b Salina, Kans, Aug 18, 27; m 52, Jurhee Galloway; c Dale D Jr, Harold & Amy (Denton). *Educ:* Univ Colo, BS, 57; Univ NMex, MS, 62, PhD(physics), 65. *Prof Exp:* Staff mem physics, Los Alamos Nat Lab, 57-80, dep group leader, 80-85, assoc div leader, 85-87. *Mem:* Am Phys Soc. *Res:* Design and development of a high intensity neutron source for simulating the radiation damage effects that will be produced in fusion reactor materials. *Mailing Add:* 13839 Elmbrook Dr Sun City West AZ 85375

ARMSTRONG, DANIEL WAYNE, PHARMACEUTICAL & BIOANALYTICAL CHEMISTRY, SEPARATIONS. *Current Pos:* CUR PROF CHEM, UNIV MO, ROLLA, 87- *Personal Data:* b Ft Wayne, Ind, Nov 2, 49; m 72, Linda M Todd; c Lincoln T, Ross A & Colleen V. *Educ:* Washington & Lee Univ, BS, 72; Tex A&M Univ, MS, 74, PhD(chem), 77. *Honors & Awards:* EAS Award Chromatography, 90; Martin Medal, 91; ISCO Award Bioanalytical Separations, 92; Midwest Award Chem, Am Chem Soc, 93; Pres Award Res & Creativity, 93; Perkin Elmer Award Capillary Electrophoresis, 94; R&D-100 Award, 95; Benedetti-Pichler Award, 96. *Prof Exp:* Asst prof chem, Bowdoin Col, 78-80 & Georgetown Univ, 80-83; from assoc prof to prof chem, Tex Tech Univ, 83-86. *Concurrent Pos:* Pharmaceut & chem consult; originator, writer & host, We're Science, Nat Pub Radio, 94. *Mem:* Am Chem Soc; AAAS. *Res:* Cyclodextrin and surfactant chemistry; macrocycle chemistry; enantiomeric separations; environmental chemistry; analytical applications of cyclodentrins and micelles; chemical evolution, macrocyclic antibiotics and chromatographic molecular weight determination of macromolecules; pharmaceutical chemistry. *Mailing Add:* 715 Oak Knoll Rd Rolla MO 65401. *Fax:* 573-341-6033

ARMSTRONG, DAVID ANTHONY, PHYSICAL CHEMISTRY. *Current Pos:* prof chem, 68-91, dean fac sci, 84-89, EMER PROF, UNIV CALGARY, 91- *Personal Data:* b Barbados, WI, Aug 27, 30; m 55, Ruth Hallam; c Graeme, Maureen & Andrew. *Educ:* McGill Univ, BSc, 52, PhD, 55. *Prof Exp:* Brotherton res lectr phys chem, Univ Leeds, 55-57; Nat Res Coun Can fel chem, Univ Sask, 57-58; from asst prof to assoc prof, Univ Alta, 58-68. *Mem:* Fel Chem Inst Can; Am Chem Soc; Sigma Xi. *Res:* Radiation chemistry; chemical kinetics; kinetics and thermodynamics of free radical reactions in water; electron-ion and ion-ion recombination; electron capture and ion transport in the gas phase. *Mailing Add:* Dept Chem Univ Calgary Calgary AB T2N 1N4 Can. *Fax:* 403-289-9488

ARMSTRONG, DAVID M(ICHAEL), MAMMALOGY, BIOGEOGRAPHY. *Current Pos:* From asst prof to assoc prof, Univ Colo, Boulder, 71-85, dir, Mus, 88-93, MUS ASSOC CUR, UNIV COLO, BOULDER, 71-, PROF NAT SCI, 85-, PROF ENVIRON POP & ORGANISMIC BIOL, 93- *Personal Data:* b Louisville, Ky, July 31, 44; div; c John D & Laura C. *Educ:* Colo State Univ, BS, 66; Harvard Univ, MA, 67; Univ Kans, PhD(systs & ecol), 71. *Concurrent Pos:* Sci collabr, Nat Park Serv, 71-76; ed, Southwestern Naturalist, 76-80 & J Mammal, 81-87; pres, Colo-Wyo Acad Sci, 91-92. *Mem:* Am Soc Mammalogists; Ecol Soc Am; Sigma Xi; Soc Conserv Biol. *Res:* Biogeography and ecology of mammals of the western United States and Middle America; history of evolutionary biology. *Mailing Add:* Environ, Population & Organ Biol Univ Colo Boulder CO 80309-0334

ARMSTRONG, DAVID THOMAS, PHYSIOLOGY, REPRODUCTIVE BIOLOGY. *Current Pos:* assoc prof, 68-69, PROF PHYSIOL, OBSTET & GYNEC, UNIV WESTERN ONT, 69-, DIR, MRC GROUP, REPRODUCTIVE BIOL, 79- *Personal Data:* b Kinburn, Ont, Nov 5, 29; m 56; c 3. *Educ:* Ont Agr Col, BSA, 51; Cornell Univ, MS, 56, PhD(physiol), 59. *Prof Exp:* Asst agr rep, Ont Dept Agr, 51-54; asst dept animal husb, Cornell Univ, 54-57; res assoc, Dept Biol, Brookhaven Nat Lab, 58-60; from res assoc to assoc anat, Sch Dent Med, Harvard Univ, 60-68. *Concurrent Pos:* Res career develop award, NIH, 63-; assoc, Med Res Coun Can, 69-; vis prof obstet & gynec, Univ Adelaide, 77-78. *Mem:* Soc Study Reproduction (pres, 77); Endocrine Soc; Am Physiol Soc; Can Physiol Soc; Int Embryo Transfer Soc. *Res:* Pituitary-gonad interrelationships; mechanism of hormone action. *Mailing Add:* Dept Obstet & Gynec Univ Western Ontario London ON N6A 5A5 Can

ARMSTRONG, DON L, chemical engineering, marine science; deceased, see previous edition for last biography

ARMSTRONG, DONALD, RETINAL DEGENERATION, OXYGEN FREE RADICALS. *Current Pos:* PROF & CHMN CLIN CHEM, PATHOPHYSIOL, VISUAL SCI, STATE UNIV NY, BUFFALO, 90-; PROF EXP PATH, ROSWELL PARK CANCER INST, 92- *Personal Data:* b Hamilton, Ont, July 20, 33; US citizen; m 54, Christine Medieros; c Donald A, David E, Dennis E, Sandra E, Kenneth L & Elizabeth M. *Educ:* San Diego State Univ, BS, 57; Univ Colo, MS, 69; Univ Tulsa, EdD, 74; Univ Oslo, PhD(biochem), 80; Charles Univ, DSc, 90. *Prof Exp:* Instr anat, San Diego State Univ, 60-62; instr neurochem, Univ Ore Sch Med, 63-67 & Univ Colo Sch Med, 67-70; instr anat & physiol, Tulsa Community Col, 71-74, asst prof neurochem & neuropath, 74-81; assoc prof opthal & comp opthal, Sch Med & Vet Med, Univ Fla, 81-86; prof & chmn clin chem, Fac Allied Health, Kuwait Univ, 86-90. *Concurrent Pos:* Dir, Clin Res Ctr, Hillcrest Med Ctr, 70-74, Allied Vet Med Lab, 75-78; prin investr, March Dimes Found, 73-74, Children's Brain Dis Found, 75-92, Am Cancer Soc, 77-78, Fight-for-Sight Inc, 78-82, Res Prevent Blindness, 78-83, Nat Eye Inst, 78-83, Univ Kuwait Health Sci Ctr, 87-91, Am Heart Asn, 92-; course dir neuroanat, Univ Colo Sch Med, 74-81; res prof, Nat Retinitis Pigmentosa Found, 75-78, chmn, Med Adv Bd, 76-78; vis prof, Johns Hopkins Univ Sch Med, 76, Eye & Ear Infirmary, Univ Chicago, 77, Harvard Med Sch, 78, Nat Vet Inst Norway, 79-82, Haddasah Univ Sch Med, 79, Massey Univ Sch Vet Med, NZ, 79, Univ London Sch Med, 80, Univ Helsinki, 80, Eye & Ear Infirmary, Univ La, 82, Slovak Acad Sci, 83, Cambridge Univ Sch Med, 83, Tokyo Metrop Inst Geront, 85, Inst Appl Biochem, 89, Univ Oslo Sch Med, 93; ed, Biol Res, J Am Aging Asn, 78-87; fel, Norweg Res Coun, 79-80; exchange scientist, Nat Acad Sci, Czech, 83 & 86; pres, Am Aging Asn, 84-85; sr scientist fel, Japan Soc Promotion Sci, 85; instr clin chem & neuroanat, Med Specialties, Kuwait Univ, 88-90; consult lab med, Kuwait Ministry Pub Health, 86-90; dir grad studies, Dept Clin Lab Sci, State Univ NY, Buffalo, 90-95, chmn, Fac Senate Res & Grad Coun, 94-; ed-in-chief, J Clin Lab Sci, 92-96; dir grad studies, Dept Exp Path, Roswell Park Cancer Inst, 93-; vis prof, Sch Med, Showa Univ, Tokyo, 95-; special for vis prof, Ministry Educ, Sci & Culture, Japan, 96. *Mem:* Am Aging Asn (pres, 84-85); Am Clin Scientists; Am Asn Clin Chem; Asn Res & Vision Opthal; Am Soc Clin Lab Sci; fel Nat Acad Clin Biochem. *Res:* Effects of lipid peroxidation on retinal pathophysiology, biochemistry, enzymology and protection by antioxidants is studied in models exposed to oxygen stress and in patients with diabetes, atherosclerosis or alcoholism. *Mailing Add:* Dept Clin Lab Sci 26 Carey Hall State Univ NY 3435 Main St Buffalo NY 14215-3005. *Fax:* 716-829-3601

ARMSTRONG, DONALD B, acoustics, crystallography, for more information see previous edition

ARMSTRONG, DONALD JAMES, PLANT HORMONE RESEARCH. *Current Pos:* from asst prof to assoc prof, 74-86, PROF, ORE STATE UNIV, 87- *Personal Data:* b Marshall Co, WVa, Mar 14, 37; m 61, 84, Mary E Kentula; c J West. *Educ:* Marshall Univ, AB, 59, MA, 61; Univ Wis, Madison, PhD(bot), 67. *Prof Exp:* Proj assoc bot, Univ Wis, Madison, 67-68; NSF fel biochem, Univ BC, 68-70; proj assoc bot, Univ Wis, Madison, 70-74. *Concurrent Pos:* NIH sr fel, Univ Calif, San Diego, 84-85. *Mem:* Am Soc Plant Physiol; Int Plant Growth Substances Asn; Int Soc Plant Molecular Biol. *Res:* Metabolism and mechanism of action of plant growth substances; plant tissue culture; regulation of plant growth and development. *Mailing Add:* Dept Bot Plant Path Ore State Univ Corvallis OR 97331. *Fax:* 541-737-3573; *E-Mail:* armstrod@bcc.orst.edu

ARMSTRONG, DWIGHT W, ANIMAL RESEARCH, NUTRITION. *Current Pos:* PRES, CARL AKEY INC, 93- *Personal Data:* b Princeton, Ky, 1950. *Educ:* Murray State Univ, BS, 71; Purdue Univ, MS, 73, PhD(animal nutrit), 75. *Prof Exp:* Asst prof animal sci, NC State Univ, 75-80, assoc prof, 80- 82. *Mem:* Am Soc Animal Sci; Am Feed Indust Asn. *Mailing Add:* Carl S Akey Inc 6531 State Rte 503 N Lewisburg OH 45338-5002

ARMSTRONG, EARLENE, ENTOMOLOGY, MICROBIOLOGY. *Current Pos:* asst prof, 76-81, ASSOC PROF ENTOM, UNIV MD, COLLEGE PARK, 81- *Personal Data:* b Wilson Co, NC, Apr 11, 47; m 80; c 2. *Educ:* NC Cent Univ, BS, 69, MS, 70; Cornell Univ, PhD(entom), 75. *Prof Exp:* Grad asst biol, NC Cent Univ, 69-70, instr, 70-71; instr, Southeastern Community Col, 71; asst prof entom, Howard Univ, 75-76. *Concurrent Pos:* Consult, Insect Control & Res, Inc, Baltimore, 78-80; invest, Marine Biol Lab, Mass, 76-79. *Mem:* Soc Invert Path; Entom Soc Am; Sigma Xi. *Res:* Protozoan pathogens of insects. *Mailing Add:* Dept Entom Univ Md College Park MD 20742-0001

ARMSTRONG, FRANK BRADLEY, JR, BIOCHEMISTRY. *Current Pos:* from asst prof to assoc prof genetics & bact, NC State Univ, 62-66, assoc prof biochem, 62-68, dir biotechnol prog, 83-86, UNIV PROF BIOCHEM, NC STATE UNIV, 68- *Personal Data:* b Brownsville, Feb 15, 28; m 58; c 3. *Educ:* Univ Tex, BS, 50, MA, 53; Univ Calif, PhD(biochem), 59. *Prof Exp:* Fel biochem & genetics, Univ Tex, 59-62. *Concurrent Pos:* Career develop award & Sigma Xi res award, 64; NSF panel, 70 & 71; vis prof, Univ Exeter, England, 76. *Mem:* AAAS; Genetics Soc Am; Am Soc Biol Chemists; Am Chem Soc; Am Inst Biol Sci; NY Acad Sci. *Res:* Biochemical studies on Salmonella typhimurium; enzymes and protein chemistry. *Mailing Add:* 2757 Toxey Dr Raleigh NC 27609-7642

ARMSTRONG, FRANK C(LARKSON FELIX), structural statigraphic evolution in the idaho-wyoming thrust belt, for more information see previous edition

ARMSTRONG, GEORGE GLAUCUS, JR, PHYSIOLOGY, AEROSPACE MEDICINE. *Current Pos:* RETIRED. *Personal Data:* b Houston, Miss, Feb 28, 24; m 48, Doris Moore; c Jennifer A & Marcia G. *Educ:* Univ Miss, BA, 48, MS, 50, BS, 52; Univ Ill, MD, 56. *Prof Exp:* Res assoc, Sch Med, Univ Miss, 48-49, instr physiol, 49-52, from asst prof to assoc prof physiol & biophys, 52-64; aerospace technologist, 64-68, chief biomed technol div, 68-70; dep chief, Med Opers Div, Johnson Space Ctr, NASA, 70-72, chief health serv div, 72-77; dir, Health Effects Div, US Environ Protection Agency, 77-80; dir, food ingredient assessment div, USDA, 80-84. *Res:* Cardiovascular reflexes; spaceborne medical systems. *Mailing Add:* 7135 Birch Dr Beaumont TX 77708-2713

ARMSTRONG, GEORGE MICHAEL, BIOLOGY, MOLECULAR BIOLOGY. *Current Pos:* ASSOC PROF BIOL, UNIV WIS, FOND DU LAC, 68- *Personal Data:* b Madison, Wis, Dec 5, 38; c Michael, Philip, Lori, Heidi & Mandy. *Educ:* Univ Wis-Madison, BS, 62; Univ Okla, MNS, 66, PhD(plant physiol), 68. *Mem:* Sigma Xi. *Res:* Phenolic compounds in plants as affected by environmental factors. *Mailing Add:* Dept Biol Univ Wis 400 Campus Dr Fond du Lac WI 54935-2950. *E-Mail:* garmstro@uwc.edu

ARMSTRONG, JAMES CLYDE, CIVIL ENGINEERING, SOIL MECHANICS. *Current Pos:* RETIRED. *Personal Data:* b Wheelock, Tex, Dec 23, 33; m 58; c 2. *Educ:* Tex A&M Univ, BS, 55, BS, 61, MS, 62, PhD(civil eng), 67. *Prof Exp:* Sr lab asst soil mech, Tex Hwy Dept, 57-59; asst res engr pavement design, Tex Transp Inst, 62-66; asst prof soil mech, Univ Mo-Rolla, 66-69; assoc prof, Univ Ark, 69-71; mem staff, Nat Soil Serv, Arlington, Tex, 75-77; mem staff, Univ Tex, Arlington, 77-89. *Concurrent Pos:* NSF res grant, 68-69; mem, Ford Found Prog Residencies Eng Pract, 70-75. *Mem:* Am Soc Civil Engrs; Nat Soc Prof Engrs; Int Soc Soil Mech & Found Engrs; Am Soc Eng Educr. *Res:* Pore pressure dissipation around piles and pile groups; comparison of particulate mechanics approaches to the action of real solid systems; soil stabilization of active clay soils. *Mailing Add:* PO Box 44 Wheelock TX 77882

ARMSTRONG, JAMES G, MEDICAL ADMINISTRATION. *Current Pos:* EMER ASST PROF MED, IND UNIV SCH MED, 80-; CHMN BD & PRES, ALEXANDER GRANT & ASSOCS INC, 80- *Personal Data:* b London, Eng, Nov 14, 24; US citizen; m 51; c 4. *Educ:* Oxford Univ, MA, 49, BM, BCh, 50; MRCS, 49; Ind Royal Col Univ, MD, 63, Physicians & Surgeons Can, cert pediat, 63; FRCPC. *Prof Exp:* House physician, St Olave's Hosp, London, Eng, 50-51, house surgeon, 51-52; colonial med officer, Nigeria, 52-55; staff physician, Alta Ment Inst, 55-56; resident, St Josephs Hosp, Toronto, Ont, 56-57; chief resident, Hosp Sick Children, 57-58; physician, Lilly Labs Clin Res, 58-66, sr physician, Lilly Res Labs, 66-68, asst dir med regulatory affairs, 68-69, dir med plans & regulatory affairs, 69-73, dir med liaison, 73-75, clin investr, 75-80. *Concurrent Pos:* Fel pediat, Hosp Sick Children, 57-58; fel pediat med, Univ Toronto, 57-58; instr, Ind Univ, 58-66, asst prof, 66-; staff physician, Dept Pediat, Marion County Gen Hosp, Indianapolis, Ind, 58-79, physician, Tumor Bd, 60-79; med consult, US Armed Forces, 75-; mem bd, US Pharmacists, 83- *Mem:* Fel Am Col Physicians; Am Asn Cancer Res; Am Fedn Clin Res; fel Royal Soc Med; Brit Med Asn. *Res:* Pediatric medicine; clinical pediatrics; cancer chemotherapy; medical research administration. *Mailing Add:* 3633 E 71st St Indianapolis IN 46220

ARMSTRONG, JOHN A, QUANTUM ELECTRONICS, LASER PHYSICS. *Current Pos:* RETIRED. *Personal Data:* b Schenectady, NY, July 1, 34; m 58, Elizabeth Saunders; c Sarah & Jennifer. *Educ:* Harvard Univ, BA, 56, PhD(appl physics), 61. *Hon Degrees:* DSc, State Univ NY, Albany. *Honors & Awards:* George E Pake Prize, Am Phys Soc, 89; Karl T Compton Vis Lectr, Mass Inst Technol, 93-94. *Prof Exp:* mem res staff, IBM Corp, 63-76, dir phys sci, Res Ctr, 76-80, mem, Corp Tech Comt, 80-81, mgr mat & technol develop, 81-83, vpres, Logic & Mem, 83-86, dir res, 86-87, vpres & dir res, 87-89, vpres sci & technol, 89-93, mem corp mgt bd, 89-93. *Concurrent Pos:* Trustee, Assoc Univs Inc, 86-97, mem, Harvard Bd Overseers, 90-96, Nat Adv Comt Semiconductors; mem, Nat Sci Bd, 96; adj prof, Univ Mass, Amherst, 96. *Mem:* Nat Acad Eng; fel Optical Soc Am; fel AAAS; fel Am Phys Soc; Royal Swedish Acad Eng Sci; Am Acad Arts & Sci. *Res:* Nonlinear optics, photon statistics; nonlinear optical pulse propagation; picosecond laser pulse techniques; laser spectroscopy of atoms; author of more than 55 publications. *Mailing Add:* PO Box 29 South Salem NY 10590. *Fax:* 413-549-1897; *E-Mail:* 71160.126@compuserve.com

ARMSTRONG, JOHN BRIGGS, PEDIATRIC NEUROLOGY, BIOCHEMISTRY. *Current Pos:* STAFF NEUROLOGIST, MONTREAL CHILDREN'S HOSP, 79-; PROF BIOL, UNIV OTTAWA. *Personal Data:* b Toronto, Ont. *Educ:* McGill Univ, BSc, 63, MD & CM, 65, PhD(neurochem), 75. *Prof Exp:* Intern med, St Paul's Hosp, Vancouver, BC, 66-67; resident, Montreal Gen Hosp, 67-68; resident neurol, Montreal Neurol Inst, 68-69, res fel neurochem, 69-71; res fel neurochem, Hosp for Sick Children, Toronto, 71-74, chief resident pediat neurol, 74-75; asst prof pediat, Univ Toronto, 75-76; assoc med dir, 76-77, med dir, Pfizer Co Ltd, 77- *Concurrent Pos:* Med Res Coun Can fel, 69-73; Muscular Dystrophy Asn Can fel, 73-74, clin fel, 74-75; staff neurologist & res assoc, Hosp for Sick Children, Toronto, 75-76. *Mem:* Can Soc Child Neurol; Am Fedn Clin Res; Am Acad Neurol; Can Neurol Soc. *Res:* Hemodynamic effects of vasodilators in congestive heart failure and hypertension; relationship of therapeutic effect to plasma levels of cyclic antidegenerants. *Mailing Add:* Dept Biol Univ Ottawa PO Box 450 Sta A Ottawa ON K1N 6N5 Can

ARMSTRONG, JOHN BUCHANAN, INTERNAL MEDICINE. *Current Pos:* RETIRED. *Personal Data:* b Toronto, Ont, Oct 19, 18; m 44, Dorothy M Green; c Robert, Stanley, Sheila & Mary. *Educ:* Univ Toronto, MD, 43; McGill Univ, dipl, 51; FRCP, 50. *Honors & Awards:* Queen Elizabeth's Silver Jubilee Medal, 77. *Prof Exp:* Sr intern & asst resident med, Royal Victoria Hosp, 46-48; fel, Duke Hosp, 48-49; registr, Post-Grad Med Sch, Hammersmith Hosp, London, 49-50; asst prof physiol & med res & spec lectr med, Univ Man, 50-56; assoc prof pharmacol, Univ Toronto, 56-69; sr lectr pharmacol, Univ Ottawa, 69-75; assoc prof prev med, Univ Toronto, 75-83, sr med consult epidemiol, Ont Ministry Health, 75-83. *Concurrent Pos:* Can Life Ins med fel, 50-52; Markle scholar, 52-56; physician, Winnipeg Munic Hosps, 51-56; chmn & mem panel shock & plasma expanders, Defense Res Bd Can, 53-68; asst physician, Winnipeg Gen Hosp, 54-56; consult, Can Forces Med Coun, 54-60; vol asst, Toronto Gen Hosp, 57-68; exec dir & chief med adv, Can Heart Found, 57-75; pres, Biol Coun Can, 71-72. *Mem:* Can Cardiovasc Soc; Can Hypertension Soc; Pharmaceut Soc Can (pres, 72-73); Can Med Asn. *Res:* Clinical cardiovascular physiology, pharmacology and epidemiology. *Mailing Add:* Apt 151 Bay St Apt 401 Ottawa ON K1R 7T2 Can

ARMSTRONG, JOHN EDWARD, quaternary geology, glacial geology; deceased, see previous edition for last biography

ARMSTRONG, JOHN MORRISON, WATER RESOURCES MANAGEMENT, COASTAL ENGINEERING. *Current Pos:* chief exec officer, 89-, PRES, TRAVERS GROUP. *Personal Data:* b Nov 11, 36; US citizen; m 58; c 4. *Educ:* Univ Mich, Ann Arbor, PhD(eng), 69. *Prof Exp:* Assoc engr systs analyst, Univ Mich, Ann Arbor, 64-66, lectr environ & water resource eng, 67-69, asst prof, 69-73, assoc prof environ & water resource eng, 74-89. *Concurrent Pos:* Dir, Mich Sea Grant Prog, Univ Mich, 70-75 & Great Lakes Resource Mgt Prog & Coastal Zone Lab, 73-; consult, UN, 74-76; mem, Adv Comt Effect Offshore Develop, NSF, 76-77; mem, Nat Tech Comt Coastal Zone Mgt, Am Soc Civil Engrs, 78- *Mem:* Sigma Xi; Am Soc Civil Engrs; AAAS. *Res:* Coastal and ocean resource management; water resource systems analysis; environmental impact analysis; resource policy analysis; engineering economics. *Mailing Add:* Travers Group 3712 Plaza Dr Ann Arbor MI 48108

ARMSTRONG, JOHN WILLIAM, ASTRONOMY, SPACE PHYSICS. *Current Pos:* RES SCIENTIST, JET PROPULSION LAB, CALIF INST TECHNOL, 77- *Personal Data:* b Roslyn, NY, Mar 15, 48; m 75. *Educ:* Harvey Mudd Col, BS, 69; Univ Calif, San Diego, MS, 71, PhD(appl physics), 75. *Prof Exp:* Res assoc astron, Nat Radio Astron Observ, 75-77. *Concurrent Pos:* Mem, Plasma Turbulence Explorer Study Group, NASA, 80; Henry G Booker fel, 20th Union Radio Sci Int Gen Assembly. *Mem:* AAAS; Am Astron Soc; Am Geophys Union. *Res:* Dynamics of interplanetary and interstellar media; wave propagation in random media, turbulence in planetary atmospheres, gravitational wave astronomy. *Mailing Add:* 601 Manzanita Ave Sierra Madre CA 91024

ARMSTRONG, JOSEPH EVERETT, MORPHOLOGY & SYSTEMATICS OF FLOWERING PLANTS. *Current Pos:* from asst prof to assoc prof, 78-89, PROF BOT, ILL STATE UNIV, 90- *Personal Data:* b Rochester, NY, Sept 18, 48; m 71; c 1. *Educ:* State Univ NY Oswego, BA, 70; Miami Univ, MA, 72, PhD(bot), 75. *Prof Exp:* Res fel wood sci, Univ Mo, Columbia, 76-78. *Mem:* Bot Soc Am; Am Inst Biol Sci; Sigma Xi; Torrey Bot Club; Asn Trop Biol. *Res:* Structure, development, and function of flowers in scrophulariaceae, solanaceae, and related families; floral biology and reproduction of primitive, beetle-pollinated, rainforest trees, Myristicaceae Eupomatiaceae; rain forest research in Australia; introduction textbook author. *Mailing Add:* Dept Biol Sci Ill State Univ Campus Box 4120 Normal IL 61790-0001

ARMSTRONG, KENNETH WILLIAM, MATHEMATICS. *Current Pos:* dir bd educ prog, 73-78, ASSOC PROF MATH, UNIV WINNIPEG, 69- *Personal Data:* b Brandon, Man, Sept 4, 35; m 61; c 2. *Educ:* Univ Man, BSc, 57, MSc, 61; McGill Univ, PhD(math), 65. *Prof Exp:* Lectr, Univ Man, 57-58, 59-60, 63-64, from asst prof to assoc prof, 64-69, asst head dept, 66-69. *Mem:* Can Math Soc. *Mailing Add:* Dept Math & Statist Univ Winnipeg 515 Portage Ave Winnipeg MB R3B 2E9 Can

ARMSTRONG, LLOYD, JR, ATOMIC PHYSICS. *Current Pos:* PROVOST & SR VPRES ACAD AFFAIRS, UNIV SOUTHERN CALIF, 93-, PROF PHYSICS, 93- *Personal Data:* b Austin, Tex, May 19, 40; m 65, Judith Glantz; c Wade M. *Educ:* Mass Inst Technol, BS, 62; Univ Calif, Berkeley, PhD(physics), 66. *Prof Exp:* Physicist, Lawrence Radiation Lab, 65-67; sr physicist, Westinghouse Res Labs, Pa, 67-68; res assoc, Johns Hopkins Univ, 68-69, from asst prof to prof physics, 69-93, chmn, Dept Physics & Astron, 85-87, dean, Sch Arts & Sci, 87-93. *Concurrent Pos:* Consult, Westinghouse Res Labs, 69-71; vis fel, Joint Inst Lab Astrophys, Boulder, Co, 78-79; prog officer, NSF, 81-83; mem, Nat Acad Sci/Nat Res Coun, Comt Recommendations for the US Army Basic Sci Res, 84-87, vchmn, Comt Atomic & Molecular Sci, 84-85 & chmn, 85-88; mem, NSF, Adv Comt Physics, 85-88; mem, adv bd phys rev A, 84-89; mem bd, Physics & Astron, Nat Acad Sci/Nat Res Coun, 90-92; mem panel, Nat Measurement Lab, Nat Inst Stand & Technol, 89-92, Joint Inst Lab Astrophys, 85-, chmn, 89-92. *Mem:* Fel Am Phys Soc. *Res:* Theoretical atomic physics, investigation of atomic shell theory through use of group theory and second quantization techniques; many body theory applied to atoms; interaction of atoms with intense laser beams; electron-atom scattering. *Mailing Add:* Univ Southern Calif Univ Park Off Provost Los Angeles CA 90089. *Fax:* 213-740-7606

ARMSTRONG, LYDIA, CYTOSKELETON. *Current Pos:* SR SCIENTIST, SCHERING-PLOUGH RES INST, 92- *Personal Data:* b Fresno, Calif, May 9, 57. *Educ:* San Diego State Univ, BS, 80; Univ Denver, MS, 85, PhD(cell biol), 82. *Prof Exp:* Res fel, Glaxo Res Inst, 89-92. *Mem:* AAAS; Am Soc Cell Biol. *Res:* Adhesion molecules. *Mailing Add:* Tumor Buol Dept Schering-Plough Res Inst K-15-4 2015 Galloping Hill Rd Kenilworth NJ 07033

ARMSTRONG, MARK L, cardiovascular disease; deceased, see previous edition for last biography

ARMSTRONG, MARTINE YVONNE KATHERINE, MICROBIOLOGY, VIROLOGY. *Current Pos:* SR RES SCIENTIST EPIDEMIOL, YALE UNIV, 75-, CHMN, ANIMAL CARE & USE COMT, 85- *Educ:* Univ London, MB & BS, 55, MD, 68. *Mem:* Am Soc Microbiol. *Res:* Parasitology. *Mailing Add:* Sch Med Yale Univ 60 College St PO Box 208034 New Haven CT 06520-8034

ARMSTRONG, MARVIN DOUGLAS, BIOLOGICAL CHEMISTRY. *Current Pos:* RETIRED. *Personal Data:* b Wilmington, NC, Apr 15, 18; m 46; c 5. *Educ:* Univ SC, BS, 38; Univ Ill, MS, 39, PhD(org chem), 41. *Prof Exp:* Asst biochem, Med Col, Cornell Univ, 41-42 & 46; from asst res prof to assoc res prof biochem, Col Med, Univ Utah, 46-57; chmn, Dept Biochem, Fels Res Inst, Ohio, 57-77, fels prof biol chem & chief, Biochem Sect, Fels Res Inst, Sch Med, Wright State Univ, 77-80. *Mem:* AAAS; Am Chem Soc; Am Soc Biol Chemists. *Res:* Chemistry and metabolism of the amino acids; metabolism of aromatic compounds; hereditary and metabolic disorders; biochemistry of mental disorders. *Mailing Add:* 1899 Arlington Dr Pocatello ID 83204-5052

ARMSTRONG, NEAL EARL, ENVIRONMENTAL ENGINEERING, POLLUTION ECOLOGY. *Current Pos:* assoc prof, 71-79, PROF CIVIL ENG, UNIV TEX, AUSTIN, 79- *Personal Data:* b Dallas, Tex, Jan 29, 41; c 3. *Educ:* Univ Tex, BA, 62, MA, 65, PhD(environ health eng), 68. *Honors & Awards:* Serv Award, Water Pollution Control Fedn, 89. *Prof Exp:* Res engr, Eng-Sci, Inc, 67-68, asst off mgr & consult sanit engr, 68-70, mgr, Washington Res & Develop Lab, 70-71. *Mem:* Ecol Soc Am; Am Soc Limnol & Oceanog; Water Pollution Control Fedn; Int Asn Water Pollution Res; Estuarine Res Fedn (vpres, 75-77); Am Soc Civil Engrs; NAm Lake Mgt Soc. *Res:* Water quality management; water quality analysis; water quality modeling. *Mailing Add:* Dept Civil Eng Univ Tex Austin TX 78712-1076

ARMSTRONG, NEIL A, AERONAUTICAL ENGINEERING. *Current Pos:* CHMN BD, AIL SYSTS, INC, 89- *Personal Data:* b Wapakoneta, Ohio, Aug 5, 30; m; c 2. *Educ:* Purdue Univ, BS, 55. *Hon Degrees:* Univ Southern Calif, MS, 70; Purdue Univ, DEng, 70 & Butler Univ, 72. *Honors & Awards:* Octave Chanute Award, Am Inst Aeronaut & Astronaut, 62; Presidential Medal for Freedom, 69; Kitty Hawk Mem Award, 69; Hubbard Gold Medal, Nat Geog Soc, 70. *Prof Exp:* Joined Lewis Flight Propulsion Lab, NASA, 55, aeronaut res pilot, High Speed Flight Sta, Edwards AFB, Calif, astronaut, 62, backup comdr, Gemini V, 65, prime comdr, Gemini VIII, 66, backup comdr, Gemini XI, 66 & Apollo VIII, 68, prime comdr, Apollo XI, 69 & first man on the moon-July 20; prof eng, Univ Cincinnati, 71-79; chmn bd, Cardwell Int Ltd, 80-82; chmn, CTA Inc, 82-92. *Mem:* Nat Acad Eng; fel Am Inst Aeronaut & Astronaut; fel Soc Exp Test Pilots. *Mailing Add:* PO Box 436 777 Columbus Ave Apt E Lebanon OH 45036

ARMSTRONG, P(AUL) DOUGLAS, HETEROCYCLIC CHEMISTRY, ORGANOFLUORINE CHEMISTRY. *Current Pos:* assoc prof, 85-88, PROF CHEM, OLIVET NAZARENE UNIV, 88- *Personal Data:* b New Albany, Ind, Jan 4, 41; m 70, Moonyean Devine; c Paul & Mary. *Educ:* Ind Univ, BS, 63; Univ Iowa, PhD(org med chem), 68. *Prof Exp:* Res assoc chem under Prof John C Sheehan, Mass Inst Technol, 68-69; asst prof chem, Mass Col Pharm, 69-74; assoc prof, Calif Baptist Col, 74-76, chmn, Div Natural Sci, 75-76; asst prof chem, Carson-Newman Col, 76-78; chemist & qual control dir, Deltona Corp, 78-81; asst prof chem, Union Univ, 81-83; assoc prof chem, Pikeville Col, 83-85. *Concurrent Pos:* Am Chem Soc Acad-Indust Polymer Educ Prog, Tenn Eastman Co, 85; Smith Kline Beckman vis res fel, Univ Iowa, 87; consult, Res Biochem Int, 92- & Jordi Assocs, Inc, 96- *Mem:* Am Chem Soc; Int Soc Heterocyclic Chem. *Res:* Organic synthesis designed to produce novel compounds and/or to elucidate organic mechanisms and/or to determine structure-activity relationships of pharmacologically active compounds. *Mailing Add:* Chem Dept Olivet Nazarene Univ Kankakee IL 60901-0592. *Fax:* 815-939-5071; *E-Mail:* darmstrg@olivet.edu

ARMSTRONG, PETER BROWNELL, CELL BIOLOGY & DEVELOPMENTAL BIOLOGY, COMPARATIVE IMMUNOLOGY. *Current Pos:* From asst prof to assoc prof, 66-79, prof zool, 79-94, PROF MOLECULAR & CELLULAR BIOL, UNIV CALIF, DAVIS, 94- *Personal Data:* b Syracuse, NY, Apr 27, 39; m 62, Margaret Tryon; c Katharine, Elisabeth & Philip. *Educ:* Univ Rochester, BS, 61; Johns Hopkins Univ, PhD(biol), 66. *Concurrent Pos:* Assoc, Clare Hall, Cambridge Univ, 73-74; mem & trustee, Corp Marine Biol Lab, Woods Hole, Mass; regular mem, Cell Biol & Physiol study sect, NIH, 86-90. *Mem:* Am Soc Cell Biol; Soc Develop Biol; Brit Soc Develop Biol; Int Soc Develop & Comp Immunol. *Res:* Physiological basis for cellular adhesion; mechanisms of morphogenetic movements; mechanisms of intercellular invasion; regulation of cell proliferation functions of the extracellular matrix; comparative immunology; alpha-2-macroglobulin. *Mailing Add:* Dept Molecular & Cellular Biol Univ Calif Davis CA 95616-8535. *Fax:* 530-752-1449; *E-Mail:* pbarmstrong@ucdavis.edu

ARMSTRONG, PHILIP E(DWARD), PHYSICAL METALLURGY. *Current Pos:* RETIRED. *Personal Data:* b St Cloud, Minn, Sept 23, 27; m 51; c 4. *Educ:* Iowa State Univ, BS, 50, MS, 52, PhD(metall), 57. *Prof Exp:* Asst, Ames Lab, Iowa State Univ, 50-57; mem staff, Los Alamos Nat Lab, 57-90. *Mem:* Am Soc Metals; Am Inst Mining, Metall & Petrol Engrs. *Res:* Elastic properties of refractory metals and graphites; mechanical properties of metals and alloys. *Mailing Add:* 127 Monte Rey Dr S Los Alamos NM 87544

ARMSTRONG, R(ONALD) W(ILLIAM), MATERIALS SCIENCE, MECHANICAL ENGINEERING. *Current Pos:* asst provost, Div Math Phys Sci & Eng, 85, PROF MAT, UNIV MD, COLLEGE PARK, 68- *Personal Data:* b Baltimore, Md, May 4, 34; m 58, Mary A Manarczyk; c Lisa J & Lori B. *Educ:* Johns Hopkins Univ, BES, 55; Carnegie Inst Technol, MSc, 57, PhD(metall eng), 58. *Hon Degrees:* MA, Brown Univ, 66. *Honors & Awards:* Hardy Gold Medal, Am Inst Mining, Metall & Petrol Engrs, 62. *Prof Exp:* Brit Dept Sci & Indust Res grant, Univ Leeds, 58-59; res metallurgist, Res Labs, Westinghouse Elec Corp, 59-65; assoc prof eng, Brown Univ, 65-68. *Concurrent Pos:* Commonwealth Sci & Indust Res Orgn fel, Australia, 64-65; sr Fulbright-Hays fel, Physics & Eng Lab, Dept Sci & Indust Res, Lower Hutt, NZ, 74; prog mgr, Div Sci Educ Resources Improvement, Directorate Sci Educ, NSF, 76-77; NATO Advan Study Inst lectr, Univ Durham, Eng, 79; US-France coop sci prog lectr, Paris, 80 & Snowmass, Colo, 83; mat sci liaison officer, Europ Sci Off, Off Naval Res, London, 82-84; vis prof, Univ Strathclyde, Scotland, 82-85; vis fel, Clare Hall, Univ Cambridge, Eng, 84; NATO advan study inst contr, Crete, Greece, 85; sabbatical visitor, Cavendish Lab, Univ Cambridge, Eng, 90; liaison scientist, Off Naval Res, Europ Off, London, 91; mem bd gov, Inst Mech & Mat, Univ Calif, San Diego, 93- *Mem:* Soc Eng Sci; fel Am Soc Metals; Am Cryst Assoc; Am Phys Soc; Mat Res Soc. *Res:* Material deformation and fracture; crystal x-ray diffraction; dislocation model calculations. *Mailing Add:* Mech Eng Dept Univ Md College Park MD 20740. *Fax:* 301-314-9477

ARMSTRONG, ROBERT A, surface physics, for more information see previous edition

ARMSTRONG, ROBERT BEALL, MUSCLE PHYSIOLOGY. *Current Pos:* prof & head, 92-95, DISTINGUISHED PROF & HEAD, DEPT HEALTH & KINESIOL, TEX A&M UNIV, 95- *Personal Data:* b Hastings, Nebr, Nov 13, 40; m 66, Ingrid Vaiciulenas; c Edwin J, Andrew N & Sarah E. *Educ:* Hastings Col, BA, 62; Wash State Univ, MS, 70, PhD(exercise physiol), 73. *Honors & Awards:* Citation, Am Col Sports Med, 97. *Prof Exp:* Asst prof biol & health sci, Boston Univ, 73-78; from assoc prof to prof physiol, Oral Roberts Univ, 78-85; prof exercise physiol, Univ Ga, 85-90, res prof, 90-92. *Concurrent Pos:* Assoc zool, Mus Comp Zool, Harvard Univ, 77-87; prin investr, NIH grant, 75-; assoc ed, Med Sci Sports Exercise, 85-87. *Mem:* Am Physiol Soc; fel Am Col Sports Med. *Res:* Skeletal muscle; utilization during locomotion and adaptation to exercise; properties and distributions of fiber types in mammalian skeletal muscles; regulation of blood flow to the muscles during physical exercise. *Mailing Add:* Dept Health & Kinesiol Tex A&M Univ 158 Read Bldg College Station TX 77843. *Fax:* 409-847-8987; *E-Mail:* rb_armstrong@hlkn.tamu.edu

ARMSTRONG, ROBERT G, polymer chemistry, analytical chemistry; deceased, see previous edition for last biography

ARMSTRONG, ROBERT JOHN, HORTICULTURE, GENETICS. *Current Pos:* RES HORTICULTURIST, LONGWOOD GARDENS, 67- *Personal Data:* b Cropsey, Ill, Feb 12, 39. *Educ:* Univ Ill, BS, 62, PhD(hort), 67; Univ Ariz, MS, 63. *Concurrent Pos:* Adj asst prof, Longwood Grad Prog, Univ Del, 68- *Mem:* Am Soc Hort Sci; Am Genetic Asn; Ecol Soc Am. *Res:* New crops research and breeding of ornamental crops; study of the effects of growth regulators and other factors on new ornamental crops, and the development and maintenance of naturalized areas. *Mailing Add:* Longwood Gardens PO Box 501 Kennet Square PA 19348

ARMSTRONG, ROBERT LEE, BIOCHEMISTRY. *Current Pos:* from asst prof to assoc prof, 74-91, PROF CHEM, ALBION COL, 92- *Personal Data:* b Xenia, Ohio, July 15, 39; m 63, Roberta Mack; c Robin M & Douglas R. *Educ:* Heidelberg Col, BS, 61; Ohio State Univ, MS, 63; Mich State Univ, PhD(biochem), 66. *Prof Exp:* NIH fel, Princeton Univ, 66-68; asst prof biochem, Univ Mich, 68-74. *Concurrent Pos:* Sabbatical MSU, 88-89 & 95-96. *Mem:* Am Soc Microbiol; Sigma Xi; AAAS. *Res:* Spore germination; ribosome biosynthesis; antibiotic resistance; in vitro protein syntheses; recombinant DNA. *Mailing Add:* Dept Chem Albion Col Albion MI 49224. *Fax:* 517-629-0509; *E-Mail:* rarustrong@albion.edu

ARMSTRONG, ROBIN L, NUCLEAR MAGNETIC RESONANCE, NEUTRON SCATTERING. *Current Pos:* from asst prof to prof physics, 62-90, from assoc chmn dept to chmn dept, 69-82, dean fac arts & sci, 82-90, PROF PHYSICS, UNIV TORONTO, 96- *Personal Data:* b Galt, Ont, May 14, 35; m 60, Karen E Hansen; c Keir G & C Drew. *Educ:* Univ Toronto, BA, 58, MA, 59, PhD(physics), 61; FRSC, 79. *Honors & Awards:* Herzberg Medal, Can Asn Physicists, 74 & Medal of Achievement, 90. *Prof Exp:* Rutherford Mem fel, Nat Res Coun Can, 61; pres & prof physics, Univ NB, 90-96. *Concurrent Pos:* Founding dir, Can Inst Advan Res, 81-82, res coun, 82-; mem coun, Natural Sci & Eng Res Coun, 91-, exec, 92-, chair, Comt Int Relations, 92-; mem comt, Div Spatially Resolved Magnetic Resonance, Ampere Soc, 93-, vpres, 94-; distinguished visitor, Univ Cordoba, Arg. *Mem:* Can Asn Physicists (pres, 90-91); Int Soc Magnetic Resonance; fel Royal Soc Can; Int Soc Magnetic Resonance Med; Can Inst Neutron Scattering (pres, 86-89). *Res:* Nuclear spin relaxation studies of molecular motions in gases and liquids; nuclear quadrupole resonance, neutron scattering and thermodynamic studies of structural phase transitions; in-vivo magnetic resonance imaging and spectroscopy of rodents; magnetic resonance imaging in material science. *Mailing Add:* Dept Physics Univ Toronto 60 St George St Toronto ON M5S 1A7 Can. *Fax:* 416-978-1547; *E-Mail:* rla@physics.utoronto.ca

ARMSTRONG, SARAH LEE, AQUATIC ECOLOGY. *Current Pos:* PROF & CHAIR BIOL, MILLSAPS COL, 85- *Personal Data:* b Joliet, Ill, Sept 23, 52. *Educ:* Univ Tex, Austin, BA, 74; Univ Calif, Los Angeles, MA, 77; Duke Univ, PhD(zool), 84. *Prof Exp:* Res assoc, Univ Calif, Los Angeles, 75-77; res fel, Smithsonian Inst, 84-85. *Concurrent Pos:* Vis prof curric develop, Rice Univ, 90-93; mem, Curric Revision Task Force, Miss Dept Educ, 94-95; consult, Abt Assoc, 96- *Mem:* Soc Integrative & Comp Biol; AAAS; Am Asn Univ Profs; Sigma Xi. *Res:* Develop science curriculum including classrooms and laboratory materials for college and precollege biology programs. *Mailing Add:* Dept Biol Millsaps Col Jackson MS 39210

ARMSTRONG, THOMAS PEYTON, SPACE PHYSICS. *Current Pos:* from asst prof to assoc prof, 68-74, PROF PHYSICS, UNIV KANS, 74- *Personal Data:* b Atchison, Kans, Nov 24, 41; m 62, Jeanette Fry; c Elizabeth & Stuart. *Educ:* Univ Kans, BS, 62; Univ Iowa, MS, 64, PhD(physics), 66. *Honors & Awards:* NASA Group Achievement for Voyager, Galileo, Ulysses. *Prof Exp:* Res assoc space physics, Univ Iowa, 66-67; res assoc plasma physics, Culham Lab, UK Atomic Energy Auth, Eng, 67-68. *Concurrent Pos:* Br chief, Magnetospheric Physics, NASA Hq, 89-90. *Mem:* AAAS; Am Phys Soc; Am Geophys Union. *Res:* Geomagnetically trapped radiation; solar cosmic ray events; magnetospheric physics; non-linear waves in plasmas; interplanetary energetic particles and plasmas; Jovian and Saturnian magneto-spheres. *Mailing Add:* Dept Physics Univ Kans Lawrence KS 66044. *E-Mail:* armstrong@kuphsx.phsx.ukans.edu

ARMSTRONG, WILLIAM DAVID, physical chemistry, for more information see previous edition

ARMSTRONG, WILLIAM LAWRENCE, ORGANIC CHEMISTRY. *Current Pos:* from asst prof to assoc prof, 65-78, PROF CHEM, 78-, CHMN DEPT, STATE UNIV NY, ONEONTA, 85- *Personal Data:* b Lorain, Ohio, Jan 14, 39; m 75, Suzanne S Beddoe; c Rebecca S, Megan F & Sally A. *Educ:* Oberlin Col, BA, 60; Univ Rochester, PhD(chem), 66. *Prof Exp:* Asst prof chem, State Univ NY Col Geneseo, 64-65. *Mem:* Am Chem Soc; Royal Soc Chem. *Res:* Synthetic organic chemistry. *Mailing Add:* Dept Chem State Univ NY Oneonta NY 13820

ARNAL, ROBERT EMILE, GEOLOGY. *Current Pos:* MEM STAFF, US GEOL SURV, 80- *Personal Data:* b Orleans, France, Sept 10, 22; nat US; m 54; c 3. *Educ:* Univ Poitiers, France, BS, 46; Univ Nancy, France, MS, 48; Univ Southern Calif, PhD(geol), 57. *Prof Exp:* Geophysicist, Cie Gen de Geophysique, France, 48-51; paleontologist, Western Gulf Oil Co, 53-58; asst prof phys sci, San Jose State Col, 58-61, assoc prof geol, 61-69; prof oceanog, Moss Landing Marine Labs, 69-80. *Mem:* Fel Geol Soc Am; Am Asn Petrol Geol; Soc Econ Paleontologists & Mineralogists. *Res:* Shallow water oceanography; micropaleontology environmental studies of recent organisms and tertiary fossils. *Mailing Add:* 170 El Caminito Rd Carmel Valley CA 93924

ARNAOUT, M AMIN, NEPHROLOGY, IMMUNOLOGY. *Current Pos:* ASSOC PROF MED, RENAL UNIT, MASS GEN HOSP, 87- *Personal Data:* b Sidon, Lebanon, Aug 8, 49; US citizen. *Educ:* Am Univ, Beirut, BS, 69, MD, 74. *Prof Exp:* Resident internal med, Am Univ Hosp, Beirut, 74-76; fel immunol, Children's Hosp, Harvard Med Sch, 76-78, fel nephrology, 78-79, instr, 79-82, from asst prof to assoc prof pediat, 82-87. *Mem:* Am Asn Immunologists; Am Soc Nephrology; Int Soc Nephrology; Soc Pediat Res; Am Soc Clin Invest. *Res:* Structure and function of leukocyte membrane molecules involved in adhesion and inflammation. *Mailing Add:* Renal Unit Dept Med Mass Gen Hosp & Harvard Med Sch 149 13th St Charlestown MA 02129-2000

ARNAS, OZER ALI, thermodynamics, heat transfer, for more information see previous edition

ARNASON, BARRY GILBERT WYATT, IMMUNOLOGY, NEUROLOGY. *Current Pos:* dir, Brain Res Inst, 85-93, PROF, DEPT NEUROL, UNIV CHICAGO, 76- *Personal Data:* b Winnipeg, Man, Aug 30, 33; m 60, Joan Morton; c Stephen, Jon & Eva. *Educ:* Univ Man, MD, 57. *Honors & Awards:* Dr Jon Stefansson Mem Prize, 55-56. *Prof Exp:* Intern, Winnipeg Gen Hosp, Man, 56-57, asst resident internal med, 56-58; Nat Mult Sclerosis Soc prin investr, Lab of Dr Pierre Grabar, Inst Sci Res Cancer, Villejuif, France, 62-64; instr, Harvard Med Sch, 64-67, assoc, 67, from asst prof to assoc prof neurol, 68-76. *Concurrent Pos:* Teaching fel neurol, Harvard Med Sch, 58-59 & 61-62, res fel, 59-61; clin & res fel, Lab of Dr Byron H Waksman, 59-61, asst, 64-66, asst neurologist, 66-68, clin fel, Hosp, 61-62; asst resident neurol, Mass Gen Hosp, 58-59, assoc neurologist, 71-76. *Mem:* Am Neurol Asn; Am Acad Neurol; Am Soc Clin Invest; Am Asn Neuropathologists; Am Asn Immunologists. *Res:* Neuroimmunology and multiple sclerosis. *Mailing Add:* Univ Chicago Dept Neurol 5841 S Maryland Ave Chicago IL 60637-2602. *Fax:* 773-702-9076

ARNAUD, CLAUDE DONALD, JR, ENDOCRINOLOGY, PHYSIOLOGY. *Current Pos:* PROF MED & PHYSIOL, UNIV CALIF, SAN FRANCISCO, 77- *Personal Data:* b Hackensack, NJ, Dec 4, 29; m 87; c 2. *Educ:* Columbia Col, BA, 51; NY Med Col, MD, 55. *Prof Exp:* Assoc prof med, Mayo Grad Sch Med, 70-74, prof, 74-77. *Concurrent Pos:* Head mineral res endocrinol, Mayo Clin, 72-74, endocrine res, 74-77; chief, Endocrine Unit, Vet Admin Med Ctr, San Francisco, 77-89; chief, Div Gerontol, Univ Calif, San Francisco, 89-, dir, Ctr Biomed Res Aging, 89- *Mem:* Am Physiol Soc; Am Soc Biol Chemists; Am Soc Clin Invest; Asn Am Physicians; Endocrine Soc; fel AAAS; fel Am Col Endocrinologists. *Res:* Minerals and bones. *Mailing Add:* Ctr Osteoporosis & Bone Health 1710 Scott St 3rd Floor San Francisco CA 94115

ARNAUD, PAUL HENRI, JR, ENTOMOLOGY. *Current Pos:* res entomologist, Calif Acad Sci, 63-64, asst cur, 64-65, assoc cur, 65-72, chmn dept, 68-78, 88-90 & 94, cur entom, 72-94, EMER CUR, CALIF ACAD SCI, 94- *Personal Data:* b San Francisco, Calif, Sept 15, 24; m 70, Madeline Milliet; c Paul Henri & Sandrine. *Educ:* San Jose State Col, AB, 49; Stanford Univ, MA, 50, PhD(biol), 61. *Prof Exp:* Syst entomologist, Bur Entom, Calif Dept Agr, 50-52, 55-56 & 57-59; prin investr med entom, Stanford Univ & Off Surgeon Gen, US Army, Japan, 54-55; entomologist, USDA at US Nat Mus, Washington, DC, 56-57; res entomologist, Calif Acad Sci, 59-61; res fel entom, Am Mus Natural Hist, NY, 61-62. *Concurrent Pos:* Mem, Sefton Found Exped, Gulf Calif, 53 & entom expeds, Baja Calif & Mex, 53, 59 & 63; grants, NSF, 60 & 72-80, USDA, 66-68 & Am Philos Soc Penrose Fund, 72 & 76; assoc, Exp Sta, Univ Calif, Albany, 66-94 & Div Biol Control, Univ Calif, Berkeley, 66-; pres, Pac Coast Entom Soc, 61, treas, 64-81, 93-94. *Mem:* Soc Syst Zool; Entom Soc Am; Am Entom Soc; Russ Entom Soc; Soc Entom France. *Res:* Classification; biology; systematics and distribution of Diptera; zoogeography; evolution. *Mailing Add:* Calif Acad Sci Golden Gate Park San Francisco CA 94118-4599. *Fax:* 415-750-7228; *E-Mail:* parnaud@calacademy.org

ARNAUD, PHILIPPE, IMMUNOCHEMISTRY, PROTEIN PURIFICATION. *Current Pos:* CONSULT, 87- *Personal Data:* b Saint-Etienne, France, Mar 30, 35; m 61, Marie-Laure Boigues; c 3. *Educ:* Faculte Des Sci, Lyon, France, BS, 55; Univ Claude Bernard, MD, 69; Med Univ SC, PhD(immunol), 77. *Prof Exp:* Resident, Med Univ, Lyon, France, 64-68; instr biochem, Univ Claude Bernard, France, 66-69, asst prof, 70-75, chef de travaux, 75-77; from asst prof to prof immunol, Med Univ SC, 77-84, dir res & develop, Dept Immunol, 85, dir, Lab Molecular Genetics, 88; vis scientist, Biochem Lab, Nat Cancer Inst, NIH, 85-87. *Concurrent Pos:* Adj prof molecular genetics, Univ Genova, Italy; inter govt personnel act, Nat Cancer Inst, 85 & 86. *Mem:* AAAS; Am Soc Human Genetics; Am Asn Immunologists; Electrophoresis Soc. *Res:* New techniques for protein isolation and purification--microheterogeneity and poly morphism of proteins and their structural basis; effect of acute-phase proteins on the immune response; regulation of acute-phase proteins; gene expression. *Mailing Add:* Dept Microbiol & Immunol Lab Molecular Genetics Med Univ SC Charleston SC 29425-0002. *Fax:* 803-792-2464; *E-Mail:* arnaudp@musc.edu

ARNBERG, ROBERT LEWIS, NONCOMMUNICATIVE RINGS, HARMONIC ANALYSIS. *Current Pos:* OR ANALYST, US GEOL SURV, 89- *Personal Data:* b San Francisco, Calif, Mar 19, 45; m 67; c Christopher. *Educ:* Univ Calif, Berkelely, AB, 67; Univ Ore, MA, 69. *Prof Exp:* Sr programmer, Consult & Designers, 75-76; teacher math, George Washington Univ, 76-78; systs analyst, Data Transformation Corp, 78-79; programmer-analyst, Nat Econ Res Assoc, 79-80; res fel, Logistics Mgt Inst, 80-88. *Concurrent Pos:* Consult, 76-78; book-film reviewer, AAAS, 76-; adj asst prof computer sci-mgt, Univ Col, Univ Md, 88-89. *Mem:* Am Math Soc; Math Asn Am; Soc Indust & Appl Math; AAAS; NY Acad Sci; Int Cong Mathematicians. *Res:* Design and development of scientific and statistical computer applications including energy modelling, logistical modelling and financial modelling; computer systems management; management control analysis of administrative information systems; management and operations of local area networks; optimization theory. *Mailing Add:* 11635 Stoneview Sq No 1B Reston VA 22091-2935. *Fax:* 703-648-7229; *E-Mail:* rarnberg@usgs.gov

ARNDT, HENRY CLIFFORD, ORGANIC CHEMISTRY. *Current Pos:* Asst res scientist, 72-73, assoc res scientist, 73-76, RES SCIENTIST CHEM, MILES LABS INC, 76- *Personal Data:* b Caldwell, Idaho, Sept 3, 45; m 69; c 2. *Educ:* Univ Idaho, BS, 67; Univ Wis-Madison, MS, 72, PhD(org chem), 76. *Mem:* Am Chem Soc. *Res:* Total synthesis of natural products and prostaglandin analogs; new methods in organic synthesis. *Mailing Add:* Miles Labs Inc PO Box 40 Elkhart IN 46515-0040

ARNDT, RICHARD ALLEN, PHYSICS. *Current Pos:* from asst prof to assoc prof, 67-78, PROF PHYSICS, VA POLYTECH INST & STATE UNIV, 78- *Personal Data:* b Cleveland, Ohio, Jan 3, 33; m 53; c 4. *Educ:* Case Inst Technol, BS, 57; Univ Calif, Berkeley, MA, 62, PhD(physics), 65. *Prof Exp:* Engr, Northrop Corp, Calif, 57-59; physicist, Lawrence Radiation Lab, Univ Calif, 59-67. *Res:* Elementary particle physics; dispersion relations in nucleon-nucleon scattering; single boson exchange contribution to nucleon-nucleon scattering. *Mailing Add:* Physics Dept Va Polytech & State Univ Blacksburg VA 24061

ARNDT, ROGER EDWARD ANTHONY, HYDROMECHANICS, HYDRAULIC ENGINEERING. *Current Pos:* dir & prof, 77-93, PROF & CHMN, FLUID MECH, ST ANTHONY FALLS HYDRAUL LAB, UNIV MINN, 93- *Personal Data:* b New York, NY, May 25, 35; m 90, Jane Pfund; c Larysa & Tanya. *Educ:* City Col New York, BCE, 60; Mass Inst Technol, SM, 62, PhD, 67. *Honors & Awards:* First Theodore Ranov Dist Lectr; Lorenz G Straub Award; Alexander Von Humboldt Sr Scientist Award; Fluids Eng Award, Am Soch Mech Engrs. *Prof Exp:* Chemist, Consol Testing Labs, 56-57; res asst hydrodyn, Mass Inst Technol, 60-62; res engr, Allegany Ballistics Lab, 62-63; sr res engr, Lockheed-Calif Co, 63-64; asst prof aerospace eng, 67-71, assoc prof, Pa State Univ, 71-77. *Concurrent Pos:* Consult, Army Aeronaut Res Lab, Ill Inst Technol Res Inst & Bell Aerospace Corp, Richards of Rockford, Yarway Corp, Wylie Labs, Off Naval Res-London, Neth Ships Model Basin, Honeywell Corp, Bolt Beranek & Newman, Inc, US Bur Reclamation, Babcock & Wilcox Co, Thermal Systs Inc, ScMed Inc, Indeco Inc, Metals Selling Corp, Henkel Corp, UN. *Mem:* Assoc fel Am Inst Aeronaut & Astronaut; Acous Soc Am; fel Am Soc Mech Engrs; Am Soc Civil Engrs; Int Asn Hydraul Res. *Res:* Cavitation in turbulent shear flows both Newtonian and non-Newtonian liquids being considered; hydraulic turbine hydrodynamics and hydropower; aerodynamic noise, especially jet noise and noise induced by other turbulent shear flows. *Mailing Add:* NSF 4201 Wilson Blvd Rm 525 Arlington VA 22230. *E-Mail:* arndt001@maroon.tc.umn.edu

ARNDT, STEPHAN, BIO-BEHAVIORAL STATISTICS, DATA QUALITY CONTROL. *Current Pos:* DIR BIOSTATIST CORE, MENT HEALTH CLIN RES CTR, 88- *Personal Data:* b New York, NY, Dec 6, 51. *Educ:* Loyola Univ, Los Angeles, BS, 74; Claremont Grad Sch, MA, 76, PhD(psychol), 80. *Prof Exp:* Coordr comput serv, Claremont Grad Sch, 77-78; res psychologist, Univ Calif, Los Angeles, 78-80, fel, 80-81; chief statist consult, Univ Notre Dame, 81-88. *Concurrent Pos:* Statist ed, Am J Ment Deficiency, 82-86 & Am J Psychiat, 93-; dir res, Jurix Graphics, 92- *Mem:* Am Statist Asn. *Res:* Applications of statistics to medical imaging of the human brain, longitudinal studies using nonparametric methods, and statistical issues in data base quality assurance for research. *Mailing Add:* MH-CRC 2911 JPP Univ Iowa Hosps & Clins 200 Hawkins Dr Iowa City IA 52242-1057. *E-Mail:* stephan_arndt@uiowa.edu

ARNELL, JOHN CARSTAIRS, PHYSICAL CHEMISTRY. *Current Pos:* RETIRED. *Personal Data:* b Halifax, NS, Apr 4, 18; m 42, 75, Celia Campbell; c Susan, Elizabeth & Peggy. *Educ:* Dalhousie Univ, BSc, 39, MSc, 40; McGill Univ, PhD(phys chem), 42. *Prof Exp:* Supt, Defence Res Chem Labs, 49-54, dir sci intel, 55-58, dir plans, 58; sci adv, Royal Can Air Force, 58-63 & Royal Can Navy, 63-64; sci dep chief logistics, eng & develop, Can Forces Hq, Ottawa, 64, sci dep chief tech serv, 64-66; asst dep minister finance, Can Dept Nat Defence, Nat Defence Hq, 66-73; prog consult, Finance Ministry, 73-76, coordr metrication, Govt Bermuda, 75-76. *Mem:* Fel Chem Inst Can; assoc fel Can Aeronaut & Space Inst; Sigma Xi. *Res:* Overall management of planning, programming budgeting and financial management systems for defense. *Mailing Add:* PO Box HM 1263 Hamilton HMFX Bermuda. *Fax:* 441-236-4646

ARNELL, WALTER JAMES, SYSTEMS & INDUSTRIAL ENGINEERING. *Current Pos:* PRES & CONSULT, LENRA ASSOCS LTD, 77- *Personal Data:* b Farnborough, Eng, Jan 9, 24; US citizen; m 55, Patricia; c Sean, Victoria & Sara. *Educ:* Univ London, BSc, 53, PhD, 67; Occidental Col, MA, 56; Univ Southern Calif, MS, 58. *Prof Exp:* Lectr mech eng, City Univ & London Polytech Cols, 48-53; instr gen & aeronaut eng, Univ Southern Calif, 54-59; from asst prof to assoc prof mech eng, Calif State Col, Long Beach, 59-66, chmn dept, 64-65, actg chmn, Div Eng, 64-66, prof mech eng, 66-71, dean, 67-69; researcher, Ctr Eng Res & mem grad affil fac, Dept Ocean Eng, Col Eng, Univ Hawaii, 70-76. *Concurrent Pos:* Dir Cannon Elec Co, Calif, 57-63; consult, Human Factors Inc, 58, Arrowhead Prod, 62-63, Taper Tubes, Inc, 64-65 & Northrup Inst Technol, 69-70; chmn & co-dir, Hawaii Simulation Lab, 71-72; mem bd dirs, Rehab Hosp of the Pac, Honolulu, 75-78; adj prof systems & indust eng, Univ Ariz, 81- *Mem:* Am Inst Aeronaut & Astronaut; Human Factors Soc; Inst Elec & Electronics Engrs; Brit Psychol Soc; Am Psychol Asn; Royal Aeronaut Soc; Ergonomics Soc. *Res:* Man-machine systems; human performance in systems; human factors. *Mailing Add:* 4491 E Ft Lowell Rd Tucson AZ 85712. *Fax:* 520-881-1710; *E-Mail:* lenra@azstarnet.com

ARNEMAN, HAROLD FREDERICK, SOILS. *Current Pos:* from instr to assoc prof, 46-61, prof, 61-80, EMER PROF SOILS, UNIV MINN, ST PAUL, 80- *Personal Data:* b Mankato, Minn, May 31, 15; c 1. *Educ:* Univ Minn, BS, 39, MS, 46, PhD, 50. *Prof Exp:* Soil surveyor, Univ Minn, 35-40; farm credit apprentice, Fed Land Bank, Minn, 40-42. *Res:* Mineralogical and physical studies of soils. *Mailing Add:* 1403 California Ave W St Paul MN 55108

ARNER, DALE H, APPLIED PLANT & BEAVER ECOLOGY, RESTORATION & MANAGEMENT OF DISTURBED ECOSYSTEMS. *Current Pos:* from asst prof to assoc prof wildlife ecol, Miss State Univ, 62-68, prof wildlife, fisheries & zool & head Dept Wildlife & Fisheries, 68-87, EMER PROF HABITAT MGT & ANALYSIS & HEAD DEPT, MISS STATE UNIV, 87- *Personal Data:* b Weissport, Pa, Feb 10, 20; m 45, Julia Bentley; c Martha J. *Educ:* Pa State Univ, BS, 49, MS, 54; Auburn Univ, PhD(wildlife mgt), 59. *Honors & Awards:* C W Watson Award, Am Fisheries Soc/Wildlife Soc. *Prof Exp:* Hatchery asst, Pa Fish Comn, 41; wildlife field supt, Md Game & Inland Fish Comn, 48-54; biologist, Soil Conserv Serv, USDA, Ala, 57-62. *Concurrent Pos:* Consult, Asplundh, Fish & Wildlife Serv, Environ Protection Agency, Dept Interior, Nat Parks, Miss, 76-78. *Mem:* Hon mem Wildlife Soc; Audubon Soc; Sigma Xi. *Res:* Beaver ecology; utility line rights-of-way management and habitat management for upland game and waterfowl; author or co-author of 70 publications. *Mailing Add:* 209 Seville Pl Starkville MS 39759

ARNESON, DORA WILLIAMS, DRUG DEVELOPMENT, PROJECT MANAGEMENT. *Current Pos:* sr chemist, Midwest Res Inst, 84-91, prin chemist, 91-92, sect head toxicol & metab, 92-95, SECT MGR CLIN SCI, MIDWEST RES INST, KANSAS CITY, MO, 95- *Personal Data:* b Fayetteville, Ark, Aug 4, 47; div. *Educ:* Univ Mo, BA, 67, PhD(anal chem), 72. *Prof Exp:* Instr analytical biochem, Ctr Health Sci, Univ Tenn, Memphis, 72-77; actg chief, Univ Tenn Ctr Health Sci, Memphis, 77-79, assoc dir clin biochem, child develop ctr, 79-83, asst prof biochem & pediat, Col Med, 77-83. *Mem:* Am Chem Soc; Soc Inherited Metab Disorders; Am Asn Cancer Res; Drug Info Asn. *Res:* Preclinical and clinical pharmaceutical development bioanalysis toxicology studies. *Mailing Add:* Midwest Res Inst 425 Volker Blvd Kansas City MO 64110. *Fax:* 816-753-8823

ARNESON, PHIL ALAN, PLANT PATHOLOGY. *Current Pos:* AT DEPT NUTRIT SERV, CORNELL UNIV. *Personal Data:* b Fergus Falls, Minn, May 17, 40; m 63; c 2. *Educ:* Carleton Col, BA, 62; Univ Wis, PhD(plant path), 67. *Prof Exp:* Plant pathologist, Trop Res Div, United Fruit Co, 67-70; asst prof, 70-76, assoc prof plant path, Cornell Univ, 76- *Mem:* Am Phytopath Soc. *Res:* Orchard replant problems; soil fumigation; nematicides; integrated pest management; computer simulation modeling; pest management curriculum development. *Mailing Add:* Plant Path Cornell Univ Main Campus 334 Plant Sci Bldg Ithaca NY 14853-0001

ARNESON, RICHARD MICHAEL, BIOCHEMISTRY. *Current Pos:* RETIRED. *Personal Data:* b Fergus Falls, Minn, Oct 18, 38; m 73, Dora Williams. *Educ:* Univ Minn, BA, 60; Duke Univ, PhD(biochem), 71. *Prof Exp:* From instr to asst prof biochem, Ctr Health Sci, Univ Tenn, Memphis, 71-79; biochemist, Oak Ridge Assoc Univs, 79-80; fel, Oak Ridge Nat Lab, 81 & Univ Ga, Athens, 82; Mid-Career Develop fel environ toxicol, Univ Iowa, Iowa City, 82-84; fel, Minneapolis Med Res Found, 85. *Mem:* Sigma Xi. *Res:* Free radical biochemistry. *Mailing Add:* 2716 Blaidell Ave S #207 Minneapolis MN 55408-1529

ARNETT, EDWARD MCCOLLIN, PHYSICAL ORGANIC CHEMISTRY. *Current Pos:* R J Reynolds Industs prof, 80-92, EMER R J REYNOLDS INDUSTS PROF, DUKE UNIV, 92- *Personal Data:* b Philadelphia, Pa, Sept 25, 22; m 51, 69, Sylvia Gettmann; c 5. *Educ:* Univ Pa, BA, 43, MS, 47, PhD(chem), 49. *Honors & Awards:* James Flack Norris Award, 77; Pittsburgh Award, 76; Kelly lectr, Purdue Univ, 77; Petrol Chem Award, Am Chem Soc, 85. *Prof Exp:* Asst instr qual, inorg, anal & org chem, Univ Pa, 43-46, 47; res dir, Max Levy & Co, 49-53; asst prof, Western Md Col, 53-55; res fel, Harvard Univ, 55-57; from asst prof to assoc prof gen & org chem, Univ Pittsburgh, 57-64, prof, 64-80. *Concurrent Pos:* Vis lectr, Univ Ill, 63; adj sr fel, Mellon Inst, 64-; distinguished lectr, Howard Univ, 66 & Guggenheim fel, 68-69; dir, Pittsburgh Chem Info Ctr, 68-; mem adv bd, Petrol Res Fund, 68-; comt chem info, Nat Res Coun, 69-; vis prof, Univ Kent, 70; sr fel, Inst Hydrocarbon Chem, Univ Southern Calif, 80-; A Cope scholar award, Am Chem Soc, 90. *Mem:* Nat Acad Sci; Fel AAAS; Am Chem Soc; Royal Soc Chem. *Res:* Acid base behavior of organic compounds; solvent effects in organic chemistry; organic monolayers; stereochemistry of aggregation. *Mailing Add:* Dept Chem Duke Univ Durham NC 27706. *Fax:* 919-660-1605

ARNETT, JERRY BUTLER, GENERAL ENGINEERING, PHYSICS. *Current Pos:* electronic engr, 77-80, SYSTS STUDY ENGR, AERONAUT SYSTS DIV, WRIGHT-PATTERSON AFB, USAF, 80- *Personal Data:* b Pike Co, Ohio, July 19, 38; m 62, Sharon Hossler; c Katherine & David. *Educ:* Ohio Univ, BS, 60, MS, 63; NMex State Univ, PhD(Physics), 67. *Prof Exp:* Res & teaching asst physics, Ohio Univ, 60-62; res engr, Los Angeles Div, NAm Aviation, 62-64; sr res scientist remote sensing & space physics, Gen Dynamics Ft Worth & Convair, 67-73; staff scientist, Technol Inc, Dayton, Ohio, 73-76; radar engr, BDM Serv Inc, Dayton, 76-77. *Concurrent Pos:* Instr, Tex Wesleyan Col, 70 & Tex Christian Univ, 70-71. *Mem:* Sigma Xi, Air Force Asn. *Res:* Innovative systems and applications directed toward near term and future Air Force aeronautical and transatmospheric missions; operational analyses of future weapon systems; application of modeling and simulation to acquisition of future aeronautical systems. *Mailing Add:* ASD/YDE Wright-Patterson AFB OH 45433-6503. *E-Mail:* arnettjb@b1b.wpafb.af.mil

ARNETT, ROSS HAROLD, JR, ENTOMOLOGY. *Current Pos:* PROF ENTOM, UNIV FLA, GAINESVILLE, 82- *Personal Data:* b Medina, NY, Apr 13, 19; m 42, Mary Ennis; c Ross H III, Michael J, Mary A, Barbara E, Frances X, Joseph A, Bernadette T & Matthew C. *Educ:* Cornell Univ, BS, 42, MS, 46, PhD(entom), 48. *Prof Exp:* Asst entom, Cornell Univ, 46-48; entomologist, Div Insects, USDA, 48-54; head dept biol, St John Fisher Col, 54-58; from assoc prof to prof biol, Cath Univ, 58-66, head dept, 63-66; prof entom, Purdue Univ, 66-70; res biologist, Tall Timbers Res Sta, 71-73; prof biol, Siena Col, NY, 73-79; prof & dir, Oxycopis Pond Res Sta, Kenderhook, NY, 79-82. *Concurrent Pos:* Asst, State Conserv Dept, NY, 42; instr, US Army Sch Malariol, CZ, 44-45; founder & ed, Coleopterists Bull; exec dir, Biol Res Inst Am, Inc, 73-80; founder & ed, Insecta Mundi, 85- *Mem:* AAAS; Am Soc Zool; Soc Syst Zool; Soc Study Evolution; hon mem Entom Soc Am; Am Inst Biol Sci; Nat Asn Biol Teachers; Bot Soc Am. *Res:* Taxonomy of Coleoptera; biology of mosquitoes; Onychophora; revision of world Oedemeridae; experimental systematic biology; desert biology. *Mailing Add:* 2406 NW 47th Terr Gainesville FL 32606. *Fax:* 352-371-0962; *E-Mail:* oedemeridae@msn.com

ARNETT, WILLIAM DAVID, ASTROPHYSICS, COMPUTATIONAL PHYSICS. *Current Pos:* PROF ASTROPHYS, UNIV ARIZ, 88-, PROF ASTRON, 95- *Personal Data:* b Williamson, WVa, May 2, 40; c 2. *Educ:* Univ Ky, BS, 61; Yale Univ, MS, 63, PhD(physics), 65. *Prof Exp:* NASA-Nat Res Coun resident res assoc, Goddard Inst Space Studies, NY, 65-67; res fel physics, Kellogg Radiation Lab, Calif Inst Technol, 67-69; asst prof space sci, Rice Univ, 69-71; assoc prof astron & physics, Univ Tex, Austin, 71-74; prof astrophys, Univ Ill, Urbana, 74-76; prof astrophys, Univ Chicago, 76-88; distinguished serv prof, Enrico Fermi Inst, 76-88. *Concurrent Pos:* Consult, Lawrence Radiation Lab, 66-67; fel, Alfred P Sloan Found, 70-72; comt space astron & astrophys, Nat Acad Sci/Nat Res Coun. *Mem:* Nat Acad Sci; Am Astron Soc; Am Phys Soc; Int Astron Union. *Mailing Add:* Stuart Observ Univ Ariz Tucson AZ 85721

ARNETT, WILLIAM HAROLD, ECONOMIC ENTOMOLOGY. *Current Pos:* asst prof & asst entomologist, Univ Nev, Reno, 60-65, assoc prof & assoc entomologist, 65-74, prof & entomologist, 74-88, EMER PROF, UNIV NEV, RENO, 88- *Personal Data:* b Louisville, Miss, June 13, 28; m 57; c 3. *Educ:* Miss State Univ, BS, 55, MS, 57; Kans State Univ, PhD(entom), 60. *Prof Exp:* Instr entom, Kans State Univ, 57-60. *Mem:* AAAS; Entom Soc Am; Sigma Xi. *Res:* Biology, ecology and control of agricultural insect pests; forage and animal insects; pollinators; pollination. *Mailing Add:* 156 Bret Harte Ave Reno NV 89509

ARNFIELD, ANTHONY JOHN, PHYSICAL GEOGRAPHY, CLIMATOLOGY. *Current Pos:* From asst prof to assoc prof, 72-90, PROF GEOG & ATMOSPHERIC SCI, OHIO STATE UNIV, 90-, ENVIRON SCI GRAD PROG, 93- *Personal Data:* b Nuneaton, Eng, Jan 2, 45; m 69. *Educ:* Univ Wales, BA, 66; McMaster Univ, MA, 68, PhD(geog), 73. *Mem:* Royal Meteorol Soc; Am Meteorol Soc; Inst Brit Geographers; Asn Am Geographers; Asn Brit Climatologists; AAAS. *Res:* Microclimatology; radiation climatology; investigation of the fluxes of energy, mass and momentum across the earth-atmosphere interface, especially as determined by surface properties; urban surface energy budgets; urban climatology. *Mailing Add:* Dept Geog Ohio State Univ 154 N Oval Mall 1036 Derby Hall Columbus OH 43210-1361. *Fax:* 614-292-6213; *E-Mail:* aja+@osu.edu

ARNHEIM, NORMAN, MOLECULAR BIOLOGY, EVOLUTION. *Current Pos:* asst prof biochem, 68-74, ASSOC PROF BIOCHEM, STATE UNIV NY, STONY BROOK, 74- *Personal Data:* b New York, NY, Dec 24, 38; m 68; c 2. *Educ:* Univ Rochester, BA, 60, MS, 62; Univ Calif, Berkeley, PhD(genetics), 66. *Prof Exp:* Res biochemist, Dept Biochem, Univ Calif, Berkeley, 67-68. *Mem:* Genetics Soc Am; Am Soc Biol Chemists; Am Soc Naturalists. *Res:* Molecular biology; multi-gene evolution. *Mailing Add:* Dept Molecular Biol Univ Southern Calif Los Angeles CA 90089-1340

ARNHEITER, HEINZ, DEVELOPMENTAL MOLECULAR GENETICS. *Current Pos:* vis scientist, Lab Molecular Genetics, Nat Inst Neurol & Commun Dis & Stroke, 86-88, CHIEF, VIRAL PATHOGENESIS SECT, LAB DEVELOP NEUROGENTICS, MAMMALIAN DEVELOP SECT, NIH, 88- *Personal Data:* b St Gallen, Switz, May 2, 51. *Educ:* Kantonsschule St Gallen, BA, 70; Univ Zurich, MD, 78. *Prof Exp:* Res fel, Inst Immunol & Virol, Univ Zurich, Switz, 77-81, Lab Molecular Genetics, NIH, 81-82, Fogarty Int fel, Nat Inst Neurol & Commun Dis & Stroke, 82-83, vis assoc, 83-84; oberassistent, Inst Immunol & Virol, Univ Zurich, 84-86. *Concurrent Pos:* Fel, Int Union Against Cancer, 79; res grant, Swiss NSF, 84; ad hoc mem, Team Prog Proj Grant, Scripps Clin, 89; ad hoc consult, Neurobiol Dis Prog Proj Rev A Comt, 89. *Mem:* Am Soc Cell Biol; Am Soc Microbiol; Am Soc Interferon Res; AAAS. *Res:* Molecular genetics of mammalian development, particularly of the vertebra and neural crest. *Mailing Add:* Lab Develop Neurogenetics Mammalian Develop Sect NINDS-NIH Bldg 36 Rm 5D04 Bethesda MD 20892. *E-Mail:* heinz@zippy.nimh.nih.gov

ARNHOLT, PHILIP JOHN, BOTANY. *Current Pos:* asst prof, 71-81, PROF BIOL, 89-, DIV CHMN BIOL, CONCORDIA UNIV, WIS, 85- *Personal Data:* b Danville, Ill, May 16, 40; m 64, Karen L Bartel; c 2. *Educ:* Eastern Ill Univ, BSEd, 63, MSEd, 67; Univ Nebr, PhD(bot), 73. *Prof Exp:* Teacher biol, Dixon High Sch, Ill, 63-67 & LaSalle-Peru Twp High Sch, Ill, 67-68. *Mem:* Bot Soc Am; Nat Asn Biol Teachers; Nat Audubon Soc. *Res:* Morphology and histochemistry of grasses. *Mailing Add:* 10910 N San Marino Dr Thiensville WI 53092

ARNISON, PAUL GRENVILLE, MOLECULAR BIOLOGY. *Current Pos:* GEN MGR, FAAR BIOTECH, 93-; PRES, BOTANICAL ALTERNATIVES INC, 93- *Personal Data:* b Clatterbridge, Eng, Aug 9, 49; Can citizen. *Educ:* McGill Univ, BSc, 70, PhD(plant physiol), 75. *Prof Exp:* Asst prof biol, Northeastern Univ, 75-78; asst prof, Dept Biol, St Francis Xavier Univ, NS, 78-79; asst prof to assoc prof, Dept Biol, Univ New Brunswick, NS, 79-81; supvr agr res, Allied Chem Can, Ltd, 81-85; res dir, Paladin Hybrids Inc, 85-90, gen mgr, 90-93. *Res:* Anther and microspore culture of Brassica Napus, Campestris and Oleracea; microscope specific gene characterization; gene regulation via antisense RNA; use of doubled-haploid hybrids in crop improvement; transformation of plants; development of new hybrid systems. *Mailing Add:* 1612 Marcoux Dr Orleans ON K1E 2K6 Can. *Fax:* 613-834-5265; *E-Mail:* faarbio1@magi.com

ARNO, STEPHEN FRANCIS, FOREST ECOLOGY. *Current Pos:* forester, 70-71, RES FORESTER, US FOREST SERV, 71- *Personal Data:* b Seattle, Wash, Oct 1, 43; m 64; c 2. *Educ:* Wash State Univ, BS, 65; Univ Mont, MF, 66, PhD(forestry, plant sci), 70. *Prof Exp:* Park ranger & naturalist, US Nat Park Serv, 63-65; instr forestry, Univ Mont, 67. *Mem:* Nat Areas Asn; Soc Am Foresters. *Res:* Phytosociology; forest succession; phytogeography; silvicultural use of prescribed fire in western forests; dendrology; effects of fire on forest and range vegetation. *Mailing Add:* Intermountain Fire Sci Lab PO Box 8089 Missoula MT 59807-8089

ARNOLD, ALLEN PARKER, ORGANIC CHEMISTRY, FUEL TECHNOLOGY. *Current Pos:* CONSULT 84- *Personal Data:* b Oshkosh, Wis, June 25, 23; m 94, Betty Brandenburg; c Gwenyth A & Deborah A (DeChavez). *Educ:* Oberlin Col, AB, 44; Case Inst Technol, MS, 57, PhD(chem), 58. *Prof Exp:* Jr analytical chemist, Shell Chem Corp, Calif, 44-45 & 46-47; res assoc org chem, Case Inst Technol, 47-48; res chemist, Cleveland Indust Res, Inc, Euclid, 48-62, asst lab dir, 62-72; group leader res & develop, Lubrizol Corp, 72-84. *Concurrent Pos:* Adj asst prof chem, Univ NC, Asheville; fuel additive sem, India, 87. *Mem:* Am Chem Soc; Sigma Xi. *Res:* Organic synthesis, particularly phosphorus chemistry. *Mailing Add:* 32 Wagon Trail Black Mountain NC 28711-2533

ARNOLD, ARTHUR PALMER, NEUROBIOLOGY. *Current Pos:* from asst prof to assoc prof, PROF PSYCHOL, UNIV CALIF, LOS ANGELES, 76- *Personal Data:* b Philadelphia, Pa, Mar 16, 46; m 67, Caroline Scheaffer; c Jennifer E & Matthew W. *Educ:* Grinnell Col, AB, 67; Rockefeller Univ, PhD(neurobiol), 74. *Prof Exp:* Instr psychol, Cent State Univ, Ohio, 68-69. *Mem:* Soc Neurosci; AAAS. *Res:* Sex differences in the brain; steroid hormone effects on neurons. *Mailing Add:* 2700 Selby Ave Los Angeles CA 90064

ARNOLD, BEN ALLEN, MEDICAL X-RAY IMAGING RESEARCH, BONE DENSITOMETRY FOR OSTEOPOROSIC EVALUATION. *Current Pos:* PRES & FOUNDER IMAGE ANALYSIS INC, 85- *Personal Data:* b Columbia, Ky, Jan 28, 45; c 3. *Educ:* Centre Col, BA, 67; Yale Univ, MS, 69; Harvard Univ, PhD(med physics), 77. *Prof Exp:* Assoc prof radiol sci, Univ Calif, Irvine, 77-79; dir physic & assoc prof, SBay Hosp, Univ Calif, Los Angeles, 79-81; vpres & dir res, Healthcare Affil, 81-84. *Res:* Medical imaging research in digital angiography and mammography; development of techniques and instrumentation for measurement of bone density as a test for osteoporosis; developed a patented technique using a ct scanner for bone densitometry of the spine and a new device for bone densitometry of the fingers. *Mailing Add:* Image Analysis Inc 1430 Burkesville Rd Columbia KY 42728. *Fax:* 502-384-6405

ARNOLD, BRADFORD HENRY, PURE MATHEMATICS. *Current Pos:* RETIRED. *Personal Data:* b Chehalis, Wash, Oct 14, 16; m 41. *Educ:* Univ Wash, BS, 38, MS, 40; Princeton Univ, PhD(math), 42. *Prof Exp:* Instr math, Purdue Univ, 42-44, 46; major aerodynamicist, Boeing Airplane Co, 44-46; asst prof, Mont State Col, 46-47; from asst prof to prof math, Ore State Univ, 47-81, asst chmn dept, 72-79, emer prog math, 82. *Concurrent Pos:* Fulbright grants, Iraq, 57-58, China, 62-63 & 69-70. *Mem:* Am Math Soc. *Res:* Topology and abstract algebra. *Mailing Add:* Holladay Park Plaza 1300 NE 16th Ave Apt 809 Portland OR 97232-1454

ARNOLD, C(HARLES) W(ILLIAM), PETROLEUM ENGINEERING. *Current Pos:* res supvr, 59-64, res mgr, 64-76, SR RES ADV, EXXON PROD RES CO, 76- *Personal Data:* b Goree, Tex, June 13, 23; m 51; c 5. *Educ:* Univ Okla, BS, 44; Univ Tex, MS, 50, PhD(chem eng), 54. *Prof Exp:* Prin & teacher pub sch, Tex, 45-46; res engr, Humble Oil & Refining Co, 54-59. *Mem:* Am Chem Soc; Soc Petrol Engrs; Am Inst Mining, Metall & Petrol Engrs; Sigma Xi. *Res:* Petroleum production research; enhanced oil recovery. *Mailing Add:* 4609 Redstart Houston TX 77035-5019

ARNOLD, CHARLES, JR, POLYMER CHEMISTRY. *Current Pos:* RETIRED. *Personal Data:* b Brooklyn, NY, May 29, 30; m 59, Claudia J Hamill; c Stephen, Joseph, Peter, Ann, Jane & Susan. *Educ:* Yale Univ, BS, 52; Purdue Univ, MS, 54, PhD(org chem), 57. *Prof Exp:* From res chemist to sr res chemist, E I du Pont de Nemours & Co, 57-67; mem staff polymer chem, Sandia Nat Labs, 67-85, distinguished mem tech staff, 85-94. *Mem:* Am Chem Soc; Soc Advan Mat & Process Engrs. *Res:* Thermal and radiative degradation of polymers; development of novel polyurethanes for encapsulation of electronic components; development of battery membranes and solid polymer electrolytes; thin films. *Mailing Add:* 3436 Tahoe St Albuquerque NM 87111-5435. *Fax:* 505-290-5712; *E-Mail:* carn789@flash.net

ARNOLD, D(ONALD) S(MITH), CHEMICAL ENGINEERING, ENVIRONMENTAL ENGINEERING. *Current Pos:* RETIRED. *Personal Data:* b Summit Co, Ohio, Sept 14, 20; m 44, Eleanor Webster; c Ann, Jane, Elaine, Dale, David & Douglas. *Educ:* Ohio State Univ, BChE, 42, MSc, 47, PhD(chem eng), 49. *Honors & Awards:* Kirkpatrick Award Chem Eng Achievement, 63. *Prof Exp:* Instr chem eng, NC State Col, 47-48, asst prof, 48-53, res engr, 51-53; supvr process develop, Nat Lead Co, Ohio, 53-54, head, Chem Dept, 54-59; head, High Energy Fuels Sect, Am Potash & Chem Corp, Calif, 59, res mgr, Trona Lab, 59-67, dir cent eng, 67-69, dir process planning & develop, 69-70; proj mgr, Kerr-McGee Corp, 70-72, consult to tech dir, 72, chief process engr, 72-78, sr proj engr, 78-79, mgr resource develop, 79-80, sr tech adv, 80-83, engr specialist, 83-91. *Concurrent Pos:* Mem, Joint Comt Uranium Concentrate Specifications, US AEC, 54-59; mem, Design Inst Phys Properties, Am Inst Chem Engrs, 80-84; mem, Tech Comt, Fractionation Res, Inc, 81-84. *Mem:* AAAS; Am Chem Soc; Am Inst Mining, Metall & Petrol Engrs; Am Soc Eng Educ; fel Am Inst Chem Engrs; Sigma Xi. *Res:* Chemical engineering operations; extraction; distillation; thermodynamics; high energy chemical fuels; uranium refining; process design and development; refining inorganic alkali and borate chemicals; fossil fuel boilers and emission controls; crystallization; carbon dioxide from flue gas. *Mailing Add:* 2005 N Briarcliff Ave Bethany OK 73008-5656

ARNOLD, DAVID M, ABELTAN GROUP THEORY. *Current Pos:* PROF MATH, NMEX STATE UNIV, 68- *Personal Data:* b Falls City, Nebr, Aug 9, 39. *Educ:* Univ Ill, PhD(math), 69. *Mem:* Am Math; Math Asn Am. *Res:* Abeltan group theory. *Mailing Add:* Dept Math Baylor Univ PO Box 97328 Waco TX 76798

ARNOLD, DAVID WALKER, CHEMICAL ENGINEERING, OPERATIONS RESEARCH. *Current Pos:* process study engr, 66-68, res proj mgr, 68-69, chief process & process study engr, 69-72, mgr process eng, 72-74, dir eng, 74-75, vpres eng, 75-81, sr vpres, 81-87, SR VPRES RES & ENG, MISS CHEM CORP, 87- *Personal Data:* b Dundee, Miss, Dec 6, 36; m 58; c 1. *Educ:* Univ Miss, BS, 58; Iowa State Univ, MS, 63, PhD(chem eng), 66. *Prof Exp:* Jr engr, Inst Atomic Res, Ames Lab, Atomic Energy Comn, Iowa State Univ, 63-66. *Mem:* Am Inst Chem Engrs; Nat Soc Prof Eng. *Res:* Applications of nuclear magnetic resonance techniques to chemical engineering problems; nonlinear optimization; resource allocation and scheduling; fertilizer technology. *Mailing Add:* Dept Chem Eng Univ Ala PO Box 870203 Tuscaloosa AL 35487-0203

ARNOLD, DEAN EDWARD, FRESHWATER FISHERIES, WATER QUALITY. *Current Pos:* asst leader, 72-80, leader, Pa Fishery Res Unit, 80-82, assoc leader fisheries, 82-93, US NAT BIOL SURV, PA COOP FISH & WILDLIFE RES UNIT, US FISH & WILDLIFE SERV, 93-; ASST LEADER FISHERIES, BIOL RESOURCES DIV, US GEOL SERV, 93- *Personal Data:* b Elmira, NY, Apr 8, 39; m 64, 80, Juliet K Johnson; c Margaret J & David E. *Educ:* Univ Rochester, AB, 61; Cornell Univ, MS, 65, DPhil(aquatic ecol), 69. *Honors & Awards:* W F Thompson Award, Am Inst Fishery Res Biologists, 74; Qual Performance Award, US Fish & Wildlife Serv, 75. *Prof Exp:* Res asst fisheries, Cornell Univ, 63-65, res assoc & asst proj leader warmwater fisheries invests, 65-66, teaching asst limnol, 66-68; asst res limnologist, Great Lakes Res Div, Univ Mich, 69-72; asst prof biol, Pa State Univ, 72-82. *Concurrent Pos:* Eng officer, Navy Oceanog Ship, 61-63; consult, Environ Res Group, Inc, Ann Arbor, Mich, 70-72; assoc ed, Am Fisheries Soc, 75-77 & 84-86; adj asst prof aquatic ecol, Pa State Univ, 82-; chmn adv bd, Sport Fishery Abstracts, 85- *Mem:* Am Fisheries Soc; Int Asn Theoret & Appl Limnol; Am Inst Fishery Res Biologists; NAm Benthological Soc. *Res:* Hydrobiological effects of acid precipitation; aquatic productivity; effects of manipulations of lakes and streams; lake restoration; pollution, conservation biology and aquatic ecology; acid mine drainage; river ecology; thermal pollution; erosion and siltation of streams. *Mailing Add:* Coop Fish & Wildlife Res Unit Merkle Lab University Park PA 16802-1100. *Fax:* 814-863-4710

ARNOLD, DONALD ROBERT, ORGANIC CHEMISTRY, PHOTOCHEMISTRY. *Current Pos:* Killam res prof, 79-84, ALEXANDER MCLEOD PROF CHEM, DALHOUSIE UNIV, 91- *Personal Data:* b Buffalo, NY, Mar 1, 35; m 55; c 6. *Educ:* Bethany Col, WVa, BS, 57; Univ Rochester, PhD(org chem), 61. *Honors & Awards:* Alfred Bader Lectr, Org Chem, Can Soc Chem, 95. *Prof Exp:* Res chemist, Union Carbide Res Inst, New York, 61-70; from assoc prof to prof chem, Univ Western Ont, 70-79. *Concurrent Pos:* Alfred P Sloan Found fel, 72-74; fel, Chem Inst Can, 74; Guggenheim Found fel, 80-81. *Mem:* Am Chem Soc; Chem Inst Can; Inter-Am Photochem Soc (pres). *Res:* Radical ions; heterocyclic compounds; small ring compounds; free radicals; synthetic applications and mechanisms of photochemistry; organic electrochemistry. *Mailing Add:* Dept Chem Dalhousie Univ Halifax NS B3H 4J3 Can. *Fax:* 902-494-1310; *E-Mail:* arnold@ac.dal.ca

ARNOLD, EMIL, SOLID STATE PHYSICS, SEMICONDUCTORS. *Current Pos:* sr physicist, Philips Labs, Div NAm Philips, 63-69, sr prog leader, 69-84, prin res scientist, 84-90, CONSULT SCIENTIST, PHILIPS LABS, DIV PHILIPS ELECTRONICS, N AM, 90- *Personal Data:* b Luck, Poland, May 20, 32; US citizen; m 65, Barbara Stearns; c Elizabeth & Rebecca. *Educ:* Dalhousie Univ, BS, 54; Yale Univ, MS, 55, PhD(phys chem), 63. *Prof Exp:* Sr physicist, Gen Instrument Corp, 55-57; sr engr, Gen Tel & Electronics Labs, 57-60. *Concurrent Pos:* Consult, Am Phys Soc, 70-91; exec comt, Am Phys Soc, NY, 87-91. *Mem:* Am Phys Soc; sr mem Inst Elec & Electronics Engrs. *Res:* Solid state electronics; transport properties of semiconductors; electrical behavior of semiconductor surfaces; electrochemistry; optoelectronics; semiconductor devices; power electronics; electronic materials. *Mailing Add:* Philips Res Briarcliff Manor NY 10510. *Fax:* 914-945-6375; *E-Mail:* exa@philabs.research.philips.com

ARNOLD, FREDERIC G, BIOLOGY, HUMAN PHYSIOLOGY. *Current Pos:* prof biol, Kean Col, NJ, 56-73, chmn dept, 69-73, prof instr, Curric & Admin, 73-86, asst dean educ, 80-86, cert officer, 93-95, EMER PROF BIOL & SCI EDUC, KEAN COL, NJ, 86- *Personal Data:* b Irvington, NJ, Jan 14, 23; m 47, Annella Biggs; c Mary A (Mueller) & Joan (Prestinari). *Educ:* Montclair State Col, BA, 46, MA, 47; Columbia Univ, EdD(prep sci teachers), 56. *Prof Exp:* Teacher high schs, NJ, 47-55. *Concurrent Pos:* Adj teaching, Kean Col, NJ, 95- *Mem:* AAAS; Nat Sci Teachers Asn. *Res:* Body fluids, blood and circulation; science education; desert biology, especially the ecology and plant life of the desert with emphasis on the cacti and succulent plants. *Mailing Add:* Seven Graymoor Rd Livingston NJ 07039-6109

ARNOLD, GEORGE W, SOLID STATE PHYSICS. *Current Pos:* PHYSICIST, SANDIA NAT LABS, 61- *Personal Data:* b Dayton, Ohio, Nov 24, 23; m 45; c 3. *Educ:* Univ Tex, BS, 48, MA, 49. *Prof Exp:* Physicist, Optical Res Lab, Univ Tex, 48-49, Nat Bur Standards, 49-50 & US Naval Res Lab, 50-61. *Concurrent Pos:* Fulbright prof, Egypt, 60-61. *Mem:* Am Phys Soc; AAAS; Mat Res Soc. *Res:* Ion implantation and radiation effects studies in inorganic solids. *Mailing Add:* 11729 S Hwy 14 Tijeras NM 87059

ARNOLD, HARVEY JAMES, MATHEMATICAL STATISTICS, APPLIED STATISTICS. *Current Pos:* RETIRED. *Personal Data:* b Niagara Falls, Ont, Can, Mar 5, 33; US citizen; m 56, Barbara Bickel; c Diane (Rodriguez), Douglas, Linda & Karen (Tomko). *Educ:* Queen's Univ, Ont, BA, 51, MA, 52; Princeton Univ, MA, 55, PhD(math), 58. *Prof Exp:* Res asst,

Princeton Univ, 57-58; asst prof, Univ Western Ont, 58-60 & Wesleyan Univ, 60-63; assoc prof, Bucknell Univ, 63-67; actg chmn dept, Oakland Univ, 70-71, from assoc prof to prof math, 70-92. *Concurrent Pos:* Vis res assoc, Princeton Univ, 62-63; statistician-in-residence, Univ Wis, 72-73. *Mem:* Am Soc Qual Control; Am Statist Asn. *Res:* Nonparametric statistics; design of experiments and statistical applications to the physical and engineering sciences; quality control. *Mailing Add:* 36 Sedilane Brevard NC 28712

ARNOLD, HENRY ALBERT, OCEAN ENGINEERING, SCIENCE POLICY. *Current Pos:* RETIRED. *Personal Data:* b Chewelah, Wash, Feb 18, 14; m 38; c 2. *Educ:* US Naval Acad, BS, 36; Mass Inst Technol, BS & MS, 41. *Prof Exp:* Res officer hydronautics, David Taylor Model Basin, US Navy, 50-53, res officer submarine res & design, 53-58, design officer, Polaris submarine, Spec Proj Off, US Navy, 58-60; asst chief sci, United Aircraft Corp, 61-70; dep dir, AID, Dept of State, 70-73, dir, Off Sci & Technol, 73-79. *Concurrent Pos:* Consult ocean eng, Off of Pres Sci Adv, 61-64; tech dir, US Navy Deep Ocean Systs Rev Task Force, 63; sr specialist ocean eng, Pres Coun Marine Resources & Eng Develop, 66-68. *Mem:* Sigma Xi. *Res:* Role and application of science and technology to the social and economic development of the lesser developed countries of the world. *Mailing Add:* 1583 Frontier Dr Melbourne FL 32940

ARNOLD, HUBERT ANDREW, mathematics; deceased, see previous edition for last biography

ARNOLD, J BARTO, III, UNDERWATER ARCHAEOLOGY. *Current Pos:* asst marine archaeologist, 72-75, STATE MARINE ARCHAEOLOGIST, TEX HIST COMN, 75- *Personal Data:* b San Antonio, Tex, Jan 9, 50; m 70, Aurora I; c Kathryn, Julia & Jessica. *Educ:* Univ Tex, Austin, BA, 71, MA, 73. *Honors & Awards:* Achievement Award for Hist Preserv, US Dept Interior, 80; Spec Achievement Award, Soc Prof Archaeologists, 90. *Prof Exp:* Res asst, Tex Archaeol Res Lab, Univ Tex, Austin, 71-72. *Concurrent Pos:* Mem, USS Monitor Tech Adv Comt, 77-90; prog chmn, 9th Conf Underwater Archaeol, 78; consult, Maritime Preserv, Nat Trust Hist Preserv, 79-; USS Monitor Proj, 87; mem, Md Gov Adv Comt Underwater Archaeol, 87-89; prog chmn underwater archaeol, First Joint Archaeol Cong, Baltimore, Md, 89. *Mem:* Soc Prof Archaeologists (secy-treas, 87-89); Soc Am Archaeol; Soc Hist Archaeol (pres, 93); Archaeol Instit Am. *Res:* Underwater archaeology, excavation of the San Esteban, a wreck of the 1554 New Spain Fleet; location and investigation of La Belle, the French explorer La Salle's wreck of 1686; surveys and recording shipwrecks in Texas; marine remote sensing surveys. *Mailing Add:* 3610 Crowncrest Dr Austin TX 78759. *Fax:* 512-463-8927; *E-Mail:* barnold@access.texas.gov

ARNOLD, JAMES DARRELL, RANGE SCIENCE, CROP PRODUCTION. *Current Pos:* dir forage lab, Tex A&M Univ-Kingsville, 76-78, assoc prof, 76-86, asst dean acad affairs, Col Agr/Home Econ & prof, 88-91, ACAD COORDR & PROF CROP SCI, 86-, PROF CROP SCI & GRAD COORDR, TEX A&M UNIV-KINGSVILLE, 91- *Personal Data:* b Emporia, Kans, Apr 21, 37; m 63; c 4. *Educ:* Panhandle State Univ, BS, 64; SDak State Univ, MS, 66; Tex Tech Univ, PhD(range sci), 73. *Prof Exp:* Res agronomist crop sci, Panhandle State Univ-Okla State Univ & assoc prof agron crop sci, Panhandle State Univ, 66-73. *Mem:* Am Soc Agron; Soc Range Mgt; Crop Sci Soc Am. *Res:* Renewable natural resources; factors relating to range improvement in tropical, subtropical and semi-arid regions. *Mailing Add:* Dept Agr Tex A&M Univ 700 Uni Blvd Kingsville TX 78363-8203. *Fax:* 512-595-3713

ARNOLD, JAMES NORMAN, engineering heat transfer, for more information see previous edition

ARNOLD, JAMES RICHARD, PLANETARY SCIENCE, SPACE APPLICATIONS. *Current Pos:* from assoc prof to prof chem, Univ Calif, San Diego, 58-83, chmn dept, 60-63, Harold C Urey Prof, 83-93, EMER PROF CHEM, CALIF, SAN DIEGO, 93- *Personal Data:* b New Brunswick, NJ, May 5, 23; m 52; c 3. *Educ:* Princeton Univ, AB, 43, MA, 45, PhD(chem), 46. *Honors & Awards:* Ernest Orlando Lawrence Award, AEC, 68. *Prof Exp:* Asst, Princeton Univ, 43 & Manhattan Proj, 43-46; fel, Inst Nuclear Studies, Univ Chicago, 46; Nat Res fel, Harvard Univ, 47; asst prof, Inst Nuclear Studies, Univ Chicago, 48-55; from asst prof to assoc prof, Princeton Univ, 55-58. *Concurrent Pos:* Dir, Calif Space Inst, 79-89, interim dir, 96-97. *Mem:* Nat Acad Sci; Am Acad Arts & Sci; AAAS; Am Chem Soc; Int Acad Astronaut; Meteoritical Soc. *Res:* Cosmic-ray produced nuclides; history of moon and meteorites; cosmochemistry; lunar resources utilization. *Mailing Add:* Dept Chem 0524 Univ Calif San Diego La Jolla CA 92093

ARNOLD, JAMES S(LOAN), APPLIED PHYSICS, ACOUSTICS. *Current Pos:* RETIRED. *Personal Data:* b Ely, Nev, Sept 27, 11; m 42, Merceda Jewett; c Richard & Elizabeth. *Educ:* Univ Calif, Los Angeles, AB, 34; NMex Col Agr & Mech Arts, MS, 51. *Prof Exp:* Prod & tool engr, Trumbull Div, Gen Elec Co, 39-43 & 45-48; assoc physicist, Phys Sci Lab, NMex Col Agr & Mech Arts, 48-53; physicist, Stanford Res Inst, 53-66; sr tech specialist, Reconnaissance Lab, McDonnell Douglas Corp, 66-69, sr group engr, 69-76. *Mem:* Sigma Xi. *Res:* Electronic instrumentation; ultrasonic methods for non-destructive testing; physics of ignition and combustion processes; sonic devices and techniques; photographic and electronic imaging systems for reconnaissance; electronic control systems. *Mailing Add:* 4948 Park Dr Carlsbad CA 92008

ARNOLD, JAMES SCHOONOVER, KIDNEY BLOOD FLOW, BONE MORPHOLOGY. *Current Pos:* CHIEF, LAB NUCLEAR MED, IRON MOUNTAIN VET ADMIN HOSP, 80- *Personal Data:* b Nov 20, 23; m 51, Martha H; c Janet, Christine, Gail, Judith, Michael, Sara & John. *Educ:* Duke Univ, MD, 48. *Concurrent Pos:* Nuclear med physician, 60- *Mem:* Soc Nuclear Med; Soc Clin Path. *Res:* Kidney blood flow & function; bone morphology. *Mailing Add:* Iron Mountain Vet Admin Hosp H St Iron Mountain MI 49801

ARNOLD, JAMES TRACY, EXPERIMENTAL PHYSICS. *Current Pos:* physicist, 58-72, SR SCIENTIST, VARIAN ASSOCS, 72- *Personal Data:* b Taiyuanfu, China, Oct 23, 20; US citizen; m 57, Marna; c Erica, Laura, David & Andrew. *Educ:* Oberlin Col, AB, 42; Stanford Univ, PhD(physics), 54. *Prof Exp:* Lab instr physics, Oberlin Col, 47-48; spec asst, Europ Ctr Nuclear Res, 54-55; res assoc physics, Stanford Univ, 55-57; asst prof, Ore State Col, 57-58. *Mem:* Sigma Xi. *Res:* High resolution nuclear magnetic resonance spectroscopy, magnetometers, mass spectroscopy, ultrasonic imaging and computer application to instruments. *Mailing Add:* PO Box 314 Los Altos CA 94023

ARNOLD, JESSE CHARLES, APPLIED STATISTICS, MATHEMATICAL STATISTICS. *Current Pos:* assoc prof, 68-74, PROF STATIST & HEAD DEPT, VA POLYTECH INST & STATE UNIV, 74- *Personal Data:* b Bowie, Tex, Sept 28, 37; m 59; c 2. *Educ:* Southeastern State Col, BS, 60; Fla State Univ, MS, 65, PhD(statist), 67. *Prof Exp:* Asst chief exp design, Ctr Dis Control, USPHS, 61-63; asst prof educ res, Fla State Univ, 67-68. *Concurrent Pos:* Va State Water Control Bd grant water qual monitoring, Va Polytech Inst & State Univ, 69-71; consult, USPHS, 71, NASA-Langley Res Ctr, 72 & USAID, 72-84; coordr Philippine Nat Nutrit Proj, Va Polytech Inst & State Univ & USAID, 74-84. *Mem:* Biomet Soc(pres, 81); fel Am Statist Asn; Int Statist Inst; Am Statist Asn. *Res:* Theory of estimation; application of statistics to environmental problems; sampling biometrics; international nutrition in the Philippines and Haiti; applications and research in quality control. *Mailing Add:* Dept Statist Va Polytech Inst & State Univ PO Box 0439 Blacksburg VA 24063-0439

ARNOLD, JIMMY THOMAS, POLYNOMIAL & POWER SERIES RINGS. *Current Pos:* From asst prof to assoc prof, 69-76, PROF MATH, VA POLYTECH INST & STATE UNIV, 77- *Personal Data:* b Crowville, La, May 31, 41; m 67, Linda Andrews; c Cindy & Pamela. *Educ:* Northeastern La State Col, BS, 63; Fla State Univ, MS, 65, PhD(algebra), 67. *Mem:* Am Math Soc; Math Asn Am. *Res:* Dimension theory in power series rings and in polynomial rings. *Mailing Add:* Dept Math Va Polytech Inst & State Univ Blacksburg VA 24061. *E-Mail:* arnold@math.vt.edu

ARNOLD, JOHN MILLER, ZOOLOGY, EMBRYOLOGY. *Current Pos:* from asst prof to assoc prof, 66-75, PROF CYTOL, PAC BIOMED RES CTR, UNIV HAWAII, MANOA, 75- *Personal Data:* b St Paul, Minn, Oct 6, 36. *Educ:* Univ Minn, BA, 58, PhD(zool), 63. *Prof Exp:* Instr zool, Oberlin Col, 60-61; res fel, Lerner Marine Lab, Am Mus Natural Hist, 63-64; asst prof, Iowa State Univ, 64-66. *Concurrent Pos:* Mem corp & trustee, Marine Biol Lab, Woods Hole; res assoc, Am Mus Natural Hist, 86; ed, J Cephalopod Biol. *Mem:* Fel AAAS; Am Soc Zool; Soc Develop Biol; Am Soc Cell Biol; Int Soc Develop Biologists; Am Malacological Union; Am Inst Biol Soc. *Res:* Embryological development; biology of cephalopods, first discovered Nautilus embryos; reproductive biology. *Mailing Add:* Pac Biomed Res Ctr Univ Hawaii Manoa Snyder Hall 209A Honolulu HI 96822

ARNOLD, JOHN RICHARD, SURFACE SCIENCE, CORROSION & ADHESION SCIENCE. *Current Pos:* DIR, TECH SERV, DYMAX CORP, 94-, PRIN INVESTR, 97- *Personal Data:* b Fort McClellan, Ala, Oct 16, 56; m 86, Katharine Cooper; c Robin. *Educ:* Univ Calif, Santa Barbara, BS, 78; Univ Calif, Irvine, PhD(chem), 84. *Prof Exp:* Engr res, Bethlehem Steel Corp, 84-89; res chemist, First Brands Corp, 89-93. *Mem:* Am Chem Soc; Am Physics Soc. *Res:* Surface analysis; adhesive joint durability in corrosive environments; coated steel products; development of ultraviolet coatings and adhesives. *Mailing Add:* 70 Lake Harwinton Rd Harwinton CT 06791. *Fax:* 860-496-0608

ARNOLD, JONATHAN, POPULATION & STATISTICAL GENETICS, GENOMICS. *Current Pos:* ASSOC PROF GENETICS, UNIV GA, 82- *Personal Data:* b New York, NY, Nov 27, 53; m 80, O'Hara. *Educ:* Yale Univ, BS, 75, MPhil, 78, PhD(statist), 82. *Prof Exp:* Adj instr statist, Rutgers Univ, 81-82. *Concurrent Pos:* Grant, NSF, 83-86 & Army Res Off, 83-85, NIH, 89-94; adj prof, Emory Univ, 84-; assoc ed, Evolution, 90-92. *Mem:* Am Statist Asn; Soc Study Evolution; Biometrics Soc; Genetics Soc Am; Inst Math Statist. *Res:* Statistical problems in population genetics, including the analysis of fitness components and the modeling of plant and animal mating systems; statistical analysis of DNA sequence data and models of molecular evolution; physical mapping of genomes. *Mailing Add:* Dept Genetics Univ Ga Athens GA 30602. *Fax:* 706-542-3910; *E-Mail:* arnold@bscr.uga.edu

ARNOLD, KEITH ALAN, ORNITHOLOGY. *Current Pos:* from asst prof to assoc prof, 66-78, PROF WILDLIFE SCI, TEX A&M UNIV, 78- *Personal Data:* b Jackson, Mich, Sept 23, 37; m 68; c 2. *Educ:* Kalamazoo Col, AB, 59; Univ Mich, MS, 61; La State Univ, PhD(zool), 66. *Prof Exp:* Instr zool, La State Univ, 65-66. *Mem:* Am Ornith Union; Soc Syst Zool; Cooper Ornith Soc; Wilson Ornith Soc; Sigma Xi. *Res:* Taxonomic, ecological and behavioral ornithology; avian ectoparasites; tropical vertebrate ecology. *Mailing Add:* Dept Wildlife & Fisheries Sci Tex A&M Univ College Station TX 77843-0100

ARNOLD, KENNETH JAMES, MATHEMATICAL STATISTICS. *Current Pos:* assoc prof statist, 52-62, prof, 62-81, chmn dept, 63-67, EMER PROF STATIST, MICH STATE UNIV, 81- *Personal Data:* b Pawtucket, RI, Aug 20, 14; m 39, Pauline Frew; c William D, Robert J & Rebecca A (Sill). *Educ:* Mass Inst Technol, BS, 37, PhD(math), 41. *Prof Exp:* Asst, Mass Inst Technol, 38-39, 40-41, instr math, 41-43; asst prof, Univ NH, 43-44; sr math statistician, Statist Res Group, Columbia Univ, 44-45; asst prof math, Univ Wis, 45-52. *Concurrent Pos:* Ed, J Soc Indust & Appl Math, 58-69. *Mem:* Math Asn Am; Inst Math Statist (secy-treas, 52-55). *Res:* Statistical theory; computational methods; spherical probability distributions. *Mailing Add:* 12 Cahoon's Hollow Chatham MA 02633

ARNOLD, LESLIE K, mathematics; deceased, see previous edition for last biography

ARNOLD, LUTHER BISHOP, JR, textile chemistry; deceased, see previous edition for last biography

ARNOLD, LYNN ELLIS, MECHANICAL METALLURGY. *Current Pos:* CONSULT, ARNOLD METALL, 89- *Personal Data:* b Cincinnati, Ohio, Nov 17, 34; m 88, Carol Bennett. *Educ:* Univ Cincinnati, MetE, 57; Univ Ill, MS, 59. *Honors & Awards:* Eisenman Award, Am Soc Metals, 79; Tech Div Award, Am Gear Mfrs Asn, 89. *Prof Exp:* Staff metallurgist, Xtek, 59-67, sr res metallurgist, 67-72, mgr metall, 72-76, tech mgr, 76-88; mgr tech servs, Am Power Equip, 88-89. *Mem:* Fel Am Soc Metals. *Res:* Mechanical metallurgy including technology of gears, forged rolls, failure analysis, heat treatment and innovative testing methods. *Mailing Add:* 6538 Kugler Mill Cincinnati OH 45236-2260

ARNOLD, MARY B, PEDIATRIC ENDOCRINOLOGY. *Current Pos:* consult biochem, 66-68, DIR PEDIAT OUTPATIENT DEPT & ENDOCRINE CLIN, 66-, CHMN DEPT PEDIAT, ROGER WILLIAMS GEN HOSP, 74- *Personal Data:* b Fitchburg, Mass, Sept 29, 24; wid; c 3. *Educ:* Vassar Col, AB, 45; Univ Vt, MD, 50; Am Bd Pediat, dipl, 56. *Hon Degrees:* Brown Univ, MA, 74. *Honors & Awards:* Carrbee Award Obstet, Univ Vt, 50. *Prof Exp:* Intern, Hartford Hosp, 50-52; asst resident pediat, Babies Hosp, 52-54; asst pediat, Sch Med, Harvard Univ, 55-57; instr, Sch Med, Univ NC, 57-59, asst prof, 59-65. *Concurrent Pos:* Res fel pediat endocrinol, Mass Gen Hosp, Boston, 54-57; lectr med sci, Brown Univ, 66-71; attend pediatrician, Roger Williams Gen Hosp, 66-; consult pediat endocrinol, Women & Infants Hosp RI, 66-; asst physician pediat & attend pediatrician, RI Hosp, 70-, dir pediat endocrinol, 71-; assoc prof pediat & dir pediat endocrinol, prog med, Brown Univ, 71- *Mem:* Sigma Xi; Endocrine Soc; Am Fedn Clin Res; AMA; Lawson Wilkins Pediat Endocrinol Soc. *Res:* Endocrine problems of childhood with particular reference to thryoid disorders and disorders of calcium and phosphorus metabolism; fetal endocrinology, and various mechanisms responsible for growth hormone release, including the role of somatostatin and somatomedin in normal growth and development. *Mailing Add:* 825 Chalkstone Ave Providence RI 02908-4728

ARNOLD, RICHARD THOMAS, physical organic chemistry, for more information see previous edition

ARNOLD, ROBERT FAIRBANKS, MATHEMATICS. *Current Pos:* From asst prof math to assoc prof, 68-76, chmn dept, 75-77, 88-90, PROF MATH, CALIF STATE UNIV, FRESNO, 76- *Personal Data:* b Gilroy, Calif, July 3, 40; m 66; c 1. *Educ:* Fresno State Col, BS, 63, MA, 64; Univ Calif, Berkeley, PhD(math), 69. *Mem:* Math Asn Am. *Mailing Add:* Dept Math Calif State Univ 5245 N Backer Ave Fresno CA 93740-8001

ARNOLD, ROLAND R, DENTAL RESEARCH, MUCOSAL IMMUNOLOGY. *Current Pos:* DENT RESEARCHER MUCOSAL IMMUNOL, DENT RES CTR, UNIV NC, 91- *Personal Data:* b Denver, Colo, Dec 18, 46. *Educ:* La State Univ, BS, 72, PhD(microbiol), 75. *Prof Exp:* Assoc dean dent res, Emory Univ, 88-91. *Concurrent Pos:* Mem study sect, NIH, 83-91. *Mem:* Am Asn Immunologists; Am Asn Dent Res. *Mailing Add:* Dent Res Ctr Rm 101 Univ NC CB 7455 Dent Res Bldg Chapel Hill NC 27599-7455

ARNOLD, ROY GARY, FOOD SCIENCE, BIOCHEMISTRY. *Current Pos:* DEAN, COL AGR SCI, ORE STATE UNIV, 87- *Personal Data:* b Lyons, Nebr, Feb 20, 41; m 63; c 2. *Educ:* Univ Nebr, BSc, 62; Ore State Univ, MS, 65, PhD(food sci), 67. *Honors & Awards:* William Cruess Award, Inst Food Technologists. *Prof Exp:* Proj leader food res, Res & Develop Lab, Fairmont Food Co, Nebr, 62-63; from asst prof to assoc prof, Univ Nebr, Lincoln, 67-74, chmn dept, 73-79, dean & dir, Agr Exp Sta, 80-82, vchancellor, Inst Agr & Natural Resources, 82-87, prof food sci & technol, 74-87. *Mem:* AAAS; Inst Food Technologists. *Res:* Flavor chemistry of foods; food lipids. *Mailing Add:* Oregon State Univ Col Agr A-624 Admin Serv Corvallis OR 97331

ARNOLD, STEPHEN, PHYSICS. *Current Pos:* from asst prof to assoc prof, 78-82, PROF, POLYTECH INST NY, 82-, THOMAS POTTS PROF PHYSICS, 93- *Educ:* Univ Toledo, BS, 64; City Univ NY, PhD(physics), 70. *Prof Exp:* Lectr, Queens Col, 64-68, instr, 70-73; res assoc, Brookhaven Nat Labs, 68-70; sr res scientist, NY Univ, 73-74, mgr, Radiation & Solid State Lab, 74-78. *Concurrent Pos:* Guest scientist, Brookhaven Nat Labs, 70-; Alfred P Sloan fel, 81. *Mem:* Fel Am Phys Soc; fel Optical Soc Am; Sigma Xi. *Res:* Organic solid state physics; microparticle photophysics. *Mailing Add:* Dept Physics Polytech Univ 333 Jay St Brooklyn NY 11201. *Fax:* 718-260-3139; *E-Mail:* arnold@photon.poly.edu

ARNOLD, VLADIMIR IGOREVICH, MATHEMATICS. *Current Pos:* PROF, STEKLOV MATH INST, 86-; PROF, UNIV PARIS-DAUPHINE, 93- *Personal Data:* b Odessa, Russia, June 12, 37; m 76, Elionova Alexandrovna Voronina; c Igor & Dimitri. *Educ:* Moscow State Univ, PhD, 59; Keldysh Appl Math Inst, DSc, 63. *Hon Degrees:* Dr, Univ P&M Curie, Paris, 78, Univ Warwick, 88, Univ Utrecht, 91, Univ Bologna, 91, Univ Complutense, Madrid, 94 & Univ Toronto, 97. *Honors & Awards:* Lenin Prize, USSR, 65; Crafoord Prize, Swed Acad Sci, 82; Lobatchevsky Prize, Russ Acad Sci, 92; Harvey Prize, Israel Inst Technol, 94. *Prof Exp:* Dozent math fac, Moscow State Univ, 63-65, prof, 65-86. *Mem:* Fel Russ Nat Sci Acad; foreign mem Am Philos Soc; fel Russ Acad Sci; foreign mem Nat Acad Sci; foreign mem Am Acad Arts & Sci; foreign mem Royal Soc London. *Res:* Mathematics; mechanics; mathematical physics; stability theory of Hamiltonian systems; hydrodynamics; singularity theory; symplectic and contact topology of caustics and wavefronts; catastrophe theory; bifurcation theory; dynamical systems; braids theory; reflection groups; optics. *Mailing Add:* Steklov Math Inst 8 Gubkina St Moscow GSP-1 Russia. *E-Mail:* arnold@genesis.mi.ras.ru, arnold@ceremade.dauphine.fr

ARNOLD, WATSON CAUFIELD, PEDIATRICS, NEPHROLOGY. *Current Pos:* DIR PEDIAT NEPHROLOGY, COOK FT WORTH CHILDREN'S MED CTR, FT WORTH, TEX, 90- *Personal Data:* b Waco, Tex, Jan 12, 45; m 75; c 2. *Educ:* Tulane Univ, BA, 66; Univ Tex, Dallas, MD, 70; Am Bd Pediat. *Prof Exp:* Intern pediat, Med Col, Univ Ark, 71, resident, 75; clin fel pediat & nephrology, Med Sch, Univ Calif, San Francisco, 75-76, NIH trainee res fel, 76-78; from asst prof to assoc prof pediat, Sch Med Sci, Univ Ark, 77-90, dir pediat Nephrology, Ark Children's Hosp, 78-90. *Concurrent Pos:* Chmn, Sect Nephrology, Am Acad Pediat. *Mem:* Am Acad Pediat; Am Soc Nephrology; Am Soc Pediat Nephrology; Am Fedn Clin Res; Am Fedn Exp Biol; Am Soc Clin Nutrit; Am Inst Nutrit. *Res:* Nutrition and kidney failure in children, including growth and development; emphasis on endocrine aspect of uremia and nutrition and in hypertension. *Mailing Add:* Cook Children's Med Ctr 801 Seventh Ave Ft Worth TX 76104

ARNOLD, WILFRED NIELS, BIOCHEMISTRY, HISTORY OF MEDICINE. *Current Pos:* assoc prof, 72-80, PROF BIOCHEM, UNIV KANS MED CTR, KANSAS CITY, 81- *Personal Data:* b Australia, May 29, 36; US citizen; m 61, Louis Merz; c Conrad. *Educ:* Univ Queensland, BS, 57; Univ Calif, Los Angeles, MA, 58; Cornell Univ, PhD(plant biochem), 62. *Prof Exp:* Res specialist air pollution, Univ Calif, Riverside, 57-58; res fel, Waite Res Inst, Univ Adelaide, 62-63; res scientist, Commonwealth Sci & Indust Res Orgn, Adelaide, Australia, 63-66; sr fel, Med Sch, Univ Wis, 66-67; asst prof biochem, Med Sch, Wayne State Univ, 67-71. *Concurrent Pos:* Mid Am State Univs lectr, 81-82; vis prof, Univ Queensland, Australia, 82; speaker, Atlantic Seaboard Circuit, Am Chem Soc, 94. *Mem:* AAAS; Am Chem Soc; Sigma Xi; Am Soc Biol Chemists. *Res:* Enzymology; structure and function of the cell envelope in yeasts; carbohydrate and amino acid metabolism in higher plants and microorganisms; history and philosophy of science; author of 80 publications. *Mailing Add:* Med Sch Univ Kans Rainbow Blvd 39th St Kansas City KS 66160-7421. *Fax:* 913-588-7440; *E-Mail:* warnold@kumc.edu

ARNOLD, WILLIAM ARCHIBALD, PLANT PHYSIOLOGY. *Current Pos:* RETIRED. *Personal Data:* b Douglas, Wyo, Dec 6, 04; m 29; c 2. *Educ:* Calif Inst Technol, BS, 31; Harvard Univ, PhD(physiol), 35. *Prof Exp:* Sheldon fel biol, Univ Calif, 35-36; Gen Educ Bd fel, Hopkins Marine Sta, Stanford Univ, 36-37, asst, 37-38, res assoc biol, 39-40 & 41, asst prof, 41-46; prin biologist, Oak Ridge Nat Lab, 46-70. *Concurrent Pos:* Rockefeller fel, Inst Theoret Physics, Copenhagen Univ, 38-39; physicist, Princeton Univ, 42; sr physicist, Eastman Kodak Co, NY, 42-44 & Tenn, 44-46; consult, 69-79. *Mem:* Nat Acad Sci; Am Phys Soc; Soc Gen Physiol; Sigma Xi. *Res:* Photosynthesis. *Mailing Add:* 102 Balsam Rd Oak Ridge TN 37830-7823

ARNOLD, WILLIAM HOWARD, NUCLEAR ENGINEERING. *Current Pos:* RETIRED. *Personal Data:* b St Louis, Mo, May 13, 31; m 52, Josephine Routheau; c William, Frances, Edward, David & Thomas. *Educ:* Cornell Univ, AB, 51; Princeton Univ, MA, 53, PhD(physics), 55. *Prof Exp:* Instr physics, Princeton Univ, 55; sr scientist reactor physics, Atomic Power Div, Westinghouse Electric Corp, 55-57, mgr reactor physics design, 57-61; dir nuclear fuel mgt, Nuclear Utility Serv, Inc, 61-62; dep mgr reactor eng, Astronuclear Lab, 62-64, Westinghouse Elec Corp, mgr test systs & opers, 64-66, dep prog mgr NERVA proj, 66-68, proj mgr, 68, mgr, Weapons Dept, Astronuclear Underseas Div, 68-70, mgr eng, 70-72, gen mgr pressurized water reactor systs, 72-80; gen mgr adv energy systs, Westinghouse Hanford Co, 86-89; pres, LA Energy Serv, 89-96. *Concurrent Pos:* Lectr, Univ Pittsburgh, 58; chmn nuclear propulsion, Inst Aeronaut & Astronaut. *Mem:* Nat Acad Eng; fel Am Nuclear Soc; Am Physics Soc; assoc fel Inst Aeronaut & Astronaut; fel AAAS. *Res:* Cosmic ray and elementary particle physics; reactor physics; nuclear engineering; author of 45 technical publications; awarded 2 patents. *Mailing Add:* 3204 Pickwick Lane Chevy Chase MD 20815. *E-Mail:* wmhowarn@aol.com

ARNOLDI, JOAN, VETERINARY MEDICINE, ANIMAL SCIENCE & NUTRITION. *Current Pos:* DEP ADMINR, VET SERV, ANIMAL & PLANT HEALTH INSPECTION SERV, US DEPT AGR, 97- *Mailing Add:* Animal & Plant Health Inspection Serv US Dept Agr 14th Independence Ave SW AG Box 3491 Washington DC 20250

ARNOLDI, ROBERT ALFRED, APPLIED MECHANICS, ACOUSTICS. *Current Pos:* RETIRED. *Personal Data:* b New York, NY, Mar 30, 21; m 43, Eleanor Pike; c Richard, Kenneth & Barbara. *Educ:* Stevens Inst Technol, ME, 42; Polytech Univ, MS, 50, PhD(appl mech), 53. *Prof Exp:* Analytical engr vibrations, Pratt & Whitney Aircraft, 42-46; instr eng physics, Stevens Inst Technol, 46-51; analytical engr aerodyn, Res Labs, United Aircraft Corp, 51-68; proj engr Aeroelasticity & Aeroacoust, Pratt & Whitney Aircraft, 68-81. *Concurrent Pos:* Adj prof appl mech, Hartford Grad Ctr, Rensselaer Polytech Inst, 55-70; mem adv subcomt fluid mech, NASA Res & Technol, 69-71. *Mem:* Am Inst Aeronaut & Astronaut. *Res:* Aerolasticity; aeroacoustics. *Mailing Add:* 108 Selden Hill Dr West Hartford CT 06107

ARNOLDI, WALTER EDWIN, MECHANICAL ENGINEERING, APPLIED MATHEMATICS. *Current Pos:* RETIRED. *Personal Data:* b New York, NY, Dec 14, 17; m 42; c 2. *Educ:* Stevens Inst Technol, ME, 37; Harvard Univ, MS, 39. *Prof Exp:* Anal engr, Hamilton Standard Div, United Aircraft Corp, 39-44, proj engr, 44-51, systs engr, 51-59, sr tech specialist advance planning, 59-60, chief adv analysis, 60-62, head prod res, 62-67, chief div res, 67-70, div tech consult, 70-77. *Concurrent Pos:* Mem subcomt vibration & flutter, Nat Adv Comt Aeronaut, 57-58. *Res:* Vibration of propellers, engines and aircraft; high speed digital computers; aerodynamics and acoustics of aircraft propellers; life support in space vehicles; composite structural materials. *Mailing Add:* 18 Avondale Rd West Hartford CT 06117-1107

ARNOLDY, ROGER L, SPACE PHYSICS. *Current Pos:* assoc prof, 67-78, PROF PHYSICS, UNIV NH, 78-, DIR SPACE SCI CTR, 74- *Personal Data:* b LaCrosse, Wis, May 30, 34; m 61; c 5. *Educ:* St Mary's Col, Minn, BS, 56; Univ Minn, MS, 60, PhD(physics), 62. *Prof Exp:* Res assoc physics, Univ Minn, 62-64; sr res scientist, Honeywell Res Ctr, Minn, 64-67. *Mem:* Am Geophys Union. *Res:* Experimentation to measure charged particle radiation in the earth's magnetosphere and in interplanetary space. *Mailing Add:* 38 Woodridge Rd Durham NH 03824

ARNON, DANIEL I(SRAEL), biochemistry; deceased, see previous edition for last biography

ARNONE, ARTHUR RICHARD, BIOCHEMISTRY. *Current Pos:* assoc prof, 73-78, PROF BIOCHEM, UNIV IOWA, 78- *Personal Data:* b Syracuse, NY, Sept 25, 42; m 66; c 2. *Educ:* Mass Inst Technol, PhD(phys chem), 70. *Prof Exp:* Fel molecular biol, Med Res Coun Lab, Cambridge, Eng, 70-73. *Concurrent Pos:* NIH res career develop award, 75. *Mem:* Am Soc Biol Chemists; Am Chem Soc; Am Crystallog Asn; Sigma Xi. *Res:* X-ray crystallographic studies of hemoglobin and other proteins. *Mailing Add:* Dept Biochem Univ Iowa Bowen Sci Bldg Iowa City IA 52242-1109

ARNOTT, HOWARD JOSEPH, BOTANY, CELL BIOLOGY. *Current Pos:* prof biol & dean, Col Sci, 74-90, Ashbell Smith prof biol, 91-95, DIR, CTR ELECTRON MICROS, UNIV TEX 85-, JENKINS GARRETT PROF, 95- *Personal Data:* b Los Angeles, Calif, Mar 9, 28; m 50, Wanda J Cross; c John J, Catherine J (Thornton), Susan L (Garrett) & Virginia A (Scott). *Educ:* Univ Southern Calif, AB, 52, MS, 53; Univ Calif, PhD(bot), 58. *Honors & Awards:* Distinguished Res Award, Univ Tex, Arlington, 84; Bessy lectr, Iowa State Univ, 93. *Prof Exp:* Asst prof biol, Northwestern Univ, 58-64; fel, Cell Res Inst, Univ Tex, Austin, 64-65, vis assoc prof bot, 65-66, from assoc prof to prof, 66-72; prof biol & chmn dept, Univ SFla, 72-74. *Concurrent Pos:* Adv ed, Protoplasma, 74-; adv ed & consult, J Calcified Tissue Res, 69-78; consult, Alcon Labs, Frito Lay Inc, Tampa Elec Co, many univ; chmn, Gordon Conf Calcium Oxalate, 89; pres, Tex Soc Electron Micros, 88; SW regional dir & bd dirs, Sigma Xi, 84-91. *Mem:* Am Soc Cell Biol; Bot Soc Am; Am Micros Soc; Sigma Xi; Am Mycological Soc; Am Soc Plant Physiol. *Res:* Biological ultrastructure; mineralization in biological systems; organic crystals in insect viruses and animals reflecting systems; calcium oxalate crystals in plants, animals and fungi; ultrastructural ecology; electron microscopy of foods. *Mailing Add:* Dept Biol Box 19498 Arlington TX 76019. *Fax:* 817-272-2855; *E-Mail:* arnott@albert.uta.edu

ARNOTT, MARILYN SUE, BIOCHEMISTRY, GENETICS. *Current Pos:* AT ASN WOMEN SCI. *Personal Data:* b Lafayette, Ind, Aug 26, 43. *Educ:* Univ Tex, Austin, BSc, 65; Univ Tex Grad Sch Biomed Sci, Houston, MSc, 67, PhD(biochem), 70. *Prof Exp:* Instr human genetics, Univ Tex Med Br Galveston, 70-74; asst prof biol, Syst Cancer Ctr, Univ Tex M D Anderson Hosp & Tumor Inst, 74- *Mem:* AAAS; Am Chem Soc; Am Soc Human Genetics; Environ Mutagen Soc; Sigma Xi. *Res:* Carcinogen metabolism; chemical carcinogenesis; protein sequence analysis; biochemical genetics. *Mailing Add:* Rd No 7 Box A1 Boyertown PA 19512

ARNOTT, ROBERT A, ENVIRONMENTAL & HEALTH PROTECTION. *Personal Data:* b Spencer, WVa, Dec 4, 41; m 63; c 2. *Educ:* WVa Univ, BS, 63; Univ Wis, PhD(phys chem), 68. *Prof Exp:* Asst prof chem, Univ Wis, Oshkosh, 68-75; dir, NSF Environ Assessment Prog, 74-75; mgr, Ambient Air Monitoring Sect, Div Air Pollution Control, Ill EPA, 75-77, mgr, air qual, 77-78; dir air mgt, Wis Dept Natural Resources, 78-80; asst dir, Colo State Dept Health, 80-86. *Concurrent Pos:* Environ intern, German Marshall Fund, 83; mem coun public health consults, NSF, 85. *Mem:* Am Chem Soc; Sigma Xi; Air Pollution Control Asn. *Res:* Environmental trace analysis; environmental regulatory approaches; European waste management. *Mailing Add:* 5301 Preserve Pkwy N Littleton CO 80111-2151

ARNOTT, STRUTHER, MOLECULAR BIOPHYSICS. *Current Pos:* PRIN, UNIV ST ANDREWS, 86- *Personal Data:* b Larkhall, Scotland, Sept 25, 34; m 70, Greta; c Aaron & Euan. *Educ:* Glasgow Univ, BSc, 56, PhD(chem), 60. *Prof Exp:* Med Res Coun, scientist, Biophys Unit, King's Col, Univ London, 60-70, dir postgrad studies, Dept Biophys, 67-70; prof biol, Purdue Univ, 70-88, head, Dept Biol Sci, 75-80, vpres res & dean, Grad Sch, 80-86. *Concurrent Pos:* Fel, Jesus Col, Oxford, 80-81; Guggenheim Mem fel, 85. *Mem:* Fel Royal Soc London. *Res:* X-ray diffraction analysis; fibrous polymers; nucleic acids; polysaccharides; proteins. *Mailing Add:* Univ St Andrews Col Gate St Andrews FiFe KY16 9AJ Scotland

ARNOVICK, GEORGE (NORMAN), COMPUTER SCIENCE, INFORMATION SCIENCE. *Current Pos:* PROF COMPUT SCI, 68-, DIR, TECH RES CTR, GRAD SCH, CALIF STATE UNIV, CHICO, 87- *Personal Data:* b Shanghai, China, Aug 22, 25; US citizen; m 56; c 3. *Educ:* Univ Southern Calif, BS, 53, MA, 59. *Prof Exp:* Instr high sch, Calif, 54-56; sr systs designer, Rand Corp, Syst Develop Corp, 56-59; consult engr electrodata div, Burroughs Corp, 59-60; mgr systs anal, EDP Div, Radio Corp Am, NJ, 60-61, engr & group leader systs eng div, Data Systs Div, Calif, 61-62; prin scientist & proj engr, Space & Info Systs Div, NAm Aviation, Inc, 62-63; asst to vpres info storage & retrieval systs, Planning Res Corp, 64-65; mgr systs eng, Informatics, Inc, 65-67; dir info systs div, Tracor Inc, 67-68; pres & chmn bd, Digital Industs Inc, 68. *Concurrent Pos:* Res eng assoc, Douglas Aircraft Corp, Calif, 55-56; NATO fels, Int Advan Study Inst on Automatic Documentation, Venice, Italy, 63 & Int Advan Study Inst on Eval Info Retrieval Systs, The Hague, 65; consult, Arnovick Assocs, Consult, 68-80 & Chico Consult Group, 80-; chmn & pres, Calif Microcomput Co, Inc, Chico, 77-80. *Mem:* AAAS; Asn Comput Mach; Am Asn Artificial Intel; Inst Elec & Electronics Engrs Computer Soc; Soc Comput Simulation; Oper Res Soc Am; Inst Mgt Sci; Am Asn Univ Professors. *Res:* Systems architecture; official information systems; management information systems; artificial intelligence software engineering; expert systems, development of case tools for system integration, Interface requirements for multiple system platforms. *Mailing Add:* 1339 Manchester Rd Chico CA 95926

ARNOW, THEODORE, GEOLOGY. *Current Pos:* CONSULT, 86- *Personal Data:* b New York, NY, July 27, 21; m 49, Lois Aileen; c Dan & Don. *Educ:* NY Univ, BA, 42; Columbia Univ, MA, 49. *Honors & Awards:* Award, US Dept Interior, 84. *Prof Exp:* Geologist, US Geol Surv, 46-66, Dist Chief, Water Resources Div, 66-86. *Mem:* Geol Soc Am. *Res:* Ground-water geology; Great Salt Lake, Utah. *Mailing Add:* 1064 Hillview Dr Salt Lake City UT 84124

ARNOWICH, BEATRICE, PHYSICAL ORGANIC CHEMISTRY. *Current Pos:* from asst prof to assoc prof, 69-81, PROF CHEM, 81-, CHAIRPERSON, QUEENSBOROUGH COMMUNITY COL, 91- *Personal Data:* b New York, NY, June 14, 30; div; c Anne. *Educ:* Vassar Col, AB, 51; Univ Mich, MS, 52; NY Univ, PhD(phys-org chem), 57. *Prof Exp:* Asst, NY Univ, 56-57; chemist, Charles Bruning Co, 57-59; sr chemist, Interchem Corp, 59-66, group leader, 66-69. *Mem:* Fel AAAS; Am Chem Soc; NY Acad Sci. *Res:* Surface chemistry; photoconductivity. *Mailing Add:* 10 E End Ave New York NY 10021-1106

ARNOWITT, RICHARD LEWIS, THEORETICAL PHYSICS. *Current Pos:* PROF PHYSICS, NORTHEASTERN UNIV, 59- *Personal Data:* b New York, NY, May 3, 28. *Educ:* Rensselaer Polytech Inst, BS & MS, 48; Harvard Univ, PhD(physics), 53. *Prof Exp:* Res assoc, Radiation Lab, Univ Calif, 52-54; mem, Inst Advan Study, 54-56; from asst prof to assoc prof, Syracuse Univ, 56-59. *Res:* Elementary particle theory; quantum field theory. *Mailing Add:* Dept Physics Tex A&M Univ College Station TX 77843

ARNS, ROBERT GEORGE, NUCLEAR PHYSICS. *Current Pos:* vpres acad affairs, 77-85, PROF PHYSICS, UNIV VT, 77-, DEAN, COL ENG & MATH, 96- *Personal Data:* b Buffalo, NY, July 24, 33. *Educ:* Canisius Col, BS, 55; Univ Mich, MS, 56, PhD(physics), 60. *Prof Exp:* Res assoc physics, Univ Mich, 59-60, instr, 60; from asst prof to assoc prof physics, State Univ NY Buffalo, 60-64; from assoc prof to prof physics, Ohio State Univ, 64-77, vice provost arts & sci, 71-73, assoc provost, 75-77. *Mem:* Am Phys Soc; Hist Sci Soc; Am Asn Physics Teachers; Soc Hist Technol. *Res:* Nuclear structure; nuclear reactions; gamma and particle-gamma directional correlations; nuclear lifetimes; energy conversion systems; management of technology; history of science; history of technology. *Mailing Add:* Dept Physics Univ Vt Burlington VT 05405. *E-Mail:* arns@emba.uvm.edu

ARNTZEN, CHARLES JOEL, CELL BIOLOGY, BIOCHEMISTRY. *Current Pos:* PRES & CHIEF EXEC OFFICER, BOYCE THOMPSON INST PLANT RES, 95-; DIR, PLANTS & HUMAN HEALTH PROG. *Personal Data:* b Granite Falls, Minn, July 20, 41; m 62, Kathleen; c Christopher J. *Educ:* Univ Minn, BS, 65, MS, 67; Purdue Univ, PhD(cell physiol), 70. *Hon Degrees:* DSc, Purdue Univ, 97. *Honors & Awards:* Charles Albert Shull Award, Am Soc Plant Physiologists, 79, Dennis Robert Hoagland Award, 94; Award Excellence, Weed Sci Soc Am, 80; USDA Superior Serv Award, 80. *Prof Exp:* NSF fel photosynthesis, C F Kettering Res Lab, 69-70; from asst prof to prof bot, Univ Ill, Urbana, 70-80, plant physiologist, Sci Educ Admin, USDA, 76-80; prof biochem & dir, Dept Energy Plant Res Lab, Mich State Univ, 80-84; dir, Plant Sci & Microbiol, Cent Res & Develop Dept, E I Du Pont de Nemours & Co, Inc, 84-87, Agr Biotechnol Res, 87-88; dep chancellor & dean agr, 88-91, Tex A&M Univ, dir, Plant Biotechnol Prog, 92-95. *Concurrent Pos:* Vis prof, Australian Nat Univ, Canberra, 81; chmn, Physiol Sect, Weed Sci Soc Am, 83-83 & Biotechnol Adv Comt to Pres Reagan's Sci Adv, Nat Acad Sci, 85; mem var sci comts & adv panels, USDA, NIH, NSF & nat socs, 82-; vis res scientist, Photosynthesis Lab, Nat Ctr Sci Res, France, 76 & Academia Sinica, Beijing, 83. *Mem:* Nat Acad Sci; Nat Acad Sci India; Am Soc Plant Physiologists (pres elect, 84-85, pres, 85-86); Am Soc Cell Biol; Am Biophys Soc; Am Soc Agron; Int Plant Molecular Biol Soc; Weed Sci Soc Am. *Res:* Plant molecular biology and protein engineering; utilization of plant biotechnology for enhancement food quality and value for expression of pharmacologically active products in transgenic plants; overcoming health and agricultural constraints in the developing world. *Mailing Add:* Boyce Thompson Inst Plant Res Tower Rd Ithaca NY 14853. *E-Mail:* cja7@cornell.edu

ARNTZEN, CLYDE EDWARD, ORGANIC CHEMISTRY. *Current Pos:* RETIRED. *Personal Data:* b Crescent City, Ill, Dec 26, 15; m 48, Lois Watson; c Linda & Bruce. *Educ:* Univ Ill, BS, 38; Iowa State Col, PhD(org chem), 42. *Prof Exp:* Engr res labs, Westinghouse Elec Corp, 42-45, engr & group leader, 45-46, mgr, Insulation Develop Sect, Mat Eng Dept, 46-48, Insulation Appln Sect, 48-52 & Chem Develop Sect, 52-53, sect mgr chem labs, 53-55, asst to mgr, Mat Eng Depts, 55-58, mgr, 58-62, mgr prog eval & div coord, Res Labs, 62-44, mgr tech serv, Res Labs, 64-76, mgr, Res & Develop Opers, 76-79. *Mem:* Am Chem Soc; Sigma Xi. *Res:* Synthetic organic chemistry; organic resins and plastics; chemical engineering; synthetic resins and plastics; radio; evaluation of technical projects; administration. *Mailing Add:* 5923 Tidewater Dr Jupiter FL 33458

ARNUSH, DONALD, THEORETICAL PHYSICS. *Current Pos:* mem tech staff, 63-72, mgr, plasma physics dept, 72-81, dir, Energy Res Ctr, Energy Tech Div, 81-89, MGR ADVAN TECHNOL, TRW, 90- *Personal Data:* b New York, NY, Feb 7, 36; m 66. *Educ:* Mass Inst Technol, SB, 57, PhD(physics), 61. *Prof Exp:* NSF fel, Max Planck Inst Physics & Astrophysics, 61-62. *Mem:* Am Phys Soc. *Res:* Theory of fundamental particles; engineering physics; electromagnetic wave propagation; ionospheric and fusion related plasma physics; technical management; theoretical physics. *Mailing Add:* 6018 Via Sonoma Rancho Palos Verdes CA 90274

ARNWINE, WILLIAM CARROL, OPERATIONS RESEARCH, INDUSTRIAL ENGINEERING. *Current Pos:* staff specialist, 72-83, PROJECT MGR, ROCKWELL INT, 83- *Personal Data:* b McCurtain, Okla, July 28, 29; m 51, 87, Juanita Smith; c William, Jean, James, Clark & Neil. *Educ:* Okla State Univ, BSIE, 54; Iowa State Univ, MSIE, 62, PhD(opers res, indust eng), 67. *Prof Exp:* Methods engr & group leader indust eng, E I du Pont de Nemours & Co, Iowa, 54-59; from instr to asst prof indust eng & opers res, Iowa State Univ, 59-66; assoc prof, Univ Ark, 66-68; prof & head dept, Univ Nebr, Omaha, 68-69 & NMex State Univ, 69-72. *Concurrent Pos:* Licensed methods-time measurement instr, MTM Asn for Stand & Res, 76-; lectr, Calif State Univ, Fullerton, 75 & Long Beach, 79; work measurement ed, Am Inst Indust Engrs Transactions, 80-85. *Mem:* Am Inst Indust Engrs; Opers Res Soc Am; fel Methods-Time Measurement Asn; Sigma Xi; Am Mgt Asn. *Res:* Allocating multiple warheads; queueing systems; sequencing problems; scheduling models; computer approaches for curve fitting; accuracy of work measurement systems. *Mailing Add:* 508 N Cornell Ave Fullerton CA 92631-2711

ARNY, DEANE CEDRIC, AGRONOMY. *Current Pos:* From instr to prof, 43-84, EMER PROF PLANT PATH, UNIV WIS, MADISON, 84- *Personal Data:* b St Paul, Minn, May 22, 17; m 47; c 5. *Educ:* Univ Minn, BS, 39; Univ Wis, PhD(agron, plant path), 43. *Honors & Awards:* Ruth Allen Award, Am Phytopath Soc, 87. *Concurrent Pos:* Vis prof, Univ Ife, Nigeria, 66-68, Andalas Univ, Indonesia, 86. *Mem:* Am Phytopath Soc; Am Soc Agron. *Res:* Diseases of field crops-corn, smallgrains, alfalfa. *Mailing Add:* 5401 Whitcomb Dr Madison WI 53711

ARNY, THOMAS TRAVIS, ASTROPHYSICS. *Current Pos:* from asst prof to assoc prof, 66-96, chmn, Five Col Astron Dept, 75-81, PROF ASTRON, UNIV MASS, AMHERST, 96- *Personal Data:* b Montclair, NJ, June 2, 40; m 68. *Educ:* Haverford Col, BA, 61; Univ Ariz, PhD(star formation), 65. *Prof Exp:* Res assoc astron, Amherst Col, 65-66. *Mem:* Am Astron Soc; Royal Astron Soc; Int Astron Union; fel AAAS. *Res:* Astronomy education; star formation. *Mailing Add:* Dept Astron GRC B Univ Mass Amherst MA 01003

AROESTY, JULIAN MAX, CORONARY ANGIOPLASTY, CARDIAC CATHETERIZATION. *Current Pos:* Instr cardiol, 66-71, asst clin prof med, 71-83, ASSOC CLIN PROF MED, HARVARD MED SCH, 83- *Personal Data:* b Rochester, NY, Sept 12, 31; m 71, Elaine Cronin; c Steven M, Marla B, David C & Adam M. *Educ:* Cornell Univ, BA, 53; State Univ NY, Syracuse, MD, 60. *Concurrent Pos:* clin asst, Harvard Med Sch, 66-71, clin assoc, 71-86. *Mem:* fel Am Col Physicians; fel Am Col Cardiol; fel Am Heart Assoc; fel Soc Cardiac Angiography & Intervention. *Res:* Cardiogenic shock, valvular and coronary heart disease, permanent pacemaker therapy, coronary angioplasty and valvuloplasty. *Mailing Add:* 330 Brookline Ave Boston MA 02215

AROIAN, LEO AVEDIS, MATHEMATICAL STATISTICS. *Current Pos:* RETIRED. *Personal Data:* b Holden, Mass, May 10, 07; m 41; c 2. *Educ:* Univ Mich, AB, 28, MA, 29, PhD, 40. *Honors & Awards:* Res Award, Am Soc Qual Control, 70. *Prof Exp:* Asst prof math, Colo State Univ, 30-39; instr, Hunter Col, 39-47, asst prof, 48-50; head math sect, Hughes Aircraft Co, 50-59, sr math consult, 59-60; mem tech staff, space technol labs, Thompson-Ramo-Wooldridge Inc, 60-67, sr staff mathematician, TRW Systs, 67-68; prof indust admin, Union Col, 68-72, res prof admin & mgt, 76-87, emer prof, 72- *Concurrent Pos:* Rackham fel, Univ Mich, 38-39; res assoc, Mtrop Life Ins Co, 43-44, Statist Lab, Univ Calif, 45; mem Nat Defense Res Comt, 45; vis prof, dept math, Western Ill Univ, 76-77. *Mem:* Am Math Soc; Math Asn Am; fel Am Soc Qual Control; fel Am Statist Asn; Inst Math Statist; Sigma Xi. *Res:* High speed computation; numerical methods; mathematical, applied and industrial statistics; reliability theory; sequential analysis; time series; security investments. *Mailing Add:* 32 Union Ave Schenectady NY 12308

ARON, GERT, HYDROLOGY, WATER RESOURCES. *Current Pos:* RETIRED. *Personal Data:* b Konigsberg, Ger, July 10, 27; US citizen; m 78; c 2. *Educ:* Univ Iowa, MS, 60; Univ Calif, PhD(hydrol), 69. *Prof Exp:* Flood control engr, Rudolf Goetze Consult, 60-61; hydraul engr, Harza Eng Co, 61-63; res engr hydraul, Univ Calif, Davis, 63-69; from asst prof to prof civil eng, Pa State Univ, 69-92. *Concurrent Pos:* Ground water specialist, UNESCO, 70-73; hydraul eng consult for various firms. *Mem:* Am Soc Civil Eng; Am Water Resources Asn; Am Geophys Union. *Res:* Water resources distribution planning; drought and flood frequencies; urban storm runoff modeling; hydrologic modeling. *Mailing Add:* 227 Kimport Rd Boalsburg PA 16827

ARON, ROBERT, AGRICULTURAL CLIMATOLOGY, MICROCLIMATOLOGY. *Current Pos:* PROF GEOG, CENT MICH UNIV, 76- *Personal Data:* m 75, I-Ming Wang; c Rebecca A. *Educ:* Univ Calif, Los Angeles, BA, 65; Calif State Univ, MA, 70; Ore State Univ, PhD(geog), 75. *Mem:* Asn Am Geographers. *Res:* Agricultural climatology; microclimatology; air pollution modeling. *Mailing Add:* 1518 Carnahan Mt Pleasant MI 48858. *Fax:* 517-774-2907

ARON, WALTER ARTHUR, THEORETICAL PHYSICS. *Current Pos:* RETIRED. *Personal Data:* b Milwaukee, Wis, Aug 30, 21; m 43, 72, Anabelle Purtell; c John A, Mary B (Cohen) & Margaret A. *Educ:* Univ Calif, PhD(physics), 51. *Prof Exp:* Physicist, Radiation Lab, Mass Inst Technol, 44-46; physicist, Radiation Lab, Univ Calif, 46-51; res assoc physics, Princeton Univ, 51-55; asst prof, Univ Va, 55-59; theoret physicist, Lawrence Radiation Lab, Univ Calif, Berkeley, 59-64; res physicist, Stanford Res Inst, 64-71; scientist, Sci Applns, Inc, 71-83; consult, 83-84. *Mem:* Sigma Xi; AAAS. *Res:* Particle interactions; data analysis; acoustics; optical transmission. *Mailing Add:* 7 Manor Pl Menlo Park CA 94025-3714

ARON, WILLIAM IRWIN, BIOLOGICAL OCEANOGRAPHY. *Current Pos:* dir, Off Ecol & Conserv, 71-78, dir, Off Marine Mammals & Endangered Species, 78-80, DIR, NORTHWEST & ALASKA FISHERIES CTR, NAT OCEANIC & ATMOSPHERIC ADMIN, 80- *Personal Data:* b Brooklyn, NY, June 26, 30; m 61; c 2. *Educ:* Brooklyn Col, BS, 52; Univ Wash, MS, 57, PhD, 60. *Prof Exp:* Biologist, Wash State Dept Fisheries, 52-53, res instr oceanog, Univ Wash, 56-60, res asst prof, 60-61; res supvry biologist, defense res labs, Gen Motors Corp, 61-67; dep head, off oceanog & limnol, Smithsonian Inst, 67-69, dir oceanog & limnol prog, 69-71. *Concurrent Pos:* Consult, Vet Corps, US Army, 56-, President's Marine Sci Comn, 68-69 & Nat Water Comn, 69-; mem gen adv comt, Mediter Marine Sorting Ctr, Tunisia, 70-; US del, Coop Invests of the Mediter, 70-; mem comt oceanog biol methods panel, Nat Acad Sci; mem bd dirs, Nat Oceanog Instrumentation Ctr. *Mem:* Fel AAAS; Am Soc Limnol & Oceanog; Am Soc Ichthyologists & Herpetologists; Soc Study Evolution; Sigma Xi; fel Am Inst Fisheries Res Biol; fel Minerals, Metals & Mat Soc. *Res:* Instrumentation for sampling; zoogeography of pelagic fish and plankton; research administration. *Mailing Add:* 11809 NE 30th Pl Bellevue WA 98005

ARONI, SAMUEL, STRUCTURES, URBAN PLANNING. *Current Pos:* actg dean, Grad Sch Archit & Urban Planning, 74-75 & 83-85, prof, 70-91, EMER PROF ARCHIT & URBAN PLANNING, UNIV CALIF, LOS ANGELES, 91-, DIR, SPEC ACAD COOP PROJ, INT STUDIES & OVERSEAS PROG, 91- *Personal Data:* b Kishinev, Romania, May 26, 27; m 56, Malca Corenfeld; c Ruth & Miriam. *Educ:* Univ Melbourne, BCE, 55; Univ Calif, Berkeley, MS & PhD(struct eng & mech), 66. *Honors & Awards:* J James R Croes Gold Medal, Am Soc Civil Engrs, 81. *Prof Exp:* Lectr civil eng, Univ Melbourne, 55-62; teaching fel & res asst struct eng & mech, Univ Calif, Berkeley, 63-66; assoc prof eng, San Francisco State Col, 66-67; res engr, Am Cement Corp, 67-70. *Concurrent Pos:* Consult, Adv Comt Dept Housing & Urban Develop, Nat Acad Sci & Nat Acad Eng, 70-73; mem exec comt, Int Tech Coop Ctr, 71-77; vpres, Urban Innovations Bd, 74-75, chmn, 83-85; mem, Comt on Socioecon Effects of Earthquake Predictions, Nat Acad Sci, 76-78; chmn, Acad Senate, Univ Calif, Los Angeles, 81-82; mem bd gov, Ben-Gurion Univ Nyev, Israel, 83-; mem, Adv Comt, NSF, 85-90; vpres, Archit Res Ctrs Consortium, 85-86. *Mem:* Am Soc Civil Engrs; Am Concrete Inst. *Res:* Cementitious materials; concrete technology; structures; earthquakes; low-cost housing, policy and technology. *Mailing Add:* Sch Art & Archit Univ Calif Los Angeles CA 90024. *E-Mail:* aroni@ucla.edu

ARONIN, LEWIS RICHARD, MATERIALS SCIENCE, PHYSICAL METALLURGY. *Current Pos:* CONSULT, ADVAN MAT DEVELOP. *Personal Data:* b Norwood, Mass, Aug 4, 19; m 47; c 2. *Educ:* Mass Inst Technol, BS, 40. *Prof Exp:* Asst res dir precision instruments, Waltham Watch Co, 40-49; staff mem, Metall Proj, Mass Inst Technol, 49-54; dept mgr, Nuclear Metals Inc, 54-66; consult econ eval, Kennecott Copper Ledgemont Lab, 66-67; mat engr res & develop, Army Mat Technol Lab, 67-90. *Mem:* Am Inst Mining, Metall & Petrol Engrs-Metall Soc; Sigma Xi; Soc Advan Mat & Process Eng; Am Soc Metals; Am Inst Aeronaut & Astronaut. *Res:* Materials research and development in aerospace and nuclear materials with emphasis on refractory metals, beryllium, and advanced composite materials. *Mailing Add:* 20 Ingleside Rd Lexington MA 02173-2522

ARONOFF, GEORGE R, NEPHROLOGY, CLINICAL PHARMACOLOGY. *Current Pos:* CHIEF, DIV NEPHROL & PROF MED & PHARMACOL, UNIV LOUISVILLE, 87- *Personal Data:* b Peoria, Ill, Mar 6, 50. *Educ:* Ind Univ, BA, 72, MS, 84 & MD, 75. *Prof Exp:* From asst prof to assoc prof med, Ind Univ, 80-87. *Mem:* Fel Am Col Physicians; AAAS; Am Soc Clin Pharmacol & Therapeut; Am Soc Nephrol; Cent Soc Clin Res. *Res:* Drug disposition in patients with renal disease; drug nephrotoxicity; artificial intelligence. *Mailing Add:* 615 S Preston St Louisville KY 40292. *Fax:* 502-852-7643

ARONOFF, SAMUEL, BIOCHEMISTRY. *Current Pos:* dean sci, 71-76, PROF CHEM, SIMON FRASER UNIV, 76- *Personal Data:* b New York, NY, Feb 27, 15; m 36; c 3. *Educ:* Univ Calif, Los Angeles, AB, 36; Univ Calif, PhD(physico-chem biol), 42. *Prof Exp:* Asst agr, Univ Calif, 41-42, res fel, 42-43; instr chem, Boston Univ, 43-44; res instr, Univ Chicago, 44-46; mem staff, Radiation Lab, Univ Calif, 46-48; from assoc prof to prof bot, Iowa State Univ, 48-60, prof biochem & biophys, 60-69; dean, Grad Sch Arts & Sci & vpres res, Boston Col, 69-71. *Concurrent Pos:* Sr fel, NSF, 57-58, prog dir molecular biol, 63-64, consult, 64-65. *Mem:* Am Chem Soc; Am Soc Plant Physiol (secy, 62-63, vpres, 64, pres, 65); Am Soc Biol Chemists; Can Soc Plant Physiol. *Res:* Plant biochemistry; photosynthesis; chlorophyll; radiobiochemistry; boron biochemistry. *Mailing Add:* 76 E Vista del Mar Camano Island WA 98292-8720

ARONOFSKY, JULIUS S, applied mathematics; deceased, see previous edition for last biography

ARONOVIC, SANFORD MAXWELL, ANALYTICAL CHEMISTRY, MICROANALYSIS. *Current Pos:* CONSULT, 81- *Personal Data:* b New York, NY, June 10, 26; m 57, Gilda Kugler; c Daniel, Allen & Diane. *Educ:* Columbia Univ, BS, 45; Univ Wis, PhD(chem), 57. *Prof Exp:* Chemist microanal, Lederle Labs Div, Am Cyanamid Co, 47-52, res chemist anal develop, Stamford Res Labs, 57-62; res asst infrared spectros, Univ Wis, 52-57; res anal chemist, Maumee Chem Co, 62-65; res scientist, Union Bag-Camp Paper Corp, 65, res chemist, Union Camp Corp, 65-68; supvr qual control, Thiokol Chem Corp, 69-72, supvr anal serv, 72-76, supvr toxicol, 76-77, coordr Environ & Regulatory Affairs, 77-81. *Mem:* Am Chem Soc. *Res:* Microanalytical chemistry; infrared spectroscopy; instrumental methods of analysis; analytical separations, identification and separations, analytical methods development; gas chromatography. *Mailing Add:* 351 Franklin Ave Princeton NJ 08540-3953

ARONOW, LEWIS, PHARMACOLOGY. *Current Pos:* PROF PHARMACOL & CHMN DEPT, UNIFORMED SERV UNIV HEALTH SCI, 76- *Personal Data:* b New York, NY, Mar 28, 27; m 53, Gladys Levy; c 4. *Educ:* City Col New York, BS, 50; Georgetown Univ, MS, 52; Harvard Univ, PhD(pharmacol), 56. *Honors & Awards:* Premio Martin Vegas, Soc Venezolana Dermat, 64; Maloney lectr, Howard Univ, 77. *Prof Exp:* Chemist, Lab Chem Pharmacol, Nat Heart Inst, 50-52; fel pharmacol, Harvard Univ, 52-56; from instr to prof, Stanford Univ, 56-76. *Concurrent Pos:* Vis prof pharmacol & chmn dept, Sch Med Jose Vargas, Univ Cent Venezuela, 62-63; Am Cancer Soc/Eleanor Roosevelt Int Cancer fel, Cambridge Univ, Eng, 70-71; actg chmn dept pharmacol, Stanford Univ, 74-76. *Mem:* Am Soc Pharmacol & Exp Therapeut; Am Asn Cancer Res. *Res:* Glucocorticoid hormones; anti-cancer drugs; biochemical and cellular pharmacology; drug metabolism. *Mailing Add:* 9100 Covered Wagon Ave Las Vegas NV 89117. *Fax:* 301-295-3220; *E-Mail:* aronow@usuhsb.usuhs.mil

ARONOW, SAUL, GEOMORPHOLOGY, SOILS. *Current Pos:* RETIRED. *Personal Data:* b Brooklyn, NY, Dec 10, 23; m 48, Judith Zuckerman; c Jessie, Kurt & Rebecca. *Educ:* Brooklyn Col, BA, 45; Univ Iowa, MS, 46; Univ Wis, PhD, 55. *Prof Exp:* Draftsman, Army Map Serv, 45; geologist, US Geol Surv, 48-52; asst geol, Univ Wis, 53-54; prof geol, Lamar Univ, 55-92. *Concurrent Pos:* Consult, Tex Bur Econ Geol, 65-70, Soil Conserv Serv, 65-, Minn Geol Serv, 72-73 & 78-80, Nat Park Serv, 79-, Corps Engrs, 84, Moore archeol consult, 88- & Archeol Res Lab, Tex A&M Univ, 89- *Mem:* AAAS; Am Geol Soc; Sigma Xi; Am Quaternary Asn; Soil Sci Soc Am. *Res:* Geomorphology; glacial geology; ground water; Pleistocene of Gulf Coast region; soils; salt domes; geoarcheology. *Mailing Add:* 5590 Frost Beaumont TX 77706

ARONOW, SAUL, BIOMEDICAL ENGINEERING, RADIOLOGICAL PHYSICS. *Current Pos:* from asst physicist to assoc appl physicist, Mass Gen Hosp, 53-68, dir med eng group, 68-72, assoc physicist, Dept Radiol, 72-82, CONSULT PHYSICS, MASS GEN HOSP, 82- *Personal Data:* b Brooklyn, NY, Oct 4, 17; m 42, Alice Pearlman; c 6. *Educ:* Cooper Union, BEE, 39; Harvard Univ, MS, 46, PhD(appl sci), 53. *Honors & Awards:* Gano Dunn Medal. *Prof Exp:* Electronics engr, Harvey Radio Labs, 46-49. *Concurrent Pos:* Prin assoc med, Harvard Med Sch, 54-; lectr, Northeastern Univ, 56- & Mass Inst Technol, 57-82; vis prof, Denmark Tech Univ, 69; consult engr, Mass; pres, Technol Med Res Inst; engr, Proj Hope, Technol Med, Inc, 82-83. *Mem:* Fel Inst Elec & Electronics Engrs; Am Asn Physicists in Med; Soc Nuclear Med; Biomed Eng Soc; Sigma Xi. *Res:* Medical applications of electronic instrumentation; nuclear medicine; radiological imaging. *Mailing Add:* 86 Crofton Rd Waban MA 02168-2115

ARONOW, WILBERT SOLOMON, INTERNAL MEDICINE. *Current Pos:* MED DIR, HEBREW HOSP HOME, BRONX, NY, 84- *Personal Data:* b New York, NY, Oct 30, 31; m 58, Ina Brody; c Janice S & Michael S. *Educ:* Queens Col, NY, BS, 53; Harvard Univ, MD, 57. *Prof Exp:* Residency internal med & cardiovascular dis, Michael Reese Hosp & Med Ctr, 57-61; chief cardiol & gen med, US Army Hosp, Ft Chaffee, Ark, 61-63; staff internist, Vet Admin Hosp, E Orange, 63-64; staff cardiologist, Vet Admin Hosp, Long Beach, 64-82, chief, Cardiovasc Sect, 73-82, asst chief med res, 75-80; prof med & chief cardiovasc res, Creighton Univ Sch Med, Omaha, Nebr, 82-84. *Concurrent Pos:* Asst clin prof med, Univ Calif Irvine, 68-72, assoc prof med, 72-75, vchief, Cardiovasc Div & chief cardiovasc res, 74-82, prof med, 75-82 & prof pharmacol & therapeut, 76-82; mem cardiovasc & renal adv comt, US Food & Drug Admin, 73-76; chmn, Cardiovasc & Pulmonary Dis Sect, Am Soc Clin Pharmacol & Therapeut, 73-74 & 75-77; distinguished lectr, Am Col Angiol, 73; consult, US Environ Protection Agency, 73 & 78-83, Calif Air Resources Bd, 73, 78, 80 & 82, NIH, 76 & 80, US Dept Justice Law Enforcement Assistance Admin, 78, Dept Health, WGer, 78, Nat Heart, Lung & Blood Inst, 79, Nat Cancer Inst, 80, Dept Health & Environ Sci, Mont, 80 & Fed Trade Comn, 80-81; consult, Dept Drugs, AMA, 3rd ed of AMA Drug Eval, 74, 4th ed, 78 & 5t ed, 82 & Nat Ctr Health Statist, 81; pres, Asn Vet Admin Cardiologists, 75-77; vis prof med, Univ Tex Southwestern Med Sch, Dallas, 76, Univ Man & Univ Toronto, 79, Rutgers Med Sch, 83 & pharmacol & therapeut, Texas Tech Univ Sch Med, Lubbock, 83; consult smoking, Am Heart Asn, 80 & mem subcomt, 80-83; guest field ed, J Pharmacol & Exp Therapeut, 81; attend physician, Geront Geriat Soct, Dept Med, Westchester County Med Ctr, Valhalla, NY, 85-87; consult, State NY Dept Health, Off Pub Health, 86; fel, Coun Geriat Cardiol; cardiol consult, Albert Einstein Col Med, 90-; attend physician, Cardiol Div, Bronx Munic Hosp Ctr, 90-; adj prof geriat & adult develop, Mt Sinai Sch Med, 92-, adj attend, 92- *Mem:* Fel Am Col Chest Physicians; Am Soc Clin Pharmacol & Therapeut; fel Am Col Physicians; fel Am Col Cardiol; fel Am Heart Asn; fel Am Geriat Soc; Am Fedn Clin Res; mem Am Med Dir Asn; fel Coun Geriat Cardiol; Geront Soc Am. *Res:* Cardiovascular diseases; geriatrics. *Mailing Add:* 23 Pebble Way New Rochelle NY 10804. *Fax:* 718-379-2751; *E-Mail:* iaronow@aol.com

ARONOWITZ, FREDERICK, QUANTUM PHYSICS. *Current Pos:* CHIEF SCIENTIST, ROCKWELL INT, 84- *Personal Data:* b New York, NY, July 3, 35; m 69, Marguerite; c Malica, Michelle & Jacqueline. *Educ:* Polytech Inst Brooklyn, BS, 56; NY Univ, PhD(physics), 69. *Honors & Awards:* Prize for Indust Applns of Physics, Am Inst Physics, 83; Elmer A Sperry Award, 84; Kirschner Award, Inst Elec & Electronics Engrs, 88; Michelson Award, Navy League, 90; Technol Achievement Award, Int Soc Optical Eng, 90. *Prof Exp:* Physicist, David Taylor Model Basin, 56; consult, Eastern Res Group, 61-62; staff scientist, Honeywell, Inc, 62-80, sect head, 80-83; mgr, Raytheon, 83-84. *Mem:* Am Phys Soc. *Res:* Quantum electronics with major emphasis of the theory and development of the laser gyroscope. *Mailing Add:* 32542 Adriatic Dr Dana Point CA 92629

ARONS, ARNOLD BORIS, OCEANOGRAPHY, PHYSICS EDUCATION. *Current Pos:* prof physics, 68-82, EMER PROF, UNIV WASH, 82- *Personal Data:* b Lincoln, Nebr, Nov 23, 16; m 42, Jean Rendall; c Marion, Janet, Kenneth & Paul. *Educ:* Stevens Inst Technol, ME, 37, MS, 40; Harvard Univ, PhD(phys chem), 43. *Hon Degrees:* AM, Amherst Col, 53; DE, Stevens Inst Technol, 82. *Honors & Awards:* Honor Medal, Stevens Inst Technol, 68; Oersted Medal, Am Asn Physics Teachers, 72. *Prof Exp:* Asst, Harvard Univ, 42-43; instr chem, Stevens Inst Technol, 37-40, from asst prof to assoc prof, 46-52; prof, Amherst Col, 52-68. *Concurrent Pos:* Res assoc, Oceanog Inst, Woods Hole, 43-72, mem corp, 63-, trustee, 64-; chief, Sect Underwater Blast Measurements, Oper Crossroads, Navy Bur Ord, 46; Guggenheim fel, 57-58; NSF fac fel, 62-63; consult, Naval Ord Lab, Waterways Exp Sta; mem, Comn Col Physics, 62-68; gov bd, Am Inst Physics, 66-72; baccalaureate degree proj, Asn Am Cols, 82-85; res comt, math, sci & technol educ, Nat Acad Sci-Nat Res Coun, 83-85; mem adv comt sci & eng educ, NSF, 84-85. *Mem:* Fel AAAS; fel Am Phys Soc; Am Asn Physics Teachers (pres, 67); Am Geophys Union; Nat Sci Teachers Asn. *Res:* Explosion phenomena; development of tourmaline piezoelectric gauges for measurement of explosion pressure waves; physical oceanography; hydrodynamics of rotating systems; science education; cognitive development. *Mailing Add:* Dept Physics 351560 Univ Wash Seattle WA 98195. *Fax:* 206-685-0635; *E-Mail:* arons@dirac.phys.washington.edu

ARONS, BERNARD S, PSYCHIATRY. *Current Pos:* DIR, CTR MENT HEALTH SERVS, SUBSTANCE ABUSE & MENT HEALTH SERVS ADMIN, US DEPT HEALTH & HUMAN SERVS, 93- *Prof Exp:* Psychiatrist, St Elizabeths Hosp, NIMH, Washington, DC, dir, Dixon Implementation Off, 80, chief clin adv, assoc dir ment health financing, 86. *Concurrent Pos:* Legis fel, Health Subcomt Ways & Means Comt; chair, Ment Health & Substance Abuse Working Group Cluster, Pres Task Force Nat Health Care Reform; psychiatrist & instr, Ctr Ment Health Inc, Washington, DC; clin prof psychiat, Sch Med, Georgetown Univ. *Res:* Concerns of individuals with mental illness and their families; persons with serious mental illnesses and health care reform. *Mailing Add:* Substance Abuse & Ment Health Serv Admin US Dept Health & Human Servs Ctr Ment Health Servs 5600 Fishers Lane Rm 13-103 Rockville MD 20857

ARONS, JONATHAN, THEORETICAL ASTROPHYSICS, THEORETICAL PLASMA PHYSICS. *Current Pos:* from asst prof to assoc prof astron, 72-82, assoc prof physics, 80-82, PROF ASTRON & PHYSICS, 82-, CHMN, ASTRON DEPT, UNIV CALIF, BERKELEY, 93- *Personal Data:* b Philadelphia, Pa, Aug 16, 43; m 74, Claire E Max; c 1. *Educ:* Williams Col, BA, 65; Harvard Univ, AM, 69, PhD(astron), 70. *Prof Exp:* Res assoc astron, Princeton Univ Observ, 70-71; mem astrophys staff, Inst Advan Study, 71-72. *Concurrent Pos:* Guggenheim Found fel, 80-81; mem, Physics Surv Subcomt, Space & Astrophys Plasmas, Nat Acad Sci, 83-84; vchmn, Astron Dept, Univ Calif, Berkeley, 84-85; Miller Found res prof, 85-86; vchmn & chmn, Astrophys Div, Am Phys Soc, 84-86; mem adv bd, Inst Theoret Physics, 88-91; actg chmn astron dept, Univ Calif, Berkeley, 90-91; mem, Plasma Sci Comt, Nat Acad Sci, 90-93. *Mem:* Am Astron Soc; fel Am Phys Soc; Am Geophys Union; Int Astron Union. *Res:* Astrophysical plasma physics; coherent radiation from plasmas; high energy astrophysics. *Mailing Add:* Dept Astron 601 Campbell Hall Univ Calif Berkeley CA 94720

ARONS, MICHAEL EUGENE, PHYSICS. *Current Pos:* VPRES ACAD AFFAIRS, LONG ISLAND UNIV, 94- *Personal Data:* b New York, NY, Mar 29, 39; m 61, Rosemarie Davoli; c David & Jennifer. *Educ:* Cooper Union, BEE, 59; Univ Rochester, PhD(theoret physics), 64. *Prof Exp:* Asst res scientist theoret physics, NY Univ, 64-66, asst prof physics, 66-70; assoc prof, City Col New York, 70-82, chmn dept, 81-87, prof, 82-, dean sci, 88-92, provost, 92-94. *Res:* Field theory and quantum electrodynamics; theories of elementary particles, including symmetries and field-theoretic models. *Mailing Add:* Univ Ctr City Long Island Univ Northern Blvd Brookville NY 11548. *Fax:* 212-650-6425; *E-Mail:* arons@scc.ccny.cuny.edu

ARONSON, A L, PHARMACOLOGY, VETERINARY MEDICINE. *Current Pos:* PROF PHARMACOL & HEAD DEPT ANAT, PHYSIOL SCI & RADIOL, NC STATE UNIV, 80- *Personal Data:* b Minneapolis, Minn, Aug 24, 33; m 56; c 3. *Educ:* Univ Minn, BS, 55, DVM, 57, PhD(pharmacol), 63; Cornell Univ, MS, 59. *Prof Exp:* Teaching asst pharmacol, Cornell Univ, 57-58; res fel, Univ Minn, 58-63, res assoc, 63-64; from asst prof to prof, State Univ NY Vet Col, Cornell Univ, 64-80. *Concurrent Pos:* Chmn, Coun Biol & Therapeut Agts, Am Vet Med Asn, 85-86. *Mem:* Am Vet Med Asn; Am Acad Vet Pharmacol & Therapeut (pres-elect, 85-87, pres, 87-89); Soc Toxicol; Am Soc Pharmacol & Exp Therapeut. *Res:* Clinical pharmacology; toxicology. *Mailing Add:* NC State Univ Col Vet Med 4700 Hillsborough St Raleigh NC 27606-1428

ARONSON, ARTHUR H, METALLURGICAL ENGINEERING. *Current Pos:* EXEC VPRES, 88-, CHIEF OPER OFFICER, ALLEGHENY LUDLUM CORP, 90- *Personal Data:* b July 9, 35; m 59, Alice Ades; c Terisa, Steven, Kristina & Betsy. *Educ:* Mass Inst Technol, BS, 58; Rensselaer Polytech Inst, PhD(metall), 65. *Prof Exp:* Pres & chief exec officer, Cold Metal Prod, 80-84; pres & chief oper officer, Lukens Steel, 84-88. *Mem:* Fel Am Soc Metals; Sigma Xi. *Res:* Metallurgical engineering. *Mailing Add:* Allegheny Ludlum Corp 1000 Six PPG Pl Pittsburgh PA 15222

ARONSON, ARTHUR IAN, MICROBIOLOGY. *Current Pos:* from asst prof to assoc prof, 60-67, PROF MICROBIOL, PURDUE UNIV, 67- *Personal Data:* b Boston, Mass, July 2, 30; m 56; c 2. *Educ:* Univ Chicago, BA, 50; Univ Mass, MS, 53; Univ Ill, PhD(microbiol), 58. *Prof Exp:* Nat Found Polio fel, 58-59; fel, Carnegie Inst, 59-60. *Concurrent Pos:* Guggenheim fel, 68-69. *Mem:* AAAS; Am Soc Microbiol; Am Soc Biol Chemists. *Res:* Molecular biology; bacterial spore formation; regulation in bacilli; structure of insect protoxin genes. *Mailing Add:* Dept Biol Sci Purdue Univ 1392 Lilly Hall West Lafayette IN 47907-1392

ARONSON, CARL EDWARD, PHARMACOLOGY, TOXICOLOGY. *Current Pos:* instr pharmacol, Sch Med, Univ Pa, 67-70, assoc, 70-71, asst prof, Sch Vet Med, 71-73, from asst prof to assoc prof pharmacol, Sch Med, 71-92, head labs pharmacol & toxicol, 72-86, ASSOC PROF TOXICOL, DEPT ANIMAL BIOL, SCH VET MED, UNIV PA, 73- *Personal Data:* b Providence, RI, Mar 14, 36; m 60, Marjorie Boutelle; c Linda & Kristen. *Educ:* Brown Univ, AB, 58; Univ Vt, PhD(pharmacol), 66. *Hon Degrees:* MA, Univ Pa, 73. *Prof Exp:* Res technician, Worcester Found Exp Biol, Shrewsbury, Mass, 58-60. *Concurrent Pos:* Fel pharmacol, Univ Pa, 65-67, Pa Plan scholar, 69-71; lectr pharmacol, Div Grad Med Educ, Sch Med, Univ Pa, 65-74, actg assoc dean stud affairs, Sch Vet Med, 74-75; Heart Asn Southeastern Pa res fel, 69-72; vis res scientist, Philadelphia Vet Admin Med Ctr, 86- *Mem:* Sigma Xi; Am Acad Vet Pharmacol & Therapeut (pres, 83-85); Am Acad Vet & Comp Toxicol; Am Soc Pharmacol & Exp Therapeut; Am Vet Med Asn. *Res:* Biochemical pharmacology and toxicology; effects of drugs and hormones on cardiac performance and metabolism; effects of drugs on neurotransmitters and their receptors in the CNS. *Mailing Add:* Dept Animal Biol Lab Pharmacol & Toxicol Sch Vet Med Univ Pa 3800 Spruce St Philadelphia PA 19104-6008

ARONSON, CASPER JACOB, PHYSICS, EXPLOSIVES. *Current Pos:* RETIRED. *Personal Data:* b Canisteo, NY, Sept 1, 16; m 43, Eleanor J Gould; c Rhyda (Conant). *Educ:* Univ Rochester, BS, 38, MS, 39. *Honors & Awards:* Flemming Award, 55. *Prof Exp:* Asst, Univ Rochester, 38-40; physicist, Carnegie Inst, 40-41 & chief, Magnetic Model Sect, 44-46 & Magnetic Fields Sect, 46-49, sr res assoc, Explosives Res Dept, 49-52, dep chief, Explosion Effects Div, 52-53, asst chief atomic tests, 53-57, chief, Explosion Res Dept, 57-74, actg assoc head chem & explosions res, US Naval Ord Lab, 74-75; scientific asst res & technol, Naval Surface Weapons Ctr, 75 & Ablard Enterprises Inc, 75-76; scientific asst res & technol, VSE Corp, 80-87. *Mem:* AAAS; Am Phys Soc; Optical Soc Am; Sigma Xi; NY Acad Sci. *Res:* Ship's magnetic fields; shock waves; effects of explosions. *Mailing Add:* 3401 Oberon St Kensington MD 20895-2935

ARONSON, DONALD GARY, MATHEMATICS. *Current Pos:* from instr to assoc prof, 57-65, PROF MATH, UNIV MINN, MINNEAPOLIS, 65- *Personal Data:* b Jersey City, NJ, Oct 2, 29; m 53; c 3. *Educ:* Mass Inst Technol, SB, 51, SM, 52, PhD(math), 56. *Prof Exp:* Res assoc digital comput lab, Univ Ill, 56-57. *Concurrent Pos:* NSF fel, 61-62; Soc Indust & Appl Math vis lectr, 64-66. *Mem:* Am Math Soc; Math Asn Am. *Res:* Partial differential equations. *Mailing Add:* Sch Math Univ Minn Inst Technol 127 Vincent Hall 206 Church SE Minneapolis MN 55455-0488

ARONSON, FREDERICK RUPP, ONCOLOGY-HEMATOLOGY, TUMOR IMMUNOLOGY. *Current Pos:* ASSOC CLIN PROF MED, SCH MED, UNIV VT, 93- *Personal Data:* b New York, NY, Nov 5, 53; m 88, Jennifer A Goldfarb; c Jonathan G & Max D. *Educ:* Johns Hopkins Univ, BA, 75; Yale Univ Sch Med, MPH & MD, 80. *Prof Exp:* Med resident, RI Hosp, Brown Univ, 80-83; fel hemat-oncol, New Eng Med Ctr, Tufts Univ, 83-86; asst prof med, Sch Med, Tufts Univ, 86-88; asst clin prof med, Univ Calif, San Francisco, 88-93. *Concurrent Pos:* Res fel, Med Found, Boston, 86-88; prin investr, Nat Cancer Inst, 88-91; consult, Chiron Corp, Calif, 88-93, Cowan & Assocs, Mass, 90-; res assoc & dir, Biol Response Modifiers Prog, Cancer Res Inst, Univ Calif, San Francisco, 88-93; consult prof, Liaoning Tumor Hosp & Inst, China, 92; vis prof, Jinzhou Med Col, China, 92; co-prin investr, NIH, 92-93. *Mem:* Fel Am Col Physicians; Am Fedn Clin Res; Am Asn Cancer Res; Am Soc Clin Oncol; Am Soc Hemat. *Res:* Physiology of interleukin-2 toxicity; clinical trials of cytokines; melanoma immunology; cancer clinical trials; interleukin-2; interleukin-6; gene therapy; melanoma; renal cell cancer. *Mailing Add:* 100 US Rte One Scarborough ME 04074-9302. *Fax:* 207-885-7610; *E-Mail:* mccm.data@office.mmc.org

ARONSON, HERBERT, EXPERIMENTAL PSYCHOLOGY. *Current Pos:* ASSOC PROF MECH ENG, NY INST TECHNOL, 64- *Personal Data:* b Braunschweig, Ger, Feb 23, 23; US citizen; m 54; c 2. *Educ:* City Col New York, BME, 49; Newark Col Eng, MSME, 54. *Prof Exp:* Liaison engr, Hydropress Co, 49-52; proj engr, Morey Mach Co, 52-53, Curtis Wright and Pratt & Whitney, 53-55, Silent Hoist & Crane Co, 55-57, Sperry Gyroscope Co, 57-59 & Am Mach & Foundry, 59-64. *Concurrent Pos:* Eng consult, 60- *Mem:* Soc Automotive Engrs; Am Soc Mech Engrs; Am Soc Safety Engrs. *Res:* Application of the detection theory model to the study of attitudinal factors in temporal integration in vision. *Mailing Add:* 101-06 67th Dr Forest Hills NY 11375

ARONSON, JAMES RIES, SPECTRAL MODEL OF REFLECTANCE EMITTANCE OF PARTICULATE MATERIALS. *Current Pos:* CONSULT, 86- *Personal Data:* b Chicago, Ill, Sept 1, 32; m 63, Rita M Cronin; c James T, Audrey M, Kathy J, Diane E & Christopher J. *Educ:* Northwestern Univ, BS, 54; Mass Inst Technol, PhD(chem), 58. *Prof Exp:* Res assoc, Mass Inst Technol, 58-59; res scientist, Arthur D Little, Inc, 59-86; res prof appl optics, Fairleigh Dickinson Univ, 87-88. *Mem:* Fel Optical Soc Am. *Res:* Infrared physics and spectroscopy; remote sensing; theory of emittance and reflectance of particulate media; optical constants of anisotropic solids; applications of spectroscopy to earth sciences and pollution; laser spectroscopy; infrared instrumentation; scientific software development. *Mailing Add:* 7 Wainwright Rd Winchester MA 01890. *E-Mail:* 71232.1271@compuserve.com

ARONSON, JAY E, MATHEMATICAL PROGRAMMING, PARALLEL NETWORKS. *Current Pos:* assoc prof mgt sci & info technol, Col Bus Admin, 87-92, ASSOC PROF MGT, TERRY COL BUS, UNIV GA, 92- *Personal Data:* b Boston, Mass, July 19, 53; m 80, Sharon Goldman; c Marla D, Michael L & Stephanie E. *Educ:* Carnegie-Mellon Univ, BS, 75, MS, 76, MS, 78, PhD(indust admin), 80. *Prof Exp:* Instr opers mgt & mgt info systs, Carnegie-Mellon Univ, 78-80; asst prof opers res & eng mgt, Southern Methodist Univ, 80-87. *Concurrent Pos:* Consult, 75-, UN, 89-92; asst prof mgt sci & comput, 84- *Mem:* Opers Res Soc Am; Inst Mgt Sci; Math Prog Soc; Decision Sci Inst. *Res:* Parallel Network Optimization; networks; large scale mathematical programming; executive information systems; decision support systems; artificial intelligence; neural networks; cluster analysis; group support systems. *Mailing Add:* Dept Mgt Terry Col Bus Univ Ga Athens GA 30602. *Fax:* 706-542-3743; *E-Mail:* aronson@phoenix.cs.uga.edu

ARONSON, JEROME MELVILLE, EXPERIMENTAL MYCOLOGY. *Current Pos:* assoc prof, 66-71, PROF BOT, ARIZ STATE UNIV, 71- *Personal Data:* b Oakland, Calif, May 20, 30; m 55; c 2. *Educ:* Univ Calif, BA, 52, PhD(bot), 58. *Prof Exp:* Lectr bot, Univ Calif, 57; NIH fel, 58-59; asst prof biol, Wayne State Univ, 59-63; lectr, Univ Calif, Berkeley, 64-66. *Concurrent Pos:* assoc ed, Exp Mycol, 79- *Mem:* Am Soc Plant Physiol; Bot Soc Am; Mycol Soc Am; Sigma Xi. *Res:* Cellwall biosynthesis, chemistry of fungal cell walls and polysaccharide storage products; biochemical systematics of fungi. *Mailing Add:* Dept Bot Ariz State Univ Tempe AZ 85287-0002

ARONSON, JOHN FERGUSON, physiology; deceased, see previous edition for last biography

ARONSON, JOHN NOEL, BIOCHEMISTRY. *Current Pos:* ASSOC PROF CHEM, STATE UNIV NY ALBANY, 65- *Personal Data:* b Dallas, Tex, Mar 15, 34; m 58; c 3. *Educ:* Rice Inst, BA; Univ Wis, MS, 55, PhD(biochem), 59. *Prof Exp:* Asst prof chem, Ariz State Univ, 59-65. *Concurrent Pos:* NIH res fel oncol, Univ Wis, 59; NSF fac fel, Ind Univ, 63-64; Am Soc Microbiol Pres fel, Univ Ill, 64. *Mem:* AAAS; Am Chem Soc; Am Soc Microbiol; Am Soc Biol Chemists; NY Acad Sci; Sigma Xi. *Res:* Biochemistry of bacterial sporulation; structure and function of proteins. *Mailing Add:* 4871 N Via Serenidad No 1 Tucson AZ 85718-5715

ARONSON, M(OSES), FLIGHT SIMULATION, MATHEMATICAL MODELING. *Current Pos:* CONSULT, ARONSON INDUSTS, 80- *Personal Data:* b New York, NY, May 2, 19; m 46, Ruth Katz; c Joel, Wayne & Helene. *Educ:* NY Univ, BAE, 40, MAE, 50, MIE, 58. *Prof Exp:* Jr Engr, Langley Aeronaut Lab, Nat Adv Comt Aeronaut, 40-41; sr aerodynamicist, Repub Aviation Corp, 45-49 & 50-51; sr proj engr electronics div, Curtiss-Wright Corp, 50; sr proj engr, Naval Training Equip Ctr, 51-56, br head eng dept, 56-60, div head aerospace syst trainers dept, 60-63, staff res engr, 63-64, head, Visual Simulation Lab, 64-73, head, Electronics Lab, 73-77, head modification eng br, 77-79. *Concurrent Pos:* Mem comt driving simulation, Transp Res Bd, 67-85; adj prof, Univ Cent Fla, 80-81; mem, Am Inst Aeronaut & Astronaut Tech Comt, Flight Simulation, 82-85. *Mem:* Assoc fel Am Inst Aeronaut & Astronaut. *Res:* Conducted training requirements analysis, experimental applications research and preliminary evaluation of potential solutions for operator training simulators and real world visual simulation devices, as well as establishing design parameters. *Mailing Add:* 3705 Wilder Lane Orlando FL 32804-3535

ARONSON, MIRIAM KLAUSNER, GERONTOLOGY. *Current Pos:* DIR, INST AGING, BERGEN PINES CO HOSP, PARAMUS, NJ, 93- *Personal Data:* b New York, NY, July 12, 40; c Eric, Andrew & Elliott. *Educ:* Barnard Col, AB, 61; Columbia Univ, EdM, 70, EdD, 80. *Honors & Awards:* Founders Award, Nat Alzheimers Dis & Related Dis, Asn, 87. *Prof Exp:* Consult, Res Geriat Facils, NY & NJ, 69-75; dir geriat prog, Soundview-Throgs Neck Community Ment Health Ctr, 78-79; dir long-term care, Geront Ctr, Albert Einstein Col Med, 79-91, from asst prof to prof neurol & psychiat, 80-90, clin assoc prof epidemiol & soc med & psychiat, 91-92. *Concurrent Pos:* Adminr,

Aging Grants, 68-70 & 74-75; dir, Task Force Long Term Care, Geront Soc Am, 81-85; prin investr senile dementias, risks & course, 84-; co-chair, Study Group on Aging, Am Orthopsychiat Soc, 88-; dir long-term care servs, Jewish Guild for Blind, Yonkers, 91-92; consult gerontologist & dir, Inst Aging, Bergen Pines Co Hosp. *Mem:* Geront Soc Am; Am Orthopsychiat Soc; Am Geriatrics Soc; Nat Alzheimers Dis & Related Dis Asn. *Res:* Geriatrics; aging. *Mailing Add:* Bergen Pines Co Hosp 230 E Ridgewood Ave Paramus NJ 07652

ARONSON, NATHAN NED, JR, BIOCHEMISTRY. *Current Pos:* from asst prof to assoc prof, 69-85, PROF BIOCHEM, PA STATE UNIV, UNIVERSITY PARK, 85- *Personal Data:* b Dallas, Tex, Dec 8, 40; m 64; c 3. *Educ:* Rice Univ, 62; Duke Univ, PhD(biochem), 67. *Prof Exp:* Guest investr cell biol, Rockefeller Univ, 66-68; fel molecular biol, Vanderbilt Univ, 68-69. *Concurrent Pos:* Helen Hay Whitney fel, 66-69; fel molecular path, Strange Ways Res Lab, Cambridge, Eng, 76-77; Brit-Am Heart fel, 76-77; Guggenheim fel, 76-77; sabbatical, Univ Calif San Diego, 84. *Mem:* Brit Biochem Soc; Am Soc Biol Chemists. *Res:* Lysosomes; membranes; glycoproteins. *Mailing Add:* Dept Biochem Univ SAla MSB 2152 Mobile AL 36688-0002. *Fax:* 334-460-6127

ARONSON, PETER S, KIDNEY & MEMBRANE PHYSIOLOGY, NEPHROLOGY. *Current Pos:* From asst prof to assoc prof med & physiol, 77-87, PROF MED & CELLULAR MOLECULAR PHYSIOL, SCH MED, 87-, CHIEF NEPHROL, YALE UNIV, 87-, CNH LONG PROF, 87- *Personal Data:* b Brooklyn, NY, Feb 3, 47; m 77, Marie L Landry; c Paul L & William L. *Educ:* NY Univ, MD, 70. *Hon Degrees:* MA, Yale Univ, 87. *Honors & Awards:* Young Investr Award, Am Soc Nephrol & Am Heart Asn, 85; Homer W Smith Award, Am Soc Nephrol & NY Heart Asn, 94. *Concurrent Pos:* Counr, Am Soc Clin Investr, 86-88. *Mem:* Am Fed Med Res; Am Physiol Soc; Asn Am Physicians; Am Soc Nephrol; Soc Gen Physiologists; Am Soc Clin Investr; fel AAAS. *Res:* Molecular mechanisms of ion transport across plasma membranes of epithelial cells. *Mailing Add:* Dept Med Sch Med Yale Univ PO Box 208029 New Haven CT 06520-8029. *Fax:* 203-785-7068; *E-Mail:* peter.aronson@yale.edu

ARONSON, RAPHAEL (FRIEDMAN), THEORETICAL PHYSICS, REACTOR PHYSICS. *Current Pos:* PROF NUCLEAR ENG & PHYSICS, POLYTECHNIC UNIV, 73- *Personal Data:* b Minneapolis, Minn, Feb 13, 28; m 58, 90; c 2. *Educ:* Univ Minn, BPhys, 47; Harvard Univ, MA, 48, PhD(physics), 52. *Prof Exp:* Sr scientist, Nuclear Develop Assocs, 51-55; sr supvry scientist, Tech Res Group, Inc, 55-63; sr res scientist, NY Univ, 63-66, prof nuclear eng, 66-73. *Mem:* Am Phys Soc. *Res:* Nuclear science; statistical mechanics; transport theory; reactor shielding. *Mailing Add:* 64 Burnett Terr West Orange NJ 07052

ARONSON, ROBERT BERNARD, BIOCHEMISTRY. *Current Pos:* RETIRED. *Personal Data:* b Seneca Falls, NY, Aug 29, 30; m 55, Edna Gray Brucks; c Myra & Evelyn. *Educ:* Harvard Univ, AB, 52; Boston Univ, AM, 58, PhD(biochem), 62. *Prof Exp:* Res assoc, Brookhaven Nat Lab, 60-62, from asst chmn to assoc chmn dept, 70-76, from asst scientist to scientist, Biochem Dept, 62-87, dep chmn, Med Dept, 76-87. *Res:* Structure, function and metabolism of collagens. *Mailing Add:* PO Box 34 Shoreham NY 11786. *E-Mail:* redarrow@worldnet.att.net

ARONSON, RONALD STEPHEN, CLINICAL CARDIOLOGY. *Current Pos:* from asst prof to assoc prof, 77-89, PROF MED, ALBERT EINSTEIN COL MED, 89- *Personal Data:* b Chicago, Ill, Mar 25, 44; m 70; c 3. *Educ:* Univ Miami, BS, 65; Univ Fla, MD, 69. *Prof Exp:* Intern med, Johns Hopkins Hosp, 69-70, resident, 70-71; fel cardiac electrophysiol, Col Physicians & Surgeons, Columbia Univ, 71-73; fel cardiol, Med Ctr, Duke Univ, 73-75; cardiologist, Andrews AFB, 75-77, dir Cardiovasc Lab, 76-77. *Concurrent Pos:* Res assoc, Rockefeller Univ, 72-73, adj fac, Cardiac Electrophysiol Lab, 83-; sr investr, NY Heart Asn, 77; estab investr, Am Heart Asn. *Mem:* Am Physiol Soc; Am Soc Clin Invest; fel Am Col Physicians; fel Am Col Cardiol; NY Acad Sci; Am Heart Asn. *Res:* Investigation of the cellular mechanisms that underlie abnormal electrical activity in the heart; electrical measurements in isolated cardiac tissues from animal models of human cardiac disease. *Mailing Add:* Dept Med Albert Einstein Col Med 110 Lockwood Ave New Rochelle NY 10801

ARONSON, SAMUEL HARRY, EXPERIMENTAL HIGH ENERGY PHYSICS. *Current Pos:* assoc physicist, 78-80, physicist, Isabelle Proj, Accelerator Dept, 80-82, PHYSICIST, BROOKHAVEN NAT LABS, 82-, ASSOC DEPT CHMN, PHYSICS DEPT, 87- *Personal Data:* b Huntington, NY, May 14, 42; m 68; c 2. *Educ:* Columbia Univ, AB, 64; Princeton Univ, PhD(physics), 68. *Prof Exp:* Res assoc high energy physics, Enrico Fermi Labs, Univ Chicago, 68-71; asst prof physics, Univ Wis, Madison, 72-77. *Mem:* Am Phys Soc. *Res:* Experimental study of fundamental processes involving elementary particles at high energies, using electronic detectors; searcher for weak new intermediate-range forces; research in novel and exotic techniques for particle acceleration. *Mailing Add:* Brookhaven Nat Labs Bldg 510C Box 5000 Upton NY 11973

ARONSON, SEYMOUR, PHYSICAL CHEMISTRY. *Current Pos:* assoc prof, 68-74, chmn dept, 78-81, PROF CHEM, BROOKLYN COL, 74- *Personal Data:* b New Britain, Conn, Jan 23, 29; m 57; c 3. *Educ:* Yeshiva Col, BA, 50; Polytech Inst Brooklyn, PhD(chem), 56; Univ Pittsburgh, MS(Math), 60. *Prof Exp:* Res chemist, Westinghouse Atomic Power Div, 54-61 & Brookhaven Nat Lab, 61-68. *Mem:* Am Chem Soc; Sigma Xi. *Res:* Thermodynamic and electrical properties of solids; kinetics of gas-solid reactions. *Mailing Add:* Dept Chem Brooklyn Col Brooklyn NY 11210

ARONSON, STANLEY MAYNARD, MEDICINE, PUBLIC HEALTH. *Current Pos:* chmn, Dept Path, 70-72, dean med, 72-81, PROF MED SCI, BROWN UNIV, 81-, EMER DEAN MED & UNIV PROF, 87- *Personal Data:* b New York, NY, May 28, 22; m 47, Betty Ellis; c Susan (Symons), Lisa (Wyland), & Sarah C. *Educ:* City Col New York, BS, 43; NY Univ, MD, 47; Brown Univ, MA, 71; Harvard Sch Pub Health, MPH, 81. *Prof Exp:* Asst instr biol, City Col New York, 43; assoc neuropath, Col Physicians & Surgeons, Columbia Univ, 52-54; assoc prof, Downstate Med Ctr, State Univ NY, 54-60, prof path & asst dean, 60-70. *Concurrent Pos:* Res assoc, Mt Sinai Hosp, NY, 51-54; attend neuropathologist, Kingsbrook Jewish Med Ctr, NY, 52-; dir labs & neuropathologist, Kings County Hosp, 54-70; consult neuropath, NIH, 62-, US Vet Admin, 63- & Brooklyn Hosp, Long Island Col Hosp, RI Hosp, Butler Hosp, Roger Williams Hosp, Mem Hosp, State Univ NY Hosp & Lutheran Med Ctr; lectr, Yale Sch Med, 64-65, Tufts Univ, 78-; pathologist-in-chief, Miriam Hosp, Providence, 70-74; prof lectr, Downstate Med Ctr, State Univ NY, 70-; mem, Nat Adv Comn Multiple Sclerosis, 74-75 & Nat Comn Control Huntington's Dis, 76-77; vis prof med, Univ NY, 81 & community med, Dartmouth Med Sch, 82-; pres, Hospice Care, RI, 89-; ed-in-chief, RI Med J, 89-; vchair, RI Bd Med Licensure & Discipline. *Mem:* Am Soc Exp Biol & Med; Am Asn Neuropath (pres, 71-72); Am Acad Neurol; Am Neurol Asn; Am Asn Path & Bact; Am Col Epidemiol; Am Pub Health Asn. *Res:* Experimental neuropathology; neuroepidemiology; population studies of vascular and aging disorders of the nervous system; sphingolipidoses. *Mailing Add:* Sch Med Brown Univ Providence RI 02912. *Fax:* 508-252-6942

ARONSTAM, ROBERT S, MEDICAL RESEARCH, MICRO-CHEMISTRY. *Current Pos:* RESEARCHER BASIC NEUROCHEM RES, GUTHRIE RES INST, 92- *Personal Data:* b Staten Island, NY, 1950. *Educ:* Columbia Univ, BA, 68; Univ Rochester, PhD(neurosci), 78. *Prof Exp:* Prof pharmacol, Med Col Ga, 80-92. *Mem:* Soc Neurosci; Am Soc Neurochem. *Mailing Add:* Guthrie Res Inst One Guthrie Sq Sayre PA 18840

ARORA, JASBIR SINGH, ENGINEERING MECHANICS, STRUCTURAL ENGINEERING. *Current Pos:* fel, 71-72, from asst prof to assoc prof mech, 72-81, PROF CIVIL & MECH ENG, UNIV IOWA, 81- *Personal Data:* b Tarn-Taran, India, Apr 13, 43; US citizen; m 72, Rita; c Ruhee. *Educ:* Univ Iowa, PhD(mech), 71. *Prof Exp:* Asst prof struct, GN Eng Col, LDH, India, 64-65; engr, Severud Asn, NY, 67. *Mem:* Am Soc Civil Engrs; Am Soc Mech Engrs; Am Acad Mech; Am Inst Aeronaut & Astronaut. *Res:* Design optimization, structural dynamics, engineering mechanics. *Mailing Add:* 1262 Oakes Dr Iowa City IA 52245

ARORA, NARINDER, RESPIRATORY MUSCLES. *Current Pos:* PVT PRAC, PULMON INTERNAL MED. *Educ:* Univ Ireland, UK, MRCP, 79. *Prof Exp:* Dr, Internal Med, Univ Va, 75-82. *Mem:* Fel Am Col Physicians. *Mailing Add:* Univ Va Pulmonary & Allergy Clin 308 Tenth St NE Suite 2 Charlottesville VA 22901-5317

ARORA, PRINCE KUMAR, neuroscience, for more information see previous edition

ARORA, SARDARI LAL, ORGANIC CHEMISTRY, LIQUID CRYSTAL MATERIAL. *Current Pos:* ASSOC PROF, CHEM DEPT, KENT STATE UNIV, STARK CAMPUS, 75- *Personal Data:* b Lahore, India, 1929. *Educ:* Lucknow Univ, BS, 51, MS, 53, PhD(org chem), 59. *Prof Exp:* Dir res liquid crystal mat, Int Liquid XTAL Co, 71-75. *Mem:* Sigma Xi; fel Am Inst Chem; Am Chem Soc; AAAS; Int Union Appl Chem. *Mailing Add:* 162 Steeplechase Ave Munroe Falls OH 44262-1745

ARORA, VIJAY KUMAR, COMPUTER-AIDED DESIGN, MICROELECTRONICS PHYSICS & TECHNOL. *Current Pos:* deans asst res & scholarly activ, 87-93, PROF ELEC ENG, WILKES COL, 85-, CO-COORDR INDUST-UNIV MICROELECTRONICS PROG, 85-, DIR, ELECTRONICS LAB, 91- *Personal Data:* b Multan, Pakistan, Nov 13, 45; m 76, Rashmi Indu-Bala; c Vineeta & Namita. *Educ:* Kurukshetra Univ, India, BSc, 65, MSc, 67; Univ Colo, Boulder, MS, 70, PhD(physics), 73; Western Mich Univ, 76. *Honors & Awards:* Appreciation Award, Inst Elec & Electronics Engrs; Distinguished Ser Award, Int Div, Am Soc Eng Educ. *Prof Exp:* Lectr physics, DAV Col, Chandigaru, India, 67-68 & eng physics, Regional Engr Col, Kurukshetra, 68; res & teaching asst eng physics, Univ Colo, Boulder, 68-73, lectr, Univ Colo, Denver, 73-74; asst prof physics, Western Mich Univ, 74-76; from asst prof to prof, King Saud Univ, Saudi Arabia, 76-85; vis assoc prof elec eng, Univ Ill, Urbana, 81-82. *Concurrent Pos:* Vis asst prof, Colo Sch Mines, 72-73; guest worker, Nat Bur Stand, 73-74; vis prof, Univ Antwerp, Belg, 80; vis assoc prof, Univ Ill, Urbana, 81-82; vis scientist, GTE Labs, 84; vis prof, Res Ctr Advan Sci & Technol, Univ Tokyo, 89-91, Dept Elec Eng, Nat Univ Singapore, 91-93. *Mem:* Sr mem Inst Elec & Electronics Engrs; Am Phys Soc; Indian Phys Soc; Sigma Xi; Am Soc Eng Educ; Nat Geog Soc; Semiconductor Soc India. *Res:* Electronic transport in quantum; well microstructures and design considerations for high speed devices; process modelling of GaAs-based microdevices; opto-electronic properties of semiconductors; physics of very large-scale integration and very-large-scale integrated circuit. *Mailing Add:* Dept Elec & Comput Eng Wilkes Univ Wilkes-Barre PA 18766. *Fax:* 717-829-2434; *E-Mail:* varora@wilkes1.wilkes.edu

AROTS, JOSEPH B(ARTHOLOMEW), CHEMICAL ENGINEERING. *Current Pos:* RETIRED. *Personal Data:* b Waterbury, Conn, Nov 23, 23; m 50; c 3. *Educ:* Northeastern Univ, BS, 44; Washington Univ, St Louis, PhD(chem eng), 50. *Prof Exp:* Sr res chem eng, Res Ctr, Hercules Inc, 50-79, res scientist, 79-86. *Mem:* Nat Asn Corrosion Engrs; Sigma Xi. *Res:* Boiler water treatment chemicals and cooling water additives; failure analysis; corrosion; cost estimating. *Mailing Add:* 726 Loveville Rd Cottage 10 Hockessin DE 19707-1504

AROYAN, H(ARRY) J(AMES), CHEMICAL ENGINEERING. *Current Pos:* VPRES CHEM, CHEVRON RES CO, 68- *Personal Data:* b Venice, Italy, Dec 10, 21; nat US; m 48; c 5. *Educ:* Univ Pa, BS, 43; Univ Mich, MS, 47, PhD(chem eng), 49. *Prof Exp:* Group supvr, Calif Res Corp, 44-46, 49-64, sr eng assoc, 64-66; mgr planning & develop, Chevron Chem Co, 66-68. *Mem:* Am Chem Soc; Am Inst Chem Engrs. *Res:* Petrochemical processes. *Mailing Add:* 6021 Shelter Bay Ave Mill Valley CA 94941-3059

ARP, ALISSA JAN, ECOLOGICAL PHYSIOLOGY, MARINE INVERTEBRATE PHYSIOLOGY. *Current Pos:* lectr & res assoc, 86-88, ASSOC PROF BIOL, SAN FRANCISCO STATE UNIV, 89- *Personal Data:* b Glendale, Calif, Apr 6, 54; m 86; c 1. *Educ:* Sonoma State Univ, BA, 77; Univ Calif, Santa Barbara, MA & PhD(biol), 82. *Prof Exp:* Postdoctoral res biochem, Scripps Inst Oceanog, 84-86; vis scientist marine biol, Moss Landing Marine Lab, 88-89. *Mem:* AAAS; Asn Women Sci; Sigma Xi; Am Soc Zoologists; Soc Conserv Biol. *Res:* Ecological physiology of marine animals; physiological adaptation to low oxygen, high sulfide habitats; function of oxygen transport proteins; hydrothermal vent biology. *Mailing Add:* Dept Biol Romberg Tiburons Ctr San Francisco State Univ 1600 Holloway Ave San Francisco CA 94132

ARP, DANIEL JAMES, MICROBIOL BIOCHEMISTRY. *Current Pos:* assoc prof, 90-92, PROF, DEPT BOT & PLANT PATH, 92-, DIR, MOLECULAR & CELLULAR BIOL PROG, ORE STATE UNIV, 93- *Personal Data:* b Sutton, Nebr, March 14, 54; m 74, Wanda Hofmann; c Sarah & James. *Educ:* Univ Nebr, Lincoln, BS, 76; Univ Wis-Madison, PhD(biochem), 80. *Prof Exp:* Res asst, Univ Wis-Madison, 76-80; NATO fel, Univ Erlangen, WGer, 81-82; from asst prof to assoc prof biochem, Univ Calif, Riverside, 82-89. *Mem:* Sigma Xi; Am Chem Soc; Am Soc Microbiol; Am Asn Adv Sci; Am Soc Biochem & Molecular Biol. *Res:* Microbiol biochemistry, enzymology, nitrogen fixation and hydrogen metabolism of microorganisms and plant-bacterial symbioses; nitrification; bioremediation. *Mailing Add:* Lab Nit Fixation Res Ore State Univ 2082 Cordley Corvallis OR 97331-2906. *Fax:* 541-737-3573; *E-Mail:* arpd@bcc.orst.edu

ARP, HALTON CHRISTIAN, ASTRONOMY. *Current Pos:* RETIRED. *Personal Data:* b New York, NY, Mar 21, 27; m 49, 62, 84, Marie H Demoulin; c Kristana, Alissa, Andrice & Delphine. *Educ:* Harvard Univ, AB, 49; Calif Inst Technol, PhD(astron), 53. *Honors & Awards:* Warner Prize, Am Astron Soc, 60; Newcomb Cleveland Prize, AAAS, 61. *Prof Exp:* Carnegie fel, Mt Wilson & Palomar Observ, 53-55; res assoc, Ind Univ, 55-57; asst astromr, Mt Wilson & Palomar Observ, 57-65, astromr, 65-69, astromr, Hale Observ, 69-81, Mt Wilson & Las Campanas Observ, 81-85. *Concurrent Pos:* Alexander von Humboldt Sr Scientist Award, WGer, 84-85; vis scientist, Max-Planck Inst Astrophys, 85-; Eminent Scientist, Riken, Japan, 96-97. *Mem:* AAAS; Am Astron Soc; Int Astron Union; Soc Sci Explor; Academia Europ, 96. *Res:* Globular clusters and globular cluster variable stars; novae; cepheids and extragalactic nebula; peculiar galaxies; formation and evolution of galaxies; quasars, compact galaxies, companion galaxies and the nature of red shifts; cosmology. *Mailing Add:* Max-Planck Inst Astrophys Karl Schwarzschild Str No 1 85748 Garching Bei Munchen Germany. *E-Mail:* arp@mpa-sgarching.mpg.de

ARP, LEON JOSEPH, INDUSTRIAL & BIOMEDICAL ENGINEERING. *Current Pos:* assoc prof, 66-70, prof indust eng & opers res, 70-77, PROF MECH ENG, VA POLYTECH INST & STATE UNIV, 71- *Personal Data:* b Norway, Iowa, June 30, 30; m 55; c 4. *Educ:* Iowa State Univ, BS, 60, MS, 63, PhD(indust educ), 66. *Prof Exp:* From instr to asst prof eng, Iowa State Univ, 60-65. *Mem:* Am Soc Eng Educ; Am Inst Indust Engrs; Sigma Xi. *Res:* Design and development of infant respiratory support equipment; extra-corporeal oxygenators; new method for replacement and attachment of detached retinas. *Mailing Add:* 1107 Highland Circle Blacksburg VA 24060

ARP, VINCENT D, APPLIED MATHEMATICS, SOFTWARE SYSTEMS. *Current Pos:* RETIRED. *Personal Data:* b Grass Valley, Calif, May 9, 30; m 56; c 3. *Educ:* Univ Calif, Berkeley, BS, 53, PhD(physics), 59. *Prof Exp:* Physicist, US Nat Bur Stand, 59-89. *Mem:* Am Phys Soc. *Res:* Superconductivity; low temperature physics; fluid dynamics; heat transfer; mechanics. *Mailing Add:* 7837 Fairview Rd Boulder CO 80303

ARPAIA, PASQUALE J, NUMBER THEORY. *Current Pos:* PROF, ST JOHN FISHER COL, 71- *Personal Data:* b Brooklyn, NY, July 21, 32; m 58, dosephine J Lepro; c Joseph, Paschal, Paul, Mary, Stephen & Edith. *Educ:* St Johns Univ, BS, 58 & MS, 61; Adelphi Univ, PhD(math), 72. *Concurrent Pos:* Vis lectr, Math Asn Am, 92-96. *Mem:* Math Asn Am; Am Math Soc. *Res:* Generating solutions for a special class of diophantine equations; distribution of prime numbers. *Mailing Add:* St John Fisher Col Rochester NY 14618-3597

ARPKE, CHARLES KENNETH, SCIENCE ADMINISTRATION. *Current Pos:* PVT CONSULT, 75- *Personal Data:* b Beatrice, Nebr, Dec 8, 21; m 50, Eileen Hepperly; c Thomas K, Douglas K & Richard K. *Educ:* Univ Nebr, AB, 48, MA, 50, PhD(chem), 62. *Prof Exp:* Asst prof air sci, Univ Nebr, 55-59, dep chief, Chem & Mat Br, USAF Rocket Propulsion Lab, 61-63; res assoc, F J Seiler Res Lab, USAF Acad, 63-64, assoc prof chem & dir chem res, 64-66, prof chem & actg head dept chem & physiol, 66-68; chief, Weapons Div, Air Force Armament Lab, 68-69, Technol Div, 69-72 & Weapons Effect Div, 72-74; chief, Anal Div, Armament Develop & Test Ctr, 74-75; publ mgr, Okla State Univ Eng Field Off, Eglin AFB, 76-85; tech dir, Datatec Inc, 85-86. *Concurrent Pos:* Consult environ sci study, Okaloosa-Walton Jr Col. *Mem:* Am Chem Soc; Am Inst Aeronaut & Astronaut; fel Am Inst Chem. *Res:* Smoke obscuration phenomena; obscuration simulation studies; toxicity of rocket propellants; high explosive thermal stability; weapons effects determinations; aeroballistic dispersion phenomena; exterior and terminal ballistics phenomena; computer simulation and modeling studies; library information management systems. *Mailing Add:* 1064 Lake Way Dr Niceville FL 32578

ARQUETTE, GORDON JAMES, PHYSICAL CHEMISTRY. *Current Pos:* DIR CORP PLANNING DEVELOP & TECHNOL, AIRCO, INC, 70- *Personal Data:* b North Lawrence, NY, Mar 3, 25; m 48; c 3. *Educ:* St Lawrence Univ, BS, 47, MS, 49; Cornell Univ, PhD(phys chem), 53. *Prof Exp:* Res assoc, Cornell Univ, 52-56; sr chemist, Cent Res Lab, Air Reduction Co, Inc, 56-57, sect head, 57-58, supvr, Chem Res Div, 58-61, assoc dir to dir res, 61-68, dir sci & eng & mem operating comt, 68-70. *Mem:* Am Chem Soc; NY Acad Sci; Am Inst Chemists; Sigma Xi. *Res:* Chemistry and physics of high polymers; phase equilibria; chemical kinetics. *Mailing Add:* 130 Christopher Circle Ithaca NY 14850-1702

ARQUILLA, EDWARD R, PATHOLOGY, IMMUNOLOGY. *Current Pos:* PROF PATH & CHMN DEPT, UNIV CALIF, IRVINE-CALIF COL MED, 68- *Personal Data:* b Chicago, Ill, Sept 10, 22; m 49; c 4. *Educ:* Northern Ill Univ, BS, 47; Univ Ill, MS, 49; Western Reserve Univ, PhD(anat), 57. *Prof Exp:* Asst Physiol, Univ Ill, 48-49; asst prof path, Univ Southern Calif, 59-61; from asst prof to assoc prof, Univ Calif, Los Angeles, 61-68. *Concurrent Pos:* USPHS grants, 57-65; Pop Coun grant, 64-65; mem coun, Midwinter Conf Immunologists, 62; mem path training comt, Nat Inst Gen Med Sci, 70- *Mem:* AAAS; Am Asn Immunol; Soc Exp Path; Am Diabetes Asn; Am Asn Path & Bact. *Res:* Immunological aspects of insulin as related to etiology and pathogenesis of diabetes; immunological properties of thyroid stimulating hormones and human chorionic gonadotropin. *Mailing Add:* Dept Path Univ Calif Col Med Surg 1 Rm 172 Irvine CA 92717-0001

ARRHENIUS, GUSTAF OLOF SVANTE, MOLECULAR BIOLOGY. *Current Pos:* vis asst res oceanogr, 52, asst res oceanogr, 53-55, assoc prof biogeochem, 55-59, PROF OCEANOG, SCRIPPS INST OCEANOG, UNIV CALIF, 59- *Personal Data:* b Stockholm, Sweden, Sept 5, 22; m 48, Jenny DeHevesy; c Susan, Thomas & Peter. *Educ:* Univ Stockholm, DSc, 53. *Honors & Awards:* Group Achievement Award, Lunar Sci Team, NASA, 73. *Prof Exp:* Geologist, Swed Skagerak Exped, 46 & Swed Deep Sea Exped, 47-48; assoc dir, Inst Pure & Appl Phys Sci, 71-92. *Concurrent Pos:* Vis res fel, Calif Inst Technol, 53-56 & Univ Brussels, 55; vis assoc prof, Int Inst Meterol, Sweden, 57-58; Guggenheim fel, Brussels & Berne, 57-58; chmn, Dept Earth Sci, Univ Calif, La Jolla, 59-61, dir, Space Res Lab, San Diego, 61-63; Perol Res Fund Award, Am Chem Soc, 60; mem, Lunar Sample Anal Team, NASA, 70-71 & Asteroid-Comet Mission Study Panel, 71-72; vis comt mem, Max Planck Soc, Ger, 75. *Mem:* Am Chem Soc; Geophys Soc; Swed Geol Soc; Swed Acad Sci; Int Acad Astronaut. *Res:* Processes of sedimentation; geochemistry; cosmochemistry; solid state chemistry; oceanography; origin of life. *Mailing Add:* 2711 Glenwick Pl La Jolla CA 92037-2040. *Fax:* 619-534-0784; *E-Mail:* arrhenius@ucsd.bitnet

ARRIGHI, FRANCES ELLEN, CELL BIOLOGY. *Current Pos:* RETIRED. *Personal Data:* b Topeka, Kans, July 24, 24. *Educ:* Marymount Col, BS, 47; La State Univ, MS, 61; Univ Tex, PhD(zool), 65. *Prof Exp:* Med technologist, Charity Hosp, New Orleans, La, 47-54, Self Mem Hosp, Greenwood, SC, 54 & Sch Med, La State Univ, 54-58; assoc biologist, Univ Tex M D Anderson Hosp & Tumor Inst Houston, 65-85. *Mem:* Tissue Cult Asn. *Res:* Cell biology, particularly nucleic acid, protein metabolism and chromosome structure. *Mailing Add:* 3036 Albans St Houston TX 77005-2146

ARRINDELL, EVAN R, SOCIAL WORK, PUBLIC HEALTH. *Current Pos:* dir state activ, Rockville, Md, 93-94, DIR, DIV SHORTAGE DESIGNATION, BUR PRIMARY HEALTH CARE, HEALTH RESOURCES, & SERV ADMIN, BETHESDA, MD, 95- *Personal Data:* b Staten Island, NY, May 6, 47. *Educ:* Richmond Col, BA, 69; Hunter Col, MSW, 72, PhD(social work), 86. *Prof Exp:* Prog consult, Ctr Studies Ment Health of Aging, NIMH, Md, 76-79; spec asst to dir, Div Alcohol, Drug Abuse & Ment Health, Pub Health Serv Region II, NY, 79-80; dep chief, Opers Support Br, Off Ambulatory Care, Bur Med Servs, Md, 80-81; chief, Patient Servs Br, Div Beneficiary Med Progs, Bur Health Care Delivery & Assistance, Md, 81-83, Support Servs Br, Nat Health Servs Corps, 83-84; social work consult, Genetic Dis Br, Div Maternal & Child Health, Md, 84-86; dep emergency coordr, Off Adminr, Health Resources & Servs Admin, Md, 86-87; dep dir, Health Care Prog Homeless, Off Dir, Bur Health Care Delivery & Assistance, Md, 87-88; chief, Spec Projs & Data Anal Br, Div Med, Bur Health Prof, Md, 88-89; liaison officer, Joint Staff Logistics Directorate, Off Dep Dir Med Readiness, Pentagon, Washington, 89-91; dep dir, Div Nat Health Serv Corps, Bur Health Care Delivery & Assistance, Health Resources & Servs Admin, Md, 91-93. *Concurrent Pos:* Opers officer, Disaster Med Assistance Team, Md, 84-89; spec asst & actg chief staff, Off Surgeon Gen, Md, 87; chief prof officer, Health Serv Officer Category, Md,

91-95. *Mem:* US Pub Health Serv Prof Asn; Asn Military Surgeons US; Nat Asn Social Workers. *Mailing Add:* Bur Primary Health Care Div Shortage Destination 4350 EW Hwy Ninth Fl Bethesda MD 20814. *Fax:* 301-594-4988

ARRINGTON, CHARLES HAMMOND, JR, PHYSICAL CHEMISTRY. *Current Pos:* RETIRED. *Personal Data:* b Rocky Mount, NC, Dec 23, 20; m 41; c 2. *Educ:* Duke Univ, BS, 41; Calif Inst Technol, PhD(phys chem), 49. *Prof Exp:* Res chemist, E I du Pont de Nemours & Co, 49-52, res supvr, 52-57, lab dir, 57-67, dir res, 67-74, asst gen dir res, Photog Prod Dept, 74-78, gen dir res, 78-84. *Mem:* AAAS; Am Chem Soc; Am Phys Soc; Sigma Xi. *Res:* Physical chemistry of solutions; photographic science; properties of macromolecules; solid state chemistry. *Mailing Add:* 711 Greenwood Rd Westover Hills Wilmington DE 19807-2935

ARRINGTON, ELAYNE, ALGEBRA, PURE MATHEMATICS. *Current Pos:* ASST PROF MATH, UNIV PITTSBURGH, 74- *Personal Data:* b Homestead, Pa, Feb 3, 40; m 64; c 2. *Educ:* Univ Pittsburgh, BS, 61; Univ Dayton, MS, 68; Univ Cincinnati, PhD(math), 74. *Prof Exp:* Aerospace engr, Foreign Technol Div, Wright-Patterson AFB, 62-66 & Parachute Br, 67-68; instr math, Univ Cincinnati, 73-74. *Mem:* Am Math Soc; Math Asn Am; Nat Asn Mathematicians. *Res:* Finite group theory, particularly formation theory and automorphisms of finite groups. *Mailing Add:* Dept Math & Statist Univ Pittsburgh 301 Thackeray Hall Pittsburgh PA 15260

ARRINGTON, JACK PHILLIP, TECHNOLOGY ACQUISITION, RESEARCH MANAGEMENT & DEVELOPMENT. *Current Pos:* Sr res chemist, Spec Assignments Group, Dow Chem Co, 70-71 & org chem res, 71-73, res specialist, Agr Synthesis Lab, 73-79, group leader organic processes, 79-81, res mgr new monomers, Cent Res, 81-83, mgr health & environ sci, 83-84, sr develop mgr, Org Chem Dept, 84-87, sr develop mgr & opers mgr, Chem & Metals Dept, 87-90, mgr technol acquisition, chem & performance prods, 90-93, MGR OPERS, CENT RES, DOW CHEM, 93- *Personal Data:* b Waterloo, Ohio, Dec 28, 42; m 67, Martha Starr; c Mark & Malia. *Educ:* Ohio Univ, BS, 65; Ind Univ, PhD(org chem), 69. *Concurrent Pos:* Chmn, Midland Sect, Am Chem Soc, 81. *Mem:* Am Chem Soc; Sigma Xi. *Res:* Technology assessment and transfer; organic synthesis; polymer synthesis; chemical development; synthesis and structure-activity relationships of agricultural chemicals. *Mailing Add:* 1100 Timber Ave Midland MI 48642. *E-Mail:* sparr@dow.com

ARRINGTON, LOUIS CARROLL, POULTRY SCIENCE. *Current Pos:* from asst to assoc prof, 66-80, PROF POULTRY SCI, UNIV WIS-MADISON, 80- *Personal Data:* b Baltimore, Md, July 5, 36; m 60; c 2. *Educ:* Univ Md, BS, 58; Univ Calif, Davis, MS, 61; Mich State Univ, PhD(poultry sci), 66. *Prof Exp:* Res asst, Univ Calif, 58-61 & Mich State Univ, 61-66. *Mem:* Poultry Sci Asn; World's Poultry Sci Asn. *Res:* Physiology of the domestic fowl; reproductive and environmental physiology of the domestic fowl; artificial insemination of poultry; poultry products technology. *Mailing Add:* Dept Poultry Sci 260 Animal Sci Univ Wis Madison WI 53706-1205

ARRINGTON, RICHARD, JR, invertebrate zoology, for more information see previous edition

ARRINGTON, WENDELL S, SCIENCE ADMINISTRATION, BIOSTATISTICS. *Current Pos:* mgr biostatist, 68-72, assoc dir sci comput appln, 72-74, DIR SCI COMPUT APPLN, WYETH LABS, DIV AM HOME PROD, 74- *Personal Data:* b Brooklyn, NY, Oct 3, 36; c 4. *Educ:* Rensselaer Polytech Inst, BS, 58, PhD(physics), 64; Temple Univ, MBA, 73. *Prof Exp:* NIH trainee biophys, Rensselaer Polytech Inst, 64-65; asst prof physics, State Univ NY Albany, 65-66; head res comput appln, Merck & Co Inc, 66-67. *Mem:* Drug Info Asn; Asn Comput Mach; Sigma Xi. *Res:* Development of new user-oriented computer programming languages and data base technology to maximize cost-effectiveness in the evaluation of biomedical research data; automation and control of biomedical research experiments and related statistical analysis of data. *Mailing Add:* Box 484 Newton Square PA 19073-0484

ARROTT, ANTHONY, MAGNETISM. *Current Pos:* chmn, 77-80, PROF PHYSICS, SIMON FRASER UNIV, 68- *Personal Data:* b Pittsburgh, Pa, Apr 1, 28; m 53; c 4. *Educ:* Carnegie Inst Technol, BS, 48, PhD(physics), 54; Univ Pa, MS, 50. *Prof Exp:* Asst prof physics, Carnegie Inst Technol, 55-56; sr scientist, Sci Lab, Ford Motor Co, 56-69. *Concurrent Pos:* Guggenheim fel, 63-64; adj prof nuclear eng, Univ Mich, 67-69; mem rev comts, Argonne Univs Assoc, 79-; mem grant selection comt, Nat Sci & Eng Res Coun, Can, 78-81; Japanese Soc Prom Sci fel, Meson Sci Lab, Univ Tokyo, 85. *Mem:* Am Phys Soc; Can Asn Physicists; Am Asn Physics Teachers; Inst Elec & Electronic Engrs; fel Royal Soc Can. *Res:* Magnetism; neutron scattering; electronic structure of metals; liquid crystal elasticity; nuclear engineering; muon spin rotation; molecular bean epitaxy; X-ray photoelectron spectroscopy. *Mailing Add:* Dept Physics Simon Fraser Univ Burnaby BC V5A 1S6 Can

ARROW, KENNETH J, OPERATIONS RESEARCH. *Current Pos:* actg asst prof, econ & statist, Stanford Univ, 49-50, assoc prof, 50-53, exec head, Dept Econ, 53-56, 62-63, prof econ, statist & opers res, 53-68, Joan Kenney prof, 79-91, EMER JOAN KENNEY PROF ECON & OPERS RES, STANFORD UNIV, 91- *Personal Data:* b Aug 23, 21; m 47, Selma Schweitzer; c David & Andrew. *Educ:* City Col New York, BS, 40; Columbia Univ, MA, 41, PhD(econ), 51. *Hon Degrees:* Numerous from US & foreign univs, 68-94. *Honors & Awards:* Nobel Mem Prize in Econ Sci, 72; John Bates Clark Medal, Am Econ Asn, 57; Marshall lectr, Cambridge Univ, 70; John R Commons Lectr Award, Omicron Delta Epsilon, 73; Tanner lectr, Harvard Univ, 85; Von Neumann Prize, Inst Mgt Sci & Opers Res Soc Am, 86. *Prof Exp:* Weather officer, USAAF Corp, 42-46; res assoc, Cowles Comn Res Econ, 47-49; asst prof econ, Univ Chicago, 48-49; James Bryant Conant Univ prof, Harvard Univ, 74-79. *Concurrent Pos:* Consult, Rand Corp, 48-; economist, Coun Econ Adv, US Govt, 62; vis prof econ, Mass Inst Technol, 66; fel, Churchill Col, Cambridge, Eng, 63-64, 70, 73 & 86. *Mem:* Nat Acad Sci; fel AAAS; fel Ctr Advan Study Behav Sci; Am Philos Soc; Inst Med; Finnish Acad Sci; Sigma Xi; Economet Soc (vpres, 55, pres, 56); fel Inst Math Statist; Am Statist Asn; Am Econ Asn (pres-elect, 72, pres, 73); Inst Mgt Sci (pres, 62); Am Acad Arts & Sci; Int Soc Inventory Res (pres, 83-); Int Econ Asn (pres, 83-86); Brit Acad. *Res:* Economic and non-economic factors and consequences of the flow of technical information among firms. *Mailing Add:* Dept Econ Stanford Univ Stanford CA 94305-6072. *Fax:* 650-725-5702; *E-Mail:* arrow@leland.stanford.edu

ARROWOOD, ROY MITCHELL, JR, MECHANICAL PROPERTIES MATERIALS, FAILURE ANALYSIS. *Current Pos:* SR RES ENGR, SOUTHWEST RES INST, 81- *Personal Data:* US citizen. *Educ:* NC State Univ, BS(mat eng) & BS(geol), 72; Univ Calif, Davis, PhD(mat sci), 81. *Mem:* Am Soc Metals; Am Ceramic Soc; Am Inst Mining, Metall & Petrol Engrs; Am Soc Mech Engrs. *Res:* Deformation and fracture behavior of metals, ceramics, rocks, and composite materials; effects of chemical and physical environment, loading rate and stress state; ceramic processing. *Mailing Add:* Dept Metall Eng Univ Tex 500 W Univ Ave El Paso TX 79968

ARROYAVE, GUILLERMO, VITAMIN DEFICIENCIES, NUTRITIONAL FOOD PROGRAMS. *Current Pos:* NUTRIT CONSULT, 87- *Educ:* Univ Rochester, NY, PhD(biochem), 53. *Prof Exp:* Nutrit consult & prof nutrit, San Diego State Univ, 82-87. *Mailing Add:* 2520 Clairemont Dr No 113 San Diego CA 92117-6616

ARSCOTT, GEORGE HENRY, POULTRY NUTRITION & MANAGEMENT. *Current Pos:* from asst prof to assoc prof, Ore State Univ, 53-59, prof poultry sci, 65-87, actg head dept, 69-70, head, Dept Poultry Sci, 70-87, EMER PROF POULTRY SCI, ORE STATE UNIV, 88- *Personal Data:* b Hilo, Hawaii, July 20, 23; m 53, Elizabeth J Mcgeary; c John A & William E. *Educ:* Ore State Col, BS, 49; Univ Md, MS, 50, PhD(poultry husb), 53. *Honors & Awards:* Poultry Scientist of Yr, Pac Egg & Poultry Asn. *Prof Exp:* Res asst, Univ Md, 49-50 & 51-53. *Concurrent Pos:* Poultry adv, Consortium Int Develop, Yemen Arab Repub, 81, 83, 85 & 86; poultry specialist, Ore Partners of the Americas, Costa Rica, 89; poultry mgt adv, Int Exec Serv Corps, Dominican Repub, 90 & 91, Peru, 93-94; vol overseas coop asst, Agr Coop Develop Int, Egypt, 95, Lithuania, 96. *Mem:* AAAS; fel Poultry Sci Asn (pres, 83-84); Am Inst Nutrit; Sigma Xi; World Poultry Sci Asn; Am Poultry Hist Soc (pres, 92-93). *Res:* Nutritional requirements of poultry and evaluation of feedstuffs; nutritional studies with dwarf layers and roosters. *Mailing Add:* 489 NW Witham Dr Corvallis OR 97330

ARSENAULT, GUY PIERRE, BIO-ORGANIC CHEMISTRY, ANALYTICAL CHEMISTRY. *Current Pos:* PROF CHEM & CHEM ENG, ROYAL MIL COL CAN, 77- *Personal Data:* b Montreal, Que, Sept 25, 30; m 55; c 2. *Educ:* Univ Toronto, BASc, 53; Ohio State Univ, PhD(org chem), 58. *Prof Exp:* From asst res officer to assoc res officer org chem, Atlantic Regional Lab, Nat Res Coun Can, 60-67; guest dept chem, Mass Inst Technol, 65-66, res chemist, 67-77. *Mem:* Am Chem Soc; Am Soc Mass Spectrometry; Chem Inst Can. *Res:* Structure of fungal and bacterial metabolites; application of mass spectrometry to organic and biological chemistry and to biomedicine and environmental research; transformation of seed oils into petroleum refinery stocks. *Mailing Add:* 2195 Middle Rd RR 2 Kingston ON K7L 5H6 Can

ARSENAULT, HENRI H, OPTICS. *Current Pos:* from asst prof to assoc prof, 70-78, PROF PHYSICS, LAVAL UNIV, 78- *Personal Data:* b Montreal, Que, Sept 29, 37; m 65; c 2. *Educ:* Laval Univ, BSc, 63, MSc, 66, PhD(physics), 69. *Prof Exp:* Scientist x-ray spectros, Aluminium Labs Ltd, 63-64; teacher physics, Col Jonquiere, 64-65; Nat Res Coun Can fel, Inst Optics, Univ Paris, Orsay, 68-70. *Concurrent Pos:* Vis prof, Stanford Univ, 78-79; asst ed, Optical Eng, 80-; prin investr contracts, Dept Nat Defense, Can. *Mem:* Fel Optical Soc Am; Can Asn Physicists; Inst Elec & Electronics Engrs; fel Int Soc Optical Eng (pres, 94-). *Res:* Optical data processing; digital image processing, holography, speckle phenomena; optical computing; neural nets. *Mailing Add:* 2625 Rue de Port Royal Sainte-Foy Quebec PQ G1V 1A5 Can

ARSENAULT, RICHARD JOSEPH, COMPOSITE MATERIALS, PLASTIC DEFORMATION & FRACTURE. *Current Pos:* assoc prof, 66-71, PROF MAT SCI & ENG, UNIV MD, 71- *Personal Data:* b Champion, Mich, June 16, 35; m 59; c 4. *Educ:* Mich Tech Univ, BS, 57; Northwestern Univ, PhD(mat sci), 62. *Honors & Awards:* DeVivo lectr, Northeastern Univ, 94. *Prof Exp:* Scientist, Oak Ridge Nat Lab, 62; hon prof, Shenyang Inst Metals, 90. *Concurrent Pos:* Vis prof, Univ Liverpool, 73-74; assoc prog dir, NSF, 78-79; prin scientist, Erich Schmid, 82; chmn nuclear mat comt, Metall Soc, 86-87; distinguished overseas mat scientist, Mat Res Lab India, 94. *Mem:* Fel Am Soc Mat Int; Metall Soc; Chinese Acad Sci. *Res:* Studies of the plastic deformation of crystalline materials; metal matrix and inter-metallic matrix composites; computer simulation of dislocation motion; FEM analysis of microdeformation of composites. *Mailing Add:* 6918 Lamont Dr Lanham MD 20706-4607. *Fax:* 301-314-9467; *E-Mail:* rja@eng.umd.edu

ARSENEAU, DONALD FRANCIS, CELLULOSE CHEMISTRY, TECHNOLOGY TRANSFER. *Current Pos:* RETIRED. *Personal Data:* b St John, NB, Mar 18, 28; m 54; c 10. *Educ:* St Francis Xavier Univ, BSc, 50; Laval Univ, DSc(chem), 55. *Honors & Awards:* Can Centennial Medal. *Prof Exp:* From assoc prof to prof chem, St Francis Xavier Univ, 55-74; prof, Col Cape Brenton, 74-88, dir, Bras D'or Inst, 75- *Mem:* Am Chem Soc; Forest Prod Res Soc; Chem Inst Can; AAAS; Sci Coun Can. *Res:* Thermal breakdown of wood; differential thermal analysis; thermal degradation of naturally occurring polymers; water quality; utilization of coal for coking; new technologies in community development. *Mailing Add:* 10 Xavier St Sydney NS B1S 2R8 Can

ARSHAM, HOSSEIN, MATHEMATICAL MODELING & DISCRETE-EVENT SYSTEMS SIMULATION, LINEAR & NETWORKS OPTIMIZATION & SENSITIVITY ANALYSIS. *Current Pos:* asst prof, 83-88, ASSOC PROF, INFO QUANT SCI, UNIV BALTIMORE, 88- *Personal Data:* b Mashad, Iran, Mar 28, 47; US citizen; m 84, Elaheh N Khoshghadam; c Aryana. *Educ:* Arya-Meher Univ Technol, Iran, BSc, 71; Cranfield Inst Technol, Eng, MSc, 78; George Washington Univ, DSc, 82; Inst Am Assembly Col Sch Bus, Info Syst, advan cert, 91. *Honors & Awards:* Sci Achievement Res Award, Black & Decker, 87 & 88. *Prof Exp:* Postdoctoral researcher, Int Water Resources Inst, Washington, DC, 82-83. *Concurrent Pos:* Lectr, Bethlehem Steel Corp, Baltimore, 83-84; grad prog dir oper & res, Univ Baltimore, 85-87; assoc ed, Comput Statist & Data Analysis, 90-; assoc fac advan studies eng, Calif Nat Univ, 91-; Comn on Off Lab Accreditation grant, 93; NSF grant, 95. *Mem:* Fel Royal Statist Soc; NY Acad Sci; fel Oper Res Soc; fel Inst Combinatories Appln; AAAS; Am Math Soc; Inst Elec & Electronics Engrs. *Res:* Genealogy of operations research and its theoretical unification; advancement in the practical implementation of, inference for stochastic processes; development of solution algorithms and optimization, sensitivity and what if analysis of discrete event computer simulation. *Mailing Add:* Dept Info & Quant Sci Univ Baltimore Baltimore MD 21201-5779. *Fax:* 410-837-5722; *E-Mail:* harsham@ubmail.ubalt.edu

ARSLANCAN, AHMET N, HEAT TRANSFER PROCESS, MICROELECTRONICS PROCESSING. *Current Pos:* engr res & develop, 83-88, DIR RES & APPLN, RADIANT TECHNOL CORP, 88- *Personal Data:* US citizen; m 85; c 1. *Educ:* Carleton Col, BA, 73; Univ Rochester, PhD(chem eng), 80. *Prof Exp:* Res assoc chem eng, Univ Rochester, 74-79; proj engr, Stress Technol Corp, 79-80; control engr, Occidental Chem Corp, 80-83. *Concurrent Pos:* Res assoc, Rochester Inst Technol, 72-73. *Mem:* Am Chem Soc; Am Inst Chem Engrs; Int Soc Hybrid Microelectronics; Int Electronics Packaging Soc; Surface Mount Technol Asn. *Res:* CERMET thick film firing; semiconductor packaging processes; polymer thick film curing; hybrid and PWB assembly by reflow soldering methods; other related microelectronics processing applications by infrared technology. *Mailing Add:* 5461 Festival Circle La Palma CA 90623

ARSOVE, MAYNARD GOODWIN, MATHEMATICS. *Current Pos:* from instr to assoc prof, 51-60, PROF MATH, UNIV WASH, 60- *Personal Data:* b Lincoln, Nebr, Mar 11, 22; m 44; c 4. *Educ:* Lehigh Univ, BS, 43; Brown Univ, ScM, 48, PhD(math), 50. *Hon Degrees:* DrEd, Saipan Univ, 46. *Prof Exp:* Fulbright scholar, Grenoble Univ, 50-51. *Concurrent Pos:* Guggenheim fel, 57-58; Fulbright fel, Univ Paris, 57-58; NATO fel, Univ Hamburg, 64-65. *Mem:* Am Math Soc. *Res:* Subharmonic function theory; potential theory; complex analysis; theory of bases. *Mailing Add:* 2035 E Newton St Univ Wash Seattle WA 98112

ART, HENRY WARREN, FOREST & COASTAL ECOLOGY, ENVIRONMENTAL BIOLOGY. *Current Pos:* Res assoc, Williams Col, 70-71, asst prof & asst dir res, Ctr Environ Studies, 71-76, actg dir, 76-79, assoc prof biol, 76-82, asst dir, 80-87, chmn, Dept biol, 81-87, pre-med adv, 88-92, chair, Sci Exec Comt, 92-93, dir, Bronfman Sci Ctr, 92-93, PROF BIOL, WILLIAMS COL, 82-, SAMUEL FESSENDEN CLARK PROF BIOL, 93- *Personal Data:* b Norfolk, Va, Sept 11, 44; m 66, Pamela Beall; c Andrew B, James B & Mattew B. *Educ:* Dartmouth Col, BA, 66; Yale Univ, MPhil, 69, PhD(forest ecol), 71. *Honors & Awards:* Quill & Trowel Award, Garden Writers Asn Am. *Concurrent Pos:* Vis prof environ studies, Univ Vt, 75 & Univ Calif, Santa Barbara, 79-80; vis fel, Corpus Christi Col & Bot Sch, Cambridge Univ, Eng, 87-88. *Mem:* Ecol Soc Am; Brit Ecol Soc; AAAS; Garden Writers Asn Am. *Res:* Biomass and productivity of ecosystems; nutrient cycling; ecosystem dynamics; land use and successional relationships; coastal ecology. *Mailing Add:* Dept Biol Williams Col Williamstown MA 01267-2606. *Fax:* 413-597-3495; *E-Mail:* hart@williams.edu

ARTEAGA, LUCIO, MATHEMATICS, STATISTICS. *Current Pos:* RETIRED. *Personal Data:* b Calatayud, Spain, May 22, 24; Can citizen; m 52; c 2. *Educ:* Univ Madrid, cert, 56; Dalhousie Univ, MSc, 59; Univ Sask, PhD(math), 64. *Prof Exp:* Statistician, NS Tumor Clin, 57-60; consult, Sask Res Coun, 60-62; asst prof math, Univ Windsor, 62-65; asst prof, Dalhousie Univ, 65-67, Univ NC, Charlotte, 67-68; from assoc prof to prof math, Wichita State Univ, 68-86; at Boeing, 86-93. *Concurrent Pos:* Nat Res Coun Can grants, 64-66. *Mem:* Am Math Soc; Math Asn Am. *Res:* Integral equations; Fourier transforms. *Mailing Add:* 2712 N Terrace Dr Wichita KS 67220

ARTEMIADIS, NICHOLAS, MATHEMATICAL ANALYSIS. *Current Pos:* EMER PROF, ACAD ATHENS, GREECE, 84- *Personal Data:* b Constantinople, Turkey, May 17, 17; US citizen; m 63, Zafiria Pyrlidis. *Educ:* Univ Thessaloniki, MS, 39; Fr Inst, Athens, dipl, 51; Univ Paris, certs, 54, 55, DSc(math), 57. *Honors & Awards:* Stavropoulos Prize, Greek Embassy Paris, 57; Hon Dipl Distinguished Serv, Greek Math Soc, 88. *Prof Exp:* From asst prof to assoc prof, Univ Wis-Milwaukee, 58-66; assoc prof, Univ Thessoloniki, 60-61; prof math, Southern Ill Univ, Carbondale, 66-77; prof math, Univ Patras, 75-84, dean, Sch Math & Physics, 75-76. *Concurrent Pos:* Vis lectr, Univ Wis, 59 & Univ Chicago, 60; res grant, US Army Math Res Ctr, 59, Univ Wis, 61; guest, French Govt, Cult Exchange Prog, Univ Paris, 81; study mission, Org Econ Coop Develop, Coop Action Prog, Paris, 81. *Mem:* Am Math Soc; Math Soc France; Greek Math Soc (pres, 85-); Sigma Xi; NY Acad Sci; hon mem Union Baleanique des Mathematiciens; Math Asn Am; Am Asn Univ Professors. *Res:* Mathematical and harmonic analysis; author of eight books in real, complex, harmonic and functional analysis; over 40 research papers and articles in scientific journals. *Mailing Add:* 169 Megalou Alexandrou St 136 71 Thrakomakedones Athens Greece

ARTERBURN, DAVID ROE, TOPOLOGY. *Current Pos:* chmn math dept, 88-91, ASSOC PROF MATH, NMEX INST MINING & TECHNOL, 67- *Personal Data:* b Norfolk, Nebr, Dec 29, 39; m 63; c 2. *Educ:* Southern Methodist Univ, BS, 61; NMex State Univ, MS, 63, PhD(functional analysis), 64. *Prof Exp:* Asst prof math, Univ Mont, 64-67. *Mem:* Math Asn Am; Sigma Xi. *Res:* Functional analysis; rings of functions; rings of operators. *Mailing Add:* Rte 1 Box 39A Lemitar NM 87823

ARTES, RICHARD H, SPEECH PATHOLOGY. *Current Pos:* PROF SPEECH PATH, BALL STATE UNIV, 52- *Personal Data:* b Ionia, Iowa, Apr 19, 26; m 52. *Educ:* Ariz State Univ, BA, 49; Univ Iowa, MA, 51, PhD(speech path), 67. *Prof Exp:* Clinician speech path, Faribault, Minn Pub Schs, 50-52. *Concurrent Pos:* Consult, Vet Admin Hosp, Marion, Ind, 78- *Mem:* Sigma Xi. *Res:* Psychological problems associated with severe language impairment subsequent to brain damage, such as aphasia. *Mailing Add:* 401 N Taft Rd Muncie IN 47304

ARTH, JOSEPH GEORGE, JR, geochemistry, for more information see previous edition

ARTHAUD, RAYMOND LOUIS, ANIMAL SCIENCE. *Current Pos:* RETIRED. *Personal Data:* b Cambridge, Nebr, Apr 21, 21; m 47; c 5. *Educ:* Univ Nebr, BSc, 47, MSc, 49; Univ Mo, PhD(animal breeding), 53. *Prof Exp:* Instr animal husb, Univ Nebr, 49; asst prof beef cattle res sta, Va Polytech Inst, 52-54; animal husbandman beef cattle breeding, Animal & Poultry Husb Res Br, Agr Res Serv, USDA, Univ Nebr, 54-59; prof animal sci, Exten, Univ Minn, 59-80. *Mem:* Am Soc Animal Sci. *Res:* Swine breeding and nutrition; beef cattle breeding and nutrition. *Mailing Add:* 2321 Cedar Ave St Paul MN 55110

ARTHUR, ALAN THORNE, reproductive biology, toxicology, for more information see previous edition

ARTHUR, JAMES ALAN, POULTRY BREEDING. *Current Pos:* Pop geneticist, 64-70, mgr appl res, 70-71, RES DIR, HY-LINE INT, 71- *Personal Data:* b Stockton, Calif, June 19, 36; m 58; c 5. *Educ:* Univ Calif, Davis, BS, 61, PhD, 65. *Mem:* Sigma Xi; Genetics Soc Am; Poultry Sci Asn. *Res:* Improvement of hybrid performance in the fowl. *Mailing Add:* Hy-Line Int PO Box 310 Dallas Center IA 50063-0310

ARTHUR, JAMES GREIG, AUTOMORPHIC FORMS, GROUP REPRESENTATIONS. *Current Pos:* prof math, 79-87, PROF, UNIV TORONTO, 87- *Personal Data:* b Hamilton, Can, May 18, 44; m 72, Dorothy Helm; c James & David. *Educ:* Univ Toronto, BSc, 66, MSc, 67; Yale Univ, PhD(math), 70. *Honors & Awards:* John L Surge Award, Royal Soc Can, 87. *Prof Exp:* Instr math, Princeton Univ, 70-72; asst prof math, Yale Univ, 72-76; prof math, Duke Univ, 76-79. *Concurrent Pos:* Vis mem, Inst Advan Studies, 77-78; mem ed adv bd, Crelles J, 85, Can J Math, 86, J Am Math Soc, 87; Sloan fel, Sloan Found; E W R Stocie fel, Nat Sci & Eng Res Coun Can, 82. *Mem:* Am Math Soc; Can Math Soc; fel Royal Soc Can; fel Royal Soc London. *Res:* Trace formula and its applications to group representations, automorphic forms, number theory and algebraic geometry. *Mailing Add:* Univ Toronto Toronto ON M5S 1A1 Can

ARTHUR, JETT CLINTON, JR, PHYSICAL & POLYMER CHEMISTRY, RADIATION CHEMISTRY. *Current Pos:* BIOMAT CONSULT, 79- *Personal Data:* b Hemphill, Tex, May 31, 18; m 41, Oma L Pitts; c James C, Martha A (Stitsinger) & Laura A (Porter). *Educ:* Stephen F Austin State Univ, BA, 39; Univ Tex, MA, 46; Environ Eng Intersoc Bd, dipl, 71. *Honors & Awards:* Am Chem Soc Southwest Regional Award, 80, Southern Chemist Award, 88; Anselme Payen Award in Cellulose, 84; Polymer Sci Pioneer, Polymer News, 85 & 93; Herty Medal, 89. *Prof Exp:* Chemist, Southern Regional Res Ctr, Agr Res Serv, USDA, 41-43 & 46-49, chemist in charge protein prod, 49-52, chemist in charge biochem, 52-56, prin chemist & head radiochem, 56-66, chief chemist, 66-79. *Concurrent Pos:* Abstractor, Chem Abstr, 46-79, ed phys org chem, 63-79; deleg, Int Atomic Energy Comn, Austria, 62; lectr, Brit Asn Radiol Res, 65; lectr, NATO Advan Study Inst, Wales, 67; deleg, Int Union Pure & Appl Chemists, Japan, 66, Can, 68, Australia, 69, UK, 78, US, 82, Fourth UN Conf Peaceful Uses Atomic Energy, Switz, 71, Pac Chem Eng Cong, Japan, 72, US, 77, Pac Chem Cong, Hawaii, 79 & 89; mem, First Chem Cong-NAm Continent, Mex, 75, Cellucon, Int Conf Cellulose, 84; chmn, res comt, Am Inst Chem Engrs, 77-78, Cellulose, Paper, Textile Div, Am Chem Soc, 85; vis prof, NWales Inst Higher Educ, UK, 78-86; macromolecular secretariat, treas, Am Chem Soc, 88-93; emer dir, Cell Div, Am Chem Soc, 94- *Mem:* Fel Cell Div Am Chem Soc; Sci Res Soc Am; fel Am Inst Chem Engrs. *Res:* Radiation chemistry and photochemistry of natural products; physical organic chemistry of natural polymers including cellulose, protein, starch and biotechnology applications; industrial chemistry; applied mathematics; macrocellulosic free radical chemistry; applications of nuclear radiation to development of fibrous cotton graft copolymers; oilseed protein products for food and industrial uses; enzymatic reactions in food technology; biotechnological uses of natural biopolymers. *Mailing Add:* 3013 Ridgeway Dr Metairie LA 70002-5053

ARTHUR, JOHN READ, JR, SURFACE PHYSICS. *Current Pos:* prof, 83-96, dir, Ctr Advan Mats Res, 92-96, EMER PROF, DEPT ELEC ENG, ORE STATE UNIV, 96- *Personal Data:* b Omaha, Nebr, Dec 17, 31; m 54, Beverly Bentzinger; c John, Stephen, Michael & Mary. *Educ:* Iowa State Univ, BS, 54, PhD(phys chem), 61. *Honors & Awards:* Morris N Liebmann Award, Inst Elec & Electronics Engrs, 82; IBM Award New Mat, Am Phys Soc, 82; Gaede-Langmuir Award, Am Vac Soc, 88. *Prof Exp:* Res asst surface chem, Inst Atomic Res, Iowa State Univ, 56-61; mem tech staff, Bell Tel Labs, 61-77; sr proj scientist, Phys Electronics Div, Perkin-Elmer Corp, 77-83. *Mem:* Am Phys Soc; fel Am Vacuum Soc (pres, 83). *Res:* Adsorption and surface reaction kinetics on semi-conductors; thin film structures and growth mechanisms; electron diffraction and auger spectroscopy; molecular beam scattering from surfaces; molecular beam epitaxy. *Mailing Add:* Dept Elec Eng Ore State Univ Corvallis OR 97331. *Fax:* 541-737-3593; *E-Mail:* jra@ece.orst.edu

ARTHUR, JOHN W, AQUATIC TOXICOLOGY, AQUATIC BIOLOGY. *Current Pos:* res aquatic biologist bioassays, Duluth, Minn, 67-70 & res team coordr, 70-74, res aquatic biologist 74-78, sta chief stream ecol, Monticello, Minn, 78-86, RES AQUATIC BIOL & TEAM LEADER, WATERSHED ASSESSMENT, US ENVIRON PROTECTION AGENCY, 86- *Personal Data:* b Superior, Wis, Sept 9, 37; m 61, Carol; c Erik, Sarah & Kirstin. *Educ:* Gustavus Adolphus Col, BS, 59; Wash State Univ, MS, 62; Univ Minn, MPH, 64. *Honors & Awards:* Bronze Medal, US Environ Protection Agency, 75. *Prof Exp:* Aquatic biologist, Upper Miss River Proj, USPHS, Minneapolis, Minn, 64-67. *Concurrent Pos:* Subcomt chmn bioassays, Environ Protection Agency Biol Methods Manual, 73; adv bd Stand Methods for Exam Water, Wastewater, 14th ed, 74-75; 15th ed, 79-80; Planning comt Midwest Conf Environ Technol, 81-85. *Mem:* NAm Benthological Soc. *Res:* Aquatic life damage; protective aquatic life criteria evaluation in lab and outdoor experimental streams, watershed criteria. *Mailing Add:* US Environ Protection Agency 6201 Congdon Blvd Duluth MN 55804

ARTHUR, MARION ABRAHAMS, PLASTICS ENGINEERING, GEOPHYSICS. *Current Pos:* RETIRED. *Personal Data:* b Port Deposit, Md, Apr 28, 11; m 34; c 3. *Educ:* Haverford Col, BS, 31; Harvard Univ, MS, 32. *Prof Exp:* Seismograph operator, Humble Oil & Refining Co, Houston, 33-34, geophys researcher, 35-42; proj supvr ballistics, Off Sci Res & Develop, Washington, DC, 42-45; res specialist geophys, Exxon Corp USA, Houston, 46-71; pres, Marion Arthur, Inc, 71-94. *Mem:* Emer mem Soc Plastic Engrs (secy-treas, 48-49, pres, 49-50). *Res:* Improvement in the art and science of acrylic embedment. *Mailing Add:* 777 N Post Oat Rd Apt 812 Houston TX 77024

ARTHUR, MICHAEL ALLAN, PALEOCEANOGRAPHY, STABLE ISOTOPE GEOCHEMISTRY. *Current Pos:* PROF & HEAD GEOSCI, PA STATE UNIV, 91- *Personal Data:* b Sacramento, Calif, June 25, 48; m 82, Janice A Jenkins; c Paige A. *Educ:* Univ Calif, Riverside, BS, 71, MS, 74; Princeton Univ, PhD(geol), 79. *Prof Exp:* Res scientist, Deep Sea Drilling, Scripps Inst Oceanog, 77-79; geologist, Br Oil & Gas Resources, US Geol Surv, 79-81; asst prof geol sci, Univ SC, 81-83; from assoc prof to prof geol oceanog, Grad Sch Oceanog, Univ RI, 83-91. *Concurrent Pos:* Geologist-WAE, US Geol Surv, 81- *Mem:* Am Asn Petrol Geologists; Am Geophys Union; fel Geol Soc Am; Soc Sedimentary Geol; Geochem Soc; Oceanog Soc. *Res:* Role of the carbon cycle in past climates; causes of global change over the past 140 million years; chemistry of ancient oceans and the sedimentary record; diagenesis of carbonate and organic-carbon rich sediments. *Mailing Add:* RR 2 Box 199 Spring Mills PA 16875-9745. *Fax:* 814-863-7823; *E-Mail:* arthur@geosc.psu.edu

ARTHUR, PAUL D(AVID), MECHANICAL ENGINEERING. *Current Pos:* prof mech eng, 68-89, EMER PROF MECH ENG, UNIV CALIF, IRVINE, 89- *Personal Data:* b Washington, DC, Feb 23, 25. *Educ:* Univ Md, BS, 44, MS, 48; Calif Inst Technol, PhD(aeronaut), 52. *Prof Exp:* Engr, Convair, 46-47; instr mech eng, Univ Md, 48-49; res engr hypersonics, Calif Inst Technol, 49-52; oper analyst, USAF, 52-53; Fulbright prof, Iraq, 53-54; syst engr, Ramo-Wooldridge, 54-56; consult, 57-65; vpres, Systs Corp Am, 58-65; prof, Univ Fla, 65-68. *Concurrent Pos:* Adj prof, Univ Southern Calif, 56-65; vis prof, Technol Univ Delft, 59 & Cairo Univ, 60; Fulbright prof, Univ Naples, 63-64. *Mem:* Am Astronaut Soc; Am Soc Mech Engrs. *Res:* Aerodynamics; orbital mechanics; fluid mechanics. *Mailing Add:* 17871 Arbor Lane Irvine CA 92715

ARTHUR, RICHARD J(ARDINE), INSTRUMENTATION. *Current Pos:* RETIRED. *Personal Data:* b Springfield, Ohio, Dec 12, 24; m 49, Marie Carmody. *Educ:* Purdue Univ, BS, 48; Univ Ill, MS, 49. *Prof Exp:* Asst math, Univ Ill, 48-51; proj aerodynamicist, Bell Aircraft Corp, 51-55, proj engr inertial instrumentation, 55-57, group leader, 57-61; head dept engr, Sperry Marine Systs Div, Sperry Rand Corp, 61-66, eng mgr, 66-71, dir eng, 71-73; div head, Naval Surface Warfare Ctr, 73-80, dep dept head, 80-86. *Res:* Inertial instrument design; gyro and accelometer design; physics; digital methods applied to instruments; servomechanisms; applied mathematics and electronics; radar systems; collision avoidance systems. *Mailing Add:* 117 Indian Spring Rd Charlottesville VA 22901

ARTHUR, ROBERT DAVID, NUTRITION. *Current Pos:* from asst prof to assoc prof, 77-88, prof & chmn, Animal Sci Food & Nutrition, 88-95, ASSOC DEAN ACAD PROG, COL AGR, SOUTHERN ILL UNIV-CARBONDALE, 95- *Personal Data:* b Union City, Ind, Oct 3, 42; m 65, Beth Miller; c 2. *Educ:* Purdue Univ, BS, 64, MS, 66; Univ Mo, PhD(agr chem), 70. *Prof Exp:* Fel, Univ Mo, 70-72; asst prof biochem, Miss State Univ, 72-77. *Concurrent Pos:* Consult, SE Asia-US Feed Grains Coun, 80, Am Soybean Asn, 81 & China-US Feed Grains Coun, 84, 85, 88 & 91, Vietnam-US Feed Grain Counc, 95. *Mem:* Am Soc Animal Sci; Sigma Xi; Am Registry Prof Animal Scientists. *Res:* Study of the factors affecting growth and development in swine with emphasis on nutritional and management practices. *Mailing Add:* Dept Animal Sci Food & Nutrit Southern Ill Univ Carbondale IL 62901. *Fax:* 618-453-2505; *E-Mail:* rarthur@siu.edu

ARTHUR, ROBERT M, ENVIRONMENTAL HEALTH ENGINEERING. *Current Pos:* PRES, ARTHUR TECHNOL, 72- *Personal Data:* b Fond du Lac, Wis, Mar 21, 24; m 65; c 1. *Educ:* Ripon Col, BA, 49; Northwestern Univ, BS, 53; Harvard Univ, MS, 56; Univ Iowa, PhD(environ health eng), 63. *Honors & Awards:* Kermit Fisher Environ Award, Instrument Soc Am, 81. *Prof Exp:* Asst city engr civil eng, City of Fond du Lac, 49-53; asst sanit engr, Chicago Pump Co, 53-55; assoc prof civil eng, Rose Polytech Inst, 56-63, prof & chmn dept biol eng, 63-72. *Mem:* Water Pollution Control Fedn; Am Soc Eng Educ; Instrument Soc Am; Int Asn Water Pollution Res; Am Soc Testing & Mat. *Res:* Research and development in operation of wastewater treatment plants including instrumentation and control; operator training. *Mailing Add:* PO Box 1236 Fond du Lac WI 54936

ARTHUR, ROBERT SIPLE, physical oceanography; deceased, see previous edition for last biography

ARTHUR, SUSAN PETERSON, BIOSTATISTICS, EPIDEMIOLOGY. *Current Pos:* statist consult, Coherent Laser Med Div, 85-87, RES SCHOLAR, INT INST APPL SYST ANALYSIS, 79-; STANFORD STATIST CONSULTS, 87- *Personal Data:* b Berkeley, Calif, June 16, 49; m 74, Brian; c 4. *Educ:* Univ Calif, Berkeley, MA, 73; Princeton Univ, PhD(math statist), 79. *Prof Exp:* Statist consult, Epidemiol Div, Col Physicians & Surgeons, Columbia Univ, 75-76. *Concurrent Pos:* Sr statistician, Univ Calif, San Francisco, 94-97. *Mem:* Am Statist Asn. *Res:* Applied mathematical statistics and probability theory; clinical trials; uncertainty of oil resource estimates. *Mailing Add:* 1060 Vernier Pl Stanford CA 94305

ARTHUR, WALLACE, NUCLEAR PHYSICS, SPACE PHYSICS. *Current Pos:* prof physics & chmn dept, 62-73, dean col sci & eng, 73-83, PROF PHYSICS, FAIRLEIGH DICKINSON UNIV, 73- *Personal Data:* b New York, NY, Nov 22, 32; m 60; c 3. *Educ:* NY Univ, BEngSc & BEE, 57, PhD(physics), 62. *Prof Exp:* Asst physics, NY Univ, 57-61; lectr physics, Rutgers Univ, 61-62. *Mem:* Am Asn Physics Teachers; Am Phys Soc. *Res:* Cosmic ray analyses; atmospheric physics and gas kinetics; low energy experimental nuclear physics; gamma ray lasers. *Mailing Add:* 22 Raymond St Harrington Park NJ 07640-1214

ARTHUR, WILLIAM BRIAN, OPERATIONS RESEARCH, ECONOMICS. *Current Pos:* MORRISON PROF ECON & POP STUDIES, STANFORD UNIV, 83- *Personal Data:* b Belfast, N Ireland, July 21, 46; m 74; c 4. *Educ:* Queen's Univ Belfast, BSc, 66; Univ Mich, Ann Arbor, MA, 69; Univ Calif, Berkeley, MA, 73, PhD(opers res), 73. *Honors & Awards:* Schumpeter Prize, Econ, 90. *Prof Exp:* Res scholar methodol, Int Inst Appl Systs Anal, 77-82. *Concurrent Pos:* Guggenheim Fel, 88-89; dir, Econ Res Prog, Santa Fe Inst, 88-90. *Mem:* Int Union for Sci Study of Pop; Am Econ Asn. *Res:* Economics; demography. *Mailing Add:* Sante Fe Inst 1660 Old Pecos Trail Suite A Santa Fe NM 87501

ARTIN, MICHAEL, MATHEMATICS. *Current Pos:* PROF MATH, MASS INST TECHNOL, 63- *Personal Data:* b June 28, 34; US citizen. *Educ:* Harvard Univ, PhD(math), 60. *Mem:* Nat Acad Sci. *Res:* Algebra. *Mailing Add:* Dept Math Rm 2-239 Mass Inst Technol Cambridge MA 02139

ARTMAN, JOSEPH OSCAR, engineering physics, solid state physics; deceased, see previous edition for last biography

ARTNA-COHEN, AGDA, INFORMATION SCIENCE, NUCLEAR PHYSICS. *Current Pos:* CONSULT, 85- *Personal Data:* b Tartu, Estonia, Oct 19, 30; US citizen; m 67; c 1. *Educ:* McMaster Univ, BSc, 57, PhD(nuclear physics), 61. *Prof Exp:* Nuclear physicist nuclear data proj, Nat Acad Sci-Nat Res Coun, 61-63, nuclear physicist nuclear data proj, Oak Ridge Nat Lab, 64-67, consult, 67-75; res physicist, Naval Res Lab, Washington, DC, 75-85. *Concurrent Pos:* Lectr, USDA Grad Sch, 62-63; assoc ed, Nuclear Data, 65-67. *Mem:* Can Asn Physicists; Am Phys Soc. *Res:* Nuclear structure physics; information retrieval and evaluation; science writings. *Mailing Add:* 8801 Mansion Farm Pl Alexandria VA 22309

ARTRU, ALAN ARTHUR, CEREBROSPINAL FLUID DYNAMICS, CEREBRAL BLOOD FLOW & METABOLISM. *Current Pos:* from asst prof to assoc prof, 80-89, PROF ANESTHESIOL, UNIV WASH, SEATTLE, 89- *Personal Data:* b Oakland, CA, Apr 30, 49; m 72, Linda M Mason; c Rebecca, Naomi, Aaron & Alana. *Educ:* Univ Calif, Santa Cruz, BA, 71; Med Col Wis, Milwaukee, MD, 75. *Prof Exp:* Intern, Univ Calif, San Francisco, 75-76, res anesthesiol, 76-78; fel neuroanesthesiol, Mayo Clin,

Rochester, 78-80, asst consult anesthesiol, 79-80. *Concurrent Pos:* Mem, Comt Neurosci & Anesthetic Action, Am Soc Anesthesiologists, 85-91; bd dirs, Soc Neurosurg Anesthesia & Critical Care, 88-94; ed lab reports, J Neurosurg Anesthesiol, 88- *Mem:* Am Soc Anesthesiol; Int Anesthesia Res Soc; Soc Neuroanesthesia & Critical Care; Int Soc Cerebral Blood Flow & Metab; Asn Univ Anesthesiol. *Res:* Effects of anesthetics and other medical treatments and drugs on cerebral blood flow, blood volume, and metabolism, cerebrospinal fluid dynamics and pressure and the electroencephalogram. *Mailing Add:* Dept Anesthesiol Univ Wash Sch Med Box 356540 Seattle WA 98195-6540. *Fax:* 206-543-2958; *E-Mail:* artruaa@u.washington.edu

ARTUSIO, JOSEPH F, JR, ANESTHESIOLOGY. *Current Pos:* from instr to assoc prof surg, Med Col, Cornell Univ, 47-57, prof anesthesiol in surg, obstet & gynec, 57-67, prof anesthesiol & chmn dept, 67-89, EMER PROF ANESTHESIOL, MED COL, CORNELL UNIV, 89- *Personal Data:* b Jersey City, NJ, Nov 26, 17; m 45; c 6. *Educ:* St Peter's Col, BS, 39; Cornell Univ, MD, 43; Am Bd Anesthesiol, dipl. *Prof Exp:* Intern, Bellevue Hosp, NY, 43-44; resident anesthesiol, NY Hosp, 46-47. *Concurrent Pos:* Asst attend anesthesiologist in chg, 48-57, anesthesiologist-in-chief, 57-89, attend anesthesiologist, 89-; ed-in-chief, Clin Anesthesia; mem, Unitarian Serv Comt to Japan, 56. *Mem:* Fel Am Col Anesthesiol; AMA; Am Soc Anesthesiol; Asn Univ Anesthetists; fel NY Acad Med. *Res:* Effect of anesthetic and muscular relaxant agents on the physiology and pharmacology of surgical patients. *Mailing Add:* Dept Anesthesiol Cornell Univ Med Ctr 525 E 68th St New York NY 10021-4899

ARTZT, KAREN, DEVELOPMENTAL GENETICS. *Current Pos:* PROF, UNIV TEX, AUSTIN, 87- *Personal Data:* b New York, NY, Sept 4, 42. *Educ:* Cornell Univ, AB, 64, PhD(genetics), 72. *Honors & Awards:* Boyer Young Investr Award, Sloan Kettering Inst, 81. *Prof Exp:* Fel immunogenetics, Pasteur Inst, Paris, 72-73; res assoc develop biol, Col Med, Cornell Univ, 73-75, asst prof, 75-76; assoc develop genetics, 76-78, assoc mem, Sloan Kettering Inst Cancer Res, 78-86. *Concurrent Pos:* Mem, Personnel Comt A, Am Cancer Soc, 82-88, Animal Resources Rev Comt, Div Res Resources, NIH, 88-92; res career develop award, Nat Cancer Inst, 76-81. *Mem:* AAAS; Genetics Soc Am; Soc Develop Biol. *Res:* Molecular biology of mammalian development; genetics of T/t complex. *Mailing Add:* Dept Zool Univ Tex Austin TX 78712-1064. *Fax:* 512-471-9651; *E-Mail:* artzt@uts.cc.utexas.edu

ARUMI, FRANCISCO NOE, THERMAL PHYSICS. *Current Pos:* res assoc physics, 70-72, asst prof archit, 71-75, assoc prof, 75-80, PROF ARCHIT, UNIV TEX, 80-, DIR RES, SCH ARCHIT & DIR, NUMERICAL SIMULATION LAB, 77- *Personal Data:* b Valparaiso, Chile, Feb 4, 40; m 63; c 2. *Educ:* Univ NC, BS, 62, MS, 64; Univ Tex, PhD(physics), 70. *Prof Exp:* Asst prof physics, Calif State Polytech Col, 64-65; vis prof, Univ Costa Rica, 65-66; regional specialist, Asn Am Univ, 66-67. *Concurrent Pos:* Fulbright fel, Comn Int Exchange of Persons, 71 & 72. *Mem:* Am Phys Soc; Int Solar Energy Soc; Am Soc Heating & Refrig Engrs; Am Asn Physics Teachers. *Res:* Thermal physics applied to energy analysis in architectural design; thermodynamic modelling of societal systems. *Mailing Add:* Dept Archit Univ Tex Austin TX 78712-1160

ARUNASALAM, VICKRAMASINGAM, PHYSICS. *Current Pos:* res assoc plasma physics, Princeton Univ, 64-67, mem res staff, 67-76, res physicist, 76-80, PRIN RES PHYSICIST, PLASMA PHYSICS LAB, PRINCETON UNIV, 80- *Personal Data:* b Jaffna, Ceylon, Aug 26, 35; m 68. *Educ:* Univ Ceylon, BS, 57; Univ Mass, Amherst, MS, 60; Mass Inst Technol, PhD(physics), 64. *Prof Exp:* Asst lectr physics, Univ Ceylon, 57-58; instr physics, Univ Mass, summer 60. *Mem:* Fel Am Phys Soc. *Res:* Plasma physics; quantum theory. *Mailing Add:* Plasma Physics Lab Princeton Univ Princeton NJ 08543

ARVAN, DEAN ANDREW, CLINICAL PATHOLOGY, BIOCHEMISTRY. *Current Pos:* PROF & ASSOC CHAIR PATH & DIR, LAB MED DIV, SCH MED & DENT, UNIV ROCHESTER, 77- *Personal Data:* b Arta, Greece, Sept 27, 33; US citizen; m 58; c 3. *Educ:* Wilkes Col, BS, 55; Hahnemann Med Col, MD, 59. *Hon Degrees:* MA, Univ Pa, 71. *Prof Exp:* Intern, St Agnes Hosp, Philadelphia, 59-60; resident path, Univ Pa Hosp, 60-64, asst instr, Sch Med, Univ Pa, 60-64, assoc, 64-69, assoc prof path, 69-77, asst dir, Chem Sect, Pepper Lab, Hosp, 67-69, dir, 69-77. *Concurrent Pos:* Attend physician, Dept Path, Vet Admin Hosp, Philadelphia, 67-77; consult biochemist, Coatesville Hosp, Pa, 68-77. *Mem:* AAAS; Am Asn Clin Chemists; Am Soc Clin Pathologists. *Res:* Clinical enzymology; use of serum and tissue enzymes in diagnosis; protein chemistry; application of new molecular techniques to diagnosis of disease. *Mailing Add:* Strong Mem Hosp Univ Rochester Med Ctr 601 Elmwood Ave Rochester NY 14642-0001

ARVAN, PETER, CELL BIOLOGY. *Current Pos:* ASST PROF ENDOCRINOL, BETH ISRAEL HOSP, HARVARD MED SCH, 88-, ASST PROF CELL & DEVELOP BIOL, MED SCH, 88- *Personal Data:* US citizen. *Educ:* Cornell Univ, AB, 77; Yale Univ, MD, 84, PhD(cell biol), 84. *Prof Exp:* Intern med, NC Mem Hosp, 84-85; postdoctoral fel cell biol, Sch Med, Yale Univ, 85-86, resident med, 86-87, fel endocrinol, 87-88. *Concurrent Pos:* Prin investr & consult endocrinol, Beth Israel Hosp, 88- *Mem:* Am Soc Cell Biol; AAAS; NY Acad Sci; Endocrine Soc; Am Thyroid Asn. *Res:* Sorting and targeting of newly-synthesized secretary proteins and peptide hormones. *Mailing Add:* Div Endocrinol Beth Israel Hosp 99 Brookline Ave Res N Boston MA 02215-5491

ARVESON, WILLIAM BARNES, MATHEMATICS. *Current Pos:* lectr, 68-69, assoc prof, 69-73, PROF MATH, UNIV CALIF, BERKELEY, 73- *Personal Data:* b Oakland, Calif, Nov 22, 34; c 3. *Educ:* Calif Inst Technol, BS, 60; Univ Calif, Los Angeles, AM, 63, PhD(math), 64. *Prof Exp:* Mathematician, US Naval Undersea Res Ctr, 60-64; actg asst prof math, Univ Calif, Los Angeles, 65; Benjamin Peirce instr, Harvard Univ, 65-68. *Concurrent Pos:* Nat Res Coun fel, Brit, 72, sr fel, 81; guest prof, Aarhus Univ, 73-74; Guggenheim fel, 76-77; assoc ed, Duke Math J, 78-87, J Operator Theory, 79-88, prin ed, 88-; Miller Res Prof, Univ Calif, Berkeley, 85-86. *Mem:* Am Math Soc. *Res:* Algebras of operators on Hilbert space; representations of Banach algebras; ergodic and prediction theory. *Mailing Add:* Dept Math Univ Calif Berkeley CA 94720-3840

ARVIDSON, RAYMOND ERNST, REMOTE SENSING. *Current Pos:* from asst prof to prof, 74-88, PROF EARTH & PLANETARY SCI DEPT, 84-, DEPT CHAIR, WASH UNIV, 91- *Personal Data:* b Brooklyn, NY, Jan 22, 48; m 69; c 2. *Educ:* Temple Univ, BA, 69; Brown Univ, MS, 71, PhD(geol), 74. *Honors & Awards:* Cushing Orator, Am Neurol Asn, 85; Pub Serv Medal, NASA, 85, 92, Group Achievement Award, 92. *Prof Exp:* Res assoc planetary geol, Brown Univ, 73. *Concurrent Pos:* Fel, McDonnel Ctr Space Sci, Wash Univ, 76-, dir, NASA Planetary Image Facil, 78-; team leader, Viking Lander Imaging Team, 78-82; mem, Space Sci Bd & chmn, Comn Data Mgt & Comput, Nat Acad Sci, 81-; assoc ed, J Geophys Res, 81-84 & Cambridge Univ Press, 83-; mem planetary rev panel, NASA, 81-, chmn, earth observation syst data panel, 84; adv, Mars Inst Planetary Soc, 83-; secy, planetary geol div, Geol Soc Am, 83-85 & planetology div, Am Geophys Union, 84-85; proj scientist, Pilot Planetary Data Syst, 85; chmn working group, Magellan Data Prod Group, 85; interdisciplinary scientist, Mars Observ, 86-; ed, Geol, 88; mem, Mars Mission Coord Implementation Team, US/USSR, 88, Joint Working Group on Solar Syst Explor; Node mgr, Planetary Geosci Node, 89-; pres, Planetary Sect, Am Geophys Union, 92- *Mem:* Am Geophys Union; Geol Soc Am; Planetary Soc. *Res:* Remote sensing of the surfaces of the terrestrial moons and planets; regional geologic studies of the earth; understanding the relationships between planetary geology records and interior evolution; investigations of the geological histories of Mars and Venus. *Mailing Add:* Wash Univ Campus Box 1169 EPSC One Brookings Dr St Louis MO 63130. *Fax:* 314-935-7361; *E-Mail:* arvidson@wunder.wustl.edu

ARY, DENNIS, PREVENTIVE MEDICINE, BEHAVIORAL MEDICINE. *Current Pos:* RES SCIENTIST BEHAV MED, ORE RES INST, 82-; PRES ORE CTR APPL SCI, 89- *Personal Data:* b Los Angeles, Calif, July 18, 50; m 83; c 2. *Educ:* Loyola Univ, BA, 72; Claremont Grad Sch, MA, 75, PhD(psychol), 80. *Prof Exp:* Mgr comput serv, Claremont Grad Sch, 74-77 & instr, grad statist, 76; res assoc, Inst Social Sci & Res, Univ Ore, 81 & Col Health & Phys Educ, 81. *Mem:* Soc Behav Med. *Res:* Primary prevention of adolescent health and problem behavior with sex, AIDS, tobacco and other drug use; predictions and risk factors for adolescent tobacco and other drug use; methodological and statistical issues in field research. *Mailing Add:* Ore Res Inst 1715 Frankland Blvd Eugene OR 97403. *E-Mail:* dennis@ori.org

ARY, T S, MINERAL EXPLORATION. *Current Pos:* RETIRED. *Personal Data:* b Eldorado, Ill, Mar 30, 25; m 45, Martha K Metz; c David. *Educ:* Stanford Univ, BS, 47. *Honors & Awards:* Distinguished Serv Award, Nat Indust Coal Operators, 88; Robert Earll McConnell Award, Am Inst Mining Engrs, 93. *Prof Exp:* Shift boss & supt, Anaconda Copper Co, 51-53; mining engr, Union Carbide Corp, 53-55, asst mgr explor, 55-57, mgr domestic explor, 57-62, land mgr, Union Carbide Nuclear Co, 62-67, vpres mineral explor, Mining & Metals Div, 67-74; vpres, Utah Int Inc, San Francisco, 74-80; pres mineral explor & pres resource div, Kerr-McGee Corp, 80-87; dir, Bur Mines, US Dept Interior, 88-93. *Concurrent Pos:* Comt chmn, Am Mining Cong, 60-88; prog chmn, Circum-Pac Coun Energy & Mineral Resources, 78-80; assoc ed, J Resource Mgt & Technol, 82-88; chmn, Nat Res Comt, Nat Asn Mfrs, 85-87; chmn, Nat Critical Mat Coun, 89-93; bd dirs, Mineral Info Inst, Denver. *Mem:* Am Inst Prof Geologists; Am Asn Prof Landmen; Am Inst Mining Engrs; Nat Asn Mfrs. *Res:* Mineral resources; public lands management; author of numerous publications. *Mailing Add:* 2901 N Green Castle St Arlington VA 22207

ARY, THOMAS EDWARD, NEUROPHARMACOLOGY, PSYCHOPHARMACOLOGY. *Current Pos:* DIR COMPLIANCE, PRACS INST, 96- *Personal Data:* b Walla Walla, Wash, Apr 30, 50. *Educ:* Wash State Univ, BPharm, 73, PhD(pharmaceut sci), 80. *Prof Exp:* Asst prof, Col Pharm, NDak State Univ, 89-96. *Concurrent Pos:* Alta Heritage fel, res asst prof, Univ Nev Sch Med; vis asst prof, Idaho State Univ. *Mem:* Am Asn Col Pharm. *Res:* Smooth muscle excitation-contraction coupling; role of prostaglandins. *Mailing Add:* Pracs Inst 2615 N Univ Dr Fargo ND 58102

ARYA, ATAM PARKASH, NUCLEAR PHYSICS. *Current Pos:* from asst prof to assoc prof, 64-74, PROF PHYSICS, WVA UNIV, 74- *Personal Data:* b Panjab, India, June 2, 34; m 61; c 2. *Educ:* Univ Rajasthan, India, BS, 53, MS, 55; Univ Panjab, India, MA, 56; Pa State Univ, PhD(physics), 60. *Prof Exp:* Vis res assoc physics, Pa State Univ, 60-62; asst prof, Univ Toledo, 62-64. *Mem:* Am Phys Soc; Am Asn Physics Teachers. *Res:* Beta and gamma spectroscopy; neutron inelastic scattering; energy and angular distribution of protons from neutron induced reactions. *Mailing Add:* Dept Physics WVa Univ PO Box 6023 Morgantown WV 26506

ARYA, SATYA PAL, METEOROLOGY, FLUID DYNAMICS. *Current Pos:* PROF METEOROL, DEPT MARINE EARTH & ATMOSPHERIC SCI, NC STATE UNIV, 81- *Personal Data:* b Mavi Kalan, India, Aug 24, 39; c Nikita, Sumita & Vishal. *Educ:* Univ Roorkee, India, BE, 61, ME, 64; Colo

State Univ, Ft Collins, PhD(fluid mech), 68. *Prof Exp:* Asst engr civil eng, Irrig Dept, India, 61-62; lectr, Univ Roorkee, India, 63-65; from res asst to res assoc fluid dynamics, Colo State Univ, Ft Collins, 65-69; from res asst prof to res assoc prof atmospheric sci, Univ Wash, Seattle, 69-76; assoc prof meteorol & geosci, NC State Univ, 76-81, prof meteorol & actg head, 81-83. *Concurrent Pos:* Vis prof, Ctr Atmospheric Sci, Indian Inst Tech, New Delhi, 83-84. *Mem:* Am Geophys Union; AAAS; Sigma Xi; Am Meteorol Soc. *Res:* Planetary boundary layers; atmospheric turbulence and diffusion; air-sea and air-sea ice interactions; micrometeorology; dispersion in complex terrain/flows; physical/fluid modeling. *Mailing Add:* Dept Marine Earth & Atmospheric Sci NC State Univ PO Box 8208 Raleigh NC 27695-8208. *Fax:* 919-515-7802

ARZBAECHER, ROBERT, ELECTRICAL ENGINEERING, BIOENGINEERING. *Current Pos:* PROF & DIR, PRITZKER INST MED ENG, ILL INST TECHNOL, 88-; RES ASSOC, PROF RANK, DEPT INTERNAL MED, UNIV CHICAGO, 81- *Personal Data:* b Chicago, Ill, Oct 28, 31; m 56; c 5. *Educ:* Fournier Inst Technol, BS, 53; Univ Ill, MS, 58, PhD(elec eng), 60. *Prof Exp:* Elec engr, Argonne Nat Lab, 54-60; from asst prof to prof elec eng, Christian Bros Col, Tenn, 60-67; from assoc prof to prof, Univ Ill, Chicago Circle, 67-76; prof & chmn, Dept Elec & Comput Eng, Univ Iowa, 76-87. *Concurrent Pos:* Mem comt electrocardiography, Am Heart Asn, 71-; prof internal med, Univ Iowa, 78-81. *Mem:* Fel Inst Elec & Electronics Engrs; fel Am Col Cardiol; fel Am Inst Med & Biol Eng. *Res:* Cardiac electrophysiology; computers in medical research. *Mailing Add:* Pritzker Inst Med Eng Lit Ctr Ill Inst Technol Chicago IL 60616

ARZOUMANIDIS, GREGORY G, HOMOGENEOUS CATALYSIS, ORGANOMETALLIC CHEMISTRY. *Current Pos:* RES ASSOC, AMOCO CHEM CO, NAPERVILLE, ILL, 79- *Personal Data:* b Thessaloniki, Greece, Aug, 16, 36; nat US; m 66; c 2. *Educ:* Univ Thessaloniki, BS & MS, 59; Univ Stuttgart, Germany, PhD(inorg chem), 64; Univ Conn, MBA, 79. *Prof Exp:* Sr res chemist, Am Cyanamid Co, Stamford, Conn, 69-72 & Stauffer Chem Co, Dobbs Ferry, NY, 72-79. *Mem:* Am Chem Soc; Sigma Xi. *Res:* Polyolefin catalysis (Ziegler-Natta). *Mailing Add:* 7 S 610 Carriage Way Naperville IL 60540-8241

ASA, SYLVIA L, ENDOCRINE PATHOLOGY. *Current Pos:* ASST PROF PATH, UNIV TORONTO-ST MICHAELS' HOSP, 84- *Personal Data:* b New York, NY, May 26, 53; m 76; c 2. *Educ:* Univ Toronto, MD, 77, PhD, 90; FRCP(C), 82, FCAP, 82. *Mem:* Int Acad Path; Am Asn Pathologists; fel Col Am Pathologists; Endocrine Soc. *Res:* Pituitary pathology; pituitary tumor tissue culture; fetal pituitary; hormone production by tumors. *Mailing Add:* Dept Path Mt Sinai Hosp 600 University Ave Toronto ON M5G 1X5 Can

ASAAD, MAGDI MIKHAEIL, PHARMACOLOGY, BIOCHEMICAL PHARMACOLOGY. *Current Pos:* RES LEADER, BRISTOL-MYERS SQUIBB PHARMACEUT RES INST, PRINCETON, NJ, 90- *Personal Data:* b Zagazig, Egypt, Sept 3, 40; US citizen; m 73. *Educ:* Cairo Univ, BPharm & Pharm Chem, 62; Univ Houston, PhD(pharmacol), 76. *Prof Exp:* Pharmacist, Zein El Abdine Pharm, Cairo, Egypt, 62-63, pharmacist in charge, 63-71; technician acad res, Dept Pharmacol, Univ Pittsburgh, 71-73; res fel indust res, Squibb Inst Med Res, Princeton, NJ, 76-78, res investr, 78-90. *Mem:* Am Pharmaceut Asn; Am Soc Pharmacol & Exp Therapeut; NY Acad Sci. *Res:* Hypertension; role of central and peripheral nervous system; renin angiotensin system, renal physiology and pharmacology; autonomic physiology and pharmacology; neuronal and receptor functions. *Mailing Add:* Bristol-Myers Squibb Pharm Res Inst PO Box 4000 Princeton NJ 08543-4000

ASADULLA, SYED, MATHEMATICS. *Current Pos:* asst prof, 68-71, ASSOC PROF MATH, ST FRANCIS XAVIER UNIV, 71- *Personal Data:* b Channapatna, India, June 3, 33; m 59. *Educ:* Cent Col, Bangalore, India, BSc, Hons, 55; Univ Karachi, MSc, 56; Univ Fla, PhD(math), 66. *Prof Exp:* Lectr math, Fed Col, Karachi, Pakistan, 55-56, head dept, 56-57, chmn fac sci, 57-61; interim instr math, Univ Fla, 61-66; asst prof, Miami Univ, 66-68. *Concurrent Pos:* Coop lectr, Univ Karachi, 57-61. *Mem:* Math Asn Am; Am Math Soc; Can Math Soc. *Res:* Number theory; quadratic forms. *Mailing Add:* St Francis Xavier Univ PO Box 5000 Antigonish NS B2G 2W5 Can

ASAI, DAVID J, CYTOSKELETON, CELL MOTILITY. *Current Pos:* asst prof, 85-89, assoc prof, 89-94, PROF BIOL, PURDUE UNIV, 94-, ASSOC DEPT HEAD, 95- *Personal Data:* b Chicago, Ill, June 7, 53; m 82, Verna S Abe. *Educ:* Calif Inst Technol, PhD(biochem), 79. *Prof Exp:* Asst res prof, Univ Calif, Santa Barbara, 82-85. *Mem:* Am Soc Cell Biol; Am Soc Biochem & Molecular Biol; Am Soc Develop Biol; Soc Protozoologists. *Res:* Structure and function of dynein heavy chain isoforms. *Mailing Add:* Dept Biol Sci Purdue Univ Lilly Hall West Lafayette IN 47907. *Fax:* 765-494-0876; *E-Mail:* dasai@bilbo.bio.purdue.edu

ASAKURA, TOSHIO, BIOCHEMISTRY, HEMATOLOGY. *Current Pos:* assoc biophysics, Johnson Res Found, 67-69, asst prof, 69-74, assoc prof pediat & biophysics, 74-76, PROF PEDIAT, BIOCHEM & BIOPHYS, UNIV PA, 76- *Personal Data:* b Osaka, Japan, Aug 21, 35; m 67; c 2. *Educ:* Kyoto Med Col, BS, 56, MD, 60; Univ Tokyo, PhD(biochem), 65; Univ Pa, MA, 74. *Prof Exp:* Intern hosp, Univ Tokyo, 60-61; asst prof biochem, Univ, 65-67. *Concurrent Pos:* Career develop award, NIH, 70-75. *Mem:* AMA; Soc Pediat Res; Am Soc Biol Chemists; Am Chem Soc. *Res:* Metabolism of red blood cells; oxygen binding properties of hemoglobin; spin-labeling of hemes and porphyrins; sickle cell disease and other hemoglobinopathies; transgenic mice. *Mailing Add:* Children's Hosp Philadelphia 34th St & Civic Ctr Blvd Philadelphia PA 19104

ASAL, NABIH RAFIA, EPIDEMIOLOGY, BIOSTATISTICS. *Current Pos:* from instr to asst prof biostatist & epidemiol, Univ Okla,68-72, epidemiologist, 69-72, assoc prof, 73-78, PROF BIOSTATIST & EPIDEMIOL & CHMN, SCH HEALTH, UNIV OKLA, 78- *Personal Data:* b Haifa, Israel, Dec 21, 38; m 66. *Educ:* William Jewell Col, AB, 63; Univ Mo, MS, 65; Univ Okla, PhD(epidemiol), 68. *Prof Exp:* Res asst epidemiol, Univ Mo, 65-66. *Concurrent Pos:* Consult, Okla Regional Med Prog, 68-, Epidemiol Div, Okla State Health Dept, US Environ Protection Agency, Am Cancer Soc, Cancer Ctr, Fed Aviation Agency & Civil Aeromed Inst. *Mem:* Soc Epidemiol Res; Am Pub Health Asn; Asn Teachers Prev Med. *Res:* Infectious and chronic disease epidemiology; cancer and cerebrovascular disease. *Mailing Add:* Pub Health Univ Okla Health Sci Ctr 941 S L Young Blvd Oklahoma City OK 73190-0001

ASANO, AKIRA, PHARMACEUTICS. *Current Pos:* group leader, 57-59, asst dir pharmaceut res, 59-65, dir prod develop, Johnson's Prof Prod Co, 65-67, asst mgr pharmaceut res, 67-77, ASST MGR BIOCHEM & BIOENG RES, JOHNSON & JOHNSON, 77- *Personal Data:* b Stockton, Calif, Jan 20, 23; m 51; c 2. *Educ:* Drake Univ, BS, 44; Univ Minn, MS, 45, PhD(pharmaceut chem), 48. *Prof Exp:* Res assoc, Merck Sharp & Dohme, 48-57. *Mem:* Am Pharmaceut Asn; Sigma Xi. *Res:* Drug formulation. *Mailing Add:* 510 Lake Dr Princeton NJ 08540-5633

ASANO, TOMOAKI, physiology, for more information see previous edition

ASANTE-DUAH, D KOFI, RISK ASSESSMENT, ENVIRONMENTAL IMPACT ASSESSMENTS. *Current Pos:* RES ASST PROF, UNIV MASS, LOWELL, 96-; ENVIRON CONSULT, CALIF. *Personal Data:* b Akim-Oda, Ghana, Nov 4, 55. *Educ:* Univ Sci & Tech, Ghana, BS, 80; Nat Univ Ireland, MS, 83; Budapest Tech Univ, PhD(hydrol & water mgt), 86; Utah State Univ, CE, 92. *Prof Exp:* Vis scientist, Civil Eng Dept, Univ Pittsburgh, 85-86; res asst, Utah State Univ, 86-88; proj engr, Environ Res Mgt, 88-89; sr proj eng CH2M Hill, 90-91, Int Technol Corp, 90-92; sr scientist, Tetra Tech Inc, 93-96. *Concurrent Pos:* Vis res asst prof, Univ Waterloo, 90-91; consult, Environ Consult, 91-93. *Mem:* Am Geophys Union; Am Soc Civil Engr; Am Water Res Asn; Asn Ground Water Scientist & Engrs; Soc Risk Anal; Nat Water Well Asn. *Res:* Effects of environmental/chemical contaminants on human health and the environment; application of multi-attribute decision analysis and utility theory in the investigation of environmental health management problems; policy analysis of tradeoffs in transfrontier movements of wastes. *Mailing Add:* 7040 Martano Pl Alta Loma CA 91701. *Fax:* 978-934-3092

ASANUMA, HIROSHI, NEUROPHYSIOLOGY. *Current Pos:* PROF NEUROPHYSIOL, ROCKEFELLER UNIV, 72- *Personal Data:* b Kobe, Japan, Aug 17, 26; m 53; c 2. *Educ:* Keio Univ, Japan, MD, 52; Kobe Med Col, DMedSci, 59. *Prof Exp:* Instr physiol, Kobe Med Col, 53-59; asst prof, Med Sch, Osaka City Univ, 59-61, 63-65; guest investr, Rockefeller Inst, 61-63; from assoc prof to prof physiol, NY Med Col, 65-72. *Mem:* Am Physiol Soc; Soc Neurosci; Harvey Soc; Physiol Soc Japan. *Res:* Physiology of mammalian motor system with reference to the function of the pyramidal tract. *Mailing Add:* Dept Motor Physiol Rockefeller Univ 1230 York Ave New York NY 10021

ASARNOW, ROBERT FRANKLIN, NEUROPSYCHOLOGY, COGNITIVE IMPAIRMENTS. *Current Pos:* PELLA MARTIN PROF PSYCHIAT, UNIV CALIF, LOS ANGELES, 80-, PROF PSYCHOL, 96- *Personal Data:* b Newark, NJ, Apr 14, 45; m 70, Joan Rosenbaum; c David & Lauren. *Educ:* Rutgers Univ, BA, 67; Wayne State Univ, PhD(clin psychol), 73. *Honors & Awards:* Merit Award, NIMH, 89. *Prof Exp:* Asst prof psychol, Univ Waterloo, 73-80. *Concurrent Pos:* Consult, WHO, 84-89; prin investr, NIMH, NIH, 86- *Mem:* Am Psychol Asn; Int Neuropsychol Soc; Soc Res Psychopath; AAAS; Am Psychopath Asn. *Res:* Detailing the cognitive/neuropsychological impairments associated with schizophrenia, Attention Deficit Hyperactivity Disorder and closed head trauma; family genetic studies of children with schizophrenia and Attention Deficit Hyperactivity Disorder; neurobehavioral sepuelae of closed head injuries in children and adults. *Mailing Add:* Dept Psychiat Univ Calif 48-240 NPI Los Angeles CA 90024. *Fax:* 310-206-4446; *E-Mail:* rasarnow@nplmain.medsch.ucla.edu

ASARO, ROBERT JOHN, METALLURGY. *Current Pos:* asst prof, 75-79, ASSOC PROF ENG, BROWN UNIV, 79- *Personal Data:* b Brooklyn, NY, Aug 29, 45; m 66; c 2. *Educ:* Stanford Univ, BS, 67, MS, 69, PhD(mat sci), 72. *Prof Exp:* Res assoc metall, Ohio State Univ, 72-73; staff scientist, Ford Motor Co, 73-75. *Concurrent Pos:* Consult, US Naval Underwater Systs Command, 80- *Mem:* Am Soc Mining & Metall Engrs. *Res:* Plasticity and fracture of solids; metal corrosion; environmental effects in material behavior; theoretical and experimental studies of the mechanics of crystals. *Mailing Add:* Eng Sci 0310 Univ Calif San Diego 9500 Gilman Dr La Jolla CA 92093

ASASHIMA, MAKOTO, BIOLOGY, DEVELOPMENTAL BIOLOGY. *Current Pos:* PROF, DEPT HEAD & DIR UNIV PRESS, UNIV TOKYO, 93- *Personal Data:* b Niigata, Japan, Sept 6, 44; m 75, Yoshiko Asashima; c Nobuko & Hiromitsu. *Educ:* Tokyo Kiyoiku Univ, BS, 67; Univ Tokyo, MS, 69, DSc, 72. *Honors & Awards:* Prize, Zool Soc Japan, 90; Siebold Prize, Ger Govt, 94; Kihara Mem Prize, 94. *Prof Exp:* Res asst, Free Univ Berlin, 72-74; assoc prof, Yokohama City Univ, 74-84, prof, 85-93. *Concurrent Pos:* Dept head & mem univ coun, Yokohama City Univ, 89-92. *Mem:* NY Acad Sci; Japanese Soc Develop Biologists; Zool Soc Japan; Int Soc Develop Biologists; Japanese Soc Cell Biol; Japanese Soc Molecular Biol. *Res:* Control of organogenesis and cell differentiation during amphibian development. *Mailing Add:* Dept Life Sci Univ Tokyo 3-8-1 Komaba Meguro-ku Tokyo 153 Japan. *Fax:* 81-3-5454-4330; *E-Mail:* cmasa@komaba.ecc.u.tokyo.ac.jp

ASATO, GORO, ORGANIC CHEMISTRY. *Current Pos:* Res chemist, 61-72, group leader, Agr Div, 72-87, MGR, METAB, RESIDUE & ENVIRON CHEM, AM CYANAMID CO, 87- *Personal Data:* b Mt View, Hawaii, May 29, 31; m 62. *Educ:* Univ Hawaii, BA, 53, MS, 58; Purdue Univ, PhD(org chem), 61. *Mem:* Am Chem Soc. *Res:* Stereochemical and optical rotatory dispersion studies of cyclohexane derivatives; synthesis of pesticides, antifungals and antibacterials; synthesis and infrared spectroscopic studies of transition metal carbonyls; animal health products. *Mailing Add:* 10 Maddock Rd Titusville NJ 08560-1309

ASATO, YUKIO, MICROBIOLOGY. *Current Pos:* from asst prof to assoc prof, 71-80, PROF MICROBIOL, SOUTHEASTERN MASS UNIV, 80- *Personal Data:* b Waipahu, Hawaii, Jan 19, 34; m 69; c 2. *Educ:* Univ Hawaii, BA, 57, MS, 66, PhD(microbiol), 69. *Prof Exp:* Microbiologist, State Dept Health, Hawaii, 61-63; asst microbiol, Univ Hawaii, 63-65; res assoc, biol adaptation br, Ames Res Ctr, NASA, 69-71. *Mem:* AAAS; Am Soc Microbiol; Genetics Soc Am. *Res:* Microbial genetics; biochemical genetics of cyanobacteria. *Mailing Add:* Dept Biol Res Bldg 205A Univ Mass 285 Old Westport Rd North Dartmouth MA 02747-2387

ASAY, KAY HARRIS, CROP BREEDING, AGRONOMY. *Current Pos:* RES GENETICIST, AGR RES SERV, USDA, 74- *Personal Data:* b Lovell, Wyo, Nov 20, 33; m 53, 83; c 4. *Educ:* Univ Wyo, BS, 57, MS, 59; Iowa State Univ, PhD(crop breeding), 65. *Prof Exp:* Instr high sch, Wyo, 59-61; res assoc crop breeding, Iowa State Univ, 61-65; from asst prof to assoc prof grass breeding, Univ Mo-Columbia, 65-74. *Res:* Development of improved range grass varieties and related basic studies. *Mailing Add:* 1655 N 1560 E Logan UT 84341

ASBRIDGE, JOHN ROBERT, SPACE PHYSICS. *Current Pos:* RETIRED. *Personal Data:* b Lakeside, Mont, Aug 26, 28; m 54, Marilyn Milburn; c Deborah L, Karen J, Mary J, Gary M & Joseph R. *Educ:* Mont State Col, BS, 53; Lehigh Univ, MS, 55, PhD(physics), 59. *Prof Exp:* Staff mem, Los Alamos Sci Lab, Univ Calif, 59-82, satellite prog mgr, 82-91. *Mem:* Am Geophys Union. *Res:* Satellite based study of space environment, the composition of the solar wind, and the earth's magnetosphere and cosmic rays. *Mailing Add:* HC75 Box 1183 Rutheron NM 87551

ASBURY, ARTHUR K, NEUROLOGY. *Current Pos:* prof, Dep. *Personal Data:* b Cincinnati, Ohio, Nov 22, 28; m 80, Carlyn H; c Dana, Patricia K & William F. *Educ:* Univ Ky, BS, 51; Univ Cincinnati, MD, 58, Am Bd Psychiat & Neurol, cert, 67. *Hon Degrees:* MA, Univ Pa, 74. *Honors & Awards:* Bernard J Alpers Lectr, Jefferson Med Col, 74; Robert B Aird Lectr, Univ Calif, 77; Simon Bruetman Mem Lectr, Rush Med Sch, 83; Charles D Aring Lectr, Univ Cincinnati, 85; Raymond D Adams Lectr, Mass Gen Hosp, 86; Frank H Netter Lectr, Am Acad Neurol, 87; Benjamin R Boshes Lectr, 88; Richard Paddison Lectr, La State Univ, 89; Eric Kugelberg Keynote Lectr, Int Cong Clin Neurophysiol, 92; Leadership Award, Peripheral Neuropathy Asn, 92. *Prof Exp:* Intern & residency med neurol & path, Mass Gen Hosp, 58-63, res & clin fel, 63-65, from asst neurol to assoc neurologist, 65-69; assoc prof neurol & path, Dept Neurol, Sch Med, Univ Calif, San Francisco, 69-73, vice-chmn, 69-74, prof residence neurol & path, 73-74. *Concurrent Pos:* Teaching fel, Harvard Med Sch, 58-63, res fel neuropath, 63-65, from instr to assoc neurol, 65-69; assoc path, Beth Israel Hosp, 66-69; chief, Neurol Serv, Vets Admin Hosp, San Francisco, 69-74, actg chief, 82-83; NIH & Nat Inst Neurol Dis & Stroke Safety Sects & Comts, 70-91; secy, Conf Comt Influenza, Dept Health Educ Welfare, 76-80; mem, Liaison Group, Neurol Soc, 81-83; James P Stephens vis prof, Univ Colo, 81; Norman J Allen vis prof, Ohio State Univ, 81; Robert A Utterback vis prof, Univ Tenn, 81; mem, Sci Prog Comt, Fifth & Sixth Int Cong Neuromuscular Dis, 82-86; vis prof neurol, Univ Calif, San Francisco, 82-83; chief ed, Ann Neurol, 84-92; co-chmn, Joint Comt, Diabetic Neuropath, 87-88, 92; Comt Vaccine Safety, Inst Med, 92-93; Harvard Longwood Neurol vis prof, 94; Jerome K Merlis vis prof, Univ Md, 95; hon prof med, Second Teaching Hosp, Shijiazhuang, 93, Hebei Med Col & Hebei Province, 95; mem, Subcomt Clin Res Ctrs, NIH Dir Comt Clin Res, 95-; chair, Inst Med Comt Eval Vet Admin Uniform Case Assessment Protocol, 97. *Mem:* Inst Med-Nat Acad Sci; Asn Am Med Cols; Am Acad Neurol; hon mem Am Neurol Asn(pres 82-83); hon mem Europ Neurol Soc; fel AAAS; Asn Univ Prof Neurol; Am Asn Neuropathologists (vpres, 83-84); Soc Neurosci; World Fedn Neurol (vpres, 89-93); Asn Res Nervous & Ment Dis. *Res:* Author of numerous publications. *Mailing Add:* Dept Neurol Med Ctr 3W Gates Bldg Univ Pa 3400 Spruce St Philadelphia PA 19104-4283

ASBURY, JOSEPH G, PHYSICS. *Current Pos:* asst physicist, 67-72, assoc physicist, 72-80, SR ECONOMIST, ARGONNE NAT LAB, 80-, DIR STRATEGIC PLANNING, 85-, DEP LAB DIR, 88- *Personal Data:* b Dayton, Ohio, Jan 15, 38; m 68; c 2. *Educ:* Univ Dayton, BS, 60; Purdue Univ, MS, 62, PhD(physics), 64. *Prof Exp:* Volkswagen fel, Deutsches Elektronen Synchroton, 65-67. *Concurrent Pos:* Mem, Ill Solid Waste Mgt Task Force, 70-73; officer & prin, Biodyne Corp, 72-74; mem, Gas Res Inst, Econ Adv Comt, 78-83; mem, Gov Sci Adv Comt, 89- *Mem:* AAAS; Am Phys Soc; Am Water Resources Asn; Sigma Xi. *Res:* Research planning and administration; research and development policy analysis; energy technology assessment. *Mailing Add:* 1322 E 56th St Chicago IL 60637

ASCAH, RALPH GORDON, PHYSICAL CHEMISTRY. *Current Pos:* RETIRED. *Personal Data:* b Montreal, Que, July 7, 18; wid; c James, Barbara & Robert. *Educ:* McGill Univ, BSc, 39; NY Univ, PhD(chem), 44. *Prof Exp:* Res chemist, Can Indust, Ltd, 43-47; from asst prof to assoc prof chem, Pa State Univ, 47-80. *Mem:* Am Chem Soc; Sigma Xi. *Res:* Photochemistry; vapor phase kinetics and low temperature calorimetry; infrared spectroscopy. *Mailing Add:* 223 Westerly Pkwy State College PA 16801

ASCARELLI, GIANNI, spectroscopy, electronic transport in semiconductors insulators & liquids; deceased, see previous edition for last biography

ASCENSAO, JOAO L, HEMATOLOGY, ONCOLOGY. *Current Pos:* PROF MED, VET ADMIN MED CTR, RENO, NEV, 91- *Personal Data:* b Maputo, Mozambique, July 6, 48; m 84. *Educ:* Univ Lisbon Sch Med, MD, 72. *Prof Exp:* Asst prof med, Univ Minn, 81-84; assoc prof med, NY Med Col, 84-91. *Concurrent Pos:* Dir CRC, NY Med Col, 86-; assoc dir, Bone Marrow Transplant, NY Med Col, 87-; dir hemat, Westchester Med Ctr, 88- *Mem:* Int Soc Experimental Hemat; Am Soc Hemat; Am Soc Clin Oncol; Am Asn Can Res; Am Fed Clin Res; Europ Soc Med Oncol. *Mailing Add:* Dept Med Div Hemat & Oncol Vet Admin Med Ctr 1000 Locust St Reno NV 89520-0102

ASCENZI, JOSEPH MICHAEL, MICROBIOLOGY. *Current Pos:* sr microbiologist, 78-82, sect head, 82-87, MGR MICROBIOL, JOHNSON & JOHNSON MED, 87- *Personal Data:* b Troy, NY, Oct 18, 49; m 71; c 1. *Educ:* Univ Dayton, BS, 71, MS, 73; Univ Cincinnati, PhD(microbiol), 77. *Prof Exp:* Res assoc microbiol, Univ Tex, 77-78. *Concurrent Pos:* Assoc referee, Asn Off Anal Chemists, 78- *Mem:* Am Soc Microbiol; AAAS; Sigma Xi; Soc Indust Microbiol. *Res:* Fatty acid biochemistry; near-ultraviolet radiation effects in bacteria; mode of action of chemo-sterilents and disinfectants. *Mailing Add:* 1908 Wimbledon Dr Arlington TX 76017

ASCH, BONNIE BRADSHAW, TUMOR BIOLOGY, CARCINOGENESIS. *Current Pos:* CANCER RES SCIENTIST, ROSWELL PARK CANCER INST, 81- *Personal Data:* m, Harold L. *Educ:* Baylor Col Med, PhD(exp biol), 76. *Prof Exp:* Res assoc, Beth Israel Hosp, Boston, MA, 78-81; asst prof, Harvard Med Sch, 80-81. *Concurrent Pos:* Res assoc prof, State Univ NY, Buffalo, 87- *Mem:* AAAS; Am Soc Cell Biol; Am Asn Cancer Res; Int Asn Breat Cancer Res. *Res:* Breast cancer; endogenous retrotransposons in mammary carcinogenesis; mammary cell biol; biomarkers for normal and malignant mammary cells. *Mailing Add:* Roswell Park Cancer Inst Carlton & Elm St Buffalo NY 14263-0001. *Fax:* 716-845-3242

ASCH, DAVID KENT, NEUROSPORA GENE CONTROL. *Current Pos:* ASST PROF, YOUNGSTOWN STATE UNIV, 92- *Personal Data:* b Neligh, Nebr, Nov 6, 58; m 81, Joanna Clement; c Jeffrey & Stephanie. *Educ:* Univ Nebr, Lincoln, BS, 81; Creighton Univ, MS, 84; Univ Kans Med Ctr, PhD(microbiol), 91. *Prof Exp:* Fel genetics, Univ Ga, 89-92. *Mem:* Am Soc Microbiol; Genetics Soc Am. *Res:* Gene control of the ga gene cluster of N crassa. *Mailing Add:* Dept Biol Sci Youngstown State Univ 410 Wick Ave Youngstown OH 44555-0001

ASCH, HAROLD LAWRENCE, MAMMARY CARCINOGENESIS. *Current Pos:* cancer res scientist cell biol, Dept Exp Path, 81, scientist adminr pancreas cancer, Organ Systs Coord Ctr, 85-89, ASST PROF EXP PATH, ROSWELL PARK MEM INST DIV, STATE UNIV NY, 81- *Personal Data:* b New York, NY, Nov 6, 43; m 68. *Educ:* Cornell Univ, BS, 66; Univ Tex, MS, 71; Rice Univ, PhD(biol), 74. *Prof Exp:* Fel biochem, Biochem Dept, Baylor Col Med, 73-77, instr, 77-78; actg dir parasitol, Ctr Trop Dis, Univ Lowell, 78-80, assoc dir, 80-81. *Concurrent Pos:* Vis scientist, Ain Shams Univ, Cairo, Egypt, 80-81. *Mem:* Am Soc Parasitologists; AAAS; Am Soc Cell Biol; Int Asn Breast Cancer Res; Am Asn Cancer Res. *Res:* Cell biology of mammmary carcinogenesis, especially the roles of retrotransposons and of cytoskeletal (Paraten) components. *Mailing Add:* Dept Exp Path Roswell Park Cancer Inst Buffalo NY 14263

ASCHBACHER, MICHAEL, FINITE GROUP THEORY. *Current Pos:* from asst prof to assoc prof, 72-76, prof, Dept Math, 76-96, SHALER ARTHUR HANISCH MEM PROF MATH, CALIF INST TECHNOL, 96- *Personal Data:* b Little Rock, Ark, Apr 8, 44. *Educ:* Calif Inst Technol, BS, 66; Univ Wis, PhD, 69. *Prof Exp:* Res fel, Univ Ill, 69-70. *Concurrent Pos:* Alfred P Sloan fel, Calif Inst Technol, 72-74. *Mem:* Nat Acad Sci; Am Math Soc (vpres). *Mailing Add:* Math Dept 253-37 Calif Inst Technol Pasadena CA 91125. *E-Mail:* asch@cco.caltech.edu

ASCHBACHER, PETER WILLIAM, ANIMAL PHYSIOLOGY. *Current Pos:* RETIRED. *Personal Data:* b Ashland, Wis, Apr 20, 28; m 55; c 3. *Educ:* Univ Wis, BS, 51, MS, 53, PhD(dairy husb), 57. *Prof Exp:* From asst prof to assoc prof dairy husb, NDak State Univ, 56-64, asst dairy husbandman, 56-61; animal physiologist, Agr Res Serv, USDA, 64-78, res leader, Metab & Radiation Res Lab, 78-93. *Concurrent Pos:* Assoc scientist, Agr Res Lab, Atomic Energy Comn, 61. *Mem:* AAAS; Am Dairy Sci Asn; Am Soc Animal Sci; Sigma Xi. *Res:* Physiology of farm animals; metabolic fate of xenobiotics in farm animals. *Mailing Add:* 97 Woodland Dr NE Fargo ND 58102-2424

ASCHER, EDUARD, PSYCHIATRY. *Current Pos:* Asst prof, 49-73, ASSOC PROF PSYCHIAT, JOHNS HOPKINS UNIV, 73-, PSYCHIATRIST, OUTPATIENT DEPT, JOHNS HOPKINS HOSP, 49- *Personal Data:* b Vienna, Austria, Nov 23, 15; nat US; m 54; c 4. *Educ:* Wash Univ, BS & MD, 42. *Concurrent Pos:* Asst clin prof, Sch Med, Univ Md, 64-69, assoc clin prof, 69-; instr, Wash Sch Psychiat, 71-90; consult, off hearings & appeals, Social Security Admin. *Mem:* Fel Am Psychiat Asn. *Res:* Psychotherapy; depressive disorders; expressive behavior; group psychotherapy. *Mailing Add:* 3601 Greenway Apt 801 Baltimore MD 21218-2439

ASCHER, MARCIA, ETHNOMATHEMATICS. *Current Pos:* from asst prof to prof, 61-97, EMER PROF MATH, ITHACA COL, 95- *Personal Data:* b New York, NY, Apr 23, 35; m 56, Robert. *Educ:* Queens Col, NY, BS, 56; Univ Calif, Los Angeles, MA, 60. *Prof Exp:* Comput analyst math, Douglas Aircraft Co, 57-60; specialist tech discipline, Gen Elec Co, 60-61. *Concurrent Pos:* Getty Scholar, 87-88. *Mem:* Math Asn Am; Can Soc Hist & Philos Math. *Res:* Applications of mathematics to anthropology; mathematical ideas of traditional cultures. *Mailing Add:* Dept Math Ithaca Col Ithaca NY 14850

ASCHER, MICHAEL S, CLINICAL & INFECTIOUS DISEASES, VIROLOGY. *Current Pos:* LECTR, UNIV CALIF, BERKELEY, 85- *Personal Data:* b Freeport, Ill, May 17, 42; m 68; c 2. *Educ:* Harvard Univ, MD, 68. *Prof Exp:* DEP CHIEF, VIRAL & RICKETTSIAL DIS LAB, CALIF DEPT HEALTH, 85- *Concurrent Pos:* US Army med res. *Mem:* Am Col Physicians; Infectious Dis Soc; Am Soc Rickettsiology; Am Asn Immunologists; Am Soc Trop & Med Hyg; Am Soc Microbiologists. *Res:* AIDS; infectious disease pathogenesis. *Mailing Add:* Virus Lab Calif Dept Health Serv 2151 Berkeley Way Berkeley CA 94704

ASCHER, NANCY L, SURGERY, TRANSPLANTATION OF KIDNEY & LIVER. *Current Pos:* PROF SURG, UNIV CALIF, 88-, VCHMN, SAN FRANCISCO MED CTR, 93- *Personal Data:* b Detroit, Mich, Mar 15, 41. *Res:* transplantation of kidney & liver; surgery. *Mailing Add:* Box 0780 Rm M-896 Univ Calif San Francisco Med Ctr 533 Parnassus Ave San Francisco CA 94143-0780

ASCHER, PHILIPPE, NEUROBIOLOGY. *Current Pos:* DIR NEUROBIOL LAB & DEPT BIOL, PARIS, FRANCE. *Honors & Awards:* Charles A Dana Ward Pioneering Achievements in Health; Inst Med-Nat Acad Sci, 94. *Mailing Add:* Ecole Normale Superievre 45 rue d'Ulm Paris 75230 Cedex 05 France

ASCHER, ROBERT, ENTNOMATHEMATICS, EXPERIMENTAL FILMMAKING. *Current Pos:* from asst prof to assoc prof, 60-66, PROF ANTHROP & ARCHAEOL, CORNELL UNIV, 66- *Personal Data:* b New York, NY, Apr 28, 31; m 50. *Educ:* Queens Col, NY, BA, 54; Univ Calif, Los Angeles, MA, 59, PhD, 60. *Prof Exp:* Asst gen anthrop, Univ Calif, Los Angeles, 57-59, instr, Exten Div, 58-60. *Mem:* AAAS; Am Anthrop Asn; Soc Visual Anthropology. *Res:* Mathematical ideas in non-Western cultures; films that translate mythology in other cultures; anthropology. *Mailing Add:* Dept Anthrop Cornell Univ 726 University Ave Ithaca NY 14853

ASCHNER, JOSEPH FELIX, SOLID STATE PHYSICS, SEMICONDUCTORS. *Current Pos:* from asst prof to prof, 62-91, EMER PROF PHYSICS, CITY COL NEW YORK, 91- *Personal Data:* b Vienna, Austria, Jan 23, 22; US citizen; m 45, 62, Helga Buchenauer; c Katherine (Debruyn). *Educ:* Univ Chicago, BS, 43; Univ Ill, PhD(physics), 54. *Prof Exp:* Asst physics, Univ Ill, 50-54; mem tech staff solid state device tech, Bell Tel Labs, 54-62. *Concurrent Pos:* Fac assoc, Boeing Co, 63-66, Gen Atomic Co, 67-68 & Zenith Radio Co, 69. *Mem:* Am Phys Soc; Sigma Xi. *Res:* Alkali halide crystals; solid state diffusion; semiconductor device technology and surfaces; radiation effects; infrared phenomena in semiconductors. *Mailing Add:* 340 E 64th St Apt 26B New York NY 10021

ASCHNER, MICHAEL, NEUROTOXICOLOGY. *Current Pos:* asst prof pharmacol & toxicol, 88-92, ASSOC PROF, PHARMACOL & TOXICOL, ALBANY MED COL, 92- *Personal Data:* b Jerusalem, Israel, Nov 11, 55; US citizen; m 79; c 4. *Educ:* Univ Rochester, NY, BS, 80, MS, 83, PhD(neurobiol & anat), 85. *Prof Exp:* Fel toxicol, Univ Rochester, 85-87. *Concurrent Pos:* Teratol Soc young investr award, 85; prin investr, NIH new res serv award, 85-87 & First award, 89-94. *Mem:* Soc Toxicol; Teratology Soc; AAAS; NY Acad Sci. *Res:* Heavy metal, transport across the blood-brain barrier and their effects on homeostasis within the central nervous system employing both in vivo and in vitro techniques. *Mailing Add:* Dept Pharmacol & Ther Albany Med Col 47 New Scotland Ave Albany NY 12208-3412

ASCOLI, MARIO, HORMONE ACTION, MOLECULAR ENDOCRINOLOGY. *Current Pos:* PROF, PHARMACOL DEPT, UNIV IOWA, 90- *Personal Data:* b Guatemala City, Guatemala, May 3, 51; US citizen; m 84, Deborah L Segaloff; c Peter A & Rachel A. *Educ:* San Carlos Univ, Guatemala, Equi, 71; Vanderbilt Univ, Nashville, PhD(biochem), 75. *Prof Exp:* Fel biochem, M D Anderson Hosp & Tumor Inst, 75-76; res assoc, Biochem Dept, Vanderbilt Univ, 76-77, res instr, 77-78, from asst prof to assoc prof biochem, Med Dept, 78-85; scientist, Pop Coun, 85-88, sr scientist, 89-90. *Concurrent Pos:* Prin investr, NIH, 78-, Biochem Endocrinol Study Sect, 93-; ed, Endocrinol, 86-89; Carver sr scientist, Univ Iowa Col Med, 90-95. *Mem:* Sigma Xi; AAAS; Endocrine Soc; Am Soc Cell Biol; Am Soc Biochem & Molecular Biol; Soc Study Reproduction. *Res:* Cellular, biochemical and molecular basis of hormone action. *Mailing Add:* Dept Pharmacol Univ Iowa Col Med Iowa City IA 52242-1109

ASCULAI, SAMUEL SIMON, AGRICULTURAL ECONOMICS, TECHNICAL MANAGEMENT. *Current Pos:* PRES & CHIEF EXEC OFFICER, HYAL PHARMACEUT CORP, 90- *Personal Data:* b Tel Aviv, Israel, Apr 13, 42; m 81, Mira E Macht; c Avra, Jon, Ben & Micalt. *Educ:* Pace Col, BSc, 65; Rutgers Univ, MSc, 70, PhD(microbiol), 73. *Prof Exp:* Res asst, Ortho Pharmaceut Corp, 65-67, asst scientist, 67-69, assoc scientist, 69-70, scientist, 70-72, sr scientist, 72-74, dir div microbiol, 74-75; mgr res & develop, Monsanto Co, 75-81; pres, Viral Genetics, Inc, 81; vpres, Enscore Biol, Inc, 82-87; pres, Firstmiss Seed Co, 88-93; independent consult, Health & Agr Biotech, 87-89. *Concurrent Pos:* Adj prof biol, Univ Mo, St Louis, 79-80; pres, Int Genetic Sci, 85-87. *Mem:* AAAS. *Res:* Antiviral agents immune modulation and reproductive physiology; immunology; hyaluronic acid and drug delivery. *Mailing Add:* Hyal Pharmaceut Corp 2425 Skymark St Mississauga ON M5C 1B5 Can. *Fax:* 416-366-6330

ASEFF, GEORGE V, METALLURGY, CHEMISTRY. *Current Pos:* MGR NOE, MGR ENG FAILURE ANALYSIS, CORPORATE MATRS CONS, LAW ENG, TESTING CO, 71- *Personal Data:* b Meridian, Miss, May 26, 21; m 46; c 3. *Educ:* Case Inst Technol, BS, 48; Ga Inst Technol, MS, 51, MS, 63. *Prof Exp:* Sr engr, Lockheed-Ga Co, 51-53, lead engr, 53-58, nuclear specialist, 58-61, scientist, 61-62, proj engr, 62-63, staff & proj engr, 63-65, res scientist & prin investr ultrasonics & metall, 65-70; adminr chem dept, Ga State Univ, 70-71. *Concurrent Pos:* Consult, Photog Assistance Corp, 64- & Minn Mining & Mfg Co, 65- *Mem:* Sr mem AAAS; Am Soc Testing & Mat; sr mem Am Soc Metals. *Res:* Development of materials and material systems for use in a variety of environments, including cryogenic temperature, very high temperature, vibration and nuclear radiation. *Mailing Add:* 1015 Avondale Ave SE Atlanta GA 30312

ASENDORF, ROBERT HARRY, THEORETICAL PHYSICS, INFORMATION SCIENCE. *Current Pos:* RETIRED. *Personal Data:* b Philadelphia, Pa, Mar 5, 27; m 53, Sylvia Schwartz; c Laura & Lonna. *Educ:* Univ Pa, BA, 47, PhD(physics), 56. *Prof Exp:* Physicist, Selas Corp Am, 52-53; asst instr physics, Bryn Mawr Col, 53-56; physicist, Westinghouse Res Labs, 56-58; sr mem tech staff, Hughes Res Labs, 58-68; with US Govt, 68-73; sr corp scientist, Systs Control, Inc, 73-75; mgr, Imagery & Intel Systs, Ford Aerospace, Western Develop Lab, 75-77; chief engr & dir res & develop, Dalmo-Victor, 77; sr staff engr, Appl Technol, 77-86; sr staff scientist, ESL Inc, 86-91. *Mem:* Am Phys Soc; Sigma Xi; NY Acad Sci; Pattern Recognition Soc. *Res:* Theoretical physics, group theory, solid state physics: architect of multi-variant adaptive computer, multivac; digital image processing system, Idims; radar signature analysis, Ipcress; signal processing using a minimum, not maximum, entropy separation algorithm, Mesa; role of linear operators in Jungian archetypal psychology. *Mailing Add:* 14510 Manuela Rd Los Altos Hills CA 94022

ASENJO, FLORENCIO GONZALEZ, MATHEMATICAL LOGIC. *Current Pos:* assoc prof, 63-66, PROF MATH, UNIV PITTSBURGH, 66- *Personal Data:* b Buenos Aires, Arg, Sept 28, 26; US citizen; m 60; c 2. *Educ:* La Plata Nat Univ, Lic math, 54, PhD(math), 56. *Prof Exp:* Res mathematician, Lab Testing Mat & Tech Invests, Arg, 48-57, head calculus & statist sect, 57-58; asst prof math, Georgetown Univ, 58-61; assoc prof math, Univ Southern Ill, 61-63. *Concurrent Pos:* Asst, La Plata Nat Univ, 53-55, instr, 55-57, titular prof, 57-58; Fulbright fel, Univ Lisbon, 70 & 85. *Mem:* Am Math Soc; Asn Symbolic Logic; Acad Sci Spain. *Res:* Formalization of internal relations; arithmetic of term-relation numbers; calculus of antinomies; theory of multiplicities; sampling processes; model theory. *Mailing Add:* Dept Math Univ Pittsburgh Pittsburgh PA 15260

ASERINSKY, EUGENE, SLEEP PHYSIOLOGY, ELECTROPHYSIOLOGY. *Current Pos:* prof & chmn physiol & pharmacol, 76-77, prof & chmn physiol, 77-86, EMER PROF PHYSIOL, SCH MED, MARSHALL UNIV, WASH, 87- *Personal Data:* b New York, NY, May 6, 21; m 42, 59, Rita Goldman; c Armond, Jill & Iris. *Educ:* Univ Chicago, PhD(physiol), 53. *Honors & Awards:* Spec Recognition Award, Sleep Res Soc, 95. *Prof Exp:* Res assoc physiol, Sch Fisheries, Univ Wash, 53-54; instr, Dept Physiol, Jefferson Med Col, 54-57, from asst prof to prof, 54-76. *Concurrent Pos:* Vis instr, Northern Ill Col Optom, 51-52; vis res scientist, Eastern Pa Psychiat Inst, Philadelphia, Pa, 63-69; vis prof, NY Sch Psychiat, 66-68 & Dept Biophys, Ramon y Cajal Inst, Spain, 71; adj prof, Dept Physiol, WVa Univ, 77-87. *Mem:* Am Physiol Soc; Soc Neurosci; Am Med Writers Asn; Am Astronaut Soc; Neuroelec Soc. *Res:* Physiological parameters of sleep; oculomotor characteristics of rapid eye movement; oculocardiac reflex, chronaxie and CNS changes subsequent to spinal hemisection. *Mailing Add:* 7370 Calle Cristobal No 115 San Diego CA 92126

ASFAHL, C RAY, SAFETY, AUTOMATED SYSTEMS & COMPUTER SCIENCE. *Current Pos:* assoc prof, 69-74, PROF INDUST ENG, UNIV ARK, 74- *Personal Data:* b Enid, Okla, Aug 31, 38; c 4. *Educ:* Okla State Univ, BS, 61; Stanford Univ, MS, 62; Ariz State Univ, PhD(indust eng), 70. *Prof Exp:* Indust engr, Ethyl Corp, 60; engr, Continental Pipeline Co, 61; asst prof indust eng, Ohio Univ, 65-67. *Mem:* Am Inst Indust Engrs; Soc Mfg Engrs; Am Soc Safety Engrs; Am Indust Hyg Asn; Am Soc Eng Educ. *Res:* Industrial safety; robotics; automated systems; reliability of automated systems. *Mailing Add:* 3130 Warwick Fayetteville AR 72703

ASGAR, KAMAL, BIOENGINEERING. *Current Pos:* from res asst to res assoc, 52-59, from asst prof to prof, 59-90, EMER PROF DENT MAT, SCH DENT, UNIV MICH, ANN ARBOR, 90- *Personal Data:* b Tabriz, Iran, Aug 28, 22; m 48, Safieh Seyedi; c Alexander & Andrew. *Educ:* Tech Col Tehran, BA, 45; Univ Mich, Ann Arbor, MS, 48, BS, 50, PhD(mat & metall), 59. *Honors & Awards:* Hollenback Award, Acad Oper Dent, 84; Nikayama Award, 88. *Prof Exp:* Pain chemist. *Concurrent Pos:* Mem, Base Metal Alloys Comt, Am Nat Stand Comt & chmn, Casting Investment Comt & Gypsum Subcomt, 73-77; mem, Consult Team, Nat Inst Dent Res; consult, Vet Admin Hosp & USN Dent, 74- *Mem:* Int Asn Dent Res; Am Soc Metallurgists; Microbeam Anal Soc. *Res:* Cast alloys used in dentistry; both noble and base metal alloys; porcelain-metal restorations; dental amalgam; dental investments. *Mailing Add:* Dept Biomat Sch Dent Univ Mich Ann Arbor MI 48109. *Fax:* 313-971-7565

ASGHAR, KHURSHEED, PHARMACOLOGY, PHARMACY. *Current Pos:* health scientist adminr, Nat Inst Drug Abuse, NIH, 81-84, pharmacologist, Div Preclin Res, Alcohol, Drug Abuse & Ment Health Admin, 84-88, chief, Extramural Policy & Proj Rev Br, Off Sci, 88-89, CHIEF, BASIC SCI REV BR, OFF EXTRAMURAL PROG REV, NAT INST DRUG ABUSE, NIH, 89- *Personal Data:* b India, Aug 16, 40; US citizen; m 69; c 3. *Educ:* Univ Panjab, BPharm, 60; Univ Calif, San Francisco, PhD(pharm chem), 66. *Prof Exp:* Res fel, Dept Pharmacol, Univ Calif, San Francisco, 65-67; lectr pharm, Univ Karachi, 67-68; res assoc pharmacol, Univ Chicago, 68-71; spec res fel toxicol, Nat Heart & Lung Inst, NIH, 71-73; pharmacologist, Bur Drugs, Food & Drug Admin, 73-74, mid-level assoc, Career Develop Prog, 74-76; health scientist adminr, Nat Inst Neurol & Commun Disorders & Stroke, NIH, 76-81. *Concurrent Pos:* Teaching & res asst, Dept Pharmaceut Chem, Univ Calif, San Francisco, 61-66. *Res:* Pharmacology; toxicology; drug abuse; policy development and management of biomedical programs. *Mailing Add:* 8 Bouldercrest Ct Rockville MD 20850. *Fax:* 301-443-0538; *E-Mail:* ka181@nih.gov

ASH, ARLENE SANDRA, HEALTH SERVICES RESEARCH, STATISTICS & BIOSTATISTICS. *Current Pos:* asst prof statist, Boston Univ, 78-84, from asst prof to assoc prof math in med, 84-97, PROF MATH IN MED, BOSTON UNIV MED SCH, 97- *Personal Data:* b Stamford, Conn, May 15, 46. *Educ:* Harvard Univ, BA, 67; Washington Univ, MS, 72; Univ Ill, PhD(math, statist), 77. *Prof Exp:* Instr math, Mindanao State Univ, 67-69; res instr, Dartmouth Col, 76-78. *Concurrent Pos:* Statist consult, Sidney Farber Inst, Boston, 78-80; statist consult in legal disputes, 78-; pres, Boston Chap, Am Statist Asn, 82-83; pres, Caucus on Women in Statist, 86. *Mem:* Am Statist Asn; Biomet Soc; Inst Math Statist. *Res:* Experimental design; design optimality; statistical aspects of case-control studies and clinical trials, public health policy; statistical methodology in discrimination litigation. *Mailing Add:* 73 Hemenway St Boston MA 02115

ASH, J MARSHALL, HARMENIC ANALYSIS. *Current Pos:* from asst prof to assoc prof, 69-74, PROF MATH, DEPAUL UNIV, 74- *Personal Data:* b New York, NY, Feb 18, 40; m 77, Alison Igo; c Michael, Garrett & Andrew. *Educ:* Univ Chicago, SB, 61, SM, 63, PhD(math), 66. *Prof Exp:* Joseph Fels Ritt instr math, Columbia Univ, 66-69. *Concurrent Pos:* Partic harmonic anal conf, Warwick Univ, 68, Williams Col, 78, Univ Md, 79 & Tohoku Univ, 90; Am Math Soc partic, Int Math Cong, 70, 74, 78, 86, 90 & 94; vis prof, Stanford Univ, 77. *Mem:* Am Math Soc; Math Asn Am; Sigma Xi. *Res:* Generalized derivatives of functions of a real variable; multiple trigonometric series; real variable; harmonic analysis; measure theory; singular integrals; Fourier series; analytic number theory. *Mailing Add:* Dept Math DePaul Univ Chicago IL 60614. *E-Mail:* mash@math.depaul.edu

ASH, KENNETH OWEN, PATHOLOGY, CLINICAL CHEMISTRY. *Current Pos:* DIR CLIN CHEM, MED CTR, UNIV UTAH, 75-, ASSOC DIR CLIN LABS, 77-, DIR CLIN CHEM GROUP, 80-, PROF PATH, UNIV UTAH, 85- *Personal Data:* b Provo, Utah, Aug 21, 36; m 56; c 4. *Educ:* Brigham Young Univ, BS, 58, PhD(biochem), 61. *Honors & Awards:* Evans Award, Acad Clin Lab Physicians & Scientists, 89. *Prof Exp:* Proj leader protein res, Gen Mills, Inc, 61-64; sr res scientist, Honeywell Regulator Co, 64-66; prin scientist, Honeywell, Inc, 66-70, tech dir clin instrumentations dept, 70-71; dir lab, A&M Labs, 71-74; dir, Br Lab, Bio-Sci Labs, 75. *Concurrent Pos:* Lab consult, Vet Admin Hosp, Salt Lake City, 75-; sr vpres, Asn Regional & Univ Pathologists, 84; exec vpres & chief opers officer, Assoc Regional & Univ Pathologists, Inc. *Mem:* Am Asn Clin Chemists; Am Soc Clin Pathologists; Nat Acad Clin Biochem; Acad Clin Lab Physicians & Scientists (pres elect, 85, pres, 86). *Res:* Cation flux; hypertension; olfaction; bilirubin; trace metal analysis. *Mailing Add:* 500 Chipeta Way Salt Lake City UT 84108

ASH, LAWRENCE ROBERT, PARASITOLOGY, TROPICAL MEDICINE. *Current Pos:* from asst prof to assoc prof infectious & trop dis, Univ Calif, Los Angeles, 67-75, chmn & assoc dean, 79-84, prof, 75-94, EMER PROF EPIDEMIOL & INFECTIOUS & TROP DIS, SCH PUB HEALTH, UNIV CALIF, LOS ANGELES, 94- *Personal Data:* b Holyoke, Mass, Mar 5, 33; m 60; c 1. *Educ:* Univ Mass, BS, 54, MA, 56; Tulane Univ, PhD(parasitol), 60. *Prof Exp:* Asst parasitologist, Univ Hawaii, 60-61; instr parasitol, Tulane Univ, 62-65; med parasitologist, NIH, 65-67. *Concurrent Pos:* Mem US panel parasitic dis, US-Japan Coop Med Sci Prog, NIH, 72-78, chmn panel, 78-84; mem adv sci bd, Gorgas Mem Inst, 74-76; mem ad hoc study group on parasitic dis, US Army Med Res & Develop Command, 75-79. *Mem:* Am Soc Parasitol; Am Soc Trop Med & Hyg; Royal Soc Trop Med & Hyg; Am Soc Clin Pathologists. *Res:* Parasitic diseases of man and animals; biology, pathology and systematics of filariae, metastrongyles, ascarids, spirurids and other helminths; diagnostic methods in parasitic diseases. *Mailing Add:* Pub Health Univ Calif 405 Hilgard Ave Los Angeles CA 90095-1772. *E-Mail:* larryash@ucla.edu

ASH, MAJOR MCKINLEY, JR, PERIODONTICS. *Current Pos:* from instr to prof periodont & oral path, 54-69, chmn dept Occlusion, 69-87, PROF PERIODONT, SCH DENT, UNIV MICH, ANN ARBOR, 87-, MARCUS L WARD PROF DENT, 86- *Personal Data:* b Bellaire, Mich, Apr 7, 21; m 47; c 4. *Educ:* Mich State Col, BS, 47; Emory Univ, DDS, 51; Univ Mich, MS, 54. *Hon Degrees:* DrMed, Univ Bern, 75. *Prof Exp:* Instr oral path, Emory Univ, 52-53; teaching fel, Sch Dent, Univ Mich, 53-54. *Concurrent Pos:* Attend physician, Vet Admin Hosp, Atlanta, Ga, 52-53; consult, Vet Admin Hosp, Ann Arbor, 61-; pres, Mich Basic Sci Bd, 66-70; consult, Catherine McAuley Health Ctr, Ann Arbor, 86- & Fed Drug Admin, 86- *Mem:* AAAS; Int Asn Dent Res. *Res:* Evaluation of electric and manual toothbrushes; telemetry of intra-oral occlusal forces, pH, muscle forces and jaw movements; evaluation of dental pain thresholds and hypersensitivity; occlusion and temporomandibular joint pathology. *Mailing Add:* 1206 Snyder Ave Ann Arbor MI 48103

ASH, MICHAEL EDWARD, APPLIED MATHEMATICS, ESTIMATION THEORY. *Current Pos:* PRIN MEM TECH STAFF, INERTIAL INSTRUMENT MODELING & PARAMETER ESTIMATION, CHARLES STARK DRAPER LAB, INC, 76- *Personal Data:* b Detroit, Mich, June 26, 37; m 63, Marta Bernal; c Arthur & Rachel. *Educ:* Mass Inst Technol, BS, 59; Princeton Univ, MA, 60, PhD(math), 63. *Prof Exp:* Instr math, Princeton Univ, 62-63; res assoc, Brandeis Univ, 63-64; mem staff celestial mech & gen relativity, Lincoln Lab, Mass Inst Technol, 64-76. *Concurrent Pos:* Lectr, Northeastern Univ Grad Eve Sch, 68-71 & Dept Comput Sci, Eve Sch, Boston Univ, 73-89; adj assoc prof, Col Eng, Boston Univ, 86-; chair, Accelerometer Comt, Inst Elec & Electronics Engrs/Aerospace & Electronics Systs Soc, Gyro Accelerometer Panel, 96- *Mem:* Assoc fel Am Inst Aeronaut & Astronaut. *Res:* Inertial instruments; filtering and estimation; data acquisition and processing; celestial mechanics. *Mailing Add:* 16 Baskin Rd Lexington MA 02173. *E-Mail:* mash@draper.com

ASH, RAYMOND H(OUSTON), CONTROL SYSTEMS, SYSTEMS ANALYSIS. *Current Pos:* group leader, Systs Anal Group, 69-75, sect head eng div, 75-78, MGR CONTROL SYSTS TECHNOL, ENG DIV, PROCTER & GAMBLE CO, 78- *Personal Data:* b Paterson, NJ, Jan 17, 39; m 60; c 3. *Educ:* Rensselaer Polytech Inst, BEE, 60, MEE, 65, PhD(elec eng), 69. *Prof Exp:* Engr, Procter & Gamble Co, Ohio, 60-64; from instr to asst prof elec eng, Rensselaer Polytech Inst, 67-69. *Mem:* Inst Elec & Electronics Engrs. *Res:* Real-time process computer control systems applications; state estimation and system identification; optimization; industrial applications of modern control theory. *Mailing Add:* Winton Hill Tech Ctr Proctor & Gamble Eng Cincinnati OH 45224

ASH, ROBERT B, MATHEMATICS. *Current Pos:* assoc prof, 63-71, PROF MATH, UNIV ILL, URBANA-CHAMPAIGN, 71- *Personal Data:* b New York, NY, May 20, 35; m 56. *Educ:* Columbia Univ, BA, 55, BS, 56, MS, 57, PhD(elec eng), 60. *Prof Exp:* From instr to asst prof elec eng, Columbia Univ, 58-62; vis asst prof, Univ Calif, Berkeley, 62-63. *Res:* Information theory; probability theory. *Mailing Add:* Univ Ill 1409 W Green St Urbana IL 61801

ASH, ROBERT LAFAYETTE, AEROSPACE ENGINEERING, FLUID MECHANICS. *Current Pos:* Asst prof thermal eng, Old Dom Univ, 67-70, from assoc prof to prof eng, 70-79, actg dean, 83-84, chmn, 84-93, EMINENT PROF ENG, MECH ENG & MECH DEPT, 79-, AEROSPACE ENG, OLD DOM UNIV, 93- *Personal Data:* b Holton, Kans, Dec 27, 41; m 69, Mary L Webb; c Susan D & Catherine P. *Educ:* Kans State Univ, BS, 63; Tulane Univ, MS, 66, PhD(mech eng), 68. *Honors & Awards:* Charles T Main Award, Am Soc Mech Engrs, 63. *Concurrent Pos:* NASA grants, 69-72 & 79- & consult, 69-72; sr resident res assoc, Jet Propulsion Lab, Calif Inst Technol, 77-79, Navy grant, 79-84; vis distinguished res engr, NASA, 92-93. *Mem:* Am Soc Mech Engrs; Am Soc Eng Educ; Am Inst Aeronaut & Astronaut; Soc Natural Philos; Soc Automotive Engrs. *Res:* Thermal sciences; heat transfer; fluid mechanics; thermodynamics; space systems. *Mailing Add:* Old Dominion Univ Aerospace Engr Dept Norfolk VA 23529. *Fax:* 757-489-8643

ASH, RONALD JOSEPH, PROTEIN SCIENCE, VIROLOGY. *Current Pos:* assoc prof, 87-95, PROF BIOL, WASHBURN UNIV, 95- *Personal Data:* b Covington, Ky, Dec 24, 41; m 70, Aleta Johnson; c Nathan, Casey & Lesley. *Educ:* Thomas More Col, Ky, BA, 61; Univ Cincinnati, MS, 64, PhD(microbiol), 68. *Prof Exp:* From instr to assoc prof microbiol, Emory Univ, 67-77; sr microbiologist, Merrell Res Ctr, 77-81, res assoc, 81-87. *Concurrent Pos:* Vis asst prof, Inst Microbiol, Univ Basel, 73-74. *Mem:* Am Soc Microbiol; Am Chem Soc. *Res:* Proteins and enzymes of plants, molecular phylogeny of oak trees. *Mailing Add:* 817 SE 43rd Terr Topeka KS 66609. *Fax:* 785-231-0189; *E-Mail:* zzash@acc.wuacc.edu

ASH, ROY PHILLIP, biochemistry, for more information see previous edition

ASH, SIDNEY ROY, GEOLOGY, PALEOBOTANY. *Current Pos:* assoc prof, Weber State Col, 70-75, chmn dept, 77-83, PROF GEOL, WEBER STATE UNIV, 75-, CHMN DEPT, 92- *Personal Data:* b Albuquerque, NMex, Nov 25, 28; m 62, Shirley M Arviso; c Kathleen E & Randolph H. *Educ:* Midland Lutheran Col, BA, 51; Univ NMex, BA, 57, MS, 61; Univ Reading, PhD, 66. *Honors & Awards:* Govs Medal Sci & Technol, 87. *Prof Exp:* Phys sci aid ground water br, US Geol Surv, NMex, 56-58, geologist, 58-61, geologist paleont & stratig br, 61-64; instr natural sci, Midland Lutheran Col, 66-67, asst prof earth sci, 67-69; asst prof geol, Ft Hays Kans State Col, 69-70. *Concurrent Pos:* US-Australia Coop Sci res grant, Mesozoic plants, 76-77; NSF grant, Mesozoic plants, 79-88; mem, State Adv Coun, Sci & Technol, 87-89. *Mem:* Bot Soc Am; Paleont Soc; Paleont Asn; Geol Soc Am. *Res:* Stratigraphy and paleobotany of the Mesozoic. *Mailing Add:* Dept Geol Weber State Univ Ogden UT 84408-2507. *Fax:* 801-626-7445; *E-Mail:* sidash@weber.edu

ASH, WILLIAM JAMES, dermatoglyphics, for more information see previous edition

ASHBROOK, ALLAN WILLIAM, inorganic chemistry, metallurgical chemistry, for more information see previous edition

ASHBURN, EDWARD V, PHYSICS, ATMOSPHERIC PHYSICS. *Current Pos:* RETIRED. *Personal Data:* b Pittsburgh, Pa, May 13, 10. *Educ:* Univ Calif-Berkeley, BS, 39; Mass Inst Tech, MS, 40. *Prof Exp:* Physicist, Naval Weapon Ctr, 46-62; res physicist, Lockheed Calif Co, 62-73. *Mem:* Fel Am Phys Soc; fel AAAS; Sigma Xi. *Mailing Add:* 26137 Village 26 Leisure Village Camarillo CA 93012

ASHBURN, WILLIAM LEE, NUCLEAR MEDICINE. *Current Pos:* PROF RADIOL & CHIEF DIV NUCLEAR MED, SCH MED, UNIV CALIF, SAN DIEGO, 68- *Personal Data:* b New York, NY, Jan 18, 33; m 60; c 3. *Educ:* Western Md Col, AB, 55; Univ Md, MD, 59; Am Bd Radiol, dipl, 66. *Prof Exp:* Intern, Ohio State Univ Hosp, 59-60; med officer, USPHS Hosp, Savannah, Ga, 60-62, resident radiol, Clin Ctr, NIH, 62-66, chief diag radioisotopes sect, Dept Nuclear Med, 66-68. *Mem:* AMA; Soc Nuclear Med. *Res:* Use of radioisotopes in medical diagnosis; development of improved techniques of radioisotopic organ visualization using computers and other electronic aids with particular emphasis on cardiopulmonary diagnosis and diseases of the central nervous system. *Mailing Add:* UCSD Sch Med Univ Hosp 225 W Dickenson St San Diego CA 92103-1910

ASHBY, B(ILLY) B(OB), PROCESS DEVELOPMENT, PROCESS DESIGN. *Current Pos:* RETIRED. *Personal Data:* b Gatesville, Tex, Mar 15, 30; m 51; c 5. *Educ:* Univ Tex, BS, 52; Univ Mich, MSE, 53, PhD(chem eng), 56. *Prof Exp:* Sr chem engr, Humble Oil & Ref Co, 58-61, staff engr, 61-63, eng supvr, 63-67; dept head, Kawasaki, Japan, 69-70; eng assoc, Exxon Chem Co Am, 70-94. *Mem:* Am Inst Chem Engrs. *Res:* Distillation; process design; process simulation and control; computer control of process equipment; environmental control; wastewater treatment; process development. *Mailing Add:* 9344 Meredith Dr Baton Rouge LA 70815

ASHBY, BRUCE ALLAN, ORGANIC CHEMISTRY. *Current Pos:* INDEPENDENT CONSULT, HERCULES, GENERAL ELECTRIC, 84- *Personal Data:* b Elmhurst, NY, Mar 28, 22; m 48, Julia Consalvo; c Melanie & Hollis. *Educ:* Rutgers Univ, BS, 48, PhD(org chem), 54; Univ Mich, MS, 49. *Prof Exp:* Chemist, Dow Chem Co, Mich, 49-50; instr chem, Rutgers Univ, 50-53; chemist, silicones, Gen Elec Co, 54-60, specialist, 60-66, mgr spec projs, Silicone Prod Div, 66-70, specialist, silicone prod div, 70-84. *Mem:* AAAS; emer mem Am Chem Soc; Am Inst Chem; emer mem Sigma Xi. *Res:* Reaction mechanisms; synthetic routes to morphine; agriculturally important sulfur-nitrogen compounds; organo-silicon chemistry; fluorine compounds; organic and organometallic polymers; platinum chemistry. *Mailing Add:* 452 Penn Ave N Forked River NJ 08731-2506

ASHBY, CARL TOLIVER, PHYSICAL CHEMISTRY. *Current Pos:* RETIRED. *Personal Data:* b Vale, Ark, June 26, 05; m 29; c 2. *Educ:* Univ Tex, AB, 29, AM, 31, PhD(phys chem), 34. *Prof Exp:* Tutor chem, Univ Tex, 27-32, instr chem, 33-34; res engr, Servel, Inc, 34-43, dir develop, 43-53, chief engr, 53-56; dir eng & pres, Conrad, Inc, Mich, 56-60; dir eng, Norge Div, Borg-Warner Corp, 60-63; adv eng, Arkla Air Conditioning Co, 63-65; res assoc agr-biochem, Univ Ariz, 65-73. *Concurrent Pos:* Consult, 73- *Mem:* Am Chem Soc; Am Soc Heating, Refrig & AirConditioning Engrs. *Res:* Absorption refrigeration; low temperature refrigeration; environmental engineering; corrosion; crystallography; hydrothermal growth of crystals. *Mailing Add:* 13755 W Kentucky Dr Lakewood CO 80228-3064

ASHBY, EUGENE CHRISTOPHER, ORGANIC CHEMISTRY, INORGANIC CHEMISTRY. *Current Pos:* asst prof chem, 63-65, from assoc prof to prof, 65-73, REGENTS' PROF CHEM, 73-, DISTINGUISHED PROF, GA INST TECHNOL, 88- *Personal Data:* b New Orleans, La, Oct 25, 30; m 52; c Chris, Steven, Terry, Marie, Julie, Angie & Rachel. *Educ:* Loyola Univ, La, BS, 51; Auburn Univ, MS, 53; Univ Notre Dame, PhD(chem), 56. *Honors & Awards:* Lavoisier Medal, French Chem Soc, 71; Herty Medal, Am Chem Soc, 84; Sigma Xi Res Award, GA Inst Technol, 69 & 75. *Prof Exp:* Res assoc, Ethyl Corp, 56-63. *Concurrent Pos:* Sloan fel, 65-67; Guggenheim fel, 78-79. *Mem:* Am Chem Soc; Sigma Xi. *Res:* Organometallic chemistry; organoaluminum, magnesium, beryllium and boron; complex metal hydrides; organometallic reaction mechanisms; stereochemistry of alkylation and reduction reactions; organic reaction mechanisms; single electron transfer; author or coauthor of over 280 research publications. *Mailing Add:* Dept Chem Ga Inst Technol Atlanta GA 30332. *Fax:* 404-894-7452

ASHBY, JON KENNETH, SPEECH-LANGUAGE PATHOLOGY, AUDIOLOGY. *Current Pos:* PROF & PROG DIR COMMUN DIS, ABILENE CHRISTIAN UNIV, 72- *Personal Data:* b Dayton, Ohio, Feb 2, 41; c 2. *Educ:* Abilene Christian Univ, BS, 64; La State Univ, MA, 66, PhD(commun disorders), 72. *Prof Exp:* Speech pathologist speech ther, Hearing & Speech Ctr, Dayton, Ohio, 64; instr & supvr speech & hearing therapy, NTex State Univ, 66-70. *Concurrent Pos:* Sect chief, WTex Rehab Ctr, 72-73, consult & clinician, 73- *Mem:* Am Speech-Language & Hearing Asn; Int Asn Logopedics & Phoniatrics. *Res:* Aging and communication disorders; gerontology; stuttering and the attitudes toward that problem; conductive hearing impairment in children; history and philosophy of the rehabilitation of the hearing impaired; differential diagnosis of aphasia. *Mailing Add:* Abilene Christian Univ Comm Box 8156 1600 Campus Ct Abilene TX 79699-0001

ASHBY, MICHAEL FARRIES, ENGINEERING, DESIGN. *Current Pos:* ROYAL SOC RES PROF, UNIV CAMBRIDGE, 75- *Personal Data:* b Bristol, Eng, Nov 20, 35; m, Maureen Stewart; c Benjamin, Zachary & Victoria. *Educ:* Univ Cambridge, BA, 61, MA, 62, PhD, 64; Harvard Univ, MA, 70. *Honors & Awards:* Von Hippel Award, Mat Res Soc, 92. *Mem:* Foreign mem Nat Acad Eng; Royal Soc; fel Royal Acad Eng; foreign mem Swedish Acad Eng; Ger Acad Sci. *Res:* Materials in design; micromechanics of solids. *Mailing Add:* 51 Maids Causeway Cambridge CB5 8DE England

ASHBY, NEIL, THEORETICAL PHYSICS. *Current Pos:* Asst prof, 61, Sheldon fel, 61-62, from asst prof to assoc prof, 62-70, PROF PHYSICS, UNIV COLO, BOULDER, 70- *Personal Data:* b Dalhart, Tex, Mar 5, 34; div; c 2. *Educ:* Univ Colo, BA, 55; Harvard Univ, MA, 56, PhD(physics), 61. *Concurrent Pos:* Chmn, Boulder fac assembly, 80-82, dept physics, Univ Colo, 84-88. *Mem:* Am Phys Soc; Asn Develop Comput-Based Instruct Syst; Int Soc Gen Relativity & Gravitation. *Res:* Transport phenomena; quantum statistical mechanics; relativity. *Mailing Add:* Dept Physics Univ Colo Box 390 Boulder CO 80309-0390

ASHBY, VAL JEAN, APPLIED PHYSICS, ELECTROOPTICS. *Current Pos:* RETIRED. *Personal Data:* b Kansas City, Mo, June 24, 23; m 48; c 3. *Educ:* Univ Kans, BS, 44; Univ Calif, PhD(nuclear physics), 53. *Prof Exp:* Physicist, Lawrence Radiation Lab, Univ Calif, 46-59; physicist, Ramo-Woodridge, 59-61; physicist, Space Technol Labs, 61-62; physicist, Litton Indust Inc, 62-88. *Mem:* Am Phys Soc; Optical Soc Am. *Res:* Signal processing for noise-limited measurement systems; random noise, correlation, filtering and Fourier analyses; multidimensional spatial filtering; geometrical and physical optics; electro-optical systems; nuclear magnetic resonance gyro; ring laser gyro. *Mailing Add:* 19465 Vintage St Northridge CA 91324

ASHBY, WILLIAM CLARK, RECLAMATION, BIOMASS PRODUCTION. *Current Pos:* from assoc prof to prof bot, 60-92, VIS RES PROF, SOUTHERN ILL UNIV, CARBONDALE, 93- *Personal Data:* b Duluth, Minn, July 6, 22; m 51, Rhoda Stratton; c Rhoda, Janet & Carol. *Educ:* Univ Chicago, SB, 47, PhD(bot), 50. *Honors & Awards:* Plass Award, Am Soc Surface Mining & Reclamation. *Prof Exp:* Plant physiologist, US Forest Serv, 50-53; res fel, Calif Inst Technol, 53-54; Fulbright res scholar, Sydney, Australia, 54-55; asst prof bot, Univ Chicago, 55-60. *Concurrent Pos:* Fac res partic, Argonne Nat Lab, 66 & 70-71; cooperator, USDA Forest Serv; bus mgr, Ecol Soc Am, 69-73. *Mem:* Fel AAAS; Ecol Soc Am (treas, 66-68); Am Soc Surface Mining & Reclamation; Am Inst Biol Sci; Soil & Water Conserv Soc; Sigma Xi. *Res:* Tree, shrub and herb establishment and growth on surface coal mines with differing rooting media, grading, ground cover, herbicides and mycorrhizae; emphasis on tree growth and root system development; silver maple production for biomass. *Mailing Add:* Dept Plant Biol Southern Ill Univ Carbondale IL 62901-6509. *Fax:* 618-453-3441; *E-Mail:* plb@gm.c-plant.siu.edu

ASHCOM, JAMES D, BIOCHEMISTRY, PROTEIN CHEMISTRY. *Current Pos:* RESEARCHER BIOCHEM RES, HOLLAND LAB, AM RED CROSS, 88- *Personal Data:* b New Castle, Pa, 1950. *Educ:* Univ Pittsburgh, BS, 75, PhD(biochem), 85. *Prof Exp:* Fel biochem, Univ Pittsburgh, 85-88. *Mem:* Am Chem Soc; Soc Cell Biol. *Mailing Add:* 20013 Hob Hill Gaithersburg MD 20879

ASHCRAFT, ARNOLD CLIFTON, JR, ORGANIC CHEMISTRY, POLYMER CHEMISTRY. *Current Pos:* MEM RES STAFF ORG & POLYMER CHEM, CHEM & PLASTICS DIV, UNION CARBIDE CORP, 63- *Personal Data:* b Lexington, Ky, Nov 1, 38; m 59; c 4. *Educ:* Univ Cincinnati, BS, 60; Univ Calif, Berkeley, PhD(org chem), 64. *Honors & Awards:* Cert Recognition, NASA, 73. *Mem:* Sigma Xi. *Res:* Synthetic organic chemistry; polymer synthesis; dielectric materials; composite materials. *Mailing Add:* 838 Perrineville Rd Perrineville NJ 08535

ASHCROFT, DALE LEROY, ELECTRICAL ENGINEERING. *Current Pos:* ELEC ENGR, PRINCETON UNIV PLASMA PHYSICS LAB, 74- *Personal Data:* b Plainview, Minn, Apr 22, 26; m 49, Patricia Walch; c Joseph & Jennifer. *Educ:* US Naval Acad, BS, 49; Univ Ill, MS, 53. *Prof Exp:* Elec engr, USAF, 49-57, Gen Elec Co, 57-62, Louis Allis Corp, 62-64, Westinghouse Elec Corp, 64-68, US Elec Motors, 68-71, Ward Leonard Elec Co, 71-74. *Mem:* Inst Elec & Electronics Engrs; Indust Appls Soc. *Res:* Energy conversion and storage; power electronics; electric motor speed control; electrical power distribution system design. *Mailing Add:* Princeton Univ Plasma Pl Box 451 Princeton NJ 08543

ASHCROFT, FREDERICK H, EXPERIMENT & INSTRUMENTATION DESIGN. *Current Pos:* PROG MGR, SCI MARINE SERV, 93- *Personal Data:* b New York, NY, July 14, 53; m 76, Christine M Hall; c John H. *Educ:* Univ Mich, Ann Arbor, BSE, 85. *Prof Exp:* Sr assoc res eng, Univ Mich, 78-91; div mgr, Ship Hydrodyn Div, Arctec Offshore Corp, 91-93. *Concurrent Pos:* Consult, FH Ashcroft, 76-91. *Mem:* Soc Naval Architects & Marine Engrs; Am Soc Naval Engrs. *Res:* Design and instrumentation of all aspects of hydrodynamic modeling including ships and marine structures; design structural monitoring systems for ships and marine structures. *Mailing Add:* 945 Park Villa Pl Escondido CA 92025. *Fax:* 760-737-0232; *E-Mail:* rashcrof@scimar.com, 2674.3001@compuserve.com

ASHCROFT, NEIL WILLIAM, THEORETICAL CONDENSED MATTER PHYSICS. *Current Pos:* DEP DIR, CORNELL HIGH ENERGY SYNCHROTRON SOURCE, 78- *Personal Data:* b London, Eng, Nov 27, 38; US citizen; m 61; c 2. *Educ:* Univ NZ, BSc, 58, MScHons, 60, & Dipl (hon); Univ Cambridge, PhD(physics), 64. *Hon Degrees:* DSc, Victoria Univ, Wellingtons, NZ, 96. *Prof Exp:* Res assoc, Univ Chicago, 64-65; from res assoc to assoc prof, Cornell Univ, 65-75, dir, Lab Atomic Solid State Physics, 79-84, prof physics, 75-89, Horace White Prof Physics, Cornell Univ, 90- *Concurrent Pos:* Sr fel, sci res coun, Cavendish Lab, 73-74; vis fel, Clare Hall, Cambridge Univ, 73-74 & Churchill Col, 84-85; consult, Los Alamos Nat Lab, 76-; mem panel High Pressure Sci & Technol, Div Mat Sci, US Dept Energy, 82; mem, NAS Panel, Condensed Matter Physics, 83; actg dir, Cornell High Energy Synchrotron Source, 83-84; vchmn, Gordon Conf, High Pressure

Physics & Chem, 84, chmn-elect, 86-; adv panel, High Flux Beam Reactor, Brookhaven Nat Lab, 84-; John Simon Guggenheim Mem fel, 84-85; Royal Soc Guest fel, Cambridge, 84-85; vchmn Div Condensed Matter Physics, Am Phys Soc, 85-86; consult, Lawrence Livermore Nat Lab, 85-; chmn, Div Condensed Matter Physics, Am Phys Soc, 86-87; chmn, Gordon Conf Res High Pressures, 86; vis comt mem, Brookhaven Nat Lab, 86; panel, High Temp Superconductivity, Nat Acad Sci, 87; hon fel, Royal Soc NZ. *Mem:* Nat Acad Sci; Am Inst Physics; fel AAAS; fel Am Phys Soc. *Res:* Properties of matter under extreme conditions, theory of disordered systems, theory of classical and quantum liquids, optical properties of solids, theory of the metallic state; numerous articles in physics journals. *Mailing Add:* Cornell Univ Clark Hall Lab Atomic SS Phys Ithaca NY 14853. *Fax:* 607-255-6428; *E-Mail:* nwa@msc.cornell.edu

ASHE, ARTHUR JAMES, III, ORGANOMETALLIC CHEMISTRY OF MAIN GROUP ELEMENTS. *Current Pos:* From asst prof to assoc prof, 66-76, chm, 83-86, PROF CHEM, UNIV MICH, 76- *Personal Data:* b New York, NY, Aug 5, 40; m 62, Penelope G Vaugan; c 2. *Educ:* Yale Univ, BA, 62, MS, 65, PhD(org chem), 66. *Concurrent Pos:* A P Sloan fel, 73; vis scholar, Phys Chem Inst, Univ Basel, 74. *Mem:* Am Chem Soc; Int Coun Main Group Chem. *Res:* Physical organic chemistry; organometallic compounds. *Mailing Add:* Dept Chem Univ Mich Ann Arbor MI 48109. *Fax:* 313-747-4865; *E-Mail:* ajashe@umich.edu

ASHE, JAMES S, SYSTEMATICS, EVOLUTION. *Current Pos:* ASSOC PROF ENTOM, SYSTEMATICS & ECOL & DIR ENTOM, UNIV KANSAS, LAWRENCE, 88- *Personal Data:* b Charlotte, NC, Feb 23, 47; m 84; c 1. *Educ:* Univ NC, BS, 69; Appalachian State Univ, MA, 72; Univ Alta, Edmonton, PhD(systematics), 82. *Prof Exp:* From asst cur to assoc cur insects, Field Mus Natural Hist, 82-88. *Concurrent Pos:* Asst cur & sessional instr, Univ Alta, 78-79; lectr biol, Field Mus Natural Hist, Chicago, 83-84, adult educ, 85-86, evol biol, Univ Chicago, 84-88; vis cur entom, Am Mus Natural Hist, 83-; div head insects, Field Mus Nat History, 85-88, actg chmn zool, 85, 87 & 88, actg div head zool, 86-87, chmn, Sci Adv Coun, 86-87; naturalist & lectr, Tour-Falkland Island, 88-; sci ed, Fieldiana, 88- *Mem:* Coleopterists Soc (pres & pres-elect, 89-90); Entom Soc Am (secy, 88-90); Soc Syst Zool; Soc Study Evolution; AAAS. *Res:* Systematics and evolution of mushroom inhabiting beetles; evolution, host relationships and ecology of parasitic staphylinid beetles and their rodent hosts. *Mailing Add:* Snow Entom Mus Snow Hall Univ Kans Lawrence KS 66045-0001

ASHE, JOHN HERMAN, NEUROPHYSIOLOGY, SYNAPTIC MECHANISMS. *Current Pos:* from asst prof to assoc prof, 80-90, PROF NEURO SCI & PHYSIOL PSYCHOL, UNIV CALIF, RIVERSIDE, 90-, CHMN, DEPT NEUROSCI PSYCHOL. *Personal Data:* b Philadelphia, Pa, Mar 27, 44; div; c 1. *Educ:* Univ Calif, Riverside, BA, 72, Irvine, PhD(biol), 77. *Prof Exp:* NIH fel neurophysiol, Med Ctr, Univ Calif, San Francisco, 77-78, NIMH fel, 78-79, asst res physiologist, 79-80. *Concurrent Pos:* Prin investr, NSF, 81-88, 90-; mem, Div Res Grants Study Sect Behav & Neurosci, NIH, 84-87; mem, Ctr Neurobiol Learning & Memory Organized Res Unit, Univ Calif, 84-; NSF adv panel, Neural Mechanisms Behav, 90- *Mem:* Soc Neurosci; Am Physiol Soc; Am Soc Cell Biol; AAAS; Int Brain Res Orgn. *Res:* Electrophysiological and neuropharmacological analysis of synaptic transmission and plasticity in the central and peripheral nervous system; neurophysiological process in learning and memory. *Mailing Add:* Dept Neurosci & Psychol Univ Calif Riverside CA 92521. *Fax:* 909-787-3985; *E-Mail:* ashe@ucracl.ucr.edu

ASHE, WARREN (KELLY), MICROBIOLOGY, BIOCHEMISTRY. *Current Pos:* instr, 71-85, ASST DEAN RES, COL MED, 71-, ASST PROF, HOWARD UNIV, 85- *Personal Data:* b Halifax, NC, Aug 20, 29; m 51; c 5. *Educ:* Howard Univ, BS, 51, MS, 62, PhD, 84. *Prof Exp:* Med biol technician, Nat Inst Dent Res, 54-56, supvr med biol technol, 56-57, from microbiologist to res microbiologist, 57-70, health scientist adminr, 70-71. *Concurrent Pos:* Spec consult to secy Dept Health, Educ & Welfare, 68; consult, NIH, 72-, Ohio State Univ, 72-74, Col Dent & dept microbiol, Grad Sch, Southern Ill Univ, 73-74 & Patent Awareness Prog, Atlanta Univ, 74-75; prin investr, biomed res support grant, 72-; mem, Spec Grants Rev Comt, Nat Inst Dent Res, 75-79; mem bd dirs, Am Heart Asn, Dallas, 83-, chmn, 86-88; prin investr, Student Res Asst Prog Grant, 78; prog dir, Howard Univ Ctr Health Sci, Div Res Resources, NIH, 77-81; consult, Nat Cancer Inst, 86- *Mem:* Int Asn Dent Res; Am Asn Lab Animal Sci; Am Soc Microbiol; Soc Exp Biol & Med; Soc Res Adminr; Sigma Xi. *Res:* Virology; immunology; pathology; the role of Herpes simplex viruses in the pathogenesis of chronic diseases, including oral facial ulcerative disorders, autoimmune diseases and vitiligo; research administration. *Mailing Add:* 5051 12th St NE Washington DC 20017-2851

ASHEN, PHILIP, INORGANIC CHEMISTRY. *Current Pos:* mgr Chem Div, 48-63, vpres, 63-77, PRES, MW HARDY & CO, INC, 77- *Personal Data:* b Brooklyn, NY, Nov 5, 15. *Educ:* City Univ New York, BA, 36; New York Univ, MBA, 57, PhD(chem), 68. *Prof Exp:* Chief chemist, Alco Mfg Corp, 36-48. *Concurrent Pos:* Gas reconnaissance officer & lectr chem warfare, US Citizens Defense Corps, 40-45; consult, 50-; lectr, Grad Sch, NY Univ, 54-56. *Mem:* Fel Am Inst Chemists; fel AAAS; NY Acad Sci; Am Chem Soc; Chem & Econ Soc. *Res:* Experimentation with plant life for pharmaceutical and industrial purposes; synthetic organic and natural products chemistry. *Mailing Add:* 2315 Ave I Brooklyn NY 11210-2825

ASHENDEL, CURTIS LLOYD, CANCER RESEARCH, CELLULAR PHYSIOLOGY. *Current Pos:* Asst prof, 82-88, ASSOC PROF MED CHEM, PURDUE UNIV, 88- *Personal Data:* b St Louis, Mo, June 20,1955; m 84; c 3. *Educ:* Mich State Univ, BS, 77; Univ Wis, PhD(oncol), 82. *Concurrent Pos:* Consult, NSF Prog Cellular Biosci, 87-91. *Mem:* Am Asn Cancer Res; Am Soc Biochem & Molecular Biol. *Res:* Molecular mechanisms of carcinogenesis and cellular signaling; the roles of oncogene-encoded proteins and protein kinase in normal and altered signal transduction. *Mailing Add:* Dept Med/Chem Purdue Univ Life Sci Res Bldg West Lafayette IN 47907-1524

ASHENHURST, ROBERT LOVETT, APPLIED MATHEMATICS, COMPUTER SCIENCES. *Current Pos:* from asst prof to assoc prof, 57-65, chmn comt info sci, 69-74, dir, Inst Comput Res, 69-78, PROF APPL MATH, GRAD SCH BUS, UNIV CHICAGO, 65- *Personal Data:* b Paris, France, Aug 9, 29; div; c 4. *Educ:* Harvard Univ, AB, 50, SM, 54, PhD(appl math), 56. *Prof Exp:* Res assoc, Harvard Comput Lab, 50-56, instr appl math, Harvard Univ, 56-57. *Concurrent Pos:* Ed-in-chief, Commun of Asn Comput Mach, 73- *Mem:* Soc Indust & Appl Math; Inst Elec & Electronics Engrs; Asn Comput Mach; Inst Mgt Sci; AAAS. *Res:* Computer and information systems and their application to scientific and management problems. *Mailing Add:* Univ Chicago 1101 E 58th St Chicago IL 60637

ASHER, DAVID MICHAEL, INFECTIOUS DISEASES, PEDIATRICS. *Current Pos:* AT DEPT PEDIAT & ONCOL, JOHNS HOPKINS UNIV. *Personal Data:* b Chicago, Ill, Nov 10, 37; m 71; c 1. *Educ:* Harvard Univ, AB, 59; Harvard Med Sch, MD, 63; Am Bd Pediat, dipl, 75. *Prof Exp:* Intern med, King County Hosp, Seattle, 63-64; jr asst resident pediat, Boston City Hosp, 64-65; jr resident, Mass Gen Hosp, Boston, 65-66; res assoc virol, Nat Inst Child Health & Human Develop, Bethesda, Md, 66-69; Nat Inst Neurol Dis & Stroke spec res fel virol, USA-USSR Health Scientist Exchange, 69-70; res med officer virol, Nat Inst Neurol & Commun Dis & Stroke, NIH, 70- *Concurrent Pos:* Instr pediat, Sch Med, Johns Hopkins Univ, 76. *Mem:* Soc Pediat Res; Infectious Dis Soc Am. *Res:* Persistent viral infections, especially pathogenesis of infections of the nervous system and the urinary tract; viral infections of children with impaired immune defenses. *Mailing Add:* Nat Inst Neuro Commun Dis 36-5821 Johns Hopkins Univ Baltimore MD 20892

ASHER, ROBERT BERNARD, ADVANCED SYSTEMS & TECHNOLOGY FOR DEFENSE APPLICATIONS. *Current Pos:* sr mem tech staff, 81-92, MGR, SPECIAL PROJ DEPT, SANDIA NAT LABS, 92- *Personal Data:* b Chicago, Ill, June 15, 41; m 65, Linda L Parker; c Heidi (Giebel), Kimberly & Christina (Buchanan). *Educ:* Okla State Univ, BS, MS, 71, PhD(eng), 74. *Prof Exp:* Mach designer, Brown Eng & Mach Co, 61-64; comput programmer, Satellite Control Facil, USAF, 64-67, tech mgr, Avionics Lab, 71-74, researcher, F J Seiler Res Lab, 74-77; prof, Tex Tech Univ, 77-78; prog mgr, Orincon Corp, 78-79; supvr, Adaptive Optics Group, Lockheed Palo Alto Res Lab, 79-81. *Concurrent Pos:* Invited lectr & vis scientist, Stanford Univ, 75; consult, Optical Sci Corp, 77-78; prin investr, Sandia Nat Labs, 81- *Mem:* Inst Elec & Electronics Engs; Optical Soc Am. *Res:* Adaptive optics, control and estimation theory, wavefront control; special technologies. *Mailing Add:* Sandia Nat Labs PO Box 5800 MS 0105 Albuquerque NM 87185. *Fax:* 505-844-9895; *E-Mail:* rbasher@sandia.gov

ASHER, SANFORD ABRAHAM, BIOPHYSICS, COLLOID SCIENCE. *Current Pos:* PROF, DEPT CHEM, UNIV PITTSBURGH, 80- *Personal Data:* b Landesburg, Ger, June 18, 47; US citizen; m 76, Nancy L Day; c Rachel, David S & Dianne. *Educ:* Univ Mo-St Louis, BA, 71; Univ Calif, Berkeley, MS, 73, PhD(chem), 77. *Honors & Awards:* Spectrochem Anal Award, Am Chem Soc, 94. *Prof Exp:* Fel, Div Appl Sci, Harvard Univ, 77-80. *Concurrent Pos:* Estab investr, Am Heart Asn, 84; NIH career develop award, NIH, 84; adj prof, Dept Chem, Carnegie-Mellon Univ, 85-; mem, Coblentz Soc Bd, 90-94, Pittsburgh Conf Comt, 90- *Mem:* Biophys Soc; Am Chem Soc; AAAS. *Res:* Raman spectroscopy; biophysical chemistry; colloids; optical devices; instrumentation; analytical chemistry; lasers, laser spectroscopy; heme proteins. *Mailing Add:* Dept Chem Univ Pittsburgh 234 Chemistry Bldg Pittsburgh PA 15260-3902. *Fax:* 412-624-0588; *E-Mail:* ashers@vms.cis.pitt.edu

ASHER, WILLIAM EDWARD, AIR-SEA GAS EXCHANGE, APPLIED LASER SPECTROSCOPY. *Current Pos:* Norcus assoc, 89-90, SR RES SCIENTIST, BATTELLE MARINE SCI LAB, 90- *Personal Data:* b Seattle, Wash, Oct 9, 58. *Educ:* Reed Col, BA 80; Ore Grad Inst, PhD(environ sci & eng), 87. *Prof Exp:* Res assoc, Rensselaer Polytech Inst, 87-89. *Res:* Understanding near-surface physico-chemcial processes affecting gas/liquid transfer rates as applied to remote estimation of air/sea gas fluxes. *Mailing Add:* Univ Wash Box 355640 Seattle WA 98195-5640. *Fax:* 425-681-3699; *E-Mail:* we_asher@ccmail.pnl.gov

ASHERIN, DUANE ARTHUR, INFORMATION SYSTEMS APPLICATIONS, ENVIRONMENTAL IMPACT ASSESSMENT. *Current Pos:* LEADER, TECH SERV SECT, MIDCONTINENT ECOL SCI CTR, US GEOL SURV, 93- *Personal Data:* b Watertown, Wis, Oct 13, 40; m 61; c 4. *Educ:* Univ Wis-Stevens Point, BS, 67; Univ Idaho, PhD(wildlife sci), 74. *Prof Exp:* Res assoc wildlife res, Nat Ecol Res Ctr, US Fish & Wildlife Serv, 71-73, res wildlife biologist, Idaho Coop Wildlife Res Unit, 73-77, wildlife data analyst, Ecol Assessment Methods Group, 77-79, group leader, Rapid Assessment Methods Group, Western Energy & Land Use Team, 79-87, sect leader, Resource Problem Anal Sect, Terrestrial Systs Br, 87-90, chief, Tech Serv Br, 90-93. *Concurrent Pos:* Field asst, Dept Natural Resources, Univ Wis, 67; wildlife asst, Idaho Dept Fish & Game, 71. *Mem:* Wildlife Soc; Nat Wildlife Fedn. *Res:* Development of a terrestrial wildlife and habitat characterization process or methodology; prescribed burning effects on nutrition, production, and big game use of key northern Idaho browse species; natural resource applications of geographic information systems; technical and information services administration. *Mailing Add:* Midcontinent Ecol Sci Ctr US Geol Surv 4512 McMurry Ave Ft Collins CO 80525-3400

ASHFORD, VICTOR AARON, XRAY IMAGING INSTRUMENTATION, EXPERIMENTAL HIGH ENERGY PHYSICS. *Current Pos:* RES SPECIALIST, UNIV CALIF, SAN DIEGO, 86- *Personal Data:* b Bremerton, Wash, Sept 12, 42; m 73; c 3. *Educ:* Long Beach State Col, BS, 65; Univ Calif, San Diego, MS, 68, PhD(physics), 73. *Prof Exp:* res assoc physics, Fermi Nat Accelerator Lab, 73-76; assoc physicist, Brookhaven Nat Lab, 76-82; res asst, Stanford Linear Accelerator Ctr, 82-86. *Mem:* Am Phys Soc. *Res:* Particles and fields; physics and society; experimental high energy elementary particle physics; x-ray imaging instrumentation for x-ray protein crystallography. *Mailing Add:* Energy Sci Lab Inc 6888 Nancy Ridge Rd San Diego CA 92121

ASHKENAZI, AVI, SIGNAL TRANSDUCTION, PROTEIN ENGINEERING. *Current Pos:* Res fel, 88-89, scientist, 89-93, SR SCIENTIST, DEPT MOLECULAR BIOL, GENENTECH, INC, 93- *Personal Data:* b Tel Aviv, Israel, Nov 29, 56; m 93, Chris D Clark; c 1. *Educ:* Hebrew Univ, Israel, PhD(biochem), 87. *Res:* Mechanisms of signal transduction by receptors and by GTP-binding proteins; use of receptor-based immunoglobulin fusion proteins as therapeutic agents in human diseases. *Mailing Add:* Genetech Inc 460 Point San Bruno Blvd South San Francisco CA 94080. *Fax:* 650-225-6443

ASHKIN, ARTHUR, EXPERIMENTAL PHYSICS. *Current Pos:* mem tech staff, Res Dept, 52-63, head, Dept Laser Sci, 63-87, MEM TECH STAFF, BELL LABS, 88- *Personal Data:* b Brooklyn, NY, Sept 2, 22; m 54; c 3. *Educ:* Columbia Col, AB, 47; Cornell Univ, PhD(physics), 52. *Honors & Awards:* Charles Hard Townes Award, Optical Soc Am, 88; Rank Prize, Quantum Electronic Award, Inst Elec & Electronics Engrs. *Prof Exp:* Staff mem, Radiation Lab, Columbia Univ, 42-46; asst, Nuclear Studies Lab, Cornell Univ, 48-52. *Mem:* Nat Acad Sci; Nat Acad Eng; fel Am Phys Soc; fel Optical Soc Am; fel Inst Elec & Electronics Engrs. *Res:* Quantum electronics; nonlinear optics; radiation pressure; optical trapping and manipulation of atoms, dielectric particles and biological particles. *Mailing Add:* AT&T Bell Labs 4E-418 Holmdel NJ 07733

ASHLEY, CHARLES ALLEN, PATHOLOGY. *Current Pos:* REFTIRED. *Personal Data:* b Bronxville, NY, Oct 10, 23; m 48, Audrey Waite; c 5. *Educ:* Cornell Univ, AB, 44, MD, 47; Univ Ill, MS, 51. *Prof Exp:* Intern, Mary Imogene Bassett Hosp, 47-49, assoc pathologist, 55-67, dir, 67-84, consult to dir, 84-88; resident path, Presby Hosp, Chicago, 49-52, asst attend pathologist, 52-53; asst chief path, Walter Reed Army Hosp, 53-55. *Concurrent Pos:* Instr, Univ Ill, 52-53; instr path, Columbia Univ, 55-62, assoc clin prof, 69-84. *Mem:* Am Asn Path; Sigma Xi. *Res:* Structural and chemical studies of muscular contractions; chemical carcinogenesis; pathology of radiation; electron microscopy. *Mailing Add:* RD No 2 Box 10 Cooperstown NY 13326

ASHLEY, DOYLE ALLEN, AGRONOMY, APPLIED PHYSIOLOGY. *Current Pos:* asst prof, 69-73, assoc prof, 73-78, PROF AGRON, UNIV GA, 78- *Personal Data:* b Collinsville, Ala, May 18, 32; m 58; c 2. *Educ:* Auburn Univ, BS, 54, MS, 57; NC State Univ, PhD(agron), 67. *Prof Exp:* Asst agron, Auburn Univ, 56-58; soil scientist, Agr Res Serv, USDA, 58-67, res soil scientist, Coastal Plains Soil & Water Conserv Res Ctr, 67-69. *Mem:* Am Soc Agron; Soil Sci Soc Am; Crop Sci Soc Am. *Res:* Nutrient and water utilization by field crops; field canopy photosynthesis of crop plants; photosynthate translocation and utilization by crop plants; plant-soil relationships. *Mailing Add:* Crop Sci Univ Ga 1180 E Broad St Athens GA 30601-3040

ASHLEY, HOLT, AERODYNAMICS, AEROELASTICITY. *Current Pos:* PROF AERONAUT & ASTRONAUT, STANFORD UNIV, 67- *Personal Data:* b San Francisco, Calif, Jan 10, 23; m 47. *Educ:* Univ Chicago, BS, 44; Mass Inst Technol, SM, 48, ScD(aeronaut eng), 51. *Honors & Awards:* Goodwin Medal, Mass Inst Technol, 53; Struct, Struct Dynamics & Mat Award, Am Inst Aeronaut & Astronaut, 69, Wright Bros Lectr, 81; 50th Anniversary Medal, Am Meteorol Soc, 71 Astronautics, 81- *Prof Exp:* From instr to prof aeronaut eng, Mass Inst Technol, 47-67. *Concurrent Pos:* Mem, Res Adv Comt Aircraft Struct, NASA, 58-, Subcomt Aircraft Struct; prof aeronaut eng & head dept, Indian Inst Technol, Kampur, India, 64-65; mem, Struct & Mat Panel, Adv Group for Aeronaut Res & Develop, 66-69; dir, Aeronaut & Astronaut Affiliates Prog, Stanford Univ; mem, USAF Sci Adv Bd; distinguished prof aerospace eng, Univ Md, 71-72; div dir, NSF, 73-74; mem bd visitors, USAF Inst Technol, 78-82. *Mem:* Nat Acad Eng; Am Inst Aeronaut & Astronaut (pres, 73); Am Meteorol Soc; Am Acad Arts & Sci; Am Soc Mech Eng. *Res:* Flutter analysis of wings; structural dynamics; unsteady aerodynamics; application of unsteady aerodynamics to stability of aircraft; wind energy conversion systems; earthquake response of structures. *Mailing Add:* Dept Aeronaut & Astronaut Stanford Univ Stanford CA 94305. *Fax:* 650-725-3377

ASHLEY, J(AMES) ROBERT, ELECTRICAL ENGINEERING, ACOUSTICS. *Current Pos:* RETIRED. *Personal Data:* b Kansas City, Mo, Oct 22, 27; m 53; c 3. *Educ:* Univ Kans, BSEE, 52, MSEE, 56; Univ Fla, PhD(elec eng), 67. *Prof Exp:* Engr klystrons, Sperry Gyroscope Co, Great Neck, NY, 52-53; instr elec eng, Univ Kans, 53-56; sr engr klystron res & develop, Sperry Electron Tube Div, Gainesville, Fla, 56-65; engr cathode ray tubes, Hewlett-Packard, Colo, 67; from assoc prof to prof, Univ Colo, Colorado Springs, 67-77; eng staff consult, Sperry Gyroscope, 77-92. *Concurrent Pos:* Res & develop consult, Sperry Microwave Electronics Div, 68-72; sci consult, Army Res Off, 72-78; res & develop consult, Koss Corp, 76-80; prof elec eng, Univ Colo, Denver, 77-81. *Mem:* Sr mem Inst Elec & Electronics Engrs; sr mem Simulation Coun; fel Audio Eng Soc. *Res:* Electron tubes; microwave noise measurements; computer aided design procedures; loudspeaker synthesis; loudspeaker crossover networks; loudspeaker placement in listening rooms; theory of musical transients; auditorium psychoacoustics; electronic warfare. *Mailing Add:* 2523 Lake Ellen Lane Tampa FL 33618

ASHLEY, KENNETH R, INORGANIC CHEMISTRY. *Current Pos:* from asst prof to assoc prof, 68-78, PROF CHEM, 78-, DEPT HEAD, EAST TEX STATE UNIV, 93- *Personal Data:* b Louisville, Ky, Nov 7, 41; m 63; c John M & Ian M. *Educ:* Southern Ill Univ, BA, 63; Wash State Univ, PhD(chem), 66. *Prof Exp:* Fel inorg chem, Univ Southern Calif, 66-68. *Mem:* Am Chem Soc; Sigma Xi. *Res:* Inorganic reaction mechanisms of transition metals; ion exchange studies. *Mailing Add:* Dept Chem E Tex State Univ Commerce TX 75428

ASHLEY, MARSHALL DOUGLAS, FOREST BIOMETRY, REMOTE SENSING. *Current Pos:* from asst prof to assoc prof, 69-77, prof forest resources & assoc dir sch forest resources, 77-, EMER PROF, UNIV MAINE, ORONO. *Personal Data:* b Portland, Maine, Apr 18, 42; m 65; c 1. *Educ:* Univ Maine, BS, 65; Purdue Univ, MS, 68, PhD, 69. *Prof Exp:* Forester, Int Paper Co, 65-66. *Mem:* Am Soc Photogram; Soc Am Foresters; Sigma Xi. *Res:* Forest sampling design; application of remote sensors to forest measurement; crop yield from satellites; insect damage from aerial photography. *Mailing Add:* 283 Main St Orono ME 04473

ASHLEY, RICHARD ALLAN, WEED SCIENCE. *Current Pos:* From asst prof to assoc prof, 68-82, PROF HORT, UNIV CONN, 82- *Personal Data:* b Wilmington, Del, Mar 20, 41; m 63; c 2. *Educ:* Univ Del, BS, 63, MS, 65, PhD(biol sci), 68. *Concurrent Pos:* Secy-treas, Northwestern Weed Sci Soc, 84-88. *Mem:* Weed Sci Soc Am; Am Soc Plasticult. *Res:* Effect of herbicides on plant-soil water relations and weed interference with crop growth; use of row covers for pest control. *Mailing Add:* Dept Plant Sci U67 Univ Conn 1376 Storrs Rd Mansfield CT 06269-0002

ASHLEY, ROGER PARKMAND, ECONOMIC GEOLOGY. *Current Pos:* Geologist, 66-79, chief, Br Western Mineral Resources, 80-84, GEOLOGIST, US GEOL SURV, 85- *Personal Data:* b Portland, Ore, Oct 1, 40; m 64; c 2. *Educ:* Carleton Col, BA, 62; Stanford Univ, PhD(geol), 67. *Mem:* AAAS; Geol Soc Am; Soc Econ Geologists; Am Geophys Union. *Res:* Geology of gold deposits in western United States; detection and mapping of hydrothermal alteration using multispectral imagery; regional geology and ore deposits of Cascade Range, Washington and Oregon. *Mailing Add:* 3114 Cowper St Palo Alto CA 94306-3001

ASHLEY, TERRY FAY, CYTOGENETICS, MEIOSIS. *Current Pos:* RES SCIENTIST, SCH MED, YALE UNIV, 93- *Personal Data:* b Mayfield, Ky, Aug 24, 42; m. *Educ:* Duke Univ, BA, 64; Fla State Univ, MS, 67, PhD(genetics), 70. *Prof Exp:* Asst prof bot, Univ Ga, 70-71; fel biol, Univ Lethbridge, 71-73; instr, Univ Calgary, 73-75; adj asst prof, Univ Denver, 75-76; res assoc anat, Med Ctr, Duke Univ, 76-79; prof, Dept Zool, Univ Tenn, 79-93. *Concurrent Pos:* Fel, Nat Res Coun Can, 71-73; NIH fel & prin investr, 76-79, 80-83 & 84-87; assoc res prof, Dept Zool, Univ Tenn, 80-; vis scientist, Genetic Inst, Uppsala, Sweden, 87, 89 & 93; consult, Oak Ridge Nat Lab; vis prof, Dept Human Genetics, Yale Univ Sch Med; NSF vis prof women, 91-93. *Mem:* Am Soc Cell Biol; Genetics Soc Am; Am Genetics Asn; Sigma Xi. *Res:* Molecular cytogenetis of meiosis: factors involved in homologous recognition of chromosomes synapsis, recombination and disjunction; how chromosome rearrangements affect fertility and speciation. *Mailing Add:* Dept Genetics Yale Univ Sch Med Newtown CT 06510

ASHLEY, WARREN COTTON, POLYMER CHEMISTRY. *Current Pos:* INDEPENDENT FORMULATOR, 69- *Personal Data:* b Yorkville, Ill, Dec 25, 04; m 29, Genevieve D Silkey; c Warren Cotton Jr & Elizabeth (Buchinger). *Educ:* Univ Ill, BS, 29, MS, 30, PhD, 35. *Honors & Awards:* George B Heckel Award, Fedn Socs Coatings Technol, 45. *Prof Exp:* Org chemist, Eastman Kodak Co, 34; res org chemist, Battelle Mem Inst, 35-38, Pyroxylin Prod, Inc, 38-62, G J Aigner Co, 62-69. *Mem:* Am Chem Soc; Fedn Socs Coatings Technol. *Res:* Emulsion and lacquer type and hot melt coatings and adhesives. *Mailing Add:* 656 S Wright St Naperville IL 60540-6734

ASHMAN, MICHAEL NATHAN, ANESTHESIOLOGY, COMPUTER SCIENCES. *Current Pos:* Instr, 69-71, ASST PROF ANESTHESIOL, SCH MED, UNIV MD, BALTIMORE CITY, 71- *Personal Data:* b Baltimore, Md, Oct 15, 40; m 66; c 2. *Educ:* Johns Hopkins Univ, BA, 60; Univ Md, MD, 64; Polytech Inst Brooklyn, MS, 69; Am Bd Anesthesiologists, dipl, 70. *Concurrent Pos:* Fel, Dept Anesthesiol, Columbia-Presby Med Ctr, NY, 67-69; consult, Ctr Educ Comput Develop, Univ Md, Baltimore City, 69-78; chmn, Anesthesiol PSG-37, Am Asn Med Systs & Informatics, 83-; mem, comt Comput Appln, Am Soc Anesthesiolgists, 85- *Mem:* Am Soc Anesthesiologists; fel Am Col Anesthesiologists; Asn Comput Mach; Am Asn Med Systs & Informatics; Asn Advan Med Instrumentation; Soc Comput Simulation. *Res:* Uptake and distribution of inhalation anesthetics; continuous system simulation; continuous system simulation languages; computer appplications in anesthesiology. *Mailing Add:* Univ Md Hosp Dept Anes 22 S Greene St Baltimore MD 21201-1544

ASHMAN, ROBERT F, RHEUMATOLOGY, INTERNAL MEDICINE. *Current Pos:* STAFF MEM, VET ADMIN HOSP, IOWA CITY, 80-; PROF RHEUMATOLOGY & MICROBIOL, UNIV IOWA, 80- *Personal Data:* b Buffalo, NY, Oct 7, 38; m 65, Claire Bergsma; c Paul, Beth (Collins) & Brian. *Educ:* Wabash Col, BA, 60; Oxford Univ, Eng, MA, 66; Col Surgeons & Physicians, Columbia Univ, MD, 66. *Prof Exp:* From asst to assoc prof microbiol & med, Univ Calif, Los Angeles, 72-80. *Mem:* Am Asn Immunologists; Am Rheumatism Asn; Am Soc Clin Invest; Am Asn Physicians. *Res:* Regulation of apoptosis in lymphocytes. *Mailing Add:* Dept Internal Med Univ Iowa Hosps & Clins 200 Hawkins Rd Iowa City IA 52242-0001. *Fax:* 319-353-6290; *E-Mail:* robert_ashman@uiowa.edu

ASHMORE, CHARLES ROBERT, biochemistry, developmental biology, for more information see previous edition

ASHOK, S, SEMICONDUCTOR DEVICES, SOLID STATE ELECTRONICS. *Current Pos:* asst prof, 78-83, assoc prof, 83-87, PROF ENG SCI, PA STATE UNIV, 87- *Personal Data:* b Coimbatore, India, July 17, 47; m 80, Lavanya Dilli; c Vivekinan. *Educ:* Univ Madras, India, BE, 68; Indian Inst Technol, MTech, 70; Rensselaer Polytech Inst, NY, PhD(elec eng), 78. *Prof Exp:* Instr & grad asst elec eng, Rensselaer Polytech Inst, NY, 70-78. *Concurrent Pos:* Instr, Indust Labor Welfare Asn, India, 68-69; mem staff, Gen Elec Res & Develop Ctr, NY, 73; adj fac, Schenectady Community Col, 75-77; fac fel, Gen Elec Res & Develop Ctr, NY, 82 & Humboldt fel, Inst Semiconductor Electronics, Tech Univ Aachen, WGer, 83; vis scientist, Indian Inst Sci, Bangalore & Uppsala Univ, Sweden, 90; vis prof, Indian Inst Sci, 96. *Mem:* Inst Elec & Electronics Engrs; Am Vacuum Soc; Electrochem Soc; Sigma Xi; Mat Res Soc. *Res:* Semiconductor surface barrier formation and transport; ion-beam and radiation effects on semiconductor devices; photovoltaics; semiconducting and insulating thin films; semiconductor surface and interface modification; ion implantation; semiconductor; surface modification; semiconductor defect engineering. *Mailing Add:* Dept Eng Sci 130 Hammond Bldg University Park PA 16802. *E-Mail:* sxa4@psu.edu

ASHOUR-ABDALLA, MAHA, PHYSICS. *Current Pos:* from asst geophysicist to res geophysicist, 76-85, PROF PHYSICS, DEPT PHYSICS & INST GEOPHYSICS & PLANETARY PHYSICS, UNIV CALIF, LOS ANGELES, 85- *Personal Data:* b Alexandria, Egypt, Sept 27, 44; c 1. *Educ:* Alexandria Univ, BSc, 64; Imp Col, DIC, 68; PhD, 71. *Prof Exp:* Teaching asst, Fac Sci, Univ Alexandria, Egypt, 64-65; res scientist, Nat Ctr Studies Telecommunications, France, 72-76. *Concurrent Pos:* Vis prof, Radio Atmospheric Sci Ctr, Japan, 84; fel Japanese Soc Foothe Prom Sci, 84. *Mem:* fel Am Phys Soc; fel Am Geophys Union; European Geophys Soc; Sigma Xi. *Mailing Add:* Inst Geophysics & Planetary Physics 405 Hilgard Ave 3863 Slichter Hall Los Angeles CA 90024

ASHRAF, MUHAMMAD, STATISTICS, QUALITY & RELIABILITY OF MATERIALS SCIENCE ENGINEERING. *Current Pos:* RES & DEVELOP ENGR, SHELDAHL INC, 96- *Personal Data:* b Pakistan, India, Jan 10, 60; m, Mary Dolliver; c Rizwan & Aisha. *Educ:* Colo State Univ, PhD(agr eng), 93. *Mailing Add:* 1285 S Fordham St Longmont CO 80503. *Fax:* 303-651-2265; *E-Mail:* ashraf@sheldahl.com, mashraff@aol.com

ASHTAKALA, BALAKRISHNAMURTHY, ROAD PAVEMENT DESIGN, COMMODITIES & HAZARDOUS MATERIAL TRANSPORTATION. *Current Pos:* ASSOC PROF CIVIL ENG, CONCORDIA UNIV, CAN, 82- *Personal Data:* b Nellore, India, Sept 28, 35; Can citizen; m 61, Devaki Bangalore; c Meena, Aruna & Venka. *Educ:* Madras Univ, India, BE, 57; Roorkee Univ, India, ME, 59; Univ Waterloo, PhD(civil eng), 69. *Honors & Awards:* Chmns Award, Roads & Transp Asn Can, 86. *Prof Exp:* Assoc prof civil eng, Punjab Univ, India, 59-65; transp planning engr, Govt Alta, Can, 69-82. *Concurrent Pos:* Chmn, Standing Comt, Transp Asn Can, 82-97; invited lectr, Univ Waterloo, 87, Kyoto Univ, Japan, 88, Indian Inst Technol, 88 & Univ Roorkee, Bangalore, 91-95. *Mem:* Am Soc Civil Engrs; Transp Asn Can. *Res:* Passenger and freight transportation modeling; road pavement design and construction, specialization pot holes; hazardous material transportation. *Mailing Add:* Dept Civil Eng Concordia Univ 1455 De Maisonneuve Blvd W Montreal PQ H3G 1M8 Can. *Fax:* 514-848-2809; *E-Mail:* ashtakal@civil.concordia.ca

ASHTEKAR, ABHAY VASANT, GENERAL RELATIVITY, QUANTUM THEORY. *Current Pos:* EBERLY PROF PHYSICS & DIR, CTR GRAVITATIONAL PHYSICS & GEOM, PA STATE UNIV, 93-, CHAIR-ELECT, GRAVITY TOPICAL GROUP, 97- *Personal Data:* b Shirpur, India, July 5, 49; m 89, Christine Clarke. *Educ:* Univ Bombay, India, BSc Hons, 69; Univ Chicago, PhD(physics), 74. *Honors & Awards:* First Gravity Prize, Gravity Res Found, 79; Andrejewski Lectr, Fed Repub Ger, 95. *Prof Exp:* Lectr, Univ Clermont, France, 78-80; prof physics, Syracuse Univ, 84-88, distinguished prof, 88-92, Erastus Fraklin Holden prof, 92-93. *Concurrent Pos:* Guest scientist, Max Planck Inst Astrophys, Ger, 76-; prin investr, Syracuse Univ, NSF, 80-93; Alfred P Sloan res fel, 81-85; prof gravitation, Univ Paris, 83-85; vis prof, Univ Poona, 85-97; coordr, Quantum Gravity Prog, Inst Theoret Physics, NSF, Santa Barbara, Calif, 86; Mem gov coun, Int Soc Gen Relativity & Gravitation; Rufus Putnam vis prof, Ohio State Univ, 89; distinguished lectr, Univ Fla, 92 & Univ Md, 94; sci dir, Workshop Quantum Gravity, Schroding Inst, Vienna, 96; chair, Special Emphasis Panel, NSF, 96; hon fel, Indian Acad Sci, 96- *Mem:* Int Soc Math Physics; Int Soc Gen Relativity & Gravitation; Am Phys Soc. *Res:* General relativity; gravitation; quantum field theory; differential geometry; quantum gravity. *Mailing Add:* Physics Dept Pa State Univ University Park PA 16802-6300. *Fax:* 814-863-9608

ASHTON, DAVID HUGH, FOOD MICROBIOLOGY. *Current Pos:* lab mgr microbiol res & develop dept, Hunt-Wesson Foods, Inc, 75-81, lab mgr prod develop, 81-83, assoc dir, 83-84, dir prod develop, 85-89, sr dir prod & process develop, Beatrice-Hunt-Wesson Inc, 89-91, SR DIR RES & DEVELOP, HUNT-WESSON INC, 91- *Personal Data:* b Rivers, Man, Nov 25, 39; m 66, Margaret-Ann Lowes; c Christopher Grant & Karen Elizabeth. *Educ:* Univ Man, BS, 62, MS, 64; NC State Univ, PhD(food sci, microbiol), 67. *Prof Exp:* Nat Acad Sci-Nat Res Coun fel, USDA, 67-69; sr res microbiologist, Campbell Inst Food Res, Campbell Soup Co, 69-72, div head microbiol res, 72-75. *Mem:* Inst Food Technol; Sigma Xi. *Res:* Heat processed microbiology; toxin detection including Clostridium botulinum and Staphylococcus aureus; tomato products, convenience and snack foods, vegetable oils, peanut butter product and process development, tomato, popcorn, oil crop and peanut improvement via biotechnology; nutrceuticals. *Mailing Add:* Hunt-Wesson Inc 1645 W Valencia Dr Fullerton CA 92833-3899. *Fax:* 714-449-5166; *E-Mail:* ashtond@class.org

ASHTON, FLOYD MILTON, PLANT PHYSIOLOGY, WEED SCIENCE. *Current Pos:* instr, Univ Calif, Davis, 56-58, from asst prof to assoc prof, 58-68, prof, 68-88, EMER PROF BOT, UNIV CALIF, DAVIS, 88- *Personal Data:* b Indianapolis, Ind, Jan 27, 22; m 42, 86, Phyllis M Randall; c Mark M. *Educ:* Univ Ill, BS, 47; Ohio State Univ, PhD, 55. *Honors & Awards:* Res Award, Weed Sci Soc Am. *Prof Exp:* Anal chemist, Presto-Lite Battery Co, Inc, 40-42; lab asst, Eli Lilly & Co, 45-46; asst biochemist exp sta, Hawaiian Sugar Planters' Asn, 47-55. *Concurrent Pos:* NIH fel, 62-63; consult, Nat Acad Sci, 67-68; hon mem, Calif Weed Conf. *Mem:* Am Soc Plant Physiol; fel Weed Sci Soc Am. *Res:* Mode of action of herbicides; weed control. *Mailing Add:* 602 12th St Davis CA 95616

ASHTON, FRANCIS T, ELECTRON MICROSCOPY, COMPUTER IMAGE PROCESSING. *Current Pos:* RES ASSOC, UNIV PA, 77- *Personal Data:* b Dec 25, 30; m 55, Nancy Kelley. *Educ:* Swarthmore Col, BA, 53; Univ Pa, PhD(gen physiol), 60. *Prof Exp:* Postdoctoral fel, 60-62; res assoc, Inst Cancer Res, 62-74, Presby Hosp, 74-77. *Mem:* Sigma Xi. *Res:* Investigating parasitic nematode neuroanatomy and function using 3-D reconstruction from serial electron micrographs and microlaser ablation; parasitology. *Mailing Add:* Dept Cell & Develop Biol 6058 Univ Pa Philadelphia PA 19104-6058. *Fax:* 215-898-9871; *E-Mail:* ashton@ivem.bio.upenn.edu

ASHTON, GEOFFREY C, GENETICS. *Current Pos:* chmn, Dept Genetics, 65-72 & 80-87, from asst vchancellor to vchancellor acad affairs, 72-79, PROF GENETICS, UNIV HAWAII, 64-, DIR, HEALTH INSTRNL RESOURCES UNIT, 86- *Personal Data:* b Croydon, Eng, July 5, 25; nat US; m 51, Kathleen J Stanley; c Carolyn, Kathryn, Melinda& Jonathan. *Educ:* Univ Liverpool, BSc, 45, PhD(genetics), 58, DSc, 67. *Prof Exp:* Asst, Univ Toronto, 48-50; sect leader, fermentation res div, Glaxo Labs, Ltd, 51-56; sr sci officer, Farm Livestock Res Ctr, Eng, 56-58; prin sci officer, div animal genetics, Commonwealth Sci & Indust Res Orgn, Australia, 58-64. *Concurrent Pos:* Mem panel blood group scientists, Food & Agric Orgn, UN, 63-68; consult, Joint Comn Rural Reconstruct, Taiwan, 70-74; mem, Health Sci Consortium, 87- *Mem:* Int Soc Myopia Res; Behav Genetics Asn; Am Soc Human Genetics; Am Soc Naturalists; Int Soc Animal Blood Group Res. *Res:* Factors maintaining protein and enzyme polymorphisms; genetic aspects of fertility and disease susceptibility; human behavioral genetics; genetics of myopia; multimedia-based instruction in health sciences. *Mailing Add:* Dept Genetics Univ Hawaii Barns Med Sch 1960 East-West Rd Honolulu HI 96822-2319. *Fax:* 808-956-5506; *E-Mail:* geoff@uhunix.uhcc.hawaii.edu

ASHTON, JOSEPH BENJAMIN, ORGANIC CHEMISTRY, MATHEMATICS. *Current Pos:* RETIRED. *Personal Data:* b Brownwood, Tex, Sept 17, 30; m 60; c 2. *Educ:* Tex Technol Col, BS, 52; Univ Tex, Austin, PhD(chem), 59. *Prof Exp:* Chemist, Res & Develop Lab, Shell Chem Co, Tex, 59-60, chemist, Shell Develop Co, Calif, 60-61, group leader indust chem, Shell Co, Tex, 61-65, proj eval mgr, Indust Chem Div, NY, 65-68, asst mgr transp & supplies, Shell Oil Co, 68-69, mgr chem plant indust, Chem Div, Shell Chem Co, Calif, 69-70, mgr, Dominguez Chem Plant, 70-71, mgr forecasting, Shell Oil Co, Houston, 71-72, mgr elastomers, 72-76, mgr planning & anal & mfg resins & solvents, 76-81, mgr gen facil support, 81-85, eng adv comput syst planning, mfg & technol, 85-90. *Mem:* Sigma Xi; Am Chem Soc. *Res:* Mechanism of attack of ozone on organic compounds; oxidation of organic compounds; forecasting of energy requirements and development of energy model for interfuel competition. *Mailing Add:* 3709 Barton Creek Blvd Austin TX 78735

ASHTON, JULIET H, CORONARY ARTERY DISEASE, THROMBOSIN. *Current Pos:* ASST PROF MED, HEALTH SCI CTR, UNIV TEX, DALLAS, 83- *Educ:* Univ Tex, Dallas, PhD(physiol), 80. *Mailing Add:* 6309 Cahoba Dr Ft Worth TX 76135-4402

ASHTON, PETER MARK SHAW, REGENERATION ECOLOGY FORESTS, DYNAMICS OF FOREST LANDSCAPES. *Current Pos:* asst prof, 91-96, ASSOC PROF SILVICULT, YALE UNIV, 95- *Personal Data:* b Brunei, Sept 23, 59; Brit citizen. *Educ:* Univ Maine, BS, 83; Yale Univ, MF, 85, PhD(forest ecol), 90. *Honors & Awards:* Leopold Schepp Award, Forest Res. *Mem:* Brit Ecol Soc; Soc Am Foresters; Ecol Soc Am; AAAS. *Mailing Add:* Marsh Hall 360 Prospect St New Haven CT 06511. *Fax:* 203-432-3809

ASHTON, PETER SHAW, BOTANY, ECOLOGY. *Personal Data:* b Boscombe, Eng, June 27, 34; m 58, Mary Spence; c Mark, Mellard & Rachel. *Educ:* Cambridge Univ, MA, 61, PhD(bot), 62. Prof. *Honors & Awards:* Environ Merit Award, Environ Protection Agency, 87. *Prof Exp:* Forest botanist, Forest Dept, Brunei, 57-62 & Sarawak, 62-66; from lectr to sr lectr, Univ Aberdeen, Scotland, 66-78; consult forest botanist, Royal Soc London, 70; consult silvi-cult botanist, Food Agr Orgn-UN Develop Prog, 66-71; co-dir, UNESCO/Man & Biosphere Prog, 74-75; mem, UK Nat Comt Man & Biosphere Prog, 74-78; vis lectr, Univ Malaya, 75; dir, Arnold Arboretum, Harvard Univ, 78-87; pres, Int Asn Bot Gardens & Arborator, 86-93. *Concurrent Pos:* Mem, Bd Govs, Nature Conser, 89-; fac assoc, Harvard Inst Int Develop. *Mem:* Brit Ecol Soc; Int Soc Trop Ecol; Asn Trop Biol; fel Royal Soc Edinburgh; fel Am Acad Arts & Sci; Bot Soc Am; AAAS. *Res:* Tropical tree taxonomy; tropical forest ecology; tropical tree evolutionary and reproductive biology. *Mailing Add:* Arnold Arboretum Harvard Univ 22 Divinity Ave Cambridge MA 02138. *Fax:* 617-495-9484

ASHUTOSH, KUMAR, EMPHYSEMA, COR PULMONALE. *Current Pos:* Fel, pulmonary dis, 72-74, from asst prof to assoc prof, 74-91, PROF MED, UPSTATE MED CTR, STATE UNIV NY, SYRACUSE, 91-, ASST ATTEND PHYSICIAN, STATE UNIV HOSP, 74- *Personal Data:* b Darbhanga, India, Feb 14, 40; US citizen; m 66, Sabiba Prasad; c Ami & Ishan. *Educ:* Darbhanga Med Col, Bihar, India, MBBS, 63, MD, 66; Am Bd Internal Med, dipl, 72, Am Bd Pulmonary Med, dipl, 74. *Concurrent Pos:* Dir respiratory care, respiratory med, Vet Admin Hosp, Syracuse, NY, 77-, chief, pulmonary sect, 80-; prin investr, Res Proj 57207, Am Heart Asn, Syracuse, 80-82 & Res Proj E81-1250-Boehringer, Ingelheim, Ridgefield, Conn, 81-83. *Mem:* Am Thoracic Soc; fel Am Col Chest Physicians; fel Am Col Physicians. *Res:* Acute and chronic respiratory failure in lung disease especially treatment of cor pulmonale; pathogenesis of emphysema and proteolytic antiproteolytic mechanisms in experimental models; pulmonary physiology. *Mailing Add:* Dept Med State Univ NY Upstate Med Ctr 155 Elizabeth Blackwell St Syracuse NY 13210

ASHWELL, G GILBERT, BIOCHEMISTRY. *Current Pos:* med dir, 50-78, chmn, 78-84, INST SCHOLAR, LAB BIOCHEM & METAB, NIH, 84-, EMER SCIENTIST, 95- *Personal Data:* b Jersey City, NJ, July 16, 16; m 42; c Jonathan D & Ariel J. *Educ:* Univ Ill, BA, 38, MS, 41; Columbia Univ, MD, 48. *Hon Degrees:* Dr, Univ Paris-Sud, 88. *Honors & Awards:* Prize for Outstanding Achievement in Field of Med Sci, Gairdner Found, 82; Merck Prize, Am Soc Biol Chemists, 84; Sr Scientist Award, Alexander von Humboldt Found, 89. *Prof Exp:* Chemist, Merck & Co, Inc, NJ, 41-44; res fel biochem, Columbia Univ, 48-50. *Concurrent Pos:* Chief, Sect Enzymes & Cellular Biochem, Arthritis Inst, NIH & chief, Lab Biochem & Metab. *Mem:* Nat Acad Sci; Am Soc Biol Chem. *Res:* Pentose metabolism; uronic acid metabolism in bacteria; sugar nucleotide biosynthesis and metabolism; mechanism of polysaccharide biosynthesis; structure and function of carbohydrate moiety of glycoproteins; receptor-mediated endocytosis of asialo glycoprotein; NCAM function in physiology. *Mailing Add:* Lab Cell Biochem & Bioeng NIH Rm 415 Bldg 8 Bethesda MD 20892. *Fax:* 301-476-9431; *E-Mail:* ga15u@nih.gov

ASHWIN, JAMES GUY, physiology, pharmacology; deceased, see previous edition for last biography

ASHWORTH, HARRY ARTHUR, ANALYTICAL CHEMISTRY. *Current Pos:* FROM ASST PROF TO PROF PHYSICS, SETON HALL UNIV, 70- *Personal Data:* b Rochester, NY, Sept 9, 43; m 66. *Educ:* Univ Rochester, BS, 65; Carnegie-Mellon Univ, MS, 67, PhD(physics), 71. *Concurrent Pos:* Vis scientist, Francis Bitter Nat Magnet Lab, 69, Dept Physics, Princeton Univ, 76-77; fel, Sandia Nat Lab, 81; consult, Inverness, Inc, 81-83, Angenics, Inc, 86-88. *Mem:* Am Phys Soc; Sigma Xi; Am Asn Physics Teachers. *Res:* Statistical methods; luminescence. *Mailing Add:* 40 Chicjon Lane East Hanover NJ 07936

ASHWORTH, T, SOLID STATE PHYSICS, THERMODYNAMICS. *Current Pos:* asst prof, 68-71, assoc prof, 72-76, PROF PHYSICS, SDAK SCH MINES & TECHNOL, 76- *Personal Data:* b Colne, Eng, Sept 18, 40; m 64; c 2. *Educ:* Univ Manchester, BSc, 61, PhD(physics), 67. *Prof Exp:* Turner & Newall res fel physics, Univ Manchester, 66-68. *Concurrent Pos:* Sr res fel, Nat Ctr Atmospheric Res, 74-75; res scientist & vis prof physics, Cornell Univ, 85-86. *Mem:* AAAS; Am Phys Soc; Brit Inst Physics. *Res:* Thermal conductivities; specific heats; condensation and coalescence; atmospheric physics. *Mailing Add:* Dept Physics SDak Sch Mines & Technol 501 E St Joseph St Rapid City SD 57701-3995

ASHWORTH, WILLIAM BRUCE, JR, SCIENTIFIC REVOLUTION, HISTORY OF ASTRONOMY. *Current Pos:* ASSOC PROF HIST SCI, UNIV MO, KANSAS CITY, 75- *Personal Data:* b Philadelphia, Pa, June 18, 43; m 80; c 1. *Educ:* Wesleyan Univ, BA, 64; Univ Wis, PhD(hist sci), 75. *Prof Exp:* Vis asst prof hist sci, Univ Wis, 77-78. *Concurrent Pos:* Consult, Linda Hall Library Sci & Technol, 78- *Mem:* AAAS; Hist Sci Soc; Am Astron Soc; Brit Soc Hist Sci; Renaissance Soc Am. *Res:* Renaissance and 17th century science, especially cosmology, natural history, geology, paleontology, and prehistory. *Mailing Add:* Dept Hist Univ Mo 5100 Rockhill Rd Kansas City MO 64110-2446

ASHY, PETER JAWAD, CHEMICAL PHYSICS, MATHEMATICS. *Current Pos:* INT CONSULT, 78-; PRES, AMAR INT, INC. *Personal Data:* b Lebanon, Aug 5, 40; US citizen; m 62, Sandra Guidry; c Jawad P, Diana L & Lara A. *Educ:* Univ Southwestern La, BS, 62; Clemson Univ, MS, 65, PhD(chem physics), 67. *Prof Exp:* Chem engr, Textile Fiber Div, E I du Pont de Nemours & Co, 63-65, res physicist, 67-68; asst prof math, Furman Univ, 68-72, chmn, Dept Comput Sci, 76-77, assoc prof comput sci-math, 72-78. *Concurrent Pos:* Consult, Philips Fibers Res Orgn, 68-, Lockwood Greene Engrs, Daniel Int, Bigelow-Sanford, Dan River, Stone Mfg Co & Fountain Industs; statist consult, Union Carbide Corp, Greenville, 73-75; Enwright assoc, 77-; mem exec bd, Southern Fedn, 77-80. *Mem:* Am Inst Chem Engrs; Am Chem Soc; Math Asn Am. *Res:* Fundamental and applied work in thermal reactions; kinetics and sorption; phenomena and intermolecular forces; structure and physical behavior of fibers; thermal diffusivity of gases; quantum theory of surface tension; application of Markov processes; chemical engineering. *Mailing Add:* PO Box 26925 Greenville SC 29616-2925. *Fax:* 803-244-4400

ASIK, JOSEPH R, AUTOMOTIVE ELECTRONICS, CONTROL SYSTEMS. *Current Pos:* PRIN STAFF ENGR, PROD & MFG STAFF, 69-, SR ENG SPECIALIST, RES STAFF, FORD MOTOR CO, DEARBORN, 93- *Personal Data:* b Lorain, Ohio, Aug 8, 37; m 59, Grace Nayper; c Jeffrey, Wendy & Charles. *Educ:* Case Inst Technol, BS, 59; Univ Ill, Urbana, MS, 61, PhD(physics), 66. *Prof Exp:* Res staff mem phys sci, T J Watson Res Ctr, IBM Corp, 66-69. *Concurrent Pos:* Adj prof elec eng, Lawrence Technol Univ, 78-; chmn, Champion Ignition Conf, 78. *Mem:* Am Phys Soc; Soc Automotive Engrs; sr mem Inst Elec & Electronics Engrs. *Res:* Control systems design; ignition systems; electronic engine controls; 9 US patents. *Mailing Add:* 776 Great Oaks Dr Bloomfield Hills MI 48304-1920. *Fax:* 313-594-4051

ASIMAKIS, GREGORY K, BIOCHEMISTRY. *Current Pos:* MEM FAC, BIOCHEM DIV, SURG RES LAB, MED BR, UNIV TEX, GALVESTON, 80- *Personal Data:* b Beaumont, Tex, Sept 23, 47. *Educ:* Rice Univ, BA, 71; Univ Tex Med Br, Galveston, PhD(biochem), 77. *Prof Exp:* Fel, Harvard Univ & Mass Gen Hosp, 77-78; res assoc biochem, Tufts Univ, 78-80. *Mem:* Sigma Xi; Biophys Soc. *Res:* Development of oxidative-phosphorylation in fetal and neotal liver; loss of mitochondrial function in ischemic or pathologic tissues; regulation of mitochondrial ion transport. *Mailing Add:* Surg Res Lab Med Br Univ Tex Galveston TX 77555-0528

ASKANAZI, JEFFREY, anesthesiology, artificial nutrition, for more information see previous edition

ASKARI, AMIR, PHARMACOLOGY, BIOCHEMISTRY. *Current Pos:* PROF & CHMN, DEPT PHARMACOL & THERAPEUT, MED COL OHIO, 75- *Personal Data:* b Ahwaz, Iran, Dec 24, 30; US citizen; m 57; c 2. *Educ:* Univ Dubuque, BS, 53; NY Univ, MS, 57; Cornell Univ, PhD(biochem), 60. *Prof Exp:* From instr to prof pharmacol, Med Col, Cornell Univ, 63-75. *Concurrent Pos:* Res fel pharmacol, Med Col, Cornell Univ, 60-63; USPHS grant, 63. *Mem:* AAAS; Am Soc Biochem & Molecular Biol; Am Soc Pharmacol & Exp Therapeut; Harvey Soc; Biophys Soc. *Res:* Mechanism of ion transport through cell membranes; effects of drugs on membranes. *Mailing Add:* Dept Pharmacol & Therapeut Med Col Ohio PO Box 10008 Toledo OH 43699-0008

ASKELAND, DONALD RAYMOND, METALLURGICAL ENGINEERING. *Current Pos:* asst prof, 70-76, ASSOC PROF METALL ENG, UNIV MO-ROLLA, 76- *Personal Data:* b Spirit Lake, Iowa, Dec 4, 42; m 65; c 1. *Educ:* Dartmouth Col, BA, 65, MS, 66; Univ Mich, PhD(metall eng), 70. *Prof Exp:* Teaching asst metall eng, Mich State Univ, 68-70. *Concurrent Pos:* Res assoc, Gen Motors Corp, 72; partner, Askeland, Kisslinger, & Wolf, Consults, 73- *Mem:* Am Inst Mining, Metall & Petrol Engrs; Am Soc Metals; Am Foundrymen's Soc; Am Welding Soc. *Res:* Effect of casting, welding and metallurgical variables on the structure and behavior of cast iron alloys; general solidification and metals casting; failure analysis. *Mailing Add:* Dept Metall Eng Univ Mo Rolla Rolla MO 65401

ASKENASE, PHILIP WILLIAM, ALLERGY, CLINICAL IMMUNOLOGY. *Current Pos:* trainee inflammatory dis, 70-71, from asst prof to assoc prof, 71-82, PROF MED & PATH, SCH MED, YALE UNIV, 83-, SECT CHIEF CLIN IMMUNOL & ALLERGY, 85- *Personal Data:* c 2. *Educ:* Brown Univ, BA, 61; Yale Univ, MD, 65. *Prof Exp:* Intern & resident med, Harvard Med Unit & Thorndike Labs, Boston City Hosp, 65-67; clin assoc arthritis & rheumatology sect, Nat Inst Allergy & Infectious Dis, NIH, 67-69. *Concurrent Pos:* British Am Heart fel, Am Heart Asn, London Hosp Med Col, 69-70; USPHS fel, 71-73; mem, NIH Immunol Sci Study Sect, 83-87; vis scientist tumor immunol, Univ Col, London, Eng, 84-85; NIH merit awardee, Nat Inst Allergy & Infectious Dis, 87- *Mem:* AAAS; Am Asn Physicians; Am Fedn Clin Res; Am Rheumatism Asn; Am Soc Clin Invest; Am Soc Trop Med & Hyg; Am Thoracic Soc; Brit Soc Immunol; Clin Immunol Soc; fel Am Acad Allergy. *Res:* Pathogenesis of cutaneous and bronchial inflammatory responses due to immunoglobulin E antibodies and T cells; a myriad of cell subsets, mediators and biologically active polypeptides, including soluble T cells receptors; cutaneous allergic disorders such as atopic dermatitis, interbronchial asthma, as well as to acquire immune deficiency syndrome and immune resistance to cancer cells. *Mailing Add:* LCI 904 Sch Med Yale Univ 333 Cedar St Box 208013 New Haven CT 06520-8013

ASKEW, ELDON WAYNE, BIOCHEMISTRY, PHYSIOLOGY. *Current Pos:* DIR, MIL NUTRIT RES, 85- *Personal Data:* b Pontiac, Ill, Aug 23, 42; m, Sharon Bess; c Debbie, Barbara, Rebecca & Jennifer. *Educ:* Univ Ill, BS, 64, MS, 66; Mich State Univ, PhD(nutrit), 70. *Prof Exp:* Biochemist, US Army Med Res & Nutrit Lab, 69-74, Lettermen Army Inst Res, 74-82; asst chief, Dept Clin Invest, Tripler Army Med Ctr, 82-85. *Concurrent Pos:* Mem nutrit adv panel, US Olympic Comt; Dept Defense rep, Interagency Comt Human Nutrit Res. *Mem:* Am Inst Nutrit; Am Col Sports Med; Sigma Xi; Asn Mil Surgeons US. *Res:* Biochemical adaptions of energy metabolism to physical training and the effect of nutrition on health and physical performance. *Mailing Add:* Div Foods & Nutrit Univ Utah 239 N-HPR Salt Lake City UT 84112. *Fax:* 508-651-5833

ASKEW, RAYMOND FIKE, SYSTEMS ENGINEERING. *Current Pos:* from asst prof to assoc prof physics, Auburn Univ, 60-71, actg dir, Nuclear Sci Ctr, 69-71, interim head mech eng, 80-82, dir, Nuclear Sci Ctr, 83-86, PROF PHYSICS, AUBURN UNIV, 71-; DIR, CTR COM DEVELOP, 87- *Personal Data:* b Birmingham, Ala, Oct 29, 35; m 81, Sherry Hoover; c Beth, Michael, Patrick, Lee, Misty, Robyn & Clay. *Educ:* Birmingham-Southern Col, BS, 56; Univ Va, MS, 58, PhD(physics), 60. *Prof Exp:* Sr physicist res lab eng sci, Univ Va, 60. *Concurrent Pos:* Consult, USAF Systs Command, Eglin AFB, Fla, 72-74. *Mem:* Am Asn Physics Teachers; Am Phys Soc; Soc Physics Students (pres, 85-87); Am Inst Aeronaut & Astronaut. *Res:* Nuclear and atomic physics; gaseous discharges; plasmas; pulsed power; space power systems. *Mailing Add:* 548 Heard Ave Auburn AL 36830-6020

ASKEW, WILLIAM CREWS, RADIATION CHEMISTRY, ANALYTICAL CHEMISTRY. *Current Pos:* DEPT CHEM ENGR, UNIV SOUTH ALA. *Personal Data:* b Athens, Ala, Jan 5, 40; m 63; c 3. *Educ:* Auburn Univ, BS, 62, MS, 63; Univ Fla, PhD(radiolysis of fluorocarbons), 66. *Prof Exp:* Res asst chem eng, Univ Fla, 63-66; asst prof chem eng, Auburn Univ, 67-80. *Concurrent Pos:* Proj leader, US AEC res grant, 69- *Mem:* Am Inst Chem Eng. *Res:* Synthesis by radiolysis, identification and purification of perfluoroalkanes. *Mailing Add:* Dept Chem Eng Univ S Ala 307 University Blvd N Mobile AL 36688-0001

ASKEY, RICHARD ALLEN, SPECIAL FUNCTION. *Current Pos:* from asst prof to assoc prof, 63-86, GABOR SZEGO PROF MATH, UNIV WIS-MADISON, 86- *Personal Data:* b St Louis, Mo, June 4, 33; m 58, Elizabeth Hill; c James & Suzanne. *Educ:* Wash Univ, AB, 55; Harvard Univ, MA, 56; Princeton Univ, PhD(math), 61. *Prof Exp:* Instr math, Wash Univ, 58-61; instr, Univ Chicago, 61-63. *Concurrent Pos:* Guggenheim fel, 69-70. *Mem:* Am Math Soc (vpres, 86-87); Math Asn Am; Soc Indust & Appl Math; fel Am Acad Arts & Sci; hon fel Indian Acad Sci. *Res:* Special functions. *Mailing Add:* Dept Math Univ Wis 480 Lincoln Dr Madison WI 53706. *Fax:* 608-263-8891; *E-Mail:* askey@math.wisc.edu

ASKILL, JOHN, SOLID STATE PHYSICS, METALLURGY. *Current Pos:* from asst prof to assoc prof, 66-84, chmn dept, 66-93, PROF PHYSICS, MILLIKIN UNIV, 85- *Personal Data:* b Kent, Eng, Apr 27, 39; c 2. *Educ:* Univ Reading, BSc, 60 & 61, PhD(physics), 64. *Prof Exp:* Fel, Univ Reading, 64-65; res physicist, Oak Ridge Nat Lab, 65-66. *Concurrent Pos:* Consult, Metals & Ceramics Div, Oak Ridge Nat Lab, 66-67. *Mem:* Am Asn Physics Teachers; Brit Inst Physics & Phys Soc. *Res:* Diffusion of metals in metals using radioactive tracers. *Mailing Add:* Dept Physics Millikin Univ Decatur IL 62522. *Fax:* 217-424-3993; *E-Mail:* jaskill@mail.millikin.edu

ASKIN, RONALD GENE, PRODUCTION CONTROL, MANUFACTURING SYSTEM MODELING. *Current Pos:* assoc prof systs & indust eng, 85-92, PROF & ASSOC DEPT HEAD, SYSTS & INDUST ENG, UNIV ARIZ, 92- *Personal Data:* b Baltimore, Md, Dec 28, 53; m 76, Jacalyn Smith; c Kenneth & Amanda. *Educ:* Lehigh Univ, BS, 75; Ga Inst Technol, MS, 76, PhD(indust & syst eng), 79. *Honors & Awards:* Am Inst Indust Engrs Transactions Develop & Appln Award, 85; Eugene L Grant Award, 86; Shingo Prize, 94. *Prof Exp:* Asst indust eng, Ga Inst, Technol, 76-79; from asst prof to assoc prof, Univ Iowa, 79-85. *Concurrent Pos:* Assoc ed, Am Inst Indust Engrs Trans, 81-87, dept ed, 87-94, ed, 95-97; NSF presidential young investr, 84. *Mem:* Inst Indust Engrs; Oper Res Soc Am; Am Soc Qual Control; Soc Mfg Engrs. *Res:* Production system design, planning and control; manufacturing facility design, multicollinearity and nonnormality in multiple linear regression models; experimental design for parameter optimization; manufacturing planning. *Mailing Add:* Dept Systs & Indust Eng Univ Ariz Tucson AZ 85721. *Fax:* 520-621-6555; *E-Mail:* ron@sie.arizona.edu

ASKINS, HAROLD WILLIAMS, JR, EDUCATIONAL ADMINISTRATION. *Current Pos:* from asst prof to assoc prof, 74-82, PROF ELEC ENG, THE CITADEL, 82-, DEPT HEAD ELEC ENG, 88- *Personal Data:* b Chesnee, SC, Sept 3, 39; m 64; c 2. *Educ:* The Citadel, BS, 61; Clemson Univ, MS, 63; Purdue Univ, PhD(elec eng), 72. *Prof Exp:* Instr elec eng, Clemson Univ, 63-64; mgr, Chesnee Tel Co, SC, 65-66; instr electronics, TEC, Spartanburg, SC, 65-66; res & develop engr elec power, Westinghouse Elec Corp, 71-74. *Concurrent Pos:* Electronics engr, Naval Electronic Systs Eng Ctr, Charleston, SC, 76-; lectr, Mod Power Syst Anal Short Course, Auburn Univ, 78-; consult, Nuclear Electromagnetic Pulse Effects, Oak Ridge Nat Lab, 83-86. *Mem:* Inst Elec & Electronics Engrs; Am Soc Eng Educ; Appl Computational Electromagnetics Soc; Sigma Xi. *Res:* Electromagnetic pulse-power system interaction; electromagnetic environmental effect on communication facilities and personnel; lightning and switching surge phenomena; insulation coordination. *Mailing Add:* The Citadel Charleston SC 29409-0001

ASLAM, MOHAMMAD, ORGANIC SULFUR CHEMISTRY, ORGANOMETALLIC CHEMISTRY. *Current Pos:* res chemist, Hoechst Celanese Corp, 86-89, sr res chemist, 89-91, group leader nitrate oxidation, 91-93, prog mgr generic pharmaceut, 93-95, PROJ LEADER, INNOVATOR DRUG PROG, HOECHST CELANESE CORP, 95- *Personal Data:* b Pilibhit, India, Jan 16, 53; m, Ambreen Musharraf; c Asra & Hira. *Educ:* AMU Aligarh, India, BS, 74, MS, 76; Univ Western Ont, PhD(org chem), 82. *Prof Exp:* Teaching asst, Univ Western Ont, 75-81; res assoc, State Univ NY, 81-86. *Mem:* Am Chem Soc. *Res:* Synthesis of generic pharmaceuticals; organo-sulfur chemistry, especially sulfenes and sulfones, sulfonyl chlorides, etc; palladium-catalyzed coupling reactions. *Mailing Add:* Hoechst Celanese PO Box 9077 Corpus Christi TX 78469. *E-Mail:* ma@corhcc1.hcc.com

ASLESON, GARY LEE, ANALYTICAL CHEMISTRY. *Current Pos:* from asst prof to assoc prof, 75-94, PROF CHEM, COL CHARLESTON, 94- *Personal Data:* b St Peter, Minn, June 14, 48; m 71, Meredith Knutson; c Kristin. *Educ:* Gustavus Adolphus Col, BA, 70; Univ Iowa, PhD(anal chem), 75. *Prof Exp:* Teaching asst chem, Univ Iowa, 70-73, res asst, 73-75. *Mem:* Am Chem Soc; Sigma Xi. *Res:* High performance liquid chromatography; gas chromatography; nuclear magnetic resonance spectrometry. *Mailing Add:* Dept Chem Col Charleston Charleston SC 29424. *Fax:* 803-953-1404; *E-Mail:* aslesong@cofc.edu

ASLESON, JOHAN ARNOLD, SOILS. *Current Pos:* RETIRED. *Personal Data:* b Stoughton, Wis, Sept 13, 18; m 43; c 3. *Educ:* Univ Wis, BS, 42, MS, 47, PhD, 57. *Prof Exp:* From asst prof to assoc prof soils, Mont State Univ, 47-54, asst to dir, Agr Exp Sta, 54-57, prof soils, 54-, from asst dir to assoc dir, 57-61, dir, Agr Exp Sta, 61-, dean, Col Agr, Mont State Univ, 65- *Mem:* Sigma Xi; Am Soc Agron; Soil Sci Soc Am. *Res:* Applied fertilizer research; agronomy and soil science; plant physiology. *Mailing Add:* 2419 Spring Creek Dr Bozeman MT 59715

ASLING, CLARENCE WILLET, GENERAL MEDICAL SCIENCES. *Current Pos:* prof anat, 66-80, EMER PROF ANAT, MED CTR, UNIV CALIF, SAN FRANCISCO, 80- *Personal Data:* b Duluth, Minn, June 17, 13; m 36, 70; c 2. *Educ:* Univ Kans, AB, 34, AM, 37, MD, 39; Univ Calif, Berkeley, PhD(anat), 47. *Prof Exp:* Asst instr anat, Univ Kans, 34-37; intern, Huntington Mem Hosp, Pasadena, Calif, 39-40; instr anat, Sch Med, Vanderbilt Univ, 40-41; instr, Univ Kans, 41-42, asst prof anat & lectr surg anat, 42-46; res asst, Univ Calif, Berkeley, 44-47, lectr anat, 45-47, from asst prof to prof, 47-66, res assoc, Inst Exp Biol, 51-58, co-chmn dept anat & physiol, 58-62. *Concurrent Pos:* Fulbright award, Eng, 53-54; Guggenheim fel, 62-63; guest prof, Univ Geneva, 62-63. *Mem:* Am Asn Anatomists; Anat Soc Gt Brit & Ireland; Teratology Soc; Am Asn Univ Professors. *Res:* Regulation of head form; endocrine and nutritional control of skeletal development; localization of radioactive minerals; teratology and congenital abnormalities. *Mailing Add:* Univ Calif San Francisco Med Ctr PO Box 0452 San Francisco CA 94143

ASMUS, JOHN FREDRICH, LASERS & APPLICATIONS, COMPUTER IMAGE PROCESSING & ART CONSERVATION. *Current Pos:* RES PHYSICIST, UNIV CALIF, SAN DIEGO, 73- *Personal Data:* b Chicago, Ill, Jan 20, 37; m 63, Barbar Flaherty; c Joanne & Rosemary. *Educ:* Calif Inst Technol, BS, 58, MS, 59, PhD(elec eng, physics), 65. *Prof Exp:* Staff assoc high energy fluid dynamics, Gen Atomic Div, Gen Dynamics Corp, 64-67; mem staff spec nuclear effects, Gulf Gen Atomic Inc, 67-69; res staff mem laser technol, Inst for Defense Anal, 69-71; vpres, Sci Applns, Inc, 71-73. *Concurrent Pos:* Assoc mem spec group on optical lasers, Dir Defense Res & Eng Adv Group Electron Devices, 69-70, mem, 70- *Mem:* Int Inst Conserv; Am Inst Conserv; Int Soc Optical Eng. *Res:* Interaction of high-power laser beams with solid surfaces; laser-induced stress wave propagation and micrometeorite generation; laser excited chemistry; computer image processing in art; plasma pinch ultraviolet radiation. *Mailing Add:* 8239 Sugarman Dr La Jolla CA 92037-2222. *Fax:* 619-534-7649; *E-Mail:* jasmus@consbio.ucsd.edu

ASMUSSEN, JES, PLASMA PROCESSING, MICROWAVE DISCHARGE PHYSICS & CHEMISTRY. *Current Pos:* From asst prof to prof, Dept Elec Eng, Mich State Univ, 67-97, assoc chair, 73-75, actg asst dir, Col Eng, 83-84, actg chair, Dept Elec Eng, 89-90, CHAIR, DEPT ELEC ENG, MICH STATE UNIV, 90-, UNIV DISTINGUISHED PROF, 97- *Personal Data:* m 87, Colleen Cooper; c Kirsten, Jes, & Stig. *Educ:* Univ Wis-Madison, BS, 60, MS, 64, PhD(elec eng), 67. *Prof Exp:* Design & develop engr, Louis Allis Co, 60-62. *Concurrent Pos:* Consult to 23 indust & govt orgns, 72-; mem, Tech Comt Elec Propulsion, Am Inst Aeronaut & Astronaut, 87- *Mem:* Fel Inst Elec & Electronics Engrs; Am Inst Aeronaut & Astronaut; Am Vacuum Soc; AAAS. *Res:* Microwave discharges as applied to microchip technology; electric propulsion engines for spacecraft propulsion; microwave plasma assisted diamond thin film disposition; granted 15 US patents. *Mailing Add:* 3811 Viceroy Dr Okemos MI 48864

ASMUSSEN, MARJORIE A, THEORETICAL EVOLUTIONARY GENETICS. *Current Pos:* From asst prof to assoc prof math & genetics, 76-90, PROF GENETICS, UNIV GA, 90- *Personal Data:* b Tacoma, Wash, June 28, 49. *Educ:* Occidental Col, BA, 71; Stanford Univ, MS, 72, PhD(math biol), 76. *Mem:* Genetics Soc Am; Soc Study Evolution; Molecular Biol & Evolution Soc; Soc Am Naturalists; AAAS. *Res:* Theoretical population genetics with particular interest in developing and applying mathematical models to the study of complex interactions in genetic systems. *Mailing Add:* Dept Genetics Univ Ga 1180 E Broad St Athens GA 30601-3040. *Fax:* 706-542-3910; *E-Mail:* marjorie@asmus1.genetics.usa.edu

ASNER, BERNARAD A, JR, APPLIED MATHEMATICS. *Current Pos:* ASSOC PROF MATH, UNIV DALLAS, IRVING, 79- *Personal Data:* b Oklahoma City, Okla, Dec 28, 33; m 60; c 2. *Educ:* Univ Okla, BS, 57; Univ Ala, MA, 64; Northwestern Univ, PhD(eng sci), 68. *Prof Exp:* Mathematician control, NASA, 60-65; assoc prof math, Bogazici Univ, Turkey, 70-72; exchange scientist, Nat Acad Sci, 72-73; assoc prof math & bus mgt, Univ Dallas, Irving, 73-78; res assoc, Systs Dynamics Lab, Marshall Space Flight Ctr, NASA, 78-79. *Concurrent Pos:* Nat Acad Sci res assoc, 78-79. *Mem:* Math Asn Am; Am Math Soc; Soc Indust & Appl Math. *Res:* Degeneracy in functional differential equations and computer science. *Mailing Add:* 8271 Navarre Pkwy Navarre FL 32566-6918

ASNES, CLARA F, MICROTUBULES. *Current Pos:* RES ASSOC CELL BIOL, UNIV ROCHESTER, 82- *Personal Data:* b Jersey City, NJ, Aug 31, 46. *Educ:* Boston Univ, PhD(biochem), 75. *Mailing Add:* Dept Biochem & Molecular Biol Wash Univ 225 McDonnell Sci Bldg Box 8231 St Louis MO 63110

ASOFSKY, RICHARD MARCY, IMMUNOLOGY, PATHOLOGY. *Current Pos:* staff assoc immunol, Nat Inst Allergy & Infectious Dis, 63-66, head exp path sect, Lab Germfree Animal Res, 65-70, asst chief, Lab Microbiol Immunity, 70-72, chief, 72-86, CHIEF, EXP PATH SECT, LAB IMMUNOL, NAT INST ALLERGY & INFECTIOUS DIS, 86- *Personal Data:* b New York, NY, Sept 25, 33; m 60; c 2. *Educ:* State Univ NY, MD, 58. *Honors & Awards:* Arthur S Fleming Award, 71. *Prof Exp:* Intern internal med, Kings County Hosp, NY, 58-59; resident, Med Ctr, NY Univ, 59-63. *Concurrent Pos:* NIH trainee path, Med Ctr, NY Univ, 59-63. *Mem:* Am Asn Immunologists; AAAS; NY Acad Sci. *Res:* Sites and control of immunoglobulin synthesis; interaction among lymphocytes in immune responses. *Mailing Add:* 8501 Pelham Rd Bethesda MD 20817

ASP, CARL W, SPEECH & HEARING SCIENCES, STATISTICS. *Current Pos:* PROF SPEECH & HEARING SCI, UNIV TENN, KNOXVILLE, 67- *Personal Data:* b Cleveland, Ohio, Aug 14, 31; m 56; c 2. *Educ:* Ohio State Univ, BS, 63, MA, 64, PhD(speech & hearing sci), 67. *Concurrent Pos:* Mem field read & site visit team, US Off Educ, 69- *Mem:* AAAS; Acoust Soc Am; Am Speech & Hearing Asn; Audio Eng Soc. *Res:* Psychoacoustics; speech communication; psychophysical experiments; perception of hearing impaired. *Mailing Add:* Dept Audiol & Speech Path Univ Tenn Knoxville 1345 Circle Park Knoxville TN 37996-0001

ASPDEN, ROBERT GEORGE, METALLURGY. *Current Pos:* RETIRED. *Personal Data:* b Geneva, Ill, May 22, 27; m 53, Hildegard Buchele; c Nancy, Heidi & Eric. *Educ:* Univ Ill, BS, 50; Univ Pittsburgh, MS, 57, DScEng, 65. *Prof Exp:* Mat engr, Westinghouse Elec Corp, 50-55, res engr, 55-60, supvr engr, 60-65, mgr, 65-68, adv engr, 68-69, mgr, 69-80, engr, 80-94. *Mem:* Am Inst Mining, Metall & Petrol Engrs; Am Soc Metals; Nat Asn Corrosion Engrs. *Res:* High temperature alloys; magnetic materials; corrosion. *Mailing Add:* 2382 Flagstaff Dr Export PA 15632

ASPELIN, GARY B, INTERNATIONAL REGULATORY AFFAIRS. *Current Pos:* PRIN CONSULT, INT ACCESS, ARLINGTON TEX, 97- *Personal Data:* b Bristol, Conn, Dec 31, 39; m 67, Janice Lund; c Sonja & Scott. *Educ:* Brown Univ, AB, 61; Univ Wis, PhD(org chem), 66. *Prof Exp:* Res chemist, Am Cyanamid Co, Bound Brook, NJ, 66-71; res scientist, Johnson & Johnson, New Brunswick, 71-76, group leader tech serv, 76-78, group mgr tech serv, 78-80; group mgr tech serv, Surgikos Inc, Arlington, Tex, 80-90; dir int tech affairs, Johnson & Johnson Med Inc, Arlington, Tex, 90-96. *Mem:* Regulatory Affairs Prof Soc. *Res:* Nonwoven fabrics; film and fabric laminates; disposable hospital packs and gowns; bacterial filtration; cold sterilant solutions; surgical gloves; wound care; international medical device registrations; CE marking for medical devices. *Mailing Add:* 3611 Lake Champlain Dr Arlington TX 76016-3504. *E-Mail:* gaspelin@startext.com

ASPEN, FRANK, PHYSICS. *Current Pos:* SR RES SPECIALIST, 3M CO, 83- *Personal Data:* b Fossom, Minn, Apr 16, 49. *Mailing Add:* 1185 Wolters Blvd Vadnais Heights MN 55110

ASPER, SAMUEL PHILLIPS, MEDICAL ADMINISTRATION, SCIENCE ADMINISTRATION. *Current Pos:* EMER PROF MED, SCH MED, JOHNS HOPKINS UNIV, 85- *Personal Data:* b Oak Park, Ill, July 14, 16; m 42, Ann Carver; c Ann & Lucy. *Educ:* Baylor Univ, AB, 36; Johns Hopkins Univ, MD, 40. *Prof Exp:* House officer med, Johns Hopkins Hosp, 40-41; res fel, Thorndike Mem Lab, Harvard Univ, 41-42 & 46-47; from instr to prof, Sch Med, Johns Hopkins Hosp, 47-85, assoc dean, 57-68, vpres med affairs, 70-73; prof internal med & dean fac med sci, Am Univ Beirut, 73-78, chief of staff, Univ Hosp, 73-78; dep exec vpres, Am Col Physicians, 79-81. *Concurrent Pos:* Pres, Educ Comn Foreign Med Grads, 82-85, emer pres, 86- *Mem:* Inst Med-Nat Acad Sci; Endocrine Soc (vpres, 66-67); Asn Am Physicians; Am Col Physicians (pres, 69-70, emer pres, 85-); Am Soc Clin Invest. *Res:* Clinical endocrinology; metabolism. *Mailing Add:* PO Box 153 Gibson Island MD 21056

ASPER, VERNON LOWELL, OCEANOGRAPHY. *Current Pos:* Res asst scientist, 86-88, asst prof, 88-92, ASSOC PROF MARINE SCI, UNIV SOUTHERN MISS, 92- *Personal Data:* b Mechanicsburg, Pa, July 17, 56; m 77, Lindell K Albin; c Alicia & Jennifer. *Educ:* Messiah Col, BA, 78; Univ Hawaii, MS, 81; Mass Inst Technol, PhD(oceanog), 86. *Mem:* Oceanog Soc; Am Geophys Union. *Res:* Marine particulate matter with emphasis on large aggregates and their role in the verticle and lateral transport of material in the oceans. *Mailing Add:* Univ Southern Miss Ctr Marine Sci Bldg 1103 Rm 102 Stennis Space Center MS 39529. *E-Mail:* vasper@whale.st.usm.edu

ASPERGER, ROBERT GEORGE, SR, CORROSION ENGINEERING, CORROSION INHIBITOR OIL & GAS PRODUCTION & REFINING. *Personal Data:* b Detroit, Mich, Oct 1, 37; m 61, Fortune; c Robert G II. *Educ:* Eastern Mich Univ, AB, 60; Univ Mich, MS, 63, PhD(chem), 65. *Honors & Awards:* Vern Stenger Prize in Anal Chem, 78; Distinguished Serv Award, Nat Asn Corrosion Engrs, 91. *Prof Exp:* Res chemist, Dow Chem Co, 65-75, sr res specialist, 75-78; assoc scientist, Phillips Petrol Co, 78-82; prin investr, Petrolite Corp, 82-91; dir corrosion sci, CLI Int, Houston, 91-95. *Concurrent Pos:* Chmn & pres, Jay Develop Inc, 80-82; vchmn, Tech Prac Comt, Nat Asn Corrosion Engrs, 87-90. *Mem:* AAAS; Nat Asn Corrosion Engrs. *Res:* Corrosion inhibitors, gas systems; coordination chemistry; surface characterization using x-ray photoelectron spectroscopy, auger spectroscopy, electron microprobe, transmission electron microscopy and scanning electron microscopy/x-ray energy dispersive spectroscopy; fundamentals of corrosion and its inhibition; inhibitor development; application of oil and gas inhibitors to carbon steel and aluminum. *Mailing Add:* Asperger Technol 5622 Yarwell Houston TX 77096. *Fax:* 713-726-0175

ASPINALL, GERALD OLIVER, ORGANIC CHEMISTRY. *Current Pos:* chmn dept, 72-79, distinguished res prof, 88-92, PROF CHEM, YORK UNIV, 72-, EMER DISTINGUISHED RES PROF, 92- *Personal Data:* b Chesham Bois, Eng, Dec 30, 24; m 53; c 2. *Educ:* Bristol Univ, BSc, 44, PhD(chem), 48; Univ Edinburgh, DSc(chem), 58. *Honors & Awards:* C S Hudson Award Carbohydrate Chem, Am Chem Soc, 86; John Labatt Ltd Award, Org/Biochem Res, Can Soc Chem, 87. *Prof Exp:* From lectr to sr lectr chem, Univ Edinburgh, 48-63, reader, 63-67; prof & chmn dept, Trent Univ, 67-72. *Mem:* Am Chem Soc; Chem Inst Can; fel Royal Soc Chem; fel Royal Soc Can. *Res:* Chemistry of carbohydrates, especially chemical methodology for structure determination of plant and microbial polysaccharides; structural characterization and synthesis of oligosaccharides as serological determinants in bacterial glycolipid and lipopolysaccharide antigens. *Mailing Add:* Dept Chem York Univ 4700 Keele St North York ON M3J 1P3 Can. *Fax:* 416-736-5936

ASPLAND, JOHN RICHARD, TEXTILE CHEMISTRY. *Current Pos:* PROF, TEXTILE CHEM, CLEMSON UNIV, 82- *Personal Data:* b Leeds, Eng, Oct 22, 36; m 61; c 1. *Educ:* Univ Leeds, BSc, 58, MSc, 60; Univ Manchester, PhD(textile chem), 64. *Prof Exp:* Prof textile chem, Inst Sci & Technol, Univ Manchester, 61-66; sr res chemist dye applns res, Southern Dyestuff Co, Martin-Marietta Corp, 66-68, group leader dye applns & eval, 68-74; textile res mgr, Reeves Bros, Inc, 74-82. *Concurrent Pos:* Examr, Soc Dyers Colourists, 60-64, chartered colourist; ed, J Coated Fabrics, 84-88. *Mem:* Fiber Soc; Am Asn Textile Chem & Colorists; fel Soc Dyers & Colourists; fel Textile Inst. *Res:* Interactions between dyestuffs and polymeric substances, particularly disperse dyes and hydrophobic fibers and reactive dyes and cellulose; instrumental color measurement and shade sorting; sulfur dyes; flame-resistant fabrics; energy conservation; coated fabrics; carpet dyeing and finishing. *Mailing Add:* Dept Textile Chem Clemson Univ Clemson SC 29634-1307. *Fax:* 864-656-5973; *E-Mail:* aj@clemson.edu

ASPLUND, JOHN MALCOLM, RUMINANT NUTRITION, NUTRITIONAL METABOLISM. *Current Pos:* RETIRED. *Educ:* Univ Wis-Madison, PhD(nutrit), 60. *Prof Exp:* Prof animal sci, Univ Mo, 69-92. *Mailing Add:* c/o Animal Sci Res Univ Mo Columbia MO 65211

ASPLUND, RUSSELL OWEN, biochemistry, for more information see previous edition

ASPNES, DAVID E, PHYSICS. *Current Pos:* PROF PHYSICS, NC STATE UNIV. *Personal Data:* b Madison, Wis, May 1, 39; wid; c James, Gary & Ann. *Educ:* Univ Wis-Madison, BS, 60, MS, 61; Univ Ill, Urbana, PhD(physics), 65. *Honors & Awards:* Wood Prize, Optical Soc Am, 87; John Yarwood Mem Medal, British Vacuum Coun, 93; Isakson Prize, Am Phys Soc, 96. *Prof Exp:* Res assoc physics, Univ Ill, Urbana, 65-66 & Brown Univ, 66-67; mem tech staff, AT&T Bell Labs, 67-83; dist res mgr, Bell Commun Res Inc, 83-92. *Concurrent Pos:* Alexander von Humboldt sr scientist award. *Mem:* Fel Am Phys Soc; fel Soc Photooptical Instrumentation Engrs; fel Optical Soc Am; Mat Res Soc; fel Am Vacuum Soc; Sigma Xi; AAAS. *Res:* Experimental solid state physics; semiconductors; surface physics; optical properties of solids and thin films; ellipsometry; crystal growth. *Mailing Add:* Dept Physics NC State Univ Campus Box 8202 Raleigh NC 27695-8202. *Fax:* 919-515-1333; *E-Mail:* aspnes@unity.ncsu.edu

ASPREY, LARNED BROWN, PHYSICAL CHEMISTRY, INORGANIC CHEMISTRY. *Current Pos:* RETIRED. *Personal Data:* b Sioux City, Iowa, Mar 19, 19; m 44, Margaret Williams; c 7. *Educ:* Iowa State Univ, BS, 40; Univ Calif, PhD(chem), 49. *Prof Exp:* Chemist, Campbell Soup Co, 40-42, Metall Lab, Univ Chicago, 44-46 & Radiation Lab, Univ Calif, 46-49; mem staff, Los Alamos Sci Lab, 49-86. *Mem:* Fel AAAS; Am Chem Soc; Sigma Xi. *Res:* Physical and inorganic chemistry of actinide and lanthanide elements; fluorine chemistry. *Mailing Add:* 1311 Lebanon Arc Las Cruces NM 88005-3749

ASPREY, WINIFRED ALICE, MATHEMATICS, COMPUTER SCIENCES. *Current Pos:* from instr to prof, Vassar Col, 45-61, chmn, Dept Math, 58-62, Elizabeth Stillman Williams chair prof math, 61-82, dir comput sci, 77-82, EMER PROF MATH & COMPUT SCI, VASSAR COL, 82- *Personal Data:* b Sioux City, Iowa, Apr 8, 17. *Educ:* Vassar Col, AB, 38; Univ Iowa, MS, 43, PhD(math), 45. *Hon Degrees:* DSc, Marist Col, Poughkeepsie, NY, 85. *Prof Exp:* Teacher, Brearley Sch, New York, 38-40 & Girls Latin Sch, Chicago, 40-42; asst math, Univ Iowa, 42-45. *Concurrent Pos:* IBM Corp indust res fel, 57-58; NSF grant, Univ Calif, Los Angeles, 62, NSF fac fel & vis scholar, 64-65; dir, Acad Year Inst Math, State Dept Educ, NY, 62-64 & Acad Year Inst Comput Math, Vassar Col, spring, 64, 66 & 67; IBM Corp exchange grant, 69-70; vis staff mem & consult, Los Alamos Nat Lab, 72-76; consult & lectr, Mount St Mary's Col, Newburgh, NY, 82; distinguished prof math & comput sci, Bethany Col, WVa, 83, Marist Col, Poughkeepsie, NY, 85, 88 & 89; prof math & comput sci, St Louis Univ, Madrid, Spain, 83, 84, 85, 86; vis prof comput sci, Vassar Col, Poughkeepsie, NY, 90. *Mem:* Fel AAAS; Nat Coun Teachers Math; Am Math Soc; Math Asn Am; Sigma Xi;

Asn Comput Mach. *Res:* Analysis and topology; families of total oscillators and their derived functions; computer languages: APL and J. *Mailing Add:* PO Box 87 Vassar Col Poughkeepsie NY 12604-0087. *E-Mail:* asprey@vassar.edu

ASQUITH, GEORGE BENJAMIN, PETROLOGY, MINERALOGY. *Current Pos:* from asst prof to assoc prof, 70-81, PROF GEOL, WEST TEX STATE UNIV, 81- *Personal Data:* b Chicago, Ill, June 23, 36; m 63; c 1. *Educ:* Tex Tech Univ, BS, 61; Univ Wis, Madison, MS, 63, PhD(geol), 66. *Prof Exp:* Instr geol, Univ Wis, Madison, 66; res geologist, Atlantic-Richfield Res Lab, 66-70. *Mem:* Soc Econ Paleontologists & Mineralogists; Clay Minerals Soc; Sigma Xi. *Res:* Igneous petrology and volcanology; sandstone and carbonate petrology and sedimentation and carbonate diagenesis. *Mailing Add:* 4407 14th St Lubbock TX 79416-4801

ASRAR, GHASSAM R, REMOTE SENSING, ENVIRONMENTAL PHYSICS. *Current Pos:* prog scientist, 87-91, CHIEF SCIENTIST, NASA, 92- *Personal Data:* b Shiraz, Pars, Persia, Oct 12, 51; US citizen; m 86, Naimeh Razzaghi. *Educ:* Pahlavi Univ, BSc, 74; Mich State Univ, MS, 78, MS, 81, PhD(environ physics), 81. *Prof Exp:* Res assoc, Kans State Univ, 81-83, asst prof, 83-87; vis sr scientist, Calif Inst Technol, 87-90, Univ Space Res Asn, 90-92. *Concurrent Pos:* Mem, Remote Sensing Comt, Am Geophys Union, 92-; mem, Exec Comt, Int Airborn Remote Sensing, 93- *Mem:* Am Meteorol Soc; Am Geophys Union; Inst Elec & Electronics Engrs Geosci & Remote Sensing Soc; Sigma Xi. *Res:* Modeling solar radiation transfer through lower atmosphere and its interactions with Earth surface; modeling exchange of energy mass and momentum between earth surface and the planetary boundary layer. *Mailing Add:* NASA Mail Code YS 300 E St SW Washington DC 20546. *Fax:* 202-358-2770; *E-Mail:* gasrar@mtpe.ha.nasa.gov

ASRAR, JAWED, REACTION-INJECTION MOLDING. *Current Pos:* RES SPECIALIST, MONSANTO CO, 83- *Personal Data:* b India, Oct 1, 49. *Educ:* Aligarh Univ, India, BS, 69, MS, 71; Moscow Inst Chem Technol, USSR, PhD(chem technol), 78. *Prof Exp:* Teaching fel chem technol, Moscow Inst Chem Technol, USSR, 78-79; res assoc, Duke Univ, Durham, NC, 79-81; res assoc polymer chem & vis lectr gen chem, Univ Lowell, Mass, 81-83. *Concurrent Pos:* Assoc sci fel, Monsanto Co. *Mem:* Am Chem Soc. *Res:* Synthesis and modification of polyester resins, reinforced plastics, liquid crystalline polymers: polyesters, polyamides, polyamide hydrazides, polyoxadiazoles, polyacylsemicarbazides and ring opening polymerization. *Mailing Add:* 14949 Royal Brook Chesterfield MO 63017-7722

ASSADOURIAN, FRED, MATHEMATICS. *Current Pos:* RETIRED. *Personal Data:* b Panderma, Turkey, Apr 13, 15; nat US; m 54, Ann Mendikian; c Gary A & Brian H. *Educ:* NY Univ, BS, 35, MS, 36, PhD(math), 40. *Prof Exp:* Instr math, Col Eng, NY Univ, 37-42; assoc prof, Tex Tech Col, 42-44; res engr, Westinghouse Res Labs, Pa, 44-46; develop engr, Fed Telecommun Labs, NJ, 46-51, proj engr, 51-56; sr engr, Radio Corp Am, NY, 56-59, leader tech staff, 59-62, sr staff scientist & head adv transmission, 62-68; from assoc prof to prof elec eng, Pratt Inst, 68-81; pres, Faha Consult Inc, 83-93. *Concurrent Pos:* Adj prof elec eng, NJ Inst Technol, 50-57 & Stevens Inst Technol, 68 & 81-82; consult, RCA Astro Electronics & GE Astro-Space, 81-92; vis prof elec eng, Pratt Inst, 81-93. *Mem:* Inst Elec & Electronics Engrs. *Res:* Almost-periodic functions; pulse transformers; equations in gas discharge; microwave transmission; reflex klystron; distortion of amplitude modulation and frequency modulation signals; special microwave components; special problems in communications systems; communications satellite systems. *Mailing Add:* 21 76th St North Bergen NJ 07047

ASSALI, NICHOLAS S, OBSTETRICS. *Current Pos:* ATTEND OBSTETRICIAN & GYNECOLOGIST, UNIV CALIF, LOS ANGELES HOSP, 61- *Personal Data:* b Lebanon, Apr 7, 16; US citizen. *Educ:* Jesuit Sch, Lebanon, BS, 32; Gymnasio Normal, Brazil, BS, 37; Univ Sao Paulo, MD, 43; Am Bd Obstet & Gynec, cert. *Prof Exp:* Intern med, Univ Hosp, Sao Paulo, 41-42, resident surg & gynec, 42-43; consult obstet & gynec, Polyclin, Sao Paulo, 44-45; fel obstet & gynec, Bethesda Hosp, Cincinnati, Ohio, 46-47; asst prof obstet, Univ Cincinnati, 48-53, dir clin res & asst attend obstetrician, Dept Obstet, Cincinnati Gen Hosp, 48-53; assoc prof, 53-57, Prof Obstet & Gyned, Univ Calif, Los Angeles, 57- *Concurrent Pos:* Consult obstet & gynec, Sao Paulo Health Serv, 44-45; dir, training prog basic sci appl to obstet & gynec, NIH, 57-71; dir, training prog reproductive physiol, USPHS, 59-71; attend obstetrician & gynecologist, Harbor County Gen Hosp, Torrance, Calif, 60-; prof physiol, Univ Calif, Los Angeles, 61-73; mem, Gen Med B Study Sect, NIH, 69-73; mem, Coun Circulation, Am Heart Asn. *Mem:* Am Fedn Clin Res; Am Gynec Soc; Am Heart Asn; Am Physiol Soc; AAAS; Biophys Soc; Soc Gynec Invest (pres, 56); Soc Exp Biol & Med; Sigma Xi; Soc Hist Med Sci. *Res:* Maternal-fetal-neonatal cardiovascular physiology; hypertensive diseases of pregnancy; maternal-fetal exchange mechanisms; author or co-author of over 180 publications. *Mailing Add:* 520 Amalfi Dr Pacific Palisades CA 90272

ASSANIS, DENNIS N, thermal sciences & systems, internal combustion engines, for more information see previous edition

ASSAYKEEN, TATIANA ANNA, PHARMACOLOGY, CARDIOLOGY. *Current Pos:* med dir, Astra Chem, Sydney, Australia, 76-80, assoc dir clin res, Astra Pharmaceut Prod, Inc, Framingham, 80-81, vpres & treas, Southboro, 82-83, PRES & TREAS, ASTRA CLIN RES ASSOC, INC, HOPKINTON, MASS, 84- *Personal Data:* b South Orange, NJ, Sept 27, 39; m 80. *Educ:* Trinity Col, DC, BA, 61; Univ Va, PhD(pharmacol), 65. *Prof Exp:* Asst prof surg & pharmacol, 67-73, adj prof surg, Sch Med, Stanford Univ, 73-76. *Concurrent Pos:* USPHS fel, Med Ctr, Univ Calif, San Francisco, 65-67; NIH res grant, 69-76. *Mem:* resigned from all the above Soc Nephrology. *Res:* Renin-angiotensin-aldosterone system; hypertension; catecholamines. *Mailing Add:* 33 Alexander Rd Hopkinton MA 01748

ASSENZO, JOSEPH ROBERT, BIOSTATISTICS. *Current Pos:* res mgr, Upjohn Co, 66-80, group mgr biostatist & info sci, 80-85, dir proj mgt, 85-90, EXEC DIR, US PHARMACEUT REGULATORY AFFAIRS, UPJOHN CO, 90- *Personal Data:* b Boston, Mass, Jan 1, 32; m 60, 90; c 2. *Educ:* Northeastern Univ, BS, 54; Harvard Univ, SM, 55; Univ Okla, PhD(biostatist), 63. *Prof Exp:* Asst engr, Camp Dresser & McKee, Mass, 51-54, engr, 54-56, proj engr, 58; instr sanit eng, Univ Okla, 58-61, instr biostatist & sanit eng, 61-63, assoc prof, 63-66. *Concurrent Pos:* Consult, Bur Water Resources Res, 58-, Civil Aeromed Res Inst, Fed Aviation Agency, 61-66, med ctr, Univ Okla, 61-66 & pub sch syst, Oklahoma City, 62-66; mem water resources develop prog, Okla, 63-66; adj prof math sci, Oakland Univ, 79-; mem, Human Subj Instnl Review Bd, Western Mich Univ, 81- *Mem:* Fel Am Statist Asn; Asn Comp Mach; Biomet Soc; Drug Info Asn; Am Soc Pharmacol & Therapeut. *Res:* Applications of statistics, biomathematics, epidemiology and computer science and laboratory and medical research and regulations and to the discovery and development of drugs for human use. *Mailing Add:* 200 N Capitol Ave Lansing MI 48933

ASSINK, ROGER ALYN, POLYMER CHEMISTRY. *Current Pos:* MEM STAFF MAT RES, SANDIA LABS, 72- *Personal Data:* b Holland, Mich, Sept 28, 45; m 67; c 2. *Educ:* Mich State Univ, BS, 67; Univ Ill, MS, 69, PhD(chem), 72. *Mem:* Am Phys Soc; Am Chem Soc. *Res:* Study of the molecular dynamics and structure of polymeric materials by nuclear magnetic resonance spectroscopy. *Mailing Add:* PO Box 5800 Albuquerque NM 87185-1407

ASSMUS, ALEXI JOSEPHINE, HISTORY OF SCIENCE & TECHNOLOGY, US HISTORY. *Current Pos:* FEL, UNIV CALIF, BERKELEY, 91-, LECTR, HIST DEPT, 93-; LECTR, HIST DEPT, PRINCETON UNIV, 95- *Personal Data:* b New York, NY, Mar 22, 62. *Educ:* Stanford Univ, BA, 84; Harvard Univ, MA, 88, PhD(hist sci), 91. *Prof Exp:* Teaching fel, Hist Sci & Physics Dept & Core Prog, Harvard Univ, 86-90. *Concurrent Pos:* NSF fel, Univ Calif, Berkeley, 91-92. *Mem:* Am Hist Asn; Hist Sci Soc. *Res:* History of post WWII; history of the physical science; development of American science; history of quantum chemistry and quantum theory; American intellectual history; United States history; several publications and presentations. *Mailing Add:* 470 Stephens Hall Univ Calif Berkeley CA 94609

ASSMUS, EDWARD F(ERDINAND), JR, ALGEBRA. *Current Pos:* from assoc prof to prof, 66-93, univ distinguished prof math, 93-94, UNIV DISTINGUISHED EMER PROF MATH, LEHIGH UNIV, 94- *Personal Data:* b Nutley, NJ, Apr 19, 31; m 61, 72, Green; c Alexi & Richard. *Educ:* Oberlin Col, AB, 53; Harvard Univ, AM, 55, PhD(math), 58. *Prof Exp:* Off Naval Res res assoc, Columbia Univ, 58-59, Ritt instr math, 59-62; lectr, Wesleyan Univ, 62-66. *Concurrent Pos:* Consult, Appl Res Lab, Sylvania Electronic Systs, 61-71; vis prof, Queen Mary Col, London Univ, 68-69; summer fac, Sandia Lab, 78; vis prof, Univ Ill, Chicago Circle, 81, Univ Rome, 83, Univ Birmingham, Eng, 85 & 87, Inst Math & Applns, Univ Minn, 88, INRIA, France, 92-93 & 95-96 & Univ Rome, Italy, 96. *Mem:* Am Math Soc; Math Asn Am; London Math Soc; Soc Indust & Appl Math; AAAS; Inst Combinations & Applns. *Res:* Homological algebra; algebraic coding theory; combinatorial mathematics. *Mailing Add:* Dept Math Lehigh Univ 14 E Packer Ave Bethlehem PA 18015-3174. *E-Mail:* efa0@lehigh.edu

ASSOIAN, RICHARD KENNETH, CELL & MOLECULAR BIOLOGY. *Current Pos:* ASST PROF CELL BIOL, UNIV MIAMI SCH MED, 92- *Personal Data:* b Englewood, NJ, June, 1954. *Educ:* Johns Hopkins Univ, BA, 75; Univ Chicago, PhD(biochem), 81. *Prof Exp:* Fel, Nat Cancer Inst, 81-83, staff fel, 83-86; asst prof biochem, Col Physicians & Surgeons, Columbia Univ, 86-92. *Mem:* Sigma Xi; Am Soc Biochem & Molecular Biol; Am Soc Cell Biol. *Res:* control of cell growth by TGT-beta and cell adhesion; growth regulatory mechanisms in normal and transformed cells. *Mailing Add:* Dept Cell Biol & Anat & Cancer Ctr Univ Miami Sch Med PO Box 016960 (R-124) Miami FL 33101. *Fax:* 305-548-4431; *E-Mail:* rassoian@mednet.med.miami.edu

ASSONY, STEVEN JAMES, ORGANIC CHEMISTRY. *Current Pos:* RETIRED. *Personal Data:* b Czech, Apr 13, 20; nat US; m 48; c 2. *Educ:* Rutgers Univ, BS, 50; Univ Southern Calif, MS, 53, PhD(chem), 57. *Prof Exp:* Analyst, Geigy Co, Inc, 49-50; assoc, Univ Southern Calif, 51-56, res asst, Off Ord Res, 52-55; asst tech dir, Am Latex Prod Corp, 56-61; dir res & develop, Upjohn Co, 61-70, head tech serv, CPR Div, 70-81, mgr tech serv & regulatory affairs, 81-84. *Mem:* Am Chem Soc; Chem Soc; NY Acad Sci; Sigma Xi. *Res:* Organic and polymer chemistry; polyurethanes and polymers of boron, phosphorus and nitrogen. *Mailing Add:* 31944 Corte Positas Temecula CA 92592-9285

AST, DAVID BERNARD, DENTISTRY, PUBLIC HEALTH ADMINISTRATION. *Current Pos:* RETIRED. *Personal Data:* b New York, NY, Sept 30, 02; m 28, Isabel Helene; c Joan F. *Educ:* NY Univ, DDS, 24; Univ Mich, MPH, 42. *Hon Degrees:* ScD, Georgetown Univ, 85. *Honors & Awards:* Gov Alfred E Smith Award, Am Soc Pub Admin, 55; Award, NY State Soc Dent Children, 63; Award, USPHS & Am Dent Asn, 66; Award, NY Acad Prev Med, 66; H Trendley Dean Award, Int Asn Dent Res, 68;

Hermann M Biggs Mem Award, NY State Pub Health Asn, 71; John W Knutson Award, Am Pub Health Asn, 82. *Prof Exp:* Pvt pract, 24-38; asst dir oral hyg, NY State Dept Health, 38-45, chief dent health sect, 45-48, dir bur dent health, 48-66, assoc dir div med serv, 66-70, asst comnr div med care serv & eval, 70-72. *Concurrent Pos:* Dept Health, Educ & Welfare grants, 45-55, 63-64 & 67-69; lectr pub health pract, Columbia Univ, 44-73; spec lectr pub health, Albany Med Col, 50-73; consult, Prof Exam Serv, Am Pub Health Asn, 50-73; mem community health proj rev comt, Dept Health, Educ & Welfare, 63-65. *Mem:* Am Dent Asn; fel Am Pub Health Asn; fel Am Col Dent; Asn State & Territorial Dent Dirs (pres, 50-51); Am Asn Pub Health Dentists (pres, 60). *Res:* Effectiveness of supplementing a fluoride deficient community water supply with a fluoride compound to bring the fluoride ion concentration up to 1.0 part per million of water to prevent dental caries; public health aspects of malocclusion; administration and medical assistance programs. *Mailing Add:* 954-A Calle Aragon Laguna Hills CA 92653

ASTARITA, GIANNI, chemical engineering; deceased, see previous edition for last biography

ASTAVANIS-TSAKONAS, SPYRIDON, MOLECULAR DEVELOPMENT GENETICS. *Current Pos:* from asst prof to prof biol, 81-90, PROF CELL BIOL, YALE UNIV SCH MED, 80-; INVESTR, HOWARD HUGHES MED INST, 90- *Personal Data:* b Athens, Greece, Oct 28, 46; Greek & US citizen. *Educ:* Fed Inst Technol Zurich, MS, 71; Univ Cambridge, PhD(molecular med), 75. *Prof Exp:* Researcher, Univ Basel, Switz, 75-78 & Biochem Dept, Stanford Univ, 79-80. *Mem:* Genetics Soc Am; Am Soc Cell Biol; Soc Develop Biol; AAAS; Inst Molecular Biol & Biotechnol; European Molecular Biol Org. *Res:* Molecular development genetics. *Mailing Add:* Dept Biol Yale Univ Sch Med Boyer Ctr Molecular Med 295 Congress Ave New Haven CT 06510

ASTBURY, ALAN, PHYSICS. *Current Pos:* R M PEARCE PROF, PHYSICS DEPT, UNIV VICTORIA, 82-; DIR, TRI-UNIV MESON FACIL, VANCOUVER, 94- *Personal Data:* b Crewe, England, Nov 27, 34; m 64, Kathleen A Stratmeyer; c Elizabeth A & Gillian M. *Educ:* Univ Liverpool, BS, PhD, 61. *Honors & Awards:* Rutherford Medal, Brit Inst Physics, 86. *Prof Exp:* Res assoc, Lawrence Radiation Lab, Berkeley, 61-63; res assoc, physicist & chmn NIMROD, Rutherford Lab, UK, 63-83. *Concurrent Pos:* Leader, UK Collab, CERN, 70-73; dir, Inst Particle Physics Can, 91- *Mem:* Fel Royal Soc Can; fel Royal Soc. *Mailing Add:* TRIUMF Labs 4004 Westbrook Mall PO Box 3055 Vancouver BC V6T 2A3 Can

ASTELL, CAROLINE R, MOLECULAR VIROLOGY. *Current Pos:* from asst prof to assoc prof, 80-90, PROF BIOCHEM, UNIV BC, 90- *Educ:* Univ BC, PhD(biochem), 71. *Honors & Awards:* Killam Res Prize, 95. *Prof Exp:* Res assoc, Banting & Best Dept Med Res/Med Genetics, Univ Toronto, 73-75; asst prof biol & med biochem, Univ Calgary, 75-78. *Mem:* Am Soc Microbiol; Am Soc Virol. *Res:* Molecular biology; DNA replication and transcription of parvoviruses. *Mailing Add:* Dept Biochem Univ BC 2146 Health Sci Mall Vancouver BC V6T 1Z3 Can. *Fax:* 604-822-5227; *E-Mail:* astell@unixg.ubc.ca

ASTER, ROBERT WESLEY, PERFORMANCE SIMULATION, PROJECT DESIGN. *Current Pos:* supvr performance analysis, 90, SUPVR PROJ ENG, SYST ENG DIV, JET PROPULSION LAB, 91- *Personal Data:* b Spokane, Wash, Feb 10, 53. *Educ:* Stanford Univ, BS & MS, 76. *Prof Exp:* Sr analyst photovoltaics, Flat Plate Solar Array Proj, Jet Propulsion Lab, 76-82, sr analyst coal mining, Advan Coal Extraction Proj, 82-83, task mgr performance analyst, FAA-Radar Weather Proj, 84-89; team leader cost analysis, NASA Info Syst Strategic Plan, 89-90; task mgr performance analysis, Space Sta Info Syst, 90-91. *Res:* National authority on photovoltaic economics; development of JPL's information system performance simulation team; developing a project engineering group to ensure JPL flight and instrument projects achieve cost/schedule goals. *Mailing Add:* 1015 Worcester Ave Pasadena CA 91104

ASTERIADIS, GEORGE THOMAS, JR, HUMAN SEXUALITY. *Current Pos:* From asst prof to assoc prof, 71-91, PROF BIOL, PURDUE UNIV, N CENT CAMPUS, 91- *Personal Data:* b Colorado Springs, Colo, May 7, 44; m 77; c 1. *Educ:* State Univ NY, BS, 66; Purdue Univ, PhD(molecular bio), 71. *Concurrent Pos:* Fel, Int Coun Sex Educ & Parenthood; infection control consult. *Mem:* Nat Sci Teachers Asn; Am Asn Sex Educr, Counr & Therapists; Asn Practr Infection Control; Am Chem Soc; Am Soc Microbiol. *Res:* Nucleic acid chemistry. *Mailing Add:* Biol Chem Sect US 421 Purdue Univ N Cent Campus Westville IN 46391

ASTHEIMER, ROBERT W, electrooptics; deceased, see previous edition for last biography

ASTILL, BERNARD DOUGLAS, BIOCHEMISTRY. *Current Pos:* CONSULT, BERNARD D ASTILL ASSOC, 87- *Personal Data:* b Nottingham, Eng, Feb 11, 25; US citizen; m 55; c 2. *Educ:* Univ Nottingham, BSc, 50, PhD(org chem), 53. *Prof Exp:* Asst anal chemist, Boots Pure Drug Co, Nottingham, Eng, 43-44; chemist, Lab Indust Med, Eastman Kodak, 55-60, sr biol chemist, 60-66, res assoc, 67-72, supvr biochem, Health & Safety Lab, 72-85, dir, Regulatory Affairs, 85-87. *Concurrent Pos:* Cerebral Palsy Found grant, Univ Rochester, 52-54, NIH fel, 54-55; clin instr, Dept Community Health & Prev Med, Univ Rochester Med Ctr, 62-76. *Mem:* Am Chem Soc; NY Acad Sci; Soc Toxicol; Am Indust Hyg Asn; Soc Environ Toxicol & Chem. *Res:* Fate of organic chemicals in mammalian and aquatic species; biological monitoring for environmental exposures; biochemical mechanism of toxicity in vitro tests for toxicity; structure-activity relationships in toxicology; environment health and safety. *Mailing Add:* 195 Lyell St Spencerport NY 14559-9536

ASTILL, KENNETH NORMAN, MECHANICAL ENGINEERING. *Current Pos:* prof mech eng, 47-90, assoc dean eng, 80-89, EMER PROF, MECH ENG, TUFTS UNIV, 91- *Personal Data:* b Westerly, RI, July 16, 23; m 48; c 2. *Educ:* Univ RI, BS, 44; Chrysler Inst Eng, MAE, 46; Harvard Univ, MS, 53; Mass Inst Technol, PhD, 61. *Honors & Awards:* Ralph R Teetor Award, 80. *Prof Exp:* Lab engr, Chrysler Corp, 44-47. *Concurrent Pos:* Instr, Northeastern Univ, 49-54; mech engr, Gen Elec Co, 48-49, Harvard Proj, Pratt & Whitney Aircraft Div, United Aircraft Corp, 51 & Cambridge Air Force Res Ctr, 52-53; consult engr, Sylvania Elec Prod Inc, 54-57, Kaye Instruments, Inc, 57-68, Cohoon & Heasley, 64-69, USMC, US Army-Natick Labs, 67-74, Kaye Instuments, Inc, 70-73, C S Draper Labs, 73- & B-D Electrodyne; vis fel, Univ Sussex, 68; vis prof, Univ Leeds, 76, Foster-Miller Assoc, 79-81, Analytix Inc, 83, Univ Sussex, 83. *Mem:* Fel Am Soc Mech Engrs; Am Soc Eng Educ. *Res:* Heat transfer and fluid mechanics. *Mailing Add:* Dept Mech Eng Col Eng Tufts Univ Medford MA 02155

ASTLEY, EUGENE ROY, NUCLEAR ENGINEERING, APPLIED PHYSICS & ENGINEERING MANAGEMENT. *Current Pos:* dir & chief exec officer, 83-91, DIR, SANDVIK SPEC METALS CORP, KENNEWICK, WASH, 91-; CHMN BD, STIRLING TECHNOL CORP; DIR, ASTLEY ENTERPRISES, 95- *Personal Data:* b Alameda, Calif, Dec 5, 26; m 48, Peggy Lund; c Clifford A, Michael J & William L. *Educ:* Univ Ore, BS, 48; Ore State Univ, MS, 50. *Prof Exp:* Physicist, Gen Elec Co, Schenectady, NY, 50-55 & Richland, Wash, 55-60, mgr maintenance & indust eng prod reactors, 60-65; dir, FFTF Dept, Pac Northwest Div, Battelle Mem Inst, Richland, Wash, 65-69, assoc dir systs & elec, 69-71; dir & vpres res, Exxon Nuclear Co Inc, Bellevue, Wash, 71-79, dir & vpres, Fuels Mfg, Richland, Wash & Lingen, Ger, 79-83; dir, Sandvik Rhenium Alloys, Inc, 89-93, Columbia Mfg, 93-95. *Concurrent Pos:* Asst prof, Univ Wash, 58; bd dir, Jersey Nuclear Avco Isotopes, Inc, 72-75, Austin-McDaniel Corp, 91-93. *Res:* Instrumentation, reactor physics; industrial engineering, technical management; nuclear reactors and laser isotope enrichment; speciality metal fabrication; granted five US patents. *Mailing Add:* 2414 Harris Ave Richland WA 99352. *Fax:* 509-375-5298

ASTLING, ELFORD GEORGE, METEOROLOGY. *Current Pos:* RES METEOROLOGIST, US ARMY DUGWAY PROVING GROUND, 84- *Personal Data:* b Sycamore, Ill, Aug 13, 37; m 71, Priscilla Crisp; c David, Mark & Stephen. *Educ:* Univ Utah, BS, 60; Univ Wis-Madison, MS, 64, PhD(meteorol), 70. *Prof Exp:* Res meteorologist, Nat Environ Satellite Ctr, Environ Sci Serv Admin, 64-66; asst prof meteorol, Fla State Univ, 69-72; asst prof geophys sci, Old Dominion Univ, 72-75; asst prof, 75-80, assoc prof meteorol, Univ Utah, 80-84. *Mem:* AAAS; Am Meteorol Soc; Am Geophys Union. *Res:* Synoptic meteorology; mesoscale meteorology, mountain meteorology, remote sensing. *Mailing Add:* 2941 Zenith Circle Univ Utah Salt Lake City UT 84106. *Fax:* 435-831-5289; *E-Mail:* astling@dugway_emh4.army.mil

ASTON, DUANE RALPH, SOLID STATE PHYSICS. *Current Pos:* RETIRED. *Personal Data:* b Strabane, Pa, Aug 3, 32; m 55; c 6. *Educ:* Brigham Young Univ, BS, 55, MS, 57; Temple Univ, PhD(physics), 69. *Prof Exp:* Engr, Gen Dynamics/Convair, 55-56 & Boeing Airplane Co, 57-58; assoc scientist, Bettis Atomic, Westinghouse Elec Corp, 58-59; instr physics, Drexel Inst Technol, 59-67; from assoc prof to prof physics, Calif State Univ, Sacramento, 68-97. *Mem:* Am Asn Physics Teachers. *Res:* Nuclear reactor calculations; nuclear shielding studies; effects of demagnetization coefficients on type II superconductors; magnetization studies on the strong-coupling Pb-In alloy systems; intermediate and mixed states in type II superconductors. *Mailing Add:* Dept Physics Calif State Univ 6000 J St Sacramento CA 95819-2605

ASTON, RICHARD, ELECTROSURGERY, COURSE DEVELOPMENT. *Current Pos:* ASSOC PROF MED INSTRUMENTATION, PA STATE UNIV, WILKES-BARRE, 84- *Personal Data:* b Wilkes-Barre, Pa, Oct 4, 36; m 65; c 3. *Educ:* Pa State Univ, BS, 61, MS, 64; Ohio State Univ, PhD(med instrumentation), 69. *Prof Exp:* Asst prof elec eng, Rochester Inst Technol, 70-72; staff engr, Hughes Aircraft Co, 72-75; design specialist, Pomona Div, Gen Dynamics, 75-78; assoc prof elec eng, Wilkes Univ, 78-64. *Concurrent Pos:* Biol med engr, Proj Hope, Millwood, Va; session chair, Am Soc Eng Educ, 90-93. *Mem:* Inst Elec & Electronics Engrs Eng Med & Biol Soc; Am Soc Eng Educ; Sigma Xi. *Res:* Surgical devices; Impatt power combiners; speech therapy instrumentation; microwave devices; medical instrumentation for hospitals; electrical circuit theory; author of books on medical instrumentation principles, laboratory manual. *Mailing Add:* 33 Barney St Wilkes-Barre PA 18702

ASTON, ROY, PHARMACOLOGY. *Current Pos:* prof physiol & pharmacol, 80-90, PROF PHARMACOL, DEPT BIOMED SCI, SCH DENT, UNIV DETROIT, MERCY, 90- *Personal Data:* b Windsor, Ont, Dec 31, 29; m 73; c 1. *Educ:* Univ Windsor, BA, 50; Wayne State Univ, MSc, 54; Univ Toronto, PhD(pharmacol), 58. *Prof Exp:* Res assoc pharmacol, Med Sch, Univ Mich, 58-59; res assoc pharmacol, Sch Med, Wayne State Univ, 59-62, from instr to asst prof, 62-70, assoc prof, 70-80. *Mem:* Am Soc Pharmacol; Pharmacol Soc Can. *Res:* Pharmacodynamics and psychopharmacology of drugs acting on the central nervous system; drug protection against pathological effects of acceleration. *Mailing Add:* Dept Biomed Sci Sch Dent Univ Detroit/Mercy 2985 E Jefferson Ave Detroit MI 48207-4282

ASTON-JONES, GARY STEPHEN, BEHAVIORAL NEUROBIOLOGY, NEUROANATOMY. *Current Pos:* assoc prof, 88-93, DIR BEHAV & NEUROBIOL LAB, 88-, HAHNEMANN UNIV, PROF, MENT HEALTH SCI, 93- *Personal Data:* b Havre de Grace, Md, Oct 25, 51; m 81; c 1. *Educ:* Univ Va, BA, 73; Calif Inst Technol, PhD(neurobiol), 80. *Prof Exp:* Fel, A V Davis Ctr Behav Neurobiol, Salk Inst, 80-82; asst prof psychol, State Univ NY, Binghampton, 82-84; asst prof biol, NY Univ, 84-88. *Mem:* AAAS; Soc Neurosci. *Res:* Physiology and anatomy of brain monoaminergic systems. *Mailing Add:* Dept Psychiat Hahnemann Univ Sch Med Broad & Vine St Philadelphia PA 19102-1178

ASTRACHAN, BORIS MORTON, PSYCHIATRY. *Current Pos:* PROF, HEAD & CHIEF PSYCHIAT, UNIV ILL, CHICAGO, 90- *Personal Data:* b New York, NY, Dec 1, 31; m 56, Batja Sanders; c David, Joseph, Michael & Ellen. *Educ:* Alfred Univ, BA, 52; Albany Med Col, MD, 56. *Honors & Awards:* Contributions to Theory & Pactice of Admin Psychiat Award, Am Psychiat Asn, 95. *Prof Exp:* Asst dir, Inpatient Psychiat Serv, Yale-New Haven Hosp, 63-66; from asst prof to assoc prof psychiat, Sch Med, Yale Univ, 65-71; chief, Day Hosp, Conn Ment Health Ctr, 66-68, dir, Gen Clin Div, 68-70, actg ctr dir, 70, dir, Conn Ment Health Ctr, 71-87; prof psychiat, Sch Med, Yale Univ, 71-90. *Concurrent Pos:* NIMH fel, Yale Univ, 61-63; mem, Res Task Panel, President's Comn Ment Health, 77-78; mem, Epidemol & Serv Comt, NIMH, 87-91, chair, 89-91. *Mem:* AAAS; fel Am Psychiat Asn; Am Pub Health Asn; fel Am Col Psychiatrists; fel Am Asn Psychiat Admin (pres, 90-91). *Res:* Organizational group dynamics; schizophrenia, clinical epidemiology and outcome; evaluation research. *Mailing Add:* Dept Psychiat 912 S Wood St MC 913 Chicago IL 60612-7325. *Fax:* 312-413-1228

ASTRACHAN, LAZARUS, BIOCHEMISTRY. *Current Pos:* from asst prof to assoc prof, 62-90, EMER PROF MICROBIOL, SCH MED, CASE WESTERN RESERVE UNIV, 90- *Personal Data:* b New York, NY, Aug 7, 25; m 45; c 2. *Educ:* City Col NY, BS, 44; Yale Univ, PhD(physiol chem), 51. *Prof Exp:* Biochemist, Biol Div, Oak Ridge Nat Lab, 54-62. *Concurrent Pos:* Fel, McCollum-Pratt Inst, Johns Hopkins Univ, 51-53, Polio Found fel, Sch Hyg & Pub Health, 54. *Mem:* Am Soc Microbiol; Am Soc Biol Chemists; Sigma Xi. *Res:* Biochemistry of nucleic acids; virology; bacterial lipids. *Mailing Add:* 2700 Colchester Rd Cleveland OH 44106-3651

ASTRAHAN, MELVIN ALAN, HYPOTHERMIA, THERMAL PHYSICS. *Current Pos:* ASSOC PROF RADIATION ONCOL, UNIV SOUTHERN CALIF, 84- *Personal Data:* b Poughkeepsie, NY, Oct 31, 52; m 76; c 3. *Educ:* Univ Calif, Irvine, BS, 74; Univ Calif, Los Angeles, MS, 78, PhD(med physics), 81. *Honors & Awards:* Silverman Award, Southern Calif Health Physics Soc, 81. *Prof Exp:* Res physicist, Vet Admin Res Serv, Brentwood, Calif, 81-84. *Mem:* Am Asn Physicists Med; NAm Hyperthermia Group. *Res:* Hyperthermia systems for adjunctive use in cancer therapy; treatment planning software for radiation therapy; thermal physics. *Mailing Add:* 11401 Kensington Rd Los Alamitos CA 90720

ASTROLOGES, GARY WILLIAM, ORGANIC CHEMISTRY. *Current Pos:* RES CHEMIST, HALOCARBON PROD CORP, 77- *Personal Data:* b Granby, Que, Oct 22, 49; US citizen. *Educ:* Mass Inst Technol, BS, 71; Univ Ill, Urbana, PhD(org chem), 77. *Mem:* Am Chem Soc; AAAS. *Res:* Organofluorine chemistry; hypervalent chemistry, especially involving sulfur and phosphorus. *Mailing Add:* Ariz Chem Co Caller Box 2447 Panama City FL 32402-2447

ASTROM, KARL JOHAN, CONTROLLED MATHEMATICS. *Current Pos:* PROF AUTOMATIC CONTROL, LUND INST TECHNOL, 65-, HEAD, DEPT AUTOMATIC CONTROL. *Personal Data:* b Ostersund, Sweden, Aug 5, 34. *Educ:* Royal Inst Technol, Stockholm, PhD(controlled math), 60. *Hon Degrees:* Dr, Nat Inst Polytech, Grenoble, 87. *Honors & Awards:* Rufus Oldenburger Medal; Quazza Medal, 87; Control Systs Sci & Eng Award, Inst Elec & Electronics Engrs, Medal of Honor, 93. *Prof Exp:* Researcher, IBM, 60-65, Res Inst Nat Defense, Stockholm. *Mem:* Nat Acad Eng; Royal Swed Acad Sci; Swed Acad Eng Sci; Royal Physiog Soc; Soc Indust & Appl Math; fel Inst Elec & Electronics Engrs. *Res:* Design and development of adaptive controllers; adaptive control covers, development of adaptive algorithms robust adaptive algorithms, automatic tuning and autonomous control. *Mailing Add:* Lund Inst Technol Box 118 Lund S-22100 Sweden. *Fax:* 46-46-138-118; *E-Mail:* kja@controlx.lth.se

ASTROMOFF, ANDREW, MATHEMATICS. *Current Pos:* From asst prof to assoc prof, 62-70, PROF MATH, SAN FRANCISCO STATE UNIV, 70- *Personal Data:* b Paris, France, Nov 30, 32; US citizen; m 57; c 3. *Educ:* Univ Calif, Berkeley, AB, 54, MA, 58, PhD(math), 63. *Mem:* Math Asn Am. *Res:* Foundations of mathematics; theory of models; general algebraic systems. *Mailing Add:* 754 Kokomo Pl Honolulu HI 96825

ASTRUC, JUAN, ANATOMY & NEUROANATOMY, NEUROLOGY & NEURO-OPTHAMOLOGY. *Current Pos:* assoc prof, 67-76, PROF ANAT & NEUROL, MED COL VA, 76- *Personal Data:* b Utrera, Spain, June 5, 33; m 61; c 7. *Educ:* Univ Granada, MD, 57, PhD, 59. *Prof Exp:* From instr to asst prof anat, Sch Med, Univ Granada, 57-61; from asst prof to assoc prof, Sch Med, Univ Navarra, 62-67. *Concurrent Pos:* asst prof, Sch Med, Lit Univ Salamanca, 58-60; Span Govt res fel, 59-60; Ger Govt res fel, 60; March Found res grant, 62-63; USPHS res fel, 63-64 & res grants, 65-67 & 69- *Mem:* Am Asn Anatomists; Soc Neurosci; Am Asn Neurol; NAm Neuro-opthal Soc. *Res:* Influence of the central nervous system upon the endocrine glands, control of the movement of the eyes; structure and connections in the central nervous system. *Mailing Add:* Dept Neurol Med Col Va Va Commonwealth Univ MCV Sta Box 599 Richmond VA 23298

ASTRUE, ROBERT WILLIAM, SOLID STATE PHYSICS. *Current Pos:* asst prof, 66-70, assoc prof, 70-77, PROF PHYSICS, HUMBOLDT STATE UNIV, 77- *Personal Data:* b San Francisco, Calif, Feb 2, 28; m 56; c 5. *Educ:* Univ Calif, Berkeley, AB, 51; Univ Wash, MS, 59; Wayne State Univ, PhD(physics), 66. *Prof Exp:* Res physicist, Ford Motor Co Sci Res Lab, 63-66. *Mem:* Am Phys Soc; Am Asn Physics Teachers; Sigma Xi. *Res:* Magnetic resonance; ferromagnetic thin films. *Mailing Add:* Dept Physics Sci Humboldt State Univ Arcata CA 95521

ASTUMIAN, RAYMOND DEAN, RELAXATION KINETICS OF MEMBRANE ENZYMES. *Current Pos:* RES CHEMIST, NAT INST STANDARDS & TECHNOL, 88- *Personal Data:* b Birmingham, Ala, Oct 3, 56. *Educ:* Univ Tex, PhD(chem & math sci), 83. *Honors & Awards:* Galvani Prize, Bioelectrochem Soc, 87. *Prof Exp:* Staff fel, NIH, 84-88. *Concurrent Pos:* Vis prof, Bielefeld Univ, Ger, 89-90. *Mem:* Am Soc Biochem & Molecular Biol; Biophys Soc; Am Chem Soc; Bioelectrochem Soc; Bioelectromagnetics Soc. *Res:* Interaction between electromagnetic fields and biomembrane macromolecules, particularly with regard to the kinetics of membrane enzymes in an AC electric field. *Mailing Add:* Univ Chicago MC 6035 5841 S Maryland Ave Chicago IL 60637

ASWAD, A ADNAN, INDUSTRIAL & SYSTEMS ENGINEERING. *Current Pos:* lectr indust eng, 65-72, PROF INDUST & SYSTS ENG & CHMN DEPT, UNIV MICH, DEARBORN, 72- *Personal Data:* b Antioch, Turkey, Dec 6, 33; US citizen; m 62; c 1. *Educ:* Robert Col, Istanbul, BSc, 55; Univ Mich, Ann Arbor, MSc, 61 & 64, PhD(indust eng), 72. *Prof Exp:* Power plant engr, Damascus Power Co, 55-56; design engr, Mech Construct Co, 56-59; stress anal engr, Int Harvester Co, 61-63. *Concurrent Pos:* Prin researcher, Kellogg Found grant, 75-77; consult, automotive indust, 70- *Mem:* Sr mem Am Inst Indust Engrs; Opers Res Soc Am; Inst Mgt Sci; Am Soc Eng Educ; Soc Mfg Engrs. *Res:* Risk analysis; management of research and development; manufacturing systems; mechanical engineering. *Mailing Add:* Dept Indust Eng Univ Mich 4901 Evergreen Rd Dearborn MI 48128-1491

ASZALOS, ADORJAN, BIO-ORGANIC CHEMISTRY, CANCER. *Current Pos:* CHIEF CELL BIOL, FOOD & DRUG ADMIN, 79- *Personal Data:* b Szeged, Hungary, May 9, 29; US citizen; m 60; c 2. *Educ:* Tech Univ Budapest, MS, 51; Tech Univ Vienna, PhD(natural prod chem), 61. *Prof Exp:* Plant engr, Hungary, 51-53; supvr, Biochem Res Inst, 53-56; res chemist, Nat Starch & Chem Co, 57-59; sr res scientist, Squibb Inst Med Res, 62-74; head biochem, Frederick Cancer Res Ctr, 74-79. *Concurrent Pos:* Fel, Rutgers Univ, 61-62, coadj prof, 71-73; res prof, Princeton Univ, 73-75. *Mem:* Am Chem Soc; NY Acad Sci; Intra Sci Found. *Res:* Isolation and structural studies of antibiotics; synthetic organic chemistry in field of carbohydrates; biochemistry; biophysics; cell biology. *Mailing Add:* 7711 Bradley Blvd West Bethesda MD 20817-1442

ATACK, DOUGLAS, PHYSICAL CHEMISTRY. *Current Pos:* RETIRED. *Personal Data:* b Wakefield, Eng, Aug 6, 23; m 50; c 1. *Educ:* Univ Leeds, BSc, 44, PhD(chem), 46. *Honors & Awards:* Weldon Medal, Can Pulp & Paper Asn, 63 & 81; Walter Brecht Medal, Soc Ger Pulp & Paper Engrs, 82. *Prof Exp:* Res assoc high pressure, PTX Data, Univ Leeds, 46-48; fel critical phenomena, Nat Res Coun Can, 48-50; fel PVI data, Univ Manchester, 50-51; res assoc, Off Naval Res Contract, Univ NC, 51-53; asst prof phys chem, Syracuse Univ, 53-54; head wood & fiber physics div, Pulp & Paper Res Inst Can, 54-67, chmn wood & fiber res dept, 67-69, dir appl physics div, 69-89, dir acad affairs, 85-89. *Concurrent Pos:* Auxillary prof mech eng, McGill Univ, 64-; fel, Asn Pulp & Paper Indust, 75. *Mem:* Am Phys Soc; fel Tech Asn Pulp & Paper Indust; Chem Soc. *Res:* High speed friction phenomena; mechanical properties of polymeric materials. *Mailing Add:* 2180 Marine Dr Suite 2204 Oakville ON L6L 5V2 Can

ATAL, BISHNU S, ACOUSTICS. *Current Pos:* res staff, 81-85, head, Res Dept, 85-90, HEAD, SPEECH RES DEPT, AT&T LABS, 90- *Personal Data:* b Kanpur, India, May 10, 33. *Educ:* Univ Lucknow, BSc, 52; Polytech Inst Brooklyn, PhD(elec eng), 68. *Honors & Awards:* Centennial Medal, Inst Elec & Electronics Engrs, Morris N Liebman Mem Field Award, 88. *Prof Exp:* Lectr acoust, Dept Elec Commun Eng, Indian Inst Sci, Bangalore, 57-80. *Mem:* Nat Acad Sci; Nat Acad Eng. *Res:* Published technical papers in architectural acoustics and speech communication. *Mailing Add:* Dept Speech Res AT&T Labs 600 Mountain Ave Murray Hill NJ 07974

ATALA, ANTHONY, PEDIATRIC UROLOGIC SURGERY, TISSUE ENGINEERING. *Current Pos:* res fel, Dept Surg, Harvard Med Sch, 90-91, clin fel, Children's Hosp, 91-92, instr, 92-93, ASST PROF SURG, CHILDRENS HOSP, HARVARD MED SCH, 94- *Personal Data:* b Lima, July 14, 58. *Educ:* Univ Miami, BA, 81; Univ Louisville, MD, 85. *Honors & Awards:* Res Award, Soc Endourology & J Endourology; First Place Award, Am Col Surgeons; Edelen Award Outstanding Surg Res; John Perry Miles Award; Cap Cure Award, Milliken Found; Res Prize, World Soc Endourology, 88; First Place Investr Award, Am Soc Plastic Surg; Basic Res Award, Am Acad Pediat & Europ Soc Pediat Urol. *Prof Exp:* Intern surg, Univ Louisville, 85-86, resident surg, 86-87, resident urol, 87-90. *Concurrent Pos:* Consult, J Urol, 92-; Von L Meyer travelling fel; bd dirs, Nat Kidney Found, 96. *Mem:* Soc Basic Urol Res; Soc Pediat Urol; Am Urol Asn; Am Acad Pediat; Am Col Surgeons; AMA; AAAS. *Res:* Urologic diseases, gene therapy and tissue engineering; author of over 108 publications; granted several patents. *Mailing Add:* 300 Longwood Ave Boston MA 02115. *Fax:* 617-355-6587

ATALAY, BULENT ISMAIL, THEORETICAL PHYSICS, NUCLEAR PHYSICS. *Current Pos:* from asst prof to assoc prof, 66-72, PROF & CHMN, MATH SCI & PHYSICS DEPT, MARY WASHINGTON COL, UNIV VA, 74- *Personal Data:* b Ankara, Turkey, June 10, 40; US citizen. *Educ:* Georgetown Univ, BS, 63, MS, 67, PhD(theoret physics), 70; Oxford Univ, MA, 72. *Prof Exp:* Instr area studies, Georgetown Univ, 63-64 & Princeton Univ, 64-65; res assoc nuclear physics, Univ Calif, Berkeley, 68-69. *Concurrent Pos:* NATO scholar, 60-68; NSF fel, 68-69; Baron Schwarchild fel, 74, 76, 78 & 79; res assoc, Dept Physics, Princeton Univ, 68-69, mem, Inst Advan Study, 74-76; fel, Dept Theoretical Phsyics, Oxford Univ, 72-73. *Mem:* Am Inst Physics. *Res:* Theoretical physics perturbation theory for projected states; nuclear structure and nuclear models. *Mailing Add:* Dept Physics Mary Wash Col 1301 College Ave Fredericksburg VA 22401-4666

ATALLA, RAJAI HANNA, CHEMICAL PHYSICS. *Current Pos:* HEAD, DIV CHEM & PULPING RES, FOREST PROD LAB, 89- *Personal Data:* b Jerusalem, Palestine, Feb 21, 35; nat US; m 63; c 2. *Educ:* Rensselaer Polytech Inst, BChE, 55; Univ Del, MChE, 58, PhD(chem eng), 61. *Prof Exp:* Res engr res ctr, Hercules Inc, 60-62, res chemist, 62-68; from assoc prof to prof chem physics & eng, Inst Paper Chem, 68-89. *Mem:* AAAS; Royal Chem Soc; Am Chem Soc; Tech Asn Pulp & Paper Indust; Sigma Xi. *Res:* Molecular structure and organization in plant cell walls; celluloses, hemi celluloses, and ligrins; vibrational spectroscopy; solid state 13C NHR spectroscopy; thermodynamics and statistical mechanics. *Mailing Add:* Forest Prods Lab One Gifford Pinchot Dr Madison WI 53705-2398

ATALLA, ROBERT E, mathematics; deceased, see previous edition for last biography

ATALLAH, MIKHAIL JIBRAYIL, ALGORITHMS, PARALLEL COMPUTATION. *Current Pos:* From asst prof to assoc prof, 82-89, PROF COMPUT SCI, PURDUE UNIV, 89- *Personal Data:* b Aleppo, Syria, Apr 19, 53; m 80, Karen A Nowakowski; c Christina & Nadia. *Educ:* Am Univ, Beirut, BS, 75; Johns Hopkins Univ, MS, 80, PhD(elec eng), 82. *Honors & Awards:* Pres Young Invest Award, NSF, 85. *Mem:* Fel Inst Elec & Electronics Engrs; Asn Comput Mach; Soc Indust & Appl Math. *Res:* Design and analysis of computer algorithms; parallel computation; computational geometry; intrusion and misuse detection in computer systems. *Mailing Add:* Dept Comput Sci Purdue Univ West Lafayette IN 47907. *Fax:* 517-494-0739; *E-Mail:* mja@cs.purdue.edu

ATAM-ALIBECKOFF, GALIB-BEY, CELLULOSE CHEMISTRY, VISCOSE CHEMISTRY. *Current Pos:* EXEC VPRES, NYLONGE CORP, 91- *Personal Data:* b Paris, France, Jan 1, 23; m 59, Nadia Vicentic; c Dominique & Tamara. *Educ:* Univ Paris, Licence Es Sci, 44. *Prof Exp:* Res chemist, French Soc Glycerin, 46-47; chemist, Bact Inst Chile, 47-49; chief chemist, Rayonhil, Chile, 49-57, Von Kohorn Int Corp, 57-66 & Chemtex Inc, 66-67; vpres, Nylonge Corp, 66-78; exec vpres, Sponge Inc, 78-90. *Mem:* Am Chem Soc; Tech Asn Pulp & Paper Indust. *Res:* Viscose rayon spinning; new products based on viscose and cellulose. *Mailing Add:* Nylonge Corp 1301 Lowell St Elyria OH 44035

ATANASOFF, JOHN VINCENT, physical mathematics, research administration; deceased, see previous edition for last biography

ATASSI, ZOUHAIR, BIOCHEMISTRY, IMMUNOLOGY. *Current Pos:* WELCH CHAIR CHEM, DEPT BIOCHEM, BAYLOR COL, 83- *Personal Data:* b Homs, Syria, Dec 20, 34; m 63, Lena Moussa-Pasha; c Shana. *Educ:* Bristol Univ, BSc, 57; Univ Birmingham, MSc, 58, PhD(chem), 60, DSc(chem), 73. *Honors & Awards:* Established investr, Am Heart Asn, 66; Harden Medal & Jubilee Lect, Biochem Soc, 87; Medico-Legal Soc Japan Distinction Award, 88; Kuwait Prize Basic Sci, 95; Commendation Outstanding Contrib, Japanese Soc Electrophonesis. *Prof Exp:* Postdoctoral res fel chem, Univ Birmingham, 60-61; res assoc biochem, Albany Med Col & postdoctoral res fel labs protein chem, Div Labs & Res, NY State Dept Health, 62-63; asst prof biochem sch med, State Univ NY Buffalo, 63-68; prof chem, Wayne State Univ, 68-75; prof biochem & immunol, Mayo Med Sch, 75-83; prof biochem & immunol, Univ Minn, Minneapolis, 75-83. *Concurrent Pos:* Grants, Off Naval Res, 64-70 & 84-90, Nat Inst Arthritis & Metab Dis, 64-, Am Heart Asn, 71-74 & 81-, Nat Inst Allergy & Infectious Dis, 74-, Welch Found, 83- & US Army Med Res & Develop Command, 89-; immunol consult, Mayo Clin, 75-83, distinguished lectr med sci; pres, Int Symposium on Immunobiol of Proteins; ed in chief, CRC Crit Reviews in Immunol & J Protein Chem; chmn, Tenth Int Conf Methods Protein Struct Analysis, 94. *Mem:* Am Soc Biol Chem; Am Asn Immunol; Brit Biochem Soc; Am Chem Soc; AAAS. *Res:* Protein structure and function; chemistry, biochemistry and molecular and cellular immunology; protein chemistry, immunochemistry and conformation; chemical modification and cleavage of proteins; organic synthesis of peptides; localization and synthesis of protein binding sites. *Mailing Add:* Dept Biochem Baylor Col One Baylor Plaza Houston TX 77030-3498

ATCHER, ROBERT W, RADIOPHARMACEUTICAL CHEMISTRY, RADIOBIOLOGY. *Current Pos:* ASSOC PROF, UNIV ALA, BIRMINGHAM, 94- *Personal Data:* b Chicago, Ill, June 12, 51; c R Andrew. *Educ:* Washington Univ, BA, 72; Univ Rochester, MS, 74, PhD(nuclear chem), 80; Univ Mo, MA, 76. *Honors & Awards:* R&D 100 Award, Res & Devel Mag, 89. *Prof Exp:* Res assoc, Harvard Med Sch & Brigham & Women's Hosp, 80-83; cancer expert, Radiation Oncol Div, Nat Cancer Inst, 83-86; group leader, Chem Div, Argonne Nat Lab, 86-93; asst prof radiation and cellular oncol, Univ Chicago, 86-94. *Mem:* Fel Am Inst Chemists; Am Chem Soc; AAAS; Fedn Am Sci; Soc Nuclear Med; NY Acad Sci; Radiation Res Soc; Sigma Xi. *Res:* Novel therapeutic uses of radioisotopes. *Mailing Add:* Univ Ala AB880 Birmingham AL 35294-0108. *E-Mail:* ratcher@aol.com

ATCHESON, J D, PSYCHIATRY. *Current Pos:* RETIRED. *Personal Data:* b London, Ont, July 27, 17; m 42; c 3. *Educ:* Univ Western Ont, MD, 41; Univ Toronto, dipl psychiat, 46; FRCP(C), 47; FRCP(C), 72. *Honors & Awards:* Centennial Medal, Dom Can, 67. *Prof Exp:* Resident, Hamilton Gen Hosp, 41-42; surgeon lieutenant comdr, Royal Can Navy, 42-45; registr, Allen Mem Inst Psychiat, McGill Univ, 44-45; teaching assoc, Univ Toronto, 47-57, from asst prof to prof, 57-83, emer prof, fac med, dept psychiat, 83-90; sr psychiatrist, Forensic Out-Patient Serv, Clarke Inst Psychiat, Univ Toronto, 71-90. *Concurrent Pos:* Dir, psychiat clin, Juv & Family Court, Toronto, 47-57; consult training schs, Dept Corrections, 49-57, dir treatment serv, 58; supt, Thistletown Children's Psychiat Hosp, 58-69; consult, Eastern Arctic, Dept Nat Health & Welfare, 65- & Ont Correctional Inst, Brampton, 74-; med dir & chief of staff, Thistletown Regional Ctr Children & Adolescents, 69-71; mem, Lieutenant Gov adv rev bd, Ont, 75- *Mem:* Hon fel Am Psychiat Asn; Can Psychiat Asn; Can Med Asn; Am Acad Psychiat & Law. *Res:* Juvenile delinquency; residential care of children; child psychiatry; forensic psychiatry; trans-cultural psychiatry, especially problems of emotional disorder in the Canadian Arctic. *Mailing Add:* 300 Mill Rd PH32 Etobicoke ON M9C 4W7 Can

ATCHISON, F(RED) STANLEY, ELECTRONICS, PHYSICS. *Current Pos:* RETIRED. *Personal Data:* b Stoddard Co, Mo, Jan 3, 18; m 40, Ethel Harty. *Educ:* Southeast Mo State Univ, AB, 38; Univ Iowa, MS, 40, PhD(physics), 42. *Prof Exp:* Instr sci, City HS, Cairo, Ill, 37-38; asst physics, Univ Iowa, 38-42; physicist, US Bur Stand, 42-53; dept head electronics, Naval Ord Lab, Corona, Calif, 53-55, tech dir, 55-68; mem res staff, Inst Defense Anal, 69-80. *Mem:* Am Phys Soc; fel Inst Elec & Electronics Engrs; AAAS; Sigma Xi. *Res:* Nuclear physics; proximity fuse development; guided missile development; microwave radar development; weapons systems analysis. *Mailing Add:* 6197 Palm Ave Riverside CA 92506

ATCHISON, THOMAS ANDREW, NUMERICAL ANALYSIS. *Current Pos:* prof math & chmn dept, 79-89, DEAN COL SCI & MATH, STEPHEN F AUSTIN STATE UNIV, 89- *Personal Data:* b Brady, Tex, July 3, 37; m 59, Elizabeth A Wash; c Michael A, Alan T & Susan E. *Educ:* Univ Tex, BA, 59, MS, 60, PhD(math), 63. *Prof Exp:* Instr math, Howard Payne Col, 59; spec instr, Univ Tex, 61-63; from asst prof to assoc prof, Tex Tech Univ, 63-66; mem staff, LTV Electrosysts, Inc, 66-67; assoc prof math, Tex Tech Univ, 67-72; prof math & head dept, Miss State Univ, 72-79. *Concurrent Pos:* Pres, ETex Coun Teachers Math, 87-89; mem, Tex Higher Educ Coord Bd Adv Comt Res Prog, 87-91; pres, Tex Asn Acad Adminr Math Sci, 89-90; mem, Res Enhancement Formula Study Comt, 91-93; chair, Res Enhancement Eval Comt, 92. *Mem:* Sigma Xi; Math Asn Am. *Res:* Numerical solutions of differential equations; extrapolation processes; complex analysis. *Mailing Add:* Col Sci & Math Stephen F Austin State Univ PO Box 13034 Nacogdoches TX 75962. *Fax:* 409-468-1226; *E-Mail:* f_atchison@titan.sfasu.edu

ATCHISON, THOMAS CALVIN, JR, MINING ENGINEERING. *Current Pos:* RETIRED. *Personal Data:* b Fremont, Ohio, June 11, 22; m 50; c 3. *Educ:* Princeton Univ, AB, 43. *Prof Exp:* Electronic technician, Palmer Lab, Princeton Univ, 43; physicist, Bur Ships, US Navy Dept, 46-49; supvr physicist, US Bur Mines, 49-70, res dir, Twin Cities Mining Res Ctr, 70-76. *Concurrent Pos:* Vis prof, Dept Civil & Mineral Eng, Univ Minn, 76- *Mem:* Sigma Xi; Int Soc Rock Mech (vpres, 79-); AAAS; Am Planning Asn; World Future Soc. *Res:* Underground space use; mining research; rock mechanics; blasting; lunar surface research. *Mailing Add:* 6512 Warren Ave Edina MN 55439

ATCHISON, WILLIAM FRANKLIN, MATHEMATICS, COMPUTER SCIENCE. *Current Pos:* RETIRED. *Personal Data:* b Smithfield, Ky, Apr 7, 18; m 47, Lois Bruinkool; c Allen, Glen, MaryBeth & David. *Educ:* Georgetown Col, AB, 38; Univ Ky, MA, 40; Univ Ill, PhD(math), 43. *Honors & Awards:* Chester Morrill Mem Award, Asn Syst Mgt, 75; Award Outstanding Contrib Comput Sci Educ, Asn Comput Math, 80, Distinguished Serv Award, 93. *Prof Exp:* Asst, Physics Lab, Georgetown Col, 36-38; asst math, Univ Ky, 39-40; asst, Univ Ill, 40-42, instr, 43-44 & 46-48, asst prof, 49-50 & 51-55; asst prof, Harvard Univ, 50-51; res assoc prof, Ga Inst Technol, 55-63, res prof, 63-66; dir, Comput Sci Ctr, Univ Md, College Park, 66-76, prof, 66-88, emer prof comput sci, 88- *Concurrent Pos:* Head prog & coding group, Rich Electronic Comput Ctr, 55-57, dir ctr, 57-66, actg dir sch info sci, 63-64. *Mem:* Asn Comput Mach; Math Asn Am; Nat Coun Teachers Math. *Res:* Digital computation; information science; numerical analysis; algebraic geometry; numerical solution of ordinary differential equations. *Mailing Add:* Dept Comput Sci Univ Md College Park MD 20742

ATCHLEY, ANTHONY A, PHYSICS, ACOUSTICS. *Current Pos:* assoc prof, 85-96, PROF & CHAIR, DEPT PHYSICS, NAVAL POST GRAD SCH, 96- *Personal Data:* b Lebanon, Jan 23, 57; c 2. *Educ:* Univ of the South, BS, 79; NMex Tech, MS, 82; Univ Miss, PhD(physics), 84. *Honors & Awards:* R Bruce Lindsay Award, 92. *Concurrent Pos:* F V Hunt postdoctoral fel, 85. *Mem:* Am Phys Soc; fel Acoust Soc Am; Am Asn Physics Teachers. *Res:* Thermoacoustics heat transport. *Mailing Add:* Dept Physics Naval Post Grad Sch Monterey CA 93943

ATCHLEY, BILL LEE, ENGINEERING MECHANICS. *Current Pos:* PRES, SCH ENG, CLEMSON UNIV, 79- *Personal Data:* b Cape Girardeau, Mo; m 52; c 3. *Educ:* Univ Mo-Rolla, BS, 57, MS, 59; Tex A&M Univ, PhD(struct mech), 65. *Prof Exp:* From instr to prof eng mech, Univ Mo-Rolla, 57-75, dir centennial events, 69-75, asst dean eng, 68-70, assoc dean, 70-75; dean & prof mech engr & mech, Col Eng, WVa Univ, 75-79. *Mem:* Am Soc Eng Educ; Am Soc Civil Engrs; Nat Soc Prof Engrs; Sigma Xi. *Res:* Dynamic properties of engineering materials and the behavior of structures under dynamic loadings. *Mailing Add:* 1 University Plaza Cape Girardeau MO 63701

ATCHLEY, WILLIAM REID, QUANTITATIVE GENETICS, DEVELOPMENTAL GENETICS. *Current Pos:* PROF GENETICS & HEAD DEPT & PROF STATIST, NC STATE UNIV, 86- *Personal Data:* b Stilwell, Okla, Sept 6, 42; m 64; c 2. *Educ:* Eastern NMex Univ, BS, 64; Univ Kans, MS, 66, PhD(entom), 69. *Prof Exp:* Teaching asst entom, Univ Kans, 64-66, NSF trainee systs & evolutionary biol, 66-69, vis asst prof entom, 70-71; from asst prof to assoc prof biol sci & statist, Tex Tech Univ, 71-77; from assoc prof to prof genetics & entom, Univ Wis-Madison, 77-86. *Concurrent Pos:* Fulbright scholar, Dept Genetics, Melbourne, 69-70; NIH fel, Dept Med Genetics, Univ Wis, 76-77; mem adv panel, NSF Syst Biol Prog, 77-81; res fel, Dept Pop Bio, Australian Nat Univ, 79-81. *Mem:* Soc Syst Zool; Soc Study Evolution; Am Soc Naturalists; Genetic Soc; fel AAAS; Soc Study Evolution; Soc Syst Zool; Am Naturalist (vpres, 87). *Res:* The origin of genetic variability during ontogeny; genetic aspects of growth and morphogenesis; the evolution of developmental processes; the evolutionary aspects of maternal effects. *Mailing Add:* Dept Genetics NC State Univ Box 7614 Raleigh NC 27695-0001

ATEMA, JELLE, SENSORY PHYSIOLOGY. *Current Pos:* assoc prof, 74-84, PROF, 84-, DIR, MARINE PROG, BOSTON UNIV, 90- *Personal Data:* b Deventer, Neth, Dec 9, 40. *Educ:* Univ Utrecht, Drs, 66; Univ Mich, PhD(biol), 69. *Prof Exp:* Res assoc, Med Sch & Sch Natural Resources, Univ Mich, 66-70; asst scientist, Woods Hole Oceanog Inst, 70-74. *Concurrent Pos:* Res assoc, Univ Hawaii, 76-77; vis prof, Univ Regensburg, WGer, 79-80; trustee, Marine Biol Lab, Woods Hole. *Mem:* Fel AAAS; Am Soc Zoologists; Animal Behav Soc; Soc Neurosci; Asn Chemoreception Sci; Crustacean Soc. *Res:* Neurophysiological and behavioral function of chemoreceptors in aquatic invertebrates and fish, their behavioral and chemical ecology and the effects of pollutants on behavior and chemoreception; physics of odor dispersal; pheromones. *Mailing Add:* Dept Biol Boston Univ Two Cummington St Boston MA 02215-2425

ATEN, CARL FAUST, JR, PHYSICAL CHEMISTRY. *Current Pos:* from asst prof to assoc prof, 62-72, PROF PHYS CHEM, HOBART & WILLIAM SMITH COLS, 72- *Personal Data:* b Lorain, Ohio, Aug 15, 32; m 55; c 4. *Educ:* Col Wooster, BA, 54; Brown Univ, PhD(phys chem), 59. *Prof Exp:* Chemist, Texaco, Inc, NY, 58-60; asst chem kinetics in shock tubes, Cornell Univ, 60-62. *Mem:* Am Chem Soc. *Res:* Agricultural and food chemistry; analysis of pesticide residues. *Mailing Add:* Hobart Col Geneva NY 14456-3191

ATENCIO, ALONZO C, BIOCHEMISTRY. *Current Pos:* ASST DEAN & ASST PROF BIOCHEM, SCH MED, UNIV NEW MEX, 70- *Personal Data:* b Ortiz, Colo, June 24, 29; m 53; c 5. *Educ:* Univ Colo, Boulder, BA, 58; Univ Colo, Denver, MS, 64, PhD(med), 67. *Prof Exp:* Res technician, Sch Med, Univ Colo, Denver, 58-67. *Concurrent Pos:* NIH fel chem, Northwestern Univ, 67-70. *Mem:* AAAS; Am Chem Soc; Am Heart Asn; Am Physiol Soc; Int Soc Thrombosis & Haemostasis. *Res:* Hormonal control of protein biosynthesis in mammals using the fibrinogen system as a model. *Mailing Add:* Dept Biochem Univ NMex Sch Med 915 Stanford NE Albuquerque NM 87106

ATERMAN, KURT, PEDIATRIC & EXPERIMENTAL PATHOLOGY. *Current Pos:* RETIRED. *Personal Data:* b Bielitz, Sept 9, 13; m 55, Rita Lawrence; c Robert, Paul & Peter. *Educ:* Charles Univ, Prague, MD, 38; Queen's Univ Belfast, MB & BCh(hons), 42, DSc, 65; Conjoint Bd, London, DCH, 43; Univ Birmingham, PhD, 59; FRC Path. *Prof Exp:* Sr lectr, Univ Birmingham, 50-58; assoc prof path, Dalhousie Univ, 58-61; prof, Woman's Med Col Pa, 61-63, State Univ NY, Buffalo & Children's Hosp, 63-67; prof path, Dalhousie Univ & I W Killiam Hosp Children, 67-79; dir, Regional Lab, Dr Everett Chalmers Hosp, NB, Can, 79-86. *Concurrent Pos:* Masaryk Found Stipendium, Commonwealth fel, Harvard & Univ Chicago. *Mem:* Am Asn Path & Bact; Am Soc Exp Path; Path Soc Gt Brit & Ireland; Ger Asn Path; Can Asn Path; Ger Histochem Soc; hon mem Ger Soc Path. *Res:* Experimental pathology of liver; history of medicine. *Mailing Add:* 5737 Southwood Dr Halifax NS B3H 1E6 Can

ATHANASIOU, KYRIACOS A, ARTICULAR CARTILAGE HEALING, CYTOMECHANICS. *Current Pos:* asst prof mech eng, 89-94, asst prof orthop, Health Sci Ctr, 89-94, DIR, ORTHOP BIOMECH LAB, UNIV TEX, SAN ANTONIO, 89-, ASSOC PROF, ORTHOP DEPT, UNIV TEX HEALTH SCI CTR, 94- *Personal Data:* b Larnaca, Cyprus, Aug 1, 60; Cyprus & US citizen; m 93, Kiley Crill. *Educ:* NY Inst Technol, BS, 84; Columbia Univ, MS, 85, PhM, 88, PhD(mecheng), 89. *Honors & Awards:* Young Scientist Award, Am Soc Biomech, 92; William J Stickel Gold Award Res, Am Podiatric Med Asn, 93. *Concurrent Pos:* Adj asst prof orthop, Audie L Murphy Mem Vet Admin Hosp, 90-; consult, Lifequest, Inc, 89, Biodynamics, Res Corp & Osteobiologics, Inc, 93-; adj asst prof biomed eng, Univ Tex, Austin, 91-; US nat deleg, 4th China-Japan US Conf Biomech, 95. *Mem:* Orthop Res Soc; Am Soc Mech Engrs; Am Soc Biomech; Biomed Eng Soc; Cyprus Asn Prof Engrs; Cyprus Soc Biomed Eng & Med Physics. *Res:* New cartilage repair processes are designed using a biodegradable carrier of bioactive agents in order to achieve biological resurfacing of large articular cartilage defects; design of diagnostic tools necessary to characterize the state of health of articular cartilage. *Mailing Add:* Dept Orthop UTHSCSA 7703 Floyd Curl Dr San Antonio TX 78284-7774

ATHANASSIADES, THOMAS J, IMMUNOPATHOLOGY. *Current Pos:* ASST PROF PATH, DOWNSTATE MED CTR, STATE UNIV NY, 65- *Educ:* Tulane Med Sch, MD, 60. *Mailing Add:* Dept Path SUNY Health Sci Ctr 450 Clarkson Ave Brooklyn NY 11203-2012

ATHANS, MICHAEL, ELECTRICAL ENGINEERING, CONTROL DESIGN. *Current Pos:* PROF ELEC ENG, MASS INST TECHNOL, 73-; CONSULT, ALPHATECH INC, 79- *Personal Data:* b Drama, Greece, May 3, 37; US citizen. *Educ:* Univ Calif, Berkeley, BS, 58, MS, 59, PhD(eng), 61. *Honors & Awards:* Eckman Award, 64; Frederick Terman Educ Award, Inst Elec & Electronics Engrs, 69. *Prof Exp:* Consult, 60-61, mem staff, 61-64, lectr, 63-64, from asst prof to assoc prof, 64-73, consult, Lincoln Lab, 64-76, dir lab info & decision systs, Mass Inst Technol, 74-81. *Concurrent Pos:* Ford Found fel, Mass Inst Technol, 64-66; consult, Bolt, Berannek & Newman, 66-68, Systs Control, Inc, 68-76, Army Mat Command, 68-74, Hamilton Standard, 68-70, Anal Sci Corp, 75-79 & Gen Motors Res Labs, 76; chmn bd, Alphatech, 78-; assoc ed, Automatica. *Mem:* Fel Inst Elec & Electronics Engrs; Sigma Xi. *Res:* Design of control systems; theory and application of optimal control; command-control and communication systems. *Mailing Add:* Dept Elec Eng Mass Inst Technol Cambridge MA 02139

ATHAR, MOHAMMED AQUEEL, MEDICAL MICROBIOLOGY, PUBLIC HEALTH. *Current Pos:* MICROBIOLOGIST, CALGARY DIAG LABS, 93- *Personal Data:* b Lucknow, India, Mar 9, 39; Can citizen; m 65, Ansa Ahmed; c Yasmin & Tanya. *Educ:* Univ Karachi, BS, 57, MS, 59; Univ Mich, MPH, 63; Univ London, PhD(med microbiol), 69. *Honors & Awards:* Fulbright Scholar, US, 62-65. *Prof Exp:* Lectr microbiol, D J Sci Col, Univ Karachi, 60-62; res asst clin microbiol, Med Ctr, Univ Mich, 63-65; bacteriologist, Holy Cross Hosp, Calgary, Can, 65-66, head, Microbiol Div, Dept Labs & Dir, Infection Control, 70-88; head microbiol lab, Calgary Dist Hosp Group, 88-93. *Concurrent Pos:* Res fel, Charing Cross Med Sch, London, Eng, 66-69; adj assoc prof microbiol, Fac Med, Univ, Univ Calgary, 70-; mem bd health, Calgary, 78-80. *Mem:* Am Soc Clin Pathologists; Am Soc Microbiol; Brit Inst Biol; Can Asn Clin Microbiol & Infectious Dis; Can Soc Int Health. *Res:* Effects of polyene antibiotics on Candida species; development of resistance in microorganisms to antibiotics; detection and control of legionella species in hopital air conditioners and hot water systems; control of hospital-associated infections. *Mailing Add:* 220 Varsity Estates Pl NW Calgary AB T3B 3B7 Can. *Fax:* 403-270-0690

ATHELSTAN, GARY THOMAS, PHYSICAL MEDICINE & REHABILITATION. *Current Pos:* from assoc prof to prof, 70-96, EMER PROF PHYS MED & REHAB & PSYCHOL, SCH MED, UNIV MINN, MINNEAPOLIS, 96-; INDEPENDENT DISABILITY EVAL CONSULT, 96- *Personal Data:* b Minneapolis, Minn, Dec 26, 36; m 60; c 2. *Educ:* Univ Minn, BA, 60, PhD(psychol), 66. *Honors & Awards:* Licht Award, Am Cong Rehab Med, 82. *Prof Exp:* Voc rehab counr, Minn Div Voc Rehab, 60-61; res psychologist, Am Rehab Found, 65-68; dir res, Occup Res Div, Inst Interdisciplinary Studies, 68-70. *Concurrent Pos:* Consult continuing educ, Am Acad Phys Med & Rehab, 69-70; sect ed, Arch Phys Med & Rehab, 74-81, assoc ed, 77-81; consult psychol, Vet Admin Hosp, Minneapolis, 73- *Mem:* Am Psychol Asn. *Res:* Development of psychosocial outcome criteria in rehabilitation; psychosocial factors related to rehabilitation success; improved methods to select, train and utilize health professionals. *Mailing Add:* 719 Fifth Ave SE Minneapolis MN 55414

ATHENS, JOHN WILLIAM, INTERNAL MEDICINE, HEMATOLOGY. *Current Pos:* RETIRED. *Personal Data:* b Buhl, Minn, Oct 2, 23; m 49; c 3. *Educ:* Univ Mich, BA, 45; Johns Hopkins Univ, MD, 48; Am Bd Internal Med, dipl. *Prof Exp:* Intern med, Peter Bent Brigham Hosp, Boston, Mass, 48-49; asst res, Univ Utah, 52-54, from res instr to asst res prof med, Col Med, 55-62, assoc prof, 62-68, prof med & head, Div Hemat & Oncol, 68- *Concurrent Pos:* AEC fel, Johns Hopkins Hosp, 49-50; Nat Cancer Inst res fel hemat, Col Med, Univ Utah, 54-56; dir outpatient dept, Salt Lake County Gen Hosp, 58-68. *Mem:* Am Fedn Clin Res; Am Col Physicians; Am Soc Clin Invest; Asn Am Physicians; Am Soc Hemat. *Res:* Leukocyte physiology; oncology. *Mailing Add:* 5735 S Oakdale Dr Holladay UT 84121

ATHERLY, ALAN G, GENETICS, MOLECULAR BIOLOGY. *Current Pos:* from asst prof to assoc prof, 68-70, chmn, 80-90, PROF GENETICS, IOWA STATE UNIV, 76- *Personal Data:* b Kalamazoo, Mich, Nov 19, 36; m 59, Mary Klitch; c Jill & Todd. *Educ:* Western Mich Univ, BS, 60; Univ NC, PhD(biochem), 65. *Prof Exp:* Fel, Dept Biol, Western Res Univ, 65-66 & Inst Molecular Biol, Univ Ore, 66-68. *Concurrent Pos:* Consult, Eni Chem Am, Princeton, NJ, 86; consult, Pioneer Hibred Int, Johnston, Iowa, 87, Biotechnol Res & Develop Corp, Peoria, Ill; ed, Genetica. *Mem:* Plant Molecular Biol Soc; Am Soc Microbiol. *Res:* Phytophthoria resistance in soybeans. *Mailing Add:* Dept Zool Iowa State Univ Ames IA 50011-2010. *Fax:* 515-294-0345; *E-Mail:* agatherl@iastate.edu

ATHERTON, DAVID L, APPLIED MAGNETICS, NON DESTRUCTIVE TESTING. *Current Pos:* assoc prof, 71-75, PROF PHYSICS, QUEEN'S UNIV, 75- *Personal Data:* b Chelsea, Eng, Feb 22, 35; m 64, Joanna M Banham; c Tamsin C & Heather J. *Educ:* Cambridge Univ, BA, 59, MA, 63. *Honors & Awards:* Ross Medal, Eng Inst Can, 79; Achievement Award, Am

Soc Non-Destructive Testing, 90. *Prof Exp:* Head superconductivity res, Ferranti-Packard Ltd, 59-71. *Concurrent Pos:* Leader, Can Magnetic Levitation Proj, 70-80; dir, Can Superconductor Cryogenics, 71-74; leader, Appl Magnetics Res Group, 80-; founding chmn, Can Asn Res Nondestructive Eval, 87-89. *Mem:* Fel Brit Inst Non-Destructive Testing; fel Royal Soc Can; Can Asn Physicists; Inst Elec & Electronics Engrs; Am Soc Nondestructive Testing; Am Phys Soc. *Res:* Non-Destructive inspection of pipelines, heat exchangers, pressure tubes and water supply pipes; author of over 200 publications on magnetics. *Mailing Add:* Dept Physics Queen's Univ Kingston ON K7L 3N6 Can. *Fax:* 613-545-6463

ATHERTON, ROBERT W, CHEMICAL ENGINEERING, SOFTWARE PATENTS. *Current Pos:* PRES, IN-MOTION TECHNOL, 85- *Personal Data:* b Auburn, Ala, Dec 20, 46; m 68; c 1. *Educ:* Rice Univ, BA, 69, MChE, 70; Stanford Univ, ChE, 72, PhD, 74. *Honors & Awards:* Donald P Eckman Award, Am Automatic Control Coun, 76. *Mem:* Am Inst Chem Engrs; Soc Indust & Appl Math; Sigma Xi. *Res:* Automatic control of manufacturing systems. *Mailing Add:* 1694 Miller Ave Los Altos CA 94024

ATHEY, ROBERT DOUGLAS, JR, COLLOID SCIENCE. *Current Pos:* CONSULT, ATHEY TECHNOL, 82- *Personal Data:* b Washington, DC, Aug 27, 36; m 58, 81, Patricia Blankenship; c Elizabeth (Jorgenson), Carol (Athey) & Jane (Satryan). *Educ:* Univ Md, BS, 64; Univ Del, PhD(org chem), 74. *Prof Exp:* Res chemist, Int Latex & Chem Corp, 64-67; sr res chemist, Scott Paper Co, 67-71 & Gen Tire & Rubber Co, 73-77; mgr proj res, Mellon Inst, 77-80; res assoc, Swedlow, Inc, 80-82. *Concurrent Pos:* Instr, Calif State Univ, Fullerton, 81-82, Univ Calif, Berkeley, 83-86 & Calif Polytech State Univ, 91. *Mem:* Am Chem Soc; Sigma Xi; Fedn Soc Coating Technol; Tech Asn Pulp & Paper Indust; Computer Press Asn. *Res:* Tailor-making polymers and formulating through use of organic and colloid chemistry, to assure the polymers utility as coating, adhesives or structural components; expert witness in trade secrets 657 product liability. *Mailing Add:* Athey Technol Drawer 7 El Cerrito CA 94530-0007. *Fax:* 510-528-3303

ATHEY, ROBERT JACKSON, ORGANIC CHEMISTRY. *Current Pos:* RETIRED. *Personal Data:* b Washington, DC, Mar 7, 25; m 49; c 3. *Educ:* Ga Inst Technol, BS, 48, MS, 50; Univ Wis, PhD(org chem), 54. *Prof Exp:* res chemist, E I du Pont de Nemours & Co, 43-86. *Mem:* Am Chem Soc. *Res:* Spectral investigation of nitryl chloride; preparation of morphine analogs; rubber chemistry; isocyanate chemistry; urethane polymers; fluoro elastomers. *Mailing Add:* 1107 Crestover Rd Graylyn Crest Wilmington DE 19803-3308

ATHOW, KIRK LELAND, PLANT PATHOLOGY. *Current Pos:* RETIRED. *Personal Data:* b Tacoma, Wash, Jan 22, 20; m 51. *Educ:* State Col Wash, BSA, 46; Purdue Univ, MS, 48, PhD(plant path), 51. *Prof Exp:* Instr plant path, Purdue Univ, West Lafayette, 49-51, asst plant pathologist, 51-56, from assoc prof bot & plant path, 56-90. *Concurrent Pos:* Mem team, Purdue-Brazilian Proj, 66-68; USAID consult, Brazil, 70, 71, 72 & 73. *Mem:* Am Phytopath Soc. *Res:* Forage crop and soybean diseases; seed treatment; disease resistance. *Mailing Add:* 1216 Farallone Ave Tacoma WA 98466

ATHREYA, KRISHNA BALASUNDARAM, PROBABILITY & STOCHASTIC PROCESSES, MATHEMATICAL STATISTICS. *Current Pos:* PROF MATH, IOWA STATE UNIV, 80- *Personal Data:* b Madras, India, Dec 12, 39; c 3. *Educ:* Madras Univ, India, BA, 59; Stanford Univ, PhD(math), 67. *Prof Exp:* From asst prof to assoc prof math, Univ Wis-Madison, 68-71; prof math, Indian Inst Sci, Bangalore, 71-79. *Concurrent Pos:* Assoc ed, Zetschrift fur Wahrscheinlihkeits Theorie, 78- & Letters Probability & Statist, 81-; vis prof, Univ Wis-Madison & Milwaukee, Univ Copenhagen & Australian Nat Univ. *Mem:* Fel Inst Math; fel Indian Acad Sci; fel Inst Math Statist. *Res:* Limit theorems for markov chains, mathematical statistics, branching processes, integral equations, stochastic modelling in applied areas. *Mailing Add:* 3219 Ross Rd Ames IA 50014

ATIA, ALI EZZ ELDIN, MICROWAVE ENGINEERING. *Current Pos:* mem tech staff, COMSAT Labs, 69-76, sr scientist, 76-80, sr dir, Satelite Syst Design, COMSAT Corp, 80-88, VPRES, SYSTS ENG, COMSAT SYSTS DIV, 88- *Personal Data:* b Cairo, Egypt, Aug 10, 41; US citizen; m 64; c 3. *Educ:* Ain Shams Univ, Cairo, MSc, 62; Univ Calif, Berkeley, PhD, 69. *Prof Exp:* Asst prof, Dept Elec Eng & Comput Sci, Univ Calif, Berkeley, 68-69. *Mem:* Fel Inst Elec & Electronics Engrs; Sigma Xi; Am Inst Aeronaut & Astronaut. *Res:* Microwave circuits; satellite communications systems; microwave filters and multiplexers; computer aided design. *Mailing Add:* 10841 Willow Run Ct Potomac MD 20854-2581

ATINMO, TOLA, nursing, for more information see previous edition

ATIYAH, MICHAEL FRANCIS, MATHEMATICS. *Current Pos:* RETIRED. *Personal Data:* b London, Eng, Apr 22, 29; m 55, Lily J Brown; c John, David & Robin. *Educ:* Trinity Col, Cambridge, BA, 52, PhD, 55. *Hon Degrees:* DSc, Warwick & Bonn, 68, Univ Durham, 77, Univ Dublin, Univ Chicago & Univ Cambridge. *Honors & Awards:* Fields Medal, Int Cong Mathematicians, Moscow, 66; DeMorgan Medal, London Math Soc, 80; Feltrinelli Prize, Accademia Nazionale dei Lincei, 82; King Faisal Found Int Prize Sci, 87, Order of Merit, 93; Benjamin Franklin Medal, Am Philos Soc, 93. *Prof Exp:* Fel, Trinity Col, Cambridge, 54-58, hon fel, 76; lectr & fel, Penbroke Col, Cambridge, 58-61, hon fel, 83; reader, Oxford Univ 61-63, Savilian prof geom, 63-69, Royal Soc res prof, & fel, St Catherines Col, 73-90; dir, Isaac Newton Inst Math Sci, Cambridge, 90-96. *Concurrent Pos:* Fel, Commonwealth Fund, Princeton, 55-56; prof, Inst Advan Study, 69-72. *Mem:* foreign mem Nat Acad Sci; foreign mem Am Acad Arts & Sci; hon mem Royal Acad Eng; fel Royal Soc (pres, 90-95); foreign mem Indian Nat Sci Acad; foreign mem Swedish Royal Acad; foreign mem Ukranian Acad Scis; foreign mem Australian Acad Sci; Int Math Union; Acad Sci; Russian Acad Sci; foreign mem Am Philos Soc. *Res:* k-theory; commutative algebra; contributed numerous articles to math journals. *Mailing Add:* Trinity Col Masters Lodge Cambridge CB2 1TQ England

ATKIN, AUDREY LYNN, REGULATION OF GENE EXPRESSION, MRNA STABILITY. *Current Pos:* ASST PROF MOLECULAR GENETICS, UNIV NEBR, 96- *Personal Data:* m, James A Williams. *Educ:* Univ Guelph, BS, 85; Univ Alta, PhD(genetics), 92. *Prof Exp:* Res asst, Nat Res Coun Can, 85, Tech Ctr, Molson Breweries Can Ltd, 85; postdoctoral fel, Univ Wis-Madison, 91-96. *Concurrent Pos:* Grad fac fel, Univ Nebr, 96, grad fac mem, 96. *Mem:* Genetics Soc Am; Ribonucleic Acid Soc; AAAS. *Res:* mRNA turnover is an important control point for the regulation of gene expression; nonsense-mediated mRNA decay pathway of the yeast Saccharomyces cerevisiae is an example of a mRNA decay pathway that recognizes and targets special mRNA's for accelerated decay; using pathway as a model system to determine how mRNA's are recognized and targeted for specialized decay. *Mailing Add:* E146 Beadle Ctr Univ Nebr Lincoln NE 68588-0666. *Fax:* 402-472-8722; *E-Mail:* aatkin@unlinfo.unl.edu

ATKIN, J MYRON, science education, science policy, for more information see previous edition

ATKIN, RUPERT LLOYD, INDUSTRIAL & MANUFACTURING ENGINEERING. *Current Pos:* RETIRED. *Personal Data:* b Madison, Ohio, June 7, 18; m 41, Anne Richards; c Terri E, Gregory L (deceased), Valerie L & William D. *Educ:* Ohio State Univ, BME, 41. *Hon Degrees:* DSc, Ohio State Univ, 79. *Honors & Awards:* Engr of Distinction, Engrs Joint Coun; Benjamin G Lamme Medal, Col Eng, Ohio State Univ, 76. *Prof Exp:* With Kelsey-Hayes Co, Mich, 46-64, chief engr, 58-64; mem staff, TRW Inc, 64-74, dir eng chassis components, 74-76, vpres eng, automotive worldwide chassis components, 76-83; dir, Davco Mfg Co, 83-90; dir, Cogsdill Tool Prod Inc, 84-93; dir, Int Tech Group Inc, 84-95. *Concurrent Pos:* Mem, res adv bd, Col Eng, Univ Detroit, 60-65; mem, indust comt, Col Eng, Univ Mich, 65-83, chmn, 75-77; mem, indust adv comt, Mech Eng Dept, Col Eng, Ohio State Univ, 76-83, mem, steering comt, 79-83. *Mem:* Nat Acad Eng; fel Soc Automotive Engrs. *Res:* Design and/or engineering direction on first vacuum power brake unit, first ventilated rotor disc brake and first power rack & pinion steering gear produced for American cars. *Mailing Add:* 1715 N River Rd Unit 50 St Clair MI 48079

ATKINS, CHARLES GILMORE, MICROBIAL GENETICS. *Current Pos:* from asst prof to assoc prof genetics & microbiol, Ohio Univ, 69-77, assoc prof zool & microbiol, 74-90, assoc dean, Col Osteop Med, 76-90, ASSOC PROF BIOMED SCI, OHIO UNIV, 90- *Personal Data:* b Stambaugh, Mich, July 4, 39; div; c Robert H, Karla M & James C. *Educ:* Albion Col, BA, 61; Eastern Mich Univ, MS, 63; NC State Univ, PhD(genetics), 69. *Prof Exp:* Teaching asst biol, Eastern Mich Univ, 62-63; instr biol, Coe Col, 63-66. *Concurrent Pos:* Lectr, Cornell Col, 64-65; dir training prog, Appalachian Life Sci Col, 72-74; clin lab officer, 291st US Army Hosp, 81-92; active duty, US Army, Gulf War, 91. *Mem:* AAAS; Genetics Soc Am; Am Soc Human Genetics; Sigma Xi. *Res:* Transductional studies and biochemical analysis of Salmonella typhimurium, Salmonella montevideo and hybrids of these species, with emphasis on the isoleucine-valine biosynthetic pathway; recombination in T-even bacteriophage; medical education, preclinical. *Mailing Add:* 356 Irvine Hall Ohio Univ Athens OH 45701. *Fax:* 740-593-0300

ATKINS, DAVID LYNN, VERTEBRATE ANATOMY, NEUROANATOMY. *Current Pos:* asst prof, 70-75, assoc prof zool, 75-81, PROF BIOL, GEORGE WASHINGTON UNIV, 81- *Personal Data:* b Wichita Falls, Tex, July 12, 35; m 59. *Educ:* Univ Tex, Austin, BA, 57; ETex State Univ, MA, 63; Tex A&M Univ, PhD(comp neuroanat), 70. *Prof Exp:* Teacher high schs, Tex, 57-59 & 61-62; asst prof zool, Tarleton State Col, 65-67. *Mem:* Am Soc Zool; Sigma Xi. *Res:* Comparative neuroanatomy; systematics; comparative ontogeny and evolution of the mammalian cerebellum, particularly related to the phylogeny of the major taxa. *Mailing Add:* 2608 Sigmona St Falls Church VA 22046-2727

ATKINS, DON CARLOS, JR, INDUSTRIAL CHEMISTRY. *Current Pos:* PRES, D C ATKINS & SON, 75-, PRES, CONTAINMENT CORP, 87-, VPRES, RESIN SUPPORT SYSTS, 85- *Personal Data:* b Denver, Colo, Apr 11, 21; m 47; c 2. *Educ:* Univ Calif, Los Angeles, BA, 43, MS, 48; Chapman Col, DSc, 76. *Honors & Awards:* Honor Scroll Award, Am Inst Chemists, 74. *Prof Exp:* Tech dir, US Chem Milling Corp, 57-62; vpres, Chem & Aerospace Prod, Inc, 62-64; vpres, Wilco Prod, Inc, 64-68; exec vpres, Sanitek Prod, Inc, 68-73; lab dir non-foods chem specialties, Hunt-Wesson Foods, 73-75. *Concurrent Pos:* Staff consult, Solder Removal Co, 70-, Inst Tricology, Inc, 72-, Chemrite Corp, 75- & Clorox Co, 75- *Mem:* Am Inst Chemists; Am Chem Soc; Am Soc Metals; Am Electroplater Soc; Sigma Xi; Am Oil Chemists Soc; Soc Cosmetic Chemists. *Res:* Interaction of chemicals to surfaces with particular emphasis on chemical specialty compounds for consumer and industrial applications; development of cleaning materials, coatings and cosmetics; special expertise in chemical milling and plating of metals onto plastics. *Mailing Add:* 11282 Foster Rd Los Alamitos CA 90720-2922

ATKINS, ELISHA, INTERNAL MEDICINE. *Current Pos:* from asst prof to prof, 55-85, EMER PROF MED, YALE UNIV, 85- *Personal Data:* b Belmont, Mass, Nov 16, 20; m 44; c 5. *Educ:* Harvard Univ, AB, 42; Univ Rochester, MD, 50. *Honors & Awards:* Bristol Award, Infectious Dis Soc Am, 85. *Prof Exp:* From intern to asst resident, Barnes Hosp, 50-52; instr med, Wash Univ, 54-55. *Concurrent Pos:* Res fel infectious dis, Wash Univ, 52-54; USPHS res grant, 57-; attend physician, Yale-New Haven Hosp, Conn, 55-; consult, Vet Admin Hosp, West Haven, Conn, 55-; sabbatical, Radcliffe Infirmary, Eng, 62-63, Scripps Clin & Res Found, Calif, 69-70 & Dept Immunol, Yale Univ, 78-79; master, Saybrook Col, Yale Univ, 75-85; exec dir, Habitat Inst Environ, Belmont, Mass, 85- *Mem:* Am Soc Clin Invest; Asn Am Physicians; Infectious Dis Soc Am; Sigma Xi. *Res:* Pathogenesis of fever, especially experimental fevers induced by microbial agents and antigens in specifically sensitized animals. *Mailing Add:* 44 Juniper Rd Belmont MA 02178

ATKINS, FERREL, MATHEMATICS. *Current Pos:* from asst prof to prof, 58-88, EMER PROF MATH, EASTERN ILL UNIV, 88- *Personal Data:* b West York, Ill, Feb 15, 24; m 55, Virginia Hogge; c Alden L & Anne F (Guettler). *Educ:* Eastern Ill State Col, BS, 45; Univ Ill, MS, 46; Univ Ky, PhD(math), 50. *Prof Exp:* Asst math, Univ Ill, 45-46; instr math, Univ Ky, 46-50; asst prof, Bowling Green State Univ, 50-52; from asst prof to assoc prof math, Univ Richmond, 52-58, chmn dept, 57-58. *Concurrent Pos:* NSF fac fel, Stanford Univ, 64-65. *Mem:* Math Asn Am. *Res:* Computer sciences; analysis. *Mailing Add:* Dept Math Eastern Ill Univ 600 Lincoln Ave Charleston IL 61920-3011. *E-Mail:* cfdfa@eiu.edu

ATKINS, GEORGE T(YNG), CHEMICAL ENGINEERING. *Current Pos:* RETIRED. *Personal Data:* b Dallas, Tex, Sept 25, 06; m 29, Frances Hann; c Frances (Gidley), Anselm, Robert & Joseph. *Educ:* Wash Univ, BS, 29. *Prof Exp:* Analytical chemist bur chem & soils, USDA, Tex, 29-30; chem engr tech serv, Humble Oil & Ref Co, 30-55, eng assoc, 56-59; consult chem engr, 59-70; partner, Atkins & McBride, Chem Engrs, 70-72, partner, Atkins, McBride & Owen, Chem Engrs, 72-82. *Mem:* AAAS. *Res:* Process design for oil refinery and petrochemical units; computer programs for physical properties in systems undergoing distillation. *Mailing Add:* 1704 California St Baytown TX 77520

ATKINS, HAROLD LEWIS, NUCLEAR MEDICINE, RADIOLOGY. *Current Pos:* from assoc scientist to scientist, 63-72, sr scientist, 72-79, RES COLLABR RADIOL NUCLEAR MED, BROOKHAVEN NAT LAB, 79- *Personal Data:* b Newark, NJ, Sept 24, 26; m 63, Beverly B Malkind; c Peter, Sue, Mathew & Michael. *Educ:* Yale Univ, BS, 48; Harvard Med Sch, MD, 52. *Honors & Awards:* Redway Award, Med Soc State NY, 79; Berson-Yelow Award, Soc Nuclear Med, 93. *Prof Exp:* Intern med, Grace-New Haven Hosp, 52-53; resident radiol, Hosp Univ Pa, 53-56; instr radiol, Sch Med, Yale Univ, 56-59; from instr to asst prof, Col Physicians & Surgeons, Columbia Univ, 59-63. *Concurrent Pos:* Am Cancer Soc fel, Hosp Univ Pa, 55-56 & Yale-New Haven Med Ctr, 56-57; from adj assoc prof to prof radiol & nuclear med, State Univ NY, Stony Brook, 68-; consult, USPHS Hosp, Staten Island, NY, 61-63, Vet Admin Hosp, Northport, 71- & St Charles Hosp, Port Jefferson, 71-93; prof radiol, Sch Med, State Univ NY, Stony Brook, 72-94, emer prof radiol, 94- *Mem:* Soc Nuclear Med (trustee, 72-76, 78-82, treas, 88-91); Radiol Soc NAm; fel Am Col Radiol. *Res:* Application of radiotracers to problems of renal transplants, gallbladder physiology and lungs; palliative treatment of pain from osseous metastases. *Mailing Add:* Med Dept Box 5000 Brookhaven Nat Lab Upton NY 11973-5000. *Fax:* 516-751-5307; *E-Mail:* atkins@mail.bnl.gov

ATKINS, HENRY PEARCE, MATHEMATICS. *Current Pos:* PROF MATH, UNIV RICHMOND, 58- *Personal Data:* b Birmingham, Ala, Jan 12, 15; m 41; c 2. *Educ:* Cornell Univ, AB, 36; Brown Univ, MSc, 37; Univ Rochester, PhD(math), 47. *Prof Exp:* Instr, Brown Univ, 38-39; asst, Univ Rochester, 39-42, from instr to assoc prof, 42-58, dean of men, 54-58. *Res:* Fractional derivatives of univalent functions and bounded functions. *Mailing Add:* 440 Lafayette Ave No A-214 Cincinnati OH 45220

ATKINS, JAMES LAWRENCE, NEPHROLOGY. *Current Pos:* ASOC PROF MED, F EDWARD HEBERT SCH MED, UNIFORMED SERV UNIV HEALTH SCI, 90- *Personal Data:* b York, Pa, Oct 10, 47; m 70; c 2. *Educ:* Univ Notre Dame, AB, 69; Univ Md, MD, 75, PhD, 78; Am Bd Internal Med, cert, 78, nephrology cert, 86. *Honors & Awards:* Leonard M Hummel Award for Excellence in Internal Med, 75. *Prof Exp:* Med intern, Univ Md Hosp, 75-76, med resident, 76-78, renal fel, 78-79; res fel, Lab Kidney & Electrolytes, NIH, 79-81, sr staff fel, 81-82. *Mem:* Fel Am Col Physicians; Am Fedn Clin Res; AAAS; Am Soc Nephrol; Int Soc Nephrol; Am Physiol Soc. *Res:* Rena physiology and causes of renal failure; hemorrhogic shock. *Mailing Add:* Dept Nephrol Walter Reed Army Inst Res Bldg 40 Rm 3029 Washington DC 20307-5100. *Fax:* 202-782-0703; *E-Mail:* col_james_atkins@wrsmtp-ccmail.army.mil

ATKINS, JASPARD HARVEY, PHYSICAL CHEMISTRY, ANALYTICAL CHEMISTRY. *Current Pos:* CONSULT, 87- *Personal Data:* b Boston, Mass, May 9, 26; m 54; c 4. *Educ:* Univ Mass, BS, 50; Rensselaer Polytech Inst, PhD(chem), 55. *Prof Exp:* Anal chemist, US Food & Drug Admin, 50-51; AEC res assoc, Rensselaer Polytech Inst, 53-56; sr scientist, Westinghouse Atomic Power Div, Bettis Atomic Power Lab, 56-57; Portland Cement Asn res fel, Nat Bur Standards, 57-59; proj mgr, Nat Res Corp, 59-61; group leader, Cabot Corp, 61-70, sr res assoc, 70-87. *Mem:* Am Chem Soc; Sigma Xi. *Res:* Physical chemistry measurement; gas-solid interfaces; vacuum techniques; gaseous kinetics; instrumentation. *Mailing Add:* 1536 High St Westwood MA 02090-3031

ATKINS, JOHN MARSHALL, MATHEMATICS. *Current Pos:* ASST PROF, WVA UNIV, 80- *Personal Data:* b Charleston, WVa, Mar 2, 41; m 68; c 1. *Educ:* Marshall Univ, BS, 65; WVa Univ, MA, 67, MS, 80; Univ Pittsburgh, PhD(math), 72. *Prof Exp:* Sr teaching fel math, Univ Pittsburgh, 68-73; asst prof math, Bethany Col, 73-80. *Mem:* Math Asn Am; Asn Comput Mach; Sigma Xi. *Mailing Add:* WVa Univ PO Box 6330 Morgantown WV 26506

ATKINS, MARVIN C(LEVELAND), PHYSICS, NUCLEAR ENGINEERING. *Current Pos:* CONSULT. *Personal Data:* b Ballinger, Tex, July 30, 31; m 55, Lois Doescher; c David & Nancy (Savoca). *Educ:* Agr & Mech Col, Tex, BS, 52; Univ Ill, MS, 53; Univ Mich, PhD(nuclear sci), 61. *Prof Exp:* Proj engr, Mat Lab, USAF, 53-57, group leader, Spec Weapons Ctr, 60-62, chief, Theoret Sect, 62-63, sr scientist, Weapons Lab, 63-64; chief, Energy Effects Sect, Res & Develop Div, Avco Corp, Mass, 64-66, asst mgr, Mat Sci Dept, Space Systs Div, 66-67, mgr, Eng Tech Dept, 67-68, dir environ sci, 68-70; asst to dep dir sci & technol, Defense Nuclear Agency, Washington, DC, 70-78, dep dir, 83-89; dir offensive & space syst, Off Undersecretary Defense for Res & Eng, 78-83; sr vpres qual rev, Sci Appln Int Corp, McLean, Va, 89-96. *Mem:* Am Nuclear Soc; Am Inst Aeronaut & Astronaut. *Res:* Shock hydrodynamics and effects; advanced materials; missile system engineering; radiation application and effects; research management. *Mailing Add:* 21779 Cove Lane Leonardtown MD 20650

ATKINS, PATRICK RILEY, ENVIRONMENTAL HEALTH ENGINEERING, ENVIRONMENTAL MANAGEMENT. *Current Pos:* mgr, 77-90, DIR ENVIRON AFFAIRS, ALUMINUM CO AM, 90- *Personal Data:* b Russellville, Ky, May 20, 42; m 65; c Lee Ann & John. *Educ:* Univ Ky, BS, 64; Stanford Univ, MS, 65, PhD(sanit eng), 68. *Prof Exp:* Asst prof civil eng, Univ Tex, Austin, 68-77. *Concurrent Pos:* Assoc adj prof, Dept Civil Eng & Grad Sch Pub Health, Univ Pittsburgh. *Mem:* Am Waste Mgt Asn; Am Soc Civil Engrs. *Res:* Air pollutant transport and dispersion; aerosol dynamics; nucleation; rainout and washout processes; air pollution control. *Mailing Add:* 1501 Alcoa Bldg Pittsburgh PA 15219

ATKINS, PAUL C, ALLERGY, IMMUNOLOGY. *Current Pos:* asst prof med, 74-80, ASSOC PROF MED, ALLERGY & IMMUNOL, SCH MED, UNIV PA, 80- *Personal Data:* b Yonkers, NY, Sept 27, 42; m 63; c 2. *Educ:* Syracuse Univ, BS, 63; NY Med Col, MD, 67; Am Bd Internal Med, cert, 74; Am Bd Allergy & Immunol, cert, 75. *Prof Exp:* Intern, Beth Israel Med Ctr, 67-68; fel allergy & immunol, Univ Pa Hosp, 70-72; chief resident med, Metrop Hosp, NY Med Col, 68-70; allergist & internist med, Madigan Army Med Ctr, 72-74. *Concurrent Pos:* Chief, Allergy & Immunology Clin, Univ Pa Hosp, 74-; consult, Vet Admin Hosp, Philadelphia, 74- *Mem:* Am Acad Allergy; Am Fedn Clin Res; Am Thoracic Soc; Am Col Physicians. *Res:* Allergy and immunology; cellular inflammatory response and mediators released during immediate hypersensitivity reactions in man. *Mailing Add:* Univ Hosp Pa 3rd Fl Silverstein Pavilion 3400 Spruce St Suite B Philadelphia PA 19104

ATKINS, RICHARD ELTON, AGRONOMY. *Current Pos:* RETIRED. *Personal Data:* b Corning, Kans, Feb 10, 19; m 59; c 3. *Educ:* Kans State Univ, BS, 41; Iowa State Univ, MS, 42, PhD(crop breeding), 48. *Prof Exp:* Res asst prof agron, Iowa State Univ, 48-50, from assoc prof to prof, 50-89. *Mem:* Am Soc Agron; Crop Sci Soc Am. *Res:* Breeding of improved varieties of small grains and grain sorghum for agronomic and disease characters and allied genetic and production studies; crop breeding. *Mailing Add:* 1225 Wisconsin Ave Ames IA 50014

ATKINS, ROBERT CHARLES, ORGANIC CHEMISTRY, HAZARDOUS MATERIALS. *Current Pos:* from asst prof to assoc prof, 71-88, PROF CHEM, JAMES MADISON UNIV, 88- *Personal Data:* b Norwood, Mass, Aug 19, 44; m 67, Mary Burke; c David & Maureen. *Educ:* Mass Inst Technol, SB, 66; Univ Wis-Madison, PhD(org chem), 70. *Prof Exp:* Assoc org chem, Columbia Univ, 70-71. *Concurrent Pos:* NIH fel, 70-71; vis fel, Nat Cancer Inst, 81. *Mem:* Am Chem Soc. *Res:* Pyrolytic reactions. *Mailing Add:* Dept Chem James Madison Univ Harrisonburg VA 22807-0002

ATKINS, ROBERT W, PSYCHIATRY, PSYCHOANALYSIS. *Current Pos:* RETIRED. *Personal Data:* b Belmont, Mass, Nov 30, 17; m 40; c 5. *Educ:* Yale Univ, BA, 40; Harvard Univ, MD, 43. *Prof Exp:* Dir, Community Ment Health Ctr Div, Dept Psychiat, Sch Med & Dent, Univ Rochester & Strong Mem Hosp, 68-72, prof psychiat, 70-80; spec consult, Vet Admin Hosp, Canandaigua, NY, 80-86. *Mem:* Fel Am Psychiat Asn. *Res:* Mental illness and unemployment; psychological effects of induced abortion and surgical sterilization in men and women; cerebral metabolic disturbances in hypothyroidism; conceptual thinking in psychiatric patients. *Mailing Add:* 260 Crittenden Blvd Rochester NY 14642

ATKINS, RONALD LEROY, organic chemistry, for more information see previous edition

ATKINS, WILLIAM M, BIOCHEMISTRY. *Current Pos:* ASST PROF, DEPT MED CHEM, UNIV WASH, SEATTLE, 91- *Educ:* Col William & Mary, BS, 80; Harvard Univ, AM, 82; Univ Ill, Urbana, PhD(biochem), 88. *Prof Exp:* NIH postdoctoral fel chem, Pa State Univ, 88-91. *Mem:* Fedn Am Socs Exp Biol. *Res:* Biophysical and biotechnical approaches to understand structure-function relationships in the mechanism and regulation of biological macromolecules; author of 20 technical publications. *Mailing Add:* Dept Med Chem Univ Wash BG-20 Seattle WA 98195

ATKINSON, ARTHUR JOHN, JR, CLINICAL PHARMACOLOGY. *Current Pos:* from asst prof to assoc prof, 70-76, PROF PHARMACOL & MED, MED SCH, NORTHWESTERN UNIV, 76- *Personal Data:* b Chicago, Ill, Mar 21, 38; m 50. *Educ:* Harvard Univ, AB, 59; Cornell Univ, MD, 63. *Honors & Awards:* Rawls Palmer Award, Am Soc Clin Pharmacol & Therapeut, 83; Herry Gold Award, Am Soc Pharmacol & Exp Therapeut, 89. *Prof Exp:* Intern, internal med, Mass Gen Hosp, 63-64, resident, 64-65; clin assoc, Nat Inst Allergy & Infectious Dis, NIH, 65-67; chief resident internal med, Passavant Mem Hosp, 67-68; fel clin pharmacol, Univ Cincinnati, 68-69, asst prof, 69; vis scientist, Karolinska Inst, 70. *Concurrent Pos:* Mem pharmacol toxicol prog comt, Nat Inst Gen Med Sci, NIH, 75-79, chmn, pharmacol sci prog comt, 84-86. *Mem:* Fel Am Col Physicians; Am Soc Pharmacol & Exp Therapeut; Asn Am Physicians; Am Soc Clin Pharmacol & Therapeut. *Res:* Clinical pharmacokinetics; drug metabolism; drug development. *Mailing Add:* Dept Pharmacol & Med Med Sch Northwestern Univ Chicago IL 60611

ATKINSON, BARBARA, CYTOPATHOLOGY, FLOW CYTOMETRY. *Current Pos:* DIR CYTOPATH, UNIV PA, 78-, ASSOC PROF PATH, 85-; ANNENBERG DEAN, M C P HAHNEMANN SCH MED, ALLEGHENY UNIV HEALTH SCI. *Educ:* Jefferson Univ, MD, 74. *Mem:* Inst Med-Nat Acad Sci. *Mailing Add:* 2900 Queen Lane Philadelphia PA 19129

ATKINSON, BURR GERVAIS, BIOCHEMISTRY, DEVELOPMENTAL BIOLOGY. *Current Pos:* from asst prof to assoc prof, 72-80, PROF ZOOL, UNIV WESTERN ONT, 80-, CHMN GENETICS, 81- *Personal Data:* b Elizabeth, NJ, Sept 17, 37; div; c 2. *Educ:* Ohio Univ, BA, 61; Univ Conn, PhD(biochem, biophys), 68. *Prof Exp:* NIH fel, Fla State Univ, 68-71, res assoc develop biochem, 71-72. *Concurrent Pos:* Lab instr, Marine Biol Labs, Woods Hole, 66-68, investr, 69; bd dir, Can Fedn Biol Sci. *Mem:* Sigma Xi; Am Soc Biol Chemists; Am Soc Cell Biol; Can Soc Cell Biol (secy, 85-); Can Fedn Biol Sci; Can Soc Genetics. *Res:* Nucleic acid biochemistry; hormone-induced synthesis of nucleic acids; tissue-specific proteins in development; tissue culture; proteins and nucleic acids of genetic machinery; molecular biology; gene expression. *Mailing Add:* Dept Zool Univ Western Ont London ON N6A 5B7 Can

ATKINSON, DALE B, AERONAUTICAL ENGINEERING. *Current Pos:* CONSULT, SURVIVABILITY & DAMAGE REPAIR, WASHINGTON. *Mailing Add:* 7703 Carrleigh Pkwy Springfield VA 22152-1305

ATKINSON, DANIEL EDWARD, BIOCHEMISTRY. *Current Pos:* from asst prof to prof, 52-91, EMER PROF CHEM, UNIV CALIF, LOS ANGELES, 91- *Personal Data:* b Pawnee City, Nebr, Apr 8, 21; m 48, Elsie Hemmingson; c Kristine, Owen, Joyce, Ellen & David. *Educ:* Univ Nebr, BS, 42; Iowa State Col, PhD(chem), 49. *Hon Degrees:* DSc, Univ Nebr, 75. *Prof Exp:* Res fel, Calif Inst Technol, 49-50; assoc plant physiologist, Argonne Nat Lab, 50-52. *Mem:* Am Chem Soc; Am Soc Microbiol; Am Soc Biol Chemists; Am Physiol Soc. *Res:* Metabolic regulation and correlation; properties of regulatory enzymes; energy metabolism; pH homeostasis. *Mailing Add:* 3123 Malcolm Ave Los Angeles CA 90034

ATKINSON, EDWARD NEELY, BIOMATHEMATICS. *Current Pos:* Res assoc, 81-84, ASST PROF, DEPT BIOMATH, M D ANDERSON HOSP, UNIV TEX, HOUSTON, 84- *Personal Data:* b Shreveport, La, Apr 29, 53; m 81. *Educ:* Rice Univ, BA, 75, MA & PhD(math sci), 81. *Mem:* Soc Indust & Appl Math; Am Math Soc; Am Statist Asn; Inst Math Statist; Biomet Soc. *Res:* Minimization of function whose evaluations are subject to stochastic error; mathematical modelling of neoplastic progression. *Mailing Add:* 1515 Holcombe Blvd Houston TX 77030

ATKINSON, EDWARD REDMOND, ORGANIC CHEMISTRY. *Current Pos:* INDUST CONSULT, 77- *Personal Data:* b Boston, Mass, Feb 15, 12; m 35, 44, Lorraine Crittendon; c Kathleen & Carol. *Educ:* Mass Inst Technol, BS, 33, PhD(org chem), 36. *Honors & Awards:* Henry A Hill Memorial Award, Am Chem Soc, 81. *Prof Exp:* Teaching fel chem, Mass Inst Technol, 33-36; instr org chem, Trinity Col, Conn, 36-38; from asst prof to assoc prof chem, Univ NH, 38-51; group leader, Dewey & Almy Chem Co, 51-57; sr chemist, Arthur D Little, Inc, 57-77. *Concurrent Pos:* Lectr, Northeastern Univ, 51-63 & Boston Univ, 64-65. *Mem:* Am Chem Soc; AAAS. *Res:* Diazonium compounds; history of chemistry; condensation polymers; antiradiation drugs; pharmaceuticals; biphenylene; chemical hazard evaluation. *Mailing Add:* 163 Gray St Amherst MA 01002-2105

ATKINSON, GEORGE FRANCIS, INSTRUMENTATION SPECTROELECTROCHEMISTRY. *Current Pos:* from lectr to assoc prof, 61-94, EMER PROF CHEM, UNIV WATERLOO, 94- *Personal Data:* b Toronto, Ont, Feb 25, 32; m 61, Lorraine J McGowan; c Sheila J, Arwen C, James C & David G. *Educ:* Univ Toronto, BA, 53, MA, 54, PhD(chem), 60; FRSC(UK), 72; FCIC, 78. *Prof Exp:* Lectr chem, Univ Western Ont, 60-61. *Concurrent Pos:* Mem sci study comt, Ont Curric Inst, 64-68; vis prof, Univ Southampton, 69-70 & 75-76, Univ E Anglia, 88-89. *Mem:* Am Chem Soc; Brit Soc Res Higher Educ; Chem Inst Can; Royal Soc Chem. *Res:* Applications of computers in analysis; instrumentation for electroanalytical and spectrophotometric methods; electrochemistry; continuous analysis and control of process streams; chemical education. *Mailing Add:* Dept Chem Univ Waterloo Waterloo ON N2L 3G1 Can. *E-Mail:* gatkinson@chemistry.watstar.uwaterloo.ca

ATKINSON, GORDON, PHYSICAL CHEMISTRY, INORGANIC CHEMISTRY. *Current Pos:* chmn dept, 71-74, grad dean, 74-78, PROF CHEM, UNIV OKLA, NORMAN, 71- *Personal Data:* b Brooklyn, NY, Aug 29, 30; m 76; c 4. *Educ:* Lehigh Univ, BS, 52; Iowa State Col, PhD(chem), 56. *Prof Exp:* Res assoc, Ames Lab, US AEC, 56-57; instr chem, Univ Mich, 57-61; from asst prof to prof, Univ Md, College Park, 61-71. *Concurrent Pos:* Fulbright Fel, 70-71; Regent's award res, 82. *Mem:* AAAS; Am Chem Soc; fel Am Inst Chem; fel NY Acad Sci. *Res:* Electrolyte solutions; conductance; ultrasonic absorption in solution; kinetics and thermodynamics of ion association; structure of aqueous solutions; chemical oceanography; oil field brines. *Mailing Add:* Dept Chem Univ Okla Norman OK 73019

ATKINSON, HAROLD RUSSELL, MATHEMATICAL ANALYSIS. *Current Pos:* Asst prof, 64-70, ASSOC PROF MATH, UNIV WINDSOR, 70- *Personal Data:* b Hamilton, Ont, Sept 25, 37; m 62, Mary Walczak; c Margaret, Sarah, Kevin, Aaron & Anna. *Educ:* Univ Western Ont, BA, 60; Assumption Univ, MSc, 61; Queen's Univ, Ont, PhD(math), 64. *Concurrent Pos:* Visitor, Dept Pure Maths, Univ Wales, Swansea, UK, 71-72; vis assoc prof, Univ BC, Vancouver, 82-83. *Mem:* Can Math Soc; Am Math Soc. *Res:* Ordered Banach spaces; spaces of affine continuous functions on compact convex sets; measure theory; Hausdorff measures; chaotic behaviour of real-valued functions. *Mailing Add:* Dept Math Univ Windsor Windsor ON N9B 3P4 Can. *Fax:* 519-971-3649; *E-Mail:* hrat@uwindsor.ca

ATKINSON, JAMES BYRON, ANATOMIC PATHOLOGY, SURGICAL PATHOLOGY. *Current Pos:* ASST PROF GEN PATH, VANDERBILT UNIV, 85- *Educ:* Vanderbilt Univ, MD & PhD(path), 81. *Mailing Add:* Dept Path C-3321 MCN Vanderbilt Univ Sch Med 1211 21st Ave S Nashville TN 37232-2561

ATKINSON, JAMES WILLIAM, MOLLUSCAN REPRODUCTION & DEVELOPMENT. *Current Pos:* From instr to prof natural sci, 68-89, PROF ZOOL, MICH STATE UNIV, 89- *Personal Data:* b Pittsburgh, Pa, Mar 15, 42; m 68; c 2. *Educ:* Kenyon Col, AB, 64; Emory Univ, MS, 66, PhD(biol), 69. *Concurrent Pos:* Adj prof zool, Mich State Univ, 83-89. *Mem:* Am Soc Zoologists; AAAS; Am Malacological Union. *Res:* Analysis of spiralian development with emphasis on the coordination of developmental events in space and time; evolutionary implications of developmental biology; history and philosophy of science; development and evolution of the nervous system in molluscs; history of biology. *Mailing Add:* Dept Zool Mich State Univ 203 Natural Sci East Lansing MI 48824-1115

ATKINSON, JOHN BRIAN, MOLECULAR SPECTROSCOPY. *Current Pos:* from asst prof to assoc prof, 72-87, PROF PHYSICS, UNIV WINDSOR, 87- *Personal Data:* b Louth, Eng, Aug 15, 42; m 70; c 1. *Educ:* Oxford Univ, BA, 63, DPhil(physics), 67. *Prof Exp:* Fel physics, Univ Windsor, 67-69, vis asst prof, 69-72; res assoc, Wayne State Univ, 69-72. *Mem:* Can Asn Physicists; Am Phys Soc. *Res:* Study of atomic collision cross-sections and atomic lifetimes using tunable dye lasers; applications of atomic properties to development of tunable lasers; molecular spectroscopy. *Mailing Add:* Dept Physics Univ Windsor Windsor ON N9B 3P4 Can

ATKINSON, JOHN PATTERSON, RHEUMATOLOGY, IMMUNOLOGY. *Current Pos:* NIH res fel, Sch Med, Washington Univ, 74-76, from asst prof to assoc prof med, 76-80, head, Div Pheumatol, 76-92, PROF MED, SCH MED, WASHINGTON UNIV, 80- *Personal Data:* b Clay Center, Kans, July 4, 43; m 64; c 3. *Educ:* Kans Univ, AB, 65, MD, 69. *Prof Exp:* Intern med, Mass Gen Hosp, 69-70, asst resident, 70-71; clin assoc, Lab Clin Ivest, Nat Inst Allergy & Infectious Dis, 71-72, chief clin assoc allergy, 72-73, staff fel, 73-74. *Mem:* Inst Med-Nat Acad Sci; Am Acad Allergy; Am Asn Immunologists; Am Fedn Clin Res. *Res:* Complement-mediated immune damage; autoimmune hemolytic anemia; hereditary angioedema; receptors on immunocompetent cells; cyclic nucleotides and the immune response. *Mailing Add:* Dept Rheumatol Sch Med Wash Univ 660 S Euclid Ave Box 8045 St Louis MO 63110-1031

ATKINSON, JOSEPH FERRIS, ENVIRONMENTAL FLUID MECHANICS, WATER QUALITY MODELING. *Current Pos:* Asst prof, 84-90, ASSOC PROF, DEPT CIVIL ENG, STATE UNIV NY, BUFFALO, 90- *Personal Data:* b San Francisco, Calif, June 9, 51; m 78, Nancy Levine; c Ariel, Ephraim & Shira. *Educ:* Harvey Mudd Col, BS, 73; Cornell Univ, MEng, 79; Mass Inst Technol, PhD(civil eng), 85. *Concurrent Pos:* Ed, Int Solar Pond Lett, Am Solar Energy Soc, 86-93; vis prof, Technion-Israel Inst Technol, 91-92; guest investr, Woods Hole Oceanog Inst, 93. *Mem:* Am Soc Civil Engrs; Am Int Solar Energy Soc; Am Geophys Union; Int Asn Great Lakes Res; Int Asn Water Sediment Sci. *Res:* Environmental fluid mechanics and water quality modeling, primarily in surface waters; dissolved oxygen modeling, sediment transport, dispersion and turbulent mixing processes, rotating stratified flow and use of global ionospheric studies with water quality modeling. *Mailing Add:* Dept Civil Eng State Univ NY Buffalo NY 14260

ATKINSON, JOSEPH GEORGE, MEDICINAL CHEMISTRY, PATENT COORDINATOR. *Current Pos:* res fel, 70-84, SR RES FEL, MERCK FROSST CAN INC, 84- *Personal Data:* b St Paul, Alta, Mar 9, 35. *Educ:* Univ Alta, BSc, 57; Mass Inst Technol, PhD(photochem), 62. *Prof Exp:* Group leader, Merck, Sharp & Dohme Can, Ltd, 62-70. *Mem:* Am Chem Soc; fel Chem Inst Can. *Res:* Organic photochemistry; synthesis of isotopically labeled organic compounds; synthesis of organometallic compounds and metal hybrides and deuterides; medicinal chemistry; organic synthesis. *Mailing Add:* 1380 Des Pins Montreal PQ H3G 1A8 Can. *Fax:* 514-428-8615; *E-Mail:* joe_atkinson@merck.com

ATKINSON, KENDALL E, NUMERICAL ANALYSIS. *Current Pos:* PROF MATH & COMPUTER SCI, UNIV IOWA, 72- *Personal Data:* b Centerville, Iowa, Mar 23, 40; m 61, Alice Morse; c Elizabeth & Kathryn. *Educ:* Iowa State Univ, BS, 61; Univ Wis-Madison, MS, 63, PhD(math), 66. *Prof Exp:* Assoc prof math, Ind Univ, Bloomington, 66-72. *Concurrent Pos:* Vis res fel, Australian Nat Univ, 70-71; vis prof, Univ New S Wales, Univ Queensland, 88 & Colo State Univ, 77, 93. *Mem:* Soc Indust & Appl Math; Australian Math Soc. *Res:* Numerical analysis; numerical solution of integral equations; mathematical computer software. *Mailing Add:* Dept Math Univ Iowa Iowa City IA 52242-1466. *Fax:* 319-335-0627; *E-Mail:* kendall_atkinson@uiowa.edu

ATKINSON, LARRY P, CHEMICAL OCEANOGRAPHY. *Current Pos:* MEM STAFF, DEPT OCEANOG, OLD DOMINION UNIV, NORFOLK, VA. *Personal Data:* b Ames, Iowa, Aug 6, 41; m 66. *Educ:* Univ Wash, BS, 63, MS, 66; Dalhousie Univ, PhD(oceanog), 73. *Prof Exp:* Res assoc oceanog, Marine Lab, Duke Univ, 66-68; res assoc, Skidaway Inst Oceanog, 72-74, from asst prof to assoc prof oceanog, 74-82. *Mem:* AAAS; Am Geophys Union; Am Soc Limnol & Oceanog. *Res:* Continental shelf oceanography. *Mailing Add:* Dept Oceanog Old Dominion Univ Norfolk VA 23529-1000

ATKINSON, LENETTE ROGERS, plant morphology; deceased, see previous edition for last biography

ATKINSON, MARK ARTHUR LEONARD, CELL BIOLOGY. *Current Pos:* assoc prof, 87-91, PROF & CHMN BIOCHEM, UNIV TEX HEALTH CTR, TYLER, 91-, ASSIST DIR RES, 95- *Personal Data:* b London, Eng, Feb 21, 52; m 84, Lynn D Morrow; c Jeremy D & Joshua A. *Educ:* Oxford Univ, BA, 74, MA, 78, DPhil(cell biol), 79. *Prof Exp:* Fel path, Sch Med, Yale Univ, 79-82; vis assoc cell biol, Nat Heart, Lung & Blood Inst, NIH, 82-87. *Concurrent Pos:* Kate Erin res scholar, Linacre Col, Oxford, 77; James Hudson Brown & Alexander B Coxe fel, Yale Univ, 81; estab investr, Am Heart Asn. *Mem:* AAAS; Biophys Soc; Am Soc Cell Biol; Am Soc Biochem & Molecular Biol; Protein Soc; Soc Leukocyte Biol. *Res:* The structure, function and regulation of non-muscle cell myosins; interrelationships of actomyosin with other cytoskeletal elements. *Mailing Add:* Dept Biochem Univ Tex Health Sci Ctr PO Box 2003 Tyler TX 75710-2003. *Fax:* 903-581-7558; *E-Mail:* mark%jason.decnet@relay.the.net

ATKINSON, PAUL H, CELL BIOLOGY, VIROLOGY. *Current Pos:* PROF DEVELOP BIOL, ALBERT EINSTEIN COL MED, 83- *Personal Data:* b Auckland, NZ, Aug 31, 43; m 67; c 2. *Educ:* Univ Auckland, PhD(cell biol), 69. *Concurrent Pos:* Asst dir, Cancer Res Ctr, RECOM, NIH Cell Physiol Study Sect, 77-83, NIH Cell Biol Study Sect, 83-86. *Res:* Specificity of intracellular sorting of viral and membrane glycoproteins especially in endoplasmic reticulum; NMR spectroscopy of glycosylation processing intermediates. *Mailing Add:* Wallaceville Animal Res Ctr PO Box 40063 Upper Hutt New Zealand. *Fax:* 64-4286605

ATKINSON, RICHARD C, SCIENCE ADMINISTRATION. *Current Pos:* chancellor, 89-95, PRES, UNIV CALIF, SAN DIEGO, 95- *Personal Data:* b Oak Park, Ill, Mar 19, 29; m 52; c 1. *Educ:* Univ Chicago, PhD, 48; Ind Univ, PhD(psychol), 55. *Hon Degrees:* Ten from US univs. *Honors & Awards:* Distinguished Res Award, Soc Sci Res Coun, 62; Distinguished Sci Contrib Award, Am Psychol Asn, 77, E L Thorndike Award, 80; William W Cook Lectr, Univ Mich, 78; Mountain in Antactica named in honor. *Prof Exp:* Lectr, Appl Math & Statist Labs, Stanford Univ, 56-57; asst prof psychol, Univ Calif, Los Angeles, 57-61; assoc prof, Stanford Univ, 61-65, prof psychol & educ & affil fac mem, Inst Eng & Econ Systs, Sch Eng, 65-80, chmn, Dept Psychol, 68-73; dir, NSF, 75-80. *Concurrent Pos:* Consult, Systs Develop Corp, 58-67, Bell Tel Labs, 61-63, Radio Corp Am, 64-68, Off Comput Activ, NSF, 68-75; assoc dir, Inst Math Studies Soc Sci, Stanford Univ, 61-75; vis prof psychol, Univ Mich, 63; ed, J Math Psychol, 63-70; dep dir, NSF, 75-76 & 77-80 & actg dir, 76-77; mem, Task Force Info Networks, Educ Comn, Inter Univ Commun Coun, 65-68; dir, Job Corps Reading Inst, Off Econ Opportunities, 66; chmn, Comt Learning & Educ Process, Soc Sci Res Coun, 66-68 & mem, 63-69; mem, Comt Technol Augmentation Cognition, Smithsonian Inst, 68-70; mem, Math Social Sci Bd, Ctr Advan Study Behav Sci, 68-72, US-USSR Joint Comn Sci & Tech Coop, 77-80, US-Peoples Repub China Joint Comn Sci & Technol Coop, 79-80, Assembly Behav & Soc Sci, Nat Res Coun & Calif Comn Indus Innovation, Exec Dept, State Calif, 81-82, Comn Educ & Pub Policy, Nat Acad Educ, 84-; chmn, Math Soc Sci Bd, Ctr Advan Study Behav Sci, 71-73; bd dirs, Am Psychol Asn, 73-76 & Whittier Inst Diabetes & Endocrinol,; adv coun, Int Asn Study Attention & Performance, 76-81; intergovt sci, Eng & Technol Adv Panel, Off Sci & Technol Policy & Federal Coun Arts & Humanities, Exec Off Pres, 77-80; mem, Nat Mus Serv Bd, Inst Mus Serv, Dept Educ, 77-80; pres comt, Nat Medal Sci, 81-84; counr, Nat Acad Sci, 82-85; chmn, Blue Ribbon Panel Info Policy, Implications Archiving Satellite Data, Nat Comn Libr & Info Sci, 83-84; adv comt, Higher Educ Policy, Online Comput Libr Ctr, 84-, Comt Sci, Eng & Pub Policy, NAS, 84-85, comt nominations, AAAS, 85-; vis comt, Dept Psychol, Harvard Univ. *Mem:* Inst Med-Nat Acad Sci; Am Acad Arts & Sci; Nat Acad Educ; Am Philos Soc; fel AAAS (pres elec, 88); Psychonomic Soc; Am Psychol Asn (pres, Div Exp Psychol, 74); Soc S Pole. *Res:* Experimental and applied mathematics, particularly with problems of memory and cognition; published over 150 scientific articles; author of 7 books in psychology. *Mailing Add:* Off Pres Univ Calif 300 Lakeside Dr Oakland CA 94612-3550. *Fax:* 510-987-9086

ATKINSON, RICHARD L, JR, MEDICINE, CLINICAL NUTRITION. *Current Pos:* PROF MED & NUTRIT SCIS, UNIV WIS, 93-, DIR, BEERS-MURPHY CLIN NUTRIT CTR, 93- *Personal Data:* b Petersburg, Va, May 15, 42; m 66, Susan Hume; c Catherine C, Barbara H & Deborah G. *Educ:* Va Mil Inst, BA, 64; Med Col Va, MD, 68. *Prof Exp:* Asst prof, Univ Va, 77-83; assoc prof internal med, Univ Calif, Davis, 83-86; prof internal med, Chief Div Clin Nutrit, Eastern Va Med Sch, 86-93; assoc chief of staff, Res & Develop, Va Med Ctr, Hampton, 86-93. *Concurrent Pos:* Comt, Mil Nutrit Res, Nat Acad Sci, 89-93; nutrit study sect, NIH, 91-95, chair, 93-95; Nat Inst Diabetes & Digestive & Kidney Nat Task Force, prev & treatment obesity, 91-95. *Mem:* Am Soc Nutrit Sci; Am Soc Clin Nutrit (vpres, 92, pres elect, 93, pres, 94); Endocrine Soc; Am Diabetes Asn; fel Am Col Physicians; NAm Asn Study Obesity (pres, 90). *Res:* Clinical nutrition; research in human and animal obesity; regulation of food intake, body weight, and energy expenditure. *Mailing Add:* Nutrit Scis Bldg Univ Wis 1415 Linden Dr Madison WI 53706. *Fax:* 608-265-5532; *E-Mail:* rla@medicine.wisc.edu

ATKINSON, ROGER, GAS KINETICS, ATMOSPHERIC CHEMISTRY. *Current Pos:* from asst res chemist to assoc res chemist, 72-78, RES CHEMIST, UNIV CALIF, RIVERSIDE, 80-, PROF, DEPT SOILS & ENVIRON SCIS, 90- *Personal Data:* b Scarborough, UK, July 30, 45; m 88; c 2. *Educ:* Cambridge Univ, BA, 66, PhD(phys chem), 69. *Prof Exp:* Res fel chem, Nat Res Coun Can, 69-71; res fel, York Univ, Can, 71-72; sr scientist, Shell Res Ltd, UK, 78-79 & ERT, Inc, Calif, 79-80. *Mem:* Am Chem Soc; Soc Environ Toxicol Chem. *Res:* Kinetics and mechanisms of gas phase reactions of atmospheric interest; radical reactions with organic compounds. *Mailing Add:* Univ Calif Soil & Environ Sci Riverside CA 92521-0001

ATKINSON, RUSSELL H, PHYSICAL CHEMISTRY, ENGINEERING MANAGEMENT. *Current Pos:* RETIRED. *Personal Data:* b Brooklyn, NY, Aug 22, 22; m 44; c 3. *Educ:* Polytech Inst Brooklyn, BS, 48, PhD(chem), 52. *Prof Exp:* Jr chemist, Manhattan Proj, Tenn Eastman Corp, 44-46; sr engr, Westinghouse Elec Corp, 51-56, sect mgr, Metals Res Group, 56-59, asst res dir, 59-61, mgr parts eng, 61-63, asst mgr, Div Eng, 63-66, mgr parts mfg, 67-69, mgr, Div Eng, 69-76, prod eng mgr, 76-79, dir res & develop, Lamp Div, 79-81. *Concurrent Pos:* Instr, Polytech Inst Brooklyn, 52-54; lectr, Calif State Polytech Univ, 82- *Mem:* Am Illum Eng Soc; Sigma Xi; Soc Advan Mat Processing Eng; Am Soc Metals. *Res:* Chemistry of refractory metals; gas-metal reactions; analysis of refractory metals; vapor deposition reactions; lamp development and materials; composites; material sciences. *Mailing Add:* 650 W Harrison Ave Claremont CA 91711-4595

ATKINSON, SHANNON K C, REPRODUCTIVE BIOLOGY & FERTILITY MANAGEMENT, BREEDING PROGRAMS FOR CAPTIVE WILDLIFE. *Current Pos:* res affil, 89-91, ASSOC RESEARCHER WILDLIFE RES, HAWAII INST MARINE BIOL, UNIV HAWAII, 91- *Personal Data:* b Honolulu, Hawaii, Dec 29, 56; m 81, Marlin J; c 2. *Educ:* Univ Hawaii, BSc, 78, MSc, 81; Murdoch Univ, PhD(vet studies), 85. *Honors & Awards:* Mary Walters Mem Bursary, Australian Fedn Univ Women, 83. *Prof Exp:* Fel endocrinol & physiol, Vet Sch, Murdoch Univ, 84-86; exp scientist, endocrinol & physiol, Commonwealth Sci & Indust Res Orgn, Australia, 86-88. *Mem:* Am Asn Zool Parks & Aquariums; Soc Marine Mammal; Endocrine & Reproductive Biol Soc (pres, 86-88). *Res:* Breeding strategies and control of fertility in wildlife species. *Mailing Add:* Hawaii Inst Marine PO Box 1346 Univ Hawaii Kaneone HI 96744. *Fax:* 808-956-3014

ATLAS, DAVID, METEOROLOGY, REMOTE SENSING. *Current Pos:* CONSULT, 84- *Personal Data:* b Brooklyn, NY, May 25, 24; m 48, Lucille Rosen; c Joan & Robert. *Educ:* NY Univ, BSc, 46; Mass Inst Technol, MSc, 51, DSc(meteorol), 55. *Honors & Awards:* Meisinger Award, Am Meteorol Soc, 57, Carl Gustav Ressby Medal, 77, Cleveland Abbe Award, 83, Remote, Sensing Award, 91; Loeser Award, Air Force Cambridge Res Labs, 57; O'Day Award, 64; Losey Award, Am Inst Aeronaut & Astronaut, 66; Outstanding Leadership Medal, NASA, 82; Symons Mem Medal, Royal Meteorol Soc, 89. *Prof Exp:* Chief weather radar br, Air Force Cambridge Res Labs, Bedford, Mass, 48-66; prof meteorol, Univ Chicago, 66-72; dir atmospheric technol div, Nat Ctr Atmospheric Res, Boulder, Colo, 72-73, dir nat hail res exp, 74-75; dir lab atmospheric sci, Goddard Space Flight Ctr, NASA, Greenbelt, MD, 77-84; sr res assoc dept meteorol, Univ Md, 85-87. *Concurrent Pos:* Assoc ed publ, Am Meteorol Soc, 57-74, counr, 61-64 & 72-74; NSF sr fel, Imp Col, London Eng, 59-60; pres inter-union comn radio meteorol, Int Radio Sci Union, 69-72; distinguished vis scientist, Jet Propulsion Lab, Calif Inst Technol, 84- & NASA Goddard Space Flight Ctr, 89-; mem US deleg to VII Cong, World Meteorol Orgn, 75; chmn, AAAS, Atmospheric Hydrospheric Sci sect. *Mem:* Nat Acad Eng; fel Am Geophys Union; fel Royal Meteorol Soc; fel AAAS; fel Am Astronaut Soc; fel Am Meteorol Soc. *Res:* Meteorology and climatology; satellite meteorology; radar meteorology; remote sensing; research management; remote measurement of rainfall both from space and from airborne and surface platforms by radar and other sensors. *Mailing Add:* 7420 Westlake Terr Bethesda MD 20817. *Fax:* 301-286-1626; *E-Mail:* datlas@gsfcmail.nasa.gov

ATLAS, RONALD M, MICROBIOLOGY, MICROBIAL ECOLOGY. *Current Pos:* from asst prof to assoc prof, 73-81, PROF BIOL, UNIV LOUISVILLE, 81-; LECTR, SIGMA XI, 81- *Personal Data:* b New York, NY, Oct 19, 46; m 70; c 2. *Educ:* State Univ NY, Stony Brook, BS, 68; Rutgers Univ, MS, 70, PhD(microbiol), 72. *Prof Exp:* Res assoc, Jet Propulsion Lab, Calif Inst Technol, 72-73. *Concurrent Pos:* Res grants, Off Naval Res, 73-79, Nat Oceanic & Atmospheric Admin, 75- & Dept Energy, 76-81; Environ Microbiol Comt, Am Soc Microbiol, 81- *Mem:* Am Soc Microbiol; AAAS; Sigma Xi; fel Am Acad Microbiol; Soc Indust Microbiol. *Res:* Microbial degradation of hydrocarbons and other organic pollutants; numerical taxonomy of marine bacteria; effects of pesticides and other organic compounds on microorganisms; ecology of soil and marine microorganisms. *Mailing Add:* Dept Biol Univ Louisville 2301 S 3rd St Louisville KY 40292-0001

ATLAS, STEVEN ALAN, HYPERTENSION, CIRCULATORY PHYSIOLOGY. *Current Pos:* ASSOC PROF MED, MT SINAI SCH MED, 93-; ATTEND PHYSICIAN, MT SINAI MED CTR, 93-; STAFF PHYSICIAN, BRONX VET AFFAIRS MED CTR, 93- *Personal Data:* b New York, NY, Sept 3, 46; m 88, Barbara R Hirsch; c Lauren S & Benjamin A. *Educ:* Johns Hopkins Univ, BA, 68, MD, 71. *Honors & Awards:* Clin Endocrinol Trust Lectr, Brit Endocrine Soc, 87. *Prof Exp:* Intern & resident, New York Hosp, Cornell Med Ctr, 71-73; res assoc pharmacol, Nat Inst Health, 73-76; from instr to assoc prof med, Cornell Univ Med Col, 76-93; assoc attend physician, New York Hosp, 82-93. *Concurrent Pos:* Asst attending physician, New York Hosp, 77-82; mem, Cardiovascular & Renal Study Sect, NIH, 84-88; mem, Coun High Blood Pressure Res, Am Heart Asn. *Mem:* Am Soc Clin Invest; Endocrine Soc; Am Heart Asn; Am Soc Hypertension; Int Soc Hypertension; NY Acad Sci; Soc Exp Biol & Med. *Res:* Biochemical endocrinology, pharmacology and physiological role of hormones involved in cardiovascular regulation, with particular expertise on the Renin-Angiotensin-Aldosterone system and on atrial natriuretic factor. *Mailing Add:* Hypertension Res Lab Vet Affairs Med Ctr 130 W Kingsbridge Rd Bronx NY 10468. *Fax:* 718-579-1635

ATLURI, SATYA N, FRACTURE MECHANICS & COMPUTATIONAL FLUID DYNAMICS, COMPUTATIONAL SOLID MECHANICS. *Current Pos:* from assoc prof to prof mech, 74-79, REGENTS PROF MECH, GA INST TECHNOL, 79-, DIR COMPUT MECH CTR, 80-, INST PROF, 91- *Personal Data:* b Gudivada, India, Oct 7, 45; US citizen; m 72, Revati Adusumilli; c Neelima & Niroupa. *Educ:* Andhra Univ, BS, 65; Indian Inst Sci, MS, 66; Mass Inst Technol, DSc, 69. *Hon Degrees:* DSc, Nat Univ Ireland, 89. *Honors & Awards:* Aerospace Struct & Mat Award, Am Soc Civil Engrs, 86; Struct, Struct Dynamics & Mat Medal, Am Inst Aeronaut & Astronaut, 88; Monie Ferst Mem Award, Sigma Xi, 88; Computational Mech Div Medal, Japan Soc Mech Engrs, 91; Tech Achievement Award, US Nat Acad Eng, 95. *Prof Exp:* Res assoc aeronaut & astronaut, Mass Inst Technol, 69-71; asst prof aeronaut & astronaut, Univ Wash, 71-74. *Concurrent Pos:* Ed, Int J Comput Mech 86-, Am Inst Aeronaut & Astronaut J, 83-87; prin investr grants, Off Naval Res, USAF, NSF, Nat Res Coun & many others; chmn Comt Comput Appl Mech, Am Soc Mech Engrs, 81-85; J C Hunsaker prof aeronaut & astronaut, Mass Inst Technol, 90-91; inst prof, Ga Tech, 91; dir, Ctr Excellence for Aging Aircraft, Fed Aviation Admin, 92- *Mem:* Fel Nat Acad Sci; fel Am Acad Mech; US Asn Comput Mech; fel Am Inst Aeronaut & Astronaut; hon fel Int Cong Fracture; fel Am Soc Mech Engrs; US Nat Acad Eng. *Res:* Computational mechanics; finite element and boundary element methods; fracture mechanics; dynamin and control; composite materials; author of over 500 articles in archival scientific literature and 30 books. *Mailing Add:* Computational Mech Ctr French Bldg Rm 225 Ga Inst Technol 237 Uncle Heinie Way Atlanta GA 30332-0356. *Fax:* 404-894-2299; *E-Mail:* satyaatluri@cad.gatech.edu

ATLURU, DURGAPRASADARAO, IMMUNOLOGY, MOLECULAR BIOLOGY. *Current Pos:* SCIENTIST, MINNEAPOLIS MED RES FOUND, 90- *Personal Data:* b Tenneru, Andhra Pradesh, India, Oct 15, 49; US citizen; m 84, Subbayamma Gorijavolu; c Sreevalli. *Educ:* Andhra Pradesh Agr Univ, DVM, 71, MSc, 74, Univ Minn, MS, 80. *Prof Exp:* Vet officer, Andhra Pradhesh Dairy Develop Corp, Hyderabad, India, 74-76; res asst, Dept Large Animal Clin Sci, Univ Minn, 77-81; res assoc, Dept Vet Microbiol, Auburn Univ, 82; vis-guest scientist, Dept Vet Microbiol, Col Vet Sci, Hyderabad, India, 82; NIH trainee, Dept Med, Univ NMex Sch Med, 83-85; instr, Dept Med, Med Col Wis, 85-87; asst prof, Dept Anat & Physiol, Kans State Univ, 87-90. *Concurrent Pos:* Prin investr, NIH, 87-93, USDA, 88-92 & Am Heart Asn, 88-90; vis-guest scientist, Dept Biol, Argonne Nat Labs, 89-90; Sandoz vis prof, Dept Surg, Univ Wis, 90. *Mem:* Am Asn Vet Immunologists; Am Asn Immunologists; Soc Leukocyte Biol; AAAS; Conf Res Workers Animal Dis. *Res:* To determine the role of leukotrienes in human lymphocyte proliferation, specially at cell growth, role on lymphocyte growth factors and on messenger KNA of these growth factors; to find out the effect of immunosuppresive agents commonly used in organ transplantation on the synthesis of the leukotrienes; published more than 40 reasarch papers in peer reviewed journals. *Mailing Add:* 653 White Birch Dr Shoreview MN 55126-1254

ATNEOSEN, RICHARD ALLEN, PHYSICS. *Current Pos:* ASSOC PROF PHYSICS & ASTRON, WESTERN WASH STATE UNIV, 68- *Personal Data:* b St James, Minn, Sept 11, 34. *Educ:* Univ Minn, BS, 56, MS, 58; Ind Univ, PhD(physics), 63. *Prof Exp:* Res assoc nuclear chem, Princeton Univ, 63-65; asst res prof physics, Mich State Univ, 65-68. *Mem:* Am Phys Soc; Am Asn Physics Teachers; Astron Soc Pacific. *Res:* Reaction mechanisms in alpha particle scattering; particle-induced fission; infrared astronomy; acoustics. *Mailing Add:* 320 Crest Ln Bellingham WA 98226

ATNIP, ROBERT LEE, ANATOMY. *Current Pos:* instr anat & pediat, 66-68, asst prof anat & child develop & res assoc pediat, 68-74, ASSOC PROF ANAT & CHILD DEVELOP, UNIV TENN MED UNITS, 74- *Personal Data:* b Bridgeport, Ala, Aug 10, 28; m 51; c 5. *Educ:* David Lipscomb Col, BA, 51; George Peabody Col, MA, 52; Univ Tenn, PhD(anat), 64. *Prof Exp:* Teacher high schs, Ga & Ala, 52-54; instr biol, Freed-Hardeman Col, 54-59. *Concurrent Pos:* Nat Inst Child Health & Human Develop fel anat, Col Med, Univ Tenn, 65-66. *Mem:* Am Soc Human Genetics; Sigma Xi. *Res:* Mammalian embryology and experimental teratology; experimentally-produced cleft palate in mice; chromosomal aberrations of malformed mentally retarded children. *Mailing Add:* 1953 Claude Capps Rd Greenfield TN 38230

ATOJI, MASAO, MATERIALS SCIENCES. *Current Pos:* ASSOC ED, CHEM ABSTR SERV AM CHEM SOC, 90- *Personal Data:* b Osaka, Japan, Dec 21, 25; US citizen; m 57, Iris Noma; c Naomi J (Walker), Cynthia A (Szubzda) & David M. *Educ:* Osaka Univ, BS, 48, PhD(chem), 56. *Prof Exp:* Res fel chem, Univ Minn, Minneapolis, 51-56; assoc res, Iowa State Univ, 56-58, asst prof, 58-60; chemist, div chem, Argonne Nat Lab, 60-69, sr chemist & group leader, neutron group, 69-81; sr staff scientist, Airtron Div, Litton Systs, 81-83; sr staff scientist, Motorola Inc, 84-87; mgr, crystal lab, Northwestern Univ, 88-90. *Mem:* AAAS; Am Crystallog Asn; Am Chem Soc; fel Am Phys Soc; Phys Soc Japan; Soc Appl Spectroscopy; Am Asn Crystal Growth; Sigma Xi; Am Translr Asn. *Res:* Crystal and magnetic structures; neutron and x-ray diffraction; crystal growth, fabrication and characterization; semiconductor and electronics materials; metallurgy, ceramics & superconductors. *Mailing Add:* 702 86th Pl Downers Grove IL 60516

ATON, THOMAS JOHN, SOLID STATE PHYSICS. *Current Pos:* SR MEM TECH STAFF, TEX INSTRUMENTS, 84- *Personal Data:* b Miami, Okla, Nov 1, 48; m 71; c 2. *Educ:* Rice Univ, BA, 70; Univ Ill, MS, 72, PhD(physics), 76. *Prof Exp:* Instr physics, Princeton Univ, 76-78; asst prof physics, Univ Va, 78-84. *Mem:* Am Phys Soc. *Mailing Add:* 15735 Daleport Circle Dallas TX 75248

ATRAKCHI, AISAR HASAN, ENVIRONMENTAL TOXICOLOGIST, NEUROTOXICOLOGIST. *Current Pos:* STAFF SCIENTIST ENVIRON TOXICOL, DYNAMAC CORP, 90- *Personal Data:* b Baghdad, Iraq, Mar 16, 55. *Educ:* Baghdad Univ, BSc, 78; Univ Missoula, MSc, 82; Univ Calif Davis, PhD(pharmacol & toxicol), 87. *Prof Exp:* Postgraduate researcher, Off Curricular Support, Univ Calif Davis, Sch Med, 85-87; postdoctoral fel free radicals, George Washington Univ, DC, 87-89; Fogarty Int fel electrophysiol, Lab Biophysics, NIH, 89-90. *Mem:* Am Soc Pharmacol & Exp Therapeut; Soc Risk Anal. *Res:* Research in pharmacology and physiology of the cardiovascular and central nervous systems; in situ, in vivo, and in vitro preparations; membrane channel activities and kinetics and toxicology. *Mailing Add:* Food & Drug Admin HFD 120 5600 Fishers Lane Rockville MD 20857. *Fax:* 301-417-9801

ATRASH, HANI K, EPIDEMIOLOGY. *Current Pos:* epidemiologist, 85-87, CHIEF, PREGNANCY & INFANT HEALTH BR, CTR DIS CONTROL, 87- *Personal Data:* b Lebanon, Feb 20, 51. *Educ:* Univ Beirut, BS, 72; Am Univ Beirut, MD, 76; Emory Univ, MPH, 85. *Prof Exp:* Epidemiologist, Bahrain, 81 & 84. *Mem:* Am Pub Health Asn; AMA; Am Col Obstetricians & Gynecologists. *Mailing Add:* Pregnancy & Infant Health Br Ctr Dis Control 4770 Buford Hwy NE MSK 23 Atlanta GA 30341. *Fax:* 770-488-5628; *E-Mail:* hkai@ccddrhi.em.cdc.gov

ATREYA, ARVIND, COMBUSTION, HEAT & MASS TRANSFER. *Current Pos:* asst prof, 83-87, ASSOC PROF THERMAL SCI, MICH STATE UNIV, 87- *Personal Data:* b Bijnor, India, Jan 15, 54; m 83; c 2. *Educ:* Indian Inst Technol, New Delhi, BTech, 75; Univ NB, Can, MScE, 77; Harvard Univ, MS, 78, PhD(eng sci), 83. *Prof Exp:* Res asst fire res, Harvard Univ, 78-83. *Concurrent Pos:* Mech engr, Nat Inst Standards & Technol, 83-84; NSF presidential young investr award, 86; consult, Hughes, Hubbard & Reed, 88-90 & Hughes Assocs Inc, 89- *Mem:* Combustion Inst; Am Soc Mech Engrs; Int Asn Fire Safety Sci; Sigma Xi. *Res:* Fire safety research including ignition, flame spread, pyrolysis and extinguishment; industrial combustion research to enhance flame radiation and reduce pollutants. *Mailing Add:* 1220 Fairmount Dr Ann Arbor MI 48105

ATREYA, SUSHIL KUMAR, ORIGIN & EVOLUTION OF PLANETARY ATMOSPHERES, ATMOSPHERIC SCIENCES. *Current Pos:* res scientist space physics, 74-78, from asst prof to assoc prof, 78-87, PROF ATMOSPHERIC & SPACE SCI, UNIV MICH, ANN ARBOR, 87-, DIR, PLANETARY SCI LAB. *Personal Data:* b Apr 15, 46; US citizen; m 70, Evelyn Bruckner; c Chloe. *Educ:* Univ Rajasthan, India, BSc, 63, MSc, 65; Yale Univ, MS, 68; Univ Mich, PhD(atmospheric sci), 73. *Honors & Awards:* Exceptional Sci Accomplishments Award, Voyager UVS Spectroscopy, NASA, Group Achievement Awards, Voyager, 81, 86 & 90, Galileo, 96. *Prof Exp:* Res fel physics, Univ Delhi, India, 65-66; res assoc physics, Univ Pittsburgh, 73-74. *Concurrent Pos:* Assoc prof physics, Univ Paris, 84-85; sci teams, Cassini-Huygens Probe/Gas Chromatograph Mass Spectrometer, Aerosol Collector Pyrolyzer, Voyager/Ultraviolet Spectrometer, Galileo/Jupiter Probe Mass Spectrometer, Comet Rendezvous Asteroid Flyby Neutral Gas & Ion Mass Spectrometer, 86-92, Mars 96 & Phobos Projs, Japanese Planet B Mars Spacecraft & Spacelab/Imaging Observ; guest investr, Hubble Space Telescope, Copernicus & Int Ultraviolet Explorer satellites; vis sr res scientist, Imp Col, London, 84; pres, Com Planetary Atmospheres & Evolution, Int Asn Meteorol & Atmospheric Sci, 86-94. *Mem:* AAAS; Am Geophys Union; Am Astron Soc; Int Astron Union; Int Asn Meteorol & Atmospheric Sci; Int Acad Astronauts. *Res:* Modelling and measurements of physical and chemical processes in the atmospheres of the planets and satellites with the goal of understanding the origin and evolution of atmospheres in the solar system. *Mailing Add:* Dept Atmospheric Oceanic & Space Sci Space Res Bldg Univ Mich Ann Arbor MI 48109-2143

ATTALLA, ALBERT, PHYSICAL CHEMISTRY, ANALYTICAL CHEMISTRY. *Current Pos:* RES SPECIALIST INSTRUMENTAL ANALYSIS, MONSANTO RES CORP, 63- *Personal Data:* b Cuyahoga Falls, Ohio, Sept 29, 31; m 56; c 3. *Educ:* Kent State Univ, BA, 55, MA, 59; Univ Cincinnati, PhD(phys chem), 62. *Prof Exp:* Sr chemist, Corning Glass Works, NY, 62-63. *Res:* Nuclear magnetic resonance and x-ray fluorescence spectroscopy; gas chromatography. *Mailing Add:* 350 Blackstone Dr Dayton OH 45459

ATTANASIO, ROBERTA, VIROLOGY, IMMUNOLOGY. *Current Pos:* ASST SCIENTIST, SW FOUND BIOMED RES, 89- *Personal Data:* b Rome, Italy. *Res:* Virology; immunology. *Mailing Add:* Yerkes Reg Primate Res Ctr Emory Univ 954 Gatewood Rd NE Atlanta GA 30329

ATTARDI, GIUSEPPE M, MITOCHONDRIA BIOGENESIS. *Current Pos:* from assoc prof to prof biol, 67-84, GRACE C STEELE PROF MOLECULAR BIOL, CALIF INST TECHNOL, 85- *Personal Data:* b Yicari, Panerio, Italy, Sept 14, 23. *Educ:* Univ Padua, MD, 47. *Honors & Awards:* Antonio Feltrinelli Int Prize for Med, 89. *Prof Exp:* Asst prof, Dept Histol & Gen Embryol, Univ Padua, Italy, 47-57; Fulbright fel, Dept Microbiol, Washington Univ, St Louis, 57-59 & Div Biol, Calif Inst Technol, 59-60; sr researcher, Lab Enzymol, Nat Ctr Sci Res & Pasteur Inst, Paris, 61-62. *Concurrent Pos:* Res fel, Inst Cell Res & Genetics, Karolinska Inst, Stockholm, Swed, 52-55; Guggenheim fel, Molecular Genetics Ctr, Nat Ctr Sci Res, France, 70-71 & 86-87. *Mem:* Nat Acad Sci. *Mailing Add:* Div Biol 156-29 Calif Inst Technol Pasadena CA 91125

ATTAS, ELY MICHAEL, RADIOCHEMICAL ANALYSIS, NUCLEAR SAFEGUARDS TECHNIQUES. *Current Pos:* res chemist, Anal Sci Br, 82-90, head, Radio Chem Anal Sect, 90-92, HEAD, PHYS-CHEM ANALYSIS SECT, ANALYTICAL SCI BR, ATOMIC ENERGY OF CAN LTD, WHITESHELL LABS, 92- *Personal Data:* b Montreal, Que, July 18, 52; m 75; c 3. *Educ:* McGill Univ, BSc, 73, MSc, 75, PhD(chem & archaeol), 83; Univ Paris XI, Orsay, Doctorat de 3E cycle, 80. *Concurrent Pos:* Tech collabr, Chem Dept, Brookhaven Nat Lab, 76-77; lectr, Classics Dept, McGill Univ, Montreal, 76, Dept Etudes Anciennes Modernes, Univ Montreal, 78, Anthrop, Pinawa Sec Sch, Man, 88-89. *Mem:* Can Nuclear Soc. *Res:* Development of instrumental methods for analysis of radioactive samples; nuclear safeguards instrumentation, including ultraviolet imaging of Cerenkov radiation from used nuclear fuel stored underwater; neutron activation analysis techniques, archaeometry and chemometrics; digital imaging. *Mailing Add:* Atomic Energy of Can Ltd Whiteshell Labs Pinawa MB R0E 1L0 Can. *E-Mail:* attasm@aecl.ca

ATTAWAY, CECIL REID, MECHANICAL ENGINEERING, MACHINE DESIGN. *Current Pos:* PRIN ENGR, NUCLEAR DIV, UNION CARBIDE CORP, 76- *Personal Data:* b Fredericksburg, Va, May 19, 40; m 69. *Educ:* Clemson Col, BS, 62; Ga Inst Technol, MS, 68, PhD(mach design), 69. *Prof Exp:* Mech engr, Cadre Corp, Ga, 66-67; dir res & develop, Gunter & Cooke Inc, 69-70; res & develop engr, Blue Bell Inc, 70-73; proj engr, Cadre Corp, 73-76. *Mem:* Am Soc Mech Engrs; Nat Soc Prof Engrs. *Res:* Design of state-of-the-art research and development, testing, and production facilities. *Mailing Add:* 724 Kimbee Rd Knoxville TN 37923

ATTAWAY, DAVID HENRY, BIOCHEMISTRY. *Current Pos:* asst dir res, Nat Sea Grant Col Prog, 86-95, PROG DIR BIOTECHNOL & SEAFOOD SCI, 72- *Personal Data:* b Sterling, Okla, June 9, 38. *Educ:* Univ Okla, BS, 60, PhD(biochem), 68. *Prof Exp:* Phys oceanogr, US Naval Oceanog Off, 62-65; res assoc org geochem, Marine Sci Inst, Univ Tex, 68-69; chief geochem, State Geol Surv, Univ Kans, 69-71; res chem oceanogr, US Coast Guard Hq, 71-72. *Concurrent Pos:* Univ Tex grad sch fel, 68-69; Cong fel, 80-81. *Mem:* AAAS; Marine Technol Soc; Am Chem Soc; Sigma Xi; Inst Food Technol; Am Geophys Union. *Res:* Comparative chemistry of natural products from marine plants and animals; toxic substances of marine origin; organic geochemistry; petroleum in marine environment; marine biotechnology policy. *Mailing Add:* 609 Seventh St NE Washington DC 20002-3713. *Fax:* 202-544-1977; *E-Mail:* dha@erols.com

ATTAWAY, JOHN ALLEN, PLANT BIOCHEMISTRY, RESEARCH ADMINISTRATION. *Current Pos:* res chemist, 59-68, DIR RES, FLA DEPT CITRUS, 68- *Personal Data:* b Atlanta, Ga, July 19, 30; m 57; c 4. *Educ:* Fla Southern Col, BS, 51; Univ Fla, MS, 53; Duke Univ, PhD(chem), 57. *Honors & Awards:* Confructa Award, Int Fedn Fruit Juice Producers. *Prof Exp:* Asst, Off Ord Res, Univ Fla, 53; asst, Duke Univ, 53-54, Off Ord Res & Off Naval Res, 54-55, fel plant biochem, 57; res chemist, Monsanto Chem Co, 57-58; res chemist org chem & biochem, Resources Res Inc, 58-59. *Mem:* Am Chem Soc; Am Soc Plant Physiologists; Inst Food Technologists; Asn Off Anal Chemists; Asn Food & Drug Off. *Res:* Chromatographic analysis; instrumentation; natural products and flavors; organic fluorine compounds; plant growth regulators; organic chemistry. *Mailing Add:* Box 205 Winter Haven FL 33882-0205

ATTEBERY, BILLY JOE, MATHEMATICS. *Current Pos:* assoc prof, 67-68, PROF MATH, LA TECH UNIV, 68- *Personal Data:* b Bearden, Ark, Dec 26, 27; m 58; c 2. *Educ:* Ark State Teachers Col, BSE, 50; Univ Ark, MA, 54; Univ Mo, PhD, 58. *Prof Exp:* Instr math, Univ Mo, 54-58; from asst prof to assoc prof, Univ Ark, 58-67. *Mem:* Math Asn Am. *Res:* Probability theory. *Mailing Add:* 3107 Bienville Ave Ruston LA 71270

ATTIE, ALAN D, LIPOPROTEINS, CHOLESTEROL. *Current Pos:* Asst prof, 82-89, ASSOC PROF BIOCHEM, DEPT COMP BIOSCI, UNIV WIS-MADISON, 89- *Personal Data:* b New York, NY, June 18, 55. *Educ:* Univ Wis-Madison, BS, 76; Univ Calif, San Diego, PhD(biol), 80. *Concurrent Pos:* Mem Arteriosclerosis Coun, Am Heart Asn; fel res award, Am Asn Study Liver Dis, 80; estab investr award, Am Heart Asn, 87. *Mem:* Am Heart Asn; Am Soc Biochem & Molecular Biol. *Res:* Structure and function of plasma lipoproteins; mutations affecting the structure and expression of apolipoproteins; cholesterol metabolism; animal models for studying lipoprotein and cholesterol metabolism. *Mailing Add:* Dept Biochem Univ Wis 420 Henry Mall Madison WI 53706-1569

ATTIG, THOMAS GEORGE, INORGANIC CHEMISTRY, ORGANOMETALLIC CHEMISTRY. *Current Pos:* res proj leader, Sohio Res, Stand Oil Co Ohio, 79-85, res assoc, 85, mgr, Process Res, 85-87, mgr process res, Chem Technol, BP Am, 88, MGR DERIVATIVES, BP CHEM, 88- *Personal Data:* b Pontiac, Ill, Oct 2, 46; m 68, Carol Klinker; c Steven & Elizabeth. *Educ:* DePauw Univ, BA, 68; Ohio State Univ, PhD(chem), 73. *Prof Exp:* Teaching asst, Ohio State Univ, 69-70, NSF trainee, 70-73; fel chem, Univ Western Ont, 73-75; asst prof chem, Univ Ky, 75-79. *Mem:* Am Chem Soc. *Res:* Hetereogenous catalysis; hydrogenation; organic synthesis. *Mailing Add:* BP Chemicals 4440 Warrensville Rd Cleveland OH 44128. *Fax:* 216-586-5030; *E-Mail:* attigtg@bp.com

ATTINGER, ERNST OTTO, BIOENGINEERING. *Current Pos:* CONSULT, 90- *Personal Data:* b Zurich, Switz, Dec 27, 22; c 3. *Educ:* Winterthur Cantonal Sch, Switz, BA, 41; Univ Zurich, MD, 48; Drexel Inst Technol, MS, 61; Univ Pa, PhD(biomed eng), 65. *Prof Exp:* Chief res, Dis of Chest, Heilstaette Du Midi, Davos, Switz, 50-52; asst res, Internal Med, Lincoln Hosp, NY, 52-53; asst prof med, Med Sch, Tufts Univ, 56-59; from asst prof to prof physiol, Sch Vet Med, Univ Pa, 61-67; res dir, Res Inst, Presby Hosp, 62-67; prof physiol & chmn biomed eng, Univ Va, 67-90, Forsyth prof appl sci, 84-90. *Concurrent Pos:* Res fels, Cardiopulmonary Lab, Nat Jewish Hosp, Denver, Colo, 43-54, Lung Sta, Boston City Hosp, Tufts Univ, 54- 59 & Res Inst, Presby Hosp, Philadelphia, 59-62. *Mem:* AAAS; Biomed Eng Soc; Inst Elec & Electronics Engrs; fel Biophys Soc; Sigma Xi; Am Physiol Soc. *Res:* Analysis of biological systems; systems analysis with particular emphasis on control hierarchies in biological and social systems; technology assessment in health care. *Mailing Add:* RR 1 Crozet VA 22932

ATTIX, FRANK HERBERT, RADIOLOGICAL PHYSICS. *Current Pos:* prof, 76-87, EMER PROF MED PHYSICS, UNIV WIS-MADISON, 87- *Personal Data:* b Portland, Ore, Apr 2, 25; m 59; c 2. *Educ:* Univ Calif, Berkeley, AB, 49; Univ Md, MS, 53. *Honors & Awards:* Appl Sci Award, Sigma Xi, 69; Distinguished Sci Achievement Award, Health Physics Soc, 87. *Prof Exp:* Res physicist, NIH, 49-50; res physicist, Nat Bur Stand, 50-57; reactor shielding physicist, ACF Industs, DC, 57-58; res physicist, Naval Res Lab, Washington, DC, 58-76, head, Dosimetry Br, 63-68, consult, Dosimetry Radiation Technol Div, 69-76. *Concurrent Pos:* Vis scientist, UK Atomic Energy Res Estab, Harwell, 68-69; consult, 87- *Mem:* Health Phys Soc; Sigma Xi; Am Asn Physicists Med. *Res:* Measurement radiation dose and related quantities; codeveloper of theory of cavity ionization and experimental verification of that theory; invented variable-length free-air ionization chamber; definitive measurement of gamma ray output of radium; measurement of dose by luminescent materials; fast-neutron dosimetry in cancer radiotherapy. *Mailing Add:* 705 Kent Oaks Way Gaithersburg MD 20878

ATTREP, MOSES, JR, RADIOCHEMISTRY, GEOCHEMISTRY. *Current Pos:* asst prof, 66-74, PROF CHEM, E TEX STATE UNIV, 74- *Personal Data:* b Alexandria, La, Jan 2, 39; m 65. *Educ:* La Col, BS, 60; Univ Ark, MS, 62, PhD(chem), 65. *Prof Exp:* Res assoc chem, Clark Univ, 65-66. *Mem:* Geochem Soc; Am Chem Soc. *Res:* Analytical chemistry; radiochemistry. *Mailing Add:* Isotope & Nuclear Chem Los Alamos Nat Lab MSJ514 Los Alamos NM 87545-0001

ATTWOOD, DAVID THOMAS, JR, ENGINEERING PHYSICS. *Current Pos:* Physicist, Lawrence Livermore Nat Lab, Calif, 72-83, PHYSICIST LAWRENCE BERKELEY NAT LAB, UNIV CALIF, 83-, PROF RESIDENCE, 89-, CHAIR APPL SCI & TECHNOL, 91- *Personal Data:* b New York, NY, Aug 15, 41; div, Linda Geniesse; c Timothy D, Courtney C & Kevin R. *Educ:* Hofstra Univ, BS, 63; Northwestern Univ, MS, 64; NY Univ, DSc(plasma physics), 72. *Concurrent Pos:* Founder & dir, Ctr X-ray Optics, Lawrence Berkeley Nat Lab; mem, Comt Optical Sci & Eng, Nat Acad Sci. *Mem:* AAAS; Am Phys Soc; fel Optical Soc Am. *Res:* X-ray optics; x-ray microscopy; synchrotrons; partially coherent x-rays; extreme ultraviolet lithography. *Mailing Add:* 20 La Sonoma Ct Alamo CA 94507-2127

ATTYGALLE, ATHULA B, CHEMICAL ECOLOGY, MASS SPECTROMETRY. *Current Pos:* DIR, MASS SPECTROMETRY FACIL, CORNELL UNIV, 91- *Personal Data:* b Galle, Sri Lanka, June 3, 50; m 84, Miho Yamakawa; c Suneth. *Educ:* Univ Ceylon, BSc, 75; Univ Sri Lanka, MSc, 77; Tokyo Inst Technol, dipl chem & chem eng, 79; Univ Keele, PhD(chem), 83. *Prof Exp:* Res fel chem, Univ Erlangen-Nurenberg, Ger, 84-87 & 88-89; fel, Univ Keele, Eng, 84; vis asst prof chem, Univ Houston, 87-88; vis assoc prof, Cornell Univ, 89-90. *Concurrent Pos:* Sr res assoc, Cornell Inst Res Chem Ecol, 91-; co-prin investr, NSF, 92-94; prin investr, USAID, 92-97; fel Alexander Von Humbolt. *Mem:* Am Chem Soc; Int Soc Chem Ecol; Am Soc Pharmacog. *Res:* Chemical communication and defense mechanisms of arthropods; structure elucidation of natural products by microchemical methods including gasphase infrared spectrometry, mass spectrometry and nuclear magnetic resonance spectrometry. *Mailing Add:* Baker Lab Dept Chem Cornell Univ Ithaca NY 14853. *Fax:* 607-255-3407; *E-Mail:* abal@cornell.edu

ATWAL, ONKAR SINGH, ULTRA STRUCTURE OF PULMONARY INTRAVASCULAR MACROPHAGES, HORMONAL MANIPULATION. *Current Pos:* from asst prof to prof, 67-94, EMER PROF ANAT, DEPT BIOMED SCI, UNIV GUELPH, 95- *Personal Data:* b Mombasa, Kenya, Sept 16, 29; Can citizen; m 60, Devinder; c Nina, Preeti, Seema & Randeep. *Educ:* Punjab Univ, BVSc, 53; Univ Calif, Davis, MS, 63, PhD(anat), 68. *Prof Exp:* Lectr vet anat, Punjab Univ, 55-61; teaching asst, Univ Calif, Davis, 61-67. *Concurrent Pos:* Consult & lectr, Cent Univ, Foreign Agr Orgn, UN, Quito, Ecuador, 69, Nat Antonomous, Univ Mex, 74, Kabul

Univ, Afghanistan, 76-78; vis prof, Univ Calif, Davis, 91-92; prof, Ross Univ, St Kitts, WI, 94- *Mem:* Am Asn Anatomists; Am Asn Invest Pathol; NY Acad Sci; Am Asn Vet Anatomists; Can Asn Anatomists; World Asn Vet Anatomists. *Res:* Pulmonary intravascular macrophages (PIMS) in the lungs of horses and goats; special properties of the surface coat of PIMS in sheep, goats, calves and horses and its composition of predominately lipoproteins at the cytochemical level; digestive metabolite, 3-methylindole (a pneumotoxic 3-carbon compound) produces acute pneumonia in cattle and leads to pulmonary hypertension and impaired funtion(s) of the pulmonary surfactant; DNase and RNase in periheral leukocytes of laboratory mammals. *Mailing Add:* 212 Dimson Ave Guelph ON N1G 3C8 Can. *E-Mail:* oatwal@uoguelph.ca

ATWATER, BEAUFORD W, OPTICAL SENSORS, PHOTOCHEMISTRY. *Current Pos:* MEM TECH STAFF, BELL COMMUN RES, 93- *Personal Data:* b Milwaukee, Wis, Feb 24, 58; m 82, Gretchen Day; c Melanie. *Educ:* Univ Nebr, Lincoln, BS, 80; Univ Kans, PhD(org chem), 86. *Prof Exp:* Fel, Fla State Univ, 85-87; sr scientist, Boc Group Tech Ctr, 87-91, lead scientist, 91-93. *Mem:* Am Chem Soc; Inter Am Photochem Soc. *Res:* Design optical sensors for indoor air quality, such as volatile organic compounds, nitrous oxide, ozone, airborne particles; designed optical sensors for biomedical applications. *Mailing Add:* Bellcore Rm 3X285 331 Newman Springs Rd Red Bank NJ 07701. *Fax:* 732-741-2891; *E-Mail:* atwater@nyquist.bellcore.com

ATWATER, EDWARD CONGDON, INTERNAL MEDICINE, HISTORY OF MEDICINE. *Current Pos:* Intern & asst resident, Univ Rochester, 55-57, chief resident, 59-60, sr instr & asst prof, 59-69, assoc prof med, Sch Med, 69-91, from asst prof to assoc prof hist med, 71-91, EMER PROF MED, UNIV ROCHESTER, 91- *Personal Data:* b Rochester, NY, Feb 6, 26; m 50, Ruth Prole; c Rebecca W & Edward W. *Educ:* Univ Rochester, BA, 50; Harvard Univ, MD, 55; Johns Hopkins Univ, MA, 74. *Concurrent Pos:* USPHS trainee arthritis & metab dis, Univ Rochester, 57-59; Macy fel, Sch Med, Johns Hopkins Univ, 70-71; from asst physician to assoc physician, Strong Mem Hosp, Rochester, 60-69, sr assoc physician, 69-84, attend physician, 84-91. *Mem:* Am Rheumatism Asn; Am Asn Hist Med. *Res:* History of American medicine and the medical profession; history of medical education. *Mailing Add:* 195 Whitewood Lane Univ Rochester Med Ctr Rochester NY 14618

ATWATER, HARRY ALBERT, solid state physics, for more information see previous edition

ATWATER, NORMAN WILLIS, ORGANIC CHEMISTRY. *Current Pos:* RETIRED. *Personal Data:* b Paterson, NJ, Mar 16, 26; m 47; c 3. *Educ:* Rensselaer Polytech Inst, BS, 49; Johns Hopkins Univ, PhD(chem), 53. *Prof Exp:* Dir qual control, G D Searle & Co, 53-76; dir overseas qual control, E R Squibb & Son, 76-88. *Mem:* AAAS; Am Chem Soc. *Res:* Steroids; terpenes. *Mailing Add:* 26 Zion Rd Hopewell NJ 08525

ATWATER, TANYA MARIA, MARINE GEOPHYSICS, TECTONICS. *Current Pos:* PROF, DEPT GEOL SCI, UNIV CALIF, SANTA BARBARA, 80- *Personal Data:* b Los Angeles, Calif, Aug 27, 42; c 1. *Educ:* Univ Calif, Berkeley, AB, 65, Univ Calif, San Diego, PhD(earth sci), 72. *Honors & Awards:* Newcomb Cleveland Prize, AAAS, 80; Encourage Award, Asn Woman Geologists, 84. *Prof Exp:* Vis res assoc seismol, Univ Chile, 66-67; res assoc paleomagnetism, Stanford Univ, 70-71; asst prof marine geophys, Univ Calif, San Diego, 72-73; Nat Acad Sci exchange scientist, USSR, 73-74; from asst prof to assoc prof marine geophys,Mass Inst Technol, 74-80. *Concurrent Pos:* Sloan fel, 75-77; nat lectr, Sigma Xi, 75-76. *Mem:* Nat Acad Sci; fel Am Geophys Union; AAAS; Am Geol Inst; Asn Women Geologists; Soc Women Geogr; fel Geol Soc Am. *Res:* Detailed tectonic nature of mid ocean ridges and the mechanisms by which ocean floor is created and modified; plate tectonic reconstructions and their implications for continental geologic structure and history. *Mailing Add:* Dept Geol Sci Univ Calif Santa Barbara CA 93106

ATWELL, CONSTANCE WOODRUFF, DEVELOPMENTAL PSYCHOBIOLOGY, SENSORY DEVELOPMENT. *Current Pos:* ASSOC DIR EXTRAMURAL ACTIV, NAT INST NEUROL DIS & STROKE, 92- *Personal Data:* b Philadelphia, Pa, Jan 27, 42; m 90, Patrick M Morris; c Catherine & Cynthia. *Educ:* Mount Holyoke Col, AB, 63; Univ Calif, Los Angeles, MA, 65, PhD(psychol), 68. *Prof Exp:* From asst prof to prof psychol, Pitzer Col & Claremeont 67-78; grants assoc, NIH, 78-79; chief, Strabismus, Amblyopia & Vision Processing Br, 81-92, dep assoc dir, Extramural & Collab Progs, Nat Eye Inst, NIH, 88-92. *Concurrent Pos:* Res assoc, Fac Med, Univ Col Nairobi, 68-69, lectr child psychol, 69; prin investr res grants, Grant Found, 75-77 & Nat Inst Child Health & Human Develop, NIH, 76-78; chief, Off Clin Applns Vision Res, Nat Eye Inst, NIH, 79-88. *Mem:* AAAS; Am Psychol Asn; Asn Res Vision & Ophthal; Asn Women Sci; Women Eye Res; Soc Neurosci. *Res:* Development of the visual system and behavior; development of vestibular responsiveness in human infants; vestibular self-stimulation in normal children. *Mailing Add:* Nat Inst Neurol Disorders & Stroke Fed Bldg 1016 7550 Wisconsin Ave Bethesda MD 20852. *Fax:* 301-402-4370; *E-Mail:* ca23c@nih.gov

ATWELL, WILLIAM ALAN, PRODUCT DEVELOPMENT, CEREAL CHEMISTRY. *Current Pos:* SR SCIENTIST, PILLSBURY CO, 79- *Personal Data:* b Baltimore, Md, Aug 26, 51; m 73; c 2. *Educ:* State Univ NY, BS, 72, MS, 76; Kans State Univ, PhD(grain sci), 78. *Prof Exp:* Teaching asst chem, State Univ NY, Oswego, 73-74; res tech, Lake Ont Environ Labs, 74-75; res asst grain sci, Kans State Univ, 76-78. *Concurrent Pos:* Consult, Magnolia Labs, 77-78. *Mem:* Am Asn Cereal Chemists. *Mailing Add:* MS 9920 330 University Ave SE Minneapolis MN 55414

ATWELL, WILLIAM HENRY, ORGANIC CHEMISTRY. *Current Pos:* Res mgr, basic intermediates, Dow Corning Corp, 69-72, silicone rubber, 72-75 & elastomers, 75-80, tech dir, basic mat, 81-83, TECH MGR, CERAMICS, DOW CORNING CORP, 83- *Personal Data:* b Milwaukee, Wis, Dec 13, 36; m 60; c 4. *Educ:* Marquette Univ, BS, 59, MS, 60; Iowa State Univ, PhD(chem), 64. *Mem:* Am Chem Soc; Sigma Xi; Am Ceramic Soc. *Res:* The use of chemical precursor to produce advanced structural ceramics; development of ceramic fibers an ceramic composites. *Mailing Add:* 1402 Wildwood St Midland MI 48642

ATWOOD, CHARLES LEROY, COMPUTER-AIDED ARCHITECTURAL DESIGN. *Current Pos:* VPRES & DIR RES & DEVELOP, FORSIGHT RESOURCES, 88- *Personal Data:* b Decatur, Ill, Dec 24, 51; m 74; c 2. *Educ:* Univ Ill, BSc, 74, MArchit, 76. *Honors & Awards:* Prize, Edward C Earl Found, 76; Award, Emerson Found, 76. *Prof Exp:* Spec teaching fel comput appln in archit, Univ Ill, 75-76; asst dir comput serv, Skidmore, Owings & Merrill, 76-81; sr vpres, Hok Comput Serv Corp, 81-84, chief exec officer & pres, 84-87. *Mem:* Asn Comput Mach; Digital Equip Comput Users Soc; Data Processing Mgt Asn; Soc Comput Appln Eng, Planning & Archit. *Res:* Computer applications for architectural design, engineering, interiors and facility management with an emphasis on integration. *Mailing Add:* 7712 N Lucerne Kansas City MO 64151

ATWOOD, DONALD J, electrical engineering; deceased, see previous edition for last biography

ATWOOD, DONALD KEITH, COASTAL OCEAN ENVIRONMENTAL QUALITY, GLOBAL CLIMATE CHANGE. *Current Pos:* DIR, OCEAN CHEM DIV, NAT OCEANIC & ATMOSPHERIC ADMIN, ATLANTIC OCEANOG & METEOROL LABS, 76- *Personal Data:* b Burlington, Vt, June 5, 33; div; c Joseph M, Janet M, Daniel J & Sarah K. *Educ:* St Michael's Col Vt, BS, 55; Purdue Univ, PhD(chem), 60. *Prof Exp:* Sr res specialist, Exxon Prod Res, 60-69; assoc prof chem oceanog, Univ PR, 69-76. *Concurrent Pos:* Subj leader chem oceanog, Coop Invest Caribbean & Adj Regions, 72-76; consult, NSF, 75-76; dir, Intergovt Oceanog Comn Regional Marine Pollution Monitoring Prog Caribbean, 78-86; adj prof, Univ Miami, 78- & Univ PR, 89-; fel, Coop Inst Marine & Atmospheric Sci, Univ Miami, 91- *Mem:* Am Chem Soc; Oceanog Soc; Am Soc Limnol & Oceanog; Am Geophys Union. *Res:* Environmental impact of anthropogenic inputs to coastal ocean; coral ecosystem health. *Mailing Add:* 575 Crandon Blvd Key Biscayne FL 33149

ATWOOD, GENEVIEVE, APPLIED GEOMORPHOLOGY, GEOGRAPHIC INFORMATION SYSTEMS. *Current Pos:* CHIEF EDUC OFFICER, EARTH SCI EDUC, 93- *Personal Data:* b Calif, May 4, 46; m 87, Don R Mabey. *Educ:* Bryn Mawr Col, BA, 68; Wesleyan Univ, MA, 73. *Honors & Awards:* Jim Bridger Award, Utah State Univ, 78; John Wesley Powell Award, US Geol Surv, 90. *Prof Exp:* Staff officer, Environ Studies Bd, Nat Acad Sci, Nat Res Coun, 72-74; mem, Utah House Rep, 74-80; geologist, Ford, Bacon & Davis, Utah, Inc, 76-81; state geologist & dir, Utah Geol Surv, 81-89. *Concurrent Pos:* Mem, President's Intergovernmental Adv Panel Sci & Technol, 76-79; mem, Comt Ground Failure Hazards, Comn Eng & Tech Systs, Nat Res Coun, 83-89. *Mem:* Asn Women Geoscientists; fel Geol Soc Am. *Res:* Geomorphology; teach teachers earth-science principles, hands-on, outdoors, in their schools and neighborhoods; processes and applied geomorphology of Great Salt Lake Utah. *Mailing Add:* Earth Sci Educ 30 U St Salt Lake City UT 84103

ATWOOD, GILBERT RICHARD, PHYSICAL CHEMISTRY. *Current Pos:* RETIRED. *Personal Data:* b Taunton, Mass, Apr 9, 28; m 55; c 2. *Educ:* Carnegie Inst Technol, BS, 49; Purdue Univ, MS, 51; Univ Pittsburgh, PhD(chem), 58. *Prof Exp:* From asst to assoc, Mellon Inst, 51-54, from jr fel to fel, 54-58; proj leader, Union Carbide Corp, 63-68, from res scientist to sr res scientist, 68-74, res assoc, 74-91. *Mem:* AAAS; Am Chem Soc. *Res:* Thermodynamics, phase equilibria; thermometry; cryoscopy; ebulliometry; calorimetry; separation and purification, gas absorption; liquid-liquid extraction and diffusion; fundamental papers and patents in environmental processes, e.g., stack gas scrubbing and removal of PCB's from transformers. *Mailing Add:* 21 Redwood Lane Briarcliff Manor NY 10510-1117

ATWOOD, GLENN A, CHEMICAL ENGINEERING, ENVIRONMENTAL ENGINEERING. *Current Pos:* CHEM & ENVIRON ENG CONSULT. *Personal Data:* b Rock Rapids, Iowa, Oct 24, 35; m 55; c 5. *Educ:* Iowa State Univ, BS, 57, MS, 59; Univ Wash, PhD(mass transfer), 63. *Prof Exp:* Res asst separation lanthanides, Ames Lab, Iowa, 57-59; instr chem eng, Univ Wash, 59-62; engr, Esso Res & Eng Co, 62-65; from asst prof to prof chem eng, Univ Akron, 65-90, assoc dean, 85-88, actg dean, 88-89; dir res & develop, Midwest Ore Processing Co, 90-93. *Concurrent Pos:* Consult, Khapp Foundry, BF Goodrich, Norton Co, Gen Tire & Rubber Co, Firestone Tire & Rubber Co, Chemstress Consult Co. *Mem:* Am Inst Chem Engrs; Sigma Xi. *Res:* Mass transfer; adsorption; process control. *Mailing Add:* Atwood Assocs 725 Ridgecrest Rd Akron OH 44303-1344. *Fax:* 330-836-2802

ATWOOD, HAROLD LESLIE, PHYSIOLOGY. *Current Pos:* from asst prof to assoc prof, 65-71, prof & chmn, Dept Physiol, 81-91, PROF ZOOL, UNIV TORONTO, 71-; PROF & DIR, MRC GROUP, 91- *Personal Data:* b Montreal, Que, Feb 15, 37; m 59, Lenore Mendelson; c David, Robert & Evan. *Educ:* Univ Toronto, BA, 59; Univ Calif, Berkeley, MA, 60; Glasgow Univ, PhD(zool), 63. *Hon Degrees:* DSc, Glasgow Univ, 79. *Prof Exp:* Res assoc biol, Univ Ore, 62-64; res fel, Calif Inst Technol, 64-65. *Mem:* Am

Physiol Soc; Can Physiol Soc; fel AAAS; fel Royal Soc Can; Soc Neurosci; Can Soc Zoologists. *Res:* Comparative and neuromuscular physiology; genetic effects on synaptic transmission. *Mailing Add:* Dept Physiol Med Sci Bldg Univ Toronto Toronto ON M5S 1A8 Can

ATWOOD, JERRY LEE, INORGANIC CHEMISTRY, PHYSICAL CHEMISTRY. *Current Pos:* From asst prof to assoc prof, 68-87, UNIV RES PROF CHEM, UNIV ALA, TUSCALOOSA, 87- *Personal Data:* b Springfield, Mo, July 27, 42; m 64, 84; c 3. *Educ:* Southwest Mo State Col, BS, 64; Univ Ill, MS, 66, PhD(inorg chem), 68. *Mem:* Am Inst Chem Eng; Am Chem Soc; Am Crystallog Asn. *Res:* Organometallic chemistry; x-ray crystallography; inclusion chemistry. *Mailing Add:* Dept Chem Univ Mo Columbia MO 65211-0336

ATWOOD, JIM D, INORGANIC CHEMISTRY, ORGANOMETALLIC CHEMISTRY. *Current Pos:* from asst prof to assoc prof, 77-88, assoc dean, Fac Natural Sci & Math, 84-85, PROF CHEM, STATE UNIV NY, BUFFALO, 89- *Personal Data:* b Springfield, Mo, June 3, 50; m 71, Mary Nichalson; c Angela, Amanda & Alanna. *Educ:* Southwest Mo State Univ, BS, 71; Univ Ill, PhD(chem), 75. *Prof Exp:* Fel, US-USSR Prog Coop Catalysis, Cornell Univ, 75-76. *Concurrent Pos:* Alfred P Sloan Found fel, 83-85; Alexander von Humboldt Found fel, 84; guest prof, Johann Wolfgang Goeth Univ, Frankfurt, 84. *Mem:* Am Chem Soc. *Res:* Reactivity and mechanisms of organometallic compounds; water-soluble organometallic compounds; modeling catalytic reactions; ligand effects; polynuclear complexes; electron transfer. *Mailing Add:* Dept Chem State Univ NY Buffalo NY 14260-3000. *Fax:* 716-645-6963; *E-Mail:* jatwood@acsu.buffalo.edu

ATWOOD, JOHN LELAND, ENGINEERING. *Current Pos:* RETIRED. *Personal Data:* b Walton, Ky, Oct 26, 04; m 72; c 1. *Educ:* Hardin Simmons Univ, AB, 26; Univ Tex, BS, 28. *Hon Degrees:* DEng, Stevens Inst Technol, 55, Carnegie-Mellon Univ, 65, Harvey Mudd Col, 79. *Honors & Awards:* H H Arnold Trophy, 70; Wright Bros Mem Lectr, 76; Wright Bros Mem Trophy; Nat Medal Technol, Pres Reagan, 84. *Prof Exp:* Jr aeroplane engr, Army Air Corps, Dayton, Ohio, 28-29; design engr, Douglas Aircraft Co, Calif, 30-34; vpres & chief engr, NAm Aviation, Inc, 34-38, vpres & asst gen mgr, 38-41, first vpres, 41, pres, 48-67, chief exec officer, 60-67, chmn bd, 62-67, pres & chief exec officer, NAm Rockwell Corp, 67-70, dir & sr consult, Rockwell Int Corp, 70-77. *Concurrent Pos:* Chmn indust adv comt, Nat Adv Comt Aeronaut, 58. *Mem:* Nat Acad Eng; hon fel Am Inst Aeronaut & Astronaut; Soc Automotive Engrs; Aerospace Indust Asn. *Mailing Add:* PO Box 1587 Vista CA 92085-1587

ATWOOD, JOHN WILLIAM, COMPUTER NETWORK PROTOCOLS, DISTRIBUTED APPLICATIONS. *Current Pos:* asst prof comput sci, 73-75, ASSOC PROF COMPUT SCI, CONCORDIA UNIV, 75- *Personal Data:* b Sherbrooke, Que, Feb 23, 41; m 70, Noreen Cain; c Tony & Christy. *Educ:* McGill Univ, BEng, 63; Univ Toronto, MASc, 65; Univ Ill, Urbana, PhD(elec eng), 70. *Prof Exp:* Res assoc elec eng, Univ Ill, Urbana, 65-70; asst prof, Univ Toronto, 70-72. *Concurrent Pos:* Consult, Metrop Toronto Police Comn, 71-72 & Amdahl Corp, 76-79; vis assoc prof comput sci, Univ Tex, Austin, 79-80; vis researcher, Centre Recherche Informatique Montreal, 86-87. *Mem:* Inst Elec & Electronics Engrs. *Res:* Design, analysis, validation, performance evaluation of high- speed computer network protocols; design, implementation, performance evaluation of distributed applications. *Mailing Add:* Dept Comput Sci Concordia Univ 1455 de Maisonneuve Blvd W Montreal PQ H3G 1M8 Can. *E-Mail:* bill@cs.concordia.ca

ATWOOD, KENNETH W, ELECTRICAL ENGINEERING. *Current Pos:* RETIRED. *Personal Data:* b Cedarview, Utah, Dec 21, 22; m 44; c 3. *Educ:* Univ Utah, BS, 50, MS, 54, PhD(elec eng), 57. *Prof Exp:* Transmitter engr, Sta KSL-KSL-TV, 49-56; from asst prof to prof elec eng, Univ Utah, 56-82. *Concurrent Pos:* Sr engr, Hanford Labs, Gen Elec Co, 62-63. *Mem:* Am Soc Eng Educ; Inst Elec & Electronics Engrs. *Res:* Solid state circuitry; digital circuitry design. *Mailing Add:* 140 W 8600 S Midvale UT 84047

ATWOOD, LINDA, BIO-ORGANIC CHEMISTRY. *Current Pos:* asst prof, 74, assoc prof, 74-84, PROF CHEM, CALIF POLYTECH STATE UNIV, SAN LUIS OBISPO, 84- *Personal Data:* b Rochester, NY, Nov 13, 46. *Educ:* Bard Col, BA, 68; Wesleyan Univ, MA, 72, PhD(chem), 74. *Prof Exp:* Teaching & res asst chem, Wesleyan Univ, 70-74. *Mem:* Am Chem Soc; AAAS. *Res:* Teaching and writing in the areas of pharmacology and nutritional biochemistry. *Mailing Add:* Dept Chem Calif Polytech State Univ San Luis Obispo CA 93407-0001

ATWOOD, MARK WYLLIE, ENTOMOLOGY, PHYSIOLOGY. *Current Pos:* MEM STAFF, AGR DIV, AM CYANAMID CO, 77- *Personal Data:* b Fairfield, Iowa, Mar 23, 42; m 62; c 2. *Educ:* Parsons Col, BS, 62; Univ Wis-Madison, MS, 65, PhD(zool), 68. *Prof Exp:* Asst prof biol, Purdue Univ, Ft Wayne, 67-70; entomologist, Iowa State Dept Agr, 70-77. *Mem:* AAAS; Am Soc Zool; Cent Plant Bd (pres, 75). *Res:* Excitation in insect visual system and use of visual information in behavior; mechanism of action of pesticides and relation of sub-lethal doses of pesticides to insect behavior. *Mailing Add:* 1359 Brentwood Rd Yardley PA 19067-3924

ATYEO, WARREN THOMAS, ENTOMOLOGY. *Current Pos:* PROF ENTOM & CUR, UNIV GA, 68- *Personal Data:* b Highland Park, Mich, Feb 15, 27; m 55; c 3. *Educ:* Western Ill Univ, BS & MS, 53; Univ Kans, PhD(entom), 59. *Prof Exp:* From asst prof to prof entom, Col Agr, Univ Nebr, 58-67, cur mus, 58-67; partic, Grants Assocs Prog, NIH, 67-68. *Concurrent Pos:* Res assoc, Field Mus Natural Hist. *Mem:* Soc Study Evolution; Entom Soc Am; Acarological Soc Am; Soc Systematic Zool; Soc Parasitol. *Res:* Acarology; systematics of Acarina: Bdelloidea, Analgoidea. *Mailing Add:* 160 Pioneer Ct Athens GA 30605

AU, CHI-KWAN, THEORETICAL PHYSICS. *Current Pos:* from asst prof to assoc prof, 75-84, PROF PHYSICS, UNIV SC, COLUMBIA, 85- *Personal Data:* b Macau, China, Jan 21, 46; nat US; m 70; c 2. *Educ:* Hong Kong Univ, BSc, 68; Columbia Univ, MA, 70, PhD(physics), 72. *Honors & Awards:* Univ SC Educ Found Res Award, 85. *Prof Exp:* Res assoc physics, Univ Ill, Urbana, 72-74; res assoc, Yale Univ, 74-75, lectr, 75. *Concurrent Pos:* Vis asst prof physics, Columbia Univ, 76, 77 & 78; mem, Inst for Theoret Physics, Santa Barbara, 81 & 88; hon lectr, Hong Kong Univ, 81-82; prin investr, NSF grants, 79-81 & 85-91, co-investr, 80-85; prin investr, Univ SC fac res & productive scholarship grant, 81-82 & 85-86; vis scientist, Harvard-Smithsonian Ctr Astrophys, Harvard Univ, 82, 83, 84, 87 & 90; partic, Lewis Ctr Physics, Del, 84 & 85; sr vis fel, City Univ, Hong Kong, 91. *Mem:* Am Phys Soc. *Res:* Theoretical astrophysics, neutron star matter; perturbation theory; atomic physics and quantum electrodynamics of simple atomic systems, interpretations of quantum mechanics. *Mailing Add:* Dept Physics & Astron Univ SC Columbia SC 29208. *Fax:* 803-777-3065; *E-Mail:* au@sc.edu

AU, WHITLOW W L, MARINE BIOACOUSTICS, DOLPHIN ACOUSTICS & SONAR. *Current Pos:* CHIEF SCIENTIST, MARINE MAMMAL RES PROG, HAWAII INST MARINE BIOL, 93- *Personal Data:* b Honolulu, Hawaii, July 31, 40; m 66, Dorothy Wagner; c Wagner, Wailani, Wesley & Wainani. *Educ:* Univ Hawaii, BS, 62; Wash State Univ, MS, 64, PhD(eng sci), 70. *Prof Exp:* Sr scientist, Naval Command, Control & Ocean Surveillence Ctr, 70-93. *Mem:* Fel Acoust Soc Am; Inst Elec & Electronics Engrs; Soc Marine Mammalogy. *Res:* Acoustic sensory and echolocation systems of dolphins and small whales. *Mailing Add:* R&D Hawaii Inst Marine Biol PO Box 1106 Kailua HI 96734. *Fax:* 808-236-7443; *E-Mail:* au@humu.nosc.mil

AUBEL, JOSEPH LEE, PHYSICS. *Current Pos:* Asst prof, 64-74, ASSOC PROF PHYSICS, UNIV SFLA, 74- *Personal Data:* b Lansing, Mich, Sept 7, 36; m 67, Elvira M Ruhlig; c Edward L. *Educ:* Mich State Univ, BS, 54, PhD(physics), 64. *Mem:* Optical Soc Am; Am Asn Physics Teachers; Am Sci Affil. *Res:* Optics; computer-based and individualized competency-based education; computer control of optical instrumentation for semiconductor characterization. *Mailing Add:* Dept Physics Univ SFla Tampa FL 33620

AUBERTIN, GERALD MARTIN, WATERSHED MANAGEMENT. *Current Pos:* ASSOC PROF FORESTRY, SOUTHERN ILL UNIV, CARBONDALE, 76- *Personal Data:* b Kankakee, Ill, Sept 23, 31; m 57; c 4. *Educ:* Univ Ill, Urbana-Champaign, BS, 58, MS, 60; Pa State Univ, PhD(agron), 64. *Prof Exp:* Asst agron, Univ Ill, 58; res asst, Pa State Univ, 64; res soil physicist & fel, Univ Calif, Riverside, 64-65; res soil scientist, US Forest Serv, Parsons, WVa, 65-76. *Concurrent Pos:* Vis prof dept earth resources, Colo State Univ, 75; vis res scientist, Pac Forest Res Ctr, Victoria, BC, 83-86; chair, Qual Assurance Steering Comt, Nat Atmospheric Deposition Prog. *Mem:* Am Soc Agron; Soil Sci Soc Am; Sigma Xi. *Res:* Watershed management; non-point pollution; forestry best management practices; stream water quality; subsurface water movement and soil macropores in forested watersheds; oxygen-salt-moisture and root relations; physical edaphology; soil structure problems; geologic/soil/water quality investigation; acid rain; atmospheric deposition; effect of forest harvesting on soil and water. *Mailing Add:* 103 S Dixon Ave Southern Ill Univ Carbondale IL 62901

AUBIN, JANE E, CELL BIOLOGY, DIFFERENTIATION. *Current Pos:* From asst prof to assoc prof, 79-88, chair, Grad Dept Dent, 89-94, PROF CELL BIOL, UNIV TORONTO, 88- *Personal Data:* b Cornwall, Ont, Mar 3, 50. *Educ:* Queen's Univ, BSc, 72; Univ Toronto, PhD(med biophy), 77. *Honors & Awards:* Oral Biol Res Award, Int Asn Dent Res, 85. *Concurrent Pos:* Mem coun, Am Soc Bone & Mineral Res, 91-94, Med Res Coun Can, 91- *Mem:* Am Soc Cell Biol; Am Soc Bone & Mineral Res; Int Asn Dental Res; Can Soc Cell Biol; Int Soc Differentiation. *Res:* Osteoblast lineage, differentiation and regulation. *Mailing Add:* Dept Anat Cell Biol Univ Toronto Fac Med One Kings Col Ctr Med Sci Bldg Rm 6255 Toronto ON M5S 1A8 Can

AUBORN, JAMES JOHN, PHYSICAL CHEMISTRY. *Current Pos:* from mem tech staff to distinguished mem tech staff, 76-87, tech supvr undersea lightwave systs, 87-89, DEPT HEAD/PROG MGR, LIGHTWAVE TRANSMISSION SYSTS, AT&T BELL LABS, 89- *Personal Data:* b Portland, Ore, Feb 21, 40; m 62; c 2. *Educ:* Ore State Univ, BS, 61, MS, 62; Univ Utah, PhD(chem), 71. *Prof Exp:* Mem tech staff electrochem, GTE Lab, Inc, Gen Tel & Electronics Corp, Bayside, NY, 71-72 & Waltham, Mass, 72-73, mem tech staff mat sci, 74-75, tech proj mgr electrochem, 75-76. *Concurrent Pos:* Instr, Northeastern Univ, 74-76; proj mgr electrochem, Off Naval Res, 84; sci tech agent, Dept Defense, 84. *Mem:* Electrochem Soc; Am Chem Soc; AAAS; Am Inst Physics; Sigma Xi; Optical Soc; Int Soc Optical Engrs. *Res:* Undersea fiber optic communications systems; chemistry and physics of inorganic non-aqueous liquids relating to electrochemical power sources; materials science and engineering; high temperature and refractory materials; electrical and optical properties of materials. *Mailing Add:* 121 Mt Horeb Rd Warren NJ 07060-5528

AUBRECHT, GORDON JAMES, II, ENERGY ISSUES, PHYSICS PEDAGOGY. *Current Pos:* from asst prof to assoc prof, 81-87, PROF PHYSICS, OHIO STATE UNIV, 87- *Personal Data:* b Bedford, Ohio, May 2, 43; m 84, Michelle Felty; c Dacia B(Jackson), Katarina P & Taryn G. *Educ:* Rutgers Univ, BA, 65; Princeton Univ, PhD(theoret physics), 71. *Honors & Awards:* Woodrow Wilson Fel, 65-66. *Prof Exp:* Res assoc high energy theory, Ohio State Univ, 70-72; vis asst prof, Inst Theoret Sci, Univ Ore, 72-75; vis assoc prof, Univ Md, 85-87. *Concurrent Pos:* Alexander von Humboldt fel, 79-80; gastdozent, Inst Theoret Physics, Univ Karlsruhe, WGer, 79-80; consult, Ctr Fac Develop, Kans State Univ, 83-86; vis fel, Am Asn Physics Teachers, Univ Md, 85-87; coordr, Conf Teaching Mod Phys, 85-88; chmn, Comt Prof Concerns, Am Asn Physics Teachers, 85-87, Metric Comt, 91-; secy, Contemporary Physics Ed Proj, 86- *Mem:* Am Phys Soc; Am Asn Physics Teachers; Sigma Xi; AAAS. *Res:* Theoretical structure of the electroweak interaction; higher symmetry; chiral group phenomenology; physics pedagogy; alteration of the introductory physics to include more contemporary physics at all levels of education. *Mailing Add:* Dept Physics Ohio State Univ 1465 Mt Vernon Ave Marion OH 43302-5695. *Fax:* 614-389-6786 Ext 6258; *E-Mail:* aubrecht@mps.ohio-state.edu

AUBREY, DAVID GLENN, MARINE SCIENCES. *Current Pos:* from asst to assoc scientist, 78-90, dir, Coastal Res Ctr, 87-92, SR SCIENTIST, WOODS HOLE OCEANOG INST, 91-; PRES, AUBREY CONSULT, 86- *Personal Data:* b Ft Sill, Okla, Aug 21, 50; m 72, Sandra; c Shelley, Andrew & Julie. *Educ:* Univ Southern Calif, BS & BS, 73; Scripps Inst Oceanog, PhD(oceanog), 78. *Concurrent Pos:* Consult, 72-; lectr, Mass Inst Technol, 84-85. *Mem:* Am Geophys Union; AAAS; Oceanog Soc. *Res:* Nearshore processes: inner shelf sediment transport; waves and currents; beach erosion; tidal waves; sea-level change; lagoons and estuaries. *Mailing Add:* Aubrey Consult Inc PO Box 10 1140 Rte 284 Cataumet MA 02534. *Fax:* 508-457-2187; *E-Mail:* daubrey@whoi.edu

AUBRY, MURIEL, MEDICAL RESEARCH, BIOCHEMISTRY. *Current Pos:* RES ASST PROF, CLIN RES INST MONTREAL, 93- *Personal Data:* b Tarbes, France, 1958. *Educ:* Univ Montreal, BS, 79, MS, 83, PhD(biochem), 87. *Prof Exp:* Fel biochem-human genetics, Montreal Gen Hosp Res Inst, 87-93. *Mem:* Am Soc Cell Biol. *Mailing Add:* Clin Res Inst Montreal 110 W Pine Ave Montreal PQ H2W 1R7 Can

AUCHAMPAUGH, GEORGE FREDRICK, EXPERIMENTAL NUCLEAR PHYSICS. *Current Pos:* RETIRED. *Personal Data:* b Chicago, Ill, Jan 19, 39. *Educ:* Univ Ill, BS, 61; Univ Calif, MS, 66, PhD(appl sci), 68. *Prof Exp:* Staff mem neutron physics, Lawrence Livermore Lab, 61-68; staff mem neutron physics, Los Alamos Sci Lab, 68- *Mem:* Am Phys Soc. *Res:* Neutron physics research with monoenergetic and continuous neutron sources; fission barrier physics; resonance region of sub threshold fission isotopes; nuclear spectroscopy of light elements from R-matrix analysis of neutron cross section data. *Mailing Add:* Los Alamos Nat Lab PO Box 1663 D436 Los Alamos NM 87545

AUCHINCLOSS, HUGH, JR, TRANSPLANT SURGERY. *Current Pos:* From instr to asst prof, 86-90, ASSOC PROF SURG, HARVARD UNIV, 90-; CHIEF PANCREAS TRANSPLANTATION, MASS GEN HOSP, 90- *Personal Data:* b New York, NY, Mar 15, 49; c 3. *Educ:* Harvard Univ, MD, 76. *Concurrent Pos:* Asst surg, 77-85, Mass Gen Hosp, 77-85. *Mem:* Transplantation Soc; Am Soc Transplant Surgeons; Am Asn Immunologists; Am Col Surgeons. *Res:* Transplantation; immunology. *Mailing Add:* Dept Surg Harvard Med Sch Mass Gen Hosp White 510B Boston MA 02114-2696

AUCHINCLOSS, JOSEPH HOWLAND, JR, INTERNAL MEDICINE. *Current Pos:* From instr to assoc prof, 51-71, PROF MED, COL MED, STATE UNIV NY UPSTATE MED CTR, 71- *Personal Data:* b Lawrence, NY, June 28, 21; m 46; c 4. *Educ:* Yale Univ, BS, 43; Columbia Univ, MD, 45. *Mem:* Am Fedn Clin Res; Am Thoracic Soc; Am Physiol Soc; Am Col Physicians; Sigma Xi. *Res:* Cardiopulmonary physiology. *Mailing Add:* 3935 Rippleton Rd Cazenovia NY 13035

AUCHMUTY, GILES, VARIATIONAL METHODS, NUMERICAL ANALYSIS. *Current Pos:* PROF MATH, UNIV HOUSTON, 82- *Personal Data:* b Dublin, Ireland, 1945; US citizen; m 81. *Educ:* Australian Nat Univ, BSc, 66; Univ Chicago, SM, 68, PhD(appl math), 70. *Prof Exp:* Res instr math, State Univ NY, Stony Brook, 70-72; from asst prof to assoc prof math, Ind Univ, Bloomington, 72-81. *Concurrent Pos:* Res fel, Math Inst, Oxford Univ, 81; vis mem, Inst Advan Study, Princeton, 89; vis prof, Tex A&M Univ, College Station, 90; managing ed, AMS Pubs in Appl Math, 87-90; managing ed, Houston Math, 93- *Mem:* Am Math Soc; Soc Indust & Appl Math; Sigma Xi; Int Asn Math Physicists. *Res:* Variational methods; bifurcation theory and partial differential equations; numerical analysis; models of rotating stars; thermodynamics; chemical equilibria; reaction diffusion problems. *Mailing Add:* Dept Math Univ Houston Houston TX 77204-3476. *Fax:* 713-743-3505; *E-Mail:* auch@uh.edu

AUCHTER, HARRY A, PHYSICS. *Current Pos:* from instr to asst prof, 53-58, assoc prof, 58-86, EMER PROF PHYSICS, CARROLL COL, WIS, 86- *Personal Data:* b St Louis, Mo, Aug 31, 20; m 54, Nancy Boefer; c Ruth (Daniel) & Mark. *Educ:* Southeast Mo State Col, AB, 42; Univ Iowa, MS, 46. *Prof Exp:* Instr physics, Kearney State Col, 46-47, Bangkok Christian Col, Thailand, 47-50 & Augustana Col (SDak), 51-53. *Mem:* Am Asn Physics Teachers. *Res:* Adiabatic compressibilities of aqueous solutions using ultrasonics. *Mailing Add:* 140 Tenny Ave Waukesha WI 53186

AUCLAIR, ALLAN NELSON DOUGLAS, GLOBAL CHANGE, CARBONDIOXIDE BUDGETS. *Current Pos:* SR SCIENTIST GLOBAL CHANGE RES, SCI & POLICY ASSOCS, INC, 90- *Personal Data:* b Montreal, Que, Sept 22, 43; c Gregory, Alexandra & Tara A. *Educ:* McGill Univ, BS, 64; Univ Wis, PhD(plant ecol), 68. *Prof Exp:* Fel bot, Univ Mo, 68-69; from asst prof to assoc prof ecol, McGill Univ, 69-79; assoc prof, George Mason Univ, 79-81; prog dir, Environ, Forestry Can, 81-90. *Concurrent Pos:* Vis scientist, Embrada, Brazil, 76 & CSIRO, Australia, 79. *Res:* Global change; missing carbon budget; role of climate change in forest dieback. *Mailing Add:* 4000 Massachusetts Ave NW Washington DC 20016. *Fax:* 202-789-1206

AUCLAIR, WALTER, DAIRY NUTRITION, GENETICS. *Current Pos:* OWNER, AUCLAIR FARMS, 66- *Personal Data:* b Manchester, NH, Sept 13, 33; m 54; c 3. *Educ:* Univ Conn, BA, 55; NY Univ, MS, 58, PhD(biol), 60. *Honors & Awards:* Nat Winner, Nat Endowment Soil & Water Conserv, 90. *Prof Exp:* NIH res fel, George Washington Univ, 60-61; from asst prof to assoc prof zool, Univ Cincinnati, 61-66; assoc prof biol, Rensselaer Polytech Inst, 66-77. *Concurrent Pos:* Investr, Zool Sta, Naples, Italy, 65-66; trustee & secy, Bermuda Biol Sta Res, Inc; NSF sci consult, India, 68-69; vis assoc prof, Cambridge Univ, England, 74, Rockefeller Univ, 74-75. *Mem:* Am Inst Biol Sci; Am Soc Cell Biol; Soc Develop Biol; Am Soc Animal Sci; Am Dairy Sci Asn. *Res:* Differentiation of cilla and other organelles in marine invertebrate embryos; renal hemopoiesis in amphibians; bovine reproductive physiology; dairy nutrition and genetics. *Mailing Add:* RD-1 Box 99 Melrose NY 12121

AUDESIRK, GERALD JOSEPH, NEUROETHOLOGY. *Current Pos:* AT DEPT BIOL, UNIV COLO. *Personal Data:* b New Brunswick, NJ, Sept 15, 48; m 70. *Educ:* Rutgers Univ, BA, 70; Calif Inst Technol, PhD(neurobiol), 74. *Prof Exp:* Fel neurobiol, Calif Inst Technol, 74-57; fel, Univ Wash, 76-78, res assoc, 78-79; asst prof neurobiol, Univ Mo-Columbia, 79- *Mem:* AAAS; Soc Neurosci; Animal Behav Soc. *Res:* Cellular basis of neurotoxicity of heavy metals especially lead; cellular basis of behavior of invertebrates. *Mailing Add:* 2317 Daisy Lane Golden CO 80401

AUDESIRK, TERESA ECK, NEUROETHOLOGY. *Current Pos:* AT BIOL DEPT, DIV NATURAL PHYS SCI, UNIV COLO, DENVER. *Personal Data:* b Washington, DC, Jan 28, 50; m 71. *Educ:* Bucknell Univ, BS, 71; Univ Southern Calif, PhD(marine physiol), 76. *Prof Exp:* Res assoc neuroethol, Univ Wash, 76-79; asst prof neuroethol & biol, Univ Mo, 79- *Mem:* Soc Neurosci; Sigma Xi; Animal Behav Soc. *Res:* Identifying neurons in simple invertebrate nervous systems which underlie production of behavior; neuronal changes which underlie learning. *Mailing Add:* Biol Dept Box 171 Univ Colo Denver PO Box 173364 Denver CO 80217-3364

AUDET, SARAH ANNE, semiconductor sensors & actuators, analytical spectroscopic instrumentation, for more information see previous edition

AUE, DONALD HENRY, ORGANIC CHEMISTRY. *Current Pos:* ASSOC PROF CHEM, UNIV CALIF, SANTA BARBARA, 68- *Personal Data:* b Columbus, Ohio, June 19, 42; m 64; c 2. *Educ:* Ohio State Univ, BSc, 63; Cornell Univ, PhD(org chem), 67. *Prof Exp:* NSF fel org chem, Columbia Univ, 67-68. *Mem:* Am Chem Soc; Brit Chem Soc. *Res:* Synthesis and properties of strained carbocyclic and heterocyclic systems; additions to strained multiple bonds; carbonium ion reactions in solution and gas phase; organic photochemistry; organic synthesis. *Mailing Add:* Dept Chem Univ Calif Santa Barbara CA 93106

AUE, WALTER ALOIS, ORGANIC CHEMISTRY, ANALYTICAL CHEMISTRY. *Current Pos:* dept chmn, 83-86, PROF CHEM, DALHOUSIE UNIV, 73- *Personal Data:* b Vienna, Austria, Jan 20, 35. *Educ:* Univ Vienna, PhD(org chem), 63. *Honors & Awards:* Fisher Award, Can, 80. *Prof Exp:* Res investr org chem, Western Reserve Univ, 63-65; asst prof anal chem, Univ Mo-Columbia, 65-69, assoc prof chem & res assoc Space Sci Ctr, 69-73. *Concurrent Pos:* USDA grant with Dr Billy G Tweedy, 67-70; USPHS grant, 67-70; NSF grant, 70-72; US Environ Protection Agency grant, 72-75; Nat Res Coun Can grant, 73-; Can Defense Res Bd grant, 74-76; Agr Can grant, 74-79; Environ Can grant, 78-80. *Res:* Pesticide residue analysis; specific detectors for gas chromatography; support-bonded chromatographic phases. *Mailing Add:* Dept Chem Dalhousie Univ Halifax NS B3H 4H6 Can

AUER, HENRY ERNEST, protein structure & stability, protein folding, for more information see previous edition

AUER, JAN WILLEM, MATHEMATICS. *Current Pos:* Lectr, 69-70, asst prof math, 70-76, ASSOC PROF MATH, BROCK UNIV, 76- *Personal Data:* b Utrecht, Neth, Apr 10, 42; Can citizen; c 2. *Educ:* McGill Univ, BEng, 64, MSc, 66; Univ Toronto, PhD(math), 71. *Mem:* Am Math Soc; Math Asn Am; Tensor Soc. *Res:* Algebraic topology and differential geometry, specifically on smooth bundles. *Mailing Add:* Brock Univ St Catharines ON Can. *E-Mail:* jauer@spartan.ac.brocku.ca

AUER, LAWRENCE H, ASTROPHYSICS. *Current Pos:* AT DIV EARTH & SPACE SCI, LOS ALAMOS SCI LAB. *Personal Data:* b Englewood, NJ, Dec 26, 41; m. *Educ:* Haverford Col, BA, 63; Princeton Univ, PhD(astron), 67. *Prof Exp:* Res assoc & fel astron, Joint Inst Lab Astrophys, Univ Colo, 66-68; from asst prof to assoc prof, Yale Univ, 68-77, dir grad studies, Watson Astron Ctr, 74-77; mem staff, Nat Ctr Atomspheric Res, 77-; assoc prof, Pa State Univ, 80- *Mem:* Am Astron Soc; Asn Comput Mach; Royal Astron Soc; Sigma Xi. *Res:* Stellar atmospheres; radiative transfer; numerical analysis. *Mailing Add:* 1202 Seventh St Los Alamos NM 87544

AUER, PETER LOUIS, PLASMA PHYSICS. *Current Pos:* prof, Grad Sch Aerospace Eng, 66-72, dir lab plasma studies, 67-74, prof, 72-95, EMER PROF, MECH & AEROSPACE ENG, CORNELL UNIV, 95- *Personal Data:* b Budapest, Hungary, Jan 12, 28; nat US; m 52, Rheta Siegel; c 4. *Educ:* Cornell Univ, BA, 47; Calif Inst Technol, PhD(chem & physics), 51. *Prof Exp:* Fel & res asst, Calif Inst Technol, 48-50; res chemist & physicist, Calif Res & Develop Co, 50-54; physicist, Gen Elec Res Lab, 54-61; head plasma physics dept, Sperry Rand Res Ctr, 62-64; dep dir ballistic missile defense, Advan Res Proj Agency, 64-66. *Concurrent Pos:* Guggenheim fel, 60-61; vis prof, Oxford Univ, 72-73. *Mem:* Fel Am Phys Soc. *Res:* Theoretical physics and chemistry; gaseous electronics. *Mailing Add:* 224 Upson Hall Cornell Univ Ithaca NY 14853-7501

AUERBACH, ANDREW BERNARD, POLYMER CHEMISTRY. *Current Pos:* sr res chemist, 81-87, staff chemist, 87-90, RES ASSOC, HOECHST CELANESE, 90- *Personal Data:* b New York, NY, Jan 23, 48; m 72; c Lee & Meredith. *Educ:* Brooklyn Col, BS, 68; City Univ New York, PhD(polymer & org chem), 75; Rutgers Univ, MBA, 80. *Prof Exp:* Res chemist, ITT Rayonier Inc, 74-81, group leader, 79-81. *Concurrent Pos:* Adj asst prof chem, Morris Co Community Col, 81-86; dir, Ctr Prof Advan, Course on Eng Plastics, 90- *Mem:* Am Chem Soc; sr mem Soc Plastics Engrs. *Res:* Polymer stabilization; computer databases for plastics formulation; liquid crystals; engineering resins including polyacetals, nylons and polyesters; crosslinking; flame retardants; polymer blends; product development. *Mailing Add:* 23 Orchard Lane Livingston NJ 07039

AUERBACH, ARLEEN D, HUMAN GENETICS, CYTOGENETICS. *Current Pos:* asst prof, Lab Invest Dermatol, 82-89, ASSOC PROF, LAB HUMAN GENETICS & HEMAT, ROCKEFELLER UNIV, 89- *Personal Data:* b New York, NY, May 24, 37; m 58, Robert; c Laura & Steven. *Educ:* William Smith Col, BA, 57; Columbia Univ, MA, 58; NY Univ, PhD(biol), 77. *Prof Exp:* Instr biol, Brearley Sch, NY, 58-59 & Dalton Sch, NY, 71; res fel, 77-78, res assoc genetics , Sloan-Kettering Inst, 78-82. *Mem:* AAAS; Am Soc Hemat; Am Soc Human Genetics. *Res:* Characterization of the molecular defect in Fanconi anemia; somatic cell genetics; molecular genetics and cytogenetics; fanconi anemia registry. *Mailing Add:* Rockefeller Univ 1230 York Ave New York NY 10021

AUERBACH, ARTHUR HENRY, PSYCHIATRY. *Current Pos:* NIMH career develop award, Dept Psychiat, 64-69, ASST PROF PSYCHIAT, SCH MED, UNIV PA, 64- *Personal Data:* b Philadelphia, Pa, Mar 12, 28. *Educ:* Jefferson Med Col, MD, 51. *Prof Exp:* Resident psychiat, St Elizabeth's Hosp, Washington, DC, 52-53; resident, West Haven Vet Admin Hosp, Conn, 53-54; resident, Hosp, Temple Univ, 56-57. *Concurrent Pos:* Consult, Magee Mem Hosp, Philadelphia, 58-68; NIMH Career Develop Award, Dept Psychiat, 64-69. *Mem:* Am Psychiat Asn; Soc Psychother Res. *Res:* Psychotherapy research. *Mailing Add:* 3600 Market St Philadelphia PA 19130-3838

AUERBACH, CLEMENS, CHEMISTRY. *Current Pos:* CONSULT. *Personal Data:* b Berlin, Ger, Nov 30, 23; US citizen; m 64; c 1. *Educ:* Robert Col, Istanbul, BS, 43; Harvard Univ, AM, 48, PhD(chem), 51. *Prof Exp:* Res fel, Univ Minn, 50-53; asst prof chem, Univ Buffalo, 53-56; from asst chemist to assoc chemist, Brookhaven Nat Lab, 56-62, scientist, Dept Nuclear Energy, 62-92. *Mem:* Am Chem Soc; Inst Nuclear Mat Mgt. *Res:* Analytical chemistry; analysis of uranium and other reactor materials; nuclear materials safeguards. *Mailing Add:* 77 S Howell Point Rd Bellport NY 11713-2621

AUERBACH, DANIEL J, SURFACE SCIENCE. *Current Pos:* staff mem, 78-83, mgr phys sci, 83-94, MGR SCI & TECHNOL, IBM ALMADEN RES CTR, 94- *Personal Data:* b New York, NY, Nov 29, 42; m 69, Valerie Waldhorn; c Jesse, Emma & Liza. *Educ:* Univ Chicago, BS, 64, MS, 68, PhD(physics), 71. *Prof Exp:* Vis scientist, Inst Atomic & Molecular Physics, Amsterdam, 71-72; teaching fel physics, Univ Western Ontario, 72-73; sr res fel, James Frank Inst, 73-75; asst prof chem, Johns Hopkins Univ, 76-77. *Mem:* Fel Am Phys Soc; Am Vacuum Soc; Am Chem Soc; Materials Res Soc. *Res:* Study of the dynamics of gas surface interaction, using a combination of surface science, molecular beam and laser techniques. *Mailing Add:* K31/802 IBM Almaden Res Ctr 650 Harry Rd San Jose CA 95120-6099. *Fax:* 408-927-4180; *E-Mail:* dja@almaden.ibm.com

AUERBACH, ELLIOT H, NUCLEAR PHYSICS, ACCELERATOR PHYSICS. *Current Pos:* staff mem, Physics Dept, 66-82, ALTERNATING GRADIENT SYNCHROTRON DEPT, BROOKHAVEN NAT LAB, 84- *Personal Data:* b New York, NY, July 21, 32; m 71, Rita Breithart. *Educ:* Columbia Univ, AB, 53, AM, 57. *Prof Exp:* Mathematician & physicist, Knolls Atomic Power Lab, Gen Elec Co, 58-61; assoc physics, Brookhaven Nat Lab, 61-64; vis res scientist, Lab Nuclear Sci, Mass Inst Technol, 64-66. *Concurrent Pos:* Vis staff mem, Los Alamos Sci Lab, 65 & 66. *Mem:* Am Phys Soc. *Res:* Nuclear structure and scattering; applications of computers to model and control accelerators. *Mailing Add:* 911-C Brookhaven Nat Lab Box 5000 Upton NY 11973. *E-Mail:* eha@bnlux1.bnl.gov

AUERBACH, IRVING, HIGH TEMPERATURE MATERIALS. *Current Pos:* STAFF MEM, SANDIA NAT LABS, 57- *Personal Data:* b Cleveland, Ohio, May 24, 19; m 69, Hertha Bienes. *Educ:* Ohio State Univ, BSc, 42, PhD(chem), 48. *Prof Exp:* Asst org chem, Res Found, Ohio State Univ, 44-46; res assoc, Cleveland Indust Res, 48-50 & Gooodyear Tire & Rubber Co, 50-57. *Concurrent Pos:* Res fel, Case Inst Technol, 48; fel & pres, NMex Acad Sci, 61-62. *Mem:* Fel AAAS; Am Chem Soc; fel Am Inst Chem; Am Inst Aeronaut & Astronaut. *Res:* Physical properties of polymers; radiation chemistry and effects of radiation on polymers; high temperature chemistry of thermal resistant materials. *Mailing Add:* 3425 Tahoe NE PO Box 5800 Albuquerque NM 87111

AUERBACH, JEROME MARTIN, PLASMA PHYSICS & FUSION, NUCLEAR ENGINEERING. *Current Pos:* PHYSICIST LASER FUSION, LAWRENCE LIVERMORE LAB, UNIV CALIF, 76- *Personal Data:* b Providence, RI, June 13, 44. *Educ:* Brown Univ, ScB, 67; Calif Inst Technol, MS, 68, PhD(eng), 75. *Prof Exp:* Nuclear engr reactor physics, Argonne Nat Lab, 75-76. *Mem:* Am Phys Soc; Am Nuclear Soc. *Res:* Physics of laser-plasma interaction; physics of laser driven thermonuclear fusion. *Mailing Add:* 823 Debra St Livermore CA 94550

AUERBACH, LEONARD B, PHYSICS. *Current Pos:* FROM ASSOC PROF TO PROF, TEMPLE UNIV, 67- *Personal Data:* b New York, NY, Aug 11, 29; m 51; c 2. *Educ:* City Col New York, BS, 51; Univ Ill, MS, 52; Univ Calif, Berkeley, PhD(physics), 62. *Prof Exp:* Res assoc particle physics, Segre Group, Lawrence Radiation Lab, 62-63; res assoc, Univ Pa, 63-65, asst prof, 65-67. *Mem:* Am Phys Soc. *Res:* Elementary and experimental high energy particle physics. *Mailing Add:* Dept Physics Temple Univ Philadelphia PA 19122

AUERBACH, MICHAEL HOWARD, INTERNATIONAL FOOD INGREDIENT REGULATORY AFFAIRS. *Current Pos:* res mgr, 76-82, asst dir spec chem res & develop, 82-92, SR ASSOC DIR, REGULATORY AFFAIRS, FOOD SCI RES & DEVELOP, PFIZER INC, 92- *Personal Data:* b Akron, Ohio, June 24, 43; m 66, Sandra Goldman; c David, Sara & Karen. *Educ:* Mass Inst Technol, BS, 64; Cornell Univ, PhD(anal chem), 69. *Prof Exp:* Sr res chemist, Hydrocarbons & Polymers Div, Monsanto Co, 69-74; res specialist, Monsanto Polymers & Petrochem Co, 74-76. *Concurrent Pos:* Guest lectr, Farleigh Dickinson Univ, 79-83. *Mem:* Am Chem Soc; Inst Food Technologists; NY Acad Sci. *Res:* Chemical applications test development; chemical product market opportunity assessment; food ingredient development. *Mailing Add:* 43 Merlino Dr Groton CT 06340-3149. *Fax:* 860-441-4289

AUERBACH, OSCAR, MEDICINE. *Current Pos:* chief lab serv, 52-59, SR MED INVESTR, VET ADMIN HOSP, EAST ORANGE, NJ, 60-, VET ADMIN DISTINGUISHED PHYSICIAN, 78- *Personal Data:* b New York, NY, Jan 1, 05; m 32; c 2. *Educ:* New York Med Col, MD, 29; Am Bd Path, dipl, 44. *Prof Exp:* Pathologist, Sea View Hosp, NY, 32-47; chief lab serv, Halloran Vet Admin Hosp, 47-51. *Concurrent Pos:* Res fel, Univ Vienna, 32; consult, Richmond Mem Hosp, 38-47, US Vet Admin Hosp, 46-47 & US Naval Hosp, 47-49; vis instr, Sch Med, Wash Univ, 44; assoc prof, New York Med Col, Flower & Fifth Ave Hosps, 49-61, prof, 61-71; prof path, Col Med & Dent, NJ, 71- *Mem:* Am Thoracic Soc; Am Asn Thoracic Surg; fel Am Col Physicians; fel NY Acad Med; hon mem Mex Tuberc Soc. *Res:* Relationship of smoking to lung cancer and other diseases both human and experimental. *Mailing Add:* Dept Path Vet Med Ctr Center & Tremont Aves Newark NJ 07019

AUERBACH, ROBERT, DEVELOPMENTAL BIOLOGY, IMMUNOLOGY. *Current Pos:* from asst prof to assoc prof, 57-65, PROF ZOOL, UNIV WIS-MADISON, 65- *Personal Data:* b Berlin, Ger, Apr 12, 29; nat; m 50; c Richard & Emily. *Educ:* Berea Col, AB, 49; Columbia Univ, AM, 50, PhD(zool), 54. *Prof Exp:* Assoc, Biol Div, Oak Ridge Nat Lab, 54-55; fel, Nat Cancer Inst, 55-57. *Concurrent Pos:* Guggenheim fel, 68; vis prof surg, Harvard Med Sch, 73-74; vis prof cell biol, Southwestern Med Sch, Dallas, 74-75; Rockefeller fel, 74-75; Harold R Wolfe prof, 83. *Mem:* Soc Develop Biol; Am Asn Invest Path; Am Asn Immunol; fel AAAS; Am Asn Cancer Res; Soc Anal Cytol; Am Soc Cell Biol; Int Soc Differentiation. *Res:* Endothelial cell heterogeneity and specificity; ontogeny of immunity; genetics and immunology of granulomatous lung disease; flow cytometry; angiogenesis; developmental aspects of hematopoietic stem cells. *Mailing Add:* Dept Zool Univ Wis Madison WI 53706. *Fax:* 608-262-1171; *E-Mail:* auerbach@macc.wisc.edu

AUERBACH, STANLEY IRVING, RADIATION ECOLOGY, SYSTEM ANALYSIS. *Current Pos:* RETIRED. *Personal Data:* b Chicago, Ill, May 21, 21; m 54, Dawn P Dauby; c Andrew, Anne, Jonathan & Alison. *Educ:* Univ Ill, BS, 46, MS, 47; Northwestern Univ, PhD(zool), 49. *Prof Exp:* Asst zool & animal ecol, Northwestern Univ, 47-48; lectr biol, Roosevelt Univ, 50-51, instr, 51-54, asst prof, 50-54; assoc scientist, Oak Ridge Nat Lab, 54-55, health physicist ecol, 54-59, scientist, 55-59, sect chief radiation ecol, 59-70, dir, Ecol Sci Div, 70-72, dir, Environ Sci Div, 72-86, sr staff adv, 86-90. *Concurrent Pos:* Lectr, Univ Tenn, 60; vis res prof, Univ Ga, 64-90; adj res prof, Univ Tenn, 65-90; dir eastern deciduous forest biomed, Int Biol Prog, 68-76, vpres US exec comt, 71-; mem bd energy studies & var subcomt, Nat Acad Sci-Nat Res Coun, 74-77; mem sci adv bd, US Environ Protection Agency, 86-92, environ adv bd, chief engrs, 89-93; mem adv comn Sci & Technol Ctr, NSF, 88-92. *Mem:* Am Inst Biol Sci; fel AAAS; Ecol Soc Am (secy, 64-69, pres, 71-72); Brit Ecol Soc; Int Union Radioecologists; Health Physics Soc. *Res:* Ecosystem analysis; radioactive waste cycling in terrestrial ecosystems. *Mailing Add:* 103 Wildwood Dr Oak Ridge TN 37830. *E-Mail:* stanauer@juho.com

AUERBACH, STEPHEN MICHAEL, CLINICAL PSYCHOLOGY, BEHAVIORAL MEDICINE. *Current Pos:* PROF PSYCHOL & DIR DOCTORAL PROG CLIN PSYCHOL, VA COMMONWEALTH UNIV, 82- *Personal Data:* b New York, NY, Nov 19, 42; c 2. *Educ:* Queens Col, CUNY, BA, 65; Fla State Univ, MS, 69, PhD(clin psychol), 71. *Prof Exp:* Asst prof psychol, NMex State Univ, 72-74; from asst prof to assoc prof, Va Commonwealth Univ, 74-82. *Concurrent Pos:* Adj prof oral & maxillofacial surg, Med Col Va, 89- *Mem:* Fel Am Psychol Asn; fel Am Psychol Soc; fel Am Asn Appl Prev Psychol. *Res:* Psychological stress, coping and stress management; development and evaluation of procedures designed to manage stresses associated with medical treatment and disease and aging. *Mailing Add:* Dept Psychol Va Commonwealth Univ PO Box 842018 Richmond VA 23284-2018

AUERBACH, VICTOR, SYNTHETIC HIGH POLYMERS, MANAGEMENT OF PATENTS & LICENSING. *Current Pos:* MGT & LICENSING CONSULT, PLAINFIELD, NJ, 81- *Personal Data:* b Philadelphia, Pa, July 4, 17; m 46, Leona Fishkin; c Burt J, Paul S & Janet L (Sherman). *Educ:* Brooklyn Col, BA, 40; Polytech Inst New York, PhD(chem), 45. *Prof Exp:* Chemist urea resins, Bakelite Co, 42-43; instr organic chem, Polytechnic Inst New York, 42-46; res assoc thin films, Nat Defense Res Coun, 43-45; group leader reactive resins, Bakelite Co, 45-55; assoc coordr patents, Union Carbide Plastics Co, 55-62, coordr patents, Plastics Div, 62-67, patent mgr chem & plastics, Union Carbide Corp, 67-79, patent mgr, Polyolefins Div, 79-81. *Res:* Thermosetting resins; thermoplastic resins; causal influence of molecular weight distribution and molecular structure on resin and end-product properties and performance. *Mailing Add:* 1218 Stillman Ave Plainfield NJ 07060-2729

AUERBACH, VICTOR HUGO, BIOCHEMISTRY. *Current Pos:* asst prof physiol chem & res pediat, Temple Univ, 58-64, assoc prof biochem & res pediat, 64-68, res prof, 68-85, sr res prof pediat, 85-92, EMER PROF, SCH MED, TEMPLE UNIV, 92- *Personal Data:* b New York, NY, Oct 2, 28; m 56, Helen M Matalas. *Educ:* Columbia Col, AB, 51; Harvard Univ, AM, 55, PhD(biochem), 57. *Prof Exp:* Asst, Col Physicians & Surgeons, Columbia Univ, 45-47; biochemist, Rheumatic Fever Res Inst, 48; asst, Columbia Univ, 48-52; res biochemist, Fleishmann Labs, 52; res assoc pediat & instr physiol chem, Univ Wis, 57-58; dir, enzyme lab & dir res chem, St Christopher's Hosp for Children, 58-85 & dept labs, 76-85. *Concurrent Pos:* Pres, Fac Sen, Temple Univ, 74-75 & Child Health Assocs, Inc, 75-80. *Mem:* Am Chem Soc; fel AAAS; Am Soc Biochem & Molecular Biol; Am Soc Clin Nutrit; Soc Pediat Res. *Res:* Mammalian amino acid metabolism; control mechanisms such as adaptive enzyme formation and negative feedback regulation of enzyme synthesis; inborn errors of metabolism and genetic disorder in man; clinical chemistry. *Mailing Add:* 1244 Hoffman Rd Ambler PA 19002-5033. *E-Mail:* vhambler@voicenet.com

AUERBACK, ALFRED, psychiatry; deceased, see previous edition for last biography

AUERSPERG, NELLY, CANCER, CELL BIOLOGY. *Current Pos:* mem staff, Cancer Res Ctr, Univ BC, 68-78, from assoc prof to prof zool, 68-77, prof anat, 78-93, HON PROF OBSTET & GYNEC, UNIV BC, 92- *Personal Data:* b Vienna, Austria, Dec 13, 28; Can citizen; m 55; c 2. *Educ:* Univ Wash, MD, 55; Univ BC, PhD(cell biol), 68. *Honors & Awards:* Distinguished Lifetime Achievement Award, Soc In Vitro Biol. *Prof Exp:* Intern med, Vancouver Gen Hosp, BC, 55-56, res asst tissue cult, 59-60; cytologist, Cytol Lab, Vancouver, 60-65. *Concurrent Pos:* Terry Fox res scientist. *Mem:* Am Asn Cancer Res; Am Soc Cell Biol; Tissue Cult Asn; Can Soc Cell Biol (pres, 78); Int Soc Differentiation; Sigma Xi. *Res:* Regulation of phenotypic expression in malignant tumors. *Mailing Add:* Dept Obstet/Gynec Univ BC 4490 Oak St Vancouver BC V6H 3V5 Can. *Fax:* 604-875-2725; *E-Mail:* auersper@unixg.ubc.ca

AUFDEMBERGE, THEODORE PAUL, PHYSICAL GEOGRAPHY, REGIONAL GEOGRAPHY. *Current Pos:* instr geog, 64-66, from asst prof to assoc prof, 66-81, PROF GEOG, CONCORDIA COL, ANN ARBOR, 81- *Personal Data:* b Winnipeg, Man, Feb 1, 34; US citizen; m 60; c 4. *Educ:* Concordia Teachers Col, BSc, 56; Wayne State Univ, MA, 64; Univ Mich, Ann Arbor, PhD(geog), 71. *Prof Exp:* Prin & teacher, Immanual Lutheran Sch, Brownton, Minn, 56-58; teacher sci & english, Trinity Lutheran Sch, Mt Clemens, Mich, 58-64. *Mem:* Creation Res Soc; Nat Coun Geog Educ. *Res:* Spatial distributions of economic activities particularly agricultural & manufacturing activities in Anglo-America; carbon dioxide as a greenhouse gas and world wide spatial distribution of carbon dioxide. *Mailing Add:* Concordia Col 4090 Geddes Rd Ann Arbor MI 48105

AUFDERHEIDE, KARL JOHN, CELL BIOLOGY & DEVELOPMENTAL BIOLOGY, LASER OPTICS. *Current Pos:* asst prof, 79-86, ASSOC PROF, TEX A&M UNIV, 86- *Personal Data:* b Minneapolis, Minn, Aug 17, 48; m 69; c 1. *Educ:* Univ Minn, BS, 70, MS, 72, PhD(cell biol), 74. *Prof Exp:* Res assoc cell biol, Ind Univ, Bloomington, 74-77; instr, Univ Iowa, 77-79. *Concurrent Pos:* NIH fel, 75-77; sr scientist, A&M Inst Develop Biol, 83-85; vis scholar, Ind Univ, 86. *Mem:* Soc Protozoologists; AAAS. *Res:* Intracellular development and differentiation; intracellular pattern formation in ciliate protozoa; developmental genetics of exocytotic organelles; formation and positioning of cytoskeletal arrays in the cell cortex; use of laser tweezers in analysis of developmental events in cilates. *Mailing Add:* Dept Biol Texas A&M Univ College Station TX 77843-3258

AUFDERMARSH, CARL ALBERT, JR, COMPOSITES, ENGINEERING PLASTICS. *Current Pos:* CONSULT POLYMER CHEM & TECHNOL, 92- *Personal Data:* b Cincinnati, Ohio, Nov 9, 32; m 55; c 4. *Educ:* Univ Cincinnati, BS, 54; Yale Univ, MS, 55, PhD(chem), 58. *Prof Exp:* Res chemist, E I du Pont de Nemours & Co, 58-82; mat engr, Schlumberger Well Serv, 83-92. *Mem:* Am Chem Soc; Am Inst Chemists; Soc Advan Mat & Process Eng. *Res:* Polymer chemistry; organic synthesis; isocyanates and polyurethanes; fluoroelastomers; advanced composites; engineering plastics. *Mailing Add:* 5 Lack Lane Asheville NC 28804. *Fax:* 704-258-1422

AUFFENBERG, WALTER, HERPETOLOGY. *Current Pos:* chmn Dept Natural Sci, 63-73, CUR HERPET, FLA STATE MUS, 73- *Personal Data:* b Dearborn, Mich, Feb 6, 28; m 49; c 4. *Educ:* Stetson Univ, BS, 51; Univ Fla, MS, 53, PhD(biol), 56. *Honors & Awards:* 1st Prize Honorarium, Am Soc Ichthyol & Herpet, 53. *Prof Exp:* Cur vert paleont, Charleston Mus, 53; asst prof biol, Univ Fla & assoc cur vert paleont, Fla State Mus, 56-59; assoc dir, Biol Sci Curric Study, Univ Colo, 59-63. *Concurrent Pos:* Res assoc, Univ Colo Mus, 59-63 & NY Zool Soc, 69-; consult, AID, India, 62 & -64 & NSF, India, 67. *Mem:* Fel AAAS; Am Soc Ichthyologists & Herpetologists; Am Soc Naturalists; Am Soc Zool; Sigma Xi. *Res:* Behavior; field biology of large reptiles; biosystematics of fossil and living land tortoises of the world. *Mailing Add:* 7008 NW 67th Ave Gainesville FL 32653

AUGELLI-SZAFRAN, CORINNE E, MEDICINAL CHEMISTRY. *Current Pos:* RES ASSOC, PARKE-DAVIS, 88- *Personal Data:* b Scranton, PA, 1958. *Educ:* Univ Pa, BS, 80; NY Univ, MS, 86, PhD(org chem), 88. *Prof Exp:* Chemist, Am Cyanamid, Princeton, 80-83. *Mem:* Am Chem Soc. *Mailing Add:* Warner Lambert Parke Davis Co Chem Dept 2800 Plymouth Rd Ann Arbor MI 48105

AUGENLICHT, LEONARD HAROLD, cancer, colon, for more information see previous edition

AUGENSEN, HARRY JOHN, ASTRONOMY, PHYSICS. *Current Pos:* PROF PHYSICS ASTRON, WIDENER UNIV, 82- *Personal Data:* b Chicago, Ill, July 18, 51; m 81, Anna DiEgidio. *Educ:* Elmhurst Col, BA, 73; Northwestern Univ, MS, 74, PhD(astron), 78. *Honors & Awards:* Harlow Shapley Lectr, 81- *Prof Exp:* lectr astron, Northwestern Univ, 78-80 & Swarthmore Col, 80-82. *Concurrent Pos:* Vis observer, Cerro Tololo Inter-Am Observ, 76-77 & 81; Goddard summer fac fel, NASA, 82, 83. *Mem:* Am Astron Soc; Royal Astron Soc; Sigma Xi; Astron Soc Pac. *Res:* High-velocity stars; galactic structure; planetary nebulae. *Mailing Add:* Dept Physics Widener Univ One Univeristy Pl Chester PA 19013. *Fax:* 215-499-4059; *E-Mail:* augensen@physics.widener.edu

AUGENSTEIN, BRUNO (WILHELM), PHYSICS, AERONAUTICS. *Current Pos:* assoc phys scientist, Rand Corp, 49-53, phys scientist, 53-56, asst head sci staff, 56-57, sr staff, 56-58, vpres, 67-71, chief scientist, 71-72, consult, 72-76, SR SCIENTIST, RAND CORP, 76- *Personal Data:* b Ger, Mar 16, 23; nat US; m 50, Kathleen Greenlaw; c Karen, Eric & Christopher. *Educ:* Brown Univ, ScB, 43; Calif Inst Technol, MS, 45. *Prof Exp:* Supvr, Aerophys Lab, NAm Aviation, Inc, 46-48; asst prof aeronaut, Purdue Univ, 48-49; consult scientist, Lockheed Missiles & Space Co, Calif, 58-59, sci adv, 59-61, dir adv planning, 61; asst dir defense res & eng, US Dept Defense, 61-65, spec asst intel reconnaissance to dir, 63-65, res adv, Inst Defense Anal, 65-67. *Concurrent Pos:* Consult, Nat Acad Sci, 65-, US Dept Defense, 78 & Off Sci Technol Policy, 78-; assoc chmn bd regents, Nat Libr Med; head, US Navy Med Rev Comt, 75; dir, Xerad, 81-83. *Mem:* AAAS; Am Phys Soc; Am Inst Aeronaut & Astronaut; Am Geog Soc. *Res:* Research and development administration; applied physics; weapon systems; operational and systems analysis; strategic policies; policy analysis; astronautics; biomedicine computers and communications. *Mailing Add:* 1144 Tellem Dr Pacific Palisades CA 90272

AUGENSTEIN, MOSHE, SOFTWARE SYSTEMS. *Current Pos:* PROF COMPUTER SCI, BROOKLYN COL, 72- *Personal Data:* b Baltimore, Md, Nov 27, 47; m 70; c 5. *Educ:* Brooklyn Col, BS, 69; NY Univ, MS, 71, PhD(opers res), 75. *Concurrent Pos:* Consult, 78- *Mem:* Asn Comput Mach. *Res:* Data structures; microcomputers; graphic display of data structures; author of several publications. *Mailing Add:* 1370 E Eighth St Brooklyn NY 11230

AUGER, PAUL EMILE, GEOLOGY. *Current Pos:* CONSULT GEOLOGIST, 79- *Personal Data:* b Ste-Croix, Lotbiniere, Sept 30, 08; m 40, Gabrielle Hebert; c Jacques, Louise & Michele. *Educ:* Laval Univ, BA, 33; Queen's Univ, BS, 36; Mass Inst Technol, DSc, 39. *Honors & Awards:* Leonard Medal, Eng Inst Can, 42. *Prof Exp:* Geologist, Dept Mines, Que, 38-41; mine geologist, Mine Sch, Valdor, Abitibi, 39-42; lectr econ geol, Sch Mines, Laval Univ, Que, 41-42, from asst prof to prof econ geol, 47-60; dep minister, Dept Mines, Que, 60-61, Dept Natural Resources, 61-71. *Concurrent Pos:* Pres & gen mgr, Molybdenite Corp Ltd, 71-73; dir, Falconbridge Copper Ltd, 71-89, Asbestos Corp Ltd, 72-87, Mineral Explor Res Inst, 71-78, Kiena Gold Mine, 75-88, New Que Raglan Mine, 75-, Soc Mineral Raglan Que, 75-, Northgate Explor Co, 79-88, Minnova Mines Inc, 86-, Soc Mineral MSV Inc, 88-; dir & pres, Lacorne Molybdenite Mine Ltd, 72-74. *Mem:* Fel, Royal Soc Can; fel, Am Inst Mining, Metall & Petrol Engrs; Geol Asn Can (pres, 62); fel, Geol soc Am; Can Inst Mining & Metall (pres-elect, 67-68, pres 68-69); Soc Econ Geol. *Res:* Spectrographic study of the minor elements in sulphides by means of grating spectrograph. *Mailing Add:* Geologue 250 Grande-Allee O 1701 Quebec PQ G1R 2H4 Can

AUGHENBAUGH, NOLAN B(LAINE), GEOLOGICAL & GEOTECHNICAL ENGINEERING, WASTE DISPOSAL. *Current Pos:* CONSULT, 60- *Personal Data:* b Akron, Ohio, July 29, 28; m 59, Barbara A Hill; c Lowell D, Amy E (Vogel) & Debra J (Butler). *Educ:* Purdue Univ, BSCE, 55, PhD(civil eng), 63; Univ Mich, MS, 59. *Honors & Awards:* Mountain & Rock Group named in honor, Anatarctica. *Prof Exp:* From instr to asst prof civil eng, Purdue Univ, 59-65; from assoc prof to prof geol eng, Univ Mo, Rolla, 66-83; dean, Sch Mineral Eng, Univ Alaska, Fairbanks, 83-84; PROF GEOL ENG, UNIV MISS, 85- *Concurrent Pos:* Lab asst geol, Purdue Univ, 54-55; chmn dept mining, petrol & geol eng, Univ Mo, Rolla, 70-80; mem, Mo Land Recalamtion Comn, 77-; deleg leader, People-to-People Tour to Europe on Underground Space Use, 78; Fulbright scholar, NZ; chmn, Miss Hazardous Waste Tech Siting Comt. *Mem:* Asn Eng Geologists; Soc Mining Engrs; Am Soc Civil Engrs; Sigma Xi; Am Underground Space Asn; Nat Soc Prof Engrs. *Res:* Agregate quality and degradation, evaluating laboratory tests with physical properties; mechanics of rock fracture; coal mine roof stability; subsidence; effects of humidity and temperature on rocks; properties and durability of shale; basic engineering properties of clay and shales; flexibility of compacted clays; durability of shales; photoelastic analysis of earth minerals; general soil and rock mechanics; author of more than 50 technical publications. *Mailing Add:* 311 Dogwood Dr Oxford MS 38655

AUGL, JOSEPH MICHAEL, ORGANIC CHEMISTRY. *Current Pos:* res chemist, Naval Ord Labs, 68-78, RES CHEMIST, NAVAL SURFACE WARFARE CTR, 78- *Personal Data:* b Pasching, Austria, Jan 8, 32; m 62; c 1. *Educ:* Univ Vienna, PhD(org chem), 59. *Honors & Awards:* Capt Walter S Diehl Award, Sci & Eng Symp, 78. *Prof Exp:* Asst prof org chem, Univ Vienna, 59-61; sr res organometallic chemist, Sohio Res Ctr, Ohio, 61-63, proj leader, 63; org chem, Melpar Inc, 63-64, res leader, 64-68. *Mem:* Am Chem Soc; Soc Adv Mat & Process Eng. *Res:* Synthesis of heterocyclic compounds; transition metal coordination compounds; synthesis of high temperature stable polymers; composite materials; material aging phenomena. *Mailing Add:* 606 W Nettle Tree Rd Sterling VA 20164-4724

AUGOOD, DEREK RAYMOND, PHYSICAL CHEMISTRY, RESEARCH ADMINISTRATION. *Current Pos:* at SCI CERT SYSTS INC, 89- *Personal Data:* b London, Eng, Mar 7, 28; nat US; m 55, Joan Pauline Jameson; c 2. *Educ:* Univ London, BSc, 49, PhD(phys org), 52; Cambridge Univ, PhD(chem eng), 55. *Honors & Awards:* Moulton Medal, Brit Inst Chem Engrs, London, 55; Neal Ricc Award, Int Briquetting Assoc, 87. *Prof Exp:* Harwell fel, UK Atomic Energy Res Estab, 54-56; engr, E I DuPont de Nemours & Co, 56-62; head sect prod develop & mgr, Res & Develop Lab, Kaiser Chem, 72-89. *Res:* Homolytic aromatic substitution; isotope separation; nylon intermediates; polyethylene, fluorocarbon and vinyl butyral polymers; isocyanates and urethanes; research and development project evaluation; manufacture and performance of extruded dielectric cables; non-bauxitic alumina processes; alumina reduction plant processes, industrial hygiene, carbon product, waste product utilization, environmental, risk assessment and life cycle assessment studies; certification of product environmental attributes, author of over 50 publications. *Mailing Add:* 151 Camino Amigo Ct Danville CA 94526

AUGSBURGER, LARRY LOUIS, DOSAGE FORM DESIGN, INDUSTRIAL PHARMACY. *Current Pos:* asst prof, 69-74, ASSOC PROF PHARMACEUT, SCH PHARM, UNIV MD, 74-, DIR, PHARMACEUT GRAD PROG, 76- *Personal Data:* b Baltimore, Md, July 1, 40; m 65; c 4. *Educ:* Univ Md, BS, 62, MS, 65, PhD(pharm), 67. *Prof Exp:* Sr res scientist, Johnson & Johnson, 67-69. *Concurrent Pos:* Consult, FMC Corp, 75-76 & 81-82, Mallincordt, Inc, 79-80, E R Squibb & Sons, 79-80 & Pharmakinetics, Inc, 80-81. *Mem:* Am Pharmaceut Asn; Acad Pharmaceut Sci; Am Asn Col Pharm; Fine Particle Soc; Sigma Xi. *Res:* Instrumentation of table presses and capsule filling machines; interplay of formulation and process variables on the performance and manufacturability of solid dosage forms; drug release from dosage forms. *Mailing Add:* Dept Pharmaceut Univ Md Sch Pharm 20 N Pine St Baltimore MD 21201-1180

AUGSPURGER, CAROL KATHLEEN, ECOLOGY, EVOLUTION. *Current Pos:* ASST PROF BOT, UNIV ILL, URBANA, 78- *Personal Data:* US citizen. *Educ:* Bowling Green State Univ, BS, 63; Univ Mich, MS, 75, PhD(biol), 78. *Mem:* Ecol Soc Am; Soc Study Evolution; Asn Trop Biol; AAAS. *Res:* Evolutionary ecology of tropical plant populations; reproductive strategies and reproductive synchrony; phenological patterns and environmental cues; life history and demography of semelparous plants; plant-animal coevolution. *Mailing Add:* Dept Plant Biol Univ Ill 505 S Goodwin Ave Urbana IL 61801-3707

AUGSTKALNS, VALDIS ANSIS, CHEMICAL ENGINEERING, POLYMER CHEMISTRY. *Current Pos:* res engr polymers, 62-63 & 65-75, sr res engr polymers, 75-79, SR TECHNOL ASSOC, E I DU PONT DE NEMOURS & CO INC, 79- *Personal Data:* b Rezekne, Latvia, Mar 31, 39; US citizen; m 86, Catherine A Ellinghausen; c Mary C. *Educ:* Univ Mass, BSChE, 61, MSChE, 63. *Prof Exp:* Res chem engr polymers & pyrotech, Chem Res & Develop Labs, Edgewood Arsenal, US Army, Md, 63-65. *Concurrent Pos:* NSF coop grad fel, Univ Mass, 61-62. *Mem:* Am Inst Chem Engrs; AAAS; Sigma Xi. *Res:* Nylon and polyester polymerization, degradation and processing; computer modeling of these. *Mailing Add:* E I du Pont de Nemours & Co Inc Wash Lab PO Box 1217 Parkersburg WV 26102

AUGUST, JOSEPH THOMAS, BIOCHEMISTRY, MOLECULAR BIOLOGY. *Current Pos:* PROF & DIR, DEPT PHARMACOL & EXP THERAPEUT, SCH MED, JOHNS HOPKINS UNIV, 76- *Personal Data:* b Whittier, Calif, Sept 19, 27; m 51; c 3. *Educ:* Stanford Univ, AB, 51, MD, 55. *Prof Exp:* Intern med, Los Angeles County Gen Hosp, 54-55; resident, Royal Infirmary, Univ Edinburgh, 55-56; resident & fel, Harvard Med Sch, 56-59; asst prof, Sch Med, Stanford Univ, 59-61; assoc prof, Sch Med, NY Univ, 61-63; from asst prof to prof molecular biol, Albert Einstein Col Med, 63-76, chmn & dir, Dept Molecular Biol & Div Biol Sci, 72-76. *Concurrent Pos:* Res fel, Am Heart Asn, 57-59; career scientist grant, Health Res Coun New York City, 62-71; Guggenheim fel, 71-72; vis prof biochem, Oxford Univ, 71-72; Merkle Scholar Med Sci, 60-65; Siegfried Ullman prof molecular biol, 68-76; Johnson & Johnson Focused Giving Award, 82-87. *Mem:* Am Soc Biol Chemists; Am Chem Soc; Am Soc Microbiol; Harvey Soc; Am Soc Pharmacol & Exp Therapeut. *Res:* Identification, purification and characterization of eukaryotic cell surface protein; immunopharmacology. *Mailing Add:* Dept Pharmacol Johns Hopkins Sch Med 725 N Wolfe St Baltimore MD 21205-2105

AUGUST, LEON STANLEY, NUCLEAR SCIENCE, RADIATION DAMAGE. *Current Pos:* CONSULT PHYSICIST, 86- *Personal Data:* b New Orleans, La, Sept 30, 26; m 52. *Educ:* La State Univ, BS, 50, PhD(physics), 57; Tulane Univ, MS, 52. *Prof Exp:* Res physicist, US Naval Res Lab, 57-86. *Concurrent Pos:* Mem cyclotron group, Univ Calif, Los Angeles, 65-66. *Mem:* Am Phys Soc; Sigma Xi; AAAS; Inst Elec & Electronics Engrs. *Res:* Radiation damage experiments in semiconductors; space dosimetry, neuron gamma, electron, proton, and heavy-ion dosimetry and spectroscopy; microdosimetry and ion-track theory as applied to semiconductor; accelerator physics. *Mailing Add:* 6920 Baylor Dr Alexandria VA 22307-1703

AUGUSTEIJN, MARIJKE FRANCINA, THEORETICAL PHYSICS. *Current Pos:* AT DEPT COMPUT SCI, UNIV COLO, 82- *Personal Data:* b Rotterdam, Neth, Mar 30, 46; m 70. *Educ:* Tech Univ Delft, Ing, 70; Ohio Univ, PhD(physics),80. *Prof Exp:* Instr physics & math, Haags Montessori Lyceum, 70-75; res fel med physics, Inst Med & Math, Ohio Univ, 80-82. *Concurrent Pos:* Vis asst prof, Math Dept, Ohio Univ, 81-82. *Mem:* Asn Comput Mach; Am Asn Artificial Intel; Inst Elec & Electronics Engrs. *Res:* Nonlinear classical mechanics; oscillatory systems; mathematical physics; intelligent training systems. *Mailing Add:* Dept Comput Sci Univ Colo PO Box 7150 Colorado Springs CO 80933

AUGUSTIN, JORG A L, FOOD SCIENCE, PLANT BIOCHEMISTRY. *Current Pos:* RETIRED. *Personal Data:* b Heerbrugg, Switz, Jan 5, 30; US citizen; m 62. *Educ:* Swiss Fed Inst Technol, dipl agrotech, 55; Univ Ill, MS, 57; Mich State Univ, PhD(food sci), 64. *Prof Exp:* Res assoc, Hero Konserven, Switz, 57-60; asst plant supt food processing, Libby, McNeil & Libby, 60; res asst food sci, Mich State Univ, 61-64; food technologist food res div, Armour & Co, 64-68, from asst sect head to sect head meat prod develop, 66-68; assoc res prof agr biochem, Br Exp Sta, Univ Idaho, 68-75, group leader & prof bact & biochem, 75-92, in chg, Food Res Ctr, 75-92. *Mem:* Inst Food Technol; Am Chem Soc; Am Asn Cereal Chemists; Sigma Xi. *Res:* Process and product development and improvement of foods, especially canned foods; studies on thermal destruction of bacterial spores; sugar beet storage; nutrient composition of fresh, stored and processed potatoes, legumes and cereal products; vitamin analysis. *Mailing Add:* 70610 E Bottle Bay Rd Sagle ID 83860

AUGUSTINE, JAMES A, BLOOD RESEARCH, CELLULAR SIGNALING. *Current Pos:* BLOOD RESEARCHER CELLULAR SIGNALING, BLOOD CTR SE WIS, 92- *Personal Data:* b Rochester, Pa, Dec 9, 53. *Educ:* Univ Pittsburgh, BS, 78, PhD(pharmacol), 87. *Prof Exp:* Fel, Mayo Clin, 87-92. *Mem:* Am Soc Biochem & Molecular Biol; Fedn Am Socs Exp Biol. *Mailing Add:* Blood Ctr SE Wisc PO Box 2178 Milwaukee WI 53201-2178

AUGUSTINE, JAMES ROBERT, NEUROANATOMY. *Current Pos:* asst prof, 76-86, ASSOC PROF ANAT, SCH MED, UNIV SC, COLUMBIA, 86- *Personal Data:* b Mascoutah, Ill, Jan 27, 46; m 70; c 3. *Educ:* Millikin Univ, BA, 68; St Louis Univ, Mo, MS, 70; Univ Ala, Birmingham, PhD(anat), 73. *Honors & Awards:* Stefan Mironescu Res Award, 85. *Prof Exp:* From instr to asst prof anat, Sch Med & Sch Dent, Univ Ala, Birmingham, 73-76. *Concurrent Pos:* Scholarly exhib, Mus Royal Col Surgeons, London, Eng. *Mem:* Am Asn Anatomists; AAAS; Cajal Club. *Res:* Primate neuroanatomy; immunocytochemistry; tissue culture. *Mailing Add:* Dept Cellular Biol & Neurosci Univ SC Sch Med Columbia SC 29208

AUGUSTINE, NORMAN R, AERONAUTICAL ENGINEERING. *Current Pos:* PRES, LOCKHEED MARTIN, 95-, CHIEF EXEC OFFICER, 96-, CHMN, 97- *Personal Data:* b Denver, Colo, July 27, 35; m, Margareta Engman; c Gregory E & Rene I. *Educ:* Princeton Univ, BScE, 57, MScE, 59. *Hon Degrees:* Dr Eng, Rensselaer Polytech Inst, 88, Western Md Col, Univ Md, 91, Stevens Inst Technol, 93 & Univ Cent Fla, 95; DSc, Univ Colo, 89; DHH, Wheeling Jesuit Col, 94; DBA, Embry-Riddle Aeronaut Univ, 92. *Honors & Awards:* Meritorious Serv Medal, Dept Defense, 70, Distinguished Serv Medal, 75; James Forrestal Mem Award, Nat Security Indust Asn; Mil Astronaut Trophy, Am Astronaut Soc; Gold Medal, Soc Mfg Engrs, 87; Goddard Medal, Am Inst Aeronaut & Astronaut, 88; Gold Medal, Am Defense Preparedness Asn, Knowles Award, John C Jones Award; Nat Eng Award, Am Asn Eng Soc; Carlton Award, Inst Elec & Electronics Engrs; Bernard Baruch Lectr, Nat Defense Univ; Bueche Award, Nat Acad Eng, 91; John R Alison Award, Air Force Asn, 92; Nat Medal of Technol, 97. *Prof Exp:* Eng exec, Douglas Aircraft, 59-65; off secy of defense, 65-70; vpres advan progs, LTV Aerospace, 70-73; asst secy, Army Res & Develop, 73-75; under secy army, 75-77; vpres tech opers, Martin Marietta Corp, 77-82, pres, Denver Aerospace, 82-85, sr vpres, 85-86, pres & chief oper officer, 86-87, chief exec officer, 87-95, chmn, 88-95. *Concurrent Pos:* Chmn, Defense Policy Adv Comt Trade; trustee, Int Acad Astronaut; mem bd dirs, Phillips Petrol Co, Procter & Gamble Corp, Riggs Nat (Bank) Corp, Ethics Resource Ctr, Atlantic Coun, Alliance to Save Energy & Wolf Trap Found; mem, President's Nat Security Telecommun Adv Comt, Chief Naval Opers Exec Panel & numerous others; chmn, Antarctic Prog, External Panel, NSF; chmn, Whitehouse Comt US Space Prof, NASA, Space Systs & Technol Adv Comt. *Mem:* Nat Acad Eng; fel Inst Elec & Electronics Engrs; Int Acad Astronaut; hon fel Soc Tech Commun; hon fel Am Inst Aeronaut & Astronaut; fel Am Astronaut Soc; Sigma Xi; fel Royal Aeronaut Soc; fel Am Acad Arts & Sci. *Mailing Add:* Lockheed Martin Corp 6801 Rockledge Dr Bethesda MD 20817

AUGUSTINE, PATRICIA C, COCCIDIOSIS, CELL CULTURE. *Current Pos:* MICROBIOLOGIST, USDA, 65- *Personal Data:* b Lanham, Md, June 7, 37; m 58; c 3. *Educ:* Univ Md, BS, 59, MS, 76, PhD(poultry sci), 80. *Prof Exp:* Microbiologist, NIH, 59-61. *Concurrent Pos:* Adj prof, Univ Md, 83- *Mem:* Am Soc Parasitologists; Poultry Sci Asn; Soc Exp Biol & Med. *Res:* Avian loccidia; mechanisms of host cell invasion by coccidia; tissue culture and hybridoma technology; pathophysiologic effects of coccidal infection in turkeys; cross-species immunity. *Mailing Add:* Parasite Biol & Epidemiol Lab, Livestock & Poultry Scis Inst USDA Bldg 1040 Rm 103 BARC-E Beltsville MD 20705. *Fax:* 301-504-5306

AUGUSTINE, ROBERT LEO, CATALYSIS ORGANIC CHEMISTRY. *Current Pos:* from asst prof to assoc prof, 61-69, chmn dept, 88-91, PROF CHEM, SETON HALL UNIV, 69- *Personal Data:* b Omaha, Nebr, Nov 15, 32; m 57, Marilyn Filippella; c Theresa M & Mary S. *Educ:* Creighton Univ, 54; Columbia Univ, MA, 55, PhD(chem), 57. *Honors & Awards:* Joseph P Hyman Award, Am Chem Soc, 88; Paul N Rylander Award, Org Reactions Catalysis Soc, 90. *Prof Exp:* From instr to asst prof chem, Univ Tex, 57-61. *Mem:* Am Chem Soc; Royal Soc Chem; Org Reactions Catalysis Soc (dir, 75-77, chmn, 84-86); NAm Catalysis Soc. *Res:* Synthetic and mechanistic applications of catalytic hydrogenation, oxidation and related reactions; development of emantioselective heterogeneous catalysts; synthetic application of catalytic reactions. *Mailing Add:* Dept Chem Seton Hall Univ South Orange NJ 07079. *Fax:* 973-761-9772; *E-Mail:* augustrl@lanmail.shu.edu

AUGUSTYN, JOAN MARY, BIOCHEMISTRY. *Current Pos:* RES ASST PROF ATHEROSCLEROSIS, ALBANY MED COL, 76- *Personal Data:* b Buffalo, NY. *Educ:* D'Youville Col, BA, 62; State Univ NY Buffalo, PhD(biochem), 69. *Prof Exp:* Trainee steroid biochem, Worcester Found Exp Biol, Shrewsbury, Mass, 69-71; RES BIOCHEMIST, RES SERV, VET ADMIN HOSP, ALBANY, 71-, CLIN CHEMIST, LAB SERV, 79- *Concurrent Pos:* Mem, Am Heart Asn. *Mem:* Tissue Cult Asn; Sigma Xi; AAAS; Am Asn Clin Chem. *Res:* Biochemical mechanisms involved in atherosclerotic heart disease. *Mailing Add:* Dept Path 47 New Scotland Ave Albany Med Col Albany NY 12208-3412

AUKERMAN, LEE WILLIAM, SOLID STATE PHYSICS. *Current Pos:* MEM TECH STAFF, AEROSPACE CORP, LOS ANGELES, 63- *Personal Data:* b North Grove, Ind, June 7, 23; m 62; c 4. *Educ:* Purdue Univ, BS, 49, MS, 53, PhD(physics), 58. *Prof Exp:* Asst, Purdue Univ, 49-58; prin physicist, Battelle Mem Inst, 58-63. *Mem:* AAAS; Am Phys Soc; Sigma Xi. *Res:* Semiconductors and insulators; radiation damage; electrical and optical properties; infrared detectors. *Mailing Add:* 220 25th St Hermosa Beach CA 90254

AUKLAND, JERRY C, SIGNAL PROCESSING DEVICES, REMOTE SENSING. *Current Pos:* RES & DEVELOP MGR, HEWLETT-PACKARD, SAN JOSE, CALIF, 84-, CUSTOMER ASSURANCE MGR. *Personal Data:* b Macedonia, Iowa, Oct 7, 31; m 51; c 4. *Educ:* Iowa State Univ, BS, 59. *Honors & Awards:* Centennial Award, Inst Elec & Electronics Engrs. *Prof Exp:* Res engr, Autonetics Div, NAm Aviat, Inc, 59-63, sr res physicist, 63-64, res specialist, 64-66; dept mgr sensor systs & instrumentation, Space Gen, 66-68; dir eng microwave sensor systs, Spectran, Inc, 68-71; group leader, Electronics Div, Rockwell Int, 71-78, mgr advan prods, 78-80, mgr microwave develop, 80-84. *Concurrent Pos:* Dir, Region 6, Inst Elec & Electronic Engrs, 91 & 92. *Mem:* Inst Elec & Electronics Engrs; fel Inst Advan Eng. *Res:* Parametric amplifiers and their applications at microwave frequencies; millimeter semiconductor devices and parametric interactions; earth resource applications; pollution detection; surface acoustic wave devices; Rf and microwave semiconductor devices and IC's. *Mailing Add:* 982 Scorpion Pl Fremont CA 94539

AUKRUST, EGIL, metallurgy, physical chemistry, for more information see previous edition

AUKSMANN, BORIS, ENGINEERING DESIGN. *Current Pos:* CONSULT MECH ENG, 70- *Personal Data:* b Tartu, Estonia, Mar 12, 27; Can citizen; m 55. *Educ:* Univ BC, BASc, 55; Calif Inst Technol, MS, 58, ME, 59, PhD(mech eng), 64. *Prof Exp:* Design engr, Can Industs Ltd, 55-56 & H A Simons, Consult Engr, 56-57; res engr, Ingersoll-Rand Co, 59-61; asst mech eng, Calif Inst Technol, 61-64, asst prof eng design, 64-70. *Mem:* Am Soc Mech Engrs; Sigma Xi. *Res:* Journal bearings; planetary gear trains; mechanical seals; engineering design; accident reconstruction and analysis. *Mailing Add:* 1816 Anita Crest Dr Arcadia CA 91006

AULD, DAVID STUART, BIOPHYSICS, METALLO BIOCHEMISTRY. *Current Pos:* from asst prof to assoc prof biol chem, 70-83, ASSOC MED, BRIGHAM & WOMENS HOSP, HARVARD MED SCH, 67-, ASSOC PROF PATH & BIOCHEM, 83- *Personal Data:* b Newton, NJ, Jan 8, 37; m 61, Loretta Patricia; c Cynthia A & Douglas S. *Educ:* Lehigh Univ, BA, 60, MS, 62; Cornell Univ, PhD(chem), 67. *Prof Exp:* Res fel biol chem, Am Cancer Soc, 67-69, assoc, 69-70. *Concurrent Pos:* Res fel, Cancer Div, NIH, 69-70, spec fel, 70-71; consult, Monsanto Res Corp, 75-77; bd tutors biochem sci, Harvard Univ, 77- *Mem:* Am Chem Soc; Am Soc Exp Biol Chemists; Sigma Xi; NY Acad Sci. *Res:* Mechanism of enzyme action; metals, particularly zinc, in biochemical processes; developed mechanistic approaches which can relate functional characteristics of an enzyme to structural features through information obtained during the reaction. *Mailing Add:* 29 Railroad Ave Bedford MA 01730. *E-Mail:* dauld@warren.med.harvard.edu

AULD, EDWARD GEORGE, NUCLEAR PHYSICS. *Current Pos:* assoc prof, 66-83, PROF PHYSICS, UNIV BC, 83-, DIR ENG PHYSICS, 81-, PROF ENG, 76- *Personal Data:* b Chilliwack, BC, Apr 27, 36; m 60; c 4. *Educ:* Univ BC, BASc, 59, MASc, 61; Univ Southampton, PhD(nuclear physics), 64. *Prof Exp:* Athlone fel, 61, sci officer, Rutherford High Energy Lab, eng, 63-64, sr sci officer, 64-66. *Concurrent Pos:* Vpres, Univ BC Res Enterprizes, technol transfer & commercialization. *Mem:* Am Asn Physics Teachers; Can Asn Physicists. *Res:* Particle physics, especially proton-antiproton interactions; nuclear physics, especially deuteron interactions; high energy physics; meson resonance and pion inelastic interactions; cyclotron magnetic design for the TRIUMF negative ion cyclotron. *Mailing Add:* Dept Physics Rastron Univ BC 2075 6224 Agr Rd Vancouver BC V6T 1Z1 Can

AULD, PETER A MCF, MEDICINE, PEDIATRICS. *Current Pos:* from asst prof to prof pediat, 62-74, PROF PEDIAT & PERINATAL MED IN OBSTET & GYNEC, MED COL, CORNELL UNIV, 74- *Personal Data:* b Toronto, Ont, Feb 5, 28; m 51; c 2. *Educ:* Univ Toronto, BA, 48; McGill Univ, MD, 52; FRCP(C), 57. *Prof Exp:* Instr pediat, Harvard Med Sch, 59-60; res assoc, McGill Univ, 60-62. *Concurrent Pos:* Res fel pediat, Harvard Med Sch, 57-59; career investr, NY Health Res Coun, 62- *Mem:* Fel Am Acad Pediat; Perinatal Res Soc; Soc Pediat Res; Am Pediat Soc. *Res:* Cardiology; cardio-pulmonary physiology; neonatal pulmonary disease. *Mailing Add:* Dept Pediat Cornell Univ Med Col 1300 York Ave New York NY 10021-4805

AULENBACH, DONALD BRUCE, ENVIRONMENTAL ENGINEERING. *Current Pos:* from asst prof to assoc prof, 60-65, chmn environ eng curric, 67-71, prof environ eng, 73-90, EMER PROF, RENSSELAER POLYTECH INST, 90- *Personal Data:* b Berwick, Pa, Mar 7, 28; m 52, Marie P (Wertz); c Louise (Trakimas), Bruce, Nancy (Baker) & Brent. *Educ:* Franklin & Marshall Col, BS, 50; Rutgers Univ, MS, 52, PhD(chem, sanit), 54. *Prof Exp:* Chemist-bacteriologist, Del Water Pollution Comn, 54-60. *Concurrent Pos:* Consult, Gen Elec Co, 65-85; invited lectr, Peoples Rupub China, 85; adj prof environ eng, Lenox Inst Water Technol, 80-91; consult over 100 cos. *Mem:* Am Chem Soc; Health Physics Soc; Water Environ Fedn; Am Water Works Asn; Asn Environ Eng Prof; Sigma Xi; Nat Soc Prof Eng. *Res:* Treatment of laundromat wastes; chemical nutrients in natural waters; fate of chemical nutrients in ground water; thermoluminescent dosimetry; effects of man's works on environment; Lake George ecosystem; removal of heavy metals in wastewaters; leachate. *Mailing Add:* 24 Valencia Lane Clifton Park NY 12065. *Fax:* 518-276-2080

AULERICH, RICHARD J, ANIMAL SCIENCE, FURBEARING ANIMAL BIOLOGY. *Current Pos:* Technician, Fur Animal Proj, 62-67, from asst prof to prof poultry sci, 67-80, PROF ANIMAL SCI, MICH STATE UNIV, 80-, ASSOC CHMN, ANIMAL SCI DEPT, 92- *Personal Data:* b Detroit, Mich, Mar 12, 36; m 63; c 3. *Educ:* Mich State Univ, BS, 58, MS, 64, PhD(poultry sci), 67. *Concurrent Pos:* Mem subcomt furbearer nutrit, Nat Res Coun, 67, univ coordr, live animal res, 87- *Mem:* Sigma Xi; Soc Environ Toxicol Chem; Am Soc Animal Sci; Comp Nutrit Soc; Int Fur Animal Sci Asn. *Res:* Nutrition, physiology, toxicology and management of furbearing animals. *Mailing Add:* Dept Animal Sci Mich State Univ East Lansing MI 48824

AULICK, LOUIS H, POST-BURN HYPERMETABOLISM, INFECTION. *Current Pos:* ASSOC PROF SURG & PHYSIOL, SCH MED, MARSHALL UNIV, 84- *Educ:* Ind Univ, PhD(physiol), 74. *Res:* Temperature regulation. *Mailing Add:* Dept Physiol Sch Med Marshall Univ 1542 Spring Valley Dr Huntington WV 25704-9588

AULL, CHARLES EDWARD, MATHEMATICS. *Current Pos:* from assoc prof to prof, 65-94, EMER PROF MATH, VA POLYTECH INST & STATE UNIV, 94- *Personal Data:* b US, Sept 1, 27. *Educ:* Columbia Univ, BS, 49; Univ Ore, MS, 53; Univ Colo, PhD(math), 62. *Prof Exp:* Asst math, Univ Ore, 52-53; instr, Univ Ariz, 53-55; instr, Univ Colo, 55-62; asst prof, Kent State Univ, 62-65. *Mem:* Am Math Soc; Math Asn Am. *Res:* Topological spaces; separation and base axioms; covering properties and sequences; algebra, especially ideal theory; analysis, especially generalized variations. *Mailing Add:* Dept Math Va Polytech Inst & State Univ Blacksburg VA 24061-0123

AULL, FELICE, PHYSIOLOGY. *Current Pos:* from instr to asst prof, 66-72, ASSOC PROF PHYSIOL, SCH MED, NY UNIV, 72-, DIR, ADV COL PROG, 91- *Personal Data:* b Vienna, Austria, Aug 12, 38; US citizen; m 62; c 1. *Educ:* Columbia Univ, AB, 60; Cornell Univ, PhD(physiol), 64. *Prof Exp:* Physiologist, Radiobiol Lab, Bur Com Fisheries, NC, 64-65. *Concurrent Pos:* USPHS fel physiol, Med Col, Cornell Univ, 65-66. *Mem:* Soc Health & Human Values; NY Acad Sci; Soc Gen Physiol; Am Physiol Soc; Biophys Soc; Assoc Women Sci. *Res:* Anion transport. *Mailing Add:* Dept Physiol & Neurosci NY Univ Sch Med 550 First Ave New York NY 10016

AULL, JOHN LOUIS, ENZYMOLOGY. *Current Pos:* from asst to assoc prof chem, 74-85, PROF CHEM, AUBURN UNIV, 85-, ACTG DEPT HEAD, 86- *Personal Data:* b Newberry, SC, May 7, 39; m 62; c 2. *Educ:* Univ NC, Chapel Hill, AB, 64; NC State Univ, PhD(biochem), 72. *Prof Exp:* Chemist, NC Dept Agr, 62-63; teaching asst, NC State Univ, 68-69, res asst, 69-72, NIH fel, 72-73; Am Cancer Soc fel, Univ SC, 73-74. *Concurrent Pos:* Line officer, US Navy, 64-67. *Mem:* Am Soc Biol Chemists & Molecular Biologists; Am Chem Soc; Sigma Xi. *Res:* Interactions of potential chemotherapeutic compounds with enzymes; enzyme mechanisms and metabolic regulation of enzymes; protein structures; function relationships; chemical modification of proteins. *Mailing Add:* Dept Chem Auburn Univ 362 Chem Bldg Auburn AL 36849-5312

AULL, LUTHER BACHMAN, III, SCIENCE ADMINISTRATION, NUCLEAR & RADIATION PHYSICS. *Current Pos:* MED PHYSICIST, SELF MEM HOSP, 85- *Personal Data:* b Greenwood, SC, Mar 1, 29; m 50, Louise Fleming; c Alyson, John F, Ginna & Debra. *Educ:* US Mil Acad, BS, 50; Univ Va, PhD(physics), 59. *Prof Exp:* Physicist nuclear weapon effects, Defense Atomic Support Agency, 59-63; physicist nuclear physics, US Army Res Off, 63-67; tech asst nuclear weapon effects, Defense Res & Eng, Off Secy Defense, 67-70; planning consult nuclear weapon progs, Combined Opers Planning Group, Union Carbide 70-73, mgr planning & spec tasks gas centrifuge develop, Nuclear Div-Separation Systs Div, 73-81, mgr, tech integration off, advan gas centrifuge prog, Nuclear Div, 81-84. *Mem:* Sigma Xi; Am Phys Soc; Am Asn Physicists Med. *Res:* Planning and coordinating continuing development program for the gas entrifuge for use in uranium isotope separation. *Mailing Add:* 1711 Hwy 34 W Ninety Six SC 29666

AULSEBROOK, LUCILLE HAGAN, ANATOMY. *Current Pos:* instr, 69-71, ASST PROF ANAT, SCH MED, VANDERBILT UNIV, 71-, ASSOC PROF, SCH NURSING, 73- *Personal Data:* b Houston, Tex, Dec 31, 25; m 52; c 4. *Educ:* Univ Tex, Austin, BA, 46, MA, 47; Univ Ark, Little Rock, PhD(anat), 66. *Prof Exp:* Instr zool, Univ Tex, Austin, 48; res assoc cancer res, M D Anderson Hosp Cancer Res, Houston, Tex, 48-50; teaching asst zool, Univ Wis, Madison, 50-53; instr biol & chem, Univ Ark, Little Rock, 57-60, teaching asst anat, Sch Med, 60-64. *Concurrent Pos:* USPHS fel, Sch Med, Vanderbilt Univ, 66-69. *Mem:* Am Asn Anat; Soc Neurosci; Sigma Xi. *Res:* Hypothalamic-endocrine interrelations, particularly neural regulation of releasing factors involved in reproduction, parturition and lactation. *Mailing Add:* 203 Cherokee Rd Nashville TN 37205

AULT, ADDISON, ORGANIC CHEMISTRY. *Current Pos:* from asst prof to assoc prof, 62-70, PROF CHEM & CHMN DEPT, CORNELL COL, 70- *Personal Data:* b Boston, Mass, July 3, 33; m 58, Janet Meade; c Margaret, Warren, Addison, Peter & Emily. *Educ:* Amherst Col, AB, 55; Harvard Univ, PhD(chem), 60. *Prof Exp:* Asst prof chem, Grinnell Col, 59-61; resident res assoc, Argonne Nat Lab, 61-62. *Concurrent Pos:* NSF sci fac fel, Pa State Univ, 68-69; consult & evaluator, NCent Asn Cols & Schs, 72-; tour speaker, Am Chem Soc, 79-81, 84, 85, 94 & 97. *Mem:* Am Chem Soc; AAAS. *Res:* Structure determination of natural products; reaction mechanisms; physical organic chemistry; nuclear magnetic resonance; sterochemistry; enzyme kinetics; chemical education; author of laboratory manuals and textbooks for organic chemistry. *Mailing Add:* Dept Chem Cornell Col Mt Vernon IA 52314. *Fax:* 319-895-4492

AULT, GEORGE MERVIN, METALLURGY, MATERIALS ENGINEERING. *Current Pos:* RETIRED. *Personal Data:* b Pomeroy, Iowa, Aug 23, 21; m 64; c 2. *Educ:* Iowa State Univ, BS, 43. *Honors & Awards:* Except Sci Achievement Medal, NASA, 68, Except Serv Medal, 76, Distinquished Serv Medal, 80. *Prof Exp:* Engr & head, Mat Res Sect, Lewis Res Ctr, NASA, 47-55, chief, 55-59, asst chief, Mat & Struct Div, 59-64, assoc chief, 64-70, dir, Power & Mat, 70-75, dir energy progs directorate, 75-81. *Concurrent Pos:* Mem mat adv bd, Nat Acad Sci & Eng, 67-70. *Mem:* Fel Am Soc Metals; Am Inst Mining, Metall & Petrol Engrs; AAAS. *Res:* Superalloys; refractory metals; ceramics and cermets; composites; thermal and mechanical fatigue; space power; terrestrial energy technology for propulsion and electric power generation. *Mailing Add:* 25920 Myrtle Ave Olmsted Falls OH 44138

AULT, JEFFREY GEORGE, BIOPHYSICS. *Current Pos:* RES SCIENTIST, DEPT STRUCT PATH, WADSWORTH CTR LABS & RES, 92- *Personal Data:* b Fargo, NDak, June 18, 53. *Res:* Biophysics. *Mailing Add:* Dept Struct Path Wadsworth Ctr Labs & Res Empire State Plaza PO Box 509 Albany NY 12201-0509

AULT, N(EIL) N(ORMAN), CERAMICS. *Current Pos:* CONSULT, 87- *Personal Data:* b Dunkirk, Ohio, Mar 31, 22; m 46, Anne Hoffman; c 3. *Educ:* Ohio State Univ, BCerE, 47, MSCerE, 48, PhD(ceramic eng), 50. *Honors & Awards:* Distinguished Ceramist of New Eng, Am Ceramic Soc, 76. *Prof Exp:* Res assoc eng exp sta, Ohio State Univ, 48-50; res ceramic engr, Norton Co, 50-57, asst dir res & develop, 57-64, dir res, Refractories & Protective Prod Div, 64-70, tech dir, Indust Ceramics Div, 70-78, res mgr technol, Indust Ceramics Div, 78-80, tech dir, 81-87. *Mem:* Distinguished mem Am Ceramic Soc; Nat Inst Ceramic Engrs. *Res:* Materials science; special refractories for high temperatures. *Mailing Add:* 52 Holden St Holden MA 01520

AULT, WAYNE URBAN, GEOCHEMISTRY. *Current Pos:* PROF GEOL, MEMPHIS STATE UNIV, 85- *Personal Data:* b Monroe Co, Mich, Jan 20, 23; m 47; c 4. *Educ:* Wheaton Col, BA, 50; Columbia Univ, MA, 56, PhD(geochem), 57. *Prof Exp:* Asst geochem, Lamont Geol Observ, 50-57; res geochemist, US Geol Surv, 57-62; sr res scientist, Isotopes, Inc, 62-64, dir tech representation, 64-68; assoc prof, Wheaton Col, 68-69; assoc prof chem, 69-70, actg chmn dept, 69, assoc prof geol, 70-72, prof geol, King's Col, NY, 72-, chmn dept, 70-; AT DEPT GEOL, NYACK COL. *Concurrent Pos:* Asst prof, Shelton Col, 52-54; asst prof, Nyack Col, 64-72, assoc prof geol, 72- *Mem:* Fel Geol Soc Am; Am Geophys Union; Am Nuclear Soc; Int Asn Geochem & Cosmochem; Sigma Xi. *Res:* Isotope geology; mass spectrometry; vacuum fusion; age determination; volcanology; volcanic fluids; subsurface tracing; radioisotope applications; environmental geology. *Mailing Add:* 595 Watson St Memphis TN 38111

AUMAN, JASON REID, ASTROPHYSICS. *Current Pos:* from asst prof to assoc prof, 68-77, PROF ASTRON, UNIV BC, 77- *Personal Data:* b High Point, NC, Feb 5, 37; m 58; c 2. *Educ:* Duke Univ, BS, 59; Northwestern Univ, PhD(astron), 65. *Prof Exp:* Res assoc astron, Princeton Univ, 64-68. *Mem:* Am Astron Soc; Int Astron Union. *Res:* Structure and evolution of stars; atmospheres of late-type stars; infrared opacity of water vapor at elevated temperatures; nucleii of galaxies. *Mailing Add:* Dept Physics & Astron Univ BC 2075 Westbrook Pl Vancouver BC V6T 1W5 Can

AUMANN, GLENN D, ECOLOGY, ETHOLOGY. *Current Pos:* assoc prof, Univ Houston, 65-70, chmn dept, 67-76, assoc dean, 76-81, interim dean, 82-83, assoc provost, 84-85, assoc vpres res, 85-90, PROF BIOL, UNIV HOUSTON, 70-, DEAN, NATURAL SCI & MATH, 90- *Personal Data:* b Elbowoods, NDak, June 17, 30; m 50; c 4. *Educ:* Wis State Univ, Eau Claire, BS, 57; Univ Wis, MS, 58, PhD(ecol), 64. *Prof Exp:* Asst prof biol, Gogebic Community Col, 57-61; NIH fel electron micros, Sch Med, Univ Wis, 64-65. *Mem:* AAAS. *Res:* Vertebrate population control mechanisms. *Mailing Add:* Biol Dept Univ Houston Houston TX 77204-0001

AUMANN, HARTMUT HANS-GEORG, SPACE SCIENCE, ASTRONOMY. *Current Pos:* SR SCIENTIST SPACE SCI, JET PROPULSION LAB, CALIF INST TECHNOL, 70- *Personal Data:* b Frankfurt, Ger, Nov 18, 40; US citizen; m 70; c 3. *Educ:* Univ Idaho, BS, 62; Univ Okla, MS, 64; Rice Univ, PhD(space sci), 70. *Prof Exp:* Res scientist physics, Esso Prod Res Co, 64-66. *Concurrent Pos:* IRAS proj scientist, Jet Propulsion Lab, 76- *Res:* Remote sounding of earth and planetary atmospheres in the infrared. *Mailing Add:* Mail Stop 100-22 4800 Oak Grove Dr Calif Inst Technol Pasadena CA 91109

AUMANN, ROBERT JOHN, GAME THEORY, MATHEMATICAL ECONOMICS. *Current Pos:* from instr to assoc prof, 56-68, PROF MATH, HEBREW UNIV, JERUSALEM, 68- *Personal Data:* b Frankfurt-am-Main, Ger, June 8, 30; US & Israeli citizen; m 55, Esther Schlesinger; c Shlomo, Tamar, Yehonatan, Miriam & Noga J. *Educ:* City Col New York, BS, 50; Mass Inst Technol, SM, 52, PhD(math), 55. *Hon Degrees:* Doctoris Rerum Politicarum, Univ Bonn, 88; Dr, Cath Univ Louvain, 89; LLD, Univ Chicago, 92. *Honors & Awards:* Harvey Prize, Israel Inst Technol, 83; Israel Prize, 94. *Prof Exp:* Res asst, Dept Math, Princeton Univ, 54-56. *Concurrent Pos:* Res assoc, Princeton Univ, 60-61; vis prof, Yale Univ, 64-65, & 89, Univ Calif, Berkeley, 71, Univ Louvain, 72, 78, 84, Stanford Univ, 75-76 & 80-81. *Mem:* Nat Acad Sci; fel Econometric Soc; foreign hon mem Am Acad Arts & Sci; Israel Acad Sci Humanities; hon mem Am Econ Asn. *Res:* Interactive decision making; general equilibrium theory; repeated games; interactive epistemology; value theory; coalitional games. *Mailing Add:* Inst Math Hebrew Univ 91904 Jerusalem Italy

AUNE, KIRK CARL, physical biochemistry, for more information see previous edition

AUNE, THOMAS M, MEDICAL RESEARCH, IMMUNOLOGY. *Current Pos:* RESEARCHER CHEM RES-DRUG DISCOVERY, MILES INC, 88- *Personal Data:* b Winona, Minn, Apr 23, 51. *Educ:* Rhoades Col, BS, 73; Univ Tenn, PhD(biochem), 76. *Prof Exp:* Researcher clin res-drug discovery, Genentech Inc, 86-88. *Mem:* Am Asn Pathologists; Am Asn Immunologists; NY Acad Sci. *Mailing Add:* Bayer Corp 400 Morgan Lane West Haven CT 06516-4134

AUNG, TAING, CYTOGENETICS, PLANT BREEDING. *Current Pos:* RES SCIENTIST, CROP RES CTR, AGR & AGR-FOOD CAN, WINNIPEG, MAN, 90- *Personal Data:* b Hmawbe, Yangon, Myanmar, July 15, 44; Can citizen. *Educ:* Univ Rangoon, Burma, BSc, 65, MSc, 72; Univ Wales, UK, MSc, 75, PhD(cytogenesis), 78. *Prof Exp:* Lect demonstrator forest ecol, Bot Dept, Univ Rangooon, 70-72, jr lectr genetics statist, 78-80; fel, Agr Bot Dept, Univ Col wales, Aberystwyth, 81-84; res assoc, Plant Sci Dept, Univ Alta, 84-87; asst prof gen genetics, plant breeding & cytogenetics, Plant Soil & Insect Sci Dept, Univ Wyo, 87-90. *Concurrent Pos:* Wyo state rep, Regional Tech Comt on Plant Germplasm, Western US, 87-90. *Mem:* Genetics Soc Can; Am Soc Agron; Crop Sci Soc Am. *Res:* Transfer of desirable genes from related and unrelated species of wheat, oat and barley into the cultivated forms through cytogenetic techniques. *Mailing Add:* 195 Dafoe Rd Winnipeg MB R3T 2M9 Can

AUNGST, BRUCE J, PHARMACOKINETICS, PHARMACEUTICS. *Current Pos:* PRIN SCIENTIST, DU PONT MERCK, 91- *Personal Data:* b Pottsville, Pa, Nov 22, 52; m 80, Judith; c Matthew, Colleen, Christopher, Keenan & Mariette. *Educ:* Pa State Univ, BS, 74, MS, 77; State Univ NY, Buffalo, PhD(pharmaceut), 81. *Prof Exp:* Prin scientist, E I Du Pont de Nemours & Co, 81-90. *Mem:* Am Asn Pharmaceut Scientists; Controlled Release Soc. *Res:* Drug Transport; drug metabolism; drug delivery; biopharmaceutics. *Mailing Add:* Du Pont Merck PO Box 80400 Wilmington DE 19880-0400. *Fax:* 302-695-1460; *E-Mail:* aungstbj@a1.lldmpc.umc.dupont.com

AUNON, JORGE IGNACIO, BIOMEDICAL ENGINEERING. *Current Pos:* PROF & HEAD DEPT ELEC ENG, COLO STATE UNIV, FT COLLINS, 88- *Personal Data:* b Havana, Cuba, Sept 2, 42; US citizen; m 65; c 4. *Educ:* George Washington Univ, BS, 67, MS, 69, ScD(eng), 72. *Honors & Awards:* Cert of Recognition, Inst Elec & Electronics Engrs, 77. *Prof Exp:* Med engr, George Washington Univ Hosp, 69-72; res assoc neurol, Children's Hosp, Washington, DC, 72-73; from asst prof to prof elec eng, Purdue Univ, West Lafayette, 73-87. *Mem:* Fel Inst Elec & Electronics Engrs. *Res:* Electroencephalography research; evoked potentials; computer processing of physiological data. *Mailing Add:* 1919 Dorset Dr Ft Collins CO 80526

AUPPERLE, ERIC MAX, COMPUTER SCIENCE, ELECTRONICS. *Current Pos:* proj leader, Merit Comput Network, Inst Sci & Technol, Univ Mich, 69-73, assoc dir, 73-74, dir, 74-78, assoc dir commun, Comput Ctr, 81-89, interim dir, Info Tech Div, Network Systs, 90-92, PRES, MERIT NETWORK INC, INFO TECH DIV, NETWORK SYSTS, UNIV MICH, 88-; RES SCIENTIST, INST SCI & TECHNOL, COOLEY ELECTRONICS LAB, 74- *Personal Data:* b Batavia, NY, Apr 14, 35; m 58, Nancy A Jach; c Bryan & Lisa. *Educ:* Univ Mich, BSEE, 57, BSE, 57, MSE, 58, InstmE, 64. *Prof Exp:* From asst res engr to res engr, Cooley Electronics Lab, 57-69, res engr, Inst Sci & Technol, 69-74. *Concurrent Pos:* Lectr, Dept Elec Eng, Univ Mich, 72, Dept Indust & Opers Eng, 73-74, mem, Univ Hierarch Comput Study Comt, 78-79, Univ Comt Comput Policy & Utilization, 79-80, chmn, 80-84; guest lectr, Comput Sci Sect, Dept Math, Wayne State Univ, 75; consult, Cholette, Perkins & Buchanan Comput Tech Mgt Servs, Reliance Elec Co, Votrax, Prentice Hall, IBM, Owens-Ill & Donnelly Mirror. *Mem:* Inst Elec & Electronics Engrs; Sigma Xi. *Res:* Systems networking. *Mailing Add:* 1499 Stark Strasse Ann Arbor MI 48105-9537

AURAND, HENRY SPIESE, JR, UNDERWATER ACOUSTICS. *Current Pos:* RETIRED. *Personal Data:* b Columbus, Ohio, Feb 24, 24; m 46; c 2. *Educ:* US Mil Acad, BS, 44; State Univ Iowa, MS, 47. *Prof Exp:* Design engr ballistic missiles, Douglas Aircraft Co, 54-56; mem tech staff weapon syst, Tech Mil Planning Oper, Gen Elec, 57-63; mgr eng develop dept, Electronics Div, Gen Mill Inc, 63; sr res engr ocean acoustics, Lockheed Missiles & Space Co, 63-69; phys sci adminr, Off Naval Res, Washington, 69-71; supvr physicist Ocean Acoust, Naval Undersea Ctr, San Diego, 71-84. *Mem:* Acoust Soc Am; Am Geophys Union; Am Soc Civil Engr. *Res:* Large scale computers and sensors in ocean acoustics. *Mailing Add:* 734 Camino Catalina Solana Beach CA 92075

AURAND, LEONARD WILLIAM, BIOCHEMISTRY OF MILK LIPIDS. *Current Pos:* RETIRED. *Personal Data:* b Shamokin Dam, Pa, Feb 5, 20; m 43, Eleanor M Nichols; c Rebecca A (Newton), Thomas J & Sarah A. *Educ:* Pa State Univ, BS, 41, PhD(biochem), 49; Univ NH, MS, 47. *Prof Exp:* From res asst prof to res assoc prof animal indust, NC State Univ, 49-60, prof food, 60-88. *Mem:* Inst Food Technol; Am Inst Nutrit. *Res:* Off-flavors in milk; enzyme chemistry; oxidation of lipids. *Mailing Add:* NC State Univ 921 Trailwood Dr Raleigh NC 27606-3708

AURELIAN, LAURE, VIROLOGY. *Current Pos:* postdoctoral fel microbiol, Johns Hopkins Sch Med, 66-67, instr, Lab Animal Med & Microbiol, 67-69, asst prof, 69-74, assoc prof, Dept Comp Med & Biophysics, 74-83, PROF, DEPT BIOCHEM, JOHNS HOPKINS MED INST, 83; PROF PHARMACOL & EXP THERAPEUT & MICROBIOL & DIR VIROL/IMMUNOL LABS, UNIV MD SCH MED, 83- *Personal Data:* b Bucharest, Rumania, June 17, 39; m 64. *Educ:* Tel Aviv Univ, MSc, 62; Johns Hopkins Univ, PhD(microbiol), 66. *Honors & Awards:* Georgian Republican & Tbilisi Sci Soc of Oricologists, Georgia, USSR; Premlo XXIV Casali, 90; Pro Loco Bronte Edizione Speciale Medicina, Catania, Sicily. *Prof Exp:* Res asst microbiol, Tel Aviv Univ, 60-62. *Concurrent Pos:* Consult, Virus Cancer Prog, 75-77; USSR prog, 79; vis prof, Univ Bologna, 80, Univ Catania, 85-90; mem, Cancer Res Manpower Rev comt, Nat Cancer Inst, 82-85, Sci Exec Comt, Mediter Soc Gynec, 88-; mem, US sci deleg epidemiol Gynec Cancer, USA. *Mem:* AAAS; Am Asn Cancer Res; Soc Exp Biol & Med; Am Soc Microbiol; Am Asn Immunol; hon mem D A Boyes Soc Gynaecol Oncol. *Res:* Biological, biochemical and biophysical properties of viruses; basis of host-range restrictions; role of viruses in cancer; author of numerous articles to professional journals. *Mailing Add:* Dept Pharmacol & Exp Therapeut Univ Md Sch Med 10 S Pine St Baltimore MD 21201

AURILIA, ANTONIO, HIGH ENERGY PHYSICS, COSMOLOGY. *Current Pos:* PROF PHYSICS, CALIF STATE POLYTECH UNIV, POMONA, 86- *Personal Data:* b Napoli, Italy, May 14, 42; nat US; m 72, Elizabeth C Adams; c Darius M & Alexandra R. *Educ:* Univ Naples, Italy, Doctor Degree(Laurea)physics, 66; Univ Wis, Milwaukee, PhD(physics), 70. *Prof Exp:* Fel, Univ Alta, Can, 70-72; res assoc, Syracuse Univ, 72-74; res scientist, Int Ctr Theoret Physics, Trieste, Italy, 74-75; sr res scientist, Nat Inst Nuclear Physics, Trieste, Italy, 75-86. *Concurrent Pos:* Vis scientist, Imp Col Sci Technol, London, UK, 77-78, Univ Alta, Can, 80-82, Univ Toronto, Can, 85-86. *Mem:* Am Phys Soc; Am Asn Physics Teachers; Sigma Xi; NY Acad Sci. *Res:* Unification of fundamental forces of nature to account for the origin and evolution of the universe. *Mailing Add:* Dept Physics Calif State Polytech Univ Pomona CA 91768. *Fax:* 909-869-4396; *E-Mail:* aaurilia@csupomona.edu

AURON, PHILIP E, MEDICAL RESEARCH, MOLECULAR BIOLOGY. *Current Pos:* ASSOC PROF PATH, CTR BLOOD RES, HARVARD MED SCH, 92- *Personal Data:* b Wilkes-Barre, Pa. *Educ:* Wilkes Col, BS, 74; Pa State Univ, PhD(biochem), 80. *Prof Exp:* Fel biol, Mass Inst Technol, 82-83; asst prof med, Tufts Univ, 83-89; molecular biologist, Mass Gen Hosp, 90-92. *Mem:* AAAS; Am Asn Immunologists. *Mailing Add:* Ctr Blood Res Harvard Med Sch Warren Alpert Bldg 200 Longview Ave Boston MA 02115

AUSICH, RODNEY L, PLANT TISSUE CULTURE, PLANT MOLECULAR BIOLOGY. *Current Pos:* Res Biol, 80-84, staff res scientist, Amoco Corp, 84-89, RES SUPVR, AMOCO TECHNOL CO, 89- *Personal Data:* b Casper, Wyo, Oct 28, 53; m 86, Rebecca Simmons; c Evan & Brandyn. *Educ:* Univ Wyo, BS, 76; Ind Univ, MA, 78, PhD(biol), 80. *Mem:* Am Soc Plant Physiologists; AAAS. *Res:* Regulation of gene activity in plant, algal and yeast cells. *Mailing Add:* 4110 Greenwood Dr Des Moines IA 50312

AUSICH, WILLIAM IRL, INVERTEBRATE PALEONTOLOGY, PALEOECOLOGY. *Current Pos:* assoc prof, 84-90, PROF, GEOL SCI DEPT, OHIO STATE UNIV, 90- *Personal Data:* b Kewanee, Ill, Feb 2, 52; m 73, Regina S Dolk; c Elizabeth C, Arlene E & Mary K. *Educ:* Univ Ill, BS, 74; Ind Univ Bloomington, AM, 76, PhD(geol, biol), 78. *Honors & Awards:* Schuchert Award, Paleont Soc, 90. *Prof Exp:* Instr geol, Indiana Univ, Bloomington, 78; asst prof, Wright State Univ, 78-82, assoc prof, 82-84; Fulbright fel, 92. *Mem:* Paleont Soc; Int Palaeont Soc; Sigma Xi. *Res:* Paleoecology, functional morphology, taxonomy, and evolution of Paleozoic crinoids; Paleozoic community paleoecology; lower Mississippian paleontology. *Mailing Add:* Geol Sci Dept Ohio State Univ 155 S Oval Mall Columbus OH 43210

AUSIELLO, DENNIS ARTHUR, MEDICINE. *Current Pos:* CHIEF, RENAL UNIT, MASS GEN HOSP, 84-, PHYSICIAN & CHIEF, 88- *Personal Data:* b Chelsea, Mass, Sept 12, 45. *Educ:* Harvard Col, BA, 67; Univ Pa, MD, 71; Am Bd Internal Med, dipl, 74; Am Bd Nephrology, dipl, 78. *Prof Exp:* Intern med, Mass Gen Hosp, 71-72, asst resident, 72-73, clin fel med-nephrology, 75-76, asst med, 76-82, asst physician, 82-84, assoc physician, 85-88; clin fel med, Harvard Med Sch, 71-73, res fel, 75-76, from instr to asst prof, 76-85, ASSOC PROF MED, HARVARD MED SCH, 85- *Concurrent Pos:* Surgeon, Pub Health Serv & staff assoc, Lab Kidney & Electrolyte Metab, Nat Heart & Lung Inst, NIH, 73-75; NIH res fel med-nephrology, Mass Gen Hosp, 76-77, attend physician, Med Serv & visit, Renal Serv, 76-; lectr & sect leader renal pathophysiol, Harvard Med Sch, 76-; res career develop award, NIH, 77-82; assoc ed, Am J Physiol, 87- *Mem:* Am Soc Nephrology; Int Soc Nephrology; Am Fedn Clin Res; Am Physiol Soc; Am Soc Clin Invest; Asn Am Physicians. *Mailing Add:* Harvard Med Sch & Renal Unit Mass Gen Hosp 149 13th St Charlestown MA 02129-2060

AUSKAPS, AINA MARIJA, DENTISTRY, BIOCHEMISTRY. *Current Pos:* CONSULT, 86- *Personal Data:* b Raiskums, Latvia, Sept 2, 21; US citizen. *Educ:* Univ Latvia, MD, 44; Ludwic Maximilian Univ, Munich, DDS, 45; Harvard Univ, DMD, 55. *Prof Exp:* Res asst physiol & dent, Sch Med, Yale Univ, 49-52; res assoc nutrit & biochem, Harvard Univ, 52-61. *Mem:* Fel AAAS; fel Am Acad Dent Sci. *Res:* Studies on bone and tooth metabolism using phosphorus-32; nutrition; fluoride metabolism. *Mailing Add:* 104 Perkins St Jamaica Plain MA 02130-4303

AUSLANDER, BERNICE LIBERMAN, MATHEMATICS. *Current Pos:* ASSOC PROF MATH, UNIV MASS, BOSTON, 71- *Personal Data:* b Brooklyn, NY, Nov 21, 30; m 50; c 2. *Educ:* Columbia Univ, AB, 51; Univ Chicago, MS, 54; Univ Mich, PhD(math), 63. *Prof Exp:* Asst prof, Wellesley Col, 65-71. *Concurrent Pos:* Fel, Radcliffe Inst Independent Study, 63-65. *Mem:* Am Math Soc; Math Asn Am. *Res:* Algebra, particularly the theory of commutative rings. *Mailing Add:* 16 Everett St Newton Center MA 02159-1939

AUSLANDER, JOSEPH, MATHEMATICS. *Current Pos:* assoc prof, 62-66, PROF MATH, UNIV MD, COLLEGE PARK, 66- *Personal Data:* b New York, NY, Sept 10, 30; m 57; c 2. *Educ:* Mass Inst Technol, SB, 52; Univ Pa, PhD(math), 57. *Prof Exp:* Asst prof math, Carnegie Inst Technol, 57-60; mem staff, Res Inst Advan Study, 60-62. *Concurrent Pos:* Res assoc, Yale Univ, 64-65; vis sr lectr, Imp Col, Univ London, 67-68. *Mem:* AAAS; Am Math Soc; Math Asn Am. *Res:* Topological dynamics; ergodic theory. *Mailing Add:* Univ Md College Park MD 20742-0001

AUSLANDER, LOUIS, MATHEMATICS. *Current Pos:* DISTINGUISHED PROF MATH, GRAD SCH & UNIV CTR, CITY UNIV NEW YORK, 65- *Personal Data:* b Brooklyn, NY, July 12, 28; m 77; c 3. *Educ:* Columbia Univ, BA, 49, MA, 50; Univ Chicago, PhD, 54. *Prof Exp:* Instr, Yale Univ, 53-55; asst prof math, Univ Pa, 56-57; from asst prof to assoc prof, Ind Univ, 57-62; prof, Purdue Univ, 62-64 & Belfer Grad Sch Sci, Yeshiva Univ, 64-65. *Concurrent Pos:* NSF fel, Inst Advan Study, 55-57; vis assoc prof, Yale Univ, 60-62; vis prof, Univ Calif, Berkeley, 63-64; Guggenheim fel, 71-72; prog mgr, Appl & Computational Math, DARPA, 89-90. *Mem:* Am Math Soc; Soc Indust & Appl Math. *Res:* Unitary representation of groups and digital signal processing. *Mailing Add:* Dept Math Grad Sch & Univ Ctr City Univ NY 33 W 42nd St New York NY 10036-8003

AUSLANDER, MARC, MATHEMATICS, OPERATING SYSTEMS. *Current Pos:* FEL, THOMAS J WATSON RES CTR, IBM, 91- *Personal Data:* b Brooklyn, NY, May 12, 42. *Educ:* Princeton Univ, AB, 63. *Mem:* Nat Acad Eng; Asn Comput Mach; sr mem Inst Elec & Electronics Engrs. *Mailing Add:* IBM Thomas J Watson Res Ctr P O Box 218 Yorktown Heights NY 10598. *E-Mail:* marc@watson.ibm.com

AUSLANDER, MAURICE, mathematics; deceased, see previous edition for last biography

AUSMAN, ROBERT K, MEDICAL ADMINISTRATION, SURGERY. *Current Pos:* PRES, MILDON CORP, 85-; PRES, CITATION PUBL CORP, 90-; CLIN PROF SURG, MED COL WIS, 96- *Personal Data:* b Milwaukee, Wis, Jan 31, 33; m 92, Christine McCann. *Educ:* Marquette Univ, MD, 57. *Prof Exp:* Intern, Univ Minn, 57-58; dir, Health Res, Inc, 61-69; mem staff, NY State Dept Health, Roswell Park Mem Inst, 69; dep dir, Fla Regional Med Prog, 69-70; dir clin res, Baxter Labs, 70-73, vpres clin res, 73-89. *Concurrent Pos:* Res fel, Univ Minn, 58-61; Damon Runyon res fel, 59-61; assoc clin prof surg, Med Col Wis. *Mem:* AAAS; Am Asn Cancer Res; Am Geriat Soc; Am Soc Clin Oncol; Sigma Xi. *Res:* Medical systems and data processing; cancer chemotherapy; public health statistics; nutrition; computer science. *Mailing Add:* Box 3538 RFD Long Grove IL 60047

AUSPOS, LAWRENCE ARTHUR, CHEMISTRY. *Current Pos:* RETIRED. *Personal Data:* b Anoka, Minn, Aug 27, 17; m 45; c 2. *Educ:* Univ Portland, BS, 40; Univ Notre Dame, MS, 41, PhD(org chem), 43. *Prof Exp:* Sr lab asst chem, Univ Portland, 39-40; lab asst, Univ Notre Dame, 40-41; instr, Holy Cross Sem, 41-42; mem staff, Pioneering Res Div, Rayon Tech Div, E I duPont de Nemours & Co, 43-50, mem staff, Textile Fibre Dept, 50-79. *Mem:* Am Chem Soc. *Res:* Synthetic plastics and fibers; preparation of fiberforming polymers; preparation of dibutyl benezenes. *Mailing Add:* 2536 Blackwood Rd Wilmington DE 19810

AUST, CATHERINE COWAN, MATHEMATICS, UNIVERSAL ALGEBRA. *Current Pos:* from asst prof to assoc prof, 75-85, PROF MATH, CLAYTON STATE COL, 85-, MATH COORDR, 77- *Personal Data:* b Atlanta, Ga, Apr 26, 46; m 67, Tomie R; c Jennifer K. *Educ:* Univ Ga, BS, 68; Emory Univ, PhD(math), 73. *Prof Exp:* From instr to asst prof math, Ga Inst Technol, 72-75. *Mem:* Am Math Soc; Math Asn Am; Am Math Asn of Two Year Cols; Asn Women in Math. *Mailing Add:* Sch Arts & Sci Clayton State Col 5900 N Lee St Morrow GA 30260-0285. *Fax:* 770-961-3700; *E-Mail:* aust@gg.csc.peachnet.edu

AUST, J BRADLEY, SURGERY. *Current Pos:* prof & chmn, Dept Surg, 66-96, DORN DISTINGUISHED PROF SURG, UNIV TEX MED SCH, SAN ANTONIO, 96- *Personal Data:* b Buffalo, NY, Sept 8, 26; m 49, Constance MacMullin; c Jay B, Bonnie J, Barbara A, Linda L, Mary L, & Tracey R. *Educ:* Univ Buffalo, MD, 49; Univ Minn, MS, 57, PhD(surg), 58; Am Bd Surg, dipl, 58; Am Bd Thoracic Surg, dipl, 65. *Prof Exp:* Res asst, Univ Minn, 53-57, from instr to prof surg, 57-66, coordr cancer res, 60-66. *Concurrent Pos:* Nat Consult surg gen, USAF, 75-77; chair bd govs, 83-85; dir, Am Bd Surg, 83-89; nat consult Vet Admin, 86- *Mem:* Soc Univ Surg; Soc Surg Oncol (pres, 88); fel Am Col Surg (vpres, 92-); Western Surg Asn (pres, 89); Am Surg Asn (vpres, 86); Sigma Xi; Soc Prog Dirs Surg (pres, 91-93). *Res:* Cancer immunity; homotransplantation; surgical oncology. *Mailing Add:* Dept Surg Univ Tex Health Sci Ctr San Antonio TX 78284

AUST, KARL T(HOMAS), PHYSICAL METALLURGY, MATERIALS SCIENCE. *Current Pos:* chmn, Mat Res Ctr, 69-74, prof, 67-91, EMER PROF METALL & MAT SCI, UNIV TORONTO, 91- *Personal Data:* b Toronto, Ont, Aug 9, 25; nat US; m 50, June Conlin; c Karen, Michael, Stephen & Richard. *Educ:* Univ Toronto, BASc, 46, MASc, 48, PhD(phys metall), 50. *Honors & Awards:* Mathewson Gold Medal, Am Inst Mining, Metall & Petrol Engrs, 61; Hoffman Mem Award, Lead Develop Asn, 71; Japan Soc Promotion Sci Award, 75 & 88; Yamada Sci Found Award, 81; Can Metal Physics Medal, 89. *Prof Exp:* Asst metallurgist, US Metals Refining Co, 46-47; res metallurgist, Kaiser Aluminum & Chem Corp, 50-52; res assoc metall, Johns Hopkins Univ, 52-55; res metallurgist, Gen Elec Co, 55-67. *Concurrent Pos:* Guggenheim fel, Ecole des Mines, Paris, France, 62-63; spec lectr, Nat Inst Nuclear Sci & Technol, Paris, 63; chmn phys metall, Gordon Res Conf, 72; vis prof, Univ Hawaii, 74, Univ Kyoto, 75, Univ Saarlandes, 81, Univ Kyoto, 81 & 88 & Univ Gottingen, 87; vis scientist, Ecole des Mines, St Etienne, France, 76; Gauss prof, Gottingen Acad Sci, 87. *Mem:* Fel Am Soc Metals; Am Inst Mining, Metall & Petrol Engrs; Hist Metall Soc; Sigma Xi. *Res:* Structure and properties of grain boundaries in metals; plastic deformation and annealing phenomena in metals; structure and properties of metals and metallic glasses; triple line defects; nanocrystals; grain boundary engineering. *Mailing Add:* Dept Metall-Mat Sci Univ Toronto Toronto ON M5S 1A4 Can. *Fax:* 416-978-4155

AUST, RICHARD BERT, CHEMICAL ENGINEERING, PHYSICAL CHEMISTRY. *Current Pos:* Sr res chemist, 64-69, RES ASSOC, EASTMAN KODAK CO, 69- *Personal Data:* b Oklahoma City, Okla, Aug 29, 38; m 68; c 2. *Educ:* Carnegie Inst Technol, BS, 60; Univ Ill, MS, 62, PhD(chem eng), 64. *Mem:* SPIE; Sigma Xi. *Res:* Properties of matter; preparation and evaluation of thin film optical coatings. *Mailing Add:* 150 Mt Airy Dr Rochester NY 14617

AUST, STEVEN DOUGLAS, BIOCHEMISTRY, TOXICOLOGY. *Current Pos:* PROF CHEM & BIOCHEM, NUTRIT & FOOD SCI, UTAH STATE UNIV, 87-, DIR, BIOTECHNOL CTR. *Personal Data:* b South Bend, Wash, Mar 11, 38; m 72; c 2. *Educ:* Wash State Univ, BS, 60, MS, 62; Univ Ill, PhD(dairy sci), 65. *Prof Exp:* Prof biochem, Mich State Univ, 67-87, dir, Ctr Study Active Oxygen in Biol & Med, 80-87. *Concurrent Pos:* USPHS fel, Karolinska Inst, Sweden, 66; Ministry Agr & Fisheries NZ fel, Ruakura Agr Res Ctr, Hamilton, NZ, 75-76; consult, Nat Ctr Dis Control & Environ Protection Agency Sci Adv Bd; mem toxicol study sect, NIH, 79-83; comnr, Mich Toxic Substance Control Comn, 79-83, chmn, 81-83. *Mem:* Soc Toxicol; Am Soc Photobiol; AAAS; Am Soc Biol Chem; Am Soc Pharmacol & Exp Therapeut; Am Chem Soc; Soc Ecotoxicol & Environ Safety. *Res:* Mixed function oxidation of drugs, the peroxidation of lipids, toxicity of halogenated aromatic hydrocarbons; biological oxidation of environmental pollutants. *Mailing Add:* Biotechnol Ctr Utah State Univ Logan UT 84322-4705

AUSTEN, K(ARL) FRANK, INTERNAL MEDICINE, ALLERGY & IMMUNOLOGY. *Current Pos:* from asst to assoc, Harvard Univ, 61-64, from asst prof to prof, 65-72, chmn Dept Rheumatology & Immunol, Brigham & Women's Hosp, Boston, 80-95, THEODORE BEVIER BALES PROF MED, MED SCH, HARVARD UNIV, 72-, DIR, INFLAMMATION & ALLERGIC DIS RES SECT, DIV RHEUMATOLOGY, ALLERGY & IMMUNOL, BRIGHAM & WOMEN'S HOSP, BOSTON, 95- *Personal Data:* b Akron, Ohio, Mar 14, 28; m 59, Joycelyn Chapman; c 4. *Educ:* Amherst Col, BA, 50; Harvard Univ, MD, 54; Am Bd Internal Med, dipl; Am Bd Allergy, dipl, 65. *Hon Degrees:* Dr, Univ Pierre Marie Curie, Paris, France, 92. *Honors & Awards:* Geigy Prize, Int League Against Rheumatism, 73; Squibb Award, Infectious Dis Soc Am, 73; Lila Gruber Award, Am Acad Dermat, 75; Marion L Sulzberger Award, Am Dermat Soc Allergy & Immunol, 79; Waterford Biomed Sci Award, 82; Distinguished Serv Award, Int Asn Allergol & Clin Immunol, 88; Paul Klemperer Award, NY Acad Med, 92; Distinguished Investr Award, Am Col Rheumatology, 93; Recognition Sci Accomplishment Award, Am Thoracic Soc, 96; Sci Achievement Award, Int Asn Allergol & Clin Immunol, 94; Lee C Howley Sr Prize, Arthritis Found, 94; Lilly Lectr, Royal Col Physicians, London, 95. *Prof Exp:* Intern med, Mass Gen Hosp, Boston, 54-55, asst resident, 55-56, sr resident, 58-59, chief resident, 61-62, asst, 62-63, asst physician, 63-66, chief, Pulmonary Unit, 64-66; captain, US Army Med Corp Div Immunochem, Walter Reed Army Inst Res, 56-58. *Concurrent Pos:* USPHS fel, Nat Inst Med Res, Eng, 59-61, USPHS res career develop award, NIH, 66; mem, Comt Drug Reactions, AMA, 63-66, sci & ed coun, Allergy Found Am, 64-, Comt Collab Res Transplantation & Immunol, NIH, 65-68, Nat Comn Arthritis & Related Musculoskeletal Dis; physician-in-chief, Robert B Brigham Hosp, 66-80; physician, Peter Bent Brigham Hosp, 66-80; mem bd dirs, Arthritis Found & chmn res comt; Am Asn Immunol rep, Nat Res Coun; mem, Am Bd Allergy & Immunol & chmn, res & develop comt; vchmn, Immunol & Microbiol Interdisciplinary Cluster, President's Biomed Res Panel, 75-76; chmn, Allergy & Immunol Res Comt, Nat Int Allergy & Infectious Dis, NIH, 76-79, mem, Adv Comt to Dir, 86-90 & Task Force Allergy & Immunol, 89-90. *Mem:* Nat Acad Sci; Inst Med-Nat Acad Sci; fel Am Acad Allergy & Immunol (pres, 81-82); Am Asn Immunologists (pres, 77-78); fel Am Acad Arts & Sci; Int Soc Immunopharmacol (pres, 94); Am Fedn Clin Res; Am Soc Clin Invest; Asn Am Physicians (pres, 89-90); Brit Soc Immunol; Am Soc Pharmacol & Exp Therapeut; Am Soc Exp Path; Am Rheumatism Asn; fel AAAS; fel Am Col Physicians; hon master Am Col Rheumatology. *Res:* Basic and clinical immunology. *Mailing Add:* Brigham & Women's Hosp 75 Francis St PBB2 Boston MA 02115

AUSTEN, W(ILLIAM) GERALD, SURGERY. *Current Pos:* assoc, 63-65, from assoc prof to prof, 65-74, EDWARD D CHURCHILL PROF SURG, MED SCH, HARVARD UNIV, 74-; CHIEF SURG SERV, MASS GEN HOSP, 69-, SURGEON-IN-CHIEF, 89- *Personal Data:* b Akron, Ohio, Jan 20, 30; m 61; c 4. *Educ:* Mass Inst Technol, BS, 51; Harvard Univ, MD, 55; Am Bd Surg, cert, 62; Am Bd Thoracic Surg, cert, 64. *Hon Degrees:* DHH, Univ Akron, 80; DSc, Univ Athens, Greece, 81, Univ Mass, 85. *Honors & Awards:* Gold Heart Award, Am Heart Asn, 80; Louis Mark Mem Lectr Award, Am Col Chest Physicians, 81. *Prof Exp:* Intern, Mass Gen Hosp, Boston, 55-56, asst resident surg, 56-59; sr registr, Kings Col Hosp, London, Eng, 59; hon sr registr, Thoracic Unit, Gen Infirmary, Univ Leeds, 59; chief resident, E Surg Serv, Mass Gen Hosp, 60-61; clin surgeon, NIH, 61-62. *Concurrent Pos:* Teaching fel surg, Med Sch, Harvard Univ, 60-61; Markle scholar acad med, 63-68; chief, Surg Cardiovasc Res Unit, Mass Gen Hosp, 63-69, vis surgeon, 66-; numerous vis prof, US & foreign; mem, Coun Cadiovasc Surg, Am Heart Asn, 69-76, chmn, 74-76; mem, Ad Hoc Policy Adv Bd Coronary Surg, NIH, 72-74, Heart & Lung Prog Proj Comt, 73-76; mem, Bd Trustees, Mass Inst Technol, 72-, chmn, 74-84; consult, Univ Mass Hosp, 76-; mem bd gov, Am Col Surgeons, 80-83; dir, Am Bd Thoracic Surg, 84-, bd dirs, 84-90; mem bd dirs, Found Biomed Res, 88. *Mem:* Inst Med-Nat Acad Sci; fel Am Acad Arts & Sci; Soc Univ Surg (secy, 67-70, pres, 72-73); Am Surg Asn (secy, 79-84, pres, 85-86); Am Heart Asn (pres, 77-78); Am Asn Thoracic Surg (vpres, 87-88, pres, 88-89); Am Col Surgeons; AAAS; Am Asn Univ Prof. *Res:* Cardiovascular physiology. *Mailing Add:* Dept Surg Interval No White 506 Mass Gen Hosp Boston MA 02114

AUSTERN, BARRY M, ANALYTICAL CHEMISTRY, BIOCHEMISTRY. *Current Pos:* RES CHEMIST, US ENVIRON PROTECTION AGENCY, 70- *Personal Data:* b New York, NY, Nov 2, 42; m 68, Susan Levin; c Heather. *Educ:* Columbia Univ, AB, 63; NY Univ, MS, 65; Univ Mass, PhD(biochem), 69. *Honors & Awards:* Bronze Medal, Environ Protection Agency, 79. *Prof Exp:* Res chemist, US Dept Interior, 69-70. *Concurrent Pos:* Abstractor, Chem Abstracts Serv, 66-77. *Mem:* Am Chem Soc; Sigma Xi; Soc Appl Spectros; Am Soc Mass Spectrometry. *Res:* Analytical chemistry and biochemistry of wastewaters and effluents; chromatography; mass spectroscopy. *Mailing Add:* Nat Risk Mgt Res Lab Environ Protection Agency Cincinnati OH 45268. *Fax:* 513-569-7105; *E-Mail:* austern.barry@epamail.epa.gov

AUSTERN, NORMAN, THEORETICAL NUCLEAR PHYSICS. *Current Pos:* from asst prof to assoc prof, 56-70, PROF PHYSICS, UNIV PITTSBURGH, 70- *Personal Data:* b New York, NY, Feb 23, 26; m 64; c 4. *Educ:* Cooper Union, BSEE, 46; Univ Wis, PhD(physics), 51. *Honors & Awards:* Fulbright lectr, 68-69. *Prof Exp:* Asst, Univ Wis, 46-48; AEC fel physics, Cornell Univ, 51-52, res assoc, 52-54; staff scientist, Comput Facil, AEC & math inst, NY Univ, 54-55. *Concurrent Pos:* Fulbright res scholar, Univ Sydney, 57-58; NSF sr fel, Inst Theoret Physics, Copenhagen Univ, 61-62; vis prof, Univ Wash, Seattle, 76-77; vis fel, Japan Soc Prom Sci, 84- *Mem:* Am Phys Soc; AAAS; Sigma Xi. *Res:* Nuclear reactions and structure, especially direct reaction theory. *Mailing Add:* Dept Physics Univ Pittsburgh Pittsburgh PA 15260. *Fax:* 412-524-9163; *E-Mail:* na@pitt.vms

AUSTIC, RICHARD EDWARD, NUTRITION. *Current Pos:* Res assoc nutrit, 68-70, asst prof animal nutrit, 70-75, ASSOC PROF ANIMAL NUTRIT, CORNELL UNIV, 75- *Personal Data:* b Ithaca, NY, Apr 10, 41; m 63; c 2. *Educ:* Cornell Univ, BS, 63; Univ Calif, Davis, PhD(nutrit), 68. *Mem:* AAAS; Poultry Sci Asn; Am Inst Nutrit; World Poultry Sci Asn; NY Acad Sci. *Res:* Poultry nutrition; amino acid requirements and interactions; hyperuricemia and gout; nutrition and embryonic development. *Mailing Add:* Dept Animal Sci Cornell Univ NYS Col Agr & Life Sci 248 Morrison Hall Ithaca NY 14853-0001

AUSTIN, ALFRED ELLS, PHYSICAL INORGANIC CHEMISTRY, SOLID STATE SCIENCE. *Current Pos:* RETIRED. *Personal Data:* b Waltham, Mass, Oct 26, 20; m 43; c 2. *Educ:* Alfred Univ, BA, 42; Yale Univ, PhD(chem), 44. *Prof Exp:* Res chemist, Corning Glass Works, 44-47; res engr, 47-56, div consult, 56-60, fel, Battelle Mem Inst, 60-82. *Concurrent Pos:* At AEC, 44. *Mem:* Am Chem Soc; Am Crystallog Asn; Am Phys Soc; Electrochem Soc; fel Am Inst Chemists. *Res:* Solid state chemistry and physics; crystallography; nonaqueous electrochemistry. *Mailing Add:* 115 Shore Dr Dunedin FL 34698-2545

AUSTIN, BERT PETER, ANATOMICAL SCIENCE, CELL BIOLOGY. *Current Pos:* asst prof, 75-83, ASSOC PROF ANAT, SCH DENT, MARQUETTE UNIV, 83- *Personal Data:* b Utica, NY, July 26, 46; m 66; c 2. *Educ:* Hobart Col, BA, 68; State Univ NY Upstate Med Ctr, Syracuse, PhD(anat), 73. *Prof Exp:* Fel, Orthop Res Labs, Vet Admin Hosp, Syracuse, 73-75. *Concurrent Pos:* NIH fel, 73, NIH Biomed Res Develop grant, investr, 77-80. *Mem:* Sigma Xi; Am Asn Anatomists. *Res:* Structural alterations in an experimentally induced arthritis; osseous reactions to dental materials. *Mailing Add:* Sch Dent Marquette Univ 604 N 16th St Milwaukee WI 53233

AUSTIN, BILLY RAY, INTEGRAL THEORY. *Current Pos:* from inst to assoc prof, 65-82, PROF & CHAIR MATH, UNIV TENN, MARTIN, 82- *Personal Data:* b Atkins, Ark, July 25, 40; m 90, Dianne Miller; c William Andrew, Bradley Ellis & Shelly Diane. *Educ:* Ark Col, BA, 62; La State Univ, MS, 64; Univ Miss, PhD(math), 76. *Prof Exp:* Instr math, Christian Bros Col, 64-65. *Mem:* Sigma Xi; Math Asn Am; Am Math Soc; Nat Coun Teachers Math. *Res:* Real variables, integration theory. *Mailing Add:* Dept Math Univ Tenn Martin TN 38238-5049

AUSTIN, CARL FULTON, MINERALOGY, EXPLOSIVES. *Current Pos:* SELF EMPLOYED CONSULT, 91- *Personal Data:* b Oakland, Calif, July 18, 32; m 53, Barbara Vest; c Miriam (Paulsey), Carl F Jr & Richard R. *Educ:* Univ Utah, BS, 54, MS, 55, PhD(geol eng), 58. *Honors & Awards:* L T E Thompson Award, 82. *Prof Exp:* Geologist, NMex Bur Mines & Mineral Resources, 58-61; res geologist, Naval Weapons Ctr, 61-86, head, Geothermal Prog Off, 86-90 & Sci Res Off, 90-91. *Concurrent Pos:* Owner/operator, Cedarsage Farm & Golden Jubilee Mining & Double Diamond Ranch. *Res:* Exploration geochemistry, geothermal deposits, lined-cavity and other impulsive loading phenomena in brittle solids; fracture and penetration of rock and concrete; sub-sea floor construction; geochemistry. *Mailing Add:* PO Box 93 Oakley ID 83346

AUSTIN, CHARLES WARD, MATHEMATICS. *Current Pos:* assoc prof, 66-71, chmn dept, 67-73, PROF MATH, CALIF STATE UNIV, LONG BEACH, 71-, ASSOC DEAN SCH LETT, 73- *Personal Data:* b Seattle, Wash, Nov 5, 32; m 55; c 4. *Educ:* Univ Wash, BS, 54, MS, 60, PhD(math), 62. *Prof Exp:* Actg instr math, Univ Wash, 61-62; asst prof, Univ Colo, Boulder, 62-66. *Mem:* Am Math Soc; Math Asn Am. *Res:* Topological algebra, especially semigroups and continuous functions on them. *Mailing Add:* Dept Math Calif State Univ 1250 Bellflower Blvd Long Beach CA 90840-1001

AUSTIN, DANIEL FRANK, EVOLUTIONARY BIOLOGY, SYSTEMATIC BOTANY. *Current Pos:* From asst prof to assoc prof, 70-78, PROF BOT, FLA ATLANTIC UNIV, 78- *Personal Data:* b Paducah, Ky, May 18, 43. *Educ:* Murray State Univ, BA, 66; Wash Univ, AM, 69, PhD(biol), 70. *Concurrent Pos:* Vis res assoc bot, Inst Pesquisas Norte, Brazil, 69; nat sci trainee, Wash Univ, 69-70; adj asst prof bot, Fla Int Univ, 73; res grants, Fla Atlantic Univ, Fla Int Univ Joint Ctr Urban & Environ Issues, 74-75, 78-79 & Off Endangered Species, Dept Interior, 78-81, Nat Geog Soc, 91-92 & NSF, 92-93; adj prof bot, Univ SFla, 79-; mem, Food & Agr Orgn, UN, 81-84; res grant, Fla Dept Transp, 85, USDA, 90, NSF, 93 & USAID, 94; adj prof, Univ Ariz, 89-90; coun, Soc Econ Bot, 93- *Mem:* Asn Trop Biol; Soc Econ Bot; Torrey Bot Club; Int Asn Plant Taxonomists; Soc Ethnobiol. *Res:* Systematic, evolutionary and ethnobotanical studies of the Morning Glory family (Convolvulaceae); ecosystem dynamics in southern Florida; economic botany. *Mailing Add:* Dept Biol Sci Fla Atlantic Univ 777 Glades Rd Boca Raton FL 33431. *E-Mail:* daustin@fau.edu

AUSTIN, DONALD GUY, mathematics, for more information see previous edition

AUSTIN, DONALD MURRAY, APPLIED MATHEMATICS. *Current Pos:* ASST DIR PLANNING, NAT COORD OFF COMPUT INFO & COMMUN, 94- *Personal Data:* b Memphis, Tenn, Aug 11, 38; m 61; c Scott & Lisa. *Educ:* Memphis State Univ, BS, 64; Iowa State Univ, PhD(physics), 69. *Prof Exp:* Fel physics, Lawrence Berkeley Lab, Univ Calif, Berkeley, 69-70, comput scientist, 70-80; mathematician math & comput sci, Dept Energy, 80-90; exec dir, Army High Performance Comput Res Ctr, Univ Minn, 90-94. *Concurrent Pos:* Mem, Gov Task Force Minn Comput Indust, 90-91; vchmn, Supercomput Activ Group, Soc Indust & Appl Math, 91- *Mem:* AAAS; Soc Indust & Appl Math. *Res:* Computational aspects of science, engineering and mathematics; massively parallel computation and graphics/visualization techniques for displaying results of scientific computation. *Mailing Add:* Nat Coord Off Comput Info & Commun 4201 Wilson Blvd Suite 665 Arlington VA 22230. *Fax:* 612-626-1596; *E-Mail:* austin@ahpcrc.umn.edu

AUSTIN, FAYE CAROL GOULD, IMMUNOLOGY, CANCER BIOLOGY. *Current Pos:* chemist, Lab Viral Carcinogenesis, Nat Cancer Inst, NIH, 76-79, microbiologist, Lab Cellular & Molecular Biol, 79-81, prog dir cellular immunol, Immunol Prog, 81-87, chief, Cancer Immunol Br, 85-90, ASSOC DIR, EXTRAMURAL RES PROG, DIV CANCER BIOL DIAG & CTRS, NAT CANCER INST, NIH, 90- *Personal Data:* b Philadelphia, Pa, Dec 3, 44; m 79, G Harris Eisenhardt; c Heather T & Jennifer L. *Educ:* Pa State Univ, BS, 62, MS, 64; George Washington Univ, PhD(microbiol), 78. *Prof Exp:* Sr chemist to res assoc, Biosci Labs, 67-70; scientist, Meloy Labs, 72-74, sr scientist, 74-76, prin scientist, 76. *Mem:* Sigma Xi; Am Asn Immunologists; Am Asn Cancer Res. *Res:* Virus-augmented skin test antigens specific for human melanoma or breast cancer; virus-augmented tumor antigens as vaccines in mice; therapeutic and diagnostic potential of monoclonal antibodies against human breast cancer. *Mailing Add:* Div Cancer Biol Nat Cancer Inst NIH 6130 Executive Blvd Suite 500 Rockville MD 20892-7380. *Fax:* 301-496-8656

AUSTIN, FRANK HUTCHES, JR, AEROSPACE MEDICINE. *Current Pos:* ASSOC CLIN PROF, SCH MED, WRIGHT STATE UNIV. *Personal Data:* b Kerrville, Tex, 1924. *Educ:* Univ Tex, MD. *Honors & Awards:* Louis H Bauer Founders Award, Aerospace Med Asn, 85; Jefferies Med Res Award, Am Inst Aeronaut & Astronaut, 91. *Prof Exp:* Intern, Long Beach Naval Hosp; resident aerospace med, Univ Calif, Berkeley, 60-63. *Mailing Add:* 1595 Brass Lantern Way Reston WA 22094-1225

AUSTIN, FRED, STRUCTURAL DYNAMICS, DYNAMIC ANALYSIS. *Current Pos:* SR STAFF SCIENTIST, GRUMMAN AEROSPACE CORP, BETHPAGE, 62- *Personal Data:* b Vienna, Austria, Apr 3, 36; US citizen; m 57, Myrna L Bogner; c Martin L & Howard B. *Educ:* Cooper Union, BME, 57; NY Univ, MME, 60, PhD(mech eng), 68. *Prof Exp:* Engr, Curtiss Wright Corp, 57, Control Instrument Co, Burroughs Corp, 57-58 & Sperry Gyroscope Co, 58-62. *Concurrent Pos:* Adj asst prof, NY Univ; lectr, Hofstra Univ, 74-81. *Mem:* Sigma Xi; Am Soc Mech Engrs. *Res:* Spacecraft structural dynamics and controls; combat analysis; structural optimization; dynamics of rotating elastic satellites; development of theory and computer program for automatically controlling fixed-wing end helicopter aircraft during dogfights; damping spacecraft structural vibration. *Mailing Add:* 5 Zinnia Ct Commack NY 11725. *Fax:* 516-575-7716

AUSTIN, GARTH E, CLINICAL PATHOLOGY, REGULATION OF TRANSCRIPTION. *Current Pos:* asst prof, 80-84, ASSOC PROF PATH, EMORY UNIV SCH MED, 84-; CHIEF CLIN PATH, ATLANTA VET ADMIN MED CTR,, 83- *Personal Data:* b Vancouver, BC, 1942; m 69, Ellen L Wogan; c Eric D & Elizabeth K. *Educ:* Univ BC, MD, 67; Univ Pa, PhD(molecular biol), 73. *Prof Exp:* Asst prof path, Univ Calif Los Angeles Sch Med, 73-80. *Concurrent Pos:* Mem NIH Study Sect OmB1, 86-91; prin investr, Va Merit Awards, 86- *Mem:* AAAS; Col Am Pathologists; Sigma Xi. *Res:* Myeloperoxidase gene expression in normal and leukemic myelois cells; animal models of prostate carcinogenesis; monitoring diabetic control. *Mailing Add:* Atlanta Vet Admin Med Ctr Dept Path Lab Serv 113 1670 Clairmont Rd Decatur GA 30033-4004

AUSTIN, GEORGE M, NEUROPHYSIOLOGY. *Current Pos:* CLIN PROF, UNIV SOUTHERN CALIF, 81- *Personal Data:* b Philadelphia, Pa, May 10, 16; m 42; c 4. *Educ:* Lafayette Col, AB, 38; Univ Pa, MD, 42; McGill Univ, MSc, 51; Am Bd Neurol Surg, dipl. *Prof Exp:* Assoc neurosurg, Univ Pa, 51-54, asst prof, 54-57; prof & head div, Med Sch, Univ Ore, 57-68; prof neurosurg & chief sect, Loma Linda Univ, 68-81; NEUROL SURGEON, SANTA BARBARA COTTAGE HOSP, 81- *Concurrent Pos:* USPHS spec fel, Dept Theoret Chem, Cambridge Univ; chief neurosurg, Philadelphia Gen Hosp & Lankenau Hosp. *Mem:* Am Physiol Soc; Am Col Surgeons; AMA; Soc Univ Surgeons; Am EEG Soc. *Res:* Brain edema and water flux in nerve cells; mechanisms of spasticity in spinal cord and brain lesions; new techniques and measurement of cerebral blood flow in conditions of cerebrovascular disease and brain edema. *Mailing Add:* Stroke Res Found 1187 Coast Village Rd Suite 1-114 Santa Barbara CA 93108-2794

AUSTIN, GEORGE STEPHEN, GEOLOGY. *Current Pos:* indust minerals geologist, 74-76, dep dir, 76-88, SR INDUST MINERALS GEOLOGIST, NMEX BUR MINES & MINERAL RES, 88- *Personal Data:* b Roanoke, Va, Mar 24, 36; m 60; c 2. *Educ:* Carleton Col, BA, 58; Univ Minn, MS, 62; Univ Iowa, PhD(geol), 71. *Prof Exp:* Teacher geol, Col of St Thomas, 62-67; stratigrapher, Minn Geol Surv, 67-69; clay mineralogist, Ind Geol Surv, 71-74. *Mem:* Soc Econ Paleontologists & Mineralogists; Clay Mineral Soc; Am Inst Mining & Petrol Engrs; Geol Soc Am. *Res:* The study of industrial minerals, especially clay and shales, potash, perlite, fluorite and coal. *Mailing Add:* NMex Bur Mines & Mineral Res Campus Sta Socorro NM 87801

AUSTIN, GEORGE T(HOMAS), chemical engineering; deceased, see previous edition for last biography

AUSTIN, HOMER WELLINGTON, MATHEMATICAL EDUCATION. *Current Pos:* from instr to assoc prof, 67-83, PROF MATH DEPT, SALISBURY STATE UNIV, 83- *Personal Data:* b Greenlee, Va, Aug 7, 44;; m 77; c 2. *Educ:* James Madison Univ, BS, 66; Univ Wyoming, MS, 68; Univ Virginia, PhD(math), 75. *Prof Exp:* PUb teacher math, Rockbridge County, Va, 66; grad asst math, Univ Wyo, 66-67; from instr to assoc prof math sci, James Madison Univ, 76-83. *Mem:* Math Asn Am. *Mailing Add:* Math Sci Dept Salisbury State Univ Salisbury MD 21801

AUSTIN, INEZ J, NUCLEAR ENGINEERING. *Current Pos:* staff engr, West Tank Farm Opers, Westinghouse Hanford Co/Rockwell Hanford Opers, Richland, Wash, sr engr, Single Emphasis Task Team, sr engr & single shell tank process, engr, phase II B/BX/BY farms cognizant engr, sr engr, Data Processing Appln, actg mgr, MEA & A, INSPECTOR QUAL CONTROL & MONITOR RADIATION, WESTINGHOUSE HANFORD CO/ROCKWELL HANFORD OPERS. *Honors & Awards:* Scientific Freedom & Responsibility Award, AAAS, 92. *Mailing Add:* 218 Atkins Ave Richland WA 99352-4431

AUSTIN, JAMES HENRY, neurology, for more information see previous edition

AUSTIN, JAMES MURDOCH, METEOROLOGY. *Current Pos:* asst, 40-41, from asst prof to prof, 41-79, dir summer session, 56-83, EMER PROF METEOROL, MASS INST TECHNOL, 79- *Personal Data:* b Dunedin, NZ, May 25, 15; US citizen; m 41, Pauline Morrow; c Doris A (Price) & Carol T (West). *Educ:* Univ NZ, BA, 35, MA, 36; Mass Inst Technol, ScD, 41. *Prof Exp:* Asst meteorologist, Apia Observ, West Samoa, 37-39. *Concurrent Pos:* Consult, USAAF, Washington, DC, 43-45; expert consult, Joint Res & Develop Bd, 47-48; consult, AEC, 47-53 & USN, 55-62; vis lectr, Harvard Univ, 55-79; mem adv coun air pollution emergencies, Dept Pub Health, Mass, 69-77. *Mem:* Fel Am Acad Arts & Sci; fel Am Meteorol Soc. *Res:* Development of quantitative forecasting methods; growth of cumulus clouds; climatology; meteorological aspects of air pollution. *Mailing Add:* 100 Keyes Rd Unit 421 Concord MA 01742

AUSTIN, JOHN H(ENRY), SANITARY ENGINEERING. *Current Pos:* US NUCLEAR REGULATORY COMN, 72- *Personal Data:* b Washington, DC, Feb 22, 29; m 56; c 4. *Educ:* Syracuse Univ, BCE, 51; Mass Inst Technol, SM, 53; Univ Calif, Berkeley, PhD(sanit eng), 63. *Prof Exp:* Asst sanit engr, Taft Ctr, USPHS, Ohio, 55-57; sanit engr, Adv to Ministry Health, Int Coop Admin, Vietnam, 57-59; sr asst sanit engr, San Francisco Bay Study, USPHS, Calif, 59; assoc air pollution, Sch Pub Health, Univ Calif, Berkeley, 59-60, lectr radiol eng, 63, res engr, Col Eng, 60-62; from asst prof to assoc prof sanit eng, Univ Ill, Urbana, 63-69; head, Dept Environ Systs Eng, Clemson Univ, 73-77, prof, 69-76; environ engr, USAID, 81-84. *Concurrent Pos:* HEW grant, 64-67; US Dept Interior Fed Water Qual Admin grants, 69-70; Environ Protection Agency grants, 71-; vis prof civil eng, Univ Md, 76-78; consult, Maxima Corp, 78-, vpres, 78-81. *Mem:* Am Water Works Asn; Water Pollution Control Fedn; Sigma Xi. *Res:* Water and wastewater treatment plant operations. *Mailing Add:* 1895 Milboro Dr Potomac MD 20854-6123

AUSTIN, JOSEPH WELLS, ANIMAL SCIENCE. *Current Pos:* AT DEPT ANIMAL & DAIRY & VET SCI, UTAH STATE UNIV. *Personal Data:* b Snowville, Utah, Mar 10, 30; m 54; c 5. *Educ:* Utah State Univ, BS, 58; Univ Tenn, MS, 61; Tex A&M Univ, PhD(physiol reprod), 67. *Prof Exp:* Res asst radiation, Tex A&M Univ, 62-65, from asst radiobiologist to assoc radiobiologist, 65-67; asst prof biol, Ill Wesleyan Univ, 67-74; area livestock specialist, Coop Exten Serv, 74- *Mem:* Am Soc Animal Sci; Sigma Xi. *Res:* Mammalian reproduction. *Mailing Add:* 22613 Elm Ave Torrance CA 50505-2923

AUSTIN, LEONARD G(EORGE), METALLURGICAL ENGINEERING, FUEL TECHNOLOGY. *Current Pos:* prof mat sci, 68-77, prof, 77-89, EMER PROF FUELS & MINERAL ENG, PA STATE UNIV, 89- *Personal Data:* b London, Eng, Oct 5, 29; m 51, 84, Sofia Barreneche; c Mark R, Timothy L & Stuart R. *Educ:* Univ London, BSc, 50; Pa State Univ, PhD(fuel technol), 61. *Honors & Awards:* Distinguished Visitors Award, Commonwealth Sci & Indust Res Orgn, SAfrica, 72; A M Gaudin Award, Soc Mining Eng, Am Inst Mining, Metall & Petrol Engrs, 84, P W Nicholls Award, 87; Babcock Power Award, Inst Energy UK, 86; Taggart Award, Soc Mining Eng, 91. *Prof Exp:* Asst chemist cent labs, Southeastern Gas Bd, Eng, 52-54; gen engr fuel technol subdiv, Chief Engrs Dept, Cent Elec Generating Bd, Eng, 54-55, asst engr, 55-57; from instr to prof fuel sci, Pa State Univ, 57-67; prof chem eng, NC State Univ, 67-68. *Concurrent Pos:* Vis prof chem eng, Durban Univ, 72-73 & Cape Town Univ, SAfrica, 92-93; ed, Powder Technol, 80-88; vis prof metallurgy, Concepcion Univ Chile, 86-87; vis prof chem eng, Tech Univ Delft, Neth, 89; vis prof mineral processing, Univ BC, Can, 89-90; fel chem eng, Univ Manchester Inst Sci & Technol, UK, 90; vis scientist, Commonwealth, Sci & Indus Res Orgn, Australia, 91. *Mem:* Am Inst Mining, Metall & Petrol Engrs; Int Comminution Res Asn. *Res:* Boiler slagging; comminution; powder technology; process design of all types of comminution devices. *Mailing Add:* Dept Mineral Eng Pa State Univ University Park PA 16802. *Fax:* 814-865-3248

AUSTIN, MAX E, HORTICULTURE. *Current Pos:* head dept, 72-85, prof hort, Coastal Plain Exp Sta, 79-93, EMER PROF, UNIV GA, 93- *Personal Data:* b Pine Grove, Pa, July 17, 33; m 53, Eleanor Fessenden; c Susan, Becky, Max Jr & Robin. *Educ:* Univ RI, BS, 55, MS, 60; Mich State Univ, PhD(hort), 64. *Honors & Awards:* Tifton Sigma Xi Outstanding Res Award; Japanese Ministry Educ Fel Award. *Prof Exp:* Jr res asst hort, Univ RI, 57-60; res assoc, Mich State Univ, 60-64, dist agt, Coop exten serv, 64-65; from asst prof to assoc prof, Va Polytech Inst & State Univ, 65-72. *Concurrent Pos:* Exchange prof, Kagoshima Univ, Japan, 81; vpres, Int Affairs Div, Am Soc Hort, Sci, 89; regional rep, Int Soc Hort Sci, 92-; hort consult, 93- *Mem:* sr mem, Am Soc Hort Sci; Am Pomol Soc; Int Hort Soc; fel Am Soc Hort Sci; Am Soc Agr Consult. *Res:* Rabbiteye blueberry breeding, production, harvest including fertility, pruning, breeding and evaluation of Southern highbush blueberries. *Mailing Add:* 2202 N Ridge Ave Tifton GA 31794-2835. *Fax:* 912-382-0399; *E-Mail:* maustin@surfsouth.com

AUSTIN, PAUL ROLLAND, ORGANIC CHEMISTRY. *Current Pos:* counsel, Tech Serv Div, 67-73, ADJ PROF MARINE CHEM, COL MARINE STUDIES, UNIV DEL, 73- *Personal Data:* b Monroe, Wis, Dec 9, 06; m 34; c 4. *Educ:* Univ Wis, AB, 27; Northwestern Univ, MS, 29; Cornell Univ, PhD(org chem), 30. *Prof Exp:* Asst chem, Cornell Univ, 28-30; Nat Res fel, Univ Ill, 30-32; res chemist, Rockefeller Inst Technol, 32-33; res chemist, Chem Dept, E I du Pont de Nemours & Co, 33-36, group leader, 36-39, asst lab dir, 39-49, dir res div, Electrochem Dept, 49-59, mgr patent & licensing div, Int Dept, 59-66. *Mem:* fel AAAS; Am Chem Soc. *Res:* Marine polymer chemistry; chitin isolates, their separation, characterization, derivatives and applications; particularly solvents, filaments, chiroptical properties and use in animal feed supplements. *Mailing Add:* 2327 W 18th St Wilmington DE 19806

AUSTIN, PAULINE MORROW, METEOROLOGY. *Current Pos:* RETIRED. *Personal Data:* b Kingsville, Tex, Dec 18, 16; m 41, James M; c Doris A (Price) & Carol T (West). *Educ:* Wilson Col, BA, 38; Smith Col, MA, 39; Mass Inst Technol, PhD(physics), 42. *Hon Degrees:* ScD, Wilson Col, 64. *Prof Exp:* Comput, Radiation Lab, Mass Inst Technol, 41-42, mem staff, 42-45, res staff, 46-53; lectr, Wellesley Col, 53-55; sr res assoc, Mass Inst Technol, 56-79. *Concurrent Pos:* Mem Comn II, Int Sci Radio Union. *Mem:* Fel Am Meteorol Soc. *Res:* Radar scattering cross sections; weather radar; propagation of electromagnetic waves in the atmosphere; precipitation physics. *Mailing Add:* 100 Keyes Rd Unit 421 Concord MA 01742

AUSTIN, ROBERT ANDRAE, PAPER CHEMISTRY, FLEXOGRAPHY. *Current Pos:* res chemist, Mead Corp, 74-77, sr res chemist, 77-78, tech dir Opas, 78-87, PROJ MGR, MEAD CORP, 87- *Personal Data:* b Wilmington, Del, Sept 26, 38; m 68, Marcia A Muldoon; c Christine S & Carolyn D. *Educ:* Bucknell Univ, BS, 61; Univ Mass, MS, 67, PhD(chem), 68. *Prof Exp:* Develop chemist, E I Du Pont de Nemours & Co, 68-74. *Mem:* Am Chem Soc; Tech Asn Pulp & Paper Indust. *Res:* Conformation of substituted indans by nuclear magnetic resonance; building products from polymers; carbonless copy papers; paper coatings; flexography. *Mailing Add:* 86 E Fourth St Chillicothe OH 45601-3312

AUSTIN, ROBERT HAMILTON, PHYSICS. *Current Pos:* from asst prof to assoc prof, 79-89, PROF PHYSICS, PRINCETON UNIV, 89- *Personal Data:* b St Charles, Ill, July 19, 46; m, Shirley S Chan; c Doug & Wayne. *Educ:* Hope Col, BA, 68; Univ Ill, Urbana, MS, 70, PhD(physics), 75. *Prof Exp:* Res fel, Univ Ill, Urbana, Max Planck Inst, WGer. *Mem:* Fel Am Phys Soc. *Res:* Protein dynamics; energy transport in biomolecules; DNA-protein interactions and topology; applications of microlithography to biology. *Mailing Add:* Dept Physics Princeton Univ Jadwin Hall Princeton NJ 08544-0708. *E-Mail:* rha@pupgg.princeton.edu

AUSTIN, SAM M, NUCLEAR PHYSICS. *Current Pos:* from assoc prof to prof physics, Mich State Univ, 65-70, assoc dir, Cyclotron Lab, 76-79, res dir, 83-85, chmn, dept physics & astron, 80-83, co-dir, Nat Superconducting Cyclotron Lab, 85-91, dir, Nat Superconducting Cyclotron Lab, 89-92, UNIV DISTINGUISHED PROF PHYSICS, MICH STATE UNIV, 90-, ACTG DEAN, COL NATURAL SCI, 94- *Personal Data:* b Columbus, Wis, June 6, 33; m 59, Mary Ellen Herb; c Laura & Sara. *Educ:* Univ Wis, BS, 55, MS, 57, PhD(physics), 60. *Prof Exp:* Res assoc physics, Univ Wis, 60; NSF fel, Oxford Univ, 60-61; asst prof, Stanford Univ, 61-65. *Concurrent Pos:* Sloan res fel, 63-66; vis scientist, Neils Bohr Inst, 70; guest prof, Univ Munich, 72-73; collaborateur etranger, CEN Saclay, 79-80; vis scientist, Lab Rene Bernas, Orsay, 80; mem, subcomt adv comt physics to Rev Nuclear Physics Labs, NSF, 79, Argonne Univs Asn Spec Comt Elec Accelerator, 81-84, nuclear sci adv comt, NSF & Dept Energy, 81-83, nuclear sci adv comt Panel Electron Accelerators, 83, Panel Solar Neutrino Prob, 85 & adv comt physics, NSF, 83-85; vis staff mem, Los Alamos Nat Lab, 81-; vchair, Div Nuclear Physics, Am Phys Soc, 81-82, chair, 82-83; Am Phys Soc Coun, 86-89; AAU vis comt, physics dept, Brookhaven Nat Lab, 86-91; ed, Phys Reviews C, 88-; mem dirs rev comt, Nuclear Sci Div, Lawrence Berkeley Lab, 89-91; mem rev comt, Physics Div, Argonne Nat Lab, 89-97; vis scientist, TRIUMF, UBC, 93-94; invited prof, Univ Paris Orsay, 96; assoc ed, Atomic Data, Nuclear Data Tables, 96-; mem comt nuclear physics, Nat Res Coun, 96- *Mem:* Fel Am Phys Soc; fel AAAS; Am Asn Physics Teachers; Fedn Am Scientists. *Res:* Experimental study of the structure of nuclei, of nuclear reaction mechanisms and of the two body force; nuclear astrophysics; nitrogen fixation. *Mailing Add:* Cyclotron Lab Mich State Univ East Lansing MI 48824. *Fax:* 517-353-3264; *E-Mail:* austin@nscl.msu.edu

AUSTIN, STEVEN ARTHUR, COAL GEOLOGY. *Current Pos:* CHMN, GEOL DEPT, INST CREATION RES, 79- *Personal Data:* b Stanford, Calif, Jan 25, 48; m 87. *Educ:* Univ Wash, BS, 70; San Jose State Univ, MS, 71; Pa State Univ, PhD(geol), 79. *Prof Exp:* Teaching asst geol, Earth & Mineral Sci, Pa State Univ, 76, res asst, 77-79. *Concurrent Pos:* Geologist, Keymar Resources Inc, 83-86. *Mem:* Geol Soc Am; Am Asn Petrol Geologists; Soc Econ Paleontologists & Mineralogists. *Res:* Modern and ancient catastrophic geologic processes, especially those that form sedimentary strata; processes at Mount St Helens and application to Grand Canyon and origin of coal. *Mailing Add:* Geol Inst Creation Res 10946 Woodside Ave N Santee CA 92071-2833

AUSTIN, T LOUIS, JR, ENGINEERING. *Current Pos:* RETIRED. *Personal Data:* b Trenton, Tenn, Mar 19, 19. *Prof Exp:* Pres, Brown & Root, 85-90. *Mem:* Nat Acad Eng. *Mailing Add:* 7352 Lane Park Ct Dallas TX 75225

AUSTIN, THOMAS HOWARD, ORGANIC CHEMISTRY, POLYURETHANE CHEMISTRY. *Current Pos:* RES CHEMIST, ARCO CHEM CO, 87- *Personal Data:* b Mt Pleasant, Tex, Aug 12, 37; m 57, 82, Lucille Carroll; c Janet & Jeffrey. *Educ:* Cent State Col, Okla, BS, 61; Okla State Univ, PhD(org chem), 65. *Prof Exp:* Asst chem, Okla State Univ, 61-65; res chemist, Jefferson Chem Co, Texaco, Inc, 65-87. *Res:* Nucleophilic reactions of organophosphorus esters; catalytic reactions of petrochemical derivatives; application research and product development of isocyanates polyisocyanurates and polyurethanes. *Mailing Add:* Arco Chem Co 3801 Westchester Pike Newtown Square PA 19073

AUSTIN, TOM AL, GROUNDWATER & SURFACE WATER HYDROLOGY, CONTAMINATE HYDROLOGY. *Current Pos:* from asst prof to assoc prof civil eng, 72-79, PROF HYDROL, IOWA STATE UNIV, 79- *Personal Data:* b Ft Worth, Tex, Nov 21, 43; m 63, Loretta A Catlett; c Lowell, Laura, Melissa, Matthew, Kathryn & Andrew. *Educ:* Tex Tech Univ, BSCE, 67, Utah State Univ, MS, 69; PhD(civil eng), 71. *Prof Exp:* Civil engr, Forest Serv, USDA, 67-69; systs engr, Tex Water Develop Bd, 71-72. *Concurrent Pos:* Exec Comt, Irrig & Drainage Div, Am Soc Civil Engrs, 84-87; bd dir, Univs Coun Water Resources, 87-90; dir, Iowa State Water Resources Res Inst, 83-90. *Mem:* Am Soc Civil Engrs; Am Water Resources Asn; Int Water Resources Asn; Nat Asn Water Inst Dirs. *Res:* Contaminate transport of organic chemicals in groundwater aquifers; fundamental studies on absorption of pesticides in groundwater aquifer materials. *Mailing Add:* 496 Town Eng Bldg Iowa State Univ Ames IA 50011. *Fax:* 515-294-8216; *E-Mail:* austin@ccelab.iastate.edu

AUSTIN, WALTER J, STRUCTURAL ENGINEERING. *Current Pos:* RETIRED. *Personal Data:* b St Louis, Mo, Feb 6, 20; m 49; c 2. *Educ:* Rice Univ, BS, 41; Univ Ill, MS, 46, PhD(civil eng), 49. *Honors & Awards:* Moisseiff Award, Am Soc Civil Engrs, 58. *Prof Exp:* Struct designer, Chicago Bridge & Iron Co, 42-46; from asst prof to assoc prof civil eng, Univ Ill, 49-60; prof, Rice Univ, 60-87, chmn dept, 63-64 & 77-82, emer prof, 87- *Concurrent Pos:* Mem, Exec Comt, Column Res Coun, 76-82. *Mem:* Am Soc Civil Engrs; Struct Stability Res Coun. *Res:* Structural analysis and design; numerical methods; plates; buckling; metal compression member design. *Mailing Add:* 5211 Rutherglenn Dr Houston TX 77096

AUSTIN, WANDA M, SPACE SYSTEMS ENGINEERING. *Current Pos:* Mem tech staff, Aerospace Corp, 79-94, systs dir, 91-94, prin dir, 94-96, GEN MGR, ELECTRONIC SYSTS DIV, AEROSPACE CORP, 96- *Educ:* Franklin & Marshall Col, BS, 75; Univ Pittsburg, MS(math) & MS(systs eng), 77; Univ Southern Calif, PhD(systs eng), 88. *Honors & Awards:* Outstanding Achievement Award, Women Aerospace, 96. *Mem:* Soc Women Engrs; assoc fel Am Inst Aeronaut & Astronaut; Int Astronaut Fedn. *Res:* Intelligent modeling and simulation. *Mailing Add:* Aerospace Corp PO Box 92957 Los Angeles CA 90009. *Fax:* 310-336-1450; *E-Mail:* wanda.austin@aero.org

AUSTIN, WILLIAM W(YATT), METALLURGY, MATERIALS & ENGINEERING SCIENCE. *Current Pos:* assoc prof & head, Dept Mech Eng, NC State Univ, 52-54, prof mineral industs, 54-70, prof mat eng & head dept, 70-79, EMER PROF, NC STATE UNIV, 79-; METALL CONSULT, RALEIGH, NC, 79- *Personal Data:* b Vicksburg, Miss, May 29, 15; m 39, Lucia Patton; c 4. *Educ:* Birmingham-Southern Col, BS, 35; Vanderbilt Univ, MS, 39, PhD(metall), 48. *Honors & Awards:* A E White Distinguished Teacher Award, Am Soc Metals Int, 81. *Prof Exp:* Inspector, Gulf States Steel Corp, Ala, 35-36; res chemist & opers foreman, Swann & Co, Birmingham, 36-38; fel metall & chem, Vanderbilt Univ, 39-41; inspection foreman & supvr metall labs, Consol Vultee Aircraft Corp, Nashville, 41-45; sr res metallurgist, Southern Res Inst, 45-52. *Concurrent Pos:* Mem exten fac, Univ Ala, 49-51. *Mem:* Am Inst Mining, Metall & Petrol Engrs; fel Am Soc Metals Int; Am Foundrymen's Soc; Am Soc Eng Educ. *Res:* Metallurgy of cast iron; phase distribution in alloy steels; direct reduction of iron ores; nondestructive testing and failure analysis; metallurgical factors in metal cutting; substitutes for manganese in steel making; metallic corrosion; metallurgy of nuclear reactor materials; accident reconstruction. *Mailing Add:* 3017 Rue Sans Famille Raleigh NC 27607. *E-Mail:* olsd529@earthlink.net

AUSTON, DAVID H, LASERS, OPTICAL SPECTROSCOPY. *Current Pos:* PROVOST & HERMAN BROWN PROF ENG, RICE UNIV, 93- *Personal Data:* b Toronto, Ont, Nov 14, 40. *Educ:* Univ Toronto, BA, 62, MA, 63; Univ Calif, Berkeley, PhD(elec eng), 69. *Honors & Awards:* R W Wood Prize, Optical Soc Am, 85; Quantum Electronics Award, Inst Elec & Electronics Engrs, 90, Morris E Leeds Award, 91. *Prof Exp:* Mem tech staff physics res, AT&T Bell Labs, Inc, 69-87, dept head, 82-87; prof elec eng & appl physics, Columbia Univ, 87-93, chair, Dept Elec Eng, 90-91, dean, Sch Eng & Appl Sci, 91-93. *Mem:* Nat Acad Sci; Nat Acad Eng; Optical Soc Am; Am Phys Soc; Am Acad Arts & Scis; Inst Elec & Electronics Engrs. *Res:* Optical and electronic properties of materials and devices using ultrashort optical and electronic pulses; femto second lasers; far-infrared and optical spectroscopy; nonlinear optics. *Mailing Add:* Off Provost Rice Univ MS-2 6100 Main St Houston TX 77005-1892. *Fax:* 713-285-5971; *E-Mail:* auston@rice.edu

AUSTRIAN, ROBERT, INTERNAL MEDICINE, BACTERIAL GENETICS. *Current Pos:* John Herr Musser prof res med & chmn dept, 62-86, EMER PROF, SCH MED, UNIV PA, 86- *Personal Data:* b Baltimore, Md, Apr 12, 16; m 63, Babette Natalie Friedmann. *Educ:* Johns Hopkins Univ, AB, 37, MD, 41; Am Bd Internal Med, dipl. *Hon Degrees:* DSc, Hahnemann Med Col & Hosp, 80, Philadelphia Col Pharm & Sci, 81, Univ Pa, 87, State Univ NY, 96. *Honors & Awards:* USA Typhus Commission Medal, 47; Maxwell Finland Lectureship Award, Infectious Diseases Soc Am, 74; Albert Lasker Clin Med Res Award, 78; James D Bruce Mem Award, Am Col Physicians, 79; Bristol Award, Infectious Dis Soc Am, 86. *Prof Exp:* Asst med, Sch Med, Johns Hopkins Univ, 42-43, instr, 43-47, instr med, 49-52; res assoc microbiol, Col Med, NY Univ, 47-48; from assoc prof to prof med, Col Med, Downstate Med Ctr, State Univ NY, 52-62. *Concurrent Pos:* Vis physician, Univ Div Med Serv, Kings County Hosp, 52-62 & Univ Pa Hosp, 62-; consult, Brooklyn & Maimonides Hosps, 53-62 & Univ Pa Hosp, 62-; vis scientist, Dept Microbial Genetics, Pasteur Inst, 60-61; trustee, Johns Hopkins Univ, 63-69; Tyndale vis lectr & prof, Col Med, Univ Utah, 64; mem study sect A, Allergy & Immunol, NIH, 65-69, mem bd sci counr, Nat Inst Allergy & Infectious Dis, 67-70, chmn, 69-70; mem subcomt streptococci & pneumococci, Int Comn Bact Nomenclature; mem comt meningococcal infections, Comn Acute Respiratory Dis, Armed Forced Epidemiol Bd, 66-72. *Mem:* Nat Acad Sci; Asn Am Physicians; Am Soc Clin Invest; master Am Col Physicians; Am Philos Soc; Infectious Dis Soc Am (pres, 71). *Res:* Infectious disease; pneumococcal transformation reactions; pneumococcal vaccines; pneumococcal epidemiology. *Mailing Add:* Dept Res Med Univ Pa Sch Med Philadelphia PA 19104-6088

AUSUBEL, FREDERICK MICHAEL, MOLECULAR GENETICS. *Current Pos:* Asst prof, 75-80, assoc prof biol, 80-, FAC MEM, SCH MED, HARVARD UNIV, 80- *Personal Data:* b New York, NY, Sept 2, 45. *Educ:* Univ Ill, Urbana, BS, 66; Mass Inst Technol, PhD(biol), 72. *Mem:* Nat Acad Sci. *Res:* Molecular genetic analysis of nitrogen-fixation; somatic cell genetics of plant cell tissue cultures. *Mailing Add:* 271 Lake Ave Newton MA 02161

AUSUBEL, JESSE HUNTLEY, EMISSION PROJECTION, TECHNOLOGICAL EVOLUTION. *Current Pos:* dir studies, Comn Sci Technol Govt, 89-93, DIR HUMAN ENVIRON PROG & SR RES ASSOC, ROCKEFELLER UNIV, 93-; PROG OFFICER, ALFRED P SLOAN FOUND, 94- *Personal Data:* b New York, NY, Sept 27, 51. *Educ:* Harvard Univ, BA, 74; Columbia Univ, MBA, 77, MIA, 77. *Prof Exp:* Resident fel, Nat Acad Sci, 77-79; res scholar, Int Inst Appl Systs Anal, 79-81; staff officer, Nat Res Coun, 81-83; spec asst to pres, Nat Acad Eng, 83-85, dir prog off, 85-89. *Concurrent Pos:* Consult, Nat Sci Bd, NSF, 83-84 & Exec Off, Rockefeller Univ, 84-88; dir studies, Carnegie Comn Sci, Technol & Govt, 89-93; fel sci & pub policy, Rockefeller Univ, 89-93; adj scientist, Woods Hole Oceanog Inst, 91-; univ fel, Resource for Future, 94- *Mem:* AAAS; Am Meteorol Soc; NY Acad Sci; Sigma Xi. *Res:* Technological change; science and technology policy; carbon dioxide; climate; atmospheric and ocean policy; environment; energy; impact assessment; general systems theory; long economic cycles; industrial evolution; author of numerous publications. *Mailing Add:* Rockefeller Univ 1230 York Ave New York NY 10021-6341

AUTENRIETH, JOHN STORK, ORGANIC CHEMISTRY. *Current Pos:* RETIRED. *Personal Data:* b Weehawken, NJ, Dec 28, 16; m 91, Janet Lawton. *Educ:* City Col New York, BS, 37; Mass Inst Technol, PhD(org chem), 41. *Prof Exp:* Res chemist, Exp Sta, Hercules Powder Co, 41-44, tech serv rep, 44-48, tech sales rep, 48-53, dist mgr, Synthetics Dept, 53-56, indust sales mgr, 56-59, mgr mkt serv, 59-61, mgr hard resin develop, Pine & Paper Chem Dept, 61-63, sales mgr resins, 63-65, mgr sales develop, 65, mgr mkt develop, 65-67, mgr tech serv pine chem, Pine & Paper Chem Dept, 67-76, mgr prod safety, Org Dept, Hercules Inc, 76-77. *Mem:* Sigma Xi; Am Chem Soc. *Res:* Identification of aromatic hydrocarbons; research on development of synthetic resins; synthetic rosin ester resins; paints; varnishes; enamels; lacquers; adhesives; printing inks; floor tiles. *Mailing Add:* 1103 Chadwick Rd Wilmington DE 19803-4111

AUTHEMENT, RAY PAUL, MATHEMATICS. *Current Pos:* assoc prof, 57-60, vpres, 66-73, PRES, UNIV SOUTHWESTERN LA, 73-, PROF MATH, 60- *Personal Data:* b Chauvin, La, Nov 19, 29; m 51; c 2. *Educ:* Southwestern La Inst, BS, 50; La State Univ, MS, 52, PhD, 56. *Prof Exp:* Instr math, La State Univ, 52-56; assoc prof, McNeese State Col, 56-57. *Concurrent Pos:* Vis prof, Univ NC, 62-63. *Mem:* Math Asn Am. *Res:* Algebraic number theory; matrix theory; Galois theory. *Mailing Add:* 200 E University Ave Lafayette LA 70503

AUTHIER, ANDRE, PHYSICS. *Current Pos:* lectr, Sci Dept, 66-71, PROF, UNIV PIERRE-ET-MARIE-CURIE, 71- *Personal Data:* b La Fleche, France, June 17, 32; m 59, 86, Irena Wawrzyniak; c Bertrand, Isabelle & Sophie. *Educ:* Ecole Normale Superieure, BS, 55; Paris Univ, PhD, 61. *Honors & Awards:* Bronze Medal, Ctr Nat Res Sci, 61; Danton Prize, Acad Sci, 63; Ancel Prize, Fr Physics Soc, 67. *Prof Exp:* Asst lab dir, Col France, 61-66. *Mailing Add:* Univ Paris et Marie Curie 4 Pl Jussieu Paris 75252 Codex 5 France

AUTIAN, JOHN, PHARMACY. *Current Pos:* PROF PHARMACEUT & DENT & DIR, MAT SCI TOXICOL LAB, COL DENT & COL PHARM, UNIV TENN, MEMPHIS, 67-, DEAN, COL PHARM, 75-, PROF ORAL PATH, 80- *Personal Data:* b Philadelphia, Pa, Aug 20, 24; m 62; c 1. *Educ:* Temple Univ, BS, 50; Univ Md, MS, 52, PhD(pharm chem), 54. *Prof Exp:* Instr pharm, Univ Md, 52-53, Franklin Sq Hosp Sch Nursing, Md, 53 & Sinai Hosp Sch Nursing, Md, 54; asst prof, Sch Pharm, Temple Univ, 54-56, Sch Pharm, Univ Md, 56-57 & Col Pharm & Rackham Sch Grad Study, Univ Mich, 57-60; assoc prof pharm, Col Pharm, Univ Tex, 60-67, dir drug-plastic res lab, 61-67. *Concurrent Pos:* Mem, Nat Formulary Adv Panel, 57; fel, Am Found Pharmaceut Educ; consult, Clin Ctr, NIH, 60- *Mem:* AAAS (vpres, 62); Am Pharmaceut Asn; Am Chem Soc. *Res:* Toxicology; plastic materials and their use in pharmacy and medicine. *Mailing Add:* 6997 Fords Station Rd Memphis TN 38138

AUTON, DAVID LEE, PHYSICS. *Current Pos:* RETIRED. *Personal Data:* b Lexington, Ky, Apr 1, 39; m 63; c 2. *Educ:* Univ Chicago, BS, 62, SM, 64, PhD(physics), 69. *Prof Exp:* Sr scientist, Anal Serv, Inc, 69-75; oper res physicist, Defense Nuclear Agency, 75-96. *Res:* Radiation transport, fallout; civil defense; civil protection; biological response; strategic studies. *Mailing Add:* 3511 Prince William Dr Fairfax VA 22031

AUTOR, ANNE POMEROY, CELL CULTURE, BIOCHEMICAL TOXICOLOGY. *Current Pos:* PROF, DEPT PATH, UNIV BC, 83- *Personal Data:* b Prince George, BC, Jan 26, 35; div; c Erik O & Kurt P. *Educ:* Univ BC, BA, 56, MSc, 57; Duke Univ, PhD(biochem), 70. *Prof Exp:* Res asst biochem, Duke Univ, 61-65; Damon Runyon fel, Univ Mich, 70-72; res assoc, Univ Iowa, 72-73, from asst prof to prof pharmacol, 73-83. *Concurrent Pos:* Career Develop award, NIH, 75-80; consult study sects, NIH, Nat Inst Environ Health Sci, Mat Res Ctr, Can, 76-; adv ministry environ, BC; bd trustees, Vancouver Art Gallery. *Mem:* Am Soc Biochem & Molecular Biol; Am Soc Pharmacol & Exp Therapeut; Int Acad Path; Oxygen Soc; Soc Tocicol Can. *Res:* Biology and toxicology of endothelial cells; oxygen and oxygen radical toxicity; biological generation of oxygen radicals; enzyme antioxidants; cell culture; toxicology of heavy metals. *Mailing Add:* Dept Path Univ BC 2211 Westbrook Mall Vancouver BC V6T 2B5 Can

AUTREY, ROBERT LUIS, ORGANIC CHEMISTRY, TECHNICAL MANAGEMENT. *Current Pos:* CORP SECY & CHIEF CHEMIST, WESTREY WINE CO, 93- *Personal Data:* b Indio, Calif, Feb 24, 32; m 55, 79; c 5. *Educ:* Reed Col, AB, 53; Harvard Univ, AM, 55, PhD(org chem), 58. *Prof Exp:* Instr chem, Reed Col, 57-58; from instr to asst prof org chem, Univ Rochester, 59-65; lectr, Harvard Univ, 65-67; assoc prof chem, Ore Grad Ctr, 67-72, chmn fac, 70-72; secy & treas, Chiron Press, Inc, 71-77; exec vpres, Baleking Systs, 78-80; mgr systs develop, Heidelberg Eastern, Inc, 81-82; mgr res & develop, NERCO, Inc, 83-92. *Concurrent Pos:* NSF fel, Imp Col, Univ London, 58-59; asst ed, Am Chem Soc Jour, 62-65. *Mem:* AAAS. *Res:* Organic chemical reactions of synthetic utility; structure and synthesis of natural products and related substances. *Mailing Add:* 705 NW Winchester Terr Portland OR 97210-2738

AUVIL, PAUL R, JR, THEORETICAL HIGH ENERGY PHYSICS, THEORETICAL CONDENSED MATTER PHYSICS. *Current Pos:* res assoc, Northwestern Univ, 64-65, asst prof, 65-68, actg chmn, Dept Physics & Astron, 78, dir, Integrated Sci Prog, 79-82, assoc chmn physics, 82-88, assoc vpres res & assoc dean grad sch, 88-93, ASSOC PROF PHYSICS, NORTHWESTERN UNIV, 68- *Personal Data:* b Charleston, WVa, Aug 4, 37; m 60, Carole Koehler; c Paul & Pamela. *Educ:* Dartmouth Col, BA, 59; Stanford Univ, PhD(physics), 62. *Prof Exp:* NSF fel physics, Imperial Col, London, 62-64. *Concurrent Pos:* Vis scientist, CERN, Switz, 69-70. *Mem:* Am Phys Soc; Sigma Xi; NY Acad Sci. *Res:* Theory of elementary particles, Coulomb corrections, current algebra, symmetry breaking and quark-gluon models; superconductor superlattice structures; Josephson radiation; transition temperatures. *Mailing Add:* Dept Physics Northwestern Univ Evanston IL 60208. *Fax:* 847-491-9982; *E-Mail:* p-auvil@nwu.edu

AUXIER, JOHN A, HUMAN RADIOBIOLOGY. *Current Pos:* PRES, AUXIER & ASSOC INC, KNOXVILLE, TENN, 92- *Personal Data:* b Paintsville, Ky, Oct 7, 25; m 48; c 2. *Educ:* Berea Col, AB, 51; Vanderbilt Univ, MS, 52; Ga Tech, PhD(nuclear eng), 72. *Hon Degrees:* PhS, Berea Col, 87. *Prof Exp:* Head, Radiobiol Lab, Dept Physics & Eng, Univ Tex, 52-55; dir, Appl Health Physics & Safety Div, Union Carbide Nuclear, 55-82; dir, Appl Sci Lab, Gulf Nuclear Corp, 83-85; dir, Radiation Sci Lab, IT Corp, 85-89, nuclear sci corp mgr, 89-92. *Concurrent Pos:* Ed, Health Physics J, 58-77; mem, Nat Coun Radiation Protection & Measurements, 73- & Staff President's Comn Accident Three Mile Island, 79; consult, Radiation Protection & Environ Assessment, 77-; corp scientist, Erc Corp, 83. *Mem:* Fel Health Physics Soc; Am Acad Health Physics (pres, 91); Int Radiation Protection Asn; Soc Risk Assessment. *Res:* Radiation measurements; instrument development; environmental assessments for radiation and radionuclides; human radiobiology; author of 100 publications. *Mailing Add:* 2532 Jones Rd Lenoir City TN 37771

AUYONG, THEODORE KOON-HOOK, PHARMACOLOGY. *Current Pos:* asst prof, 63-72, ASSOC PROF PHARMACOL, SCH MED, UNIV N DAK, 72- *Personal Data:* b Honolulu, Hawaii, Jan 18, 25; m 70. *Educ:* Univ Mo, Kansas City, BSc, 54, MSc, 55; Univ Mo, Columbia, PhD(pharmacol), 62. *Prof Exp:* Res assoc pharmacol, Univ Mo, Kansas City, 55-56; instr, Univ Mo, Columbia, 62-63. *Concurrent Pos:* Consult community physicians on drug interactions. *Mem:* Sigma Xi; Int Soc Biochem Pharmacologists. *Res:* Isolation of pharmacologically active extracts of plants and determination of its mechanism of action; structure-function relationships of drugs; mechanism of renal toxicity by lithium. *Mailing Add:* 3614 11th Ave N Grand Forks ND 58203-2009

AVADHANI, NARAYAN G, BIOCHEMISTRY, MOLECULAR GENETICS. *Current Pos:* res investr, 72-73, from asst prof to assoc prof, 73-82, PROF BIOCHEM, UNIV PA, 82- *Personal Data:* b Honavar, India, Jan 28, 41; m 72; c 1. *Educ:* Karnatak Univ, India, BSc, 61; Univ Bombay, PhD(biochem), 69. *Prof Exp:* Res assoc physiol, Univ Ill, Urbana, 69-70, res asst prof, 70-72. *Concurrent Pos:* Consult, Vet Admin Hosp, Coatesville, Pa, 73- *Mem:* Am Chem Soc; Brit Biochem Soc; Am Soc Biol Chem. *Res:* Biogenesis of mitochondria with special reference to the information contents and the expression of the mitochondrial genome in normal and tumor cells. *Mailing Add:* 313 Josephs Way Media PA 19063

AVAKIAN, PETER, POLYMER PHYSICS. *Current Pos:* RES PHYSICIST, CENT RES & DEVELOP DEPT, E I DU PONT DE NEMOURS & CO, 61- *Personal Data:* b Tabriz, Iran, May 15, 33; US citizen; m 57; c 2. *Educ:* Univ Rochester, BS, 55; Mass Inst Technol, PhD(physics), 60. *Prof Exp:* Res physicist, Lab Insulation Res, Mass Inst Technol, 60. *Concurrent Pos:* Fulbright fel, Univ Stuttgart, 60-61. *Mem:* AAAS; fel Am Phys Soc; Optical Soc Am; Sigma Xi. *Res:* Morphology, structure, molecular motions, and structure-property relationships in polymers; dielectric and optical properties of polymers, organic crystals and insulating inorganic crystals; electronic excitation energy transfer in organic crystals. *Mailing Add:* 6515 Limestone Rd Hockessin DE 19707-9173

AVANT, PATRICIA KAY COALSON, PARENT-CHILD NURSING. *Current Pos:* ASSOC PROF NURSING, AUSTIN SCH NURSING, UNIV TEX, 78-, CHAIR, PARENT-CHILD NSG DIV. *Personal Data:* b Dallas, Tex, Aug 15, 41; m 63, Gayle R; c Samantha G & Celia K. *Educ:* Tex Christian Univ, BS, 63; Univ NC, Chapel Hill, MS, 65, Tex Womans Univ, PhD(nursing), 78. *Prof Exp:* Asst prof nursing, Georgetown Univ, 65-67, Miami Univ, Ohio, 70-71; instr nursing, McLennan Community Col, 71-76. *Concurrent Pos:* Chair, Taxonomy Comn, NAm Nursing Diag Asn, 90-94; Fulbright prof nursing sci, Univ Olso, Norway, 92-93. *Mem:* Fel Am Acad Nursing; NAM Nursing Diag Asn; Am Nurses Asn; Asn Women's Health Obstet & Neonatal Nursing; Nat League Nursing. *Res:* Psychophysiologic factors affecting the adaptation to parenthood and health promot ion behaviors of working parents. *Mailing Add:* 7601 Tallahassee Waco TX 76712. *Fax:* 512-471-4910; *E-Mail:* snae331@utxvm.utexas.edu

AVAULT, JAMES W, JR, BIOLOGY. *Current Pos:* from asst prof to assoc prof, 66-75, PROF FISHERIES, SCH FORESTRY, WILDLIFE & FISHERIES, LA STATE UNIV, BATON ROUGE, 75- *Personal Data:* b East St Louis, Ill, May 20, 35; m 66; c 2. *Educ:* Univ Mo, BS, 61; Auburn Univ, MS, 63, PhD(fisheries), 66. *Prof Exp:* Res asst fish parasitol, Auburn Univ, 61-63 & biol weed control, 63-66. *Concurrent Pos:* Ed, J World Maricult Soc, 70-86; consult, govt Philipines, 77, Dominican Republic, 78 & Sierra Rutile Ltd, Sierra Leone, 87- *Mem:* Am Fisheries Soc; World Maricult Soc (secy-treas, 70-71, vpres, 74, pres, 75); Int Asn Astacology (pres, 74-). *Res:* Fish culture; marine fisheries; ichthyology; fishery biology; author of numerous publications in various journals. *Mailing Add:* Sch Forestry Wildlife La State Univ Baton Rouge LA 70803-0001

AVCIN, MATTHEW JOHN, JR, ECONOMIC GEOLOGY, STRATIGRAPHY. *Current Pos:* CONSULT, 95- *Personal Data:* b Pittsburgh, Pa, June 8, 43; m 75. *Educ:* Lafayette Col, BA, 65; Univ Ill, Urbana, MS, 69, PhD(geol), 74. *Prof Exp:* Res asst geol, Ill State Geol Surv, 69-73; chief coal sect geol, Iowa State Geol Surv, 73-90; geologist, Coleman Co, Wichita, 90-95. *Mem:* Soc Econ Paleontologists & Mineralogists; Paleont Res Inst; Sigma Xi; AAAS. *Res:* Coal research and the practical applications of stratigraphy, biostratigraphy and paleobotany. *Mailing Add:* 202 N Rock Rd Apt 310 Wichita KS 67206-2225

AVEGEROPOULOS, G, PROCESSING, PROCESS ENGINEERING & DESIGN. *Current Pos:* DIR TECHNOL RES & DEVELOP & QUAL, RM ENG PROD-INTERTECH, 87- *Personal Data:* b Phthiotis, Greece, Jan 25, 34; US citizen; m 64; c 3. *Educ:* Nat Univ Athens, Greece, MA, 61; Wayne State Univ, Detroit, MS, 67, PhD(theoret physics), 68. *Prof Exp:* Postdoctoral statist thermodyn, Univ Ga, 68; sr res scientist polymer physics, Firestone Cent Res, 68-78; tech dir polymer physics, Stand Prod Co, 79-83; dir technol polymer eng, Gen Corp-EED, 83-87. *Concurrent Pos:* Consult process eng, 77-88; chmn, Akron Sect, Am Chem Soc, 78. *Mem:* Am Phys Soc; AAAS; Soc Rheol; Am Inst Chemists; Am Inst Chem Engrs; Am Soc Testing Mat. *Res:* Morphology of elastomers and elastomeric blends; physical characterization of polymers and blends; laminated reinforced composites with continuous and discontinuous fibers; mechanical modeling of molecules and engineering systems; antivibration systems; molded and extruded product studies. *Mailing Add:* Ariston Inc 13 Chalyn Dr Charleston SC 29407

AVE LALLEMANT, HANS GERHARD, STRUCTURAL ANALYSIS, TECTONOPHYSICS. *Current Pos:* from asst prof to assoc prof, 70-81, PROF GEOL, RICE UNIV, 81- *Personal Data:* b Benkulen, Indonesia, May 2, 38; m 66; c 2. *Educ:* State Univ Leiden, BSc, 60, MSc, 64, PhD(struct petrol), 67. *Honors & Awards:* Basic Res Award, US Nat Comn Rock Mech, 81. *Prof Exp:* Res staff geologist, Yale Univ, 67-70. *Concurrent Pos:* Vis assoc prof, State Univ NY, Stony Brook, 76-77; assoc ed technophysics, 80-; vchmn, Dept Geol & Geophys, Rice Univ, 80-83, chmn, 86-89; vis prof, Univ Pierre, Mary Curie, Paris, 84-85. *Mem:* Am Geophys Union; fel Geol Soc Am; Am Asn Petrol Geologists; corresp mem Royal Dutch Acad Arts & Sci. *Res:* Structural analysis in fold and thrust belts and wrench fault zones in Alaska, Yukon Territory, California, Honduras and Venezuela. *Mailing Add:* Dept Geol & Geophys Rice Univ Dept MS126 Houston TX 77005-1892

AVELLON, GUY THOMAS, FASTENER TECHNOLOGY & BOLTING MATERIALS, METAL COATING. *Current Pos:* MGR ENG & QUAL CONTROL, KAR PROD, 93- *Personal Data:* b Cleveland, Ohio, Dec 19, 45; m 77, Linda Buck; c Guy Jr, Kimberly & Kelley. *Educ:* Purdue Univ, BS, 67. *Prof Exp:* Engr metal coating, Repub Steel Res Ctr, 67-69; sales engr, Therm-O-Disc Inc, 69-73; mat engr, Lea-Ronal Inc, 73-75; consult, Bowman & Barnes Group Inc, 75-92; chief engr, GT Tech Consults, 92-93. *Concurrent Pos:* Consult & lectr, Amusement Indust Mfg & Suppliers Int, 84- *Mem:* Soc Automotive Engrs; Am Welding Soc; Am Soc Testing & Mat. *Res:* Ion beam vapor deposition of aluminum to steel; produced enhanced adhesion and regeneration cycles to electroless nickel plating; fastener assembly, failure analysis and welding. *Mailing Add:* 712 Grand Blvd Wauconda IL 60084-1514. *Fax:* 847-796-6046; *E-Mail:* gt-roadracer@juno.com

AVELSGAARD, ROGER A, ALGEBRA. *Current Pos:* RETIRED. *Personal Data:* b Minneapolis, Minn, Jan 5, 32; m 63; c Sarah A. *Educ:* Univ Minn, Minneapolis, BChE, 54, MA, 63; Univ Iowa, PhD(math), 69. *Prof Exp:* Teaching assoc math, Univ Minn, 59-63; from asst prof to prof math, Bemidji State Univ, 64-93. *Mem:* Am Math Soc; Math Asn Am. *Res:* Cohomology of non-associative algebra. *Mailing Add:* Rte 1 Box 5640 Solway MN 56678

AVEN, MANUEL, MATERIALS SCIENCE. *Current Pos:* res phys chemist, Lamp Develop Lab, Gen Elec Co, Cleveland, Ohio, 55-59, phys chemist, Res Lab, Schenectady, NY, 59-68, mgr luminescence br, Gen Elec Res & Develop Ctr, 68-72, mgr phys chem lab, 72-82, mgr mat labs, Gen Elec Res & Develop Ctr, 82-86, phys chemist, 86-88, mgr power syst prog, 88-89, mgr mat res prog, 89-92, CONSULT, INT TECH INTEGRATION, GEN ELEC CO, SCHENECTADY, 92- *Personal Data:* b Tallinn, Estonia, Dec 25, 24; nat US; m 47, Sylvia Kaar; c Peter & Michael. *Educ:* Univ Pittsburgh, BS, 51, PhD(phys chem), 55. *Prof Exp:* Chemist, Mercy Hosp, 50-51; res asst, Univ Pittsburgh, 51-55, lectr, 54. *Mem:* Am Chem Soc; Am Phys Soc; Mat Res Soc. *Res:* Consulting on research in material science and solid state physics in the US and Europe. *Mailing Add:* 38 Forest Rd Burnt Hills NY 12027

AVEN, MICHAEL R, FORMULATION RESEARCH, INFLUENCE OF FORMULATION ON PERFORMANCE OF CROP PROTECTION AGENTS. *Current Pos:* LAB HEAD, CYANAMID FORSCHUNG GMBH, 91- *Personal Data:* b Schenectady, NY, Oct 4, 60; m 92, Linda York. *Educ:* Univ Vt, BS, 82; Cornell Univ, MS, 86, PhD(chem eng), 89. *Prof Exp:* Teaching asst statist, Univ Vt, 80-82; teaching asst chem eng, Cornell Univ, 82-84; res asst polymer sci, Ger Plastics Inst, 84-85; postdoctoral res assoc polymer sci, Max Planck Inst Polymer Res, 89-91. *Res:* Maximize activity of crop protection formulations while minimizing any negative impact to the environment of the active ingredient in the formulations. *Mailing Add:* Rathenaustr 8 55131 Mainz Germany. *Fax:* 6130-911113; *E-Mail:* york-aven@t-online.de

AVEN, RUSSELL E(DWARD), CHEMICAL ENGINEERING. *Current Pos:* assoc prof, 56-66, PROF CHEM ENG, SCH ENG, UNIV MISS, 66- *Personal Data:* b Water Valley, Miss, Feb 18, 23; m 54, Delma Barber; c Debra (Swartzendruber) & Anson A. *Educ:* Univ Miss, BSE, 44, MA, 50; Univ Tenn, PhD, 63. *Prof Exp:* Lab chemist, E I du Pont de Nemours & Co, Tex, 46-48; develop engr, Oak Ridge Nat Lab, Tenn, 51-56. *Mem:* AAAS; Am Chem Soc; Am Inst Chem Engrs; Sigma Xi. *Res:* Heat transfer; nuclear engineering. *Mailing Add:* PO Box 68 University MS 38677-0068

AVENI, ANTHONY, ASTRONOMY, ARCHAEOASTRONOMY. *Current Pos:* From instr to asst prof, 63-68, assoc prof, 68-73, PROF ASTRON, COLGATE UNIV, 74-, R B COLGATE PROF ASTRON & ANTHROP, 88- *Personal Data:* b New Haven, Conn, Mar 5, 38; m 59; c 2. *Educ:* Boston Univ, AB, 60; Univ Ariz, PhD(astron), 65. *Concurrent Pos:* NSF grants, 66-71; vis assoc prof, Univ SFla, 71; consult, Ferson Optical Div, Bausch & Lomb. *Mem:* AAAS; Am Astron Soc. *Res:* Galactic structure; star formation; works on observational evidence relating to formation of stars in low mass primary condensations; archaeoastronomy of Mesoamerica; studies on orientation of buildings in Maya and Zapotec zone of Mexico/Peru. *Mailing Add:* Dept Physics & Astron Colgate Univ Hamilton NY 13346

AVENS, JOHN STEWART, FOOD MICROBIOLOGY & SAFETY. *Current Pos:* from instr to assoc prof, 67-82, PROF FOOD SCI & ANIMAL SCI, COLO STATE UNIV, 82- *Personal Data:* b Geneva, NY, Mar 23, 40; m 63; c Audrey, Alan & Heather. *Educ:* Syracuse Univ, BS, 62; Colo State Univ, MS, 69, PhD(animal sci), 72. *Prof Exp:* Res technician hemat, NY Univ Med Ctr, 62-63; res scientist food microbiol, Syracuse Univ Res Corp, 63-65; sr microbiologist, Food & Drug Admin, Buffalo, 65-67. *Concurrent Pos:* Consult, Agr & Food Indust, 77- *Mem:* Soc Qual Assurance; Inst Food Technologists; Coun Agr Sci & Technol; Sigma Xi; Nat Registry Microbiologists. *Res:* Improvement of microbiological analytical methodology for food; microbiology related to food safety in food production and processing and food service establishments; coauthor of textbook on poultry science and production; author of chapter in textbook on food safety; efficacy and safety testing of animal pharmaceuticals. *Mailing Add:* Dept Food Sci & Human Nutrit Colo State Univ Ft Collins CO 80523. *Fax:* 970-491-7252; *E-Mail:* avens@cahs.colostate.edu

AVENT, JON C, GEOLOGY. *Current Pos:* From asst prof to assoc prof, 65-77, PROF GEOL, CALIF STATE UNIV, FRESNO, 77- *Personal Data:* b Billings, Mont, July 4, 34. *Educ:* Univ Colo, BA, 56; Univ Wash, Seattle, MS, 62, PhD(phys stratig), 65. *Mem:* Geol Soc Am; Am Asn Petrol Geol. *Res:* Cenozoic stratigraphy and structure; trace element distribution in basalt flows. *Mailing Add:* Dept Geol Calif State Univ 2345 E San Ramon Fresno CA 93740-8031

AVENT, ROBERT M, OCEANOGRAPHY-BIOLOGICAL. *Current Pos:* oceanographer, Bur Land Mgt, 81-82, OCEANOGRAPHER, MINERALS MGT SERV, US DEPT INTERIOR, 82- *Personal Data:* b Jacksonville, Fla, Feb 24, 42; div; c 2. *Educ:* Jacksonville Univ, BA, 67; Fla State Univ, MS, 70, PhD(oceanog), 73. *Prof Exp:* Oceanographer, Harbor Br Found, 73-77 & Tex Instruments, Inc, 78; marine biologist, Tex Parks & Wildlife Dept, 79; oceanographer, Nat Oceanic & Atmospheric Admin/Nat Marine Fisheries Serv, 79-81. *Concurrent Pos:* Adj prof oceanog, Fla Inst Technol, 73-74. *Res:* Biological effects of elevated hydrostatic pressure, physiography and fauna of continental shelf and slope, distribution and abundance of penaeid shrimps, and biology of deep shelf coral habitats. *Mailing Add:* Minerals Mgt Serv 1201 Elmwood Park Blvd New Orleans LA 70123-2394

AVERA, FITZHUGH LEE, FOOD SCIENCE, CHEMISTRY. *Current Pos:* RETIRED. *Personal Data:* b Pocahontas, Ark, July 4, 06; m 50; c 1. *Prof Exp:* Sales mgr, Skippy CPC Int Inc, 26-38, chief chemist, 38-43, dir res, Best Foods Peanut Butter Div, 46-69; consult chem engr, 69. *Concurrent Pos:* Mem, Food & Agr Orgn, UN survey West Indies; bd dirs, Driwater Inc, 90. *Mem:* Nat Soc Prof Engrs; Am Oil Chem Soc; NY Acad Sci; Sigma Xi. *Res:* Edible fats and oils; quantal chemical analysis; food products; numerous industrial process patents. *Mailing Add:* 1809 Yale Dr Alameda CA 94501-1607

AVERBACH, B(ENJAMIN) L(EWIS), METALLURGY. *Current Pos:* asst, 45-47, from asst prof to assoc prof, 47-60, PROF METALL, MASS INST TECHNOL, 60- *Personal Data:* b Rochester, NY, Aug 12, 19; m 47. *Educ:* Rensselaer Polytech Inst, BS, 40, MS, 42; Mass Inst Technol, ScD(metall), 47. *Honors & Awards:* Am Welding Soc Prize, 45; Howe Medal, Am Soc Metals, 49. *Prof Exp:* Chief metallurgist, US Radiator Corp, NY & Mich, 43-45; metallurgist, Gen Elec Co, NY, 45. *Concurrent Pos:* Past pres, Int Cong Fracture; deleg, Int Inst Welding. *Mem:* Am Inst Mining, Metall & Petrol Engrs; fel Am Soc Metals; Am Phys Soc; Am Crystallog Soc; fel Inst Metals. *Res:* Physical metallurgy; solid state physics; x-ray diffraction; neutron diffraction; phase transformations; thermodynamics; fracture correlations; structure of liquids; magnetic materials; theory of alloys. *Mailing Add:* 165 Somerset St Belmont MA 02178

AVERETT, JOHN E, systematic botany, for more information see previous edition

AVERILL, BRUCE ALAN, inorganic chemistry, biological chemistry, for more information see previous edition

AVERILL, FRANK WALLACE, QUANTUM MECHANICS, APPLIED MATHEMATICS. *Current Pos:* PROF MATH & PHYSICS, JUDSON COL, 73- *Personal Data:* b Anniston, Ala, June 4, 45. *Educ:* Univ Fla, BS, 67, PhD(physics), 71. *Prof Exp:* Res assoc quantum mech, Univ Fla, 72; res assoc, Northwestern Univ, 72-73. *Concurrent Pos:* Consult, Oak Ridge Nat Lab, 81- *Mem:* Math Asn Am; Am Phys Soc. *Res:* Developing computer programs which produce approximate total energies and forces for large molecules and atom clusters. *Mailing Add:* 1151 N State St Elgin IL 60123

AVERILL, SEWARD JUNIOR, RUBBER CHEMISTRY. *Current Pos:* RETIRED. *Personal Data:* b Punxsutawney, Pa, Jan 5, 21; m 43; c 3. *Educ:* Kent State Univ, BS, 42. *Prof Exp:* Instr chem, Williams Col, Mass, 43-45; res chemist, B F Goodrich, 46-49, mgr raw mat develop, 59-70, sr develop engr, 70-76, mgr gen chem lab, 76-80. *Concurrent Pos:* Consult, Sprague Elec Co, 43-45. *Res:* Rubber reinforcement and natural rubber technical characterization; rubber compounding; organo-metallics; synthesis and reactions of vinylidene cyanide; plasticizers for vinyl polymers. *Mailing Add:* 71 Colony Dr Hudson OH 44236

AVERRE, CHARLES WILSON, III, PLANT PATHOLOGY. *Current Pos:* PROF PLANT PATH, NC STATE UNIV, 68- *Personal Data:* b Puerto Castilla, Honduras, June 3, 32; US citizen; m 55; c 2. *Educ:* NC State Univ, BS, 55, MS, 60; Purdue Univ, PhD(plant path), 63. *Prof Exp:* Asst plant pathologist, Subtrop Exp Sta, Univ Fla, 63-67; asst prof plant path, Ga Exp Sta, 67-68. *Concurrent Pos:* Consult, Int Biol Ser, Inc, 73, Catie-MIP Turrialba, Costa Rica; ed, Fungicide & Nematicide Tests, Am Phytopath Soc, 74-79. *Mem:* Am Phytopath Soc. *Res:* Extension; diseases of vegetable crops; disease control systems; evaluation of fungicides and nematicides; plant disease diagnoses. *Mailing Add:* 2730 Van Dyke Ave Raleigh NC 27607

AVERY, BYLLYE YVONNE, PSYCHOLOGY, SPECIAL EDUCATION. *Current Pos:* exec dir & founder, 82-90, FOUNDING PRES, CHIEF SPOKESPERSON & BD MEM, NAT BLACK WOMEN'S HEALTH PROJ, ATLANTA, 90- *Educ:* Talladega Col, BA, 59; Univ Fla, MEd, 69. *Hon Degrees:* LHD, Thomas Jefferson Univ, 90, State Univ NY, Binghamton, 90 & Bowdoin Col, 93; LLD, Bates Col, 95. *Honors & Awards:* Trend Setters Award, Nat Health Coun, 93; Gustav O Lienhard Award, Inst Med, 94; Presidential Citation, Am Pub Health Asn, 95. *Prof Exp:* Occup recreational & ther aide, Northeast Fla State Hosp, Macclenny, 59-65; resource teacher emotionally disturbed, Richard L Browm Elem Sch, Jacksonville, 66-68; learning disabilities resource teacher, Waldo Community Sch, Fla, 69-70; head teacher, Children's Ment Health Units & instr, Dept Psychiat, Univ Fla, Gainesville, 70-76; co-founder & dir educ, Birthplace: An Alternate Birth Environ, 76-80, dir pub rels, Gainesville, 78-80; dir comprehensive employ training prog, Santa Fe Community Col, Gainesville, 80-82. *Concurrent Pos:* bd dirs, Nat Women's Health Network, 76-81, New World Found, 86-91, W K Kellog Int Fel Prog, 89-94 & Boston Women's Health Book Collective, 90-92; consult, Univ West Indies, St Michael's, Barbados, 86, Belize Rural Women's Asn, Belize City, 87-88, Provincial Church Kenya, World Coun Churches, Kisumu Kenya, 88, John D & Catherine MacArthur Found, 89, Geledes Black Women's Inst, Sao Paulo, Brazil, 89-93 & Kellog Int Leadership Prog, W K Kellog Found, 89-94; John D & Catherine T MacArthur Found fel, 89; bd visitors, Tucker Found, Dartmouth Col, 90-; mem, Women's Cancer Bd, Dana Farber Cancer Ctr, Boston; vis fel, Dept Health & Social Behav, Sch Pub Health, Harvard Univ, 91-93. *Res:* Contributed several articles to professional journals. *Mailing Add:* PO Box 535 Swarthmore PA 19081

AVERY, CHARLES CARRINGTON, FOREST HYDROLOGY. *Current Pos:* assoc prof, 74-80, PROF FORESTRY, NORTHERN ARIZ UNIV, 80- *Personal Data:* b Syracuse, NY, July 22, 33; m 61; c 4. *Educ:* Utah State Univ, BS, 61; Duke Univ, MF, 63; Univ Wash, PhD(hydrol), 72. *Prof Exp:* Forester, Wenatchee Nat Forest, US Forest Serv, 61-64, forest hydrologist, Med Bow Nat Forest, 64-66, res hydrologist, Rocky Mountain Forest Exp Sta, 68-74. *Mem:* Am Geophys Union; Soc Am Foresters; Sigma Xi; Am Inst Hydrol; NY Acad Sci. *Res:* The relationships between forest practices and water quantity and quality. *Mailing Add:* Box 22514 Flagstaff AZ 86002-2514

AVERY, DONALD HILLS, accident reconstruction, for more information see previous edition

AVERY, GORDON B, MEDICINE, EMBRYOLOGY. *Current Pos:* Dir clin res ctr, Children's Hosp DC, 66-71, DIR NEWBORN NURSERY, CHILDREN'S HOSP DC, 63-, PROF CHILD HEALTH, SCH MED, GEORGE WASHINGTON UNIV, 71- *Personal Data:* b Beirut, Lebanon, Dec 10, 31; US citizen; m 54; c 3. *Educ:* Harvard Univ, AB, 53; Univ Pa, MD, 58, PhD(embryol), 59; Am Bd Pediat, dipl. *Honors & Awards:* Leavonson Prize, 57; Pepper Prize, 58. *Concurrent Pos:* Grants, Gen Res Support, 63-65, Children's Bur, 65-67, NSF, 65-67 & Clin Res Ctr, 66-73; consult, Wash Hosp Ctr, Bethesda Naval Hosp & Nat Inst Child Health & Human Develop, 64-; assoc prof pediat, Sch Med, George Washington Univ, 67-71; mem comt ment retardation res & training, NIH, 69- *Mem:* AMA; Am Acad Pediat; Transplantation Soc; Soc Pediat Res; Am Pediat Soc. *Res:* Pediatrics; neonatology; pulmonology; nutrition. *Mailing Add:* Dept Child Health Develop Childrens Hosp Nat Med Ctr 111 Mich Ave Washington DC 20010-2916

AVERY, HOWARD S, metallurgy & physical metallurgical engineering, mining engineering; deceased, see previous edition for last biography

AVERY, JAMES KNUCKEY, EMBRYOLOGY, ANATOMY. *Current Pos:* from asst prof to assoc prof dent, Sch Dent, 54-63, assoc prof anat, Sch Med, 61-71, dir, Dent Res Inst, 75-89, prof anat, 77-89, PROF DENT, SCH DENT, UNIV MICH, ANN ARBOR, 63-, EMER PROF, SCH MED & DENT. *Personal Data:* b Holly, Colo, Aug 6, 21; m 50; c Nancy, David & Robert. *Educ:* Univ Kansas City, DDS, 45; Univ Rochester, BA, 48, PhD(anat), 52. *Honors & Awards:* Acad Dent Med Award; Pulp Biol IADR Award. *Prof Exp:* Res assoc & instr, Univ Rochester, 52-54. *Concurrent Pos:* Res & educ consult, Ann Arbor Vet Admin Hosp, 63-; consult, Dent Training Comt, NIH, 64-68, Sci Sessions of Am Dental Assoc, 60-70, Coun on Dent Educ & Accreditation, 75-80. *Mem:* Fel AAAS (chmn sect dent, 75-76); fel Am Col Dent; Int Asn Dent Res (pres, 74-75); Am Asn Anat; Electron Micros Soc Am; Sigma Xi; Teratology Soc. *Res:* Embryology of teeth, jaws, and face, comparative and human; histology and histochemistry of oral and related structures; in vivo and in vitro study of developing organs and structures; cytology of formative cells by means of light, phase, interference and electron microscopy; immunochemical technologies. *Mailing Add:* Rm 5213 Univ Mich Sch Dent Ann Arbor MI 48109. *Fax:* 313-764-7406

AVERY, LEON, NEUROGENETICS, CAENORHABDITIS ELEGANS. *Current Pos:* asst prof biochem, 90-, ASSOC PROF MOLECULAR BIOL & ONCOL UNIV TEX SOUTHWESTERN MED CTR, DALLAS. *Educ:* Cornell Univ, BS, 76; Stanford Univ, PhD(biochem), 83. *Prof Exp:* Fel, Mass Inst Technol, 84-87; vis, Lab Molecular Biol, Med Res Coun, 87-90. *Mem:* Genetics Soc Am; Soc Neurosci. *Res:* Genetics and neurobiology of feeding in the nematode caenorhabditis elegans; how excitable cells in the pharynx work to produce feeding behavior and the molecular genetic basis for the properties of the excitable cells. *Mailing Add:* Dept Molecular & Oncol Univ Tex Southwestern Med Ctr 5323 Harry Hines Blvd Dallas TX 75235-9148. *Fax:* 214-648-8856; *E-Mail:* leon@eatworms.swmed.edu

AVERY, MARY ELLEN, MEDICINE, PEDIATRICS. *Current Pos:* THOMAS MORGAN ROTCH PROF PEDIAT, HARVARD MED SCH, 74- *Personal Data:* b Camden, NJ, May 6, 27. *Educ:* Wheaton Col, BA, 48; Johns Hopkins Univ, MD, 52; Am Bd Pediat, cert, 59. *Hon Degrees:* MA, Harvard Univ, 74; DSc, Wheaton Col, 74, Univ Mich, 75, Med Col Pa & Trinity Col, 76, Albany Med Col, 77, Med Col Wis & Radcliffe Col, 78, Russell Sage Col, 83, Mem Univ Nfld, 93; LHD, Emmanuel Col, 79. *Honors & Awards:* Nat Medal of Sci, 91; Wall-Copeland lectr, Georgetown Univ, 81; Arthur McElfresh lectr, St Louis Univ, 81; John Howland lectr, Johns Hopkins Univ, 81, Anna Baetjer Lectr, 91; Theodore L Badger lectr, Harvard Med Sch, 83; Harry Bawkin Mem lectr, 84; Edward Livingston Trudeau Medal, Am Lung Asn, 84; Charles McNeil lectr, Royal Col Physicians, Scotland, 88; Donald F Eagan Mem lectr, New Orleans, 90; Vickers lectr, London, 92; Bradford lectr, Cincinnati, 93; Bradford lectr, Children's Mercy Hosp, Kansas City, 93. *Prof Exp:* From asst prof to assoc prof pediat, Johns Hopkins Univ, 61-69; prof, Montreal Children's Hosp, McGill Univ, 69-74; physician-in-chief, Children's Hosp, Boston, 74-85. *Concurrent Pos:* Res fel pediat, Harvard Med Sch, 57-59; Nat Inst Neurol Dis & Blindness spec trainee, 57-60; fel, Sch Med, Johns Hopkins Univ, 59-60; USPHS res grants, 61-; Markle scholar med sci, 61-66; pediatrician in chg newborn nurseries, Johns Hopkins Hosp, 61-69; consult, US HEW, 64; mem, Med Res Coun Can, 70-74, adv comt, NIH & Robert Wood Johnson Found; bd dirs, AAAS, 88-; consult, Food & Drug Admin, 89-; chair, Fedn Pediat Orgn, 90-; mem, Comt Health & Human Rights, Inst Med, 90- *Mem:* Nat Acad Sci; Inst Med-Nat Acad Sci; Soc Pediat Res (pres, 72); Am Pediat Soc (pres-elect, 89, pres, 90); Am Physiol Soc; fel Am Acad Arts & Sci; fel AAAS; fel Am Acad Pediat. *Res:* Respiratory problems of the newborn infant; pulmonary surfactant; control of breathing; prevention of hyaline membrane disease with antenatal glucorticoids and postnatal surfactant replacement; author and editor in pediatric medicine. *Mailing Add:* Children's Hosp 300 Longwood Ave Boston MA 02115. *Fax:* 617-732-4151

AVERY, ROBERT, THEORETICAL & REACTOR PHYSICS. *Current Pos:* RETIRED. *Personal Data:* b Ft Worth, Tex, Sept 7, 21. *Educ:* Univ Ill, BS, 43; Univ Wis, MS, 47, PhD(physics), 50. *Prof Exp:* Mem, Naval Reactor Div, Argonne Nat Lab, 50-56, sect head, Theoret Reactor Physics Sect, Reactor Eng Div, 56-63, dir, Appl Physics Div, 63-73, dir, Reactor Analysis & Safety Div, 73-86, sr physicist, 86- *Mem:* Nat Acad Eng; fel Am Nuclear Soc; fel Am Phys Soc. *Res:* Nuclear reactor theory. *Mailing Add:* Reactor Analysis & Safety Div Argonne Nat Lab 9700 S Cass Ave Argonne IL 60439

AVERY, SUSAN KATHRYN, ATMOSPHERIC DYNAMICS. *Current Pos:* ASSOC PROF ELEC ENG, UNIV COLO, 85-, ASSOC DEAN RES & GRAD EDUC, 90- *Personal Data:* b Detroit, Mich, Jan 5, 50; m 72; c 1. *Educ:* Mich State Univ, BS, 72; Univ Ill, MS, 74, PhD(atmospheric sci), 78. *Prof Exp:* Asst prof atmospheric dynamics elec eng, dept elec eng, Univ Ill, 78-83. *Concurrent Pos:* Mem, Int Comn Meteorol Upper Atomosphere, Working Group Tides in the Mesosphere & Lower Thermosphere, 81-86; fel, Coop Inst Res Environ Sci, 83-; mem adv panel, NSF, 85-88; mem, Comt Solar-Terrestrial Res, Nat Res Coun, 87-90, Comt Educ & Human Res, Am Geophys Union, 88-, Comt Middle Atmosphere, Am Meteorol Soc, 90-93, Steering Comt, Equatorial Middle Atmosphere Dynamics & Mesosphere-Lower Thermosphere Network, Int STEP Prog, 90-; mem-at-large, Int Union Radio Sci, Nat Res Coun, 91-93, mem, Comns F & G; bd trustees, Univ Corp Atmospheric Res, 91-93. *Mem:* Am Meteorol Soc; Am Geophys Union; Inst Elec & Electronics Engrs; Sigma Xi; Union Radio Sci Int. *Res:* Dynamics of the mesosphere and stratosphere; unifying observational analyses and theoretical studies; modeling large scale atmospheric waves; ground based measurement techniques to observe the atmosphere. *Mailing Add:* Elec & Computer Eng Univ Colo Campus Box 425 Boulder CO 80309

AVERY, WILLIAM HINCKLEY, PHYSICAL CHEMISTRY, PHYSICS. *Current Pos:* RETIRED. *Personal Data:* b Ft Collins, Colo, July 25, 12; m 38, Helen W Palmer; c Christopher & Patricia (Bartlett). *Educ:* Pomona Col, AB, 33; Harvard Univ, AM, 35, PhD(photochem), 37. *Honors & Awards:* President's Cert Merit, 47; Hickman Medal, 50; Sir Alfred C Egerton Gold Medal, Combustion Inst, 71. *Prof Exp:* Asst chem, Harvard Univ, 34-39; res chemist, Shell Oil Co, 39-43; res assoc & chief propellants div, Nat Defense Res Comt, Allegany Ballistics Lab, 43-46; res assoc, A D Little, Inc, 46-47; res assoc, Appl Physics Lab, Johns Hopkins Univ, 47-50, supvr launching & propulsion, 50-54, res & develop, 54-60 & appl res, 60-73, asst dir explor develop, Appl Physics Lab, 73-78, supvr, Aeronaut Div, 61-80, dir, Ocean Energy Progs, 73-89. *Concurrent Pos:* Mem res adv comt air breathing propulsion systs, NASA; mem advan systs panel, Hwy Res Bd, 70-75; mem, Sr Adv Comt, Cent Energy & Environ Res, Univ Puerto Rico, 77-84. *Mem:* Am Chem Soc; Am Inst Aeronaut & Astronaut; Combustion Inst; AAAS; Int Hydrogen Energy Asn; Marine Technol Soc. *Res:* Photochemistry; spectroscopy; molecular structure; chemical kinetics rocket propellants and internal ballistics; ramjet propulsion; combustion; urban transportation; ocean thermal energy conversion; renewable energy from the ocean; ocean energy, ocean thermal energy conversion. *Mailing Add:* 724 Guilford Ct Silver Spring MD 20901-3218. *Fax:* 301-953-5850; *E-Mail:* william.avery@apljhu.edu

AVGEROPOULOS, GEORGE N, PHYSICAL CHEMISTRY, QUANTUM CHEMISTRY. *Current Pos:* RES & DEVELOP DIR, RM ENGINEERED PROD INC, 87- *Personal Data:* b Greece, Jan 25, 34; m 64; c 1. *Educ:* Nat Univ Athens, MA, 61; Wayne State Univ, MSc, 67, PhD(quantum chem), 68. *Prof Exp:* Chief res chemist, Michaelides Food Indust, Greece, 61-62; asst chem, Wayne State Univ, 62-68; eng scientist, Cent Res Labs, Firestone Tire & Rubber Co, 68-72, polymer physicist-rheologist, 72-78; tech dir, Standard Prod Co, 78-83; dir technol, Diversitech-Gen Corp, 83-87. *Mem:* Am Chem Soc; Am Phys Soc; Soc Rheol; AAAS; Am Inst Chemists; Am Soc Testing Mat; Soc Automotive Engr; Soc Mining Engr; Am Inst Chem Engr. *Res:* Applied mathematics; rheology of polymers and polymeric blends; mechanical properties and characterization of polymers; morphology of heterogeneous blends; mathematical models for the study of synthesis and characterization of polymers; processing of polymers, extrusion moldings & coating. *Mailing Add:* Ariston Inc 13 Charlyn Dr Charleston SC 29407-3724

AVIADO, DOMINGO MARIANO, TOXICOLOGY, CLINICAL PHARMACOLOGY. *Current Pos:* PRES, ATMOSPHERIC HEALTH SCI INC, 80- *Personal Data:* b Manila, Philippines, Aug 28, 24; m 53, Asuncion Guevara; c Maria C (Gentile), Carlos, Domingo & Maria A. *Educ:* Univ Pa, MD, 48. *Prof Exp:* From asst instr to instr pharmacol, Sch Med, Univ Pa, 48-50, assoc, 50-52, from asst prof to prof, 52-77; sr dir biomed res, Allied Chem Corp Med Affairs, 77-80. *Concurrent Pos:* NIH res fel, 48-50; Guggenheim Found fel, 62-63; assoc ed, Circulation Res, 58-62; treas sect pharmacol, Int Union Physiol Sci, 59-61; adj prof pharmacol, NJ Col Med & Dent, 77-83; mem clear air sci adv comt, Environ Protection Agency, 78-82; ed, Inhalation Toxicol & Path Sect, Environ Path & Toxicol, 79-82. *Mem:* AMA; Am Soc Clin Pharmacol & Therapeut; Am Soc Pharmacol & Exp Therapeut; Am Physiol Soc; Soc Toxicol; Am Col Toxicol. *Res:* Respiratory and circulatory reflexes; physiology and pharmacology of pulmonary circulation; clinical pharmacology; environmental toxicology; occupational medicine. *Mailing Add:* Atmospheric Health Sci Inc 225 Hartshorn Dr Short Hills NJ 07078-3225. *Fax:* 973-564-9156

AVIGAD, GAD, BIOLOGICAL CHEMISTRY, CARBOHYDRATE BIOCHEMISTRY. *Current Pos:* assoc prof, 70-79, PROF BIOCHEM, RUTGERS UNIV & R W JOHNSON MED SCH, 79- *Personal Data:* b Jerusalem, Israel, Apr 30, 30; nat US; m 65, Lois Schwartz; c Rachel T. *Educ:* Hebrew Univ Jerusalem, MSc, 55, PhD(biochem), 58. *Honors & Awards:* Israel Sci Prize, 58. *Prof Exp:* Asst biochem, Hadassah Med Sch, Hebrew Univ Jerusalem, 54-57, instr, 57-59; res fel, Med Col, NY Univ, 59-61; sr lectr,

Hebrew Univ Jerusalem, 61-65, assoc prof, 65-69. *Concurrent Pos:* Vis scientist, Carlsberg Labs, Copenhagen, Denmark, 58; Jane Coffin Childs Mem Fund fel, 60-61; vis asst prof, Albert Einstein Col Med, 64, vis assoc prof, 67-70, vis res scientist, 88; vis prof, Parana State Univ, Brazil, 72. *Mem:* Soc Gen Microbiol; NY Acad Sci; Am Chem Soc; Am Soc Microbiol; Am Soc Biol Chem; Soc Glycoconjugate Res. *Res:* Carbohydrate chemistry; biosynthesis and degradation of polysaccharides and complex glycosides; mechanisms of enzyme action; sugar metabolism. *Mailing Add:* Dept Biochem Univ Med & Dent NJ R W Johnson Med Sch PO Box 101 Piscataway NJ 08854-5635. *Fax:* 732-235-4783

AVIGAN, JOEL, LIPIDS, NUCLEIC ACIDS. *Current Pos:* RES SCIENTIST, KENNEDY KRIEGER INST, 90- *Personal Data:* b Warsaw, Poland, Jan 8, 20; m 48, Vita Poznansky; c Mark I, Ruth Z & David E. *Educ:* Hebrew Univ, Israel, MSc, 43; McGill Univ, PhD(biochem), 54. *Prof Exp:* Res chemist, Israel Res Coun, 50-52; vis scientist, Bio-Med Res, Lab Metab, Nat Heart, Lung & Blood Inst, 55-64, res chemist, Lab Cellular Metab, 64-91. *Concurrent Pos:* Vis fel, Hadassah Med Sch, Hebrew Univ, 63; vis scientist, Lab Chem Enzymol, Shell Res Ltd, Eng, 63; mem coun arteriosclerosis, Am Heart Asn. *Mem:* Am Soc Biochem & Molecular Biol; Am Heart Asn Coun Arteriosclerosis. *Res:* Biochemistry of sterols, fatty acids and metabolism of plasma lipoproteins in relation to atherosclerosis; molecular mechanisms of hormonal effects on mammalian cells. *Mailing Add:* 816 Kersey Rd Silver Spring MD 20902-3004

AVIGNONE, FRANK TITUS, III, ELEMENTARY PARTICLE PHYSICS. *Current Pos:* From asst prof to assoc prof physics, 65-73, PROF PHYSICS & ASTRON, UNIV SC, 73- *Personal Data:* b New York, NY, May 9, 32; m 54; c 2. *Educ:* Ga Inst Technol, BS, 60, MS, 62, PhD(physics), 65. *Res:* Experimental elementary particle physics. *Mailing Add:* Dept Physics Univ SC Columbia SC 29208

AVILA, CHARLES FRANCIS, MILITARY CAMERA DESIGN. *Current Pos:* RETIRED. *Personal Data:* b Taunton, Mass, Sept, 17, 06; m 34; c 2. *Educ:* Harvard Univ, BS, 29. *Hon Degrees:* LLD, Univ Mass, 63. *Honors & Awards:* Edison Medal, Inst Elec & Electronics Engrs, 68. *Prof Exp:* Eng mgt, Boston Edison Co, 29-60, pres & chmn, 60-71; dir, Liberty Mutual Ins Co, 60-70, Liberty Mutual Fire Ins Co, 69-78, Chas T Main, Inc, 77-84, C T M Ltd, Bermuda, 80-84. *Concurrent Pos:* Consult, Shawmut Bank Boston, 58-79, Raytheon Co, 62-78, John Hancock Mutual Life Ins Co, 64-74, Shawmut Corp, 65-79; chief exec officer, Boston Edison Co, 60-70, consult, 60-75; New Eng award, Eng Socs New Eng Inc, 83. *Mem:* Emer mem Nat Acad Eng; fel Am Inst Elec & Electronics Engrs. *Res:* Study and design or redesign of various plant and equipment of a major utility including management. *Mailing Add:* 10 Longwood Dr Westwood MA 01907

AVILA, JESUS, MICROTUBULE PROTEINS. *Current Pos:* SCI COORDR, SCI INVEST, 90- *Personal Data:* b Madrid, Spain, Dec 12, 45; m 80, Nieves Villanueva; c Marina. *Educ:* Univ Complutense Madrid, Master, 67, PhD(chem), 71. *Prof Exp:* Res fel, Molecular Biol Lab, NIH, Bethesda, 72-75; mem staff res, Inst Biol Develop (CSIC), 75-76; head Microtub Lab, Molecular Biol Ctr (CSIC-UAM), 76-84, head struct unit, 84-86, dir, 86-88; br pres, Nat Agency Perspective Eval, 88-90. *Mem:* Am Soc Cell Biol; Int Union Biol Sci. *Res:* Structure and function of microtubule proteins in neural cells. *Mailing Add:* Ctr Molecular Biol Univ Autonoma Fac Sci Canto Blanco Madrid 28049 Spain

AVILA, VERNON LEE, COMPARATIVE ENDOCRINOLOGY, CELL BIOLOGY. *Current Pos:* asst prof, 73-76, ASSOC PROF BIOL, SAN DIEGO STATE UNIV, 76- *Personal Data:* b Segundo, Colo, Apr 5, 41; m, Patricia G Frye; c Pamela, Paula, Patrick & Raquel. *Educ:* Univ NMex, BS, 62; Northern Ariz Univ, MA, 66; Univ Colo, PhD(biol), 73. *Prof Exp:* Teacher, Los Lunas High Sch, 62-65 & Valley High Sch, 65-71; lectr biol, Univ Colo, 72-73. *Concurrent Pos:* Sci adv, Goodyear Publ Co, 74-77; sci consult, Scott Foresman & Co Publ, 75-; expert consult & health scientist adminr, Nat Cancer Inst, NIH, 78-79; admin fel, Col Sci, San Diego State Univ, 80-81; prof biol & asst dean, Col Natural Sci, Univ PR, Rio Piedras, 85-87; expert consult & health scientist adminr, Div Res Resources, NIH, 87-88; pres, Bookmark Publ, 90- *Mem:* AAAS; Am Soc Zoologists; Animal Behav Soc; Am Inst Biol Sci. *Res:* Endocrinological aspects of behavior in teleost fishes; behavior in aquatic frogs; hormonal aspects of behavior in vertebrates. *Mailing Add:* Dept Biol San Diego State Univ 500 Campanile Dr San Diego CA 92182-0057. *Fax:* 619-669-1461; *E-Mail:* vavila@sunstroke.sdsu.edu

AVILES, JOSEPH B, THEORETICAL PHYSICS. *Current Pos:* CONSULT PHYSICIST, 87- *Personal Data:* b Atlantic City, NJ, Aug 21, 27; m 59; c 2. *Educ:* Rutgers Univ, BS, 50; Johns Hopkins Univ, PhD, 58. *Prof Exp:* Theoret physicist & head, Radiation Matter Interactions Br, US Naval Res Lab, 56-87. *Mem:* Am Phys Soc. *Res:* Radiation-matter interactions; nuclear physics; explosive initiation. *Mailing Add:* 710 W Tantallon Dr Ft Washington MD 20744

AVILES, RAFAEL G, PHYSICAL CHEMISTRY, POLYMER CHEMISTRY. *Current Pos:* sr scientist coatings res, Rohme & Haas Co, 80-84, res sect mgr indust coatings res, 84-87, res sect mgr trade sales coatings res, 87-89, RES MGR FORMULATION CHEM, ROHM & HAAS CO, 89- *Personal Data:* b Mexico City, Mex, April 28, 52; m 82; c Michael & Katharine. *Educ:* Univ Guanajuato, Mex, BChemE, 74; Univ Nev, Reno, PhD(phys chem), 79. *Prof Exp:* Res asst phys chem, Univ Nev, Reno, 75-79; fel, Cornell Univ, 79-80. *Concurrent Pos:* Adj prof, Philadelphia Col Textiles & Sci, 84- *Mem:* Am Chem Soc. *Res:* Kinetics and photophysics of aromatic polymers; gas phase kinetics; laser initiated reactions; energy transfer; structure-property relationships in polymeric systems; design of latex polymers; physic chemical properties of polyelectrolytes. *Mailing Add:* Rohm & Haas Co 727 Norristown Rd Spring House PA 19477. *Fax:* 215-619-1636; *E-Mail:* rscrga@rohmhaas.com

AVIOLI, LOUIS, NUCLEAR MEDICINE, ENDOCRINOLOGY. *Current Pos:* asst prof, 66-70, PROF MED, MED SCH, WASH UNIV, 70-; CHIEF ENDOCRINOL & METAB, JEWISH HOSP ST LOUIS, 66- *Personal Data:* b Coatesville, Pa, Apr 13, 31; m 55; c 5. *Educ:* Princeton Univ, AB, 53; Yale Univ, MD, 47. *Prof Exp:* From intern to resident med, NC Mem Hosp, 57-59; clin investr, NIH, 59-61; from instr to asst prof med, Seton Hall Col Med, 61-66, dir isotope lab & asst sci dir clin res ctr, 61-66. *Concurrent Pos:* Grants, Nat Inst Arthritis & Metab Dis, 60-67, AEC, 62-67 & NIH, 65-70; attend physician, Jersey City Med Ctr, 62-66. *Mem:* AAAS; Soc Nuclear Med; Radiation Res Soc; Am Nuclear Soc; Am Fedn Clin Res. *Res:* Metabolism; radioactive isotopes. *Mailing Add:* Schoenberg Prof Med Div Bone & Mineral Dis Wash Univ Sch Med 216 S Kings Hwy Blvd St Louis MO 63110

AVIRAM, ARI, ORGANIC CHEMISTRY, CHEMICAL PHYSICS. *Current Pos:* RES STAFF MEM ORG & THEORET CHEM, T J WATSON RES LAB, IBM CORP, 68- *Personal Data:* b Braila, Romania, Aug 18, 37; m 59; c 3. *Educ:* Israel Inst Technol, BSc, 65; NY Univ, MSc, 71, PhD(theoret chem), 75. *Prof Exp:* Synthetic chemist pharmaceut, Ayerst Lab, Can, 67-68. *Mem:* Am Chem Soc; Am Physics Soc. *Res:* The ability of molecules to perform device functions; molecular rectifiers and molecular memory elements; theoretical and synthetic aspects. *Mailing Add:* 444 Bramble Bush Croton-on-Hudson NY 10520

AVIS, KENNETH EDWARD, PHARMACEUTICS, PARENTERAL TECHNOLOGY. *Current Pos:* from assoc prof to prof, Univ Tenn, Memphis, 61-77, vchmn dept, 68-77, dir Div Parenteral Medications, 72-83, Goodman prof pharmaceut, 68-88, chmn dept, 83-88, EMER PROF PHARMACEUT, COL PHARM, UNIV TENN, MEMPHIS, 88- *Personal Data:* b Elmer, NJ, June 3, 18; m 43, Irma J Hildreth; c Carolyn, John & Beverly. *Educ:* Philadelphia Col Pharm, BSc, 42, MSc, 47, DSc(pharm), 56. *Honors & Awards:* Parenteral Drug Asn Res Award, 71, 74, & 79; Schaufus Parenteral Technol Achievement Award, 76; Spec Recognition Lifetime Achievement, Parental Drug Asn, 96- *Prof Exp:* From instr to assoc prof pharm, Philadelphia Col Pharm, 46-61. *Concurrent Pos:* Consult, Nat Cancer Inst, 66-67, Food & Drug Admin, 68-, Vet Admin Hosp, Memphis & over 50 pharmaceut co, 60-; dir, Parenteral Drug Asn, 60-77, pres, 68-69; mem, Nat Formulary Comt on Specif, 70-74; mem, nat coord comt on large vol parenterals, US Pharmacopeia & Food & Drug Admin. 72-76; consult, Pan-Am Health Orgn, 79 & 83. *Mem:* Am Soc Hosp Pharmacists; Am Pharmaceut Asn; Am Asn Cols Pharm; fel Acad Pharmaceut Sci; Parenteral Drug Asn (pres, 68 & 69); fel Am Asn Pharm Scientists, 86- *Res:* Sterile pharmaceutical products; formulation, evaluation of effects of environmental and processing factors on sterile products; radiopharmaceuticals; use of principles of aerobiology to evaluate potential for contamination of containers and systems. *Mailing Add:* Col Pharm Univ Tenn 874 Union Ave Memphis TN 38163. *Fax:* 901-448-6940

AVISE, JOHN C, EVOLUTIONARY GENETICS. *Current Pos:* From asst prof to prof, 75-87, RES PROF GENETICS, UNIV GA, 87- *Personal Data:* b Grand Rapids, Mich, Sept 19, 48. *Educ:* Univ Mich, BS, 70; Univ Tex, MA, 71; Univ Calif, Davis, PhD(genetics), 75. *Mem:* Nat Acad Sci; Am Acad Arts & Sci. *Res:* Ecology and evolution of natural populations. *Mailing Add:* Dept Genetics Rm C-228-A Univ Ga Athens GA 30602

AVISSAR, RONI, BOUNDARY-LAYER METEOROLOGY, LAND-ATMOSPHERE INTERACTIONS. *Current Pos:* PROF ATMOSPHERIC SCI, RUTGERS UNIV, 89- *Personal Data:* b Paris, France, Jan 11, 53; French & Israeli citizen; m 75, Patricia L Tebeka; c Naomi & Daniel. *Educ:* Hebrew Univ Jerusalem, BSc, 80, MSc, 82, PhD(mesoscale meteorol), 87. *Prof Exp:* Res asst, Hebrew Univ Jerusalem, 79-84, instr soil & water sci, 84-86; res assoc, Colo State Univ, 86-89. *Concurrent Pos:* Prin investr, NSF, 90-, NASA, 91-, Dept Energy, 92-, Nat Oceanic & Atmospheric Admin, 93-; mem, Panel Atmospheric Processes, Global Energy & Water Exp, Continental-Scale Int Proj, 92-95; ed, J Geophys Res Atmospheres, 96. *Mem:* Am Meteorol Soc; Am Geophys Union. *Res:* Develop parameterizations of subgrid-scale processes in atmospheric models, with special emphasis on land-atmosphere interactions. *Mailing Add:* Dept Enivron Sci Cook Col Rutgers Univ New Brunswick NJ 08903

AVITZUR, BETZALEL, MECHANICAL ENGINEERING. *Current Pos:* RETIRED. *Personal Data:* b Haifa, Israel, May 7, 25; m 55; c 4. *Educ:* Israel Inst Technol, BSc & Dipl Ing, 49; Univ Mich, MS, 56, PhD(mech eng), 60. *Prof Exp:* Res & develop engr, Ministry of Defence, Israel, 49-54; dept mgr indust eng, Vulcan Foundries, Israel, 54-55; res & develop engr, Micrometrical Develop Corp, Mich, 56-58; res engr, Sci Lab, Ford Motor Co, 59-61; sr lectr mech eng, Israel Inst Technol, 61-64; from assoc prof to prof metall & mat sci, Lehigh Univ, 64-95, dir inst metal forming, 70-95. *Concurrent Pos:* Guest lectr, Univ Mich, 61. *Mem:* Am Soc Mech Engrs; Am Soc Metals; Am Soc Mfg Engrs. *Res:* Design of mechanical instruments; metal behavior undergoing gross plastic deformations. *Mailing Add:* 1427 Bedford Circle Allentown PA 18104

AVIV, ABRAHAM, ION TRANSFER, HYPERTENSION. *Current Pos:* PROF & DIR, DIV HYPERTENSION, NJ MED SCH, 87- *Personal Data:* b Israel. *Res:* Nephrology; pediatrics; ion transfer; hypertension. *Mailing Add:* Hypertension Res Ctr Univ Med & Dent NJ Med Sch 185 S Orange Ave Newark NJ 07103

AVIZIENIS, ALGIRDAS, COMPUTER SCIENCE. *Current Pos:* asst prof eng, 62-68, assoc prof comput sci, 68-76, PROF ENG & APPL SCI, UNIV CALIF, LOS ANGELES, 76- *Personal Data:* b Kaunas, Lithuania, July 8, 32; US citizen; m 62; c 1. *Educ:* Univ Ill, BS, 54, MS, 55, PhD(elec eng), 60. *Honors & Awards:* Apollo Achievement Award, NASA, 69. *Prof Exp:* Res engr, Jet Propulsion Lab, Calif Inst Technol, 55-56; staff engr, Barnes & Reinecke, Inc, Ill, 58-60; sr res engr, Jet Propulsion Lab, Calif Inst Technol, 60-68, mem tech staff, 68-76. *Concurrent Pos:* Mem adv panel comput sci & comput eng, NSF, 71- *Mem:* Asn Comput Mach; Inst Elec & Electronics Engrs. *Res:* Information systems engineering; digital computer system architecture; theory of digital arithmetic; fault-tolerant and self-repairing digital systems. *Mailing Add:* Dept Comput Sci Univ Calif Boelter Hall 4731 Los Angeles CA 90095

AVIZONIS, PETRAS V, LASERS, PHYSICAL OPTICS. *Current Pos:* sr proj scientist, 62-68, tech dir laser div, 68-71, TECH DIR, ADVAN RADIATION TECHNOL OFF, US AIR FORCE WEAPONS LAB, 71- *Personal Data:* b Lithuania, Aug 17, 35; US citizen; m 59; c 2. *Educ:* Duke Univ, BS, 57; Univ Del, MS, 59, PhD(phys chem), 62. *Honors & Awards:* Arthur S Flemming Award, Civil Serv Comn, Washington, DC, 71. *Prof Exp:* Chemist, Sun Oil Co, Pa, 61-62. *Mem:* Am Phys Soc; Am Optical Soc. *Res:* High energy lasers; optical systems; excited state chemistry and physics. *Mailing Add:* Strategic Defense Ctr SZ-15 2800 Westminster Blvd PO Box 3089 Seal Beach CA 90740

AVNER, BARRY P, MONOCLONAL ANTIBODIES, HOSPITAL ADMINISTRATION. *Current Pos:* DIR IMMUNOL ONCOL LAB, BAPTIST HOSP MIAMI, 88- *Personal Data:* b Chicago, Ill, June 19, 44. *Educ:* State Univ NY, Buffalo, PhD(biochem pharmacol), 70; Univ Miami, MBA, 92. *Prof Exp:* Asst vpres sci affairs & dir res, Summa Med Corp, Albuquerque, NMex, 81-85; dir Antibody Proj, Biotherapeutics, Inc, 85-88. *Mem:* NY Acad Sci; Am Asn Cancer Res; Am Soc Pharmacol & Exp Therapeut; Am Col Health Care Execs; Soc Anal Cytol. *Res:* Technology assessment and acquisition; monoclonal antibodies; development of reference clinical laboratory for esoteric oncology testing and therapeutics. *Mailing Add:* 8499 NW 14th Ct Coral Springs FL 33071. *Fax:* 305-598-5952

AVNER, ELLIS DAVID, PEDIATRIC NEPHROLOGY, DEVELOPMENTAL BIOLOGY. *Current Pos:* PROF PEDIAT, UNIV WASH, 88-; DIR, DIV NEPHROLOGY, CHILDREN'S HOSP, SEATTLE, 88- *Personal Data:* b Pittsburgh, Pa, June 12, 48; m 70; c 2. *Educ:* Princeton Univ, AB, 70; Univ Pa, MD, 75. *Honors & Awards:* Basil O Connor Res Award, 82; New Investr Res Award, NIH, 84-87. *Prof Exp:* Resident pediat, Children's Hosp, Boston, Mass, 75-78, clin fel nephrology, 78-79, res fel, 79-80; from asst prof to assoc prof pediat, Sch Med, Univ Pittsburgh, 80-88. *Concurrent Pos:* Scholar, Woodrow Wilson Nat Fel, 70; staff nephrologist, Children's Hosp, Pittsburgh, 80-88, dir, Organ Cult Lab, 81-88; med adv, Nat Kidney Found, Western Pa, 81-88; prin investr, NIH, 87-91, 91-; coun mem, Int Soc Pediat Nephrology, 86-92 & Soc Pediat Res, 88-91. *Mem:* Int Soc Pediat Nephrology; Soc Pediat Res; Am Soc Cell Biol; Am Fedn Clin Res; Am Soc Nephrology; Am Pediat Soc. *Res:* Use of tissue and organ culture models to study normal and abnormal mammalian kidney development; pathophysiology of renal cystic maldevelopment. *Mailing Add:* Pediat Dept Rainbow Babies & Children's Hosp 11100 Euclid Ave MC 6003 Cleveland OH 44106-6003

AVONDA, FRANK PETER, ORGANIC CHEMISTRY. *Current Pos:* PROF CHEM, NICHOLLS STATE UNIV, 69-, HEAD DEPT, 76- *Personal Data:* b New York, NY, Nov 26, 24; m 56; c 4. *Educ:* City Col New York, BS, 48; Columbia Univ, AM, 49; Ohio State Univ, PhD(chem), 53. *Prof Exp:* Res assoc org fluorides, Duke Univ, 53-54; res chemist, Hooker Electrochem Co, 54-56; instr org chem, Univ Tampa, 56-58; asst prof, Univ Md, 58-59 & Seton Hall Univ, 59-61; proj leader res & develop, Maxwell House Div, Gen Foods Corp, 61-62; prof Am indust technol, Ger Employees Acad, 62-63; sr res chemist, Allied Chem Corp, NJ, 63-64; assoc prof chem, Northern State Col, 64-65; prof, Nicholls State Col, 65-67; chmn div sci & math, Southern State Col, SDak, 67-68; prof chem & asst dean arts & sci, Delgado Col, 68-69. *Concurrent Pos:* NSF grant, 70-72. *Mem:* Am Chem Soc. *Res:* Synthesis and chemistry of organic fluorine compounds. *Mailing Add:* PO Box 1041 Thibodaux LA 70302-1041

AVOURIS, PHAEDON, CHEMISTRY METAL SURFACES. *Current Pos:* mgr, 78-84, MGR CHEM PHYSICS, IBM RES DIV, THOMAS J WATSON RES CTR, 84- *Personal Data:* b Athens, Greece, June 16, 45; US citizen; m 76; c 1. *Educ:* Aristotelian Univ, Greece, BS, 68; Mich State Univ, PhD(phys chem), 74. *Prof Exp:* Fel, Univ Calif, Los Angeles, 75-77; res assoc, AT&T Bell Labs, 77-78. *Mem:* Fel Am Phys Soc; Am Chem Soc; Mat Res Soc; Am Vacuum Soc. *Res:* Experimental and theoretical studies of the electronic structure and reactivity of atoms and molecules on semiconductor and metal surfaces; mechanisms and dynamics of particle/photon-surface interactions; scanning tunneling microscopy; charge and energy transfer processes at surfaces. *Mailing Add:* IBM Thomas J Watson Res Ctr PO Box 218 Yorktown Heights NY 10598

AVRETT, EUGENE HINTON, ASTROPHYSICS. *Current Pos:* PHYSICIST, SMITHSONIAN ASTROPHYS OBSERV, 62- *Personal Data:* b Atlanta, Ga, Oct 28, 33; m 61; c 2. *Educ:* Ga Inst Technol, BS, 57; Harvard Univ, PhD(physics), 62. *Concurrent Pos:* Lectr, Harvard Univ, 64- *Res:* Radiative transfer in stellar atmospheres; spectral line formation; applied mathematics. *Mailing Add:* 36 Andover St Andover MA 01810

AVRIN, WILLIAM F, SUPERCONDUCTING TECHNOLOGIES, MAGNETIC MEASUREMENTS. *Current Pos:* RES PHYSICIST, QUANTUM MAGNETICS, INC, 87- *Personal Data:* b Pomona, Calif, June 5, 53. *Educ:* Univ Calif, San Diego, BA, 75; Cornell Univ, MS, 79, PhD(physics), 91. *Prof Exp:* Res physicist, Standard Oil, Ohio, 83-85 & Quantum Design, Inc, 85-87. *Concurrent Pos:* Prin investr, NSF, 90. *Res:* New measurement instruments involving magnetic sensors, superconductivity and superconducting quantum interference devices: optically pumped magnetometers, Josephson-junction voltage standards, seismometers, nuclear magnetic resonance and nondestructive inspection. *Mailing Add:* Quantum Magnetics Inc 7740 Kenamar Ct San Diego CA 92121-2425

AVRUCH, JOSEPH, MEDICINE. *Current Pos:* from asst prof to assoc prof, 72-88, PROF MED, HARVARD MED SCH, 88-; CHIEF, DIABETES UNIT, MASS GEN HOSP, 79- & PHYSICIAN, 86- *Personal Data:* b New York, NY, Apr 13, 41. *Educ:* Brooklyn Col, BS, 61; Wash Univ, MD, 65; Am Bd Internal Med, dipl, 75. *Prof Exp:* Intern, Ward Med, Barnes Hosp, St Louis, Mo, 65-66, asst resident, 68-69, chief resident, 71-72; res fel biol chem & med, Harvard Med Sch & Mass Gen Hosp, Boston, 69-71; asst med, Mass Gen Hosp, 72-75, asst physician, 75-80, assoc physician, 80-85. *Concurrent Pos:* Clin assoc, Metab Study Sect, Geront Res Ctr, NIH, 66-68; instr med, Sch Med, Wash Univ, 71-72; investr, Howard Hughes Med Inst, 74-89; lectr, 74-; mem, Comt Res & Prog Comt, Am Diabetes Asn, 79-82; assoc ed, J Clin Invest, 82-86; vis scientist, Molecular Biol Dept, Mass Gen Hosp & Dept Genetics, Harvard Med Sch, 85-86; vchmn, comt res, Mass Gen Hosp, 88-91, chmn, Subcomt Res Bldgs, 88-, dir, Endocrine Div, 89- & chmn, comt res, 91-; spec lectr, Swed Diabetes Asn, 89 & 33rd Gen Assembly, Japan Diabetes Soc, 90. *Mem:* AAAS; Am Diabetes Asn; Am Soc Clin Invest; Endocrine Soc; Am Soc Biol Chemists; Asn Am Physicians. *Res:* Insulin action; hormonal control of protein phosphorylation; author of numerous publications. *Mailing Add:* Dept Med Mass Gen Hosp E Bldg 149 8th Floor 13th St Charlestown MA 02129-2060

AWAD, ALBERT T, NATURAL PRODUCTS CHEMISTRY, PHARMACOGNOSY. *Current Pos:* assoc prof, 66-71, PROF PHARMACOG, COL PHARM, OHIO NORTHERN UNIV, 71- *Personal Data:* b Cairo, Egypt, Nov 25, 28; m 58; c 3. *Educ:* Cairo Univ, BSc, 52, MSc, 60; Ohio State Univ, PhD(pharmacog), 66. *Prof Exp:* instr & researcher pharmacog, Col Pharm, Cairo Univ, 56-61; teacher & res asst, Col Pharm, Ohio State Univ, 61-66. *Concurrent Pos:* Lederle pharm fac award, 67; Gilford instrument apparatus grant, 68; NSF col sci improvement grant, 69-73. *Mem:* Am Asn Col Pharm; Am Soc Pharmacog; Acad Pharmaceut Sci; Marine Technol Soc; Sigma Xi. *Res:* Medicinal plant alkaloids and glycosides; study of active principles in medicinal plants, including the screening, isolation and characterization of these co nstituents which might possess certain pharmacological and clinical activities in treatment. *Mailing Add:* Col Pharm Ohio Northern Univ 525 S Main St Ada OH 45810-1555

AWAD, ATIF B, MEMBRANES, LIPIDS. *Current Pos:* ASSOC PROF NUTRIT & DIR, NUTRIT PROG, SCH HEALTH RELATED PROFESSIONALS, STATE UNIV NY, BUFFALO, 85-, ASSOC PROF BIOCHEM, SCH MED, 87- *Personal Data:* US citizen; m 74; c 4. *Educ:* Ain Shams Univ, Cairo, BS, 59, MS, 66; Rutgers Univ, PhD(nutrit), 74. *Prof Exp:* Fel biochem, Univ Iowa, 74-76; asst prof biochem, Kirksville Col Osteop Med, 76-80, assoc prof, 80-85. *Concurrent Pos:* Prin investr, Kirksville Col Osteop Med, NIH, 78-80, Am Osteop Asn, 81-83, USDA, 81-84; adj asst prof, Northeast Mo State Univ, 76-80, adj assoc prof, 80-85. *Mem:* Am Inst Nutrit; Am Diet Asn; Am Oil Chemists Soc; Am Soc Biol Chemists. *Res:* The effect of dietary fats on structure and function of mammalian cell membranes; the role of saturated fatty acids in the inhibition of hormone-stimulated lipolysis in adipose tissue; nutrition and cancer. *Mailing Add:* Nutrit Prog 301 Parker Hall State Univ NY 3435 Main St Buffalo NY 14214

AWAD, ELIAS M, EXPERT SYSTEMS, STRUCTURED SYSTEMS DESIGN. *Current Pos:* PROF INFO SYSTS, UNIV VA, 82- *Personal Data:* b Latakia, Syria, Oct 06, 34; US citizen; m 70; c 3. *Educ:* Geneva Col, BA, 56; Tulsa Univ, MBA, 58; Northwestern Univ MA, 66; Univ Ky, PhD(personnel info), 75. *Prof Exp:* Asst prof computer systs, Rochester Inst Tech, 60-65; asst prof info systs, DePaul Univ, 67-75; prof info systs, Ball State Univ, 75-77 & Fla Int Univ, 77-82. *Concurrent Pos:* Consult, Awad & Assoc Inc, 67-; personnel dir, First Nat Bank SMiami, 78-82, dir, 83-88; vis prof, Dartmouth Col, 86-87. *Mem:* Asn Comput Mach; Data Processing Mgt Asn. *Res:* Author of 19 textbooks on management information systems, system design and database design; published over 20 papers and presented over 50 papers in National Conferences on computer systems. *Mailing Add:* McIntire Sch Com Univ Va Charlottesville VA 22903

AWAD, ESSAM A, RHEUMATOLOGY & MUSCULOSKELTAL MEDICINE. *Current Pos:* prof & clin chief, Dept Phys Med & Rehab, 87-93, EMER PROF, PHYS MED & REHAB, UNIV MINN MED SCH, 93- *Personal Data:* b Cairo, Egypt, Mar 5, 32; m 65; c 4. *Educ:* Cairo Univ, MD, 57; Univ Minn, PhD(phys med rehab), 64. *Honors & Awards:* Gold Medal Award, Am Acad Phys Med & Rehab, 66. *Prof Exp:* Instr, 64, prof, 69-80, clin prof phys med & rehab, Univ Minn, Minneapolis, 80-87; from asst prof to assoc prof, Temple Univ, 65-67; lectr, Med Sch, Al-Azhar Univ, 67-68; med dir, phys med & rehab dept, United Hosp, St Paul, Minn, 80-86. *Concurrent Pos:* Private pract, Southgate Clinic, Bloomington, Minn. *Mem:* Am Cong Rehab Med; NY Acad Sci; Am Acad Phys Med; Am Asn Orthop Med. *Res:* Neuromuscular diseases; electromyography and nerve conduction studies; rheumatology. *Mailing Add:* 9912 Dellridge Rd Bloomington MN 55425. *Fax:* 612-881-4349; *E-Mail:* awadx001@maroon.tc.umn.edu

AWAD, WILLIAM MICHEL, JR, INTERNAL MEDICINE, HEMATOLOGY. *Current Pos:* from asst prof to assoc prof, 65-78, dir PhD-MD prog, 73-88, PROF MED, UNIV MIAMI, 78-, PROF BIOCHEM & MOLECULAR BIOL, 79- *Personal Data:* b Shanghai, China, Nov 5, 27; US citizen; m 57, 93, Josephine A Davis; c Lily & William III. *Educ:* Manhattan Col, BS, 50; State Univ NY, MD, 54; Univ Wash, PhD(biochem), 65. *Prof Exp:* Intern med, Kings County Hosp, Brooklyn, NY, 54-55; asst resident path, St Vincent's Hosp, Manhattan, 55-56; asst resident med, Bronx Munic Hosp Ctr, 56-57; fel med, Univ Minn Hosps, 57-58; fel cardiol, New York Hosp, 58-59; physician, NY Tel Co, 59-60; Damon Runyon fel, 60-63; Nat Cancer Inst fel, Univ Wash, 63-64. *Mem:* Am Soc Biol Chem; Am Asn Oncol Soc; Am Chem Soc; Biochem Soc; Am Soc Hemat. *Res:* Protein and peptide chemistry; biosynthesis of methyl containing metabolites; macrophage function. *Mailing Add:* Dept Med Univ Miami Sch Med R-123A PO Box 016960 Miami FL 33101. *Fax:* 305-243-4975

AWAPARA, JORGE, BIOCHEMISTRY. *Current Pos:* assoc prof biol, 57-62, PROF BIOCHEM, RICE UNIV, 62- *Personal Data:* b Arequipa, Peru, Dec 15, 18; nat US; m 61; c 1. *Educ:* Mich State Univ, BS, 41, MS, 42; Univ Southern Calif, PhD(biochem), 47. *Prof Exp:* Biochemist, Univ Tex M D Anderson Hosp & Tumor Inst, 48-57, assoc biochemist, 57-74. *Mem:* AAAS; Am Soc Biol Chemists. *Res:* Intermediary metabolism of amino acids; metabolism of amino acids in the brain; mechanism of enzymatic decarboxylation of amino acids in the brain; sulfur metabolism. *Mailing Add:* 3426 Deal St Houston TX 77025-3708

AWASTHI, YOGESH C, BIOLOGICAL CHEMISTRY. *Current Pos:* sr res assoc, 74-76, from asst prof to assoc prof, 76-84, PROF HUMAN GENETICS, UNIV TEX MED BR, GALVESTON, 84- *Personal Data:* b July 13, 39; Indian citizen; m 61; c 4. *Educ:* Univ Lucknow, India, BS, 57, MS, 59, PhD(chem), 67. *Prof Exp:* Jr res fel plant chem, 59-60, from sr sci asst to jr sci officer, 60-70, sr sci officer plant chem, Nat Bot Gardens, Lucknow, India, 70-76. *Concurrent Pos:* Fel biol sci, Purdue Univ, 68-70; res assoc hemat, City of Hope Nat Med Ctr, Duarte, Calif. *Mem:* Am Soc Biol Chemists; Am Soc Human Genetics; Biochem Soc London. *Res:* Biochemical genetics of Tay-Sach's disease and other lysosomal storage diseases; red cell metabolism with particular Glutathione metabolism and defense mechanisms against xenobiotics and oxidative stress; chemoprevention of cancer; protein chemistry and enzymology. *Mailing Add:* Dept Human Biol Chem & Genetics Univ Tex Med Br 7-138 Med Res Bldg Galveston TX 77555-1067. *Fax:* 409-772-6603

AWBREY, FRANK THOMAS, BIOLOGY. *Current Pos:* from asst prof to assoc prof, 64-79, PROF BIOL, SAN DIEGO STATE UNIV, 79- *Personal Data:* b Carlsbad, NMex, Oct 16, 32; m 56; c 3. *Educ:* Univ Calif, Riverside, AB, 60; Univ Tex, MA, 63, PhD(bioacoust), 65. *Concurrent Pos:* NSF res grant, 65-67 & 76-; sr res fel, Hubbs/SeaWorld Res Inst. *Mem:* AAAS; Soc Study Evolution; Am Soc Ichthyologists & Herpetologists; Sigma Xi; Acoust Soc Am; Soc Marine Mammal. *Res:* Biological significance of vocalization in amphibians and marine mammals; effects of noise on animals. *Mailing Add:* Dept Biol San Diego State Univ San Diego CA 92182-0057. *Fax:* 619-594-5676; *E-Mail:* fawbrey@sunstroke.sdsu.edu

AWRAMIK, STANLEY MICHAEL, PALEOBIOLOGY. *Current Pos:* from lectr to assoc prof, 80-85, PROF GEOL, UNIV CALIF, SANTA BARBARA, 85- *Personal Data:* b Lynn, Mass, Aug 11, 46; m 85, Jacqueline K Greenshields; c Jennifer. *Educ:* Boston Univ, AB, 68; Harvard Univ, PhD(geol), 73. *Prof Exp:* Res fel biol, Harvard Univ, 73-74. *Mem:* Fel AAAS; Sigma Xi; Soc Econ Paleontologists & Mineralogists; Paleont Soc; Int Soc Study Origin of Life. *Res:* Precambrian microbial evolution; role of cyanobacteria in sedimentary constructions; Phanerozoic algal-invertebrate interactions; early earth history; stromatolites. *Mailing Add:* Dept Geol Sci Univ Calif 552 University Ave Santa Barbara CA 93106-0001. *Fax:* 805-893-2314

AXE, JOHN DONALD, CHEMICAL PHYSICS. *Current Pos:* MEM RES STAFF, BROOKHAVEN NAT LAB, 69-, ASSOC DIR, 90- *Personal Data:* b Denver, Colo, Sept 6, 33; m 63. *Educ:* Univ Denver, BS, 55; Univ Calif, Berkeley, PhD(chem), 60. *Honors & Awards:* Warren Award, Am Crystallog Soc, 73. *Prof Exp:* NSF res fel, Dept Physics, Johns Hopkins Univ, 61-62; mem res staff, Thomas J Watson Res Ctr, Int Bus Mach Corp, 62-69. *Mem:* Fel Am Phys Soc. *Res:* Neutron spectroscopy; lattice dynamics; structural phase transformations in solids; x-ray scattering; surface structure. *Mailing Add:* Brookhaven Nat Lab Bldg 510A Upton NY 11973-5000

AXEL, LEON, RADIOLOGY, MEDICAL PHYSICS. *Current Pos:* From asst prof to assoc prof, 81-90, PROF RADIOL, UNIV PA, 90- *Personal Data:* b Lakewood, NJ, Nov 1, 47; c 1. *Educ:* Syracuse Univ, BS, 67; Princeton Univ, PhD(astrophys), 71; Univ Calif, San Francisco, MD, 76. *Concurrent Pos:* Vis prof, Stanford Univ, 88; acad vis, Imperial Col, 95. *Mem:* Radiol Soc N Am; Soc Magnetic Resonance in Med; Soc Magnetic Resonance Imaging; Am Asn Physicists Med; Asn Univ Radiologists; Am Col Radiol. *Res:* Magnetic resonance imaging, particularly for the study of blood flow and the heart. *Mailing Add:* Dept Radiol Univ Pa Hosp 3400 Spruce St Philadelphia PA 19104-4219

AXEL, RICHARD, MOLECULAR BIOLOGY. *Current Pos:* resident, Dept Path, Col Physicians & Surgeons, Columbia Univ, 70-71, fel, Inst Cancer Res, 71-72, asst prof, Dept Path, 74-78, prof, Dept Path & Biochem, 78-83, actg dir, Inst Cancer Res, 83-85, HIGGINS PROF BIOCHEM & MOLECULAR BIOL, COLUMBIA UNIV, 83-, PROF PATH, 83-; INVESTR, HOWARD HUGHES MED INST, 84- *Personal Data:* b Brooklyn, NY, July 2, 46; m 75. *Educ:* Columbia Univ, AB, 67; Johns Hopkins Sch Med, MD, 70. *Honors & Awards:* Alan T Waterman Award, 82; Eli Lilly Award, 83; Harvey lectr, Rockefeller Univ, 83; NY Acad Sci Award Biol & Med Sci, 84; Chipperfield lectr, Mass Inst Technol 86; Chiron lectr, Univ Calif, Berkeley, 87; Richard Lounsbery Award, Nat Acad Sci, 89. *Prof Exp:* Res assoc, NIH, 72-74. *Concurrent Pos:* Vis fel, Dept Path, Columbia Univ, 71-72; asst ed, Cell, 76-, Neuron, 87; young scientist award, Passano Found, 79; sci adv bd, Israel Cancer Res Fund, 84, Cancer Res Inst, 86- *Mem:* Nat Acad Sci; Am Acad Arts & Sci. *Res:* Control of gene expression in normal and transformed cells; published numerous articles in various journals. *Mailing Add:* Howard Hughes Med Inst Columbia Univ 701 W 168th St New York NY 10032

AXELRAD, ARTHUR AARON, HEMATOLOGY & IMMUNOLOGY, CELL BIOLOGY. *Current Pos:* asst prof anat & histol, 56-57, assoc prof med biophys, 57-66, head, Div Histol, 66-85, PROF ANAT, UNIV TORONTO, 66-; HON STAFF, DEPT MED, MT SINAI HOSP, TORONTO, 81- *Personal Data:* b Montreal, Que, Dec 30, 23; m 60; c 3. *Educ:* McGill Univ, BSc, 45, MD & CM, 49, PhD(anat), 54. *Honors & Awards:* Thomas W Eadie Medal, Royal Soc Can, 88. *Prof Exp:* Demonstr zool, McGill Univ, 43-44, comp anat, 44-45, med histol, 46 & exp morphol, 52-54. *Concurrent Pos:* Nat Cancer Inst Can fel, 50-57 & Inst Cell Res & Genetics, Karolinska Inst, Sweden, 54-56; scientist & head, Subdiv Immunogenetics & Cytol, Ont Cancer Inst, Toronto, 57-68; mem, Inst Med Sci, Univ Toronto, 67-; mem, res adv group, Nat Cancer Inst Can, 68-74; Chercheur assoc, Nat Ctr Sci Res, Inst Pasteur, 76-77; Michael Sela fel, Weizmann Inst Sci, Israel, 77. *Mem:* Asn Cancer Res; Can Soc Cell Biol; Int Soc Exp Hemat; Am Soc Hemat; Can Asn Anatomists; fel Royal Soc Can. *Res:* Leukemia, genetics and virology; gene control of hemopoietic stem and progenitor cell proliferation and differentiation. *Mailing Add:* Dept Anat & Cell Biol Med Sci Bldg Univ Toronto Toronto ON M5S 1A8 Can

AXELRAD, D(AVID) R(OBERT), MICROMECHANICS, RHEOLOGY. *Current Pos:* prof, 64-70, Thomas Workman prof, 70-89, EMER PROF MECH ENG, MCGILL UNIV, 89- *Personal Data:* b Vienna, Austria, Apr 24, 10; Brit citizen; m 47; c 1. *Educ:* Vienna Tech Univ, Dipl Ing, 36, DEngSc, 63; Univ Sydney, MEngSc, 59. *Prof Exp:* Sr lectr mech eng, Univ Sydney, 54-64. *Concurrent Pos:* Alexander von Humboldt fel, Inst Theoret Physics, Aachen, Ger, 63; vis prof, Univ Ill, Urbana, 64; mem, Can Nat Comt, Int Union Theoret & Appl Mech, 66-70. *Mem:* Am Soc Mech Engrs; Brit Inst Mech Engrs; Soc Rheology; Soc Eng Sci; NY Acad Sci. *Res:* Response behavior of solid matter to external fields; theoretical analysis; random theory of deformation of solids; thermodynamic aspects; experimental work concerned with stress holographic interferometry; x-ray holography. *Mailing Add:* 239 Kensington No 905 Montreal PQ H3Z 2H1 Can

AXELRAD, GEORGE, ORGANIC CHEMISTRY. *Current Pos:* from asst prof to assoc prof, 61-81, chmn dept, 80-94, PROF CHEM, QUEENS COL, 81- *Personal Data:* b Trutnov, Czech, Oct 3, 29; US citizen; m 62, Beate Artmann; c Penina & Joy. *Educ:* City Col New York, BS, 54; Univ Kans, PhD(org chem), 60. *Prof Exp:* Fel chem, Ohio State Univ, 60-61. *Mem:* Am Chem Soc; Royal Soc Chem; NY Acad Sci. *Res:* Synthetic organic chemistry; reaction mechanisms. *Mailing Add:* Dept Chem & Biochem Queens Col Flushing NY 11367. *E-Mail:* axelrad@qcvaxa.acc.qc.edu

AXELROD, ARNOLD RAYMOND, HEMATOLOGY. *Current Pos:* instr clin med, 49-51, asst prof med, 51-53, from asst prof to assoc prof clin med, 53-70, PROF MED, COL MED, WAYNE STATE UNIV, 70-, CHMN DEPT MED, SINAI HOSP, 74- *Personal Data:* b Cleveland, Ohio, Jan 1, 21; m 43; c 3. *Educ:* Ohio Univ, AB, 41; Wayne Univ, MD, 44; Am Bd Internal Med, dipl, 51. *Prof Exp:* Intern, Billings Hosp, Chicago, 44-45; first asst resident med, Detroit Receiving Hosp, 48-49. *Concurrent Pos:* Teaching fel hemat, Col Med, Wayne Univ, 45-48. *Mem:* Am Fedn Clin Res; Cent Soc Clin Res; fel Am Col Physicians (gov, 82); Int Soc Hemat; Am Soc Hemat. *Mailing Add:* Dept Med Harper Hosp 3990 John R St Detroit MI 48201-2018

AXELROD, BERNARD, BIOCHEMISTRY. *Current Pos:* from assoc prof to prof biochem, 54-84, head dept, 65-75, EMER PROF BIOCHEM, PURDUE UNIV, WEST LAFAYETTE, 84- *Personal Data:* b New York, NY, Oct 16, 14; m 34, Sara Feingersh; c Eugene & Judith A (Weitzman). *Educ:* Wayne Univ, BS, 35; George Washington Univ, MS, 39; Georgetown Univ, PhD(biochem), 43. *Hon Degrees:* PhD(sci), Purdue Univ, 89. *Prof Exp:* Chemist, USDA, Washington, DC, 38-43 & Calif, 43-50, chief enzyme sect, Western Regional Res Lab, Bur Agr & Indust Chem, 52-54. *Concurrent Pos:* Sr res fel, Calif Inst Technol, 50-52; NSF sr fel, Carlsberg Lab, Copenhagen, 60-61; NSF sr res fel, Univ Calif, Santa Cruz, 70-71; adj prof biochem, Sch Med, Indiana Univ, 71. *Mem:* Am Chem Soc; Am Soc Biochem & Molecular Biol; Am Soc Plant Physiol. *Res:* Enzymology; molecular biology; plant biochemistry; lipoxygenase. *Mailing Add:* Dept Biochem Purdue Univ West Lafayette IN 47907. *Fax:* 765-494-7897

AXELROD, DANIEL, BIOPHYSICS, PHYSICS. *Current Pos:* asst prof & asst res scientist, 77-81, assoc prof & assoc res scientist, 81-87, PROF & RES SCIENTIST, DEPT PHYSICS & BIOPHYS RES DIV, UNIV MICH, 87- *Personal Data:* b Brooklyn, NY, Mar 15, 48. *Educ:* Brooklyn Col, BS, 68; Univ Calif, Berkeley, PhD(physics), 74. *Prof Exp:* NIH fel biophys, Cornell Univ, 74-77. *Mem:* Biophys Soc. *Res:* Biophysics of membranes and cell surfaces; development of nerve/muscle synapses; fluorescence spectroscopy. *Mailing Add:* Biophys Res Div Univ Mich 930 N University St Ann Arbor MI 48109-1055

AXELROD, DANIEL ISAAC, PALEOBOTANY. *Current Pos:* PROF BOT, UNIV CALIF, DAVIS, 68- *Personal Data:* b Brooklyn, NY, July 16, 10; m 85, Marilyn Gayles; c 1. *Educ:* Univ Calif, AB, 33, MA, 36, PhD(paleobot), 38. *Honors & Awards:* Fel Medal Cal Acad Sci, 81, Int Medal, Palaeobot Soc, 85; Sir Albert Charles Seward Mem Lectr, India, 86; Paleont Soc Medal, 90. *Prof Exp:* Technician, Calif Forest & Range Exp Sta, 34, jr forester, 36; Nat Res fel, US Nat Mus, 39-41; asst cur, Carnegie Inst, 41-42 & 46; from asst prof to prof geol, Univ Calif, Los Angeles, 46-68. *Concurrent Pos:* John Simon Guggenheim fel, 52-53. *Mem:* Fel Geol Soc Am; Paleont Soc; Soc Study Evolution; AAAS; fel Am Acad Arts & Sci. *Res:* Tertiary paleobotany; evolution of vegetation; paleoecology; paleoclimate; plate tectonics and angiosperm evolution; evolution of Madrean-Tethyan Sclerophyll vegetation; biogeography. *Mailing Add:* Dept Botany Univ Calif Davis CA 95616

AXELROD, DAVID, health administration; deceased, see previous edition for last biography

AXELROD, DAVID E, CELL & MOLECULAR BIOLOGY, CANCER CELLS. *Current Pos:* asst prof, 70-75, ASSOC PROF BIOL, RUTGERS UNIV, 76- *Personal Data:* b Chicago, Ill, Aug 25, 40; m 72, Helena Rettig; c Daniel C. *Educ:* Univ Chicago, BS, 62; Univ Tenn, PhD(radiation biol), 67. *Prof Exp:* Nat Cancer Inst fel develop biol & cancer, Albert Einstein Col Med, 68-70. *Concurrent Pos:* Res biologist, Nat Heart & Ling Inst, NIH, 76 & 77; prin investr, NJ Cancer Comt Res Grant, 84-88, Nat Cancer Inst, 86-90, Coun Tobacco Res, 90-92 & Peterson Trust, 93-94; prin investr, USPHS Res Grant, Rutgers Univ, 86-89, NSF Res Grant, 75-77, 78-80 & 80-83; prin investr, NJ Cancer Comt Res Group, 94-96 & 96-97. *Mem:* Am Soc Cell Biol; Am Soc Microbiol; Genetics Soc Am; Am Asn Cancer Res. *Res:* Molecular cell genetics, oncogenes and anti-oncogenes; cell cycle, genome dynamics; breast cancer; image cytometry. *Mailing Add:* Waksman Inst Rutgers Univ PO Box 759 Piscataway NJ 08855-0759. *Fax:* 723-445-5735; *E-Mail:* axelrod@mbcl.rutgers.edu

AXELROD, JULIUS, BIOCHEMICAL PHARMACOLOGY. *Current Pos:* biochemist, Nat Heart Inst, 49-55, chief, Sect Pharmacol, Lab Clin Sci, 55-84, guest worker, 84-96, EMER GUEST WORKER, LAB CELL BIOL, NIMH, 96- *Personal Data:* b New York, NY, May 30, 12; m 38; c 2. *Educ:* City Col New York, BS, 33; NY Univ, MS, 41; George Washington Univ, PhD(chem pharmacol), 55. *Hon Degrees:* DSc, Univ Chicago, 66, NY Univ & Med Col Wis, 71; LLD, George Washington Univ, 71, City Col New York, 72 & Med Col Pa, 74; Dr, Univ Panama, 72, Tel Aviv Univ, 86, Ripon Col, 84. *Honors & Awards:* Nobel Prize in Med Physiol, 70; Otto Loewi Mem Lectr, Med Sch, NY Univ, 64; Gardner Award, 67; Albert Einstein Award, Yeshiva Univ, 71; Parkinson Lectr, Columbia Univ, 71; Hodge Lectr, Rochester Univ, 71. *Prof Exp:* Chemist, Lab Indust Hyg, Inc, NY, 35-45; res assoc, Res Div, Goldwater Mem Hosp, Welfare Island, NY Univ, 45-49. *Concurrent Pos:* Lectr, NIH, 67; Claude Bernard prof, Univ Montreal, 69. *Mem:* Sr mem Inst Med-Nat Acad Sci; AAAS; fel Am Acad Arts & Sci; hon mem Am Psychophysiol Asn; Am Soc Pharmacol & Exp Therapeut; foreign mem Royal Soc; foreign mem Ger Acad Sci; Int Brain Res Orgn. *Res:* Biochemical mechanisms of drug and hormone action; drug and hormone metabolism; enzymology. *Mailing Add:* 10401 Grosvenor Pl Rockville MD 20852

AXELROD, LLOYD, ENDOCRINOLOGY, METABOLISM. *Current Pos:* from instr to asst prof med, 73-83, ASSOC PROF MED, HARVARD MED SCH, 83-; CHIEF, JAMES HOWARD MEANS FIRM, MASS GEN HOSP, 89- *Personal Data:* b Brooklyn, NY, July 29, 42; div; c 1. *Educ:* Princeton Univ, AB, 63; Harvard Med Sch, MD, 67. *Prof Exp:* Intern med, Peter Bent Brigham Hosp, 67-68, jr resident, 68-69, res fel, 69-70, asst med, 70-72; resident, Mass Gen Hosp, 70-71, clin & res fel, 71-72, chief resident, 73. *Concurrent Pos:* Res fel med, Harvard Med Sch, 71-72; Daland fel, Am Philos Soc, 74-77; asst med, Mass Gen Hosp, 74-78, asst physician, 78-80, assoc physician, 81-89, physician, 89-; mem, US Med Deleg to People's Repub China, 75; chief md unit, Mass Eye & Ear Infirmary, 77-85. *Mem:* Am Diabetes Asn; Am Fedn Clin Res; NY Acad Sci; AAAS; Endocrine Soc; fel Am Col Physicians. *Res:* Role of prostaglandins in the regulation of lipolysis and ketogenesis; prostaglandin production by adipose tissue in vitro and in vivo; role of prostaglandins in the pathogenesis of diabetic microvascular disease and diabetic ketoacidosis; role of Omega-3 fatty acids in patients with diabetes mellitus. *Mailing Add:* Mass Gen Hosp Boston MA 02114

AXELROD, NORMAN NATHAN, OPTICS & OPTICAL SENSING, VISION SYSTEMS. *Current Pos:* PRES, NORMAN N AXELROD ASSOC, 72- *Personal Data:* b New York, NY, Aug 26, 34; m 75; c 2. *Educ:* Cornell Univ, AB, 54; Univ Rochester, PhD(physics, optics), 60. *Prof Exp:* Aerospace scientist, Goddard Space Flight Ctr, NASA, 59-60; res fel, Univ London, 60-61; asst prof physics, Univ Del, 61-65; mem tech staff, Bell Tel Labs, 65-72. *Concurrent Pos:* Univ res found grant, Univ Del, 63-64, Off Naval Res grant, 64-65; dir, World Resources Develop Co, 71-; consult, Gen Elec, 73-, Recognition Equip Inc, 74-, Timex, 74-, Konishiroku, 76-, Picker, 77-, Wall St J, 78-, Timken Res, 78-, Polychrome, 79-, ITT, 80-, Thatcher Glass, 80-, Am Cyanamid Co, 81-, Torrington, 81, Perkin-Elmer, 82, Comput Scan, 82, IBM, 83, Becton-Dickenson, 83, Firestone, 84, RCA, 84, Johnson & Johnson, 85, Emhart, 85, Gen Foods, 86, Celanese, 87-, Medtronic, 88-, Conrail, 89, Bausch & Lomb, 89-, Wesley-Jesson Universal Instrument, 91, Iomega, 91, Labatt, 92, Color PLC, 92 & Lear Siegler, 93. *Mem:* Inst Elec & Electronics Engrs; fel AAAS; NY Acad Sci; Am Phys Soc; Optical Soc Am. *Res:* Optical-electronic and laser measurement, control, and display systems and techniques; dynamic materials characterization; Pattern recognition; non-contact defect detection, metrology, and alignment; applications to industrial, consumer and professional products. *Mailing Add:* 445 E 86th St New York NY 10028

AXELROD, STEVE, SENSOR DEVELOPMENT. *Current Pos:* from sr physicist to sr staff physicist, 85-96, PRIN PHYSICIST & HEAD, ISD MEASUREMENT SYSTS DEPT, HONEYWELL-MEASUREX, 96- *Personal Data:* b Astoria, NY, Feb 18, 54; m 89, Kimberly A Larson; c Haley D & Lindsay A. *Educ:* Univ Conn, BSc, 76; Yale Univ, PhD(physics), 85. *Prof Exp:* Res assoc, Stanford Univ, 85-88. *Mem:* Am Phys Soc. *Res:* Applied research and development of sensors and scanners used in sheet process industries. *Mailing Add:* 106 Lockhart Lane Los Altos CA 94022. *E-Mail:* axelrod_s@measurex.com

AXELSON, JOHN F, NEUROANATOMY, HORMONES & BEHAVIOR. *Current Pos:* Asst prof, 82-83, ASSOC PROF PSYCHOL, HOLY CROSS COL, 83- *Personal Data:* m 92, Mary Beth Keating. *Educ:* Pac Lutheran Univ, BA, 75; Tulane Univ, MS, 78, PhD(psychol), 80. *Prof Exp:* Fel, Emory Sch Med, 80-82. *Concurrent Pos:* Res physiologist, Vet Admin Med Ctr, Boston, 83-85; vis scientist, Neth Inst Brain Res, 88-89; adj fac, Med-Physiol Dept, Univ Mass, 86- *Res:* Biological basis of behavior focusing on hormonal control of behavior; sexual differentiation of brain and behavior. *Mailing Add:* Psychol Dept Holy Cross Col PO Box 155A 1 College St Worcester MA 01610

AXELSON, MARTA LYNNE, FOOD RELATED BEHAVIOR. *Personal Data:* b Lewiston, Idaho, March 5, 53; m 87, David Brinberg; c Isaac & Miriam. *Educ:* Fla State Univ, BS, 75; Univ Tenn, Knoxville, PhD(food sci), 79; State Univ NY, Albany, MS, 91. *Prof Exp:* Res asst, Univ Tenn, Knoxville, 75-79; fac intern, Univ Md, College Park, 81, assoc prof food sci, 79-87; researcher, State Univ NY, 88-91; assoc ed, J Nutrit Educ, 94-95. *Mem:* Inst Food Technologists. *Res:* Food related behavior of elderly people living independently, incidence and duration of breast feeding among women, food classification systems, dietary fiber intake and measurement issues of nutrition knowledge. *Mailing Add:* 2321 Woodland Hills Dr Blacksburg VA 24060

AXEN, DAVID, NUCLEAR PHYSICS. *Current Pos:* Nat Res Coun Can-NATO res fel physics, 65-68, asst prof, 68-74, ASSOC PROF PHYSICS, UNIV BC, 74- *Personal Data:* b Brackendale, BC, Aug 6, 38; m 65. *Educ:* Univ BC, BASc, 60, PhD(physics), 65. *Res:* A polarized helium-3 ion source. *Mailing Add:* Dept Physics Univ BC Hennings Bldg 6224 Agricultural Rd Vancouver BC V6T 1Z1 Can

AXEN, KENNETH, PULMONARY PHYSIOLOGY. *Current Pos:* Asst prof, 79-85, ASSOC PROF PHYSIOL, INST REHAB MED, NEW YORK UNIV, 85- *Personal Data:* b New York, NY, Mar 23, 43. *Educ:* New York Univ, PhD(biomed eng), 72. *Mailing Add:* New York Univ Med Ctr Inst Rehab Med 400 E 34th St New York NY 10016-4901

AXEN, UDO FRIEDRICH, ORGANIC CHEMISTRY. *Current Pos:* head res to res mgr, Upjohn Co, 74-81, group mgr, 81-83, dir, 83-85, SCIENTIST, UPJOHN CO, 66-, VPRES, RES & DEVELOP, JAPAN, 85- *Personal Data:* b Siegburg, Ger, Sept 10, 35; m 62; c 2. *Educ:* Univ Bonn, Dipl Chem, 61, Dr rer nat(org chem), 63. *Prof Exp:* Res assoc org chem, Mass Inst Technol, 64-66. *Mem:* Am Chem Soc. *Res:* Structure elucidation of natural products; saponines; macrolides; prostaglandin synthesis. *Mailing Add:* 2207 Aberdeen Kalamazoo MI 49008-1729

AXENROD, THEODORE, ORGANIC CHEMISTRY. *Current Pos:* from asst prof to assoc prof, 61-72, PROF CHEM & CHMN DEPT, CITY UNIV NEW YORK, 72- *Personal Data:* b New York, NY, Aug 27, 35; m 61; c 1. *Educ:* NY Univ, BA, 56, PhD(chem), 61. *Prof Exp:* Res fel, Univ Wis, 60-61. *Mem:* Am Chem Soc; Brit Chem Soc. *Mailing Add:* Dept Chem City Univ NY 138th St & Convent Ave New York NY 10031-9198

AXFORD, ROY ARTHUR, NUCLEAR ENGINEERING, THEORETICAL PHYSICS. *Current Pos:* assoc prof, 66-68, PROF NUCLEAR ENG, UNIV ILL, URBANA-CHAMPAIGN, 68- *Personal Data:* b Detroit, Mich, Aug 26, 28; m 54; c 3. *Educ:* Williams Col, BA, 52; Mass Inst Technol, SB, 52, SM, 55, ScD(nuclear eng), 58. *Prof Exp:* Supvr theoret physics group, Atomics Int Div, NAm Aviation, Inc, 58-60; assoc prof, Tex A&M Univ, 60-62, prof, 62-63; assoc prof, Northwestern Univ, 63-66. *Concurrent Pos:* Consult, United Nuclear Corp, 63, Los Alamos Sci Lab, 63- & Argonne Nat Lab, 64-66. *Mem:* Am Nuclear Soc; Am Soc Mech Engrs; Am Inst Aeronaut & Astronaut. *Res:* Theoretical reactor physics; transport theory; reactor heat transfer; thermoelasticity; nuclear reactor design; plasma physics. *Mailing Add:* 2017 S Cottage Grove Ave Urbana IL 61801

AXLER, DAVID ALLAN, VIROLOGY. *Current Pos:* assoc prof microbiol, 75-79, PROF & CHMN, DEPT MICROBIOL, IMMUNOL & PATH, PA COL PODIATRIC MED, 79-, VPRES RES & DEAN FOR EDUC AFFAIRS, 84- *Personal Data:* b Philadelphia, Pa, Feb 6, 42; m 65; c 1. *Educ:* Pa State Univ, BS, 63; Hahnemann Med Col, MS, 66, PhD(virol), 69. *Prof Exp:* Asst prof vet path, Ohio State Univ, 70-73; prin virologist, Battelle Mem Inst, 73-75. *Mem:* AAAS; Am Soc Microbiol; Tissue Cult Asn; Sigma Xi. *Res:* Mechanism of carcinogenesis induced by viruses and development of methods for extraction and in vitro assay in tumor specific transplantation antigens; in vitro and in vivo assays of antifungal agents; susceptibility to infection in the diabetic. *Mailing Add:* 716 Suffolk Rd Jenkintown PA 19046

AXLEY, JOHN HAROLD, SOILS. *Current Pos:* RETIRED. *Personal Data:* b Butternut, Wis, June 2, 15; m 38, Nita Lyans; c John Jr, Thomas & James. *Educ:* Univ Wis, BA, 37, PhD(soil chem), 45. *Prof Exp:* Mem staff, Riverside Exp Sta, Univ Calif, 46; agronomist, Zeloski Potato Farm, 47; assoc prof soils, Univ Md, College Park, 48-68, prof agron, 68-85. *Concurrent Pos:* Chmn phosphorus & lime work group, Regional Soil Nitrogen Proj & mem soil test work group, Northeast Soil Res Comt; emer fac, Univ Md, 88- *Mem:* Am Soc Agron; Soil Sci Soc Am; Potato Asn Am; Sigma Xi. *Res:* Response of Maryland tobacco to liming; clay separation and identification by a density gradient method; chemistry and phytotoxicity of arsenic in soils--arsenic soil test correlation; technique for determining phototoxicity of water extracts of plants; nitrogen removal from sewage waters by soils and plants. *Mailing Add:* 2184 Cedar Rd PO Box 184 Port Republic MD 20676

AXSMITH, BRIAN J, BOTANY. *Current Pos:* PROF, PLANT BIOL DEPT, OHIO STATE UNIV. *Honors & Awards:* Isabel C Cookson Paleobot Award, Bot Soc Am, 93. *Mailing Add:* Dept Plant Biol Ohio State Univ 1735 Nell Ave Columbus OH 43210

AXTELL, DARRELL DEAN, INORGANIC CHEMISTRY, CHEMICAL EDUCATION. *Current Pos:* AT UNITED WORLD COL,. *Personal Data:* b Grants Pass, Ore, July 27, 44; m 69; c 1. *Educ:* Linfield Col, BA, 67; Ore State Univ, PhD(chem), 73. *Prof Exp:* Fel chem, Univ Ariz, 73-74; fel & lectr chem, Tex A&M Univ, 75-77; asst prof chem, Eastern Mont Col, 77- *Mem:* Am Chem Soc; Am Asn Univ Professors; Sigma Xi. *Res:* Inorganic coordination chemistry; chemical education; self-paced instruction; microforms. *Mailing Add:* Dept Chem St Martins Col Lacey WA 98503

AXTELL, JOHN DAVID, PLANT BREEDING. *Current Pos:* from asst prof to prof, 67-82, LYNN DISTINGUISHED PROF AGRON, PURDUE UNIV, 82- *Personal Data:* b Minneapolis, Minn, Feb 5, 34; m 57; c 3. *Educ:* Univ Minn, BS, 57, MS, 65; Univ Wis, PhD(genetics), 67. *Honors & Awards:* Crop Sci Award, Crop Sci Soc Am, 77; Alexander von Humboldt award, 76. *Prof Exp:* Res asst genetics, Univ Wis, 59-65, res assoc, 67. *Concurrent Pos:* Proj leader, USAID res grants, 72-79, 79- & 82; sci liaison officer, USAID & Int Crops Res Inst Semi-Arid Tropics, Hyderabad, India, 84-86; chmn, Agr Sci Sect, Nat Acad Sci, 87-90; mem, Expert Panel USAID Biotechnol Res, Nat Acad Sci, 90, Sci Coun Plant Gene Expression Ctr, 90 & Comt Plant Sci, 90. *Mem:* Nat Acad Sci; Genetics Soc Am; Am Soc Agron; Am Genetic Asn; Crop Sci Soc Am; AAAS. *Res:* Controlling elements in maize; paramutation in maize; chemical paramutagenesis; mutagenesis in higher plants; regulation of gene action in higher plants; plant genetics and breeding; genetic improvement of protein quality in cereals. *Mailing Add:* Dept Agron Rm 2-318 Purdue Univ 1150 Lilly Hall Sci Bldg West Lafayette IN 47907-1150

AXTELL, RALPH WILLIAM, VERTEBRATE ZOOLOGY. *Current Pos:* asst prof zool, Southern Ill Univ, Edwardsville, 60-65, assoc prof biol, 65-70, chmn fac biol sci, 65-67, PROF BIOL, SOUTHERN ILL UNIV, EDWARDSVILLE, 70- *Personal Data:* b Norfolk, Nebr, Apr 20, 28; m 67; c 1. *Educ:* Univ Tex, BA, 53, MA, 54, PhD, 58. *Honors & Awards:* Student Paper Award, Am Soc Ichthyol & Herpet, 57. *Prof Exp:* Res sci zool, Univ Tex, 55-57; instr biol, ETex State Col, 57-58; asst prof, Sul Ross State Col, 58-60. *Concurrent Pos:* Herpet ed, Copeia, Am Soc Ichthyologists & Herpetologists, 68- *Mem:* Fel AAAS; Am Soc Ichthyologists & Herpetologists; Soc Study Evolution; Soc Syst Zool; Am Inst Biol Sci. *Res:* North American herpetology and zoogeography; lizard genus Holbrookia; lizard family Iguanidae; reptilian evolution. *Mailing Add:* Dept Biol Sci Southern Ill Univ 60 Hairpin Dr Edwardsville IL 62026-0001

AXTELL, RICHARD CHARLES, MEDICAL ENTOMOLOGY. *Current Pos:* from asst prof to assoc prof, 62-68, PROF ENTOM, NC STATE UNIV, 68- *Personal Data:* b Medina, NY, Aug 4, 32; m 61; c 2. *Educ:* State Univ NY Albany, BS, 54, MS, 55; Cornell Univ, PhD(entom), 62. *Prof Exp:* Vis instr zool, Col Agr, Univ Philippines, 55-56. *Concurrent Pos:* Consult, Nat Develop Co, Philippines, 55-56; prin investr, USPHS Grant, 63-70; dir, NIH med entom training grant, 66-73; Sigma Xi res award, NC State Univ, 69; Off Naval Res contract, 70-75; dir dept com, Nat Oceanic & Atmospheric Admin sea grant proj, 70-76; prin investr, NIH grant, 83- *Mem:* AAAS; Entom Soc Am; Am Mosquito Control Asn (vpres, 80, pres, 82); Acarological Soc Am. *Res:* Medical and veterinary entomology; biology and control of Diptera; mosquito control; arthropod sensory structures and behavior; biological control; poultry pest management. *Mailing Add:* Dept Entom NC State Univ Raleigh NC 27695-7613. *Fax:* 919-515-7746

AXTHELM, DEON D, WATER MANAGEMENT. *Current Pos:* asst prof irrig, coop Exten SErv, 56-65, from assoc prof to prof, 66-80, EMER PROF AGR ENG & WATER RESOURCES, UNIV NEBR, LINCOLN, 80-; WATER CONSULT, 80- *Personal Data:* b Hallam, Nebr, Mar 6, 20; c 3. *Educ:* Univ Nebr, BS, 41, BS, 48, MA, 65. *Prof Exp:* Agr exten asst, Coop Exten Serv, Clay County, Nebr, 48-49; self employed, 50-55. *Concurrent Pos:* Mem water develop comt, Great Plains Coun, 68-, mem feedlot pollution res comt, 69-71; consult, Com Water Measurement Mfg Firms, Demonstration & Sales. *Mem:* Am Soc Agr Engrs. *Res:* Groundwater management and related administrative-political systems. *Mailing Add:* 3731 S Glenstone No 1L Springfield MO 65804

AXTMANN, ROBERT CLARK, APPLIED PHYSICS, CHEMICAL ENGINEERING. *Current Pos:* assoc prof chem eng, Princeton Univ, 59-65, chmn, prog nuclear studies, 60-68, chmn coun environ studies, 70-73, PROF CHEM ENG, PRINCETON UNIV, 65- *Personal Data:* b Youngstown, Ohio, Feb 25, 25; m 49; c 3. *Educ:* Oberlin Col, AB, 47; Johns Hopkins Univ, PhD(phys chem), 50. *Prof Exp:* Instr org chem, Johns Hopkins Univ, 48-49; res physicist, Ballistic Res Lab, Aberdeen Proving Ground, Md, 50; res physicist, E I du Pont de Nemours & Co, 50-53, res supvr reactor physics, 53-54, area tech supvr reactor physics & eng, 55-56, sr res supvr chem physics, 57-59. *Concurrent Pos:* Vis fel, Israel AEC, 64 & Nat Comn Nuclear Energy, Mex, 69; mem, NJ Comn Radiation Protection, 66-70; mem vis comt, Brookhaven Nat Lab, 68-71; vis scientist, Dept Sci & Indust Res, Govt NZ, 74 & 79-80 & Inst Invests Elec, Mex, 84-85; mem, Rev Comt, Argonne Nat Lab, 75-79; mem Adv Comt Geothermal Energy, US Dept Energy, 76-80 & Adv Comt Reactor Safeguards, US Nuclear Regulatory Comn, 81-85. *Mem:* AAAS; Am Phys Soc; Am Chem Soc; Am Inst Chem Eng. *Res:* Nuclear fusion technology; geothermal energy; radiation chemistry; nuclear reactor physics; Mossbauer effect; nuclear magnetic resonance; environmental effects of geothermal power; desilication of geothermal fluids. *Mailing Add:* 346 Burnt Hill Rd Skillman NJ 08558-9408

AYALA, FRANCISCO JOSE, GENETICS, EVOLUTION. *Current Pos:* assoc prof, Univ Calif, Davis, 71-74, prof genetics, 74-87, dir, Inst Ecol, 77-81, distinguished prof biol sci, 87-89, DONALD BREN PROF BIOL SCI, UNIV CALIF, IRVINE, 89- *Personal Data:* b Madrid, Spain, Mar 12, 34; m 85, Hana Lostakova; c Francisco J & Carlos A. *Educ:* Univ Madrid, BS, 55; Lit Univ Salamanca, STL, 60; Columbia Univ, MA, 63, PhD(genetics), 64. *Hon Degrees:* Dr, Univ Leon, 82, Univ Madrid, 86 & Univ Barcelona, 86, Univ Athens, 91, Univ Vigo, Spain, 96. *Honors & Awards:* Medal, Col France, 79; W E Key Award, Am Gen Asn, 85; Sci Freedom & Responsibility Award, Amer Asn Adv Sci, 87. *Prof Exp:* Res assoc genetics, Rockefeller Inst, 64-65; prof biol, Providence Col, 65-67; asst prof, Rockefeller Univ, 67-71. *Concurrent Pos:* Guggenheim fel, 77-78; assoc ed, Molecular Evolution & Paleobiol; mem, Nat Adv Coun, Nat Inst Gen Med Sci; mem exec comt, Sci Adv Bd, Environ Protection Agency; Fulbright fel, 79 & 81; assoc ed, Biol & Philos; chmn, Sect Pop Biol, Evolution & Ecol, Nat Acad Sci, 83-86; mem, Comn Life Sci, Nat Res Coun, 84-91, chmn, Bd Basic Biol, 85-91; coun, Nat Acad Sci, 86-89; bd dir, AAAS, 89-93, chmn, 95; mem, Adv Comm Ed Hum Res, Nat Sci Found, 89-92. *Mem:* Nat Acad Sci; Am Acad Arts & Sci; AAAS (pres-elect, 93, pres, 94); Genetics Soc Am; Soc Study Evolution (vpres, 72, pres, 79-80); Am Philos Soc; hon mem Fedn Yugoslavian Genetics Socs; hon mem Genetics Soc Spain; foreign mem Royal Acad Sci Spain; foreign mem Rus Acad Natural Sci; foreign mem Mex Acad Sci. *Res:* Evolution; population genetics, fitness of natural and experimental populations; reproductive isolation and origin of species; biochemical variation and molecular evolution; philosophy of science. *Mailing Add:* Dept Ecol & Evolutionary Biol Univ Calif Irvine CA 92697-2525

AYALA, NELSON PAUL, INORGANIC PHOTOCHEMISTRY, COMPUTER INTERFACING. *Current Pos:* RES & DEVELOP CHEMIST, WESTWOOD CHEMICAL CO, 88- *Personal Data:* m 89, Ines; c Kristina & Daniel. *Educ:* City Univ NY, BS, 79; Stony Brook Univ, MS, 82; Univ Va, PhD(chem), 88. *Prof Exp:* Res & develop technician, Lever Bros, 76-78. *Concurrent Pos:* Adj prof chem, Orange Community Col, 96- *Mem:* Am Chem Soc; Soc Cosmetic Chemists. *Res:* Spectroscopic, kinetic, mechanistic, structural studies of inorganic polymers and their uses in personal care industry. *Mailing Add:* 167 South St Middletown NY 10940. *E-Mail:* nelsona53@aol.com

AYARS, JAMES EARL, ENGINEERING, AGRICULTURE. *Current Pos:* RES AGR ENGR, AGR RES SERV, USDA, 80- *Personal Data:* b Penns Grove, NJ, Jan 28, 43; m 69; c 2. *Educ:* Cornell Univ, BSAgE, 65; Colo State Univ, MS, 73, PhD(eng), 76. *Prof Exp:* Asst prof eng, Univ Md, 76-80. *Mem:* Sigma Xi; Am Soc Agr Engrs; Am Soc Agron. *Res:* Groundwater hydrology; irrigation water management; drainage water reuse; drainage system design and management. *Mailing Add:* 3056 E Vartikian Fresno CA 93710

AYCOCK, BENJAMIN FRANKLIN, TEXTILE CHEMISTRY. *Current Pos:* RETIRED. *Personal Data:* b Washington, DC, May 18, 22; m 48; c 5. *Educ:* Univ NC, BS, 42; Univ Ill, MS, 45, PhD(org chem), 47. *Prof Exp:* Asst, Nat Defense Res Comt, Univ Ind, 44-45; res assoc, Explosives Res Lab, Carnegie Inst Technol, 45; from instr to asst prof chem, Univ Wis, 47-50; chemist, Rohm and Haas Co, Pa, 50-59, sect head, Redstone Arsenal Res Div, 59-69; head, Chem Dept, Burlington Idust Res Ctr, 69-72, sr scientist, 72-80, mgr res & develop, 80-84. *Mem:* Am Chem Soc; Swiss Chem Soc; Am Asn Textile Chemists & Colorists. *Res:* Chemistry of natural products; nitrogeneous resins; plasticizers; propellant chemistry; textile chemistry. *Mailing Add:* 2310 N Elm St Greensboro NC 27408-5120

AYCOCK, MARVIN KENNETH, JR, PLANT BREEDING, PLANT GENETICS. *Current Pos:* from asst prof to prof, 66-87, prof & chmn, 87-91, PROF PLANT BREEDING, DEPT AGRON, UNIV MD, COLLEGE PARK, 91- *Personal Data:* b Warrenton, NC, Nov 12, 35; m 60, Barbara Howard; c Amy V & Marvin K III. *Educ:* NC State Univ, BS, 59, MS, 63; Iowa State Univ, PhD(plant breeding), 66. *Honors & Awards:* Res Award, Am Soc Agron, 82. *Prof Exp:* Teacher, Bear Grass High Sch, 59-60. *Mem:* Am Soc Agron; Crop Sci Soc Am; Am Genetic Asn. *Res:* Effects of a male-sterile cytoplasm in Nicotiana tabacum and inbreeding depression in Medicago sativa; developing new and improved varieties of Maryland tobacco through conventional breeding and tissue culture procedures. *Mailing Add:* Dept Agron Univ Md College Park MD 20742

AYCOCK, ROBERT, PHYTOPATHOLOGY. *Current Pos:* RETIRED. *Personal Data:* b Lisbon, La, Dec 23, 19; m 41; c 2. *Educ:* La State Univ, BS, 40, NC State Col, MS, 42, PhD(plant path), 49. *Prof Exp:* Assoc plant pathologist, 49-55, Clemson Col; res assoc prof, NC State Univ, 55-61, prof plant path, 61-84, head dept, 73-84. *Concurrent Pos:* Ed-in-chief, Phytopathology, Am Phytopath Soc, 70-72. *Mem:* Fel Am Phytopath Soc (pres, 75-76). *Res:* Plant disease diagnosis and diseases of ornamental crops. *Mailing Add:* 2001 Manuel St Raleigh NC 27612

AYDELOTTE, MARGARET BEESLEY, BIOCHEMISTRY. *Current Pos:* asst prof, 81-89, ASSOC PROF BIOCHEM, COL MED, RUSH UNIV, 89- *Personal Data:* b London, Eng, June 1, 34; m 61; c 3. *Educ:* Cambridge Univ, BA, 56, MA, 60, PhD(physiol), 61. *Honors & Awards:* Carol Nachman Prize in Rheumatol, 87. *Prof Exp:* Demonstr physiol, Cambridge Univ, 59-63; assoc prof biol, Tarkio Col, Mo, 64-68; fel anat, Col Med, Univ Iowa, 69-70, asst prof, 71-75; assoc prof biol, Franklin Col, 75-78; asst prof anat, Sch Med, Ind Univ, 78-81. *Concurrent Pos:* Vis physiologist, Univ Calif, San Francisco, 61. *Mem:* Am Asn Anatomists; Tissue Cult Asn; AAAS; Am Soc Cell Biol; Orthop Res Soc. *Res:* Morphological and biochemical studies of connective tissues; cartilage matrix synthesis and degradation by articular chondrocytes. *Mailing Add:* Dept Biochem Rush-Presbyterian-St Luke's Med Ctr 1653 W Congress Pkwy Chicago IL 60612-3833. *Fax:* 312-942-3053

AYDELOTTE, MYRTLE K, NURSING. *Current Pos:* dir, dean & prof, Col Nursing, 49-57, prof, 57-62 & 64-76, dir nursing, 68-76, PROF & EMER DEAN, UNIV IOWA, 76- *Personal Data:* b May 31, 17; m 56; c 2. *Educ:* Univ Minn, BS, 39, MA, 48, PhD(educ admin & educ psych), 55. *Hon Degrees:* DS, Univ Nebr, 81. *Honors & Awards:* Luther Christman Award, 77; Elizabeth Soule lectr, Univ Wash, 81; Levery Legend Award, Am Acad Nursing, 95. *Prof Exp:* Head nurse, Charles T Miller Hosp, St Paul, 39-41; surgical teaching supvr, St Mary's Hosp, Sch Nursing, Minn, 41-42; asst chief nurse, Army Nurse Corps, 26th Gen Hosp, Europ Theatre, 42-45, chief nurse, 52nd Sta Hosp, 45; instr, Univ Minn, 45-49; assoc chief nursing, Res Nursing, VA Hosp, Iowa, 63-64, chief nursing, Nursing Res, 64; clin prof, Yale Univ, 83-85. *Concurrent Pos:* Mem, Nat Acad Sci Comt Study of Health Care Resources, Va, 75-77, Comn Nursing Servs, Am Nurses Asn, 76-77, Nat Comn Nursing, 80-83; exec dir, Am Nurses Asn, Kans, 77-81; vis prof, Univ Ill, Col Nursing, 82-; actg exec dir, Ctr Nursing Innovation, New Haven, Conn, 83-84. *Mem:* Inst Med-Nat Acad Sci; Am Acad Nursing; Am Nurses Asn. *Res:* Structural arrangements and financial mechanisms for delivery of nursing services; author of 2 articles and 48 publications. *Mailing Add:* 308 Montclair Park 201 N First Ave Iowa City IA 52245

AYDLETT, LOUISE CLATE, OPERATIONS RESEARCH. *Current Pos:* RETIRED. *Personal Data:* b Elizabeth City, NC, Aug 04, 41. *Educ:* Duke Univ, AB, 62; E Carolina Univ, MA, 66. *Prof Exp:* Prof math, Col Albemarle, 64-91. *Mem:* Math Asn Am. *Mailing Add:* 6 Gardner Pt Elizabeth City NC 27909

AYE, MAUNG TIN, EXPERIMENTAL HEMATOLOGY, CELL BIOLOGY. *Current Pos:* RETIRED. *Personal Data:* b Rangoon, Burma, Aug 9, 41; Can citizen; c 2. *Educ:* Univ Cambridge, Eng, BChir, MB & MA, 66; Univ Toronto, PhD(med sci), 74, FRCP, 81. *Prof Exp:* House physician & surgeon, Hereford Gen Hosp, UK, 66-67; sr house officer, St Thomas' Hosp, London, 67-68; resident hemat & internal med, Ottawa Gen Hosp, 68-70; assoc prof & scholar, Res Coun, Dept Med & Physiol, 74-91; nat dir serv, Red Cross Can, 91-96. *Concurrent Pos:* Fel, Med Res Coun, Ont Cancer Inst, 70-74, scholar, 76-81, grant, 74-; Nat Cancer Inst Can grant, 77-81; chmn, Comt Human Experimentation, Ottawa Gen Hosp, 77- *Mem:* Am Soc Hemat; Can Soc Hemat; Can Soc Cell Biol. *Res:* Regulation of cell proliferation and differentiation in mammalian hemopoietic systems. *Mailing Add:* 50 Whitemarl Dr Rockliffe Park ON K1L 8J6 Can

AYEN, RICHARD J(OHN), CHEMICAL ENGINEERING. *Current Pos:* sr res engr, Stauffer Chem Co, 68-70, supvr, Richmond Res Ctr, 70-74, sect mgr, 74-79, sr sect mgr, 79-81, dept mgr, Eastern Res Ctr, 81-88, DIR CHEM PROCESS DEVELOP, CHEM WASTE MGT, STAUFFER CHEM CO, 88- *Personal Data:* b Loyal, Wis, June 8, 38; m 63; c 2. *Educ:* Univ Wis, BS, 60; Univ Ill, MS, 61, PhD(chem eng), 64. *Prof Exp:* Asst prof chem eng, Univ Calif, Berkeley, 64-68, consult, 65-67. *Mem:* Am Inst Chem Engrs. *Res:* Catalyzed reactions of nitrogen oxides; gas-solids fluidization; scaleup of processes for sulfur and phosphorus-containing compounds; chemical waste treatment. *Mailing Add:* 230 Royal Oaks Dr Anderson SC 29625

AYENGAR, PADMASINI (MRS FREDERICK ALADJEM), BIOCHEMISTRY, MICROBIOLOGY. *Current Pos:* RETIRED. *Personal Data:* b Bangalore, India, July 31, 24; m 57; c 1. *Educ:* Travancore Univ, India, BSc, 44; Univ Wash, St Louis, PhD, 53. *Prof Exp:* Fel enzymechem, Enzyme Inst, Univ Wis, 53-54; res assoc biochem, City of Hope Med Ctr, Calif, 54-56; vis scientist, Nat Inst Arthritis & Metab Dis, NIH, Md, 57; res assoc immunochem, Dept Med Microbiol, Sch Med, Univ Southern Calif, 58-76, res assoc microbiol, 76-92. *Mem:* Am Chem Soc; Am Soc Biol Chem. *Res:* Microbial fermentation; growth factors and inhibitors; biosynthesis and metabolism of phosphodiester of serine and ethanolamine; enzymes; purification; properties and mechanism of action. *Mailing Add:* 845 Las Palmas Rd Pasadena CA 91105-1230

AYENI, BABATUNDE J, RESERVOIR ENGINEERING, STATISTICS. *Current Pos:* lead statistician, 88-91, STATIST SPECIALIST, 3M CO, ST PAUL, MINN, 91- *Personal Data:* b Lagos, Nigeria, May 29, 54; m 78, Flora Olubunmi; c Tina A, Louis O, Lawrence C, Philip B & Andrew O. *Educ:* Univ Southwestern La, BS, 80, MS, 81, PhD(statistics), 84. *Prof Exp:* Lectr, Petroleum Eng, Univ Southwestern Univ, La, 81-84; asst prof, Southern Univ, New Orleans, 84-85, dir technol, 85-88. *Mem:* Soc Petrol Engrs; Am Statist Asn; Am Soc Qual Control. *Res:* Petroleum reserves analysis; property evaluation; pressure transient analysis; forecasting; estimation in a mixture of distribution; arima modeling; quality and process improvements, design of experiment and response surface methodology. *Mailing Add:* 3M Co Bldg 224-4S-19 St Paul MN 55144-1000. *Fax:* 612-737-4836

AYER, HOWARD EARLE, INDUSTRIAL HYGIENE. *Current Pos:* PROF ENVIRON HYG, UNIV CINCINNATI, 72- *Personal Data:* b Brookings, SDak, July 28, 24; m 47, Elsie Donaldson; c Mitchell, Gus, Matthew & Elzabeth (Garvin). *Educ:* Univ Minn, BChE, 48; Harvard Univ, SM, 55. *Honors & Awards:* Borden Award, Am Indust Hyg Asn, 96. *Prof Exp:* Engr, Div Occup Health, US Pub Health Serv, 48-64; asst dir field studies, Nat Inst Occup Safety & Health, 64-72. *Concurrent Pos:* Chmn, Am Conf Govt Indust Hygienists, 71-72. *Mem:* Am Indust Hyg Asn; Health Physics Soc; Brit Occup Hyg Soc; Am Pub Health Asn. *Res:* Behavior of aerosols in environment and health effects; methods of measurement which relate to these effects on worker health. *Mailing Add:* 2812 Linwood Ave Cincinnati OH 45208

AYER, WILLIAM ALFRED, NATURAL PRODUCTS. *Current Pos:* from asst prof to prof, 58-91, UNIV PROF CHEM, UNIV ALTA, 91- *Personal Data:* b Sackville, NB, July 4, 32; m 54, Dorothy K Monteith; c 6. *Educ:* Univ NB, BSc, 53, PhD(chem), 56. *Honors & Awards:* Merck Sharp & Dohme Award, Chem Inst Can, 70; John Labatt Award, Chem Inst Can, 81; Van Cleave Lectr, Univ Sask, Regina, 85; E W R Steacie Award, Can Soc Chem, 94. *Prof Exp:* Res assoc, Harvard Univ, 57-58. *Concurrent Pos:* Fel, Alfred P Sloan Found, 65-67; vis prof, Japan Soc Prom Sci, 76; org chem ed, Can J Chem, 76-83, sr ed, 83-88; Job vis prof, Mem Univ Nfld, 83. *Mem:* Sr mem Am Chem Soc; fel Chem Inst Can; fel Royal Soc Can; sr mem Can Soc Chem (pres, 88-89). *Res:* Structural and synthetic studies of naturally occurring substances. *Mailing Add:* Dept Chem Univ Alta Edmonton AB T6G 2G2 Can

AYERS, ALVIN DEARING, SOIL SCIENCE, PLANT PHYSIOLOGY. *Current Pos:* CONSULT, 73- *Personal Data:* b Alvin, Tex, Apr 27, 09; m 39; c 2. *Educ:* Univ Ariz, BS, 32, MS, 34; Univ Calif, PhD(soil sci), 39. *Prof Exp:* Asst agr chemist, Exp Sta, Univ Ariz, 32; chemist, Salt River Valley Water Users Asn, Ariz, 34 & Asn Lab, Calif, 35; asst plant nutrit, Univ Calif, 36-37; agent, Salinity Lab, USDA, 38-41, asst chemist, 41-42; chemist, Calif Inst Technol, 42-43; supvr safety & personnel, 43-45; assoc chemist, Salinity Lab, USDA, 45-48, chemist, 48-50, agriculturist field comt, Ark White & Red Basins Inter-Agency Comt, Okla, 51-53, soil scientist, US Salinity Lab, 53-59, asst dir, Europ Res Off, Agr Res Serv, Italy, 59-62, dir, Far Eastern Regional Res Off, 62-66; soil & water mgt specialist, Agr & Rural Develop Serv, War on Hunger, AID, 66-70 & Off Agr & Fisheries Tech Assistance Bur, 70-73. *Mem:* Fel Soil Sci Soc Am; Am Soc Agron. *Res:* Agricultural research administration; soil salinity and alkali; salt tolerance of plants; soil moisture-plant relationships; soil chemistry. *Mailing Add:* 5621 Del Rio Ct Cape Coral FL 33904

AYERS, ARTHUR RAYMOND, PLANT MOLECULAR BIOLOGY, PLANT DISEASE RESISTANCE. *Current Pos:* DIR GENETIC ENG TECHNOL PROG, CEDAR CREST COL, ALLENTOWN, PA, 86- *Personal Data:* b San Diego, Calif, Sept 28, 47; m 84; c 3. *Educ:* Univ Calif, San Diego, BA, 69; Univ Colo, Boulder, PhD(molecular cell develop biol), 75. *Prof Exp:* Guest researcher biomass conversion, Swedish Forest Prods Res Labs, Stockholm, Sweden, 75-77; res asst phytopath, dept plant path, Univ Mo, Columbia, 77-79, & plant cell cult, Kans State Univ, Manhattan, 79-80; asst prof cell & develop biol, Harvard Univ, 81-86. *Concurrent Pos:* Consult, Vital Technol Inc, Cambridge, 83-85; consult Agr Diag Assoc Inc, Cinnaminson, NJ, 86-; assoc ed, J Pa Acad Sci, 88- *Mem:* Am Soc Plant Physiologists; Am Phytopath Soc; Sigma Xi; Phytochem Soc NAm. *Res:* Molecular basis of plant disease resistance using monoclonal antibodies to identify pathogen and host molecules that mediate race-cultivar specificity; immunodiagnostics for plant pathogens. *Mailing Add:* Dept Natural Sci Albertson Col 2112 Cleveland Blvd Caldwell ID 83605-4494

AYERS, CARLOS R, INTERNAL MEDICINE. *Current Pos:* DIR, VA HEART RES LAB, 69- *Personal Data:* b Oakvale, WVa, Apr 2, 32; m 58; c 3. *Educ:* Lincoln Mem Univ, BS, 53; Univ Va, MD, 58. *Prof Exp:* Intern med, Univ Va, 58-59; resident univ affil hosp, Univ Utah, 61-62; resident, 63-64, from instr to assoc prof internal med, 64-75, PROF INTERNAL MED, SCH MED, UNIV VA, 75- *Concurrent Pos:* Fel cardiol, Univ Hosp, Univ Va, 62-63; mem coun high blood pressure res, Am Heart Asn; Va Heart Asn res prof cardiol, 68- *Mem:* Am Fedn Clin Res; fel Am Col Physicians. *Res:* Peripheral vascular disease; hypertension; aldosterone metabolism; renin; angiotensin metabolism. *Mailing Add:* Hypertension Unit Univ Va Sch Med Univ VA Hosp Box 146 Charlottesville VA 22908

AYERS, CAROLINE LEROY, PHYSICAL CHEMISTRY, SCIENCE EDUCATION. *Current Pos:* from asst prof to assoc prof, 67-84, chmn dept, 83-88, PROF CHEM, E CAROLINA UNIV, 84-, ADJ PROF SCI EDUC, 91-, INTERIM ASST VCHANCELLOR ACAD AFFAIRS, 95- *Personal Data:* b Augusta, Ga, Oct 30, 41; m 63, Paul W; c Paul W & Eulalia. *Educ:* Univ Ga, BS, 62, PhD(phys chem), 66. *Prof Exp:* Asst prof chem, Portland State Col, 66-67. *Mem:* Am Chem Soc; Sigma Xi. *Res:* Chemical education. *Mailing Add:* Dept Chem ECarolina Univ Greenville NC 27858-4353. *E-Mail:* chayers@ecuvm.cis.ecu.edu

AYERS, JACK DUANE, PHYSICAL METALLURGY, SOLIDIFICATION PROCESSING. *Current Pos:* METALLURGIST, NAVAL RES LAB, 71- *Personal Data:* b Nampa, Idaho, Feb 25, 41; m 63, Sharon A Denny; c Gayle M, Bryan D & Stuart D. *Educ:* Univ Wash, BS, 66; Carnegie-Mellon Univ, PhD(metall & mat sci), 70. *Prof Exp:* NATO fel, Univ Oxford, 70-71. *Mem:* Am Inst Mining, Metall & Petrol Engrs Metall Soc; Am Soc Metals. *Res:* Kinetics and crystallography of solid state phase transformations; solidification processing of metals with the objective of improving their physical properties. *Mailing Add:* Code 6320 Naval Res Lab Washington DC 20375-5000. *Fax:* 202-767-2623

AYERS, JERRY BART, SCIENCE EDUCATION. *Current Pos:* prof sci educ & assoc dean educ, 70-94, ASSOC VPRES RES, TENN TECHNOL UNIV, 95- *Personal Data:* b Atlanta, Ga, Apr 17, 39; m 71, Mary C Nesbiji. *Educ:* Oglethorpe Univ, BS, 60; Univ Ga, MEd, 66, EdD(sci educ), 67. *Prof Exp:* Assoc physicist, Union Carbide Nuclear-Oak Ridge Nat Labs, 60-61; instr chem, Lenoir Rhyne Col, 64-65; asst prof sci educ, Univ Ga, 67-70. *Mem:* Am Chem Soc; Nat Sci Teachers Asn. *Res:* Preparation of improved teaching materials for use at the college level in training teachers; evaluation of science teaching; scientific information retrieval. *Mailing Add:* Off Res Tenn Tech Univ Box 5012 Cookeville TN 38505-0001

AYERS, JOHN E, PLANT PATHOLOGY, PLANT GENETICS. *Current Pos:* From asst prof to assoc prof, 69-80, PROF PLANT PATH, PA STATE UNIV, UNIVERSITY PARK, 80- *Personal Data:* b Indianapolis, Ind, Dec 20, 41; m 88; c 5. *Educ:* Purdue Univ, BS, 63, MS, 65; Pa State Univ, PhD(genetics), 69. *Mem:* Am Phytopath Soc. *Res:* Nature and inheritance of disease resistance in plants. *Mailing Add:* Dept Plant Path Pa State Univ 121 Buckhout Lab University Park PA 16802-4506. *Fax:* 814-863-7217; *E-Mail:* jayers@psupem.psu.edu

AYERS, JOSEPH LEONARD, JR, NEUROPHYSIOLOGY, COMPARATIVE PHYSIOLOGY. *Current Pos:* ASST PROF BIOL, NORTHEASTERN UNIV, 78- *Personal Data:* b Long Beach, Calif, Nov 14, 47. *Educ:* Univ Calif, Riverside, AB, 70; Univ Calif, Santa Cruz, PhD(biol), 75. *Prof Exp:* Res asst neurophysiol, Univ Calif, Santa Cruz, 70-75; fels, Nat Ctr Sci Res, Marseille, France, 75-76 & Univ Calif, San Diego, 76-78. *Mem:* Soc Neurosci; AAAS; Int Union Physiologists. *Res:* Neurophysiology, neural control at locomotion, neuroethology, cellular mechanisms underlying behavior, pattern generation, computer applications in neurosciences. *Mailing Add:* Dept Biol Northeastern Univ 360 Huntingten Ave Boston MA 02115-5096

AYERS, JOSEPH W, GRINDING PROCESS DEVELOPMENT FOR NUT SHELL PRODUCTS. *Current Pos:* pres, 39-76, CHMN, AGRASHELL INC, LOS ANGELES, 76-; CHMN, AYERS CO, 71- *Educ:* Cornell Univ, BS, 27. *Prof Exp:* Res dir, P K Williams & Co, 30-48, vpres, 48-62; gen mgr, Mem Div, Pfizer, New York City, 62-68, pres, 68-69; pres, Calcium Chem, Adams, Mass, 37-48, J W Ayers & Co, Easton, Pa, 55-61, Josheph Ayers Inc, 73-86. *Concurrent Pos:* Dir, New Eng Lime Co, Foote Min Co; chmn, Pa Hosp & Health Coun, 71-74; vpres, N County Citizens Reg Progress, 72-78. *Mem:* Fel Am Inst Chemists; fel NY Acad Sci. *Mailing Add:* 1325 Kirklord Village Gate Bethlehem PA 18017

AYERS, ORVAL EDWIN, ORGANIC CHEMISTRY, TECHNICAL MANAGEMENT. *Current Pos:* RETIRED. *Personal Data:* b Grant, Ala, Mar 29, 32; m 52, Masiel Deweese; c Karen, Lisa & Sylvia. *Educ:* Berea Col, Ky, BA, 55; Auburn Univ, MS, 58; Univ Ala, Tuscaloosa, PhD(org chem), 73. *Honors & Awards:* Army Res & Develop Achievement Awards, Dept Army, 75. *Prof Exp:* Chemist qual control, Nat Cash Regist Co, Dayton, Ohio, 55-56; res chemist propellant res, Res, Develop & Eng Ctr, US Army Missele Command, Redstone Arsenal, Ala, 59-86, supvry aerospace engr, 86-88, dep dir propulsion directorate, 88-95. *Mem:* Am Chem Soc (treas, 75-76). *Res:* Technical management of the development and evaluation of propellants and rocket motors for application as propulsion systems in US Army Missile systems. *Mailing Add:* 7805 Martha Dr SE Huntsville AL 35802-2458

AYERS, PAUL WAYNE, PHYSICAL ORGANIC CHEMISTRY. *Current Pos:* asst prof, 67-73, ASSOC PROF CHEM, E CAROLINA UNIV, 73- *Personal Data:* b Winter Garden, Fla, Oct 18, 36; m 63. *Educ:* David Lipscomb Col, BA, 60; Univ Ga, MS, 62, PhD(chem), 66. *Prof Exp:* Asst prof chem, Portland State Col, 66-67. *Mem:* Am Chem Soc. *Res:* Free radical rearrangements and oxidation processes *Mailing Add:* Dept Chem ECarolina Univ Greenville NC 27834

AYERS, RAYMOND DEAN, MUSICAL ACOUSTICS. *Current Pos:* From asst prof to assoc prof, 67-79, PROF PHYSICS & ASTRON, CALIF STATE UNIV, LONG BEACH, 79- *Personal Data:* b Ossining, NY, July 11, 40; m 89, Patricia Kling. *Educ:* Calif Inst Technol, BS, 63, MS, 64; PhD(mat sci), 71. *Mem:* Am Asn Physics Teachers; Acoust Soc Am. *Res:* Acoustics of wind instruments; acoustical imaging; experimental solid state physics. *Mailing Add:* Dept Physics & Astron Calif State Univ 1250 Bellflower Blvd Long Beach CA 90840

AYERS, WILLIAM ARTHUR, MICROBIOLOGY. *Current Pos:* RETIRED. *Personal Data:* b Highgrove, Calif, Dec 22, 24; m 51, Adelia Romeieh; c Kathy (Traber) & Susan (Hampton). *Educ:* Univ Calif, Los Angeles, AB, 49; Rutgers Univ, MS, 51; Univ Wis, PhD(bact), 54. *Prof Exp:* Asst bact, Rutgers Univ, 49-51 & Univ Wis, 51-54; asst prof, Univ NH, 54-59; microbiologist, Brooklyn Bot Garden, 59-62; microbiologist, USDA, 62-84. *Mem:* Am Soc Microbiol. *Res:* Soil microbiology; ecology and physiology of soilborne plant pathogenic fungi. *Mailing Add:* 11472 Chelsea Ct Fredericksburg VA 22407

AYLER, MAYNARD FRANKLIN, MINE-ASSISTED RESIDUAL OIL RECOVERY. *Current Pos:* MINING CONSULT, 52-; PRES, OIL MINING CORP, 54- *Personal Data:* b Tacoma, Wash, Oct 15, 22; m 45, Ann L; c Corliss A (Scully) & David F. *Educ:* Colo Sch Mines, E of M, 45, MS, 63. *Prof Exp:* Geologist, US Bur Reclamation, 45-47, Calif Co, 47-52; instr mining, Colo Sch Mines, 58-63; mining engr, US Bur Mines, 60-77. *Concurrent Pos:* Chief, Libyan Geol Surv, USAID & Govt Libya, 64-66; instr geol, Univ Md, 65-66; pres, Oil Mining Energy Co, 93- *Mem:* Am Asn Petrol Geologists. *Res:* Developing and patenting a safe system and needed equipment for mine-assisted mobile residual oil recovery; recipient of 2 US and 3 Canadian, 1 Venzuelan, 1 Argentine and 1 Mexican patents. *Mailing Add:* 1315 Normandy Rd Golden CO 80401. *Fax:* 303-205-1204

AYLES, GEORGE BURTON, FISH GENETICS, AQUACULTURE. *Current Pos:* Res scientist, Dept Fisheries & Oceans, 72-80, regional planning officer, 80-82, dir res, 82-86, dir res, Fisheries Habitat Mgt, Cent Arctic Region, 86-95, REGIONAL DIR, MERGER & PROG REV, DEPT FISHERIES & OCEANS, 95- *Personal Data:* b Prince Albert, Sask, Nov 28, 45. *Educ:* Univ BC, BSc, 67, MSc, 69; Univ Toronto, PhD(zool), 72. *Concurrent Pos:* Adj prof, Dept Zool, Univ Man, 77- *Mem:* Aquacult Asn Can; Can Soc Zoologists; Can Genetics Soc; Am Genetics Soc. *Res:* Fish genetics and fish culture; management techniques of rainbow trout culture in small lakes and in tanks using recirculated water and waste heat; quantitative genetics of rainbow trout and Arctic char. *Mailing Add:* Dept Fisheries & Oceans 501 University Crescent Winnipeg MB R3T 2N6 Can

AYLESWORTH, THOMAS GIBBONS, ZOOLOGY. *Current Pos:* RETIRED. *Personal Data:* b Valparaiso, Ind, Nov 5, 27; m 49, Virginia Boelter; c Carol J & Thomas P. *Educ:* Ind Univ, AB, 50, MS, 53; Ohio State Univ, PhD(sci educ), 59. *Prof Exp:* Asst prof sci educ, Mich State Univ, 57-62; lectr sci & sr ed, Current Sci, Wesleyan Univ, 62-65; sr ed sci bks, Doubleday & Co, 65-80; ed in chief, Bison Books Ltd, 80-86. *Concurrent Pos:* Vis fac mem, Ohio State Univ, 62, Wis State Univ, Whitewater, 64, Fairfield Univ, State Univ NY, 80 & Western Conn State Univ, 81-; New Eng ed, Am Biol Teacher, 62-64. *Mem:* Nat Asn Biol Teachers; Nat Asn Sci Writers; Nat Sci Teachers Asn; Nat Asn Res Sci Teaching; NY Acad Sci. *Res:* Critical thinking and its applications in the field of teaching; uses of printed materials in the teaching of science; author of 61 science trade books. *Mailing Add:* 48 Van Rensselaer Stamford CT 06902

AYLING, JUNE E, BIOCHEMISTRY, PHARMACOLOGY. *Current Pos:* PROF PHARMACOL, UNIV SALA, MOBILE, 81- *Personal Data:* b US citizen. *Educ:* Univ Calif, Berkeley, BS, 63, PhD(biochem), 66. *Prof Exp:* Fel biochem, Univ Calif, 66-67, Max Planck Inst, Munich, 67-69; asst prof, Univ Calif, Los Angeles Sch Med, 69-76; assoc prof biochem, Univ Tex, San Antonio, 76-81. *Concurrent Pos:* Fel, Am Cancer Soc, 67-69; prin investr res grant, Nat Cancer Inst, NIH, Dept Health & Human Resources, 74-87, Robert A Welch Found, 78-81, Nat Inst Gen Med Sci, 80-, Nat Inst Neurol & Commun Dis & Stroke, 84- & Ciba Geigy, 85- *Mem:* Am Soc Biol Chemists; Am Chem Soc; AAAS; Am Soc Pharmacol & Exp Therapeut; Soc Neurosci. *Res:* Mechanism of enzyme action; coenzyme catalysis; structure function relationship; physical and chemical properties of enzymes; regulation of enzyme activity; role of tetrahydrobiopterin in regulation of neurotransmitter biosynthesis. *Mailing Add:* Pharmacol Dept Col Med Univ S Ala Mobile AL 36688. *Fax:* 334-460-6798; *E-Mail:* jayling@jaguar1usouthal.edu

AYLOR, DONALD EARL, BIOPHYSICS, MICROMETEOROLOGY. *Current Pos:* Asst scientist, 69-75, chief scientist biophys, Dept Ecol & Climat, 76-83, CHIEF SCIENTIST, DEPT PLANT PATH & ECOL, CONN AGR EXP STA, 84- *Personal Data:* b Hunt, NY, Dec 22, 40; m 64, Ruthann Brody; c Adam & Rachel. *Educ:* State Univ NY, Stony Brook, BES, 64, MES, 66, PhD(mech eng), 70. *Concurrent Pos:* Mem comt aerobiol, Nat Res Coun, 76-80; Guggenheim fel, 80. *Mem:* Fel Am Meteorol Soc; fel Am Phytopath Soc; fel AAAS. *Res:* Turbulent dispersion of particles and gases in the atmosphere and of solutes in rivers; plant disease epidemiology; noise propagation outdoors; mechanics of plant cells. *Mailing Add:* Dept Plant Path & Ecol PO Box 1106 New Haven CT 06504

AYLOR, JAMES HIRAM, ELECTRICAL ENGINEERING, COMPUTER ENGINEERING. *Current Pos:* Res engr, 73-78, PROF ELEC ENG, UNIV VA, 78-, CHMN, 96- *Personal Data:* b Charlottesville, Va, May 30, 46; m 73; c 2. *Educ:* Univ Va, BSEE, 68, MSEE, 71, PhD(elec eng), 77. *Concurrent Pos:* Consult, Gen Elec Co, 74, Alert Commun Corp, & Va Hwy & Transp Res Coun, 77-; vis scientist, Fed Sys Div, IBM, 82-83. *Mem:* Inst Elec & Electronics Engrs; Inst Elec & Electronics Engrs Comput Soc; AAAS. *Res:* Computer and microprocessor applications; pattern recognition; rehabilitation engineering; very large scale integration systems; test technology. *Mailing Add:* Dept Elec Eng Univ Va Charlottesville VA 22903-2442

AYNARDI, MARTHA WHITMAN, CELL & MOLECULAR BIOLOGY, GENETICS. *Current Pos:* ASST PROF BIOL, PA STATE UNIV, 84- *Educ:* Carnegie Mellon Univ, PhD(intermediate filaments), 82. *Mailing Add:* 1512 Concord Rd Wyomissing PA 19610-1106

AYO, DONALD JOSEPH, AGRONOMY, HORTICULTURE. *Current Pos:* from instr to prof plant sci, Nicholls State Univ, 58-67, head dept agr, 66-68, dean div sci, 68-69, dean div life sci & technol, 69-77, ALCEE FORTIER DISTINGUISHED HONOR PROF PLANT SCI, NICHOLLS STATE UNIV, 67-, VPRES, 71-, PROVOST, 75- *Personal Data:* b Bourg, La, Apr 1, 34; m 58; c 2. *Educ:* La State Univ, BS, 56, MS, 58, PhD, 64. *Prof Exp:* Asst prof hort, La State Univ, 58. *Concurrent Pos:* Asst ed, Nat Asn Col Teachers Am J, 63-65. *Mem:* Am Soc Hort Sci; Am Soc Agron; Soil Sci Soc Am; NY Acad Sci; Am Inst Biol Sci. *Res:* Dormancy and rest periods in deciduous plants. *Mailing Add:* Nicholls State Univ 906 E First St Thibodaux LA 70310-2001

AYOUB, AYOUB BARSOUM, ALGEBRAIC NUMBER THEORY. *Current Pos:* from asst prof to assoc prof, 83-97, PROF MATH, PA STATE UNIV, 97- *Personal Data:* b Cairo, Egypt, May 22, 31; US citizen; m 72, Germaine Saad; c Sameh & Mariane. *Educ:* Ain-Shams Univ, Cairo, BSc, 51; Temple Univ, MA, 77, PhD(math), 80. *Prof Exp:* Asst prof math, Ain-Shams Univ, 80-82. *Concurrent Pos:* Vis prof math, Temple Univ, Philadelphia, 82-83. *Mem:* Math Asn Am; Am Math Asn Two Yr Cols; Nat Coun Teachers Math. *Res:* Number theory; special functions; algebra; calculus; differential equations; numerical analysis and geometry. *Mailing Add:* Pa State Univ 1600 Woodland Rd Sutherland Bldg Abington PA 19001. *Fax:* 215-881-7317; *E-Mail:* aba2@psu.edu

AYOUB, CHRISTINE WILLIAMS, MATHEMATICS. *Current Pos:* RETIRED. *Personal Data:* b Cincinnati, Ohio, Feb 7, 22; m 50, Raymond G; c Cynthia (Harris) & Daphne (Schreiber). *Educ:* Bryn Mawr Col, AB, 42; Radcliffe Col, AM, 43; McGill Univ, MA, 44; Yale Univ, PhD(math), 47. *Prof Exp:* Fel, Inst Advan Study, Off Naval Res, 47-48; instr math, Cornell Univ, 48-51; from instr to prof math, Pa State Univ, 53-84; prof, King Saud Univ, 84-85; vis lectr, Bethlehem Univ, West Bank, 86-87. *Concurrent Pos:* Res asst, Radcliffe Col, 51-52; NSF sci fac fel, 66-67; vis prof, Univ Frankfurt, 66-67 & Univ Warwick, 79-80; Fulbright fel, Monocco, 88 & Jordan, 95. *Mem:* Am Math Soc; Math Asn Am; Asn Women Mathematicians. *Res:* Theory of groups and normal chains; modern algebra; constructive algebra. *Mailing Add:* 500 E Marylyn Ave State College PA 16801

AYOUB, ELIA MOUSSA, PEDIATRICS. *Current Pos:* PROF PEDIAT, COL MED, UNIV FLA, 69- *Personal Data:* b Haifa, Palestine, Apr 12, 28; m 54; c 5. *Educ:* Am Univ Beirut, BS, 49, MD, 53; Am Bd Pediat, dipl. *Prof Exp:* Intern, Am Univ Beirut, 53; physician in-chg, Qaisumah Hosp, Beirut, 53-56; resident pediat, Univ Wis, 56-57; from instr to prof, Univ Minn, 59-69. *Concurrent Pos:* Fel, Col Med, Univ Minn, 57-58, res fel, 58-59; Helen Hay Whitney res fel, 60-63; guest investr, Rockefeller Univ, 63-65; estab investr, Helen Hay Whitney Res Found, 63-68; fac res award clin sci, 87. *Mem:* AAAS; Am Soc Microbiol; Soc Pediat Res; Am Asn Immunol; Am Acad Pediat. *Res:* Studies on the pathogenesis of rheumatic fever; genetic susceptibility. *Mailing Add:* Dept Pediat Univ Fla Med Ctr Box 100296 Gainesville FL 32610. *Fax:* 904-392-0481

AYOUB, MAHMOUD A, OCCUPATIONAL SAFETY & HEALTH. *Current Pos:* asst prof, 71-75, assoc prof, 75-80, PROF INDUST ENG, NC STATE UNIV, 80- *Personal Data:* b Cairo, Egypt, Jan 1, 42; US citizen. *Educ:* Cairo Univ, BS, 64; Tex Tech Univ, MS, 69, PhD(indust eng), 70. *Honors & Awards:* Phil Carrol Award, Am Inst Indust Engrs, 80. *Prof Exp:* Field engr, Egypt, 64-65; instr civil eng, Cairo Univ, 65-66; res asst indust eng, Tex Tech Univ, 67-69. *Concurrent Pos:* Assoc dir syst safety eng, Nat Inst Occup Safety & Health, 71-; adj asst prof environ sci, Univ NC, Chapel Hill, 73-; prin investr, NIH biomed sci grant, 74-75, NSF, 74-76 & NC Dept Transp, 75-76; partic, Pres Comt on Employ of Handicapped, 79; consult, Reynolds Metals Co, 79-80 & Hanes Knitwear, 80-; dir develop support mat for training naval aviation personnel, US Navy, 80- *Mem:* Am Inst Indust Engrs; Human Factors Soc; Ergonomics Res Soc. *Res:* Evaluating manual lifting hazards and developing recommended solutions; defining an acceptable solution to the tendonitis problem; simulation modeling. *Mailing Add:* Indust Sci Box 7906 NC State Univ Main Campus Raleigh NC 27695-0001

AYOUB, MOHAMED MOHAMED, INDUSTRIAL ENGINEERING. *Current Pos:* from asst prof to prof indust eng, 61-69, prof indust eng & statist, 69-76, prof, 76-78, HON PROF INDUST ENG & BIOMED ENG, TEX TECH UNIV, 78- *Personal Data:* b Tanta, Egypt, Feb 17, 31; US citizen; m 69; c 2. *Educ:* Cairo Univ, BS, 53; Univ Iowa, MS, 55, PhD(indust eng), 64. *Honors & Awards:* Paul Fitts Award, Human Factors Soc, 75; David Baker Research Award, Am Inst Indust Engrs, 81. *Prof Exp:* Indust engr, Maytag Co, Iowa, 56-58, planning engr, 58-61. *Mem:* Am Inst Indust Eng; Am Indust Hyg Asn; Human Factors Soc; Ergonomics Res Soc; Am Soc Eng Educ; Sigma Xi. *Res:* Ergonomics, with particular interest in occupational biomechanics and work physiology; contributions of these areas to occupational safety and health. *Mailing Add:* Dept Indust Eng Tex Tech Univ Lubbock TX 79409

AYOUB, RAYMOND G DIMITRI, MATHEMATICS. *Current Pos:* from asst prof to prof, 66-84, EMER PROF MATH, PA STATE UNIV, 84- *Personal Data:* b Sherbrooke, Can, Jan 2, 23; m 50; c 2. *Educ:* McGill Univ, BSc, 43, MSc, 46; Univ Ill, PhD(math), 50. *Prof Exp:* Lectr math, McGill Univ, 47-49; Pierce instr, Harvard Univ, 50-52. *Mem:* Am Math Soc; Math Asn Am. *Res:* Analytic theory of numbers; theory of algebraic numbers. *Mailing Add:* 500 E Marylyn Apt 1142 State College PA 16801

AYRAL-KALOUSTIAN, SEMIRAMI, ORGANIC SYNTHESIS, ORGANIC PHOTOCHEMISTRY, PEPTIDOMIMETICS. *Current Pos:* sr res chemist, 82-88, proj leader, 88-93, group leader, AM CYANAMID CO, 93- *Personal Data:* b Istanbul, Turkey; m 69, Moses. *Educ:* Am Univ, Beirut, BS, 66; Univ Calif, Los Angeles, PhD(org chem), 73. *Honors & Awards:* Sci Achievement Award, Am Cyanamid Co, 87 & 92. *Prof Exp:* Asst prof org chem, Haigazian Col, Beirut, 72-73; asst prof chem & thermodynamics, Lebanese Univ, 73-74; res assoc, Rockefeller Univ, 75-78, asst prof org chem, 78-82. *Concurrent Pos:* Teaching assoc, Univ Calif, Los Angeles, 66-69, res assoc, 69-71; res asst, Imp Col Sci & Technol, London, 72; chairperson, NY Acad Scis, 93- *Mem:* Am Chem Soc; NY Acad Scis. *Res:* Synthesis, photolysis and thermolysis of organic compounds; investigations in the photochemistry of epoxy and cyclopropyl ketones; synthesis of fructose bisphophate analogs as potential antidiabetic agents; synthesis of immunostimulants and peptide mimics. *Mailing Add:* Wyeth-Ayerst Res N Middletown Rd Pearl River NY 10965. *Fax:* 914-732-5519

AYRES, DAVID SMITH, EXPERIMENTAL HIGH ENERGY PHYSICS. *Current Pos:* res assoc, 69-70, from asst physicist to physicist, 71-84, SR PHYSICIST, ARGONNE NAT LAB, 84- *Personal Data:* b Boston, Mass, June 14, 39; m 65. *Educ:* Williams Col, BA, 61; Univ Calif, Berkeley, MA, 63, PhD(physics), 68. *Prof Exp:* US Peace Corps lectr physics, Univ Nigeria, 63-65; res asst physics, Univ Calif, Berkeley, 65-68, res assoc, Lawrence Berkeley Lab, 68-69. *Mem:* Fel Am Phys Soc; AAAS. *Res:* Planning, execution, and analysis of experiments in elementary particle physics, with emphasis on hadron-hadron colliding beams at very high energies, nucleon decay, and other underground experiments. *Mailing Add:* Argonne Nat Lab Bldg 362 Argonne IL 60439. *E-Mail:* ayres@hep.anl.gov

AYRES, GILBERT HAVEN, ANALYTICAL CHEMISTRY. *Current Pos:* from assoc prof to prof, 47-74, chmn dept chem, 50-52, grad adv, 57-61 & 65-69, EMER PROF CHEM, UNIV TEX, AUSTIN, 74- *Personal Data:* b Upland, Ind, Aug 29, 04; m 26; c 2. *Educ:* Taylor Univ, AB, 25; Univ Wis, PhD(chem), 30. *Prof Exp:* Instr chem, Taylor Univ, 25-27; asst, Univ Wis, 27-30, instr, 30-31; from asst prof to assoc prof, Smith Col, 31-47. *Mem:* AAAS; Am Chem Soc. *Res:* Spectrophotometric methods of analysis; analytical chemistry of platinum elements. *Mailing Add:* 2101 Butts Dr Arlington TX 76012-1820

AYRES, JAMES WALTER, PHARMACOKINETICS, BIOPHARMACEUTICS. *Current Pos:* PROF PHARMACOKINETICS & BIOPHARMACEUT, ORE STATE UNIV, 70- *Personal Data:* b Boise, Idaho, Apr 14, 42; m 64; c 2. *Educ:* Idaho State Univ, BS, 65; Univ Kans, PhD(org med chem), 70. *Honors & Awards:* Inst Food Technol Indust Achievement Award, 82. *Concurrent Pos:* Scholar pharmacokinetics & biopharmaceut, Univ Mich, 77; scholar pharmaceut, Glaxo, UK, 90. *Mem:* Acad Pharmaceut Sci; fel Am Pharmaceut Asn; Am Asn Cols Pharm; fel Am Asn Pharmaceut Sci. *Res:* Drug product formulation and evaluation; biopharmaceutics; pharmacokinetics. *Mailing Add:* Ore State Univ Sch Pharm Corvallis OR 97331-3507

AYRES, JOSE MARCIO CORREA, CONSERVATION BIOLOGY, PRIMATOLOGY. *Current Pos:* assoc researcher, 86-96, SR RESEARCHER, MUSEU PARAENSE EMILIO GOELDI, BRAZIL, 96-; SR CONSERV ZOOLOGIST, WILDLIFE CONSERV SOC, NY, 90- *Personal Data:* b Feb 21, 54; Brazilian citizen; div, Deborah De Magalhaes; c Daniel & Lucas. *Educ:* Univ Sao Paulo, Brazil, BSc, 76; Nat Inst Amazonian Res, Brazil, MSc, 81; Univ Cambridge, UK, PhD(primatology), 86. *Honors & Awards:* Gold Medal, World Wide Fund Nature, 92; Augusto Ruschi Prize, Brazilian Acad Sci, 95. *Prof Exp:* Asst researcher, Nat Inst Amazonian Res, Brazil, 77-86. *Concurrent Pos:* Mem, Primate Specialist Group, Int Union Conserv Nature & Natural Resources, 77-, Sci Comt, Nat Inst Amazonian Res, Brazil, 91-; prof primatology & field ecol, Fed Univ Paraguay, 89-; gen coordr, Mamiraua Proj, Nat Res Coun, 90-; dir ecosyst, Nat Environ Agency Brazil, 91-92; dep-chmn, Species Survival Comn, World Conserv Union, 97- *Mem:* Brazilian Acad Sci; fel Linnean Soc; Sociedade Civil Mamiraua. *Res:* Field ecology of Amazonian primates; investigate basic ecological features of wildlife and ecosystems in order to understand the factors that limit distribution and population size of fungivores in tropical rainforests; conservation of Amazonian fauna; establishment of conservation strategies for biodiversity by means of protected areas. *Mailing Add:* Wildlife Conserv Soc Bronx Zoo Bronx NY 10460. *Fax:* 55-91-2496369

AYRES, KATHLEEN N, DEVELOPMENTAL BIOLOGY, CELL BIOLOGY. *Current Pos:* CONSULT, 90- *Educ:* Univ Chicago, PhD(cell & develop biol), 76. *Prof Exp:* Peace Corps, 62-65; fel, Ohio State Univ, 77-78; res assoc, Univ Chicago, 78-80, 88-90 & Univ Ill Med Ctr, 82-85; asst prof cell & molecular biol, Ill Benedictine Col, 91-92. *Mem:* Am Soc Cell Biol. *Mailing Add:* 6708 Meadowcrest Dr Downers Grove IL 60516-3546

AYRES, ROBERT U, TECHNOLOGY, ECONOMICS & ENVIRONMENT. *Current Pos:* AT INSEAD, 92-, SANDOZ PROF ENVIRON & MGT. *Personal Data:* b Plainfield, NJ, June 29, 32; m 54, Leslie Wentz; c Jennifer L. *Educ:* Univ Chicago, BS, 54; Univ Md, MS, 56; Univ London, PhD(math physics), 58. *Prof Exp:* Res assoc physics, Univ Md, 58-60, G C Dewey Corp, NY, 60-61 & Grad Sch Sci, Yeshiva Univ, 61-62; mem res staff, Hudson Inst, 62-67; vis scholar, Resources for the Future, 67-68; vpres, Int Res & Technol Corp, 69-75, chmn, 76; vpres & dir, Delta Res Corp, 76-78; prof eng & pub policy, Carnegie-Mellon Univ, 79-92. *Concurrent Pos:* Chmn, Vari-Flex Corp, 69-87; mem, Hwy Res Bd Comt on New Transp Systs & Technol, 71-, Nat Acad Sci Comt Technol & Water, Comt Alternatives for Reduction Chlorofluorocarbon Emissions, Nat Mat Adv Bd Comt Tech Aspects Strategic & Critical Mat; prin consult, UN Statist Off, 74-78; dep prog leader, Int Inst Appl Sci Anal, 86-90. *Mem:* Soc Hist Technol; Am Econ Asn; fel AAAS; Asn Environ Resource Economists; Schumpeter Soc. *Res:* Resource and environmental economics and technology; technology and economics systems modelling and forecasting; evolutionary economics; environmental indicators; industrial metabolism; industrial ecology. *Mailing Add:* INSEAD Blvd d'Constance 77305 Fountainebleu Cedex France. *Fax:* 33-1-6072; *E-Mail:* ayres@insead.fr

AYRES, STEPHEN MCCLINTOCK, INTERNAL MEDICINE. *Current Pos:* DEAN, MED COL VA, 85- *Personal Data:* b Elizabeth, NJ, Oct 29, 29; m 55; c 3. *Educ:* Gettysburg Col, BA, 51; Cornell Univ, MD, 55. *Honors & Awards:* Phoenix Award, Found Critical Care Med, 83. *Prof Exp:* Dir cardiopulmonary lab, St Vincent's Hosp, New York, 63-73; prof med, Med Sch Univ Mass, 73-75; prof int med & chmn dept, St Louis Univ Sch Med, 75-85. *Concurrent Pos:* Chmn, Pulmonary Dis Adv Comt, 76 & 79-80. *Mem:* Soc Critical Care Med (pres, 79); Am Lung Asn; Am Soc Clin Invest; Asn Am Prof; Am Col Cardiol. *Mailing Add:* Va Commonwealth Univ Sch Med MCV Sta Box 565 Richmond VA 23298-0565

AYRES, WESLEY P, PHYSICS. *Current Pos:* INDEPENDENT MGT CONSULT, 75- *Personal Data:* b Los Angeles, Calif, Sept 26, 24; m 48; c 2. *Educ:* Fresno State Col, BS, 51; Stanford Univ, MS, 53, PhD(physics), 54. *Prof Exp:* Sr engr, Electronic Defense Lab, Sylvania Elec Prod, Gen Tel & Electronics Corp, 54-56; vpres eng, Melabs, Inc, 56-69; dir systs eng, Bus Equip Div, SCM Corp, 69-73, mgr consult, 73-75. *Mem:* Am Phys Soc; Inst Elec & Electronics Engrs; Sigma Xi. *Res:* Application of solid state physics at microwave frequencies to achieve new devices; study and design of microwave systems; study and development of systems engineering techniques to office equipment research and development. *Mailing Add:* 12760 Camino Medio Ln Los Altos Hills CA 94022

AYROUD, ABDUL-MEJID, CHEMISTRY, PULP & PAPER. *Current Pos:* RETIRED. *Personal Data:* b Aleppo, Syria, Nov 24, 26; nat Can; m 54, Suzanne Vincent; c Mejid, Yasmine & Mouna (Westergard). *Educ:* Univ Lille, ChE, 49; Fr Sch Paper Making, Papermaking E, 50; Univ Grenoble, PhD(chem), 53. *Honors & Awards:* First Prize, Grenable Univ, France, 53. *Prof Exp:* Head, Res Dept, Fr Sch Paper Making, 53-57; chem engr, Pulp & Paper Res Inst Can, 57-58; sr res chemist, Res Ctr, Consol Paper Corp, Ltd, 58-60, leader chem pulping, 60-66, sect chief, Res & Develop Ctr, 66-67, mgr chem pulping & bleaching, Res & Develop Ctr, Consol-Bathurst Ltd, 67-71, asst dir, Res & Tech Serv, 71-84, dir res, Consul-Bathurst Ltd, 84-89. *Concurrent Pos:* Lectr, Univ Laval & Univ Que; consult, 89-; pres, AMA Paper Tech Inc; mem, Res Comt, Can Pulp & Paper Asn Tech Sect. *Mem:* Tech Asn Pulp & Paper Indust; Can Pulp & Paper Asn. *Res:* Applied chemistry; wood chemistry; pulp and paper technology; pollution abatement; administration. *Mailing Add:* 31 Dr Rigby Lachute PQ J8H 4A2 Can

AYUSO, KATHARINE, FOOD SCIENCE. *Current Pos:* RETIRED. *Personal Data:* b New York, NY, June 25, 18. *Educ:* St Lawrence Univ, BS, 40. *Prof Exp:* Asst chief chemist, Great Atlantic & Pac Tea Co, 42-65; assoc res dir, Foster D Snell, Inc, Booz Allen & Hamilton, 65-73; dir food sci, Rosner-Hixson Labs, 73-78; dir, Food Prod Develop, Herbert V Shuster, Inc, 78-85. *Mem:* Am Inst Chemists; Am Asn Cereal Chemists; Inst Food Technologists; Am Chem Soc; Am Asn Candy Technologists. *Res:* New product development, product reformulation, utilization of by-products; development of foods for the future; consumer evaluation studies. *Mailing Add:* 8 Plympton St No 32 Cambridge MA 02138

AYVAZIAN, L FRED, internal medicine, for more information see previous edition

AYYAGARI, L RAO, DNA REPLICATION, BIOLOGY EDUCATION. *Current Pos:* from asst prof to assoc prof, 83-91, PROF BIOL, LINDENWOOD COL, ST CHARLES, 91- *Personal Data:* b Mogallu, India, Dec 30, 40; US citizen; m 72; c 2. *Educ:* Bombay Univ, India, BSc, 60, MSc, 65; Loyola Univ Chicago, MS, 69, PhD(biochem), 72. *Prof Exp:* Postdoctoral fel, Univ Calif, Davis, 72-77; res scientist, Mich Cancer Found, 77-79; instr chem, Univ Mich, Dearborn, 79-82. *Concurrent Pos:* Vis res fel, Dept Biochem & Biophys, Wash Univ Med Sch, 90- *Mem:* AAAS; Am Arachnological Soc; Int Soc Chem Ecol; Nat Asn Biol Teachers. *Res:* Pheromones in invertebrates; DNA replication, especially fidelity in yeasts; radioactive waste disposal. *Mailing Add:* Dept Math & Sci Lindenwood Col 209 S Kings Hwy St Charles MO 63301-1695

AYYANGAR, KOMANDURI M, PHYSICS, MEDICAL PHYSICS. *Current Pos:* PROF & CHIEF PHYSICS, DEPT RADIATION THER, MED COL OHIO, TOLEDO, 92- *Personal Data:* b Andhra, India, Jan 13, 40; m 70; c 2. *Educ:* Andhra Univ, India, BSc, 58, MSc, 60, PhD(nuclear physics), 65. *Prof Exp:* Res fel nuclear physics, Andhra Univ, India, 60-66; res fel med physics, Physics Res Lab, Mass Gen Hosp, Boston, MA, 66-69; sci officer, Div Radiol Protection, Bhabha Atomic Res Ctr, Bombay, India, 70-74; trainee, Thomas Jefferson Univ Hosp, 75, from asst prof to assoc prof, 76-92, prof med physics, Dept Radiation Ther & Nuclear Med, 90-92. *Mem:* Am Asn Physicists in Med; Sigma Xi; Am Col Med Physics; Am Soc Ther Radiol; Radiol Soc NAm. *Res:* Nuclear medicine; radiation physics; radiation therapy physics; nuclear cardiology; radiation dosimetry. *Mailing Add:* Med Col Ohio Dept Radiation Ther 3000 Arlington Ave Toledo OH 43699-0008. *Fax:* 419-382-3040; *E-Mail:* komanduri@opus.mco.edu

AYYASWAMY, PORTONOVO S, APPLIED MECHANICS, MECHANICAL ENGINEERING. *Current Pos:* from asst prof to assoc prof, 74-87, PROF MECH ENG, UNIV PA, 87. *Personal Data:* b Bangalore, India, Mar 21, 42; US citizen; m 75; c 2. *Educ:* Univ Mysore, BE, 62; Columbia Univ, MS, 65, ME, 67; Univ Calif, Los Angeles, PhD(eng), 71. *Prof Exp:* Postdoctoral fel geophysics, Inst Geophys & Planetary Phys, 71-72, postdoctoral scholar mech eng, Univ Calif, Los Angeles, 72-74. *Concurrent Pos:* Consult, Nat Air Oil Burner Co, Inc, Philadelphia, 76- & Combustion Unlimited Inc, Jenkintown, Pa, 78-; electric power res inst grant, 75-77; NSF grant, 78; NIH grants, 81-, Battelle, NC, 84-; US deleg, Nuclear reactor safety to People's Repub of China, 85; key note lectr, Nat Heat & Mass Transfer Conf, India, 85; invited lectr Condensation Theory, Cavendish Labs, Univ Cambridge, Eng, 86; invited lectr Condensation Theory, Royal Inst Technol, Stockholm, Sweden, 86; invited lectr Condensation Theory, Danish Ctr Appl Math & Mech, Lyngby, Denmark, 86; mem, eval panel for award-NSF, 87, mem, panelist Workshop Combustion, Sandia Nat Labs, 88. *Mem:* Am Soc Mech Engrs; Am Nuclear Soc; Radiation Res Soc. *Res:* Stability of fluid motion, natural convection flow and stability, two-phase flows condensation, evaporation, combustion, plasma heat transfer and stability; nuclear reactor safety analysis, solar energy heat collection and utilization; bioheat transfer. *Mailing Add:* Dept Mech Eng SEAS Univ Pa Philadelphia PA 19104

AZAD, ABDU F(ARHANG), PARASITOLOGY, TROPICAL MEDICINE. *Current Pos:* Fel, 76-78, from asst prof to assoc prof, 78-89, PROF MICROBIOL, DEPT MICROBIOL, SCH MED, UNIV MD, 90- *Personal Data:* b Iran, Nov 9, 42; US citizen; m 71; c 1. *Educ:* Univ Tehran, DrPhar, 66, MPH, 69; Johns Hopkins Univ, PhD(parasitol), 76. *Concurrent Pos:* Team-leader, Iran-WHO, 68-69; vis scientist USSR, Nat Acad Sci, 71; mem field team, Ethiopia, Burma, Pakistan & Iran, 76-78; consult, WHO, 76-78 & Med Serv Consult, 79-; mem expert comt rodent-borne dis, WHO, 73-77; mem NIH Alaska-hemorraghic fever proj, Univ Md, 81. *Mem:* AAAS; Am Soc Trop Med & Hyg; Am Soc Ricketsiology & Rickettsial Dis (pres, 92-); Am Soc Microbiol. *Res:* Vector biology; transmission dynamics of arthropods-borne diseases; host immunological resposes to insect bitos; host-parasite interactions; reactivation of latent infection by artificial stress. *Mailing Add:* Dept Microbiol & Immunol Sch Med Univ Md 660 W Redwood St Baltimore MD 21201

AZAD, HARDAM SINGH, ENVIRONMENTAL ENGINEERING, CHEMICAL ENGINEERING. *Current Pos:* dir environ projs, 75-77, dir eng, 77-81, GEN MGR, HOUSTON ENG DIV, NUS CORP, 81- *Personal Data:* b Abohar, India, Aug 10, 38; m 65; c 2. *Educ:* Punjab Univ, BA, 60; Kans State Univ, BS, 64; Univ Mo-Columbia, MS, 65; Univ Mich, PhD(environ eng), 68. *Prof Exp:* Water resources engr, Irrigation Dept, Punjab Govt, 58-62; res asst, Univ Mo, 64-65; teaching fel & res assoc, Univ Mich, 65-68; supvr pollution control res & develop lab & mgr water pollution control plant, Abbott Labs, 68-70; sr res group leader, Monsanto Biodize Systs, Inc, 70-71; indust develop mgr, Monsanto Envirochem Systs Inc, 71-72; mgr environ control, McKee Corp, 72-75. *Mem:* Water Pollution Control Fedn; Am Inst Chem Engrs. *Res:* Biochemical wastewater treatment processes; activated carbon adsorption; chemical oxidations; ecological and eutrophication investigation; water renovation and reuse; recovery and recycling in industrial pollution control. *Mailing Add:* 8730 Memorial Dr Houston TX 77024

AZAM, FAROOQ, MICROBIAL ECOLOGY. *Current Pos:* res biologist, Scripps Inst Oceanog, Univ Calif, San Diego, 69-73, res biologist marine microbial ecol, Inst Marine Resources, PROF MARINE BIOL, SCRIPPS INST OCEANOG, UNIV CALIF, LA JOLLA, 88- *Personal Data:* b Lahore, Pakistan. *Educ:* Panjab Univ, BSc, 61, MSc, 63; Czech Acad Sci, Prague, CSc(microbiol), 68. *Honors & Awards:* Rosenstiel Award, Marine Sci, 84. *Prof Exp:* Res assoc anal biochem, West Regional Labs, Coun Sci & Indust Res, Pakistan, 63-65; fel biochem, State Univ NY Stony Brook, 68-69. *Mem:* AAAS; Am Soc Microbiol; Am Soc Limnol Oceanog. *Res:* Biochemistry; role of bacteria in marine food webs; transport of sugars and amino acids in marine bacteria; metabolic regulation in marine bacteria. *Mailing Add:* 12936 Longboat Way Del Mar CA 92014

AZAR, HENRY A, PATHOLOGY. *Current Pos:* PROF PATH, COL MED, UNIV S FLA, 72-; CHIEF LAB SERV, 72-83, CHIEF ANAT PATH, VET JAMES A HALEY HOSP, TAMPA, 83- *Personal Data:* b Heliopolis, Egypt, Dec 21, 27; US citizen; m 60; c 2. *Educ:* Am Univ Beirut, BA, 48, MD, 52; Am Bd Path, dipl, cert anat path, 58, cert clin path, 74, cert hematol, 76. *Prof Exp:* Asst prof path, Am Univ Beirut, 58-60; from asst prof to assoc prof, Col Physicians & Surgeons, Columbia Univ, 60-70; prof path & dir surg path, Univ Kans Med Ctr, Kansas City, 70-72. *Concurrent Pos:* Assoc dir path, Francis Delafield Hosp, 68-70; assoc attend pathologist, Presby Hosp, 68-70. *Mem:* Col Am Path; Harvey Soc; Int Acad Path; Arthur Purdy Stout Soc Surg Path. *Res:* Lymphomas; myeloma; human tumor xenografts. *Mailing Add:* Dept Path Univ SFla Col Med Tampa FL 33620

AZAR, JAMAL J, DRILLING ENGINEERING, SOLID MECHANICS & STRUCTURAL ANALYSIS. *Current Pos:* asst prof struct dynamics & vehicle struct, 65-68, assoc prof mech & aerospace eng, 68-73, PROF PETROL ENG & DIR DRILLING RES PROJS, UNIV TULSA, 74- *Personal Data:* b Tripoli, Lebanon, sept 19, 37; US citizen; m 61, Jean Bradshaw; c Scott & Steven. *Educ:* Univ Okla, BS, 61, MS, 62, PhD(mech eng), 65. *Prof Exp:* Sr res engr, Okla Univ Res Inst, 61-65. *Concurrent Pos:* Consult var cos & govt orgns; int lectr drilling eng. *Mem:* Soc Petrol Engrs; Am Soc Mech Engrs; Int Asn Drilling & Contractors. *Res:* Drilling-bit mechanics; wellbore hydraulics; drillstring mechanics; wellbore mechanics. *Mailing Add:* Dept Petroleum Eng Univ Tulsa Tulsa OK 74104. *Fax:* 918-631-3125, 492-2878

AZAR, MIGUEL M, IMMUNOLOGY, PATHOLOGY. *Current Pos:* asst prof lab med & dir blood bank, 69-70, assoc prof lab med & dir clin lab, 70-75, PROF LAB MED, DIR LABS & DIR GRAD STUDIES LAB MED & PATH, VET ADMIN HOSPS, SCH MED, UNIV MINN, MINNEAPOLIS, 75- *Personal Data:* b Cordoba, Arg, Oct 21, 36; m 60; c 6. *Educ:* Nat Col Dean Funes, Arg, BA, 53; Cordoba Nat Univ, MD, 58; Univ Tenn, PhD(path), 65. *Prof Exp:* Assoc physician, Children's Hosp, Cordoba, 58-60; intern, Mercy Hosp, Des Moines, Iowa, 60-61; resident pediatrician, Med Units, Univ Tenn, 61-63, res assoc, 66-67. *Concurrent Pos:* Nat Inst Allergy & Infectious Dis spec fel immunol, Sch Med, Univ Minn, Minneapolis, 67-69; vis prof path, Harvard Med Sch, 87-89; USA rep, Allergy & Immunol Divs, Asn Latin Am Pediat; allergy & immunol ed, Medico; ed, (Immunossuppression) Immunol Res. *Mem:* Am Asn Immunol; Soc Exp Biol & Med; Am Soc Exp Path; Asn Latin Am Pediat. *Res:* Pediatric pathology; immunopathology; allergy. *Mailing Add:* 6609 Field Way Minneapolis MN 55436. *Fax:* 612-725-2079; *E-Mail:* azarx001@staff.tc.umn.edu

AZARI, PARVIZ, BIOCHEMISTRY. *Current Pos:* Asst prof chem & physiol, 63-70, assoc prof biochem, 70-75, PROF BIOCHEM, COLO STATE UNIV, 75- *Personal Data:* b Baku, Russia, Feb 3, 30; US citizen; m 55; c 5. *Educ:* Univ Calif, AB, 55; Univ Nebr, MS, 58, PhD(chem), 61. *Concurrent Pos:* USPH fel, 61-63, grant, 64- *Mem:* AAAS; Am Soc Biol Chem; Sigma Xi; Am Soc Biochem Molecular Biol. *Res:* Biochemical and molecular mechanisms of aging lens. *Mailing Add:* Colo State Univ Ft Collins CO 80523-1870. *E-Mail:* pazari@vines.colostate.edu

AZARNOFF, DANIEL LESTER, CLINICAL PHARMACOLOGY. *Current Pos:* PRES, D L AZARNOFF ASSOC, 86- *Personal Data:* b Brooklyn, NY, Aug 4, 26; m 51, Joanne Stokes; c Rachel, Richard & Martin. *Educ:* Rutgers Univ, BS, 47, MS, 48; Univ Kans, MD, 55. *Honors & Awards:* Res Achievement Award Clin Sci, Am Asn Pharmaceut Sci; Oscar B Hunter Award. *Prof Exp:* Res assoc, Univ Kans, 49-52, intern, 55-56; asst prof med, Sch Med, St Louis Univ, 60-62; from asst prof to assoc prof med & dir, Clin Pharmacol Study Unit, Med Ctr, Univ Kans, 64-68, prof med & pharmacol, 68-73, distinguished prof med & pharmacol, 73-78; sr vpres, G D Searle & Co, 78-79, pres res & develop, 79-85; prof path & clin prof pharmacol, Northwestern Univ Med Sch, 78-86. *Concurrent Pos:* USPHS res fel med, Univ Kans, 56-58; Nat Inst Neurol Dis & Blindness spec trainee, Sch Med, Wash Univ, 58-60; John & Mary R Markle scholar acad med, 62-67; Burroughs-Wellcome scholar clin pharmacol, 64-69; Fulbright scholar, Karolinska Inst, Sweden, 68; mem, Drug Res Bd, Nat Res Coun, Adv Coun & Pharmacol-Toxicol Prog Adv Comt, Nat Inst Gen Med Sci & Comt Revision, US Pharmacopoeia; ed, Rev Drug Interactions & Year Bk Drug Ther; clin prof med, Univ Kans Med Sch. *Mem:* Inst Med Nat Acad Sci; fel Am Col Physicians; Brit Pharmacol Soc; Am Soc Pharmacol & Exp Therapeut; fel NY Acad Sci; fel Am Asn Pharmaceut Scientists; fel AAAS; Am Soc Clin Pharmaceut Therapeuts. *Res:* Lipid metabolism; drug development. *Mailing Add:* DL Azarnoff Assoc 433 Airport Blvd Suite 419 Burlingame CA 94010-2014. *Fax:* 650-340-1510; *E-Mail:* diazai@sirius.com

AZAROFF, LEONID VLADIMIROVICH, X-RAY CRYSTALLOGRAPHY. *Current Pos:* PROF PHYSICS & DIR INST MAT SCI, UNIV CONN, 66- *Personal Data:* b Moscow, Russia, June 19, 26; nat US; m 46, 71. *Educ:* Tufts Univ, BS, 48; Mass Inst Technol, PhD(crystallog), 54. *Prof Exp:* Asst res engr, Raytheon Mfg Co, 41-44; asst, Mass Inst Technol, 50-52; assoc, 52-53; assoc physicist, Armour Res Found, 53-55, res physicist, 55-56, sr scientist, 56-57; from assoc prof to prof metall eng, Ill Inst Technol, 57-66. *Concurrent Pos:* Guest physicist, Brookhaven Nat Lab, 61-64. *Mem:* Am Phys Soc; Am Crystallog Asn; Mineral Soc Am; Am Inst Min, Metall & Petrol Eng; Am Soc Eng Educ. *Res:* Physics of metals; x-ray diffraction; soft x-ray spectroscopy; liquid-crystal polymers. *Mailing Add:* 5555 Heron Point Dr Naples FL 33963

AZBEL, MARK, RANDOM SYSTEMS. *Current Pos:* prof physics, 73-87, CHAIR THEORET PHYSICS, TEL-AVIV UNIV, ISRAEL, 88. *Personal Data:* b Poltava, USSR, May 12, 32; Israel citizen; c Vadim & Julia. *Educ:* Kharkov Univ, USSR, MA, 53, PhD, 55; Inst Phys Prob, Moscow DSc(physics), 57. *Honors & Awards:* Lomonosov Prize; Landau Prize; Christopher Award. *Prof Exp:* Prof physics, Kharkov State Univ, USSR, 57-65, Moscow State Univ & Landau Inst Theoret Phys, 65-72. *Concurrent Pos:* Consult, AT&T Bell Labs, IBM, 78-; adj prof, Univ Pa, Philadelphia, 80-; chmn theoret physics, Univ Lousanne, Switz, 81-82. *Mem:* Israeli Phys Soc; fel Am Phys Soc; Europ Phys Soc; NY Acad Sci. *Res:* Predictions of cyclotron resonance in metals; Kantor set-type spectrum; theory of the helix coil transition in DNA and of resonance tunneling in random systems. *Mailing Add:* Sch Physics & Astron Tel-Aviv Univ Tel-Aviv Israel. *Fax:* 972-3-6422979

AZBELL, WILLIAM, PHYSICS. *Current Pos:* ASSOC PROF PHYSICS & HEAD DEPT, WARTBURG COL, 52- *Personal Data:* b Manito, Ill, Jan 1, 06; m; c Marilyn, Bonnie & Norman. *Educ:* Ill State Norm Univ, BS, 33; Univ Ill, AM, 34. *Prof Exp:* Pub sch instr, Ill, 34-41; instr physics, Exten Div, Univ Ill, 41-43, Army Specialized Training Prog, Ball State Teachers Col, 43-44, Navy V-12, DePauw Univ, 44-45 & Univ Ill, 45-46; asst prof, Bradley Univ, 46-52. *Mem:* Am Asn Physics Teachers. *Res:* Atomic physics. *Mailing Add:* 502 Fourth St SW Waverly IA 50677

AZEN, EDWIN ALLAN, HEMATOLOGY, MEDICINE. *Current Pos:* Asst prof, 63-69, assoc prof, 69-74, PROF MED, UNIV WIS-MADISON, 74-, PROF MED GENETICS, 81- *Personal Data:* b Pittsburgh, Pa, March 13, 31; c 4. *Educ:* Univ Chicago, BA, 51; Univ Pittsburgh, MD, 55. *Mem:* AAAS; Am Fedn Clin Res; Am Soc Hematol; Am Soc Human Genetics. *Res:* Genetic research on human salivary proteins; genetic polymorphisms of salivary proteins using electrophoretic and recombinant DNA techniques. *Mailing Add:* Dept Med Hemat Univ Wis Hosp Madison WI 53706

AZHAR, SALMAN, REPRODUCTIVE ENDOCRINOLOGY, HORMONE METABOLISM. *Current Pos:* BIOCHEMIST, VET ADMIN MED CTR, 80- *Educ:* La, Kampur Univ, India, PhD(biochem), 73. *Mailing Add:* GRECC Vet Admin Hosp 3801 Miranda Ave Palo Alto CA 94304-1207. *Fax:* 650-855-9437

AZIZ, ABDUL, DRUG ANALYSIS, HIGH PERFORMANCE LIQUID CHROMATOGRAPHY. *Current Pos:* DIR LAB, HALSEY DRUG CO, INC, 94- *Personal Data:* m 64, Joan Forman; c Mariam & Frederick. *Educ:* Karachi Univ, BS, 50; pharm dipl, 57; Long Island Univ, MS, 65; Univ Pittsburgh, PhD(pharmaceut sci), 69. *Prof Exp:* Analytical chemist, NYSCO Lab Inc, 61-65; proj coordr, Julius Schmid Labs Inc, 65-67; mgr lab, NYSCO Lab, 69-70; asst prof, Arnold & Marie Schwartz Col Pharm, 70-78; dir lab, Zenith Lab, 78-86 & Ambix Lab, 88-93. *Concurrent Pos:* Pharmacist, Guvenier Hosp, 72-78. *Mem:* Am Chem Soc; Am Pharm Asn; Am Inst Chemists. *Res:* Development of analytical methods for new and generic drugs; new high-performance liquid chromatography methods for different drug products; good manufacturing practices in drug industry; technical writing. *Mailing Add:* 82-67 Austin St Apt 412 Kew Gardens NY 11415

AZIZ, KHALID, CHEMICAL ENGINEERING, PETROLEUM ENGINEERING. *Current Pos:* assoc dean res, Sch Earth Sci, Stanford Univ, 83-86, chmn petrol eng, 86-91, actg chmn, 93-94, chmn petrol eng, 94-95, PROF PETROL ENG, STANFORD UNIV, 82-, OTTO N MILLER PROF EARTH SCI, 89- *Personal Data:* b Pakistan, Sept 29, 36; Can citizen; m 62, Mussarrat Rizwani; c Natasha & Imraan. *Educ:* Univ Mich, BSE, 55; Univ Alta, BSc, 58, MSc, 61; Rice Univ, PhD(chem eng), 66. *Honors & Awards:* Gold Medal, Asn Prof Engrs Alta, 58; Cedric K Ferguson Cert Award, Soc Petrol Engrs, 79; Reservoir Eng Award, Soc Petrol Engrs, 87, Lester C Uren Award, 88, Distinguished Achievement Award, 90; Peter the Great Medal, Russia, 96, Kapitsa Medal, 96. *Prof Exp:* Jr design engr, Massey-Ferguson, 55-56; distribution engr, 58-59, Karachi Gas Co, chief engr, 62-63; from instr to asst prof petrol eng, Univ Alta, 60-62; from asst prof to prof chem & petrol eng, Univ Calgary, 65-82. *Concurrent Pos:* Vis scientist, Inst Francais Petrol, 70; vis scholar, Stanford Univ, 71; Killam resident fel, Univ Calgary, 77; mem, US Nat Comt World Petrol Cong, 83-; dir, Golden Gate Sect Soc Petrol Eng, 86-88; assoc fac, Sci Comput & Comput Math Prog, Comput Sci Dept, Stanford Univ, 88-; vis prof, Mining Univ, Leoben, Austria, 89; hon prof, Univ Calgary, 94-; exed ed, Soc Petrol Engrs J Univ. *Mem:* Nat Acad Eng; Soc Petrol Engrs; Sigma Xi; Am Inst Chem Engrs; Soc Indust & Appl Math; hon mem Am Inst Mining, Metall & Petrol Engrs; hon mem Soc Petrol Engrs; fel Chem Inst Can; foreign mem Russ Acad Nat Sci. *Res:* Multiphase and single phase flow of oil, gas and their mixtures in pipes and design of innovative oil and gas transportation and production systems; reservoir simulation and the use of innovative technologies for the development of oil and gas fields; natural gas engineering and hydrocarbon fluid phase behavior; author of numerous publications. *Mailing Add:* 112 Peter Coutts Circle Stanford CA 94305-2170. *Fax:* 650-725-2099

AZIZ, PHILIP MICHAEL, physical chemistry, for more information see previous edition

AZIZ, RONALD A, CHEMICAL PHYSICS. *Current Pos:* from asst prof to assoc prof, Univ Waterloo, 58-67, assoc dean grad studies, Fac Sci, 76-81, prof, 67-91, DISTINGUISHED EMER PROF PHYSICS, UNIV WATERLOO, 91- *Personal Data:* b Toronto, Ont, Sept 27, 28; m 59, Joan Ferguson; c Andrew, Diana & Jeffrey. *Educ:* Univ Toronto, BA, 50, MA, 51, PhD(physics), 55. *Prof Exp:* Lectr physics, Royal Mil Col, Can, 55-57; asst prof, Univ Windsor, 57-58. *Concurrent Pos:* Heinemann Found scholar, 65-66. *Mem:* Fel Am Phys Soc. *Res:* Low temperature physics; solidified inert gas solids; intermolecular potentials; thermodynamic and transport properties. *Mailing Add:* Dept Physics Univ Waterloo Waterloo ON N2L 3G1 Can. *Fax:* 519-888-3456 Ext 2727; *E-Mail:* aziz@watvm.uwaterloo.ca

AZMANOV, ISKREN DENEV, COMMUNIST CONFLICTS IN SCIENCE, TWENTIETH-CENTURY SCIENCE HISTORY. *Current Pos:* VIS RESEARCHER HIST SCI, UNIV CALIF, SANTA BARBARA, 95- *Personal Data:* b Sofia, Bulgaria, Feb 1, 48; m 79, Elena Todorova; c Elisabeth, Vangelia & Iana. *Educ:* Agr Inst Sofia, Bulgaria, BS, 76; Inst Genetics, MS, 77; Bulg Acad Sci, Sofia, PhD(hist), 89. *Hon Degrees:* Dr, NY Acad Sci, 91. *Prof Exp:* Dir youth house, Blagoevgrad District Comsomol, 77-79; secy dist comt, Bulgarian-Soviet, 80-82; researcher, Dept Sci Knowledge, Bulg Acad Sci, 82-91. *Concurrent Pos:* sci secy, Comn Presidium, Bulg Acad Sci, 88-90; newsp publ, Bulgarian Nat Front, 90-94. *Mem:* AAAS; Am Asn Advan Slavic Studies; Agr Hist Soc; Hist Sci Soc. *Res:* History of agricultural science, Russian science and East-European relationships; history of phytopathology and genetics; using the ocean; actual plant protection; science and religions relationship. *Mailing Add:* 414 W Canon Perdido St Santa Barbara CA 93101. *Fax:* 805-899-4663

AZOFF, EDWARD ARTHUR, MATHEMATICS. *Current Pos:* from asst prof to assoc prof, 75-84, PROF MATH, UNIV GA, 85- *Personal Data:* b Chicago, Ill, Oct 4, 45. *Educ:* Univ Chicago, BS, 67; Univ Mich, MS, 69, PhD(math), 72. *Prof Exp:* Res assoc math, Univ Ga, 72-73, vis asst prof, 73-74; asst prof, Univ Iowa, 74-75. *Concurrent Pos:* Res assoc, NSF, 73-74, prin investr, 75, co-prin investr, 76-85. *Mem:* Am Math Soc. *Res:* Operator theory; operator algebras; measurable selections. *Mailing Add:* Univ Ga Athens GA 30602-7403

AZPEITIA, ALFONSO GIL, MATHEMATICS. *Current Pos:* PROF MATH, UNIV MASS, BOSTON, 65- *Personal Data:* b Madrid, Spain, Feb 22, 22; nat US. *Educ:* Univ Madrid, BA, 39, MA, 46, PhD, 52. *Prof Exp:* Res assoc, Nat Res Coun, Spain, 52-55; res assoc, Brown Univ, 55-57; from instr to prof math, Univ Mass, Amherst, 57-65. *Concurrent Pos:* Fulbright lectr, 69-70. *Mem:* Am Math Soc; Math Asn Am; Soc Indust & Appl Math; Opers Res Soc Am. *Res:* Theory of functions; linear and mathematical programming. *Mailing Add:* 135 Pleasant St 602 Brookline MA 02146

AZUMAYA, GORO, ALGEBRA. *Current Pos:* vis prof, 65-66, EMER PROF MATH, IND UNIV, BLOOMINGTON, 68- *Personal Data:* b Yokohama, Japan, Feb 26, 20; m 50; c 1. *Educ:* Tokyo Univ, BS, 42; Nagoya Univ, PhD(math), 49. *Honors & Awards:* Chunichi Cultural Prize, Japan, 49. *Prof Exp:* From lectr to asst prof math, Nagoya Univ, 45-53; prof, Hokkaido Univ,

53-68. *Concurrent Pos:* Fel math, Off Naval Res, Yale Univ, 56-58; NSF fel, Northwestern Univ, 58-59; vis prof, Univ Mass, 64-65; vis prof, Univ Munich, 75-76; fel math, ETH Zurich, 83-84. *Mem:* Math Soc Japan; Am Math Soc. *Res:* Ring theory; number theory; homological algebra. *Mailing Add:* Ind Univ Bloomington IN 47405-4301

AZZAM, RASHEED M A, ELLIPSOMETRY, THIN FILMS. *Current Pos:* from assoc prof to prof, 79-82, DISTINGUISHED PROF ELEC ENG, UNIV NEW ORLEANS, 82- *Personal Data:* b Elminia, Egypt, Mar 9, 45; m 74, Fatema Elmoursi; c Reem, Omar, Adel, Yousef, Kareem & Yahya. *Educ:* Cairo Univ, Egypt, BSc, 67; Univ Nebr, Lincoln, PhD(elec eng), 71. *Honors & Awards:* Photonics Circle Excellence Award, Photonics Spectrom Mag, 93; Res & Develop 100 Awards, Res & Develop Mag, 93. *Prof Exp:* Fel elec eng, Univ Nebr, Lincoln, 72-74, assoc prof eng & med, 74-79. *Concurrent Pos:* Researcher eng & med, Med Ctr, Univ Nebr, Omaha, 74-79; prin investr, NSF grant, Univ New Orleans, 81-83, 86-89 & 93-; sr Fulbright scholar, Univ Provence, 85-86; topical ed, J Optical Soc Am, 85-89, Appl Optics, 93- *Mem:* Fel Optical Soc Am; fel Soc Photo-Optical Instrumentation Engrs; Sigma Xi. *Res:* Surface science and thin-film optics; electrical engineering; polarization optics. *Mailing Add:* Dept Elec Eng Univ New Orleans Lakefront New Orleans LA 70148. *E-Mail:* rmaee@uno.edu

AZZARO, ALBERT J, NEUROPHARMACOLOGY. *Current Pos:* DIR CLIN PSYCHOPHARMACOL LAB SERV, CHESTNUT RIDGE HOSP, MORGANTOWN, WVA, 89-; PROF, DEPT NEUROL, PHARMACOL/TOXICOL & BEHAV MED/PSYCHIAT, HEALTH SCI CTR, WVA UNIV, MORGANTOWN, 83- *Personal Data:* b Apr 27, 43; m, Beverly Z Hummel; c James, Christopher, Laura Hummel & Christopher Hummel. *Educ:* Wheeling Jesuit Col, BS, 65; WVa Univ, PhD(pharmacol), 70. *Prof Exp:* Instr high sch biol & chem, Bishop Donahue High Sch, WVa, 65-66; fel pharmacol, Health Sci Ctr, Univ Colo, Denver, 70-71; from asst prof to prof, Dept Neurol & Pharmacol/Toxicol, Health Sci Ctr, WVa Univ, Morgantown, 71-83. *Concurrent Pos:* Grant reviewer, NSF, 75-85, Nat Inst Drug Abuse, 75 & US-Israel Binat Sci Found, 88- *Mem:* Sigma Xi; Soc Neurosci; AAAS; Am Soc Pharmacol & Exp Therapeut; Am Acad Neurol; NY Acad Sci. *Res:* Monoamine Oxidase-B inhibitors in the treatment of Parkinson's Disease; neurobiology and pharmacology of anxiety disorders. *Mailing Add:* Clin Develop Somerset Pharmaceut Inc 5415 W Laurel St Tampa FL 33607

B

BAAD, MICHAEL FRANCIS, PLANT TAXONOMY, ECOLOGY. *Current Pos:* assoc prof, 69-80, PROF BIOL SCI, CALIF STATE UNIV, SACRAMENTO, 80- *Personal Data:* b Hillsdale, Mich, Jan 5, 41; m 65, 79; c 1. *Educ:* Univ Mich, BS, 63, MS, 66; Univ Wash, PhD(bot), 69. *Mem:* Ecol Soc Am; Am Soc Plant Taxon; Int Soc Plant Taxon; Soc Study Evolution; Am Inst Biol Sci; Sigma Xi. *Res:* Taxonomy of the Caryophyllaceae; pollination ecology; plant succession; genecology; floristics of Central Sierra Nevada. *Mailing Add:* Dept Biol Sci Calif State Univ 6000 J St Sacramento CA 95819-2605

BAADSGAARD, HALFDAN, GEOCHEMISTRY. *Current Pos:* from asst prof to assoc prof, 57-66, PROF GEOCHEM, UNIV ALTA, 66- *Personal Data:* b Minneapolis, Minn, Apr 16, 29; Can citizen; m 57; c 5. *Educ:* Univ Minn, BS, 51; Swiss Fed Inst Technol, PhD, 55. *Prof Exp:* Sr res assoc, Univ Minn, 55-57. *Concurrent Pos:* NATO exchange prof, Copenhagen Univ, 64; vis fel, Res Sch Earth Sci, Australian Nat Univ, 82-83. *Mem:* Geochem Soc; Am Geophys Union; fel Geol Asn Can. *Res:* Methods of geologic dating; geochronology; trace elements in geochemical research. *Mailing Add:* Dept Geol Univ Alta Edmonton AB T6G 2M7 Can

BAALMAN, ROBERT J, BOTANY, ECOLOGY. *Current Pos:* from asst prof to assoc prof, 65-74, PROF BIOL, CALIF STATE UNIV, HAYWARD, 74- *Personal Data:* b Grinnell, Kans, Oct 28, 39; m 64, Judith A Oates; c Janet, Joseph & Gary. *Educ:* Ft Hays Kans State Univ, BS, 60, MS, 61; Univ Okla, PhD(bot), 65. *Prof Exp:* Teaching asst bot, Ft Hays Kans State Col, 60-61; teacher, High Sch, Kans, 61-62; teaching asst bot, Univ Okla, 62-64. *Mem:* AAAS; Ecol Soc Am; Am Forestry Asn; Am Inst Biol Sci. *Res:* Plant succession; fire as a successional factor; seed dissemination and germination; saline plant communities in inland and coastal areas; plant competition. *Mailing Add:* 24827 St Luke Ct Hayward CA 94541. *E-Mail:* rbaalman@csuhayward.edu

BAARDA, DAVID GENE, ORGANIC CHEMISTRY, ENVIRONMENTAL CHEMISTRY. *Current Pos:* from asst prof to assoc prof, 65-74, PROF CHEM, GA COL, 74- *Personal Data:* b Newton, Iowa, Apr 23, 37; m 62, Elizabeth Traylor; c JoAnne, Mary E & Laura J. *Educ:* Cent Col, Iowa, BA, 59; Univ Fla, MS, 60, PhD(org chem), 62. *Prof Exp:* Res asst chem, Univ Fla, 62-63; chemist, Texaco, Inc, 63-64, sr chemist, 64-65. *Concurrent Pos:* Danforth assoc, 70. *Mem:* Am Chem Soc. *Res:* Use of laboratory investigation and computerized data handling to teach chemistry at the undergraduate level. *Mailing Add:* Dept Chem Ga Col CPO Box 82 Milledgeville GA 31061

BAARS, DONALD LEE, STRATIGRAPHY, SEDIMENTARY PETROLOGY. *Current Pos:* RETIRED. *Personal Data:* b Oregon City, Ore, May 27, 28; m 97, Renate Henseik; c Karla, Jodi & Cayli. *Educ:* Univ Utah, BS, 52; Univ Colo, Boulder, PhD(geol), 65. *Honors & Awards:* Am Asn Petrol Geol Jour Award, 97. *Prof Exp:* Explor geologist, Shell Oil Co, 52-61; res geologist, Continental Oil Co, 61-62; assoc prof geol, Wash State Univ, 65-68; assoc prof, Ft Lewis Col, 68-70, prof geol, 70-80; consult petroleum geologist, 80-88; res petrol geologist, Kans Geol Surv, 88-96. *Concurrent Pos:* Proj dir, NSF Res Grant, 68-71; dir short course for col teachers proj, NSF, 70-71. *Mem:* Am Asn Petrol Geol; Fel Geol Soc Am; Soc Econ Paleont & Mineral. *Res:* Paleozoic stratigraphy of Colorado Plateau; carbonate sedimentation and sedimentary petrology; early Paleozoic paleotectonic history of the ancestral Rockies and related tectonic system; basement and early Paleozoic paleotectonic history of southern midcontinent. *Mailing Add:* 2939 Wellington Ave Grand Junction CO 81504-5362

BAASEL, WILLIAM DAVID, CHEMICAL ENGINEERING. *Current Pos:* asst prof, Ohio Univ, 62-66, assoc prof, 66-70, prof, 70-93, EMER PROF CHEM ENG, OHIO UNIV, 93- *Personal Data:* b Chicago, Ill, Mar 18, 32; m 60, 90, Arlene; c 3. *Educ:* Northwestern Univ, BS, 54, MS, 56; Cornell Univ, PhD(chem eng), 62. *Honors & Awards:* Fritz & Dolores Russ Res Award, 81. *Prof Exp:* Asst prof chem eng, Clemson Col, 59-62. *Concurrent Pos:* Mem, NSF Summer Inst, Mich Technol Univ, 63, US Environ Protection Agency, 78-80 & Coop Agreement, 80-83; Ford Found res eng practice, Dow Chem Co, Mich, 65-66, consult, 66-68; instr, Petaling Jaya Community Col, Petaling Jaya Malaysia, 86; actg chmn chem eng, Ohio Univ, 88-90. *Mem:* AAAS; Sigma Xi. *Res:* Environmental assessment, air pollution abatement, acid rain; plant design; author of three books. *Mailing Add:* 63 Mulligan Rd Athens OH 45701. *Fax:* 740-593-0873

BABA, ANTHONY JOHN, RADIATION PHYSICS. *Current Pos:* RETIRED. *Personal Data:* b Bethleham, Pa, May 2, 36; m 59; c 6. *Educ:* Georgetown Univ, BS, 57. *Prof Exp:* Physicist, Nat Bur Stand, 58-60; res physicist, Harry Diamond Labs, 60-, supvr physicist. *Concurrent Pos:* Lectr, Trinity Col, DC, 63-69; assoc mem, Adv Group Electron Devices, Dept Defense, 72-79. *Mem:* Sr mem Inst Elec & Electronics Engrs. *Res:* Chemical vapor depositions for silicon integrated circuit applications; transient radiation effects on integrated circuits; thermal radiation effects on materials. *Mailing Add:* 37 Kate Wagner Rd Westminster MD 21158

BABA, PAUL DAVID, CERAMICS. *Current Pos:* RETIRED. *Personal Data:* b Elizabeth, NJ, Dec 15, 32; m 59; c 2. *Educ:* Rutgers Univ, BS, 54, PhD(ceramics), 60; Golden Gate Univ, MBA, 80. *Prof Exp:* Mem tech staff, Bell Tel Labs Inc, 60-65; head ferrite res group, Ampex Corp, 65-68, mgr ferrite res sect, 68-72, mgr ferrite mat dept, 72-78, gen mgr mat & devices group, 78-80, dir bus mgt, Magnetic Tape Div, 80-81, dir res & develop eng, 81-84, dir, Media Technol Lab, 84-91; dirr, Data Tapes, Santa Clara Fac, 91-93. *Mem:* Inst Elec & Electronics Engrs; KERAMOS; Soc Photo-Optical Instrumentation Engrs. *Res:* Electronic materials, devices such as ferromagnetics, ferroelectrics, insulators, semiconductors, and magnetic tapes; optical recording media. *Mailing Add:* 142 Coronado Ave San Carlos CA 94070

BABAD, HARRY, ORGANIC CHEMISTRY, NUCLEAR CHEMISTRY & NUCLEAR WASTE MANAGEMENT. *Current Pos:* fel scientist, 80-87, MGR, RES DEPT, ROCKWELL HANFORD CO, 77-, PRIN SCIENTIST, BASALT WASTE ISOLATION PROJ, 80- *Personal Data:* b Vienna, Austria, Mar 12, 36; US citizen; m 65, Joan K; c Bruce & Nachael. *Educ:* Polytech Inst Brooklyn, BS, 56; Univ Ill, MS & PhD(org chem), 61. *Prof Exp:* Fel org chem, Mass Inst Technol, 61-62; res assoc, Univ Chicago, 62-63; asst prof, Univ Denver, 63-67; group leader new prod res, Ott Chem Co, 67-69, head, Sect Res & Develop, 69-74; mgr, Chem Technol Lab, Atlantic Richfield Hanford Co, 74-77. *Concurrent Pos:* Consult, Colo Int, 74- & Argent Chem, 79-; adv chemist, Westinghouse, Co, 87-97. *Mem:* AAAS; Am Chem Soc; NY Acad Sci; fel Am Inst Chemists; Am Nuclear Soc; Sigma Xi. *Res:* Areas of chemical and environmental sciences aimed at nuclear waste treatment, immobilization and isolation as well as aspects of chemical processing of nuclear materials; multidisciplinary technical integration. *Mailing Add:* 2540 Cordoba Ct Babau Tech Serv Richland WA 99352. *E-Mail:* hbabad@oneworld.owt.com

BABAYAN, VIGEN KHACHIG, food science, lipid chemistry, deceased, see previous edition for last biography

BABB, ALBERT L(ESLIE), CHEMICAL ENGINEERING, BIOMEDICAL ENGINEERING. *Current Pos:* from asst prof to prof chem eng & nuclear eng, Univ Wash, 52-91, chmn, Nuclear Eng Group, 56-65, dir, Nuclear Reactor Labs, 61-73, chmn, Dept Nuclear Eng, 65-81, actg chmn, Dept Chem Eng, 85, actg chmn, Dept Nuclear Eng, 84-87, EMER PROF CHEM & NUCLEAR ENG, UNIV WASH, 91- *Personal Data:* b Vancouver, BC, Nov 7, 25; US citizen; m 72, Marion A Standahl; c 3. *Educ:* Univ BC, BASc, 48; Univ Ill, MS, 49, PhD(chem eng), 51. *Honors & Awards:* Dialysis Pioneer Award, Nat Kidney Found, 82; Noteworthy Achievement in Sci Award, Sigma Xi, 82. *Prof Exp:* Res engr, Rayonier, Inc, Wash, 51-52. *Concurrent Pos:* Consult, Puget Sound Bridge & Dry Dock Co, Seattle, 58-65, R W Beck & Assocs, 63-67, Swed Hosp, Seattle, 65-67, AEC, 65-70, Kidney Dis Br, USPHS & Nat Inst Arthritis & Metab Dis, 66-, Physio Control Corp, 68-70, Seattle Res Ctr, Battelle Mem Inst, 69- & Nat Heart, Lung & Blood Inst, NIH, 91-; mem bd dirs & consult, Thermo-Dynamics Inc, 67-74, Sweden Freezer, 72-78, Biomedics, 78-81, Renal Devices, Inc, 79-81, Meridian Med Corp, 86-91; adj prof bioeng, Univ Wash, 85-91; vpres res, Meridian Med Group, Seattle, Wash, 91- *Mem:* Nat Acad Eng; Inst Med-Nat Acad Sci; fel Am Inst Chem Engrs; fel Am Nuclear Soc; sr mem Biomed Eng Soc; fel Am Inst Med & Biol Eng; fel Am Inst Chemists. *Res:* Engineering of hemodialysis systems; membrane transplant processes; dynamics of soluble gas interactions in human airways; author and co-author of about 170 publications; granted 21 patents. *Mailing Add:* Dept Chem Eng Univ Wash BF-20 Seattle WA 98195-1750. *Fax:* 206-685-3451

BABB, DANIEL PAUL, INORGANIC CHEMISTRY. *Current Pos:* assoc prof, 75, asst dean, Col Sci, 86-90, PROF CHEM, MARSHALL UNIV 72-, CHMN DEPT, 90- *Personal Data:* b Red Wing, Minn, Aug 1, 39. *Educ:* Mankato State Col, BA, 63; Univ Idaho, PhD(inorg chem), 68. *Prof Exp:* Asst prof chem, Kearney State Col, 67-68; asst scientist, Inorg Chem Inst, Univ Gottingen, 68-69; asst prof, Va Polytech Inst, 70-72. *Concurrent Pos:* Vis assoc prof, Univ Idaho, 77-78. *Mem:* Am Chem Soc. *Res:* Fluorine and inorganic synthesis chemistry. *Mailing Add:* Dept Chem Marshall Univ Huntington WV 25755-2520

BABB, DAVID DANIEL, ELECTROMAGNETISM. *Current Pos:* RETIRED. *Personal Data:* b Saugus, Mass, Sept 20, 28; m 49. *Educ:* Mass Inst Technol, BS & MS, 50, MS, 58. *Prof Exp:* Student engr, Philco Corp, 47-49; proj engr, Radio Div, Bendix Corp, 49-52; res asst atomic physics, Mass Inst Technol, 55-58; sr nuclear engr, Gen Dynamics, Ft Worth, 58-61; sr res physicist, Dikewood Corp, NMex, 61-66, head, Physics Div, 66-68, physics prog mgr, 68-69, prog mgr theoret res, 69-70; pres, Albuquerque Res Assocs, Inc, 70-73; sr res physicist, Dikewood Corp, NMex, 73-78; eng mgr, Babb Sound Corp, Tex, 78-80; sr elec engr, Holmes & Narver Inc, Nev, 80-93. *Mem:* Am Phys Soc; Inst Elec & Electronics Engrs; Sigma Xi. *Res:* Nuclear weapons effects, including electromagnetic pulse, neutron and gamma transport and x-ray vulnerability; air and space borne reactor hazards, including reactor shielding and space radiation; atomic frequency standards; radio design; lasers, loudspeakers, electrical power distribution. *Mailing Add:* 3901 Embudito Dr NE Albuquerque NM 87111-4371

BABB, JOHN, PHARMACY. *Current Pos:* PHARMACIST/ADMINR, PUB HEALTH SERV, 89-, DIR, PHARM PROG, FED BUR PRISONS, WASHINGTON, DC. *Educ:* Univ Tenn, BSPh, 68; Univ Memphis, MPA, 93. *Prof Exp:* Community pharmacist, 68-89. *Mailing Add:* Fed Bur Prisons 320 First St NW Rm 1000 Washington DC 20001

BABB, ROBERT MASSEY, ORGANIC CHEMISTRY, SAFETY & HEALTH. *Current Pos:* group leader, Dyestuffs & Chem Div, 72-75, staff chemist, 75-76, group leader, 76-77, safety supt, Agr Div, 77-87, sr staff chemist, 88-96, SAFETY SPECIALIST, CIBA-GEIGY CORP, 96- *Personal Data:* b Durham, NC, Apr 24, 38; m 66; c 1. *Educ:* Univ NC, Chapel Hill, BS, 60; Univ Utah, PhD(org chem), 69. *Prof Exp:* Jr chemist, Merck Sharp & Dohme Res Labs, NJ, 60-63; res chemist, Res Ctr, Burlington Industs, Inc, NC, 68-72. *Mem:* Am Chem Soc; Am Inst Chem Eng. *Res:* Reactions of cyclopropenes and methylenecyclopropanes; organophosphorus chemistry; textile chemistry; pesticides and process development; chemical permeation of protective clothing; chemical spill mitigation; emergency modeling of gaseous chemical releases. *Mailing Add:* PO Box 749 St Gabriel LA 70776-0749

BABBITT, DONALD GEORGE, MATHEMATICAL PHYSICS. *Current Pos:* From asst prof to assoc prof, 62-73, assoc dean, Grad Div, 90-92, PROF MATH, UNIV CALIF, LOS ANGELES, 73- *Personal Data:* b Detroit, Mich, Feb 24, 36; m 86, Berit Rignor; c Donald G III & David T. *Educ:* Univ Detroit, BS, 57, Univ Mich, MA, 58, PhD(math), 62. *Concurrent Pos:* Mem, Inst Advan Study, 70-71; managing ed, Pac J Math, 79-85; exec ed, Math Reviews, 92- *Mem:* Am Math Soc. *Res:* Study of mathematical structures which arise in theoretical physics. *Mailing Add:* Math Reviews 201 Charles St Providence RI 02940-6248. *E-Mail:* dgb@math.ams.org

BABBOTT, FRANK LUSK, JR, EPIDEMIOLOGY. *Current Pos:* RETIRED. *Personal Data:* b New York, NY, Feb 6, 19; m 73, Cynthia Holly; c Barbara, Anne & Frank. *Educ:* Amherst Col, BA, 47; State Univ NY, MD, 51; Harvard Univ, MPH, 53, MS, 54; Am Bd Prev Med, dipl. *Honors & Awards:* Distinguished Serv Award, Am Col Prev Med, 86. *Prof Exp:* Instr epidemiol, Sch Pub Health, Harvard Univ, 54-55, assoc, 55-58; asst prof prev med, Sch Med, Univ Pa, 58-62; vis fel epidemiol, Pub Health Lab Serv, London, Eng, 62-63; assoc prof epidemiol, Col Med, Univ Vt, 63-91. *Concurrent Pos:* Vchmn, Am Bd Prev Med, 74-79. *Mem:* Fel Am Pub Health Asn; fel Am Col Prev Med; Am Epidemiol Soc; Asn Teachers Prev Med; AAAS. *Mailing Add:* Fox Run Webster Rd Shelburne VT 05482

BABBS, CHARLES FREDERICK, CARDIOVASCULAR PHYSIOLOGY, HEAT THERAPY FOR CANCER. *Current Pos:* instr biol sci & res assoc, 74-80, ASSOC RES SCHOLAR BIOMED ENG, PURDUE UNIV, 80-; INSTR FAMILY MED, IND UNIV SCH, 80- *Personal Data:* b Toledo, Ohio, July 6, 46; m 81; c 3. *Educ:* Yale Univ, BA, 68; Baylor Col Med, MD, 74 & MS, 75; Purdue Univ, PhD(pharmacol), 77. *Honors & Awards:* James R MacKenzie Award, Univ Asn Emergency Med, 84. *Prof Exp:* Instr anat, Baylor Col Med, 71-73. *Mem:* Nat Soc Med Res; Asn Advan Med Instrumentation; Am Heart Asn; Soc Acad Emergency Med. *Res:* Cardiopulmonary resuscitation, pathophysiology of tissue ischemia and reperfusion; free radicals in medicine and biology; heat therapy for cancer; drug effects upon all of the foregoing; computer modeling of complex biological systems; digital imaging methods for breast cancer detection. *Mailing Add:* 804 Cumberland Ave West Lafayette IN 47906. *Fax:* 765-494-1193; *E-Mail:* babbs@ecn.purdue.edu

BABCOCK, ANITA KATHLEEN, COMPUTER MODELING & SIMULATION. *Current Pos:* SR PHYSICIST, VITRO CORP, 80- *Personal Data:* b Tucson, Ariz, Sept 2, 48. *Educ:* Pomona Col, BS, 70; State Univ NY, Buffalo, PhD (biophysics), 76. *Prof Exp:* Res asst, Mich State Univ, 72-73 & State Univ NY, Buffalo, 73-76; staff fel, Nat Cancer Inst, NIH, 76-79; res assoc, Georgetown Univ, 79-80. *Concurrent Pos:* Vchmn, Vitro Tech J, 88, chmn, 89- *Res:* Computer systems development, simulation and modeling; applied mathematics; network analysis; statistics; Kalman filtering; system-level test tolerance derivation. *Mailing Add:* Anita Kathleen Babcock PO Box 9517 Silver Spring MD 20916-9517

BABCOCK, BYRON D(ALE), CHEMICAL ENGINEERING. *Current Pos:* RETIRED. *Personal Data:* b Wilmington, Del, Mar 17, 31; m 61, Anna Latsha; c Alison & Gregg. *Educ:* Univ Del, BChE, 52; Univ Wis, MS, 53, PhD(chem eng), 55. *Prof Exp:* Res supvr, Sabine River Works, E I DuPont de Nemours & Co, 61-62, asst supt, 62-64, tech supt, Victoria Plant, 64-68, lab supt, Washington Works, 68-74, dir planning & develop, Mexico City, 75-76, mgr mfg & res, 77-87, prog mgr, 87-92. *Mem:* Am Chem Soc; Am Inst Chem Eng. *Mailing Add:* 738 Taunton Rd Tavistock Wilmington DE 19803. *E-Mail:* USSB75A@prodigy.com

BABCOCK, DALE F, nuclear engineering; deceased, see previous edition for last biography

BABCOCK, DANIEL LAWRENCE, engineering management, systems engineering; deceased, see previous edition for last biography

BABCOCK, DONALD ERIC, ELECTRO ORGANIC CHEMISTRY. *Current Pos:* RETIRED. *Personal Data:* b Canton, Ohio, Nov 10, 07. *Educ:* Ohio State Univ, BS, 31, MS, 33, PhD(chem), 35. *Prof Exp:* Consult, Repub Steel Corp, 31-73. *Concurrent Pos:* Consult prof engr; tech consult adv, UN. *Mem:* Am Chem Soc; hon fel Am Soc Metals; Am Inst Mining Metall & Petrol Engrs. *Mailing Add:* 2501 Westerland Dr Houston TX 77063

BABCOCK, ELKANAH ANDREW, STRUCTURAL GEOLOGY, REMOTE SENSING. *Current Pos:* SCI ADV, IDRC, 93- *Personal Data:* b Elizabeth, NJ, Nov 23, 41; m 64; c 1. *Educ:* Union Col, NY, BS, 63; Syracuse Univ, MS, 65; Univ Calif, Riverside, PhD(geol), 69. *Prof Exp:* Asst prof geol, Univ Alta, 69-75; dir, Alta Res Coun, 75-80, vpres, Natural Resources Div, 80-90; head, Geol Surv Can, 90-93. *Mem:* AAAS; Geol Asn Can; Can Soc Petrol Geologists. *Res:* Structural geology of the Salton Trough, Southern California; terrain analysis and geologic mapping applications of remote sensing; study of fracture phenomena in rock. *Mailing Add:* 655 Richmond Rd No 8 Ottawa ON K2A 3Y3 Can

BABCOCK, GARY G, muscle research & cell motility, for more information see previous edition

BABCOCK, GERALD THOMAS, BIOPHYSICAL CHEMISTRY, PHYSICAL CHEMISTRY. *Current Pos:* from asst prof to assoc prof chem, 76-84, PROF CHEM, MICH STATE UNIV, 84-, CHMN, DEPT CHEM, 90- *Personal Data:* b Minneapolis, Minn, Feb 9, 46; m 76; c 2. *Educ:* Creighton Univ, BS, 68; Univ Calif, Berkeley, PhD(chem), 73. *Honors & Awards:* Phillips Lectr, Haverford Col, 90. *Prof Exp:* Fel chem, Univ Calif, Berkeley, 73-74; NIH fel biochem, Rice Univ, 74-76. *Concurrent Pos:* Vis prof, Col de France, 90. *Mem:* Am Chem Soc; Biophys Soc; Fedn Am Soc Exp Biol. *Res:* Physical chemistry of bioenergetic reactions; electron transfer kinetics in photosynthesis associated with water oxidation; cytochrome oxidase-structure and function. *Mailing Add:* 1028 Chesterfield Pkwy East Lansing MI 48223

BABCOCK, HORACE W, ASTRONOMY. *Current Pos:* RETIRED. *Personal Data:* b Pasadena, Calif, Sept 13, 12; m 40, 58; c Ann L, Bruce H & Kenneth L. *Educ:* Calif Inst Technol, BS, 34; Univ Calif, PhD(astron), 38. *Hon Degrees:* DSc, Univ Newcastle-upon-Tyne, 65. *Honors & Awards:* US Navy Bur Ord Develop Award, 46; Draper Medal, Nat Acad Sci, 57; Eddington Medal, Royal Astron Soc, 58, Gold Medal, 70; Bruce Gold Medal, Astron Soc of the Pac, 69; Hale Prize, Am Astron Soc, 92. *Prof Exp:* Asst, Lick Observ, Univ Calif, 38-39; instr, McDonald Observ, Univ Chicago & Univ Tex, 39-41; res assoc, Radiation Lab, Mass Inst Technol, 41-42; res assoc, Rocket Proj, Calif Inst Technol, 42-46; staff mem to dir, Mt Wilson & Palomar Observ, 46-74; dir observ site-surv & construct, Las Campanas Observ, Chile, Carnegie Inst Wash, 63-78. *Concurrent Pos:* Counr, Am Astron Soc, 52-53 & Nat Acad Sci, 73-76. *Mem:* Nat Acad Sci; Am Astron Soc; Am Acad Arts & Sci; Int Astron Union; Am Philos Soc. *Res:* Rotation and mass distribution of spiral galaxy in Andromeda (M31); stellar spectroscopy; diffraction gratings; adaptive optics; astronomical instrumentation; magnetic fields of sun and stars; telescope design (engineering). *Mailing Add:* 2189 N Altadena Dr Altadena CA 91001-3533

BABCOCK, LOREN EDWARD, GEOLOGY, PALEONTOLOGY. *Current Pos:* ASST PROF GEOL SCI, OHIO STATE UNIV, 90- *Personal Data:* b Buffalo, NY, May 26, 61; m 85; c 1. *Educ:* State Univ NY, Fredonia, BS, 83; Kent State Univ, MS, 86; Univ Kans, PhD(geol), 90. *Concurrent Pos:* Res assoc, Cleveland Mus Natural Hist, 93- & Byrd Polar Res Ctr, 94- *Mem:* Paleont Soc; Soc Sedimentary Geol; Geol Soc Am. *Res:* Paleobiology, paleobiogeography and evolution of Paleozoic arthropods (principally trilobites) and some problematic fossils; Late Proterozoic through Paleozoic geology; evolutionary history of handedness; paleobioloby and taphonomy of early metazoans. *Mailing Add:* Dept Geol Sci Ohio State Univ 125 S Oval Mall Columbus OH 43210-1308. *Fax:* 614-292-1496; *E-Mail:* lbabcock@orton.mps.ohio-state.edu

BABCOCK, LYNDON ROSS, (JR), ENVIRONMENTAL MANAGEMENT, ENVIRONMENTAL EDUCATION. *Current Pos:* from assoc prof to prof, Univ Ill, 70-90, dir, 79-84, assoc dean, 84-85, EMER PROF, ENVIRON & OCCUP HEALTH SCI PROG, SCH PUB HEALTH, UNIV ILL, 90- *Personal Data:* b Detroit, Mich, Apr 8, 34; m 57, Betty I Immonen; c 4. *Educ:* Mich Technol Univ, BS, 56; Univ Wash, MS, 58, PhD(environ eng), 70. *Prof Exp:* Chem engr polymers, Shell Chem Co, 58-67.

Concurrent Pos: Consult, Ill Inst Natural Resources, 70-71 & 76- & Oak Ridge & Argonne Nat Labs, 71-75; consult & proj mgr, Indust Environ Res Lab, US Environ Protection Agency, 72-80; sr lectr, Fulbright-Hays Prog, Turkey & India, 75-76, Mex, 86-87 & 92-93; mem, Nat Air Conserv Comn, 77-82, WHO, 85, Los Alamos Nat Lab, 90-91 & Interam Develop Bd, 90-91. *Mem:* Air & Waste Mgt Asn; Nat Asn Environ Prof. *Res:* Environmental management especially in developing countries; environmental education, air quality characterization, control and health effects; land use; urban transportation, environmental policy and analysis. *Mailing Add:* 4934 Wildwood Dr Bridgman MI 49106-3553. *Fax:* 312-996-1374; *E-Mail:* u40701@uicvm.uic.edu

BABCOCK, MALIN MARIE, TOXICOLOGY. *Current Pos:* FISHERY RES BIOLOGIST HISTOL & PHYSIOL, AUKE BAY LAB, NAT MARINE FISHERIES SERV, 69- *Personal Data:* b Juneau, Alaska, Oct 31, 39; c 2. *Educ:* Ore State Univ, BS, 62; Univ Alaska, MS, 69. *Prof Exp:* Arctic physiologist, Arctic Health Res Ctr, HEW, 66-69. *Mem:* Am Fisheries Soc; Am Inst Fishery Res Biologists; Crustacean Soc; Nat Shellfisheries Asn. *Res:* Histopathology and physiology of fish and invertebrates exposed to stress and pollutants. *Mailing Add:* 17525 Point Lena Loop Rd Juneau AK 99801

BABCOCK, PHILIP ARNOLD, PHARMACOGNOSY, BOTANY. *Current Pos:* Asst prof, 62-66, ASSOC PROF PHARMACOG, COL PHARM, BUSCH CAMPUS, RUTGERS UNIV, 66- *Personal Data:* b Clinton, Mass, May 11, 32; m 59; c 2. *Educ:* Mass Col Pharm, BS, 54, MS, 59; Univ Iowa, PhD(pharm), 62. *Concurrent Pos:* Dir, Scholastic Standing & Student Recs. *Mem:* Acad Pharmaceut Sci; Am Pharmaceut Asn; Am Soc Pharmacog; Soc Econ Bot. *Res:* Biosynthesis of drugs in plants; tissue culture of medicinal plants; chemotaxonomy. *Mailing Add:* Dept Pharm Rutgers Univ New Brunswick NJ 08903

BABCOCK, ROBERT E, THERMODYNAMICS. *Current Pos:* from asst prof to assoc prof, 65-77, asst dean res, 69-77, RES COORDR, UNIV ARK, FAYETTEVILLE, 71-, DIR, WATER RESOURCES RES CTR & PROF CHEM ENG, 77-, HEAD, DEPT CHEM ENG, 94- *Personal Data:* b Chicago, Ill, Oct 10, 37; m 59; c 2. *Educ:* Univ Okla, BS, 59, MChE, 62, PhD(heat transfer), 64. *Prof Exp:* Sr res engr, Esso Prod Res Co, 64-65. *Mem:* Am Inst Chem Engrs; Am Inst Mining, Metall & Petrol Engrs; Am Soc Eng Educ. *Res:* Transport properties; irreversible thermodynamics; heat transfer; fluid flow; petroleum reservoir engineering. *Mailing Add:* Dept Chem Eng Univ Ark Main Campus Bell 3202 Fayetteville AR 72701-1202

BABCOCK, ROBERT FREDERICK, ANALYTICAL CHEMISTRY, ENVIRONMENTAL ANALYSIS. *Current Pos:* SR RES CHEMIST, AMOCO CORP, 82- *Personal Data:* b Ft Wayne, Ind, Feb 26, 30; m 53; c 2. *Educ:* DePauw, BA, 51; Ind Univ, PhD(anal chem), 58. *Prof Exp:* From proj chemist to sr proj chemist, Am Oil Co, Whiting, Ind, 57-74; res chemist, Stand Oil Co (Ind), 74-82. *Mem:* Am Chem Soc; Am Soc Testing Mat; Sigma Xi. *Res:* Development of analytical methods; spectrophotometry; environmental analytical research. *Mailing Add:* 26 W 270 Durfee Rd Wheaton IL 60187-7841

BABCOCK, WILLIAM EDWARD, VETERINARY MEDICINE. *Current Pos:* RETIRED. *Personal Data:* b Buhl, Idaho, Oct 15, 22; m 45; c 4. *Educ:* State Col Wash, BS, 44, DVM, 45; Ore State Col, MS, 51. *Prof Exp:* Assoc vet, Dept Vet Med, Ore State Col, 49-63; res vet, Agr Res Dept, Pfizer, Inc, 63, mgr, 63-65, asst dir, 65-68. *Mem:* Am Vet Med Asn; Poultry Sci Asn; Am Asn Avian Path. *Res:* Poultry diseases. *Mailing Add:* 69 Allendale Terre Haute IN 47802

BABEL, FREDERICK JOHN, FOOD MICROBIOLOGY. *Current Pos:* res assoc prof, 47-50, prof, 50-78, EMER PROF DAIRY & FOOD MICROBIOL, PURDUE UNIV, LAFAYETTE, 78- *Personal Data:* b Traverse City, Mich, Oct 22, 11; m 39, Marcella Ewing. *Educ:* Mich State Univ, BS, 35; Purdue Univ, MS, 36; Iowa State Univ, PhD(dairy bact), 39. *Honors & Awards:* Paul-Lewis Pfizer Award, 61. *Prof Exp:* Res chemist & bacteriologist, NAm Creameries, Inc, Minn, 39-40; res assoc dairy bact, Iowa State Univ, 40-43, asst prof, 43-44, res assoc prof, 44-47. *Concurrent Pos:* Consult, C Hansen's Lab, Milwaukee & Kraft, Inc, Glenview, Ill. *Mem:* Am Dairy Sci Asn; Int Asn Milk & Food Sanitarians. *Res:* Microbiology and enzymology of dairy products; bacteriophage; flavor of cultured dairy products; milk-coagulating enzymes; dairy plant sanitation. *Mailing Add:* 519 Parkridge Dr West Lafayette IN 47906. *Fax:* 765-494-7953; *E-Mail:* foodsci@fsmail.foodsci.purdue.edu

BABER, BURL B, JR, FUEL TECHNOLOGY & PETROLEUM ENGINEERING. *Current Pos:* RETIRED. *Personal Data:* b Wellston, Okla, June 15, 28; m 49; c 3. *Educ:* Okla State Univ, BS, 51. *Prof Exp:* Prod tester, Int Havester Co, Ind, 51-53; from res engr to sr res engr, Southwest Res Inst, 53-60, sect mgr, Appl Lubrication Sect, 60-69, asst dir, Div 02, 69-89. *Mem:* Am Soc Lubrication Eng; Am Soc Testing Mat. *Res:* Applied lubrication of gears and bearings, primarily as used in aircraft and aerospace applications; use of methanol fluid (M85) in various current engine designs as observed from active fleet tests.. *Mailing Add:* PO Box 9 Kingsland TX 78639

BABERO, BERT BELL, PARASITOLOGY. *Current Pos:* STAFF MEM, SCH NURSING, GRAMBLING STATE UNIV, 90- *Personal Data:* b St Louis, Mo, Oct 9, 18; m 50; c 2. *Educ:* Univ Ill, BS, 49, MS, 50, PhD, 57. *Prof Exp:* Med parasitologist, USPHS, Alaska, 50-53; asst parasitol, Univ Ill, 54-57; prof zool & head dept, Ft Valley State Col, 57-59; prof, Southern Univ, 59-60; lectr, Fed Emergency Sci Scheme, Lagos, Nigeria, 60-62; parasitologist, Col Med, Univ Baghdad, Iraq, 62-65; from assoc prof to prof, Univ Nev, Las Vegas, 65-85, prof biol sci, 87-90. *Concurrent Pos:* Fulbright-Hayes fel, US Dept State, Iraq, 63-65; La State Univ fel, 68; prof, Grambling State Univ, 87-89. *Mem:* Soc Syst Zool; Soc Protozool; Am Soc Parasitol; Wildlife Dis Asn; Am Micros Soc. *Res:* Animal and human parasitology; ascariasis; diphyllobothriasis; echinococcosis; zoonotic diseases; author of approximately 100 scientific publications. *Mailing Add:* Biol Sci Grambling State Univ 99 S Main St Grambling LA 71245-3099

BABES-DORNEA, ELENA, ELECTROCHEMISTRY, CATALYSIS. *Current Pos:* MGR, ELECTROCHEM DEPT, SYPROTEC INC, 87- *Personal Data:* b Turda, Romania, Mar 29, 43; Can & Romanian citizen; m 75, Traian. *Educ:* Univ Babes-Bolyai, Romania, Bs, 64, MS, 65, PhD(phys chem), 80. *Prof Exp:* Researcher, Inst Environ Protection, Romania, 65-67; prof phys chem, Univ Oradea, Romania, 71-75, Univ Babes-Bolyai, Napoca, Romani, 75-82; researcher, Inst Appl Electrochem, Setif, Algeria, 84-86. *Concurrent Pos:* Consult sanit & environ eng, Inst Energetics, Romania, 77-82; vis prof phys chem, Univ Batna, Algeria, 82-84, Tech Univ, Setif, Algeria, 84-86. *Mem:* Electrochem Soc. *Res:* Dynamics of interfacial phenomena correlated with catalyst and electrocatalyst bulk structure and performance; new composite (metallic, polymer, silicats) materials with improved efficiency and selectivity for electrochemical energy conversion and sensing. *Mailing Add:* 4931 Ste Suzanne Pierre Fonds PQ H8Y 2A2 Can. *Fax:* 514-684-5250

BABIC, DUBRAVKO IVAN, SEMICONDUCTOR MODELING & DEVELOPMENT. *Current Pos:* MEM TECH STAFF, HEWLETT-PACKARD LABS, PALO ALTO, CALIF, 95- *Personal Data:* b Zagreb, Croatia, May 29, 59. *Educ:* Univ Zagreb, Croatia, dipl, 82; Univ Calif, Santa Barbara, MS, 84, PhD(elec & comput eng), 95. *Prof Exp:* Design engr II, Advan Bipolar Prod Res & Develop, Avantek Inc, Calif, 85-88, sr design engr, 88-89; vis researcher, Semiconductor Fabrication Div, Radio Indust Zagreb, Croatia, 89; tech consult, FEI Microwave, Calif, 89-90. *Mem:* Inst Elec & Electronics Engrs; Optical Soc Am; Mat Res Soc; Croatian Soc Control, Measurement, Electronics, Comput & Commun. *Res:* Vertical-cavity semiconductor lasers for optical communication applications; laser design, fabrication processes and analysis modeling. *Mailing Add:* PO Box 60861 Palo Alto CA 94306

BABICH, HARVEY, TISSUE CULTURE, IN VITRO ASSAYS. *Current Pos:* PROF BIOL, STERN COL, YESHIVA UNIV, 87- *Personal Data:* b Brooklyn, NY, Mar 19, 47. *Educ:* Yeshiva Col, BA, 68; Long Island Univ, MS, 71; NY Univ, PhD(biol), 76. *Prof Exp:* Adj asst prof gen biol, NY Univ, 76-79, sr res scientist, 80-84; sr staff scientist, Environ Law Inst, 79-80; sr res assoc, Rockefeller Univ, 84-91. *Mem:* AAAS; Am Soc Microbiol; Tissue Culture Asn; fel Am Acad Microbiol. *Res:* In vitro cytotoxicity testing using cultured human cells. *Mailing Add:* Sci Stern Col for Women 245 Lexington Ave New York NY 10016-4605. *Fax:* 212-340-7788

BABICH, MICHAEL WAYNE, PHYSICAL INORGANIC CHEMISTRY, SOLID STATE CHEMISTRY. *Current Pos:* from asst prof to assoc prof, 71-85, chmn chem prog, 85-87, PROF & HEAD DEPT CHEM, FLA INST TECHNOL, 87-, CO-CHAIR BIOCHEM PROG, 88- *Personal Data:* b Milwaukee, Wis, Sept 23, 45; m 73, Cynthia Charusch; c Jessica & Ashley. *Educ:* Univ Wis-Madison, BS, 67; Univ Nev, Reno, PhD(inorg chem), 74. *Honors & Awards:* Outstanding Chemist, Orlando Sect, Am Chem Soc, 95. *Prof Exp:* Teaching fel chem, Univ Nev, Reno, 70-74; res assoc, Iowa State Univ-Ames Lab, US Dept Energy, 74-76; vis asst prof, Ohio Wesleyan Univ, 76-77 & Univ Del, 77-78. *Concurrent Pos:* Prin investr, NSF-ISEP, 80-83, NSF-CIP, 82-84, Am Chem Soc-PRF, 84-86, Am Chem Soc-PRF-SRF, 85, Fla Solar Energy Ctr, 87-97; chmn, Grad Educ, Coun Chem Res; bd dirs, Joint Ctr Advan Ther & Biomed Res, Holmes Regional Med Ctr & Fla Inst Technol. *Mem:* Am Chem Soc; Sigma Xi; fel Am Inst Chemists; NAm Thermal Anal Soc; Int Confedn Thermal Anal. *Res:* Solid phase reaction kinetics; crystallography of inorganic complexes; synthetic inorganic chemistry; thermal analysis; DSC and TG. *Mailing Add:* Dept Chem Fla Inst Technol Melbourne FL 32901-6988. *E-Mail:* babich@fit.edu

BABIN, SERGEY, ELECTRICAL ENGINEERING, MICROLITHOGRAPHY. *Current Pos:* SR STAFF ENGR, ETECh SYSTS INC, 96- *Personal Data:* b Russia, May 3, 57; m 85, Viktoria Boldyreva; c Ivan & Polina. *Educ:* Moscow State Univ, MsSci, 80 PhD(physics), 88. *Prof Exp:* Scientist, Inst Microelectronic Technol, Russia, 82-91 & Inst Physics & Technol, Russia, 91-93. *Concurrent Pos:* Consult, Airspace Univ, Russia, 90-92 & Set-Serv, 94-95; vis scientist & Alexander von Humboldt Fel, Ger, 93-94, Sci Ctr Ger Telekom, 95. *Res:* Investigations of physical effects involved in electron beam lithography and photolithography; creation of new computer generated refractive and diffractive optical elements for X-ray to IR wavelength range; author 50 publications; patentee in field. *Mailing Add:* 26460 Corporate Ave Hayward CA 94545. *E-Mail:* babin@etec.com

BABINEAU, G RAYMOND, PSYCHIATRY. *Current Pos:* PVT PRACT. *Personal Data:* b New York, NY, Apr 8, 37; m 60; c 3. *Educ:* Bowdoin Col, BA, 59; Harvard Med Sch, MD, 63. *Prof Exp:* Chief ment hyg psychiat, US Army Hosp, Berlin, Ger, 67-70; asst prof & sr assoc psychiat, Univ Health Serv, Univ Rochester, 70-, chief, Ment Health Sect, 73- *Mem:* Am Psychiat Asn; Am Col Health Asn. *Res:* Psychological problems of university students. *Mailing Add:* Strong Mem Hosp Box 617 Rochester NY 14642-0001

BABIOR, BERNARD M, BIOCHEMISTRY, HEMATOLOGY. *Current Pos:* HEAD DIV BIOCHEM, DEPT MOLECULAR & EXP MED & STAFF PHYSICIAN, DEPT MED, SCRIPPS CLIN RES FOUND, 86- *Personal Data:* b Los Angeles, Calif, Nov 10, 35; m 61; c 2. *Educ:* Univ Calif, San Francisco, MD, 59; Harvard Univ, PhD(biochem), 65. *Prof Exp:* Asst prof med, Harvard Med Sch, 69-71, assoc prof, 71-72; from assoc prof to prof med, Sch Med, Tufts Univ, 72-86. *Mem:* AAAS; Am Soc Biol Chem; Am Soc Clin Invest. *Res:* Mechanism of action of coenzyme B12; granulocyte physiology. *Mailing Add:* Div Biochem Dept Molecular & Exp Med Scripps Res Inst 10550 N Torrey Pines Rd La Jolla CA 92037

BABISH, JOHN GEORGE, TOXICOLOGY, CELL BIOLOGY. *Current Pos:* EXEC VPRES RES, BIOSIGNAL LTD, BROOKTONDALE, NY, 97- *Personal Data:* b Johnstown, Pa, Dec 10, 46; div; c Aeden & Brendan. *Educ:* Pa State Univ, BS, 68; Cornell Univ, PhD(food chem & toxicol), 76. *Prof Exp:* Res assoc, Pesticide Res Lab, Pa State Univ, 68-71; toxicologist, Food & Drug Res Lab, 76-78; asst prof toxicol, Dept Prev Med, Cornell Univ, 78-85, assoc prof, Dept Pharmacol, 85-92; pres & chief exec officer, Paracelsian Inc, 92-97. *Mem:* Soc Toxicol; AAAS. *Res:* Interaction of xenobiotics and expression of cyclin dependent kinases. *Mailing Add:* Bio Signal Ltd 508 White Church Rd Brooktondale NY 14817

BABIUK, LORNE A, VIROLOGY, IMMUNOLOGY. *Current Pos:* from asst prof to assoc prof, 73-79, PROF VIROL, UNIV SASK, 79- *Personal Data:* b Canora, Sask, Jan 25, 46; m 73; c 2. *Educ:* Univ Sask, BSA, 67, MSc, 69, PhD(virol), Univ BC, 72. *Hon Degrees:* DSc, Univ Sask, 87. *Honors & Awards:* Award, Am Asn Vet Immunologists, 92; Xerox Can Award, 93; Emerging Sci & Technol Award, 95. *Prof Exp:* Fel virol, Univ Toronto, 72-73. *Concurrent Pos:* Consult, Molecular Genetic, Inc, 80-85, Genentech Inc, 81-85, Biostar, 84-95; vchmn, Can Soc Microbiol, 80-82, chmn, 82-84; assoc dir res, Vet Infectious Dis Orgn, 84-93, dir res, 93-; chmn, Strategic Grants Biotechnol, Natural Sci & Eng Res Coun Can, 85-88; mem, Biohazards Comt, Med Res Coun, 86-, coun mem, 96- *Mem:* Am Soc Microbiol; Can Soc Microbiol; Am Soc Virol; Can Soc Microbiol. *Res:* Virus cell interactions molecular level and host response to virol pathogenesis, Bovine Rotavirus, Coronavirus and herpes virus; immune responses and modulation by lymphokines. *Mailing Add:* Vet Infectious Disease Orgn 120 Veterinary Rd Saskatoon SK S7N 5E3 Can. *Fax:* 306-966-7478

BABLANIAN, ROSTOM, VIROLOGY, BIOLOGY. *Current Pos:* from asst prof to prof, 66-95, EMER PROF MICROBIOL & IMMUNOL, STATE UNIV NY DOWNSTATE MED CTR, 95- *Personal Data:* b Addis-Ababa, Ethiopia, Nov 24, 29; US citizen; m 55; c 1. *Educ:* Am Univ Cairo, BS, 53, BA, 55; NY Univ, MS, 59, PhD(cell biol), 64. *Prof Exp:* Res assoc virol, Rockefeller Univ, 64-65. *Mem:* Am Soc Microbiol. *Res:* Mechanisms of animal virus-induced cell damage. *Mailing Add:* Dept Microbiol & Immunol Downstate Med Ctr 450 Clarkson Box 44 Brooklyn NY 11203

BABLER, JAMES HAROLD, SYNTHETIC ORGANIC CHEMISTRY. *Current Pos:* From asst prof to assoc prof, 70-85, PROF CHEM, LOYOLA UNIV, CHICAGO, 85- *Personal Data:* b Evanston, Ill, June 14, 44. *Educ:* Loyola Univ, Ill, BS, 66; Northwestern Univ, PhD(chem), 71. *Mem:* AAAS; Am Chem Soc; Sigma Xi. *Res:* Natural products; new synthetic methodology; chemicals controlling insect behavior; allylic rearrangements; synthesis of retinoids and carotenoids. *Mailing Add:* Loyola Univ Dept Chem 6525 N Sheridan Rd Chicago IL 60626. *Fax:* 773-508-3086; *E-Mail:* jbabler@luc.edu

BABOIAN, ROBERT, electrochemistry, corrosion, for more information see previous edition

BABRAUSKAS, VYTENIS, fire protection engineering, instrument development, for more information see previous edition

BABROV, HAROLD J, MOLECULAR SPECTROSCOPY, ATMOSPHERIC CHEMISTRY & PHYSICS. *Current Pos:* RETIRED. *Personal Data:* b New York, NY, Apr 21, 26; m 52; c 4. *Educ:* Univ Calif, Los Angeles, AB, 50, MA, 51; Univ Pittsburgh, PhD(physics), 59. *Prof Exp:* Physicist, US Naval Ord Test Sta, 50; asst, Inst Geophys, Univ Calif, 51; physicist, Knolls Atomic Power Lab, Gen Elec Co, 51-54; asst, Univ Pittsburgh, 54-60; sr physicist, Control Instrument Div, Warner & Swasey Co, NY, 60-63, chief physicist, 63-68; assoc prof physics, Ind Univ, South Bend, 68-72; mem tech staff, Rockwell Int Space Div, 72-79; mem tech staff, Aerospace Corp, 79-85; mem tech staff, Rockwell Int, 85-88. *Concurrent Pos:* Cottrell grant, Res Corp, 69. *Mem:* Fel Optical Soc Am; Am Phys Soc; Sigma Xi. *Res:* Infrared physics; intensity spectra of small molecules and atoms, especially the broadening of spectral lines and determination of transition probabilities; applications of intensity spectroscopy to problems of radiant energy transfer. *Mailing Add:* 9881 Cheshire Ave Westminster CA 92683

BABSON, ARTHUR LAWRENCE, CLINICAL CHEMISTRY. *Current Pos:* RETIRED. *Personal Data:* b Orange, NJ, Mar 3, 27; m 50, 71, Susan Rader; c Betsy & James. *Educ:* Cornell Univ, BA, 50; Rutgers Univ, MS, 51, PhD(physiol, biochem), 53. *Honors & Awards:* Bernard F Gerault Mem Award, Am Asn Clin Chemists, 75. *Prof Exp:* Res assoc, Radiation Res Lab, Univ Iowa, 53-54; sr res assoc biochem, Warner-Lambert Res Inst, 54-66, dir, Dept Diag Res, 66-76, vpres res & develop, Gen Diag Div, 76-80; pres, Babson Res Labs, 80-88; founder, pres & chmn, Cirrus Diag Inc, 87-92, chief scientist, DPC Cirrus. *Mem:* AAAS; Am Asn Clin Chemists; Am Chem Soc; NY Acad Sci; Can Soc Clin Chemists. *Res:* Blood coagulation; diagnostic enzymology; immanoassay; medical and laboratory instrumentation. *Mailing Add:* 47 Old Mill Rd Chester NJ 07930

BABU, GADDAM N, ADHESIVES, PHOTOPOLYMERS. *Current Pos:* sr res chemist, 85-87, res specialist, 87-92, SR RES SPECIALIST, 3M RES CTR, 92- *Personal Data:* b Pushadam, India, Mar 21, 50; m 75, Padma; c Neelima. *Educ:* Indian Inst Technol, New Delhi, PhD(polymer sci), 77. *Prof Exp:* Res assoc, Indian Inst Technol, New Delhi, 77-79, assoc prof, Bombay, 79-85. *Concurrent Pos:* Res assoc, Univ Mass, 81-84; consult, Hindusian Lesers, India, 84-85. *Mem:* Am Chem Soc. *Res:* Examine effect of the type of catalysts on stereo chemistry of polydefins; determine effect of copolymer sequence of silicones on adhesive properties; synthesis of new photochemical monomers and their polymerization rates in copolymers; published over 90 papers, 15 patents issued and several pending. *Mailing Add:* 9446 Hillingdom Rd Woodbury MN 55125

BABU, SURESH PANDURANGAM, CHEMICAL ENGINEERING, BIOFUELS CONVERSION. *Current Pos:* res supvr, Inst Gas Technol, 73-77, mgr process develop, 79-84, assoc dir process develop, 84-87, dir process res, 88-90, DIR, LICENSING & COMMERCIALIZATION, INST GAS TECHNOL, 90-, DIR, INTELLECTUAL PROPERTY. *Personal Data:* b Secunderabad, India, July 15, 41; US citizen; m 70. *Educ:* Osmania Univ, Hyderabad, India, BS, 62; Indian Inst Technol, Kharagpur, India, MS, 63; Ill Inst Technol, PhD(gas eng), 71. *Prof Exp:* Sr res fel coal conversion, Regional Res Labs, Coun Sci & Indust Res, Hyderabad, India, 63-65; asst prof mineral processing, WVa Univ, 71-73. *Concurrent Pos:* Vis expert, UN Indust Develop Orgn, Vienna, Austria, 81, USAID, Bandung, Indonesia, 82 & UN Develop Progs, India, 85; task leader, Int Energy Agency, Thermal Gasification Proj, 89-91. *Mem:* Am Inst Chem Engrs; Am Chem Soc; Lic Exec Soc. *Res:* Development of substitute fuel production processes from fossil fuels and renewable resources and process modeling. *Mailing Add:* Inst Gas Technol 1700 S Mt Prospect Rd Des Plaines IL 60018

BABU, UMA MAHESH, diagnostics, biologicals, for more information see previous edition

BABUSKA, IVO MILAN, NUMERICAL ANALYSIS, APPLIED MATHEMATICS. *Current Pos:* RES PROF MATH, UNIV MD, 69- *Personal Data:* b Prague, Czech, Mar 22, 26. *Educ:* Tech Univ Prague, PhD(civil eng), 51; Czech Acad Sci, PhD(math), 55, DSc(math), 60. *Honors & Awards:* Czechoslovak State Award, Math, 68. *Prof Exp:* Res scientist math, Math Inst, Czech Acad Sci, 50-69. *Concurrent Pos:* Alexander von Humboldt sr scientist award, 77. *Mem:* Am Math Soc; Soc Indust Appl Math. *Res:* Numerical analysis of partial differential equations; applied mathematics related to continuum theory. *Mailing Add:* Res Prof Phys Sci Rm 4309 Bldg 224 Univ Md College Park MD 20742

BACA, GLENN, PHYSICAL INORGANIC CHEMISTRY, ELECTROCHEMISTRY. *Current Pos:* RETIRED. *Personal Data:* b Socorro, NMex, Nov 22, 43. *Educ:* NMex State Univ, BS, 65, MS, 67, PhD(inorg chem), 69. *Prof Exp:* Teaching asst chem, NMex State Univ & Rose-Hulman Inst Technol, 65-69; asst prof chem, Mercer Co Community Col, 69-70; assoc prof chem, Rose-Hulman Inst Technol, 70-83. *Mem:* Sigma Xi; Am Chem Soc. *Res:* The determination of transference numbers in non-aqueous solvents in conjunction with the development and construction of batteries in water-like solvents. *Mailing Add:* PO Box 2135 Mesilla Park NM 88047

BACA, OSWALD GILBERT, MICROBIOLOGY, BIOLOGY. *Current Pos:* from asst prof to assoc prof, 76-86, assoc dean grad studies, 86-88, PROF BIOL, UNIV NMEX, 86-, RES PROF MICROBIOL, SCH MED, 88- *Personal Data:* b Belen, NMex, July 6, 42; m 63; c 2. *Educ:* Univ NMex, BS, 66, MS, 69; Univ Kans, PhD(microbiol), 73. *Honors & Awards:* Res & Develop 100 Award, Res & Develop Mag. *Prof Exp:* Fel biochem, Friedrich Miescher Inst, Basel, Switz, 73-75; res assoc biochem, Univ Minn, Minneapolis, 75-76. *Concurrent Pos:* Prin investr, NSF, Univ NMex, 77-79 & 77-80 & NIH, 93- *Mem:* Am Soc Microbiol; AAAS; Am Soc Rickettsiology & Rickettsial Dis; Fedn Am Soc Exp Biol. *Res:* Host parasite interactions at the biochemical & molecular level. *Mailing Add:* Dept Biol Univ NMex Main Campus 1 Univ Campus Albuquerque NM 87131-0001. *Fax:* 505-277-0304

BACANER, MARVIN BERNARD, PHYSIOLOGY, MEDICINE. *Current Pos:* PROF PHYSIOL, UNIV MINN, MINNEAPOLIS, 61- *Personal Data:* b Chicago, Ill, Mar 18, 23; m 48; c 4. *Educ:* Boston Univ, MD, 53. *Honors & Awards:* William & Dorothy Fish Kerr Award, San Francisco Heart Asn, 57. *Prof Exp:* Intern path, Boston City Hosp, Mass, 53-54; resident internal med, Cambridge City Hosp, 54-55 & Mt Sinai Hosp, New York, 55-56; res fel cardio-pulmonary physiol, Stanford Univ, 57-59; res physician biophys & physiol, Donner Lab, Lawrence Radiation Lab, Univ Calif, Berkeley, 59-61. *Concurrent Pos:* Percy Klingenstein fel cardiol, Mt Sinai Hosp, New York, 56-57; USPHS res fel, Med Sch, Stanford Univ, 57-59; Burroughs-Wellcome fel, Rambam Hosp, Haifa, Israel, 68-69. *Mem:* Am Physiol Soc. *Res:* Metabolic determinants of heart performance; development of bretylium tosylate antiarrhythmic drug; in-vivo methods of measuring intestinal circulation; x-ray microanalysis of deep frozen tissue with the scanning electron microscope; electron optical imaging of deep-frozen muscle; voltage clamp studies of antifibrillatory drugs. *Mailing Add:* 4401 Fremont Ave Minneapolis MN 55409

BACASTOW, ROBERT BRUCE, NATURAL CARBON CYCLE, OCEAN CHEMISTRY. *Current Pos:* assoc specialist, 74-76, SPECIALIST, SCRIPPS INST OCEANOG, 76- *Personal Data:* b Kearny, NJ, June 4, 30; m 76, Wanda C Dalbridge; c Eddie Dalbridge, Kathleen Dalbridge, Robbie & Rebecca. *Educ:* Mass Inst Technol, BS, 52, MS, 54; Univ Calif, Berkeley,

PhD(physics), 63. *Prof Exp:* Asst prof physics, Univ Calif, Riverside, 65-69, assoc res physicist, San Diego, 69-70. *Mem:* Am Geophys Union; AAAS; Sigma Xi. *Res:* Modeling the natural carbon cycle in the world oceans; uptake of anthropogenic carbon dioxide by the oceans. *Mailing Add:* 1031 Sea Village Dr Cardiff CA 92007-1433

BACCANARI, DAVID PATRICK, ENZYMOLOGY. *Current Pos:* SR RES MICROBIOLOGIST, WELLCOME RES LAB, 73- *Personal Data:* b Wilkes-Barre, Pa, Apr 15, 47; m 68; c 2. *Educ:* Wilkes Col, BS, 68; Brown Univ, PhD(biochem), 72. *Prof Exp:* Fel, Brown Univ, 72-73. *Mem:* Am Soc Microbiol; Am Soc Biol Chem; Am Asn Cancer Res. *Res:* Comparative enzymology and its relationship to chemotherapy. *Mailing Add:* Dept Cancer Biol Glaxo Wellcome 5 Moore Dr Research Triangle Park NC 27709-5206

BACCEI, LOUIS JOSEPH, POLYMER CHEMISTRY. *Current Pos:* res & develop chemist, Loctite Corp, 72-73, sr chemist, 74-75, res assoc, 75-78, MGR ANAEROBIC CHEM, LOCTITE CORP, 78-, SR VPRES RES & DEVELOP. *Personal Data:* b Torrington, Conn, Dec 16, 41; m 64; c 4. *Educ:* Cent Conn State Col, BS, 63; Univ Md, PhD(org chem), 70. *Prof Exp:* Res & develop chemist monomer polymers, Am Cyanamid Co, 69-72. *Mem:* Am Chem Soc. *Res:* Monomer and polymer synthesis; study of structure-property relationships; free radical chemistry. *Mailing Add:* 64 Hunters Crossing Burlington CT 06013

BACCHETTI, SILVIA, VIROLOGY, CANCER RESEARCH. *Current Pos:* from asst prof to assoc prof, 75-82, PROF, MCMASTER UNIV, 82- *Personal Data:* b Rome, Italy, Sept 20, 39; m 68. *Educ:* Univ Rome, Laurea, 61. *Prof Exp:* Fel, Univ Rome, 61-64, researcher, 64-65; fel, Ont Cancer Inst, 66-68; vis scientist, Argonne Nat Lab, 68-70; asst prof, Univ Leiden, Holland, 70-74. *Concurrent Pos:* Res scholar, Nat Cancer Inst, Can, 76-82, res assoc, 82-85, Terry Fox cancer res scientist, 85- *Res:* Mechanisms of mammalian cell transformation by DNA tumor virus; induction of genetic damage by viral oncogenes; characterization of viral functions involved in DNA metabolism. *Mailing Add:* Dept Path Rm 4H30 McMaster Med Ctr Hamilton ON L8N 3Z5 Can

BACCHUS, HABEEB, INTERNAL MEDICINE, ENDOCRINOLOGY. *Current Pos:* assoc prof med, 69-79, PROF MED, SCH MED, LOMA LINDA UNIV, 79-; ASSOC CHIEF INTERNAL MED, RIVERSIDE GEN HOSP, 69-, CHIEF ENDOCRINOL & METAB, 84-, CHIEF MED, 87- *Personal Data:* b Triumph, Brit Guiana, Oct 15, 28; US citizen; m 65, Frances Solarczyk; c Paula, Andree, Jeanne, David, Michael & Julie. *Educ:* Howard Univ, BS, 47; George Washington Univ, MS, 48, PhD(physiol), 50, MD, 54; Am Bd Internal Med, dipl, 63 & 74, cert endocrinol & metab, 75. *Prof Exp:* Res assoc physiol, George Washington Univ, 51-54, asst res prof, 54-57, asst clin prof, 57-59; prin investr, Res Labs Biochem, Providence Hosp, Washington, DC, 60-65, dir metab lab & sr attend physician internal med, 65-69, res mem dept path, 65-67, chief res div, 67-69. *Concurrent Pos:* Clin assoc, Nat Cancer Inst, 57-59; coordr health serv, Am Univ, 68-69; med consult, Vet Admin, 61-; assoc clin pathologist, Riverside Gen Hosp, 70-80. *Mem:* Am Col Physicians; Endocrine Soc; Am Fedn Clin Res; Am Physiol Soc; Am Asn Clin Endocrinologists. *Res:* Pituitary-adrenal axis; ascorbic acid adrenal hormone formation and breakdown; ascorbic acid and intermediary metabolism; adrenogenital syndromes; metabolic diseases; Marfan's syndrome; connective tissue diseases; hypertensive vascular disease; experimental hypertension; glycoprotein markers in malignant neoplastic disorders; disorders of calcium metabolism; vitamin D hormones; thyroid stimulating immunoglobulins; insulin resistance phenomena. *Mailing Add:* Riverside Gen Hosp Loma Linda Univ 9851 Magnolia Ave Riverside CA 92503-3588

BACH, DAVID RUDOLPH, NUCLEAR PHYSICS, REACTOR PHYSICS. *Current Pos:* CONSULT, LAWRENCE LIVERMORE NAT LAB, 86- *Personal Data:* b Shimonoseki, Japan, Apr 24, 24; US citizen; m 48, 75; c 4. *Educ:* Univ Mich, BA, 48, MS, 50, PhD(physics), 55. *Prof Exp:* Res assoc physics, Knolls Atomic Power Lab, Gen Elec Co, NY, 55-58, mgr flexible plastic reactor, 58-64; from assoc prof to prof nuclear eng, Univ Mich, Ann Arbor, 64-79; res physicist, Los Alamos Nat Lab, 79-84, consult, 84-88. *Concurrent Pos:* Consult, Knolls Atomic Power Lab, 65-69, Lawrence Livermore Nat Lab, 86- *Mem:* Am Phys Soc. *Res:* Experimental nuclear and reactor physics; neutron physics, especially pulsed neutron research; plasma physics, especially laser interaction with dense plasmas; inertial confinement fusion. *Mailing Add:* 3142 Grove St Ventura CA 93003

BACH, ERIC, NUMBER-THEORETIC ALGORITHMS, COMPLEXITY THEORY. *Current Pos:* Asst prof, 84-89, ASSOC PROF COMPUT SCI, UNIV WIS-MADISON, 89- *Personal Data:* b Chicago, Ill, Nov 30, 52. *Educ:* Univ Mich, BA, 74; Univ Calif, Berkeley, PhD(comput sci), 84. *Concurrent Pos:* NSF presidential young investr, 86; vis assoc prof, Univ Paris-Sud, Orsay, 89; mem, Spec Interest Group Automata & Computability Theory, Asn Comput Mach. *Mem:* Asn Comput Mach; Am Math Soc; Math Asn Am. *Res:* Design and analysis of algorithms for algebraic and number-theoretic problems; computer algebra; cryptography; pseudo-random number generation. *Mailing Add:* Dept Comput Sci Comp Sci-5355 Univ Wis 1210 W Dayton St Madison WI 53706-1685

BACH, FREDERICK L, ORGANIC CHEMISTRY. *Current Pos:* RETIRED. *Personal Data:* b Corning, NY, Feb 5, 21; m 47; c 2. *Educ:* Univ Md, BS, 43; NY Univ, MS, 57, PhD(chem), 63. *Prof Exp:* Sr res chemist, Lederle Labs Div, 49-71, dir Tech Regulatory Affairs, Am Cyanamid, 71-78. *Concurrent Pos:* Lectr org chem, NY Univ, 63-73. *Mem:* AAAS; Am Chem Soc; Brit Chem Soc; Brit Inst Regulatory Affairs. *Res:* Tuberculostatic agents; tropical diseases; cardiovascular drugs; hypocholesteremic agents; free radical chemistry; computer solutions of photochemical mechanisms. *Mailing Add:* 44 Sunrise Dr Montvale NJ 07645-1030

BACH, HARTWIG C, POLYMER CHEMISTRY. *Current Pos:* RETIRED. *Personal Data:* b Kiel, Ger, May 24, 30; m 57. *Educ:* Kiel Univ, BS, 54, MS, 57, PhD(org chem), 59. *Prof Exp:* Res assoc fels, org chem, Univ SC, 59-60 & Fla State Univ, 60-61; res specialist polymer chem, Chemstrand Res Ctr, Inc, 61-69, sr res specialist nylon res, 69-71, sci fel nylon res, 71-81, sr sci fel adv technol, Monsanto Co, 81-89. *Mem:* Am Chem Soc. *Res:* Organic chemistry; catalysis; polymer chemistry; synthetic fibers; solution and melt spinning. *Mailing Add:* 11416 High Springs Rd Pensacola FL 32534

BACH, JOHN ALFRED, MICROBIOLOGY. *Current Pos:* RETIRED. *Personal Data:* b Detroit, Mich, July 26, 35; m 57; c 3. *Educ:* Mich State Univ, BS, 58, MS, 61, PhD(microbiol), 63. *Prof Exp:* Sr microbiologist, Bristol Labs, NY, 63-67; assoc scientist, Upjohn Co, 67-88. *Mem:* Am Soc Microbiol. *Res:* Physiology of bacterial endospores; antibiotics; chemotherapy; fluorescent antibody techniques; fermentation microbiology. *Mailing Add:* 521 Cherokee St Apt 303 Kalamazoo MI 49006-2851

BACH, MARILYN LEE, SCIENCE POLICY. *Current Pos:* ASSOC PROF, DIV HEALTH SERV RES & POLICY, SCH PUB HEALTH, 82- *Personal Data:* b Lynn, Mass, Apr 24, 37; m 58; c 3. *Educ:* Simmons Col, BS, 58; NY Univ, PhD(biochem), 66. *Honors & Awards:* Gold Medal Award, Am Inst Chemists, 58; Fac Res Award, Am Cancer Soc, 71. *Prof Exp:* Fel oncol, Univ Wis, 66-67, proj assoc, Dept Genetics, 67-68, res assoc, 68-70, from asst prof to assoc prof, Dept Pediat, 70-78; fel sci policy, Brookings Inst, 81-82; assoc prof, Dept Lab Med/Path & Health Serv Res Ctr, Univ Minn, Minneapolis, 78- *Concurrent Pos:* Vis prof, Univ Leiden, Netherlands, 73; mem, Nat Adv Allergy & Infectious Dis, 74-77 & Basil O'Connor Starter Res Grant Panel, Nat Found, 74-77; sci liaison, Off Med Applications Res, 79-80; spec asst to dir, Nat Inst Allergy & Infectious Dis, NIH, 80-81; exec dir, Minnesota Coun on Biotechnol, 85-87. *Mem:* Transplantation Soc; Am Asn Immunologists; AAAS. *Res:* Relationships between academia, industry and government, focusing on work in recombinant DNA, hybridomas, and vaccine development. *Mailing Add:* 1743 Forssa Way St Paul MN 55122

BACH, MICHAEL KLAUS, biochemistry, immunology; deceased, see previous edition for last biography

BACH, RICARDO O, BIOINORGANIC CHEMISTRY. *Current Pos:* PRES, BACH ASSOCS, INC, 83- *Personal Data:* b Ulm, Ger, Dec 25, 17; US citizen; m 45, Ida Kopp; c Jose A, Claudia (Goldman) & Charles R. *Educ:* Univ Zurich, PhD(phys chem), 42. *Prof Exp:* Dir res electrometall & inorg chem, Meteor Est Met, Buenos Aires, Arg, 42-54; res investr, Cent Res Labs, Am Smelting & Ref Co, NJ, 54-59; dir inorg res, Lithium Corp Am, Inc, 59-67, mgr res dept, 67-82. *Mem:* Am Chem Soc; Am Inst Mining, Metall & Petrol Engrs; fel Am Inst Chem; Sigma Xi. *Res:* Extractive metallurgy of lithium; biochemistry of antiviral compounds. *Mailing Add:* 44 Old Post Rd Lake Wylie SC 29710-8944

BACH, SHIRLEY, BIOMEDICAL ETHICS. *Current Pos:* from instr to assoc prof, 74-81, PROF NATURAL SCI, WESTERN MICH UNIV, 81- *Personal Data:* b Williston Park, NY, Nov 22, 31; m 54; c 2. *Educ:* Queens Col, NY, BS, 53; Univ Wis, PhD(org chem), 57. *Mem:* Am Chem Soc; AAAS. *Res:* Chemical reactions in monomolecular layers; natural product chemistry; human serum complement genetics. *Mailing Add:* Dept Philos Western Mich Univ Kalamazoo MI 49008-3804

BACH, WALTHER DEBELE, JR, ATMOSPHERIC DYNAMICS. *Current Pos:* METEOROLOGIST, US ARMY RES OFF, 83- *Personal Data:* b Pensacola, Fl, Apr 11, 39; m 61; c 3. *Educ:* Ga Inst Technol, BS, 61; Univ Okla, MS, 66, PhD(meteorol), 70. *Prof Exp:* Res meteorologist, Res Triangle Inst, 69-82. *Concurrent Pos:* Vis assoc prof, NC State Univ, 81-82; vis fac assoc, Savannah River Lab, 82; consult meteorologist, 82- *Mem:* Am Meteorol Soc. *Res:* Manager of basic research program in dynamics of the planetary boundary layer for Army Research Office. *Mailing Add:* 68 Kimberly Dr Durham NC 27707

BACHA, JOHN D, ORGANIC CHEMISTRY, DISTILLATE & RESIDUAL PETROLEUM FUELS. *Current Pos:* sr res chemist, Chevron Res & Technol Co, 85-87, sr res assoc, 87-91, res scientist, 91-92, sr staff scientist, 92-96, CONSULT SCIENTIST, CHEVRON PRODS CO, 96- *Personal Data:* b Minneapolis, Minn, Aug 21, 41; m 66, Jane Downey; c Jeffrey, Jay, Joel & Jennifer. *Educ:* St Mary's Col, Minn, BA, 63; Case Inst Technol, PhD(chem), 67. *Prof Exp:* Res chemist, Gulf Res & Develop Co, 67-72, sr res chemist, 72-78, res assoc, 78-85. *Mem:* Am Chem Soc; Am Inst Mining, Metall & Petrol Engrs; Metall Soc; Am Carbon Soc; Am Soc Test & Mat; Int Asn Stability & Handling Liquid Fuels. *Res:* Free radical chemistry; carbonium ion chemistry and aromatic substitution; metal catalysis of organic reactions; solvent effects upon organic reactions; monomers for high performance polymers; carbon products and their precursors; distillate and residual petroleum fuels. *Mailing Add:* Chevron Prod Co PO Box 1627 Richmond CA 94802-0627

BACHA, WILLIAM JOSEPH, JR, PARASITOLOGY. *Current Pos:* from instr to assoc prof, Rutgers Univ, Camden, 59-70, actg dean, 69-70, chmn, Dept Biol & dir grad prog, 71-74, PROF BIOL, RUTGERS UNIV, CAMDEN, 70- *Personal Data:* b US, Mar 1, 30; m 53, 79, 92, Linda M Wood; c Alison, Anne, Darcy, Jessie & Kevin. *Educ:* Long Island Univ, BS, 51; NY Univ, PhD(biol), 59. *Prof Exp:* Asst biol, NY Univ, 51-54 & 56-58; lectr, City Col New York, 58-59. *Concurrent Pos:* Adj prof, Univ Pa Sch Vet Med. *Mem:* Sigma Xi; Am Soc Parasitol; Am Micros Soc. *Res:* Biology; life cycles, behavior and development of trematodes. *Mailing Add:* Rutgers Univ Camden Campus 311 N Fifth St Rutgers Univ Camden NJ 08102-1205

BACHARACH, MARTIN MAX, BIOLOGY, GENETICS. *Current Pos:* supvr info serv, William D McAdams, Inc, New York, 66-82 CONSULT 82- *Personal Data:* b Munich, Germany, Dec 18, 25; nat US. *Educ:* Rutgers Univ, BS, 50; Univ Wis, MS, 52, PhD(poultry genetics), 55. *Prof Exp:* Asst, Univ Wis, 50-55, assoc, 55-57; cytologist, Tumor Res, Vet Admin Hosp, Hines, Ill, 57-58; instr biol, NCent Col, Ill, 59; geneticist, Honegger Farms Co, Inc, Ill, 59-60; res nutritionist & librn, Dawe's Labs, Inc, Chicago, 60-62; info res scientist, Squibb Inst Med Res, NJ, 62-64; mem staff, Med Serv Dept, Sandoz, Inc, NJ, 64; dir sci info, Cortez F Enloe, Inc, NY, 65-66. *Res:* Immuno-genetics of species and species hybrids; developmental genetics; physiological reactions of normal and malignant cells; literature research. *Mailing Add:* 390 Prospect Ave Hackensack NJ 07601-2547

BACHE, ROBERT JAMES, CORONARY ARTERY DISEASE, ISCHEMIC HEART DISEASE. *Current Pos:* PROF MED, UNIV MINN, 76- *Personal Data:* b 1938; m 71, Elaine Anderson; c Elizabeth, Christian & Matthew. *Educ:* Harvard Univ, MD, 64. *Honors & Awards:* Distinguished Achievement Award, Coun Circulation, Am Heart Asn, 95. *Prof Exp:* Assoc prof med, Duke Univ, 73-76. *Mem:* Am Soc Clin Invest; Asn Univ Cardiologists; Am Physiol Soc; fel Am Col Cardiol; Am Fedn Clin Res; Asn Am Physicians. *Res:* Cardiovascular physiology; control of blood flow, contractile function and energy metabolism in the ischemi heart; development and function of coronary collateral vasculature. *Mailing Add:* Univ Minn Hosp Minneapolis MN 55455. *Fax:* 612-626-3579; *E-Mail:* bache001@maroon.tc.umn.edu

BACHELET, DOMINIQUE, SIMULATION MODELING. *Current Pos:* ASST PROF, DEPT BIORESOURCE ENG, ORE STATE UNIV, 89- *Personal Data:* b Arras, France, July 16, 57; m 88, Steven Wondzell. *Educ:* Univ des Scis et Tech, Lille I, France, DEUG B, 76; Licence, 77, Maitrise, 78; Univ de Paris XI, DEA, 79; Colo State Univ, PhD(bot & plant path), 83. *Prof Exp:* Lab tech plant path, WVa Univ, 80; teaching asst, Dept Bot & Plant Path, Colo State Univ, 80, res asst, Natural Resource Ecol Lab, 81-83, teaching asst, Agron Dept, 82; res asst, soil & environ scis, Univ Calif, Riverside, 84-86; res specialist, Biol Dept, NMex State Univ, 86-87, Agron Dept, 88. *Concurrent Pos:* Quantitative ecologist, Mantech Environ Tech Inc, 88-94. *Mem:* Fel AAAS; fel Ecol Soc Am; fel Sol Sci Soc Am; fel Int Soc Ecol Modelling; fel Int Asn Ecol. *Res:* Climate change impacts on vegetation distribution C and N cycle, methane emissions, large scale simulation. *Mailing Add:* FSL 3200 SW Jefferson Way Corvallis OR 97331. *Fax:* 541-750-7329; *E-Mail:* bachelet@fsl.orst.edu.gov

BACHELIS, GREGORY FRANK, ANALYSIS OF ALGORITHMS, PARALLEL ALGORITHMS. *Current Pos:* assoc prof math, 71-79, PROF MATH, WAYNE STATE UNIV, 79- *Personal Data:* b Los Angeles, Calif, Mar 9, 41; m; c 1. *Educ:* Reed Col, BA, 62; Univ Ore, MA, 63, PhD(math), 66. *Prof Exp:* Asst, Univ Ore, 62-63 & 64-66; asst prof math, State Univ NY, Stony Brook, 66-70; vis assoc prof, Kans State Univ, 70-71. *Concurrent Pos:* Programmer & analyst, Ford Motor Co, 82-83; adj prof comput sci, Wayne State Univ, 88- *Mem:* Am Math Soc; Math Asn Am; Asn Comput Mach; Soc Indust & Appl Math. *Mailing Add:* Dept Math Wayne State Univ Detroit MI 48202-9861

BACHELOR, FRANK WILLIAM, ORGANIC CHEMISTRY. *Current Pos:* AT FWB CHEM CONSULT LTD, 89- *Personal Data:* b New York, NY, Nov 2, 28; m 55; c 3. *Educ:* Univ Calif, Berkeley, BS, 51; Mass Inst Technol, PhD(org chem), 60. *Prof Exp:* Asst chemist, Merck & Co, Inc, NJ, 51-54; NSF fel, Inst Org Chem, Munich Tech Univ, 60-61; res assoc org chem, Johns Hopkins Univ, 61-63; from asst prof to assoc prof org chem, Univ Calgary, 63-89. *Mem:* Am Chem Soc; Brit Chem Soc; fel Chem Inst Can. *Res:* Structure and synthesis of natural products; organic reaction mechanisms; chemistry of coal and asphaltenes. *Mailing Add:* FWB Chem Consult Ltd 118-339 50th Ave SE Calgary AB T2G 2B3 Can. *Fax:* 403-253-7072

BACHENHEIMER, STEVEN LARRY, ANIMAL VIROLOGY. *Current Pos:* asst prof, 75-80, ASSOC PROF ANIMAL VIROL, DEPT MICROBIOL & IMMUNOL, UNIV NC CHAPEL HILL, 80- *Personal Data:* b Chicago, Ill, Sept 19, 45; m 67, 86; c 2. *Educ:* Univ Ill, Urbana, BS, 67; Univ Chicago, PhD(microbiol), 72. *Prof Exp:* From res assoc to lectr animal virol, Columbia Univ, 72-74; fel, Rockefeller Univ, 74-75. *Concurrent Pos:* Damon Runyon fel, 72-74; NIH res fel. *Mem:* Am Soc Microbiol; AAAS; Am Soc Virol. *Res:* Genetics of assembly of herpesvirus nucleoeapsids; modification of cell-cycle check points by HSV; regulation of HSV transcription. *Mailing Add:* Univ NC Chapel Hill Sch Med Univ NC Chapel Hill NC 27599-7290

BACHER, ANDREW DOW, NUCLEAR PHYSICS. *Current Pos:* from asst prof to assoc prof, 70-77, PROF PHYSICS, IND UNIV, BLOOMINGTON, 77- *Personal Data:* b Ithaca, NY, Sept 5, 38; m 62. *Educ:* Harvard Univ, AB, 60; Calif Inst Technol, PhD(nuclear physics), 67. *Prof Exp:* Res fel physics, Calif Inst Technol, 66-67; NSF fel, Lawrence Radiation Lab, Univ Calif, 67-68, res physicist, 68-70. *Mem:* Am Phys Soc. *Res:* Nuclear astrophysics. *Mailing Add:* Dept Physics Ind Univ Bloomington IN 47401

BACHER, FREDERICK ADDISON, PHYSICAL CHEMISTRY. *Current Pos:* RETIRED. *Personal Data:* b Northampton, Mass, July 18, 15; m 44, 54, Angela Bornn; c Beatrice E, Edward V & Judith A. *Educ:* Harvard Univ, SB, 36; Rutgers Univ, MSc, 45. *Prof Exp:* Asst chemist, Plastics Dept, E I Du Pont de Nemours & Co, Inc, Mass, 36-38; chemist, Merck Sharp & Dohme Res Labs, 39-57, mgr new prod control, 57-70, dir pharmaceut anal, 70-80. *Mem:* Fel AAAS; Am Chem Soc; Sigma Xi. *Res:* Stability-indicating assays for drug formulations; purity of organic compounds; analytical methods; bio-availability of drug dosage forms. *Mailing Add:* 321 45th Pl W Sea Isle City NJ 08243-1847

BACHER, ROBERT FOX, HIGH ENERGY PHYSICS, NUCLEAR ENERGY. *Current Pos:* chmn, Div Physics, Math & Astron, Calif Inst Technol, 49-62, prof, 49-76, provost, 62-70, EMER PROF PHYSICS, CALIF INST TECHNOL, 76- *Personal Data:* b Loudonville, Ohio, Aug 31, 05; m 30; c 2. *Educ:* Univ Mich, BS, 26, PhD(physics), 30. *Hon Degrees:* ScD, Univ Mich, 48; LLD, Claremont Grad Sch, 75. *Honors & Awards:* Medal for Merit. *Prof Exp:* Nat res fel physics, Calif Inst Technol, 30-31 & Mass Inst Technol, 31-32; Lloyd fel, Univ Mich, 32-33; instr, Columbia Univ, 34-35; from instr to prof, Cornell Univ, 35-49, dir, Nuclear Studies Lab, 46; res assoc, Radiation Lab, Mass Inst Technol, 41-45; head, Exp Physics Div, Atomic Bomb Proj, Los Alamos Lab, 43-44 & Bomb Physics Div, 44-45; mem, US AEC, 46-49. *Concurrent Pos:* Sci adv to US Rep UN AEC, 46-49; trustee, Assoc Univs, 46, 62-66, 70-73, Rand Corp, 50-60, Carnegie Corp, 59-76 & Univ Res Assoc, 65-75, chmn, 70-73, pres, 73-74; mem, Pres Sci Adv Comt, 53-55, 57-60 & Naval Res Adv Comt, 57-62; bd fels, Claremont Univ Ctr, 71-88. *Mem:* Nat Acad Sci; AAAS; Am Phys Soc (pres, 64); Am Philos Soc; Int Union Pure & Appl Physics (vpres, 66-69, pres, 69-72). *Res:* High energy physics; photoproduction of mesons; nuclear physics; atomic energy. *Mailing Add:* 300 Hot Springs Rd No 12 Montecito CA 93108

BACHEVALIER, JOCELYNE H, BRAIN DEVELOPMENT, LEARNING & MEMORY. *Current Pos:* ASSOC PROF NEUROBIOL-ANAT, UNIV TEX MED SCH, HOUSTON, 91- *Personal Data:* b Hussein Dey, Algeria, Jan 28, 47; Can citizen. *Educ:* Univ Montreal, BS, 71, PhD(clin sci), 81; Univ Provence, MS, 72; Univ Paris, PhD(psychobiol), 75. *Prof Exp:* Res asst, Clin Res Inst Montreal, 75-80; guest researcher, NIMH, 81-83, vis scientist, 83-88 & 90-91; res assoc prof, George Washington Univ, 89-90. *Concurrent Pos:* Guest researcher, NIMH, 91- *Mem:* AAAS; Soc Neurosci; Int Brain Res Orgn; Am Psychol Soc; Advan Women Sci. *Res:* Maturation of the brain in relation to maturation of learning and memory processes; social behavior and emotion in primates. *Mailing Add:* Univ Tex Med Sch 6431 Fannin St Houston TX 77030-1501. *Fax:* 713-792-5795; *E-Mail:* bachera@nba19.med.uth.tmc.edu

BACHINSKY, DAVID ROBERT, MOLECULAR GENETICS. *Current Pos:* RES ASSOC, DEPT GENETICS, HARVARD MED SCH, 95- *Personal Data:* b Abington, Pa, Apr 10, 58. *Educ:* LaSalle Univ, BS, 80; Univ Mass, Lowell, MS, 83; St Louis Univ, PhD(biochem & molecular biol), 90. *Prof Exp:* Res fel genetics, Harvard Med Sch, 90-91, path, 91-93; res fel molecular biol, Mass Gen Hosp, 90-91, path, 91-93; instr, Dept Med, Div Nephrology, New Eng Med Ctr, Tufts Univ Sch Med, 94-95. *Concurrent Pos:* Nat Res Serv Award, NIH, 91-93; employee, Howard Hughes Med Inst, 95- *Mem:* Am Soc Human Genetics; Genetic Soc Am; Am Soc Cell Biol; Am Soc Microbiol; NY Acad Sci; assoc mem Am Soc Biochem & Molecular Biol. *Res:* Cellular manifestations of autosomal dominant polycystic kidney disease; characterization of GP330 a member of the LO6 receptor gene family and an antigen in the rat autoimmune disease, Heymann Nephritis. *Mailing Add:* Dept Genetics Harvard Med Sch 200 Longwood Ave Boston MA 02115. *Fax:* 617-956-1355

BACHKOSKY, JOHN M (JACK), NUCLEAR DEFENSE. *Current Pos:* CORP VPRES ADVAN TECH, SYSTEM PLANNING CORP. *Personal Data:* b Taylor, Pa, Nov 1, 39; m, Helen Bachkosky; c Arlene, Janice, Karen & John. *Educ:* Pa State Univ, BEng. *Prof Exp:* Aircraft engr, USN, 63-82; from tech & mgt to chief of staff, Defense Nuclear Agency, Washington, 86-91; tech dir direct energy weapon develop & dir advan tech, Dept Defense Res & Eng, Pentagon, Wash, 82-86, dep dir, Off Dir Defense Res & Eng, 91-95. *Res:* Defense research and engineering. *Mailing Add:* Syst Planning Corp 1000 Wilson Blvd Suite 3100 Arlington VA 22209

BACHMAN, BONNIE JEAN WILSON, MECHANICS, SURFACE PHYSICS. *Current Pos:* PRES, ADVAN CONCEPTS, 96- *Personal Data:* b Mt Pleasant, Iowa, Sept 20, 50; c Chad M. *Educ:* Ill Benedictine Col, BS, 79; Rutgers Univ, MS, 87, PhD, 95. *Honors & Awards:* Outstanding Achievement Award, Soc Plastics Engrs, 91 & 93; Outstanding Serv Award, NAm Thermal Anal Soc, 93. *Prof Exp:* Lab supvr, Norplex Div, UOP, 79-80; mem tech staff, AT&T Bell Labs, 81-91; vis scientist, Solar Energy Res Inst, 91-92; lab mgr, Empak, 92-93, res & develop mgr, 93-96. *Concurrent Pos:* Mem, Gov Task Force Recycling, Colo. *Mem:* Soc Plastics Engrs (treas, 90, 2nd vpres, 91, 1st vpres, 92, pres-elect, 93, pres, 94, past pres, 95, prior past pres, 96); NAm Thermal Anal Soc (secy, 85-87, vpres, 88, pres, 89); Am Chem Soc; Sigma Xi; Am Soc Metals Int; Inst Elec & Electronics Engrs. *Res:* Developing polymers and their processing conditions for electronic, microelectronic and optoelectronic applications; property-structure relationships of high temperature polymers; polymer-metal interface studies; contamination control for ultraclean application; friction and wear properties; triboelectric charging effects; particle size and distribution studies; characterization of polymers. *Mailing Add:* 7020 Johnson Circle Niwot CO 80503-7506. *Fax:* 303-652-1360; *E-Mail:* bbachman@adv-concepts

BACHMAN, GEORGE, MATHEMATICS. *Current Pos:* from asst prof to assoc prof, 60-65, PROF MATH, POLYTECH INST BROOKLYN, 65- *Personal Data:* b New York, NY, Jan 17, 29. *Educ:* NY Univ, BEE, 50, MS, 52, PhD(math), 56. *Honors & Awards:* Distinguished Teacher Award, Polytech Inst NY, 74. *Prof Exp:* From instr to asst prof math, Rutgers Univ, 57-60. *Mem:* Am Math Soc; Math Asn Am; Math Soc France; Indian Math Soc; Can Math Cong; Sigma Xi. *Res:* Functional analysis; algebraic number theory; topological measure theory. *Mailing Add:* 27 Summit Rd Riverside CT 06878

BACHMAN, GEORGE O, ROCKY MOUNTAIN, DESERT REGIONS. *Current Pos:* RETIRED. *Personal Data:* b Wichita, Kans, Aug 4, 20. *Educ:* Univ NMex, BA, 48. *Prof Exp:* Geologist, US Geol Surv, 48-78; independent consult, 78-88. *Mailing Add:* 4008 Hannett Ave NE Albuquerque NM 87110

BACHMAN, GEORGE S(TRICKLER), CERAMICS. *Current Pos:* RETIRED. *Personal Data:* b Lebanon, Pa, Jan 6, 15; m 50. *Educ:* Pa State Col, BS, 36, MS, 38; Univ Mich, BSE, 43; Univ Ill, PhD, 47. *Prof Exp:* Ceramic engr, Owens-Ill Glass Co, 37-42; res ceramist, Pittsburgh Plate Glass Co, 47-52, dir, Res Fiberglass Div, 52-57, asst dir res, Gen Ceramics Corp, 57-62, mfr thermoelements, 62-69, proprietor patent referencing serv, 69-80. *Mem:* Am Chem Soc; Am Ceramic Soc; Am Inst Chem. *Res:* Glass compositions; thermoelectric materials. *Mailing Add:* Redfield Village 16 B 3 Edison NJ 08837

BACHMAN, GERALD LEE, ORGANIC CHEMISTRY. *Current Pos:* RETIRED. *Personal Data:* b Alton, Ill, Oct 6, 32; m 57; c 2. *Educ:* Univ Ill, BS, 54; Washington Univ, PhD(org chem), 63. *Prof Exp:* Res chemist biochem, Monsanto Co, 56-58, res chemist explor synthesis, 63-80, sr res group leader, 80-84, res mgr, 84-86, mgr res & develop, 86-87, res dir, 87-95. *Res:* Chemistry of carbenes, particularly phenylcarbene; synthesis of heterocyclic compounds; amino acid chemistry; asymmetric hydrogenation; protein purification. *Mailing Add:* 1627 Dunmorr Des Peres MO 63131-3830

BACHMAN, HENRY L(EE), ENGINEERING MANAGEMENT. *Current Pos:* prod line dir radio navig, Hazeltine Corp, 70-71, dir qual & logistics eng, 71-75, vpres qual & customer serv, 76-78, vpres opers, 79-89, vpres eng, 86-89, vpres mkt planning, 89-91, vpres spec proj, 92-95, SR CONSULT ENGR, HAZELTINE CORP, 96- *Personal Data:* b New York, NY, Apr 29, 30; m 51, Doris Engelhardt; c Steven, Diane & Lorraine. *Educ:* Polytech Univ, BEE, 51, MEE, 54. *Honors & Awards:* Centennial Medal, Inst Elec & Electronics Engrs, Haradan Pratt Medal. *Prof Exp:* Elec engr, Wheeler Labs, Inc, 51-61, asst chief engr, 62-68, pres, 68-70. *Concurrent Pos:* Bd dir, Inst Elec & Electronics Engrs; bd trustees, Polytechnic Univ. *Mem:* Fel Inst Elec & Electronics Engrs (exec vpres, 84, treas 85, pres-elect, 86, pres, 87); fel AAAS. *Res:* Antennas and microwave components; manufacturing technology. *Mailing Add:* GEC-Marconi Hazeltine Corp Greenlawn NY 11740. *Fax:* 516-262-8400; *E-Mail:* h.bachman@ieee.org

BACHMAN, KENNETH CHARLES, PHYSICAL CHEMISTRY, FUEL SCIENCE. *Current Pos:* RETIRED. *Personal Data:* b West New York, NJ, Mar 1, 22; m 51, Dorothy Jessee; c 3. *Educ:* Rutgers Univ, BS, 44, MS & PhD(phys chem), 50. *Honors & Awards:* Arch T Colwell, Soc Automotive Eng, 66. *Prof Exp:* Chemist, Benzol Prod Co, 44 & 46; asst, Rutgers Univ, 46-49, res asst, 49-50; res chemist, M W Kellogg Co, 51-55; res chemist, Esso Res & Eng Co, Standard Oil Co NJ, 55-66, sr chemist, 66-70, res assoc, Exxon Res & Eng Co, Exxon Corp, Linden, 70-84. *Mem:* Am Chem Soc; Sigma Xi. *Res:* Cause of and control methods for ignitions induced by static discharges during fuel transfer, such as truck loading and aircraft fueling; methods for control of automotive exhaust emissions, particularly sulphates; combustion, particularly residual fuels. *Mailing Add:* 404 Wells St Westfield NJ 07090-1338

BACHMAN, MARVIN CHARLES, MICROBIOLOGY. *Current Pos:* RETIRED. *Personal Data:* b Decorah, Iowa, Feb 8, 21; m 44; c 3. *Educ:* Luther Col, BS, 42; Okla State Univ, MS, 47. *Prof Exp:* Chemist, E I du Pont de Nemours & Co, 42-44; teaching fel, Okla State Univ, 46-47; microbiologist, Com Solvents Corp, 47-51, dir microbiol res, 51-56, lab res, 56-62, dir res, 62-75; dir res & develop, IMC Chem Group, Int Min & Chem Corp, 75-79, dir life sci, 79-82. *Mem:* Am Soc Microbiol; Soc Chem Indust; Am Soc Testing & Mat; Agr Res Inst. *Mailing Add:* 2931 Placita Nublada Green Valley AZ 85614

BACHMAN, RICHARD THOMAS, GEOACOUSTICS, GEOTECHNOLOGY. *Current Pos:* OCEANOGR, NAVAL OCEAN SYSTS CTR, 67- *Personal Data:* b Los Angeles, Calif, May 10, 43; m 67; c 2. *Educ:* San Diego State Univ, AB, 66. *Mem:* Fel Geol Soc Am. *Res:* Measurement of physical properties of marine sediments and rocks which control elastic wave propagation; generalization and prediction of acoustic properties; integration of sediment acoustics with general studies of oceanic sound propagation. *Mailing Add:* NCCOSC Base RDTE Div D881 49575 Gate Rd Rm 170 San Diego CA 92152-6435

BACHMANN, BARBARA JOYCE, microbial genetics, for more information see previous edition

BACHMANN, FEDOR W, INTERNAL MEDICINE, HEMATOLOGY. *Current Pos:* Prof, Univ Lausanne, 77-92, actg chmn, Dept Med, 80-81, provost, 87-91, EMER PROF, MED SCH, UNIV LAUSANNE, 92-, SCI ADV, THROMBOSIS RES INST, LONDON, 95- *Personal Data:* b Zurich, Switz, May 23, 27; US & Swiss citizen; m 57, Edith Derendinger; c Christian. *Educ:* Gym Zurich, Matura, 46; Univ Zurich, Switz, MD. *Honors & Awards:* BIANNUAL PRIZE, INT COMT FIBRINOLYSIS, 88. *Prof Exp:* Internship, Univ Lausanne Med Sch; resident, Univ Zurich Med Sch, 56-61; trainee enzym, Wash Univ, St Louis, Mo, 61-64, instr, 63, asst prof med & asst chief med serv, 64-69; dir, Thrombolysis & Coagulation Lab, St Louis, Mo, 64-69; chief, Coagulation & Thrombosis Res Lab, Rush Presby-St Luke's Med Ctr, Chicago, Ill, 69-73, attend physician, 69-72; assoc prof med, Abraham Lincoln Sch Med, Univ Ill, 69-71 & Rush Med Sch, Chicago, 71-74; consult staff, Grant Hosp Chicago Med, 71-73; sr attend physician, Presby-St Luke's Hosp, Chicago, Ill, 72-74; dir med res, Schering-Plough, US, Lucerne, 73-77; head, Div Hemat, Dept Med & Cent Hemat Lab, Univ Med Ctr, Lausanne Univ, Switz, 77-92, consult, Health Mgt Inst, 92-95. *Concurrent Pos:* Grant, Emil Barrell Found, 55-57, NIH, USPHS, 61-73, Swiss Nat Sci Found, 77-92, Roche Found, 79-80, Swiss Cancer League, 79-84, Sandoz Found, 81-82, Thrombosis & Atherosclerosis Found, 83-92, Swiss Cardiol Found 86-87; chmn, Med Adv Bd, Nat Hemophilia Found, 66-68, Nursing Serv Comt, Dept Health & Hosps, St Louis, Mo, 67-68, Int Comt Thrombosis & Hemostatis, 84-86, Coun Thrombosis, Int Soc & Fedn Cardiol, 94-; mem, Manpower Comt, Bi-Stat Regional Health Prog, St Louis, Mo, 68-69, Med Adv Bd, Nat Hemophilia Soc, Switz, 77-85, Sci Coun, Swiss Cancer Inst, 80-88 & Coun Thrombosis, Am Heart Asn, 80-; vchmn, Med Adv Bd, Nat Hemophilia Found, Midwest Chap, 71-73; vis assoc prof, Rush Med Col, Chicago, Ill, 74-78; vis scholar, Path Dept, Stanford Univ Sch Med, 86; vis prof, Univ Paris VI, 91-94. *Mem:* Am Heart Asn; fel Am Col Physicians; Am Soc Hemat; Am Physiol Soc; Cent Soc Clin Res; Sigma XI; NY Acad Sci; Int Soc Hemat; Swiss Med Soc; Int Soc Thrombosis & Hemostasis. *Res:* Hematology, particularly hemostasis, thrombosis and fibriolysis; author of over 200 publications. *Mailing Add:* Hopital Nestle 2077 Lausanne Univ Med Ctr LeMont 1052 Switzerland. *Fax:* 41-21-653-7788; *E-Mail:* fedor.bachmann@dmed.unic.ca

BACHMANN, JOHN HENRY, JR, CARBON BLACK, RUBBER COMPOUNDING. *Current Pos:* GROUP LEADER, ANAL LAB, CONTINENTAL GEN TIRE, INC, 95- *Personal Data:* b Akron, Ohio, Nov 27, 44; m 82, Jean Wenum; c Brittany. *Educ:* Ohio State Univ, BS, 66; Univ Chicago, MS, 69. *Prof Exp:* Teacher chem & math, Revere Local Sch Dist, Revere High Sch, Bath, Ohio, 68-72; compounder, Firestone Tire & Rubber Co, 72-76, mgr chem labs, 76-83; mgr, Res Ctr, Sid Richardson Carbon Co, 83-95. *Mem:* Am Chem Soc; Am Chem Soc Rubber Div. *Res:* Carbon black and rubber compounding. *Mailing Add:* Continental Gen Tire Inc 1800 Continental Blvd Charlotte NC 28273. *Fax:* 704-583-3975; *E-Mail:* jbachmann@gentire.com

BACHMANN, KENNETH ALLEN, PHARMACOLOGY. *Current Pos:* ASSOC PROF PHARMACOL, COL PHARM, UNIV TOLEDO, 73- *Personal Data:* b Columbus, Ohio, Mar 21, 46; m 69. *Educ:* Ohio State Univ, BS, 69, PhD(pharmacol), 73. *Mem:* AAAS; NY Acad Sci; Sigma Xi. *Res:* Pharmacokinetic aspects of oral anticoagulant-drug interactions; influence of environmental chemical exposure and disease upon oral anticoagulant disposition. *Mailing Add:* 285 Cedar Ridge Ct Perrysburg OH 43551-2844

BACHMANN, ROGER WERNER, LIMNOLOGY. *Current Pos:* VIS PROF, UNIV FLA, GAINESVILLE. *Personal Data:* b Ann Arbor, Mich, Dec 11, 34; m 60; c 2. *Educ:* Univ Mich, 56, PhD(zool), 62; Univ Idaho, MS, 58. *Prof Exp:* Res zoologist, Univ Calif, Davis, 62-63; from asst prof to assoc prof, Iowa State Univ, 63-71, prof limnol, 71- *Concurrent Pos:* Assoc ed, Ecol & Ecol Monogr, 77-82; mem, Iowa Gov Sci Adv Coun, 77-82; ed, J Iowa Acad Sci, 83- *Mem:* AAAS; Am Soc Limnol & Oceanog; Ecol Soc Am; Am Fisheries Soc. *Res:* Biological productivity of lakes; aquatic mineral cycles. *Mailing Add:* Dept Fishery & Aquatic Sci Univ Fla 7922 NW 71 St Gainesville FL 32003

BACHOP, WILLIAM EARL, GROSS ANATOMY, DEVELOPMENTAL BIOLOGY. *Current Pos:* asst prof & actg chmn, Nat Col Chiropractic, 74-75, assoc prof, 76-80, chmn dept, 76-86, prof, 80-95, EMER PROF ANAT NAT COL CHIROPRACTIC, LOMBARD, 95- *Personal Data:* b Youngstown, Ohio, Aug 31, 26; m 58, Annabelle Adams; c Alice M & Margaret A. *Educ:* Western Res Univ, AB, 50; Ohio State Univ, MSc, 58, PhD(zool), 63. *Prof Exp:* Asst prof biol, Univ Omaha, 63-65; training prog fel develop biol res, Sch Med, Univ Wash, 65-69; asst prof zool, Clemson Univ, 69-73. *Mem:* Am Anatomists Asn; Hist Sci Soc; Am Asn Clin Anatomists. *Res:* Ossified transforaminal ligaments of human lumbar spine; giant nuclei in yolk sac syncytium of oviparous bony fishes. *Mailing Add:* Dept Anat Nat Col Chiropractic 200 E Roosevelt Rd Lombard IL 60148

BACHRACH, ARTHUR JULIAN, EXPERIMENTAL PSYCHOLOGY. *Current Pos:* CONSULT, 87- *Personal Data:* b New York, NY, Mar 20, 23; m 54; c 2. *Educ:* Col City New York, BS, 47; Western Reserve Univ, MA, 50; Univ Va, PhD(educ & psychol), 52. *Honors & Awards:* Award for Sci, Underwater Soc Am, 73; Greenstone Award Contrib Diving Safety, Nat Asn Underwater Instrs, 83; Shilling Award, Undersea & Hyperbaric Med Soc, 86. *Prof Exp:* From instr to assoc prof neurol & psychiat, Sch Med, Univ Va, 50-62, dir, div clin & med psychol, 50-58, dir, div behav sci, 58-62; prof psychol & chmn dept, Ariz State Univ, 62-69; chmn, Dept Behav Sci, Naval Med Res Inst, 69-79, dir, Environ Stress Prog Ctr & chmn, Sci Psychophysiol, 79-87. *Concurrent Pos:* Adj prof med psych, Uniformed Serv Univ Health Sci, 78-87; chmn, bd adv, Col Oceaneering, 83-87; mem, bd adv, Op Raleigh, US, 84-88. *Mem:* Undersea Med Soc (pres, 76-77); fel Am Psychol Asn; fel

AAAS; Am Littoral Soc; Human Factors Soc; Royal Soc Med. *Res:* Stress physiology and behavior under conditions of environmental extremes of cold, heat, and underwater; effects of protection equipment such as garments and masks. *Mailing Add:* PO Box 3600 Taos NM 87571-3600

BACHRACH, CHRISTINE A, POPULATION DYNAMICS. *Current Pos:* Statician, 88-92, CHIEF, DEMOG & BEHAV SCI BR, NAT INST CHILD HEALTH & HUMAN DEVELOP, CTR POP RES, NIH, 92- *Personal Data:* b New York, NY, May 28, 50. *Educ:* Radcliffe Col, BA, 72; Georgetown Univ, MA, 74; Johns Hopkins Univ, PhD(pop dynamics), 79. *Prof Exp:* Statistician, Nat Ctr Health Statist, 79-88. *Concurrent Pos:* Bd dir, Pop Asn Am, 97. *Mem:* Pop Asn Am; Nat Coun Family Relations; Soc Study Social Biol; Am Sociol Asn. *Mailing Add:* NICHH-NIH Rm 8B13 6100 Executive Blvd Bethesda MD 20892. *Fax:* 301-496-0962; *E-Mail:* bachracc@hd01.nichd.nih.gov

BACHRACH, HOWARD L, MOLECULAR VIROLOGY, SUB-UNIT VACCINES. *Current Pos:* chief scientist & head biochem & phys invest, 53-81, res chemist, 81-85, CONSULT-COLLABR, PLUM ISLAND ANIMAL DIS CTR, USDA, 85- *Personal Data:* b Faribault, Minn, May 21, 20; m 43, Shirley Lichterman; c Eve E & Harrison J. *Educ:* Univ Minn, BA, 42, PhD(biochem), 49. *Honors & Awards:* US Pres Citation, 65; Theobald Smith Lectr, Am Soc Microbiol, 81; Newcomb Cleveland Prize, AAAS, 82; Kenneth A Spencer Medal, Am Chem Soc, 82; Nat Medal Sci, President Ronald Reagan, 83; Alexander von Humboldt Award, 83; Nat Award Agr Excellence, 83; USDA Agr Res Serv Hall Fame, 87. *Prof Exp:* Res asst, Explosives Res Lab, Nat Defense Res Comt Proj, Carnegie Inst Technol, 42-45; biochemist, Foot & Mouth Dis Res Mission, USDA, Denmark, 49-50; res biochemist, Biochem & Virus Lab, Univ Calif, Berkeley, 50-53. *Concurrent Pos:* Chemist, Jos Seagram & Co, Lawrenceburg, Ind, 42; consult, Walter Reed Army Inst Res, 81-84, Am Chem Soc Spencer Awards Comt, 83-85, Nat Acad Sci, 84-91, Off Tech Assessment, US Cong, 84-85, Nat Cancer Inst, 84-87, Inst Biosci & Technol, Tex A&M Univ, 87-89 & var industs, 83- *Mem:* Nat Acad Sci; fel NY Acad Sci; hon mem Am Col Vet Microbiologists; Am Chem Soc; Am Soc Virol. *Res:* Structure and function of animal viruses; viral replication strategies; cloned viral protein vaccines; immunology; immunization with a capsid protein of foot and mouth disease virus; structure and molecular biology of viruses; first production through gene splicing of an effective vaccine against any disease of animals or humans; first purification and electron microscopic identification of poliovirus and foot-and-mouth disease virus. *Mailing Add:* 355 Dayton Rd PO Box 1054 Southold NY 11971

BACHRACH, JOSEPH, CARBOHYDRATE CHEMISTRY. *Current Pos:* prof chem, 66-89, chmn dept, 77-88, EMER PROF, NORTHEASTERN ILL UNIV, 89- *Personal Data:* b Ger, Feb 9, 18; US citizen; m 58. *Educ:* Queen's Univ (Ont), BA, 44, MA, 45; Purdue Univ, PhD(bio-org-chem), 50. *Prof Exp:* Asst prof chem, Concord Col, 50-53; from asst prof to assoc prof, Univ Ill, Chicago Circle, 53-66. *Mem:* Am Chem Soc; Sigma Xi. *Res:* Carbohydrates; hemicelluloses. *Mailing Add:* 6744 Trumbull Lincolnwood IL 60645-3740

BACHRACH, ROBERT ZELMAN, solid state physics, for more information see previous edition

BACHUR, NICHOLAS R, SR, BIOCHEMISTRY, PHARMACOLOGY. *Current Pos:* dir res, 82-94, PROF UNIV MD CANCER CTR, 82- *Personal Data:* b Baltimore, Md, July 21, 33; m 52; c 3. *Educ:* Johns Hopkins Univ, AB, 54; Univ Md, MD & PhD(biochem), 61. *Honors & Awards:* Commendation Medal, USPHS, 80. *Prof Exp:* Res asst biochem, McCollum-Pratt Inst, Johns Hopkins Univ, 51-55; instr biochem, Univ Md, 61, intern med, Univ Hosp, 61-62; res biochemist, Lab Clin Biochem, Nat Heart Inst, 62-65; chief, lab clin biochem, Baltimore Cancer Res Ctr, Nat Cancer Inst, 66-85. *Concurrent Pos:* Actg dir, Univ Md Cancer Ctr, 85-87. *Mem:* AAAS; Am Soc Pharmacol & Exp Therapeut; Am Soc Clin Onocol; Am Asn Cancer Res. *Res:* Drug mechanism of action; biochemical mechanisms and molecular disease mechanisms; clinical pharmacology; drug design. *Mailing Add:* Cancer Res Ctr Univ Md 655 W Baltimore St Baltimore MD 21201. *Fax:* 410-328-6559

BACHVAROFF, RADOSLAV J, IMMUNOGENETICS, HISTOCOMPATIBILITY ANTIGENS. *Current Pos:* res internal med, 86-88, chief resident internal med, 88-90, NEPHROLOGY FEL, NASSAU COUNTY MED CTR, 90-; ATTEND PHYSICIAN & CLIN INSTR, FLUSHING HOSP MED CTR, 90-; ATTEN PHYSICIAN, PARKWAY HOSP, 93- *Personal Data:* b Blagoevrad, Bulgaria, Nov 5, 35; US citizen; m 65; c 4. *Educ:* Med Acad Sofia, Bulgaria, MD, 59. *Prof Exp:* Resident, Alexandrov Hosp, Sofia, 59-61; res assoc immunol, Inst Microbiol & Epidemiol, Sofia, 61-63; guest investr biochem & immunol, Immunol Lab, Nat Inst Allergy & Infectious Dis, NIH, 63-64 & biochem, Rockefeller Univ, 64; Eleanor Roosevelt fel cancer res, Inst Biol & Med Chem, Acad Med Sci, Moscow, 65-66; res assoc immunol, Biochem Lab, Pasteur Inst, Paris, 67-69, Rockefeller Univ, 69-70; res assoc immunol & transplantation, Med Ctr, NY Univ, 71-73, asst prof, 73-77; from assoc prof to prof, depts surgery & path, State Univ NY, Stony Brook, 77-85. *Mem:* Am Asn Immunologists; Transplantation Soc; Soc Exp Biol & Med; NY Acad Sci; Harvey Soc; AAAS; Am Col Physicians. *Res:* Transplantation biology; lymphocyte differentiation in the immune response; histocompatibility testing; immunogenetics; nephrology; kidney and bone marrow transplantation. *Mailing Add:* Flushing Hosp Med Ctr 56-28 Francis Lewis Blvd Bayside NY 11364

BACHVAROVA, ROSEMARY FAULKNER, EMBRYOLOGY, MOLECULAR BIOLOGY. *Current Pos:* Res fel, 70-72, from instr to assoc prof anat, 73-90, PROF CELL BIOL, MED COL, CORNELL UNIV, 90- *Personal Data:* b Brookline, Mass, Oct 2, 38; div; c 3. *Educ:* Radcliffe Col, BA, 61; Rockefeller Univ, PhD(molecular embryol), 66. *Mem:* Soc Develop Biol; Sigma Xi. *Res:* Oogenesis and early embryological development, especially in mammals. *Mailing Add:* Dept Biol Cornell Univ Med Col 1300 York Ave New York NY 10021

BACHYNSKI, MORREL PAUL, PLASMA PHYSICS. *Current Pos:* FOUNDER & PRES, MPB TECHNOLOGIES INC, 77- *Personal Data:* b Bienfait, Sask, July 19, 30; m 59, Slava Krkovic; c Caroline Dawn & Jane Diane. *Educ:* Univ Sask, BEng, 52, MSc, 53; McGill Univ, PhD(physics), 55. *Hon Degrees:* LLD, Waterloo Univ, 93, Concordia Univ, 97; DSc, McGill Univ, 94. *Honors & Awards:* David Sarnoff Gold Medal, 77; Prix Sci du Quebec, 77; Achievement in Physics Medal, Can Asn Physicists, 87; Res & Develop Award, Can Res Mgt Asn, 88; Medal Indust & Appl Physics, Can Asn Physicists, 95. *Prof Exp:* Res assoc, Eaton Electronics Lab, McGill Univ, 55; mem sci staff, Res Labs, RCA Corp, 55-57, assoc labs dir, 58-59, dir microwave & plasma physics labs, 59-65, dir res, RCA Ltd, 65-72, dir res & develop, 72-75, vpres res & develop, RCA Ltd, 75-76. *Concurrent Pos:* Pres, Asn Sci, Eng & Tech Community of Can, 74-75; mem, Sci Coun Can; vpres, Acad III Royal Soc Can, 82-83; mem bd dirs, Commun Res Ctr, 93-; chmn, Fac Sci Adv Bd, McGill Univ, 93-, Que Govt Comt Space Sci & Technol, 94-, Citec Comt Indust/Univ Interaction, 94- *Mem:* Fel Inst Elec & Electronics Engrs; fel Am Phys Soc; fel Can Aeronaut & Space Inst; fel Royal Soc Can (vpres, 81-82); Can Asn Physicists (pres, 68-69); hon mem Eng Inst Can; fel Can Acad Eng; assoc fel Am Inst Aeronaut & Astronaut. *Res:* Electromagnetic wave propagation; microwave optics; plasma physics; geophysics and space physics; plasma and laser technology, including controlled fusion and communications. *Mailing Add:* MPB Technol Inc 151 Hymus Blvd Pointe Claire Dorval PQ H9R 1E9 Can. *Fax:* 514-695-7492; *E-Mail:* bachynsu@mpb.tech.qc.ca

BACH-Y-RITA, PAUL, neurophysiology, rehabilitation; deceased, see previous edition for last biography

BACK, BIRGER BO, EXPERIMENTAL NUCLEAR PHYSICS. *Current Pos:* asst physicist, 77-81, PHYSICIST, NUCLEAR PHYSICS, ARGONNE NAT LAB, 81- *Personal Data:* b Copenhagen, Denmark, Mar 26, 46; m 73, Ulla O Ebberup; c Henning O, Niklas O & Christoffer O. *Educ:* Univ Copenhagen, MS, 70, PhD(nuclear physics), 74. *Prof Exp:* Res asst, Univ Copenhagen, 70-71; vis staff mem, Los Alamos Sci Lab, 71-72; fel, Univ Copenhagen, 72-77; vis staff mem, Los Alamos Sci Lab, 77. *Mem:* Am Phys Soc. *Res:* Nuclear fission and heavy ion reactions. *Mailing Add:* Argonne Nat Lab 9700 S Cass Argonne IL 60439. *Fax:* 630-252-6210; *E-Mail:* back@anlphy.phy.anl.gov

BACK, KENNETH CHARLES, MEDICAL SCIENCES. *Current Pos:* CO-OWNER, INT TOXICOL CONSULTS, 87- *Personal Data:* b Wharton, NJ, Nov 17, 25; m 50, 81; c 9. *Educ:* Muhlenberg Col, BS, 51; Univ Okla, MS, 54, PhD(med sci), 57. *Prof Exp:* Sr scientist, Warner-Lambert Res Inst, 57-58; pharmacologist, Pitman-Moore Co, 58-60; pharmacologist-toxicologist, Wright-Patterson AFB, 60-66, supvry pharmacologist-toxicologist & chief toxicol br, 6570th Aerospace Med Res Labs, 66-82; prof prev med & biomet, Uniformed Serv Univ Health Sci, Bethesda, Md, 82-87. *Concurrent Pos:* Adj prof biol sci, Wright State Univ, 73-; mem, Am Conf Govt Indust Hygienists. *Mem:* Sigma Xi; Soc Toxicol; Am Soc Pharmacol & Exp Therapeut; NY Acad Sci. *Res:* General pharmacology; intermediary metabolism; aerospace toxicology; propellant toxicology. *Mailing Add:* 125 Upgang Lane North Yorks Y0213J2 England

BACK, MARGARET HELEN, PHYSICAL CHEMISTRY. *Personal Data:* b Ottawa, Ont, Dec 7, 29; m 54, Robert; c Roberta & Michael. *Educ:* Acadia Univ, BSc, 50; McGill Univ, MSc, 54, PhD(chem), 59. *Honors & Awards:* Clara Benson Award, 96. *Prof Exp:* Fel chem, Nat Res Coun Can, 59-61; res assoc, Univ Ottawa, 61-65, from asst prof to prof, 65-95. *Concurrent Pos:* Nat Res Coun Can res grants, 63-; Ont Res Found grant, 64-67; natural sci & eng res grants, Res Coun Can, 79-95. *Mem:* Fel Chem Inst Can. *Res:* Kinetics of gas phase reactions; formation of carbon from hydrocarbons; reactions of carbon. *Mailing Add:* 546 Queen Elizabeth Driveway Ottawa ON K1S 3N4 Can

BACK, NATHAN, PHARMACOLOGY. *Current Pos:* PROF BIOCHEM PHARMACOL, STATE UNIV NY BUFFALO, 64- *Personal Data:* b Philadelphia, Pa, Nov 30, 25; m 51; c 5. *Educ:* Pa State Univ, BS, 48; Philadelphia Col Pharm, MS, 52, DSc(pharmacol), 55. *Honors & Awards:* E K Frey Medal, 70. *Prof Exp:* Asst admin & tech orgn med labs, Israel, 48-49; biochemist, Wyeth Inst, 50-51, pharmacologist, 51-52; res asst pharmacol, Philadelphia Col Pharm, 52-54, instr, 54-55; cancer res scientist, Roswell Park Mem Inst, 55-58, sr cancer res scientist, 58-66. *Concurrent Pos:* Res fel, State Univ NY Buffalo, 56-58, from asst prof to prof pharmacol, Sch Pharm, 56-64, prof, Grad Sch Arts & Sci, 64-, from actg chmn to chmn dept biochem pharmacol, 67-71; vis prof & actg dir sch pharm, Fac Med, Hebrew Univ, Jerusalem, 69-71, vis prof, 71-; exec ed, Pharmacol Res Commun; chmn, State Univ Task Force on Israel Progs; UN expert pharmacol, 75-; UN Sci Expert, Jerusalem, Israel, 76-77; vis prof, Weizman Inst Sci, 85-86. *Mem:* Fel AAAS; Am Soc Hemat; Int Soc Hemat; Fedn Am Soc Exp Biol; fel Am Soc Clin Pharmacol & Therapeut; fel Royal Soc Med; fel NY Acad Sci; Am Soc Exp Pharmacol. *Res:* Chemotherapy of cancer; alkylating agents; physiology and pathology of blood and blood-forming organs; pharmacology of fibronolytic agents and anticoagulants; extracorporeal circulation; thrombo-embolic phenomena; mechanisms of drug resistance; shock mechanisms; vasoactive polypeptides; atherosclerosis; biochemical pharmacology; angiogenesis; Kallikrein-Kininogen-Kinin system; proteases and protease inhibitors. *Mailing Add:* Dept Biochem Pharmacol Rm H347 Hochstetter Hall State Univ NY Buffalo Amherst NY 14260-0001

BACK, THOMAS GEORGE, ORGANIC SYNTHESIS, ORGANOSULFUR & ORGANOSELENIUM CHEMISTRY. *Current Pos:* from asst prof to assoc prof, 78-87, PROF CHEM, UNIV CALGARY, 87- *Personal Data:* b Prague, Czech, Sept 11, 47; Can citizen; m 78, Gisele Villeneuve. *Educ:* McGill Univ, BSc, 68, MSc, 71, PhD(chem), 74; Imperial Col, UK, DIC, 76. *Prof Exp:* Res chemist, Frank W Horner Ltd, 68-69; res assoc, Nat Res Coun Can, 76-78. *Concurrent Pos:* Mem exec org div, Can Soc Chem, 81-86, chmn, 84-85; vis scholar, Stanford Univ, 85. *Mem:* Fel Can Soc Chem; Am Chem Soc; Royal Soc Chem. *Res:* Novel structures, reactions and synthetic methods based on organosulfur and organoselenium chemistry; synthesis of steroids, antibiotics, anticancer agents, plant growth promoters and other biologically active compounds. *Mailing Add:* Dept Chem Univ Calgary Calgary AB T2N 1N4 Can. *Fax:* 403-289-9488; *E-Mail:* TGBACK@ACS.UCALGARY.CA

BACK, WILLIAM, HYDROGEOLOGY. *Current Pos:* geologist, Calif, 50-54, GEOLOGIST, WATER RESOURCES DIV, US GEOL SURV, VA, 54- *Personal Data:* b East St Louis, Ill, Aug 9, 25; m 50; c 4. *Educ:* Univ Ill, AB, 48; Univ Calif, MS, 55; Harvard Univ, MPA, 56; Univ Nev, Reno, PhD(chem hydrogeol), 69. *Honors & Awards:* O E Meinzer Award, Geol Soc Am, 73; Distinguished Lectr in Hydrogeol, Geol Soc Am, 78-79. *Prof Exp:* Asst, Ill State Geol Surv, 45-48; asst geol, Univ Calif, 49-50. *Concurrent Pos:* Instr hist & Eng, Fla Mil Acad, 47; asst geol, Harvard Univ, 56-57; lectr, Am Univ, 57-59; vis scholar, Desert Res Inst, Nev, 66-68; continuing FAO adv to Israel, 67; USAID adv to Pakistan, 71; UNDP consult, Costa Rica, 71, Bolivia, 77, Turkey, 85; Dept Interior adv to Poland, 74; prin investr, NSF grant, Mexico, 75-77 & US-Spain Proj, 84-; adj prof, George Washington Univ, 75- *Mem:* Int Asn Hydrogeologists; Geol Soc Am; Am Geophys Union; Geochem Soc. *Res:* Isotopes and geochemistry of ground water; regional ground water systems; Karst processes. *Mailing Add:* 4100 Nellie Custis Dr Arlington VA 22207

BACKAITIS, STANLEY HEROLD, BIOMECHANICAL ENGINEERING, SAFETY STANDARDS ENGINEERING. *Current Pos:* br chief, 68-76, PRIN ENGR, NAT HWY TRAFFIC SAFETY ADMIN, 76- *Personal Data:* b Kaunas, Lithuania, Sept 10, 29; US citizen; m 56, Aloona A; c Nida, Virginia & Audra. *Educ:* Rensselaer Polytech Inst, BSME, 53; Calif Western Univ, PhD(biomech eng), 78. *Hon Degrees:* DSc, Kans Univ Technol, 95. *Honors & Awards:* Spec Achievement Award, Nat Hwy Traffic Safety Admin, 85 & 90; Arch T Colwell Award, Soc Automotive Engrs, 89; Ministry of Transp Award, Repub Lithuania, 91. *Prof Exp:* Engr-in-training, Chrysler Eng, 53-55, proj engr, 55-62; proj managing engr, Chrysler Defense-Space Eng, 62-68. *Concurrent Pos:* Chmn, Truck Ride & Vibrations Comt, Soc Automotive Engrs, 63-68, organizer, Passenger Protection Comt, 86- *Mem:* Soc Automotive Engrs; Int Stand Orgn; Am-Lithuanian Soc Engrs. *Res:* Development of human mechanical simulations and human injury tolerances to impact. *Mailing Add:* PO Box 558 Great Falls VA 22066. *E-Mail:* sbackaitis@nhtsa.dot.gov, bstays@aol.com

BACKER, DONALD CHARLES, ASTRONOMY. *Current Pos:* RES ASTRONR, RADIO ASTRON LAB, UNIV CALIF, BERKELEY, 75-, PROF, ASTRON DEPT, 90- *Personal Data:* b Plainfield, NJ, Nov 9, 43; m; c 1. *Educ:* Cornell Univ, BEP, 66, PhD(astron), 71; Univ Manchester, MSc, 69. *Prof Exp:* Res asst, Nat Radio Astron Observ, 71-73; res assoc, Goddard Space Flight Ctr, NASA, 73-75. *Concurrent Pos:* Mem vis comt, Nat Radio Astron Observ, 78-81. *Mem:* Am Astron Soc; AAAS; Int Astron Union; Union Radio Sci Int. *Res:* Pulsars; interstellar scattering; extragalactic radio sources. *Mailing Add:* 1592 Euclid Ave Berkeley CA 74708

BACKER, RONALD CHARLES, TOXICOLOGY. *Current Pos:* ASST PROF PATH, UNIV NMEX SCH MED, ALBUQUERQUE, NMEX, 88- *Personal Data:* b Newark, NJ, May 3, 43; c 5. *Educ:* Univ Ariz, BA, 64, PhD(pharmaceut chem), 70; Am Bd Forensic Toxicol, dipl. *Prof Exp:* Asst chief forensic chem, Milwaukee Health Dept, 69-74; asst toxicol, Off Chief Med Examr, State Md, 74-76; chief toxicol, Off Chief Med Examr, State W Va, 76-88; bur chief toxicol, Sci Lab Div, State Health & Environ Dept, Albuquerque, NMex, 88. *Concurrent Pos:* Instr toxicol, Dept Path, Div Forensic Path, Univ Md, Baltimore City, 74-76; supvr toxicol, Cent Labs Assoc Md Pathologists, Ltd, 74-76; lectr toxicol, Sch Pub Health & Hyg, Johns Hopkins Univ, 74-76. *Mem:* Soc Forensic Toxicologists; Am Acad Forensic Sci. *Res:* Improvement and development of analytical procedures for drugs from biological specimens. *Mailing Add:* 3811 Suncrest Midland TX 79707

BACKES, PAUL GREGORY, ROBOTICS, AUTOMATION. *Current Pos:* TECH GROUP LEADER, JET PROPULSION LAB, 91- *Personal Data:* m 93, Barbara Kohl; c Laura, Kelly & Kevin. *Educ:* Univ Calif, Berkeley, BSME, 82; Purdue Univ, MSME, 85, PhD(mech eng), 87. *Concurrent Pos:* Asst prof, Calif State Univ, Los Angeles, 91; assoc ed, Robotics & Automation Soc Mag, Inst Elec & Electronics Engrs, 93- *Mem:* Inst Elec & Electronics Engrs. *Res:* Robotics and automation; intelligent control systems for telerobotic systems and autonomous vehicles; distributed operations and remote operations. *Mailing Add:* Jet Propulsion Lab 4800 Oak Grove Dr M/S 198-219 Pasadena CA 91109

BACKMAN, KEITH CAMERON, MOLECULAR BIOLOGY, GENETICS. *Current Pos:* AT OMNI GENE INC, 85- *Personal Data:* b Utica, NY, Feb 22, 47; m 79; c 1. *Educ:* Univ Chicago, BS, 69; Harvard Univ, PhD(biophys), 77. *Prof Exp:* Helen Hay Whitney fel, Univ Calif, San Francisco, 77-79 & Mass Inst Technol, 79-80; Charles A King mem trust fel, Mass Inst Technol, 80-82; sr scientist, Biotechnica Int, Inc, 82-85, vpres res & develop, 85. *Concurrent Pos:* Consult, Genentech, Inc, 78-81. *Mem:* AAAS. *Res:* Genetic engineering of micro-organisms for the purpose of altering their physiology toward the production of useful and valuable compounds. *Mailing Add:* 53 A Rd Apt 53B Bedford MA 01730

BACKMAN, PAUL ANTHONY, PHYTOPATHOLOGY. *Current Pos:* ASSOC PROF PLANT PATH, AUBURN UNIV, 71- *Personal Data:* b Shrewsbury, Eng, Nov 7, 44; US citizen. *Educ:* Univ Calif, Davis, BS, 66, PhD(plant path), 70. *Prof Exp:* Fel mycotoxins, NC State Univ, 70; res plant pathologist, US Dept Agr, 70-71. *Concurrent Pos:* Assoc ed, Plant Dis Reporter, 74-77; consult, Off Technol Assessment, US Cong, 78 & Food & Agr Orgn, UN, 78-79; assoc ed, Peanut Sci, 81- *Mem:* Am Phytopath Soc; AAAS; Sigma Xi; NY Acad Sci. *Res:* Control of diseases of peanuts and soybeans, including loss estimation, optimization of pesticide programs, seed bacterization and post harvest diseases; sugar beet and peach diseases. *Mailing Add:* Plant Path Auburn Univ Auburn AL 36849-3501

BACKOFEN, WALTER A, MATERIALS SCIENCE ENGINEERING, METALLURGY & PHYSICAL METALLURGICAL ENGINEERING. *Current Pos:* Prof, 50-80, EMER PROF ENG, MASS INST TECHNOL, 80- *Personal Data:* b Bockville, Conn, Dec 8, 25. *Educ:* Mass Inst Technol, SB, 46, ScD, 50. *Mem:* Fel Am Soc Metals. *Res:* Social history with a numerical taxonomic bias. *Mailing Add:* HC 64 Box 201 Lebanon NH 03766

BACKUS, CHARLES E, SOLAR ENERGY, ELECTRICAL ENGINEERING. *Current Pos:* from asst prof to assoc prof, 68-76, PROF ENG, ARIZ STATE UNIV, 76-, ASST DEAN, COL ENG & APPL SCI, 79-, DIR, CTR FOR RES, 80- *Personal Data:* b Wadestown, WVa, Sept 17, 37; m 57; c 3. *Educ:* Univ Ohio, BSME, 59; Univ Ariz, MS, 61, PhD(nuclear eng), 65. *Prof Exp:* Res asst nuclear eng, Univ Ariz, 62-65; supvr systs dynamics, Westinghouse Astronuclear Lab, 65-68. *Concurrent Pos:* Vis staff mem, Los Alamos Sci Lab, 69-; dir, Advan Energy Conversion Short Course, 69-; consult to various industs and govt; dir, Photovoltaics Short Course, 80- *Mem:* Am Nuclear Soc; Am Soc Eng Educ; fel Inst Elec & Electronics Engrs; Am Soc Mech Engrs; AAAS. *Res:* Sunlight concentration onto solar cells; photovoltaics; solar thermal power generation; solar energy utilization. *Mailing Add:* Col Eng & Appl Sci Ariz State Univ Tempe AZ 80004

BACKUS, ELAINE ATHENE, INSECT-HOST PLANT INTERACTIONS, VECTORS OF PLANT PATHOGENS, INSECT FEEDING BEHAVIOR. *Current Pos:* Asst prof, 84-90, ASSOC PROF, DEPT ENTOM, UNIV MO, COLUMBIA, 90- *Personal Data:* m 88, Ned M Gruenhagen. *Educ:* Brigham Young Univ, BS, 78; Univ Calif, Davis, PhD(entom), 83. *Prof Exp:* Researcher, Dept Entom, Univ Calif, Davis, 83-84. *Concurrent Pos:* Prin investr, USDA, 88-; vis prof, Dept Entom, Univ Calif, Riverside, 91-92. *Mem:* AAAS; Entom Soc Am; Asn Women Sci; Micros Soc Am. *Res:* Feeding behavior of Empoasca leafhoppers to better diagnose, breed and genetically engineer crops to resist it. *Mailing Add:* Entom 1-87 Agr Bldg Univ Mo Columbia MO 65211-0001. *Fax:* 573-882-1469

BACKUS, GEORGE EDWARD, GEOPHYSICS. *Current Pos:* assoc prof, 60-62, PROF GEOPHYS, UNIV CALIF, SAN DIEGO, 62- *Personal Data:* b Chicago, Ill, May 24, 30; m 77, Varda Peller; c Benjamin, Brian & Emily. *Educ:* Univ Chicago, BS, 48, MS, 50 & 54; PhD(physics), 56. *Hon Degrees:* Dr, Inst Physique Du Globe Paris, Univ Paris, 96. *Honors & Awards:* Gold Medal, Royal Astron Soc; John Adam Fleming Medal, Am Geophy Union. *Prof Exp:* Physicist, Proj Matterhorn, Princeton Univ, 57-58; from asst prof to assoc prof math, Mass Inst Technol, 58-60. *Concurrent Pos:* Guggenheim Mem fel, 63 61 & 70-71; mem comt on sci & pub policy, Nat Acad Sci, 70-73, mem report rev comt, 73-76, chmn Day fund selection comt, 75-78, co-chmn, Int Working Group on Magnetic Field Satellites, 83-90; foreign assoc, Fr Acad Sci; investr, Proj Orsted, 94- *Mem:* Nat Acad Sci; fel Am Geophys Union; Royal Astron Soc; Soc Indust & Appl Math; Am Acad Arts & Sci; Royal Soc Arts. *Res:* Origin of geomagnetic field; normal modes of elastic-gravitational oscillation of the earth; general theory of geophysical inverse problems; lower mantle electrical conductivity; fluid motion in earth's core; analysis of satellite magnetic data. *Mailing Add:* Inst Geophys & Planetary Phys Univ Calif San Diego La Jolla CA 92093-0225

BACKUS, JOHN, FUNCTIONAL PROGRAMMING. *Current Pos:* CONSULT, 91- *Personal Data:* b Philadelphia, Pa, Dec 3, 24; m 68, Barbara Una Stannard; c Karen & Paula. *Educ:* Columbia Univ, BS, 49, AM, 50. *Hon Degrees:* Dr, Univ York, England, 85; DSc, Univ Ariz, 88; Dr Hon Causa Use, Univ de Nancy I, France, 89; DSc, Ind Univ, 92. *Honors & Awards:* W W McDowell Award, Inst Elec & Electronics Engrs, 67; Nat Medal Sci, 75; A M Turing Award, Asn Comput Mach, 77; Charles Stark Draper Prize, Nat Acad Eng, 94. *Prof Exp:* programmer, Pure & Appl Sci Depts, IBM Corp, 50-53, mgr, Prog Res Dept, 54-58, res staff mem, Thomas J Watson Res Ctr, 59-63, IBM fel, 63-64, IBM fel, Almaden Res Ctr, 65-91, mgr, Functional Prog, 73-91. *Concurrent Pos:* Mem, Working Group 2.2, Int Fedn Info Processing, 65-91, Working Group 2.8, 88; vis prof, Univ Calif, Berkeley, 80. *Mem:* Nat Acad Sci; Nat Acad Eng; fel Am Acad Arts & Sci. *Res:* Programming languages, their syntax and semantics; functional programming and its algebra of programs; program optimization. *Mailing Add:* 91 St Germain Ave San Francisco CA 94114

BACKUS, JOHN KING, PHYSICAL CHEMISTRY, POLYMER CHEMISTRY. *Current Pos:* CONSULT, 90- *Personal Data:* b Buffalo, NY, May 22, 25; m 50; c 4. *Educ:* Hamilton Col, AB, 47; Cornell Univ, MS, 50, PhD(phys chem), 52. *Prof Exp:* Res chemist, Procter & Gamble Co, 52-53; res chemist, O-Celo Dept, Gen Mills, Inc, 53-56, res supvr, 56-61; res specialist, Mobay Corp, 62-63, group leader, 64-67, sr group leader, 67, coordr regulatory affairs, Ind Hyg Med Serv, 71-77, mgr, 67-90. *Concurrent Pos:* Chmn, Gordon Conf Chem & Physics of Cellular Mat, 70; comt Toxicol & Indust Health, Int Isocyante Inst, 74-80, ad hoc comt Criteria Doc, 74 & 78; bd dirs, Western Pa Safety Coun, 75-90, SPE Div Thermoplastic Mat & Forms 76-79; chmn, Tech Conf, Urethane Div, SPI, 77, Urethane Div Flammability Comm, 73, Isocyanate Shipping Comm, 74; mem, Comt Environ Improv, Am Chem Soc, 90-, chmn, Pittsburgh Sect, 93. *Mem:* AAAS; NY Acad Sci; Sigma Xi; Am Chem Soc. *Res:* Physical polymer chemistry; flammability; degradation; molecular structure; health effects; government regulation; safety; polymer physics; author and co-author of numerous publications; patents. *Mailing Add:* 9441 Katherine Dr Allison Park PA 15101-2020

BACKUS, MILO M, GEOPHYSICS. *Current Pos:* DISTINGUISHED CHAIR GEOPHYS, SHELL OIL CO, 92- *Personal Data:* b Ill, May 3, 32; m 52, Barbara Carns; c Colleen, Marcia, Stephen (deceased), Kurt & Kathleen. *Educ:* Mass Inst Technol, BS, 52, PhD(geophys), 56. *Honors & Awards:* Conrad Schlumberger Award, Europ Asn Explor Geophys, 76; Maurice Ewing Medal, Soc Explor Geophys, 90. *Prof Exp:* From res physicist to vpres, Geophys Serv Inc, 56-74; consult, 74-75; Wallace E Pratt prof geophys, Univ Tex, Austin, 75-80, Dave P Carlton prof geophys, 80-92. *Mem:* Soc Explor Geophysicists (vpres, 77, pres, 80); Europ Asn Geophysicists; Am Asn Petrol Geologists. *Res:* Petroleum exploration; geophysical data inversion and imaging. *Mailing Add:* 6606 Mesa Dr Sci Univ Tex PO Box 7909 Austin TX 78731

BACKUS, RICHARD HAVEN, MARINE BIOLOGY. *Current Pos:* res assoc marine biol, 52-59, marine biologist, 59-63, chmn dept biol, 70-74, SR SCIENTIST, WOODS HOLE OCEANOG INST, 63- *Personal Data:* b Rochester, NY, Dec 5, 22; m 49; c 3. *Educ:* Dartmouth Col, BA, 47; Cornell Univ, MS, 48, PhD(ichthyol), 53. *Prof Exp:* Supvry res assoc oceanog, Cornell Univ, 51-52. *Mem:* AAAS; Ecol Soc Am. *Res:* Biology of marine vertebrates, especially mesopelogic fishes; marine biogeography. *Mailing Add:* 244 Woods Hole Rd Falmouth MA 02540

BACLAWSKI, LEONA MARIE, ORGANIC CHEMISTRY. *Current Pos:* STAFF, FLEXSYS AM, LP, AKRON, 95- *Personal Data:* b Akron, Ohio, Dec 26, 45. *Educ:* Univ Akron, BS, 67, PhD(chem), 74. *Prof Exp:* Fel org chem, State Univ NY Col Environ Sci & Forestry, Syracuse Univ, 74; fel chem, 75, lab dir org chem, Bucknell Univ, 75-77; mem staff, Monsanto Akron Res Ctr, 77-95. *Mem:* Sigma Xi; Am Chem Soc. *Res:* Diaziridine chemistry; 1,3-dipolar addition; heterocyclic chemistry; carbanion synthesis; rubber chemicals; thermal analysis. *Mailing Add:* 137 Quaker Ridge Dr Akron OH 44313-3524

BACON, ARTHUR LORENZA, PROTOZOOLOGY, EMBRYOLOGY. *Current Pos:* PROF BIOL, TALLADEGA COL, 80-, CHMN, DEPT BIOL & DIV NATURAL SCI & MATH, 69-, DIR, BIOMED RES, 73- *Personal Data:* b West Palm Beach, Fla, Sept 22, 37. *Educ:* Talladega Col, AB, 61; Howard Univ, MS, 63, PhD, 67. *Honors & Awards:* Armstrong Award for Creative Ability, 59. *Prof Exp:* Instr protozool, Howard Univ, 63-65, res assoc, 65-67, asst prof, 67-68. *Concurrent Pos:* Fel, Univ Miami, 68-69; presentor, President's Cancer Panel, 84; consult, Div Res Resources, NIH, Nat Inst Gen Med Sci. *Mem:* Soc Protozoologists; Am Soc Zoologists; AAAS; Sigma Xi. *Res:* Studies of the effects of certain food and drug additives on development in sea urchins and protozoan morphology. *Mailing Add:* Dean Sci Talladega Col 627 W Battle St Talladega AL 35160-2354

BACON, CHARLES WILSON, MYCOLOGY, BOTANY. *Current Pos:* RES MICROBIOLOGIST, AGR RES SERVS, USDA & ASST PROF PLANT PATH, UNIV GA, ATHENS, 72-; RES LEADER, TOXICOL & MYCOTOXINS RES UNIT, RUSSELL RES CTR, ATHENS, 96- *Personal Data:* b Bradenton, Fla; m 68; c 2. *Educ:* Clark Col, BS, 65; Univ Mich, PhD(bot), 72. *Prof Exp:* Res assoc biochem, 71-72. *Mem:* Mycological Soc Am; Am Soc Microbiol; Agron Soc Am; Ga Asn Plant Pathologists. *Res:* Fungal physiology and biochemistry; mycotoxicology and plant pathology. *Mailing Add:* 125 Plantation Dr Athens GA 30605

BACON, DAVID W, CHEMICAL ENGINEERING, STATISTICS. *Current Pos:* assoc prof chem eng, 68-73, dean, Fac Appl Sci, 80-90, PROF CHEM ENG, QUEEN'S UNIV, ONT, 73- *Personal Data:* b Peterborough, Ont, Sept 12, 35; m 63, Lucille A Parks; c Ann M & David E. *Educ:* Univ Toronto, BASc, 57; Univ Wis, MS, 62, PhD(statist), 65. *Honors & Awards:* Shewell Award, Am Soc Qual Control, 84. *Prof Exp:* Comput analyst, Can Gen Elec Co, Ont, 57-61; comput programmer, Math Res Ctr, Univ Wis-Madison, 61-63; statist & math group leader, Du Pont Can, Ont, 65-67. *Concurrent Pos:* Vis assoc prof, Univ Wis-Madison, 69-70; vis lectr, Univ Sydney, 76-77; chmn, Nat Comt Deans Eng & Appl Sci, 82-83 & Comt Ont Deans Eng; vis scholar, Stanford Univ, 85-86. *Mem:* Fel Chem Inst Can; Can Soc Chem Eng; Royal Statist Soc; Statist Soc Can; Can Res Mgt Asn; fel Am Statist Asn. *Res:* Statistical process control; mathematical modeling of processes; design of experimental programs; on-line optimization. *Mailing Add:* RR 1 Picton ON K0K 2T0 Can. *Fax:* 613-545-6637; *E-Mail:* bacond@qucdn.queensu.ca

BACON, EDMOND JAMES, AQUATIC ECOLOGY. *Current Pos:* asst prof, 74-80, ASSOC PROF BIOL, UNIV ARK, MONTICELLO, 80- *Personal Data:* b Chidester, Ark, Jan 10, 44; m 73. *Educ:* Southern State Col, Ark, BS, 66; Univ Ark, MS, 68; Univ Louisville, PhD(biol), 73. *Prof Exp:* From teaching asst to res asst zool, Univ Ark, 66-68; technician radiation, Univ Louisville, 68-70, res asst water resources, 72-74. *Concurrent Pos:* Environ consult, Aquatic Control, Inc & Dames & Moore, 72-74; ichthyologist, Water Resources Lab, Univ Louisville, 73-74; proj engr, E D'Appolonia Consult Engrs, 74. *Mem:* Am Soc Limnol & Oceanog; Int Soc Limnol; Am Fisheries Soc; Brit Freshwater Biol Asn; assoc Sigma Xi. *Res:* Environmental deterioration appraisal and the impact of costly restoration efforts; natural history of lower vertebrates of Arkansas and primary productivity, water quality and limiting factors in oxbow lakes. *Mailing Add:* Math & Sci Univ Ark Monticello AR 71655

BACON, EGBERT KING, chemistry; deceased, see previous edition for last biography

BACON, FRANK RIDER, PHYSICAL INORGANIC CHEMISTRY. *Current Pos:* RETIRED. *Personal Data:* b Wilton, Iowa, Apr 28, 14; m 38, Eleanor Bennett; c John B, George W & Katherine Z (Endersbe). *Educ:* Iowa State Univ, BS, 35; Washington Univ, MS, 37. *Prof Exp:* Asst chem, Washington Univ, 35-37; res chemist, Owens-Ill Glass Co, 37-58; chief surface chem, Glass Container Div, Owens-Ill, Inc, 58-82. *Mem:* Am Chem Soc; fel Am Ceramic Soc; Sigma Xi. *Res:* Chemical durability of glass; light transmission of glass; strength of glass. *Mailing Add:* 3153 Darlington Rd Toledo OH 43606

BACON, GEORGE EDGAR, PEDIATRIC ENDOCRINOLOGY. *Current Pos:* from instr to prof, 63-95, EMER PROF PEDIAT, UNIV MICH, ANN ARBOR, 95- *Personal Data:* b New York, NY, Apr 13, 32; m 56; c 3. *Educ:* Wesleyan Univ, BA, 53; Duke Univ, MD, 57; Univ Mich, MS, 67. *Prof Exp:* Intern pediat, Duke Hosp, 57-58; resident, Columbia Presby Med Ctr, 61-63; prof & chair, dept pediat, Tex Tech Univ, Lubbock, 86-89. *Concurrent Pos:* Fel physiol, Univ Mich, Ann Arbor, 65, fel pharmacol, 65-67; pediat endocrinologist, Univ Pittsburgh, 70; dir med educ & res, Butterworth Hosp, Grand Rapids, 90-95, hon attending physician, 95- *Mem:* Soc Pediat Res; Endocrine Soc; Am Pediat Soc; Am Fedn Clin Res; Am Acad Pediat; Pediat Endocrin Soc; Am Diabetes Asn. *Res:* Adrenal disorders, particularly modes of therapy and metabolic effects of treatment in congenital adrenal hyperplasia; diabetes mellitus. *Mailing Add:* 3911 Waldenwood Ann Arbor MI 48105

BACON, LARRY DEAN, GENETICS, IMMUNOGENETICS. *Current Pos:* IMMUNOGENETICIST, USDA, AGR RES SERV AVIAN DIS & ONCOL LAB, 78- *Personal Data:* b Topeka, Kans, Jan 24, 38; m 69, Patricia Gaskins; c Keith & Andrew. *Educ:* Kans State Univ, BS, 61, MS, 67, PhD(genetics), 69. *Prof Exp:* Instr path, NY Med Col, 69-72; asst prof microbiol, Sch Med, Wayne State Univ, 72-77. *Concurrent Pos:* NIH fel, NY Med Col, 69-71. *Mem:* Fedn Am Soc Exp Biol; Am Asn Immunol; Poultry Sci Asn. *Res:* Immunological responses to sex-linked histocompatibility antigens in chickens; genetics of autoimmune disease and the relationship of alloantigens to autoimmunity, tumor regression and disease resistance. *Mailing Add:* USDA Agr Res Serv 3606 E Mt Hope Rd East Lansing MI 48823-5338

BACON, LYLE C(HOLWELL), JR, ELECTRONICS. *Current Pos:* res scientist, 78-86, ADVAN DECISION SYSTS, LOCKHEED PALO ALTO RES LAB, 86- *Personal Data:* b Los Angeles, Calif, June 23, 31. *Educ:* Pomona Col, BA, 53; Stanford Univ, MS, 54, PhD(elec eng), 58. *Prof Exp:* Mem tech staff, Gen Elec Microwave Lab, 58-62; sr engr, Electromagnetic Technol Corp, 62-66; mem staff, Develco, Inc, 66-78. *Mem:* AAAS; Inst Elec & Electronics Engrs; Sigma Xi. *Res:* Microwave electronics; active and passive microwave devices; electromagnetic field theory; systems and circuit analysis; antennas and propagation; computer analyses; expert systems; image processing. *Mailing Add:* 205 Golden Oak Dr Portola Valley CA 94025-7762

BACON, MARION, MEDICAL MICROBIOLOGY, ENTOMOLOGY. *Current Pos:* RETIRED. *Personal Data:* b Hemingford, Nebr, May 26, 14; m 50, Roma Fulberg. *Educ:* Iowa State Univ, BSc, 50; Wash State Univ, MS, 52, PhD(bact), 56. *Prof Exp:* Asst entomol, Wash State Univ, 50-52; med entomologist, Ctr for Dis Control, USPHS, 52-53; asst bact, Wash State Univ, 53-56; from instr to asst prof microbiol, Univ Nebr, 56-59; from assoc prof to emer prof biol, Eastern Wash Univ, 59-79. *Mem:* Am Soc Microbiol; Sigma Xi; Nature Conservancy. *Res:* Diseases of nature communicable to man; medical entomology; bacterial indicators of fecal pollution. *Mailing Add:* 2808 Bancroft Missoula MT 59801

BACON, MERLE D, ENGINEERING MECHANICS, AERONAUTICAL ENGINEERING. *Current Pos:* EXEC VPRES, INT EDUC FOUND, 86- *Personal Data:* b Dacoma, Okla, Nov 28, 31; m 51; c 1. *Educ:* Wichita State Univ, BS, 54; Univ Okla, MS, 61, PhD(eng mech), 66. *Prof Exp:* Liaison engr, Beech Aircraft Corp, 51-53; structural engr, 53-54; USAF, 54-, proj engr, Armament Ctr, Elgin AFB, 54-55, interceptor pilot, 57-60, from instr to assoc prof eng mech, USAF Acad, 61-63 & 65-69, Air Liaison Off, Vietnam, 69-70; chief, Laser Effects Br, Laser Div, Air Force Weapons Lab, 70-75; comdr & assoc prof eng mech, Frank J Seiler Res Lab, USAF Acad, 75-79, dir fac res, 79-81; dir training, Bechtel Corp, Saudi Arabia, 81-84; proj mgr, Nat Educ Corp, Newport Beach, Calif, 84-86. *Mem:* Am Inst Aeronaut & Astronaut; Soc Exp Stress Anal; Am Soc Eng Educ. *Res:* Structural dynamics; aircraft structures; stress analysis. *Mailing Add:* 6265 Altman Dr Colorado Springs CO 80918

BACON, MICHAEL E, PHYSICS. *Current Pos:* DOCTOR, DEPT PHYSICS, THIEL COL, 81- *Personal Data:* b Bulawayo, Zimbabwe. *Educ:* Colo State Univ, PhD(laser plasma prod), 69. *Mailing Add:* Dept Physics Thiel Col Greenville PA 16125

BACON, OSCAR GRAY, ENTOMOLOGY. *Current Pos:* assoc div entom, Univ Calif, Davis, 46-47, sr lab technician, 47-48, instr econ entom & jr entomologist, 48-50, from asst prof to assoc prof econ entom, 50-63, chmn, Dept Entom, 67-74, PROF ECON ENTOM & ENTOMOLOGIST, EXP STA, UNIV CALIF, DAVIS, 63- *Personal Data:* b Sanger, Calif, Nov 8, 19; m 45; c 2. *Educ:* Fresno State Col, AB, 41; Univ Calif, MS, 44, PhD(entom), 48. *Prof Exp:* Field aide, Div Fruit Insects, Bur Entom & Plant Quarantine, USDA, 41-43. *Mem:* Entom Soc Am. *Res:* Economic entomology; biology and control of insect pests of field crops; small seeded legumes for seed; field corn and grain sorghums; insect pests of potato; insect pests of cereal grains. *Mailing Add:* 615 Cordova Pl Davis CA 95616-0414

BACON, ROBERT ELWIN, PHOTOGRAPHIC SCIENCE, TECHNOLOGY ASSESSMENT COMPETITIVE INTELLIGENCE. *Current Pos:* Sr chemist, Eastman Kodak Co, 60-64, res assoc, 65-73, lab head res, 73-79, sr lab head, 79-84, sr tech aassoc, 84-90, MGR TECH ASSESSMENT, EASTMAN KODAK CO, 91- *Personal Data:* b Lansdowne, Pa, Apr 24, 34; m 57, Sally Myers; c Elizabeth & Jeffrey. *Educ:* Univ Mich, BSChem, 56, BSChE, 56; Mass Inst Technol, PhD(phys chem), 60. *Concurrent Pos:* Fel, Dept Mat Sci, Stanford Univ, 70-71. *Mem:* Soc Imaging Sci & Technol. *Res:* Physical and chemical aspects of photographic response in silver halides; process engineering and research; internal corporate venturing. *Mailing Add:* 6 Marks Hill Lane Rochester NY 14617

BACON, ROGER, MATERIALS SCIENCE. *Current Pos:* SR RES ASSOC, AMOCO PERFORMANCE PROD, INC, 86-; CONSULT. *Personal Data:* b Cleveland, Ohio, Apr 16, 26; m 72; c 2. *Educ:* Haverford Col, AB, 51; Case Inst Technol, MS, 53, PhD, 56. *Prof Exp:* Res physicist, Union Carbide Corp, 55-62, group leader carbon fiber develop, 62-86. *Mem:* Am Phys Soc; Am Carbon Soc; Soc Advan Mat & Process Eng. *Res:* Studies of structure and properties of graphite crystals, whiskers and fibers; experimental demonstration of extremely high strength and stiffness inherent in oriented graphite structures; development of processes for producing high performance carbon fibers from organic precursors; development of carbon-carbon composites. *Mailing Add:* Amoco Performance Prod Inc Res & Develop Ctr 4500 McGinnis Ferry Rd Alpharetta GA 30202-3944

BACON, VINTON WALKER, CIVIL ENGINEERING, WATER POLLUTION CONTROL. *Current Pos:* prof, 70-82, EMER PROF CIVIL ENG, UNIV WIS- MILWAUKEE, 82- *Personal Data:* b Estelline, SDak, Dec 21, 16; m 40; c 4. *Educ:* Univ Calif, Berkeley, BS, 40; Am Acad Environ Engrs, dipl, 56. *Honors & Awards:* Awards, Am Soc Civil Engrs, 56, 67. *Prof Exp:* Engr, East Bay City Sewage Disposal Surv, Berkeley, 40-41; designer, Los Angeles County Sanit Dist, 41-43 & 46; office engr, Orange County Sewerage Surv, Calif, 46-49; exec officer, Calif State Water Pollution Control Bd, 50-56; exec secy, NW Paper & Pulp Asn, Tacoma, Wash, 56-62; gen supt, Metrop Sanit Dist Greater Chicago, 62-70. *Concurrent Pos:* Consult civil eng; chmn, Wis Gov Solid Waste Recycling Task Force, 71-76; mem, Wis Solid Waste Recycling Authority, 74-76; city councilman, Mill Creek, Wash, 92-96. *Mem:* Nat Acad Eng; Am Pub Health Asn; Water Pollution Control Fedn; Am Water Works Asn. *Res:* Originator deep tunnel project. *Mailing Add:* 2616 143 Rd Pl SE Mill Creek WA 98012

BACON, WILLIAM EDWARD, INORGANIC CHEMISTRY, PHYSICAL ORGANIC CHEMISTRY. *Current Pos:* PRES, PORTAGE TECH CONSULTS, KENT, OH, 85- *Personal Data:* b Dansville, NY, Dec 12, 17; m 48, Mary Swain; c Roger, Rebecca, Margaret, James & George. *Educ:* St Lawrence Univ, BS, 42; Ind Univ, Bloomington, MA, 50; Kent State Univ, PhD(inorg chem), 67. *Prof Exp:* Chemist, E I du Pont de Nemours & Co, 43-47; res supvr chem, Lubrizol Corp, 50-61; sr res fel chem, Liquid Crystal Inst, Kent State Univ, 67-84. *Concurrent Pos:* Consult, Gen Tire & Rubber Co, Akron, 72; prin investr, NSF, 74-78, US Army Res Off, 75 & Air Force Off Sci Res, 76; co-chmn, Fifth Int Liquid Crystal Conf, Kent State Univ, 76; Sigma Xi lectr, NCent Chap, 81-84; NASA summer fac fel, Lewis Res Ctr, 84. *Mem:* Am Chem Soc; AAAS. *Res:* Structure and properties of thermotropic and lyotropic liquid crystalline substances; study of chemical reactions within these media; comparison of kinetics of isomerizations, polymerizations and hydrolysis in anisotropic and isotropic solvents. *Mailing Add:* 1010 S Willow St Kent OH 44240

BACOPOULOS, NICHOLAS G, NEUROPHARMACOLOGY, RECEPTOR REGULATION. *Current Pos:* asj assoc prof pharmacol & psychiat, 83-88, DIR, DEPT CANCER & NEUROSCI, PFIZER CENT RES, 83- *Personal Data:* b Athens, Greece, Mar 13, 49; US citizen; m 80. *Educ:* Cornell Col, BA, 71; Univ Iowa, PhD(pharmacol), 76. *Prof Exp:* Fel pharmacol, Yale Univ, 76-79; asst prof pharmacol & psychiat, Med Sch, Dartmouth Col, 79-83. *Concurrent Pos:* Prin investr res grant, NIMH, 81-83; ad hoc mem, Neurol Sci Initial Rev Group, NIH, 81; mem Tech Adv Bd, Chicago Consortium Psychiat Res. *Mem:* Am Soc Pharmacol & Exp Therapeut; Soc Exp Biol & Med; Soc Neurosci; NY Acad Sci; Sigma Xi; Col Int Neuropsychopharm; Am Asn Cancer Res. *Res:* Regulation of dopamine receptors in mammalian brain; mechanisms of drug-induced tolerance and supersensitivity; mechanism of acute and chronic effects of antipsychotic drugs. *Mailing Add:* Dept Pharmacol & Psych Pfizer Cent Res Eastern Paint Rd Groton CT 06385-5196

BACSKAI, BRIAN JAMES, flourescence imaging microscopy, for more information see previous edition

BACSKAI, ROBERT, ORGANIC CHEMISTRY, POLYMER CHEMISTRY. *Current Pos:* RETIRED. *Personal Data:* b Ujpest, Hungary, Feb 17, 30; US citizen; m 56, Judith A Dan; c Dorothy & Sandra. *Educ:* Eotvos Lorand Univ, Budapest, dipl, 52. *Prof Exp:* Res chemist, Plastics Res Inst, Budapest, Hungary, 52-56; res assoc polymer chem, Princeton Univ, 57-60; from res chemist to sr res chemist, Chevron Res & Technol Co, 60-68, sr res assoc polymer chem, 68-89, res scientist, 89-90, consult scientist, Petrochem Group, 90-92. *Mem:* Am Chem Soc. *Res:* Ferrocene chemistry; hydrogen bonding; water soluble, stereoregular, cationic, anionic and free radical polymers; nuclear magnetic resonance of polymers; lactam polymerization; high activity catalysts; corrosion inhibitors; reactive processing. *Mailing Add:* 254 Stanford Ave Berkeley CA 94708-1104

BACUS, JAMES NEVILL, BACTERIOLOGY, FOOD SCIENCE. *Current Pos:* PRES, DIVERSITECH, INC, 87- *Personal Data:* b Ft Worth, Tex, Jan 8, 48; m 70; c 3. *Educ:* Univ Evansville, BA, 70; Univ Wis, MS, 72, PhD(bact), 73. *Prof Exp:* Res asst microbiol, Food Res Inst, 70-73; res scientist processed meats, Swift & Co, 74-75; vpres prod develop, ABC Res Corp, 75-85; vpres, Qual Sausage, 85-87. *Mem:* Inst Food Technologists; Am Soc Microbiol; Am Meat Sci Asn; Am Meat Inst; Am Chem Soc. *Res:* Meat and poultry, especially formulation of processing and characteristics. *Mailing Add:* 5306 NW 67th St Gainesville FL 32653

BACUS, JAMES WILLIAM, bioengineering, physiology, for more information see previous edition

BADA, JEFFREY L, COSMOGEOCHEMISTRY, GEOCHRONOLOGY. *Current Pos:* asst prof oceanog, 70-74, assoc prof, 74-80, PROF MARINE CHEM, SCRIPPS INST OCEANOG, UNIV CALIF, SAN DIEGO, 80-, DIR RES & TRAINING EXO-BIOL, NASA SPEC CTR, 96- *Personal Data:* b San Diego, Calif, Sept 10, 42; c 2. *Educ:* San Diego State Univ, BS, 65; Univ Calif, San Diego, PhD(chem), 68. *Prof Exp:* Instr chem, Univ Calif, San Diego, 68-69; res fel geophys & environ chem, Harvard Univ, 69-70. *Concurrent Pos:* Res grants, NSF, 70-71, 73-75, 75-79 & 88-, Petrol Res Fund, 70-73, 84-87 & NIH, 77-85; Alfred P Sloan res fel, 75-79; Off Naval Res, 75-82 & 86- *Mem:* AAAS; Am Chem Soc; Geochem Soc; Int Soc Study Origin Life. *Res:* Organic chemistry of natural waters, sediments and fossils; stability of organic compounds on the primitive earth; geochemical implications of the kinetics of reactions involving biologically produced organic compounds; biochemistry of fishes. *Mailing Add:* Scripps Inst Oceanog Univ Calif San Diego La Jolla CA 92093-0212

BADALAMENTE, MARIE ANN, ORTHOPAEDIC BIOMEDICAL RESEARCH. *Current Pos:* PROF, DEPT ORTHOP, STATE UNIV NY, STONY BROOK, 79- *Personal Data:* b Bronx, NY, July 17, 49. *Educ:* Long Island Univ, BA, 71, MS, 73; Fordham Univ, PhD(cell biol), 77. *Honors & Awards:* Hunterian Award, Royal Col Surgeons, Eng, 81. *Prof Exp:* Instr, Dept Biol, City Univ New York, Bronx, 74-75; asst prof, Dept Biol, Long Island Univ, 75-78, Dept Anat/Cell Biol, State Univ NY, Brooklyn, 78-79. *Concurrent Pos:* Prin investr, Muscular Dystrophy Asn, 79-81, Orthop Res & Ed Found, 81-84 & 85-87, NIH, 85-88, 88-91 & 92-94, Food & Drug Admin, 91-94. *Mem:* Orthop Res Soc; Am Soc Surg Hand; NY Acad Sci; Brit Orthop Res Soc; AAAS; Sigma Xi. *Res:* Neuromuscular recovery after peripheral microsurgical nerve repair. *Mailing Add:* Dept Orthop State Univ NY Health Sci Col Med 100 Nicolls Rd Stony Brook NY 11794-0001. *Fax:* 516-444-7671

BADALAMENTI, ANTHONY FRANCIS, BIOMATHEMATICS, PROBABILITY. *Current Pos:* RES SCIENTIST, NATHAN KLINE INST, 76- *Personal Data:* b Bronx, NY, Feb 2, 43; m 68; c 1. *Educ:* Manhattan Col, BS, 64; Stevens Inst Technol, MS, 67; Brooklyn Polytech Inst, PhD(math), 70. *Honors & Awards:* Merit Award, Soc Psychoanal Psychother. *Prof Exp:* Mem tech staff, Bell Tel Labs, 64-70; asst prof math & comput sci, Fairleigh Pickinson Univ, 70-72; mem tech staff, Gen Res Corp, 72-74; dir revenue modeling, Western Union Tel Corp, 74-75. *Concurrent Pos:* Consult, Clin Concepts, Teanech, NJ, 80-86. *Mem:* Am Math Soc; Asn Comput Mach; Soc Indust & Appl Math; Soc Psychoanal Psychother; NY Acad Sci. *Res:* Quantifying the study of psychotherapy and of human emotional communication; research in number theory; modelling for artificial intelligence. *Mailing Add:* 19 Crest St Apt 3B Westwood NJ 07675-3128

BADASH, LAWRENCE, HISTORY OF MODERN PHYSICS, SCIENCE & SOCIETY. *Current Pos:* from asst prof to assoc prof, 66-79, PROF, HIST SCI, UNIV CALIF, SANTA BARBARA, 79- *Personal Data:* b Brooklyn, NY, May 8, 34. *Educ:* Rensselaer Polytech Inst, BS, 56; Yale Univ, PhD(hist sci), 64. *Prof Exp:* Instr hist sci, Yale Univ, 64-65, res assoc, 65-66. *Concurrent Pos:* NATO fel, Cambridge Univ, 65-66, prin investr, NSF grant, 69-70, 90-92; dir sem, Global Security & Arms Control, Univ Calif, 83 & 86; Guggenheim fel, 84-85; chair, Div Hist Physics, Am Phys Soc, 88-89. *Mem:* Hist Sci Soc; fel Am Phys Soc; fel AAAS; Fedn Am Scientists. *Res:* History of radioactivity and nuclear physics; history of the nuclear arms race and arms control; science and society; science and social responsibility. *Mailing Add:* Dept Hist Univ Calif Santa Barbara CA 93106

BADDER, ELLIOTT MICHAEL, GENERAL SURGERY, VASCULAR SURGERY. *Current Pos:* asst prof, 77-79, ASSOC PROF SURV, UNIV MD HOSP, 80-; CHIEF SURG, MERCY HOSP, BALTIMORE, 84- *Personal Data:* b Philadelphia, Pa, Feb 7, 43; div, Marianne Pasekiewicz; c Nathaniel, Anastasia & Carla. *Educ:* Univ Pa, BA, 63; Thomas Jefferson Univ, MD, 67. *Prof Exp:* Asst prof surg, Pa State Univ, 75-77; asst chief surg, Mercy Hosp, Baltimore, 77-83, actg chief, 83. *Concurrent Pos:* Inst gen surg, Frances

Delafield Hosp, New York, NY, 72; asst attend surgeon, Vanderbilt Clin, Presby Hosp, New York, 72; co-investr, NIH Grant, Cardiovasc Determinants of Catecholamine Release, 76-83. *Mem:* Am Fedn Clin Res; Asn Acad Surg; fel Am Col Surgeons; Am Asn Endocrine Surgeons; Soc Univ Surgeons. *Res:* Catecholamines under conditions of stress. *Mailing Add:* 301 St Paul Pl Baltimore MD 21202

BADDILEY, JAMES, MICROBIAL BIOCHEMISTRY. *Current Pos:* RETIRED. *Personal Data:* b Manchester, Eng, May 15, 18; m 44, Hazel M Townsend; c Christopher J. *Educ:* Univ Manchester, BSc, 41, PhD(chem), 44, DSc, 53; Univ Cambridge, ScD, 86. *Hon Degrees:* DSc, Heriot-Watt, Edinburgh, 79, Bath, 86. *Honors & Awards:* Meldola Medal, Royal Soc Chem, 47, Corday-Morgan Medal, 52, Tilden Medal, 59, Pedler Medal, 78; Leeuwenhoek Lectr, Royal Soc, 67, Davy Medal, 74. *Prof Exp:* Imp Chem Industs res fel, Pembroke Col, Cambridge, 45-49; staff mem biochem, Lister Inst Prev Med, Univ London, 49-54; prof org chem, Newcastle upon Tyne Univ, 54-77, prof chem microbiol, 77-83. *Concurrent Pos:* Rockefeller fel, Mass Gen Hosp, Harvard Med Sch, 54; Karl Folkers vis prof, Univ Ill, 62; head, Sch Chem, Newcastle upon Tyne Univ, 68-78, dir, Microbiol Chem Res Lab, 77-83; sr fel, Sci & Eng Res Coun, Univ Cambridge, 81-84; fel, Pembroke Col, Cambridge, 81-84, emer fel, 84- *Mem:* Fel Royal Soc UK; Royal Soc Chem; hon mem Am Soc Biochem & Molecular Biol; fel Royal Soc Edinburgh; Biochem Soc; Soc Gen Microbiol. *Res:* Chemical structure and synthesis of nucleotide coenzymes as ATP, coenzyme A; discovery, isolation, structure of bacterial cell-wall polymers including the teichoic acids and lipoteichoic acids in gram positive bacteria; biosynthesis and function of these polymers. *Mailing Add:* Dept Biochem Univ Cambridge Tennis Court Rd Cambridge CB2 1QW England

BADDING, JOHN VICTOR, SOLID STATE CHEMISTRY, HIGH PRESSURE SCIENCE. *Current Pos:* ASST PROF CHEM, PA STATE UNIV, UNIVERSITY PARK, 91- *Personal Data:* b Buffalo, NY, May 6, 62; m 93, Mizue Abe. *Educ:* Manhattan Col, BS, 84; Univ Calif, Berkeley, PhD(chem), 89. *Prof Exp:* Postdoctoral fel, Geophys Lab, Carnegie Inst Washington, 89-91. *Concurrent Pos:* Packard fel, 93; NSF Young Investr Award, 93. *Mem:* Am Chem Soc; Sigma Xi; AAAS. *Res:* Solid state chemistry; high pressure chemistry; thermoelectric materials; novel carbon-based covalently bonded networks. *Mailing Add:* Dept Chem Pa State Univ 152 Davey University Park PA 16802

BADDING, VICTOR GEORGE, ORGANIC CHEMISTRY. *Current Pos:* from asst prof to assoc prof, 65-90, PROF CHEM, MANHATTAN COL, 90- *Personal Data:* b Buffalo, NY, Dec 15, 35; m 61; c 2. *Educ:* Canisius Col, BS, 57; Univ Notre Dame, PhD(org chem), 61. *Prof Exp:* Fel, Univ Wis, 61-62; res chemist, Silicones Div, Union Carbide Corp, 62-65. *Concurrent Pos:* Fel, State Univ NY Buffalo, 65. *Mem:* Am Chem Soc; Royal Soc Chem; Sigma Xi; NY Acad Sci. *Res:* Chemistry of acetals; polymer stereochemistry; intermolecular interactions in polymer blends. *Mailing Add:* 10 Lake Rd Peekskill NY 10566-6414

BADDOUR, RAYMOND F(REDERICK), CHEMICAL ENGINEERING. *Current Pos:* from asst prof to prof, 51-63, head dept, 69-76, dir, Environ Lab, 70-76, Lammont Du Pont prof, 73-97, EMER LAMMOT DU PONT PROF CHEM ENG, MASS INST TECHNOL, 97- *Personal Data:* b Laurinburg, NC, Jan 11, 25; m 54; c 3. *Educ:* Univ Notre Dame, BS, 45; Mass Inst Technol, MS, 49, ScD, 51. *Honors & Awards:* P C Reilley Lectr, Univ Notre Dame, 65. *Prof Exp:* Asst dir, Eng Practice Sch, Tenn, 48-49. *Concurrent Pos:* Co-founder & dir, Amgen, Inc, Enterprise Mgt Corp, & Tekmat, Inc. *Mem:* Fel Am Acad Arts & Sci; NY Acad Sci; Am Chem Soc; fel Am Inst Chem Engrs; fel Am Inst Chem. *Res:* Chemical reactions in plasmas; diffusion in adsorptive solids; preparation and properties of selected sorbents and membranes; chromatography; ion exchange. *Mailing Add:* Dept Chem Eng Rm 66-350 Mass Inst Technol Cambridge MA 02139-3561

BADE, MARIA LEIPELT, SCIENCE EDUCATION. *Current Pos:* VIS SCIENTIST, MASS INST TECHNOL, 93- *Personal Data:* b Hamburg, Ger, Dec 13, 25; US citizen; m 49; c W Chris. *Educ:* Univ Nebr, BS, 51, MS, 54; Yale Univ, PhD(biochem), 60. *Prof Exp:* Fel biochem, Harvard Univ, 60-62, fel, Sch Med, 63-64; USPHS fel, Mass Inst Technol, 64-65, res assoc, 65-67; asst prof biol, Boston Col, 67-72, assoc prof, 72-93. *Mem:* Am Inst Chemists; Am Chem Soc; Am Soc Zool; Am Physiol Soc; Am Soc Biol Chem; Sigma Xi. *Res:* Biochemistry and structure of arthropod cuticle; chitin structure and enzymology; enzymology of molting in arthropods and its inhibition; plastics pollution and water pollution and its mitigation. *Mailing Add:* 4 Bowser Rd Lexington MA 02173

BADE, WILLIAM GEORGE, MATHEMATICS. *Current Pos:* from asst prof to assoc prof, 55-64, PROF MATH, UNIV CALIF, BERKELEY, 64- *Personal Data:* b Oakland, Calif, May 29, 24; m 52; c 6. *Educ:* Calif Inst Technol, BS, 45; Univ Calif, Los Angeles, MA, 48, PhD(math), 51. *Prof Exp:* Instr math, Univ Calif, 51-52 & Yale Univ, 52-55. *Concurrent Pos:* NSF sr fel, 58-59. *Mem:* Am Math Soc. *Res:* Functional analysis. *Mailing Add:* Dept Math Univ Calif Berkeley CA 94720-0001

BADEER, HENRY SARKIS, MEDICAL PHYSIOLOGY. *Current Pos:* prof physiol & pharmacol, 67-76, prof physiol, 76-91, EMER PROF PHYSIOL, SCH MED, CREIGHTON UNIV, 91- *Personal Data:* b Mersine, Turkey, Jan 31, 15; nat US; m 48, Mariam Kassarjian; c Gilbert H & Danial H. *Educ:* Am Univ Beirut, MD, 38. *Honors & Awards:* Golden Apple, 75. *Prof Exp:* Asst physiol, Am Univ Beirut, 38-41, instr, 41-45, from adj prof to asst clin prof, 45-51, from assoc prof to prof, 51-65, actg head dept, 51-56, chmn dept, 56-65; vis prof physiol, State Univ NY Downstate Med Ctr, 65-67. *Concurrent Pos:* Rockefeller res fel physiol, Harvard Med Sch, 48-49; vis prof, Univ Iowa, 57-58; actg chmn dept physiol & pharmacol, Creighton Univ, 71-72. *Mem:* AAAS; Am Physiol Soc; Int Soc Heart Res; Int Soc Adaptive Med. *Res:* Hypothermia on heart; ventricular fibrillation after coronary occlusion; myocardial oxygen uptake; cardiac hypertrophy and hemodynamics; author text. *Mailing Add:* 2808 S 99th Ave Omaha NE 68124-2603. *Fax:* 402-280-2690

BADEN, ERNEST, anatomic pathology, oral pathology, for more information see previous edition

BADEN, HARRY CHRISTIAN, ANALYTICAL CHEMISTRY. *Current Pos:* IND CONSULT, 84- *Personal Data:* b Brooklyn, NY, Oct 22, 23; m 47; c 2. *Educ:* Col Educ Albany, BA, 48, MA, 49; Rensselaer Polytech Inst, PhD(chem), 55. *Prof Exp:* Teacher, High Sch, NY, 48-50; asst chem, Rensselaer Polytech Inst, 50-52, asst chem physics, 52-54; analytical chemist, Eastman Kodak Co, Rochester, 54-58, sr analytical chemist, 58-64, tech assoc, Photog Technol Div, 65-83. *Mem:* Am Chem Soc; Sigma Xi. *Res:* Explosive oxidation of boron hydrides; instrumental analysis; infrared spectra; gas chromatography; photographic chemistry. *Mailing Add:* 205 Curtice Park Webster NY 14580-3422

BADEN, HOWARD PHILIP, DERMATOLOGY. *Current Pos:* DERMATOLOGIST, MASS GEN HOSP, 80- *Personal Data:* b Boston, Mass, Feb, 23, 31; m 81; c 3. *Educ:* Harvard Univ, AB, 52; Harvard Med Sch, MD, 56. *Prof Exp:* Intern med, Peter Bent Brigham Hosp, Boston, 56-57; asst resident dermat, Mass Gen Hosp, Boston, 59-60, clin fel, 60-61; assoc dermatologist, Mass Gen Hosp, 76-80; res assoc, 62-63, instr, 63-64, assoc, 64-67, from asst prof in assoc prof, 67-75, mem fac; Ctr Human Genetics, 71-75, PROF DERMAT, HARVARD MED SCH, 75- *Concurrent Pos:* NIH fel, Res Lab, Harvard Med Sch, Dept Dermat, Mass Gen Hosp & Grad Dept Biochem, Brandeis Univ, 61-62; clin assoc, Mass Gen Hosp, Boston, 62-64, asst, 64-67, from asst dermatologist to dermatologist, 67-75; mem, Gen Med A Study Sect, NIH, 69-73; Am Cancer Soc-Eleanor Roosevelt int cancer fel, Galton Lab, Univ Col, Univ London, 70-71; ed, Progress in Dermat, 71-74; assoc ed, J Soc Invest Dermat, 72-77. *Mem:* Am Fedn Clin Res; Soc Invest Dermat; Am Soc Human Genetics; AAAS; Am Soc Clin Invest; Fedn Am Soc Exp Biol. *Res:* Differentiation of epidermal tissues with emphasis on the structural proteins; diagnosis and management of genetic disorders of keratinization. *Mailing Add:* Dept Dermat Mass Gen Hosp E CBRC Charlestown MA 02129

BADENHUIZEN, NICOLAAS PIETER, botany; deceased, see previous edition for last biography

BADER, HENRY, ORGANIC CHEMISTRY. *Current Pos:* RETIRED. *Personal Data:* b Warsaw, Poland, Apr 26, 20; nat US; m 50; c 2. *Educ:* Univ Strasbourg, Ing Chem, 40; Univ Paris & Univ Montpellier, LSc, 42; Univ London, PhD(chem), 48, Imperial Col, dipl, 48. *Prof Exp:* Res chemist, Beecham Res Labs, Eng, 48-50 & May & Baker, Ltd, 50-51; group leader & sr chemist, Dominion Tar & Chem Co, Can, 51-53; sr res assoc, Ortho Res Found, Raritan, NJ, 53-61 & Am Cyanamid Co, Bound Brook, 61-63; dir labs, Aldrich Chem Co, 63-66; sr scientist, Polaroid Corp, 66, group leader, 67-69, sr group leader, 70-77, res fel, 77-82; res assoc, Dana Farber Cancer Inst, Boston, 82-95. *Concurrent Pos:* Expert, UN Chem Indust Develop Orgn, Cuba, 82. *Mem:* Am Chem Soc; Chem Soc. *Res:* Synthetic organic chemistry; acetylenes and heterocyclics; chemotherapy; process research. *Mailing Add:* 254 Del Pond Dr Canton MA 02021

BADER, HERMANN, CIRCULATION, MEMBRANE TRANSPORT. *Current Pos:* prof & dept head, 72-96, EMER PROF PHARMACOL & TOXICOL, UNIV ULM, 96- *Personal Data:* b Furtwangen, Ger, Nov 23, 27; m 58, Gertraude Haack; c Sylvia M, Andreas A, Raoul G, Maureen P, Gregor D, Oliver T, Niklas T, Matthias W & Dominik M. *Educ:* Univ Munich, MD, 55. *Prof Exp:* Asst, Physiol Inst, Univ Munich, 54-56, med apprentice, Med Outpatient Dept, 56-57, Ger Res Asn scholar, Physiol Inst, 57-58, sci asst, 60-61; instr, Dept Physiol, Vanderbilt Univ, 59-60, asst prof, 60 & 63-66; sci asst, Physiol Inst, Univ Wurzburg, 61-63; res fel, Biochem Inst, Univ Strassburg, Frankreich, 62; assoc prof, Dept Pharmacol & Toxicol, Sch Med, Univ Miss, 66-70, prof, 70-72. *Concurrent Pos:* Prorector & chmn senate, Univ Ulm, 73, dean, Fac Theoret Med, 74-75, prodekan, 75-77, chmn, Ctr Biol & Theoret Med, 74-79, dean, Fac Theoret Med, 79-83. *Mem:* Ger Physiol Soc; Ger Soc Biol Chem; Ger Soc Biophysics; Biophys Soc; Am Soc Pharmacol & Exp Therapeut; Ger Pharmacol Soc. *Res:* Blood pressure regulation; active transport; ethics in medicine. *Mailing Add:* Neue Welt 6 89269 Vohringen-Illerberg Germany

BADER, KENNETH L, AGRONOMY, ACADEMIC ADMINISTRATION. *Current Pos:* CHIEF EXEC OFFICER, AM SOYBEAN ASN, 76- *Personal Data:* b Carroll, Ohio, May 4, 34; m 55; c 2. *Educ:* Ohio State Univ, BSc, 56, MSc, 57, PhD(agron), 60. *Prof Exp:* Asst agron, Ohio State Univ, 56-57, from instr to prof agron, 57-72, actg asst dean col agr & home econ, 63-64, asst dean col agr, 64-68, from assoc dean students to dean students, 68-72; prof agron & vchancellor student affairs, Univ Nebr, Lincoln, 72-76. *Concurrent Pos:* Am Coun Educ fel acad admin, 67-68. *Mem:* Am Soc Agron; Sigma Xi; Agr Coun Am. *Res:* Grass physiology and turf management; business administration. *Mailing Add:* 1635 Trotting Trail Rd Chesterfield MO 63005

BADER, RICHARD FREDERICK W, THEORETICAL CHEMISTRY. *Current Pos:* assoc prof, 63-66, PROF CHEM, McMASTER UNIV, 66- *Personal Data:* b Kitchener, Ont, Oct 15, 31; m 58; c 3. *Educ:* McMaster Univ, BSc, 53, MSc, 55; Mass Inst Technol, PhD(chem), 58. *Honors & Awards:* JC Polamyi Lectr Award, CSC, 97. *Prof Exp:* Fel chem, Mass Inst Technol, 58, Univ Cambridge, UK, 58-59; from asst prof to assoc prof, Univ Ottawa, 59-63. *Concurrent Pos:* A P Sloan res fel, Sloan Found, 64-66; E W R Steacie mem fel, Nat Res Coun Can, 67-69; Guggenheim Mem Found fel, 79-80. *Mem:* Royal Soc Can; Chem Inst Can; Am Phys Soc. *Res:* Development of a theory that quantifies the chemical concepts of atoms, bonds, structure and reactivity. *Mailing Add:* Dept Chem McMaster Univ Hamilton ON L8S 4M1 Can

BADER, ROBERT SMITH, evolutionary biology, taxonomy, for more information see previous edition

BADER, SAMUEL DAVID, PHYSICAL CHEMISTRY, SOLID STATE PHYSICS. *Current Pos:* Appointee superconductivity,Argonne Nat Lab, 74-76, asst physicist, 76-79, physicist, 79-87, sr physicist, 90, GROUP LEADER, MAT SCI, ARGONNE NAT LAB, 87- *Personal Data:* b New York, NY, Feb 4, 47; wid; c Ari & Danya. *Educ:* Univ Calif, Berkeley, BS, 67, PhD(chem), 74. *Concurrent Pos:* Assoc ed, Applied Physics Lett; adv ed, J Magnetism & Magnetic Mat. *Mem:* Fel Am Phys Soc; Am Vacuum Soc; Am Phys Soc Div Mat Physics (secy/treas, 96-99). *Res:* Experimental surface science; electron spectroscopies; surface magnetism; magneto-optics; magnetic superlattices. *Mailing Add:* Mat Sci Div Argonne Nat Lab Bldg 223 Argonne IL 60439. *E-Mail:* bader@anl.gov

BADERTSCHER, ROBERT F(REDERICK), AERONAUTICAL & ASTRONAUTICAL ENGINEERING. *Current Pos:* RETIRED. *Personal Data:* b Cincinnati, Ohio, June 4, 22; m 46; c 4. *Educ:* Ohio State Univ, BAAE & MSc, 50. *Prof Exp:* Engr, Aeroprod Div, Gen Motors Co Corp, 50-52; engr, Columbus Labs, Battelle Mem Inst, 52-60, chief aerospace mech res group, 60-74, prog mgr, 74-76, assoc dir, 76-78, proj mgr, Battelle Advan Systs Lab, 79- *Mem:* Assoc fel Am Inst Aeronaut & Astronaut; Am Defense Preparedness Asn. *Res:* General aeropsace vehicle design and development problems; aircraft and missile systems analysis; armored combat vehicle systems assessment and related technologies; technology assessment. *Mailing Add:* 218 Kenbrook Dr Columbus OH 43085

BADGER, ALISON MARY, IMMUNOBIOLOGY. *Current Pos:* sr investr, Smith Kline & French, 79-82, asst dir, 82-90, RES FEL, SMITHKLINE BEECHAM PHARMACEUT, PHILADELPHIA, 90- *Personal Data:* b Croyden, Eng, Nov 25, 35; US citizen; m 61; c 2. *Educ:* Univ London, BSc, 58; Boston Univ, PhD(microbiol), 72. *Prof Exp:* Res asst microbiol, United Fruit Co, Boston, 58-64; res asst biochem, Blood Res Inst, Boston, 66-68; res assoc microbiol, Sch Med, Boston Univ, 68-73, from instr to asst prof, 73-77, asst prof surg, 75-77, assoc prof microbiol, 77-79. *Mem:* Am Asn Immunologists. *Res:* Cellular immunology. *Mailing Add:* Smithkline Beecham Pharmaceut 709 Swedeland Rd King of Prussia PA 19406

BADGER, RODNEY ALLAN, ORGANIC CHEMISTRY. *Current Pos:* PROF CHEM, SOUTHERN ORE STATE COL, 69- *Personal Data:* b Fullerton, Calif, Feb 7, 43; div. *Educ:* Ore State Univ, BA & BS, 64; Univ Calif, Berkeley, MS, 66, PhD(chem), 68. *Prof Exp:* Asst chemist, Univ Hawaii, 68-69. *Concurrent Pos:* Vis assoc prof chem, Univ BC, 76-77; vis prof chem, Ore State Univ, 83-84 & Univ Victoria, 90-91; indust consult, 83-; sr proj scientist, Axys Group, 90-91. *Mem:* Am Chem Soc; Sigma Xi; Carr Soc Chem. *Res:* Isolation and synthesis of natural products; isolation and structure determination of pharmacologically-active compounds. *Mailing Add:* Dept Chem Southern Ore State Col Ashland OR 97520. *Fax:* 541-552-6415; *E-Mail:* badger@wpo.sosc.osshe.edu

BADGER, THOMAS MARK, ENDOCRINOLOGY OF GROWTH & REPRODUCTION, EFFECTS OF NUTRITION ON ENDOCRINOLOGY & METABOLISM. *Current Pos:* PROF, UNIV ARK MED SCI, 86- *Personal Data:* b Modesto, Calif, Mar 21, 45; m 67, Cheryl A Jordan; c Mark J. *Educ:* Calif State Univ, Fresno, BS, 68; Univ Mo, Columbia, MS, 70, PhD(nutrit & biochem), 73. *Prof Exp:* From asst prof to assoc prof, Harvard Med Sch, 76-86. *Concurrent Pos:* Dir res, Vincent Mem Res Labs, 78-86, Dept Pediat, 86-; dir, Ark Childrens Hosp Res Inst, 91- *Mem:* Am Inst Nutrit; Endocrine Soc; Int Soc Neuroendocrinol; Soc Neurosci; Res Soc Alcohol; Int Brain Res Orgn. *Res:* Laboratory has studied the neuro-regulation of growth and reproduction; have developed techniques to treat central disorders of reproduction and growth; study the effects of nutrition, alcohol and various drug and toxicants on hormones and metabolic processes. *Mailing Add:* Dept Pediat Slot 512B 4301 W Markham Little Rock AR 72205

BADGETT, ALLEN A, BIOCHEMICAL GENETICS, HUMAN GENETICS. *Current Pos:* ASSOC PROF GENETICS, SOUTHWESTERN OKLA STATE UNIV, 73- *Personal Data:* b Van Nuys, Calif, Sept 8, 43; m 68, Darlene Dameron; c Blake, Mark & Matt. *Educ:* Humboldt State Univ, AB, 67, MS, 68; Utah State Univ, PhD(genetics), 73. *Concurrent Pos:* Instnl res grant, Southwestern Okla State Univ, 74-80; vis prof, Ctr Excellence Molecular Med & Univ Okla Health Sci Ctr, 93-; grantee, NSF & Eisenhower Telecommun. *Mem:* Genetics Soc Am; Am Statist Soc. *Res:* Regulation of gene activity and how it relates to biochemical and cytogenetic parameters; isolation, cloning and sequencing of the TAM-horse field gene; DNA sequencing; polymerase chain reaction. *Mailing Add:* Dept Biol Sci Southwestern Okla State Univ 100 Campus Dr Weatherford OK 73096

BADGLEY, FRANKLIN ILSLEY, METEOROLOGY. *Current Pos:* from instr to assoc prof, 50-67, PROF METEOROL, UNIV WASH, 67-, PROF ATMOSPHERIC SCI, 73-, DEPT CHMN, 77- *Personal Data:* b Mansfield, Ohio, Dec 20, 14; m 43; c 2. *Educ:* Univ Chicago, BS, 35; NY Univ, MS, 49, PhD(meteorol), 51. *Prof Exp:* Chemist, Swift & Co, 36-42; meteorologist, Trans World Airlines, Inc, 47. *Concurrent Pos:* Assoc dir, Quarternary Res Ctr, Univ Wash, 73-76. *Mem:* AAAS; Am Meteorol Soc; Am Geophys Union; Sigma Xi. *Res:* Atmospheric turbulence. *Mailing Add:* 13749 41st Ave NE Seattle WA 98125-3820

BADHWAR, GAUTAM D, RADIATION PHYSICS, CROP MONITORING USING SATELLITE DATA. *Current Pos:* mem staff, 72-90, HEAD, SPACE RADIATION & SR SCIENTIST, NASA JOHNSON SPACE CTR, HOUSTON, 90- *Personal Data:* b New Delhi, India, Nov 8, 40; US citizen; m 70; c 2. *Educ:* Agra Univ, BS, 59; Univ Rochester, PhD(physics), 67. *Prof Exp:* Asst prof physics, Univ Rochester, 67-72. *Concurrent Pos:* Lectr, Univ Houston, 76-90. *Res:* Radiation monitoring; astronaut health; crop identification; orbital monitoring. *Mailing Add:* Code SN NASA Johnson Space Ctr Houston TX 77058

BADIN, ELMER JOHN, PHYSICAL ORGANIC CHEMISTRY. *Current Pos:* SELF EMPLOYED. *Personal Data:* b Canonsburg, Pa, Aug 21, 17. *Educ:* Cooper Union, BChE, 42; Princeton Univ, MA, 44, PhD(org chem), 45. *Prof Exp:* Res assoc combustion chem, Princeton Univ, 45-46, instr chem, 46-50; sr res chemist, Celanese Corp Am, 56-59; prof chem & chmn dept, Union Col, NJ, 59-63; combustion chemist, 63-65; sr res chemist, Cities Serv Oil Co, 65-72; combustion chemist, 72-74; staff mem, Mitre Corp, 74-76; combustion chemist, 76-78; mgr combustion chem, Tenn Valley Authority, 78-82; Combustion Chem Bk, 82-96. *Concurrent Pos:* Consult, Wesco Paint Co, 45-47; assoc, US Navy Proj Squid, Princeton Univ, 45-47; researcher, Univ Calif, Berkeley, 49-50. *Mem:* Am Chem Soc; Combustion Inst; Sigma Xi. *Res:* Inorganic-organic-physical organic chemistry; combustion-oxidation; petroleum and polymer chemistry; coal science and energy; synthesis and chemical mechanisms. *Mailing Add:* 91 Castleton Rd Princeton NJ 08540-1637

BADLER, NORMAN IRA, HUMAN MOVEMENT, COMPUTER GRAPHICS. *Current Pos:* From asst prof to assoc prof, 74-86, chairperson, 90-94, PROF COMPUT SCI, UNIV PA, 87- *Personal Data:* b Los Angeles, Calif, May 3, 48; m 68, Virginia; c Jeremy & David. *Educ:* Univ Calif, Santa Barbara, BA, 70; Univ Toronto, MS, 71, PhD(comput sci), 75. *Concurrent Pos:* Prin investr, NSF grants, 75- & ARO grants, NASA, 82-; consult, 76-; vchair, Spec Interest Group on Comput Graphics, Asn Comput Mach, 79-82; sr ed, Comput Graphics & Image Processing, 81-90, Graphical Models & Image Processing, 90-; mem, Comput Soc, Inst Elec & Electronics Engrs, assoc ed, Comput Graphics & Appln, 84-90. *Mem:* Asn Comput Mach (vchmn, 79-82); Inst Elec & Electronics Engrs; Asn Comput Ling; Am Asn Artificial Intelligence; Cognitive Sci Soc; Human Factors & Ergonomics Soc. *Res:* The computer representation, simulation, animation, analysis and description of human movement; the understanding and processing of movement concepts in natural languages; interactive and graphics system design; archaeological site reconstruction. *Mailing Add:* Dir Comput & Info Sci Univ Pa Philadelphia PA 19104-6389. *Fax:* 215-898-0587; *E-Mail:* badler@central.cis.upenn.edu

BADONNEL, MARIE-CLAUDE H M, TISSUE TYPING, TEACHING. *Current Pos:* ASST PROF PATH, UNIV MASS MED CTR, 78-, ASSOC DIR, TISSUE TYPING LAB/BLOOD BANK, 87- *Personal Data:* b France, 39. *Educ:* Univ Geneva, Switzerland, PhD(exp path), 75. *Mem:* Am Soc Histocompatibility & Immunogenetics; Am Asn Path; AAAS; Am Heart Asn. *Mailing Add:* Univ Mass Med Ctr HLA Blood Bank 55 Lake Ave N Worcester MA 01655-0007

BADOYANNIS, HELEN LITMAN, MOLECULAR NEUROBIOLOGY, DEVELOPMENTAL NEUROBIOLOGY. *Current Pos:* RETIRED. *Personal Data:* b New York, NY, Apr 16, 59; m 89, Steven; c 2. *Educ:* Smith Col, AB, 81; NY Med Col, MS, 88, PhD(neurosci), 91. *Prof Exp:* Teaching asst psychol, Smith Col, 81-82; teaching assoc psychol, Univ Mass, 81-82; teaching asst histol, NY Med Col, 86 & 87, teaching asst neurosci, 88 & 89; post doctoral fed neurobiol, State Univ Ny, Stony Brook, 91-92. *Mem:* Soc Neurosci; Soc Cell Biol; AAAS; Am Women Sci; NY Acad Sci. *Res:* Molecular and cellular neurobiology; examining various growth factors and cell-cell contact alone or in combination for their ability to alter catecholaminergic phenotypic expression in the neural crest derived PC12 cell line. *Mailing Add:* 65 Shore Rd East Setauket NY 11733

BADR, MOSTAFA, pharmacology, toxicology, for more information see previous edition

BADRE, ALBERT NASIB, INFORMATION SCIENCE. *Current Pos:* asst prof, 73-79, ASSOC PROF, SCH INFO & COMPUT SCI, GA INST TECHNOL, 79- *Personal Data:* b Beirut, Lebanon, Aug 15, 45; US citizen; m 69; c 1. *Educ:* Univ Iowa, BA, 68; Univ Mich, Ann Arbor, MA, 71, PhD(behav sci), 73. *Prof Exp:* Soc worker, New York City Dept Soc Serv, 68-69; asst res, Ment Health Res Inst, Univ Mich, 70-71, res asst comput applns, 71-73. *Mem:* AAAS; Am Asn Univ Prof; Am Soc Info Sci; Am Educ Res Asn; Am Psychol Asn; Sigma Xi. *Res:* The study, design, and analysis of man-computer problem-solving, information-processing, learning, pattern recognition, memory and decision processing systems. *Mailing Add:* Dept Comput Eng Ga Inst Technol 225 North Ave NW Atlanta GA 30332-0001

BAE, JAE HO, CHEMICAL ENGINEERING. *Current Pos:* RES CONSULT, CHEVRON PETROL TECHNOL CO, 92- *Personal Data:* b Taegu, Korea, Dec 11, 39; m 68; c 3. *Educ:* Seoul Nat Univ, BSE, 62; Univ Fla, MSE, 64, PhD(chem eng), 66. *Prof Exp:* Engr, Cheil Sugar Indust Co, 62-63; res engr, Gulf Res & Develop Co, 66-73, sr res engr, 73-78, res assoc, 78-81, dir chem recovery processes, 81-85; sect supvr mobility control/chem flooding, Chevron Oil Field Res Co, 85-92. *Concurrent Pos:* Lectr chem eng, Carnegie-Mellon Univ, 67-68. *Mem:* Am Inst Chem Engrs; Soc Petrol Engrs. *Res:* Thermal recovery of crude oil; underground oxidation of hydrocarbons; enhanced oil recovery by surfactant flooding; alkaline flooding; polymer flooding; fluid flow in porous media; reservoir management. *Mailing Add:* PO Box 446 La Habra CA 90631. *Fax:* 562-694-7228; *E-Mail:* jhba@chevron.com

BAECHLER, CHARLES ALBERT, MEDICAL & PHARMACEUTICAL INFORMATION, INDUSTRIAL & MANUFACTURING ENGINEERING. *Current Pos:* microbiologist-tech serv, Merck & Co, Inc, 78-80, appln develop engr, 80-85, mgr ed & labeling, 85-87, MGR MED INFO MGT SYSTS, MERCK SHARP & DOHME, 87- *Personal Data:* b Lima, Ohio, Dec 15, 34; m 57, Nancy Grim; c 3. *Educ:* Ohio State Univ, BScEduc, 57; Univ Toledo, MS, 64; Wayne State Univ, PhD(med microbiol), 71. *Prof Exp:* Teacher biol & chem, Libby High Sch, Toledo, Ohio, 60-63; teacher chem, Sylvania High Sch, 63-64; microbiol res specialist, Parke-Davis & Co, 64-71; res assoc, Sch Med, Wayne State Univ, 71-74, asst prof physiol, 74-78. *Concurrent Pos:* Lectr, Univ Toledo Community Col, 64; consult electron micros, Parke-Davis & Co, 71-78. *Mem:* Soc Exp Biol & Med; Sigma Xi. *Res:* Function, structure and developmental aspects of blood and cardiovasculature interactions and microbial interactions at the ultrastructural level; technical services-vaccine and biological development; development of computer systems for scientific and industrial laboratory and production applications. *Mailing Add:* 250 Hampshire Dr Chalfont PA 18914-2344

BAECHLER, RAYMOND DALLAS, ORGANIC CHEMISTRY. *Current Pos:* from asst prof to assoc prof, 74-82, chmn, Dept Chem, 83-86 & 90-93, PROF CHEM, RUSSELL SAGE COL, 82- *Personal Data:* b Brooklyn, NY, Mar 11, 45; m 67, Carol Denig; c Michael D & Dawn M. *Educ:* Fordham Univ, BS, 66; Princeton Univ, MA, 68, PhD(chem), 71. *Prof Exp:* Instr, Princeton Univ, 71-73; teaching fel, Miami Univ, 73-74. *Mem:* Am Chem Soc. *Res:* Elucidation of reaction mechanisms; correlations between structure and reactivity; conformational processes of bond torsion and pyramidal inversion; silicon, phosphorus and sulfur chemistry; thermal rearrangements; unstable intermediates. *Mailing Add:* Dept Chem Russell Sage Col Troy NY 12180. *E-Mail:* baechr@sage.edu

BAEDECKER, MARY JO, ORGANIC GEOCHEMISTRY. *Current Pos:* res chemist, Water Resources Div, 74-92, supvry hydrologist, 92-96, ASST CHIEF HYDROLOGIST RES, US GEOL SURV, RESTON, VA, 96- *Personal Data:* b Richmond Ky, Nov 6, 41. *Educ:* Vanderbilt Univ, BS, 64; Univ Ky, MS, 67; George Wash Univ, PhD(geochem), 85. *Honors & Awards:* Super Serv Award, Dept Interior, 88, Meritorious Serv Award, 91. *Prof Exp:* Chemist, Inst Geophys & Planetary Physics, Univ Calif, Los Angeles, 68-73. *Concurrent Pos:* Adj prof, George Washington Univ, 87- *Mem:* Geol Soc Am; Geochem Soc; Am Geophys Union; Am Chem Soc; Nat Well Water Asn. *Res:* Organic-inorganic interactions in aquifers and recent sediments; degradation of natural and man-made organic materials and compounds in sub-surface environments; analytical methods for analyses of organic and inorgainc compounds. *Mailing Add:* 436 Nat Ctr Reston VA 20192

BAEDECKER, PHILIP A, RADIOCHEMISTRY-ACTIVATION ANALYSIS, TRACE ELEMENT GEOCHEMISTRY. *Current Pos:* chief, Anal Chem Br, US Geol Surv, 81-86, chmn, Effects Mat Task Group, Nat Acid Precipitation Assessment Prog, 86-90, res chemist, 74-96, EMER SCIENTIST, US GEOL SURV, 96- *Personal Data:* b East Orange, NJ, Dec 19, 39; m 66, Mary Jo LaFuze; c Cheryl E. *Educ:* Ohio Univ, BS, 61; Univ Ky, MS, 64, PhD(inorg & radiochem), 67. *Prof Exp:* Res assoc nuclear chem, Mass Inst Technol, 67-68; asst res chemist, Univ Calif, Los Angeles, 68-73, asst prof in residence, 70-71. *Mem:* AAAS; Am Chem Soc; Meteoritical Soc; Sigma Xi. *Res:* Application of nuclear analytical methods to problems in geochemistry; computer methods in gamma-ray spectroscopy and activation analysis; effects of acidic deposition on carbonate stone. *Mailing Add:* 11314 Handlebar Rd Reston VA 20191-3910

BAEDER, DONALD L(EE), CHEMICAL ENGINEERING, CHEMISTRY. *Current Pos:* CHMN, BAEDER NERUDA INTERESTS INC, 85- *Personal Data:* b Cleveland, Ohio, Aug 23, 25; m 52, Barbara Ayres; c Donald Scott, David Arthur, Ellen Jane Brda, Richard Lee & James Douglas. *Educ:* Baldwin-Wallace Col, BA, 49; Carnegie Inst Technol, BS, 51. *Prof Exp:* Group head process res, Esso Res & Eng Co, 53-55, asst sect head, explor & fundamental res, 55-56, sect head, 56-58, asst dir process res div, 58-62, dir, cent basic res lab & spec proj unit, 62-63; mgr res & develop, Humble Oil & Ref Co, 64-66, mgr plastics div, Enjay Chem Co Div, 66-68; vpres corp & govt res, Esso Res & Eng Co, 69-75; exec vpres res & develop, Occidental Petrol Corp, 75-77; pres, Hooker Chem Co, 77-81; exec vpres sci & technol, Occidental Petrol Corp, 81-84. *Concurrent Pos:* Mem div sci & technol, Am Petrol Inst. *Mem:* Am Chem Soc; fel Am Inst Chem Engrs; Sigma Xi. *Res:* Kinetics of thermal and catalytic reactions; radiation initiation of free radical reactions. *Mailing Add:* 307 Sugarberry Circle Houston TX 77024-7245. *Fax:* 713-783-8878; *E-Mail:* dlbaeder@aol.com

BAEKELAND, FREDERICK, PSYCHIATRY. *Current Pos:* From instr to asst prof, 64-71, ASSOC PROF PSYCHIAT, STATE UNIV NY DOWNSTATE MED CTR, 71- *Personal Data:* b Bronxville, NY, Sept 3, 28; m 50; c 2. *Educ:* Columbia Univ, BS, 51; Yale Univ, MS, 54, MD, 58; State Univ NY Downstate Med Ctr, DMSc(psychiat), 67. *Mem:* Asn Psychophysiol Study Sleep; fel Am Psychiat Asn. *Res:* Sleep: effects of drugs, physiology, dream content, requirements; alcoholism; correlates of treatment outcome; psychology of art. *Mailing Add:* 155 W 68th St Apt 28A New York NY 10023-5835

BAENZIGER, NORMAN CHARLES, PHYSICAL CHEMISTRY. *Current Pos:* from asst prof to assoc prof, 49-57, PROF PHYS CHEM, UNIV IOWA, 57- *Personal Data:* b New Ulm, Minn, Sept 23, 22; m 44; c 4. *Educ:* Hamline Univ, BS, 43; Iowa State Col, PhD(phys chem), 48. *Prof Exp:* Assoc chemist, Manhattan Proj & AEC, Iowa State Col, 44-48; instr phys chem, 46-48; fel, Mellon Inst, 48-49. *Mem:* Am Chem Soc; Am Crystallog Asn. *Res:* X-ray crystallography; intermetallic compounds; metal-olefin complexes. *Mailing Add:* 1960 Elm Ridge Rd NE North Liberty IA 52317

BAENZIGER, PETER STEPHEN, STRESS TOLERANCE, ADAPTATION. *Current Pos:* from assoc prof to prof, Dept Agron, 86-96, EUGENE W PRICE DISTINGUISHED PROF TECHNOL, UNIV NEBR, 93- *Personal Data:* b Toronto, Ont, Apr 25, 51; US citizen; m 76, Marsha Lois Sims; c Peter E & Aubrie A. *Educ:* Harvard Univ, BA, 72; Purdue Univ, MS, 74, PhD(plant breeding & genetics), 75. *Honors & Awards:* Young Crop Scientist Award, Crop Sci Soc Am, 87. *Prof Exp:* Res geneticist, USDA, 76-83; res mgr, Monsanto Agr Prod Co, 83-86. *Concurrent Pos:* Hon prof, Ningxia Acad Agr & Forestry Sci, 92; interim head, Dept Agron, Univ Nebr, 93-96, chancellor, Search Comt, 95, Speaker's Bur, 96-97. *Mem:* Fel Am Soc Agron; fel Crop Sci Soc Am; fel AAAS. *Res:* Development of new winter wheat, barley, and triticale cultivars and germplasm; biotechnology (gene transfer and molecular mapping), disease and stress resistance/tolerance and advanced statistical design for efficient experimental line selection; improved end-use quality and how to best adapt cultivars for agricultural ecosystems. *Mailing Add:* Dept Agron Univ Nebr 330 Keim Lincoln NE 68583-0915. *Fax:* 402-472-7904; *E-Mail:* agrol04@unlvm.unl.edu

BAER, ADELA (DEE), GENETICS. *Current Pos:* ADJ PROF, DEPT ZOOL, ORE STATE UNIV, CORVALLIS, 84- *Personal Data:* b Blue Island, Ill, Apr 4, 31; c 2. *Educ:* Univ Ill, BS, 53; Purdue Univ, 54-56; Univ Calif, Berkeley, PhD(genetics), 63. *Prof Exp:* From asst prof to prof biol, San Diego State Univ, 62-83, chmn dept, 75-78. *Concurrent Pos:* Fulbright prof genetics, Univ Malaysia, 67-68; res scientist, Int Ctr Med Res, Inst Med Res, Malaysia, 71-72; vis prof genetics, Univ Calif, Berkeley, 75 & 81; vis prof, Ctr Theoret Studies, Indian Inst sci, Bangalore, India, 78 & 89; instr, Ore State Univ, 84- *Mem:* Am Soc Human Genetics; Sigma Xi. *Res:* Human ecological and biochemical genetics. *Mailing Add:* 42220 Marks Ridge Rd Sweet Home OR 97386

BAER, ADRIAN DONALD, SOLID STATE PHYSICS. *Current Pos:* res physicist, 74-79, OPER RES ANALYST, NAVAL WEAPONS CTR, 79- *Personal Data:* b St Louis, Mo, Nov 3, 42; m 64; c Adrian, Michael & Sarah. *Educ:* Univ Denver, BS, 64; Stanford Univ, MS, 65, PhD(elec eng), 71. *Prof Exp:* Res assoc physics, Mont State Univ, 71-73 & Stanford Univ, 73. *Mem:* Sigma Xi. *Res:* Measuring various electron emission and optical spectra and utilizing these spectra to study electronic states at surfaces and interfaces, and in thin films. *Mailing Add:* 1539 N China Lake Blvd No 212 Ridgecrest CA 93555

BAER, DONALD RAY, SURFACE SCIENCE, SOLID STATE PHYSICS. *Current Pos:* res scientist, 76-80, SR RES SCIENTIST, SURFACE SCI GROUP, MAT DEPT, PAC NORTHWEST DIV, BATTELLE MEM INST, 80-, STAFF SCIENTIST & INTERPHASE GROUP LEADER, MOLECULAR SCI RES CTR, MAT & INTERFACE PROG, 93- *Personal Data:* b Warren, Ohio, Nov 12, 47; w; c 2. *Educ:* Carnegie-Mellon Univ, BS, 69; Cornell Univ, PhD(physics), 74. *Prof Exp:* Res assoc physics, Mat Res Lab & Dept Physics, Univ Ill, Urbana, 74-76. *Concurrent Pos:* Vis res fel, Dept Mat Sci & Eng, Univ Surrey, Eng, 84-85; adj fac chem, Wash State Univ; assoc ed, Surface Sci Spectron. *Mem:* Am Phys Soc; Am Soc Testing & Mat; Electrochem Soc; Am Vacuum Soc; AAAS; Am Sci Affil. *Res:* Surface and interface science; oxide and mineral surfaces; high temperature corrosion; amorphous materials; surface reactivity; aqueous corrosion; auger electron spectroscopy; x-ray photo-electrons spectroscopy; ion beam materials analysis; metals physics; low temperature physics. *Mailing Add:* Battelle NW Labs Mat Dept Box 999 K893 Richland WA 99352. *Fax:* 509-376-2837

BAER, ERIC, POLYMER PHYSICS & CHEMISTRY. *Current Pos:* PROF ENG, CASE WESTERN RESERVE UNIV, 66- *Personal Data:* b Nieder-Weisel, Germany, July 18, 32; US citizen; m 56; c 2. *Educ:* Johns Hopkins Univ, MA, 53, PhD(chem eng), 57. *Honors & Awards:* McGraw Award, Am Soc Eng Educ, 68; Int Award, Soc Plastics Engrs, 80; Borden Award, Am Chem Soc, 81. *Prof Exp:* Res engr, Polychem Dept, E I Du Pont de Nemours & Co, 57-60; asst prof chem eng, Univ Ill, 60-62; assoc prof, 62-66, prof-in-chg polymer sci & eng, 62-66, chmn, Dept Macromolecular Sci, 67-78,; dean, 78-83, prof, Case Inst Technol, 83- *Concurrent Pos:* Indust consult ed, Polymer Eng & Sci. *Mem:* Am Inst Chem Engrs; Am Soc Mech Engrs; Am Chem Soc; fel Am Phys Soc; fel Am Inst Chemists; Sigma Xi. *Res:* Physical behavior and structure of polymers; engineering design for plastics; reactions on polymer crystal surfaces; properties of polymeric materials under high pressure and at cryogenic temperatures; nucleation phenomena in phase changes; heat transfer during condensation. *Mailing Add:* Dept Macromolecular Sci Case Western Reserve Univ Cleveland OH 44106-2699

BAER, FERDINAND, METEOROLOGY, NUMERICAL WEATHER PREDICTION. *Current Pos:* dir meteorol prog, Univ Md, 77-79, chmn, Dept Meteorol, 79-87, dir coop inst climate studies, 84-89, PROF METEOROL, UNIV MD, COLLEGE PARK, 77- *Personal Data:* b Dinkelsbuhl, Ger, Aug 30, 29; US citizen; m, Karen Klein; c Darius, Robin, Jason & Gavin. *Educ:* Univ Chicago, AB, 50, MS, 54, PhD(geophys sci), 61. *Prof Exp:* Asst atmospheric physics, Univ Ariz, 55-56; asst meteorol, Univ Chicago, 56-61; from asst prof to assoc prof atmospheric sci, Colo State Univ, 61-71; prof atmospheric sci, Univ Mich, 72-77. *Concurrent Pos:* Vis res fel, Geophys Fluid Dynamics Lab, Princeton Univ, 68-69; consult, McGraw Hill Info Systs, 71-79; vis prof, Stockholm Univ, 74-75 & Frie Univ, Berlin, 75; mem rep, Univ Corp for Atmospheric Res, 77-90; mem comt on atmospheric sci, Nat Acad Sci, 80-82; mem, Bd Atm Sci & Climate, Nat Res Coun, 82-85; trustee, Univ Corp Atmospheric Res, 85-91; sci team mem, ARM, Dept Energy, 90- & CHAMMP, 91-; prof, Inst Atmosphere Univ Md, College & Climate Studies, Park, 92-94; chair, Sect Atmospheric & Hydrosphin Sci, AAAS, 94-95. *Mem:* Fel Am Meteorol Soc; Am Geophys Union; fel Royal Meteorol Soc; AAAS; Can Meteorol & Oceanog Soc. *Res:* Dynamics of the atmosphere; expansion of atmospheric space variables in series of orthogonal polynominals; numerical analysis of atmospheric space fields; normal mode analysis; initialization. *Mailing Add:* Dept Meteorol Univ Md College Park MD 20742. *Fax:* 301-314-9482; *E-Mail:* bagr@atmos.umd.edu

BAER, GEORGE M, epidemiology, virology, for more information see previous edition

BAER, HANS HELMUT, ORGANIC CHEMISTRY, CARBOHYDRATE CHEMISTRY. *Current Pos:* from assoc prof to prof chem, 61-92, chmn dept, 69-75, HON RES PROF, UNIV OTTAWA, 93- *Personal Data:* b Karlsruhe, Ger, July 3, 26; Can citizen; m 56, Gertrud Mackprang; c Thomas & Nicole. *Educ:* Karlsruhe Tech Univ, cand chem, 47; Univ Heidelberg, dipl chem, 50, Dr rer nat(chem), 52. *Honors & Awards:* C S Hudson Award, Am Chem Soc, 75. *Prof Exp:* Res assoc chem, Max Planck Inst Med Res, Heidelberg, 52-57; vis scientist biochem, Univ Calif, Berkeley, 57-59; vis scientist chem, Nat Inst Arthritis & Metab Dis, 59-61. *Mem:* Am Chem Soc; Chem Inst Can; Soc Ger Chemists. *Res:* Chemistry of natural products, especially carbohydrates; general synthetic organic chemistry. *Mailing Add:* 54 Rothwell Dr Ottawa ON K1J 7G6 Can. *Fax:* 613-564-6793

BAER, HAROLD, ALLERGY, IMMUNOLOGY. *Current Pos:* RETIRED. *Personal Data:* b New York, NY, Oct 3, 18; m 46; c 2. *Educ:* Brooklyn Col, BA, 38; Columbia Univ, MA, 40; Harvard Univ, MA, 42, PhD(chem), 43. *Prof Exp:* From asst to res assoc, Col Physicians & Surgeons, Columbia Univ, 43-50; from asst prof to assoc prof, Med Sch, Tulane Univ, 50-60; chief sect allergenic prod, Div Biol Stand, NIH, 60-71, chief, Lab Bact Prod, 71-74, dir allergenic prod, Bur Biol, Food & Drug Admin, 74-88. *Concurrent Pos:* Instr, City Col New York, 48-50. *Mem:* AAAS; Sigma Xi; Can Soc Allergy & Clin Immunol; Am Acad Allergy. *Res:* Allergen chemistry and standardization of allergenic extracts; delayed contact sensitivity. *Mailing Add:* 11420 Strand Dr No 306 Rockville MD 20852

BAER, HELMUT W, nuclear physics, for more information see previous edition

BAER, HERMAN, MEDICAL MICROBIOLOGY. *Current Pos:* asst prof, 66-70, ASSOC PROF IMMUNOL & MED MICROBIOL, COL MED, UNIV FLA, 70-, ASSOC PROF PATH, 74-, DIR, CLIN MICROBIOL LAB, 66- *Personal Data:* b Uetikon, Switz, Sept 11, 33; US citizen; c 3. *Educ:* Univ Basel, Switz, MD, 60; Am Acad Med Microbiol, dipl med bact, 69. *Prof Exp:* Fel, Inst Med Microbiol, Sch Med, Univ Zurich, 60-62, head, Diag Unit, 62-63; fel, Div Infectious Dis, Dept Med, Med Sch, Univ Pittsburgh, 63-64 & Dept Bact, Div Natural Sci, 65-66. *Mem:* Am Soc Microbiol. *Res:* Role of hand contamination of personnel in the epidemiology of gram negative nosocomal infections; role of airborne contamination in orthopedic surgery. *Mailing Add:* Dept Pathol Col Med Univ Fla Gainesville FL 32611-2002

BAER, HOWARD A, PHENOMENOLOGY, COMPUTER SIMULATIONS. *Current Pos:* asst res scientist, 87-90, ASST PROF THEORET PARTICLE PHYSICS, FLA STATE UNIV, 90- *Personal Data:* b Milwaukee, Wis, Nov 4, 57. *Educ:* Univ Wis, BS, 79, MS, 81, PhD(physics), 84. *Prof Exp:* Researcher theoret particle physics, Europ Orgn Nuclear Res, 84-85, Argonne Nat Lab, 85-87. *Mem:* Am Phys Soc. *Res:* Theoretical physics of elementary particles; interface of experiment and theory; phenomenology; search for supersymmetry; new quarks and leptons; perturbative quantum chromodynamics; computer simulation of particle scattering. *Mailing Add:* Physics Dept Fla State Univ Keen Bldg Tallahassee FL 32306

BAER, JAMES L, PALEOECOLOGY, STRUCTURAL GEOLOGY. *Current Pos:* asst prof, 69-74, ASSOC PROF GEOL, BRIGHAM YOUNG UNIV, 74- *Personal Data:* b Van Wert, Ohio, Oct 6, 35; m 61; c 4. *Educ:* Ohio State Univ, BS, 57; Brigham Young Univ, MS, 62, PhD(paleoecol), 68. *Prof Exp:* Asst prof geol, Northeast La State Col, 68-69. *Mem:* Geol Soc Am; Paleont Soc. *Res:* Paleoecology of ancient lake sediments; structural evolution of western United States; continental drift; geochemistry of sediments. *Mailing Add:* Dept Geol Brigham Young Univ 258 Esc Provo UT 84602-1022

BAER, JOHN ELSON, PHARMACOLOGY, DRUG METABOLISM. *Current Pos:* RETIRED. *Personal Data:* b Cleveland, Ohio, Apr 25, 17; m 47; c 4. *Educ:* Swarthmore Col, AB, 38; Univ Pa, MS, 40, PhD(org chem), 48. *Honors & Awards:* Albert Lasker Spec Award, Lasker Found, 75. *Prof Exp:* Chemist, Med Sch, NY Univ, 43-46; instr chem, Haverford Col, 47-48; asst prof, Carleton Col, 48-51; res assoc, Pharmacol Sect, Sharp & Dohme Div, Merck & Co, 51-58, dir pharmacol chem, Merck Inst, 58-69, assoc dir, Merck Inst Therapeut Res, 69-71, sr dir, 71-76, exec dir drug metab, 76-81, staff executive, Merck Sharp & Dohme Res Labs, 81-84. *Mem:* AAAS; Am Soc Pharmacol & Exp Therapeut; Am Soc Nephrology; Am Soc Clin Chemists. *Res:* Chemical methods for analysis of compounds in biological systems; pharmacology of diuretics and saluretics. *Mailing Add:* 1308 Brittany Pt Estates Lansdale PA 19446-6520

BAER, LEDOLPH, PHYSICAL OCEANOGRAPHY. *Current Pos:* dir oceanog serv, Nat Oceanic & Atmospheric Admin, 74-78, dir policy & long range planning, 78-80, oceanog sci adv & mgr coastal waves prog, 80-82, spec asst off chief scientist, 82-89, chief, Phys Oceanog Div, 89-93, CHIEF, OCEAN OBSERVATIONS DIV, NAT OCEAN SERV, NAT OCEANIC & ATMOSPHERIC ADMIN, 93- *Personal Data:* b Monroe, La, Nov 21, 29; m 57, Inge Rosenbaum; c Teresa, Margaret & Leonard. *Educ:* La Polytech Inst, BS, 50; Tex Agr & Mech Col, MS, 55; NY Univ, PhD(ocean waves), 62. *Prof Exp:* Meteorologist, Gulf Consult, Tex, 55-56; res specialist, Lockheed Missiles & Space Co, 59-62, res & develop scientist, Lockheed-Calif Co, 62-66, mgr, Ocean Sci Dept, Lockheed Ocean Lab, 66-74. *Mem:* AAAS; Am Meteorol Soc; Am Geophys Union. *Res:* Surface wave forecasting; physical oceanography; oceanographic statistics; quality assurance of oceanic data and products; synoptic oceanography. *Mailing Add:* 9920 Bedfordshire Ct Potomac MD 20854. *Fax:* 301-713-4494; *E-Mail:* lbaer@noaa.gov

BAER, NORBERT SEBASTIAN, ENVIRONMENTAL SCIENCE, MATERIALS DEGRADATION. *Current Pos:* from instr to prof, 69-86, actg dir admin, 78-79, HAGOP KEVORKIAN PROF CONSERV, INST FINE ARTS, NY UNIV, 86- *Personal Data:* b New York, NY, June 6, 38; m 59, Janet L Depold; c Diana M (O'Neill) & Norbert S Jr. *Educ:* Brooklyn Col, BSc, 59; Univ Wis, MSc, 62; NY Univ, PhD(phys chem), 69. *Prof Exp:* Physicist, Control Instrument Div, Warner & Swasey Co, 62-63; researcher sci bks, Sci Lib, Bk Div, Time Inc, 63-64; lectr chem, Queensborough Community Col, 67-68, asst prof, 68-69. *Concurrent Pos:* Ed adv & assoc ed, Studies Conserv, 71-87; mem, Exec Comt, Nat Conserv Adv Coun, 72-79; co-chmn, Conserv Ctr, Inst Fine Arts, NY Univ, 75-83, Dahlan Conf, Conserv Hist Stone Struct, 95-97; US coordr, Conserv Workshops Indo-US Subcomt Educ & Cult, 78-; US exec ed, Butterworth-Heinemann Series Conserv Arts, 79-; chmn, Comt Conserv Historic Stone Bldg & Monuments, Nat Mat Adv Bd, Nat Acad Sci, 80-82; chmn, Adv Comt, Nat Archives & Records Serv, 80-; mem, Vis Comt, Dept Objects Conserv, Metropoliton Mus Art, 80-, chmn, 85-90; John Simon Guggenheim Mem Found fel, 83-84; chmn, Rev Panel Progs Dry Depostion & Mat Effects, Environ Protection Agency, 85; tech adv, Comt Preserv Hist Rec, Nat Mat Adv Bd, Nat Acad Sci, 85-86; mem, Nat Mat Adv Bd, Nat Acad Sci, 86-93, Comt Natural Disasters, 88-; mem, Book Preserv Technol Adv Panel, Off Technol Assessment, 87-88, Comn Sistine Chapel, 87- *Mem:* Am Chem Soc; fel Am Inst Chemists; sr mem, Instrument Soc Am; Air Pollution Control Asn; Sigma Xi. *Res:* Application of physiochemical methods to the examination and preservation of artistic and historic works; effects of air pollution on materials. *Mailing Add:* Conserv Ctr Inst Fine Arts 1 E 78th St New York NY 10021. *Fax:* 212-772-5851; *E-Mail:* baer@is2.nyu.edu

BAER, PAUL NATHAN, PERIODONTOLOGY. *Current Pos:* PROF PERIODONT, SCH DENT MED, STATE UNIV NY, STONY BROOK, 73-; ED PERIODONT CLIN INVEST. *Personal Data:* b New York, NY, Oct 13, 21; m 50, Claire Greenland; c 1. *Educ:* Brooklyn Col, BA, 42; Columbia Univ, DDS, 45; Am Bd Periodent, dipl, 56. *Honors & Awards:* William J Gies Award, 82; Silver Medal, Turkish Soc Periodont, 90. *Prof Exp:* Asst prof periodont, Univ Southern Calif, 55-56; peridontist, Nat Inst Dent Res, 56-70, chief adolescent periodont unit, 70-73. *Concurrent Pos:* Pres, Greater Wash Soc Periodontists, 59-61, Northeastern Soc Periodontists, 81-82 & NY State Soc Periodontists, 84-86; Irwin Scopp fel, Northeastern Soc Periodont, 92. *Mem:* Am Dent Asn; Am Acad Periodont; Int Asn Dent Res; hon mem Colombia Soc Periodont; Int Acad Periodent; Hon mem, Turkish Soc Periodontists; Northeastern Soc Periodontists. *Res:* Periodontal disease. *Mailing Add:* Dept Periodont State Univ NY Sch Dent Med Stony Brook NY 11794-8703. *Fax:* 516-632-7130

BAER, RALPH NORMAN, UNDERWATER ACOUSTICS, ACOUSTIC PROPAGATION. *Current Pos:* Mathematician, 74-80, SUPVR MATHEMATICIAN, US NAVAL RES LAB, 80- *Personal Data:* b Flushing, NY, Jan 2, 48. *Educ:* Rensselaer Polytech Inst, BS, 68, MS, 70, PhD(appl math), 74. *Honors & Awards:* R Bruce Lindsay Award, Acoust Soc Am. *Concurrent Pos:* Sci officer, Off Naval Res, 90- *Mem:* Acoust Soc Am; Soc Indust & Appl Math; Am Math Soc; Math Asn Am. *Res:* Basic research in underwater acoustic propagation, scattering, and signal processing; acoustic computer-based model development. *Mailing Add:* 1250 Fourth St SW Apt 707 Washington DC 20024-2362

BAER, RICHARD, MICROBIOLOGY. *Current Pos:* ASST PROF MICROBIOL, UNIV TEX SOUTHWESTERN MED CTR, DALLAS, 87- *Personal Data:* b Aug 29, 53. *Educ:* Rutgers Univ, BA, 76, PhD(microbiol), 81. *Prof Exp:* Postdoctoral fel, Lab Molecular Biol, MRC, Cambridge, Eng, 80-83 & 84-87, Mem Sloan-Kettering Cancer Ctr, NY, 83-84. *Concurrent Pos:* Damon Runyon/Walter Winchell Cancer Fund fel, 80-82 & Lady Tata Mem Trust fel, 82-85; jr fac res award, Am Cancer Soc, 90-92. *Mailing Add:* Dept Microbiol Univ Tex Southwestern Med Sch 6000 Harry Hines Blvd Dallas TX 75235-9140. *Fax:* 214-684-7955

BAER, ROBERT LLOYD, MECHANICAL ENGINEERING. *Current Pos:* RETIRED. *Personal Data:* b New York, NY, Jan 29, 31; m 76; c 2. *Educ:* Clarkson Col Technol, BME, 52; Rensselaer Polytech Inst, MSME, 58. *Prof Exp:* Engr, Nuclear Div, Pratt & Whitney Aircraft Div, United Aircraft Corp, 54-57, sr engr, 57-59; eng specialist, Nuclear Div, Martin Co, 59-61, proj engr, 61-63; chief reactor systs, Hittman Assoc, Inc, 63-67, dept mgr, 67-70; sr proj mgr, AEC, 71-74; sect leader, Nuclear Regulatory Comn, 74-76, br chief, 76-96. *Concurrent Pos:* Lectr, Cath Univ, 63-76. *Mem:* Am Soc Mech Engrs; Am Nuclear Soc. *Res:* Nuclear power plant design, development and operation; safety, systems and economic analysis of large central station power plants; heat transfer and flow analysis of nuclear reactor cores. *Mailing Add:* 2844 Blue Spruce Lane Silver Spring MD 20906

BAER, ROBERT W, CARDIOVASCULAR & CORONARY PHYSIOLOGY. *Current Pos:* asst prof, 82-89, ASSOC PROF PHYSIOL, KIRKSVILLE COL OSTEOP MED, 89- *Personal Data:* b Minneapolis, Minn, Nov 8, 48; m 79, Diane Draper; c Kristin M & Lauren A. *Educ:* Carleton Col, BA, 71; Johns Hopkins Univ, PhD(physiol), 79. *Prof Exp:* Res fel physiol, Cardiovasc Res Inst, Univ Calif, San Francisco, 79-82. *Mem:* Am Physiol Soc; Am Heart Asn. *Res:* Control of coronary blood flow and myocardial oxygen delivery; transmural distribution of myocardial blood flow; cardiac function during respiratory maneuvers. *Mailing Add:* Dept Physiol Kirksville Col Osteop Med Kirksville MO 63501. *Fax:* 660-626-2965; *E-Mail:* baer@fileserver5.kcom.edu

BAER, RUDOLF L, DERMATOLOGY, IMMUNOLOGY. *Current Pos:* asst prof clin dermat & syphil, Postgrad Med Sch, 49-50, from assoc prof to prof, 50-61, chmn dept, 61-81, PROF DERMAT, SCH MED, NY UNIV, 61- *Personal Data:* b Strasbourg, Alsace-Lorraine, July 22, 10; nat US; m 41; c 2. *Educ:* Univ Frankfurt, Basel, MD, 34; Am Bd Dermat, dipl, 40. *Hon Degrees:* Dr Med, Univ Munich, WGer, 81. *Honors & Awards:* Dohi Mem Medal, Japanese Dermat Soc, 65; Hellerstrom Medal-Karolinska Inst, Sweden, 70; Stephen Rothman Medal, Soc Invest Dermat, 73; Alfred Marchionini Gold Medal, XV Int Cong of Dermat, 77; Gold Medal, Am Acad Dermat, 78; M H Samitz lectr, Univ Pa, 79; Nomland-Carney lectr, Univ Iowa, 79; Barrett Kennedy Mem lectr, La Dermat Soc, 80; A Harvey Neidoff Lectr, Am Asn Clin Immunol Allergy, 85-; Morrow-Miller-Taussig Mem Lectr, San Francisco Dermat Soc, 61; Leo Ritter von Zumbusch Mem Lectr, Univ Munich, 67; Ferdinand von Hebra Lectr, Austrian Soc Dermat & Venerology, 88. *Prof Exp:* Teacher dermat allergy, Med Sch, Columbia Univ, 39-46, instr dermat & syphil, 46-48, asst clin prof, Postgrad Med Sch & Hosp, 48. *Concurrent Pos:* Consult, Med Adv Panel on Hazardous Substances, US Dept Health, Educ & Welfare, 61, Nat Inst Allergy & Infectious Dis, 68; chmn Dermat Sect, AMA, 66, bd, Dermat Found, 74-78; founder & mem bd trustees, Rudolf L Baer Found Skin Dis, Inc, 75-; mem comt cutaneous dis, Armed Forces Epidemiol Bd, 67-72; consult, Surgeon Gen, US Army, 67; mem, Int Comt Dermat, 67-82, pres, 72-77; consult, Food & Drug Admin, 69; mem comt on revision, US Pharmacopeia, 70; mem, Am Bd Dermat, 64-72, pres, 70-; O'Leary lectr, Mayo Clin, Rochester, Minn, 71; Robinson lectr, Univ Md, 72; Barrett Kennedy Mem lectr, SCent Dermat Soc, 73; Duhring lectr, Pa Acad Dermat, 74; Bluefarb lectr, Chicago Dermat Soc, 75; Dome lectr, Am Acad Dermat, 76; F C Novy vis scholar, Univ Calif, Davis, 78. *Mem:* AAAS; fel Am Acad Allergy; fel & hon mem Am Acad Dermat (pres, 74-75); fel Am Col Allergists (vpres, 54); hon mem Am Dermat Asn (pres, 77); hon mem Soc Invest Dermat (pres, 64); hon mem Int Dermat Socs; Brazilian Nat Acad Med. *Res:* Immunology and allergy cutaneous aspects; cutaneous aspects; cross-sensitization; photobiology of the skin; biology of fungous infections of the skin; Langerhans cells; contact sensitization. *Mailing Add:* 1185 Park Ave New York NY 10128-1308

BAER, THOMAS STRICKLAND, NUCLEAR & ENVIRONMENTAL ENGINEERING. *Current Pos:* VPRES, NUCLEAR FUEL SERV INC. *Personal Data:* b Huntington, WVa, May 24, 42; m 64, Margaret Durkin; c Kathleen & Thomas. *Educ:* US Naval Acad, BS, 64; Univ Cincinnati, MS, 71, PhD, 73; US Naval War Col, MA, 91. *Prof Exp:* Sta engr, Metrop Edison Co, 73-74; vpres & gen mgr, Protective Packaging Inc, 74-76; vpres, Nuclear Eng Co, 76-81; mgr health physics-environ safety, Formerly Utilized Sites Remedial Action Prog, Bechtel Nat, Inc, 81-83, proj mgr, Hazardous Chem Waste Dept, 83-85, proj mgr, 85-86; sr vpres, US Ecol Inc, 86-91; vpres, PAI Corp, 91-93; oper dir, Automated Sci Group, Inc, 94. *Mem:* Am Nuclear Soc; Health Physics Soc; Soc Am Mil Engrs; Am Soc Eng Mgt; Am Soc Naval Engrs. *Res:* Evaluation and development of methods to treat, handle, transport, and dispose of hazardous chemical and radioactive wastes; methods for processing nuclear fuel. *Mailing Add:* Nuclear Fuel Serv Inc 621 Summit Lake Ct Knoxville TN 37922

BAER, TOMAS, CHEMICAL PHYSICS, CHEMICAL DYNAMICS. *Current Pos:* from asst prof to prof, 70-92, KENAN PROF CHEM, UNIV NC, CHAPEL HILL, 92- *Personal Data:* b Zurich, Switz, Aug 27, 39; US citizen; m 62, Carol; c 3. *Educ:* Lawrence Univ, BA, 62; Wesleyan Univ, MA, 64; Cornell Univ, PhD(chem), 69. *Honors & Awards:* Lucia R Briggs Distinguished Achievement Award, Lawrence Univ, 93. *Prof Exp:* Fel chem, Northwestern Univ, 69-70. *Concurrent Pos:* J S Guggenheim fel, Univ Paris, 76-77; vis prof, Univ Paris, 79; ed bd, Int J Mass Spectrom Ion Proc, 86-; organizing comt, Symp Synchroton Radiation, 87; exec comt, Advan Light Source Synchroton, 87-; chmn, Gordon Conf Multiphoton Processes, 97. *Mem:* Am Chem Soc; fel Am Phys Soc; Am Soc Mass Spectrometry. *Res:* Photoion-photoelectron coincidence spectroscopy used to study the dissociation rates of energy selected ions and the role of ion internal energy in ion-molecule reactions; use of synchrotron radiation and multiphoton ionization; laser spectroscopy. *Mailing Add:* Dept Chem Univ NC Chapel Hill NC 27599-3290. *Fax:* 919-962-2388; *E-Mail:* baer@unc.edu

BAER, WALTER S, TELECOMMUNICATIONS, INFORMATION TECHNOLOGY. *Current Pos:* consult & sr scientist, 70-78, dir energy policy prog, 78-81, DEP VPRES, RAND CORP, 90- *Personal Data:* b Chicago, Ill, July 27, 37; m 88, Jeri Weiss; c Alan & David. *Educ:* Calif Inst Technol, BS, 59; Univ Wis, PhD(physics), 64. *Honors & Awards:* Preceptor Award, Broadcast Indust Conf, 74. *Prof Exp:* Mem tech staff, Bell Tel Labs, 64-66; White House fel, Off of Vice President, 66-67; staff mem, Off Sci & Technol, Exec Off of President, 67-69; dir advan technol, Times Mirror Co, 81-89. *Concurrent Pos:* Mem comput sci & eng bd, Nat Acad Sci, 69-72; consult, maj US corps & govt agencies, 70-; mem cable TV adv comt, Fed Commun Comn, 72-74; dir, Aspen Cable Workshop, 72-73; mem adv coun, Electric Power Res Inst, 86-92; mem adv bd, Int Inst Appl Systs Anal, Columbia Univ; mem, Govs Coun on Info Techology; Inst Tele-Info UCSB Dept Commun; mem vis comt, Dept Eng & Pub Policy, Carnegie Mellon Univ. *Mem:* AAAS; Am Phys Soc; Inst Elec & Electronics Engrs; Int Inst Commun. *Res:* Science, technology, and public policy; telecommunications and information technology; technical management. *Mailing Add:* Rand Corp 1700 Main St Santa Monica CA 90401. *Fax:* 310-451-6942; *E-Mail:* boer@rand.org

BAERG, DAVID CARL, MEDICAL ENTOMOLOGY. *Current Pos:* ENVIRON & ENERGY CONTROL OFFICER, OFF CANAL IMPROV, PANAMA CANAL COMN, 78- *Personal Data:* b Dinuba, Calif, June 23, 38; m 62; c 2. *Educ:* Univ Calif, Davis, BS, 64, MS, 65, PhD(entom), 67. *Prof Exp:* Res asst mosquito res, Univ Calif, Davis, 64-67; res entomologist, Gorgas Mem Lab, 67-76; clin asst prof & assoc mem grad fac trop med & med parasitol, La State Univ Med Ctr, New Orleans, 73-76; environ health inspection, CZ Health Bur, 76-78. *Mem:* Audubon Soc; Animal Welfare Inst. *Res:* Mosquito biology and ecology; transmission, development and chemotherapy of malarias. *Mailing Add:* PAC 0636 PO Box 37301 Washington DC 20013

BAERG, WILLIAM, ELECTRONICS ENGINEERING, MATERIALS SCIENCE ENGINEERING. *Current Pos:* sr staff engr, 72-80, PRIN ENGR, INTEL CORP, 80- *Personal Data:* b Fayetteville, Ark, Oct 16, 38; m 60, 72, Marti Peck; c 3. *Educ:* Stanford Univ, BS, 60, PhD(chem eng), 65. *Prof Exp:* NSF fel eng & appl math, Harvard Univ, 65-66; sr scientist, chem lab, Aeronutronic Div, Philco-Ford Corp, 66-68; private res, 68-69; vpres, Linviron Corp, 69-72. *Mem:* Inst Elec & Electronics Engrs. *Res:* Acoustics and turbulence; plasma physics; reverse osmosis and module design; home water purification devices; semiconductor technology. *Mailing Add:* Intel Corp RN3-24 2200 Mission College Blvd Santa Clara CA 95052. *E-Mail:* bill_baerg@ccm.hf.intel.com

BAERNSTEIN, ALBERT, II, MATHEMATICAL ANALYSIS. *Current Pos:* assoc prof, 72-74, PROF MATH, WASH UNIV, 74- *Personal Data:* b Birmingham, Ala, Apr 25, 41; m 62; c 2. *Educ:* Cornell Univ, AB, 62; Univ Wis, MA, 64, PhD(math), 68. *Prof Exp:* Cost analyst, Prudential Ins Co, 62-63; instr math, Wis State Univ, Whitewater, 66-68; asst prof, Syracuse Univ, 68-72. *Concurrent Pos:* Fulbright-Hays sr res scholar, Imp Col, Univ London, 76-77. *Mem:* Am Math Soc. *Res:* Complex analysis and related areas. *Mailing Add:* Dept Math Wash Univ St Louis MO 63130

BAERTSCH, RICHARD D, ELECTRICAL ENGINEERING. *Current Pos:* ELEC ENGR, GEN ELEC RES & DEVELOP CTR, 65- *Personal Data:* b Robbinsdale, Minn, Mar 14, 36; m 60; c 2. *Educ:* Univ Minn, BSEE, 59, MSEE, 61, PhD(elec eng), 64. *Mem:* Sr mem Inst Elec & Electronics Engrs. *Res:* Noise in semiconductor devices; semiconductor physics and detectors; surface charge transport; integrated circuit design and process. *Mailing Add:* Gen Elec Res & Develop Ctr PO Box 8 Schenectady NY 12301

BAERWALD, JOHN E(DWARD), TRANSPORTATION & TRAFFIC ENGINEERING. *Current Pos:* from asst prof to prof, transp & traffic eng, 55-83, dir Hwy Traffic Safety Ctr, 61-83, EMER PROF, UNIV ILL, URBANA-CHAMPAIGN, 83- *Personal Data:* b Milwaukee, Wis, Nov 2, 25; m 48, 75, Donna L Granger; c Thomas J, James K & Barbara L (Bowman. *Educ:* Purdue Univ, BSCE, 49, MSCE, 50, PhD(civil eng), 56. *Honors & Awards:* Award, Inst Transp Engrs, 53, Matson Award, 88. *Prof Exp:* Instr, surv lab, Valparaiso Univ, 47-48; res asst traffic eng, Purdue Univ, 49-52, res engr, 52-55. *Concurrent Pos:* Consult transp & traffic engr, 52-; mem, Traffic Conf Exec Comt, Nat Safety Coun, 62-81, bd dirs, 75-80; chmn adv comt ambulance design criteria, Nat Acad Eng, 68-69; tech adv, tech comt traffic & safety, Pan Am Hwy Cong, 68-74; mem group 3 coun, oper & mgt serv & maintenance facil, Transportation Res Bd, Nat Res Coun-Nat Acad Sci, 69-73; mem, Bd Trustees, Champaign-Urbana, 73-83, chmn transit dist, 75-83; mem, tech adv comt, Ill Transportation Study Comn, 77-81; chair, Expert Witness Coun, Inst Transp Engrs, 89, Transp Safety Coun, 94. *Mem:* Fel Inst Transp Engrs (int pres, 70); fel Am Soc Civil Engrs; Am Road & Transp Builders Asn (pres, 79); Sigma Xi. *Res:* Traffic safety; traffic planning and administration; transportation and traffic engineering; traffic accident reconstruction. *Mailing Add:* RR 2 Box 927 Santa Fe NM 87505. *Fax:* 505-473-0742

BAES, CHARLES FREDERICK, JR, SEPARATION SCIENCE, AQUEOUS CHEMISTRY. *Current Pos:* res chemist, 51-87, CONSULT, OAK RIDGE NAT LAB, 88- *Personal Data:* b Cleveland, Ohio, Dec 2, 24; m 48; c 3. *Educ:* Rutgers Univ, BSc, 46; Univ Southern Calif, MSc, 48, PhD(phys inorg chem), 50. *Prof Exp:* Fel metal, Columbia Univ, 50-51. *Concurrent Pos:* Vis prof chem, Col William & Mary, 72-73. *Mem:* Fel AAAS; Am Chem Soc; Sigma Xi. *Res:* Solution chemistry; thermodynamics; solvent extraction chemistry; environmental chemistry; high temperature aqueous chemistry. *Mailing Add:* 102 Berwick Dr Oak Ridge TN 37830

BAETKE, EDWARD A, ENVIRONMENTAL ANALYSIS. *Current Pos:* LAB DIR, CORY LABS INC, 70- *Personal Data:* b Marinette, Wis, March 3, 37; m 58; c 2. *Educ:* St Norbert Col, BS, 59; Northwestern Univ, MS, 62. *Prof Exp:* Res chemist, Central Soya, 60-62, The Ansul Co, 62-70. *Mem:* Am Chem Soc. *Mailing Add:* 4000 Irving St Marinette WI 54143-1045

BAETZ, ALBERT L, VETERINARY MICROBIOLOGY. *Current Pos:* RES CHEMIST, NAT ANIMAL DIS CTR, AGR RES SERV, USDA, 66- *Personal Data:* b Cleveland, Ohio, Dec 25, 38; m 89, Laura McCollum; c Brad. *Educ:* Purdue Univ, BS, 61; Iowa State Univ, MS, 63, PhD(analytical chem) 66. *Mem:* AAAS; Am Chem Soc; Am Asn Vet Physiologists & Pharmacologists; Sigma Xi. *Res:* Purification and characterization of protein antigens from Listeria Monocytogenes in order to elucidate their roles in animal disease. *Mailing Add:* Nat Animal Dis Ctr PO Box 70 Ames IA 50010. *Fax:* 515-239-8458; *E-Mail:* abaetz@nodc.ars.usda.gov

BAETZOLD, ROGER C, PHYSICAL CHEMISTRY, CHEMICAL PHYSICS. *Current Pos:* Sr res chemist, 66-71, res assoc, 71-84, SR RES ASSOC, EASTMAN KODAK CO, NY, 84- *Personal Data:* b Warsaw, NY, Feb 26, 42; m 64, Gail Petz; c 4. *Educ:* Univ Buffalo, BA, 63; Univ Rochester, PhD(chem), 67. *Mem:* Am Chem Soc; Am Phys Soc. *Res:* Experimental and theoretical kinetics of chemical reactions; molecular orbital calculations; solid state chemistry. *Mailing Add:* 1188 Clarkson Parma TL Rd Brockport NY 14420-9417

BAEUMLER, HOWARD WILLIAM, MATHEMATICS, ELECTRICAL ENGINEERING. *Current Pos:* ASSOC PROF MATH, OLD DOMINION UNIV, 65- *Personal Data:* b Buffalo, NY, Sept 29, 21. *Educ:* State Univ NY, Teachers Col, Buffalo, BS, 43; Univ Buffalo, MA, 50; Ohio State Univ, PhD(elec eng), 64. *Prof Exp:* Instr math & sci, Park Sch, Buffalo, 43-44; instr math, Univ Buffalo, 46-53; asst prof, Marshall Univ, 54-55; asst instr, Ohio State Univ, 55-56, res assoc elec eng, Res Found, 56-61, instr univ, 59-64. *Concurrent Pos:* Lectr, Va High Sch Vis Scientist Prog, 66-67. *Mem:* AAAS; Am Soc Eng Educ; Asn Comput Mach; Inst Elec & Electronics Engrs; Math Asn Am. *Res:* Electromagnetic field theory; numerical methods, computation and analysis; Boolean algebra and Boolean matrices; electronic and mechanical switching circuits; symbolic binary and ternary logic; computer science, programming languages and non-numerical applications. *Mailing Add:* Dept Math Old Dominion Univ Norfolk VA 23529-1000

BAEZ, ALBERT VINICIO, PHYSICS, ENVIRONMENTAL EDUCATION & ETHICS. *Current Pos:* chmn 79-84, EMER CHMN, COMN EDUC, INT UNION CONSERV NATURE & NATURAL RESOURCES, GLAND, SWITZ, 84-; PRES, VIVAMOS MEJOR/USA, 86- *Personal Data:* b Puebla, Mex, Nov 15, 12; nat US; m 35, Joan Bridge; c Pauline, Joan & Mimi. *Educ:* Drew Univ, BA, 33; Syracuse Univ, MA, 35; Stanford Univ, PhD, 50. *Hon Degrees:* Dr, Open Univ, Gt Brit, 74; LHD, Drew Univ, 91. *Honors & Awards:* Dennis Gabor Award, Int Soc Optical Eng, 91. *Prof Exp:* Instr physics & math, Morris Jr Col, 36-38; instr math, Drew Univ, 38-40; from instr math to prof physics, Wagner Col, 40-44; instr, Stanford Univ, 44-45, actg instr math, 45-46, res asst physics, 46-49; physicist, Aeronaut Lab, Cornell Univ, 49-50; prof physics, Univ Redlands, 51-56, physicist, Film Group, Phys Sci Study Comt, 58-60; assoc prof physics, Harvey Mudd Col, 60-61; dir div sci teaching, UNESCO, 61-67; consult sci & technol educ, UN, NY & UNESCO, Paris, 67-74; assoc, Lawrence Hall Sci, Univ Calif, Berkeley, 74-78. *Concurrent Pos:* Prof, Col Arts & Sci, Univ Baghdad & head, UNESCO Tech Asst Mission, 51-52; vis prof, Stanford Univ, 56-58; physicist, Smithsonian Astrophys Observ, Cambridge, Mass, 60-61; sci dir, Physics Loop Film Proj, Encycl Britannica, 67-75; hon res assoc, Dept Physics, Harvard Univ, 70-71; consult int sci educ, NSF, 70-; vchmn, Comt Teaching Sci, Int Coun Sci Unions, 70-74, chmn, 74-78; vis prof, Open Univ, Gt Brit, 71-72, Univ Md, 73 & Inst Politecnico Nacional, Mex, 74; mem, Bd Int Orgns & Progs, Nat Acad Sci, 74-76; proj head, Inst Elec Electronics, Algeria, 76-78. *Mem:* Fel AAAS; Am Phys Soc; Am Asn Physics Teachers. *Res:* Absolute intensity of x-ray radiation; x-ray optics and microscopy; x-ray optical images; holography; science and environmental education; instrumentation for x-ray astronomy. *Mailing Add:* 58 Greenbrae Boardwalk Greenbrae CA 94904. *Fax:* 415-461-2082; *E-Mail:* baezav@aol.com

BAEZ, SILVIO, PHYSIOLOGY. *Current Pos:* assoc prof, 61-69, PROF ANESTHESIOL, ALBERT EINSTEIN COL MED, 69- *Personal Data:* b July 6, 15; US citizen; m 50; c 3. *Educ:* Nat Univ Paraguay, BS, 35, MD, 42. *Prof Exp:* Res assoc, Cornell Univ, 48-52, asst prof, 52-58; asst prof anesthesiol, NY Univ, 58-61. *Concurrent Pos:* Fel physiol, Int Training Admin, Cornell Univ, 44, res fel med, Med Col, 45-48; hon prof, Univ Montevideo, 68. *Mem:* AAAS; Am Heart Asn; Am Physiol Soc; Harvey Soc; NY Acad Sci. *Res:* Peripheral vascular physiology; shock; hypertension; adaptation; anesthesiology. *Mailing Add:* Albert Einstein Col Med 1300 Morris Park Ave Bronx NY 10461

BAG, JNANANKUR, MOLECULAR BIOLOGY, BIOCHEMISTRY. *Current Pos:* assoc prof, 85-93, PROF MOLECULAR BIOL & GENETICS, UNIV GUELPH, 93- *Personal Data:* b Calcutta, India, Oct 17, 47; m 74, Bishnapriya Lahiry; c Kheya & Diya. *Educ:* Univ Calcutta, India, PhD(biochem), 73. *Prof Exp:* Asst prof, Mem Univ Nfld, 81-85. *Mem:* Am Soc Cell Biol; Can Biochem Soc; Can Cell Biol Soc. *Res:* Regulation of gene expression in muscle cells; post-transcriptional control of gene expression; use of antisense technology to block specific gene expression. *Mailing Add:* Dept Molecular Biol & Genetics Univ Guelph Guelph ON N1G 2W1 Can. *Fax:* 519-837-2075

BAGASRA, OMAR, CELLULAR & CLINICAL IMMUNOLOGY, IMMUNOPATHOLOGY. *Current Pos:* DIR, MOLECULAR RETRO-VIROL, DIV INFECTIOUS DIS, THOMAS JEFFERSON UNIV, 91- *Personal Data:* b Bagasra, India, Oct 9, 48; US citizen; c Alexander & Anisah. *Educ:* Karachi Univ, Pakistan, BSc, 68, MSc, 70; Univ Louisville, Ky, PhD(microbiol & immunol), 79; Autonomous City Univ, Juarez, Mex, MD, 85. *Prof Exp:* Chief biochemist, Sind Flour Mills Co, Karachi, Pakistan, 68-72; med technologist, Clark Co Mem Hosp, Jeffersonville, Ind, 74-79; teaching fel, dept clin microbiol, Div Infectious Dis, Albany Med Col, NY, 80; sr instr & dir, Treponemal Res Sect, Dept Med, Hahnemann Med Col, 80-82, from asst prof to assoc prof, Dept Pathol & Lab Med, 86-87. *Concurrent Pos:* Grad student asst scholar, dept microbiol & immunol, Sch Med, Univ Louisville, 76-79; instrnl grant, Hahnemann Univ, 81; Am Cancer Soc grant, 82-83; adj asst prof pediat & immunol, St Christopher's Hosp & Sch Med, Temple Univ, Philadelphia, 85- *Mem:* Am Asn Immunologists; AAAS; fel Sigma Xi; Am Asn Immunol. *Res:* Immunobiology of syphilitic hamsters; immunobiology of congenital syphilis in Syrian hamsters; immunobiology of experimental alcoholism in rat model; in vitro cloning of tumors in soft agarose and its use in chemotherapy; preparation of monoclonal antibodies to various tumor and cellular antigens; effect of Cis-platinum, cyclophosphamide and irradiation on the immune system; preparation of HIV-1 neuratizers as a possible alternate to vaccine; natural immunity against HIV-1; discoverer of molecular immunity against HIV-1/retroviruses. *Mailing Add:* Dept Med Thomas Jefferson Univ 1020 Locust St 329 JAH Philadelphia PA 19107

BAGBY, FREDERICK L(AIR), AEROSPACE & MECHANICAL ENGINEERING. *Current Pos:* res engr, 46-48, asst div chief, 48-55, div chief, 55-60, assoc mgr, mech eng dept, 60-66, mgr, 66-70, asst dir, Columbus Div, 70-76, dir, Advan Concepts Lab, 76-78, SR PROG MGR, BATTELLE MEM INST, 78- *Personal Data:* b Salt Lake City, Utah, Aug 2, 20; m 43; c 3. *Educ:* Univ Utah, BS, 42. *Prof Exp:* Prod design engr, Curtis-Wright Corp, Columbus, 42-46. *Mem:* AAAS; Am Soc Mech Engrs; Am Inst Aeronaut & Astronaut; Sigma Xi. *Res:* Aeronautical sciences; astronautics; fluid mechanics; combat and tactical vehicle engineering; thermodynamics; high temperature technology; propulsion technology; combustion physics; aircraft and missile engineering; military weapons technology; inter and multi disicplinary program management; applications of technology to contemporary social problems. *Mailing Add:* 1714 Church View Lane Columbus OH 43220

BAGBY, GREGORY JOHN, METABOLIC REGULATION DURING INFECTIONS. *Current Pos:* PROF PHYSIOL, LA STATE UNIV MED CTR, 75- *Educ:* Wash State Univ, PhD(phys educ), 76. *Mem:* Am Physiol Soc; Am Col Sports Med; Shock Soc; Am Heart Asn; Endotoxin Soc. *Res:* Regulation of carbohydrate/lipid metabolism during infection by macrophage derived cytokines and its impart on host defense. *Mailing Add:* Physiol Dept La State Univ Med Ctr 1901 Perdido St New Orleans LA 70112-1394

BAGBY, GROVER CARLTON, HEMATOLOGY, ONCOLOGY. *Current Pos:* Resident med, Ore Health Sci Univ, 70-72, fel hematol, 74-76, instr, 75-76, from asst prof to assoc prof, 76-79, PROF MED & MED GENETICS & HEAD, DIV HEMAT & ONCOL, ORE HEALTH SCI UNIV, 85-, DIR, ORE CANCER CTR, 91- *Personal Data:* b Summit, NJ, July 15, 42; m 67, Susan Pound; c 2. *Educ:* Pomona Col, BS, 64; Baylor Col Med, MD, 68. *Honors & Awards:* Med Res Found Discovery Award; Kendall Award. *Concurrent Pos:* Prin investr, Vet Admin, 76-81, 82-85 & NIH, 84-87; vis prof, Good Samaritan & St Joseph's Hosp, Phoenix, 78; dir res, E E Osgood Leukemia Ctr, 79-; clin investr, Vet Admin Med Ctr, 80-83; mem, Hemat Study Sect, NIH, 84-88 & 90-94, chmn, 88. *Mem:* Am Soc Clin Invest; fel Am Col Physicians; Am Soc Hematol; Int Soc Exp Hematol; Am Soc Clin Oncol; Am Asn Cancer Res. *Res:* Cellular and molecular regulation of growth and differentiation of hematopoietic cells in normal humans and in patients with leukemia, preleukemia, and other disorders of marrow function including Fanconi anemia. *Mailing Add:* Vet Admin Med Ctr 3710 SW US Vet Hosp Rd Portland OR 97201

BAGBY, JOHN R, JR, PUBLIC HEALTH, BIOLOGY. *Current Pos:* RETIRED. *Personal Data:* b Aurora, Mo, Mar 3, 19; m 43, Billie Hudson; c Caroline, John & Thomas. *Educ:* Univ Ark, BS, 54, MS, 55; Emory Univ, PhD(parasitol), 62. *Honors & Awards:* Walter F Snyder Award, Environ Health, 83. *Prof Exp:* Malaria control aid, USPHS, 46-51, info officer, Econ Stabilization Agency, 51-53, vector control specialist, 55-59, asst to chief, Tech Br, 59-62, asst chief, Tech Br, 62-63 & 64-66, dep chief, Tech Br, 63-64, dept dir, Nat Commun Dis Ctr, 66-69; dir, Inst Environ Health & head, Dept Microbiol, Colo State Univ, 69-84; dir, Div Environ Health & Epidemiol, Mo Dept Health, 84-88, dir, 89-93. *Concurrent Pos:* Consult, NASA, Jet Propulsion Lab & Am Inst Biol Sci; mem, Armed Forces Epidemiol Bd; chmn, Comt Energy Related Epidemiol Res. *Mem:* NY Acad Sci; Nat Environ Health Asn; Am Soc Trop Med & Hyg; Sigma Xi. *Res:* Parasitology; entomology; bacteriology; serology; control of vectors; reservoirs; etiologic agents of communicable diseases; health effects of dioxin; cancer epidemiology. *Mailing Add:* 5315 Foxfire Lane Lohman MO 65053

BAGBY, MARVIN ORVILLE, ORGANIC CHEMISTRY, NATURAL PRODUCTS CHEMISTRY. *Current Pos:* Org chemist, Nat Ctr Agr Utilization Res, Agr Res Serv, USDA, 57-75, res leader, 75-81, mgr, Northern Agr Energy Ctr, 81-85, RES LEADER, OIL CHEM RES, USDA, 85- *Personal Data:* b Macomb, Ill, Sept 27, 32; m 57, Mary J Jennings; c Gary L & Gordon E. *Educ:* Western Ill Univ, BS & MS, 57. *Hon Degrees:* LHD, Western Ill Univ, 92. *Honors & Awards:* Cert Merit, Am Paper Indust, 88; ARS Technol Transfer Award, 90; Domestic Mkt Award, Am Soybean Asn, 90; Fed Lab Consortium Award, 91; Distinguished Serv Award, USDA, 92. *Concurrent Pos:* Tech adv, technologies fiber uses, Sci & Educ Admin,

USDA, 75-81, technologies indust uses plant & animal prods (hydrocarbon plants), 80-81, Great Lakes Gov Regional Biomed Energy, 84-; team leader utilization fibrous mat, Bilateral Res & Educ Proj, Am Chem Soc/Egyptian Nat Res Ctr, 77; mem, Secy Agr Task Force Critical Mat, 83-85; res assoc grant, 90. *Mem:* AAAS; Am Chem Soc; Am Oil Chem Soc; Tech Asn Pulp & Paper Indust; NY Acad Sci; Am Soc Agr Eng. *Res:* Natural products; lipids, especially isolation, characterization, and reactions of fatty acids and sugars; annual plants for pulp and paper raw materials; plant biomass for energy and strategic materials; hydrocarbon plants; vegetable oils as alternative fuels; industrial materials from soybean oil and other seed oils; alternative industrial crops. *Mailing Add:* 209 S Louisiana Morton IL 61550-2705. *Fax:* 309-681-6686

BAGBY, ROLAND MOHLER, IMMUNOFLUORESCENCE, THREE DIMENSIONAL RECONSTRUCTION. *Current Pos:* PROF PHYSIOL, UNIV TENN, 66- *Educ:* Univ Ill, Urbana, PhD(physiol & biophys), 64. *Mailing Add:* Dept Biochem Univ Tenn Knoxville TN 37996-0840

BAGCHI, AMITABHA, SOLID STATE PHYSICS, SURFACE PHYSICS. *Current Pos:* ASST PROF, DEPT MECH ENG, CLEMSON UNIV, 90- *Personal Data:* b Calcutta, India, June 12, 45; m 74. *Educ:* Calcutta Univ, BSc, 64; Univ Calif, San Diego, MS, 67, PhD(physics), 70. *Prof Exp:* Res assoc physics, Univ Ill, Urbana, 70-71; res assoc surface physics, James Franck Inst, Univ Chicago, 71-73; res fel physics, Battelle Mem Inst, Columbus, Ohio, 73-74; asst prof physics, Univ Md, 74-80; dept physics, Zerox Corp, 80-; at AT&T Bell Labs. *Mem:* Am Phys Soc; Am Vacuum Soc. *Res:* Electronic properties of metal surfaces including chemisorption and photoemission and optical reflectance from clean and adsorbate-covered surfaces; excitation spectrum of He3-He4 mixtures. *Mailing Add:* 2G-230 AT&T Bell Labs Crawfords Corner Rd Holmdel NJ 07733

BAGCHI, MIHIR, CELL BIOLOGY, OPHTHALMOLOGY. *Current Pos:* asst prof, 75-81, ASSOC PROF ANAT, SCH MED, WAYNE STATE UNIV, 81- *Personal Data:* b Ranchi, India, Nov 28, 38; m 72, Champa Sanyal; c Atasi, Aditi & Ankoor. *Educ:* Univ Bihar, BS, 59; Univ Ranchi, MS, 62; Univ Vt, PhD(zool), 69. *Prof Exp:* Res asst biol, Ciba Res Ctr, India, 63-65; res assoc, Oakland Univ, 63-75. *Concurrent Pos:* NIH spec fel, 73-75; NIH grants, 76-91. *Mem:* Am Soc Cell Biol; Sigma Xi; Am Asn Anatomists; Asn Res Vision & Ophthal. *Res:* Biochemistry and morphology of mammalian lens in culture. *Mailing Add:* Dept Anat Wayne State Univ Sch Med 540 E Carfield Ave Detroit MI 48201

BAGCHI, PRANAB, COLLOID CHEMISTRY, SURFACE CHEMISTRY. *Current Pos:* Sr res chemist, 70-80, RES ASSOC, EASTMAN KODAK CO, 80- *Personal Data:* b Calcutta, India, Jan 14, 46. *Educ:* Jadavpur Univ, India, BSc, 65; Univ Southern Calif, PhD(phys chem), 70. *Mem:* Am Chem Soc; AAAS; NY Acad Sci; The Chem Soc; Fedn Am Scientists. *Res:* Investigation of the mechanism of the stability of lyophobic dispersions in nonaqueous media and in the presence of nonionic surfactants; long chain nonionic molecules and polymeric nonionic molecules, both experiment and theory considered; surface colloidal properties and stability of silver salts in nonaqueous media; interfacial behavior of model polymer colloids; interactions of immunoproteins at latex/water interface; rheology of concentrated dispersions. *Mailing Add:* Res Lab Eastman Kodak Co Rochester NY 14650. *Fax:* 716-872-5748; *E-Mail:* bagchip@kodak.com, bgchip@vivanet.com

BAGCHI, SAKTI PRASAD, NEUROSCIENCE, PHARMACOLOGY. *Current Pos:* SR RES SCIENTIST, NY STATE DEPT MENT HYG, NATHAN KLINE INST, 73- *Personal Data:* b Tatanagar, India, Dec 26, 31; US citizen; m 59, Preeti; c Arnab K & Kunal S. *Educ:* Univ Calcutta, BS, 51, MS, 54, PhD(biochem), 59. *Prof Exp:* Res assoc biochem, Okla State Univ, 59-60; jr res biochemist, Sch Med, Univ Calif, San Francisco, 60-62; res assoc, Kinsmen Lab of Neurol Dis, Univ BC, 63-66; res biochemist, Psychiat Res Unit, Dept Pub Health, Univ Hosp, 66-73. *Mem:* AAAS; Int Soc Neurochem; Int Brain Res Orgn; Am Soc Neurochem; Soc Neurosci. *Res:* Neuropharmacology; psychotropic drug action; neurological diseases; neurotoxicology. *Mailing Add:* 51 Minuteman Circle Orangeburg NY 10962. *Fax:* 914-365-6107; *E-Mail:* bagchi@nki

BAGDASARIAN, ANDRANIK, BIOCHEMISTRY. *Current Pos:* res mgr, protein res labs, 80-83, ASSOC DIR RES, HYLAND THERAP LABS, 84- *Personal Data:* b Tehran, Iran, Dec 5, 35; m 69; c 3. *Educ:* Univ Tehran, BS, 60, DrPharm, 61; Univ Louisville, PhD(biochem), 67. *Prof Exp:* Fel protein chem, Calif Inst Technol, 67-68; fel enzymol, Syntex Res, Palo Alto, 68-70; res fel plasma proteases, Mass Gen Hosp, Harvard Med Sch, 70-73; res assoc plasma proteases, Univ Pa, 73-75, res asst prof biochem, dept med, 75-78; sr res scientist, Hyland Div, Travenol Labs, Inc, 78-80. *Concurrent Pos:* NIH award studies prekallikrein activation, 71; Nat Cancer Inst & Am Cancer Soc grant kinin pathway normal & malignant tissue, 75. *Mem:* Sigma Xi; Am Chem Soc; Am Soc Biol Chemists. *Res:* Purification and characterization of proteases and protease inhibitors involved in the kallikrein-kinin, coagulation and fibrinolysis systems of human plasma, platelets and normal and malignant tissue; hemoglobin-structure/function relationship; stroma free hemoglobin as a blood substitute. *Mailing Add:* Res & Develop Dept Alpha Therapeut Corp 5555 Valley Blvd Los Angeles CA 90032-3548

BAGDON, ROBERT EDWARD, pharmacology, for more information see previous edition

BAGDON, WALTER JOSEPH, TOXICOLOGY, PHARMACOLOGY. *Current Pos:* Sr res toxicologist, 64-68, res fel, 68-74, sr res fel, 74-79, dir, toxicol & path, 79-86, SR INVESTR, MERCK INST THERAPEUT RES, 86- *Personal Data:* b Camden, NJ, Apr 22, 38; m 62, Jeanette Freeman; c Theresa, Marianne & Lara. *Educ:* Philadelphia Col Pharm, BS, 59; Temple Univ, MS, 61, PhD(pharmacol), 64. *Mem:* AAAS; Soc Toxicol; Am Pharmaceut Asn; Sigma Xi; Dipl Am Bd Toxicol. *Res:* Safety evaluation of current and potential therpeutic agents; evaluation of clinical tests concerning normal body function of animals. *Mailing Add:* Merck Inst Therapeut Res West Point PA 19486. *Fax:* 215-652-7758

BAGG, THOMAS CAMPBELL, information systems, photo optical; deceased, see previous edition for last biography

BAGGENSTOSS, ARCHIE HERBERT, PATHOLOGY. *Current Pos:* Consult path anat, 38-52, head sect Exp & Anat Path, 55-68, prof path, 52-75, EMER PROF PATH, MAYO GRAD SCH MED, UNIV MINN, 75-, SR CONSULT, MAYO CLIN, 68- *Personal Data:* b Richardton, NDak, Apr 13, 08; m 34; c 3. *Educ:* Univ NDak, AB, 30, BS, 31; Univ Cincinnati, BM, 33, MD, 34; Univ Minn, MS, 38. *Mem:* Fel AMA; fel Am Soc Clin Path; Am Asn Path & Bact; Am Gastroenterol Asn; Am Asn Study Liver Dis (pres, 68-69). *Res:* Pathologic anatomy; liver; pancreas; gastrointestinal tract. *Mailing Add:* 211 NW Second St Rochester MN 55901-2485

BAGGERLY, LEO L, PHYSICS. *Current Pos:* RETIRED. *Personal Data:* b Wichita, Kans, Mar 13, 28; m 66; c 5. *Educ:* Calif Inst Technol, BS, 51, MS, 52, PhD(physics), 56. *Prof Exp:* Sr res engr, Jet Propulsion Lab, Calif, 55-56; from asst prof to prof, Tex Christian Univ, 59-69; assoc prog dir, NSF, 69, prog dir, 70-71; vis fel, Cornell Univ, 71-72; prof physics, Calif State Col, Bakersfield, 72-75; vis prof physics, Pomona Col, 75-76; vis prof, Harvey Mudd Col, 76-77; sr consult, Milco Int, 76-77; sr mem tech staff, TRW Inc, 77-93. *Concurrent Pos:* Fulbright lectr physics, Univ Ceylon, 56-59; sr scientist, Res Ctr Div, Ling-Temco-Vought Corp, 63-64. *Mem:* AAAS; Am Asn Physics Teachers; Sigma Xi. *Res:* Electromagnetic properties of materials; science education; radiation physics. *Mailing Add:* 550 Orpheus Ave Leucadia CA 92024-2660. *E-Mail:* 74144.2134@compuserve.com

BAGGEROER, ARTHUR B, MARINE ENGINEERING. *Current Pos:* From asst prof to assoc prof, 68-80, PROF, DEPT OCEAN & ELEC ENG, MASS INST TECHNOL, 80-, FORD PROF ENG, 91- *Personal Data:* b Weymouth, Mass, June 9, 42; c 4. *Educ:* Purdue Univ, BSEE, 63; Mass Inst Technol, SM, 65, DSc, 68. *Concurrent Pos:* Consult, Chief Naval Res, NATO Supreme Allied Comdr Atlantic, asst secy, War Ctr, Italy, 77; chief scientist, Fram II & Fram IV Ice Sta, Off Naval Res, 80, 82, Marginal Ice Zone Exp, 83 & 84, Cearex Exp, 88-89, RV Cory Chouest, 92; mem, Panel Navy Long Range, Deep Ocean Technol, Nat Res Coun, 81-82, Naval & Ocean Studies Bd, 90, 92 & 93; dir, Woods Hole Joint Prog Oceanog & Oceanog Eng, 83-88; Green scholar, Scripps Inst Oceanog, Inst Geophysics & Planetary Sci, 90; consult, Navy Ocean Systs Ctr, San Diego, Mass Inst Technol Lincoln Lab, Lexington, Avco, Wilmington, Atlantic Aerospace Electronics, Waltham. *Mem:* Nat Acad Eng; fel Inst Elec & Electronics Engrs; fel Acoust Soc Am; Am Geophys Union; Sigma Xi; Am Inst Physics. *Mailing Add:* Mass Inst Technol Rm 5-204 Cambridge MA 02139

BAGGETT, BILLY, BIOCHEMICAL ENDOCRINOLOGY. *Current Pos:* chmn dept, 69-78, PROF BIOCHEM, MED UNIV SC, 69-, PROF OBSTET & GYNEC, 80- *Personal Data:* b Oxford, Miss, Oct 23, 28; m 90, Elvira Castro; c Sallie (Moore), William, Mary, Teresa & H Lane. *Educ:* Univ Miss, BA, 47; St Louis Univ, PhD(biochem), 52. *Prof Exp:* Instr biochem, Harvard Med Sch, 52-57; asst, Mass Gen Hosp, 52-57; from asst prof to prof pharmacol & biochem, Univ NC, Chapel Hill, 57-69. *Concurrent Pos:* USPHS sr res fel, Univ NC, Chapel Hill, 57-62; consult, Res Triangle Inst, 66-71, NIH, 80-82. *Mem:* AAAS; Endocrine Soc; Am Soc Biol Chemists; Am Chem Soc; Am Asn Cancer Res; Soc Study Reproduction; Am Fertility Soc. *Res:* Metabolism and actions of steroid hormones. *Mailing Add:* Dept Obstet & Gynecol Med Univ SC 171 Ashley Ave Charleston SC 29425. *Fax:* 803-792-0533; *E-Mail:* baggettb@musc.edu

BAGGETT, JAMES RONALD, HORTICULTURE. *Current Pos:* From asst prof to assoc prof, 56-71, PROF HORT, ORE STATE UNIV, 71- *Personal Data:* b Boise, Idaho, Apr 24, 28; m 51; c 2. *Educ:* Univ Idaho, BS, 52; Ore State Col, PhD(hort), 56. *Mem:* Am Soc Hort Sci. *Res:* Genetics and breeding of disease resistance in vegetables. *Mailing Add:* Hort Dept Ore State Univ 4017 Agr Life Sci Corvallis OR 97331-7304

BAGGETT, LAWRENCE W, MATHEMATICS. *Current Pos:* From asst prof to assoc prof, 66-77, dept chmn, 84-87, PROF MATH, UNIV COLO, BOULDER, 77- *Personal Data:* b Morehead, Miss, Mar 3, 39; m 79; c 2. *Educ:* Davidson Col, BS, 60; Univ Wash, Seattle, PhD(math), 66. *Concurrent Pos:* NSF grant, 67-88. *Mem:* Am Math Soc. *Res:* Topological groups and their representations; ergodic theory. *Mailing Add:* Dept Math Univ Colo PO Box 395 Boulder CO 80309-0395

BAGGETT, LESTER MARCHANT, NUCLEAR PHYSICS, HYDRODYNAMICS. *Current Pos:* RETIRED. *Personal Data:* b Oakland, Calif, Nov 28, 20; m 51; c 2. *Educ:* Rhodes Col, BA, 43; Ga Inst Technol, MS, 48; Rice Univ, PhD(physics), 51. *Prof Exp:* Assoc div leader, Los Alamos Sci Lab, 51-84. *Mem:* Am Phys Soc. *Res:* Energy levels of light nuclei. *Mailing Add:* 996 Nambe Pl Los Alamos NM 87544

BAGGETT, NEIL VANCE, PHYSICS. *Current Pos:* PHYSICIST DIRECTORATE, SUPER CONDUCTING SUPER COLLIDER LAB, 89- *Personal Data:* b DeRidder, La, Aug 12, 38. *Educ:* Tulane Univ, BS, 60; Univ Md, PhD(physics), 69. *Prof Exp:* Physicist heat transfer & nuclear physics, Nat Bur Stand, 60-66; res assoc high energy physics, Inst Hochenergiephysik, Univ Heidelberg, 69-71; res asst high energy physics, Imp Col, London, 71-73; proj assoc high energy physics, Purdue Univ, 73-77; physicist, Div High Energy Physics, US Dept Energy, 77-80, physicist & spec asst to assoc dir high energy physics, 80-89. *Mem:* Am Phys Soc; AAAS. *Res:* Experimental high energy physics; science communications; scientific computing; weak decays; neutrino interactions; hadronic interactions. *Mailing Add:* 1703 Creekhaven Dr Duncanville TX 75137. *E-Mail:* baggett@sscvx1

BAGGI, DENIS LOUIS, COMPUTER SCIENCE, ELECTRICAL ENGINEERING. *Current Pos:* AT DEPT CENT RES & COMPUT SCI, METTLER INSTRUMENTE AG, 88- *Personal Data:* b Zurich, Switz, Feb 10, 45; c 2. *Educ:* Swiss Fed Inst Technol, Dipl Ing elec eng, 69; Polytech Inst, New York, MS, 71; Univ Calif, Berkeley, PhD(elec eng, comput sci), 74. *Prof Exp:* Instr comput sci, Univ Calif, Berkeley, 73-74; asst prof elec eng & comput sci, Polytech Inst, New York, 74-76; consult speech synthesis, Bell Tel Labs, Murray Hill, 75-77; asst prof comput sci, Queens Col NY, 87- *Concurrent Pos:* Actg res prof, USAF, Rome, NY, 77-80; vpres, XI Comput Corp, Irvine, Calif; pres, Ventur Tech, SA, Lupano, Switz; vis prof, Univ Calif, Berkeley, 85 & 88. *Mem:* Inst Elec & Electronics Engrs; Asn Comp Mach; Swiss Soc Comp Music. *Res:* Software engineering and reliability; artificial intelligence applied to music composition; modeling of social systems; speech synthesis; expert systems. *Mailing Add:* Xi Comput Corp 980 Negocio San Clemente CA 92672

BAGGOT, J DESMOND, CLINICAL PHARMACOKINETICS, ANTIMICROBIOL THERAPY. *Current Pos:* DEPT PRE-CLIN VET STUDIES, UNIV ZIMBABWE, 96- *Personal Data:* b Ireland, Oct 11, 39; m 65; c 2. *Educ:* Nat Univ Ireland, Dublin, BSc, 62; Vet Col Ireland, Dublin, 66; Nat Univ Ireland, Dublin, MVM, 68; Ohio State Univ, PhD(biochem pharmacol), 71, DSc, 80. *Prof Exp:* Prof clin pharmacol & chmn vet pharmacol & toxicol, Univ Calif, Davis, 81-86, res prof clin pharmacol, 86-; dir, Irish Equine Ctr, Johnstown, Co Koldare, Ireland, 86-96. *Concurrent Pos:* Vet consult, Alza Corp, Palo Alto, Calif, 84- *Mem:* Am Soc Pharmacol & Exp Therapeut; Controlled Release Soc; fel Am Col Clin Pharmacol; Europ Asn Vet Pharmacol & Toxicol. *Res:* Drug bioavailability and disposition kinetics in animals and humans; influence of disease conditions on drug disposition and dosage; species variations in drug response. *Mailing Add:* Dept Pre-Clin Vet Studies Univ Zimbabwe PO Box MP167 Mt Pleasant Harare Zimbabwe

BAGGOTT, JAMES PATRICK, BIOCHEMISTRY. *Current Pos:* Sr instr, Hahnemann Univ, 68-71, asst prof, 71-78, asst dean student affairs, 78-84, ASSOC PROF BIOCHEM, HAHNEMANN UNIV SCH MED, 78- *Personal Data:* b Milwaukee, Wis, Jan 19, 41; m 66; c 7. *Educ:* Marquette Univ, BS, 62; Johns Hopkins Univ, PhD(biochem), 66. *Concurrent Pos:* Fel biol chem, Univ Utah, 66-68. *Mem:* Am Chem Soc. *Res:* Medical education; development and evaluation of computer based learning. *Mailing Add:* Dept Biol Chem Allegheny Univ Health Sci Broad & Vine St Philadelphia PA 19102-1192

BAGINSKI, F(RANK) C(HARLES), CHEMICAL ENGINEERING. *Current Pos:* RETIRED. *Personal Data:* b Holyoke, Mass, Oct 6, 23; m 51; c 6. *Educ:* Worcester Polytech Inst, BS, 44; Yale Univ, DEng, 52. *Prof Exp:* Res chem engr, Monsanto Chem Co, 46-47; lab asst units oper lab, Yale Univ, 48-49; res engr, E I du Pont de Nemours & Co Inc, 51-53, res supvr polymer mfg, 53-56, res supvr cellophane mfg, 56-68, from plant supt polyethylene film mfg res & develop to tech supt, Spruance Film Plant, 58-66, prod mgr polyolefin films mfg, 66-68, mfg supt, 68-71, tedlar plant supt, Yerkes Plant, 71-84. *Mem:* AAAS; Am Chem Soc. *Res:* Research and development in films manufacturing in polyvinyl fluoride, cellophane and polyethylene films. *Mailing Add:* 123 Meadow View Lane Williamsville NY 14221

BAGLEY, BRIAN G, ELECTRONIC & PHOTONIC MATERIALS SCIENCE, THIN FILMS. *Current Pos:* NEG ENDOWED CHAIR & PROF PHYSICS, UNIV TOLEDO, 91-; DIR EITEL INST, 91- *Personal Data:* b Racine, Wis, Nov 20, 34; div; c Brian J, James D & Kristin M. *Educ:* Univ Wis-Madison, BS, 58, MS, 59; Harvard Univ, AM, 64, PhD(appl physics), 68. *Prof Exp:* Mem res staff, Univ Wis, 59-60; mem tech staff, Bell Labs, Murray Hill, NJ, 67-83, Bell Commun Res, Red Bank, NJ, 84-91. *Mem:* Am Phys Soc; Mat Res Soc; Sigma Xi. *Res:* Thin films and coatings; glasses for photonic applications; integrated optics; flat panel displays. *Mailing Add:* Dept Physics & Astron Univ Toledo 2801 W Bancroft St Toledo OH 43606-3390. *Fax:* 419-530-2723; *E-Mail:* bgb@physics.utoledo.edu

BAGLEY, CLYDE PATTISON, ANIMAL SCIENCE & NUTRITION, AGRONOMY. *Current Pos:* assoc prof, 80-88, RESIDENT DIR ANIMAL SCI, ROSEPINE RES STA, LA STATE UNIV, 80-; PROF, 80-; EXT SPECIALIST & HEAD, NMISS RES & EXT CTR, 89- *Personal Data:* b Shreveport, La, Dec 19, 51; m 75; c 2. *Educ:* La State Univ, BS, 72, MS, 75; Va Tech Univ, PhD(animal sci), 78. *Honors & Awards:* Merit Award, Am Forage & Grassland Coun. *Prof Exp:* Res asst animal sci, La State Univ, 74-75; asst prof, WLa Exp Sta, 78-80. *Mem:* Am Soc Animal Sci; Am Forage & Grassland Coun; Am Soc Agron; Sigma Xi; Coun Agr Sci Technol; Soc Range Mgt. *Res:* Beef cattle production using existing forage resources; evaluation of systems to optimize beef cattle performance, using high quality forages. *Mailing Add:* NMiss Res & EXt Ctr PO Box 456 Verona MS 38879. *Fax:* 601-566-2257

BAGLEY, GEORGE EVERETT, POLYMER CHEMISTRY. *Current Pos:* Res chemist, Armstrong World Industs, Inc, 58-69, res suprv, 69-70, sr res scientist, 70-77, res assoc, 77-89, SR PRIN SCIENTIST, ARMSTRONG WORLD INDUSTS, INC, 90- *Personal Data:* b Corry, Pa, Feb 14, 33; m 56, Gail Wooster; c Daniel M, Deborah L (Sylvia), Douglas E & Jonathan D. *Educ:* Houghton Col, BS, 54; Univ Pa, PhD(phys chem), 59. *Mem:* Am Chem Soc; Soc Plastics Engrs; Soc Photog Scientists & Engrs; Rad Tech Int; Oil & Color Chemists Asn; Am Soc Testing & Mat. *Res:* Inorganic synthesis and inorganic polymers; polyvinyl chloride technology; radiation curable polymers; elastomers. *Mailing Add:* 2425 Mayfair Dr Lancaster PA 17603-4135. *Fax:* 717-396-5006

BAGLEY, JAY M(ERRILL), HYDRAULIC ENGINEERING. *Current Pos:* asst prof civil & irrig eng, Utah State Univ, 54-60, assoc prof, Dept Civil Eng & Utah Water Res Lab, 60-66, prof, Dept Civil Eng & Dir Utah Water Res Lab, 66-76, PROF CIVIL & ENVIRON ENG, UTAH STATE UNIV, 78- *Personal Data:* b Koosharem, Utah, Oct 14, 25; m 47; c 5. *Educ:* Utah State Univ, BS, 52, MS, 53; Stanford Univ, PhD(hydraul eng), 64. *Prof Exp:* Engr, Irrig Equip Co, Ore & Colo, 52-53; field engr, Farm Improv Co, 53-54; gen mgr, West Irrig Co, 54; vis scientist, Inst Water Resources, CEngrs, Ft Belvoir, Va, 76-78. *Concurrent Pos:* Consult, Sprinkler Irrig Assocs, 55, Plantacoes do Mucoso, Port WAfrica, 55, Foreign Agr Serv, 56, Gunnison Irrig Co, 57, Resources Co, 64, United Park City Mines Co, Atlantic Refining Co, Anaconda Co, Ralph M Parsons Co, US Agency Int Develop, Nat Oceanic & Atmospheric Admin, US Dept Agr & var assignments to Africa, Vietnam & China. *Mem:* Am Soc Civil Engrs; Nat Soc Prof Engrs; Int Asn Sci Hydrol; Am Geophys Union; Sigma Xi. *Res:* Water resource development; irrigation and drainage; hydrology; fluid mechanics; watershed and river basin modeling; water resources planning methodology; hydrologic processes; extending utility of water supplies; legal and institutional impediments to effective water use. *Mailing Add:* Utah Water Res Lab Utah State Univ Logan UT 84322-8200

BAGLEY, JOHN D(ANIEL), COMPUTER SCIENCES. *Current Pos:* SUPVR SYSTS ENG, INDIAN HILL LAB, BELL TEL LABS, 77- *Personal Data:* b Chicago, Ill, Oct 2, 35; m 58; c 5. *Educ:* Univ Notre Dame, BSEE, 57; Univ Ill, Urbana-Champaign, MS, 58; Univ Mich, AM, 63, PhD(commun sci), 67. *Prof Exp:* Mem staff, Systs Develop Div, IBM Corp, 59, Advan Systs Develop Div, 59-61 & 65-67 & Res Div, NY, 67-76, adv programmer, Gen Systs, 76-77. *Mem:* Inst Elec & Electronics Engrs; Asn Comput Mach. *Res:* Adaptive systems; simulation of biological systems; digital computer operating system and architecture; voice and graphical input to digital computers; digital computer simulation of continuous systems; distributed computer systems; computer networking; unix operating system. *Mailing Add:* AT&T Bell Labs 2000 N Naperville Rd Naperville IL 60566

BAGLEY, ROBERT WALLER, MATHEMATICS. *Current Pos:* assoc prof, 63-64, PROF MATH, UNIV MIAMI, 64- *Personal Data:* b Wesson, Miss, Apr 14, 21; m 44; c 3. *Educ:* Univ Mich, BS, 47; Tulane Univ, MS, 49; Univ Fla, PhD(math), 54. *Prof Exp:* Asst prof math, Univ Ky, 54-55; assoc res scientist, Lockheed Missile Systs, 55-58; prof math, Miss Southern Univ, 58-60 & Univ Ala, 60-63. *Concurrent Pos:* Consult, Grad Sch Bus, Stanford Univ, 57. *Mem:* Am Math Soc; Math Asn Am. *Res:* Topological groups. *Mailing Add:* 14451 SW 146th Pl Miami FL 33186

BAGLI, JEHAN FRAMROZ, PHARMACEUTICAL & MEDICINAL CHEMISTRY. *Current Pos:* sr res scientist, 60-69, sr res adv, 69-79, assoc dir chem, 79-95, DISTINGUISHED RES FEL, WYETH-AYERST RES, 95- *Personal Data:* b Bombay, India, Sept 25, 28; m 56, Freny Marshall; c Darius B & Shiraz B. *Educ:* Univ Bombay, BSc, 49 & 51; Univ London, PhD(pharmaceut chem), 55. *Prof Exp:* Fel, Johns Hopkins Univ, 55-59; Nat Res Coun Can fel, Laval Univ, 59-60. *Mem:* Am Chem Soc; Royal Soc Chem; fel Can Inst Chem. *Res:* Elucidation of structure and stereochemistry of natural products; mechanism of the organic reactions and the biogenesis of the sterolds and terpenoids; mechanism and pharmacological profile of drug molecules. *Mailing Add:* Chem Res Dept Wyeth Ayerst Res 61 Sayre Dr Princeton NJ 08540

BAGLIN, JOHN EDWARD ERIC, RADIATION EFFECTS IN SOLIDS, THIN FILM PHYSICS. *Current Pos:* res staff mem, T J Watson Res Ctr, IBM, 72-87, mgr mat physics, 88-94, RES STAFF MEM, IBM ALMADEN RES CTR, 94- *Personal Data:* b Melbourne, Australia, Oct 22, 36; m 70, Coral Chesterfield. *Educ:* Univ Melbourne, Australia, BSc, 57, MSc, 59, PhD(physics), 63. *Prof Exp:* Asst prof physics, Iowa State Univ & assoc physicist, Ames Lab, US AEC, 63-65 & 70-72; res assoc, Yale Univ, 65-70. *Concurrent Pos:* Assoc ed, Mat Lett, 85-89 & J Adhes Sci Technol, 89-95; ed, J Mat Educ, 96- *Mem:* Fel Am Phys Soc; Mat Res Soc (vpres, 86-87, pres, 88); Mat Educ Coun; Am Soc Metals Int. *Res:* Ion beam modification of materials and surfaces; thin film and interface interactions; ion beam analysis; physics of adhesion. *Mailing Add:* IBM Almaden Res Ctr 650 Harry Rd, K19/D1 San Jose CA 95120. *E-Mail:* baglin@almaden.ibm.com

BAGLIN, RAYMOND EUGENE, JR, FISHERIES SCIENCE. *Personal Data:* b Hartford, Conn, Aug 26, 44; m 66; c 2. *Educ:* Univ Hartford, BA, 66; Univ Ark, MS, 68; Univ Okla, PhD(fisheries), 75. *Prof Exp:* Fishery biologist, US Army Corps Engrs, 69-71; from aquatic ecologist to sr aquatic ecologist, Off Environ Planning, NY State Pub Serv Comn, 72-74; fishery biologist, Nat Marine Fisheries Serv, US Dept Com, 74-95. *Mem:* Am Fisheries Soc; Am Inst Fishery Res Biologists. *Res:* Reproduction, migration, age and growth, and stock structure of fishes. *Mailing Add:* 86 Exeter Rd Hampton Falls NH 03844

BAGLIO, JOSEPH ANTHONY, PHYSICAL CHEMISTRY. *Current Pos:* SR ENG SPECIALIST, OSRAM SYLVANIA, 93- *Personal Data:* b New York, NY, May 16, 39; m 60, Helen Peters; c Frances (Beeber) & Christine (Williamson). *Educ:* Rutgers Univ, PhD(phys chem), 65. *Prof Exp:* Chemist, Atomic Energy Comn, 60 & David Sarnoff Res Ctr, Radio Corp Am Inc, 61; prin mem tech staff, GTE Labs Inc, 65-93. *Concurrent Pos:* Dupont teaching fel; NSF fel; NIH fel. *Mem:* Am Chem Soc; Electrochem Soc; Sigma Xi. *Res:* Development of catalysts for removal of sulfur dioxide, hydrogen sulfide and carbon sulfide compounds from plant stacks; development of amorphous and crystalline materials for magnetic bubble memory applications; precious metal replacement in materials for the communications industry; plasma chemistry, luminescent and catalytic materials research; correlation of crystal structure with solid state properties; x-ray diffraction and knudsen cell mass spectrometry; investigation of semiconductors for applications in liquid-junction solar cells; physics and chemistry of III-IV semiconductor surfaces for applications in metal insulator semiconductor field effect transistor devices; solid state chemistry of high temperature materials; thermodynamics of high temperature materials; plasma-enhanced chemical vapor deposition of diamond films, lights; chemistry of light sources. *Mailing Add:* 8 Forest Hill Dr Andover MA 01810. *Fax:* 978-750-1795; *E-Mail:* baglio@rd.sylvania.com

BAGLIONI, CORRADO, CELL BIOLOGY. *Current Pos:* prof & chmn dept, 73-75, assoc dean, Sch Health Sci, 85-88, LEADING PROF BIOL, STATE UNIV NY, ALBANY, 76- *Personal Data:* b Rome, Italy, Aug 1, 33; m 57, Tina Rangoni; c Adriano, Alessandra & Gianluca. *Educ:* Univ Rome, MD, 57. *Prof Exp:* Vis lectr biochem, Mass Inst Technol, 59-61, asst prof genetics, 61-62; Ital Nat Res Coun intern genetics, Biophys Lab, 62-66; assoc prof biol, Mass Inst Technol, 67-73. *Concurrent Pos:* Mem dir, Ital Asn Biophys & Molecular Biol, 64-66; mem, Immunol & Allergy Study Sect, NIH, 67-71; mem, Cell & Develop Biol Study Sect, Am Cancer Soc, 81-85; Rockfeller & Foggarty scholar. *Mem:* Europ Molecular Biol Orgn. *Res:* Genetic control of protein structure; action of suppressor genes in Drosophila; human abnormal hemoglobins; mechanism of assembly of hemoglobin and immunoglobulin peptide chains; genetic basis of antibody variability; regulation of histone synthesis; mechanisms of action of interferon and tumor nerosis factor. *Mailing Add:* Bi-225 State Univ NY 1400 Washington Ave Albany NY 12222. *Fax:* 518-442-4767; *E-Mail:* cb252@cmunix.albany.edu

BAGLIVO, JENNY ANTOINETTE, MATHEMATICS. *Current Pos:* Asst prof, 76-81, ASSOC PROF MATH, FAIRFIELD UNIV, 81- *Personal Data:* b New York, NY, Nov 7, 48. *Educ:* Fordham Univ, BA, 70; Syracuse Univ, MA, 72, MS, 76, PhD(math), 76. *Mem:* Am Math Soc; Math Asn Am. *Res:* Topology; transformation groups. *Mailing Add:* Dept Math Boston Col Chestnut Hill MA 02167-3806

BAGNALL, LARRY OWEN, AGRICULTURAL ENGINEERING. *Current Pos:* from asst prof to assoc prof, 69-81, PROF AGR ENG, UNIV FLA, 81- *Personal Data:* b Enumclaw, Wash, Dec 19, 35; m 58, Shirley A VonAhn; c Juanita, Mark & Edith. *Educ:* Wash State Univ, BS, 57; Cornell Univ, PhD(agr eng), 67. *Prof Exp:* Trainee, Allis-Chalmers, 57-58, eng scientist, 58-66, res engr, 66-68. *Concurrent Pos:* Long-term techn adv & prof, Univ Ctr Dschang, Cameroon, 89-92. *Mem:* Am Soc Agr Engrs; Sigma Xi; Am Soc Eng Educ. *Res:* Aquatic plant harvesting, processing, utilization; forage harvesting, processing; aquaculture; biomass energy; appropriate technology. *Mailing Add:* Dept Agr & Bio Eng Univ Fla Gainesville FL 32611-0570. *E-Mail:* gagnall@agen.ufl.edu

BAGNALL, RICHARD HERBERT, PLANT PATHOLOGY. *Current Pos:* RETIRED. *Personal Data:* b Hazel Grove, PEI, Feb 23, 23; m 52; c 4. *Educ:* Prince of Wales Col, jr col dipl, 44; McGill Univ, BSc, 46, MSc, 49; Univ Wis, PhD, 56. *Prof Exp:* Agr scientist, Can Agr Res Ctr, NB, 46, res scientist, Plant Path Lab, 46-85, res scientist plant virol, 85- *Mem:* Am Phytopath Soc; Potato Asn Am. *Res:* Epidemiology, resistance, serology of potato viruses. *Mailing Add:* Agr & Agri-Food Can Res Ctr PO Box 20280 Fredericton NB E3B 4Z7 Can

BAGNARA, JOSEPH THOMAS, EMBRYOLOGY, ENDOCRINOLOGY. *Current Pos:* from instr to prof zool, 56-64, prof biol sci & anat, 64-, dept head gen biol, 80-83, EMER PROF, UNIV ARIZ. *Personal Data:* b Rochester, NY, July 26, 29; m 55. *Educ:* Univ Rochester, BA, 52; Univ Iowa, PhD, 56. *Honors & Awards:* Myron Gordon Award, 86. *Prof Exp:* Lab instr, Univ Iowa, 52-56, res asst, 55. *Concurrent Pos:* Fulbright res scholar, Univ Paris, 64 & Zool Sta, Naples, 69-70; managing ed, Am Zoologist, Am Soc Zool, 71-75; res scholar, Japan Soc Prom Sci, 79; ed in chief, Pigment Cell Res, 86- *Mem:* Am Soc Zool; Am Asn Anat; Soc Develop Biol; Am Soc Cell Biol. *Res:* Experimental embryology of amphibia; endocrinology; physiology of pigmentation; growth factors; cell culture. *Mailing Add:* Dept Anat Cell Biol Univ Ariz Tucson AZ 85724-0001

BAGNELL, CAROL A, REPRODUCTIVE ENDOCRINOLOGY. *Current Pos:* asst prof, 88-94, ASSOC PROF, DEPT ANIMAL SCI, RUTGERS UNIV, 94-, ASSOC CHAIR, 95- *Personal Data:* b Avenel, NJ, July 10, 52; m 91; c 2. *Educ:* Glassboro State Col, BA, 74; WVa Univ, Morgantown, MS, 76; Med Col Ga, PhD(endocrinol), 83. *Prof Exp:* Res fel, Dept Anat, Univ Hawaii, 83-84, asst researcher, 84-85, assoc researcher, 85-88. *Mem:* Sigma Xi; Endocrine Soc; Soc Study Reproduction. *Res:* Paracrine control of follicular development, ovulation and luteal function; interaction of local hormones within the ovary; elucidation of the source, biological action and receptors for relaxin in ovarian tissue. *Mailing Add:* Dept Animal Sci Rutgers Univ New Brunswick NJ 08903-0231

BAGRODIA, SHRIRAM, FIBER SCIENCE-DEVELOPMENT & FLUID MANAGEMENT IN FIBROUS STRUCTURES, POLYMER STRUCTURE & PROPERTY RELATIONSHIPS. *Current Pos:* PRIN RES CHEM ENGR, EASTMAN CHEM CO, 91- *Personal Data:* b Gwalior, India, Sept 24, 52; US citizen; m 78, Rajni Khemka; c Mridula & Aditya. *Educ:* Indian Inst Technol, Kanpur, BTech, 73; Princeton Univ, MS, 75; Va Polytech Inst & State Univ, PhD(chem eng), 84. *Honors & Awards:* Best Paper Award, Am Chem Soc, Rubber Div, 95. *Prof Exp:* Plant engr, Orient Paper Mills, India, 75-80; sr res engr, Monsanto, 84-86; from res chem engr to sr res chem engr, Eastman Kodak, 86-91. *Concurrent Pos:* Adj prof, Clemson Univ, 93- *Mem:* Am Chem Soc; Soc Plastics Eng; Fiber Soc. *Res:* Structure-property relationships in polymeric materials; novel fiber products and processes; invented spontaneously wettable fibers; fluids management in fibrous structures; blends of engineeering thermoplastic polymers. *Mailing Add:* Eastman Chemical Co PO Box 1972 Kingsport TN 37662-5150. *Fax:* 423-224-0637

BAGSHAW, JOSEPH CHARLES, GENE STRUCTURE & FUNCTION. *Current Pos:* PROF, DEPT BIOL & BIOTECHNOL, WORCESTER POLYTECH INST, 84- *Personal Data:* b Niagara Falls, NY, Sept 2, 43; m 71; c 2. *Educ:* Johns Hopkins Univ, BA, 65; Univ Tenn, PhD(biochem), 69. *Prof Exp:* From asst prof to assoc prof biochem, Sch Med, Wayne State Univ, 71-84. *Concurrent Pos:* Res fel, Harvard Med Sch-Mass Gen Hosp, Boston, 70-71; dir, Worcester Consortium PhD Prog Biomed Sci, 84- *Mem:* AAAS; Am Soc Biol Chemists; Am Soc Cell Biol. *Res:* Transcriptional regulation in eukaryotes; gene structure and expression; cloning and characterization of histone and tubulin genes. *Mailing Add:* Dept Biol & Biotechnol Worcester Polytech Inst 100 Institute Rd Worcester MA 01609. *Fax:* 508-831-5936; *E-Mail:* jbagshaw@wpi.edu

BAGSHAW, MALCOLM A, RADIOTHERAPY, RADIOBIOLOGY. *Current Pos:* From instr to assoc prof, 55-69, PROF RADIOL, SCH MED, STANFORD UNIV, 69-, CHMN DEPT, 72-, DIR DIV RADIOTHER, 60- *Personal Data:* b Adrian, Mich, June 24, 25; m 48; c 3. *Educ:* Wesleyan Univ, BA, 46; Yale Univ, MD, 50. *Concurrent Pos:* Consult, Vet Admin Hosp, Palo Alto, 60- *Mem:* Am Col Radiol; Asn Univ Radiol; Radiol Soc NAm; Radiation Res Soc; Am Soc Therapeut Radiol; Am Asn Cancer Res. *Mailing Add:* Radiol/Oncol Stanford Univ Sch Med Stanford Univ Hosp Stanford CA 94305

BAGUS, PAUL SAUL, SOLID STATE PHYSICS, QUANTUM CHEMISTRY. *Current Pos:* PROF STAFF MEM, INT BUS MACH RES LAB, 68- *Personal Data:* b New York, NY, Nov 19, 37; m 81; c 1. *Educ:* Univ Chicago, BS & MS, 58, PhD(physics), 65. *Prof Exp:* Fel, Argonne Nat Lab, 62-64, res assoc physics, Solid State Sci Div, 64-66; assoc prof, Fac Sci, Univ Paris, 66-67; res assoc physics, Univ Chicago, 67-68. *Concurrent Pos:* Consult, Lockheed Missiles & Space Corp, 62-63; US sr scientist, Alexander von Humboldt Found, 80-81. *Mem:* Fel Am Phys Soc; Am Vacuum Soc. *Res:* Ab initio calculation of the electronic structure of atoms and molecules to determine properties of atoms, molecules, solids and surfaces; application to the theory of x-ray photo-electron spectroscopy and related matters; use of cluster models to determine the nature of the interaction of adsorbates with surfaces. *Mailing Add:* IBM Res Lab K31/802 650 Harry Rd San Jose CA 95120

BAGWELL, ERVIN EUGENE, PHARMACOLOGY. *Current Pos:* From asst prof to assoc prof pharmacol, 65-75, PROF PHARMACOL, MED UNIV SC, 75- *Personal Data:* b Honea Path, SC, Jan 24, 36; m 58; c 2. *Educ:* Furman Univ, BS, 58; Med Univ SC, MS, 60, PhD, 63. *Mem:* Am Soc Pharmacol & Exp Therapeut. *Res:* Autonomic and cardiovascular drugs; electropharmacology of antiarrhythmic drugs. *Mailing Add:* 1735 Clark Hills Circle Johns Island SC 29445

BAHADUR, BIRENDRA, LIQUID CRYSTALS, DISPLAYS. *Current Pos:* mgr res & develop, 85-95, SR STAFF SCI, LITTON SYST, CAN, 95- *Personal Data:* b Gorakhpur, India, July 1, 49; m 70, Urmila Srivastva; c Shivendra & Shachindra. *Educ:* Gorakhpur Univ, BSc, 67, MSc, 69, PhD(physics), 76. *Honors & Awards:* Spec Recognition Award, Soc Info Display, 93. *Prof Exp:* Res fel physics, Gorakhpur Univ, India, 69-76, asst prof, 76-77; sr sci officer res & develop, Nat Phys Lab, New Delhi, India, 77-81; vpres & dir res & develop, Data Images Inc, Ottawa, 81-85. *Concurrent Pos:* Chairperson, Liquid Crystal Technol Comt, Soc Info Display, 96-97. *Mem:* Inst Physics UK; Soc Phys Chem France; Soc Info Displays; Int Liquid Crystal Soc. *Res:* Developed manufacturing process & technology for LCDS; author of over 60 research papers, review articles & three books on LCDS and liquid crystals; liquid crystals and liquid crytal display. *Mailing Add:* Litton Systs Can Ltd 25 City View Dr Etobicoke ON M9W 5A7 Can. *Fax:* 416-246-2090; *E-Mail:* bahadurb@littonlsl.com

BAHADUR, RAGHU RAJ, MATHEMATICAL STATISTICS. *Current Pos:* RETIRED. *Personal Data:* b Delhi, India, Apr 30, 24; m 50, Thelma Clark; c Sekhar & Sheila. *Educ:* Univ Delhi, BA, 43, MA, 45; Univ NC, Chapel Hill, PhD(math statist), 50. *Prof Exp:* Instr statist, Univ Chicago, 50-51, asst prof, 54-56; prof, Indian Coun Agr Res, 51-52; asst prof math statist, Columbia Univ, 52-53; prof statist, Indian Statist Inst, 56-61; assoc prof, Statist, Univ Chicago, 62-64, prof, 65-91. *Mem:* Fel Inst Math Statist (pres, 74-75); fel Int Statist Inst; fel Nat Inst Sci India; fel Am Acad Arts & Scis; Sigma Xi; fel Indian Acad & Arts & Sci; Indian Acad Scis. *Res:* Theory of statistical tests and decisions; approximations to classical distributions; large sample theory. *Mailing Add:* 1700 E 56th St No 2402 Chicago IL 60637

BAHAL, SURENDRA MOHAN, PHYSICAL PHARMACY & FORMULATION OF LIQUIDS. *Current Pos:* res pharmacist, Wyeth Labs, Inc, 64-72, supvr, Oral Liquids & Top Prod Unit, Inc, 73-88, res assoc, Oral Parenteral & Top Prod, E I Dupont de Nemours & Co, Inc, 88-90, res mgr, liquids & top prod, 91-93, PRIN RES SCIENTIST, LIQUIDS & TOP PROD, DUPONT MERCK PHARMACEUT CO, 94- *Personal Data:* b India, July 1, 35; m 61, Chander K Chowdhary; c Neeta (O'Mara) & Neelam. *Educ:* Univ Bombay, BS, 54, BS, 56, MS, 59; Temple Univ, PhD(phys pharm), 65. *Honors & Awards:* Lunsford-Richardson Pharm Award, Eastern Region, Richardson Merrell Co, Inc, 65; Pharmaceut Res Discussion Group Award, 70. *Prof Exp:* Instr pharm, Dept Chem Technol, Univ Bombay, 58-61. *Mem:* Am Asn of Pharm Scientists; Parenteral Drug Asn. *Res:* Excretion kinetics of drugs as modified by protein binding and renal tubular secretion; antiinfective agents; powder caking; antacid technology; effect of sugars on penicillin degradation kinetics; stabilization of pharmaceutical formulations; drug stabilization patents; inhalation aerosol technology; author of several publications and patents. *Mailing Add:* 650 Timber Dr Wayne PA 19087. *Fax:* 302-695-7592

BAHAM, ARNOLD, DAIRY NUTRITION. *Current Pos:* from asst prof to assoc prof, 74-79, PROF DAIRY SCI, LA STATE UNIV, 91- *Personal Data:* b Folsom, La, Oct 7, 43; m 68, Patricia L Lord; c Christopher K & Kimberly D. *Educ:* La State Univ, Baton Rouge, BS, 66, MS, 68; Auburn Univ, PhD(dairy nutrit), 71. *Prof Exp:* Asst dairy sci, La State Univ, 66-68; asst dairy nutrit, Auburn Univ, 68-71; asst prof agr, Southeastern La Univ, 71-74. *Concurrent Pos:* Transp chmn, Am Dairy Sci Asn Meeting, 81; pres, Noba-Atlantic-LABC Affil Breeders, 82; secy fedn coun, Atlantic-LABC-Eastern AI, 85; mgr, La Animal Breeders Coop, 77- *Mem:* Am Dairy Sci Asn; Nat Asn Animal Breeders. *Res:* Nutrition and reproduction of dairy animals. *Mailing Add:* Dairy Sci La State Univ Baton Rouge LA 70803-0001. *Fax:* 504-388-3235

BAHAR, EZEKIEL, ELECTROMAGNETIC PROPAGATION, REMOTE SENSING. *Current Pos:* from assoc prof to prof, 67-80, REGENTS PROF, DURHAM PROF ELEC ENG & GEORGE HOLMES DISTINGUISHED PROF, UNIV NEBR, LINCOLN, 80- *Personal Data:* b Bombay, India, May 23, 33; US citizen; m 57; c 3. *Educ:* Israel Inst Technol, BSc, 58, MSc, 60; Univ Colo, PhD(wave propagation), 64. *Prof Exp:* Teaching asst elec eng, Israel Inst Technol, 58-60, instr, 60-62; res assoc, electromagnetic model studies, Univ Colo, 62-64, asst prof elec eng, 64-67. *Concurrent Pos:* Res grants, Adv Res Projs Agency, 62-67 & Off Naval Res & NSF, 66-67, 72-78 & 87-; Environ Sci Serv Admin, US Dept Com, 70-71, Army Res Off, 76-79, 82-86 & 87-, Air Force, 81-83, NSF, 85- *Mem:* Fel Inst Elec & Electronics Engrs; Int Union Radio Sci. *Res:* Electromagnetic theory; propagation in general multimode waveguide structures; electromagnetic modelling techniques; synthesis of waveguide junctions; propagation in inhomogeneous anisotropic media; scattering, depolarization and diffraction by irregular media; generalized field transform techniques for nonuniform boundary value problems; scattering depolarization by random rough surfaces; remote sensing. *Mailing Add:* Dept Elec Eng Univ Nebr Lincoln NE 68588-0511

BAHAR, LEON Y, APPLIED MECHANICS. *Current Pos:* assoc prof, 66-79, PROF APPL MECH, DREXEL UNIV, 79- *Personal Data:* b Turkey, Apr 4, 28; US citizen; m 65; c 3. *Educ:* Robert Col, Istanbul, BS, 50; Lehigh Univ, MS, 59, PhD(mech), 63. *Prof Exp:* Instr mech, Lehigh Univ, 57-63; asst prof eng, City Univ New York, 63-66. *Concurrent Pos:* Consult, Data Processing Div, IBM Corp, NY, 65, United Engrs & Constructors, Inc, 74-75, Gulf Res & Develop Corp & Western Res & Develop, 74, INA Corp, 76, George M Ewing Co, 76, Hudson Int, 90. *Mem:* Am Soc Mech Engrs; Am Acad Mech; Sigma Xi; fel NY Acad Sci. *Res:* Dynamics and stability of constrained dynamical systems and interaction with control theory. *Mailing Add:* Dept Mech Eng Drexel Univ 3141 Chestnut St Philadelphia PA 19104-2875

BAHARY, WILLIAM S, POLYMER PHYSICAL CHEMISTRY. *Current Pos:* SCIENTIST-ENTREPRENEUR, 96- *Personal Data:* b Kermanshah, Iran, Jan 20, 36; US citizen; m 79, Susan C Kurshan. *Educ:* Harvard Univ, AB, 57; Columbia Univ, AM, 58, PhD(chem), 61. *Prof Exp:* Sr res chemist, Tex-US Chem Co, 61-68; vis asst prof chem, Fairleigh Dickinson Univ, 68-73; res scientist, Stevens Inst Technol, 73-75, adj asst prof chem, 75-79; consult chemist, Wallace Clark Co, 75-79; eng supvr, Duracell, Inc, 79-88; res scientist, Unilever, Inc, 89-96. *Mem:* Am Chem Soc. *Res:* Structure and properties of synthetic and biological macromolecules; viscoelasticity of concentrated polymer solutions; structure and function of polysaccarides of dental plaque; chemistry of biomimetic blood anticoagulation; battery research and technology; characterization, including light scattering GPC and EM of solutions of polymers and biopolymers; materials science and process engineering; household and personal products research and development. *Mailing Add:* 325 E 79th St New York NY 10021-0900. *E-Mail:* wsbahary@worldnet.att.net

BAHCALL, JOHN NORRIS, ASTROPHYSICS. *Current Pos:* mem, 68-70, PROF NATURAL SCI, INST ADVAN STUDY, 71- *Personal Data:* b Shreveport, La, Dec 30, 34; m 66, Neta Assaf; c 3. *Educ:* Univ Calif, Berkeley, BA, 56; Univ Chicago, MA, 57; Harvard Univ, PhD(physics), 61. *Honors & Awards:* Warner Prize, Am Astron Soc, 70; Shulamet Goldhaber lectr, Tel Aviv Univ, 87; James Arthur Prize lectr, Harvard-Smithsonian Ctr Astrophys, 88; Danz lectr, 92; D Heinnemann Prize, Am Inst Physics, 94. *Prof Exp:* Res fel physics, Ind Univ, 60-62; res fel physics, Calif Inst Technol, 62-63, sr res fel, 63-65, from asst prof to assoc prof theoret physics, 65-70. *Concurrent Pos:* Sloan found fel, 68-71; vis lectr, Dept Astron, Princeton Univ, 71-; mem, Physics Adv Panel, NSF, 72-75; comt mem, Div High Energy Astrophys, Am Astron Soc, 72-74; chmn, Sect Astron, Nat Acad Sci, 80-83, Astron & Astrophys Decode Surv Comt, 89-91; regent's fel, Smithsonian Inst, 86-89; mem, Astrophys Mgt Opers Working Group, 87. *Mem:* Nat Acad Sci; Am Acad Arts & Sci; fel Am Phys Soc; Am Astron Soc (pres-elect, 89-90, pres, 90-92). *Res:* Theoretical calculations of solar neutrino expectations; quasar absorption lines and lensing; construction of models of distribution of stars in galaxy. *Mailing Add:* Sch Natural Sci Inst Advan Study Olden Lane Princeton NJ 08540

BAHCALL, NETA ASSAF, ASTROPHYSICS, ASTRONOMY. *Current Pos:* PROF, DEPT ASTROPHYS SCI, PRINCETON UNIV, 90- *Personal Data:* b Tel-Aviv, Israel, Dec 16, 42; m 66; c 3. *Educ:* Hebrew Univ, Jerusalem, BSc, 63; Weizmann Inst Sci, Israel, MSc, 65; Tel-Aviv Univ, PhD(astrophys), 70. *Prof Exp:* Res asst astrophys, Calif Inst Technol, 65-66, res fel, 70-71; res assoc, Princeton Univ Observ, 71-74, res staff mem, 74-75, res astronr, 75-79, sr res astronr,; off head sci prog, Space Telescope Sci Inst, 79-90. *Mem:* Nat Acad Sci; Am Astron Soc. *Res:* Galactic and extra-galactic astronomy; properties of galaxies and clusters of galaxies; structure of universe; dark matter; cosmology. *Mailing Add:* Dept Astro-Phys Sci Princeton Univ Peyton Hall Princeton NJ 08544

BAHE, LOWELL W, physical chemistry; deceased, see previous edition for last biography

BAHILL, A(NDREW) TERRY, EXPERT SYSTEMS, MODELING PHYSIOLOGICAL SYSTEMS. *Current Pos:* PROF SYSTS & INDUST ENG, UNIV ARIZ, 84- *Personal Data:* b Washington, Pa, Jan 31, 46; m 71, Karen Swain; c Alex & Zach. *Educ:* Univ Ariz, BSEE, 67; San Jose State Univ, MSEE, 70; Univ Calif, Berkeley, PhD(elec eng & comput sci), 75. *Prof Exp:* Asst prof elec eng & bioeng, Carnegie-Mellon Univ, 76-81, assoc prof, 81-84. *Concurrent Pos:* From asst to assoc prof neurol, Sch Med, Univ Pittsburgh, 77-84. *Mem:* Fel Inst Elec & Electronics Engrs; Sigma Xi; Soc Neurosci; Nat Coun Syst Eng. *Res:* Experiments and modeling analysis of human head and eye movements, with applications to the science of baseball; computer techniques for validating decision support systems; systems engineering design. *Mailing Add:* Systs & Indust Eng Univ Ariz Tucson AZ 85721-0020. *Fax:* 520-621-6555; *E-Mail:* terry@tucson.sie.arizona.edu

BAHL, INDER JIT, MICROWAVE TECHNOLOGY, MICROWAVE INTEGRATED CIRCUITS. *Current Pos:* EXEC SCIENTIST, ITT GALLIUM ABSENIDE TECHNOL CTR, 81- *Personal Data:* b Punjab, India, Jan 27, 44; US citizen; m 68; c 2. *Educ:* Punjab Univ, India, BS, 65; Birla Inst Technol & Sci, India, MS, 67, MS, 69; Indian Inst Technol, PhD(elec eng), 75. *Prof Exp:* Res engr, Indian Inst Technol, India, 69-78; res assoc microwave, Univ Ottawa, Can, 79-81; res scientist, Defense Res Estab, Can, 81. *Concurrent Pos:* Assoc ed, Int J Microwave & Millimeter-Wave Comput-Aided Eng, 90- *Mem:* Fel Inst Elec & Electronics Engrs; Electromagnetics Acad. *Res:* Advanced state-of-the-art in the areas of microwave and millimeter-wave integrated circuits including antennas; author of five books and numerous publications. *Mailing Add:* ITT Gallium Absenide Technol Ctr 7670 Enon Dr Roanoke VA 24019

BAHL, LALIT R(AI), COMMUNICATIONS & COMPUTER SCIENCE. *Current Pos:* RES STAFF MEM COMPUT SCI, 68-, MGR NATURAL LANG SPEECH RECOGNITION, IBM CORP RES CTR. *Personal Data:* b Shekhupura, India, July 30, 43; m 68; c 3. *Educ:* Indian Inst Technol, Kharagpur, BTech, 64; Univ Ill, Urbana-Champaign, MS, 66, PhD(elec eng), 68. *Concurrent Pos:* Adj assoc prof, dept elec eng & comput sci, Columbia Univ, 70-75. *Mem:* Inst Elec & Electronics Engrs. *Res:* Coding theory for reliable transmission; information theory; speech recognition. *Mailing Add:* IBM Corp Watson Res Ctr Div Natural Lang Speech Recognition PO Box 704 Yorktown Heights NY 10598

BAHL, OM PARKASH, CHEMISTRY. *Current Pos:* from asst prof to assoc prof, State Univ NY, 66-71, prof, Dept Chem, 71-74, prof & dir, Div Cell & Molecular Biol, 74-78, chmn Dept Biol Scis, 76-83, PROF, DEPT BIOL SCIS, STATE UNIV NY, BUFFALO, 76- *Personal Data:* b Lyallpur, Punjab, India, Jan 10, 27; m 52; c 3. *Educ:* Punjab Univ, India, MSc, 50; Univ Minn, PhD, 62. *Honors & Awards:* Schoellkopf Award, Am Chem Soc, 78; Med & Life Sci Award, Nat Coun Asian Indian Orgn NAm, 82. *Prof Exp:* Lectr chem, Arya Col, Ludhiana, India, 50-52 & Govt Col, 52-57; res assoc biochem, Univ Minn, 62-63 & Univ Calif, 63-64; Am Cancer Soc career investr & Dernham fel, Univ Southern Calif, 64-65, asst prof biochem, 65-66. *Concurrent Pos:* Nat Found res grant, 65-66; Am Cancer Soc career develop award, 65-66, 69-82; USPHS res grant, 66-92. *Mem:* Am Chem Soc; Am Soc Biol Chemists; Brit Chem Soc; NY Acad Sci; Endocrine Soc; AAAS; Am Soc Cell Biol. *Res:* Proteins and enzymes; polysaccharides; glycoproteins; hormones and receptors. *Mailing Add:* Dept Biol Sci 347 Cooke Hall State Univ NY Buffalo Amherst Campus Buffalo NY 14260-1300. *Fax:* 716-645-2975; *E-Mail:* cambobahl@ubvms.cc.buffalo.edu

BAHLER, THOMAS LEE, ZOOLOGY. *Current Pos:* from asst prof to assoc prof, 49-59, prof zool & physiol, 59-73, PROF BIOL, UTAH STATE UNIV, 73- *Personal Data:* b Walnut Creek, Ohio, Feb 1, 20; m 48; c 2. *Educ:* Col Wooster, BA, 43; Univ Wis, PhD(zool), 49. *Prof Exp:* From res asst to teaching asst, Univ Wis, 44-49. *Concurrent Pos:* NSF fac fel, 58-59. *Res:* Physiology of parasites; physiological effects of insecticides; physiology of eosinophils. *Mailing Add:* 1246 Island Dr Logan UT 84321

BAHN, ARTHUR NATHANIEL, MICROBIAL PATHOGENSIS, ORAL MICROBIOL. *Current Pos:* RETIRED. *Personal Data:* b Boston, Mass, Jan 5, 26; m 84; c 5. *Educ:* Boston Univ, AB, 49; Univ Kans, MA, 52; Univ Wis, PhD(microbiol), 56. *Prof Exp:* Asst bacteriologist, Kans State Bd Health,

51-52; asst bact, Univ Wis, 55-66; instr, Sch Dent Med, Univ Ill, 56-58; assoc prof, Sch Dent, Northwestern Univ, 58-71; prof & sect head microbiol, Sch Dent Med, Southern Ill Univ, Alton, 71- *Concurrent Pos:* Proj asst, Univ Wis, 52-56; adj prof oral path, Med Univ SC, 68-; adj prof, Univ NMex, 69-79; mem, Am Bd Med Microbiol, 70-; consult, Food & Drug Admin Oral Cavities Prod Panel, 74-80; Sr Fulbright fel, 78. *Mem:* Fel AAAS; fel Am Soc Microbiol; Int Asn Dent Res. *Res:* Caries vaccine using glucosy/transfreance as an enzyme; developer of the agar replica method; molecular biology of oval protozoa. *Mailing Add:* Sch Dent Med So Ill Univ 2800 College Ave Alton IL 62002. *Fax:* 618-474-7150

BAHN, EMIL LAWRENCE, JR, INORGANIC CHEMISTRY, NUCLEAR CHEMISTRY. *Current Pos:* RETIRED. *Personal Data:* b Cape Girardeau, Mo, Sept 6, 24; m 49; c 2. *Educ:* Mo Sch Mines, BSChE, 46; Washington Univ, MSChE, 49, MA, 61, PhD(chem), 62. *Prof Exp:* Prof chem, Southeast Mo State Col, 62-73, head dept, 62-73. *Mem:* AAAS; Am Chem Soc; Am Nuclear Soc; Health Physics Soc; Soc Appl Spectros. *Res:* X-ray fluorescence; trace elements emitted from coal burning; utilization of drinking water and waste water sludges. *Mailing Add:* 6094 State Hwy 177 Cape Girardeau MO 63701

BAHN, GILBERT S(CHUYLER), ENGINEERING, MATHEMATICAL MODELING. *Current Pos:* RETIRED. *Personal Data:* b Syracuse, NY, Apr 25, 22; wid; c Gilbert K. *Educ:* Columbia Univ, BS, 43; Rensselaer Polytech Inst, MS, 65; Columbia Pacific Univ, PhD, 79. *Prof Exp:* Chem engr sci prog, Chem Dept, Gen Elec Co, 46-48, develop engr, Thermal Power Systs Div, 48-53; sr thermodyn engr, Marquardt Aircraft Co, 53-54, from res specialist to res consult, Marquardt Corp, 54-70; eng specialist, Hampton Tech Ctr, LTV Aerospace Corp, 70-88. *Concurrent Pos:* Chmn, Nat Conf Performance of High Temperature Systs, 59-68; ed, Pyrodynamics, 63-69; mem performance stand working group, JANNAF Interagency Propulsion Comt, 66-84, thermochem working group, 67-72; free-lance hist res proj, 88- *Mem:* Am Soc Mech Engrs; Combustion Inst. *Res:* High-temperature thermodynamics; kinetics, and thermal power performance analysis; documentation; environmental research with remotely-sensed digital imagery; statistical inference of undefined populations; analysis of aberrant engineering data. *Mailing Add:* 4519 N Ashtree St Moorpark CA 93021

BAHN, ROBERT CARLTON, pathology, coronary circulation; deceased, see previous edition for last biography

BAHNER, CARL TABB, ORGANIC CHEMISTRY, BIOMEDICAL ENGINEERING. *Current Pos:* DIR, CANCER CHEMOTHER PROJ, CARSON-NEWMAN COL. *Personal Data:* b Conway, Ark, July 14, 08; m 31, Mary C Garrott; c Thomas M, Mary C & Frances J. *Educ:* Hendrix Col, AB, 27; Univ Chicago, MS, 28; Southern Baptist Theol Sem, ThM, 31; Columbia Univ, PhD(chem eng), 36. *Prof Exp:* Asst prof chem & head, Dept Physics, Union Univ, Tenn, 36-37; prof chem, Carson-Newman Col, 37-73, res coordr, 67-73; from assoc prof to prof chem, 73-78, Walters State Community Col, 78-81; prof chem, Bluefield Col, 79-91. *Concurrent Pos:* Consult, Tenn Valley Authority, 42-45, Carbide & Carbon Chem Corp, 48-79, Oak Ridge Inst, 50-78, Roswell Park Mem Hosp, 56, Chester Beatty Res Inst, 57. *Mem:* AAAS; Am Chem Soc; Am Asn Cancer Res; fel Am Inst Chem. *Res:* Reactions of aliphatic nitro compounds and of organic halides; amines; heterocyclic nitrogen compounds; protein extraction; immersion freezing solutions; hydrotropic solutions; organic complexes of radioisotopes; cancer chemotherapy; nitrites in saliva. *Mailing Add:* 424 Buckingham Dr Jefferson City TN 37760

BAHNFLETH, DONALD R, APPLIED ENGINEERING PROBLEM SOLVING, SYSTEM ANALYSES. *Current Pos:* tech dir, 71-76, exec vpres, 76-84, PRES, ZBA, INC, 84- *Personal Data:* b West Chicago, Ill, July 16, 27; m 51; c 3. *Educ:* Univ Ill, BSME, 52, MSME, 56. *Honors & Awards:* Distinguished Serv Award, Am Soc Heating, Refrig & Air Conditioning Engrs, 76; First Outstanding Achievement Award, Nat Air Filtration Asn, 90. *Prof Exp:* Res asst prof, Univ Ill, 55-60; ed, Heating/Piping/Air Conditioning, 60-70, ed dir, 70-71. *Concurrent Pos:* Mgt rep, Automated Procedures Eng Consults. *Mem:* Nat Soc Prof Engrs; fel Am Soc Heating Refrig & Air Conditioning Engrs; Air Pollution Control Asn; Sigma Xi; Am Consult Engrs Coun; Automated Procedures Eng Consults. *Res:* Applied research identifying thermal and hydraulic system deficiencies in large scale central steam, high temperature water and chilled water generation and distribution systems. *Mailing Add:* 7466 Glenover Dr Cincinnati OH 45236

BAHNG, JOHN DEUCK RYONG, astronomy, for more information see previous edition

BAHNIUK, EUGENE, BIOMECHANICS. *Current Pos:* assoc prof eng, 69-70, assoc prof mech eng, 71-76, ASST PROF ORTHOP SURG, CASE WESTERN RES UNIV, 71-, PROF MECH ENRG, 77- *Personal Data:* b Weirton, WVa, Mar 10, 26; m 77, Margaret Hilton; c Douglas, Joy, Barbera, Becky & David. *Educ:* Case Inst Technol, BSME, 50, MS, 61; Case Western Res Univ, PhD(eng), 70. *Honors & Awards:* Award of Merit, Am Soc Testing & Mat; Venor Award. *Prof Exp:* Develop engr, NY Air Brake Co, 50-54; proj engr, Lear Siegler Inc, 54-56; supvr, Borg-Warner Corp, 56-61; res & develop mgr, Weatherhead Co, 61-69. *Concurrent Pos:* Res assoc, Vet Admin, Cleveland, 76-; fel, NIH; fel, NSF; vis prof & fel, NASA Langley. *Mem:* Am Soc Biomechanics; fel Am Soc Testing & Mat; Sigma Xi; Int Soc Ski Safety. *Res:* Biomechanics of bone; sports trauma; cervical spinal cord trauma; loosening of orthopedic implants; mathematical modeling of the human neuromuscular system; mechanical design. *Mailing Add:* 7629 Cairn Ln Gates Mills OH 44040. *Fax:* 440-423-3459; *E-Mail:* exb9@po.cwru.edu

BAHNS, MARY, MICROBIOLOGY, MOLECULAR BIOLOGY. *Current Pos:* PROF OFF, NAT SCI FOUND, 90- *Educ:* Univ Va, PhD(cell biol), 85. *Prof Exp:* Asst prof biol, Briar Cliff Col, 83-; asst prof sci educ, Tex Christian Univ, 86-90. *Mailing Add:* 9324 Arlington Blvd Fairfax VA 22031-1929

BAHR, CHARLES CHESTER, SURFACE CHEMISTRY, SURFACE MORPHOLOGY. *Current Pos:* Mem tech staff, AT&T Eng Res Ctr, 86-88, MEM TECH STAFF, AT&T BELL LABS, LUCENT TECHNOL, 88- *Personal Data:* b Orange, Tex, Apr 2, 58; m 89, Gail Fine; c Jackson. *Educ:* Tex A&M Univ, BS, 80; Univ Calif, Berkeley, PhD(phys chem), 86. *Mem:* Am Phys Soc. *Res:* Dynamics of surface chemical reactions to develop novel and technologically important materials in electronic and optical applications. *Mailing Add:* Bell Labs Lucent Technol 600 Mountain Ave Murray Hill NJ 07974-0636. *E-Mail:* ccb@clockwise.lucent.com

BAHR, DONALD WALTER, GAS TURBINE ENGINE COMBUSTION & EMISSION ABATEMENT TECHNOLOGY. *Current Pos:* RETIRED. *Personal Data:* b Chicago, Ill, Dec 13, 27; m 60, Mary E Zieverink; c Donald W Jr & Susan M. *Educ:* Univ Ill, BS, 49; Ill Inst Technol, MS, (chem eng) & MS (gas technol), 51. *Honors & Awards:* Perry T Egbert Award for Eng Achievement, Gen Elec Co, 82; Air Breathing Propulsion Award, Am Inst Aeronaut & Astronaut, 83. *Prof Exp:* Aeronaut res scientist jet engine combustion, NACA Lewis Flight Propulsion Lab, Cleveland, 51-54; first lt, Environ Health Lab, Wright Patterson AFB, Ohio, 54-56; combustion chem engr, GE Aircraft Engines, 56-59, mgr aerothermochem, 59-60, mgr combustion appl res, 60-62, mgr propulsion equip eng, GE Missile & Space Div, 62-68, mgr combustion & emission control, 68-86, mgr combustion & heat transfer technol, 86-92, mgr combustion technol, 92-94. *Concurrent Pos:* Chmn, Aircraft Engine Emissions Comt, Aerospace Industs Asn, 71-96; vchmn, Ad Hoc Panel Jet Engine Hydrocarbon Fuels, NASA, 73-76; tech rep, Comt Aircraft Fuel Conserv, Nat Acad Eng, 75-78; indust deleg, Comt Aircraft Engine Emissions, Int Civil Aviation Orgn, 78-95; mem, Aircraft Fuel, Lubricant & Equip Res Comt, Coord Res Coun, Inc, 78-94; vchmn, Combustion & Fuels Comt, Am Soc Mech Engrs, 85-87, chmn, 87-89; mem bd governors, Combustion Inst, 86-95, chmn comt sect, 95-, Mem High Speed Res Comt, 96-; Panel On Atmospheric Effects Aviation, 95-, Nat Res Coun. *Mem:* Nat Acad Eng; fel Am Inst Aeronaut & Astronaut; Combustion Inst; fel Am Soc Mech Engrs. *Res:* Design and development of high-performance, long-life, low-pollutant emmision and fuel-flexible combustion systems for both aircraft and industrial gas turbine engines. *Mailing Add:* 6576 Branford Ct Cincinnati OH 45236. *Fax:* 513-793-6506

BAHR, GUSTAVE KARL, RADIOLOGICAL PHYSICS, NUCLEAR MEDICINE. *Current Pos:* radiol physicist, 58-59, from instr to asst prof, 59-70, ASSOC PROF RADIOL, COL MED, UNIV CINCINNATI, 70- *Personal Data:* b Chicago, Ill, Mar 7, 29; m 61; c 2. *Educ:* Xavier Univ, Ohio, BS, 51; Univ Cincinnati, MS, 59, PhD(physics), 64; Am Bd Radiol, dipl, 66. *Prof Exp:* Instrumentation engr, Keleket Instrument Co, Ohio, 51-53; exp physicist, Ohmart Corp, 53-54; res asst appl mech, Univ Cincinnati, 54-56; tech engr, Gas Turbine Div, Gen Elec Co, 56-58. *Concurrent Pos:* Adj prof physics, Xavier Univ Ohio, 65-; lectr eng physics, Eve Col, Univ Cincinnati, 66-; consult, Bur Dis Prev & Environ Control, Nat Ctr Radiol Health, 66-, Christian Holmes Hosp & Good Samaritan Hosp, Cincinnati, 68- *Mem:* AAAS; Am Asn Physicists in Med; Am Col Radiol. *Res:* Application of digital computer techniques to radiation therapy planning and nuclear medicine diagnostic techniques; application of linear programming to radiation therapy; application of stochastic simulation of radiation to radiologic physics problems. *Mailing Add:* 2743 Bentley Ct Cincinnati OH 45244

BAHR, JAMES THEODORE, PLANT PHYSIOLOGY. *Current Pos:* mgr, plant growth regulators, 85-88, MGR HERBICIDE DISCOVERY PROJS, FMC CORP, 88- *Personal Data:* b East Orange, NJ, Nov 19, 42; m 66; c 3. *Educ:* Mass Inst Technol, BS, 64; Univ Pa, PhD(biophys), 71. *Prof Exp:* Res assoc chem, Univ Ariz, 71-76; sr res biologist, Mobil Chem Co, 76-80, assoc biol & crop chem, 80-81; res mgr, Agrochem Div, Rhone-Poulenc Inc, 81-85. *Res:* Regulation of photosynthetic carbon metabolism; regulation and mechanism of ribulose diphosphate carboxylase-oxygenase; cyanide-insensitive respiration in plant mitochondria; yield enhancement and plant growth regulators in soybeans; herbicidal agrochemicals. *Mailing Add:* 68 Featherbed Lane Hopewell NJ 08525

BAHR, JANICE M, ANIMAL SCIENCE PHYSIOLOGY. *Current Pos:* endocrinol trainee, Dept Physiol, 70-72, from asst prof to assoc prof, 74-83, PROF ANIMAL SCI & PHYSIOL, UNIV ILL, URBANA, 83-, ASSOC VCHANCELLOR RES, 96- *Personal Data:* b LaCrosse, Wis, Feb 14, 35. *Educ:* Viterbo Col, BA, 64; Univ Ill, Urbana, MSc, 68, PhD(physiol), 74. *Prof Exp:* Instr biol, Viterbo Col, LaCrosse, Wis, 68-70. *Concurrent Pos:* NSF, NIH & USDA res grants, 74-; NIH vis scientist, Univ Krakow, Poland, 77; asst ed, Biol Reproduction, 77-81; mem, Prog Site Visit Team, NIH, 78 & 89-90, Panel Rev Competitive Grants Regulatory Biol, NSF, 81-84, Animal Welfare Comt, Endocrine Soc, 86-90, Panel Animal Sci Competitive Grants Prog, USDA, 87, Reproductive Biol Study Sect, NIH, 88-92 & Panel Rev Progs Biol, Behav & Social Sci, NSF, 89-90; chair, Sci Sessions Endocrine Soc, Soc Study Reproduction & Poultry Sci Asn, 80-; mem, Develop Comt, Soc Study Reproduction, 83-86, bd dirs, 84-87; assoc, Ctr Advan Study, 90. *Mem:* Fel AAAS; Am Physiol Soc; Am Soc Animal Sci; Endocrine Soc; Soc Study Fertil; Poultry Sci Asn; Soc Study Reproduction; Sigma Xi; World Poultry Sci Asn. *Res:* Author of more than 150 refereed publications; regulatioon of the ovary and the role of estrogen in regulating the male reproduction tract. *Mailing Add:* 326 Animal Sci Lab Univ Ill 1207 W Gregory Urbana IL 61801. *Fax:* 217-333-8286; *E-Mail:* j-bahr@uiuc.edu

BAHR, KARL EDWARD, automation equipment design, process development, for more information see previous edition

BAHR, LEONARD M, JR, SYSTEMS ECOLOGY. *Current Pos:* res assoc, Ctr Wetland Resources, 73-75, asst prof, 75-79, assoc prof coastal ecol, 79-84, PUBL, CITY FITNESS MAG, DEPT MARINE SCI, LA STATE UNIV, 87- *Personal Data:* b Baltimore Md, June 17, 40; m 79; c 1. *Educ:* Univ Md, BS, 63; Univ Richmond, MS, 68; Univ Ga, PhD(zool & ecol), 74. *Prof Exp:* Res asst, Chesapeake Biol Lab, Univ Md, 63-66. *Res:* Coastal systems ecology, especially as relating to resource management; energetics of ecosystems; identification of the functional roles of organisms within ecosystems, particularly estuarine epifauna, including oyster reef inhabitants. *Mailing Add:* 5544 Melrose Blvd Baton Rouge LA 70806

BAHR, THOMAS GORDON, LIMNOLOGY. *Current Pos:* DIR, WATER RESOURCES RES INST, NMEX STATE UNIV, 78- *Personal Data:* b La Crosse, Wis, Apr 17, 40; m 60; c 1. *Educ:* Univ Idaho, BS, 63; Mich State Univ, MS, 66, PhD(limnol, physiol), 68. *Prof Exp:* Asst prof zool, Colo State Univ, 68-70; from asst dir to dir, Inst Water Res, Mich State Univ, 70-78. *Mem:* AAAS; Am Soc Limnol & Oceanog. *Res:* Applied limnology; water management in arid regions; nutrient cycling; waste water management; dynamics of toxic materials in natural systems. *Mailing Add:* 3135 Southwind Rd Las Cruces NM 88005

BAI, MAO, RESERVOIR MECHANISM, NUMERICAL ANALYSIS OF GEOLOGICAL SCIENCES IN SUBSURFACE ENGINEERING. *Current Pos:* RES ASSOC, ROCK MECH INST, UNIV OKLA, 92- *Personal Data:* b Beijing, China, Apr 16, 52; m, Nai Zhang; c Andi. *Educ:* Xian Mining Inst, dipl, 77; Cent Coal Mining Inst, Beijing, MEng, 82; Newcastle Univ Upon Tyne, Eng, MSc, 86; Pa State Univ, PhD(mineral eng), 91. *Prof Exp:* Asst engr, Xian Coal Mine Design & Res Inst, China, 77-79; res engr, Cent Coal Mining Res Inst, China, 82-85; postdoctoral fel, Sch Petrol & Geol Eng, Univ Okla, 91-92; engr, Agapito & Assoc, Inc, 92. *Concurrent Pos:* Co-prin investr, Rock Mech Res Ctr, Univ Okla, 95-; adj asst prof, Dept Civil & Environ Eng, Univ Mass, Lowell, 96-; assoc, Weir Int Mining Consults, Ltd, 96-; prin investr, Sino-US Collab Res, Univ Okla, 96- *Mem:* Am Geophys Union; Am Rock Mechs Asn; Int Rock Mech Soc; Int Asn Comput Methods & Advan Geomech. *Res:* Analytical and numerical modeling of fluid flow and contaminant transport in fractured, deformable porous media under nonlinear or nonisothermal conditions. *Mailing Add:* 2057 W Lindsey Apt G Norman OK 73069. *Fax:* 405-325-7511; *E-Mail:* mao@rmg.uoknor.edu

BAI, ZHI DONG, STATISTICS. *Current Pos:* SR FEL, DEPT MATH, NAT UNIV SINGAPORE, 97- *Personal Data:* b Leting Cty, China, Nov 27, 43; m 72; c 2. *Educ:* China Univ Sci & Technol, BS, 68, PhD (statist), 82. *Prof Exp:* Assoc prof math, China Univ Sci & Technol, 82-84; res assoc statist, Dept Math, Univ Pittsburgh, 84-88, Univ Philadelphia, 88-97. *Mem:* Chinese Soc Math; Chinese Soc Probability & Statist. *Res:* Density and nonparametric regression estimation; limiting theorems; model selection; multivariate analysis; nonparametric discrimination and prediction; spectral analysis of random matrices and signal processing; author of 80 papers. *Mailing Add:* Dept Math Nat Univ Singapore Philadelphia PA 19122

BAIAMONTE, VERNON D, PHYSICAL CHEMISTRY. *Current Pos:* assoc prof, 67-69, PROF CHEM, MO SOUTHERN STATE COL, 70-, HEAD DEPT, 69- *Personal Data:* b Greeley, Colo, Apr 29, 34; m 58; c 4. *Educ:* Colo State Col, AB, 59, MA, 60; Univ Ind, PhD(phys chem), 66. *Prof Exp:* Instr chem, Ball State Univ, 60-62; fel phys chem, Los Alamos Sci Lab, 66-67. *Mem:* Am Chem Soc. *Res:* Kinetic spectroscopy, especially the fast reactions initiated by flash photolysis and detected by spectroscopic methods. *Mailing Add:* Dept Chem Mo Southern State Col 3950 E Newman Rd Joplin MO 64801-1595

BAIARDI, JOHN CHARLES, HEMATOLOGY, PHYSIOLOGY. *Current Pos:* RETIRED. *Personal Data:* b Brooklyn, NY, Feb 9, 18; m 43, Rosalind Castaldi; c 2. *Educ:* St Francis Col, NY, BS, 40; Brooklyn Col, MA, 43; NY Univ, PhD(biol), 53. *Prof Exp:* Instr biol, St Francis Col, NY, 42-43, asst prof & chmn dept, 46-48; assoc prof, St John's Univ, NY, 48-54; prof biol, Long Island Univ, 54-70, chmn dept, 54-62, assoc dean sci, 58-62, vpres & provost, 62-67, vchancellor, 67-70; pres, Affil Cols & Univs, Inc, 70-82; dir, NY Ocean Sci Lab, Montauk, 70-82. *Concurrent Pos:* Mem med adv bd, Cooley's Anemia Found, NY, vchmn, 63-75. *Mem:* Fel NY Acad Sci. *Res:* Research administration; blood and hemopoietic organs of mammals, fish and invertebrates. *Mailing Add:* 9930-4 Eagles Pt Circle Port Richey FL 34668

BAICH, ANNETTE, BIOCHEMISTRY. *Current Pos:* assoc prof, 69-74, PROF BIOCHEM, SOUTHERN ILL UNIV, EDWARDSVILLE, 74-, CHMN, BIOL DEPT, 84- *Personal Data:* b Chicago, Ill, Mar 2, 30; m 50. *Educ:* Roosevelt Univ, BS, 51; Univ Ore, MS, 54, PhD(chem), 60. *Prof Exp:* Asst chem, Univ Ore, 51-54, instr, 55-56, asst, 56-57; lab technician, Agr Exp Sta, Univ Calif, 54-55; fel biochem, Ore State Univ, 60-61; fel microbiol, Rutgers Univ, 61-62; asst prof biochem, Ore State Univ, 63-69. *Concurrent Pos:* NIH career develop award, 65-69. *Mem:* AAAS; Am Chem Soc; Am Soc Biol Chemists. *Res:* The relation and response of an organism to its environment and how this relationship may be explained in chemical terms. *Mailing Add:* Dept Biol Sci Southern Ill Univ Edwardsville IL 62025-1651

BAID, KUSHALKUMAR MOOLCHAND, POLYMER FILMS, POLYMER PROCESSING. *Current Pos:* Sr res mgr & tech dir polymer eng & labeling film, 87-91, TECH DIR, MARKING FILMS DIV, AVERY DENNISON CORP, 91- *Personal Data:* b Jodhpur, India, Apr 12, 43; US citizen; m 70, Jyoti Kothari; c Smita & Vineet. *Educ:* Bombay Univ, BChem Eng, 65; Ill Inst Technol, MS, 67; Univ Del, PhD(chem eng), 73. *Prof Exp:* Sr chem engr polymer processing, Films Packaging Div, Union Carbide Corp, 67-69; res fel, Univ Del, 69-70 & 70-72; tech specialist & proj mgr III chem eng & polymer processing, Xerox Corp, 73-79; from sr staff engr to sr group leader polymer eng, packaging films, St Regis Corp, 79-84; mgr & sr staff sci chem eng & polymer eng, Champion Int, 84-86. *Mem:* Am Inst Chem Engrs; Soc Plastics Engrs. *Res:* Directing and leading research and development aimed at the development of new and improved polymer films and adhesives for label, signage and decorative applications. *Mailing Add:* PO Box 5093 Mentor OH 44061. *Fax:* 440-639-3708

BAIDINS, ANDREJS, COLLOID & SURFACE CHEMISTRY. *Current Pos:* RETIRED. *Personal Data:* b Dauguli, Latvia, Dec 16, 30; US citizen; m 60, Dzintra Vaivars; c Juris & Andris. *Educ:* Franklin & Marshall Col, BS, 54; Rutgers Univ, PhD(phys chem), 58. *Prof Exp:* Chemist, Res Div, Chem & Pigments Dept, E I Du Pont De Nemours & Co, Inc, 58-93. *Concurrent Pos:* Abstractor, Chem Abstr Serv, 59-81. *Mem:* AAAS; Am Chem Soc. *Res:* Kinetics of decomposition of light and heat sensitive compounds; physical and chemical properties of inorganic crystal surfaces and solid-liquid interfaces. *Mailing Add:* 1104 Windon Dr Wilmington DE 19803-3339

BAIE, LYLE FREDRICK, EXPLORATION GEOLOGY, OCEANOGRAPHY. *Current Pos:* staff geologist, 74-77, geol supvr, Cent Gulf Mexico Area, 77-78, MGR GEOL RES EXPLOR, CITIES SERV CO, 78- *Personal Data:* b Rockford, Ill, Dec 14, 42; m 69; c 4. *Educ:* Univ Notre Dame, BA, 64; Tex A&M Univ, MS, 67, PhD(oceanog), 70. *Honors & Awards:* Sr Geol Assoc, Cities Serv Co, 77. *Prof Exp:* Geologist explor, Texaco, Inc, 70-74. *Mem:* Am Asn Petrol Geologists. *Mailing Add:* 2310 Ivy Glen Dr Houston TX 77077

BAIER, ROBERT EDWARD, SURFACE CHEMISTRY, BIOMATERIALS. *Current Pos:* res prof & dir biomat, Ctr Advan Technol, Health-Care Instruments & Devices Inst, State Univ NY, 85-89, co-dir, 88-92, assoc prof, 89-93, DIR, NSF INDUST/UNIV COOP RES CTR BIOSURFACES, STATE UNIV NY, BUFFALO, 93-, PROF 94- *Personal Data:* b Buffalo, NY, Oct 31, 39; m 61, Corinne M Bonglovanni; c Valerie A & Anne M. *Educ:* Cleveland State Univ, BES, 62; State Univ NY, Buffalo, PhD(biophys), 66. *Hon Degrees:* Dr odontol, Lund Univ, Sweden, 94. *Honors & Awards:* Union Carbide Chem Award, Am Chem Soc, 71; Clemson Award Basic Res, Soc Biomat, 83; Distinguished Serv Award, Soc Appl Spectros, 87; Award Innovation Med Devices, 87. *Prof Exp:* Res asst, Buffalo Gen Hosp, 59-60; nucleonics engr, Electromech Res Lab, Repub Steel Corp, 61-62; res chemist & Nat Res Coun-Nat Acad Sci fel surface chem, Naval Res Lab, 66-68; prin physicist, Cornell Aeronaut Lab, 68-71, head, Chem Sci Sect, 71-74; mem tech staff, Calspan Corp, 74-77, staff scientist, 77-84. *Concurrent Pos:* Guest worker, Nat Heart & Lung Inst, 68; mem, Adv Bd, Prog Biomed Eng, Clemson Univ, 70-82; consult, Roswell Park Mem Inst, NY, 70-89; chmn, Columbia Univ Biomat Sem, 71-72; adj assoc prof chem eng, Cornell Univ, 71-76; res assoc prof biophys, State Univ NY, Buffalo, 71-, Dent Mat, 75-88, res prof biophys sci, 83-, assoc prof oral path, 84-88; consult biomat develop & environ quality control; vpres eng, B/A/I/E/R Inc, 81-; chmn, Gorden Conf Biomed & Biocompatibility, 88-89; pres, Niagara Frontier Asn Res & Develop Dir, 93-94. *Mem:* Soc Biomat (pres, 92-93); Am Soc Artificial Internal Organs; Biophys Soc; Am Chem Soc; Am Soc Cell Biol; Soc Am Mil Engrs; fel Am Inst Med & Biol Engrs (vpres, 95-96). *Res:* Interdisciplinary studies in surface chemistry and physics of materials at liquid-gas, solid-gas and solid-liquid interfaces, including biomedical and environmental systems. *Mailing Add:* Ctr Biosurfaces 110 Parker Hall State Univ NY Buffalo NY 14214. *Fax:* 716-835-4872; *E-Mail:* baier@acsu.buffalo.edu

BAIER, WILLIAM H, SOLID MECHANICS, ELECTRONICS. *Current Pos:* LECTR, DU PAGE COL, 83- *Personal Data:* b Chicago, Ill, Oct 1, 22; m 58. *Educ:* Ill Inst Technol, BS, 44 & 49, MS, 50, PhD(mech eng), 58. *Prof Exp:* Instr mech, Ill Inst Technol, 47-49; designer fluid power, Hannifin Corp, 49-51; design engr, Askania Regulator Co, 51-53; mgr space systs, IIT Res Inst, 53-63; mgr aerospace mech, Emerson Elec Co, 64-66; dir res, Thor Power Tool Co, 66-68; dir res & eng, Cenco Instruments Corp, 68-76; vpres res & eng, Cent Sci Co, 76-78; dir eng, Fitzpatrick Co, 78-83. *Concurrent Pos:* Lectr, Ill Inst Technol, 55-57; pres, DuPage Inst Res & Educ, 69-; mem, bd standardization, Am Soc Mech Eng, 70- *Mem:* Am Inst Physics; Am Soc Testing & Mat; Am Vacuum Soc; Am Soc Mech Engrs; Am Inst Aeronaut & Astronaut. *Res:* Lunar surface petrographic analyzers; physics educational instrumentation; in-space rendezvous mechanisms and systems; vacuum systems; portable tools for industrial and extraterrestrial use; fluid power mechanisms and systems; fluidized beddryers. *Mailing Add:* 3624 Creekwood Ct Downers Grove IL 60515

BAIER, WOLFGANG, AGRICULTURAL METEOROLOGY. *Current Pos:* RETIRED. *Personal Data:* b Liegnitz, Ger, Dec 10, 23; nat US; m 50; c 2. *Educ:* Hohenheim Agr Univ, Dipl, 49, Dr Agr, 52; Univ Pretoria, MSc, 64. *Honors & Awards:* Patterson Medal, Can, 75. *Prof Exp:* Officer in charge agrometeorol sect, Agr Res Inst Highveld Region, SAfrican Dept Agr, 55-64; res scientist agrometeorol sect, Plant Res Inst, Agr Can, 64-69, chief sect, Res Br, 69-73, head agrometeorol res & serv, Agrometeorol Sect, Chem & Biol Res Inst, 73-78, head agrometeorol sect & asst dir, Land Resource Res Inst, Agr Can, 78-90. *Concurrent Pos:* Secy, Can Comt Agr Meteorol; pres, Comn Agr Meteorol, World Meteorol Orgn, 71- *Mem:* Am Meteorol Soc; Can Meteorol Soc; Int Soc Biometeorol. *Res:* Problems related to the impact of weather and climate on agricultural crops and production; development and application of computer models to evaluate plant-weather relationships. *Mailing Add:* 55 Pemberton Crescent Nepean ON K2G 4Y9 Can

BAIERLEIN, RALPH FREDERICK, THEORETICAL PHYSICS. *Current Pos:* from asst prof to prof, 66-77, CHARLOTTE AYRES PROF PHYSICS, WESLEYAN UNIV 77- *Personal Data:* b Springfield, Mass, Dec 19, 36; m 65, Jean Lennox; c Eric & Jeffrey. *Educ:* Harvard Univ, AB, 58; Princeton Univ, PhD(gen relativity), 62. *Prof Exp:* Instr physics, Harvard Univ, 62-65. *Concurrent Pos:* Res assoc, Smithsonian Astrophys Observ, 65-66; rev ed, Am J Physics, 88-96. *Mem:* Fel Am Phys Soc; Am Asn Physics Teachers. *Res:* Star formation and turbulence; nonlinear aspects of superfluid helium films. *Mailing Add:* Dept Physics Wesleyan Univ Middletown CT 06457. *E-Mail:* rbaierlein@wesleyan.edu

BAIG, MIRZA MANSOOR, biochemistry, for more information see previous edition

BAILAR, BARBARA ANN, STATISTICS. *Current Pos:* EXEC DIR, AM STATIST ASN, 88- *Personal Data:* b Monroe, Mich, Nov 24, 35; m 66, John; c Pamela (Monaco) & Melissa. *Educ:* State Univ NY Albany, AB, 56; Va Polytech Inst, MS, 65; Am Univ, PhD(statist), 72. *Prof Exp:* Math statistician, Bur Census, 58-72, chief, Res Ctr Measurement Methods, 72-79; assoc dir, Statist Stand & Methodology, 79-87. *Concurrent Pos:* Chmn rev comt for grant to Am Statist Asn from NSF, 75-76; chmn, Dept Math & Statist, USDA Grad Sch, 75-87. *Mem:* Fel Am Statist Asn; Int Asn Surv Statisticians; Am Asn for Pub Opinion Res; AAAS; Int Statist Inst; Int Asn Survey Samples (pres, 90-91). *Res:* Effect of different methods of measurement on final published statistics. *Mailing Add:* NORC 1155 E 60th St Chicago IL 60637. *Fax:* 703-684-2037; *E-Mail:* barbarab@asa.mhs.compuserve.com

BAILAR, JOHN CHRISTIAN, III, RESEARCH ADMINISTRATION, BIOSTATISTICS. *Current Pos:* CHAIR & PROF, DEPT HEALTH STUDIES, UNIV CHICAGO, 95- *Personal Data:* b Urbana, Ill, Oct 9, 32; m 66; c 4. *Educ:* Univ Colo, BA, 53; Yale Univ, MD, 55; Am Univ, PhD, 73. *Honors & Awards:* McArthur Fel, 90-95. *Prof Exp:* Field investr cancer res, Nat Cancer Inst, 56-62, head, Demog Sect, 62-70, dir, Third Nat Cancer Surv, 67-70; dir, Res Serv, US Vet Admin, 70-72; dep assoc dir cancer control, Nat Cancer Inst, 72-74, sr consult coop studies & ed-in-chief, jour, 74-80; prof biostatist, Harvard Sch Pub Health, 80-87; prof epidemiol & biostatist, Fac Med, McGill Univ, 88-95. *Concurrent Pos:* Lectr, Sch Med, Yale Univ, 59-; assoc ed, J Nat Cancer Inst, 64-66; instr, Grad Sch, USDA, 66-76; assoc ed, Cancer Res, 68-72; mem, Task Force Cancer of Prostate & Bladder, 68-70 & Clin Cancer Training Grants Comt, 69-73; vis prof, State Univ NY, Buffalo, 74-82; ed-in-chief, J Nat Cancer Inst, 74-80; instr, George Washington Univ, 75-80; vis prof, Harvard Univ, 76-79; statist consult, New Eng J of Med, 80-; pres, Coun Biol Ed, 87-88. *Mem:* Inst Med-Nat Acad Sci; fel Am Statist Asn; Biomet Soc; Coun Biol Eds; Soc Risk Anal; Int Statist Inst. *Res:* Administration of medical research; cancer epidemiology; randomized clinical trials; development of related statistical methods and theory; risk assessment and environmental epidemiology. *Mailing Add:* Dept Health Sci Univ Chicago 5841 S Maryland Ave MC 2007 Chicago IL 60637

BAILDON, JOHN DAVID, CONVEXITY, STARSHAPED SETS. *Current Pos:* From instr to asst prof, 70-77, ASSOC PROF MATH, PA STATE UNIV, WORTHINGTON SCRANTON CAMPUS, 77- *Personal Data:* b Johnstown, Pa, Nov 14, 43; m 68, Rachel P Winlock; c Thomas E & Carolyn P. *Educ:* Lafayette Col, BS, 65; Rutgers Univ, MS, 67; State Univ NY, Binghamton, PhD(math), 71. *Concurrent Pos:* Reviewer, Math Reviews, 78-, NSF, 91-92; vis assoc prof math, Univ Okla, 85-86. *Mem:* Sigma Xi; Am Math Soc; Math Asn Am. *Res:* Studies in convexity on visibility problems concerning conditions under which sets will be star shaped or unions of star shaped sets; light open maps on 2-manifolds. *Mailing Add:* Worthington Scranton Campus Pa State Univ Dunmore PA 18512. *E-Mail:* jdb8@psu.edu

BAILE, CLIFTON AUGUSTUS, III, NUTRITION, PHYSIOLOGY. *Current Pos:* DIST FEL & DIR RES & DEVELOP, AM SCI DIV, MONSANTO CO, 82- *Personal Data:* b Warrensburg, Mo, Feb 8, 40; m 60, Beth L Hoover; c Christopher A & Marisa. *Educ:* Cent Mo State Col, BS, 62; Univ Mo, PhD(nutrit), 64; Univ Pa, MA, 79. *Honors & Awards:* Nutrit Res Award, Am Feed Mfgrs Asn & Am Dairy Sci Asn, 79; Animal Growth & Develop Award, Am Soc Animal Sci, 89. *Prof Exp:* NIH fel, Sch Pub Health, Harvard Univ, 64-66, from instr to asst prof nutrit, 66-71; sr investr res & develop, Animal Health Prod Div, Smith Kline & French Labs, 71-73, mgr neurobiol res, 73-75; from assoc prof to prof nutrit, Dept Clin Studies, Sch Vet Med, Univ Pa, 75-82. *Concurrent Pos:* Lectr, Univ Pa & res assoc, Monell Chem Senses Ctr, 71-75; adj assoc prof, Pa State Univ, 71-81, adj prof, 81- & adj prof, Wash Univ, 82- *Mem:* Am Physiol Soc; Am Inst Nutrit; Am Dairy Sci Asn; Am Soc Animal Sci. *Res:* Regulatory mechanisms for control of food intake and energy balance. *Mailing Add:* Grad Studies Res Ctr Univ Ga 708 Boyd Athens GA 30602. *Fax:* 314-537-7002; *E-Mail:* cabail@ccmail.monsanto.com

BAILES, GORDON LEE, ARTIFICIAL INTELLIGENCE, SOFTWARE ENGINEERING. *Current Pos:* Asst prof, ETenn State Univ, 72-77, chmn & assoc prof, 77-83, chmn, 83-96, PROF COMPUT SCI, ETENN STATE UNIV, 96- *Personal Data:* b Greenwood, SC, Apr 18, 46; m 96, Lisa Wilson; c John, Jeff, Tonya & Nichole. *Educ:* Clemson Univ, BS, 68, MS, 69, PhD(math sci), 72. *Concurrent Pos:* Tech chair, Comput Sci Conf, Asn Comput Mach, 88-89, abstr chair, 89-91 & 90-92, publicity chair, 89-91; team chair, Comput Sci Accreditation Comn, 89- *Mem:* Asn Comput Mach; Inst Elec & Electronics Engrs; Am Asn Artificial Intel; Spec Interest Group Artificial Intel; Spec Interest Group Comput Sci Educ; Inst Elec & Electronics Engrs Comput Sci. *Res:* Authored a book on computer organization and assembly language. *Mailing Add:* ETenn State Univ Box 70711 Johnson City TN 37614-0711. *Fax:* 423-439-4227; *E-Mail:* bailes@etsu.tn.edu

BAILEY, ALFRED, HISTORY & PHILOSOPHY OF SCIENCE. *Current Pos:* EMER PROF, DEPT HIST, UNIV NEW BRUNSWICK. *Mailing Add:* Univ New Brunswick Res 2 Acacia Ct Fredericton NB E3B 1Y7 Can

BAILEY, ARTHUR W, RANGE SCIENCE. *Current Pos:* From asst prof to prof, 66-97, EMER PROF PLANT SCI, UNIV ALTA, 97- *Personal Data:* b Chilliwack, BC, July 22, 38; m 62; c 3. *Educ:* Univ BC, BSA, 60; Ore State Univ, MS, 63, PhD(range mgt), 66. *Concurrent Pos:* Grants, Can Dept Agr, 66-, Alta Agr Res Trust, 67-82, Nat Res Coun Can, 69-78 & Alta Farming Future, 79-; vis prof, Tex Tech Univ, 72-83 & Univ Natal, SAfrica, 81-82, Univ Witwatersrand, SAfrica, 88-89. *Mem:* Soc Range Mgt; Agr Inst Can. *Res:* Range ecology; brush control; rangeland fire; grazing effects on vegetation. *Mailing Add:* Agr Food & Nutrit Sci 4-10 Agr Forestry Ctr Edmonton AB T6G 2P5 Can

BAILEY, BRUCE M(ONROE), MECHANICAL ENGINEERING. *Current Pos:* RETIRED. *Personal Data:* b Stoneham, Mass, Nov 5, 28; m 51; c 3. *Educ:* Worcester Polytech Inst, BS, 51; Northeastern Univ, MS, 75. *Prof Exp:* Aeronaut res scientist, Nat Adv Comt Aeronaut, Langley Field, Va, 51-53; sr mech engr, Arthur D Little, Inc, 53-59; sr scientist, Air Prod, Inc, 59-60; chief mech engr, Lab Nuclear Sci, Mass Inst Technol, 60-89. *Concurrent Pos:* Lectr, Northeast Univ, 64-65; mech engr consult. *Mem:* Am Soc Mech Engrs; Am Vacuum Soc. *Res:* Low-temperature thermodynamics applications; high-vacuum techniques; gas separation processes. *Mailing Add:* 41 Woodland St Sherborn MA 01770

BAILEY, BYRON JAMES, OTOLARYNGOLOGY. *Current Pos:* assoc prof, 64-70, PROF OTOLARYNGOL, WEISS PROF & CHMN DEPT, UNIV TEX MED BR GALVESTON, 70- *Personal Data:* b Oklahoma City, Okla, Apr 5, 34; m 57; c 5. *Educ:* Univ Okla, BA, 55, MD, 59. *Honors & Awards:* Mosher Award, Am Caryngol, Rhinologic & Otologic Soc; Harvey W Wiley Medal, US Food & Drug Admin; De Roaldes Medal, Laryngol Asn. *Prof Exp:* Surg intern, Univ Calif, Los Angeles, 59-60, asst resident gen surg, 60-61, resident head & neck surg, 61-62. *Concurrent Pos:* USPHS fel, Univ Calif, Los Angeles, 62-64; NIH res grant, 67-; bd dirs, Am Coun Otolaryngol, 73- & Am Bd Otolaryngol, 76-; mem, Residency Rev Comt Otolaryngol, 73-79; consult, Fed Drug Admin Panel Classification of Ear, Nose & Throat Devices, 77-80; chmn, Commun Sci Study Sect, NIH, 77-79; past pres, Am Acad Otalaryngol Head & Neck Surg, Am Soc Head & Neck Surg, Am Laryngol Asn & Am Bd Otolaryngol. *Mem:* AAAS; Soc Univ Otolaryngol (pres, 76-77); fel Am Acad Ophthal & Otolaryngol; fel Am Col Surg; fel Am Soc Head & Neck Surg; Sigma Xi. *Res:* Laryngeal reconstruction; tracheal transplantation. *Mailing Add:* Dept Otolaryngol Univ Tex Med Br Galveston TX 77550

BAILEY, CARL LEONARD, physics, for more information see previous edition

BAILEY, CARL WILLIAMS, III, WOOD CHEMISTRY, PAPER CHEMISTRY. *Current Pos:* From res chemist to sr res chemist, Westvaco Corp, 68-73, group leader res lignin chem, 73-74, group leader res tall oil chem, 74-79, SECT LEADER RES, CHARLESTON RES CTR, WESTVACO CORP, 79- *Personal Data:* b New Haven, Conn, Feb 7, 41; m 63; c 2. *Educ:* State Univ NY Col Environ Sci & Forestry & Syracuse Univ, BS, 63, MS, 65, PhD(pulp & paper), 68. *Mem:* Am Oil Chem Soc. *Res:* Preparation of derivatives of rosin and fatty acids; characterization of these products and finding commercial areas where they can be utilized. *Mailing Add:* Westvaco Corp PO Box 70848 Charleston Heights SC 29415-0848

BAILEY, CARROLL EDWARD, solid state physics, for more information see previous edition

BAILEY, CATHERINE HAYES, POMOLOGY. *Current Pos:* Tech asst, Agr Exp Sta, Rutgers Univ, 48-54, res assoc, 54-57, asst prof pomol, 57-66, assoc res prof, 66-72, prof, 72-80. *Personal Data:* b New Brunswick, NJ, May 9, 21. *Educ:* Douglass Col, BA, 42; Rutgers Univ, PhD(fruit breeding), 57. *Concurrent Pos:* Exchange scientist, Res Sta, Can Dept Agr, BC, 65-66. *Mem:* Am Soc Hort Sci; Am Pomol Soc; Torrey Bot Club; Int Soc Hort Sci. *Res:* Fruit breeding; breeding for disease resistance; peaches, apricots, apples; inheritance of season of ripening in progenies from certain early ripening peach varieties and selections. *Mailing Add:* 71 Mountain Terr Bristol VT 05443

BAILEY, CECIL DEWITT, DYNAMICS. *Current Pos:* from assoc prof to prof, 67-85, EMER PROF AERONAUT & ASTRONAUT ENG, OHIO STATE UNIV, 85- *Personal Data:* b Ayers, Miss, Oct 25, 21; m 42, Myrtis Taylor; c Marilyn & Beverly. *Educ:* Miss State Univ, BS, 51; Purdue Univ, MS, 54, PhD(trapezoidal plates), 62. *Prof Exp:* Instr B-47 bomber sch, USAF, 51-52, eng mech & aircraft structure, Air Force Inst Technol, 54-56, asst prof, 56-58, chief aerospace res, Air Force Systs Command Off, Langley Res Ctr, NASA, 59-63, aeronaut engr, Hq Air Force Systs Command, 64-65, assoc prof mech, Air Force Inst Technol, 66-67. *Concurrent Pos:* Dir, USAF-ASEE Summer Fac Res Prog, Wright-Patterson AFB, Ohio, 76-78. *Mem:* Soc Exp Stress Anal; Am Soc Eng Educ; Am Acad Mech. *Res:* Alternatives to the theory of differential equations; systems dynamics; particles, rigid and deformable body mechanics; dynamics of thermally stressed structures. *Mailing Add:* Dept Aeronaut Eng Ohio State Univ Columbus OH 43210

BAILEY, CHARLES BASIL MANSFIELD, ANIMAL PHYSIOLOGY, NUTRITION. *Current Pos:* RETIRED. *Personal Data:* b Vancouver, BC, Feb 10, 30; m 57; c 3. *Educ:* Univ BC, BSA, 54, MSA, 56; Univ Reading, PhD(animal physiol), 59. *Honors & Awards:* Can Asn Animal Breeders Medal, 83. *Prof Exp:* Res scientist animal physiol, Can Dept Agr, 59-90. *Concurrent Pos:* Nat Res Coun Can fel, 59-60. *Mem:* Can Soc Animal Sci; Brit Nutrit Soc. *Res:* Renal physiology, particularly urinary calculi formation in cattle; effect of diet on muscle protein synthesis in cattle. *Mailing Add:* 4235 Frederick Rd RR 2 C-18 Armstrong BC V0E 1B0 Can

BAILEY, CHARLES EDWARD, PHYSICAL CHEMISTRY. *Current Pos:* RETIRED. *Personal Data:* b Johnson City, Tenn, May 25, 32; m 58; c 3. *Educ:* Univ Tenn, BS, 53, MS, 55, PhD(phys chem), 58. *Prof Exp:* Sr physicist, Polymer Intermediates Dept, Savannah River Lab, E I du Pont de Nemours & Co, Inc, 58-69, sr res supvr comput appln div, 69-74, staff chemist, Environ Anal Planning Div, Savannah River Lab, 74-90. *Mem:* Am Chem Soc; Am Nuclear Soc. *Res:* Environmental management; nuclear reactor safety; environmental sciences. *Mailing Add:* 563 Coker Spring Rd SW Aiken SC 29801-4841

BAILEY, CHARLES LAVON, medical entomology, for more information see previous edition

BAILEY, CHARLES W, MATHEMATICS. *Current Pos:* Instr, 65-77, PROF, MESA STATE COL, 77- *Personal Data:* b Paonia, Colo, 36. *Educ:* Univ Northern Colo, MA, 62. *Mem:* Math Asn Am; Nat Coun Teachers Math. *Res:* Mathematics. *Mailing Add:* 302 Country Club Park Grand Junction CO 81503-1613

BAILEY, CLAUDIA F, TELEOST NEURULATION, ENDOCYTOSIS. *Current Pos:* ASSOC PROF ZOOL, UNIV ARK, 70- *Educ:* Bryn Mawr Col, PhD(develop biol), 70. *Mailing Add:* Dept Biol Sci SE632 Univ Ark Fayetteville AR 72701

BAILEY, CLETA SUE, veterinary medicine, for more information see previous edition

BAILEY, CURTISS MERKEL, ANIMAL BREEDING. *Current Pos:* From asst prof to assoc prof, 60-71, prof & geneticist, 71-90, EMER PROF ANIMAL SCI, UNIV NEV, RENO, 90- *Personal Data:* b Cleveland, Ohio, Aug 31, 27; m 54; c 4. *Educ:* Univ Wis, BS, 52, PhD(genetics, animal husb), 60; Tex A&M Univ, MS, 54. *Concurrent Pos:* Ed-in-chief, J Animal Sci. *Mem:* Am Genetic Asn; Am Soc Animal Sci; Sigma Xi. *Res:* Selection responses; crossbreeding; bull beef concept; total life-cycle beef systems. *Mailing Add:* 5100 Twin Springs Rd Reno NV 89510

BAILEY, DANA KAVANAGH, GEOPHYSICS, SYSTEMATIC BOTANY. *Current Pos:* RES ASSOC, UNIV COLO MUS, 72- *Personal Data:* b Clarendon Hills, Ill, Nov 22, 16. *Educ:* Univ Ariz, BS, 37; Oxford Univ, BA, 40, MA, 43, DSc, 67. *Honors & Awards:* US Antarctic Serv Medal, 47. *Prof Exp:* Observ asst, Steward Observ, Univ Ariz, 33-37; astronr, Hayden Planetarium, Am Mus Natural Hist, New York, 37; physicist, Anarctic Serv, US Dept Interior, 40-41; proj engr, Rand, Douglas Aircraft Co, Calif, 46-48; consult to chief, Cent Radio Propagation Lab, Nat Bur Stand, 48-55; sci dir, Page Commun Engrs, Inc, DC, 55-59; consult, Space Environ Lab, Environ Res Labs, Nat Oceanic & Atmospheric Admin, 59-78. *Concurrent Pos:* Mem, Hayden Planetarium-Grace Eclipse exped, Peru, 37 & US Antarctic exped, 40-41; chmn, Int Study Group Ionospheric Radio Progagation, Int Radio Consult Comt, Int Telecommun Union, 56-; hon res assoc, Rhodes Univ, 70-71. *Mem:* Am Astron Soc; fel Am Phys Soc; Am Geophys Union; fel Royal Geog Soc; fel Royal Astron Soc; Sigma Xi. *Res:* Solar terrestial relationships; cosmic ray physics; ionosphere; radio wave propagation; phytogeography; dendrochronology; systematic and evolutionary aspects of gymnosperms. *Mailing Add:* 624 Pearl St No 403 Boulder CO 80302-5073

BAILEY, DAVID GEORGE, LEATHER CHEMISTRY, WASTE TREATMENT. *Current Pos:* Res chemist, 67-80, SUPR RES CHEMIST, AGR RES SERV, USDA, PA, 80- *Personal Data:* b New York, NY, Feb 21, 40; m 61; c 3. *Educ:* Univ Del, BS, 63, MS, 64; Univ Vt, PhD(biochem), 67. *Mem:* Am Chem Soc; Am Leather Chemists Asn. *Res:* Chemistry of conversion of rawhides to leather; anaerobic treatment of tannery waste. *Mailing Add:* 600 E Mermaid Lane Philadelphia PA 19118-2551

BAILEY, DAVID H, COMPUTER SCIENCE. *Current Pos:* COMPUT SCIENTIST, AMES RES CTR, NASA, MOFFETT FIELD, CALIF, 84- *Personal Data:* c 4. *Educ:* Brigham Young Univ, BS, 72; Stanford Univ, PhD(math), 76. *Honors & Awards:* Chauvenet Prize, Math Asn Am, 93; Merten Hasse Prize, 93; Sidney Fernbach Award, Inst Elec & Electronics Engrs, 93. *Prof Exp:* Comput scientist, US Govt, Ft Meade, Md, 76-80, TRW/ESL Inc, Sunnyvale, Calif, 80-84 & SRI/Int, Menlo Park, Calif, 81-84. *Mem:* Inst Elec & Electronics Engrs; Asn Comput Mach; Soc Indust & Appl Math. *Res:* Contributed numerous articles to professional journals. *Mailing Add:* Ames Res Ctr NASA Mail Stop T27A-1 Moffett Field CA 94035-1000

BAILEY, DAVID NELSON, CLINICAL TOXICOLOGY, LABORATORY MEDICINE. *Current Pos:* from asst prof to assoc prof, Univ Calif, San Diego, 77-86, head, Div Lab Med, 83-89, vchmn, 85-86, actg chmn, 86-88, DIR CLIN LABS, UNIV CALIF, SAN DIEGO, 82-, PROF PATH, DEPT PATH, 86-, CHMN, 88-, HEAD, DIV LAB MED, 94- *Personal Data:* b Anderson, Ind, June 21, 45. *Educ:* Indiana Univ, BS, 67; Yale Univ, MD, 73. *Honors & Awards:* Gerald T Evans Award, Acad Clin Lab Physicians & Scientists. *Prof Exp:* Clin fel, Dept Lab Med, Yale Univ, 73-75; asst resident clin path, Yale-New Haven Hosp, 75-76, chief resident, 76-77. *Concurrent Pos:* Clin instr, Dept Lab Med, Yale Univ, 76-77; pres, Calif Asn Toxicol, 81-82. *Mem:* AAAS; Am Chem Soc; Am Asn Clin Chem; Acad Clin Lab Physicians & Scientists (pres, 88-89); Asn Path Chmn (secy-treas, 96-). *Res:* Clinical pharmacology of drugs of abuse; epidemiology of drug overdose; pharmacology of cocaine and its homologs-analytical toxicology. *Mailing Add:* Dept Path Univ Calif Med Ctr 200 W Arbor Dr San Diego CA 92103-8320. *Fax:* 619-543-3730

BAILEY, DAVID NEWTON, ANALYTICAL CHEMISTRY. *Current Pos:* PROF CHEM, ILL WESLEYAN UNIV, 80- *Personal Data:* b Pittsburgh, Pa, Dec 1, 41; m 61, Sara Yost; c Glenn, Lauren & Allan. *Educ:* Juniata Col, BS, 63; Mass Inst Technol, PhD(analytical chem), 68. *Prof Exp:* Asst prof anal chem, Gustavus Adolphus Col, 68-71; from asst prof to assoc prof anal chem, Lebanon Valley Col, 71-80. *Concurrent Pos:* Consult, State Farm Ins Co. *Mem:* Sigma Xi; Am Chem Soc. *Res:* Drug analysis; computer applications to chemistry. *Mailing Add:* Dept Chem Ill Wesleyan Univ Bloomington IL 61702-2900

BAILEY, DAVID TIFFANY, ORGANIC CHEMISTRY, BIOCHEMISTRY. *Current Pos:* MGR NAT PROD RES, HAUSER CHEM RES INC. *Personal Data:* b Olney, Tex, Aug 26, 42; m 66. *Educ:* Univ Colo, Boulder, BA, 64; Iowa State Univ, PhD(org chem), 68. *Prof Exp:* NIH res fel & assoc chem, Yale Univ, 68-69; from asst prof to prof chem, Calif State Univ, Fullerton, 69-79; prof chem, Flathead Valley Community Col, 80- *Mem:* AAAS; Am Chem Soc. *Res:* Organic chemistry and biosynthesis of natural products. *Mailing Add:* PO Box 4989 Boulder CO 80306-4989

BAILEY, DENIS MAHLON, ORGANIC CHEMISTRY. *Current Pos:* RETIRED. *Personal Data:* b St Louis, Mo, Aug 14, 35; m 61; c 4. *Educ:* Washington Univ, BA, 57, PhD(org chem), 61; Rensselaer Polytech Inst, MBA, 85. *Prof Exp:* NIH fel, Stanford Univ, 62-63; res assoc, Sterling Winthrop Res Inst, 63-65, group leader, 65-68, sr res chemist, 68-74, sect head, 68-76, sr res assoc, 74-77, dir med chem, 77-82, vpres chem, 82-84, exec vpres drug discovery, 84-94. *Concurrent Pos:* Ed-in-chief, Ann Reports Med Chem. *Mem:* Am Chem Soc; AAAS; Am Soc Pharmacol & Exp Therapeut; Soc Magnetic Resonance Med. *Res:* Medicinal chemistry; cardiovascular and metabolic diseases; central nervous system, analgesic, antiinflammatory and antiinfective agents; diagnostic imaging agents. *Mailing Add:* 200 Country Lane Phoenixville PA 19460

BAILEY, DON MATTHEW, AEROSPACE. *Current Pos:* secy & vpres corp develop, 80-92, PRES & CHIEF EXEC OFFICER, COMARCO INC, 92- *Personal Data:* b Pittsburgh, Pa, Jan 2, 46; m 67, Linda Reed; c Don M Jr, Kirsten P & Terrance R. *Educ:* Drexel Univ, BSME, 68; Univ Southern Calif, MS, 71; Pepperdine Univ, MBA, 86. *Prof Exp:* Programmer, Naval Air Systs Command, Washington, 63-69; engr, Rockwell Int, 69-71; prog mgr, Logicon, Inc, 71-80. *Concurrent Pos:* Mem bd dirs, Develop Disabilities Ctr Orange Co, Calif & Perspective Instruct Commun, San Diego. *Res:* Operations research; aerospace. *Mailing Add:* Comarco Inc 22800 Savi Ranch Pkwy Yorba Linda CA 92667

BAILEY, DONALD ETHERIDGE, SCIENCE EDUCATION, BIOLOGY. *Current Pos:* prof sci educ, 61-69, dean gen col, 69-90, PROF SCI EDUC, E CAROLINA UNIV, 90- *Personal Data:* b Moore Co, NC, May 4, 31; m 54; c 2. *Educ:* Univ NC, BS, 53, MEd, 58, EdD(sci educ), 62. *Prof Exp:* Teacher pub schs, NC, 53-54 & 56-60. *Mem:* Nat Sci Teachers Asn. *Res:* Incidence and prevalence of misconceptions of matters scientific in secondary schools of North Carolina. *Mailing Add:* 214 York Rd Greenville NC 27858

BAILEY, DONALD FOREST, MATHEMATICS. *Current Pos:* assoc prof, 83-91, PROF MATH, TRINITY UNIV, 91- *Personal Data:* b Cliffside, NC, Apr 10, 39; m 61, Elaine Byassee; c Matthew F & G David. *Educ:* Wake Forest Univ, BS, 61; Vanderbilt Univ, MA, 63, PhD(math), 65. *Prof Exp:* Assoc prof math, Cornell Col, 69-78, prof, 78-83. *Mem:* Math Asn Am; Am Math Soc; Sigma Xi; Nat Coun Teachers Math. *Res:* Elementary number theory. *Mailing Add:* 210 Ranger Dr Boerne TX 78006. *E-Mail:* dbailey@trinity.edu

BAILEY, DONALD LEROY, organic chemistry; deceased, see previous edition for last biography

BAILEY, DONALD WAYNE, DEVELOPMENTAL GENETICS, IMMUNOGENETICS. *Current Pos:* from staff scientist to sr staff scientist, 67-90, EMER SCIENTIST, JACKSON LAB, 90- *Personal Data:* b Hutchinson, Kans, Feb 28, 26; m 82, Patricia Ward. *Educ:* Univ Calif, AB, 49, PhD(genetics), 53. *Prof Exp:* Fel, USPHS, Jackson Lab, 53-55, lab fel, 55-56, staff scientist, 56-57; asst prof, Univ Kans, 57-59; geneticist, Lab Aids Br, NIH, 59-61; assoc res geneticist, Univ Calif, San Francisco, 61-67; emer prof, 90- *Mem:* Genetics Soc Am. *Res:* Development of methodologies that use recombinant-inbred and bilineal congenic strains of mice to analyze complexly inherited traits, such as morphogenesis and disease resistance. *Mailing Add:* Jackson Lab 600 Main St Bar Harbor ME 04609

BAILEY, DONALD WYCOFF, physiology, for more information see previous edition

BAILEY, DUANE W, COMPUTER NETWORKS. *Current Pos:* from asst prof to assoc prof, 63-71, chmn dept, 67-72, PROF MATH, AMHERST COL, 71- *Personal Data:* b Moscow, Idaho, Sept 22, 36; m 59; c 3. *Educ:* Wash State Univ, BA, 57; Univ Ore, MA, 59, PhD(math), 61. *Hon Degrees:* MA, Amherst Col, 71. *Prof Exp:* Instr math, Yale Univ, 61-63. *Concurrent Pos:* Vis prof, Univ Tex, Austin, 84-85. *Mem:* Am Math Soc; Math Asn Am; London Math Soc; Soc Indust Appl Math. *Res:* Banach and topological algebras. *Mailing Add:* Amherst Col Amherst MA 01002-5002

BAILEY, EDWARD D, ANIMAL BEHAVIOR. *Current Pos:* RETIRED. *Personal Data:* b Port Clinton, Pa, Sept 22, 31. *Educ:* Mont State Univ, BS, 58, MS, 60; Pa State Univ, PhD(zool), 63. *Prof Exp:* Instr zool, Mont State Univ, 63-64; asst prof, Ont Agr Col, 64-69; assoc prof zool, Univ Guelph, 69-95, emer prof, 95. *Mem:* Fel AAAS; Animal Behav Soc; Am Orinthologist Union. *Res:* Social behavior in wild mammals and birds; development of communication and early learning. *Mailing Add:* Dept Zool Univ Guelph Guelph ON N1G 2W1 Can

BAILEY, EVERETT MURL, JR, VETERINARY TOXICOLOGY. *Current Pos:* from asst prof to assoc prof, 70-81, PROF PHYSIOL & PHARMACOL, COL VET MED, TEX A&M UNIV, 81- *Personal Data:* b Big Spring, Tex, Mar 24, 40; c 2. *Educ:* Tex A&M Univ, DVM, 64; Iowa State Univ, MS, 66, PhD(physiol), 68; Am Bd Vet Toxicol, dipl, 72. *Honors & Awards:* Comnr Spec Citation, FDA. *Prof Exp:* Staff pathologist, US Army Inst Environ Med, 68-70. *Concurrent Pos:* Vis prof, Food & Drug Admin, 81; chmn, IRB, 88- *Mem:* Am Vet Med Asn; Am Acad Vet & Comp Toxicol; Am Asn Vet Physiol & Pharmacol; Am Bd Vet Toxicol (pres, 79-82). *Res:* Chemical restraining agents in horses; experimental surgery; toxicology; anesthesiology; toxic plants; treatment of intoxications; pesticides. *Mailing Add:* 12492 Old Wellborn Rd College Station TX 77845. *Fax:* 409-845-6544; *E-Mail:* mbailey@vthvax.tamu.edu

BAILEY, F WALLACE, PHYSICAL CHEMISTRY, POLYMER PROCESSING. *Current Pos:* RETIRED. *Personal Data:* b Britt, Iowa, Nov 6, 29; m 50; c 3. *Educ:* Univ Okla, BS, 53, MS, 54. *Prof Exp:* Chemist, Silicones Div, Union Carbide Corp, 54-61_& Res & Develop Dept, Phillips Petrol Co, 61-91. *Mem:* Soc Plastics Engrs. *Res:* Product development and application research of polymers. *Mailing Add:* 6001 SE Harvard Bartlesville OK 74006

BAILEY, FRED COOLIDGE, MECHANICS, ENGINEERING. *Current Pos:* RETIRED. *Personal Data:* b Claremont, NH, Oct 5, 25; m 48, Mary Cunningham; c 2. *Educ:* Mass Inst Technol, SB, 48, SM, 49. *Honors & Awards:* Linnard Prize, Soc Naval Archit & Marine Engrs, 71. *Prof Exp:* Res engr, Caterpillar Tractor Co, 49-52; actg tech dir, comt ship steel & ship struct design, Nat Acad Sci, 52-55; pres, Lessells & Assocs, 55-66 & Teledyne Mat Res Co, 66-76; pres, Teledyne Eng Serv, Teledyne Inc, 76-87, group exec, 83-87, consult, 87-89. *Mem:* Hon mem Soc Exp Stress Anal (treas, 61-65, vpres, 65-67, pres, 67-69); Am Soc Mech Engrs; Am Welding Soc; Soc Naval Archit & Marine Engrs. *Res:* Theoretical and experimental stress analysis; metals engineering; applied mechanics. *Mailing Add:* 48 Coolidge Ave Lexington MA 02173

BAILEY, FREDERICK EUGENE, JR, PHYSICAL CHEMISTRY. *Current Pos:* res chemist, 52-59, group leader, 59-61, asst dir res & develop dept, Chem Div, 61-69, tech mgr calendering, flooring & rec prod dept, Plastics Div, 64-65, tech mgr vinyl resins, 65-68, mgr mkt res, 69-71, SR RES SCIENTIST POLYMER SCI, UNION CARBIDE CORP, 71- *Personal Data:* b Brooklyn, NY, Oct 8, 27; m 79. *Educ:* Amherst Col, AB, 48; Yale Univ, MS, 50, PhD(chem), 52. *Honors & Awards:* Chem Pioneers Award, Am Inst Chem, 87; Sci Achievement Award, Kanawha Valley Sect, Am Chem Soc, 88. *Prof Exp:* Asst, Yale Univ, 50-52. *Concurrent Pos:* Lectr, Kanawha Valley Grad Ctr, WVa Univ, 59-60 & Morris Harvey Col, 61-62, 65-66; chmn, Gordon Res Conf Polymers, 72 & 84, Gordon Res Conf Forms, 90 & 92; adj prof chem, Marshall Univ, 75-; prof chem eng, WVa Col Grad Studies, 81-; chmn, Div Polymer Chem, Am Chem Soc, gen secy, Macromolecular Secretariat, 78, counr, 78-89, exec-officer counr, 90-, bd dirs, 90-93. *Mem:* Fel AAAS; Am Chem Soc; Am Phys Soc; fel NY Acad Sci; fel Am Inst Chem; Am Chem Soc. *Res:* Polymer chemistry and physics; polymer morphology-property relationships and polymer synthesis, polyurethanes; author of twenty-one publications, three books, sixty-eight technical articles and sixty patents. *Mailing Add:* 848 Beaumont Rd Charleston WV 25314

BAILEY, FREDRIC NELSON, CONTROL SYSTEMS, MOTION CONTROL. *Current Pos:* from asst prof to assoc prof, 64-90, PROF ELEC ENG, UNIV MINN, MINNEAPOLIS, 90- *Personal Data:* b Toledo, Ohio, Jan 5, 32; div; c 5. *Educ:* Purdue Univ, BSEE, 53; Univ Mich, MSE, 60, PhD(elec eng), 64. *Prof Exp:* Asst res engr, Cooley Electronics Lab, Univ Mich, 57-62, assoc res eng, 62-64. *Concurrent Pos:* Consult, Unisys Corp, 66-84, Cimcorp Inc, 85-88, Graco Inc, 89; vis assoc prof, Inst Automation, Tech Univ Warsaw, 73, 74 & 77, Univ Budapest, 80; assoc ed, Trans Automatic Control, 82-84; vis scientist, Dept Comput Sci, Tech Univ Madrid, 86, 87, 88 & 91. *Mem:* Sr mem Inst Elec & Electronics Engrs; Soc Indust & Appl Math; Int Fedn Automatic Control. *Res:* Analog and digital control systems; computer aided design of control systems; industrial applications of control in manufacturing; machine tools and robotics. *Mailing Add:* Dept Elec Eng Univ Minn 200 Union St SE Minneapolis MN 55455. *Fax:* 612-625-4583; *E-Mail:* bailey@ee.umn.edu

BAILEY, GEORGE WILLIAM, ENVIRONMENTAL QUALITY. *Current Pos:* supvry res soil phys chemist, Southeastern Environ Lab, US Environ Protection Agency, 70-74, supvry res soil phys chemist, 74-76, assoc dir rural lands res, 76-85, RES SOIL PHYS CHEMIST, ENVIRON RES LAB, US ENVIRON PROTECTION AGENCY, ATHENS, GA, 85- *Personal Data:* b Des Moines, Iowa, Oct 30, 33; m 58, 77; c 4. *Educ:* Iowa State Univ, BS, 55; Purdue Univ, MS, 58, PhD(soil chem, mineral), 61. *Honors & Awards:* Bronze Medal, Environ Protection Agency. *Prof Exp:* Soil surveyor, Soil Conserv Serv, 55-56; NIH res fel, Purdue Univ, 61-64; soil-pesticide chemist, Div Water Supply & Pollution Control, USPHS, 64-66; soil phys chemist, Fed Water Pollution Control Admin, US Dept Interior, 66-70, Fed Water Qual Admin,. *Mem:* AAAS; fel Am Soc Agron; fel Soil Sci Soc Am; Am Chem Soc; Sigma Xi. *Res:* Soil pesticide chemistry; water quality; clay and soil mineralogy; mathematical modeling and simulation of the transformation, transport and fate of pesticides, plant nutrients, hazardous wastes and toxics from agricultural and rural land; fate and transport of metals in the environment; surface chemistry of metal interactions; redox reactions at mineral surfaces. *Mailing Add:* 4135 Old Lexington Rd Athens GA 30605

BAILEY, GLENN CHARLES, SOLID STATE PHYSICS. *Current Pos:* physicist, 85-87, CONSULT, SACHS/FREEMAN ASSOC, LANDOVER, MD, 87- *Personal Data:* b Pekin, Ill, Aug 21, 30; m 58; c 5. *Educ:* Univ Ill, BS, 52; Univ Wis, MS, 54; Cath Univ Am, PhD(physics), 65. *Prof Exp:* Physicist, Caterpillar Tractor Co, Ill, 55-57; res physicist, Condensed Matter & Radiation Sci Div, US Naval Res Lab, 57-85. *Mem:* Am Phys Soc. *Res:* Microwave interactions in materials and non-equilibrium superconductivity; ferromagnetic resonance of thin films and single crystals; radiation damage in semiconductors, ferrites and thin films; x-ray diffraction and fluorescent analysis; residual stresses in metals. *Mailing Add:* 1915 Taylor Ave Ft Washington MD 20744

BAILEY, GORDON BURGESS, BIOCHEMISTRY. *Current Pos:* PROF BIOCHEM, MOREHOUSE SCH MED, 76- *Personal Data:* b Worcester, Mass, Feb 13, 34; m 58; c 3. *Educ:* Brown Univ, BA, 56; Univ Mass, MA, 61; Univ Fla, PhD(biochem), 66. *Prof Exp:* Vis prof biochem, Field Staff, Rockefeller Found, 66-73; dep dir, Anemia & Malnutrition Res Ctr, Fac Med, Chiang Mai Univ, Thailand, 73-76. *Concurrent Pos:* Vis prof, Mahidol Univ, Bangkok, 66-73; consult human reproduction unit, WHO, 75-76. *Mem:* AAAS; Am Soc Cell Biol; Am Soc Microbiol; Am Soc Parasitol; Soc Protozool. *Res:* Motility and cytopathogenicity of Entamoeba. *Mailing Add:* Dept Biochem Morehouse Sch Med 720 Westview Dr Atlanta GA 30310-1495

BAILEY, HAROLD EDWARDS, PHARMACOGNOSY. *Current Pos:* asst prof biol sci & pharmacog, Wayne State Univ, 47-53, assoc prof biol sci, 53-58, prof pharmacog, 59-74, EMER PROF PHARMACOG, WAYNE STATE UNIV, 74- *Personal Data:* b Salt Lake City, Utah, July 26, 06; m 33, Virginia Edith Long. *Educ:* Univ Calif, Los Angeles, AB, 30, PhD(microbiol), 35. *Prof Exp:* Teaching fel bot, Univ Calif, Los Angeles, 31-34; asst forester, Nat Park Serv, 35-38, jr park naturalist, 39-42; instr bot, Univ Tenn, 38; res asst, Parke Davis & Co, 42-47. *Mem:* AAAS; Am Pharmaceut Asn; Am Soc Pharmacog; Soc Econ Bot; Acad Pharmaceut Sci. *Res:* Antibiotics; physiology of fungi; chemotaxonomy. *Mailing Add:* 4727 Second Detroit MI 48201-1244

BAILEY, HAROLD STEVENS, II, PHARMACEUTICAL CHEMISTRY. *Current Pos:* asst prof pharmacol, SDak State Univ, 51-52, from assoc prof to prof pharmaceut chem, 52-73, dean acad affairs, 61-73, dean grad sch, 65-76, vpres acad affairs, 73-85, VPRES EMER & DISTINGUISHED PROF HIGHER EDUC, SDAK STATE UNIV, 85- *Personal Data:* b Springfield, Mass, Apr 18, 22; m 46; c 5. *Educ:* Mass Col Pharm, BS, 44, MS, 48; Purdue Univ, PhD(pharmaceut chem), 51. *Prof Exp:* Asst chem, Mass Col Pharm, 46-48. *Concurrent Pos:* Ed, Pharm Sect, SDak J Med & Pharm, 53-61. *Mem:* Fel AAAS; Sigma Xi; fel Am Found Pharm Educ. *Res:* Application of biochemical research to pharmacology and radiation biology; dental research. *Mailing Add:* 336 Eastern Ave Brookings SD 57006

BAILEY, HERBERT R, MATHEMATICS. *Current Pos:* prof & chmn dept, 66-75, vpres acad affairs & dean fac, 75-77, PROF MATH, ROSE-HULMAN INST TECHNOL, 77- *Personal Data:* b Denver, Colo, Nov 2, 25; m 51; c 5. *Educ:* Rose Polytech Inst, BS, 45, 46; Univ Ill, MS, 47; Purdue Univ, PhD(math), 55. *Prof Exp:* Instr math, Gen Motors Inst, 47-49; mathematician, US Naval Ord Plant, Ind, 49-55 & Denver Res Ctr, Ohio Oil Co, 56-62; assoc prof math, Colo State Univ, 62-66. *Mem:* Math Asn Am. *Res:* Differential difference equations; fluid flow and diffusion. *Mailing Add:* Math Dept 219 Gardendale Rd Terre Haute IN 47803

BAILEY, IAN L, VISION SCIENCE, ILLUMINATING ENGINEERING. *Current Pos:* PROF OPTOM, UNIV CALIF, BERKELEY, 76- *Personal Data:* b Melbourne, Australia, Dec 22, 40; m 63; c 2. *Educ:* Victorian Col Optom, LOSc, 62; Univ Melbourne, B App Sc, 63; City Univ London, FBOA HD, 67; Ind Univ, MS, 71. *Honors & Awards:* Glen A Fry Award, Am Acad Optom, 86. *Prof Exp:* Lectr optom, Victorian Col Optom, Univ Melbourne, 68-74; sr res officer, Nat Vision Res Inst Australia, 75-76. *Concurrent Pos:* Gov, Asn Blind, Melbourne, Australia, 75; rep comt vision, Nat Acad Sci/Nat Res Coun, Am Acad Optom, 85-; chair, Low Vision Sect, Am Acad Optom, 85-86. *Mem:* Am Acad Optom; Am Optom Asn; Asn Res Vision & Ophthal. *Res:* Low vision; clinical assessment of vision; visual ergonomics; visual optics. *Mailing Add:* 5708 Thornhill Dr Oakland CA 94611

BAILEY, J EARL, AERONAUTICS, ASTRONAUTICS. *Current Pos:* RETIRED. *Personal Data:* b State College, Miss, Apr 16, 33; m 58; c 2. *Educ:* Miss State Univ, BS, 55, MS, 58. *Prof Exp:* Sr aerophys engr, Gen Dynamics, Ft Worth, 58-62; assoc prof aerospace eng, Univ Ala, Tuscaloosa, 63-81, prof, 81-92, dir, Flight Dynamics Lab, 77-92. *Concurrent Pos:* NSF fac fel, Mass Inst Technol, 66-69; sabbatical leave, Boeing Com Airplane Co, 85-86. *Mem:* Am Inst Aeronaut & Astronaut; Soc Automotive Engrs. *Res:* Flight dynamics; automatic control of aircraft and space vehicles; aeroelasticity; flight simulation. *Mailing Add:* PO Box 1000 Brierfield AL 35035

BAILEY, JACK CLINTON, II, ENTOMOLOGY. *Current Pos:* CONSULT, 89- *Personal Data:* b Austin, Tex, Aug 10, 36; m 61; c 2. *Educ:* Tex A&M Univ, BS, 59; Miss State Univ, MS, 65, PhD(entom), 67. *Prof Exp:* Jr entomologist, Tex Agr Exp Sta, Weslaco, 59-63; res entomologist, Soybean Insects, Agr Res Serv, USDA, 67-71 & res leader quarantine insects res, 71-77, res entomologist, cotton host plant resistance, 78-89. *Concurrent Pos:* Adj assoc prof entom & assoc mem grad coun, Miss State Univ, 68- *Mem:* Sigma Xi; Entom Soc Am. *Res:* Biological control both of plants and insects; pest management systems. *Mailing Add:* 520 N 38th Ave Apt 73 Hattiesburg MS 39401-5745

BAILEY, JAMES ALLEN, UNGULATE MANAGEMENT. *Current Pos:* from asst prof to assoc prof, 69-77, prof wildlife biol, 80-94, EMER PROF, COLO STATE UNIV, 94-; ASST DIV CHIEF, CONSERV SERV DIV, DEPT GAME & FISH, NMex, 94- *Personal Data:* b Chicago, Ill, May 14, 34; m 59; c 2. *Educ:* Mich Technol Univ, BS, 56; State Univ NY Col Forestry, MS, 58, PhD(zool), 66. *Prof Exp:* Res assoc ecol, Ill Natural Hist Surv, 64-68; asst prof wildlife biol, Univ Mont, 68-69. *Mem:* Wildlife Soc. *Res:* Population dynamics; ungulate behavior, foraging efficiency; habitat requirements of mountain ungulates. *Mailing Add:* Conserv Serv Div Dept Game & Fish 141 E DeVargas Santa Fe NM 87501

BAILEY, JAMES E(DWIN), CHEMICAL ENGINEERING. *Current Pos:* CHEM ENGR, INST BIOTECHNOL, ZURICH, SWITZ, 92- *Personal Data:* b Great Falls, Mont, Feb 28, 44; m 66; c 1. *Educ:* Rice Univ, BA, 66, PhD(chem eng), 69. *Hon Degrees:* Dr, Univ Brussel, 88. *Honors & Awards:* Allan T Colburn Award, Am Inst Chem Eng, 79, Prof Progress Award, 87; Curtis W Mc Graw Award, Am Soc Eng Educ, 83; Marvin J Johnson Award, Am Chem Soc, 90; Cert of Recognition, NASA, 90; John C & Florence W Holtz Lectr, Johns Hopkins Univ, 90; Merck Distinguished Lectr, Rutgers Univ, 91. *Prof Exp:* Engr, Shell Develop Co, Calif, 69-71; from asst prof to prof chem eng, Univ Houston, 71-80, assoc dean fac res, 76-78; prof, Calif Inst Technol, Pasadena, 80-92, Chevron prof, 89-92. *Concurrent Pos:* Distinguished biotechnol lectr, Univ Fla, 88; distinguished vis lectr, Univ Alta, 88. *Mem:* Nat Acad Eng; Am Inst Chem Engrs; Sigma Xi; Am Chem Soc; fel AAAS. *Res:* Enzyme and microbial reaction engineering; catalytic reactor dynamics. *Mailing Add:* Inst Biotechnol ETH Honnerberg HPThnol CH 8093 Zurich Switzerland

BAILEY, JAMES EDWARD, INDUSTRIAL ENGINEERING. *Current Pos:* PROF INDUST ENG, ARIZ STATE UNIV, 74- *Personal Data:* b Detroit, Mich, Jan 16, 42; m 66; c 2. *Educ:* Wayne State Univ, BS, 64, MS, 66, PhD(indust eng), 75. *Prof Exp:* Mfg engr, Gen Motors Corp, 65-67; staff engr, Nat Bank Detroit, 67-69; instr, Wayne State Univ, 69-72, dir co-op educ, 72-74. *Concurrent Pos:* Mem bd & actg chief exec officer, Kurta Corp, 81. *Mem:* Am Inst Indust Engrs (vpres); Inst Mgt Sci; Soc Info Mgt. *Res:* Concurrent engineering; production control; data systems management; data systems analysis; expert systems. *Mailing Add:* Dept Indust Eng Ariz State Univ PO Box 875960 Tempe AZ 85287-5906

BAILEY, JAMES L, APPLIED MATHEMATICS. *Current Pos:* RETIRED. *Personal Data:* b Tiffin, Ohio, Mar 21, 30; m 52; c 3. *Educ:* Heidelberg Col, BS, 52; Mich State Univ, MS, 54, PhD(math), 58. *Prof Exp:* Instr math, Mich State Univ, 58; asst prof, Case Inst Technol, 58-63; from assoc prof to prof math, Univ Toledo, 63-94. *Mem:* Math Asn Am. *Res:* Mechanics. *Mailing Add:* 2423 Middlesex Dr Toledo OH 43606

BAILEY, JAMES STEPHEN, ELECTRICAL ENGINEERING, PHYSICS. *Current Pos:* CONSULT DEFENSE INDUST, 78- *Personal Data:* b Paris, Tex, Oct 3, 42. *Educ:* Univ Tex, BS, 65, MS, 68, PhD(elec eng), 71; Southern Methodist Univ, MS, 82. *Prof Exp:* Aerosysts engr analog comput, Gen Dynamics Corp, 64-66; res engr microwave res, Collins Radio Co, 67-68; eng specialist high frequency technol, Vought Corp, 73-78. *Concurrent Pos:* Res scientist & adj prof, Strategic Defense Initiate Prog, Univ Tex, Arlington, 85-89; proj engr advan avionics, A-12 Navy Stealth Aircraft Prog, Gen Dynamics, Ft Worth, 89-91. *Mem:* Inst Elec & Electronics Engrs; Am Inst Physics. *Res:* Microwave devices; electromagnetic wave propagation and antenna theory; radar systems; electronic warfare systems; stealth technology. *Mailing Add:* 4401 Bellaire Dr Suite 226 Ft Worth TX 76109

BAILEY, JOHN ALBERT, METALLURGY, METALLURGICAL ENGINEERING. *Current Pos:* assoc prof, 67-72, PROF MECH ENG, NC STATE UNIV, 72-, HEAD DEPT MECH & AERO ENG, 84- *Personal Data:* b Liverpool, Eng, June 8, 37; m 63. *Educ:* Univ Col Swansea, Wales, BSc, 60, PhD(metall), 63. *Prof Exp:* Res asst metall, Imp Chem Industs, Ltd, Eng, 56-57 & Univ Col Swansea, Wales, 57-63; from asst prof to assoc prof mech eng, Ga Inst Technol, 63-67. *Mem:* Brit Inst Metall; fel Inst Metallurgists; Soc Mfg Engrs; Metals Soc. *Res:* Properties of materials at elevated temperatures; mechanics of metal machining; wear, surface integrity in machining; friction. *Mailing Add:* Dept Mech Eng NC State Univ Box 7910 Raleigh NC 27695-0001

BAILEY, JOHN CLARK, SURFACE CHEMISTRY, ELECTROCHEMISTRY. *Current Pos:* TECH ASSOC BATTERY PRODS, UNION CARBIDE CORP, 76- *Personal Data:* b Newport, Vt, Aug 25, 42; m 88, Jean Boyd; c 5. *Educ:* Cornell Univ, BA, 64; Duke Univ, PhD(phys chem), 69. *Prof Exp:* Asst, Manchester Univ, 69-71; asst prof chem, Univ NC, Charlotte, 74-75 & Swarthmore Col, 75-76. *Mem:* Electrochem Soc. *Res:* Battery research and development. *Mailing Add:* Eveready Battery Co PO Box 45035 Westlake OH 44145

BAILEY, JOHN MARTYN, BIOCHEMISTRY. *Current Pos:* from asst prof to assoc prof, 59-69, PROF BIOCHEM, SCH MED, GEORGE WASHINGTON UNIV, 69- *Personal Data:* b Hawarden, Eng, May 13, 29; US citizen; m 63; c 3. *Educ:* Univ Wales, BSc, 49, PhD(biochem), 52. *Hon Degrees:* DSc, Univ Wales, 70. *Prof Exp:* Res assoc, Iowa State Univ, 54-55; res assoc physiol chem, Johns Hopkins Univ, 55-56, res assoc biochem, Dept Surg, Med Sch, 56-59. *Concurrent Pos:* Fel chem, Prairie Regional Lab, Nat Res Coun Can, 52-54; USPHS career develop award, 63-73; consult, Div Res Grants, USPHS, 69- & NSF, 74-; fel coun arteriosclerosis, Am Heart Asn, 69-, prog comnr, 75-77; vis prof biochem, Univ Miami Sch Med, 71, 78 & 85; pres, Convirex Inc. *Mem:* Am Heart Asn; AAAS; Am Soc Biol Chem; Soc Exp Biol & Med. *Res:* Lipid and lipoprotein metabolism in cultured mammalian cells, genetic disorders, essential fatty acids, prostaglandins and thromboxanes; experimental atherosclerosis; immune cell functions; anti-viral drugs. *Mailing Add:* Dept Biochem George Washington Univ Sch Med 2300 I St NW Washington DC 20037-2337. *Fax:* 202-994-8974

BAILEY, JOSEPH RANDLE, ZOOLOGY. *Current Pos:* from instr to prof, 46-83, EMER PROF ZOOL, DUKE UNIV, 83- *Personal Data:* b Fairmont, WVa, Sept 17, 13; m 46; c 2. *Educ:* Univ Mich, AB, 35, PhD(zool), 40; Haverford Col, MA, 37. *Prof Exp:* Int exchange fel, Brazil, 40-41 & fel, 41-42. *Concurrent Pos:* Fulbright lectr, Sao Paulo Univ, 61-62; Guggenheim Mem Found fel, 53-54; Fulbright sr scholar, James Cook Univ NQueensland, Townsville, 71. *Mem:* Soc Study Amphibians & Reptiles; Herpetologists League; AAAS; Am Soc Ichthyol & Herpet (pres, 72). *Res:* Systematics; life history and distribution of herpetology and ichthyology; zoogeography. *Mailing Add:* Dept Zool Duke Univ Durham NC 27706-0325

BAILEY, JOSEPH T(HOMAS), CERAMICS ENGINEERING. *Current Pos:* proj engr,3M Corp, Chattanooga, 60-64, res supvr oxide mat, 66-74, tech dir, Tech Ceramic Prod Div, 74-81, dept mgr, Tech Ceramic Resources Dept, 81-82, dept mgr, Ceramic Mat Dept, 83-89, VPRES RES & DEVELOP, I & E SECTOR, 3M CORP, ST PAUL, 89- *Personal Data:* b Clemson, SC, Oct 16, 37; m 62. *Educ:* Clemson Univ, BS, 59, MS, 60; Ohio State Univ, PhD(ceramic eng), 66. *Prof Exp:* Metallurgist, Savannah River Lab, E I Du Pont de Nemours & Co, 60. *Concurrent Pos:* Mem, indust adv comt, Dept Ceramic Eng, Ohio State Univ. *Mem:* Fel Am Ceramic Soc; Nat Inst Ceramic Engrs; Sigma Xi; Int Soc Hybrid Microelectronics. *Res:* Electronic materials; ceramic substrates; mechanical ceramics; polymeric inorganic composites; technical management; ceramic fibers; sol-gel ceramics. *Mailing Add:* 3M Ctr Bldg 220-4E-01 St Paul MN 55144-1000

BAILEY, KINCHEON HUBERT, JR, RADIO FREQUENCY COMMUNICATION, MICROWAVES. *Current Pos:* Instr, 67-92, head, Elec Eng Dept, 78-92, EMER INSTR ELECTRONIC ENG, WAKE TECH COMMUNITY COL, 92- *Personal Data:* b Zebulon, NC, Dec 21, 21; m 48, Tommye L Williams; c Kincheon H III, Linda (Hux), Beth E, Laura J & Nancy M (Brodd). *Educ:* US Mil Acad, West Point, BS, 45; Pa State Univ, MEE, 67; NC State Univ, EdD, 75. *Honors & Awards:* Wiley Award, Am Soc Eng Educ, 88. *Concurrent Pos:* Consult, John Wiley Publ, 70-, MacMillan, McGraw-Hill Publ, 80-92, Prentice-Hall Publ, 82-92 & Charles E Merrick Publ, 82-92. *Mem:* Inst Elec & Electronics Engrs; Am Soc Eng Educ. *Res:* Radio frequency communication; microwaves. *Mailing Add:* 701 Currituck Dr Raleigh NC 27609. *E-Mail:* bert-b@usa.ngwb47.@usa.ng

BAILEY, LEO L, HORTICULTURE, ENTOMOLOGY. *Current Pos:* EMER PROF TEX A&M UNIV, KINGSVILLE, 88- *Personal Data:* b Blossom, Tex, Jan 17, 22; m 45; c 4. *Educ:* Tex A&M Univ, BS, 43; Sam Houston State Teachers Col, MS, 49; La State Univ, PhD(hort), 54. *Honors & Awards:* Hon Agr Educ Award, Am Soc Hort Sci. *Prof Exp:* Instr voc agr, Red River Co Voc Sch, Tex, 46-48; instr hort, Sam Houston State Teachers Col, 48-49; from asst prof to prof, Tex A&I Univ, 49-74, for student adv, 65-73, teacher agr, 75-88. *Mem:* Am Soc Hort Sci. *Res:* Maturity test for vegetable crops; propagation of ornamental plants; teaching techniques. *Mailing Add:* 431 W King Kingsville TX 78363

BAILEY, LEONARD CHARLES, PHARMACEUTICAL CHEMISTRY. *Current Pos:* ASST PROF PHARMACEUT CHEM, RUTGERS UNIV, NEW BRUNSWICK, 73- *Personal Data:* b Jersey City, NJ, Feb 5, 36; m 64; c 2. *Educ:* Fordham Univ, BS, 57; Rutgers Univ, MS, 65, PhD(pharmaceut sci), 69. *Prof Exp:* Sci drug analyst, Ortho Pharmaceut Corp, 69-73. *Mem:* Am Pharmaceut Asn; Am Chem Soc; Sigma Xi. *Res:* Application of modern chromatographic techniques to the analysis of drugs in formulations and in biological fluids. *Mailing Add:* 4321 Larchwood Ave Philadelphia PA 19104-3903

BAILEY, LEONARD LEE, CARDIO-THORACIC SURGERY. *Current Pos:* ASST PROF SURG, ASST PROF PEDIAT & DIR PEDIAT CARDIAC SURG, MED CTR, LOMA LINDA UNIV, 76- *Personal Data:* b Takoma Park, Md, Aug 28, 42; m 66. *Educ:* Columbia Union Col, BS, 64; Loma Linda Univ, MD, 69. *Mem:* Am Col Surgeons. *Res:* Transplant whole organ grafting, such as heart, lung and kidney. *Mailing Add:* Dept Cardio-Thoracic Surg Rm 2560 Loma Linda Univ Med Ctr Loma Linda CA 92354

BAILEY, LESLIE EDGAR, PHARMACOLOGY. *Current Pos:* PROF PHARMACOL, UNIV HAWAII, 80- *Personal Data:* b Los Angeles, Calif, Oct, 25, 31. *Educ:* Utah State Univ, BS, 59; Univ Utah, PhD(pharmacol & biophys), 66. *Prof Exp:* Asst pharmacologist, Riker Labs, 59-60; asst statistician, Thiokol Chem Corp, 60-61; postdoctoral pharmacol, Univ Man, 66-68, from assoc prof to assoc prof, 68-76; from assoc prof to prof, Dalhousie Univ, 76-80. *Concurrent Pos:* Res fel, Can Heart Found, 68-71, res scholar, 71-76, mem, Sci Subcomt, 74-80, chmn, Personnel Support Comt, 75-79, vchmn, Sci Res Comt, 77-80; counr, Pharmacol Soc Can, 76-79 & Western Pharmacol Soc, 83-85; mem, Prog Comt, Am Soc Pharmacol & Exp Therapeut, 76-84 & Pulmonary & Cardiovasc Study Sect, 77; field ed, J Pharmacol & Exp Therapeut, 77 & 84-; Med Res Coun vis prof, Univ BC, 79. *Mem:* Am Soc Pharmacol & Exp Therapeut; Int Soc Heart Res; Can Cardiovasc Soc. *Res:* Author of numerous technical publications. *Mailing Add:* Dept Pharmacol Sch Med Univ Hawaii 1960 East-West Rd Honolulu HI 96822-2319

BAILEY, LORAINE DOLAR, SOIL CHEMISTRY, PLANT NUTRITION. *Current Pos:* Res scientist soil-plant relationship, Brandon Res Sta, Agr Can, 66-78, head plant & soil sci res, 78-93, assoc dir, 91-93, SR RES SCIENTIST, BRANDON RES STA, AGR CAN, 93- *Personal Data:* b St Vincent, Wis, Sept 5, 36; Can citizen; m 62; c 3. *Educ:* Univ Man, BSA, 65, MSc, 67; Univ Guelph, PhD(soil-plant relationship), 71. *Concurrent Pos:* Assoc ed, Can J Plant Sci, 86. *Mem:* Can Soc Soil Sci; Int Soc Soil Sci; Am Soc Agron; Am Soc Soil Sci; Agr Inst Can; Can Soc Agron (pres, 91-93). *Res:* Nitrogen fixation by legumes and the value of fixed nitrogen to cereals; placement of phosphorus with crop seeds and the residual value of fertilizer phosphorus; efficient use of fertilizer materials and pen manure; heavy metal contaminants in cereals and oilseeds. *Mailing Add:* Brandon Res Sta Agr Can Box 1000A RR No 3 Brandon MB R7A 5Y3 Can. *Fax:* 204-728-3858

BAILEY, LYNN BONNETTE, HUMAN NUTRITION. *Current Pos:* ASST PROF NUTRIT, UNIV FLA, 77- *Personal Data:* b Charleston, SC, Aug 25, 48; m 70. *Educ:* Winthrop Col, BA, 70; Clemson Univ, MS, 72; Purdue Univ, PhD(nutrit), 75. *Prof Exp:* Res asst nutrit, Clemson Univ, 70-73; res instr, Purdue Univ, 73-75. *Concurrent Pos:* Assoc, Dept Nutrit, Purdue Univ, 75-76; affil asst prof, Col Health Related Professions, Univ Fla, 77- *Mem:* Assoc Am Inst Nutrit; Am Dietetic Asn; Inst Food Technologists; Sigma Xi. *Res:* Evaluation of the etiology of nutritional anemia in low-income adolescent and elderly people. *Mailing Add:* Dept Food Sci & Human Nutrit Univ Fla Gainesville FL 32611

BAILEY, MARION CRAWFORD, ELECTROMAGNETICS, ANTENNAS. *Current Pos:* RETIRED. *Personal Data:* b Carrollton, Miss, Oct 26, 37; m 63; c 2. *Educ:* Miss State Univ, BS, 64; Univ Va, MS, 67; Va Polytech Inst & State Univ, PhD(eng), 72. *Honors & Awards:* Sci Achievement Medal, NASA. *Prof Exp:* res engr electromagnetics, NASA, 64-82. *Concurrent Pos:* Vis prof, Univ Miss, 78-79. *Mem:* Inst Elec & Electronics Engrs. *Res:* Antennas; microwaves. *Mailing Add:* 108 King Forest Lane Newport News VA 23602

BAILEY, MAURICE EUGENE, SCIENCE EDUCATION, MINING. *Current Pos:* RETIRED. *Personal Data:* b Portsmouth, Ohio, Mar 14, 16; m 37, 74, 96, Georgia Maynard; c James C, Susan (Levi), F Stephen & Christopher M. *Educ:* Ohio Wesleyan Univ, AB, 37; Purdue Univ, MS, 39, PhD, 41. *Prof Exp:* Res chemist, Purdue Univ Res Found, 40-41; res chemist, Allied Chem Corp, 41-55, mgr appln res, 55-59, tech liaison, 59-63, chem planning, 63-68, dir res, 68-70; dir mining technol & chmn, Div Sci & Technol, Pikeville Col, 71-81, prof chem, 70-87; dir coal develop, Ky Dept Energy, 81-82; environ engr, Ky Partners, 88-92. *Concurrent Pos:* Consult, Ky Coun Pub Higher Educ, 75. *Mem:* AAAS; Am Chem Soc. *Res:* Author of 85 publications; polyurethanes. *Mailing Add:* 100 Poplar St Pikesville KY 41501-1122

BAILEY, MICHAEL JOHN, COMPUTER GRAPHICS, COMPUTER AIDED DESIGN. *Current Pos:* MGR SCI VISUALIZATION, SAN DIEGO SUPERCOMPUTER CTR, 89- *Personal Data:* b Philadelphia, Pa, Oct 16, 53. *Educ:* Purdue Univ, BSME, 75, MSME, 76, PhD, 79. *Honors & Awards:* Ralph Teetor Award, Soc Automotive Engrs, 83. *Prof Exp:* Tech staff, Sandia Nat Labs, 79-81; assoc prof comput graphics, Purdue Univ, 81-85; dir advan develop, Megatek Corp, 85-89. *Concurrent Pos:* Sr instr, Interactive Comput Systs, 81-; assoc adj prof, Univ Calif, San Diego, 89- *Mem:* Asn Comput Mach; Am Soc Mech Eng; Soc Mfg Engrs. *Res:* Creation and use of high performance computer graphics displays to solve scientific visualization problems, particularly in mechanical engineering and the physical sciences. *Mailing Add:* San Diego Supercomputer Ctr PO Box 85608 San Diego CA 92186-9784

BAILEY, MILTON, INDUSTRIAL CHEMISTRY, LEATHER CHEMISTRY. *Current Pos:* SELF-EMPLOYED, 89- *Personal Data:* b New York, NY, May 20, 17; m 54, Lucille Rubin; c Joseph A. *Educ:* City Col NY, BA, 40, MS, 49; Pratt Inst, cert, 51. *Prof Exp:* Ed newspaper & educr, Adj Gen Off, US Dept Army, 41-43; chem supt, Ruderman, Inc, NY, 46-52; leather chemist, US Naval Supply Res & Develop Facil, NJ, 52-66, footwear specialist, 66-67; leather chemist & opers res analyst, US Naval Clothing Res & Develop Unit, Mass, 67; leather chemist, footwear specialist & phys scientist, US Navy Clothing & Textile Res Facil, 67-89; expert witness, 58-93. *Concurrent Pos:* Lectr, City Col NY, 51-52 & NY Community Col, 53-61; arbitrator, Am Arbit Asn, 73-; chmn elec hazard & conductive safety shoe comt, Am Nat Stand Inst, 73-; chmn, safety & traction for footwear, Am Soc Testing & Mat, 78-82. *Mem:* Am Leather Chem Asn; Am Soc Testing & Mat; Am Nat Stand Inst; Nat Fire Protection Asn. *Res:* Impregnation of leather and protein fibers; coloring of hair and protein fibers; instrumentation; leather and footwear technology; chemical specialties; static electricity; conductive rubber; personnel protection asbestos fibers; traction; slips and falls; athletic and general footwear; walkways; environmental health; human factors. *Mailing Add:* 18 Bayfield Rd Wayland MA 01778

BAILEY, MILTON (EDWARD), FOOD CHEMISTRY. *Current Pos:* asst prof animal husb, 58-60, assoc prof food sci & nutrit, 60-69, PROF FOOD SCI & NUTRIT, UNIV MO-COLUMBIA, 69- *Personal Data:* b Shreveport, La, June 7, 24; m 58. *Educ:* Tulane Univ, BS, 49; La State Univ, MS, 53, PhD(biochem), 58. *Prof Exp:* Res assoc, La State Univ, 53-58. *Concurrent Pos:* Fulbright-Hays fel, Agr Res Serv, USDA, 74-75 & Univ Col Cork, Ireland, 75-76. *Mem:* Am Chem Soc; Inst Food Technologists. *Res:* Muscle physiology and biochemistry; flavoring constituents of foods; enzymology. *Mailing Add:* 21 Agr Bldg Food Sci & Nutrit Columbia MO 65211

BAILEY, ORVILLE TAYLOR, PATHOLOGY. *Current Pos:* prof neurol, Univ Ill, 59-70, prof neurol surg, 70-72, prof neuropath, 72-77, EMER PROF NEUROPATH, ABRAHAM LINCOLN SCH MED, UNIV ILL COL MED, 77-, DISTINGUISHED PROF PATH, RUSH MED COL, 77- *Personal Data:* b Jewett, NY, May 28, 09. *Educ:* Syracuse Univ, AB, 28; Albany Med Col, MD, 32. *Prof Exp:* Rotating intern, Albany Hosp, NY, 32-33; house officer path, Peter Bent Brigham Hosp, Boston, 33-34; resident, Children's Hosp, 34-35; from instr path to asst prof path, Harvard Med Sch, 35-51; prof neuropath, Sch Med, Ind Univ & chief neuropath, Larue Carter Mem Hosp, 51-59. *Concurrent Pos:* Guggenheim fel, Univ Cambridge, 46-47; resident, Peter Bent Brigham Hosp, 35-37, assoc pathologist, 40-43, assoc pathologist neuropath, 46-51; jr fel, Soc Fels, Harvard Univ, 37-40; lectr, Lowell Inst, 40; mem, Off Sci Res & Develop, 41-46; neuropathologist & vchmn, Neurol Inst, Children's Hosp, 47-51; chmn deleg & vpres, US Int Cong Neuropath, 59-67. *Mem:* Am Asn Neurol Surgeons; AMA; Am Asn Pathologists; Sigma Xi. *Res:* Dural sinus thrombosis; alloxan diabetes; myelin degeneration; brain tumors; radioactive materials in brain; pediatric neuropathology; hydrocephalus. *Mailing Add:* PO Box 2517 Chicago IL 60690-2517

BAILEY, PAUL TOWNSEND, physics; deceased, see previous edition for last biography

BAILEY, PHILIP SIGMON, ORGANIC CHEMISTRY. *Current Pos:* RETIRED. *Personal Data:* b Chickasha, Okla, June 9, 16; m 41, 73; c 3. *Educ:* Okla Baptist Univ, BS, 37; Univ Okla, MS, 40; Univ Va, PhD(org chem), 44. *Prof Exp:* Asst chem, Univ Okla, 37-40; chemist, Halliburton Oil Well Cementing Co, Okla & Kans, 40-41; asst under contract, Off Sci Res & Develop, 42-45; from asst prof to prof, Univ Tex, Austin, 45-84, emer prof chem, 84. *Concurrent Pos:* Fulbright res award, Univ Karlsruhe, WGer, 53-54; consult. *Mem:* Am Chem Soc. *Res:* Reactions of ozone with organic compounds. *Mailing Add:* PO Box 4827 Lago Vista TX 78645

BAILEY, R L, AVIAN PHYSIOLOGY, VETERINARY ANATOMY. *Current Pos:* RETIRED. *Personal Data:* b Trenton, Tenn, Sept 14, 16; m 44; c 1. *Educ:* Tenn State Univ, BS, 42; Iowa State Univ, MS, 46, PhD(avian physiol, vet anat), 50. *Prof Exp:* Instr animal husb, Tenn State Univ, 42-45; instr poultry husb, WVa State Col, 46-48, asst prof, 50-53; prof, Agr & Tech Col, NC, 53-58; prof poultry husb, Grambling Col, 58-76, head dept agr, 63-83, prof biol sci, 76-83. *Mem:* Am Inst Biol Sci; Poultry Sci Asn; World Poultry Sci Asn. *Res:* Reproduction in the male animal. *Mailing Add:* PO Box 35 Grambling LA 71245

BAILEY, R V, ECONOMIC GEOLOGY. *Current Pos:* PRES, ASPEN EXPLORATION CORP, 80- *Personal Data:* b Hanna, Wyo, Sept 16, 32. *Educ:* Univ Wyo, BS, 56. *Prof Exp:* Geologist uranium geol, Utah Int, 59-64; geologist coal geol, Page T Jenkins, Geologist, 64-65; dist geologist uranium, Union Carbide Corp, 65-68; independent consult geol, 68-71; pres, Aquarius Resources Corp, 71-73; pres, Power Resources Corp, 73-79. *Mem:* Soc Econ Geol; Soc Mining Engrs; Am Asn Petrol Geologists; Can Inst Mining. *Mailing Add:* PO Box 1420 Castle Rock CO 80104

BAILEY, RAYMOND VICTOR, CHEMICAL ENGINEERING. *Current Pos:* head dept, 51-72, head, Eng Res Inst, 53-72, asst dean eng & grad prog, 70-73, PROF CHEM ENG, TULANE UNIV, 51-, ASSOC DEAN ENG, 73- *Personal Data:* b Strong, Ark, Nov 22, 23; m 43; c 3. *Educ:* La Polytech Inst, BS, 44; La State Univ, MS, 48, PhD(chem eng), 49. *Prof Exp:* Asst chem, La Polytech Inst, 41-44; chemist, Cities Serv Ref Corp, 44-45; asst chem eng, La State Univ, 46-48; assoc prof, Univ Miss, 48-51. *Mem:* Sr mem Am Chem Soc; Am Inst Chem Engrs; Am Soc Eng Educ. *Res:* Distillation heat transmission; fluid dynamics. *Mailing Add:* Dept Chem Eng Tulane Univ La New Orleans LA 70118

BAILEY, RICHARD ELMORE, MEDICINE. *Personal Data:* b Cleveland, Ohio, Nov 4, 29; m 53; c 4. *Educ:* Stanford Univ, BA, 51, MD, 55. *Honors & Awards:* Ayerst-Squibb Res Award, Endocrine Soc, 69; Estab Investigatorship Award, Am Heart Asn, 70. *Prof Exp:* Trainee diabetes & metab dis, Sch Med, Stanford Univ, 57-59; trainee steroid biochem training prog, Clark Univ & Worcester Found Exp Biol, 60-61; dir res training prog diabetes & metab, Med Sch, Univ Ore, 61-71, asst prof, 61-66, assoc prof med, 66-73; assoc prof med, Col Med, Univ Utah, 73-86. *Concurrent Pos:* Fel diabetes, Sch Med, Univ Southern Calif, 56-57; NASA fac fel award, 69; USPHS spec res fel, Case Western Res Univ, 69-70; asst prof biochem, Case Western Reserve Univ, 69-70. *Mem:* Endocrine Soc; Am Diabetes Asn; Am Fedn Clin Res; AMA; Am Physiol Soc. *Res:* Metabolic diseases; hypertension; endocrinology and diabetes. *Mailing Add:* 1977 E 10980 S Sandy UT 84092

BAILEY, RICHARD HENDRICKS, INVERTEBRATE PALEONTOLOGY. *Current Pos:* Asst prof, 72-80, ASSOC PROF GEOL, NORTHEASTERN UNIV, 80- *Personal Data:* b Rocky Mt, NC, Oct 30, 46; m 72; c 3. *Educ:* Old Dominion Univ, BS, 68; Univ NC, MS, 71, PhD(geol), 73. *Mem:* Soc Econ Paleontologists & Mineralogists. *Res:* Cenozoic molluscan communities from Atlantic Coastal Plain; systematic and evolutionary studies of Cenozoic Mollusca; stratigraphy and depositional history of Avalonian rocks of Eastern Massachusetts. *Mailing Add:* Dept Geol Northeastern Univ 360 Huntington Ave Boston MA 02115-5096

BAILEY, ROBERT CLIFTON, STATISTICS. *Current Pos:* STATIST ADV TO DIR, BUR HEALTH STANDARD QUAL, HEALTH CARE FINANCING ADMIN, 88- *Personal Data:* b Richmond, Va, Mar 29, 41; m 65, Susan Goodman; c Alice K & Linda C. *Educ:* Randolph-Macon Col, BS, 62; Iowa State Univ, MS, 64; Emory Univ, PhD(biomet), 72. *Prof Exp:* Res asst physics, Iowa State Univ, 62-64; assoc prof statist, Morris Brown Col, 67-73; math statistician, Food & Drug Admin, 73-75; statistician & head biomet, Naval Med Res Inst, 75-80; statistician, Off Water Regulations & Standards, Environ Protection Agency, 80-88. *Concurrent Pos:* Statist consult, Asn Off Anal Chemists, 74-75; mem prof adv comt, Food & Drug Admin, 75-78; mem human relations comt, Naval Med Res Ins, Bethesda, Md, 79-80, guest scientist, 84-91; lectr decision sci, George Mason Univ, 85; chair, Am Statist Asn Rep to AAAS, 81-86, co-chair, 86-91; chair comt reps to AAAS for the comt of pres of Statist Soc, 87-91, secy statist sect, 91-; guest lectr, Uniformed Servs Univ Health Sci, 93 & 94. *Mem:* Fel AAAS; Am Statist Asn; Biomet Soc; Sigma Xi; Soc Math Biol; Inst Math Statist; Math Asn Am; Am Soc Qual Control. *Res:* Mathematical and statistical models for data analysis and quality improvement of health care and medical outcomes and design of sampling studies and systems; environmetrics. *Mailing Add:* 6507 Divine St McLean VA 22101-4620

BAILEY, ROBERT E, NUCLEAR ENGINEERING. *Current Pos:* AT DEPT NUCLEAR ENG, OHIO STATE UNIV. *Personal Data:* b Lafayette, Ind, Dec 28, 31; m 53; c 2. *Educ:* Univ Ill, BS, 55, MS, 56; Purdue Univ, PhD(nuclear eng), 63. *Prof Exp:* Asst chem engr, Argonne Nat Lab, 56-59; from instr to assoc prof nuclear eng, Purdue Univ, 59-71, prof, 71-80. *Concurrent Pos:* Ford Found res specialist, Atomics Int Div, NAm Aviation, Inc, 64-65; mem, Adv Comt Civil Defense, Nat Acad Sci. *Mem:* AAAS; Am Nuclear Soc; Am Soc Eng Educ. *Res:* Nuclear kinetics and controls, sociotechnical problems and interdisciplinary studies. *Mailing Add:* Dept Nuclear Eng Ohio State Univ 206 W 18th Ave Columbus OH 43210-1189

BAILEY, ROBERT LEROY, BIOMETRICS, FORESTRY. *Current Pos:* MEM STAFF, SCH FOREST RESOURCES, UNIV GA, 80- *Personal Data:* b Carrollton, Miss, Oct 16, 40; m 64; c 2. *Educ:* Miss State Univ, BS, 62; Univ Ga, MS, 68, PhD(biomet), 72. *Prof Exp:* Math statistician, USDA Forest Serv, 71-74; biometrician, Weyerhaeuser Co, 74-76, res mgr, 76-78, sr biometrician, 78-80. *Concurrent Pos:* Assoc ed, Forest Sci, Soc Am Foresters, 76- *Mem:* Biomet Soc; Soc Am Forestry; Am Statist Asn; Am Forestry Asn. *Res:* Mathematical and statistical models as applied to forest growth, yield and inventory; experimental design in forestry and biology. *Mailing Add:* Sch Forest Resources Univ Ga 1180 E Broad St Athens GA 30601-3040

BAILEY, RONALD ALBERT, COORDINATION CHEMISTRY, MOLTEN SALTS. *Current Pos:* from asst prof to assoc prof, 61-71, PROF INORG CHEM, RENSSELAER POLYTECH INST, 71- *Personal Data:* b Winnipeg, Man, June 2, 33; m 61. *Educ:* Univ Man, BSc, 56, MSc, 57; McGill Univ, PhD(radiochem), 60. *Prof Exp:* NATO sci fel, Univ Col, Univ London, 60-61. *Mem:* Am Chem Soc; Brit Chem Soc. *Res:* Preparation and characterization of coordination complexes; chemistry of metal compounds in melter salt solutions especially electrochemistry and electroplating. *Mailing Add:* Dept Chem Rensselaer Polytech Inst Troy NY 12180-3590

BAILEY, ROY ALDEN, MINERALOGY & PETROLOGY, VOLCANOLOGY. *Current Pos:* geologist, 53-55 & 57-95, Pecora fel, 95-97, EMER SCIENTIST, US GEOL SURV, 97- *Personal Data:* b Providence, RI, July 28, 29; m 58, Patrice Kelly; c Tara, Deirdre & Moana. *Educ:* Brown Univ, AB, 51; Cornell Univ, MSc, 54; Johns Hopkins Univ, PhD, 78. *Concurrent Pos:* Fulbright scholar, Auckland Univ, NZ, 56; coodinator US Geol Surv, Volcano Hazards Prog, 80-83; vis sci, NZ Geol Surv, 89. *Mem:* Geol Soc Am; Mineral Soc Am; Am Geophys Union; Sigma Xi; Int Asn Volcanology. *Res:* Volcanology, petrology of igneous rocks, volcano tectonics, geothermal resources, Jemez Mountains, New Mexico, Long Valley Caldera, eastern California, New Zealand volcanism. *Mailing Add:* US Geol Survey MS-910 345 Middlefield Rd Menlo Park CA 94025. *Fax:* 650-329-5203; *E-Mail:* rbailey@mojave.wr.usgs.gov

BAILEY, ROY HORTON, JR, PHYSICAL ORGANIC CHEMISTRY. *Current Pos:* RETIRED. *Personal Data:* b Maxton, NC, Nov 7, 21; m 47; c 3. *Educ:* Univ NC, BS, 48, PhD(chem), 58. *Prof Exp:* Asst analytical chem, Univ NC, 48-53; asst prof chem, King Col, 53-57, prof & chmn dept, 57-63; from asst prof to assoc prof chem, Clemson Univ, 63-88. *Mem:* Am Chem Soc. *Res:* Heterocyclic reaction kinetics; analytical instrumentation. *Mailing Add:* 105 Carolus Dr Clemson SC 29631

BAILEY, SAMUEL DAVID, PHYSICAL CHEMISTRY. *Current Pos:* RETIRED. *Personal Data:* b Cedar Falls, Iowa, July 14, 15; m 42, Ouida Frances Lowry; c Lawrence David. *Educ:* Univ Northern Iowa, BA, 37; Univ Iowa, MS, 40, PhD(phys chem), 42. *Prof Exp:* From instr to asst prof chem, Univ Northern Iowa, 41-42 & 46-48; res chemist, Rohm and Haas Co, 42-46; head phys chem sect, Smith Kline & French Lab, 48-51; dir, Pioneering Res Lab, Army Natick Res & Develop Labs, 51-74, Food Sci Lab, 74-81 & Sci & Advan Technol, 81. *Mem:* AAAS; Am Chem Soc; Am Inst Chemists. *Res:* Physical and optical properties of matter; research administration; radiation and flavor chemistry; photochemistry; food chemistry; pollution abatement; food nutrition and microbiology; behavioral sciences. *Mailing Add:* 901 N Abrego Dr Green Valley AZ 85614-3331

BAILEY, STURGES WILLIAMS, clay mineralogy, crystallography; deceased, see previous edition for last biography

BAILEY, SUSAN GOODMAN, ENVIRONMENTAL SCIENCES. *Current Pos:* CHEMIST, ASCI CORP, 89- *Personal Data:* b Washington, DC, Aug 5, 40; m 65; c 2. *Educ:* Vassar Col, BA, 62; Iowa State Univ, MS, 65; Emory Univ, PhD(inorg chem), 69. *Prof Exp:* Instr chem, Ga State Col, 65, Northern Va Community Col, 73-74 & Marshall Adult Ctr, 86-87; chemist, Ctr Dis Control, 69; tutor chem, 87-88. *Res:* Environmental remediation work; quality assurance audits of environmental research laboratories. *Mailing Add:* 6507 Divine St McLean VA 22101

BAILEY, THOMAS DANIEL, ORGANIC CHEMISTRY. *Current Pos:* dir com develop, 84-89, VPRES TECHNOL CORP DEVELOP, REILLY INDUST, 89- *Personal Data:* b Birmingham, Ala, July 15, 45; m 66; c 1. *Educ:* Univ Montevallo, BS, 69; Univ Ala, PhD(chem), 74. *Prof Exp:* Res chemist, Reilly Tar & Chem Corp, 75-79, assoc dir res, 80-83. *Mem:* Am Chem Soc. *Res:* Synthesis of heterocyclic compounds; synthesis and chemistry of heterocyclic-N-oxides; process development. *Mailing Add:* Reilly Indust Inc 300 N Meridian St Suite 1500 PO Box 41076 Indianapolis IN 46241-0076

BAILEY, THOMAS L, III, CHEMICAL PHYSICS. *Current Pos:* Asst res elec eng, 53-54, asst res prof, 54-57, from assoc prof to prof, 57-87, EMER PROF PHYSICS, CHEM & ELEC ENG, UNIV FLA, 87- *Personal Data:* b Newnan, Ga, Dec 24, 23; m 55, Elinor Williams; c Krista & Ruth (Corey). *Educ:* Carnegie Inst Technol, BS, 49; Univ Chicago, SM, 50, PhD(chem), 53. *Concurrent Pos:* Guggenheim fel, 59-60. *Mem:* Fel Am Phys Soc. *Res:* Molecular and atomic structure; experimental mass spectroscopy; collisions of positive ions, negative ions and electrons with atoms and molecules; applied physics. *Mailing Add:* 2619 NW 63rd St Gainesville FL 32606

BAILEY, VERNON LESLIE, JR, PLASMA PHYSICS. *Current Pos:* STAFF PHYSICIST, PULSE SCI INC, SAN LEANDRO, 82- *Personal Data:* b St Louis, Mo, Apr 27, 41; m 65; c 2. *Educ:* Northwestern Univ, BSME, 63, PhD(plasma physics), 68. *Prof Exp:* Tech staff mem fluid mech, Sandia Corp, 68-70; dep dept mgr theoret groups plasma physics, Physics Int Co, 70-82. *Mem:* Am Phys Soc. *Res:* Application of relativistic electron beams to controlled thermonuclear fusion (steady state tokamaks, low aspect ratio tokamaks, linear systems, tandem mirror and inertial confinement), ion acceleration, and inductive storage. *Mailing Add:* 2047 Westbrook Lane Livermore CA 94550

BAILEY, WAYNE LEWIS, MISSION PLANNING, SPACE ENVIRONMENT. *Current Pos:* SR SYSTS ANALYST, PHYSICS, TELEDYNE BROWN ENG, 77- *Personal Data:* b Woodbury, NJ, Dec 12, 42; m, Eileen Reed; c Jeffrey W & Victoria J. *Educ:* Rutgers Univ, BS, 65; Univ Ariz, PhD(physics), 71. *Prof Exp:* Asst prof geosci, Jersey City State Col, 72-77. *Mem:* Am Phys Soc; Am Astronaut Soc; Am Inst Astronaut & Aeronaut; Royal Astronaut Soc. *Mailing Add:* 12003 Pulaski Pike Toney AL 35773

BAILEY, WILFORD SHERRILL, VETERINARY PARASITOLOGY. *Current Pos:* prof path & parasitol, 74-84, PROF, AUBURN UNIV, 84- *Personal Data:* b Somerville, Ala, Mar 2, 21; m 42; c Edward, Margaret, Joe & Sarah. *Educ:* Auburn Univ, DVM, 42, MS, 46; Johns Hopkins Univ, ScD(hyg), 50. *Hon Degrees:* DHH, Auburn Univ, 84. *Prof Exp:* From instr to assoc prof, Sch Vet Med, Auburn Univ, 42-48, head prof, 50-62, res prof parasitol & assoc dean grad sch & coordr res, 62 66, vpres acad affairs, 66-69, vpres acad & admin affairs, 69-72, pres, 83-84; health scientist adminr, Nat Inst Allergy & Infectious Dis, 72-74. *Concurrent Pos:* NSF sci fac fel, 59; mem, Nat Res Coun, 63-69; mem comt vet med educ & res, Nat Acad Sci, 68-70; mem, Nat Adv Allergy & Infectious Dis Coun, NIH, 71-72 & 75-78; pres, Nat Col Athletic Asn, 87-88. *Mem:* Am Soc Parasitol (pres, 71); Am Vet Med Asn; Am Soc Trop Med & Hyg (pres, 77); World Asn Advan Vet Parasitol. *Res:* Life cycle and immunity to Hymenolepis nana; immunology and pathology of Cooperia punctata and ruminant stomach worms; toxic hepatitis in dogs; life cycle and pathology of Spirocerca lupi and its relationship to neoplasia; prevalence of Pneumocystis carinii in dogs and cats; biology and life cycle of Cryptosporidium in man and animals. *Mailing Add:* 778 Moores Mill Rd Auburn AL 36830. *Fax:* 334-844-3697

BAILEY, WILLIAM C, PULMONARY DISEASES. *Current Pos:* asst prof to assoc prof, 73-79, PROF MED, SCH MED, UNIV ALA, BIRMINGHAM, 79- *Personal Data:* b Jacksonville, Fla, Aug 4, 39; m 63; c 3. *Educ:* Washington & Lee Univ, BA, 61; Tulane Univ, MD, 65. *Prof Exp:* Dir, Bur Tuberculosis Control, City New Orleans Health Dept, 70-73; asst prof med, Sch Med, Tulane Univ, 72-73. *Concurrent Pos:* Med dir, Bur Commun Dis, Jefferson County Health Dept, 73-78; assoc chief staff educ, Vet Admin Med Ctr, Birmingham, Ala & chief pulmonary dis med sect, 73-; tuberculosis coordr, Ala Dept Public Health, Birmingham, 73-; consult, Bur Commun Dis, Jefferson County Health Dept, 78- *Mem:* Am Col Chest Physicians; Am Col Physicians; Am Thoracic Soc; Int Union Against Tuberculosis. *Res:* Clinical pulmonary disease; occupational pulmonary disease; tuberculosis control. *Mailing Add:* Univ Ala Univ Hosp Univ Ala Birmingham Med Ctr Birmingham AL 35294

BAILEY, WILLIAM CHARLES, NUCLEAR MAGNETIC RESONANCE. *Current Pos:* ASST PROF PHYSICS, KEAN COL, 83- *Personal Data:* b Albany, NY, Aug 21, 39. *Educ:* Siena Col, BS, 63; State Univ NY Albany, MS, 66, PhD(physics), 71. *Prof Exp:* Res assoc physics, State Univ NY, Albany, 71-80; fel mat sci & eng, Univ Pa, 80-82. *Concurrent Pos:* J Corbett fel physics, Atomic Energy Comn, State Univ NY, Albany, 71-73, fel, Inst Study of Defects in Solids, 75-80, instr phys sci, Educ Opportunities Prog, 75-80. *Mem:* Am Phys Soc; Am Asn Physics Teachers. *Res:* Ion diffusion in superionic conducting solids such as sodium beta alumina. *Mailing Add:* Chem Phys Dept Kean Col NJ Morris Ave Union NJ 07083-9982

BAILEY, WILLIAM FRANCIS, ORGANIC CHEMISTRY. *Current Pos:* from asst prof to assoc prof, 75-85, PROF CHEM, UNIV CONN, 85- *Personal Data:* b Jersey City, NJ, Dec 8, 46. *Educ:* St Peter's Col, NJ, BS, 68; Univ of Notre Dame, PhD(chem), 73. *Prof Exp:* Post doc assoc chem, Univ NC, 73 & Yale Univ, 73-75. *Concurrent Pos:* Fac summer fel, Univ Conn, 76; co-chmn, Int Conf Conformational Anal, 81; vis prof, Nat Polytech Inst Mex, 81, Oxford Univ, 83. *Mem:* Am Chem Soc; Sigma Xi. *Res:* Synthetic methods; molecular structure and energetics; group I organometallic chemistry; chemistry of organolithium compounds. *Mailing Add:* Dept Chem Univ Conn Box U60 Storrs CT 06269-3060

BAILEY, WILLIAM T, MATHEMATICS. *Current Pos:* Instr statist, 60-64, PROF MATH, STATE UNIV NY, COL BUFFALO, 64- *Personal Data:* b Buffalo, NY, Apr 4, 36; m 83; c 2. *Educ:* State Univ, NY Buffalo, BA, 59, MA, 62, EdD(math educ), 71. *Concurrent Pos:* Mem, Nat Coun Teachers Math. *Mem:* Math Asn Am; Sch Sci & Math Asn. *Res:* Group reaction to and productivity on a mathematical task involving productive thinking. *Mailing Add:* 3300 Indian Meadow Dr Blacksburg VA 24060

BAILEY-BROCK, JULIE HELEN, INVERTEBRATE ZOOLOGY, POLYCHAETE BIOLOGY. *Current Pos:* From asst prof to assoc prof, 69-85, PROF ZOOL, UNIV HAWAII, 85- *Personal Data:* b Birmingham, Eng; US citizen; m 70. *Educ:* Univ Wales, BSc, 64, PhD(zool), 69. *Honors & Awards:* Fulbright-Hays Res Abroad Award, SE Asia & E Australia, 77; First Prize, Polaroid Int Photomicrography Competition Life Sci, 91. *Concurrent Pos:* Vis scholar, dept zool, Univ Wash, Seattle, 73-74; vis researcher, Lizard Island Res Sta, 77, Univ Malaysia, 77, Marine Lab, Univ Guam, 81; res assoc, Bernice P Bishop Museum, Honolulu, 83- *Mem:* Sigma Xi; Am Soc Zoologists; Int Polychaete Soc; Int Bryzool Asn. *Res:* Polychaete communities of coral reefs; polychaete fauna of Hawaii & West Pacific Islands; deep sea polychaetes; Serpulidae and Spirorbidae; polychaetes as pollution indicators; coral reef bryozoans; benthic community development on artificial reefs; benthic communities near sewage outfalls in Hawaii. *Mailing Add:* Dept Zool Univ Hawaii 2538 The Mall Honolulu HI 96822. *Fax:* 808-956-9812; *E-Mail:* brock@zoogate.zoo.hawaii.edu

BAILEY-SERRES, JULIA, PLANT MOLECULAR BIOLOGY, PLANT GENETICS. *Current Pos:* res assoc, 86-90, ASST PROF GENETICS, DEPT BOT & PLANT SCI, UNIV CALIF, RIVERSIDE, 90- *Personal Data:* b Redwood City, Calif, July 9, 58. *Educ:* Univ Utah, BS, 82; Univ Edinburgh, PhD(plant biol), 86. *Prof Exp:* Res assoc, Univ Edinburgh, 84-86, postdoctoral res assoc, 86. *Concurrent Pos:* Fels & res grants, several insts & schs, 86- *Mem:* Am Soc Plant Physiologists; Maize Genetics Coop. *Res:* Plant response to environmental stress; molecular genetic analysis of the response of maize to hypoxia and ozone stress; analysis of isozyme expression in tissues of maize. *Mailing Add:* Dept Bot & Plant Sci Univ Calif 900 University Ave Riverside CA 92521-0101

BAILIE, GEORGE RUSSELL, CLINICAL NEPHROLOGY, PHARMACOKINETICS. *Current Pos:* Assoc prof, 88-91, PROF PHARM PRACT, ALBANY COL PHARM, 91- *Personal Data:* b Belfast, N Ireland, Mar 5, 55; div; c Caragh & Orla R. *Educ:* Queen's Univ, Belfast, BSc (Hons), 77; Strathclyde Univ, Glasgow, MSc, 78; Univ Minn, PharmD, 83; Univ Wales, PhD(clin pharm), 92. *Prof Exp:* Staff pharmacist, Southern Gen Hosp, 79-81; fel infectious dis & pharmacokinetics, Univ Minn, 83-84; dir pharm servs, Hope Hosp, Salford, Eng, 84-88. *Concurrent Pos:* Lectr hosp pharm, Univ Manchester, Eng, 84-88; vis prof, Univ Minn, 89; consult, Am Soc Hosp Pharmacists' Found, 92- *Mem:* Fel Am Col Clin Pharm; Nephrol Pharmacists' Asn; Am Soc Nephrol; Int Soc Peritoneal Dialysis. *Res:* Disposition of drugs in patients undergoing hemo- or peritoneal dialysis or in end-stage renal disease; clinical and microbiology studies of treatment of peritoneal dialysis-associated peritonitis. *Mailing Add:* Dept Pharm Albany Col Pharm 106 New Scotland Ave Albany NY 12208. *Fax:* 518-445-7202; *E-Mail:* bailieg@panther.acp.edu

BAILIE, MICHAEL DAVID, PEDIATRICS, PHYSIOLOGY. *Current Pos:* PROF PEDIAT, UNIV ILL, 91- *Personal Data:* b South Bend, Ind, Sept 27, 36; m 58; c 2. *Educ:* Ind Univ, Bloomington, AB, 59, MA, 60, PhD(physiol), 66; Ind Univ, Indianapolis, MD, 64. *Prof Exp:* From asst prof to prof human develop & physiol, Dept Human Develop, Col Human Med, Mich State Univ, 70-79 & assoc chmn, 78-79; prof pediat & chmn, Univ Conn Health Ctr, 79-91. *Concurrent Pos:* Fel, Univ Tex Southwestern Med Sch Dallas, 68-70. *Mem:* Am Fedn Clin Res; Am Soc Nephrology; Int Soc Nephrology; Soc Pediat Res; Am Physiol Soc. *Res:* Renal physiology, specifically, control of renal hemodynamics; relation of renin-angiotensin system to renal hemodynamics; intra renal actions and formation of angiotensin II; development of renal function; renal metabolism. *Mailing Add:* Dept Pediat Univ Ill Med Col Box 1649 Peoria IL 61656-1649

BAILIE, RICHARD COLSTEN, CHEMICAL ENGINEERING. *Current Pos:* PROF CHEM ENG, WVA UNIV, 65- *Personal Data:* b Chicago, Ill, July 4, 28; m 63; c 4. *Educ:* Ill Inst Technol, BS, 51; Wayne State Univ, MS, 57; Iowa State Univ, PhD(chem eng), 65. *Prof Exp:* Jr engr, Victor Chem Works, 51-53; res & develop chem engr, US Rubber Co, Joliet Arsenal, 53; instr chem eng, Wayne State Univ, 56-57; partic, Int Sch Nuclear Sci & Eng, Argonne Nat Lab, 57-58; asst prof nuclear eng, Kans State Univ, 58-61, assoc prof, 61-65. *Mem:* Am Inst Chem Engrs; Am Chem Soc; Am Soc Eng Educ; Sigma Xi. *Res:* Gasification, including combustion and pyrolysis in fluidized beds; kinetics of solid-gas reactions. *Mailing Add:* RR 2 Morgantown WV 26505

BAILIE, WAYNE E, VETERINARY MICROBIOLOGY. *Current Pos:* assoc prof infectious diseases, 71-81, PROF LAB MED, KANS STATE UNIV, 81- *Personal Data:* b Bondurant, Iowa, Aug 28, 32; m 55; c 3. *Educ:* Kans State Univ, BS & DVM, 57, PhD(path), 69; Am Col Vet Microbiologists, cert, 80. *Prof Exp:* Vet, self-employed, Nebr, 57-64; instr path, Kans State Univ, 64-69; assoc prof, SDak State Univ, 69-70 & Ahmadu Bello Univ, Nigeria, 70-72. *Mem:* Am Vet Med Asn; Am Soc Microbiol. *Res:* Infectious diseases of domestic animals; taxonomy of unnamed species of bacteria associated with domestic animals. *Mailing Add:* 1615 Cedar Crest Dr Manhattan KS 66503

BAILIN, GARY, BIOCHEMISTRY. *Current Pos:* asst prof, 77-79, ASSOC PROF BIOCHEM, UNIV MED & DENT NJ-SCH OSTEOP MED, 79- *Personal Data:* b New York, NY, Apr 2, 36; m; c 2. *Educ:* City Col New York, BS, 58; Adelphi Univ, PhD(biochem), 65. *Prof Exp:* Res asst, Adelphi Univ, 59-61; res assoc protein chem, Inst Muscle Dis, 64-74, asst prof biochem, Mt Sinai Sch Med, 74-77. *Concurrent Pos:* Adj asst prof, Brooklyn Col, 68-75. *Mem:* Am Soc Biochemists & Molecular Biologists; Biophys Soc. *Res:* Regulation of muscle contraction by muscle and membrane proteins; correlation of structure and function of muscle contractile and membrane proteins. *Mailing Add:* Dept Molecular Biol Univ Med & Dent NJ-Sch Osteop Med 2 Med Ctr Dr Stratford NJ 08084. *E-Mail:* bailinga@umdnj.edu

BAILIN, LIONEL J, PHYSICAL INORGANIC CHEMISTRY. *Current Pos:* res scientist, 62-73, staff scientist, Chem Dept, 74-78, SR STAFF SCIENTIST, PALO ALTO RES LAB, LOCKHEED MISSILES & SPACE CO, 78- *Personal Data:* b New York, NY, Oct 28, 28; m 58; c 4. *Educ:* NY Univ, BA, 49; Polytech Inst Brooklyn, MS, 52; Tulane Univ, PhD(inorg chem), 58. *Prof Exp:* Develop chemist, Am Cyanamid Co, 51-52; phys chemist chem warfare, US Army Edgewood Arsenal, Md, 52-54; chemist pigment technol, E I Du Pont de Nemours & Co, 57-62. *Mem:* Am Chem Soc; Am Soc Metals; fel Am Inst Chemists; Sigma Xi; Electrochem Soc Am. *Res:* Materials science and engineering; inorganic and modified inorganic materials; protective coatings technology, coatings for anticorrosion applications on metals; reactions at polymer-metal interfaces. *Mailing Add:* 740 Crane Ave Foster City CA 94404-1313

BAILIT, HOWARD L, PUBLIC HEALTH. *Current Pos:* PROF & DIR, HEALTH POLICY & PRIMARY CARE RES CTR, UNIV CONN HEALTH CTR, 96-; RES ASSOC, SLOAN MANAGED CARE INDUST CTR, HARVARD UNIV, 96- *Personal Data:* b Boston, Mass, Dec 17, 37. *Educ:* Tufts Dent Sch, DMD, 62; Harvard Univ, PhD, 67. *Prof Exp:* From asst prof to prof & head, Dept Behav Sci & Community Health, Univ Conn Health Ctr, 67-82; prof & head, Dept Healthcare Admin, Sch Pub Health & Med, Columbia Univ, 83-86; sr vpres med policies & progs, Aetna Life & Casualty, 86-95. *Concurrent Pos:* Mem, Study Sect, Nat Ctr Health Serv Res, 78-82 & 86-, Nat Affairs Comt, Am Asn Dent Res, 78-82, Future Dent Comn, Am Dent Asn, 83 & Comt Cost Mgt Systs, Inst Med Nat Acad Sci, 87-90; consult, Rand Health Ins Exp, 79-86 & Off Qual Assurance, Am Dent Asn, 83-; mem, Comt Cost Mgt Systs, Inst Med-Nat Acad Sci, 87-90, Comt Physician Supply, 95; bd mem, Asn Found Health Serv Res, 89-95; mem, Qual Mgt Comt, Group Health Asn Am, 91-95. *Mem:* Nat Acad Sci; Inst Med-Nat Acad Sci; Am Col Dentists; Sigma Xi. *Res:* Health services, research and policy; author of 112 publications. *Mailing Add:* Univ Conn Health Ctr 263 Farmington Ave Farmington CT 06030-1910. *E-Mail:* bailit@nsol.uchc.edu

BAILLARGEON, VICTOR PAUL, RESEARCH ADMINISTRATION. *Current Pos:* sr res assoc, 88-89, dir, Int Res & Develop, 89-91, MGR KNOWLEDGE TRANSFER, BUCKMAN LABS INT, 91- *Personal Data:* b Dover, NH, Apr 4, 58; m 83. *Educ:* Univ NH, BS, 80; Colo State Univ, PhD(chem), 85. *Prof Exp:* Res chemist, Humko Chem Div, Witco Corp, 85-88. *Mem:* Am Chem Soc; Tech Asn Pulp & Paper Indust; Int Mgt Coun; Am Mgt Asn. *Res:* Corporate knowledge base management. *Mailing Add:* 6399 Thistle Point Cove Bartlett TN 38135

BAILLE, DAVID L, BIOLOGY. *Current Pos:* PROF, DEPT BIOL, SIMON FRASER UNIV, BURNABY, CAN. *Honors & Awards:* Luigi Provasoli Award, Phycol Soc Am, 90. *Mailing Add:* Dept Biol Simon Fraser Univ Burnaby BC V5A 1S6 Can

BAILLIE, ANDREW DOLLAR, BASIN ANALYSIS. *Current Pos:* RETIRED. *Personal Data:* b Dollar, Scotland, Nov 20, 12; m 46, Margaret Purvis; c John R. *Educ:* Univ Man, BSc, 49, MSc, 50; Northwestern Univ, PhD(geol), 53. *Honors & Awards:* Spencer Gold Medal, Univ Man, 53; Medal Merit, Alta Soc Petrol Geol, 55. *Prof Exp:* Geologist, Mines Br, Man, 50-53; Can Gulf Oil Co, 53-57; from regional geologist to res geologist, Brit Am Oil Co, 57-70; dir res geol, Gulf Oil Can, 70-72, mgr geol serv, 72-78. *Concurrent Pos:* Vis prof basin studies, Univ Alta, 77-85; consult int training basin anal, 78-90. *Mem:* Hon mem Am Asn Petrol Geologists; fel Geol Soc

Am; hon mem Soc Econ Paleont & Mineral; fel Geol Asn Can; hon mem Can Soc Petrol Geol. *Res:* Sedimentary basin analysis and oil occurrence. *Mailing Add:* 917 Rideau Rd Calgary AB T2S 0S3 Can. *E-Mail:* 102545.327@compuserve.com

BAILLIE, PRISCILLA WOODS, ESTUARINE ECOLOGY, MICROALGAL ECOLOGY. *Current Pos:* PRIN INVESTR, MARINE & FRESH WATER RES SERV, 83- *Personal Data:* b Buffalo, NY, Jan 18, 35; m 53. *Educ:* Univ Hartford, BS, 74; Univ Conn, MS, 78, PhD, 83. *Mem:* Aquatic Plant Mgt Soc; NAm Lake Mgt Soc; Sigma Xi. *Res:* Eutrophication problems associated with perturbations of estuarine, lacustrine, and wetlands ecosystems. *Mailing Add:* 276 State St Guilford CT 06437-2407

BAILLIE, THOMAS ALLAN, DRUG METABOLISM, MASS SPECTROMETRY. *Current Pos:* from asst prof to assoc prof, 81-88, PROF MED CHEM, UNIV WASH, 88-, VPRES DRUG METAB, 95- *Personal Data:* b Isle-of-Islay, Scotland, May 30, 48. *Educ:* Univ Glasgow, Scotland, BSc, 70, PhD(chem), 73, DSc, 92; Univ London, Eng, MSc, 78. *Prof Exp:* Fel, Karolinska Inst, Sweden, 73-75; lectr, Royal Postgrad Med Sch, Eng, 75-78; asst prof pharmaceut, Univ Calif, San Francisco, 78-81. *Concurrent Pos:* Sci adv, Food & Drug Admin, San Francisco, 80-81; Fogarty sr int fel, 88-89. *Mem:* Royal Soc Chem; Am Soc Mass Spectrometry; Am Chem Soc; Int Isotope Soc. *Res:* Application of stable isotope labelling techniques and mass spectrometry to studies of pathways of drug metabolism and their relationship to drug-induced toxicities; toxicology. *Mailing Add:* Merck Res Sumney Town West Point PA 19486. *Fax:* 206-685-3252

BAILLOD, CHARLES ROBERT, CIVIL ENGINEERING, ENVIRONMENTAL ENGINEERING. *Current Pos:* From asst prof to assoc prof civil eng, 68-78, dir, Environ Eng Ctr Water & Waste Mgt, 82-91, PROF CIVIL & ENVIRON ENG, MICH TECHNOL UNIV, 82-, HEAD DEPT, 91- *Personal Data:* b Milwaukee, Wis, Mar 21, 41; c 3. *Educ:* Marquette Univ, BCE, 63; Univ Wis, MSCE, 65, PhD(civil eng), 68. *Concurrent Pos:* Vis prof civil eng, Univ Wis-Madison, 77-78, Rogaland Regional Col, Stavanger, Norway, 83. *Mem:* Am Soc Civil Engrs; Am Inst Chem Engrs; Water Pollution Control Fedn; Asn Environ Eng Professors (pres, 91-92); Am Acad Environ Engrs; Air & Waste Mgt Asn. *Res:* Biological waste treatment; hazardous waste destruction processes; clean technologies; pollution prevention; environmental engineering education. *Mailing Add:* Civil & Environ Eng Mich Technol Univ Houghton MI 49931

BAILY, EVERETT M, RESEARCH & DEVELOPMENT, MANUFACTURING. *Current Pos:* mem staff reliability, design eng & mfr, 74-84, prod eng mgr, 84-87, SR MFR DEVELOP ENGR, BOISE DIV, HEWLETT-PACKARD, 87- *Personal Data:* b Twin Falls, Idaho, June 9, 38; m 61, Donna R Larson; c Susan G (Ehrstine) & Brian C. *Educ:* Univ Idaho, BS, 61, MS, 64; Stanford Univ, PhD(network theory), 68. *Prof Exp:* Instr elec eng, Univ Idaho, 61-64, asst prof, 64-70, assoc prof, 70-74. *Concurrent Pos:* Am Soc Eng Educ & Dow Chem Co Pac Northwest faculty award, 70. *Mem:* Inst Elec & Electronics Engrs; Am Soc Eng Educ; Soc Mfg Engrs; Sigma Xi. *Res:* Remote sensing; control systems; printer mechanisms; laser printers. *Mailing Add:* Hewlett-Packard Co MS 541 PO Box 15 11311 Chinden Blvd Boise ID 83707. *Fax:* 208-396-5559

BAILY, WALTER LEWIS, JR, MATHEMATICS. *Current Pos:* from asst prof to assoc prof, 57-63, PROF MATH, UNIV CHICAGO, 63- *Personal Data:* b Waynesburg, Pa, July 5, 30; c 1. *Educ:* Mass Inst Technol, SB, 52; Princeton Univ, MA, 53, PhD(math), 55. *Prof Exp:* Instr math, Princeton Univ, 55-56 & Mass Inst Technol, 56-57. *Concurrent Pos:* Mathematician, Bell Tel Labs, 57-58; NSF sr fel, 65-66. *Mem:* Am Math Soc; Math Soc Japan. *Res:* Algebraic groups; modular forms; arithmetic properties of automorphic forms. *Mailing Add:* Dept Math Univ Chicago 5734 S University Ave Chicago IL 60637-1404

BAILYN, MARTIN H, PHYSICS. *Current Pos:* From asst prof to assoc prof, 58-66, PROF PHYSICS, NORTHWESTERN UNIV, 66- *Personal Data:* b Conn, June 24, 28. *Educ:* Williams Col, BA, 48; Harvard Univ, PhD, 56. *Mem:* Am Phys Soc. *Res:* Magnetism in metals. *Mailing Add:* Dept Physics Northwestern Univ Evanston IL 60208

BAIN, BARBARA, EXPERIMENTAL MEDICINE. *Current Pos:* RES ASSOC HEMAT, ROYAL VICTORIA HOSP, 68- *Personal Data:* b Montreal, Que, May 8, 32. *Educ:* McGill Univ, BSc, 53, MSc, 57, PhD(exp med), 65. *Prof Exp:* Res asst hemat, Royal Victoria Hosp, 65-68; demonstr, 65-67, lectr, 67-68, ASST PROF EXP MED, McGILL UNIV, 68- *Concurrent Pos:* Med Res Coun Can scholar, 66-71, grant, 70- *Mem:* Tissue Cult Asn; Transplantation Soc; Can Soc Immunol; Can Soc Cell Biol; Am Soc Cell Biol. *Res:* Lymphocyte transformation to blast cells in vitro, using allogenic leukocytes and other stimuli; application of mixed leukocyte reaction to histocompatibility testing; mechanisms of blast cell transformation. *Mailing Add:* 201 Huron St London ON N6A 5B7 Can

BAIN, GORDON ORVILLE, pathology; deceased, see previous edition for last biography

BAIN, JAMES ARTHUR, BIOCHEMICAL PHARMACOLOGY. *Current Pos:* chmn, Dept Pharmacol, Emory Univ, 57-62, dir, Div Basic Health Sci, 60-76, prof pharmacol, 54-88, exec assoc dean, sch med, 65-88, EMER PROF PHARMACOL, EMORY UNIV, 88- *Personal Data:* b Langdon, NDak, May 22, 18; m 47; c 2. *Educ:* Univ Wis, BS, 40, PhD(physiol), 44. *Prof Exp:* Asst, Univ Wis, 40-44; res assoc psychiat & pharmacol, Med Sch, Univ Ill, 47-50, from asst prof to assoc prof, 50-54. *Concurrent Pos:* Consult, gov & indust. *Mem:* AAAS; Am Chem Soc; Am Soc Pharmacol & Exp Therapeut. *Res:* Biochemical basis of drug action; epilepsy; carcinogenesis; neurochemistry. *Mailing Add:* 2275 Tanglewood Dr Decatur GA 30033-1915. *Fax:* 404-727-0365

BAIN, LEE J, MATHEMATICAL STATISTICS. *Current Pos:* From asst prof to assoc prof, 63-73, PROF MATH, UNIV MO-ROLLA, 73- *Personal Data:* b Newkirk, Okla, Jan 11, 39; m 62, Harriet H Bu; c Patrick, Robert, Kelly, Jennifer & William. *Educ:* Okla State Univ, BS, 60, MS, 62, PhD(math), 63. *Concurrent Pos:* Co-ed, Commun in Statist, Series E, 81-88. *Mem:* Fel Am Statist Asn. *Res:* Statistical inference concerning life-testing distribution and reliability problems. *Mailing Add:* Dept Math Univ Mo-Rolla 1101 McCutcheon Rd Rolla MO 65401-2631

BAIN, ROGER J, GEOLOGY. *Current Pos:* asst prof, 70-74, ASSOC PROF GEOL, UNIV AKRON, 74- *Personal Data:* b Kenosha, Wis, Mar 29, 40; m 66; c 2. *Educ:* Univ Wis, BS, 62, MS, 64; Brigham Young Univ, PhD(geol), 68. *Prof Exp:* Asst prof geol, Univ RI, 67-68 & Univ Va, 68-70. *Concurrent Pos:* Res grants, 68-70, 71, 73, 75, 76-81, 83, 90-91; consult, NAm Explor, 70. *Mem:* Int Asn Sedimentologists; Soc Econ Paleont & Mineral; Am Asn Petrol Geologists; Geol Soc Am. *Res:* Sedimentary geology; sedimentology; carbonate petrology; paleoecology; paleoenvironments. *Mailing Add:* 3436 Yellow Creek Rd Akron OH 44333

BAIN, WILLIAM MURRAY, MICROBIAL PHYSIOLOGY. *Current Pos:* From asst prof to prof, 59-91, EMER PROF BACT, UNIV MAINE, 91- *Personal Data:* b Indianapolis, Ind, Dec 28, 28; m 64; c 2. *Educ:* Ind Univ, AB, 51, MA, 53, PhD(bact), 59. *Mem:* AAAS; Am Soc Microbiol; Sigma Xi. *Res:* Endogenous metabolism of bacteria; survival of bacteria, terrestial and aquatic bacteria. *Mailing Add:* 8 Edgewood Dr Orono ME 04473

BAINBOROUGH, ARTHUR RAYMOND, pathology, for more information see previous edition

BAINBRIDGE, KENNETH TOMPKINS, nuclear physics; deceased, see previous edition for last biography

BAINE, WILLIAM BRENNAN, INFECTIOUS DISEASE, EPIDEMIOLOGY. *Current Pos:* asst prof, Southwestern Med Sch & Southwestern Grad Sch Biomed Sci, 81-88, assoc prof internal med & microbiol, 81-92, CLIN ASSOC PROF INTERNAL MED, SOUTHWESTERN MED SCH, UNIV TEX, 92- *Personal Data:* b Washington, DC, Aug 10, 45; m 69, Martha Scott; c Britton A. *Educ:* Princeton Univ, AB & cert, 66; Vanderbilt Univ, MD, 70. *Prof Exp:* Intern med, Cleveland Metrop Gen Hosp, 70-71, resident, 71-72; Epidemic Intel Serv officer, Bact Dis Div, Epidemiol Prog, Ctr Dis Control, Atlanta, 72-74; resident internal med, Parkland Mem Hosp, Dallas, 74-75; fel infectious dis, Univ Tex Health Sci Ctr at Dallas, 75-77; med epidemiologist, Bact Dis Div, Epidemiol Prog, Ctr Dis Control, Atlanta, 77-79, Epidemiol Prog Off, 79-81. *Concurrent Pos:* Guest, Lab Epidemiol & Biostatist, Superiore di Sanita, Rome, Italy, 79-81. *Mem:* Fel Am Col Epidemiol; fel Am Col Physicians; Am Fedn Clin Res; Am Soc Microbiol; fel Infectious Dis Soc Am; Soc Epidemiol Res. *Res:* Infectious disease clinical practice and epidemiology. *Mailing Add:* 8210 Walnut Hill Lane Ste 700 LB 59 8210 Walnut Hill Lane Suite 700 LB59 Dallas TX 75231. *Fax:* 214-691-3967

BAINES, A D, PHYSIOLOGY, CLINICAL BIOCHEMISTRY. *Current Pos:* BIOCHEMIST-IN-CHIEF, TORONTO GEN HOSP, 84-, TORONTO HOSP, 87- *Personal Data:* b Toronto, Ont, July 17, 34; c 2. *Educ:* Univ Toronto, MD, 59, PhD(path chem), 65; FRCP(c), 88. *Prof Exp:* Assoc prof path chem, 68-72, prof clin biochem, Univ Toronto, 72-, dept chmn, 88- *Concurrent Pos:* Res fel, Dept Med, Univ NC, Chapel Hill, 65-67; res fel, Dept Physiol, AEC, France, 67-68; mem, Inst Biomed Eng & lectr, Dept Med, Univ Toronto, 72-; assoc physician, Toronto Gen Hosp, 72-; prin, New Col, Univ Toronto, 74- & Dept Clin Biochem, Oxford Univ, Eng, 80-81. *Res:* Normal and abnormal renal physiology; cellular transport mechanisms; histochemistry. *Mailing Add:* Dept Clin Biochem Banting Inst Univ Toronto Rm 2113 Med Sci Bldg 1 Kings College Cir Toronto ON M5G 2C4 Can

BAINES, KIM MARIE, ORGANOSILICON CHEMISTRY, ORGANOGERMANIUM CHEMISTRY. *Current Pos:* asst prof, 88-94, ASSOC PROF CHEM, UNIV WESTERN ONT, 94- *Personal Data:* b Halifax, NS, Oct 6, 60. *Educ:* St Mary's Univ, BSc, 82; Univ Toronto, PhD(chem), 87. *Honors & Awards:* John C Polanyi Prize, Govt Ont, 88. *Prof Exp:* Postdoctoral fel chem, Dortmund Univ, 87-88. *Mem:* Am Chem Soc; Chem Inst Can; Soc Chem. *Res:* Synthesis of novel organosilicon and organogermanium compounds; germasilenes; siladigermiranes; silylgermanes. *Mailing Add:* Dept Chem Univ Western Ont London ON N6A 5B7 Can. *Fax:* 519-661-3022; *E-Mail:* kbaines2@julian.uwo.ca

BAINES, WILLIAM DOUGLAS, FLUID MECHANICS, HEAT TRANSFER. *Current Pos:* assoc prof, Univ Toronto, 59-65, dean grad studies, 70-71, chmn dept, 71-76, dir cont studies, 85-86, PROF MECH ENG, UNIV TORONTO, 65- *Personal Data:* b Edmonton, Alta, Feb 11, 26; m 50; c 4. *Educ:* Univ Alta, BSc, 47; Univ Iowa, MS, 48, PhD(hydraul), 50. *Prof Exp:* Asst prof civil eng, Mich State Univ, 50-51; res officer mech eng, Nat Res Coun Can, 51-59. *Res:* Viscous flow; turbulence; flow processes of paper manufacture; heat and mass transfer. *Mailing Add:* Dept Mech Eng Univ Toronto Toronto ON M5S 3G8 Can

BAINS, MALKIAT SINGH, PHYSICAL INORGANIC CHEMISTRY. *Current Pos:* assoc prof, 68-73, PROF GEN & INORG CHEM, SOUTHERN UNIV, 73- *Personal Data:* b Montgomery, India, Jan 29, 32; m 66; c 3. *Educ:* Panjab Univ, India, BSc, 55, MSc, 57; Univ London, PhD(inorg chem), 59; Atomic Energy Estab, Trombay, Bombay, cert radiation nuclear chem, 63. *Prof Exp:* Nat Res Coun Can fel, Univ Western Ont, 59-61; lectr inorg chem, Panjab Univ, India, 61-65; reader, Marathwada Univ, India, 65-66; Nat Acad Sci-Nat Res Coun resident res assoc inorg free radicals & electron spin resonance, Agr Res Serv, USDA, 66-68. *Concurrent Pos:* New Delhi Univ Grants Comn grant, 64-66. *Mem:* Am Chem Soc; Sigma Xi; The Chem Soc; life mem Indian Chem Soc. *Res:* Coordination chemistry of metal alkoxides and metal carboxylates; flame retardation; inorganic free radicals in solution; application of nuclear magnetic resonance and electron spin resonance to biomedical problems; synthesis of transition metal compounds; metalloporphysins. *Mailing Add:* 5742 E Louis Prima Dr New Orleans LA 70128

BAINTON, CEDRIC R, ANESTHESIOLOGY. *Current Pos:* resident anesthesia, Univ Calif, San Francisco, 62-66, asst clin prof anesthesia, 66-74, from assoc prof to prof in residence, 74-85, PROF ANESTHESIA & PHYSIOL & CHIEF ANESTHESIA SERV, GEN HOSP, UNIV CALIF, SAN FRANCISCO, 85-, CHMN, DEPT ANESTHESIA, 86- *Educ:* Oberlin Col, BA, 53; Univ Rochester, MD, 58; Am Bd Anesthesiol, cert, 67. *Prof Exp:* Intern, Strong Mem Hosp, 58-60; surgeon, Heart Dis Control Prog, Seattle Health Dept, USPHS, 60-62. *Concurrent Pos:* Fel anesthesia, Cardiovasc Res Inst, Univ Calif, San Francisco, 63-65; guest referee ed, Am J Physiol, 67 & J Appl Physiol, 67-; NIH career develop award, 69-74; clin investr, Vet Admin Med Ctr, 74-77, asst chief anesthesiol serv & dir, Anesthesia Res Labs, 77-85, chief inhalation ther, 79-80 & 83-85, dir, Anesthesia Clin Blood-Gas Lab, 77-85; consult, Children's Hosp, Palo Alto, Calif, 75-78; chmn, Sci Session, Am Soc Anesthesiologists, 76 & Am Physiol Soc, 77 & 79-80, Sci Adv Bd, Asn Univ Anesthetists, 89-90. *Mem:* Am Heart Asn; Am Soc Anesthesiologists; Am Physiol Soc; Asn Univ Anesthetists. *Res:* Author of more than 60 technical publications. *Mailing Add:* Prof & Chmn 50 Ventura San Francisco CA 94116

BAINTON, DOROTHY FORD, PATHOLOGY, INTERNAL MEDICINE. *Current Pos:* from asst prof to prof, 66-94, chmn, 86-94, PROF PATH & VICE CHANCELLOR ADMIN, SCH MED, UNIV CALIF, SAN FRANCISCO, 94- *Personal Data:* b Magnolia, Miss, June 18, 33; m 59; c 3. *Educ:* Millsaps Col, BS, 55; Tulane Univ, MD, 58; Univ Calif, San Francisco, MS, 66. *Honors & Awards:* Phyllis Bodel Med Lectr, Yale Univ, 79. *Prof Exp:* Intern med, Strong Mem Hosp, Univ Rochester, 58-59, resident internal med, 59-60; resident hemat, Sch Med, Univ Wash, 60-62. *Concurrent Pos:* NIH career develop award, 70-75; mem, Hemat Study Sect, NIH, 76-78, Subcomt Res Needs Hemat, Nat Inst Arthritis, Metab, Digestive Dis, 78-81, comt, 78-81, Spec Grants Rev Comt, Nat Inst Arthritis, Diabetes, Digestive & Kidney Dis, 85-87; mem coun, Am Asn Pathologists, 77-80; mem coun, Am Soc Cell Biol, 77-80, Nat Pub Policy Comt, 81-84, Publ Comt, 84-87; vis prof cell biol, Univ Tex, Dallas, 83; lectr, Royal Micros Soc, Eng, 83; NIH merit award, 86-; mem, Sci Adv Bd, Armed Forces Inst Path, 89-; mem, Vascular Biol Res Study Comt, Am Heart Asn, 89-; mem, Health Sci Policy Comt, Inst Med-Nat Acad Sci, 90- *Mem:* Inst Med-Nat Acad Sci; Am Soc Cell Biol; AAAS; Am Soc Hemat; Am Soc Histochemists & Cytochemists; Am Asn Pathologists (pres, 90-91); Am Asn Physicians; Am Heart Asn. *Res:* Hematology and cell biology; leukocyte maturation and function using the light and electron microscopes, histochemistry and cell fractionation procedures. *Mailing Add:* Sch Med Univ Calif 513 Parnassies Ave Rm 5-115 San Francisco CA 94143-0400

BAINUM, PETER MONTGOMERY, SPACECRAFT SYSTEMS, STABILITY THEORY. *Current Pos:* assoc prof, Howard Univ, 69-73, dir grad studies, Dept Mech Eng, 74-84, prof aerospace eng, 73-90, GRAD PROF, HOWARD UNIV, 76-, DISTINGUISHED PROF AEROSPACE ENG, 90- *Personal Data:* b St Petersburg, Fla, Feb 4, 38; m 68, Carmen C Perez; c David P. *Educ:* Tex A&M Univ, BS, 59; Mass Inst Technol, SM, 60; Cath Univ Am, PhD(aerospace eng), 67. *Honors & Awards:* Teetor Award, Soc Automotive Engrs, 71; Dirk Brouner Award, Am Astronaut Soc, 90. *Prof Exp:* Asst engr, Naval Supersonic Lab, Mass Inst Technol, 59-60; sr engr, Martin Marietta Corp, 60-62; staff engr, Space Systs Ctr, IBM Fed Syst Div, 62-65; sr staff engr, Appl Physics Lab, Johns Hopkins Univ, 65-69. *Concurrent Pos:* Consult, Appl Physics Lab, Johns Hopkins Univ, 69-72; NASA-Am Soc Eng Educ fac fel, Goddard Spaceflight Ctr, NASA, 70-71; prin investr res grantee, NASA, 71-, USAF, 88-; vpres & res consult, WHF & Assoc, Inc, 77-86; Outstanding Res, Howard Univ, 80-81. *Mem:* Fel Am Astronaut Soc; fel Am Inst Aeronaut & Astronaut; fel Brit Interplanetary Soc; Sigma Xi; Int Acad Astronaut; fel AAAS. *Res:* Analysis of passive and active satellite control systems, as applied to proposed large space structural systems where both shape and orientation control are required. *Mailing Add:* 9804 Raleigh Tavern Ct Bethesda MD 20814

BAIR, EDWARD JAY, PHYSICAL CHEMISTRY, ANALYTICAL CHEMISTRY. *Current Pos:* from instr to prof, 54-90, EMER PROF CHEM, IND UNIV, BLOOMINGTON, 90- *Personal Data:* b Ft Collins, Colo, June 30, 22; m 58, Dorothy Bimson. *Educ:* Colo Agr & Mech Col, BS, 43; Brown Univ, PhD(chem), 49. *Prof Exp:* Chemist, Manhattan Proj, Tenn Eastman Corp, 44-46; res assoc chem, Univ Wash, 49-54. *Mem:* Am Chem Soc; Am Phys Soc. *Res:* Photochemistry; spectroscopy; kinetics of atmospheric and combustion reactions; solar dynamic power. *Mailing Add:* Dept Chem Ind Univ Bloomington IN 47401

BAIR, HARVEY EDWARD, THERMAL PHYSICAL PROPERTIES OF MATERIALS. *Current Pos:* assoc mem tech staff, 65-75, MEM TECH STAFF, AT&T BELL LABS, 75- *Personal Data:* b Williamsport, Pa, June 6, 36; m 58; c 4. *Educ:* Dickinson Col, BS, 58; Pa State Univ, MS, 62. *Honors & Awards:* Mettlar Award in Thermal Anal, NAm Thermal Anal Soc, 87. *Prof Exp:* Res training fel, Gen Elec Res Lab, 62-64; assoc chemist, Appl Physics Lab, Johns Hopkins Univ, 64-65. *Concurrent Pos:* Guest fac mem, Polymer Res Inst, Polytech Univ, NY, 90-91. *Mem:* Fel NAm Thermal Anal Soc (pres, 84); fel Am Phys Soc; Am Chem Soc. *Res:* Application of thermoanalytical techniques to characterize the structure and behavior of polymeric materials, especially multicomponent blends, reactive polymer systems, and materials containing additives or contaminants. *Mailing Add:* 7E Lucent Technol Bell Labs Murray Hill NJ 07974. *Fax:* 908-582-5570; *E-Mail:* heb@bell-labs.com

BAIR, JOE KEAGY, NUCLEAR PHYSICS. *Current Pos:* RETIRED. *Personal Data:* b Massillon, Ohio, Mar 10, 18; m 41; c 1. *Educ:* Rice Inst, BA, 40. *Prof Exp:* Asst physics, Columbia Univ, 40-41; physicist, Naval Ord Lab, 41-47 & Fairchild Eng & Airplane Co, 47-51; Physicist, Oak Ridge Nat Lab, 51-80. *Concurrent Pos:* Civilian technician, Naval Mine Modification Unit, 44-45. *Mem:* Am Phys Soc. *Res:* Low energy nuclear physics. *Mailing Add:* 200 W Fairview Rd Oak Ridge TN 37830

BAIR, KENNETH WALTER, SYNTHETIC ORGANIC CHEMISTRY. *Current Pos:* EXEC DIR PRE-CLINICAL ONCOLOGY, SANDOZ PHARMACEUT CO, 94- *Personal Data:* b Detroit, Mich, Mar 20, 48; m 69, 79; c 1. *Educ:* Wayne State Univ, BS, 70, MS, 73; Brandeis Univ, PhD(org chem), 76. *Prof Exp:* Lab technician clin chem, Clin Chem Lab, Harper Hosp, 69-72; res assoc enzyme chem, Dept Internal Med, Hutzel Hosp, 72-73; res assoc org chem, Wayne State Univ, 73; res assoc org chem, Brandeis Univ, 73-76; Damon Runyon-Walter Winchell res fel, Mass Inst Technol, 76-78; sr rec chemist, Burroughs-Wellcome Co, 78-94. *Mem:* Am Chem Soc; The Chem Soc. *Res:* Synthesis of medicinally important compounds, development of new synthetic methods. *Mailing Add:* Sandoz Pharmaceut Co Bldg 405 4th Floor 59 Rte 10 East Hanover NJ 07936-1080

BAIR, THOMAS DE PINNA, PARASITOLOGY, PHYSIOLOGY & MEDICAL ENTOMOLOGY. *Current Pos:* RETIRED. *Personal Data:* b New York, NY, Mar 19, 22; m 84, Sonia Legayada; c Hudson & John. *Educ:* DePauw Univ, AB, 46; Ind Univ, MA, 47; Univ Ill, PhD(zool, physiol), 51. *Prof Exp:* Asst zool, Ind Univ, 47; asst zool & physiol, Univ Ill, 47-49, vet parasitol, 49-50; instr biol, Utica Col, Syracuse Univ, 50-53; instr physiol, Albany Med Col, 53-56; from asst prof to prof zool, Calif State Univ, Los Angeles, 56-88. *Concurrent Pos:* Vis asst prof, Calif Col Med, 58-64; lectr & consult, Gormac Polygraph Inst, 59-; sr lectr, Univ Southern Calif, 64-; Fulbright prof, Nangrahar Med Fac, Jalalabad, Afghanistan, 70-71 & India, 77-78; fel trop med, La State Univ Sch Med, USPHS, fel physiol, Univ Calif, Los Angeles. *Mem:* Indian Soc Parasitol; AAAS; Am Soc Parasitol; Sigma Xi; fel Linnean Soc London. *Res:* Comparative physiology; parasitology; history and philosophy of science; physiology of parasites. *Mailing Add:* 1240 Journey's End Dr La Canada CA 91012

BAIR, THOMAS IRVIN, POLYMER CHEMISTRY, PHYSICAL ORGANIC CHEMISTRY. *Current Pos:* Res chemist, 65-69, sr res chemist, 69-72, supvr res & develop, 72-77, RES ASSOC, E I DU PONT DE NEMOURS & CO, 77- *Personal Data:* b Grier City, Pa, Feb 12, 38; m 66. *Educ:* Pa State Univ, BS, 60; Univ Wis, PhD(electrophilic substitution), 66. *Mem:* Am Chem Soc; Sigma Xi; NY Acad Sci. *Res:* Cyclopropanol chemistry; nuclear magnetic resonance spectroscopy of cyclopropane compounds; electrophilic substitution at saturated carbon; synthesis and characterization of condensation polymers; fiber technology; rubber reinforcing materials; adhesives and finishes. *Mailing Add:* 4 Little Leaf Ct Foulk Woods Wilmington DE 19810-3702

BAIR, WILLIAM J, RADIOBIOLOGY, RADIOLOGICAL HEALTH. *Current Pos:* mgr inhalation toxicol sect, Biol Dept, Battelle Mem Inst, 56-68, mgr Biol Dept, 68-74, dir, Life Sci Prog, 73-75, mgr, Biomed & Environ Res Prog, 75-76, mgr, Environ Health & Safety Res Prog, 76-86, mgr, Life Sci Ctr, 86-93, SR ADV HEALTH PROTECTION RES, PAC NORTHWEST LABS, BATTELLE MEM INST, 93- *Personal Data:* b Jackson, Mich, July 14, 24; m 52, Barbara Sites; c William J, Michael B & Andrew E. *Educ:* Ohio Wesleyan Univ, BA, 49; Univ Rochester, PhD(radiation biol), 54. *Honors & Awards:* E O Lawrence Mem Award, US AEC, 70. *Prof Exp:* Nat Res Coun-AEC fel, Univ Rochester, 49-50, res assoc, 50-54; biol scientist, Hanford Labs, Gen Elec Co, Richland, Wash, 54-56. *Concurrent Pos:* Lectr radiation biol, Joint Ctr Grad Study, Richland, Wash, 55-; mem subcomt on inhalation hazards, Comt on Path Effects of Atomic Radiation, Nat Acad Sci, 57-64; Japan AEC invited lectr, Nat Radiol Health Inst, Chiba, 69, Radiation Effects Res Found, Hiroshima, 89; chmn, task force, Int Comn Radiol Protection, 70-79, ad hoc comt hot particles, 74-75 & task group respiratory tract model, 84-; mem, Sci Comt Radionuclides, Int Coun Radiol Protection, 70-77, Comt Internal Radiation, 73-, Nat Coun Radiation Protection & Measurements, 74-91, hon mem, 91-, Comt Basic Radiation Protection, 75-91 & bd dirs, 76-82, Presidents Comn Accident Three Mile Island, 79-80; consult, Adv Comt Reactor Safeguards, Nuclear Regulatory Comn, 71-87; chmn, Transuranium Tech Group, Am Inst Biol Sci-AEC- Energy Res & Develop Admin, 72-75; mem ad hoc comt on hot particles of subcomt biol effects of ionizing radiation, Nat Acad Sci-Nat Res Coun, 74-76 & vchmn, comt on biol effects of ionizing radiation, Beir IV alpha radiation, 85-88, Beir VI-Radon, 94-; chmn, Marshall Islands radiol adv group, Dept Energy, 78-81; lectr, SAfrican Asn Physicists in Med & Biol, Pretoria, 80; invited lectr, NChina Inst Radiation Protection, 84; guest scientist, USSR Meeting Med Consequences Chernobyl Accident, 88. *Mem:* Fel AAAS; Radiation Res Soc; fel Health Physics Soc (pres-elect, 83-84, pres, 84-85); Sigma Xi. *Res:*

Radiation biology of inhaled radionuclides; health and environmental effects of transuranium elements; establishment of radiation protection criteria and standards for radionuclides. *Mailing Add:* 102 Somerset Richland WA 99352-1966

BAIRD, ALFRED MICHAEL, TARGET SIGNATURE ANALYSIS. *Current Pos:* DIV DIR, ANALYTICS INC, 85- *Personal Data:* b Philadelphia, May 29, 48; m 70; c 2. *Educ:* St Joseph's Col, BS, 70; Dartmouth Col, PhD(physics), 77. *Prof Exp:* Lead scientist, Analytics Inc, 78-83; lead engr, Raytheon Co, 83-85. *Mem:* Optical Soc Am. *Res:* Analysis and simulation of electromagnetic signatures of military targets and performance evaluation of autonomous acquisition sensors. *Mailing Add:* 2418 Rocky Shores Dr Niceville FL 32578

BAIRD, BARBARA A, CELL SURFACE RECEPTORS. *Current Pos:* from asst prof to assoc prof, 80-91, PROF CHEM, CORNELL UNIV, 91- *Personal Data:* b Decatur, Ill, June 8, 51; m 79, David Holowka; c 3. *Educ:* Knox Col, BA, 73; Cornell Univ, MS, 75, PhD(chem), 79. *Honors & Awards:* Lamport Award Young Investr Biophys, NY Acad Sci, 87. *Prof Exp:* Fel immunol, Nat Cancer Inst, 78-80. *Concurrent Pos:* J S Guggenheim fel, 93-94. *Mem:* Am Soc Biol Chemists; Biophys Soc; Am Chem Soc. *Res:* Biophysical chemistry; structure and function of cell membrane receptor proteins involved in immunological responses. *Mailing Add:* Box 555 Lab Chem Cornell Univ Ithaca NY 14853-1301. *Fax:* 607-255-4137; *E-Mail:* bab13@cornell.edu

BAIRD, BRIDGET B, COMPUTER SCIENCE, MATHEMATICS. *Current Pos:* PROF MATH, CONN COL, NEW LONDON. *Concurrent Pos:* Fulbright grantee comput sci, Univ Americas, Pueblo, Mex, 96-97. *Res:* Virtual reality as applied to art and music. *Mailing Add:* Dept Math Conn Col New London CT 06320

BAIRD, CHARLES ROBERT, CONTROL SYSTEMS THEORY, OPTIMAL SYSTEMS THEORY. *Current Pos:* From asst prof to assoc prof, 74-79 & 81-86, PROF & HEAD, ELEC ENG DEPT, TECH UNIV NS, 86- *Personal Data:* b Windsor, NS, Nov 2, 35; m 62; c 6. *Educ:* Tech Univ NS, BEng, 57; Univ BC, MASc, 62; Univ NB, PhD(elec eng), 74. *Concurrent Pos:* Dir & prin investr, Vehicle Safety Res Team, TUNS for Transp Can, 75-; adj prof elec eng, USN Postgrad Sch, 79-81; pres, Synergetic Eng Assoc Inc, 84-; mem bd examiners, Asn Prof Eng NS, 89-92. *Mem:* Soc Automotive Engrs; Am Asn Automotive Med. *Res:* Identification and estimation theory applied to optimal control systems; knowledge based intelligent controllers; vehicle safety research. *Mailing Add:* Univ NS PO Box 1000 Halifax NS B3J 2X4 Can

BAIRD, CRAIG RISKA, ENTOMOLOGY, WILDLIFE BIOLOGY. *Current Pos:* asst prof, 74-80, PROF ENTOM & EXTEN ENTOMOLOGIST, UNIV IDAHO, 80- *Personal Data:* b Woodland, Utah, May 6, 39; m 63; c 6. *Educ:* Utah State Univ, BS, 67, MS, 70; Wash State Univ, PhD(entom), 73. *Prof Exp:* Sr sci aide entom, Wash State Univ, 72-73, pest mgt specialist, Dept Entom, 73-74. *Mem:* Entom Soc Am; Entom Soc Can; Soc Vector Ecologists. *Res:* Life history and biology of rodent and rabbit botflies; livestock parasites and control; alfalfa seed production and pest management; leafcutting bee management; ecology of wildlife ectoparasites; hops insects and pest management. *Mailing Add:* 9556 Gloria Rd Middleton ID 83644

BAIRD, D C, LOW TEMPERATURE PHYSICS. *Current Pos:* Lectr, Royal Mil Col Can, 52-54, from asst prof to assoc prof, 54-65, head dept, 72-78, PROF PHYSICS, ROYAL MIL COL CAN, 65-, DEAN SCI, 80- *Personal Data:* b Edinburgh, Scotland, May 6, 28; m 54; c 4. *Educ:* Univ Edinburgh, BSc, 49; Univ St Andrews, PhD(physics), 52. *Concurrent Pos:* Defence Res Bd Can res grant, 58- *Res:* Low temperature physics; magnetic properties of superconductors. *Mailing Add:* Dept Physics Royal Mil Col Kingston ON K7K 5L0 Can

BAIRD, DONALD, VERTEBRATE PALEONTOLOGY. *Current Pos:* RETIRED. *Personal Data:* b Pittsburgh, Pa, May 12, 26; m 48; c 2. *Educ:* Univ Pittsburgh, BS, 48; Univ Colo, MS, 49; Harvard Univ, PhD(biol), 55. *Hon Degrees:* MS, Wagner Free Inst Sci, 90. *Prof Exp:* Asst geologist, Pa Topog & Geol Surv, 47-48; cur, Univ Mus, Univ Cincinnati, 49-51; asst cur vert paleont, Mus Comp Zool, Harvard Univ, 54-57; from asst cur to assoc cur, Mus Natural Hist, Princeton Univ, 57-67, cur, 67-73, dir, 73-88. *Concurrent Pos:* Res assoc, Am Mus Natural Hist, 64-, Acad Natural Sci, Philadelphia, 84-, Carnegie Mus Natural Hist, 84-; pres, Princeton Jr Mus, 68-70. *Mem:* Soc Vert Paleont; Paleont Soc; Hist Earth Sci Soc; Soc Hist Archaeol; Brit Palaeont Asn; Sigma Xi. *Res:* Carboniferous, Triassic and Cretaceous reptiles, amphibians and footprints. *Mailing Add:* 4 Ellsworth Terr Pittsburgh PA 15213

BAIRD, DONALD HESTON, PHYSICS & CHEMISTRY OF THIN FILMS. *Current Pos:* MEM TECH STAFF, GEN TEL & ELECTRONICS LABS, INC, 50- *Personal Data:* b Milwaukee, Wis, July 3, 21; m 51; c 2. *Educ:* Haverford Col, BS, 43; Harvard Univ, MA, 50, PhD(phys chem), 50. *Prof Exp:* Asst, Manhattan Proj, 43-46. *Mem:* Am Phys Soc; Inst Elec & Electronics Engrs; AAAS. *Res:* Fundamental development of materials for thin film electroluminescent services, for magnetic bubble memories and other magnetic devices and for various types of opto-electronic devices. *Mailing Add:* 31 Locke Rd Newton MA 02168-1415

BAIRD, GORDON CARDWELL, HISTORICAL GEOLOGY. *Current Pos:* AT DEPT GEOL, STATE UNIV NY, FREDONIA. *Personal Data:* b Rochester, NY, Oct 6, 46. *Educ:* Earlham Col, BA, 69; Univ Nebr-Lincoln, MS, 71; Univ Rochester, PhD(geol), 75. *Prof Exp:* Res assoc geol sci, State Univ NY Binghamton, 75-76; asst curator, Field Mus Natural Hist, 76- *Mem:* AAAS; Paleontological Soc; Soc Econ Paleontologists & Mineralogists; Sigma Xi. *Res:* Paleoecology-sedimentary geology; animal-sediment relationships in ancient deposits in order to do paleocommunity-paleoenvironmental reconstructions. *Mailing Add:* Dept Geosci State Univ NY Fredonia NY 14063

BAIRD, HERBERT WALLACE, STRUCTURAL CHEMISTRY. *Current Pos:* from asst prof to assoc prof, 63-75, PROF CHEM, WAKE FOREST UNIV, 75- *Personal Data:* b Morganton, NC, Sept 2, 36; m 58; c 2. *Educ:* Berea Col, BA, 58; Univ Wis, PhD(chem), 63. *Prof Exp:* Asst chem, Univ Wis, 59-60. *Mem:* Am Chem Soc; Am Crystallog Asn. *Res:* X-ray diffraction structure analysis. *Mailing Add:* 5845 Sullivan Town Rd Walkerton NC 27051-0849

BAIRD, JACK R, ELECTRICAL ENGINEERING. *Current Pos:* PRES, VIDEO ACCESSORIES CORP, BOULDER, 80- *Personal Data:* b Colchester, Ill, May 1, 31; m 54; c 3. *Educ:* Univ Ill, BS, 58, MS, 59, PhD(elec eng), 63. *Prof Exp:* Res assoc elec eng, Univ Ill, 63-64, asst prof, 64-68; from assoc to prof, Univ Colo, Boulder, 68-80. *Mem:* Inst Elec & Electronics Engrs. *Res:* Millimeter and submillimeter wave length generation, transmission, detection and optical communication systems. *Mailing Add:* 129 High Country Ct Lafayette CO 80026

BAIRD, JACK VERNON, SOIL SCIENCE. *Current Pos:* exten agronomist soil sci, 64-71, actg head dept, 70-71, EXTEN PROF SOIL SCI, NC STATE UNIV, 71- *Personal Data:* b Grand Island, Nebr, July 7, 28; m 49; c 3. *Educ:* Univ Nebr, BS, 49, MS, 51; Wash State Univ, PhD(soil sci), 55. *Prof Exp:* Exten agronomist soil mgt, Univ Ill, 58-60; gen agron, Kans State Univ, 61-64. *Mem:* Am Soc Agron; Soil Sci Soc Am. *Res:* Soil fertility problems in North Carolina; proper fertilizer usage and soil management. *Mailing Add:* 3730 Swift Dr Raleigh NC 27606

BAIRD, JAMES CLYDE, PHYSICAL CHEMISTRY. *Current Pos:* from asst prof to assoc prof chem, 62-71, PROF CHEM & PHYSICS, BROWN UNIV, 71- *Personal Data:* b Montgomery, Ala, Oct 26, 31; m 59; c 1. *Educ:* Stanford Univ, BS, 53; Rice Inst, PhD(chem), 59. *Prof Exp:* Fel chem, Harvard Univ, 58-60; res chemist, Calif Res Corp, 60-62. *Concurrent Pos:* Res assoc, Univ Calif, Berkeley, 60-62; Alfred Sloan fel, 65-67; vis fel, Joint Inst Lab Astrophys, Univ Colo, 70-71. *Mem:* Am Phys Soc. *Res:* Atomic and molecular physics and chemistry; radio frequency spectroscopy. *Mailing Add:* Dept Chem Brown Univ Providence RI 02912-9127

BAIRD, JAMES KERN, DIFFUSION, CRYSTAL GROWTH. *Current Pos:* chmn dept, 82-90, PROF CHEM, UNIV ALA, HUNTSVILLE, 82- *Personal Data:* b Pittsburgh, Pa, Aug 24, 41; m 67, Peggy Flanagan; c David. *Educ:* Yale Univ, BS, 63; Harvard Univ, AM, 65, PhD(chem physics), 69. *Honors & Awards:* Cert of Achievement, Test Command, Defense Atomic Support Agency, 70; Charles H Stone Award, Am Chem Soc, 91. *Prof Exp:* Capt & dep test group coordr, Test Command, Defense Atomic Support Agency, Sandia Base, US Army, NMex, 69-70; physicist, Oak Ridge Nat Lab, Tenn, 70-81; mgr, Radiochem Unit, Knolls Atomic Power Lab, Schenectady, NY, 81-82. *Concurrent Pos:* Adj assoc prof, Dept Physics, Univ Kans, Lawrence, 77-80; prin sci adv, Consortium Mat Develop Space, Univ Ala, 85-; consult, Chrysler Corp, 88, Sci Comput, Inc, 88, Morton Thiokol, 88-89; dir, Univ Ala Syst Joint PhD Prog Mat Sci, 92-95; distinguished summer fac res fel, Naval Res Lab, Washington, DC, 93. *Mem:* Am Phys Soc; Am Chem Soc; Mat Res Soc. *Res:* Theoretical chemistry with emphasis on problems in diffusion, crystal growth, plasmas, heat transfer and shock waves. *Mailing Add:* Dept Chem Univ Ala Huntsville AL 35899. *Fax:* 205-890-6441; *E-Mail:* jkbaird@matsci.uah.edu

BAIRD, JAMES LEROY, JR, COMPARATIVE PHYSIOLOGY. *Current Pos:* DIR, AVERY POINT CAMPUS, UNIV CONN, 75- *Personal Data:* b Bridgeport, Conn, Aug 5, 34; m 56, 93, Margaret S Pollard; c Elizabeth, Margaret & James III. *Educ:* Tufts Univ, BS, 56; Univ Minn, MS, 59; Univ Conn, PhD(zool), 64. *Prof Exp:* Res entomologist, US Forest Serv, 59; instr biol, Conn Col, 62-63 & zool, Univ Conn, 63-64; asst prof, Lafayette Col, 64-71, actg dean studies, 71; assoc prof biol & head dept, Rochester Inst Technol, 71-74, fac assoc student affairs, 74-75. *Concurrent Pos:* Lectr physiol & neurobiol. *Mem:* Entom Soc Am; Am Soc Zoologists. *Res:* Comparative physiology of insect flight; insect neuromuscular biology; biological control systems; arthropod behavior. *Mailing Add:* Provost/Dir Univ Conn Avery Point 1084 Shennecossett Rd Groton CT 06340. *Fax:* 860-443-3498

BAIRD, JOHN JEFFERS, NEUROEMBRYOLOGY. *Current Pos:* from asst prof to prof embryol, Calif State Univ, 56-67, chmn, Dept Biol, 61-67, Univ chancellors off assoc dean acad planning, 67-73, dep dean, 73-78, prof biol, 78-84, actg chmn dept, 81-82, EMER PROF, CALIF STATE UNIV, LONG BEACH, 84- *Personal Data:* b North English, Iowa, Jan 1, 21; m 45, Geraldine Garner; c Stephanie (Williams). *Educ:* Iowa State Teachers Col, AB, 48; Univ Iowa, MS, 53, PhD, 57. *Prof Exp:* Teacher high sch, Iowa, 48-54; instr, Univ Iowa, 54-56. *Mem:* AAAS; Am Soc Zool; Sigma Xi. *Res:* Peripheral control of development of motor and sensory elements of central nervous system. *Mailing Add:* Dept Biol 1250 Bellflower Blvd Long Beach CA 90840

BAIRD, KENNETH MACCLURE, PHYSICS. *Current Pos:* RETIRED. *Personal Data:* b Hawaiking Fu, China, Jan 23, 23; Can citizen; m 51; c 4. *Educ:* Univ New Brunswick, BSc, 43; Univ Bristol, PhD(physics), 53. *Prof Exp:* Prin res scientist, Nat Res Labs, 43-48 & 50-81. *Mem:* Optical Soc Am. *Res:* Optics; interferometry. *Mailing Add:* 25 Rothwell Dr Gloucester ON K1J 7G5 Can

BAIRD, LISA MORRISON, PLANT DEVELOPMENT, MOLECULAR BIOLOGY. *Current Pos:* assoc prof, 88-94, CHAIR BIOL, UNIV SAN DIEGO, 91-, PROF BIOL, 94- *Personal Data:* b Lawrence, Kans, Sept 16, 54; m 77, Steven Lowrance Morrison. *Educ:* Smith Col, AB, 76; Univ Calif, Davis, MS, 78, PhD(bot), 80. *Prof Exp:* NSF fel, Univ Calif, Davis, 80-81, res agronomist, 81-83; asst prof bot, Conn Col, 83-88. *Concurrent Pos:* Res fel biol, Yale Univ, 87-89; chair, Biol Div, Coun Undergrad Res, 95-97. *Mem:* Am Soc Plant Physiologists. *Res:* Development/function of symbiosis for nitrogen fixation in legumes; factors limiting reproduction in crop plants; abscission/senescence in plants. *Mailing Add:* Dept Biol Univ San Diego San Diego CA 92110. *Fax:* 619-260-6804; *E-Mail:* baird@acusd.edu

BAIRD, MALCOLM HENRY INGLIS, CHEMICAL ENGINEERING. *Current Pos:* assoc prof, 67-73, chmn dept, 82-85, PROF CHEM ENG, MCMASTER UNIV, 73- *Personal Data:* b London, Eng, July 2, 35; Can & Brit citizen; m 65, Jean Lawrie; c Iain & Kenneth. *Educ:* Univ Glasgow, BSc, 57; Univ Cambridge, PhD(chem eng), 60. *Prof Exp:* Res engr, Can Industs Ltd, 60-63; teaching fel chem eng, Univ Edinburgh, 63-65, lectr, 65-67. *Concurrent Pos:* Assoc ed, Can J Chem Eng, 69-73, 74-76 & 81-84; vis fel, Univ Queensland, Australia, 73-74, Robinson Col, Cambridge, UK, 94; vis prof, Univ Bradford, UK, 85; assoc ed, Chem Eng Res & Design, 90- *Mem:* Can Soc Chem Eng. *Res:* Mass transfer and fluid mixing processes such as mixing, solvent extraction and gas absorption; oscillation flow phenomena; modelling of pyrometallurgical processes. *Mailing Add:* Chem Eng Dept McMaster Univ Hamilton ON L8S 4L7 Can. *Fax:* 905-521-1350

BAIRD, MELLON CAMPBELL, JR, ELECTRONICS. *Current Pos:* PRES, CHIEF EXEC OFFICER & CHMN BD DIRS, DELFIN SYSTS, SUNNYVALE, CALIF, 90- *Personal Data:* b Corsicana, Tex, Feb 24, 31; m 56, Mary Beth Norman. *Educ:* NTex State Univ, BBA, 57, MBA, 61. *Prof Exp:* Admin asst, Varo Inc, Garland, Tex, 57-59, western region mgr, Los Angeles, 59-61, dir mkt, Santa Barbara, Calif, 61-63; exec vpres & pres, F & M Systs Co, Dallas, 63-74; pres & bd dir, Fed Systs Group, Sanders Assocs Inc, Nashua, NH, 74-81; pres, Defense & Electronics Group, Eaton Corp, Cleveland, 81-86; pres, chief oper officer & bd dirs, Tracor Inc, Austin, Tex, 86-87, pres & chief exec officer, 88-89. *Concurrent Pos:* Mem bd dirs, Software Spectrum Inc & Edo Corp. *Mem:* Nat Security Indust Asn; Armed Forces Commun & Electronics Asn. *Mailing Add:* Delfin Systs 3000 Patrick Henry Dr Santa Clara CA 95054-1814

BAIRD, MERTON DENISON, ORGANIC CHEMISTRY, NMR & COMPUTERS IN CHEMICAL EDUCATION. *Current Pos:* From asst prof to assoc prof, 68-80, chmn dept, 74-77, PROF CHEM, SHIPPENSBURG UNIV, 80- *Personal Data:* b Ft Wayne, Ind, Sept 9, 40; m 67, Shirley Gorden; c Alan & Katherine. *Educ:* Purdue Univ, BS, 62; Univ Wis-Madison, PhD(org chem), 69. *Mem:* Am Chem Soc. *Res:* Synthesis of organic compounds related to natural products; applications of nuclear magnetic resonance and computational methods to conformational analysis of molecules and correlations of structure and reactivity; synthesis of silicon containing anticonvulsants. *Mailing Add:* Dept Chem Shippensburg Univ 1871 Old Main Dr Shippensburg PA 17257. *Fax:* 717-530-4048; *E-Mail:* mdbair@ark.ship.edu

BAIRD, MICHAEL JEFFERSON, CATALYST EVALUATIONS. *Current Pos:* PROJ MGR, US DEPT ENERGY, 87- *Personal Data:* b New Orleans, La, Oct 21, 39; m 67; c 4. *Educ:* Tex A&M Univ, BS, 63, PhD(phys chem), 71; Univ Pittsburgh, MS, 79. *Prof Exp:* Process engr, E I Du Pont, Chattanooga, 63-64; res chemist, US Bur Mines, Minneapolis, 71-74; supvry chem engr, Pittsburgh Energy Res Ctr, US Dept Energy, 74-79; sr res chemist res & develop, Ashland Oil, 79-80; staff res engr hydrotreating process develop, Amoco Oil, Naperville, Ill, 80-87. *Concurrent Pos:* Adj prof chem eng, Ill Inst Technol, 81 & Univ Ill, Chicago, 82 & 84. *Mem:* Am Chem Soc. *Res:* Pilot plant evaluations of hydrotreating and hydrocracking catalysts; catalyst preparation of new hydrotreating catalysts; catalyst regeneration processes. *Mailing Add:* US Dept Energy PO Box 10940 Pittsburgh PA 15236-0940

BAIRD, NORMAN COLIN, PHYSICAL CHEMISTRY. *Current Pos:* asst prof to assoc prof, 68-78, PROF PHYS CHEM, UNIV WESTERN ONT, 78- *Personal Data:* b Montreal, Que, May 22, 42; c 1. *Educ:* McGill Univ, BSc, 63, PhD(phys chem), 67. *Prof Exp:* Robert A Welch fel, Univ Tex, 66-68. *Res:* Quantum-mechanical investigations of the structure, energy and chemical bonding in molecules. *Mailing Add:* Dept Chem Univ Western Ont London ON N6A 5B7 Can

BAIRD, PATRICIA A, MEDICAL GENETICS. *Current Pos:* instr pediat, Univ BC, 68-72, from asst prof to prof, 72-82, head, 79-89, actg dir, Ctr Molecular Genetics, 82-87, PROF MED GENETICS, UNIV BC, 82-, UNIV KILLAM DISTINGUISHED PROF, 94-, VPRES CAN INST ADVAN RES, 91- *Personal Data:* b Rochdale, Eng; Can citizen; m 64; c 3. *Educ:* McGill Univ, BS, 59, MD & CM, 63. *Hon Degrees:* DSc, McMaster Univ, 91, Dr, Univ Ottawa, 91. *Honors & Awards:* Women Distinction Award, YWCA, 88; Osler lectr, Vanouver Med Asn, 91; Commemorative Medal 125th Anniv, Can Confedn, 92. *Prof Exp:* Head med genetics, Grace & Children's Univ Hosps, BC, 81-89; chair, Fed Royal Comn New Reproductive Technol, 89-93. *Concurrent Pos:* Med consult, Health Surveillance Registry BC, 77-90; mem, Bd Gov, Univ BC, 84-90; vpres, Can Col Med Geneticists, 84-86; mem, Nat Consult Comt Epidemiol Ment Retardation, Can, 84-87; mem, Nat Adv Bd Sci & Technol, Fed govt, 87-91; Coun mem, Med Res Coun can, 87-90, FIGO Comm Study Ethical Aspects Human Reproduction, 94; mem ethics panel, Int Pediat Asn, 90-; co-chair, Nat Forum Sci & Technol Councils, 91-95. *Mem:* Am Soc Human Genetics; Genetics Soc Can; Royal Col Physicians Can; Can Col Med Geneticists. *Res:* Use of population-based data on genetic and handicapping conditions to provide insights and information useful in clinical counselling and program planning; natural history of genetic disorders; biological background and mechanisms responsible for some congenital disorders; social and ethical implications of appling scientific knowledge about genetics and reproductive biology to people. *Mailing Add:* Dept Med Genetics Univ BC 222-6174 Univ Blvd Vancouver BC V6T 1Z3 Can

BAIRD, QUINCEY LAMAR, REACTOR SAFETY. *Current Pos:* RETIRED. *Personal Data:* b Hoschton, Ga, Mar 22, 32; m 56; c 4. *Educ:* Berry Col, AB, 52; Emory Univ, MS, 54; Vanderbilt Univ, PhD(physics), 58. *Prof Exp:* Teacher pvt sch, Tenn, 52-53; physicist, Argonne Nat Lab, 58-63; engr, Nuclear Technol Div, Idaho Opers Off, US AEC, 63-66; sr res scientist, Pac Northwest Lab, Battelle Mem Inst, 66-70; sr res scientist, Wadco Corp, Westinghouse-Hanford Co, 70-74, prin engr & tech assoc, 74-92. *Mem:* Am Phys Soc; Am Nuclear Soc. *Res:* Experimental reactor physics related to power reactor design and operation; nuclear engineering aspects of system design; liquid metal and fast breeder reactor safety, design requirements and operations analysis. *Mailing Add:* 1710 Alder Ave Richland WA 99352-2739

BAIRD, RAMON CONDIE, PHYSICS, ELECTRICAL ENGINEERING. *Current Pos:* RETIRED. *Personal Data:* b Ogden, Utah, May 25, 29; m 61; c 4. *Educ:* Brigham Young Univ, BS, 55, MS, 57; Univ Colo, PhD(physics), 65. *Prof Exp:* Proj leader mm-wave interferometry, Microwave Physics Sect, Radio Physics Div, Nat Bur Stand, 57-66, sect chief antenna measurements, antenna systs metrol, Electromagnetic Fields Div, 66-87, div chief, Nat Inst Stand & Technol, 87- *Concurrent Pos:* Chmn, Sub-Comt Measurements & Instrumentation & mem, Comt Radiation Hazards, Am Nat Stand Inst, 70-; chmn US Comn Electromagnetic Metrol, Int Union Radio Sci, 78- *Mem:* Am Nat Standards Inst; Int Union Radio Sci; Inst Elec & Electronics Engrs. *Res:* Millimeterwave measurements of the speed of light and refractive indices of gases; near-field antenna measurement techniques; metrology for satellite communication systems. *Mailing Add:* 1112 Barberry Ct Boulder CO 80303

BAIRD, RICHARD, POLYMER CHEMISTRY. *Current Pos:* RETIRED. *Personal Data:* b Sioux City, Iowa, Aug 15, 31; m 59, Janet S Morton; c Bruce A & Catherine A. *Educ:* Reed Col, BA, 53; Univ Calif, Los Angeles, PhD, 58. *Prof Exp:* Instr chem, Yale Univ, 58-60, asst prof, 60-63, lectr, 63-64; res chemist, Cent Res Dept, E I Du Pont de Nemours & Co, 64-69, Elastomers Dept, 69-73, develop supvr, 73-74, div head, Elastomers Dept, 74-79, res mgr, Polymer Prod Dept, 79-80, tech mgr, 80-81, res mgr, Fabricated Prod Dept, 82-88, tech mgr Technol Acquisition, 88-90. *Mem:* Am Chem Soc. *Res:* Physical organic chemistry; coordination chemistry; polymer chemistry. *Mailing Add:* 8 Aldrich Way Wilmington DE 19807

BAIRD, RONALD C, EDUCATION ADMINISTRATION, ECOLOGY. *Current Pos:* vpres & exec vpres, 79-84, PRES, SCHUSTER CORP, 85-; DIR CORP RELS, WORCESTER POLYTECH INST, 91- *Personal Data:* b New Albany, Ind, Apr 1, 36; m 62, Kay Schuster; c Susanna & Lesley. *Educ:* Yale Univ, BS, 58; Univ Tex, MA, 65; Harvard Univ, PhD, 69. *Prof Exp:* Asst cur, Mus Comp Zool, 68-69; from asst prof to assoc prof marine sci, Univ SFla, 70-78. *Concurrent Pos:* Dir res, Geo-Marine, Inc, 76-79; courtesy prof marine sci, Univ SFla, 79-; trustee, Worcester Hort Soc, 89-94; chmn, Nat Sea Grant Rev panel, 90-; mem, Gulf Maine Regional Res Bd, 92- *Mem:* AAAS; Am Soc Limnol & Oceanog; Am Soc Naturalists; Am Soc Eng Educ; Am Soc Zoologists; Am Soc Ichthyologists & Herpetologists. *Res:* Biology of deep-sea ecosystems, oceanic ichthyology and coastal resource management. *Mailing Add:* Nat Sea Grant Col Prog NOAA 1315 East-West Hwy Rm 11716 Silver Spring MD 20910

BAIRD, RONALD JAMES, CARDIOVASCULAR SURGERY. *Current Pos:* PROF SURG, UNIV TORONTO, 72- *Personal Data:* b Toronto, Ont, May 3, 30; m 55; c 3. *Educ:* Univ Toronto, MD, 54, BSc, 56, MSurg, 64; FRCS(C), 59, cert cardiovasc & thoracic surg, 64. *Honors & Awards:* Royal Col Surg Medal, 69. *Prof Exp:* Dir surg res, Univ & Toronto Gen Hosp, 72-77, cardiovasc surg, 77-88. *Concurrent Pos:* Res assoc, Ont Heart Found, 64-; dir, Can Heart Found, 67- & Ont Heart Found, 67-; assoc ed, Can J Surg, 67-; mem, Med Res Coun Can, 67-; chief cardiovasc surg, Toronto Western Hosp, 72-77. *Mem:* Can Cardiovasc Soc (secy-treas, 70-73); fel Am Col Surg; Int Cardiovasc Soc (vpres, 73-75); Am Surg Asn; Soc Univ Surg; Int Soc Cardiovasc Surg (pres, 88-89). *Res:* Cardiovascular surgery and physiology; surgery of the ischemic heart and the ischemic limb. *Mailing Add:* Toronto Hosp 200 Elizabeth St-Eaton N Rm 14-218 Toronto ON M5G 1L5 Can

BAIRD, TROY ALAN, EVOLUTION OF SOCIAL BEHAVIOR IN VERTEBRATES, REPRODUCTIVE ECOLOGY OF VERTEBRATES. *Current Pos:* ASST PROF BIOL, ZOOL & ANIMAL BEHAV, UNIV CENT OKLA, 89- *Personal Data:* b Pomona, Calif, Dec 29, 54; m 79, Teresa Baird. *Educ:* Calif State Univ, San Diego, BS, 78, MS, 80; Univ BC, PhD(zool), 89. *Prof Exp:* Postdoctoral res assoc, Marine Sci Ctr, Ore State Univ, Hatfield, 88-89. *Concurrent Pos:* Adj fac, Dept Zool, Okla State Univ. *Mem:* Am Soc Zoologists; Am Soc Ichthyologists & Herpetologists; Sigma Xi; Southwestern Asn Naturalists. *Res:* Evolution of social systems; adaptive significance of group living, individual use of space, reproductive patterns and both intra- and inter-specific social interactions. *Mailing Add:* Dept Biol Univ Cent Okla 100 N University Dr Edmond OK 73034

BAIRD, WILLIAM C, ORGANIC CHEMISTRY, CATALYSIS. *Current Pos:* Exxon Res & Eng Co, 61-68, res assoc, 68-72, res assoc, Exxon Res & Develop Lab, 72-75, SR RES ASSOC, EXXON RES & DEVELOP LAB, 75- *Personal Data:* b McKeesport, Pa, Sept 23, 33; m 61; c 2. *Educ:* Pa State Univ, BS, 55; Univ Iowa, PhD(chem), 59. *Prof Exp:* Am Chem Soc-Petrol Res Fund fel, Swiss Fed Inst Technol, 59-60; NSF fel, La State Univ, 60-61; chemist catalysis. *Mem:* Am Chem Soc. *Res:* Organometallic chemistry; homogeneous catalysis; heterogeneous catalysis; refining processes. *Mailing Add:* 5905 Bennington Ave Baton Rouge LA 70808-3508

BAIRD, WILLIAM MCKENZIE, CHEMICAL CARCINOGENESIS. *Current Pos:* assoc prof, 80-82, PROF MED CHEM, PURDUE UNIV, 82-, DIR, PURDUE CANCER CTR, 86-, GLENN L JENKINS PROF MED CHEM, 89- *Personal Data:* b Philadelphia, Pa, Mar 23, 44; m 69; c 3. *Educ:* Lehigh Univ, BS, 66; Univ Wis, PhD(oncol), 71. *Prof Exp:* Fel, Inst Cancer Res, London, 71-73; from asst prof to assoc prof, Wistar Inst, 73-80. *Concurrent Pos:* Fac partic, Biochem Prog, Purdue Univ, 80- & Purdue Univ Cancer Ctr, 80-; adv comt, Biochem & Chem Carcinogenesis, Am Cancer Soc, 83-86; mem, Chem Path Study Sect, NIH, 86-90. *Mem:* Am Asn Cancer Res; Am Chem Soc; Am Soc Biochem & Molecular Biol; Environ Mutagen Soc; Soc Toxicol; Sigma Xi. *Res:* Metabolism of polycyclic aromatic hydrocarbons; interactions of chemical carcinogens with nucleic acids; use of cells in culture for studies on carcinogenesis; environmental carcinogenesis; chemoprevention of cancer; genetic toxicology; DNA repair. *Mailing Add:* Dept Med Chem & Pharmacog Hansen Life Sci Res Bldg Sch Pharm & Pharm Sci Purdue Univ West Lafayette IN 47907-1524

BAISDEN, CHARLES ROBERT, MEDICINE, PATHOLOGY. *Current Pos:* prof path, 84, DIR CLIN LABS, MED COL GA HOSP & CLINS, 79- *Personal Data:* b Logan, WVa, Apr 23, 39; m 62; c 3. *Educ:* WVa Univ, AB, 61, MD, 65. *Prof Exp:* Intern med, WVa Univ Hosp, 65-66, resident path, 66-68; resident, Baptist Mem Hosp, Memphis, Tenn, 68-70; asst prof lab med, Sch Med, Johns Hopkins Univ & pathologist, Johns Hopkins Hosp, 70-79. *Concurrent Pos:* Path consult, Vet Admin Hosp, Perry Point, Md, 70-79; dir clin labs, Franklin Sq Hosp, Baltimore, 72-76; consult, Vet Admin Hosp, Augusta, Ga, 79- *Mem:* Am Soc Clin Path. *Res:* Types of bisalbuminemia and methods of detection; cancer detection with ultraviolet microscopy. *Mailing Add:* Dept Path Med Col Ga Augusta GA 30912

BAISDEN, PATRICIA ANN, FISSION PROPERTIES, HEAVY-ION REACTIONS. *Current Pos:* staff scientist, 76-81, GROUP LEADER NUCLEAR CHEM, LAWRENCE LIVERMORE NAT LAB, 81- *Personal Data:* b Montgomery, WVa, July 10, 49; m 78. *Educ:* Fla State Univ, BS, 71, PhD(chem), 75. *Prof Exp:* Res assoc chem oceanog, Univ Puerto Rico, 71; res chemist spectros, Procter & Gamble, 75-76. *Concurrent Pos:* Consult, Int Atomic Energy Agency, 80- *Mem:* Am Chem Soc; Am Phys Soc; Sigma Xi. *Res:* Measurment of heavy element fission properties using both chemical and on-line techniques; solution of chemistry of lanthanide and actinide elements; heavy ion collisions leading to complete or incomplete fusion. *Mailing Add:* Lawrence Livermore Nat Lab Univ Calif PO Box 808 L-326 Livermore CA 94550

BAISDEN, RONALD HUBERT, NEURAL TRANSPLANTATION, NEURAL PLASTICITY. *Current Pos:* from asst prof to assoc prof, 78-87, PROF, DEPT ANAT & CELL BIOL, E TENN STATE UNIV, 87- *Personal Data:* wid; c Ronald H Jr, Tiffany A & Stacey N. *Educ:* Univ Fla, Bs, 68, PhD(med sci/anat), 73. *Prof Exp:* Postdoctoral instr, State Univ NY, Syracuse, 73-75; asst prof, Univ Ill, Chicago, 75-77. *Mem:* Soc Neurosci; Am Asn Anatomists; Am Soc Neural Transplantation; Int Brain Res Orgn; Fedn Am Socs Exp Biol. *Res:* Response of the cenral nervous system to damage; cellular events following axonal disruption; structure, development and functional effects of fetal neural transplantation in animal models. *Mailing Add:* Dept Anat & Cell Biol E Tenn State Univ Johnson City TN 37614. *Fax:* 423-461-7040; *E-Mail:* baisden@access.easttnstuniv-tn.edu

BAISH, JAMES WILLIAM, BIOHEAT TRANSFER. *Current Pos:* asst prof, 86-92, ASSOC PROF, BUCKNELL UNIV, 92- *Personal Data:* b Carlisle, Pa, Nov 2, 57. *Educ:* Bucknell Univ, BSME, 79; Univ Pa, MSE, 83, PhD (mech eng & appl mech), 86. *Prof Exp:* Edison engr, Space Div, Gen Elec, 79-81. *Concurrent Pos:* NSF presidential young investr, 90. *Mem:* Am Soc Mech Engrs; Inst Elec & Electronics Engrs; Am Soc Eng Educ; Biomed Eng Soc. *Res:* Heat and mass transport in biological tissues; transport in multiphase media; mathematical modeling of tree structures; control theory; application of engineering to medicine and biology. *Mailing Add:* Dept Mech Eng Bucknell Univ Lewisburg PA 17837. *E-Mail:* baish@bucknell.edu

BAISTED, DEREK JOHN, BIOCHEMISTRY. *Current Pos:* NIH fel, 63-64, USPHS career develop award, 65-70, from asst prof to assoc prof, 65-81, PROF BIOCHEM, ORE STATE UNIV, 81- *Personal Data:* b London, Eng, Oct 5, 34; m 60; c 2. *Educ:* Exeter Univ, BSc, 57, PhD(org chem), 60. *Prof Exp:* USPHS trainee steroid biochem, Clark & Worcester Found Exp Biol, 60-62; NSF fel, Ind Univ, 62-63. *Mem:* Fedn Am Soc Exp Biol; Royal Soc Chem; Am Soc Plant Physiologists. *Res:* Biosynthesis and metabolism of lipids; membrane-associated enzymes. *Mailing Add:* 835 NW Conifer Blvd Corvallis OR 97330

BAITINGER, WILLIAM F, TEXTILE CHEMISTRY. *Current Pos:* VPRES TECH, WESTEX INC, 84- *Personal Data:* b Bridgeton, NJ, Nov 24, 35; m 85, Sheila Moran; c Andrew, Leslie & Dawn. *Educ:* Albright Col, BS, 58; Princeton Univ, MA, 62, PhD(chem), 64. *Prof Exp:* Chemist, Am Cyanamid Co, 58-60, res chemist, 63-66, group leader textile chem, 66-71, sr res scientist, 71-74; mgr fire retardant res, Cotton, Inc, 74-78, assoc dir prod safety res, 78-79, dir, 80-84. *Mem:* Am Chem Soc; Am Soc Testing & Mat; Am Asn Textile Chemists & Colorists. *Res:* Synthesis of aromatic and aliphatic light stabilizers; effects of ultra-violet light on polymers and organic compounds; chemistry of textile wet processing. *Mailing Add:* Westex Inc 2845 W 48th Pl Chicago IL 60632-2012. *Fax:* 773-523-0965

BAIZER, JOAN SUSAN, NEUROPHYSIOLOGY, VISION. *Current Pos:* ASSOC PROF PHYSIOL, STATE UNIV NY, BUFFALO, 76-, ASSOC PROF NEUROBIOL, DEPT PHYSIOL. *Personal Data:* b New York, NY, Sept 12, 46. *Educ:* Bryn Mawr Col, BA, 68; Brown Univ, MS, 70, PhD(psychol), 73. *Prof Exp:* Fel neurophys, Lab Neurobiol, NIMH, 73-76. *Concurrent Pos:* Nat Inst Neurol & Commun Disorders & Stroke fel, 73-75; NIMH fel, 75-76; Nat Eye Inst res grant, 77-80. *Mem:* Asn Res Vision & Ophthal; Soc Neurosci; Asn Women Sci. *Res:* Neurophysical vision system; prestriate cortex; eye movements. *Mailing Add:* Dept Physiol 124 Sherman State Univ NY Buffalo Sch Med 3435 Main St Buffalo NY 14214-3001

BAJAJ, JAGMOHAN, SEMICONDUCTORS, INFRARED IMAGING. *Current Pos:* MEM TECH STAFF, ROCKWELL INT SCI CTR, 81- *Personal Data:* b New Delhi, India, Mar 12, 54; US citizen; m 83; c 2. *Educ:* Univ Delhi, India, BSc, 73, MSc, 75; Northwestern Univ, Evanston, PhD(solid state physics), 81. *Mem:* Am Phys Soc. *Res:* HgCdTe alloy semiconductor based materials and device physics for development of infrared imaging. *Mailing Add:* Rockwell Int Sci Ctr 1049 Camino Dos Rios Thousand Oaks CA 91360

BAJAJ, PREM NATH, MATHEMATICAL ANALYSIS, TOPOLOGY. *Current Pos:* asst prof, 68-72, ASSOC PROF MATH, WICHITA STATE UNIV, 72- *Personal Data:* b Ferozepur City, India, Oct 6, 32; m 56; c Ashok, Ravi, Arvind, Ajay & Anta. *Educ:* Punjab Univ, India, BA, 51, MA, 54; Case Western Reserve Univ, MS, 67, PhD(math), 68. *Prof Exp:* Teacher, 51-52; lectr, RKSD Col, Kaithal, 54-57 & DAV Col, Jullundur, 57-65; vis asst prof, Case Western Reserve Univ, 68. *Concurrent Pos:* Mem, Vishveshvaranand Vedic Res Inst; chair, Kans sect Math Asn Am, 95-96. *Mem:* Math Asn Am; Indian Math Soc. *Res:* Ordinary differential equations; dynamical systems; topology. *Mailing Add:* Dept Math Wichita State Univ Wichita KS 67260-0033. *Fax:* 316-978-3748

BAJAJ, RAM, METALLURGY, RADIATION EFFECTS. *Current Pos:* FEL ENGR MAT SCI, BETTIS ATOMIC POWER LAB, WESTINGHOUSE ELEC CORP, 74- *Personal Data:* b Sukkur, Pakistan, May 15, 46; m 74; c 3. *Educ:* Indian Inst Technol, Bombay, BTech, 68; Univ Mo-Rolla, MS, 70; Iowa State Univ, PhD(metall), 75. *Concurrent Pos:* Mem task group, Nat Alloy Develop Prog, Dept Energy, 76- *Mem:* Metall Soc. *Res:* Alloy development; mechanical properties of high temperature alloys; radiation damage; refractory materials; macro and micro analytical techniques; electron microscopy; corrosion; ceramics. *Mailing Add:* 886 Freightner Rd Greensburg PA 15601

BAJAJ, S PAUL, BIOCHEMICAL HEMOSTASIS. *Current Pos:* assoc prof, 85-89, PROF MED & BIOCHEM, MED CTR, ST LOUIS UNIV, 89- *Personal Data:* b Punjab, Pakistan, Nov 12, 46; m, Maclhu Aggavwal; c Renata L. *Educ:* Univ Minn, PhD(biochem), 74. *Prof Exp:* Asst prof med, Univ Calif, San Diego, 78-85. *Concurrent Pos:* Estab investr, Am Heart Asn; vis prof, Dept Chem, Mich State Univ, 94-95. *Mem:* Am Soc Hemat; Int Soc on Thrombosis & Hemostasis; Am Heart Asn; Am Soc Biochem & Molecular Biol; Protein Soc. *Res:* Biochemical regulation of thrombosis. *Mailing Add:* Dept Hematol Med Path & Biochem St Louis Univ Sch Med 3635 Vista PO Box 15250 St Louis MO 63110-2500

BAJARS, LAIMONIS, chemical engineering, applied industrial catalysis; deceased, see previous edition for last biography

BAJCSY, RUZENA K, COMPUTER SCIENCE. *Current Pos:* asst prof, 72-77, assoc prof, 77-84, PROF COMPUT & INFO SCI, UNIV PA, 84, DEPT CHAIR, 85-, DIR, GEN ROBOTICS ACTIVE SENSORY PERCEPTION LAB, 85- *Personal Data:* b Czech, May 28, 33; c 2. *Educ:* Slovak Tech Univ, Bratislava, PhD(elec eng), 67; Stanford Univ, PhD(comput sci), 72. *Honors & Awards:* Von Neuman Award, Inst Elec & Electronics Engrs. *Prof Exp:* Comput engr, Comput Ctr, Slovak Tech Univ, Bratislava, 62-64, asst prof comput sci, 64-67; res assoc, Stanford Univ, 67-72. *Concurrent Pos:* NSF res grant, 74; vis prof, Univ Pisa, 88, Univ Copenhagen, Denmark, 88; vis scientist, Queens Univ, Can, ATR Commun Syst Res, Japan, 90 & Electro Tech Lab, Japan, 95; consult. *Mem:* Nat Acad Eng; fel Inst Med-Nat Acad Sci; fel Asn Comput Mach; fel Inst Elec & Electronics Engrs; fel Am Asn Artificial Intel. *Res:* Artificial intelligence; scene analysis; pattern recognition of outdoor scenes; analysis of biological images. *Mailing Add:* Dept Comput Sci Univ Pa 3401 Walnut St Rm 303C Philadelphia PA 19104

BAJEMA, CARL J, HUMAN ECOLOGY, BIOLOGICAL ANTHROPOLOGY. *Current Pos:* from asst prof to assoc prof, 64-72, PROF BIOL, GRAND VALLEY STATE UNIV, 72- *Personal Data:* b Plainwell, Mich, May 25, 37; m 59, 78; c 4. *Educ:* Western Mich Univ, BS, 59, MA, 61; Mich State Univ, PhD(zool), 63. *Prof Exp:* Instr sci, Grand Rapids Pub Sch Syst, Mich, 59-60; asst zool, Mich State Univ, 62-63; asst prof biol, Mankato State Col, 63-64. *Concurrent Pos:* Pop Coun sr fel demog & pop genetics, Univ Chicago, 66-67; res assoc pop studies, Ctr Pop Studies, Harvard Univ, 67-73, vis prof anthrop, 74-75. *Mem:* Hist Sci Soc; Forest Hist Soc; Am Inst

Biol Sci; Nat Asn Biol Teachers; Sigma Xi. *Res:* Measurement of natural selection in human populations; interactions between genetic and cultural systems for adapting to the environment; history of evolutionary thought; teaching of human ecology and evolution; environmental history of Michigan forests. *Mailing Add:* Dept Biol Grand Valley State Univ 1 Campus Dr Allendale MI 49401-9401

BAJER, ANDREW, CELL BIOLOGY. *Current Pos:* assoc prof, 64-69, PROF BIOL, UNIV ORE, 69- *Personal Data:* b Czestochowa, Poland, Jan 3, 28; US citizen; m 51; c 2. *Educ:* Jagiellonian Univ, MA, 49, PhD(cytol), 50, DSc, 56. *Honors & Awards:* Sci Award, Alfred Jurzykowski Found, 74. *Prof Exp:* Asst cytol, Jagiellonian Univ, 48, assoc prof, 56-63; assoc prof, Polish Acad Sci, 63-64. *Concurrent Pos:* NIH career develop award, 67-72. *Mem:* AAAS; Am Soc Cell Biologists; Bot Soc Fund; Int Soc Cell Biol; Am Sci Film Asn; Sigma Xi. *Res:* Physiology of cell division and mechanism of chromosome movements; mitosis and meiosis, especially microcinematrographic technique on plant endosperm; developed technique permitting study of the same cell with light microscopy and electron microscopy. *Mailing Add:* Dept Biol Univ Ore Eugene OR 97403

BAJIKAR, SATEESH, MICROELECTRONICS PROCESSING, MICROMACHINING & MICROMECHANICS. *Current Pos:* res asst, 89-91, TEACHING ASST PHYSICS, UNIV WIS-MADISON, 91-; POSTDOCTORAL, ARGONNE NAT LABS, 96- *Personal Data:* b Mangalore, India, Sept 24, 65. *Educ:* Univ Poona, BE, 87; Univ Louisville, MS, 88; Univ Wis-Madison, MS, 90. *Prof Exp:* Teaching asst chem, Univ Louisville, 87-89. *Mem:* Am Inst Chem Engrs. *Res:* Deep ultraviolet and x-ray resist technology for micromachining application and the application of the micromachining process to the development of vacuum microelectronics and field emission devices. *Mailing Add:* Argonne Nat Labs 9700 S Caff Ave Bldg 401 Rm B-3191-B Argonne IL 60439

BAJOREK, CHRISTOPHER HENRY, APPLIED PHYSICS, MAGNETISM. *Current Pos:* Res staff mem & var mgt positions, Thomas J Watson Res Ctr, IBM, Yorktown Heights, NY, 71-81, dir storage systs & technol, Almaden Ctr, San Jose, Calif, 81-83, dir technol develop, GPD, San Jose, Calif, 83-86, dir Rochester storage prod, ABS, Rochester, Minn, 87-90, dir tech strategy develop, IBM Hq, Armonk, NY, 90-91, VPRES TECHNOL, IBM SSD DIV, SAN JOSE, CALIF, 91- *Personal Data:* b Tel Aviv, Palestine, Nov 26, 43; US citizen; m 65, Janet Fullmer; c Peter & Jennifer. *Educ:* Calif Inst Technol, BS, 67, MS, 68, PhD(elec eng), 71. *Concurrent Pos:* Mem, Tech Acad, IBM. *Mem:* Sigma Xi; fel Inst Elec & Electronics Engrs. *Res:* Thin film magnetic recording heads and storage media; magnetic bubble devices and materials; ferromagnetic resonance; thin film magnetic materials for general use; bipolar semiconductor devices and materials; semiconductor packaging design and materials. *Mailing Add:* 120 Clover Way Los Gatos CA 95032-5621

BAJPAI, PRAPHULLA K, PHYSIOLOGY, IMMUNOLOGY. *Current Pos:* instr physiol, Univ Dayton, 64-66, asst prof physiol & immunol, 66-70, assoc prof, 70-77, PROF PHYSIOL & IMMUNOL, UNIV DAYTON, 77- *Personal Data:* b Charkhari, India, Sept 24, 36; m 66. *Educ:* Agra Univ, BVSc, 58, MVSc, 60; Ohio State Univ, MSc, 63, PhD(avian physiol), 65. *Honors & Awards:* C W Hall, Outstanding Publ Award, Acad Surg Res USA, 88, C William Hall Res Award, Southern Biomed Eng Conf, 90; C P Sharma Award, Soc Biomat & Artificial Organs of India, 92; A F vonRecum Award, Acad Surg Res, 93. *Prof Exp:* Vet surgeon, Govt India, 58. *Concurrent Pos:* Res assoc & fel, Reprod Endocrinol Prog, Dept Path, Univ Mich, Ann Arbor, 72-73; adj assoc prof, 75-77, adj prof, Sch Med & Sch Sci & Eng, Wright State Univ, 77- *Mem:* Am Fedn Clin Res; Am Physiol Soc; Soc Study Reprod; Fedn Am Socs Exp Biol; Soc Biomat. *Res:* Physiology and immunology of heart, reproductive system and bone. *Mailing Add:* Dept Biol Univ Dayton 300 College Park Dayton OH 45469-2320

BAJPAI, RAKESH KUMAR, BIOTECHNOLOGY, FERMENTATION TECHNOLOGY & BIOREMEDIATION. *Current Pos:* from asst prof to assoc prof, 82-93, PROF CHEM ENG, UNIV MO, COLUMBIA, 93- *Personal Data:* b Kanpur, India, Dec 24, 50; US citizen; m 77, Sunita Misra; c Ambareesh & Ashish. *Educ:* Kanpur Univ, BSc, 69; Indian Inst Technol, MTech, 72, PhD(chem eng), 76. *Prof Exp:* Lectr chem eng, Indian Inst Technol, New Delhi, 76-79; wissenschaftlicher mitarbeiter, Microbiol Inst, Swiss Fed Inst Technol, 78 & Inst Garungsgewerbe & Biotechnol, WBerlin, 79-82. *Mem:* Am Chem Soc; Am Inst Chem Engrs. *Res:* Study of growth and product formation in bioprocesses; design and scale-up of bioreactors; hydrodynamics in bioreactors; shear sensitive organisms; fermentation; production of biological insecticides and pharmaceuticals; delivery of nutrients to biologically active zones in subsurfaces; bioremediation. *Mailing Add:* Chem Eng Dept Univ Mo 2030 Eng Bldg E Columbia MO 65211. *Fax:* 573-884-4940; *E-Mail:* bajpai@ecvax2.ecn.missouri.edu

BAJZAK, DENES, REMOTE SENSING, FOREST ENGINEERING. *Current Pos:* prof remote sensing & measurements, 69-71, PROF ENG & APPL SCI, MEM UNIV NFLD, 71-, FORESTRY PROG COORDR, 87- *Personal Data:* b Cegled, Hungary, Dec 25, 33; Can citizen; m 62, Daphne King; c Denes & Krisztina. *Educ:* Univ BC, BSF, 58, MF, 60; Syracuse Univ, PhD(photogram), 67. *Prof Exp:* Forest res off, Forestry Br, Can Dept Northern Affairs & Nat Resources, 61-62; res scientist, Forest Res Lab, Can Dept Forestry, Nfld, 66-69. *Concurrent Pos:* Assoc prof, Engrs & Geoscientists Nfld; chmn, Nfld Sect, Can Inst Forestry, 92-93. *Mem:* Am Soc Photogram; Can Inst Forestry; Sigma Xi; Can Remote Sensing Soc. *Res:* Land and forest site classification research in Newfoundland; application of remote sensing techniques for forest insect detection, bird and animal census and mapping of thermal pollution; the effect of flooding in reservoirs of hydroelectric power development in Labrador; snow-water equivalent using multi-channel radar. *Mailing Add:* Dept Eng Mem Univ Nfld St John's NF A1B 3X5 Can. *Fax:* 709-737-4042; *E-Mail:* dbajzak@kean.ucs.mun.ca

BAJZER, WILLIAM XAVIER, ORGANIC CHEMISTRY. *Current Pos:* Chemist, Dow Corning Corp, 63-65, res chemist, 69-70, supvr chem, 70-73, develop mgr, 73-75, res sect mgr, 75-77, sr res specialist, 77-81, process eng sect mgr, 81-91, PROCESS CONSULT & COMMERCIALIZATION LEADER & PROCESS ENG SCIENTIST, DOW CORNING CORP, 91- *Personal Data:* b Cleveland, Ohio, June 17, 40; m 63, Elizabeth Mocnik; c Christopher, Cheryl, Michael & Susan. *Educ:* Case Inst Technol, BS, 63; Ohio State Univ, MS, 66, PhD(org chem), 68. *Mem:* Am Chem Soc; NY Acad Sci; Sigma Xi. *Res:* Chemistry of fluorinated compounds; methods of fluorine introduction in organic molecules; synthesis and chemistry of fluoroalkylsilicon compounds and polymers derived therefrom; fluoroalkyl triazine chemistry; biocompatible polymers and elastomers; flexible silicone contact lens; biologically active compounds containing silicon; polymer bound drugs; chemical process research and development on speciality silane chemicals. *Mailing Add:* 4201 McKeith Rd Midland MI 48642-3863. *Fax:* 517-496-6243; *E-Mail:* wxbajzer@dcrn.e-mail.com

BAK, CHAN SOO, LIQUID CRYSTALS, HOLOGRAMS. *Current Pos:* RETIRED. *Personal Data:* b Chun-nam, Korea, June 15, 36; US citizen; m 66, Kyung J Choi; c James H & David H. *Educ:* Seoul Nat Univ, BS, 59; Univ Pittsburgh, PhD(solid state physics), 70. *Prof Exp:* Commun officer, Korean Air Force, 60-64; res assoc liquid crystals, State Univ NY, Stony Brook, 70-72, Univ Mass, 72-73 & Temple Univ, 73-76; sr physicist res & develop, Spectro-Systs Inc, 76-80; mem staff, Hughes Res Lab, Malibu, Calif, 80- *Concurrent Pos:* Lectr, George Washington Univ & Northern Va Community Col, 78-80. *Mem:* Am Phys Soc; Sigma Xi; Soc Info Display; Int Soc Optical Eng; Mats Res Soc. *Res:* Liquid crystals; critical phenomena in liquid mixtures; laser light scattering study; pyroelectricity in polymers; geothermal energy; silicon on insulators; holographic optical elements; artificial neural networks; CRT phosphors; low temperature ceramics by Sol-Gel; chemical sensors for automobile exhaust; new materials by reactive atmosphere process, catalysis. *Mailing Add:* 641 Lois Ave Newbury Park CA 91320. *Fax:* 310-317-5483; *E-Mail:* 0065883@msgate.emis.hac.com

BAK, DAVID, PHYSICAL CHEMISTRY, ORGANIC CHEMISTRY. *Current Pos:* from asst prof to assoc prof, 66-77, chmn dept, 74-85, PROF CHEM, HARTWICK COL, 77- *Personal Data:* b Yankton, SDak, Feb 6, 39; div; c 2. *Educ:* Augustana Col, BA, 61; Kans State Univ, PhD(org chem), 66. *Prof Exp:* Res assoc org chem, Mich State Univ, 65-66. *Concurrent Pos:* Am Chem Soc-Petrol Res Fund res grant, 67-69; vis prof, NTex State Univ, 77-78; sr res scientist, AKZO, 87-88; res assoc, Hoffman-LaRoche, 90. *Mem:* Am Chem Soc. *Res:* Reactions of cyclooctatetraenyl dianion; electron transfer reactions; small ring ketone photochemistry; synthetic organic electrochemistry. *Mailing Add:* Dept Chem Hartwick Col Oneonta NY 13820-1757

BAK, PER, PHASE TRANSITIONS, DYNAMICAL SYSTEMS. *Current Pos:* res assoc physics, 74-76, head, Condensed Matter Theory Group, 84-87, SCIENTIST, BROOKHAVEN NAT LAB, 83- *Personal Data:* b Bronderslev, Denmark, Dec 8, 47; wid; c Jakob, Tine & Thomas. *Educ:* Tech Univ Denmark, PhD(physics), 74; Univ Copenhagen, DPhil, 82. *Prof Exp:* Asst prof, Nordita, Copenhagen, 76-78; vis scientist, T J Watson Res Ctr, IBM, 78-79; assoc prof physics, Univ Copenhagen, 79-83. *Mem:* Fel AAAS. *Res:* Theoretical condensed matter physics; statistical mechanics; dynamical systems; theory of chaos; incommensurate structures; quantum mechanical tunneling; surface transitions; self-organized criticality. *Mailing Add:* Dept Physics Brookhaven Nat Lab Upton NY 11973. *Fax:* 516-282-2918; *E-Mail:* bak@bnlux1.bnl.gov

BAKAC, ANDREJA, KINETICS & MECHANISMS, FREE RADICAL CHEMISTRY. *Current Pos:* Res assoc, 76-79, from asst chemist to assoc chemist, 79-84, CHEMIST AMES LAB, IOWA STATE UNIV, 84- *Personal Data:* b Varazdin, Croatia. *Educ:* Univ Zagreb, BS, 68, MS, 72 & PhD(chem), 76. *Mem:* Am Chem Soc; AAAS; Sigma Xi. *Res:* Kinetic and mechanistic studies of chemical and photochemical reactions of transition metal complexes, organometallics, free radicals and oxygen intermediates. *Mailing Add:* 1432 Breckinridge Ct Ames IA 50010. *Fax:* 515-294-5233; *E-Mail:* bakac@ameslab.gov

BAKAL, ABRAHAM I, FOOD SCIENCE, CHEMICAL ENGINEERING. *Current Pos:* PRES, ABIC INT CONSULTS, INC, 78- *Personal Data:* b Bagdad, Iraq, July 5, 36; US citizen; m 66, Frida Shomer; c Gil & Amir. *Educ:* Israel Inst Technol, BSc, 62, MSc, 64; Rutgers Univ, NB, PhD(food sci), 70. *Prof Exp:* Tech head food & chem engr, Israel Indust Adv Sta, 63-66; asst prof food sci, Univ Sask, 67-68; assoc res dir food consult, Booz, Allen & Hamilton, Inc, 70-73; tech dir food & cosmetics, Centro Indust Exp Para la Exportacion, Venezuelan Corp Develop, 73-75; prin, Booz, Allen & Hamilton, Inc, 75-78. *Concurrent Pos:* Vis scientist, Nat Ctr Sci Res, France, 65; res asst, Rutgers Univ, NB, 68-70. *Mem:* NY Acad Sci; Inst Food Technologists. *Res:* Product development, process development, mostly in the food and nutrition field with emphasis on system innovation. *Mailing Add:* Ten Stafford Rd Parsippany NJ 07054

BAKANOWSKI, STEPHEN MICHAEL, MICROWAVE PHYSICS, THERMOGRAPHY & EXPERIMENTAL METHODS. *Current Pos:* PHYSICIST, GEN ELEC CO, 77- *Personal Data:* b Washington, DC, May 28, 45; m 67, Claudia R Stengs; c Brigid A, Greta M, Eva E, Carl A & Antony E. *Educ:* Rutgers Univ, BA, 66; Temple Univ, PhD(physics), 75. *Prof Exp:* NSF fel, Temple Univ, 75-76; asst prof physics, Calif State Univ, Fullerton, 76-77. *Concurrent Pos:* Vis prof, Physics Dept, Univ Louisville, 78- *Mem:* Am Phys Soc. *Res:* Instrumentation and techniques to solve problems with and improve performance of appliances; apply principles of microwave physics and develop experimental techniques to expand knowledge of microwave oven operation; apply engineering mechanics principles to reduce noise and vibrations in consumer products; experimental methods. *Mailing Add:* 1908 Warrington Way Louisville KY 40222. *Fax:* 502-452-7881

BAKAY, LOUIS, NEUROSURGERY, NEUROPHYSIOLOGY. *Current Pos:* PROF SURG, SCH MED, STATE UNIV NY BUFFALO, 61- *Personal Data:* b Pozsony, Hungary, June 18, 17; US citizen; m 54; c 2. *Educ:* Univ Budapest, MD, 41. *Prof Exp:* Asst prof surg, Univ Budapest, 45-47; clin asst neurosurg, Serafimer Hosp, Stockholm, Sweden, 47-48; instr neurosurg, Harvard Med Sch, 53-61. *Concurrent Pos:* Res fel, Harvard Univ, 48-50; clin assoc, Mass Gen Hosp, Boston, 52-61; chief neurosurg serv, E J Meyer Mem Hosp, Buffalo Gen Hosp & Children's Hosp, Buffalo, 61-87. *Mem:* Am Col Surg; Harvey Cushing Soc; Am Acad Neurol. *Res:* Surgery of pituitary tumors and cervical spine; cerebral circulation and metabolism; hydrodynamics of cerebrospinal fluid; blood-brain barrier; radioactive isotopes in nervous system; cerebral edema; head injuries; medical history. *Mailing Add:* 152 Bryant St Buffalo NY 14222

BAKELMAN, ILYA J(ACOB), differential geometry; deceased, see previous edition for last biography

BAKER, A LEROY, BIOCHEMISTRY, CHROMATOGRAPHY. *Current Pos:* Res assoc, 78-88, SR RES SCI, ELI LILLY & CO, 88- *Personal Data:* b Hagerstown, Md, Oct 9, 39; m 60; c 2. *Educ:* Bridgewater Col, BA, 61; Va Polytech Inst, PhD(biochem), 64. *Mem:* Am Soc Biochem & Molecular Biol. *Mailing Add:* Eli Lilly & Co Indianapolis IN 46285-0001

BAKER, ADOLPH, PHYSICS. *Current Pos:* prof, 63-86, EMER PROF PHYSICS & APPL PHYSICS, UNIV LOWELL, 86- *Personal Data:* b Russia, Nov 15, 17; US citizen; m 42, Dora Krugman; c Linda, Daniel & Ellen. *Educ:* City Col New York, BA, 38, MS, 39; Polytech Inst Brooklyn, BME, 46; NY Univ, MS, 49; Brandeis Univ, PhD(physics), 64. *Prof Exp:* Stress analyst, Repub Aviation Corp, NY, 46-47; sr engr, Ranger Aircraft Engines, 47-48; mem staff, Int Bus Mach Corp, 48-50; sr engr, Raytheon Co, Mass, 50-55; mgr airborne digital comput develop, Radio Corp Am, 55-59, consult, 59-65. *Concurrent Pos:* Sr Fulbright-Hays scholar, USSR, 74-75. *Mem:* Am Phys Soc. *Res:* Scattering theory; high energy electron scattering from nuclei; potential scattering theory; digital computers; optical image enhancement. *Mailing Add:* 7 Gage Rd Wayland MA 01778. *E-Mail:* bakerad@woods.ulowell.edu

BAKER, ALAN GARDNER, engineering physics, for more information see previous edition

BAKER, ALAN PAUL, PRODUCT ACQUISITION & LICENSING. *Current Pos:* ASST VPRES, LICENSING & NEW BUS PLANNING, WYETH-AYERST LABS, 87- *Personal Data:* b Saltsburg, Pa, Aug 6, 38; m 61, Morgan; c Alexandra & Morgan P. *Educ:* Philadelphia Col Pharm, BSc, 60; Hahnemann Med Col, PhD(biochem), 64. *Prof Exp:* Damon Runyon Mem Fund fel cancer res, Royal Univ Umea, Sweden, 64-66; fel enzymol, Brandeis Univ, 66-67; sr chemist, Wyeth Labs, 67-68; sr scientist, Smith Kline & French Labs, 68-71, sr investr, 71-79, asst dir pharmacol, 79-81, assoc dir new compound eval, 81-84, dir, R & D Licensing, 84-86. *Mem:* Am Chem Soc; Licensing Exec Soc; Am Soc Biol Chemists. *Res:* Structure and function of myeloperoxidase; uterine peroxidase; eosinophils; mast cells; electron spin resonance of flavin enzymes; microbial cell wall synthesis; mucopolysaccharides; immunopharmacology; respiratory pharmacology; regulation of biosynthesis and secretion of respiratory mucus; reaginic antibody production. *Mailing Add:* Licensing & New Business Planning Wyeth Ayerst Labs PO Box 8299 Philadelphia PA 19101-8299. *Fax:* 610-995-4801

BAKER, ALLAN JOHN, MOLECULAR SYSTEMATICS & EVOLUTION, POPULATION GENETICS. *Current Pos:* from asst prof to assoc prof, 76-88, PROF ZOOL, UNIV TORONTO, 89-; CUR-IN-CHG ORINTHOL, ROYAL ONT MUS, 81-, DIR, CTR BIODIVESITY & CONSERV GENETICS, 94- *Personal Data:* b Westport, Buller, NZ, July 9, 43; Can & NZ citizen; m 70, Susan M Cato; c Daniel & Benjamin. *Educ:* Univ Canterbury, BS, 66, MS, 69, PhD(systematics), 72. *Prof Exp:* Asst cur orinthol, Royal Ont Mus, 72-78, assoc cur, 78-82. *Concurrent Pos:* Fel, Am Orinthol Union, 88. *Mem:* Soc Study Evolution; Soc Systematic Biol; Am Soc Naturalists; Soc Molecular Biol & Evolution; Am Orinthologists Union. *Res:* Sequence evolution in mtDNA of vertebrates, mechanisms of speciation of vertebrates, linkage between microevolution and macroevolution, molecular systematics, molecular evolution, molecular population structure of species. *Mailing Add:* Royal Ont Mus 100 Queen's Park Toronto ON M5S 2C6 Can. *Fax:* 416-586-5863; *E-Mail:* allanb@zoo.utoronto.ca

BAKER, ALLEN JEROME, ENGINEERING, FLUID MECHANICS. *Current Pos:* assoc prof, 75-80, PROF ENG SCI, UNIV TENN, KNOXVILLE, 80- *Personal Data:* b Buffalo, NY, Oct 19, 36; m 61; c 4. *Educ:* Union Col, BS, 58; State Univ NY Buffalo, MSc, 68, PhD(eng sci), 70. *Prof Exp:* Engr, Linde Div, Union Carbide Corp, 58-64; lectr eng sci, State Univ NY Buffalo, 65-70; prin scientist res, Bell Aerospace Div, Textron, 70-74; vis prof mech eng, Old Dominion Univ, 74-75. *Concurrent Pos:* Digital analyst, Bell Aerospace Div, Textron, 66-70; pres, Computational Mech Corp, 75-; IBM professorship, Univ Tenn, 83-86, Chancellor's res scholar, 88. *Mem:* Am Inst Aeronaut & Astronaut; Am Acad Mech; Am Soc Eng Educ. *Res:* Computational fluid dynamics, finite element analysis, turbulent flows; large scale fluid dynamics computer codes; parallel processing. *Mailing Add:* 2321 Craig Cove Rd Knoxville TN 37919

BAKER, ANDREW NEWTON, JR, AERONAUTICAL & ASTRONAUTICAL ENGINEERING, PHYSICS. *Current Pos:* dep chief engr, Lockhead Corp, 68-70, dir res, 70-72, dir develop planning, 72-73, dir res, 73-77, dir res & planning, 77-85, dep dir technol, 85-87 dir Eng-Aero Systems, Lockheed Corp, 87-90, ENG CONSULT, 91- *Personal Data:* b Wellington, Kans, Oct 21, 28; m 51; c 2. *Educ:* Univ Rochester, BS, 49; Univ Calif, Los Angeles, MS, 51, PhD(physics), 54. *Prof Exp:* Assoc physics, Univ Calif, Los Angeles, 52-54; mem tech staff, Bell Tel Labs, 54-60; head solid state lab, Lockheed-Calif Co, 60-63, mgr phys sci, 64-66; Sloan exec fel, Stanford Univ, 66-67. *Mem:* Am Phys Soc; Am Inst Aeronaut & Astronaut; Sigma Xi. *Res:* Infrared spectroscopy; hydrogen bonds; semiconductors and semiconductor devices; electro-optics and ferroelectrics; titanium metallurgy and corrosion; CAD/CAM; low observables technology; aircraft safety. *Mailing Add:* 12324 Woodley Ave Granada Hills CA 91344. *Fax:* 818-832-9263

BAKER, ARTHUR A, geology; deceased, see previous edition for last biography

BAKER, BARTON SCOFIELD, AGRONOMY. *Current Pos:* From asst prof to prof agron, 69-87, dir, Allegheny Highlands Proj, 78-80, DIR, DIV PLANT & SOIL SCI, 87- *Personal Data:* b Paint Bank, Va, Oct 4, 41; m 64. *Educ:* Berea Col, BS, 64; WVa Univ, MS, 66, PhD(agron), 69. *Mem:* Am Soc Agron; Am Forage & Grassland Coun. *Res:* Influence of environmental conditions on the growth and composition of forage crops. *Mailing Add:* Dept Plant Sci WVa Univ Box 6108 Morgantown WV 26506-0001

BAKER, BERNARD S, RESEARCH ADMINISTRATION, TECHNICAL MANAGEMENT. *Current Pos:* PRES, ENERGY RES CORP, 70- *Personal Data:* b Philadelphia, Pa, June 26, 36; m 59; c 4. *Educ:* Univ Pa, BS, 57, MS, 59; Ill Inst Technol, PhD(chem eng), 69. *Prof Exp:* Sr scientist electrochem, Lockheed Missiles & Space Co, 60-62 & Electrochem Corp, 62; from mgr energy conversion res to dir basic sci, Int Gas Technol, 62-70. *Concurrent Pos:* Chmn steering comt, Intersoc Energy Conversion Eng Conf, 72. *Mem:* Electrochem Soc; Am Inst Chem Engrs. *Res:* Energy conversion research, especially electrochemical power sources such as fuel cells and batteries. *Mailing Add:* Energy Res Corp Three Great Pasture Rd Danbury CT 06813

BAKER, BRENDA SUE, COMPUTER SCIENCE. *Current Pos:* MEM TECH STAFF, BELL LABS LUCENT TECHNOL, 91- *Personal Data:* b Oakland, Calif, Dec 19, 48; m 82; c 2. *Educ:* Radcliffe Col, BA, 69; Harvard Univ, MS, 70, PhD(appl math), 73. *Prof Exp:* Res fel comput sci, Harvard Univ, 73-74; mem tech staff comput sci, Bell Labs, 74-78, mem staff, 80-86; asst prof comput & commun sci, Univ Mich, 78-79. *Concurrent Pos:* Vis lectr, Univ Calif, Berkeley, 77-78. *Mem:* Asn Comput Mach; AAAS. *Res:* Theoretical computer science. *Mailing Add:* 140 North Rd Berkeley Heights NJ 07922

BAKER, BRUCE S, MOLECULAR BIOLOGY. *Current Pos:* PROF, DEPT BIOL SCI, STANFORD UNIV. *Honors & Awards:* Molecular Biol Award, Nat Acad Sci, 92; Genetic Soc Medal, 91. *Mem:* Nat Acad Sci. *Res:* Biological sciences. *Mailing Add:* Dept Biol Sci Stanford Univ Stanford CA 94305

BAKER, BRYAN, JR, ANIMAL HUSBANDRY, ANIMAL PHYSIOLOGY. *Current Pos:* from assoc prof to prof, 56-88, head dept, 78-88, EMER PROF, ANIMAL SCI, MISS STATE UNIV, 88- *Personal Data:* b Grenada, Miss, Feb 24, 23; m 46; c 1. *Educ:* Miss State Univ, BS, 47, BS, 48, MS, 52; Univ Ill, PhD(animal sci), 55. *Prof Exp:* Teacher voc agr, Biggersville High Sch, 48-51; asst animal husb, Miss State Univ, 51-52; asst animal sci, Univ Ill, 52-55; assoc prof animal husb, Va Polytech Inst, 55-56. *Mem:* AAAS; Am Soc Animal Sci; Sigma Xi. *Res:* Effect of environmental factors on physiology of reproduction of sheep, cattle and swine. *Mailing Add:* 11 Talley Ho Dr Starkville MS 39759

BAKER, CARL GWIN, RESEARCH ADMINISTRATION. *Current Pos:* RETIRED. *Personal Data:* b Louisville, Ky, Nov 27, 20; m 49, 75, Catherine Smith; c Cathy, Jeannette, David, Robert, Bruce & Kathleen. *Educ:* Univ Louisville, AB, 41, MD, 44; Univ Calif, MA, 49. *Hon Degrees:* DSc, 80, Univ Louisville. *Honors & Awards:* Meritorious Serv Medal, Pub Health Serv, 66. *Prof Exp:* Intern, Milwaukee County Gen Hosp, 44-45; physician, US Navy, 45-46; Childs fel, Pub Health Serv, 46-48; sr asst surgeon to med dir, Nat Cancer Inst, 49-55, asst dir, 58-61, actg sci dir, 60-61, assoc dir prog, 61-67, sci dir etiology, 68-69, dir, 69-72; asst to dir intramural res, NIH, 56-58; asst surgeon gen, Pub Health Serv, 70-96. *Concurrent Pos:* Spec fel, Nat Cancer Inst, 49; assoc ed, Jour Nat Cancer Inst, 54-55; spec lectr, Sch Med,

Georgetown Univ, 54-64; mem subcomt amino acids, Comt Biochem, Nat Res Coun, 56-58; mem planning comt, Nat Cancer Conf, 62-64; mem ed adv bd, Cancer, 65-73; dir, Am Cancer Soc, 69-72; vpres, Tenth Int Cancer Cong, 70; mem sci adv comt, Ludwig Inst Cancer Res, 71-85; pres & sci dir, Hazelton Labs, 72-73; mem bd dirs, Am Asn Cancer Res, 73-76; consult, Res Admin, 73-75; dir prog policy staff, Health Resources Admin, HEW, 75-77; med dir, Ludwig Inst Cancer Res, Switz, 77-82, emer med dir, 82-, consult, 85-87; adj instr, Columbia Union Col, 88-, Univ Md Univ Col, 91- *Mem:* Am Chem Soc, Div Biol Chem (secy, 54-57); Soc Exp Biol & Med; Am Soc Biochem & Molecular Biol; Am Asn Cancer Res; Sigma Xi. *Res:* Evaluation of the introduction of strategic systems planning into the administration of the broad; multidiscipline cancer research programs at the National Cancer Institute. *Mailing Add:* 19408 Charline Manor Rd Olney MD 20832

BAKER, CARLETON HAROLD, CARDIOVASCULAR PHYSIOLOGY, MICROCIRCULATION & SHOCK. *Current Pos:* RETIRED. *Personal Data:* b Utica, NY, Aug 2, 30; m 63, Sara Johnson; c Elizabeth & Janet. *Educ:* Syracuse Univ, BA, 52; Princeton Univ, MA, 54, PhD(biol), 55. *Prof Exp:* Asst instr biol, Princeton Univ, 52-54, asst res biol, 54-55; from asst prof to prof physiol, Med Col Ga, 55-67; prof physiol & biophys, Sch Med, Univ Louisville, 67-71; chmn, Dept Physiol & Biophys, Univ SFla, Tampa, 71-92, prof physiol, Col Med, 71-95, dep dean res grand affairs, 80-82, prof surg, 92-95. *Concurrent Pos:* Prin investr, NIH, 58-95; vis prof physiol, Univ SC, 93- *Mem:* AAAS. *Res:* Adrenal cortex; blood volume regulation; cardiovascular system; microcirculation; vascular control in shock; hemorrage, endotoxemia; role of endothelium. *Mailing Add:* 4039 Old Waynesboro Rd Augusta GA 30906. *Fax:* 813-974-3079

BAKER, CHARLES CLAYTON, FUSION REACTOR TECHNOLOGY DEVELOPMENT, FUSION REACTOR SYSTEMS ANALYSIS. *Current Pos:* US HOME TEAM LEADER, INT THERMONUCLEAR EXP REACTOR, UNIV CALIF, 94- *Personal Data:* b Racine, Wis, Mar 13, 43; m 65, Susan S Beyer; c Michael & Andrew. *Educ:* Univ Wis, BS, 66, MS, 67, PhD(nuclear eng), 72. *Prof Exp:* Dept mgr fusion, Gen Atomics Co, 72-77; prog dir, Argonne Nat Lab, 77-89; assoc div dir, Oak Ridge Nat Lab, 89-93, res prog dir, 93-94. *Concurrent Pos:* Ed, Fusion Eng & Design, 90-; mem, Nuclear Eng Vis Comt, Mass Inst Technol, 93- *Mem:* Fel Am Nuclear Soc. *Res:* Engineering development of magnetic fusion reactor concepts. *Mailing Add:* ITER Univ Calif La Jolla CA 92093-0035

BAKER, CHARLES EDWARD, PHYSICAL CHEMISTRY. *Current Pos:* RETIRED. *Personal Data:* b Manchester, Ky, Nov 8, 31; m 52; c 4. *Educ:* Berea Col, BA, 53; Univ Fla, PhD(phys chem), 60. *Prof Exp:* Chemist, Res Div, Monsanto Chem Co, Ohio, 53-54; asst, Univ Fla, 56-60; sr res engr, Gen Dynamics/Convair, Calif, 60-62; aeronaut res scientist, Lewis Res Ctr, NASA, 62-84. *Mem:* AAAS; Am Chem Soc; Sigma Xi. *Res:* Atmospheric chemistry; low-energy scattering of negative-ion beams; thermal conductivities of ordinary and isotopically substituted polar gases; diffusion of polar gases; recombination of atoms; combustion fundamentals; alternate fuels. *Mailing Add:* 510 Wyleswood Dr Berea OH 44017-2229

BAKER, CHARLES H, AGRICULTURAL SCIENCE. *Current Pos:* staff mem, 72-81, DIR, ROHM & HAFF SEED CO, 81-; DIR, NAM PLANT BREEDERS, 81-; PRES, BIOTECHNICA AGR INC, 87- *Prof Exp:* Staff mem, NAm Plant Breeders, 72-81. *Res:* Plant breeding. *Mailing Add:* 4305 W 111th St Shawnee Mission KS 66211

BAKER, CHARLES P, accelerator design; deceased, see previous edition for last biography

BAKER, CHARLES RAY, APPLIED MATHEMATICS, ENGINEERING. *Current Pos:* assoc prof, 68-73, PROF STATIST, UNIV NC, CHAPEL HILL, 73-; PRES, CAROLINIAN SYSTS RES CORP, 89- *Personal Data:* b Pine Bluff, Ark, May 22, 32; m 52; c 1. *Educ:* Univ Southwestern La, BS, 57; Univ Calif, Los Angeles, MS, 63, PhD(eng), 67. *Prof Exp:* Staff engr, Land-Air, Inc, Holloman Air Develop Ctr, NMex, 57-59; engr, Aerospace Systs Div, Bendix Corp, Mich, 59-60, sr engr, Electrodynamics Div, Calif, 60-67, eng res specialist, 67-68. *Mem:* Inst Elec & Electronics Engrs; Inst Math Statist; Am Math Soc; Soc Indust & Appl Math. *Res:* Statistical communication theory; probability theory; stochastic processes and applications to communication systems. *Mailing Add:* Dept Statist Univ NC Chapel Hill NC 27599-3260

BAKER, CHARLES TAFT, ELECTROCHEMISTRY, EPOXY POLYMERS. *Current Pos:* Mem tech staff, Mat Sci & Res Lab, Cent Res, Tex Instruments Inc, 66-70, sect leader, 70-72, mgr qual reliability assurance, Anal Serv Lab, 72-84, mgr qual reliability assurance, Eng Labs, Semiconductor Group, 84-87, sr mem tech staff/VLSI QRA eng mgr, 87-93, SR MEM TECH STAFF/ASP QRE ASSEMBLY-PACKAGE TECHNOL, TEX INSTRUMENTS INC, 93- *Personal Data:* b Carbondale, Ill, Aug 29, 39; m 62, Paula J Mackey; c Gregory T, Ondria S & Robert N. *Educ:* Southern Ill Univ, BA, 61; Univ Ill, MS, 64, PhD(chem), 66. *Res:* Semiconductor device material reliability evaluation and qualification; electromigration; metal migration; plating processes and organic polymer encapsulation compounds; analytical characterization techniques; ion-selective electrodes; anodization of (Hg, Cd)Te; low-temperature kinetics of battery electrodes. *Mailing Add:* 7631 El Pensador Dr Dallas TX 75248

BAKER, CHARLES WESLEY, CARBOHYDRATE CHEMISTRY PROCESSING, SENIOR MANAGEMENT. *Current Pos:* VPRES SCI AFFAIRS, SUGAR ASN INC, 90- *Personal Data:* b Binghamton, NY, May 29, 45; m 67, Margaret E Bottum; c Christopher W & Douglas L. *Educ:* Northeastern Univ, BA, 67; Purdue Univ PhD(biochem), 73. *Prof Exp:* Asst prof cereal chem, NDak State Univ, 73-77; mgr res & develop, Pabst Brewing Co, 77-80; mgr tech ctr, Jos Schlitz Brewing Co, 80-82; dir tech ctr, Stroh Brewery Co, 82-86, dir tech serv, 86-90. *Concurrent Pos:* Mem bd adv, Stedman Nutrit Ctr, Duke Univ Med Sch; corp affil, Dept Foods & Nutrit, Purdue Univ. *Mem:* Am Soc Brewing Chemists (pres, 86-88); Am Asn Cereal Chemists; Inst Food Technologists; NAm Asn Study Obesity; Am Chem Soc. *Res:* Defining role of sucrose in diet and health; development of sucrose-based specialty chemicals/products. *Mailing Add:* Sugar Asn Inc 1101 15th St NW Suite 600 Washington DC 20005-5002. *Fax:* 202-785-5019; *E-Mail:* sugar@sugar.org

BAKER, D(ALE) B(URDETTE), CHEMICAL ENGINEERING. *Current Pos:* asst ed, 46-50, assoc ed, 51-57, dir chem abstr, 58-86, EMER DIR, AM CHEM SOC, 86- *Personal Data:* b Bucyrus, Ohio, Sept 19, 20; m 47; c 3. *Educ:* Ohio State Univ, BChE, 42, MS, 48. *Hon Degrees:* PhD, Ohio State Univ, 86. *Honors & Awards:* Austin Patterson-Crane Award, Am Chem Soc, 79, Herman Skolnik Award, 86. *Prof Exp:* Chemist supvr, E I du Pont de Nemours & Co, 42-45. *Concurrent Pos:* Mem bd, Nat Fedn Sci Abstr & Indexing Serv; mem planning & steering comt, abstr bd, Int Coun Sci Unions; comt int sci & tech info progs, Nat Acad Sci, 73-; mem bd visitors, grad sch libr & info sci, Univ Pittsburgh, 76-82 & Case-Western Reserve Univ. *Mem:* Nat Acad Sci; AAAS; Am Chem Soc; Am Inst Chem Engrs; Am Soc Info Sci. *Res:* Chemical literature, documentation, communication, research, development and planning. *Mailing Add:* 64 W Dunedin Rd Columbus OH 43214-4002

BAKER, D(ONALD) JAMES, PHYSICAL OCEANOGRAPHY. *Current Pos:* ADMINR UNDER SECY FOR OCEANS & ATMOSPHERE, NAT OCEANIC & ATMOSPHERIC ADMIN, US DEPT COM, 93- *Personal Data:* b Long Beach, Calif, Mar 23, 37; m 68, Emily Lind. *Educ:* Stanford Univ, BS, 58; Cornell Univ, PhD(physics), 62. *Hon Degrees:* LHD, Nova Univ, 93. *Prof Exp:* Res assoc oceanog, Univ RI, 62-63; NIH fel biophys, Univ Calif, Berkeley, 63-64; res fel geophys fluid dynamics, Harvard Univ, 64-66, asst prof oceanog, 66-70, assoc prof phys oceanog, 70-73; from res assoc prof to res prof oceanog, Appl Physics Lab, 75-79, group leader deep-sea physics, Pac Marine Environ Lab, Univ Wash-Nat Oceanic & Atmospheric Admin, 77-79, chmn, Dept Oceanog, Univ Wash, 79-81, prof, Sch Oceanog, 79-86, dean, Col Ocean & Fishery Sci, 81-83, adj prof, Dept Atmospheric Sci, 79-86; pres, Joint Oceanog, Inc, 83-93. *Concurrent Pos:* Vis scholar, Woods Hole Oceanog Inst, 70; chmn, Joint Polar Exp Panel, Nat Res Coun, 73-79, co-chmn, Int Southern Ocean Studies Prog, 74-84 & mem, Climate Dynamics Panel, US Global Atmospheric Res Prog, Nat Acad Sci, 76-78; consult, Polar Exp, World Meteorol Orgn, 75-79; Univ Wash/Nat Oceanic & Atmospheric Admin & Univ Hawaii/Nat Oceanic & Atmospheric Admin sr fels, Joint Insts Study of Atmospheres & Oceans & Marine & Atmospheric Res, 77-83; mem bd gov, Joint Oceanog Inst, Inc, 79-83; mem, Ocean Studies Bd, Nat Res Coun, 79-91, Space Sci Bd, 84-87, Climate Res Comt, 79-90, Space & Earth Sci Adv Comt, NASA, 82-86, Earth Syst Sci Comt, 83-87, environ panel, Navy Res Adv Comt, 83-85, Comt Global Change, Nat Res Coun, 87-93, Panel on Climate & Global Change, Nat Oceanic & Atmospheric Admin, 87-93; distinguished vis scientist, Jet Propulsion Lab, Calif Inst Techno, 82-93; officer, Joint Sci Comt, World Climate Res Prog, 87-93; co-chmn, World Ocean Circulation Exp Sci Steering Group, 88-93; chmn, Comt Ocean Processes & Climate, Intergov Oceanog Comn, 89-93, Panel Rev Earth Observing Syst, Nat Res Coun, 89-90; mem bd dirs, Coun Ocean Law, 89-91; mem, Comt Future US Space Prog, NASA, 90-92; actg chmn, Coun Environ Qual, 93-94; mem, Pres Comn Sustainable Develop, 93- & Comt Int Sci Eng & Technol, Nat Sci & Tech Coun, 93- *Mem:* Am Geophys Union; Am Asn Univ Profs; Fel AAAS; Am Meteorl Soc; Sigma Xi; Marine Technol Soc; Oceanog Soc (pres, 88-92). *Res:* Physical oceanography, physics of large-scale ocean circulation and climate; ocean instrumentation; ocean measurements from satellites, research management; co-awardee of one patent; author of one book. *Mailing Add:* 4531 28th St NW Washington DC 20008

BAKER, DALE E, AGRONOMY, SOIL CHEMISTRY. *Current Pos:* from asst prof to assoc prof, 61-91, dir, Soil & Environ Chem Lab, 74-91, EMER PROF SOIL CHEM, PA STATE UNIV, 91- *Personal Data:* b Marble Hill, Mo, May 5, 30; m 49; c 3. *Educ:* Univ Mo, BS, 57, MS, 58, PhD(soils), 60. *Prof Exp:* Agronomist, NE Exp Sta, Duluth, Minn, 60-61. *Concurrent Pos:* Consult, Amax, Inc, 72-75 & Food & Drug Admin, Dept Health, Educ & Welfare, 74; pres, Land Mgt Decisions, Inc, 89- *Mem:* Fel Am Soc Agron; fel Soil Sci Soc Am; fel AAAS; Sigma Xi. *Res:* Physical and colloidal chemistry of soils, soil testing and genetic control of physiological processes in plants in relation to ion uptake, environmental quality and production of field crops; land management. *Mailing Add:* Environ Resources Res Inst Pa State Univ Land & Water Bldg University Park PA 16802

BAKER, DANIEL NEAL, SPACE PLASMA PHYSICS. *Current Pos:* DIR, LAB ATMOSPHERIC & SPACE PHYSICS, UNIV COLO, 94-, PROF, ASTROPHYS & PLANETARY SCI, 94- *Personal Data:* b Postville, Iowa, Nov 10, 48; m 71, A Victoria Vaughan; c Kirsten A. *Educ:* Univ Iowa, BA, 69, MS, 73, PhD(physics), 74. *Prof Exp:* Res assoc physics, Univ Iowa, 74-75; res fel, Calif Inst Technol, 75-77; staff mem space physics, Los Alamos Nat Lab, Univ Calif, 77-81, leader, Space Plasma Physics Group, 81-87; dir, Lab Extraterrestrial Physics, NASA, 87-94. *Concurrent Pos:* Fel, Dept Physics, Math & Astron, Calif Inst Technol, 75-77; prin investr, NASA, basic energy sci, Dept Energy & Inst Geophys Progs, Univ Calif, 81-; chmn, Data Systs Users Working Group, NASA, 82-90; mem, Comt Solar & Space Physics, Nat Acad Sci, 84-87 & Bd Atmospheric Sci, Climate Panel Long-term Observ,

Nat Res Coun, 85-88 & Mgt & Opers Comt, NASA; assoc ed, Geophys Res Letters, 85-88; mem, Comt Data Mgt & Comput, Nat Acad Sci, 85-89; organizer, Coord Data Anal Workshop Prog, NASA-ESA, 85-; US mem comn D, Int Asn Geomagnetism & Aeronomy, 86-; US rep, Int Sci Comt Solar-Terrestrial Physics Res, 87-; consult, Los Alamos Nat Lab, Univ Calif, 87-; mem, Geospace Environ Modeling Steering Comt, NSF, 88-, Space Sci & Appln Adv Comt, NASA, 88-92; proj scientist, Small Explorer Prog, NASA, 88- & US Solar Terrestrial Energy Prog, 89-; mem, External Adv Comt, Boston Univ, Univ Md & External Rev Bd, Can Centers Excellence; magnetospheric secy, Am Geophys Union, 88-90. *Mem:* Fel Am Geophys Union; Sigma Xi; AAAS; Int Acad Astronaut. *Res:* Magnetospheric physics, energetic particle and cosmic ray physics, solar-terrestrial relationships; space plasma physics; study of planetary magnetospheres; solar planetary relationships; plasma astrophysics. *Mailing Add:* Lab Atmospheric & Space Physics Univ Colo Boulder CO 80309. *Fax:* 303-492-6444; *E-Mail:* baker@orion.colorado.edu

BAKER, DAVID A, VIROLOGY, SEXUALLY TRANSMITTED DISEASES. *Current Pos:* asst prof, 79-85, ASSOC PROF OBSTET GYNEC, STATE UNIV NY, STONYBROOK, 85- *Personal Data:* b Brooklyn, NY, Aug 1, 45; m 72, Eileen; c Dara, Dawn & Erica. *Educ:* Brooklyn Col, BS, 67, State Univ NY, Brooklyn, MD, 73; Univ Rochester, MS, 69. *Prof Exp:* Instr obstet gynec, Med Ctr, Univ Vt, 77-79. *Mem:* Am Soc Microbiol; Asn Reproductive Health Profs; Soc Gynec Invest. *Res:* Immunology and molecular biology of sexually transmitted diseases. *Mailing Add:* Obstet/Gynec State Univ NY Health Sci Col Med 100 Nicolls Ave Stonybrook NY 11794-0001. *Fax:* 516-444-7740

BAKER, DAVID BRUCE, PLANT PHYSIOLOGY. *Current Pos:* from asst prof to assoc prof biol, 66-76, DIR WATER QUAL LAB, HEIDELBERG COL, 76- *Personal Data:* b Akron, Ohio, May 29, 36; m 60; c 1. *Educ:* Heidelberg Col, BS, 58; Univ Mich, MS, 60, PhD(bot), 63. *Prof Exp:* Asst prof bot, Rutgers Univ, 63-66. *Concurrent Pos:* NSF fel, 63-64. *Mem:* Am Soc Plant Physiol. *Res:* Effects of agricultural land use on water quality; large scale agri-eco system research. *Mailing Add:* Water Qual Lab Heidelberg Col Tiffin OH 44883-2460

BAKER, DAVID H, ANIMAL NUTRITION. *Current Pos:* from asst prof to assoc prof, 67-74, PROF NUTRIT, UNIV ILL, URBANA-CHAMPAIGN, 74- *Personal Data:* b DeKalb, Ill, Feb 26, 39; m 57, 81, Norraine; c 3. *Educ:* Univ Ill, BS, 61, MS, 63, PhD(animal nutrit), 65. *Honors & Awards:* Res Award, Am Soc Animal Sci, 71; Nutrit Res Award, Am Feed Mfrs Asn, 73; Paul A Funk Award, 77; Merck Award, 77; Broiler Res Award, 83; Gustav Bohstedt Award, 85; Borden Award, Am Inst Nutrit, 86; Distinguished Serv Award, USDA, 87. *Prof Exp:* Res asst nutrit, Univ Ill, 61-65; sr scientist, Greenfield Labs, Eli Lilly & Co, Ind, 65-67. *Mem:* Am Soc Animal Sci; Poultry Sci Asn; Am Inst Nutrit. *Res:* Amino acid nutrition and metabolism; trace minerals. *Mailing Add:* Dept Animal Sci Univ Ill Urbana IL 61801. *Fax:* 217-333-7861

BAKER, DAVID H, pediatrics, radiology, for more information see previous edition

BAKER, DAVID KENNETH, SOLID STATE PHYSICS. *Current Pos:* RETIRED. *Personal Data:* b Glasgow, Scotland, Oct 2, 23; nat US; m 47, Vivian Perry; c Richard R. *Educ:* McMaster Univ, BSc, 46; Univ Pa, PhD, 53. *Prof Exp:* Instr physics, Univ Pa, 52-53; prof, Union Col, 53-65; prof personnel & univ rels, Res & Develop Ctr, Gen Elec Co, 65-67; vpres & dean, St Lawrence Univ, 67-76; pres, Harvey Mudd Col, 76-88. *Mem:* Am Phys Soc; Am Asn Physics Teachers; Sigma Xi. *Res:* Semiconductors and solid state physics. *Mailing Add:* 3088 Fairway Woods Carolina Trace Sanford NC 27330

BAKER, DAVID THOMAS, NUCLEAR PHYSICS, SCIENCE EDUCATION. *Current Pos:* RETIRED. *Personal Data:* b Granite Falls, Minn, June 27, 25; m 64, Mary Eldredge; c 3. *Educ:* US Mil Acad, BS, 46; Purdue Univ, MS, 51; Am Univ, MS, 71. *Prof Exp:* US Army, 46-70, instr nuclear physics & elec eng, US Mil Acad, 51-54, asst prof nuclear physics, 54-55, res & develop officer, nuclear weapons, Army Artil & Guided Missile Off, Ft Sill, Okla, 56-58, nuclear weapons effects, Atomics Off, Off Chief Res & Develop, Hq Dept Army, 60-64, dir Nuclear Weapons Assembly Dept, Army Sch Europe, Ger, 65-66, develop officer, Nuclear Weapons Req Div, US Army Mobility Equip Res & Develop Ctr, 69-71; master instr physics, Culver Mil Acad, 71-93. *Res:* Nuclear weapons, their development, testing, effects and employment. *Mailing Add:* 1300 Academy Rd Culver IN 46511

BAKER, DAVID WARREN, STRUCTURAL GEOLOGY, TECTONOPHYSICS. *Current Pos:* OWNER, LITTLE BELT CONSULT SERV, 84- *Personal Data:* b Great Falls, Mont, Nov 9, 39; m 62; c Erik, Andrew & Paula. *Educ:* Mass Inst Technol, BS, 61; Swiss Fed Inst Technol, Dipl Nat Sci, 64; Univ Calif, Los Angeles, PhD(geol), 69. *Prof Exp:* Asst prof geol sci, Univ Ill, 70-76, res geologist, Gulf Res, 76-83. *Concurrent Pos:* Res geophysicist, Inst Geophys & Plantetary Physics, Univ Calif, Los Angeles, 69-70; res geologist, Dept Geol & Geophys, Yale Univ, 70. *Mem:* Am Geophys Union; Swiss Mineral & Petrog Soc; Geol Soc Am. *Res:* X-ray petrofabric analysis of deformed rocks; deep-seated thrust zones; seismic velocity anisotropy in the upper mantle; plate and regional tectonics; central Montana alkalic igneous province; origin of Montana sapphires; debunking creationist claims of a young Earth. *Mailing Add:* PO Box 906 Monarch MT 59463

BAKER, DENNIS JOHN, COMMUNICATION, SIMULATION. *Current Pos:* RES PHYSICIST, NAVAL RES LAB, 67- *Personal Data:* b Detroit, Mich, July 25, 40; m 70; c 5. *Educ:* Univ Detroit, BS, 63; Univ Mich, PhD(physics), 73. *Prof Exp:* Res physicist, US Army Tank Plant, 66. *Concurrent Pos:* Consult, Gen Dynamics, 68. *Res:* Distributed simulation; communication network design; software systems; co-originator of the linked cluster architecture for mobile, broadcast radio networks. *Mailing Add:* US Naval Res Lab Code 5521 4555 Overlook SW Washington DC 20375-5000

BAKER, DON H(OBART), JR, extractive & chemical metallurgy; deceased, see previous edition for last biography

BAKER, DON ROBERT, ORGANIC CHEMISTRY. *Current Pos:* SR RES ASSOC, ZENECA AG PROD, 87- *Personal Data:* b Salt Lake City, Utah, Apr 6, 33; m 94, Shirlee Ann Lundberg; c Robert D, David J, Barbara S & George C. *Educ:* Sacramento State Col, AB, 55; Univ Calif, PhD(chem), 59. *Honors & Awards:* Petersen Award, 91. *Prof Exp:* Sr res chemist, Stauffer Chem Co, 58-72, res assoc, 72-74, supvr, 74-85, sr res assoc, 85-87. *Concurrent Pos:* Counr, Am Chem Soc, 70-; ed, Calif Chemists Alert, 86-, Synthesis & Chem of Agrochem, 87, 91, 92, & 95; vchmn, Agrochem Div, Am Chem Soc, 93, chmn-elect & prog chair, 94, chmn, 95. *Mem:* Fel Am Chem Soc; Plant Growth Regulator Soc; Am Orchid Soc. *Res:* Organic synthesis; agricultural chemistry; microbiology; computer applications; mineralogy; 200 patents. *Mailing Add:* 15 Muth Dr Orinda CA 94563

BAKER, DONALD GARDNER, MICROCLIMATOLOGY. *Current Pos:* Asst soils, 49-51, 53-58, from instr to assoc prof, 58-69, PROF SOILS, UNIV MINN, ST PAUL, 69- *Personal Data:* b St Paul, Minn, July 20, 23; m 53; c 1. *Educ:* Univ Chicago, prof cert, 44; Univ Minn, BS, 49, MS, 51, PhD(soils), 58. *Honors & Awards:* Spec Serv Award, Nat Weather Serv, Nat Oceanic & Atmospheric Admin, 86. *Concurrent Pos:* Weather forecaster, 44-46 & 51-52. *Mem:* Fel AAAS; Am Meteorol Soc; Am Geophys Union; Soil Sci Soc Am; Royal Meteorol Soc, London; fel Am Soc Agron. *Res:* Agricultural meteorology and climatology. *Mailing Add:* Dept Soil Sci 429 Borlaug Hall Univ Minn Inst Agr St Paul MN 55108

BAKER, DONALD GRANVILLE, PHYSIOLOGY. *Current Pos:* RETIRED. *Personal Data:* b Toronto, Ont, Oct 19, 24; m 52; c 2. *Educ:* Univ Toronto, BA, 51, MA, 52, PhD(physiol), 55. *Prof Exp:* Res assoc, Banting & Best Dept Med Res, Univ Toronto, 55-62, lectr, Sch Hyg, 58-64, from asst prof to assoc prof physiol & spec lectr zool & radiobiol, 59-64; radiobiologist, Biol Div, Brookhaven Nat Lab, 64-68; radiobiologist, Claire Zellerbach Saroni Tumor Inst, Mt Zion Hosp & Med Ctr, 68-77; assoc prof, Div Radiation Oncol, Univ Va Hosp, 77- *Mem:* Radiation Res Soc; NY Acad Sci; Am Soc Therapeut; Am Asn Cancer Res; Am Sci Affil. *Res:* Radiation injury; radiation biology; hyperthermia anti tumor biology. *Mailing Add:* Dept Radiol Div Radiation Oncol Univ Va Hosp Box 395 Med Ctr Charlottesville VA 22908-0001

BAKER, DONALD ROY, ORGANIC GEOCHEMISTRY, PETROLEUM GEOLOGY. *Current Pos:* assoc prof, Rice Univ, 66-72, chmn dept, 77-80, prof, 72-96, EMER PROF GEOL, RICE UNIV, 97- *Personal Data:* b Norfolk, Va, May 8, 27; m 48; c 2. *Educ:* Calif Inst Technol, BS, 50; Princeton Univ, PhD(geol), 55. *Prof Exp:* Instr petrol & chem geol, Northwestern Univ, 54-56; sr res geologist, Denver Res Ctr, Marathon Oil Co, 56-66. *Mem:* Geol Soc Am; Am Asn Petrol Geol; Soc Econ Paleontologists & Mineralogists; Geochem Soc; Am Geophys Union; Europ Asn Org Geochemists; Int Asn Geochem & Cosmochem. *Res:* Organic and stable isotope geochemical research with focus on problems related to petroleum evolution and sedimentary petrology. *Mailing Add:* Dept Geol & Geophys MS 126 Rice Univ 6100 S Main Houston TX 77005-1892

BAKER, DORIS, analytical chemistry, cereal chemistry, for more information see previous edition

BAKER, DUDLEY DUGGAN, III, UNDERWATER ACOUSTICS. *Current Pos:* VPRES MKTG, NAT INSTRUMENTS, 87- *Personal Data:* b Seguin, Tex, Feb 1, 36; m 59; c 3. *Educ:* Univ Tex, BS, 57, MA, 58. *Prof Exp:* Res scientist assoc, Defense Res Lab, Univ Tex, Austin, 59-67, head, Electroacoust Div, 67-76, asst dir, 78-81, head, Acoust Measurement Div, 81-84, res assoc, Appl Res Labs, 84-87. *Mem:* Acoust Soc Am; Sigma Xi. *Res:* Underwater acoustical measurements, especially related to sonar transducer testing. *Mailing Add:* 8804 Silverarrow Ct Austin TX 78759

BAKER, DURWOOD L, VETERINARY MEDICINE. *Current Pos:* From instr to prof vet med, 47-89, from asst dean to assoc dean, Col Vet Med, 64-89, EMER PROF, IOWA STATE UNIV, 89- *Personal Data:* b Algona, Iowa, June 16, 19; m 45; c 4. *Educ:* Iowa State Univ, DVM, 43. *Mem:* Am Vet Med Asn. *Res:* Small animal medicine and surgery. *Mailing Add:* 3910 Stone Brooke Circle Ames IA 50010

BAKER, EARL WAYNE, ORGANIC CHEMISTRY. *Current Pos:* dean col sci, 77-83, PROF CHEM, FLA ATLANTIC UNIV, 77- *Personal Data:* b Lewistown, Mont, Sept 26, 28; m 49; c 3. *Educ:* Mont State Univ, BS, 52; Johns Hopkins Univ, MA, 62, PhD(org chem), 64. *Prof Exp:* Jr chemist, Lago Oil & Transport Co, Ltd, Aruba, 52-60; chemist, Stand Oil Co, NJ, 53-60; instr chem, Johns Hopkins Univ, 60-63, Petrol Res Found fel, 63-64; res fel petrol chem, Mellon Inst, 64-70; assoc prof chem, Univ Pittsburgh, 69-70; prof chem & head dept, Northeast La Univ, 70-76. *Concurrent Pos:* Am Chem Soc grant & lectr, Carnegie-Mellon Univ, 67-69; mem adv panel, Joint

Oceanog Inst for Deep Earth Sampling, 68-83; mem, US Nat Comt Geochem, Nat Acad Sci, 76-79; vchmn, Conf Org Geochem, Gordon Res Conf, 77-78, chmn, 79-80; secy-treas, Div Geochem, Am Chem Soc, 79-, vchmn, 80, chmn, 81 & alt counr, 82-; ed-in-chief, Org Geochem, 81- *Mem:* AAAS; Am Chem Soc; NY Acad Sci. *Res:* Synthesis, reactions and spectrometry of the transition metal porphyrins and related materials; biogeochemistry of tetrapyrrole pigments. *Mailing Add:* Col Sci Chem Fla Atlantic Univ Boca Raton FL 33431

BAKER, EDGAR GATES STANLEY, BIOLOGY. *Current Pos:* from assoc prof to prof, 50-74, head dept, 51-70, EMER PROF ZOOL, DREW UNIV, 74- *Personal Data:* b Peotone, Ill, June 7, 09; m 35, 88; c 3. *Educ:* DePauw Univ, AB, 31; Stanford Univ, PhD(biol), 43. *Prof Exp:* From instr to asst prof zool, Wabash Col, 32-38, actg head dept, 38-39; asst biol, Stanford Univ, 39-42; head biol sect, Del Mar Col, 46; asst prof biol, Cath Univ Am, 46-50; instr, Cath Sisters Col, 47-50. *Concurrent Pos:* Consult surv physiol sci, Am Physiol Soc, 52-54; NSF sci fac fel, 57-58; chief reader biol, Adv Placement Prog, Col Entrance Exam Bd, 64-67; staff biologist, Comn on Undergrad Educ in Biol Sci, 67-68. *Mem:* Fel AAAS; Am Soc Zool; Sigma Xi. *Res:* Physiology of protozoan populations; bacteria-free cultures; effects of nutrition on rate of growth. *Mailing Add:* 1400 N Drake Rd Apt 369 Kalamazoo MI 49006-1970

BAKER, EDWARD L(AMAR), JR, OCCUPATIONAL MEDICINE & SAFETY. *Current Pos:* ASST SURGEON GEN & DIR, DEPT HEALTH & HUMAN SERV, CTR DIS CONTROL, 90- *Personal Data:* b Chattanooga, Tenn, Nov 18, 46. *Educ:* Vanderbilt Univ, BA, 68; Baylor Col, MD, 72; Harvard Univ, MPH, 79, MSc, 80. *Prof Exp:* Assoc prof occup med, Harvard Univ Sch Pub Health, 82-85; asst dir, Nat Inst Occup Safety & Health, 85-87, actg dep, 87-88, dep dir, 89-90. *Concurrent Pos:* Dir, Occup Med Residency Prog, Harvard Sch Pub Health, 81-85; vis prof occup med, Royal Soc Med, London, 89-90. *Mem:* Am Pub Health Asn; Am Col Occup & Environ Med. *Res:* Author of more than 100 articles in journals. *Mailing Add:* Dept Health & Human Serv K-36 1600 Clifton Rd NE Atlanta GA 30333. *Fax:* 470-488-2420

BAKER, EDWARD THOMAS, OCEANOGRAPHY, MARINE GEOLOGY. *Current Pos:* AFFIL ASSOC PROF, DEPT OCEANOG, UNIV WASH, 85- *Personal Data:* b Chicago, Ill, May 21, 45; m 70; c 3. *Educ:* Univ Notre Dame, BS, 67; Univ Wash, MS, 69, PhD(oceanog), 73. *Prof Exp:* oceanogr, pac marine environ lab, Nat Oceanic & Atmospheric Admin, dept com, 76- *Mem:* AAAS; Am Geophys Union; Oceanog Soc. *Res:* Geological and geochemical oceanography; composition, distribution and transport of particulate matter in the ocean; submarine hydrothermal processes. *Mailing Add:* NOAA/PMEL 7600 Sandpoint Wy NE Seattle WA 98115-0070

BAKER, EDWARD WILLIAM, acarology, for more information see previous edition

BAKER, ELIZABETH MCINTOSH, INVERTEBRATE ZOOLOGY. *Current Pos:* CHMN, DEPT BIOL, BELMONT ABBEY COL, 78-, CHMN MATH & NATURAL SCI DIV, 81- *Personal Data:* b Washington, DC, Sept 30, 45; div. *Educ:* George Washington Univ, BA, 67; Univ Mich, MS, 68; Univ Va, PhD(develop biol), 73. *Prof Exp:* Vis asst prof, 75, electron micros technician biol, Univ NC, Charlotte, 75-77; adj prof, Sacred Heart Col, 77-78. *Res:* Insectan prothoracic gland development and function. *Mailing Add:* Dept Biol Belmont Abbey Col 100 Belmont Mt Holly Belmont NC 28012-2702

BAKER, FRANCIS EDWARD, JR, STATIC MAGNETIC FIELD ANALYSIS. *Current Pos:* head, Surface Warfare Anal Off, 84-88, Naval Surface Warfare Ctr, head, Combat Engr & Assignment Div, 89-91, S&T Adv CNO dir Surface Warfare, 92-93, SR SCIENTIST, THEATER WARFARE & ANALYSIS, NAVAL SURFACE WARFARE CTR, 96- *Personal Data:* b Baltimore, Md, Nov 9, 44; m 66, Honora Lewis; c Michael, Jennifer & Timothy. *Educ:* Va Polytech Inst & State Univ, BS, 67, MS, 69, PhD(elec eng), 71; Mass Inst Tech, SM, 89. *Prof Exp:* Instr elec eng, Va Polytech Inst & State Univ, 70-71; asst dir sci & technol, chief Naval Opers Exec Panel. *Concurrent Pos:* Vis assoc prof physics, US Naval Acad, Md, 80; adj prof, Univ Md Univ Col, 91-; tech dir Prog Exec Off, Theater Air Defense, 94-95. *Mem:* Sigma Xi; Inst Elec & Electronics Engrs; Am Soc Naval Engr. *Res:* Static and low frequency electromagnetic field phenomena; electroacoustic phenomena; circuit analysis; electric power system design. *Mailing Add:* 1501 Kingsway Dr Gambrills MD 21054. *Fax:* 540-653-5478; *E-Mail:* fbaker@relay.nswc.navy.mil

BAKER, FRANCIS TODD, NUCLEAR PHYSICS. *Current Pos:* from asst prof to assoc prof, 74-89, PROF PHYSICS, DEPT PHYSICS & ASTRON, UNIV GA, 89-, HEAD, 91- *Personal Data:* b Chicago, Ill, Feb 22, 42; m 64, 83; c 3. *Educ:* Miami Univ, AB, 63, MA, 64; Univ Mich, PhD(physics), 70. *Prof Exp:* Asst prof, Carroll Col, Wis, 66-68 & St Lawrence Univ, 70-71; res assoc, Univ Mich, 71 & Rutgers Univ, 71-74. *Mem:* Am Phys Soc. *Res:* Experimental nuclear physics, particularly nuclear structure and reactions. *Mailing Add:* Dept Physics Univ Ga Athens GA 30602. *E-Mail:* baker@uscn

BAKER, FRANK, PSYCHOSOCIAL ONCOLOGY. *Current Pos:* DIR, BEHAV RES CTR, AM CANCER SOC, 95- *Personal Data:* b Dallas, Tex, Feb 28, 36; m 60, Adrienne Polland; c Steven, David & Julie. *Educ:* Vanderbilt Univ, BA, 58; Northwestern Univ, MA, 62, PhD(psychol), 64. *Prof Exp:* Lectr psychol, Northwestern Univ, 61-62; asst prof social psychol, Lehigh Univ, 63-65, psychiat, Harvard Med Sch, 65-74; prof psychol, social & prev med, Med Sch, State Univ NY, Buffalo, 74-85; prof & chmn, Dept Behav Sci, Johns Hopkins Sch Hyg & Pub Health, 85-87, prof health psychol environ health sci, 87-95. *Concurrent Pos:* Dir, Div Community Psychiat, Med Sch, State Univ NY, Buffalo, 74-85; vis lectr psychiat, Harvard Med Sch, 81-82. *Mem:* Sigma Xi; fel Am Psychol Asn; Am Pub Health Asn; AAAS; fel Am Orthopsychiat Asn; Soc Behav Med. *Res:* Psychosocial factors and quality-of-life of cancer patients; case management systems and community adjustment of the severely mentally ill; new techniques for health program evaluation; work stress and immunomodulation. *Mailing Add:* Behav Res Ctr Am Cancer Soc 1599 Clifton Rd NE Atlanta GA 30329-4251. *Fax:* 410-955-1811

BAKER, FRANK HAMON, animal science; deceased, see previous edition for last biography

BAKER, FRANK SLOAN, JR, ANIMAL HUSBANDRY, ANIMAL NUTRITION. *Current Pos:* RETIRED. *Personal Data:* b Brownwood, Tex, May 20, 21; m 42; c 3. *Educ:* Agr & Mech Col Tex, BS, 42; Univ Fla, MSA, 57. *Prof Exp:* From asst animmal husbandman to assoc animal husbandman, NFla Exp Sta, Univ Fla, Quincy, 45-63, animal husbandman & prof animal sci, Agr Res & Educ Ctr, Inst Food & Agr Sci, 63-89. *Mem:* Am Soc Animal Sci; Am Dairy Sci Asn. *Res:* Production of beef cattle; beef cattle nutrition and finishing. *Mailing Add:* PO Box 470 Quincy FL 32353

BAKER, FRANK WEIR, organic chemistry, for more information see previous edition

BAKER, FRANK WILLIAM, ELECTROCHEMISTRY, FINISHING TECHNOLOGY. *Current Pos:* develop engr process develop, 59-73, sect head, 73-78, SR TECH SUPVR PROCESS METALL, ALUMINUM CO AM, 78- *Personal Data:* b Kittanning, Pa, Oct 17, 35; m 58; c 3. *Educ:* Grove City Col, BS, 57. *Prof Exp:* Scientist phys chem, Allegheny Ludlum Steel Corp, 57-59. *Mem:* Am Electroplaters Soc; Electrochem Soc; Sigma Xi. *Res:* Metal finishing including mechanical, chemical, electrochemical and applied finishing treatments; aluminum reduction processes. *Mailing Add:* 445 Chester Dr Lower Burrell PA 15068-3301

BAKER, FREDERICK CHARLES, enzymology, insect biochemistry, for more information see previous edition

BAKER, GEORGE ALLEN, MATHEMATICAL STATISTICS. *Current Pos:* from instr math & jr statistician to prof math & statistician, 37-74, EMER PROF MATH, UNIV CALIF, DAVIS, 71- *Personal Data:* b Robinson, Ill, Oct 31, 03; m 30; c 2. *Educ:* Univ Ill, BS, 26, PhD(math statist), 29. *Prof Exp:* Assoc statistician, USPHS, 29; Milbank Mem Fund fel, Columbia Univ, 29-30; statistician, State Dept Health, NY, 30-31; head dept math, Shurtleff Col, 31-34; prof & head dept, Miss Woman's Col, 34-36; with consumers purchase study, Bur Home Econ, USDA, 36-37. *Concurrent Pos:* Fac Res Lectr, 56. *Mem:* Am Math Soc; Math Asn Am; fel Inst Math Statist; Am Statist Asn; Biomet Soc (vpres, 50); fel AAAS. *Res:* Application of field trials and growth curves; selection, prediction and transformation of data; random sampling from nonhomogeneous populations; taste-testing; factor analysis; applications to astronomy, physics and education. *Mailing Add:* Dept Math Univ Calif Davis CA 95616-5224

BAKER, GEORGE ALLEN, JR, STATISTICAL MECHANICS, APPLIED MATHEMATICS. *Current Pos:* MEM STAFF, LOS ALAMOS NAT LAB, 75- *Personal Data:* b Alton, Ill, Nov 25, 32; m 90; c 3. *Educ:* Calif Inst Technol, BS, 54; Univ Calif, Berkeley, PhD(physics), 56. *Prof Exp:* NSF fel, Columbia Univ, 56-57; mem staff, Los Alamos Sci Lab, 57-66; physicist, Brookhaven Nat Lab, 66-71, sr physicist, 71-75. *Concurrent Pos:* Assoc res physicist, Univ Calif, San Diego, 61-62; vis prof, Kings Col, Univ London, 64-65, Univ Nice, 70 & Cornell Univ, 71-72, Univ New S Wales, 85; assoc ed, J Math Physics & J Statist Physics; assoc group leader, 76-81, Los Alamos Fel, Los Alamos Nat Lab, 83-; vis physicist, serv physic theory, Saclay Ctr Nucl Study; vis lectr, Princeton Univ, 83. *Mem:* Fel Am Phys Soc; Int Asn Math Physics. *Res:* Statistical mechanics; mathematical methods of theoretical physics; quantum theory; field theory; nuclear physics. *Mailing Add:* 115 La Senda Los Alamos NM 87544

BAKER, GEORGE SEVERT, SOLID STATE PHYSICS. *Current Pos:* asst dean, Col Eng & Appl Sci, 72-76, PROF, DEPT MAT, UNIV WIS-MILWAUKEE, 67-, CHMN DEPT, 78- *Personal Data:* b Chicago, Ill, Aug 2, 27; m 59, Shari Jennings; c Gail & Geoffrey. *Educ:* Purdue Univ, BS, 50; Univ Ill, PhD(physics), 57. *Prof Exp:* Res assoc metall, Univ Ill, 56-57; asst prof physics, Univ Utah, 57-62; tech specialist, Aerojet Gen Corp, Calif, 62-67. *Mem:* Am Soc Metals. *Res:* Defect properties of crystals; mechanical properties; refractory metals; forging; manufacturing processes. *Mailing Add:* Univ Wis Milwaukee Milwaukee WI 53201. *Fax:* 414-229-6958; *E-Mail:* gsbaker@csd4.vwm.edu

BAKER, GEORGE THOMAS, III, BIOMEDICAL, GERONTOLOGY. *Current Pos:* PRES, BAKER & ASSOCS, 86- *Personal Data:* b Waterbury, Conn, Sept 10, 40; m, Nicole J Aguet; c Patrick T & Nicolas G. *Educ:* Univ Conn, BA & BS, 65; Univ RI, MS, 69; Univ Miami, PhD(physiol & biophys), 71. *Honors & Awards:* Swiss Am Found Award, 73. *Prof Exp:* Res assoc biochem, Cancer Res Inst, New Eng Deaconess Hosp & Harvard Med Sch, Boston, 65-66; instr anat & physiol, Registr Nurse Prog, RI Hosp, Univ RI,

66-67; res physiologist, Naval Submarine Med Ctr, Groton, Conn, 67-69; res assoc, dept physiol & biophys, Univ Miami, 69-70, instr gen physiol, 71-73; vis prof biochem genetics, Univ Zurich, 73-75; vis scientist molecular biol, Max Planck Inst, Tubingen, Ger, 75-76; dir med & physiol, Inst Aging, Drexel Univ, 76-82; dir biomed, Ctr Aging, Univ Md, College Park, 82-86. *Concurrent Pos:* Consult, space re-entry div, Gen Elec, Valley Forge, Pa, 79-84, GTE Serv Corp, Stamford, Conn, 82- & Milnor Fenwick, 83-; mem adv bd, nat community educ proj, Nat Coun Aging, 82-84 & technol & aging, Am Soc Aging, 82-85; consult, Nat Inst Aging/NIH, 86-87, Bessmer Carraway Med Ctr, Bessmer Ala, 86-, Montgomery Gen Hosp, Md, 86-87, Travelers Ins, Off Technol Assessment, US Cong, Am Asn Homes Aging, 87, Nat Oceanic & Atmospheric Admin, 89-; guest researcher, Gerontol Res Ctr, Nat Inst Aging/NIH, 89-; pres, Nathan Shock Aging Res Found. *Mem:* Fel Geront Soc Am (vpres, 80-81); AAAS; Sigma Xi; Am Aging Asn (pres, 85-); NY Acad Sci; Am Asn Advan Health Care Res. *Res:* Molecular-genetic mechanisms of aging,; impact of technology on older Americans health care issues and delivery systems; biomarkers of aging development and marketing of products and services for mature individuals. *Mailing Add:* 14628 Carona Dr Silver Spring MD 20907

BAKER, GLADYS ELIZABETH, BOTANY. *Current Pos:* vis prof, 61-62, prof, 63-73, EMER PROF BOT, UNIV HAWAII, 73- *Personal Data:* b Iowa City, Iowa, July 22, 08. *Educ:* Univ Iowa, AB, 30, MS, 32; Washington Univ, PhD(mycol), 35. *Prof Exp:* Asst bot, Washington Univ, 35-36; instr biol, Hunter Col, 36-40; from instr to prof plant sci, Vassar Col, 40-63, chmn dept, 48-60. *Concurrent Pos:* Vassar Col fac fel, Stanford Univ, 45 & Univ Calif, 54; grants, NSF, Sigma Xi, Smith Kline-French. *Mem:* Fel AAAS; Mycol Soc Am; Sigma Xi; Brit Mycol Soc. *Res:* Cytology and morphology of myxomycetes, lichens and basidiomycetes; cytogenetics of imperfect fungi; distribution of fungi. *Mailing Add:* 158 Sierra Winds 17300 N 88th Ave Peoria AZ 85382

BAKER, GLEN BRYAN, NEUROCHEMISTRY & ANALYTICAL CHEMISTRY, DRUG METABOLISM. *Current Pos:* from asst prof to assoc prof, 77-85, hon asst prof, 79-81, HON PROF, FAC PHARM & PHARMACEUT SCI, PROF PSYCHIAT, DEPT PSYCHIAT, UNIV ALTA, 85- *Personal Data:* b Watrous, Sask, July 26, 47; m 75, Judith Slingsby. *Educ:* Univ Sask, BSP, 70, MSc, 72, PhD(biol psychiat), 74. *Prof Exp:* Fel, Med Res Coun Neuropharmacol Unit, Univ Birmingham, UK, 74-77. *Concurrent Pos:* From asst dir to assoc dir, Neurochem Res Unit, Univ Alta, 79-90, co-dir, 90- *Mem:* Can Col Neuropsychopharm; Int Soc Neurochem; Pharmacol Soc Can; Europ Soc Neurochem; Soc Neurosci. *Res:* Biochemical bases of psychiatric disorders; modes of action of antidepressant, neuroleptic and antianxiety drugs; development of assays for biogenic amines, psychotropic drugs and their metabolites. *Mailing Add:* Neurochem Res Unit Dept Psychiat MacKenzie Ctr Univ Alta Edmonton AB T6G 2B7 Can. *Fax:* 403-492-6841; *E-Mail:* glen.baker@ualberta.ca

BAKER, GRAEME L, ANALYTICAL CHEMISTRY. *Current Pos:* chmn dept, 68-78, PROF CHEM, UNIV CENT FLA, 68- *Personal Data:* b Kalispell, Mont, Mar 7, 25; m 49; c 3. *Educ:* Mont State Univ, BSc, 47, MS, 53, PhD(chem), 59. *Prof Exp:* Instr chem, Mont State Col, 49-51; assoc state feed control chemist, State Dept Agr, Mont, 51-52; asst chem, Mont State Col, 52-53, from instr to prof, 53-68. *Mem:* Am Chem Soc; Sigma Xi. *Res:* Lipids of insect origin; protective coatings and corrosion. *Mailing Add:* 914 Arabian Lane Libby MT 59923-9537

BAKER, GRIFFIN JONATHAN, entomology; deceased, see previous edition for last biography

BAKER, HAROLD NORDEAN, BIOCHEMISTRY, ATHEROSCLEROSIS. *Current Pos:* RES SCIENTIST, ABBOTT LAB, 87- *Personal Data:* b Iowa City, Iowa, May 18, 43; c 4. *Educ:* Lamar Univ, BS, 65; Tulane Univ, PhD(org chem), 70. *Prof Exp:* Robert A Welch Found fel, Univ Tex M D Anderson Hosp, Houston, 69-71, res assoc protein struct, 71; res assoc, Baylor Col Med, 71-72, from instr to asst prof, 72-76; asst prof, Univ Minn, 76-78; asst prof lipoproteins in atherosclerosis, La State Univ Med Ctr, 78-87. *Concurrent Pos:* Dir, Lipid Res Clin, Core Lab, 72-76. *Mem:* Am Chem Soc. *Res:* Protein structure; metabolic basis of atherosclerosis; lipid transport; development of immunochemical assays; reproductive endocrinology. *Mailing Add:* Abbott Labs Dept 9FA Bldg AP31 Abbott Park IL 60064

BAKER, HAROLD REID, AGRICULTURE. *Prof Exp:* Fel, Agr Inst Can, 94. *Mailing Add:* Ext Div Univ Sask Kirk Hall Rm 132 Saskatoon SK S7N 0W0 Can

BAKER, HAROLD WELDON, ANALYTICAL CHEMISTRY. *Current Pos:* RETIRED. *Personal Data:* b Lincoln, Nebr, Jan 23, 31; m 57; c 2. *Educ:* Nebr Wesleyan Univ, BA, 54; Purdue Univ, MS, 56; Univ Iowa, PhD, 61. *Prof Exp:* Instr chem, Butler Univ, 56-57; from assoc prof to prof, Parsons Col, 59-62; from asst prof to assoc prof chem, Sch Pharm, Temple Univ, 62-74, prof, Sch Pharm, 74- *Mem:* Am Chem Soc. *Res:* Atomic absorption and fluorescence; trace analysis of metals; air and water pollution; heavy metal toxicity of life systems; pharmaceutical analysis; clinical chemistry. *Mailing Add:* c/o Suzanne Butler Dept Pharm Temple Univ 3307 N Broad St Philadelphia PA 19140

BAKER, HERBERT GEORGE, EVOLUTION, ECOLOGY. *Current Pos:* dir bot garden, Univ Calif, Berkeley, 57-69, assoc dir, 69-74, assoc prof, 57-60, PROF BOT, UNIV CALIF, BERKELEY, 60- *Personal Data:* b Brighton, Eng, Feb 23, 20; m 45; c 1. *Educ:* Univ London, BSc, 41, PhD, 45. *Honors & Awards:* Merit Award, Am Bot Soc. *Prof Exp:* Res chemist & plant physiologist, Hosa Res Labs, 40-45; lectr bot, Univ Leeds, 45-54; sr lectr, Univ Col Gold Coast, 54-55, prof & head dept, 55-57. *Concurrent Pos:* Res fel, Carnegie Inst, 48-49; assoc ed, Evolution, 56-59, 62-65 & Ecology, 63-66; res prof, Miller Inst, 66-67 & 88; mem bd gov, Orgn Trop Studies, 64-76; distinguished econ botanist, Soc Econ Bot. *Mem:* Am Bot Soc (vpres, 77, pres, 79); Soc Study Evolution (secy, 67-69, pres, 69); Ecol Soc Am; Int Asn Bot Gardens (vpres, 64-69); fel AAAS; fel Am Acad Arts & Sci; fel Asn Trop Biol; Am Philos Soc; hon mem Brit Ecol Soc. *Res:* Ecology and evolution of higher plants, especially on reproductive biology; palynology; cytogenetics; history of biology; general tropical botany; nectar and pollen chemistry; weed evolution. *Mailing Add:* 635 Creston Rd Berkeley CA 94708-1239

BAKER, HERMAN, METABOLISM, NUTRITION. *Current Pos:* Assoc prof med, 60-70, PROF MED & PREV MED & DIR DIV NUTRIT & PREV MED, UNIV MED & DENT NJ, 70- *Personal Data:* b New York, NY, Jan 22, 26; m 52; c Elliott & Joel. *Educ:* City Col New York, BS, 46; Emory Univ, MS, 48; NY Univ, PhD(metab), 56; Am Bd Nutrit, dipl, 68. *Honors & Awards:* Hans Selye Award, 79. *Concurrent Pos:* Mem, Coun Nutrit & pres Prev Med Sect, Pan Am Med Asn. *Mem:* Soc Exp Biol & Med; Am Soc Clin Nutrit; Pan Am Med Asn; fel Am Col Nutrit. *Res:* Vitamin metabolism; nutrition and analysis. *Mailing Add:* Dept Prev Med Pub Health Univ Med & Dent NJ Med Sch 185 S Orange Ave Newark NJ 07103

BAKER, HOUSTON RICHARD, PHARMACOLOGY, PHYSIOLOGY. *Current Pos:* bus exec, Am Soc Plant Physiologists, 74-77, EXEC OFFICER, AM SOC PHARMACOL & EXP THERAPEUT, 77- *Personal Data:* b Pittsfield, Mass, Aug 27, 40; m 66; c 2. *Educ:* Harvard Col, BA, 63; Ohio State Univ, PhD(physiol), 69. *Prof Exp:* Res asst physiol, Physiol Inst, Univ Saarlandes, 69-70; res assoc cryobiol, Blood Res Lab, Am Nat Red Cross, 70-74. *Concurrent Pos:* Ed, Newsletter, Am Soc Plant Physiologists, 74-77 & Pharmacologist, 77-; publ, What's New in Plant Physiol, 76- *Mem:* Am Soc Pharmacol & Exp Therapeut; Coun Eng & Sci Soc Execs; Soc Cryobiol; Am Soc Plant Physiologists; fel AAAS. *Res:* Muscle contraction; electrophysiology; freezing injury and mitigation; plant hardiness; scientific society management; scientific journal publishing and management. *Mailing Add:* Biophysics Sec 9411 Warfield Rd Gaithersburg MD 20882-4215

BAKER, HOWARD CRITTENDON, THEORETICAL PHYSICS. *Current Pos:* HEAD, DEPT PHYSICS & ASTRON, BUTLER UNIV, 90- *Personal Data:* b Lexington, Ky, Sept 4, 43; m 67. *Educ:* Berea Col, BA, 65; Washington Univ, St Louis, MA, 67, PhD(physics), 72. *Prof Exp:* From asst prof to prof physics, Berea Col, 72-90. *Concurrent Pos:* Vis asst prof physics, Univ Conn, 74-75; NSF fel, Oakridge Nat Lab, 79; vis res fel, Johns Hopkins Univ, 80; mem tech staff, Rocketdyne Div, Rockwell Int, 85-86. *Mem:* Am Phys Soc; Am Asn Physics Teachers. *Res:* Field theory quantum measurement, decay theory and nonlinear optics. *Mailing Add:* Dept Physics & Astron Box 209 Butler Univ Indianapolis IN 46208. *Fax:* 317-940-9950; *E-Mail:* hbaker@butler.edu

BAKER, JAMES ADDISON, COMPUTER SCIENCE. *Current Pos:* RETIRED. *Personal Data:* b Eugene, Ore, Aug 20, 22; m 46; c 1. *Educ:* Pomona Col, AB, 44. *Prof Exp:* Head math & comput, Lawrence Berkeley Lab, Univ Calif, Berkeley, 52-58; head data systs div, Broadview Res Corp, 58-61; head math & comput group, Lawrence Berkeley Lab, Univ Calif, Berkeley, 61-84; consult, Sci Comput Systs Corp, 84-88 & Silicon Mgt Group, 88-90. *Concurrent Pos:* Consult, Comt Uses of Comput, Nat Acad Sci, 63; lectr elec eng, comput sci, indust eng, opers res & transp eng, Univ Calif, Berkeley, 63-; vis scholar, Europ Orgn Nuclear Res, Geneva, 74-75; mem, Am Nat Stand Comt, X3 Info Processing. *Mem:* Asn Comput Mach; Inst Elec & Electronics Engrs Comput Soc. *Res:* Simulation of communications systems; programming systems; mass storage systems; network analysis. *Mailing Add:* 131 Avenida Dr Berkeley CA 94708

BAKER, JAMES BERT, ECOLOGY, SILVICULTURE. *Current Pos:* Res forester silvicult, USDA Forest Serv, 62-71, res soil scientist forest soils, 71-78, supvry res forester, Southern Forest Exp Sta, 78-90, RES TEAM LEADER, SOUTHERN RES STA, USDA FOREST SERV, 90- *Personal Data:* b Bernice, La, Feb 7, 39; m 60; c James C & Terrell S. *Educ:* Univ Ark, Monticello, BSF, 61; Duke Univ, MF, 62; Miss State Univ, PhD(forest soils), 70. *Mem:* Soc Am Foresters; Sigma Xi. *Res:* Uneven-aged management; development of silvicultural systems; forest management; multi-resource management. *Mailing Add:* 230 Tracy Dr Monticello AR 71655

BAKER, JAMES E, SCIENTIFIC ADMINISTRATION, SPEECH RECOGNITION. *Current Pos:* prof & head elec eng, 84-93, EMER PROF, OKLA STATE UNIV, 93- *Personal Data:* b Columbus, Ohio, Apr 16, 31; m 58, Thelma; c Karen (Voorhees) & Kurt. *Educ:* US Naval Acad, BS, 54; Okla State Univ, BS & MS, 62, PhD(elec eng), 71. *Prof Exp:* Dir, Satellite Commun Prog, USAF, 74-77, dir elec systs, Hq, Systs Command Prog, 77-79, comdr, Geophysics Lab, 79-81, dir, Off Sci Res, 81-84. *Concurrent Pos:* US rep, Res Panel Physics & Electronics, NATO, 81-84. *Mem:* Inst Elec & Electronics Engrs; Sigma Xi; Nat Soc Prof Engrs. *Res:* Speech processing for recognition by machines; scientific disciplines. *Mailing Add:* 2809 N Husband St Stillwater OK 74075

BAKER, JAMES GILBERT, OPTICAL PHYSICS, ASTRONOMY. *Current Pos:* Res fel, Harvard Univ, 42-45, dir, Optical Res Lab, 43-45, assoc prof, Harvard Observ, 46-48, res assoc, 49-62, ASSOC, HARVARD OBSERV, HARVARD UNIV, 62- *Personal Data:* b Louisville, Ky, Nov 11, 14; m 38; c 4. *Educ:* Univ Louisville, AB, 35; Harvard Univ, MA, 36, PhD(astron, astrophys), 42. *Hon Degrees:* ScD, Univ Louisville, 48. *Honors & Awards:* Lowell Lectr, 40; Adolph Lomb Medal, 42; Presidential Medal of Merit, 47; Magellanic Medal, Am Philos Soc, 53; Exceptional Civilian Serv Award, USAF, 57; Elliott Cresson Medal, Franklin Inst, 62; Frederick Ives Medal, Optical Soc Am, 65; Alan Gordon Award, Soc Photooptical Instrumentation Engrs, 76, Gold Medal, 78; Int Lens Design Conf Award, 90; Fraunhofer Award, Optical Soc Am, 91. *Concurrent Pos:* res assoc, Lick Observ, 48-60; consult optical physics & aerial photog, US Air Force, 49-57, mem, Sci Adv Bd, 52-57; chmn, US Nat Comn, Int Comn Optics, 56-59, vpres, 59-62; assoc, Ctr Astrophys, Harvard & Smithsonian Observs, 66-; consult optical physics & astron, Aerospace Corp, 66-75, photog physics, Polaroid Corp, 66-; trustee, Perkin Fund, 70- *Mem:* Nat Acad Sci; Nat Acad Eng; Am Astron Soc; fel Optical Soc Am (pres, 60); Am Acad Arts & Sci; Am Philos Soc. *Res:* Instrumentation and optical design; astrophysics. *Mailing Add:* 14 French Dr Bedford NH 03102

BAKER, JAMES HASKELL, MARINE ZOOLOGY, MARINE SCIENCES. *Current Pos:* SR ENVIRON SCIENTIST, TETRA-TECH ENVIRON MGT INC, 94- *Personal Data:* b Ft Worth, Tex, Sept 8, 40. *Educ:* Tex Christian Univ, BA, 62, MS, 65; Univ Houston, PhD(biol), 75. *Prof Exp:* Mus technician, Smithsonian Oceanog Sorting Ctr, 67; res assoc aquatic biol, Res Found, Tex Christian Univ, 68-70; sr res scientist aquatic biol, Southwest Res Inst, 73-80, Imco Serv, 81-84, Rollins Environ Serv, 84-89, Fluon Daniel, 89, ENSR Consult & Eng, 89-93; sr res scientist, J K Enterprises, 93-96. *Concurrent Pos:* Pres & bd mem, Tex Asn Environ Profs. *Mem:* Soc Wetland Scientists; Nat Asn Environ Profs. *Res:* Ecology and systematics of marine invertebrates. *Mailing Add:* Tetra-Tech Environ Mgt Inc 3334 Richmond Ave Suite 200 Houston TX 77098

BAKER, JAMES LEROY, PHYSICAL CHEMISTRY, AGRICULTURAL ENGINEERING. *Current Pos:* Asst chem, Iowa State Univ, 66-71, agr engr, 71-73, from asst prof to assoc prof, 73-82, PROF AGR ENG, IOWA STATE UNIV, 82- *Personal Data:* b Chamberlain, SDak, Apr 25, 44; m 65, Margery Walless; c Chad & Leslie. *Educ:* SDak Sch Mines & Technol, BS, 66; Iowa State Univ, PhD(phys chem), 71. *Honors & Awards:* Joan Hodges Queneau Palladium Metal, 89. *Mem:* Soil & Water Conserv Soc; Am Soc Agr Engrs; Am Soc Agron; Soil Sci Soc Am. *Res:* Effects of farm management practices on the efficient use of pesticides and nutrients by agriculture, with emphasis on losses to the environment. *Mailing Add:* Dept Agr Iowa State Univ Ames IA 50011-2010. *Fax:* 515-294-2552

BAKER, JAMES R, PRODUCTION, AGRICULTURE FINANCE & CREDIT. *Current Pos:* ADMINR, GRAIN INSPECTION PACKERS & STOCKYARDS ADMIN, US DEPT AGR, 94- *Personal Data:* b Glenwood, Ark, Aug 3, 46; m 71, Linda Nelson; c Monica & Jason. *Educ:* Southern State Col, BS, 68. *Prof Exp:* Vpres, Cent Ark Prod Credit Asn, 68-83; mgr, Lewis Livestock Co, Conway, Ark, 83-94. *Concurrent Pos:* Bd dirs, Faulkner Co Farm Bur, 73-, pres, 86-97; chmn, Ark Livestock & Poultry Comn, 83-94; bd mem, Ark Farm Bur, bd dirs, 89-94. *Res:* Trial and error in production agriculture. *Mailing Add:* Grain Inspection Packers & Stockyards Admin Stop 3601 1400 Independence Ave SW Washington DC 20250-3601

BAKER, JAMES ROBERT, ENTOMOLOGY. *Current Pos:* Exten entomologist, NC Agr Exten Serv, 72-81, PROF EXTEN ENTOMOLOGY, NC STATE UNIV, 81- *Personal Data:* b Urbana, Ill, Apr 20, 41; m 66; c 3. *Educ:* NC State Univ, BS, 66, MS, 68; Univ Kans, PhD(entom), 72. *Mem:* Entom Soc Am; Sigma Xi. *Res:* Mealybugs infesting ornamental plants in North Carolina, identification and control. *Mailing Add:* 3025 Pleasant Plains Rd Apex NC 27502

BAKER, JEFFREY JOHN WHEELER, DEVELOPMENTAL BIOLOGY. *Current Pos:* sr fel, sci soc prog, 75-82, LECTR SCI, WESLEYAN UNIV, 69- *Personal Data:* b Montclair, NJ, Feb 2, 31; m 55, Barbara Bernache; c 4. *Educ:* Univ Va, BA, 53 & MS, 59. *Prof Exp:* Supvr qual control, Libby, McNeill & Libby Food Co, Inc, 53-54; teacher biol, Mt Hermon, Mass, 54-62; lectr sci, Wesleyan Univ, 62-66; vis assoc prof biol, George Washington Univ, 66-68; prof, Univ PR, 68-69. *Concurrent Pos:* Staff biologist & educ dir, Comn Undergrad Educ Biol Sci, 66-68; vis prof biol, Washington Univ, St Louis, Mo, 85; scientist scholar, Res Dept Religious Studies, Charlottesville, Va. *Mem:* AAAS; Am Inst Biol Sci; Nat Asn Sci Writers; Soc Sci Study Sex. *Res:* Amphibian development; religion and science; science writing. *Mailing Add:* Box 205 Ivy VA 22945

BAKER, JOFFRE BERNARD, CARDIOVASCULAR RESEARCH. *Current Pos:* sr scientist, 88-90, ACTG DIR, DEPT CARDIOVASC RES, GENENTECH, INC, 90- *Personal Data:* b Alameda, Calif, Dec 23, 47. *Educ:* Univ Calif, San Diego, BA, 71; Univ Hawaii, PhD(biochem), 77. *Prof Exp:* Postdoctoral fel, Dept Med Microbiol, Univ Calif, Irvine, 77-79; from asst prof to assoc prof, Dept Biochem, Univ Kans, 79-88. *Concurrent Pos:* NIH & Am Heart Asn grants, 80-88; NIH res career develop award, 83-88. *Mem:* Am Soc Cell Biol; Am Soc Biochem & Molecular Biol; Sigma Xi. *Res:* Interactions of protein hormones with cells; cellular regulation of protease activity; control of proliferations of eukaryotic cells and biochemistry of cell membranes. *Mailing Add:* Sr Sci Genentech Inc 460 Pt San Bruno Blvd South San Francisco CA 94080-4980

BAKER, JOHN ALEXANDER, ANALYSIS & FUNCTIONAL EQUATIONS. *Current Pos:* from asst prof to prof, 68-96, ADJ PROF MATH, UNIV WATERLOO, 96- *Personal Data:* b Stratford, Ont, Apr 11, 39; m 65, Donna Barradell; c Sean & Laurel. *Educ:* Univ Sask, BA, 60, MA, 63; Univ Waterloo, PhD(math), 68. *Prof Exp:* Instr math, Can Serv Col Royal Roads, 64-65; lectr, Univ Sask, 65-66. *Mem:* Can Math Soc; Math Asn Am. *Res:* Analytic aspects of the theory of functional equations; regularity properties; stability and techniques of solution involving differential equations; distribution theory and functional analysis; expository writing in calculus. *Mailing Add:* Dept Pure Math Univ Waterloo Waterloo ON N2L 3G1 Can. *E-Mail:* jabaker@math.uwaterloo.ca

BAKER, JOHN BEE, JR, PLANT PHYSIOLOGY, WEED SCIENCE. *Current Pos:* RETIRED. *Personal Data:* b Clarksdale, Miss, Mar 30, 27; m 56, Mildred M Bullock; c Susan R & Joan B. *Educ:* Miss State Col, BS, 50; Univ Wis, MS, 51, PhD(bot), 55. *Prof Exp:* Asst prof plant path & asst pathologist weed control, La State Univ, Baton Rouge, 53-59, assoc prof bot & plant path, 59-66, prof plant path & crop physiol, 66-90, chmn dept, 90-92. *Mem:* Am Soc Plant Physiol; fel Weed Sci Soc Am. *Res:* Mechanism of action of herbicides and growth regulators; autecology of weeds; weed control in rice. *Mailing Add:* 5789 Hyacinth Baton Rouge LA 70808

BAKER, JOHN CHRISTOPHER, LARGE ANIMAL INTERNAL MEDICINE, VIROLOGY. *Current Pos:* From asst prof to assoc prof, 84-93, PROF, MICH STATE UNIV, 93- *Personal Data:* b Warren, Ohio, Feb 25, 52; m 79, Terese B Heineman; c Trevor C & Justin L. *Educ:* Ohio State Univ, BS, 73, MS, 75, DVM, 80; Univ Minn, PhD(vet med), 84; Am Col Vet Internal Med, dipl, 85. *Mem:* Am Vet Med Asn; Res Workers Animal Dis; Am Soc Virol; Am Soc Microbiol. *Res:* Bovine respiratory disease, specifically the epidemiology pathogenesis of respiratory syncytial virus infection. *Mailing Add:* Dept Large Animal Clin Sci Vet Clin Ctr Mich State Univ East Lansing MI 48824-1314. *Fax:* 517-336-1042; *E-Mail:* baker@cvm.msu.edu

BAKER, JOHN D, RADIOCHEMISTRY, SEPARATIONS CHEMISTRY. *Current Pos:* scientist, 80-83, sr scientist, 83-88, SCI SPECIALIST, EG&G, IDAHO, INC, 88- *Personal Data:* b Columbus, Ohio, Aug 9, 49; m 80; c 2. *Educ:* Northern Ill Univ, BS, 72; Univ Idaho, MS, 80. *Prof Exp:* Assoc chemist, Allied Chem Corp, 73-78; group leader, Exxon Nuclear Corp, 78-80. *Mem:* Am Chem Soc. *Res:* Applying chemical separation techniques, such as high performance liquid chromatography solvent extraction to the rapid radiochemical separation of short lived fission products; basic solvent extraction processes; automating chemical separations; radioisotope production. *Mailing Add:* EG&G Idaho TRA 604 PO Box 1625 Idaho Falls ID 83415-7111

BAKER, JOHN KEITH, MEDICINAL CHEMISTRY, PHYSICAL CHEMISTRY. *Current Pos:* From asst prof to assoc prof 70-79, PROF MED CHEM, UNIV MISS, SCH PHARM, 79- *Personal Data:* b San Antonio, Tex, Dec 1, 42; m 65; c 2. *Educ:* Univ Tex, Austin, BS, 66; Univ Calif, San Francisco, PhD(pharmaceut chem), 70. *Concurrent Pos:* Sr fel, Nat Inst Health, 85-86. *Mem:* Am Pharmaceut Asn; Am Chem Soc. *Res:* Application of spectroscopic methods in molecular pharmacological studies; thermodynamic studies of the interaction of adenosine triphosphate; drug metabolism; high pressure liquid chromatography; quantitative drug analysis. *Mailing Add:* 5217 Starry Ct Ft Worth TX 76123

BAKER, JOHN M, SURFACE OXIDATION. *Current Pos:* RES STAFF MEM, MFG RES DEPT, T J WATSON RES CTR, 71- *Educ:* Harvard Univ, AB, 64; Cornell Univ, PhD(appl physics), 70. *Res:* Monitoring semiconductor manufacturing processes with emphasis on residual Gas Analyzer sensors; surface analysis; thin film deposition plasma oxidation and effects of sputtering with plasmas on the properties of surfaces. *Mailing Add:* 1455 Hayes Dr Yorktown Heights NY 10598

BAKER, JOHN P, EQUINE NUTRITION & MANAGEMENT. *Current Pos:* RETIRED. *Personal Data:* b Aledo, Tex, Jan 31, 23; m 44; c 3. *Educ:* Univ Ill, PhD(animal sci), 60. *Prof Exp:* Prof animal sci, Univ Ky, 67- *Concurrent Pos:* Assoc prof animal sci, Univ Idaho, 60-67. *Mem:* Equine Nutrit & Physiol Soc; Am Inst Nutrit; Am Soc Animal Sci. *Res:* Equine nutrition and exercise physiology. *Mailing Add:* 982 Maywick Dr Lexington KY 40504

BAKER, JOHN ROWLAND, DENTISTRY, BIOCHEMISTRY. *Current Pos:* assoc prof, 72-80, PROF DENT, UNIV ALA, BIRMINGHAM, 80-, PROF BIOCHEM, 82- *Personal Data:* b Hadleigh, Essex, Eng, Sept 26, 34. *Educ:* Univ Reading, Eng, BSc Hons, 56, PhD(physiol chem), 59. *Hon Degrees:* MA, Trinity Col, Dublin, 67. *Prof Exp:* Postdoctoral fel, Dept Biochem & Biophys, Univ Calif, Davis, 59-61; res assoc, Queen Charlotte's Hosp, London, Eng, 62-63; lectr biochem, Trinity Col, Univ Dublin, Ireland, 63-72. *Concurrent Pos:* USPHS int fel, 68; sabbatical leave, Dept Pediat, Univ Chicago, 68-70; sr scientist, Diabetes Res & Training Ctr, Univ Ala, Birmingham; comt mem, Brit Biochem Soc, 70-72. *Mem:* Biochem Soc; Sigma Xi; assoc Royal Inst Chem; Soc Complex Carbohydrates; Fedn Am Socs Exp Biol. *Res:* Problems of proteoglycan structures and biosynthesis; structure of proteoglycans from other connective tissues; interaction of proteoglycans with other connective tissue macromolecules; immunological changes in proteoglycans in disease. *Mailing Add:* Dept Biochem Univ Ala UAB Sta 1808 Seventh Ave S Birmingham AL 35294-0012

BAKER, JOHN WARREN, FUNCTIONAL ANALYSIS, TOPOLOGY. *Current Pos:* asst prof, 73-75, ASSOC PROF MATH, KENT STATE UNIV, 75- *Personal Data:* b El Paso, Tex, Aug 24, 36; m 70. *Educ:* Hardin-Simmons Univ, BS, 58; Univ Tex, Austin, MA, 65, PhD(math), 68. *Prof Exp:* Asst prof math, Fla State Univ, 68-73. *Concurrent Pos:* Undergrad coordr, Dept Math, Kent State Univ, 74-76; colloquium chmn math sci, Kent State Univ, 81- *Mem:* Asn Comput Mach; Math Asn Am. *Res:* Computer algebra; spaces of continuous functions; projections in Banach spaces; zero-dimension topological spaces. *Mailing Add:* Dept Math & Comput Sci 233 MSB Kent State Univ Main Campus Kent OH 44242

BAKER, JOSEPH WILLARD, ORGANIC CHEMISTRY, PROCESS DEVELOPMENT. *Current Pos:* CONSULT, 85- *Personal Data:* b Luray, Va, Sept 15, 24; m 52; c 2. *Educ:* Bridgewater Col, BA, 45; Univ Va, MS, 49, PhD(org chem), 52. *Prof Exp:* Instr, Univ Va, 51-52; res chemist, 52-56, res group leader, 56-72, sr res group leader, Monsanto Co, 72-85,. *Mem:* Am Chem Soc; Sigma Xi. *Res:* Organophosphorus chemistry; agricultural chemicals; food and fine chemicals; pharmaceuticals; bacteriostats; plasticizers; functional fluids; amino acids, ketones and alcohols; organic heterocycles; catalytic reductions and chemical process development; antioxidants; pharmaceuticals. *Mailing Add:* 421 Greenleaf Dr St Louis MO 63122-4451

BAKER, JUNE MARSHALL, ANALYTICAL CHEMISTRY, INSTRUMENTAL CHEMISTRY. *Current Pos:* RETIRED. *Personal Data:* b Napton, Mo, Nov 11, 22; m 47, Jane B Laye; c Nancy J, Paul E & Janna A (Poole). *Educ:* Mo Valley Col, BA, 44; Ohio State Univ, MSc, 50; Univ Mo, PhD(chem), 55. *Prof Exp:* Instr chem, Mo Valley Col, 47-49; analyst, Univ Mo, 52-55; asst prof, Tenn Polytech Univ, 55-56; assoc prof, Eastern Ill State Col, 56-57; from assoc prof to prof chem, Auburn Univ, 57-88. *Concurrent Pos:* Consult, Orradio Industs, Auburn Res Found & Southwire; pres, Auburn Sect, Am Chem Soc, 63, secy, 64-89. *Mem:* Am Chem Soc; Sigma Xi. *Res:* Ion-exchange method for study of chemical reactions; determinations for chromium; trace element contamination; spectrophotometry. *Mailing Add:* 950 Terrace Acres Dr Auburn AL 36830

BAKER, KAY DAYNE, METEOROLOGY, ELECTRICAL ENGINEERING. *Current Pos:* dir, Space Sci Lab, 70-79, dept head, Elec Engr, 72-77, dir, Ctr Atmospheric & Space Sci, 81-83, PROF ELEC & PHYSICS, UTAH STATE UNIV, 70- *Personal Data:* b Escalante, Utah, Jan 31, 34; m 55; c 3. *Educ:* Univ Utah, BS, 56, MS, 57, PhD(elec eng), 66. *Honors & Awards:* Alexander von Humboldt Found sr scientist award. *Prof Exp:* Res asst, Upper Air Res Lab, Univ Utah, 54-57, res engr, 57-62, asst dir lab, 62-69, dir lab, 69-70. *Concurrent Pos:* Mem Comn 3, Inst Sci Radio Union, 67- *Mem:* Am Geophys Union. *Res:* Development of measuring techniques and investigations of the upper atmosphere of the earth, with special emphasis on ionospheric auroral measurements. *Mailing Add:* Physics Utah State Univ Logan UT 84322-0001

BAKER, KENNETH FRANK, phytopathology, soil microbiology; deceased, see previous edition for last biography

BAKER, KENNETH L(EROY), MECHANICAL ENGINEERING. *Current Pos:* RETIRED. *Personal Data:* b Inwood, Ind, Feb 3, 19; m 45; c 2. *Educ:* Purdue Univ, BSME, 42. *Prof Exp:* Mech engr, US Naval Surface Weapons Ctr, Silver Spring, 43-79. *Res:* Naval ordnance. *Mailing Add:* 9104 49th Ave College Park MD 20740

BAKER, KENNETH MELVIN, EXPERIMENTAL BIOLOGY. *Current Pos:* ASSOC PROF MED, THOMAS JEFFERSON SCH MED, PHILADELPHIA, PA, 89- *Personal Data:* b Harrisburg, Pa, Oct 30, 47; m; c 1. *Educ:* Lebanon Valley Col, BS, 69; Temple Univ, MD, 74. *Prof Exp:* Med residency, Temple Univ Hosp, Philadelphia, Pa, 74-77, clin instr & chief med resident, 77-78; cardiol fel & res fel hypertension & pharmacol, Univ Va Hosp, Charlottesville, 78-81; from asst prof to assoc prof med, Milton S Hershey Med Ctr, Pa, 81-87; asst dir, Cardiovasc Non-Invasive Lab, 81-86, assoc, dept cardiol, Geisinger Med Ctr, Danville, Pa, 81-, staff scientist, Weis Ctr Res, Geisinger Clin, 87- *Concurrent Pos:* Emergency Rm physician, Germantown Hosp, Charlottesville, Va, 77-78; co-investr & prin investr, var insts, 78-; mem, Sci Res Comt, 84-88 & Hazardous Waste Comt, 90-; fel, Coun High Blood Pressure Res, Am Heart Asn, 90, estab investr, Asn, 91 & mem, Coun Basic Sci. *Mem:* Am Soc Cell Biol; fel Am Col Cardiol; assoc mem Am Col Physicians; AMA; Am Heart Asn; Am Fedn Clin Res; Am Physiol Soc. *Mailing Add:* Geisinger Clin Weis Ctr Res 100 N Academy Ave Danville PA 17822-2611. *Fax:* 717-271-6701

BAKER, KIRBY ALAN, MATHEMATICS. *Current Pos:* from asst prof to assoc prof, 68-76, PROF MATH, UNIV CALIF, LOS ANGELES, 76- *Personal Data:* b Boston, Mass, June 17, 40; m 66, 80, Glenda Howell; c Elizabeth (Leavy) & Edwin. *Educ:* Harvard Univ, AB, 61, PhD(math), 66. *Prof Exp:* Ford Found res fel math, Calif Inst Technol, 66-68. *Mem:* Am Math Soc; Math Asn Am. *Res:* Lattice theory and partial order; algebraic systems. *Mailing Add:* Dept Math Univ Calif 405 Hilgard Ave Los Angeles CA 90095-1555

BAKER, LAURENCE HOWARD, HEMATOLOGY, ONCOLOGY. *Current Pos:* fel oncol, Wayne State Univ, 70-72, from asst prof to prof med, Dept Oncol, 72-93, assoc chmn, Dept Oncol, 80-82, dir, Div Oncol, Dept Internal Med, 82-86, dir, Div Hemat & Oncol, 86-93, ASST DEAN CANCER PROGS, WAYNE STATE UNIV, 88- *Personal Data:* b Brooklyn, NY, Jan 14, 43; m 64, Maxine V Friedman; c Mindy & Jennifer. *Educ:* City Col New York, BA, 62, Univ Osteop Med & Surg, Des Moines, DO, 66; Am Bd Internal Med, dipl. *Prof Exp:* Rotating intern, Flint Osteop Hosp, Mich, 66-67; med resident, Detroit Osteop Hosp, 67-69. *Concurrent Pos:* Mem bd dirs, Meyer L Prentis Comp Cancer Ctr Metrop Detroit, Childrens Leukemia Soc Mich, Mich Cancer Consortium, Dept Pub Health, Mich Cancer Found & US Biosci Sci Bd; assoc chmn, SW Oncol Group; consult, Upjohn Co, 86, USPC, 86, Univ Chicago Clin Ctr, 86 & Nat Cancer Inst, 87; investr several grants, 86- *Mem:* Am Soc Cancer Res; Am Soc Clin Oncol; Am Soc Clin Pharmacol & Therapeut; Am Asn Clin Res; Am Asn Cancer Educ; Am Col Osteop Internists. *Res:* Cancer. *Mailing Add:* Harper Hosp 3990 John R St Detroit MI 48201-2018

BAKER, LEE EDWARD, PHYSIOLOGY, ELECTRICAL ENGINEERING. *Current Pos:* prof elec eng & dir biomed eng prof, 75-82, ROBERT L PARKER SR PROF ELEC & DIR BIOMED ENG PROG, UNIV TEX, AUSTIN, 82- *Personal Data:* b Springfield, Mo, Aug 31, 24; m 48; c 2. *Educ:* Univ Kans, BS, 45; Rice Univ, MS, 60; Baylor Col Med, PhD(physiol), 65. *Prof Exp:* Design engr, Radio Corp Am, 46-47; consult engr, 47-51; chief engr & part owner, Radio Sta KDKD, Mo, 53-54; owner & mgr, Radio Sta KOKO, 54-55; from instr to asst prof elec eng, Rice Univ, 55-65; from asst prof to assoc prof physiol, Baylor Col Med, 65-75. *Concurrent Pos:* Consult, Sci Res Ctr, Int Bus Mach Corp, 66-67 & Southwest Res Inst, 82-84. *Mem:* Am Inst Elec & Electronics Eng; Asn Advan Med Instrumentation; Biomed Eng Soc; Am Physiol Soc; NY Acad Sci. *Res:* Use of electrical impedance for the measurement of physiological events. *Mailing Add:* Dept Biomed Eng Univ Tex Eng Sci Bldg 610 Austin TX 78712

BAKER, LENOX DIAL, orthopaedic surgery; deceased, see previous edition for last biography

BAKER, LEONARD MORTON, ORGANIC CHEMISTRY, POLYMER CHEMISTRY. *Current Pos:* Chemist, Plastics Div, Union Carbide, 59-62, proj scientist, 62-64, group leader, 64-69, assoc dir res & develop chem & plastics, 69-74, dir, 74-77, vpres res & develop, 77-84, corp dir, 84-92, corp vpres technol, 84-92, VPRES TECHNOL, PRAXAIR INC, 92- *Personal Data:* b Medford, Mass, Oct 2, 34; m 58; c 3. *Educ:* Harvard Univ, AB, 56; Mass Inst Technol, PhD(org chem), 59. *Concurrent Pos:* Mem gov bd, Coun Chem Res, 89- *Mem:* Nat Acad Sci; Am Chem Soc; Am Inst Chem Engrs; Indust Res Inst; NY Acad Sci; Coun Chem Res. *Res:* Catalysis; process research and development; polymer applications development. *Mailing Add:* Praxair Inc 39 Old Ridgebury Rd Danbury CT 06817-0001

BAKER, LESTER, PEDIATRIC DIABETES. *Current Pos:* instr, 66-70, from asst prof to assoc prof, 66-76, PROF PEDIAT, UNIV PA SCH MED, 76- *Personal Data:* June, 30, 30; m 60, Liesel Gutman; c Deborah A, Herbert P. *Educ:* Columbia Univ, BA, 51; Sch Law & Higher Studies, France, MA, 52; Col Physicians & Surgeons, MD, 59. *Prof Exp:* Rotating internship, Hosp Univ Pa, 59-60, pediat residency, 60-62; NIH trainee metab dis, Childrens Hosp, Philadelphia, 62-65, sr physician, 71. *Concurrent Pos:* Dir, Clin Res Ctr, Childrens Hosp Philadelphia, 70-94; actg dir, Div Endocrin & Diabetes, Childrens Hosp Philadelphia, 77-78, dir, 78-; Fogarty sr int fel, 83; asst dir, Diabetes Res Ctr, 85-89; Henry Evans traveling fel, Columbia Univ. *Mem:* Soc Pediat Res; Am Pediat Res; Am Diebetes Asn. *Res:* Pediatric medicine; diabetes; metabolic diseases; author of over 100 publications. *Mailing Add:* Children's Hosp Philadelphia Div Endocrinology 34th & Civic Center Blvd Philadelphia PA 19104. *Fax:* 215-590-3053

BAKER, LOUIS, PHYSICAL CHEMISTRY. *Current Pos:* assoc chemist, 58-70, SR CHEMIST, ARGONNE NAT LAB, 70- *Personal Data:* b Chicago, Ill, Dec 31, 27; m 51; c 4. *Educ:* Ill Inst Technol, BS, 49, MS, 51, PhD(chem), 55. *Honors & Awards:* E O Lawrence Award, US AEC, 73. *Prof Exp:* Aeronaut res scientist, Lewis Lab, Nat Adv Comt Aeronaut, 54-58. *Mem:* Am Chem Soc; Am Nuclear Soc. *Res:* Reactor safety; chemical kinetics and heat transfer. *Mailing Add:* 760 61st St Downers Grove IL 60516-1935

BAKER, LOUIS COOMBS WELLER, STRUCTURAL INORGANIC CHEMISTRY, HETEROPOLY COMPLEXES. *Current Pos:* chmn dept, 62-84, prof, 62-92, EMER PROF CHEM, GEORGETOWN UNIV, 92- *Personal Data:* b New York, NY, Nov 24, 21; m 64, Violet E Simmons; c William W S & Godfrey A S. *Educ:* Columbia Univ, AB, 43; Univ Pa, MS, 47, PhD(chem), 50. *Hon Degrees:* LHD, Georgetown Univ, 88. *Honors & Awards:* Tchugaev Medal, USSR Acad Sci, 73. *Prof Exp:* Asst instr chem, Univ Pa, 43-50, instr, 45-50, assoc, Johnson Found, 50-51; from asst prof to assoc prof & head inorg div, Boston Univ, 51-62. *Concurrent Pos:* Co-proj dir, Off Prod Res & Develop, 43-46; instr, Pa Area Cols, 45-49; external examr for doctorate, Univ Calcutta, 56-; consult, Various Petrochem Co, 57-, John Wiley & Sons, 68- & Nat Res Coun, 69-; Guggenheim fel, 60-; fel, Wash Acad Sci, 64-; lectr, Tour Univs, Romanian Ministry Educ, 73; Univs & Res Insts, USSR Acad Sci, 73; Plenary lectr, XV Int Conf on Coord Chem, 73; chmn, Comt Recommendations US Army Basic Sci Res, Nat Acad Sci, 74-78; consult sci educ, Ferdowsi Univ, Iran, 75-77; mem comt, Accreditation Cols & Univs, Middle States Asn, 75-80. *Mem:* Am Chem Soc; Sigma Xi (past pres). *Res:* Structures, properties and syntheses of heteropoly molybdates, tungstates and vanadates; coordination complexes; electron exchange and delocalization, magnetochemistry; high thermal efficiency engines; multinuclear nuclear magnetic resonance; synthetic inorganic chemistry; academic administration. *Mailing Add:* Dept Chem Georgetown Univ Washington DC 20057. *Fax:* 202-687-6209

BAKER, MALCHUS BROOKS, JR, HYDROLOGY, FORESTRY. *Current Pos:* HYDROLOGIST WATERSHED MGT, ROCKY MOUNTAIN FOREST & RANGE EXP STA, 69- *Personal Data:* b Alton, Ill, June 19, 41; m 70; c 3. *Educ:* Southern Ill Univ, BS, 64; Yale Univ, MF, 65; Univ Minn, PhD(forestry), 71. *Mem:* Am Geophys Union; Sigma Xi; Soc Am Foresters; Am Water Resources Asn. *Res:* Quantify the effects of vegetation manipulation upon stream flow, water quality and sediment yield. *Mailing Add:* 29 W Silver Spruce Ave Flagstaff AZ 86001-1354

BAKER, MARSHALL, PHYSICS. *Current Pos:* assoc prof physics, 62-66, PROF PHYSICS, UNIV WASH, 66- *Personal Data:* b Boston, Feb 12, 32. *Educ:* Harvard Univ, AB, 53, PhD, 57. *Prof Exp:* Res assoc physics, Stanford Univ, 57-59, asst prof, 59-62. *Concurrent Pos:* Vis prof, Univ Buenos Aires, 60 & 63, Univ Rome, 63-64, 79- 80, Tohoku Univ, Sandai, Japan, 64, Consumer Educ Resource Network, 74 & 80, Univ Paris, Orsay, 85-86; res sci, Nat Acad Sci, Lesedev physical guest, Moscow, 66, Inst Theoret Exp Physics, Moscow, 66, 70, 73-74; fel, John Simon Guggenheim Mem Found, 79-80. *Res:* Physics; published numerous articles. *Mailing Add:* Dept Physics Univ Wash Seattle WA 98195

BAKER, MARY ANN, MAMMALIAN PHYSIOLOGY, NEUROSCIENCES. *Current Pos:* assoc prof, 76-81, interirm dir, Biomed Sci Prog, 92-95, PROF BIOMED SCI, UNIV CALIF, RIVERSIDE, 81- *Personal Data:* b Los Angeles, Calif, Oct 11, 40; m 82, V H Shoemaker. *Educ:* Univ Redlands, BA, 61; Univ Calif, Santa Barbara, MA, 64; Univ Calif, Los Angeles, PhD(anat), 68. *Prof Exp:* Bank of Am-Giannini Found res fel, 68-69; NIH trainee physiol & biophys, Univ Wash, 69-70; asst prof, Sch Med, Univ Southern Calif, 70-73, assoc prof physiol, 73-76. *Mem:* Am Physiol Soc. *Res:* Mammalian thermoregulation and water balance. *Mailing Add:* Div Biomed Sci Univ Calif Riverside CA 92521. *Fax:* 909-787-5504; *E-Mail:* mary.baker@ucr.edu

BAKER, MAX LESLIE, RADIOBIOLOGY, BIOPHYSICS. *Current Pos:* Instr radiol, 69, instr radiobiol, 70-71, asst prof radiobiol, 71-77, assoc prof radiol, 77-86, PROF RADIOL, UNIV ARK, LITTLE ROCK, 86-, PROF PHYSIOL & BIOPHYS, MED SCI, 88- *Personal Data:* b Batesville, Ark, Aug 4, 43; m 69; c 3. *Educ:* Ark Col, BA, 65; Univ Ark, Little Rock, MS, 67, PhD(physiol, biophys), 70. *Concurrent Pos:* Fel biol, Univ Tex M D Anderson Hosp & Tumor Inst Houston, 69-70. *Mem:* Radiation Res Soc; Sigma Xi; Health Physics Soc. *Res:* Radiobiological basis of radiation therapy; radioprotective drugs; radiation safety. *Mailing Add:* Dept Radiol Univ Ark Med Sci 4301 W Markham Little Rock AR 72205-7101. *Fax:* 501-686-8136; *E-Mail:* mlbaker@life.uams.edu

BAKER, MERL, MECHANICAL ENGINEERING, ENGINEERING MANAGEMENT. *Current Pos:* provost prof eng, 82-85, DIR PRO CAREER ENHANCEMENT & PROF ENG, UNIV TENN, 82- *Personal Data:* b Cadiz, KY, July 11, 24; m 46, Emily Wilson; c Merl W & Marilyn R. *Educ:* Univ Ky, BS, 45; Purdue Univ, MS, 48, PhD, 52. *Honors & Awards:* Award, Am Soc Heating, Refrig & Air-Conditioning Engrs, 59. *Prof Exp:* Asst, Purdue Univ, 46-48; from asst prof mech eng to prof, Univ Ky, 48-63, exec dir res found, 53-63, res dir, Overseas prog, 56-63; dean of fac, sch mines & metall, Univ Mo-Rolla, 63-64, chancellor, 64-73; spec asst to pres, Univ Mo Syst, 74-77; lab wide coordr energy conserv, Oak Ridge Nat Labs, 77-79, energy mgt res specialist, Oak Ridge Nat Lab, 79-82. *Mem:* Am Soc Mech Engrs; fel Am Soc Eng Educ; Am Soc Eng Mgt; Sigma Xi. *Res:* Engineering management and management of technology; refrigeration; air conditioning; heat transfer; energy policy, legal and ethical issues in engineering. *Mailing Add:* Univ Tenn 615 McCallie Ave Chattanooga TN 37403-2598. *Fax:* 423-755-5229

BAKER, MICHAEL ALLEN, HEMATOLOGY, CANCER. *Current Pos:* assoc med, 72-73, from asst prof to assoc prof, 73-82, ASSOC, INST MED SCI, SCH GRAD STUDIES, UNIV TORONTO, 74-, PROFMED, 82-, ASSOC CHAIR, DEPT MED, 92-, DIR, ONCOL PROG & DEPT HEMAT, TORONTO GEN HOSP, 84-; PRES, NAT CANCER INST CAN, 91-; PHYSICIAN-IN-CHIEF, TORONTO HOSP, 92- *Personal Data:* b Toronto, Ont, Jan 24, 43; m 67, Barbara Woods; c Jeffrey & Jillian. *Educ:* Univ Toronto, MD, 66; FRCP(C), cert clin haematol, 71 & internal med, 74; Am Bd Internal Med, dipl & cert hemat, 72. *Honors & Awards:* William Goldie Prize, Univ Toronto, 75. *Prof Exp:* Intern, Toronto Gen Hosp, 66-67; asst resident internal med, Mt Sinai Hosp, New York, 67-69, chief resident med & clin resident hemat, 69-70, chief resident hemat, 70-71, res fel, 70-72; clin hematologist & oncologist, Div Hemat Oncol, Toronto Western Hosp, 72-84. *Concurrent Pos:* Asst med, Mt Sinai Sch Med, 67-69, instr, 69-72; Med Res Coun Can fel, 71-72; assoc, Ont Cancer Treatment & Res Found, 73-; dir, Interdept Dev Oncol, Toronto Western Hosp, 77-84, Div Hemat, Dept Med, 80-84, Div Hemat, Dept Med, Univ Toronto, 83-92, oncology prog, Toronto Hosp, 84-95 & Div Med Oncol, Toronto Gen Hosp, 84-87; consult, Princess Margaret Hosp, 78-96, Clin Inst, Addiction Res Found, Toronto, 86-96; vis prof, Univ Western Ont, 79, Eighth Ann Journee Hematologique, Univ Montreal, 81; head, Dept Hemat Labs, Toronto Gen Hosp, 85-87 & Div Hemat-Oncol, Toronto Hosp, 87-92; chmn, Subcomt Neoplasia, Am Soc Haematology, 85; bd dirs, Can Found AIDS Res, 87-92, Nat Cancer Inst Can, 89-95; assoc physician-in-chief, Toronto Hosp, 90-92; bd trustee, Toronto Hosp, 90-92, Toronto Hosp Foudn, 92-94; pres, Nat Cancer Inst, 91-94; interim clin head, Princess Margaret Comprehensive Cancer Ctr, 96- *Mem:* Am Fedn Clin Res; Am Soc Hemat; fel Am Col Physicians; Can Soc Clin Invest; AAAS; Can Oncol Soc; Am Soc Clin Oncol; Can Med Asn; Am Asn Cancer Res. *Res:* Studies of cell membrane changes in acute and chronic leukemia; clinical trials of treatment for leukemia; author of numerous publications. *Mailing Add:* Toronto Hosp 585 University Ave BW1-639 Toronto ON M5G 2C4 Can. *Fax:* 416-340-3545; *E-Mail:* mbaker@forhosp.toronto.on.ca

BAKER, MICHAEL H, APPLIED CHEMISTRY, CHEMICAL ECONOMICS. *Current Pos:* chmn, 80-93, PRES, CHEM/SERV INC, 51- *Personal Data:* b Roanoke, Va, Oct 25, 16; m 40; c 3. *Educ:* Pratt Inst, ChE, 38; Va Polytech Inst, BS, 39, MS, 40; Univ Md, cert, 42. *Honors & Awards:* Albert Einstein Award, Am Technicon Soc, 85. *Prof Exp:* Owner, Chem Prod Distrib Co, 37-40; plant-prod chem engr, Joseph Seagram Sons Co, 40-42; field develop engr, Davison Chem Co, 42-47; head chem prod eval, Gen Mills Inc, 47-51. *Concurrent Pos:* Ed, Minn Chemist, 60-62; consult, Vols Int Tech Asst; ed, Chem Distribr, 78-80. *Mem:* AAAS; Am Inst Chemists; Am Chem Soc; Inst Food Technol; Am Inst Chem Eng. *Res:* Application of raw materials of a chemical nature in the production of food products, paints, paper, cosmetics and related industries; chemical economics. *Mailing Add:* 715 SE Eighth St Minneapolis MN 55414

BAKER, NEAL KENTON, SOLAR PHYSICS, METEOROLOGY. *Current Pos:* Mem tech staff solar physics, Aerospace Corp, 68-71, mem techstaff optics, 75-79, proj engr, 79-83, SYST DIR, AEROSPACE CORP, 83- *Personal Data:* b Boston, Mass, Mar 20, 45; m 68. *Educ:* Harvard Univ, AB, 67; Pa State Univ, PhD(astron), 75. *Mem:* Am Astron Soc; Am Soc Photogram; Sigma Xi; Optical Soc Am. *Res:* Solar radio astronomy-microwave bursts, solar flares; image processing; meteorology. *Mailing Add:* 22468 Paul Revere Dr Calabasas CA 91302-5108

BAKER, NORMAN HODGSON, ASTROPHYSICS. *Current Pos:* from asst prof to assoc prof, 65-71 chmn, Dept Astron, 72-76, PROF ASTRON, COLUMBIA UNIV, 71- *Personal Data:* b Fergus Falls, Minn, Oct 23, 31; m 76, Doris B Nagel. *Educ:* Univ Minn, BA, 52; Cornell Univ, PhD(physics), 59. *Prof Exp:* Vis fel, Max Planck Inst, Munich, 59-61; res fel, NASA Goddard Inst, 61-64; res assoc, NY Univ, 64-65. *Concurrent Pos:* Mem, Inst F Advan Study, 62-63; co-ed, Astron J, 67-79 & ed, 79-84, Bulletin Am Astron Soc, co-ed, 69-79 & ed, 79-83. *Mem:* Am Phys Soc; Am Astron Soc; Royal Astron Soc; Int Astron Union. *Res:* Stellar structure and evolution; theory of stellar pulsation; convection in stars. *Mailing Add:* Dept Astron Columbia Univ 538 W 120th St New York NY 10027. *Fax:* 212-316-9504; *E-Mail:* nbaker@columbia.edu

BAKER, PAUL, JR, ASTROPHYSICS. *Current Pos:* RETIRED. *Personal Data:* b Ashland, Ky, Feb 10, 21; m 48, Iantha Dunton; c Paul M, Miriam A (Hatcher) & Jon C. *Educ:* Washington & Lee Univ, BA, 42; US Mil Acad, BS, 45; NC State Univ, MS, 52; Univ Denver, PhD(physics), 66. *Prof Exp:* Proj officer nuclear propulsion, Directorate Requirements, Hq, USAF, 52-56, chief tech br, Hartford Area, US AEC, 56-61, from instr to prof physics, USAF Acad, 61-67, head dept, 64-65, res assoc, 65-66, dir fac res, 66-67, chief, Tech Div, Directorate Space, Pentagon, 67-71, prog mgr, Defense Advan Res Proj Agency, Va, 71-75; consult, Nuclear Regulatory Comm, 75-76, res projs mgr, 76-85, sr safeguards scientist, 85-92. *Res:* Cosmic rays. *Mailing Add:* 4404 Random Ct Annandale VA 22003

BAKER, PAUL THORNELL, BIOLOGICAL ANTHROPOLOGY. *Current Pos:* res assoc, Biophys Lab, Pa State Univ, 57-58, from asst prof to prof anthrop, 58-68, actg head, Dept Sociol & Anthrop, 64-65, prof, Dept Anthrop, 64-80, exec officer, Anthrop Br, 65-68, actg head, Dept Anthrop, 68-69, head dept, 80-85, Evan Pugh prof, 81-87, EVAN PUGH EMER PROF ANTHROP, PA STATE UNIV, UNIVERSITY PARK, 88- *Personal Data:* b Burlington, Iowa, Feb 28, 27; m 49, Thelma Shoher; c Deborah, Amy, Joshua & Felicia. *Educ:* Univ NMex, BA, 51; Harvard Univ, PhD(anthrop), 56. *Honors & Awards:* Distinction in Soc Sci Award, Pa State Univ, 77; Huxley Mem Lectr & medallist, Royal Anthrop Inst, Gt Brit & Ireland, 82; Gorjanovic-Krambergeri Medal, Univ Zagreb, Yugoslavia; Gandhi Freedom Award, 91; Distinguished Serv Award, Am Anthrop Asn, 92; Darwin Lifetime Achievement Award, Am Asn Phys Anthropologists, 93; Fulbright Lectr, Brazil. *Prof Exp:* Res phys anthropologist, Environ Protection & Res Div, US Army Qm Res & Develop Ctr, 52-57. *Concurrent Pos:* res scholar, Peru, 62; US Army grant, 62-68; mem, NIH Behav Sci Fels Rev Comt, 65-69; prog dir, US Int Biol Prog Biol Human Pop at High Altitude, 65-74, mem, US Exec Comt Int Biol Prog, 70-74; NATO sr sci fel, Oxford Univ, 68; Nat Inst Gen Med Sci grant, 69-79; mem, Int Coun Sci Unions Comn Predictive World Ecosysts, 71-72; NSF grant, 71-74; ed, Am Anthropologist, 73-76; Guggenheim fel, 74-75; chmn, US Man & Biosphere Prog 12 Directorate, 75-77; consult, UNESCO, 75 & 79-, UN Environ Prog, 79; Nat Inst Child Health & Human Develop grant, 75-77; mem, Adv Coun Bd Trustees, Wenner-Gren Found Anthrop Res, Inc, 80-84; chmn, US Man & Biosphere Prog, 83-85; chair, Anthrop Sect, Nat Acad Sci, 84-87 & US Deleg, Int Cong Anthrop & Ethnol Sci, 88. *Mem:* Nat Acad Sci; fel Am Anthrop Asn; Am Asn Phys Anthropologists (pres, 69-71); Int Asn Human Biologists (pres, 80-); fel AAAS; Human Biol Coun (pres, 74-77); Int Union Anthrop & Ethnol Sci (vpres, 88-90, sr vpres, 93-98). *Res:* Adaptation to high altitude; biological effects of modernization in human populations; environmental health. *Mailing Add:* 47-450 Lulani St Kaneohe HI 96744. *Fax:* 808-239-8029; *E-Mail:* pbaker@uhunix

BAKER, PETER C, NEUROBIOLOGY, EMBRYOLOGY. *Current Pos:* RETIRED. *Personal Data:* b San Francisco, Calif, Feb 14, 33; m, Cecilie Goodrich; c Howard, Leslie, Jennifer & Michael. *Educ:* Univ Calif, Berkeley, AB, 56, MA, 61, PhD(zool), 66. *Prof Exp:* Instr biol, City Col San Francisco, 66-67; from asst prof to prof biol, Cleveland State Univ, 67-94. *Concurrent Pos:* Lectr genetics, Dept Biol, San Francisco State Col, 66-67. *Mem:* AAAS; Sigma Xi; Am Soc Zool; Nat Ctr Sci Educ; Am Inst Biol Sci. *Res:* Maturation of indoleamines in the mouse brain; mammals; drug affects on the maturing brain. *Mailing Add:* 39 Oakshore Dr Bratenahl OH 44108-1118

BAKER, PHILLIP JOHN, MICROBIOLOGY, IMMUNOLOGY. *Current Pos:* MICROBIOLOGIST, LAB MICROBIAL IMMUNITY, NIH, 70- *Personal Data:* b East Chicago, Ind, Aug 21, 35; m 67; c 2. *Educ:* Ind State Univ, BA, 60; Univ Wis, MS, 62, PhD(bact), 65. *Prof Exp:* Res asst bact, Univ Wis, 60-65. *Concurrent Pos:* USPHS fel immunol, Lab Immunol, NIH, 65-67, staff fel microbiol & immunol, Lab Germfree Animal Res, 67-69, sr staff fel, Lab Microbial Immunity, 69-70, res microbiologist, 70-76, head microbiol & immunol sect, 76-; chmn, Immunol Div, Am Soc Microbiol, 83-85. *Mem:* AAAS; Am Asn Immunologists; Reticuloendothelial Soc; Am Soc Microbiol; Sigma Xi. *Res:* Antibody formation at cellular level, particularly microbial antigens or microbial products; initiation of antibody synthesis and tolerance to microbial polysaccharide antigens; factors related to virulence of bacteria; regulation of antibody responses; suppressor T cells; genetics of the immune response. *Mailing Add:* Div Microbiol & Infectious Dis Nat Inst Allergy & Infectious Dis NIH 10006 Frederick Ave Kensington MD 20895-3401

BAKER, R RALPH, PLANT PATHOLOGY, MYCOLOGY. *Current Pos:* PROF BOT & PLANT PATH, COLO STATE UNIV, 54- *Personal Data:* b Houston, Tex, Aug 31, 24; wid; c 6. *Educ:* Colo Agr & Mech Col, BS, 48, MS, 50; Univ Calif, Berkeley, PhD(plant path), 54. *Honors & Awards:* Florists Mutual Award, 59; Pennock Distinguished Serv Award, 65; Apollo Prog Group Achievement Award, NASA, 73, Group Achievement Award, US-USSR Biol Satellite Mission, 76-; Sci Achievement Medal, Colo State Univ, 76. *Concurrent Pos:* Assoc ed, Phytopath, 61-63 & 76-79, sr ed, 79-81; mem comt control soil borne pathogens, Nat Acad Sci, 62-; asst dir biol res, Res Found, 62-64; vis prof, Univ Calif, Berkeley, 63-64; chmn comt planning manned orbital res & lab exp in space biol, Am Inst Biol Sci, 65-68, chmn Study Group II, 69-70, comt study role of the lunar receiving lab in the post Apollo biol & biomed activities; mem plant sci comt, Comn Undergrad Educ Biol Sci, 66, partic workshop for teaching biol to nonsci majors, Bar Harbor, 68; NSF sr fel & vis prof, Cambridge Univ, 68-69; Lunar Sample Rev Bd, 70-73; mem bd govs, Am Inst Biol Sci, 71-75, mem educ comt, 74-; partic, USA/Repub of China Coop Sci Prog, 75; chmn fungal antagonists group, Fungal Biocontrols Workshop, Am Inst Biol Sci-Environ Protect Agency, Univ Ark, 75; mem space processing payload adv subcomt, NASA, 75-76; NSF partic, US-USSR Coop Symp, 76; Sigma Xi lectr, 76-78; mem study group recombinant DNA, Environ Protection Agency, 77; mem Adv Comt concerned with treatment of returned Mars (NASA-JPL) samples; mem, IR4-Biorational Workshop; sr ed, Can J Microbiol, 87-; assoc ed, Crop Protection, 87-; mem, Subcomt Biol Control, Exp Stas Comt Organized Policy, 88- *Mem:* Fel AAAS; fel Am Phytopath Soc. *Res:* Ecology of soil microorganisms; physiology of sexual reproduction in fungi; mathematical biology; ornamental pathology; space biology; biological control. *Mailing Add:* Dir Phys Plant Colo State Univ Ft Collins CO 80523-0001

BAKER, RALPH ROBINSON, SURGERY. *Current Pos:* From instr to prof, 62-75, PROF ONCOL, SCH MED, JOHNS HOPKINS UNIV, 75- *Personal Data:* b Baltimore, Md, Dec 30, 28; m 53; c 4. *Educ:* Johns Hopkins Univ, AB, 50, MD, 54. *Concurrent Pos:* Am Cancer Soc adv clin fel, 65-68; consult, US Vet Admin Hosp, Perry Point & Loch Raven, Md, 64-68. *Mem:* Am Surg Asn; Am Asn Thoracic Surg; Soc Surg Alimentary Tract; Soc Univ Surg; Asn Acad Surg. *Res:* Academic surgery; cancer and transplantation research. *Mailing Add:* Surg Johns Hopkins Univ Med Sch 720 Rutland Ave Baltimore MD 21205-2109

BAKER, RALPH STANLEY, WEED SCIENCE, COTTON. *Current Pos:* RETIRED. *Personal Data:* b LeRaysville, Pa, Aug 1, 27; m 54; c 2. *Educ:* Univ Del, BS, 57; Purdue Univ, MS, 59, PhD(plant physiol), 61. *Prof Exp:* Researcher weed sci, Delta Br, Miss Agr & Forestry Exp Sta, 61-91. *Mem:* Weed Sci Soc Am; Sigma Xi; Coun Agr & Sci Technol. *Res:* Weeds, herbicides and cultural methods for controlling weeds in cotton. *Mailing Add:* 409 N Deer Creek Dr W Leland MS 38756

BAKER, RALPH THOMAS, HOMOGENEOUS CATALYSIS. *Current Pos:* RES CHEMIST, E I DUPONT DE NEMOURS & CO, INC, 81- *Personal Data:* b Penticton, BC, Apr 10, 53; m 78; c 2. *Educ:* Univ BC, BSc, 75; Univ Calif, Los Angeles, PhD(chem), 80. *Prof Exp:* Lab asst, BC Govt Lab, 75; teaching asst, Univ Calif, Los Angeles, 75-76; fel, Pa State Univ, 80-81. *Mem:* Am Chem Soc. *Res:* Metalloborane and carborane synthesis; metal atom synthesis; homogeneous catalysis; multinuclear nuclear magnetic resonance; early transition metal diorganophosphide synthesis; early-late phosphide-bridged heterobimetallic synthesis; fluoroorganometallic synthesis; transition metal-catalyzed hydroboration. *Mailing Add:* Los Alamos Nat Lab CST-18 MS-J514 Los Alamos NM 87545

BAKER, RAYMOND MILTON, SOMATIC CELL GENETICS, EXPERIMENTAL THERAPEUTICS. *Current Pos:* ASSOC RES PROF PHARMACOL, STATE UNIV NY, BUFFALO, 81- *Personal Data:* b Kansas City, Mo, Nov 7, 40; m 78, Lynette A Spencer; c Samuel E & Joseph R. *Educ:* Yale Univ, BS, 62; Univ Calif, Berkeley, PhD(biophys), 69. *Prof Exp:* USPHS fel med biophys, Univ Toronto-Ont Cancer Inst, 69-70; staff scientist, Ont Cancer Inst, 71-74 & Hosp Sick Children, Toronto, 73-74; from asst prof to assoc prof genetics, Dept Biol & Ctr Cancer Res, Mass Inst Technol, 74-81; assoc chief cancer res scientist, Dept Exp Therapeut, Roswell Park Cancer Inst, 81-96. *Concurrent Pos:* From lectr to asst prof med biophys, Univ Toronto, 71-74; prin investr, NIH, 74-94, mem, Exp Therapeut-2 Study Sect, 85-90; consult, Elket Assocs, Buffalo, 94- *Mem:* AAAS; Am Asn Cancer Res; Genetics Soc Am. *Res:* Genetics of cellular drug resistances including, clinical drug resistances, transient phenotypes, membrane mutants, repair and recombination. *Mailing Add:* 123 Wesley Ave Buffalo NY 14214-1655. *Fax:* 716-832-4312; *E-Mail:* elket@ix.netcom.com

BAKER, REES TERENCE KEITH, KINETICS, CATALYSIS. *Current Pos:* PROF CHEM, NORTHEASTERN UNIV, BOSTON, 96- *Personal Data:* b Coventry, UK, Nov 24, 38; m 90, Nelly Rodriguez; c Gail E & Lois M. *Educ:* Liverpool Polytech, ARIC, 63, ARC, 64; Univ Wales, PhD(chem), 66, DSc, 78. *Honors & Awards:* Graffin lectr, Am Carbon Soc, 85-86, Pettinos Award, 87; Light Metals Award, Minerals, Metals & Mat Soc, 93. *Prof Exp:* Sr scientific res officer, Atomic Energy Res Estab, 68-75; sr res assoc, Exxon Res & Eng Co, 75-86; prof, Chem Eng Dept, Auburn Univ, Ala, 86-92; prof mat, Pa Sate Univ, 92-96. *Concurrent Pos:* Hougen prof, Univ Wis-Madison, 88; distinguished vis prof, Kyushu Univ, Japan, 93. *Mem:* Am Carbon Soc; Am Chem Soc; Mat Res Soc; NAm Catalysis Soc. *Res:* Examination of various aspects of reaction involving gas and solid systems, with the emphasis on the catalytic behavior of metals and metal oxides during carbon deposition and carbon gasification. *Mailing Add:* 12 Old Stable Dr Mansfield MA 02048

BAKER, RICHARD A, ELECTRICAL ENGINEERING. *Current Pos:* from asst prof to assoc prof, 61-77, PROF ELEC ENG, WASH STATE UNIV, 77- *Personal Data:* b Enumclaw, Wash, Mar 13, 34; m 55; c 3. *Educ:* Wash State Univ, BS, 56; NY Univ, MEE, 59; Univ Calif, Berkeley, PhD(elec eng), 67. *Prof Exp:* Mem tech staff, Bell Tel Labs, 56-60; sr proj engr, AC Spark Plug Div, Gen Motors Corp, 60-61. *Concurrent Pos:* Guest prof, Brown Boveri Res Ctr, Baden, Switz, 80-81, Asea Brown Boveri, 87-88. *Mem:* Inst Elec & Electronics Engrs; Sigma Xi. *Res:* System theory and control theory, principally, stability analysis; power systems. *Mailing Add:* Elec Eng & Comput Sci Wash State Univ 1 SE Stadium Way Pullman WA 99164-0001

BAKER, RICHARD DEAN, chemistry; deceased, see previous edition for last biography

BAKER, RICHARD FRELIGH, biophysics, for more information see previous edition

BAKER, RICHARD GRAVES, PALYNOLOGY, QUATERNARY GEOLOGY. *Current Pos:* from asst prof to assoc prof, 70-82, PROF GEOL, UNIV IOWA, 82-, DEPT CHMN, 92-, PROF BIOL SCI. *Personal Data:* b Merrill, Wis, June 12, 38; m 90, Debby J (Zieglowski); c Kristina, James & Charity. *Educ:* Univ Wis-Madison, BA, 60; Univ Minn, Minneapolis, MS, 64; Univ Colo, Boulder, PhD(geol), 69. *Prof Exp:* Res assoc, Ctr Climatic Res, Univ Wis-Madison, 69-70. *Mem:* AAAS; Geol Soc Am; Am Quaternary Asn; Am Asn Stratig Palynologists; Ecol Soc Am. *Res:* Quaternary palynology and plant macrofossil analysis in the Rocky Mountains and Midwest. *Mailing Add:* Dept Geol Univ Iowa Iowa City IA 52242

BAKER, RICHARD H(OWELL), ELECTRONICS ENGINEERING, INFORMATION SYSTEMS ARCHITECTURE. *Current Pos:* electronic syst consult, 51-68, mgt consult, 58-76, CONSULT, 76- *Personal Data:* b Long Beach, Calif, Jan 5, 21; m 47; c Douglas B & Gwendolyn (Scott). *Prof Exp:* Prototype engr, Lockheed Aircraft Corp, 41-43; res engr, Northrop Aircraft Corp, 47-48, chief, Electronic Comput Opers, 48-50; proj engr, Bill Jack Sci Instrument Co, 50-51. *Concurrent Pos:* Chief engr, Digital Control Systs, Inc, 51-53; lectr eng & head dept, USN Elec Eng & Radio Mat Sch, Tex; consult, Stanford Res Inst, 54-58, head electronics indust res, 54-58; consult to chief sig off, US Army, 53; chmn bd dirs & vpres, ABL, Inc, 62-68. *Mem:* Sigma Xi. *Res:* Electronic computer and control systems; communications system design; electronics management and marketing; magnetic recording technique; system architect, video-graphic data systems and hardware design; long term information and energy systems. *Mailing Add:* PO Box 420245 San Diego CA 92142

BAKER, RICHARD H, GENETICS. *Current Pos:* FLA MED ENTOM LAB, UNIV FLA. *Personal Data:* b Hayfield, Minn, Sept 14, 36; m 61; c 2. *Educ:* Univ Ill, BS, 59, MS, 62, PhD(zool, genetics), 65. *Prof Exp:* Res assoc mosquito genetics, Univ Ill, 65; res assoc, 65-66, asst prof mosquito genetics, 66-69, assoc prof int med, Sch Med, Univ Md, Baltimore, dir, Pakistan Med Res Ctr, Lahore, Pakistan, 69-79, prof & dir, Int Health Prog, Univ Md, Baltimore, 82- *Concurrent Pos:* Consult, WHO, 65. *Mem:* Genetics Soc Am; Entom Soc Am; Am Soc Trop Med & Hyg; Am Genetic Asn; Am Mosquito Control Asn; Sigma Xi. *Res:* Mosquito genetics and cyto-genetics. *Mailing Add:* Fla Med Entom Lab 200 Ninth St SE Vero Beach FL 32962-4657

BAKER, RICHARD WILLIAM, PHYSICAL CHEMISTRY, POLYMER CHEMISTRY. *Current Pos:* AT MEMBRANE TECHNOL & RES. *Personal Data:* b Boreham Wood, Eng, Aug 18, 41; m 68. *Educ:* London Univ, BS, 63, DIC, 65, PhD(phys chem), 66. *Prof Exp:* Sr chemist, Amicon Corp, 66-68; res fel, Polymer Res Inst, Brooklyn Polytech Inst, 68-70; sr scientist, Alza Corp, 70-74; dir res, Bend Res Inc, 74- *Mem:* Royal Soc Chem; AAAS; Am Chem Soc. *Res:* Physical chemistry of synthetic polymer membranes as applied to separation processes such as ultrafiltration and reverse osmosis, and the application of membranes to sustained release drug-delivery systems. *Mailing Add:* Membrane Technol & Res 1360 Willow Rd Suite 103 Menlo Park CA 94025-1516

BAKER, ROBERT ANDREW, ENVIRONMENTAL SCIENCES. *Current Pos:* RETIRED. *Personal Data:* b Lakewood, Ohio, Sept 8, 25; m 47, Peggy Plummer. *Educ:* NC State Univ, BS, 49; Villanova Univ, MS, 55 & 58; Univ Pittsburgh, DSc(environ health eng), 69. *Honors & Awards:* Award of Merit, Am Soc Testing & Mat, 68, Max Hecht Award, 70 & Award Sensory Res, 73; Eng of Distinction, Eng Joint Coun, 70; Buswell-Porges Award, Inst Advan Sanitation Res, 72; Larry Cecil Environ Award, Am Inst Chem Engrs, 84; Res Award, AWWA, 85. *Prof Exp:* Chem engr, Atlantic Refining Co, 49-57; sr staff eng environ sci, Franklin Inst, 57-64; sr fel, Mellon Inst Sci, 64-70; dir environ sci, Teledyne Brown Eng, 71-73; regional res hydrologist & chief, Gulf Coast Hydro-Sci Ctr, US Geol Surv, 73-91. *Concurrent Pos:* Consult, Gulf Mex Prog Tech Comts. *Mem:* Am Chem Soc; Am Water Works Asn; fel Am Soc Testing & Mat; fel AAAS; fel Am Inst Chem Engrs; Int Soc Water Pollution & Control. *Res:* Direction of interdisciplinary research involving various aspects of the hydrological cycle with personal emphasis on trace organic contaminants in the environment. *Mailing Add:* US Geol Surv Bldg 2101 Stennis Space Center MS 39529

BAKER, ROBERT CARL, FOOD SCIENCE. *Current Pos:* from asst prof to assoc prof, 49-56, dir food sci & mkt, 69-75, PROF FOOD SCI, CORNELL UNIV, 57-, CHMN, DEPT POULTRY & AVIAN SCI, 79- *Personal Data:* b Newark, NY, Dec 29, 21; m 44; c 5. *Educ:* Cornell Univ, BS, 43; Pa State Univ, MS, 49; Purdue Univ, PhD(food sci), 58. *Prof Exp:* Asst prof poultry exten, Pa State Univ, 46-49. *Concurrent Pos:* Inst Am Poultry Industs food res award, 59; mem, Comt Animal Prod, Nat Acad Sci, 65-68. *Mem:* AAAS; Sigma Xi; Poultry Sci Asn; Inst Food Technologists. *Res:* Bacteriology; microbiology of eggs; new poultry meat and egg products; new fish products; biochemistry. *Mailing Add:* 112 Rice Hall Cornell Univ Ithaca NY 14853-5601

BAKER, ROBERT CHARLES, ECOLOGY, SCIENCE EDUCATION. *Current Pos:* RETIRED. *Personal Data:* b Blackduck, Minn, June 17, 30; m 54; c 6. *Educ:* Bemidji State Col, BS, 54; Univ NDak, MSEd, 55; Ore State Univ, MS, 63. *Prof Exp:* Teacher high sch, 55-56; instr sci & math, Lab Sch, 56-68, actg prin, 59-62, asst prof sci educ, 63-65, Minn State Col Bd fel, 65-66; asst prof sci educ, Bemidji State Univ, 66-67, dir continuing educ, 67-68, assoc prof, 67-81, prof biol & sci educ, 81-91. *Concurrent Pos:* Adv, State Curric Environ Educ Kindergarten to 12th grade, 70- *Mem:* AAAS; Am Inst Biol Sci; Nat Soc Stud Educ; Nat Asn Biol Teachers; Nat Sci Teachers Asn. *Res:* Environmental pollution, especially solutions to land use problems and waste disposal; statistical evaluation of general biology program, traditional versus experimental; biological and attitudinal analysis of Upper Mississippi, especially Iowa-Itasca. *Mailing Add:* 1005 17th Ave N St Cloud MN 56303

BAKER, ROBERT DAVID, EPITHELIAL PHYSIOLOGY. *Current Pos:* From instr to asst prof, 59-64, ASSOC PROF PHYSIOL, UNIV TEX, MED BR, GALVESTON, 64- *Personal Data:* b Chicago, Ill, July 7, 29; div; c 4. *Educ:* Iowa Wesleyan Col, BS, 54; Univ Iowa, MS, 57, PhD(physiol), 59. *Concurrent Pos:* USPHS grants, 60-64 & 68-75. *Mem:* AAAS; Am Physiol Soc; Biophys Soc. *Res:* Intestinal absorption; transport of materials across biological membranes. *Mailing Add:* Dept Physiol & Biophys Univ Tex Med Sch Galveston 301 University Blvd Galveston TX 77550-2708

BAKER, ROBERT DONALD, FOREST MANAGEMENT, REMOTE SENSING. *Current Pos:* PROF FOREST MGT, TEX A&M UNIV, 75- *Personal Data:* b Chico, Calif, Dec 7, 27; m 58, Mary A Brooks; c Allison. *Educ:* Univ Calif, BS, 51, MF, 52; State Univ NY, PhD, 57. *Honors & Awards:* Res Award, Tex Forestry Asn. *Prof Exp:* From asst prof to prof forest mgt, Stephen F Austin State Univ, 56-74. *Concurrent Pos:* Nat dir, Am Soc Photogram, 75-77. *Mem:* Fel Soc Am Foresters; emer mem Am Soc Photogram. *Res:* Forest mensuration; remote sensing; forest history. *Mailing Add:* Dept Forest Sci Tex A&M Univ College Station TX 77843-2135. *Fax:* 409-845-6049

BAKER, ROBERT FRANK, MOLECULAR BIOLOGY, GENETICS. *Current Pos:* from asst prof to assoc prof, 68-83, PROF MOLECULAR BIOL, UNIV SOUTHERN CALIF, 83- *Personal Data:* b Weiser, Idaho, Apr 9, 36; m 65, Mary Murphy; c Allison L & Steven M. *Educ:* Stanford Univ, BS, 59; Brown Univ, PhD(biol), 66. *Prof Exp:* Fel microbial genetics, Stanford Univ, 66-68. *Concurrent Pos:* Vis prof, Harvard Med Sch, 75-76; genetics study sect, NIH, 77-79, 82; dir, Molecular Biol Div, Univ Southern Calif, 78-80, mem, Univ Southern Calif Med Sch, Comprehensive Cancer Ctr, 84- *Mem:* Am Soc Microbiol; Am Soc Zoologists; Sigma Xi. *Res:* Gene regulation in eucaryotic cells; molecular oncology. *Mailing Add:* Molecular Biol Univ Southern Calif Los Angeles CA 90089-1340. *Fax:* 213-740-0863; *E-Mail:* baker@molbio.usc.edu

BAKER, ROBERT G, BIOPHYSICS, NUCLEAR PHYSICS. *Current Pos:* RETIRED. *Personal Data:* b Kindersley, Sask, Dec 17, 18; m 42; c 4. *Educ:* Univ Sask, BA, 50, MA, 52; Univ Toronto, PhD(physics), 60. *Prof Exp:* Res officer radiol, Nat Res Coun Can, 52-54; physicist radiation ther, Ont Cancer Found, 54-58; physicist isotopes, Ont Cancer Inst, 60-68; asst prof med biophys, Univ Toronto, 62-68; chief physicist, Ont Cancer Found, Ottawa Civic Hosp, 68-81. *Mem:* Can Asn Physicists; Soc Nuclear Med. *Res:* Medical biophysics; instrumentation and application of isotopes to diagnosis and treatment of disease, especially cancer. *Mailing Add:* 181 Freeland Dr Stratford ON N4Z 1H2 Can

BAKER, ROBERT GEORGE, NEUROBIOLOGY. *Current Pos:* PROF PHYSIOL & BIOPHYS, MED CTR, NY UNIV, 76- *Personal Data:* b Streator, Ill, Sept 1, 40; m 64; c 2. *Educ:* NCent Col, BA, 62; Univ Ill, PhD(pharmacol), 67. *Prof Exp:* Fel pharmacol, Univ Ill, Nat Inst Neurol Dis & Blindness, 67-68; USPHS spec fel neurobiol, Inst Brain Res, Univ Tokyo, 68-69; asst prof, Dept Neurobiol, Inst Biomed Res, Am Med Asn, 69-70; asst prof physiol & biophysics, Div Neurobiol, Univ Iowa, 70-73, assoc prof, 73-76. *Concurrent Pos:* Vis prof, Physiol du Travail Ergonomie Conservatone Nat des Artsetmetiels, Paris, France, 71, Reg Primate Res Ctr, Univ Wash, 73; consult, Commmun Sci Study Sect, NIH, 76-80. *Mem:* Fedn Am Scientists; AAAS; Soc Neurosci; Am Physiol Soc; Int Brain Res Orgn. *Res:* Physiological organization of eye movements with emphasis on synaptic mechanisms in the brainstem and cerebellum of vertebrates. *Mailing Add:* Dept Physiol & Biophys Med Ctr NY Univ 550 First Ave New York NY 10016-6402

BAKER, ROBERT HENRY, COMPUTER SCIENCES. *Current Pos:* RETIRED. *Personal Data:* b Lexington, Ky, Apr 5, 34; m 57; c 3. *Educ:* Trinity Col, Conn, BS, 56; Ind Univ, PhD(biochem), 60. *Prof Exp:* NSF fels, Univ Wis, 60-62; res assoc phys & anal chem, Upjohn Co, 61-66, sect head comput systs, Res Comput Ctr, 66-69, mgr comput systs res & develop, 69-72, mgr admin, Comput Ctr, 72-79, mgr, Future Technologies Res & Develop, 79-90. *Mem:* Am Chem Soc. *Res:* Computer and telephone systems resource management. *Mailing Add:* 5147 Colony Woods Dr Kalamazoo MI 49009-9735

BAKER, ROBERT J(ETHRO), JR, CERAMIC ENGINEERING, CHEMISTRY. *Current Pos:* PRES, RATHBONE PROD, 77- *Personal Data:* b Dayton, Ohio, June 10, 38; m 61; c 3. *Educ:* Univ Ill, MS, 63, PhD(ceramic eng), 64; Mass Inst Technol, SM, 72. *Prof Exp:* Res scientist, Hanford Labs, Gen Elec Co, 64-65; res scientist, Pac Northwest Labs, Battelle Mem Inst, 65-66, mgr mat process develop, 66-67, mgr, Battelle Develop Corp, Washington/Ohio, 67-74; founder, Venture Resources Int, Ohio, 74- *Mem:* Sigma Xi; Am Ceramic Soc; Nat Inst Ceramic Engrs; Newcomen Soc. *Res:* Materials and process research, development and application; high temperature materials; characterization of powders, microstructure analysis and correlation with properties and behavior. *Mailing Add:* 2901 Berwick Blvd Columbus OH 43209

BAKER, ROBERT JOHN, PLANT BREEDING, QUANTITATIVE GENETICS. *Current Pos:* sr res scientist, 78-87, PROF, UNIV SASK, 87- *Personal Data:* b Cold Lake, Alta, June 10, 38; m 60; c 2. *Educ:* Univ Sask, BSA, 61, MSc, 62; Univ Minn, PhD(genetics), 66. *Prof Exp:* Res scientist plant breeding, Can Dept Agr, 66-78. *Mem:* Crop Sci Soc Am; Agr Inst Can; fel Am Soc Agron; fel Crop Sci Soc Am. *Res:* Methods of improving quantitative characteristics in self-pollinated species. *Mailing Add:* Dept Crop Sci Univ Sask 51 Campus Dr Saskatoon SK S7N 5A8 Can

BAKER, ROBERT M L, JR, DESIGN OF INTERNET SYSTEMS, DESIGN & FABRICATION OF WIND-MILL ELECTRICAL SYSTEMS. *Current Pos:* PRES & CHIEF EXEC OFFICER, KRELL LABS, 97- *Personal Data:* b Los Angeles, Calif, Sept 1, 30; m 64, Bonnie S Vold; c Randy, Robert M L III & Robin M L. *Educ:* Univ Calif, Los Angeles, BA, 54, MA, 56, PhD(eng & astron), 58. *Honors & Awards:* Dirk Brouwer Award for Outstanding Contribs Astrodyn & Flight Mechs, Am Inst Aeronaut & Astronaut, 76. *Prof Exp:* Asst prof, Dept Eng, Univ Calif, Los Angeles, 58-64; head, Astrodyn Res Ctr, Lockheed Aircraft, 62-64; assoc mgr math anal, Comput Sci Corp, 64-80; pres & chief exec officer, West Coast Univ, 80-97. *Concurrent Pos:* Ed, Astronaut Sci, Am Astronaut Soc, 59-63; chmn bd, Transp Sci Corp, 65- *Mem:* Assoc fel AAAS; fel Am Astronaut Soc; fel Am Inst Aeronaut & Astronaut; fel Inst Navig. *Res:* Development of networks and devices for the Internet-alternate linking intercom control; research and development of vertical-axis windmill electricity generators. *Mailing Add:* 8123 Tuscany Ave Playa del Rey CA 90293. *Fax:* 310-821-1694; *E-Mail:* bakerjr@gte.net

BAKER, ROBERT NORTON, MEDICINE. *Current Pos:* prof neurol, Med Ctr, Univ Nebr, Omaha, 70-72, chief neurol serv, Creighton-St Joseph Hosp, 74-76, PROF NEUROL & PATH, UNIV NEBR & CREIGHTON COL MED, 72-, EMER PROF NEUROL, UNIV NEBR, 77- *Personal Data:* b Inglewood, Calif, Mar 25, 23; m 71, Noreen J Isaak; c Mark, Kent & Melanie. *Educ:* Park Col, BA, 44; Univ Southern Calif, MD, 50. *Prof Exp:* Lab asst comp anat, Univ Mo, 42-43; asst biochem, Univ Southern Calif, 46-48, asst anat, 49-50, instr neuroanat, 50-53; from instr to assoc prof med neurol, Med Ctr, Univ Calif, Los Angeles, 53-70. *Concurrent Pos:* Chief, Neurol Sect, Vet Admin Ctr, Gen Med & Surg Hosp, 53-54 & 56-70; Vet Admin liaison, Neurol A Study Sect, NIH, 71-75. *Mem:* AMA; Am Acad Neurol; Am Asn Neuropath; Am Neurol Asn; Col Med Soc. *Res:* Experimental neuropathology; electron microscopic studies of cerebral vascular disease especially cerebral edema, hypertensive encephalopathy and cerebral embolism; clinical and pathological studies of cerebral vascular diseases and their metabolic aspects. *Mailing Add:* 555 Prospect Ave PO Box 1349 Estes Park CO 80517-1349

BAKER, ROLLIN HAROLD, ZOOLOGY. *Current Pos:* CUR, PRAIRIE EDGE MUS, EAGLE LAKE, TEX, 83- *Personal Data:* b Cordova, Ill, Nov 11, 16; m 39, Mary E Waddell; c Elizabeth A, Bruce R & Byron L. *Educ:* Univ Tex, BA, 37; Tex A&M Univ, MS, 38; Univ Kans, PhD(zool), 48. *Prof Exp:* Field biologist, State Coop Wildlife Res Unit, Tex, 38-39; wildlife biologist, State Game, Fish & Oyster Comn, 39-43; vis investr, Rockefeller Inst, 44; asst instr zool, Univ Kans, 46-48; from instr to assoc prof & asst cur mammals, Mus Natural Hist, 48-55; prof zool, Fish & Wildlife & dir mus, Mich State Univ, 55-83. *Concurrent Pos:* Leader, Mus Expeds, Latin Am, 50-82. *Mem:* AAAS; Am Soc Mammal; Wildlife Soc; Soc Study Evolution; Ecol Soc Am; Am Ornith Union. *Res:* Mammalian taxonomy, distribution and ecology; author of 160 publications on vertebrate zoology mostly mammals. *Mailing Add:* 302 N Strickland St Eagle Lake TX 77434

BAKER, RONALD G, HISTORY OF MATH. *Current Pos:* PROF MATH & CHMN, DEPT MATH & COMPUT SCI, EDINBORO UNIV PA, 85- *Personal Data:* b Erie, Pa, Mar 21, 39; m 61; c 5. *Educ:* Edinboro Univ, Pa, BS, 60; State Univ NY, Albany, MD, 65; State Univ NY, Buffalo, DEduc, 71. *Mem:* Math Asn Am; Data Processing Mgt Assoc. *Res:* History of mathematics. *Mailing Add:* Dept Math & Comput Sci Edinboro Univ 219 Meadville St Edinboro PA 16444-0001

BAKER, SAMUEL I, radiation physics, for more information see previous edition

BAKER, SAUL PHILLIP, geriatrics, cardiology; deceased, see previous edition for last biography

BAKER, SHIRLEY MARIE, bivalve physiology, for more information see previous edition

BAKER, STEPHEN DENIO, PHYSICS. *Current Pos:* Res assoc & lectr, 63-66, from asst prof to assoc prof, 66-73, PROF PHYSICS, RICE UNIV, 73- *Personal Data:* b Durham, NC, Nov 30, 36; m 62; c 2. *Educ:* Duke Univ, BS, 57; Yale Univ, MS, 59, PhD(physics), 63. *Mem:* Am Phys Soc; Am Asn Physics Teachers; AAAS. *Mailing Add:* Dept Physics Rice Univ PO Box 1892 Houston TX 77251

BAKER, STEPHEN PHILLIP, BIOCHEMICAL PHARMACOLOGY. *Current Pos:* from asst prof to assoc prof, 79-89, PROF, DEPT PHARMACOL & INTERIM CHMN, DEPT PHARMACOL & THERAPEUT, COL MED, UNIV FLA, GAINESVILLE, 89- *Personal Data:* b Auburn, NY, Nov 20, 48; c 1. *Educ:* Univ Mass, BA, 71; Univ Aston, Birmingham, Eng, PhD(biochem pharmacol), 76. *Prof Exp:* Res technician, Dept Pharmacol, Sch Med, Univ Rochester, 71-72; res asst, Dept Pharmacol, Univ Aston, Birmingham, Eng, 72-73; res assoc, Dept Pharmacol, Univ Miami, 76-79. *Concurrent Pos:* Prin investr, NIH, 80-91, Am Heart Asn, 80-92 & Am Fedn Aging Res, Inc, 85; consult, Brain Inst, Mt Sinai Med Ctr & Univ Miami, 80 & NIH, 88; mem, Peer-Rev Comt, Am Heart Asn, 82-87, Cardiovasc & Renal Rev Group, NIH, 88 & Neurol Sci Study Sect, NIH, 89. *Mem:* Am Soc Pharmacol & Therapeut; Soc Neurosci. *Res:* Author of numerous technical publications; awarded one US patent. *Mailing Add:* Dept Pharmacol Univ Fla Col Med JHMHC Box J-267 Gainesville FL 32610-0267

BAKER, SUSAN PARDEE, EPIDEMIOLOGY, INJURY CONTROL. *Current Pos:* PROF HEALTH POLICY & MGT, SCH HYG & PUB HEALTH, JOHNS HOPKINS UNIV, 68- *Personal Data:* b Atlanta, Ga, May 31, 30; m 51, Timothy D; c 3. *Educ:* Cornell Univ, BA, 51; Johns Hopkins Univ, MPH, 68. *Honors & Awards:* Prince Bernhard Medal for Dissertation in Traffic Med, 74; Stone Lectr, Am Trauma Soc, 85; Charles A Dana Award, 89. *Concurrent Pos:* Res assoc, Off Chief Med Exam Md, 68-81; mem bd dirs, Baltimore Safety Coun, 69-74; adj asst prof prev med, Sch Med, Univ Md, 79-; chmn, Nat Accident Sampling Syst Rev Bd, 76-80; co-chmn, Nat Symp Injury Control, 81; vchmn trauma comt, Nat Res Coun, 84-85; mem, Adv Comt Injury Control, Ctr Dis Control, 89. *Mem:* Am Asn Automotive Med (pres, 74-75); Am Trauma Soc (bd dirs, 72-); Am Pub Health Asn. *Res:* Injury epidemiology and prevention; burns; driver and pedestrian fatalities; alcohol; drowning; carbon monoxide poisoning; emergency medical services; evaluation; falls in the elderly; injury severity scoring; aviation safety and occupational safety. *Mailing Add:* Sch Hyg & Pub Health Johns Hopkins Univ 624 N Broadway Baltimore MD 21205

BAKER, THEODORE PAUL, COMPUTER SCIENCE. *Current Pos:* MEM FAC, DEPT COMPUT SCI, FLA STATE UNIV, 80- *Personal Data:* b Abington, Pa, Dec 15, 49; m 73, Syauchen Chang; c 3. *Educ:* Cornell Univ, AB, 70, PhD(comput sci), 74. *Prof Exp:* Asst prof comput sci, Fla State Univ, 73-79; assoc prof, Univ Iowa, 79-80. *Concurrent Pos:* Vis prof, Univ Wash, 84-85; vis scientist, Statist Eng Inst, Carnegie Mellon Univ, 91-92. *Mem:* Asn Comput Mach; Inst Elec & Electronics Engrs Comput Soc; Sigma Xi. *Res:* Ada programming language; real-time systems; operating systems; compilers. *Mailing Add:* 1304 Leewood Dr Tallahassee FL 32312-2525

BAKER, THOMAS, NEUROMUSCULAR JUNCTION, PERIPHERAL NERVES. *Current Pos:* dir res, Dept Anesthesiol, 90-95, DIR RES, DEPT MED EDUC, MONMOUTH MED CTR, 95- *Personal Data:* b Mineola, NY, Sept 19, 33; m 51, Marion Whitaker; c 6. *Educ:* City Univ NY, BA, 68; Cornell Univ, MS, 71. *Prof Exp:* Res asst pharmacol, Cornell Univ, 62-68, res assoc, 68-76, asst prof pharmacol, Med Col, 76-81, asst prof, Grad Sch Med, 77-81, assoc res prof pharmacol, Med Col, 81-82; dir res anesthesiol, St Joseph's Hosp & Med Ctr, Paterson, NJ, 83-90. *Concurrent Pos:* Co-investr, Nat Inst Neurol & Commun Dis & Stroke grants, 70-82, Nat Inst Gen Med, 78-79; vis assoc prof pharmacol, Col Pharm, Rutgers Univ, 85- *Mem:* Am Soc Anesthesiologists; Am Soc Pharmacol & Exp Therapeut; NY Acad Sci; Soc Neurosci; Soc Toxicol; Soc Exp Biol & Med. *Res:* Effects of drugs and toxic agents on the motor nerve endings of the mammalian neuromuscular junction. *Mailing Add:* Dept Med Educ Monmouth Med Ctr 300 Second Ave Long Branch NJ 07740-6393

BAKER, THOMAS IRVING, MICROBIOLOGY, BIOCHEMISTRY. *Current Pos:* asst prof, 67-74, ASSOC PROF MICROBIOL, SCH MED, UNIV NMEX, 74- *Personal Data:* b La Rue, Ohio, Sept 28, 31; m 53; c 4. *Educ:* Kent State Univ, BS, 54; Ohio State Univ, MS, 56; Western Res Univ, PhD(microbiol), 65. *Prof Exp:* Assoc chemist fermentation lab, Northern Utilization Res & Develop Div, USDA, 57-60. *Concurrent Pos:* Res fel microbiol, Western Res Univ, 65-67. *Mem:* Genetics Soc Am; Am Soc Microbiol; AAAS. *Res:* Microbiol genetics, specifically gene-enzyme interrelationships; molecular genetics; DNA repair. *Mailing Add:* Dept Microbiol Univ NMex Sch Med 1 Univ Campus Albuquerque NM 87131-0001

BAKER, TIMOTHY D, PREVENTIVE MEDICINE. *Current Pos:* prof int health & pub health admin, asst dean curric & assoc dir dept int health, 59-72, PROF INT HEALTH, OCCUP HEALTH & HEALTH POLICY & MGT, JOHNS HOPKINS UNIV, 72- *Personal Data:* b Baltimore, Md, July 4, 25; m 51; c 3. *Educ:* Johns Hopkins Univ, BA, 48, MPH, 54; Univ Md, MD, 52; Am Bd Prev Med, dipl, 59. *Prof Exp:* Intern, Univ Baltimore Hosp & pub health resident, NY State, 52-54; clinician, Med Care Clin, Johns Hopkins Univ, 53-54; NY State actg dist health officer, Geneva, 54-56; from asst chief to actg chief health div, Tech Coop Mission, India, 56-58; asst prof prev med, State Univ NY Upstate Med Ctr, 58-59; NY State Syracuse Dist Health Officer, 58-59. *Concurrent Pos:* Consult health manpower, Taiwan, Thailand, Indonesia & US Dept Health, Educ & Welfare; consult health planning, Brazil, Saudi Arabia, El Salvador, Burma & Sri Lanka; consult med educ, Peru & Saudi Arabia; vpres & dir, Univ Assocs Inc, dir, Intermed Inc, 72-74; asst secy-treas, Am Bd Prev Med; treas & dir, Pan Am Health Educ Found. *Mem:* Fel AAAS; fel Am Pub Health Asn; Am Soc Trop Med & Hyg; Am Col Prev Med; Nat Coun Int Health. *Res:* Health manpower and planning; medical education; international health and population dynamics; public health administration; medical care; epidemiology. *Mailing Add:* Sch Hyg & Pub Health Johns Hopkins Univ 615 N Wolfe St Baltimore MD 21205-2103

BAKER, TIMOTHY STANLEY, CRYO-ELECTRON MICROSCOPY OF BIOLOGICAL MACROMOLECULES, IMAGE ANALYSIS OF ELECTRON MICROGRAPHS. *Current Pos:* PROF BIOL, PURDUE UNIV, 83- *Personal Data:* b Hackensack, NJ, July 1, 49; m 87, Beverly J Brassie; c Lindsay B, Colby H & Mekrae L. *Educ:* Duke Univ, BS, 71; Univ Calif, Los Angeles, CPhil, 74, PhD(biochem), 76. *Prof Exp:* Jane Coffin Childs fel, Med Res Coun Lab Molecular Biol, Eng, 76-78; NIH fel, Rosenstiel Ctr, Brandeis Univ, 79-80, Med Found fel, 80-82, sr res assoc, 82-83. *Concurrent Pos:* Assoc ed, J Ultrastructure Res, 76-86; prin investr, Purdue Univ, 83- *Mem:* Micros Soc Am. *Res:* Structure determination of biological macromolecules, in particular animal, plant and bacterial viruses, studied by cryo-electron microscopy and image reconstruction techniques. *Mailing Add:* Dept Biol Sci Purdue Univ West Lafayette IN 47907-1968. *Fax:* 765-496-1189; *E-Mail:* tsb@bragg.bio.purdue.edu

BAKER, VICTOR RICHARD, PALEOHYDROLOGY, PLANETARY, GEOMORPHOLOGY. *Current Pos:* PROF GEOSCI, UNIV ARIZ, TUCSON, 81-, PROF PLANETARY SCI, LUNAR & PLANETARY LAB, 82-, REGENTS PROF, DEPT GEOSCI & DEPT PLANETARY SCI, 88-, REGENTS PROF & HEAD DEPT HYDROL & WATER RESOURCES, 96- *Personal Data:* b Waterbury, Conn, Feb 19, 45; m 67, Pauline M Heaton; c Trent H & Theodore W. *Educ:* Rensselaer Polytech Inst, BS, 67; Univ Colo, PhD(geol), 71. *Honors & Awards:* David Linton Award, Brit Geomorphol Res Group, 95. *Prof Exp:* Geophysicist hydrol, US Geol Surv, 67-69; city geologist urban geol, Boulder, Colo, 69-71; asst prof geol sci, Univ Tex, Austin, 71-76, assoc prof, 76-81, prof, 81. *Concurrent Pos:* Res scientist, Bur Econ Geol, Univ Tex, 73; mem, NASA Viking Orbital Imaging Team, 77-79; vis res fel, Australian Nat Univ, 79-80; Fulbright-Hays sr res scholar, 79-80; mem, Nat Res Coun Comt & Panels, 79-; prin investr, NASA grants, 73- , NSF grants, 78-85, 88-, US Dept Interior grants, 80-86; consult, NASA, 82, US Dept Energy, 83-92 & US Bur Reclamation, 89-; mem Magellan Space Mission Team, 83-94; vis res fel, Nat Inst Hydrology, India, 87-88; vis fel, Univ Adelaide, Australia, 88; chmn, Planetary Geol Div, Geol Soc Am, 86, Quaternary Geo & Geomorphol Div, 87; mem, Panel Global Surficial Geofluxes, Nat Res Coun, 88-93, chmn, US Nat Comn Int Union Quaternary Res, 91-96, Global Chg Comt Working Group on Solid Earth Processes, 90-92, Panel Sci Responsibility & Conduct of Res, 90-92; assoc ed, J Geophys Res, 89-91; chair, Sect Geol & Geog, AAAS, 92-93, counr, 93-94; treas, Int Asn Geomorphologists, 93-97; Hydrol Scis Panel, NSF, 93-96; fel, Udall Ctr Studies Pub Policy, 94-95; distinguished lectr, Binghampton Univ, 95; pres, Comn Global Continental Paleohydrology. *Mem:* Fel Geol Soc Am(vpres, 96-97); Am Geophys Union; fel AAAS; Am Quaternary Asn; Sigma Xi; Nat Asn Geol Teachers; foreign mem Polish Acad Scis. *Res:* Geomorphology; paleohydrology; quaternary geology; natural hazards; geology of Mars and Venus; fluvial geomorphic studies in western United States, Australia, India, Israel and South America; flood geomorphology; philosophy of earth and planetary sciences. *Mailing Add:* Dept Hydrology & Water Resources Univ Ariz Tucson AZ 85721-0011. *Fax:* 520-621-1422; *E-Mail:* baker@hwr.arizona.edu

BAKER, WALTER L(OUIS), ELECTRONICS ENGINEERING, ACOUSTICS. *Current Pos:* RETIRED. *Personal Data:* b Earlton, NY, Aug 7, 24; m 44, Janet K Sprague; c Laurence, Linda L & Louis M. *Educ:* Clarkson Col Technol, BEE, 44; Pa State Univ, MS, 54, EE, 55. *Honors & Awards:* Navy Meritorious Pub Serv Citation, USN, 75. *Prof Exp:* Tech asst, Tenn Eastmn Corp, 44-45; sr engr, Philco Corp, 45-49; from res assoc to prof, Pa State Univ, 49-82, sr mem grad fac, 65-82; pres, Baker Eng Co, 80-93. *Concurrent Pos:* Consult, John I Thompson & Co, 52-68, Sparton Elec Corp, 60-61, HRB-Singer Corp, 58-67, USMC, 65, DSI, 79-84, Woods Hole Oceanog Inst, 80-, Vitro Corp, 81, SRM, 84-86 & BB&N, Inc, 86-93. *Mem:* Sr mem Inst Elec & Electronics Engrs; NY Acad Sci; Acoust Soc Am; Sigma Xi. *Res:* Underwater acoustics; signal processors; data processing; computer systems; weapon system feasibility studies; methodology and digital simulation. *Mailing Add:* 22 Oliver Hazard Perry Rd Portsmouth RI 02871

BAKER, WALTER WOLF, neuropharmacology; deceased, see previous edition for last biography

BAKER, WARREN J, CIVIL ENGINEERING, SOIL MECHANICS. *Current Pos:* PRES, CALIF POLYTECH STATE UNIV. *Personal Data:* b Fitchburg, Mass, Sept 5, 38; m 62; c 2. *Educ:* Univ Notre Dame, BSCE, 60, MSCE, 62; Univ NMex, PhD(civil eng), 66. *Prof Exp:* Proj engr, C E

Williams & Assoc, Inc, 59-62; res asst engr, Air Force Shock Tube Facility, 62-65, res assoc engr, 65-66; asst prof civil eng, Univ Detroit, 66-67, assoc prof, 67-, acad vpres, 76- *Concurrent Pos:* Lectr, Univ NMex, 65-66; consult, Woodward, Clyde & Assoc, 62-65, E H Wang Civil Eng Res Facility, 67- & Off Civil Defense, Dept Defense Mem Instrumentation panel, Defense Atomic Support Agency, 63-65; mem, Nat Sci Bd, 85- *Mem:* Nat Soc Prof Engrs; Am Soc Civil Engrs; Am Soc Eng Educ; Int Soc Soil Mech & Found Eng. *Res:* Soil dynamics; foundation vibrations; shock loading response of earth masses; wave propagation in non-linear materials; foundation engineering. *Mailing Add:* Off Pres Chancellor Calif Polytech State Univ 1 Polyview Dr San Luis Obispo CA 93407-0001

BAKER, WILLIAM KAUFMAN, GENETICS. *Current Pos:* chmn dept, 77-80, prof biol, 80-85, EMER PROF, UNIV UTAH, 85- *Personal Data:* b Portland, Ind, Dec 2, 19; m 44, Margaret Stewart; c Bruce, Ann & Brian. *Educ:* Col of Wooster, BA, 41; Univ Tex, MS, 43, PhD(genetics), 48. *Hon Degrees:* DSc, Col of Wooster, 84. *Prof Exp:* Nat Res Coun fel, Univ Tex, 46-48; asst prof zool, Univ Tenn, 48-52; from biologist to sr biologist, Oak Ridge Nat Lab, 51-55; assoc prof zool, Univ Chicago, 55-59, chmn, dept biol, 68-72, prof biol, 59-76. *Concurrent Pos:* NSF sr fel, 63-64; co-ed, Am Naturalist, 65-70; NIH spec fel, 72-73. *Mem:* Am Soc Naturalists (secy, 62-64, vpres, 76); Genetics Soc Am (pres, 80); Soc Study Evolution. *Res:* General genetics and development of Drosophila. *Mailing Add:* Rte 33 Box 86WB Santa Fe NM 87505. *E-Mail:* wbaker19@aol.com

BAKER, WILLIAM OLIVER, PHYSICAL CHEMISTRY, POLYMER SCIENCE. *Current Pos:* RETIRED. *Personal Data:* b Chestertown, Md, July 15, 15; m 41; c Wendy (deceased) & Joseph. *Educ:* Wash Col, BS, 35; Princeton Univ, PhD(phys chem), 38. *Hon Degrees:* 26 from US and foreign univs, 57-93. *Honors & Awards:* Honor Scroll, Am Inst Chemists, 62, Gold Medal, 75; Perkin Medal, 63; Priestley Medal, Am Chem Soc, 66, Charles Lathrop Parsons Award, 76, J Willard Gibbs Medal, 78; Edgar Marburg Award, 67; Indust Res Inst Medal, 70; Frederik Philips Award, Inst Elec & Electronics Engrs, 72; Procter Prize, Sigma Xi, 73; James Madison Medal, Princeton Univ, 75; Mellon Inst Award, 75; Franklin Inst Fahrney Medal, 77; V Bush Award, NSF, 81; Pres Nat Security Medal, 83; co-recipient, Nat Medal of Technol, 85; Thomas Alva Edison Medal, 87; Nat Medal Sci, 88. *Prof Exp:* Mem tech staff, Bell Labs, 39-51, asst dir chem & metall res, 51-54, dir res phys sci, 54-55, vpres res, 55-73, pres, AT&T Bell Labs, 73-79, chmn, 79-80. *Concurrent Pos:* mem, Nat Sci Bd, 60-66; mem, Sci Info Coun, NSF, 58-61, chmn, 59-61; consult, US Dept Defense, 58-71, spec asst sci & technol, 63-73; chmn, Nat Res Coun, 64-78, mem, Comn Sociotech Systs, 63-70, mem, Comt Phys Chem, Div Chem & Chem Technol, 63-70; consult, Panel Opers Eval Group, USN, 60-62 & Nat Sci Bd, 60-66; mem bd visitors, USAF Systs Command, 62-73; mem bd visitors, Tulane Univ, 63-80; mem, Liaison Comt Sci & Technol, Libr Cong, 63-73, Comt Sci & Technol, US Chamber of Com, 63-66, Coun Trends & Perspective, 66-74; mem bd regents, Nat Libr Med, 69-73; chmn, Adv Tech Panel, Nat Bur Stand & Nat Acad Sci-Nat Res Coun, 69-78; mem coun, Nat Acad Sci, 69-72 & Inst Med, 73-75; mem mgt adv coun, Oak Ridge Nat Lab, 70-, chmn, Andrew W Mellon Found, 70-90, emer chmn, 90-, trustee, Rockefeller Univ, 60-90, chmn, 80-90, emer chmn, 90-; mem, Nat Comn Libr & Info Sci, 71-75; mem, Nat Policy Panel on Future UN Role in Sci & Technol, UN Asn, 72-, Nat Coun Educ Res, Nat Inst Educ, 73-75, Energy Res & Develop Adv Coun, Energy Policy Off, 73-75, Comn on Critical Choices for Am, 73-75, Proj Independence Adv Comt, Fed Energy Admin, 74-75, Nat Cancer Adv Bd, 74-80, Governor's Comn Evaluate Capital Needs NJ, 74-75; mem gov bd, Nat Enquiry Into Scholarly Commun, 75-; bd overseers, Col Eng & Appl Sci, Univ Pa, 75-; consult, Nat Security Agency, 76-; vchmn, Pres Comt Sci & Technol, Off Sci & Technol Policy, 76-77, Nat Comt Excellence in Educ, 81-84. *Mem:* Nat Acad Sci; Nat Acad Eng; Inst Med-Nat Acad Sci; fel Am Inst Chemists; fel Am Phys Soc; Am Acad Arts & Sci; Am Chem Soc; Sigma Xi; Am Philos Soc. *Res:* Study of solid state materials and macromolecules; dielectric and dynamic mechanical properties of crystals and glasses; information processing; photonics; author of approximately 95 papers; holder of 13 patents. *Mailing Add:* 600 New York Ave Murray Hill NJ 07974

BAKER, WILLIE ARTHUR, JR, INORGANIC CHEMISTRY. *Current Pos:* PROF CHEM & DEAN GRAD SCH, UNIV TEX, ARLINGTON, 70-, VPRES ACAD AFFAIRS, 72- *Personal Data:* b San Antonio, Tex, Nov 7, 33; m 54; c 2. *Educ:* Tex Col Arts & Indust, BS, 55; Univ Tex, PhD(chem), 59. *Prof Exp:* From asst prof to prof chem, Syracuse Univ, 59-70, chmn dept, 66-70. *Mem:* AAAS; Am Chem Soc; The Chem Soc; Sigma Xi. *Res:* Coordination compounds; magnetic properties; spectra structure. *Mailing Add:* PO Box 19065 Chem Univ Tex Arlington TX 76019-0001

BAKER, WINSLOW FURBER, HIGH ENERGY PHYSICS, ELEMENTARY PARTICLE PHYSICS. *Current Pos:* PHYSICIST, FERMI LAB, UNIV RES ASN, 69- *Personal Data:* b Brockton, Mass; m 67; c 2. *Educ:* Bowdoin Col, AB, 50; Columbia Univ, MA, 53, PhD(physics), 57. *Hon Degrees:* DSc, Allegheny Col, 75. *Prof Exp:* Res assoc physics, Columbia Univ, 57-59; physicist, Brookhaven Nat Lab, 59-64, Europ Orgn Nuclear Res, 64-69. *Mem:* Am Phys Soc. *Res:* Strong interactions at high energies; backward scattering, baryon exchange, elastic scattering, total cross sections; direct photons. *Mailing Add:* Fermi Lab PO Box 500 Batavia IL 60510

BAKERMAN, SEYMOUR, biophysics, pathology; deceased, see previous edition for last biography

BAKHIET, ATEF, MAINTENANCE, QUALITY CONTROL. *Current Pos:* PVT CONSULT, 90-; OWNER, GROUP GAMU. *Personal Data:* b El Minia, Egypt, Apr 21, 41; Can citizen; m 68; c 2. *Educ:* El Minia Univ, BSc, 66; Turin Univ, Italy, dipl, 70. *Prof Exp:* Maintenance supt, Egyptian Co Metall Construct, 66-71; plant supvr, Oxygen Plant, Egyptian Co & Steel & Iron, 71-74; proj engr, Que Iron & Titanum, Soul, Que, 76-83; maintenance consult, Ministry Recreation, Hunting & Fishing, Que, 83-85; mgr mfg serv, Simonds Industs Inc, 85-87, mgr eng & mfg serv, 87-90. *Mem:* Stand Coun Can; Indust Admin Clubs Can; Asn Can Mfg. *Res:* General maintenance and quality control. *Mailing Add:* 588 Des Mouettes Granby PQ J2H 1S6 Can

BAKHRU, HASSARAM, NUCLEAR & SOLID STATE PHYSICS. *Current Pos:* asst prof, 70-73, PROF PHYSICS, STATE UNIV NY ALBANY, 73-, DIR, ACCELERATOR LAB, 72- *Personal Data:* b Rohri, India, June 2, 37; c 2. *Educ:* Banaras Hindu Univ, India, BS, 58, MS, 60; Calcutta Univ, PhD(nuclear physics), 64. *Honors & Awards:* Frederick Gardner Cottrell Res Award, Res Corp, 71. *Prof Exp:* Fel, Heavy Ion Accelerator, Yale Univ, 65-69, res staff fel nuclear physics, 65-66, res assoc & assoc dir, 66-69. *Concurrent Pos:* USAEC res grant, 71- *Mem:* Am Phys Soc. *Res:* Nuclear reactions and spectroscopy; new isotopes; heavy ion and neutron induced reactions; x-ray spectroscopy; modification of surface sensitive properties of metals using MeV ions; research on fatigue, corrosion, wear and hardness of metals, analysis using microbeams, materials characterization using MeV ions. *Mailing Add:* Dept Physics State Univ NY 1400 Washington Ave Albany NY 12222-1000

BAKHSHI, NARENDRA NATH, CHEMICAL ENGINEERING. *Current Pos:* from asst prof to assoc prof, 64-74, PROF CHEM & CHEM ENG, UNIV SASK, 74- *Personal Data:* b New Delhi, India, July 27, 28; Can citizen; m 51, Nirmal Viran; c Ranju, Neena, Aron & Rajesh. *Educ:* Benares Hindu Univ, BSc, 46, MSc, 48; Va Polytech Inst, PhD(chem eng), 57. *Prof Exp:* Lectr chem, Yuvraj Dutta Col, India, 48-49 & Dayanand, India, 49-50; asst, Nat Phys Lab, 50-53; process develop engr, Hydrocarbon Res, Inc, 56-59; process engr, Air Prod & Chem, Inc, Pa, 59-60; sr chem engr, Air Prod Ltd, Eng, 60-63; sr process engr, Brit Oxygen Co, Ltd, 63-64. *Concurrent Pos:* Spec lectr chem eng, Univ Sask, 63-64. *Mem:* Fel Chem Inst Can; Can Soc Chem Eng; Asn Prof Engrs Sask; Am Chem Soc; Am Inst Chem Engrs. *Res:* Heterogeneous catalysis; chemical reactor design; biomass pyrolysis; upgrading of biomass-derived oils to fuels and chemicals. *Mailing Add:* Dept Chem Eng Univ Sask Saskatoon SK S7N 5C9 Can

BAKHSHI, VIDYA SAGAR, APPLIED MATHEMATICS. *Current Pos:* from assoc prof to prof, 68-83, OPERS RES ANALYST, VA STATE COL, 91-, PROF, VA STATE UNIV. *Personal Data:* b India, Sept 23, 39; m; c 2. *Educ:* Univ Delhi, BA, 59, MA, 63; Ore State Univ, PhD(math), 68. *Prof Exp:* Lectr math, Kurukshetra Univ, India, 63-65; teaching asst, Ore State Univ, 65-68. *Concurrent Pos:* Special assignment, prov fel; US Army, 83-90. *Mem:* Math Asn Am. *Res:* Fluid dynamics and mathematical seismology; two and three dimensional boundary layer problems. *Mailing Add:* 121 Stratford Dr Colonial Heights VA 23834-1919

BAKHT, BAIDAR, CIVIL ENGINEERING. *Current Pos:* ADJ PROF CIVIL ENG, UNIV TORONTO & DALHOUSIE UNIV, 91-; PRES JMB STRUCTURES RES INC, TORONTO, 97- *Personal Data:* b Delhi, India, Sept 4, 40; m 68, Anita Das; c Natasha & Sacha. *Educ:* Aligarh Univ, India, BSc, 62; Imp Col, London, MSc, 72; London Univ, DSc, 90. *Honors & Awards:* Moisseif Award, Am Soc Civil Engrs, 82; Gzowski Medal, Eng Inst Can, 83; President's Medal, Rd & Transp Asn Can, 85; Pratley Award, Can Soc Civil Eng, 88 & 94, Vance Award, 96. *Prof Exp:* Asst engr, Heavy Engr Corp, Ranchi, India, 62-66; engr, Dept Environ, London, 67-73. *Mem:* Fel Inst Engrs India; Can Soc Civil Eng; Eng Inst Can. *Res:* Contributor of over 200 articles on structural engineering; co-inventor of unique deck slab of bridges; inventor of stressed-log bridge. *Mailing Add:* 21 Whiteleaf Crescent Scarborough ON M1V 3G1 Can

BAKIS, RAIMO, PHYSICS. *Current Pos:* Assoc physicist res ctr, 59, staff physicist, 59-60, res staff mem speech recognition, 60-61, res staff mem pattern recognition, 61-66, res staff mem speech processing res lab, Ruschlikon ZH, Switz, 66-68, RES STAFF MEM, IMAGE PROCESSING, RES CTR, INT BUS MACH CORP, 68- *Personal Data:* b Tartu, Estonia, May 7, 33; US citizen; m 65; c 2. *Educ:* Sterling Col, BA, 54; Kans State Univ, MS, 56, PhD(physics), 59. *Mem:* AAAS. *Res:* Speech processing--automatic recognition of continuous speech. *Mailing Add:* 204 Ridge Top Lane Brewster NY 10509

BAKISH, ROBERT, PHYSICAL METALLURGY. *Current Pos:* PRES, BAKISH MAT CORP, 64- *Personal Data:* b Sofia, Bulgaria, Jan 5, 26; US citizen; m 59, Ellen Katholm Udsen; c Robert Marc. *Educ:* Columbia Univ, BSMetEng, 52; Yale Univ, MEng, 53, DEng(metall), 55. *Prof Exp:* Sr metallurgist, Sprague Elec Co, Mass, 55-57; consult phys metall, Rare Metals Div, Ciba Corp, Switz, 57-59; vpres res & develop, Alloyd Electronics Corp, Mass, 59-62; exec vpres, Electronics & Alloys, Inc, NJ, 62-64. *Concurrent Pos:* Lectr, Rensselaer Polytech Inst, 56-57, Univ Calif, Los Angeles, 64-68 & Am Welding Soc, 66-; consult, Repub Foil, Inc, Conn, 60-, vpres res & develop, 66-70; chmn, Int Conf Electron & Ion Beams in Sci & Technol, 63-83; prof, Fairleigh Dickinson Univ, 64-80; dir, St Croix Corrosion Installation, 70-80; pres, Int Desalination Environ Asn, 78-81; chmn, Electron Beam Melting & Refining State of the Art, 83-94, Laser vs Electron Beam, 85-93. *Mem:* Inst Mining, Metall & Petrol Engrs; Am Welding Soc; Nat Asn Corrosion Engrs; Am Vacuum Soc; Am Soc Metals; Sigma Xi. *Res:* Corrosion; electron beam technology; metals processing; various publications regarding electron beam and vacuum technology and desalination; over 100 publications including contribution & editor to 35 volumes dealing with electron beam technology. *Mailing Add:* 171 Sherwood Pl PO Box 148 Englewood NJ 07631

BAKKE, JEROME E, BIOCHEMISTRY. *Current Pos:* RES BIOCHEMIST RADIATION & METAB LAB, USDA, 64- *Personal Data:* b Mapes, NDak, July 14, 31; m 54; c 2. *Educ:* NDak State Univ, BS & MS, 56; Univ NDak, PhD(biochem), 60. *Prof Exp:* Chemist, Lignite Res Lab, US Bur Mines, NDak, 55-58; res biochemist, Lipid Sect, Fundamental Food Res Dept, Gen Mills, Inc, Minn, 60-61, Natural Prod Sect, 61-63, Explor Food Res Dept, 63-64; asst prof biochem, NDak State Univ, 68-73. *Concurrent Pos:* Adj prof biochem, NDak State Univ, 73- *Mem:* Int Soc Study Xenobiotics. *Res:* Natural product isolation, identification and synthesis; lipid metabolism; food research; insecticide metabolism in the animal. *Mailing Add:* 301 15th Ave N Fargo ND 58102

BAKKEN, AIMEE HAYES, CELL BIOLOGY, DEVELOPMENTAL BIOLOGY. *Current Pos:* asst prof, 73-78, ASSOC PROF ZOOL, UNIV WASH, 79- *Personal Data:* b Camden, NJ, Oct 18, 41; m 63; c 1. *Educ:* Univ Chicago, BA, 63; Univ Iowa, PhD(zool), 70. *Prof Exp:* Res asst reprod biol, Dept Obstet & Gynec, Univ Chicago, 63-66; investr, Biol Div, Oak Ridge Nat Lab, 70-72; res assoc biol, Yale Univ, 72-73. *Concurrent Pos:* NSF res grant, 74-82, 89-, NIH grant, 80- *Mem:* AAAS; Am Soc Cell Biol. *Res:* Regulation of RNA genes; correlation of chromosome and nucleolar structure and function in eukaryotic germ cells, embryonic cells and somatic cells, using molecular and cytogenetic techniques. *Mailing Add:* Dept Zool NJ-15 Univ Wash Seattle WA 98195-1800

BAKKEN, ARNOLD, ZOOLOGY. *Current Pos:* teaching, 53-55, from assoc prof to prof, 55-83, EMER PROF BIOL, UNIV WIS, EAU CLAIRE, 83- *Personal Data:* b Antelope, Mont, Feb 19, 21; m 47, Charlotte M Toelle; c Barbara M & Deborah A. *Educ:* Univ Mont, BA, 43; Univ Wis, MS, 49, PhD(zool, mammal, ecol), 53. *Prof Exp:* Teaching & res zool & anat, Reed Col, 52-53. *Concurrent Pos:* Fulbright grant, Norway, 51-52; NSF award, 58. *Mem:* AAAS; Am Inst Biol Sci; Animal Behav Soc; Am Soc Mammal; Ecol Soc Am; Sigma Xi. *Res:* Behavior and interrelationships between fox squirrels and grey squirrels in mixed populations; population problems of Norwegian lemmings; microclimate and behavior. *Mailing Add:* 500 Big Flat Rd Missoula MT 59804

BAKKEN, EARL E, RESEARCH ADMINISTRATION. *Current Pos:* Partner, Medtronic Inc, 49-57, chief exec officer & chmn bd, 57-76, sr chmn bd, 76-89, FOUNDER & EMER DIR, MEDTRONIC INC, 89- *Personal Data:* b Minneapolis, Minn, 1924. *Educ:* Univ Minn, BEE, 48. *Hon Degrees:* DSc, Univ Minn, 88, Tulane Univ, 88, Univ Minn, 88, Albany Col Pharm, 95. *Honors & Awards:* Eng for Gold Award, Nat Soc Prof Engrs, 84; Centennial Medal, Inst Elec & Electronics Engrs, 84, Eli Lilly Award, 94; Distinguished Serv Award, NAm Soc Pacing & Electrophysiol, 85; Officer in the Order of Orange-Nassau, Neth, 89. *Concurrent Pos:* Chmn bd dirs, Archaeus Proj & Bakken, pres bd dirs, Pavek Mus Broadcasting, mem bd dirs, Children's Heart Fund, Med Graphics Corp & NHawaii Community Hosp. *Mem:* Nat Acad Eng; fel Inst Elec & Electronics Engrs; fel Instrument Soc Am; Am Antiquarian Soc; Asn Advan Med Instrumentation; assoc mem NAm Soc Pacing & Electrophysiol; hon fel Am Col Cardiol; hon fel Int Col Surgeons. *Res:* Bioengineering; developed the first weavable, external, battery powered transistorized pacemaker; author of several professional papers and delivered numerous speeches to medical, technical, educational and business groups. *Mailing Add:* Medtronic Inc 7000 Central Ave NE Minneapolis MN 55432

BAKKEN, GEORGE STEWART, PHYSIOLOGICAL ECOLOGY. *Current Pos:* res assoc, Div Biol Sci, 73-75, from asst prof to assoc prof, 75-83, PROF LIFE SCI, IND STATE UNIV, 83-, DIR, CTR BIODIVERSITY STUDIES, 94- *Personal Data:* b Denver, Colo, Feb 17, 43; m 73, Laura E Coons; c Anne Marie & David. *Educ:* NDak State Univ, BS, 65; Rice Univ, MA, 67, PhD(physics), 70. *Prof Exp:* Res assoc physics, Rice Univ, 69-70; fel physiol ecol biophys, Mo Bot Garden, 70-71, Univ Mich, 71-73. *Mem:* AAAS; Am Ornithol Union; Ecol Soc Am; Brit Ecol Soc; Soc Integrative & Comp biol; Soc Conserv Biol. *Res:* Energy and mass flow between organisms and their physical environment and the consequences for physiology, ecology, behavior and evolution; biological, physical and mathematical methods are employed. *Mailing Add:* Dept Life Sci Ind State Univ Terre Haute IN 47809. *Fax:* 812-237-4480; *E-Mail:* lsgb@scifac.ind state.edu

BAKKER, CORNELIS BERNARDUS, PSYCHIATRY. *Current Pos:* MED DIR, DEPT PSYCHIAT, SACRED HEART MED CTR, SPOKANE, WASH, 84-; CLIN PROF, DEPT PSYCHIAT & BEHAV SCI, UNIV WASH SCH MED, SEATTLE, WASH, 85-, ASSOC RESIDENCY TRAINING DIR, 91- *Personal Data:* b Rotterdam, Holland, Jan 6, 29; US citizen; m 55, Marianne K Rabdau; c Paul, James & Gabrielle. *Educ:* State Univ Utrecht, MD, 52. *Honors & Awards:* Significant Achievement Award, Am Psychiat Asn, 75. *Prof Exp:* Intern, Clin of Rotterdam, Holland, 52-53; intern, Sacred Heart Hosp, Spokane, Wash, 53-54; resident psychiat, Eastern State Hosp, Medical Lake, 54-56; resident, Psychiat Clin, State Univ Utrecht, 56-57; resident, Med Sch, Univ Mich, Ann Arbor, 57-59, res assoc ment health res inst, 58-60, instr, 59-60; from instr to assoc prof, Univ Wash, 60-72, dir adult psychiat inpatient serv, Univ Hosp, 61-68, dir adult prog, Univ Hosp, Univ Wash, 68-79, actg chmn psychiat, Sch Med, 69-70, prof psychiat, Sch Med, 72-79; prof, Dept Psychiat, Univ Ill Col Med, Peoria, 79-84. *Concurrent Pos:* Fulbright & Comt Int Exchange Persons grant, 53; Fogarty sr fel, Univ Leuven, Belg, 77-78; psychiat consult, Soc See Hearing & Appeals, 63-79; Ketchikan Community Ment Health Ctr, 72-77. *Mem:* Am Psychiat Asn; Am Col Psychiat; Am Asn Dirs Psychiat Residency Training. *Res:* Behavior change techniques; human territoriality. *Mailing Add:* Dept Psychiat Sacred Heart Med Ctr PO Box 2555 Spokane WA 99220-2555. *Fax:* 509-455-4890

BAKKER, GERALD ROBERT, ORGANIC CHEMISTRY. *Current Pos:* RETIRED. *Personal Data:* b Chicago, Ill, May 16, 33; m 57, Barbara Verbridge; c Anne (Gras) & Mark. *Educ:* Calvin Col, AB, 55; Univ Ill, PhD(chem), 59. *Prof Exp:* Res assoc chem, Univ Kans, 58-59; from asst prof to prof, Earlham Col, 59-71, consult teaching & learning, 75-77, actg provost, 88-89, prof chem, 71-, assoc acad dean, 86-88 & 89- *Mem:* AAAS; Am Chem Soc; Sigma Xi. *Res:* Organic chemistry; cytochrome c electrochemistry. *Mailing Add:* 12785 Lakeshore Dr Grand Haven MI 49417. *Fax:* 765-983-1497; *E-Mail:* jerryb@earlham.edu

BAKKER, JAAP JELLE, CIVIL & TRANSPORTATION ENGINEERING. *Current Pos:* from asst prof to assoc prof, 59-76, PROF TRANSP, UNIV ALTA, 76- *Personal Data:* b Kerkrade, Netherlands, Dec 12, 29; Can citizen; m 56; c 5. *Educ:* Glasgow Univ, BSc, 54; Imp Col Sci & Technol, Univ London, dipl, 55; Purdue Univ, MSCE, 57. *Prof Exp:* Instr graphics, Purdue Univ, 55-57; design engr, City of Moose Jaw, Sask, 57-58, city engr, 58-59. *Concurrent Pos:* Transp consult to City of Edmonton, 60-77; univ rep, Transp Res Bd, Nat Acad Sci-Nat Res Coun, 71- *Mem:* Can Soc Civil Engrs. *Res:* Traffic and transit; long-range transit planning; transportation prediction and performance; geometric design. *Mailing Add:* 4119 Reid Rd PO Box 247 Eagle Bay BC V0E 1T0 Can

BAKKER, MARTIN GERARD, ELECTRON PARAMAGNETIC RESONANCE SPECTROSCOPY. *Current Pos:* ASST PROF PHYS CHEM, UNIV ALA, 90- *Personal Data:* b Rottendam, Neth, Feb 19, 59; m 94, Deborah Hughes; c Isadora. *Educ:* Univ Canterbury, NZ, BS Hons, 80, PhD(chem), 85. *Prof Exp:* Fel, Australian Inst Nuclear Sci & Eng, 85-88, Argonne Nat Lab, 88-90. *Mem:* Int Electron Paramagnetic Resonance Soc; Am Chem Soc. *Res:* Application of electron paramagnetic resonance to the study of reactions in cyclodextrins, binding of metals in zeolites, interactions of surfactants and polymers on surfaces, and motions of electrons in conducting polymers. *Mailing Add:* Dept Chem Univ Ala Tuscaloosa AL 35487-9671. *E-Mail:* bakker@ualvm.ua.edu

BAKKER, ROBERT T, PALEONTOLOGY. *Personal Data:* b Ridgewood, NJ, 1945; m, Constance Clark. *Educ:* Yale Univ, BA, 68. *Prof Exp:* Prof, Johns Hopkins Univ, Baltimore, 71-84. *Mailing Add:* Univ Colo Mus Broadway between 15th & 16th Sts Boulder CO 80309

BAKKER-ARKEMA, FREDERIK WILTE, AGRICULTURAL ENGINEERING. *Current Pos:* Asst, 57-63, from asst prof to assoc prof, 63-71, PROF AGR ENG, MICH STATE UNIV, 71- *Personal Data:* b Groningen, Neth, Aug 18, 32; m 57; c 3. *Educ:* Mich State Univ, BS, 59, MS, 61, PhD(agr eng), 64. *Mem:* Am Soc Agr Engrs. *Res:* Bioengineering; mass and heat transfer in biological products; drying and processing of biological products; digital computer techniques in agriculture. *Mailing Add:* Dept Agr Eng Mich State Univ 101 Farrell Hall East Lansing MI 48824-1323

BAKKUM, BARCLAY W, CHIROPRACTIC. *Current Pos:* instr, 89-92, asst prof, 92-95, ASSOC PROF, NAT COL CHIROPRACTIC, 95- *Personal Data:* b Manchester, Iowa, Apr 10, 57; m 91, Wendy Birch; c Brittany. *Educ:* Wartburg Col, BA, 78; Palmer Col Chiropractic, DC, 81; Univ Ill, Chicago, PhD(anat), 91. *Prof Exp:* Chiropractor, Breitbach Chiropractic Off, Charles City, Iowa, 81-85. *Mem:* Soc Neurosci. *Res:* Clinical anatomy of the region of the intervertebral foramen including gross anatomical, histological and in vivo imaging techniques. *Mailing Add:* Anat Dept Nat Col Chiropractic 200 E Roosevelt Rd Lombard IL 60148. *Fax:* 630-889-6554; *E-Mail:* bbakkum@national.chiropractic.edu

BAKOS, JACK DAVID, JR, STRUCTURAL MECHANICS, TRANSPORTATION. *Current Pos:* Assoc prof, 69-80, PROF & CHAIR, CIVIL ENG DEPT, YOUNGSTOWN STATE UNIV, 80- *Personal Data:* b Robins, Ohio, Nov 7, 40; m 71, Patsy Napolitano; c Christine A & Jason D. *Educ:* Univ Akron, BSCE, 63; WVa Univ, MSCE, 65, PhD(civil eng), 67. *Honors & Awards:* Watson Merit Award, 83; Outstanding Civil Engr, Am Soc Civil Engrs, 85; Outstanding Eng Educ Award, Am Soc Automotive Engrs. *Prof Exp:* Eng aide, Hwy Eng Dept, City of Akron, Ohio, 60-62; instr civil eng, WVA Univ, 64-67; prog eng, US Army Corp Engrs, 67-69. *Concurrent Pos:* Consult, Republic Steel Corp & Com Shearing, Inc, 77- *Mem:* Am Soc Civil Engrs; Nat Soc Prof Engrs; Sigma Xi; Am Soc Eng Educ. *Res:* Highway impact attenuators; low density concrete; freeze-thaw protection of concrete; flexural/torsimal buckling. *Mailing Add:* Dept Civil Environ Eng Youngstown State Univ Youngstown OH 44555

BAKSAY, LASZLO ANDRAS, INSTRUMENTATION, DETECTOR DEVELOPMENT. *Current Pos:* ASSOC PROF, UNIV ALA, 91- *Personal Data:* b Budapest, Hungary, July 22, 45; m 83, 92, Judit Tormassy; c Ruth, Laszlo, Emese, & Atilla. *Educ:* Rheinisch-Westfälische Technische Hochschule Aachen, WGer, dipl physics, 72, Dr rer nat, 78, Staats examen, 79. *Prof Exp:* Researcher, Centre Europ Recherche Nucleaire, 72-75; sci collabr, Rheinisch-Westflisch Technische Hochschule Aachen, WGer, 75-78; asst prof physics, Northeastern Univ, 78-82; staff scientist, Univ Calif, Berkeley, 82-83; assoc prof, Univ Dallas, 83-85; assoc prof, Union Col, 85-90; guest scientist, Brookhaven Nat Lab, 86-90. *Concurrent Pos:* Vis scientist, Stanford Univ, 78-82; rev panelist, NSF, 87-88, US Dept Ed, 87-89; prin investr, NSF, 87-90, Res Corp, 87-88; vis prof, Hungarian Acad Sci, 88-; hon mem, Maifhe; prin investr, US Dept Energy, 91-; guest prof, Tech Univ Budapest, 92-93. *Mem:* Am Asn Physics Teachers; Am Phys Soc; Europ Phys Soc; NY Acad Sci; Soc Col Sci Teachers; Ger Phys Soc; hon mem Int Asn Physics Studies. *Res:* Experimental elementary particle physics; L3 experiment at LEP, CERN; instrumentation for high energy physics; astronomy; high pressure research; international physics education. *Mailing Add:* Dept Physics & Astron Univ Ala Tuscaloosa AL 35487. *Fax:* 205-348-9792; *E-Mail:* lbaksay@ualvm.ua.edu

BAKSHI, PRADIP M, THEORETICAL PHYSICS. *Current Pos:* assoc prof, 70-75, PROF PHYSICS, BOSTON COL, 75- *Personal Data:* b Baroda, India, Aug 21, 36; m 67, Hansika Parekh; c Vaishali & Ashesh. *Educ:* Univ Bombay, BSc, 55; Harvard Univ, AM, 57, PhD(physics), 62. *Prof Exp:* Res fel physics, Harvard Univ, 63; res physicist, Air Force Cambridge Res Labs, 63-66; sr res assoc physics, Brandeis Univ, 66-68, assoc prof, 68-70. *Mem:* Am Phys Soc. *Res:* New techniques in mathematical physics; quantum field theory; plasma physics; low dimensional solid state systems. *Mailing Add:* Dept Phys Boston Col Chestnut Hill MA 02167. *Fax:* 617-552-8478; *E-Mail:* bakshi@bcvms.bc.edu

BAKSHI, TRILOCHAN SINGH, ECOLOGY. *Current Pos:* prof, 70-90, EMER PROF BIOL, ATHABASCA UNIV, 96- *Personal Data:* b Lonavla, India, Sept 13, 25; Can citizen; div; c 3. *Educ:* Univ Bombay, BSc, 47; Univ Saugar, MSc, 49; Wash State Univ, PhD(bot), 58. *Prof Exp:* Asst prof bot, Birla Col, India, 50-52; lectr, Univ Delhi, 52-53; head, Dept Biol, SNat Col, India, 54; asst bot, Wash State Univ, 54-58; fel ecol & anat, Univ Sask, 58-59; syst botanist & ecologist, Ministry Nat Resources, Sierra Leone, WAfrica, 60-63; lectr bot, Univ Ghana, 63-64; from assoc prof to prof biol, Notre Dame Univ, BC, 64-73. *Concurrent Pos:* Fulbright travel grantee, 54-58; Nat Res Coun Can study grants plant ecol southeast BC; vis prof bot, Univ WIndies, 78, Indira Gandhi Nat Open Univ, India, 86-87, Univ of South Pacific, Fiji, 87; Lady Davis vis prof agr eng, Technion-Israel Inst Technion, 81-82; vis prof, distance educ, Deakin Univ, Australia, 91-94, Charles Sturt Univ, Australia, 95. *Mem:* Int Soc Plant Morphol; Indian Bot Soc. *Res:* Ecology of vascular plants; distance education; plant taxonomy. *Mailing Add:* 1904 Kramer Way NW Edmonton AB T6L 6Z7 Can

BAKSI, SAMARENDRA NATH, BIOCHEMICAL PHARMACOLOGY, ENDOCRINOLOGY. *Current Pos:* SUPVRY VET MED OFFICER, USDA, 89- *Personal Data:* b Rajshahi, India, Dec 28, 40; US citizen; m 71, Shila Mandel; c Samudra N & Subir K. *Educ:* Bihar Vet Col, India, BVSc, 60; Univ Mo, Columbia, MS, 67, PhD(endocrinol), 71. *Prof Exp:* Vet surg, Govt Bihar, India, 60-66; res asst endocrinol, Univ Mo, Columbia, 67-71; res fel, Worcester Found Exp Biol, 71-72; vis fel environ toxicol, NIH, 72-74; res assoc, Univ Tex Med Br, Galveston, 75-76; res assoc pharmacol, Sch Med, Tex Tech Univ, 76-79, res assoc physiol, Health Sci Ctr, 80-84; asst prof, Dept Vet Comp Anat, Pharmacol & Physiol, Wash State Univ, 84-89. *Mem:* Endocrine Soc; Am Soc Pharmacol & Exp Therapeut; Am Physiol Soc; Am Soc Bone & Mineral Res. *Res:* Endocrine aspects of calcium metabolism; pharmacology of calcemic hormones; regulation of vitamin D metabolism; neurotransmitter physiology; dietary calcium and hypertension Angiotensin II receptor bindings; veterinary public health and food safety. *Mailing Add:* NW 210 Dillon St Pullman WA 99163

BAKULE, RONALD DAVID, TECHNOLOGY PROTECTION. *Current Pos:* chemist, 62-73, proj leader, 73-80, res sect mgr, 80-87, RES PATENT LIAISON, ROHM & HAAS CO, 87- *Personal Data:* b Chicago, Ill, Nov 19, 36; m 68; c 2. *Educ:* Ill Inst Technol, BS, 57; Cornell Univ, PhD(phys chem), 62. *Mem:* Am Chem Soc. *Res:* Polymer chemistry. *Mailing Add:* Res Labs Rohm & Haas Co Spring House PA 19477. *Fax:* 215-641-7027; *E-Mail:* rsrrdb@rohmhaas.com

BAKUN, ANDREW, physical oceanography, fisheries, for more information see previous edition

BAKUN, WILLIAM HENRY, EARTHQUAKE PREDICTION. *Current Pos:* RES GEOPHYSICIST, US GEOL SURV, 73- *Personal Data:* b Seattle, Wash, Dec 23, 41; m 70; c 2. *Educ:* Univ Wash, BS, 64; Univ Calif, Berkeley, MA, 66, PhD(geophys), 70. *Concurrent Pos:* Chief scientist, Parkfield Earthquake Prediction Proj, 85- *Mem:* Seismol Soc Am; Am Geophys Union. *Res:* Earthquake prediction in California; work in California and the People's Republic of China on earthquake magnitude and seismic scales and source mechanics; earthquake source mechanics. *Mailing Add:* 8 Patricia Pl Menlo Park CA 94025

BAKUS, GERALD JOSEPH, MARINE ECOLOGY. *Current Pos:* ASSOC PROF BIOL & CUR SPONGES, ALLAN HANCOCK FOUND, UNIV SOUTHERN CALIF, 67-, RES FEL, INST MARINE & COASTAL STUDIES, 81-, PROF BIOL, 86- *Personal Data:* b Thorpe, Wis, Dec 5, 34; m 53; c 2. *Educ:* Calif State Univ, Los Angeles, BA, 55; Univ Mont, MA, 57; Univ Wash, PhD(zool), 62. *Prof Exp:* Asst prof biol, Calif State Univ, Northridge, 61-62; asst prof & asst cur, Allan Hancock Collections, Univ Southern Calif, 62-67; chief biologist, Tetra Tech, Inc, Calif, 76-79. *Concurrent Pos:* NSF & Cocos Found grants, Fanning Island Exped, 63; NSF grant, 64-66; NIH biomed sci grant, 68-70; staff officer, Div Biol & Agr, Nat Acad Sci, 69-70; mem, Mirex Comt, Environ Protection Agency, 71-72; chmn comt marine biol, Orgn Trop Studies, 72-; various environ contracts, 74-; prin biologist, Tetra Tech Inc, Calif, 74-75, consult, 75-; hon mem, Great Barrier Reef Comt, Univ Queensland, Australia, 76; Off Naval Res grant, 84-92; mem, Indo-US Marine Bioactive Substances Prog, 84-92; Fulbright fel, Chile, 87; mem, Indo-US Marine Biofoulong Prog, 90-92; Fulbright distinguished fel, Thailand, Philippines, Malaysia & Indonesia, 96. *Mem:* Fel AAAS; Ecol Soc Am; Int Soc Chem Ecol; Pac Sci Asn. *Res:* Natural toxins as chemical defense mechanisms in marine organisms; bioactive substances; biology of sponges; author of 4 books and more than 150 papers. *Mailing Add:* Dept Biol Sci 0371 Univ Southern Calif University Park Los Angeles CA 90089-0371. *Fax:* 213-740-8123; *E-Mail:* bakus@mizar.usc.edu

BAKUZIS, EGOLFS VOLDEMARS, FOREST ECOLOGY. *Current Pos:* res fel forest ecol, Sch Forestry, Univ Minn, 56-59, res assoc, 59-61, asst prof forest synecol, 61-63, from assoc prof to prof, 63-82, EMER PROF FOREST ECOSYSTS, SCH FORESTRY, UNIV MINN, ST PAUL, 82- *Personal Data:* b Kuldiga, Latvia, May 27, 12; US citizen; m 40; c 6. *Educ:* Univ Latvia, ForestE, 35; Univ Minn, PhD(forestry), 59. *Prof Exp:* Instr forest mgt, Sch Forestry, Acad Agr Jelgava, 40-41; asst forest growth & yield, Eberswalde Forest Acad, Ger, 44-45; lectr forest mensuration, valuation & mgt, Baltic Univ, Ger, 47-50. *Concurrent Pos:* Assoc mem, Forest Res Inst Latvia, 36-44; res grant, Univ Minn, 60-63; NSF travel grant, Int Union Forest Res Orgn Cong, Vienna, Austria, 61, Munich, Ger, 67 & Gainesville, Fla, 71; Int Bot Cong, Seattle, Wash, 69. *Mem:* Fel AAAS; Ecol Soc Am; Soc Am Foresters; Soil Sci Soc Am; Am Inst Biol Sci; Sigma Xi. *Res:* Forest measurements and silviculture; forest ecology, particularly theoretical aspects of forest ecosystems; growth and yield studies; systems ecology. *Mailing Add:* Univ Minn Forestry 1530 W Cleveland Ave St Paul MN 55108

BAL, ARYA KUMAR, CELL BIOLOGY. *Current Pos:* from asst prof to assoc prof, 69-77, PROF BIOL, MEM UNIV NFLD, 77- *Personal Data:* b Jorhat, India, Aug 24, 34; c 1. *Educ:* Univ Calcutta, BSc, 51, MSc, 53, PhD(bot), 60. *Prof Exp:* Lectr bot, Bangabasi Col, India, 54-58; res asst cytol, Carnegie Inst Genetics Res Unit, 58-60; lectr bot, Bangabasi Col, India, 60-62; fel biol, Brown Univ, 62-65; res assoc anat, McGill Univ, 65-66; res assoc biol, Univ Montreal, 66-69. *Concurrent Pos:* Nat Res Coun Can grants, 68- *Mem:* Am Soc Cell Biol; Can Soc Cell Biol; Electron Micros Soc Am; Micros Soc Can. *Res:* Cell biology of symbiotic nitrogen fixation; cell biology of the potato wart disease. *Mailing Add:* Dept Biol Mem Univ Nfld St John's NF A1B 3X9 Can

BALA, SHUKAL, PARASITE IMMUNOLOGY, NUTRITION IMMUNOLOGY. *Current Pos:* MICROBIOLOGIST PARASITE-IMMUNOL, FOOD & DRUG ADMIN, 91- *Personal Data:* b New Delhi, India, Nov 27, 51. *Educ:* Univ Delhi, BSc, 73, MSc, 75; All India Inst Med Sci, PhD, 81. *Prof Exp:* Jr res fel immunol filariasis, All India Inst Med Sci, 75-76, sr res fel, 76-81, res officer immunol filariasis & brain tumor, 81-86, sr res officer, molecular biol HSV, HPV cancer cervix, 86-87; res assoc bact-immunol, Ala State Univ, Montgomery, 87-88; res assoc nutrit-immunol, US Dept Agr, 88-90. *Mem:* Assoc mem Am Inst Nutrit; Sigma Xi; Indian Immunol Soc; Indian Asn Med Microbiologists; Indian Asn Pathologists & Microbiologists. *Res:* Opportunistic parasites in patients with AIDS; cryptosporidium; toxoplasmosis; pneumocystis; giardia; leishmaniasis. *Mailing Add:* Div Antiviral Drug Prod FDA HFD-530 5600 Fishers Lane Rockville MD 20857-0001

BALABA, WILLY MUKAMA, TRIBOMECHANICAL PROPERTIES OF POLYMERS, POLYMERS IN ELECTRONIC PACKAGING. *Current Pos:* scientist, Surface & Polymer Div, 85-86, sr scientist, Packaging Div, 86-89, STAFF SCIENTIST, SURFACE TECHNOL DIV, ALCOA TECH CTR, 89- *Personal Data:* b Uganda, May 5, 53. *Educ:* Makerere Univ, Kampala, BS, 76; Univ Wash, MS, 80; Wash State Univ, PhD(eng sci), 84. *Prof Exp:* Spec asst, Chem Dept, Makerere Univ, 76-78; res asst, Forestry Dept, Univ Wash, 78-80, mat sci & eng, Wash State Univ, 80-84. *Res:* Application of polymers in electronic packaging and in tribological settings. *Mailing Add:* 2210 Stone Cliff Dr Monroeville PA 15146

BALABAN, CAREY D, NEUROSCIENCE. *Current Pos:* ASST PROF SCI, UNIV PITTSBURGH, 88- *Personal Data:* b New York, NY, July 20, 54. *Educ:* Mich State Univ, BS, 75; Univ Chicago, PhD(anat), 79. *Prof Exp:* Fac mem, Hershey Med Ctr, 82-88. *Mem:* Am Asn Anat; AAAS; Am Physiol Soc; Am Acad Sci; Am Inst Chemists. *Mailing Add:* Dept Otolaryngol Univ Pittsburgh Eye & Ear Inst Pittsburgh PA 15213

BALABAN, MARTIN, ZOOLOGY. *Current Pos:* from asst prof to assoc prof, 64-71, PROF ZOOL, MICH STATE UNIV, 71- *Personal Data:* b New York, NY, Oct 5, 30; m 50; c 3. *Educ:* Univ Chicago, BA, 50, PhD(biopsychol), 59. *Prof Exp:* USPHS fel neurochem, Univ Ill, 59-61; USPHS fel neuroembryol, Univ Wash, St Louis, 61-62, res assoc, 61-64. *Mem:* AAAS; Am Soc Zoologists. *Res:* Behavioral biology; neuroembryology; ontogeny of behavior; ontogeny of central nervous system development. *Mailing Add:* Dept Zool Mich State Univ 203 Natural Sci Bldg East Lansing MI 48824-1115

BALABAN, MURAT OMER, SUPERCRITICAL FLUID EXTRACTION, OHMIC HEATING & THAWING OF BIOLOGICAL MATERIALS. *Current Pos:* asst prof, 86-91, ASSOC PROF FOOD ENG, UNIV FLA, 91- *Personal Data:* b Ankara, Turkey, Feb 5, 52; US citizen; m 77, Canan Bayezit; c Denis T. *Educ:* Middle East Tech Univ, Turkey, BSc, 76; Univ Wash, PhD(food sci & technol), 84. *Prof Exp:* Independent software consult, Wash, 84-85; res assoc, Rutgers Univ, 85-86. *Concurrent Pos:* Mem, Opers Anal Group, Singleton Seafood, Tampa; grantee, Gulf & S Atlantic Fisheries Develop Found, 86-87, Am Alligator Farmers Asn, 87-88, Food Mach Corp, 88-90, Fla Sea grant, Fla Dept Educ, Nat Coastal Res Inst, USDA; mem, Sci Adv Bd Food Mach Corp, 91- *Mem:* Inst Food Technologists; Am Soc Agr Engrs. *Res:* Food safety and quality by food engineering; extraction with supercritical fluids, effects on microorganisms and enzymes; automated ohmic thawing of foods; machine vision and automation for quality evaluation of foods. *Mailing Add:* Food Sci & Human Nutrit Univ Fla PO Box 110370 Gainesville FL 32611-0370. *Fax:* 904-392-9467; *E-Mail:* mob@gnv.ufl.ifas.edu

BALABAN, ROBERT S, HEART & KIDNEY PHYSIOLOGY, BIOENERGETICS. *Current Pos:* Staff fel, 81-85, res physiologist, 85-88, CHIEF, LAB CARDIAC ENERGETICS, NAT HEART, LUNG & BLOOD INST, NIH, 88- *Personal Data:* b Los Angeles, Calif, May 9, 53; m. *Educ:* Duke Univ, PhD(physiol & pharmacol), 79. *Concurrent Pos:* NATO postdoctoral fel, Oxford, Eng. *Mem:* Soc Gen Physiologists; Am Physiol Soc; Biophys Soc; Soc Magnetic Resonance Med. *Mailing Add:* Nat Heart Lung & Blood Inst NIH Bldg 10 Rm B1D61 Bethesda MD 20892-0001

BALABANIAN, NORMAN, ELECTRICAL ENGINEERING. *Current Pos:* COURTESY PROF, UNIV FLA, 91- *Personal Data:* b New London, Conn, Aug 13, 22; c 4. *Educ:* Aleppo Col, Syria, Sci Dipl, 42; Syracuse Univ, BEE, 49, MEE, 51, PhD(elec network synthesis), 54. *Honors & Awards:* Centennial Award, Inst Elec & Electronics Engrs, 84. *Prof Exp:* Instr English, Aleppo Col, Syria, 42-43; from instr to assoc prof elec eng, Syracuse Univ, 49-91, chmn elec & comput eng, 83-90, emer prof elec eng, 91. *Concurrent Pos:* Mem tech staff, Bell Labs, 56; consult ed, Allyn & Bacon Elec Eng Serv, 59-74; dir, Syracuse Electronics Corp, 63-65; mem, Develop Lab, Int Bus Mach Corp, 63; ed, Trans Circuit Theory, 63-65, Trans on Commun, 76 & Technol & Soc Mag, 76, 79-86 & 93-; vis prof, Univ Colo, 65 & Univ Calif, Berkeley, 65-66; consult, UNESCO, 66; mem vis comt, Engrs Coun Prof Develop, 67-70; specialist in tech teacher training, UNESCO, Nat Polytech Inst, Mex, 69-70; sr Fulbright fel, Univ Zagreb, Yugoslavia, 74-75; dir eng & pub affairs, Syracuse Univ, 75-77; consult, UNESCO, Paris, 76; Nat Inst Elec & Electronics Engrs, Algeria, 77-78; vis scholar elec eng, Tufts Univ, 90-, Sci Tech & Soc Prog, Mass Inst Technol, 90- *Mem:* Fel AAAS; fel Inst Elec & Electronics Engrs; Am Soc Eng Educ; Inst Elec & Electronics Engrs Soc Implications Technol (pres, 89-91). *Res:* Electric network theory; network synthesis; linear network analysis; programmed learning; engineering and public affairs; telecommunications policy; technology and society; active network design. *Mailing Add:* 6232 NW 34th Dr Gainesville FL 32653. *Fax:* 617-627-3220

BALACHANDRAN, KASHI RAMAMURTHI, OPERATIONS RESEARCH, APPLIED PROBABILITY. *Current Pos:* mgt consult cost mgt systs & dir, Doctoral Prog, 79-95, PROF BUS, NY UNIV, 95- *Personal Data:* b Madras, India, June 16, 41; m 69, Rajini Sarma; c Siddharth & Sumitra. *Educ:* Univ Madras, India, BE, Hons, 62; Univ Calif, MS, 64; Univ Calif, Berkeley, PhD(opers res), 68; Inst Mgt Acct, CMA, 76. *Prof Exp:* Field engr, Neyveli Lignite Corp, India, 62; designer mech eng, Qual Casting Systs, 63; mem opers res staff planning, Gen Mills, Inc, 63; opers res analyst planning & designing, Nat Cash Regist Co, 67-68; asst prof mgt sci, Univ Wis-Milwaukee, 68-72; assoc prof, Ga Inst Technol, 72-76; assoc prof bus, Univ Ky, 76-79. *Concurrent Pos:* Res fel, Univ Wis, 69; mem, Gov's Comn Educ, Wis, 69-70; assoc ed, J Oper Res Soc India, 75-84; vis prof, Univ Kans, 76, Bolloni Univ, Italy, 94-96 & Int Univ Japan, 96; assoc ed, J Acct, Auditing & Finance. *Mem:* Inst Mgt Sci; Opers Res Soc Am; Oper Res Soc India; Am Acct Asn; Inst Mgt Acct. *Res:* Individual and collective optima in queues; operations research applications; cost allocations and efficient usage of scarce resources; transfer pricing under uncertainty; cost management systems for new manufacturing environemnt; supplier-manufacturer relationships. *Mailing Add:* Stern Sch Bus 434 Tisch Hall NY Univ New York NY 10012-1118. *Fax:* 212-995-4004; *E-Mail:* kbalacha@stern.nyu.edu

BALADY, MICHAEL A, pharmacology, toxicology, for more information see previous edition

BALAGNA, JOHN PAUL, ANALYTICAL CHEMISTRY, RADIOCHEMISTRY. *Current Pos:* RETIRED. *Personal Data:* b Florence, Colo, Aug 19, 20; m 49; c 2. *Educ:* Holy Cross Col, Colo, AB, 41. *Prof Exp:* Chemist, Chem Warfare Serv, US Army, 43-44; staff mem anal chem, Manhattan Dist, Corps Engrs, 44-47; staff mem radiochem, Los Alamos Nat Lab, 47-74, assoc group leader, 74-86. *Concurrent Pos:* Consult, 66-69. *Mem:* AAAS; Inst Elec & Electronics Engrs; Am Chem Soc. *Res:* Design of ultra low level gas filled proportional counters; laboratory scale electromagnetic isotope separation. *Mailing Add:* 223 Rio Bravo Dr Los Alamos NM 87544

BALAGUER, JOHN P, MANUFACTURING, SPACE PROPULSION. *Current Pos:* Flight test engr, Sikorsky Aircraft Div, United Technologies, 60-80, vpres S-76 prog, 80-82, exec vpres mfg div, Pratt & Whitney, East Hartford, Conn, 82-85, PRES, GOVT ENGINES & SPACE PROPULSION DIV, UNITED TECHNOLOGIES, PRATT & WHITNEY, WEST PALM BEACH, 85- *Personal Data:* b Paris, France, July 1, 35; m, Veronica Glasser; c John & Michelle. *Res:* Aerospace engineering. *Mailing Add:* 4971 Ravenel Pl Jacksonville FL 32225

BALAGURA, SAUL, NEUROSURGERY, PHYSIOLOGICAL PSYCHOLOGY. *Current Pos:* RETIRED. *Personal Data:* b Cali, Colombia, Jan 11, 43; US citizen; m 64. *Educ:* Univ Valle, Colombia, MD, 64; Princeton Univ, MA, 66, PhD(psychol), 67, Am Bd Neurol Surgery, 83. *Prof Exp:* Asst prof psychol, Univ Chicago, 67-71; assoc prof, Univ Mass, Amherst, 71-73; resident neurosurg, Downstate Med Ctr, Brooklyn, 73-76; resident neurosurg, Albert Einstein Sch Med, Yeshiva Univ, 76-80; assoc prof clin, Univ Ill, Champaign, 83-88; pvt neurosurg, Victoria, Tex, 88-94. *Concurrent Pos:* NIMH res grant, 67-71. *Mem:* Fel Am Phycol Asn; Am Physiol Soc; Soc Neurosci; Cong Neurol Surg; Am Asn Neurol Surg; fel Am Psychol Asn. *Res:* Neurophysiological and endocrine regulation of feeding behavior; recovery of function after brain injury; feedback systems involved in the control of food intake. *Mailing Add:* PO Box 508 Tesuque NM 87574

BALAGURU, PERUMALSAMY N, STRUCTURAL ANALYSIS & DESIGN, REINFORCED & PRESTRESSED CONCRETE. *Current Pos:* from asst prof to assoc prof, 77-87, PROF CIVIL ENG, RUTGERS, STATE UNIV NJ, 88- *Personal Data:* b Tamil Nadu, India, Mar 26, 47; m 74, Suryaprabha V Sulu; c Bala S & Bala M. *Educ:* Univ Madras, BE Hons, 68; Indian Inst Sci, ME, 70; Univ Ill, Chicago, PhD(struct eng), 77. *Prof Exp:* Assoc lectr civil eng, Univ Madras, 70-73. *Concurrent Pos:* Assoc grad dir, Rutgers, State Univ NJ, 80-86; consult, DuPont de Nemours & Co, 87-89 & Allied Signal, Inc, 87-; vis prof, Northwestern Univ, 90. *Mem:* Am Concrete Inst; Am Soc Civil Engrs. *Res:* Reinforced and prestressed concrete; new construction materials; construction management; computer aided analysis and design; fiber reinforced cement composites and ferrocements; author of 150 publications. *Mailing Add:* Rutgers Univ New Brunswick NJ 08903

BALAJEE, SHANKVERM R, METALLURGICAL ENGINEERING. *Current Pos:* res engr, 71-72, SR RES ENGR METALL ENG, RES DEPT, INLAND STEEL CO, 75- *Personal Data:* b Chikkaballupur, India, Feb 3, 39; m 69; c 2. *Educ:* Univ Nagpur, India, BSC, 58, MSc, 60; Univ Minn, MS, 68; Univ Wis, PhD(metall eng), 71. *Prof Exp:* Sr tech asst mineral technol, Indian Bur Mines, Nagpur, India, 61-62, sr ore dressing off, 62-65. *Concurrent Pos:* Guest lectr, Purdue Univ, 81. *Mem:* Am Inst Mining, Metall & Petrol Engrs; Soc Mining Engrs; Am Soc Metals. *Res:* Process metallurgy dealing with benefication and agglomereter areas dealing with steel plant. *Mailing Add:* 9401 Verbena Dr Munster IN 46321

BALAKRISHNAN, A V, ENGINEERING. *Current Pos:* assoc prof eng, Univ Calif, Los Angeles, 61-62, prof, 62-65, prof math & eng, 65-76, chmn, Dept Syst Sci, 69-76, PROF MATH & PROF ENG & APPL SCI, UNIV CALIF, LOS ANGELES, 76- HEAD, INFO SYSTS DIV, DEPT ENG, 64- *Personal Data:* b Palghat, India, Dec 4, 22; US citizen; m 52; c 4. *Educ:* Univ Madras, BSc, 43, MA, 47; Univ Southern Calif, AM & MS, 50, PhD(math), 54. *Prof Exp:* Sr engr, Radio Corp Am, NJ, 54-56; asst prof math, Univ Southern Calif, 56-57; asst prof math, Univ Calif, Los Angeles, 57-59; sr staff engr systs & res, Space Technol Labs, Inc, 59-61. *Concurrent Pos:* Consult, NASA, 64; consult ed, Syst Sci Series, McGraw-Hill Book Co, 64; chief ed, J Comput & Syst Sci; mem, US Comn 6, Union Radio Sci Int, 63; chmn, Int Symposium Info Theory, 66. *Mem:* Am Math Soc; Inst Math Statist; fel Inst Elec & Electronics Engrs. *Res:* Communication theory; control theory; systems optimization theory. *Mailing Add:* Dept Elec Eng Univ Calif Los Angeles CA 90095-1594

BALAKRISHNAN, KRISHNA, MONOCLONAL ANTIBODIES, IMMUNOCHEMISTRY. *Current Pos:* dir hybridoma sci, 85-88, vpres res & develop, 88-96, VPRES TECHNOL, BERKELEY ANTIBODY CO, RICHMOND, 96- *Personal Data:* b Chelakkara, Kerala, India, June 30, 55; m 84, Sheela Kalyanakrishnan; c Karthik & Purnima. *Educ:* Indian Inst Technol, Kanpur, MSc, 77; Stanford Univ, PhD(biophys chem), 82. *Prof Exp:* Res asst, Chem Dept, Stanford Univ, 77-82; staff scientist, DNAX, Palo Alto, 82-85. *Mem:* AAAS; Am Chem Soc. *Res:* Development and use of monoclonal antibodies for established as well as new applications such as immunoassays, catalytic antibodies and receptor research. *Mailing Add:* 6087 Monterey Richmond CA 94805. *Fax:* 510-442-8940; *E-Mail:* balki@babco.com

BALAKRISHNAN, NARAYANA SWAMY, NUCLEAR MAGNETIC RESONANCE SPECTROSCOPY, CHEMICAL KINETICS. *Current Pos:* AT DEPT CHEM, UNIV GUAM. *Personal Data:* b Madras, India. *Educ:* Univ Madras, BS, 65; Indian Inst Technol, MS, 67; Univ Hawaii, PhD(chem), 78. *Prof Exp:* Instr, Univ Hawaii, 74-81; res scientist & tech sales dir, Indust Anal Lab, Inc, 82- *Concurrent Pos:* Vis prof, Hawaii Loa Col, 80-81. *Mem:* Am Chem Soc. *Res:* Rotational dynamics and geometries in the liquid state; nuclear magnetic resonance in liquid crystal solvents to probe the details of the liquid state. *Mailing Add:* Univ Guam PO Box 5034 Mangilao GU 96923-5034

BALAKRISHNAN, NARAYANASWANY, ORDER STATISTICS, STATISTICAL INFERENCE. *Current Pos:* postdoctoral fel, McMaster Univ, Hamilton, Can, 82-83 & 84, univ res fel, 85-86, from asst prof to assoc prof, 86-95, PROF STATIST, MCMASTER UNIV, HAMILTON, CAN, 95- *Personal Data:* b Tamil Nadu, India, May 2, 56; Can citizen; m 85, Colleen D Cutler; c Sarah M & Julia L. *Educ:* Univ Madras, India, BSc, 76, MSc, 78; Indian Inst Technol, Kanpur, India, PhD(statist), 82. *Prof Exp:* Lectr statist, Indian Inst Technol, Delhi, 81-82; postdoctoral fel, Univ Man, Winnipeg, Can, 83 & Univ Guelph, Can, 84-85. *Concurrent Pos:* Assoc ed, Selected Tables in Math Statist, 90- & Commun Statist, 90-, Comput Statist & Data Anal, Am Jj Math & Mgt Sci, JJ Appl Statist Sci, Parisankkyan Samikka, IIE Transactions, 95-, Appl Probability, 97-; consult & proprietor, Statpro Consult, 91-; vis prof, Univ Waterloo, Waterloo, Can, 92-93 & 96-97. *Mem:* Int Statist Inst; Inst Math Statist; fel Am Statist Asn; Statist Soc Can; Am Soc Qual Control; fel Royal Statist Soc. *Res:* Order statistics; inference for life-testing and reliability models; robust inference; classification theory; statistical quality control; characterizations of statistical distributions; logistic model and inference; regression problems; censoring and truncation; statistical distribution theory; outliers and related issues. *Mailing Add:* Dept Math & Statist McMaster Univ Hamilton ON L8S 4K1 Can. *Fax:* 905-522-1676; *E-Mail:* bala@mcmail.cis.mcmaster.ca

BALAKRISHNAN, V K, COMBINATORIAL & DISCRETE MATHEMATICS. *Current Pos:* From asst prof to assoc prof, 70-81, PROF MATH, UNIV MAINE, 81- *Personal Data:* b India; US citizen. *Educ:* Univ Wis, MS, 65; State Univ NY, Stony Brook, PhD(math), 70. *Concurrent Pos:* Vis fel, Yale Univ, 77-78; assoc dean, Univ Maine, 80-81. *Mem:* Am Math Soc; Soc Indust & Appl Math; Oper Res Soc Am; Asn Comput Mach. *Res:* Graph Theory network flows combinatorial optimization and linear programming; writer of books on discrete mathematics and discrete optimization. *Mailing Add:* Math Dept Univ Maine Orono ME 04469-5752

BALAM, BAXISH SINGH, ANALYTICAL CHEMISTRY, ENVIRONMENTAL CHEMISTRY. *Current Pos:* PROF CHEM, MISS VALLEY STATE UNIV, 69-, CHMN, NATURAL SCI & ENVIRON HEALTH, 96- *Personal Data:* b Kukar Pind, India, Aug 16, 30; US citizen; m 65, Marilyn Cogswell; c Elisabeth, Gabrielle & Bryan. *Educ:* Punjab Univ, India, BSc, 51, MSc, 53; Ohio State Univ, PhD(soil chem), 65. *Prof Exp:* Agr asst soil chem, Dept Agr, Punjab, 53-55; asst prof chem, Col Agr, Univ Nagpur, 55-56 & Univ Jabalpur, 56-58; from asst prof to assoc prof, Punjab Univ, India, 58-66; res assoc agron, Ohio State Univ, 66; adv chem, Int Atomic Energy Agency, UN, 66-68. *Concurrent Pos:* Consult, Govt Iran, Ministry Agr & Rural Develop, 77-78; fac res intern, Environ Protection Agency, 87-89. *Mem:* Am Soc Agron; Soil Sci Soc Am; Am Chem Soc. *Res:* Availability, plant uptake and interactions of soil and fertilizer phosphates; fertilizer technology; assessment of fertilizer requirements; radioisotopes in agricultural research; partial acidulation of rock phosphate; soil salinity and alkalinity; radioactive waste management. *Mailing Add:* 123 Bluebird Dr Greenwood MS 38930. *Fax:* 601-254-3392; *E-Mail:* mamp2@cypress.mcsr.olemiss.edu

BALAMUTH, DAVID P, NUCLEAR PHYSICS. *Current Pos:* assoc prof, 75-80, chmn dept, 92-95, PROF PHYSICS, UNIV PA, 80-, ASSOC DEAN, SCH ARTS & SCI, 95- *Personal Data:* b New York, NY, Nov 4, 42; m 69, Margaret Gordon. *Educ:* Harvard Col, AB, 64; Columbia Univ, PhD(physics), 68. *Prof Exp:* Res assoc physics, Univ Pa, 68-70, asst prof, 70-74; prog officer nuclear physics, NSF, 74-75. *Mem:* Fel Am Phys Soc; AAAS; Sigma Xi. *Res:* Nuclear structure and nuclear reaction mechanisms in light nuclei; study of formation and decay of continuum states using coincidence techniques; use of computers in experimental nuclear physics data acquisition and analysis; spectroscopy of nuclei far from stability. *Mailing Add:* Dept Physics Univ Pa 209 S 33rd St Philadelphia PA 19104-6396. *Fax:* 215-898-2010; *E-Mail:* balamuth@dept.physics.upenn.edu

BALANDRIN, MANUEL F, PHARMACEUTICAL CHEMISTRY, DRUG DESIGN. *Current Pos:* RES SCIENTIST, 89-96, SR RES SCIENTIST MED CHEM, NPS PHARMACEUT, INC, 96- *Personal Data:* b Havana, Cuba, Oct 5, 52, US citizen; m 77, Donna J Barnow; c David E. *Educ:* Univ Ill, BS, 77; PhD(pharmacog), 82. *Honors & Awards:* Platinum Award, Agri Food Chem Am, Chem Soc, 96. *Prof Exp:* Scientist natural prod chem, Native Plants, Inc, 82-83, coordr phytochem, 83-88, sr res scientist natural prod chem, 83-88. *Concurrent Pos:* Consult, Stand Oil, Ohio, 82-85; prin investr, Dept Energy, 83; US Dept Agr, 83-85, NSF, 84 & 86. *Mem:* Am Chem Soc; Am Pharmaceut Asn; Am Soc Pharmacog; Int Soc Chem Ecol; Acad Pharmaceut Res & Sci. *Res:* Isolation and structure elucidation of biologically active natural plant products used as chemotherapeutic and insect control agents; quinolizidine alkaloids, saponins, terpenoids, tannins; drug design; structure-activity relationships of medicinal agents. *Mailing Add:* NPS Pharmaceut Inc Univ Res Park 420 Chipeta Way Salt Lake City UT 84108. *Fax:* 801-583-4961; *E-Mail:* mbalandrin@npsp.com

BALANIS, CONSTANTINE A, ELECTRICAL ENGINEERING. *Current Pos:* prof, Dept Elec Eng, Col Eng & Appl Sci, 83-91, REGENTS' PROF, 91-, DIR, TELECOMMUNICATIONS RES CTR, ARIZ STATE UNIV, 88- *Personal Data:* b Trikala, Thessalia, Greece, Oct 29, 38; m 72, Helen Jouaras; c Erini & Stephanie. *Educ:* Va Polytech Inst, BSEE, 64; Univ Va, MEE, 66; Ohio State Univ, PhD(elec eng), 69. *Honors & Awards:* Individual Achievement Award, Region 6, Inst Elec & Electronics Engrs. *Prof Exp:* Engr, Langley Res Ctr, NASA, Hampton, Va, 64-70; from vis assoc prof to assoc prof elec eng, WVa Univ, 70-76, prof, 76-83. *Concurrent Pos:* Asst prof lectr, George Washington Univ, 68-70; consult, Nat Radio Astron Observ, 72-74 & Naval Air Test Ctr 76-, Nat Inst Occup Safety & Health, 80-81, Southwest Res Inst, 81-84, Motorola Inc, 84-, Loral Syst Group, 86-88 & Gen Dynamics, 86; grants, NASA, Dept Trans, Fed Aviation Admin, NSF, Naval Air Test Ctr, Army Res Off, Energy Res Develop Admin, Dept Energy, Motorola Inc, Boeing Helicopters, IBM, McDonnell Douglas, Silorsky Aircraft, Rockwell Int, Gen Dynamics, US Bur Mines; assoc ed, Inst Elec & Electronics Engrs Trans Geosci & Remote Sensing, Inst Elec & Electronics Engrs Trans Antennas Propagation. *Mem:* Fel Inst Elec & Electronics Engrs; Am Soc Eng Educ; Sigma Xi. *Res:* Computational electromagnetics, electromagnetic wave radiation, propagation and scattering; electromagnetic wave propagation in microwave integrated circuit lines. *Mailing Add:* Dept Elec Eng Ariz State Univ Tempe AZ 85287-7206. *Fax:* 602-965-8325; *E-Mail:* balanis@asu.edu

BALANTEKIN, AKIF BAHA, THEORETICAL PHYSICS AT THE INTERFACE OF NUCLEAR PHYSICS, PARTICLE PHYSICS & ASTROPHYSICS. *Current Pos:* from asst prof to assoc prof, 86-92, PROF PHYSICS, UNIV WIS-MADISON, 92- *Personal Data:* b Ankara, Turkey, 1954. *Educ:* Middle East Tech Univ, BS, 75; Yale Univ, PhD(physics), 82. *Honors & Awards:* Presidential Young Investr, NSF, 87; Jefferson Cup, Martin Marietta Corp, 86; Alexander Von Humboldt Sr US Scientist Award, 96. *Prof Exp:* Res assoc, Mass Inst Technol, 82-84; E P Wigner fel, Oak Ridge Nat Lab, 84-86. *Concurrent Pos:* Mem exec comt, Div Nuclear Physics, Am Phys Soc, 94-96; sr fel, Japan Soc Prom Sci, 94. *Mem:* Fel Am Phys Soc. *Res:* Theoretical physics at the interface of particle physics, nuclear physics and astrophysics; neutrino astrophysics. *Mailing Add:* Dept Physics Univ Wis 1150 University Ave Madison WI 53706. *Fax:* 608-262-8628; *E-Mail:* baha@nucth.physics.wisc.edu

BALAS, EGON, MATHEMATICAL PROGRAMMING. *Current Pos:* Ford distinguished res prof, Carnegie-Mellon Univ, 67-68, GSIA alumni chair prof, 80-97, PROF INDUST ADMIN & APPL MATH, CARNEGIE-MELLON UNIV, 68-, UNIV PROF, 90-, THOMAS LORD PROF OPER RES, 97- *Personal Data:* b Cluj, Romania; US citizen; c 2. *Educ:* Bolyai Univ, Romania, dipl licentiae econ; Univ Brussels, DScEc; Univ Paris, DrSci(math). *Honors & Awards:* John Von Neumann Theory Prize, 95. *Prof Exp:* Lectr, Inst Econ Sci & Planning, Bucharest, 49-58; res assoc, Inst Econ Res Romanian Acad, 56-58; proj engr, Designing Inst Forestry & Timer Indust, 59-61, head, Math Prog Group, 62-64; head, Math Prog Sect, Ctr Math Statist Romanian Acad, 64-65; res fel, Int Comput Ctr, Rome, 66. *Concurrent Pos:* Vis prof opers res, Univ Toronto & Stanford Univ, 67 & vis prof systs eng, Fed Energy Admin, 76; assoc ed, Opers Res, 67-, Annals Opers Res, 83- & Naval Res Logistics Quart, 79-89, ed assoc, Europ J Oper Res, 76-; var res grants, NSF, Off Naval Res, NATO & Air Force Off Sci Res, 67-; mem, Comt Recommendations US Army Basic Res, Nat Res Coun, 77-80; consult, var indust co & govt agencies. *Mem:* Opers Res Soc Am; Soc Indust & Appl Math; Math Prog Soc; Am Math Soc; Inst Mgt Sci. *Res:* Integer programming; combinatorial optimization; network models; polyhedral theory; projection methods; scheduling and sequencing; distribution and location theory; author or co-author of over 140 publications; developer of scheduling system for steel rolling. *Mailing Add:* Carnegie Mellon Univ GSIA Pittsburgh PA 15213

BALASINSKI, ARTUR, PROCESS-RELATED DEFECTS IN SILICON DIOXIDE. *Current Pos:* STAFF ENGR, CYPRESS SEMI CONDUCTOR, 97- *Personal Data:* b Warsaw, Poland, June 30, 57; m 83; c 1. *Educ:* Warsaw Univ Technol, MS, 80, PhD(elec eng), 86. *Prof Exp:* Res scientist elec eng, Warsaw Univ Technol, 87-88, asst prof, 88-89; assoc elec eng, Yale Univ, 89-93, res assoc, 89-93; sr engr, SGS Thomson Microelectronics, 93-97. *Mem:* Electrochem Soc; Inst Elec & Electronics Engrs. *Res:* Investigation of radiation and hot-electron effects in metal-oxide-semiconductor capacitors and transistors; properties of dielectric layers (silicon dioxide, diamond like carbon, etc); charge trapping; studies of work function difference; experimental work involving device fabrication and measurements. *Mailing Add:* 9990 N Scottsdale Rd Paradise Valley AZ 85253. *Fax:* 972-466-7582

BALASKO, JOHN ALLAN, AGRONOMY, CROP PHYSIOLOGY. *Current Pos:* Asst prof agron, 70-74, assoc prof, 74-78, PROF AGRON, WVA UNIV, 78- *Personal Data:* b Morgantown, WVa, July 16, 41; m 63; c 3. *Educ:* WVa Univ, BS, 63, MS, 67; Univ Wis, Madison, PhD(agron), 71. *Mem:* Crop Sci Soc Am; Am Soc Agron; Am Forage & Grassland Coun. *Res:* Carbohydrate metabolism in perennial forage plants; forage management and forage quality. *Mailing Add:* Div Plant Sci WVa Univ PO Box 6108 Morgantown WV 26506-0001

BALASUBRAHMANYAN, VRIDDHACHALAM K, physics, astrophysics, for more information see previous edition

BALASUBRAMANIAN, KRISHNAN, THEORETICAL CHEMISTRY, RELATIVISTIC QUANTUM CHEMISTRY. *Current Pos:* asst prof 83-86, ASSOC PROF CHEM, ARIZ STATE UNIV, 87- *Personal Data:* b Bangalore, India, Apr 10, 56; m 82; c 1. *Educ:* Birla Inst Technol & Sci, MSc, 77; Johns Hopkins Univ, MA, & PhD, 80. *Prof Exp:* Res assoc chem phys, Lawrence Berkeley Lab, Univ Calif, Berkeley, 80-82, vis lectr chem, 83. *Concurrent Pos:* Alfred P Sloan fel, Sloan Foundation, 84-; panelist, Air Force Off Sci Res, Chem Sci Panel, Nat ACad Sci, 88- *Mem:* NY Acad Sci; Am Chem Soc. *Res:* Theoretical and computer chemistry; relativistic quantum chemistry; chemical applications of group theory and graph theory; artificial intelligence. *Mailing Add:* Ariz State Univ Tempe AZ 85287-0002

BALATSKY, ALEXANDER V, SUPERCONDUCTIVITY IN STRONGLY CORRELATED SYSTEMS. *Current Pos:* Jr Oppenheimer fel, 91-94, STAFF MEM, LOS ALAMOS NAT LAB, 94- *Personal Data:* m 88, Galya Martemyanova; c Kirill & Darya. *Educ:* Landau Inst Theoret Physics, PhD(superfluidity), 87. *Prof Exp:* Res scientist, Landau Inst, 87-89; postdoctoral, Univ Ill, Urbana, 89-90, vis res asst prof, 90-91. *Res:* Effects of strong correlations and quantum fluctuations on properties of metals and superconductors. *Mailing Add:* Theory Div B262 Los Alamos Nat Lab Los Alamos NM 87545

BALAZOVICH, KENNETH J, PEDIATRICS. *Current Pos:* res fel, 84-87, asst res scientist, Dept Pediat, 87-96, ASST RES SCIENTIST, DEPT BIOL, MED SCH, UNIV MICH, 97- *Personal Data:* b Detroit, Mich, Dec 21, 54; m. *Educ:* Wayne State Univ, BS, 79; Univ Miami, PhD(human anat & cell biol), 84. *Prof Exp:* Res technician, Wayne State Univ, 80-81; teaching asst, Sch Med, Univ Miami, 83. *Concurrent Pos:* First award, NIH, 88- & 91- *Mem:* Am Soc Cell Biol; Electron Micros Soc Am; NY Acad Sci; Sigma Xi; Am Soc Hemat; Am Fedn Clin Res. *Mailing Add:* Dept Biol Univ Mich 3103 Natural Sci Bldg Ann Arbor MI 48109

BALAZS, ENDRE ALEXANDER, BIOCHEMISTRY. *Current Pos:* PRES, BIOMATRIX INC, 81- *Personal Data:* b Budapest, Hungary, Jan 10, 20; nat US; m 45; c 2. *Educ:* Univ Budapest, MD, 43. *Hon Degrees:* MD, Royal Univ Uppsala, 67. *Honors & Awards:* Friedenwald Award, Asn Res Vision & Ophthal, 63. *Prof Exp:* Res asst histol, biol & embryol, Univ Budapest, 40-43, asst prof, 43-44, asst prof pharmacol, 45; dir, Lab Biol Anthrop, Mus Natural Hist, Budapest, 45-47; assoc exp histol, Karolinska Inst, Sweden, 48-51; assoc dir, Retina Found-Int Biol & Med Sci, 51-62, pres, 62-63 & 65-68, vpres, 63-65, dir dept connective tissue res, 62-69; res dir, Dept Connective Tissue Res, Boston Biomed Res Inst, 69-76, exec dir, 74-75; Malcolm P Aldrich prof ophthal, Col Physicians & Surgeons, Columbia Univ, 76-, dir res, 76- *Concurrent Pos:* Vis scientist, Swed Inst, 47; instr, Harvard Med Sch, 51-56, lectr, 56-, mem bd freshman adv, 57-61; Mass Eye & Ear Infirmary fel ophthal, 51-56, biochemist, 56-6S; co-ed-in-chief, Exp Eye Res, 62-; Guggenheim fel, 68-69; vis scientist, Dept Tumor Biol, Karolinska Inst, Sweden, 68-69; vis prof chem, Univ Salford, Eng, 69-76; mem, Coun Biol

Educ. *Mem:* Reticuloendothelial Soc; fel Geront Soc; Asn Res Vision & Ophthal; fel NY Acad Sci; Int Soc Eye Res (pres 74-78). *Res:* Biochemistry and physiology of connective tissues, especially of the eye and joint; molecular biology of the intercellular matrix; physical biochemistry of glycosaminoglycans. *Mailing Add:* Matrix Biol Inst 65 Railroad Ave 2nd Floor Ridgefield NJ 07657-0174

BALAZS, LOUIS A P, THEORETICAL HIGH ENERGY PHYSICS. *Current Pos:* assoc prof, 70-78, PROF PHYSICS, PURDUE UNIV, 78- *Personal Data:* b Tsing-Tao, China, July 31, 37; US citizen; m, Beth A Winebrenner. *Educ:* Univ Calif, Berkeley, BA, 59, PhD(physics), 62. *Prof Exp:* Mem, Sch Math, Inst Advan Study, 62-63; res fel, Calif Inst Technol, 63-64; vis prof, Tata Inst Fundamental Res, India, 64-65; asst prof, Univ Calif, Los Angeles, 65-70. *Concurrent Pos:* Alfred P Sloan Found fel, 67-69; visitor, Imp Col, London, 68-69, Fermi Nat Accel Lab, 76 & Univ Pierre et Marie Curie, Paris, 79 & 81. *Mem:* Fel Am Phys Soc. *Res:* Relativistic non-perturbative model calculations in elementary-particle theory for the self-consistent amplitude-unitarization dynamical generation of electroweak-theory symmetry-breaking light bound-state neutral Higgs scalars. *Mailing Add:* Dept Physics Purdue Univ Sch Sci West Lafayette IN 47907

BALAZS, NANDOR LASZLO, THEORETICAL PHYSICS. *Current Pos:* PROF PHYSICS, STATE UNIV NY, STONY BROOK, 61- *Personal Data:* b Budapest, Hungary, July 7, 26; nat US; c 1. *Educ:* Univ Budapest, MSc, 48; Univ Amsterdam, PhD(physics), 51. *Honors & Awards:* Schrodinger Mem lectr, Zurich & Dublin, 76; J L Synge Jubilee lectr, Dublin, 82. *Prof Exp:* Fel, Dublin Inst Advan Study, 51-52; Nat Res Coun Can fel, 52; mem, Inst Advan Studies, Princeton Univ, 53; vis assoc prof physics, Univ Ala, 53, assoc prof, 53-54; sr theoret physicist, Am Optical Co, 55-56; res assoc, Enrico Fermi Inst Nuclear Studies, Chicago, 56-59; mem res staff, Plasma Physics Lab, Princeton Univ, 59-61. *Concurrent Pos:* Consult, Gen Atomics, La Jolla, Calif, 59, Am Optical Co, Mass, 60 & Dept Chem, Univ Calif, San Diego, 62; NSF grants, 62-64 & 64-; consult comt col physics, 63 & 65, Gen Tel & Electronics, Bayside, NY, 63-65 & Laser Inc, 66-67; vis prof, Univ Wash, 65, Dublin Inst Advan Study, 67, 70 & 71, Univ Cambridge, 68, Oxford Univ, 72, Max-Planck-Inst Nuclear Physics, Heidelberg, 76 & 78, Inst Theor Phys, Tech Univ Munich, 77-79, 81 & 89, Centre d'Etudes Nucleaire, Saclay, 80 & 84, Inst Nuclear Physics, Kernforschungsanlage, Julich, 81 & Inst Phys Nucleaire, Orsay, 84; State of NY distinguished fac res fel, 68; exchange visit, Nat Acad Sci, Budapest, 80 & NSF, 81, 82 & 84; vis prof Theor Physics Serv, CEN-Saclay & Inst Nuclear Physics, Orsay, 84-88 & 86-90; vis prof, Los Alamos Nat Lab, 90, consult, 92- *Mem:* Am Phys Soc. *Res:* Statistical mechanics; relativity theory; quantum mechanics. *Mailing Add:* Dept Physics State Univ NY Stony Brook NY 11794. *E-Mail:* balazs@nuclear.physics.sunysb.edu

BALAZS, TIBOR, TOXICOLOGY. *Current Pos:* RETIRED. *Personal Data:* b Sarbogard, Hungary, Mar 1, 22; US citizen; m 49; c 1. *Educ:* Univ Agr Sci, Hungary, Vet Surg, 45, DMV, 49; Pazmany Peter Univ, MPharm, 48. *Honors & Awards:* Arnold J Lehman Award, Soc Toxicol. *Prof Exp:* Asst prof pharmacol, Univ Agr Sci, Hungary, 46-50; sr biologist, Nat Inst Pub Health, Hungary, 50-56; res toxicologist, Ayerst Lab Div, Am Home Prod Co, Quebec, 57-59; res toxicologist, Food & Drug Directorate, Can Dept Nat Health & Welfare, 59-63; res pharmacologist, Lederle Labs Div, Am Cyanamid Co, 63-67, group leader toxicol, 67-69; asst dir toxicol, Smith Kline & French Labs, Pa, 69-71; chief Drug Toxicol Br, Div Drug Biol Ctr Drugs & Biologics, Food & Drug Admin, 71-88. *Concurrent Pos:* Adj prof, Dept Pharmacol, Sch Med, Howard Univ, Washington, DC. *Mem:* Vet Med Asn; Soc Toxicol; Am Soc Pharmacol & Exp Therapeut; Soc Toxicol Path; fel Acad Vet & Comparative Toxicol; Acad Toxicol Sci. *Res:* Drug toxicology; pharmacology; experimental pathology. *Mailing Add:* 5500 Friendship Blvd No N22 Chevy Chase MD 20815-7219

BALBES, RAYMOND, MATHEMATICS. *Current Pos:* from asst prof to assoc prof, 66-78, PROF MATH, CHMN DEPT & COORDR SEC MATH, UNIV MO, ST LOUIS, 78- *Personal Data:* b Los Angeles, Calif, Dec 14, 40; m 62; c 2. *Educ:* Univ Calif, Los Angeles, BS, 62, MA, 64, PhD(math), 66. *Prof Exp:* Asst math, Univ Calif, Los Angeles, 62-66. *Concurrent Pos:* Consult microcomput graphics. *Mem:* Math Asn Am; Am Math Soc. *Res:* Lattice theory, particularly distributive lattices and Boolean algebras; projective and injective distributive lattices; order sum of distributive lattices; representation theory for prime and implicative semi-lattices. *Mailing Add:* Dept Math Univ Mo St Louis St Louis MO 63121-4499

BALBINDER, ELIAS, GENETICS, MOLECULAR BIOLOGY. *Current Pos:* adj prof genetics, 82-93, RES PROF, DEPT BIOCHEM, BIOPHYS & GENETICS, UNIV COLO HEALTH SCI CTR, 93- *Personal Data:* b Warsaw, Poland, Jan 22, 26; US citizen; m 55; c 2. *Educ:* Univ Mich, BS, 49; Ind Univ, PhD(cytogenetics), 57. *Prof Exp:* Res assoc & instr zool, Univ Pa, 56-57; res assoc genetics, Carnegie Inst, 57-60; Am Cancer Soc fel biol, Univ Calif, La Jolla, 60-63; vis investr Fulbright travel grant, Univ Buenos Aires, 63; from asst prof to prof genetics, Syracuse Univ, 63-76; dir genetics & carcinogenesis res, AMC, Cancer Res Ctr, 76-82. *Concurrent Pos:* Adj prof microbiol, Univ Colo Med Sch, 76-; mem, NSF genetics panel, 77-79; vis prof Fulbright fel, Univ Los Andes, Bogota, Colombia, 81. *Mem:* Fel AAAS; Am Soc Microbiol; Genetics Soc Am; Environ Mutagen Soc. *Res:* Evolution of tryptophan synthetase; mutation and recombination in bacteria; fine structure genetics; regulation of gene expression; carcinogenesis. *Mailing Add:* Dept Biochem Biophys & Genetics Univ Colo Health Sci Ctr 4200 E Ninth Ave B-121 Denver CO 80262. *Fax:* 303-270-8215; *E-Mail:* elias.balbinder@uchsc.edu

BALBONI, EDWARD RAYMOND, INSECT PHYSIOLOGY. *Current Pos:* From instr to asst prof, 62-69, ASSOC PROF BIOL SCI, HUNTER COL, 69- *Personal Data:* b Springfield, Mass, Dec 7, 30; m 54. *Educ:* Boston Univ, AB, 57, AM, 58; Univ Mass, PhD(entom), 62. *Concurrent Pos:* NSF grant, 65-70. *Mem:* AAAS; Entom Soc Am; Am Soc Zool; NY Acad Sci; Sigma Xi. *Res:* Insect flight muscle metabolism. *Mailing Add:* 201E 17th St Apt 8F New York NY 10003-3635

BALBUS, STEVEN ANDREW, ASTROPHYSICAL GAS DYNAMICS, MAGNETOHYDRODYNAMICS. *Current Pos:* res asst prof, 85-87, from asst prof to assoc prof, 87-97, PROF ASTRON, UNIV VA, 97- *Personal Data:* b Philadelphia, Pa, Nov 23, 53; m 80, Barbara Small; c Adam Andrew & Ian Alexander. *Educ:* Mass Inst Technol, BS(math) & BS(physics), 75; Univ Calif, Berkeley, PhD(physics), 81. *Prof Exp:* Res fel, Mass Inst Technol, 81-83 & Princeton Univ, 83-85. *Mem:* Am Astron Soc; Int Astron Union. *Res:* Astrophysical gas dynamics; contributions to the subfields of thermal conduction in plasmas, thermal instabilities in hot plasmas, galactic structure and accretion disk theory. *Mailing Add:* Astron Dept Univ Va Charlottesville VA 22903. *Fax:* 804-924-3104

BALCER-BROWNSTEIN, JOSEFINE P, ENVIRONMENTAL PHYSIOLOGY, PUBLIC HEALTH. *Current Pos:* EVALUATOR, DIV CHRONIC DIS, COMMUNITY HEALTH PROM BR, CTRS DIS CONTROL, 90-, HEALTH EDUC SPECIALIST. *Personal Data:* b Augsburg, Ger, Mar 19, 48; m; c 1. *Educ:* Univ Calif, Santa Barbara, PhD(environ physiol), 77. *Prof Exp:* Assoc res coordr, Sch Med, La State Univ, 79-86. *Mem:* Am Pub Health Asn; Am Soc Training & Develop; Nat Soc Performance & Instr. *Mailing Add:* Ctr Dis Control MS K-45 4770 Buford Hwy NE Atlanta GA 30341-3724

BALCERZAK, MARION JOHN, MECHANICAL ENGINEERING. *Current Pos:* FOUNDER, M T BALCERZAK & ASSOCS, 90- *Personal Data:* b Baltimore, Md, Oct 28, 33; m 58; c 4. *Educ:* Univ Detroit, BME, 56; Northwestern Univ, Evanston, MSME, 58, PhD(mech eng), 61. *Honors & Awards:* Charles T Main Award, Am Soc Mech Engrs, 56. *Prof Exp:* Res engr, R C Ingersol Res Ctr, Borg Warner Corp, 60-62; res engr, Gard, Inc, 62-64, dir appl mech, 65-68, tech dir, 69-76, vpres & gen mgr, 77-80, pres & dir res & develop Gard Inc, GATX Corp, 80-84; group vpres technol group, Chamberlain Mfg Corp, Unit Duchossois Indust Inc, 84-90. *Mem:* Am Soc Mech Engrs; Am Inst Aeronaut & Astronaut; Am Soc Testing & Mat; Am Mgt Asn. *Res:* Management of research and development subsidiary which provides advanced design, analysis and application engineering services to industry and the government. *Mailing Add:* 2750 Crabtree Lane Northbrook IL 60062

BALCERZAK, STANLEY PAUL, INTERNAL MEDICINE, HEMATOLOGY & ONCOLOGY. *Current Pos:* assoc prof, 67-71, dir, Div Hemat-Oncol, 69-94, PROF MED, OHIO STATE UNIV, 71-, DEP DIR, COMPREHENSIVE CANCER CTR, 84- *Personal Data:* b Pittsburgh, Pa, Apr 27, 30; m 53; c 8. *Educ:* Univ Pittsburgh, BS, 53; Univ Md, Baltimore, MD, 55. *Prof Exp:* Instr med, Univ Chicago, 59-60; consult hemat & med, Walter Reed Army Inst, 60-62; from instr to asst prof med, Univ Pittsburgh, 62-67. *Concurrent Pos:* Consult hemat, Dayton Vet Admin Hosp, 67- & Wright Patterson Air Force Hosp, 67- *Mem:* Am Col Physicians; Cent Soc Clin Res; Am Fedn Clin Res; Am Soc Hemat; AMA; Am Soc Clin Oncol; Am Asn Cancer Res. *Res:* Iron metabolism; oxygen transport; abnormal hemoglobins; tumor immunology; clinical trials in new drug development; magnetic resonance imaging and spectroscopy as applied to sickle cell disease and cancer. *Mailing Add:* Div Hemat Oncol N-1021 Ohio State Univ Hosp 410 W Tenth St Columbus OH 43210-1236

BALCH, ALAN LEE, INORGANIC CHEMISTRY. *Current Pos:* Asst prof chem, Univ Calif, Los Angeles, 66-70, from asst prof to assoc prof, 70-77, PROF CHEM, UNIV CALIF, DAVIS, 77-, CHAIR, CHEM, 94- *Personal Data:* b Pottstown, Pa, Aug 21, 40, m 61, Paula Burnett; c Kimberly, Tamara & Rudolph. *Educ:* Cornell Univ, BA, 62; Harvard Univ, PhD(chem), 67. *Honors & Awards:* Creativity Award, Nat Sci Found; Reiley lectr, Univ Notre Dame. *Mem:* Chem Soc London; Am Chem Soc. *Res:* Synthesis, structure and reactions of transition metal complexes; reactions of metalloporphyrins; oxidation catalysts, fullereness. *Mailing Add:* Dept Chem Univ Calif Davis CA 95616. *Fax:* 530-752-8995; *E-Mail:* albalch@ucdavis.edu

BALCH, ALFRED HUDSON, GEOPHYSICS. *Current Pos:* MEM STAFF, US GEOL SURV, DENVER, COLO, 74- *Personal Data:* b Manhattan, Kans, May 22, 28; m 53; c 3. *Educ:* Stanford Univ, BS, 50; Colo Sch Mines, DSc(geophys), 64. *Prof Exp:* Asst petrol eng, Stanford Univ, 50-52; seismic computist, Phillips Petrol Co, 55-57 & Chevron Oil Co div, Stand Oil Co Calif, 57-58; asst, Colo Sch Mines, 58-63; adv res geophysicist, Marathon Oil Co, 63-71; assoc prof geophys, Colo Sch Mines, 71-74. *Mem:* AAAS; Soc Explor Geophys; Am Geophys Union; Sigma Xi; Europ Asn Explor Geophys. *Res:* Wave propagation; geophysical data analysis techniques from random noise theory. *Mailing Add:* 919 Homestake Dr Golden CO 80401

BALCH, CHARLES MITCHELL, SURGICAL ONCOLOGY, IMMUNOLOGY. *Current Pos:* head, div surg & chmn, Dept Gen Surg, 86-93, VPRES, HOSP & CLINICS (AD INTERIM), M D ANDERSON CANCER CTR, 93- *Personal Data:* b Milford, Del, Aug 24, 42; m 66; c 4. *Educ:* Univ Toledo, BS, 63, Columbia Univ, MD, 67. *Prof Exp:* Intern surg, Med Ctr, Duke Univ, 67-68; prog specialist, Gen Clin Res Ctr Br, NIH, 68-70; resident gen surg, Med Ctr, Univ Ala, Birmingham, 70-71 & 73-75; fel immunol, Scripps Clin & Res Found, 71-73; from asst prof to assoc prof surg,

Med Ctr, Univ Ala, Birmingham, 75-81, prof, 81-, assoc prof microbiol, 81- *Concurrent Pos:* Scientist, Comprehensive Cancer Ctr, 75-; Am Cancer Soc jr fac fel, 76-79. *Mem:* Soc Univ Surgeons; Asn Acad Surg; Am Asn Immunologists; Am Asn Cancer Res. *Res:* Human cellular immunobiology; tumor immunology; adjunctive therapy for neoplast disease. *Mailing Add:* M D Anderson Cancer Ctr 1515 Holcombe Blvd Houston TX 77030

BALCH, DONALD JAMES, ANIMAL BREEDING. *Current Pos:* RETIRED. *Personal Data:* b Hanover, NH, July 15, 22; m 46, Mary Sawyer; c Brenda Charron & Brian. *Educ:* Univ NH, BS, 48, MS, 52; Va Polytech Inst, PhD(animal breeding), 62. *Prof Exp:* Instr animal husb, Univ NH, 50-51; from instr to emer prof animal sci, Univ Vt, 52-90, dir, Morgan Horse Farm, 72-85. *Mem:* Am Soc Animal Sci. *Mailing Add:* PO Box 85 Underhill VT 05489

BALCH, WILLIAM E, MOLECULAR BIOLOGY, BIOCHEMISTRY. *Current Pos:* ASSOC MEM, DEPT CELL & MOLECULAR BIOL, SCRIPPS RES INST, 88- *Personal Data:* b Corvallis, Ore, Feb 22, 49. *Educ:* Portland State Univ, BSc, 71; Univ Ill, PhD(microbiol), 79. *Prof Exp:* Res asst & res assoc, Dept Biol, Portland State Univ, 71-73 & Dept Microbiol, Univ Ill, 73-79; NIH postdoctoral scholar, Dept Biochem, Stanford Univ, 79-83; from asst prof to assoc prof, Dept Molecular Biophys & Biochem, Yale Univ, 83-88. *Mem:* Fedn Am Socs Exp Biol. *Res:* In vitro reconstitution of vesicular trafficking in the secretory pathway; biochemical and molecular characterization of vesicle fission and fusion events regulating endoplasmic reticulum to Golgi protein transport; author of 27 technical publications. *Mailing Add:* Dept Molecular & Cellular Biol Scripps Res Inst 10550 N Torrey Pines Rd La Jolla CA 92037-1092

BALCHUM, OSCAR JOSEPH, internal medicine, pulmonary diseases; deceased, see previous edition for last biography

BALCZIAK, LOUIS WILLIAM, EDUCATIONAL STATISTICS. *Current Pos:* from asst prof to assoc prof, 50-63, PROF CHEM, MANKATO STATE UNIV, 63- *Personal Data:* b Duluth, Minn, Feb 11, 18; m 46; c 1. *Educ:* Duluth State Teachers Col, BS, 40; Univ Minn, AM, 49, PhD(ed statist), 53. *Prof Exp:* Instr chem, Duluth State Teachers Col, 41-44 & 46-47 & Duluth Br, Univ Minn, 47-48. *Concurrent Pos:* Mem, NSF Summer Insts, 59-65. *Mem:* Am Chem Soc. *Res:* Inorganic chemistry; nuclear chemistry. *Mailing Add:* 1114 Anderson Dr Mankato MN 56001

BALD, KENNETH CHARLES, PHYSICAL CHEMISTRY. *Current Pos:* res chemist,69-82, MGR COATING DEVELOP, RIEGEL PROD CORP, 82-; SR PROD TECHNOLOGIST, JAMES RIVER GRAPHICS. *Personal Data:* b Rock Island, Ill, Oct 27, 30; m 65; c 4. *Educ:* St Ambrose Col, AB, 52; St Louis Univ, PhD(phys chem), 62. *Prof Exp:* Chemist, Callery Chem Co, 52-57; teaching fel, St Louis Univ, 57-62; res chemist, M W Kellogg Co, 62-69; res chemist, Riegel Prod Corp, 69-82, mgr coating develop, 82- *Mem:* Am Chem Soc; Tech Asn Pulp & Paper Indust; Am Soc Qual Eng. *Res:* Development of electrochemical processes for industrial applications; development of electrophotographic products, cured release products, and other specialty coated papers; development of coated printable decorative products; quality assurance decorative products. *Mailing Add:* 160 N Main St South Hadley MA 01075-1714

BALDA, RUSSELL PAUL, ANIMAL ECOLOGY. *Current Pos:* From asst prof to prof, 66-88, REGENT'S PROF BIOL, NORTHERN ARIZ UNIV, 88- *Personal Data:* b Oshkosh, Wis, June 14, 39; m 87; c 3. *Educ:* Univ Wis, Oshkosh, BS, 61; Univ Ill, MS, 63, PhD(zool), 67. *Mem:* Ecol Soc Am; Am Ornith Union; Cooper Ornith Soc (secy, 75-76); Wilson Ornith Soc; Asn Study Animal Behav; Sigma Xi. *Res:* Spatial memory in seed caching birds; social behavior of birds. *Mailing Add:* Dept Biol Sci Northern Ariz Univ Flagstaff AZ 86011-0001

BALDAUF, GUNTHER H(ERMAN), CHEMICAL ENGINEERING, INDUSTRIAL CHEMISTRY. *Current Pos:* PAPER CONSULT, 86- *Personal Data:* b Munich, Ger, May 20, 23; nat US; m 48; c 4. *Educ:* Mass Inst Technol, 44, MS, 46, DSc, 49. *Prof Exp:* Chem engr, Godfrey L Cabot, Inc, 45-47 & Ecusta Paper Div, Olin Mathieson Chem Corp, 49-59; res mgr, Allied Paper Corp, 59-63; consult, Nadelman-Baldauf & Assocs, Inc, 63-65; mgr cent tech serv, Simpson Paper Co, 65-86. *Mem:* Am Soc Qual Control; Tech Asn Pulp & Paper Indust; Paper Mgt Asn. *Res:* Adhesives; pulp and paper manufacture; paper coating; process and quality control; copier technology. *Mailing Add:* 609 Fleetwood Dr Modesto CA 95350

BALDER, JAY ROYAL, CHEMICAL ENGINEERING. *Current Pos:* CONSULT MGR, ENG EVAL, ENG SERV DIV, E I DU PONT DE NEMOURS & CO, INC, 85- *Personal Data:* b Bridgeport, Conn, Feb 4, 41; c 2. *Educ:* Univ Del, BChE, 63; Univ Calif, Berkeley, PhD(chem eng), 67. *Mem:* Am Inst Chem Engrs. *Mailing Add:* 104 Fox Lane Newark DE 19711

BALDESCHWIELER, JOHN DICKSON, BIOCHEMISTRY, CHEMICAL PHYSICS. *Current Pos:* prof, 73-96, J STANLEY JOHNSON PROF CHEM, CALIF INST TECHNOL, 96- *Personal Data:* b Elizabeth, NJ, Nov 14, 33; c 3. *Educ:* Cornell Univ, BChemE, 56; Univ Calif, Berkeley, PhD(phys chem), 59. *Honors & Awards:* Am Chem Soc Award, 67; Am Acad Arts & Sci Award, 72. *Prof Exp:* Lectr chem, Harvard Univ, 60, instr, 60-62, asst prof, 62-65; assoc prof, Stanford Univ, 65-67, prof, 67-71; dep dir, Off Sci & Technol, Washington, DC, 71-73. *Concurrent Pos:* Consult, Ballistic Res Labs, Aberdeen Proving Grounds, Md, 60-, Monsanto Chem Co, Mo & Res Systs, Inc, Mass; Alfred P Sloan Found fel, 62-66; mem, Army Sci Adv Panel, 66-69; mem, President's Sci Adv Comt, 69-; vis scientist, Nat Cancer Inst, 73; consult, NSF, Nat Security Coun, Nat Cancer Inst & Merck Sharp & Dohme, 73-; chmn, Bd Dirs, Vestar Res Inc; mem, Biophys Chem Study Sect, NIH, 84-86; vis prof, E T H, Zurich, Switz, 85. *Mem:* Nat Acad Sci; Am Inst Physics; Am Chem Soc; Am Acad Arts & Sci; Am Philos Soc. *Res:* Molecular structure and spectroscopy, including nuclear magnetic resonance, nuclear spectroscopy, mass spectroscopy, x-ray diffraction and applications of these methods to biological systems. *Mailing Add:* Div Chem & Chem Eng Calif Inst Technol Pasadena CA 91125

BALDESSARINI, ROSS JOHN, PHARMACOLOGY, PSYCHIATRY. *Current Pos:* PROF PSYCHIAT & NEUROSCI, MAILMAN RES CTR, MCLEAN HOSP, 77- *Personal Data:* b Sept 30, 37; m 68; c Anne R & John W. *Educ:* Johns Hopkins Univ, MD, 63. *Hon Degrees:* MA, Harvard Univ, 77, DSc, N Adams State Col, 95, DSc, John Hopkins Scholars, 95. *Honors & Awards:* Efron Res Prize, Am Col Neuropsychopharmacol. *Mem:* Soc Neurosci; Am Col Neuropsychopharmacol; Am Soc Pharmacol & Exp Therapeut; Soc Neurochem; Am Psychiat Asn. *Res:* Pharmacology of antipsychotic drugs and of dopamine system in the brain. *Mailing Add:* Mailman Res Ctr McLean Hosp Belmont MA 02178. *Fax:* 617-855-3479

BALDICK, ROSS, ELECTRICAL ENGINEERING, OPERATIONS RESEARCH & ELECTRIC TRANSMISSION POLICY. *Current Pos:* ASST PROF ELEC & COMPUT ENG, UNIV TEX, AUSTIN, 94- *Personal Data:* b Sydney, Australia, 1962. *Educ:* Univ Sydney, Australia, BSc, 83, BE, 85; Univ Calif, Berkeley, MS, 88, PhD(elec eng & comput sci), 90. *Prof Exp:* Prof eng, Elec Comn NSW, Australia, 85-86; postdoctoral fel, Lawrence Berkeley Lab, Calif, 91-92; asst prof, Worcester Polytech Inst, 92-93. *Concurrent Pos:* Prin investr, Univ Tex, NSF, 94- *Mem:* Inst Elec & Electronics Engrs; Soc Indust & Appl Math. *Res:* Interaction of technical, economic and public policy issues in electric power deregulation, electric transmission; optimization of power systems operation; very-large-scale integration inter-connect design. *Mailing Add:* Dept Elec & Comput Eng Univ Tex Austin TX 78712-1084

BALDINI, JAMES THOMAS, nutrition; deceased, see previous edition for last biography

BALDINO, FRANK, JR, ELECTROPHYSIOLOGY, MOLECULAR NEUROBIOLOGY. *Current Pos:* OWNER, CEPHALONS INC, 90- *Personal Data:* b Passaic, NJ, May 13, 53; m 76; c 2. *Educ:* Muhlenberg Col, BS, 75; Temple Univ, PhD(pharmacol), 79. *Prof Exp:* Teaching fel pharmacol, Sch Med, Rutgers Univ, 79-80, instr, 80-81; prin scientist neurobiol, E I du Pont de Nemours, 81-90. *Concurrent Pos:* Adj asst prof, Dept Pharmacol, Sch Med, Temple Univ, 81- *Mem:* AAAS; Soc Neurosci. *Res:* Multidisciplinary approach to the function and regulation of neuropeptides in the central nervous system; trophic influences on gene expression of hypothalamic peptides. *Mailing Add:* 24 Middleton Lane Landenberg PA 19350

BALDOCCHI, DENNIS D, CANOPY MICROMETEOROLOGY, BIOPHYSICAL ECOLOGY. *Current Pos:* PHYS SCIENTIST, ATMOSPHERIC TURBULENCE DIFFUSION DIV, NAT OCEANIC & ATMOSPHERIC ADMIN, 86- *Personal Data:* b Antioch, Calif, Apr 12, 55; m 84, Nicole Lepoutre; c Ian. *Educ:* Univ Calif, Davis, BS, 77; Univ Nebr, Lincoln, MS, 79, PhD(bioenviron eng), 82. *Honors & Awards:* Silver Medal, US Dept Com, 96. *Prof Exp:* Postdoctoral fel, Oak Ridge Assoc Univ, 82-83, biometeorologist, 83-86. *Concurrent Pos:* Mem, Comt Agr Forest Meteorol, Am Meteorol Soc, 85-88 & Comt Biometeorol, 90-93; vis scientist, Meterol Dept, Univ Stockholm, 90, Univ Tuscia, India, 93. *Mem:* Am Meteorol Soc; Am Geophys Union. *Res:* Experimental and theoretical studies on the physical, biological and chemical processes affecting trace gas exchange between vegetation and the atmosphere. *Mailing Add:* NOAA-ATDD PO Box 2456 Oak Ridge TN 37831-2456. *Fax:* 423-576-1327; *E-Mail:* baldocchi@atdd.noaa.gov

BALDONI, ANDREW ATELEO, ORGANIC CHEMISTRY. *Current Pos:* RETIRED. *Personal Data:* b Pekin, Ill, May 16, 16; m 42, Marjorie Eisele; c Andrew & William. *Educ:* Bradley Univ, BS, 47; Univ Notre Dame, PhD(chem), 51. *Prof Exp:* Chemist, Control Lab, Am Distilling Co, 37-42; res chemist & group leader, Ringwood Chem Corp, 50-56, dir res, 57; asst dir res, Morton Chem Co, 58-64, dir tech serv, 64-67; dir res, Simoniz Co, 67-70; dir corp res, Morton Int, Inc, 70-72, dir res & develop dyes, 72-74, dir new prod res, 74-79, vpres res, Morton Chem Co, 79-85. *Mem:* Am Chem Soc. *Res:* Organic research. *Mailing Add:* 344 Hilkert Ct Crystal Lake IL 60014-5814

BALDRIDGE, ROBERT CRARY, BIOCHEMISTRY. *Current Pos:* RETIRED. *Personal Data:* b Herington, Kans, Jan 9, 21; m 43; c 5. *Educ:* Kans State Univ, BS, 43; Univ Mich, MS, 48, PhD(biol chem), 51. *Prof Exp:* Instr biol chem, Univ Mich, 51-53; from asst prof to prof biochem, Sch Med, Temple Univ, 53-70, assoc dean grad sch, 65-70; dean, Col Grad Studies, Thomas Jefferson Univ, 70-81, prof biochem, Jefferson Med Col, 70-86. *Mem:* Am Soc Biol Chem. *Res:* Amino acid metabolism; biochemical genetics; histidinemia; steroid hormone receptors. *Mailing Add:* 101 Woodland Rd Wyncote PA 19095-1323

BALDRIDGE, WARREN SCOTT, IGNEOUS PETROLOGY, REGIONAL GEOLOGY. *Current Pos:* fel, 78-80, GEOLOGIST, LOS ALAMOS NAT LAB, 80- *Personal Data:* b Lyons, NY, Jan 7, 45; m 74; c 1. *Educ:* Hamilton Col, AB, 67; Calif Inst Technol, MS, 70, PhD(geol), 79. *Prof Exp:* Res asst geophys, Mass Inst Technol, 69-72. *Concurrent Pos:* Fulbright fel exp petrol, Univ Gottingen, 67-68; vis assoc prof, Hebrew Univ, Jerusalem, 84-85; adj prof, Univ NMex, 92-; Fulbright sr res scholar, Univ Oslo, 96-97. *Mem:* Sigma Xi; fel Geol Soc Am; Am Geophys Union. *Res:* Petrologic and geochemical studies of mafic volcanic rocks; mantle xenoliths; petrogenesis of rift zone igneous rocks; evolution and regional tectonic studies of Rio Grande rift. *Mailing Add:* Earth & Environ Sci Div MS D462 Los Alamos Nat Lab Los Alamos NM 87545. *Fax:* 505-665-3285; *E-Mail:* sbaldridge@lanl.gov

BALDUCCI, LODOVICO, GERIATRICS, NUTRITION. *Current Pos:* ASSOC PROF MED, UNIV SFLA, 87- *Personal Data:* b Borgonovo, Italy, Apr 7, 44; nat US; m 71; c 1. *Educ:* Catholic Univ Sch Med Rome, Italy, MD, 68. *Prof Exp:* Resident med, Univ Miss, 73-76, fel med & oncol, 76-78, asst prof, 78-84, assoc prof med, 84-87. *Concurrent Pos:* Staff oncologist, Jackson Vet Admin, Jackson, Miss, 78-87; chief hemat & oncol, Buy Pines Vet Admin, Fla, 87- *Mem:* Am Assoc Cancer Res; Am Soc Hemat; Am Soc Clin Oncol; Am Col Physicians; Am Cancer Soc. *Res:* Cancer in the elderly, geriatric oncology; prostate cancer; hemopoiesis and cancer. *Mailing Add:* James A Haley VA Med Ctr 13000 Bruce B Downs Blvd Tampa FL 33612-4745

BALDUS, WILLIAM PHILLIP, INTERNAL MEDICINE, GASTROENTEROLOGY. *Current Pos:* instr, 65-68, asst prof, 68-78, ASSOC PROF GASTROENTEROL, MAYO GRAD SCH MED, UNIV MINN, 78- *Personal Data:* b Milwaukee, Wis, Mar 11, 32; m 56; c 5. *Educ:* Marquette Univ, BS, 54, MD, 57; Univ Minn, MS, 64. *Prof Exp:* Intern, Boston City Hosp, 57-58; resident, Univ Minn Hosps, 58-61. *Mem:* Am Gastroenterol Asn; fel Am Col Physicians; Am Fedn Clin Res. *Res:* Renal failure and disturbances of water and electrolyte metabolism in liver disease. *Mailing Add:* 1234 19th Ave NE Rochester MN 55906-4306

BALDWIN, ANN LINDA, TRANSVASCULAR TRANSPORT MECHANISMS, MECHANISMS OF ATHERO GENESIS. *Current Pos:* res assoc, 83-85, res asst prof, 86-91, asst prof, 91-94, ASSOC PROF PHYSIOL, UNIV ARIZ, 94- *Personal Data:* b London, Eng, Aug 16, 54; m 84, Timothy Secomb; c 2. *Educ:* Univ Bristol, UK, BSc, 75; Univ London, UK, MSc, 76, PhD(physiol), 79. *Honors & Awards:* Lamport Award, Am Physiol Soc, 86. *Prof Exp:* Res asst, Imp Col, Univ London, UK, 79-81; res assoc, Columbia Univ, 81-83. *Concurrent Pos:* Robert S Flinn merit award, Ariz Affil, Am Heart Asn, 87-89; Whitaker Found res award, 89-92; mem, Coun Circulation, Am Circulation, Am Heart Asn. *Mem:* Am Physiol Soc; Microcirculation Soc; Biomed Eng Soc; fel Int Soc Biorheology; Am Heart Asn. *Res:* Understanding the mechanisms by which water and macromolecules are exchanged between blood and tissue across large arteries and microvessels; changes in endothelial fenestrae and in the endothelial cytoskeleton are being investigated as possible mechanisms for permeability regulation. *Mailing Add:* Dept Physiol Col Med Univ Ariz Tucson AZ 85724-0001. *Fax:* 520-629-1801; *E-Mail:* a160854@ccit.arizona.edu

BALDWIN, ARTHUR DWIGHT, JR, HYDROLOGY & WATER RESOURCES. *Current Pos:* Assoc prof, Miami Univ, 66-79, dep dir affairs, Inst Environ Sci, 77-79, prof & chmn dept, 79-87, PROF GEOL, MIAMI UNIV, 87- *Personal Data:* b Boston, Mass, Oct 28, 38; m 62; c 2. *Educ:* Bowdoin Col, BA, 61; Univ Kans, MA, 63; Stanford Univ, PhD(geol), 67. *Mem:* Geol Soc Am; AAAS; Nat Water Well Asn; Sigma Xi. *Res:* Problems related to finding sufficient water, both in quantity and in quality, to satisfy our nation's increasing needs. *Mailing Add:* Dept Geol Miami Univ 500 E High St Oxford OH 45056-1618

BALDWIN, ARTHUR RICHARD, CHEMISTRY. *Current Pos:* RETIRED. *Personal Data:* b Palmyra, Mich, Feb 20, 18; m 42, Eleanor A Warner; c Eleanor L, Arthur C & Richard L. *Educ:* Stetson Univ, BS, 40; Univ Pittsburgh, PhD(biochem), 43. *Honors & Awards:* Normann Medal, Ger Oil Sci Soc, 51; Alton E Bailey Award, Am Oil Chem Soc, 63; Chevreul Medal, Groupement Technique des Corps Gras, 65; A Richard Balwin Award, Am Oil Chem Soc, 81. *Prof Exp:* Lab asst chem, Univ Pittsburgh, 40-42, Swift & Co fel, 43, Nutrit Found fel, 44; sect leader food & lipid chem, Corn Prod Refining Co, 44-54; dir res, Cargill, Inc, 54-64, vpres & exec dir res, 64-83, secy, Cargill Long Range Planning Comt, 68-83. *Concurrent Pos:* Ed, J Am Oil Chem Soc; mem space applns bd, Nat Acad Eng, 73 & 78; dir, Agribus Coun, 71-; mem, Joint Res Coun, Bd Int Food & Agr Develop, 78- & Joint Coun Food & Agr Sci, USDA, 78-; chmn, World Conf Vegetable Food Proteins, 78 & World Conf Emerging Technol on Fats & Oils; ed, Nine World Conf Proceedings; mem, Res Adv Comt of AID, 82-89; bd trustees, Pan Am Sch Agr, 82-; chmn, Minn Coun Biotechnol, 85-87 & Minn Comt Sci & Technol, 87. *Mem:* Am Chem Soc; Am Oil Chem Soc; Inst Food Technologists; Am Asn Cereal Chem. *Res:* Purification of inositol and phytates; fat and oil analyses recoveries and processing; development of food products; fat digestibilities and metabolism; compounding hydrogenated shortening; preparation of synthetic lipids; carbohydrate oxidations; new packaged food products; plant breeding; feed and animal nutrition research; drying oils and protection coatings; plant biology; agricultural research management. *Mailing Add:* 4854 Thomas Ave S Minneapolis MN 55410

BALDWIN, BARRETT S, JR, AERONAUTICS, ASTRONAUTICS. *Current Pos:* RES SCIENTIST, NASA, 58- *Personal Data:* b Bakersfield, Calif, July 22, 21; m 43; c 2. *Educ:* Univ Calif, BS, 43; Stanford Univ, MS, 51, PhD(aeronaut, astronaut), 62. *Prof Exp:* Teaching asst physics, Stanford Univ, 48-51; res scientist, Nat Adv Comt Aeronaut, 51-58. *Mem:* Am Phys Soc; Am Inst Aeronaut & Astronaut; Am Geophys Union. *Res:* Wind tunnel wall interference in airfoil testing; behavior of radiating gas flows; application of aeronautical technology to interpretation of meteor phenomena; computational fluid dynamics and turbulence modeling. *Mailing Add:* 2468 Whitney Dr Mountain View CA 94043

BALDWIN, BERNARD ARTHUR, PHYSICAL CHEMISTRY, MOLECULAR SPECTROSCOPY. *Current Pos:* SR RES CHEMIST, PHILLIPS PETROL CO, 68- *Personal Data:* b Chicago, Ill, Sept 7, 40; m 92; c Kimberly, Wendy & Minda. *Educ:* La Verne Col, BA, 62; San Diego State Col, MS, 65; Univ Calif, Santa Barbara, PhD(phys chem), 68. *Honors & Awards:* Walter D Hodson Award, 77; Capt Alfred E Hunt Award, 87. *Prof Exp:* Asst chem, San Diego State Col, 62-64, asst phys chem, 63-65; asst chem, Univ Calif, 65-66, asst phys chem, 66-67. *Mem:* Am Soc Lubrication Engrs; Soc Core Analysts; Soc Petrol Engr. *Res:* Perturbation effects on the population and depopulation processes of electronically excited molecules; chemical character of natural adsorbates and mechanism for adsorption of molecular species on solid surfaces; chemical characterization of surfaces, adsorbed molecular species and their reaction products; mechanism(s) responsible for boundary lubrication of metals; petrophysical properties of fluids in porous media; nuclear magnetic resonance imaging of fluids in porous media; 50 technical publications and 16 patents. *Mailing Add:* Phillips Petrol Co 103 GB Bartlesville OK 74004. *Fax:* 918-662-2047; *E-Mail:* babaldw@ppco.com

BALDWIN, BERNELL ELWYN, NEUROPHYSIOLOGY. *Current Pos:* instr physiol, Loma Linda Univ, 63-67, asst prof physiol & biophys, 67-69, asst prof physiol, Sch Med, 69-77, ASSOC PROF APPL PHYSIOL, SCH HEALTH, LOMA LINDA UNIV, 77- *Personal Data:* b Angwin, Calif, Jan 21, 24; m 60, Marjorie Jacobs. *Educ:* Columbia Union Col, BA, 56; George Washington Univ, MA, 58, PhD, 63. *Prof Exp:* Teaching asst, George Washington Univ, 63. *Concurrent Pos:* Mem staff, Appl Physiol Lab, Wildwood Lifestyle Ctr Hosp; grants brain & heart, NIH & Int Nutrit Lab. *Mem:* Am Physiol Soc; NY Acad Sci. *Res:* Effects of combined exercise, metabolic alteration and stress control on human lipid profiles and on blood pressure; frontal lobe contribution to autonomic nervous system dynamics and feeding behavior. *Mailing Add:* Appl Physiol Lab Wildwood Sanitarium & Hosp Wildwood GA 30757-0109. *Fax:* 706-820-1474

BALDWIN, BREWSTER, GEOLOGY. *Current Pos:* RETIRED. *Personal Data:* b Brooklyn, NY, Nov 10, 19; m 46; c 4. *Educ:* Williams Col, Mass, AB, 41; Columbia Univ, AM, 44, PhD(geol), 51. *Prof Exp:* Jr geologist, US Geol Surv, 42-44; instr geol, Univ SDak, 47-51; econ geologist, Bur Mines, NMex, 51-58; from asst prof to prof geol, Middlebury Col, 58-89,. *Concurrent Pos:* Mem, Coun Educ in Geol Sci, 67-70 & New Eng Sect, Correlation Stratig Units NAm. *Mem:* Geol Soc Am; Soc Econ Paleontologists & Mineralogists; Nat Asn Geol Teachers. *Res:* Sedimentology of Taconics; environmental geology; curriculum philosophy; rates of sedimentation. *Mailing Add:* 17 Buttolph Dr Middlebury VT 05753

BALDWIN, BRUCE GREGG, BOTANY. *Current Pos:* CUR, JEPSON HERBARIUM & ASST PROF-IN-RESIDENCE, DEPT INTEGRATIVE BIOL, UNIV CALIF, BERKELEY, 94- *Personal Data:* b San Luis Obispo, Calif, Oct 24, 57. *Educ:* Univ Calif, Santa Barbara, BA, 81; Univ Calif, Davis, MS, 85, PhD(bot), 89. *Honors & Awards:* George R Cooley Award, Am Soc Plant Taxonomists, 93; Nat Young Investr, NSF, 94. *Prof Exp:* NSF postdoctoral fel, Univ Ariz, Tucson, 90-92; asst prof, Dept Bot, Duke Univ, 92-94. *Concurrent Pos:* Arts & sci res coun grantee, Duke Univ, 93-94; grantee, Div Environ Biol Res, NSF, 94-97; Mellon vis scholar, Rancho Santa Ana Bot Garden, 94; rare plant consult, US Fish & Wildlife Serv, Calif Dept Fish & Game & Calif Native Plant Soc. *Mem:* Am Soc Plant Taxonomists. *Res:* Plant systematics, phylogenetics, plant cytogenetics and chromosome evolution; plant speciation; California floristics; phytogeography; insular evolution; contributor of articles to professional journals. *Mailing Add:* Dept Integrative Biol Univ Calif Berkeley Jepson Herbarium 1001 Valley Life Sci Bldg 2465 Berkeley CA 94720-2465

BALDWIN, CHANDLER MILNES, ELECTRONICS ENGINEERING, ELECTROMAGNETISM. *Current Pos:* prin engr media develop, 83-85, mgr, 85-89, DIR DEVELOP, CENSTOR CORP, 89- *Personal Data:* b Oakland, Calif, Nov 22, 51; m 82; c 2. *Educ:* Univ Calif, Los Angeles, BS, 74, MS, 75, PhD(eng), 79. *Honors & Awards:* Grad Res Award, Electrochem Soc, 78. *Prof Exp:* Engr develop, Menorex Corp, 78-79, sr engr advan thin film, 79-81; prin engr process develop, Exxon Enterprises, 81-82. *Mem:* Inst Elec & Electronics Engrs Magnetics Soc. *Res:* Development and characterization of glassy BeF_2 based materials; magnetic recording industry primarily thin film device development. *Mailing Add:* 1205 Monte Verde Ct Los Altos CA 94024

BALDWIN, CHARLES M, ORGANIC CHEMISTRY, BIOCHEMISTRY. *Current Pos:* assoc prof chem, 70-81, PROF CHEM & CHMN, DEPT CHEM & PHYSICS, UNION UNIV, JACKSON TENN, 88- *Personal Data:* b Oct 22, 40; m, Janice A Perry; c Lisa R (Galleta) & Michelle D. *Educ:* Univ Corpus Christi, Tex, BA, 62, PhD, 70. *Prof Exp:* Field chemist, Halliburton Co, Corpus Christi, Tex, 61-64; high sch teacher math & physics, Earth-Springlake High Sch, Earth, Tex, 64-65; teaching asst & res fel, Tex Tech Univ, 65-69, instr org chem, 69-70; prof chem, chmn, Dept Phys Sci & chmn, Div Sci & Math, Howard Payne Univ, Brownwood, Tex, 81-83; prof chem & phys sci, Wayland Baptist Univ, Plainview, Tex, 83-88. *Concurrent Pos:* Robert A Welch res fel, 67-69; adj asst prof, Dept Med Chem, Col Pharm, Univ Tenn, Memphis, 79-81. *Mem:* Am Chem Soc; AAAS; Sigma Xi; Nat Sci Teachers Asn; Soc Col Sci Teachers. *Res:* Chemistry and physics; published several articles. *Mailing Add:* 48 Sandpiper Cove Jackson TN 38305

BALDWIN, DAVID ELLIS, PLASMA PHYSICS. *Current Pos:* SR VPRES, GEN ATOMICS. *Personal Data:* b Bradenton, Fla, June 12, 36; m 61, Eleanore Haggard; c Kenneth B & Johanna D. *Educ:* Mass Inst Technol, BSc, 58, PhD(physics), 62. *Prof Exp:* Res assoc physics, Stanford Univ, 62-64 & Theory Div, Culham Lab, Eng, 64-66; from asst prof to assoc prof appl sci, Yale Univ, 66-70; res physicist, Lawrence Livermore Lab, 70-78, dep theory prog leader, 78-84, from dep assoc dir to actg assoc dir, 84-88; dir, Inst Fusion Studies & prof physics, Univ Tex, Austin, 88-91; assoc dir magnetic fusion energy, Lawrence Livermore Nat Lab, 91-92, assoc dir energy, 92- *Mem:* Fel Am Phys Soc. *Res:* Theoretical plasma physics; controlled thermonuclear fusion. *Mailing Add:* Fusion Group Gen Atomics PO Box 85608 13/216A San Diego CA 92186

BALDWIN, DAVID HALE, METALLURGY. *Current Pos:* SR ENGR, SPACE NUCLEAR ENG & TECHNOL, 87-96. *Personal Data:* b Manchester, Conn, Dec 4, 36; m 59; c Jennifer, Rebecca & Jonathan. *Educ:* Univ Fla, BME, 59, MSE, 61, PhD, 66. *Prof Exp:* Asst prof metall eng, Univ Fla, 66-77; engr, Mat & Processes Lab, Gen Elec Co, 77-87. *Mem:* Am Soc Metals; Am Inst Mining, Metall & Petrol Engrs; Sigma Xi. *Res:* Mechanical properties of superalloys; fabrication of nuclear hardware for space applications. *Mailing Add:* 6036 Loma Prieta Dr San Jose CA 95123-3931

BALDWIN, ELDON DEAN, AGRICULTURAL ECONOMICS. *Current Pos:* asst prof, 74-80, assoc prof, 80-90, PROF AGR ECON, OHIO STATE UNIV, 90- *Personal Data:* b Ashley, Ohio, Sept 23, 39; m 64, Judy Fogel; c Jeffrey & Amy. *Educ:* Ohio State Univ, BS, 63; Univ Ill, MS, 67, PhD(agr econ), 70. *Honors & Awards:* Cert Excellence, Soc Agr, 92; Distinguished Individual Exten Prog Award, Am Agr Econ Asn, 92, Qual Commun Award, 93. *Prof Exp:* Agr statistician, Bur Census, US Dept Com, 63-65; res asst agr econ, Univ Ill, 65-69; asst prof econ, Eastern Ill Univ, 69-70 & Miami Univ, 70-74. *Concurrent Pos:* Consult nat & int firms. *Mem:* Am Agr Econ Asn. *Res:* Analyze and model structures and performance variables for grain markets; electronic marketing of livestock, application and its impact on future market price and marketing costs and performance for cash markets. *Mailing Add:* 4324 Hollandia Ct Westerville OH 43081

BALDWIN, EWART MERLIN, GEOLOGY. *Current Pos:* RETIRED. *Personal Data:* b Pomeroy, Wash, May 17, 15; m 42; c 2. *Educ:* State Col Wash, BS, 38, MS, 39; Cornell Univ, PhD(geol), 43. *Prof Exp:* Asst, State Col Wash, 38-39 & Cornell Univ, 40-43; from asst geologist to geologist, Ore Dept Geol & Mining Industs, Portland, 43-47; from asst prof to prof, Univ Ore, 47-80, emer prof geol, 81- *Concurrent Pos:* Fulbright award, Dacca, EPakistan, 59-60; Arnold vis prof, Whitman Col, 81. *Mem:* Fel Geol Soc Am; Am Asn Petrol Geologists; Paleont Soc; Sigma Xi. *Res:* Oregon coast range stratigraphy; Coos Bay coal fields; Hambaek coal field of Korea; geology of Oregon and parts of Washington and Idaho; regional geology of Oregon, in particular the Oregon Coast Range and Klamath Mountains. *Mailing Add:* Univ Oregon PO Box 3966 Eugene OR 97403-0966

BALDWIN, GEORGE C, ULTRASHORT WAVELENGTH LASERS. *Current Pos:* from adj prof to prof nuclear eng & sci, 61-77, EMER PROF NUCLEAR ENG & SCI, RENSSELAER POLYTECH INST, 77- *Personal Data:* b Denver, Colo, May 5, 17; m 44, 52, Winifred Gould; c George, John & Celia. *Educ:* Kalamazoo Col, BA, 39; Univ Ill, MA, 41, PhD(physics), 43. *Prof Exp:* Instr physics, Univ Ill, 43-44; res physicist, Gen Elec Co, 44-55, physicist, Aircraft Nuclear Propulsion Dept, 55-57; mgr, Argonaut Reactor, Argonne Nat Lab, 57-58; appl physicist, Adv Tech Labs, Gen Elec Co, 58-65, sr physicist, 65-67; mem staff, Los Alamos Sci Lab, 77-87; pres, Baldwin Sci Inc, 87-92. *Concurrent Pos:* Vis mem staff, Los Alamos Sci Lab, 75-77 & 96-; vis lectr, Naval Res Lab, 88; consult, systomation, Inc 70-72, US Army Ballistic Rscr Lab, 73-75; Keytech, 85-87. *Mem:* AAAS; fel Am Phys Soc. *Res:* Nuclear photo-effect; high energy radiation and neutron physics; nuclear instrumentation; reactor kinetics and physics; nuclear and ion propulsion; particle accelerators; stimulated emission devices; electron collision spectrometry of molecules; nuclear lasers. *Mailing Add:* 1016 Calle Bajo Santa Fe NM 87501

BALDWIN, HARRY L, JR, MATHEMATICS. *Current Pos:* RETIRED. *Personal Data:* b Oklahoma City, Okla, 30. *Educ:* Univ NMex, BS, 50; Col Sch Mines, MS, 60. *Prof Exp:* prof math, San Diego City Col, 63-93. *Mem:* Am Math Asn. *Res:* Mathematics. *Mailing Add:* 3490 Lockwood Dr San Diego CA 92123-2620

BALDWIN, HOWARD WESLEY, INORGANIC CHEMISTRY. *Current Pos:* RETIRED. *Personal Data:* b Winnipeg, Man, June 11, 28; m 58; c 3. *Educ:* Univ Sask, BA, 50, MA, 51; Univ Chicago, PhD(chem), 59. *Prof Exp:* Asst prof, Univ Western Ont, 59-67, asst dean fac grad studies, 69-78, assoc prof chem, 69-95, asst provost & univ res officer, 78-92. *Mem:* Chem Inst Can. *Res:* Kinetic and isotopic studies of reactions of complex ions in solution. *Mailing Add:* 75 Friars Way London ON N6G 2B1 Can

BALDWIN, JACK TIMOTHY, COMPUTER SCIENCE. *Current Pos:* ASSOC PROF, DEPT MATH, UNIV ILL, CHICAGO CIRCLE, 80- *Personal Data:* b Abilene, Tex, Oct 6, 45; m 67. *Educ:* Univ Tex, Austin, BA, 67, PhD(comput sci), 76. *Prof Exp:* Programmer-technician, IBM, 67-69; teaching asst comput sci, Univ Tex, Austin, 69-72; asst prof comput sci, Univ Nebr, Omaha, 75-80. *Mem:* Asn Comput Mach. *Res:* Programming techniques; artificial intelligence; computer assisted instruction. *Mailing Add:* Dept Math M/C 249 Univ Ill 851 S Morgan St Chicago IL 60607-7045

BALDWIN, JAMES GORDON, plant nematology, plant pathology, for more information see previous edition

BALDWIN, JAMES W(ARREN), JR, CIVIL ENGINEERING, MATERIALS. *Current Pos:* RETIRED. *Personal Data:* b Peoria, Ill, June 29, 29; m 58; c 2. *Educ:* Univ Ill, BS, 51, MS, 56, PhD(mech), 61. *Prof Exp:* Res asst theoret & appl mech, Univ Ill, 55-56, instr, 57-60; assoc prof, Univ Mo, Columbia, 60-66, chmn dept, 67-72, PROF CIVIL ENG, 66- *Concurrent Pos:* Comt mem, Hwy Res Bd, Nat Acad Sci-Nat Res Coun; sr design engr, Rust Eng, 65-66; vis prof, Univ Warwick, Coventry, Eng, 72. *Mem:* Am Concrete Int; Am Soc Civil Engrs; Am Soc Eng Educ; Sigma Xi. *Res:* Fatigue, fracture and field testing of structures; structure monitoring; motor vehicle roll over; failure analysis. *Mailing Add:* 2010 Ivy Way Columbia MO 65203

BALDWIN, JOHN CHARLES, EXPERIMENTAL BIOLOGY. *Current Pos:* PROF SURG & CHIEF CARDIOTHORACIC SURG, SCH MED & CARDIOTHORACIC SURGEON-IN-CHIEF, NEW HAVEN HOSP, YALE UNIV, 88- *Personal Data:* b Ft Worth, Tex, Sept 23, 48. *Educ:* Harvard Univ, BA, 71; Stanford Univ, MD, 75; Am Bd Internal Med, cert; Am Bd Surg, cert; Am Bd Thoracic Surg, cert. *Hon Degrees:* MA, Yale Univ, 89. *Honors & Awards:* Medaille de la Ville de Bordeaux, French Thoracic Soc, 87. *Prof Exp:* Clin fel med, Med Sch, Harvard Univ, 75-77, clin fel surg, 77-81; asst prof & physician specialist cardiovasc surg, Sch Med, Stanford Univ, 84-85, asst prof & dir, Transplantation Res Lab, 85-87. *Concurrent Pos:* Prin investr, Stanford Univ Med Ctr, 81-88, Datascope Corp, 85-87 & 88-90, Cystic Fibrosis Found, 86-88 & Upjohn Corp, 87-; attend surgeon cardiovasc & thoracic surg serv, Stanford Univ Med Ctr, 84-87, head, Heart-Lung Transplant Prog, 85-87; mem, Res Grant Peer Rev Subcomt, Am Heart Asn, 84-87, Prog Comt, Int Soc Heart Transplantation, 84-85 & 87, Comt Organ Transplantation, Pan Am Med Asn, 85-, Clin Res Comt Ad Hoc Res Grant Rev, Cystic Fibrosis Found, 86- & Adv Comt Issues, Am Soc Transplant Surgeons, 89-; assoc ed, J Appl Cardiol, 85-; chmn, Comt Heart Transplantation, Am Soc Transplant Surgeons, 86-89, mem, 90-93, chmn, Subcomt Heart Transplantation, 89-; Royal Col Surgeons Eng traveling lectr, 88; mem, bd gov, Am Col Surgeons, 93-97, Evarts A Graham Mem traveling fel comt, Am Asn Thoracic Surg, 93-97; chmn, Task Force Cardiac Donor Procurement, Am Col Cardiol Bethesda Conf, Best Doc Am-Woodward/White Survey, 93-94. *Mem:* Am Asn Thoracic Surg; fel Am Col Angiol; fel Am Col Cardiol; fel Am Col Chest Physicians; fel Am Col Physicians; fel Am Col Surgeons; Am Heart Asn; AMA; Am Organ Transplant Soc; Am Physiol Soc. *Res:* Control of pulmonary vascular resistance; author of more than 350 technical publications. *Mailing Add:* Dept Surg Baylor Col Med One Baylor Plaza Houston TX 77030-3498

BALDWIN, JOHN E, PHYSICAL ORGANIC CHEMISTRY. *Current Pos:* PROF CHEM, SYRACUSE UNIV, 84- *Personal Data:* b Berwyn, Ill, Sept 10, 37; m 61, Anne K Nordlander; c Claire M, John N & Wesley H. *Educ:* Dartmouth Col, AB, 59; Calif Inst Technol, PhD, 63. *Prof Exp:* From instr to assoc prof chem, Univ Ill, 62-68; prof chem, Univ Ore, 68-84, dean, Col Arts & Sci, 75-80. *Concurrent Pos:* Alfred P Sloan res fel, 66-68; Guggenheim Mem Found fel, 67; consult, Stauffer Chem Co & Off Sci & Technol; mem bd ed, Org Reactions & Chem Rev; Alexander von Humboldt Found Sr US scientist award, 74-75; Jubileums prof, Chalmers Univ Technol, Goteborg, Sweden, 90. *Mem:* Am Chem Soc. *Res:* Stereochemistry; reaction mechanisms; molecular rearrangements; cycloadditions; stereochemical definition of reaction paths for hydrocarbon molecular rearrangements and fragmentations. *Mailing Add:* Dept Chem Syracuse Univ Syracuse NY 13244-4100. *Fax:* 315-443-4070; *E-Mail:* jbaldwin@syr.edu

BALDWIN, JOHN THEODORE, MATHEMATICAL LOGIC. *Current Pos:* asst prof, 73-77, ASSOC PROF MATH, UNIV ILL, CHICAGO CIRCLE, 77- *Personal Data:* b Danbury, Conn, Aug 14, 44; m 65; c 1. *Educ:* Mich State Univ, BSc, 66; Univ Calif, Berkeley, MS, 67; Simon Fraser Univ, PhD(math), 71. *Prof Exp:* Res assoc math, Mich State Univ, 71-73. *Mem:* Am Math Soc; Asn Symbolic Logic; Math Asn Am. *Res:* Model theory; universal algebra. *Mailing Add:* Dept Math Univ Ill 851 S Morgan St Rm 417 Chicago IL 60607

BALDWIN, JOHN TIMOTHY, BIOENGINEERING. *Current Pos:* RES ENGR, CARBOMEDICS INC, 91- *Personal Data:* b Chicago, Ill, Feb 7, 62. *Educ:* Va Polytech Inst & State Univ, BS, 85; Pa State Univ, MS, 87, PhD(biol eng), 90. *Mem:* Am Soc Mech Engrs; Biomed Eng Soc; Sigma Xi. *Mailing Add:* CarboMedics Inc 1300-A E Anderson Lane Austin TX 78752-1793

BALDWIN, KATE M, CELL COMMUNICATIONS, CELL MEMBRANES. *Current Pos:* Asst prof, 72-84, ASSOC PROF ANAT, COL MED, HOWARD UNIV, 84- *Personal Data:* b Seattle, Wash, July 12, 40. *Mem:* Am Soc Cell Biol; Am Asn Anatomists. *Mailing Add:* Dept Anat Howard Univ Col Med 520 W St NW Washington DC 20059-0001

BALDWIN, KEITH MALCOLM, PHYSICS, ELECTRONICS. *Current Pos:* PRES, KMB/TECH, 86- *Personal Data:* b Buffalo, NY, May 25, 28; m 51; c 4. *Educ:* Mich State Univ, BS, 50; Univ Maine, MS, 55. *Prof Exp:* Assoc scientist, Raytheon Mfg Co, 55-57; assoc scientist, Res & Adv Develop Div, Avco Corp, 57-59, from sr scientist to sr proj scientist, 59-63; assoc prof physics, Mich Technol Univ, 63-86. *Mem:* AAAS; Am Asn Physics Teachers; Sigma Xi. *Res:* Analysis of properties of ionized gas by microwave, optical and ultrasonic diagnostic techniques; microwave transmission through ionized air during missile re-entry; electronic instrumentation. *Mailing Add:* Point Mills Box 440 Dollar Bay MI 49922

BALDWIN, KENNETH M, MUSCLE PHYSIOLOGY. *Current Pos:* PROF PHYSIOL & BIOPHYS, UNIV CALIF, IRVINE, 78- *Personal Data:* b Leominster, Mass, Apr 25, 42. *Educ:* Univ Iowa, PhD(exercise sci), 70. *Concurrent Pos:* Sr assoc dean, Col Med. *Mem:* Am Physiol Soc; Am Col Sports Med; Am Heart Asn. *Mailing Add:* Dept Physiol Univ Calif Irvine CA 92717-0001

BALDWIN, LIONEL V, CHEMICAL ENGINEERING. *Current Pos:* PRES, NAT TECHNOL UNIV, 84- *Personal Data:* b Beaumont, Tex, May 30, 32; m 55; c 4. *Educ:* Univ Notre Dame, BS, 54; Mass Inst Technol, SM, 55; Case Inst Technol, PhD(chem eng, phys chem), 59. *Prof Exp:* Res engr, Nat Adv Comt Aeronaut, Ohio, 55-59; unit head, NASA, 59-61; assoc prof eng, Colo State Univ, 61-64, actg dean, 64-65, dean col eng, 65-84. *Concurrent Pos:* Off Naval Res, NIH & NASA eng res grants; asst engr, E I du Pont de Nemours & Co, Tex, 51-53; jr engr, W R Grace & Co, NY, 54. *Mem:* Am Soc Mech Engrs; Am Inst Chem Engrs; Am Inst Aeronaut & Astronaut; Am Soc Eng Educ. *Res:* Engineering science; turbulent fluid flow and diffusion; heat transfer in rarefied gas flows; low density, high energy plasma research. *Mailing Add:* Nat Technol Univ 700 Centre Ave Ft Collins CO 80526

BALDWIN, MARK PHILLIP, RESEARCH ADMINISTRATION. *Current Pos:* POSTDOCTORAL ASSOC, NORTHWEST RES ASSOC, 87- *Personal Data:* b Schenectady, NY, Mar 4, 58; m 82. *Educ:* State Univ NY, Albany, BS, 80, MS, 81; Univ Wash, MS, 85, PhD(atmospheric sci), 87. *Mem:* Am Meteorol Soc. *Res:* Dynamics of stratosphere and trosposphere; observational studies of wave propagation, wave-mean flow interaction and sudden strastospheric warning; relation of polar strastospheric flow to tropospheric and tropical flow. *Mailing Add:* 2360 Squak Mountain Loop SW Issaquah WA 98027

BALDWIN, RANSOM LELAND, ANIMAL SYSTEMS, RUMINANT NUTRITION. *Current Pos:* Asst prof animal husb, 62-70, chmn dept, 78-81, PROF ANIMAL SCI, UNIV CALIF, DAVIS, 70-, CESSNON CHAIR, DEPT ANIMAL SCI, 92- *Personal Data:* b Meriden, Conn, Sept 21, 35; m 57; c 3. *Educ:* Univ Conn, BS, 57; Mich State Univ, MS, 58, PhD(biochem), 62. *Honors & Awards:* Am Feed Mfrs Award, 70; Borden Award, 80. *Concurrent Pos:* Guggenheim Mem Found fel, 68-69; assoc ed, J Nutrit, 76-79 & 84-89; Fulbright fel, UK, 83-84. *Mem:* Nat Acad Sci; Am Dairy Sci Asn; Am Inst Nutrit; Am Soc Animal Sci; AAAS. *Res:* Ruminant digestion; physiology of lactation; nutritional energetics; mechanisms and quantitative aspects of regulation of animal and tissue metabolism; computer simulation modeling of animal systems. *Mailing Add:* Dept Animal Sci Univ Calif Davis CA 95616

BALDWIN, RICHARD H(AROLD), CHEMICAL ENGINEERING. *Current Pos:* RETIRED. *Personal Data:* b Mich, Aug 7, 27. *Educ:* Ill Inst Technol, BS, 50. *Prof Exp:* Chem engr, Res Dept, Standard Oil Co, Ind, 53-54, asst proj engr, 54-57, proj chem engr, 57-59, group leader, 59-61; group leader, Res Dept, Amoco Chem Corp, 61-65, sect leader, 65-67, asst div dir, 67-69, dir, 69-77, mgr, Chem Intermediates Process Design & Econ Anal, 77-81, mgr process eng, Eng Dept, 81-92. *Mem:* Sigma Xi. *Res:* Chemical engineering fundamentals; fluid mixing. *Mailing Add:* 1945 N Mohawk St Chicago IL 60614

BALDWIN, ROBERT CHARLES, risk assessment, analytical chemistry, for more information see previous edition

BALDWIN, ROBERT LESH, PHYSICAL BIOCHEMISTRY, PROTEIN FOLDING. *Current Pos:* assoc prof, 59-64, PROF BIOCHEM, STANFORD UNIV, 64- *Personal Data:* b Madison, Wis, Sept 30, 27; m 65, Anne Norris; c David & Eric. *Educ:* Univ Wis, BA, 50; Oxford Univ, PhD, 54. *Honors & Awards:* Stein & Moore Award, Protein Soc, 92. *Prof Exp:* From asst prof to assoc prof biochem, Univ Wis, 55-59. *Concurrent Pos:* Rhodes scholar, 50-53, Guggenheim fel, 58-59, NIH sr fel, 63-64; mem, USPHS Fel Comt Biochem & Molecular Biol, 69-71; vis prof, Col de France, Paris, 71, NIH Adv Panel Molecular & Cell Biophysics, 84-88; sabbatical, Institut Pasteur, Dept Molecular Biol, Paris, 71-72, MRC Lab Molecular Biol, Cambridge, Eng, 78-79; mem, NSF Adv Panel Biochem & Biophys, 74-76; coun mem, Protein Soc, 93- *Mem:* Nat Acad Sci; Am Soc Biol Chemists; Biophys Soc; Am Chem Soc; Am Acad Arts & Sci; Protein Soc. *Res:* Mechanism of protein folding; alpha-helix formation by peptides; author of numerous articles and publications. *Mailing Add:* Dept Biochem Stanford Univ Stanford CA 94305-5307. *Fax:* 650-723-6783

BALDWIN, ROBERT MILTON, FUELS SCIENCE, CATALYSIS & REACTION ENGINEERING. *Current Pos:* From asst prof to assoc prof, 75-85, PROF CHEM ENG, COLO SCH MINES, 85-, HEAD DEPT, 90- *Personal Data:* m 74, Linda J Siegel; c Lindy & Ross. *Educ:* Iowa State Univ, BS, 69, MS, 72; Colo Sch Mines, PhD(chem eng), 75. *Mem:* Am Chem Soc; Am Inst Chem Engrs. *Res:* Fuels science; catalysis; reaction engineering; synthesis of novel additives and oxygenates; catalytic combustion; catalytic membranes and membrane reactors. *Mailing Add:* Dept Chem Eng Colo Sch Mines Golden CO 80401. *Fax:* 303-273-3730; *E-Mail:* rbaldwin@mines.edu

BALDWIN, ROBERT RUSSEL, BIOCHEMISTRY. *Current Pos:* RETIRED. *Personal Data:* b Chicago, Ill, Nov 15, 16; m 44; c 2. *Educ:* DePauw Univ, AB, 38; Iowa State Univ, PhD(plant chem), 43. *Prof Exp:* Instr chem, Iowa State Col, 39-43, assoc chemist, Manhattan Dist Proj, 43-46; biophys sect head, Gen Foods Corp, NY, 46-48, dir biochem lab, 48-56 & chem res lab, 56-61; res supvr, Continental Baking Co, 61-66, assoc dir res, ITT Continental Baking Co, 66-74; vpres & dir res & develop, Morton Frozen Foods, Del Monte Frozen Foods, 74-81. *Concurrent Pos:* Mem, Nat Res Coun Comt Civil Defense, 56. *Mem:* AAAS; fel Am Inst Chem; fel Inst Food Technol; Am Asn Cereal Chem; NY Acad Sci; Am Chem Soc. *Res:* Physico-chemical studies; carbohydrates, fats and proteins; toxicology; quality control; product development. *Mailing Add:* 105 Wilson Ct Charlottesville VA 22901-2941

BALDWIN, ROBERT WILLIAM, TUMOR IMMUNOLOGY, CLINICAL IMMUNOLOGY & IMMUNOPATHOLOGY. *Current Pos:* VPRES RES, ALLERGENE, SAN MATEO, CALIF, 92- *Personal Data:* b Huddersfield, Mar 12, 27; m 52, Lilian Haston; c Robert Neil. *Educ:* Univ Birmingham, UK, BSc, 48, PhD, 51; Royal Col Pathologists, UK, MRC Path, 66; FRC Path, 73. *Honors & Awards:* Almroth-Wright Award, St Mary's Hosp Med Sch, London, 75; Harold Dorn Mem lectr, XIIth Int Cancer Cong, Buenos Aires, 78. *Prof Exp:* Dir oncol, Cancer Res Labs, Univ Nottingham, UK, 60-92, Gibbs sr res fel oncol, Can Res Campaign Labs, 71-92. *Concurrent Pos:* Prof tumour biol oncol, Cancer Res Campaign Labs, Univ Nottingham, UK, 72-92; chmn, Europ Orgn Res, Treatment of Cancer, Tumour Immunol, 72-75; counr, Sci Adv Bd, NY Cancer Res Inst Inc, 72-89 & MRC Leukaemic Steering Comt, 82-90; mem sub-comt on biol, Comt Safety of Med, London, UK, 92-; vis prof, Dept Surg, Univ Hosp, Nottingham, UK, 92- *Mem:* Am Asn Cancer Res; Am Asn Immunologists; Europ Asn Cancer Res (pres, 73-79); Royal Col Pathologists; Royal Inst Biol; Brit Soc Allergy & Clin Immunol. *Res:* Immunology related to human diseases including cancer, infectious diseases and allergies; clinical investigations aimed at developing immunotherapy in cancer and allergic diseases; immunotoxicology and environmental health assessment; carcinogenesis. *Mailing Add:* Dept Surg Floor E W Block Univ Hosp-Queen's Med Ctr Nottingham NG7 2UH England

BALDWIN, ROGER ALLAN, ORGANIC CHEMISTRY, FUEL SCIENCE. *Current Pos:* group leader, 69-78, MGR PROCESS CHEM, KERR MCGEE CORP, 78- *Personal Data:* b Decatur, Ill, June 2, 31; m 54; c 2. *Educ:* Millikin Univ, BS, 53; Mich State Univ, MS, 56, PhD(chem), 59. *Prof Exp:* Asst, Mich State Univ, 53-59; sr res chemist, Am Potash & Chem Corp, 59-60, res proj chemist, 60-63, group leader, 63-64, head org sect, 64-69. *Mem:* Am Chem Soc; The Chem Soc. *Res:* Phosphorus and boron chemistry; azide chemistry; thiophene and sulfur chemistry; solvent extraction; coal conversion. *Mailing Add:* 5908 NW 72nd St Oklahoma City OK 73132-5703

BALDWIN, RONALD MARTIN, RADIOCHEMISTRY. *Current Pos:* Proj chemist, Medi-Physics Inc, 74-76, res scientist, 76-79, sr res scientist, 79, proj mgr, 79-82, DEVELOP MGR, MEDI-PHYSICS INC, 82- *Personal Data:* b Argentina, June 6, 47; US citizen; m 77. *Educ:* Univ Calif, Berkeley, BS, 69, PhD(org chem), 74. *Mem:* Am Chem Soc; Soc Nuclear Med; Sigma Xi; AAAS. *Res:* Development of derivatives of short-lived radioisotopes for use as radiodiagnostic agents in nuclear medicine; iodine 123 labeled amines for brain imaging and iodine 123 labeled fatty acids for heart imaging, and 99 Tc complexes. *Mailing Add:* 73 Brookwood Rd Guilford CT 06437

BALDWIN, THOMAS O, SOLID STATE PHYSICS. *Current Pos:* MGT CONSULT, BOULDER CONSULT GROUP, 80- *Personal Data:* b Ironton, Mo, Sept 18, 38; m 61; c 2. *Educ:* Univ Mo, BS, 59, MS, 61, PhD(physics), 64. *Prof Exp:* Res physicist, Solid State Div, Oak Ridge Nat Lab, 64-69; assoc prof physics, Southern Ill Univ, Edwardsville, 69-72, chmn dept physics, 71-74, prof physics, 72-80. *Concurrent Pos:* Consult, Oak Ridge Nat Lab, 69-72. *Mem:* Am Chem Soc; Am Asn Physics Teachers. *Res:* Debye-Waller factors; expansion coefficients in ionic crystals; anomalous transmission in perfect metal crystals; x-ray studies of defects and radiation damage in crystals. *Mailing Add:* 5124 Williams Fork Trail 210 Boulder CO 80301

BALDWIN, THOMAS OAKLEY, BIOCHEMISTRY, MOLECULAR BIOLOGY & PROTEIN CHEMISTRY. *Current Pos:* assoc prof, 81-86, PROF BIOCHEM & CHEM, TEX A&M UNIV, COLLEGE STATION, 86-, DIR, CTR MACROMOLECULAR DESIGN, 91- *Personal Data:* b Jackson, Miss, June 3, 47; m 67, 78, Miriam M Ziegler; c Amanda, Rebecca & Ruth. *Educ:* Univ Tex, Austin, BS, 69, PhD(zool), 71. *Prof Exp:* Fel biochem, Harvard Univ, 72-75; asst prof biochem, Univ Ill, Urbana, 75-81. *Concurrent Pos:* Mem corp & instr physiol, Marine Biol Lab, 77- *Mem:* AAAS; Biophys Soc; Am Chem Soc; Am Soc Biochem & Molecular Biol; Am Soc Photobiol; Am Soc Microbiol; Protein Soc. *Res:* Structure and function of proteins; structure of bacterial luciferase; analysis of the structures of mutant forms of bacterial luciferase; mechanism of protein folding and assembly of multimeric structures; mechanism of quorum sensing in gram negative bacteria. *Mailing Add:* Dept Biochem & Biophys Tex A&M Univ College Station TX 77843-2128. *Fax:* 409-845-4946; *E-Mail:* baldwin@bioch.tamu.edu

BALDWIN, VIRGIL CLARK, JR, GROWTH & YIELD PREDICTION OF PINE STANDS, ECOLOGICAL & PHYSIOLOGICAL MODELING. *Current Pos:* res forester, 78-90, SUPVRY RES FORESTER, SOUTHERN RES STA, USDA FOREST SERV, 90- *Personal Data:* b Salt Lake City, Utah, Jan 15, 40; m 64, Patricia A Williams; c David, Anna, Jane, Jason, Lance, Adam, Daniel & Amie. *Educ:* Univ Utah, BS, 67; Colo State Univ, MS, 69; Duke Univ, PhD(forest biomet), 75. *Prof Exp:* Res scientist, Maritimes Forest Res Ctr, Can Forestry Serv, 72-75; asst prof forestry, Wash State Univ, 75-78. *Concurrent Pos:* Consult, Ouzinkie Native Corp, 76; prin investr, US Dept Energy grant, 78 & US Bur Indian Affairs grant, 78; instr statist, Northwestern State Univ La, 81; sabbatical, Univ Ga, 90-91. *Mem:* Soc Am Foresters; Resource Modeling Asn. *Res:* Modeling physiological processes; modeling forest stand growth and yield in terms of weight and volume for selection of optimum management practices under specified conditions; silviculture and ecology of forest stands. *Mailing Add:* USDA Forest Serv Southern Res Sta 2500 Shreveport Hwy Pineville LA 71360. *Fax:* 318-473-7117

BALDWIN, W GEORGE, INORGANIC CHEMISTRY. *Current Pos:* from asst prof to assoc prof, 68-84, PROF INORG CHEM, UNIV MAN, 84- *Personal Data:* b Winnipeg, Man, May 3, 38; m 65; c 2. *Educ:* Univ Man, BSc, 59, MSc, 61; Univ Melbourne, PhD(chem), 66. *Prof Exp:* Fel, Univ Adelaide, 66 & Royal Inst Technol, Sweden, 66-68. *Mem:* Chem Inst Can. *Res:* Thermodynamic and kinetic studies of complex ions. *Mailing Add:* Dept Chem Univ Man Winnipeg MB R3T 2N2 Can

BALDWIN, WENDY HARMER, RESEARCH ADMINISTRATION, DEMOGRAPHY. *Current Pos:* Health scientist adminr, Behav Sci Br, Ctr Pop Res, Nat Inst Sci Child Health & Human Develop, NIH, 73-79, chief, Demog & Behav Br, 79-91, dep dir, 91-94, actg dep dir extramural res, NIH, 93-94, DEP DIR EXTRAMURAL RES, NIH, 94- *Personal Data:* b Philadelphia, Pa, Aug 29, 45; m, Delbert H Futrell; c Michele, Michael & Robin. *Educ:* Stetson Univ, BA, 67; Univ Ky, MA, 70, PhD(social/demog), 73. *Honors & Awards:* Superior Serv Award, USPHS, 85, Sr Exec Serv Award, 92; Carl S Schults Award, Am Pub Health Asn, 86. *Concurrent Pos:* Mem, Panel Adolescent Pregnancy & Childbearing, Nat Acad Sci, 84-87. *Mem:* Pop Asn Am (second vpres, 84, first vpres, 86); Am Pub Health Asn; Soc Res Child Develop; Am Psychol Soc; Am Social Asn; AAAS. *Res:* Areas of fertility trends, especially related to adolescents. *Mailing Add:* 11765 Gainsborough Rd Potomac MD 20854-3247. *Fax:* 301-402-3469; *E-Mail:* baldwinw@nih.gov

BALDWIN, WILLIAM RUSSELL, OPTOMETRY, EDUCATION ADMINISTRATION. *Current Pos:* RETIRED. *Personal Data:* b Danville, Ind, July 29, 26; m 47; c 1. *Educ:* Pac Univ, BS, 49, OD, 51; Ind Univ, MS, 56, PhD(phys optics), 64. *Hon Degrees:* LHD, New Eng Col Optom, 82. *Prof Exp:* Dir, Optom Clin, Ind Univ, 59-63; dean, Col Optom, Pac Univ, 63-69; pres, New Eng Col Optom, 69-79; dean, Col Optom, Univ Houston, 79-90; pres, River Blindness Found, 90-96. *Concurrent Pos:* Pvt pract optom, Beech Grove & Bloomington, Ind, 51-63; mem bd dirs, Am Optom Found, 70-74; mem bd, Nat Soc Prevent Blindness, 88- *Mem:* Am Optom Asn; Asn Schs & Cols Optom (pres, 73-75); Am Acad Optom; AAAS. *Res:* Mechanisms of refractive change of the eye; myopia and physiological and behavioral correlates; optometric education. *Mailing Add:* 5 Meeting House Lane Wilbraham MA 01095

BALDWIN, WILLIAM WALTER, MICROBIOLOGY, BIOCHEMISTRY. *Current Pos:* ASSOC PROF MICROBIOL, MED SCH, IND UNIV NORTHWEST, 73- *Personal Data:* b Ft Wayne, Ind, July 27, 40. *Educ:* Ind Cent Col, AB, 62; Ind Univ, MSEd, 67, PhD(microbiol), 73. *Mem:* AAAS; Am Soc Microbiol; Can Soc Microbiol. *Res:* Antitumor agents; cellular energy metabolism and osmolarity responses. *Mailing Add:* Micro & Immuno Ind Univ Sch Med 3400 Broadway Gary IN 46408

BALDY, MARIAN WENDORF, GENETICS, ENOLOGY. *Current Pos:* from asst prof to assoc prof plant sci, 71-80, spec asst to dean, Sch Agr & Home Econ, 80-83, PROF AGR, CALIF STATE UNIV, CHICO, 80- *Personal Data:* b Cleveland, Ohio, June 18, 44; m 65, Richard W. *Educ:* Univ Calif, Davis, AB, 65, PhD(genetics), 68. *Prof Exp:* Res assoc biochem, Med Sch, Univ Ore, Portland, 69-70, NIH fel, 70; inst agr, Butte Community Col, 73. *Concurrent Pos:* Winemaker, Butte Creek Vineyards, Inc, 72-76; dir, Univ Hons Prog, Calif State Univ, Chico, 90-92. *Mem:* Soc Wine Educrs; Am Wine Soc. *Mailing Add:* Sch Agr Calif State Univ Chico 101 Orange St Chico CA 95929-0001. *Fax:* 916-898-4675

BALDY, RICHARD WALLACE, AGRICULTURE. *Current Pos:* PROF POMOL & VITICULTURE, CALIF STATE UNIV, CHICO, 70- *Personal Data:* b Madena, Calif, Jan 15, 42; m 65. *Educ:* Univ Calif, Davis, BS, 64, PhD(plant physiol), 68. *Prof Exp:* Sloan fel biol, Reed Col, 68-70. *Mem:* Am Soc Hort Sci; Appl Econ Entomologist. *Res:* Integrated crop and pest management. *Mailing Add:* Dept Agr Calif State Univ Chico 101 Orange St Chico CA 95929-1000

BALE, HAROLD DAVID, X-RAY CRYSTALLOGRAPHY. *Current Pos:* from asst prof to prof, 59-92, actg chmn dept, 63-67, EMER PROF PHYSICS, UNIV NDAK, 92- *Personal Data:* b Fargo, NDak, Oct 3, 27; m 54, Beverly Bolme; c 4. *Educ:* Concordia Col, BA, 50; Univ NDak, MS, 53; Univ Mo, PhD, 59. *Prof Exp:* Phys sci aide, US Bur Mines, 50-53; instr physics, Univ NDak, 53-55 & Univ Mo, 55-59. *Concurrent Pos:* Fel, Univ Mo, 69-70, vis prof, 78 & 84. *Res:* Small angle x-ray scattering. *Mailing Add:* PO Box 8008 Grand Forks ND 58202. *Fax:* 701-777-3650; *E-Mail:* hbale@sage.und.nodak.edu

BALES, BARNEY LEROY, BIOPHYSICS. *Current Pos:* assoc prof, 75-80, PROF PHYSICS, CALIF STATE UNIV, NORTHRIDGE, 80- *Personal Data:* b Amarillo, Tex, Jan 4, 39. *Educ:* Univ Colo, BS, 62, PhD(physics), 68. *Prof Exp:* Staff scientist biophys, Nat Inst Sci Res, Venezuela. *Mem:* Am Phys Soc; Sigma Xi. *Res:* Structure and dynamics of the biological membrane and of liquid crystals; micelles. *Mailing Add:* Physics & Astron Dept Calif State Univ Northridge CA 91330-0001

BALES, CONNIE WATKINS, BIOLOGY OF AGING, CLINICAL NUTRITION. *Current Pos:* PROF NUTRIT, CTR AGING, DUKE UNIV. *Personal Data:* b Morristown, Tenn, Oct 21, 54; m 75. *Educ:* Univ Tenn, Knoxville, BS, 76, PhD(nutrit sci), 81. *Prof Exp:* Therapeut Nutritionist, St Mary's Med Ctr, Knoxville, Tenn, 76-77; res asst, Univ Tenn, Knoxville, 77-81; asst prof nutrit foods, Univ Tex, Austin, 81- *Mem:* Am Dietetic Asn; Am Geront Soc; AAAS; Am Home Econ Asn; Am Col Nutrit. *Res:* Relationships between nutrition and aging, including prolongation of lifespan by dietary restriction; protein and mineral status of the elderly; trace mineral metabolism. *Mailing Add:* Ctr Aging Duke Univ Med Ctr 3003 Duke Hosp S Durham NC 27710-0001

BALES, HOWARD E, spectroscopy, research administration, for more information see previous edition

BALES, VIRGINIA SHANKLE, CHRONIC DISEASE, PUBLIC HEALTH. *Current Pos:* Pub health analyst & actg chief training unit, Tuberculosis Control Div, Ctr Dis Control, 71-74, pub health adv, Prog Develop Br, Environ Health Servs Div, 74-79, opers officer consol surveillance & commun activ, Bur Epidemiol, 79-81, asst to dep dir, 81-83, asst dir prog opers, Ctr Health Prom & Educ, 83-87, dep dir, 88, DEP DIR, NAT CTR CHRONIC DIS PREV & HEALTH PROM, CTR DIS CONTROL & PREV, GA, 88- *Educ:* Emory Univ, BA, 71, MPH, 77. *Honors & Awards:* Presidential Meritorious Exec Rank Award, 94; Jeffrey P Koplan Award, 95. *Concurrent Pos:* Actg dir, Off Smoking & Health, Ctr Dis Control, 91-92 & Nat Ctr Chronic Dis Prev & Health Prom, 94-95. *Mem:* Am Pub Health Asn. *Mailing Add:* Nat Ctr Chronic Dis Prev & Health Prom Rhodes Bldg Koger Ctr 3005 Chamglee-Tucker Rd Atlanta GA 30341-3724

BALFOUR, HENRY H, JR, PEDIATRICS, VIROLOGY. *Current Pos:* from asst prof to assoc prof, 72-79, PROF LAB MED & PATH & PEDIAT, UNIV MINN, 79-, DIR, DIV CLIN MICROBIOL, 74- *Personal Data:* b Jersey City, NJ, Feb 9, 40; m 67; c 3. *Educ:* Princeton Univ, BA, 62; Columbia Univ Col Physicians & Surgeons, MD, 66. *Prof Exp:* Attend pediatrician, Wright-Patterson AFB, Ohio, 68-70. *Concurrent Pos:* Prin investr, NIH grant, 76-, Ctr Dis Control grant, 77-79 & Wellcome Found grant, 78-, NIH NIAID-Funded Aids Clin Trials Univ, MN, 87-; proj dir NIH grant, 77- *Mem:* Am Soc Microbiol; Soc Exp Biol & Med; Soc Pediat Res; Infectious Dis Soc Am; Am Pediat Soc. *Res:* Pathogenesis and treatment of herpes virus diseases and AIDS. *Mailing Add:* Mayo Univ Minn Hosp PO Box 437 Minneapolis MN 55458-0137. *Fax:* 612-625-5468; *E-Mail:* balfoool@tc.umn.edu

BALFOUR, WALTER JOSEPH, MOLECULAR SPECTROSCOPY, PHYSICAL CHEMISTRY. *Current Pos:* from asst prof to assoc prof, 69-81, PROF CHEM, UNIV VICTORIA, BC, 81- *Personal Data:* b Hilton, Scotland, May 1, 41; Can citizen; m 74, Rosemary Picozzi; c Annemarie C & Jennifer R. *Educ:* Aberdeen Univ, BSc, 63, DSc, 85; Mc Master Univ, PhD(chem), 67. *Prof Exp:* Nat Res Coun Can fel physics, 67-69. *Concurrent Pos:* Vis scientist, Nat Sci Res Ctr, Orsay, France, 75-76, Inst Physics, Univ Stockholm, Sweden, 82-83 & Nat Res Coun Can, 89-90. *Mem:* Can Asn Physicists; Can Inst Chem; fel Chem Inst Can. *Res:* Spectroscopy and structure of diatomic and small polyatomic molecules. *Mailing Add:* Dept Chem Univ Victoria Victoria BC V8W 3P6 Can. *Fax:* 250-721-7147; *E-Mail:* balfour@uvvm.uvic.ca

BALFOUR, WILLIAM MAYO, PHYSIOLOGY. *Current Pos:* asst prof physiol, Univ Kans, 57, res assoc, 59-64, assoc prof, 62-66, dean student affairs, 68-70, vchancellor student affairs, 68-70, PROF PHYSIOL & CELL BIOL, SCH MED, UNIV KANS, 66- *Personal Data:* b Pasadena, Calif, Nov 26, 14; m 39; c 4. *Educ:* Univ Minn, MD, 40, MS, 48. *Prof Exp:* Intern internal med, Univ Rochester, 39-40, resident path, 40-42; consult, Mayo Clin & Mayo Found, 48-56. *Concurrent Pos:* Fel internal med, Mayo Found, 42-48, instr, Univ Minn, 50-56; USPHS fel, Univ Kans, 57-59. *Mem:* AAAS; Am Diabetes Asn; AMA; Am Physiol Soc; NY Acad Sci. *Res:* Cerebral energy metabolism; cellular structure and function of brain; endocrine physiology. *Mailing Add:* PO Box 117 Lawrence KS 66044

BALGOOYEN, THOMAS GERRIT, ORNITHOLOGY. *Current Pos:* ASSOC PROF BIOL, SAN JOSE STATE UNIV, 75- *Personal Data:* b Grand Haven, Mich, July 5, 43; c 1. *Educ:* San Jose State Univ, BA, 66; MA, 67; Univ Calif, Berkeley, PhD(zool), 72. *Prof Exp:* Fel ornith, Univ Calif, Berkeley, 72-74. *Mem:* Am Ornithologists Union; Cooper Ornith Soc; Wilson Ornith Soc; Sigma Xi. *Res:* Adaptive strategies of raptorial birds in terms of time and energy; interactions of avian behavior and ecology. *Mailing Add:* Dept Biol Sci San Jose State Univ 1 Washington Sq San Jose CA 95192-0001

BALIGA, B JAYANT, SEMICONDUCTOR DEVICES, SEMICONDUCTOR TECHNOLOGY. *Current Pos:* PROF ELEC ENG, NC STATE UNIV, 88-; DIR, POWER SEMICONDUCTOR RES CTR, 91- *Personal Data:* b Madras, India, Apr 28, 48; m 75; c 2. *Educ:* Indian Inst Technol, Madras, BTech, 69; Rensselaer Polytech Inst, NY, MS, 71, PhD(elec eng), 74. *Honors & Awards:* Newell Award, Inst Elect & Electronics Engrs, 91, Liebmann Award, 93. *Prof Exp:* Staff mem, Gen Elec Res Ctr, 74-79, mgr, 79-88. *Concurrent Pos:* Adj prof, Rensselaer Polytech Inst, NY, 74-80; mem, Electron Mat Comt, Am Inst Mech Eng, 78-, Int Electron Devices Meeting, Inst Elec & Electronics Engrs, 82-; UN consult, Cent Electron Eng Res Inst, 79-80; Coolidge Mem Found fel. *Mem:* Nat Acad Eng; fel Inst Elec & Electronics Engrs. *Res:* Power semiconductor devices; smart power integrated circuits; process/materials technology; author or co-author of over 400 publications, author of 6 books and contributor to 18 books. *Mailing Add:* PO Box 7924 NC State Univ Centennial Campus Raleigh NC 27695-7924

BALIGA, B SURENDRA, BIOCHEMISTRY, NUTRITION. *Current Pos:* ASSOC PROF BIOCHEM NUTRIT & DIR NUTRIT LAB, MED CTR, UNIV S ALA, 78- *Personal Data:* b Bangalore, India, Jan 12, 35; US citizen; m 64; c 2. *Educ:* Poona Univ, BSc Hons, 56, MSc, 58; Indian Inst Sci, Bangalore, PhD(biochem), 63. *Prof Exp:* Fel biochem, Indian Inst Sci, Bangalore, 63-64 & Med Ctr, Tufts Univ, Boston, 65-66; res assoc biochem nutrit, Mass Inst Technol, 67-68. *Mem:* Am Soc Biol Chemists; Am Inst Nutrit. *Res:* Regulatory mechanisms in eucaryotic systems. *Mailing Add:* Dept Pediat Univ SAla Med Ctr 2451 Fillingim St Mobile AL 36617-2293

BALIGA, SHANKAR B, ELECTRO-OPTICS, INFRARED & UTRAVIOLET PHYSICS. *Current Pos:* RES SCIENTIST, GEN MONITORS INC, 95- *Personal Data:* b Lucknow, India, Nov 19, 57; US citizen. *Educ:* Indian Inst Technol, Kanpur, MS, 79; Ohio State Univ, PhD(physics), 86. *Prof Exp:* Mem tech staff, Hypres Inc, 86-88; sr engr, Servo Corp Am, 88-95. *Mem:* Inst Elec & Electronics Engrs; Am Phys Soc; Int Soc Optical Eng; sr mem Instrument Soc Am. *Res:* Electro-optics leading to products for combustible and toxic gas detection using optical methods; electro-optics for flame detection via optical methods; design and fabrication of infrared detectors and systems. *Mailing Add:* 424 E Yale Loop Irvine CA 92614. *Fax:* 714-581-8253

BALIN, ARTHUR KIRSNER, DERMATOLOGY, AGING RESEARCH. *Current Pos:* ASST PROF & ASSOC PHYSICIAN, ROCKEFELLER UNIV, NY, 81- *Personal Data:* b Philadelphia, Pa, June 17, 48. *Educ:* Northwestern Univ, BA, 70; Univ Pa, MD, 74, PhD(biochem), 76, Am Bd Internal Med, dipl, 79, Am Bd Dermat, dipl, 80, Am Bd Path, Dermatopathology, dipl, 81. *Honors & Awards:* Wilton M Earle Award, Tissue Cult Asn, 75. *Prof Exp:* Resident internal med, Hosp Univ Pa, 76-78; resident dermat, Sch Med, Yale Univ, 79-80, res dermatopathology, 80-81. *Concurrent Pos:* Assoc scientist aging res, Wistar Inst Anat & Biol, 76-78; adj asst prof dermat, Sch Med, Cornell Univ, 81-; asst attend physician, New York Hosp, 81-; fel Am Acad Dermat; fel Col Am Pathologists; fel Am Soc Dermatologic Surg. *Mem:* Am Chem Soc; AMA; Am Geriat Soc; Geront Soc; Tissue Cult Asn; fel Am Soc Dermatopath. *Res:* Biology of aging; molecular biology, clinical; photobiology, radiation biology; oxygen toxicity, free radical biology, cell cycle, cell culture; dermatology. *Mailing Add:* 2129 Providence Ave Chester PA 19103-5506

BALINSKI, MICHEL LOUIS, MATHEMATICS OF DECISION SCIENCES, MATHEMATICAL PROGRAMMING. *Current Pos:* DIR RES, NAT CTR SCI RES, LAB ECON, ECOLE POLYTECH, PARIS, FRANCE, 83-, DIR, LAB D'ECONOMETRIE, 89-, CO-DIR PHD PROG OPTIMIZATION, GAMES & ECON MODELS, UNIV PARIS 6, 89- *Personal Data:* b Geneva, Switz, Oct 6, 33; US citizen; m 57, 93, Assieh Majidi; c Maria L & Marta A. *Educ:* Williams Col, BA, 54; Mass Inst Technol, MS, 56; Princeton Univ, PhD(math), 59. *Hon Degrees:* MA, Yale Univ, 78. *Honors & Awards:* Lanchester Prize, Opers Res Soc Am, 65; Lester R Ford Award, Math Asn Am, 75; Spec Serv Award, Math Prog Soc, 82. *Prof Exp:* Instr math, Princeton Univ, 59-61, lectr & res assoc, 61-63; assoc prof econ, Univ Pa, 63-65; from assoc prof to prof math, Grad Ctr, City Univ NY, 65-77; prof admin sci, Yale Univ, 78-80; prof, Inst August Comte, Paris, France, 80-81 & Ecole Polytech, 81-82; prof appl math, statist & econ, State Univ NY, Stony Brook, 83-89. *Concurrent Pos:* Consult, Mathematica, 59-74, Rand Corp, 60-66 & Mobil Oil Res Labs, 66-69; lectr, Univ Mich Summer Eng Conf, 62-69; mem, Opers Res Coun Adv Body, Mayor, City New York, 67-70; prof fel, IBM Corp World Trade Corp, Paris, 69-70; founding ed-in-chief, Math Prog & Math Prog Studies, 70-80; consult, Off Radio-diffusion TV, France, 71; vis prof, Swiss Fed Inst Technol, Lausanne, 72-73 & Univ Grenoble, 74-75; chmn, Syst & Decision Sci Area, Int Inst Appl Systs Anal, Laxenburg, Austria, 75-77; sr consult econ, 78-80; chmn, Math Prog Soc, 86-89; founder & dir, Inst Decision Sci, State Univ NY, Stony Brook, 86-89. *Mem:* Math Prog Soc; Soc Indust Appl Math; Opers Res Soc Am. *Res:* Mathematical programming; combinatorial applied mathematics; decision sciences; mathematical methods in the social sciences; equity and apportionment. *Mailing Add:* Lab d'Econometrie Ecole Polytech 1 Rue Descartes Paris 75005 France. *Fax:* 33-1-46343428; *E-Mail:* balinski@poly. polytechnique.fr

BALINSKY, DORIS, CANCER RESEARCH, NUTRITION. *Current Pos:* RETIRED. *Personal Data:* b Frankfurt, Ger, Dec 3, 34; c 2. *Educ:* London Univ, PhD(biochem), 59. *Prof Exp:* Prof biochem, Iowa State Univ, 81-85; prog adminr, USDA, 85-88; prog dir, Nat Heart, Lung & Blood Inst, NIH, 88-91, mem tech staff, 91-94. *Mem:* Am Asn Cancer Res; Am Soc Biol Chemists. *Mailing Add:* 4024 Thornton Ct Annandale VA 22003

BALINT, FRANCIS JOSEPH, MATHEMATICS. *Current Pos:* RETIRED. *Personal Data:* b Johnstown, Pa, Mar 2, 32; m 56; c 6. *Educ:* Indiana Univ Pa, BS, 54; Univ Pittsburgh, MS, 59. *Honors & Awards:* US Dept Com Silver Medal, 71. *Prof Exp:* Customs engr, IBM Corp, 54-55; programmer, Gulf Res & Develop Co, 55-60, opers leader, 60-62, sr proj engr, 63-65; chief, Mgt & Prog Br, US Weather Bur, Nat Oceanic & Atmospheric Admin, 65-66, chief, Mgt & Planning Br, 66-70, chief, Mgt Systs Div, 70-72, dir, Off Info & Mgt Serv, 78-84, dep dir, Off Mgt & Comput Systs, 72-93; dir, Off Info Systs, US Dept Com, 84-93. *Concurrent Pos:* Instr, Ind State Col Pa, 62; mem exec bd, Share, Inc, 68-69, mgr, Basic Systs Div, 72-73; Nat lectr, Asn Comput Mach. *Mem:* NY Acad Sci; Asn Comput Mach; AAAS. *Res:* Application of supercomputers for scientific and engineering problem solutions. *Mailing Add:* 2400 Jackson Pkwy Vienna VA 22180

BALINT, JOHN ALEXANDER, MEDICINE. *Current Pos:* assoc prof, 63-68, chmn, Dept Med, 81-88, PROF MED & GASTROENTEROL, ALBANY MED COL, 68-, RICHARD T BEEBE PROF MED, 88- *Personal Data:* b Budapest, Hungary, Feb 11, 25; m 49; c 2. *Educ:* Univ Cambridge, BA, 45, MB, BCh, 48; FRCP(UK), 76. *Prof Exp:* Fel gastroenterol, Col Med, Univ Cincinnati, 58-59; fel med, Sch Med, Johns Hopkins Univ, 59-60; asst prof med & gastroenterol, Med Col Ala, 60-63. *Concurrent Pos:* NIH trainee lipid biochem, Sinai Hosp, Baltimore, 59-60. *Mem:* Am Fedn Clin Res; Am Physiol Soc; Am Soc Clin Invest; Brit Med Asn; fel Royal Soc Med; Sigma Xi; Am Gastroenterol Asn; Am Asn Study Liver Dis; Am Clin & Climat Asn. *Res:* Lipid metabolism in relation to fat absorption and intrahepatic phospholipid metabolism; lipid and protein disorders in hereditary lipid storage diseases. *Mailing Add:* Dept Med Albany Med Ctr A-153 45 New Scotland Ave Albany NY 12208

BALIS, JOHN ULYSSES, LUNG PATHOLOGY. *Current Pos:* PROF PATH, COL MED, UNIV SFLA, 78- *Personal Data:* b July 7, 32; m; c 1. *Educ:* Nat Univ Athens, MD, 57. *Mem:* Am Asn Pathologists; Int Acad Path. *Res:* Lung surfactant system. *Mailing Add:* Dept Path Univ SFla Col Med Box 11 12901 Bruce B Downs Blvd Tampa FL 33612-4799

BALIS, MOSES EARL, BIOCHEMISTRY. *Current Pos:* RETIRED. *Personal Data:* b Philadelphia, Pa, June 19, 21; m 45, Bernice Lamborg; c Andrea & Ellen. *Educ:* Temple Univ, BA, 43; Univ Pa, MA, 47, PhD(org chem), 49. *Honors & Awards:* USPHS Res Career Award, 63. *Prof Exp:* Assoc, 49-54, Sloan-Kettering Inst Cancer Res, assoc mem, 54-65, mem, 65-87, chief div cell metab, 71-87, prof biochem, Sloan-Kettering Div, Cornell Univ, 66-87; consult, 87-92. *Concurrent Pos:* Assoc prof biochem, Sloan-Kettering Div, Cornell Univ, 54-56, chmn dept, 69-72; chmn biochem unit, Sloan-Kettering Inst Cancer Res, 69-71, 77-79, mem ed adv bd, Cancer Res, 70-73, assoc ed, 69-81; partic, Nat Cancer Planning Prog, 72; mem adv comt pathogenesis, Am Cancer Soc; mem rev comt, Nat Large Bowel Cancer Proj, 76-81. *Mem:* Am Chem Soc; Am Soc Biol Chem; Harvey Soc; Am Asn Cancer Res; Sigma Xi. *Res:* Biochemistry of differentiation and malignancy; regulation of enzyme function; purine metabolism; action of antimetabolites; genetic defects; mechanisms of carcinogenesis. *Mailing Add:* 146 Byrdcliffe Rd Woodstock NY 12498-1026

BALISH, EDWARD, MICROBIOLOGY, BIOCHEMISTRY. *Current Pos:* assoc prof, 70-77, PROF MED MICROBIOL & SURG, MED SCH, UNIV WIS-MADISON, 78- *Personal Data:* b Scranton, Pa, Apr 23, 35; m 61; c 1. *Educ:* Univ Scranton, BS, 57; Syracuse Univ, MS, 59, PhD(microbiol), 63. *Prof Exp:* Asst, Syracuse Univ, 57-60, res assoc, 62-63; resident res assoc, Argonne Nat Lab, 63-65; res scientist-microbiologist, Oak Ridge Assoc Univs, 66-70. *Mem:* AAAS; Am Soc Microbiol; Radiation Res Soc; Can Soc Microbiol; Int Soc Human & Animal Mycol; Sigma Xi. *Res:* Microbial biochemistry; enzymology; gnotobiology; mechanism of pathogenicity of fungi, particularly Candida albicans. *Mailing Add:* Dept Surg Univ Wis Med Sch 1300 Univ Ave 4638 MSC Madison WI 53706-1532

BALIUNAS, SALLIE LOUISE, SOLAR VARIABILITY & TERRESTRIAL CLIMATE CHANGE, MAGNETIC FIELDS OF STARS & SUN. *Current Pos:* ASTROPHYSICIST, HARVARD SMITHSONIAN CTR ASTROPHYS, 80-; DEP DIR, MOUNT WILSON OBSERV, 91- *Personal Data:* b New York, NY, Feb 23, 53. *Educ:* Villanova Univ, BS, 74; Harvard Univ, AM, 75, PhD(astron), 80. *Honors & Awards:* Newton-Lacy Pierce Prize, Am Astron Soc, 88. *Concurrent Pos:* Vis prof, Ctr Excellence Info Systs , Tenn State Univ, 90-; vis scholar, Dartmouth Col, 90; Wesson fel, Hoover Inst, Stanford Univ, 93-94. *Mem:* Astron Soc Pac; Am Astron Soc; Am Geophys Union; Int Astron Union; Am Phys Soc; Sigma Xi. *Res:* Research of magnetism of the sun and sun-like stars; solar variability and terrestrial climate change; evolution of sun and life on Earth; adaptive optics; astronomical images for classroom education; robotic and remote-control telescopes. *Mailing Add:* Harvard Smithsonian Ctr Astrophys 60 Garden St, MS 15 Cambridge MA 02138. *Fax:* 617-495-7049; *E-Mail:* baliunas@cfa. harvard.edu

BALK, PIETER, MICROELECTRONICS, SEMICONDUCTOR DEVICE TECHNOLOGY. *Current Pos:* DIR & PROF SEMICONDUCTOR ELEC, DELFT INST MICROELECTRONICS & SUBMICRON TECHNOL, TECH UNIV, 88- *Personal Data:* b Breukelen, Neth, Dec 27, 24; m 53, Cornelia B; c 3. *Educ:* State Univ, Utrecht, MSc, 53; Free Univ, Amsterdam, PhD(chem physics), 57. *Prof Exp:* Res fel, Nat Res Coun, Ottawa, Can, 57-58; res staff mem, IBM Res Ctr, NY, 59-72; prof semiconductor elec, Tech Univ, Aachen, 72-87. *Concurrent Pos:* Staff, Dimes, Tu Delft, 88-93, dir, 93- *Mem:* Fel Inst Elec & Electronics Engrs; Electrochem Soc; Ger Physics Soc. *Res:* Physics and technology of mos devices and III-V devices. *Mailing Add:* Dimes Tech Univ Delft Univ Feldmanweg 17 PO Box 5053 Delft 2600 Ga Netherlands. *Fax:* 31-15-262-2163

BALKA, DON STEPHEN, MATHEMATICS, MATHEMATICS EDUCATION. *Current Pos:* from asst prof to assoc prof, 74-87, PROF MATH, ST MARY'S COL, 88- *Personal Data:* b South Bend, Ind, Aug 14, 46; m 69, Sharon J Albert; c Stephen & Paige. *Educ:* Mo Valley Col, BS, 68; Ind Univ, MS, 70; St Francis Col, MS, 71; Univ Mo, Columbia, PhD(math educ), 74. *Honors & Awards:* Maria Piata Award. *Prof Exp:* Jr high sch teacher math, Plymouth Community Sch Corp, 68-69; sr high sch teacher math, Union-North United Sch Corp, 69-71; lectr math educ, Univ Mo, Columbia, 73-74. *Concurrent Pos:* Math consult, Creative Publ, Inc, 74-, Didax Educ Resources & Cuisenaire Co Am, 87- & Harcourt Braces & Co. *Mem:* Nat Coun Teachers Math; Sch Sci & Math Asn; Nat Educ Asn; Math Asn Am. *Res:* Mathematics manipulatives in the classroom; creativity in mathematics; handheld calculators in classrooms; problem solving; analysis of Indiana high school math contest results for gender differences. *Mailing Add:* Dept Math St Mary's Col 218 Madelena Notre Dame IN 46556. *Fax:* 219-284-4716

BALKANY, THOMAS JAY, OTOLOGY. *Current Pos:* Resident otolaryngol, 73-76, chief resident, 76-77, ASST PROF OTOL, UNIV COLO, MED CTR, 77-, DIR SECT PEDIAT OTOLARYNGOL, 72-, VCHMN, DEPT OTOLARYNGOL. *Personal Data:* b Miami, Fla; m 70; c 1. *Educ:* Univ Miami, MD, 72; Am Bd Otolaryngol, cert. *Concurrent Pos:* Chmn, Dept Otolaryngol, Denver Children's Hosp, 79- *Mem:* Fel Am Acad Otolaryngol; Soc Univ Otolaryngologists; fel Am Col Surgeons; fel Int Col Surgeons. *Res:* Electrical cochlear prosthesis for the profoundly deaf; etiology, diagnosis and treatment of otitis media; developmental delays in Down's Syndrome children due to hearing loss. *Mailing Add:* Dept Otolaryngol D4S Univ Miami Sch Med 1600 NW 10th Ave Miami FL 33136-1015

BALKE, BRUNO, PHYSIOLOGY. *Current Pos:* RETIRED. *Personal Data:* b Braunschweig, Ger, Sept 6, 07; US citizen; m 35; c 4. *Educ:* Acad Phys Educ, Ger, dipl, 31; Univ Berlin, MD, 36; Univ Leipzig, Dr med habil, 45. *Prof Exp:* Consult sports med, Univ Berlin, 36-42; head dept performance physiol, Med Sch Ger Army Mt Corps, 42-45; physiologist, Sch Aviation Med, US Air Force, 50-60; chief biodynamics br, Civil Aeromed Res Inst, Fed Aviation Agency, 60-64; from prof to emer prof phys educ & physiol, Univ Wis-Madison, 64-92. *Concurrent Pos:* Assoc prof, Air Univ, 58-60; prof, Col Med, Univ Okla, 60-; attend physician, Vet Admin Hosp, 60-; ed, J Med & Sci in Sports, 69-73; consult, Colo Govt Coun Phys Fitness, Health & Tennis Corp Am, Longevity Ctr, Santa Barbara & Health Enhancement & Lifestyle Med Inst, Palm Springs, Calif; dir, Aspen Cardio-Pulmonary Rehab Unit, 73-92. *Mem:* Soc Exp Biol & Med; Aerospace Med Asn; Am Physiol Soc; Am Col Sports Med (pres, 65). *Res:* Medical and physiological research applied to human stress tolerance under condition of exercise, climate, altitude and high speed flying; role of exercise in cardiac rehabilitation. *Mailing Add:* 2821 1/2 Elm Ave Grand Junction CO 81501-4907

BALKE, NELSON EDWARD, PLANT PHYSIOLOGY, WEED SCIENCE. *Current Pos:* Asst prof, 77-83, ASSOC PROF AGRON, UNIV WIS-MADISON, 83- *Personal Data:* b Edwardsville, Ill, Mar 28, 49. *Educ:* Univ Ill, BS, 71; Purdue Univ, MS, 74, PhD(plant physiol), 77. *Mem:* Am Soc Plant Physiologists; Weed Sci Soc Am; Am Soc Agron; Crop Sci Soc Am; Coun Agr Sci & Technol; AAAS. *Res:* Absorption and metabolism of organic molecules by plant cells; enzymatic detoxication of xenobiotics by plants. *Mailing Add:* 259 Moore Hall Univ Wis 1575 Linden Dr Madison WI 53706-1597

BALKISSOON, BASDEO, CARDIOVASCULAR PHYSIOLOGY. *Current Pos:* Resident surg, 53-58, asst prof, 59-62, ASST PROF SURG & PHYSIOL, COL MED, HOWARD UNIV, 65-; PVT PRACT GEN SURG, 65- *Personal Data:* b Trinidad, WI, July 29, 22; US citizen; m 53, Gloria; c Jaikrishna & Indira. *Educ:* Univ London, Inter BA, 46; Howard Univ, BS, 48, MD, 52, MS, 56, PhD(physiol & surg), 64; Am Board Surg, dipl, 1959. *Mem:* Fel Am Col Surgeons; Am Physiol Soc; AMA; Nat Med Asn; Pan Am Med Asn; Am Heart Asn. *Res:* Liver transplanted dogs and pigs. *Mailing Add:* Howard Univ Col Med Washington DC 20017-2596

BALKO, BARBARA ANN, PHOTOLUMINESCENCE FROM SEMICONDUCTORS, ELECTROCHEMISTRY. *Current Pos:* ASST PROF CHEM, LEWIS & CLARK COL, 93- *Personal Data:* b Passaic, NJ, Apr 24, 62. *Educ:* Bryn Mawr Col, AB, 84; Univ Calif, Berkeley, PhD(phys chem), 91. *Prof Exp:* Fel, Univ Ore, 91-93. *Mem:* Am Chem Soc; Am Phys Soc. *Res:* Dynamics of the photo-dissociation of acetylene and ethylene as well as reactions with hot D atoms using a molecular beam machine; rate of photoluminescence decay from gallium arsenic; photoluminescence from colloidal film electrodes. *Mailing Add:* Dept Chem, Lewis & Clark Col Olin Portland OR 97219. *Fax:* 503-768-7369; *E-Mail:* balko@lclark.edu

BALKWILL, DAVID LEE, MICROBIOLOGY. *Current Pos:* from asst prof to assoc prof, 82-90, PROF, DEPT BIOL SCI, FLA STATE UNIV, 90- *Personal Data:* b Sheboygan, Wis, Jan 19, 49. *Educ:* Univ Wis-Madison, BS, 71; Pa State Univ, MS, 73, PhD(microbiol), 77. *Prof Exp:* Asst prof, dept microbiol, Univ NH, 77-82. *Mem:* Am Soc Microbiol; US Fedn Cult Collections; AAAS. *Res:* Natural ecology of aquifer and other subsurface sediment; physiological and phylogenetic characteristics of micro-organisms in substance sediments. *Mailing Add:* Dept Biol Sci Fla State Univ Tallahassee FL 32306-1096. *Fax:* 850-644-4865; *E-Mail:* balkwill@bio.fsu.edu

BALL, ALEXANDER KEITH, NEUROSCIENCES, ANATOMY. *Current Pos:* From asst prof to assoc prof, 84-94, PROF & CHAIR, DEPT BIOMED SCI, MCMASTER UNIV, 94- *Personal Data:* b Sydney, NS, Sept 2, 55; m 77, Thelma Christina Burns; c Elizabeth J & Katherine M. *Educ:* Dalhousie Univ, BSc, 73, PhD(anat), 77. *Concurrent Pos:* Vis assoc prof, Univ Mich, 93. *Mem:* Can Asn Anatomists; Micros Soc Can; Asn Res Vision & Opthal; Sigma Xi. *Res:* Retina anatomy, physiology & pharmacology; neural plasticity and adaption; cell to cell coupling and gap junctions; nerve regeneration; immunohistochemistry; fluorescence and laser scanning confocal microscopy. *Mailing Add:* Health Sci-IRI McMaster Univ Hamilton ON L8N 3Z5 Can. *Fax:* 905-525-7400; *E-Mail:* akball@fhs.csu.mcmaster.ca

BALL, BILLIE JOE, ELECTRICAL ENGINEERING. *Current Pos:* assoc prof, 63, PROF ELEC ENG, MISS STATE UNIV, 80-, HEAD DEPT, 64- *Personal Data:* b Louin, Miss, Apr 8, 29; m 54; c 2. *Educ:* Miss State Univ, BS(chem eng) & BS(elec eng), 56, MS, 59; Tex A&M Univ, PhD(elec eng), 62. *Prof Exp:* Engr, Westinghouse Elec Corp, 55 & Reynolds Metals Co, 56 & 57; instr elec eng, Miss State Univ, 57-59; from instr to assoc prof, Tex A&M Univ, 59-63. *Mem:* Inst Elec & Electronics Engrs; Am Soc Eng Educ; Nat Soc Prof Engrs; Instrument Soc Am. *Mailing Add:* PO Box 2848 Mississippi State MS 39762

BALL, BILLY JOE, MATHEMATICS. *Current Pos:* RETIRED. *Personal Data:* b Crowell, Tex, Nov 29, 25; m 47; c 1. *Educ:* Univ Tex, BA, 48, PhD(math), 52. *Prof Exp:* Instr pure math, Univ Tex, 49-52; actg asst prof math, Univ Va, 52-53, asst prof, 53-59; head dept math, Univ Ga, 63-69, from assoc prof to prof math, 59-86. *Mem:* Am Math Soc; Math Asn Am. *Res:* Point set topology. *Mailing Add:* 3304 Glen Rose Dr Austin TX 78731

BALL, CARROLL RAYBOURNE, ANATOMY. *Current Pos:* from asst prof to assoc prof, 63-71, PROF ANAT, SCH MED, UNIV MISS, 71- *Personal Data:* b Leakesville, Miss, Oct 11, 25; div; c 3. *Educ:* Univ Miss, BA, 47, MS, 48, PhD(anat), 63. *Prof Exp:* Asst zool, Univ Miss, 46-48; asst, Duke Univ, 48-50, instr, 50-51; instr micros & gross anat, Med Sch, WVa Univ, 51-57; asst prof biol, Univ Southern Miss, 57-60, instr anat, 62-63. *Mem:* Am Asn Anat; Am Soc Exp Path; Soc Exp Biol & Med; Sigma Xi. *Res:* Experimental pathology; nutrition; cardiovascular disease; hepatic liposis. *Mailing Add:* Dept Anat Univ Miss Sch Med 2500 N State St Jackson MS 39216-4505

BALL, DAVID RALPH, INDUSTRIAL ORGANIC CHEMISTRY, FUEL SCIENCE. *Current Pos:* SCIENTIST INDUST GRAPHITE RES & DEVELOP, PARMA TECH CTR, UNION CARBIDE CORP, 73- *Personal Data:* b Swansea, Wales, July 20, 40; m 64; c 3. *Educ:* Univ Leeds, Eng, BSc, 64, PhD(coal chem), 69. *Prof Exp:* Chem engr & group leader, Brit Acheson Electrodes Ltd, 68-73. *Mem:* Brit Inst Fuel; Soc Chem Indust. *Res:* Preparation, composition, structure, chemical reactivity, carbonisation and pyrolysis of fossil fuel derivatives. *Mailing Add:* Parma Tech Ctr Union Carbide Corp 12900 Snow Rd Parma OH 44130

BALL, DEREK HARRY, CARBOHYDRATE CHEMISTRY. *Current Pos:* res chemist, Org Chem, US Army Natick Res & Develop Ctr, 60-72, head org chem group, Pioneering Res Lab, 72-74, res chemist, Food Sci Lab, 74-83, HEAD, BIOTECHNOL BR, SCI & ADV TECH LAB, US ARMY NATICK RES & DEVELOP CTR, 83- *Personal Data:* b London, Eng, Sept 1, 31; m 65, Eleanor J Fischer; c Derek M, Douglas H & Edward W. *Educ:* Bristol Univ, BSc, 53; Queen's Univ, Ont, PhD(chem), 56. *Prof Exp:* Res fel carbohydrate chem, Div Appl Biol, Nat Res Coun Can, 56-58; fel catalysis, State Univ NY Col Ceramics, Alfred Univ, 59-60. *Mem:* Am Chem Soc; fel Brit Chem Soc. *Res:* Selective substitution of carbohydrates; branched chain sugars; sucrochemistry; H-1 and C-13 nmr of carbohydrates; liquid chromatographic methods for the analysis of free sugars in foods. *Mailing Add:* 15 Keith Rd Wayland MA 01778

BALL, DONALD LEE, CHEMISTRY. *Current Pos:* RETIRED. *Personal Data:* b Kalamazoo, Mich, June 9, 31; m 69. *Educ:* Kalamazoo Col, AB, 53; Brown Univ, PhD(chem), 56. *Prof Exp:* Proj assoc chem, Univ Wis, 56-57; sr res chemist res labs, Gen Motors Corp, Mich, 57-67; chief phys chem prog, Chem Sci Directorate, Air Force Off Sci Res, 67-70, prog mgr chem energetics, 70-73, dir chem & atmospheric sci, 73-94. *Mem:* Am Chem Soc; Sigma Xi. *Res:* Physical and inorganic chemistry. *Mailing Add:* 8207 Toll House Rd Annandale VA 22003

BALL, DOUGLAS, GEOLOGY. *Current Pos:* PRES, BALL ASN, 57-, INTERSTATE SERV CORP, 60- *Personal Data:* b Cheyenne, Wyo, Mar 5, 20; m; c Richard, Denver, Michael & Anna (Berlin). *Educ:* Colo Sch Mines, PE(EE Petrol), 43. *Prof Exp:* Natural gas eng, Phillips Petrol Co, 46-49. *Concurrent Pos:* Prof, Clear Creek Co Metal Mining Asn, 88-90. *Mem:* Fel Geol Soc Am; Soc Petrol Engrs; Am Asn Petrol Geologists. *Res:* Natural gases in carbonate reservoirs. *Mailing Add:* PO Box 122 Rollinsville CO 80474

BALL, EDWARD D, HEMATOLOGY, IMMUNOLOGY. *Current Pos:* PROF MED, SCH MED, UNIV PITTSBURGH, 91- *Personal Data:* b Syracuse, NY, Mar 15, 50. *Educ:* Case Western Reserve Univ, MD, 76. *Prof Exp:* Instr med, Case Western Reserve Univ, 79-81; instr, Sch Med, Dartmouth Univ, 81-82, from asst prof to assoc prof med, 82-91. *Concurrent Pos:* Scholar Leukemia Soc Am, Stohlman Scholar. *Mem:* Am Soc Hemat; Am Asn Immunologists; AAAS; Am Fedn Clin Res; Am Soc Clin Invest; Am Soc Clin Oncol. *Res:* Tumor antigens; bone marrow transplantation; leukemia biology; immunotherapy. *Mailing Add:* Div Hemat/Bone Marrow Univ Pittsburgh Med Ctr 200 Lothrop St Pittsburgh PA 15213-3241. *Fax:* 412-648-6393; *E-Mail:* balled@novell1.dept_med.pitt.edu

BALL, EDWARD JAMES, TRANSPLANTATION IMMUNOLOGY, TCELL ANTIGEN RECEPTOR. *Current Pos:* DIR TRANSP IMMUNOL, HISTOCOMPATIBILITY LAB, DAYTON COMMUNITY BLOOD CTR, 88- *Personal Data:* b Ashtabula, Ohio, May 6, 48; m 71; c 2. *Educ:* Cleveland State Univ, BS, 70; Incarnate Word Col, San Antonio, MS, 75; Univ Cincinnati, (microbiol), 79. *Prof Exp:* From instr to asst prof internal med transp, Univ Tex Southwestern Med Sch Dallas, 85-88. *Mem:* Am Asn Immunologists; Am Soc Histocompatibility & Immunogenetics. *Res:* Human major histocompatibility complex (HLA) D-region polymorphism and recognition by alloreactive and antigen-specific T cells; poloymorphism and structure of human T cell antigen reception. *Mailing Add:* Community Blood Ctr 349 S Main St Dayton OH 45402-2736

BALL, FRANCES LOUISE, ORGANIC CHEMISTRY, ELECTRON MICROSCOPY. *Current Pos:* RETIRED. *Personal Data:* b Murfreesboro, Tenn, Oct 6, 24. *Educ:* Mid Tenn State Col, BS, 45; Vanderbilt Univ, MS, 48. *Honors & Awards:* Distinguished Serv Award, Micros Soc Am, 92. *Prof Exp:* Jr chemist, E I du Pont de Nemours & Co, 45; instr high sch, Tenn, 45-46; instr chem, Limestone Col, 48-49; chemist, Oak Ridge Gaseous Diffusion Plant, Oak Ridge Nat Lab, Union Carbide Corp,49-68, physicist, Molecular Anat Prog, 68-75, res staff mem, Anal Chem Div, 75-83. *Mem:* Electron Micros Soc Am (secy, 75-84); Am Chem Soc. *Res:* Beckmann rearrangement of oximes; oxidation of single crystals of copper; structure and reactions of thin metal films. *Mailing Add:* 1128 E Northfield Blvd Murfreesboro TN 37130

BALL, FRANK JERVERY, ORGANIC CHEMISTRY, WOOD CHEMISTRY. *Current Pos:* RETIRED. *Personal Data:* b Charleston, SC, Jan 29, 19; m 50, Mary E Furtwangler; c Frank J Jr, Stuart F, Bruce D & Steven M. *Educ:* Univ South, BS, 41; Univ Rochester, PhD(org chem), 44. *Prof Exp:* Res chemist, 44-46; group leader, 46-53; dir, Charleston Res Ctr, Westvaco Corp, 53-75, dir, Tyrone Res Lab, 58-60, assoc corp res dir, 75-84. *Concurrent Pos:* Pres, Empire State Pulp Res Assocs, 74-78. *Mem:* Am Chem Soc; Tech Asn Pulp & Paper Industs; Can Pulp & Paper Asn; Am Soc Magnesium Res; NY Acad Sci. *Res:* Sulfate lignin chemicals; fatty and rosin derived surfactants and chemicals from tall oil; activated carbon; pulping, bleaching and chemical recovery; air pollution control; nutrition; medical chemistry. *Mailing Add:* 4 Atlantic St Charleston SC 29401

BALL, GENE V, INTERNAL MEDICINE. *Current Pos:* from instr to assoc prof, 65-71, interim dir, 95-96, PROF INTERNAL MED, MED CTR, UNIV ALA, BIRMINGHAM, 71-, CHIEF, CLIN SERV, CLIN IMMUNOL & RHEUMATOLOGY. *Personal Data:* b Rivesville, WVa, June 28, 31; m 59, Sara J Clark; c Rebecca A & Hillary E. *Educ:* WVa Univ, BS, 57; Vanderbilt Univ, MD, 59; Am Bd Internal Med, dipl; Am Bd Rheumatol, dipl. *Prof Exp:* Intern, Cincinnati Gen Hosp, 59-60; resident, Hosp Univ Pa, 60-61, Jackson Mem Hosp, 61-64; pract internal med, Univ Miami, 64-65. *Concurrent Pos:* Fel, Jackson Mem Hosp, 61-64; assoc ed, Arthritis & Rheumatism, 75-80; mem, Subspecialty Sect Rheumatol, Am Bd Internal Med; mem, Arthritis Adv Coun, Food & Drug Admin, 89-92; mem, Rheumatology Sect, MKSAP, Am Col Physicians; consult, Accreditation Coun Grad Med Educ. *Mem:* Fel Am Col Physicians; Am Rheumatism Asn. *Res:* Gout; Saturnine gout; systemic lupus erythematosus. *Mailing Add:* Dept Internal Med Univ Ala Med Ctr Birmingham AL 35294

BALL, GEORGE A(PPLETON), ENGINEERING, APPLIED PHYSICS. *Current Pos:* RETIRED. *Personal Data:* b Philadelphia, Pa, Apr 12, 21; m 45, Mary Jane Bickford; c George A Jr, Janet (Delaney), David & Lucinda (Eby). *Educ:* Harvard Univ, BS, 42, MS, 43, PhD(appl physics), 51. *Prof Exp:* Engr, Chance Vought Aircraft, 43-46; res engr, Ethyl Corp, 51-56; res engr, Chrysler Corp, 56-87. *Mem:* Combustion Inst; Soc Automotive Engrs. *Res:* Development of gas turbine components for automotive use. *Mailing Add:* 17198 Buckingham Beverly Hills MI 48025

BALL, GEORGE EUGENE, SYSTEMATICS. *Current Pos:* From asst prof to prof, 54-91, dept chmn, 73-83, EMER PROF ENTOM, UNIV ALTA, 92- *Personal Data:* b Detroit, Mich, Sept 25, 26; m 49; c 2. *Educ:* Cornell Univ, AB, 49, PhD, 54; Univ Ala, MS, 50. *Honors & Awards:* Gold Medal, Entom Soc Can, 80. *Mem:* Soc Syst Zoologists; Soc Study Evolution; Royal Entom Soc London. *Res:* Systematic entomology, especially classification, way of life and geographical distribution of beetles of the family Carabidae. *Mailing Add:* Dept Biol Scis Univ Alta Edmonton AB T6G 2E9 Can. *Fax:* 403-492-1767

BALL, GEORGE WILLIAM, SOFTWARE ENGINEERING, PROGRAMMING LANGUAGES. *Current Pos:* ASSOC PROF MATH, ALFRED UNIV, 68- *Personal Data:* b Warren, Pa, Apr 3, 41; m 78, 84, Rita Burns; c Derrick, Douglas, Jolene, Janice, Tobias, Christopher, Thomas & Timothy. *Educ:* Union Col, NY, BS, 63; Syracuse Univ, MS, 65, PhD(math), 72; Rochester Inst Technol, MS, 88. *Mem:* Asn Comput Mach. *Res:* Computer science education. *Mailing Add:* Div Math & Comput Sci Alfred Univ Saxon Dr Alfred NY 14802-1205. *E-Mail:* gball@cs.alfred.edu

BALL, GORDON CHARLES, nuclear structure, nuclear chemistry, for more information see previous edition

BALL, GREGORY FRANCIS, NEUROETHOLOGY, BEHAVIORAL NEUROENDOCRINOLOGY. *Current Pos:* asst prof, 91-94, ASSOC PROF PSYCHOL, JOHNS HOPKINS UNIV, BALTIMORE, MD, 94- *Personal Data:* b Washington, DC, May 6, 55; m 93, Margaret M McCarthy. *Educ:* Columbia Univ, BA, 77; Rutgers Univ, PhD(psychobiol), 83. *Prof Exp:* Fel behav neuroendocrinol, Rockefeller Univ, New York, NY, 83-86, asst prof animal behav, 86-88, asst dir animal behav, Field Res Ctr, Millbrook, NY, 86-88; asst prof psychol, Boston Col, Chestnut Hill, Mass, 88-91. *Concurrent Pos:* Adj asst prof, Rockefeller Univ, New York, NY, 89; adj assoc prof, Johns Hopkins Sch Hyg & Pub Health, 95- *Mem:* Soc Neurosci; Animal Behav Soc; Am Soc Zoologists; Int Soc Neuroethology; Am Ornithologists Union. *Res:* Interaction of hormones, brain and behavior in birds; steroid hormones regulate the production and acquisition of birdsong; environmental stimuli regulate seasonal reproduction in birds; hormones influence the development of sex differences in the brain. *Mailing Add:* Dept Psychol Johns Hopkins Univ Charles & 34th St Baltimore MD 21218. *Fax:* 410-516-6205; *E-Mail:* gball@jhuvms.ucf.jhu.edu

BALL, HAROLD JAMES, INSECT PHYSIOLOGY. *Current Pos:* from asst prof to prof entom, 51-89, EMER PROF ENTOM, UNIV NEBR, LINCOLN, 89- *Personal Data:* b Beaver Dam, Wis, Mar 13, 19; m 60, Ellen Moorhead; c Pamela. *Educ:* Univ Wis, BA, 43, MA, 46, PhD(entom), 51. *Prof Exp:* Asst prof naval sci & tactics, Univ SC, 46. *Mem:* Entom Soc Am. *Res:* Insect photoreceptors; insecticide resistance; photo periodism effects in insects. *Mailing Add:* 102 Plant Indust Bldg Univ Nebr Lincoln NE 68583-0721

BALL, IRVIN JOSEPH, WATERFOWL ECOLOGY. *Current Pos:* ASST LEADER, MONT COOP WILDLIFE RES UNIT, UNIV MONT, MISSOULA, 79- *Personal Data:* b Peoria, Ill, Oct 17, 44; m 77; c 3. *Educ:* Utah State Univ, BS, 66; Univ Minn, MS, 71, PhD(wildlife), 73. *Prof Exp:* From asst prof to assoc prof, Zool Dept, Wash State Univ, 74-79. *Mem:* Wildlife Soc. *Res:* Ecology, behavior and management of gallinaceous birds and waterfowl; habitat use, movements, population dynamics, nesting ecology and effects of exploitation. *Mailing Add:* 35 Pearl St Libby MT 59923

BALL, JAMES BRYAN, NUCLEAR CHEMISTRY. *Current Pos:* Resident res assoc, Oak Ridge Nat Lab, 58-59, dir, Holifield Heavy Ion Res Facil, 74-83, dir, Physics Div, 83-94, PHYSICIST, OAK RIDGE NAT LAB, 59-, DEP ASSOC LAB DIR ADVAN MAT, PHYSICAL & NEWTON SCI, 95- *Personal Data:* b Portland, Ore, Oct 2, 32; m 60, Jacqueline Snyder; c Michaela & Jason. *Educ:* Ore State Col, BS, 54; Univ Wash, PhD, 58. *Concurrent Pos:* Mem, nuclear sci adv comt, Dept Energy-NSF, 80-82 & 90-91; chmn, Div Nuclear Physics, Am Phys Soc, 90-91. *Mem:* Fel AAAS; fel Am Phys Soc. *Res:* Nuclear structure with direct reactions, two-nucleon transfer reactions, shell-model theory of nuclear structure, heavy-ion reactions and accelerator physics. *Mailing Add:* 110 Berwick Dr Oak Ridge TN 37830. *Fax:* 423-574-0323; *E-Mail:* balljb@ornl.gov

BALL, JAMES STUTSMAN, PHYSICS. *Current Pos:* assoc prof, 68-72, PROF PHYSICS, UNIV UTAH, 72- *Personal Data:* b Reno, Nev, Sept 13, 34; m 57; c 1. *Educ:* Calif Inst Technol, BS, 56; Univ Calif, Berkeley, PhD(physics), 60. *Prof Exp:* Res assoc physics, Lawrence Radiation Lab, Univ Calif, Berkeley, 60, asst res physicist, La Jolla, 60-63, asst prof physics, Los Angeles, 63-68. *Mem:* Am Phys Soc. *Res:* Elementary particle physics; structure of elementary particles based on quantum-chromodynamics. *Mailing Add:* Dept Physics 201 JFB Univ Utah Salt Lake City UT 84112

BALL, JOHN ALLEN, RADIO ASTRONOMY, ASTROPHYSICS. *Current Pos:* CHIEF TELESCOPE OPERS, HAYSTACK OBSERV, MASS INST TECHNOL, 84- *Personal Data:* b Ravenna, Nebr, Dec 8, 35; m 55, Audrey A Roth; c Fifine D, Desiree B, Laurie G & Kevin D. *Educ:* Univ Nebr, BSEE, 57; Harvard Univ, PhD(astron), 69. *Honors & Awards:* Rumford Award, Am Acad Arts & Sci, 71. *Prof Exp:* Staff mem, Haystack Observ, Mass Inst Technol, 64-69; res fel, 69-73, res assoc & lectr, 73-77, dir radio astron facil & lectr, Harvard Col Observ, 77-84. *Mem:* Inst Elec & Electronics Engrs; Am Astron Soc; Int Astron Union; Am Asn Physics Teachers; Sigma Xi; Int Union Radio Sci. *Res:* Studies of the interstellar medium and circumstellar clouds using radio-frequency atomic and molecular spectral lines; studies of circumstellar molecular masers using very-long-baseline interferometry; data-acquisition and data-reduction techniques in radio astronomy. *Mailing Add:* 85 Oak Hill Rd Harvard MA 01451-1744. *Fax:* 781-981-0590; *E-Mail:* jball@wells.haystack.edu

BALL, JOHN R, HEALTH SERVICES. *Current Pos:* exec vpres, actg pres, chief exec officer, 95-96, PRES & CHIEF EXEC OFFICER, PA HOSP, PHILADELPHIA, 96- *Personal Data:* b Opelika, Ala, Jul 16, 44. *Educ:* Emory Univ, AB, 66; Duke Univ, JD, 71, MD, 72. *Prof Exp:* Res asst, Dept Community Health Sci, Duke Univ Sch Med, Durham, NC, 71-72; asst dir, Off Qual Stand, Off Asst Secy Health, Rockville, Md, 74-76, chief, Med Audit Br, Div Peer Rev, Bur Qual Assurance, 76-77; sr policy analyst, Off Sci & Technol Policy, Exec Off President, Washington, DC, 78-81; assoc exec vpres health & pub policy, Am Col Physicians, Philadelphia, Washington & Philadelphia, 81-86, exec vpres, 86-94; sr scholar Asn Acad Health Ctrs, 94-95. *Concurrent Pos:* Mem numerous panels & comts, US cols & orgns. *Mem:* Inst Med-Nat Acad Sci; fel Am Col Legal Med; fel Am Col Physicians; AMA; Am Clin & Climat Asn; Am Bar Asn; Soc Med Adminr. *Mailing Add:* Pa Hosp 800 Spruce St Philadelphia PA 19107

BALL, JOHN SIGLER, PETROLEUM CHEMISTRY. *Current Pos:* RETIRED. *Personal Data:* b Hamlin, Tex, Aug 2, 14; m 38, Virginia N; c 6. *Educ:* Tex Tech Col, BS, 34, MS, 36. *Prof Exp:* Jr chem engr petrol & oil-shale exp sta, US Bur Mines, 38-42, asst chemist, 42-43, assoc petrol chemist, 43-44, chemist, 44-45, head petrol chem & refining sect & shale oil res & anal sect, 45-56, chief br petrol, Region III, 56-58, projs coordr petrol res, 58-63, dir, Am Petrol Inst Projs, 48-63, res dir, Bartlesville Energy Res Ctr, US Dept Energy, 63-78; consult, 78-88. *Mem:* Fel AAAS; fel Am Inst Chemists; Am Chem Soc; Soc Petrol Engrs. *Res:* Sulfur and nitrogen compounds of petroleum; composition of shale oil; analytical methods for petroleum. *Mailing Add:* 5934 Cornell Dr Bartlesville OK 74006

BALL, JOSEPH ANTHONY, OPERATOR & SYSTEM THEORY. *Current Pos:* From asst prof to assoc prof, 73-82, PROF MATH, VA TECH, 82- *Personal Data:* b Washington, DC, June 4, 47; m 82, Amelia Sullivan. *Educ:* Georgetown Univ, BS, 69; Univ Va, MS, 70, PhD(math), 73. *Mem:* Am Math Soc; Soc Indust & Appl Math; Inst Elec & Electronics Engrs. *Res:* Matrix and operator valued functions; interpolation; robust control theory. *Mailing Add:* Dept Math Va Polytech Inst & State Univ Blacksburg VA 24601

BALL, KENNETH STEVEN, TURBULENCE, COMPUTATIONAL FLUID DYNAMICS & HEAT TRANSFER. *Current Pos:* asst prof, 89-94, ASSOC PROF MECH ENG, UNIV TEX, AUSTIN, 94- *Personal Data:* b Philadelphia, Pa, Sept 10, 60; m 83, Sandra R Eck; c Steven J, Owen M, Aidan A & Colin P. *Educ:* Lehigh Univ, BSME, 82; Drexel Univ, MSME, 84, PhD(mech eng), 87. *Honors & Awards:* NSF Young Investr Award, 92. *Prof Exp:* Res assoc appl math, Ctr Fluid Mech, Brown Univ, 87-89. *Mem:* Am Soc Mech Engrs; Am Phys Soc; Am Soc Eng Educ; Am Inst Aeronaut & Astronaut; Sigma Xi. *Res:* Computational fluid dynamics and heat transfer; hydrodynamic stability; transition; turbulence; buoyancy induced flow; thermal radiation heat transfer; transport phenomena in manufacturing and materials processing. *Mailing Add:* Dept Mech Eng Univ Tex Austin TX 78712

BALL, LAURENCE ANDREW, ANIMAL VIROLOGY. *Current Pos:* PROF MICROBIOL, UNIV ALA, BIRMINGHAM, 87- *Personal Data:* b York, Yorkshire, Eng, July 9, 44; m 68, 87, Gail W Wertz; c Jennifer Susan & Katherine Sarah. *Educ:* Oxford Univ, Eng, BA, 66, MA, 69, PhD(biochem), 69. *Prof Exp:* Fel biochem, Univ Wis-Madison, 69-71; staff scientist, Nat Inst Med Res, Mill Hill, London, Eng, 72-74; from asst prof to assoc prof microbiol, Univ Conn, Storrs, 74-79; from assoc prof to prof biochem, Univ Wis-Madison, 79-87. *Concurrent Pos:* Res career develop award, NIH, 79-84, mem, Study Sect Virol, 80-83, Merit Award, 87-; assoc ed, Acad Press, Inc, 80-83 & J Interferon Res, Liebert, 80-82; ed-in-chief, Virus Res, 87- *Mem:* Am Soc Microbiol; Am Soc Virol; Am Soc Biochem & Molecular Biol. *Res:* Control of gene expression in animal cells infected with viruses; molecular biology of pox viruses. *Mailing Add:* Microbiol Dept Univ Ala Birmingham UAB Sta Birmingham AL 35294. *Fax:* 205-934-1636; *E-Mail:* andy_ball@micro.microbio.uab.edu

BALL, LAWRENCE ERNEST, POLYMER CHEMISTRY, ORGANIC CHEMISTRY. *Current Pos:* Proj assoc, Stand Oil Co, 61-64, proj leader, 64-68, res assoc Polymer Synthesis, 68-89, RES SCIENTIST, RES LAB, BP RES, 89- *Personal Data:* b Akron, Ohio, Nov 11, 35; m 79, Mary Jo Howes; c Hope C. *Educ:* Univ Akron, BS, 57, MS, 58, PhD(polymer org chem), 61. *Mem:* Am Chem Soc; Soc Petrol Engrs. *Res:* Polymer synthesis; structure and property relations in polymers specialty; acrylonitrile; nylon; water soluble polymers; 27 patents; 7 publications. *Mailing Add:* 4288 W Bath Rd Akron OH 44333-1112

BALL, M ISABEL, BIO-ORGANIC CHEMISTRY. *Current Pos:* PROF CHEM, OUR LADY OF LAKE UNIV, 75-, CHMN DEPT, 68-, DIR, DIV SCI & MATH, 73-, DEAN, COL ARTS & SCI, 80- *Personal Data:* b Elmendorf, Tex, June 1, 29. *Educ:* Our Lady of the Lake Univ, BA, 50; Univ Tex, MA, 63, PhD, 69. *Prof Exp:* Teacher parochial sch, Okla, 52-54; from instr to asst prof chem, Our Lady of the Lake Univ, 54-65; res assoc, Clayton Found Biochem Inst, Univ Tex, 65-68. *Concurrent Pos:* AEC res partic, Oak Ridge Nat Lab, 69. *Mem:* Am Chem Soc; Nat Sci Teachers Asn. *Res:* Synthesis and assay of analogs of metabolites; studies of Aspergillus niger using purine analogs and derivatives; metabolic changes caused by phthalic acid esters in mice and bacteria. *Mailing Add:* Dept Chem 411 SW 24th St San Antonio TX 78285

BALL, MAHLON M, GEOPHYSICS, PETROLEUM GEOLOGY. *Current Pos:* EMER GEOHPYSICIST, ENERGY RESOURCES TEAM, DENVER, 95- *Personal Data:* b Lawrence, Kans, Apr 7, 31; m 53, Marilyn Ringler; c Jon M & Jeffrey R. *Educ:* Univ Kans, BSc, 53, MSc, 58, PhD(geol), 60; Univ Birmingham, UK, MSc, 59. *Prof Exp:* Geologist, Shell Develop Co, 59-62, res geologist, 62-63, sr geologist, Shell Oil Co, 63-65, div geologist, Shell Develop Co, 65-66, res assoc, 66-67; assoc prof geophys, Rosenstiel Sch Marine & Atmospheric Sci, Univ Miami, 67-70, res geophysicist, Inst Marine Sci, 67-75, prof geophys, 70-75; geophysicist, Woods Hole Oceanographic Inst, 75-89 & Petrol Geol Br, US Geol Surv, Denver, 89-94. *Concurrent Pos:* Mem geol adv comt, USAF Weapons Res, 73; mem site surv comt, Int Prog Ocean Drilling, 74; chair, Pollution Prev & Safety Panel, Joint Oceanog Inst, 85- *Mem:* Geol Soc Am; Soc Econ Paleontologists & Mineralogists; Am Geophys Union; Soc Explor Geophys; Am Asn Petrol Geologists; Am Scismol Soc. *Res:* Recent carbonate sediments; marine geophysical investigations of the Bahamas, Caribbean and equatorial Atlantic Ocean; US and international petroleum geology. *Mailing Add:* US Geol Surv Petrol Geol Br PO Box 25046 MS 939 Denver CO 80225. *Fax:* 303-236-8822

BALL, MARION J, MEDICAL & HEALTH SCIENCES. *Current Pos:* PROF, DEPT EPIDEMIOL & PREV MED, UNIV MD SCH MED, 85-; DIR, WHO COLLABORATING CTR HEALTH INFORMATICS, 93-; VPRES, FIRST CONSULT GROUP, 96- *Educ:* Univ Ky, BA, 61, MA, 65; Temple Univ, EdD(curric & instr), 78. *Honors & Awards:* Comput in Healthcare Pioneer Award, 92; President's Award, Am Med Informatics Asn, 95. *Prof Exp:* Programmer & instr, Dept Behav Sci & Dept Comput Sci, Univ Ky Med Ctr, 65-68; from asst dir to dir, Health Sci Ctr, Temple Univ, 68-85, lectr, 68-85, asst prof med physics & biometrics, 68-81, assoc prof family pract & med physics, 81-84, assoc prof, Dept Med, Health Sci Ctr, 84-85; dir acad comput, Univ Md, Baltimore, 85-87, assoc vpres info resources, 85-91, vpres, 91-94, chief info officer, 94-96. *Concurrent Pos:* Math teacher, Bryan Sta High Sch, Lexington, 61-62; adj prof, Univ Md Baltimore Sch Nursing, 86-; res prof, Div Dent Informatics, Univ Md, Baltimore Col Dent Surg Dent Sch, 89-93; mem, Technol Subcomt, Comt Improving Patient Record, Inst Med, 89-91; assoc ed, Int J Biomed Comput, 89-96. *Mem:* Inst Med-Nat Acad Sci; hon mem Int Med Informatics Asn; hon mem Med Libr Asn; Am Acad Med Adminrs; Am Asn Med Systs & Informatics; Am Hosp Asn; Asn Comput Mach. *Res:* Contributor of numerous publications. *Mailing Add:* First Consult Group 2 Hamill Rd Quadrangle West 359 Baltimore MD 21210

BALL, MARY UHRICH, ENVIRONMENTAL EDUCATION. *Current Pos:* assoc prof, 85-93, PROF BIOL, CARSON-NEWMAN COL, 93- *Personal Data:* b Pittsburg, Kans, May 26, 44; m 62, Raiford M; c Linda, Ginger, Ralph, Dana & Jeremy. *Educ:* Trinity Univ, BS, 66; Tex A&M Univ, MS, 72, PhD(genetics), 74. *Prof Exp:* Asst prof zool-entom, Auburn Univ, 74-85. *Mem:* Nat Sci Teachers Asn. *Res:* Science education; genetics. *Mailing Add:* Carson-Newman Col Box 72044 Jefferson City TN 37760

BALL, MICHAEL OWEN, OPERATIONS RESEARCH. *Current Pos:* from asst prof to assoc prof, 78-90, PROF OPER RES, COL BUS & MGT & SYST RES CTR, UNIV MD, 90- *Personal Data:* b Washington, DC, July 20, 50; m; c 3. *Educ:* Johns Hopkins Univ, BES, 72, MSE, 73; Cornell Univ, PhD(oper res), 77. *Prof Exp:* Mem tech staff comput networks, Bell Labs, 76-78. *Mem:* Opers Res Soc Am; Math Prog Soc; Inst Elec & Electronics Engrs; Soc Indust & Appl Math. *Res:* Operations research especially in the areas of computer and transportation networks. *Mailing Add:* 1012 S Manison Dr Silver Spring MD 20902

BALL, MILLICENT (PENNY), MULTIMEDIA DEVELOPMENT. *Current Pos:* CHIEF EXEC OFFICER & PROJ DIR, MJB CONSULT, 94- *Personal Data:* b Buffalo, NY, Sept 15, 39; div. *Educ:* Antioch Col, BS, 61; Univ Md, PhD(physics), 69. *Prof Exp:* Res assoc, Univ Heidelberg, 69-71; sr programmer, Imp Col, 72-73; asst prof comput prog, Purdue Univ, 73-77; systs analyst, Calculon Corp, 78-80; comput analyst, Brookhaven Nat Lab, 80-90; data mgt group leader, SSC Lab, 90-94. *Mem:* Asn Comput Mach; Asn Women Sci. *Res:* Development of computer multimedia tutorials for technical subjects. *Mailing Add:* 1415 Country Ridge Dr Dallas TX 75115. *Fax:* 972-709-7561; *E-Mail:* penny@acm.org

BALL, RAIFORD MILL, SOLID STATE PHYSICS, SCIENCE EDUCATION. *Current Pos:* ASSOC PROF PHYS, E TENN STATE UNIV, 87- *Personal Data:* b Bryan, Tex, Nov 16, 41; m 62; c 3. *Educ:* Trinity Univ, BS, 64; Tex A&M Univ, MS, 71, PhD(physics), 75. *Prof Exp:* Physics teacher, Auburn City Sch, Ala, 75-85; assoc prof physics & phys sci, E Tenn State Univ, 85-87; instr, Morristown Col, Tenn, 87-88. *Concurrent Pos:* Teaching asst, Physics Dept, Tex A&M Univ, 69-75; adj asst prof, physics dept, Auburn Univ, Ala, 80-85. *Mem:* Am Asn Physics Teachers; Am Phys So. *Mailing Add:* 344 Summitt Heights Dr Jefferson City TN 37760

BALL, RALPH WAYNE, MATHEMATICS. *Current Pos:* prof math, 66-85, EMER PROF MATH, NMEX INST MINING & TECHNOL, 85- *Personal Data:* b Los Angeles, Calif, Oct 14, 25. *Educ:* Pomona Col, BA, 47; Univ Southern Calif, MA, 52; NMex State Univ, MS, 63, PhD(math), 64. *Prof Exp:* Teacher, Los Angeles City Schs, 49-59; secy curric coord, Inyo Co Schs, Calif, 59-61; instr math, NMex State Univ, 61-64; assoc prof, Appalachian State Univ, 64-66. *Mem:* Am Math Soc; Math Asn Am. *Res:* Group theory, particularly infinite symmetric groups. *Mailing Add:* 2097 Heather Way Woodburn OR 97071

BALL, RICHARD WILLIAM, mathematics, for more information see previous edition

BALL, RUSSELL MARTIN, REACTOR PHYSICS, NUCLEAR PHYSICS. *Current Pos:* SUPVR, BABCOCK & WILCOX, 55- *Personal Data:* b Chicago, Ill, Oct 28, 27; m 55; c 3. *Educ:* Univ Ill, BS, 49, MS, 50; Univ Va, PhD, 70. *Prof Exp:* Process engr, Elec Storage Battery Co, 46-47; asst, Univ Ill, 47-50; chief engr, Nuclear Instrument & Chem Corp, 50-55; staff mem, Oak Ridge Sch Reactor Technol, 55. *Concurrent Pos:* Lectr, Univ Wis. *Mem:* Am Phys Soc; Am Asn Physics Teachers; Inst Elec & Electronics Engrs; Am Nuclear Soc. *Res:* Isometric transitions; radiation detectors and computers; industrial application of nucleonics and isotopes; nuclear instrumentation; process control; computers. *Mailing Add:* 1620 Belfield Pl Lynchburg VA 24503-3102

BALL, STANTON MOCK, GEOLOGY. *Current Pos:* geologist, Pan Am Petrol Corp, 64-70, res scientist, Okla, 70-74, RES SCIENTIST, AMOCO PRODS CO, TEX, 74- *Personal Data:* b Lawrence, Kans, Aug 20, 33; m 55; c 2. *Educ:* Univ Kans, BS, 56, MS, 58, PhD(geol), 64. *Prof Exp:* Geologist, Kans State Geol Surv, 57-64. *Mem:* Geol Soc Am; Am Asn Petrol Geologists; Soc Econ Paleont & Mineral; Sigma Xi. *Res:* Stratigraphy and carbonate petrology. *Mailing Add:* 7709 Marble Canyon Ct Ft Worth TX 76137-4150

BALL, TERRY BRIGGS, PHYTOLITH SYSTEMATICS, IMAGE ANALYSIS. *Current Pos:* ASST PROF ANCIENT SCRIPTURE, BRIGHAM YOUNG UNIV, 92- *Personal Data:* b Pocatello, Idaho, May 25, 55; m 77, DeAnna Hill; c Camillia, Christopher, Carla, Daniel, Cody & Alexander. *Educ:* Brigham Young Univ, BS, 79, MA, 90, PhD(bot), 92. *Prof Exp:* Prin, LDS Church Educ Syst, 79-91. *Mem:* Soc Am Archaeol; Micros Soc Am; Soc Phytolith Res; Sigma Xi; AAAS. *Res:* Development of phytolith systematics using computer-assisted image analysis and electron microscopy for application in paleoecological and archaeobotanical research. *Mailing Add:* 321 E 60 N Lindon UT 84042-2043. *Fax:* 801-378-5980; *E-Mail:* ballt@reli.byu.edu

BALL, TIMOTHY K, PLANT MOLECULAR BIOLOGY, POLYMER-FIBER SCIENCE. *Current Pos:* FEL, MONSANTO, 90- *Personal Data:* b Lamesa, Tex, Dec 15, 57; m 83, Diana Parse; c Alisha & Brinna. *Educ:* Univ Tex, Austin, BA, 83; Tex A&M Univ, PhD(microbiol), 90. *Mem:* Am Soc Metals; Soc Indust Microbiol; Am Chem Soc; AAAS. *Res:* Analysis of expression in plants of DNA sequences encoding repetitive amino acid sequences. *Mailing Add:* 2268 Oberhelman Foristell MO 63348

BALL, WILBUR PERRY, AGRICULTURE. *Current Pos:* RETIRED. *Personal Data:* b Briggsdale, Colo, Jan 2, 23; m 48; c 3. *Educ:* Colo State Univ, BS, 48, MEd, 53; Iowa State Univ, PhD(agr), 56. *Prof Exp:* Teacher pub sch, Colo, 48-53; instr agr mech, Iowa State Univ, 53-56; consult agr educ, Stanford Univ Contract, Int Coop Admin, Philippines, 56-58; from asst prof to assoc prof agr educ, Calif State Univ, Fresno, 58-68, grad coordr, Sch Agr & Sch Supvr Teacher Educ, 65-77, prof agr & educ, 78-83, prof int agr & educ, 85- *Concurrent Pos:* Consult rural educ, Calif State Univ, Fresno, contract, US AID, Sudan, 61-63; vis prof agr educ, Ohio State Univ, 67-68; res assoc, Nat Ctr Voc & Tech Educ, 67-68; instr hist, AIMS Community Col, Greeley, Colo. *Mem:* Assoc Am Soc Agr Eng; Soc Int Agr. *Res:* Agricultural engineering; international agriculture; author of ten books about Colorado history. *Mailing Add:* 330 Cherry Ave Eaton CO 80615

BALL, WILLIAM DAVID, DEVELOPMENTAL BIOLOGY, PROTEIN SECRETION. *Current Pos:* ASSOC PROF ANAT, COL MED, HOWARD UNIV, 78- *Personal Data:* b Newark, NJ, July 22, 37; m 75; c 3. *Educ:* Univ Wis, BS, 58, MS, 61; Univ Chicago, PhD(zool), 65. *Prof Exp:* Proj asst zool, Univ Wis, 58-61; res assoc biochem, Univ Ill, 65; res assoc, Univ Wash, 65-67, asst prof zool, 67-73, res assoc zool, 73-75; assoc prof oral biol, Sch Dent, Univ Colo, 75-78. *Concurrent Pos:* NIH res grant, 69-72 & 83-91; Cystic Fibrosis Found grant, 77-79, NSF grant, 79-82. *Mem:* Am Soc Cell Biologists; Am Soc Zoologists; Soc Develop Biol; Int Asn Dent Res; Am Asn Anatomists. *Res:* Epithelio-mesenchymal interactions in development of rat salivary glands; formation of specific proteins in embryonic tissues; secretory proteins as markers for cellular differentiation in salivary glands. *Mailing Add:* Dept Anat Col Med Howard Univ 520 W St NW Washington DC 20059. *Fax:* 202-265-7055

BALL, WILLIAM E(RNEST), INTELLIGENT DATABASE SYSTEMS. *Current Pos:* RETIRED. *Personal Data:* b Emporia, Kans, May 26, 30; m 53, Eva S Ross; c Susan & Steven. *Educ:* Washington Univ, BS, 52, DSc(chem eng), 58. *Prof Exp:* Instr, Washington Univ, 54-56; appl sci rep, Int Bus Mach Corp, 57; mathematician, Monsanto Co, 58-62; assoc prof, Washington Univ, 62-67, prof comput sci, 67-95, chmn, Dept Appl Math & Comput Sci, 70-74. *Mem:* Am Asn Artificial Intel; Asn Comput Mach; Inst Elec & Electronics Engrs. *Res:* Knowledge-based information systems; object oriented database systems; object oriented analysis and design methodologies. *Mailing Add:* 5256 88th St E Bradenton FL 34202. *E-Mail:* weball@surfer.pcsonline.com

BALL, WILLIAM HENRY WARREN, electrical engineering; deceased, see previous edition for last biography

BALL, WILLIAM JAMES, JR, BIOCHEMISTRY. *Current Pos:* asst prof, 77-84, ASSOC PROF, COL MED, UNIV CINCINNATI, 84- *Personal Data:* b New York, NY, Sept 5, 42; m, Elvira Ponce; c Valerie & Darek. *Educ:* San Diego State Univ, BS, 66, MS, 68; Univ Calif, Los Angeles, PhD(biochem), 72. *Prof Exp:* Fel, Sloan-Kettering Cancer Ctr, 72-75; instr, Baylor Col Med, 75-77. *Concurrent Pos:* Estab investr, Am Heart Asn; immunol trainee, Columbia Univ, 78. *Mem:* NY Acad Sci; Biophys Soc; Am Soc Biochem & Molecular Biol; Am Heart Asn. *Res:* Mechanisms of enzyme regulation; utilization of immunological techniques to study sodium potassium, adenosine triphosphatase-ligand interactions; isolation of and characterization of monoclonal antibodies. *Mailing Add:* Dept Pharmacol & Cell Biophysics Col Med Univ Cincinnati 231 Bethesda Ave ML 575 Cincinnati OH 45267. *Fax:* 513-558-1169

BALL, WILLIAM PAUL, NUCLEAR PHYSICS, RADIATION SCIENCE. *Current Pos:* RETIRED. *Personal Data:* b San Diego, Calif, Nov 16, 13; m 41, Edith Lucille March; c Lura I (Raplee) & Roy E. *Educ:* Univ Calif, Los Angeles, AB, 40; Univ Calif, Berkeley, PhD(physics), 53. *Prof Exp:* High sch teacher math & phys educ, Montebello Unified Sch Dist, 41-42; instr math & physics, Santa Ana Army Air Base, 42-43; physicist, Radiation Lab, Univ Calif, 43-58 & Ramo Wooldridge Corp, 58-59; sr scientist & mgr nuclear technol staff, Hughes Aircraft Co, 59-64; sr scientist engr space & nuclear physics, TRW Systs & Energy, 64-83; staff engr, Hughes Aircraft Co, 83-86. *Concurrent Pos:* Bd dirs, S Dist, Los Angeles Chapter ARC, 79-86, Torrance, Calif Area Chamber of Commerce, 76-83; Consult, 86- *Mem:* AAAS; Am Phys Soc; Am Nuclear Soc; NY Acad Sci; Sigma Xi. *Res:* Space and nuclear radiation environments and lasers and their effects on properties and responses of materials, sensors, electronics and systems. *Mailing Add:* 209 Via El Toro Redondo Beach CA 90277

BALLAL, DILIP RAMCHANDRA, MECHANICAL ENGINEERING. *Current Pos:* PROF MECH ENG, UNIV DAYTON, OHIO, 83-; CONSULT, GM RES LABS & GE AIRCRAFT, WARREN, CINCINNATI, 87- *Personal Data:* b Nagpur, India, Jan 16, 46; m 75, Shubhangi Sadashiv Ayachit; c Rahul & Deepti. *Educ:* Col Eng, Bhopal, India, BSME, 67; Cranfield Inst Technol, UK, PhD, 72. *Hon Degrees:* DSc, Cranfield Inst Technol, UK, 83. *Honors & Awards:* Best Res Award, Am Soc Mech Engrs, 86 & 92, Leadership Award, 96; Energy Syst Award, Am Inst Aeronaut & Astronaut, 93. *Prof Exp:* Lectr mech eng, Cranfield Inst Technol, 72-79; sr staff engr, GM Res Labs, Warren, Mich, 79-83. *Concurrent Pos:* Chmn, Propellants & Combustion Comt, Am Inst Aeronaut & Astronaut, 88-92, Combustion & Fuels Comt, Am Soc Mech Engrs, 95-97. *Mem:* Fel Am Soc Mech Engrs; fel Am Inst Aeronaut & Astronaut; Combustion Inst. *Res:* Patents on ignitor plug for jet engine combustor; contributor of 130 articles on combustion, turbulence, heat transfer and pollution to professional journals. *Mailing Add:* 5519 Knollcrest Ct Dayton OH 45429-5913. *Fax:* 937-229-3885; *E-Mail:* ballal@udri.udayton.edu

BALLAL, S K, BOTANY, PHYSIOLOGY. *Current Pos:* from asst prof to assoc prof biol, 65-74, admin asst to chancellor, 89, PROF BIOL, TENN TECHNOL UNIV, 74- *Personal Data:* b Trichur, Kerala, India, Dec 31, 38; m, Katherine; c Meera & Matthew. *Educ:* Univ Madras, BS, 59, MS, 61; Univ Tenn, PhD(bot), 64. *Prof Exp:* Asst bot, Univ Tenn, 61-64. *Concurrent Pos:* Shell Merit fel, Stanford Univ, 70. *Mem:* AAAS; Bot Soc Am; Am Inst Biol Sci. *Res:* Plant growth regulations. *Mailing Add:* Dept Biol Tenn Tech Univ Cookeville TN 38505-0001

BALLAM, JOSEPH, ELEMENTARY PARTICLE PHYSICS. *Current Pos:* from assoc prof to prof, 61-87, assoc dir res div, Linear Accelerator Ctr, 61-82, EMER PROF PHYSICS, STANFORD UNIV, 87- *Personal Data:* b Boston, Mass, Jan 2, 17; m 38, Ethel Hirsh; c John J & Denise C (Clark). *Educ:* Univ Mich, BS, 39; Univ Calif, PhD, 51. *Prof Exp:* Physicist, US Navy Dept, 41-45; asst physics, Univ Calif, 45-46, physicist, Radiation Lab, 46-48, asst physics, 48-51; asst, Princeton Univ, 51-52, instr, 52-53, res assoc, 53-56; from assoc prof to prof, Mich State Univ, 56-61. *Concurrent Pos:* Res collabr, Brookhaven Nat Lab, 56-; Ford Found fel, Europ Orgn Nuclear Res, 60-61; Guggenheim Found fel, 71-72; coun fel sci res, Imperial Col, London, 80; vis prof, Polytechnic Sch, Paris, 81. *Mem:* Fel Am Phys Soc. *Res:* Elementary particles; cosmic rays; high energy physics; laboratory scientific administration; experimental physics; astroparticle physics. *Mailing Add:* Stanford Linear Accelerator Ctr Stanford Univ PO Box 4349 Stanford CA 94309. *E-Mail:* jballam@slac.stanford.edu

BALLANTINE, C S, MATHEMATICS, MATRIX THEORY. *Current Pos:* from instr to assoc prof, 60-72, PROF MATH, ORE STATE UNIV, 72- *Personal Data:* b Seattle, Wash, Aug 27, 29; wid. *Educ:* Univ Wash, BS, 53; Stanford Univ, PhD(math), 59. *Prof Exp:* Asst math, Stanford Univ, 56-58; actg instr, Univ Calif, 58-59, instr, 59-60. *Mem:* Am Math Soc; Sigma Xi. *Res:* Matrix theory. *Mailing Add:* Dept Math Ore State Univ Corvallis OR 97331-4605

BALLANTINE, LARRY GENE, AGRICULTURAL CHEMISTRY. *Current Pos:* HAZLETON LABS, MADISON, WI. *Personal Data:* b Webster City, Iowa, July 6, 44; m 73; c 2. *Educ:* Iowa State Univ, BS, 66; Univ Mass, PhD(soil chem), 71. *Prof Exp:* Teacher chem, Essex Agr & Tech Inst, 71-73; asst prof soil chem, State Univ NY Agr & Tech Col, Cobleskill, 73-74; environmentalist, Ciba-Geigy Corp, 74-80, mgr environ invests, 80- *Mem:* Am Chem Soc; Am Soc Agron; Sigma Xi; Soc Environ Chem & Toxicol. *Res:* Environmental research; emphasis on pesticide usage. *Mailing Add:* 2876 Forest Down Madison WI 53711

BALLANTYNE, BRYAN, TOXICOLOGY. *Current Pos:* DIR TOXICOL, UNION CARBIDE CORP, 78- *Personal Data:* b Halifax, Eng, Sept 11, 34; m 67; c 4. *Educ:* Univ Leeds, BSc, 58, MB & ChB, 61, PhD(histochem), 68, MD, 71, DSc, 78; Royal Col Pathologists, MRCPath, 71, FRCpath, 73; Am Col Toxicol Sci, dipl, 82. *Prof Exp:* House surgeon, Gen Infirmary, Leeds Univ, 61-62; house physician, Bradford Royal Infirmary, 62-63; lectr anat & hist, Sch Med, Univ Leeds, 63-68; sr med officer, Chem Defense Estab, 68-78. *Concurrent Pos:* Mem, Sci Subcomt Pesticides, Mininstry Agr, Fisheries & Food, 69-78, Comt Experts Pesticides, Coun Europe, 76-78, Intergovn Maritime Consult Orgn, 77-; ed, Forensic Toxicol, 74, Current Approaches Toxicol, 77, Respiratory Protection, 81; adj prof toxicol, Univ Pittsburgh & Univ WVa, 81-; ed, Perspecher Basic & Appl Toxicol, 88, Clin & Exp Toxicol Cyanides, 87. *Mem:* Royal Col Physicians; Soc Toxicol; Europ Soc Toxicol; Am Acad Occup Med; Am Occup Med Asn; Fac Occup Med; fel Am Acad Clin Toxicol; Am Col Toxicol; Sigma Xi; Brit Pharmacol Soc. *Res:* Acute toxicity; primary irritancy; ophthalmic toxicology; application of histochemical methods; toxicology of cyanides and cyanogens; evaluation of potential human health hazards from chemicals; clinical toxicology. *Mailing Add:* Union Carbide Corp P2594 39 Old Ridgebury Rd Danbury CT 06817

BALLANTYNE, CATHERINE COX, development of thin film products, standardize safety compliance testing of semiconductor manufacturing equipment, for more information see previous edition

BALLANTYNE, DAVID JOHN, HORTICULTURE, PLANT PHYSIOLOGY. *Current Pos:* asst prof, 62-68, assoc prof, 68-96, EMER ASSOC PROF PLANT PHYSIOL, UNIV VICTORIA, BC, 96- *Personal Data:* b Victoria, BC, May 1, 31; m 62, Mary Hamilton; c Sara (Brant), Janet (Petrillo) & John. *Educ:* Univ BC, BCom, 54; Wash State Univ, MS, 57; Univ Md, PhD(hort), 60. *Prof Exp:* Nat Res Coun Can fel, 60-61; res officer plant physiol, Exp Farm, Can Dept Agr, 61-63. *Mem:* Am Soc Plant Physiol; Am Soc Hort Sci; Can Soc Plant Physiol. *Res:* Effect of air pollutants on plant metabolism; photosynthesis, growth and development of Rhododendron. *Mailing Add:* Dept Biol Univ Victoria Victoria BC V8W 2Y2 Can. *Fax:* 250-721-7120

BALLANTYNE, DONALD LINDSAY, TRANSPLANTATION BIOLOGY, MICROSURGERY. *Current Pos:* from asst prof to assoc prof, NY Univ Med Ctr, 62-75, res assoc tissue transplantation, 54-62, prof, 75-90, EMER PROF EXP SURG, INST RECONSTRUCT PLASTIC SURG, NY UNIV MED CTR, 90- *Personal Data:* b Peking, China, Nov 8, 22; m 63; c 3. *Educ:* Princeton Univ, AB, 45; Cath Univ Am, MS, 48, PhD(biol), 52. *Honors & Awards:* Edmund Lyon Mem Lectr, Nat Inst Deaf, Rochester Inst Technol. *Prof Exp:* Parasitologist, E R Squibb & Sons, 51-53 & Ill State Psychopath Inst, 53-54. *Concurrent Pos:* Dir, Microsurgical Res & Training Labs, NY Univ Med Ctr, 78- *Mem:* AAAS; Transplantation Soc; Sigma Xi; Found Sci & Handicapped (pres, 84-86). *Mailing Add:* 59 Dalebrook Rd Bloomfield NJ 07003

BALLANTYNE, GARTH H, COLON & RECTAL SURGERY, GASTROINTESTINAL PHYSIOLOGY. *Current Pos:* CHIEF GEN SURG, VET ADMIN CTR, WEST HAVEN, CONN, 84- *Personal Data:* b Mineola, NY, June 4, 51; m 75; c 5. *Educ:* Harvard Col, AB, 73; Col Physicians & Surgeons Columbia Univ, MD, 77. *Prof Exp:* ASST PROF SURG, YALE UNIV SCH MED, 84- *Mem:* Asn Acad Surg; Am Soc Colon & Rectal Surgeons; Am Asn Gastrointestinal Endoscopists; Sigma Xi. *Res:* Mechanisms of release of putative colonic hormones and their modulation of proximal gastrointestinal function; downstaging colorectal cancers by endoscopic surveillance of high risk populations. *Mailing Add:* W Haven Va Med Ctr Dept Surg No 112 Branford CT 06516

BALLANTYNE, JAMES STUART, MITOCHONDRIA, FISH & MOLLUSC METABOLISM. *Current Pos:* asst prof, 85-92, ASSOC PROF, UNIV GUELPH, 92- *Personal Data:* b Smiths Falls, Ont, Oct 21, 52. *Educ:* Univ Guelph, BSc, 73, MSc, 76; Univ BC, PhD(zool), 81. *Res:* Environmental adaptation of marine invertebrates and fish; biochemical strategies of adaptation; membrane structure and function; metabolism and membranes of elasmobranch fishes; metabolism and membranes of arctic fishes. *Mailing Add:* Dept Zool Univ Guelph Guelph ON N1G 2W1 Can. *Fax:* 519-767-1656; *E-Mail:* jballant@uoguelph.ca

BALLANTYNE, JOSEPH M(ERRILL), SEMICONDUCTOR OPTICAL DEVICES. *Current Pos:* asst prof, Cornell Univ, 64-68, assoc prof elec eng, 68-71, actg dir, Nat Res & Resource Facil, Submicron Struct, 77-88, dir, Sch Elec Eng, 80-84, PROF ELEC ENG, CORNELL UNIV, 71-, VPRES, RES & ADVAN STUDIES, 84- *Personal Data:* b Tucson, Ariz, Dec 16, 34; m 61; c 8. *Educ:* Univ Utah, BS & BSEE, 59; Mass Inst Technol, SM, 60, PhD(elec eng), 64. *Prof Exp:* Asst elec eng, Mass Inst Technol, 60-61, staff mem & consult, Lincoln Lab, 61, res asst & staff mem, Lab Insulation Res, 62-63. *Concurrent Pos:* NSF sr fel, Stanford Univ, 70-71; consult, Mat Technol Inc, 62-63, Gen Tel & Electronics Lab, 65, Int Bus Mach Corp, 66, 78 & 79, Sandia Corp, 67-70, Cayuga Assocs, 68-69, Battelle Mem Inst, 68-69 & 76-78, Eastman Kodak & Schlumberger, 81-, McDonald Douglas Astron Ctr, 88; mem, adv comt, Sherman Fairchild Lab, Lehigh Univ, 78-; external adv comt, Elec Eng Dept, Univ Del, 79-; policy bd, Nat Nanofabrication Facil, Cornell Univ, 78-; MIT Whitney fel, Schlumberger fel, 59-63. *Mem:* Fel Am Phys Soc; Inst Elec & Electronics Engrs; Am Vacuum Soc; Asn Inst Mech Engrs; Metall Soc Am Inst Mining Metall & Petrol Engrs. *Res:* Ferroelectricity; infrared and optical properties of solids; quantum electronics; magnetic thin films; far infrared spectroscopy; solid state electronic devices; optical semiconductor devices; microfabrication technology. *Mailing Add:* 116 Kelvin Pl Ithaca NY 14850

BALLARD, HAROLD NOBLE, ATMOSPHERIC PHYSICS. *Current Pos:* RES PHYSICIST, UNIV TEX, EL PASO, 81- *Personal Data:* b Little Rock, Ark, Feb 11, 19; m 45, 60; c 4. *Educ:* Univ Tex, El Paso, BS, 48; Tex A&M Univ, MS, 50. *Prof Exp:* Res physicist, NMex Inst Mining & Technol, 50; asst prof physics, Univ Tex, El Paso, 50-54; physicist, Los Alamos Sci Lab, 54-57; res physicist, Univ Tex, El Paso, 57-64; res physicist, Atmospheric Sci Lab, US Army Electronics Command, White Sands Missile Range, 64-79. *Concurrent Pos:* Mem, Joint Comt Space Environ Forecasting, 68-; assoc prof & lectr, physics, Univ Tex, El Paso, 70. *Mem:* Am Phys Soc; Am Meteorol Soc; Am Geophys Union; AAAS. *Res:* Composition and thermal structure of stratosphere; multiple instrument balloon-borne experiments; development of rocket and balloon-borne atmospheric sensory instruments. *Mailing Add:* 239 El Puente St El Paso TX 79912

BALLARD, JAMES ALAN, SEISMIC STRATIGRAPHY. *Current Pos:* CONSULT, 91- *Personal Data:* b Rockingham, NC, Aug 13, 29; m 53; c 4. *Educ:* Univ NC, BS, 53, MS, 59, PhD(oceanog), 79. *Prof Exp:* Geophysicist oil explor, Independent Explor Inc, 53-54; oceanographer geol & geophysic oceanog, Naval Oceanog Off, 59-64, supvr, 64-68, res scientist, 68-76; res scientist marine geophys, Naval Ocean Res & Develop Activ, 76-79, prog mgr, 79-88; prin scientist oceanog/geophys, MAR, Inc, 88-90; sci consult, Environ Protection Agency, 90-91. *Concurrent Pos:* Lectr, Univ NC, 56-58; tech adv, Md Geol Surv, 75-76; tech prog chmn, US Navy Soc Explor Geophysicists Joint Tech Symp, 78, 80, 82, 84, 86 & 90. *Mem:* Soc Explor Geophysicists; Sigma Xi. *Res:* Development, installation and operation of a broad band marine bore hole seismograph station; instrumentation, techniques and applications of seismic stratigraphy to naval problems; geohazards analysis. *Mailing Add:* 1520 W Fourth Ave Picayune MS 39466

BALLARD, KATHRYN WISE, cardiovascular physiology; deceased, see previous edition for last biography

BALLARD, KENNETH J, PHARMACY. *Current Pos:* RETIRED. *Personal Data:* b Highland Park, Ill, Jan 22, 30; m 56; c 2. *Educ:* Univ Calif, Berkeley, BA, 50, BSc, 54, PharmD, 55. *Prof Exp:* Staff pharmacist, USPHS Hosp, San Francisco, 55-57; sr asst pharmacist, Div Biologics Stand, Lab Blood & Blood Prod, NIH, 57-58; asst prof pharm, Sch Pharm & Grad Div Arts & Sci, Univ Buffalo, 58-60; assoc prof, Col Pharm, Northeastern Univ, 60-64; res assoc, Allergan Pharmaceut, 64-66; dir pharm serv, Student Health Serv, Univ Calif, Los Angeles, 66-70; asst clin prof pharm & dir clin pharm serv, Los Angeles Co/Univ Southern Calif Med Ctr, 70-91; staff mem, Little Co of Mary Hosp. *Mem:* Am Pharmaceut Asn; Am Soc Hosp Pharmacists. *Res:* Developing innovations in delivery of clinical pharmacy services; education of clinical pharmacists; electronic data processing of pharmacy drug and information systems; drug product development. *Mailing Add:* 2808 Colby Ave Los Angeles CA 90064

BALLARD, LEWIS FRANKLIN, POLLUTION CONTROL INSTRUMENTATION. *Current Pos:* CONSULT, 85- *Personal Data:* b Mooresville, NC, Dec 17, 34; m 61; c 3. *Educ:* NC State Univ, BS, 58; Duke Univ, MS, 67, PhD(elec eng), 69. *Prof Exp:* Rocket engr, Thiokol Chem Corp, 58-59; nuclear engr, Res Triangle Inst, 59-65, staff scientist, 65-69, supvr Anal Chem & Physics Sect, 69-73; pres, Nutech Corp, 73-85. *Mem:* Inst Elec & Electronics Engrs; Am Phys Soc. *Res:* Electrical and optical properties of insulators, semiconductors, and organometallics; design of radiation detectors; applications of nuclear techniques in industry and highway engineering; ambient air monitoring instrumentation; gas chromatography, mass spectrometry. *Mailing Add:* 11019 Governors Dr Chapel Hill NC 27514

BALLARD, MARGUERITE CANDLER, INTERNAL MEDICINE, HEMATOLOGY. *Current Pos:* CLIN INSTR & ASSOC, DEPT MED, EMORY UNIV SCH MED, 54- *Personal Data:* b Atlanta, Ga, June 14, 20; m 73, George Speights Jr. *Educ:* Vassar Col, BA, 42; Emory Univ, MS, 43, MD, 48. *Prof Exp:* Bacteriologist, US War Dept, 43-44; intern & med resident, Md Gen Hosp, 48-51; exam physician, Lockheed Aircraft Corp, 51-52; hemat fel, Emory Clin, 52-54; comn officer, Ctr Dis Control, USPHS, 54-85. *Concurrent Pos:* Auth, Lab Techniques in Central of Anticoaqulent Therapy, 63, Atlas of Blood Cell Morphol, 87; consult & maj contr, Third Ed Am Soc Hemat Slide Bank, 90. *Mem:* AAAS; fel Int Soc Hemat; AMA; Sigma Xi; fel Am Soc Hemat. *Res:* Standardization of hematological laboratory procedures; development and presentation of lectures and bench training; photomicrographer of blood cells in health and disease for publication of Atlas. *Mailing Add:* 3092 Argonne Dr NW Atlanta GA 30305-1950

BALLARD, NEIL BRIAN, ZOOLOGY, PARASITOLOGY. *Current Pos:* Assoc prof, 68-80, PROF BIOL, MANKATO STATE UNIV, 80- *Personal Data:* b Mankato, Minn, Jan 26, 38. *Educ:* Mankato State Col, BS, 59; Colo State Univ, MS, 65, PhD(zool), 68. *Concurrent Pos:* Brown-Hazen Fund grant, 69-70. *Mem:* Soc Protozool; Am Soc Parasitol; Wildlife Disease Asn. *Res:* Host-specificity and immunity phenomena with regard to coccidian infections in rodents. *Mailing Add:* Dept Biol Sci Mankato State Univ 515 Malin St Mankato MN 56001-6001

BALLARD, RALPH CAMPBELL, ENTOMOLOGY, PHYSIOLOGY. *Current Pos:* from assoc prof to prof biol, 58-88, dir Toxicol Grad Prog, 77-88, EMER PROF BIOL, SAN JOSE STATE UNIV, 88- *Personal Data:* b Washington, DC, Jan 4, 26; m 51, 80; c 2. *Educ:* George Washington Univ, BS, 51; Ohio State Univ, MS, 53; Rutgers Univ, PhD(entom), 56. *Prof Exp:* Assoc prof biol, Pac Union Col, 56-58. *Concurrent Pos:* Environ toxicol fel, Univ Calif, Davis, 75-76. *Mem:* AAAS; Am Indust Hyg Asn; Entom Soc Am; Am Chem Soc; Soc Risk Anal; Col Toxicol. *Res:* Toxicology; general physiology. *Mailing Add:* 127 Altura Vista Los Gatos CA 95030

BALLARD, ROBERT D, PLATE TECTONICS. *Current Pos:* PRES, INST EXPLOR. *Personal Data:* b Wichita, Kans, June 30, 42; m 91, Barbara Earle; c Douglas M. *Educ:* Univ Calif, Santa Barbara, BS(chem & geol), 65; Univ Hawaii, BS(oceanog & marine geol), 66; Univ Southern Calif, BS(marine geol & geophys), 67; Univ RI, PhD(marine geol & geophys), 74. *Hon Degrees:* DSc, Clark Univ, 86; Univ RI, 86; Southern Mass Univ, 86; Long Island Univ, 87; Univ Bath, Eng, 88; Tufts Univ, 90. *Honors & Awards:* Newcomb Cleveland Prize, AAAS, 81; Cutty Sark Award, Sci Dig, 82; Westinghouse Award, AAAS, 90; William Proctor Award, Sigma Xi, 90; Am Geol Inst Award, 90. *Prof Exp:* Res assoc ocean eng, Woods Hole Oceanog Inst, 69-74, asst scientist geol & geophys, 74-76, assoc scientist, 76-78, assoc scientist, Ocean Eng Dept, 78-79 & 80-83, sr scientist & head, Deep Submergence Lab, Ocean Eng Dept, 83- *Concurrent Pos:* Vis scholar, Geol Dept, Stanford Univ, 79-80, consult prof, 80-81; pvt consult, Benthos, Inc, Mass, 82-83; consult, Dep Chief Naval Oper Submarine Warfare, 84-, Marine Bd, Nat Res Coun, Comn Eng & Tech Systs, 84-87; dir, Ctr Marine Explor, Woods Hole Oceanog Inst, 87-; founder, Jason Found Educ. *Mem:* Geol Soc Am; Marine Technol Soc; Explorers Club; Am Geophys Union. *Res:* Development of advanced deep water technology aimed at better understanding of the ocean floor with special emphasis on the Mid-Ocean Ridge; deep diving submersibles. *Mailing Add:* Inst Explor 55 Coogan Blvd Mystic CT 06355

BALLARD, STANLEY SUMNER, PHYSICS, OPTICS. *Current Pos:* prof physics, 58-78, chmn dept physics & astron, 58-71, dir div phys & math sci, 68-71, distinguished serv prof physics, 78-81, EMER PROF PHYSICS, UNIV FLA, 82- *Personal Data:* b Los Angeles, Calif, Oct 1, 08; m 35, 74; c 2. *Educ:* Pomona Col, AB, 28; Univ Calif, MA, 32, PhD(physics), 34. *Hon Degrees:* DSc, Pomona Col, 74. *Honors & Awards:* Pegram Award, Am Phys Soc, 81; Oersted Medal, Am Asn Physics Teachers, 85. *Prof Exp:* Asst physics, Dartmouth Col, 28-30; asst, Univ Calif, 30-34, res fel, 34-35; from instr to asst prof, Univ Hawaii, 35-41; prof physics & chmn dept, Tufts Univ, 46-54; res physicist, Scripps Inst, Univ Calif, 54-58. *Concurrent Pos:* Consult exp sta, Hawaiian Sugar Planters Asn, 37-40; collabr, Hawaii Agr Exp Sta & res assoc, Hawaii Nat Park, 39-41; consult physicist, Polaroid Corp, Mass, 46-54 & Baird Assocs, Inc, 46-51; US deleg int comn optics, Int Union Pure & Appl Physics, Delft, 48, London, 50, Madrid, 53, Cambridge, Mass, 56, Stockholm, 59, Munich, 62, Paris, 66, Reading, Eng, 69, Calif, 72, Czech, 75 & Madrid, 78 & Graz, Austria, 81, vpres, 48-56, pres, 56-59, chmn, US Nat Comt, 48-56; consult, Rand Corp, 52-53, physicist, 53-54, consult, 54-71; mem vision comt, Armed Forces-Nat Res Coun, exec secy, 56-59; consult, Inst Sci & Technol, Univ Mich, 57-65, Bendix Systs Div, 57-59, Perkin-Elmer Corp, 60-62 & Atlantic Missile Range, 60-63; consult astrionics div, Aerojet-Gen Corp, 61-66; mem bd dirs, Am Inst Physics, 62-65 & 67-73; mem phys sci div, Nat Res Coun, 63-65; consult, Douglas Advan Res Labs, 66-70, Aerospace Corp, 67-70 & Honeywell Radiation Ctr, 69. *Mem:* AAAS (secy physics sect, 60-67, vpres, 68); fel Am Phys Soc; fel Optical Soc Am (pres, 63); Am Asn Physics Teachers (pres, 68-69); fel Brit Phys Soc; fel Soc Photo-Optical Instrumentation Engrs. *Res:* Spectroscopy; optical and infrared instrumentation; properties of optical materials. *Mailing Add:* 4320 NW 17th Pl Gainesville FL 32605

BALLAS, ZUHAIR K, ALLERGY IMMUNOLOGY. *Current Pos:* Asst prof, 80-86, ASSOC PROF MED, UNIV IOWA, 86- *Educ:* Am Univ Beirut, Lebanon, MD, 74. *Mailing Add:* Dept Internal Med Univ Iowa Col Med SE621 GH 200 Hawkins Dr Iowa City IA 52242-1081

BALLATO, ARTHUR, ELECTROPHYSICS, ELECTRONICS ENGINEERING. *Current Pos:* PRIN SCIENTIST, ELECTRONICS POWER SOURCES DIRECTORATE, USAR LAB, MONMOUTH, NJ, 90- *Personal Data:* b Astoria, NY, Oct 15, 36; m 59; c 2. *Educ:* Mass Inst Technol, SB, 58; Rutgers Univ, MS, 62; Polytech Inst Brooklyn, PhD(electrophys), 72. *Honors & Awards:* C B Sawyer Mem Award, Sawyer Res Prod Inc, 78; H Jacobs Award, 85. *Prof Exp:* Electronics engr, 58-86, res phys scientist, US Army Electronics Technol & Devices Lab, NJ, 86-90. *Concurrent Pos:* Adj prof, Monmouth Col, NJ, 83-; tech adv group TC-49, Int Electrotech Comn, 83-; nat lectr, Inst Elec & Electronics Engrs, Sonics & Ultrasonics Group, 84-85. *Mem:* Sigma Xi; Am Phys Soc; fel Inst Elec & Electronics Engrs; Inst Elec Engrs London. *Res:* Piezoelectric crystal resonators and filters; crystal physics; stacked crystal filters; surface acoustic waves; stress effects in crystal plates; temperature compensated acoustic devices; frequency control devices; author of over 250 technical articles and patents. *Mailing Add:* 75 Algonquin Ave Oceanport NJ 07757-1611. *Fax:* 732-544-3733; *E-Mail:* a.ballato@ieee.org

BALLENGER, JAMES CAUDELL, PSYCHIATRY, CLINICAL PSYCHOPHARMACOLOGY. *Current Pos:* dir inpatient serv, 79-81, PROF & DIR RES BEHAV MED & PSYCHIAT, UNIV VA MED CTR & WESTERN STATE HOSP, 79-, HEAD DIV PSYCHOPHARMACOLOGY, 81-; CHMN DEPT PSYCHIAT & BEHAV SCI & DIR, INST PYSCHIAT, MED UNIV SC, 88- *Personal Data:* b Raleigh, NC, Mar 2, 44; m 69; c 2. *Educ:* Univ NC, AB, 66; Duke Univ, MD, 70. *Prof Exp:* Intern internal med, Duke Univ Med Ctr, 70-71; resident psychiat, Harvard Med Sch, Mass Gen Hosp, Boston, 71-74; pvt pract adult gen psychiat, Boston, Mass, 74-76; staff psychiatrist, Nat Naval Med Ctr, Bethesda, Md, 76-77; ward chief, 3 West Clin Res Unit, Inst Mental Health, 77-79. *Concurrent Pos:* Mem & co-chmn, publ comt, Am Col Neuropsychiat Pharmacol, 87. *Mem:* Fel Am Psychiat Asn; Soc Biol Psychiat; fel Am Col Psychiatrists. *Res:* Clinical psychological and biological interfaces in patients with spectrum of psychiatric problems, especially anxiety, manic-depressive illness, schizophrenia, alcoholism and personality disorders; relationship between biological factors and manifest psychopathology; biological and psychological relationships in normals; clinical psychopharmacology. *Mailing Add:* Dept Psychiat & Behav Sci Med Univ SC 171 Ashley Ave Charleston SC 29425-0001

BALLENTINE, ALVA RAY, PHYSICAL ORGANIC CHEMISTRY, SYNTHETIC ORGANIC CHEMISTRY. *Current Pos:* from asst prof to assoc prof, 56-68, PROF CHEM, THE CITADEL, 68- *Personal Data:* b Irmo, SC, Feb 19, 31. *Educ:* Univ SC, BS, 50, MS, 52, PhD(org chem), 56. *Prof Exp:* Asst prof chem, Presby Col, SC, 55-56. *Mem:* Am Chem Soc; Sigma Xi. *Res:* Reaction mechanisms; organic synthesis. *Mailing Add:* 1825 St Julian Pl 12G Columbia SC 29204

BALLENTINE, LESLIE EDWARD, QUANTUM MECHANICS. *Current Pos:* from asst prof to assoc prof, 67-73, PROF PHYSICS, SIMON FRASER UNIV, 73- *Personal Data:* b Wainwright, Alta, Apr 19, 40; c 2. *Educ:* Univ Alta, BSc, 61, MSc, 62; Cambridge Univ, PhD(physics), 66. *Prof Exp:* Fel, Theoret Phys Inst, Univ Alta, 65-67. *Mem:* Can Asn Physicists; Am Phys Soc. *Res:* Foundations of quantum mechanics; dynamical chaos and quantum mechanics. *Mailing Add:* Dept Physics Simon Fraser Univ Burnaby BC V5A 1S6 Can. *E-Mail:* ballenti@sfu.ca

BALLENTINE, ROBERT, BIOCHEMISTRY, MICROBIAL ECOLOGY. *Current Pos:* assoc prof, 49-81, EMER PROF BIOL, JOHNS HOPKINS UNIV, 81- *Personal Data:* b Orange, NJ, Mar 6, 14; m 68, Dorothy Dauner. *Educ:* Princeton Univ, AB, 37, PhD(biol), 40. *Prof Exp:* Proctor fel, Princeton Univ, 40-41; Nat Res fel zool, Rockefeller Inst, 41-42; lectr, Columbia Univ, 42-43, instr, 43-48; scientist, Brookhaven Nat Lab, 48-49. *Concurrent Pos:* Guggenheim fel, Calif Inst Technol, 47; assoc res specialist, Rutgers Univ, 48-49. *Mem:* Fel AAAS; Am Chem Soc; Soc Gen Physiol; Inst Elec & Electronics Engrs Computer Soc; Asn Computer Mach. *Res:* Computer information science; radioisotope assay; inorganic ion accumulation; surface colonization by bacteria in estuarine environments; chaos theory in population/evolution dynamics. *Mailing Add:* Dept Biol Johns Hopkins Univ Charles & 34th St Baltimore MD 21218

BALLENTINE, RUDOLPH MILLER, holistic medicine, for more information see previous edition

BALLERINI, ROCCO, EXTREME VALUE THEORY, TIME SERIES ANALYSIS. *Current Pos:* ASST DIR BIOSTATIST, NY COL MED, 95- *Personal Data:* b Pittsburgh, Pa, June 24, 58; m 89; c 1. *Educ:* Pa State Univ, BS, 80; Colo State Univ, MS, 83, PhD(statist), 85. *Prof Exp:* From asst prof to assoc prof statist, Univ Fla, 85-95. *Mem:* Am Statist Asn; Inst Math Statist; Am Geophys Union. *Res:* Extreme value theory; time series analysis; geophysical applications. *Mailing Add:* NY Col Med 466 Devon Park Dr Wayne PA 19087

BALLESTERO, THOMAS P, GROUNDWATER, HYDROLOGIC SIMULATION. *Current Pos:* ASST PROF CIVIL ENGR, UNIV NH, 83-, DIR, WATER RESOURCES RES CTR, 86- *Personal Data:* b Saratoga Springs, NY, Aug 10, 53; m 79; c 3. *Educ:* Pa State Univ, BS, 75 & MS, 77; Colo State Univ, PhD(civil eng), 81. *Prof Exp:* Inst civil eng, Pa State Univ, 77-78; div mgr, Simons, Li & Assoc, 80-83. *Concurrent Pos:* Pvt consult, 77- *Mem:* Am Geophys Union; Am Inst Hydrol; Am Water Resources Asn; Am Water Works Asn; Nat Water Well Asn. *Res:* Computer simulation of hydrologic phenomena and field measurement of parameters of such models; new methodologies for field measurements in which the areas of interest include groundwater, flow and bioremediation. *Mailing Add:* 236 Kingsbury Hall Durham NH 03824

BALLEW, DAVID WAYNE, NUMBER THEORY. *Current Pos:* asst prof, 67-75, dept head, 81-86, PROF MATH, SDAK SCH MINES & TECHNOL, 75- *Personal Data:* b Mangum, Okla, Aug 20, 40; m 60, Mary Lou Wilson; c Lawrence & Diana. *Educ:* Univ Okla, BA, 62, MA, 64; Univ Ill, PhD(math), 69. *Prof Exp:* Asst math, Univ Okla, 62-64 & Univ Ill, 64-67. *Mem:* Am Math Soc; Math Asn Am; Am Soc Eng Educ; Asn Comput Mach; Inst Elec & Electronics Engrs. *Res:* Software engineering; programming languages; computer science education. *Mailing Add:* Dept Comput Sci Western Ill Univ Macomb IL 61455. *Fax:* 309-298-2302; *E-Mail:* davidballew@ccmail.wiu.edu

BALLHAUS, WILLIAM F(RANCIS), AERONAUTICAL & ASTRONAUTICAL ENGINEERING. *Current Pos:* RETIRED. *Personal Data:* b San Francisco, Calif, Aug 15, 18; m 44; c 4. *Educ:* Stanford Univ, BS, 40, ME, 42; Calif Inst Technol, PhD(aerodyn, math), 47. *Hon Degrees:* LLD, Pepperdine Univ, 80. *Prof Exp:* Chief engr, Northrop Corp, 53-57, vpres & gen mgr, Nortronics Div, 57-61, exec vpres & dir corp, 61-64; pres & dir, Beckman Instruments, Inc, 65-82, chief exec off, 83-84, consult, 84-93. *Concurrent Pos:* Mem, Nat Adv Comt Aeronaut, 54-57; mem, Tech Adv Panel Aeronaut, Off Secy Defense, 54-60; adv, Off Critical Tables, Nat Acad Sci. *Mem:* Nat Acad Eng; fel Am Inst Aeronaut & Astronaut. *Mailing Add:* 1293 S Beverly Glen Blvd No 408 Los Angeles CA 90024-5236

BALLHAUS, WILLIAM FRANCIS, JR, COMPUTATIONAL AERODYNAMICS. *Current Pos:* pres civil space & commun, 90-93, pres, aero & naval systs, 93-94, VPRES SCI & ENG, LOCKHEED MARTIN CORP, 94- *Personal Data:* b Los Angeles, Calif, Jan 28, 45; m 83, Jane Kerber; c William L, Michael F, Jennifer & Benjamin. *Educ:* Univ Calif, Berkeley, BS, 67, MS, 68, PhD(mech eng), 71. *Honors & Awards:* Lawrence Sperry Award, Am Inst Aeronaut & Astronaut, 80; Arthur S Flemming Award, 80. *Prof Exp:* Dir astron, NASA, Ames Res Ctr, 71-78, res scientist computational aerodyn, US Army Aviation Res Develop Comn & Ames Res Ctr, 71-79, chief, Appl Computational Aerodyn Br & Ames Res Ctr, NASA & US Army Aviation Res & Develop Comn, 79-84, dir, Ames Res Ctr, 84-89 & actg assoc adminr, Aeronaut & Space Technol, 88-89. *Mem:* Nat Acad Eng; fel Am Inst Aeronaut & Astronaut (pres, 88-89); Int Acad Astronaut; Int Asn Astronaut; Indust Res Inst; fel Royal Aeronaut Soc; AAAS. *Res:* Computational simulation of fluid flows about aerodynamic configurations; transonic regime; applied mathematics. *Mailing Add:* 6801 Rockledge Blvd Bethesda MD 20817

BALLHAUSEN, LENNART, PHYSICAL CHEMISTRY. *Current Pos:* CHMN BD & MEM BD DIRS, CARLSBERG LABS, 92- *Personal Data:* b Copenhagen, Denmark, Apr 4, 26. *Educ:* Univ Copenhagen, MS, 54, DSc(chem), 58. *Prof Exp:* Prof chem & dept chair, Univ Parken, 59-96. *Mem:* Nat Acad Sci; Royal Danish Soc Arts & Letters; Danish Chem Soc. *Mailing Add:* Carlsberg Lab G1 Carlsbergvej 8-10 Copenhagen 2500 Valby Denmark

BALLIF, JAE R, SOLAR PHYSICS, TERRESTRIAL PHYSICS. *Current Pos:* From asst prof to assoc prof, 62-70, PROF PHYSICS, BRIGHAM YOUNG UNIV, 70-, DEAN PHYS & MATH SCI, 74- *Personal Data:* b Provo, Utah, July 5, 31; m 53; c 7. *Educ:* Brigham Young Univ, BS, 53; Univ Calif, Los Angeles, MA, 61, PhD(atmospheric physics), 62. *Concurrent Pos:* Provost & acad vpres, Brigham Young Univ, 80-89. *Mem:* Am Geophys Union. *Res:* Atmospheric airglow, particularly nocturnal emission of sodium and hydroxyl emissions; interplanetary magnetic field structure, its solar origin and terrestrial effects. *Mailing Add:* Dept Physics & Astron Brigham Young Univ 296 Esc Provo UT 84602-1022

BALLINA, RUDOLPH AUGUST, ORGANIC CHEMISTRY. *Current Pos:* RETIRED. *Personal Data:* b New York, NY, Nov 30, 34; m 67; c 5. *Educ:* St John's Univ, NY, BS, 56, MS, 61, PhD(org chem), 65. *Prof Exp:* Anal chemist, US Treas Dept, 59-60; prod develop chemist, Toms River Chem Corp, 65-77, asst dept head, 77-92. *Mem:* Am Chem Soc. *Res:* Natural products, specifically peptides and polypeptides; organic synthesis; dyestuffs. *Mailing Add:* 30 Smith Rd Toms River NJ 08755

BALLING, JAN WALTER, ANIMAL BEHAVIOR. *Current Pos:* PROF BIOL, CALIF STATE COL, PA, 66- *Personal Data:* b Louisville, Ky, Apr 8, 34. *Educ:* Univ Louisville, BA, 56, PhD(radiation biol), 64; Purdue Univ, MS, 57. *Prof Exp:* Instr biol, Univ Louisville, 60-64; dir labs, Cent State Hosp, Louisville, 64-65; asst prof biol, George Peabody Col, 65-66. *Mem:* Am Soc Parasitol; Am Nuclear Soc; Am Soc Ichthyologists & Herpetologists; Animal Behav Soc; Sigma Xi. *Res:* Turtle ethology; operant behavior of rats; trematode systematics; chemical protection of cold-blooded vertebrates against radiation damage; operant behavior of chronic schizophrenics. *Mailing Add:* PO Box 576 California PA 15419-0576

BALLINGER, CARTER M, ANESTHESIOLOGY. *Current Pos:* prof, 79-93, EMER PROF ANESTHESIOL, SCH MED, UNIV COLO, 93- *Personal Data:* b Lewistown, Mont, Mar 9, 22; m 47, Doris L Ziebell; c Steven, Jane, John, Bruce & Mary. *Educ:* Univ Iowa, BA, 43, MD, 45; Univ Pa, MMedSci, 61; Am Bd Anesthesiol, dipl, 55. *Prof Exp:* Intern, Fresno County Gen Hosp, Calif, 45-46; asst resident surg, Crile Vet Admin Hosp, Cleveland, Ohio, 48-50; resident anesthesiol, Columbia Univ, 51-53, instr, 53-54; chmn div anesthesiol, Univ Utah, 54-73, anesthesiologist-in-chief, 65-73, assoc prof anesthesiol, 54-76; prof anesthesiol & chmn dept, NJ Med Sch, Col Med & Dent, 76-78. *Concurrent Pos:* Asst attend, Presby Hosp, NY, 53-54; chmn div anesthesiol, Salt Lake County Hosp, Utah, 54-65; consult, Salt Lake Vet Admin Hosp, 54-75, Shriners Hosp, 57-72; secy-treas, Biennial Western Conf Anesthesiol, 61-65, pres, 65-67, prog chmn, 67-69; NIH spec fel neurophysiol, Univ Wis, 62-63; pres, Guedel Mem Anesthesia Libr, San Francisco, Calif, 68-70; sr staff mem anesthesiol, Martland Hosp, Newark, 76-78; sr staff anesthesiol, Univ Hosp, Denver, 79-93. *Mem:* Sigma Xi; AMA; Am Soc Anesthesiol; Asn Univ Anesthetists; Int Asn Study Pain. *Res:* Antiemetic and anesthetic agents in dogs and man; blood transfusion and intravenous therapy; mechanism of action anesthetic agents; treatment of chronic pain; training of general practitioners in anesthesiology; development of a disposable anesthesia bacterial filter system; continuing medical education in anesthesiology. *Mailing Add:* Univ Colo Med Ctr Box B-113 4200 E Ninth Ave Denver CO 80262-0001. *Fax:* 303-372-6315; *E-Mail:* cmballinger@skiuhcolorado.edu

BALLINGER, PETER RICHARD, ORGANIC CHEMISTRY. *Current Pos:* RETIRED. *Personal Data:* b London, Eng, Oct 15, 32; US citizen; m 59, 70; c 3. *Educ:* Univ London, BSc, 54, PhD(org chem), 57. *Prof Exp:* Fel phys org chem, Cornell Univ, 57-58, instr chem, 58-59; res chemist petrol prod, Calif Res Corp, 59-64, sr res chemist, 64-67, sr res assoc petrol prod, Chevron Res Co, 67-87. *Concurrent Pos:* AEC fel, 57-59. *Mem:* NY Acad Sci; Am Chem Soc. *Res:* Chemistry of air pollution; composition of automobile exhaust; mechanism of detergency; detailed analysis of hydrocarbon fuels. *Mailing Add:* 963 Peralta Ave Albany CA 94706

BALLINGER, ROYCE EUGENE, EVOLUTIONARY ECOLOGY, VERTEBRATE ZOOLOGY. *Current Pos:* assoc prof ecol, Sch Biol Sci, Univ Nebr, Lincoln, 76-82, vdir, Sch Life Sci, 77-82, prof ecol & dir, 82-90, PROF, SCH BIOL SCI, UNIV NEBR, LINCOLN, 90-, ASSOC VCHANCELLOR RES & DIR, NEBR EXP PROG STIMULATE COMPETITIVE RES, 93- *Personal Data:* b Burkburnett, Tex, Feb 21, 42; m 76, Ruth A Hamslat; c Bevia, Ryan, Mike (Dempsey), Karen (Metz) & David (Dempsey). *Educ:* Univ Tex, Austin, BA, 64; Tex Tech Univ, MS, 67; Tex A&M Univ, PhD(ecol), 71. *Prof Exp:* Res asst ecol, Ctr Biol Nat Systs, Wash Univ, 66-67; instr biol, Angelo State Univ, 67-71, from asst prof to assoc prof, 71-76. *Concurrent Pos:* NSF grant, 72-76, 78-80 & 93-; Dept Interior Water Resources grant, 77-79; panel mem, NSF, 78-79; bd gov, Ctr Great Placing Studies, 80-88; ecol ed, Copeia, Am Soc Ichthyologists & Herpetologists, 84-87; proj specialist, Chinese Provincial Univ Dev Proj, Guilin, Peoples Repub China, 88; res grants, Dept Defense Exp Prog Stimulate Competitive, 93 & Dept of Energy, 93; EPSCOR grant, NSF, 93-97. *Mem:* Herpetologist League; Sigma Xi; Soc Study Amphibians & Reptiles. *Res:* Evolutionary ecology of life history and reproductive strategies of lizards; ecology of natural selection and the importance of demographic and competitive environments to ecological adaptations; reptile thermoregulation; prairie ecology. *Mailing Add:* 8140 Dorset Dr Lincoln NE 68510. *E-Mail:* royceb@forager.unl.edu

BALLINGER, WALTER ELMER, HORTICULTURE. *Current Pos:* RETIRED. *Personal Data:* b Burlington, NJ, Jan 22, 26; m 62; c 3. *Educ:* Rutgers Univ, BS, 52; Mich State Univ, MS, 55, PhD(hort), 57. *Prof Exp:* Res asst, Mich State Univ, 54-57; from asst prof to prof hort, NC State Univ, 57-87, coordr acad affairs, Dept Hort Sci, 73-87. *Concurrent Pos:* Guest lectr, Peach Cong, Verona, Italy, 65 & Univ Berlin, 65. *Mem:* Am Soc Hort Sci. *Res:* Pre- and post-harvest physiology of blueberries and grapes, especially anthocyanin characterization, physical and chemical measurement of quality and maintenance of quality. *Mailing Add:* 5612 Winthrop Dr Raleigh NC 27612

BALLINGER, WALTER F, II, SURGERY. *Current Pos:* chmn dept, 67-78, Bixby prof surg, 67-92, EMER PROF SURG, SCH MED, WASH UNIV, 92-, LECTR HEALTH ADMIN PROG, 92- *Personal Data:* b Philadelphia, Pa, May 16, 25; m 53, 80, Mary R Dickson; c Walter F III, Christopher & David G. *Educ:* Univ Pa, MD, 48. *Prof Exp:* From asst to assoc prof surg, Jefferson Med Col, 56-64; assoc prof, Sch Med, Johns Hopkins Univ, 64-67. *Concurrent Pos:* Markle scholar acad med, 61-66; surgeon-in-chief, Barnes & Allied Hosps, 67-78, surgeon, 78-; ed-in-chief, Surgery, 71- *Mem:* Am Col Surg; Soc Univ Surg; Soc Clin Surg; Soc Vascular Surg. *Res:* Gastrointestinal, vascular and metabolic research. *Mailing Add:* Wash Univ Sch Med 4547 Clayton Ave St Louis MO 63110

BALLMANN, DONALD LAWRENCE, GEOLOGY. *Current Pos:* LICENSING DIR, PA LOW-LEVEL WASTE PROJ, CHEM-NUCLEAR SYSTS, INC, 93- *Personal Data:* b Dayton, Ohio, Apr 25, 27; m 72, Miriam Nelson. *Educ:* St Joseph's Col, Ind, AB, 54; Univ Ill, BS, 55, MS, 56, PhD(geol), 59. *Prof Exp:* Asst prof geol, St Joseph's Col, Ind, 56-63, dir geol field camp, 56-60, dir undergrad res, 58-60, asst dir develop, 61-62, exec asst to pres, 62-63, assoc prof geol, 63-72, acad dean, 63-68, dir develop found & govt rels, 68-72; proj mgr to assoc, Dames & Moore, 73-82; sr licensing adv, Battelle, 83-89, tech admin, off Low-Level Waste Technol, 89-90, Geosci Mgr, Conn Low-Level Waste Proj, 91-92. *Mem:* Am Asn Petrol Geol; Geol Soc Am; Am Inst Prof Geologists; Soc Econ Paleontologists & Mineralogists; Sigma Xi; AAAS; Am Nuclear Soc. *Res:* Areal geology; geomorphology; historical geology; engineering geology; soil mechanics; facility siting. *Mailing Add:* 871 Zermatt Dr Hummelstown PA 17036

BALLOU, CLINTON EDWARD, BIOCHEMISTRY. *Current Pos:* asst res biochemist, 52-55, from asst prof to assoc prof biochem, 55-61, chmn dept, 64-68, PROF BIOCHEM, UNIV CALIF, BERKELEY, 61- *Personal Data:* b King Hill, Idaho, June 18, 23; m 49; c 2. *Educ:* Ore State Col, BS, 44; Univ Wis, MS, 48, PhD(biochem), 50. *Honors & Awards:* Claude Hudson Award, 81. *Prof Exp:* USPHS res fels, Univ Edinburgh, 50-51 & Univ Calif, Berkeley, 51-52. *Concurrent Pos:* NSF sr fel, 61-62; Guggenheim fel, Kyoto & Paris, 68-69; vis scientist, Basel Inst Immunol, 75-76, Imp Col London & Nat Ctr Sci Res, Grenoble, 82-83. *Mem:* Nat Acad Sci; AAAS; Am Chem Soc; Am Soc Biol Chemists. *Res:* Structure and biosynthesis of complex polysaccharides, lipids and lipopolysaccharides and the role these substances play in the biochemistry of the cell envelope; glycoproteins. *Mailing Add:* Div Biochem & Molecular Biol Barker Hall Univ Calif Berkeley CA 94720

BALLOU, DAVID PENFIELD, BIOCHEMISTRY, ENZYMOLOGY. *Current Pos:* Asst res biochemist, 71-72, from instr to assoc prof biochem, 72-87, PROF BIOCHEM, UNIV MICH, ANN ARBOR, 87- *Personal Data:* b New Britain, Conn, Aug 25, 42; m 72; c 2. *Educ:* Antioch Col, BS, 65; Univ Mich, MS, 67, PhD(chem), 71. *Concurrent Pos:* Consult, Henry Ford Hosp, Detroit, 72- *Mem:* AAAS; Am Soc Biol Chemists. *Res:* Study of oxygen activation in biological systems; reactions of oxygen with flavins, nonheme iron proteins and cytochromes employing computerized rapid kinetics, absorption, fluorescence and magnetic resonance spectroscopy; development of instrumentation for the above. *Mailing Add:* Dept Biol Chem Univ Mich Ann Arbor MI 48109-0606

BALLOU, DONALD HENRY, MATHEMATICS. *Current Pos:* from asst prof math to prof, 42-64, Beman prof, 64-71, Charles A Dana prof, 71-73, head dept, 54-68, CHARLES A DANA EMER PROF MATH, MIDDLEBURY COL, 73- *Personal Data:* b Chester, Vt, Mar 28, 08; m 33, Dorothy Pollard; c Donald P. *Educ:* Yale Univ, AB, 28; Harvard Univ, AM, 31, PhD(math), 34. *Prof Exp:* Instr, Harvard Univ, 33-34; instr math, Ga Inst Technol, 34-35, asst prof, 35-42. *Concurrent Pos:* Vis assoc prof, Yale Univ, 51-52. *Mem:* Am Math Soc; Math Asn Am. *Res:* Laplace transforms; roots of polynomial equations. *Mailing Add:* 27 Weybridge St Middlebury VT 05753-1024

BALLOU, DONALD POLLARD, MANAGEMENT SCIENCE. *Current Pos:* asst prof math, State Univ NY, Albany, 70-76, lectr mgt sci, 76-81, chmn, Mgt Sci & Info Systs Dept, 87-88, ASSOC PROF MGT SCI, STATE UNIV NY, ALBANY, 81- *Personal Data:* b Atlanta, Ga, Sept 30, 40; m 69, Rhonda Bartsch; c Jeffrey & Lisa. *Educ:* Harvard Col, BA, 62; Univ Mich, MA, 63, PhD(math), 68. *Prof Exp:* Res assoc math, Brown Univ, 69-70. *Concurrent Pos:* Prin or co-prin investr, NSF, 76-78, US Dept Transp, 77-79, 79-80 & 83-85, USCG, 87-88 & 88-89. *Mem:* Asn Comput Mach; Sigma Xi. *Res:* Mathematical modeling of non-linear wave phenomona, transportation flows, production systems and decision making; quality of information; information resource management. *Mailing Add:* 3 Rita Ct Delmar NY 12054. *E-Mail:* dpb67@cnsibm.albany.edu

BALLOU, JOHN EDGERTON, INHALATION TOXICOLOGY. *Current Pos:* RETIRED. *Personal Data:* b King Hill, Idaho, Oct 25, 25; m 52; c 4. *Educ:* Ore State Col, BS, 50; Univ Rochester, PhD(toxicol), 69. *Prof Exp:* Biol scientist, Hanford Atomic Prod Oper, Gen Elec Co, 51-64; biol scientist, Pac Northwest Lab, Battelle Mem Inst, 65-69, staff scientist, 69-88. *Mem:* Am Chem Soc; Health Physics Soc. *Res:* Absorption, distribution and retention of inhaled radioisotopes. *Mailing Add:* 1628 Butternut Richland WA 99352

BALLOU, NATHAN ELMER, SEPARATIONS SCIENCE, MASS SPECTROSCOPY. *Current Pos:* sr res mgr, 69-87, LEAD SCIENTIST, PAC NORTHWEST LABS, BATTELLE MEM INST, 87- *Personal Data:* b Rochester, Minn, Sept 28, 19; m 45, 73, Elaine Chapman; c Robert K & Douglas P. *Educ:* Minn State Teachers Col, BS, 41; Univ Ill, MS, 42; Univ Chicago, PhD(chem), 47. *Prof Exp:* Asst chem, Univ Ill, 41-42; asst, Metall Lab, Univ Chicago, 42-43; asst, Clinton Labs, Oak Ridge, 43-44, assoc chemist, 45-46; res chemist, Hanford Eng Works, Wash, 44-45; assoc, Radiation Lab, Univ Calif, 47-48; head nuclear chem br, Naval Radiol Defense Lab, 48-69. *Concurrent Pos:* Head chem dept, Belgian Nuclear Ctr, 59-60; mem comt nuclear sci, Nat Acad Sci-Nat Res Coun, chmn subcomt radiochem, 62-66; mem exec comt, Div Nuclear Chem & Technol, Am Chem Soc, 69-77, counr, 81-83. *Mem:* AAAS; Am Chem Soc. *Res:* Fission process; radiochemical techniques; ultrasensitive analytical techniques. *Mailing Add:* Pac-Northwest Lab PO Box 999 P7-07 Richland WA 99352-0999

BALLUFFI, R(OBERT) W(EIERTER), PHYSICAL METALLURGY. *Current Pos:* PROF MAT SCI & ENG, MASS INST TECHNOL, 78- *Personal Data:* b Bayshore, NY, Apr 18, 24; c 3. *Educ:* Mass Inst Technol, BS, 47, DSc, 50. *Honors & Awards:* David Adler Lectr, Am Phys Soc, 89; Von Hippel Award, Mat Res Soc, 90. *Prof Exp:* Sr engr, Sylvania Elec Prod, Inc, 50-54; res assoc, Columbia Univ, 54; prof mat sci & eng, Univ Ill, 54-64 & Cornell Univ, 64-78. *Mem:* Nat Acad Sci; fel Am Inst Mining, Metall & Petrol Engrs; Metall Soc; Brit Inst Metals; fel Am Acad Arts & Sci; fel Am Phys Soc. *Res:* Diffusion in metals; radiation damage; crystal imperfections. *Mailing Add:* Dept Mat Sci & Eng Bldg 13 Rm 5078 Mass Inst Technol Cambridge MA 02139

BALLY, ALBERT WALTER, STRUCTURAL, PETROLEUM. *Current Pos:* PROF GEOL, RICE UNIV, 81- *Personal Data:* b The Hague, Holland, Apr 21, 25. *Educ:* Univ Zurich, PhD(geol), 52. *Prof Exp:* Chief geologist, Shell Oil Co, 77-81. *Mem:* Fel Geol Soc Am; Am Asn Petrol Geologists. *Mailing Add:* Dept Geol Rice Univ 6100 Main St Houston TX 77005-1827

BALMAIN, KEITH GEORGE, ELECTROMAGNETICS. *Current Pos:* from asst prof to assoc prof, 66-73, PROF ELEC ENG, UNIV TORONTO, 73-, NAT SCI & ENG RES COUN/BELL CAN INDUST RES CHAIR ELECTROMAGNETICS, 91- *Personal Data:* b London, Ont, Aug 7, 33; m 58, J Shirley. *Educ:* Univ Toronto, BASc, 57; Univ Ill, Urbana-Champaign, MS, 59, PhD(elec eng), 63. *Prof Exp:* Res asst elec eng, Univ Ill, Urbana-Champaign, 61-63, res assoc, 63-64, asst prof, 64-66. *Concurrent Pos:* Chmn, Div Eng Sci, Univ Toronto, 85-87, chmn, Res Bd, 87-90. *Mem:* Fel Inst Elec & Electronics Engrs; Can Asn Physicists. *Res:* Antennas in plasmas; broadband antennas; spacecraft electrostatic charging and discharging; electromagnetic compatibility; electromagnetic theory; electrostatic discharge simulation. *Mailing Add:* Univ Toronto Dept Elec & Comput Eng 10 Kings College Rd Toronto ON M5S 3G4 Can

BALMER, CLIFFORD EARL, ORGANIC CHEMISTRY, POLYMER CHEMISTRY. *Current Pos:* RETIRED. *Personal Data:* b Brownstown, Pa, Sept 17, 21; m 44, Irene C Fisher; c David C, Donald K & Deborah E. *Educ:* Albright Col, BS, 47. *Prof Exp:* Org chemist, Pioneer Res Labs, US Army Qm Depot, 47-53; chemist, Appln Labs, Rohm & Haas Co, 53-59, tech sales, 59-68, tech sales rep, Resins Dept, 68-70, tech sales rep, Indust Chem Dept, 70-73, tech sales rep, Plastics Int Dept, 73-78, tech sales rep, Plastics Dept, 78-82. *Mem:* Soc Plastics Engrs; Am Chem Soc. *Res:* Development of plasticizers and modifiers for polyvinyl chloride. *Mailing Add:* PO Box 562 8 Lord Jeffrey Dr Amherst NH 03031-0562

BALMER, ROBERT THEODORE, THERMODYNAMICS, RHEOLOGY. *Current Pos:* from asst prof to assoc prof, Univ Wis-Milwaukee, 69-79, chair, Mech Eng Dept, 72-74 & 89-93, eng res coordr, Grad Sch, 84-87, PROF TEACHING & RES, UNIV WIS-MILWAUKEE, 79-, DIR, CAE LAB, 90-, ASSOC DEAN ACAD PROGS & RES, 94- *Personal Data:* b Chelsea, Mich, Nov 26, 38; m 61, Mary A Sorensen; c Christine, Robert & Theodore. *Educ:* Univ Mich, BSE, 61, BSE, 64, MSE, 63; Univ Va, ScD, 68. *Honors & Awards:* Teetor Award, Soc Automotive Engrs, 66. *Prof Exp:* NATO vis prof res, Univ Naples, Italy, 68-69. *Concurrent Pos:* Vis prof, Tech Univ, Budapest, Hungary, 90. *Mem:* Am Soc Mech Engrs; Soc Rheology; Am Soc Eng Educ; Am Asn Higher Educ. *Res:* Authored an engineering thermodynamics textbook (1990) and over 50 research papers in the areas of fluid flow, bioengineering, thermodynamics, history of technology and engineering education; developed nonequilibrium thermodynamic theory of static charge generation in flowing fluids. *Mailing Add:* Mech Eng Dept Univ Wis-Milwaukee Shorewood WI 53211. *Fax:* 414-229-6958; *E-Mail:* balmer@watt.cae.uwm.edu

BALMFORTH, DENNIS, CHEMISTRY. *Current Pos:* RETIRED. *Personal Data:* b Pudsey, Eng, Apr 29, 30; m 56; c 3. *Educ:* Univ Leeds, BSc, 54, PhD(colour chem, dyeing), 61. *Prof Exp:* Res chemist, James Anderson & Co, Ltd, Scotland, 54-56; chemist, Courtaulds Ltd, Eng, 57-58 & 61-63; supvr dyeing res, Chemstrand Co, 63-67; dir, Chem & Environ Res & Serv Dept, Inst Textile Technol, 67-97. *Mem:* Royal Inst Chem; Brit Soc Dyers & Colourists. *Res:* Color chemistry; fine structure of fibrous materials and its influence on dyeing and finishing behavior. *Mailing Add:* Inst Textile Technol 2551 Ivy Rd Charlottesville VA 22903

BALOG, GEORGE, LASERS. *Current Pos:* RETIRED. *Personal Data:* b Gunn, Wyo, Oct 12, 28; m 51; c 4. *Educ:* Univ Wyo, BS, 50; Ill Inst Technol, MS, 54, PhD(chem), 58. *Prof Exp:* Mem staff, Los Alamos Sci Lab, 56-90. *Mem:* Am Chem Soc. *Res:* Polarographic studies in non-aqueous solvents; refractory materials, specifically the thermionic emission microscopy; high temperature x-ray studies; chemical lasers; dye lasers and laser dye development. *Mailing Add:* Four Erie Lane Los Alamos NM 87544

BALOGH, CHARLES B, MATHEMATICS. *Current Pos:* asst prof, 64-68, ASSOC PROF MATH, PORTLAND STATE UNIV, 68- *Personal Data:* b Beled, Hungary, Sept 13, 29; US citizen; m 54; c 1. *Educ:* Eotvos Lorand Univ, Budapest, Ms, 54; Ore State Univ, PhD(math), 65. *Prof Exp:* Res fel, Astrophys Observ, Budapest, 54-56; instr math, Jr Col, Austria, 57-58 & Univ Portland, 59-61; asst, Ore State Univ, 61-64. *Mem:* Am Math Soc; Soc Indust & Appl Math. *Res:* Asymptotic solutions of differential equations; special functions; computer languages. *Mailing Add:* Dept Math Portland State Univ PO Box 751 Portland OR 97207-0751

BALOGH, KAROLY, PATHOLOGY, HISTOCHEMISTRY. *Current Pos:* PATHOLOGIST, NEW ENG DEACONESS HOSP, 77-; ASSOC PROF PATH, HARVARD MED SCH, 77- *Personal Data:* b Budapest, Hungary, Sept 24, 30; m 55; c 3. *Educ:* Med Univ Budapest, MD, 54. *Prof Exp:* Resident path anat, Univ Budapest, 54-56; dir otolaryngol path, Mass Eye & Ear Infirmary, 62-68; asst prof path, Sch Med, Harvard Univ, 68; from assoc prof to prof, Sch Med, Boston Univ, 68-75, chief path, Univ Hosp, 68-74; sr staff mem, Mallory Inst Path, 74-75; chief path, Worcester City Hosp, 75-77; prof, Sch Med, Univ Mass, 75-77. *Concurrent Pos:* Rockefeller fel, Sch Med, Tulane Univ, 57-58; USPHS trainee path, Mass Gen Hosp, Boston, 58-61. *Mem:* Am Asn Path & Bact; Int Acad Path; Histochem Soc; Ger Path Soc. *Res:* Pathological anatomy; pediatric pathology; bone pathology; enzyme histochemistry; histochemistry of calcified tissues; histochemistry of the inner ear. *Mailing Add:* New Eng Deaconess Hosp Dept Path 185 Pilgrim Rd Boston MA 02215-5399

BALON, EUGENE KORNEL, EPIGENETICS. *Current Pos:* from assoc prof to prof, 72-96, EMER PROF ZOOL, UNIV GUELPH, ONT, 96- *Personal Data:* b Orlova, Czechoslovakia, Aug 1, 30; Can citizen; c 1. *Educ:* Charles Univ, Prague, RNDr, 53, CSc(zool), 62. *Prof Exp:* Res biologist, Lab Ichthyol, Bratislava, 54-67; fish biologist fishery sci, UN Develop Prog, Food & Agr Orgn UN, Res Inst, Chilanga, Zambia, 67-71. *Concurrent Pos:* Vis prof, Forschungsinstitut Senckenberg, Frankfurt, 76, 79 & 84; vis fel, JLB Smith Inst Ichthyol, Grahamstown, 86 & 87; res assoc, Royal Ont Mus, Toronto, 72-; ed-in-chief, Int Environ Biol Fishes, 76-; Hugh Kelly fel, 87. *Mem:* Am Soc Zool; Am Soc Ichthyologists & Herpetologists; Am Fisheries Soc; Can Soc Zoologists; Europ Ichthyol Union; Sigma Xi. *Res:* Ecology, developmental and evolutionary biology; patterns and mechanisms of fish reproduction, early life history, epigenesis, and their applications to evolution and aquaculture; philosophy and metatheoretical aspects of science; comparative ontogeny and epigenetics. *Mailing Add:* Dept Zool Inst Ichthyol Univ Guelph Guelph ON N1G 2W1 Can

BALON, THOMAS WILLIAM, EXERCISE PHYSIOLOGY, PHYSICAL EDUCATION. *Current Pos:* ASST RES SCIENTIST, CITY OF HOPE NAT MED CTR, 92- *Personal Data:* b Albany, NY, Mar 3, 52; m 93, Emilia Cavaco; c Tanya. *Educ:* State Univ NY, BS, 75; Ball State Univ, MA, 76; Univ Toledo, PhD(physiol), 83. *Prof Exp:* Lab technician, Ball State Univ, 75-76; grad teaching asst anat & physiol, Univ Toledo, 77-81, fel, 81-83; fel endocrinol, Boston Univ Sch Med, 83-86; asst prof exercise sci, Univ Iowa, 86-92. *Mem:* Fel Am Col Sports Med; Am Physiol Soc; Am Diabetes Asn; fel Am Heart Asn; AAAS. *Res:* To account, describe and explain the changes and adaption that occur in skeletal muscles and endocrine organs as a result of acute and chronic exercise. *Mailing Add:* Dept Diabetes City of Hope Nat Med Ctr 1500 Duarte Rd Duarte CA 91010-3000. *Fax:* 626-301-8489

BALOUN, CALVIN H(ENDRICKS), CORROSION, MATERIALS SCIENCE. *Current Pos:* from asst prof to assoc prof, 61-71, chmn dept, 72-77, PROF CHEM ENG, OHIO UNIV, 71- *Personal Data:* b Chicago, Ill, Apr 14, 28; m 51. *Educ:* Univ Cincinnati, ChE, 54, MS, 57, PhD(metall eng), 62. *Prof Exp:* Instr metall eng, Univ Cincinnati, 60-61. *Concurrent Pos:* Corrosion consult, 64-; vis prof metall eng, Univ Cincinnati, 65 & 68; vis fac mem, Esso Res & Eng Co, 68. *Mem:* Nat Asn Corrosion Engrs; Am Inst Mining, Metall & Petrol Engrs; Am Soc Metals; Am Soc Testing & Mat; Am Inst Chem Engrs. *Res:* Corrosion science; corrosion engineering; physical metallurgy. *Mailing Add:* Dept Chem Eng Ohio Univ Athens OH 45701-2979

BALOW, JAMES E, NEPHROLOGY, INTERNAL MEDICINE. *Current Pos:* CLIN DIR, NAT INST DIABETES, DIGESTIVE & KIDNEY DIS, NIH, 88- *Personal Data:* b Wabasha, Minn, Nov 6, 42. *Educ:* Col St Thomas, BS, 64; Univ Minn, MD, 68. *Mem:* Am Soc Nephrology; Am Asn Immunobiol; Nat Kidney Found; Am Col Physicians. *Mailing Add:* Clin Dir NIH Bldg 10 Rm 9N222 Bethesda MD 20892-0001

BALPH, MARTHA HATCH, ORNITHOLOGY, ANIMAL BEHAVIOR. *Personal Data:* b Boston, Mass, May 27, 43; wid, David F (deceased); c David C. *Educ:* Wellesley Col, BA, 65; Univ Wyo, MS, 69; Utah State Univ, PhD(biol), 75. *Honors & Awards:* Carnes Award, Am Ornithologists Union, 79. *Prof Exp:* Mus technician & biol illusr ichthyol, Nat Mus Natural Hist Smithsonian Inst, Washington, DC, 67-70; res asst prof, Utah State Univ, 75-80, res assoc prof fisheries & wildlife, 80-95. *Concurrent Pos:* Biol consult, White River Oil Shale Proj, 74-77; F M Chapman grants, Am Mus Natural Hist, NY, 76-77 & 78-79; second vpres, Western Bird Banding Asn, 77-78, first vpres, 78-79, pres, 79-81; bd dirs, Cooper Ornith Soc, 84-87. *Mem:* Am Ornithologists Union; Cooper Ornith Soc; Asn Field Ornithologist; Wilson Ornith Soc. *Res:* Avian social behavior and behavioral ecology, especially communication and social organization in winter-flocking passerines. *Mailing Add:* P O Box 68 Millville UT 84326-0068

BALSANO, JOSEPH SILVIO, POPULATION BIOLOGY, SCIENCE EDUCATION. *Current Pos:* assoc prof, 74-84, PROF BIOL SCI, UNIV WIS-PARKSIDE, 84- *Personal Data:* b Kenosha, Wis, Apr 19, 37; m 60; c 5. *Educ:* Marquette Univ, BS, 59, MS, 62, PhD(biol), 68. *Prof Exp:* From instr to assoc prof biol, Dominican Col, Wis, 61-68; asst prof, Marquette Univ, 68-69. *Mem:* AAAS; Am Inst Biol Sci; Am Soc Ichthyologists & Herpetologists; Nat Sci Teachers Asn; Sigma Xi. *Res:* Ecological genetics of fish populations; use of electrophoretic analyses and tissue transplantation to assay variation in bisexual/unisexual complexes of molly fishes. *Mailing Add:* Dept Biol Sci Univ Wis-Parkside Box 2000 Kenosha WI 53141-2000

BALSBAUGH, EDWARD ULMONT, JR, ENTOMOLOGY. *Current Pos:* PROF ENTOM, N DAK STATE UNIV, 76- *Personal Data:* b Harrisburg, Pa, Jan 12, 33; m 68; c 2. *Educ:* Lebanon Valley Col, BS, 55; Pa State Univ, MS, 61; Auburn Univ, PhD(entom), 66. *Prof Exp:* Entomologist, Bur Plant Indust, Pa Dept Agr, 58-62; assoc prof entom, SDak State Univ, 65-76. *Concurrent Pos:* Consult, Am Mus Nat Hist, 82, US Army Corps Engrs, 90; ed, Schafer-Post Series NDak Insects, 76- *Mem:* Coleopterists Soc; Entom Soc Am; Sigma Xi. *Res:* Taxonomy, biology, ecology, evolution and zoogeography of Coleoptera, especially Chrysomelidae. *Mailing Add:* 3208 Elm St Fargo ND 58102

BALSLEY, BEN BURTON, ATMOSPHERIC PHYSICS, IONOSPHERIC PHYSICS. *Current Pos:* SR RES FEL, COOP INST RES ENVIRON SCI, UNIV COLO, BOULDER, 85-, RES PROF ELEC & COMPUT ENG, 91- *Personal Data:* b Santa Monica, Calif, Apr 23, 32; m 93, Loys A Lavender; c Christopher, Tobin & Debora. *Educ:* Calif State Polytech Univ, BSc, 57; Univ Colo, MSc, 64, PhD(elec eng), 67. *Honors & Awards:* Gold Medal, US Dept Com, 74. *Prof Exp:* Physicist & engr ionospheric studies, Jicamarca Observ, Peru, 60-69; supvry physicist atmospheric studies, Aeronomy Lab, Nat Oceanic Atmospheric Admin, Boulder, Colo, 69-90. *Concurrent Pos:* Adj prof elec eng, Univ Colo & Geophys Inst, Univ Alaska; prin investr various sci res proj. *Mem:* Sigma Xi; Am Meteorol Soc; Am Geophys Union; Int Union Radio Sci. *Res:* Investigations of neutral atmospheric dynamics in the troposphere, stratosphere and mesosphere by radar techniques; similar studies of small-scale ionospheric irregularity structure in the E and F regions at both equatorial and auroral latitudes. *Mailing Add:* 7240 Terrace Pl Boulder CO 80303-4638. *Fax:* 303-492-1149; *E-Mail:* balsley@terra.colorado.edu

BALSTER, CLIFFORD ARTHUR, GEOLOGY, GEOMORPHOLOGY-SOILS. *Current Pos:* RETIRED. *Personal Data:* b Monmouth, Iowa, Feb 27, 22; m 43, Norma A Petersen; c Steven W, Linda J (King), Gwen K (Hoffman) & Kenneth L. *Educ:* Iowa State Univ, BS, 48, MS, 50. *Prof Exp:* Geologist, Pure Oil Co, 51-53, div stratigrapher, 53-54; stratigrapher, Am Stratig Co, 54-56, mgr, Northern Div, 56-60; group leader carbonate res, Continental Oil Co, 60-61; area geologist, Soil Conserv Serv, USDA, 61-67; from asst prof to assoc prof geol, Mont Col Mineral Sci & Technol, 67-74; consult geologist, 74-78; explor mgr, Burlington Northern, 78-79; pres, Cana Corp, 81-88; consult geologist, 88-94. *Concurrent Pos:* Asst prof, Ore State Univ, 61-67; res petrol geologist, Mont Bur Mines & Geol, 67-74. *Mem:* Fel Geol Soc Am; Am Asn Petrol Geol; Am Inst Prof Geologists; Sigma Xi. *Res:* Petrology of sedimentary rocks, especially carbonate rocks; geology of soils and soil genesis, particularly weathering and geomorphology; energy mineral resources and supplies. *Mailing Add:* 318 W 13th St Laurel MT 59044

BALSTER, ROBERT L(OUIS), BEHAVIORAL PHARMACOLOGY. *Current Pos:* from asst prof to assoc prof, 73-84, dir, grad studies, 80-87, PROF PHARMACOL & TOXICOL, MED COL VA, VA COMMONWEALTH UNIV, 84-, DIR, CTR DRUG & ALCOHOL STUDIES, 93- *Personal Data:* b St Cloud, Minn, Oct 12, 44; m 66; c 1. *Educ:* Univ Minn, BA, 66; Univ Houston, PhD(psychol), 70. *Prof Exp:* Teaching fel psychiat & pharmacol, Univ Chicago, 70-72; asst prof psychiat, Sch Med, Duke Univ, 72-73. *Concurrent Pos:* Prin investr, Environ Protection Agency, Nat Inst Environ Health Sci & Nat Inst Drug Abuse, 76-; pres, Int Study Group Invest Drugs as Reinforcers, 79-81; mem, Drug Adv Comt, Food & Drug Admin, 80-84, chmn, 83-84; pres-elect, Col Probs Drug Dependence, 87-; mem, Bd Sci Affairs, Am Psychol Asn, 89-90. *Mem:* Fel Am Psychol Asn; Soc Stimulus Properties Drugs (pres, 84-85); fel Am Col Neuropsychopharmacol; Am Soc Pharmacol & Exp Therapeut; Behav Pharmacol Soc; fel Col Problems Drug Dependence. *Res:* Effects of drugs of abuse, particularly phencyclidine and volatile solvents, on learned behavior of animals; drug self-administration and drug discrimination; behavioral toxicology of inhalants. *Mailing Add:* Dept Pharmacol Med Col Va Box 980310 MCV Station Richmond VA 23298-0310. *Fax:* 804-371-7519; *E-Mail:* balster@gems.vcu.edu

BALTACIOGLU, MEHMET NECIP, SOFTWARE SYSTEMS. *Current Pos:* PRES, WINSOFT SOFTWARE INC, OTTAWA, 90- *Personal Data:* b Ankara, Turkey, Sept 4, 54; m 77, Yaprak Erem; c Sinan A. *Educ:* Mid Tech Univ, Ankara, BS, 76; Bhosporous Univ, MS, 77; Carleton Univ, PhD, 86. *Honors & Awards:* Whitman Wright Excellence in CAD Design Award, Can Soc Civil Eng, 92. *Prof Exp:* Struct engr, Cag Ltd, Istanbul, 77-80; pres, Cube Systs Inc, Ottawa, 86-90. *Concurrent Pos:* Grantee, Nat Res Coun Can, 88. *Mem:* Can Soc Civil Eng. *Res:* Polarized three dimensional vision drivers; stereoscopic vision drivers using bi-coloured lenses; author of several publications. *Mailing Add:* Winsoft Software Inc PO Box 187 Sta B Ottawa ON K1P 6C4 Can

BALTAY, CHARLES, NUCLEAR PHYSICS. *Current Pos:* EUGENE HIGGINS PROF PHYSICS, YALE UNIV, 88-, CHMN DEPT, 95- *Personal Data:* b Budapest, Hungary, Apr 15, 37; US citizen; m 61, Virginia; c 5. *Educ:* Union Col, BS, 58; Yale Univ, MS, 59, PhD(physics), 63. *Prof Exp:* Res physicist, Yale Univ, 63-64; from instr to prof physics, Columbia Univ, 64-88, dir, Nevis Labs, 79-88. *Concurrent Pos:* Alfred P Sloan fel, 66-68; CERN fel, 80. *Mem:* Fel Am Phys Soc. *Res:* Elementary particle physics. *Mailing Add:* Physics Dept Yale Univ New Haven CT 06520

BALTAZZI, EVAN S, ORGANIC CHEMISTRY, MATERIALS SCIENCE ENGINEERING. *Current Pos:* RETIRED. *Personal Data:* b Izmir, Turkey, Apr 11, 19; US citizen; m 45, Nellie Bioriaro; c A Vittoria, James P & Maria I. *Educ:* Univ Paris, DSc(phys sci), 49; Oxford Univ, PhD(org reaction mechanisms), 54. *Honors & Awards:* Distinguished Serv Award in Sci, 65. *Prof Exp:* Head org chem res, French Nat Res Ctr, 46-59; group leader org synthesis, Nalco Chem Co, 59-61; mgr org res, IIT Res Inst, 61-63; dir org res, Multigraphics Develop Ctr, Addressograph Multigraph Corp, 63-66, dir phys & chem res, 66-70, dir appl sci, 70-77; pres, Evanel Assocs, 77-78; eng consult, Am Europ Japanese Cos, Toshiba, 78-88. *Concurrent Pos:* Brit Coun Exchange scholar, Oxford Univ, 52-54; Can Nat Res Coun fel, 55-56; chmn, Gordon Res Conf Photoconductors, 76; mem, Comt US currency, Nat Res Coun, 85-87. *Mem:* Sr mem Am Chem Soc; fel Chem Soc; fel Soc Chem Indust; sr mem French Chem Soc; sr mem Soc Photog Scientists & Engrs; Inst Elec & Electronics Engrs; Tech Asn Pulp & Paper Indust. *Res:* Heterocyclic chemistry; synthetic methods; biologically active compounds; photosensitive compounds; photocopying and duplicating materials and systems. *Mailing Add:* 825 Greengate Oval Sagamore Hills OH 44067-2311. *Fax:* 216-467-1750

BALTENSPERGER, ARDEN ALBERT, PLANT BREEDING. *Current Pos:* RETIRED. *Personal Data:* b Kimball, Nebr, Dec 25, 22; m 47, Elsie Schlossen; c Bruce, Cathey, Paul & Carl. *Educ:* Univ Nebr, BS, 47, MS, 49; Iowa State Col, PhD(agron), 58. *Prof Exp:* Jr agronomist field crop res, Agr Exp Sta, Agr & Mech Col, Tex, 52-54; instr agron, Iowa State Col, 54-56, res assoc, 56-58; asst plant breeder sorghum res, Univ Ariz, 58-59, assoc prof & assoc agronomist grass breeding, 59-62, prof & agronomist, 62-63; head dept, NMex State Univ, 63-77, prof, 63-88, emer prof agron, 89-; dir, Turfgrass Res, Farmers Mkt Corp, 89- *Mem:* Fel Am Soc Agron (pres, 90); fel Crop Sci Soc Am. *Res:* Grass, corn and sorghum breeding and production; bermudagrass breeding for improved seed propagated cultivars. *Mailing Add:* 1807 Half Moon Dr Las Cruces NM 88005

BALTENSPERGER, DAVID DWIGHT, PROSO MILLET BREEDING. *Current Pos:* assoc prof, 89-95, PROF AGRON, UNIV NEBR, 95- *Personal Data:* b Kimball, Nebr, Dec 28, 53; m 76, Jeanne R Larson; c Stacey, Robert & Katie. *Educ:* Nebr Wesleyan Univ, BS, 76; Univ Nebr, MS, 78; NMex State Univ, PhD(agron), 80. *Prof Exp:* From asst prof to assoc prof, Univ Fla, 81-89. *Mem:* Am Soc Agron; Crop Sci Soc Am; Soc Range Mgt; Sigma Xi. *Res:* Proso millet breeding and alternative crop development for dryland production in Western Nebraska; emphasis on mineral oil seeds, millets and amaranth; irrigated turfgrass seed production. *Mailing Add:* 4502 Ave I Scottsbluff NE 69361. *Fax:* 308-632-1365; *E-Mail:* agr037@unlvm.edu

BALTHASER, LAWRENCE HAROLD, GEOLOGY. *Current Pos:* Asst prof geol, Southampton Col, Long Island Univ, 67-69, assoc prof, 69-76, PROF PHYSICS, CALIF STATE POLYTECH COL, SAN LUIS OBISPO, 77- *Personal Data:* b Camden, NJ, Feb 19, 37; m 67; c 1. *Educ:* Rutgers Univ, BA, 60; Ind Univ, Bloomington, MA, 63, PhD(geol), 69. *Concurrent Pos:* E R Cumings award, Ind Univ, 70; map draftsman, Sun Oil Co, field asst, NJ Agr Exp Sta & teaching asst, Indiana Univ, 75- *Mem:* Soc Econ Paleont & Mineral. *Res:* Sedimentary petrology and paleoecology of carbonate rocks; paleocurrent analysis of Franciscan and Great Valley sequence rocks. *Mailing Add:* Dept Physics Calif Poly State Univ 1 Poly View Dr San Luis Obispo CA 93407-0001

BALTHAZAR, EMIL JACQUE, GASTROINTESTINAL RADIOLOGY, ABDOMINAL IMAGING. *Current Pos:* PROF RADIOL, NY UNIV, TISCH-BELLEVUE MED CTR, 80- *Educ:* Sch Med, Bucharest, Rumania, MD, 59; Am Bd Radiol, dipl, 68. *Honors & Awards:* R Marshak Award, Am Col Gastroenterol, 76. *Concurrent Pos:* Attend radiol, NY Univ, Tisch Med Ctr, Bellevue Med Ctr & Manhattan Vet Admin Med Ctr, 80-; examnr gastrointestinal radiol, Am Bd Radiol, Louisville, Ky, 82-85. *Mem:* Radiol Soc NAm; fel Am Col Radiol; Soc Gastrointestinal Radiologists; fel Am Col Gastroenterol; Soc Computed Body Tomography; Am Roentgen Ray Soc. *Res:* Author of various publications. *Mailing Add:* Radiol Dept NY Univ Sch Med 550 First Ave New York NY 10016-6481. *Fax:* 212-263-7666

BALTHAZOR, TERRELL MACK, ORGANIC CHEMISTRY. *Current Pos:* DIR RES, MONSANTO CO, 75- *Personal Data:* b Hays, Kans, Aug 25, 49; m 68, Kay Marcell; c Troy. *Educ:* Ft Hays Kans State Col, BS, 71; Univ Ill, PhD(org chem), 75. *Mem:* Am Chem Soc. *Res:* Discovery of bioactive molecules. *Mailing Add:* 7208 Chamberlain University City MO 63130-3014

BALTIMORE, DAVID, VIROLOGY, BIOCHEMISTRY. *Current Pos:* assoc prof microbiol, Mass Inst Technol, 68-72, Am Cancer Soc Prof Microbiol, 73-84, prof biol, 72-90, IVAN R COTTRELL PROF MOLECULAR BIOL & IMMUNOL, MASS INST TECHNOL, 94- *Personal Data:* b New York, NY, Mar 7, 38; m 68; c 1. *Educ:* Swarthmore Col, BA, 60; Rockefeller Inst, PhD(biol), 64. *Hon Degrees:* DSc, Swarthmore Col, 76; DSc, Mt Holyoke Col, 87. *Honors & Awards:* Nobel Prize in Physiol & Med, 75; Gustav Stern Award Virol, 70; Warren Trienniel Prize, Mass Gen Hosp, 71; Eli Lilly Award, 71; US Steel Found Award, Molecular Biol, Nat Acad Sci, 74. *Prof Exp:* Fel microbiol, Mass Inst Technol, 63-64; fel molecular biol, Albert Einstein Col Med, 64-65; res assoc virol, Salk Inst Biol Studies, 65-68; pres, Rockefeller Univ, 90-91. *Concurrent Pos:* Bd govs, Weizmann Inst Sci, Israel, 79-; bd mem, Life Sci Res Found, 81-; co-chmn, Comt Nat Strategy AIDS, Nat Acad Sci & Inst Med, 86; bd mgrs, Swarthmore Col; NIH ad hoc prog adv comt complex genomes; dir, Whitehead Inst, 82-90. *Mem:* Inst Med-Nat Acad Sci; AAAS; Am Soc Microbiol; Am Soc Biol Chem; Pontif Acad Sci; Am Acad Arts & Sci; foreign mem Royal Soc Eng. *Mailing Add:* Mass Inst Technol Bldg 68 Rm 380 77 Mass Ave Cambridge MA 02139

BALTIMORE, ROBERT SAMUEL, PEDIATRICS, INFECTIOUS DISEASES. *Current Pos:* from asst prof to assoc prof, 76-95, PROF PEDIAT & EPIDEMIOL, YALE UNIV SCH MED, 95- *Personal Data:* b New York, NY, Nov 3, 42; m 78, Katalin Radnay; c Gwen & Richard. *Educ:* Univ Chicago, AB, 64; State Univ NY, Buffalo, MD, 68. *Hon Degrees:* MA, Yale Univ, 96. *Prof Exp:* Fel med off, Walter Reed Army Inst Res, 71-74; fel infectious dis, Channing Lab, Harvard Med Sch, 74-75, instr pediat, 75-76. *Concurrent Pos:* Prin investr, Cystic Fibrosis Found, 78-81, USPHS, 81-84; assoc hosp epidemiologist, Yale-New Haven Hosp, 97- *Mem:* Fel Infectious Dis Soc Am; fel Soc Pediat Res; fel Pediat Infectious Dis Soc; fel Am Acad Pediat; Soc Hosp Epidemiol Am; Am Pediat Soc. *Res:* Predisposing factors for infections of infants and children; immunologic studies of susceptibility to bacterial infections and epidemiology of infection acquisition in infants. *Mailing Add:* 333 Cedar St New Haven CT 06520-8064. *Fax:* 203-785-7194; *E-Mail:* robert.baltimore@yale.edu

BALTRUSAITIS, ROSE MARY, ELEMENTARY PARTICLE PHYSICS. *Current Pos:* MEM STAFF, STANFORD LINEAR ACCELERATOR CTR, STANFORD UNIV, 80-; SECT LEADER, LOS ALAMOS NAT LAB, 92- *Personal Data:* b Saginaw, Mich, Aug 28, 50. *Educ:* Northwestern Univ, BA, 71; Princeton Univ, PhD(physics), 77. *Prof Exp:* Res assoc physics, Fermi Nat Accelerator Lab, 77-80; at physics dept, Univ Utah, 83-87. *Mem:* Am Phys Soc. *Mailing Add:* B220 Los ALmosa Nat Lab PO Box 1663 Los Alamos NM 87545

BALTZ, ANTHONY JOHN, THEORETICAL NUCLEAR PHYSICS. *Current Pos:* From res assoc to assoc physicist, 71-76, PHYSICIST, BROOKHAVEN NAT LAB, 76- *Personal Data:* b Indianapolis, Ind, Mar 10, 42; m 68, Marie Lepri; c Edward & William. *Educ:* Spring Hill Col, BS, 66; Case Western Res Univ, MS, 68, PhD(physics), 71. *Concurrent Pos:* Detailee, US Dept Energy, 84-85. *Mem:* Am Phys Soc; fel AAAS. *Res:* Theoretical nuclear physics especially in the areas of relativistic heavy ion reactions and solar neutrino matter oscillation effects; relativistic atomic collisions. *Mailing Add:* Dept Physics Brookhaven Nat Lab Upton NY 11973. *E-Mail:* baltz@bnl.gov

BALTZ, HOWARD BURL, APPLIED STATISTICS, MANAGEMENT SCIENCES. *Current Pos:* assoc prof, 68-76, PROF STATIST, UNIV MO-ST LOUIS, 76- *Personal Data:* b St Louis, Mo, July 27, 30; m 68; c 3. *Educ:* Baylor Univ, BBA, 55, MS, 56; Okla State Univ, PhD(econ statist), 64. *Prof Exp:* Instr statist, Baylor Univ, 57-59, asst dir Bur Bus & Econ Res, 58-59; teaching asst, Okla State Univ, 59-62; asst prof statist & dir Comput Ctr, Midwestern Univ, 62-64; asst prof, Univ Tex, Austin, 64-68. *Concurrent Pos:* Coordr, Sci Quant Mgt Sci Group, Univ Mo, 68-73. *Mem:* Am Statist Asn; Am Inst Decision Sci. *Res:* Applied forecasting. *Mailing Add:* Dept Bus Admin Univ Mo St Louis 8001 Natural Bridge St Louis MO 63121-4401

BALTZELL, JANET K, human nutrition, for more information see previous edition

BALTZER, OTTO JOHN, PHYSICS. *Current Pos:* CONSULT, 81- *Personal Data:* b St Louis, Mo, Dec 24, 16; m 81; c 4. *Educ:* Washington Univ, AB, 38, MS, 39, PhD(physics), 41. *Prof Exp:* Res assoc radiation lab, Mass Inst Technol, 41-45; asst dir & supvr, Defense Res Lab, Tex, 45-56; pres & tech dir, Textran Corp, 56-62, prin scientist, Tracor, Inc, 62-80. *Mem:* Am Phys Soc. *Res:* Electromagnetic propagation; guided missile research and development; precision timing; navigation. *Mailing Add:* 11805 Arabian Trail Austin TX 78759

BALTZER, PHILIP KEENE, PHYSICS. *Current Pos:* RETIRED. *Personal Data:* b Quincy, Mass, Feb 11, 24; m 44; c 4. *Educ:* Northeastern Univ, SB, 52; Mass Inst Technol, SM, 55; Rutgers Univ, PhD, 63. *Prof Exp:* Draftsman, Fore River Shipyard, Mass, 46-47; student engr, Charles T Main, Inc, 48-52; res staff magnetic mat, Digital Comput Lab, Mass Inst Technol, 52-55; mem res staff, RCA Sarnoff Res Labs, 55-67, dir res, RCA Labs, Tokyo, 67-72, staff scientist, 72-76, group head, LSI Systs Design & Appln, RCA Sarnoff Res Labs, 76-86. *Mem:* Sigma Xi. *Res:* Solid state physics; magnetic materials. *Mailing Add:* 6128 Weobley Lane Raleigh NC 27614

BALUDA, MARCEL A, VIROLOGY, ONCOLOGY. *Current Pos:* PROF VIROL ONCOL, UNIV CALIF, LOS ANGELES, 66- *Personal Data:* b France, June 30, 30; nat US; c 3. *Educ:* Univ Pittsburgh, BS, 51, MS, 53; Calif Inst Technol, PhD(virol, chem), 56. *Prof Exp:* Res assoc pediat, City of Hope Med Ctr, 56-62, sr virologist, Biol Dept, 62-66. *Concurrent Pos:* Dep dir, Jonsson Comprehensive Cancer Ctr, 81- *Mem:* Am Soc Microbiol; Am Asn Cancer Res; AAAS. *Res:* Tumor viruses; leukemia; oncogenesis and cellular differentiation. *Mailing Add:* Dept Path Univ Calif Sch Med Los Angeles 10833 Le Conte Ave Los Angeles CA 90024-1300

BALWANZ, WILLIAM WALTER, engineering, physical science; deceased, see previous edition for last biography

BALWIERCZAK, JOSEPH LEONARD, CARDIOVASCULAR PHARMACOLOGY. *Current Pos:* sr scientist, 87-90, RES SCIENTIST II, DEPT CARDIOVASC RES, PHARMACEUT DIV, CIBA-GEIGY CORP, 91- *Personal Data:* b Staten Island, NY, Apr 4, 54. *Educ:* State Univ NY, Buffalo, BS, 76, PhD(biochem pharmacol), 83. *Prof Exp:* Fel, Dept Pharmacol & Cell Biophys, Sch Med, Univ Cincinnati, 83-85, res assoc, 85-87. *Mem:* Am Soc Pharmacol & Exp Therapeut; NY Acad Sci. *Res:* Ion channel activity and regulation; receptor classification: receptor binding, in vitro organ studies; receptor activated messenger systems: cyclic nucleotides, inositol phosphates. *Mailing Add:* Cardiovasc Pharmacol Dept Novartis Pharmaceut Div 556 Morris Ave Bldg LSB Rm 2281 Summit NJ 07901-1398

BALZHISER, RICHARD E(ARL), ENERGY RESEARCH, ENVIRONMENTAL RESEARCH. *Current Pos:* Dir, Fossil Fuel & Adv Syst, Elec Power Res Inst, 73-79, vpres res & develop, 79-83, sr vpres, 83-87, exec vp, 87-88, pres & chief exec officer, 88-96, EMER PRES, ELEC POWER RES INST, 96- *Personal Data:* b Elmhurst, Ill, May 27, 32; m 51, Christine; c Gary, Robert, Patricia & Michele. *Educ:* Univ Mich, BSE, 55, MSE, 56, PhD(chem eng), 61. *Honors & Awards:* Charles M Schwab Mem lectr, Am Iron & Steel Inst. *Prof Exp:* Prof chem eng, Univ Mich, 60-70, chmn chem eng, 70-71; asst dir, Off Sci & Technol, White House, 71-73. *Concurrent Pos:* Consult, Allegany Ballistics Lab, 61-62 & E I du Pont de Nemours & Co Inc, 67-70; White House fel, 67-68; consult prof, Stanford Univ, 74-79; mem adv bd, Univ Calif, Berkeley, 74-77, Argonne Nat Lab, 74-80, Oak Ridge Nat Lab, 76-79, Cal Tech Energy Comt, 76-78, Gas Res Inst, 79-82; Nat Res Coun Bd Sustainable Develop, 94-; bd dirs, Houston Indust, 96- *Mem:* Nat Acad Eng; Am Inst Chem Engrs; Am Inst Mining, Metall & Petrol Engrs; AAAS; Sigma Xi. *Res:* Heat transfer; thermodynamics studies in liquid metal systems; direct research in generation, delivery and use of electrical energy including environmental and economic consideration; electric power. *Mailing Add:* Elec Power Res Inst 3412 Hillview Ave PO Box 10412 Palo Alto CA 94304-1395. *Fax:* 650-855-2090; *E-Mail:* rbalzhis@epri.com

BAMBACH, RICHARD KARL, PALEOECOLOGY, MACROEVOLUTION. *Current Pos:* asst prof, 70-81, PROF PALEONT, DEPT GEOL SCI, VA POLYTECH INST & STATE UNIV, 81- *Personal Data:* b Cincinnati, Ohio, May 18, 34; m 59, Susan Fennell; c Margaret Ann (Moore) & Catharine Larece. *Educ:* Johns Hopkins Univ, BA, 57; Yale Univ, MS, 64, PhD(geol), 69. *Honors & Awards:* Raymond C Moore Medal, Soc Sedimentary Geol, 98. *Prof Exp:* Mus aide, Dept Geol, US Nat Mus Natural Hist, 57-58 & 61-62; ens & ltjg, USN, 58-61; asst prof & lectr, Dept Geol, Smith Col, 67-70. *Concurrent Pos:* Vis assoc prof paleont, Univ Chicago, 78-79; vis prof geol, Utah State Univ, 81, biol, Marine Prog, Boston Univ, 90 & Harvard Univ, 95. *Mem:* Paleont Soc; Ecol Soc Am; Marine Biol Asn UK; Soc Study Evolution; Geol Soc Am; Soc Sedimentary Geol. *Res:* Community paleoecology, functional morphology of fossil marine invertebrates; patterns of diversity change over time, changes in the marine ecosystem through time and paleobiogeography and paleogeography. *Mailing Add:* 601 Broce Dr NW Blacksburg VA 24060. *Fax:* 540-231-3386; *E-Mail:* bambachr@vt.edu

BAMBARA, ROBERT ANTHONY, BIOCHEMISTRY, MOLECULAR BIOLOGY. *Current Pos:* from asst prof to assoc prof, 77-089, PROF ONCOL BIOCHEM, UNIV ROCHESTER, 89- *Personal Data:* b Chicago, Ill, Jan 3, 49; m 74, Bonnie Messersmith; c Rebecca & Bradley. *Educ:* Northwestern Univ, BA, 70; Cornell Univ, PhD(biochem), 74. *Honors & Awards:* Faculty Res Award, Am Cancer Soc. *Prof Exp:* Fel biochem, Stanford Univ, 74-76. *Mem:* Am Asn Biochem & Molecular Biol. *Res:* Mechanism of DNA synthesis in procaryotes and eukaryotes; inhibition of DNA polymerases and replication proteins by anti-tumor drugs; replication of human immunodeficiency virus; hormonal regulation of gene expression. *Mailing Add:* Cancer Ctr & Dept Biochem Univ Rochester 601 Elmwood Ave Rochester NY 14642-0001. *Fax:* 716-271-2683

BAMBECK, GREGORY SCOTT, GEL ELECTROPHORESIS, COMPUTERIZED DENSITOMETRY. *Current Pos:* VPRES RES & DEVELOP, ZAXIS INC, 89- *Personal Data:* John Goodland. *Educ:* Kent State Univ, BA, 76, PhD(molecular biol), 81. *Prof Exp:* Mgr res & develop, Isolab Inc, 79-81; vpres res & develop, Separation Sci Inc, 81-84 & Geltech Inc, 85-89. *Concurrent Pos:* Consult, Seragen Inc, 83, Framingham Study, 96-97. *Mem:* AAAS; Am Chem Soc; Am Asn Clin Chem; Electrophonesis Soc. *Res:* Designing and producing precast gels for DNA sequencing, DNA fingerprinting, protein separation, electrophoresis and genomics; designing reagent and equipment systems for using said gels. *Mailing Add:* Z Axis Inc 1890 Georgetown Rd Hudson OH 44236. *Fax:* 216-650-2024; *E-Mail:* zbec@1x.netcom.com

BAMBERGER, CARLOS ENRIQUE LEOPOLDO, PHYSICAL INORGANIC CHEMISTRY. *Current Pos:* chemist, 66-80, chem div, 80-85, SR STAFF MEM, CHEM DIV, OAK RIDGE NAT LAB, 85- *Personal Data:* b Offenbach, Ger, Mar 26, 33; m 59, Elena R Gidekel; c Gustavo E, S Karen & Roberto H. *Educ:* Univ Buenos Aires, Licenciado, 57, Dr en Quimica, 58. *Honors & Awards:* Martin-Marietta Energy Systs Inventor Award, 85. *Prof Exp:* Chemist, Nat Atomic Energy Comn, Arg, 57-60, head lab, 60-63, head div beryllium chem, 63-66. *Concurrent Pos:* Int Atomic Energy Agency fel, 61-63. *Mem:* Am Chem Soc; Sigma Xi; Am Ceramic Soc; fel AAAS. *Res:* Beryllium chemistry; preparation of high purity compounds, solvent extraction, stability of complexes; molten (fluorides) salts physical chemistry; actinide chemistry in molten salts; inorganic chemistry for the development of thermochemical cycles for hydrogen production; nuclear waste chemistry; synthesis of advanced ceramics. *Mailing Add:* Chem & Anal Sci Div Oak Ridge Nat Lab PO Box 2008 Oak Ridge TN 37831-6119

BAMBERGER, CURT, ANTHRAQUINONE INTERMEDIATES & DYES. *Current Pos:* CHEM CONSULT, 71- *Personal Data:* b Stettin, Ger, Jan 8, 00; nat US; m 30; c 2. *Educ:* Univ Wurzburg, PhD(chem), 23. *Prof Exp:* Asst, Univ Wurzburg, 23-25; res chemist, I G Farbenindust AG, Works Elberfeld & Leverkusen, 25-39; res & develop chemist, Union Chimique Belge, Brussels, 39-40, Nat Aniline Div, Allied Chem & Dye Corp, 41-42 & Patent Chem, Inc, 43-68; sr res chemist, Morton Chem Co Div, Morton-Norwich Prod Inc, 68-71. *Mem:* Am Chem Soc; fel Am Inst Chemists. *Res:* Inorganic salts and organic pesticides; intermediates and dyestuffs of the anthraquinone series; fast wool dyes; vat dyes; fast pigments; oil soluble colors dyestuffs for plastics; fluorescent dyes of the anthraquinone series. *Mailing Add:* 1050 George St Apt 11-L New Brunswick NJ 08901

BAMBURG, JAMES ROBERT, BIOCHEMISTRY, NEUROSCIENCES. *Current Pos:* from asst prof to assoc prof, Colo State Univ, 71-81, interim chmn dept, 82-85 & 88-89, assoc dir neurol growth develop, 86-90, dir neurol growth develop, 90-96, PROF BIOCHEM, COLO STATE UNIV, 81-, ASSOC CHAIR BIOCHEM, 96- *Personal Data:* b Chicago, Ill, Aug 20, 43; m 70, 85, Laurie S Minamide; c Eric & Leslie. *Educ:* Univ Ill, Urbana, BS, 65; Univ Wis-Madison, PhD(biochem), 69. *Prof Exp:* From res asst biochem to res assoc physiol chem, Univ Wis-Madison, 65-69; fel biochem, Med Sch, Stanford Univ, 69-71. *Concurrent Pos:* Acad coordr, Grad Prog Cellular & Molecular Biol, Colo State Univ, 75-76, chmn elect, 82; vis scientist, MRC Lab Molecular Biol, Univ Postgrad Med Sch, Cambridge, Eng, 78-79; J S Guggenheim Mem fel, 78-79; vis scientist, M R C Cell Biophys, London, Eng & sr int fel, Fogarty Ctr, 85-86, 92-93; W Evans vis fel, Univ Otago, Dunedin, NZ, 91; vis scientist, Children's Med Res Inst, Sydney, Australia, 92-93. *Mem:* Sigma Xi; Am Chem Soc; Int Soc Neurochem; Am Soc Cell Biol; Am Soc Biol Chem & Molecular Biol. *Res:* Structural and functional role of microtubules, microfilaments and other proteins on the processes of nerve growth, cytoplasmic transport, secretion and mitosis. *Mailing Add:* Dept Biochem Colo State Univ Ft Collins CO 80523. *E-Mail:* jbamburg@vines.colostate.edu

BAME, SAMUEL JARVIS, JR, SPACE PHYSICS. *Current Pos:* Mem staff, Space Physics Group, 51-80, LAB FEL, SPACE PLASMA GROUP, LOS ALAMOS NAT LAB, 80- *Personal Data:* b Lexington, NC, Jan 12, 24; m 56; c 3. *Educ:* Univ NC, BS, 47; Rice Univ, AM, 49, PhD(physics), 51. *Concurrent Pos:* Prin investr, Int Sun Earth Explorer Mission & Ulysses Int Solar Polar Mission. *Mem:* Fel AAAS; fel Am Phys Soc; fel Am Geophys Union; Am Astron Soc. *Res:* Light particle reactions; neutron physics; particles and radiations in space. *Mailing Add:* 164 Dos Brazos Los Alamos Nat Lab Los Alamos NM 87544

BAMFORD, ROBERT WENDELL, ECONOMIC GEOLOGY, GEOCHEMISTRY. *Current Pos:* CONSULT, 80- *Personal Data:* b Glendale, Calif, July 13, 37. *Educ:* Univ Wash, BSc, 59; Stanford Univ, PhD(geol geochem), 70. *Prof Exp:* Res chem engr by-prod chem res, Ga Pac Corp, 60-63; res geologist geol & geochem res, 70, chief site geologist ore deposit eval, 71, sr res geologist geol & geochem, Kennecott Explor, Inc, 72-77; sr geochemist & proj mgr geochem res, Earth Sci Lab, Univ Utah Res Inst, 77-80. *Concurrent Pos:* Consult specializing in applns & technique develop for mineral & geothermal explor, 77- *Mem:* Soc Econ Geologists; Geol Soc Am; Mineral Soc Am; Soc Mining Engrs; Am Inst Mining & Metall Engrs. *Res:* Development of ore deposit and geothermal system empirical models, chemical and mineralogical, and of new or refined techniques in exploration geochemistry. *Mailing Add:* 2315 26th Ave E Seattle WA 98112

BAMFORTH, BETTY JANE, ANESTHESIOLOGY. *Current Pos:* assoc prof, 54-64, actg chmn dept, 69-71, PROF ANESTHESIOL, SCH MED, UNIV WIS, MADISON, 64-, ASST DEAN EDUC ADMIN, 73- *Personal Data:* b New Britain, Conn, Jan 20, 23. *Educ:* Bates Col, BS, 44; Boston Univ, MD, 47. *Prof Exp:* Intern, Mt Auburn Hosp, 48; resident, Univ Wis Hosp, 51; asst prof anesthesiol, Sch Med, Univ Okla, 51-54. *Concurrent Pos:* Consult, Madison Vet Admin Hosp, 54-; mem anesthetic & respiratory adv comt, Food & Drug Admin, 73- *Mem:* Am Soc Anesthesiol; Int Anesthesia Res Soc; Asn Univ Anesthesiol. *Res:* Medical education. *Mailing Add:* Univ Hosps Clins Univ Wis 600 Highland Ave Madison WI 53792-0001

BAMFORTH, STUART SHOOSMITH, PROTOZOOLOGY. *Current Pos:* from instr to assoc prof, 57-72, PROF BIOL, NEWCOMB COL, TULANE UNIV, 72- *Personal Data:* b White Plains, NY, Oct 23, 26; m 52; c 2. *Educ:* Temple Univ, AB, 51; Univ Pa, AM, 54, PhD(zool), 57. *Prof Exp:* Asst instr biol, Univ Pa, 51-57. *Mem:* Am Soc Zoologists; Soc Study Evolution; Soc Protozool; Am Soc Limnol & Oceanog; Sigma Xi. *Res:* Ecology of protozoa and plankton. *Mailing Add:* EEO Biol Dept Tulane Univ New Orleans LA 70118

BAMRICK, JOHN FRANCIS, BIOLOGY, GENETICS. *Current Pos:* From instr to assoc prof biol, 55-70, PROF BIOL, LARAS COL, 70- *Personal Data:* b Rockwell, Iowa, Dec 15, 26; m 56; c 3. *Educ:* Loras Col, BS, 53; Marquette Univ, MS, 56; Iowa State Univ, PhD(zool), 60. *Mem:* AAAS; Soc Invert Path; Sigma Xi. *Res:* Disease resistance; insect pathology. *Mailing Add:* Dept Biol Laras Col 1450 Alta Vista Dubuque IA 52003

BAN, STEPHEN DENNIS, TRANSPORT PHENOMENA, PROCESS RESEARCH. *Current Pos:* vpres, Gas Reg Inst, 81-85, sr vpres res & develop opers, 85-86, exec vpres, 86-87, PRES & CHIEF EXEC OFFICER, GAS RES INST, CHICAGO, 87- *Personal Data:* b Gary, Ind, Dec 16, 40; m 66; c 3. *Educ:* Rose Polytech Inst, BSME, 62; Case Inst Technol, MSME, 64, PhD(fluid, thermal & aero sci eng), 67. *Prof Exp:* Res engr, Battelle Mem Inst, 67-68, sr res engr, 68-69, sr proj leader, 69-70, assoc chief, Fluid & Gas Dynamics Div, 70-71, chief, 71-77; dir & vpres res & develop, Develop & Testing Lab, Bituminous Mat Co, 77-80. *Concurrent Pos:* Adj prof mech eng, Rose Hulman Inst Technol, 80- *Mem:* Am Inst Aeronaut & Astronaut; Sigma Xi. *Res:* Fluid mechanics; heat transfer in gases and liquids; singular parabolic differential equations; boundary layer mechanics; applying research and development to real industrial processes; gas utilization technology, cooperative research management. *Mailing Add:* 8600 W Bryn Mawr Gas Res Inst 11th floor Chicago IL 60631

BAN, THOMAS ARTHUR, PSYCHOPHARMACOLOGY, PSYCHIATRIC NOSOLOGY. *Current Pos:* PROF PSYCHIAT, VANDERBILT UNIV, 76- *Personal Data:* b Budapest, Hungary, Nov 16, 29; Can citizen; m 63, Joan E Valley; c Christopher. *Educ:* Med Univ Budapest, MD, 54; McGill Univ, dipl, 60. *Honors & Awards:* McNeil Award, Can Psychiat Asn. *Prof Exp:* Demonstr, McGill Univ, 60-63, lectr, 64-65, asst prof, 65-70, assoc prof psychiat, 71-76, dir div psychopharmacol, Dept Psychiat, 70-76. *Mem:* AAAS; Am Psychiat Asn; fel Am Col Neuro-Psychopharmacol; Collegium Int Neuro-Psychopharmacologicum; Am Psychopath Asn. *Res:* Psychopharmacology and the classification of psychiatric disorders; composite diagnostic evaluation of psychiatric disorders. *Mailing Add:* 2304 Valley Brook Rd Nashville TN 37215

BAN, VLADIMIR SINISA, SOLID STATE SCIENCE, TIBEROPHIC DEVICES. *Current Pos:* PRES, PD-LD INC, PRINCETON, 93- *Personal Data:* b Bjelovar, Croatia, Sept 7, 41; US citizen; m, Edith Sayer; c Sasha & Sophie. *Educ:* Univ Zagreb, dipl Eng, 64; Pa State Univ, PhD(solid state sci), 69. *Prof Exp:* Res asst solid state sci, Mat Res Lab, Pa State Univ, 64-69; mem tech staff solid state sci, Mat Res Lab, RCA Lab, Princeton, NJ, 69-79, group head, Videodisc Mat & Diag, 79-84; exec vpres, Epitaxx Inc, Princeton, 84-93. *Concurrent Pos:* Vis fel, Imp Col, Univ London, 72. *Mem:* Electrochem Soc; Am Crystal Growth Soc; Sigma Xi; Mat Res Soc; Am Chem Soc. *Res:* Chemical vapor deposition of semiconducting films; fundamental research on thermodynamics and kinetics of vapor deposition of semiconductors and the subsequent optimization of their synthesis; laser solid interactions; high temperature mass spectrometry; videodisc materials; polymer surfaces; fiber optic components; science entrepreneur; started two successful high-tech companies. *Mailing Add:* 1061 The Great Rd Princeton NJ 08540

BANAKAR, UMESH VIRUPAKSH, PHARMACEUTICAL TECHNOLOGY, DRUG PRODUCT DEVELOPMENT & CLINICAL DRUG DEVELOPMENT. *Current Pos:* PROF PHARMACEUT TECHNOL, ST LOUIS COL PHARM, 90- *Personal Data:* b Solapur, India, Dec 4, 56; m 84, Suneeta Kaura; c Kapil. *Educ:* Bombay Univ, India, BPharm, 78; Duquesne Univ, Pittsburgh, PhD(pharmaceut sci), 85. *Honors & Awards:* Keck Award, 86; Pete Ellerbeck Mem Award, 88; Kenetick Award, 89; Foxmeyer Award, 94. *Prof Exp:* Prod chemist trainee, Roussel Pharmaceut Ltd, Bombay, 78-79; lectr pharmaceut technol, J N Med Col, India, 80; instr-in-charge, Sch Pharm, Duquesne Univ, Pittsburgh, 81-84; assoc prof pharmaceut sci, Sch Pharm, Creighton Univ, 85-90. *Concurrent Pos:* Book rev ed, BioPharm Mfg J, 87; expert, WHO, 87-; mem, Int Exec Serv Corps, 89-; dir res, St Louis Col Pharm, St Louis, 90-96. *Mem:* Am Asn Pharmaceut Scientists; Sigma Xi; Am Pharmaceut Asn; Am Asn Cols Pharm. *Res:* Controlled release technology; pharmaceutical product development; dissolution technology; bioavailability-bioequivalence; transdermal drug delivery; prolonged release pharmaceuticals; biopharmaceutics; novel drug delivery systems; pharmaceutical technology; technology transfer through education. *Mailing Add:* St Louis Col Pharm 4588 Parkview Pl St Louis MO 63110. *Fax:* 314-367-2784, 527-2203

BANASCHEWSKI, BERNHARD, MATHEMATICS. *Current Pos:* chmn, 61-67 & 82-87, PROF, DEPT MATH, MCMASTER UNIV, 55- *Personal Data:* b Munich, Ger, 26. *Educ:* Hamburg Univ, Dr Res Nat (math), 53. *Prof Exp:* Asst, Dept Math, Hamburg Univ, 53-55. *Mem:* Fel Royal Soc Can; Nat Sci & Eng Res Coun Can. *Res:* Mathematics. *Mailing Add:* McMaster Univ BSB Rm 227 1280 Main St McMaster Univ Hamilton ON L8S 4K1 Can

BANASIAK, DENNIS STEPHEN, ORGANIC CHEMISTRY, AGRICULTURAL CHEMICALS. *Current Pos:* Res chemist, Phillips Petrol Co, 77-81, mkt develop mgr, Phillips Chem Co, 82-85, MGR TECHNOL PLANNING, PHILLIPS PETROL CO, 93- *Personal Data:* b Chicago, Ill, June 3, 50; m 73; c 2. *Educ:* DePaul Univ, BS, 72; Iowa State Univ, PhD(org chem), 77. *Concurrent Pos:* Mgr, Enzymes & Pheromone Prog, Provesta Corp, 85-88; pres, Agrisense, 88-93. *Mem:* Am Chem Soc; Am Mgt Asn; Am Semiochemicals Asn; Entom Soc Am. *Res:* Organometallic chemistry, organosilicon chemistry, biotechnology, enzymatic chemistry, agricultural chemicals, specialty chemicals and fermentation chemicals. *Mailing Add:* 2740 Braddock Bartlesville OK 74006

BANASIK, ORVILLE JAMES, BIOCHEMISTRY. *Current Pos:* RETIRED. *Personal Data:* b Wales, NDak, Nov 17, 19; m 47; c 4. *Educ:* NDak State Univ, BS, 43, MS, 46. *Prof Exp:* Lab asst & fel, NDak State Univ, 46-47, asst cereal technologist, 47-58, assoc cereal technologist, 58-63, assoc prof cereal technol, 63-70, prof cereal chem & technol, 70-85, chmn dept, 71-85. *Mem:* Am Asn Cereal Chem; Am Soc Brewing Chem; Sigma Xi; Am Chem Soc. *Res:* Cereal research, especially barley; development of testing methods and basic research; durum wheat and pasta quality research. *Mailing Add:* 2406 Tenth St N Fargo ND 58102

BANASZAK, LEONARD JEROME, CRYSTALLOGRAPHY, BIOCHEMISTRY. *Current Pos:* Asst prof physiol & biophys, 66-71, assoc prof biol chem, 71-75, PROF BIOL CHEM, SCH MED, WASH UNIV, 75- *Personal Data:* b Milwaukee, Wis, Feb 1, 33; m; c 4. *Educ:* Univ Wis, Madison, BS, 55; Loyola Univ, Chicago, MS, 60, PhD(biochem), 61. *Concurrent Pos:* USPHS fels biochem, Ind Univ, 61-63 & Med Res Coun Lab Molecular Biol, Eng, 63-65; USPHS career develop award, 69-74. *Mem:* AAAS; Am Chem Soc; Am Crystallog Asn. *Res:* Structure of enzymes and the relationship of these structures to biological function. *Mailing Add:* Dept Biochem 4-225 Millard Wash Univ Sch Med 435 Delaware St Minneapolis MN 55455-0347

BANAUGH, ROBERT PETER, COMPUTER SCIENCES, GEOPHYSICS. *Current Pos:* dir, Comput Ctr, 64-72, chmn dept, 67-80, PROF COMPUT SCI, UNIV MONT, 64- *Personal Data:* b Los Angeles, Calif, Oct 27, 22; m 46; c 8. *Educ:* Univ Calif, Berkeley, AB, 46, MA, 52, PhD(eng sci), 62. *Prof Exp:* High sch teacher, Calif, 47-50; mathematician, Calif Res & Develop Corp, 52-54; aeronaut engr, Pioneer Industs, Nev, 54-55; theoret physicist, Lawrence Radiation Lab, Univ Calif, 55-62; head appl math group, Ventura Div, Northrop Corp, 62-64. *Concurrent Pos:* Consult, Air Force Shock Tube Facility, Univ NMex, 65-66, Boeing Co, 65-68, Appl Theory, Inc, 70-76 & USDA, Forest Serv, 75-; vis prof, Col Natural Resources, Univ Calif, Berkeley, 78-79; vis prof, Dept Comput Sci, Univ Wollongong, Wollongong, Australia, 85-86. *Mem:* AAAS; Am Geophys Union; Seismol Soc Am. *Res:* Computer based methods of analysis of biological and physical systems; educational uses of computers in science; computer modeling; computational methods in linear and nonlinear ware interaction phenomena; quantitative ecology. *Mailing Add:* 9401 Upper Miller Creek Rd Missoula MT 59803

BANAVAR, JAYANTH RAMARAO, STATISTICAL PHYSICS, COMPUTATIONAL PHYSICS. *Current Pos:* assoc prof physics & mat res, 88-91, PROF PHYSICS, PA STATE UNIV, 91- *Personal Data:* b Bangalore, Karnataka, India, Oct 8, 53; m 82, Suchitra; c Samhita. *Educ:* Bangalore Univ, India, BSc Hons, 72, MSc, 74; Univ Pittsburgh, MS, 75, PhD(physics), 78. *Prof Exp:* Res assoc physics, Univ Chicago, 78-81; mem tech staff, Bell Labs,

81-83; mem prof staff, Schlumberger-Doll Res, 83-88. *Concurrent Pos:* Vis prof, Univ Paris & Univ Padova; Fulbright fel, 95; vis scientist, NEC Res. *Mem:* Fel Am Phys Soc. *Res:* Theoretical condensed matter physics; statistical mechanics. *Mailing Add:* Dept Physics Davey Lab Pa State Univ University Park PA 16802. *Fax:* 814-865-3604; *E-Mail:* jayanth@phys.psu.edu

BANAY-SCHWARTZ, MIRIAM, BIOCHEMISTRY, ORGANIC CHEMISTRY. *Current Pos:* SR RES SCIENTIST, NY STATE RES INST NEUROCHEM & DRUG ADDICTION, 68- *Personal Data:* b Sibiu, Rumania, Oct 9, 29; US citizen; m 51; c 2. *Educ:* Hebrew Univ, Jerusalem, MSc, 54, PhD(biochem), 61. *Prof Exp:* Instr biochem, 62-68, ASST PROF BIOCHEM, ALBERT EINSTEIN COL MED, 68- *Mem:* Am Soc Neurochem; Int Soc Neurochem; NY Acad Sci; Am Inst Chemists. *Res:* Electron transport; intermediate metabolism. *Mailing Add:* Ctr Neurochem The Nathan S Kline Inst Psychiat Res Orangeburg NY 10962

BANCHERO, J(ULIUS) T(HOMAS), PROCESS DESIGN. *Current Pos:* prof & head dept, 59-79, EMER PROF CHEM ENG, UNIV NOTRE DAME, 81- *Personal Data:* b New York, NY, June 18, 14; wid; c Julia A, Mary G & Barbara A. *Educ:* Columbia Univ, AB, 33, BS, 35, ChE, 36; Univ Mich, PhD(chem eng), 50. *Prof Exp:* Chem engr prod dept, Carbide & Carbon Chem Corp, 36-38; instr, Univ Detroit, 38-41; from instr chem eng to prof, Univ Mich, 43-59. *Mem:* Am Chem Soc; Am Inst Chem Engrs; Am Soc Eng Educ. *Res:* Kinetics of epoxide-alcohol reactions; chemical engineering process design. *Mailing Add:* 202 S Jacob St South Bend IN 46615-1002

BANCHERO, NATALIO, CARDIOVASCULAR RESPIRATORY PHYSIOLOGY. *Current Pos:* PROF PHYSIOL, SCH MED, UNIV COLO, 77- *Personal Data:* b Lima, Peru, June 6, 35. *Educ:* San Marcos Univ, MD, 62. *Mem:* Am Physiol Soc; Int Soc Oxygen Transport Tissues; Microcirulatory Soc; Soc Exp Biol & Med. *Mailing Add:* Dept Physiol Univ Colo Health Sci Ctr C240 4200 E Ninth Ave Denver CO 80262-0001

BANCROFT, DENNISON, physics, for more information see previous edition

BANCROFT, GEORGE MICHAEL, PHYSICAL INORGANIC CHEMISTRY. *Current Pos:* from asst prof to assoc prof, 70-74, PROF CHEM, UNIV WESTERN ONT, 74-, CHMN, 86- *Personal Data:* b Saskatoon, Sask, Apr 3, 42; m 67, Joan MacFarlane; c David & Catherine. *Educ:* Univ Man, BSc, 63, MSc, 64; Univ Cambridge, PhD(chem), 67. *Hon Degrees:* MA & ScD, Univ Cambridge, 70. *Honors & Awards:* Harrison Mem Prize, Brit Chem Soc, 72; Meldola Medal, Royal Inst Chem, 72; Rutherford Medal, Royal Soc Can, 80; Alcan Lectr Award, Can Soc Chem, 90; Herzberg Award, Can Spectros Soc, 92; Medal, Chem Inst Can, 96. *Prof Exp:* Demonstr & teaching fel chem, Univ Cambridge, 67-70. *Concurrent Pos:* Prin investr, NASA, 70-72; E W Steacie mem fel, Nat Res Coun Can, 73-76; vis investr, Phys Sci Lab, Univ Wis, 75-76; mem, Int Comn Applns Mossbauer Effect, 75-; Guggenheim fel, 82-83. *Mem:* The Chem Soc; Chem Inst Can; Am Chem Soc; fel Royal Soc Can. *Res:* High resolution photoelectron auger and absorption spectroscopy of inorganic and organometallic gases using resonance lamps and synchrotron radiation; adsorption and leaching of ions from minerals and glasses with particular application to nuclear waste disposal; NAXAFS, EXAFS of coals and antiwear films. *Mailing Add:* Dept Chem Univ Western Ont London ON N6A 5B8 Can

BANCROFT, HAROLD RAMSEY, ENTOMOLOGY. *Current Pos:* Asst prof, 62-66, ASSOC PROF BIOL, MEMPHIS STATE UNIV, 66- *Personal Data:* b Meridian, Miss, May 3, 32; m 59, Bettye J McCaskill; c Harold & Pamela D (Morrow). *Educ:* Miss State Univ, BS, 58, MS, 59, PhD(entom), 62. *Concurrent Pos:* Consult entomologist, Univ Memphis. *Mem:* Entom Soc Am; Am Registry Prof Entomologists. *Res:* Insect resistance to pesticides; pest control research. *Mailing Add:* Dept Biol Univ Memphis Memphis TN 38152

BANCROFT, JOHN BASIL, BIOLOGY. *Current Pos:* prof plant sci & chmn dept, 73-78, DEAN SCI & FAC SCI, UNIV WESTERN ONT, 78- *Personal Data:* b Vancouver, BC, Can, Dec 31, 29; m 54; c 4. *Educ:* Univ BC, BA, 52; Univ Wis, PhD(plant path), 55. *Prof Exp:* From asst prof to prof bot & plant path, Purdue Univ, 55-70; prof & head, John Innes Inst, 70-73. *Mem:* Am Phytopath Soc; fel Royal Soc Can; Sigma Xi. *Res:* Biological and biophysical characteristics of certain simple plant viruses and their assembly. *Mailing Add:* 21 Scarlett Ave London ON N6G 1Z3 Can. *Fax:* 519-661-3935

BANCROFT, LEWIS CLINTON, ELECTRICAL ENGINEERING. *Current Pos:* RETIRED. *Personal Data:* b Reading, Mass, Jan 1, 29; m 51, 62, Shirley Simonton; c Stephen, Ellen, Betsey, Thomas, Jay, Donald Foster, Fay (Felty) & Frances (Fosselman). *Educ:* Princeton Univ, BSE, 50, MSE, 52. *Prof Exp:* Res mgt, Nuclear Reactor Instrumentation, Microwave Heating, Photopolymer & Silver Halide Chem, E I Du Pont de Nemours & Co, 51-83, mgr, Patents & Contracts, DuPont Photosystems & Electronic Prods, 83-85. *Concurrent Pos:* Sayre Fel, Princeton Univ, 51. *Mem:* Sigma Xi. *Res:* Physics and chemistry of magnetic recording materials, especially chromium dioxide. *Mailing Add:* 12 Red Oak Rd Wilmington DE 19806

BANCROFT, RICHARD WOLCOTT, AEROSPACE PHYSIOLOGY. *Current Pos:* RETIRED. *Personal Data:* b Denver, Colo, Mar 28, 16; m 87, Ivy E Walker. *Educ:* Stanford Univ, BA, 38; Univ Southern Calif, MS, 47, PhD(physiol), 51. *Prof Exp:* Res asst aviation physiol, Sch Aerospace Med, US Air Force, 47-48, physiologist, 50-68, chief, Appl Physiol Br, 68-72. *Mem:* Fel Aerospace Med Asn; Am Physiol Soc; Soc Exp Biol & Med; fel Royal Soc Med London. *Res:* Aerospace physiology; respiration; circulation. *Mailing Add:* 1022 E Southwind Lane Unit 1064 Scottsdale AZ 85262-4667

BAND, DAVID LOUIS, HIGH ENERGY ASTROPHYSICS. *Current Pos:* ASST RES PHYSICIST, CTR ASTROPHYS & SPACE SCI, UNIV CALIF, SAN DIEGO, 91- *Personal Data:* b Boston, Mass, Jan 9, 57; m 79, Debra B Levy; c Zvi & Gabriel. *Educ:* Mass Inst Technol, BS, 79; Harvard Univ, MA, 80, PhD(physics), 85. *Prof Exp:* Fel, Inst Geophys & Planetary Physics, Lawrence Livermore Nat Lab, 85-88, Dept Astron, Univ Calif, Berkeley, 88-90. *Res:* Spectroscopy of gamma ray bursts. *Mailing Add:* CASS0111 Univ CalifSan Diego 9500 Gilman Dr La Jolla CA 92093-0111. *Fax:* 619-534-2294; *E-Mail:* dlbbat@cass09.ucsd.edu

BAND, HANS EDUARD, PHYSICS, ATOMIC & MOLECULAR PHYSICS. *Current Pos:* RETIRED. *Personal Data:* b Vienna, Austria, Oct 14, 24; US citizen; m 48, Elizabeth Harford; c Richard, Charles & Peter. *Educ:* Harvard Univ, AB, 47; Boston Univ, AM, 53. *Prof Exp:* Elec engr, Gen Elec Co, 48-52; mem staff, Lincoln Lab, Mass Inst Technol, 52-53; lit analyst, Gillette Safety Razor Co, 53-56; sr res engr, Melpar, Inc, 56-57; opers analyst, Tech Opers, Inc, 57-58; staff physicist, Pickard & Burns, Inc, 58-61; sr res scientist, Raytheon Co, 61-63; optical physicist, Concord Radiance Lab, Utah State Univ, 63-66; prin res scientist, Avco Everett Res Lab, Mass, 66-67; physicist, Army Mat & Mech Res Ctr, 68-80, electronics engr, US Army Electronics Command, 80-83; electronics engr, USAF, 83-87, Defense Logistics Agency, 87-89, Electronic Systs Div, 89-90. *Concurrent Pos:* Math & physics tutor, Middlesex Community Col, 90- *Mem:* Am Phys Soc; Am Sci Affil. *Res:* Optical and radiation physics; atomic spectroscopy; radio communication; solid state physics; materials science and electronics engineering. *Mailing Add:* 22 Reeves Rd Bedford MA 01730-1335

BAND, PIERRE ROBERT, MEDICAL ONCOLOGY. *Current Pos:* AT CANCER CONTROL AGENCY, BC. *Personal Data:* b Paris, France, June 23, 35; Can citizen; m 60; c 4. *Educ:* Col Stanislas Montreal, BA, 57; Univ Montreal, MD, 62; FRCP(C), 68. *Prof Exp:* Assoc prof, Dept Med, Univ Alta, 70-76; dir clin res oncol, Inst Cancer Montreal, 76-; prof med, Univ Montreal, 76- *Concurrent Pos:* McEachern fel, Can, 64-65; NIH fel, 67-68; prin investr, Eastern Coop Oncol Group, 71-; mem, Breast Cancer Task Force, Combination Chemother Subcomt, NIH, 73-74; prin investr, Europ Orgn Res & Treat Cancer, 73-; chmn, Working Group Lung Cancer, Cancer Res Coord Comt, Can, 77- *Mem:* Am Asn Cancer Res; Am Soc Clin Oncol; Int Asn Study Lung Cancer. *Res:* Phase I-II-III investigation of antineoplastic agents; epidemiology of lung cancer in uranium workers. *Mailing Add:* Environ Health Ctr Rm 109 Health Protection Br Health Canada Tunney's Pasture Ottawa ON V5Z 4E6 Can

BAND, RUDOLPH NEAL, ZOOLOGY. *Current Pos:* from asst prof to assoc prof, 63-69, PROF ZOOL, MICH STATE UNIV, 69- *Personal Data:* b Oakland, Calif, Aug 2, 29; m 55. *Educ:* Univ San Francisco, BS, 52, MS, 54; Univ Calif, Berkeley, PhD(zool), 59. *Prof Exp:* NIH fel, Amherst Col, 58-59; from instr to asst prof, 59-63. *Concurrent Pos:* USPHS spec res fel, physiol lab, Cambridge Univ, 65-66 & Dept Zool, Univ Calif, Berkeley, 72-73. *Mem:* Soc Protozool; Am Soc Parasitol; Am Soc Cell Biologists. *Res:* Biochemistry and physiology of protozoan organelles; locomotion; phagocytosis; physiology and biochemistry of amoebae. *Mailing Add:* Dept Zool Mich State Univ East Lansing MI 48823

BAND, WILLIAM, physics; deceased, see previous edition for last biography

BAND, YEHUDA BENZION, ATOMIC PHYSICS, QUANTUM PHYSICS. *Current Pos:* PROF, DEPT CHEM, BEN-GURION UNIV, 78- *Personal Data:* b Munich, Ger, Dec 1, 46; US citizen; m 70; c 4. *Educ:* Cooper Union, BS, 68; Univ Chicago, MS, 70, PhD(physics), 73. *Honors & Awards:* Allied-Signal Inventor Award. *Prof Exp:* Fel chem physics, Univ Chicago, 73-75; asst scientist physics, Argonne Nat Lab, 75-78. *Concurrent Pos:* Res scientist, Allied-Signal Inc; Barecha fel, outstanding young scientists, 78-81. *Mem:* Am Inst Physics; fel Am Phys Soc; Israel Chem Soc. *Res:* Collision theory; charge exchange processes; dissociation of molecules; surface phenomena; many body physics; laser physics; nonlinear optics; transport processes. *Mailing Add:* Dept Chem Ben-Gurion Univ Beer-Sheva Israel. *E-Mail:* band@bgumail.bgu.ac.il

BANDA, SIVA S, CONTROL SYSTEMS. *Current Pos:* AEROSPACE ENGR, FLIGHT CONTROL, FLIGHT DYNAMICS LAB, WRIGHT PATTERSON AFB, OHIO, 81-, CHIEF, CONTROL DYNAMICS BR, WRIGHT LAB, 94- *Personal Data:* b Vijayawada, India, Mar 28, 51; US citizen; m 94, Erna Kuhn; c Kevin, Ryan Moore & Erin Moore. *Educ:* Regional Eng Col, Warangal, India, BS, 74; Indian Inst Sci, Bangalore, MS, 76; Wright State Univ, Ohio, MS, 78; Univ Dayton, PhD(aerospace eng), 80. *Concurrent Pos:* Adj assoc prof elec eng & adj asst prof math, Wright State Univ, 78-89; mgr, Air Force Basic Res Task 2304N2, 84-; adj assoc prof aerospace eng, Univ Dayton, 88-90; fel, Wright lab, Wright-Patterson AFB. *Mem:* Assoc fel Am Inst Aeronaut & Astronaut; Inst Elec & Electronics Engrs. *Res:* Reconfigurable flight control; tailless aircraft control and control of uninhabited aerial vehicles. *Mailing Add:* WL/FIGC Wright Patterson AFB OH 45433

BANDEEN, WILLIAM REID, METEOROLOGY, SPACE SCIENCE. *Current Pos:* RETIRED. *Personal Data:* b Escanaba, Mich, Oct 11, 26; m 60, Joan Sleeper; c Kevin, Karen & Keith. *Educ:* US Mil Acad, BS, 48; NY Univ, MS, 55. *Prof Exp:* Meteorologist, Meteorol Br, NASA, 59-65, head Planetary Radiations Br, 65-72, asst chief, Lab Meteorol & Earth Sci, 72-74, chief, Atmospheric & Hydrospheric Appln Div, 74-77, assoc chief, Lab Atmospheric Sci, 77-86, assoc dir, Space & Earth Sci, Goddard Space Flight Ctr, 86-89. *Mem:* Fel Am Meteorol Soc; fel AAAS; fel Am Geophys Union. *Res:* Radiation budget of the earth from remotely sensed measurements from satellites; remote sensing of atmospheric parameters from space; radiative transfer in the atmosphere. *Mailing Add:* 12 Brinkwood Rd Brookeville MD 20833

BANDEL, HERMAN WILLIAM, PLASMA PHYSICS. *Current Pos:* RETIRED. *Personal Data:* b Great Falls, Mont, Sept 23, 16; m 45. *Educ:* Univ Calif, Berkeley, AB, 47, PhD(physics), 54. *Prof Exp:* Sr engr, Appl Physics Sect, Electron Defence Lab, Sylvania Elec Prod, Inc, 54-57, adv res physicist, Microwave Physics Lab, 57-63; res scientist, Lockheed Missiles & Space Co, 63-76. *Mem:* Am Phys Soc. *Res:* Discharge through gases. *Mailing Add:* 1753 Mayflower Ct Mountain View CA 94040

BANDEL, VERNON ALLAN, AGRONOMY, PLANT PHYSIOLOGY. *Current Pos:* Asst prof soils, 64-69, assoc prof, 69-77, PROF SOILS, UNIV MD, COLLEGE PARK, 77-, EXTEN SOILS SPECIALIST, 64- *Personal Data:* b Baltimore, Md, May 8, 37; m 59; c 2. *Educ:* Univ Md, BS, 59, MS, 63, PhD(agron, soil fertil), 65. *Mem:* Fel Am Soc Agron; Soil Sci Soc Am; Coun Soil Testing & Plant Anal; Am Forage & Grassland Coun. *Res:* Soil fertility; nutrient balance in plants; micro-nutrient fertilization of corn, soybeans; nitrogen fertilization of corn and small grains; no-tillage and conventional tillage corn fertilization; soil test-plant response; nutrient management. *Mailing Add:* 14668 Mustang Path Glenwood MD 21738-9517

BANDER, MYRON, THEORETICAL PHYSICS. *Current Pos:* assoc prof physics, 66-72, dean, Sch Phys Sci, 80-86, PROF PHYSICS, UNIV CALIF, IRVINE, 72- *Personal Data:* b Belzyce, Poland, Dec 11, 37; US citizen; m 67, Carol J Helmberg. *Educ:* Columbia Univ, BA, 58, MA, 59, PhD(physics), 62. *Prof Exp:* NSF fel, 62-63; res assoc theoret physics, Linear Accelerator Ctr, Stanford Univ, 63-66. *Concurrent Pos:* Sloan Found fel, 67-69. *Mem:* Fel Am Phys Soc. *Res:* Elementary particle physics. *Mailing Add:* Dept Physics Univ Calif Irvine CA 92717. *Fax:* 714-824-2174; *E-Mail:* mbander@uci.edu

BANDERET, LOUIS EUGENE, EXPERIMENTAL PSYCHOLOGY & PSYCHOLOGICAL ASSESSMENT, BIOMEDICAL RESEARCH. *Current Pos:* Animal res psychologist, US Army Res Inst Environ Med, 70-75, simulation res psychologist, 76-79, assessment res psychologist, 80-90, RES PSYCHOLOGIST SOLDIER CAPABILITIES, US ARMY RES INST ENVIRON MED, NATICK, MASS, 91- *Personal Data:* b Des Moines, Iowa, Aug 9, 43; m 97, Marilyn Alice Betz; c Paul M, Tanya L & Suszanne M. *Educ:* Concordia Col, BA, 65; Wash State Univ, MS, 68, PhD(exp psychol), 70. *Concurrent Pos:* Sr lectr psychol, Northeastern Univ, 70-, Quinsigamond Community Col, 86-88 & 93-; consult, Enterprise Systs, 93-; grantee, Defense Women's Health Res Prog, 96; co-ed, J Mil Psychol, 97. *Mem:* Sigma Xi. *Res:* Assess the behavior and performance of soldiers and animals exposed to environmental extremes; use of verbal and other responses for noninvasive assessment of active soldiers; biomedical research. *Mailing Add:* Attn: MCMR-UE-MPD US Army Res Inst Environ Med Natick MA 01760-5007. *Fax:* 508-233-4195; *E-Mail:* lbanderet@natick-ccmail.army.mil

BANDES, DEAN, MATHEMATICS, SOFTWARE SYSTEMS. *Current Pos:* MEM STAFF, CREDENCE SYSTS CORP, 88- *Personal Data:* b New York, NY, Jan 16, 1944; m 68; c 2. *Educ:* Williams Col, BS, 65; Brandeis Univ, MA, 67, PhD(math), 74. *Prof Exp:* Asst prof math, Univ Mass, Boston, 74-76; mem staff, Parke Math Labs, 76-79; mem staff, LTX Corp, 79-88. *Res:* Topology-knot theory; computer combinatorics; partitions, transportation problem; ray-tracing; real-time control. *Mailing Add:* 225 Cypress St Newton MA 02159-2226

BANDES, HERBERT, ELECTROCHEMISTRY. *Current Pos:* dean admin affairs, 69-84, ADJ PROF, MANCHESTER COMMUNITY COL, 84- *Personal Data:* b New York, NY, May 23, 14; m; c 3. *Educ:* Univ Mich, BS, 35, MS, 36, PhD(electrochem), 38. *Prof Exp:* Res chemist, Alrose Chem Co, RI, 39; plant chemist, Cohn & Rosenberger, Inc, 40; physicist, Brooklyn Naval Shipyard, Bur Ord, 40-43; electrochemist, Kellex Corp, NY, 43-44; sr engr, Sylvania Elec Prod, Inc, 44-50, mgr chem lab, Cent Res Labs, 50-55, chief engr, Semiconductor Div, 55-58; mem sr staff & dir res, Western Div, Arthur D Little, Inc, 58-63; dir res, Eitel-McCullough, Inc, Calif, 63-65; chief engr, Electronics Dept, Hamilton Stand Div, United Aircraft Corp, 65-69. *Mem:* Am Chem Soc; Electrochem Soc; Sigma Xi. *Res:* Kinetics of electrode reactions; mechanism of electrodeposition; solid state chemistry. *Mailing Add:* 35 London Rd Hebron CT 06248-1028

BANDICK, NEAL RAYMOND, HUMAN PHYSIOLOGY, MEDICAL EDUCATION. *Current Pos:* assoc prof, 70-81, PROF BIOL, ORE COL EDUC, WESTERN ORE STATE COL, 81- *Personal Data:* b Orange, Calif, Mar 29, 38; m 63; c 2. *Educ:* Univ Calif, Davis, BS, 60; Trinity Univ, MS, 65; Univ Mich, EdD(physiol), 70. *Prof Exp:* Instr physiol, Univ Mich, 69-70. *Mem:* Am Physiol Soc. *Res:* Cardiovascular physiology; visco-elastic and contractile properties of arterial walls during hypothermia. *Mailing Add:* Dept Sci & Math Western Ore State Col 345 Monmouth Ave Monmouth OR 97361

BANDLER, JOHN WILLIAM, ELECTRICAL ENGINEERING. *Current Pos:* PRES, OPTIMIZATION SYSTS ASSOCS, 83- *Personal Data:* b Jerusalem, Nov 9, 41; Can citizen; m, Beth M Budd; c Lydia & Zoe. *Educ:* Imperial Col, Univ London, BSc(eng), 63, DIC & PhD, 67. *Hon Degrees:* DSc, Univ London, 76. *Prof Exp:* Engr, elec eng, Mullard Res Labs, Eng, 66-67; lectr & fel, Univ Man, 67-69. *Concurrent Pos:* Assoc ed, IEEE trans on microwave theory and tech, 69-74, guest ed, 74, 92 & 97. *Mem:* Fel Inst Elec & Electronics Engrs; fel Inst Elec Engrs UK; Can Asn Prof Engrs; fel Royal Soc Can; Electromagnetics Acad. *Res:* Integrated circuits and systems; computer-aided design; optimization methods; microwave circuits; engineering design; power systems; CAD/CAE software systems; optimization with tolerances; computer methods; electronic circuit fault diagnosis; author of more than 290 technical papers; engineering design centering. *Mailing Add:* Dept Elec & Comput Eng McMaster Univ Hamilton ON L8S 4L7 Can

BANDMAN, EVERETT, MOLECULAR BIOLOGY. *Current Pos:* fel zool, Univ Calif, Berkeley, 76-78, asst res zoologist, 78-81, from asst prof to assoc prof, 81-90, PROF, UNIV CALIF, DAVIS, 90- *Personal Data:* b New York, NY, June 29, 47; m 82, Elizabeth Burrill; c Sherri L & Evan D. *Educ:* City Col New York, BS, 69; Univ Calif, Berkeley, PhD(molecular biol), 74. *Honors & Awards:* Nat Res Serv Award, NIH, 76; George M Strathearn Mem Res Award, 86. *Prof Exp:* Res fel surg, Mass Gen Hosp, 74-76; fel biochem, Harvard Med Sch, 74-76. *Concurrent Pos:* Res technician biochem, Sloan Kettering Inst, 69; USPHS traineeship, 69-74; fel, Shriner's Burn Inst, 74-76. *Mem:* AAAS; Am Soc Cell Biol; NY Acad Sci; Inst Food Technologists. *Res:* Molecular biology of muscle development; functional analysis of myosin protein diversity. *Mailing Add:* Dept Food Sci & Technol Univ Calif Davis CA 95616

BANDONI, ROBERT JOSEPH, MYCOLOGY. *Current Pos:* from asst prof to EMER PROF MYCOL, UNIV BC, 58- *Personal Data:* b Weeks, Nev, Nov 9, 26; Can citizen; m 88, Alice A Webb; c 1. *Educ:* Univ Nev, BSc, 53; Univ Iowa, MSc, 56, PhD(mycol), 57. *Honors & Awards:* George Lawson Award, Can Bot Asn, 90. *Prof Exp:* Instr, Univ Wichita, 57-58. *Concurrent Pos:* Gertrude S Burlingham fel mycol, New York Bot Garden, 56; vis prof, Fac Sci, Mahidol Univ, Bangkok, 93. *Mem:* Fel Japanese Soc Prom Sci; Mycol Soc Am; Brit Mycol Soc; Japanese Mycol Soc. *Res:* Studies of leaf-decay fungi; taxonomic studies of lower Basidiomycetes; systematic studies of lower basidiomycetes. *Mailing Add:* Bot Dept Univ BC 6270 University Blvd No 3529 Vancouver BC V6T 1Z4 Can. *Fax:* 604-822-6089; *E-Mail:* robert_j.bandoni@mtsg.ubc.ca

BANDRAUK, ANDRE D, THEORETICAL CHEMISTRY, MATHEMATICAL CHEMISTRY. *Current Pos:* from asst prof to assoc prof, 70-80, PROF THEORET CHEM, UNIV SHERBROOKE, 80- *Personal Data:* b Berlin, Ger, 41. *Educ:* Univ Montreal, BSc, 61; Mass Inst Technol, MSc, 63; McMaster Univ, PhD(chem physics), 68. *Honors & Awards:* Herzberg Medal, Can Spectros Soc, 89. *Concurrent Pos:* Killam res fel, Can Coun, 82-84; vis fel, Los Alamos Nat Lab, 83-84. *Mem:* Royal Soc Can; Am Phys Soc; Soc Indust Appl Math; Can Soc Chem. *Res:* Theoretical and Mathematical Chemistry. *Mailing Add:* Chem Dept Sci Fac Univ Sherbrooke Sherbrooke PQ J1K 2R1 Can

BANDURSKI, ROBERT STANLEY, PLANT BIOCHEMISTRY. *Current Pos:* from assoc prof to prof, 54-63, DISTINGUISHED PROF BOT, MICH STATE UNIV, 63- *Personal Data:* b Chicago, Ill, May 11, 24; m 44; c 1. *Educ:* Univ Chicago, BS, 46, PhD(plant physiol), 49. *Hon Degrees:* DSc, Copernicus Univ, Poland, 87. *Prof Exp:* Instr bot, Univ Chicago, 48-49; Nat Res Coun fel biol, Calif Inst Technol, 49-50, res fel, 50-52, sr res fel, 52-53; asst biochem, Mass Gen Hosp, 53-54. *Mem:* Fedn Biol Chem; Am Soc Plant Physiol. *Res:* Plant pigments; respiratory enzymes; auxins; chemistry of plant hormones and enzymes of sulfur metabolism. *Mailing Add:* Dept Bot Mich State Univ East Lansing MI 48824-1312

BANDY, ALAN RAY, ATMOSPHERIC, PHYSICAL & ANALYTICAL CHEMISTRY. *Current Pos:* assoc prof, 75-82, PROF CHEM, DREXEL UNIV, 82- *Personal Data:* b Indiahoma, Okla, Sept 13, 40; m 63; c 4. *Educ:* Okla State Univ, BS & MS, 64; Univ Fla, PhD(chem), 68. *Prof Exp:* Res assoc chem, Univ Md, College Park, 68-70; from asst prof to assoc prof, Old Dom Univ, 70-75. *Mem:* Am Chem Soc; Am Geophhys Union; AAAS. *Res:* Photochemistry of trace atmospheric constituents; atmospheric chemistry of atmospheric sulfur and nitrogen compounds. *Mailing Add:* Dept Chem Drexel Univ 3141 Chestnut St Philadelphia PA 19104-2816

BANDY, PERCY JOHN, ZOOLOGY. *Current Pos:* RETIRED. *Personal Data:* b Mexico City, Mex, Aug 13, 27; Can citizen; m 52; c 3. *Educ:* Univ BC, BA, 52, MA, 55, PhD(zool), 65. *Prof Exp:* Regional wildlife biologist, 58-62, wildlife res biologist, 62-73, asst dir, BC Fish & wildlife Br, 73-88. *Concurrent Pos:* Chmn, Nat Adv Comt Land Capability Classification for Wildlife, 66; chmn, BC Wildlife & Recreation Comt, Can Land Inventory, 66-71: hon lectr fac agr, Univ BC, 67-71, res assoc inst animal resource ecol, 69-71; ed, Fish & Wildlife Publ, 70-73, prog eval, 81-87. *Res:* Wildlife management research of various types including population dynamics, diseases, parasites and nutrition. *Mailing Add:* 4580 Torquay Dr Victoria BC V8N 3L7 Can

BANDYOPADHYAY, AMITABHA, CONSTRUCTION ENGINEERING & MANAGEMENT, CONSTRUCTION PRODUCTIVITY. *Current Pos:* ASSOC PROF & CHMN, STATE UNIV NY, 90- *Personal Data:* b Calcutta, India, Dec 25, 54; US citizen; m 88, Aditi Chattopadhyay. *Educ:* Univ

Calcutta, BEng, 75; Pa State Univ, MS, 87, PhD(civil eng), 91. *Prof Exp:* Struct engr, M N Dastur & Co Ltd, 76-80; lead anal engr, United Engrs & Constructor, 80-84; instr gen eng & civil eng, Pa State Univ, 84-90. *Concurrent Pos:* Consult var construct & eng cos, 84-; prin investr, NY State, 91-93 & 93-95. *Mem:* Am Soc Civil Engrs; Am Soc Eng Educ; NY Acad Sci; AAAS. *Res:* Application of Bayesian statistics in handling uncertainty in construction management, automated field data collection, material testing and construction engineering; expert systems application in construction management; field construction improvement and human factors in construction engineering. *Mailing Add:* Dept Construction Lupton Hall State Univ NY Farmingdale NY 11735. *Fax:* 516-420-2194; *E-Mail:* bandyoa@snyfarva.cc.farmingdale.edu

BANE, GILBERT WINFIELD, MARINE ECOLOGY, BIOLOGICAL OCEANOGRAPHY. *Current Pos:* PROF BIOL, KODIAK COL, 88- *Personal Data:* b San Diego, Calif, Dec 11, 31; m 70; c 3. *Educ:* San Jose State Col, BA, 54; Cornell Univ, MS, 61, PhD(vert zool), 63. *Prof Exp:* From jr scientist to sr scientist, Inter-Am Trop Tuna Comn, 55-58; scientist, Starkist Foods, Inc, 59-60; lab asst vert zool, Conserv Dept, Cornell Univ, 60-63; asst prof marine biol, Univ PR, Mayaguez, 63-65 & Univ Calif, Irvine, 65-69; assoc prof, Southampton Col, LI Univ, 69-73; chmn marine & natural sci, St Francis Col, Maine, 73-75; dir marine sci & environ studies, Univ NC, Wilmington, 75-80; dir marine sci wetland res, La Univ, 80-88. *Concurrent Pos:* Danforth assoc, Danforth Found, 68. *Mem:* Am Fisheries Soc; Am Soc Ichthyol & Herpet; Am Soc Mammal; Am Soc Limnol & Oceanog; Am Soc Zool. *Res:* Biology and population studies of marine fishes, especially sharks; environmental stresses on coastal fishes, especially offshore petroleum operations and coastal nuclear facilities; fishes of southern Mexico. *Mailing Add:* Dept Biol Kodiak Col 117 Benny Benson Dr Kodiak AK 99615

BANE, JOHN MCGUIRE, JR, PHYSICAL OCEANOGRAPHY. *Current Pos:* from asst prof to assoc prof phys oceanog & physics, 76-86, PROF PHYS OCEANOG, GEOL & ENVIRON SCI ENG, UNIV NC, CHAPEL HILL, 87- *Personal Data:* b Kalamazoo, Mich, May 3, 46; m 93, Sharon McBride; c Jeffrey, Darcy & Shannon. *Educ:* Western Mich Univ, BS, 70; Fla Atlantic Univ, ME, 71; Fla State Univ, PhD(phys oceanog), 75. *Mem:* Am Geophys Union; Am Meteorol Soc; Oceanog Soc. *Res:* Theoretical and observational studies of western boundary current dynamics and ocean circulation; air-sea interaction; coastal meteorology; aircraft environmental sensing systems. *Mailing Add:* Dept Marine Sci Univ NC Chapel Hill NC 27599-3300. *Fax:* 919-962-1259; *E-Mail:* bane@marine.unc.edu

BANERJEE, AMIYA KUMAR, BIOCHEMISTRY, MOLECULAR BIOLOGY. *Current Pos:* from asst mem to mem molecular biol, 70-87, CHMN, DEPT MOLECULAR BIOL, ROCHE INST MOLECULAR BIOL, 87-; VCHMN, RES INST, CLEVELAND CLIN FOUND, 90-; PROF, DEPT BIOCHEM, CASE WESTERN RES UNIV, CLEVELAND, OHIO, 93- *Personal Data:* b Rangoon, Burma, May 3, 36; nat US; m 65, Sipra Datta; c Antara & Arjun. *Educ:* Univ Calcutta, BS, 55, MS, 58, PhD(biochem), 64. *Hon Degrees:* DSc, Univ Calcutta, 70. *Honors & Awards:* Phoebe Weinstein Award, Negative Strand Virus Res, 77. *Prof Exp:* Res assoc molecular biology, Albert Einstein Col Med, 66-69. *Concurrent Pos:* Vis prof, Wellcome Found, 92. *Mem:* Am Soc Microbiol; AAAS; Harvey Soc; Am Soc Biochem & Molecular Biol; Am Soc Virol; NY Acad Sci. *Res:* Gene expression of negative strand RNA viruses using vesicular stomatitis virus and human parainfluenza virus as prototype viruses; studies on the structure and function of the virion- associated RNA polymerase. *Mailing Add:* Dept Molecular Biol Res Inst Cleveland Clin Found 9500 Euclid Ave Cleveland OH 44195-0001. *Fax:* 216-444-0512; *E-Mail:* banerja@ccsmtp.ccf.org

BANERJEE, CHANDRA MADHAB, RESPIRATORY PHYSIOLOGY. *Current Pos:* prof, 74-95, EMER PROF PHYSIOL, SCH MED, SOUTHERN ILL UNIV, 95- *Personal Data:* b Calcutta, India, Aug 28, 32; m 66, Janet Woolley; c Kyle, Aaron, Dean & Neal. *Educ:* Univ Calcutta, MB & BS, 55; Med Col Va, PhD(physiol), 67. *Prof Exp:* Clin asst med, Calcutta Nat Med Col, 55-56, house surgeon venereal dis, 56-57; med officer leprosy, Cent Leprosy Teaching & Res Inst, India, 57-58; rotating intern, St Vincent's Hosp, NY, 59; intern, St Mary's Hosp, 59-60; staff scientist respiratory physiol, Hazleton Labs Inc, Va, 67-68; from asst prof to assoc prof physiol & anesthesiol, Jefferson Med Col, Pa, 68-74. *Concurrent Pos:* Fel & asst, Dept Med, Med Col Va, 60-66. *Mem:* AAAS; Am Physiol Soc; NY Acad Sci; Am Heart Asn. *Res:* Air pollution; myocardial infarction; pulmonary edema; right duct lymph; cardiovascular physiology. *Mailing Add:* Dept Physiol Sch Med Southern Ill Univ Carbondale IL 62901. *Fax:* 618-453-1517; *E-Mail:* cbannerjee@som.siu.edu

BANERJEE, DEBENDRANATH, ANIMAL & PLANT PHYSIOLOGY. *Current Pos:* Teaching fel, 72-74, res assoc, 76-78, assoc investr, 78-87, INVESTR, NY BLOOD CTR, 87- *Personal Data:* b Calcutta, India, Sept 10, 35; m 70; c 1. *Educ:* Univ Calcutta, BSc, 57, MSc, 59; Univ Nebr, PhD(biol), 72. *Mem:* Am Soc Cell Biol; NY Acad Sci. *Res:* Cellular mechanisms governing the biosynthesis, intracellular movement, secretion and regulation of secretory proteins; studies involve small laboratory animals, a variety of biochemical techniques, electron microscopy, gene cloning and the use of monoclonal antibodies. *Mailing Add:* Membrane Biochem New York Blood Ctr 310 E 67th St New York NY 10021-6295

BANERJEE, DIPAK KUMAR, GLYCOPROTEINS, BIOMEMBRANES. *Current Pos:* assoc prof, 86-94, PROF, UNIV PR SCH MED, 94- *Personal Data:* b Pakshi, Bangladesh, Jan 5, 47; m 79; c 1. *Educ:* Univ Calcutta, BSc, 66, MSc, 68, PhD(biochem), 76. *Honors & Awards:* Inventor's Award, US Dept Com. *Prof Exp:* Sr sci asst, 69-75, jr sci officer, Inst Nuclear Med & Allied Sci, 75-79; postdoctoral fel, Univ Md Med Sch, 79-82; biochemist, NIH, 83-86. *Concurrent Pos:* Jr & sr res fel, Christian Med Col Hosp, 72-75; postdoctoral fel, NIH, 82-83; vis prof, Ctr Cancer Res, Mass Inst Technol, 95- *Mem:* Biochem Soc London; Am Soc Biochem & Molecular Biol; NY Acad Sci; Sigma Xi; Soc Glycobiol; Am Cell Biol. *Res:* Angiogenesis; capillary proliferation; biochemical molecular mechanism of the angiogenic process; signal transduction mechanism of asparagine-linked glycoprotein; homeostasis; hemophilia A antigen gene expression. *Mailing Add:* Dept Biochem & Nutrit Univ Puerto Rico Sch Med GPO Med Sci Campus San Juan PR 00936-5067. *Fax:* 787-274-8724; *E-Mail:* d.banerjee@rcmca.upr.clu.edu

BANERJEE, KALI SHANKAR, MATHEMATICAL STATISTICS, THEORY OF INDEX NUMBERS WEIGHING DESIGN. *Current Pos:* RETIRED. *Personal Data:* b Dacca, Bangladesh, Sept 1, 14; m, Niti; c Gwapna (Mukhertee). *Educ:* Univ Calcutta, BA, 35, MA, 37, PhD(statist), 50. *Honors & Awards:* Distinguished Scientist Award, Sigma Xi, 75. *Prof Exp:* Sr asst statistician, Cent Sugarcane Res & Develop, Pura Bihor, India, 42-44, statistician, 46-51; statist officer, Govt of Orissa, India, 44-46; dep dir, State Statist Bur, WBengal, 57-62, 63-64 & 66, addn dir, 66-67: vis assoc prof, Cornell Univ, 62-63; vis prof, 65-66, prof, Kans State Univ, 68-69; addn dir eval develop & planning dept, WBengal, India, 67-68; prof statist, Univ Del, 69-74, H Rodney Sharp prof, 74-80, emer prof, 80-; mem fac, Dept Math & Comput Sci, Univ Md, Baltimore County Campus, 80-86. *Concurrent Pos:* Fulbright travel grant assistance, 62-63; NSF grants, 64-66, 68-69 & 71-74. *Mem:* Int Statist Inst; fel AAAS; fel Royal Statist Soc; fel Am Statist Asn; fel Inst Math Statist. *Res:* Weighing designs; index numbers and quadratic forms; design of experiments in general; more than one hundred research publications and five published monographs. *Mailing Add:* 66 Eighth Ave Kings Park NY 11754

BANERJEE, MANOJ K, PHYSICS. *Current Pos:* vis prof, 66-67, PROF PHYSICS, UNIV MD, 67- *Personal Data:* b May 25, 31. *Educ:* Patna Univ, India, BSc, 49; Calcutta Univ, 51, PhD, 56. *Prof Exp:* Lectr, Saha Inst Nuclear Physics, 52-57, reader, 57-60, prof, 60-66; vis fel, Princeton Univ, 55-57, res assoc, 59-60. *Concurrent Pos:* Vis prof, Univ Manchester, England, 73-74, Univ Wash, 80-81, State Univ NY, Stony Brook, 87-88. *Mem:* Fel Am Phys Soc; fel Indian Acad Sci. *Mailing Add:* Dept Physics & Astron Univ Md College Park MD 20742

BANERJEE, MIHIR R, GENETICS CELLULAR & MOLECULAR BIOLOGY, MAMMARY GLAND RESEARCH. *Current Pos:* assoc prof zool, Sch Life Sci, 67-71, PROF GENETICS, CELLULAR & MOLECULAR BIOL, SCH BIOL SCI, UNIV NEBR, LINCOLN, 71- *Personal Data:* b Calcutta, India, Oct 24, 27. *Educ:* Univ Calcutta, BSc, 49, MSc, 51, PhD(zool), 59. *Prof Exp:* Lectr zool, City Col, Calcutta, India, 53-59; res fel, Cancer Res Lab, Univ Calif, Berkeley, 60-62, Dept Exp Path & Biol, City of Hope Med Ctr, Duarte, Calif, 62; vis res scientist, Div Biol, Inst Cancer Res, Fox Chase, Philadelphia, Pa, 63-64; vis scientist, Carcinogenesis Area, Nat Cancer Inst, NIH, 64-67. *Concurrent Pos:* Fulbright scholar, 60-63; grants, USPHS-NIH, 68-78, 78-81, 79-82, 83-86 & 86-90, HEW-NIH, 68-78, Univ Res Coun, 83, 84, 86 & 87; chmn, Cell Biol & Genetics Sect, Sch Life Sci, Univ Nebr, Lincoln, 74-77; mem, Prog Comt, Tissue Cult Asn, 74-76; mem, Chem Path Study Sect, NIH, 75 & 81, Breast Cancer Task Force, Nat Cancer Inst, 79-84; mem, Cell & Molecular Biol Prog, NSF, 78-; UNESCO consult, Cell & Molecular Biol Prog, Dept Zool, Univ Calcutta, India, 83-84. *Mem:* Am Asn Cancer Res; Am Soc Biol Chemists; Am Soc Cell Biol; Tissue Cult Asn. *Res:* Molecular biology of hormone regulated development of the mammary gland and breast cancer; culture model of the whole mammary organ; development of neoplastic transformation model in the whole mammary organ in vitro; cloning of the milk-protein genes. *Mailing Add:* 2621 Wimbleton Ct Lincoln NE 68506

BANERJEE, MUKUL RANJAN, RESPIRATORY PHYSIOLOGY. *Current Pos:* assoc prof, 77-79, PROF PHYSIOL, MEHARRY MED COL, 79- *Personal Data:* b Dacca, India, Jan 3, 37; US citizen; m 68; c 2. *Educ:* Univ Calcutta, BVSc, 57; La State Univ, PhD(physiol), 64. *Prof Exp:* Res assoc, Ind Univ, Bloomington, 64-65, from instr to asst prof, 66-72; NIH res fel, Univ Fla, 73-74; assoc prof, Tenn State Univ, 75-76. *Mem:* Am Physiol Soc; Int Soc Biometeorol; Sigma Xi. *Res:* Respiratory physiology; environmental physiology. *Mailing Add:* Dept Physiol Meharry Col Sch Med 1005 Dr D B Todd Blvd Nashville TN 37208-3501

BANERJEE, PAPIA T, MOLECULAR BIOLOGY. *Current Pos:* sr scientist, 92-, PRIN INVESTR, BIO-TRANSPLANT INC, 97- *Personal Data:* b Calcutta, India, May 20, 51. *Educ:* Calcutta Univ, India, BA, 70, MS, 73, PhD(biochem), 79. *Honors & Awards:* Am Cancer Soc Award, 81. *Prof Exp:* Asst prof med, Harvard Med Sch, 84-92. *Mem:* Am Soc Biochem & Molecular Biol; AAAS. *Mailing Add:* Molecular Biol Bldg 96 Bio-Transplant Inc 13th St Charlestown MA 02129

BANERJEE, PARTHA, FUNGI-ALPHA & OMEGA-SYSTEMATICS, STRUCTURAL BOTANY. *Current Pos:* CURATORIAL ASST BIOL SURVEY, NY STATE MUS, 92- *Personal Data:* b Calcutta, India, Apr 25, 56; m 82, Mukti Bhattacharyya; c Nandini R. *Educ:* Univ Calcutta, BSc(Hons), 77, MSc, 79; Ill State Univ, MS, 87; Southern Ill Univ, Carbondale, PhD(plant biol), 92. *Prof Exp:* Undergrad lectr bot, Univ Calcutta, 81-85; teaching asst bot & biol, Ill State Univ, 85-87 & Southern Ill Univ, 88-91; lectr mycol, Union Col, Schenectady, NY, 92. *Concurrent Pos:* Res asst bot, Southern Ill Univ, 90-91; lectr bot & plant morphol, State Univ NY, Albany, 93- *Mem:* Mycol Soc Am; Am Phytopath Soc; Sigma Xi. *Res:* Systematics and evolutionary studies of higher fungi using both traditional and non-traditional methods. *Mailing Add:* 1 Latham Village Lane Latham NY 12110. *Fax:* 518-473-8496

BANERJEE, PRASANTA KUMAR, COMPUTATIONAL MECHANICS, ENGINEERING MECHANICS. *Current Pos:* PROF CIVIL ENG, STATE UNIV NY, BUFFALO, 80-; PROJ DIR, NASA PROGS, 83- *Personal Data:* b Feb 1, 41; m 71, Barbara Shaw; c Nina, Sara & Lisa. *Educ:* Jadavpur Univ, India, BCE, 63, Southampton Univ, UK, PhD (civil eng), 70. *Prof Exp:* Prin sci officer bridges, Dept Transp London, 70-73; sr lectr civil & struct eng, Univ Wales, 73-80. *Concurrent Pos:* Pres, Boundary Element Software Technol Corp, Getzville, NY. *Mem:* Am Soc Civil Engrs; Am Soc Mech Engrs; US Asn Computational Mechs. *Res:* Development of boundary element method in engineering mechanics, development of computational mechanics, mechanical behavior of materials, dynamic as well as seismic behavior of foundations, specifically piled foundations. *Mailing Add:* Dept Civil Eng State Univ NY Ketter Hall Buffalo NY 14260-0001

BANERJEE, PRITHVIRAJ, PARALLEL ALGORITHMS AND ARCHITECTURES. *Current Pos:* Res asst, Coord sci lab, 81-84, from asst prof to assoc prof, 85-93, PROF, ELEC ENG, UNIV ILL, URBANA-CHAMPAIGN, 93- *Personal Data:* b Khartoum, Sudan, July 17, 60; Indian citizen; m 84, Swati; c Siraj. *Educ:* Indian Inst Technol, India, BTech, 81; Univ Ill, Urbana-Champaign, MS, 82; PhD(elec Eng), 84. *Honors & Awards:* Presidential Young Investr Award, NSF, 87. *Concurrent Pos:* Consult, Westinghouse Corp, Baltimore, 86-87, Jet Propulsion Lab, Pasadena, 88-, Res Triangle Inst, NC, 88-; prog comt, Int Fault-Tolerant Comput Symp, Japan, 88, organizing comt, Chicago, 89. *Mem:* Inst Elec & Electronics Engrs; Asn Comput Mach. *Res:* Developing parallel algorithms for very large scale integrated circuits computer aided design applications and distributed memory parallel architectures. *Mailing Add:* Dept Elec Eng Univ Ill Urbana 1406 W Green St Urbana IL 61801-2918. *E-Mail:* banerjee@crhc.uiuc.edu

BANERJEE, R L, SOLID STATE PHYSICS. *Current Pos:* asst prof, 69-70, assoc prof, 71-77, PROF PHYSICS, UNIV MONCTON, 78- *Personal Data:* b Bengal, India, Mar 1, 33; m 66, Jharna Chatterjee; c Ranendra L. *Educ:* Univ Calcutta, BSc, 53, MSc, 56; Univ Paris, Sorbonne, DSc(physics), 66. *Prof Exp:* Jr lectr physics, Univ Calcutta, 57; res fel, Bengal Eng Col, Calcutta, 57-58; crystallog, Univ Madrid, 58-60; from jr researcher to full researcher physics, Univ Paris, Sorbonne, 60-67; sr lectr, Univ WIS, 67-69. *Concurrent Pos:* Nat Res Coun Can Res grants, 69-76. *Mem:* Fr Soc Mineral & Crystallog. *Res:* Clay-mineral contents of Indian soils; polymorphic transitions in single crystals; thermal diffuse scattering of x-rays from molecular crystals; lattice dynamics; Compton scattering of x-rays; structures and properties of metals. *Mailing Add:* Dept Physics Univ Moncton Moncton NB E1A 3E9 Can

BANERJEE, RANJIT, MOLECULAR ONCOLOGY, MOLECULAR VIROLOGY. *Current Pos:* ASST PROF, DEPT MICROBIOL & IMMUNOL, NY MED COL. 95- *Personal Data:* b Calcutta, India, June 6, 48; US citizen; m 84, Marilyn A De Sciscio; c Christopher P & Victoria G. *Educ:* Univ Calcutta, India, BS Hons, 69, MS, 71; NY Univ, MS, 79, PhD(genetics), 81. *Prof Exp:* Res fel cell & molecular biol, Dept Path, Sch Med, Temple Univ, 81-83; res scientist, Inst Cancer Res, Col Physicians & Surgeons, Columbia Univ, 83-86; asst prof, Dept Neoplastic Dis, Mt Sinai Sch Med, 86-94. *Concurrent Pos:* NIH grant. *Mem:* Am Asn Cancer Res; AAAS; Am Soc Microbiol. *Res:* Molecular biology of gene expression in normal and transformed cells; effect of cofactors in carcinogenesis and viral gene expression; role of transcription factors and cytokines in regulation of human immunodeficiency virus and hepatitis B virus gene expression. *Mailing Add:* Dept Microbiol & Immunol NY Med Col BSB 340 Valhalla NY 10595. *E-Mail:* r_banerjee@nymc.edu

BANERJEE, SANJAY KUMAR, SEMICONDUCTOR DEVICE & PROCESS PHYSICS, LOW TEMPERATURE SEMICONDUCTOR CRYSTAL GROWTH. *Current Pos:* from asst prof to assoc prof, 87-93, PROF ELEC & COMPUT ENG, UNIV TEX, AUSTIN, 93-, ASSOC DIR, MICROELECTRONICS RES CTR, 96- *Personal Data:* b Khartoum, Sudan, Feb 24, 58; m 83, Jaba Chatterjee; c Anupam & Anurag. *Educ:* Indian Inst Technol, Kharagpur, BTech (Hons), 79; Univ Ill, Urbana-Champaign, MS, 81, PhD (elec), 83. *Prof Exp:* Res asst elec, Coord Sci Lab, Univ Ill, 79-83; mem tech staff, Very Large Scale Integration Circuits Design Lab, Tex Instruments, 83-87. *Concurrent Pos:* Vis asst prof elec eng, Univ Ill, 83; NSF presidential young investr, 88; Tex Atomic Energy Centennial fel, 93. *Mem:* Fel Inst Elec & Electronics Engrs; Am Phys Soc; Mat Res Soc; Am Soc Eng Educ. *Res:* Semiconductor physics, devices, and processes; device modeling; very low temperature semiconductor crystal growth; 3-D integrated circuits using polysilicon; drams; author of over 200 publications; awarded nine US patents. *Mailing Add:* Elec & Computer Eng MER 1 606C/R 9900 Univ Tex Austin TX 78712-1084. *Fax:* 512-471-5625; *E-Mail:* banerjee@ece.utexas.edu

BANERJEE, SIPRA, MOLECULAR GENETICS OF CANCER. *Current Pos:* ASSOC STAFF, CLEVELAND CLIN FOUND, 88-, ASST STAFF, DEPT CANCER BIOL, 93- *Personal Data:* b Calcutta, WBengal, Feb 20, 39; US citizen; m 65, Amiya K; c Riny & Arjun. *Educ:* Presidency Col, Calcutta, India, BS, 58; Calcutta Univ, MS, 60, PhD(biochem), 65. *Prof Exp:* Fel biochem, Dept Biochem, Albert Einstein Col Med, 66-69; res biochemist, NY Med Col, 69-70; fel, Hoffmann LaRoche Inc, 72-73; assoc res scientist, Inst Environ Med, Sch Med, NY Univ, 74-78, asst prof, 78-85, assoc res prof, 85-87. *Mem:* Am Asn Cancer Res; NY Acad Sci; Am Soc Biochem & Molecular Biol; AAAS. *Res:* Biochemical studies of molecular mechanism of chemical carcinogenesis with the emphasis on the metabolic pathways, enzymes, DNA damage and repair, and oncogenes. *Mailing Add:* Dept Molecular Biol Cleveland Clin Found Res Inst 9500 Euclid Ave NC2-118 Cleveland OH 44195-5108. *Fax:* 440-466-0631

BANERJEE, SUBIR KUMAR, GEOMAGNETISM, ROCK MAGNETISM. *Current Pos:* assoc prof geophys, 71-74, PROF GEOPHYS, UNIV MINN, MINNEAPOLIS, 74- *Personal Data:* b Jamshedpur, India, Feb 19, 38; m 63, 90; c 3. *Educ:* Univ Calcutta, BSc, 56; Indian Inst Technol, Kharagpur, MTech, 59; Univ Cambridge, PhD(geophys), 63. *Hon Degrees:* DSc, Univ Cambridge, 83. *Prof Exp:* Res physicist magnetism of ferrites, Mullard Res Labs, Redhill, Eng, 63-64; sr res assoc rock magnetism, Dept Geophys & Planetary Physics, Univ Newcastle, 64-66, univ lectr geophys, 66-69; sr staff scientist geophys & magnetic mat, Dept Mat Sci & Eng, Franklin Inst Res Labs, Philadelphia, 69-71. *Concurrent Pos:* Consult, Atomic Energy Res Estab, Eng, 65-69; mem res staff, Ampex Corp & res assoc, Stanford Univ, 67-68; lectr, Univ Pa, 69-71; vis sr res assoc, Lamont-Doherty Geol Observ, Columbia Univ, 70-71; adj prof Middle-Eastern & Islamic Studies, Univ Minn, Minneapolis, 76-; vis prof geophys, Stanford Univ & Univ Calif, Berkeley, vis scholar, Off for Hist of Sci & Technol, 77-78; vis prof geophys & vis scholar hist sci & technol, Univ Calif, Berkeley, 84-85; chmn, Int Asn Geomagnetism & Aeronomy's Working Group on Rock Magnetism, 83-87; pres, Geomag & Paleomag Sect, Am Geophys Union, 86-88; mem, Adv Panel Earth Sci, Nat Sci Found. *Mem:* Fel Am Geophys Union. *Res:* Rock magnetism-magnetism of natural and synthetic minerals relevant to geomagnetism and paleomagnetism; magnetic records of climatic and environmental change; geomagnetic field fluctuations; correlations between climate and geomagnetism; continental drift and sea floor spreading; magnetism of lunar samples, meteorites, recording tapes, ferrites and permanent magnets; history of medieval Arabic-Islamic science. *Mailing Add:* Dept Geol 106 Pillsbury Hall Univ Minn 310 Pillsbury Dr SE Minneapolis MN 55455-0219. *Fax:* 612-624-1333

BANERJEE, SURATH KUMAR, CLINICAL CHEMISTRY. *Current Pos:* ASSOC PROF PATH, WAYNE STATE UNIV, 80-, CHIEF CHEM, VET MED CTR, 83- *Personal Data:* b West Bengal, India, Nov 3, 38; m 70, Cynthia L Saylor; c Ronadip R. *Educ:* Calcutta Univ, India, BSc, 59 & MSc, 61; Jadavpur Univ, PhD(chem), 66. *Prof Exp:* Res assoc, Univ Ariz, 67-69 & 70-74, res asst prof, Dept Internal Med & Biochem, 74-80; res assoc, Purdue Univ, 69-70. *Mem:* Am Soc Biochem & Molecular Biol; Am Asn Clin Chemists; Am Chem Soc. *Res:* Contractile protein chemistry; cardiac myosin gene expression; drug effects on myosin genes; heart nuclear thyroid hormone receptors. *Mailing Add:* Lab Serv Vet Med Ctr 4646 John R St Detroit MI 48201

BANERJEE, SUSHANTA KUMAR, AGRONOMY, ENVIRONMENTAL HEALTH. *Current Pos:* from asst prof to assoc prof, 67-72, chmn, Biol Sci Dept, 71-73, PROF BIOL SCI & PUB HEALTH, POINT PARK COL, 72- *Personal Data:* b Ranchi, India, Sept 25, 27; m 52; c 2. *Educ:* Patna Univ, BS, 48; Tex A&M Univ, MS, 57, PhD(plant & soil sci), 64; Univ Pittsburgh, MPH, 80. *Prof Exp:* Owner & mgr, Liluah Dairy Farm, India, 48-50; asst storage & transp off, Govt WBengal, 50-55, subdiv agr off, 55-57; supt agr, Govt India, 57-60; instr biol, Mitchell Col, Conn, 64-67. *Concurrent Pos:* Mem, Bd Dir, Allegheny Co Environ Coalition, Pittsburgh, Pa, 72-75; dir, Point Park Col Chapter Inst Human Ecol Southwestern Pa, 72-76; chmn, Bd Dir, India Asn, Pittsburgh, Pa, 73; pres, Bengali Asn, Pittsburgh, Pa, 81-82; vis prof, Visva Bharati Univ, Santiniketan, West Bengal, India, 88. *Mem:* Soc for Environ Geochem & Health. *Res:* Soil fertility and plant nutrition; response of rice crop to fertilizers; protective effects of chemicals on radiation damage of plants. *Mailing Add:* Dept Natural Sci Point Park Col 201 Wood St Pittsburgh PA 15222-1912

BANERJEE, TAPAS KUMAR, neurology, clinical neurophysiology, for more information see previous edition

BANERJEE, UMESH CHANDRA, ENVIRONMENTAL BIOLOGY & POLLUTION, TISSUE CULTURE. *Current Pos:* ASSOC PROF BIOL & ENVIRON BIOL, NC CENT UNIV, DURHAM, 81- *Personal Data:* b Aligarh, India, July 15, 37; US citizen; c Sonali R. *Educ:* Muslim Univ, India, BSc, 58, MSc, 61; Univ Mass, Amherst, MS, 66; Harvard Univ, PhD(biol), 72. *Prof Exp:* Res assoc electron micros, Dept Biol, Yale Univ, 66-68; electron microscopist lunar res, NASA Proj, Harvard Univ, 68-69 & 71-73, res assoc & fel biol, 73-74; asst prof biol, Boston Univ, 74-75; lectr, Univ Mass, Boston, 75-78; asst prof & dir, Electron Microscope Ctr, NTex State Univ, Denton, 78-81. *Concurrent Pos:* Dir, Boston Univ Herbarium, 74-75, Benjamin Harris Herbarium, NTex State, Univ, 78-81 & Tissue Cult Labs, NC Cent Univ, 81-; fel biol, Harvard Univ, 75-78; asst dir, Electron Microscope & Immunol Ctr, NC Cent Univ, 81-; hon vpres res & develop, Agri-Horti Biotech, Inc, 93- *Mem:* Bot Soc Am; Am Asn Stratig Palynology; Indian Palynological Soc; Int Asn Aerobiol; Electron Micros Soc Am. *Res:* Biotechnology of guayule rubber, a native species of North America; allergenic pollen grains and spores; electron microscopy, transmission, scanning electron microscopy and X-ray analysis; tissue culture; origin of corn; medicinal plants; systematic biology. *Mailing Add:* Dept Biol NC Central Univ 1801 Fayetteville St Durham NC 27707-3129

BANERJEE, UTPAL, PARALLEL PROCESSING. *Current Pos:* SR RES, INTEL CORP, 89- *Personal Data:* b Howrah, India, Aug 4, 42; m 69; c 1. *Educ:* Calcutta Univ, India, BSc, 61, MSc, 63; Carnegie-Mellon Univ, MS, 67, PhD(math), 70; Univ Ill, Urbana-Champaign, MS, 76, PhD(comput sci), 79. *Prof Exp:* Asst prof math, Univ Cincinnati, 69-75; prin analyst, Large Info Systs Div, Honeywell Corp, Phoenix, 79-81; mem res staff, Fairchild Advan Res Lab, Calif, 81-82; consult, Sunnyvale Develop Div, Control Data Corp, 82-89. *Concurrent Pos:* Vis sr software engr, Ctr Supercomputing Res & Develop, Univ Ill, Urbana-Champaign, 86- *Mem:* Am Math Soc; Math Asn Am; Asn Comput Mach; Inst Elec & Electronics Engrs; Sigma Xi. *Mailing Add:* Intel Corp RN6-35 2200 Mission College Blvd Santa Clara CA 95052-8119

BANERJI, RANAN BIHARI, ENGINEERING, COMPUTER SCIENCE. *Current Pos:* EMER PROF COMPUT SCI, ST JOSEPH'S UNIV, 82- *Personal Data:* b Calcutta, India, May 5, 28; m 54, Purnima Purkayastha; c Aninclita (Spielberg) & Sunandita (Ogawa). *Educ:* Patna Univ, BSc, 47; Univ Calcutta, MSc, 49, DPhil(physics), 56. *Prof Exp:* Vis asst prof eng res, Pa State Univ, 53-56; lectr radio eng, Univ Calcutta, 56; maintenance engr comput sect, Indian Statist Inst, 56-58; res assoc opers res, Case Inst Technol, 58-59; asst prof eng, Univ NB, 59-61; from asst prof to prof, Case Western Res Univ, 61-73; prof comput sci, Temple Univ, 73-81. *Concurrent Pos:* Res asst, Ling Data Processing Sem, Ind Univ, 64; consult, Smith Electronics, Ohio, 62, RCA, 67, GE, 73, Analytics, Inc, 80, Chase Financial, 90 & Philips Res, 90; vis prof, Univ Paris, 77, Univ Calcutta, 76, Univ Vienna, 85, 91, Univ Sydney, 90 & Univ Prague, 93. *Mem:* Asn Comput Mach; sr mem Inst Elec & Electronics Engrs; Math Asn Am; Am Assoc Artificial Intel. *Res:* Statistics of radio wave fluctuations; information theory and coding; automata and linguistics; artificial intelligence. *Mailing Add:* 7612 Woodlawn Ave Elkins Park PA 19027-2911. *E-Mail:* rbanerji@sju.edu

BANERJI, SHANKHA K, CIVIL ENGINEERING, ENVIRONMENTAL ENGINEERING. *Current Pos:* PROF CIVIL ENG, UNIV MO-COLUMBIA, 75- *Personal Data:* b Lucknow, India, Jan 25, 36; m 64, Zarrine Kerravala; c 3. *Educ:* Univ Calcutta, BE, 57; Univ Ill, Urbana, MS, 62, PhD(sanit eng), 65. *Prof Exp:* Asst engr, Hindustan Steel Ltd, India, 57-60; asst prof sanit eng, Univ Ill, Urbana, 65-66; asst prof, Univ Del, 66-70, res grant, Water Resources Ctr, 67-68; consult engr, Kidde Consults, Inc, 70-75. *Concurrent Pos:* Consult, Stauffer Chem Co, Del, 66-67; Kent Country Sewer Study Comt, 67; Del Pub Serv Comn, 68-70; consult, Kidde Consults Inc, Baltimore, Md, 75-81, R W Booker & Assoc, St Louis, Mo, US Corp Engrs, St Louis, Mo, Shell Engr & Assoc, Columbia, Mo, 75 & St Louis Co Water Co, Sugar Creek, Mo. *Mem:* Int Asn Water Pollution Res; Am Soc Civil Engrs; Am Water Works Asn; Water Pollution Control Fedn; Am Chem Soc; Air & Waste Mgt Asn. *Res:* Biological treatment of waste water and stream pollution control; water quality control facility design; sludge stability analysis; waste stabilization; pond effluent polishing; hazardous waste bioremediation; ground water bioremediation. *Mailing Add:* Dept Civil Eng Univ Mo E209-EBE Columbia MO 65211. *Fax:* 573-882-4784

BANERJI, TAPAN KUMAR, ENDOCRINOLOGY, MICROANATOMY. *Current Pos:* res assoc, 77, fac assoc, 77-78, from asst prof to prof, 78-87, PROF ANAT, UNIV TEX MED BR, GALVESTON, 87- *Personal Data:* b Calcutta, India, July 12, 40; m 74, Sutapa Banerjec; c Soumo. *Educ:* Univ Calcutta, BSc Hons, 61, MSc, 63, PhD(endocrinol), 70. *Honors & Awards:* S P Basu Mem Medal, Zool Soc, 68. *Prof Exp:* Asst prof biol sci, Himachal Pradesh Univ, Simla, India, 72-74; fel neuroendocrinol, Waisman Ctr, Univ Wis-Madison, 74-77. *Mem:* Fel Zool Soc; NY Acad Sci; Am Asn Anatomists; Int Brain Res Org. *Res:* Neuroendocrinology, comparative endocrinology, biogenic amines, ultrastructure and rhythmic body functions; reproduction biology, psychopharmacology. *Mailing Add:* Dept Anat Sch Med Univ Tex Med Br Galveston TX 77550-1069. *Fax:* 409-772-3222

BANES, ALBERT JOSEPH, MICROBIOLOGY, BIOCHEMISTRY. *Current Pos:* res assoc biochem, 77-78, ASSOC PROF SURG, UNIV NC, 78- *Personal Data:* b McKeesport, Pa, Aug 26, 47; m 68; c 2. *Educ:* Lehigh Univ, BA, 69; Univ Richmond, MS, 71; Va Commonwealth Univ, PhD(microbiol), 75. *Prof Exp:* Fel microbiol, Duke Univ, 74-76; res assoc, Va Commonwealth Univ, 76-77. *Concurrent Pos:* Asst dir res, J C Burn Ctr, Univ NC, 78-, mem, Dent Res Ctr, 78- *Mem:* Fedn Am Soc Exp Biol; Am Burn Asn; Am Asn Dent Res; Am Soc Bone & Mineral Res. *Res:* Developmental biology and biochemistry; identification of the molecular mechanisms underlying disease, scar, mechanical. *Mailing Add:* Dept Surg Univ NC Burnett-Womack Rm 254 Chapel Hill NC 27599-7050

BANEY, RONALD HOWARD, INDUSTRIAL CHEMISTRY, SILICONE MATERIALS. *Current Pos:* RES SCIENTIST, DEPT MAT SCI & ENG, UNIV FLA, GAINESVILLE, FLA, 97- *Personal Data:* b Alma, Mich, Nov 26, 32; m 55, Mary J Wallace; c Ellen. *Educ:* Alma Col, BS, 55; Univ Wis, PhD(inorg chem), 60. *Prof Exp:* Group leader, Dow Corning Corp, 60-74, assoc scientist, 74-83, res scientist, 83-92, asst res dir & sr res scientist, Dow Corning Asia Ltd, Yamakita, Japan, 92-96. *Concurrent Pos:* Vis indust scientist, Nagoya Univ, 86-87. *Mem:* Am Chem Soc; Sigma Xi; Am Ceramic Soc; Mat Res Soc. *Res:* Physical organic chemical investigations, especially organosilicon chemistry; development of new silicone materials; ceramic materials; superconductors; sol/gel materials; ormosils. *Mailing Add:* Dow Corning Corp Midland MI 48640. *Fax:* 352-392-6359

BANFIELD, ALEXANDER WILLIAM FRANCIS, environmental impact assessment, mammalogy; deceased, see previous edition for last biography

BANFIELD, WILLIAM GETHIN, EXPERIMENTAL PATHOLOGY. *Current Pos:* RETIRED. *Personal Data:* b Hartford, Conn, Mar 2, 20; m 44, Joan Sanders; c Sandy, Peter & Sarah. *Educ:* RI State Col, BS, 41, MS, 43; Yale Univ, MD, 46; Am Univ, Washington, DC, JD, 74. *Prof Exp:* Am Cancer Soc fel, Yale Univ, 49-52, from instr to asst prof path, 52-54; pathologist, Nat Cancer Inst, NIH, 54-80. *Concurrent Pos:* Assoc pathologist, Grace-New Haven Community Hosp, 52-54. *Res:* Connective tissues; viruses; transmission and scanning electron microscopy; electron probe analysis. *Mailing Add:* 15715 Avery Rd Rockville MD 20855

BANG, NILS ULRIK, MEDICINE, HEMATOLOGY. *Current Pos:* CHIEF HEMAT SERV, LILLY LAB CLIN RES, WISHARD MEM HOSP, 66- *Personal Data:* b Copenhagen, Denmark, Sept 24, 29; m 60; c 3. *Educ:* Copenhagen Univ, MD, 55. *Prof Exp:* Intern, Munic Hosp, Copenhagen, 55-56; resident, Univ Hosp, Univ of Copenhagen, 57; resident cardiol, Mem Ctr Cancer & Allied Dis, Med Col, Cornell Univ, 57-58; NIH res trainee enzymol, Sch Med, Wash Univ, 59-61; asst prof med, NY Hosp-Cornell Med Ctr, 62-66; assoc prof, 66-72, PROF MED, SCH MED, IND UNIV, INDIANAPOLIS, 72-, PROF PATH, 80- *Concurrent Pos:* Spec fel enzymol, Munic Hosp, Copenhagen, 56; res fel, Sloan-Kettering Inst Cancer Res, 58-S9; fel couns thrombosis, stroke & arteriosclerosis, Am Heart Asn. *Mem:* AAAS; Harvey Soc; Am Fedn Clin Res; fel Am Col Cardiol; Am Hemat Soc; Sigma Xi. *Res:* Biochemistry of blood coagulation and platelet function. *Mailing Add:* Lilly Res Lab Eli Lilly & Co DC 0812 Lilly Corp Ctr 1001 W Tenth St Indianapolis IN 46285

BANGA, HARJIT SINGH, CARDIOVASCULAR RESEARCH, METABOLIC DESEASES. *Current Pos:* sr scientist & proj leader, Dept Cardiovasc Res, 90-91, assoc res investr, 91-93, CLIN DOC SPECIALIST, HOFFMAN-LA ROCHE, 93- *Personal Data:* b Ambala, Punjab, India, July 15, 56. *Educ:* Panjab Univ, BS, 75; MS Univ, India, MS, 77, PhD(biochem), 85. *Honors & Awards:* Young Scientist Travel Award, Fidia Res Found, Italy, 85, 87 & 89. *Prof Exp:* Jr res fel biochem, MS Univ, India, 77-78, teaching asst, 78-80, lectr, 81-84; res asst physiol chem, Ohio State Univ, 80; res fel med, Harvard Med Sch, Brigham & Women's Hosp, 85-86; res assoc biochem, Univ Vt, 86-88; res fel pharmacol, Univ Conn Health Ctr, 88, asst prof, 88-90. *Concurrent Pos:* Adv biomed sci-pharmacol, Univ Conn, 89, res initiation grant, Health Ctr, 89-90. *Mem:* Am Soc Biochem & Molecular Biol; Am Heart Asn; Int Soc Neurochem; Neurosci Soc India. *Res:* Endogenous ADP-ribosylation of a unique protein in rabbit and rat heart membranes; development of high-flux screens for testing compounds; novel endogenous ADP-ribosylation of proteins in transformed cells. *Mailing Add:* Hoffman-La Roche Inc Bldg 719 Rm 518 340 Kingsland St Nutley NJ 07110-1199. *Fax:* 973-235-3569

BANGDIWALA, ISHVER SURCHAND, STATISTICS METHODOLOGY, APPLIED RESEARCH. *Current Pos:* dir res & consult statistician, 58-66, prof, 66-82, EMER PROF STATIST & RES, UNIV PR, RIO PIEDRAS, 82- *Personal Data:* b Surat, India, Jan 9, 22; US citizen; m 47; c 2. *Educ:* Bombay, BSc, 43, MSc, LLB, JD, 46; Univ NC, MS, 50, PhD(exp statist, math statist), 58. *Prof Exp:* Head statist sect & legal adv, K A Pandit, Actuary, India, 44-48; head statist dept, Agr Exp Sta, Univ PR, 52-58. *Concurrent Pos:* Prof & consult, Inst Statist, Univ PR, 53-66, Col Agr & Mech Arts, 59-82, Med Sch, 69-82. *Mem:* Fel Royal Statist Soc; Inst Math Statist; Biomet Soc; fel Int Statist Inst; emer Sigma Xi; Int Asn Survey Statisticians; Int Asn Off Statist. *Res:* Statistical methodology; sampling; experimental designs; educational and social science research; medical science research; evaluation design and statistical analysis. *Mailing Add:* Calle Cisne 792 URB Dos Pinos Rio Piedras PR 00923-2792

BANGDIWALA, SHRIKANT I, BIOSTATISTICS. *Current Pos:* RES ASSOC PROF BIOSTATIST, UNIV NC, 90- *Personal Data:* b PR. *Educ:* Univ NC, PhD(biostatist), 80. *Mailing Add:* Dept Biostatist Univ NC PO Box 2688 Chapel Hill NC 27515

BANGE, DAVID W, GRAPH THEORY. *Current Pos:* PROF MATH, UNIV WIS, 70- *Personal Data:* b St Louis, Mo, Apr 29, 45. *Educ:* St Louis Univ, BS, 67; Colo State Univ, MS, 69 &, PhD(math), 71. *Mem:* Am Math Soc. *Mailing Add:* Dept Math Univ Wis La Crosse WI 54601-3767

BANGERT, JOHN T(HEODORE), COMMUNICATION ENGINEERING. *Current Pos:* RETIRED. *Personal Data:* b Chicago, Ill, Jan 8, 19; m 50, Doris Lambert; c John Jr & Barbara. *Educ:* Univ Mich, BS, 42; Stevens Inst Technol, MS, 47. *Prof Exp:* Dir, Carrier Transmission Lab, AT&T Bell Labs, Inc, 68-75, dir, Transmission Technol Lab, 62-68 & 76-79, dir, Transmission Develop Planning Lab, 79-81. *Mem:* Fel Inst Elec & Electronics Engrs. *Res:* Transient and steady state analysis and synthesis of active and passive networks; time domain equalization; time varying networks; computer aided design; pulse code modulation systems; coaxial cable systems; international standards; applications of early transistors; aerial electronics; granted 12 patents. *Mailing Add:* 75 Dascomb Rd Andover MA 01810

BANGERTER, ROGER ODELL, PHYSICS, HEAVY ION FUSION. *Current Pos:* physicist elem particle physics, 69-74, PHYSICIST, FUSION ENERGY RES, LAWRENCE BERKELEY LAB, 90- *Personal Data:* b Salt Lake City, Utah, Mar 9, 39; m 65, Sharon Wilkey; c Jamie, Boyd, Megan, Neal, Robyn & Jeana. *Educ:* Univ Utah, BA, 63; Univ Calif, Berkeley, PhD(physics), 69. *Prof Exp:* Physicist inertial confinement fusion, Lawrence Livermore Lab, 74-81 & 84-90; physicist, Los Alamos Nat Lab, 81-84. *Mem:* Fel Am Phys Soc. *Res:* Inertial confinement fusion; specifically, the use of heavy ion accelerators for inertial confinement fusion. *Mailing Add:* Lawrence Berkeley Lab Fusion Energy Res Berkeley CA 94720. *Fax:* 510-486-5392; *E-Mail:* bangerter@lbl.gov

BANGHART, FRANK W, BIOSTATISTICS. *Current Pos:* RETIRED. *Personal Data:* b Michael, Ill, Oct 30, 23; m 46; c 2. *Educ:* Quincy Col, AB, 49; Drake Univ, MA, 50, EdD(statist), 57. *Prof Exp:* Instr psychol, Quincy Col, 49-52; asst instr ed, Univ Va, 55-56, instr, 56-57, from asst prof to assoc prof biostatist, 57-65; prof educ mgt system, Fla State Univ, 65-89. *Concurrent Pos:* Prin investr, Off Naval Res, 57-61; Air Force Syst Command

Hqs, 57-; mem adv comt new educ media, US Health, Educ & Welfare Dept, 61- *Mem:* AAAS; Am Statist Asn; Biomet Soc; NY Acad Sci. *Res:* Statistical methodology, research designs. *Mailing Add:* 3374 Lakeshore Dr Tallahassee FL 32312

BANGS, LEIGH BUCHANAN, SURFACE CHEMISTRY, COLLOID CHEMISTRY. *Current Pos:* PRES, BANGS LAB INC, 88- *Personal Data:* b Marblehead, Mass, Oct 9, 36; m 59, Sonia E; c Mark, Adam & Alex. *Educ:* Colby Col, BA, 58; Mass Inst Technol, SM, 62, PhD(metall), 65. *Prof Exp:* Spec assignments chemist, Dow Chem Co, 64-66, res chemist, Dow Chem USA, 66-68, res specialist, 68-81, nat serv mgr, Div Dow Chem, Photovolt Corp, prod mgr, Dow Inst & Reagents, 82-83; prod mgr, Seradyn Diag Inc, 83-85, bus mgr, 85-88. *Mem:* Am Chem Soc; Sigma Xi; AAAS; Am Asn Clin Chem. *Res:* Surface chemistry; colloid chemistry; uniform latex particles applications; diagnostic chemistry. *Mailing Add:* Bangs Lab Inc 9025 Technology Dr Fishers IN 46038-2886. *Fax:* 317-570-7034; *E-Mail:* leigh@bangslabs.com

BANICK, WILLIAM MICHAEL, ANALYTICAL CHEMISTRY. *Current Pos:* Anal proj chemist, 57-65, sr res chemist, 66-68, GROUP LEADER, AM CYANAMID CO, 68- *Personal Data:* b Scranton, Pa, Feb 6, 32; m 56; c 3. *Educ:* Kings Col, BS, 53; Univ Ill, PhD(chem), 57. *Mem:* Am Chem Soc. *Res:* Analytical chemistry of basic intermediates; rubber chemicals; brighteners; ultraviolet absorbers; antioxidants, especially acid-base behavior, thin-layer and liquid chromatography. *Mailing Add:* 119 W High St Somerville NJ 08876-2108

BANIGAN, THOMAS FRANKLIN, POLYMER CHEMISTRY, ORGANIC CHEMISTRY. *Current Pos:* VPRES, ANVER BIOSCI DESIGN, 77- *Personal Data:* b Dover, NJ, Sept 22, 20; m 46; c 1. *Educ:* Univ Notre Dame, BS, 42, MS, 43, PhD(org chem), 46. *Prof Exp:* Chemist, Sinclair Refining Co, Ind, 46-48; res chemist, rubber res sta, USDA, 48-53; sr res chemist, Tide Water Oil Co, 53-57; chemist, Arthur D Little, Inc, 57-61; vpres & dir res, Ben Holt Co, 62-65; tech dir, Pilot Chem Co, 65-68; mgr chem res, Avery Prod Corp, 68-70; tech dir, Pilot Chem Co, 70-73; assoc, Chem Res & Develop Co, 74-76. *Mem:* Am Chem Soc; Consult Chemists Asn. *Res:* Natural resources; detoxification of plant materials, adhesive and detergent chemicals; protective coatings. *Mailing Add:* 403 Bougainvillea Lane Glendora CA 91740-2667

BANIJAMALI, ALI REZA, METABOLISM OF AGRICULTURAL CHEMICALS IN ANIMALS & PLANTS, METABOLISM CHEMISTRY. *Current Pos:* res chemist, 87-90, RES SCIENTIST, UNIROYAL CHEM CO, 90- *Personal Data:* b Arak, Iran, Mar 10, 53; m, Sohiela Shaficazad; c Sahar & Bobak. *Educ:* Mass Col Pharm & Allied Health Scis, PhD(med chem), 84. *Prof Exp:* Fel, Univ Conn, 85-87. *Concurrent Pos:* Adj prof, Univ Conn, 87- *Mem:* Am Chem Soc; Int Soc Study Xenobiotics. *Res:* Investingating the metabolism of agricultural chemicals in animals and plants; Use of mass spectrometry and nuclear magnetic resonance for identification of metobolites. *Mailing Add:* Uniroyal Chem Co R-1-2 Middlebury CT 06749-9805. *Fax:* 203-573-3660

BANIK, NARENDRA LAL, NEUROCHEMISTRY. *Current Pos:* res assoc, 76-77, asst prof neurol & biochem, 77-80, ASSOC PROF NEUROL, MED UNIV SC, 80- *Personal Data:* b Ganganagar, India, Jan 2, 38; m 68; c 2. *Educ:* Univ Calcutta, BSc, 59; Univ London, MSc, 66, PhD(biochem), 70. *Prof Exp:* Res asst biochem, Inst Psychiat, London, 61-65; res asst, Charing Cross Hosp Med Sch, London, 65-71; lectr neurochem, Inst Neurol, London, 71-74; res assoc neurol, Sch Med, Stanford Univ, 74-76. *Mem:* Biochem Soc London; Soc Neurosci; AAAS; Int Soc Neurochem; Am Soc Neurochem; Am Soc Biol Chem. *Res:* Brain development process of myelination and dissolution of the myelin membrane in demyelinating diseases; metabolism and function of membranes and isolated myelin-forming cells. *Mailing Add:* Dept Neurol Med Univ SC 171 Ashely Ave Charleston SC 29425-2232

BANISTER, ERIC WILTON, ERGONOMICS, SPORTS MEDICINE. *Current Pos:* asst prof physiol exercise, Phys Develop Studies, 67-69, assoc prof physiol exercise, Kinesiology, 69-72, chmn physiol exercise, 1st Dept Kinesiology NAm, 70-82, dir physiol exercise, Sch Kinesiology, 87-88, PROF PHYSIOL EXERCISE, KINESIOLOGY, SIMON FRASER UNIV, 72- *Personal Data:* b Barrow-in-Furness, Lancashire, Eng, May 18, 32; Can citizen; m 60; c 3. *Educ:* Manchester Univ, Eng, BSc, 53; Loughborough Univ, Eng, DPE, 54; Univ BC, Can, MPE, 62; Univ Ill, PhD(phys ed & physiol), 64. *Prof Exp:* Asst prof physiol exercise, Dept Phys Ed, Univ BC, 64-67; vis prof res, Dept Naval & Aviation Med, Karolinska Inst, Stockholm, 69-70, Dept Physiol, Sch Med, Univ Hawaii, 75-76 & Royal Postgrad Med Sch, Univ London, Eng, 76. *Concurrent Pos:* Prin investr, Submissions to Can Natural Sci & Eng Res Coun Funded, 67-; exec, Can Asn Sport Sci, 78-81, pres, 79-80; coun mem, Can Sports Med Coun, 79-82, vpres, 80-81; ed, Can J Appl Sport Sci, Can Asn Sport Sci, 80-83; ed-in-chief, J Sports Med, Training & Rehab, Gordon, Breach Harwood Sci Publ, NY, USA, 89-; guest ed, Int J Sports Med, Ger, Vol II, Suppl 2, 90- *Mem:* Can Asn Sport Sci (pres, 79-80); fel Am Asn Sports Med; AAAS; Undersea Med Soc. *Res:* Researcher and writer in contemporary health issues, mathematically modeling human physical performance and topics which include occupational health and safety, ergonomics and toxicology of the silviculture industry and optimization of the athletic potential. *Mailing Add:* Dept Kinesiology Simon Fraser Univ Burnaby BC V5A 1S6 Can

BANITT, ELDEN HARRIS, ORGANIC CHEMISTRY. *Current Pos:* res specialist, 65-75, sr res specialist, Riker Labs, 75-89, DIV SCIENTIST, 3M PHARMACEUT, 89- *Personal Data:* b Red Wing, Minn, Apr 7, 37; m 59; c 2. *Educ:* St Olaf Col, BA, 59; Univ Wis, PhD(org chem), 64. *Prof Exp:* Fel, Univ Calif, Berkeley, 64-65. *Mem:* Am Chem Soc; Int Soc Heterocylic Chem; NY Acad Sci. *Res:* Synthetic medicinal chemistry. *Mailing Add:* 3772 Village Ct Woodbury MN 55125-9365

BANK, ARTHUR, HEMATOLOGY. *Current Pos:* PROF MED & GENETICS, COLUMBIA UNIV, 70- *Personal Data:* b New York, NY, Apr 20, 35; m; c 2. *Educ:* Harvard Univ, MD, 60. *Concurrent Pos:* Dir hemat & clin path, Presby Hosp. *Mem:* Am Soc Hemat; Am Asn Physicians; Am Soc Biol Chemists. *Res:* Globin gene regulation; gene transfer and gene therapy. *Mailing Add:* 701 W 168th St HHSC 1604 Columbia Univ New York NY 10032-2704

BANK, HARVEY L, cryobiology, cell biology, for more information see previous edition

BANK, NORMAN, NEPHROLOGY. *Current Pos:* assoc prof, 71-73, PROF MED, ALBERT EINSTEIN SCH MED, 73- *Personal Data:* b New York, NY, Oct 19, 25; m 54; c 2. *Educ:* NY Univ, AB, 49; Columbia Univ, MD, 53. *Prof Exp:* From instr to assoc prof med, Sch Med, NY Univ, 60-71. *Concurrent Pos:* Life Ins Med Res Found res fel, New Eng Med Ctr, Tufts Univ, 57-59; assoc attend physician, NY Univ Med Ctr, 68-71, attend physician, 71-; chief nephrology, Montefiore Hosp, 71- *Mem:* Am Soc Clin Invest; Asn Am Physicians; Am Physiol Soc; Am Fedn Clin Res; Am Soc Nephrology. *Res:* Regulation of acid secretion by kidney; renal concentrating defects in hypercalcemia; renal function in pyelonephritis and mercury poisoning; regulation of sodium transport; renal function in diabetes. *Mailing Add:* Montefiore Hosp Dept Nephrol Albert Einstein Col Med 111 E 210th St Bronx NY 10467

BANK, SHELTON, ORGANIC & ENVIRONMENTAL CHEMISTRY. *Current Pos:* assoc prof chem, 66-72, PROF CHEM, STATE UNIV NY, ALBANY, 72-, PROF ENVIRON HEALTH & TOXICOL, GRAD SCH PUB HEALTH SCI, 85- *Personal Data:* b New York, NY, Jan 28, 32; m 57; c 2. *Educ:* Brooklyn Col, BS, 54; Purdue Univ, PhD(phys chem), 60. *Prof Exp:* Res fel, Harvard Univ, 60-61; res chemist, Esso Res & Eng Co, 61-64, sr res chemist, 64-66. *Concurrent Pos:* Consult, Col Chem Consults, Am Chem Soc, 72-, Tour Speaker, 84- *Mem:* Am Chem Soc; Chem Soc Brit. *Res:* Clay catalysed organic reactions; solid state NMR; chemistry of environmental pollutants; nuclear magnetic resonance method in environmental chemistry; multinuclear NMR spectroscopy. *Mailing Add:* Dept Chem State Univ NY Albany NY 12222

BANK, STEVEN BARRY, mathematics; deceased, see previous edition for last biography

BANKER, GARY A, CELLULAR NEUROBIOLOGY, DEVELOPMENTAL NEUROBIOLOGY. *Current Pos:* PROF NEUROSCI, UNIV VA, 89- *Personal Data:* b Seattle, Wash, July 1, 46. *Educ:* Univ Wash, BS, 68; Univ Calif, Irvine, PhD(neurobiol), 73. *Prof Exp:* Prof neurosci, Albany Med Col, 76-89. *Res:* Neurosciences. *Mailing Add:* Dept Neurosci Univ Va Med Ctr MR-4 Box 5148 Charlottesville VA 22908. *Fax:* 804-982-4380

BANKER, GILBERT STEPHEN, PHARMACY. *Current Pos:* DEAN & DISTINGUISHED PROF DRUG DELIVERY, UNIV IOWA, IOWA CITY, 92- *Personal Data:* b Tuxedo Park, NY, Sept 12, 31; m 56, Gwen Hughes; c Stephen R, Susan R, David W & William G. *Educ:* Albany Col Pharm, Union Univ (NY), BS, 53; Purdue Univ, MS, 55, PhD(pharm), 57. *Honors & Awards:* Lederle Fac Res Award, 61; Am Pharm Asn Indust Pharm Award, 71. *Prof Exp:* From asst prof to assoc prof pharm, Purdue Univ, 57-64, prof indust pharm, 64-85, head, Dept Indust & Phys Pharm, 66-85; dean & prof pharm, Univ Minn, Minneapolis, 85-92. *Concurrent Pos:* Consult, G D Searle, 76-, Richardson Merrell, 74- & FMC Corp, 79- *Mem:* Fel AAAS; Am Pharmaceut Asn; Am Chem Soc; fel Am Asn Pharmaceut Sci; fel Acad Pharmaceut Sci (vpres, 70-71). *Res:* Quantitative evaluations of pharmaceutical unit operations; applications of radioactive tracer techniques to the evaluation of pharmaceutical products; emulsion and suspension rheology; applications of polymers to pharmaceutical product development and controlled drug and chemical agent release. *Mailing Add:* Col Pharm Univ Iowa Iowa City IA 52242. *Fax:* 319-353-5594; *E-Mail:* gilbert-banker@uiowa.edu

BANKERT, RALPH ALLEN, ORGANIC CHEMISTRY. *Current Pos:* RETIRED. *Personal Data:* b York, Pa, Jan 19, 18; m 46; c 2. *Educ:* Gettysburg Col, BA, 40; Pa State Col, MS, 41, PhD(org chem), 44. *Prof Exp:* Res chemist, Res Ctr, B F Goodrich Co, 43-50 & Res Ctr, Hercules Inc, 50-82. *Mem:* Am Chem Soc. *Res:* Antioxidants; preparation of aliphatic ketimines; reactions of N-monochloramines; terpenes; amine chemistry; peroxides; polymers. *Mailing Add:* 726 Loveville Rd Hockessin DE 19707

BANKERT, RICHARD BURTON, VETERINARY MEDICINE. *Current Pos:* CANCER RES SCIENTIST IMMUNOL, ROSWELL PARK MEM INST, 73-, ASSOC CHIEF, MOLECULAR IMMUNOL, 83- *Personal Data:* b St Louis, Mo, Apr 22, 40; m 70; c 3. *Educ:* Gettysburg Col, BA, 62; Univ Pa, VMD, 68, PhD(immunol), 73. *Concurrent Pos:* Res fel, Sch Vet Med,

Univ Pa, 68-70 & 70-73; res prof, Dept Microbiol/Immunol & Molecular Biol, State Univ NY, Buffalo; mem, Immunobiology Study Sect, NIH, 84-88, NIH Reviewers Reserve, 88-92. *Mem:* Am Asn Immunologists; AAAS; Sigma Xi. *Res:* Membrane events associated with lymphocyte function; molecular genetics of the expression and regulation of the B-cell repertoire; human tumor cell biology. *Mailing Add:* Dept Molecular Immunol Roswell Park Cancer Inst Elm & Carlton Sts Buffalo NY 14263-0001

BANKOFF, S(EYMOUR) GEORGE, CHEMICAL ENGINEERING. *Current Pos:* prof chem eng, 59-73, Walter P Murphy prof chem, mech & nuclear eng, 73-92, EMER PROF, NORTHWESTERN UNIV, 92- *Personal Data:* b New York, NY, Oct 7, 21. *Educ:* Columbia Univ, BS, 40, MS, 41; Purdue Univ, PhD(chem eng), 52. *Honors & Awards:* Wolfson Lectr, Sch Chem Eng, Technion, Israel, 70; Max Jacob Mem Award, 87; Robert E Wilson Nuclear Chem Eng Award, Am Inst Chem Engrs, 94, Donald Q Kern Award, 96. *Prof Exp:* Chem engr, Sinclair Refining Co, East Chicago, 41-42, E I du Pont de Nemours & Co, Ala, 42-43; res assoc, Manhattan Proj, Univ Chicago, 43-44; chem engr, Hanford Eng Works, Washington, 44-45, NJ, 45-48; from asst prof to prof & head dept, Rose Polytech Inst, 48-59. *Concurrent Pos:* NSF fel, Calif Inst Technol, 58-59; Guggenheim fel, 66-67; Shell vis prof, Imp Col, Univ London, 67; Fulbright intercountry exchange lectr, Scandinavia & Israel, 67; consult, Los Alamos Nat Lab, Argonne Nat Lab & various co; chmn, Energy Eng Coun, Northwestern Univ, 75-79; vis res scientist, Centre d'Etudes Nucleaires, Comn Atomic Energy, Grenoble, France, 80; fel, Int Ctr Heat & Mass Transfer, Belgrade, Yugoslavia, 83; mem, Organizing Comt, Int Symp Multi-phase Transport, 86 & US Team, Seminar Two-Phase Flow, 88; pres, SGB Assocs, 86-; chmn, Heat Transfer & Energy Conversion Div, Am Inst Chem Engrs, 87; co-chmn, US Sci Comt, Int Heat Transfer Conf, 87- *Mem:* Nat Acad Eng; Am Nuclear Soc; fel Am Soc Mech Engrs; fel Am Inst Chem Engrs. *Res:* Two-phase flow and heat transfer; nuclear reactor safety; vapor explosions. *Mailing Add:* 5030 Arbor Lane Northfield IL 60093

BANKOWSKI, RAYMOND ADAM, VETERINARY MEDICINE. *Current Pos:* assoc, Agr Exp Sta, 40-42, asst prof vet sci & asst vet, 46-52, assoc prof & assoc vet, 52-57, prof vet med & vet, 57-78, EMER PROF, EXP STA, UNIV CALIF, DAVIS, 78- *Personal Data:* b Chicago, Ill, Feb 4, 14; m 40; c 2. *Educ:* Mich State Col, DVM, 38; Univ Calif, MS, 40, PhD(comp path), 46. *Honors & Awards:* Mark Morris Found Award, 61; Am Vet Med Asn Res Award, 71; Vet Med Res Award, 71; K F Meyer Gold Cane Award, 85; E P Pope Diagnosticians Award, 85; Fulbright Award, 57 & 58. *Prof Exp:* Asst, Univ Calif, Berkeley, 38-40. *Concurrent Pos:* Collabr bur animal indust, USDA, Mex, 48-49; pres, Conf Vet Lab Diag, 59-60; mem bd dirs, Am Col Vet Microbiologists, 66-70, pres, 69-70; mem virus study sect, NIH, 68-70; consult animal & plant health inspection serv, USDA, 68-85, consult, Plum Island Animal Dis Res Ctr, 78-81. *Mem:* Fel Am Acad Microbiol; Am Vet Med Asn; Am Asn Avian Path; Sigma Xi. *Res:* Virus diseases, especially vesicular and myxovirus groups; diagnosis; prevention and control of diseases of animals. *Mailing Add:* 3119 Evening Bay Pl Davis CA 95616

BANKS, ARTHUR L, PUBLIC HEALTH & EPIDEMIOLOGY. *Current Pos:* DIR, RETAIL FOOD PROTECTION BR, FOOD & DRUG ADMIN, 80- *Personal Data:* b Ind, Nov 23, 40. *Educ:* Southern Ill Univ, BA, 65. *Prof Exp:* Environ health adminr, Monroe County Health Dept, 65-72; sr food & milk specialist, NY, Field Off, 72-77. *Mailing Add:* Ctr Food Safety & Appl Nutrit FDA MS HFS-627 200 C St SW Washington DC 20204. *Fax:* 202-205-5560; *E-Mail:* alb@fdacf.ssw.dhhs.gov

BANKS, DALLAS O, APPLIED MATHEMATICS. *Current Pos:* from asst prof to assoc prof, 59-70, PROF MATH, UNIV CALIF, DAVIS, 70- *Personal Data:* b Campbell, Nebr, Oct 21, 28; m 52; c 3. *Educ:* Ore State Univ, BS, 50, MS, 52; Carnegie Mellon Univ, PhD(math), 59. *Prof Exp:* Math asst, Gen Elec Co, Wash, 52-54. *Concurrent Pos:* Grant, Air Force Off Sci Res, 62-65; consult, Lawrence Livermore Lab, 78- *Mem:* Math Asn Am; Am Math Soc; Soc Indust & Appl Math. *Res:* Differential equations of engineering and physics; mathematical modelling in engineering. *Mailing Add:* Dept Math Univ Calif Davis CA 95616-5224

BANKS, DONALD JACK, BOTANY, PLANT TAXONOMY. *Current Pos:* prof agron, 77-90, EMER PROF AGRON, OKLA STATE UNIV, 90- *Personal Data:* b Sentinel, Okla, July 11, 30; m 52; c Michael & Sandra. *Educ:* Okla State Univ, BS, 53, MS, 58; Univ Ga, PhD(bot), 63. *Honors & Awards:* Nat Peanut Coun Res & Educ Award, 91. *Prof Exp:* Instr agron, Auburn Univ, 58-60; asst prof biol, Stephen F Austin State Col, 63-66; res geneticist, Plant Sci Res Div, Agr Res Serv, USDA, 66-90. *Concurrent Pos:* Assoc prof agron, Okla State Univ, 68-77. *Mem:* Bot Soc Am; Am Soc Plant Taxon; Crop Sci Soc Am; Sigma Xi; AAAS; fel Am Peanut Res & Educ Soc. *Res:* Plant taxonomy, agrostology, cytology, genetics and breeding; speciation in genus Paspalum; studies in the Paspalum setaceum Michaux complex; breeding, genetics, cytology, speciation and evolution of peanuts. *Mailing Add:* PO Box 2286 Stillwater OK 74076-2286

BANKS, EPHRAIM, inorganic chemistry; deceased, see previous edition for last biography

BANKS, GRACE ANN, PHYSICAL CHEMISTRY. *Current Pos:* ASSOC PROF CHEM & PHYS, CHESTNUT HILL COL, 79- *Personal Data:* b Philadelphia, Pa, Apr 1, 42. *Educ:* Chestnut Hill Col, BS, 72; Univ NC, Chapel Hill, MS, 75, PhD(chem), 78. *Prof Exp:* Teacher physics, chem, Notre Dame High Sch, Easton, Pa, 70-73; teaching asst chem, Univ NC, 73-75, res asst, 75-77; asst prof, St Augustine's Col, 77-79. *Mem:* Am Chem Soc; Nat Soc Teachers Asn. *Res:* Nuclear magnetic resonance spin lattice relaxation in low temperature organic solids. *Mailing Add:* Chestnut Hill Col Philadelphia PA 19118-2693

BANKS, HARLAN PARKER, PLANT MORPHOLOGY & ANATOMY, PALEOBOTANY. *Current Pos:* from assoc prof to prof, Cornell Univ, 49-77, head, Dept Bot, 52-61, Liberty Hyde Bailey prof bot, 77-78, EMER PROF BOT & EMER LIBERTY HYDE BAILEY PROF BOT, CORNELL UNIV, 78- *Personal Data:* b Cambridge, Mass, Sept 1, 13; m 39; c 2. *Educ:* Dartmouth Col, AB, 34; Cornell Univ, PhD(bot), 40. *Honors & Awards:* Int Medal, Paleont Asn India, 91. *Prof Exp:* Instr bot, Dartmouth Col, 34-36; asst, Cornell Univ, 37-39, instr, 39-40; from instr to assoc prof biol, Acadia Univ, 40-47; asst prof bot, Univ Minn, 47-49. *Concurrent Pos:* Fulbright res scholar, Univ Liege, 57-58; Guggenheim fel, 63-64; fel, Clare Hall, Cambridge, 68-; lectr, Am Inst Biol Sci Vis Biologists Prog, 69-70 & 71-73; mem, Paleont Res Inst. *Mem:* Nat Acad Sci; Bot Soc Am (secy pro-tem, 52-53, treas, 64-67, vpres, 68, pres, 69); Torrey Bot Club; Int Orgn Paleobot (vpres, 64-69, pres, 69-75); foreign mem Geol Soc Belg. *Res:* Paleobotany, origin and early evolution of land plants (Devonian and other early Paleozoic Periods). *Mailing Add:* Plant Biol 228 Plant Sci Bldg Cornell Univ Ithaca NY 14853

BANKS, HAROLD DOUGLAS, ORGANIC CHEMISTRY. *Current Pos:* RES CHEMIST, US ARMY CHEM RES, DEVELOP & ENG CTR, ABERDEEN PROVING GROUND, 86- *Personal Data:* b Brooklyn, NY, Apr 28, 43; m 67, Vivian Youmans; c Alison & Matthew. *Educ:* Brooklyn Col, BS, 63, MA, 65; Cornell Univ, PhD(org chem), 70. *Prof Exp:* Assoc prof chem, Univ Bridgeport, 70-81; assoc prof chem, Atlanta Univ, 81-86. *Concurrent Pos:* Am Chem Soc Petrol Res Fund grant, Univ Bridgeport, 70; sabbatical leave, Nat Inst Arthritis, Metabolism, & Digestive Dis, NIH, 79-80. *Mem:* Am Chem Soc. *Res:* Synthesis of substituted piperidines and other heterocycles. *Mailing Add:* US Army Edgewood Res Develop & Eng Ctr Aberdeen Proving Ground MD 21010-5423. *Fax:* 410-671-2107; *E-Mail:* hdhanks@cdbcom.apgea.army.mil

BANKS, HARVEY OREN, civil engineering, water resources; deceased, see previous edition for last biography

BANKS, HENRY H, ORTHOPEDIC SURGERY. *Current Pos:* dean, 83-90, prof, 70-90, CHMN DEPT, SCH MED, TUFTS UNIV, 70-, ASSOC DEAN AFFIL HOSPS, 72-, EMER DEAN & EMER PROF ORTHOP SURG, 90- *Personal Data:* b Boston, Mass, Mar 9, 21; m 45; c 3. *Educ:* Harvard Univ, BA, 42; Tufts Univ, MD, 45; Am Bd Orthop Surg, cert, 56. *Prof Exp:* Geogr, Peter Brent Brigham Hosp, 53-70. *Concurrent Pos:* Asst clin prof orthop surg, Harvard Med Sch, 65-70; head div orthop, Peter Bent Brigham Hosp, 68-70; surgeon-in-charge pediat orthop surg, New Eng Med Ctr Hosps, 70-71; dir orthop surg, Boston City Hosp, 70-75, chmn surg serv, 61-73; consult orthop surg, numerous hosps. *Mem:* Am Orthop Asn; Am Acad Orthop Surg; Int Soc Orthop Surg & Traumatology; Orthop Res Soc; Am Acad Cerebral Palsy (past pres); Am Bd Orthop Surg(secy-treas, 75-78, pres, 78-79). *Mailing Add:* Sch Med Tufts Univ 136 Harrison Ave Boston MA 02111-1800

BANKS, JERRY, INDUSTRIAL ENGINEERING, OPERATIONS RESEARCH SIMULATION. *Current Pos:* Asst prof indust eng, 65-66, assoc prof, 70-93, PROF INDUST & SYSTS ENG, GA INST TECHNOL, 93- *Personal Data:* b Birmingham, Ala, Apr 23, 39; m 88, Nancy Singer; c David & Susan. *Educ:* Univ Ala, BS, 61, MS, 63; Okla State Univ, PhD(indust eng), 66. *Mem:* Am Inst Indust Engrs; Opers Res Soc Am; Soc Mfg Engrs; Soc Comput Simulation; Int Test & Eval Asn. *Res:* Knowledge based on line simulation. *Mailing Add:* Sch Indust Eng Ga Inst Technol 225 North Ave NW Atlanta GA 30332-0001

BANKS, KEITH L, immunopathology, for more information see previous edition

BANKS, NORMAN GUY, GEOLOGY, VOLCANOLOGY. *Current Pos:* Geologist ore deposits, US Geol Surv, Ariz & Wash, 67-78, Volcanoes-Hawaii, 78-85, Mt St Helens, 80, Pagan Mariana Islands, 81, Indonesia, 83, Papua New Guinea & Mayon, Philippines, 83-84, Latin Am, 85-92, US Embassy sci officer, Chile, 92-94, GEOLOGIST, US GEOL SURVEY, CENT & SAM, 85- *Personal Data:* b Philadelphia, Pa, Feb 19, 40; m, Jane M Buchanan; c Adna (Sydelle) & Janet L. *Educ:* NMex Inst Mining & Technol, BS, 62; Univ Calif, San Diego, MS, 65, PhD(geol), 67. *Mem:* Soc Econ Geologists; Int Asn Genesis Ore Deposits; AAAS; Geol Soc Am; Int Asn Volcanology & Chem Earths Interior; Am Geophys Union; Northwest Mining Asn; Am Geophys Inst. *Res:* Geologic mapping; economic geology; petrology; geochemistry; volcanology, domestic and international; petrology of porphyry copper deposits, Arizona and Washington; volcano hazards mitigation and crisis management. *Mailing Add:* Cascades Volcano Observ US Geol Surv 5400 MacArthur Blvd Vancouver WA 98661. *Fax:* 206-696-7866; *E-Mail:* hbanks@mallvan.wr.usgs.gov

BANKS, PETER MORGAN, SPACE PLASMA SCIENCE, ACTIVE EXPERIMENTS IN SPACE. *Current Pos:* PRES & CHIEF EXEC OFFICER, EVIRON RES INST MICH, ANN ARBOR, 95- *Personal Data:* b San Diego, Calif, May 21, 37; m 60, 83, Paulett M Behanna; c Kevin, Michael, Steven & David. *Educ:* Stanford Univ, MS, 60; Pa State Univ, PhD(physics), 65. *Honors & Awards:* Appleton Prize, Royal Soc London, 78; Space Sci Award, Am Inst Aeronaut & Astronaut, 81; Distinguished Pub Serv Medal, NASA, 86; Nicolet lectr, Am Geophys Union, 91; Waynick Mem lectr, 92. *Prof Exp:* Res asst physics, Pa State Univ, 63-65; res assoc aeronomy, Inst Space Aeronomy, Brussels, Belg, 65-66; from asst prof to prof electrophys, Univ Calif, San Diego, 66-76; prof & head, Dept Physics, Utah State Univ, 76-81; prof elec eng & dir, Space, Telecommun & Radiosci Lab, Stanford Univ, 81-90; dean & prof, Col Eng, Univ Mich, 90-95. *Concurrent Pos:* prin investr, Vehicle Charging & Potential Exp, NASA, 78-84, Shuttle

Electrodynamic Tether Syst, 85-; fel, Pa State Univ, 81; mem, Space Sci Adv Comt, 83-87; chmn, Task Force on Sci Uses of Space Sta, NASA, 83-87; mem bd dirs, Ctr Space & Applns Technol, Fairfax, Va, 88-94, Indust Technol Inst, Ann Arbor, Mich, 90- & Mich Instrnl Television Network, 91-92; mem adv group, Aspen Global Cahnge Inst, 88-93; mem sci bd, Innovare, SRL, Naples, Italy, 89-; mem bd dir, Space Dynamic Labs Inc, Logan, Utah, 89, Tecumseh Prod Inc, Mich, 91-, Ford Design Inst, Dearborn, Mich, 91-95, Res Environ Ind Corp, Cleveland, Ohio, 92-96, CIESIN, Saginaw, Mich, 94- *Mem:* AAAS; fel Am Geophys Union; Int Sci Radio Union; Soc Automotive Engrs; Nat Acad Eng. *Res:* Structure of the upper atmosphere; aeronomy; magnetospheric physics. *Mailing Add:* Environ Res Inst Mich PO Box 134001 Ann Arbor MI 48113-4001. *Fax:* 313-994-6070; *E-Mail:* peter_banks@erim.org

BANKS, PHILIP ALAN, WEED SCIENCE, SOIL-HERBICIDE INTERACTIONS. *Current Pos:* PRES, MARATHON AGR & ENVIRON CONSULT INC, 90- *Personal Data:* b Sentinel, Okla, Jan 12, 52; div; c 2. *Educ:* Okla State Univ, BS, 74, MS, 76; Tex A&M Univ, PhD(agron), 78. *Honors & Awards:* Outstanding Young Scientist Award, Weed Sci Soc Am, 88. *Prof Exp:* Instr agron, Tex A&M Univ, 77-78; from asst prof to prof agron, Univ Ga, 79-90. *Concurrent Pos:* Lectr, Fed Rural Univ Pernambues, Brazil, 87. *Mem:* Weed Sci Soc Am; Am Soc Agron. *Res:* Weed biology, herbical persistence in soils; evaluation of general weed control practices in agronomic crops. *Mailing Add:* 2649 Navajo Rd Las Cruces NM 88005-5227

BANKS, PHILIP OREN, GEOLOGY, GEOCHEMISTRY. *Current Pos:* Asst prof, 63-80, ASSOC PROF GEOL, CASE WESTERN RES UNIV, 68- *Personal Data:* b Palo Alto, Calif, Jan 31, 37. *Educ:* Mass Inst Technol, BS, 58; Calif Inst Technol, PhD(geochem), 63. *Mem:* AAAS; Geol Soc Am; Mineral Soc Am; Am Geophys Union; Sigma Xi. *Res:* Geochronology; isotope geochemistry. *Mailing Add:* Dept Geol Case Western Res 10900 Euclid Ave Cleveland OH 44106-7216

BANKS, RICHARD C, ORGANIC CHEMISTRY. *Current Pos:* Asst prof org chem to assoc prof, 68-77, PROF CHEM, BOISE STATE UNIV, 78-, CHMN DEPT, 88- *Personal Data:* b Green Bay, Wis, Aug 19, 40; m 65; c 2. *Educ:* Col Idaho, BS, 63; Ore State Univ, PhD(org chem), 68. *Mem:* Am Chem Soc; Sigma Xi. *Res:* Isolations and identification problem on terpenes and terpene derivatives; synthesis of stable isotope labeled metabolites. *Mailing Add:* Chem Dept Boise State Univ Boise ID 83725-1010

BANKS, RICHARD CHARLES, ORNITHOLOGY, MAMMALOGY. *Current Pos:* ZOOLOGIST, PATUXENT WILDLIFE RES CTR, US GEOL SURV, 95- *Personal Data:* b Steubenville, Ohio, Apr 19, 31; m 67, Gladys Sparks; c Randall C & David R. *Educ:* Ohio State Univ, BS, 53; Univ Calif, Berkeley, MS, 58, PhD(zool), 61. *Prof Exp:* NSF grant & res biologist, Birds & Mammals, Calif Acad Sci, 61-62; cur & ed, San Diego Nat Hist Mus, 62-66; chief, Bird Sect, Bird & Mammal Labs, US Fish & Wildlife Serv, 66-71, dir, 71-73, staff specialist, Div Wildlife Res, 73-78, zoologist, Biol Surv Sect, NERC, 78-93, Denver Wildlife Res Ctr, Nat Biol Surv, 93-95. *Concurrent Pos:* Res assoc, Dept Vert Zool, Smithsonian Inst, 67- *Mem:* Am Ornithologists Union (secy, 69-73, vpres, 86-87, pres elect, 92-94, pres, 94-96); Am Soc Mammal; Cooper Ornith Soc; Wilson Ornith Soc (2nd vpres, 87-89, 1st vpres, 89-91, pres, 91-93); Asn Field Ornith. *Res:* Systematics, distribution, molt and hybridization of American birds; endangered species; biology of introduced species. *Mailing Add:* Biol Res Div US Geol Surv Nat Mus Natural Hist Washington DC 20560

BANKS, ROBERT B(LACKBURN), FLUID MECHANICS. *Current Pos:* CONSULT, 85- *Personal Data:* b Wichita, Kans, Oct 12, 22; m 60; c 2. *Educ:* Northwestern Univ, BSCE, 47, MS, 49; Univ Calif, PhD(fluid mech), 51; Univ London, DIC, 52. *Hon Degrees:* DTech, Asian Inst Technol, 84. *Prof Exp:* Res engr, Univ Calif, 49-51; develop engr fluid mech res, Infilco, Inc, 52-54; lectr civil eng, Northwestern Univ, 54-55, assoc prof civil eng & sci eng, 55-59, chmn sci-eng comt, 55-57 & Dept Civil Eng, 56-58, prof eng sci, 59-61, 56-58, asst dean res & grad studies, 60-61; prof eng & dir res, Asian Inst Technol, Bangkok, 61-63; prof eng sci & dean eng, Univ Ill, Chicago, 63-67; prog adv sci & technol, Ford Found, Mexico, 67-76; prof eng, Nat Autonomous Univ Mex, 67-76; pres, Asian Inst Technol, Bangkok, 76-83; exec officer, Int Serv for Nat Agr Res, The Hague, 83-85. *Mem:* Am Soc Eng Educ; AAAS; Am Geophys Union. *Res:* Fluid mechanics; biomathematics; environmental engineering; scientific and engineering education; international education. *Mailing Add:* 400 Prospect St Apt 232 La Jolla CA 92037

BANKS, ROBERT O, RENAL HEMODYNAMICS, ATRIAL NATRIURETIC FACTOR. *Current Pos:* ASSOC PROF PHYSIOL, COL MED, UNIV CINCINNATI, 70- *Educ:* State Univ NY, Buffalo, PhD(physiol), 68. *Mailing Add:* Dept Physiol & Biophys Univ Cincinnati Col Med 231 Bethesda Ave Cincinnati OH 45267-0576

BANKS, ROBERT R(AE), CHEMICAL ENGINEERING, METALLURGY. *Current Pos:* CONSULT ENG, 86- *Personal Data:* b New York, NY, Oct 19, 25; m 61; c 2. *Educ:* Columbia Univ, BS, 44, MS, 46, PhD(chem eng), 50. *Prof Exp:* Assoc chem engr, Armour Res Found, 50-51, res metallurgist, 51-53; sr engr, Air Reduction Co, Inc, 53-54, sect head, 54-56, supvr, 56-59, proj engr, Air Reduction Sales Co, 59-60, engr, 60-63, supvr, Air Reduction Co, Inc, 63-67, mgr develop, Pittsburgh Metall Co Div, 67-69, mem staff, Airco Alloys, NY, 69-76; mgr res & develop, Wheelabrator-Frye Inc, 76-86. *Mem:* Am Chem Soc; Am Inst Chem Engrs; Iron & Steel Soc; Am Soc Metals; Air & Waste Mgt Asn; Am Filtration Soc. *Res:* Ferroalloys; piloting of smelting processes; electron beam equipment; cryogenic engineering; brazing, high vacuum equipment; inorganic chemical processes; air pollution control equipment. *Mailing Add:* 1817 Tilton Dr Pittsburgh PA 15241-2636

BANKS, RONALD ERIC, CHEMISTRY. *Current Pos:* PROF CHEM, UNIV MANCHESTER, ENG. *Honors & Awards:* Creative Work in Flourine Chem Award, Am Chem Soc, 93. *Mailing Add:* Dept Chem Univ Manchester P O Box 88 Sackville St Manchester M6O 1QD England

BANKS, THOMAS, STRING THEORY, QUANTUM FIELD THEORY. *Current Pos:* PROF PHYSICS, RUTGERS UNIV, 89- *Personal Data:* b New York, NY, Apr 19, 49; m 69; c 2. *Educ:* Reed Col, BA, 69; Mass Inst Technol, PhD(physics). *Prof Exp:* Fel physics, Tel Aviv Univ, Israel, 73-75, lectr, 75-77, sr lectr, 77-80, from assoc prof to prof, 80-85; prof physics, Univ Calif, Santa Cruz, 86-89. *Concurrent Pos:* Mem, Inst Advan Study, 76-78, Einstein fel, 83-84; vis prof, Stanford Univ, 82-86. *Mem:* Am Phys Soc. *Res:* Theory of elementary particles; quantum field theory; renormalization group; string theory; quantum cosmology. *Mailing Add:* Dept Phys & Astron PO Box 849 Piscataway NJ 08855-0849

BANKS, WILLIAM JOSEPH, JR, veterinary histology, veterinary gross anatomy; deceased, see previous edition for last biography

BANKS, WILLIAM LOUIS, JR, ONCOLOGY, NUTRITION. *Current Pos:* from asst prof to prof biochem, 65-74, co-dir Cancer Ctr, 74-88, PROF BIOCHEM/MOLECULAR BIOPHYS & SURG, MED COL VA, 74-, DIR, NUTRIT SCI CTR, 88- *Personal Data:* b Paterson, NJ, Mar 25, 36; m 65, Sharon Hazelton; c Heather. *Educ:* Rutgers Univ, BS, 58, PhD(physiol, biochem), 63; Bucknell Univ, MS, 61. *Prof Exp:* Clin lab officer, USAF Sch Aerospace Med, 63-65. *Concurrent Pos:* Lectr, St Mary's Univ, Tex, 64-65. *Mem:* Am Asn Cancer Res; Am Chem Soc; Am Inst Nutrit; NY Acad Sci; AAAS; Fedn Soc Exp Biol & Med. *Res:* Diet and cancer; cancer education; nutrition and cancer therapy. *Mailing Add:* Dept Biochem & Molecular Biophys Med Col Va Richmond VA 23298-0614. *Fax:* 804-828-8530; *E-Mail:* banks@gems.vcu.edu

BANKS, WILLIAM MICHAEL, ZOOLOGY. *Current Pos:* from asst prof to assoc prof, 61-67, PROF ZOOL, HOWARD UNIV, 70- *Personal Data:* b New York, NY, Jan 10, 14; m 43; c 1. *Educ:* Univ Iowa, BA, 42; Ohio State Univ, MA, 49, PhD, 53. *Prof Exp:* From assoc prof to prof biol, Agr & Technol Col NC, 52-56; assoc prof, Grambling Col, 56-58; prof & chmn dept, Clark Col, 58-61. *Mem:* AAAS; Am Micros Soc; Am Soc Zool; Entom Soc Am; Am Inst Biol Soc. *Res:* Taxonomy; life cycles and nutritional requirements of trematodes; invertebrate physiology; carbohydrases; composition of hemolymph; cardiology of cockroaches; characterization and biological effects of bacterial toxins. *Mailing Add:* 4207 Blagden Ave NW Washington DC 20011

BANKS, WILLIAM PREAS, PERCEPTION, COGNITION. *Current Pos:* PROF PSYCHOL, POMONA COL, 69- *Personal Data:* div; c Joshua & Abigail. *Educ:* St Johns Col, BA, 64; Johns Hopkins Univ, MA, 66, PhD(psychol), 68. *Res:* Attention and the relation between attention and perception. *Mailing Add:* Dept Psychol Pomona Col 333 N College Way Claremont CA 91711-6301. *E-Mail:* wbanks@pomona.claremont.edu

BANK-SCHLEGEL, SUSAN PAMELA, CELL BIOLOGY, TUMOR BIOLOGY. *Current Pos:* SR STAFF FEL, NAT CANCER INST, 80- *Educ:* Northwestern Sch Med, PhD(microbiol), 73. *Mailing Add:* Div Lung Dis Airways Biol & Dis Br Nat Heart Lung & Blood Inst 2 Rockledge Ctr Suite 10018 6701 Rockledge Dr Bethesda MD 20892-7920. *Fax:* 301-496-9886

BANKSON, DANIEL DUKE, CANCER PREVENTION, CLINICAL CHEMISTRY. *Current Pos:* ASST CHIEF CLIN CHEM, VET AFFAIRS MED CTR, SEATTLE, WASH, 93- *Personal Data:* b Moscow, Idaho, June 27, 56; m 82; c 1. *Educ:* Univ BC, BSc, 78; Mass Inst Technol, SM, 82, PhD(nutrit), 85. *Honors & Awards:* Young Investr Award, Acad Clin La Physicians & Scientists, 87; Travel Award, Am Asn Clin Chem, 87. *Prof Exp:* Res asst nutrit, Univ BC, 78 & Mass Inst Technol, 79-82; sr res asst nutrit, Tufts Univ, 82-85, res assoc, 85-86; fel clin chem, NC Mem Hosp, 86-88; res fel endocrin, Univ NC, 88-89; assoc cancer prev, Fred Hutchinson Cancer Res Ctr, 89-93. *Concurrent Pos:* Dipl, Am Bd Clin Chem, 90; asst prof, Lab Med, Univ Wash, 93- *Mem:* Am Asn Clin Chem (treas, 90-92); Fedn Am Socs Exp Biol; Am Inst Nutrit; Am Soc Clin Nutrit; Am Asn Cancer Res; Nat Acad Clin Biochem. *Res:* Cancer prevention research: how nutrition may help prevent cancer; role of vitamin A in health and disease. *Mailing Add:* Dept Clin Chem Vet Admin Med Ctr 1660 S Columbian Way 113 Seattle WA 98108. *Fax:* 206-764-2001

BANN, ROBERT (FRANCIS), ORGANIC CHEMISTRY. *Current Pos:* RETIRED. *Personal Data:* b New Baden, Ill, June 30, 21; m 60, Elizabeth Squier; c Charles, Robert, James & Kenneth. *Educ:* Univ Ill, BS, 43; Rutgers Univ, MS, 59. *Prof Exp:* Sect chief chemist, Am Cyanamid Co, 56-65, chief chemist, 65-68, gen supt, Dyes Mfg, 68-73, mgr, Dyes & Chem Intermediates Prod, Dyes Dept, Org Chem Div, 73-76, plant mgr, 76-89. *Mem:* Am Chem Soc; Am Asn Textile Chemists & Colorists. *Res:* Azo dyes and intermediates; triphenylmethane dyes; dyes for synthetic fibers. *Mailing Add:* 119 Meadow Lane Marietta OH 45750-1345

BANNAI, EICHI, COMBINATORICS MATHEMATICS. *Current Pos:* PROF MATH, OHIO STATE UNIV, 74- *Personal Data:* b Tokyo, Japan, Feb 07, 46. *Educ:* Tokyo Univ, PhD(math), 74. *Mem:* Am Math Soc; Japanese Math Soc. *Mailing Add:* Kyushu Univ Grad Sch Math Hakozaki 6-10-1 Fukuoka 812 Japan

BANNAN, ELMER ALEXANDER, MICROBIOLOGY. *Current Pos:* RETIRED. *Personal Data:* b Wilmington, Del, Sept 5, 28; m 58; c 3. *Educ:* Univ Mich, BS, 58, MS, 60. *Prof Exp:* Microbiologist, Procter & Gamble, Co, 60-73, mgr dermal safety testing, 73-87, mgr qual assurance, 88-94. *Mem:* Am Soc Microbiol; Soc Indust Microbiol; Soc Qual Assurance. *Res:* Bacterial physiology, the ultra structure of bacterial spores; antimicrobial cleansing products; skin degerming; human skin response to cleaning products. *Mailing Add:* 9492 Shamrock West Chester OH 45069

BANNARD, ROBERT ALEXANDER BROCK, ORGANIC CHEMISTRY. *Current Pos:* RETIRED. *Personal Data:* b Edmonton, Alta, Apr 28, 22; m 46; c 2. *Educ:* Queen's Univ, BSc, 45, MSc, 46; McGill Univ, PhD(chem), 49. *Prof Exp:* Jr res officer, Atomic Energy Proj, Nat Res Coun Can, 49-50, asst res officer, Div Appl Chem, 50-51; Sci Serv Officer, Defense Res Estab Ottawa, Defense Res Bd, 52-86. *Mem:* Am Chem Soc; fel Chem Inst Can; Royal Soc Chem; fel Royal Inst Chem. *Res:* Stereochemistry; organophosphorus chemistry; heterocyclics; alicyclic compounds; gas-liquid chromatographic separations and analysis. *Mailing Add:* 152 Robertlee Dr PO Box 219 Carp ON K0A 1L0 Can

BANNER, DAVID LEE, PHYSICS. *Current Pos:* NON PROLIFERATION ARMS CONTROL, INT SECURITY DEPT, LAWRENCE LIVERMORE NAT LAB. *Personal Data:* b St Joseph, Mo, Jan 7, 42; m 86; c 2. *Educ:* Purdue Univ, BS, 64; Univ Ill, MS, 66, PhD(physics), 72. *Prof Exp:* Res physicist mat studies, B-Div, Lawrence Livermore Lab, Univ Calif, 72, group leader, 73-75, proj mgr lab liaison with Air Force, D-Div, 75-77, asst assoc prog leader laser fusion, Y Div, 77-81; mgr, Advan Technol, FMC Corp, San Jose, Calif, 81-82; group leader appl technol, Z Div, 82-90; head, Physics Sect, Dept Res & Isotopes, IAEA, Vienna, Austria, 90- *Mem:* Am Phys Soc. *Res:* Weak interactions of elementary particles; material properties of materials under high pressure and high rates of strain; inertial confinement fusion using lasers as the driver. *Mailing Add:* Lawrence Livermore Nat Lab PO Box 808 L-183 Livermore CA 94550

BANNERMAN, DOUGLAS GEORGE, TEXTILE CHEMISTRY. *Current Pos:* ENVIRON CONSULT, NEMA, 83- *Personal Data:* b Calgary, Alta, Can, Feb 22, 17; US citizen; m 42; c 4. *Educ:* Beloit Col, BS, 39; Colo Col, MA, 41; Mass Inst Technol, PhD(chem), 45. *Prof Exp:* Instr chem, Colo Col, 39-41 & Mass Inst Technol, 42-45; asst prof, Colo Col, 45-46; res chemist, E I du Pont De Nemours & Co, 45-56, merchandising mgr, 56-60, mkt develop mgr, 60-78; adv toxic substances, US Environ Protection Agency, 78-82. *Mem:* Am Chem Soc. *Res:* Organic research in heterocyclic chemistry; high polymer chemistry; synthetic fiber research; textile development; synthetic fiber paper; toxic substances regulation. *Mailing Add:* 1250 Washigton St Apt 404 Alexandria VA 22314

BANNERMAN, JAMES KNOX, PHYSICAL CHEMISTRY. *Current Pos:* RETIRED. *Personal Data:* b Houston, Tex, Sept 11, 46. *Educ:* Houston Baptist Univ, BA, 68; Baylor Univ, PhD(chem), 73. *Prof Exp:* Pres, Bannerman & Assoc, Specialty Chem & Minerals, 84-89. *Mem:* Am Chem Soc; Am Inst Chemists; Mineral Soc Am; Clay Minerals Soc. *Res:* Clay mineral syntheses; clay surface modification; water-soluble polymer chemistry. *Mailing Add:* 4635 Banning Dr Houston TX 77027

BANNING, JON WILLROTH, regulatory affairs, for more information see previous edition

BANNING, LLOYD H(AROLD), METALLURGY. *Current Pos:* RETIRED. *Personal Data:* b St Lawrence, SDak, Feb 21, 09; m 35; c 1. *Educ:* SDak Sch Mines & Technol, BS, 31. *Prof Exp:* Assayer, Canyon Corp, 35-38; Gilt Edge Mining Co, 38-39; chemist, Bald Mountain Mining Co, 39-42; mine mgr, Va Hardwood Lumber Co, 42; metallurgist, Bur Mines, Md, 42-47; asst plant supt, Titanium Dioxide Plant, Chem & Pigment Co, 47-48; metallurgist, Bur Mines, US Dept Interior, 48-52, proj coordr, Pyometallurgic Lab, 52-65, Scrap Utilization Lab, 65-67, metallurgist, 67-74. *Mem:* Am Inst Mining, Metall & Petrol Engrs; Sci Res Soc Am. *Res:* Recovery of copper, nickel, chromium and titanium from low-grade ores and tin, copper and iron from municipal incinerator residues. *Mailing Add:* 4779 Independence Dr Bradenton FL 34210

BANNISTER, BRIAN, ORGANIC CHEMISTRY. *Current Pos:* proj leader, Dept Chem, 54-73, SR SCIENTIST, DEPT INFECTIOUS DIS, UPJOHN CO, 73- *Personal Data:* b Gateshead, Eng, Mar 10, 26; m 57, Mary Jo Shea. *Educ:* Oxford Univ, BA, 47, BSc, 47, MA & DPhil(org chem), 50. *Prof Exp:* Nuffield Found res fel, Dyson Perrins Lab, Univ Oxford, 50-52; Alumni Res Found fel, Univ Wis, 52-53, NSF fel, 53-54. *Mem:* Am Chem Soc; The Chem Soc. *Res:* Degradative and synthetic investigations in field of natural products, with major emphasis on antibiotics. *Mailing Add:* 4150 E Hillandale Dr Upjohn Co Henrietta St Kalamazoo MI 49008-3138

BANNISTER, BRYANT, DENDROCHRONOLOGY. *Current Pos:* Lab asst dendrochronology, Univ Ariz, 51-53, res asst, 53-54, cur archaeol collections, 54-59, from instr to prof dendrochronology, 59-89, dir, Lab Tree Ring Res, 64-82, asst dean, Col Earth Sci, 71-72, actg dean, 72, assoc dean, 72-82, EMER DIR, LAB TREE RING RES, UNIV ARIZ, 82-, EMER PROF DENDROCHRONOLOGY, 89- *Personal Data:* b Phoenix, Ariz, Dec 2, 26; m 51; c 2. *Educ:* Yale Univ, BA, 48; Univ Ariz, MA, 53, PhD(anthrop), 60. *Concurrent Pos:* Ed, Tree-Ring Bull, 58-69; collabr, Nat Park Serv, 60-; res assoc, Mus Northern Ariz, 60-77. *Mem:* Fel AAAS; fel Am Anthrop Asn; Soc Am Archaeol; Tree-Ring Soc. *Res:* Derivation and application of archaeological tree-ring dates. *Mailing Add:* Lab Tree-Ring Res Univ Ariz Tucson AZ 85721

BANNISTER, PETER ROBERT, physics, mathematics, for more information see previous edition

BANNISTER, ROBERT GRIMSHAW, TEXTILE CHEMISTRY, TEXTILE EQUIPMENT. *Current Pos:* res chemist textile chem, E I du Pont de Nemours & Co, Inc, 51-53, patent chemist, 53-63, sr patent specialist, 63-79, PATENT ASSOC TEXTILE CHEM, E I DU PONT DE NEMOURS & CO, INC, 79- *Personal Data:* b Terre Haute, Ind, Oct 27, 25; m 56; c 4. *Educ:* Rose Polytech Inst, BS, 46; Univ Ill, MS, 48, PhD(org chem), 51. *Prof Exp:* Chemist anal chem, Com Solvents Corp, 47-48. *Mem:* Am Chem Soc. *Res:* Fiber forming polymers; fiber structure; industrial fibers; textile machinery; chemical and textile patents. *Mailing Add:* 2103 Largo Rd Wilmington DE 19803-2307

BANNISTER, THOMAS TURPIN, BIOLOGY. *Current Pos:* instr biol, 58-60, from asst prof to assoc prof, 61-69, chmn Dept Biol, 69-75, PROF RADIATION BIOL & BIOPHYS, UNIV ROCHESTER, 69- *Personal Data:* b Orange, NJ, Apr 20, 30; m 53; c 2. *Educ:* Duke Univ, BS, 51; Univ Ill, MS, 53, PhD(biophys), 58. *Prof Exp:* Res asst, Duke Univ, 48-51 & Univ Ill, 51-53, 55-58. *Concurrent Pos:* NIH res fel, Nat Cent Sci Res, France, 62-63. *Mem:* Am Soc Plant Physiol; Biophys Soc. *Res:* Photosynthesis; photochemistry of chlorophyll and energy transfer; plant and cell physiology; biophysics; ecology of algae. *Mailing Add:* Dept Biol Univ Rochester 500 Joseph C Wilson Rochester NY 14627-9000

BANNISTER, WILLIAM WARREN, PHYSICAL ORGANIC CHEMISTRY & COMBUSTION CHEMISTRY, FIRE FIGHTING TECHNOLOGIES. *Current Pos:* PROF CHEM, UNIV LOWELL, 67- *Personal Data:* b Terre Haute, Ind, Feb 24, 29; m 52; c 5. *Educ:* Purdue Univ, BS, 53, PhD(org chem), 61. *Prof Exp:* Chemist, Miami Valley Labs, Procter & Gamble Co, Ohio, 60-65; asst prof org chem, Tenn Tech Univ, 65-66; asst prof, Univ Cincinnati, 66-67. *Concurrent Pos:* Res grants, Sigma Xi, 66, NSF, 67 & 68, US Navy, 75, 76 & 79-80, Environ Protection Agency, 77 & 78, USAF/AFESC, 85- *Mem:* Am Chem Soc; Sigma Xi. *Res:* Structure-property correlations of organic compounds; acidities of organic compounds; organic reaction mechanisms; environmental chemistry with regard to inland, coastal and ocean waterways; fire initiation mechanisms. *Mailing Add:* One University Ave Lowell MA 01854-2881

BANNON, JAMES ANDREW, CLINICAL RESEARCH, POST-MARKETING SURVEILLANCE. *Current Pos:* Clin instr, 80-83, CLIN ASST PROF, PHILADELPHIA COL PHARM & SCI, 83-, SR VPRES MED RES, 92- *Personal Data:* b Philadelphia, Pa, June 17, 53; m 76; c 2. *Educ:* Philadelphia Col Pharm & Sci, BSc, 76, PharmD, 81. *Concurrent Pos:* Clin pharmacist, Temple Univ Hosp, 76-79, clin instr, Temple Univ Sch Pharm, 76-79; clin res assoc, Philadelphia Asn Clin Trials, 81-82, asst dir clin res, 82-86, vpres clin res, 86-92. *Mem:* Am Soc Clin Pharmacol & Therapeut; Am Soc Hosp Pharmacists; Am Heart Asn; Drug Info Asn. *Res:* The planning, conduct and analysis of large-scale post-marketing drug surveillance studies (up to 75,000 patients) and other peri-approval studies to treat patients not well studied in the phases of clinical drug development (e.g. elderly). *Mailing Add:* 150 Radnor Corp Ctr Radnor PA 19087

BANNON, ROBERT EDWARD, ophthalmology, optometry; deceased, see previous edition for last biography

BANOVITZ, JAY BERNARD, IMMUNOCHEMISTRY. *Current Pos:* RETIRED. *Personal Data:* b Los Angeles, Calif, Nov 10, 25. *Educ:* Univ Ill, BS, 46; Univ Wis, PhD(zool), 58. *Prof Exp:* Asst immunochem, Calif Inst Technol, 48-52; asst zool, Univ Wis, 52-57; res assoc biochem, Inst Cancer Res, Pa, 57-60; res immunologist, Nat Jewish Hosp, 60-66 & Childrens Asthma Res Inst & Hosp, 66-69; mgr immunol proj, Smith Kline Instruments, Inc, 70-73; mgr immunochem, Oxford Labs, 73-74; consult, 75-77; dept head immunochem, Antibodies Inc, 77-81, staff immunochemist & mgr regulatory affairs, 81-90. *Mem:* Am Asn Clin Chem; Am Asn Immunologists; Am Chem Soc. *Res:* Immunodiagnostic product development; immunochemistry and immunochemical product development. *Mailing Add:* 211 Ipanema Pl Davis CA 95616-0253

BANSAL, NAROTTAM PRASAD, GLASSES, CERAMIC MATRIX COMPOSITES. *Current Pos:* Sub-proj mgr, 94-96, RES SCI, NASA LEWIS RES CTR, 90- *Personal Data:* b Narnaul (Haryana) India, Sept 26, 46; m 74, Shashi Gupta; c Gaurav & Saurabh. *Educ:* Panjab Univ, BS, 65; Birla Inst Technol Sci, MS, 68; Delhi Univ, PhD(electrochem), 72. *Prof Exp:* Head qual control, Royal Pharmaceut, 68-69; res fel, Delhi Univ, 69-72, asst prof chem, 71-82; fel, Univ Alta, 75-77; res assoc, Rensselaer Polytech Inst, 77-78, 80, 82-85; sr res assoc, Nat Res Coun/NASA, 85-87; prin res sci, Case Western

Res Univ/NASA, 87-90. *Concurrent Pos:* Mem, Tech Comt 18, Int Comn Glass, 85-; secy, Northern Ohio Sect, Am Ceramic Soc, 92-93, vpres, 93-94, pres, 94-95. *Mem:* Fel Am Ceramic Soc. *Res:* Ceramic matrix composites for high-temperature turbine engine applications; high-temperature superconductors; sol-gel processing; chemical durability of glasses and ceramics; kinetics of phase transformation; awarded 4 US patents. *Mailing Add:* 25003 Tara-Lynn Dr North Olmsted OH 44070. *Fax:* 216-433-5544; *E-Mail:* narottam.p.bansal@lerc.nasa.gov

BANSCHBACH, MARTIN WAYNE, BIOCHEMISTRY, LIPID BIOCHEMISTRY. *Current Pos:* ASSOC PROF BIOCHEM, OKLA COL OSTEOP MED, TULSA, 80-, DIR, MOLECULAR MED RES CTR, 81- *Personal Data:* b Glen Cove, NY, July 5, 46; m 68; c 2. *Educ:* Susquehanna Univ, BA, 68; Va Polytech Inst & State Univ, MS, 71, PhD(biochem), 72. *Prof Exp:* NIH trainee, Univ Wis-Madison, 72-74, NIH fel, 74-75; asst prof biochem, Sch Med, La Univ, Shreveport, 75-80; assoc mem, Sch Grad Studies, La Univ Med Ctr, 75-80. *Concurrent Pos:* Special lectr biochem, Centenary Col, La, 77-80. *Mem:* AAAS; Am Chem Soc; Soc Exp Biol & Med; NY Acad Sci; Sigma Xi. *Res:* Lipid metabolism; role of membrane lipids in regulating calcium transport; role of prostaglandins in the regulation of cellular activity and the induction of human disease; calcium metabolism in patients with cystic fibrosis. *Mailing Add:* Okla Col Osteop 1111 W 17th St Tulsa OK 74107-1800

BANSE, KARL, BIOLOGICAL OCEANOGRAPHY, HYDROBIOLOGY. *Current Pos:* From asst prof to prof, 60-95, EMER PROF OCEANOG, UNIV WASH, 95- *Personal Data:* b Koenigsberg, Ger, Feb 20, 29. *Educ:* Univ Kiel, PhD(oceanog zool), 55. *Hon Degrees:* Dr, Univ Kiel, 95. *Mem:* AAAS; Am Soc Limnol & Oceanog; Marine Biol Asn UK; fel Marine Biol Asn India; Ger Zool Soc; Am Geophys Union. *Res:* Marine plankton production; Arabian Sea; remote sensing. *Mailing Add:* Sch Oceanog Univ Wash Box 357940 Seattle WA 98195-7940. *Fax:* 206-543-6073; *E-Mail:* banse@u.washington.edu

BANSIL, ARUN, CONDENSED MATTER PHYSICS. *Current Pos:* From asst prof to assoc prof, 76-87, PROF PHYSICS, NORTHEASTERN UNIV, 87- *Personal Data:* b New Delhi, India, Sept 16, 48; m, Rama; c Nisha, Amit & Rajat. *Educ:* Univ Delhi, BSc, 67; Stony Brook Univ, MA, 68; Harvard Univ, PhD(physics), 74. *Concurrent Pos:* Sci consult, Neth Energy Res Found, Holland, 87-; hon prof, Tampere Univ Technol, Finland, 89-; resident assoc, Argonne Nat Lab, 91-; mem, comn charge, spin & momentum densities, Int Union Crystallog, 93- *Mem:* Fel Am Phys Soc. *Res:* Electronic structure and properties of ordered and disordered materials; high-technetium superconductors and other complex systems. *Mailing Add:* Dept Physics Northeastern Univ Boston MA 02115. *Fax:* 617-373-8277; *E-Mail:* bansil@neu.edu

BANSIL, RAMA, POLYMER PHYSICS, STATISTICAL MECHANICS. *Current Pos:* res asst prof, 76-77, asst prof, 77-84, ASST PROF, DEPT PHYSIOL, SCH MED, BOSTON UNIV, ASSOC PROF PHYSICS, 84- *Personal Data:* b Bilaspur, India, Oct 29, 47; US citizen; m 72, Arun; c Nisha, Amit & Rajat. *Educ:* Delhi Univ, India, BSc Hons, 67, MSc, 69; Univ Rochester, PhD(physics), 75. *Prof Exp:* Res assoc, Harvard Univ, 74-75 & Mass Inst Technol, 75-76. *Concurrent Pos:* Sci scholar fel, Bunting Inst, Radcliffe Col, 93-94. *Mem:* Am Phys Soc; Am Chem Soc. *Res:* Physics of gels and polymers using light scattering techniques to study diffusion and phase separation kinetics related phenomena; computer simulation of gels; bio-macromolecule structure, phase transitions in membranes and biological gels; structure and gelation of mucin from stomach. *Mailing Add:* Physics Dept Boston Univ Boston MA 02215-2507. *Fax:* 617-353-9393; *E-Mail:* rb@buphy.bu.edu

BANTA, JAMES E, EPIDEMIOLOGY. *Current Pos:* prof epidemiol & dean, 75-87, ADJ PROF APPL HEALTH SCI, SCH PUB HEALTH & TROP MED, TULANE UNIV, 89-; CLIN PROF EPIDEMIOL, GEORGETOWN UNIV SCH MED, 90-; ADJ PROF HEALTH SERVS, GEORGE WASHINGTON UNIV MED SCH, 92. *Personal Data:* b Tucumcari, NMex, July 1, 27; m 50; c 2. *Educ:* Marquette Univ, MD, 50; Johns Hopkins Univ, MPH, 54; Am Bd Prev Med, dipl, 60. *Prof Exp:* Intern, Hosp Good Samaritan, US Navy, Los Angeles, Calif, 50-51, epidemiologist, US Naval Med Sch, 51-52 & Streptococcal Dis Res Unit, Naval Training Ctr, Md, 52-53, prev med officer, Third Marine Div, Far East, 54-55, sr investr, Virol Sect, Naval Res Inst, Md, 55-57, chief, Virol Sect, US Naval Med Res Unit, Egypt, 57-59, chief mil med, Naval Dispensary, Va, 59-60; chief coronary artery dis unit, USPHS, 60-62, dir, Ecol Field Sta, Univ Mo, Columbia, 62-63, dir & dep dir, Med Prog Div, Peace Corps, 63-65, head spec int progs, Off Int Res, NIH, 65-68; assoc prof, Sch Med, Georgetown Univ, 68-69, clin assoc prof, 69-70; prof pub health, Univ Hawaii, Manoa, 70-73; dep dir, Off Health, US AID, 73-75; prof pub health epidemiol, Univ Hawaii, Manoa, 87-88. *Concurrent Pos:* Lectr, US Naval Med Sch, 56-57; mem subcomt criteria & methodology, Comt Epidemiol, Am Heart Asn, 61-63; clin asst prof, Univ Mo, 62-68; chronic dis adv, WHO-Pan-Am Health Orgn, 69-70; fel Philadelphia Col Physicians; fel Am Col Epidemiol. *Mem:* Fel AAAS; fel Am Pub Health Asn; fel Am Col Prev Med; fel Am Heart Asn; Am Col Epidemiol. *Res:* Research epidemiology in infectious and chronic disease; epidemiologic studies ischemic heart disease; hypertension; environmental health; public health operations; international health. *Mailing Add:* 146 G St SW Washington DC 20024-4303

BANTA, MARION CALVIN, PHYSICAL CHEMISTRY, ANALYTICAL CHEMISTRY. *Current Pos:* asst prof, 68-77, assoc prof, 77-, PROF, SAM HOUSTON STATE UNIV. *Personal Data:* b Marshall, Tex, July 19, 34; m 61; c 2. *Educ:* NTex State Univ, BS, 56, MS, 57; Univ Tex, Austin, PhD(chem), 63. *Prof Exp:* Res chemist, Tracor, Inc, Tex, 60-61; sr res scientist, Esso Prod Res Co, 62-66; asst prof chem, ETex Baptist Col, 66-68. *Mem:* Am Chem Soc. *Res:* Electrochemical kinetics; kinetics of reaction in solution. *Mailing Add:* Dept Chem Sam Houston State Univ Huntsville TX 77340

BANTA, WILLIAM CLAUDE, INVERTEBRATE ZOOLOGY. *Current Pos:* ASSOC PROF BIOL, AM UNIV, 70- *Personal Data:* b Long Beach, Calif, Nov 13, 41; m 65; c Claude E, Joshua A & Jessica S. *Educ:* Univ Calif, Berkeley, BA, 63; Univ Southern Calif, PhD(biol), 69. *Prof Exp:* Res fel, Div Invert Paleont, Smithsonian Inst, 69-70. *Concurrent Pos:* Assoc ed, Chesapeake Sci, 75-; res prof, Univ Sydney, Australia, 77; vis prof, US Naval Acad, 86; fel, Am Soc Eng Educ, David Taylor Lab, Annapolis, 87, 88. *Mem:* NY Acad Sci; Sigma Xi; Am Micros Soc; Am Soc Zoologists. *Res:* Recent cheilostome and ctenostome Bryozoa; biological assessment of water quality; salt marshes; fouling. *Mailing Add:* Dept Biol Am Univ 4400 Massachusetts Ave NW Washington DC 20016-8001. *Fax:* 202-885-2182; *E-Mail:* wcbanta@american.edu

BANTER, JOHN C, PHYSICAL CHEMISTRY. *Current Pos:* assoc prof, 66-69, asst dean col sci, 89-95, PROF CHEM, FLA ATLANTIC UNIV, 69- *Personal Data:* b Marion, Ind, Dec 25, 31; m 83, Gail Sky; c Todd, Susan, Steven & Jeffrey. *Educ:* DePauw Univ, BA, 54; Western Res Univ, MS, 56, PhD(chem), 57. *Prof Exp:* Sr res chemist, Oak Ridge Nat Lab, Union Carbide Nuclear Corp, 57-66. *Concurrent Pos:* Consult, Metals & Ceramics Div, Oak Ridge Nat Lab, 67-69, Van Prod Corp, Chem Form Div, KMS Industs, Int Bus Mach Corp & City of Boca Raton, Fla, 68-69. *Mem:* Am Chem Soc; Electrochem Soc; Sigma Xi. *Res:* Kinetics and mechanisms of metallic corrosion; anodization of metals; solid state electrochemistry; thin oxide films; spectroscopy applied to the study of thin dielectric films. *Mailing Add:* 1150 NW 13th St No 1506 Boca Raton FL 33486-4797

BANTLE, JOHN ALBERT, CELL BIOLOGY, DEVELOPMENTAL BIOLOGY. *Current Pos:* asst prof, 76-80, assoc prof zool, 81-87, ASST PROF CELL BIOL, DEPT CELL MOLECULAR & DEVELOP BIOL, OKLA STATE UNIV, 76-, PROF ZOOL, 87-, ASSOC DEAN RES, 91- *Personal Data:* b Detroit, Mich, Jan 20, 46; m 69, Donetta L Lee; c Kelly & John. *Educ:* Eastern Mich Univ, BA, 68, MS, 70; Ohio State Univ, PhD(zool), 73. *Honors & Awards:* MASUA Hon lectr, 87. *Prof Exp:* Fel cell biol, Anat Dept, Univ Colo Med Ctr, 73-76. *Concurrent Pos:* NSF grant, 77-81, March Dimes Birth Defects Found, 81-87, USDA Coop Agreement, 84-92, US Army Biomed Res & Develop Command, 86- & USAF, 91- *Mem:* Am Soc Cell Biol; Am Soc Testing & Mat; Soc Environ Toxicologists & Chemists. *Res:* Regulation and expression of the animal genome; reproductive and developmental toxicology; mutagenesis and teratogenesis. *Mailing Add:* Dept Zool Okla State Univ Stillwater OK 74074. *Fax:* 405-744-7074

BANTTARI, ERNEST E, PLANT PATHOLOGY. *Current Pos:* From asst prof to assoc prof, 63-73, PROF PLANT PATH, UNIV MINN, ST PAUL, 73- *Personal Data:* b Bismarck, NDak, Aug 2, 32. *Educ:* Univ Minn, BS, 54, MS, 59, PhD(plant path), 62. *Mem:* Am Phytopath Soc. *Res:* Plant virology. *Mailing Add:* Dept Plant Path Univ Minn St Paul 1991 Upper Buford Cr 495 Borlaugh Hall St Paul MN 55108-6024

BANUCCI, EUGENE GEORGE, ORGANIC POLYMER CHEMISTRY. *Current Pos:* AT AM CYANAMID CO, 80- *Personal Data:* b Racine, Wis, June 5, 43; m 66; c 3. *Educ:* Beloit Col, BA, 65; Wayne State Univ, PhD(org chem), 70. *Prof Exp:* Staff chemist, Polymer Plastic Div, Gen Elec Corp, 70-75, tech coordr, Phys Chem Lab, Res & Develop Ctr, 75-76, mgr advan develop, Lexan Prod Dept, Plastics Div, 77-78, mgr, Arnox Prod Sect, 78-80. *Mem:* Am Chem Soc. *Res:* Heterocyclic chemistry; cycloaddition reactions; condensation polymers; high temperature materials; cyanopolymers. *Mailing Add:* 106 Adams Lane New Canaan CT 06840-6003

BANVILLE, BERTRAND, physics, for more information see previous edition

BANVILLE, MARCEL, theoretical physics; deceased, see previous edition for last biography

BANWART, GEORGE J, FOOD MICROBIOLOGY. *Current Pos:* prof food microbiol, 69-88, EMER PROF, OHIO STATE UNIV, 88- *Personal Data:* b Algona, Iowa, Sept 15, 26; m 55, Sally Foss; c Deborah J & Geoffrey D. *Educ:* Iowa State Univ, BS, 50, PhD(bact), 55. *Prof Exp:* Asst prof food technol, Univ Ga, 55-57; head egg prod sect, USDA, 57-62; assoc prof bact, Purdue Univ, 62-65; res microbiologist, Plant Indust Sta, USDA, Md, 65-69. *Mem:* Inst Food Technologists. *Res:* Salmonella in foods; methodology of Salmonella; methods to destroy Salmonella; egg products; food spoilage; public health organisms. *Mailing Add:* 262 Highgate Worthington OH 43085

BANWART, WAYNE LEE, SOILS. *Current Pos:* from asst prof to assoc prof soils, 75-84, PROF SOIL SCI, UNIV ILL, 84-, ASST DEAN, 95- *Personal Data:* b West Bend, Iowa, Jan 9, 48; m 70, Charlen Schrock; c Krista, Kara & Neil. *Educ:* Iowa State Univ, BS, 69, MS, 72, PhD(soil fertil), 75. *Honors & Awards:* George D Scarseth Award, Am Soc Agron, 74. *Prof Exp:* Res asst soil fertil, Iowa State Univ, 69-72, res assoc, 72-75. *Mem:* Fel Am Soc Agron;

fel Soil Sci Soc Am; fel Nat Asn Cols & Teachers Agr. *Res:* Factors affecting ionic balance of plants; sorption of organic compounds by soils, including herbicides; organic transformations of sulfur in soils and other natural systems; characterization of natural organics in soil rhizospheres; effect of acid rain on agricultural crops; bioremediation of chemically contaminated soils. *Mailing Add:* AW-101 Turner Univ Ill 1102 S Goodwin Urbana IL 61801. *Fax:* 217-333-9817; *E-Mail:* wayneb@ccmail.agn.uiuc.edu

BANWELL, JOHN G, MEDICINE, PHYSIOLOGY. *Current Pos:* PROF MED, GASTROENTEROL DIV, CASE WESTERN RES UNIV, 81- *Personal Data:* b Pegu, Burma, Aug 2, 30; US citizen; m 61; c 4. *Educ:* Oxford Univ, BA, 53, MD, 56, DM, 63. *Prof Exp:* Resident, Middlesexon Hosp, London, 56-59; fel, Johns Hopkins Univ Hosp, 59-61, asst prof, Dept Med, 66-72; prof med & chief gastroenterol, Dept Med, Med Ctr, Univ Ky, 72-81. *Mem:* Am Fedn Clin Res; Am Gastroenterol Asn; Am Col Physicians. *Res:* Intestinal function, scentern and absorptive junction; plant lectins. *Mailing Add:* Case Western Res Univ Sch Med 2119 Abington Cleveland OH 44106-2333

BANZETT, ROBERT B, RESPIRATORY PHYSIOLOGY. *Current Pos:* Asst prof, 80-85, ASSOC PROF PHYSIOL, SCH PUB HEALTH, HARVARD UNIV, 85- *Personal Data:* b Englewood, NJ, Aug 16, 47. *Educ:* Univ Calif, Davis, PhD(physiol), 74. *Mem:* Am Physiol Soc. *Res:* Respiratory sensation; avian respiration. *Mailing Add:* Dept Environ Health Sch Pub Health Harvard Univ 665 Huntington Ave Boston MA 02115-6021

BAO, JIAN-ZHONG, COMPUTER SIMULATION & SIGNAL PROCESSING ELECTROMAGNETIC PULSES. *Current Pos:* SR RES ENGR, MCKESSON BIOSERVS, 94- *Personal Data:* b Beijing, China, May 18, 58; m 88, Xiao Yue Yang; c Emily H. *Educ:* Northwestern Univ, China, BS, 82; Univ Md, PhD(chem physics), 91. *Prof Exp:* Res asst, Univ Md, 92-94. *Mem:* Am Phys Soc; sr mem Inst Elec & Electronics Engrs; sr mem Biophys Soc; Bioelectromagnetics Soc; Comput Soc. *Res:* Computer modeling of electromagnetics with the finite-difference-time-domain method using object-oriented methodologies; signal processing of pico second electromagnetic pulses; complex dielectric measurements and analysis of materials, including biological material, liquid, gel and solid. *Mailing Add:* 4041 Medical Dr No 319 San Antonio TX 78229. *E-Mail:* jzbao@aol.com

BAO, JUN, FIBEROPTICS, INSTRUMENTATION. *Current Pos:* SR ENGR, NOYES FIBER SYSTS, 96- *Personal Data:* b Shanghai, China, Jul 5, 62; m 90, Beihna Zhao; c Kevin Z. *Educ:* Shanghai Jiao Tong Univ, China, BS, 84, MS, 87; Univ RI, PhD(elec eng), 94. *Prof Exp:* Lectr, optoelectronics res, Shanghai Inst Mech Eng, 87-90; res engr, Optigain, 94, sr res engr, 94-96. *Mem:* Inst Elec & Electronics Engrs; Optical Eng Soc. *Res:* New fiber optic technology for implementation in optical fiber test equipment design. *Mailing Add:* PO Box 398 Laconia NH 03247. *Fax:* 603-528-1878; *E-Mail:* junbao@hstmail.com

BAO, QINGCHENG, MICROCHEMICAL SENSOR & INSTRUMENTATION, OPTICAL ENGINEERING. *Current Pos:* RES SPECIALIST DESIGN & MFG, DEPT CHEM, ARIZ STATE UNIV, 88- *Personal Data:* b Jinan, China, Feb 15, 48; m 74; c 2. *Educ:* Tsing Hua Univ, Beijing, China, BS, 70; Semiconductor Inst, Beijing, China, MS, 82; Chinese Univ Technol & Sci, PhD(solid state physics), 86. *Prof Exp:* Mfg engr semiconductor, Changchun Semiconductor Device Co, China, 70-79; res asst laser diode, Semiconductor Inst, Beijing, China, 79-82; res assoc laser spectroscopy, Changchun Physics Inst, China, 82-86; postdoctoral mod optics, Chem Dept, Univ Rochester, NY, 86-88. *Concurrent Pos:* Pres, Silverdow Corp, 90-, prin investr, 91-; chief scientist, Endetec Ltd, 91- *Mem:* Am Vacuum Soc. *Res:* Non-linear optics; high density excitation; laser holographic technology and spectroscopy; acoustic generation; dynamic chemistry; surface science; thin film technology; device design and processing development. *Mailing Add:* 1904 E El Parque Dr Tempe AZ 85282

BAPATLA, KRISHNA M, PHARMACEUTICS, PHARMACEUTICAL CHEMISTRY. *Current Pos:* DIR, PHARMACEUT TECH AFFAIRS, ALCON LABS, 78- *Personal Data:* b Guntur, India, Feb 18, 36; nat US; m 67; c 1. *Educ:* Andhra Univ, India, BPharm, 55, MPharm, 59; Univ Southern Calif, PhD(pharmaceut chem), 66; Fairleigh-Dickinson Univ, MBA, 76. *Honors & Awards:* Gold Medal. *Prof Exp:* Lectr pharm, Andhra Univ, India, 59-60; asst, Univ Southern Calif, 60-66; asst prof pharm, SDak State Univ, 66-69; res assoc, State Univ Ny, Buffalo, 70-71; sr scientist, Warner-Lambert Res Inst, 71-76; section head, Cooper Labs, 76-78. *Concurrent Pos:* Res fel pharmaceut chem, Cancer Chemother Nat Serv Ctr, Univ Ariz, 66; Syntex Res Ctr, Calif, 69-70. *Mem:* Am Pharm Asn; fel Am Inst Chem; Sigma Xi; Am Asn Pharmaceut; Parenteral Drug Asn; Regulatory Affairs Professionals Soc. *Res:* Synthesis of organic medicinal compounds; biopharmaceutics; research and development of new drug products; regulatory affairs; project management. *Mailing Add:* 6932 Sanday Pl Ft Worth TX 76133

BAPTIST, JAMES (NOEL), MICROBIAL BIOCHEMISTRY. *Current Pos:* SELF-EMPLOYED, 77- *Personal Data:* b Shelbyville, Ill, June 6, 30. *Educ:* Case Inst Technol, BS, 52; Univ Ill, PhD(biochem), 57. *Prof Exp:* Chemist, Phillips Petrol Co, Okla, 52-54; Damon Runyon Fund fel enzymatic study omega oxidation, Univ Mich, 57-59; biochemist, W R Grace & Co, Md, 59-63; microbiologist, Int Minerals & Chem Co, Ill, 63-65; self-employed, Fla, 65-68; res assoc biol, Univ Tex M D Anderson Hosp, & Tumor Inst, 68-69, from asst to assoc biologist, 69-77. *Mem:* Am Chem Soc; Sigma Xi. *Res:* Isozymes; metabolism of chemical carcinogens; protein purification methods; aquatic biology. *Mailing Add:* 2620 Lake Victoria Dr El Paso TX 79936-3107

BAPTISTA, JOSE ANTONIO, CARBOHYDRATE ANALYSIS, OLIGONUCLEOTIDE SYNTHESIS. *Current Pos:* RES ASSOC ANALYTIC BIOCHEM, FAC MED, UNIV TORONTO, CAN, 88- *Personal Data:* b Azores, Portugal, Jan 30, 39; Can citizen; m 67; c 1. *Educ:* Univ Porto, Portugal, Bachelor, 64; Univ Coimbra, Portugal, Master, 70; Columbia P Univ, PhD(anal chem), 85. *Prof Exp:* Researcher org chem, Fac Sci, Univ Porto, Portugal, 70-80; physico-chem specialist anal chem, Ludwig Inst Cancer Res, 80-88. *Concurrent Pos:* Dir, Analytic Biochem Lab, Carbohydrate Res Ctr, Fac Med, Univ Toronto, 88-91. *Res:* Separation and analysis of mixtures of natural and synthetic products; purification of chemical and biochemical substances; quantitative and qualitative analysis of carbohydrates of biological specimens using HPLC and GC techniques. *Mailing Add:* 93 Ambleside Ave Toronto ON M8Z 2H9 Can

BAPTISTA, LUIS FELIPE, AVIAN TOXONOMY & SYSTEMATICS, ETHOLOGY & BIOACOUSTICS. *Current Pos:* chair & assoc cur, 80-87, CHAIR & CURATOR ORNITH & MAMMOL, CALIF ACAD SCI, SAN FRANCISCO, 87- *Personal Data:* b Hong Kong, Aug 9, 41; US citizen. *Educ:* Univ San Francisco, BS, 65, MS, 68; Univ Calif, Berkeley, PhD(zool), 71. *Prof Exp:* Cur asst bot, Calif Acad Sci, 65-67; cur asst ornith, Mus Vert Zool, Univ Calif, Berkeley, 67-70, actg asst prof zool, 71-72, asst cur, 71; from asst prof & cur to assoc prof biol & cur, Moore Lab Zool, Occidental Col, Los Angeles, 73-80. *Concurrent Pos:* Max Planck Soc fel, Max Planck Inst Physiol & Behav, 71-72 & NATO fel, 72-73; referee, NSF Grant Proposals, 75-; adj prof biol, San Francisco State Univ, 80-; Am rep, Int Ornith Comt, 82- *Mem:* Fel Am Ornithologists Union; Cooper Ornith Soc; Wilson Ornith Soc; Animal Behav Soc. *Res:* Taxonomy and systematic relationships using morphology, behavior and biochemical characters; song development and regional song dialects of birds in the USA and the neotropics; conservation programs with Mexican biologists; authored and co-authored over 90 publications and one book on ornithology. *Mailing Add:* Ornith & Mammol Calif Acad Sci Los Angeles CA 90041

BAQUET, CLAUDIA, CANCER RESEARCH. *Current Pos:* FAC, UNIV MD, SCH MED, 92- *Educ:* Meharry Med Col, MD, 77; Johns Hopkins Univ, MPH, 83. *Honors & Awards:* W S Quinland Prize, Meharry Med Col, 76; ONI Award, Int Black Womens Health Cong, 88. *Prof Exp:* Pvt gen pract, Los Angeles, 79-80, St Louis, Mo, 80-82; parochial sch physician, Sch Health Prog, City St Louis, 80-82; dir, Cancer Prog & Epidemiologist/Cancer Control Specialist, Provident Hosp Inc, 83-84; expert, Nat Cancer Ctr, 84-87, chief, Spec Pop Studies Br, 87-89, assoc dir, Cancer Control, Sci Prog, Div Cancer Prev & Control, 89-92. *Concurrent Pos:* Consult, Mo Div Health, Bur Chronic Dis, St Louis, 81-82, Charles R Drew Postgrad Med Sch, Los Angeles, 83-84, Hanes Group, Winston-Salem, NC, 83-84, Richmond Community Hosp, 83-84, Provident Hosp, 84; mem, Nat Adv Comt on Cancer in Minorities, Am Cancer Soc, 82-86, Nat Subcomt Cancer in Econ Disadvantaged Patient, 85-86; bd dirs, Pub Educ Comt, Am Cancer Soc, 83-86; chairperson, Community Med & Pub Health Sect, Nat Med Asn, 85-, fac, Cancer Prev Fel Prog, Nat Cancer Inst, 86- *Mem:* Am Soc Clin Path; Am Pub Health Asn; Am Soc Prev Oncol; Nat Med Asn. *Res:* Preventive oncology; nutrition as an etiologic and preventive factor and cancer; public education for cancer; epidemiologic methods; breast cancer in young women; aged populations and cancer; cancer in racial/ethnic minorities; numerous technical publications. *Mailing Add:* Univ Md Bressler Bldg Rm 14011 Baltimore MD 21201

BAR, ROBERT S, ENDOCRINOLOGY. *Current Pos:* from asst prof to assoc prof, 77-86, PROF, DEPT MED, UNIV IOWA, IOWA CITY, 86-, DIR, DIABETES-ENDOCRINOL RES CTR, 86-, DIR, VET ADMIN, DIABETES RES CTR, 96- *Personal Data:* b Gainesville, Tex, Dec 2, 43; m 70, Laurel E Burns; c Katharine J & Matthew T. *Educ:* Tufts Univ, BS, 64; Ohio State Univ, MS & MD, 70. *Prof Exp:* Med intern, Pa Hosp, Philadelphia, 70-71; med resident, Ohio State Univ, Columbus, 71-72. *Concurrent Pos:* Nat res serv award endocrinol, 84-; mem study sect, Nat Vet Admin, 84-87; dir, Div Endocrinol & Metab, Univ Iowa, 85-; vpres res, Nat Am Diabetes Asn, 87-88; ed, Endocrinol, 87-89, Advan Endocrinol & Metab, 89-95. *Mem:* Am Diabetes Asn; Am Soc Clin Invest; Asn Am Physicians; Endocrine Soc; Sigma Xi. *Res:* Endocrinology and metabolism; diabetes. *Mailing Add:* Univ Iowa Hwy 6 West 3E19 VA Iowa City IA 52246

BARABINO, GILDA A, CHEMICAL & BIOMEDICAL ENGINEERING. *Current Pos:* ASST PROF CHEM ENG, NORTHEASTERN UNIV, 89- *Personal Data:* b Anchorage, Alaska. *Educ:* Xavier Univ, New Orleans, BS, 78; Rice Univ, PhD(chem eng), 86. *Prof Exp:* Res engr, Rohm & Haas, 86-89. *Mem:* Am Inst Chem Engrs; Am Chem Soc. *Mailing Add:* Northeastern Univ 342 Snell Eng Bldg 360 Huntington Ave Boston MA 02115. *E-Mail:* barabino@mit.edu

BARACH, JOHN PAUL, LIVING STATE PHYSICS, PLASMA PHYSICS. *Current Pos:* From asst prof to assoc prof, 61-73, dir undergrad study, 79-83, PROF PHYSICS, VANDERBILT UNIV, 73- *Personal Data:* b New York, NY, Dec 21, 35; m 57, Carol Menuez; c 2. *Educ:* Princeton Univ, BA, 57; Univ Md, PhD(physics), 61. *Mem:* Am Phys Soc; Sigma Xi. *Res:* Experiments on biomagnetism, electromagnetic shock tubes; magnetic interactions; spectroscopy; function of nerves; computer modeling of non-linear wayes. *Mailing Add:* Dept Physics Vanderbilt Univ 2201 W End Ave Nashville TN 37240-0001

BARAC-NIETO, MARIO, RENAL FUNCTION, EXERCISE & FITNESS. *Current Pos:* assoc prof, 80-85, assoc prof & sr scientist, 85-89, PROF PEDIAT, UNIV ROCHESTER, NY, 89- *Personal Data:* b Bogotá, Colombia, DE, Jan 1, 40; m 64; c 2. *Educ:* Univ Javeriana, Bogotá, MD, 62; Univ

Rochester, NY, PhD(physiol), 68. *Prof Exp:* Teaching asst physiol, Univ Javeriana, Bogota, Colombia, 59, instr biol, 60-61; res asst biol, Univ los Andes, Bogota, Colombia, 60-62; from asst prof to prof physiol, Univ Valle, Cali, Colombia, 60-80. *Concurrent Pos:* Fel, Rockefeller Found, 63-65, dept med, Buswell, Univ Rochester, 67-68, Monroe Co Chap, Am Heart Asn, 66-67; vis scientist, Venezuela Inst Sci Res, 74-75; vis prof, Max Planck Inst Biophys, Frankfurt, 77-78, dept physiol, Med Col Wis, 78-80. *Mem:* Am Physiol Soc; Am Soc Nephrol; Am Col Sports Med; Am Soc Renal Biochem & Metab; NY Acad Sci. *Res:* Renal trasport and metabolism of nutrients; influence of nutrition on renal function, body composition and physical work capacity as influenced by development and aging. *Mailing Add:* Dept Physiol Albert Einstein Col Med 1410 Pelham Pkwy Bronx NY 10461

BARACOS, ANDREW, CIVIL ENGINEERING, GEOLOGICAL ENGINEERING. *Current Pos:* Prof civil eng, 67-78, head dept, 78-83, PROF GEOL ENG, UNIV MAN, 83- *Personal Data:* b Calgary, Alta, May 10, 25; m 51; c 3. *Educ:* Univ Alta, BSc, 47, MSc, 49. *Concurrent Pos:* Vis prof, Chiang Mai Univ, Thailand, 86. *Mem:* Fel Eng Inst Can; Can Geotech Soc. *Res:* Geological engineering environmental impact; overburden stabilization for mining clays. *Mailing Add:* 4200 Palamos Close Victoria BC V8N 6H3 Can

BARAFF, GENE ALLEN, SOLID STATE PHYSICS. *Current Pos:* PHYSICIST, SOLID STATE THEORY, BELL TEL LABS, 61- *Personal Data:* b Washington, DC, Dec 27, 30; m 58; c 3. *Educ:* Columbia Univ, AB, 52; NC State Col, MS, 56; NY Univ, PhD(physics), 61. *Prof Exp:* Reactor physicist, Astra Assocs, Inc, 56-58. *Mem:* Fel Am Phys Soc. *Res:* Electronic properties of metals, semimetals, semiconductor surfaces and point defects. *Mailing Add:* Bell Labs 600 Mountain Ave Rm 1D-333 Murray Hill NJ 07974

BARAGAR, WILLIAM ROBERT ARTHUR, GEOLOGY, PETROLOGY. *Current Pos:* tech off, geologist & res scientist, 57-91, EMER RES SCIENTIST, GEOL SURV CAN, 91- *Personal Data:* b Brandon, Man, Mar 7, 26; m 55, Dorothy; c Geoffrey & Marc. *Educ:* Univ BC, BASc, 50; Queen's Univ, Ont, MSc, 52; Columbia Univ, PhD, 59. *Honors & Awards:* Career Achievement Award, Volcanology Div, Geol Asn Can, 93. *Prof Exp:* Geologist, Falconbridge Nickel Mines Ltd, 52-54. *Concurrent Pos:* Assoc ed, Canadian J Earth Science, 81-91; chmn, publ comt, Geol Asn Can, 88-91. *Mem:* Geol Soc Am; Geol Asn Can; Mineral Asn Can; Mineral Soc Am. *Res:* Petrology; petrology of basic igneous rocks; petrochemistry of the Troodos ophiolite, Cyprus; petrochemistry and emplacement major dyke swarms; petrology romatiitic lavas. *Mailing Add:* Geol Survey Can Geol Survey Bldg 601 Booth St Ottawa ON K1A 0E8 Can. *Fax:* 613-995-9273

BARAGI, VIJAYKUMAR M, IMMUNOLOGY & PHARMACOLOGY. *Current Pos:* Sr scientist, 86-92, GROUP LEADER ARTHRITIS CELL BIOL, PARKE-DAVIS WARNER-LAMBERT CO, 92- *Personal Data:* b Beelad, Bagewadi, India, May 17, 54. *Educ:* Bangladesh Sch Sci, BS, 75, MS, 78; Auburn Univ, PhD(cell biol), 84; Tufts Univ, MD, 87. *Mem:* Am Soc Cell Biol; Arthritis Soc; Inflammation Soc. *Mailing Add:* Dept Immunopharmacol Parke-Davis Pharmaceut Res 2800 Plymouth Rd Ann Arbor MI 48105-2495

BARAJAS, LUCIANO, PATHOLOGY. *Current Pos:* from instr to asst prof path, Sch Med, 61-69, assoc prof zool, Univ, 69-74, PROF PATH, UNIV CALIF, LOS ANGELES & HARBOR HOSP, TORRANCE, 74- *Personal Data:* b Santa Cruz de Tenerife, Canary Islands, Spain, Oct 10, 33; m 60; c 3. *Educ:* Univ Madrid, MD, 56. *Prof Exp:* Rotating intern med, Alexian Bros Hosp, Elizabeth, NJ, 57-58; res path, Malmonides Hosp, Brooklyn, NY, 58-59; res path, Barnes Hosp, Wash Univ, 59-61, USPHS trainee exp path, 59-60 & Nat Cancer Inst trainee, 60-61. *Concurrent Pos:* NIH spec fel, 66-69. *Mem:* Am Soc Cell Biol; Am Asn Anat; Soc Exp Biol & Med; Am Asn Pathologists; Int Acad Path. *Res:* Normal and pathologic anatomy of the kidney. *Mailing Add:* Dept Path Univ Calif Los Angeles Med Ctr Harbor Hosp 1000 W Carson St Torrance CA 90509-2069

BARAK, ANTHONY JOSEPH, BIOCHEMISTRY. *Current Pos:* From instr to assoc prof, 53-77, PROF BIOCHEM, UNIV NEBR MED CTR, 77- *Personal Data:* b Petersburg, Nebr, July 18, 22; m 50; c 5. *Educ:* Creighton Univ, BS, 48, MS, 50; Univ Mo, PhD(biochem), 53. *Concurrent Pos:* Biochemist, Vet Admin Hosp, Omaha, 56- *Res:* Alcohol metabolism; liver disease. *Mailing Add:* Dept Med Univ Nebr Med Ctr Omaha NE 68105

BARAK, EVE IDA, CELL BIOLOGY. *Current Pos:* from asst prog dir to assoc prog dir, 86-92, PROG DIR CELL BIOL, NSF, 92- *Personal Data:* b New York, NY, Jan 28, 48; m 70, 90, Eugene A Davidson. *Educ:* Brown Univ, AB, 68; Rockefeller Univ, PhD(cell biol), 74. *Prof Exp:* Postdoctoral fel, Sch Med, Wash Univ, 74-78, Univ Ala, Birmingham, 78-79; asst prof anat, Univ Ala, Birmingham, 79-82, tumor biol, Univ Tex Syst Cancer, 83-86. *Mem:* Am Soc Cell Biol; Soc Complex Carbohydrates. *Res:* Cell biology; microbiology; biochemistry. *Mailing Add:* NSF Rm 655 4201 Wilson Blvd Arlington VA 22230. *Fax:* 703-306-0355; *E-Mail:* ebarak@nsf.gov

BARAKAT, HISHAM A, BIOCHEMISTRY, MICROBIOLOGY. *Current Pos:* res assoc, 73-75, from asst prof to assoc prof, 75-86, PROF BIOCHEM, MED SCH, E CAROLINA UNIV, 87- *Personal Data:* b Sept 22, 43; m 69; c 2. *Educ:* Am Univ Beirut, BSc, 65, MSc, 67; Univ Mass, PhD(microbiol), 72. *Prof Exp:* Instr sci, Teacher-Training Inst, Siblin, Lebanon, 67-68; fel biochem, Baylor Col Med, 72-73. *Mem:* Soc Exp Biol & Med; Am Physiol Soc; Am Heart Asn; Am Diabetes Asn. *Res:* Metabolism of plasma lipoproteins in obese subjects and subjects with diabetes mellitus. *Mailing Add:* Dept Biochem Sch Med E Carolina Univ Greenville NC 27858-4354

BARALD, KATE FRANCESCA, NEUROBIOLOGY, DEVELOPMENTAL BIOLOGY. *Current Pos:* asst prof, 81-90, ASSOC PROF ANAT & CELL BIOL, MED SCH, UNIV MICH, ANN ARBOR, 90- *Personal Data:* b May 11, 45; US citizen; m 71, Douglas M Jewett; c Ethan M. *Educ:* Bryn Mawr Col, AB, 67; Univ Wis-Madison, MS, 69, PhD(oncol immunol), 74. *Prof Exp:* NIH fel neurobiol, Cornell Univ, 75; MDA fel biol & neurobiol, Univ Calif, San Diego, 75-78; NIH fel biol, Stanford Univ, 78-81. *Concurrent Pos:* Mem, Develop Biol Panel, NSF, 83-86, Develop Neurosci Panel, 90-; consult, univs & indust; Fulbright sr fel, Univ Sydney, Australia & Children's Med Res Inst, Syndney, 90-91; mem, biol-2 study sect, NIH, 93- *Mem:* Soc Neurosci; Am Soc Cell Biol; Am Soc Develop Biol; Sigma Xi; AAAS. *Res:* Developmental neurobiology and molecular biology; cell-cell interactions in the formation of specific connections in the nervous system; neural crest; development and regeneration of muscle. *Mailing Add:* Univ Mich Med Sch Dept Anat & Cell Biol 5740 MSII PO Box 0616 Ann Arbor MI 48109-0616. *Fax:* 313-763-1166; *E-Mail:* katebarald@um.cc.umich.edu

BARAN, GEORGE ROMAN, DENTAL MATERIALS. *Current Pos:* PROF DENT, SCH DENT, TEMPLE UNIV, PA, 78- *Personal Data:* b Philadelphia, Pa, Nov 3, 50. *Educ:* Univ Mich, BSE, 72, MSE, 73, PhD(mat sci eng), 76. *Prof Exp:* Res fel, Free Univ Berlin, 77-78. *Concurrent Pos:* Res fel, Alexander von Humboldt Found, 77; consult. *Mem:* Am Asn Dent Res; Am Ceramic Soc; Am Asn Dent Sch; AAAS; Am Soc Testing & Mat. *Res:* Properties of casting alloys that may be used as alternatives to high gold content alloys in dentistry; enameling; wear; polymer composites. *Mailing Add:* Dept Oper Dent Sch Dent Temple Univ 3223 N Broad St Philadelphia PA 19140

BARAN, JOHN STANISLAUS, ORGANIC CHEMISTRY, BIOLOGICAL CHEMISTRY. *Current Pos:* RETIRED. *Personal Data:* b Chicago, Ill, Feb 7, 29; m 54; c 2. *Educ:* Univ Chicago, BA, 51, MSc, 53; Univ Wis, PhD(chem), 55. *Prof Exp:* Res investr, G D Searle & Co, Inc, 56-59, sr res investr, 59-66, res fel, 66-88, sr res fel, 89-94. *Concurrent Pos:* Fel, Univ Wis, 56; vis lectr, Univ Southern Calif, 68. *Mem:* Am Chem Soc; AAAS; NY Acad Sci. *Res:* Medicinal chemistry; biological chemistry; synthetic, organic and natural products. *Mailing Add:* 659 Locust St Winnetka IL 60093

BARAN, PAUL, COMPUTER SCIENCE. *Current Pos:* FOUNDER & CHMN BD, COM21 INC, 92-; CHMN BD, ALOHA NETWORKS, 97- *Personal Data:* b Poland, Apr 29, 26; US citizen; m 55, Evelyn Murphy; c David. *Educ:* Drexel Univ, BSEE, 49; Univ Calif, Los Angeles, MS, 59. *Hon Degrees:* DSc, Drexel Univ, 97. *Honors & Awards:* Edwin H Armstrong Award, Commun Soc, Inst Elec & Electronics Engrs, 87; First Annual Award, Asn Comput Mach 89; Centennial 100 Medal, Drexel Univ, 92; Pioneer Award, Electron C Frontier Found, 93; Alexander Graham Bell Medal, Inst Elec & Electronics Engrs, 90; Comput & Commun Found Award, 96. *Prof Exp:* Technician, Eckert Mauchly Comput Co, 49-50; staff, Raymond Rosen Eng Prod Co, 50-55, Hughes Aircraft Co, 55-59 & Rand Corp, 59-68; co-founder, Inst Future, 68-72; founder, Cable Data Assoc, 72-80, Packet Technol, 80-85, Metricom, 85-92 & Interfax, 90-92. *Concurrent Pos:* Marconi Int fel, 91. *Mem:* Nat Acad Eng; fel Inst Elec & Electronics Engrs; fel AAAS. *Res:* ATM based cable modem system technology; designed equipment for interactive TV control and high speed transmission of packetized voice and data over T1 links; packet switching and its engineering implications. *Mailing Add:* 83 James Ave Atherton CA 94027-2009. *Fax:* 650-323-2056; *E-Mail:* paul@baran.com

BARANCZUK, RICHARD JOHN, ENDOCRINOLOGY, CLINICAL CHEMISTRY. *Current Pos:* INSTR BIOCHEM, AVILA COL, 76-; DIR ENDOCRINOL & LAB SCI DIR CLIN CHEM, PHYSICIANS REF LAB, 76- *Personal Data:* b Hrubieszow, Poland, Nov 15, 43; US citizen; m 67; c 2. *Educ:* Loyola Univ, BS, 65; Northern Ill Univ, MS, 67; Med Col Ga, PhD(endocrinol), 72. *Prof Exp:* Co-investr obstet & gynec, Univ Kans Med Ctr, 73-76, asst prof, 75-76, res assoc endocrinol, 76-77. *Concurrent Pos:* Fel, Ford Found, 71-73; fel, USPHS, 71-73; instr, Univ Kans Med Ctr, 73-75; prin investr, SBIR Awards & Res Contract, Nat Cancer Inst, 81- *Mem:* Endocrine Soc; Soc Study Reproduction. *Res:* Reproductive endocrinology, clinical chemistry. *Mailing Add:* 10127 Horton Shawnee Mission KS 66207

BARANGER, ELIZABETH UREY, THEORETICAL PHYSICS. *Current Pos:* assoc dean, 73-78, dean grad studies in arts & sci, 78-89, PROF PHYSICS, UNIV PITTSBURGH, 73-, VICE PROVOST GRAD STUDIES, 89- *Personal Data:* b Baltimore, Md, Sept 18, 27; m 51; c 3. *Educ:* Swarthmore Col, BA, 49; Cornell Univ, MA, 51, PhD, 54. *Prof Exp:* Res fel, Calif Inst Technol, 53-55; res fel, Univ Pittsburgh, 55-58, from asst prof to prof, 58-69; res assoc, Mass Inst Technol, 69-73. *Mem:* Fel Am Phys Soc; fel AAAS. *Res:* Theoretical nuclear physics. *Mailing Add:* Dept Physics Univ Pittsburgh Pittsburgh PA 15260. *E-Mail:* eub@vms.cis.pitt.edu

BARANGER, MICHEL, CLASSICAL & QUANTUM CHAOS, COMPLEX SYSTEMS. *Current Pos:* PROF PHYSICS, MASS INST TECHNOL, 69- *Personal Data:* b Le Mans, France, July 31, 27; nat US; m 51; c Martin, Harold & Anne. *Educ:* Ecole Normale Superieure, Paris, 45-49; Cornell Univ, PhD(physics), 51. *Prof Exp:* Res assoc physics, Cornell Univ, 51-53; res fel, Calif Inst Technol, 53-55; res physicist, Carnegie Inst Technol, 55-56, from asst prof to assoc prof, 56-64, prof, 64-69. *Concurrent Pos:* NSF sr fel, Univ Paris, 61-62. *Mem:* Fel Am Phys Soc. *Res:* Many-body physics; quantal-classical connection; Poincare's dream; far-from-equilibrium thermodynamics. *Mailing Add:* Mass Inst Technol Rm 6-312 77 Massachusetts Ave Cambridge MA 02139-4307. *Fax:* 617-253-8674; *E-Mail:* baranger@ctp.mit.edu

BARANKIEWICZ, JERZY ANDRZEJ, PURINE BIOCHEMISTRY, NUCLEOTIDE BIOCHEMISTRY & CELL BIOLOGY. *Current Pos:* ASST DIR PHARM, ST MARCOS, 95- *Personal Data:* b Warsaw, Poland, July 27, 42; c 2. *Educ:* Univ Warsaw & Univ Lodz, MS, 68; Inst Biochem & Biophys, Polish Acad Sci, PhD(biochem), 73. *Honors & Awards:* Award of Pres, Polish Acad Sci, 77. *Prof Exp:* Jr asst biochem, Polish Acad Sci, 68-69, asst lectr, 69-73, adj, 73-75 & 77-81; postdoctoral fel, Univ Alta Cancer Res Unit, 75-77; sr scientist, Dir Immunol, Res Inst, Hosp Sick Children, Can, 81-88. *Concurrent Pos:* Postdoctoral fel, Univ Alta, 75. *Mem:* Polish Biochem Soc; Polish Bot Soc; Europ Acad Sci & Humanities; Europ Soc Nuclear Methods Agr; NY Acad Sci; Europ Soc Purine Pyrimidine Res. *Res:* Purine and pyrimidine; anticancer drugs and immunomodulation; comparative and evolutionary biochemistry; experimental chemotherapy; cardiovascular and cerebrovascular research; inflammation. *Mailing Add:* 12457 Carmel Cape San Diego CA 92130

BARANOWSKI, RICHARD MATTHEW, ENTOMOLOGY. *Current Pos:* From asst entomologist to entomologist, Sub Trop Exp Sta, 58-84, CTR DIR, TROP RES & EDUC CTR, UNIV FLA, 84- *Personal Data:* b Utica, NY, Mar 1, 28; m 51; c 3. *Educ:* Syracuse Univ, BA, 51; Univ Conn, MS, 53, PhD, 59. *Concurrent Pos:* Tech adv, Animal Plant Health Inspection Serv, Nat Biol Control Prog, USDA, 80-82. *Mem:* Entom Soc Am; Int Org Biol Control. *Res:* Economic entomology; biology of hemiptera; biological control. *Mailing Add:* 26000 SW 197th Ave Homestead FL 33031

BARANOWSKI, ROBERT LOUIS, BIOCHEMISTRY, PATHOPHYSIOLOGY. *Current Pos:* RES ASST RENAL PHYSIOL & PROF MED, UNIV UTAH, 83- *Educ:* Univ Ill, Chicago, PhD(human physiol), 79. *Mailing Add:* Dept Med Div Nephrol Vet Admin Med Ctr 500 Foothill Blvd 11H Salt Lake City UT 84148-0001

BARANOWSKI, TOM, HEALTH PSYCHOLOGY, HEALTH EDUCATION. *Current Pos:* PROF, DEPT BEHAV SCI, MD ANDERSON CANCER CTR, UNIV TEX, 96- *Personal Data:* b Brooklyn, NY, Dec 3, 46; m 90, Janice Carlson; c Tanya & Todd. *Educ:* Princeton Univ, AB, 68; Univ Kans, MA, 70, PhD(social psychol), 74. *Prof Exp:* Res scientist, Health Care Study Ctr, Battelle Mem Inst, 74-76; asst prof health educ, WVa Univ Med Ctr, 76-80; assoc prof prev med, Univ Tex Med Br, Galveston, 80-90; prof pediat & dep dir, Ga Prev Inst, 90-92; prof health behav, Div Behav Sci & Health Educ, Emory Univ Sch Pub Health, 92-96. *Concurrent Pos:* Prin investr, Nat Heart, Lung & Blood Inst, 78-80, 83-86 & 92-96, Moody Found, 81-84, Nat Cancer Inst, 86-87, 93-97 & 96-99. *Mem:* Am Pub Health Asn; Am Psychol Soc; Am Heart Asn; Soc Behav Med; Am Psychol Asn; Am Soc Prev Oncol. *Res:* Behavioral determinants of cancer risk factors; behavioral change for cancer risk reduction; ethnic group differences in health related behaviors; measurement of health related behaviors and cognitions. *Mailing Add:* 1515 Holcom be Blvd Box 243 Houston TX 77030. *E-Mail:* tbaranow@notes.mdacc.tmc.edu

BARANSKI, MICHAEL JOSEPH, FIELD BOTANY, PLANT ECOLOGY. *Current Pos:* from asst prof to assoc prof, 74-85, PROF BIOL, CATAWBA COL, 86- *Personal Data:* b Wheeling, WVa, Dec 8, 46; m 69, Julia Rafa; c Christopher & Amanda. *Educ:* Liberty State Col, BS, 68; NC State Univ, PhD(bot), 74. *Prof Exp:* Instr bot, NC State Univ, 73-74. *Concurrent Pos:* Vis instr, Rocky Mountain Biol Lab, 75; vis asst prof, Duke Univ, 78-79, NC State Univ, 82; consult, Highlands Biol Sta, 96-97. *Mem:* Sigma Xi; Am Soc Plant Taxonomists; Am Inst Biol Sci; Ecol Soc Am. *Res:* Vegetation ecology; floristics; dendrology; natural areas; land management. *Mailing Add:* Dept Biol Catawba Col Salisbury NC 28144. *Fax:* 704-637-4204; *E-Mail:* mbaransk@catawba.edu

BARANWAL, KRISHNA CHANDRA, polymer science, for more information see previous edition

BARANY, FRANCIS, PROTEIN ENGINEERING. *Current Pos:* asst prof, 85-90, ASSOC PROF MICROBIOL, CORNELL UNIV MED COL, 90- *Personal Data:* b Afula, Israel, Apr 4, 57. *Educ:* Univ Ill, Chicago Circle, BA, 76; Rockefeller Univ, PhD(microbiol), 81. *Prof Exp:* Fel, Rockefeller, Univ, 81-82,John Hopkins Univ Sch Med, 82-85. *Concurrent Pos:* Adj asst prof, Rockefeller Univ, 86-, adj assoc prof, 90- *Mem:* Sigma Xi; Am Soc Microbiol; Fed Am Soc Exp Biol. *Res:* Using protein engineering, Tag I mutants with alatered cleavage properties are being constructed,these mutant proteins are being characterized via star reaction, nuclear magnetic resonance spectroscopy and x-ray crystallography; developed ligase chain reaction (LCR) for detection of single base genetic diseases using cloned thermostable ligase. *Mailing Add:* Dept Microbiol Rm B-406 Box 62 Cornell Univ Med Col 1300 York Ave New York NY 10021-4896

BARANY, GEORGE, PEPTIDE SYNTHESIS, ORGANOSULFUR CHEMISTRY. *Current Pos:* from asst prof to assoc prof, 80-91, PROF CHEM, UNIV MINN, 91- *Personal Data:* b Budapest, Hungary, Feb 19, 55; US citizen; m 86, Barbara Goldenberg; c Michael J & Deborah A. *Educ:* Rockefeller Univ, PhD(biochem), 77. *Honors & Awards:* Vincent du Vigneaud Award, Am Peptide Soc, 94. *Prof Exp:* USPHS fel peptide synthesis, Rockefeller Univ, 78-80. *Concurrent Pos:* Searle Scholar, 82; USPHS res career develop award, 82-87; consult, peptide synthesis. *Mem:* Sigma Xi; AAAS; Am Peptide Soc; NY Acad Sci; Am Chem Soc; Am Soc Biochem & Molecular Biol. *Res:* Peptide synthesis, particularly the solid-phase method; protecting groups for organic fuctionalities with an emphasis on the concept of orthogonality; chemistry of thiols, disulfides and polysulfanes; biochemistry of garlic. *Mailing Add:* Dept Chem Univ Minn 207 Pleasant St SE Minneapolis MN 55455-0431. *Fax:* 612-626-7541; *E-Mail:* barany@maroon.tc.umn.edu

BARANY, JAMES W, INDUSTRIAL ENGINEERING. *Current Pos:* from instr to assoc prof, 58-69, PROF INDUST ENG, PURDUE UNIV, 69-, ASSOC HEAD DEPT, 70- *Personal Data:* b South Bend, Ind, Aug 24, 30; m 60; c 1. *Educ:* Univ Notre Dame, BS, 53; Purdue Univ, MS, 58, PhD(indust eng), 61. *Prof Exp:* Jr engr, Bendix Aviation Corp, 53-54, prod liaison engr, 55-56. *Concurrent Pos:* Instr, Training Prog, Western Elec Co, Inc, 61-; res grants, NSF, 61-62, NIH, 63- & Easter Seal Found, 64-; consult, Int Coop Admin, China Productivity & Trade Ctr, 61-62. *Mem:* Fel Am Inst Indust Engrs; Human Factors Soc; Am Soc Eng Educ. *Res:* Human factors engineering pertaining to the assessment of the degree of handicap of hemiplegic patients; the application of job design principals for rehabilitation. *Mailing Add:* 101 Andrew Pl Apt 201 Lafayette IN 47906-3928

BARANY, KATE, MYOSIN LIGHT CHAIN PHOSPHORYLATION. *Current Pos:* PROF PHYSIOL & BIOPHYS, DEPT PHYSIOL & BIOPHYS, COL MED, UNIV ILL, 74- *Personal Data:* m 49, Michael; c George & Francis. *Educ:* Goethe Univ, PhD(phys chem), 59. *Prof Exp:* Staff, Inst Muscle Dis, NY. *Mem:* Biophys Soc; Am Physiol Soc. *Res:* Physical-chemical characterization of proteins; physiology of muscle contraction; protein phosphorylation. *Mailing Add:* Dept Physiol & Biophys M/C 901 Col Med Univ Ill Chicago IL 60612-7342. *Fax:* 312-996-1414; *E-Mail:* kbarany@uic.edu

BARANY, MICHAEL, MUSCLE BIOCHEMISTRY, IN VIVO MAGNETIC RESONANCE SPECTROSCOPY. *Current Pos:* PROF BIOL CHEM, COL MED, UNIV ILL, 74- *Personal Data:* b Budapest, Hungary, Oct 29, 21; nat US; m 49, Kate Foti; c George & Francis. *Educ:* Univ Budapest, MD, 51, PhD(biochem, physiol), 56. *Prof Exp:* Lectr gen biochem, Inst Biochem, Univ Budapest, 51-56; intermediate scientist protein chem, Weizman Inst, 56-57; assoc mem muscle biochem, Max Planck Inst, 58-60; mem contractile proteins, Inst Muscle Dis, Inc, 61-74. *Mem:* Am Soc Biol Chem; Am Physiol Soc; Am Chem Soc; Biophys Soc; Magnetic Resonance Med. *Res:* Contractile proteins of muscle; actin and myosin, isolation, characterization and mechanism of their interaction; muscle contraction; protein phosphorylation in smooth muscle, hereditary muscular dystrophy; nuclear magnetic resonance of intact muscle and live human patients; editor of book on smooth muscle contraction. *Mailing Add:* Dept Biol Chem M/C 536 Chicago Col Med Univ Ill Chicago IL 60612-7334. *Fax:* 312-413-0364; *E-Mail:* mbarany@uic.edu

BARANY, RONALD, PHYSICAL CHEMISTRY. *Current Pos:* RETIRED. *Personal Data:* b Bronx, NY, Mar 11, 28; m 60; c 4. *Educ:* City Col NY, BS, 49; NY Univ, MS, 51; Yale Univ, PhD(chem), 55. *Prof Exp:* Phys chemist thermochem measurements, US Bur Mines, 55-67; sr math analyst, Kaiser Engrs Div, Kaiser Indust Corp, 67-72; sr engr, Bechtel Corp, 72-81, sr analyst, 81-86; sr analyst, Lawrence Livermore Nat Lab, 87-89. *Mem:* Am Chem Soc; Asn Comput Mach. *Res:* Thermochemistry and thermodynamics; data processing; theoretical chemistry. *Mailing Add:* 6553 Chabot Rd Oakland CA 94618

BARASCH, GUY ERROL, ATMOSPHERIC PHYSICS. *Current Pos:* staff scientist atmospheric physics, 71-77, GROUP LEADER, ATMOSPHERIC NUCLEAR WEAPONS EFFECTS GROUP, LOS ALAMOS SCI LAB, UNIV CALIF, 78- *Personal Data:* b Baltimore, Md, Aug 28, 37; m 77; c 2. *Educ:* Johns Hopkins Univ, AB, 58, PhD(physics), 65. *Prof Exp:* Staff scientist atmospheric physics, Los Alamos Sci Lab, Univ Calif, 65-69; sci specialist weapon physics, Santa Barbara Opers, EG&G, Inc, 69-71. *Mem:* Sigma Xi; Optical Soc Am. *Res:* Physics of atmospheric nuclear detonations; light emission and propagation in highly dosed air; production and dispersal of pollutants due to nuclear, chemical and natural sources. *Mailing Add:* 2805 Glade Vale Way Vienna VA 22181

BARASCH, WERNER, PLASTICS CHEMISTRY. *Current Pos:* CONSULT, 79- *Personal Data:* b Breslau, Ger, May 27, 19; nat US. *Educ:* Univ Calif, AB, 47; Mass Inst Technol, SM, 49; Univ Colo, PhD(org chem), 52. *Prof Exp:* Asst chem, Mass Inst Technol, 47-49 & Univ Colo, 49-52; res chemist, Olin Industs, Inc, 52-56; chief chemist resins, US Plywood Corp, 56-62; dir chem res, Plastomeric, Inc, 62-67 & Becton, Dickinson of Calif, Inc, 67-79. *Concurrent Pos:* Study supvr, Harvard Univ, 49; consult, 79- *Mem:* Am Chem Soc; Sigma Xi. *Res:* Carbohydrate chemistry; mechanisms of organic reactions; polymers. *Mailing Add:* 23049 Santa Cruz Hwy Los Gatos CA 95030-9012

BARASH, MOSHE M, MACHINE DESIGN. *Current Pos:* PROF INDUST ENG, PURDUE UNIV, 63- *Personal Data:* b Lwow, Poland, Apr 5, 22; m 49; c 3. *Educ:* Israel Inst Technol, BSc & Dipl Ing, 47, BSc, 50; Univ Manchester, PhD(mech eng), 58. *Prof Exp:* Sci officer mech eng, Israel Ministry Defence, 48-51, sect head, 51-53; sr engr, ATA Textile Co, Israel, 53-55; lectr mech eng, Univ Manchester, 56-63. *Concurrent Pos:* Consult eng, Pergamon Press, 60-62; contrib ed, Machinery, 65-70. *Mem:* Am Soc Mech Engrs; sr mem Am Inst Indust Engrs; Am Soc Eng Educ; Sigma Xi. *Res:* Materials processing; kinematics and dynamics of machines; synthesis of mechanisms; theory and effect of metal working processes on machined parts; computerized automation; reliability of systems; manufacturing science. *Mailing Add:* 124 Pawnee Dr West Lafayette IN 47906-2114

BARASH, PAUL G, ANESTHESIOLOGY. *Current Pos:* From instr to asst prof, 72-77, ASSOC PROF ANESTHESIOL, SCH MED, YALE UNIV, 78- *Personal Data:* b Brooklyn, NY, Feb 22, 42; m 67; c 2. *Educ:* City Col New York, BA, 63; Univ Ky, MD, 67. *Concurrent Pos:* Attend physician, Yale New Haven Hosp, 73-74, asst clin dir anethesiol, 74-, dir surg intensive care unit, 74- *Mem:* Int Anesthesia Res Soc; fel Am Col Anesthesiol; Am Soc Anesthesiol; Soc Comput Med. *Res:* Critical care medicine; cardiovascular and respiratory physiology; pharmacology of cocaine; computer applications in medicine. *Mailing Add:* Yale-New Haven Hosp Yale Univ Sch Med 867 Robert Treat Ext Orange CT 06477

BARATTA, ANTHONY J, RADIATION DAMAGE, ENGINEERING MANAGEMENT. *Current Pos:* from asst prof to assoc prof, 78-89, PROF NUCLEAR ENG, PA STATE UNIV, 89- *Personal Data:* b Bayonne, NJ, Dec 24, 45; m 68, Barbara K Hill; c Jaime L & Anthony J III. *Educ:* Columbia Univ, BA & BS, 68; Brown Univ, MS, 70, PhD(physics), 78. *Prof Exp:* Proj engr, Div Naval Reactors, US Dept Energy, 69-71, proj officer, 71-74, refueling engr, 74-75, proj mgr, 74-78; res assoc, US Naval Res Lab, 78. *Concurrent Pos:* Consult, US Dept Energy, 79-80, US Naval Res Lab, 79-, Lom Tech, 85-90, Vollian Enterprises, 90- & Escom, Johannesberg, 88-; vis prof, Vrije Univ, Amsterdam, 86; vis scientist, US Nat Res Coun, 93. *Mem:* Am Nuclear Soc; Am Phys Soc; Inst Elec & Electronics Engrs. *Res:* Neutron transport; nuclear reactor safety analysis; thermal hydraulic analysis; severe accident analysis; radiation damage to semiconductor devices and materials. *Mailing Add:* Dept Nuclear Eng Pa State Univ 231 Sackett Bldg University Park PA 16802-1408. *Fax:* 814-865-8499; *E-Mail:* ab2@psuvm.psu.edu

BARATTA, EDMOND JOHN, ANALYTICAL CHEMISTRY, RADIOCHEMISTRY. *Current Pos:* chief radionuclide sect, 72-85, nat expert radioactivity, Winchester Eng & Analysis Ctr, 85-88, RADIATION SAFETY OFFICER, FOOD & DRUG ADMIN, 86-, INT EXPERT RADIOACTIVITY, 88- *Personal Data:* b Somerville, Mass, June 22, 28; m 53, Marie Doucette; c Susan. *Educ:* Northeastern Univ, BSc, 53. *Prof Exp:* Chemist, Control Lab, Shell Oil Co, 53-56; chemist, Petrol Lab, Naval Supply Depot, US Navy, 57-59; sr prof biol & med, Nat Lead Co, Inc, 59-61, chief anal serv, 61-68; chief anal qual control serv, Bur Radiol Health, USPHS, 68-70; chief radiation off, Environ Protection Agency, 71-72. *Mem:* Am Chem Soc; Health Physics Soc; fel Asn Off Analytical Chem. *Res:* Development, testing and standardization of methods for various radionuclides in environmental media; quality control for radionuclides in environment from fallout, nuclear reactors and fuel processing plants; radiopharmaceutical methodology investigations. *Mailing Add:* Winchester Eng & Analysis Ctr 109 Holton St Winchester MA 01890. *Fax:* 617-728-5700, 729-5702

BARATZ, ROBERT SEARS, ORAL & EMERGENCY MEDICINE, MEDICINE & MEDICAL DEVICES. *Current Pos:* EMERGENCY PHYSICIAN, CARNEY HOSP, BOSTON, 91-; PRES, INT MED CONSULT SERVS, INC, 92-; ASST CLIN PROF MED, BOSTON UNIV, 93-; DIR, URGENT CARE DEPT, HARBOR HEALTH SERVS, 94- *Personal Data:* b New London, Conn, July 15, 46; m 75, Robin Sokoloff; c Beth & Adam. *Educ:* Boston Univ, AB, 69, MD, 87; Northwestern Univ, DDS, 72, PhD(anat & cell biol), 75; Am Bd Oral Med, dipl, 88. *Prof Exp:* Nat Inst Dent Res fel, 72-74; instr anat, Med Sch, Northwestern Univ, 74-76; asst prof anat, Sch Grad Dent, Boston Univ, 76-83, asst res prof oral & maxillofacial surg, 77-86, asst res prof dermat, Sch Med, 83-86; resident internal med, Carney Hosp, Boston, 87-91; asst res prof oral med, Tufts Univ, 87-91. *Concurrent Pos:* Staff dentist, Harvard Community Health Plan, 81-83; consult USAF, 83-84, Am Dent Asn, 85-, Food & Drug Admin, 91 & states of Calif, Colo & NY; indust consult Biomed Devices, 82-; med dir, Thermedics Inc, 85-87; physician & res scientist, Boston Vet Admin Med Ctr, 88-94. *Mem:* Am Soc Cell Biol; AAAS; Int Asn Dent Res; Am Dent Asn; Am Col Physicians; Am Med Assn. *Res:* Keratinization; oral mucosa in health and disease; biomedical devices; wound healing; allergic responses to biomedical materials. *Mailing Add:* Harbor Health Serv 159 Bellevue St Newton MA 02158. *E-Mail:* 102073.1044@compuserve.com

BARB, C RICHARD, REPRODUCTIVE PHYSIOLOGY, NEUROENDOCRINOLOGY. *Current Pos:* biol lab tech, 76-85, RES PHYSIOLOGIST, RUSSELL RES CTR, USDA, AGR RES SERV, ATHENS, GA, 85- *Personal Data:* b Washington, DC, July 19, 48; m 70; c 3. *Educ:* Univ Md, BS, 75; Univ Ga, MS, 80, PhD(neuroendocrin), 85. *Prof Exp:* Biol lab tech, Beltsville Agr Res Ctr, USDA, Agr Res Serv, Beltsville, Md, 70-76. *Concurrent Pos:* Vis scientist, Inst Animal Husb & Animal Behav, Fed Agr Res Ctr, Mariensee, Fed Repub Ger, 86 & Univ Hohenheim, Stuttgart, Fed Repub Ger, 86; adj asst prof, Animal & Dairy Sci Dept, Univ Ga, 88- *Mem:* Am Soc Animal Sci; Soc Study Reproduction; Soc Neurosci; Soc Exp Biol & Med. *Res:* Neuropeptide and metabolite regulation of pituitary hormone secretion changes during different physiological states; identified site of action of these peptides on modulating pituitary hormone secretion. *Mailing Add:* Russell Res Ctr Animal Physiol Unit USDA-Agr Res Serv PO Box 5677 Athens GA 30613. *Fax:* 706-546-3586; *E-Mail:* rbarb@uga.cc.uga.edu

BARBA, WILLIAM P, II, PEDIATRICS. *Current Pos:* actg asst dean, Temple Univ, 65-67, assoc dean, 67-69, actg dean, 69-71, assoc vpres, 71-87, ASSOC PROF PEDIAT, SCH MED, TEMPLE UNIV, 64- *Personal Data:* b Philadelphia, Pa, Sept 25, 22; m 47; c 4. *Educ:* Princeton Univ, BA, 44; Univ Pa, Med Sch, MD, 46. *Prof Exp:* Intern, Pa Hosp, 46-47; Univ Pa, Md, 46; pediat resident, Res & Educ Hosp, Univ Ill, 49-51, instr pediat, 51-52; instr, Sch Med, Temple Univ, 52-54, assoc attend pediatrician, 57-61; dir med educ, Babies Unit, United Hosps, Newark, NJ, 61-64. *Concurrent Pos:* Mem adv comt, Child Guid Clin, 62-64; assoc attend pediatrician, St Christopher's Hosp Children, 64-87. *Mem:* Asn Am Med Cols; AAAS. *Res:* Pediatrics and medical education; systems of providing health care. *Mailing Add:* 326 Summit Ave Jenkintown PA 19046

BARBACCI, MARIO R, SOFTWARE ENGINEERING, REALTIME & DISTRIBUTED SYSTEMS. *Current Pos:* Res assoc, Sch Comput Sci, Carnegie-Mellon Univ, 74-77, res comput scientist, 77-82, dir, Technol Explor Dept, Software Eng Inst, 85-86, proj leader, 86-90, prof dir, 91-94, SR RES COMPUT SCIENTIST, SCH COMPUT SCI, CARNEGIE-MELLON UNIV, 82- *Personal Data:* b Lima, Peru, Aug 28, 45; US citizen. *Educ:* Univ Eng, Lima, BS, 66, EE, 68; Carnegie-Mellon Univ, PhD(comput sci), 74. *Honors & Awards:* Silver Core Award, Int Fed Info Processing, 86; Outstanding Contrib Award, Inst Elec & Electronics Engrs Comput Soc, 88 & 90. *Concurrent Pos:* Consult, Naval Res Lab, 75-77, Digital Equip Corp, 76-77 & Bendix Corp, 78-80, ITT, 82-84, Wright Patterson Labs, USAF, 82-84; assoc ed hardware, Comput Reviews, Asn Comput Mach, 79-84, assoc ed software, 86-93; chmn, IFIP Working Group 10.2, 79-84; bd gov, Inst Elec & Electronics Engrs Comput Soc, 86-90 & 91-, vpres tech activ, 90-91. *Mem:* Fel Inst Elec & Electronics Engrs; Asn Comput Mach; Sigma Xi; fel Inst Elec & Electronics Engrs Comput Soc (secy, 93-94, pres, 96). *Res:* Computer architecture; design automation; programming languages and environments; real-time and distributed systems; software architecture, realtime and distributed systems, software quality attributes. *Mailing Add:* Software Eng Inst Carnegie Mellon Univ Pittsburgh PA 15213-3890

BARBACK, JOSEPH, MATHEMATICS. *Current Pos:* assoc prof math, 69-72, PROF MATH, STATE UNIV NY COL BUFFALO, 72- *Personal Data:* b Buffalo, NY, Oct 27, 37; m; c 1. *Educ:* Univ Buffalo, AB, 59; Rutgers Univ, MS, 61, PhD(math), 64. *Prof Exp:* Asst prof math, Univ Pittsburgh, 63-65 & State Univ NY Buffalo, 65-67; vis asst prof, Ariz State Univ, 67-68; NIH fel biostatist, Stanford Univ, 68-69. *Mem:* Asn Symbolic Logic; Am Math Soc. *Res:* Recursive function theory; theory of computation; isols. *Mailing Add:* Dept Math Buffalo State Col 1300 Elmwood Ave Buffalo NY 14222-1004

BARBAN, STANLEY, BIOCHEMISTRY. *Current Pos:* biochemist, Nat Inst Allergy & Infectious Dis, 54-78, SCIENTIST-ADMINR, OFF RECOMBINANT DNA ACTIV, NAT INST ALLERGY & INFECTIOUS DIS, NIH, 78- *Personal Data:* b New York, NY, Mar 16, 21; m 50; c 2. *Educ:* City Col New York, BS, 43; Univ Mich, MS, 49; Wash Univ, PhD(bact & biochem), 52. *Prof Exp:* Bacteriologist, Dept Health, Syracuse, NY, 50; instr bact, Med Col, State Univ NY, 52-53. *Concurrent Pos:* USPHS fel, 53-54. *Mem:* Am Soc Microbiol; Am Soc Biol Chem. *Res:* Tissue cell culture metabolism; bacterial metabolism; enzymology; experimental chemotherapy; molecular biology of tumor viruses; recombinant DNA. *Mailing Add:* 6603 Pyle Rd Bethesda MD 20817-5453

BARBARO, RONALD D, ENVIRONMENTAL SCIENCES. *Current Pos:* PROF CHEM & ENVIRON SCI, NORTHERN VA COMMUNITY COL, 74- *Personal Data:* b Brooklyn, NY, Aug 5, 33; m 56, Ellen Lydon; c 4. *Educ:* Providence Col, BA, 56; Univ RI, MS, 60; Rutgers Univ, PhD(environ sci), 66. *Prof Exp:* Technician, Gen Dynamics/Elec Boat Div, 59; lit scientist, Stamford Res Lab, Am Cyanamid Corp, 60; chief recreation-water qual unit, Southeast Water Lab, Fed Water Pollution Control Admin, US Dept Interior, 66-68; scientist adminr extramural prog br, Off Manpower Develop, Nat Air Pollution Control Admin, 68-70; vpres & dir, Princeton Aqua Sci, Inc, 70-72. *Concurrent Pos:* Mgr air & water qual progs, Glass Container Mfrs Inst, 72; pres, GBC Assocs Inc-Environ Consult, 72- *Mem:* Am Chem Soc; Water Pollution Control Fedn; Sigma Xi. *Res:* Administration of programs with scientific orientation; water pollution control equipment design, development; pollution control consulting; educational program development; hazardous waste management; patent water filtration. *Mailing Add:* 7036 Lee Park Ct Falls Church VA 22042-3937. *Fax:* 703-237-0575

BARBAS, JOHN THEOPHANI, FREE RADICAL CHEMISTRY. *Current Pos:* PROF CHEM, VALDOSTA STATE COL, GA, 82- *Personal Data:* b Kyrenia, Cyprus; US citizen; m 70; c 2. *Educ:* Bob Jones Univ, BS, 66; Univ Ga, PhD(org chem), 71. *Prof Exp:* Res assoc chem, Fla State Univ, 70-72; prof, Lane Col, Jackson, Tenn, 72-78, Univ Montevallo, Ala, 79-82. *Concurrent Pos:* Fulbright scholar, 66; vis res prof, Fla State Univ, 73-76. *Mem:* Am Chem Soc. *Res:* Free radical mechanisms in solution and on surfaces; electron transfer reactions; photochemistry; chemically induced dynamic nuclear polarization. *Mailing Add:* 2616 Quincy Circle Valdosta GA 31602-1591

BARBE, DAVID FRANKLIN, ELECTRONIC DEVICES, INTEGRATED CIRCUITS. *Current Pos:* assoc dir, 85-87, PROF ELEC ENG, UNIV MD, 85-, EXEC DIR, ENG RES CTR, 87- *Personal Data:* b Webster Springs, WVa, May 26, 39; c John D & Jane S. *Educ:* WVa Univ, BS, 62, MS, 64; Johns Hopkins Univ, PhD(elec eng), 69. *Honors & Awards:* VHSIC Pioneer Award, 87. *Prof Exp:* Instr elec eng, WVa Univ, 62-65; engr res & develop, Westinghouse Elec Corp, 69-71; br head, Naval Res Lab, 71-79; asst for electronics & phys sci, Off Asst Secy Navy for res, Eng & Systs, 79-83, dir submarine & anti-submarine systs, 83-85. *Mem:* Fel Inst Elec & Electronics Engrs. *Res:* Charge coupled devices for imaging; infrared imaging and signal processing; very large scale integrated circuits, semiconductor processing; university industry cooperative research programs. *Mailing Add:* Exec Dir Eng Res Ctr Univ Md College Park MD 20742. *Fax:* 301-403-4105; *E-Mail:* d_barbe@umail.umd.edu

BARBEAU, EDWARD JOSEPH, JR, PURE MATHEMATICS. *Current Pos:* from asst prof to assoc prof, 67-88, PROF MATH, UNIV TORONTO, 88- *Personal Data:* b Toronto, Ont, June 25, 38; m 61; c 2. *Educ:* Univ Toronto, BA, 60, MA, 61; Univ Newcastle, PhD(semialgebras), 64. *Honors & Awards:* David Hilbert Award, World Fedn Nat Math Competion; Andrien Pouliot Award, Can Math Soc. *Prof Exp:* Lectr math, Univ Newcastle, 63-64;

asst prof, Univ Western Ont, 64-66. *Mem:* Am Math Soc; Math Asn Am; Can Math Soc; Can Soc Hist & Philos Math; Nat Coun Teachers Math. *Res:* History of analysis (17th and 18th centuries); elementary number theory; optimization. *Mailing Add:* Dept Math Univ Toronto Toronto ON M5S 3G3 Can

BARBEE, R WAYNE, CARDIOLOGY. *Current Pos:* ASST PROF, DEPT PHYSIOL, MED SCH, LA STATE UNIV, 88- *Personal Data:* b Greensboro, NC, Feb 6, 56; m 81. *Educ:* Univ NC, Wilmington, BS, 77, BA, 78; Univ Fla, Gainesville, MS, 81; La State Univ, New Orleans, PhD(physiol), 86. *Prof Exp:* Res asst, Dept Physiol, Univ Fla, 79-80, teaching asst, 80-81; postdoctoral fel, Dept Hypertension Res, 86-88, staff res scientist, 88-90, STAFF RES SCIENTIST, CARDIOL SECT, DEPT MED, ALTON OCHSNER MED FOUND, 90- *Concurrent Pos:* Sigma Xi res award, 85-86; innovative res am grant award, 85-86; adj asst prof, Dept Physiol, Tulane Sch Med, 88-; mem, Safety Comt, Alton Ochsner Med Found, 88-90, chmn, Animal Care & Use Comt, 89; mem, Coun Circulation & Res Peer Rev Comt, Am Heart Asn, 89- *Mem:* Am Fedn Clin Res; Am Heart Asn; Am Physiol Soc; AAAS; Int Soc Heart Res; Sigma Xi. *Res:* Skeletal muscle efficiency and acid-base metabolism; cardiovascular changes during shock and diabetes; atrial natriuretic peptides; endothelial derived contracting and relaxing factors; author of various publications. *Mailing Add:* Div Res Alton Ochsner Med Found 1520 Jefferson Hwy New Orleans LA 70121-2429

BARBEHENN, ELIZABETH KERN, BIOCHEMISTRY. *Current Pos:* PHARMACOLOGIST, DIV METAB, FOOD & DRUG ADMIN, 85- *Personal Data:* b Washington, DC, June 21, 33; m 57; c 3. *Educ:* Cornell Univ, BS, 55; Wash Univ, PhD(biochem pharmacol), 74. *Prof Exp:* Staff fel, NIH, 74-80, expert, 80-85. *Mem:* Fed Am Soc Exp Biol. *Res:* Metabolism of retina; micromethods of analysis; enzymatic assays. *Mailing Add:* 8208 Thoreau Dr Bethesda MD 20817

BARBEHENN, KYLE RAY, VERTEBRATE ECOLOGY. *Current Pos:* RETIRED. *Personal Data:* b Cumberland, Md, Dec 24, 28; m 56, Elizabeth Rosenthal; c Raymond, Katherine & Micheal. *Educ:* Rutgers Univ, BS, 50; Cornell Univ, MS, 52, PhD(vert zool), 55. *Prof Exp:* Biologist, Nat Res Coun, 57-58; res fel, NIMH, 59-62; prin investr, NSF grant, 62-64; lectr biol, Univ Pa, 64-65; dir field ctr, Smithsonian Inst, 65-68; res fel, Ctr for Biol Natural Systs, Wash Univ, 68-74; proj mgr, Off Spec Pesticide Rev, US Environ Protection Agency, 74-89. *Mem:* AAAS; Fel Am Soc Mammal; Ecol Soc Am; Am Soc Naturalists; Wildlife Soc; Sigma Xi. *Res:* Intraspecific and interspecific behavioral relationships among small mammals and their relevance to population dynamics; urban rat ecology; management of vertebrate pest species by ecological methods; pharmacodynamics of pesticides. *Mailing Add:* 8208 Thoreau Dr Bethesda MD 20817

BARBENEL, JOSEPH CYRIL, TISSUE MECHANICS, CELLULAR ENGINEERING. *Current Pos:* PROF & HEAD DEPT BIOENG, UNIV STRATHCLYDE, 85- *Personal Data:* b London, Jan 2, 37; m, Lesley M Jowett; c Rachel, David & Daniel. *Educ:* Univ London, BDS, 60; Univ St Andrews, BSc, 66; Univ Strathclyde, MSc, 67, PhD(bio eng), 79. *Honors & Awards:* Medal, Soc Cosmetic Scientists, 94. *Prof Exp:* House surgeon, London Hosp, 60; lt/capt, Royal Army Dent Corp, 60-62; gen dent pract, Nat Health Serv, UK, 62-63; lectr dent, prosthetics, Univ Dundee, 67-69. *Concurrent Pos:* Vis prof, Nat Eng Univ, Lima, Peru, 79, Chongqing Univ, China, 86-, Dept Electronics & Elec Eng, Tech Univ Vienna, 87 & Dept Med, Univ Dundee, 89-93. *Mem:* Fel Biol Eng Soc UK (pres, 90-92); Soc Tissue Viability (pres, 88-92); fel Royal Soc Med; Int Fedn Med & Biol Eng; fel Inst Physics; fel Inst Biol; fel Royal Soc Edinburgh. *Res:* Biomedical systems and materials, particularly natural body cells tissues and organs; mechanical, optical and thermal behavior of tissues and the relationship between structure, composition, and mechanical properties; ex vivo, haemo and bio compatibility studies; cellular engineering and hybrid devices. *Mailing Add:* Univ Strathclyde Glasgow G4 ONW Scotland. *Fax:* 44-141-552-6098

BARBER, ALBERT ALCIDE, CELL BIOLOGY. *Current Pos:* RETIRED. *Personal Data:* b Providence, RI, July 13, 29; m 56; c 2. *Educ:* Univ RI, BS, 50, MS, 52; Duke Univ, PhD, 58. *Prof Exp:* Assoc, Duke Univ, 57-58; from instr to assoc prof zool, Univ Calif, Los Angeles, 58-68, prof, 68-91, assoc vchancellor res, 71-91. *Concurrent Pos:* Consult, NIH, 73-75. *Mem:* Am Soc Biol Chemists; AAAS; Am Soc Zoologists; Am Physiol Soc. *Res:* Cell membranes; aging and antioxidant activity. *Mailing Add:* PO Box 2260 Middleburg VA 22117

BARBER, BRIAN HAROLD, MOLECULAR IMMUNOLOGY. *Current Pos:* ASSOC PROF IMMUNOL, DEPT IMMUNOL, UNIV TORONTO, 76- *Educ:* Univ Toronto, PhD(med biophys), 74. *Res:* Viral vaccines; histocompatibility antigens. *Mailing Add:* Dept Immunol Univ Toronto Med Sci Bldg Toronto ON M5S 1A8 Can

BARBER, DONALD E, HEALTH PHYSICS, INDUSTRIAL HYGIENE. *Current Pos:* assoc prof, 66-74, head, Environ & Occup Health Div, 81-89, PROF ENVIRON HEALTH, SCH PUB HEALTH, UNIV MINN, MINNEAPOLIS, 74- *Personal Data:* b Harrisburg, Pa, Apr 1, 31; div; c 3. *Educ:* Dickinson Col, BS, 53; Univ Mich, MPH, 59, PhD(environ health), 61. *Prof Exp:* Health physicist, Elec Boat Div, Gen Dynamics Corp, 54-55; asst prof environ health, Univ Mich, 61-66. *Concurrent Pos:* Chmn, Sci Comt, 45, Nat Coun Radiation Protection & Measurements, 83-89; cert health physicist; cert safety prof. *Mem:* Health Physics Soc; Am Indust Hyg Asn. *Res:* Occupational and environmental radiation dosimetry; environmental radioactivity. *Mailing Add:* 909 Dartmouth Pl SE Minneapolis MN 55414. *Fax:* 612-626-0650; *E-Mail:* dbarber@mail.eoh.umn.edu

BARBER, EUGENE DOUGLAS, TOXICOLOGY, GENETIC. *Current Pos:* SR RES CHEMIST, EASTMAN KODAK CO, 72-, MGR GENETIC TOXICOL, 78- *Personal Data:* b Philadelphia, Pa, Jan 20, 43; c 1. *Educ:* Drexel Univ, BS, 65; Univ Pa, PhD(biochem), 70; Am Bd Toxicol, dipl, 87. *Prof Exp:* NIH fel lipid chem, Univ Mich, 70-72. *Mem:* Soc Toxicol; Environ Mutagen Soc; Genetic Toxicol Asn. *Res:* Metabolism of foreign compounds; mutagenicity of chemicals; composition and function of biological membranes; in vitro percutaneous absorption studies; toxicity of phthalate esters. *Mailing Add:* Eastman Kodak Co Kodak Park Bldg 320 Rochester NY 14652-6272. *Fax:* 716-722-7561

BARBER, EUGENE JOHN, chemistry of fluorine & uranium compounds; deceased, see previous edition for last biography

BARBER, FRANKLIN WESTON, FOOD SCIENCE. *Current Pos:* RETIRED. *Personal Data:* b New York, NY, July 3, 12; m 37, Natalie Eaton; c Susan. *Educ:* Aurora Col, BS, 34; Univ Wis, MS, 42, PhD(agr bact), 44. *Prof Exp:* Lab technician, H P Hood & Sons, Boston, 37-40; instr bact, Univ Wis, 40-44; asst, Golden State Co, Ltd, San Francisco, 44-45; new prod develop, Res & Develop Div, Kraftco Corp, 45-46, bacteriologist & head, Dept Bact Res, 46-53, sr scientist & chief div fundamental res, 53-57, assoc mgr fundamental res, Ill, 58-60, div res dir, 60-64, asst mgr patents & regulatory compliance, 64-66; from mgr to dir regulatory compliance, 66-75; consult, Food Regulations & Qual Control, 75-80. *Concurrent Pos:* Chmn, Food & Agr Orgn-WHO Joint Expert Comt Milk Hyg, Geneva, 59; mem, Expert Adv Panel Environ Health, WHO, 59-78; secy-treas, Fla Asn Milk, Food & Environ Sanitarians, 81-89. *Mem:* Am Soc Microbiol; Am Dairy Sci Asn; Inst Food Technologists; hon mem Int Asn Milk, Food & Environ Sanitarians (pres, 58-59). *Res:* Dairy bacteriological research; factors affecting accuracy of the phosphatase test; dissociation in lactobacilli; coliform bacteria in ice cream; psychrophilic bacteria in dairy products; milk plate count media; millipore filter techniques; patent and regulatory problems in dairy and food products. *Mailing Add:* 464 Bouchelle Dr No 305 New Smyrna Beach FL 32169-5414

BARBER, GEORGE ALFRED, BIOCHEMISTRY. *Current Pos:* PROF BIOCHEM, OHIO STATE UNIV, 68- *Personal Data:* b New York, NY, May 7, 25. *Educ:* Rutgers Univ, AB, 51; Columbia Univ, PhD(plant physiol, chem), 55. *Prof Exp:* Jr asst res biochemist, Univ Calif, Berkeley, 55-57; asst biochemist, Conn Agr Exp Sta, 57-59; biochemist, Stanford Res Inst, 59-60; asst res biochemist, Univ Calif, Berkeley, 60-65; assoc prof biochem, Univ Hawaii, 65-68. *Mem:* Am Soc Biol Chemists. *Res:* Intermediary metabolism of higher plants. *Mailing Add:* Dept Biochem Ohio State Univ 484 W 12th Ave Columbus OH 43210-1292

BARBER, GEORGE ARTHUR, SCIENTIFIC DRILLING MANAGEMENT, MINERAL EXPLORATION & EVALUATION. *Current Pos:* INDEPENDENT RESOURCE ANALYST/MINERALS CONSULT, 89- *Personal Data:* b Chicago, Ill, Dec 6, 29; m 52, Elvira M Glad; c Timothy, Jennifer (Watson), Susan & Patrick. *Educ:* Univ Ariz, BS, 51. *Hon Degrees:* ME, Univ Ariz, 66. *Honors & Awards:* Marsden Award, Soc Econ Geologists, 97. *Prof Exp:* Field geologist, Anaconda Co, 51-66, chief geologist, SW region, 66-71, explor mgr, Prime Metals Div, 71-73, vpres geol & explor, 73-74, vpres geol & technol, 74-77; vpres explor & geol, Anaconda Minerals-Atlantic Richfield Co, 77-82, vpres minerals adv, 82-85; pres & chief exec officer, Deep Observ & Sampling Earths Continental Crust, Inc, 85-89. *Concurrent Pos:* Film ed, Geophys Film Comt, Nat Acad Sci-Nat Res Coun, 81-86, mem comt global & int geol, 82-85, mem Panel Mineral Res, 83-87 & mem comt hydrocarbon res drilling, 87-; mem, Prog Comt, Am Mining Cong, 82-85 & Resources for the future Policy Adv Comt, 83-; panel chmn, Comt Status & Res Objectives Sun Earth Sci, Nat Acad Sci, 87-93; 28th intern, Geol Congress, 89-; chmn, US Nat Comt Geol, 93- *Mem:* Soc Econ Geologists (vpres, 84, pres, 90-); Geol Soc Am; Soc Mining Engrs; Int Asn Genesis Ore Deposits; Asn Geoscientists Int Develop; Soc Geol Appl Mineral Deposits. *Res:* Organization and management of national continental scientific drilling program; world wide exploration for base and precious metal, energy resources, and non-metallic minerals; evaluation & publication of various project results; coordination with other nation's scientific drilling programs. *Mailing Add:* 5800 Morning Glory Lane Littleton CO 80128-2708. *Fax:* 303-730-2111

BARBER, J(AMES) C(ORBETT), CHEMICAL ENGINEERING. *Current Pos:* CONSULT, JAMES C BARBER & ASSOCS, 76- *Personal Data:* b Ruskin, Ga, Nov 28, 16; m 46; c 3. *Educ:* Ga Inst Technol, BS, 38. *Prof Exp:* Chief plant chem control br, Tenn Valley Authority, 38-63, staff chem engr & off mgr, Off Agr & Chem Develop, 63-76. *Concurrent Pos:* Mem comt med & biol effects environ pollutants, Nat Res Coun, 76-77. *Mem:* Fel Am Chem Soc; Am Inst Chem Engrs. *Res:* Development of processes for production of phosphate fertilizers by the electric furnace method; environmental control for fertilizer operations; development of new fertilizer production processes; elemental phosphorus production; biomass utilization. *Mailing Add:* Courtview Towers Suite 115 201 N Pine St Florence AL 35630-5434

BARBER, JAMES RICHARD, CONTACT MECHANICS, THERMOELASTICITY. *Current Pos:* assoc prof, 81-85, PROF MECH ENG & APPL MECH, UNIV MICH, 85- *Personal Data:* b High Wycombe, UK, Apr 15, 42; c 2. *Educ:* Univ Cambridge, BA, 63, MA, 67 & PhD(eng), 68. *Prof Exp:* Tech asst, British Rail, 63-69; lectr mech eng, Univ Newcastle Upon Tyne, 69-81, reader solid mech, 81. *Mem:* Inst Mech Engrs. *Res:* Elasticity and thermoelasticity, particularly in systems where thermal distortion affects the static or sliding contact of elastic bodies; engine-generator brakes, seals, heat transfer between contacting bodies, thermally driven fracture; solidification of castings. *Mailing Add:* Dept Mech Eng 2250 GGB Univ Mich Main Campus 2351 Herbert Ave Ann Arbor MI 48109-2125

BARBER, JOHN THRELFALL, PLANT PHYSIOLOGY. *Current Pos:* asst prof, 69-71, ASSOC PROF BIOL, TULANE UNIV, 71- *Personal Data:* b Lancaster, Eng, Mar 13, 37; m 61; c 2. *Educ:* Univ Liverpool, BSc, 58 & 59, PhD(plant physiol), 62. *Prof Exp:* Res assoc, Lab Cell Physiol, Growth & Develop, Cornell Univ, 62-69. *Mem:* Sigma Xi; Am Soc Plant Physiol; Am Mosquito Control Asn. *Res:* Plant proteins in relation to growth, development and morphogenesis; ecology of mucilaginous plant seeds. *Mailing Add:* Dept Ecol Tulane Univ 6823 St Charles Ave New Orleans LA 70118-5665

BARBER, M(ARK) R, ELECTRONICS. *Current Pos:* mem tech staff, Semiconductor Electronics, 61-64, TECH MGR, AT&T BELL LABS, 64- *Personal Data:* b Wellington, NZ, July 23, 31; US citizen; m 78, Roberta E DiMenna. *Educ:* Univ Auckland, BSc, 54, BE, 55; Cambridge Univ, PhD(eng), 59. *Prof Exp:* Res engr, Naval Res Lab, NZ, 59-61. *Concurrent Pos:* Mem, Testing Comt, SEMATECH, 93- *Mem:* Fel Inst Elec & Electronics Engrs. *Res:* Electrocardiography; medical electronics; high power electron guns; processing signals from underwater acoustic arrays; solid state microwave switching networks; tunnel diode amplifiers and frequency converters; microwave solid state oscillators; semiconductor memories; integrated circuits; automated test equipment for integrated circuits. *Mailing Add:* Lucent Technols 555 Union Blvd Allentown PA 18103

BARBER, MARY COMBS, LINKING SCIENCE TO NEEDS OF DECISION MAKERS. *Current Pos:* ACTG EXEC DIR, ECOL SOC AM, 94- *Personal Data:* b Vienna, Austria, July 26, 49; US citizen; m 85, Curtis E von Kann; c Marieke, Kathryn & Harry. *Educ:* Vassar Col, BA, 71; Johns Hopkins Univ, PhD(ecol & evolutionary biol), 82. *Prof Exp:* Policy analyst policy & planning, Nat Oceanic & Atmospheric Admin, 83-86; staff scientist, Oceanic Soc, 86-87; prog mgr, NSF, 88-90; sr environ scientist, Sci & Policy Assocs Inc, 90-94. *Mem:* Womens Aquatic Network; Asn Women Sci (pres, 81-); Ecol Soc Am; Am Inst Biol Sci; AAAS. *Res:* Use of scientific information by decision makers and policy makers; interest and support of women in science and other technical fields. *Mailing Add:* Ecol Soc Am 2010 Massachusetts Ave Suite 400 Washington DC 20036. *Fax:* 202-789-1206

BARBER, MICHAEL JAMES, METALLOENZYMES. *Current Pos:* from asst prof to assoc prof, 83-91, PROF BIOCHEM, COL MED, UNIV SFLA, 91- *Personal Data:* b UK, Aug 8, 50; m 82, Janet Forrester; c Nicholas. *Educ:* Univ Kent, BSc, 72, MSc, 73; Univ Sussex, DPhil(biochem), 76. *Prof Exp:* Teaching fel biochem, Univ Sussex, 75-77; lectr phys sci, Open Univ, 76-77; res assoc biochem, Duke Univ Med Ctr, 77-83. *Concurrent Pos:* Assoc mem, H Lee Moffitt Comprehensive Cancer Center & Res Inst, 94-; assoc dir, Inst Biomolecular Sci, 94-96; mem, NIH Phys Biochem Study Sec, 95-99; vis prof biochem, New Col, Sarasota, Fla, 96. *Mem:* Am Soc Biol Chemists; Inst Biomolecular Sci. *Res:* Structure and function of metalloenzymes with special emphasis on those containing molybdenum; mechanism of action of nitrate reductase; use of spin-labels in biochemistry; structure and function of flavoproteins protein engineering. *Mailing Add:* Dept Biochem MS MDC7 Univ SFla Col Med Tampa FL 33612. *Fax:* 813-974-5798; *E-Mail:* mbarber@nick.med.usf.edu

BARBER, PATRICK GEORGE, PHYSICAL CHEMISTRY & LIQUID CRYSTALS. *Current Pos:* assoc prof chem, 78-85, PROF CHEM & DIR CHEM PROG, DEPT NATURAL SCI, LONGWOOD COL, 85- *Personal Data:* b Santa Barbara, Calif, Dec 14, 42; m 67, Patricia Price; c David & Dawn. *Educ:* Stanford Univ, BS, 64; Cornell Univ, PhD(phys chem), 69. *Prof Exp:* Res technician radiol chem, US Naval Radiol Defense Lab, 63; res assoc chem, Duke Univ, 69-71; asst prof chem & math, Daniel Campus, Southside Va Community Col, 71-75, chmn, Div Arts & Sci, 73-75, prof chem, 75-78. *Concurrent Pos:* NSF prof develop grant, Duke Univ, 77; summer fac fel, Lewis Res Ctr, NASA, 76 & 77, Langley Res Ctr, 83, 84, 87 & 88, res scientist, 84-85 & 87-91; summer fac fel, David W Taylor Naval Ship Res & Dev Ctr, 81 & 83; researcher crystal growth, Spain, 90, liquid crystal res, Halle, Ger, 91. *Mem:* Am Chem Soc; Am Crystallog Asn; Sigma Xi; fel Am Inst Chem; Am Asn Crystal Growth. *Res:* Crystallographic studies on derivatives of Gramicidin-S; structure and properties of liquid crystalline compounds; crystal growth in gels; alkaline-zinc battery for electric car; computer generated displays and computer software; conformation of polymers in the solid state; crystal growth of semiconductor crystals, etches for semiconductor crystals; x-ray crystallography. *Mailing Add:* Rte 2 Box 29B Keysville VA 23947. *Fax:* 804-395-2652; *E-Mail:* pbarber@longwood.lwc.edu

BARBER, RICHARD T, OCEANOGRAPHY. *Current Pos:* from assoc prof to prof, 70-87, HARVEY W SMITH PROF BIOL OCEANOG, DUKE UNIV, 87- *Personal Data:* b Bridgeton, NJ, Apr 3, 38. *Educ:* Utah State Univ, BS, 62; Stanford Univ, PhD(biol sci), 67. *Honors & Awards:* Creativity Award, NSF, 84; John Hollard Martin Medal Excellence, 94. *Prof Exp:* Postdoctoral fel, Woods Hole Oceanog Inst, 67, asst scientist, 68-69. *Concurrent Pos:* Mem, Comt Water Qual, Nat Acad Sci, 71-73, Int Ocean Sci Policy Comt, 83-85 & Comt Ocean's Role Global Change, 89-92 & Fleet Improvement Comt, Univ Nat Oceanog Lab Systs, 87-90; nat coordr, Coastal Upwelling Ecosystem Anal, 72-80; exec dir, Monterey Bay Aquarium Res Inst, 87-90; counr, Oceanog Soc, 92-96; actg dir, Duke Univ NC Oceanog Consortium. *Mem:* Fel AAAS; fel Am Geophys Union; Am Soc Limnol & Oceanog (pres, 86-88). *Res:* Causes and consequences of large scale variability in oceanic productivity; author of numerous publications. *Mailing Add:* Marine Lab Duke Univ 135 Duke Marine Lab Rd Beaufort NC 28516. *Fax:* 919-504-7648; *E-Mail:* rbarber@acpub.duke.edu

BARBER, ROBERT CHARLES, PHYSICS. *Current Pos:* from asst prof to assoc prof, 65-75, head dept, 87-96, PROF PHYSICS, UNIV MAN, 75- *Personal Data:* b Sarnia, Ont, Apr 20, 36; m 62; c 3. *Educ:* McMaster Univ, BSc, 58, PhD(physics), 62. *Prof Exp:* Fel physics, McMaster Univ, 62-65. *Concurrent Pos:* Sabbatical leave, Sch Physics, Univ Minn, Minneapolis, 71-72; mem, Int Union Pure & Appl Physics, Comn C13 on Atomic Massas & Fundamental Constants, 72-75, secy, 75-78, Comn C2 on Symbols, Units, Nomenclature, SUN-AMCO, secy, 78-84, chmn, 86-90, mem, 90-93. *Mem:* Can Asn Physicists; Can Asn Univ Teachers. *Res:* Determination of atomic mass differences by high resolution mass spectrometer. *Mailing Add:* Dept Physics Univ Man Winnipeg MB R3T 2N2 Can. *Fax:* 204-269-8489

BARBER, ROBERT EDWIN, organic rankine engines, low specific turbine design & analysis, for more information see previous edition

BARBER, SAUL BENJAMIN, ZOOLOGY, INVERTEBRATE NEUROPHYSIOLOGY. *Current Pos:* from asst prof to prof, 56-85, chmn, Biol Dept, 65-72, 74-76 & 78-80, assoc dean, Col Arts & Sci, 76-77, dean pro-tem, 77-78, EMER PROF BIOL, LEHIGH UNIV, 85- *Personal Data:* b Somerville, Mass, Sept 3, 20; m 55; c 3. *Educ:* RI State Col, BS, 41; Yale Univ, PhD(zool), 54. *Prof Exp:* Instr zool, RI State Col, 46-48; instr biol, Williams Col, 52-54; instr zool, Smith Col, 54-55; res assoc, Narragansett Marine Lab, Univ RI, 55-56. *Concurrent Pos:* NIH res contract; Nat Inst Neurol Dis & Blindness spec res fel zool, Oxford, 63-64. *Mem:* AAAS; Am Soc Zoologists; Electron Micros Soc Am; Sigma Xi; Am Asn Univ Professors. *Res:* Chemoreception and proprioception in the horseshoe crab; fish sound production; physiology of insect flight and muscle. *Mailing Add:* 1021 W Yarmouth Rd Yarmouth Port MA 02675-1946

BARBER, SHERBURNE FREDERICK, MATHEMATICS. *Current Pos:* RETIRED. *Personal Data:* b Nunda, NY, Oct 25, 07; m 44, Virginia L Roy; c John, David & Andrew. *Educ:* Univ Rochester, AB, 29, AM, 30; Univ Ill, PhD(math), 33. *Prof Exp:* Nat res fel, Johns Hopkins Univ, 33-34 & Princeton Univ & Inst Advan Study, 34-35; assoc math, Univ Iowa, 35-37; tutor, City Col New York, 37-40, from instr to prof math, 40-76, from asst dean to dean, Col Lib Arts & Sci, 53-71. *Mem:* Am Math Soc. *Res:* Cremona and birational transformations; algebraic geometry. *Mailing Add:* 211 Applewood Southbury CT 06488

BARBER, STANLEY ARTHUR, SOIL CHEMISTRY, SOIL FERTILITY. *Current Pos:* from asst prof to prof, 49-91, EMER PROF SOILS, PURDUE UNIV, WEST LAFAYETTE, 91- *Personal Data:* b Wolseley, Can; Mar 29, 21; nat; m 50; c 2. *Educ:* Univ Sask, BSA, 45, MSc, 47; Univ Mo, PhD(soils), 49. *Hon Degrees:* LLD, Univ Sask, 86. *Honors & Awards:* Soil Res Award, Am Soc Agron, 74, Agron Res Award, 83, Agron Achievement Award, 84; Bouyoucos Distinguished Career Award, Soil Sci Soc Am, 85; Alexander von Humboldt Found Award, 86. *Prof Exp:* Instr soils, Univ Sask, 45-47. *Concurrent Pos:* Vis prof, Univ Calif, Berkeley, 61 & Univ Adelaide, 68-69; NSF sr fel, 68-69; vis prof, Cornell Univ, 79; Can Indust Ltd distinguished vis lectr, Univ Sask, 87. *Mem:* Nat Acad Sci; fel Am Soc Agron; fel Soil Sci Soc Am; Int Soc Soil Sci; Am Soc Plant Physiol. *Res:* Mechanisms for the movement of nutrients through the soil to the plant root; influence of the plant root on the soil; soil nutrients availability and crop growth. *Mailing Add:* Dept Agron Purdue Univ West Lafayette IN 47907-1150

BARBER, THOMAS JOSEPH, COMPUTATIONAL FLUID DYNAMICS, PROPULSION. *Current Pos:* PROF MECH ENG, HARTFORD GRAD CTR, 69-; MGR, UNITED TECHNOL RES CTR, 83- *Personal Data:* b Warwick, Eng, Nov 3, 42; US citizen; m 66, Lorraine J; c Michelle S & Jeffrey S. *Educ:* NY Univ, BS, 64, MS, 65, PhD(aeronaut eng), 68. *Prof Exp:* Res engr, Pratt & Whitney Aircraft, 68-83. *Concurrent Pos:* Assoc ed, J Propulsion Power, Am Inst Aeronaut & Astronaut, 92-95. *Mem:* Assoc fel Am Inst Aeronaut & Astronaut; Am Soc Mech Engrs. *Res:* Developed and applied computational analysis to investigate internal and external flow problems; mix-up enhancement concepts in propulsion applications, leading to the development of low-noise and low-observable engine exhaust systems. *Mailing Add:* 411 Silver Lane East Hartford CT 06108. *Fax:* 860-610-2108; *E-Mail:* barbertj@utrc.utc.com

BARBER, THOMAS KING, DENTISTRY. *Current Pos:* assoc dean, 78-80, 81-83, prof, 69-97, EMER PROF PEDIAT, SCH MED & PEDIAT DENT, SCH DENT, UNIV CALIF, LOS ANGELES, 97- *Personal Data:* b Highland Park, Mich, Sept 26, 23; m 47; c 3. *Educ:* Mich State Col, BS, 45; Univ Ill, BS, 47, DDS & MS, 49. *Honors & Awards:* Hon Mem Award, Peruvian Dent Soc, 68; Hon Mem Award, Soc Dent Children, 70; Award of Excellence, Am Soc Dent Children, 81. *Prof Exp:* Instr pedodontics, Marquette Univ, 50-51; from instr to prof, Univ Ill, 51-69. *Concurrent Pos:* Consult, Coun Dent Educ, Am Dent Asn, Am Fund Dent Health & Educ Testing Serv; actg dean, Univ Calif, Los Angeles, 80-81. *Mem:* Fel Am Col Dent; Am Dent Asn; Am Soc Dent for Children; Am Acad Pedodontics. *Res:* Pedodontics, especially growth and dental development of children and minor orthodontics in children; educational research in dentistry. *Mailing Add:* 2570 Bayside Pl Arroyo Grande CA 93420-6515

BARBER, THOMAS LYNWOOD, SCIENCE EDUCATION, ANIMAL DISEASE RESEARCH. *Current Pos:* RETIRED. *Personal Data:* b Dothan, Ala, Feb 4, 34; div; c 3. *Educ:* Auburn Univ, DVM, 58; Cornell Univ, MS, 61, PhD, 69. *Prof Exp:* Res vet, Plum Island Animal Dis Ctr, 58-69; vet med officer agr res, Arthropod-Borne Animal Dis Res Lab, Agr Res Serv, USDA, 69-85; consult, 85. *Concurrent Pos:* Fac affil, Colo State Univ, 73-88. *Mem:* US Animal Health Asn; Am Vet Med Asn. *Res:* Arthropod borne diseases of animals; bluetongue virus vaccine development for sheep and cattle. *Mailing Add:* 7855 Armadillo Trail Evergreen CO 80439

BARBER, WILLIAM AUSTIN, physical chemistry, for more information see previous edition

BARBER, WILLIAM J, MICROCIRCULATION. *Current Pos:* ASSOC RES PROF, CTR BIOMED ENG, UNIV KY, 90- *Educ:* Univ Ky, PhD(biol sci), 76. *Prof Exp:* Assoc prof physiol, Med Col Wis, 80-90. *Mailing Add:* 1330 River Rd Nicholasville KY 40356-9649

BARBERO, GIULIO J, PEDIATRICS, GASTROENTEROLOGY. *Current Pos:* RETIRED. *Personal Data:* b Mt Vernon, NY, Oct 13, 23; m 47, Margaret Goff; c 6. *Educ:* Univ Maine, BS, 43; Univ Pa, MD, 47. *Honors & Awards:* Abraham Levi Int Award Cystic Fibrosis, 96. *Prof Exp:* Sr physician, dir div gastroenterol & cystic fibrosis res group, Children's Hosp Philadelphia, 59-67; prof pediat & chmn dept, Hahnemann Med Col, 67-73 & Sch Med, Univ Mo, Columbia, 73-90; prof pediat & chmn dept, Sch Med, Univ Mo-Columbia, 73-90. *Concurrent Pos:* Chmn, gen med & sci adv coun, Nat Cystic Fibrosis Res Found, 71-74; mem, Coun Heart, Lung & Blood Inst, NIH. *Mem:* Soc Pediat Res; Am Acad Pediat; Am Gastroenterol Asn; Am Psychosom Soc; Soc Pediat Gastroenterol. *Res:* Cystic fibrosis; gastrointestinal disturbances of children; psychosomatic aspects of gastrointestinal disorders of childhood. *Mailing Add:* Sch Med Univ Mo Columbia MO 65201. *Fax:* 573-882-2742

BARBIN, ALLEN R, MECHANICAL ENGINEERING. *Current Pos:* RETIRED. *Personal Data:* b Beaumont, Tex, July 3, 34; m 54; c 2. *Educ:* Lamar State Col, BS, 55; Tex A&M Univ, MS, 59; Purdue Univ, PhD(mech eng), 61. *Prof Exp:* Asst prof mech eng, Lamar State Col, 56-58; assoc prof, Auburn Univ, 61-67, prof mech eng, 67-87. *Concurrent Pos:* Consult, Reactor Div, Oak Ridge Nat Lab, 63- *Mem:* Assoc mem Am Soc Mech Engrs; Sigma Xi. *Res:* Turbulent flow in tubes; jet flows; forced turbulent boundary layers; fluid jet amplifiers. *Mailing Add:* Rte 1 Box 160 Fea Rd Buna TX 77612

BARBO, DOROTHY M, NUTRITION. *Current Pos:* PROF OBSTET & GYNEC, UNIV NMEX, SCH MED, 91- *Personal Data:* b River Falls, Wis, May 28, 32. *Educ:* Asbury Col, Wilmore, Ky, AB, 54; Univ Wis-Madison, MD, 58. *Hon Degrees:* DSc, Asbury Col, 81. *Prof Exp:* Instr obstet & gynec, Med Col Wis, 62-66, asst prof, 66-67; assoc prof obstet & gynec, Ludhiana Christian Med Col, Punjab, India, 68-72, actg chmn dept, 70, chief gynec oncol, 69-72, chief family planning, 70-72; coordr & clin dir, Med Col Pa, 73-77, dir gynec oncol, 75-85, assoc prof obstet & gynec, 72-78, dir, Ctr Mature Women, 83-91, prof obstet & gynec, 88-91. *Concurrent Pos:* Sr clin trainee obstet & gynec, USPHS CA Control, 63-65; mem bd dirs, Ludhiana Christian Med Col, NY, 73-, Am Cancer Soc, Philadelphia Div, 80-86 & Serv Master Co LP, Chicago, 82-91; consult, Vet Admin Hosp, Philadelphia, 75-85; examr, Am Bd Obstet & Gynec, 84-; mem, Dept Health Human Serv, Fed Drug Admin Fertil & Maternal Health Drug Adv Comn, 86-91. *Mem:* Am Col Obstet & Gynec; Am Col Surgeons; AMA; Am Soc Colposcopy & Cervical Path; Am Women's Med Asn; NAm Menopause Soc. *Res:* Gynecological oncology in the areas of prevention, screening techniques and early diagnosis; gynecological surgery and care of the post-menopausal woman with emphasis on menopausal problems; prevention, early diagnosis and treatment of post-menopausal osteoporosis. *Mailing Add:* Dept Obstet/Gynec Univ NMex Sch Med One Univ Campus Albuquerque NM 87131-0001

BARBORAK, JAMES CARL, MECHANISTIC ORGANOMETALLIC CHEMISTRY, CATALYSIS. *Current Pos:* from asst prof to assoc prof chem, 72-80, PROF CHEM, UNIV NC, GREENSBORO, 80- *Personal Data:* b Moulton, Tex, Sept 8, 41; m 69, Shirley Heczko. *Educ:* Univ Tex, Austin, BS, 63, PhD(chem), 68. *Prof Exp:* Res scientist, Uniroyal, Inc, 68-69; fel, Princeton Univ, 69-70, instr chem, 70-72. *Concurrent Pos:* Vis res prof, Univ NC, Chapel Hill, 90. *Mem:* Am Chem Soc. *Res:* Organic synthesis of strained ring systems; organometallic chemistry applied to organic synthesis; rearrangements of olefin systems induced by iron carbonyl catalysts and the mechanism of these rearrangements; organic polymer chemistry; catalysis of polymerization. *Mailing Add:* Dept Chem Univ NC Greensboro NC 27412

BARBORIAK, JOSEPH JAN, BIOCHEMICAL PHARMACOLOGY, ALCOHOLISM. *Current Pos:* assoc prof, 62-71, PROF PHARMACOL & TOXICOL, MED COL WIS, 71-, PROF PREV MED, 79- *Personal Data:* b Slovakia, Feb 19, 23; nat US; m 56; c 3. *Educ:* Inst Technol, Bratislava, BS, 44; Swiss Fed Inst Technol, ScD(nutrit biochem), 53. *Prof Exp:* Res assoc, Swiss Fed Inst Technol, 47-53; res assoc, Yale Univ, 54-58; group leader, Mead Johnson & Co, 59-61. *Concurrent Pos:* Chief biochem sect, Res Serv, Vet Admin Ctr, 61- *Mem:* AAAS; Am Soc Pharmacol & Exp Therapeut; Am Inst Nutrit; Am Acad Allergy & Immunol; Soc Exp Biol & Med; Am Col Epidemiol; fel Am Col Clin Nutrit; fel Soc Behav Med; Am Col Epidemiol. *Res:* Lipid metabolism; pharmacology of alcoholism; nutrition; epidemiology of cardiac risk factors. *Mailing Add:* Dept Pharmacol Med Col Wis 8701 Watertown Plank Rd Milwaukee WI 53226-4801

BARBOSA-CANOVAS, GUSTAVO VICTOR, FOOD PROCESS ENGINEERING, PHYSICAL PROPERTIES OF FOODS. *Current Pos:* asst prof, 90-94, ASSOC PROF, FOOD ENG, WASH STATE UNIV, 94- *Personal Data:* b Minas, Lavalleja, Uruguay, Nov 1, 49; US citizen; m 81, Ana M Rodriquez-Vivaldi; c Juan M & Gabriela M. *Educ:* Univ Uruguay, BS, 77; Univ Mass, MS, 82, PhD(food eng),85. *Honors & Awards:* Scholarly Productivity Award, NSF, 88-89. *Prof Exp:* Asst prof mech eng, Univ Uruguay, 74-80, chem eng, Univ PR, 85-90; res asst, Univ Mass, 80-85. *Concurrent Pos:* Mech engr, Uruguayan Brewery, 77-78, Uruguay River Dam Proj, 78-80; nat rep, Sci & Technol for Develop, 87-; vis prof, Univ Chihuahua, Mex, 92-, Univ de las Am-Puebla, Mex, 93-; hon prof, Univ Uruguay, 93. *Mem:* Sigma Xi; Inst Food Technologists; Am Inst Chem Engrs; Am Soc Mech Engrs; Am Soc Agr Engrs; Am Filtration Soc. *Res:* Preservation of food by non-thermal processes which include pulsed electrical fields, oscillating magnetic fields and high hydrostatic pressure; physical properties of foods, controlled released and powder technology. *Mailing Add:* Biol Syst Eng Wash State Univ Pullman WA 99164-0001. *Fax:* 509-335-2722; *E-Mail:* Bitnet: barbosa@wsuvmi

BARBOUR, CLYDE D, ICHTHYOLOGY. *Current Pos:* ASSOC PROF BIOL, WRIGHT STATE UNIV, 75- *Personal Data:* b New York, NY, Oct 30, 35; m 62; c 2. *Educ:* Stanford Univ, AB, 58; Tulane Univ, PhD(zool), 66. *Prof Exp:* Asst prof biol, Univ Utah, 66-72 & Tuskegee Inst, 74-75; vis scientist, Mus Zool, Univ Mich, 72-73; vis asst prof, Miss State Univ, 73-74; asst prof biol, Tuskegee Inst, 74-75. *Mem:* AAAS; Am Soc Ichthyologists & Herpetologists; Soc Study Evolution; Soc Syst Zool. *Res:* Ichthyology, including systematics, zoogeography and ecology. *Mailing Add:* Dept Biol Sci Wright State Univ 3640 Colonel Glenn Dayton OH 45435-0001

BARBOUR, MICHAEL G, ECOLOGY, BOTANY. *Current Pos:* From asst prof to prof bot, 67-93, PROF ENVIRON HORT, UNIV CALIF, DAVIS, 93- *Personal Data:* b Jackson, Mich, Feb 24, 42; m 87, Valerie Whitworth; c Julie (Neal), Steven (Whitworth) & Alan. *Educ:* Mich State Univ, BSc, 63; Duke Univ, PhD(bot), 67. *Concurrent Pos:* NSF grants, Study Coastal Vegetation, 69-71, Study Beach Vegetation, 73-75 & Study Montane Forests, 89-91; NSF/Int Biol Prog grant desert vegetation in NAm & SAm, 70-73; Univ Calif sea grant mgt dune vegetation, 74-76; fed & state grants to study salt marshes, 77-80, grasslands and meadows, 84-87; Fullbright fel, Univ Adelaide, Australia, 64; Guggenheim fel, 78; vis prof bot, Hebrew Univ, Israel, 79-80, La State Univ, 83. *Mem:* Am Inst Biol Sci; Ecol Soc Am; Brit Ecol Soc; Sigma Xi; Bot Soc Am. *Res:* Physiological ecology; ecological life histories of coastal, desert and mountain plant species; community ecology of California vegetation. *Mailing Add:* Dept Bot Univ Calif Davis CA 95616

BARBOUR, MICHAEL THOMAS, DEVELOPMENT OF BIOASSESSMENT APPROACHES. *Current Pos:* SR SCIENTIST, EA ENG, SCI & TECHNOL, 77- *Personal Data:* b Stockbridge, Mich, Sept 21, 47; m 69; c 2. *Educ:* Eastern Mich Univ, BS, 70, MS, 72. *Prof Exp:* Biol tech, US Fish & Wildlife Serv, 70-72; instr zool, Eastern Mich Univ, 72; assoc biologist, NALCO Chem Co, 72-74; assoc ecologist, NUS Corp, 74-77. *Concurrent Pos:* Treas, Atlantic Estuarine Res Soc, 86-88; chmn, Exec Comt, N Am Benthological Soc, 89-90. *Mem:* Estuarine Res Fedn; Soc Toxicol & Chem; N Am Benthological Soc. *Res:* Development of bioassessment approaches for evaluating pollutant effects on indigenous aquatic communities; concept of an integrated assessment utilizing habitat quality; physicochemical measurements and biological condition indices. *Mailing Add:* 3457 Augusta Rd Manchester MD 21102

BARBUL, ADRIAN, SURGERY. *Current Pos:* ASST SURGEON-IN-CHIEF, SINAI HOSP, BALTIMORE, 82- *Personal Data:* b Bucharest, Romania, Jan 11, 50; US citizen; m; c 2. *Educ:* City Col New York, BS, 69; Gen Sch Med, Bucharest, Romania, MD, 74; Am Bd Surg, dipl, 83. *Honors & Awards:* Mead-Johnson Excellence of Res Award, 77; Resident Res Award, Asn Acad Surg, 82. *Prof Exp:* Surg resident, Albert Einstein Col Med, 74-76, NIH res trainee trauma & burns, 76-78; surg resident, Sinai Hosp, Baltimore, 78-82; asst prof, 83-87, ASSOC PROF, DEPT SURG, JOHNS HOPKINS UNIV, 87- *Concurrent Pos:* Mem, Comt Infections, Sinai Hosp, 83-, Tissue Comt, 85-, Nutrit Care Comt, 86-88, chmn, 89-, mem, Animal Care Comt, 88-, Inst Rev Bd, 88-; prin investr, NIH, 87-92, Johnson & Johnson Patient Care, Inc, 88-90; rep to Nat Asn Biomed Res, Soc Univ Surgeons, 90-91, counr- at-large, 91-93. *Mem:* Fel Am Col Surgeons; Soc Univ Surgeons; Am Soc Parenteral & Enteral Nutrit; Asn Acad Surg; Am Inst Nutrit; Am Soc Clin Nutrit; fel Am Col Nutrit; AAAS; NY Acad Sci; Soc Crit Care Med. *Res:* Studies on nutritional modification of the deleterious effects of trauma and tumors on protein metabolism; wound healing and immunity. *Mailing Add:* Dept Surg Sinai Hosp 2401 W Belvedere Ave Baltimore MD 21215-5271

BARCELLONA, WAYNE J, ELECTRON MICROSCOPY. *Current Pos:* asst prof, 73-79, chmn dept, 81-87, ASSOC PROF BIOL, TEX CHRISTIAN UNIV, 79- *Personal Data:* b Chicago, Ill, Sept 22, 40; m 70, Joan M Gabriele; c Mario & Margo. *Educ:* Univ Southern Calif, AB, 62, MS, 65, PhD(biol), 70. *Prof Exp:* Fel biol, Sect Cell Biol, M D Anderson Hosp & Tumor Inst, Univ Tex, 70-72; res assoc, Univ Tex Med Br, 72-73. *Mem:* Am Soc Androl; AAAS; Am Inst Biol Sci; Am Soc Cell Biol; Soc Study Reproduction. *Res:* Reproductive biology; differentiation; control and regulation of cell division and mammalian spermatogenesis. *Mailing Add:* Dept Biol Tex Christian Univ 298860 Ft Worth TX 76129-0000

BARCELLOS-HOFF, MARY HELEN, RADIATION BIOLOGY, EXTRACELLULAR MATRIX. *Current Pos:* Res, 86-88, STAFF SCIENTIST, LAWRENCE BERKELEY LAB, UNIV CALIF, 88- *Personal Data:* b Verdun, France, May 10, 55. *Educ:* Univ Chicago, BA, 78; Univ Calif, San Francisco, PhD(exp pathol), 86. *Concurrent Pos:* Adj asst prof, Colo State Univ, Ft Collins, 91-; adj assoc prof anat, Univ Calif, San Francisco, 93- *Mem:* Am Soc Cell Biol; Radiation Res Soc; AAAS. *Res:* Studies of irradiated tissue cell and molecular responses of the murine mammary gland to ionizing radiation; mechanisms of tissue damage and relationship to carcinogenesis. *Mailing Add:* Bldg 74 Lawrence Berkeley Lab One Cyclotron Rd Berkeley CA 94720-0001. *Fax:* 510-486-6746; *E-Mail:* mhbh@ux5.lbl.gov

BARCELO, RAYMOND, PHYSIOLOGY, BIOCHEMISTRY. *Current Pos:* asst prof, 62-70, ASSOC PROF MED, UNIV MONTREAL, 71-, CHIEF SERV NEPHROLOGY, MAISONNEUVE HOSP, 64- *Personal Data:* b Montreal, PQ, July 14, 31; m 54; c 4. *Educ:* Univ Montreal, BSc, 50, MD, 57; Univ Pa, DSc(biochem), 60; FRCPC, 62. *Prof Exp:* Intern, Hosp Necker, Paris, France, 60-61. *Concurrent Pos:* Head dept, Clin & Res Lab, Maisonneuve Hosp, 67-70. *Mem:* Am Soc Clin Res; Can Soc Clin Res; Can Soc Immunol; Can Soc Nephrol; Int Soc Nephrology. *Res:* Protein biochemistry; immunochemical studies of serum and urinary proteins; plasma seromucoids in various inflammatory conditions; perfusion of isolated kidney; diuretics; antibiotics; antihypertensive drugs. *Mailing Add:* Dept Nephrology Maisonneuve Hosp Montreal PQ H3C 3J7 Can

BARCELONA, MICHAEL JOSEPH, GROUNDWATER GEOCHEMISTRY, ENVIRONMENTAL ANALYTICAL CHEMISTRY. *Current Pos:* RES PROF, CIVIL & ENVIRON ENG, UNIV MICH, 93- *Personal Data:* b Chicago, Ill, Aug 20, 49; m 72; c 3. *Educ:* St Mary's Col, Minn, BA, 71; Northeastern Univ, MS, 74; Univ PR, PhD(marine chem), 77. *Prof Exp:* Environ sect head, OMNI Res, Inc, 73-75; instr chem oceanog, Univ PR, 75-76; res assoc environ eng, Keck Lab Environ Eng Sci, 77 & Calif Inst Technol, 78-79; assoc prof sci, Water Surv Div, Ill Dept Energy & Natural Resources, 79-80, aquatic chem sect head, 80-90; dir & prof chem, Inst Water Scis, Western Mich Univ, 89-93; ed, Ground Water Monitoring & Remediation, 92- *Mem:* Am Chem Soc; Nat Ground Water Asn. *Res:* Chemistry of environmental processes in natural waters; sediments; temporal and spatial variability in geochemical conditions. *Mailing Add:* Dept Civil & Environ Eng 1221 Ist Bldg Univ Mich 2099 Bonisteel Blvd Ann Arbor MI 48109-2099. *Fax:* 313-763-6513

BARCHAS, JACK D, BEHAVIORAL NEUROCHEMISTRY. *Current Pos:* ASSOC DEAN NEUROSCI, SCH MED, UNIV CALIF, LOS ANGELES, 90-, PROF PSYCHIAT BEHAV SCI, 90- *Personal Data:* b Los Angeles, Calif, Nov 2, 35. *Educ:* Pomona Col, BA, 56; Yale Univ, MD, 61. *Prof Exp:* Intern psychiat, Pritzker Sch Med, Univ Chicago, 61-62; res assoc, NIH, 62-64; res prof, Stanford Univ, 64-67, Nancy Friend Pritzer prof, 67-89. *Mem:* Inst Med-Nat Acad Sci; Am Soc Neurochem; Am Soc Pharmacol; AAAS; Am Chem Soc. *Mailing Add:* Dept Neurosci MS 107 Univ Calif Sch Med 10833 Le Conte Ave Los Angeles CA 90024-1722

BARCHET, WILLIAM RICHARD, WIND ENERGY, CLOUD PHYSICS. *Current Pos:* sr res scientist atmospheric sci, 79-91, staff scientist, 91-93, mgr boundary layer meteorol, 93-94, MGR ATMOSPHERIC SCI, BATTELLE PAC NW LAB, 94- *Personal Data:* b Baltimore, Md, June 24, 43; m 68, Doris T Rodenbuecher; c Christopher & Alexander. *Educ:* Drexel Inst Technol, BS, 66; Colo State Univ, MS, 68, PhD(atmospheric sci), 71. *Prof Exp:* Asst prof physics, Univ Northern Ariz, 70-71; vis asst prof meteorol, Univ Wis, Madison, 71-72, asst prof, 72-78. *Concurrent Pos:* Affil prof, Wash State Univ, Tricities. *Mem:* Am Meteorol Soc. *Res:* Atmospheric processes affecting the fate of pollutants; cloud modeling, microphysics and weather modification; wind energy resource assessment and data analysis; regional air quality model evaluation; airborne measurements environmental assessments. *Mailing Add:* 308 Scot St Richland WA 99352

BARCHFELD, FRANCIS JOHN, MECHANICAL ENGINEERING. *Current Pos:* MGR, LTV, 84- *Personal Data:* b Pittsburgh, Pa, Sept 12, 35; m 58; c 1. *Educ:* Carnegie-Mellon Univ, BS, 58. *Prof Exp:* Engr, US Steel Corp, 58-60; engr, Hagan Controls Corp, 60-61; dir control res, Jones & Laughlin Steel Corp, 61-84. *Mem:* Asn Iron & Steel Engrs; Instrument Soc Am; Am Soc Nondestructive Testing. *Res:* Design of automatic inspection equipment. *Mailing Add:* 1788 Farr's Garden Path Westlake OH 44145

BARCHI, ROBERT LAWRENCE, NEUROSCIENCE, CLINICAL NEUROLOGY. *Current Pos:* asst prof biochem, Med Sch, Univ Pa, 74-75, from asst prof to assoc prof neurol & biochem, 75-81, chmn, Neurosci Grad Prog, 83-89, dir, Mahoney Inst Neurol Sci, 83-96, vdean res, Sch Med, 89-91, PROF NEUROL & BIOCHEM, SCH MED, UNIV PA, 81-, DAVID MAHONEY PROF & CHAIR, DEPT NEUROL & NEUROSCI, 92- *Personal Data:* b Philadelphia, Pa, Nov 23, 46; m 76, Joan E Mollman; c Jonathan R & Jennifer E. *Educ:* Georgetown Univ, BS, 68, MS, 69; Univ Pa, PhD(biochem), 72, MD, 73; Am Bd Psychiat & Neurol, dipl. *Honors & Awards:* Javits Award, NIH, 85. *Prof Exp:* Resident neurol, Univ Pa Hosp, 73-75. *Concurrent Pos:* Mem, Med Adv Bd, Muscular Dystrophy Asn, 82- *Mem:* Inst Med-Nat Acad Sci; fel Am Acad Neurol; Am Neurol Asn; Biophys Soc; Soc Neurosci; Am Soc Clin Invest; Asn Am Physicians. *Res:* Structure and function of voltage-dependent sodium channels, regulation of channel gene expression and channel mutations causing human disease. *Mailing Add:* Univ Pa David Mahoney Inst Neurol Sci 215 Stemmler Hall Eleminitt 452 Med Educ Bldg Philadelphia PA 19104. *Fax:* 215-573-2015

BARCILON, ALBERT I, DYNAMIC METEOROLOGY. *Current Pos:* asst prof meteorol & res assoc, 68-72, assoc prof, 72-80, PROF METEOROL, FLA STATE UNIV, 81- *Personal Data:* b Alexandria, Egypt, July 21, 37; m 61, Michelle M Perez; c Jolelyn E & Danielle R. *Educ:* McGill Univ, BEngPhysics, 60; Harvard Univ, MA, 61, PhD(fluid dynamics), 65. *Prof Exp:* Res assoc, Meteorol Dept, Mass Inst Technol & Harvard Univ, 65-66; scientist, Space Sci Lab, Gen Elec Co, Philadelphia, 66-68. *Concurrent Pos:* Adj asst prof, Physics Dept, Drexel Inst & Villanova Univ, 66-68; consult, Naval Res Lab, Washington, DC, 70-; liaison scientist, Off Naval Res, London, 75-77. *Mem:* Am Meteorol Soc. *Res:* Dynamics of intense atmospheric vortices; geophysical fluid dynamics, internal gravity waves, nearshore circulations; turbulence; nonlinear baroclinic waves; moist flow over topography; blocking; low-frequency atmospheric flows; predictability. *Mailing Add:* Geophys Fluid Dynam Inst Fla State Univ Tallahassee FL 32306. *Fax:* 850-644-8972

BARCILON, VICTOR, APPLIED MATHEMATICS, FLUID DYNAMICS. *Current Pos:* PROF MATH, DEPT GEOPHYS SCI, UNIV CHICAGO, 72- *Personal Data:* b Alexandria, Egypt, Oct 10, 39; m 61; c 1. *Educ:* McGill Univ, BSc, 59; Harvard Univ, AM, 60, PhD(math), 63. *Prof Exp:* Res assoc meteorol & oceanog, Harvard Univ, 63-64; fel meteorol, Univ Oslo, 64-65; res assoc, Mass Inst Technol, 65-66, asst prof appl math, 66-69; assoc prof math, Univ Calif, Los Angeles, 69-72. *Concurrent Pos:* Ed, J Soc Indust & Appl Math, 75- *Mem:* Soc Indust & Appl Math; Royal Astron Soc; Am Geophys Union. *Res:* Inverse problems of geophysics; dynamics of rotating/stratified flows. *Mailing Add:* Dept Geol Sci Univ Chicago Chicago IL 60637-1404

BARCLAY, ALEXANDER PRIMROSE HUTCHESON, ELECTRICAL ENGINEERING, COMMUNICATIONS ENGINEERING. *Current Pos:* RETIRED. *Personal Data:* b Glasgow, Scotland, Apr 19, 13; Can citizen; wid; c William A & Susan E. *Educ:* McMaster Univ, BA, 35; Cornell Univ, MSc, 36. *Prof Exp:* Engr radio, Can Westinghouse Ltd, 36-38; engr commun, Northern Elec Ltd, 38-41; mgr radar, Res Enterprises Ltd, 41-45; gen mgr, Philips Electronics Indust Ltd, 45-71; gen mgr res, Ryerson Appl Res Ltd, 71-73; mgr elec, Can Post, 73-78. *Concurrent Pos:* Fel, Postal Eng, 78. *Mem:* Inst Elec & Electronics Engrs. *Res:* Communications; general electronics; microwave, radar; closed circuit television and mobile radio. *Mailing Add:* Valley View Apts No 913 240 Scarlet Rd York Toronto ON M6N 4X4 Can

BARCLAY, ARTHUR S, PLANT TAXONOMY. *Current Pos:* RETIRED. *Personal Data:* b Minneapolis, Minn, Aug 5, 32. *Educ:* Univ Tulsa, BS, 54; Harvard Univ, MA, 58, PhD(biol), 59. *Prof Exp:* Res botanist, New Crops Res Br, USDA, 59-72, Med Plant Resources Lab, 72-78, Econ Bot Lab, 78-79. *Res:* Evolution; economic botany; cancer. *Mailing Add:* 8455 Greenbelt Rd No 101 Greenbelt MD 20770-2528

BARCLAY, FRANCIS WALTER, THERMALHYDRAULICS, REACTOR PHYSICS. *Current Pos:* RETIRED. *Personal Data:* b Vancouver, BC, Apr 11, 31; m 55; c 3. *Educ:* Univ BC, BA, 55. *Prof Exp:* Shift supvr reactor opers, Atomic Energy Can, Ltd, 58-63, reactor physicist opers, 63-66, res officer reactor physics & econ studies, 66-76, res officer exp thermalhydraul, 76-80, res officer analytic thermalhydraul, 80-90. *Res:* Analytical thermalhydraulics; validation of the two-fluid thermalhydraulics code ATHENA against experimental data; use of the code, primarily for reactor accident analysis calculations. *Mailing Add:* Box 313 Pinawa MB R0E 1L0 Can

BARCLAY, HUGH JOHN, MODELLING THE DYNAMICS OF INSECT PEST CONTROL METHODS, MODELLING FOREST ECOSYSTEMS. *Current Pos:* RES SCIENTIST, PAC FOREST CTR, CAN FOREST SERV, 81- *Personal Data:* m 77, Masami Makino. *Educ:* Univ BC, BSc, 64; Univ Victoria, MSc, 73, PhD(pop ecol), 78. *Prof Exp:* Res assoc ecol, Simon Fraser Univ, 78-80; asst prof, Dalhousie Univ, 80-81. *Concurrent Pos:* Adj assoc prof biol, Univ Victoria, 87-, lectr quantitative ecol, 87 & biomet, 91; lectr, Int Biomet Asn, 88, Agr Biotechnol, 88, Int Orgn Biol, Spain, 90. *Mem:* Soc Pop Ecol; Resource Modelling Asn; Entom Soc Can. *Res:* Investigation of the population dynamic characteristics of several pest control methods, both singly and more especially in various combinations to ascertain which ones work well in combination using modelling methods. *Mailing Add:* Pac Forestry Ctr 506 W Burnside Rd Victoria BC V8Z 1M5 Can. *Fax:* 250-363-0775; *E-Mail:* hbarclay@pfc.forestry.ca

BARCLAY, JACK KENNETH, CARDIOVASCULAR PHYSIOLOGY, SKELETAL MUSCLE PHYSIOLOGY. *Current Pos:* FROM ASST PROF TO PROF PHYSIOL, UNIV GUELPH, 71- *Personal Data:* b July 27, 38; c 2. *Educ:* Univ Mich, PhD(physiol), 69. *Concurrent Pos:* Vis prof physiol, Monash Univ, 77-78; vis prof physiol, Mich State Univ, 84-85. *Mem:* Am Physiol Soc; Can Physiol Soc; Sigma Xi; NY Acad Sci; fel Am Col Sports Med. *Res:* muscle fatigue; local blood flow regulation; skeletal muscle function and physiology. *Mailing Add:* Dept Human Biol Univ Guelph Guelph ON N1G 2W1 Can

BARCLAY, JOHN ARTHUR, THERMODYNAMICS, SOLID STATE PHYSICS. *Current Pos:* DIR CRYOFUEL SYST GROUP, PROF MECH ENG, UNIV VICTORIA, 92-, INDUST RES CHAIR. *Personal Data:* b Beach, NDak, Apr 30, 42; m 69; c 5. *Educ:* Univ Notre Dame, BS, 64; Univ Calif, Berkeley, PhD(chem-physics), 69; Monash Univ, Australia, dipl tertiary educ, 72. *Prof Exp:* Fel physics, Australian Inst Nuclear Sci & Eng, Monash Univ, 69-71, lectr, Monash Univ, 71-75, sr lectr, 76-77; staff scientist physics, Los Alamos Sci Lab, 77-85; dir, Technol Ctr, Astronaut Tech Ctr, 85-90. *Concurrent Pos:* Consult-vis scientist, Los Alamos Sci Lab, 75-76; chmn bd dirs, Cryogenic Eng Cont, Inc, 97. *Mem:* Am Phys Soc; Sigma Xi; Am Soc Mech Eng; Int Inst Refrig; Int Mats Soc; Int Natural Gas Vehicle Asn. *Res:* Refrigeration; magnetism of solids; energy systems; cryogenic engineering; refrigeration; magnetism and its applications; recipient of one US patent. *Mailing Add:* Cryofuel Syst Univ Victoria PO Box 3055 Victoria BC V8W 3P6 Can. *E-Mail:* jbarclay@me.uvic.ca

BARCLAY, LAWRENCE ROSS COATES, ORGANIC CHEMISTRY. *Current Pos:* from asst prof to prof, Mt Allison Univ, 51-67, head dept, 67-82, Carnegie prof chem, 67-94, UNIV RES PROF, MT ALLISON UNIV, 94- *Personal Data:* b Wentworth, NS, Oct 24; 28; m 50, Helen M Fraser; c Gregor F, Michael R & Nancy J (Tregunno). *Educ:* Mt Allison Univ, BSc, 50, MSc, 51; McMaster Univ, PhD(org chem), 57. *Honors & Awards:* Syntex Award for Distinguished Contrib to Med Chem, Can Soc Chem, 92. *Prof Exp:* Vis lectr, McMaster Univ, 55-56. *Concurrent Pos:* Grants, Am Chem Soc Petrol Res Fund, 59-61, Res Corp, 60 & Nat Res Coun Can; mem, Nat Sci & Eng

Res Coun Can & Network Ctrs Excellence. *Mem:* Fel Chem Inst Can; fel Japanese Soc Prom Sci. *Res:* Orthodiquaternary aromatic compounds; solvolysis hindered benzyl compounds; chemistry of crowded and sterically hindered aromatics; photochemistry of aryl-nitro, nitroso, and halo compounds; hindered aryl radicals; autoxidation of biomembranes; free radical rearrangements. *Mailing Add:* Dept Chem Mt Allison Univ Sackville NB E0A 3C0 Can. *E-Mail:* rbarclay@mta.ca

BARCLAY, ROBERT, JR, INDUSTRIAL ORGANIC CHEMISTRY, POLYMER CHEMISTRY. *Current Pos:* RETIRED. *Personal Data:* b Mt Vernon, NY, Apr 1, 28. *Educ:* Cornell Univ, AB, 48; Univ Md, PhD(chem), 57. *Prof Exp:* Patent chemist, Barrett Div, Allied Chem Corp, 48-51; res chemist, Am Cyanamid Co, 51-52; res chemist, Union Carbide Corp Plastics Div, 56-60, proj scientist, 60-69; sr res chemist, Chem Div, Thiokol Corp, 69-71, res specialist, 71-73, res scientist, 73-75, sr res scientist, 75-79; sr process develop specialist, Hydrocarbon Res Inc, 79-81, sect head, 81-86; consult, Amoco Performance Prod, Inc, 86-90. *Mem:* Am Chem Soc. *Res:* Photocurable polymers; condensation polymers and monomers. *Mailing Add:* 6 Berrywood Dr Hamilton NJ 08619-1906

BARCLAY, STANTON DEWITT, mechanical engineering; deceased, see previous edition for last biography

BARCLAY, W(ILLIAM) J(OHN), ELECTRICAL ENGINEERING. *Current Pos:* res engr, 54, assoc tech dir, Eng Res Dept, 57-58, assoc prof, 54-58, PROF ELEC ENG, NC STATE UNIV, 58- *Personal Data:* b Corvallis, Ore, Nov 18, 12; m 39; c 2. *Educ:* Ore State Col, BS, 39; Stanford Univ, EE, 41, PhD, 49. *Prof Exp:* Asst prof elec eng, Stanford Univ, 42-45; res engr, Loran Pro, 45-46, assoc prof, 47; instr, Heald Eng Col, 47-48; asst prof, Ore State Col, 49-54. *Concurrent Pos:* Field engr, Western Elec Co, 55; res engr, Autonetics Div, NAm Aviation Co, 59; partic, Radio Propagation Course, Cent Radio Propagation Lab, Nat Bur Stand, 62. *Mem:* Sr mem Inst Elec & Electronics Engrs; Sigma Xi. *Res:* Electronic instrumentation and measurements; microwave theory, devices and components; radiation; propagation; antennas. *Mailing Add:* Elec/Comput Eng Dept NC State Univ PO Box 7911 Raleigh NC 27695

BARCLAY, WILLIAM R, MEDICINE. *Current Pos:* RETIRED. *Personal Data:* b Golden, BC, May 25, 19; m 44; c 2. *Educ:* Univ BC, BA, 41; Univ Alta, MD, 45. *Prof Exp:* Instr biochem, Univ Alta, 42; mem, Dept Nat Health & Welfare, Can, 46-47; asst, Dept Med, Univ Chicago, 48-49; mem, Dept Nat Health & Welfare, Can, 49-51; instr med, Univ Chicago, 51-52, asst prof chest dis, 52-56, assoc prof, 56-64, prof med, 64-70; dir sci activ & asst exec vpres, AMA, 70-75, vpres, 75-91. *Concurrent Pos:* Palmer sr fel, Univ Chicago, 54-56; instr surg, Univ Alta, 50-51; bd mem, Nat Tuberc & Respiratory Dis Asn, 70; chmn tuberc panel, US-Japan Med Sci Prog, 70; mem adv comt to dir, NIH, 70. *Mem:* Am Thoracic Soc (pres, 63-64); fel NY Acad Sci; Am Col Chest Physicians; Am Soc Clin Invest. *Res:* Metabolic studies of tubercle bacillus. *Mailing Add:* 247 Elm Park Ave Elmhurst IL 60126

BAR-COHEN, AVRAM (AVRAM MARKOWITZ), COOLING OF ELECTRONICS, BOILING HEAT TRANSFER. *Current Pos:* assoc profmech eng, Univ Minn, 89-91, dir, Thermodyn & Heat Transfer Div, Dept Mech Eng, 92-97, assoc dir, Ctr Develop Technol Leadership, 95-97, PROF MECH ENG, UNIV MINN, MINNEAPOLIS, 92-, DIR, CTR DEVELOP TECHNOL LEADERSHIP, 97- *Personal Data:* b Brooklyn, NY, Jan 19, 46; m 66, Annette Pavony; c Barak, Raanan & Talia Dvora. *Educ:* Mass Inst Technol, SB, 68, SM, 68, PhD, 71. *Honors & Awards:* Edwin F Church Medal, Am Soc Mech Engrs, 94. *Prof Exp:* Assoc engr, Missile Systs Div, Raytheon Co, 68-69, engr, 69-72, sr engr & sect mgr, 72-73; lectr mech eng, Ben Gurion Univ, Israel, 73-75, sr lectr, 75-81, assoc prof, 81-84, prof, 88; vis assoc prof, Univ Minn, Minneapolis, 84-85; gen mgr & exec consult corp res & eng, Control Data Corp, 85-89. *Concurrent Pos:* Vis assoc prof, Mass Inst Technol, Cambridge, 77-78; distinguished lectr, Am Soc Mech Engrs, 94-97, mem, Bd Res & Technol Develop, 95-; ed-in-chief, Inst Elec & electronics Trans Components, Packaging & Mfg Technol, 95-; mem bd govs, Components, Packaging & Mfg Technol Soc, Inst Elec & Electronics Engrs, 95-; assoc ed, Appl Mech Rev, Am Soc Mech Engrs, 85-; sr assoc ed, Trans Components, Hybrids & Mfg Technol, 87- *Mem:* NY Acad Sci; Sigma Xi; fel Am Soc Mech Engrs; fel Inst Elec & Electronics Engrs. *Res:* Thermal management and packaging of electronic components and systems. *Mailing Add:* 1440 Utah Ave S Minneapolis MN 55426-1922. *Fax:* 612-624-7510, 624-5230; *E-Mail:* abc@me.umn.edu

BAR-COHEN, YOSEPH, NONDESTRUCTIVE EVALUATION SPECIALIST, COMPOSITE MATERIALS. *Current Pos:* MEM TECH STAFF, NONDESTRUCTIVE EVAL & ADVANCED ACTUATORS PRIN INVESTR, JET PROPULSION LAB, PASADENA, 91- *Personal Data:* b Baghdad, Iraq, Sept 3, 47; US citizen; c 2. *Educ:* Hebrew Univ, Jerusalem, Israel, BS, 71, MS, 73, PhD(physics), 79. *Prof Exp:* Consult nondestructive eval, Israel Aircraft Co, 71-72, sr specialist, 72-79; fel nondestructive eval, NRC Award, Air Force Mat Lab, 79-80; sr physicist nondestructive eval, Systs Res Lab, Dayton, Ohio, 80-83; prin specialist nondestructive eval, McDonnell Douglas Corp, Long Beach, 83-91. *Concurrent Pos:* Comt mem, Aerospace & Sonics, Am Soc Nondestructive Testing, 81-, vchair, Ultrasonics; adj prof, Mane Dept, Univ Calif, Los Angeles, 89- *Mem:* Am Soc Mech Engrs; Am Soc Testing & Mat; fel Am Soc Nondestructive Testing. *Res:* Nondestructive evaluation technology for characterization of defects and determination of properties of aerospace material and structures; ultrasonic polar backscattering and leaky lamb wave for nondestructive evaluation of composite materials; author of 118 publications; granted seven patents; ultrasonic motors, piezooelectric pumps; electroactive polymer actuators and medical ultrasonics. *Mailing Add:* 3721 Fuchsia St Seal Beach CA 90740. *E-Mail:* yosi@jpl.nasa.gov

BARCOS, MAURICE P, PATHOLOGY, HEMATOPATHOLOGY. *Current Pos:* assoc clin prof, 80-93, CLIN PROF PATH, STATE UNIV NY, BUFFALO, 93-; ACTG CHIEF PATH, ROSWELL PARK CANCER INST, 90-, PROF PATH, 93- *Personal Data:* b Medellin, Colombia, Jan 13, 35; US citizen; m, Jacqueline M; c Jacqueline L, Carolina A & Michael A. *Educ:* McGill Univ, BS, 55; Dalhousie Univ, MD, 62; Univ Chicago, PhD(biophysics), 75. *Prof Exp:* Res assoc biophysics, Univ Chicago, 63-65, resident & Seymour Coman fel path, 65-69, instr & fel hematopath, 69-70; asst prof path, Univ Southern Calif Sch Med, 70-73; asst clin prof, Roswell Park Cancer Ctr, 74-80, cancer res pathologist, 73-81, assoc chief path, 81-90. *Concurrent Pos:* Fel hematopath, Univ Southern Calif, 70-72; dir clin path lab, East Los Angeles Child & Youth Clin, 72; mem, Cancer Regional Studies Rev Comt, 82-84, Cancer Clinical Invest Rev Comt, 84-86, Nat Path Panel Lymphoma Clin Studies, NIH, 80-88; chmn, Path Comt, Cancer & Leukemia Group B, 79-, Sci Rev Comt, Roswell Park Cancer Inst, 88- *Mem:* US Can Acad Path; Am Soc Hematology. *Res:* Neoplastic hematopathology; immunologic phenotyping of lymphomas. *Mailing Add:* Dept Path Roswell Park Cancer Inst Elm & Carlton Sts Buffalo NY 14263. *Fax:* 716-845-8077

BARCUS, WILLIAM DICKSON, JR, MATHEMATICS. *Current Pos:* assoc prof, 61-66, PROF MATH, STATE UNIV NY, STONY BROOK, 66- *Personal Data:* b Mineola, NY, Mar 19, 29; m 55; c 2. *Educ:* Mass Inst Technol, SB, 50; Oxford Univ, DPhil(math), 55. *Prof Exp:* Instr, Princeton Univ, 55-56; from instr to asst prof, Brown Univ, 56-61. *Concurrent Pos:* Vis sr res fel, Jesus Col, Oxford Univ, 65-66 & Math Inst, 68-69. *Mem:* Am Math Soc. *Res:* Algebraic topology. *Mailing Add:* Dept Math State Univ NY Stony Brook 100 Nicholls Rd Stony Brook NY 11794-0001

BARD, ALLEN JOSEPH, ELECTROANALYTICAL CHEMISTRY, PHYSICAL CHEMISTRY. *Current Pos:* from instr to assoc prof chem, Univ Tex, Austin, 58-67, Jack S Josey prof energy studies, 80-82, Norman Hackerman prof chem, 82-85, PROF CHEM, UNIV TEX, AUSTIN, 67-, HACKERMAN-WELCH REGENTS CHAIR, 85- *Personal Data:* b New York, NY, Dec 18, 33; m 57, Fran; c Eddie & Sarah. *Educ:* City Col NY, BS, 55; Harvard Univ, MA, 56, PhD(chem), 58. *Hon Degrees:* Dr, Univ Paris, 86. *Honors & Awards:* Harrison Howe Award, Am Chem Soc, 80, Willard Gibbs Award, 87, Analytical Chem Award Electrochem, 88; Carl Wagner Mem Award, Electrochem Soc, 81, Henry Linford Award, 86, Olin-Palladium Medal, 87; Bruno Breyer Mem Medal, Royal Australian Chem Inst, 84; Fisher Award, Am Chem Soc, 84; Charles N Reilley Award, Soc Electroanal Chem, 84; Iddles lectr, Univ NH, 85; Baker lectr, Cornell Univ, 87; Priestly lectr, Pa State Univ, 88; Woodward Vis lectr, Harvard Univ, 88; Mack Mem Award lectr, Ohio State Univ, 89; W Heinlen Hall Lect Ser, Bowling Green State Univ, 89; Venable Lectr, Univ SC, Chapel Hill, 89; Hill Mem lectr, Duke Univ, 90; Mary E Kapp lectr, Va Commonwealth Univ, 90; HM Clark Lectr, San Jose State Univ, 90; Gooch-Stephens lectr, Baylor Univ, Joel Brogerg lectr, NDak State Univ, Linus Pauling Distinguished lectr, Ore State Univ, Milton Kahn lectr, Univ NMex & Samuel Ruben lectr, Reed Col, 91; GM Kosolapoff lectr, Auburn Univ, 92; WR Grace lectr, Univ Md & SM McElvain Anal Sci lectr, Univ Wis-Madison, 93. *Prof Exp:* Anal chemist, Gen Chem Co Res Lab, 55. *Concurrent Pos:* Consult, E I Du Pont de Nemours & Co, Solar Energy Res Inst & Air Force Off Sci Res; Fulbright prof, Univ Paris, 73-74; Sherman Mills Fairchild scholar, Calif Inst Technol, 77; assoc ed, J Am Chem Soc, 80-81, ed-in-chief, 82-; centenary lectr, Royal Soc Chemists, UK, 88; co-chmn, Chem Sci & Technol Bd, Nat Acad Sci. *Mem:* Nat Acad Sci; fel Am Acad Arts & Sci; Am Chem Soc; Int Soc Electrochem; AAAS; Int Union Pure & Appl Chem (vpres, 90-91, pres, 91-93); fel Electrochem Soc. *Res:* Electro-organic chemistry; kinetics and mechanisms of electrode reactions; semiconductor electrodes for solar energy conversion, electrogenerated chemiluminescence; electrochemical techniques and instrumentation; photoelectrochemistry; electroanalytical chemistry; electron spin resonance; high resolution electrochemistry. *Mailing Add:* Dept Chem Univ Tex Austin TX 78712

BARD, CHARLETON CORDERY, PHOTOGRAPHIC CHEMISTRY. *Current Pos:* RETIRED. *Personal Data:* b Chicago, Ill, Feb 2, 24; m 46; c 4. *Educ:* Univ Chicago, PhB & BS, 46, MS, 48, PhD, 50. *Prof Exp:* Instr, Wilson Jr Col, 47-49; org chemist, Photog Technol Div, Eastman Kodak Co, 49-68, supvr, Processing Chem Sect, 68-86. *Concurrent Pos:* Consult, Image Conserv. *Mem:* Am Chem Soc; Soc Photog Sci & Eng; Int Color Coun; fel Soc Imaging Sci & Technol; Soc Motion Picture & TV Engrs. *Res:* Infrared spectroscopy and molecular structure; physical organic chemistry; conservation of images; environmental chemistry; photographic processing chemistry. *Mailing Add:* 74 Cornwall Lane Rochester NY 14617-2531

BARD, DAVID S, GYNECOLOGIC ONCOLOGY. *Current Pos:* PROF GYNEC ONCOL, COL MED, UNIV ARK, 78- *Personal Data:* b Columbua, Ohio, May 31, 35; m 81; c 4. *Educ:* J B Stetson Univ, BS, 57; Columbia Col Physicians & Surgeons, MD, 61. *Prof Exp:* Clin assoc surg, Nat Cancer Inst, NIH, 63-65; intern & jr resident surg, Univ Hosp, Columbus, Ohio, 61-63; residency obstet & gynec, Boston Hosp Women, 65-68; fel gynec oncol, M D Anderson Hosp, Houston, Tex, 69-70; asst prof, Col Med, Univ Fla, 70-76; assoc prof, Med Sch, Univ Tenn, 76-78. *Concurrent Pos:* Consult, Little Rock Vet Admin Hosp, 76- *Mem:* Soc Gynec Oncologists; fel Am Col Obstet & Gynec; Int Soc Obstet & Gynec Path. *Res:* Biological behavior of ovarian neoplasmas and other neoplasmas of female genital tract. *Mailing Add:* Dept Obstet-Gynec 4301 W Markham St Univ Ark Med Sci Little Rock AR 72205-7107

BARD, ENZO, MOLECULAR BIOLOGY, MOLECULAR PATHOLOGY. *Current Pos:* asst prof, Sch Med, 82-93, sch grad studies, 83-93, ASSOC PROF PATH, SCH MED, HEALTH SCI CTR BROOKLYN & SCH GRAD STUDIES, STATE UNIV NY, 94- *Personal Data:* b Luis Palacios, Santa Fe,

Arg, Oct 18, 38; m 65, Maria J dos Reis; c Fabio D, Dario P & Hugo F. *Educ:* La Plata Nat Univ, Arg, BPharm, 60, MSc, 63, PhD(biochem), 72. *Prof Exp:* Head instr inorg chem, Sch Agron, La Plata Nat Univ, 65-66, head instr biochem, Sch Exact Sci, 68-72; fel molecular biol, Inst Cancer Res, Fox Chase Md, 72-74; vis prof molecular biol, Dept Biol, Univ Ottawa, Ont, 75-77; res asst prof cell biol, NY Univ Med Ctr, 77-81. *Concurrent Pos:* Head, Vaccine Control Sect, Biol Inst, Ministry Health, Buenos Aires, Arg, 60-62 & Div Biol Control, 63-67; Damon Runyon Cancer Fund fel, 72-73 & 73-74; res consult cell biol, NY Univ Med Ctr, 75; dir clin chem, State Univ Hosp, State Univ NY, Health Sci Ctr Brooklyn, 81-83, dir clin virol, 81-87; dir molecular diag, 93- *Mem:* AAAS; Am Soc Cell Biol; Am Soc Microbiol; NY Acad Sci (vchmn, biol sci sect, 88, chmn, 89-90); Sigma Xi; Int Soc Molecular Morphol. *Res:* Mucosal immunity in HIV infection; vertical transmission of HIV. *Mailing Add:* Dept Path Health Sci Ctr Brooklyn State Univ NY 450 Clarkson Ave Box 25 Brooklyn NY 11203-2098. *Fax:* 718-270-3313

BARD, EUGENE DWIGHT, SCIENCE EDUCATION. *Current Pos:* RETIRED. *Personal Data:* b Blackwell, Okla, Nov 8, 28; m 50; c 4. *Educ:* Okla A&M Col, BS, 50, MS, 54; Univ Northern Colo, EdD(sci educ), 74. *Prof Exp:* Teacher phys sci, Planeview Pub Sch, 54-55; teacher phys sci, Pueblo Pub Sch, 55-65, dept head sci, 58-65, curric specialist math-sci, 63-65; instr chem, Southern Colo State Col, 65-66, from instr to assoc prof physics, 66-74; from assoc prof to prof physics, Univ Southern Colo, 74-87. *Mem:* Am Asn Physics Teachers. *Res:* Development and evaluation of non-traditional teaching materials and techniques. *Mailing Add:* 11595 US Highway 50 Howard CO 81233

BARD, FREDERIQUE, CELL BIOLOGY. *Current Pos:* SCIENTIST CELL BIOL, ATHENA NEUROSCI CORP, 89- *Personal Data:* b Paris, France, Mar 3, 57. *Educ:* Univ Paris, BS, 78, MS, 79, PhD(cell biol), 84. *Prof Exp:* Fel cell biol, Univ Paris, 85-89. *Mem:* AAAS; Cell Biol Soc. *Mailing Add:* Athena Neurosci Corp 800 Gateway Blvd South San Francisco CA 94080

BARD, JAMES RICHARD, PHYSICAL CHEMISTRY, SPECTROSCOPY. *Current Pos:* PROF CHEM, PENN VALLEY COMMUNITY COL, 70- *Personal Data:* b Chelsea, Okla. *Educ:* Univ Okla, BS, 59; Univ Ark, MS, 64; Univ Mo, Kansas City, PhD(chem), 77. *Prof Exp:* Res chemist, Shell Chem Co, 62-67 & Vet Admin, 67-70. *Mem:* Am Chem Soc; Sigma Xi. *Res:* Infrared and Raman spectra of polyatomic molecules; application of magnetic resonance to structure and equilibria of complex ions in mixed solvents; enzyme kinetics; electrochemistry; development of industry related laboratory experiments. *Mailing Add:* Penn Valley Community Col Kansas City MO 64111

BARD, JOHN C, FOOD SCIENCE. *Current Pos:* RETIRED. *Personal Data:* b Huron, SDak, Apr 7, 25; m 47; c 3. *Educ:* Huron Col, SDak, BS, 49; Iowa State Univ, MS, 50. *Prof Exp:* Technologist, Meat Prod Control, Oscar Mayer & Co, 51-52, head dept, 52-58, gen dept head, 58-61, dir res, Meat Prod & Packaging, 61-75, vpres res, 75-78, gen mgr, Sci Protein Labs, 78-83. *Concurrent Pos:* Mem sci adv comt, Am Meat Inst, 66-; mem liaison panel, Food & Nutrit Bd, Nat Acad Sci, coun mem, 74, vchmn coun, 75- *Mem:* Inst Food Technologists; Am Chem Soc. *Res:* Product, package and processing developments of application to meat industry, particularly an improved control of quality, costs and sanitation. *Mailing Add:* 603 Owen Rd Monona WI 53716-3441

BARD, MARTIN, GENETICS. *Current Pos:* asst prof, 75-79, assoc prof, 79-, PROF BIOL, IND UNIV-PURDUE UNIV, INDIANAPOLIS. *Personal Data:* b New York, NY, Dec 3, 42; m; c 2. *Educ:* City Col NY, BS, 65; Univ Calif, Berkeley, PhD(genetics), 71. *Prof Exp:* Fel genetics, Univ Sheffield, 71-73, State Univ NY, Albany, 73-74 & Univ Calif, Santa Cruz, 74-75. *Concurrent Pos:* Merck Sharp & Dohme Res Lab, 84-87, NIH, 86-88 & Eli Lilly & Co, 88- *Mem:* Am Soc Microbiol; AAAS. *Res:* Molecular genetics; sterol synthesis, cloning and regulation in Saccharomyces cerevisiae and candida albicans. *Mailing Add:* Dept Biol Ind Univ-Purdue Univ Indianapolis IN 46202-2880

BARD, RAYMOND CAMILLO, MICROBIOLOGY. *Current Pos:* RETIRED. *Personal Data:* b New Britain, Conn, Aug 26, 18; m; c 5. *Educ:* City Col New York, BS, 38; Ind Univ, MA, 47, PhD(bact), 49; Am Bd Microbiol, dipl. *Prof Exp:* Med technologist, St John's Hosp, New York, 38-40 & St Joseph's Hosp, 40-42; from instr to asst prof bact, Ind Univ, 49-53; head microbiol sect, Smith Kline & French Labs, 53-56, assoc dir res & develop, 56-60; res dir, Nat Drug Co, 60-62; prof dent, Univ Ky, 62-65, prof cell biol, 65-67, dir res, Sch Dent, 62-63, asst dean, 63-64, asst vpres res & exec dir univ res found, 64-67; vpres, Col, 67-72, actg dean 68-72, emer prof cell & molecular biol & dean, Sch Allied Health Sci, Med Col Ga, 72-88. *Concurrent Pos:* Assoc prof, Hahnemann Med Col, 54-62 (part-time). *Mem:* Fel AAAS; fel Am Acad Microbiol; Am Soc Microbiol; fel Am Soc Allied Health Profs. *Res:* Microbiological metabolism; chemotherapy; dental research. *Mailing Add:* 4275 Owens Rd Evans GA 30809-8604

BARD, RICHARD JAMES, PHYSICAL CHEMISTRY. *Current Pos:* RETIRED. *Personal Data:* b Mt Kisco, NY, July 19, 23; m 46; c 3. *Educ:* Univ Mich, BS, 44, MS, 48, PhD(chem), 51. *Prof Exp:* Instr colloid & surface chem, Univ Mich, 50-51; mem staff, Phys Chem Res, 51-56; group leader uranium chem group, Los Alamos Sci Lab, 53-73, leader phys chem & metall group, 73-82, asst div leader nuclear mat, 82-83. *Mem:* Am Chem Soc; Sigma Xi. *Res:* Physical and inorganic chemistry; gas-solid reaction kinetics; uranium processing; development of coated nuclear fuel particles; studies of pyrolytic carbons. *Mailing Add:* 975 Nambe Loop Los Alamos NM 87544-3204

BARDACH, JOHN E, AQUATIC ECOLOGY, FISH BIOLOGY. *Current Pos:* RETIRED. *Personal Data:* b Vienna, Austria, Mar 6, 15; US citizen; m 47. *Educ:* Queen's Univ, Ont, BA, 46; Univ Wis, MSc & PhD(zool), 49. *Prof Exp:* From instr to asst prof biol, Iowa State Teachers Col, 49-53; from asst prof to prof fisheries zool, Univ Mich, 53-71; dir, Hawaii Inst Marine Biol, Univ Hawaii, 71-77; res assoc & asst dir acad affairs, East West Ctr, Resource Syst Inst, 77-85. *Concurrent Pos:* Dir, Fisheries Res Prog, Bermuda Govt, 55-58; adv, Royal Cambodian Govt, 58-59; ecol adv, UN Mekong Comt; sr vis fel sci, OEEC, 61; independent investr, Int Indian Ocean Exped, 64; rep, Nat Acad Sci Coun, Pac Sci Asn, 78-; res fel, Bellagio, 79; adj prof geog & oceanog, Univ Hawaii, 78-85. *Mem:* Fel AAAS; Ecol Soc Am; Am Soc Limnol & Oceanog; Am Soc Zoologists; Am Fisheries Soc. *Res:* Aquaculture; physiology and behavior of fishes; coral reef fishes; the senses of fishes; fisheries development; natural resources ecology; resource management. *Mailing Add:* 2979 Kalakaua Ave Honolulu HI 96815

BARDACK, DAVID, VERTEBRATE PALEONTOLOGY, ICHTHYOLOGY. *Current Pos:* from asst prof to assoc prof, 64-75, assoc dean, Grad Col, 75-81, PROF BIOL SCI, UNIV ILL, CHICAGO, 75- *Personal Data:* b New York, Apr 11, 32; m 60, Elizabeth; c 2. *Educ:* Columbia Univ, AB, 54, AM, 55; Univ Kans, PhD(zool), 63. *Prof Exp:* Asst zool, Columbia Univ, 55-56; vert paleontologist & ichthyologist, Am Mus Natural Hist, 56-58; instr zool, Hunter Col, 57-58; asst, Univ Kans, 59-62, curatorial asst vert paleont, Mus Natural Hist, 63, res assoc, 63-64. *Concurrent Pos:* Res assoc, Field Mus Natural Hist. *Mem:* AAAS; Soc Vert Paleont; Am Soc Ichthyologists & Herpetologists; Am Soc Zoologists; Paleont Soc. *Res:* Anatomy and evolution of living and fossil paleoniscoid and teleostean fishes. *Mailing Add:* Dept Biol Sci MC/066 Univ Ill Chicago 845 W Taylor Chicago IL 60607-7060. *Fax:* 312-413-2435; *E-Mail:* david.bardack@uic.edu

BARDANA, EMIL JOHN, JR, ALLERGY, IMMUNOLOGY. *Current Pos:* from asst prof to assoc prof, 71-79, vchmn, 80-94, PROF MED & HEAD DIV ALLERGY & CLIN IMMUNOL, ORE HEALTH SCI UNIV, 80- *Personal Data:* b New York, NY, May 21, 35; m 60, Norma J Olson; c Anthony J & Anne M. *Educ:* Georgetown Univ, BS, 57; McGill Univ, MD, CM, 61. *Prof Exp:* Intern gen med, Univ Calif Med Ctr, San Francisco, 61-62; gen med officer, Bremerton Naval Hosp, US Navy, Wash, 62-64, US Marine Corps, S Vietnam, 65; from resident med to instr med allergy immunol, Univ Ore Health Sci Ctr, 65-69; res trainee, Dept Allergy & Immunol Clin, Nat Jewish Hosp & Res Ctr, Denver, 69-71. *Concurrent Pos:* Allergy Found Am training grant, 68-70; Am Acad Allergy travel grant, 69; dir, Am Bd Allergy & Immunol, 89-94. *Mem:* Fel Am Col Physicians; fel Am Acad Allergy & Immunol; Am Thoracic Soc; fel Am Col Allergy & Immunol; Am Col Legal Med; fel Am Col Chest Physicians. *Res:* Development of better understanding of the immunopathogenesis of mycotic hypersensitivity disorders of the lung; establishment of sensitive radioassays which will permit their earlier diagnosis; occupational lung diseases; development of better understanding of occupational hypersensitivity diseases of the lung and a better understanding of indoor air quality and health. *Mailing Add:* Ore Health Sci Univ Physicians Pavilion 3181 SW Sam Jackson Park Rd PV320 Portland OR 97201-3098. *Fax:* 503-494-4323; *E-Mail:* bardanae@ohsu.edu

BARDASIS, ANGELO, SOLID STATE PHYSICS. *Current Pos:* From asst prof to assoc prof, 63-88, PROF PHYSICS, UNIV MD, COLLEGE PARK, 88- *Personal Data:* b New York, NY, Nov 26, 36. *Educ:* Cornell Univ, AB, 57; Univ Ill, MS, 59, PhD(physics), 62. *Concurrent Pos:* NSF fel, 61-63. *Mem:* Am Phys Soc. *Res:* Superconductivity; helium three; helium four; semiconductors. *Mailing Add:* 2100 Washington Ave Silver Spring MD 20910

BARDASZ, EWA ALICE, CHEMICAL ENGINEERING, SURFACE CHEMISTRY. *Current Pos:* proj mgr, 88-93, GROUP LEADER, LUBRIZOL CORP, 93- *Personal Data:* b Warsaw, Poland; US citizen. *Educ:* Warsaw Tech Univ, MS, 67; Case Western Reserve Univ, PhD(chem eng), 74. *Prof Exp:* Asst, Case Western Reserve Univ, 71-73; engr, Exxon Res & Eng Co, 73-74, res engr, 74-77, sr res engr chem eng, 77-79, sr staff engr, 79-81, eng assoc, 81-83; sr res engr, Union Camp Corp, 84-88. *Mem:* NY Acad Sci; Am Inst Chem Engrs; AAAS; Am Chem Soc; Nat Asn Corrosion Engrs. *Res:* Lubrication, absorption, corrosion prevention, monolayers and thin films; interfaces in composite materials; adhesion; catalysis. *Mailing Add:* 6900 Weatherby Dr Mentor OH 44060-8408

BARDAWIL, WADI ANTONIO, PATHOLOGY. *Current Pos:* assoc head dept, 80-83, PROF PATH, UNIV ILL, COL MED AT CHICAGO, 77- *Personal Data:* b Mexico, May 13, 21; nat US; m 47; c 6. *Educ:* Nat Univ Mex, MD, 46; Am Bd Path, dipl. *Prof Exp:* Instr path, Univ Vt, 50-52; asst, Med Sch, Harvard Univ, 52-53, instr, 53-57; from asst prof to assoc prof path, Tufts Univ, 57-71, from asst prof to prof obstet & gynec, 57-73, prof path, 71-73, chmn dept, 73-77. *Concurrent Pos:* Pathologist, Robert Breck Brigham Hosp & asst, Peter Bent Brigham Hosp, 54-55; res assoc, Med Sch, Harvard Univ, 57-59; dir, Dept Path & Med Res, St Margaret's Hosp, 57-74. *Mem:* Am Soc Exp Path; fel Col Am Pathologists; AMA. *Res:* Gynecological and obstetrical research; regression of trophoblast and possible immune reactions involved; pathogenesis of collagen diseases and pathogenesis of vascular pathology. *Mailing Add:* 5400 S Hyde Park Blvd Chicago IL 60615

BARDE, YVES-ALAIN, NEUROSCIENCE. *Current Pos:* DIR, DEPT NEUROBIOCHEM, MAX-PLANCK INST PSYCHIAT, GER. *Honors & Awards:* Charles A Dana Award for Pioneering Achievements in Health, Inst Med-Nat Acad Sci, 94. *Mailing Add:* Max-Planck Inst Psychiat Kraepelinstr 2 & 10 80804 Munich Germany

BARDEEN, JAMES MAXWELL, THEORETICAL ASTROPHYSICS. *Current Pos:* from asst prof to assoc prof astron, 66-72, PROF PHYSICS, UNIV WASH, 76- *Personal Data:* b Minneapolis, Minn, May 9, 39; m 68. *Educ:* Harvard Univ, AB, 60; Calif Inst Technol, PhD(physics), 65. *Prof Exp:* Res assoc physics, Calif Inst Technol, 65; res physicist, Univ Calif, Berkeley, 66; from assoc prof to prof physics, Yale Univ, 74-76. *Concurrent Pos:* NSF res grants, 67-76; Sloan fel, 68-72; Fairchild fel, Calif Inst Technol, 77. *Mem:* AAAS; Am Phys Soc; Am Astron Soc; Int Astron Union. *Res:* Astrophysics of black holes and compact x-ray sources; stability of disks; dynamics of spiral structure in galaxies. *Mailing Add:* Dept Physics Univ Wash PO Box 351560 Seattle WA 98195

BARDEEN, WILLIAM A, THEORETICAL & PARTICLE PHYSICS. *Current Pos:* PHYSICIST, FERMI NAT ACCELERATOR LAB, 75-93 & 94- *Personal Data:* b Washington, Pa, Sept 15, 41; m 61, Marjorie Gaylord; c Charles & Karen. *Educ:* Cornell Univ, AB, 62; Univ Minn, Minneapolis, PhD(physics), 68. *Honors & Awards:* J J Sakurai Prize, Am Phys Soc, 96. *Prof Exp:* Res assoc physics, State Univ NY Stony Brook, 66-68; mem, Inst Advan Study, 68-69; from asst prof to assoc prof physics, Stanford Univ, 69-75; head theoret physics, SSC Lab, 93-94. *Concurrent Pos:* Vis scientist, Europ Coun Nuclear Res, 71-72, Max-Planck Inst, Munich, 77, 86, Res Inst Fundamental Physics, Kyoto, 85; Sloan Found fel, 71-74; Alexander von Humboldt Found sr US scientist award, 77; Guggenheim Found fel, 85-86. *Mem:* Am Phys Soc. *Res:* Theoretical particle physics and quantum field theory. *Mailing Add:* Theory Group Fermilab MS 106 PO Box 500 Batavia IL 60510

BARDELL, DAVID, virology, for more information see previous edition

BARDELL, EUNICE BONOW, PHARMACY. *Current Pos:* From instr to prof pharm, 48-73, EMER PROF PHARM & HEALTH SCI, UNIV WIS-MILWAUKEE, 73- *Personal Data:* b Milwaukee, Wis, Feb 8, 15; m 72. *Educ:* Univ Wis, BS, 38, MS, 49, PhD(pharm), 52. *Mem:* Am Pharmaceut Asn; Am Inst Hist Pharm. *Res:* History of pharmacy. *Mailing Add:* 1539 N 51st St Milwaukee WI 53208

BARDEN, JOHN ALLAN, HORTICULTURE. *Current Pos:* from asst prof to assoc prof, 63-81, PROF HORT, VA POLYTECH INST & STATE UNIV, 82- *Personal Data:* b Providence, RI, Oct 30, 36; m 58, Irma Miller; c Cynthia & John. *Educ:* Univ RI, BS, 58; Univ Md, MS, 61, PhD(hort), 63. *Prof Exp:* Instr hort, Univ Md, 63. *Mem:* Fel Am Soc Hort Sci; Int Soc Hort Sci; Sigma Xi; Int & Dwarf Fruit Tree Asn. *Res:* Horticultural physiology; fruit tree physiology with emphasis on apple production intensification, including size controlling rootstocks, tree spacing, pruning and manipulation of fruiting. *Mailing Add:* Dept Hort Va Polytech Inst & State Univ Blacksburg VA 24061-0327. *Fax:* 540-231-3083; *E-Mail:* bardenja@vt.edu

BARDEN, LAWRENCE SAMUEL, FOREST ECOLOGY. *Current Pos:* from asst prof to assoc prof, 70-88, PROF BIOL, UNIV NC, CHARLOTTE, 88- *Personal Data:* b Little Rock, Ark, Nov 12, 42; m 64; c 1. *Educ:* Hendrix Col, BA, 64; Univ Maine, Orono, MS, 68; Univ Tenn, Knoxville, PhD(ecol), 74. *Prof Exp:* Park ranger, Nat Park Serv, 68-70. *Concurrent Pos:* Grants, Found Univ NC, Charlotte, 75-89, Highlands Biol Sta, 76-79 & Southern Regional Educ Bd, 78-81 & NSF, 80. *Mem:* Ecol Soc Am; Southern Appalachian Bot Club. *Res:* Tree species replacement in old-growth forest; effects of fire on forest succession; competition of Lonicera Japonica with ground flora; ecology of Microstegiuan Vimineum. *Mailing Add:* Dept Biol Univ NC Charlotte 9201 University City Charlotte NC 28223-0001

BARDEN, NICHOLAS, NEUROENDOCRINOLOGY. *Current Pos:* fel, Dept Physiol, 70-73, from asst prof to assoc prof, 73-82, PROF NEUROENDOCRINOL, LAVAL UNIV, 82- *Personal Data:* b Rotherham, Eng, July 8, 46; Can citizen; c 4. *Educ:* Aberdeen Univ, BSc, 67; Sussex Univ, PhD(biochem), 70. *Concurrent Pos:* Sr mem, Med Res Coun Group, 73-86; vis scientist, NIH, 80-81, Duke Univ Med Ctr, 81. *Mem:* Endocrine Soc; Int Soc Neuroendocrinol; Can Soc Biochem; Soc Neurosci. *Res:* Control of neuropeptide gene expression; molecular genetics of affective disorders. *Mailing Add:* Le Centre Hospitalier de l'Univ Laval Ste-Foy PQ G1V 4G2 Can. *Fax:* 418-654-2748

BARDEN, ROLAND EUGENE, BIOCHEMISTRY, SURFACTANT CHEMISTRY. *Current Pos:* vpres acad affairs, 89-94, PRES, MOORHEAD STATE UNIV, 94- *Personal Data:* b Powers Lake, NDak, Sept 11, 42; m 67, Carolyn; c 3. *Educ:* Univ NDak, BS, 64; Univ Wis-Madison, MS, 66, PhD(biochem), 69. *Prof Exp:* Fel biochem, Case Western Res Univ, 68-70, sr instr, 70-71; from asst prof to prof chem & biochem, Univ Wyo, 71-89, dept head, 80-83, assoc dean arts & sci, 83-84, assoc vpres Acad Affairs, 84-89. *Concurrent Pos:* NIH fel, Case Western Res, 68-70; res career develop award, Nat Inst Gen Med Sci, Univ Wyo, 76-80. *Mem:* Am Chem Soc; Am Soc Biol Chemists. *Res:* Enzyme chemistry, lipid enzymology, affinity labels, physical properties of detergent solutions, micelles, organic geochemistry. *Mailing Add:* Moorhead State Univ Moorhead MN 56563. *E-Mail:* pres@mhd1.moorhead.msus.edu

BARDIN, CLYDE WAYNE, BIOMEDICAL RESEARCH. *Current Pos:* vpres, 78-95, DIR, CTR BIOMED RES, POPULATION COUN, 78-; PRES, BARDIN LLC, 96- *Personal Data:* b McCamey, Tex, Sept 18, 34; m 87; c Charlotte & Stephanie. *Educ:* Rice Univ, BA, 57; Baylor Univ, MS & MD, 62. *Hon Degrees:* Dr, Univ Caen, France, 90, Univ Pierre, Marie Curie Paris, 97. *Honors & Awards:* Commander of the Order of the Lion, Finland, 83; Serono Award for Outstanding Contrib in the Field of Male Reproductive Endocrinol, Am Soc Andrology, 84, Distinguished Andrologist Award, 92; David Rabin Lectr, Vanderbilt Med Sch, 85; Gregory Pincus Mem Lectr, Laurentian Hormone Conf, 86; Shirley & Maurice Saltzman Med Lectr, Mt Sinai Med Ctr, 87; Transatlantic Medalist, Brit Endocrine Socs, 88; Moritmer B Lipsett Mem Lectr, NIH, 90; Ramon Guiteras Lectr, Am Urol Asn, 90; Joji Ishigami Lectr, Kobe, Japan, 91. *Prof Exp:* Intern & asst resident med, NY Hosp-Cornell Med Ctr, New York, 62-64; clin assoc, Endocrinol Br, Nat Cancer Inst, 64-67, sr investr, 67-70; from assoc prof to prof med, Milton S Hershey Med Ctr, Pa State Univ, 70-78, chief, Div Endocrinol, 70-78, assoc physiol, Dept Physiol, 70-78. *Concurrent Pos:* Ayerst travel award, 65; assoc ed, J Nat Cancer Inst, 69-70; consult physician, Lebanon Vet Admin Hosp, Pa, 70-78; mem, Contract Rev Panel Fertil Regulating Methods, Eval Br, Nat Inst Child Health & Human Develop, NIH, 71-76, Contract Rev Panel Contraceptive Develop Br, 73-76; mem, Task Force Pop Control: Use of Antihormones, 72-73, Sperm Maturation, 74-75; mem, Nat Prostate Cancer Task Force, Nat Cancer Inst, 73-78; coun mem, Endocrine Soc, 76-79, Soc Study Reproduction, 79-82, Am Soc Andrology, 84-87, exec coun, Int Soc Andrology, 81-85; Josiah Macy Jr Found scholar, 76-77; chmn, Int Comt Contraceptive Res, 78-95; adj prof, Rockefeller Univ, NY, 78-; Oynd vis prof endocrinol & metab, Univ Rochester, NY, 81; co-chmn, Gorden Res Conf on Hormone Action, 84-85; adj prof med, Cornell Univ Med Col, 85-; endocrinologist, Nat Inst Child Health & Human Develop, NIH, 96- *Mem:* Inst Med-Nat Acad Sci; fel AAAS; Am Asn Physicians; Am Fedn Clin Res; Am Physiol Soc; Am Soc Andrology (vpres, 87-88, pres, 88-89); Am Soc Clin Invest; NY Acad Sci; Endocrine Soc; Soc Study Reproduction. *Res:* Reproductive medicine; endocrinology; contraceptive development; author of over 500 publications. *Mailing Add:* 910 Park Ave New York NY 10021. *Fax:* 212-327-7678

BARDIN, RUSSELL KEITH, INSTRUMENTATION PHYSICS. *Current Pos:* res scientist physics, 67-74, staff scientist, 74-84, SR STAFF SCIENTIST, LOCKHEED PALO ALTO RES LAB, 84- *Personal Data:* b Fresno, Calif, Mar 22, 32; m 65; c 2. *Educ:* Calif Inst Technol, BS, 53, PhD(physics), 61. *Prof Exp:* Res fel, Calif Inst Technol, 61-62; res assoc, Columbia Univ, 62-67. *Mem:* Am Phys Soc. *Res:* Applications of nuclear and electronic techniques to instrumentation specialized to high-speed pulse measurement, signal and data processing systems; specialized high-speed pulse measurement, signal and data processing systems. *Mailing Add:* Lockheed Res Lab Bldg 251 Dp 97-80 PO Box 3504 Sunnyvale CA 94088-3504

BARDIN, TSING TCHAO, NUCLEAR PHYSICS. *Current Pos:* consult, 68-87, RES SCIENTIST, PALO ALTO RES LAB, LOCKHEED CORP, 87- *Personal Data:* b Tsintao, China, July 31, 38; US citizen; m 65; c 2. *Educ:* Univ London, BS & ARCS, 61; Columbia Univ, PhD(physics), 66. *Prof Exp:* Res asst physics, Columbia Univ, 62-66; asst prof, Haverford Col, 66-67; assoc, Univ Pa, 67. *Mem:* Am Phys Soc. *Res:* Experimental physics in nuclear spectroscopy and nuclear structure studies and application to solid state material sciences. *Mailing Add:* 120 Bear Gulch Dr Portola Valley CA 94025

BARDO, RICHARD DALE, QUANTUM CHEMISTRY. *Current Pos:* RES CHEMIST, NAVAL SURFACE WEAPONS CTR, 77- *Personal Data:* b Garner, Iowa. *Educ:* Univ Wyo, BS, 66; Iowa State Univ, PhD(phys chem), 73. *Prof Exp:* Res assoc, Dept Chem, Univ Calif, Irvine, 73-77. *Mem:* Am Phys Soc. *Res:* Electronic structure calculations on explosive molecules; calculations of chemical reaction rates and electronic spectra at high pressure. *Mailing Add:* 10413 Tullymore Dr Hyattsville MD 20783

BARDOLIWALLA, DINSHAW FRAMROZE, POLYMER CHEMISTRY, PLASTICS ENGINEERING. *Current Pos:* TECH DIR, JOHN C DOLPH CO, MONMOUTH JUNCTION, NJ, 96- *Personal Data:* b Bombay, India, Jan 19, 45; m 71, Hutoxi Madon; c Nenshad & Shanaz. *Educ:* Univ Bombay, BS, 65, 68; Univ Lowell, MS, 71, PhD(polymer sci), 74; Rutgers Univ, MBA, 86. *Prof Exp:* Polaroid fel, Dept Chem, Univ Lowell, 71-74; res chemist polymer chem, Am Cyanamid Co, Stamford, Conn, 74-80, sr res chemist, 80-82; mgr polymer chem, Diamond Shamrock Corp, Morristown, NJ, 82-85, mgr develop, 85-87; tech dir, Oakite Prods Inc, Berkeley Heights, NJ, 87-88, vpres res & technol, 88-93, corp vpres qual mgt, 93-95. *Mem:* Am Chem Soc; Am Mgt Asn; Com Develop Asn. *Res:* Rheology modifiers for paints, associative thickeners, adhesives, corrosion protection coatings for automotive, aircrafts and aerospace applications; pretreatment of plastics prior to painting and decoration, plastics recycling; synthetic coolants and lubricants for metalworking operations; flame retardant acrylic polymers; cleaners and lubricants for computer discs; Insulating varnishes, potting and encapsulating compounds for electric and electronic industries. *Mailing Add:* Three Darlene Ct Randolph NJ 07869-2948. *Fax:* 732-329-1143; *E-Mail:* dfbardoli@aol.com

BARDON, MARCEL, PHYSICS ADMINISTRATION. *Current Pos:* DIR, DIV PHYSICS, NAT SCI FOUND, 88- *Personal Data:* b Paris, France, Sept 16, 27; US citizen; m 64; c 3. *Educ:* Univ Paris, dipl, 52; Columbia Univ, MA, 56, PhD(physics), 61. *Prof Exp:* Instr physics, Columbia Univ, 59-63, res assoc & asst dir, Nevis Labs, 63-64, assoc dir, 64-66, sr res assoc, 64-70, dep dir, 66-70; prog dir, Phys Sect, Nat Sci Found, 70-71, head, Physics Sect, 71-75, dep div dir physics, 75-77, dir, Physics Div, 77-79, asst dir, 82-85; sci-officer, US deleg UNESCO, 79-81; dep asst secy gen sci, NATO, 86-88. *Mem:* Fel AAAS; fel Am Phys Soc; Sigma Xi. *Res:* Intermediate and high energy physics. *Mailing Add:* 1051 Waverly Way McLean VA 22101

BARDOS, DENES I(STVAN), BIOMATERIALS, METALLURGY. *Current Pos:* vpres res & develop, 83-84, vpres res & regulatory, 84-88, VPRES SCI AFFAIRS, SMITH & NEPHEW RICHARDS, INC, 88- *Personal Data:* b Budapest, Hungary, Feb 24, 38; US citizen; m 56, Agota Szabo; c 10. *Educ:* Univ Ill, BS, 62, MS, 63, PhD(metall eng), 66. *Prof Exp:* Res assoc magnetism, Argonne Nat Lab, 65-66, appointee, 66-67, metallurgist, 67-69; chief metallurgist & res dir, Ft Wayne Metals, Inc, 69-72; res dir, Essex Int, 70-72; mat res dir, Zimmer, Inc, 72-75, tech affairs dir, 75-77, dir res, 77-83. *Concurrent Pos:* Am Soc Metals Scholar; adj prof, Memphis State Univ, 88- *Mem:* Am Soc Metals; Soc Biomat; Ortho Res Soc; Int Soc Fracture Repair. *Res:* Theory of alloying behavior and magnetic phenomena; crystal chemistry of intermetallic compounds; wire technology; superalloys; orthopaedic implant materials; composite materials for total joint prostheses; development of hot isostatically pressed cobalt alloy for surgical implants; titanium alloys for medical applications; ceramics for surgical implants; zirconium for orthopaedic prosthesis. *Mailing Add:* 2043 Dowden Ct Memphis TN 38139

BARDOS, THOMAS JOSEPH, MEDICINAL CHEMISTRY. *Current Pos:* prof, 60-93, EMER PROF MED CHEM, STATE UNIV NY, BUFFALO, 93- *Personal Data:* b Budapest, Hungary, July 20, 15; nat US; wid. *Educ:* Tech Univ Budapest, ChE, 38; Univ Notre Dame, PhD(chem), 49. *Hon Degrees:* Gold Dipl, Tech Univ Budapest, 89. *Honors & Awards:* Ebert Prize, Am Pharmaceut Asn, 71; Schoellkopf Medal, Am Chem Soc, 74. *Prof Exp:* Chem engr, Vacuum Oil Co, 38-46; res fel, Biochem Inst, Univ Tex, 48-51; res chemist, Armour & Co, 51-55, sect head, 55-59, lab head, 59-60. *Concurrent Pos:* Consult, Roswell Park Mem Inst, 60-90 & Walter Reed Army Inst Res, 79-81. *Mem:* Fel AAAS; Am Chem Soc; fel NY Acad Sci; fel Acad Pharmaceut Sci; Am Soc Biol Chemists; hon mem Hungarian Acad Sci. *Res:* Organic synthesis; isolation and identification of natural growth factors and inhibitors; biosynthetic pathways; design of antimetabolites; chemotherapy; synthesis of anticancer agents; modification of nucleic acids; antitemplates. *Mailing Add:* Dept Med Chem State Univ NY Buffalo NY 14260. *Fax:* 716-645-2393

BARDSLEY, CHARLES EDWARD, SOIL CHEMISTRY, PLANT PHYSIOLOGY. *Current Pos:* RETIRED. *Personal Data:* b Newport, RI, Apr 23, 21; m 46; c 1. *Educ:* Univ RI, BS, 48; Miss State Univ, MS, 50, PhD(soils), 59. *Prof Exp:* Soil conservationist, Soil Conserv Serv, USDA, 50-52, soil scientist, Res Serv, 52-61; assoc prof soils, Clemson Univ, 61-68; res assoc, Am Can Co, 68-72; vpres, Agritec Co, 72-75; prin investr, Mallinckrodt, Inc, 75-80, res assoc prod develop, 80-82, mgr, speciality agr technol, 83- *Mem:* Am Soc Agron; Soil Sci Soc Am; Weed Sci Soc Am; AAAS; Entomol Soc Am. *Res:* Pesticide and fertilizer formulation; synthetic soils for horticulture and forestry; environmental fate and behavior of pesticides and plant nutrients. *Mailing Add:* 1724 Sandpiper Lane Ocean Springs MS 39564

BARDSLEY, JAMES NORMAN, ATOMIC & MOLECULAR COLLISIONS, SHORT PULSE LASERS. *Current Pos:* ASSOC DIV LEADER, LAWRENCE LIVERMORE NAT LAB, 87- *Personal Data:* b Ashton-U-Lyne, Eng, May 10, 41; US citizen; m 65; c 3. *Educ:* Cambridge Univ, BA, 61, MA, 65; Manchester Univ, PhD(physics), 65. *Prof Exp:* Lectr physics, Univ Manchester, 65-69; asst prof, Univ Tex, Austin, 69-70; prof, Univ Pittsburgh, 70-87. *Concurrent Pos:* Vis fel, Joint Inst Lab Astrophys, Boulder, 74-75 & 85-86; vis astrom, Observatoire Paris, Meudon, 81; prog dir, NSF, 84-85; secy, Int Conf Physics Electronic & Atomic Collisions, 89-95. *Mem:* Fel Am Phys Soc. *Res:* Atomic and molecular collisions; physics of short-pulse lasers; gas discharges; pulsed-power systems; plasma processing; effluent gas cleaning; ion-surface interactions. *Mailing Add:* L-2014 Lawrence Livermore Nat Lab PO Box 808 Livermore CA 94550

BARDUHN, ALLEN J(OHN), CHEMICAL ENGINEERING. *Current Pos:* RETIRED. *Personal Data:* b Seattle, Wash, Aug 24, 18; m 46, Mary Wickson; c Patricia & Casey. *Educ:* Univ Wash, BS, 40, MS, 42; Univ Tex, PhD(chem eng), 55. *Prof Exp:* Jr engr, Tide Water Oil Co Assocs, Calif, 41-44, engr, 44-47, sr engr, 47-49; prof chem eng, Syracuse Univ, 54-86. *Concurrent Pos:* UNESCO expert chem eng, Indust Univ Santander, 69-70; consult various industs & govt; vis prof, Shiraz Tech Inst, Iran, 77-78. *Mem:* Am Chem Soc; fel Am Inst Chem Engrs. *Res:* Thermodynamics and kinetics of gas hydrate systems and their use in desalting sea water and waste water; growth rate of ice crystals. *Mailing Add:* 4600 Broad Rd Syracuse NY 13215

BARDWELL, GEORGE, MATHEMATICS, STATISTICS. *Current Pos:* RETIRED. *Personal Data:* b Denver, Colo, Jan 6, 24; m 46; c 5. *Educ:* Univ Colo, BS, 44, MS, 49, PhD(math), 61, MAA, 65; Bowdoin Col & Mass Inst Technol, certs, 45. *Prof Exp:* Res technician, Philadelphia Navy Yard, 46-47; instr statist, Univ Colo, 48-49; res assoc, Bur Bus & Social Res, Univ Denver, 49-54, asst prof statist & res, 54-61, assoc prof & chmn dept, 61-62, joint assoc prof math & statist, 63-71, prof math, 71-90. *Concurrent Pos:* Gulf Oil Co fac res grant, 61; consult, indust firms & govt agencies; impartial labor arbitrator, 62-; mem, Fed Mediation & Conciliation Serv. *Mem:* Am Math Asn; Am Statist Asn; Inst Math Statist; Am Arbit Asn. *Res:* Mathematical analysis of discrete probability distributions; sampling theory; social and economic research. *Mailing Add:* 2201 S Harrison Denver CO 80210

BARDWELL, JENNIFER ANN, ELECTROCHEMISTRY, SURFACE ANALYSIS. *Current Pos:* res assoc, 85-86, RES OFFICER, NAT RES COUN CAN, 86- *Personal Data:* b Saskatoon, Sask, Oct 3, 57; m 81, Roland Rotondo; c Emma M & Laura N. *Educ:* Univ Sask, BSc, 78; Univ Western Ont, PhD(chem), 83. *Honors & Awards:* Young Authors Award, Electrochem Soc, 88, Lash Miller Award, 91. *Prof Exp:* Res fel, Univ Toronto, 83-85. *Mem:* Am Chem Soc; Electrochem Soc. *Res:* Spectroscopic and electrochemical properties of thin solid films; oxide films on semiconductors. *Mailing Add:* Inst Microstruct Sci Nat Res Coun Can Ottawa ON K1A 0R6 Can. *E-Mail:* jennifer.bardwell@nrc.ca

BARDWELL, JOHN ALEXANDER EDDIE, PHYSICAL CHEMISTRY. *Current Pos:* RETIRED. *Personal Data:* b Appin, Ont, Dec 25, 21; m 54, Millicent Morgan; c Jennifer A, James C & Vivian J. *Educ:* Univ Western Ont, BA, 44, MSc, 46; McGill Univ, PhD(chem), 48; Oxford Univ, DPhil, 50. *Prof Exp:* Spec lectr chem, Univ Sask, 50-51, from asst prof to prof chem, 51-84, asst dean arts & sci, 61-67, univ secy, 68-74, asst to pres, 67-84, dir res admin, 78-84. *Mem:* Chem Inst Can. *Res:* Polymers; combustion of hydrocarbons; radiation chemistry. *Mailing Add:* Box 97 Cochin SK S0M 0L0 Can

BARDWELL, STEVEN JACK, plasma physics, continuum mechanics, for more information see previous edition

BARE, BARRY BRUCE, FOREST MANAGEMENT, FOREST VALUATION. *Current Pos:* from asst prof to assoc prof forest resources, 69-82, chmn quant ecol & resource mgt, Interdisciplinary Grad Prog, 90-93, PROF FOREST MGT & QUANT ANALYSIS, UNIV WASH, 83-, DIR, CTR QUANT SCI, 96- *Personal Data:* b South Bend, Ind, Apr 24, 42; c 2. *Educ:* Purdue Univ, BSF, 64, PhD(quant methods), 69; Univ Minn, MS, 65. *Prof Exp:* Res asst, Univ Minn, 64-65; res asst, Purdue Univ, 66 & 68, instr forest financial mgt, 68-69. *Res:* Application of operations research to forest production processes; application of financial management principles to forestry-oriented problems; forest taxation; biometry, modeling. *Mailing Add:* Col Forest Resources Univ Wash Seattle WA 98195. *Fax:* 206-685-0790; *E-Mail:* bare@u.washington.edu

BARE, CHARLES L, FUEL TECHNOLOGY, PETROLEUM ENGINEERING. *Current Pos:* RETIRED. *Personal Data:* b Oklahoma City, Okla, Apr 22, 32; m 53; c 2. *Educ:* Univ Okla, BS, 54. *Prof Exp:* Engr, Mobil Oil, 54-61; res scientist, Conoco Inc, 61-67, mgr comput applns, 67-71, mgr planning & admin, 71-80, oper mgr, Far East & Africa, 80-84; dir & gen mgr planning & admin, Conoco Ltd, London, 84-90, mgr bus develop & indust rels, Conoco Inc, 90-92. *Concurrent Pos:* Dir, Soc Petrol Engrs, UK, 87- *Mem:* Soc Petrol Engrs (treas, 77-78 & pres, 79); Soc Petrol Engrs UK; Am Inst Mining Engrs. *Mailing Add:* 15902 N Barkers Landing Houston TX 77079

BARE, THOMAS M, SYNTHETIC ORGANIC CHEMISTRY & MEDICINAL CHEMISTRY, CENTRAL NERVOUS SYSTEM RESEARCH. *Current Pos:* PRIN RES CHEMIST, BIOMED RES DEPT, ICI PHARMACEUT GROUP, 76- *Personal Data:* b Lancaster, Pa, Nov 24, 42; m 67; c 3. *Educ:* Pa State Univ, BS, 64; Mass Inst Technol, MS, 66, PhD(org chem), 68. *Prof Exp:* Sr res chemist, Lakeside Labs Div, Colgate-Palmolive Co, 69-75; sr chemist, Morton Chem Co Div, Morton-Norwich Prod, Inc, 75-76. *Mem:* Am Chem Soc; Sigma Xi; Int Soc Heterocyclic Chem. *Res:* Synthesis and design of novel therapeutic agents for diseases of the central nervous system; natural products chemistry. *Mailing Add:* 1057 Windy Knoll Rd West Chester PA 19382

BAREFIELD, EDWARD KENT, INORGANIC CHEMISTRY, ORGANOMETALLIC CHEMISTRY. *Current Pos:* assoc prof, 76-82, actg dir, Sch Chem & Biochem, 89-93, PROF CHEM, GA INST TECHNOL, 82- *Personal Data:* b Hopkinsville, Ky, Feb 26, 43; m 66, Kaye Porter; c Karen L & Stephen H. *Educ:* Western Ky Univ, BS, 65; Ohio State Univ, PhD(chem), 69. *Prof Exp:* Assoc, Cent Res Dept, E I du Pont de Nemours & Co, Inc, 69-70; asst prof chem, Univ Ill, Urbana, 70-76. *Concurrent Pos:* IDA appointment, Chem Div, NSF, 91-92. *Mem:* Am Chem Soc; Sigma Xi. *Res:* Inorganic and organometallic synthesis; homogeneous catalysis. *Mailing Add:* Sch Chem Ga Inst Technol Atlanta GA 30332. *Fax:* 404-894-7452; *E-Mail:* kent.barefield@chemistry.gatech.edu

BAREFOOT, ALDOS CORTEZ, JR, WOOD SCIENCE & TECHNOLOGY. *Current Pos:* assoc prof to prof wood technol, NC State Univ, 62-86, leader wood prod exten, 71-75, head, div univ studies, 75-82, prof univ studies, 75-86, EMER PROF, NC STATE UNIV, 86- *Personal Data:* b Angier, NC, Feb 25, 27; m 49, Naomi; c AC III, James & Rebecca. *Educ:* NC State Univ, BS, 50; MWT, 51; Duke Univ, DF(wood anat), 58. *Prof Exp:* Qual control engr, Henry County Plywood Corp, Va, 51-52; asst exp statistician, NC State Univ, 52-54, technologist, 54, asst prof, 54-59; forestry adv, Int Coop Admin, Pakistan, 59-61; chief of party, Reforestation Proj, Sri Lanka, 82-84. *Concurrent Pos:* Fulbright-Hays fel, Univ Oxford, 73-74; consult, 86- *Mem:* Int Asn Wood Anatomists; Forest Prod Res Soc; fel Brit Inst Wood Sci; Tree-Ring Soc. *Res:* Wood anatomy; tropical woods; statistical quality control; dendrochronology. *Mailing Add:* 3401 Hampton Rd Raleigh NC 27607-3131

BAREIS, DAVID W(ILLARD), CHEMICAL ENGINEERING. *Current Pos:* RETIRED. *Personal Data:* b Irondequoit, NY, Feb 9, 22; m 47; c 4. *Educ:* Univ Rochester, BS, 43; Mass Inst Technol, MS, 47. *Prof Exp:* Assoc, Chem Warfare Develop Lab, Mass Inst Technol, 43-44 & Dept Chem Eng, 46-47; assoc, Dept Metall, US Bur Ships Proj, 44-46; group leader chem processing group, Nuclear Eng Dept, Brookhaven Nat Lab, 47-53; supvr separations chem group, Atomic Energy Res Dept, NAm Aviation, Inc, 53-56, supvr process develop group, Reactor Develop Dept, Atomics Int Div, 56-58, res specialist, 58-60; res scientist, Nuclear Syst Div, Marquardt Corp, 60-61, mgr, Nuclear Res Dept, Astro Div, 61-63 & nuclear prod, Power Syst Div, 63-64; consult, 64-65; staff engr, Agbabian Assocs Inc, 65-67, tech adminr, 67-70, prin engr, 70-72; exec vpres, ATSA Calif, Inc, 82-86; consult engr, Regist Nuclear Engr, Calif, 86- *Mem:* AAAS; Am Nuclear Soc. *Res:* Energy conversion; dynamic systems; direct conversion systems; nuclear reactor, radioisotope and chemical heat sources; salt water conversion; power generation; radioisotope propulsion; radioisotope sterilization; nuclear systems design. *Mailing Add:* 31912 Kingspark Ct Westlake Village CA 91361

BAREIS, DONNA LYNN, MEDICAL PRODUCT DEVELOPMENT, BIOMEDICAL RESEARCH MANGEMENT. *Current Pos:* SR SCI, DIV MGR & ASST VPRES, MED CHEM DEFENSE & VPRES, BIOMED SCI GROUP, SCI APPLN INT CORP, FREDERICK, MD, 83- *Personal Data:* b Abington, Pa, May 1, 54; m 81, Paul Joseph Amico. *Educ:* Pa State Univ, BS, 75; Duke Univ, PhD(pharmacol), 79. *Prof Exp:* Res assoc, Lab Clin Sci, Sect Pharmacol, NIH, 79-81; prin investr pharmacol, US Army Med Res Inst Chem Defense, Aberdeen Proving Ground, 81-82, mgr Super-fund Occup Health Proj, US Army Corp Engrs, Washington, DC, 82-83. *Concurrent Pos:* Bd dir, Suburban Md High Technol Coun, 96- *Mem:* AAAS; Sigma Xi; Am Chem Soc; Soc for Risk Anal. *Res:* Mechanisms of toxicity of chemical warfare agents and antidotes, worker health and safety procedures for handling hazardous materials; biochemical mechanisms of receptor activation. *Mailing Add:* 8805 Blue Sea Dr Columbia MD 21046. *E-Mail:* bareisd@cpva.saic.com

BAREISS, ERWIN HANS, APPLIED MATHEMATICS, COMPUTER SCIENCES. *Current Pos:* vis lectr, Northwestern Univ, 69-70, prof elec eng & comput sci, appl math & eng sci & nuclear eng, 70-93, dir tech comput, 88-89, EMER PROF, NORTHWESTERN UNIV, 93- *Personal Data:* b Schaffhausen, Switz, May 10, 22; US citizen; m 60, Doris L Wicky; c John F & Peter A. *Educ:* Schaffhausen Teachers Col, BA, 43; Univ Zurich, PhD(math), 50; Lehigh Univ, MS, 52. *Prof Exp:* Mem staff, C H Knorr, Switz, 43-45; instr math, Schaffhausen Teachers Col & Winterthur Tech Col, 45-51; mathematician, Naval Res & Develop Ctr, Washington, DC, 52-54, specialist math physics, 54-56, consult numerical anal, 56-57; consult appl math, Argonne Nat Lab, 57-63. *Concurrent Pos:* Janggen-Pohen fel, 49-50; Baldwin Res fel, 51-52; lectr, Univ Md, 55-56; sr mathematician, Argonne Nat Lab, 63-76; vis lectr, Harvard Univ, 64; chmn comput sci prog, Northwestern Univ, 77-88. *Mem:* Am Math Soc; Sigma Xi; Soc Indust & Appl Math; Swiss Math Soc. *Res:* Function theory of a hypercomplex variable; theoretical and applied mechanics; applied mathematics and numerical analysis; mathematical structure and methods of transport theory; design of CRD comupter. *Mailing Add:* ECE Northwestern Univ Evanston IL 60208

BAREL, MONIQUE, IMMUNOLOGY. *Current Pos:* Sr researcher, 82-86, MEM STAFF, NAT INST HEALTH & MED RES, ST-ANTOINE, PARIS, 87- *Personal Data:* b Boulogne, France, Mar 8, 52; m 74; c 2. *Educ:* Univ Sci, Paris, MSc, 73, PhD(biochem), 87. *Mem:* Am Asn Immunologists. *Res:* Structure and function of gp140, the receptor for c3d fragment of complement and for Epstein-Barr virus, expressed on human B lymphocytes. *Mailing Add:* Centre INSERM U354 Hospital St-Antoine 184 rue du Faubourg St Antoine Paris 75571 France

BARENBERG, ERNEST J(OHN), CIVIL ENGINEERING. *Current Pos:* from res asst to res assoc, 60-65, from asst prof to assoc prof, 64-71, assoc head civil eng, 80-85, PROF CIVIL ENG, UNIV ILL, URBANA-CHAMPAIGN, 71- *Personal Data:* b Herndon, Kans, Apr 9, 29; m 53; c 6. *Educ:* Kans State Univ, BS, 53; Univ Kans, MS, 58; Univ Ill, PhD(civil eng), 65. *Prof Exp:* Engr, Cessna Aircraft Co, 53; instr eng drawing, Univ Kans, 55-56, from instr to asst prof civil eng, 56-60. *Concurrent Pos:* Mem, Hwy Res Bd, Nat Acad Sci-Nat Res Coun; indust consult, 58-; consult, Nat Technol Comt Pozzolanic Pavements, 65-, US Army Corps Engrs, 71-74, US Air Force, 71-75 & Fed Aviation Admin, 74-; Paul Kent fac travel award, 78. *Mem:* Am Soc Civil Engrs; Am Soc Eng Educ; Nat Soc Prof Engrs; Am Soc Testing & Mat. *Res:* Structural engineering; pavement behavior analysis and pavement design; paving materials. *Mailing Add:* Dept Civil Eng Univ Ill Urbana Campus 208 N Romine St Urbana IL 61801-2374

BARENBERG, SUMNER, BIOMEDICAL & PACKAGING MATERIALS, ENGINEERING PLASTICS. *Current Pos:* PRES & CHIEF EXEC OFFICER, BERNARD TECHNOL, CHICAGO, ILL, 94- *Personal Data:* b Boston, Mass, May 11, 45; m 70, Sally Viden. *Educ:* Case Inst Technol, BS, 67; Case Western Res Univ, MS, 70, PhD(macromolecular sci), 76; Northwestern Univ, MBA, 91. *Prof Exp:* Chief operating officer, Cambridge Chem Co, Inc, 70-74; biomat proj dir, Cleveland Clin Found, 75-76; fac, Univ Mich, Ann Arbor, 77-80; bus mgr, E I du Pont & Co, Inc, 80-88; dir res, Baxter Health Care, 88-90; vpres & chief tech officer, Pca (Tenneco), 91-94. *Concurrent Pos:* Consult, 70-; adj staff scientist, Dept Path, Cleveland Clin, 76-83; prin investr, NIH grants, 76-80; mem, bd dirs, Soc Biomat, 81-; asst ed, J Biomed Mat Res, 82- & J Bioactive & Compatible Polymers, 86-; chmn, Nat Res Coun Comt Biomat; NIH fel, Cleveland Clin. *Mem:* Sigma Xi; Soc Biomat; NY Acad Sci; AAAS; Am Chem Soc; Am Phys Soc; Am Soc Artificial Intern Organs; Intern Soc Artificial Organs; Tech Asn Pulp & Paper Indust. *Res:* Biomedical materials; engineering plastics; membranes; polymer structure property relationships; interfacial phenomena; biotechnology; surface science; materials science engineering; packaging; biodegradable materials; environmentally compatible materials; disease control, biological control using conmoled release recynol. *Mailing Add:* 222 E Chestnut St Chicago IL 60611. *Fax:* 312-337-0505; *E-Mail:* sfsgata@prodigy.com

BARENBLATT, GRIGORY ISAAKOVICH, APPLIED MECHANICS. *Current Pos:* vis prof, 96-97, PROF RESIDENCE, DEPT MATH, UNIV CALIF, BERKELEY, 97-; G I TAYLOR PROF FLUID MECH, UNIV CAMBRIDGE, 94-,. *Personal Data:* b July 10, 27; m 52, Iraida N Kochina; c Nadeshda & Vera. *Educ:* Moscow Univ, 50, PhD, 53, DSc, 57; Cambridge Univ, MA, 93. *Hon Degrees:* Dr Technol, Royal Inst Technol, Stockholm, Swed, 89. *Honors & Awards:* G I Taylor Lectr, Cambridge, Eng, 89, Minneapolis, Minn, 91; L S G Kovasznay Lectr, Houston, Tex, 91; Modesto Panetti Prize & Medal, 95. *Prof Exp:* From res scientist to sr res scientist, Inst Petrol, USSR Acad Sci, 53-61, head, Theoret Dept, Inst Oceanology, 75-92; head, Dept Mech Solids, Inst Mech, Moscow Univ, 61-75; G I Taylor prof fluid mech, Univ Cambrige, 92-94. *Concurrent Pos:* Vis prof, Univ de Paris VI, Pierre et Marie Curie, 90, Univ Rome Tor Vergata, 92, Univ Autonoma de Madrid, Spain, 93 & 95-96, Univ Minn, Minneapolis, 94, Univ Ill, Urbana-Champaign, 95, Dept Mech Eng, Stanford Univ, 96-97; lectr, Sec Int Cong Indust & Appl Math, Washington, DC, 91, XVIII IUTAM Cong, Haifa, Israel, 92, Ital Nat Cong Theoret Appl Mech, Trento, Italy, 92, Dutch Nat Symp, 93, Int Conf, Como, Italy, 93, IUTAM Symp, Brisbane, Australia, 93, Acad Nazzionale dei Lincei, Rome, 95; quatercentenary vis fel, Emmanuel Col, Univ Cambridge, UK, 92; fel, Gonville & Caius Col, Cambridge, 94. *Mem:* Foreign assoc Nat Acad Sci; foreign assoc Nat Acad Eng; foreign hon mem AAAS; foreign mem Danish Ctr Appl Math & Mech; foreign mem Polish Soc Theoret & Appl Mech; fel Cambridge Philos Soc; Acad Europ. *Res:* Fracture mechanics; theory of fluid and gas flows in porous media; mechanics of non-classical deformable solids; turbulence; self-similarities, nonlinear waves and intermediate asymptotics; author of many publications. *Mailing Add:* Dept Math Univ Calif Berkeley 735 Evans Berkeley CA 94720. *Fax:* 510-542-8204

BARENDREGT, RENE WILLIAM, soil micromorphology, for more information see previous edition

BARENGOLTZ, JACK BENNETT, PLANETARY PROTECTION. *Current Pos:* MEM TECH STAFF, JET PROPULSION LAB, CALIF INST TECHNOL, 70- *Personal Data:* b Pittsburgh, Pa, July 23, 44. *Educ:* Carnegie-Mellon Univ, BS, 65; Univ Ill, Chicago, MS, 67, PhD(physics), 70. *Mem:* Am Phys Soc; Sigma Xi; Inst Environ Sci; Am Inst Aeronaut & Astronaut. *Res:* Contributed numerous articles to publications. *Mailing Add:* 3610 Mesa Lila Lane Glendale CA 91208

BARER, RALPH DAVID, PHYSICAL METALLURGY. *Current Pos:* RETIRED. *Personal Data:* b Bruk, Austria, July 8, 22; Can citizen; m 50; c 5. *Educ:* Univ BC, BASc, 45; Mass Inst Technol, SM, 48. *Honors & Awards:* Int Galvanizers Award, 61. *Prof Exp:* Observer, McKinnon Indust, Ltd, 45-46; metallurgist, Polymer Corp, 46-47; instr phys metall, Univ BC, 48-50; metallurgist, Consol Mining & Smelting Co, 50-52; sect head mat eng, Defence Res Estab Pac, 52-88. *Mem:* BC Asn Prof Engrs; Am Soc Metals. *Res:* Metal failures; problems associated with marine boilers; applications of non-destructive testing; marine corrosion. *Mailing Add:* 2123 Sandowne Rd Victoria BC V8R 3J2 Can

BARER, SOL JOSEPH, BIOTECHNOLOGY. *Current Pos:* vpres technol, 87-90, EXEC VPRES & GEN MGR, CELGENE, 90- *Personal Data:* b Windsheim, Ger, Apr 20, 47; m 69, Meri I; c Jennifer, Lori, Ilyssa & Joshua. *Educ:* City Univ New York, BS, 68; Rutgers Univ, MS & PhD, 74. *Prof Exp:* Sr res chemist, Celanese Co, Summit, NJ, 74-78, supvr res & develop, 78-82, mgr chem res & develop, 82-84, dir chem systs, Tarrytown, NY, 84-87. *Mem:* Am Chem Soc; Am Soc Microbiol. *Res:* Chemical and biological development. *Mailing Add:* 625 Westfield Ave Westfield NJ 07090-3313

BARES, WILLIAM G, CHEMICAL ENGINEERING. *Current Pos:* Process develop engr, Lubrizol Corp, 63-67, group leader pilot plant, 67-71, asst dept head, 71-72, dept head, 72-78, asst to pres, 78, vpres, 78-80, exec vpres, 80-82, PRES & DIR, LUBRIZOL CORP, 82-, CHIEF OPERATING OFFICER, 87- *Personal Data:* b 1941; m. *Res:* Chemical engineering. *Mailing Add:* Lubrizol Corp 29400 Lakeland Blvd Wickliffe OH 44092-2298

BARESI, LARRY, BIOTECHNOLOGY BIOINSTRUMENTATION. *Current Pos:* Sr scientist, biotechnol group, 80-82, MEM TECH STAFF, BIOTECHNOL GROUP, JET PROPULSION LAB, 82- *Personal Data:* b Glendale, Calif; m 75; c 2. *Educ:* Cal State Univ, BA, 69, MS, 72; Univ Cal, PhD(environ nutrit), 78. *Concurrent Pos:* Postgrad researcher I & II, Univ Col, Los Angeles, 72-78; res assoc, Dept Microbiol, Univ Ill, 78-80. *Mem:* Sigma Xi; Am Soc Microbiol. *Mailing Add:* 25523 Meadow Mont Valencia CA 91355-2942

BARFIELD, BILLY JOE, HYDROLOGY, SEDIMENTOLOGY. *Current Pos:* HEAD BIOSYST & AGR ENG, OKLA STATE UNIV, 92- *Personal Data:* b Logansport, La, Oct 8, 38; m 65; c 2. *Educ:* Tex A&M Univ, BS(civil eng) & BS(agr eng), 61, PhD(agr eng), 68. *Honors & Awards:* Outstanding Young Researcher, Am Soc Agr Engrs, 78. *Prof Exp:* Res asst agr eng, Tex A&M Univ, 64-68; from asst prof to assoc prof, Univ Ky, 68-77, prof agr eng, 77-, dir, Ky Water Resources Res Inst, 88- *Concurrent Pos:* Vis agr engr, Snake River Res Ctr, Agr Res Serv, USDA, Idaho, 74-75. *Mem:* Am Soc Agr Engrs. *Res:* Sedimentology of surface mined lands; channel erosion; non point source pollution control; reparion vegetation impacts on pollution; frost protection. *Mailing Add:* Dept Biosyst & Agr Eng Okla State Univ Stillwater OK 74078

BARFIELD, MICHAEL, PHYSICAL CHEMISTRY. *Current Pos:* from asst prof to assoc prof, 65-72, PROF CHEM, UNIV ARIZ, 72- *Personal Data:* b Charleston, SC, Oct 14, 34; m 60, Ariel Foote; c Eric M, David E & Julia. *Educ:* San Diego State Col, BA, 57; Univ Utah, PhD(chem), 62. *Honors & Awards:* US Sr Scientist Award, Alexander von Humboldt Found, 86-87. *Prof Exp:* Eng chemist, Gen Dynamics/Astronaut, Calif, 57-59; res fel, Harvard Univ, 62-63; asst prof chem, Univ SFla, 63-65. *Concurrent Pos:* Fulbright-Hays scholar, Australia, 76-77; US Ed, Magnetic Resonance Chem, 90. *Mem:* Sigma Xi; Am Chem Soc; Int Soc Magnetic Resonance. *Res:* Application of molecular quantum mechanics to problems in nuclear magnetic resonance spectroscopy and molecular structures. *Mailing Add:* Dept Chem Univ Ariz Tucson AZ 85721-0001

BARFIELD, ROBERT F(REDRICK) (BOB), MECHANICAL ENGINEERING. *Current Pos:* from assoc prof to prof, 67-82, dean, 84-94, EMER DEAN ENG, UNIV ALA, 94- *Personal Data:* b Thomaston, Ga, Feb 8, 33; m; c 2. *Educ:* Ga Inst Technol, BME, 56, MSME, 58, PhD(mech eng), 65. *Prof Exp:* Preliminary design engr, AiRes Mfg Co Div, Garrett Corp, Calif, 57-58; from instr to asst prof mech eng, Ga Inst Technol, 58-65; corp staff engr, Thomaston Mills Corp, Ga, 65-67. *Concurrent Pos:* Fac fel, NSF, 62-63; vis prof & consult to fac eng, Kabul Univ, Afghanistan, 63, mech eng & chmn dept, Univ Petrol & Minerals, Saudi Arabia, 71-73; E I Dupont fel, Mech Eng, 64, Am Soc Eng Educ/NASA fel 67-68; sr adv, Shiraz Tech Inst, Iran, 75-77; cultural specialist, Dept State, Univ Jordan, 81. *Mem:* Am Soc Eng Educ; fel Am Soc Mech Engrs; fel Am Soc Prof Engrs; Sigma Xi. *Res:* Thermal and fluid sciences; energy conversion. *Mailing Add:* 703 Shallow Creek Rd Tuscaloosa AL 35406

BARFIELD, WALTER DAVID, APPLIED THEORETICAL PHYSICS, COMPUTATIONAL PHYSICS. *Current Pos:* staff mem, Los Alamos Sci Lab, 68-90, GUEST SCIENTIST, LOS ALAMOS NAT LAB, 90- *Personal Data:* b Gainesville, Fla, Nov 25, 28. *Educ:* Univ Fla, BS, 50, MS, 51; Rice Univ, PhD(physics), 61. *Prof Exp:* Asst, Theoret Physics Div, Los Alamos Sci Lab, 51-53, mem staff, 53-63; mem tech staff, Res Eng Support Div, Inst Defense Anal, 63-67. *Mem:* Am Phys Soc. *Res:* Detonations, nuclear weapons effects; radiation transfer; opacities; fluid dynamics; nuclear physics; numerical methods; gamma ray spectroscopy. *Mailing Add:* 4647 Ridgeway Dr Los Alamos NM 87544

BARFORD, ROBERT A, CHROMATOGRAPHY. *Current Pos:* RES LEADER, AGR RES SERV, USDA, 85- *Personal Data:* b Philadelphia, Pa, Feb 27, 36; m; c 2. *Educ:* Temple Univ, BS, 65. *Mem:* Am Chem Soc; AAAS. *Res:* The structure and function of food biopolymers and their aggregates; development of rapid cost effective methods for detection of toxic residues in foods. *Mailing Add:* PO Box 247 Alma CO 80420

BARFUSS, DELON WILLIS, RENAL PHYSIOLOGY. *Current Pos:* ASST PROF HUMAN PHYSIOL, GA STATE UNIV, 85- *Personal Data:* b Glendale, Calif, Dec 20, 42. *Educ:* Univ Ariz, Tucson, PhD(human physiol), 75. *Prof Exp:* Res asst prof human physiol, Univ Ala, 75-85. *Mailing Add:* Biol Dept Ga State Univ University Plaza Atlanta GA 30303

BARGELLINI, P(IER) L(UIGI), ELECTRICAL ENGINEERING. *Current Pos:* ADJ PROF ELEC ENG, UNIV PA, 87- *Personal Data:* b Florence, Italy, Feb 7, 14; nat US; m 41, Anna Cioni; c Clara, Angela & Leonard M. *Educ:* Univ Florence, Dipl, 34; Polytech Inst Turin, Dr Ing, 37; Cornell Univ, MEE, 49. *Honors & Awards:* Columbus Award, Int Commun, 75; Columbus Gold Medal, Genoa, Italy, 87. *Prof Exp:* Engr, Italoradio, Italy, 37-41; head spec tests lab, Fivre, 41-44; researcher, Microwave Res Ctr, Ital Nat Res Coun, 47-50; from instr to assoc prof, Moore Sch Elec Eng, Univ Pa, 50-68; sr scientist, Comsat Labs, 68-83. *Concurrent Pos:* Consult, RCA Corp, 53- & Aerospace Corp, 62-; lectr, Inst Humanistic Studies for Execs, Univ Pa, 57; vis prof, Pahlavi Univ, Iran, 66-67; consult, Comsat Labs, 84- *Mem:* Fel Inst Elec & Electronics Engrs; assoc fel Am Inst Aeronaut & Astronaut; Sigma Xi. *Res:* Theory of communication; electronics; satellite and space communications. *Mailing Add:* PO Box 256S Clarksburg MD 20871

BARGER, A(BRAHAM) CLIFFORD, physiology, medicine; deceased, see previous edition for last biography

BARGER, JAMES DANIEL, PATHOLOGY. *Current Pos:* PROF LAB MED & PATH, UNIV NEV, RENO, 81-; SR CONSULT, LAB MED COUSULTS, LAS VEGAS, 81- *Personal Data:* b Bismarck, NDak, May 17, 17; m 52, 71, 80; c 4. *Educ:* Univ NDak, AB & BS, 39; Univ Pa, MD, 41; Univ Minn, MS, 49. *Prof Exp:* Dir labs, Pima Co Hosp, Tucson, Ariz, 49-50 & Maricopa Co Hosp, Phoenix, 50-51; med dir, Southwest Blood Bank Ariz, 51-64; dir clin path, Sunrise Hosp, 64-69, chmn, Dept Path, 64-81. *Concurrent Pos:* Dir labs, Good Samaritan Hosp, Ariz, 51-63; gov, Col Am Pathologists, 66-71; asst clin prof path, Univ Nev, Reno, 74-; quondam chmn, Dept Path, Sunrise Hosp, 81-; consult, US Vet Admin, USPHS Indian Hosp & St Luke's Hosp, Phoenix; distinguished practr med, NAP, 83. *Mem:* Fel AAAS; Am Soc Clin Path; Am Asn Pathologists; sr mem Am Soc Qual Control; AMA; Col Am Pathologists (secy-treas, 71-79, vpres, 79-81, pres, 81-83); corresp mem Europ Acad Humanities, Arts & Sci. *Res:* Blood group serology and clinical biochemistry as related to hematologic diseases; quality management methods for medicine. *Mailing Add:* 3196 S Maryland Pkwy No 402 Las Vegas NV 89109

BARGER, JAMES EDWIN, ACOUSTICS. *Current Pos:* Sr consult appl physics, 64-68, VPRES, BOLT BERANEK & NEWMAN, INC, 68-, CHIEF SCIENTIST, 75- *Personal Data:* b Manhattan, Kans, Dec 28, 34; m 57, Mary E Rupp; c Elaine (Fleckenstein), Carolyn (Hanson), James & Corinne (Noordzij). *Educ:* Univ Mich, BS, 57; Univ Conn, MS, 60; Harvard Univ, MA, 62, PhD(appl physics), 64. *Mem:* Fel Acoust Soc Am; fel AAAS; Inst Noise Control Eng; Marine Technol Soc. *Res:* Underwater sound; acoustic cavitation in water; sonar development; medical ultra sonics; active noise and vibration control. *Mailing Add:* 3 Lakeview Rd Winchester MA 01890-3801. *E-Mail:* jbarger@bbn.com

BARGER, SAMUEL FLOYD, COMBINATORICS MATHEMATICS, GRAPH THEORY. *Current Pos:* PROF MATH, YOUNGSTOWN STATE UNIV, 70- *Personal Data:* b Butler County, Pa, July 12, 36. *Educ:* Clarion Univ, BS, 60; Univ Minn, MS, 68 &, PhD(math), 70. *Mem:* Am Math Soc; Math Asn Am. *Mailing Add:* 3855 Chaucer Lane Youngstown OH 44511-2545

BARGER, VERNON DUANE, THEORETICAL HIGH ENERGY PHYSICS. *Current Pos:* Res assoc theoret physics, Univ Wis-Madison, 63-65, from asst prof to prof physics, 65-83, Hilldale prof, 87-91, JH VAN VLECK PROF, UNIV WIS-MADISON, 83-, DIR, INST ELEM PARTICLE PHYSICS RES, 84-, VILAS PROF, 91- *Personal Data:* b Curllsville, Pa, June 5, 38; m 67, Mable A McLeod; c Victor, Amy & Andrew. *Educ:* Pa State Univ, BS, 60, PhD(physics), 63. *Concurrent Pos:* Vis prof, Univ Hawaii, 70, 79 & 82, Univ Durham, 83; vis scientist, Europ Orgn Nuclear Res, Switz & Rutherford Labs, Eng, 72 & Stanford Linear Accelerator Ctr, Stanford, Calif, 75; Guggenheim fel, 72; sr vis fel, Brit Sci-Eng Res Coun, 83-84. *Mem:* Fel Am Phys Soc. *Res:* Fundamental particle theory; elementary particle physics; achievements include classifications of hadrons as Regge recurrences; analysis of neutrino scattering and oscillations; weak boson, Higgs bason and heavy quark production; electroweak models. *Mailing Add:* Dept Physics Univ Wis Madison WI 53706

BARGERON, CECIL BRENT, PHYSICS, SURFACE SCIENCE. *Current Pos:* PHYSICIST, APPL PHYSICS LAB, JOHNS HOPKINS UNIV, 71- *Personal Data:* b Provo, Utah, May 8, 43; m 66; c 5. *Educ:* Brigham Young Univ, BS, 67; Univ Ill, MS, 68, PhD(physics), 71. *Prof Exp:* Teaching asst physics, Univ Ill, 67-68, res asst, 68-71. *Concurrent Pos:* NSF fel, 67-71; Woodrow Wilson hon fel. *Mem:* Am Phys Soc. *Res:* Surface physics and chemistry, electrochemistry (corrosion), infrared laser damage to biological tissue; light scattering from biological and related systems; high temperature physics. *Mailing Add:* Appl Physics Lab Johns Hopkins Univ Johns Hopkins Rd Laurel MD 20723-6099

BARGERON, LIONEL MALCOLM, JR, PEDIATRICS, CARDIOLOGY. *Current Pos:* instr pediat, 56-58, asst prof, 58-59, assoc prof pediat cardiol, 60-66, PROF PEDIAT, SCH MED, UNIV ALA, 66-, ASSOC PROF SURG, 77- *Personal Data:* b Savannah, Ga, Nov 4, 23; m 50; c 3. *Educ:* Univ Ala, BS, 48; Med Col Ala, MD, 52; Am Bd Pediat, dipl & cert cardiol. *Prof Exp:* Intern, Jefferson-Hillman Hosp, Birmingham, Ala, 52-53, resident, 53; asst resident, Babies Hosp, Columbia-Presby Med Ctr, NY, 54-55, sr resident, 55. *Concurrent Pos:* USPHS res fel pediat cardiol, 55-57. *Mem:* Fel Am Acad Pediat. *Res:* Pediatric cardiology. *Mailing Add:* Univ Ala Hosp Birmingham Univ Ala Univ Sta Birmingham AL 35294

BARGHUSEN, HERBERT RICHARD, PALEOZOOLOGY, ANATOMY. *Current Pos:* RETIRED. *Personal Data:* b Englewood, NJ, July 9, 33; m 57; c 2. *Educ:* Lafayette Col, AB, 55; Univ Chicago, PhD(paleozool), 60. *Prof Exp:* Asst prof zool, Smith Col, 61-64; instr anat, Stritch Sch Med, Loyola Univ, Ill, 64-67; from asst prof to prof anat & oral anat, Col Med & Col Dent, Univ Ill Med Ctr, 67-87. *Concurrent Pos:* NSF fel, 60-61; res grants, Loyola Univ, Ill, 64-67 & Univ Ill, 67-70; NSF grant, 73-75; vis prof anat, Univ Chicago, 78-79. *Mem:* AAAS; Soc Vert Paleont. *Res:* Biomechanics of vertebrate feeding mechanism; evolutionary origin of mammals and the mammalian feeding mechanism. *Mailing Add:* 1166 E 53rd St Chicago IL 60615

BARGMANN, ROLF ERWIN, MATHEMATICAL STATISTICS. *Current Pos:* PROF STATIST, UNIV GA, 65- *Personal Data:* b Glueckstadt, Ger, May 13, 21; nat; m 49; c 4. *Educ:* Univ NC, PhD(math statist), 57. *Prof Exp:* Head dept statist, Inst Educ Res, Frankfurt, 52-55; asst, Psychomet Lab, Univ NC, 55-57; from assoc prof to prof statist, Va Polytech Inst, 58-61; mgr appl math & info sci, Systs Develop div, Thomas J Watson Res Ctr, Int Bus Mach Corp, 61-65. *Concurrent Pos:* Vis lectr, Columbia Univ, 63-64, Univ Paris, 65, Univ Ill, 66, Univ Erlangen, 78 & Univ Dortmund, 80; assoc ed, J Statist Comp. *Mem:* Fel AAAS; fel Am Statist Asn; Economet Soc; Psychomet Soc; Sigma Xi. *Res:* Multivariate analysis; statistical computation. *Mailing Add:* Dept Statist Univ Ga Athens GA 30602-1952

BARGON, JOACHIM, PHYSICAL CHEMISTRY. *Current Pos:* AT INST PYHS CHEM, UNIV BONN. *Personal Data:* b Wiesbaden, Ger, Apr 13, 39; m 63; c 3. *Educ:* Darmstadt Tech Univ, BS, 61, MS, 65, PhD(physics), 68. *Prof Exp:* Staff mem spectros, Ger Plastics Inst, Darmstadt, 65-69; fac mem org chem, Calif Inst Technol, 69-70; staff mem gen chem, Res Div, Yorktown, NY, IBM Corp, 70-71, staff mem, 71-74, mgr radiation chem, 74-76, dep mgr chem, San Jose Res Lab. *Concurrent Pos:* Consult chem & plastics indust. *Mem:* Ger Phys Soc; Am Phys Soc; Am Chem Soc. *Res:* Materials science, new polymers, polymer modification, lithography, reaction mechanisms in radiation, free radical and organo-mettalic chemistry using spectroscopic techniques. *Mailing Add:* Univ Bonn Inst Phys Chem Wegelerstr 12 53115 Bonn Germany

BARHAM, WARREN SANDUSKY, PLANT BREEDING, HORTICULTURE. *Current Pos:* RETIRED. *Personal Data:* b Prescott, Ark, Feb 15, 19; m 40; c 4. *Educ:* Univ Ark, BSA, 41; Cornell Univ, PhD, 50. *Prof Exp:* Asst, Fruit & Truck Exp Sta, Univ Ark, 41-42, supt, 45-46; asst, Cornell Univ, 46-49; from asst prof to assoc prof hort, NC State Col, 49-58; dir raw mat res & seed prod, Basic Veg Prod, Inc, 58-76; head, Hort Sci Dept, Tex A&M Univ, 76-80, prof hort, 76-89. *Mem:* Fel Am Soc Hort Sci (pres, 81); Am Genetic Asn; Am Inst Biol Sci; AAAS. *Res:* Plant physiology, genetics and breeding; onions, watermelons, cantaloupes, tomatoes and garlic; disease and insect resistance; quality characteristics; seed production problems. *Mailing Add:* 7401 Crawford Dr Gilroy CA 95020-5421

BARI, ROBERT ALLAN, SOLID STATE PHYSICS, NUCLEAR ENGINEERING. *Current Pos:* SR PHYSICIST & DEP CHMN, DEPT ADVAN TECHNOL, BROOKHAVEN NAT LAB, 74- *Personal Data:* b Brooklyn, NY, Sept 3, 43; m 66; c 2. *Educ:* Rutgers Univ, AB, 65; Brandeis

Univ, PhD(physics), 70. *Prof Exp:* Physicist solid state physics, Lincoln Lab, Mass Inst Technol, 69-71; asst physicist, Brookhaven Nat Lab, 71-73; vis asst prof physics, State Univ NY, Stony Brook, 73-74. *Concurrent Pos:* Prin investr, NSF res grant, 73-74; adj assoc prof mech eng, Manhattan Col, 78-; adj prof nuclear eng, Polytech Inst NY, 78- *Mem:* Am Phys Soc; fel Am Nuclear Soc. *Res:* Nuclear reactor safety analysis; condensed matter physics; reliability and risk assessment. *Mailing Add:* Brookhaven Nat Lab PO Box 5000 Upton NY 11973-5000

BARI, WAGIH A, PATHOLOGY. *Current Pos:* DIR HEMAT PATH, ST JOHN'S MERCY MED CTR, 68- *Mailing Add:* 805 S McKnight Rd St Louis MO 63124

BARIA, DORAB NAOROZE, HAZARDOUS WASTE MANAGEMENT, LOW-RANK COAL UTILIZATION. *Current Pos:* PROF CHEM ENG, UNIV MINN, DULUTH, 85- *Personal Data:* b Bombay, India, Apr 5, 42. *Educ:* Univ Bombay, BChem Eng, 64; Northwestern Univ, MS, 68, PhD(chem eng), 71. *Prof Exp:* Assoc chem eng, Ames Lab, Iowa State Univ, 72-73; from asst prof to prof, Univ NDak, 73-85. *Mem:* Am Inst Chem Engrs; Am Soc Eng Educ; Nat Soc Prof Engrs; Sigma Xi. *Res:* Beneficiation of low-rank coals, removal of sodium, water and sulfur; flue gas desulfurization; hazardous waste management. *Mailing Add:* Chem Eng Dept Univ Minn 10 University Dr Duluth MN 55812

BARIC, LEE WILMER, MATHEMATICS. *Current Pos:* RETIRED. *Personal Data:* b Carlisle, Pa, Nov 19, 32; m 56; c 3. *Educ:* Dickinson Col, BSc, 56; Lehigh Univ, MSc, 62, PhD(math), 66. *Prof Exp:* Instr math, Lafayette Col, 58-63; mathematician, McCoy Electronics, Pa, 63-64; from asst prof to prof math, Dickinson Col, 64-95, chmn dept, 74-77. *Concurrent Pos:* Consult, McCoy Electronics, 64-90. *Mem:* Am Math Soc. *Res:* Schauder bases in Banach spaces; summability theory. *Mailing Add:* 645 Belvedere St Carlisle PA 17013-3508

BARICA, JAN M, LIMNOLOGY, AQUATIC ECOLOGY. *Current Pos:* RETIRED. *Personal Data:* b Varin, Czech, Feb 10, 33; m 60; c 3. *Educ:* Univ Bratislava, MSc, 57; Univ Prague, PhD(ecol), 67; Charles Univ, DSc, 88. *Prof Exp:* Vis scientist, Inst Limnol, Univ Freiburg, 68-69; res scientist fish ecol, Freshwater Inst, Winnipeg, 69-80; reg mgr aquatic ecol, Nat Water Res Inst, Burlington, Ont, 80-86, sr scientist, Lake Res Br, 87-97. *Concurrent Pos:* UN expert, UN Develop Prog, SChina Sea Fisheries Prog, 75; Humboldt fel, Federal Republic Germany. *Mem:* Int Soc Limnol; Soc Can Limnologists; Asn Great Lakes Res; Water Studies Inst; Can Asn Water Pollution Res. *Res:* Characterization of hypereutrophic ecosystems; instability of algal (cyanophyte) blooms, their collapses and ecological impact; predictive models for summer and winter fish kills in hypereutrophic lakes; manipulation of algal bloom composition by selective nutrient additions; ammonia contamination; Great Lakes areas of concern rehabilitation; environmental sustainability. *Mailing Add:* Nat Water Res Inst PO Box 5050 Burlington ON L7R 4A6 Can

BARIE, PHILIP S, SURGICAL CRITICAL CARE. *Current Pos:* asst prof surg, Cornell Univ Med Col, 84-89, ATTEND SURGEON & DIR, SURG INTENSIVE CARE UNIT, NY HOSP-CORNELL MED CTR, 84-, ASSOC PROF SURG, CORNELL UNIV MED COL, 89- *Personal Data:* b Buffalo, NY, Aug 18, 53; m 81, Elaine Dash; c Catherine, Steven & Alexandra. *Educ:* Boston Univ, MD, 77 Am Bd Surg, dipl, 85 & 87. *Honors & Awards:* Peter C Canizaro Award, Am Asn Surg Trauma, 92; Res Award, Soc Critical Card Med, 97. *Prof Exp:* Instr physiol, Albany Med Col, 80-81. *Concurrent Pos:* Consult surg, Cath Med Ctr, NY, 85-; consult, Critical Care Therapeut, US Pharmacopeal Conv, 91; consult specialist & mem, Med Control Bd, Health Ins Plan Greater NY, 92. *Mem:* Fel Am Col Surgeons; NY Acad Sci; Asn Acad Surg; Surg Infection Soc; Soc Critical Care Med; Am Physiol Soc; Shock Soc; Am Asn Surg Trauma; Soc Univ Surgeons; Societe Internationale de Chirurgie; Am Acad Med, fel Am Col Critical Care Med. *Res:* Pathophysiology respiratory failure, pulmonary transvascular fluid and protein exchange; clinical epidemiology of multiple organ dysfunction syndrome. *Mailing Add:* Dept Surg Med Ctr NY Hosp-Cornell Univ 525 E 68th St New York NY 10021

BARIE, WALTER PETER, ORGANIC POLYMER CHEMISTRY. *Current Pos:* RETIRED. *Personal Data:* b Pittsburgh, Pa, Oct 28, 26; m 64, Catherine; c Walter G. *Educ:* Duquesne Univ, BS, 50, MS, 51; Pa State Univ, PhD(chem), 54. *Prof Exp:* Asst, Duquesne Univ, 50-51; res chemist, Gulf Res & Develop Co, 54-67, sr res chemist, 67-75, res assoc, 75-83; tech mgr resins, Sterling Div, Reichold Chem, Inc, 83-87. *Concurrent Pos:* Consult, 87-90. *Mem:* AAAS; Am Chem Soc. *Res:* Monomers; electrical-electronic coatings, adhesives and potting compounds; high temperature polymers. *Mailing Add:* 213 Amherst Rd Glenshaw PA 15116-1303

BARIL, ALBERT, JR, RESEARCH ADMINISTRATION. *Current Pos:* RETIRED. *Personal Data:* b New Orleans, La, Aug 19, 26; m 49; c 6. *Educ:* Loyola of the South, BS, 49; Tulane Univ, MS, 52. *Prof Exp:* Dir mfg photog, Kalvar Corp, La, 62-66; dir spec prod res, Allied Paper Co, Mich, 66-67; res physicist textiles, Mach Develop, Agr Res Serv, USDA, 67-73, res leader, New Systs Res, 73-74, chief res admin, Cotton Textile Processing Lab, Southern Regional Res Ctr, 74-88. *Mem:* Electrostatic Soc Am; Am Soc Mech Engrs; Sigma Xi; Am Asn Textile Chemists & Colorists; Inst Elec & Electronics Engrs. *Res:* New systems for textile processing, particularly, integrated system, producing yarn continuously from a supply of fibers by one machine; electrostatic manipulation of fibers; electrostatic spinning of yarns; agri-particulates analysis and control. *Mailing Add:* 6300 Ackel St Metairie LA 70003

BARIL, EARL FRANCIS, BIOCHEMISTRY. *Current Pos:* RETIRED. *Personal Data:* b Claremont, NH, Apr 23, 30; m 65. *Educ:* St Anselms Col, AB, 59; Univ Houston, MS, 61; Univ Conn, PhD(biochem), 66. *Prof Exp:* NIH fel biochem, Univ Wis, 66-69; asst prof pharmacol, Med Sch, Duke Univ, 69-72; sr scientist, Worcester Found Exp Biol, 72-86, prin scientist, 86-95. *Concurrent Pos:* Exchange scientist to Poland, Nat Cancer Inst, 77; mem, Physiol Chem Study Sect, NIH, 84-88; prof pharmacol, Med Sch, Univ Mass, 84-95, prof biochem, 86-95. *Mem:* AAAS; Am Asn Cancer Res; Am Chem Soc; Am Soc Biol Chemists; Biophys Soc; Protein Soc; fel Am Inst Chem. *Res:* Regulatory control mechanisms; enzymology of DNA replication in eucaryotes. *Mailing Add:* 6500 N Fishcreek Rd Wilson WY 83014-0917

BARILE, DIANE DUNMIRE, ENVIRONMENTAL SYSTEMS ANALYSIS, COASTAL & ESTUARINE PLANNING. *Current Pos:* ENVIRON PLANNER, CITY PALM BAY, FLA, 76-; EXEC DIR, MARINE RESOURCES COUN, EFLA, 83- *Personal Data:* b Beaver Falls, Pa, July 1, 40; m 64, Tony M; c Michael A, Peter J, Daniel T, Catherine A & Elizabeth A. *Educ:* Univ Fla, BS, 62; Fla Inst Technol, MS, 76. *Honors & Awards:* Cauler Award Spec Recognition. *Prof Exp:* Teacher biol sci, Broward Co, Fla, 62-63; grad asst sci educ, Univ Miami, 63-64; adj fac urban planning, Fla Inst Technol, 76-, grad fac coastal mgt, 85- *Concurrent Pos:* Dir, Initiative to Manage Fla Indian River Lagoon, 77-78, implementation of local manatee proj prog, Nat Oceanic & Atmospheric Admin, 77-79; dir, Coastal Mgt Prog, Fla Inst Technol, 83-84, Vol Prog Habitat Restoration & NAtlantic Right Whale Tracking. *Mem:* Am Planning Asn; Am Water Resources Asn. *Res:* Environmental and urban systems; analysis of hydrological, biological and physical parameters translated into programs for enhancement of natural function for sound resource management for man's use; public awareness, education and policy implimentation. *Mailing Add:* PO Box 4123 Palm Bay FL 32905. *Fax:* 407-952-0103

BARILE, MICHAEL FREDERICK, MYCOPLASMOLOGY & IMMUNOLOGY. *Current Pos:* bacteriologist, NIH, 58-62, res bacteriologist, 62-68, chief sect Mycoplasma, 68-72, CHIEF LAB MYCOPLASMA, 72- *Personal Data:* b Bound Brook, NJ, Jan 9, 24; m 46, Grace Price; c Michael F II, Sondra J, Karin J & Deborah A. *Educ:* Univ Ga, BS, 49; Univ Mich, MS, 51, PhD(bact), 54. *Honors & Awards:* Presidential Citation Award, Int Organ Mycoplasmol, 84. *Prof Exp:* Instr microbiol, Univ Mich, 54; bacteriologist, 406th Gen Med Lab, 54-56; supvry bacteriologist, Med Lab, Tokyo, Japan, 56-57. *Mem:* AAAS; Am Acad Microbiol; Tissue Cult Asn; Int Soc Mycoplasm; Am Soc Microbiol; Soc Exp Biol & Med. *Res:* Non-gonococcal urethritis; penile lesions caused by herpesvirus, S pallidum and H ducreyi; immunization against neonatal tetanus; tetanus toxin neutralization test; diphtheria toxin for the Schick test; M pneumoniae as cause of primary typical pneumonia; etiology of recurrent aphthous stomatitis, rheumatoid arthritis and Wegener's granulomatosis; pathogenicity of Mycoplasma pneumoniae, M hominis, M genitalium, and Ureaplasma urealyticum; Mycoplasma-induced septic arthritis in patients and experimentally-induced septic arthritis in chimpanzees by M hominis, M pneumoniae and U urealyticum; M genitalium induced urogenital infections in chimpanzees and in new and old world monkeys; development of an acellular M pneumoniae vaccine containing virulence/immunogenic attachment, ciliotoxic and leukocyte recruitment factors; potency assays to evaluate M pneumoniae vaccines; other mycoplasma virulence factors; specific IgA proteases of U urealyticum; characteristics of U urealyticum urease mycoplasma lipoglycans; monoclonal antibodies to surface components of M hominis and M pneumoniae; sialic acid-containing glycoconjugates and sulfated glycolipids receptor sites for M pneumoniae; guinea pig, monkey and chimpanzee animal models to study mycoplasma disease; ocular pathology induced in hamsters and rats by Spiroplasma mirum, SMCA; cause of epidemic caprine keratoconjunctivitis contamination of cell culture. *Mailing Add:* 9716 Kensington Pkwy Kensington MD 20895

BARILE, RAYMOND CONRAD, PHYSICAL CHEMISTRY, INORGANIC CHEMISTRY. *Current Pos:* asst, 59-60, from instr to asst prof, 60-68, ASSOC PROF CHEM, MANHATTAN COL, 68- *Personal Data:* b New York, NY, June 30, 36; m 59; c 2. *Educ:* Manhattan Col, BS, 58; Fordham Univ, MS, 60, PhD(phys chem), 65. *Prof Exp:* Asst chem, Fordham Univ, 58-59. *Concurrent Pos:* Res assoc, Brookhaven Nat Lab, 66-67; fels, NSF & Atomic Energy Comn. *Mem:* Am Chem Soc. *Res:* Kinetics and mechanism of reactions of transition metal complexes, electron transfer, formation reaction and characterization of polymers. *Mailing Add:* Dept Chem 4513 Manhattan Col Bronx NY 10471-4097

BARINGER, J RICHARD, NEUROLOGY, PATHOLOGY. *Current Pos:* asst prof, 69-75, PROF NEUROL & PATH, UNIV CALIF, SAN FRANCISCO, 75-; CHIEF NEUROL, VET ADMIN HOSP, SAN FRANCISCO, 69- *Personal Data:* b Columbus, Ohio, Jan 19, 35; c 3. *Educ:* Ohio State Univ, BSc, 55; Western Reserve Univ Sch Med, MD, 59. *Honors & Awards:* Med Investr Award, Vet Admin, 71-75; Sr US Scientist Award, Alexander von Humboldt Found, 77. *Prof Exp:* Intern, Mass Gen Hosp, 59-60, resident, 60-61, asst resident, 64-65, fel, 66-69. *Concurrent Pos:* Vchmn, Dept Neurol, Univ Calif, San Francisco, 74-; chmn sci adv comt, Nat Multiple Sclerosis Soc, 76-78; mem path A study sect, NIH, 76-; Fulbright grant, 77-; med investr award, Vet Admin, 71-75. *Mem:* Am Asn Neuropathologists; Am Soc Cell Biologists; Electron Micros Soc Am; Am Neurol Asn; Am Soc Clin Invest. *Res:* Viral diseases of the central nervous system; mechanisms of viral persistence; slow virus diseases of the nervous system. *Mailing Add:* Dept Neurol Univ Utah Med Ctr Salt Lake City UT 84132

BARIOLA, LOUIS ANTHONY, ECONOMIC ENTOMOLOGY. *Current Pos:* entomologist, Entom Res Div, Tex, 62-69, RES ENTOMOLOGIST, WESTERN COTTON RES LAB, AGR RES SERV, USDA, ARIZ, 69- *Personal Data:* b Lake Village, Ark, July 7, 32; m 59; c 2. *Educ:* Univ Ark, Fayetteville, BSA, 58, MS, 62; Tex A&M Univ, PhD(entom), 69. *Prof Exp:* Res assoc entom, Univ Ark, Fayetteville, 59-62. *Mem:* Entom Soc Am; Sigma Xi. *Res:* Ecology of cotton insects; control of cotton insects using alternative methods, such as non-insecticides, cultural or biological methods; biology of cotton insects in the arid West, with major emphasis on the pink bollworm, cotton leafperforator, cotton bollworm and lygus bugs. *Mailing Add:* 2149 W Cheyenne Dr Chandler AZ 85224

BARISAS, BERNARD GEORGE, JR, CELL SURFACE BIOPHYSICS, MICROCALORIMETRY. *Current Pos:* assoc prof, 81-87, assoc dean, Col Nat Sci, 90-96, PROF CHEM & MICROBIOL, COLO STATE UNIV, 87- *Personal Data:* b Shreveport, La, July 16, 45; m 81, Deborah A Roess; c Derek A. *Educ:* Univ Kans, BA, 65; Oxford Univ, BA, 67, MA, 83; Yale Univ, MPhil, 69, PhD(chem), 71. *Honors & Awards:* Burlington Northern Fac Achievement Award. *Prof Exp:* Rhodes scholar, Oxford Univ, 67-69; NIH fel, Yale Univ, 71-72; NIH fel, Univ Colo, 73-75, lectr, 75; assoc prof biochem, Sch Med, St Louis Univ, 75-81. *Concurrent Pos:* Prin investr, NIH, NSF, March of Dimes, Am Heart Asn, 75-; mem, Midwest & Northwest Regional Rhodes Scholar Select Comts, 76-81, 82-; res career develop award, NIH, 78; Fulbright sr fel, Gottingen, 85; Max Varon vis prof, Weizmann Inst Sci, Relovoth, Israel, 95. *Mem:* Am Soc Biol Chemists; Am Asn Immunologists; Biophys Soc; Am Chem Soc; Sigma Xi. *Res:* Laser optical techniques for analysis of cell surface molecular motions; fluorescence photobleaching recovery; molecular rotation in membranes; reaction microcalorimetry and differential scanning calorimetry of biological systems; cellular immunology. *Mailing Add:* Dept Chem Colo State Univ Ft Collins CO 80523. *Fax:* 970-491-1801

BARISH, BARRY C, HIGH ENERGY PHYSICS. *Current Pos:* res fel physics, 63-66, from asst prof to assoc prof, 66-72, PROF PHYSICS, CALIF INST TECHNOL, 72- *Personal Data:* b Omaha, Nebr, Jan 27, 36; m 60; c 2. *Educ:* Univ Calif, Berkeley, AB, 57, PhD(physics), 62. *Prof Exp:* Physicist, Radiation Lab, Univ Calif, 62-63. *Mem:* Fel Am Phys Soc. *Res:* Experimental elementary particle physics; studies of neutrino interactions at high energies; production of short lived weakly decaying states by hadrons; investigation of high energy electron-positron annihilations; non-accelerator physics. *Mailing Add:* Dept Physics Calif Inst Technol HEP 256-48 Pasadena CA 91125

BARISH, LEO, MICROSCOPY, TEXTILE CHEMISTRY. *Current Pos:* sr res assoc, Fabric Res Labs, Inc, 56-72, sr res assoc, 72-79, SR MICROSCOPIST, ALBANY INT RES CO, MANSFIELD, 79- *Personal Data:* b New Bedford, Mass, Jan 19, 30; m 52; c 2. *Educ:* Southeastern Mass Univ, BS, 52; Univ Lowell, MS, 54. *Prof Exp:* Cost-finder, Dartmouth Finishing Co, Mass, 51-52; res fel, Am Asn Textile Chemists & Colorists, 53-54. *Concurrent Pos:* Bd dirs, McCrone Res Inst. *Mem:* Electron Micros Soc Am; Fiber Soc. *Res:* Optical and scanning electron microscopy; fiber structure; polymer morphology; scientific photography; textile mechanics; literature searches; fire resistant fabrics evaluation and development; stereoscopy; optical analysis; composite structures. *Mailing Add:* 2 Pole Plain Rd Sharon MA 02067. *Fax:* 508-339-4996

BARISH, ROBERT JOHN, RADIOLOGICAL PHYSICS, MEDICAL PHYSICS. *Current Pos:* CHIEF RADIOTHER PHYSICIST & ADMIN COORDR CANCER INST, DIV CATH MED CTR OF BROOKLYN & QUEENS, NY, MARY IMMACULATE HOSP, 91- *Personal Data:* b Newark, NJ, May 14, 46. *Educ:* NY Univ, BS, 68, MEng, 70; Univ London, PhD(med physics), 76; Am Bd Radiol, cert; Am Bd Health Physics, cert; Am Bd Med Physics, cert. *Prof Exp:* Clin instr radiol physics, State Univ NY, Downstate Med Ctr, 70-73; res student, Inst Cancer Res Royal Marsden Hosp, 73-76; from asst prof to assoc prof, NY Univ Med Ctr, 76-91. *Concurrent Pos:* Consult physicist, Maimonides Med Ctr, Coney Island Hosp Affil, 71-73, Booth Mem Med Ctr, 80-82, Hackensack Hosp, 81-83, Westchester Sq Hosp, 82-85, Cabrini Med Ctr, 83-85, Mary Immaculate Hosp, 81-91. *Mem:* Am Asn Physicists Med; Health Physics Soc; Am Soc Ther Radiol & Oncol. *Res:* Radiation dosimetry; physics applications in radiology. *Mailing Add:* 211 E 70th St New York NY 10021. *Fax:* 718-658-4631

BARK, LAURENCE DEAN, AGRICULTURAL METEOROLOGY. *Current Pos:* RETIRED. *Personal Data:* b Chanute, Kans, Mar 18, 26; m 64; c 3. *Educ:* Univ Chicago, BSc, 48, MSc, 50; Rutgers Univ, PhD(agron), 54. *Honors & Awards:* Nat Weather Serv Centennial Medallion. *Prof Exp:* Asst, Rutgers Univ, 51-54; bioclimatologist, US Weather Bur, 55; assoc prof physics & assoc climatologist, Agr Exp Sta, Kans State Univ, 56-67, prof climat & climatologist, 67-90. *Mem:* AAAS; Am Meteorol Soc; Am Soc Agron; Crop Sci Soc Am. *Res:* Relation of weather to the life processes of plants, animals and humans. *Mailing Add:* 1741 Fairview Ave Manhattan KS 66502

BARKA, TIBOR, EXPERIMENTAL MEDICINE. *Current Pos:* res assoc, 58-62, asst attend pathologist, 62-64, assoc attend pathologist, Mt Sinai Hosp, 64-80, prof anat & chmn dept, 67-86, PROF ANAT, MT SINAI SCH MED, 86-, PROF PATH, 66- *Personal Data:* b Debrecen, Hungary, Mar 31, 26; US citizen; m 57, Katalin Szalay. *Educ:* Debrecen Univ, MD, 50. *Prof Exp:* Asst, Inst Histol & Embryol, Med Univ Budapest, 51-54; res assoc, Inst Exp Med, Hungarian Acad Sci, 54-56; res assoc, Inst Cell Res & Genetics, Karolinska Inst, Sweden, 56-58. *Concurrent Pos:* Ed-in-chief, J Histochem & Cytochem, 65-73; prof path, Mt Sinai Sch Med, 66- *Mem:* Histochemical Soc; Am Asn Path; Am Soc Cell Biol; Am Asn Anat. *Res:* Histochemistry; experimental pathology; cell biology. *Mailing Add:* Dept Cell Biol & Anat Mt Sinai Sch Med Box 1007 New York NY 10029-6504

BARKAI, AMIRAM I, NEUROTRANSMITTERS, DRUG EFFECTS. *Current Pos:* RES SCIENTIST & ASSOC PROF PSYCHIAT, NY STATE PSYCHIAT INST, 72- *Personal Data:* b June 20, 36; m; c 2. *Educ:* Hebrew Univ, Israel, PhD(physiol), 70. *Concurrent Pos:* Med entomol; pub health serv grants. *Mem:* Am Soc Neurochem; Am Soc Pharmacol & Exp Therapeut. *Res:* Neuroscience, neurochemistry, neuropharmacology. *Mailing Add:* 214 Hilltop Lane Nyack NY 10960

BARKALOW, DEREK TALBOT, MOLECULAR BIOLOGY. *Current Pos:* asst prof, 78-87, ASSOC PROF BIOL, STETSON UNIV, 87-, CHAIRPERSON, 90- *Personal Data:* b New York, NY, May 25, 51. *Educ:* Univ Wis, Madison, BS, 73; Rutgers Univ, MS, 74, PhD(physiol), 78. *Prof Exp:* Res asst physiol, Marine Biol Lab, Mass, 75-78. *Concurrent Pos:* Res fel cell physiol, Sch Med, Wash Univ, 81; res fel cell biol, Princeton Univ, 85, Emory Univ, 92. *Mem:* AAAS; Am Soc Zoologists; Am Inst Biol Sci. *Res:* Membrane transport; intestinal absorption; cell physiology. *Mailing Add:* Dept Biol Stetson Univ 421 N Woodland Blvd De Land FL 32720-3799. *Fax:* 904-822-8832

BARKALOW, FERN J, CELL ADHESION, EXTRACELLULAR MATRIX BIOLOGY. *Current Pos:* RES FEL, BRIGHAM & WOMEN'S HOSP, BOSTON, MA, 93- *Personal Data:* b Aug 25, 60. *Educ:* Rutgers Univ, BA, PhD(microbiol), 88. *Prof Exp:* Teaching asst introductory genetics, Biol Dept, State Univ NY, Binghamton, 82; fel, Dept Molecular Biol, Princeton Univ, 88-93. *Concurrent Pos:* Nat Cancer Inst nat res serv award, 90-92. *Mem:* Am Soc Cell Biol; AAAS. *Res:* Author of eight technical publications. *Mailing Add:* Dept Path Div Vascular Res LMRC Rm 404 Brigham Women's Hosp 221 Longwood Ave Boston MA 02115

BARKAN, P(HILIP), mechanical engineering design, manufacturability; deceased, see previous edition for last biography

BARKAUSKAS, ANTHONY EDWARD, GRAPH THEORY. *Current Pos:* From asst prof to assoc prof, 72-82, PROF MATH, UNIV WIS-LA CROSSE, 82- *Personal Data:* b Seattle, Wash, Jan 30, 46; m 70; c 3. *Educ:* Whitman Col, AB, 68; Duke Univ, MA, 70, PhD(math), 72. *Mem:* Am Math Soc; Math Asn Am; Soc Indust & Appl Math. *Res:* Graph theory, specifically dominating sets, graph reconstruction and graph labeling. *Mailing Add:* Univ Wis La Crosse La Crosse WI 54601-3767

BARKAUSKAS, VIOLET H, NURSING. *Current Pos:* ASST PROF, SCH NURSING UNIV MICH, 80- *Educ:* St Joseph Col, BS, 62; Univ Mich, MPH, 68; Johns Hopkins Univ, CNM, 69; Univ Ill, PhD(nursing Sci), 80. *Prof Exp:* Pub health nurse & team leader, Waterbury Vis Nurse Asn, 62-65; staff & charge nurse, Waterbury Hosp, 67; asst nursing coordr, Boston City Dept Health & Hosps, 69-71; instr, Col Nursing, Univ Ill, 71-73, asst prof & coordr, Family Nurse Practr Prog, 73-76, instr, 76-80. *Concurrent Pos:* Grantee, HEW, 73-76 & 76-80, Dept Health & Human Servs, 83-86; fel, Univ Ill, 76-77; nurse fel, Nat Res Service Award, Dept HEW, 78-80; prin investr, Am Pub Health Asn, 85 & Univ Mich Sch Nursing, 85-86; J William Fulbright fel, 95; vis fac mem, Vilnius Univ & Kaunas Med Acad, 95. *Mem:* Fel Am Acad Nursing; Home Health Care Nurses Asn. *Res:* Home health care nursing practice, education and research; public health nursing interventions for health promotion and disease prevention of elderly populations; national perspective on home health trends: present and future. *Mailing Add:* Sch Nursing Univ Mich 400 N Ingalls Ann Arbor MI 48109-0482

BARKDOLL, BRIAN DAVID, SEDIMENT TRANSPORT, HYDRAULICS. *Current Pos:* ASST PROF CIVIL ENG, UNIV MISS, 86- *Personal Data:* b Wabash, Ind, Dec 1, 62; m 93; c 2. *Educ:* Univ Akron, BS, 85; Univ Cincinnati, MS, 92; Univ Iowa, PhD(civil & environ eng), 97. *Concurrent Pos:* Civil & sanitary engr, US Peace Corps, 85-89; civil engr, NE Ohio Regional Sewer Dist, 89-90; consult, Water Dist Syst, Univ Cincinnati, 90-91. *Mem:* Am Soc Civil Engrs; Int Asn Hydraulic Res; Am Water Works Asn; Am Water Res Asn; Am Soc Eng Educ. *Res:* Sediment transport mechanics, measurement of sediment discharge, sediment behavior in diversion flows; water distribution system hydraulic behavior; contaminant behavior, contaminant adherence to soil particles, bridge pier scour. *Mailing Add:* Dept Civil Eng Univ Miss University MS 38677. *Fax:* 601-232-7191; *E-Mail:* cvbark@olemiss.edu

BARKE, HARVEY ELLIS, economic entomology, botany; deceased, see previous edition for last biography

BARKELEW, CHANDLER H(ARRISON), CHEMICAL ENGINEERING, PROCESS CONTROL. *Current Pos:* RETIRED. *Personal Data:* b Fresno, Calif, Oct 12, 19; m 47, Virginia Koorn; c Claire (Depenbrock), James & Julia (Smith). *Educ:* Pomona Col, BA, 41; Univ Calif, Berkeley, PhD(chem), 44. *Prof Exp:* Engr chem eng, Shell Develop Co, 45-85. *Concurrent Pos:* Lectr, Univ Calif, 70- *Mem:* Am Chem Soc; Am Inst Chem Engrs; Instrument Soc Am; Soc Comput Simulation; Am Inst Chemists. *Res:* Reaction engineering; control theory; thermodynamics; simulation; chemical kinetics. *Mailing Add:* 1110 Spyglass Dr Eugene OR 97401

BARKER, ALFRED STANLEY, JR, EFFICIENT USE OF ENERGY, SOLAR & WIND ENERGY SOURCES. *Current Pos:* PROF PHYSICS, TRINITY WESTERN UNIV, 81- *Personal Data:* b Vancouver, BC, Dec 18, 33; m 55; c 3. *Educ:* Univ BC, BA, 55, MSc, 57; Univ Calif, PhD(physics),

62. *Prof Exp:* Mem tech staff physics, AT&T Bell Labs, 62-79; vis prof physics, Simon Fraser Univ, 79-81. *Concurrent Pos:* Vis lectr, NSF, 69-70; vis prof physics, Univ Southern Calif, 70; consult, Energy Study Panel, Am Phys Soc, 74-; adv, USAF Study Panel, 75-; adj prof, Energy Res Inst, Simon Fraser Univ, 80-85. *Mem:* Fel Am Phys Soc. *Res:* Lattice vibrations in solids; alternate energy sources (solar, wind, fuel cells, energy conservation). *Mailing Add:* 32-4001 Old Clayburn Rd Abbotsford BC V3G 1C5 Can

BARKER, ALLEN VAUGHAN, PLANT PHYSIOLOGY, SOIL SCIENCE. *Current Pos:* from asst prof to assoc prof, 67-76, PROF PLANT & SOIL SCI, UNIV MASS, AMHERST, 76- *Personal Data:* b McLeansboro, Ill, Aug 15, 37; m 67, Elaine Chomyn; c 2. *Educ:* Univ Ill, BS, 58; Cornell Univ, MS, 59, PhD(agron), 62. *Honors & Awards:* Dow Chem Co Environ Qual Res Award, 75; Marion Meadows Award, Am Soc Hort Sci, 77. *Prof Exp:* Fel soil sci, NC State Univ, 62-64; asst prof plant physiol, Univ Mass, 64-66 & Mich State Univ, 66-67. *Concurrent Pos:* Plant physiologist, Agr Res Serv, USDA, 66-67. *Mem:* Crop Sci Soc Am; Am Soc Agron; Soil Sci Soc Am; Am Soc Hort Sci. *Res:* Ammonium toxicity in plants; nitrate and heavy metal accumulation in vegetables. *Mailing Add:* Dept Plant & Soil Sci Univ Mass Amherst MA 01003. *Fax:* 413-545-0260; *E-Mail:* barker@pssci.umass.edu

BARKER, BARBARA ELIZABETH, HEMATOLOGY, LYMPHOCYTES. *Current Pos:* assoc dir path, 81-, SCI DIR, CELL MARKER LAB UNIV RI. *Educ:* Univ RI, PhD(cell biol), 65. *Prof Exp:* assoc dir hemat, RI Hosp, 56-; assoc dir path, Brown Univ, 74- *Res:* Immunology. *Mailing Add:* Dept Spec Hemat RI Hosp 593 Eddy St Providence RI 02902-0001

BARKER, BEN D, DENTISTRY. *Current Pos:* from instr to assoc prof fixed prosthodontics, Univ NC, Chapel Hill, 58-65, assoc prof prev dent & dent sci, 65-69, asst dean, 68-69, prof & assoc dean, 69-75, prof & dean, Sch Dent, 81-89, PROF, DEPT DENT ECOL, SCH DENT, UNIV NC, CHAPEL HILL, 89- *Personal Data:* b Burlington, NC, Dec 19, 31; m; c 3. *Educ:* Davidson Col, BS, 54; Univ NC, DDS, 58; Duke Univ, MED. *Prof Exp:* Prog dir, W K Kellogg Found, 75-81. *Concurrent Pos:* Mem, Coun Dent Educ, Am Dent Asn, 71-, Coun Int Rels, 79-83, Bd Health Care Serv, Nat Acad Sci, 87-, Comt Estab Res Agenda Aging & Comt Health Prom & Disability Rev, 88-90; vis prof, New Cross Hosp, London, 72-73. *Mem:* Inst Med-Nat Acad Sci; fel Am Col Dentists; fel Int Col Dentists. *Mailing Add:* Sch Dent 310 Braver Hall Univ NC CB 7450 Chapel Hill NC 27599-7450

BARKER, C(ALVIN) L R, THERMAL SCIENCES & FLUID MECHANICS. *Current Pos:* from assoc prof to prof, 60-94, assoc dean eng, 74-80, EMER PROF MECH ENG, UNIV TEX, ARLINGTON, 94- *Personal Data:* b Dallas, Tex, Nov 25, 30; m 52, Francis McMahon; c Leigh A (Traylor) & Karen D (Bogen). *Educ:* Univ Tex, Austin, BS, 53; Calif Inst Technol, MS, 54, PhD(mech eng), 58. *Prof Exp:* Lab res asst, Defense Res Lab, Univ Tex, 53; res engr, Jet Propulsion Lab, Calif Inst Technol, 54-58; sr propulsion engr, Gen Dynamics/Ft Worth, 58-60. *Mem:* Am Soc Mech Engrs. *Res:* Thermodynamics; gas dynamics; fluid mechanics. *Mailing Add:* 1602 Wagon Wheel Trail Pantego TX 76013-3142. *Fax:* 817-860-0353; *E-Mail:* cbarker@arlington.net

BARKER, CLYDE FREDERICK, SURGERY, IMMUNOLOGY. *Current Pos:* assoc, 64-68, from asst prof to assoc prof, 68-73, PROF SURG, SCH MED, UNIV PA, 73-, ASSOC MED GENETICS, 66-, CHMN, DEPT SURG, 83-, DIR, HARRISON DEPT SURG RES. *Personal Data:* b Salt Lake City, Utah, Aug 16, 32; m 56, Dorothy J Bicler; c Frederick G II, John R, William S & Elizabeth D. *Educ:* Cornell Univ, BA, 54, MD, 58; Am Bd Surg, dipl, 65. *Honors & Awards:* Merit Award, NIH, 87-94. *Prof Exp:* Intern, Hosp Univ Pa, 58-59, from asst resident to chief resident surg, 59-64. *Concurrent Pos:* Fel, Harrison Dept Surg Res, Sch Med, Univ Pa, 59-64, Am Cancer Soc fel, 61-62, USPHS fel med genetics, 65-66; Hartford fel vascular surg, Hosp Univ Pa, 64-65; Markle Found scholar acad med, 68; attend surgeon & assoc chief sect vascular surg, Hosp Univ Pa, 66-82, chief sect renal transplantation, 69-, chief sect vascular surg, 82-, chief surg, 83-; chief surg, Hosp Univ Pa, 83- *Mem:* Inst Med-Nat Acad Sci; Transplantation Soc; Soc Univ Surgeons; Soc Vascular Surg; Am Surg Asn; Soc Clin Surg; Am Soc Transplant Surgeons. *Res:* Gastrointestinal and cardiovascular physiology; transplantation biology; immunologically privileged sites; microvascular transplantation surgery; transplantation of pancreatic islets; clinical renal pancreas and liver transplantation; immunological aspects of diabetes and pathogenesis of diabetes. *Mailing Add:* 3 Coopertown Rd Haverford PA 19041

BARKER, COLIN G, ORGANIC GEOCHEMISTRY. *Current Pos:* from asst prof to assoc prof, 69-76, PROF GEOSCI, UNIV TULSA, 76-, CHMN, GEOSCI DEPT, 87- *Personal Data:* b Plymouth, Eng, Aug 3, 39; m 65; c 2. *Educ:* Oxford Univ, BA, 62, DPhil(geol), 65. *Honors & Awards:* Matson Award, Am Asn Petrol Geologists, 78 & 82; Esso Distinguished lectr, Univ Sydney, Australia, 85. *Prof Exp:* Res fel geol, Univ Tex, Austin, 65-67; sr res chemist, Esso Prod Res Co, Tex, 67-69. *Concurrent Pos:* Consult, Amoco Prod Res Co, 70-75, Sun Oil Co, 74-75, Agrico, 74, Rockwell Int, 75, CONOCO, 76- & Gulf Oil Co, 77; Res Corp grant; NASA grants; NSF grant, 73, 92-; assoc ed, Geochem & Cosmochem Acta, 78-85 & Bull Am Asn Petrol Geologists, 80-86; distinguished lectr, Am Asn Petrol Geologists, 80-81; Dept Energy grants, 81-94; assoc, Oil & Gas Consults Int. *Mem:* Geochem Soc; Europ Asn Org Geochemists; Am Asn Petrol Geologists. *Res:* Ultradeep gas and mass spectrometric analysis of gases in fluid inclusions; generation and migration of petroleum; pyrolysis; abnormal subsurface pressures. *Mailing Add:* Dept Geosci Univ Tulsa 600 S College Tulsa OK 74104-3126. *Fax:* 918-631-2091; *E-Mail:* geos_cgb@vaxi.utulsa.edu

BARKER, DANIEL STEPHEN, IGNEOUS PETROLOGY, VOLCANOLOGY. *Current Pos:* from asst prof to assoc prof, 63-72, PROF GEOL, UNIV TEX, AUSTIN, 72- *Personal Data:* b Waltham, Mass, Feb 27, 34; div; c 2. *Educ:* Yale Univ, BS, 56; Calif Inst Technol, MS, 58; Princeton Univ, PhD(geol), 61. *Prof Exp:* Res assoc geol, Cornell Univ, 61-62; res assoc, Yale Univ, 62-63. *Concurrent Pos:* Fulbright-Hays res fel, 74. *Mem:* Fel Geol Soc Am; fel Mineral Soc Am; Am Geophys Union. *Res:* Genesis of carbonatites and alkalic igneous rocks; volcanology. *Mailing Add:* Dept Geol Sci Univ Tex Austin TX 78712-1026. *Fax:* 512-471-9425; *E-Mail:* barker@maestro.geo.utexas.edu

BARKER, DAVID LOWELL, NEUROBIOLOGY. *Current Pos:* AT MARINE SCI CTR, ORE STATE UNIV. *Personal Data:* b Price, Utah, May 3, 41; m 64; c 1. *Educ:* Calif Inst Technol, BS, 63; Brandeis Univ, PhD(biochem), 69. *Prof Exp:* Res fel neurobiol, Harvard Med Sch, 69-71; asst prof biol, Univ Ore, 71-80; mem fac, dept zool, Univ Iowa, 80- *Mem:* Soc Neurosci; AAAS. *Res:* Identification of neurotransmitters in individual invertebrate neurons; analysis of biochemical control mechanisms that regulate neurotransmitter metabolism and electrical activity in single cells and in interconnected neurons generating motor patterns. *Mailing Add:* 4 Santa Cruz Lane Foster City CA 94404

BARKER, DEE H(EATON), CHEMICAL ENGINEERING, EDUCATION. *Current Pos:* prof, 59-90, EMER PROF CHEM ENG, BRIGHAM YOUNG UNIV, 90- *Personal Data:* b Salt Lake City, Utah, Mar 28, 21; m 45; c 5. *Educ:* Univ Utah, BS, 48, PhD(chem eng), 51. *Prof Exp:* Res engr, Eng Res Lab, E I du Pont de Nemours & Co, 51-54, engr, 54-59. *Concurrent Pos:* Fulbright fel, Chonnam Nat Univ, Kuang Ju, Korea, 80-81. *Mem:* Fel Am Inst Chem Engrs; Am Soc Eng Educ. *Res:* Heat transfer; fluid flow; particle dynamics; automatic control and process dynamics; atmospheric pollution; dust and mist collection. *Mailing Add:* 1398 Cherry Lane Provo UT 84604

BARKER, DONALD YOUNG, PHARMACY. *Current Pos:* prof, 60-89, EMER PROF PHARM, UNIV PAC, 89- *Personal Data:* b Glenboro, Man, Apr 4, 25. *Educ:* Univ Man, BS, 49; Purdue Univ, MS, 53, PhD(pharm), 55. *Prof Exp:* Instr pharm, Univ Man, 49-53. *Mem:* Am Pharmaceut Asn; Soc Cosmetic Chem; Royal Soc Health; Sigma Xi. *Res:* Pharmaceutical education; product development; dermatological vehicles; emulsion technology. *Mailing Add:* 4629 Lemmore Pl Stockton CA 95207

BARKER, EARL STEPHENS, INTERNAL MEDICINE. *Current Pos:* Asst instr pharmacol, 48-49, from asst instr to instr, 51-53, assoc, 53-55, asst prof, 55-61, ASSOC PROF MED, SCH MED, UNIV PA, 61-, DIR, DIAG CLIN, 70- *Personal Data:* b Salt Lake City, Utah, Sept 21, 20. *Educ:* Univ Utah, BA, 41; Univ Pa, MD, 45. *Concurrent Pos:* Godey-Seger fel med, Univ Pa, 49-51; NIH res fel, 51-53; asst attend physician, Univ Hosps, 51-55, attend physician, 55-; investr, Am Heart Asn, 55-60. *Mem:* Fel Am Col Physicians; Am Fedn Clin Res; Am Soc Clin Invest. *Res:* Renal physiology; tubular transport mechanisms; acid-base balance; electrolyte excretion; oxygen metabolism of kidney. *Mailing Add:* 3400 Spruce St Philadelphia PA 19104-4219

BARKER, EDWIN STEPHEN, PLANETARY ASTRONOMY. *Current Pos:* SR SCIENTIST, SOLAR SYSTS EXPLOR, NASA. *Personal Data:* b Santa Fe, NMex, Oct 22, 40; m 62, 89; c 5. *Educ:* NMex State Univ, BS, 62; Univ Kans, MA, 64; Univ Tex, Austin, PhD(astron), 69. *Prof Exp:* Staff astron planetary, Univ Tex McDonald Observ, 69-75; staff astron Copernicus, Princeton Univ, 75-77; staff astron, Univ Tex McDonald Observ, 77-78, res astron planetary, 78-79, res staff, 79-88, supt, 88- *Mem:* Am Astron Soc; Int Astron Union. *Res:* Planetary atmospheres; cometary spectroscopy and spectrophotometry; space astronomy: Copernicus observations of planets; reflectance spectroscopy of outer planets, satellites and asteroids. *Mailing Add:* Dept Astron Univ Tex Austin TX 78712

BARKER, FRANKLIN BRETT, RADIOCHEMISTRY. *Current Pos:* RETIRED. *Personal Data:* b Shawnee, Okla, Nov 12, 23; m 51; c 1. *Educ:* Univ Okla, BA, 44; Univ NMex, PhD(chem), 54. *Prof Exp:* Asst chemist, Cities Serv Oil Co, 44-45, control chemist, 45-46; mem staff, Los Alamos Sci Lab, 47-51; res asst, Univ NMex, 51-54; chemist, US Geol Surv, Colo, 54-57, res chemist & proj chief, 57-61; sr scientist, Bettis Atomic Power Lab, Westinghouse Elec Corp, 61-67, fel scientist, 67-78, adv scientist, 78-89. *Mem:* AAAS; Am Chem Soc; Am Inst Chemists; Sigma Xi. *Res:* Mass spectrometry of reactor materials; automatic control and data acquisition; computer programming; radiochemical analysis; gamma-ray spectroscopy; nuclear fuel burn-up measurement; reactor plant radiochemistry; environmental radiochemistry. *Mailing Add:* 4327 Rosecliff Ave NW Albuquerque NM 87114

BARKER, FRED, GEOLOGY. *Current Pos:* geologist, 54-93, EMER SCIENTIST, US GEOL SURV, 93- *Personal Data:* b Seekonk, Mass, Nov 4, 28; m 61, Margaret W; c 3. *Educ:* Mass Inst Technol, BS, 50; Calif Inst Technol, MS, 52 PhD, 54. *Prof Exp:* Fel, Harvard Univ, 57. *Concurrent Pos:* Vis res fel, Univ Witwatersrand, 74; adj prof Univ Wyo, 88-91. *Mem:* Fel Geol Soc Am; Am Geophys Union. *Res:* Petrology and geochemistry: trondhjemites, igneous rocks of accreted terranes; geology of Precambrian rocks; origin of granitic batholiths. *Mailing Add:* US Geol Surv Box 25046 Stop 973 Denver CO 80225

BARKER, GEORGE EDWARD, CHEMICAL ENGINEERING. *Current Pos:* RETIRED. *Personal Data:* b Detroit, Mich, Apr 3, 28; m 52, Theresa McVeigh; c Alan, Glenn & Kenneth. *Educ:* Univ Mich, BSE, 50, MSE, 51, PhD(chem eng), 52. *Prof Exp:* Chem engr, Monsanto Co, 52-55 & Process Res Sect, 57-59, res group leader, 59-62, Monsanto fel, 62-70, sr Monsanto fel, 70-91. *Mem:* Am Chem Soc; Am Inst Chem Engrs; AAAS. *Res:* Chemical reaction kinetics; process instrumentation and control; automation by computer; mammalian cell culture. *Mailing Add:* 1616 Red Gate Lane St Louis MO 63146

BARKER, HAL B, ANIMAL PHYSIOLOGY, ANIMAL NUTRITION. *Current Pos:* Assoc prof dairying, La Tech Univ, 49-58, head, Dept Animal Indust, 53-64, dean, Sch Agr & Forestry, 64-71, prof animal husb, 58-88, dean, Col Life Sci, 71-88, EMER PROF, LA TECH UNIV, 88- *Personal Data:* b Palmer, Tenn, Feb 5, 25; m 52; c 2. *Educ:* Tenn Polytech Inst, BS, 47; Iowa State Col, MS, 49; Ala Polytech Inst, PhD, 59. *Mem:* AAAS; Am Soc Animal Sci; Am Dairy Sci Asn. *Res:* Milkfat replacements in rations for dairy calves; physiology of reproduction. *Mailing Add:* 2802 Lakeview Dr Ruston LA 71270

BARKER, HAROLD CLINTON, ORGANIC CHEMISTRY, POLYMER CHEMISTRY. *Current Pos:* RETIRED. *Personal Data:* b Akron, Ohio, Aug 6, 22; m 44; c 3. *Educ:* Univ Akron, BS, 44; Ohio State Univ, MSc, 48, PhD(org chem), 51. *Prof Exp:* Res chemist, E I du Pont de Nemours Inc, 51-54, sales technologist, 54-59, indust specialist, 59-71, sales develop plastic pipe, 71-74, mkt develop polyimide plastics, 74-78, mkt develop polyvinyl butyral sheeting, 78-82. *Mem:* Sigma Xi. *Res:* Organic free radical chemistry; degradation of polymers present; sales development of polyolefin plastics; market development of glass reinforced thermoplastics. *Mailing Add:* 3204 Tanya Dr Delwynn Wilmington DE 19803-1937

BARKER, HAROLD GRANT, SURGERY. *Current Pos:* from asst prof to prof clin surg, 53-88, CLIN SURG, COL PHYSICIANS & SURGEONS, COLUMBIA UNIV, 68-, EMER PROF SURG, 88- *Personal Data:* b Salt Lake City, Utah, June 10, 17; m 49, Kathleen Butler; c Douglas R & Janet (Pinkney). *Educ:* Univ Utah, AB, 39; Univ Pa, MD, 43; Am Bd Surg, dipl. *Prof Exp:* Intern, Hosp Univ Pa, 43-44, asst instr pharmacol, Med Sch, 46-47, asst instr surg, 47-51, instr, 51-52, assoc surg, 52-53. *Concurrent Pos:* Res fel pharmacol, Univ Pa, 46-47, Harrison res fel surg, 47-51 & Runyon res fel, 51-52; asst resident surg, Hosp, Univ Pa, 47-51, sr resident, 51-52, asst attend surgeon, 52-53; from asst attend surgeon to attend surgeon, Presby Hosp, 53-, dir med affairs, 74-82. *Mem:* Am Surg Asn; Soc Univ Surgeons; Soc Surg Alimentary Tract; Am Col Surgeons; Halsted Soc. *Res:* Surgical physiology of gastrointestinal tract. *Mailing Add:* One Forest Ave Rye NY 10580

BARKER, HORACE ALBERT, BIOCHEMISTRY. *Current Pos:* instr soil microbiol, Univ Calif & jr soil microbiologist, Agr Exp Sta, 36-41, asst prof & asst soil microbiologist, 41-45, assoc soil microbiologist, 45-46, prof, 46-51, microbiologist, 46-75, prof plant biochem, 51-59, prof biochem, 59-75 chmn dept biochem, 62-64, EMER PROF BIOCHEM, AGR EXP STA, UNIV CALIF, BERKELEY, 75- *Personal Data:* b Oakland, Calif, Nov 29, 07; m 33, Margaret McDowell; c Barbara (Friede), Elizabeth (Mark) & Robert H. *Educ:* Stanford Univ, AB, 29, PhD(chem), 33. *Hon Degrees:* ScD, Western Res Univ, 64; Dr, Munich Univ, 90. *Honors & Awards:* Sugar Res Award, 45; Carl Neuberg Medal, 59; Borden Award, 62; F G Hopkins Medal, Brit Biochem Soc, 67; Nat Medal Sci, 68. *Prof Exp:* Asst zool, Univ Chicago, 30-31; Nat Res Coun fel, Hopkins Marine Sta, Pac Grove, 33-35; Gen Educ Bd fel, Technol Univ Delft, 35-36. *Concurrent Pos:* Guggenheim fel, 41-42 & 62; assoc ed, Ann Rev Microbiol; dir, Ann Rev, Inc, 46-62. *Mem:* Nat Acad Sci; Am Soc Microbiol; Am Chem Soc; Am Soc Biol Chem; Brit Biochem Soc; Am Acad Arts & Sci. *Res:* Soil microbiology; physiology and biochemistry of microorganisms; vitamin B-12 coenzymes. *Mailing Add:* H A Barker Hall Univ Calif Berkeley CA 94720

BARKER, JAMES CATHEY, AGRICULTURAL WASTE MANAGEMENT, WATER POLLUTION ABATEMENT SYSTEMS. *Current Pos:* exten asst prof, 74-79, exten assoc prof, 79-85, PROF & EXTEN SPECIALIST, NC STATE UNIV, 85- *Personal Data:* b Mt Pleasant, Tenn, Oct 30, 45. *Educ:* Univ Tenn, BS, 67, MS, 69, PhD(agr eng), 73. *Honors & Awards:* Aerovent Young Exten Worker Award, Am Soc Agr Engrs, 84, Gunlogson Coungtryside Eng Award, 96. *Prof Exp:* Res asst, Univ Tenn, 67-73; res assoc, Univ Ga, 73-74. *Concurrent Pos:* Engr consult, RI Dept Environ Mgt, 83, Neuhoff Farms, Inc, 83-84, John A Lut & Son, Inc, 84, Nat Fertilizer Serv, 87, Shimar Farms, 87, US Feed Grains Coun-Taiwan, 89, Am Asn Swine Practitioners, 89, Agrocarne, SA, 90, Phillips Dairy Farm, 90, Newsham Hybrids Inc, 92, US Feed Grains Coun, Korea, 92, Coun Indust & Com Develop, Taiwan, 93, Lianing Comn Sci & Technol, Peoples Repub of China, 93, UN-FAO, Beijing, China, 94 & UN-FAO, Kuala Lumpur, Malaysia, 95. *Mem:* Am Soc Agr Engrs; Water Environ Fedn; Coun Agr Sci & Technol. *Res:* Develop educational programs and foster the advancement of technology for systems of agricultural waste management and water quality protection; organic by-product utilization and land application; preservation of rural environmental quality. *Mailing Add:* NC State Univ Box 7625 Raleigh NC 27695-7625

BARKER, JAMES J(OSEPH), CHEMICAL ENGINEERING, NUCLEAR ENGINEERING. *Current Pos:* CONSULT ENGR, 59- *Personal Data:* b Elmhurst, NY, Apr 15, 22; m 45, 79; c 3. *Educ:* NY Univ, BChE, 43, MChE, 50, DESc(chem eng), 59. *Prof Exp:* Jr engr, Kellex Corp, 43-45 & Hydrocarbon Res Inc, 47-48; sewer cleaner, Roto-Rooter, 49; engr, Atomic Energy Div, H K Ferguson Co, 49-52; mgr, Process Dept, Walter Kidde Nuclear Labs, Inc, 52-57; assoc prof nuclear eng, NY Univ, 57-62. *Concurrent Pos:* Consult, Res Div, W R Grace & Co, 67, AiRes Mfg, 79-80 & 83-85 & Atlantic Richfield Corp, 80-82; prof physics, C W Post Col, Long Island Univ, 67-70; chmn, Dept Chem Eng, Manhattan Col, 75-76; CSULB, SJSU, De Anza Community Col, 86-88; prin engr, Westinghouse Hanford Co, 89- *Mem:* AAAS; Am Nuclear Soc; Am Inst Chem Engrs; Am Chem Soc; NY Acad Sci; Am Phys Soc; Sigma Xi. *Res:* Mass transfer in agitated liquids; isotope separation; radioisotopes; nuclear engineering; mathematics. *Mailing Add:* 1211 George Washington Way Apt G Richland WA 99352

BARKER, JANE ELLEN, DEVELOPMENTAL BIOLOGY, HEMATOLOGY. *Current Pos:* staff scientist, Jackson Lab, 80-91, assoc dir training & educ, 83-85, assoc dir res support, 90-93, SR STAFF SCIENTIST, JACKSON LAB, 91- *Personal Data:* b Bangor, Maine, June 21, 35. *Educ:* Univ Maine, BA, 57; Wellesley Col, MA, 59; Univ Wis, PhD(zool), 67. *Prof Exp:* Asst investr, Inst Med Res, Putnam Mem Hosp, 69-73; sr staff fel, Clin Hemat Br, NIH, 73-78, sr investr, 78-80. *Concurrent Pos:* Fel develop genetics, Univ Wis, 66-67; fel develop hemat, Jackson Lab, 67-69; grad fac, Univ Maine, 81-, adj prof, 90- *Mem:* AAAS; Soc Develop Biol; Am Soc Hemat; Am Soc Cell Biol. *Res:* Embryonic development of mouse hematopoietic system; cellular and molecular defects in mice with hereditary anemias; gene transfer. *Mailing Add:* Jackson Lab Bar Harbor ME 04609

BARKER, JEFFERY LANGE, NEUROBIOLOGY, NEUROPHARMACOLOGY. *Current Pos:* res assoc neurobiol, Nat Inst Neurol Dis & Stroke, 69-72, spec fel, 72-73, med officer neurobiol, Nat Inst Child Health & Human Develop, 73-76, MED OFFICER, LAB NEUROL & COMMUN DIS & STROKE, 76-, CHIEF MED DIR, PUBLIC HEATH SERV, LAB NEUROPHYSIOL, NAT INST NEUROL & COMMUN DISORDER & STROKE, NIH. *Personal Data:* b New York, NY, Jan 29, 43; m 70; c 2. *Educ:* Harvard Col, BA, 64; Boston Univ, MD, 68. *Prof Exp:* Intern surg, Boston Univ Hosp, 68-69. *Concurrent Pos:* NSF grants res consult neurobiol, 75- *Mem:* AAAS; Soc Gen Physiologists; Soc Neurosci; Am Physiol Soc; Am Soc Neurochem. *Res:* Physiological roles of peptides and neurotransmitters in neuronal function; cellular mechanisms of neuropharmacologic agents, such as anesthetics and convulsants; biophsyical mechanisms of neuronal pacemaker activity; function of rapidly transported proteins in axons. *Mailing Add:* Lab Neurophysiol Nat Inst Neurol Dis & Stroke NIH Bldg 36 Rm 2C02 Bethesda MD 20892-0001

BARKER, JOHN L, JR, EARTH SCIENCES, REMOTE SENSING. *Current Pos:* PHYS SCIENTIST, GODDARD SPACE FLIGHT CTR, NASA, 74-, NASA LANDSAT ASSOC, PROJECT SCI, 81- *Personal Data:* b New York, NY, Sept 4, 37; m 59; c 2. *Educ:* Johns Hopkins Univ, AB, 58; Univ Chicago, MS, 62, PhD(phys chem), 67. *Prof Exp:* Res assoc chem, Univ Chicago, 67-68; asst prof, Univ Md, College Park, 68-72; radiochemist, US Geol Surv, 72-73. *Concurrent Pos:* Nat Acad Sci sr fel, 73 & 74. *Mem:* Am Chem Soc. *Res:* Earth resources; applications of remote sensing from satellites; evaluation and improvement of digital image processing of imagery from scanners and linear array sensors; identifying requirements for future satellite sensors; renewable resources; satellite performance simulation; spectral analysis for global habitability. *Mailing Add:* 9102 Tuckahoe Lane Adelphi MD 20783-1438

BARKER, JOHN ROGER, CHEMICAL KINETICS. *Current Pos:* CHEMIST CHEM KINETICS, SRI INT, 74- *Personal Data:* b Sewanee, Tenn, Oct 17, 43; m 72. *Educ:* Hampden-Sydney Col, BS, 65; Carnegie-Mellon Univ, MS, 69, PhD(chem), 70. *Prof Exp:* Res assoc chem kinetics, Univ Wash, 69-71; res assoc, Brookhaven Nat Lab, 71-73; sr res assoc, Yeshiva Univ, 73-74. *Concurrent Pos:* Asst ed, Int J Chem Kinetics, 74-76. *Mem:* Am Chem Soc; AAAS; Sigma Xi. *Res:* Gas phase chemical kinetics; inter- and intra-molecular energy transfer processes; laser-induod chemistry and photophysics. *Mailing Add:* Chem Dept Univ Mich Rm 1539 Atmospheric Ocean & Space Sci Ann Arbor MI 48109-2143

BARKER, JUNE NORTHROP, PHYSIOLOGY. *Current Pos:* RES ASSOC, DEPT CHEM, RUTGERS UNIV. *Personal Data:* b Milwaukee, Wis, June 29, 28; m 51. *Educ:* Univ Rochester, BS, 52; Duke Univ, MA, 54, PhD(physiol), 56. *Prof Exp:* Instr physiol, Med Sch, Duke Univ, 57-58; from instr to asst prof, Jefferson Med Col, 58-64. *Mem:* AAAS; Am Physiol Soc; Biomed Eng Soc; Am Soc Neurochem. *Res:* Developmental and cerebrovascular physiology. *Mailing Add:* 115 Barbertown Pt Breeze Rd Frenchtown NJ 08825

BARKER, KENNETH LEROY, MOLECULAR & REPRODUCTIVE BIOLOGY, ENDOCRINOLOGY. *Current Pos:* PROF BIOCHEM & PROF OBSTET & GYNEC, TEX TECH UNIV HEALTH SCI CTR, LUBBOCK, 81-, VPRES RES & ACAD AFFAIRS & ASSOC DEAN GRAD STUDIES, 89- *Personal Data:* b Columbus, Ohio, July 15, 39; m 64, Dorothy S Baughman; c Karen S. *Educ:* Ohio State Univ, BS, 60, MS, 62, PhD(biochem), 64. *Prof Exp:* Res asst dairy sci, Ohio State Univ, 61-64; res assoc obstet & gynec, Univ Kans, 65-66; from instr to res prof obstet & gynec & from instr to prof biochem, Univ Nebr Med Ctr, Omaha, 66-81, dean grad studies & res, 79-81. *Concurrent Pos:* Fel biochem, Univ Kans, 65-66; Pop Coun res grant, 67; Nat Inst Child Health & Human Develop res grant, 67-; NIH res career develop award, 68-73; guest scientist, Biol Div, Oak Ridge Nat Lab, 70; Nat Acad Sci exchange fel, Inst Molecular Biol, Moscow, USSR, 73; mem, Reproductive Biol Study Sect, NIH, 75-79 & chmn, 85-87; mem, Pop Res Comt, Nat Inst Child Health & Human Develop, 92- *Mem:* Endocrine Soc; Soc Gynec Invest; Am Physiol Soc; Soc Study Reproduction; Am Soc Biochem Molecular Biol; Am Chem Soc. *Res:* Investigations of hormonal control mechanisms in the mammalian uterus, translational and transcriptional control of uterine, protein synthesis and enzyme activities. *Mailing Add:* Dept Biochem State Univ NY Health Sci Ctr 750 E Adams St Syracuse NY 13210-2339. *E-Mail:* acaklb@tthsc4.hsc.ttu.edu

BARKER, KENNETH NEIL, PHARMACY ADMINISTRATION, HOSPITAL PHARMACY. *Current Pos:* CHMN, DEPT PHARM ADMIN & ALUMNI PROF PHARM ADMIN, AUBURN UNIV, 75- *Personal Data:* b Spring Valley, Ohio, Mar 25, 37; m 57; c 3. *Educ:* Univ Fla, BS, 59, MS, 61; Univ Miss, PhD(pharm admin), 70. *Honors & Awards:* Res Award, Am Soc Hosp Pharmacists, 73, 85, 87 & Whitney Award, 81. *Prof Exp:* Residency, Hosp Pharm, Univ Fla, 61; proj coordr, Hosp Systs Res, Sch Pharm, Univ Miss, 67-70; dir admin res, US Pharmacopeial Conv, Inc, 70-72; assoc dir res inst & assoc prof pharm admin, Sch Pharm, Northeast La Univ, 72-75. *Concurrent Pos:* Mem vis scientist prog, Am Asn Col Pharm, 70-72; consult & ed dir, Health Care Facil Serv, Health Resources Admin, Dept Health, Educ & Welfare, 70-73; mem adv panel hosp pharm res needs, Am Soc Hosp Pharmacists, 73; proj dir & chmn, Nat Coord Comt Large Volume Parenterals, 72-80; consult, Bd Trustees, US Pharmacopeial Conv, Inc, 74-75. *Mem:* Acad Pharmaceut Sci; Am Asn Col Pharm; Am Soc Hosp Pharmacists; Am Pharmaceut Asn. *Res:* Socioeconomics of health care with emphasis on pharmacy services; hospital medication systems, errors; co-originator of unit-dose concept; organizational research; utilization of pharmacists: design of hospital pharmacy facilities; future of pharmacy. *Mailing Add:* Dept Pharm Auburn Univ Main Campus Auburn AL 36849-3501

BARKER, KENNETH RAY, SPERM CELL MORPHOLOGY, BIOLOGY OF AMPHIUMA. *Current Pos:* PROF ZOOL, D'YOUVILLE COL, 86- *Personal Data:* b Memphis, Tenn, Oct 30, 39; m 71; c 2. *Educ:* Southwestern at Memphis, BS, 61; Univ Miss, MS, 63; Univ Tex, PhD(zool), 66. *Prof Exp:* Instr zool, Univ Tex, 66, NIH fel, 66-67; res fel embryol, Univ Witwatersrand, 67-68; asst prof biol, Canisius Col, 69-79; instr, Wood Jr Col, 84. *Concurrent Pos:* Mem fertilization & gamete physiol prog, Woods Hole, Mass, 63; vis prof, Univ Tex, Austin, 76-77. *Mem:* Am Soc Cell Biologists. *Res:* Ultrastructure of sperm and sperm formation of decapods, insects and urodeles; molecular control of eucaryotic cells. *Mailing Add:* Dyouville Col Dept Math & Sci 320 Porter Ave Buffalo NY 14201-1032

BARKER, KENNETH REECE, PLANT PATHOLOGY, NEMATOLOGY. *Current Pos:* assoc prof, 66-71, PROF PLANT PATH, NC STATE UNIV, 71- *Personal Data:* b Roaring River, NC, Feb 1, 32; m 58, Betty Flynt; c Elizabeth B (Owens) & Nicole J. *Educ:* NC State Col, BS, 56, MS, 59; Univ Wis, PhD(plant path), 61. *Prof Exp:* Asst prof, Univ Wis-Madison, 61-66. *Concurrent Pos:* Ed-in-chief, J Nematol, 75-78. *Mem:* Fel Am Phytopath Soc; hon mem Soc Nematologists (vpres, 78-79, pres, 79-80). *Res:* Ecology and physiology of plant parasitic nematodes and their interaction with other plant pathogens. *Mailing Add:* Dept Plant Path NC State Univ Box 7616 Raleigh NC 27695-0001. *Fax:* 919-515-7716; *E-Mail:* krbpp@ncsu.edu

BARKER, LAREN DEE STACY, VERTEBRATE PHYSIOLOGY. *Current Pos:* assoc prof, 69-76, PROF BIOL, SOUTHWEST STATE UNIV, 76- *Personal Data:* b Honolulu, Hawaii, Mar 1, 42; m 64; c 4. *Educ:* Univ Minn, BS, 64, MS, 66; Pa State Univ, PhD(physiol), 69. *Prof Exp:* Res asst dairy husb, Univ Minn, 64-66. *Mem:* Soc Study Reproduction; Am Inst Biol Sci; Brit Soc Study Fertil. *Res:* Physiology of the male reproductive system; epididymal physiology; immunoreproduction. *Mailing Add:* Dept Biol Southwest State Univ Marshall MN 56258-1598

BARKER, LEE RANDOL, INFECTIOUS DISEASE. *Current Pos:* Chief resident & instr med, 73-74, from asst to assoc prof, 74-95, PROF MED, JOHNS HOPKINS UNIV, 95-; DIR, MED HOUSE STAFF PRACT, JOHNS HOPKINS MED CTR, BALTIMORE, 74-, MED DIR, MED CLIN, 77-, DIR, DIV INTERNAL MED, 79- *Personal Data:* b Baltimore, Md, Dec 2, 39; m 67, Marie Claire Palisse; c Marie Annick, Isabelle Virginie & Carolyn Margaret. *Educ:* Harvard Col, BA, 62; Johns Hopkins, MD, 66, MSc, 76; Am Bd Internal Med, cert, 72. *Prof Exp:* Intern, Bellevue Hosp, 66-67, asst resident, 67-68; res assoc, Nat Inst Allergy & Infectious Dis, NIH, 68-70; clin scholar fel, Johns Hopkins, Carnegie-Commonwealth/Robert Wood Johnson, 70-72. *Concurrent Pos:* Dir, Hypertension Clin, Baltimore City Hosps, 74-86; J William Fulbright sr lectr, Inst Health Studies, 95-96. *Mem:* Soc Gen Int Med. *Res:* Evaluation of teaching-skills modules for general internal medicine faculty and fellows: outcomes on knowledge, skills and satisfaction; recognition and communiction of medication side-effects by older patients; management of hypertension; published 22 articles. *Mailing Add:* Johns Hopkins Bayview Med Ctr 4940 Eastern Ave Baltimore MD 21224

BARKER, LEROY N, AGRONOMY, PLANT BREEDING. *Current Pos:* RICE RES CONSULT, 92- *Personal Data:* b Brigham City, Utah, Oct 18, 28; m 56; c 5. *Educ:* Utah State Univ, BS, 53, MS, 57; Univ Wis, PhD(agron), 64. *Prof Exp:* Plant breeder & res sta mgr, Asgrow Seed Co, Wis, 60-65; from asst prof to prof agron, Calif State Univ, Chico, 65-92. *Concurrent Pos:* Vis prof, US AID, Univ Wis Proj, Univ Ife, Nigeria, 68-70; plant breeder & consult, Rice Researchers, Inc, 74- *Mem:* Am Soc Agron; Crop Sci Soc Am. *Res:* Breeding of cowpeas, peppers and rice; agronomic research on cowpeas and tomatoes; basic genetic studies on cowpeas; field crop yield and fertilizer trials and genetic studies; variety development, agronomic research and extension service on rice. *Mailing Add:* 2502 N Valmet Ave Meridian ID 83642

BARKER, LOUIS ALLEN, PHARMACOLOGY, NEUROCHEMISTRY. *Current Pos:* assoc prof, 82-86, PROF PHARMACOL, LA STATE UNIV MED CTR, 86- *Personal Data:* b Charleston, WVa, Nov 23, 41; m 66; c 1. *Educ:* WVa Univ, BSc, 64; Tulane Univ, PhD(pharmacol), 68. *Prof Exp:* Grant researcher biochem, Queens Col, NY, 70-72, adj asst prof psychol, 72; from instr to assoc prof pharmacol, Mt Sinai Med Sch, 72-82. *Concurrent Pos:* Nat Inst Neurol Dis & Stroke fel, NY State Inst Basic Res Ment Retardation, 68-70. *Mem:* Am Soc Pharmacol & Exp Therapeut; Shock Soc. *Mailing Add:* Dept Pharmacol La State Univ Med Ctr 1100 Florida Ave New Orleans LA 70119

BARKER, LYNN MARSHALL, VISAR INSTRUMENTATION FOR SHOCKS IN CONDENSED MATERIALS. *Current Pos:* PRES, VALYN INT, 90- *Personal Data:* b Florence, Ariz, Apr 4, 28; m 64, Valeri Brown; c Scott T & Zane B. *Educ:* Univ Ariz, BS, 54, MS, 55. *Prof Exp:* Staff mem, Sandia Labs, 55-74; sr staff consult, Terra Tek, Inc, 74-81; distinguished mem tech staff, Sandia Labs, 81-90. *Concurrent Pos:* Consult, Sandia Labs, 90- *Mem:* Fel Am Phys Soc; Soc Exp Mech. *Res:* Shock waves in condensed matter; originator of VISAR laser interferometer instrumentation; in fracture mechanics originator of Am Standards Testing Mat-standardized chevron-notched short rod test method for measuring fracture toughness; nine patents. *Mailing Add:* 13229 Circulo Largo NE Albuquerque NM 87112-3771

BARKER, MARVIN, CHEMISTRY. *Current Pos:* ADMIN VPRES ACAD AFFAIRS, TENN TECHNOL UNIV, 93- *Personal Data:* b Flora, Ill, 1936. *Educ:* Southern Ill Univ, Carbondale, BA, 58; Duke Univ, MA, 60, PhD(chem), 63. *Prof Exp:* Dean, Col Arts & Sci, Univ Mo, Rolla, 89-93. *Mem:* Am Chem Soc; AAAS; Sigma Xi. *Mailing Add:* 747 Timber Lane Cookeville TN 38501-2818

BARKER, MORRIS WAYNE, APPLIED FISHERIES MANAGEMENT. *Current Pos:* Fish biologist III, 78-79, fish biologist IV, 79-80, ASST CHIEF I, DEPT FISHERIES, WASH STATE, 80- *Personal Data:* b Astoria, Ore, May 31, 45; m 66; c 2. *Educ:* Ore State Univ, BS, 72, MS, 74; Univ Wash, PhD(fisheries), 79. *Concurrent Pos:* Vis lectr, Univ Alaska, 77-78; consult, Peter Pan Seafoods & Nichiro Pac Ltd, 78. *Mem:* Pac Fisheries Biologists; Am Inst Fishery Res Biologists. *Res:* Fishing gear efficiencies and economics; population dynamics of sport exploited near shore ground fish, including fishing and natural mortality rates; growth rate estimates; tagging studies. *Mailing Add:* 8608 Ninth Way SE Lacey WA 98503

BARKER, NORVAL GLEN, nutritional biochemistry; deceased, see previous edition for last biography

BARKER, PETER EUGENE, CANCER RESEARCH, CYSTIC FIBROSIS. *Current Pos:* RES CHEMIST, NAT INST STAND & TECHNOL, 97- *Personal Data:* b Ithaca, NY; m 83; c 1. *Educ:* Cornell Univ, BA, 73; Univ Tex, PhD(cell & molecular biol), 81. *Prof Exp:* Fel, Yale Univ, 80-85; asst prof med genetics & biochem, Univ Ala, Birmingham, 85-91; vis scientist, Ger Cancer Res Ctr, Heidelberg, 91-93; staff scientist, Cold Spring Harbor Lab, 93-96. *Concurrent Pos:* Fel, Yale Univ, 80-85. *Mem:* Sigma Xi; fel Muscular Dystrophy Asn. *Res:* Human cancer genetics. *Mailing Add:* CSTL/NIST/ Div 831 US Dept Com Bldg 222/A353 Gaithersburg MD 20899

BARKER, PHILIP SHAW, ENTOMOLOGY, INSECT TOXICOLOGY. *Current Pos:* RES SCIENTIST, AGR CAN, 65- *Personal Data:* b Queretaro, Mex, Aug 2, 33; c 3. *Educ:* Univ Calif, Berkeley, MSc, 60; McGill Univ, PhD, 65. *Mem:* Entom Soc Am; Entom Soc Can; Sigma Xi. *Res:* Control of insects and mites in stored cereals; effect of freezing temperatures on fumigants; life histories of mites; statistical programs for calculators. *Mailing Add:* 59 Acadia Bay Winnipeg MB R3T 3J1 Can

BARKER, RICHARD CLARK, APPLIED PHYSICS, ELECTRONICS. *Current Pos:* From instr to assoc prof, 52-74, PROF APPL SCI, YALE UNIV, 74-, DIR UNIV RES CONTRACTS, 50- *Personal Data:* b Bridgeport, Conn, Mar 27, 26; m 48; c 2. *Educ:* Yale Univ, BE, 50, ME, 51, PhD(elec eng), 55. *Honors & Awards:* Alexander von Humboldt Found Sr Am Scientist Award, 75. *Concurrent Pos:* Consult, Naval Ord Lab, 62-68, Sandia Corp, 63-68, AMP Inc, 72-, Echlin Mfg Co, 76- & Rockwell Int, 78- *Mem:* AAAS; fel Inst Elec & Electronics Engrs; Am Phys Soc. *Res:* Basic theory of nonlinear magnetic devices; physics of magnetic materials; ferromagnetic resonance in metals; electron tunneling in semiconductors; semimetals; superconductors; metals; semiconductor device physics. *Mailing Add:* Yale Univ PO Box 20-8284 New Haven CT 06520-8284

BARKER, RICHARD GORDON, PAPER SCIENCE & TECHNOLOGY. *Current Pos:* Res scientist, Union Bag-Camp Paper Corp, 62-69, group leader, Union Camp Corp, 69-72, sect leader, 72-74, dir res & develop projs, 74-79, lab dir corp res & develop, 79-85, CORP DIR RES & DEVELOP, UNION CAMP CORP, 85- *Personal Data:* b Rochester, NY, Feb 8, 37; m 57, 95, Mary K Simpson; c Laurie, Richard Jr & Jonathan. *Educ:* Hamilton Col, BA, 58; Lawrence Univ, MS, 60, PhD(org chem), 63. *Concurrent Pos:* Mem, Indust Liaison Comt, Forest Prod Lab, 74-77; chmn, Res Steering Comt, Empire State Paper Res Inst; chmn, Res Adv Comt, Inst Paper Chem, 87-88; pres, Espra, 91-96; trustee, Miami Univ, Ohio & Univ Maine; pres bd trustees, Miami Pulp & Paper Found, 96- *Mem:* Am Chem Soc; fel Tech Asn Pulp & Paper Indust (vpres, 97-). *Res:* Chemical wood pulping processes; bleaching processes; pulp and paper. *Mailing Add:* Union Camp Corp Box 3301 Princeton NJ 08543-3301. *Fax:* 609-844-7366

BARKER, ROBERT, BIOCHEMISTRY. *Current Pos:* dir, Div Biol Sci, Cornell Univ, 80-83, vpres res & advan studies, 83-84, provost, 84-95, EMER PROF BIOL & EMER PROVOST, CORNELL UNIV, 95- *Personal Data:* b Bedlington, Eng, Sept 21, 28; m 55; c 2. *Educ:* Univ BC, BA, 52, MA, 53; Univ Calif, Berkeley, PhD(biochem), 58. *Prof Exp:* Atlas Powder Co fel chem, Washington Univ, 58-59; vis scientist, NIH, 59-60; from asst prof to assoc prof biochem, Univ Tenn, 60-64; from assoc prof to prof, Univ Iowa, 64-74, assoc dean med, 70-74; prof biochem & chmn dept, Mich State Univ, 74-80. *Concurrent Pos:* Mem, Biochem Training Comt, Nat Inst Gen Med Sci, NIH, 65-69, chmn, 69-70, mem, Med Scientist Training Comt, 70-73, Cellular &

Molecular Basis Dis Rev Comt, 77-78; vis prof, Duke Univ, 70-71; chmn, Biochem Test Comt, Nat Bd Med Examr, 73-76; mem, Merit Rev Bd Basic Sci, Vet Admin, 73-78, chmn, 76-78; mem, Exec Comt, Nat Bd Med Examr, 77-80; chmn, Panel Res Needs Basic Biomed Sci, Nat Acad Sci-Nat Res Coun, 79-84 & mem, Comt Nat Needs Biomed & Behav Res Personnel, 79-87; mem bd dirs, Corning Glass Works, 87-; mem, Adv Coun, Oak Ridge Nat Lab, 88- *Mem:* AAAS; Am Soc Biol Chemists; Am Chem Soc. *Res:* Effects of configuration and substitution on reactions of carbohydrates; solution structures of mono and oligosaccharides. *Mailing Add:* 295 Sudden Valley Bellingham WA 98226

BARKER, ROBERT EDWARD, JR, POLYMER PHYSICS, INSULATION SCIENCE. *Current Pos:* chmn Eng Sci Prog, 69-73, assoc prof, 67-80, PROF MAT SCI, UNIV VA, 80- *Personal Data:* b Bonifay, Fla, Oct 8, 30; m 81, Betty Harris; c Ann Marie (Barker-Schwartz) & Philip Pate Barker. *Educ:* Univ Ala, BS, 52, MS, 54, PhD(physics), 60. *Prof Exp:* High sch teacher, Fla, 50-51; physicist, US Navy Mine Defense Lab, 54 & 55; engr, Hayes Aircraft Corp, Ala, 56 & 57, scientist, 58; from instr to asst prof physics, Univ Ala, 58-60; physicist, Gen Elec Res Lab, 60-67. *Concurrent Pos:* Consult, Hayes Aircraft Corp, 56-59; mem exec bd & mem tech adv comt, Conf Elec Insulation & Dielectric Phenomena, Nat Acad Sci; vis scientist, Xerox Res Ctr, 73-74; mem, Inst Elec & Electronics Engrs. *Mem:* fel Am Phys Soc; Am Asn Physics Teachers; Am Chem Soc; Soc Plastics Eng; Sigma Xi. *Res:* Thermomechanical properties of solids; radiation damage of polymers; electron spin resonance; nucleation and growth of microstructures by generalized stresses; thermodynamics; thermal conductivity; diffusion; ionic mobility; glass transition phenomena in polymers; developed theory of the correlation of activation entropy with conformational entropy for structure controlled rate processes; insulation science; dielectric and ferraelectric polymers and composites. *Mailing Add:* Dept Mat Sci & Eng Univ Va Thorton Hall Charlottesville VA 22903-2442. *Fax:* 804-982-5660; *E-Mail:* reb@virginia.edu

BARKER, ROBERT HENRY, SCIENCE POLICY, POLYMER CHEMISTRY. *Current Pos:* VPRES, AM FIBER MFRS ASN, 88- *Personal Data:* b Washington, DC, Aug 17, 37; div; c 3. *Educ:* Clemson Col, BS, 59; Univ NC, PhD(org chem), 63. *Prof Exp:* From instr to asst prof org chem, Tulane Univ, 62-67; assoc prof textiles & chem, Clemson Univ, 67-74, J E Sirrine prof textile & polymer chem, 74-84; sci adv & chief staff, Hon Judd Gregg, US House Rep, 83-88. *Concurrent Pos:* Nat Res Coun-Nat Acad Sci Eval Panel, Ctr Fire Res, Nat Bur Stand, 76-82; Am Chem Soc Cong Sci fel, 81-82; consult, Fiber Indust, Inc, 81-83. *Mem:* Am Chem Soc; Am Asn Textile Chem & Colorists; Fiber Soc. *Res:* Chemistry of fibers; polymer pyrolysis and combustion; textile flammability; science policy. *Mailing Add:* 3516 S Ninth St Arlington VA 22204. *Fax:* 202-296-3052

BARKER, ROY JEAN, ENTOMOLOGY. *Current Pos:* PVT CONSULT, 80- *Personal Data:* b Norborne, Mo, July 9, 24; m 48, 71, Marylou Criss; c Jeffrey S & Brian L (deceased). *Educ:* Univ Mo, BS, 48; Univ Ill, PhD(entom), 53. *Prof Exp:* Asst entom, Univ Ill, 48-50 & Ill State Natural Hist Surv, 50-53; entomologist, E I Du Pont de Nemours & Co, 53-55; sr insect physiologist, Pioneering Lab, USDA, Md, 55-64; entomologist, Res Labs, Rohm and Haas Co, Pa, 64-67; res entomologist, USDA, 67-79. *Mem:* Am Chem Soc. *Res:* Pesticide trouble shooting; insect physiology and biochemistry; pheromones for pest control. *Mailing Add:* 4620 N Calle Altivo Tucson AZ 85718-5810

BARKER, SAMUEL BOOTH, PHYSIOLOGY, PHARMACOLOGY. *Current Pos:* dir grad studies, 65-70, prof, 65-76, dean, Grad Sch, 70-78, DISTINGUISHED PROF PHYSIOL & BIOPHYS, UNIV ALA, BIRMINGHAM, 76-, EMER DEAN, GRAD SCH, 78- *Personal Data:* b Montclair, NJ, Mar 3, 12; wid. *Educ:* Univ Vt, BS, 32; Cornell Univ, PhD(physiol), 36. *Hon Degrees:* ScD, Univ Ala, 79, Univ Vt, 84. *Prof Exp:* Asst physiol, Med Col, Cornell Univ, 37-40; from instr to asst prof physiol, Col Med, Univ Tenn, 41-44; from asst prof to assoc prof, Col Med, Univ Iowa, 44-52; prof pharm, Med Col & Sch Dent, Med Ctr, Univ Ala, 52-62; prof, Col Med, Univ Vt, 62-65. *Concurrent Pos:* Fel med, Cornell Univ, 38-41; Krichesky fel, Univ Calif, Los Angeles, 51-52, USPHS spec fel, 61-62, career res award, 62-65; pres, Am Thyroid Asn, 71. *Mem:* Fel AAAS; Am Soc Exp Pharmacol & Therapeut; Am Physiol Soc; Soc Exp Biol & Med; Endocrine Soc; Am Thyroid Asn. *Res:* Fat, carbohydrate and protein metabolism; tissue metabolism; effect of endocrines on metabolism; thyroid and iodine; endocrinology. *Mailing Add:* Dept Physiol Univ Ala Birmingham AL 35294-4410

BARKER, SAMUEL LAMAR, RADIOPHARMACEUTICAL CHEMISTRY, CLINICAL CHEMISTRY. *Current Pos:* Res scientist, E R Squibb & Sons, 69-72, sr res scientist, 72-73, sect head radiopharmaceut res, 73-75, Squibb mgt develop prog, 75-77, dir parenteral mfg, 77-78, ASSOC DIR SQUIBB INST & DIR DIAG RES & DEVELOP, E R SQUIBB & SONS, 78- *Personal Data:* b Pine Bluff, Ark, Sept 22, 42; m 63; c 2. *Educ:* Henderson State Col, BS, 64; Univ Ark, MS, 66; Purdue Univ, PhD(bionucleonics), 69. *Concurrent Pos:* USPHS radiol health fel, Univ Ark, 64-65 & Purdue Univ, 66-69. *Mem:* Soc Nuclear Med; Am Asn Clin Chemists; Clin Radioassay Soc; Parenteral Drug Asn. *Res:* Chemistry of technetium complexes and radioimmunoassay methodology as applied to medical diagnosis. *Mailing Add:* Univ Ala Physiol Dept Birmingham AL 35294-4410

BARKER, WILEY FRANKLIN, SURGERY, PERIPHEUAL VASCULAR SURGERY. *Current Pos:* asst, Univ Calif, Los Angeles, 49-51, clin instr, 51-54, chief, Div Gen Surg, 54-76, from asst prof to prof, 54-86, EMER PROF SURG, SCH MED, UNIV CALIF, LOS ANGELES, 86- *Personal Data:* b Santa Fe, NMex, Oct 16, 19; m 43, Nancy K; c Robert L, Jonathan S & Christina L. *Educ:* Harvard Univ, BS, 41, MD, 44; Am Bd Surg, dipl, 53. *Prof Exp:* Intern & resident surg, Peter Bent Brigham Hosp, 44-46. *Concurrent Pos:* Jr assoc, Peter Bent Brigham Hosp, 48-49; resident surg, Vet Admin Hosp, Los Angeles, 49-51, attend physician, 54-; chief gen surg sect & asst chief gen surg serv, Wadsworth Vet Admin Hosp, 51-54; mem bd trustees, Am Bd Surg, 64-70; chief staff, Sepulveda Vet Admin Ctr, 78-83. *Mem:* Fel Am Col Surg; Soc Univ Surg; Soc Vascular Surg; Am Surg Asn; Soc Clin Surg; Southern Surg Asn. *Res:* Clinical surgical aspects of arteriosclerosis and genesis of arterbiolerosis gastroenterological disease and aseptic technique. *Mailing Add:* 13216 Dobbins Pl West Los Angeles CA 90049. *E-Mail:* wbarker@vcia.edu

BARKER, WILLIAM ALFRED, PHYSICS. *Current Pos:* prof, 64-88, chmn dept, 69-73, EMER PROF PHYSICS, UNIV SANTA CLARA, 88- *Personal Data:* b Los Angeles, Calif, May 9, 19; m 41, 85; c 5. *Educ:* Yale Univ, BA, 41; Calif Inst Technol, MS, 48; St Louis Univ, PhD(physics), 52. *Prof Exp:* Instr, St Louis Univ, 52-55, from asst prof to prof, 55-64. *Concurrent Pos:* Res theoret physics, Swiss Fed Inst Technol, 53-55; consult, Argonne Nat Lab, 58-63, McDonnell Aircraft Corp, 60-, Hewlett-Packard, NASA-Ames, 68-77. *Mem:* Am Phys Soc; Am Asn Physics Teachers. *Res:* Nuclear orientation; quantum electronics; solid state; photoelectron spectroscopy; atmospheric physics; interaction physics; cosmology; acoustics; theory of the magnetic monopole; radioactive half lives, fusion. *Mailing Add:* 185 N El Monte Ave Los Altos CA 94022

BARKER, WILLIAM GEORGE, plant physiology, for more information see previous edition

BARKER, WILLIAM HAMBLIN, II, OPERATIONS RESEARCH, PURE MATHEMATICS. *Current Pos:* mathematician, 75-80, SR ASSOC, DANIEL H WAGNER ASSOCS, 80- *Personal Data:* b Albuquerque, NMex, Aug 10, 48. *Educ:* Univ Calif, Santa Barbara, BA, 70; Stanford Univ, MS, 72, PhD(math), 75. *Prof Exp:* Res asst math, Ames Res Ctr, NASA, 69-72, consult, 73; mathematician & asst, Stanford Univ, 70-75. *Mem:* Am Math Soc; Acoust Soc Am; Soc Indust & Appl Math. *Res:* Theory of search; theory of surveillance; complex analysis, conformal mappings; calculus of variations, hyperelliptic Reimann surfaces. *Mailing Add:* 907 Hillsboro Ave Sunnyvale CA 94086

BARKER, WILLIAM T, SYSTEMATIC BOTANY. *Current Pos:* Assoc prof, 68-80, PROF BOT, NDAK STATE UNIV, 80- *Personal Data:* b Larned, Kans, Aug 3, 41; m 62; c 2. *Educ:* Kans State Teachers Col, BA, 63, MA, 67; Univ Kans, PhD(bot), 68. *Honors & Awards:* Outstanding Achievement Award, Soc Range Mgt. *Mem:* Am Soc Plant Taxon; Int Asn Plant Taxon; Soc Range Mgt. *Res:* Floristic studies of the United States prairies and plains; grazing management. *Mailing Add:* Dept Bot NDak State Univ Fargo ND 58105. *E-Mail:* barker@badlands.nodak.edu

BARKER, WINONA CLINTON, MOLECULAR EVOLUTION. *Current Pos:* ASSOC DIR RES, NAT BIOMED RES FOUND, GEORGETOWN UNIV, 73-, VPRES, 87- *Personal Data:* b New York, NY, Sept 5, 38; m 59; c 2. *Educ:* Conn Col, BA, 59; Univ Chicago, PhD(physiol), 66. *Prof Exp:* Sr res technician physiol, Univ Chicago, 65-66, trainee comt math, 66-67, res assoc med, 67-68. *Concurrent Pos:* Staff scientist, Atlas Protein Sequence & Struct, 68-; lectr, Sch Med, Georgetown Univ, 72-, assoc mem grad fac, 74-; NIH res grant, 75-88; proj dir, Protein Identification Resource, 84-; mem, task group, comt data sci & technol. *Mem:* Biophys Soc (secy, 79-87); Am Soc Biol Chemists; Am Soc Cell Biol; AAAS; Protein Soc. *Res:* Analysis of domains in proteins; evolutionary history, function, genetic basis, role in human development, differentiation and oncogenesis; computer analysis of related proteins; protein and nucleic acid sequence databases. *Mailing Add:* Nat Biomed Res Found Med Ctr 3900 Reservoir Rd W Washington DC 20007-2195. *Fax:* 202-687-1662; *E-Mail:* barker@nbrf.georgetown.edu

BARKEY, KENNETH THOMAS, ORGANIC CHEMISTRY. *Current Pos:* RETIRED. *Personal Data:* b Auburn, Wash, Dec 29, 16; m 51, Virginia R Nablo; c K Larry & Ann L. *Educ:* Univ Wash, BS, 38, MS, 40; Mass Inst Technol, PhD(org chem), 43. *Prof Exp:* Oceanog chemist, Univ Wash, 36-38; supvr, Eastman Kodak Co, 43-79, sr tech assoc, 75-79. *Mem:* Am Chem Soc. *Res:* Cellulose esters; plasticizers; polyesters; air pollution abatement. *Mailing Add:* 14 Midlakes Dr Canandaigua NY 14424-1044

BARKIN, STANLEY M, MATERIALS SCIENCE. *Current Pos:* ENVIRON SCIENTIST, ENVIRON PROTECTION AGENCY, 94- *Personal Data:* b New York, NY, July 19, 26; div; c Diane & Nina. *Educ:* Brooklyn Col, BS, 50; Polytech Inst Brooklyn, MS, 55, PhD(polymer chem), 57. *Prof Exp:* Anal chemist, Lucius Pitkin Inc, 48-50; control chemist, Davis & Geck, Inc, 50-53; res asst, Polymer Inst Brooklyn, 53-57; res chemist, Tex-US Chem Co, 57-58; mgr, Ethicon, Inc, 58-63; sect head, Colgate-Palmolive Co, 63-70; sect supvr, US Steel Corp, 70-75; assoc dir, Nat Mat Adv Bd, Nat Acad Sci, 75-92. *Concurrent Pos:* Adj prof, Dept Math, Seton Hall Univ, 61-70; lectr, Dept Chem, George Wash Univ, 76-88; adj prof, Col Arts & Sci, Marymount Univ, 88-93, Mt Vernon Col, 96- *Mem:* Am Chem Soc; AAAS. *Res:* Solution properties of macromolecules; characterization techniques for polymers. *Mailing Add:* 4141 N Henderson Rd No 616 Arlington VA 22203-2463. *Fax:* 703-603-9104; *E-Mail:* barkin.stan@epamail.epa.gov

BARKLEY, DWIGHT G, HORTICULTURE. *Current Pos:* from asst prof to assoc prof, 68-71, PROF AGR, EASTERN KY UNIV, 71-, CHMN DEPT, 77- *Personal Data:* b Indiana, Pa, Nov 13, 32; m 59; c 2. *Educ:* Pa State Univ, BS, 55; Va Polytech Inst, MS, 63, PhD(seed germination), 69. *Prof Exp:* Instr hort, Va Polytech Inst, 63-68. *Mem:* Am Soc Agron; Crop Sci Soc Am. *Res:* Microclimate and microenvironment as they affect germination of grass and woody plant seeds; nursery crop production; turf-grass management. *Mailing Add:* Dept Agr Eastern Ky Univ 521 Lancaster Ave Richmond KY 40475-3100

BARKLEY, JOHN R, POLYMER COMPOSITES & STRUCTURE, FINE PARTICLES. *Current Pos:* Res physicist, Cent Res Dept, 66-81, SR RES ASSOC, ELECTRONICS DEPT, E I DU PONT DE NEMOURS & CO, INC, 81- *Personal Data:* b Oswego, NY, Aug 22, 38; m 96, Elaine Carpenter; c 3. *Educ:* LeMoyne Col, BS, 60; Ohio Univ, MS, 63, PhD(physics), 66. *Res:* Low loadings of inorganic particulates that affect the physical and electrical properties of polymer composites and topography of polymer films; understanding relationships among process, structure and functioning of polyester films. *Mailing Add:* E I du Pont de Nemours & Co Inc PO Box 89 Circleville OH 43113. *Fax:* 740-474-0244

BARKLEY, LLOYD BLAIR, ORGANIC CHEMISTRY. *Current Pos:* RETIRED. *Personal Data:* b Ellwood City, Pa, Mar 10, 25; m 50; c 1. *Educ:* Pa State Univ, BS, 47; Univ Pittsburgh, MS, 50, PhD(org chem), 52. *Prof Exp:* Res chemist, Monsanto Chem Co, 52-56, res group leader, 56-61; dir res & vpres, Pa Indust Chem Corp, 62-69; mgr res, Newport Div, Tenneco Inc, 69-74; mem res staff, Southern Resins, Inc, 74-80. *Mem:* Am Chem Soc. *Res:* Carbon to carbon condensations; steroids; polymers. *Mailing Add:* 166 Hardwood Rd Pelzer SC 29669

BARKLEY, THEODORE MITCHELL, SYSTEMATIC BOTANY. *Current Pos:* PROF BOT & CUR HERBARIUM, KANS STATE UNIV, 61- *Personal Data:* b Modesto, Calif, May 14, 34; m 81. *Educ:* Kans State Univ, BS, 55; Ore State Univ, MS, 57; Columbia Univ, PhD(bot), 60. *Honors & Awards:* Gleason Award, 87. *Prof Exp:* Instr biol, Occidental Col, 60-61. *Concurrent Pos:* Mem, Ed Comt, Flora NAm Proj. *Mem:* Am Soc Plant Taxon; Bot Soc Am; Int Asn Plant Taxon. *Res:* Monographic studies of the genus Senecio; floristics of the Central Great Plains; flora of North America. *Mailing Add:* 1414 McCain Lane Manhattan KS 66502-4621. *Fax:* 785-532-6653; *E-Mail:* herbksc@ksu.edu

BARKMAN, ROBERT CLOYCE, COMPARATIVE PHYSIOLOGY. *Current Pos:* from asst prof to assoc prof biol, 69-82, PROF BIOL, SPRINGFIELD COL, 82- *Personal Data:* b Massillon, Ohio, Oct 10, 42; m 65; c 2. *Educ:* Wittenburg Univ, BA, 64; Univ Cincinnati, MS, 66, PhD(zool), 69. *Prof Exp:* Teaching asst biol, Univ Cincinnati, 64-66, 68-69. *Concurrent Pos:* Res biologist, US Environ Res Lab; fel NASA. *Mem:* Am Soc Zoologists; Am Inst Biol Sci; Sigma Xi; Fedn Am Scientists. *Res:* Development of culture methods for all life stages of the Atlantic silverside, Menidia; varying temperature, salinity and plankton on growth of otolith daily rings of marine fish; new ways to teach science. *Mailing Add:* Chem & Biol Dept Springfield Col 263 Alden St Springfield MA 01109-3707

BARKO, JOHN WILLIAM, AQUATIC ECOLOGY. *Current Pos:* RES BIOLOGIST, WATERWAYS EXP STA, US ARMY CENGRS, 75- *Personal Data:* b Detroit, Mich, June 28, 47; m 68; c 1. *Educ:* Mich State Univ, BS, 72, PhD(bot), 75. *Prof Exp:* Teaching asst biol, 72-75, asst prof bot, Mich State Univ, 75. *Mem:* Int Asn Aquatic Vascular Plant Biologists; Am Inst Biol Sci; Am Soc Limnol & Oceanog; Ecol Soc Am. *Res:* Physiological ecology of vascular aquatic plants; ecosystem metabolism (fresh water). *Mailing Add:* Waterways Exp Sta US Army CEngrs 3909 Halls Ferry Rd Vicksburg MS 39180-6199

BARKS, PAUL ALLAN, ORGANIC CHEMISTRY, CHEMICAL EDUCATION. *Current Pos:* HEAD DEPT CHEM, NORTH HENNEPIN COMMUNITY COL, 71- *Personal Data:* b Ft Morgan, Colo, May 28, 36; m 60, Nancy Egbert; c Karen, Cynthia & Erica. *Educ:* Grinnell Col, BA, 58; Iowa State Univ, PhD(org chem), 63. *Prof Exp:* Instr chem, Hamline Univ, 63-64; asst prof, St Norbert Col, 64-68; asst prof, Monmouth Col, Ill, 68-71. *Concurrent Pos:* NSF undergrad instr equip grant, 65-, res participation for chem teachers grant, 65-67; vis prof, Univ Ky, 80, Macalester Col, 83-88 & Carleton Col, 87-88. *Mem:* Am Chem Soc. *Res:* Photochemical reactions of organic chemicals and natural products, particularly amino acids; effectual teaching; manuscript reviewer of chemistry textbooks. *Mailing Add:* Dept Chem North Hennepin Community Col Minneapolis MN 55445. *Fax:* 612-424-0929; *E-Mail:* pbarks@nh.cc.mn.us

BARKSDALE, CHARLES MADSEN, PHARMACOKINETICS, DRUG METABOLISM. *Current Pos:* scientist pharmacokinetics & drug metabolism, 88-90, sr scientist, 90-94, RES ASSOC, PARKE DAVIS PHARMACEUT RES DIV, WARNER LAMBERT CO, 94- *Personal Data:* b San Diego, Calif, June 20, 47. *Educ:* Univ Calif, San Diego, BA(chem) & BA(math), 70; Columbia Pac Univ, MS, 82, PhD(chem), 83. *Prof Exp:* Res neurochemist, Dept Psychiat, Vet Admin Hosp, Madison, Wis, 82-88; res assoc, Dept Psychiat, Univ Wis-Madison, 85-86, sr res assoc, 86-87, res scientist, 87-88. *Concurrent Pos:* NIH res fel, Dept Psychiat, Univ Wis-Madison, 83-86. *Mem:* Endocrine Soc; Soc Neurosci; Int Soc Psychoneuroendocrinol; Soc Adolescent Med; AAAS; fel Royal Entom Soc London. *Res:* Development of radioimmunoassays in both academic and industrial positions; psychoneuroendocrine research in plasma, CSF, and urine of human and research animals; RIA development of drugs, hormones and other substances; author of various publications. *Mailing Add:* Parke-Davis Pharmacokinetics 2800 Plymouth Rd Ann Arbor MI 48105-2430

BARKSDALE, JAMES BRYAN, JR, MATHEMATICS. *Current Pos:* asst prof, 68-73, PROF MATH, WESTERN KY UNIV, 73- *Personal Data:* b Blytheville, Ark, Dec 29, 40; m 72. *Educ:* Univ Ark, BA, 64, MS, 66, PhD(math), 69. *Prof Exp:* Instr high sch, 63-64. *Concurrent Pos:* Mu Alpha Theta vol lectr, 69- *Mem:* AAAS; Math Asn Am; Am Math Soc. *Res:* Analysis in normed vector spaces, especially research involving integrals and differentials of vector functions. *Mailing Add:* Western Ky Univ Bowling Green KY 42101-3576

BARKSDALE, LANE W, MICROBIOLOGY. *Current Pos:* from asst prof to assoc prof microbiol, 54-69, PROF MICROBIOL, SCH MED, NY UNIV, 69- *Personal Data:* b Emporia, Va, Nov 23, 14; m. *Educ:* Univ NC, AB, 38, MA, 40; NY Univ, PhD(microbiol), 53. *Prof Exp:* Chief bact, 406 Med Gen Lab, Tokyo, 46-49; fel, Pasteur Inst, Paris, 53-54. *Concurrent Pos:* Vis prof, Osaka, 60-61; Guggenheim fel, 70-71; chmn subcomt Corynebacterium & Related Organisms, Int Comt Systematic Bact, 74- *Mem:* Am Soc Microbiol; Soc Gen Physiol; Harvey Soc; NY Acad Med; Am Acad Microbiol. *Res:* Biology of Corynebacterium, Mycobacterium, Nocardia group and its viruses. *Mailing Add:* Dept Microbiol NY Univ Sch Med 550 First Ave Med Sci Bldg 147 New York NY 10016-6451

BARKSDALE, RICHARD DILLON, CIVIL ENGINEERING, GEOTECHNICAL ENGINEERING. *Current Pos:* from asst prof to assoc prof, 65-76, PROF CIVIL ENG, GA INST TECHNOL, 76- *Personal Data:* b Orlando, Fla, May 2, 38; m 62, Bonnie McClung; c Cheryl L & Richelle D. *Educ:* Ga Inst Technol, BCE, 62, MS, 64; Purdue Univ, PhD(civil eng), 66. *Honors & Awards:* Norman Medal, Am Soc Civil Eng. *Prof Exp:* Spec lectr civil technol, Southern Technol Inst, 58-60. *Concurrent Pos:* Mem, Comt Mechanics Earth Masses & Layered Systs, Hwy Res Bd, Nat Acad Sci-Nat Res Coun, chmn, Comt Strength & Deformation Characteristics Pavement Sect, 72-78, mem, 72-; vpres & consult, Soil Systs Inc, 74-80; mem, Comt Placement Improvement Soils & Pavement Design, Am Soc Civil Engrs. *Mem:* Int Soc Soil Mech & Found Eng; Am Soc Civil Engrs. *Res:* Stress distribution in earth masses; soil-structure interaction; development of a rational pavement design procedure. *Mailing Add:* Sch Civil Eng Ga Inst Technol Atlanta GA 30332-0001. *Fax:* 404-894-2281

BARKWORTH, MARY ELIZABETH, PLANT TAXONOMY. *Current Pos:* asst prof, 79-85, dir, Intermountain Herbarium, 80-82 & 84, ASSOC PROF BIOL, UTAH STATE UNIV, 82- *Personal Data:* b Marlborough, UK, Aug 5, 41; Can citizen. *Educ:* Univ BC, BSc, 61; Western Wash Univ, MEd, 70; Wash St Univ, PhD(bot), 75. *Prof Exp:* Res scientist Taxon Can Grasses, Biosysts Res Inst Agr Can, 75-79. *Mem:* Int Asn Plant Taxon; Am Soc Plant Taxonomists. *Res:* Taxonomy of North American Gramineae; evolutionary relations within the Gramineae, particularly members of Stipeae and Triticeae. *Mailing Add:* Dept Biol Utah State Univ Logan UT 84322-5305

BARLAS, JULIE S, COMPUTER SECURITY, COMPUTER-AIDED SOFTWARE ENGINEERING TOOLS. *Current Pos:* MEM TECH STAFF COMPUTER SCI, MITRE CORP, 86- *Personal Data:* b Eugene, Ore, Sept 15, 44; m 74. *Educ:* Univ Ore, BA, 65; Univ Pittsburgh, MLS, 67; Harvard Univ, MS, 85. *Prof Exp:* Librn educ, Harvard Univ, 67-70, appl sci, 70-86. *Res:* Supervision of computer security aspects of software acquired on contract by the federal government; computer-aided software engineering tools; formal verification of software; user interfaces. *Mailing Add:* 360 Littleton Rd Apt 18B Chelmsford MA 01824

BARLETTA, MICHAEL ANTHONY, PHARMACOLOGY, TOXICOLOGY. *Current Pos:* ASSOC PROF, COL PHARM, ST JOHN'S UNIV, 73-; LECTR PHARMACOL, USPHS PHYSICIANS ASST PROG, 77- *Personal Data:* b Brooklyn, NY, July 15, 42; m 66; c 2. *Educ:* St John's Univ, BS, 65, MS, 70; NY Med Col, PhD(pharmacol), 73. *Concurrent Pos:* Consult pharmacologist, Queens Gen Med Ctr, 75- & Cath Med Ctr Brooklyn & Queens, 76- *Mem:* Am Col Clin Pharmacol; Am Pharmaceut Asn; Am Soc Hosp Pharmacists. *Res:* Cardiovascular pharmacology; establishing animal models for myocardial infarction, ischemic coronary vascular disturbances, atherosclerosis; testing known and unknown drugs against these models in an effort to diminish or prevent these conditions. *Mailing Add:* Dept Pharm St John's Univ 8000 Utopia Pkwy Jamaica NY 11439

BARLOW, ANTHONY, polymer chemistry, for more information see previous edition

BARLOW, CHARLES F, MEDICINE. *Current Pos:* PROF NEUROL, HARVARD MED SCH, 63- *Personal Data:* b Mason City, Iowa, Nov 10, 23; m 53; c 3. *Educ:* Univ Chicago, SB, 45, MD, 47. *Prof Exp:* Intern, Johns Hopkins Hosp, 47-48; jr asst resident, Boston Children's Hosp, 48-49; resident neurol, Clins Univ Chicago, 51-53, instr, 53-55, asst prof, 55-63. *Concurrent Pos:* Emer chief neurologist, Children's Hosp, Med Ctr, Boston, emer dir, Ment Retardation Res Prog; consult, Peter Bent Brigham Hosp, Boston Hosp Women & Beth Israel Hosp, Boston. *Mem:* Am Acad Neurol; Am Asn Neuropath; Am Neurol Asn. *Res:* Clinical neurology of children; blood-brain barrier with isotope labeled compounds; neuropathology. *Mailing Add:* 300 Longwood Ave Harvard Med Sch Boston MA 02115-5737

BARLOW, CLYDE HOWARD, BIOMEDICAL SPECTROSCOPY, BIOINORGANIC CHEMISTRY. *Current Pos:* MEM FAC, DEPT CHEM, EVERGREEN STATE COL, 81- *Educ:* Ariz State Univ, PhD(chem), 73. *Mailing Add:* Evergreen State Col Olympia WA 98505-0001

BARLOW, EDWARD J(OSEPH), ELECTRONICS, COMPUTER SCIENCE. *Current Pos:* RETIRED. *Personal Data:* b East Orange, NJ, Sept 5, 20; m 46; c 3. *Educ:* Cooper Union, BEE, 42. *Honors & Awards:* Inst Radio Engrs Award, 49; Public Serv Award, NASA, 88. *Prof Exp:* Mem staff, Rand Corp, 48-58, dir, Interdiv projs, 58-60; vpres & opers gen mgr, Aerospace Corp, 60-68; group vpres int, Varian Assocs, 68-69, group vpres instruments, 69-76, group pres, instruments, 76-78, vpres, res & develop, 78-84. *Concurrent Pos:* Mem tech capabilities panel, President's Sci Adv Comt, 54, adv panel aeronaut, Off Secy Defense, 59; chmn aerospace vehicle panel, Air Force Sci Adv Bd, 60; mem large launch vehicle planning group, NASA Dept Defense, 61; mem report review comt, Nat Acad Sci, 74-91. *Mem:* Nat Acad Eng. *Res:* General engineering. *Mailing Add:* 334 Langton Ave Los Altos CA 94022

BARLOW, GEORGE, PHYSIOLOGY. *Current Pos:* assoc prof, 64-66, PROF BIOL, HEIDELBERG COL, 66- *Personal Data:* b Springfield, Mass, Dec 13, 26; m 51; c 2. *Educ:* Syracuse Univ, AB, 50; Princeton Univ, MS, 52, PhD, 53. *Prof Exp:* Instr physiol, Col Med, Univ Tenn, 53-57, asst prof, 57-63, instr clin physiol, 53-55, from asst prof to assoc prof, 55-63, asst dir clin physiol labs, 57-63. *Concurrent Pos:* Nat Acad Sci-Nat Res Coun travel award, Int Cong Physiol Sci, Buenos Aires, Arg, 58; Rockefeller Found travel award, Latin Am, 59; vis prof, Univ Valle, Colombia, 60-61; consult, John Gaston Hosp, Tenn. *Mem:* AAAS; Am Physiol Soc; Sigma Xi. *Res:* Adrenal cortex, water and electrolyte metabolism; capillary permeability; circulation and renal physiology. *Mailing Add:* 21 Walnut St Tiffin OH 44883

BARLOW, GEORGE WEBBER, ANIMAL BEHAVIOR, ICHTHYOLOGY. *Current Pos:* assoc prof, Univ Calif, Berkeley, 66-70, Miller prof, 70-71, prof, 70-92, EMER PROF ZOOL, UNIV CALIF, BERKELEY, 93- *Personal Data:* b Long Beach, Calif, June 15, 29; m 55, Gerta Offczarczyk; c Linda A (Kelly), Bicka A & Nora G. *Educ:* Univ Calif, Los Angeles, AB, 51, MA, 55, PhD(zool), 58. *Prof Exp:* From asst prof to assoc prof zool, Univ Ill, Champaign, 60-66. *Concurrent Pos:* NIMH fel, Max Planck Inst Physiol Behav, Ger, 58-60; mem, NSF Adv Panel Psychobiol, 65-68; Am Inst Biol Sci vis biologist, 69; US rep, Int Ethology Comt, 69-75; fel, Calif Acad Sci, 76; resident scholar, Ctr Interdisciplinary Res, Univ Bielefeld, 77-78; ed, Cambridge Studies Behav Biol; consult ed, J Comp Psychol. *Mem:* Fel AAAS; Am Soc Zoologists; Am Soc Ichthyologists & Herpetologists; fel Animal Behav Soc (pres elect, 77, pres, 79); Sigma Xi. *Res:* Lab and field studies on social behavior of New World cichlid fishes; eco-ethology of coral-reef fishes; nature of patterned movements; biology of social systems. *Mailing Add:* Dept Integrative Biol Univ Calif Berkeley CA 94720-3160. *E-Mail:* barlowgw@garnet.berkeley.edu

BARLOW, HORACE BASIL, PHYSIOLOGY. *Current Pos:* RETIRED. *Personal Data:* b Chesham Bois, Eng, Dec 8, 21; m 80, Miranda Weston-Smith; c Oscar, Ida, Pepita, Rebecca, Natasha, Naomi & Emily. *Educ:* Cambridge Univ, BA, 43; Harvard Univ, MD, 46; Univ Col Hosp London, MBB, 47. *Honors & Awards:* Edward D Tillyer Award, Optical Soc Am, 92; Crook Medal, Worshipful Co Spectacle Makers, 93; Australia Prize, 93; Royal Medal, Royal Soc London, 93. *Prof Exp:* Fel, Trinity Col, 50-54; demonstr & asst dir, Res Physiol Lab, King's Col, 54-63; prof physiol optics, Univ Calif, Berkeley, 63-73; Royal Soc res prof, Cambridge Univ, 73-87. *Concurrent Pos:* Ed, J Physiol, 72-77. *Mem:* Physiol Soc; Exp Psychol Soc; Brain Res Asn. *Res:* Contributed articles to professional journals. *Mailing Add:* Univ Cambridge Physiol Lab Downing St Cambridge CB2 1EW England

BARLOW, JAMES A, JR, PHYSICAL GEOLOGY. *Current Pos:* GEOLOGIST, BARLOW & HAUN, INC, 57- *Personal Data:* b Englewood, NJ, Sept 4, 23; m 46; c 2. *Educ:* Middlebury Col, BA, 49; Univ Wyo, MA, 50, PhD(geol), 53. *Prof Exp:* Geologist, Ohio Oil Co, 52-53 & Forest Oil Corp, 53-57. *Mem:* Fel Geol Soc Am; Am Asn Petrol Geologists. *Res:* Oil and gas exploration, stratigraphy and structure. *Mailing Add:* 1420 S David St Casper WY 82601

BARLOW, JOEL WILLIAM, CHEMICAL ENGINEERING, POLYMER ENGINEERING. *Current Pos:* from asst prof to prof, 73-84, Z D Bonner prof, 84-90, CULLEN PROF CHEM ENG, UNIV TEX, AUSTIN, 90- *Personal Data:* b Burbank, Calif, May 2, 42; m 65; c 2. *Educ:* Univ Wis, BS, 64, MS, 65, PhD(chem eng), 70. *Prof Exp:* Fel mat & thermodyn, Wash Univ, 68-70; res engr plastics, Union Carbide Corp, Bound Brook, NJ, 70-73. *Concurrent Pos:* Asst chmn, Dept Chem Eng, Univ Tex, Austin, 86-90, grad adv chem eng, 90- *Mem:* Am Chem Soc; Am Inst Chem Engrs; Soc Plastics Engrs. *Res:* Polymer processing and physics; thermodynamics of polymer blends; polymer flammability characterization; reaction injection molding; selective laser sintering. *Mailing Add:* Chem Eng Dept Univ Texas Austin TX 78712-1026

BARLOW, JOHN SUTTON, NEUROPHYSIOLOGY, BIOPHYSICS. *Current Pos:* Asst neurol, 57-61, NEUROPHYSIOLOGIST, NEUROL SERV, MASS GEN HOSP, 61- *Personal Data:* b Raleigh, NC, June 10, 25; m 50, Sibylle Jahrreiss; c Thomas W, Robert S & Lisa K. *Educ:* Univ NC, BS, 44, MS, 48; Harvard Univ, MD, 53. *Concurrent Pos:* Clin & res fel neurol, Mass Gen Hosp, 53-57; res assoc, Mass Inst Technol, 54-64, res affil, 64-; asst, Harvard Med Sch, 57-61, res assoc, 61-69, prin res assoc, 69-78, sr res assoc, 79-; spec trainee, Nat Inst Neurol Dis & Stroke, 58-61, res career development award, 62-71, res grant, 62-88; consult, Vet Admin Med Ctr, Boston, Jamaica Plain, Dept Neurol, 79-89, part-time staff, 89-; consult staff, Dept Neruol, New Eng Med Ctr, 79-; consult ed, EEG Clin Neurophysiol, 70-85; mem, Panel Neurocommunication & Biophys, Int Brain Res Orgn; mem, Panel Rev Neurol Devices, Fed Drug Admin, 74-76; Fogarty sr int fel, 79; US sr scientist award, Alexander von Humboldt Found, Ger, 79; consult staff, New Eng Med Ctr, Dept Neurol, 79-; vis scientist, Nat Prog Comt Scholar Commun People's Repub China, 88, sci visitor, USSR, 81, 82 & 88, NAS-USSR Acad Exchange Prog; sci visitor, Nat Acad Sci-USSR Acad Exchange Prog, USSR, 81, 82 & 88; vis scientist, Nat Prog Comt Scholar Commun, Peoples Repub of China, 88. *Mem:* Am Clin Neurophys Soc (pres, 75-76); Am Neurol Asn; Am Acad Neurol; Am Geophys Union; Soc Neurosci. *Res:* Electrical activity of the nervous system in man; computer design and development; medical geography and geophysics; animal navigation. *Mailing Add:* Mass Gen Hosp Boston MA 02114

BARLOW, JON CHARLES, ORNITHOLOGY. *Current Pos:* from asst prof to assoc prof, 65-80, dir, Mus Studies Prog, Sch Grad Studies, 89-95, PROF ZOOL, UNIV TORONTO, 80-, ASSOC DIR, GRAD COORDR, MUS STUDIES PROG, 95-; CUR, CTR BIODIVERSITY & CONSERV BIOL, ROYAL ONT MUS, 65- *Personal Data:* b Jacksonville, Ill, Oct 31, 35; m 81, Margaret L May; c Melinda, Tim, Amy, Deron & Ella. *Educ:* Knox Col, Ill, BA, 57; Univ Kans, MA, 60, PhD(zool), 65. *Prof Exp:* Res chemist, Corn Prod Refining Co, 57-58; teaching asst zool, Univ Kans, 58-62 & 63-64; field assoc mammal, Am Mus Natural Hist, NY, 62-63; asst prof biol, Rockhurst Col, 64-65. *Concurrent Pos:* head, Dept Ornith, Royal Ont Mus, 65-76; ed, Wilson Bull, 78-84; counr, Am Ornithologists Union, 80-83; chmn bd dirs, Metrop Toronto Zool Soc, 85-; mem manage bd, Metro Toronto Zoo, 92- *Mem:* Fel AAAS; fel Am Ornithologists Union; Cooper Ornith Soc (vpres, 83-85); Am Soc Zoologists; Animal Behav Soc; Wilson Ornith Soc (vpres, 85-87, pres, 89-91); Soc Can Ornith (pres-elect, 87-89, pres, 89-91). *Res:* Avian systematics and mammalian ecology and zoogeography; avian behavior, especially of vireos; introduced passer vocalizations evolutionary genetics. *Mailing Add:* CBCB Royal Ont Mus Toronto ON M5S 2C6 Can. *Fax:* 416-586-5863; *E-Mail:* jonb@rom.on.ca

BARLOW, MARK OWENS, MISSILE GUIDANCE, ANALOG & DIGITAL. *Current Pos:* HEFU ENGR, HERCULES INC/ALLIANT TECHSYSTS, 90- *Personal Data:* b Salt Lake City, Utah, July 24, 46; m 74, Carroll M Kerske; c Marie, Miriam, Thomas, Carl, Laura, James & Michael. *Educ:* Univ Utah, BS, 71, ME, 72. *Prof Exp:* Missile guidance engr, Boeing, Aerospace Co, 72-78; software engr, TRW, 78-81; elec engr, Diasonics Inc, 81-84, Cordin Co, 84-90. *Concurrent Pos:* Consult, 90- *Res:* ECM resistant high altitude guidance. *Mailing Add:* 6750 N 6500 W American Fork UT 84003-9735. *Fax:* 801-251-2639; *E-Mail:* mark_barlow@atk.com (work), bhontl@utah.uswest.net (home)

BARLOW, RICHARD EUGENE, MATHEMATICAL STATISTICS. *Current Pos:* assoc prof opers res & statist, 63-69, PROF OPERS RES & STATIST, UNIV CALIF, BERKELEY, 69- *Personal Data:* b Galesburg, Ill, Jan 12, 31; m 56; c 4. *Educ:* Knox Col, BA, 53; Univ Ore, MA, 55; Stanford Univ, PhD, 60. *Prof Exp:* Adv res engr math, Sylvania Electronic Defense Lab, Gen Tel & Electronics Corp, 57-60, mem tech staff, Res Labs, 61-62; mem tech staff, Inst Defense Analysis, 60-61. *Concurrent Pos:* Dir opers res ctr, Univ Calif, Berkeley; consult, Rand Corp, Calif, 63-69; vis prof statist, Fla State Univ, 75-76; assoc ed, J Inst Math Statist, 75- *Mem:* Fel Inst Math Statist; fel Am Statist Asn. *Res:* Statistics; probability theory and its applications, especially mathematical theory of reliability. *Mailing Add:* IEOR Dept Univ Calif 4135 Etcheverry Hall Berkeley CA 94720-0001

BARLOW, ROBERT BROWN, neurophysiology, for more information see previous edition

BARLOZZARI, TERESA, EXPERIMENTAL BIOLOGY. *Current Pos:* SR SCIENTIST, BASF BIORES CORP. *Personal Data:* b Masmassamartana, Italy, May 23, 54. *Mailing Add:* BASF Biores Corp 100 Research Dr Worcester MA 01605-4314. *Fax:* 617-876-8706

BARMACK, NEAL HERBERT, NEUROBIOLOGY, NEUROPHYSIOLOGY. *Current Pos:* SR SCIENTIST & CHMN, R S DOW NEUROL SCI INST, 82- *Personal Data:* b New York, NY, Aug 23, 42; m 64; c 2. *Educ:* Univ Mich, BS, 63; Univ Rochester, PhD, 70. *Prof Exp:* Asst lectr psychol, Univ Rochester, 68-69; from res assoc to sr res assoc neurophysiol, Dept Ophthal, Good Samaritan Hosp & Med Ctr, Portland, assoc scientist, 75-80, sr scientist, Neurol Sci Inst, 80-81; assoc prof biol sci, Univ Conn, 81-82. *Mem:* Soc Neurosci; Am Physiol Soc; Int Brain Res Orgn. *Res:* Neural control of eye movements; plasticity of reflexive eye movements; the cellular and biochemical basis of cerebellar modulation of reflex function. *Mailing Add:* R S Dow Neurol Sci Inst Good Samaritan Hosp & Med Ctr Portland OR 97209. *Fax:* 503-229-7229; *E-Mail:* barmackn@ohsu.edu

BARMAN, SUSAN MARIE, NEUROPHYSIOLOGY, AUTONOMIC PHYSIOLOGY. *Current Pos:* Res assoc, 75-77, from instr to assoc prof, 77-96, PROF NEUROPHYSIOL, MICH STATE UNIV, 96- *Personal Data:* b Joliet, Ill, Aug 28, 49. *Educ:* Loyola Univ, Chicago, BS, 71, PhD(physiol), 76. *Honors & Awards:* Merit Award, NIH. *Concurrent Pos:* Sci consult, study sect, NIH, 84-; NIH res grant, 85-; prof, Dept Physiol, Mich State Univ. *Mem:* Soc Neurosci; Am Physiol Soc; AAAS; Sigma Xi; Int Soc Autonomic Nerv Syst. *Res:* Neural control of circulation; identification of areas of brain which are involved in control of blood pressure and heart rate. *Mailing Add:* Dept Pharmacol & Toxicol Mich State Univ East Lansing MI 48824-1317. *Fax:* 517-353-8915; *E-Mail:* barman@pilot.msu.edu

BARMATZ, MARTIN BRUCE, ACOUSTICS, MICROWAVE MATERIAL PROCESSING & LOW TEMPERATURE PHYSICS. *Current Pos:* MEM TECH STAFF & TECH GROUP LEADER, PHYS ACOUST & CONTAINERLESS SCI GROUP, JET PROPULSION LAB, 78- *Personal Data:* b Los Angeles, Calif, May 25, 38; m 61; c 2. *Educ:* Univ Calif, Los Angeles, BA, 60, MA, 62, PhD(physics), 66. *Prof Exp:* Asst prof physics in residence, Univ Calif, Los Angeles, 66-67; mem tech staff, Condensed State Physics Res Dept, Bell Tel Labs 67-78. *Concurrent Pos:* Consult, Technol Unlimited. *Mem:* Acoust Soc Am; Am Phys Soc; Mat Res Soc; Am Ceramic Soc. *Res:* Critical point phenomena; sound velocity, sound attenuation, sound dispersion measurement and nonlinear acoustics; microwave processing of materials. *Mailing Add:* Jet Propulsion Lab 4800 Oak Grove Dr Pasadena CA 91109. *Fax:* 818-393-4878; *E-Mail:* barmatz@squid.jpl.nasa.gov

BARMBY, DAVID STANLEY, PHYSICS. *Current Pos:* ASSOC, HYDROCARBON ENG ASSOCS, INC, PA, 93- *Personal Data:* b Hull, Eng, Mar 4, 28; m 57, Drusilla A Brook; c Jonathan, Gillian & Sarah. *Educ:* Univ Leeds, BSc, 49, PhD(physics), 54. *Prof Exp:* Physicist, Wool Industs Res Asn, Eng, 54-57; physicist, Sun Co, Inc, 57-66, chief petrol processing sect, Basic Res Div, 66-70, chief explor petrol res, Corp Res Div, 70-75, mgr technol assessment, 75-84, dir advan technol, corp hq, Randor, Pa, 84-88. *Mem:* Am Phys Soc. *Res:* Solid state physics and catalysis; paraffin wax structures and phase transitions; correlations between physical properties and structure of solids; infrared spectroscopy of polymers; fuel technology; alternative energy technology. *Mailing Add:* 1237 Hunt Club Lane Media PA 19063

BARMBY, JOHN G(LENNON), SYSTEMS ENGINEERING. *Current Pos:* ENG & MGT CONSULT, 90- *Personal Data:* b Lawrence, Mass, Oct 22, 22; m 55, Ellaveen Childress; c John S & Grant C. *Educ:* Mass Inst Technol, BS, 44; Middlebury Col, AB, 44; George Washington Univ, MA, 51; Am Univ, PhD(pub admin), 57. *Prof Exp:* Aeronaut res scientist, Langley Lab, NASA, 44-48; aeronaut res engr, Bur Aeronaut, US Navy Dept, 48-57, asst br head, 57-59; mem tech staff, Systs & Opers Anal, Weapons Systs Eval Div, Inst Defense Anal, 59-62; mem staff systs anal, Bellcomm, Inc, Am Tel & Tel Co, 62-64; sr staff assoc, Ill Inst Technol Res Inst, 64-71; sr tech adv nat security, US Gen Acct Off, 71-90. *Concurrent Pos:* Adj prof, Univ Va, 69-81, Marymount Univ, 93- *Mem:* Assoc fel Am Inst Aeronaut & Astronaut; Am Soc Pub Admin; Inst Elec & Electronics Engrs; Am Eng Asn. *Res:* Engineering management; pioneer in guided missiles; systems analysis and research and development management of space and weapons programs; trade-off studies of the technical performance of various systems with cost, schedule and reliability factors. *Mailing Add:* 924 Fairway Dr NE Vienna VA 22180

BARMORE, FRANK E, PHYSICS. *Current Pos:* lectr, 77-83, asst prof, 83-86, ASSOC PROF, DEPT PHYSICS, UNIV WIS-LA CROSSE, 86- *Personal Data:* b Manhattan, Kans, June 20, 38; m 67, Irene E Wilcox; c Nathaniel & Christopher. *Educ:* Wash State Univ, BS, 60; Univ Wis-Madison, MS, 63, PhD(physics), 73. *Prof Exp:* Sr technician, Thule Field Sta, Greenland, Am Geog Soc, 61-62; teaching asst, Dept Physics, Univ Wis-Madison, 66; asst prof natural sci & actg chmn interdisciplinary div, Milton Col, 70-73; proj assoc, Dept Physics, Univ Wis-Madison, 73-74; asst prof physics, Mid-East Tech Univ, Ankara, 74-76; res assoc, Dept Physics, Univ Calgary, 76-77; proj scientist, Ctr Res Exp Space Sci, York Univ, 77-78. *Mem:* Optical Soc Am; AAAS; Am Geophys Union; Am Asn Physics Teachers; Sigma Xi; Soc Archit Historians. *Res:* Minor atmospheric constituents by ground-based spectroscopic techniques; modern optics; application of high resolution-luminosity interferometers to studies in astronomy and aeronomy; archaeoastronomy. *Mailing Add:* Dept Physics Cowley Hall Univ Wis La Crosse La Crosse WI 54601. *Fax:* 608-785-8403

BARNA, GABRIEL GEORGE, PROCESS OPTIMIZATION, PLASMA PROCESSING. *Current Pos:* TI FEL, TEX INSTRUMENTS INC, 72- *Personal Data:* b Mar 13, 46; US citizen; m 71, Betty L Collier; c Andrew & Adrienne. *Educ:* McGill Univ, BSc, 68, PhD(chem), 73. *Mem:* Electrochem Soc; Am Vacuum Soc. *Res:* Passive display technology; liquid crystal and electrochromic displays; fuel cells; plasma processing in semiconductor manufacturing; model-based process control; multivariate fault detection. *Mailing Add:* 1613 Morningstar Trail Richardson TX 75081. *Fax:* 972-995-1916; *E-Mail:* barna@spdc.ti.com

BARNAAL, DENNIS E, SOLID STATE PHYSICS. *Current Pos:* From asst prof to assoc prof, 64-74, PROF PHYSICS, LUTHER COL, 74-, HEAD DEPT, 86- *Personal Data:* b Sacred Heart, Minn, Jan 5, 36; m 62; c 3. *Educ:* Univ Minn, BS, 58, MS, 62, PhD(physics), 65. *Concurrent Pos:* Consult, Am Inst Prof Educ, 77-82, Oper Rec Inc, 79-81, Kaman Sci Corp, 80. *Mem:* Am Phys Soc; Am Asn Physics Teachers. *Res:* Pulsed nuclear magnetic resonance in solids; ice physics; wind energy research. *Mailing Add:* Dept Physics Luther Col Decorah IA 52101

BARNABEO, AUSTIN EMIDIO, ORGANIC CHEMISTRY, POLYMER CHEMISTRY. *Current Pos:* Chemist, 56-62, proj scientist, 62-69, res scientist, 69-81, SR RES SCIENTIST, UNION CARBIDE CORP, 81- *Personal Data:* b New York, NY, Feb 7, 33; m 56; c 2. *Educ:* Queens Col, BS, 54; Brooklyn Col, MS, 60. *Mem:* Am Chem Soc; Sigma Xi. *Res:* Polyhydroxyethers; epoxies; polyesters; polyethylene for wire and cable applications; cellular products. *Mailing Add:* 533 Spring Valley Dr Bridgewater NJ 08807

BARNABY, BRUCE E, PHYSICS, ELECTRICAL ENGINEERING. *Current Pos:* RETIRED. *Personal Data:* b Milwaukee, Wis, Sept 24, 29; m 57; c 6. *Educ:* DePaul Univ, BS, 51; Univ Notre Dame, PhD(physics), 60. *Prof Exp:* Res physicist, Eitel-McCullough, Inc, 60-63, proj engr, 63-65; sr proj engr, Eimac Div, Varian Assocs, 65-67; staff mem, Los Alamos Sci Lab, 67-70; dir supvr, Tube Develop Div, Sandia Labs, 70- *Mem:* Am Soc Testing & Mat; Am Nuclear Soc. *Res:* Electron physics technology, especially use of technology in industry. *Mailing Add:* 1828 Dartmouth Dr Albuquerque NM 87106

BARNARD, ADAM JOHANNES, PLASMA PHYSICS. *Current Pos:* from asst prof to assoc prof, 59-68, PROF PHYSICS, UNIV BC, 68- *Personal Data:* b Murraysburg, SAfrica, June 9, 29; m 57; c 4. *Educ:* Univ SAfrica, BSc, 49, MSc, 51; Glasgow Univ, PhD(physics), 54. *Prof Exp:* Sr lectr, Univ Natal, 54-59. *Mem:* Am Phys Soc; Can Asn Physicists. *Res:* Spectroscopic investigation of plasmas. *Mailing Add:* Dept Physics & Astron Univ BC 6224 Agr Rd Vancouver BC V6T 1Z1 Can

BARNARD, ANTHONY C L, COMPUTER SCIENCE. *Current Pos:* assoc prof biomath, 68-71, chmn dept comput & info sci, 72-78, assoc vpres acad affairs, 79-84, PROF COMPUT & INFO SCI, UNIV ALA, BIRMINGHAM, 71-, ASSOC PROF PHYSICS, 76-, DEAN GRAD SCH, 84- *Personal Data:* b Birmingham, Eng, Apr 30, 32; m 64; c 2. *Educ:* Univ Birmingham, Eng, BSc, 53, PhD(nuclear physics), 57, DSc(physics), 74, Univ Ala, Birmingham, MBA, 79. *Prof Exp:* Res physicist, Res Lab, Assoc Elec Industs, Ltd, 56-58; res assoc physics, Univ Iowa, 58-60; from instr to asst prof, Rice Univ, 60-66; mgr physics dept, Int Bus Mach Sci Ctr, 66-68. *Mem:* Am Phys Soc; Asn Comput Mach; Data Processing Mgt Asn; Inst Elec & Electronics Engrs Comput Soc. *Res:* Medical applications of physics and computer science. *Mailing Add:* Dept Comput Sci Univ Ala 1717 Seventh Ave S Birmingham AL 35294-0001

BARNARD, DONALD ROY, MEDICAL & VETERINARY ENTOMOLOGY, PEST-MANAGEMENT. *Current Pos:* res entomologist, 79-85, SUPVRY RES ENTOMOLOGIST, AGR RES SERV, USDA, 85- *Personal Data:* b Santa Ana, Calif, June 7, 46; m 67, Priscilla M Grier; c Jennifer E & David M. *Educ:* Calif State Univ, BS, 69, MA, 72; Univ Calif-Riverside, PhD(entom), 77. *Prof Exp:* Fel, Dept Zool-Entom, Col State Univ, 77-79. *Concurrent Pos:* Consult, US AID, Somali Dem Repub, 81-83, World Health Orgn, 82-85, Dept Defense, Armed Forces Pest Mgt Bd, 85-, Repub S Africa, Karoo Paralysis Proj, 88-; adj asst prof, Dept Entom, Okla State Univ, 85-; adj assoc prof, Dept Entom-Nemat, Univ Fla, 89-; mem, Fla Coord Coun Mosquito Control, 90- *Mem:* Entom Soc Am; Entom Soc Can; Ecol Soc Am; Am Mosquito Control Asn; Soc Vector Ecol. *Res:* Integrated pest management and population ecology of arthropod pests of humans and domestic livestock. *Mailing Add:* 4403 NW 77th Terr Gainesville FL 32606. *Fax:* 352-374-5922; *E-Mail:* drbarn@nervm.nerdc.ufl.edu

BARNARD, GARLAND RAY, acoustics; deceased, see previous edition for last biography

BARNARD, JOHN J, ASTROPHYSICS. *Current Pos:* PHYSICIST, HEAVY ION FUSION PROJ, LAWRENCE LIVERMORE NAT LAB, 87- *Educ:* Calif Inst Technol, BS, 77; Univ Calif Berkeley, MA, 79, PhD(astron), 84. *Prof Exp:* Nat Res Coun resident res assoc, NASA, Goddard Space Flight Ctr, Greenbelt, MD, 84-86. *Mem:* Am Astron Soc; Am Phys Soc. *Res:* Heavy ion beam-driven inertial fusion; accelerator physics; physics of beams; astrophysical plasma physics. *Mailing Add:* Lawrence Livermore Nat Lab L-440 Livermore CA 94550

BARNARD, JOHN WESLEY, HEALTH PHYSICS, CRITICALITY SAFETY. *Current Pos:* HEALTH PHYSICIST, RADIATION APPL RES BR, WHITESHELL NUCLEAR RES ESTAB, ATOMIC ENERGY CAN LTD, 80- *Personal Data:* b St Thomas, Ont, Dec 26, 46, Canadian; m 71; c 1. *Educ:* McMaster Univ, BSc, 69; Univ Man, PhD, 76. *Prof Exp:* Res scientist, Man Inst Cell Biol, Man Cancer Treatment & Res Found, 77-80. *Concurrent Pos:* Fel, Dept Physics, Univ Man, 76-77; asst prof, Dept Internal Med, Univ Man, 77-80. *Mem:* Health Physics Soc. *Res:* Nuclear physics; health physics, including radiation dose control; external dosimetry, shielding and critical safety assessment; biosphere modeling for nuclear waste management and safety assessment; industrial radiation process development. *Mailing Add:* Box 1215 Lac du Bonnet MB R0E 1A0 Can

BARNARD, KATHRYN E, NURSING. *Current Pos:* assoc prof, 65-69, PROF NURSING, UNIV WASH, 72- *Personal Data:* b Omaha, Nebr, Apr 16, 38. *Educ:* Univ Nebr, Omaha, BS, 60; Boston Univ, MS, 62; Univ Wash, Seattle, PhD(nursing), 72. *Hon Degrees:* DSc, Univ Nebr, 90. *Honors & Awards:* Jessie M Scott Award, Am Nurses Asn, 82; Martha May Eliot Award, Am Pub Health Asn, 83. *Prof Exp:* Actg instr nursing, Univ Nebr-Omaha, 60-61 & Univ Wash, Seattle, 63-65. *Concurrent Pos:* Prin investr or co-investr grants, 72-; vis prof, Sch Nursing, Univ Ala, 81; mem bd dirs, Nat Ctr Clin Infant Progs, 81-; adj prof psychol, Univ Wash, 85-, assoc dean acad progs, 87-; mem, Adv Group Prev Res, NIMH, 90- *Mem:* Inst Med-Nat Acad Sci; Am Nurses Asn; Am Asn Univ Professors; Am Asn Ment Deficiency; fel Am Acad Nursing; Am Pub Health Asn; World Asn Infant Psychiat & Allied Disciplines. *Mailing Add:* Univ Wash Box 357920 Seattle WA 98195-7920

BARNARD, R JAMES, GLUCOSE TRANSPORT, DEGENERATIVE DISEASE PREVENTION. *Current Pos:* fel, Sch Med, Univ Calif, Los Angeles, 68-71, asst res cardiologist, 71-73, assoc res cardiologist, 73-79, assoc prof, Dept Kinesiol, 73-79, res cardiologist, Sch Med, 79-88, PROF KINESIOL, UNIV CALIF, LOS ANGELES, 79-, PROF MED, DIV CLIN NUTRIT, SCH MED, 88- *Personal Data:* b July 4, 37; m 78; c 1. *Educ:* Kent State Univ, BS, 59, MA, 63; Univ Iowa, PhD, 68. *Prof Exp:* Teacher, Hawthorne, Calif, 59-61. *Concurrent Pos:* Muscular Dystrophy Asn fel, 70-71; res career develop award, USPHS, 75-80; mem bd dirs & dir res, Nathan Pritkin Res Found, 81-88; mem, Coun Circulation, Am Heart Asn; mem, Coun Exercise & Nutrit. *Mem:* Am Col Sports Med (vpres, 74-75); Am Physiol Soc; Am Heart Asn; Am Diabetes Asn. *Res:* Exercise physiology; mechanisms responsible for adaptations associated with exercise and diet; regulation of glucose transport in skeletal muscle; value of diet and exercise as preventive measures for degenerative diseases. *Mailing Add:* Dept Physiol Sci Med Univ Calif 405 Hilgard Ave Los Angeles CA 90024-1568. *Fax:* 310-206-9184; *E-Mail:* jbarnard@physci.ucla.edu

BARNARD, ROBERT D(ANE), JR, ELECTRICAL ENGINEERING, COMPUTER ENGINEERING. *Current Pos:* assoc prof, 61-62, PROF ENG, WAYNE STATE UNIV, 65- *Personal Data:* b Chicago, Ill, Mar 17, 29; m 49; c 4. *Educ:* Polytech Inst Brooklyn, BEE, 52, MEE, 55; Case Inst Technol, PhD(solid state physics), 59. *Prof Exp:* Instr elec eng, Polytech Inst Brooklyn, 53-55 & Case Inst Technol, 55-59; mem tech staff, Bell Tel Labs, Inc, 59-65. *Mem:* Ind Math Soc; Am Math Soc; Inst Elec & Electronics Engrs; Soc Indust & Appl Math. *Res:* Systems and computer science; applied mathematics. *Mailing Add:* Col Eng Wayne State Univ Detroit MI 48202

BARNARD, ROGER W, COMPLEX ANALYSIS. *Current Pos:* PROF MATH TEX TECH UNIV, 73- *Personal Data:* b One, Ohie, Sept 20, 42. *Educ:* Kent State Univ, BS, 65 & MS, 68; Univ Md, PhD(math), 71. *Mem:* Am Math Soc; Soc Indust & Appl Math. *Mailing Add:* Dept Math Tex Tech Univ Lubbock TX 79409

BARNARD, WALTHER M, MINERALOGY, GEOCHEMISTRY. *Current Pos:* asst prof to assoc prof, 64-77, actg chmn, 86-87, PROF GEOL, STATE UNIV NY COL FREDONIA, 77-, CHMN, 87- *Personal Data:* b Hartford, Conn, May 30, 37. *Educ:* Trinity Col, Conn, BS, 59; Dartmouth Col, AM, 61; Pa State Univ, PhD(mineral), 65. *Concurrent Pos:* Res Corp res grant, 65-66; State Univ NY Res Found res grants-in-aid, 65-66, 67-68, 69-70 & 72-73; res grant, Energy & Resources Develop Agency, 75-77; res consult, Res Corp, Univ Hawaii, 81-82; collab res grant, SUNY Buffalo, 87-89. *Mem:* Geochem Soc; Am Asn Univ Professors; Am Chem Soc; fel Geol Soc Am; Mineral Soc Am; Am Geophys Union. *Res:* Environmental geochemistry; Hawaiian volcanic activity and history. *Mailing Add:* Dept Geoscis State Univ NY Fredonia NY 14063. *Fax:* 716-673-3405; *E-Mail:* barnard@fredonia.bitnet

BARNARD, WILLIAM SPRAGUE, PHYSICAL CHEMISTRY. *Current Pos:* RETIRED. *Personal Data:* b Hillsboro, Ill, May 20, 25; m 48, 75; c 3. *Educ:* Harvard Univ, AB, 47; Princeton Univ, PhD(phys chem), 51. *Prof Exp:* With res dept, Nat Lead Co, 50-53; group leader res div, Chicopee Mfg Corp, 53-57, dir woven prod, 57-64, dir res & develop, 64-69, mem bd dirs, 69-80, vpres res, 69-80, vpres sci affairs, 80-90. *Concurrent Pos:* Chmn exec comt, Textile Res Inst. *Mem:* Am Chem Soc; Am Asn Textile Chemists & Colorists. *Res:* Textile chemistry and resin technology; fibers and finishes; non-woven fabric technology. *Mailing Add:* 326 Ridgeview Rd Princeton NJ 08540-7627

BARNARTT, SIDNEY, ELECTROCHEMISTRY, CORROSION. *Current Pos:* RETIRED. *Personal Data:* b Toronto, Ont, July 31, 19; nat US; m 43, Charlotte Fox; c Sharon N & Elaine R. *Educ:* Univ Toronto, BA, 41, MA, 42, PhD(chem), 44. *Honors & Awards:* Bronze Medal, Brit Asn Advan Sci, 41. *Prof Exp:* Asst, Univ Toronto, 41-43; res chemist, Westinghouse Res Labs, 46-56, adv chemist, 56-62, mgr electrochem sect, 62-64; res chemist, Fundamental Res Lab, US Steel Corp, 64-72; dir electrochem res, Technicon Instruments Corp, 72; adv scientist, Westinghouse Bettis Atomic Power Lab, 72-84; consult chemist, 84-85. *Concurrent Pos:* Instr, Carnegie Inst Technol, 54. *Mem:* Am Chem Soc; Electrochem Soc; fel Am Inst Chemists; Nat Asn Corrosion Eng. *Res:* Adsorption; batteries; electrodeposition; electrode kinetics; corrosion. *Mailing Add:* 1358 Hillsdale Dr Monroeville PA 15146

BARNAWELL, EARL B, COMPARATIVE ENDOCRINOLOGY. *Current Pos:* RETIRED. *Personal Data:* b Maryville, Tenn, Nov 26, 22; m 46, Barbara Warr; c Eric B & Sean C. *Educ:* Univ Calif, Berkeley, AB, 51, MA, 54, PhD(endocrinol, zool), 64. *Prof Exp:* Exp animal biologist, Univ Calif, Berkeley, 54-60; asst prof, Univ Nebr, Lincoln, 64-69, dir inst cellular res, 66-71, assoc prof, Sch Biol Sci, 69-91. *Mem:* Sigma Xi. *Res:* Physiology and comparative endocrinology; organ culture. *Mailing Add:* 3400 J St Lincoln NE 68510. *E-Mail:* ebb@unlinfo.unl.edu

BARNEKOW, RUSSELL GEORGE, JR, BACTERIOLOGY, BACTERIAL PHYSIOLOGY. *Current Pos:* DEAN GRAD SCH & PROF LIFE SCI, SOUTHWEST MO STATE UNIV, 76- *Personal Data:* b Cleveland, Ohio, Jan 26, 32; m 57; c 4. *Educ:* Miami Univ, AB, 55; Kans State Univ, MS, 61, PhD(bact), 67. *Prof Exp:* From asst prof to assoc prof bact, Univ Mo-Kansas City, 62-76, from asst dean to assoc dean, Sch Grad Studies, 68-76, lectr, Sch Med, 75-76. *Mailing Add:* Dept Biol SW Mo State Univ 901 S Nat Springfield MO 65804-0027

BARNER, HENDRICK BOYER, SURGERY. *Current Pos:* from instr to assoc prof, 65-73, assoc dir, Div Cardiothoracic Surg, 87-91, PROF SURG, ST LOUIS UNIV, 73-, DIR CARDIOTHORACIC SURG RES, 87-; PROF SURG, WASHINGTON UNIV, 93- *Personal Data:* b Seattle, Wash, Feb 23, 33; m 61, Mechthild Boehnke; c Boyer H, Bjorn O & Bela M. *Educ:* Univ Wash, BS, 54, MD, 57; Am Bd Surg, dipl, 67; Am Bd Thoracic Surg, dipl, 68. *Prof Exp:* Instr surg, Univ Rochester, 64-65; chief, Div Cardiothoracic Surg, Long Island Jewish Med Ctr & prof surg, Albert Einstein Col Med, 91-93. *Concurrent Pos:* USPHS res fel, 64-65, fel cardiovasc surg, 65-66. *Mem:* Am Col Surg; AMA; Am Surg Asn; Am Asn Thoracic Surg; Soc Univ Surg; Soc Thoracic Surg. *Res:* Cardiovascular surgery and physiology. *Mailing Add:* Physicians Off Bldg No 2 11125 Dunn Rd Suite 211 St Louis MO 63136. *Fax:* 314-355-6573

BARNES, AARON, PLASMA ASTROPHYSICS. *Current Pos:* Res fel, 66-67, RES SCIENTIST, NASA-AMES RES CTR, 67- *Personal Data:* b Shenandoah, Iowa, May 9, 39; m 62, Barbara J Dean; c Christopher & Stephen. *Educ:* Univ Chicago, SB, 61, SM, 62, PhD(physics), 66. *Honors & Awards:* Except Sci Achievement Medal, NASA, 82; Sackler Distinguished lectr, Tel Aviv Univ, 86. *Concurrent Pos:* Vis scientist, Max-Planck Inst Physics & Astrophysics, 73; prin investr plasma analyzers, Pioneer 10 & 11 & Pioneer Venus Orbiter, NASA-Ames Res Ctr, 80-97. *Mem:* Am Phys Soc; Am Geophys Union; Am Astron Soc; AAAS; Sigma Xi; Int Astron Union; Astron Soc Pac. *Res:* Theoretical and observational investigation of the physics of interplanetary plasma and magnetic field; development of the theory of hydromagnetic waves and turbulence in collisionless plasmas; hydromagentic waves and turbulence. *Mailing Add:* 245-3 NASA Ames Res Ctr Moffett Field CA 94035-1000. *Fax:* 650-604-6779

BARNES, ALLEN LAWRENCE, PETROLEUM & MECHANICAL ENGINEERING. *Current Pos:* MGR RESERVOIR RES ENG, ATLANTIC RICHFIELD CO, 73- *Personal Data:* b Wooster, Ohio, Sept 28, 32; m 58; c 3. *Educ:* Ohio State Univ, BPetE, 55; Pa State Univ, MS, 60; Okla State Univ, PhD(mech eng), 68. *Prof Exp:* Engr, Magnolia Petrol Co, 55-57 & 57-58; res asst petrol eng, Pa State Univ, 58-59; res engr, Sinclair Res, Inc, 59-65, sect head reservoir & recovery eng, 66-68; teaching asst petrol eng, Okla State Univ, 65-66; tech asst, Explor & Prod Dept, Ashland Oil & Refining Co, 68-69, mgr tech serv, 69-71, energy specialist planning dept, Ashland Oil Inc, 71-73. *Mem:* Soc Petrol Engrs; Opers Res Soc Am. *Res:* New secondary recovery methods of economically extracting oil from natural reservoirs; use of heating techniques for the extraction of mineral wealth; mathematical simulation of hydraulic petroleum reservoir and network problems; risk analysis and economic analyses; managing production research programs. *Mailing Add:* 370 Forest Oaks Fairview TX 75069

BARNES, ARNOLD APPLETON, JR, METEOROLOGY, ATMOSPHERIC PHYSICS. *Current Pos:* res scientist, Meteorol Develop Lab, Tech Br, 61-62, res scientist, Meteorol Res Lab, Upper Atmosphere Br, 62-63, res scientist, Meteorol Lab, 63-71, res scientist, Weather Radar Br, 71-74, chief, Convective Cloud Physics Br, Meteorol Div, Air Force Cambridge Res Labs, 74-82, Chief, Cloud Physics Br, 82-87, sr scientist, Atmospheric Sci Div, Air Force Geophys Lab, 82-96, SR SCIENTIST, OPTICAL EFFECTS DIV, PHILLIPS LAB, HANSCOM AFB, 96- *Personal Data:* b Charleston, WVa, June 10, 30; m 60, Sally N Spall; c Judith B (Ball), Arnold A III & Amy B (Hurley). *Educ:* Princeton Univ, AB, 52; Mass Inst Technol, MSc, 57, PhD(meteorol), 62. *Prof Exp:* Asst meteorol, Mass Inst Technol, 56-61. *Concurrent Pos:* Consult, Allied Res Corp, 59-60; Dept Defense team leader, Nat Storm Prog, 83-85. *Mem:* AAAS; Am Meteorol Soc; Am Geophys Union. *Res:* Large scale dynamics of the atmosphere; transport of water vapor; numerical weather prediction; radar meteor trail winds and densities; radar acoustic low level temperature soundings; weather radar; cloud physics; aircraft icing; cirrus clouds; millimeter wave precipitation attenuation; mesoscale modelling; lighting and atmospheric electricity. *Mailing Add:* 32 Bradyll Rd Weston MA 02193-1711. *E-Mail:* barnes@plh.af.mil

BARNES, ASA, JR, PATHOLOGY, HEMATOLOGY. *Current Pos:* ASSOC PATHOLOGIST & DIR BLOOD BANK, LONG BEACH MEM MED CTR, 77-; CLIN PROF PATH, COL MED, UNIV CALIF, IRVINE, 77- *Personal Data:* b Cape Girardeau, Mo, Jan 30, 33; m 57; c 4. *Educ:* Univ Ky, BA, 55; Yale Univ, MD, 59. *Honors & Awards:* US Maj Gary Wratten Award, Asn Mil Surg, 69. *Prof Exp:* Intern, Univ Hosps, Cleveland, Ohio, 59-60; resident anat path, Grace-New Haven Community Hosp, New Haven, Conn, 63-65; resident clin path, Walter Reed Gen Hosp, Washington, DC, 65-67, asst chief, 67; blood prog officer, US Army, Vietnam, 67-68; pathologist, Armed Forces Inst Path, Washington, DC, 69-70; prof path, Sch Med, Univ Mo, Columbia, 70-77; chief clin path, Ellis Fischel Cancer Hosp, 74-76; sr scientist, Cancer Res Ctr, 74-76. *Mem:* AMA; Am Soc Clin Path; Asn Mil Surg; Am Asn Blood Banks; Col Am Pathologists. *Res:* Blood banking; morphologic hematology; clinical and anatomical pathology. *Mailing Add:* Dept Path 2801 Atlantic Ave Long Beach CA 90801

BARNES, BRUCE HERBERT, COMPUTER SCIENCE, MATHEMATICS. *Current Pos:* VPRES, SOFTWARE PRODUCTIVITY CONSORTIUM, 86- *Personal Data:* b Minneapolis, Minn, May 28, 31; m 53; c 3. *Educ:* Mich State Univ, BS, 53, MS, 58, PhD(math), 60. *Prof Exp:* Teaching asst math, Mich State Univ, 56-58, res instr comput sci, 58-60; sr res engr, Jet Propulsion Labs, 60-61; asst prof math, Pa State Univ, 61-65, assoc prof, 65-68; vis assoc prof, Univ Iowa, 68-69; assoc prof comput sci, Pa State Univ, 69-74; prog dir, Comput Sci Sect, NSF, 74-86. *Mem:* Am Math Soc; Asn Comput Mach; Inst Elec & Electronics Engrs Comput Soc. *Res:* Automata theory; numerical solution of ordinary differential equations; software engineering, especially decision tables and computer science education. *Mailing Add:* 40692 Manor House Rd Leesburg VA 20175-6515

BARNES, BURTON VERNE, FORESTRY, BOTANY. *Current Pos:* from asst prof to assoc prof, 63-70, PROF FORESTRY, SCH NATURAL RESOURCES, UNIV MICH, ANN ARBOR, 70-, FOREST BOTANIST, BOT GARDEN, 67- *Personal Data:* b Bloomington, Ill, Nov 4, 30; m 57; c 3. *Educ:* Univ Mich, BSF, 52, MF, 53, PhD(forestry), 59. *Honors & Awards:* Distinguished Serv Award, Univ Mich, 67. *Prof Exp:* Forester, Region VI, US Forest Serv, 53-59, res forester, Intermountain Forest & Range Exp Sta, 59-63. *Concurrent Pos:* NSF fel, Ger, 63-64; Danforth assoc, 69-; mem staff, Syst-Geobot Inst, Univ Gottingen, 70. *Mem:* Ecol Soc Am; Soc Am Foresters. *Res:* Forest ecology; dendrology; genecology; forest genetics; silviculture; biosystematics of Populus and Betula. *Mailing Add:* Sch Natural Resources Dana Bldg Univ Mich Main Campus 430 E University Ave Ann Arbor MI 48109-1115

BARNES, BYRON ASHWOOD, PHARMACOLOGY. *Current Pos:* head dept pharmacol & physiol, 57-70, dean, 70-89, EMER DEAN PHARM, ST LOUIS COL, 89- *Personal Data:* b Peoria, Ill, Mar 14, 27; m 48; c 2. *Educ:* St Louis Col Pharm, BS, 51; Univ Fla, MS, 53, PhD(pharmacol), 54. *Prof Exp:* Lab instr pharm, St Louis Col Pharm, 49-51; instr, Clin Lab, Sch Aviation Med, US Air Force, Gunter Air Force Base, 54-57. *Concurrent Pos:* Ed, Pharmaceut Trends; ed-in-chief, Rx Sat Continuing Educ Pharmacist Series. *Mem:* Am Pharmaceut Asn; Am Asn Cols Pharm; Royal Soc Health; Sigma Xi. *Res:* Continuing pharmacy education; drug abuse. *Mailing Add:* 10232 Richview Dr St Louis MO 63127

BARNES, C(ASPER) W(ILLIAM), JR, ELECTRICAL ENGINEERING. *Current Pos:* assoc prof, 67-69, PROF ENG, UNIV CALIF, IRVINE, 69- *Personal Data:* b Leesburg, Fla, Nov 24, 27; m 47. *Educ:* Univ Fla, BE, 50; Stanford Univ, PhD(elec eng), 54. *Prof Exp:* Engr, Sylvania Microwave Tube Lab, 54-56; sr res engr, Stanford Res Inst, 56-67. *Mem:* Am Phys Soc; Inst Elec & Electronics Engrs. *Res:* Digital signal processing; image processing; applied mathematics. *Mailing Add:* Dept Elec Eng Univ Calif Irvine CA 92717-0001

BARNES, CARL E, chemistry, for more information see previous edition

BARNES, CARL ELDON, AGRONOMY, FIELD CROPS. *Current Pos:* asst agronomist, 65-68, asst prof agron, 68-75, ASSOC PROF AGRON, NMEX STATE UNIV, 75-, SUPT CROPS RES, SOUTHEASTERN BR EXP STA, 68- *Personal Data:* b Clovis, NMex, June 9, 36; m 54; c 2. *Educ:* NMex State Univ, BS, 59, MS, 60. *Prof Exp:* Asst miller, Western Wheat Qual Lab, 60-61; res asst crops, Kans State Univ, 61-63; asst agronomist, Colo State Univ, 63-65. *Mem:* Am Soc Agron. *Res:* Crop production research; cotton breeding; water requirements. *Mailing Add:* 1904 W Briscoe Ave Artesia NM 88210

BARNES, CHARLES A, NUCLEAR ASTROPHYSICS, NUCLEAR PHYSICS. *Current Pos:* res fel, Calif Inst Technol, 53-55, sr res fel, 56-57, assoc prof, 57-62, prof, 62-92, EMER PROF PHYSICS, CALIF INST TECHNOL, 92- *Personal Data:* b Toronto, Ont, Dec 12, 21; nat US; m 50; c 2. *Educ:* McMaster Univ, BA, 43; Univ Toronto, MA, 44; Cambridge Univ, PhD(physics), 50. *Prof Exp:* Res physicist, Can-Brit Atomic Energy Proj, 44-46; instr physics, Univ BC, 50-53. *Concurrent Pos:* NSF sr fel, Niels Bohr Inst, Copenhagen, Denmark, 62-63; guest prof, Nordita, Copenhagen, Denmark, 73-74; Alexander von Humboldt sr fel, 86, Max Planck Inst, Heidelberg & Univ Munster, Ger, 87-88. *Mem:* Fel Am Phys Soc; AAAS. *Res:* Astrophysical nuclear reactions; nuclear structure physics; application of nuclear and accelerator techniques to other sciences and technologies. *Mailing Add:* Div Physics Math & Astron Calif Inst Technol Pasadena CA 91125. *Fax:* 626-564-8708

BARNES, CHARLES DEE, NEUROPHYSIOLOGY. *Current Pos:* PROF & CHMN VCAPP DEPT, WASH STATE UNIV, 84- *Personal Data:* b Carroll, Iowa, Aug 17, 35; m 57, Leona Wohler; c Tara, Teagen, Kalee & Kyler. *Educ:* Mont State Col, BS, 58; Univ Wash, MS, 61, Univ Iowa, PhD(physiol), 62. *Honors & Awards:* Career Develop Award, USPHS, 67. *Prof Exp:* Fel, Univ Calif, 62-64; from asst prof to assoc prof physiol, Ind Univ, 64-71; prof life sci, Ind State Univ, Terre Haute, 71-75; prof & chmn physiol, Tex Tech Univ Sch Med, 75-83. *Concurrent Pos:* Vis scientist, Inst Physiol, Univ Pisa, 68-69; prof physiol, Sch Med, Ind Univ, 71-75. *Mem:* Int Brain Res Orgn; Am Physiol Soc; Am Soc Pharmacol & Exp Therapeut; Radiation Res Soc; Soc Neurosci; fel AAAS. *Res:* Neurophysiology, neuropharmacology and radiation effects on the nervous system; interaction of different levels of the central nervous system, particularly brain stem-spinal cord. *Mailing Add:* Dept Pharmacol & Physiol Wash State Univ Pullman WA 99164-6520. *Fax:* 509-335-4650

BARNES, CHARLES M, VETERINARY MEDICINE, MEDICAL PHYSICS. *Current Pos:* RETIRED. *Personal Data:* b Rising Star, Tex, July 21, 22; m 43, Anna L Rose; c Polly, Molly, John & James. *Educ:* Tex A&M Univ, DVM, 44; Univ Calif, PhD(comp path), 57. *Prof Exp:* Pvt pract, 44-47; livestock inspector, Comn Eradication Foot & Mouth Dis, USDA, 47-50; base vet, USAF, 50-52, res radiobiologist, Hanford Atomic Prod Oper, Gen Elec Co, 52-54, life sci proj officer, Aircraft Nuclear Propulsion Off, US AEC, 56-60, safety officer, Systs Nuclear Auxiliary Power Prog, 60-62, pathologist, Armed Forces Inst Path, 62-66, dir vet med serv, Air Proving Ground Ctr & Spec Air Warfare Ctr, Eglin AFB, Fla, 66-68; mgr radiol health & pub health ecol, L B Johnson Space Ctr, NASA, 68-71, mgr health appln off, 71-78, mgr radiation protection, space shuttle, 78-82; regional supvr, Cent Am & Colombia Animal Plant Health Inspection Serv, USDA, 82-85; consult, USAID, Pakistan, Afghanistan, 86 & environ sci, 87-93. *Concurrent Pos:* Mem, Nat Comt Radiation Protection & Measurements, 60-66; mem, Subcomt Livestock Damage, Adv Comt Civil Defense, Nat Acad Sci-Nat Res Coun, 61-62; prof comp path, Grad Sch Biomed Sci; chmn bd dirs, Int Vet Med Found, 73-, mgr animal geriat res, 85-93. *Mem:* Am Vet Med Asn. *Res:* Remote sensing; radiation toxicology; radiation biology; geographic pathology; use of aircraft and spacecraft remote sensor data in application to public health; environmental science; growing conditions - shiitake mushrooms; science exchange; veterinary medicine executives. *Mailing Add:* 133 Crystal Springs Dr Georgetown TX 78628. *Fax:* 512-931-0975; *E-Mail:* cowbarnes@aol.com

BARNES, CHARLES WINFRED, OBLIQUE-SLIP FAULTING, FORCED-DRAPED FOLDING. *Current Pos:* from asst prof to assoc prof geol, Northern Ariz Univ, 68-74, chair, Dept Geol, 79-84, assoc dean sci, 84-92, PROF GEOL, NORTHERN ARIZ UNIV, 74-, DIR HONORS PROG, 96- *Personal Data:* b Oklahoma City, Okla, Oct 21, 34; m 58, Charlotte E Coe; c Kelly, Elizabeth, Amy & Susan. *Educ:* Univ Okla, BS, 57; Univ Idaho, MS, 62; Univ Wis, PhD(geol), 65. *Prof Exp:* Asst prof geol, Eastern NMex Univ, 65-68. *Concurrent Pos:* Res prof, Univ Wyo, 66-68; prin investr, NSF, 68-76 & NASA, 83-86; chair fac, Northern Ariz Univ, 73-74; sci preceptor, Nat Col Hons Coun, 77; sr geologist, Berge Explor, 77-79; fac assoc, Danforth Found, 78; res geologist, US Geol Surv, 80-81; prin investr, NASA, 93- *Mem:* Geol Soc Am; Sigma Xi; assoc mem Am Mus Natural Hist; Hist Earth Sci Soc. *Res:* Dynamics of planetary surfaces; energetics of planets; science administration; science education; history of geology. *Mailing Add:* 250 N Circle Dr Flagstaff AZ 86001. *Fax:* 520-523-5689; *E-Mail:* chuck.barnes@nau.edu

BARNES, CHARLIE JAMES, PHYSICAL CHEMISTRY, ORGANIC CHEMISTRY. *Current Pos:* ANALYTICAL CHEMIST, FOOD & DRUG ADMIN, 63- *Personal Data:* b Greenville, NC, Aug 23, 30; m 57; c 1. *Educ:* Va Union Univ, BS, 51; Va State Col, MS, 57; Howard Univ, PhD, 59. *Prof Exp:* Phys & org chemist, Res & Develop Dept, US Naval Propellant Plant, 59-63. *Mem:* Am Chem Soc. *Res:* Development of pesticide reference standards; stability of pesticide materials; analysis of food additives; drugs in edible animal tissue. *Mailing Add:* 2203 Piermont Dr Ft Washington MD 20744

BARNES, CHRISTOPHER RICHARD, PALEONTOLOGY. *Current Pos:* DIR, CTR EARTH & OCEAN RES, UNIV VICTORIA, 89-, DIR, SCH EARTH & OCEAN SCI, 91- *Personal Data:* b Nottingham, UK, Apr 20, 40; Can citizen; m 61, Susan Miller; c Penelope J, Joanne H & Allison L. *Educ:* Birmingham Univ, UK, BSc, 61; Univ Ottawa, Can, PhD(geol), 64. *Honors & Awards:* Past Pres Medal, Geol Asn Can, 77; Bancroft Award, Royal Soc Can, 82. *Prof Exp:* NATO res fel geol, Univ Wales, 64-65; from asst prof to prof & chmn dept, Univ Waterloo, 65-81; prof & head geol, Mem Univ Nfld, 81-87; dir, Gen Sedimentary & Marine Geosci Br, Geol Surv Can, 87-89. *Concurrent Pos:* Lectr, Geol Asn Can, 78; chmn, Coun Chmn Can Earth Sci Dept, 83-85 & 95-97; group chmn, Earth Sci & Interdisciplinary, Natural Sci & Eng Res Coun Can, 87-90; mem, Sch Coun, Brit Col, 90-95. *Mem:* Fel Royal Soc Can; fel Geol Asn Can (pres, 83-84); Can Soc Petrol Geologists; fel Geol Soc Am; Paleont Soc; Paleont Asn; Can Geosci Coun (pres, 79); Acad Sci Royal Soc Can (vpres, 87-88, pres, 90-93). *Res:* Evolution; biostratigraphy; paleoecology and paleobiogeography of lower Paleozoic conodonts; lower paleozoic stratigraphy, paleoceanography and paleoclimatology. *Mailing Add:* Ctr Earth & Ocean Res Univ Victoria PO Box 3055 Victoria BC V8W 3P6 Can. *Fax:* 250-721-6200

BARNES, CLIFFORD ADRIAN, oceanography; deceased, see previous edition for last biography

BARNES, CRAIG ELIOT, ORGANOMETALLIC CHEMISTRY, CATALYSIS. *Current Pos:* asst prof, 84-90, ASSOC PROF CHEM, UNIV TENN, KNOXVILLE, 90- *Personal Data:* b Berkeley, Calif, June 17, 55; m 92, Christiane Otto. *Educ:* Harvey Mudd Col, BS, 77; Stanford Univ, PhD(chem), 82. *Prof Exp:* Postdoctoral fel res, Alexander von Humbolt Found, 82-83 & NATO, 83-84. *Mem:* Am Chem Soc. *Res:* Roles transition metals play in both homogeneous and heterogeneous catalytic systems; techniques of solid state nuclear magnetic resonance, x-ray crystallography and extended x-ray absorption fine structure spectroscopy to study known catalytic systems and develop new ones. *Mailing Add:* Dept Chem Univ Tenn Knoxville TN 37996-1600. *Fax:* 423-974-3454; *E-Mail:* barnes@novell.chem.utk.edu

BARNES, DANIEL C, COMPUTATIONAL PLASMA PHSYICS, NONNEUTRAL PLASMA & PHYSICS. *Current Pos:* staff mem, Los Alamos Nat Lab, 74-78, asst group leader, 78-80, group leader, 89-93, RES SCIENTIST PLASMA THEORY, LOS ALAMOS NAT LAB, 93- *Personal Data:* b Beech Grove, Ind, Aug 11, 43; m 66, Phyllis J Roch; c Joseph & Anna. *Educ:* Purdue Univ, BS, 65, MS, 69, PhD(appl math), 75. *Prof Exp:* Res assoc, Inst Fusion Studies, Univ Tex, 80-84; off mgr, Sci Applns Int Corp, 84-89. *Concurrent Pos:* Chief scientist, NembeTech Inc, 90- *Mem:* Am Phys Soc; fel Am Phys Soc. *Res:* Application of advanced numerical algorithms to plasma physics; experimental studies of non equilibrium, non neutral plasmas. *Mailing Add:* Los Alamos National Lab B-217 Los Alamos NM 87545. *Fax:* 505-665-5757; *E-Mail:* dbarnes@penning.lanl.gov

BARNES, DAVID FITZ, GEOPHYSICS. *Current Pos:* geophysicist, 58-90, EMER GEOPHYSICIST, US GEOL SURV, 90- *Personal Data:* b Boston, Mass, May 23, 21; m 66, Ann Tyndale-Biscoe; c Tamlynn C (Lynch) & Gretchen M (Cox). *Educ:* Harvard Univ, BS, 43, MA, 55. *Prof Exp:* Asst marine geophysics, Woods Hole Oceanog Inst, 43-49; geophysicist, US Geol

Surv, 49-54 & Air Force Cambridge Res Ctr, 56-58. *Mem:* Am Geophys Union; Soc Explor Geophys; fel Arctic Inst NAm; Geol Soc Am. *Res:* Application of geophysics to Arctic research; Alaskan regional gravity; precision gravimetry; Alaskan aeromagnetics; permafrost; perennially frozen lakes; infrared luminescence. *Mailing Add:* US Geol Surv Br Geophys 345 Middlefield Rd MS 989 Menlo Park CA 94025

BARNES, DEREK A, PLASMA PHYSICS, FLUID DYNAMICS. *Current Pos:* assoc prof, 64-66, chmn dept, 66-75, prof physics, 66-80, PROF MATH & COMPUT SCI, MONMOUTH COL, 80- *Personal Data:* b Sussex, Eng, Sept 10, 33; US citizen; m 58; c 2. *Educ:* Oxford Univ, BA, 56 & 57, MA, 60, PhD(plasma physics), 63. *Prof Exp:* Theoret physicist, UK Atomic Energy Authority, 58-60; res scientist, Courant Inst Math Sci, NY Univ, 60-61; mem tech staff, Bell Tel Labs, Inc, 61-64. *Concurrent Pos:* Consult, Aeronaut Res Assocs Princeton, Inc, 64-68 & Corp Comput Systs, Inc, 81- *Mem:* AAAS; Am Phys Soc; Am Inst Aeronaut & Astronaut. *Res:* Laminar to turbulent transition and jet impingement; macro processors. *Mailing Add:* Dept Comput Sci Monmouth Univ 400 Cedar Ave West Long Branch NJ 07764-1804

BARNES, DONALD KAY, GENETICS, PLANT BREEDING. *Current Pos:* prof, 68-95, EMER PROF AGRON & PLANT GENETICS, UNIV MINN, ST PAUL, 95- *Personal Data:* b Minneapolis, Minn, Jan 15, 35; div; c 3. *Educ:* Univ Minn, BS, 57, MS, 58; Pa State Univ, PhD(genetics), 62. *Prof Exp:* Res geneticist, Regional Pasture Res Lab, Agr Res Serv, USDA, Pa, 62-63, res geneticist, Fed Exp Sta, PR, 63-65 & Plant Indust Sta, Md, 65-68, res geneticist, 68- *Mem:* Fel Am Soc Agron; fel Crop Sci Soc Am. *Res:* Alfalfa genetics; breeding for disease and insect resistance; breeding for improved nitrogen fixation potential; alfalfa germplasm evaluation and coordination. *Mailing Add:* 8307 Miner Rd Minocqua WI 54548

BARNES, DONALD MCLEOD, VETERINARY PATHOLOGY, MICROBIOLOGY. *Current Pos:* Instr vet diag, 55-63, from asst prof to assoc prof, 63-72, PROF VET PATH, UNIV MINN, ST PAUL, 72- *Personal Data:* b New Lisbon, Wis, Sept 25, 21; m 49; c 2. *Educ:* Univ Minn, BSc, 53, DVM, 55, PhD(vet med), 63; Am Col Vet Path, dipl. *Mem:* Wildlife Disease Asn; Am Vet Med Asn; Sigma Xi. *Res:* Wildlife disease. *Mailing Add:* RR 2 Box 151AA Aitkin MN 56431-9802

BARNES, DONALD WESLEY, TOXICOLOGY, IMMUNOTOXICOLOGY. *Current Pos:* asst prof, 71-82, ASSOC PROF PHARMACOL, E CAROLINA UNIV, 82- *Personal Data:* b Norfolk, Va, June 28, 44; m 69; c 2. *Educ:* Univ Richmond, BS, 66, Med Col Va, PhD(pharmacol), 71. *Prof Exp:* Grad asst pharmacol, Med Col Va, 70-71. *Concurrent Pos:* External expert, consult & reviewer, Environ Protection Agency, 79. *Mem:* Int Soc Study Xenobiotics; Reticuloendothelial Soc; Sigma Xi; Am Soc Exp Pharmacol & Therapeut. *Res:* Biochemical and immunological mechanisms for the inhibition of drug metabolizing enzymes by immunomodulators; environmental toxicology: drinking water contaminant effects on immune systems and mixed-function oxidases. *Mailing Add:* Dept Pharmacol Sch Med E Carolina Univ Greenville NC 27858-4853

BARNES, EARL RUSSELL, MATHEMATICS. *Current Pos:* PROF INDUST ENG, GA INST TECH, 88- *Personal Data:* b Bennettsville, SC, May 2, 42; m 66. *Educ:* Morgan State Col, BS, 64; Univ Md, PhD(math), 68. *Prof Exp:* Res mathematician, IBM Watson Res Ctr, 68-88. *Concurrent Pos:* Adj assoc prof, Columbia Univ. *Mem:* Am Math Soc; Soc Indust & Appl Math; Inst Elec & Electronics Engrs. *Res:* Variational analysis and differential equations. *Mailing Add:* Sch Indust & Syst Eng Atlanta GA 30332-0205

BARNES, EDWIN ELLSWORTH, LIQUID CHROMATOGRAPHY, THERMAL ANALYSIS. *Current Pos:* RETIRED. *Personal Data:* b Kinzua, Ore, Sept 1, 29; m 52, Joan Harrison; c Michael, Belinda & Christopher. *Educ:* Univ Puget Sound, BS, 51; Univ Wash, PhD(chem), 61. *Prof Exp:* Chemist, Hooker Chem Corp, 51-53; res chemist, Am Marietta Co, 60-62; prof spec phys chem, Weyerhaeuser Co, 62-68, sci specialist, 68-77, scientist 5, 77-90. *Mem:* Am Chem Soc. *Res:* Properties of forest products and synthetic polymers. *Mailing Add:* 17158 Sixth Pl SW Seattle WA 98166

BARNES, EUGENE MILLER, JR, BIOCHEMISTRY, MOLECULAR NEUROBIOLOGY. *Current Pos:* From asst prof to assoc prof, 71-85, PROF BIOCHEM, PHYSIOL, MOLECULAR BIOPHYS & NEUROSCI, BAYLOR COL MED, 86- *Personal Data:* b Versailles, Ky, Dec 9, 43; m 69. *Educ:* Univ Ky, BS, 65; Duke Univ, PhD(biochem), 70. *Concurrent Pos:* Am Cancer Soc fels, Nat Heart & Lung Inst, 69-70 & Roche Inst Molecular Biol, Nutley, NJ, 70-71; NIH res career develop award, 75-80; Vis prof, Univ Louis Pasteur, Strasbourg, France, 79-80; NIH Neurol Dis Prog Proj Rev B Comt, 86-90. *Mem:* AAAS; Am Soc Biolchem & Molecular Biol; Int Soc Neurochem; Soc Neurosci. *Res:* Regualtion of the function, number, and suballular distribution of gamma-aminobutyric acid/benzodiazepine receptors on cortical and cerebellar neurons; mechanisms of receptor down-regulation, phosphorylation and dephosphorglation. *Mailing Add:* Dept Biochem Baylor Col Med Tex Med Ctr One Baylor Plaza Houston TX 77030-3498

BARNES, FRANK STEPHENSON, ELECTRICAL ENGINEERING, PHYSICS. *Current Pos:* assoc prof, 59-65, chmn dept, 64-81, PROF ELEC ENG, UNIV COLO, BOULDER, 65- *Personal Data:* b Boulder, Colo, July 31, 32; m 55, Gay Dirstine; c 2. *Educ:* Princeton Univ, BS, 54; Stanford Univ, MS, 56, PhD(elec eng), 58. *Honors & Awards:* Curtis McGraw Res Award, Am Soc Eng Educ, 65; Stearns Award, 80; Centennial Award, Inst Elec & Electronics Engrs; Leon Mongomery Award, Int Commun Asn. *Prof Exp:* Fulbright prof elec eng, Col Eng, Baghdad, 57-58; physicist, US Nat Bur Stand, Boulder, 59-62. *Concurrent Pos:* Exec ed, Ann Rev Telecommun; mem bd dirs, Bioelectromagnetics Soc. *Mem:* Fel Inst Elec & Electronics Engrs; Am Phys Soc; fel AAAS; Am Soc Educ Advan; Bioelectromagnetics Soc. *Res:* Applications of electromagnetic fields, ultrasonics and lasers to medicine and biology; electron devices; microwave devices. *Mailing Add:* Dept Elec Eng Univ Colo Campus Box 425 Boulder CO 80309. *Fax:* 303-492-2758; *E-Mail:* barnes@boulder.colorado.edu

BARNES, FREDERICK WALTER, JR, MEDICINE, NATURE OF HUMAN INTERACTION. *Current Pos:* PROF MED SCI, DIV MED SCI, BROWN UNIV, 62- *Personal Data:* b Cleveland, Ohio, Mar 3, 09; m 40; c 2. *Educ:* Yale Univ, BA, 30; Johns Hopkins Univ, MD, 34; Columbia Univ, PhD(chem), 43. *Prof Exp:* Intern med, Johns Hopkins Hosp, 34-35, pediat, 35-36; resident, Children's Hosp, Boston, 36-37, asst physician, 37-38; asst biochem, Col Physicians & Surgeons, Columbia Univ, 40-41; asst prof pediat, Col Med, Univ Cincinnati, 42-46, biol chem, 42-46; assoc prof med & physiol chem, Sch Med, Johns Hopkins Univ, 46-62. *Concurrent Pos:* Vis researcher, Oxford Univ, Eng, 70. *Mem:* Am Soc Biol Chem; Soc Pediat Res; Am Heart Asn; fel Am Col Physicians; Physicians for Social Responsibility; Am Lung Asn. *Res:* Protein regeneration and interaction after harmful stimuli; development immunologic theory; detoxification dysentery vaccine; evolution of the immune system. *Mailing Add:* Med Sci Brown Univ Providence RI 02912-0001

BARNES, GARRETT HENRY, JR, ORGANIC CHEMISTRY. *Current Pos:* CONSULT, 81- *Personal Data:* b Akron, Ohio, Mar 7, 26; m 57; c 3. *Educ:* Case Inst Technol, BS, 51; Pa State Univ, PhD(chem), 54. *Prof Exp:* Dow-Corning fel, Mellon Inst, 54-66; res chemist, Dow Corning Corp, 66-68, sr res chemist, 68-75, proj engr, 76-81. *Res:* Organosilicon compounds. *Mailing Add:* 1325 S Portofino No 306 Sarasota FL 34242

BARNES, GENE A, solid state physics, for more information see previous edition

BARNES, GEORGE, SCIENCE EDUCATION. *Current Pos:* from assoc prof to prof, 57-83, EMER PROF PHYSICS, UNIV NEV, RENO, 83- *Personal Data:* b Denver, Colo, May 27, 21; m 44; c 3. *Educ:* Pomona Col, AB, 42; Univ Colo, MS, 46; Ore State Univ, PhD(physics), 55. *Prof Exp:* Instr physics, Pomona Col, 43; jr physicist, US Naval Res Lab, 43-44; asst physics, Univ Colo, 44-45, instr eng math, 45-47; teacher, Taft Jr Col, 47-48; from asst prof to assoc prof physics, Linfield Col, 48-55; asst prof, Humboldt State Col, 55-57. *Mem:* Am Asn Physics Teachers; Sigma Xi. *Res:* The physics of biological systems; the physics of heat engines. *Mailing Add:* 1452 Lolinda Dr Lake San Marcus CA 92069

BARNES, GEORGE EDGAR, CARDIOVASCULAR PHARMACOLOGY, OCULAR PATHOPHYSIOLOGY-PHARMACOLOGY. *Current Pos:* SCIENTIST II & III, 85-90, PRIN SCIENTIST, ALCON LABS, 91- *Personal Data:* b San Antonio, Tex, Jan 27, 43; m 60; c 2. *Educ:* Southwest Tex State Univ, BS, 67, MA, 69; Univ Tex Med Sch, San Antonio, PhD(pharmacol), 74. *Prof Exp:* Am Heart Asn fel, Univ Miss, 73-75, instr physiol, Med Ctr, 74-75; asst prof pharmacol, Col Med, Tex A&M Univ, 75-85. *Concurrent Pos:* co-investr, NIH grant, 77-; prin investr, Am Heart Asn & NIH grant. *Mem:* Am Heart Asn; Microcirculatory Soc; Soc Exp Med & Biol; Sigma Xi; Am Soc Pharmacol Exp Therapeut; Asn Res Vision & Opthal. *Res:* Pathophysiology of cerebral edema; basic mechanisms of edema formation to provide better understanding of how to treat cerebral or brain edema; synthesis and testing of blood pressure control drugs; cardiovascular physiology; pathophysiology of degenerative diseases of the eye; testing of ophthalmic drugs. *Mailing Add:* Glaucoma Res Dept Alcon Labs Inc Ft Worth TX 76134-2099

BARNES, GEORGE LEWIS, ENTOMOLOGY. *Current Pos:* from asst prof to prof, 58-86, EMER PROF PLANT PATH, OKLA STATE UNIV, 86- *Personal Data:* b Detroit, Mich, Aug 21, 20; m 47, Phyllis Dollarhite; c William, Jeffrey, Gregory & Susan. *Educ:* Mich State Univ, BS, 48, MS, 50; Ore State Univ, PhD(plant path), 53. *Prof Exp:* Res asst, Ore State Univ, 50-53; res assoc, Ohio State Univ, 53-55; plant pathologist, Olin Mathieson Chem Corp, 55-58. *Concurrent Pos:* Plant pathologist, Agr Res Serv, USDA, 58-61; consult, Allergy Labs, Inc, 75-82. *Mem:* Sigma Xi; Am Phytopath Soc. *Res:* Fungicides; mycology; entomology; fungus physiology; peanut mold fungi; diseases of pecans and alfalfa; insect pathology. *Mailing Add:* 424 N Donaldson Dr Stillwater OK 74075

BARNES, GERALD JOSEPH, AUTOMOTIVE ENGINEERING. *Current Pos:* Sr res engr combustion, Gen Motors Res Labs, 62-70, sr res engr catalysts, 70-76, emissions engr, 76-78, STAFF ENGR AUTO EMISSION CONTROL, ENVIRON ACTIV STAFF, GEN MOTORS CORP, 78- *Personal Data:* b Beech Grove, Ind, May 7, 36; m 57; c 2. *Educ:* Purdue Univ, BS, 58, MS, 60, PhD(mech eng), 63. *Mem:* Soc Automotive Engrs; Combustion Inst. *Res:* Combustion in spark ignition and diesel engines; emission control; catalytic control of auto emissions. *Mailing Add:* 405 Applehill Lane Rochester Hills MI 48306

BARNES, GLOVER WILLIAM, IMMUNOLOGY, BACTERIOLOGY. *Current Pos:* RES CONSULT IMMUNOL, VA MASON RES CTR, 78- *Personal Data:* b Birmingham, Ala, Sept 7, 23; m 52; c 2. *Educ:* Univ Akron, BSc, 49; Univ Buffalo, MA, 56, PhD(bact, immunol), 62. *Prof Exp:* Asst cancer res scientist, Roswell Park Mem Inst, 55-58; res assoc bact & immunol & asst prof path, State Univ NY Buffalo, 61-63, from instr to asst prof path, 63-69; assoc prof, 69-76, prof urol & lectr microbiol, Univ Wash, 76- *Concurrent Pos:* Res consult, Millard Fillmore Hosp, 60-64. *Mem:* Sigma Xi; AAAS; Soc Study Reproduction; Am Soc Primatologists; Am Fertil Soc. *Res:* Immunologic studies on the organ-specific character and function of the male reproductive system. *Mailing Add:* 3415 S McClellan St Seattle WA 98144-5612

BARNES, H VERDAIN, ADOLESCENT MEDICINE, ENDOCRINOLOGY. *Current Pos:* PROF MED, PEDIAT, FAMILY PRACT & CHAIR, DEPT INTERNAL MED & DIR, CTR GENERALISM & PRIMARY CARE, EASTERN VA SCH MED, 94- *Personal Data:* b Borger, Tex, Nov 20, 35; m 57; c 4. *Educ:* McMurry Col, Abilene, Tex, BA, 58; Yale Univ, MD, 61; Vanderbilt Sch Med, Nashville, Tenn, MD, 65. *Honors & Awards:* Schweikert Award Distinguished Clin Res, Johns Hopkins Sch Med, 71; Bella Schick lectr, Brookdale Hosp, New York, 77; Robert Ward Mem lectr, Los Angeles Children's Hosp, Univ Southern Calif, 84; Mead Johnson Award, Soc Adolescent Med, 87; Adele Hofmann Award, Am Acad Pediat, 90. *Prof Exp:* Med intern, Vanderbilt Hosp, 65-66; asst resident, Johns Hopkins Hosp, 68-69, fel adult & pediat endocrinol & Metab, 69-71, chief resident med, 71-72, asst prof med & pediat, 72-75, dir adolescent med, 72-75, asst prof radiol, 73-75; assoc prof med & pediat & dir introd clin med & adolescent med, Univ Iowa Hosps & Clins, 75-78; prof med & pediat & chmn, Dept Internal Med, Col Med, Univ Tenn, Chattanooga, 78-83; prof med & pediat & chmn, Dept Internal Med, Sch Med, Wright State Univ, 83-84. *Concurrent Pos:* Vis prof at numerous univs; mem, Comp II Comt, 85-92, Nat Bd Med Examrs, 77-83; mem, Adolescent Training Grant Guidelines Comt, Maternal & Child Health, Health Educ & Welfare, 78-79; mem, Coun Socs, Am Col Physicians, 79-; ed-in-chief, J Adolescent Health Care, 79-89; Wyeth vis prof, 86-87; chmn, Am Col Physicians Coun Med Soc, Am Col Physicians Bd of Regents. *Mem:* Am Fedn Clin Res; fel Soc Adolescent Med (pres, 67-68 & 77-78); Am Diabetes Asn; fel Am Col Physicians; fel Am Acad Pediat; Endocrine Soc; Asn Profs Med; AAAS. *Res:* Adolescent growth and development; adolescent endocrinology; therapy of hyperthyroidism; thyroid dysfunction in puberty; thyroid hormone physiology; medical education. *Mailing Add:* PO Box 927 Dayton OH 45401-0927

BARNES, HERBERT M, ANIMAL SCIENCE. *Current Pos:* RETIRED. *Personal Data:* b Paulding, Ohio, Mar 27, 18; m 45; c 2. *Educ:* Ohio State Univ, BSc, 40. *Prof Exp:* assoc prof & exten specialist animal sci, Ohio State Univ, 46-86. *Mem:* Am Soc Animal Sci. *Res:* Swine production; nutrition; physiology; swine husbandry. *Mailing Add:* 524 Glenmont Ave Columbus OH 43214

BARNES, HOWARD CLARENCE, ELECTRICAL ENGINEERING. *Current Pos:* RETIRED. *Personal Data:* b Terre Haute, Ind, May 28, 12; m 32; c 3. *Educ:* Rose Polytech Inst, BSEE, 34. *Hon Degrees:* DEng, Rose Polytech Inst, 77. *Honors & Awards:* Habirshaw Award, 80. *Prof Exp:* Elec engr, Wheeling Steel Corp, 36-39 & Ohio Power Co, 39-44; from engr to asst vpres, Am Elec Power Serv Corp, 44-75; vpres power & environ systs, Charles T Main, Inc, 75-77, chief engr, 77-78, sr vpres, 77-82, dir, 78-82. *Concurrent Pos:* Vpres, Charles T Main, NY & Charles T Main Int; dir, Main Engenharia, Brazil; vis prof, Mass Inst Technol; lectr, Univ Tex, Chalmers Univ, Univ Denmark & Ohio State Univ; consult, ERDA; mem & vpres, Int Conf Large Elec Systs High Tension; vpres & dep chief engr, Am Elec Power Serv Corp, 39-74. *Mem:* Nat Acad Eng; fel AAAS; fel Inst Elec & Electronics Engrs; NY Acad Sci. *Mailing Add:* 209 Le Huerta Green Valley AZ 85614

BARNES, HOYT MICHAEL, WOOD SCIENCE & TECHNOLOGY, WOOD PRESERVATION. *Current Pos:* From asst prof to assoc prof, 71-85, PROF WOOD SCI & TECHNOL, FOREST PROD UTILIZATION LAB, MISS STATE UNIV, 85- *Personal Data:* b Long Beach, Calif, June 9, 43; m 64, Martha Lasyone; c 4. *Educ:* La State Univ, BSF, 65, MS, 68; State Univ NY, PhD(wood prod eng), 73. *Concurrent Pos:* Consult wood preserv, 81-; vis prof, Dept Biol, Imperial Col Sci & Technol, London, 88-89; fel, Inst Wood Sci. *Mem:* Forest Prod Soc; Soc Wood Sci & Technol; Am Wood-Preservers' Asn; AAAS; Railway Tie Asn; Int Res Group Preserv. *Res:* Wood preservation; wood modification; wood physics; biodeterioration of wood; treated wood products; fire retardants. *Mailing Add:* 506 Greensboro St Starkville MS 39759. *Fax:* 601-325-8126

BARNES, HUBERT LLOYD, HYDROTHERMAL PROCESSES. *Current Pos:* from asst prof to prof, 60-90, chmn, Geochem & Mineral Grad Progs, 74-78, DIR, ORE DEPOSITS RES SECT, PA STATE UNIV, UNIVERSITY PARK, 69-, DISTINGUISHED PROF GEOCHEM, 90- *Personal Data:* b Chelsea, Mass, July 20, 28; m 50, Mary T Westergaard; c Ray M & Catherine P. *Educ:* Mass Inst Technol, BS, 50; Columbia Univ, PhD(geol), 58. *Honors & Awards:* Lindsley lectr, Soc Econ Geol; Sr Humboldt Prize, Univ Munich, 87-88; Davidson Mem lectr, St Andrews, 71; Crosby lectr, Mass Inst Technol, 83. *Prof Exp:* Res geologist, Peru Mining Co, 50-52; lectr geol, Columbia Univ, 52-54; fel, Geophys Lab, Carnegie Inst Washington, 56-60. *Concurrent Pos:* Guggenheim fel, Geochem Inst, Univ Goettingen, 66-67; vis prof, Univ Heidelberg, 74; exchange scientist, USSR Acad Sci, 74; chmn, US Nat Comt Geochem, Nat Acad Sci, 76-78, Nat Res Coun Geophys Res Bd, 76-80; bd dirs, Sci Systs, Inc, 69-; mem, US Geodynamics comt, 77-80, counr, Soc Econ Geol, 80-82; gov bd, Am Geol Inst, 81-83; vis prof, Academia Sinica, China, 83; mem, US Nat Comt Geol, Nat Res Coun, 83-86; mem, US Dept Energy Mat Rev, 85-88; distinguished vis prof, Univ Sydney, 87; chmn, NATO Advan Study Inst, Geochm Hydrothermal Ore Deposits, Spain, 87; chmn, Sec Int Symp Hydrothermal Reactions, Pa State Univ, 88; gen chmn, Goldschmidt Conf, 88, 94- *Mem:* Geochem Soc (pres, 82-85); fel Soc Econ Geol; fel Geol Soc Am; Am Geophys Union; fel Mineral Soc Am. *Res:* Geochemistry of hydrothermal processes in geothermal systems and in the formation of ore deposits. *Mailing Add:* 213 E Mitchell Ave State College PA 16803. *Fax:* 814-863-2001; *E-Mail:* barnes@geosc.psu.edu

BARNES, JAMES ALFORD, LITHIUM BATTERIES, ELECTROCHEMISTRY. *Current Pos:* res chemist electrochem, 82-93, BR HEAD, ELECTROCHEM BR, NAVAL SURFACE WARFARE CTR, 93- *Personal Data:* b Charlotte, NC, Aug 20, 44; m 66, Helen Scroggins; c Mary A & Curtis C. *Educ:* Davidson Col, BS, 66; Univ NC, Chapel Hill, PhD(inorg chem), 70. *Prof Exp:* Teaching assoc inorg chem, Southampton Univ, Eng, 70-71; NIH res assoc, Univ SC, 71-72; vis asst prof chem, Western Md Col, 72-73; assoc prof, Austin Col, Sherman, Tex, 73-83. *Concurrent Pos:* Res chemist phys chem, Shell Develop Corp, 76, inorg chem, Tex Instruments, 80, environ, Southwest Res Inst, 81 & inorg chem, Naval Res Lab, 81-82. *Mem:* Am Chem Soc; Electrochem Soc; Royal Soc Chem; AAAS. *Res:* Lithium batteries; electrochemical power sources; corrosion. *Mailing Add:* Naval Surface Warfare Ctr Code 683 9500 MacArthur Blvd West Bethesda MD 20817-5700. *E-Mail:* barnesja@oasys.dt.navy.mil

BARNES, JAMES ALLEN, PHYSICS. *Current Pos:* RETIRED. *Personal Data:* b Denver, Colo, Dec 7, 33; m 59; c 3. *Educ:* Univ Colo, BS, 56, PhD(physics), 66; Stanford Univ, MS, 58; Denver Univ, MBA, 79. *Honors & Awards:* Silver Medal Award, US Dept Com, 65, Gold Medal Award, 75. *Prof Exp:* Physicist, Atomic Frequency & Time Interval Stand Sect, 56-65, from actg sect chief to sect chief, 65-67, chief Time & Frequency Div, Nat Bur Stand, 67-81; dir, Res & Develop, Austron Inc, 82-88. *Concurrent Pos:* Mem comn, Int Sci Radio Union; mem study group VII, Int Radio Consultative Comt; consult, comn 31, Int Astron Union, 72- *Mem:* Fel Inst Elec & Electronics Engrs. *Res:* Atomic and molecular spectroscopy; noise limitations of devices; statistics. *Mailing Add:* 350 Ponca Pl Apt 464 Boulder CO 80301

BARNES, JAMES MILTON, PHYSICS. *Current Pos:* RETIRED. *Personal Data:* b Ypsilanti, Mich, July 5, 23; m 49. *Educ:* Eastern Mich Univ, BS, 48; Mich State Univ, MS, 50, PhD(physics), 55. *Prof Exp:* From asst prof to assoc prof, Eastern Mich Univ, 55-62, head dept, 61-74, prof physics, 62-88. *Mem:* AAAS; Am Asn Physics Teachers; Acoust Soc Am; Nat Sci Teachers Asn. *Res:* Ultrasonics in glass by optical methods. *Mailing Add:* 4872 N Whitman Circle Ann Arbor MI 48103-9774

BARNES, JAMES RAY, AQUATIC ECOLOGY. *Current Pos:* Asst prof, 69-73, ASSOC PROF ZOOL, BRIGHAM YOUNG UNIV, 73- *Personal Data:* b Woodland, Calif, Feb 16, 40; m 62; c 3. *Educ:* Brigham Young Univ, BS, 63; Ore State Univ, MS, 66, PhD(zool), 72. *Concurrent Pos:* Adj prof, Kellogg Biol Sta, Mich State Univ, 75. *Mem:* AAAS; Ecol Soc Am; Am Soc Limnol & Oceanog; NAm Benthol Soc; Orgn Inland Biol Field Sta. *Res:* Terrestrial litter decomposition in lakes and streams; annual reproductive cycles of marine and freshwater invertebrates. *Mailing Add:* Dept Zool Brigham Young Univ 575 Widb Provo UT 84602-1049

BARNES, JEFFREY KARL, INSECT SYSTEMATICS, INSECT BIONOMICS. *Current Pos:* SR SCIENTIST ENTOM, BIOL SURV, NY STATE MUS, 80- *Personal Data:* b Batavia, NY, May 29, 50. *Educ:* Univ Rochester, BS, 72; Cornell Univ, MS, 76, PhD(entom), 79. *Concurrent Pos:* Res assoc, Fla State Collection Arthropods, 87- *Mem:* Entom Soc Am. *Res:* Curation of entomology collection; systematics biology and immature stages of two-winged flies (Diptera); forensic applications of entomological data; history of American entomology. *Mailing Add:* Biol Survey 3140 Cult Educ Ctr Albany NY 12230. *E-Mail:* jabarnes@museum.nysed.gov

BARNES, JEFFREY LEE, GLOMERLONEPHRITIS. *Current Pos:* ASST PROF PATH, HEALTH SCI CTR, UNIV TEX, 78- *Educ:* Univ Md, PhD(path), 78. *Mailing Add:* Dept Med Renal Div Univ Tex Health Sci Ctr 7703 Floyd Curl Dr San Antonio TX 78284-7750

BARNES, JOHN DAVID, POLYMER PHYSICS. *Current Pos:* PHYSICIST POLYMER PHYSICS, POLYMERS DIV, NAT INST STAND & TECHNOL, 64- *Personal Data:* b Allentown, Pa, Aug 12, 39; m 65. *Educ:* DePauw Univ, BA, 60; Univ Md, MS, 65; Cath Univ Am, PhD(physics), 72. *Prof Exp:* Physicist ceramics, Eastern Res Ctr, US Bur Mines, College Park, Md, 61-64. *Mem:* Am Phys Soc; AAAS; Mat Res Soc; Am Crystallog Asn. *Res:* Permeation, diffusion, and solubility of gases, vapors and liquids in polymers; x-ray diffraction and scattering from polymers. *Mailing Add:* 224 A209 Nat Inst Stand & Technol Rte 270 & Quince Orchard Rd Gaithersburg MD 20899

BARNES, JOHN FAYETTE, ATOMIC PHYSICS. *Current Pos:* RETIRED. *Personal Data:* b Santa Cruz, Calif, Jan 28, 30; m 55; c 2. *Educ:* Univ Calif, Berkeley, BA, 51; Univ Denver, MS, 52; Univ NMex, PhD(physics), 63, MMS, 81. *Prof Exp:* Staff mem, Los Alamos Nat Lab, 53-68, asst group leader, 68-71, alt group leader, 71, group leader, 71-77, asst theoret div leader, 76-77, assoc theoret div leader, 77-80, dep theoret div leader, 80-81, dep assoc dir energy, 81-82, dep assoc dir physics & math,82-83, appl theoret physics div leader, 83-85, sr scientist & actg group leader, 85-87, lab assoc, 87- *Concurrent Pos:* Adj instr, Univ NMex, 85-, coordr Math & Tech Progs, 87-;

adj instr, Santa Fe Community Col, 87- *Mem:* Am Phys Soc. *Res:* Thomas-Fermi theory; atomic structure; solid state physics; hydrodynamics; equation of state and opacity research for applied problems. *Mailing Add:* 2213 Calle Cacique Santa Fe NM 87505

BARNES, JOHN MAURICE, PLANT PATHOLOGY. *Current Pos:* plant pathologist, Coop State Res Serv, 67-75, coordr, Corn Blight Info Ctr, 71-72, pesticide coordr, Off Secy, 75-77, pesticide impact assessment coordr, Sci & Educ Admin, 77-80, PRIN PLANT PATHOLOGIST, COOP STATE RES SERV, USDA, 80- *Personal Data:* b Washington, DC, Apr 22, 31; m 57; c 5. *Educ:* Univ Md, BS, 54; Cornell Univ, MS, 57, PhD(plant path), 60. *Prof Exp:* Opers analyst, Opers Res Off, Johns Hopkins Univ, 60-63; plant scientist, Hazleton Labs, TRW Systs, 63-67. *Concurrent Pos:* Mem, acid rain competitive grant mgt; co-ed, Appl Bot, Crop Sci, Acad Press; cert merit, USDA, 72, 84, 86 & 88. *Mem:* Am Phytopath Soc; Sigma Xi; Soc Nematologists; AAAS. *Res:* Coordination and policy planning relative to agricultural pest control. *Mailing Add:* Coop State Res Serv USDA 8th Floor 901 D St SW Washington DC 20250-2200

BARNES, KAREN LOUISE, NEUROPHYSIOLOGY & NEUROANATOMY, RESEARCH ADMINISTRATION. *Current Pos:* STAFF DOCTOR, RES ADMIN & NEUROL, CLEVELAND CLIN FOUND, 76-, DIR, RES PROGS DEVELOP, 96-; PROF, DEPT PHYSIOL, OHIO STATE UNIV, COL MED, 94- *Personal Data:* b Cleveland, Ohio, Feb 24, 42; m 73, William E Garapick. *Educ:* Mt Holyoke Col, AB, 63; Univ Mich, Ann Arbor, AM, 65; Case Western Reserve Univ, PhD(exp psychol), 70. *Prof Exp:* Asst prof psychol, John Carroll Univ, 69-73; res psychologist med res, Cleveland Vet Admin Hosp, 73-75; asst prof neurosurg & biomed eng, Sch Med, Case Western Reserve Univ, 75-83, adj assoc prof biomed eng & neurol, 83-90; head, Sect Neurol, Cleveland Clin Found, 80-90. *Concurrent Pos:* Mem, Prog Advan Training Biomed Res Mgt, Sch Pub Health, Harvard Univ, 89. *Mem:* Soc Neurosci; Am Heart Asn; Am Physiol Soc; Am Acad Neurol; Sigma Xi. *Res:* Interactions of peptides and transmitters on neurons; neuronal actions of angiotensin and substance P in pathways of the medulla that subserve cardiovascular function; neuroanatomy of dorsal medulla cardiovascular pathways. *Mailing Add:* Res Inst NC11 9500 Euclid Ave Cleveland OH 44195-5070. *Fax:* 216-444-3279; *E-Mail:* barnesk@cesmtp.ccf.org

BARNES, LARRY D, PROTEIN-LIGAND INTERACTION, DINUCLEOSIDE POLYPHOSPHATES. *Current Pos:* PROF, HEALTH SCI CTR, UNIV TEX, 76- *Personal Data:* m 68, Sandra Bachman; c Jaime & Brian. *Educ:* Rice Univ, BA, 66; Univ Calif, Los Angeles, PhD(biochem), 70. *Mem:* Am Soc Biochem & Molecular Biol; Am Soc Cell Biol; Biochem Soc. *Res:* Metabolic regulation by nucleotides; yeast. *Mailing Add:* Dept Biochem Health Sci Ctr Univ Tex 7703 Floyd Curl Dr San Antonio TX 78284-7760. *Fax:* 210-567-6595; *E-Mail:* barnesl@uthscsa.edu

BARNES, LAWRENCE GAYLE, VERTEBRATE PALEONTOLOGY, MAMMALOGY. *Current Pos:* assoc cur, 72-75, CUR VERT PALEONT, NATURAL HIST MUS LOS ANGELES COUNTY, 75- *Personal Data:* b Portsmouth, Va, Dec 26, 45; m 67; c 1. *Educ:* Univ Calif, Berkeley, BA, 67, MA, 69, PhD(paleont), 72. *Prof Exp:* Mus asst paleont, Univ Calif, Berkeley, 67-69, mus preparator, 69-72, teaching asst, 71-72. *Concurrent Pos:* Res assoc, Mus Paleont, Univ Calif, Berkeley, 74- *Mem:* Soc Vert Paleont; Am Soc Mammal; Soc Syst Zool; Soc Marine Mammal. *Res:* Paleontology of fossil marine vertebrates, mainly marine mammals of Tertiary age. *Mailing Add:* 4431 Melbourne Ave Los Angeles CA 90027

BARNES, MARTIN MCRAE, ECONOMIC ENTOMOLOGY. *Current Pos:* Jr entomologist, 46-49, from asst entomologist to assoc entomologist, 49-61, ENTOMOLOGIST, UNIV CALIF, RIVERSIDE, 61-, PROF ENTOM, 63- *Personal Data:* b Calgary, Alta, Aug 3, 20; US citizen; wid; c 4. *Educ:* Univ Calif, Berkeley, BS, 41; Cornell Univ, PhD(entom), 46. *Concurrent Pos:* Chmn, Dept Entom, Univ Calif, Riverside, 88. *Mem:* Fel AAAS; Entom Soc Am; Can Entom Soc; Mex Soc Entom. *Res:* Biology, ecology and management of insects and mites of deciduous fruit and nut orchards and vineyards. *Mailing Add:* Entom Univ Calif 1946 Prince Albert Dr Riverside CA 92507-5836

BARNES, MARY WESTERGAARD, PHYSICAL CHEMISTRY, MATERIALS SCIENCE. *Current Pos:* RETIRED. *Personal Data:* b Champaign, Ill, May 20, 27; m 50; c 2. *Educ:* Swarthmore Col, BA, 48; Pa State Univ, PhD(phys chem), 66. *Prof Exp:* Res asst gen chem, Mass Inst Technol, 48-50; from tech asst to tech staff assoc electron devices, Bell Tel Labs, 52-56; chemist, Nat Bur Standards, 56-60; proj assoc water struct, Pa State Univ, 67-69, proj assoc nuclear waste disposal, 77-81, proj coordr, Mat Res Lab, 81-95. *Concurrent Pos:* Fel, Max Planck Inst Phys Chem, Gottingen, WGer, 66-67. *Mem:* Am Chem Soc; Mat Res Soc; Am Ceramic Soc; Geochem Soc. *Res:* Physical chemistry: interactions between nuclear waste and rock; water and groundwater; chemistry of cement and its application to waste disposal; statistical thermodynamics; materials for electron devices; phase chemistry of calcium aluminate silicate hydrates; calcium phosphates. *Mailing Add:* 213 E Mitchell Ave State College PA 16803-3655

BARNES, NORMAN P, SOLID STATE LASERS, NONLINEAR OPTICS. *Current Pos:* AEROSPACE TECHNOLOGIST, NASA LANGLEY RES CTR, 86- *Personal Data:* b Cleveland, Ohio; m 65, Barbara Jon Osterman; c Adam, Matthew & Cherie. *Educ:* Ohio State Univ, BS, 65, MS, 67, PhD(elec eng), 69. *Prof Exp:* Mem tech staff, Texas Instruments, 69-72, Martin Marietta, 72-75 & Los Alamos Nat Labs, 75-86. *Mem:* Fel Optical Soc Am. *Res:* Research and develops novel laser systems for remote sensing applications. *Mailing Add:* 103 Stone Lake Ct Yorktown VA 23693. *Fax:* 757-864-8809

BARNES, PAUL RICHARD, SPACE PHYSIOLOGY. *Current Pos:* CONSULT, AMES BIOMED DIV, NASA, 81- *Personal Data:* b San Francisco, Calif, May 1, 36; m 64; c 3. *Educ:* San Francisco State Univ, BA, 60, MA, 63; Univ Kans, PhD(biochem & physiol), 69. *Prof Exp:* Asst microbiol, Sch Med, Univ Kans, 69-71; asst pharmacol, Sch Med, Univ Md, 71-72; asst biochem, Univ Southern Calif, 72-73; lectr, 73-75, from asst prof to assoc prof, 75-83, prof biol, San Francisco State Univ, 83- *Mem:* Am Physiol Soc; Am Chem Soc; Sigma Xi. *Res:* Human physiological changes associated with space flight; alterations in body fluid composition and volumes; electrolyte-balance; hormone levels; blood pressure control mechanisms in the absence of gravity. *Mailing Add:* Dept Biol San Francisco State Univ 1600 Holloway Ave San Francisco CA 94132

BARNES, PETER DAVID, NUCLEAR & PARTICLE PHYSICS, SCIENCE ADMINISTRATION. *Current Pos:* dir, Meson Physics Accelerator, 91-93, DIR, PHYSICS DIV, LOS ALAMOS NAT LAB, 93- *Personal Data:* b Garden City, NY, Oct 10, 37; m 61, Angela Laguardia; c Alexa, Peter Jr & Diana. *Educ:* Univ Notre Dame, BS, 59; Yale Univ, MS, 60, PhD(physics), 65. *Prof Exp:* Fel nuclear physics, Niels Bohr Inst, Copenhagen, Denmark, 64-66 & Los Alamos Sci Lab, 66-68; from assoc prof to prof physics, Carnegie-Mellon Univ, 68-91. *Concurrent Pos:* NATO fel, 65-66; vis scientist, Los Alamos Sci Lab, 73-74 & Centre Etude Nucleaire, France, 78-79; mem, Nuclear Sci Adv Comt, USA, 77-80, chmn electromagnetic interactions, 81-82; assoc ed, Phys Rev C, 80-82. *Mem:* Fel Am Phys Soc; Sigma Xi. *Res:* Strong electromagnetic and weak interactions in atomic, nuclear and elementary particle systems; kaonic, antiprotonic and sigma atoms, few nucleon and complex nuclei, lamda hypernuclei, antiproton, kaon physics. *Mailing Add:* Physics Div MS/D434 Los Alamos Nat Lab Los Alamos NM 87545

BARNES, RALPH CRAIG, PUBLIC ENTOMOLOGY, PUBLIC HEALTH. *Current Pos:* RETIRED. *Personal Data:* b Summerfield, Ohio, May 4, 14; m 86; c 1. *Educ:* Ohio Univ, BS, 39; NC State Col, MS, 41. *Prof Exp:* Eng aide. Commun Dis Ctr, 42-43, asst sanitarian, 43-44, sr asst sanitarian, 44-47, sr asst scientist, 47-48, scientist, 48-52, sr scientist, 52-56, scientist dir, 56-70, regional prog dir, Ctr Dis Control, 70-74, dir Div Prev, Public Health Serv, US Dept Health, Educ & Welfare, Reg VIII, 74-78. *Concurrent Pos:* Part-time instr biol, Metrop State Col, Denver, 78-83. *Mem:* Entom Soc Am; Am Pub Health Asn. *Res:* Ecology of mosquitoes; medical entomology; communicable disease control. *Mailing Add:* 14300 E Marina Dr Apt 602 Aurora CO 80014

BARNES, RALPH W, ELECTRICAL ENGINEERING. *Current Pos:* res assoc, Sonic Lab, 69, res instr ultrasound, 70, from res asst prof to res assoc prof med sonics, 70-84, PROF NEUROL, BOWMAN GRAY SCH MED, 85-; DIR RES, AUTREC, WINSTON-SALEM, NC, 84- *Personal Data:* b New York, NY, Nov 28, 36; c 2. *Educ:* Duke Univ, BSEE, 58, PhD, 69; Univ Pa, MSE, 65. *Honors & Awards:* Small Bus Innovative Res Award, NIH. *Prof Exp:* Design engr, Radio Corp Am, Camden & Moorestown, NJ, 58-62; sr engr, Motorola, Chicago, 63-64; instr elec eng, Duke Univ, 64-65, NSF trainee, 65 & 66, teaching intern, 65-66, trainee, Div Biomed Eng, 66-69. *Concurrent Pos:* NC Heart Asn res grant; consult, NIH & NSF; prin investr grants & contracts, NIH. *Mem:* Am Inst Ultrasound Med; Inst Elec & Electronics Engrs; Sigma Xi. *Res:* Ultrasound; diagnostic data processing; biomedical instrumentation; industrial instrumentation; research and development. *Mailing Add:* Dept Neurol Bowman Gray Sch Med 300 S Hawthorne Rd Winston-Salem NC 27157-0002

BARNES, RAMON M, ANALYTICAL CHEMISTRY. *Current Pos:* from asst prof to assoc prof, 69-80, PROF ANALYTICAL CHEM, UNIV MASS, AMHERST, 80- *Personal Data:* b Pittsburgh, Pa, Apr 24, 40; m 69, Dorothy M Soja. *Educ:* Ore State Univ, BS, 62; Columbia Univ, AM, 63; Univ Ill, Urbana-Champaign, PhD(analytical chem), 66. *Prof Exp:* Spectrochemist, NASA Lewis Res Ctr, Ohio, 67-68, mat engr, 68-69; assoc anal chem, Iowa State Univ, 68-69. *Concurrent Pos:* Lectr chem, Baldwin-Wallace Col, 67-68; ed & publ, ICP Info Newslett; chmn, Winter Conf Plasma Spectrochem, 80, 82, 84, 86, 88, 90, 92, 94, 96 & 98; consult. *Mem:* Am Chem Soc; Soc Appl Spectros; Spectros Soc Can; Optical Soc Am; Sigma Xi; Royal Soc Chem; Soc Environ Geochem & Health; fel AAAS; Am Soc Mass Spectrometry. *Res:* Chemical reactions in high energy spectroscopic discharges, including sparks and radio frequency, induction heated plasmas for spectrochemical analysis; applications of atomic and mass spectroscopy with plasma sources for spectrochemical analyses and chromatographic detection. *Mailing Add:* Dept Chem Univ Mass 701 Lederle GRC Towers PO Box 34510 Amherst MA 01003-4510. *Fax:* 413-545-4490; *E-Mail:* ramon.m.barnes@chemistry.umass.edu

BARNES, RICHARD G, SOLID STATE PHYSICS. *Current Pos:* RETIRED. *Personal Data:* b Milwaukee, Wis, Dec 12, 22. *Educ:* Univ Wis, BA, 48; Dartmouth Col, MS, 49; Harvard Univ, PhD(physics), 52. *Honors & Awards:* Alexander von Humboldt Sr Scientist Award, 75. *Prof Exp:* Prog dir, Solid State Physics, Nat Sci Lab, 88-90; prof, 56-88, emer prof physics, Iowa State Univ, 90-92. *Mem:* Am Phys Soc. *Mailing Add:* 8 Lockwood Dr Kennebunk ME 04043

BARNES, RICHARD N, ECOLOGY. *Current Pos:* from asst prof to prof, 62-94, EMER PROF BIOL, BEREA COL, 94- *Personal Data:* b Washington, DC, Dec 10, 28; m 57, Mary E DeLauter; c Kathryn A & Marcia L. *Educ:* Univ Calif, Berkeley, AB, 52; Univ Calif, Davis, MA, 57, PhD(zool), 62. *Prof Exp:* Instr biol, Sacramento State Col, 57-62. *Mem:* Sigma Xi. *Res:* Limnology; aquatic ecology; entomology. *Mailing Add:* Dept Biol Berea Col Berea KY 40404

BARNES, ROBERT DRANE, invertebrate zoology; deceased, see previous edition for last biography

BARNES, ROBERT F, AGRONOMY, CROP SCIENCE. *Current Pos:* EXEC VPRES, AM SOC AGRON, CROP SCI SOC AM & SOIL SCI SOC AM, 86- *Personal Data:* b Estherville, Iowa, Feb 6, 33; m 55, Betty J Burrell; c Bradley, Rebecca (Reindale), Roberta (Nixon) & Brian. *Educ:* Estherville Jr Col, AA, 53; Iowa State Univ, BS, 57; Rutgers Univ, MS, 59; Purdue Univ, PhD(agron), 63. *Honors & Awards:* Medallion Award, Am Forage Grassland Coun, 81. *Prof Exp:* Res agronomist, Ind, USDA, 59-70, res agronomist, Pa, 70-75, dir, US Regional Pasture Res Lab, 70-75, staff scientist forage, range, plant & entom sci, Nat Prog Staff, Agr Res Serv, 75-79, assoc regional adminr, Agr Res Serv, Southern Region, 79-82, regional adminr, 82-86. *Concurrent Pos:* From instr to assoc prof, Purdue Univ, 59-70; adj prof, Pa State Univ, 70-76; partic, Int Grassland, Cong, Helsinki, Finland, 66, Surfer's Paradise, Australia, 70, Moscow, USSR, 73, Leipzig, EGer Dem Repub, 77, Lexington, Ky, 81 & Kyoto, Japan, 85, Nice France, 89, New Zealand, 93; Int Crop Sci Cong, Ames, Iowa, 92, New Delhi, India, 96. *Mem:* Fel AAAS; fel Am Soc Agron; Am Soc Animal Sci; Am Forage & Grassland Coun; fel Crop Sci Soc Am; Soil Sci Soc Am. *Res:* Forage, pasture, range and turfgrass breeding, production and utilization; crop physiology; development and application of forage evaluation and utilization techniques; biochemistry of forage and range plants; agricultural research priorities, program planning and leadership; administration of and writing for agronomy, crop science and soil science. *Mailing Add:* Am Soc Agron 677 S Segoe Rd Madison WI 53711. *Fax:* 608-273-2021; *E-Mail:* rbarnes@agronomy.org

BARNES, ROBERT LEE, PHARMACEUTICALS, MATERIALS SCIENCE. *Current Pos:* sect head chromatography, E R Squibb, 82-84, dept head, Chem Control, 84-87, dir prod qual control, 87-89, dir worldwide tech serv, 89-93, dir prod qual control, 93-95, DIR WORLDWIDE TECH SERV, BRISTOL MYERS SQUIBB, NEW BRUNSWICK, NJ, 95- *Personal Data:* b Niagara Falls, NY, Aug 1, 35; m 67, Barbara Gross. *Educ:* Hamilton Col, BA, 57; Pa State Univ, MS, 60, PhD(chem, 63). *Prof Exp:* Res fel chem. Harvard Univ, 63-65; staff scientist, Aerospace Div, Res Ctr, Gen Precision, Inc, Little Falls, 65-69, res mgr, Chem Dept, Singer-Gen Precision Kearfott Res Ctr, 69-74; mgr inorg chem, US Testing Co, Hoboken, NJ, 74-76; mgr anal labs, Booz, Allen & Hamilton, Foster D Snell Div, Florham Park, NJ, 76-80; mgr, Chem & Anal Serv, Case Consult Labs, Inc, Whippany, NJ, 80-82. *Mem:* Am Chem Soc; AAAS; Am Asn Pharmaceut Scientist; Parenteral Drug Asn. *Res:* Electron deficient compounds, especially boron hydrides and metal alkyls; mechanism of inorganic reactions; synthesis of inorganic materials; organometallics; adhesives; chemiluminescence; analytical chemistry; pharmaceutical analysis; environmental analysis; quality control. *Mailing Add:* 48 High Ridge Rd Randolph NJ 07869. *Fax:* 732-519-3875

BARNES, RODERICK ARTHUR, ORGANIC CHEMISTRY. *Current Pos:* PROF, FED UNIV RIO DE JANEIRO, 75- *Personal Data:* b Madison, Wis, June 21, 20; div; c Carolyn E (Proenca). *Educ:* Univ Wis, BS, 39; Univ Minn, PhD(org chem), 43. *Honors & Awards:* Fulbright lectr, Sao Paulo, 62-63. *Prof Exp:* Asst chem, Univ Minn, 39-42, instr & fel, 44-45; instr, Columbia Univ, 45-47; asst prof, Rutgers Univ, 47-53, from assoc prof to prof, 53-63; prof, Fla Atlantic Univ, 63-67; coordr res & grad prog, Engenharia Mil Inst, 70-75. *Concurrent Pos:* NSF sr fel, 57-58; Conselho Nacional de Pesquisas fel, Brazil, 57-58; vis prof, Brazil, 63-65; temp prof, Univ Rio de Janeiro, 67. *Mem:* Am Chem Soc; Pharmaceut Soc Japan; Brazilian Chem Soc. *Res:* Biogenesis of natural products; reaction mechanisms; alkaloids; determination of structure of new natural products; chemical transformations of abundant natural products; synthesis of natural products and analogues. *Mailing Add:* CCS-NPPN Fed Univ Rio De Janeiro Rio de Janeiro 21941-590 Brazil. *Fax:* 55-21-270-2683

BARNES, RONNIE C, ASTROPHYSICS. *Current Pos:* chmn, Div Natural Sci, 81-83, DIR, M D ANDERSON PLANETARIUM, LAMBUTH COL, 75-, PROF ASTRON, 85- *Personal Data:* b Union City, Tenn, Sept 10, 41; m 66; c 1. *Educ:* Vanderbilt Univ, BA, 63; Ind Univ, AM, 66, PhD(astrophys), 68. *Prof Exp:* From instr to asst prof physics & astron, Univ Mo, Columbia, 68-75. *Concurrent Pos:* Summer fac fel, George C Marshall Spaceflight Ctr, NASA, 79-80. *Mem:* Am Astron Soc; fel Royal Astron Soc; Astron Soc Pac. *Res:* Close binary systems; cosmology. *Mailing Add:* Dept Sci Lambuth Univ 705 Lambuth Blvd Jackson TN 38301-5296

BARNES, ROSS OWEN, marine & sedimentary geochemistry, for more information see previous edition

BARNES, THOMAS GROGARD, PHYSICS. *Current Pos:* VPRES, GEO-SPACE RES & EXPLOR FOUND, 85- *Personal Data:* b Blanket, Tex, Aug 14, 11; m 38; c 4. *Educ:* Hardin-Simmons Col, AB, 33; Brown Univ, ScM, 36. *Hon Degrees:* ScD, Hardin-Simmons Col, 60. *Prof Exp:* Asst physics, Brown Univ, 35-36; teacher high sch, Tex, 36-38; instr math & physics, Col Mines & Metall, Univ Tex, El Paso, 38-43; elec engr, Div Phys War Res, Duke Univ, 43-45; dean, Grad Sch, Inst Creation Res, El Cajon, Calif, 81-83; dir Schellenger Res Labs, 55-65, from asst prof to prof, 45-81, emer prof physics, Univ Tex, El Paso, 81- *Concurrent Pos:* Vis fel, Brown Univ, 52-53; consult physicist, US Army Res Off, Durham, 63; consult, Res Adv Proj Div, Globe Universal Sci, 65-77. *Mem:* Am Asn Physics Teachers; fel Creation Res Soc (pres, 73-77). *Res:* Electromagnetism; acoustics; atmospheric physics; electronic instrumentation; relativity. *Mailing Add:* Dept Physics Univ Tex 500 W University Ave El Paso TX 79968-0151

BARNES, VIRGIL EVERETT, GEOLOGY. *Current Pos:* geologist, Bur Econ Geol, Univ Tex, 35-77, assoc dir, 61-68, prof dept geol sci, 61-77, SR RES SCI, UNIV TEX, AUSTIN, 73-, EMER PROF GEOL, 77- *Personal Data:* b Chehalis, Wash, June 11, 03; m 32, Mildred L Adlof; c Virgil E Jr, Louise & Elizabeth (Thompson). *Educ:* State Col Wash, BS, 25, MS, 27; Univ Wis, PhD(geol), 30. *Honors & Awards:* Barringer Award, Meteoritical Soc, 89; Pub Serv Award, Am Asn Petrol Geologists, 93. *Prof Exp:* Cur dept geol, Univ Wis, 27-29; res fel, Am Petrol Inst, 30-31 & US Geol Surv, 33-35. *Concurrent Pos:* NSF grants study of origin & compos of tektites, 60-75; mem, Am Comn Stratig Nomenclature, 70-76; dir, Tektite Res, 60- *Mem:* Fel Geol Soc Am; fel Mineral Soc Am; Asn Petrol Geologists; Geochem Soc; Soc Econ Paleontologists & Mineralogists; fel AAAS. *Res:* Cambrian, Ordovician and Devonian stratigraphy; geophysics; mineralogy; world wide occurrence of tektites; Lunar glass; meteorites; economic geology of Texas. *Mailing Add:* Bur Econ Geol Box X Univ Sta Austin TX 78713-7508

BARNES, VIRGIL EVERETT, II, HIGH ENERGY PARTICLE PHYSICS. *Current Pos:* assoc prof, 69-79, asst dean, Sch Sci, 74-78, PROF PHYSICS, PURDUE UNIV, WEST LAFAYETTE, 79- *Personal Data:* b Galveston, Tex, Nov 2, 35; m 57, 70, Linda T; c Virgil E III, Christopher D, C Jeffrey & Daniel W. *Educ:* Harvard Univ, AB, 57; Cambridge Univ, PhD(physics), 62. *Honors & Awards:* Perkin Elmer Prize, Harvard Univ, 56. *Prof Exp:* Res assoc, Brookhaven Nat Lab, 62-64, from asst physicist to assoc physicist, 64-69. *Concurrent Pos:* Spokesman, Dept Energy, High Energy Physics Contract, Task G. *Mem:* Am Phys Soc; NY Acad Sci; AAAS; Sigma Xi. *Res:* Experimental elementary particle physics, currently collaborator on collider detector at Fermilab, 1.8 trillion eV antiproton-proton collisions; author or coauthor of over 166 publications. *Mailing Add:* 801 N Salisburg Lafayette IN 47906. *E-Mail:* barnes@physics.purdue.edu

BARNES, WAYNE MORRIS, BIOCHEMISTRY, MOLECULAR BIOLOGY. *Current Pos:* ASST PROF BIOCHEM, WASHINGTON UNIV SCH MED, 77- *Personal Data:* b Riverside, Calif, Sept 30, 47; m 74; c 2. *Educ:* Univ Calif, Riverside, AB, 69; Univ Wis-Madison, PhD(biochem), 74. *Prof Exp:* Fel, MRC Lab Molecular Biol, Cambridge, Eng, 75-77. *Concurrent Pos:* Fel, Am Cancer Soc, 75-76 & jr fac res award, 78-81; NSF fel, 76-77. *Mem:* Sigma Xi. *Res:* DNA sequence and mechanism of action of genetic control signals. *Mailing Add:* Dept Biochem Washington Univ Sch Med 660 S Euclid Ave St Louis MO 63110-1010

BARNES, WILFRED E, ALGEBRA. *Current Pos:* head dept, 66-82, prof, 66-94, EMER PROF MATH, IOWA STATE UNIV, 94- *Personal Data:* b Oak Park, Ill, June 3, 24; m 46; c 2. *Educ:* Univ Chicago, BS, 49, MS, 50; Univ BC, PhD(math), 54. *Prof Exp:* From instr to prof math, Wash State Univ, 54-66. *Mem:* Am Math Soc; Math Asn Am; Sigma Xi. *Res:* Algebra; theory of rings and ideals. *Mailing Add:* 35102 Riverside Dr Albany OR 97321

BARNES, WILLIAM CHARLES, GEOLOGY. *Current Pos:* asst prof, 68-77, ASSOC PROF GEOL, UNIV BC, 77- *Personal Data:* b Chicago, Ill, Dec 12, 34; m 67; c 1. *Educ:* Colo Sch Mines, Geol E, 56; Univ Wyo, MS, 58; Princeton Univ, PhD(geol), 63. *Prof Exp:* Geologist, Humble Oil & Ref Co, 58-59; asst prof geol, Ore State Univ, 63-67; geologist, US Geol Surv, 67-68. *Mem:* Geol Soc Am; Geol Asn Can. *Res:* Sedimentology; organic geochemistry of recent marine and lacustrine sediments; overthrust fault mechanics. *Mailing Add:* Dept Earth & Ocean Sci Univ BC 6339 Stores Rd Vancouver BC V6T 1W5 Can

BARNES, WILLIAM GARTIN, MICROBIOLOGY, BIOLOGY. *Current Pos:* PROF PATH, SCH MED, UNIV MO, KANSAS CITY, 83; DIR MICROBIOL, TRUMAN MED CTR, KANSAS CITY, MO, 83- *Personal Data:* b Leavenworth, Kans, June 13, 27; m 55, Roberta Long; c Eric, Kris & Neal. *Educ:* Univ Kans, BA, 50, PhD(microbiol), 68; Univ Kansas City, MA, 60. *Honors & Awards:* C Herrick Award, Eli Lilly Lab, 68; Sci Exhibit Award, Am Acad Dermat, 71; Gold Award, Am Soc Clin Pathologists, 72. *Prof Exp:* Tech rep pharmaceut, Winthrop Labs, Kansas City, 53-58; instr biol, Kansas City Jr Col, 60-63; instr microbiol, Sch Dent, Univ Mo, 64-65, asst prof, 65-69; chief microbiologist, Gen Hosp, Kansas City, 69-74; dir microbiol, Vet Admin Hosp, 74-83; from asst prof to assoc prof path, Sch Med, Univ Kans, 79-82. *Concurrent Pos:* Consult microbiologist. *Mem:* Am Soc Microbiol; Am Asn Bioanal; Am Soc Clin Path; fel Am Acad Microbiol; fel Infectious Dis Soc Am. *Res:* Medical-clinical microbiology; host-parasite relationships. *Mailing Add:* 15513 Floyd Overland Park KS 66223

BARNES, WILLIAM SHELLEY, FOOD MUTAGENS. *Current Pos:* asst prof, 84-87, assoc prof, 87-, PROF BIOL, CLARION UNIV, PA. *Personal Data:* b Wallingford, Conn, Feb 15, 47; m 70; c 2. *Educ:* Marietta Col, Ohio, BA, 69; Univ Mass, Amherst, PhD(bot), 80. *Prof Exp:* Res demonstr genetics, Univ Wales, UK, 78-79; res fel carcinogenesis, BC Cancer Res Ctr, Vancouver, 80-81; sr res fel, Am Health Fedn, Valhalla, NY, 81-82, assoc, 82-84. *Concurrent Pos:* Consult, Am Health Found, 84-86. *Mem:* Environ Mutagenesis Soc; AAAS. *Res:* Dietary origin of cancer; carcinogens formed in meat during cooking, their metabolism and genotoxic effects in vivo. *Mailing Add:* Dept Biol Clarion Univ Clarion PA 16214-1232

BARNES, WILLIAM WAYNE, MEDICAL ENTOMOLOGY, INSECT TOXICOLOGY. *Current Pos:* RETIRED. *Personal Data:* b Amsterdam, Ohio, May 26, 27; m 50; c 3. *Educ:* Ohio State Univ, BSc, 50, MSc, 58, PhD(insect toxicol), 64. *Prof Exp:* Entomologist, US Army, 52-70, chief med entom div, 66-70; chief environ biol br, Tenn Valley Auth, 70-89. *Mem:* Am Mosquito Control Asn. *Res:* Medical acarology; insect pathology; insect ecology; epidemiology of arthropod-borne diseases. *Mailing Add:* 706 Riverview Dr Florence AL 35630

BARNESS, LEWIS ABRAHAM, NUTRITION, PEDIATRICS. *Current Pos:* prof & chmn dept, 72-88, PROF PEDIAT, COL MED, UNIV S FLA, TAMPA, 92- *Personal Data:* b Atlantic City, NJ, July 31, 21; m 87, Enid F Gilbert; c Carol, Mary, Laura, Elizabeth, Joseph, Jennifer & Rebecca. *Educ:* Harvard Univ, AB, 41, MD, 44. *Hon Degrees:* MA, Univ Pa, 71. *Honors & Awards:* Borden Award Nutrit, Am Acad Pediat, 72, Jacobi Award, 91; Noer Distinguished Professor, Univ SFla, 80; Goldberger Award Clin Nutrit, AMA, 84; Joseph St Geme Leadership Award, 7 Pediat Socs, 91; John Howland Award, Am Pediat Soc, 93; Med Educ Lifetime Achievement Award, Am Acad Pediat, 95. *Prof Exp:* From instr to prof pediat, Med Sch, Univ Pa, 51-72; vis prof pediat, Univ Wis-Madison, 87-92. *Concurrent Pos:* Res fel, Children's Med Ctr, Boston, 47-50. *Mem:* AAAS; Soc Pediat; Am Pediat Soc; Am Acad Pediat; Am Inst Nutrit; Am Col Nutrit. *Res:* Metabolic diseases; liver necrosis; nitrogen requirements of infants. *Mailing Add:* Dept Pediat Univ SFla Col Med Box 15 Tampa FL 33606. *Fax:* 813-272-2749

BARNET, ANN B, PEDIATRIC NEUROLOGY. *Current Pos:* from asst prof to assoc prof, 67-84, PROF NEUROL & CHILD HEALTH & DEVELOP SCH MED, GEORGE WASHINGTON UNIV, 84-; DIR, EEG RES LAB & EVOKED RESPONSE LAB, DEPT NEUROL, CHILDREN'S HOSP, NAT MED CTR, 65- *Personal Data:* b Chicago, Ill; m 53; c 3. *Educ:* Sarah Lawrence Col, AB, 51; Harvard Univ, MD, 55. *Prof Exp:* Trainee ment health, Seizure Unit, Children's Med Ctr, Boston, Mass, 52; asst pediat, US Army 130th Field Hosp, Heidelberg, Ger, 56-57; clin dir, Child Develop Clin, Cambridge, Mass, 58-61; res assoc exp psychophysiol, Walter Reed Army Inst Res, 61-73. *Concurrent Pos:* Guest physician, Nerve Clin, Heidelberg Univ, 57; asst physician, Wrentham State Sch, Mass, 58; fel pediat, Mass Gen Hosp, Boston, 58-61; prin investr, Army Med Res & Develop Command Contract, 61-64; res assoc, Wash Sch Psychiat, 61-65; consult, Dept Neurol, Walter Reed Army Hosp, 61-65 & Children's Bur Proj 237, DC, 64-66; deleg, Conf Young Deaf Child, Toronto, Ont, 64 & Int Cong Physiol, Moscow, USSR, 66; USPHS grant, 64-78; mem, Int Elec Response Audiometry Study Group; NIMH res scientist develop award, 70-75; W T Grant Found res grant, 73-75; mem, NIH Commun Sci Study Sect, 73-77; consult, Va Comn Visually Handicapped, 77-80, UN Develop Prog, 77-83 & Food Drug Admin, 78-83; Nat Found, March of Dimes grants, 78-; Children's Hosp Res Found grant, 81-84; pres, The Family Place, Inc; proj dir, Better Babies, 83-85. *Mem:* AAAS; Soc Neuroscience. *Res:* Research on development of sensory and perceptual processes in normal and abnormal infants and young children using the method of computer analysis of electroenchephalographic responses to sensory stimuli; research in methods of reducing the incidence of low birth weight infants born to high risk women. *Mailing Add:* Dept Neurol Children's Hosp Nat Med Ctr 111 Michigan Ave NW Washington DC 20010

BARNET, HARRY NATHAN, BIOCHEMISTRY. *Current Pos:* RETIRED. *Personal Data:* b San Diego, Calif, Apr 30, 23; m 46; c 2. *Educ:* San Diego State Col, AB, 47; Univ Southern Calif, MS, 50, PhD(biochem), 53. *Prof Exp:* Asst, Med Sch, Univ Southern Calif, 49-53; res assoc, Scripps Metab Clin, 53-57; from asst prof to prof chem, US Int Univ, 57-75; prof chem, Palomar Col, 75-90. *Mem:* AAAS; Am Chem Soc; Sigma Xi. *Res:* tracer carbohydrate metabolism; serum protein chemistry; erythrocyte metabolism; blood storage. *Mailing Add:* 6036 La Jolla Blvd La Jolla CA 92037

BARNETT, ALLEN, NEUROPHARMACOLOGY. *Current Pos:* PHARMACOLOGIST, SCHERING CORP, 66- *Personal Data:* b Newark, NJ, May 5, 37; m 65; c 2. *Educ:* Rutgers Univ, BS, 59; State Univ NY Buffalo, PhD(pharmacol), 65. *Prof Exp:* Pharmacologist, Hoffman-La Roche Inc, 65-66. *Mem:* AAAS; Am Chem Soc; Am Soc Pharmacol & Exp Therapeut; sr mem Acad Pharmaceut Sci; Am Pharmaceut Asn. *Res:* Central nervous system dopamine receptors; analgesics. *Mailing Add:* Dept Pharmacol Schering-Plough Res 2000 Galloping Hill Rd Kennilworth NJ 07003

BARNETT, ALLEN M, ELECTRICAL ENGINEERING. *Current Pos:* PRES, ASTROPOWER, INC, 89-, PROF ELEC ENG, UNIV DEL, 76- *Personal Data:* b Oklahoma City, Okla, June 20, 40; m 68; c 3. *Educ:* Univ Ill, Urbana, BSEE, 62, MS, 63; Carnegie Inst Technol, PhD(elec eng), 66. *Honors & Awards:* IR-100 Awards, 70, 73, 74 & 79. *Prof Exp:* Proj engr, Electronics Lab, Gen Elec Co, 66-69, physicist, Res & Develop Ctr, 69-76; pres, XCITON Corp, 71-75; dir, Inst Energy Conversion, Univ Del, 76-79; gen mgr, Astro Power Div, Astro Systs, Inc, 83-89. *Concurrent Pos:* Consult, Technol & Mktg Assessment, 75- *Mem:* Am Phys Soc; Inst Elec & Electronics Engrs; Int Solar Energy Soc. *Res:* Solar energy, solar cells, especially development of record energy conversion efficiencies for thin-film solar cells; invention of thin film crystalline silicon solar cells on low cost substrates; energy storage; energy systems; energy conservation; development of planar processing technology for compound semiconductors. *Mailing Add:* Astropower Del Solar Park 461 Wyoming Rd Newark DE 19716-2000

BARNETT, AUDREY, GENETICS, PROTOZOOLOGY. *Current Pos:* ASSOC PROF ZOOL, UNIV MD, COLLEGE PARK, 71- *Personal Data:* b Somerset, Pa, May, 1933. *Educ:* Wilson Col, AB, 55; Ind Univ, MA, 57, PhD(genetics), 62. *Prof Exp:* Asst, Ind Univ, 55-58; asst prof biol, Western Col, 61-63; NIH vis fel, Princeton Univ, 63-65; asst prof, Bryn Mawr Col, 65-70. *Concurrent Pos:* NIH spec res fel, 68-69; vis scientist, Argonne Nat Lab, 68-70; guest worker, NIH & Nat Inst Arthritis, Metab & Digestive Dis, 77-78. *Mem:* AAAS; Soc Protozool; Genetics Soc Am; Sigma Xi. *Res:* Genetics of mating types and circadian rhythm of mating type reversals in Paramecium multimicronucleatum; cell surface antigens. *Mailing Add:* Dept Zool Univ Md College Park MD 20742-0001

BARNETT, BILL B, VIROLOGY, IMMUNODIAGNOSTICS. *Current Pos:* PROF, UTAH STATE UNIV, 77- *Personal Data:* b Pendelton, Ore, Jan 14, 46. *Educ:* Wash State Univ, BS, 68; Utah State Univ, PhD(biochem), 75. *Prof Exp:* Radiochemist, US Atomic Energy Comn, 68-71; NIH trainee, Utah State Univ, 71-75; sr scientist, Becton-Dickinson, Inc, 75-77. *Concurrent Pos:* Tech adv, Int Atomic Energy Agency, Vienna, 81- *Mem:* Am Soc Microbiol; Sigma Xi; Soc Exp Biol & Med; AAAS. *Res:* Arena viruses; bunyaviruses; detection procedures for viruses and antibodies; vaccine development; monoclonal antibodies and their application to virology; antiviral drugs. *Mailing Add:* Dept Biol Utah State Univ Logan UT 84322-0001

BARNETT, BRUCE A, PHYSICS. *Current Pos:* PROF & CHMN, DEPT PHYSICS & ASTRON, JOHNS HOPKINS UNIV, 76- *Personal Data:* b Ohio, Nov, 43; c 1. *Educ:* Harvard Univ, BA, 65; Univ Md, PhD(physics), 70. *Prof Exp:* Res assoc, Univ Md, 70-72, asst prof, 72-76. *Concurrent Pos:* Mem, Collider Detector Fermilab, 89- *Mem:* Fel Am Phys Soc (secy). *Res:* Research has covered a large variety of areas within particle physics; author of over 100 publications. *Mailing Add:* Henry A Rowland Dept Physics & Astron Johns Hopkins Univ 34th Charles St Baltimore MD 21218

BARNETT, CHARLES JACKSON, PROCESS RESEARCH. *Current Pos:* Sr org chemist, 69-75, from res scientist to sr res scientist, 75-93, RES ADV, ELI LILLY & CO, 94- *Personal Data:* b Chattanooga, Tenn, Feb 15, 42; m 70, Sharon Tankersley; c Jennifer L & Elizabeth A. *Educ:* Vanderbilt Univ, BA, 64; Rice Univ, PhD(org chem), 69. *Mem:* Am Chem Soc; Int Soc Heterocyclic Chem. *Res:* Heterocylic synthesis; new synthetic methods; asymmetric synthesis; process research; chemistry and synthesis of antifolate antitumor drugs. *Mailing Add:* 7540 N Pennsylvania St Indianapolis IN 46240. *Fax:* 317-276-4507

BARNETT, CLAUDE C, THEORETICAL PHYSICS. *Current Pos:* Instr, 57-58, from asst prof to assoc prof, 58-64, PROF PHYSICS, WALLA WALLA COL, 64-, CHMN DEPT, 61- *Personal Data:* b Woodinville, Wash, Nov 8, 28; m 51; c 2. *Educ:* Walla Walla Col, BS, 52; Wash State Univ, MS, 56, PhD(physics), 60. *Mem:* Am Phys Soc; Am Asn Physics Teachers; Sigma Xi. *Res:* Electroluminescence; quantum hydrodynamics; relativity; bio-electronics; radar; many-body problem; modelling and simulation. *Mailing Add:* 704 SW Evans College Place WA 99324-1435

BARNETT, DAVID, GEOMETRY. *Current Pos:* from asst prof to assoc prof, 67-76, PROF MATH, UNIV CALIF, DAVIS, 76- *Personal Data:* b Arlington, Wash, Sept 4, 40; m 65. *Educ:* Univ Wash, BS, 64, MS, 66, PhD(math), 67. *Prof Exp:* Asst prof, Western Wash State Col, 67. *Concurrent Pos:* NSF res grant, Univ Calif, Davis, 68- *Mem:* Math Asn Am. *Res:* Combinatorial structure of convex polytopes, particularly problems dealing with the relationships between the numbers of faces of different dimensions of convex polytopes. *Mailing Add:* Dept Math Univ Calif Davis CA 95616

BARNETT, DAVID M, APPLIED MECHANICS, MATERIALS SCIENCE. *Current Pos:* from asst prof to assoc prof, 69-78, PROF MAT SCI & APPL MECH, STANFORD UNIV, 78- *Personal Data:* b Washington, DC, Nov 16, 39; m 72, Muriel Melcher; c Rachel & Elisabeth. *Educ:* Rice Univ, BA, 61, MS, 63; Stanford Univ, PhD(mat sci), 67. *Prof Exp:* NATO fel, Inst Theoret Physics, Clausthal Tech Univ, 67-68; staff scientist, Sci Labs, Ford Motor Co, Mich, 68-69. *Concurrent Pos:* Vis scientist, Physics Inst, Oslo Univ, Norway, 74; consult, Sandia Labs, Calif, 77-80, IBM, 83-85 & Intel, 84-86. *Mem:* Int Soc Interaction Mech & Math. *Res:* Defects in anisotropic elastic solids; surface waves in anisotropic elastic and piezoelectric solids; non-destructive testing; mechanics of thin films. *Mailing Add:* Dept Mat Sci & Eng Stanford Univ Stanford CA 94305-2205. *Fax:* 650-725-4034; *E-Mail:* barnett@leland.stanford.edu

BARNETT, DON(ALD) R(AY), HUMAN & BIOCHEMICAL GENETICS, MEDICAL GENETICS EDUCATION. *Current Pos:* ASSOC PROF, DEPT CELLULAR & STRUCT BIOL, HEALTH SCI CTR, UNIV TEX, SAN ANTONIO, 82- *Personal Data:* b Morton, Tex, Oct 19, 35. *Educ:* Univ Tex, Austin, BA, 67; Univ Tex, Galveston, MA, 69, PhD(human genetics), 71. *Honors & Awards:* Award for Excellence in Res, Sigma Xi, 72. *Prof Exp:* Res scientist assoc biochem genetics, Dept Zool, Univ Tex, Austin, 62-63 & 65-68; res asst, Dept Genetics, Rockefeller Inst, 63-65; res scientist, Med Br & Grad Sch Biomed Sci, Univ Tex, Galveston, 68-71, from instr to assoc prof biochem genetics, 71-82. *Concurrent Pos:* Nat Found March of Dimes & Cystic Fibrosis Found grants, Med Br, Univ Tex, Galveston, 74-76, USPHS grant, 74-88; mem, Res Comt, Nat Cystic Fibrosis Found, 75-79; pres, Tex Genetics Soc, 89, ed, 90-97. *Mem:* AAAS; Am Soc Human Genetics; Soc Cellular Biol; Sigma Xi. *Res:* Biochemical basis for inherited disease; genetic control of protein and DNA structure and function; med genetics education. *Mailing Add:* Dept Cellular & Struct Biol Health Sci Ctr Univ Tex Health Sci Ctr 7703 Floyd Curl Dr San Antonio TX 78284-7762. *Fax:* 210-567-3803

BARNETT, DOUGLAS ELDON, ENTOMOLOGY, INTERNATIONAL ORGANIZATIONS IN AGRICULTURE. *Current Pos:* agriculturist-entomologist, Animal & Plant Health Inspection Serv, 76-92, ASST DIR OPER SUPPORT, INT SERV, USDA, 92- *Personal Data:* b Walnut Ridge, Ark, Feb 11, 44; m 73, Rosa E Lacy. *Educ:* Ark State Univ, BSE, 67; Northwestern State Univ, MS, 70; Univ Ky, PhD(entom), 74. *Prof Exp:* Lab asst biol, Northwestern State Univ, 67-68; sci instr, Maynard Pub Schs, 68-69; instr biol, Paragould Pub Schs, Ark, 69-70; researcher systs, Dept Entom, Univ Ky, 70, surv entomologist, 71-76. *Concurrent Pos:* Chmn sect E, Entom Soc Am. *Mem:* Entom Soc Am; Sigma Xi. *Res:* Revision of various genera in the Cicadellidae; taxonomic methods, cave ecology, pest detection; pest risk analysis. *Mailing Add:* Rm 5C70 4700 River Rd Riverdale MD 20737. *Fax:* 301-436-8318

BARNETT, GUY OCTO, INFORMATION SCIENCE & SYSTEMS, INTELLIGENT SYSTEMS. *Current Pos:* PHYSICIAN, MASS GEN HOSP, 79-; PROF MED, HARVARD MED SCH, 80- *Personal Data:* b Chula Vista, Calif, Sept 18, 30; m 58; c 3. *Educ:* Vanderbilt Univ, BA, 52; Harvard Univ, MD, 56. *Prof Exp:* Med resident, Peter Bent Brigham Hosp, 56-61; clin assoc, Nat Heart Inst, 58-60; estab investr, Am Heart Assoc, 61-67. *Concurrent Pos:* lectr elec eng, Mass Inst Technol, 72-; bd dirs, Am Med Informatics Asn, 84- *Mem:* Fel Inst Med-Nat Acad Sci; Inst Elec & Electronics Engrs; Asn Comput Mach; Biomed Eng Soc; Am Col Physicians. *Res:* Computer applications in patient care; computer-aided instruction in medical education. *Mailing Add:* Lab Comput Sci Mass Gen Hosp Boston MA 02114

BARNETT, H J M, NEUROLOGY. *Current Pos:* prof, 69-, EMER PROF CLIN NEUROL SCI & CHMN DEPT, UNIV WESTERN ONT. *Personal Data:* b Newcastle-on-Tyne, Eng, Feb 10, 22; Can citizen; m 46; c 4. *Educ:* Univ Toronto, MD, 44; FRCP(C), 52. *Prof Exp:* Assoc prof neurol, Univ Toronto, 67-69. *Mailing Add:* John P Robards Res Inst PO Box 5015 100 Perth Dr London ON N6A 5K8 Can

BARNETT, HENRY LEWIS, PEDIATRICS, PEDIATRIC NEPHROLOGY. *Current Pos:* prof & head dept, Albert Einstein Cool Med, 55-69, assoc dean clin affairs, 69-72, Univ prof, 72-81, EMER PROF PEDIAT, ALBERT EINSTEIN COL MED, 81-; MED DIR, CHILDREN'S AID SOC, 81- *Personal Data:* b Detroit, Mich, June 25, 14; m 40, Shirley Blanchard; c Judy & Martin. *Educ:* Washington Univ, St Louis, BS, 34, MD, 38. *Honors & Awards:* Mead-Johnson Award, 49; David Hume Award, 77; John Howland Award & Medal, 84; John P Peters Award, 88; Trustees Award, Children's Aid Soc, 92; Kidney Award, Am Acad Pediat. *Prof Exp:* Instr pediat, Sch Med, Washington Univ, 41-43; from asst prof to assoc prof, Med Col, Cornell Univ, 46-55. *Concurrent Pos:* Vis pediatrician, Bronx Munic Hosp Ctr, 55- *Mem:* Inst Med-Nat Acad Sci; Am Soc Clin Invest; Am Pediat Soc (pres, 81-82); Am Soc Pediat Nephrology; Soc Ped Res (pres, 59-60); Asn Am Physicians. *Res:* Physiology of infants and children with particular reference to kidney physiology and electrolyte metabolism as affected by growth; pediatric clinical epidemiology; pediatric and medical education; child welfare. *Mailing Add:* Children's Aid Soc 150 E 45th St New York NY 10017. *Fax:* 212-986-9635

BARNETT, HERALD ALVA, SPECTROSCOPY. *Current Pos:* RETIRED. *Personal Data:* b Orlando, WVa, Oct 2, 23; m 47, Eleanor Whitman; c Brend B, Colijn & Bruce B. *Educ:* Salem Col, BS, 44; WVa Univ, MS, 50. *Prof Exp:* Sect supvr anal chem, chromatography & spectrometry, Tech Ctr, US Steel Corp, 50-84, res mgr, Tech Serv, 82-86. *Concurrent Pos:* Treas, Pittsburgh Con Anal Chem & Applc Spectros, 93, vpres, 94, pres, 95. *Mem:* Am Chem Soc; Am Soc Testing & Mat; Coblentz Soc; Soc Appl Spectros. *Res:* Applications of mass spectrometry; absorption and fluorescence spectrophotometry; atomic absorption spectrometry; applications of gas chromatography analytical chemistry, x-ray and optical emission spectrometry to coal-chemical recovery processes, steel-making processes and air and water pollution abatement studies. *Mailing Add:* 4133 Dundee Dr Murrysville PA 15668. *Fax:* 412-825-3224

BARNETT, JAMES P, PLANT PHYSIOLOGY, FORESTRY. *Current Pos:* RES FORESTER, SOUTHERN FOREST EXP STA, US FOREST SERV, 57- *Personal Data:* b Mena, Ark, May 19, 35; m 65; c 2. *Educ:* La State Univ, BSF, 57, MF, 63; Duke Univ, DF, 68. *Mem:* Soc Am Foresters; Am Soc Plant Physiol. *Res:* Seed dormancy and physiology in the genus Pinus; artificial regeneration of forest stands; vegetation control; silviculture of Pinus. *Mailing Add:* 3783 S Loop Pineville LA 71360

BARNETT, JEFFREY CHARLES, MATHEMATICS EDUCATION. *Current Pos:* PROF CURRIC & INSTR & DEAN, COL EDUC, UNIV WIS, 89- *Personal Data:* b Philadelphia, Pa, Oct 24, 46; m; c 1. *Educ:* Shippensburg State Col, BSEd, 67; Bucknell Univ, MS, 69; Pa State Univ, PhD(math educ), 74. *Prof Exp:* Instr math, Neshaminy High Sch, 69-70 & Williamsport Area Community Col, 70-71; asst math educ, Pa State Univ, 71-74; asst prof math, Northern Ill Univ, 74-78; from asst prof to prof math & comput sci, Ft Hays State Univ, 78-89. *Concurrent Pos:* NSF grant co-researcher, Northern Ill Univ, 77-79; pres elect, Wis Asn Col Teacher Educ, 92-; dir, Wis Instr Technol Resource Ctr, 93- *Mem:* Nat Coun Teachers Math; Am Educ Res Asn; Int Coun Technol in Educ. *Res:* Mathematics education, particularly problem solving, use of manipulatives and the role of visual abilities; teaching heuristics. *Mailing Add:* Col Educ Univ Wis 800 W Main Whitewater WI 53190-1705

BARNETT, JOHN BRIAN, IMMUNOTOXICOLOGY. *Current Pos:* PROF & CHMN, DEPT MICROBIOL/IMMUNOL, WVA UNIV, 92- *Personal Data:* b Cardston, Alta, Apr 17, 45; US citizen; m 66, Cecilia Dannis; c John & Cynthia. *Educ:* Mont State Univ, BS, 67, MS, 69; Univ Louisville, PhD(microbiol), 73. *Honors & Awards:* Young Investr Award, Am Lung Asn, 75. *Prof Exp:* From asst prof to prof, Dept Pharm/Toxicol, Univ Ark, 75-92, prof, Dept Microbiol/Immunol, 88-92. *Concurrent Pos:* NIH fel, Dept Microbiol, Univ Tenn, 73-75, lectr, 74-75. *Mem:* Am Asn Immunologists; Am Soc Microbiol; Sigma Xi; Soc Toxicol; AAAS. *Res:* Immunotoxic consequences of exposure to xenobiotic compounds. *Mailing Add:* 3607 Monarch Ct Morgantown WV 26505. *Fax:* 304-293-7823; *E-Mail:* jbarnett@wvu.edu

BARNETT, JOHN DEAN, high pressure, critical phenomena, for more information see previous edition

BARNETT, JOHN WILLIAM, TOXICOLOGY, ENTOMOLOGY. *Current Pos:* res specialist, Ciba-Geigy Corp, 73-75, toxicologist, 75-77, sr toxicologist, 78-79, mgr toxicol, 79-80, dir, Safety Evals, 80-89, EXEC DIR, SAFETY EVALS, CIBA-GEIGY CORP, 89- *Personal Data:* b Gadsden, Ala, Sept 17, 41; m 62; c 2. *Educ:* Auburn Univ, BS, 62, MS, 64, PhD(entom), 69. *Prof Exp:* Asst prof entom, Univ Fla, 69-70; exten entomologist, Auburn Univ, 70-72. *Mem:* Entom Soc Am; AAAS; Soc Toxicol; Soc Environ Toxicol & Chem; Sigma Xi. *Res:* Animal toxicology; insect physiology and biochemistry; pesticide development; agricultural pest management. *Mailing Add:* 3202 Cabarrus Dr Greensboro NC 27407

BARNETT, KENNETH WAYNE, INORGANIC CHEMISTRY, POLYMER CHEMISTRY. *Current Pos:* AT ASHLAND CHEM CO, 79- *Personal Data:* b Mobile, Ala, Apr 8, 40; m 67; c 2. *Educ:* Univ Tex, Arlington, BS, 63; Univ Wis, PhD(inorg chem), 67. *Prof Exp:* Res chemist, Shell Develop Co, 67-70; asst prof chem, Univ Mo-St Louis, 70-76, assoc prof, 76-79. *Mem:* Am Chem Soc; Am Foundrymen's Soc. *Res:* Organometallic chemistry of the transition elements; organic reactions catalyzed by transition metals; inorganic photochemistry; polymer chemistry; adhesives and coatings; foundry technology. *Mailing Add:* Ashland Chem Co PO Box 2219 Columbus OH 43216-2219

BARNETT, LELAND BRUCE, zoology, ecology, for more information see previous edition

BARNETT, LEWIS BRINKLEY, PHYSICAL BIOCHEMISTRY. *Current Pos:* asst prof, 63-67, ASSOC PROF BIOCHEM & NUTRIT, VA POLYTECH INST & STATE UNIV, 67-, ASST DEAN, COL ARTS & SCI, 84- *Personal Data:* b Lexington, Ky, Jan 29, 34; m 56, Charlotte Barnes; c Elizabeth, William, Charles & Catherine. *Educ:* Univ Ky, BS, 55; Univ Iowa, MS, 57, PhD(biochem), 59. *Prof Exp:* NSF fel phys chem, Univ Wis, 59-60, univ res fel, 60-61; Am Heart Asn advan res fel, Van't Hoff Lab, Neth, 61-63. *Concurrent Pos:* Mem, Blacksburg town coun, 86- *Mem:* Am Chem Soc; Am Soc Biol Chem; Sigma Xi. *Res:* Protein chemistry. *Mailing Add:* 236 Burruss Hall Va Polytech Inst & State Univ Blacksburg VA 24061. *E-Mail:* lbb@vt.edu

BARNETT, MARK, COMPUTATIONAL FLUID DYNAMICS. *Current Pos:* assoc res engr, 84-87, RES ENGR, UNITED TECHNOL RES CTR, 87- *Personal Data:* b Amityville, NY, Mar 1, 57; m 87; c 1. *Educ:* Univ Cincinnati, BS, 79, MS, 81, PhD(aerospace eng), 84. *Prof Exp:* Aerospace engr, NASA Ames Res Ctr, Univ Cincinnati, 77-79. *Concurrent Pos:* Treas, Am Inst Aeronaut & Astronaut, Conn Sect, 86-; adj prof, Hartford Grad Ctr, Rensellear Polytech Inst, 88- *Mem:* Am Inst Aeronautics & Astronaut; Sigma Xi. *Res:* Computational fluid dynamics; viscous flows in turbomachinery; strong viscous/inviscid interactions in internal and external flows; boundary layer theory. *Mailing Add:* 50 Brainard Rd West Hartford CT 06117

BARNETT, MICHAEL PETER, litigation & computing, programming languages, for more information see previous edition

BARNETT, NEAL MASON, PLANT PHYSIOLOGY. *Current Pos:* asst prof, 68-75, ASSOC PROF PLANT PHYSIOL, UNIV MD, COLLEGE PARK, 75- *Personal Data:* b Lafayette, Ind, May 31, 37; m 60, Linda Boliek; c William & John. *Educ:* Purdue Univ, BS, 59; Duke Univ, PhD(bot), 66. *Prof Exp:* Res assoc plant physiol, Purdue Univ, 65-67. *Concurrent Pos:* NIH fel, Mich State Univ & AEC Plant Res Lab, 67-68. *Mem:* AAAS; Am Soc Plant Physiol; Am Inst Biol Sci. *Res:* Biochemistry of water stress in plants; plant cell wall protein; nitrogen assimilation. *Mailing Add:* Dept Bot Univ Md College Park MD 20742. *Fax:* 301-314-9082; *E-Mail:* nb2@umail.umd.edu

BARNETT, ORTUS WEBB, JR, PLANT VIROLOGY, PLANT PATHOLOGY. *Current Pos:* PROF & HEAD, DEPT PLANT PATH, NC STATE UNIV, 92- *Personal Data:* b Pine Bluff, Ark, July 2, 39; m 64, Phyllis G McFarland; c 3. *Educ:* Univ Ark, BSA, 61, MS, 65; Univ Wis, PhD(plant path), 69. *Prof Exp:* Sr sci officer, Scottist Crop Res Inst, 68-69; from asst prof to prof plant path & physiol, Clemson Univ, 69-92. *Concurrent Pos:* Collabr, USDA, 69-92; joint appointment, Dept Microbiol, 72-92; assoc ed, Phytopath, 80-82, sr ed, 85-87; Fulbright travel Award, Waite Agr Res Inst, Australia, 82-83; mem plant virus subcomt, Int Comt Taxon Viruses, 87-96. *Mem:* Am Phytopath Soc (secy, 86-89, vpres, 90, pres-elect, 91, pres, 92); Int Soc Plant Path; Am Soc Virol. *Res:* White clover viruses; virus purification and serology; plant virus inactivation in vitro; relationships of plant viruses by complementary DNA probes; plant virus epidemiology; plant virus taxonomy; tobacco viruses. *Mailing Add:* Dept Plant Path NC State Univ Raleigh NC 27695-7616

BARNETT, PAUL EDWARD, FOREST GENETICS. *Current Pos:* SCIENTIST, BECHTEL NAT INC, 89- *Personal Data:* b Jerryville, WVa, Mar 19, 36; m 59; c 2. *Educ:* WVa Univ, BS, 64; Univ Tenn, MS, 67, PhD(genetics), 72. *Prof Exp:* Res asst forest genetics, Forestry Dept, Univ Tenn, 64-69; botanist forest physiol, Tenn Valley Authority, 69-73, staff forester forest genetics, 73-74, staff forester & proj leader forest genetics, Div Forestry, Fisheries & Wildlife Develop, 74-79, staff forester, Forest & Biomass Harvesting Opers, 79-88. *Mem:* Sigma Xi. *Res:* Genetics and breeding of forest trees with superior growth and form; geographic and altitudinal variation; establishment of seed production areas and hardwood plantation establishment and growth; investigation of equipment and methods to improve quantity and efficiency of recovery in forest harvesting operations; harvesting biomass plantations. *Mailing Add:* 9301 Carlton Circle Knoxville TN 37922

BARNETT, R(ALPH) MICHAEL, SUPERSYMMETRY, QUANTUM CHROMODYNAMICS. *Current Pos:* staff scientist, 84-89, SR SCIENTIST, LAWRENCE BERKELEY NAT LAB, 90- *Personal Data:* b Gulfport, Miss, Jan 25, 44; m 80, Suzanne Hamilton; c Leilani, Julia & Russell. *Educ:* Antioch Col, BS, 66; Univ Chicago, PhD(physics), 71. *Prof Exp:* Fel physics, Univ Calif, Irvine, 72-74; res fel, Harvard Univ, 74-76; res assoc physics, Stanford Linear Accelerator Ctr, 76-83; vis physicist, Inst Theoret Physics, Univ Calif, Santa Barbara, 83- 84. *Concurrent Pos:* Head, Particle Data Group, Lawrence Berkeley Lab; vpres, Contemp Physics Educ Proj; pub info coordr, Am Phys Soc; educ coordr, Div Particles & Fields, ATLAS Exp, Large Hadron Collider. *Mem:* Fel Am Phys Soc. *Res:* Standard Model and its extensions, including nature and validity of quantum chromodynamics; neutral current couplings; properties, production, and decays of supersymmetric particles, Higgs bosons and heavy quarks; physics education and outreach; detector requirements for observation of physics processes; science education. *Mailing Add:* Lawrence Berkeley Nat Lab MS 50-308 1 Cyclotron Rd Berkeley CA 94720. *Fax:* 510-486-5401; *E-Mail:* barnett@lbl.gov

BARNETT, RONALD DAVID, AGRONOMY, PLANT GENETICS. *Current Pos:* PROF AGRON, UNIV FLA, 70- *Personal Data:* b Texarkana, Ark, Nov 20, 43; m 61; c 3. *Educ:* Univ Ark, BS, 65, MS, 68; Purdue Univ, PhD(genetics, plant breeding), 70. *Mem:* Am Soc Agron; Crop Sci Soc Am; Am Genetic Asn; AAAS; Coun Agr Sci & Technol. *Res:* Plant breeding and genetics with emphasis on varietal development in wheat, triticale, rye and oats. *Mailing Add:* N Fla Res & Educ Ctr Univ Fla Rte 3 Box 4370 Quincy FL 32351

BARNETT, RONALD E, PHYSICAL ORGANIC CHEMISTRY, ENZYMOLOGY. *Current Pos:* DIR, FUNDAMENTAL SCI, BORDEN INC, 89- *Personal Data:* b Pueblo, Colo, Dec 26, 42; m 63; c 1. *Educ:* Univ Colo, BA, 65; Brandeis Univ, PhD(biochem), 68. *Honors & Awards:* Merck Co Found Faculty develop award, 69. *Prof Exp:* Res assoc biochem, Stanford Univ, 68-69; asst prof chem, Univ Minn, Minneapolis, 69-76; assoc prof biochem & nutrit, Va Polytech Inst & State Univ, 76-80; Prin scientist, Gen Foods, 80-88; Group mgr ingredient res, Pepsico, 88-89. *Concurrent Pos:* NSF fel, 68-69; NIH res grant, 70- *Mem:* Fedn Am Soc Exp Biol; Am Chem Soc; Am Soc Biochem & Molecular Biol; Am Asn Cereal Chemists. *Res:* Carbonyl and acyl group reactions with diffusion limited rate determining steps; models for enzymatic reactions; conformational changes in enzymes; mechanisms of active transport of cations through cell membranes; author of 39 publications; 46 patents on high intensity sweeteners, sweetener inhibitors & food ingredients. *Mailing Add:* Campbell Soup Co Campbell Pl Box 66Z Camden NJ 08103

BARNETT, SAMUEL C(LARENCE), MECHANICAL ENGINEERING. *Current Pos:* RETIRED. *Personal Data:* b Chatsworth, Ga, May 10, 22; m 50; c 1. *Educ:* Ga Inst Technol, BIE, 48, MS, 56, PhD(mech eng), 62. *Prof Exp:* From asst prof to prof mech eng, Ga Inst Technol, 56-80, asst dir sch mech eng, 62-68, assoc dean undergrad div, 68-72; mgr educ assistance prog, Inst Nuclear Power Opers, Atlanta, Ga, 80-90. *Mem:* Am Soc Mech Engrs. *Res:* Heat transfer; fluid mechanics; thermodynamics; power production; air conditioning; refrigeration. *Mailing Add:* 1938 Gotham Way NE Atlanta GA 30324

BARNETT, SCOTT A, THIN FILM PHYSICS, SURFACE SCIENCE. *Current Pos:* from asst prof to assoc prof, 86-95, PROF MAT SCI, NORTHWESTERN UNIV, 95- *Personal Data:* b July 6, 54; m 89, Joann; c Katrina, Jessica & Emily. *Educ:* Univ Ill, BS, 76, PhD(metall), 82. *Honors & Awards:* Young Invest Award, Off Naval Res, 86. *Prof Exp:* Res asst, Univ Ill, 76-82; vis scientist, Univ Ill, 82-85, Linkoping Univ, 85-86. *Mem:* Am Vacuum Soc. *Res:* Deposition and properties of thin films by techniques such as molecular beam epitaxy and sputter deposition. *Mailing Add:* Dept Mat Sci Mat & Life Sci Bldg Northwestern Univ Evanston IL 60208

BARNETT, STANLEY M(ARVIN), BIOCHEMICAL & SEPARATIONS ENGINEERING, POLUTION PREVENTION. *Current Pos:* PROF CHEM ENG, UNIV RI, 69-, CHMN DEPT, 88-, DIR, RI CTR POLLUTION PREVENT, 92- *Personal Data:* b New York, NY, Apr 8, 36; m 59; c 1. *Educ:* Columbia Univ, BA, 57, BS, 58; Lehigh Univ, MS, 59; Univ Pa, PhD(chem eng), 63. *Honors & Awards:* Save The Bay Environ Achievement Award, 95. *Prof Exp:* Chem engr, Elec Boat Div, Gen Dynamics Corp, 59-61; engr, Process Res Div, Esso Res & Eng Co, 63-64 & Plastics Technol Ctr, Shell Chem Co, 64-69. *Concurrent Pos:* Mem adv bd, RI Solid Waste Mgt Corp, 74-; chmn, Food Pharmaceut & Bioeng Div, Am Inst Chem Engrs, 83. *Mem:* Am Inst Chem Engrs; Soc Indust Microbiologist; Am Chem Soc; NAm Membrane Soc. *Res:* Separations; alternate sources of chemicals, food and energy; waste minimization; pollution prevention; membrane and electrokinetic separations for biological and environmental applications, especially pollution prevention; foam and photosynthetic bioreactor development; alternate sources of chemicals and energy. *Mailing Add:* Dept Chem Eng Univ RI Kingston RI 02881-0806. *Fax:* 401-782-1180; *E-Mail:* barnett@egr.uri.edu

BARNETT, THOMAS BUCHANAN, MEDICINE, PHYSIOLOGY. *Current Pos:* from instr to assoc prof, 52-64, PROF INTERNAL MED, SCH MED, UNIV NC, CHAPEL HILL, 64- *Personal Data:* b Lewisburg, Tenn, May 27, 19; m 44, Anne Daughtry; c William Buchanan, Richard Kirkpatrick & Susan (Norton). *Educ:* Univ Tenn, BA, 44; Univ Rochester, MD, 49. *Prof Exp:* Instr internal med, Univ Rochester, 51-52. *Concurrent Pos:* Vis prof & researcher, Copenhagen Univ, 66-67, 75-76 & 82-83. *Mem:* Am Thoracic Soc; Am Col Physicians; Am Clin & Climat Asn; Am Fedn Clin Res; Am Physiol Soc. *Res:* Pulmonary diseases and clinical pulmonary physiology; disorders of control of respiration. *Mailing Add:* Sch Med 724 Burnett-Womack Bldg CB No 7020 Univ NC Chapel Hill NC 27599-7020

BARNETT, TIM P, METEOROLOGY. *Current Pos:* RES MARINE PHYSICIST & ACAD ADMINR, SCRIPPS INST OCEANOG, 71-, PRIN SCIENTIST & CO-ORIGINATOR, FIRST US EXP CLIMATE FORECASTER CTR, 81- *Educ:* Pomona Col, BA, 60; Scripps Inst Oceanog, La Jolla, MS, 62, PhD(phys oceanog), 66. *Honors & Awards:* Spec Creativity Award, NSF, 91 & 92; Harald Ulrick Sverdrup Gold Medal, Am Meteorol Soc, 93. *Prof Exp:* Res asst, Scripps Inst Oceanog, La Jolla, 60-64; oceanographer, US Naval Oceanog Off, Washington, 64-66; sr scientist & mgr ocean physics, Westinghouse Ocean Res Lab, San Diego, 66-71. *Concurrent Pos:* Oceanogr & consult, Marine Adv, La Jolla, 61-64; co-originator & US lead partic, Joint NSea Wave Proj, 68-72, Sea Wave Modeling Proj, 79-81; mem, Comt Tides & Mean Sea Level, Int Asn Phys Sci of the Ocean, 83-86. *Mem:* Fel Am Meteorol Soc; Int Asn Phys Sci of the Ocean. *Res:* Meteorology and oceanography. *Mailing Add:* Scripps Inst Oceanog Climate Res Div Univ Calif San Diego Mail Code 0224 La Jolla CA 92093-0224

BARNETT, WILLIAM ARNOLD, ECONOMIC STATISTICS, MATHEMATICAL STATISTICS. *Current Pos:* PROF ECON, WASHINGTON UNIV. *Personal Data:* b Boston, Mass, Oct 30, 41; div. *Educ:* Mass Inst Technol, BS, 63; Univ Calif, Berkeley, MBA, 65; Carnegie-Mellon Univ, PhD(statist), 74. *Prof Exp:* Res engr, Rocketdyne Div, Rockwell Int Corp, 63-69; res economist, Bd Govs, Fed Res Syst, 73-81; prof econ, Univ Tex, Austin, 82- *Concurrent Pos:* Res assoc, Univ Chicago, 77-80; prin investr, NSF, 77-80; vis lectr, Univ Aix-Marsielle, 79; vis prof, Johns Hopkins Univ, 80; ed, J Econometrics, 80; assoc ed, J Bus & Econ Statist, 81-; ed, Cambridge Univ Press. *Mem:* Sigma Xi; Am Statist Asn; Econometric Soc; Am Econ Asn; Fedn Am Scientists. *Res:* Development of asymptotic theory of inference with nonlinear models; demand theory and empirical systems of consumer demand functions; construction of monetary asset demand and aggregation model; monetary theory and policy. *Mailing Add:* Econ Campus Washington Univ Box 1208 1 Brookings Dr St Louis MO 63130-4862

BARNETT, WILLIAM EDGAR, MOLECULAR BIOLOGY. *Current Pos:* RETIRED. *Personal Data:* b Kempner, Tex, Aug 10, 34; m 54; c 3. *Educ:* Southwestern Univ, Tex, BS, 56; Northwestern Univ, MS, 57; Fla State Univ, PhD(biol genetics), 61. *Prof Exp:* Instr genetics, Fla State Univ, 61; USPHS fel, Oak Ridge Nat Lab, 61-63, biologist, 63-69, sci dir genetics & develop biol, 69-79; prof, Biomed Sci, Univ Tenn, 79-86. *Concurrent Pos:* Vis lectr, Univ Tenn, 62-67, prof, 67-; dir, Grad Sch Biomed Sci, 77- *Mem:* AAAS; Genetics Soc Am; Am Soc Biol Chemists. *Res:* Genetic translational apparatus of cellular organelles. *Mailing Add:* 2520 Lavendusky Temple TX 76501

BARNETT, WILLIAM OSCAR, surgery; deceased, see previous edition for last biography

BARNEY, ARTHUR LIVINGSTON, POLYMER CHEMISTRY. *Current Pos:* RETIRED. *Personal Data:* b Homer, Minn, Apr 4, 18; m 42, Jossalyn Gordy; c Raymond L, David M, Rodney C & Anne H. *Educ:* Middlebury Col, BS, 38; Syracuse Univ, MS, 40; Purdue Univ, PhD(org chem), 43. *Prof Exp:* Asst chem, Syracuse Univ, 38-40 & Purdue Univ, 40-41; res chemist, Cent Res Dept, E I Du Pont de Nemours & Co, Inc, 42-61, res assoc, Elastomer Chem Dept, 61-62, res mgr, Polymer Prod Dept, Elastomer Div, 62-81. *Mem:* Am Chem Soc; Sigma Xi. *Res:* Organic synthesis; fluorine chemistry; chemistry of high polymers; catalysis. *Mailing Add:* 2723 Shipley Rd Rm 610 Wilmington DE 19810

BARNEY, CHARLES WESLEY, FOREST ECOLOGY, SILVICULTURE. *Current Pos:* from asst prof to prof, 47-85, head dept forest mgt & utilization, 53-65, EMER PROF SILVICULTURE, COLO STATE UNIV, 85- *Personal Data:* b Brewster, NY, Apr 17, 15; m 43, Frances Johnson; c 3. *Educ:* Syracuse Univ, BS, 38; Univ Vt, MS, 39; Duke Univ, DF(root growth), 47. *Prof Exp:* Asst agr aide, Soil Conserv Serv, USDA, 41. *Mem:* Soc Am Foresters; Soil Conserv Soc Am; Am Soc Photogram & Remote Sensing; Forest Hist Soc; Sigma Xi. *Res:* Arid zone forestry; seed physiology; hosts of mistletoe (Viscum album L). *Mailing Add:* 1001 W Mulberry Ft Collins CO 80521

BARNEY, CHRISTOPHER CARROLL, TEMPERATURE REGULATION, WATER BALANCE. *Current Pos:* from asst prof to assoc prof, 80-92, PROF BIOL, HOPE COL, 92-, CHAIR BIOL, 96- *Personal Data:* b Sept 20, 51; m 73, Julie A Surface; c Christopher J & Kara L. *Educ:* Wright State Univ, Dayton, Ohio, BS, 73; Ind Univ, Bloomington, PhD(physiol), 77. *Prof Exp:* Assoc physiol & pharmacol, Univ Fla, 79-89. *Concurrent Pos:* Postdoctoral traineeships, NIH, 73-79; vis asst prof pharmaceut biol, Univ Fla, 84; Rol Award, Nat Inst Diabetes & Digestive & Kidney Dis, NIH, 87-89; REU Awards, Nat Sci Found, 88, 89, 90 & 94. *Mem:* Sigma Xi; AAAS; Am Physiol Soc; Coun Undergrad Res. *Res:* Regulatory physiology; heat stress and thirst; hypertension and temperature regulation; endocrine/metabolic effects of food and water deprivation. *Mailing Add:* Dept Biol Peale Sci Ctr Hope Col Holland MI 49423-9000. *Fax:* 616-395-7125; *E-Mail:* barney@hope.edu

BARNEY, DUANE LOWELL, electrochemistry; deceased, see previous edition for last biography

BARNEY, GARY SCOTT, PHYSICAL INORGANIC CHEMISTRY. *Current Pos:* RES STAFF CHEMIST, ATLANTIC RICHFIELD HANFORD CO, 68- *Personal Data:* b Monroe, Utah, Sept 17, 42; m 63; c 4. *Educ:* Brigham Young Univ, BS, 64, PhD(inorg chem), 70. *Mem:* Am

Chem Soc. *Res:* Plutonium process chemistry; development of chemical processes for conversion of radioactive wastes from nuclear fuel processing to forms which can be safely stored. *Mailing Add:* 105903 N Harrington Rd West Richland WA 99353

BARNGROVER, DEBRA ANNE, HIGH DENSITY MAMMALIAN CELL CULTURE, RECOMBINANT PROTEIN PRODUCTION. *Current Pos:* SR SCIENTIST, GENZYME CORP, 88- *Personal Data:* b Denver, Colo. *Educ:* Colo State Univ, BS, 77; Cornell Univ, PhD(nutrit biochem), 82. *Prof Exp:* Postdoctoral fel, Mass Inst Technol, Cambridge, 81-83; asst dir, Elf Biorecherches, Toulouse, France, 83-85; staff scientist, Integrated Genetics, Inc, 85-88. *Concurrent Pos:* Adj prof chem eng, Worcester Polytech Inst, 86- *Mem:* Am Chem Soc; Am Inst Nutrit; Int Soc Pharmaceut Eng. *Res:* Scale-up and production of therapeutic proteins using mammalian cells; bioreactor technology; automated control and monitoring systems for pilot plant fermentations; modeling of cellular energy metabolism; serum-free media. *Mailing Add:* PO Box 9322 Framingham MA 01701-9322

BARNHARD, HOWARD JEROME, MEDICINE, RADIOLOGY. *Current Pos:* chmn dept, 60-73, dir planning, 73-77, PROF RADIOL, MED CTR, UNIV ARK, LITTLE ROCK, 60- *Personal Data:* b New York, NY, July 18, 25; m 47; c 3. *Educ:* Univ Miami, BS, 44; Med Col SC, MD, 49; Am Bd Radiol, dipl, 55. *Prof Exp:* Intern, US Naval Hosp, Charleston, SC, 49-50; resident radiol, Roper Hosp, 50-51; radiologist, US Naval Hosp, Quantico, Va, 52-53; resident radiol, Roper Hosp, 53-54; from instr to asst prof radiol, Med Ctr, Univ Ark, 54-59; asst prof, Hahnemann Med Col, 59-60. *Concurrent Pos:* Teaching fel radiol, Med Col SC, 53-54; attend radiologist, Vet Admin Hosp, Little Rock, Ark, 54-59, consult, 60- *Mem:* Radiol Soc NAm; fel Am Col Radiol; Asn Univ Radiol; Am Roentgen Ray Soc; Sigma Xi. *Res:* Osseus system; medical computer applications. *Mailing Add:* 20703 River Vista Circle Roland AR 72135-9623

BARNHARDT, ROBERT ALEXANDER, TEXTILE SCIENCE. *Current Pos:* DEAN, COL TEXTILE, NC STATE UNIV, 87- *Personal Data:* b Jenkins Twp, Pa, Sept 21, 37; m 61. *Educ:* Philadelphia Col Textiles & Sci, BSTE, 59; Inst Textile Technol, MS, 61; Univ Va, EdD, 73. *Prof Exp:* Assoc prof textile mat, Philadelphia Col Textiles & Sci, 61-64, chmn, Dept Textiles, 64-66; dean, Inst Textile Technol, 66-75, vpres res & educ, 75-87. *Mem:* Nat Coun Textile Educ; Am Soc Eng Educ. *Res:* Research projects related to textile science including raw material research, energy and environmental research, flammability research. *Mailing Add:* Dept Textile Eng NC State Univ PO Box 8301 Raleigh NC 27695-8302

BARNHART, BARRY B, CURRICULUM DEVELOPMENT, COMPUTERS. *Current Pos:* PROF CHEM, PA STATE UNIV, HARRISBURG. *Personal Data:* b Dallastown, Pa, Oct 7, 36; m 58; c 2. *Educ:* Lebanon Valley Col, BS, 58; Univ NH, MS, 68. *Prof Exp:* Teacher chem, Palurgra Aneot High Sch, 58-66 & Manheim Twp High Sch, 66-71; prof chem, Harrisburg Area Community Col, 71- *Concurrent Pos:* Dir, Regional Comput Resource Ctr, 84-; pres, Comput Consult Serv, 84-; adj prof, Clarion State Univ Pa Grad Sch, 84-; PSTA fel, 90. *Mem:* Am Chem Soc; Asn Supv & Curric Develop. *Res:* Microcomputer impact on delivery strategies and learning by objective mastery; electrolytic initiation of cold fusion. *Mailing Add:* Pa State Univ Harrisburg 777 W Harrisburg Pike Middletown PA 17057-4846

BARNHART, BENJAMIN J, GENETICS. *Current Pos:* WITH LIFE SCI DEPT, MIDWEST RES INST. *Personal Data:* b Winchester, Ind, July 27, 35; m 57; c 2. *Educ:* Ind Univ, AB, 58, AM, 59; Johns Hopkins Univ, ScD(biochem), 62. *Prof Exp:* Teaching asst zool, Ind Univ, 58-59; NIH trainee biochem, Johns Hopkins Univ, 62-63; Nat Inst Allergy & Infectious Dis fel, Lab Genetics, Univ Brussels, Belg, 63-64. *Concurrent Pos:* Nat Acad Sci-Nat Res Coun travel grant, Int Biophys Cong, Austria, 66. *Mem:* Am Soc Microbiol; fel Am Inst Chemists; Am Soc Cell Biologists. *Res:* Mutagenesis; microbial genetics; mammalian cell genetics; cell biology. *Mailing Add:* 8808 Waxwing Terr Gaithersburg MD 20879

BARNHART, CHARLES ELMER, ANIMAL NUTRITION. *Current Pos:* instr, Univ Ky, 48-50, from asst prof to prof animal husb, 50-88, from assoc dir to dir agr exp sta, 62-88, assoc dean, Col Agr, 66-69, dean & dir, 69-88, EMER PROF ANIMAL HUSB & EMER DEAN, COL AGR, UNIV KY, 88- *Personal Data:* b Windsor, Ill, Jan 25, 23; m 46, 73, Jean Haendiges; c John D, Charles E III & Norman R. *Educ:* Purdue Univ, BS, 45; Iowa State Univ, MS, 48, PhD(animal nutrit), 54. *Prof Exp:* Instr, Iowa State Univ, 47-48. *Concurrent Pos:* Bd dirs, Ky Bd Agr, 67-88, Ky State Fair & Expos Ctr, 69-88, Farm Credit Servs MidAm, 88-93. *Mem:* Dm Soc Animal Sci; Sigma Xi. *Res:* Swine management, production, breeding and nutrition research; specialties: baby pig nutrition, gestating sow nutrition, carcass quality of swine. *Mailing Add:* 1017 Turkey Foot Rd Lexington KY 40502

BARNHART, CYNTHIA, NETWORK & LARGE SCALE OPTIMIZATION, TRANSPORTATION SYSTEMS. *Current Pos:* ASST PROF CIVIL & ENVIRON ENG, MASS INST TECHNOL, 92- *Personal Data:* b West Point, NY, July 23, 59; m 82, Mark Baribeau; c Olivia Baribeau. *Educ:* Univ Vt, BS, 81; Mass Inst Technol, MS, 85, PhD(transp & opers res), 88. *Prof Exp:* Sch engr, Bechtel Inc, 81-84; asst prof opers res, Ga Inst Techol, 88-92. *Concurrent Pos:* Mem coun, Transp Sci Sect, Opers Res Soc Am & Inst Mgt Sci, 90; panelist, Nat Res Coun, 90; NSF presidential young investr, 90; assoc ed, Transp Sci, Opers Res, Mgt Sci. *Mem:* Opers Res Soc Am; Inst Mgt Sci; Math Prog Soc; Am Asn Univ Women. *Res:* Apply operations research methods to large-scale problems arising in transportation, communications and productions; solution methods include decomposition, column-generation and branch-and-price techniques. *Mailing Add:* Dept Civil Eng Mass Inst Technol 77 Massachusetts Ave Cambridge MA 02139-4307. *Fax:* 617-258-5942; *E-Mail:* cbarnhar@athena.mit.edu

BARNHART, JAMES LEE, MAGNETIC RESONANCE IMAGING. *Current Pos:* ADJ ASSOC PROF, UNIV CALIF, SAN DIEGO, 78- *Educ:* Kans State Univ, PhD(physiol), 71. *Res:* Physiology; biochemistry. *Mailing Add:* Imaging Div Dept Res & Develop 10030 Barnes Canyon Rd San Diego CA 92121-2789

BARNHILL, MAURICE VICTOR, III, THEORETICAL PARTICLE PHYSICS. *Current Pos:* from asst prof to assoc prof, 68-87, PROF PHYSICS, UNIV DEL, 87- *Personal Data:* b Rocky Mount, NC, Mar 16, 40. *Educ:* Univ NC, Chapel Hill, BS, 62; Stanford Univ, MS, 65, PhD(physics), 67. *Prof Exp:* Res assoc physics, Univ Va, 67-68. *Mem:* Am Phys Soc; Am Asn Physics Teachers; AAAS. *Res:* High energy theory; bag models, including electromagnetic form factors and recoil, and in fermion mass matrices. *Mailing Add:* Dept Physics Univ Del Newark DE 19716

BARNHILL, ROBERT E, MATHEMATICAL ANALYSIS & APPLIED MATHEMATICS, COMPUTER AIDED GEOMETRIC DESIGN. *Current Pos:* PROF COMPUT SCI, ARIZ STATE UNIV, 86-, VPRES RES, 91- *Personal Data:* b Lawrence, Kans, Oct 31, 39; m 63, 83, Marigold L Linton; c John Ellis & Margaret Suzanne. *Educ:* Univ Kans, BA, 61; Univ Wis, MA, 62, PhD(math), 64. *Honors & Awards:* John Gregory Award Comput Aided Geometric Design. *Prof Exp:* From asst prof to prof math, Univ Utah, 64-86. *Mem:* Soc Indust & Appl Math; Asn Comput Mach. *Res:* Numerical analysis; computer aided geometric design; representation and approximation of free form curves, surfaces and volumes in an interactive computer graphics environment. *Mailing Add:* Vprovost Res PO Box 872703 Tempe AZ 85287-2703. *Fax:* 602-965-8293; *E-Mail:* barnhill@asu.edu

BARNHISEL, RICHARD I, SOIL MINERALOGY. *Current Pos:* Asst prof soil mineral, 64-69, assoc prof, 69-77, PROF SOIL MINERAL, UNIV KY, 77- *Personal Data:* b Peru, Ind, Mar 1, 38; m 58; c 1. *Educ:* Purdue Univ, BS, 60; Va Polytech Inst, MS, 62, PhD(soil mineral), 65. *Mem:* Am Soc Agron; Soil Sci Soc Am; Clay Minerals Soc. *Res:* Formation and stability of hydroxy-aluminum interlayers in clay minerals; weathering of primary minerals in clay formation; reclamation methods of surface-mined coal spoils. *Mailing Add:* Agron Univ Ky 500 S Limestone St Lexington KY 40506-0001

BARNICKI, STEVEN L, BIOMEDICAL ENGINEERING. *Current Pos:* ASST PROF BIOMED ENG, MILWAUKEE SCH ENG, 91- *Personal Data:* b Cleveland, Ohio, July 22, 61. *Educ:* Ohio State Univ, BS, 82, MS, 84, PhD(biomed eng), 89. *Prof Exp:* Res fel biomed eng, Ohio State Univ, 89-91. *Mem:* Inst Elec & Electronics Engrs; Biomed Eng Soc. *Mailing Add:* Elec Eng Dept Milwaukee Sch Eng PO Box 644 Milwaukee WI 53201-0644

BARNOFF, ROBERT MARK, CIVIL ENGINEERING. *Current Pos:* from instr to assoc prof, 55-70, head, 80-85, PROF CIVIL ENG, PA STATE UNIV, 70-, CONSULT ENGR, 85- *Personal Data:* b Punxsutawney, Pa, Aug 28, 26; m 54, Norma Guglielmi; c Joni L, Janice A, Mark E & Joseph R. *Educ:* Pa State Univ, BS, 51, MS, 56; Carnegie Inst Technol, PhD(civil eng), 66. *Prof Exp:* Bridge designer, Gannett, Fleming, Corddrg & Carpenter, 53-54. *Concurrent Pos:* NSF fel, Carnegie Inst Technol, 63-; consult eng, 56-; mem trans res bd, Nat Acad Sci. *Mem:* Fel Am Soc Civil Engrs; Am Soc Eng Educ; Am Concrete Inst; Am Soc Testing & Mat; Sigma Xi. *Res:* Static and fatigue strength of structures; structural behavior of prestressed concrete. *Mailing Add:* 606 Nimitz Ave State College PA 16801. *E-Mail:* rmbi@psu.edu

BARNOSKI, MICHAEL K, solid state physics, for more information see previous edition

BARNOTHY, JENO MICHAEL, nuclear physics, astrophysics; deceased, see previous edition for last biography

BARNS, ROBERT L, CRYSTALLOGRAPHY. *Current Pos:* mem tech staff, Phys Chem Res Dept, 55-60, mem tech staff, Crystal Chem Res Dept, 60-83, MEM TECH STAFF, OPT MAT RES DEPT, BELL LABS, 83- *Personal Data:* b Wichita, Kans, Mar 11, 27; m 55; c 1. *Educ:* Wichita State Univ, BS, 49, MS, 51. *Prof Exp:* Res chemist, Found Indust Res, Wichita State Univ, 50-55. *Mem:* Am Crystallog Asn; Am Asn Crystal Growth; AAAS. *Res:* Combustion; electrical contacts; crystal growth; imperfections in crystals; crystal characterization; x-ray diffraction; petrography; superconductivity; semiconductors. *Mailing Add:* 63 Martins Lane Berkeley Heights NJ 07922

BARNSLEY, ERIC ARTHUR, microbial physiology, for more information see previous edition

BARNSTEIN, CHARLES HANSEN, PHARMACEUTICAL CHEMISTRY. *Current Pos:* sr scientist, 75-78, DEP DIR, DRUG STAND DIV, US PHARMACOPEIAL CONV, INC, 78- *Personal Data:* b Newton, Wis, June 25, 25; m 54, Beatrice L Kimber; c Brian, Eric & Chris. *Educ:* Univ Wis, BSc, 52, MSc, 55, PhD(pharm), 60. *Prof Exp:* From instr to assoc prof pharm, Idaho State Col, 56-63; assoc prof, Univ Wis-Milwaukee, 63-70; assoc dir, Nat Formulary, Am Pharmaceut Asn, 70-75. *Mem:* AAAS; Am Chem Soc; Am Pharmaceut Asn; Acad Pharmacuet Sci. *Res:* Organic analytical chemistry; physical pharmacy and chemistry; chemical kinetics. *Mailing Add:* 16900 Freedom Way Rockville MD 20853-1121

BARNTHOUSE, LAWRENCE WARNER, ECOLOGY. *Current Pos:* RES ASSOC AQUATIC ECOL, OAK RIDGE NAT LAB, 76- *Personal Data:* b Cincinnati, Ohio, Oct 19, 46. *Educ:* Kenyon Col, AB, 68; Univ Chicago, PhD(biol), 76. *Mem:* AAAS; Ecol Soc Am; Am Soc Limnol & Oceanog; Sigma Xi. *Res:* Application of ecological theory to environmental impact assessment. *Mailing Add:* 1069 W Outer Dr Oak Ridge TN 37830-8635

BARNUM, DENNIS W, CHEMISTRY. *Current Pos:* from asst prof to assoc prof, 64-75, PROF CHEM, PORTLAND STATE UNIV, 75- *Personal Data:* b Portland, Ore, June 30, 31; div; c 2. *Educ:* Univ Ore, BA, 53, MA, 55; Iowa State Univ, PhD(chem), 57. *Prof Exp:* Chemist, Shell Develop Co, 57-64. *Mem:* Am Chem Soc. *Res:* Coordination chemistry; geochemistry; soils. *Mailing Add:* Dept Chem Portland State Univ PO Box 751 Portland OR 97207-0751

BARNUM, DONALD ALFRED, VETERINARY SCIENCE, MICROBIOLOGY. *Current Pos:* lectr bact, 45-47, from asst prof to prof, 47-84, head, Dept Vet Bact, 64-69, chmn, Dept Vet Microbiol & Immunol, 69-80, EMER PROF BACT, ONT VET COL, UNIV GUELPH, 84- *Personal Data:* b Ont, June 20, 18; m 42, Arleen Young; c David, John & Ardeth. *Educ:* Ont Vet Col, DVM, 41; Univ Toronto, DVPH, 49, DVSc, 52. *Prof Exp:* Bacteriologist, Ont Dept Health Labs, 41-43. *Mem:* Am Soc Microbiol; fel Am Acad Microbiol; Can Vet Med Soc; Can Soc Micro; Can Pub Health Asn. *Res:* Veterinary bacteriology and mycology; bacterial infections of animals, especially of the mammary glands of dairy cattle and gastrointestinal tract of the young. *Mailing Add:* 28 Colborn Guelph ON N1G 2M5 Can. *Fax:* 519-767-0809

BARNUM, EMMETT RAYMOND, ORGANIC CHEMISTRY. *Current Pos:* res supvr, 52-73, dept mgr, 73-75, CHEM PROD, OPTICAL PROD, SHELL DEVELOP CO, 77- *Personal Data:* b Rushville, Nebr, May 4, 13; m 41; c 1. *Educ:* Nebr State Teachers Col, BS, 37; Univ Nebr, MS, 39, PhD(org chem), 42. *Prof Exp:* Asst, Univ Nebr, 37-38; Park Davis fel, 38-42. *Mem:* Am Chem Soc. *Res:* Organic synthesis; lubrication and industrial oil; sulfur compounds to reduce wear in lubricating oils; synthetic lubricants; polymers; petrochemicals; chemical intermediates; polymers for contact lens. *Mailing Add:* 6100 Estates Dr Oakland CA 94611

BARNUM, JAMES ROBERT, RADAR ENGINEERING, OVER-THE-HORIZON RADAR. *Current Pos:* res engr, 70-74, sr res engr, 74-81, prog mgr, 81-89, staff scientist, 89-91, PRIN SCIENTIST, SRI INT, 91- *Personal Data:* b Palo Alto, Calif, Feb 19, 44; m 68, Patricia Drew; c David & Cherie. *Educ:* Stanford Univ, BS, 65, MS, 67, Eng, 69, PhD(elec eng), 70. *Prof Exp:* Res asst elec eng, Stanford Univ, 65, res assoc radiosci, 70. *Mem:* sr mem Inst Elec & Electronics Engrs. *Res:* High frequency backscatter from sea and land; ionospheric propagation; polarization of radio waves; antenna theory; wide-aperature antennas; detection of aircraft, ships, and storms at sea by backscattering of high frequency radio waves; ocean surveillance; multiple-sensor interaction; high frequency-radar systems engineering and development. *Mailing Add:* SRI Int Bldg 301-77 Menlo Park CA 94025. *E-Mail:* barnum@sri.com

BARNWELL, FRANKLIN HERSHEL, COMPARATIVE PHYSIOLOGY, BIOLOGICAL RHYTHMS. *Current Pos:* from asst prof to assoc prof, 70-84, PROF ECOL, UNIV MINN, MINNEAPOLIS, 84-, HEAD, DEPT ECOL, EVOLUTION & BEHAV, 86- *Personal Data:* b Chattanooga, Tenn, Oct 14, 37; m 59; c 1. *Educ:* Northwestern Univ, BA, 59, PhD(biol sci), 65. *Prof Exp:* Instr biol sci, Northwestern Univ, 64, res assoc, 65-67; asst prof, Univ Chicago, 67-70. *Concurrent Pos:* Mem fac, Orgn Trop Studies, Costa Rica, 66, 69-71 & 85; bd dirs, Orgn Trop Studies, 85-; gov bd, Nat Conferences Undergrad Res, 90- *Mem:* Am Soc Zoologists; Crustacean Soc (secy, 91-); Int Soc Chronobiol; Soc Res Biol Rhythms; fel Linnean Soc. *Res:* Persistent daily and tidal rhythms; invertebrate behavior; biochemical systematics, zoogeography and functional morphology of marine crustacea. *Mailing Add:* Dept Ecol Evolution & Behav Univ Minn 1987 Upper Buford Cir St Paul MN 55108

BARNWELL, JOHN WESLEY, MALARIA PARASITE BIOLOGY & IMMUNOBIOLOGY, HOST-PARASITE RECEPTOR INTERACTIONS & RELATIONSHIPS. *Current Pos:* asst prof, 83-90, ASSOC PROF TROP MED, PARISITOL, MOLECULAR & CELL BIOL, SCH MED, NY UNIV, 90- *Personal Data:* b Salem, Ore, May 6, 48; m 91, Mary R Galinski; c Geoffrey & Christy. *Educ:* Ore State Univ, BS, 74, Univ Hawaii, MPH, 76, PhD(trop med), 80. *Prof Exp:* Res asst, Univ Hawaii, 76-80; sr staff fel, NIH, 80-83. *Concurrent Pos:* Prin investr, NIH, 86-; consult, WHO, 88-91; scholar, Irma T Hirschl Trust, 91. *Mem:* Am Soc Trop Med & Hyg; NY Acad Sci; AAAS; Brit Soc Parasitol. *Res:* Biological and molecular characterization of the receptor components of malaria parasites that influence host cell invasion and pathogenesis; characterization of parasite induced modifications of host cells. *Mailing Add:* 3 Washington Sq Village No 10D New York NY 10012. *Fax:* 212-263-8116, 263-7475; *E-Mail:* john.barnwell@ccmail.med.nyu.edu

BARNWELL, THOMAS OSBORN, JR, HYDROLOGY & WATER RESOURCES, COMPUTER SCIENCES. *Current Pos:* Sanit engr, Surveillance & Anal Div, Region IV, 71-77, civil engr, Assessment Br, Environ Res Lab, Off Res & Develop, 77-95, ASST LAB DIR, NAT EXPOSURE RES LAB, US ENVIRON PROTECTION AGENCY, 95- *Personal Data:* b Charleston, SC, Mar 12, 47; m 72, Gilda Turner; c Courtney C. *Educ:* Clemson Univ, BS, 69, MS, 71. *Mem:* Am Soc Civil Engrs; Int Asn Water Pollution Res & Control; Water Pollution Control Fedn; Am Geophys Union; Int Soc Econ Modeling. *Res:* Water quality modeling and management technology; nonpoint source pollution control; expert systems. *Mailing Add:* US Environ Protection Agency Environ Res Lab 960 College Station Rd Athens GA 30605-2700. *Fax:* 706-355-8440; *E-Mail:* barnwell.thomas@epamail.epa.gov

BAROCZY, CHARLES J(OHN), MECHANICAL ENGINEERING. *Current Pos:* RETIRED. *Personal Data:* b New York, NY, Apr 21, 24; div; c John, Susan, Lily & Nancy. *Educ:* Pratt Inst, BME, 47; Harvard Univ, MS, 48. *Prof Exp:* Design engr, Ebasco Serv, Inc, 48-50; develop engr anal & develop, Gen Elec Co, 50-57; self employed, 57-58; res specialist, Atomics Int Div, NAm Aviation, Inc, 58-70, mem tech staff, NAm Rockwell Corp, 70-73; reactor engr, US Atomic Energy Comn, 73-74; staff engr, Gen Atomic Co, 74-83; sr engr, S Cal Edison, 84-85. *Mem:* Am Soc Mech Engrs. *Res:* Steam generators; heat exchangers; heat transfer and fluid flow in two phase flow, boiling and condensing. *Mailing Add:* 13735 Franciscan Dr Sun City West AZ 85375

BARON, ARTHUR L, MATERIALS SCIENCE ENGINEERING, ORGANIC CHEMISTRY. *Current Pos:* VPRES RES & DEVELOP, ATOCHEM NAM, 90- *Personal Data:* b New York, NY; m 65; c 2. *Educ:* Columbia Univ, BA, 57; Purdue Univ, MS, 59; Univ Hamburg, WGermany, PhD(chem), 63. *Prof Exp:* Res chemist, Exxon Corp, 63-66; group leader, Celanese Corp, 66-72; dir, res & develop, Mobay Chem Corp, 72-84; vpres res & develop, Pennwalt Corp, 84-89. *Mem:* Am Chem Soc; WGerman Chem Soc; Soc Plastics Engrs; Soc Chem Indust; Asn Res Dirs. *Res:* Polymer science and technology; thermoplastic, thermosetting and elastomeric materials; coatings and adhesives; composites. *Mailing Add:* 30 Randwood Dr Getzville NY 14068-1335

BARON, CARL BARRY, MEMBRANE BIOCHEMISTRY, THIN LAYER CHROMATOGRAPHY. *Current Pos:* res asst prof, 85-92, SR RES INVESTR, UNIV PA, 92- *Personal Data:* b Brooklyn, NY, May 1, 43. *Educ:* State Univ NY, Stony Brook, BS, 64; Univ Colo, PhD(biochem), 72. *Prof Exp:* Res asst prof, Dept Ophthol, Scheie Eye Inst, 77-79. *Mem:* Am Physiol Soc; NY Acad Sci. *Res:* Signal transduction in tracheal smooth muscle; enzyme isolation, metabolite quantitation; correlation of biochemical events with contraction. *Mailing Add:* Dept Physiol Univ Pa Philadelphia PA 19104-6085. *E-Mail:* cbaron@mail.med.upenn.edu

BARON, DAVID ALAN, PHYSIOLOGY & PHARMACOLOGY. *Current Pos:* RES SCIENTIST PATH, SEARLE RES & DEVELOP, 89- *Personal Data:* b Chicago, Ill, Aug 14, 51; m 83; c 2. *Educ:* Univ Chicago, BA, 72, PhD(anat), 79. *Prof Exp:* Postdoctoral fel path, Med Univ SC, 79-82; res scientist pharmacol, Drug Sci Found, 82-84; asst prof pharmacol, Med Univ SC, 84-89. *Mem:* AAAS; Am Soc Cell Biol; Electron Micros Soc Am. *Res:* Quantitative morphologic analysis of cardiovascular and gastrointestinal cell physiology and pharmacology; electron microscopy of target organs in drug toxicology studies. *Mailing Add:* Dept Path Box K341 Searle Res & Dev 4901 Searle Pkwy Skokie IL 60077-2980

BARON, HAZEN JAY, DENTAL PRODUCT DEVELOPMENT, CLINICAL RESEARCH. *Current Pos:* CONSULT, 91- *Personal Data:* b Detroit, Mich, March 12, 34; m 54, Julie C Enders; c Hazen L & Melvin P. *Educ:* Wayne State Univ, BS, 55; Northwestern Univ, DDS, 58, PhD(path), 68. *Prof Exp:* Lectr path, Northwestern Univ, 62-64; asst dir dent therapeut, Warner-Lambert Co, 64-69, dir dent sci, 69-80; dir dent care, Johnson & Johnson Co, 80-87, vpres dent res & develop, 87-91. *Concurrent Pos:* Consult, Am Dent Asn, 72-89. *Mem:* Am Dent Asn; Am Asn Dent Res; Am Acad Oral Path; Am Acad Periodont. *Res:* Consumer and professional oral hygiene products designed to prevent dental diseases. *Mailing Add:* 41 Springbrook Rd Morristown NJ 07960. *Fax:* 973-540-9103

BARON, JEFFREY, TOXICOLOGY, DRUG & XENOBIOTIC METABOLISM. *Current Pos:* from asst prof to assoc prof, 72-80, PROF PHARMACOL, UNIV IOWA, 80- *Personal Data:* b Brooklyn, NY, July 10, 42; m 65, Judith C Rothberg; c Stephanie A, Leslie B & Melissa L. *Educ:* Univ Conn, BS, 65; Univ Mich, PhD(pharmacol), 69. *Prof Exp:* Res fel biochem, Southwestern Med Sch, Univ Tex, Dallas, 69-71, res asst prof biochem & pharmacol, 71-72. *Concurrent Pos:* Res Career Develop Award, Nat Inst Arthritis, Diabetes, Digestive & Kidney Dis, NIH, 75-80; mem, chem path study sect, NIH, 83-87, environ health sci rev comt, Nat Inst Environ Health Sci, 90-94. *Mem:* AAAS; Am Soc Pharmacol & Exp Therapeut; Am Soc Biochem & Molecular Biol; Am Asn Cancer Res; Soc Toxicol; Int Soc Study Xenobiotics. *Res:* Biochemical pharmacology and toxicology; immunohistochemistry of xenobiotic-metabolizing enzyme systems; histopathologic toxicology. *Mailing Add:* Dept Pharmacol Univ Iowa 2-270 Bowen Sci Bldg Iowa City IA 52242. *Fax:* 319-335-8930; *E-Mail:* jeffrey_baron@uiowa.edu

BARON, JUDSON R(ICHARD), GAS DYNAMICS, AEROTHERMODYNAMICS. *Current Pos:* res staff, Supersonic Lab, Mass Inst Technol, 48-52, asst, Dept Aeronaut, 52-56, from asst prof to prof, 56-89, sr lectr, 89-93, EMER PROF AERONAUT & ASTRONAUT, MASS INST TECHNOL, 89- *Personal Data:* b New York, NY, July 28, 24; m 49, Selma F Wasserman; c Jason R & Jeffrey S. *Educ:* NY Univ, BAeroE, 47; Mass Inst Technol, SM, 48, ScD, 56. *Prof Exp:* Engr, Chance Vought Aircraft, Stratford, Conn, 47. *Concurrent Pos:* Res staff, Lincoln Lab, Lexington, Mass, 72; mem, USAF Sci Adv Bd, 87-91; assoc ed, Am Inst Aeronaut & Astronaut J, 89-96. *Mem:* Fel Am Inst Aeronaut & Astronaut; Sigma Xi. *Res:* Gas dynamics; aerothermodynamics; computational fluid dynamics; test facilities. *Mailing Add:* Dept Aeronaut & Astronaut 9-465 Mass Inst Technol Cambridge MA 02139-4307. *E-Mail:* jrbaron@mit.edu

BARON, LOUIS SOL, MICROBIAL GENETICS. *Current Pos:* RETIRED. *Personal Data:* b New York, NY, Jan 2, 24; m 61; c 1. *Educ:* City Col New York, BS, 47; Univ Ill, MS, 48, PhD(bact), 51. *Prof Exp:* Asst bact, Univ Ill, 49-52; bacteriologist, Walter Reed Army Inst Res, 52-56, chief, Dept Bact Immunol, Div Immunol, 56-93. *Concurrent Pos:* Squibb & Sons fel, 51; President's fel, Soc Bact, 57; Army rep, Genetics Study Sect, USPHS, 58-; spec lectr, Dept Microbiol, Sch Med, George Washington Univ, 61; res fel, Stanford Univ, 61-62; mem subcomt maintenance of genetic stocks, NSF, 64-68, chmn, 68-72; ed, J Bact, 65-70 & Proc Soc Exp Biol Med, 65-72; mem genetics fac, Grad Prog, NIH, 67-69; mem adv comt, Am Type Cult Collection, 69-; prof lectr, Sch Med, Georgetown Univ, 69-75; Coun biol ed. *Mem:* Am Soc Microbiol; Am Asn Immunologists; Biophys Soc; Am Soc Molecular Biol & Biochem; Am Acad Microbiol. *Res:* Bacterial genetics, virulence and immunology; enteric diseases; molecular biology. *Mailing Add:* 713 Horton Dr Silver Spring MD 20902

BARON, MELVIN L(EON), applied mechanics, structural engineering; deceased, see previous edition for last biography

BARON, ROBERT, PHYSICS OF INFRARED DETECTORS, CURRENT TRANSPORT IN SEMICONDUCTORS. *Current Pos:* SR SCIENTIST, SOLID STATE PHYSICS, HUGHES RES LABS, 62- *Personal Data:* b Chicago, Ill, May 16, 32; div; c 2. *Educ:* Univ Chicago, BA, 52, MS, 55, PhD(physics). 62. *Mem:* Am Inst Physics; Am Phys Soc; Inst Elec & Electronics Engrs. *Res:* Behavior of insulators and semi-insulators under high injection current conditions; physics of ion-implanted layers in semiconductors; physics of current transport and materials for extrinsic infrared detectors. *Mailing Add:* 1425 Stanford St 3 3011 Malibu Canyon Rd Santa Monica CA 90404

BARON, ROBERT WALTER, IMMUNOLOGY, PARASITOLOGY. *Current Pos:* prog leader, 87-90, RES SCIENTIST IMMUNO, AGR CAN, 78- *Personal Data:* b Winnipeg, Man, Aug 6, 47; m 70; c 3. *Educ:* Univ Man, BSc, 68, MSc, 71; McGill Univ, PhD(immmunoparasitol), 76. *Prof Exp:* Res assoc immunol, Univ Man, 76-78. *Mem:* Am Soc Parasitologists; Can Asn Advan Vet Parasitol; Can Asn Lab Animal Sci. *Res:* Characterization of immune response to arthropods; development of vaccines for protection of livestock against arthropod infestation. *Mailing Add:* Agr & Agri-Food Can Res Ctr PO Box 3000 Lethbridge AB T1J 4B1 Can. *Fax:* 403-382-3156

BARON, SAMUEL, EXPERIMENTAL ONCOLOGY, INTERFERON. *Current Pos:* CHMN, DEPT MICROBIOL, MED BR, UNIV TEX, GALVESTON, 75- *Personal Data:* b New York, NY, July 27, 28; m 49; c 5. *Educ:* New York Univ, BA, 48, MD, 52. *Honors & Awards:* USPHS Meritorious Serv Award, NIH, 70. *Prof Exp:* Intern, Montefiore Hosp, New York, 53; asst virol, Univ Mich, Ann Arbor, 55; sect head cell virol, NIH, Bethesda, Md, 68-75. *Concurrent Pos:* Ed, Tex Reports, Med Br, Univ Tex, 77-86 & med microbiol, Churchill Livingston Inc, New York, NY, 91- *Mem:* Am Asn Immunologists; Soc Exp Biol & Med; Am Soc Microbiol; Infectious Dis Soc Am; Asn Med Sch Microbiol Chmn; Soc Gen Microbiol; Sigma Xi. *Res:* Host defenses against viruses and cancer; virology; cancer; interferon; immunity. *Mailing Add:* Dept Microbiol Univ Tex Med Br 11th St & Mechanic Ave Galveston TX 77555-1019

BARON, SEYMOUR, ENGINEERING MANAGEMENT, RESEARCH DEVELOPMENT. *Current Pos:* DIR SPEC PROGS, MED UNIV SC, 94- *Personal Data:* b New York, NY, Apr 5, 23; m 50, Florence Chill; c Richard M & Paul L. *Educ:* Johns Hopkins Univ, BS, 44, MS, 47; Columbia Univ, PhD(chem eng), 50. *Prof Exp:* Lab researcher, US Indust Chem Co, 44-47; chief engr, Burns & Roe, Inc, 50-64, vpres, 64-75, sr vpres, 75-76, sr corp vpres eng & technol, 76-84; assoc dir, Brookhaven Nat Lab, 84-94. *Concurrent Pos:* Adj prof, Columbia Univ & Polytech Inst Brooklyn, 66-68; mem bd trustees, Argonne Univ Asn, 76-, bd liaison, Reactor & Safety Anal, 76- & Ad Hoc Comt, 80-; mem, NJ Comn Radiation Protection, 78-; lectr, Univ Fla, 80- *Mem:* Nat Acad Eng; fel Am Soc Mech Engrs; Am Nuclear Soc; fel Am Soc Nuclear Engrs; Am Inst Chem Engrs; fel AAAS. *Res:* Energy conversion; advanced power technology; electric power plant design; net energy analysis; economics; transfer of technology to developing countries. *Mailing Add:* Med Univ SC 159 1/2 Rutledge Ave Charleston SC 29403. *Fax:* 803-792-0235

BARON, WILLIAM ROBERT, HISTORICAL CLIMATOLOGY, HISTORICAL NATURAL DISASTER IMPACT ASSESSMENT. *Current Pos:* CUR, HIST CLIMATE RECORDS OFF, NORTHERN ARIZ UNIV, 88-, ASST PROF HIST & QUATERNARY STUDIES, 89- *Personal Data:* b Providence, RI, May 22, 47; m 72. *Educ:* Allegheny Col, BA, 69; Univ RI, MA, 70; Univ Maine, Orono, PhD(interdisciplinary), 80. *Prof Exp:* Res assoc quaternary studies, Univ Maine, 78-82; sr res assoc, Ctr Colo Plateau Studies, 83-91; res fel hist climat, Old Sturbridge Village, Mass, 90. *Concurrent Pos:* Adj res assoc, Inst Quaternary Studies, Univ Maine, 83-91. *Mem:* Asn Am Geographers; Am Soc Environ Hist; Agr Hist Soc; Am Hist Soc; Orgn Am Historians. *Res:* Reconstruction of historical world climates using instrument and qualitative data; environmentally induced stress on society; environmental and earth science records from historical data. *Mailing Add:* Dept Hist Northern Ariz Univ PO Box 6023 Flagstaff AZ 86011-0001

BARONA, NARSES, CHEMICAL ENGINEERING. *Current Pos:* RES ENGR & CONSULT, ETHYL CORP, 63- *Personal Data:* b Cali, Colombia, Feb 14, 32; m 58; c 2. *Educ:* Univ Valle, Colombia, ChE, 53; Carnegie Inst Technol, MSc, 56; Univ Houston, PhD(chem eng), 64. *Prof Exp:* Prof chem eng, Univ Valle, Colombia, 53-61, secy, Sch Chem Eng, 56-57, head dept, 58-61. *Concurrent Pos:* Hon prof, Cent Univ Ecuador, 60; prof, Am Inst Chem Engrs, 83- *Mem:* Am Chem Soc; fel Am Inst Chem Engrs; Colombian Inst Chem Engrs; Peruvian Inst Chem Engrs. *Res:* Reaction kinetics; mass transfer; process design and evaluation; mass transfer with chemical reaction; mathematical modeling and simulation of chemical processes; physical properties of materials; batch processing (chemical engineering). *Mailing Add:* 2947 Myrtle Ave Baton Rouge LA 70806

BARONDES, SAMUEL HERBERT, PSYCHIATRY, NEUROBIOLOGY & CELL BIOLOGY. *Current Pos:* chmn, Dept Psychiat, 86-94, PROF PSYCHIAT & NEUROSCI, UNIV CALIF, SAN FRANCISCO, 86-, DIR, CTR NEUROBIOL & PSYCHIAT, 94-, JEANNE & SANFORD ROBERTSON PROF NEUROBIOL & PSYCHICT, 96- *Personal Data:* b Brooklyn, NY, Dec 21, 33; wid; c Elizabeth F & Jessica G. *Educ:* Columbia Col, AB, 54; Columbia Univ, MD, 58. *Honors & Awards:* J Elliott Royer Award, 90; Stillmark Mem Medal, USSR, 90. *Prof Exp:* From intern to asst resident, Peter Bent Brigham Hosp, 58-60; clin assoc, NIH, 60-63; resident, McLean & Mass Gen Hosps, 63-66; from asst to assoc prof psychiat & molecular biol, Albert Einstein Col Med, 66-69; prof psychiat, Univ Calif, San Diego, 69-86. *Concurrent Pos:* NIH fel, 60-63; teaching fel psychiat, Harvard Med Sch, 63-66; NIH career develop award, 66-69; mem alcoholism & alcohol probs rev comt, NIMH, 67-70; mem neurobiol rev comt, NSF, 70-73; assoc ed, J Neurobiol, 70-77; mem neurobiol merit rev bd, Vet Admin Cent Off, 72-75; mem bd dirs, Found Fund for Res in Psychiat, 74-76; scholar rev comt, McKnight Found, 76-89; Fogarty Int scholar-in-residence, NIH, 79-; coun mem, Am Soc Cell Biol, 81-84; bd dir, McKnight Endowment Fund Neurosci, 86-; dir, Langley Porter Psychiat Inst, Univ Calif, San Francisco, 86-94, pres, McKnight Endowment Fund Neurosci, 89-; sci adv comn, Charles E Culpeper Found, 87- *Mem:* Inst Med-Nat Acad Sci; Am Soc Cell Biol; Soc Neurosci; Am Soc Biol Chemists; Psychiat Res Soc; fel Am Col Neuropsychopharm; fel AAAS. *Res:* Endogenous lectins; cell adhesion; genetics of mental illness. *Mailing Add:* Dept Psychiat Univ Calif San Francisco CA 94143-0984. *Fax:* 415-476-7320

BARONDESS, JEREMIAH A, INTERNAL MEDICINE. *Current Pos:* PRES, NY ACAD MED, 90- *Personal Data:* b New York, NY, June 6, 24; m 52; c 1. *Educ:* Johns Hopkins Univ, MD, 49; Am Bd Internal Med, dipl, 56 & 75. *Hon Degrees:* DSc, Albany Med Col, 78, Med Col Pa, 86. *Honors & Awards:* Alfred E Stengel Award, Am Col Physicians, 83. *Prof Exp:* Intern, Johns Hopkins Hosp, 49-50, asst med, 50-51; res fel, Dept Virol, Sch Med, Univ Pa, 51-53; asst resident med, New York Hosp, 53-54, chief resident, 54-55; instr med, Med Col, Cornell Univ, 54-59, from asst prof to assoc prof clin med, 59-71, clin prof med, 71-79, prof clin med, 79-86, assoc chmn, Dept Med, 82-90. *Concurrent Pos:* Attend physician, NY Hosp, 71-, chief, Pvt Med Serv, 73-82; vis prof med, Univ PR, 72, Univ Ill, 74, Univ Va, 76, Mayo Med Sch & Found, 78, Univ Iowa, 79, Univ Tex, Houston, 86-91 & NY Med Col, 91; vchmn bd gov, Am Col Physicians, 72-73, chmn, 73-74; trustee, Johns Hopkins Univ, 77-; chief consult, Med Necessity Prog, Nat Blue Cross/Blue Shield Asn, 83-86; Irene F & I Roy Psaty distinguished prof clin med, Med Col, Cornell Univ, 86-89, William T Foley distinguished prof, 89-90, adj prof, 90- *Mem:* Inst Med-Nat Acad Sci; Am Clin & Climat Asn; master Am Col Physicians (pres-elect, 77-79, pres, 78-79); Am Fedn Clin Res; fel AAAS; Am Pub Health Asn; Asn Am Physicians; NY Acad Sci; Int Soc Internal Med; fel Royal Soc Med London. *Res:* Medical education and training. *Mailing Add:* NY Acad Med 1216 Fifth Ave New York NY 10029

BARONE, FRANK CARMEN, NEUROSCIENCE, PHYSIOLOGY. *Current Pos:* SCIENTIST & ASSOC FEL, SMITH KLINE BEECHAM PHARMACEUT, 82- *Personal Data:* b Syracuse, NY, July 5, 49; div; c 2. *Educ:* Syracuse Univ, BA, 73, PhD(biopsychol), 78. *Prof Exp:* USPHS trainee & res asst, Syracuse Univ, 73-77, res assoc, Brain Res Lab, 77-82, asst prof psychol, 78-82. *Concurrent Pos:* Vis researcher, NSF Joint US-Repub China Res Proj, 77-; res assoc, NIH grant, 78-82; ed assoc sci journals, Brain Res Publ, Inc, 78-82; adj asst prof physiol, Temple Univ Sch Med, 87. *Mem:* Soc Neurosci; Am Physiol Soc; Am Gastroenterol Asn. *Res:* Neurophysiology and behavior; gastrointestinal pharmacology; cerebrovascular diseases; development of animal models of CNS ischemia/CNS trauma in order to discover drugs that can be useful as therapy in man. *Mailing Add:* Dept Cardiovasc Pharmacol Smith Kline Beecham Pharmaceut 709 Swedeland Rd PO Box 1539 King of Prussia PA 19406-0939

BARONE, JOHN A, ORGANIC CHEMISTRY. *Current Pos:* from instr to assoc prof, 50-62, dir, NSF In-Serv Inst, 61-68, dir res & grad sci, 63-66, vpres planning, 66-70, PROF CHEM, FAIRFIELD UNIV, 62-, PROVOST, 70- *Personal Data:* b Dunkirk, NY, Aug 30, 24; m 47. *Educ:* Univ Buffalo, BA, 44; Purdue Univ, MS, 48, PhD(chem), 50. *Prof Exp:* Asst chem, Purdue Univ, 47-48. *Concurrent Pos:* Dir, Jesuit Res Coun Am, 63-70, chmn, 68-70; consult, Conn Regional Med Prog, 70-76; proj mgr, Housing & Urban Develop-New Rural Soc Contracts, 72-76; Dir, Blue Cross-Blue Shield Conn, 73; mem, Statewide Health Coord Coun, 79-87, chmn, 83-87; mem, Conn Health & Educ Facil Auth, 87- *Mem:* AAAS; Am Chem Soc; Sigma Xi. *Res:* Heterocyclic and medicinal chemistry; organohalogen compounds; academic and research administration; resource management. *Mailing Add:* 1283 Round Hill Rd Fairfield CT 06430

BARONE, JOHN B, ECOLOGY. *Current Pos:* proj mgr, 81-87, TECH DIR, WESTON, 87- *Personal Data:* US citizen. *Educ:* Kent State Univ, BS, 72; Univ Calif, Davis, PhD(ecol), 80. *Prof Exp:* Environ engr, Firestone Tire & Rubber Co, 72-73; environ specialist, Ohio Environ Protection Agency, 73-74; res asst, Crocker Nuclear Lab, Univ Calif, Davis, 74-79, lectr meteorol, Land, Air & Water Resources Dept, 79-80. *Mem:* Air Pollution Control Asn. *Res:* Ambient air monitoring and emission testing; collection techniques and analysis of fine aerosols; statistical analysis of environmental data; evaluation of transport and disperson of air pollutants; meteorological monitoring, measurement and data analysis; micro and mesoscale meteorological studies. *Mailing Add:* Weston One Weston Way Bldg 5 West Chester PA 19380-1499

BARONE, LEESA M, MOLECULAR BIOLOGY. *Current Pos:* postdoctoral fel, Children's Hosp & Med Ctr, Univ Mass, 88-90, INSTR BONE & CARTILAGE DEVELOP, UNIV MASS, MED CTR, 90- *Personal Data:* b Fitchburg, Mass, Feb 15, 58. *Educ:* Smith Col, BA, 80; Boston Univ, PhD(biochem), 87. *Prof Exp:* Postdoctoral fel osteoarthritis, Med Ctr, Tufts Univ, 87-88. *Concurrent Pos:* Grant, Orthop Res & Educ Found, 88-90. *Mem:* Am Soc Cell Biol; Am Soc Bone & Mineral Res; Orthop Res Soc. *Mailing Add:* 1 Mountain Rd Framingham MA 01701

BARONE, LOUIS J(OSEPH), PRINCIPAL LICENSING ENGINEERING. *Current Pos:* CONSULT, 90- *Personal Data:* b Brooklyn, NY, Oct 10, 29; m 59; c 2. *Educ:* Polytech Inst Brooklyn, BChE, 51, NY Univ, MS, 58, MChE, 58. *Prof Exp:* Chem engr, res & develop, Cent Res Lab, Allied Chem & Dye Corp, 51-54; sr res engr, Stauffer Chem Co, 54-72, sr proj engr, 72-79, prin licensing engr, 80-90. *Mem:* Am Chem Soc; Am Inst Chem Engrs. *Res:* Plant design; process development. *Mailing Add:* 23 Biltom Rd White Plains NY 10607

BARONE, MILO C, ANIMAL PHYSIOLOGY. *Current Pos:* ASST PROF BIOL, FAIRFIELD UNIV, 68- *Personal Data:* b Throop, Pa, Dec 4, 41; m 82. *Educ:* Univ Scranton, BS, 63; John Carroll Univ, MS, 65; St Bonaventure Univ, PhD(physiol), 68. *Mem:* AAAS; NY Acad Sci. *Res:* Reptilian hematology; seasonal variations in serum proteins and other blood properties in Pseudemys and Chrysemys turtles. *Mailing Add:* 1242 Old Academy Rd Fairfield CT 06430-5195

BARONET, CLIFFORD NELSON, MECHANICAL ENGINEERING. *Current Pos:* RETIRED. *Personal Data:* b Quebec, Que, Oct 17, 34; m 60; c 1. *Educ:* Laval Univ, BS, 59, MS, 61; Rensselaer Polytech Inst, PhD(appl mech), 66. *Honors & Awards:* Ralph Teetor Award, Soc Automotive Engrs, 70. *Prof Exp:* From instr to assoc prof mech eng, Laval Univ, 66-70; dir, Mech Div, Que Indust Res Ctr, 70-71, mech & mat div, 71-76 & res & develop, 76-82, vpres opers, Montreal, 82-85, exec vpres, 88-92; vpres, Indust Res Assistance Prog, Nat Res Coun, 92-95. *Mem:* Soc Mfr Engrs; Can Soc Mech Engrs. *Res:* Machine design. *Mailing Add:* 167 Dunbarton Ct Ottawa ON K1K 4L7 Can

BARONI, TIMOTHY J, SYSTEMATICS OF FUNGI, ULTRASTRUCTURE OF FUNGAL PROPAGULES & EXTRACELLULAR PRODUCTS. *Current Pos:* from asst prof to assoc prof, 80-89, PROF BIOL & MYCOL, STATE UNIV NY, CORTLAND, 89- *Personal Data:* b Ft Bragg, Calif, Jan 25, 49; m 87, Lynda K Sweet. *Educ:* Humboldt State Univ, BA, 72, MA, 74; Univ Mass, Amherst, PhD(bot), 79. *Prof Exp:* Cryptogamic botanist, Harvard Univ, 79-80. *Concurrent Pos:* Vis prof environ sci & forestry, State Univ NY, 82 & Univ Tenn, 87; prin investr, State Univ NY, 83, 84 & 92, Buffalo Mus Sci, 86, 87, 89 & 90, Highlands Biol Sta, 87 & NY State Mus, 88; res assoc mycol, Buffalo Mus Sci, NY, 84- *Mem:* Mycol Soc Am (treas, 92-95); Brit Mycol Soc; Sigma Xi; AAAS. *Res:* Biology and biosystematics of Agaricales (mushrooms) and Boletales (boletes) with emphasis on monographic and floristic studies; morphology and ultrastructure of basidiospores and extracellular hyphal materials. *Mailing Add:* Dept Biol Sci State Univ NY Col Cortland PO Box 2000 Cortland NY 13045-0900. *Fax:* 607-753-2927; *E-Mail:* baronitj@snycorva.cortland.edu

BAROSS, JOHN ALLEN, MARINE MICROBIOLOGY. *Current Pos:* res assoc, 70-77, ASST PROF & SR RESEARCHER, MARINE MICROBIOL, ORE STATE UNIV, 77- *Personal Data:* b San Francisco, Calif, Aug 27, 41; m 67. *Educ:* San Francisco State Univ, BS, 63, MA, 65; Univ Wash, PhD(marine microbiol), 72. *Prof Exp:* Res asst marine microbiol, Col Fisheries, Univ Wash, 66-70. *Mem:* Am Soc Microbiol; AAAS; Soc Indust Microbiol; Sigma Xi; Audubon Soc. *Res:* Effects of temperature, pressure and salinity on the physiology and molecular biology of inshore and deepsea marine bacteria; incidence, pathogenicity and possible significance of genetic exchange among in-shore marine vibrio populations, including the human pathogen, Vibrio parahaemolyticus. *Mailing Add:* Sch Oceanog WB-10 Univ Wash Box 357940 Seattle WA 98195

BAROUDY, BAHIGE M, MOLECULAR VIROLOGY, RECOMBINANT DNA. *Current Pos:* DIR, DIV MOLECULAR VIROL, JAMES N GAMBLE INST MED RES, 89- *Personal Data:* b Beruit, Lebanon, July 1, 50; nat US. *Educ:* Am Univ, Beirut, BSc, 72; Georgetown Univ, PhD(biochem), 78. *Prof Exp:* Res asst, dept biochem, Georgetown Univ, 74-78; vis fel scientist, Lab Biol Viruses, Nat Inst Allergy & Infectious Dis, NIH, 79-81; fel, div molecular genetics, Lombardi Cancer Ctr, Georgetown Univ Med Ctr, 82; vis assoc scientist, Lab Molecular Oncol, Nat Cancer Inst, NIH, 82-83, Lab Infectious Dis, Nat Inst Allergy & Infectious Dis, 83-85; res assoc prof, Div Molecular Virol & Immunol, Dept Microbiol, Georgetown Univ, 85-89. *Concurrent Pos:* Guest scientist, Lab Immunopath, Nat Inst Allergy & Infectious Dis, NIH, 85-87; assoc mem, Lombardi Cancer Res Ctr, Georgetown Univ Med Ctr, 86-89. *Mem:* Am Soc Biochem & Molecular Biol; Am Soc Microbiol; Am Soc Virol; Sigma Xi; Am Soc Study Liver Dis. *Res:* Molecular virology of retroviruses with emphasis on murine leukemic viruses and human immunodeficiency virus; molecular virology of delta hepatitis and its interaction with hepatitis B and the molecular virology of hepatitis C virus. *Mailing Add:* K-15-4-4650 Schering Plough Res Inst 2015 Galloping Hill Rd Kenilworth NJ 07033-0539

BAROUKI, ROBERT, GENE REGULATION IN THE LIVER, HORMONE & DRUG ACTION. *Current Pos:* RES SCIENTIST MOLECULAR BIOL, UNIT 99, NAT INST HEALTH & MED RES, CRETEIL, FRANCE, 86- *Personal Data:* b Beirut, Lebanon, Apr 7, 57; French citizen; m 83; c 2. *Educ:* Univ Paris, MD, 83, PhD(pharmacol), 83, Habilitation, 91. *Prof Exp:* Postdoctoral molecular biol, Sch Med, Johns Hopkins, 83-85. *Mem:* Am Soc Cell Biol; French Soc Endocrinol. *Res:* Hormonal regulation of the promoter of aspartate aminotransferase gene: glucocorticoid, CAMP and insulin effects; DNA-protein interactions; physiopathological regulation of the human isoenzymes in the liver and serum. *Mailing Add:* INSERM Univ 99 Hosp Henri Mondor Creteil 94010 France

BARPAL, ISAAC RUBEN, RESEARCH ADMINISTRATION. *Current Pos:* SR VPRES & TECHNOL OFFICER, ALLIEDSIGNAL INC, 93- *Personal Data:* b Argentina, Feb 21, 40; c 3. *Educ:* Calif State Polytech Univ, BS, 67; Univ Calif, Santa Barbara, MS, 68, PhD(elec eng), 70. *Prof Exp:* Sr engr, Minicars Inc, 68-70; teaching, res, Univ Calif, Santa Barbara, 70-71; engr mgr, Westinghouse Transp, 71-74, gen mgr, Brazil, 74-80; pres, Westinghouse Int, Latin Am, 80-87; vpres, Westinghouse Sci & Technol Ctr, 87-93. *Concurrent Pos:* Mem, Indust Sci & Technol, Nat Sci Found, 88- *Mem:* Fel Inst Elec & Electronics Engrs; Soc Am Eng. *Mailing Add:* 25 Glimpsewood Ln Morristown NJ 07960

BARR, ALFRED L, AGRICULTURAL ECONOMICS, AGRICULTURAL ADMINISTRATION. *Current Pos:* RETIRED. *Personal Data:* b Rig, WVa, Jan 17, 33; m 59, Eva J Elwell; c Belinda L & Frederick E. *Educ:* WVa Univ, BS, 55; Univ Okla, MS, 57; Okla State Univ, PhD(agr econ), 60. *Prof Exp:* Agr economist, Res Serv, USDA, WVa, 60-61; agr economist, WVa Univ, 61-70, chmn, Div Animal Vet Sci, Col Agr, 70-80; assoc dir, WVa Agr Forestry Exp Sta, 80-97. *Mem:* Prof Agr Econ Asn. *Mailing Add:* 1080 Windsor Ave Morgantown WV 26505

BARR, ALLAN RALPH, medical entomology; deceased, see previous edition for last biography

BARR, CHARLES (ROBERT), PHOTOGRAPHIC CHEMISTRY. *Current Pos:* RETIRED. *Personal Data:* b Altoona, Pa, Mar 21, 22; m 43; c 4. *Educ:* St Vincent Col, BS, 46. *Prof Exp:* Res chemist, Remington-Rand, Inc, 46-48; res chemist, Eastman Kodak Co, 48-57, sr res chemist, 57-62, res assoc, 62, asst to div head, Color Photog Div, 62-65, head exp color photog lab, 65-75, dir info serv, 75-84. *Mem:* Am Chem Soc; Soc Photog Sci & Eng. *Res:* Synthesis of organic compounds for use in color photography; color and constitution of indoaniline dyes; new color photographic products and processes. *Mailing Add:* 18410 129th Ave Sun City West AZ 85375

BARR, CHARLES E, CELL PHYSIOLOGY. *Current Pos:* assoc prof, 68-74, PROF BIOL, STATE UNIV NY COL BROCKPORT. 74- *Personal Data:* b Chicago, Ill, Sept 20, 29; m 56; c 2. *Educ:* Iowa State Col. BS. 54; Univ Calif, Berkeley, PhD(plant physiol), 61. *Prof Exp:* Trainee biophys, Sch Med, Univ Md, 61-63, instr, 63-64; asst prof biol, Duquesne Univ, 64-68. *Mem:* Sigma Xi. *Res:* Electrophysiology and ion transport in plant cells; origin of the resting potential in Nitella. *Mailing Add:* Dept Biol Sci State Univ Col Brockport NY 14420

BARR, CHARLES RICHARD, BIOCHEMISTRY. *Current Pos:* from asst prof to assoc prof, 62-72, PROF CHEM, AUSTIN COL, 72- *Personal Data:* b Dakota, Ill, May 16, 32. *Educ:* NCent Col, BA, 54; Mich State Univ, MS, 57, PhD, 60. *Prof Exp:* Asst Mich State Univ, 54-58; asst prof, Dubuque Univ, 58-62. *Mem:* Am Chem Soc. *Res:* Isolation and synthesis of biologically active compounds; binding of metals in enzymes; Mossbauer spectroscopy. *Mailing Add:* Austin Col Suite 61612 900 North Grand Sherman TX 75090-4440

BARR, DAVID JOHN, REMOTE SENSING, GEOGRAPHIC INFORMATION SYSTEMS. *Current Pos:* chmn dept, 88-92, PROF GEOL ENG, UNIV MO, ROLLA, 72- *Personal Data:* b Evansville, Ind, Mar 5, 39; m 66, Kay A; c Joh M. *Educ:* Purdue Univ, MSCE, 64, PhD(geol eng), 68. *Concurrent Pos:* Dir, Mo Mining & Mineral Resources, Res Inst, 80-88; asst vchancellor for academic comput, Univ Mo, Rolla, 86-87. *Mem:* Am Soc Civil Engrs; Am Soc Photogrammetry & Remote Sensing; Asn Eng Geol; Soc Mining Engrs; Nat Soc Prof Engrs. *Res:* Use of expert systems and geographic information systems for thematic map creation and compilation; remote sensing and digital image processing for minerals; exploration and/or environmental site evaluation. *Mailing Add:* 11454 Cedar Grove Lane Univ Mo Rolla Rolla MO 65401. *Fax:* 573-341-6935; *E-Mail:* davebarr@umr.edu

BARR, DAVID ROSS, MATHEMATICAL STATISTICS. *Current Pos:* RETIRED. *Personal Data:* b Madison, Wis, Aug 21, 32; m 57; c 2. *Educ:* Miami Univ, BA & MA, 54, MS, 57; Univ Iowa, PhD(math), 64. *Prof Exp:* Programmer, Appl Math Lab, Eglin AFB, USAF, 55-57, instr math, USAF Acad, 59-62, asst prof, 62, res math statistician, Aerospace Res Labs, 64-68, asst prof math, USAF Inst Technol, 68-97. *Mem:* Inst Math Statist; Am Statist Asn; Math Asn Am. *Res:* Power function of the likelihood ratio test and ranking and selection problems of the uniform distribution and related distribution. *Mailing Add:* 2278 Yorkshire Pl Dayton OH 45419

BARR, DAVID WALLACE, BIOGEOGRAPHY. *Current Pos:* Curatorial asst, Royal Ont Mus, 68-69, asst cur, 69-73, assoc cur, 73-76, assoc cur-in-charge, 76-80, cur-in-charge entom, 80-84, assoc dir curatorial, 84-89, cur-in-charge, 89-90, assoc dir proj mgt, 91-92, CURATOR, INVERT ZOOL, ROYAL ONT MUS, 93- *Personal Data:* b Toronto, Ont, Jan 1, 43. *Educ:* Univ Toronto, BSc, 65; Cornell Univ, PhD(entom), 69. *Concurrent*

Pos: Asst prof zool, Univ Toronto, 73-78, assoc prof, 78- *Res:* Evolution and comparative biology of Mollusca. *Mailing Add:* Ctr Bio-Diversity & Conserv Biol Royal Ont Mus 100 Queen's Park Toronto ON M5S 2C6 Can. *Fax:* 416-586-5863; *E-Mail:* 71276.15@compuserve.com; davebar@io.org

BARR, DENNIS BRANNON, PHYSICS, ELECTRON MICROSCOPY. *Current Pos:* res physicist, 73-76, SR RES PHYSICIST ELECTRON MICROSCOPY, EASTMAN CHEM DIV, 76- *Personal Data:* b Bonham, Tex, Apr 23, 43; m 65; c 3. *Educ:* Tex A&M Univ, BS, 65, MS, 67, PhD(physics), 71. *Prof Exp:* Physicist electron microscopy, Army Mat & Mech Res Ctr, 71-73. *Mem:* Electron Microscopy Soc Am. *Res:* Industrial microscopy; polymer physics, polymer morphology. *Mailing Add:* 5329 Kiowa St Kingsport TN 37664

BARR, DONALD EUGENE, CHEMISTRY IN MICROELECTRONICS. *Current Pos:* adv engr, IBM Corp, 80, mgr, 81-84, sr eng mgr mat sci, 84-86, area mgr & mat eng, 86-95, SR TECH STAFF MEM, IBM CORP, 95- *Personal Data:* b June 30, 34; US citizen; m 56, Edythe Cloak; c Debra & Daniel. *Educ:* Elizabethtown Col, BS, 56; Bucknell Univ, MS, 61; Univ Mass, PhD(chem), 65. *Prof Exp:* Mem staff, Bucknell Univ, 61; res chemist, Chem Res Div, Armstrong Cork Co, 65-69; res specialist new imaging processes res, GAF Corp, 69-71, mgr photoimaging, 71-74, mgr, Raw Mat Qual Assurance Dept, 74-76, staff mgr photog prod, 76-78, tech dir res & develop, 78-80, Mgr Mat Sci & Eng, 81-95. *Mem:* Am Chem Soc; Soc Photog Sci & Eng. *Res:* Seven-azabenzonorbornadiene synthesis; polyvinyl chloride polymerization, characterization and stabilization; high resolution nuclear magnetic resonance, polyvinyl chloride and model compounds; photosensitive compounds and polymeric coatings for microelectronics industry; electronic packaging (computers); microelectronics reliability; materials science. *Mailing Add:* 1508 Drexel Dr Vestal NY 13850-4013. *E-Mail:* barrde@vnet.ibm.com

BARR, DONALD JOHN STODDART, MYCOLOGY. *Current Pos:* RETIRED. *Personal Data:* b Surrey, Eng, Sept 18, 37; Can citizen; m 61; c Christina & Heidi. *Educ:* McGill Univ, BSc, 60, MSc, 62; Univ Western Ont, PhD(mycol, phycol), 65. *Prof Exp:* Res scientist mycol, Plant Res Inst, Can Dept Agr, 65-73, Sr res scientist, Biosysts Res Inst, 73-81, prin res scientist, Biosysts Res Inst, 81-96. *Mem:* Mycol Soc Am (pres, 90-91); Can Phytopath Soc; Int Soc Evolutionary Protistology (pres, 90-92). *Res:* Fungal parasites of freshwater algae; taxonomy, ecology and physiology of the Mastigomycotina, particularly the Chytridiomycetes; virus transmission by zoosporic fungi; beneficial fungi in the rumen. *Mailing Add:* Biosysts Res Inst Can Dept Agr Ottawa ON K1A 0C6 Can

BARR, DONALD R, MATHEMATICAL STATISTICS. *Current Pos:* vis prof, 92-93, PROF SYSTS ENG, US MIL ACAD, 93- *Personal Data:* b Durango, Colo, Dec 10, 38; m 58, Loudan Suttle; c Mark E & Bryan M. *Educ:* Whittier Col, BA, 60; Colo State Univ, MS, 62, PhD(statist), 65. *Prof Exp:* Instr math. Colo State Univ, 63-65; asst prof, Wis State Univ, Oshkosh, 65-66; from asst prof to assoc prof opers res, Naval Postgrad Sch, 66-77, prof opers res & statist, 77-87, prof math, 90-93; vpres, Eval Technol Inc, 87-89. *Concurrent Pos:* Consult, Litton Mellonics, 67-77, Braddock, Dunn & McDonald, Inc, 71-76, Dynamic Sci, Inc, 77-80, ORI, Inc, 81-87; vis prof, Ministry Nat Defense, Thailand, 70, Tamkang Col, Taiwan, 75; liaison scientist, Off Naval Res, London, 82-84. *Mem:* Am Statist Asn; Int Test & Eval Asn; Opers Res Soc Am; Math Asn Am. *Res:* Statistical theory; sequential decision theory; reliability growth and classification models; test and evaluation, data analysis; systems engineering; simulation. *Mailing Add:* PO Box 439 Ft Montgomery NY 10922. *E-Mail:* fd4168@trotter.usma.edu

BARR, DONALD WESTWOOD, NUCLEAR CHEMISTRY. *Current Pos:* RETIRED. *Personal Data:* b Worcester, Mass, May 6, 32; m 54; c 4. *Educ:* Univ Mass, BS, 54; Univ Calif, Berkeley, PhD(nuclear chem), 57. *Honors & Awards:* E O Lawrence Award, Dept Energy, 80. *Prof Exp:* Staff mem, Los Alamos Nat Lab, 57-71, assoc group leader, 71-72, dep group leader, 72-82, fel, 81-82, assoc div leader, 82-84, div leader, 84-90. *Mem:* Am Chem Soc. *Res:* Neutron physics and radiochemistry. *Mailing Add:* PO Box 178 Jemez Springs NM 87025

BARR, E(RNEST) SCOTT, SCIENTIFIC BIOGRAPHICAL DATA. *Current Pos:* prof, 42-72, EMER PROF PHYSICS, DEPT PHYSICS & ASTRON, UNIV ALA, 72- *Personal Data:* b Lincolnton, NC, Nov 27, 05; m 31, Phoebe Baughan. *Educ:* Univ NC, BA, 26, AM, 33, PhD(physics), 36. *Prof Exp:* From instr to assoc prof physics, Tulane Univ, 36-47; sr physicist, Appl Physics Lab, Johns Hopkins Univ, 45-46. *Concurrent Pos:* Consult, Redstone Arsenal, 52-65. *Mem:* Fel AAAS; fel Am Phys Soc; fel Optical Soc Am; Am Asn Physics Teachers; Am Inst Physics; Sigma Xi. *Res:* Spectroscopic studies in infrared region, particularly chromatic aberration on free liquids, instructional aspects of optics. *Mailing Add:* PO Box 40194 East Side Sta Tuscaloosa AL 35404

BARR, FRED S, MEDICAL MICROBIOLOGY. *Current Pos:* RETIRED. *Personal Data:* b Benhams, Va, Jan 22, 26; m 50; c 2. *Educ:* Univ Tenn, BS, 52; Tenn State Univ, MA, 57. *Prof Exp:* Prod asst, S E Massengill Co, Tenn, 52-53, res bacteriologist, 53-60, res assoc microbiol & biochem, 60-70, sect head biopharmaceut res, 70-71; mgr microbiol sect, Beecham Labs, 71-88. *Mem:* AAAS; Am Soc Microbiol; Am Soc Trop Med & Hyg; Am Chem Soc. *Res:* Antibiotic isolation, identification and purification; antibiotic combinations in human and animal medications; microbiological diagnostic reagents for clinical use; drug levels in body tissues and fluids; drug metabolism and absorption-excretion kinetics. *Mailing Add:* 1760 Overhill Rd Bristol VA 24201

BARR, FREDERIC G, CANCER BIOLOGY, MOLECULAR PATHOLOGY. *Current Pos:* ASST PROF PATH & LAB MED, UNIV PA, 92-, ADJ PROF PATH PEDIAT, 92- *Personal Data:* b Baltimore, Md, Sept 28, 58. *Educ:* Williams Col, BA, 80; Washington Univ, St Louis, MD & PhD(molecular biol), 87. *Honors & Awards:* Pincus Mem Fund Award, Fedn Am Soc Exp Biol, 91; Exp Pathologist-in-Training Award, Am Soc Investigative Path, 91; Arthur Purdy Stout Soc Prize, Arthur Purdy Stout Soc Surg Pathologist, 96; Benjamin Castleman Award, US & Can Acad Pathol, 96. *Concurrent Pos:* Adj asst prof, Winstar Inst, 92- *Mem:* Am Soc Investigative Path; Am Asn Cancer Res; AAAS; Am Molecular Path; Am Soc Microbiol; US & Can Acad Path. *Res:* Chromosomal rearrangements in cancer; moleuclar biologic basis of specific cancer-associated translocations and the clinical utiltiy of detection of these arrangements in the diagnosis and management of these cancers. *Mailing Add:* Dept Path Univ Pa Philadelphia PA 19104-6082. *Fax:* 215-898-4227; *E-Mail:* barrfg@mail.med.upenn.edu

BARR, GEORGE E, APPLIED MATHEMATICS. *Current Pos:* MEM TECH STAFF APPL MATH, SANDIA LAB, 65- *Personal Data:* b Milwaukee, Wis, Oct 16, 37; wid. *Educ:* Univ Wis-Madison, BA, 58; Ore State Univ, PhD(theoret physics), 64. *Prof Exp:* Jr res assoc math physics, Brookhaven Nat Lab, 62-63. *Mem:* Soc Indust & Appl Math; Am Math Soc. *Res:* Special functions; theory of diffraction; fluid dynamics of viscous media; nuclide transport in geologic media. *Mailing Add:* Sandia Nat Lab Orgn 6312 MS 1326 Albuquerque NM 87185

BARR, HARRY L, REPRODUCTIVE PHYSIOLOGY, GENETICS. *Current Pos:* From instr to asst prof physiol, 55-67, assoc prof, 67-71, PROF DAIRY SCI, OHIO STATE UNIV, 71-, SPECIALIST, COOP EXTEN SERV, 67- *Personal Data:* b Bethesda, Ohio, Feb 15, 22; m 44; c 4. *Educ:* Ohio State Univ, BSc, 54, MS, 55, PhD(genetics), 60. *Concurrent Pos:* Vis prof, Cornell Univ, 70. *Mem:* Am Dairy Sci Asn; Am Soc Animal Sci. *Res:* Reproductive physiology and population genetics. *Mailing Add:* Dept Animal Scis 190 Noval Mall Columbus OH 43210-1321

BARR, JOHN BALDWIN, PHYSICAL CHEMISTRY, CARBON FIBER SCIENCE. *Current Pos:* CONSULT, RES OPPORTUNITIES INC, ALPHARETTA, GA, 96- *Personal Data:* b Niagara Falls, NY, Nov 8, 32; m 54, Patricia Kromer; c Mark, John, Kathryn & Karen. *Educ:* Univ Buffalo, BA, 54; Univ Mich, MS, 56; Pa State Univ, PhD(phys chem), 61. *Prof Exp:* Sr chemist, Corhart Refractories Div, Corning Glass Works, NY, 60-62; sr res chemist, Union Carbide Corp, 62-71, res scientist, Carbon Prod Div, 71-82, sr res scientist, Specialty Polymers & Composites Div, Res Lab, Union Carbide Corp, Parma, 82-86; sr res scientist, Parma, Ohio, 87-90; sr res scientist, Amoco Performance Prods Inc, Alpharetta, Ga, 90-91, assoc res scientist, 91-95. *Mem:* Am Chem Soc; Sigma Xi; Am Carbon Soc; NAm Thermal Anal Soc; Soc Advan Mat & Process Eng. *Res:* Carbon fibers; refractory compounds; carbon and graphite chemistry; boron halide reactions; high temperature chemistry; thermal management materials. *Mailing Add:* Amoco Performance Prod Inc 4500 McGinnis Ferry Rd Alpharetta GA 30202-3944

BARR, KEVIN PATRICK, heat transfer systems engineering, for more information see previous edition

BARR, LAWRENCE DALE, ASTRONOMY ENGINEERING, MECHANICAL ENGINEERING. *Current Pos:* CONSULT, 90- *Personal Data:* b Adelanto, Calif, Nov 5, 30; m 51; c Julie, Lawrence Jr, Jeffrey, Evelyn, Della & Ralph. *Educ:* Univ Wis, BS, 57; Rensselaer Polytech Inst, MS, 60. *Prof Exp:* Develop engr & dept mgr plastics, Monsanto Corp, 57-64; eng mgr, Celanese Corp, 64-66; gen mgr res & develop, Container Corp Am, 66-68; sr engr 4m telescope, Kitt Peak Nat Observ, 68-70, eng mgr astron, Nat Optical Astron Observ, 70-90. *Concurrent Pos:* Consult engr mult mirror telescope, Univ Ariz, Smithsonian Inst, 73-76, 3.6m Canada-France-Hawaii telescope & Univ Calif 10 meter telescope, 3m IR telescope facil, Keck Observ. *Mem:* Optical Soc Am; Int Soc Optical Eng; Am Soc Precision Engrs. *Res:* Large telescope design, including the 8 meter and 15 meter National New Technology Telescopes which were an outgrowth of earlier Next Generation Telescope studies; instrumentation for astronomy and diffraction grating ruling engines; large optics fabrication; medical research instrumentation for blood treatment. *Mailing Add:* 1167 N Winstel Blvd Tucson AZ 85716. *Fax:* 520-327-0421

BARR, LLOYD, PHYSIOLOGY. *Current Pos:* PROF PHYSIOL & BIOPHYS, UNIV ILL, URBANA-CHAMPAIGN, 70- *Personal Data:* b Chicago, Ill, Dec 27, 29. *Educ:* Univ Chicago, BS, 54; Univ Ill, MS, 56, PhD(physiol), 58. *Prof Exp:* Instr physiol, Univ Mich, 58-61, from asst prof to assoc prof, 61-65; prof, Med Col Pa, 65-70. *Concurrent Pos:* Spec fel, USPHS, 63-64; vis prof, Physiol Inst, Ud Saarlandes, 63-64, 72, Baumfield Marine Lab, State Univ NY, Stony Brook, 77. *Mem:* Fel AAAS; Soc Gen Physiol; NY Acad Sci; Biophys Soc; Sigma Xi. *Res:* Electrophysiology; cellular transport processes; kinetics and thermodynamics. *Mailing Add:* Lab Molecular Biol Univ Ill 900 S Ashland Ave Urbana IL 60612

BARR, MARTIN, PHYSICAL PHARMACY. *Current Pos:* EXEC VPRES, CORP BUS & MED DEVELOP, MICH HEALTH CARE CORP, 87- *Personal Data:* b Philadelphia, Pa, Nov 11, 25; m 51; c 4. *Educ:* Temple Univ, BSc, 46; Philadelphia Col Pharm, MSc, 47; Ohio State Univ, PhD, 50. *Prof Exp:* Asst pharm, Ohio State Univ, 47-49, instr, 50; from asst prof to prof, Philadelphia Col Pharm, 50-61; chmn dept, Wayne State Univ, 61-64, dean, Col Pharm, 64-72, vis lectr pharm, Col Med, 64-72, vpres spec assignments, 72-78, vpres health affairs & dep provost, 78-82, dean, Col Pharm, 82-87. *Mem:* Am Pharmaceut Asn. *Res:* Clays; ion exchange; emulsions; ointments; colloids; product development; aerosols; health care delivery systems. *Mailing Add:* 7430 Tall Timbers West Bloomfield MI 48322

BARR, MASON, JR, PEDIATRICS, TERATOLOGY. *Current Pos:* Rotating intern, 61-62, resident, 62-64, from instr to assoc prof, 66-83, PROF PEDIAT, UNIV MICH, 83-, PROF PATH, 87-, PROF OBSTET, 88- *Personal Data:* b Washington, DC, June 15, 35. *Educ:* Haverford Col, BA, 57; George Washington Univ, MD, 61. *Concurrent Pos:* Fel embryol, Univ Mich, 66-68; fel teratology, Thomas Jefferson Univ, 68-69; vis prof path, Children's Hosp Mich, 77-78; rev ed, 79-83, sect ed, J Teratology, 83-; coun mem, Teratology Soc, 84-87. *Mem:* Soc Pediat Res; Teratology Soc; Am Acad Pediat; Soc Pediat Path; Soc Perinatal Obstet. *Res:* Perinatal pathology; teratology; birth defects rehabilitation. *Mailing Add:* Dept Pediat Univ Mich D1109 MPB Box 0718 Ann Arbor MI 48109

BARR, MICHAEL, MATHEMATICS. *Current Pos:* assoc prof, 68-72, PROF MATH, MCGILL UNIV, 72- *Personal Data:* b Philadelphia, Pa, Jan 22, 37; m 64, Marcia Linden; c 3. *Educ:* Univ Pa, AB, 59, PhD(math), 62. *Prof Exp:* Instr, Columbia Univ, 62-64; from asst prof to assoc prof, Univ Ill, Urbana, 64-68. *Concurrent Pos:* Guest, Res Inst Math, Swiss Fed Inst Technol, 67 & 75-76; res assoc, Math Inst, Univ Fribourg, 70-71; vis prof, Univ Pa, 89-90. *Mem:* Math Asn Am; Can Math Soc. *Res:* Categorical algebra, especially the study of those aspects of mathematical structures describable in terms of mapping properties; applications to theoretical computer science. *Mailing Add:* Dept Math McGill Univ 805 Rue Sherbrooke Ouest Montreal PQ H3A 2K6 Can. *Fax:* 514-398-3899; *E-Mail:* barr@math.mcgill.ca

BARR, MURRAY LLEWELLYN, genetics, neurosciences; deceased, see previous edition for last biography

BARR, NATHANIEL FRANK, RADIATION CHEMISTRY, RISK ANALYSIS. *Current Pos:* mgr, Health & Environ Risk Analysis Prog, 78-83, BIOPHYSICIST, US DEPT ENERGY, 83- *Personal Data:* b Union City. NJ, Dec 28, 27; m 56, Cora J Bidwell; c Linda, Maria & Elizabeth. *Educ:* Queens Col, NY, BS. 50; Columbia Univ, PhD(chem). 54. *Prof Exp:* Asst, Columbia Univ, 51-54; res assoc, Brookhaven Nat Lab, 54-56; asst, Div Biophys, Sloan Kettering Inst, 56-61; biophysicist, US AEC, 61-62, chief, Radiol Physics & Instrumentation Br, Div Biol & Med, 62-67, tech adv to asst gen mgr res & develop, 67-69, asst dir, Div Biol & Med, 69-75; dir, Div Technol Overview, US Energy Res & Develop Admin, 76-77. *Concurrent Pos:* Asst prof, Med Sch, Cornell Univ & lectr, Columbia Univ, 58-61; prof, Southeastern Univ, 80-81. *Mem:* Radiation Res Soc (pres, 71-72); Health Physics Soc; AAAS. *Res:* Dosimetry and properties of ionizing radiation; risk analysis. *Mailing Add:* 1023 S 23rd St Arlington VA 22202. *Fax:* 301-903-8521

BARR, RICHARD ARTHUR, PLANT PHYSIOLOGY, PHYTOCHEMISTRY. *Current Pos:* assoc prof, 68-72, prof, 72-, EMER PROF BIOL, SHIPPENSBURG UNIV. *Personal Data:* b Southport, NY, Mar 12, 25; m 61; c 2. *Educ:* Univ Vt, BS, 50, MS, 55; Cornell Univ, PhD(plant physiol), 63. *Prof Exp:* Res assoc plant physiol, Cornell Univ, 61-63, asst prof, 64-66; asst prof biol, Univ Mo-St Louis, 66-68. *Res:* Growth of intact plants from cell suspensions; tissue culture; somatic cell fusion. *Mailing Add:* 55 Rich's Dr Shippensburg PA 17257

BARR, RITA, PLANT PHYSIOLOGY. *Current Pos:* Fel genetics, 60-62, res asst plant physiol, 63-65, ASSOC BIOL SCI, PURDUE UNIV, 65- *Personal Data:* b Riga, Latvia, Sept 30, 29. *Educ:* Northern Ill Univ, BS, 54, MS, 56; Purdue Univ, PhD(genetics), 60. *Mem:* Sigma Xi; Am Soc Plant Physiol; Am Soc Cell Biol. *Res:* Electron transport reactions of isolated plasma membranes in plants; transmembrane ferricyanide reduction in cultured carrot cells; plant growth regulator effects upon plasma membrane redox and concomitant proton secretion. *Mailing Add:* Dept Biol Sci Purdue Univ Lafayette IN 47907-1901

BARR, ROBERT ORTHA, JR, CONTROL SYSTEMS, COMPUTER SCIENCE. *Current Pos:* asst prof systs sci, 66-69, assoc prof elec eng & systs sci, 69-87, ASSOC CHAIR ELEC ENG, MICH STATE UNIV, 87- *Personal Data:* b Lima, Ohio, Jan 4, 40; m 64; c 2. *Educ:* Univ Mich, BSE, 61, MSE, 62, PhD(info & control eng), 66. *Prof Exp:* Res asst optimal control, Univ Mich, 65-66. *Mem:* Inst Elec & Electronics Engrs; Soc Indust & Appl Math. *Res:* Interactive computing procedures for optimal control problems; control and optimization applications to environmental systems. *Mailing Add:* Dept Elec Eng Mich State Univ 260 Engineering Blvd East Lansing MI 48824-1226

BARR, ROGER COKE, BIOMEDICAL ENGINEERING, COMPUTER SCIENCE. *Current Pos:* Res assoc, 68-69, from asst prof to assoc prof, 69-79, PROF BIOMED ENG, DUKE UNIV, 79-, ASSOC PROF PEDIAT, 72- *Personal Data:* b Jacksonville, Fla, Feb 21, 42; m 67; c 2. *Educ:* Duke Univ, BS, 64, PhD(elec eng), 68. *Mem:* Am Heart Asn; Am Col Cardiol; Inst Elec & Electronics Engrs; Sigma Xi. *Res:* Electrocardiology; electrophysiology of the heart; digital computing. *Mailing Add:* Dept Biomed Eng Duke Univ Durham NC 27706-8001

BARR, RONALD DUNCAN, HEMATOLOGY, ONCOLOGY. *Current Pos:* assoc prof, 77-81, PROF PEDIAT, MCMASTER UNIV, CAN, 81-, PROF PATH & MED, 85- *Personal Data:* b Cardross, Scotland, May 28, 43; m 70; c 2. *Educ:* Univ Glasgow, Scotland, MB & ChB, 66, MD, 77. *Prof Exp:* Res scholar hemat, Univ Glasgow, 67-68; lectr internal med, Univ Nairobi, Kenya, 70-72; lectr hemat, Univ Aberdeen, Scotland, 73-77. *Concurrent Pos:* Vis scientist, Nat Cancer Inst, NIH, 74-76. *Mem:* Fel Royal Col Physicians; Royal Col Pathologists; fel Am Col Physicians; Am Soc Hemat; Int Soc Exp Hemat. *Res:* Interaction of cellular and humoral mechanisms in the regulation of normal hemopiesis with particular reference to the roles of lymphocyte subpopulations and their ontogenesis. *Mailing Add:* Dept Pediat Fac Health Sci Rm 3N27B McMaster Univ 1200 Main St W Hamilton ON L8N 3Z5 Can. *Fax:* 905-521-1703

BARR, RONALD EDWARD, BIOPHYSICS, BIOENGINEERING. *Current Pos:* ASSOC VPRES RES, ARIZ STATE UNIV, 86- *Personal Data:* b St Louis, Mo, Sept 9, 36; m 64; c 4. *Educ:* St Louis Univ, BS, 58, MS, 63, PhD(physics), 66. *Prof Exp:* Res asst, St Louis Univ, 61-65; res fel biophys, Space Sci Res Ctr, Univ Mo-Columbia, 65-66, asst prof radiol, 66-74, assoc prof ophthalmol, 74-77, assoc dean, Grad Sch, 77-79; assoc provost, Ohio Univ, 79-86. *Concurrent Pos:* NIH spec fel, Cambridge Univ, 69-70. *Mem:* AAAS; Am Phys Soc; Nat Coun Univ Res Admin; Soc Univ Patent Adminr. *Res:* Oxygen transfer properties of the cornea and other ocular tissues; development of long term stability for oxygen, pH and pCO2 electrodes; research and graduate education administration. *Mailing Add:* PO Box 872703 Ariz State Univ Tempe AZ 85287-2703

BARR, SUMNER, METEOROLOGY. *Current Pos:* group leader atmospheric physics, 77-81, assoc group leader atmospheric sci, 81-84, STAFF MEM, LOS ALAMOS SCI LAB, 72-, PROJ MGR, ATMOSPHERIC STUDIES & OIL SHALE, 84- *Personal Data:* b Worcester, Mass, July 12, 38; m 61, Joan Copeland; c Dean & Cynthia. *Educ:* Univ Mass, BS, 60; Mass Inst Technol, SM, 65; Univ Utah, PhD(meteor), 69. *Prof Exp:* Weather officer, USAF, 60-63; scientist meteorol, GCA Corp, 64-68; asst prof physics, Drexel Univ, 69-72. *Mem:* Am Meteorol Soc; Am Geophys Union. *Res:* Physics of transport and diffusion in the atmospheric boundary layer over non-homogeneous surfaces. *Mailing Add:* 605 Meadow Lane Los Alamos NM 87544. *E-Mail:* barr@kokopelli.lanl.gov

BARR, SUSAN HARTLINE, BIOLOGICAL EDITING, RADIATION BIOLOGY. *Current Pos:* Sci asst, Argonne Nat Lab, Ill, 67-69, tech ed, 80-83, managing tech ed, 83-90, USER PROG ADMINR, ARGONNE NAT LAB, 90- *Personal Data:* b Findlay, Ohio, June 23, 42; m 66; c 2. *Educ:* Bowling Green State Univ, BA, 64; Univ Mich, Ann Arbor, MS, 65, PhD(radiation biol), 67. *Concurrent Pos:* Mem, Coun Biol Ed. *Mem:* Soc Tech Commun. *Res:* Carcinogenesis; biophysics; radiation biology; toxicology. *Mailing Add:* 22 W 517 Tamarack Dr Glen Ellyn IL 60137

BARR, TERY LYNN, CHEMICAL PHYSICS, SURFACE CHEMISTRY. *Current Pos:* PROF MAT & SURFACE STUDIES, DEPT MAT & LAB SURFACE SCI, UNIV WIS MILWAUKEE, 85- *Personal Data:* b Renova, Pa, Feb 9, 39; m 59, Alice E; c Brenda, Kevin, Kristina & Bryan. *Educ:* Univ Va, BS, 60; Univ SC, MS, 62; Univ Ore, PhD(chem), 68. *Prof Exp:* Res chemist, Union Oil Co, 63-64 & Shell Develop Co, 69-71; vis asst prof chem, Univ Calif, Berkeley, 71; asst prof, Harvey Mudd Col, 71-73; asst prof, Claremont Men's Col, 73-74; sr res chemist, 74-80, res specialist, Corp Res Ctr, UOP, Inc, 80-84, assoc res scientist, Signal Res Inc, 84-85. *Concurrent Pos:* Res assoc, Univ Wash, 68-69; consult, R&D Assoc, 72-74; vis prof chem, Harvey Mudd Col, 74-75; adj assoc prof, Univ Ill, 78-79, adj prof chem, Chicago Circle, 79-86; vis prof, Univ Messina, Italy, 83; vis prof, Inst Physics, Univ Uppsala, Sweden, 85; consult, Signal Res Ctr Inc, 85-, S C Johnson Co Res Ctr, 86-; Fulbright vis prof, Dept Chem, Univ Cambridge, Eng, 92-93; ed, Vacuum, 93- *Mem:* Sigma Xi; Am Phys Soc; Am Vacuum Soc; Soc Electron Spectros (pres, 75-); Am Soc Testing & Mat; Mats Res Soc; Am Soc Mats. *Res:* X-ray photoelectron spectroscopy; surface chemistry and physics; quantum mechanics; spectroscopic characterization of materials; catalysts, composites, and thin films; corrosion science; oxides, high Tc superconductivity, ion beam deposition; chemical interaction biocells doing silicats surfaces. *Mailing Add:* Dept Mat Col Eng & Appl Sci Univ Wis Milwaukee WI 53201. *Fax:* 414-229-6958; *E-Mail:* terybare@csd.uwm.edu

BARR, THOMAS ALBERT, JR, PLASMA PHYSICS. *Current Pos:* RES PROF, DEPT PHYSICS, UNIV ALA, HUNTSVILLE, 81- *Personal Data:* b Chattanooga, Tenn, Aug 18, 24; m 49; c 5. *Educ:* Univ Chattanooga, BS, 47; Vanderbilt Univ, MS, 50, PhD(physics), 53. *Prof Exp:* Mem staff, Vanderbilt Univ, 50-51; asst prof physics, Univ Ga, 51-56; supvy res physicist, high energy lasers, US Army Missile Res & Develop Command, Redstone Arsenal, 56-81. *Concurrent Pos:* Govt liaison rep, Plasma Phenomena Comt, AIAA, 60. *Mem:* Fel AAAS; Am Phys Soc; assoc fel Am Inst Aeronaut & Astronaut; Sigma Xi; fel Optical Soc Am. *Res:* Investigation of the properties of metal membranes; x-ray and neutron dosimetry; basic and applied research on partially and fully ionized gases; chemical and high power gas lasers. *Mailing Add:* Dept Phys Col Sci Univ Ala Huntsville AL 35899

BARR, WILLIAM A(LEXANDER), MECHANICAL ENGINEERING. *Current Pos:* ASSOC PROF MECH ENG, US NAVAL ACAD, 58- *Personal Data:* b Boston, Mass, Jan 9, 21; m; c 4. *Educ:* St John's Col, Md, BA, 42; Univ Va, BSME, 48; Va Polytech Inst & State Univ, MS, 51. *Prof Exp:* Lab technician plastic testing, Libbey-Owens-Ford Glass Co, 43; instr mech eng, Va Polytech Inst, 48-50, asst prof, 50-51; develop engr, Metal Prod Div, Koppers Co, 51-53, staff mech engr, 54; sr engr, Kaiser Aluminum & Chem Co, 55-56; plant engr, Crown Cork & Seal, 57, mgr equip eng, 57-58. *Mem:* Nat Soc Prof Engrs. *Res:* Heat transfer; design and evaluation of mechanical equipment; waste disposal problems. *Mailing Add:* Jorrick Rd Gibson Island MD 21056

BARR, WILLIAM FREDERICK, ENTOMOLOGY, TAXONOMY OF BEETLES. *Current Pos:* RETIRED. *Personal Data:* b Oakland, Calif, Oct 20, 20; m 46; c 3. *Educ:* Univ Calif, BS, 45, MS, 47, PhD(syst entom), 50. *Prof Exp:* Teaching asst entom, Univ Calif, 45-47; asst entomologist, Exp Sta, Univ

Idaho, 47-53, asst prof entom, 48-53, assoc prof & assoc entomologist, 53-58, prof & entomologist, 58-82, head, Dept Entom, 78-82. *Concurrent Pos:* NSF fac fel, 59-60. *Mem:* Pac Coast Entom Soc. *Res:* Systematic entomology; distribution and biology of Coleoptera; biological control of weeds; insects affecting range plants. *Mailing Add:* 1415 Borah Ave Moscow ID 83843

BARR, WILLIAM J, energy conversion; deceased, see previous edition for last biography

BARR, WILLIAM LEE, ATOMIC & MOLECULAR PHYSICS. *Current Pos:* PLASMA PHYSICS, LAWRENCE LIVERMORE NAT LAB, 57- *Personal Data:* b Wilbur, Wash, Feb 17, 25; m 52; c 3. *Educ:* Univ Wash, BS, 50; Univ Calif, PhD(physics), 57. *Mem:* Am Phys Soc. *Res:* Atomic spectroscopy; plasma physics. *Mailing Add:* 1274 Madison Ave Livermore CA 94550

BARRACK, CARROLL MARLIN, ELECTRICAL ENGINEERING, OPERATIONS RESEARCH. *Current Pos:* RETIRED. *Personal Data:* b Baltimore, Md, Mar 15, 27; m 49; c 3. *Educ:* Johns Hopkins Univ, BE, 50, DE, 56, MS, 65. *Prof Exp:* Sr design engr, Aircraft Armaments Inc, 54-57; res assoc res div, Electronic Commun Inc, 57-58; mgr, Electronics Dept, Miller Res Corp, Md, 58-59; prin develop engr, AAI Corp, 59-68; sr staff engr, Appl Physics Lab, Johns Hopkins Univ, 68-93. *Concurrent Pos:* Treas, E Coast Conf Aerospace & Navig Electronics, 58-61, vchmn, 61-62, chmn, 62-63; vchmn, Balto Sect, Inst Elec & Electronics Engrs, 67-68, chmn, 68-69. *Mem:* Inst Elec & Electronics Engrs; Sigma Xi. *Res:* Operations analysis in radar and missile systems; system analysis in electronic simulation, electronic warfare and digital systems; electromagnetic backscattering; applied statistics; experimental design. *Mailing Add:* 4817 Lauren Ct Ellicott City MD 21043-7420

BARRACK, EVELYN RUTH, NORMAL & ABNORMAL PROSTATE GROWTH. *Current Pos:* ASSOC DIR RES, BRADY UROL INST, JOHNS HOPKINS HOSP, 80- *Educ:* Johns Hopkins Univ, PhD(pharmacol), 75. *Prof Exp:* asst prof urol, Sch Med, Johns Hopkins Univ, 80- *Res:* Nuclear matrix. *Mailing Add:* Dept Urol Johns Hopkins Univ Sch Med 600 N Wolfe St Marburg 115 Baltimore MD 21287

BARRACLOUGH, CHARLES ARTHUR, ENDOCRINOLOGY. *Current Pos:* assoc prof, sch med, Univ Md, Baltimore City, 62-65, actg chmn dept, 71-72, prof physiol, 65-94, dir, ctr studies reproduction, 84-94, EMER PROF, UNIV MD, BALTIMORE CITY, 94- *Personal Data:* b Vineland, NJ, July 13, 26; m 52; c 2. *Educ:* St Joseph's Col, Pa, BS, 47; Rutgers Univ, MS, 51, PhD(zool), 52. *Honors & Awards:* Res Award, Soc Study Reproduction, 84, Carl Hartman Award, 90. *Prof Exp:* Asst, Rutgers Univ, 50-53; jr res anatomist, Sch Med, Univ Calif, Los Angeles, 53-54, from instr to asst prof, 54-61. *Concurrent Pos:* Spec res fel, Cambridge Univ, 61-62, Univ Milan, 69-70; consult res div, Vet Admin Hosp, Calif, 59-61; mem reproductive biol study sect, NIH, 66-68 & 70-74, chmn, 73-74. *Mem:* Fel AAAS; Soc Exp Biol Med; Int Brain Res Orgn; Am Physiol Soc; Soc Study Reproduction (dir, 71-73); Soc Neurosci; Endocrine Soc. *Res:* Reproductive physiology; neuroendocrinology. *Mailing Add:* 704 Saylor Ct Townson MD 21286

BARRACO, I ROBIN A, NEUROCHEMISTRY, NEUROPHARMACOLOGY. *Current Pos:* res assoc, 70-71, from asst prof to assoc prof, 72-87, PROF, WAYNE STATE UNIV, 87- *Personal Data:* b Detroit, Mich, Mar 24, 45; m 91, Leslie A Mohr; c Nina M. *Educ:* Georgetown Univ, BA, 66; Wayne State Univ, PhD(physiol), 71. *Prof Exp:* Res fel, NSF, 67-69 & DeVlieg Found. *Concurrent Pos:* Mem study sect, Minority Biomed Res Support Prog, NIH, 92- *Mem:* Am Physiol Soc; Soc Neurosci; Am Soc Neurochem; Int Soc Neurochem; Int Behav Neurosci Soc. *Res:* Role of neurotransmitters and neuromodulators in brain function, especially in the regulation of viscerobehavioral response patterns. *Mailing Add:* Dept Physiol Wayne State Univ Sch Med 540 E Canfield 6213 Scott Hall Detroit MI 48201-1908. *Fax:* 313-577-5494; *E-Mail:* rbarrac@cms.cc.wayne.edu

BARRADAS, REMIGIO GERMANO, PHYSICAL CHEMISTRY. *Current Pos:* RETIRED. *Personal Data:* b Hong Kong, Oct 23, 28; Can citizen; m 53; c 3. *Educ:* Univ Liverpool, BSc, 52; Royal Col Sci & Technol, Scotland, dipl, 53; Univ Ottawa, PhD(electrochem), 60. *Prof Exp:* Govt chemist, Govt Lab, Hong Kong, 53-56; chemist inspection serv, Chem Div, Dept Nat Defence, Can, 56-57; demonstr phys chem, Univ Ottawa, 57-60; res fel chem, Royal Mil Col, Can, 60-62; from asst prof to assoc prof, Univ Toronto, 62-68; prof chem, Carleton Univ, Ont, 68-95. *Mem:* Electrochem Soc; Chem Inst Can; fel Royal Inst Chem; Brit Polarographic Soc. *Res:* Theoretical electroanalytical chemistry; electrochemistry of transition metal ion complexes including photocatalytic and spectroscopic studies; battery systems and related power sources; photogalvanic cells; surface electrochemistry; electrocrystallization; electro-organic chemistry. *Mailing Add:* 1231 Woodside Dr Ottawa ON K2C 2H1 Can

BARRALL, EDWARD MARTIN, II, ANALYTICAL CHEMISTRY. *Current Pos:* res chemist, 69-80, mgr org & polymer anal, Gen Prod Div, 80-85, MGR, MAT LAB, SYSTS STORAGE PROD DIV, IBM CORP, 85- *Personal Data:* b Louisville, Ky, Dec 8, 34; m 77, Maryann Field; c Edward M III, Geoffrey A & Jennifer E (Peterson). *Educ:* Univ Louisville, BS, 55, MS, 57; Mass Inst Technol, PhD(analytical chem), 61. *Honors & Awards:* Mettler Award, NAm Thermal Anal Soc, 73. *Prof Exp:* Instr analytical chem, Univ Ga, 57-58; asst, Mass Inst Technol, 58-60; mem part-time staff, Dewey & Almy Chem Co Div, W R Grace Corp, 60-61; anal chemist, Chevron Res Co, Va, 61-69. *Concurrent Pos:* Mem part-time staff, E I du Pont de Nemours & Co, Inc, 57-59; vis prof, Univ Conn, 74-75; thesis adv, Univ Conn, 75-, Univ Southern Miss, 76- & Univ Calif, Berkeley, 79-81. *Mem:* AAAS; fel NAm Thermal Analytical Soc; Int Confedn Thermal Anal. *Res:* Thermal methods of analysis; gas chromatography; polymer characterization; thermodynamics of mesophase transitions; physics of polymers; thermal properties of organic compounds; thermal properties of cross linked systems. *Mailing Add:* 5878 Allen Ave San Jose CA 95193

BARRALL, RAYMOND CHARLES, RADIATION PHYSICS, HEALTH PHYSICS. *Current Pos:* dir radiation protection, 84-90, DIR ENVIRON HEALTH & SAFETY, UNIV ILL, CHICAGO, 90- *Personal Data:* b Philadelphia, Pa, Jan 4, 30; m 53, Shirley M Cloudt; c James DC, George E, Glenn E, Janet L & Scott R. *Educ:* Western NMex Univ, BS, 55; Univ Rochester, MS, 57. *Prof Exp:* Radiation physics fel, Brookhaven Nat Lab, 57; supv health physicist, Mare Island Naval Shipyard, 57-59; chief health physicist, IIT Res Inst, 59-65; dir health physics & safety, Stanford Univ, 65-75; dir res ctr, King Faisal Spec Hosp, 75-81, asst dir, Cancer Ther Inst, 81-83. *Concurrent Pos:* AEC radiol physics fel, 56-57. *Mem:* Am Soc Testing & Mat; Am Asn Physicists Med; Health Physics Soc; Am Nuclear Soc. *Res:* Radiation measurements, especially neutron cross-sections, flux and fluence with activation and moderator techniques; evaluation of radioactive impurities in radiopharmaceuticals; nuclear technology and applications. *Mailing Add:* 8001 Winter Circle Downers Grove IL 60516. *Fax:* 312-996-8776; *E-Mail:* rcb@uic.edu

BARRAN, LESLIE ROHIT, AGRICULTURAL MICROBIOLOGY. *Current Pos:* res scientist agr microbiol, Plant Res Ctr, 71-96, RES STA AGR CAN, STE FOY, 96- *Personal Data:* b Berbice, Guyana, July 29, 39; Can citizen; m 61, Mary Ann Simpkins; c Craig. *Educ:* McGill Univ, BSc, 63, MSc, 65; Mich State Univ, PhD(biochem), 69. *Mem:* Am Soc Microbiol. *Res:* Molecular genetics of nitrogen fixing bacteria. *Mailing Add:* 7 Jardins Merici Apt 1202 Quebec PQ G1S 4N8 Can

BARRANCO, SAM CHRISTOPHER, III, radiobiology, cancer; deceased, see previous edition for last biography

BARRANGER, JOHN ARTHUR, BIOCHEMISTRY, PEDIATRICS. *Current Pos:* clin assoc, 76-77, CHIEF, SECT CLIN INVEST, NAT INST NEUROL & COMMUN DIS, NIH, 77-, CHIEF, MOLECULAR & MED GENETICS SECT, DEVELOP & METAB NEUROL BR, NAT INST NEUROL & COMMUN DIS & STROKE, 82-, ASSOC CHIEF, DEVELOP & METAB NEUROL BR, 83- *Personal Data:* b Baltimore, Md, Aug 5, 45; m 69; c 3. *Educ:* Loyola Col, Baltimore, BS, 67; Univ Southern Calif, PhD(biochem), 73, MD, 74. *Honors & Awards:* Arthur S Fleming Award, 85. *Prof Exp:* Intern, Univ Minn, 74-75, resident, 75-76. *Concurrent Pos:* Res trainee, Univ Md, 67-69; res fel, Univ Southern Calif, 69-72, teaching asst, 72-74; clin assoc, develop & metab neurol, NIH, 76-77; clin staff, Clin Ctr, NIH, 76-78; Phillips Aull scholar; ed, Biochem Med. *Mem:* Sigma Xi; AAAS; NY Acad Sci; Soc Inherited Metabolic Dis; Am Soc Biol Chemists. *Res:* Inborn errors of metabolism; molecular genetics; enzymology; lysosomal storage disorders. *Mailing Add:* Dept Human Genetics Univ Pittsburgh E 1651 Biomed Sci Tower Bethesda PA 15261

BARRANGER, JOHN P, INSTRUMENTATION. *Current Pos:* RES ENGR, LEWIS CTR, NASA, 63- *Personal Data:* b Worcester, Mass, June 26, 30; m 56; c 8. *Educ:* George Washington Univ, BS, 57; Purdue Univ, MS, 60; Case Western Res Univ, PhD(eng), 69. *Prof Exp:* Engr, ITT Fed, 57-60 & Delco Electronics, 60-63. *Concurrent Pos:* Consult to various orgn, 70- *Mem:* Inst Elec & Electronics Engrs; Am Soc Nondestructive Testing; British Inst Nondestructive Testing. *Res:* Magnetics; magnetic measurements; material losses; network theory, eddy current and capacitance sensors; jet engine instrumentation; high temperature technology; strain gages. *Mailing Add:* NASA 21000 Brookpark Rd Cleveland OH 44126

BARRANTE, JAMES RICHARD, PHYSICAL CHEMISTRY, X-RAY CRYSTALLOGRAPHY. *Current Pos:* asst prof phys chem, 66-69, assoc prof chem, 69-76, PROF PHYS CHEM, SOUTHERN CONN STATE UNIV, 76- *Personal Data:* b Torrington, Conn, Apr 30, 38; m 65, Marlene Buccos; c Sharon, Stephen & Kimberly. *Educ:* Univ Conn, BA, 60; Harvard Univ, MA, 62, PhD(chem), 64. *Prof Exp:* Sr res chemist, Olin-Mathieson Chem Corp, Conn, 64-66. *Concurrent Pos:* Instr, Eve Sch, Southern Conn State Univ, 65-66; consult, Macdermid Corp, 81-83. *Mem:* Am Chem Soc. *Res:* Nuclear magnetic resonance studies of inorganic polymers; x-ray crystal structure analysis; theoretical chemistry. *Mailing Add:* Dept Chem Southern Conn State Univ 501 Crescent St New Haven CT 06515-1330

BARRAR, RICHARD BLAINE, MATHEMATICS. *Current Pos:* PROF MATH, UNIV ORE, 68- *Personal Data:* b Dayton, Ohio, Oct 12, 23; m 47; c 4. *Educ:* Univ Mich, MS, 48, PhD(math), 53. *Prof Exp:* Res assoc, Harvard Univ, 51-52; head theoret dept, McMillan Lab, 52-54; res physicist, Hughes Aircraft Co, 54-57; head, Antenna Group, Hoffman Lab, Inc, 57-58; sr opers res scientist, Syst Develop Corp, 58-66, sr scientist, 66-68. *Mem:* Am Math Soc; Soc Indust & Appl Math; Inst Elec & Electronics Engrs; Asn Comput Mach; Am Astron Soc. *Res:* Electromagnetic theory; existence theorems for partial differential equations; system analysis; celestial mechanics. *Mailing Add:* Univ Ore Eugene OR 97403-1222

BARRAS, DONALD J, PHYSIOLOGY, BIOCHEMISTRY. *Current Pos:* assoc prof, 70-78, PROF PHYSIOL, TROY STATE UNIV, 78-, CHMN, DEPT BIOL SCI, 76-; COLLAB RES EXPERT BIOL CONTROL, AGR RES SERV, USDA, 70- *Personal Data:* b St Martinsville, La, Jan 11, 32; m 61; c 3. *Educ:* Univ Southwestern La, BS, 54; Univ Miss, MS, 64; Miss State Univ, PhD(physiol), 70. *Prof Exp:* Teaching assoc physiol, Univ Miss, 62-64; res assoc biol warfare, Univ Okla, 64-65; asst prof physiol, Nicholls State Col, 65-67; res assoc, Miss State Univ, 67-70; prof biol, Norman Col, 70. *Mem:* Sigma Xi. *Res:* Biochemical and physiological studies of parasitoids in the use of biological control of harmful insects. *Mailing Add:* Dept Biol Sci Troy State Univ Main Campus University Ave Troy AL 36082-0001

BARRAS, STANLEY J, FOREST ENTOMOLOGY. *Current Pos:* asst dir, 80-, RES PLANT PATH, SOUTHERN FOREST EXP STA, USDA, 96- *Personal Data:* b New Orleans, La, Jan 4, 36. *Educ:* La State Univ, BS, 59, MS, 61; Univ Wis, PhD(entom), 65. *Prof Exp:* Res entomologist, Southern Forest Exp Sta, US Forest Serv, 65-75, proj leader, 75-76, forest insect & dis res staff, 76-80. *Mem:* Entom Soc Am; Soc Am Foresters; Sigma Xi. *Res:* Fungal repositories and associated microorganisms of bark beetles; interactions between bark beetle symbiotic fungi; ecology of symbiotic associations in pine phloem. *Mailing Add:* USDA Forest Serv FIDR PO Box 96090 Auditory Bldg 1 SW Washington DC 20090-6090. *Fax:* 504-589-3961

BARRAT, JOSEPH GEORGE, PLANT PATHOLOGY. *Current Pos:* RETIRED. *Personal Data:* b New Haven, Conn, May 30, 22; m 48; c 3. *Educ:* RI State Col, BS, 48; Univ RI, MS, 51; Univ NH, PhD(bot, plant path), 58. *Prof Exp:* Exten specialist entom & plant path, State Agr Exten Serv, Univ RI, 48-50; plant pathologist, Nursery Improv Prog, Dept Hort, State Dept Agr, Washington, 50-55; state exten specialist plant path, Coop Exten Serv, WVa Univ, 58-70, assoc prof, 67-70, supt exp farm, 70-80, prof plant path, 70-88, State Exten Specialist Plant Path, 80-88. *Mem:* Am Phytopath Soc. *Res:* Stone and pome fruit disease and insect control; virus diseases of stone and pome fruits. *Mailing Add:* Falling Spring Farm Shepherdstown WV 25443

BARRATT, MICHAEL GEORGE, PURE MATHEMATICS. *Current Pos:* PROF MATH, NORTHWESTERN UNIV, 72- *Personal Data:* b London, Eng, Jan 26, 27; m 52; c 5. *Educ:* Oxford Univ, BA, 48, MA, 52, DPhil, 52; Manchester Univ, MSc, 68. *Prof Exp:* Jr lectr math, Oxford Univ, 50-52, fel, 52-56; lectr, Brasenose Col, 55-59; sr lectr, Manchester Univ, 59-63, reader, 63-64, prof pure math, 64. *Concurrent Pos:* Vis asst prof, Princeton Univ, 56-67; prof, Univ Chicago, 63-64 & Northwestern Univ, 69-70. *Mem:* Am Math Soc. *Res:* Algebraic topology, particularly homotopy theory; homological algebra; topology of manifolds. *Mailing Add:* Dept Math Northwestern Univ Lunt Bldg Rm 310 Evanston IL 60208-2730

BARRATT, RAYMOND WILLIAM, MICROBIAL GENETICS. *Current Pos:* PROF BIOL & DEAN, SCH SCI, HUMBOLDT STATE UNIV, 70-, DIR FUNGAL GENETICS STOCK, 65- *Personal Data:* b Holyoke, Mass, May 4, 20; div; c 2. *Educ:* Rutgers Univ, BSc, 41; Univ NH, MSc, 43; Yale Univ, PhD(microbiol), 48. *Prof Exp:* Asst plant path & hort, Univ NH, 43-44; res assoc, Crop Protection Inst & asst plant pathologist, Conn Agr Exp Sta, 44-46; res assoc biol, Stanford Univ, 48-53, res biologist & actg asst prof, 53-54; asst prof bot, Dartmouth Col, 54-57, prof, 58-62, prof biol, 62-70, lectr microbiol, Med Sch, 61-70, chmn, Dept Biol Sci, 65-69. *Concurrent Pos:* USPHS spec fel, 61-62. *Mem:* Am Inst Biol Sci; Genetics Soc Am; Sigma Xi. *Res:* Genetics and biochemistry of microorganisms. *Mailing Add:* 6949 Fickle Hill Rd Arcata CA 95521-8299

BARRE, REMI ABDON ANDRE, ECONOMICS. *Current Pos:* DIR, OBSERV SCI & TECH, 90- *Personal Data:* b Boulogne-Sur-Seine, France, Apr 7, 48; m 77, Marie-Daniele Fichet; c Julien, Pierre & Flora. *Educ:* Ecole des Hautes Etudes, dipl, MA & PhD(econ). *Honors & Awards:* Decorated Knight Nat Order Merit. *Prof Exp:* Teaching asst, Univ NC, Chapel Hill, 74-75; asst, Resources Planning Assocs, 75-77; dir, Groupe d-Etudes Ressources Planification Amenagement, 77-81; lectr & researcher, Dept Econ & Mgt, Conservatoire Nat Des Arts et Metiers, 82-89. *Concurrent Pos:* Agent to minister, Res & Technol, 83-86. *Mailing Add:* Obseratoire Des Sci et des Tech 93 rue de Vaugirard Paris 75006 France

BARREKETTE, EUVAL S, ELECTROOPTICS, APPLIED MECHANICS. *Current Pos:* ENG CONSULT, 86- *Personal Data:* b New York, NY, Feb 18, 31; m 56; c 3. *Educ:* Columbia Univ, AB, 52, BS, 53, MS, 56, PhD(appl mech), 59. *Prof Exp:* Asst prof civil eng, Columbia Univ, 59-60; mem tech staff, IBM Corp, 60-63, tech asst to dir res, 63, mgr tech studies, 64-65, explor systs, 65-66, electrooptical technol, 67-71, prog dir advan eng, Corp Staff, 71-72, mgr advan technol, Res Div, 73-76, asst dir appl res, 76-81, asst dir comput sci, 81-84, prog dir optical technol, Corp Staff, 84-86. *Concurrent Pos:* Adj assoc prof, Columbia Univ, 60-70. *Mem:* Am Inst Aeronaut & Astronaut; Am Soc Civil Eng; Optical Soc Am; Soc Eng Sci; Inst Elec & Electronics Engrs; Sigma Xi; Nat Soc Prof Engrs. *Res:* Optical information processing; laser applications; microwave acoustics; computer printer and display technologies; semiconductor lasers. *Mailing Add:* 90 Riverside Dr New York NY 10024-5306

BARRER, DANIEL EDWARD, SYNTHETIC ORGANIC & NATURAL PRODUCTS CHEMISTRY, PATENT CHEMIST. *Current Pos:* PATENT CHEMIST, 89- *Personal Data:* b Oelwein, Iowa, Aug 24, 49; m 77, Audrey Rast; c Andry & Ryan. *Educ:* Loras Col, BS, 71; John Carroll Univ, MS, 74. *Prof Exp:* Process develop chemist, Gen Elec Co, 73-74; res chemist, Lubrizol Corp, 74-79 & 83-89, proj mgr, 79-83. *Mem:* Am Chem Soc. *Res:* Synthetic lubricants and lubricant additives; fuel conserving motor oil additives; synthetic overbased detergents for motor oil and specialty chemical applications; awarded 3 US patents. *Mailing Add:* 786 Kenbridge Dr Richmond Heights OH 44143-1931

BARRERA, CECILIO RICHARD, MICROBIAL PHYSIOLOGY. *Current Pos:* asst prof, 75-81, assoc prof biol, NMex State Univ, 81-, ASSOC DEAN GRAD SCH, 94. *Personal Data:* b Rio Grande City, Tex, Nov 30, 42; m 70; c 2. *Educ:* Univ Tex, Austin, BA, 65, MA, 67, PhD, 70. *Honors & Awards:* Founder Award, Soc Advan Chicanos & Native Americans Sci. *Prof Exp:* Fel biochem, Clayton Found Biochem Inst, Univ Tex, Austin, 70, res assoc, 70-75. *Concurrent Pos:* Served on var eval panels, NIH & NSF. *Mem:* Am Soc Microbiol; AAAS; Sigma Xi; Soc Advan Chicanos & Native Americans Sci (vpres). *Res:* Enzyme isolation and characterization; regulation of enzyme activity; microbiol ultrastructure. *Mailing Add:* Grad Sch NMex State Univ PO Box 30001 Las Cruces NM 88003. *Fax:* 505-646-5665

BARRERA, FRANK, PHYSIOLOGY. *Current Pos:* RETIRED. *Personal Data:* b Havana, Cuba, Nov 7, 17; m 49; c 5. *Educ:* Belen Col, BS, 34; Univ Havana, MD, 41. *Honors & Awards:* Tamayo Award, 52-59; Farinas Award, 58. *Prof Exp:* Instr med, Sch Med, Univ Havana, 46-47; from instr to assoc prof physiol, Sch Med, Temple Univ, 55-73, from asst prof to assoc prof med, 63-73; chief Respiratory Serv, Am Hosp, 73-85. *Concurrent Pos:* Chief clin & cardio-respiratory physiol dept, Inst Cardiovasc & Thoracic Surg, Cuba, 51-60. *Mem:* Am Physiol Soc; Sigma Xi. *Res:* Cardiopulmonary physiology. *Mailing Add:* 7095 Sunset Dr Miami FL 33143-4326

BARRERA, JOSEPH S, solid state physics, for more information see previous edition

BARRERAS, RAYMOND JOSEPH, ORGANIC CHEMISTRY. *Current Pos:* prof med educ & dir admis, 80-84, SPEC ASST TO DEAN & RES RESOURCES COORDR, MOREHOUSE SCH MED, 84- *Personal Data:* b Albuquerque, NMex, June 8, 40; m 59; c 5. *Educ:* Univ NMex, BS, 61; Mich State Univ, PhD(chem), 66. *Prof Exp:* From asst prof to assoc prof chem, Tuskegee Inst, 66-74; prof natural sci & head div, Navajo Community Col, Tsaile, Ariz, 74-78; prof biochem & dir tutorial prog, Sch Med, Morehouse Col, 78-80. *Concurrent Pos:* Res Corp Cottrell grant, 67-68; consult, Los Alamos Sci Lab, Univ Calif. *Mem:* AAAS; Am Chem Soc; Royal Soc Chem. *Res:* Synthesis of important organic intermediates; stereochemistry; reaction mechanisms; photochemistry; use of computers in education; medical data bases. *Mailing Add:* 989 Drewry St NE Atlanta GA 38306

BARRERE, CLEM A, JR, CHEMICAL ENGINEERING. *Current Pos:* DIR TECH SERV, BARRERE CO VENTURES, 89- *Personal Data:* b Bradford, Pa, Jan 5, 39; m 69. *Educ:* Yale Univ, BEng, 60; Rice Univ, PhD(chem eng), 65. *Prof Exp:* Res group leader, Continental Oil Co, 65-69, sr staff engr, 69-70, dir tech serv, 70-89. *Mem:* Am Inst Chem Engrs. *Res:* Thermodynamics; phase behavior of vapor-liquid and vapor-solid systems; adsorption; chromatography; absorption. *Mailing Add:* 5430 Lynbrock Houston TX 77056

BARRETO, ERNESTO, ELECTRODYNAMICS, FLUID DYNAMICS. *Current Pos:* SR RES ASSOC, ATMOSPHERIC SCI RES CTR, STATE UNIV NY, ALBANY, 69- *Personal Data:* b Colombia, SAm, Nov 9, 34; US citizen; m 60; c 2. *Educ:* NY Univ, BA, 58, MS, 60. *Prof Exp:* Res assoc physics, Dept Indust Med, NY Univ-Bellevue Med Ctr, 59-60; sci dir physics, Marks Polarized Corp, 60-64; proj engr, Curtiss-Wright Corp, 64-69. *Concurrent Pos:* Consult, Mobil Res Labs & US Coast Guard, 72-; mem comt hazardous mat, Nat Res Coun, 74-76; comt mem, Subcomn IV, Ions-Aerosols-Radioactivity, Int Comn Atmospheric Elec, 74- *Mem:* Am Phys Soc; Am Geophys Union; Am Inst Aeronaut & Astronaut; Elec Soc Am. *Res:* Transformation of stored electrical energy into heat in electrical discharges; oil transportation hazards, lightning studies, charged aerosol physics. *Mailing Add:* Atmospheric Sci Res Ctr State Univ NY 100 Fuller Rd Albany NY 12205

BARRETT, ANTHONY GERARD MARTIN, HETEROCYCLIC NATURAL PRODUCT CHEMISTRY. *Current Pos:* PROF CHEM, COLO STATE UNIV, 90- *Personal Data:* b Exeter, Eng, Mar 2, 52; m 73; c 2. *Educ:* Imp Col London, BSc, 73, PhD(org chem) & DIC(org chem), 75. *Honors & Awards:* Meldola Medal, Royal Soc Chem, London, 80, Harrison Medal, 82; Arthur C Cope Scholar Award, Am Chem Soc, 86; Corday Morgan Medal, Royal Soc Chem, London, 86. *Prof Exp:* From lectr to sr lectr org chem, Imp Col, 75-83; prof chem, Northwestern Univ, 83-90. *Concurrent Pos:* Consult, W R Grace, 80, G D Searle, 84 & B F Goodrich, 85, NIH Medicinal Chem, 86, Amoco, 88; Camille & Henry Dreyfus Teacher Scholar Award, 87; Japan Soc Promotion of Sci Fel, 89. *Mem:* Royal Soc Chem, London; Am Chem Soc. *Res:* The development of novel synthetic methods and their application to the total synthesis of bioactive natural products; design of host guest ensembles; discovery of versatile organometallic reagents; total synthesis. *Mailing Add:* Dept Chem Colo State Univ Ft Collins CO 80523

BARRETT, BRUCE RICHARD, THEORETICAL NUCLEAR PHYSICS. *Current Pos:* from asst prof to assoc prof, 70-76, PROF PHYSICS, UNIV ARIZ, 76- *Personal Data:* b Kansas City, Kans, Aug 19, 39; m 79, Joan F Livermore. *Educ:* Univ Kans, BS, 61; Stanford Univ, MS, 64, PhD(physics), 67. *Honors & Awards:* Alexander von Humboldt Sr Scientist Award, 83. *Prof Exp:* Res fel physics, Weizmann Inst Sci, Israel, 67-68; Andrew Mellon res fel, Univ Pittsburgh, 68-69, res assoc, 69-70. *Concurrent Pos:* Alfred P Sloan

Found res fel, 72-76; Alexander von Humboldt fel, 76-77; Fundamental Onderzoek der Materie fel, Neth, 80; Alexander von Humboldt Sr US Scientist Award, 83-84; prog dir, Theoret Physics Div, NSF, 85-87. *Mem:* Fel Am Phys Soc; Sigma Xi. *Res:* Structure of finite nuclei; particle-hole and particle-particle states with realistic nuclear forces; effective interaction calculations with realistic nuclear forces; exact reaction matrix calculations; real nuclear three-body forces; microscopic theory of nuclear collective motion; interacting Boson model of nuclear collective properties. *Mailing Add:* Dept Physics Bldg 81 Univ Ariz Tucson AZ 85721. *Fax:* 520-621-4721

BARRETT, C BRENT, pharmacology, for more information see previous edition

BARRETT, CHARLES SANBORN, materials science, physical metallurgy; deceased, see previous edition for last biography

BARRETT, CRAIG R, SEMICONDUCTOR TECHNOLOGY. *Current Pos:* reliability eng mgr, Intel Corp, 75-77, dir qual assurance, 77-80, gen mgr spec components oper, 80-83, dir components assembly, 83-84, vpres & dir components die prod, 84-85, gen mgr, Components Technol & Mfg Group, 85-87, co-mgr, Microcomput Components Group, 89-90, exec vpres, 90-92, mem bd dirs, 92, CHIEF OPER OFFICER, INTEL CORP, 93-, PRES, 97- *Personal Data:* b San Francisco, Calif, 1939; m, Barbara McConnell; c Dawn & Scott. *Educ:* Stanford Univ, BS, 61, MS, 63, PhD(mat sci), 64. *Prof Exp:* Assoc prof, Stanford Univ, 65-74. *Concurrent Pos:* Mem bd dirs, Intel Corp, 92. *Mem:* Nat Acad Eng. *Mailing Add:* Intel Corp 500 W Chandler Blvd Chandler AZ 85226

BARRETT, DENNIS, DEVELOPMENTAL BIOLOGY, BIOCHEMICAL GENETICS. *Current Pos:* asst prof, 73-77, ASSOC PROF BIOL SCI, UNIV DENVER, 77- *Personal Data:* b Philadelphia, Pa, Feb 13, 36; wid; c Alysoun. *Educ:* Univ Pa, AB, 57; Calif Inst Technol, PhD(biochem), 63. *Prof Exp:* USPHS res fel biochem, Univ Calif, Berkeley, 63-65; asst prof zool, Univ Calif, Davis, 65-73. *Concurrent Pos:* Spec consult, US AID Mission, Tunisia, 69; instr physiol, Marine Biol Lab, Woods Hole, 72-76; vis prof, Univ Edinburgh, 83-84; vis scientist, Bodega Marine Lab Univ Calif, Davis, 92-93. *Mem:* AAAS; Am Soc Zoologists; Soc Develop Biol. *Res:* Developmental biochemistry; control of gene expression in development; substrate specificity of proteases; sea urchin larval development. *Mailing Add:* Dept Biol Sci Univ Denver 2101 E Wesley Ave Denver CO 80210-5210. *Fax:* 303-871-3471; *E-Mail:* dbarrett@du.edu

BARRETT, EDWARD J, SCIENCE ADMINISTRATION. *Current Pos:* USCG, 66-, chief aeronaut, Eng Div, 88-90, comndg officer, 90-93, chief opers, Atlantic Area, 93-94, chief, Off Eng Logistics & Develop, 94-96, CHIEF SYSTS, USCG HQ, WASHINGTON, DC, 96- *Personal Data:* b Poughkeepsie, NY; m, Anne Stokley; c Wendy, Jennifer & Julie. *Educ:* Purdue Univ, MS, 75. *Mailing Add:* USCG 2100 Second St S Washington DC 20593-0001

BARRETT, EDWARD JOSEPH, organic chemistry, for more information see previous edition

BARRETT, ELLEN FAYE, NEUROBIOLOGY & NEUROSCIENCES, PHYSIOLOGY. *Current Pos:* from asst prof to assoc prof, 78-90, PROF PHYSIOL & BIOPHYS, UNIV MIAMI, 90- *Personal Data:* b Ontario, Ore, Nov 17, 44; m 68; c 2. *Educ:* Univ Wash, BS, 66, PhD(physiol & biophysics), 72. *Honors & Awards:* Javits Neuroscience Investr Award, NIH, 86. *Prof Exp:* NIH fel neurophysiol, Med Sch, Univ Colo, 72-73; fel neurobiol, Harvard Med Sch, 73; asst prof neurobiol & zool, Univ Iowa, 74. *Concurrent Pos:* Prin investr, NIH grant, 75-93; co-prin investr, Nat Parkinson Found grant, 78-79. *Mem:* Am Physiol Soc; AAAS; Soc Neurosci. *Res:* Mechanisms of transmitter release from nerve terminals; electrical properties of myelinated axons and motor nerve terminals. *Mailing Add:* Dept Physiol & Biophys Sch Med Univ Miami PO Box 016430 Miami FL 33101-6430

BARRETT, EUGENE J, DIABETES. *Current Pos:* PROF, UNIV VA, CHARLOTTESVILLE, 91-, DIR DIABETES CTR, 91- *Personal Data:* b Jersey City, NJ, May 22, 46; m 76, Paul M Quiricani; c Nora & Matthew. *Educ:* St Peters Col, BS, 68; Univ Rochester, MD & PhD, 75. *Prof Exp:* Asst prof, Yale Univ, 80-85, assoc prof, 85-91, dir diabetes unit, Sch Med, 87-91. *Concurrent Pos:* Res career award, NIH, 81-85; estab investr, Am Heart Asn, 86-90. *Mem:* Am Diabetes Asn; Am Heart Asn; Am Fedn Clin Res. *Res:* Diabetes; author of over 70 publications. *Mailing Add:* Sch Health Sci Ctr Univ Va MR4 Box 5116 Charlottesville VA 22908

BARRETT, GARY WAYNE, ECOLOGY. *Current Pos:* from asst prof to prof zool, Miami Univ, 68-86, actg dir, Inst Environ Sci, 70-71, dep dir, 71-77, dep dir res, 77-81, coordr environ educ, 76-77, CO-DIR, ECOL RES CTR, UNIV MIAMI, 77-, DISTINGUISHED PROF ECOL, 86-; ODUM PROF ECOL. *Personal Data:* b Princeton, Ind, Jan 3, 40; m 69; c 1. *Educ:* Oakland City Col, Ind, BS, 61; Marquette Univ, MS, 63; Univ Ga, PhD(zool), 67. *Hon Degrees:* DSc, Oakland City Col, 87. *Honors & Awards:* Award of Distinction, Inst Environ Sci, 77. *Prof Exp:* Asst prof biol, Drake Univ, 67-68. *Concurrent Pos:* NSF grants, 70, 71, 75, 78-79, 80-84, 85 & 89-93; adv, Citizens Task Force on Environ Protection, 71-72; Environ Protection Agency Grant, 80; dir ecol prog, NSF, 81-83; Earthwatch grants, 86, 87 & 88. *Mem:* Fel AAAS; Ecol Soc Am; Am Soc Mammal; Wildlife Soc; Am Inst Biol Sci; Sigma Xi; Am Soc Naturalists; Asn Ecosyst Res Ctrs; Int Asn Ecol; Int Soc Behav Ecol. *Res:* Pesticide stresses on total ecosystems; mammalian population regulation and dynamics; species diversity in nature; bioenergetics of small mammal populations; importance of ecotone areas in relation to agricultural productivity. *Mailing Add:* Inst Ecol Univ Ga Athens GA 30602-2202

BARRETT, HARRISON HOOKER, MEDICAL INSTRUMENTATION, OPTICS. *Current Pos:* assoc prof, 74-76, PROF, RADIOL DEPT & OPTICAL SCI CTR, UNIV ARIZ, 76- *Personal Data:* b Springfield, Mass, July 1, 39; m 59; c 2. *Educ:* Va Polytech Inst, BS, 60; Mass Inst Technol, SM, 62; Harvard Univ, PhD(appl physics), 69. *Prof Exp:* From res scientist to prin res scientist, Res Div, Raytheon Co, 62-74. *Concurrent Pos:* Alexander von Humboldt award. *Mem:* Am Phys Soc; fel Optical Soc Am. *Res:* Instrumentation for radiology and nuclear medicine; medical ultrasound; optical data processing. *Mailing Add:* Dept Radiol Univ Ariz Col Med Tucson AZ 85724

BARRETT, IZADORE, MARINE FISHERIES. *Current Pos:* RETIRED. *Personal Data:* b Vancouver, BC, Oct 4, 26; m 58, Fulvia Quesada; c Marcus, Byron, Norman & Dora. *Educ:* Univ BC, BA, 47, MA, 49; Univ Wash, PhD, 80. *Prof Exp:* Biologist, Trout Hatcheries, BC Game Comn, 52-56; scientist fishery biol, Inter-Am Trop Tuna Comn, 56-61, sr scientist tuna physiol, 61-67, ed, Bull, 64-65; chief fishery biologist, Inst Fishery Develop, Food & Agr Orgn, Chile, 67-69; asst dir, Fishery-Oceanog Ctr, US Dept Com, 70-72, dep dir, 72-77, dir, 77-88, dir sci & res, Southwest Region, Nat Marine Fisheries Serv, Nat Oceanic & Atmospheric Admin, 88-92. *Concurrent Pos:* Marine fisheries adv, Govt Chile, Food & Agr Orgn of UN, 69-70; res assoc, Scripps Inst Oceanog, 77- *Mem:* Am Inst Fishery Res Biologists (vpres, 73-74); Western Soc Naturalists. *Res:* Management and administration of marine fisheries research. *Mailing Add:* 4452 Camrose Ave San diego CA 92122. *E-Mail:* ibarrett@ucsd.edu

BARRETT, J(AMES) CARL, CANCER, CELL BIOLOGY. *Current Pos:* CHIEF, LAB MOLECULAR CARCINOGENESIS, NAT INST ENVIRON HEALTH SCI, NIH, 87-, ACTG DIR, ENVIRON CARCINOGENESIS PROG, 92- *Personal Data:* b Portsmouth, Va, Dec 28, 46; m 68; c 3. *Educ:* Col William & Mary, BS, 69; Johns Hopkins Univ, PhD(biophys chem), 74. *Prof Exp:* Res assoc chem carcinogenesis, Johns Hopkins Univ, 74-77. *Concurrent Pos:* Adj prof, Univ NC, 78- *Mem:* Am Asn Cancer Res; Am Chem Soc; Tissue Culture Asn; AAAS. *Res:* Cellular and molecular mechanisms of carcinogenesis with particular emphasis on chemical carcinogenesis, the relationship between carcinogenesis and mutagenesis, tumors suppressor genes and oncogenes. *Mailing Add:* Nat Inst Environ Health Sci NIH 111 Alexander Dr Research Triangle Park NC 27709

BARRETT, JAMES E, DRUG ABUSE, NEUROCHEMISTRY. *Current Pos:* HEAD, CENT NERV SYST RES, LEDERLE LABS, 92- *Personal Data:* b Camden, NJ, Aug 9, 42; m 62, Maura Bird; c Jennifer, Andrea & Stephanie. *Educ:* Pa State Univ, PhD, 72. *Honors & Awards:* Solvay-Duphar Award. *Prof Exp:* Prof psychiat pharmacol & med psychol, Uniformed Serv Univ Health Sci, 79-91, Lilly Res Lab, 91-92. *Concurrent Pos:* Consult, NASA Life Sci Space Lab; ed, Advances Behav Pharmacol & J Exp Anal Behav; mem sci adv bd, NE Regional Primate Res Ctr, Harvard Med Sch, Drug Abuse Ctr, Bowman Gray Sch Med. *Mem:* Soc Neurosci; AAAS; Behav Pharmacol Soc; Fed Am Soc Exp Biol; Am Soc Pharmacol & Exp Therapeut; Am Col Neuropsychopharmacol. *Res:* Behavioral and neurochemical effects of drugs; particularly those used in treating anxiety and drugs of abuse; also in dynamic interactions between behavior and neurochemistry; neurodegenerative disorders; Alzheimer's disease. *Mailing Add:* Central Nervous Syst Div Wyeth-Ayerst Res CN 8000 Princeton NJ 08543-8000. *Fax:* 914-732-5537; *E-Mail:* barrett@pr.cyanamid.com

BARRETT, JAMES MARTIN, PROTOZOOLOGY. *Current Pos:* from instr to prof, 51-86, EMER PROF BIOL, MARQUETTE UNIV, 86- *Personal Data:* b Chippewa Falls, Wis, July 4, 20; m 47; c 5. *Educ:* Marquette Univ, BS, 47, MS, 49; Univ Ill, PhD(zool), 53. *Prof Exp:* Asst zool, Marquette Univ, 47-48; asst, Univ Ill, 48-50. *Mem:* Soc Protozool; Am Soc Zool; Sigma Xi. *Res:* Biology of protozoa. *Mailing Add:* 1607 S 57th St West Allis WI 53214

BARRETT, JAMES PASSMORE, FORESTRY. *Current Pos:* from asst prof forestry to assoc prof, 62-75, PROF FOREST BIOMET, UNIV NH, 75- *Personal Data:* b Atlanta, Ga, June 20, 31; m; c 2. *Educ:* NC State Univ, BS, 54; Duke Univ, MF, 57, PhD(forest mensuration), 62. *Prof Exp:* Forest researcher, US Forest Serv, 57-62. *Mem:* Soc Am Foresters. *Res:* Applications of mathematical and statistical techniques in forestry. *Mailing Add:* Nat Res Univ NH James Hall Durham NH 03824-4724

BARRETT, JAMES R, MEDICAL IMAGING, PROCESS ANALYSIS. *Current Pos:* ASST PROF BIOMED ENG, UNIV VA, 88- *Personal Data:* b Pittsburgh, Pa, 1950. *Educ:* Pa State Univ, BS, 72, PhD(ecol), 79. *Prof Exp:* Sr software engr, Comput Vision Inc, 83-88. *Mem:* Inst Elec & Electronics Engrs; Asn Comput Mach; Biomed Eng Soc. *Mailing Add:* Univ Va Sch Med Hospital Dr Charlottesville VA 22908-0001

BARRETT, JAMES THOMAS, IMMUNOLOGY, MICROBIOLOGY. *Current Pos:* from asst prof to prof, 57-94, EMER PROF MICROBIOL, SCH MED, UNIV MO, COLUMBIA, 69-94. *Personal Data:* b Iowa, May 20, 27; m 49, 67, Barbro A L Nilsson; c Sara, Robert, Annika & Nina. *Educ:* Univ Iowa, BA, 50, MS, 51, PhD, 53. *Hon Degrees:* MD, Univ Repub Uruguay. *Prof Exp:* Asst prof microbiol, Sch Med, Univ Ark, 53-57. *Concurrent Pos:*

NIH spec fel, Sweden, 63-64; sabbatical, Dept Immunol, Med Microbiol Inst, Fac Med, Gothenberg Univ, 70-71; Nat Acad Sci exchange scientist, Romanian Acad Sci, 71; sabbatical, Inst Med Microbiol, Vet Fac, Ludwig Maximilians Univ, Munich & NIH Fogarty sr int fel, 77-78 & Univ Murcia, Spain, 86-87; Fulbright Scholar, Univ Repub Montevideo, 84; vis prof, Univ Autonoma of Guadalajara, Mex, 86- *Mem:* Am Asn Immunol; Am Soc Microbiol; Sigma Xi. *Res:* Immunological nature of proenzyme-enzyme pairs; spider venoms and ultrasound. *Mailing Add:* Dept Path-Microbiol St Georges Univ Sch Med Box 7 St Georges Grenada 65203

BARRETT, JERRY WAYNE, HISTORY & PHILOSOPHY OF SCIENCE, SCIENCE EDUCATION & POLICY. *Current Pos:* sr lectr chem, Hong Kong Baptist Col, 77-84, head dept, 80-84, dean sci, 82-88, ACAD VPRES, HONG KONG BAPTIST COL, 88- *Personal Data:* b Marshall, Tex, Apr 29, 36; m 59; c 2. *Educ:* ETex Baptist Col, BS, 61; Baylor Univ, PhD(chem), 68. *Prof Exp:* From asst prof to prof chem, Samford Univ, 66-76. *Mem:* Am Chem Soc; Sigma Xi; Hong Kong Chem Soc; fel Royal Soc Chem. *Res:* Electrodeposition, corrosion, electrodissolution and chemical plating of metals; electroanalytical methods; electrode kinetics and electrode reaction mechanism studies; philosophy of science. *Mailing Add:* Off Acad VPres Hong Kong Baptist Univ 224 Waterloo Rd Kowloon Tong Hong Kong People's Republic of China

BARRETT, JOHN HAROLD, THEORETICAL SOLID STATE PHYSICS. *Current Pos:* RETIRED. *Personal Data:* b Springfield, Mo, Oct 9, 26; m 52; c 1. *Educ:* Rice Inst, BS, 48, MA, 50, PhD(physics), 52. *Prof Exp:* Eli Lilly fel physics, Mass Inst Technol, 52-53; asst prof, NC State Col, 53-56 & La State Univ, 56-59; physicist, Oak Ridge Nat Lab, 59-78, sr res staff mem, 78-90. *Concurrent Pos:* Consult, 90- *Mem:* Am Phys Soc; AAAS. *Res:* Particle-solid interactions. *Mailing Add:* 827 W Outer Dr Oak Ridge TN 37831-8413

BARRETT, JOHN NEIL, NEUROSCIENCES & NEUROBIOLOGY, PHYSIOLOGY. *Current Pos:* from asst prof to assoc prof, 74-85, PROF PHYSIOL & BIOPHYS, UNIV MIAMI, 85- *Personal Data:* b Rochester, Minn, June 1, 43; m 68; c 2. *Educ:* St Mary's Col, Minn, BA, 65; Univ Wash, PhD(physiol & biophys), 72. *Prof Exp:* Res assoc neuroanat, Med Ctr, Univ Colo, 72-73; fel neurobiol, Harvard Med Sch, 73 & Univ Iowa, 74. *Concurrent Pos:* Prin investr, NIH grants, 75-93; co-prin investr, Nat Parkinson Found grant, 78-79 & 85-88; Javits Neurosci Investr Award. *Mem:* Soc Neurosci. *Res:* Trophic control of dopaminergic and cholinergic mammalian centrol neurons; neuronal cell culture; neuronal membrane electrical properties; physiology. *Mailing Add:* Dept Physiol & Biophys R5029 Univ Miami 1600 NW Tenth Ave Miami FL 33136-1015

BARRETT, JOSEPH JOHN, QUANTUM OPTICS, MOLECULAR SPECTROSCOPY. *Current Pos:* sr physicist, 70-80, mgr laser instrumentation, 80-85, SR RES ASSOC, ALLIED-SIGNAL CORP, 85- *Personal Data:* b Scranton, Pa, Mar 11, 36; m 67; c 2. *Educ:* Univ Scranton, BS, 58; Fordham Univ, MS, 60, PhD(physics), 64. *Honors & Awards:* Williams-Wright Award, 86. *Prof Exp:* Res asst physics, Fordham Univ, 62-64; sr scientist physics, Perkin-Elmer Corp, 64-70. *Mem:* Optical Soc Am; Am Phys Soc; Sigma Xi. *Res:* Lasers for spectroscopic applications with emphasis on the generation and analysis of coherent Raman radiation; laser imaging research. *Mailing Add:* 18 Forest Dr Morris Plains NJ 07950

BARRETT, LIDA KITTRELL, MATHEMATICS, EDUCATION. *Current Pos:* SR ASSOC, PLANNING & EXTERNAL AFFAIRS, EDUC & HUMAN RESOURCES, NSF, 91- *Personal Data:* b Houston, Tex, May 21, 27; wid; c John K, Maibel H & Mary L (Miller). *Educ:* Rice Inst, BA, 46; Univ Tex, MA, 49; Univ Pa, PhD(math), 54. *Prof Exp:* Mathematician, Schlumberger Well Surv Corp, 46-47; teacher math, Tex State Col Women, 47-48; res mathematician, Defense Res Lab, Univ Tex, 49-50; asst instr math, Univ Pa, 53-54; instr, Univ Conn, 55-56; lectr, Univ Utah, 56-61; from assoc prof to prof math, Univ Tenn, Knoxville, 61-80, head dept, 73-80; prof math & assoc provost, Northern Ill Univ, 80-87; prof math & statist & dean, Col Arts & Sci, Miss State Univ, 87-91. *Concurrent Pos:* Vis lectr, Univ Wis, 59-60; consult, Oak Ridge Nat Lab, 64-75. *Mem:* Am Math Soc; Math Asn Am (pres, 89-90); Soc Indust & Appl Math; Sigma Xi; Nat Coun Teachers Math. *Res:* Point set topology; applications of topology in metallurgy; mathematics education. *Mailing Add:* 729 Hewitt Lane New Windsor NY 12553. *Fax:* 540-667-7425; *E-Mail:* lbarrett@nsf.gov

BARRETT, LOUIS CARL, MATHEMATICS. *Current Pos:* prof & head dept, 67-72, PROF MATH, MONT STATE UNIV, 72- *Personal Data:* b Murray, Utah, Jan 23, 24; m 47; c 4. *Educ:* Univ Utah, BS, 48, MS, 51, PhD(appl math), 56. *Prof Exp:* Instr math, Univ Utah, 53-56; assoc prof math & physics, Ariz State Univ, 56-57; from assoc prof to prof math, SDak Sch Mines & Technol, 57-65, head dept, 60-65; prof & chmn dept, Clarkson Col Technol, 65-67. *Concurrent Pos:* Res mathematician, Holloman Air Develop Ctr, NMex, 55, math consult, 56; res mathematician, US Naval Ord Test Sta, Calif, 57, 58, 63-64, consult, 63-64; lectr, Ariz State Univ, 57 & NSF Inst, SDak, 59; mem anal panel, NSF Modules & Monographs Undergrad Math & Its Appln Proj, Educ Develop Ctr, Newton, Mass, 78. *Mem:* Am Math Soc; Math Asn Am; Soc Indust & Appl Math. *Res:* Eigenvalue problems; differential equation theory; boundary value problems; optimization problems; Ordinary & Interface Strum-Liouville Systems; linear algebra; statistics; probability, mathematical physics and analysis; calculus variations; advanced engineering mathematics. *Mailing Add:* 1721 S Wilson Bozeman MT 59715-5551

BARRETT, O'NEILL, JR, HEMATOLOGY, ONCOLOGY. *Current Pos:* undergrad distinguished adj prof pharm & grad prof med, 77-80, asst dean acad affairs, Sch Med, 80-87, PROF MED, UNIV SC, 80-, CHMN, DEPT MED, 87- *Personal Data:* b Baton Rouge, La, Mar 21, 29; m 52; c 3. *Educ:* La State Univ, BS, 49, MD, 53; Baylor Univ, MSc, 58. *Prof Exp:* Clin investr hemat & asst dir basic sci course, Walter Reed Army Inst Res, 59-60, chief gen med & hemat, Madigan Gen Hosp, 60-62, dep chief dept med, Letterman Gen Hosp San Francisco, Calif, 63-68, chief dept med, Tripler Gen Hosp, Honolulu, 68-71, chief dept med, Walter Reed Gen Hosp, 71-77; prof med, Col Med, Univ S Fla, 73-77, prof comprehensive med & chmn dept, 74-77. *Concurrent Pos:* Clin asst prof, Sch Med, Univ Calif, San Francisco, 63-68; clin prof, Sch Med, Univ Hawaii, 69-71. *Mem:* Fel Am Col Physicians; Am Soc Hemat; Am Fedn Clin Res; Am Soc Clin Oncol; AMA; fel Am Col Pharm Ther. *Mailing Add:* Univ S Carolina Sch Med Two Richland Med Park Suite 502 Columbia SC 29203

BARRETT, PAUL E, HIGH ENERGY ASTROPHYSICS, INTERACTING BINARY STARS. *Current Pos:* RES SCIENTIST, UNIVS SPACE R ES ASN, 90- *Personal Data:* b Whittier, Calif, Nov 22, 57; m 90, Catherine M Anderton; c Robert & Alexandra J. *Educ:* Ga Inst Technol, BS, 79; La State Univ, PhD(physics), 85. *Prof Exp:* Postdoctoral researcher, Univ Cape Town, 85-87; res fel SAfrican Astron Observ, 87-90. *Mem:* Am Astron Soc; Am Phys Soc; Int Astron Union. *Res:* Multiwavelength studies of magnetic cataclysmic variables; development of scientific data analysis environments. *Mailing Add:* Goddard Space Flight Ctr NASA Code 660 1 Greenbelt MD 20771

BARRETT, PAUL HENRY, physics, for more information see previous edition

BARRETT, PETER FOWLER, INORGANIC CHEMISTRY. *Current Pos:* from asst prof to assoc prof, Trent Univ, 67-84, actg chmn, Dept Chem, 75-76, chmn, 83-86, assoc dean sci, 88-93, PROF INORG CHEM, TRENT UNIV, 84- *Personal Data:* b Port Dover, Ont, May 27, 39; m 65; c 2. *Educ:* Queen's Univ, Ont, BSc, 61, MSc, 62; Univ Toronto, PhD(inorg chem), 65. *Prof Exp:* Nat Res Coun overseas fel, 65-67. *Mem:* Chem Inst Can. *Res:* Kinetics and mechanisms of reactions of transition metal carbonyl complexes; energy storage by supercooling of liquid salt hydrates. *Mailing Add:* Dept Chem Trent Univ Peterborough ON K9J 7B8 Can. *E-Mail:* pbarrett@trentu.ca

BARRETT, PETER VAN DOREN, INTERNAL MEDICINE, GASTROENTEROLOGY. *Current Pos:* DIR MED EDUC, ST MARY MED CTR, LONG BEACH, CALIF, 75- *Personal Data:* b Los Angeles, Calif, Oct 22, 34; m 59; c 3. *Educ:* Univ Calif, Los Angeles, BA, 56; Harvard Med Sch, MD, 60; Am Bd Internal Med, dipl & cert internal med & gastroenterol. *Prof Exp:* From intern to asst resident med, Mass Gen Hosp, Boston, 60-62; clin assoc, NIH, 62-65; resident, Mass Gen Hosp, Boston, 65-66; asst prof med, Sch Med, Univ Calif, Los Angeles, 67-71; assoc chief, Div Gastroenterol, Harbor Gen Hosp, Torrance, 67-75; assoc prof, 71-79, prof med, Sch Med, Univ Calif, Los Angeles, 79- *Concurrent Pos:* Fel gastroenterol, Wadsworth Vet Admin Hosp, Los Angeles, 66-67; NIH res grants, 67-76. *Mem:* Am Gastroenterol Asn; fel Am Col Physicians; Am Fedn Clin Res. *Res:* Hepatic physiology and bile pigment metabolism. *Mailing Add:* St Mary Med Ctr Univ Calif Los Angelea Sch Med Long Beach CA 90801

BARRETT, RICHARD JOHN, TECHNICAL ASSESSMENT, NUCLEAR REACTOR SAFETY. *Current Pos:* NUCLEAR ENG, US NUCLEAR REGULATORY COMN, 82- *Personal Data:* b West Pittston, Pa, Mar 28, 45; m 69; c 2. *Educ:* Univ Scranton, BS, 67; Univ Va, PhD(physics), 73. *Prof Exp:* Res assoc, Case Western Reserve Univ, 72-75; mem staff, Theoret Div, Los Alamos Nat Lab, 75-79, Systs Anal Div, 79-82. *Concurrent Pos:* Res prog analyst, Off Energy Res, US Dept Energy, 80- *Mem:* Am Nuclear Soc. *Res:* Formal analytical techniques to evaluate the technical, economic and safety performance of advanced energy technologies; identify areas of needed research. *Mailing Add:* 7501 Mill Run Dr Derwood MD 20855

BARRETT, RICHARD JOHN, PHARMACOLOGY. *Current Pos:* sr res biologist, 85-87, RES ASSOC, A H ROBINS CO, 87- *Personal Data:* b Newark, NJ, Oct 10, 49; m 71; c 2. *Educ:* Villanova Univ, BS, 71; Fairleigh Dickinson Univ, MS, 79; Univ Houston, PhD(pharmacol), 82. *Prof Exp:* Asst scientist I, Hoffmann La Roche Inc, 71-75; lab supvr, Hoechst-Roussell Pharmaceut Div, Am Hoechst Co, 75-79; teaching training, Univ Houston, 79-82; res pharmacologist, Stuart Pharmaceut Div, ICI Am, Inc, 82-85. *Concurrent Pos:* Adj asst prof pharmacol & toxicol, Philadelphia Col Pharm & Sci, 82-85; mem coun, High Blood Pressure Res & Kidney & Cardiovasc Dis, Am Heart Asn. *Mem:* Am Soc Pharmacol & Exp Therapeut; Soc Neurosci; Am Soc Hypertension; Am Heart Asn. *Res:* Cardiovascular pharmacology and physiology; renal and neural actions of drugs in the therapy of cardiovascular diseases. *Mailing Add:* 14406 Oak Knoll Circle Midlothian VA 23112-2406

BARRETT, ROBERT, NEUROPHYSIOLOGY. *Current Pos:* NIMH fel, Brain Res Inst, 69-70, dir, 70-85, EMER DIR, DEPT ENG & SCI, EXTEN & LECTR BIOL, UNIV CALIF, LOS ANGELES, 85- *Personal Data:* b Los Angeles, Calif, Jan 4, 14; m 38; c 1. *Educ:* Univ Calif, Los Angeles, BA, 34, MA, 65, PhD(zool), 69. *Prof Exp:* Tutor & instr sociol, Harvard Univ, 34-36; mem, NSF Cetacean Exped, Tierra del Fuego, 68. *Mem:* Am Inst Biol Sci; Soc Neurosci; Am Soc Zool. *Res:* Sensory physiology, particularly in areas of heat sensing, olfaction and taste; comparative neurophysiology. *Mailing Add:* 498 Drexel Dr Santa Barbara CA 93103-2145

BARRETT, ROLIN F(ARRAR), MECHANICAL ENGINEERING. *Current Pos:* CONSULT, 80- *Personal Data:* b White Sulphur Springs, WVa, Aug 25, 37; m 60; c 2. *Educ:* NC State Univ, BS, 59, MS, 62, PhD(mech eng), 65. *Honors & Awards:* Centennial Award, Am Soc Mech Engrs; Ralph Teetor Award, Soc Automotive Engrs. *Prof Exp:* Consult engr, L E Wooten & Co, 59-60; from instr to assoc prof mech eng, NC State Univ, 62-76, prof & asst admin dean res, 76-80. *Concurrent Pos:* Shell Oil fel. *Mem:* Soc Automotive Engrs; Am Inst Aeronaut & Astronaut; Am Soc Mech Engrs; Sigma Xi; Am Soc Metals; Am Soc Testing & Mat. *Res:* High speed mass transportation; turbine engine diagnostic techniques; mechanical design; transportation; automobile engineering; highway safety. *Mailing Add:* 3701 National Dr Suite 202 Raleigh NC 27612-4843

BARRETT, SEAN ERIC, OPTICALLY PUMPED NUCLEAR MAGNETIC RESONANCE. *Current Pos:* ASST PROF PHYSICS & APPL PHYSICS, YALE UNIV, 94- *Personal Data:* b Yonkers, NY, Aug 20, 65; m 92, Nancy Elizabeth Vergara; c Caitlin & Andrew. *Educ:* Princeton Univ, AB, 87; Univ Ill, Urbana, MS, 88, PhD(physics), 92. *Prof Exp:* Mem tech staff, AT&T Bell Labs, 92-94. *Mem:* Am Physics Soc; AAAS. *Res:* Use of optically pumped nuclear magnetic resonance to study the physics of electrons in the quantum hall regimes. *Mailing Add:* Physics Dept Yale Univ PO Box 208120 New Haven CT 06520-8120

BARRETT, SPENCER CHARLES HILTON, EVOLUTION & ECOLOGY OF PLANT REPRODUCTION, GENETICS & ECOLOGY OF WEED INVASIONS. *Current Pos:* PROF BOT, UNIV TORONTO, 77- *Personal Data:* b Bushey, Hertfordshire, Eng, June 7, 48; m 73, Suzanen Whittaker; c Rowan & Seth. *Educ:* Univ Reading, UK, BSc Hons, 71; Univ Calif, Berkeley, PhD(bot), 77. *Prof Exp:* Weed biologist, Commonwealth Develop Corp, 69-70; lectr biol, Univ Calif, Santa Cruz, 76. *Concurrent Pos:* Vis res scientist, Commonwealth Sci & Indust Res Orgn, Australia, 83-84; chmn & mem Pop Biol Grants Panel, Res Coun Can, 84-; E W R Steacie mem fel, Nat Sci & Eng Res Coun Can, 88-89; assoc ed, J Evolution, 89-92. *Mem:* Soc Study Evolution; Brit Ecol Soc; Bot Soc Am; Genetics Soc. *Res:* Evolution and genetics of plant mating systems; function and evolution of heterostyly; evolution of self-fertilization; evolution of gender polymorphisms; conservation biology. *Mailing Add:* Dept Bot Univ Toronto Toronto ON M5S 3B2 Can

BARRETT, WALTER EDWARD, MEDICAL SCIENCES GENERAL, TOXICOLOGY. *Current Pos:* CONSULT, PHARMACEUT INDUST, 95- *Personal Data:* b Stamford, Conn, May 26, 21; m; c 4. *Educ:* Columbia Univ, AB, 44; Princeton Univ, MA, 57, PhD, 58. *Prof Exp:* From asst pharmacologist to sr pharmacologist, Ciba Pharm Co, 44-61, assoc dir gen pharmacol, 62-64, head, 64-66, from asst dir macrobiol to dir pharmacol, 66-69; dir pharmacol, Parke, Davis & Co, 69-70; clin res assoc, Sandoz Res Inst, Sandoz Pharmaceut Corp, 71-72, head short term res & develop, 72-73, dir short term res & develop, Pharmaceut Res & Develop, 74-83, dir med res, 83-86; pres, Web Int Res Corp, 87-94. *Concurrent Pos:* Mem, Med Adv Bd, Coun High Blood Pressure Res, Am Heart Asn; mem comt, Am Soc Clin Pharmacol & Therapeut. *Mem:* Am Soc Pharmacol; NY Acad Sci; Sigma Xi; Am Soc Clin Pharmacol & Therapeut. *Res:* Mechanism of action of autonomic drugs; cardiovascular drugs; clinical pharmacology and research; biopharmaceutics. *Mailing Add:* 4 Hoffman Ct Convent Station NJ 07960-6041

BARRETT, WILLIAM AVON, COMPUTER SCIENCE, ELECTRICAL ENGINEERING. *Current Pos:* ASST PROF COMPUT ENG, SAN JOSE STATE UNIV, 96- *Personal Data:* b Central City, Nebr, Nov 8, 30; m 76; c 2. *Educ:* Univ Nebr, BS, 52, MS, 53; Univ Utah, PhD(physics), 57. *Prof Exp:* Mem tech staff devices, Bell Tel Labs, 57-63; asst prof physics, Muhlenberg Col, 63-66; assoc prof elec eng, Lehigh Univ, 66-74; staff mem comput, Hewlett Packard Co, 74-84; dir software, Lasa Indust, Inc, 86-93, appl scanning tech, 94-96. *Concurrent Pos:* Consult, Bell Tel Labs, 64-74, RCA Astro-Electronics, 71, Comput Ctr, Lehigh Univ, 72 & Int Tel & Tel Corp, 73. *Mem:* Inst Elec & Electronics Engrs; Asn Comput Mach. *Res:* LR(1) parser error recovery; fault detection and diagnosis; memory test systems; magnetic memory models. *Mailing Add:* 2797 Lena Dr San Jose CA 95124-1931

BARRETT, WILLIAM LOUIS, SOLID STATE PHYSICS, NUCLEAR ENGINEERING. *Current Pos:* asst prof, 68-71, ASSOC PROF PHYSICS, WESTERN WASH UNIV, 71-, CHMN, DEPT PHYSICS & ASTRON, 75- *Personal Data:* b Phoenix, Ariz, June 3, 33; m 76; c 3. *Educ:* Univ Idaho, BS, 56; Univ Wash, MS, 61, PhD(physics), 68. *Prof Exp:* Res engr, Boeing Co, Wash, 61-64. *Mem:* AAAS; Am Inst Physics; Am Phys Soc. *Res:* Ferromagnetic resonance in metals; crystal growth; nuclear rocket concepts. *Mailing Add:* Phys & Astron Western Wash Univ Bond Hall No 152 Bellingham WA 98225

BARRETT-CONNOR, ELIZABETH L, EPIDEMIOLOGY. *Current Pos:* from asst prof to assoc prof, 70-81, PROF MED & COMMUNITY MED, UNIV CALIF, SAN DIEGO, 81-, CHMN, DEPT COMMUNITY & FAMILY MED, 82- *Personal Data:* b Evanston, Ill, April 8, 35; m 65; c 3. *Educ:* Mt Holyoke Col, BA, 56; Med Col, Cornell Univ, MD, 60; London Sch Hyg & Trop Med, dipl, 65. *Hon Degrees:* DSc, Mt Holyoke Col, 85. *Honors & Awards:* Living Legacy Award, 84; Alexander D Langmuir Lectr, 85; Katherine Boucut Sturgis Lectr, 86; Kelly West Mem Lectr, 87; John Rankin Lectr, 89; Dan McLeod Mem Lectr, 90; Elizabeth Blackwell Lectr, 91; Wade Hampton Frost Lectr, Am Pub Health Asn, 93; Leonard M Schuman Lectr, 93; James D Bruce Mem Award, Am Col Physicians, 94. *Prof Exp:* Instr med, Univ Miami, 65-68, asst prof, 68-70. *Concurrent Pos:* comt mem, Nat Inst Allergies & Infectious Dis, 78-83; adv mem, Walter Reed Army Inst Res, 79-83, Nat Ctr Health Statist, 83-87; consult, Nat Inst Med, 78, Med Res Labs, Dept Defense, 80-83; mem, Nat Diabetes Adv Bd, 90-94. *Mem:* Inst Med-Nat Acad Sci; Royal Soc Health; Soc Epidemiol Res; Infectious Dis Soc Am; Am Heart Asn; Am Epidemiol Soc; Am Diabetes Asn; Nat Diabetes Adv Bd; Am Venereal Dis Asn. *Res:* Epidemiology of tropical medicine, tuberculosis, nosocomial infection, sickle cell anemia, cardiovascular disease, osteoporosis and diabetes mellitus in adults; geriatrics. *Mailing Add:* Dept Family & Prev Med 0628 Univ Calif San Diego CA 92093

BARRETTE, DANIEL CLAUDE, RUMINANT FEEDING & HUSBANDRY, SWINE FEEDING. *Current Pos:* asst prof nutrit, 72-78, assoc prof nutrit & animal sci, Fac Vet Med, 77-78, PROF NUTRIT & ANIMAL SCI, UNIV MONTREAL, 88- *Personal Data:* b Berthierville, Que, Apr 22, 43; m 67. *Educ:* Univ Montreal, BA, 62, DMV, 66; Univ Laval, MSc, 70. *Prof Exp:* Asst prof physiol, fac agri sci & nutrit, Univ Laval, Que, 70-72. *Concurrent Pos:* Lectr, fac agr sci & nutrit, Univ Laval, 72-81; vpres, coun animal prod, Que Dept Agr, 83-85, pres, 85-87; mem expert comt pet food, Can Vet Med Asn, 85- *Mem:* Nutrit Today Soc; Am Asn Bovine Practrs; Asn Am Vet Med Col; French Can Asn Advan Sci. *Res:* Evaluating metabolic and zootechnic effects of different levels of alimentary fiber and protein on growth, gestation and lactation in Beagle dogs; dog and cat feeding; small animal feeding and nutrition. *Mailing Add:* Fac Vet Med CP 5000 St Hyacinthe PQ J2S 7C6 Can

BARRETTE, JEAN, NUCLEAR STRUCTURE. *Current Pos:* PROF PHYSICS, MCGILL UNIV, 87-, DIR, FOSTER RADIATION LAB, 88- *Personal Data:* b Montreal, Que, May 1, 46. *Educ:* Univ Montreal, BSc, 67, MSc, 68, PhD(nuclear physics), 74. *Prof Exp:* Postdoctoral fel nuclear physics, Max Planck Inst Nuclear Physics, Heidelberg, Ger, 74-76; asst physicist, Brookhaven Nat Lab, 76-78, assoc physicist, 78-80, physicist, 80-82; engr/physician nuclear physics, Commissariat a L'Energie Atomique, France, 82-87. *Mem:* Am Phys Soc; Can Asn Physics. *Res:* Nucleus-nucleus reactions & heavy-ion physics with particular interest in the study of reaction mechanism at intermediate and relativistic bombarding energies. *Mailing Add:* Foster Radiation Lab McGill Univ 3600 University St Montreal PQ H3A 2T8 Can. *Fax:* 514-398-7022; *E-Mail:* barrette@physics.mcgill.ca

BARRICK, DONALD EDWARD, ELECTRICAL ENGINEERING. *Current Pos:* CHIEF SEA STATE STUDIES PROG, ENVIRON RES LABS, NAT OCEANIC & ATMOSPHERIC ADMIN, 77- *Personal Data:* b Tiffin, Ohio, Nov 7, 38; m 61; c 2. *Educ:* Ohio State, BSEE & MSc, 61, PhD(elec eng), 65. *Prof Exp:* Res assoc electromagnetic theory, electrosci lab, Ohio State Univ, 63-65; fel, Battelle-Columbus Labs, 65-69; adj asst prof, Ohio State Univ, 69-77. *Concurrent Pos:* Mem Comn II, Int Sci Radio Union, 69-77. *Mem:* AAAS; Inst Elec & Electronics Engrs. *Res:* Electromagnetic theory; radar systems; scattering from rough surfaces; radar signal processing; antenna and phased array theory; radar cluttering and clutter rejection; radar scattering theory. *Mailing Add:* 632 Lakeview Way Redwood City CA 94062-3323

BARRICK, ELLIOTT ROY, ANIMAL SCIENCE. *Current Pos:* RETIRED. *Personal Data:* b Worthington, Minn, Feb 7, 15; m 45; c 3. *Educ:* Okla State Univ, BS, 38; Purdue Univ, MS, 41, PhD(animal nutrit), 47. *Prof Exp:* Asst prof animal husb, Purdue Univ, 47-48; assoc prof, Univ Tenn, 48-49; assoc prof animal indust, NC State Univ, 49-54, head animal husb sect, 54-67, prof animal sci, 54-80. *Mem:* Am Soc Animal Sci; Am Dairy Sci Asn. *Res:* Animal production and nutrition. *Mailing Add:* 5310 Old Stage Rd Raleigh NC 27603

BARRICK, P(AUL) L(ATRELL), CHEMICAL ENGINEERING, ORGANIC CHEMISTRY. *Current Pos:* RETIRED. *Personal Data:* b Villa Grove, Ill, Aug 22, 14; m 47, Mildred Daub; c Sandra, Paige & Brenda. *Educ:* Univ Ill, BS, 35; Cornell Univ, PhD(org chem), 39. *Prof Exp:* Asst org chem, Cornell Univ, 35-38; res chemist, Exp Sta, E I DuPont de Nemours & Co, 39-48; prof chem eng, Univ Colo, Boulder, 48-85. *Mem:* Am Chem Soc; Soc Plastics Engrs; Am Inst Chem Engrs; Am Soc Eng Educ. *Res:* Synthetic polymers; catalysis; cryogenics; phase equilibria. *Mailing Add:* 360 18th St Boulder CO 80302

BARRIE, LEONARD ARTHUR, wet & dry removal processes, gas pollutant transformation aerosols, for more information see previous edition

BARRIE, ROBERT, THEORETICAL PHYSICS. *Current Pos:* from instr to assoc prof, 57-64, PROF PHYSICS, UNIV BC, 64- *Personal Data:* b Newmains, Scotland, Sept 19, 27; m 54. *Educ:* Univ Glasgow, BSc, 49, PhD(physics), 54. *Prof Exp:* From sci officer to sr sci officer, Servs Electronics Res Lab, Baldock, Herts, Eng, 53-57. *Res:* Electronic properties of solids. *Mailing Add:* 4056 W 33rd Ave Vancouver BC V6N 2G1 Can

BARRIENTOS, CELSO SAQUITAN, OCEANOGRAPHY, OCEAN REMOTE SENSING. *Current Pos:* res materologist, Tech Develop Lab, Nat Weather Serv, 69-81, SUPVRY PHYS SCIENTIST, NAT ENVIRON SATELLITE DATA & INFO SERV, NAT OCEANIC & ATMOSPHERIC ADMIN, 81- *Personal Data:* b Cavite, Philippines, Jan 9, 36; m 59, Pag-Asa C Baltazar; c Briccio & Beatriz. *Educ:* Feati Univ, Philippines, BSc, 60; NY Univ, MSc, 65, PhD(meteorol), 69. *Prof Exp:* Asst res scientist, Geophys Sci Lab, NY Univ, 62-66; res scientist, Isotopes, Inc, 66-68 & Geophys Sci Lab, NY Univ, 68-69. *Mem:* AAAS; Am Meteorol Soc; Am Geophys Union; foreign mem Royal Meteorol Soc; Meteorol Soc Japan; Philippine Am Acad Sci & Eng. *Res:* Hurricane dynamics and structures; tropical meteorology;

atmospheric diffusion; turbulence; micrometeorology; ocean waves; air-sea interactions; marine environmental predictions; oil spill trajectory forecasts; environmental monitoring and management; satellite oceanography; coastal processes. *Mailing Add:* 16609 Cutlass Drive Rockville MD 20853. *E-Mail:* cbarrientos@nesdis.noaa.gov

BARRIER, J WAYNE, RENEWABLE FUELS, BIOMASS CONVERSION. *Current Pos:* Chem engr, Tenn Valley Authority, 76-82, proj mgr biomass prog, 82-86, mgr biomass res & develop, 86-90, MGR BIOCONVERSIONS RES & DEVELOP, TENN VALLEY AUTHORITY, 90- *Personal Data:* b Savannah, Tenn, June 17, 49; m, Janet Putram; c James, Jennifer, Joseph & Jeremy. *Educ:* Univ Tenn, Knoxville, BS, 72, MS, 75. *Prof Exp:* Chem engr, Monsanto, 72-76. *Concurrent Pos:* Instr sci & mgt, Faulkner Univ, 80- *Res:* Manager of national program to develop and introduce technologies for production of liquid fuels and chemicals from renewable materials; author of over 100 articles and reports on renewable fuels from biomass. *Mailing Add:* 3000 County Rd 10 Florence AL 35633

BARRIGA, OMAR OSCAR, PARASITOLOGY, IMMUNOBIOLOGY. *Current Pos:* assoc prof, 80-95, MEM GRAD FAC, DEPT VET PREV MED, OHIO STATE UNIV, 80-, PROF, 95- *Personal Data:* b Santiago, Chile, Mar 1, 38; m 60, Ines Guirland; c Omar A & Alvaro G. *Educ:* Univ Chile, BA, 58, DVM, 63; Univ Ill, PhD(parasitol-immunol), 72. *Prof Exp:* Small animal vet, 63; asst prof parasitol, Sch Med, Univ Chile, 64-71, prof immunol, Grad Sch Med & assoc prof parasitol, Schs Med & Pub Health, 72; asst prof parasitol, Sch Vet Med, Univ Pa, 73-80. *Concurrent Pos:* Ed, J Chilean Soc Vet Med, 66-67; int consult immunoparasitol, Grad Sch, Porto Alegre, Brazil, 77-78; vis prof immunoparasitol, Mex, 82 & Dominican Repub, 84, Costa Rica, 88, Morocco, 89, Brazil, 90; Fulbright scholar, 91; chair, Dept Parasitol, Med Sch, Univ Chile, 96- *Mem:* Am Asn Vet Parasitologists; Am Asn Vet Immunologists; Am Asn Parasitologists; Am Soc Trop Med & Hyg. *Res:* Immunity to parasitic infections; modifications of the immune response by parasitic infections; immunodiagnosis and vaccination of parasitic infections; immunological control of arthropod infestations. *Mailing Add:* Dept Vet Prev Med Ohio State Univ 1900 Coffey Rd Columbus OH 43210. *Fax:* 614-292-4142; *E-Mail:* barriga.2@osu.edu

BARRIGA, RAMIRO PATRICIO, DEVICE & COMPONENT TESTING, CARDIOVASCULAR BIOPROSTHESIS & TRANSDUCERS DESIGN & TESTING. *Current Pos:* RES ENGR, SULZER CARBOMEDICS INC, 90- *Personal Data:* b Quito, Ecuador, Oct 30, 60. *Educ:* Politechnie ESPE, Ecuador, BS, 86; Univ Tex, Austin, MS, 96. *Prof Exp:* Res prof, Politechnie ESPE, 86-89. *Mem:* Soc Exp Mech; Am Ceramic Soc. *Res:* Design of thermal transducers to measure biological properties. *Mailing Add:* 1300 E Anderson Lane Austin TX 78752. *E-Mail:* tamiro.barriga@mail.utexas.edu

BARRINGER, DONALD F, JR, METABOLISM, ISOTOPICALLY LABELED COMPOUNDS. *Current Pos:* res chemist, 60-76, SR RES CHEMIST, AM CYANAMID CO, 76- *Personal Data:* b Cleveland, Ohio, June 3, 32; m 58, Ruth E Dempsey; c 4. *Educ:* Denison Univ, BS, 54; Ohio State Univ, PhD(org chem), 60. *Prof Exp:* Res chemist, E I duPont de Nemours & Co, 59-60. *Mem:* Am Chem Soc; Int Isotope Soc. *Res:* Metabolism of pesticides and veterinary drugs in plants, animals and the environment; synthesis and characterization of isotopically labeled compounds. *Mailing Add:* 7 Stonicker Dr Lawrenceville NJ 08648-3246. *E-Mail:* barringerd@pt.cyanamid.com

BARRINGER, WILLIAM CHARLES, INFORMATION SCIENCE & SYSTEMS. *Current Pos:* Develop chemist, 57-75, group leader preformulation chem, 75-78, SR RES CHEMIST, LEDERLE LAB DIV, AM CYANAMID CO, 78- *Personal Data:* b Cleveland, Ohio, Feb 28, 34; m 55, Evelyn Dodge; c Laura, Donna, Mary & Judy. *Educ:* Denison Univ, BS, 56; NY Univ, MS, 64, PhD(photochem), 68. *Concurrent Pos:* Prof chem, The King's Col, 69-71. *Mem:* Am Chem Soc; Am Asn Pharmaceut Scientists; NY Acad Sci. *Res:* The relationship between the physical and chemical properties of chemical compounds and their performance in pharmaceutical formulations; stability evaluation of potential market products. *Mailing Add:* Am Cyanamid Co Lederle Lab N Middletown Rd Pearl River NY 10965. *Fax:* 914-732-5692

BARRINGTON, A(LFRED) E(RIC), ELECTRONICS, APPLIED PHYSICS. *Current Pos:* CHIEF, SAFETY & ENVIRON TECHNOL DIV, RES & SPECIAL PROGS ADMIN, JOHN A VOLPE TRANSP SYSTS CTR, DEPT TRANSP, 70- *Personal Data:* b Vienna, Austria, Mar 22, 21; wid; c 1. *Educ:* London Univ, BSc, 47, PhD(elec eng), 50. *Prof Exp:* Design engr vacuum tubes, Machlett Labs, Conn, 50-52; sr sci officer microwave tubes, serv electronics res lab, Brit Admiralty, 52-54; Harwell res fel & lectr elec eng, Queen Mary Col, London, 55-57; lectr appl physics, Harvard & res fel physics, Cambridge Electron Accelerator, 57-60; dept mgr vacuum physics, Varian Assoc, Calif, 60-62; mgr ion physics dept, Geophys Corp Am, 62-66; head astrophys br, instrumentation lab, electronics res ctr, NASA, 66-68; div chief, 68-70. *Mem:* Inst Elec & Electronics Engrs; Am Vacuum Soc. *Res:* Microwave tubes; exploding wires; electron accelerators; ion pumps; mass spectrometers; ultra-high vacuum; analytical instruments. *Mailing Add:* John A Volpe Nat Transp Syst Ctr Kendall Sq Cambridge MA 02142

BARRINGTON, DAVID STANLEY, BOTANY. *Current Pos:* asst prof, 77-83, CUR PRINGLE HERBARIUM, UNIV VT, 74-, ASSOC PROF BOT, 83- *Personal Data:* b Boston, Mass, Sept 4, 48. *Educ:* Bates Col, BS, 70; Harvard Univ, PhD(biol), 75. *Mem:* Bot Soc Am; Am Soc Plant Taxonomists; Am Fern Soc; Soc Study Evolution; AAAS. *Res:* Systematics and evolution of tropical American ferns; anatomy of the fossil tree fern stems of the Cyatheaceae and Dicksoniaceae. *Mailing Add:* Dept Bot Univ Vt Marsh Life Sci Burlington VT 05405-0001

BARRINGTON, GORDON P, AGRICULTURAL ENGINEERING. *Current Pos:* From assoc prof to prof agr eng, 52-77, prof agr & life sci, 77-88, EMER PROF AGR & LIFE SCI, UNIV WIS-MADISON, 88- *Personal Data:* b Dayton, Wis, Apr 14, 23; m 48; c 1. *Educ:* Univ Wis, BS, 49, MS, 51. *Mem:* Am Soc Agr Engrs. *Res:* Forage seeding and harvesting machinery, forage preservation; separation of protein from plant materials. *Mailing Add:* 26 Shadow Woods Lane Waupaca WI 54981

BARRINGTON, RONALD ERIC, physics, for more information see previous edition

BARRIOS, EARL P, HORTICULTURE. *Current Pos:* from instr to assoc prof, 58-77, PROF HORT, LA STATE UNIV, BATON ROUGE, 77- *Personal Data:* b New Orleans, La, Dec 14, 17; m 46. *Educ:* La State Univ, PhD(bot, hort), 60. *Prof Exp:* Chief, Nebr Potato Develop Div, State Dept Agr & Univ Nebr, 48-54; sales mgr agr chem, P V Fertilizer Co, 54-57. *Mem:* Am Soc Hort Sci. *Res:* Breeding and genetics of horticultural crops, especially vegetables. *Mailing Add:* 1420 Aster Baton Rouge LA 70802

BARROIS, BERTRAND C, DEFENSE. *Current Pos:* RES STAFF, INST DEFENSE ANALYSIS, 78- *Personal Data:* b Princeton, NJ, Nov 10, 52. *Educ:* Mass Inst Technol, BS, 73; Caltech, PhD(physics), 79. *Mem:* Am Phys Soc. *Res:* Electronic warfare. *Mailing Add:* Inst Defense Analysis SED 1801 N Beauregard St Alexandria VA 22311. *E-Mail:* bbarrois@ida.org

BARRON, ALMEN LEO, medical microbiology, chlamydia, for more information see previous edition

BARRON, BRUCE ALBRECHT, OBSTETRICS & GYNECOLOGY. *Current Pos:* PROF OBSTET & GYNEC, SCH MED, NY UNIV, 97-, ATTEND PHYSICIAN, MED CTR, 97- *Personal Data:* b New York, NY, Nov 3, 34; m 75, Mary Cahill; c 1. *Educ:* Allegheny Col, AB, 55; Yale Univ, MPH, 60, PhD(biomet), 65; NY Univ, MD, 71. *Prof Exp:* Res asst, Dept Surg, Bellevue Med Ctr, NY Univ, 56-57; biochemist, Walter Reed Army Inst Res, 57-59; res assoc biomet, Rockefeller Univ, 65-67, asst prof, 67-74; intern, Dept Med, Bellevue Med Ctr, 71-72, asst res obstet & gynec, 72-73, chief res, 73-74; assoc prof obstet & gynec, Col Physicians & Surgeons, Columbia Univ, 74-96. *Concurrent Pos:* Consult, Biomed Div, Population Coun, 65-71; sr attend physician, Sloan Hosp Women, Presby Med Ctr, 74-96; chmn & bd dir, New York City Health & Hosp Corp, 80- *Mem:* AAAS; Biomet Soc; Am Statist Asn; Harvey Soc; Sigma Xi. *Res:* Mathematical models in carcinogenesis. *Mailing Add:* NY Univ Med Ctr 550 First Ave New York NY 10019

BARRON, CHARLES, CHEMICAL ENGINEERING, POLYMER REACTORS. *Current Pos:* prof eng & head dept, 87-94, PROF CHEM ENG, CLEMSON UNIV, 87- *Personal Data:* b Seneca, SC, Apr 18, 37. *Educ:* Clemson Univ, BS, 50; Univ Va, DSc, 63. *Prof Exp:* Prin consult chem reactor eng, DuPont, 74-87. *Mem:* Am Inst Chem Engrs; Am Chem Soc; Am Soc Eng Educ. *Mailing Add:* Dept Chem Eng Clemson Univ 125 Earle Hall Clemson SC 29634

BARRON, CHARLES IRWIN, aerospace medicine; deceased, see previous edition for last biography

BARRON, EDWARD J, clinical biochemistry; deceased, see previous edition for last biography

BARRON, EMMANUEL NICHOLAS, OPTIMAL CONTROL THEORY, HAMILTON-JACOBI EQUATIONS. *Current Pos:* PROF MATH, LOYOLA UNIV, CHICAGO, 80- *Personal Data:* b Lodi, Calif, Oct 14, 49. *Educ:* Univ Ill Chicago, BS, 70; Northwestern Univ, MS, 72 & PhD(math), 74. *Prof Exp:* Asst prof math, Ga Inst Technol, 74-80. *Concurrent Pos:* Mem tech staff, AT&T Bell Labs, 78-80. *Mem:* Soc Indust & Appl Math. *Res:* Optimal control theory and non-linear partial differential equations; stochastic processes and its applications to financial economics. *Mailing Add:* Dept Math Sci Loyola Univ Lakeshore Campus 6525 N Sheridan Rd Chicago IL 60626-5311

BARRON, ERIC JAMES, PALEOCLIMATOLOGY, PALEOCEANOGRAPHY. *Current Pos:* DIR EARTH SYST SCI CTR & ASSOC PROF GEOSCI, PA STATE UNIV, 86- *Personal Data:* b Lafayette, Ind, Oct 26, 51; m 82; c 2. *Educ:* Fla State Univ, BS, 73; Univ Miami, MS, 76, PhD(geophys), 80. *Prof Exp:* Fel, Nat Ctr Atmospheric Res, 80-81, scientist, 81-85; assoc prof marine geol & geophys, Univ Miami, 85-86. *Concurrent Pos:* Co-ed-chief, Paleogeog, Paleoclimat & Palaecol Geol, Geol Soc Am, 85-; chmn, Int Geol Correl Prog, 82-87, Climate Variations Comt, Am Meteorol Soc, 88-, Paleoceanog Comt, Am Geophys Union, 87-88. *Mem:* Am Geophys Union; Geol Soc Am; Soc Econ Paleontologists & Mineralogists; Am Meterol Soc; Am Asn Petrol Geologists; Asn Am Geographers. *Res:* Global change, specifically numerical models of the climate system and the study of climate change throughout Earth history. *Mailing Add:* Geosci Dept Penn State Univ University Park PA 16802-1009

BARRON, EUGENE ROY, SYNTHETIC FIBERS, TIRES. *Current Pos:* from res chemist to sr res chemist, 67-78, from res assoc to sr res assoc, 78-93, PRES FEL, E I DUPONT DE NEMOURS & CO, INC, 93- *Personal Data:* b Somerset, Pa, Sept 10, 41; m 63, Kay A Shunk; c Christine A (Arenson) & Kenneth E. *Educ:* Univ Md, BS, 63, PhD(chem), 67. *Res:* Nylon, Kevlar aramid and Dacron polyester for industrial applications such as tires, mechanical rubber goods, industrial fabrics, ropes and sewing thread; industrial applications research including tire cord adhesives and treating technology. *Mailing Add:* 9208 Tamara Lane Chattanooga TN 37421. *Fax:* 423-875-7551

BARRON, JOHN ARTHUR, GEOLOGY, PALEONTOLOGY. *Current Pos:* GEOLOGIST, US GEOL SURV, 74- *Personal Data:* b Omaha, Nebr, Oct 22, 47. *Educ:* Univ Calif, Los Angeles, BS, 69, PhD(geol), 74. *Honors & Awards:* Schuchert Award Paleont, 86. *Concurrent Pos:* Comt mem, Int Geol Correlations Prog, UNESCO, 76-; Int Symposium Living & Fossil Diatoms, 76, 80, 82, 84, 86, 88, 90. *Mem:* Geol Soc Am; Soc Econ Petrol Mineralogists; Am Geophys Union. *Res:* Marine diatom and silicoflagellate biostratigraphy and paleoecology of the Cenozoic. *Mailing Add:* US Geol Surv P&S Br MS 910 345 Middlefield Rd Menlo Park CA 94025

BARRON, JOHN ROBERT, entomology, taxonomy, for more information see previous edition

BARRON, KEVIN D, NEUROLOGY & NEUROPATHOLOGY. *Current Pos:* chmn, Dept Neurol, 69-93, PROF NEUROL & PROF PATH, ALBANY MED COL, 69- *Personal Data:* b St John's, Nfld, Apr 21, 29; US citizen; m 56, Elizabeth Grossman; c Kevin & Sheila. *Educ:* Dalhousie Univ, MD & CM, 52. *Honors & Awards:* Sr US Scientist Award, (Humboldt Award), 77. *Prof Exp:* Resident internal med, Victoria Gen Hosp, Halifax, Nova Scotia & Queen Mary Vet Hosp; neurol resident & neuropath fel, Montefiore Med Ctr, 54-59; instr neurol, Col Physicians & Surgeons, Columbia Univ, 57-59; assoc neurol & psychiat, Med Sch, Northwestern Univ, 59-61, from asst prof to prof, 61-69. *Concurrent Pos:* USPHS fel neuropath, Montefiore Hosp, NY, 56-59; USPHS grants, 60-; Nat Multiple Sclerosis Soc grant, 61-63, 79-81; hon Fulbright fel, 76. *Mem:* Am Neurol Asn; Can Asn Neuropath; fel Am Acad Neurol; Am Asn Neuropath. *Res:* Histochemistry and cytology; electron microscopy of the nervous system; neuroenzymology, particularly hydrolytic enzymes; neuropathology. *Mailing Add:* Dept Neurol Albany Med Col Albany NY 12208. *Fax:* 518-262-5041

BARRON, MACE GERALD, AQUATIC TOXICOLOGY. *Current Pos:* MGR & DIR AQUATIC TOXICOL, ENVIRON SCI ENG, 90- *Personal Data:* b Memphis, Tenn, Aug 19, 58. *Educ:* Ore State Univ, BS, 80; Univ Minn, MS, 82; Wash State Univ, PhD(pharmacol), 86. *Prof Exp:* Assoc drug metabolism in aquatic animals, Univ Fla, 86-87; indust assoc, Dow Chem Co, 87-88, proj leader global res & develop prog on bioaccumulation, 88-90. *Concurrent Pos:* Fac mem, Envirovet, 91-; adj prof med chem, Univ Fla, 92- *Mem:* Soc Environ Toxicol & Chem; Soc toxicol. *Res:* Determinants of chemical accumulation, metabolism and pharmacokinetics in aquatic animals. *Mailing Add:* PO Box 1661 Longmont CO 80502. *Fax:* 352-333-6622

BARRON, RANDALL F(RANKLIN), MECHANICAL ENGINEERING, CRYOGENICS & HEAT TRANSFER. *Current Pos:* assoc prof mech eng, 65-70, dir div eng res, Col eng, 76-80, dir eng res & grad studies, 80-89, PROF MECH ENG, LA TECH UNIV, 70- *Personal Data:* b Many, La, May 16, 36; m 58, Shirley McDuffie; c Randall F Jr, Donna (Ellard), Steven D & Brian R. *Educ:* La Polytech Inst, BSME, 58; Ohio State Univ, MSc, 61, PhD(mech eng), 64. *Honors & Awards:* Res Award, Sigma Xi, 71. *Prof Exp:* From instr to asst prof mech eng, Ohio State Univ, 58-65. *Concurrent Pos:* Consult, CryoVac, Inc, Ohio, 63-65; mem, Cryogenic Eng Conf Comt, 77-83; consult, Riley-Beaird, 66-86; mem, La Bd Regist Prof Engrs & Land Surv, 88-93. *Mem:* AAAS; Am Soc Mech Engrs; Am Soc Eng Educ; Cryog Soc Am. *Res:* Heat transfer; thermodynamics; design in cryogenic engineering systems; noise control. *Mailing Add:* Dept Mech Eng La Tech Univ 305 Wisteria St Ruston LA 71272-0001. *Fax:* 318-257-2562; *E-Mail:* rbarron@latech.edu

BARRON, RONALD MICHAEL, COMPUTATIONAL FLUID DYNAMICS, TRANSONIC AERODYNAMICS. *Current Pos:* Postdoctoral fel, 74-75, from asst prof to assoc prof, 75-84, PROF MATH, UNIV WINDSOR, 84- *Personal Data:* b Windsor, Ont, July 12, 48; m 69, Coral Mailloux; c 1. *Educ:* Univ Windsor, BA, 70, MS, 71; Carleton Univ, PhD(appl math), 74; Stanford Univ, MS, 82. *Concurrent Pos:* Vis scientist, Dept Aeronaut & Astronaut, Stanford Univ, 81; dept head, Dept Math & Statist, Univ Windsor, 86-89, dir, Fluid Dynamics Res Inst, 87-89 & 93-; vis prof, UGC-DSA Ctr Fluid Mech, Bangalore Univ, India, 89-90. *Mem:* Assoc mem Am Inst Aeronaut & Astronaut; Can Aeronaut & Space Inst; Am Acad Mech; Can Appl Math Soc. *Res:* Navier-Stokes; transonic full potential; Euler solvers; grid generation; automotive applications of CFD. *Mailing Add:* Dept Math & Statist Univ Windsor Windsor ON N9B 3P4 Can. *Fax:* 519-973-7050

BARRON, SAUL, THERMODYNAMICS, MATERIALS SCIENCES. *Current Pos:* RETIRED. *Personal Data:* b New York, NY, Feb 24, 17; m 41, Phyllis Levin; c Elaine, Martin & Dean. *Educ:* Lafayette Col, BS, 41; Ohio State Univ, MS, 48, PhD(chem eng), 54. *Prof Exp:* Architect & engr, Bur Ships, USN, Pa, 41-43; mech engr, US Govt, Wright-Patterson AFB, 46-51; design engr, Martin-Marietta Corp, Md, 54-56; sr scientist, Avco Mfg Corp, Mass, 56-57; dir res, Thiokol Chem Corp, Pa, 58-59 & Bell Aerosysts Co, NY, 60-64; prof chem, State Univ NY, Buffalo, 64-85. *Concurrent Pos:* Consult, Marine Trust Co, NY, 64- & Conax Corp, 65-; vis prof, Inst Chem, Hebrew Univ, Israel, 82; consult, 85- *Mem:* Am Chem Soc; NY Acad Sci; Sigma Xi; fel Am Inst Chemists. *Res:* Oxide ceramics; volume and phase chemical equilibria, especially critical region, using multi-component mixtures; chemical thermodynamics; thermal effects upon polymers; materials sciences. *Mailing Add:* 2638 NW 104th Ave Apt 302 Sunrise FL 33322

BARROSO, MARGARIDA MARIA R, PROTEIN TRAFFICKING & ENDOCYTIC PATHWAY, POLARITY & EPITHELIA. *Current Pos:* RES ASSOC, DEPT MOLECULAR BIOL, PRINCETON UNIV, 91- *Personal Data:* b Lisbon, Port, Nov 9, 63. *Educ:* Univ Lisbon, Port, PhD(molecular biol), 91. *Mem:* Am Soc Cell Biol. *Res:* Mechanisms that regulate vesicle traffic between lateral and apical plasma membrane domain in polarized epithelia; observed a trimeric G-protein involvement in the regulation of the last step of the pathway; the fusion of vesicles with apical membrane. *Mailing Add:* Dept Biol Univ Va McCormick Rd Gilmer Hall Charlottesville VA 22903-2477. *E-Mail:* mbarroso@watson.princeton.edu

BARROW, EMILY MILDRED STACY, BIOCHEMISTRY. *Current Pos:* Grad asst bot, 50-52, res technician path, 53-56, res asst path, 56-59, asst physiol, 59-62, res assoc path, 62-69, from assoc prof to prof, 69-82, EMER PROF PATH, UNIV NC, CHAPEL HILL, 82- *Personal Data:* b Washington, DC, July 2, 27; div; c David, Randall & Michael. *Educ:* Meredith Col, AB, 50; Univ NC, Chapel Hill, AM, 52, PhD(physiol), 63. *Res:* Biochemical genetics of blood coagulation disorders. *Mailing Add:* 209 Barclay Rd Chapel Hill NC 27516

BARROW, GORDON M, physical chemistry, for more information see previous edition

BARROW, JAMES HOWELL, JR, PROTOZOOLOGY, PARASITOLOGY. *Current Pos:* chmn dept, 57-71, PROF BIOL, HIRAM COL, 57-, DIR BIOL STA, 70- *Personal Data:* b West Point, Ga, June 28, 20; m 50. *Educ:* Emory Univ, BA, 43; Yale Univ, PhD(zool), 51. *Prof Exp:* Instr, Emory Univ, 43-44; asst, Yale Univ, 44-47; lectr biol, Albertus Magnus Col, 47-48; prof biol & chmn dept, Huntingdon Col, 48-57. *Concurrent Pos:* Ford Found fel, Cambridge Univ, 53-54; vis prof protozool, biol sta, Univ Mich, 56-64. *Mem:* Wildlife Disease Asn; Soc Protozool; Am Micros Soc; AAAS; Sigma Xi. *Res:* Trypanosomes of poikilothermic vertebrates; haemosporidians of waterfowl and invertebrates; avian behavior and parasitism. *Mailing Add:* 1118 Immaculate Lane Cincinatti OH 45255

BARROW, ROBERT E, PHYSIOLOGY. *Current Pos:* ASSOC PROF TOXICOL, UNIV TEX MED BR, 74- *Personal Data:* b Chicago, Ill, Mar 4, 34. *Educ:* Wayne State Univ, BS, 61, MS, 63, PhD(human physiol), 67. *Mem:* Am Chem Soc; Sigma Xi; Am Heart Asn; AAAS; Am Physiol Soc; Am Chemists Soc. *Mailing Add:* 18060 S Term Rd Galveston TX 77554

BARROW, THOMAS D, PETROLEUM GEOLOGY, MINERAL EXPLORATION. *Current Pos:* SR CHMN, GEOQUEST INT, HOLDINGS, INC, 89-; PRES, THOMSON-BARROW CORP, 90-; PRES, TECOLOTTITA, INC, 90-, PRES, T-BAR-X LTD CO, 95- *Personal Data:* b San Antonio, Tex, Dec 27, 24; m 50, Janice Hood; c Theodore Hood, Barbara B (McCelvey), Kenneth Thomson & Elizabeth B (Brueggeman). *Educ:* Univ Tex, BS, 45, MA, 48; Stanford Univ, PhD(geol), 53. *Prof Exp:* Jr geologist, Humble Oil & Refining Co, Calif, 51-55, area explor geologist, 55-58, div explor geologist, La, 59-61, regional explor mgr, 62-64, exec vpres & dir, Esso Explor, Inc, NY, 64-65, dir, Humble Oil & Ref Co, Houston, 65-72, pres, 70-72; sr vpres & dir, Exxon Corp, 72-78; chmn & chief exec officer, Kennecott Copper Corp, 78-81; vchmn, Stand Oil Co, Ohio, 81-85. *Concurrent Pos:* Mem, Oceanog Adv Comt, 68; mem, Sea Grant Adv Panel, 69; comn natural resources, Nat Res Coun, 73-78, Bd Earth Sci, 82-84, comn phys sci, math & nat resource, 84-87; Task Force US Energy Policy, 74; chmn, PI/Dwights, 77-, GX Technol Corp, 90-; investment consult, Houston, 85-, mem, Comt Eng Int Enterprise, Nat Acad Eng, 90-91. *Mem:* Nat Acad Eng; Am Geophys Union; Am Geog Soc; Am Asn Petrol Geologists; Am Inst Mining, Metall & Petrol Engrs; Geol Soc Am; AAAS; fel NY Acad Sci; Sigma Xi. *Res:* Petroleum exploration. *Mailing Add:* 911 Briar Ridge Dr Houston TX 77057

BARROWS, AUSTIN WILLARD, APPLIED PHYSICS. *Current Pos:* BR CHIEF APPL PHYSICS ADMIN, COMBUSTION & PROPULSION BR, BALLISTIC RES LABS, 71- *Personal Data:* b Addison, Vt, July 3, 37; m 60; c 4. *Educ:* Univ Vt, BA, 60, MS, 61; Univ Ky, PhD(physics), 65. *Prof Exp:* Res assoc nuclear physics, Univ Ky, 65; res physicist, US Army Nuclear Defense Lab, 66-67, br chief, 67-70; asst to dir admin, US Army Ballistic Res Lab, 70-71. *Mem:* Am Phys Soc; AAAS; Combustion Inst; Am Defense Preparedness Asn; Sigma Xi. *Res:* The phenomena of combustion of propellants and interior ballistics of guns and rockets. *Mailing Add:* 3103 Whitefield Rd Churchville MD 21028-1304

BARROWS, EDWARD MYRON, BEHAVIORAL ECOLOGY, ENTOMOLOGY. *Current Pos:* Asst prof, 75-81, ASSOC PROF BIOL, GEORGETOWN UNIV, 81- *Personal Data:* b Detroit, Mich, Aug 8, 46; m 79; c 2. *Educ:* Univ Mich, BS, 68; Univ Kans, PhD(entom), 75. *Mem:* AAAS; Entom Soc Am; Animal Behavior Soc; Ecol Soc Am; Soc Study Evol; Orgn Trop Studies. *Res:* Reproductive strategies in insects; behavior ecology and evolution of insects in urban ecosystems. *Mailing Add:* 6677 MacArthur Blvd Bethesda MD 20816-2247

BARROWS, JOHN FREDERICK, AERODYNAMICS, MANUFACTURING. *Current Pos:* PROF & DIR, MFG ENG PROG, SYRACUSE UNIV, 85- *Personal Data:* b Detroit, Mich, Dec 26, 28; m 51; c 3. *Educ:* Univ Mich, BSME, 51, MSE, 59, PhD(mech eng), 62. *Prof Exp:* Proj engr, Allison Div, Gen Motors Corp, 51-58; lectr fluid mech & thermodyn, Univ Mich Dearborn Ctr, 60-62; asst prof mech eng, Cornell Univ, 62-67; sr engr, Res Div, Carrier Corp, 67-70, chief engr, 70-78, asst dir, Res Labs, 78-85. *Mem:* Am Soc Mech Engrs; Soc Mfg Engrs; Am Soc Eng Educ. *Res:* Aerodynamics; applied thermodynamics; fluid mechanics; design for manufacturing. *Mailing Add:* Col Eng Syracuse Univ Syracuse NY 13244

BARRUETO, RICHARD BENIGNO, BIOCHEMISTRY, ORGANIC CHEMISTRY. *Current Pos:* PRES, CARL F MILLER & CO, INC, 75- *Personal Data:* b Guatemala City, Guatemala, Feb 16, 28; US citizen; m 54; c 3. *Educ:* Norm Sch, Guatemala, AB, 46; Eastern Nazarene Col, BS, 52; Boston Univ, MA, 54. *Prof Exp:* Res chemist, Sch Med, Boston Univ, 52-54; asst biochemist, US Qm Res & Eng Command, US Army, Mass, 54-60, res biochemist, Army Inst Environ Med, 60-62; bioscientist, Biotech Sect, Aerospace Div, Boeing Co, 62-65, sr bioscientist, 65-75. *Mem:* Am Sci Affil; Am Inst Chemists; Sigma Xi. *Res:* Life support and protection problems associated with man in a space vehicle; high altitude chamber; space-suit-vehicle integration; closed environment toxicological problems; optimizing man-machine interface in missile systems from psycho-physiological viewpoint. *Mailing Add:* 5155 NE Laurelcrest Lane Seattle WA 98105-5247

BARRY, ARTHUR JOHN, ORGANIC CHEMISTRY, PHYSICAL CHEMISTRY. *Current Pos:* RETIRED. *Personal Data:* b Buffalo, NY, Mar 11, 09; m 36; c 3. *Educ:* State Univ NY Col Forestry, BS, 32, PhD(org chem), 36. *Prof Exp:* Actg prof org chem & carbohydrate chem, State Univ NY Col Forestry, 36-37; res chemist, Dow Chem Co, 37-47; res group supvr, 47-50, assoc dir res, 50-65; dir chem res, Dow Corning Corp, 65-70, res consult, 70-74. *Concurrent Pos:* Vis scholar dept chem, Univ Ariz, 74-83, adj prof, 83- *Mem:* AAAS; Am Chem Soc. *Res:* Preparation of cellulose derivatives; plastics; reactions in liquid ammonia, metallo-organic chemistry; synthesis of organosilicon compounds; investigation of polysiloxane resins, fluids and elastomers. *Mailing Add:* 9102 N Riviera Dr Tucson AZ 85737

BARRY, ARTHUR LELAND, MICROBIOLOGY, BACTERIOLOGY. *Current Pos:* PRES & DIR CLIN MICROBIOL INST & CLIN PROF MICROBIOL, ORE HEALTH SCI UNIV, 82- *Personal Data:* b Spokane, Wash, Aug 2, 32; m 55, Diane Hollingsworth; c Karen, Kathleen, William & Brian. *Educ:* Gonzaga Univ, BS, 55; St Lukes Sch Med Technol, MT, 55; Wash State Univ, MS, 57; Ohio State Univ, PhD(microbiol), 62. *Prof Exp:* Chief microbiologist, Clin Lab Med Group, Los Angeles, 64-66; med microbiologist, Los Angeles Co Gen Hosp, 66-68; asst clin prof microbiol, Sch Med, Univ Calif, Davis, 67-68, prof clin microbiol, 68-82. *Concurrent Pos:* NIH trainee clin microbiol, Univ Wash Hosp, 62-64; sr ed, Am J Med Technol, 68-74; dir, Microbiol Labs, Sacremento Med Ctr, 68-82, Clin Microbiol Inst, 82- *Mem:* Am Soc Med Technol; Am Soc Microbiol; Infectious Dis Soc Am. *Res:* Methods for rapid identification of bacterial pathogens; antimicrobic susceptibility tests; quality control in microbiology. *Mailing Add:* Clin Microbiol Inst PO Box 947 Tualatin OR 97062. *Fax:* 503-692-6189

BARRY, B(ENJAMIN) AUSTIN, CIVIL ENGINEERING. *Current Pos:* From instr to assoc prof, 43-70, head dept, 62-71, prof civil eng, 70-88, EMER PROF CIVIL ENG, MANHATTAN COL, 88- *Personal Data:* b Newburgh, NY, July 23, 17. *Educ:* Cath Univ, AB, 37; Rensselaer Polytech Inst, BCE, 42; NY Univ, MCE, 49. *Honors & Awards:* Surv & Mapping Award, Am Soc Civil Engrs, 70; Hon Mem, Am Soc Civil Engrs, 87; WS Dix Award, Am Cong Surv & Mapping. *Concurrent Pos:* Consult to obtain secure water supply, Rongai Village, USAID, 77. *Mem:* Am Soc Civil Engrs; hon mem Am Cong Surv & Mapping (pres, 61-62); Am Soc Eng Educ (vpres, 69-71). *Res:* Surveying and mapping; photogrammetry; transportation engineering. *Mailing Add:* Dept Civil Eng Manhattan Col Parkway Bronx NY 10471-4098

BARRY, DANA MARIE, SCIENCE COMMUNICATIONS. *Current Pos:* TECH WRITER, ED & ADMINR, CLARKSON UNIV, 93- *Personal Data:* b Utica, NY, May 26, 49; m 71, James F; c James D, Brian P, Daniel T & Eric M. *Educ:* State Univ NY, Potsdam, BA, 71, MS, 72; Clarkson Univ, MS, 74, PhD(educ), 85. *Prof Exp:* Chem consult, Corning Glass Works, 85-86; fac mem sci educ, State Univ NY, Potsdam, 87-89; chem teacher, Lisbon Cent Sch, 91-92. *Concurrent Pos:* Ed consult, Abstracting J, 86-; prin investr, Am Chem Soc, 95-96; co-producer & host, Sensational Sci, 96- *Mem:* Am Chem Soc; Am Inst Chemists; Nat Sci Teachers Asn. *Res:* Author of numerous featured articles in national and international journals, science books for children, encyclopedia entries, television scripts and lyrics to science songs. *Mailing Add:* 46 Farmer St Canton NY 13617. *Fax:* 315-268-7615; *E-Mail:* dmbarry@agent.clarkson.edu

BARRY, DAVID WALTER, INFECTIOUS DISEASES. *Current Pos:* CHIEF EXEC OFF & CHMN, TRIANGLE PHARMACEUT, 95- *Personal Data:* b Nashua, NH, July 19, 43; m, Gracia Chen; c Christopher & Jennifer. *Educ:* Yale Col, BA, 65; Yale Univ, MD, 69. *Prof Exp:* From intern to resident, Yale-New Haven Hosp, 62-72, staff assoc, dir & actg dep dir, Div Virol, Bur Biologics, Fed Drug Admin, 72-77; head, Anti-infectives Sect, Wellcome Clin Invest, Med Div, Burroughs Wellcome Co, 77-85, head, Dept Virol, Wellcome Res Labs, 83-89, dir, Div Clin Invest, 85-86, vpres res, 86-89, vpres res develop & med affairs, 89-95. *Concurrent Pos:* Sr surgeon, USPHS, 72-77; vis fel, Univ Md, 75-76; dir, Influenza Vaccine Task Force, Bur Biologics, Fed Drug Admin, 76-77; adj prof, Sch Med, Duke Univ, 77-; mem, Comt Pub-Pvt Sectors Rel Vaccine Innovation, Inst Med NAS, 83, Acquired Immune Deficiency Syndrome Task Force, NIH, 86, roundtable drugs & vaccines against Acquired Immune Deficiency Syndrome, 89 & Indust Liaison Panel, 92; dean coun, Yale Sch Med, 89-; bd dirs, Burroughs Wellcome Fund, Wellcome Found, Family Health Int. *Mem:* Fel Am Col Physicians; Infectious Dis Soc Am; Royal Soc Med; AAAS; AMA; Am Soc Virol; Am Soc Microbiol; Am Fedn Clin Res; Pharm Mfrs Asn. *Res:* Acquired Immune Deficiency Syndrome; virology; infectious diseases; 12 patents for treatment of viral infections. *Mailing Add:* Triangle Pharmaceut 4 University Pl 4611 University Dr Durham NC 27707

BARRY, DON CARY, astronomy, for more information see previous edition

BARRY, EDWARD GAIL, GENETICS. *Current Pos:* from asst prof to assoc prof, 62-75, PROF BOT, UNIV NC, CHAPEL HILL, 75- *Personal Data:* b Butte, Mont, May 4, 33; m 58, 84; c 3. *Educ:* Dartmouth Col, AB, 55; Stanford Univ, PhD(biol), 61. *Prof Exp:* USPHS trainee genetics, Yale Univ, 60-62. *Mem:* Genetics Soc Am; Genetical Soc Gt Brit. *Res:* Microbial genetics; cytogenetics of Neurospora. *Mailing Add:* Dept Biol Univ NC Chapel Hill Chapel Hill NC 27599-3280

BARRY, HENRY F, CHEMICAL ENGINEERING, PHYSICAL CHEMISTRY. *Current Pos:* VPRES, SHATTUCK CHEM CO, 83- *Personal Data:* b Detroit, Mich, June 25, 23; m 47; c 6. *Educ:* Stanford Univ, BS, 50; Univ Mich, MS, 52, MBA, 78. *Prof Exp:* Sr engr, Standard Oil Co, Ind, 52-60; dir spec chem, Haviland Prod Co, 60-62; res assoc chem, Climax Molybdenum Co, 62-65, supvr chem res, 65-67, dir chem res, 67-75, dir chem develop, 75-82. *Mem:* Am Chem Soc; Am Soc Lubrication Engrs; Nat Soc Prof Engrs; Am Inst Chem Engrs; Soc Plastics Engrs. *Res:* Solid lubricants; catalysts; petroleum processing; engineering research; molybdenum chemistry; environmental sciences. *Mailing Add:* 5337 W Iliff Dr No 101 Lakewood CO 80227-3991

BARRY, HERBERT, III, PSYCHOPHARMACOLOGY. *Current Pos:* res assoc prof pharmacol, 63-70, PROF ANTHROP, SCH PHARM, UNIV PITTSBURGH, 70-, PROF PHARMACEUT SCI, 95- *Personal Data:* b New York, NY, June 2, 30. *Educ:* Harvard Col, BA, 52; Yale Univ, MS, 53, PhD(psychol), 57. *Honors & Awards:* Distinguished Scientist Award, Soc Stimulus Properties & Drugs, 86. *Prof Exp:* From instr to asst prof psychol, Yale Univ, 58-61; asst prof, Univ Conn, 61-63. *Concurrent Pos:* NIMH fel, Yale Univ, 57-59; res sci develop award, NIMH, 67-77; consult, Nat Inst Alcohol Abuse & Alcoholism, 72-76; managing ed, Psychopharmacol, 74-84, field ed, 85-92. *Mem:* Am Psychol Asn; Am Anthrop Asn; Soc Cross-Cult Res (pres, 73-74); Am Soc Pharmacol & Exp Therapeut; Soc Stimulus Properties Drugs (pres, 80-81); Am Col Neurophsychopharmacol. *Res:* Psychopharmacology, testing effects of drugs, especially alcohol and other sedatives; cross-cultural research, correlating child training practices with other customs; relationships of birth order and sharing parent's first name to personality characteristics. *Mailing Add:* Sch Pharm Univ Pittsburgh Pittsburgh PA 15261-1954. *Fax:* 412-648-2116; *E-Mail:* barryh@vms.cis.pitt.edu

BARRY, JAMES DALE, SPACE PHYSICS, LASERS. *Current Pos:* sr scientist, Space Commun, Hughes Aircraft Co, 78-81, sr scientist, Electro-Optical Div, 81-86, prog mgr, electro-optical/Computer Data Processing, 86-91, PROG MGR, ELECTRO-OPTICAL SYSTS, HUGHES AIRCRAFT CO, 91- *Personal Data:* b Washington, DC, Feb 8, 42; m 64, Karen Ingram; c Diane & David. *Educ:* Univ Calif, Los Angeles, BS, 64, PhD(space physics), 69; Calif State Col, Los Angeles, MS, 66. *Prof Exp:* Asst high energy physics, Univ Calif, Los Angeles, 64-65, res asst space physics, 65-68, res geophysicist, 68-69; laser scientist, Air Force Atomics Lab, 69-73, tech dir, Space Laser Commun, 73-75, sr scientist, Tech Div, Air Force Space & Missiles Orgn, 75-76, sr scientist, Space Laser Commun, Air Force Space & Missiles Systs Orgn, 76-78. *Mem:* Am Geophys Union; Inst Elec & Electronics Engrs; Sigma Xi. *Res:* Interplanetary particles and fields; ionosphere; magnetosphere; wave-particle interactions; stimulated emission; gaseous lasers; space laser communications; laser design and theory, medical applications of lasers; author of over seventy-five technical articles. *Mailing Add:* Hughes Aircraft Co EDSG/E51/A290 PO Box 902 El Segundo CA 90245. *Fax:* 310-616-4130

BARRY, JOAN, cardiovascular research, for more information see previous edition

BARRY, KEVIN GERARD, INTERNAL MEDICINE. *Current Pos:* PRES & CLIN DIR, BIO-MED INC, 76- *Personal Data:* b Newton, Mass, May 12, 23; m 42; c 4. *Educ:* Georgetown Univ, MD, 49; Am Bd Internal Med, dipl, 56. *Prof Exp:* Intern, Walter Reed Gen Hosp, Washington, DC, US Army, 49-50, mem staff internal med, Soldiers Home Hosp, 50-51 & 98th Gen Hosp, Munich, Ger, 51-52, resident internal med, Walter Reed Gen Hosp, 53-56, batallion surgeon, 43rd Combat Engrs, 52-53, chief med serv, Army Hosp, NY, 56-58; instr med, Sch Med, Georgetown Univ, 58-63, clin asst prof, 63-69, assoc prof, 69-76. *Concurrent Pos:* Res internist, Walter Reed Army Inst Res, 58-61, chief dept metab, Inst & chief med sect, Hosp, 61-65, dir div med, Inst, 65-66; dir med educ & chief, Renal & Metab Sect, Wash Hosp Ctr, 66-69; chief, DC Gen Hosp, Med Div, Georgetown Univ, 69-71; med dir, Morris Cafritz Mem Hosp, 71-74. *Mem:* Fel Am Col Physicians; fel Am Col Clin Pharmacol & Chemother; AMA; Am Fedn Clin Res; Am Soc Artificial Internal Organs. *Res:* Renal, water and electrolyte metabolism; prevention and therapy of acute renal failure in man and animals; pathogenesis of acute renal failure in animals; peritoneal membranes used as absorptive surfaces. *Mailing Add:* 1295 Lavall Dr Davidsonville MD 21035-1135

BARRY, MICHAEL ANHALT, REGENERATION, COMPARATIVE NEUROBIOLOGY. *Current Pos:* asst prof, 88-97, ASSOC PROF NEUROSCI, SCH DENT MED, UNIV CONN HEALTH CTR, 97- *Personal Data:* b Atlanta, Ga, July 11, 53; m 77, Erika Friedmann; c Miriam & Samuel. *Educ:* Univ Pa, BA, 75; Univ Hawaii, MS, 78; Univ Del, PhD(life & health sci), 85. *Prof Exp:* Postdoctoral fel neurosci, Albert Einstein Col Med, 85-88. *Concurrent Pos:* Grass fel, 87. *Mem:* Am Soc Zoologists; Soc Neurosci; Asn Chemoreception Sci; AAAS; Int Behav Neurosci Soc. *Res:* Response and regeneration of taste system following nerve injury in mammals; comparative neurobiology of auditory, lateral line and gustatory systems; fish neurobiology; anatomy; electrophysiology; behavior. *Mailing Add:* Dept Biostruct & Function Univ Conn Health Ctr Farmington CT 06030. *Fax:* 860-679-2910; *E-Mail:* barry@neuron.uchc.edu

BARRY, MICHAEL LEE, electronics engineering, for more information see previous edition

BARRY, ROGER DONALD, ORGANIC CHEMISTRY, BIOCHEMISTRY. *Current Pos:* PROF CHEM & HEAD DEPT, NORTHERN MICH UNIV, 66- *Personal Data:* b Columbus, Ohio, Nov 26, 35; m 57; c 4. *Educ:* Univ Cincinnati, BS, 57, PhD(org chem), 60. *Prof Exp:* Res fel, Ohio State Univ, 60-61, from instr to asst prof obstet & gynec, Col Med, 61-66. *Concurrent Pos:* Comnr, Accrediting Bur Med Lab Schs, 69- *Mem:* Am Chem Soc; Sigma Xi. *Res:* Organic synthesis; spectroscopy; steroid chemistry and biochemistry; gas chromatography; analytical organic chemistry; chemical education. *Mailing Add:* Dept Chem Northern Mich Univ 1401 Presque Isle Ave Marquette MI 49855-5301

BARRY, ROGER GRAHAM, CLIMATOLOGY, SNOW & ICE. *Current Pos:* assoc prof, 68-71, PROF GEOG, UNIV COLO, BOULDER, 71-, FEL, COOP INST RES ENVIRON SCI, 81-, DIR, WORLD DATA CTR-A GLACIOL, 76- *Personal Data:* b Sheffield, Eng, Nov 13, 35; m 91, Natalya Shapalina; c Rachel, Christina & Nina. *Educ:* Univ Liverpool, BA, 57; McGill Univ, MSc, 59; Univ Southampton, PhD(geog), 65. *Honors & Awards:* Honors Award, Asn Am Geogr, 86. *Prof Exp:* Lectr geog, Univ Southampton, 60-66; res scientist climat, Geog Br, Dept Energy, Mines & Resources, Ont, 66-67; lectr geog, Univ Southampton, 67-68. *Concurrent Pos:* Mem glaciol panel, Comt Polar Res, Nat Acad Sci, 73-77; J S Guggenheim fel, 82-83; mem, Comt Arctic Ocean Info Systs, Marine Bd, Nat Acad Sci, 85-87; mem, Polar Res Bd, Nat Acad Sci, 88-92. *Mem:* Am Meteorol Soc; Am Quaternary Asn; Asn Am Geogr; Int Mountain Soc (secy, 81-); Am Geophys Union. *Res:* Climates of arctic and mountain regions; climatic change, interrelations between snow and ice cover and climate. *Mailing Add:* Coop Inst Res Environ Sci Univ Colo Boulder CO 80309-0449. *E-Mail:* rbarr@kryosicolorado.edu

BARRY, RONALD A, IMMUNOLOGY. *Current Pos:* IMMUNOLOGIST & MICROBIOLOGIST, DEPT VET AFFAIRS MED CTR, 86-; ASST PROF, DEPT MICROBIOL & IMMUNOL, ORE HEALTH SCI UNIV, PORTLAND, 89- *Personal Data:* b Twin Falls, Idaho, Feb 19, 50; m. *Educ:* Col Idaho, BS, 72; Univ Md, MD, 73; Navy Med Technol Sch, MT, 74; Wash State Univ, MS, 81, PhD, 83. *Prof Exp:* Clin bact instr, Nat Naval Med Ctr, 74; clin microbiologist, Navy Med Hosp, Guam, 75-76, San Diego, Calif, 76-77; teaching asst, Wash State Univ, 78-82, res asst, 79-81; res fel, Univ Calif, San Francisco, 83-86. *Concurrent Pos:* Immunol instr, Sch Med, Ore Health Sci Univ, Portland, Ore, 88; res rep, Libr Comt, Vet Admin Med Ctr, Portland, Ore, 88-, mem, Inst Animal Care & Use Subcomt, 88-89, chmn, 89-92. *Mem:* Am Soc Clin Pathologists; Am Soc Microbiologists; Am Soc Virol; Am Asn Immunologists; AAAS. *Res:* Immune T cell phenotypes in the expression of immunity and delayed-type hypersensitivity to Listeria monocytogenes and mycobacterian tuberculosis; T cell phenotypes in antilisterial and antimycobacterial immunity. *Mailing Add:* Va Hosp 3710 US Veterans Hospital Rd Portland OR 97201-2999

BARRY, RONALD EVERETT, JR, MAMMALOGY, VERTEBRATE ECOLOGY. *Current Pos:* from asst prof to assoc prof, 84-93, PROF BIOL, FROSTBURG STATE UNIV, 93- *Personal Data:* b Great Barrington, Mass, Jan 4, 47; m 69, Elaine A DeConti; c Pamela J & Lisa M. *Educ:* Univ Conn, BA, 68; Ind State Univ, MA, 74; Univ NH, PhD(zool), 78. *Prof Exp:* Res asst biochem, Health Ctr, Univ Conn, 68-73; instr biol, Bates Col, 77-78; teaching fel, WVa Univ, 79-80; asst prof zool, Unity Col, 80-84. *Concurrent Pos:* Fel & fac mem mammal, Mountain Lake Biol Sta, Univ Va, 80; prin invest, NSF Cause grant, 83-84; Fulbright Sr res grant, 91; Nat Geog Soc res grant, 91. *Mem:* AAAS; Am Soc Mammalogists; assoc mem Sigma Xi. *Res:* Habitat selection in small mammals; gastrointestinal morphology of small mammals; orientation, navigation and spatial resource partitioning in small mammals; competition in small mammals; population biology of African hyraxes. *Mailing Add:* Dept Biol Frostburg State Univ Frostburg MD 21532-1099. *Fax:* 301-689-3034; *E-Mail:* rbarry@fre.fsu.umd.edu

BARRY, WILLIAM EUGENE, MEDICINE. *Current Pos:* from instr to assoc prof, 61-72, PROF MED, MED CTR, TEMPLE UNIV, 72- *Personal Data:* b Staten Island, NY, Aug 29, 28; m 54; c 5. *Educ:* Villanova Univ, BS, 50; NY Med Col, MD, 54; Am Bd Internal Med, dipl, 61, cert hemat, 74. *Prof Exp:* Asst resident internal med & resident, Health Ctr, Ohio State Univ, 57-59, sr asst resident hemat & chief resident, 59-61. *Concurrent Pos:* Am Col Physicians Brower travelling scholar, 65; res fel, Div Hemat, Univ Wash, 69-70. *Mem:* Am Fedn Clin Res; fel Am Col Physicians; Am Soc Hemat. *Res:* Clincial hematology; iron metabolism. *Mailing Add:* Temple Univ Hosp 3400 N Broad St Philadelphia PA 19140-5104

BARRY, WILLIAM JAMES, TERRESTRIAL ECOLOGY, ENVIRONMENTAL IMPACT ASSESSMENT. *Current Pos:* DIR, ENVIRON SERV, VANASSE HANGEN BRUSTLIN,INC, 97- *Personal Data:* b Hudson, NY, May 14, 48; m 72; c 1. *Educ:* Cornell Univ, BS, 70; Mich State Univ, MS, 71, PhD(zool), 74. *Prof Exp:* Asst prof zool, Conn Col, 75-80; prin scientist, Normandeau Assocs, 81-97. *Concurrent Pos:* Consult environ, 81- *Mem:* Animal Behav Soc; Am Soc Mammalogists; Wildlife Soc; Ecol Soc Am. *Res:* The effect of photoperiod, temperature and other environmental factors on food hoarding behavior in small mammals, especially deermice; the study of the ecological relationships of small mammals on tidal marshes; environmental impacts on wildlife. *Mailing Add:* 23 Forest Dr Bedford NH 03110

BARS, ITZHAK, ELEMENTARY PARTICLE PHYSICS. *Current Pos:* PROF PHYSICS, UNIV SOUTHERN CALIF, 83- *Personal Data:* b Izmir, Turkey, Aug 31, 43; US citizen; m 93, Annie Rosenschein; c Julie & Jamie. *Educ:* Robert Col, BS, 67; Yale Univ, MPhil, 69, PhD(physics), 71. *Honors & Awards:* First Award, Gravity Res Found, 88. *Prof Exp:* Res assoc physics, Univ Calif, Berkeley, 71-73; asst prof, Stanford Univ, 73-75; from asst prof to assoc prof, Yale Univ, 75-83. *Concurrent Pos:* Fel, A P Sloan Found, 76-80; vis prof, Harvard Univ, 78, Inst Advan Study, 79 & 90, Inst Theoret Physics, Univ Calif, Santa Barbara, 86; jr fac fel, Yale Univ 78; prin investr, Univ Southern Calif, 83-; outstanding jr investr, Dept Energy, 83. *Mem:* Am Phys Soc; NY Acad Sci. *Res:* Formulated, developed and applied symmetry and supersymmetry principles in unified gauge theories, composite models of quarks and leptons, nuclear supersymmetries, feeble forces, superstring and supermembrane theories. *Mailing Add:* Dept Physics Univ Southern Calif Los Angeles CA 90089-0484. *Fax:* 213-740-6653; *E-Mail:* bars@physics.usc.edu

BARSCH, GERHARD RICHARD, SOLID STATE PHYSICS. *Current Pos:* sr res assoc appl physics, 62-64, assoc prof solid state sci, 64-70, PROF PHYSICS, PA STATE UNIV, 70- *Personal Data:* b Berlin, Ger, June 22, 27; m 59; c 3. *Educ:* Tech Univ Berlin, MS, 51; Univ Gottingen, PhD(theoret physics), 55. *Prof Exp:* Mem sci staff theoret physics, Battelle Inst, Ger, 56-62. *Mem:* Sigma Xi. *Res:* Lattice dynamics of anharmonic properties and crystal defects; nonlinear crystal elasticity; high pressure physics. *Mailing Add:* 107 Mater Res Lab Pa State Univ University Park PA 16802

BARSCHALL, HENRY HERMAN, nuclear science; deceased, see previous edition for last biography

BARSDATE, ROBERT JOHN, GEOCHEMISTRY. *Current Pos:* from asst prof to assoc prof, 63-72, PROF MARINE SCI, UNIV ALASKA, 72- *Personal Data:* b Richmond Hill, NY, Sept 4, 34; m 59; c 2. *Educ:* Allegheny Col, BS, 59; Univ Pittsburgh, PhD(geochem), 64. *Concurrent Pos:* Vis prof, Swiss Fed Inst Water Resources, 73-74. *Mem:* AAAS; Am Soc Limnol & Oceanog; Geochem Soc; fel Arctic Inst NAm; Soc Int Limnol; Sigma Xi. *Res:* Biologically mediated movement of trace metals in natural waters. *Mailing Add:* 99708-0174 College AK 99708-0174

BAR-SHAVIT, RACHEL, GROWTH FACTORS. *Current Pos:* RES ASSOC, JEWISH HOSP ST LOUIS, 85- *Personal Data:* b Hadera, Israel, Dec 1, 53. *Educ:* Bar-Ilan, Israel, PhD(biochem), 83. *Mailing Add:* Hadassah Med Sch Dept Oncol Hebrew Univ PO Box 1200 Jerusalem 91120 Israel

BAR-SHAVIT, ZVI, CELL BIOLOGY. *Current Pos:* PROF CELL BIOLOGY, RES ASST & LECTR, DIV CELL BIOL, SCH DENT MED, WASH UNIV, 83- *Educ:* Weizmann Inst, Israel, PhD(membrane res), 81. *Mailing Add:* Hubert H Humphrey Ctr Exp Med & Cancer Res Hebrew Univ PO Box 12272 Jerusalem 91020 Israel

BARSHAY, JACOB, NUMBER THEORY. *Current Pos:* from asst prof to assoc prof, 72-90, CHMN, MATH DEPT, CITY UNIV NEW YORK, 86-, PROF MATH, 90- *Personal Data:* b New York, NY, Apr 7, 40; m 64, Barbara Pearl; c Berna G. *Educ:* Princeton Univ, AB, 61; Brandeis Univ, MA, 63 & PhD(math), 66. *Prof Exp:* From instr to asst prof math, Northeastern Univ, 65-70; vis prof math, Univ Aarhus, Denmark, 70-71, Univ Genoa, Italy, 71-72. *Mem:* Am Math Soc; Math Assoc Am. *Res:* Commutative ring theory. *Mailing Add:* City Col NY New York NY 10031-9100. *Fax:* 212-690-4117; *E-Mail:* mathjb@conyvme

BARSIS, EDWIN HOWARD, APPLIED PHYSICS, COMPUTER & INFORMATION SCIENCE. *Current Pos:* PARTNER CONSULT FIRM, BMU ASSOCS, ALBUQUERQUE, NMEX, 96- *Personal Data:* b Brooklyn, NY, June 28, 40; div; c James & Ben. *Educ:* Cornell Univ, BEP, 63, MS, 65, PhD(appl physics), 67. *Prof Exp:* Mem tech staff, Device Studies Div, Livermore, Calif, 68-71, supvr, 71-78, supvr, Advan Develop Div, 78-79; mgr, Electronics Subsysts Dept, Sandia Nat Labs, Albuquerque, 79-86, dir comput sci & math, 86-96, dir eng sci, 89-96. *Concurrent Pos:* Consult, Air Force Weapons Lab, 94. *Mem:* Am Phys Soc. *Res:* Ionic conductivity; dielectric relaxation; defects in insulators; radiation-induced optical properties; piezoresistivity; optical computing; parallel computing; computer architectures; intelligent machines; computer science. *Mailing Add:* 1538 Catron Ave SE Albuquerque NM 87123. *E-Mail:* ebarsis@bmu.com

BARSKE, PHILIP, WILDLIFE MANAGEMENT & WETLANDS. *Current Pos:* RETIRED. *Personal Data:* b Fairfield, Conn, Jan 12, 17; m 48; c 1. *Educ:* Univ Conn, BS, 40; Univ Mich, MS, 43; Union Grad Sch, Ohio PhD(appl ecol), 76. *Hon Degrees:* DSc, Univ Bridgeport, 77. *Honors & Awards:* Am

Motors Award, 63; Cert of Recognition, Wildlife Soc, 67, John Pearce Mem Award, 75. *Prof Exp:* Game biologist, Conn State Bd Fish & Game, 42-43 & 46; field conservationist, Wildlife Mgt Inst, Washington, DC, 46-, environ consult, Wetlands Specialty. *Concurrent Pos:* Consult environ systs to several major indust concerns, 70-; mem, Gov Coun Environ Qual, Conn. *Mem:* Wildlife Soc; Soil Conserv Soc Am; Nat Asn Environ Prof; Soc Am Foresters; Soc Wetland Scientists; Natl Asn State Wetland Mgrs. *Res:* Applied habitat development; wildlife areas and natural areas development and wetland evaluation and development. *Mailing Add:* 240 Massapoag Ave North Easton MA 02356

BARSKY, BRIAN ANDREW, COMPUTER GRAPHICS. *Current Pos:* Asst prof, 81-86, ASSOC PROF COMPUT SCI, UNIV CALIF, BERKELEY, 86- *Personal Data:* b Montreal, Que, Sept 17, 54. *Educ:* McGill Univ, DCS, 73, BSc, 76; Cornell Univ, MS, 78; Univ Utah, Salt Lake City, PhD(comput sci), 81. *Concurrent Pos:* Presidential young investr, NSF, 83; consult, 81-; adj asst prof, Univ Waterloo, Ont, 82-; prin investr, NSF grants, 82- & MICRO grant, 84-85; vis researcher, Nat Advan Sch Telecommun, Paris, 85-86; fac develop award, IBM, 85. *Mem:* Asn Comput Mach; Nat Comput Graphics Asn; Inst Elec & Electronics Engrs; Can Man-Comput Commun Soc; Soc Indust & Appl Math. *Res:* Interactive three-dimensional computer graphics, concentrating on various aspects of the realistic image synthesis problem; computer aided geometric design and modelling concentrating on mathematical techniques for curve and surface representation; development of the Beta-splire representation and Liang-Barsky clipping algorithms; computer aided geometric design and modelling. *Mailing Add:* Comput Sci Div Univ Calif 519 Evans Hall Berkeley CA 94720-0001

BARSKY, CONSTANCE KAY, POLYMER SCIENCE, GLASS CHEMISTRY. *Current Pos:* admin mgr, Dept Chem, 87-91, asst to dean, Col Math & Physical Sci, 90-91, DIR SCI EDUC, DEPT PHYSICS, OHIO STATE UNIV, 91- *Personal Data:* b Newark, NJ, Nov 3, 44; m 74, Steven G Katz. *Educ:* Denison Univ, BS, 66; Wash Univ, PhD(geochem), 75. *Prof Exp:* Res assoc geochem petrol, Univ Mo, Columbia, 71-77; advan scientist, Owens-Corning Fiber Glass Corp, 77-78, supvr mat anal lab, 78-81, supvr, Indust Operating Div Prod Develop Lab, 81-85, supvr, Inorg & Surface Technol Lab, 85-86; admin dir, Ohio Statewide Syst Initiative, 93-96. *Concurrent Pos:* Dir, Learning by Redesign, 96- *Mem:* Sigma Xi; Am Asn Higher Educ; Am Women Sci. *Res:* Analysis and implementation of systemic reforms in education; applications of electron beam microanalysis to problems in glass chemistry, metallurgy environmental analysis, and glass composites; major and trace element geochemistry of igneous rocks applied to problems of magma origin and evolution; diversification projects related to inorganic and surface technology of glass forming; development of polymeric coatings for continuous and chopped fibrous glass products used as reinforcements; applications of chemical microanalysis and microscopy to glass composites and metals. *Mailing Add:* 221 Elm St Granville OH 43023. *Fax:* 614-292-3221; *E-Mail:* barsky.1@osu.edu

BARSKY, ISAAK YA, BIOMEDICAL RESEARCH. *Current Pos:* jr sci worker, 59-69, sr sci worker, 69-85, PRIN RES ASSOC, SI VAVILOV STATE OPTICAL INST, 85- *Personal Data:* b Leningrad, Russia, Feb 19, 34; m 61, Tatiana Valerian Kirillo; c Michael Kirillov & Olga Kirillova. *Educ:* S I Vavilov State Optical Inst, Leningrad, PhD, 64. *Honors & Awards:* Frauhofer/Barsky Prize, Optical Soc Am, 94. *Prof Exp:* Sr technician, Botanical Inst Acad Sci, USSR, 56-59. *Concurrent Pos:* Lectr, Leiden Univ, Neth, 93 & Kardinska Inst, Stockholm, 94. *Res:* Developed new apparatus and methods of luminescence microscopy; luminescence medicine devices for diagnostics of cancer and tissue vitality; contributed over 150 articles to professional journals. *Mailing Add:* SI Vavilov State Optical Inst Birzhevaya 14 St Petersburg 199164 Russia

BARSKY, JAMES, INFORMATION SCIENCE. *Current Pos:* RETIRED. *Personal Data:* b Regina, Sask, Nov 28, 25; US citizen; m 57; c 2. *Educ:* Univ Sask, BA, 46; Univ Toronto, MA, 51; Northwestern Univ, PhD(biochem), 58. *Prof Exp:* Asst biochem, Univ Sask, 46-48; fel physiol chem, Univ Calif Col Med, Ment Health Prog & Vet Admin Ctr, Los Angeles, 58-60; mgr dept biochem, Res Div, Ethicon, Inc, 60-63; biol sci ed, Acad Press Inc, 63- 67, exec ed, 67-68, vpres ed, 68-73, sr vpres, 73-78, pres, 78-87; sr vpres, Harcourt Brace Jovanovich, 81-87. *Concurrent Pos:* Doctoral fel, Univ Calif, Los Angeles; mem adv panel, NSF Off Sci Info Serv, 75 & adv comt, Nat Comn Libr & Info Sci, 75-87; mem bd dirs, Copyright Clearance Ctr, 77-87; chmn, Academic Press, 85. *Mem:* AAAS; Am Chem Soc; Am Asn Clin Chem; Biochem Soc, UK; NY Acad Sci; Sigma Xi. *Res:* Enzymology; scientific technical, medical and scholarly publications. *Mailing Add:* 53 Rosemont Terr West Orange NJ 07052

BARSOM, JOHN M, MATERIALS SCIENCE ENGINEERING. *Current Pos:* sr res consult & chief mat, Technol Div, 67-83, RES FEL, US STEEL CORP, 83- *Educ:* Univ Pittsburgh, BS, 60, MS, 62, PhD(mech eng), 69. *Honors & Awards:* Award of Merit, Am Soc Testing & Mat, 77. *Prof Exp:* Sr res engr, Pittsburgh Plate Glass Indust, 60-67. *Concurrent Pos:* Adj prof, Civil Eng Dept, Univ Pittsburgh; chmn, Comt E-24 Fracture Mat, Am Soc Testing Mat, Transp Strut Subcomt, Am Iron & Steel Inst; mem, Comt E-9, Am Soc Testing Mat, Subcomt F-704 Hydrogen Embrittlement, Ship Res Comt, Maritime Transp Res Bd, adv mem steel, Indust Coun, Advan Steel Bridge Technol, Am Inst Steel Construct Subcomt Brittle Fracture. *Mem:* Fel Am Soc Metals; fel Am Soc Testing & Mat. *Res:* Material selection; prediction of behavior of fabricated components in structures; fracture and fatigue prevention; structural reliability; failure analysis; accident reconstruction; numerous publications. *Mailing Add:* US Steel Corp 600 Grant St Rm 2300 Pittsburgh PA 15219

BARSS, WALTER MALCOMSON, PHYSICS. *Current Pos:* RETIRED. *Personal Data:* b Corvallis, Ore, Jan 29, 17; nat Can; m 47; c 1. *Educ:* Univ BC, BA, 37, MA, 39; Purdue Univ, PhD(physics), 42. *Prof Exp:* Asst, Univ BC, 38-39 & Purdue Univ, 40-42; res physicist, Nat Res Coun Can, 42-52 & Atomic Energy Can Ltd, 52-64; assoc prof physics, Univ Victoria, 64-82. *Concurrent Pos:* Can Asn Physicists; Acoust Soc Am. *Res:* Acoustics, especially reverberation problems in rooms and in underwater sound using laboratory models. *Mailing Add:* 3915 St Georges Lanes Apt 205 Victoria BC V8N 4E3 Can

BARSTON, EUGENE MYRON, APPLIED MATHEMATICS. *Current Pos:* assoc prof, 72-77, PROF MATH, UNIV ILL, CHICAGO CIRCLE, 72- *Personal Data:* b Chicago, Ill, Aug 7, 35; m 62; c 2. *Educ:* Calif Inst Technol, BS, 57, MS, 58; Stanford Univ, PhD(physics), 64. *Prof Exp:* Math physicist, Stanford Res Inst, 63-65; assoc res scientist, Courant Inst Math Sci, 65-67, from asst prof to assoc prof math, NY Univ, 67-72. *Mem:* Soc Indust & Appl Math. *Res:* Stability theory; fluid mechanics; plasma physics. *Mailing Add:* Dept Math Univ Ill 851 S Morgan St Chicago IL 60607-7045

BARSTOW, DAVID ROBBINS, AUTOMATIC PROGRAMMING. *Current Pos:* SCI ADV, SCHLUMBERGER LAB COMPUT SCI, 89- *Personal Data:* b Middletown, Conn, Aug 5, 47; m 70; c 2. *Educ:* Carleton Col, BA, 69; Stanford Univ, MS, 71, PhD(comput sci), 77. *Prof Exp:* J W Gibbs instr comput sci, Yale Univ, 77-79, asst prof, 79-80; prog leader software res, Schlumberger-Doll Res, Ridgefield, Conn, 80-87, sci adv, 87-89. *Mem:* Asn Comput Mach; Inst Elec & Electronics Engrs-Comput Soc; Am Asn Artificial Intel. *Res:* Applications of artificial intelligence techniques to software engineering; automatic programming; programming environments; models of parallel computation. *Mailing Add:* 107 Laura Lane Austin TX 78746

BARSTOW, LEON E, ORGANIC CHEMISTRY, BIOCHEMISTRY. *Current Pos:* PRES, PROTEIN THERAPEUT, 96- *Personal Data:* b Union City, Pa, Dec 14, 40; div; c 5. *Educ:* Edinboro State Col, BS, 62; Syracuse Univ, PhD(chem), 66. *Honors & Awards:* IR-100 Award, 82; Award of Excellence, Soc Tech Commun, 84. *Prof Exp:* Asst prof chem, Robert Col, Istanbul, 66-69; res assoc, Univ Ariz, 69-72, res asst prof biochem, 72-89; chmn, Protein Technol Inc, 89-96. *Concurrent Pos:* NIH postdoctoral fel, Univ Ariz, 71-72; consult, Vega Eng, 72-75; pres & gen mgr, Vega Biochem, 74-79, pres & chief exec officer, Vega Biotechnologies, Inc, 79-85; pres & chief exec officer, Protein Technol, Inc. *Mem:* Am Chem Soc; AAAS; Sigma Xi. *Res:* Preparation of semi-synthetic analogs of proteins for structure-function studies; synthesis of peptide hormones with novel biological activity; development of peptide substrates for various enzymes. *Mailing Add:* 70 Calle Encanto Tucson AZ 85716

BART, GEORGE RAYMOND, MATHEMATICAL PHYSICS, ELEMENTARY PARTICLE PHYSICS. *Current Pos:* assoc prof, 74-81, chmn, Nat Sci Dept, 81-86, PROF PHYSICS & MATH, HARRY S TRUMAN COL, 81-, CHMN, PHYSICS SCI & ENG DEPT, 86- *Personal Data:* b Oak Park, Ill; m 61; c 2. *Educ:* Loyola Univ, Chicago, BS, 61; Ill Inst Technol, PhD(theoret physics), 70. *Prof Exp:* Physicist & mgr crystal contracts, Electronics & Res Ctr, Victor-Comptometer Corp, 63-66; resident assoc, High Energy Physics Div, Argonne Nat Lab, 67-69; asst prof physics, Loyola Univ, Chicago, 69-70; asst prof physics & math, Mayfair Col, 70-74. *Concurrent Pos:* Fac res prog, Accelerator Res Fac Div, Argonne Nat Lab, 79- *Mem:* Am Phys Soc; Am Asn Physics Teachers. *Res:* Theories of elementary particles; null-plane quantum field theories; S-matrix theory; dispersion relations; analysis of non-linear equations; soliton theory; integral equations. *Mailing Add:* Dept Physics Sci Truman Col 1145 W Wilson Ave Chicago IL 60640-5616

BARTA, OTA, VETERINARY IMMUNOLOGY. *Current Pos:* PROF, DEPT BIOMED SCI & PATH, VA TECH, 87- *Personal Data:* b Ostrava, Czech, Aug 18, 31; US citizen; m 56, Vera Dadakova; c Tomas & Marketa. *Educ:* Univ Vet Med, Brno, Czech, MVDr, 55, CSc, 63; Univ Guelph, PhD(immunolo microbiol), 69. *Honors & Awards:* Fulbright sr lectr, 81, 94 & 95; Small Animal Award, Ralston-Purina, 85. *Prof Exp:* Asst prof animal hyg, Univ Vet Med, Brno, Czech, 55-61; scientist animal hyg, Cent Res Inst Animal Husb, Prague-Uhrineves, Czech, 61-64 & Inst Vet Med Res, Brno, 64-69; from asst prof to assoc prof immunol, Dept Microbiol, Okla State Univ, 69-75; from assoc prof to prof, Sch Vet Med, La State Univ, Baton Rouge, 75-87. *Concurrent Pos:* Res assoc, Ont Vet Col, Univ Guelph, 67-69. *Mem:* Am Asn Immunologists; Am Asn Vet Immunologists; World Asn Vet Microbiologists. *Res:* Immunology, research of the complement system; immunochemistry; clinical veterinary immunology; infectious diseases. *Mailing Add:* Va-Md Regional Col Vet Med Va Tech Dept Pathobiol Blacksburg VA 24061-0442

BARTAL, ARIE H, MONOCLONAL ANTIBODIES & HYBRIDOMAS, CANCER INVESTIGATION. *Current Pos:* SCI DIR, IMMUNOSCI INC, 88- *Personal Data:* b Iasi, Romania, Feb 9, 47; Israel citizen; m 69; c 2. *Educ:* Hebrew Univ, Jerusalem, MD, 72; Technion Israel Inst Technol, DSc(immunol), 85. *Honors & Awards:* Oncol Award, Israel Med Asn, 79. *Prof Exp:* Head, Hybridoma Lab, Ramborn Med Ctr, Inst Oncol, Haifa, Israel, 82-86; div chief, Biotherapeutics, Franklin, Tenn, 87-88. *Concurrent Pos:* Assoc researcher, Ramborn Med Ctr, Israel, 74-75, Sloan Kettering Cancer Ctr, NY, 79-82; vis scientist, Sloan Kettering Cancer Ctr, NY, 84, Nat Cancer Inst, 84; asst prof, Fac Med, Technion Inst Technol, Haifa, Israel, 86; co-ed, Method of Hybridoma Formation, 87. *Mem:* Am Soc Clin Oncol; Am Asn Cancer Res; Am Fedn Clin Res; Am Asn Immunol; Fed Am Socs Exp Biol; Tissue Cult Asn. *Res:* Oncology; basic and applied research; immunology and biological response modifiers; hybridome and monoclonal antibody generation and characterization; immunopathology; tumor markers and prognostic factors; adoptive immunotherapy. *Mailing Add:* 546 Plainview Rd Plainview NY 11803

BARTEAU, MARK ALAN, SURFACE SCIENCE, CATALYSIS. *Current Pos:* asst prof chem eng, 82-87, from assoc prof to prof chem eng & chem, 87-94, ROBERT L PIGFORD PROF CHEM ENG, UNIV DEL, 94-, DIR, CTR CATALYTIC SCI & TECHNOL, 96- *Personal Data:* b St Louis, Mo, Sept 8, 56; m 83; c 2. *Educ:* Washington Univ, 76; Stanford Univ, MS, 77, PhD(chem eng), 81. *Honors & Awards:* Victor K LaMer Award, Am Chem Soc, 82, Ipatieff Prize, 95; Innovation Recognition Award, Union Carbide Corp, 88 & 89; Allan P Colburn Award, Am Inst Chem Engrs, 91; Paul H Emmett Award, Catalysis, Soc, 93. *Prof Exp:* NSF fel, Physics Dept, Tech Univ Muenchen, 81-82. *Concurrent Pos:* Assoc dir, Ctr Catalytic Sci & Technol, Univ Del, 82-; presidential young investr award, NSF, 85; vis prof, Dept Chem Eng, Univ Pa, 91-92. *Mem:* Am Inst Chem Engrs; Am Chem Soc; Catalysis Soc; Mat Res Soc; AAAS. *Res:* Synthesis of new catalytic materials; reactivity of metal oxides; surface science studies of intermediates and pathways in alcohol and hydrocarbon synthesis; applications of scanning probe microscopies. *Mailing Add:* 4 Littlebrook Dr Wilmington DE 19807. *Fax:* 302-831-2085; *E-Mail:* barteau@che.udel.edu

BARTEL, ALLEN HAWLEY, BIOCHEMISTRY. *Current Pos:* from asst prof to assoc prof biol, Univ Houston, 58-67, prof biophys sci & chmn dept, 67-79, prof biochem & biophys sci & dir, Flow Cytometry Lab, 79-87, chmn & prof biochem & biophys sci, 87-91, EMER PROF, UNIV HOUSTON, 92- *Personal Data:* b San Diego, Calif, July 26, 23; m 51; c 4. *Educ:* Univ Calif, AB, 47, MS, 49, PhD, 54. *Prof Exp:* Instr biol sci, Univ Calif, 55-56; res fel chem, Calif Inst Technol, 56-58. *Mem:* Am Soc Biochem & Molecular Biol; Am Chem Soc; AAAS. *Res:* Computational biochemistry; comparative biochemistry. *Mailing Add:* Dept Biochem & Biophys Sci Univ Houston Houston TX 77204. *Fax:* 713-743-8351; *E-Mail:* bartel@uh.edu

BARTEL, DONALD L, MECHANICAL ENGINEERING. *Current Pos:* ASST PROF MECH ENG, CORNELL UNIV, 69- *Personal Data:* b Peoria, Ill, June 5, 39; m 62; c 4. *Educ:* Univ Ill, BS, 61, MS, 63; Univ Iowa, PhD(mech), 69. *Prof Exp:* Asst prof eng, Black Hawk Col, 63-65. *Concurrent Pos:* NSF res grant, 70-71. *Mem:* Soc Indust & Appl Math; Am Soc Mech Engrs. *Res:* Optimum design of mechanical systems and components; application of mechanics principles to problems in orthopedic surgery. *Mailing Add:* Sch Mech Eng Cornell Univ 105 Upson Hall Ithaca NY 14853-1501

BARTEL, FRED F(RANK), CIVIL ENGINEERING. *Current Pos:* RETIRED. *Personal Data:* b Milwaukee, Wis, Nov 4, 17; m 43, Ann Staudacher; c Susan, Mary J, Robert & Betty J (Kennedy). *Educ:* Univ Wis, BS, 40; Univ Md, MS, 42. *Prof Exp:* Asst dir eng, Nat Sand & Gravel Asn, 46-49; chief engr, Tews Lime & Cement Co, 49-75, pres, 75-83; trustee in bankruptcy, 4x Corp, 85. *Concurrent Pos:* Chmn bd, Nat Ready Mixed Concrete Asn, 79-80; hon mem, Comt C-9, Am Soc Testing & Mat; hon dir, Nat Ready-Mixed Conrete Asn. *Mem:* Am Soc Civil Engrs; Am Soc Testing & Mat. *Res:* Portland cement concrete; aggregates for concrete and bituminous construction. *Mailing Add:* 5421 N Shoreland Ave Milwaukee WI 53217-5132

BARTEL, HERBERT H(ERMAN), JR, CIVIL ENGINEERING. *Current Pos:* chmn, 72-78, prof, 78-91, EMER PROF CIVIL ENG, UNIV TEX, EL PASO, 91- *Personal Data:* b Dallas, Tex, Mar 31, 24; m 50, Dorothy Angus; c Peggy J (Hunter) & Kathy (Najera). *Educ:* Southern Methodist Univ, BS, 44; Tex Univ, MS, 50; Tex A&M Univ, PhD(civil eng), 62. *Honors & Awards:* Excellence Eng Teaching Award, Gen Dynamics, 69. *Prof Exp:* Instr civil eng, Southern Methodist Univ, 46-53, from asst prof to prof, 53-72, chmn, Dept Civil & Environ Eng, 69-72. *Concurrent Pos:* Assoc pastor, Coronado Christian Church, El Paso, Tex. *Mem:* Am Soc Eng Educ; Am Soc Civil Engrs; Nat Soc Prof Engrs. *Res:* Highway illumination; highway traffic operation and pavement design. *Mailing Add:* 5801 Kingsfield Ave El Paso TX 79912-4815

BARTEL, LAVON L, LIPID METABOLISM, HUMAN NUTRITIONAL HEALTH. *Current Pos:* DIR, COOP EXTEN, UNIV MAINE, 96- *Personal Data:* b Salem, Ore, Nov 12, 51; m, David Struck. *Educ:* Ore State Univ, BS, 73, MS, 75; Univ Wis, Madison, PhD(nutrit), 79. *Prof Exp:* Res asst med sci, Med Sch, Univ Ore, 72; res asst, Dept Zool, Ore State Univ, 73, teaching asst, 73-75; res asst, Dept Nutrit Sci & Med, Univ Wis, Madison, 75-79; chair asst prof, Dept Home Econ Nutrit & Food Sci, Whittier Col, 79-82; assoc dir, Exten Syst, Univ Vt, 89-96, nutrit specialist, 87-89, fac nutrit sci. *Concurrent Pos:* Teaching asst, Dept Nutrit Sci, Univ Wis, Madison, 77; dir dietetics & speaker, Speakers Bur, Whittier Col, 79-; consult, Pico Rivera Health Ctr, 79-; nutrit consult, Area Health Educ Coun, Univ Southern Calif & San Gabriel Health Educ Adv Bd, 81- *Mem:* AAAS; Am Dietetic Asn; Asn Women Sci; Inst Food Technologists; Am Asn Pub Health; Am Asn Family & Consumer Scientists. *Res:* Lipid metabolism and carnitine levels in hemodialysis patients and development of a rat model and rabbit model; management of obesity through nutrition education and behavior modification techniques. *Mailing Add:* UMCE-Univ Maine 5471 Libby Hall Orono ME 04496-5741. *E-Mail:* lbartel@umce.umext.maine.edu

BARTEL, LEWIS CLARK, GEOPHYSICS, THEORETICAL SOLID STATE PHYSICS. *Current Pos:* CONSULT, 96- *Personal Data:* b Hillsboro, Kans, Dec 5, 34; m 56; c 2. *Educ:* Univ Kans, BS, 58; Iowa State Univ, PhD(physics), 64. *Prof Exp:* Asst prof physics, Colo State Univ, 64-67; staff mem physics res, Sandia Labs, 67-96. *Concurrent Pos:* Consult, PEC Res Assocs, 65-67. *Mem:* Soc Explor Geophys. *Res:* Engineering and mining geophysics, electrical and electromagnetic geophysical methods; theoretical solid state physics, magnetism and ferroelectics. *Mailing Add:* 6005 Carruthers Albuquerque NM 87111

BARTEL, MONROE H, HUMAN BIOLOGY. *Current Pos:* from asst prof to assoc prof, 63-71, PROF BIOL, MOORHEAD STATE UNIV, 71- *Personal Data:* b Newton, Kans, Oct 3, 36; m 57; c 3. *Educ:* Tabor Col, AB, 58; Kansas State Univ, MS, 60, PhD(parasitol), 63. *Prof Exp:* Instr zool, Kans State Univ, 62-63. *Concurrent Pos:* Fel trop med, Sch Med, La State Univ, 66 & Histochem Inst, 67, Acarology Prog, Ohio State Univ, 78; sabbatical, Mont State Univ, 88-89. *Mem:* Am Soc Parasitol; AAAS; Sigma Xi; Am Sci Affil. *Mailing Add:* Dept Biol Moorhead State Univ Moorhead MN 56563

BARTEL, NORBERT, RADIO ASTRONOMY. *Current Pos:* PROF, DEPT PHYSICS & ASTRON, YORK UNIV, 92- *Personal Data:* b Wettendorf, Ger, Feb 24, 50; m 74, Joan Corliss; c Hanna & Robert. *Educ:* Univ Bonn, diplom physik, 75, PhD(radio astron), 78. *Honors & Awards:* Otto Hahn Medal, Max-Planck Soc, 79. *Prof Exp:* Res assoc, Max-Plank Inst Radio Astron, 78-80, Harvard Univ, 82-92; vis scientist, Mass Inst Technol, 80-82. *Concurrent Pos:* Lectr astron, Harvard Univ, 86-92; mem, Managing Group Al Gonguin Radio Observ, Inst Space & Terrestrial Sci, 92-; coordr, Space & Commun Sci Prog, York Univ, 95- *Mem:* Am Astron Soc; Int Astron Union; Int Union Radio Sci; Ger Astron Soc. *Res:* Astronomical and astrometric investigations of compact radio sources primarily with very long baseline interferometer techniques; determinations of distances to pulsars and supernovae; imaging and proper motion measurements of radio shows; supernovae and active galactic nuclei; reference frames; tests of general relativity. *Mailing Add:* York Univ 4700 Keele St Toronto ON M3J 1P3 Can

BARTELINK, DIRK JAN, SOLID STATE ELECTRONICS. *Current Pos:* MGR METAL-OXIDE-SEMICONDUCTOR TECHNOL, HEWLETT PACKARD LABS, 80-, PROG LIAISON MGR, 96- *Personal Data:* b Heumen, Neth, Oct 28, 33; Can citizen; m 57; c 2. *Educ:* Univ Western Ont, BSc, 56; Stanford Univ, MS, 59, PhD(elec eng), 62. *Prof Exp:* Mem tech staff solid state electronics res, Bell Labs, NJ, 61-66, supvr semiconductor devices, 66-73; mgr device physics, Palo Alto Res Ctr, Xerox Corp, 73-80. *Mem:* Inst Elec & Electronics Engrs. *Res:* Fundamental and applied phenomena in semiconductor and dielectrics and interfaces between these. *Mailing Add:* Hewlett Packard Lab 3500 Deer Creek Rd Palo Alto CA 94304

BARTELL, CLELMER KAY, COMPARATIVE ANIMAL PHYSIOLOGY. *Current Pos:* ASSOC PROF ZOOL, UNIV NEW ORLEANS, 69-, ASSOC CHAIR BIOL SCI, 87- *Personal Data:* b Kingstree, SC, Nov 1, 34. *Educ:* Davidson Col, BS, 57; Univ Tenn, MS, 63; Duke Univ, PhD(zool), 66. *Prof Exp:* Res assoc, Tulane Univ, 66-69. *Mem:* Am Soc Zoologists. *Res:* Neuro-endocrine mechanisms in Crustacea; control of dermal chromatophores; Osmoregulation in animals. *Mailing Add:* Dept Biol Sci Univ New Orleans Lake Front New Orleans LA 70148. *Fax:* 504-280-6121

BARTELL, DANIEL P, ENTOMOLOGY. *Current Pos:* DEAN, SCH AGR SCI & TECHNOL, CALIF STATE UNIV, FRESNO. *Personal Data:* b St Paul, Minn, Mar 30, 44. *Educ:* Eastern Ill Univ, BSEd, 66; Purdue Univ, MS, 68, PhD(entom), 73. *Prof Exp:* Instr biol, parasitol, Davis & Elkins Col, 68-71; res assoc entom, Ill Nat Hist Surv, 73-75; asst prof, Ill Nat Hist Surv & Univ Ill, 75-76; asst prof, Tex Tech Univ, 76-78, assoc prof entom, 78-; at Col Agr Sci, Mont State Univ. *Mem:* Entom Soc Am; Entom Soc Can; Am Inst Biol Sci; Southwestern Entom Soc; Sigma Xi. *Res:* Pest management strategies for vegetable insects; host/parasite interactions; natural enemies of the red imported fire ant. *Mailing Add:* Agr Sci & Technol Calif State Univ 2415 E San Ramon Ave M/S 79 Fresno CA 93740-8033

BARTELL, LAWRENCE SIMS, PHYSICAL CHEMISTRY, CHEMICAL DYNAMICS. *Current Pos:* prof, 65-94, Philip J Elving col chair, 87-93, EMER PROF CHEM, UNIV MICH, ANN ARBOR, 94- *Personal Data:* b Ann Arbor, Mich, Feb 23, 23; m 52, Joy Keer; c Michael K. *Educ:* Univ Mich, BS, 44, MS, 47, PhD(chem), 51. *Honors & Awards:* Creativity Award, NSF, 82. *Prof Exp:* Res asst, Manhattan Proj, Univ Chicago, 44-45; Rackham fel, Univ Mich, 51-52, res assoc, 52-53; from asst prof to prof chem, Iowa State Univ, 53-65. *Concurrent Pos:* Consult, Gillette Co, Ill, 56-62 & Mobil Oil Corp, NJ, 60-84; chemist, AEC, 56-65; assoc ed, J Chem Physics, 63-65; mem, Comm Electron Diffraction, Inat Union Crystallog, 66-75; mem adv bd, Petrol Res Fund, 70-73; vis prof, Moscow State Univ, 72, Univ Paris XI, 73 & Univ Tex, Austin, 78 & 86; chmn, Div Chem-Phys, Am Phys Soc, 77-78. *Mem:* Am Chem Soc; Am Crystallog Asn; fel Am Phys Soc; fel AAAS. *Res:* Atomic and molecular structure by electron diffraction; surface and quantum chemistry; structure of molecular liquids and clusters; nucleation; dynamics of phase transitions; electron holography. *Mailing Add:* Dept Chem Univ Mich Ann Arbor MI 48104. *Fax:* 313-764-8776

BARTELL, MARVIN H, VERTEBRATE ZOOLOGY, ENDOCRINOLOGY. *Current Pos:* asst prof, 68-72, assoc prof, 72-81, PROF BIOL, CONCORDIA COL, 81- *Personal Data:* b Wanatah, Ind, Sept 16, 38; m 63; c 3. *Educ:* Concordia Teachers Col, Ill, BS, 61; Univ Mich, MS, 62, PhD(zool), 69. *Prof Exp:* Instr biol, Concordia Teachers Col, Ill, 62-64; lectr endocrinol, Univ Mich, 67. *Mem:* AAAS; Am Soc Microbiol; Sigma Xi. *Res:* Developmental endocrinology; control of carbohydrate metabolism in lower vertebrates; medical microbiology. *Mailing Add:* Dean Arts & Sci Concordia Univ 7400 Augusta St River Forest IL 60305-1402

BARTELL, STEVEN MICHAEL, SYSTEMS DESIGN, HYDROLOGY-WATER RESOURCES & ENVIRONMENTAL SCIENCE. *Current Pos:* VPRES SENES, OAK RIDGE, INC-ENVIRON CONSULT, 93- *Personal Data:* b Beaver Dam, Wis, Oct 25, 48. *Educ:* Lawrence Univ, BA, 71; Univ Wis, MS, 73, PhD(limnol & oceanog), 78. *Prof Exp:* Res assoc, Savannah River Ecol Lab, 78-80; adj asst prof, Inst Ecol, Univ

Ga, 78-80; res staff, Environ Sci Div, Oak Ridge Nat Lab, 80- *Concurrent Pos:* Panel mem, Fel Prog Rev, NSF, NATO, 81 & Competitive Grant Proposal Rev Comt, US Environ Protection Agency, 82; co-ed, Savannah River Ecol Lab, 80- *Mem:* Ecol Soc Am; Int Soc Ecol Modelling. *Res:* Development and evaluation of simulation models that predict transport, accumulation and biological effects of toxicants in aquatic systems; ecological and human health risk analysis; global resource risk analysis. *Mailing Add:* RR 1 Wartburg TN 37887

BARTELS, DAVID M, RADIATION CHEMISTRY, PHOTOCHEMISTRY. *Current Pos:* Res assoc fel, 82-85, SCIENTIST CHEM DIV, ARGONNE NAT LAB, 85- *Personal Data:* b Grand Haven, Mich, July 10, 55; m 77, Valerie A Winslow; c Kenneth W & Michelle J. *Educ:* Hope Col, BA, 77; Northwestern Univ, PhD(phys chem), 82. *Honors & Awards:* Alfred T Gordey Prize. *Concurrent Pos:* NSF grad fel, 77-80. *Mem:* Am Chem Soc; lifetime mem Am Phys Soc. *Res:* Work performed in collaboration with the radiation chemistry group. *Mailing Add:* 702 80th St Downers Grove IL 60516

BARTELS, GEORGE WILLIAM, JR, ORGANIC CHEMISTRY. *Current Pos:* RETIRED. *Personal Data:* b Hershey, Pa, June 23, 28; m 51, Helen MacFarland; c George T, Jeffrey W & Jennifer A (Haughton). *Educ:* Lebanon Valley Col, BS, 50; Univ Del, MS, 51, PhD(org chem), 53. *Prof Exp:* Asst chem, Univ Del, 50-51, Armstrong res fel, 51-53; res chemist org chem, E I du Pont de Nemours & Co, 53-58, from res supvr to sr res supvr, 58-65, tech supt, 65-67, process supt dacron, 67-69, indust prod supt, 69-72, asst to mfg dir, Dacron Div, Textile Fibers Dept, 72-79, mgr, specialty prod div, F&F Dept, 79-83, mgr, electronic prods, P&EP Dept, 83-85. *Mem:* AAAS; Am Chem Soc; Sigma Xi. *Res:* Organic research in linear high polymers; synthetic fibers; spun-bonded nonwoven fabrics. *Mailing Add:* 707 Severn Rd Wilmington DE 19803

BARTELS, PAUL GEORGE, PLANT PHYSIOLOGY. *Current Pos:* from asst prof to prof, 66-85, assoc biologist, Exp Sta, 70-78, PROF PLANT SCI, UNIV ARIZ, 78- *Personal Data:* b Yuma, Colo, Apr 9, 34; m 56; c 2. *Educ:* Vanderbilt Univ, PhD(biol), 64. *Prof Exp:* NIH fel, 64-65. *Concurrent Pos:* NSF grant, 67-69. *Mem:* Am Soc Plant Physiol. *Res:* Plant cell physiology; inhibition of chloroplast development by herbicides. *Mailing Add:* 2365 E Agaphanthus St Tucson AZ 85737

BARTELS, PETER H, OPTICS, COMPUTER SCIENCE. *Current Pos:* assoc prof, 66-70, comt comput sci, 70-76, PROF MICROBIOL & MED TECHNOL, UNIV ARIZ, 70-, OPTICAL SCI CTR, 70- *Personal Data:* b Danzig, Ger, Jan 25, 29; US citizen; m 54; c 3. *Educ:* Univ Gottingen, PhD(biophys), 54; Univ Giessen, Dr Habil, 58. *Prof Exp:* Asst prof, Univ Giessen, 54-58; dir res, E Leitz, Optical Co, Inc, 58-66. *Concurrent Pos:* Assoc prof obstet & gynec, Univ Chicago, 67-69, prof, 69- *Mem:* Hon fel Inst Acad Cytol. *Res:* Image processing; pattern recognition; objectivation of diagnostic procedures through self learning computer programs; machine recognition of tumor cells. *Mailing Add:* Dept Path Univ Ariz Col Med 1501 N Campbell Ave Tucson AZ 85724-0001

BARTELS, RICHARD ALFRED, SOLID STATE PHYSICS, ATMOSPHERIC PHYSICS. *Current Pos:* from asst prof to assoc prof, 66-75, PROF PHYSICS, TRINITY UNIV, TEX, 75- *Personal Data:* b Saginaw, Mich, May 10, 38; m 59, Shirley Wolfgang; c Steven E, Keith A & Janet L. *Educ:* Case Inst Technol, BS, 60, MS, 63, PhD(physics), 65. *Honors & Awards:* Distinguished Serv Award, Am Asn Physics Teachers, 87. *Prof Exp:* Sloan fel, Princeton Univ, 64-66. *Mem:* Am Asn Physics Teachers; Nat Sci Teachers Asn. *Res:* Effects of high pressures on the physical properties of solids; elastic and dielectric constants of solids; radiation and the atmosphere; physics pedagogy. *Mailing Add:* Dept Physics Trinity Univ 715 Stadium Dr San Antonio TX 78212. *Fax:* 210-736-8264

BARTELS, RICHARD HAROLD, COMPUTER SCIENCE. *Current Pos:* assoc prof, 80-85, PROF COMPUT SCI, UNIV WATERLOO, 85- *Personal Data:* b Ann Arbor, Mich, Jan 10, 39; m 68. *Educ:* Univ Mich, BS, 61, MS, 63; Stanford Univ, PhD, 68. *Prof Exp:* Asst prof comput sci, Univ Tex, Austin, 68-74; asst prof math sci, Johns Hopkins Univ, 74-77, assoc prof, 77-80. *Mem:* Soc Indust & Appl Math; Asn Comput Mat; Spec Interest Group Numerical Math; Spec Interest Group Comput Graphics & Interactive Tech. *Res:* Numerical data fitting; splines in computer graphics. *Mailing Add:* Dept Comput Sci Univ Waterloo Waterloo ON N2L 3G1 Can

BARTELS, ROBERT CHRISTIAN FRANK, MATHEMATICS. *Current Pos:* from asst prof to prof, 45-76, dir, Comput Ctr, 59-76, EMER PROF MATH, UNIV MICH, ANN ARBOR, 76- *Personal Data:* b New York, NY, Oct 24, 11; m 38; c 1. *Educ:* Univ Wis, PhB, 33, PhM, 36, PhD(math), 38. *Prof Exp:* Asst math, Univ Wis, 33-36, 37-38; instr, Univ Mich, 38-42; aeronaut engr, Bur Aeronaut, USN, 42-45. *Concurrent Pos:* Res partic, Oak Ridge Inst Nuclear Studies, 54; mem, Comput Res Study Sect, NIH, 62- *Mem:* AAAS; Soc Indust & Appl Math; Asn Comput Mach; Am Math Soc; Math Asn Am; Sigma Xi. *Res:* Mathematical theory of elasticity; hydrodynamics; dynamics of compressible fluid; applied mathematics; Saint-Venant's flexure problem for the regular polygon; numerical analysis; magneto hydrodynamics. *Mailing Add:* 1214 Red Oak Rd Ann Arbor MI 48103-3062

BARTELT, JOHN ERIC, ELECTRON-POSITRON COLLISIONS, UNDERGROUND DETECTORS. *Current Pos:* ASST PROF PHYSICS, VANDERBILT UNIV, 90- *Personal Data:* b Milwaukee, Wis, Aug 11, 55; m 89, Lucy Huntzinger. *Educ:* Univ Wis, BS, 77; Univ Minn, PhD(physics), 84. *Prof Exp:* Teaching assoc astron, Univ Minn, 77-79, res asst, 79-83; res assoc, Stanford Linear Accelerator Ctr, Stanford Univ, 83-89. *Mem:* Am Phys Soc. *Res:* High energy physics research using electron-positron colliding beams; detector construction and data analysis; charm meson spectroscopy; asymmetric B-Factory research and development. *Mailing Add:* Dept Physics & Astron Vanderbilt Univ PO Box 1807 Sta B Nashville TN 37235. *E-Mail:* bartlet@phyv02.phy.vanderbilt.edu

BARTELT, MARTIN WILLIAM, NUMERICAL ANALYSIS, APPROXIMATION THEORY. *Current Pos:* PROF MATH, CHRISTOPHER NEWPORT COL, NEWPORT NEWS, VA, 75- *Personal Data:* b Brooklyn, NY, Apr 4, 41; m 65, Gay Penfield; c Margaret Helen & Andrew William. *Educ:* Hofstra Univ, BA, 63; Univ Wis, MA, 65, PhD(math), 69. *Prof Exp:* Asst prof math, Rensselaer Polytech Inst, 69-75. *Concurrent Pos:* Vis asst prof, Univ RI, 73-74. *Mem:* Am Math Soc. *Res:* Approximation theory; strong unicity; Lipschitz conditions. *Mailing Add:* 465 Winterhaven Dr Newport News VA 23606

BARTER, JAMES T, psychiatry, for more information see previous edition

BARTFELD, HARRY, IMMUNOLOGY, CELL BIOLOGY. *Current Pos:* HEAD IMMUNOL, CONNECTIVE TISSUE SECT, ST VINCENTS HOSP & MED CTR, 64- *Personal Data:* b New York, NY, May 8, 13. *Educ:* NY Univ, AB, 36; NY Med Col, MD, 44. *Prof Exp:* Trainee tissue cult, Crocker Inst Cancer Res, Columbia Univ, 38-39; res asst animal oncol, Cancer Study Group, Post-grad Med Sch, 40, asst prof clin med, 50-56, assoc prof clin med, Med Ctr, NY Univ, 57- *Concurrent Pos:* Fel med, Med Ctr, NY Univ, 48-49; dir lab connective tissue dis, Sch Med, NY Univ, 57-64; co-chmn conf rheumatoid factors & their biol significance, NY Acad Sci, 69; mem adv comt fundamental res related to multiple sclerosis, Nat Multiple Sclerosis Soc, 69-72; mem conf orgn comt, NY Acad Sci; dir, Anyotrophic Lateral Sclerosis Res Ctr, St Vincent's Hosp & Med Ctr, 74- *Mem:* Am Soc Cell Biol; Soc Exp Biol & Med; Am Fedn Clin. *Res:* Am Asn Immunologists. Res: Cell biology studies of immunopathological phenomena associated with experimental and natural autoimmune disease. *Mailing Add:* St Vincent's Hosp & Med Ctr 153 W 11th St New York NY 10011-8397

BARTH, CHARLES ADOLPH, PHYSICS. *Current Pos:* assoc prof, 65-67, PROF ASTRO-GEOPHYS, UNIV COLO, BOULDER, 67-, DIR LAB ATMOSPHERIC & SPACE PHYSICS, 65- *Personal Data:* b Philadelphia, Pa, July 12, 30; m 54; c 4. *Educ:* Lehigh Univ, BS, 51; Univ Calif, Los Angeles, MA, 55, PhD(physics), 58. *Prof Exp:* Res geophysicist, Inst Geophys, Univ Calif, Los Angeles, 57-58; res physicist, Jet Propulsion Lab, Calif Inst Technol, 58-65. *Concurrent Pos:* NSF fel, Bonn, Ger, 58-59. *Mem:* AAAS; Am Astron Soc; Am Geophys Union. *Res:* Aeronomy; planetary atmospheres. *Mailing Add:* 370 Hopi Pl Boulder CO 80303

BARTH, DELBERT SYLVESTER, ENVIRONMENTAL STUDIES. *Current Pos:* vis prof biophysics, Univ Nev, Las Vegas, 78-82, sr scientist, Environ Res Ctr, 82-88, dir, 89-92, PROF, ENVIRON STUDIES PROG, UNIV NEV, LAS VEGAS, 92- *Personal Data:* b Lawrenceburg, Ind, June 25. *Educ:* US Mil Acad, BS, 46; Ohio State Univ, MS, 52; Stevens Inst Technol, MS, 60, PhD(biophysics), 62. *Prof Exp:* Asst prof, Dept Physics & Chem, US Mil Acad, Wes Point, 56-60; staff officer, Eval & Planning Sect, Res Br Div Radiol Health, US Pub Health Serv, Dept Health Educ & Welfare, 60-61; investr & staff officer, Exp Radiobiol Prog Res Br, DRH, 62-63; dir, Bioenviron Res Prog Southwestern Radiol Health Lab, US Pub Health Serv, 63-69, Bur Criteria & Stands, Nat Am Pollution Sci, Res Triangle Pk, NC, 71, Nat Environ Res Ctr, 71-72 & Las Vegas, 72-76; dep asst adminstr health & ecol effects, ORD US Environ Protection Agency, 76-78. *Concurrent Pos:* Mem, Environ Comt Ecol Sci Div, Inst Environ Sci; mem, Army Sci Bd, 84-90. *Mem:* AAAS; Sigma Xi. *Res:* Environmental studies; physics; biophysics; chemistry; radiology. *Mailing Add:* 1577 Deer Meadow Dr Henderson NV 89012-2413

BARTH, HOWARD GORDON, ANALYTICAL CHEMISTRY. *Current Pos:* staff mem, 88-96, SR RES ASSOC, DUPONT CENT RES & DEVELOP, 96- *Personal Data:* b Boston, Mass, Nov 21, 46; m 72, Nedda; c Alens, Samara & Abram. *Educ:* Northeastern Univ, BA, 69, PhD(anal chem), 73. *Prof Exp:* Res assoc clin chem, Hahnemann Med Col & Hosp, 73-74; res chemist, Hercules Res Ctr, 74-79, sr res chemist, 79-86, res scientist, 86-88, group leader, 83-88; asst prof chem, Northeastern Univ, 81. *Concurrent Pos:* Ed, Del-Chem Bull, 78-80; assoc ed, J Appl Polymer Sci, 85-88; Instrumental Adv Panel, Anal Chem, 86-88; chmn & cofounder, Int Symp Polymer Anal & Characterization, 87-; chmn, Del Sect, Am Chem Soc, 88; ed-in-chief, Int J Polymer Anal & Characterization, 95- *Mem:* Am Chem Soc; Soc Plastics Eng; Am Inst Chemists. *Res:* Polymer characterization; solution properties of polymers; separation science; high performance liquid chromatography. *Mailing Add:* Du Pont Co Exp Sta PO Box 80228 Wilmington DE 19880-0228

BARTH, KARL FREDERICK, MATHEMATICAL ANALYSIS. *Current Pos:* from asst prof to assoc prof, 66-77, PROF MATH, SYRACUSE UNIV, 77- *Personal Data:* b Houston, Tex, Sept 25, 38; m 82, Lois Black; c Justine & Clea. *Educ:* Rice Univ, BA, 60, MA, 62, PhD(math), 64. *Prof Exp:* Res mathematician, Ballistic Res Labs, 64-66. *Concurrent Pos:* Sr vis fel, Brit Sci Res Coun, 75-76 & 87. *Mem:* Am Math Soc; Math Asn Am; London Math Soc. *Res:* Functions of a complex variable; potential theory. *Mailing Add:* Dept Math Syracuse Univ Syracuse NY 13244-1150

BARTH, KARL M, ANIMAL NUTRITION. *Current Pos:* from asst prof to assoc prof, 65-79, PROF ANIMAL NUTRIT, UNIV TENN, KNOXVILLE, 79- *Personal Data:* b Elizabeth, NJ, Dec 19, 27. *Educ:* Del Valley Col, BS, 56; Rutgers Univ, MS, 58, PhD(nutrit), 64; WVa Univ, MS, 62. *Prof Exp:* Instr, Del Valley Col, 62; res assoc, Purdue Univ, 64-65. *Mem:* Am Inst Nutrit; Am Soc Animal Sci. *Res:* Forage evaluation; non-protein nitrogen utilization. *Mailing Add:* 4206 Taliluna Ave Knoxville TN 37919

BARTH, ROBERT HOOD, JR, BEHAVIOR-ETHOLOGY. *Current Pos:* asst prof, 65-70, ASSOC PROF ZOOL, UNIV TEX, AUSTIN, 70-, DIR FAC & STAFF, 73- *Personal Data:* b Midland, Mich, Feb 10, 34; div. *Educ:* Princeton Univ, AB, 56; Harvard Univ, AM, 59, PhD(biol), 62. *Prof Exp:* Instr biol, Harvard Univ, 61-63, lectr, 63-64; NSF fel zool, Univ Sheffield, 64-65. *Concurrent Pos:* NSF res grants develop & regulative biol, 61-64, 66-80. *Mem:* Am Ornithologists Union; Animal Behav Soc. *Res:* Avain behavioral ecology; mating systems; reproductive biology; neotropical ornithology; conservation biology. *Mailing Add:* Dept Zool Univ Tex Austin TX 78712-1064. *Fax:* 512-471-9651; *E-Mail:* 6.barth@mail.vtexas.edu

BARTH, ROLF FREDERICK, PATHOLOGY, IMMUNOLOGY. *Current Pos:* PROF PATH, COL MED, OHIO STATE UNIV, 79- *Personal Data:* b New York, NY, Apr 4, 37; m 65, Christine Ferguson; c Suzanna, Alison, Rolf & Christopher. *Educ:* Cornell Univ, AB, 59; Columbia Univ, MD, 64; Am Bd Path, dipl, 70. *Prof Exp:* Intern surg, Columbia-Presby Hosp, NY, 64-65; fel tumor immunol, Dept Tumor Biol, Karolinska Inst, Sweden, 65-66; res assoc immunol, Nat Inst Allergy & Infectious Dis, NIH, 66-68, resident path, Path Br, Nat Cancer Inst, 68-70; from asst prof to prof, Med Ctr, Univ Kans, Kansas City, 70-77; clin prof, Sch Med, Univ Wis-Madison & Med Col Wis, Milwaukee, 77-79, clin prof path, Univ Wis Col Med, 78-79. *Concurrent Pos:* grantee, Nat Cancer Inst, Dept Energy. *Mem:* Am Asn Immunologists; Am Asn Exp Path; Am Asn Cancer Res; Soc Exp Biol Med; Asn Univ Path; Am Asn Univ Profs. *Res:* Innovative approaches to the treatment of brain tumors including boron neutron capture therapy and gene therapy. *Mailing Add:* Dept Path 165 Hamilton Hall Ohio State Univ 1645 Neil Ave Columbus OH 43210-1239. *Fax:* 614-292-7072; *E-Mail:* rbarth.1@osu.edu

BARTHA, RICHARD, AGRICULTURAL ECOLOGY, MICROBIAL ECOLOGY. *Current Pos:* res assoc, 64-66, from asst prof to assoc prof, 66-73, PROF MICROBIOL, RUTGERS UNIV, 73- *Personal Data:* b Budapest, Hungary, Nov 14, 34; US citizen; m 67, Susi Fels; c Miriam & Doris. *Educ:* Eotvos Lorand Univ, Budapest, 52-56; Univ Gottingen, PhD(microbiol), 61. *Prof Exp:* USPHS fel microbiol, Univ Wash, 62-64. *Mem:* Am Soc Microbiol; fel AAAS; fel, Am Acad Microbiol, 95. *Res:* Chemoautotrophic bacteria; microbial degradation of pesticides and oil pollutants; microbial ecology. *Mailing Add:* Dept Biochem & Microbiol Rutgers Univ New Brunswick NJ 08903

BARTHAKUR, NAYANA N, AGRICULTURAL PHYSICS & METEOROLOGY, BIOMETEOROLOGY. *Current Pos:* From asst prof to assoc prof, 66-69, PROF AGR PHYSICS, MACDONALD CAMPUS, MCGILL UNIV, 90- *Personal Data:* b Assam, India, Mar 2, 36; c 2, Dolly Thakur; c Bonnie & Ankur. *Educ:* Cotton Col, India, BSc, 56; Univ Allahabad, MSc, 59; Univ Sask, PhD(atmospheric physics), 65. *Prof Exp:* Demonstr chem, Assam Med Col, India, 56-57; lectr physics, St Anthony's Col, 59-61. *Mem:* Int Soc Biometeorol (secy); Am Inst Biomed Climat; Can Soc Agr Meteorol. *Res:* Agricultural meteorology; plant-water relations using nuclear techniques; electrohydrodynamics; chemical analyses of tropical fruits; ultra-violet B radiation effects on biologial organisms. *Mailing Add:* Dept Natural Resources Sci Macdonald Campus-McGill Univ Ste Anne de Bellevue PQ H9X 3V9 Can. *Fax:* 514-398-7990; *E-Mail:* 28@musica.mcgill.ca

BARTHEL, HAROLD O(SCAR), AERONAUTICAL ENGINEERING. *Current Pos:* RETIRED. *Personal Data:* b Milledgeville, Ill, Sept 17, 25; m 62; c 2. *Educ:* Univ Ill, BS, 50, MS, 51, PhD(mech eng), 57. *Prof Exp:* Res assoc, Univ Ill, Urbana-Champaign, 54-57, res asst prof, 57-61, assoc prof aeronaut & astron eng, 61-91. *Mem:* Sigma Xi; Am Phys Soc. *Res:* Unsteady gas dynamics of weak and strong shock waves; shock tube flows; second shock initiation in spherical shock tubes. *Mailing Add:* 2108 Burlison Dr Urbana IL 61801

BARTHEL, ROMARD, ULTRASOUND. *Current Pos:* From instr to assoc prof physics, 47-57, chmn div physics & natural sci, 54-68, PROF PHYSICS, ST EDWARD'S UNIV, 57- *Personal Data:* b Evansville, Ind, Apr 8, 24. *Educ:* Univ Notre Dame, BS, 47; Univ Tex, PhD(physics), 51. *Mem:* Am Asn Physics Teachers; Sigma Xi. *Res:* Ultrasonic interferometers; theory of solutions; philosophy of science; atomic and nuclear physics and electronics. *Mailing Add:* St Edward's Univ Austin TX 78704

BARTHEL, WILLIAM FREDERICK, AGRICULTURAL CHEMISTRY. *Current Pos:* RETIRED. *Personal Data:* b Arbutus, Md, Mar 12, 15; m 38; c 1. *Honors & Awards:* Serv Awards, USDA, 58 & 60. *Prof Exp:* Chemist, USDA, 40-45; chief chemist insecticide div, Victor Prods Corp, 46-48; chief chemist & vpres, Edco Corp, 48; chief chemist in-chg develop insecticide div, Innis Speiden & Co, 49-50; owner, W F Barthel Chem Co, 50-51; chemist pesticide chem res lab, USDA, 51-57, chemist-in-chg chem lab, Plant Pest Control, 58-62 & Methods Improv Labs, 62-67, supvry chemist, Pesticides Lab, Nat Commun Dis Ctr, 67-68, chief toxicol lab, 68; supvry res chemist, Pesticides Div, Atlanta Toxicol Br, US Food & Drug Admin, 68-71; toxicologist, Ctr Dis Control, 71-74. *Mem:* AAAS; Am Chem Soc; Entom Soc Am; Asn Official Agr Chem; Am Inst Chem. *Res:* Organic insecticides; structural studies of pyrethrins; cinerins; Barthel rearrangement; Barthrin and related insecticides of low mammalian toxicity. *Mailing Add:* 1189 Abbe Hills Rd Mt Vernon IA 52314-9802

BARTHOLD, LIONEL O, ELECTRICAL ENGINEERING. *Current Pos:* vchmn, 69-86, CHMN, POWER TECHNOLS INC, 86- *Personal Data:* b Great Barrington, Mass, Mar 20, 26; m; c 2. *Educ:* Northwestern Univ, BA, 50. *Honors & Awards:* Power Life Award, Power Eng Soc & Inst Elec & Electronics Engrs, 89; Philips Spore Award, CIGRE, 91. *Prof Exp:* Mgr eng, Gen Elec Co, 64-69. *Mem:* Nat Acad Eng; fel Inst Elec & Electronics Engrs. *Mailing Add:* Power Technols Inc 1482 Erie Blvd Schenectady NY 12305

BARTHOLD, STEPHEN WILLIAM, VETERINARY PATHOLOGY. *Current Pos:* from asst prof to assoc prof, 74-89, PROF COMP MED, SCH MED, YALE UNIV, 89- *Personal Data:* b San Francisco, Calif, Nov 10, 45; m 71; c 1. *Educ:* Univ Calif, Davis, BS, 67, DVM, 69; Univ Wis-Madison, MS, 73, PhD(vet sci), 74. *Prof Exp:* Chief animal care, US Army Res Inst Environ Med, 69-71; res asst vet path, Univ Wis-Madison, 71-74. *Mem:* Am Vet Med Asn; Am Col Vet Path; Am Asn Lab Animal Sci. *Res:* Comparative pathology; laboratory animal pathology; infectious disease; lyme disease. *Mailing Add:* Sect Comp Med Sch Med Yale Univ 333 Cedar St PO Box 208016 New Haven CT 06520-8016

BARTHOLMEY, SANDRA JEAN, NUTRITION RESEARCH & INFANT NUTRITION, DIETARY SURVEY. *Current Pos:* MGR NUTRIT, RES DIV, GERBER PRODS CO, 86- *Personal Data:* b Chicago, Ill, Mar 22, 42; c 2. *Educ:* Univ Ill, Urbana, BS, 62, PhD(food & nutrit), 86; Sangamon State Univ, MA, 76. *Mem:* Am Inst Nutrit; Sigma Xi; Inst Food Technologists. *Res:* Iron bioavailability from cereals; dietary patterns of infants to 18 months of age-toddlers. *Mailing Add:* Nutrit Sci Res Ctr Gerber Prods Co Fremont MI 49413-0001

BARTHOLOMEW, CALVIN HENRY, CATALYSIS, AIR POLLUTION CONTROL. *Current Pos:* from asst prof to assoc prof, 73-82, PROF CHEM ENG, BRIGHAM YOUNG UNIV, 82- *Personal Data:* b Mt Pleasant, Utah, Mar 7, 43; m 65; c 5. *Educ:* Brigham Young Univ, BES, 68; Stanford Univ, MS, 70, PhD(chem eng), 72. *Honors & Awards:* Utah Award, Am Chem Soc, 91. *Prof Exp:* Sr chem eng automotive emissions control, Corning Glass Works, 72-73. *Concurrent Pos:* Pvt consult, Bartholomew Consult Serv, Inc, 73-; founder & head, Catalysis Lab, Brigham Young Univ, 73-; assoc dir, Adv Combustion Eng Res Ctr, 86-; ed, Proc Fifth Int Catalysis Deactivation Meeting, 90-91. *Mem:* Am Chem Soc; Sigma Xi. *Res:* Research in catalysis, combustion and thermodynamics; investigator or co-investigator on over 40 grants and contracts; supervised more than 60 research students; author or co-author of over 175 technical publications, reports and proceedings of meetings. *Mailing Add:* 440 N 600 E Orem UT 84057-4206

BARTHOLOMEW, DUANE P, AGRONOMY, CROP & WHOLE-PLANT PHYSIOLOGY. *Current Pos:* from asst agronomist to assoc agronomist, 66-83, AGRONOMIST, UNIV HAWAII, 83-, DEPT CHMN, 94- *Personal Data:* b Fargo, NDak, Sept 25, 34; m 56; c 3. *Educ:* Calif State Polytech Col, BS, 61; Iowa State Univ, PhD(plant physiol), 65. *Prof Exp:* Assoc plant physiologist, Pineapple Res Inst, 65-66. *Mem:* Am Soc Hort Sci; Crop Sci Soc Am; Am Soc Agron. *Res:* Physiology of the pineapple; plant-water relations; plant-environment relations; computer modeling of development. *Mailing Add:* Dept Agron & Soil Sci Univ Hawaii Manoa 1910 East-West Rd Honolulu HI 96822. *Fax:* 808-956-6539; *E-Mail:* duaneb@hawaii.edu

BARTHOLOMEW, GEORGE ADELBERT, ZOOLOGY, ECOLOGICAL PHYSIOLOGY. *Current Pos:* from instr to prof, 47-87, EMER PROF ZOOL, UNIV CALIF, LOS ANGELES, 87- *Personal Data:* b Independence, Mo, June 1, 19; m 42; c 2. *Educ:* Univ Calif, AB, 40, MA, 41; Harvard Univ, PhD(zool), 47. *Hon Degrees:* DSc, Univ Chicago, 88. *Prof Exp:* Asst, Mus Vert Zool, Univ Calif, 40-41; asst zool & comp anat, Harvard Univ, 45-47. *Mem:* Nat Acad Sci; Ecol Soc Am; Am Soc Mammal; Am Ornith Union; Cooper Ornith Soc; Am Soc Zool; Am Acad Arts & Sci. *Res:* Ecology and physiology of vertebrates and energetics of insects. *Mailing Add:* 663 Chicago Ave Stockton CA 95206

BARTHOLOMEW, GILBERT ALFRED, NUCLEAR PHYSICS, NEUTRON SOURCES. *Current Pos:* RETIRED. *Personal Data:* b Nelson, BC, Apr 8, 22; m 52. *Educ:* Univ BC, BA, 43; McGill Univ, PhD(physics), 48. *Prof Exp:* Res officer nuclear physics, Atomic Energy Can Ltd, 48-62, head neutron & solid state physics br, 62-71, dir physics div, 71-83. *Concurrent Pos:* Mem, Int Union Pure & Appl Physics Comn Nuclear Physics, 78-87, secy, 81-87; chmn, Int Adv Comt Tokamak de Varennes, Hydro Quebec, Varennes, Que, 82- *Mem:* Fel Am Phys Soc; Can Asn Physicists; Sigma Xi; fel Royal Soc Can; fel AAAS; Can Nuclear Soc. *Res:* Neutron capture gamma rays; low energy nuclear physics; nuclear structure; neutron sources; electronuclear breeding of fissile material. *Mailing Add:* PO Box 150 Lions Bay BC V0N 2E0 Can

BARTHOLOMEW, JAMES COLLINS, CELL BIOLOGY. *Current Pos:* SR STAFF CELL BIOLOGIST, LAWRENCE BERKELEY LAB, UNIV CALIF, 72- *Personal Data:* b Dec 18, 42; m 65; c 2. *Educ:* Hobart Col, BS, 65; Cornell Univ, PhD(biochem), 70. *Prof Exp:* Am Cancer Soc res fel, The Salk Inst, 70-72. *Concurrent Pos:* Dep dir, Lab Chem Biodynamics, 81- *Mem:* AAAS; Am Soc Cell Biol. *Res:* Regulation of growth of mammalian cells in cultures and the factors that affect this regulation such as serum, viruses and chemical carcinogens. *Mailing Add:* Lawrence Berkeley Nat Labs 1 Cyclotron Rd MS-Calvin Lab Berkeley CA 94720-0001

BARTHOLOMEW, LLOYD GIBSON, INTERNAL MEDICINE, GASTROENTEROLOGY. *Current Pos:* from instr to prof, 53-94, Mayo Med Sch, Univ Minn, Sr Consult Gastroenterol, Mayo Clin, 78-94, EMER PROF MED, MAYO MED SCH, UNIV MINN, 94- *Personal Data:* b Whitehall, NY, Sept 15, 21; m 43, Elisabeth Thrall; c Suzanne, Lynne, Lloyd Jr, Deborah & Douglass. *Educ:* Union Col, BA, 41; Univ Vt, MD, 44; Univ Minn, MS, 52. *Hon Degrees:* LHD, Green Mountain Col, Vt, 84. *Honors & Awards:* Woodbury & Carbee Prizes, 44; Distinguished Serv Award, Green Mountain Col, 95. *Prof Exp:* Asst, Div Med, Mayo Clin, 49-50, 52, staff, 52-53. *Concurrent Pos:* Attend physician, St Mary's Methodist & assoc hosps, 53-; head dept gastroenterol, Mayo Clinic, 67-77; deleg, Minn Med Asn, AMA, 78-93. *Mem:* AMA; Am Gastroenterol Asn; Am Bd Internal Med; Sigma Xi; Soc Med Consults Armed Forces. *Res:* Pancreatic and liver diseases. *Mailing Add:* Mayo Clin 200 First St SW Rochester MN 55905

BARTHOLOMEW, MERVIN JEROME, TECTONICS. *Current Pos:* PROF GEOL, EARTH SCI & RESOURCE INST, UNIV SC, 92- *Personal Data:* b Altoona, Pa, Nov 22, 42. *Educ:* Va Polytech State Univ, PhD(geol), 71. *Prof Exp:* chief geol, Mont Bur Mines & Geol, 83-92; prof geol, Mont Tech, 83-92. *Mem:* Fel Geol Soc Am. *Mailing Add:* 774 W Five Notch Rd North Augusta SC 29841

BARTHOLOMEW, ROGER FRANK, PHYSICAL CHEMISTRY. *Current Pos:* from res chemist to sr res chemist, 64-73, RES ASSOC CHEM, TECH STAFFS DIV, CORNING GLASS WORKS, 73- *Personal Data:* b Workington, Eng, May 21, 37; m 61; c 3. *Educ:* Univ London, BSc, 58, PhD(phys chem), 61. *Honors & Awards:* Eugene C Sullivan Award, Am Chem Soc, 81. *Prof Exp:* Res fel, Nat Res Coun Can, 61-63. *Concurrent Pos:* Chmn, Coun Comt Technician Activ, Am Chem Soc, 84-86. *Mem:* Am Chem Soc; fel Am Ceramic Soc; Royal Soc Chem. *Res:* Ion-exchange and diffusion studies in glasses and naturally occurring aluminosilicates; flow of gases through microporous activated carbon plugs; physical chemistry of molten salts in particular molten nitrates; low temperature glass forming systems; high energy battery systems; sodium-sulphur cells; application and development of ceramic materials for electronic devices; fluoride glasses for optical waveguides; erbium optical amplifiers. *Mailing Add:* 8 Overbrook Rd Painted Post NY 14870-1398. *Fax:* 607-974-3675

BARTHOLOW, GEORGE WILLIAM, PSYCHIATRY. *Current Pos:* assoc clin dir adult inpatient serv, Nebr Psychiat Inst, 61-74, from asst prof to assoc prof, 61-74, PROF PSYCHIAT, COL MED, UNIV NEBR, OMAHA, 74-,. *Personal Data:* b Yale, Iowa, July 28, 30; c 3. *Educ:* Univ Iowa, BS, 51, MD, 55. *Prof Exp:* Intern, Wayne County Gen Hosp, Eloise, Mich, 55-56; resident psychiat, Univ Iowa, 56-59. *Concurrent Pos:* Chief psychiat serv, Vet Admin Hosp, Omaha, 62-; consult, 66-; prof psychiat, Creighton Univ Col Med, 78. *Mem:* Am Psychiat Asn. *Res:* Vocational rehabilitation of the mentally ill; suicidology; adult inpatient psychiatry. *Mailing Add:* Norfolk Regional Ctr Box 1209 Norfolk NE 68702-1209

BARTHOLOW, LESTER C, NUTRITIONAL BIOCHEMISTRY. *Current Pos:* EXEC VPRES & VPRES RES & DEVELOP, KABI PHARMACIA INC, 83- *Personal Data:* b San Diego, Calif, Sept 29, 36. *Educ:* Stanford Univ, BS, 63; Bemidji State Univ, MA, 73; Mass Inst Technol, MS, 74; Harvard Univ, DSc(nutrit biochem), 81. *Prof Exp:* Mem staff, Int Bus Mach Corp, 66-69, Xerox Data Systs, 69-70, Youngstown State Univ, 74-77 & Kellogg Co, 81-83. *Mem:* Am Inst Nutrit; Am Soc Oil Chemists. *Res:* Lipid biochemistry; parenteral and enteral nutrition; parenteral product development; physical chemistry; drug delivery. *Mailing Add:* Kabi Inc Hwy 70 E PO Box 597 Clayton NC 27520-0597

BARTILUCCI, ANDREW J, PHARMACY. *Current Pos:* asst dean, Col Pharm, St Johns Univ, NY, 52-56, dean, Col Pharm & Allied Health Professions, 56-88, vpres health professions, 80-91, actg dean, Col Lib Arts & Sci, 89-91, PROF PHARM, ST JOHNS UNIV, NY, 52-, EXEC VPRES, 91- *Personal Data:* b New York, NY, Nov 29, 22; m 50, Lucy A Fulvio; c Mary A (Matterni), Phyllis E & Eugenie M. *Educ:* St John's Univ, NY, BS, 44; Rutgers Univ, MS, 49; Univ Md, PhD(pharm), 53. *Hon Degrees:* DSc, Union Univ, 90. *Honors & Awards:* Distinguished Serv Profile Award, Am Found Pharmaceut Educ. *Prof Exp:* Anal chemist, US Armed Serv Med Procurement Off, 47-48; assoc res pharmacist, Merck & Co, 49-50. *Concurrent Pos:* Mem, NY State Bd Pharm, 81- *Mem:* AAAS; Am Col Apothecaries; Am Pharmaceut Asn; fel NY Acad Sci; Sigma Xi. *Res:* Pharmaceutical formulation and analysis. *Mailing Add:* Exec vpres St Johns Univ Jamaica NY 11439

BARTIMES, GEORGE F, plastics recycling, electromechanical systems; deceased, see previous edition for last biography

BARTIS, JAMES THOMAS, ENERGY POLICY, RESEARCH PLANNING. *Current Pos:* CONSULT, 97- *Personal Data:* b Pawtucket, RI, Oct 22, 45; m 84; c 2. *Educ:* Brown Univ, ScB, 67; Mass Inst Technol, PhD(chem physics), 72. *Prof Exp:* Asst prof chem, Cornell Univ, 74-75; mem, Inst Defense Anal, 75-78; res chemist, Off Energy Res, US Dept Energy, 78-79, dir, Off Planning & Technol Assessment, 79-81, dir fossil energy policy, 81-82; dir & vpres, EOS Technol Inc, 82-92; pres, Fossil Energy Technol Div, Sci Applns Int Corp, 92-97. *Concurrent Pos:* Vis scientist, Weizmann Inst, 72; fel, NATO, 72 & Cornell Univ, 72-74. *Mem:* Am Phys Soc; Am Chem Soc; AAAS. *Res:* Transport properties of fluids, theory of chemical reactions and properties of multicomponent solutions; defense systems evaluation and analysis; energy research and technology policy; coal, oil, gas and synthetic fuel policy; assessment of advanced coal technologies. *Mailing Add:* 6960 Kyleakin Ct McLean VA 22101

BARTISH, CHARLES MICHAEL, INORGANIC CHEMISTRY, CATALYSIS. *Current Pos:* Res chemist, Corp Res Dept, Air Prod & Chem Inc, 73-76, group leader,76-77, sect mgr carbon monoxide chem, 77-79, sect mgr amines res, 79-81, tech mgr, Indust Chem Div, 81-85, mgr res, Polyurethane Chem Technol, 85-93, MGR PROD STEWARDSHIP & REGULATORY AFFAIRS, AIR PROD & CHEM INC, 93- *Personal Data:* b Easton, Pa, June 4, 47; m 69; c 2. *Educ:* Villanova Univ, BS, 69; Lehigh Univ, PhD(chem), 73. *Mem:* Am Chem Soc; Sigma Xi; Catalysis Soc; Soc Plastics Indust. *Res:* Carbon monoxide chemistry; homogeneous and heterogeneous catalysis; organometallic chemistry; industrial chemistry; process development; research management; polyurethanes. *Mailing Add:* Air Prod & Chem Inc 7201 Hamitton Blvd Allentown PA 18195-1501

BARTKE, ANDRZEJ, REPRODUCTIVE PHYSIOLOGY, ENDOCRINOLOGY. *Current Pos:* PROF & CHMN DEPT PHYSIOL, SCH MED, SOUTHERN ILL UNIV, CARBONDALE, 84- *Personal Data:* b Krakow, Poland, May 23, 39; m 66. *Educ:* Jagiellonian Univ, MSc, 62; Univ Kans, PhD(zool), 65. *Prof Exp:* Vis scientist, Inst Cancer Res, Philadelphia, 65; asst prof dept animal genetics, Jagiellonian Univ, 65-67; fel, 67-69, staff scientist, 69-72, sr scientist, Worcester Found Exp Biol, 72-78; from assoc prof to prof obstet & gynec, Univ Tex Health Sci Ctr, San Antonio, 78-84. *Concurrent Pos:* Res career develop award, NIH, 72-77. *Mem:* AAAS; Soc Study Reproduction; Endocrine Soc; Brit Soc Endocrinol; Am Soc Andrology; Soc Study Fertility; Int Soc Neuroendocrinol. *Res:* Pituitary control of testicular steroidogenesis; role of prolactin in the male; effects of cannabinoids in the male; transgenic animals; seasonal breeding. *Mailing Add:* Dept Physiol Sch Med Southern Ill Univ Carbondale IL 62901-6512

BARTKO, JOHN JAROSLAV, MATHEMATICAL STATISTICS. *Current Pos:* RES MATH STATISTICIAN, NIMH, 62-, INSTR, FOUND ADVAN EDUC IN SCI, INC, NIH GRAD SCH, 63-, CHMN, DEPT STATIST, 65- *Personal Data:* b Massillon, Ohio, Nov 17, 37. *Educ:* Univ Fla, BA, 59; Va Polytech Inst, MS, 61, PhD(math statist), 62. *Concurrent Pos:* Consult int pilot study schizophrenia, WHO, Geneva, Switz, 69- *Mem:* Fel Am Statist Asn; Biomet Soc. *Res:* Statistical theory and methodology; application of statistics in the life and behavioral sciences; research in reliability. *Mailing Add:* 5712 Roosevelt St Bethesda MD 20817

BARTKOSKI, MICHAEL JOHN, JR, MANUFACTURING VETERINARY BIOLOGICALS. *Current Pos:* VPRES OPERS, BIOMINE CO, 91-; SCHERING-PLOUGH ANIMAL HEALTH, ELKHART, IN. *Personal Data:* b Kansas City, Kans, July 1, 45; m 68, Carolyn S Pearson; c Michele L & Michael J III. *Educ:* Kans State Univ, BS, 67; Univ Mo, Kansas City, MS, 72; Univ Okla, PhD(microbiol), 74. *Prof Exp:* Postdoctoral, Univ Chicago, 75-77; asst prof microbiol, Uniformed Serv Univ, 77-82; proj leader, Tech Am Group Inc, 82-83, dir res & develop, 83-85, vpres oper, 85-87; vpres biol, Fermenta Animal Health, 82-91. *Mem:* Am Soc Microbiol. *Res:* Regulation of nuclei acid synthesis; animal health product vaccine and diagnosis. *Mailing Add:* 11822 Woolworth Ave Omaha NE 68144. *Fax:* 913-894-0236

BARTKUS, EDWARD PETER, INFORMATION SCIENCE, CHEMICAL ENGINEERING. *Current Pos:* PRES/OWNER, EXEC INFO MGT, 82- *Personal Data:* b Thomas, WVa, Jan 29, 20; m 46, Margaret Ann Curry; c David. *Educ:* WVa Univ, BS, 41, MSChE, 46, MSChE, 47, PhD(chem eng), 50. *Prof Exp:* From instr to asst prof chem eng, WVa Univ, 47-51; eval engr chem processes, Eng Serv Div, E I du Pont de Nemours & Co Inc, 51-52, field res supvr pigment processes, 52-54, field sect mgr eng, 54-57, mgr eng comput & math applns, 57-61, mgr new eng prod, Eng Res Div, 61-66, spec asst mgr new info serv, Info Systs Div, Secy Dept, 66-74, mgr info resources, Info Systs Dept, 74-82. *Concurrent Pos:* Mem, Nat Res Coun, Numerical Data Adv Bd, 72-78 & Nat Comt for Codata, 78-83, Del State Tech Serv Adv Comt, 70-80, Nat Res Coun-Nat Acad Sci-Nat Acad Eng Comt Energy Data, 80-82; consult, publ comt, Am Soc Testing & Mat, 71-89; exec info systs consult, 82- *Mem:* Am Chem Soc; fel Am Inst Chem Engrs; Am Soc Eng Educ; Nat Soc Prof Engrs; Sigma Xi. *Res:* Engineering economics; systems engineering; operations research; information storage and retrieval, systems and processing; records management; futures issues research; office automation; competitor studies. *Mailing Add:* 4830 Kennett Pike Wilmington DE 19807-1843

BARTL, PAUL, BIOPHYSICS. *Current Pos:* CONSULT, 88- *Personal Data:* b Prague, Czech, Apr 8, 28; m 53; c 1. *Educ:* Prague Tech Univ, MA, 51; Czech Acad Sci, PhD(phys chem), 54. *Prof Exp:* Scientist, Inst Org Chem & Biochem, Prague, 54-64; vis scientist, Inst Cancer Res, Villejuif, France, 65; fel biophys, Johns Hopkins Univ, 66-67, vis assoc prof, 67-68; sr scientist, Hoffmann-La Roche, Inc, 68-71; asst dir sci affairs, Roche Inst Molecular Biol, 71-78; assoc dir, Athymic Mouse Res Ctr, Univ Calif, San Diego, 78-80, acad adminr dept chem, 80-82. *Concurrent Pos:* Vpres MeDiCa, Calif, 79-92, chmn bd, 93- *Res:* High resolution electron microscopy of nucleic acids; water-miscible embedding media for electron microscopy; physical chemistry of nucleic acids and their constituents; immunodiagnostics; research administration. *Mailing Add:* 3305 Piragua Carlsbad CA 92009-7842

BARTLE, ROBERT GARDNER, ANALYSIS & FUNCTIONAL ANALYSIS. *Current Pos:* from asst prof to prof, 55-90, EMER PROF MATH, UNIV ILL, URBANA-CHAMPAIGN, 90-; PROF MATH, EASTERN MICH UNIV, YPSILANTI, 90- *Personal Data:* b Kansas City, Mo, Nov 20, 27; m 51, 82, Carolyn Orban; c James & John. *Educ:* Swarthmore Col, BA, 47; Univ Chicago, SM, 48, PhD(math), 51. *Prof Exp:* AEC fel, Yale Univ, 51-52, instr math, 52-55. *Concurrent Pos:* Vis prof math, Ga Inst Technol, 75-76, 84; exec ed, Math Reviews, 76-78, 86-90. *Mem:* Am Math Soc; Math Asn Am; London Math Soc. *Res:* Functional analysis; real analysis; integration theory. *Mailing Add:* 3340 Alpine Dr Ann Arbor MI 48108-1704. *E-Mail:* mth_bartle@online.emich.edu

BARTLE, STEVEN JON, RUMINANT NUTRITION, BEEF CATTLE MANAGEMENT. *Current Pos:* MGR BEEF NUTRIT RES, MOORMANS INC, 94- *Personal Data:* b Fargo, NDak, May 1, 51; m 85, Roene Travis. *Educ:* NDak State Univ, BS, 73; Mont State Univ, MS, 75; Wash State Univ, PhD(animal sci), 82. *Prof Exp:* Assoc, Univ Nebr, 82-84; res scientist, Tex Tech Univ, 84-94. *Mem:* Am Soc Animal Sci; Am Inst Nutrit; Soc Range Mgt; AAAS. *Res:* Feedlot nutrition and management; cow/calf nutrition and management; mineral and protein supplementation. *Mailing Add:* MoorMans Inc 1000 N 30th Quincy IL 62305-3115. *Fax:* 217-222-1794

BARTLES, JAMES RICHARD, CELL BIOLOGY. *Current Pos:* AT NORTHWESTERN UNIV MED SCH, 87- *Educ:* Wash Univ, St Louis, PhD(Biochem), 81. *Prof Exp:* Res assoc cell biol, John's Hopkins Univ, Sch Med, 81-87. *Mailing Add:* Dept Cell Molecular & Struct Biol Northwestern Univ Med Sch 303 E Chicago Ave Chicago IL 60611-3072

BARTLESON, JOHN DAVID, CHEMISTRY. *Current Pos:* RETIRED. *Personal Data:* b Detroit, Mich, Mar 17, 17; m 40; c 2. *Educ:* Mich State Univ, BS, 38, MS, 39; Western Res Univ, PhD(org chem), 45. *Prof Exp:* Asst chem, Mich State Univ, 38-39; sect leader, Chem Res Div, Standard Oil Co, Ohio, 39-52; proj leader, Ethyl Int, 52-58, mgr antioxidant sale, 58-66, mgr new area develop, Petrol Chem Div, 81-82,. *Mem:* Am Chem Soc; Am Soc Testing & Mat; Chem Develop Asn; Chem Mkt Res Asn; Independent Oil Compounders Asn. *Res:* Lubricating oil additives; antioxidants and cetane improvers; engine evaluation of fuels and lubricants; refining, compounding and testing of lubricants; United States and international technical sales management; commercial development; market research; corporate planning; acquisition studies. *Mailing Add:* Box 137 Franklin MI 48025

BARTLETT, ALAN C, GENETICS. *Current Pos:* geneticist, Boll Weevil Res Lab, Entom Res Div, 62-67 & Western Cotton Insects Invests, 69-70, GENETICIST, WESTERN COTTON RES LAB, AGR RES SERV, USDA, 70- *Personal Data:* b Price, Utah, June 17, 34; m 56, Vanice Baker; c Ravae (Johnson), Denice (Hardman), LeIsle (Jacobson) & Trace A. *Educ:* Univ Utah, BA, 56, MS, 57; Purdue Univ, PhD(pop genetics), 62. *Prof Exp:* Instr pop genetics, Purdue Univ, 61-62. *Mem:* Entom Soc Am; Am Genetic Asn; Genetics Soc Am. *Res:* Radiation genetics of Drosophila, Tribolium castaneum and Anthonomus grandis; population genetics, selection and reproduction; genetic techniques for insect control and eradication; genetics and biology of pink bollworm; heliothis and boll weevil; whitefly molecular biology. *Mailing Add:* Western Cotton Res Lab 4135 E Broadway Phoenix AZ 85040. *Fax:* 602-379-4509; *E-Mail:* abartlett@assrr.arsusda.gov

BARTLETT, ALBERT ALLEN, PHYSICS. *Current Pos:* from asst prof to prof, 50-88, EMER PROF PHYSICS, UNIV COLO, BOULDER, 88- *Personal Data:* b Shanghai, China, Mar 21, 23; US citizen; m 46, Eleanor F Roberts; c Carol L, Jane E, Lois J & Nancy M. *Educ:* Colgate Univ, BA, 44; Harvard Univ, MA, 48, PhD(physics), 51. *Honors & Awards:* Distinguished Serv Citation, Am Asn Physics Teachers, 70, Robert A Millikan Award, 81, Melba Phillips Award, 90. *Prof Exp:* Mem staff, Los Alamos Sci Lab, 44-46; teaching fel, Harvard Univ, 48-49. *Concurrent Pos:* Res vis, Nobel Inst Physics, Sweden, 63-64. *Mem:* Fel Am Phys Soc; Am Asn Physics Teachers (vpres, 76, pres-elect, 77, pres, 78); Sigma Xi; fel AAAS; Am Asn Univ Professors. *Res:* Nuclear physics; arithmetic population and energy; consequences of growth of populations and growth in rates of consumption of resources. *Mailing Add:* Box 390 Dept Physics Univ Colo Boulder CO 80309. *Fax:* 303-492-3352; *E-Mail:* bartleta@stripe.colorado.edu

BARTLETT, CHARLES SAMUEL, JR, GEOLOGY, PETROLEUM EXPLORATION. *Current Pos:* CHIEF GEOLOGIST, BARTLETT GEOL CONSULTS, ABINGDON, VA, 78- *Personal Data:* b Asheville, NC, Oct 20, 29; m 51, Jean Schaefer; c Katherine M (Kukor) & Linda C (Moore). *Educ:* Univ NC, BS, 51, MS, 67; Univ Tenn, PhD(geol), 73. *Honors & Awards:* Sullivan Award, Univ NC, 51. *Prof Exp:* Field geologist, Gulf Oil Corp, 55-61; area geologist, J M Huber Corp, 61-65; instr geol, Pembroke State Univ, 66-67; from asst prof to assoc prof, Emory & Henry Col, 67-78. *Concurrent Pos:* Adj prof, King Col, 67-69; field geologist, Va Div Mineral Resources, 69-75; adj prof, Emory & Henry Col, 79-; sci adv bd, Va Mus Natural Hist, 86-88 & Va Cave Bd, 85-90; pres, Archeol Soc, Va, 95-96; pres, Southern Applin Geo Asn, 96-; mem, Karak Resources Proj, Jordan, 96. *Mem:* Am Asn Petrol Geologists; Geol Soc Am; Nat Asn Geol Teachers; Am Inst Prof Geologists. *Res:* Natural gas exploration; space imagery applications in mineral exploration; antarctic meteorites recovery; environmental effects of coal extraction; geological archeology; archeology and geology of Jordan. *Mailing Add:* Bartlett Geol Consults 586 E Main St Abingdon VA 24210

BARTLETT, DAVID FARNHAM, GRAVITY, ELECTROMAGNETISM. *Current Pos:* assoc prof, 71-82, PROF PHYSICS, UNIV COLO, BOULDER, 82- *Personal Data:* b New York, NY, Dec 13, 38; m 60; c 4. *Educ:* Harvard Univ, AB, 59; Columbia Univ, AM, 61, PhD(physics), 65. *Prof Exp:* From instr to asst prof physics, Princeton Univ, 64-71. *Mem:* Fel Am Phys Soc; Am Asn Physics Teachers; AAAS. *Res:* Study of gravity and electromagnetism using cryogenic techniques. *Mailing Add:* Dept Phys Univ Colo Boulder CO 80309

BARTLETT, DONALD, JR, PHYSIOLOGY. *Current Pos:* from asst prof to assoc prof, 71-78, PROF PHYSIOL, DARTMOUTH MED SCH, 78-, ANDREW C VAIL PROF & CHMN, DEPT PHYSIOL, 89- *Personal Data:* b Hanover, NH, Aug 4, 37; m 65, Christine A LaPointe; c Mark, David & Curt. *Educ:* Dartmouth Col, AB, 59; Dartmouth Med Sch, BMS, 61; Harvard Med Sch, MD, 64. *Hon Degrees:* MA, Dartmouth Col, 93. *Prof Exp:* Intern, Internal Med, Strong Mem Hosp, Rochester, NY, 64-65, asst res, 65-66; physician, Epidemiol Sect, Field Studies Br, Div Air Pollution, USPHS, 66-67; chief med res sect, Health Effects Prog, Nat Ctr Air Pollution Control, 67-68. *Concurrent Pos:* USPHS res fel physiol, Dartmouth Med Sch, 68-71. *Mem:* Am Physiol Soc; Soc Neurosci. *Res:* Respiratory and comparative physiology. *Mailing Add:* Dept Physiol Dartmouth Med Sch Lebanon NH 03756-0001. *Fax:* 603-650-6130

BARTLETT, EDWIN S(OUTHWORTH), METALLURGY. *Current Pos:* metallurgist, Batelle Mem Inst, 56-61, res assoc, 61-70, tech adv, 70-81, SR RES SCIENTIST, BATTELLE MEM INST, 80- *Personal Data:* b Detroit, Mich, Nov 4, 28; m 51; c 7. *Educ:* Mich Technol Univ, BS, 50; Ohio State Univ, MS, 59. *Prof Exp:* Res engr, Hoskins Mfg Co, 50-56. *Mem:* Am Inst Mining, Metall & Petrol Engrs; Am Soc Metals; Metall Soc. *Res:* Physical and mechanical metallurgy; special metalworking practices and techniques; refractory metals; nickel alloys; coatings; titanium. *Mailing Add:* 7868 Worthington Galena Rd Columbus OH 43085

BARTLETT, FRANK DAVID, SOILS, AGRICULTURE. *Current Pos:* RETIRED. *Personal Data:* b Clarksburg, WVa, Nov 6, 28; m 50; c 4. *Educ:* Univ WVa, BS, 50, MS, 51; Univ Fla, PhD(soils), 55. *Prof Exp:* Conserv aid, USDA, 47-51, lab asst res, Fla Agr Exp Sta, 51-55, soil scientist, 55-58, supvry soil scientist, 58-62, soil scientist, Ark River Basin, 62-72, resource conservationist, 72-77, resource data specialist, River Basin Planning, Soil Conserv Serv, 77-83. *Concurrent Pos:* Cert herbicide applicator. *Res:* Soil hydrology and soil-water-plant relationships; environmental affairs watershed planning. *Mailing Add:* 2803 Hilltop Rd Alexander AR 72002

BARTLETT, FRED MICHAEL PEARCE, CIVIL ENGINEERING. *Current Pos:* ASST PROF CIVIL ENG, UNIV WESTERN ONT, 95- *Personal Data:* b Ottawa, Can, Oct 29, 57; m 82, Doreen Joan. *Educ:* Queens Univ, Kingston, BS, 79; Univ Waterloo, Ont, MApplSci, 82; Univ Alta, PhD, 94. *Honors & Awards:* Andrew Stewart Mem Grand Prize, 92; Le Prix P L Pratley Award, Can Soc Civil Eng, 92; Isaac Walton Killam Mem Scholar, The Killam Trust, 93. *Prof Exp:* From engr-in-training to proj eng, Buckland & Taylor Ltd, NVancouver, Can, 82-89. *Concurrent Pos:* Mem, Can Hwy Bridge Design Code Subcomt Eval & Rehab. *Mem:* Am Soc Civil Engrs; Can Soc Civil Eng; Am Concrete Inst. *Res:* Contributor of numerous articles to professional journals. *Mailing Add:* 44 Mayfair Dr London ON N6A 2M6 Can

BARTLETT, GERALD LLOYD, PATHOLOGY. *Current Pos:* PROF PATH & CHAIR DEPT, UNIV ILL COL MED, PEORIA, 89- *Personal Data:* b Portland, Ore, July 24, 39; m 65; c 3. *Educ:* Seattle Pac Univ, BA, 61; Univ Wash, MD, 66; Univ Pa, PhD(path), 72. *Prof Exp:* Res assoc, Inst Cancer Res, Philadelphia, 66-70 & Nat Cancer Inst, Bethesda, Md, 70-72; from asst prof to prof path & immunol, Hershey Med Ctr, Pa State Univ, 72-89. *Concurrent Pos:* Ad hoc site vis mem, NIH, 71-91; mem, Tech Rev Comt, NIH, 72-78; mem, Test Mat Div Comt, Nat Bd Med Examrs, 95-97. *Mem:* AAAS; Am Asn Pathologists; Am Asn Immunologists; Am Asn Cancer Res. *Res:* Pathology education. *Mailing Add:* Dept Path Univ Ill Col Med PO Box 1649 Peoria IL 61656-1649. *Fax:* 309-671-8513; *E-Mail:* jlb@uic.edu

BARTLETT, J FREDERICK, SOFTWARE ENGINEERING. *Current Pos:* APPL SCIENTIST, FERMI NAT ACCELERATOR LAB, 78- *Personal Data:* b Ft Wayne, Ind, Aug 18, 36; m 84, Linda G Stutte. *Educ:* Yale Univ, SB, 58; Calif Inst Technol, MS, 61. *Prof Exp:* Staff astron, Calif Inst Technol, 68-69, comput, 69-70, physics, 70-78. *Mem:* Asn Comput Mach; Inst Elec & Electronics Engrs Comput Soc. *Res:* Design and implementation of a large, distributed computer control system for the Fermilab particle accelerator; technical management of software engineering; neutrino structure functions. *Mailing Add:* 42 W540 Hidden Springs Dr St Charles IL 60175. *E-Mail:* bartlett@fnal.fnal.gov

BARTLETT, JAMES HOLLY, MECHANICS. *Current Pos:* from asst prof to prof, 30-65, EMER PROF PHYSICS, UNIV ILL, URBANA, 65-; EMER PROF PHYSICS, UNIV ALA, 75- *Personal Data:* b Brooklyn, NY, Nov 2, 04; m 32, 65, Renote Oppenlander; c Ann, Jane, Susan, Evelyn & James H. *Educ:* Northeastern Univ, BCE, 24; Harvard Univ, AM, 26, PhD, 30. *Prof Exp:* Prof physics, Univ Ala, 65-75. *Concurrent Pos:* Fel, Rockefeller Found, 40-41; consult, Lockheed Aircraft Corp, 58-59; exchange prof to USSR, 61-63. *Mem:* Fel Am Phys Soc; Electrochem Soc; Biophys Soc; Am Astron Soc. *Res:* Ionization; quadrupole radiation; chemical valency; nuclear structure; properties of fast electrons; biophysics; dissolution of metals; anodic oxidation; passivity; stability of orbits; artificial intelligence. *Mailing Add:* Dept Physics & Astron Univ Ala Box 870324 Tuscaloosa AL 35487-0324

BARTLETT, JAMES KENNETH, CHEMISTRY. *Current Pos:* RETIRED. *Personal Data:* b Lynden, Wash, Feb 2, 25; m 48; c 1. *Educ:* Willamette Univ, BS, 49; Stanford Univ, PhD(chem), 55. *Prof Exp:* Instr chem, Univ Santa Clara, 53-54; asst prof, Long Beach State Col, 54-56; asst prof, Southern Ore State Col, 56-63, prof, 63-, chmn dept, 76- *Mem:* Am Chem Soc. *Res:* Colorimetric methods of analysis. *Mailing Add:* 1235 Ceder Ridge Dr Eugene OR 97401

BARTLETT, JAMES WILLIAMS, JR, psychiatry, for more information see previous edition

BARTLETT, JANETH MARIE, PHARMACEUTICAL SCIENCES. *Current Pos:* SR SCIENTIST, MOLECULAR BIOSYSTS INC, 93- *Personal Data:* b Cooperstown, NY, Sept 10, 46. *Educ:* Temple Univ, BS, 69, MS, 71; Rutgers Univ, PhD(pharm sci), 81. *Prof Exp:* Res assoc, E R Squibb & Sons, Inc, 70-74, asst res investr, 74-81; asst prof nuclear pharm, Purdue Univ, 81-86; res assoc, Dow Chem Co, 86-92. *Mem:* Am Asn Pharmaceut Scientists; Sigma Xi. *Res:* Radiopharmaceutical and novel drug delivery systems. *Mailing Add:* 15535 Caldas de Reyes San Diego CA 92128-4459

BARTLETT, JOHN W(ESLEY), CHEMICAL & NUCLEAR ENGINEERING. *Current Pos:* PRES, BARTLETT CO, 93- *Personal Data:* b Camden, NJ, Oct 18, 35; m 57, Elaine Wepplo; c Larah & Tanya. *Educ:* Univ Rochester, BS, 57; Rensselaer Polytech Inst, MChE, 59, PhD(chem eng), 62. *Honors & Awards:* Robert E Wilson Award, Am Inst Chem Engrs. *Prof Exp:* Engr coolant technol, Knolls Atomic Power Lab, Gen Elec Co, 57-62; asst prof chem eng, Univ Rochester, 62-68; eng assoc, Pac Northwest Labs, Battelle Mem Inst, 68-69, mgr sodium coolant studies, 69-70, mgr chem systs technol, 70-73; pres interchange exec, Nat Bur Stand, 73-74; mgr process eval, Pac Northwest Labs, Battelle Mem Inst, 74-78; div dir, Anal Sci Corp, 78-89; dir, Off Civilian Radioactive Waste Mgt, US Dept Energy, 90-93. *Concurrent Pos:* Fulbright prof, Istanbul Univ, Turkey, 68-69; adj prof, Joint Ctr Grad Study, 71-78. *Mem:* Am Inst Chem Engrs; Am Nuclear Soc. *Res:* Radioactive waste management; energy systems analysis; effluent control technology; transport processes. *Mailing Add:* 2151 Wolftrap Ct Vienna VA 22182-5188. *Fax:* 703-207-9023

BARTLETT, MAURICE S, BIOMATHEMATICS, STATISTICIAN. *Current Pos:* prof, 67-75, EMER PROF BIOMATH, UNIV OXFORD, 75- *Personal Data:* b London, Eng, June 18, 10. *Educ:* Univ London, BS, 31, DSc, 37; Queens Col, BA, 32. *Honors & Awards:* Guy Silver Medal, Royal Statist Soc, 52, Guy Gold Medal, 69. *Prof Exp:* Asst lectr, Univ Col London, 33-34; statistician, Imp Chem Indust, Ltd, 34-38; lectr math, Univ Cambridge, 38-47; prof math & statist, Univ Manchester, 47-90; prof statist, Univ Col London, 60-67. *Mem:* Nat Acad Sci; Int Statist Soc; Biometric Soc. *Mailing Add:* Univ Oxford S Parks Rd Oxford OX1 3QO England

BARTLETT, NEIL, INORGANIC CHEMISTRY. *Current Pos:* prof chem, 69-92, PRIN INVESTR, CHEM SCI DIV, LAWRENCE BERKELEY LAB, UNIV CALIF, BERKELEY, 69-; ASSOC, INST JOZEF STEFAN SLOVENIA, 74- *Personal Data:* b Newcastle-upon-Tyne, Eng, Sept 15, 32; m 57, Christina I Cross; c Jeremy, Jane, Christopher & Robin. *Educ:* Univ Durham, BSc, 54, PhD(inorg fluorine chem), 58. *Hon Degrees:* DSc, Univ Waterloo, 68, Colby Col, Maine, 72 & Univ Newcastle, Tyne, 81, McMaster Univ, 92; Hon Dr, Univ Bordeaux, 76; Univ Ljubljana, 89, Univ Nantes, 90; LLD, Simon, Fraser Univ, 93. *Honors & Awards:* Corday-Morgan Medal, Chem Soc, 62; Noranda Award, Chem Inst Can, 63; Steacie Prize, 65; Res Corp Plaque & Prize, 65; William Lloyd Evans Mem lectr, 66; Cresson Medal, Franklin Inst, Pa, 68; Kirkwood Medal & Award, 69; Inorg Chem Award, Am Chem Soc, 70, W H Nichols Medal, 83, Distinguished Serv Award, Advan Inorg Chem, 89, Pauling Medal, Pac NW Sect, 89, Creative Work Flourine Chem, 92; Dannie-Heineman Prize, Gottingen Acad, 71; 20th G N Lewis Mem lectr, Univ Calif, Berkeley, 73; Robert A Welch Award, 76; Alexander von Humboldt US Sr Scientist Award, 77; Werner lectr, Univ Kans, 77; R T Major Mem lectr, Univ Conn, 85; Prix Moissan, Paris, 88; Bonner Chemiepreis, Univ Bonn, 92. *Prof Exp:* Sr chem master, Duke's Sch, Eng, 57-58; lectr chem, Univ BC, 58-59, from instr to prof chem, 59-66; prof chem, Princeton Univ, 66-69; staff scientist, Bell Labs, Murray Hill, NJ, 66-69. *Concurrent Pos:* Steacie Mem fel, 64-66; Sloan fel, 64-; Miller vis prof, Univ Calif, Berkeley, 67-68; vis Erskine fel, Univ Canterbury, NZ, 83; vis fel, All Souls Col, Oxford, 84. *Mem:* Foreign assoc Nat Acad Sci; Gottingen Acad Sci; fel Am Acad Arts & Sci; fel Royal Soc London; assoc mem Acad Sci France. *Res:* Fluorine inorganic chemistry; noble gas chemistry; high-energy oxidizers; x-ray crystallography; solid-state chemistry; nonaqueous solvent chemistry; thermochemistry. *Mailing Add:* Dept Chem Latimer Hall Univ Calif Berkeley CA 94720

BARTLETT, PAUL A, BIO-ORGANICCHEMISTRY, ORGANIC SYNTHESIS. *Current Pos:* PROF CHEM, UNIV CALIF, BERKELEY, 73- *Personal Data:* b Trenton, NJ, Jan 5, 48. *Educ:* Harvard Univ, AB & AM, 69; Stanford Univ, PhD(org chem), 72. *Honors & Awards:* Arthur C Cope Scholar Award, Am Chem Soc. *Mem:* fel Am Acad Arts & Sci. *Res:* Application of organic synthesis to the understanding of biological problems. *Mailing Add:* Dept Chem Univ Calif Berkeley CA 94720-1460

BARTLETT, PAUL DOUGHTY, ORGANIC CHEMISTRY. *Current Pos:* RETIRED. *Personal Data:* b Ann Arbor, Mich, Aug 14, 07; m 31; c 3. *Educ:* Amherst Col, BA, 28; Harvard Univ, PhD(chem), 31. *Hon Degrees:* ScD, Amherst Col, 53 & Univ Chicago, 54; Dr, Univ Montpellier, 67, Univ Paris, 69 & Univ Munich, 77. *Honors & Awards:* Pure Chem Award, Am Chem Soc, 38, Willard Gibbs Medal & Roger Adams Medal, 63, James Flack Norris Award, 69 & 78; August Wilhelm von Hofmann Medal, Ger Soc Chem, 62; Theodore William Richards Medal, 66; Nat Medal Sci, 68; John Price Wetherill Medal, Franklin Inst, 70; Linus Pauling Medal, 75; Nichols Medal, 76; Alexander von Humboldt Sr Scientist Award, Freiburg, 76 & Munich, 77; Max Tishler Award, 81; Robert A Welch Award, 81. *Prof Exp:* Nat Res fel chem, Rockefeller Inst & Columbia Univ, 31-32; instr org chem, Univ Minn, 32-34; from instr to prof chem, Harvard Univ, 34-48, Erving prof, 48-75, chmn dept, 51-54; Robert A Welch res prof, Tex Christian Univ, 74-85, Robert A Welch res emer prof chem, 85; Erving emer prof chem, Harvard Univ, 75-85. *Concurrent Pos:* Numerous lectureships US & abroad, 35-78; off invester, Nat Defense Res Comt, 41-45; vis prof, Univ Calif, Los Angeles, 50, Univ Chicago, 71, Univ Tex, Austin, 75 & Univ Munich, 77; Guggenheim fel, 57 & 71-72. *Mem:* Nat Acad Sci; hon mem Royal Soc Chem; hon mem Swiss Chem Soc; hon mem Chem Soc Japan; Am Acad Arts & Sci; fel AAAS; Am Philos Soc; Franklin Inst. *Res:* Stereochemistry; kinetics and mechanism of organic reactions; polymerization; Walden inversion; molecular rearrangements; paraffin alkylation; highly branched compounds; free radicals; reactions of sulphur; cycloaddition; organdithium reactions; photo-oxidation; specially hindered olefins. *Mailing Add:* Brookhaven Lexington Amherest No A-311/1010 Waltham St Lexington MA 02173

BARTLETT, PAUL EUGENE, EDUCATIONAL ENGINEERING ADMINISTRATION. *Current Pos:* Instr appl math, Univ Colo, Denver, 51-56, from asst prof to prof civil eng, 56-66, from asst dean to assoc dean, Col Eng, 62-71, vprovost, 70-71, asst vpres, 71-73, from assoc dean to dean, Col Eng, 73-89, actg vchancellor acad affairs, 90-91, EMER DEAN, COL ENG & EMER PROF CIVIL ENG, UNIV COLO, DENVER, 89- *Personal Data:* b Denver, Colo, Nov 21, 26; m 79, Mary Corbly; c Lorna K & Randy P. *Educ:* Univ Colo, BS(civil eng) & BS(bus mgt), 51, MS(civil eng), 56. *Concurrent Pos:* Consult, Martin-Marietta Corp, 58-62. *Mem:* Fel hon mem Am Soc Civil Engrs; Am Soc Eng Educ; Nat Soc Prof Engrs. *Res:* Hydraulics; applied fluid mechanics; engineering education. *Mailing Add:* Col Eng Campus Box 104 Univ Colo PO Box 173364 Denver CO 80217-3364

BARTLETT, R(OBERT) W(ATKINS), METALLURGY, MINERAL ENGINEERING. *Current Pos:* DEAN, COL MINES, UNIV IDAHO, 87- *Personal Data:* b Salt Lake City, Utah, Jan 8, 33; m 54, Betty Cameron; c 4. *Educ:* Univ Utah, BS, 53, PhD(metall), 61. *Honors & Awards:* Turner Award, Electrochem Soc; Extractive Metall Technol Award, Am Inst Mining, Metall & Petrol Engrs, 75, McConnell Award; McConnell Award, Am Inst Mech Engrs, 85; Wadsworth Award, Soc Mfg Engrs, 96. *Prof Exp:* Sr scientist, Ford Aeronutronic, 61-65; sr scientist, Stanford Res Inst, 65-67, assoc prof, Dept Mineral Eng, Stanford Univ, 67-74; pres, Hydrotek Mining Inc, 73-77; mgr hydrometall dept, MMD Res Ctr, Kennecott Copper Corp, 74-77; mgr mats res group, SRI INT, 77-80; vpres, Avacada Minerals Co, 80-86. *Concurrent Pos:* Dir, Idaho Geol Surv & Idaho Mining & Mineral Resources Res Inst; exec met distinguished lectr, Minerals, Metals & Mat Soc, 97. *Mem:* Nat Acad Eng; Minerals Metals & Mats Soc (pres, 89); Soc Mining Metall & Explor. *Res:* Extractive metallurgy; hydrometallurgy; corrosion; high temperature materials; metallurgical process kinetics; process engineering research; solution mining. *Mailing Add:* Univ Idaho Moscow ID 83844-3025

BARTLETT, RAYMOND C, MICROBIOLOGY. *Current Pos:* DIR GRAD MED EDUC, HARTFORD CONN HOSP. *Honors & Awards:* Becton Dickinson Award, Am Soc Microbiol, 94. *Mailing Add:* Dept Path Hartford Hosp 80 Seymour St Hartford CT 06115

BARTLETT, RICHMOND J, SOIL & WATER CHEMISTRY, PLANT NUTRITION. *Current Pos:* RETIRED. *Personal Data:* b Columbus, Ohio, Sept 23, 27; wid; c Amy, Anne, Ellen & Samuel. *Educ:* Ohio State Univ, BA, 49, PhD(soil chem), 58. *Prof Exp:* Newspaper reporter, 50-52; promotional writer, 52-55; asst soils, Ohio State Univ, 55-58; from asst prof to prof soil, Univ Vt, 58-97. *Mem:* Fel AAAS; fel Am Soc Agron; fel Soil Sci Soc Am; Int Soc Soil Sci; Int Humic Acid Soc. *Res:* Soil and water chemistry in relation to agriculture and environmental health; chemistry of root, soil, water and air interfaces; metal organic interactions; redox. *Mailing Add:* Dept Plant & Soil Sci Univ Vt Burlington VT 05405

BARTLETT, RODNEY JOSEPH, CHEMICAL PHYSICS, COMPUTER APPLICATIONS. *Current Pos:* prof chem & physics, 81-88, GRAD RES PROF CHEM & PHYSICS, QUANTUM THEORY PROJ, UNIV FLA, 89- *Personal Data:* b Memphis, Tenn, Mar 31, 44; m 66, Beverly Featherstone; c Robert D & Ronald E. *Educ:* Millsaps Col, BS, 66; Univ Fla, PhD(theoret chem), 71. *Prof Exp:* NSF fel theoret chem, Aarhus Univ, Denmark, 71-72; res assoc chem, Johns Hopkins Univ, 72-74; sr res scientist, Battelle Pac Northwest Lab, 74-77, sr res scientist & group leader chem physics, Battelle Columbus Lab, Battelle Mem Inst, 77-81. *Concurrent Pos:* Prin investr, Air Force Off Sci Res, 78-, Off Naval Res, 79- & Army Res Off, 79-87; consult, Molecular Sci Res Ctr, Battelle, Pac Northwest Lab, 85-88, sr affil scientist, 89-; Guggenheim fel, Harvard Univ & Univ Calif, Berkeley, 87; chmn, Subdiv Theoret Chem, Am Chem Soc, 85. *Mem:* Am Chem Soc; Sigma Xi; fel Am Phys Soc. *Res:* Development of the theory and applications of quantum mechanics in chemistry; correlation problem, particularly many-body, diagrammatic perturbation theory and coupled-cluster theory; studies of large molecules of biological interest; molecular structure and spectra; flame chemistry; analytical gradient and hessian methods; molecular hyperpolarizabilities. *Mailing Add:* Quantum Theory Proj Williamson Hall Univ Fla Gainesville FL 32611. *Fax:* 904-392-8277; *E-Mail:* bartgff@qtp.ufl.edu

BARTLETT, ROGER JAMES, SOLID STATE PHYSICS. *Current Pos:* staff mem low temperature physics, 72-79, STAFF MEM OPTICAL PROPERTIES MAT, LOS ALAMOS NAT LAB, 79- *Personal Data:* b Ft Madison, Iowa, Mar 19, 42; m 69; c 2. *Educ:* Iowa State Univ, BS, 64, MS, 68, PhD(physics), 70. *Prof Exp:* Fel optical physics, Ga Inst Technol, 70-72. *Mem:* Am Phys Soc. *Res:* Optical properties of materials with emphasis on atomic & solid state effects in the soft x-ray energy range; superconductivity with emphasis on critical current and current and field profiles in superconductors. *Mailing Add:* Los Alamos Nat Lab P-22 MS D410 PO Box 1663 Los Alamos NM 87545. *Fax:* 505-667-7684; *E-Mail:* rbartlett@lanl.gov

BARTLETT, WILLIAM ROSEBROUGH, ORGANIC CHEMISTRY. *Current Pos:* from asst prof to assoc prof, 78-85, PROF CHEM, FT LEWIS COL, 85- *Personal Data:* b St Louis, Mo, July 25, 43; m 64; c 3. *Educ:* Luther Col, BA, 65; Stanford Univ, PhD(org chem), 69. *Prof Exp:* NIH fel, Columbia Univ, 69-71; asst prof, Hamline Univ, 71-75 & St John's Univ, Minn, 75-78. *Concurrent Pos:* Res Corp Cottrell grant, Hamline Univ, 73-75 & St John's Univ, 76-77; Am Chem Soc-Petrol Res Fund grant, Ft Lewis Col, 79-82, 87-89 & 90-; NSF minigrant, 83; vis sr res assoc, Stanford Univ, 86-87; NSF-ROA, 86-87; chem sci eval panel, NRC, 86-89; ILIP grant, NSF, 89- *Mem:* Am Chem Soc; AAAS. *Res:* Synthesis of biologically-active compounds, insect pheromones. *Mailing Add:* Dept Chem Ft Lewis Col Durango CO 81301

BARTLEY, EDWARD FRANCIS, MATHEMATICS. *Current Pos:* RETIRED. *Personal Data:* b Scranton, Pa, June 24, 16; m 40; c 2. *Educ:* Univ Scranton, BA, 38; Columbia Univ, MA, 56. *Prof Exp:* Pub sch teacher, Pa, 39-43; assoc prof & chmn dept, Univ Scranton, 46-68, prof math, 68- *Concurrent Pos:* Consult, Scranton Schs. *Mem:* Math Asn Am. *Res:* Algebra; secondary school curriculum. *Mailing Add:* 1115 Fisk St Scranton PA 18509

BARTLEY, JOHN C, METABOLISM. *Current Pos:* STAFF SCIENTIST, LAWRENCE BERKELEY LAB, 82- *Personal Data:* b Pueblo, Colo, Apr 30, 32. *Educ:* Colo State Univ, BS, 54, DVM, 56; Univ Calif, Davis, PhD(animal physiol), 63- *Prof Exp:* Assoc dir res, Children's Hosp Med Ctr N Calif, 68-78; res scientist, Peralha Cancer Res Inst, 78-82. *Mem:* Am Soc Biol Chemists; Biochem Soc; Am Soc Cell Biol; AAAS. *Mailing Add:* Lawrence Berkeley Lab Bldg 90 Lawrence Berkeley Lab Berkeley CA 94720-0001

BARTLEY, JOHN MICHAEL, TECTONICS. *Current Pos:* from asst to assoc prof, 85-91, PROF, DEPT GEOL & GEOPHYS, UNIV UTAH, 91-, DEPT CHAIR, 95- *Personal Data:* b Seattle, Wash, June 12, 52. *Educ:* Univ Wash, Seattle, BS, 76; Mass Inst Technol, PhD(geol), 81. *Prof Exp:* Instr, Univ NC, Chapel Hill, 80-81, asst prof, 81-85. *Concurrent Pos:* Fel, Am-Scand Found, 79; grantee, NSF, 81-83, 83-85, 86-88, 89, 89-91, 90-92, 92-94, 96-98, Am Chem Soc Petrol Res Fund, 83-85, 90-92, Utah Geol & Mineral Surv, 89-90. *Mem:* Fel Geol Soc Am; Am Geophys Union; Sigma Xi. *Res:* Author of several publications. *Mailing Add:* Dept Geol & Geophysics Univ Utah Salt Lake City UT 84112. *Fax:* 801-581-7065

BARTLEY, MURRAY HILL, JR, ANATOMY, ORAL PATHOLOGY. *Current Pos:* assoc prof, Univ Ore, 69-77, chmn dept, 72-76, prof path, Dent Sch, 77-95, chmn dept, 80-95, EMER PROF PATH, UNIV ORE, 95- *Personal Data:* b Jamestown, NY, June 15, 33; m 56; c 3. *Educ:* Univ Ore, DMD, 58, cert, 65; Univ Utah, PhD(anat), 68. *Prof Exp:* Asst oral path, Univ Ore, 62-64; assoc dir res, D N Sharp Hosp, San Diego, 64-65; actg assoc prof oral biol, Sch Dent, Univ Calif, Los Angeles, 68-69. *Concurrent Pos:* Univ Ore & NIH teaching grants, 61-64; resident, Providence Hosp, 61-62; consult, Vet Admin, 70, Madigan Army Med Ctr, 76- & Coun Hosp Dent, Am Dent Asn, 77-79. *Mem:* AAAS; Am Dent Asn; Sigma Xi; Am Acad Oral; NY Acad Sci. *Res:* Cortisol effects on bone; immunopathology of oral lesions; aging in skeletal tissues determined by densitometric or histological methods; aging in skeletal tissues of anthropological material; heritable and metabolic diseases of the hard dental tissues. *Mailing Add:* 6020 SW Arrow Wood Lane Portland OR 97223

BARTLEY, WILLIAM CALL, HIGH-TECHNOLOGY INTERNATIONAL MARKETING & TRADE ENERGY, BIO-AGRICULTURE. *Current Pos:* CHMN & CHIEF EXEC OFFICER, BARTLEY TECHNOL INC & WM C BARTLEY & ASSOC, 95- *Personal Data:* b Mason, Mich, Dec 4, 32; m 56, W Dee Gray; c Carol, Gregory & Christopher. *Educ:* Mich State Univ, BS, 55, MS, 59. *Honors & Awards:* Award for Development of Satellite Aspect Comput, NASA, 74. *Prof Exp:* Asst elec eng, Mich State Univ, 55, instr, 58-59; mgn engr, Apparatus Div, Tex Instruments, 59-60, mkt engr, Semiconductor Div, 60, design engr, 60-61, br mgr, 61-63; res sci & mgr, Radiation Exp Develop Lab, Univ Tex, Dallas, 63-67; exec secy, US Comt Solar Terrestrial Res & Study, dir, Comt Biol & Climate Effects Emmissions Stratosphere, Inst Med-Nat Acad Sci, 67-74; sr staff, White House , Off Sci & Tech Policy ,74-77, asst dir energy res, Dept Energy, 77-80, assoc dir energy res, 80-82, minister counsr sci health , Dept Health & Human Serv, US Dept State, US Mission, Geneva, Switz, 82-88, special asst, Off Comnr Food & Drugs, 88-89; sr policy adv & dir energy trade policy, Off US Trade Rep, White House, 89-91; sr adv directories sci technol & health, Oceans & Environ & Sci Affairs Bur, US Dept State, 91-95. *Concurrent Pos:* Sr investr, NASA res conttracts, 63-67; staff dir, study on photovoltaics & photosynthesis, 69 & study on space sci properties & life sci, Space Sci Bd, 70-72, dir study biol & med effects of nitrogen & oxide emmisions, Nat Acad Sci, 76-78; sr policy analyst, Sci Technol & Int Affairs Directorate, NSF, 75-76; exec secy & mem, Fed Coord Coun for Sci, Eng & Technol of President, 76-78; prin staff person, Energy Res Adv Bd, Dept Energy, 78-80, US liaison, UN WHO Europ Orgn Nuclear Res, 81-88; vpres's competitiveness coun working groups on orphan drugs & drug approval, biotechnol working group, 89-91, US Japan joint working group on opto-electronics, 92-95, OECD Comt S&T Mega-Sci Forum, 92-95, State Dept negotiator US participation CERN accellorator, 94-95, Org Comt St Mary's Univ for Inter-Am Conf Com Arbitration, San Antonio, Tx, 95. *Mem:* Am Geophys Union; Inst Elec & Electronics Engrs; NY Acad Sci. *Res:* Experimental radiation research using accelerators and detectors on satellites; commercialization of emerging information/computer technologies; energy, space and enviromental foreign policy with Russia and China; White House information superhighways & adavanced energy programs. *Mailing Add:* PO Box 2246 Bandera TX 78003. *Fax:* 830-796-8468; *E-Mail:* bartley@connecti.com

BARTLEY, WILLIAM J, INDUSTRIAL CHEMISTRY, HETEROGENEOUS CATALYSIS. *Current Pos:* SR RES SCIENTIST, UNION CARBIDE CORP, 62- *Personal Data:* b Richfield, Utah, Feb 27, 35; m 56, Erika-Marie Sagebiel; c William B, Brian S & Christopher P. *Educ:* Brigham Young Univ, BS, 57, MS, 58; Univ Wash, PhD(org chem), 62. *Mem:* Am Chem Soc. *Res:* Heterogeneous catalysis; new process development. *Mailing Add:* 500 Sheridan Circle Charleston WV 25314. *Fax:* 304-747-4623; *E-Mail:* wjb@medinah.atc.ucarb.com

BARTLING, JUDD QUENTIN, physics, electro-optics & i r signal processing, for more information see previous edition

BARTLIT, JOHN R(AHN), CHEMICAL ENGINEERING, CRYOGENICS. *Current Pos:* STAFF MEM, 62-, DEP PROJ MGR, TRITIUM SYSTS TEST ASSEMBLY, LOS ALAMOS NAT LAB, 82- *Personal Data:* b Chicago, Ill, June 1, 34; m 61; c 2. *Educ:* Purdue Univ, BSChE, 56; Princeton Univ, MSE, 57; Yale Univ, DEng, 63. *Honors & Awards:* Technol Utilization Award, 71. *Prof Exp:* Instr, Yale Univ, 60-61. *Concurrent Pos:* Consult, Georgetown Univ, Nat Coal Policy Proj, 76-78. *Res:* Cryogenic engineering; heat transfer to cryogenic fluids; tritium handling; cryogenic distillation of hydrogen isotopes. *Mailing Add:* 113 Monte Rey Dr S Los Alamos NM 87544

BARTLOW, THOMAS L, HISTORY OF MATHEMATICS. *Current Pos:* Instr, 68-69, ASST PROF MATH, VILLANOVA UNIV, 69- *Personal Data:* b Johnson City, NY, May 14, 42; m 71; c 3. *Educ:* State Univ NY Albany, BS, 63; State Univ NY Buffalo, MA, 66, PhD(math), 69. *Mem:* Math Asn Am; Can Soc Hist & Philos Math. *Res:* History of mathematics, especially relations of mathematics to social sciences. *Mailing Add:* Dept Math Villanova Univ Villanova PA 19085. *Fax:* 610-519-6428

BARTNICKI-GARCIA, SALOMON, MYCOLOGY. *Current Pos:* asst microbiologist & lectr, Univ Calif, Riverside, 62-68, assoc prof & microbiologist, 68-71, prof plant path & microbiologist, 71-94, chmn, Dept Plant Path, 89-92, EMER PROF PLANT PATH & MICROBIOLOGIST, UNIV CALIF, RIVERSIDE, 94- *Personal Data:* b Mexico City, Mex, May 18, 35; m 61, Ildiko Nagy; c Linda & David. *Educ:* Nat Polytech Inst, Mex, prof degree, 57; Rutgers Univ, PhD(microbiol), 61. *Honors & Awards:* New York Bot Garden Award, Bot Soc Am, 75; Ruth Allen Award Outstanding Contrib Plant Path, Am Phytopath Soc, 83; L Pasteur Medal, Mex Soc Microbiol, 89; Distinguished Mycologist, Mycol Soc Am, 94. *Prof Exp:* Res assoc microbiol, Rutgers Univ, 61-62. *Concurrent Pos:* NIH grant, 63-; vis prof, Org Chem Inst, Univ Stockholm, 69-70; NSF grant 71-; lectr, Mycol Soc Am, 78; vis prof, French Ministry Educ, Univ Grenoble, France, 89; fac res lectr, Univ Calif, Riverside, 89. *Mem:* Fel AAAS; Am Soc Microbiol; fel Am Phytopath Soc; hon mem Brit Mycol Soc; Am Soc Biol Chem; fel Am Phytopath Soc. *Res:* Microbial biochemistry; biochemistry of morphogenesis; physiology of fungi; cell wall structure and biosynthesis; biochemistry of parasitism; mathematical and computer models of fungal development. *Mailing Add:* Dept Plant Path Univ Calif Riverside CA 92521. *Fax:* 909-787-4294; *E-Mail:* bart@ucrac1.ucr.edu

BARTNIKAS, RAY, DIELECTRICS & ELECTRICAL DISCHARGES. *Current Pos:* sr res scientist, Mat Res Dept, 68-70, dept dir, 70-82, DISTINGUISHED SR SCIENTIST, INST RES HYDRO QUE, 82- *Personal Data:* b Kaunas, Lithuania, Jan 25, 36; Can citizen; m 67, Margaret McLachlan; c Andrea & Thomas. *Educ:* Univ Toronto, BASc, 58; McGill Univ, MEng, 62, PhD(elec eng), 64. *Honors & Awards:* Thomas Dakin Distinguished Sci Achievement Award, Inst Elec & Electronics Engrs, 80, Centennial Medal, 84, Whitehead Mem Award, 87, Morris Leeds Award, 89, McNaughton Gold Medal, 93; Charles Dudley Medal, Am Soc Testing & Mat, 85, Arnold Scott Award & Award of Merit, 85; Award of Merit, Can Stand Asn, 86, John Jenkins Award, 89; J P Carrier Award, Stand Coun Can, 92; Urgel-Archambault Prize, Asn Can France Advan Sci, 93; T W Eadie Medal, Royal Soc Can, 94. *Prof Exp:* Develop engr, Cable Labs, Northern Elec Co, Que, 58-63; mem sci staff, Phys Sci Dept, Bell-Northern Res Labs, Ont, 63-68. *Concurrent Pos:* Auxiliary prof, McGill Univ, Can, 69-76; adj prof, Univ Waterloo, 69-, Sandford-Fleming vis fel, 81-; adj prof, Polytech, Univ Montreal, 80-; vis prof, Univ Rome, 95. *Mem:* Fel Inst Elec & Electronics Engrs; fel Am Soc Testing & Mat; Int Electrotech Comn; Can Stand Asn; Can Elec Asn; Order Engrs Can; fel Inst Physics, UK; fel Royal Soc Can. *Res:* Electrical discharges, conduction and loss mechanisms in dielectric materials; insulating systems of electrical apparatus, cables and devices. *Mailing Add:* Inst de Recherche Hydro-Quebec 1800 Montee Ste-Julie Varennes PQ J3X 1S1 Can. *Fax:* 514-652-8435

BARTNOFF, SHEPARD, technical management, nuclear engineering, for more information see previous edition

BARTOCHA, BODO, SCIENCE POLICY. *Current Pos:* vis scholar & assoc dir, Off Int Progs, Univ Ariz, 86-88, dir, 88-89, prof arid lands, 89-92, ADJ PROF, ARIZ RES LABS, UNIV ARIZ, 93- *Personal Data:* b Wroclaw, Poland, Dec 26, 28; m 57, Elisabeth Kieckhoefer. *Educ:* Philipps Univ, Marburg/Lahn, Ger, BS, 51, MS, 53, PhD(inorg chem), 56. *Prof Exp:* Milton fel postgrad res & teaching, Harvard Univ, 56-58; head, Propellant Br, Res US Naval Ord Lab, Corona, Calif, 58-61, dir res & actg dir develop, Res & Develop Mgt, Propellant Plant, Indian Head, Md, 61-64, dep chief scientist, Int Res & Develop Mgt, Off Naval Res, London, UK, 64-66, asst tech dir advan planning & develop, Naval Ord Sta, Indian Head, 66-67; staff assoc & dep head, Off Planning & Policy Studies, Policy Anal, NSF, 67-70, dep exec secy, Exec Coun, Mgt, 70-71, exec asst to asst dir, Nat & Int Progs, 71, dir,

Div Int Progs, Int Res & Develop Mgt, 72-86. *Concurrent Pos:* Sr vpres, S&T Technol Enterprise Corp, Washington, DC. *Mem:* Fel AAAS. *Res:* Synthetic organo-metal chemistry; reaction kinetics; solid propellants; weapons systems analysis; science policy; planning; resources allocation; technological forecasting; technology assessment; international research and development cooperation. *Mailing Add:* 1305 E Moonridge Rd Tucson AZ 85718-1142. *E-Mail:* bartocha@ccit.arizona.edu, 73347.154@compuserve.com

BARTOK, WILLIAM, PHYSICAL CHEMISTRY, CHEMICAL & ENVIRONMENTAL ENGINEERING. *Current Pos:* CONSULT, ENVIRON TECHNOL, WILLIAM BARTOK, INC, 93- *Personal Data:* b Budapest, Hungary, May 1, 30; US citizen; m 57, Susan V Roth; c Michael, Sylvia & Richard. *Educ:* McGill Univ, BEng, 54, PhD(phys chem), 57. *Honors & Awards:* Award in Chem Contemp Technol Probs, Am Chem Soc, 87. *Prof Exp:* From res chemist to sci adv, Exxon Res & Eng Co, 57-86, head, Nitrogen Oxide Projs, 70-75, group head, Combustion Sci, 75-83, coordr, 83-86; sr vpres, Energy & Environ Res Corp, 86-91; sr vpres, Technol Res, Cottrell Cos, 91-92. *Concurrent Pos:* Mem, ad hoc Panel Nitrogen Oxide Emission Control, Nat Res Ctr, Nat Acad Sci, Nat Acad Eng, 71-72 & Adequacy of Sulfur Oxide Emission Control Technol Comt, 75-78, Peer Rev Comt, Environ Protection Agency, 83, Dept Energy, 84, Sandia Nat Lab, 86, Combustion Sci & Tech; bd dirs, Combustion Inst, 80-92. *Mem:* Am Chem Soc; Am Inst Chem Eng; Combustion Inst. *Res:* Combustion; nitrogen oxides formation and control; air pollution control; kinetics and catalysis; free radical processes in oxidation and high temperature chemistry; rheology of disperse systems. *Mailing Add:* 956 Wyandotte Trail Westfield NJ 07090. *E-Mail:* wbartok@ix.netcom.com

BARTOLINI, ROBERT ALFRED, ELECTROOPTICS. *Current Pos:* Mem tech staff, 66-80, res leader electrooptics, 80-83, group head optoelectroncis, 83-89, DIR, INTEGRATED CIRCUIT LAB, DAVID SARNOFF RES CTR, 89- *Personal Data:* b Waterbury, Conn, Apr 4, 42; m 64; c 3. *Educ:* Villanova Univ, BS, 64; Case Inst of Technol, MS, 66; Univ Pa, PhD(elec eng), 72. *Honors & Awards:* Centennial Medal, Inst Elec & Electronics Engrs, 84. *Concurrent Pos:* Lectr, LaSalle Univ, Philadelphia, 72-83, chmn dept, 83-90. *Mem:* Fel Inst Elec & Electronics Engrs; fel Optical Soc Am; Am Inst Physics; Sigma Xi. *Res:* Development of materials and systems suitable for optical applications such as information storage and retrieval systems, holography and optical wave guides. *Mailing Add:* 14 Darvel Dr Rte 4 Robbinsville NJ 08691-9555

BARTON, ALEXANDER JAMES, ECOLOGY, HERPETOLOGY. *Current Pos:* RETIRED. *Personal Data:* b Mt Pleasant, Pa, May 9, 24; m 45, Arlene Arment; c Sandra (Stinnett), Lynne (Bier) & Alexander J III. *Educ:* Franklin & Marshall Col, BS, 46; Univ Pittsburgh, MS, 56. *Honors & Awards:* Silver Honor Medal, Am Rose Soc, 84. *Prof Exp:* Park naturalist, Riverview Park, Pa, 45-46; herpetologist, Highland Park Zool Gardens, 46-52; instr biol, Stony Brook Sch, NY, 52-63, dir admis & financial aid, 57-63; dir, Savannah Natural Hist Mus, Ga, 57; from asst prof to assoc prof, Undergrad Educ Sci Div, Col Sci, NSF, 63-70, prog dir, Undergrad Instrnl Progs, 70-73, prog mgr, Student-Oriented Progs, 73-75, prog dir, Sci Educ Develop Prog, 76-84, prog dir, Instrumentation Prog, 84-88. *Concurrent Pos:* Pres, Asn Admis Officers Independent Sec Schs, 59-62; adj asst prof, C W Post Col, Long Island Univ, 61-63; consult, Doubleday & Co, 62-64; mem, Inst Serv Subcomt, Col Entrance Exam Bd, 62-65, 62-65, Col Scholar Serv Comt, 65-68; chmn, Schs Scholar Serv, 62-63; mem comt endangered reptiles & amphibians, Int Union Conserv of Nature, 67-74; life-judge, Am Rose Soc, 70-, dir, 85-; mem environ educ subcomt, Fed Interagency Comt Educ, 74-, chmn, 81-82; chmn, Fed Interagency Subcomt, Int Environ Educ, 76-78; mem, US Deleg Intergovt Conf Environ Educ, Tbilisi, USSR, 78; naval mem on Secy Defense, ROPMA, steering group staff, 81-; serv to capt, USNR. *Mem:* Fel Explorers Club; Herpetologists League; Soc Study Amphibians & Reptiles. *Res:* Ecology and classification of amphibians and reptiles, especially turtles and salamanders; environmental education; design of programs for improving education in science. *Mailing Add:* PO Box 100 Monterey VA 24465

BARTON, BEVERLY E, CYTOKINE IMMUNOLOGY, BIOLOGY OF IL-GESIX. *Current Pos:* sr scientist, 87-90, PRIN SCIENTIST, SCHERING-PLOUGH RES, SCHERING-PLOUGH CORP, 90-; ADJ ASSOC PROF, UNIV MED & DENT, DEPT PATH, NEWARK, NJ, 97- *Personal Data:* b New York, NY, May 6, 54; m 78; c 2. *Educ:* Johns Hopkins Univ, BA, 76, ScM, 79; Stanford Univ, PhD(med microbiol), 84. *Prof Exp:* Sr prof, Allergan Pharmaceut, Inc, 84-85, scientist, 85-87. *Mem:* Am Asn Immunologists; NY Acad Sci; Soc Exp Biol & Med; Int Cytokine; Am Soc Microbiol. *Res:* Roles of interleukin 6 in septic shock, endotoxemia and multiple myeloma; discovering compounds which inhibit IL-6 synthesis in vivo and prevent symptoms of septic shock and endotoxemia; role of IL-6 family of cytokines in cachexia. *Mailing Add:* Dept Immunol Schering-Plough Res 2015 Galloping Hill Rd Kennilworth NJ 07033

BARTON, CHARLES JULIAN, SR, ENVIRONMENTAL HEALTH. *Current Pos:* RETIRED. *Personal Data:* b Jellico, Tenn, Jan 16, 12; m 40; c 3. *Educ:* Univ Tenn, BS, 33, MS, 34; Univ Va, PhD(anal chem), 39. *Prof Exp:* Jr phys sci aide, Tenn Valley Authority, 34-36; chemist, Chesapeake & Ohio Rwy Co, 39-40, Nat Aluminate Corp, 40 & Indust Rayon Corp, 40-47; res chemist & group leader, Int Minerals & Chem Corp, 47-48; res staff mem, Oak Ridge Nat Lab, 48-77. *Concurrent Pos:* Consult, Sci Applns, Inc, 77- & Evaluation Res Corp. *Mem:* Am Chem Soc; Am Nuclear Soc. *Res:* Photoelectric spectrophotometry applications in analytical chemistry; phase studies; plutonium chemistry; nuclear safety studies; radiological considerations in nuclear gas well stimulation; health effects of non-radioactive pollutants and radionuclides from uranium mill tailings; results of radiological surveys. *Mailing Add:* 237 Outer Dr Oak Ridge TN 37830

BARTON, CLIFF S, ENGINEERING MECHANICS, EDUCATIONAL CONSULTANT. *Current Pos:* assoc prof, 59-62, chmn dept, 63-69, PROF CIVIL ENG, BRIGHAM YOUNG UNIV, 62-, ASST DEAN, COL ENG SCI & TECHNOL, 77- *Personal Data:* b Preston, Idaho, July 18, 19; m 42; c 5. *Educ:* Utah State Univ, BSCE, 47; Rensselaer Polytech Inst, MCE, 53, PhD(eng mech), 59. *Prof Exp:* Design layout engr, Lockheed Aircraft Co, 41-45; instr appl mech, Rensselaer Polytech Inst, 47-53, asst prof mech, 53-59. *Concurrent Pos:* Consult, Watervliet Arsenal, 57-60; assoc ed, Am J Phys Anthrop, 83; contrib ed, Quar Rev Archaeol, 87. *Mem:* AAAS; Am Soc Civil Engrs; Soc Exp Stress Anal (pres, 69-70); Am Soc Eng Educ; Sigma Xi. *Res:* Wave motion in continous media; viscoelastic studies; development and utilization of residual stresses; effects of high pressure on material properties; experimental mechanics. *Mailing Add:* 1101 Elm Ave Provo UT 84604

BARTON, DAVID KNOX, ELECTRICAL ENGINEERING. *Current Pos:* EXEC VPRES, ANRO ENG, 84- *Personal Data:* b Greenwich, Conn, Sept 21, 27; m 49; c 8. *Educ:* Harvard Col, AB, 49. *Honors & Awards:* David Sarnoff Award, RCA Corp, 58; M Barry Carlton Award, Inst Elec & Electronics Engrs, 62. *Prof Exp:* Electronic engr, Signal Corps Eng Labs, 49-55 & RCA Corp, 55-63; consult scientist, Raytheon Co, 63-84. *Mem:* Nat Acad Eng; fel Inst Elec & Electronics Engrs. *Res:* Radar systems engineering and wave propagation effects on radar. *Mailing Add:* Anro Eng Inc 63 Great Rd Maynard MA 01754. *E-Mail:* anroma@aol.com

BARTON, DEREK HAROLD RICHARD, CHEMISTRY. *Current Pos:* Prof, 57-78, EMER PROF ORG CHEM, IMP COL, UNIV LONDON, 78-; DOW DISTINGUISHED PROF CHEM INVENTION, TEX A&M UNIV, 86- *Personal Data:* b Gravesend Eng, Sept 8, 18. *Educ:* Univ London, BSc, 40, PhD(org chem), 42. *Hon Degrees:* Numerous from US & foreign univs, 49-91. *Honors & Awards:* Nobel Prize in Chem, 69; Fritzsche Medal, Am Chem Soc, 56, Roger Adams Medal, 59, Second Centennial of the Priestly Chem Award, 74, Creativity in Org Synthesis Award, 89, Priestley Medal, 95; Davy Medal, Royal Soc, 61, Royal Medal, 72, Copley Medal, 80; Order of the Rising Sun, Emperor of Japan, 72; Order of Chevalie de la Legion d'Honneur, 74; First May & Baker Award, Royal Soc Chem, 87; First Goto Mem lectr, Nagolia Univ, Japan, 92; Nobel Lectr, Pohang Inst Sci & Technol, Korea, 92; First Fred Pattison Sr Lectr, Univ Western Ont, Can, 93; Ninth Archer lectr, Rensselaer Polytech Inst, 93; Rayson Huang lectr, Univ Hong Kong, 94; Patrick lectr, Kans State Univ, 94; Warner-Lambert lectr, Mich State Univ, 94; Ira Kukin lectr, Yeshiva Univ, NY, 94; Stork lectr, Columbia Univ, 95; Dakin lectr, Adelphi Univ, 95; Henri Moissan lectr, Inst Univ France, 96; Andrew J Moyer lectr, US Dept Agr, 97; Kolb lectr, Bradley Univ, 97. *Concurrent Pos:* Vis prof & lectr, numerous US & foreign univs, 45-; dir, Inst Chem Natural Substances, Nat Ctr Sci Res, 77-85, hon dir, 86- *Mem:* Foreign assoc Nat Acad Sci; foreign hon mem Am Acad Arts & Sci; Int Union Pure & Appl Chem (pres, 69-72); hon mem Acad Pharmaceut Sci; hon fel Royal Soc Chem; foreign fel Am Chem Soc; hon mem Chem Soc Japan; hon foreign mem Russ Acad Sci; hon mem Kitasato Inst; hon foreign mem Chinese Acad Sci; hon mem Korean Chem Soc; hon mem Pharmaceut Soc Japan; hon mem Arg Soc Org Chem. *Res:* Invention of new reactions in natural products chemistry. *Mailing Add:* Dept Chem Texas A&M Univ College Station TX 77843-3255

BARTON, DONALD WILBER, PLANT BREEDING. *Current Pos:* assoc prof, Cornell Univ, 51-59, head dept, 59-60, prof veg crops, 59-84, dir, NY State Agr Exp Sta & assoc dir res, Col Agr, 60-84, EMER PROF VEG CROPS, CORNELL UNIV, 84- *Personal Data:* b Fresno, Calif, June 12, 21; m 44; c 4. *Educ:* Univ Calif, BS, 46, PhD(genetics), 49. *Prof Exp:* Asst genetics, Univ Calif, 46-49; asst prof, Univ Mo, 50-51. *Concurrent Pos:* AEC fel, Univ Mo, 49-50, res grant genetics, 50-51; vis prof, Ore State Col, 59-60; res grant hort, Northwest Canners & Freezers Asn, 59- *Mem:* Genetics Soc Am; Am Soc Hort Sci; Sigma Xi. *Res:* Breeding and genetics of horticultural crops; genetic disease resistance. *Mailing Add:* 15 Whites Point Geneva NY 14456

BARTON, EVAN MANSFIELD, INTERNAL MEDICINE, RHEUMATOLOGY. *Current Pos:* PROF MED, RUSH MED COL, 71- *Personal Data:* b Chicago, Ill, Nov 7, 03; wid; c 2. *Educ:* Williams Col, AB, 24; Johns Hopkins Univ, MD, 29; Am Bd Internal Med, dipl, 42. *Prof Exp:* Intern, Presby Hosp, Chicago, 29-30; asst, Rush Med Col & Presby Hosp, 31-34; clin prof med, Med Col, Univ Ill, 51-71. *Concurrent Pos:* Fel path, Rush Med Col & Presby Hosp, 31-34, fel internal med, 36; vol asst path, Hamburg, Ger, 31; vol asst med res lab, Royal Infirmary, Aberdeen, Scotland, 35; attend physician, Presby-St Luke's Hosp, 36-; consult, rheumatol, Vet Admin Hosp, Hines, Ill, 46- *Mem:* Fel AMA; fel Am Col Physicians; Am Col Rheumatology. *Res:* Rheumatic diseases. *Mailing Add:* 1725 W Harrison St Chicago IL 60612-3828

BARTON, FRANKLIN ELLWOOD, PHYSICAL ORGANIC CHEMISTRY, PHYSICAL CHEMISTRY. *Current Pos:* Res chemist, 71-77, SUPV RES CHEMIST, RUSSELL RES CTR, SCI EDUC ADMIN, USDA, 77- *Personal Data:* b Baltimore, Md, Aug 4, 42; m 65; c 2. *Educ:* NGa Col, BS 64; Univ Ga, PhD(chem), 69. *Concurrent Pos:* Fel, Univ Ga, 70-71. *Mem:* Am Chem Soc; The Chem Soc; Am Oil Chemists Soc; Soc Appl Spectros. *Res:* Spectroscopic and chromatographic studies of the structure and association of plant polysaccharides and polyphenols and their utilization by ruminant animals. *Mailing Add:* Dept Agr RB Russell Agr Res Ctr PO Box 5677 Athens GA 30613-6199

BARTON, FURMAN W(YCHE), ENGINEERING MECHANICS, STRUCTURAL ENGINEERING. *Current Pos:* assoc prof appl mech, 67-78, PROF CIVIL ENG, UNIV VA, 78- *Personal Data:* b Greenville, SC, Sept 22, 32; m 63; c 2. *Educ:* Univ Va, BCE, 54; Univ Ill, MS, 59, PhD(struct mech), 62. *Prof Exp:* From res asst to res assoc struct, Univ Ill, 57-62, asst prof struct mech, 62-64; asst prof, Duke Univ, 64-67. *Mem:* AAAS; Am Soc Civil Engrs; Am Soc Mech Engrs; Am Acad Mech. *Res:* Structural dynamics; dynamic stability; discrete field mechanics; computer methods of structural analysis; systems analysis; finite element applications; nonlinear analysis. *Mailing Add:* Dept Civil Eng Thornton Hall Univ Va Charlottesville VA 22903

BARTON, GERALD BLACKETT, APPLIED CHEMISTRY. *Current Pos:* RETIRED. *Personal Data:* b Arco, Idaho, Oct 16, 17; m 43; c 6. *Educ:* Brigham Young Univ, BS, 39, MS, 41; Ohio State Univ, PhD, 50. *Prof Exp:* Chemist, Am Smelting & Refining Co, Utah, 41-43, res investr, NJ, 43-45; asst chem, Ohio State Univ, 45-48; chemist, Gen Elec Co, 48-65; sr res scientist, Chem Dept, Pac Northwest Lab, Battelle Mem Inst, 65-70; res scientist, Westinghouse Hanford Co, 70-81. *Mem:* Am Chem Soc. *Res:* Chemical processing of nuclear reactor fuels; disposal of radioactive wastes; analysis for trace impurities in gases; stress corrosion cracking of stainless steel. *Mailing Add:* 7707 W 12th Ave Kennewick WA 99337

BARTON, HARVEY EUGENE, SYSTEMATIC ENTOMOLOY, ECONOMIC ENTOMOLOGY. *Current Pos:* From asst prof to prof, 67-91, EMER PROF ZOOL, ARK STATE UNIV, 91- *Personal Data:* b Couch, Mo, Aug 26, 36; m 54; c 5. *Educ:* Ark State Univ, BSE, 62, MSE, 63; Iowa State Univ, PhD(entom), 69. *Mem:* Entom Soc Am; Sigma Xi; Lepidoptera Res Found; Lepidopterists Soc; Coleopterists Soc. *Res:* Systematics and morphology of heteroptera; dynamics of flying insect populations. *Mailing Add:* 909 Chestnut St Jonesboro AR 72401

BARTON, HENRY RUWE, JR, high energy physics; deceased, see previous edition for last biography

BARTON, JACQUELINE K, BIOPHYSICAL CHEMISTRY, BIOINORGANIC CHEMISTRY. *Current Pos:* PROF CHEM, CALIF INST TECHNOL, 89- *Personal Data:* b New York, NY, May 7, 52; m 90, Peter B Dervan; c Elizabeth E. *Educ:* Barnard Col, BA, 74; Columbia Univ, PhD(chem), 79. *Hon Degrees:* DSc, Knox Col, 91, Williams Col, 92, NJ Inst Technol, 93, Kenyon Col, 93. *Honors & Awards:* Alan T Waterman Award, NSF, 85; Nat Fresenius Award, Phi Lambda Upsilon, 86; Eli Lilly Award, Biol Chem, Am Chem Soc, 87, Award in Pure Chem, 88, Baekel and Medal, 91, Garvan Medal, 92; Tolman Medal, 95; Havinga Medal, 95; Karrer Medal. *Prof Exp:* Fel phys biochem, Dept Molecular Biol & Biochem, Yale Univ, 79-80; asst prof chem & biochem, Hunter Col, City Univ New York, 80-82; from asst prof to prof, chem & biol sci, Columbia Univ, 83-89. *Concurrent Pos:* Bd dirs, Dow Chem Co, 93-, Cortech Inc, 93-95. *Mem:* Am Chem Soc; fel AAAS. *Res:* Metal complex interactions with nucleic acids; biophysical probes of DNA structure and conformation; design of metal complexes as probes of DNA electron transfer. *Mailing Add:* Chem Div Calif Inst Tech 127-72 Pasadena CA 91125. *Fax:* 626-577-4976

BARTON, JAMES BROCKMAN, ELECTRONICS ENGINEERING. *Current Pos:* Mem tech staff, Cent Res Labs, 72-76, sect mgr, Charge Coupled Device Mem Design, 76-79, BR MGR, COMPLIMENTARY METAL OXIDE SEMICONDUCTOR TECHNOL DEVELOP, TEXAS INSTRUMENTS, 79- *Personal Data:* b Lubbock, Tex, July 12, 44. *Educ:* Univ Tex, Austin, BS & BA, 66; Mass Inst Technol, PhD(physics), 71. *Mem:* Inst Elec & Electronics Engrs. *Res:* Complimentary metal oxide semiconductor manufacturing processes and design methodologies for very large-scale integrated circuits. *Mailing Add:* Texas Instruments MS 446 PO Box 655474 Dallas TX 75265

BARTON, JAMES DON, JR, PLANT ECOLOGY. *Current Pos:* RETIRED. *Personal Data:* b Anna, Ill, Oct 25, 29; m, Grace E Valentine; c Jayne D & Diana J. *Educ:* Northern Ill Univ, BS, 52, MS, 53; Purdue Univ, PhD(plant ecol), 56. *Prof Exp:* Instr sci, Boston Univ Jr Col, 56-58; asst prof ecol, Boston Univ Grad Sch, 58-63; assoc prof ecol & dir Div Nat Sci, Southampton Col, Long Island Univ, 63-66, dean col, 66-68; prof bot, provost & vpres acad affairs, Alfred Univ, 68-75, prof spec environ studies, 75-76; dir inst res, State Univ NY Agr & Tech Col Alfred, 76-81, registr, 82-86. *Concurrent Pos:* Consult, Appel & Assocs & Southampton Town Conserv Comn. *Mem:* Ecol Soc Am; Sigma Xi. *Res:* Forest ecology; preparation of computer data base of all trees for 20 acres of Donaldsons Woods, Mitchell, Indiana, 20 year follow up, 1974, 30 year follow up, 1984, 40 year follow-up-1994; application of SPSS to ecological and environmental research problems. *Mailing Add:* RR1 Box 2344 Newfane VT 05345

BARTON, JANICE SWEENY, BIOPHYSICAL CHEMISTRY, PROTEINS & MICROTUBULES. *Current Pos:* assoc prof, 82-87, PROF CHEM, WASHBURN UNIV, 88-, CHAIR, 91- *Personal Data:* b Trenton, NJ, Mar 22, 39; m 67, Keith. *Educ:* Butler Univ, BS, 62; Fla State Univ, PhD(chem), 70. *Prof Exp:* Assoc res chemist, Eli Lilly & Co, 62-65; NIH fel, Johns Hopkins Univ, 70-72; asst prof chem, ETex State Univ, 72-78 & Tex Woman's Univ, 78-82. *Concurrent Pos:* Res grants, NSF, 75, 77-79, 86 & 95, Petrol Res Fund, 84-86 & NIH, 85-; coordr, Meeting in Miniature, Dallas-Fort Worth, Am Chem Soc, 81; mem, Comt Educ Health Prof, Am Chem Soc, 84-89; coun, Kans Acad Sci, 87-90; mem, NSF Rev Panel, Undergrad Fac Enhancement, 90, ILI panel, 92, 96; pres-elect, Kans Acad Sci, 91, pres, 92. *Mem:* Am Chem Soc; Biophys Soc; Sigma Xi. *Res:* The role and properties of proteins that undergo self-assembly into functional cellular macrostructures; the mechanism of tubulin assembly into microtubules; role of the nucleotide binding site of tubulin in assembly; characterization of tubulin's nucleotide site; nuclear magnetic resonance studies of nucleotide binding to tubulin. *Mailing Add:* 3401 SW Oak Pkwy Topeka KS 66614. *E-Mail:* zzbart@acc.wuacc.edu

BARTON, JEFFREY W, alcohol liver disease, for more information see previous edition

BARTON, JOHN R, INSTRUMENTATION. *Current Pos:* CONSULT. *Personal Data:* US citizen. *Educ:* Ga Inst Technol, BS, 49. *Prof Exp:* Physicist flight res lab, Off Air Res, US Air Force, 51-53; physicist, Statham Labs, 53-54; physicist, Southwest Res Inst, 49-51 & 54-59, sr res engr, Dept Electronics & Elec Eng, 59-61, mgr nondestructive eval, 61-68, dir, 69-72, tech vpres & dir, 72-74, vpres instrumentation res div, 75-85. *Mem:* Sigma Xi; fel Am Soc Nondestructive Testing. *Res:* New methods of nondestructive material evaluation; ultrasonics; eddy current; x-ray; gamma backscatter; new magnetic field perturbation methods. *Mailing Add:* 2962 Barton Hill Dr Bulverde TX 78163

BARTON, JOHN ROBERT, MATERNAL-FETAL MEDICINE. *Current Pos:* DIR ANTENATAL DIAGNOSTICS, CENT BAPTIST HOSP, 91- *Personal Data:* b Lexington, Ky, Aug 1, 57; m 86, Lisa Stephens; c Lucy & William. *Educ:* Centre Col Ky, BS, 79; Univ Ky, MS & MD, 85. *Prof Exp:* Fel maternal-fetal med, Univ Tenn, Memphis, 89-91. *Mem:* Am Col Obstet & Gynec; Soc Perinatal Obstetricians; AMA. *Res:* Pathophysiology of pre-eclampsia; management of disorders of pregnancy. *Mailing Add:* Cent Baptist Hosp 1740 Nicholasville Rd Lexington KY 40503. *Fax:* 606-275-6649

BARTON, KENNETH ALLEN, PLANT & MAMMALIAN GENETICS, GENETIC ENGINEERING. *Current Pos:* RES DIR DIS CONTROL, MONSANTO, 97- *Personal Data:* b Columbia, Mo, Jan 30, 51; m 87, Mary Allen; c Jessica. *Educ:* Bucknell Univ, BS, 73; Purdue Univ, PhD(plant physiol & biochem), 77. *Prof Exp:* Res fel, Cornell Univ, 78-80, Wash Univ, 80-82; scientist, Agracetus, Inc, 82-85, sr scientist, 85-90, vpres res & develop, 90-96, gen mgr, 96. *Concurrent Pos:* Lectr, Univ Wis, 82-, bd vis, 96-99; prin investr, USDA, NSF & Dept Energy, 84-; consult, UN Indust Develop Orgn-Int Ctr Genetic Eng & Biotechnol, 85. *Mem:* AAAS; Int Soc Plant Molecular Biol. *Res:* Developed technology for genetic engineering of plants and animals; managed research programs in human gene therapy; managed chemical and biotechnology crop disease protection research. *Mailing Add:* 4919 Hickory Trail Middleton WI 53562. *E-Mail:* kkbart@monsanto.com

BARTON, KENNETH RAY, WATER-BORNE POLYMERS, TEXTILE SIZES. *Current Pos:* CONSULT, 96- *Personal Data:* b Elberton, Ga, July 12, 36; m 63, Peggy Norton; c Stephen & Penny. *Educ:* Wofford Col, BS, 58; Univ Tenn, MS, 60, PhD(chem), 63. *Prof Exp:* Res chemist, Tenn Eastman Co, 64-66, sr res chemist, 66-75, res assoc, 76-87, tech assoc, Eastman Chem Div, 87-89, develop assoc, Eastek Inks, Eastman Kodak Co, 90-92, sr assoc, 93-96. *Mem:* Am Chem Soc; Am Asn Textile Chemists & Colorists; Tech Asn Pulp & Paper Indust. *Res:* Textile applications of water-dispersible polyesters; thermal bonding of non-woven fabrics; synthetic fiber lubricants, adhesives, coatings, textile sizes; aqueous inks. *Mailing Add:* 346 Round Ridge Rd Spartanburg SC 29302. *E-Mail:* kbarton@spartanburg.net

BARTON, LARRY LUMIR, MICROBIOLOGY, BIOCHEMISTRY. *Current Pos:* from asst prof to assoc prof, 72-93, PROF MICROBIOL, DEPT BIOL, UNIV NMEX, 93- *Personal Data:* b West Point, Nebr, May 13, 40; m 66, Sandra; c Brian & Gregory. *Educ:* Univ Nebr, BSc, 62, MS, 66, PhD(microbiol, biochem), 69. *Prof Exp:* Res assoc biochem, Univ Ga, 69-71; asst prof microbiol, Dept Pathobiol, Sch Health & Hyg, Johns Hopkins Univ, 71-72. *Concurrent Pos:* Assoc biochemist, Leonard Wood Mem Leprosy Found, 71-72; prin investr, NMex Energy Res Inst, 74-77, US Dept Interior through NMex Water Resources Res Inst, 74-79, NSF, 77-78, NIH, 79-85 & Dept Energy through Waste Mgr Educ Res Consortium, 91-93. *Mem:* Am Soc Microbiol; Sigma Xi; AAAS. *Res:* Metabolism of sulfur by microorganisms, especially energetics of sulfide formations; biotechnology; interaction of soil organic acids and microorganisms; metal metabolism. *Mailing Add:* Dept Biol Univ NMex Main Campus One Univ Campus Albuquerque NM 87131-0001. *Fax:* 505-277-0304; *E-Mail:* lbarton@triton.unm.edu

BARTON, LAWRENCE, INORGANIC CHEMISTRY. *Current Pos:* from asst prof to assoc prof, 66-86, PROF CHEM, UNIV MO, ST LOUIS, 86-, CHMN DEPT, 80- *Personal Data:* b Preston, Eng, Aug 5, 38; m 64, Patricia J Heppenstall; c 3. *Educ:* Univ Liverpool, BSc, 61, PhD(chem), 64. *Honors & Awards:* St Louis award, Am Chem Soc, 91. *Prof Exp:* Res assoc chem, Cornell Univ, 64-66. *Concurrent Pos:* Petrol Res Fund award, 67-69 & 96-; NSF awards, 69-72, 84, 87, 88, 93-97; sr res fel, Explosives Res & Develop Estab, Waltham, Abbey, Eng, 70-71; vis assoc prof, Washington Univ, 77 & Ohio State Univ, 77-78; chmn, St Louis Sect, Am Chem Soc, 80. *Mem:* Am Chem Soc; Royal Soc Chem; Am Asn Univ Prof. *Res:* Boranne and metallaborane clusters; lower boranes metalla and related compounds; organometallic chemistry. *Mailing Add:* Dept Chem Univ Mo St Louis MO 63121

BARTON, MARK Q, PHYSICS. *Current Pos:* RETIRED. *Personal Data:* b Kansas City, Mo, June 5, 28; m 54; c 2. *Educ:* Cent Methodist Col, AB, 50; Univ Ill, PhD(physics), 56. *Prof Exp:* Asst physics, Univ Ill, 50-55; physicist, Brookhaven Nat Lab, 56-74, chmn, Accelerator Dept, 74-78, tech dir Isabelle proj, 78-79, dep chmn, Nat Synchrotron Light Source, 84-86; res staff mem, Thomas J Watson Res Ctr, IBM, 89-91. *Mem:* Fel Am Phys Soc; fel Inst Elec & Electronics Engrs. *Res:* Intensity limitations of particle accelerators; accelerator design and development. *Mailing Add:* 6 Academy Lane Bellport NY 11713

BARTON, META PACKARD, FINANCIAL PLANNING. *Current Pos:* pres, 81-94, CHMN, FRIENDS RES CTR INC, BALTIMORE, 94-; PRES, NAMASTE ENTERPRISES INC, BALTIMORE, 87- *Personal Data:* b Baltimore, MD, Dec 2, 28; div; c Blair (Lee), Meta (Walker), Priscilla (Taylor) & Emilie Packard. *Educ:* Vassar Col, AB, 50; Loyola Col, MA, 77. *Prof Exp:* Bus res, Baltimore Asn Com, 50-51; fac, Bryn Mawr Sch, 52-62; staff psychologist, Epoch House, Essex, Md, 73-81; employee benefits coordr, profit sharing plan adminr & treas, Barton-Gillet Co, Baltimore, 80-90. *Mem:* Am Psychol Asn. *Mailing Add:* 6507 Montrose Ave Baltimore MD 21212

BARTON, PAUL, PETROLEUM. *Current Pos:* RETIRED. *Personal Data:* b Heckscherville, Pa, July 9, 36; m 57; c 5. *Educ:* Pa State Univ, BS, 57, MS, 60, PhD(chem eng), 63. *Prof Exp:* From res asst to res assoc, Pa State Univ, 57-68, asst prof chem eng, 68-94, sr tech specialist, Penntap, 85-89. *Concurrent Pos:* Consult, Am Aniline Prod, Inc, 66-67, Westvaco, 68, Union Carbide Corp, 70-71, Ventron Corp, 74-75, Argonne Nat Lab, 75, C-COR Electronics, Inc, 76-77, Baeuerle & Morris, Inc, 78-81, A M Todd Co, 80-81, 87-91, Leaf Protein Concentrate, Inc, 82-83, IGI Fermentation, Inc, 84, David Michael & Co, 84, Wm Wrigley Jr Co, 90, McCormick & Co, 90, Siemens Automotive, 90; vis scientist, Argonne Nat Lab, 71-72; sr prin engr, Air Products, 84-85. *Mem:* Am Inst Chem Engs; Am Chem Soc. *Res:* Phase equilibria; distillation; liquid extraction; dewaxing; supercritical extraction; pilot plant design; separational processes. *Mailing Add:* 696 Buffalo Run Rd Bellefonte PA 16823

BARTON, PAUL BOOTH, JR, GEOLOGY, MINERALOGY-PETROLOGY. *Current Pos:* GEOLOGIST, US GEOL SURV, 55- *Personal Data:* b New York, NY, Sept 30, 30; m 55, Martha Ashby; c Mark & John. *Educ:* Pa State Univ, BS, 52; Columbia Univ, AM, 54, PhD(geol), 55. *Honors & Awards:* Roebling Medal, Mineral Soc Am, 84. *Concurrent Pos:* Chmn, Geol Sect, Nat Acad Sci, 85-88. *Mem:* Nat Acad Sci; fel Mineral Soc Am (pres, 86); fel Geol Soc Am; Geochem Soc; Soc Econ Geol (pres, 79); Mineral Asn Can. *Res:* Genesis of mineral deposits; chemical and physical nature of ore forming fluids; phase relations between minerals; thermodynamic properties of minerals; long range availability of resources; geochemistry. *Mailing Add:* US Geol Surv 959 National Ctr Reston VA 22092

BARTON, RANDOLPH, JR, PHYSICAL CHEMISTRY, CRYSTALLOGRAPHY. *Current Pos:* Res chemist, 67-80, sr res chemist, 80-88, RES ASSOC, TEXTILE FIBERS DEPT, E I DU PONT DE NEMOURS & CO, INC, 88- *Personal Data:* b Wilmington, Del, Aug 15, 41; m 63, Margaret Peemoeller; c Randolph. *Educ:* Princeton Univ, AB, 63; Johns Hopkins Univ, MA, 65, PhD(phys chem), 68. *Mem:* Am Crystallog Asn; Am Phys Soc; Am Chem Soc. *Res:* Polymer structure and morphology. *Mailing Add:* 905 Edgehill Rd Wilmington DE 19807-3028. *Fax:* 302-695-9811; *E-Mail:* bartonr@csoc.dnet.dupont.com

BARTON, RICHARD DONALD, nuclear physics, for more information see previous edition

BARTON, RICHARD J, PHYSICAL CHEMISTRY, PHYSICAL METALLURGY. *Current Pos:* ASSOC PROF PHYSICS, UNIV REGINA, 65- *Personal Data:* b Painesville, Ohio, Aug 2, 28; m 55; c 3. *Educ:* Ohio Univ, BS, 50; Iowa State Univ, PhD(chem), 56. *Prof Exp:* Sr scientist, Mat Lab, Wright Air Develop Ctr, Wright Patterson AFB, Ohio, 57-61; asst prof metall, Colo Sch Mines, 61-65. *Mem:* Am Chem Soc; Electrochem Soc; Am Crystallogr Asn. *Res:* Structure and thermodynamic properties of non-stoichiometric compounds; electrochemical phenomena; structure of charge transfer compounds and organometallic compounds; crystallography; x-ray. *Mailing Add:* Dept Physics & Astron Univ Regina Regina SK S4S 0A2 Can. *Fax:* 306-585-4894; *E-Mail:* barton@meena.cc.uregina.ca

BARTON, RUSSELL RICHARD, DESIGN OF EXPERIMENTS, METAMODEL-BASED OPTIMIZATION. *Current Pos:* ASSOC PROF INDUST ENG, PA STATE UNIV, 90- *Personal Data:* b Buffalo, NY, Aug 11, 51; m 75, Robin Holliday; c 2. *Educ:* Princeton Univ, BS, 73; Cornell Univ, MS, 75, PhD(opers res), 78. *Prof Exp:* Mem tech staff, RCA David Sarnoff Res Ctr, 78-86; vis assoc prof opers res, Cornell Univ, 86-90. *Mem:* Inst Elec & Electronics Eng; Am Soc Eng Educ; Am Soc Qual Control; Inst Opers Res & Mgt Sci. *Res:* Statistics, simulation and optimization; use of network flow models to predict casting defects; multivariate statistical process control methods; metamodels for efficient yield prediction; stochastic optimization. *Mailing Add:* Pa State Univ 207 Hammond Bldg University Park PA 16802. *Fax:* 814-863-4745; *E-Mail:* barton@simplex.psu.edu

BARTON, STUART SAMUEL, surface chemistry; deceased, see previous edition for last biography

BARTON, THOMAS J, ORGANIC CHEMISTRY. *Current Pos:* instr, 67-69, from asst prof to prof, 69-83, DISTINGUISHED PROF ORG CHEM, IOWA STATE UNIV, 84-, DIR, MAT CHEM PROG, AMES LAB, 86- *Personal Data:* b Dallas, Tex, Nov 5, 40; m 66. *Educ:* Lamar State Col, BS, 62; Univ Fla, PhD(chem), 67. *Honors & Awards:* Frederic Stanley Kipping Award, Am Chem Soc, 82. *Prof Exp:* NIH fel chem, Ohio State Univ, 67. *Concurrent Pos:* Nat Acad Sci exchange scientist, Soviet Union, 75; NATO collab scientist, France 76; Japan Soc Prom Sci, 81; exchange prof, Nat Ctr Sci Res, Univ Montpellier, 83; res fel, Royal Chem Soc, 83. *Mem:* Am Chem Soc; Mat Res Soc. *Res:* Synthetic and mechanistic organosilicon chemistry; high temperature gas-phase molecular rearrangements; generation of reactive intermediates; synthesis of novel precursors for chemical vapor deposition amorphous silicon and silicon-based ceramics; synthesis of conducting organic polymers. *Mailing Add:* Iowa State Univ Ames Lab Ames IA 50011

BARTON, WALTER E, PSYCHIATRY. *Current Pos:* assoc prof, 52-63, CLIN PROF PSYCHIAT, SCH MED, BOSTON UNIV, 64-; EMER PROF PSYCHIAT, DARTMOUTH MED SCH, 74- *Personal Data:* b Oak Park, Ill, July 29, 06; wid; c John A (deceased), Gail M & Paul B. *Educ:* Univ Ill, BS, 28, MD, 31; Am Bd Neurol & Psychiat, dipl. *Hon Degrees:* DSc, Univ Ill, 75. *Honors & Awards:* Salmon Medal, NY Acad Med, 74; Distinguished Serv Award, Am Psychiat Asn, 73, Award in Admin Psychiat, 83. *Prof Exp:* Intern, West Suburban Hosp, Ill, 30-31; resident psychiat, Worcester State Hosp, 31-34, sr psychiatrist, 34-38, asst supt, 38-42; supt, Boston State Hosp, 45-63; med dir, Am Psychiat Asn, 63-74; sr physician, Vet Admin Gen Hosp, White River Junction, 74-77. *Concurrent Pos:* Lectr, Simmons Col, 36-37, Smith Col, 37-42, Clark Univ, 40-42, Columbia Univ & Yale Univ, 56-59, Med Sch, Tufts Univ, 58 & Med Sch, Georgetown Univ, 63-74; mem staff neurol, Nat Hosp, Eng, 38; assoc prof, 52-63, clin prof psychiat, Sch Med, Boston Univ, 64-; dir, Am Bd Neurol & Psychiat, 63-70; consult, NIMH & NIH, mem bd trustees, Joint Comn Ment Illness & Health & Joint Comn Ment Health of Children; mem spec res projs comt, NIMH & adv comt, Neurol-Psychiat Div, Vet Admin. *Mem:* Fel AMA; fel Am Psychiat Asn (pres, 61-62); fel Am Col Physicians; fel Am Col Psychiatists; Am Col Ment Health Adminr (pres, 80-81). *Res:* Mental health administration; ethics; forensic psychiatry; history of psychiatry; published 12 books and 175 articles in journals. *Mailing Add:* RFD 1 Box 188 Hartland VT 05048

BARTOO, JAMES BREESE, mathematics; deceased, see previous edition for last biography

BARTOS, DAGMAR, clinical biochemistry, for more information see previous edition

BARTOSHUK, LINDA MAY, TASTE PSYCHOPHYSICS, SENSORY PROCESSES. *Current Pos:* PROF SENSORY PROCESSES & NUTRIT, YALE UNIV & FEL, PIERCE FOUND, 70- *Educ:* Brown Univ, PhD(psychol), 65. *Mailing Add:* Dept Surg & Otolaryngol Yale Univ Sch Med PO Box 208062 New Haven CT 06520-8062

BARTOSIK, ALEXANDER MICHAEL, AGRICULTURAL ENGINEERING. *Current Pos:* AGR SUPV, WAIAWA CORRECTIONAL FAC, 92- *Personal Data:* b Warsaw, Poland, Sept 14, 24; US citizen; m 50. *Educ:* Akademia Rolnicza, Poland, MS, 50, PhD(agr technol), 56. *Prof Exp:* Prof agr eng, Univ Mosul, Iraq, 71-74, Am Univ Beirut, 74-75; res assoc, Univ Hawaii, 75-77; prof, Univ Federal, Brazil, 77-79; farm coordr, Hawaiian Community, Waimanalo, 80; consult, Trop Agr Adv Serv, Honolulu, 80-81; prof agr eng, Am Univ, Beirut, 81-82. *Concurrent Pos:* Assoc researcher, Indust Bastifiber Inst, Poznan, Poland, 51-59; asst prof, Col Eng, Poznan, Poland, 59-60 & 61-71; vis prof, Univ Ill, Urbana-Champaign, 60-61. *Mem:* Am Soc Agr Engrs. *Res:* Development of international agriculture by promoting agricultural engineering or mechanization; author or coauthor of 100 publications. *Mailing Add:* 911141 Kamaaha Loop Kopeli HI 96707

BARTOSIK, DELPHINE, OBSTETRICS & GYNECOLOGY. *Current Pos:* DIR, DIV REPRODUCTIVE ENDOCRINOL, DEPT OBSTET & GYNEC, HAHNEMANN UNIV, 78- *Personal Data:* b Chicago, Ill, Nov 22, 37. *Educ:* Univ Chicago, BS, 57; Women's Med Col, MD, 61. *Mem:* Endocrine Soc; Am Physiol Soc; Soc Endocrinol Great Britain; Am Fertil Soc. *Mailing Add:* 245 N Broad St Philadelphia PA 19107-1522

BARTOVICS, ALBERT, POLYMER CHEMISTRY. *Current Pos:* RETIRED. *Personal Data:* b Roosevelt, NY, Dec 1, 16; m 44, Helen Foster; c Albert & William. *Educ:* Polytech Univ, BS, 37, MS, 39, PhD(chem), 43. *Prof Exp:* Asst chem, Polytech Univ, 37-39; analyst, Shellac Res Bur, 39-40; res chemist, Firestone Tire & Rubber Co, 43-50 & Armstrong Cork Co, 50-52; from develop chemist to prod develop mgr, Borg Fabric Div, Amphenol-Borg Electronics Corp, 52-64; sr res chemist, Textile Res Lab, E I du Pont de Nemours & Co, 64-79. *Mem:* Am Chem Soc; Am Inst Chemists. *Res:* Viscometric and osmotic molecular weight studies; chlorination of synthetic polymers; polyvinyl chloride and related copolymers for various applications; development of pile fabrics from natural and synthetic fibers; end-use research on synthetic fibers. *Mailing Add:* 707 Potter Dr Cedarcroft Kennett Square PA 19348-1642

BARTRAM, JAMES F(RANKLIN), SIGNAL PROCESSING. *Current Pos:* RETIRED. *Personal Data:* b Brooklyn, NY, Mar 18, 26; m 47; c 2. *Educ:* Yale Univ, BE, 50, MEng, 51. *Prof Exp:* Mem tech staff tel commun, Bell Tel Labs Inc, 51-56; sr assoc weapons systs studies, G C Dewey & Co Inc, 56-59; fel engr, air arm div, Westinghouse Elec Corp, 59-61; prin engr, Submarine

Signal Div, Raytheon Co, 61-63; mem tech staff commun satellites, IT&T Co, 63-64; consult engr, Submarine Signal Div, Raytheon Co, 64-92. *Concurrent Pos:* Assoc ed, Acoust Signal Processing, J Acoust Soc Am, 80-83. *Mem:* Sr mem Inst Elec & Electronics Engrs; fel Acoust Soc Am. *Res:* Space-time signal processing in communications, radar and sonar fields. *Mailing Add:* 94 Kane Ave Middletown RI 02840

BARTRAM, RALPH HERBERT, SOLID STATE PHYSICS. *Current Pos:* from asst prof to assoc prof, Univ Conn, 61-71, prof physics, 71-92, dept head, 86-92, EMER PROF PHYSICS, UNIV CONN, 92- *Personal Data:* b New York, NY, Aug 16, 29; m 53, Ellen A Devlin; c Ellen B (Colburn) & Robert A. *Educ:* NY Univ, BA, 53, MS, 56, PhD(physics), 60. *Prof Exp:* Adv res physicist, Gen Tel & Electronics Labs, Inc, NY, 53-61. *Concurrent Pos:* Guest assoc physicist, Brookhaven Nat Lab, 66-71, consult, 71-85; tech adv, Gen Telephone & Electronics 61-, US Army, 66-70, Am Optical Co, 66-78, Timex Corp, 81-82 & Polaroid Corp, 87-88; res assoc, Theoret Physics Div, Atomic Energy Res Estab, Harwell, Eng, 67-68; vis prof, Clarendon Lab, Oxford Univ, Eng, 78; sr vis fel, Univ Strathclyde, Scotland, 93. *Mem:* Fel Am Phys Soc; Optical Soc Am. *Res:* Theory of color centers, luminescent centers and radiation damage in solids; theory of radiationless transitions in solids. *Mailing Add:* Dept Physics Univ Conn Storrs CT 06268. *Fax:* 860-486-3346

BARTSCH, GLENN EMIL, BIOSTATISTICS. *Current Pos:* ASSOC PROF BIOSTATIST, UNIV MINN, MINNEAPOLIS, 65- *Personal Data:* b Mankato, Minn, Sept 11, 28. *Educ:* Univ Minn, BS, 50, MA, 51; Johns Hopkins Univ, ScD, 57. *Prof Exp:* Asst, Univ Minn, 50-51 & Johns Hopkins Univ, 51-54; biostatistician, Army Chem Ctr, US Dept Army, 54-56; asst, Johns Hopkins Univ, 56-57, res assoc, 57-58; NIH fel, 58-59; asst prof biostatist, Western Reserve Univ, 60-65. *Mem:* Am Statist Asn; Sigma Xi. *Res:* Effects of non-normality upon common statistical tests; statistical techniques as applied to biological research. *Mailing Add:* 4735 Upton Ave S Minneapolis MN 55416

BARTSCH, RICHARD ALLEN, ORGANIC CHEMISTRY, SEPARATION SCIENCE. *Current Pos:* from assoc prof to prof, 74-88, PAUL WHITFIELD HORN PROF CHEM, TEX TECH UNIV, 88- *Personal Data:* b Portland, Ore, June 7, 40; m 66, Nadine L Putnam; c Robert & Lisa. *Educ:* Ore State Univ, BA, 62, MS, 63; Brown Univ, PhD(org chem), 67. *Prof Exp:* Instr chem, Univ Calif, Santa Cruz, 66-67; NATO fel, Univ Wurzburg, 67-68; asst prof chem, Wash State Univ, 68-73; asst prog adminr, Petrol Res Fund, 73-74. *Concurrent Pos:* Nat Acad Sci vis scientist, Czech, 78. *Mem:* Am Chem Soc; Royal Soc Chem; Sigma Xi. *Res:* Organic reaction mechanisms and synthesis; molecular and ionic recognition; crown ethers and other cation carriers; chromogenic ligands; synthetic polymeric ionomer membranes; metal ion extraction and transport; templated polymers. *Mailing Add:* Dept Chem & Biochem Tex Tech Univ Lubbock TX 79409-1061. *Fax:* 806-742-1289

BARTSCHMID, BETTY RAINS, ANALYTICAL CHEMISTRY. *Current Pos:* ASST PROF ANALYTICAL CHEM, VA POLYTECH INST & STATE UNIV, 75- *Personal Data:* b Shreveport, La, Dec 27, 49. *Educ:* Univ Tex, Austin, BS, 70; Univ Houston, PhD(anal chem), 74. *Prof Exp:* Fel anal chem, Colo State Univ, 74-75. *Mem:* Am Chem Soc; Optical Soc Am; Soc Appl Spectros. *Res:* Atomic absorption, fluorescense and emission applied to practical problems of trace metal analysis; development of a versatile, automatic background correcting atomic fluorescence system; molecular emission techniques to determine non-metals. *Mailing Add:* 104 Maywood St Blacksburg VA 24060

BARTUSKA, DORIS G, ENDOCRINOLOGY, METABOLISM. *Current Pos:* Asst prof med & clin path, Women's Med Col Pa, 66-71, assoc prof, Med Col Pa, 71-77, assoc dean curric, 74-76, actg dir, Ctr Women Med, 76-77, dir, Div Endocrinol & Metab, 73-95, prof med, 77-96, consult endocrinol, Pa Geriat Ctr, 82-85, EMER PROF MED, MED COL PA, 96- *Personal Data:* b Nanticoke, Pa, Apr 18, 29; m 51, Anthony; c Ann, Kathy, Lisa, Karen, Christine & Mia. *Educ:* Bucknell Univ, BS, 49; Woman's Med Col Pa, MD, 54. *Honors & Awards:* Father Clarence Shaffrey Award, St Joseph's Univ; Lindback Award, Am Med Womens Asn. *Concurrent Pos:* Consult endocrinol, Vet Admin Hosp, 70-; deleg, AMA; vchair, Educ & Sci Trust, Pa Med Soc. *Mem:* Am Thyroid Asn; Endocrine Soc; Asn Women Sci; fel Am Col Physicians; Am Asn Cancer Edu; Am Med Asn; Am Med Women's Asn. *Res:* Behavioral and genetic aspects of the endocrine diseases; endocrinology of aging-osteoperosis and altered thyroid function; influence of progesterone on human thyroid function; estrogen assay of malignant tumor tissue of the breast, effects of testosterone and estrogen on the mammary glands of iodine deficient rats; author or co-author of over 25 publications. *Mailing Add:* Allegheny Univ Health Sci Med Col Pa 3300 Henry Ave Philadelphia PA 19129

BARTZ, JERRY A, PLANT PATHOLOGY. *Current Pos:* asst prof, 69-75, ASSOC PROF PLANT PATH, UNIV FLA, 75- *Personal Data:* b Fond du Lac, Wis, Mar 4, 42; m 68; c 2. *Educ:* Univ Wis-Madison, BS, 64, MS, 66, PhD(plant path), 68. *Prof Exp:* Res fel, Environ Sci Prog, Univ Calif, Riverside, 68-69. *Concurrent Pos:* Vis prof, Univ Wis, 82; sr ed, Plant Dis, 86- *Mem:* Am Phytopath Soc; Int Soc Plant Path. *Res:* Mode of action of fungicides; treatment and prevention of post-harvest diseases of vegetables. *Mailing Add:* Dept Plant Path Univ Fla PO Box 110680 Gainesville FL 32611-2002

BARTZ, WARREN F(REDERICK), CHEMICAL ENGINEERING. *Current Pos:* RETIRED. *Personal Data:* b Sheldon, Iowa, Mar 18, 13; m 40, Alice Pugh; c W Fred Jr & John D. *Educ:* Iowa State Col, BS, 35; Univ NC, PhD(chem), 39. *Prof Exp:* Asst, Univ NC, 35-39; chem engr, Barrett Div, Allied Chem Corp, Pa, 40-43; chemist, Rohm and Haas Co, 43-75. *Mem:* Am Chem Soc. *Res:* Resins; phenolics; urea formaldehyde; alkyds; ion exchange. *Mailing Add:* 1515 The Fairway No 304 H Rydal PA 19046-1633

BARUA, ARUN B, RETINOID-SUGAR CONJUGATES, CHEMISTRY & ANALYSIS OF CAROTENOIDS. *Current Pos:* assoc scientist, 86-91, SCIENTIST, IOWA STATE UNIV, 91- *Personal Data:* b Shillong, India, Jan 1, 39; m 67, Kobita Sarma; c Bonali & Manali. *Educ:* Gauhati Univ, India, BSc(Hons), 57, MSc, 60, PhD(chem), 65. *Prof Exp:* From asst prof to assoc prof org chem, Gauhati Univ, 65-80; vis scientist, Iowa State Univ, 80-86. *Concurrent Pos:* vis scientist, Queen Mary Col, Univ London, 74. *Mem:* Am Soc Biochem & Molecular Biol; Am Chem Soc. *Res:* Chemical synthesis and study of bioactivity, metabolism and clinical usefulness of water-soluble sugar-conjugates of vitamin A; development of newer methods for the analysis of retinoids, carotenoids and tocopherols by high-performance liquid chromatography. *Mailing Add:* Dept Biochem Biophys Iowa State Univ 3256 Molecular Biol Bldg Ames IA 50011-0001. *Fax:* 515-294-4141; *E-Mail:* varg@molecbio.iastate.edu

BARUCH, JORDAN J(AY), INSTRUMENTATION, COMPUTER SCIENCE. *Current Pos:* PRES, JORDAN BARUCH ASSOCS, 81- *Personal Data:* b New York, NY, Aug 21, 23; m 44, Rhonda Wasserman; c Roberta, Marjory & Lawrence. *Educ:* Mass Inst Technol, BS & SM, 48, ScD, 50. *Hon Degrees:* LLD, Franklin Pierce Law Ctr, 81. *Prof Exp:* Vpres, Bolt Beranek & Newman, Inc, 49-66, dir, 49-77; gen mgr, Medinet Dept, Gen Elec Co, 66-68; pres, Educom, 68-70; independent consult, 70-71; lectr bus admin, Harvard Univ, 70-74; prof, Tuck Sch Bus & Thayer Sch Eng, Dartmouth Col, 74-77; asst secy sci & technol, US Dept Com, 77-81. *Concurrent Pos:* Asst prof, Mass Inst Technol, 50-53, lectr, 54-70; dir, Boston Broadcasters, 63-77 & 81-83, Baupost Group, 84-, Navig Sci Inc, 84-86, Gold Corp, 85-88; dir & treas, Inst Ment Health Initiatives, 82-; mem, Bd Sci & Technol Int Develop, Nat Res Coun; adv, US/Israel Hightech Comn; founder, Nat Ctr Indust Sci & Technol, China. *Mem:* Fel Nat Acad Eng; fel NY Acad Sci; fel Acoust Soc Am; fel Inst Elec & Electronics Engrs; fel Am Acad Arts & Sci; fel AAAS; Sigma Xi. *Res:* Computers in communication; acoustics; technology management. *Mailing Add:* Jordan Baruch Assocs 1200 18th St NW No 610 Washington DC 20036

BARUCH, MARJORY JEAN, ALGEBRA. *Current Pos:* ASST PROF MATH, HAMILTON COL, 81- *Personal Data:* b Boston, Mass, May 8, 51; m 79; c 1. *Educ:* Univ Chicago, BA, 72; Univ Pa, MA, 75, PhD(math), 79. *Prof Exp:* Res assoc math, Mich State Univ, 79-81. *Mem:* Sigma Xi. *Mailing Add:* 106 Cammot Lane Fayetteville NY 13066-1426

BARUCH, SULAMITA B, PHYSIOLOGY, MEDICINE. *Current Pos:* ASSOC ATTEND EMERGENCY RM DIR, DEPT MED, LAGUARDIA HOSP. *Personal Data:* b Medellin, Colombia, Jan 6, 36. *Educ:* Univ Valle, Colombia, MD, 59; Cornell Univ, PhD(physiol), 63. *Prof Exp:* Intern, Univ Hosp, Sch Med, Univ Valle, Colombia, 57-58, instr physiol sci, Sch Med, 59-60, asst prof, 63-65; asst prof physiol, Med Col, Cornell Univ, 65-70, assoc prof, 70-80. *Concurrent Pos:* Estab investr, Am Heart Asn, 67-72; adj assoc prof physiol, Med Col, Cornell Univ, 80- *Mem:* Am Soc Nephrology; Int Soc Nephrology; Am Physiol Soc. *Res:* Metabolic activity of the kidney as influenced by acid-base balance of the body; excretion of ammonia by the kidney; transport in isolated kidney membranes; renal handling of organic acids. *Mailing Add:* Emergency Dept LaGuardia Hosp 102-01 66th Rd Forest Hills NY 11375-2054

BARUSCH, MAURICE R, CHEMISTRY. *Current Pos:* RETIRED. *Personal Data:* b Yokohama, Japan, Sept 21, 19; m 42, Phyllis Roos; c Lawrence R & Ronald C. *Educ:* Stanford Univ, AB, 40, MA, 41, PhD(org chem), 44. *Honors & Awards:* Midgley Award, 77. *Prof Exp:* Res chemist, Calif Res Corp, 43-52, sr res chemist, 52-57, group supvr, 57-59, res assoc, 59-61, sr res assoc, 61-63, supvr, Fuel Additives Sect, 63-67, mgr, Fuel Additives Div, 67-69, mgr, Grease & Indust Oils Div, 69-73, mgr, Lubricating Oil Additives Div, 73-79, vpres, Lubricants Res Dept, Chevron Res Co, 79-82. *Mem:* Am Chem Soc; Combustion Inst. *Res:* Combustion of hydrocarbons; fuel and lubricating oil additives. *Mailing Add:* 651 Cypress Point Rd Richmond CA 94801

BARUT, ASIM ORHAN, theoretical physics, elementary particles; deceased, see previous edition for last biography

BARWICK, STEVEN WILLIAM, RADIOACTIVITY, HIGH ENERGY NUCLEAR PHYSICS. *Current Pos:* ASSOC RES PHYSICIST, UNIV CALIF, BERKELEY, 86-88. *Personal Data:* b Neenah, WI, Sept 16, 59; m 84. *Educ:* Mass Inst Technol, BA, 81; Univ Calif, Berkeley, MA, 83 & PhD(physics), 86. *Mem:* Am Phys Soc. *Mailing Add:* Dept Physics Univ Calif Irvine CA 92717

BAR-YAM, ZVI H, ELEMENTARY PARTICLE PHYSICS, HIGH ENERGY PHYSICS. *Current Pos:* COMMONWEALTH PROF PHYSICS, SOUTHEASTERN MASS UNIV, 72- *Personal Data:* b Krakow, Poland, Apr 12, 28; US & Israeli citizen; m 51, Miriam Mark; c Aureet, Yaneer & Sageet. *Educ:* Mass Inst Technol, BS, 58, MS, 59, PhD(physics), 63. *Prof Exp:* Res asst high energy physics, Synchrotron Lab, Mass Inst Technol, 57-63, staff mem, Lab Nuclear Sci, 63-64; from assoc prof to prof physics, Southeastern

Mass Univ, 64-70; assoc prof, Israel Inst Technol, 70-72 & 77-78. *Concurrent Pos:* Vis scientist, Div Sponsored Res, Mass Inst Technol, 64-65; prin investr, Cambridge Electron Accelerator, 65-71; vis scientist, Brookhaven Nat Lab, 73-, prin investr, 75- *Mem:* Am Phys Soc; Am Asn Physics Teachers. *Res:* Strong and electromagnetic interactions at high energies. *Mailing Add:* 19 Jordan Rd Brookline MA 02146. *Fax:* 617-738-8722; *E-Mail:* zbaryam@umassd.edu

BAR-YISHAY, EPHRAIM, RESPIRATORY PHYSIOLOGY. *Current Pos:* SR LECTR PHYSIOL, HEBREW UNIV, JERUSALEM, 94- *Personal Data:* b Hertzlia, Israel, June 28, 48; m 71, Hanna Zacks; c 3. *Educ:* Newark Col Eng, BSc, 73; Univ Minn, PhD(biomed eng), 78. *Prof Exp:* Jr engr, Eng Develop Ctr, Johnson & Johnson Co, New Brunswick, NJ, 72; res asst, Dept Mech Eng, NJ Inst Technol, Newark, 72; res asst biomed eng, Univ Minn, 72-78; head, Pulmonary Function Lab & Pediat Pulmonary Res Lab, Hadassah Univ Hosp, Mt Scopus, Jerusalem, Israel, 78-90; Park B Francis fel pulmonary res, Dept Thoracic Dis & Physiol, Mayo Clin, Rochester, Minn, 82-83; asst prof physiol, Mayo Med Sch, Univ Minn, Rochester, 83; asst prof pediat, Fac Med, Ohio State Univ, Columbus, 89-91. *Concurrent Pos:* Res scholar, Div Pulmonary Med, Childrens Hosp, Columbus, Ohio, 89-91; sect leader, Task Force Infant Pulmonary Function Testing, Am Thoracic Soc, 90-92; dir, Pulmonary Function Labs, Hadassah Univ Hosp, Hebrew Univ, Jerusalem, Israel, 91. *Mem:* Am Thoracic Soc; Am Physiol Soc; Int Biomed Eng Fedn; Europ Respiration Soc; Israel Soc Physiol & Parmacol (treas). *Res:* Respiratory physiology and mechanics; lung function testing in infants; whole body plethysmography; airway hyperreactivity and bronchial provocation tests; exercise-induced asthma; pulmonary function testing and instrumentation; respiratory muscle fatigue and EMG. *Mailing Add:* Pulmonary Function Lab Hadassah Univ Hosp Kiryat Hadassah PO Box 12000 Jerusalem 91120 Israel. *Fax:* 972-643-5897; *E-Mail:* emphraimb@cc.huji.ac.il

BARZEL, URIEL S, ENDOCRINOLOGY & METABOLISM, GERIATRICS. *Current Pos:* clin instr, 66-69, clin assoc, 69-71, from asst prof to assoc prof, 71-83, PROF MED, ALBERT EINSTEIN COL MED, 83- *Personal Data:* b Jerusalem, Israel, July 26, 29; US & Israeli citizen; m 52, Aviva; c Semadar, Eyal & Roney. *Educ:* Hebrew Univ, MA, 51; Columbia Univ, BSc, 54, MD, 58. *Prof Exp:* Intern, Montefiore Hosp, Bronx, NY, 58-59, trainee, Metab Ward, 59-61; sr resident & chief resident, Beilinson Hosp, Israel, 62-64; instr med, Tel Aviv Univ, 63-66. *Concurrent Pos:* Attend physician endocrinol & metab, Montefiore Med Ctr; physician & consult, Montefiore Med Group; book rev ed, J Am Geriat Soc. *Mem:* Fel Geront Soc Am; fel Am Geriat Soc; Endocrine Soc; Am Soc Bone & Mineral Res; NY Acad Sci. *Res:* Endocrinological and metabolic problems of aging; osteoporosis; disorders of calcium metabolisn in the elderly; abnormalities of calcium and thyroid metabolism. *Mailing Add:* Dept Med Albert Einstein Col Med 1300 Morris Park Ave Bronx NY 10461-1926

BARZILAI, JONATHAN, DECISION ANALYSIS, OPTIMIZATION. *Current Pos:* assoc prof, 87-90, DIR, SCH COMPUT SCI, TECH UNIV NS, 87-, PROF, 90- *Personal Data:* b Tel Aviv, Israel, June 2, 45; Can & Israeli citizen; m 72, Rachel Taase; c Dan. *Educ:* Technion Univ, Israel, BSc, 67, MSc, 78, DSc(appl math), 81. *Prof Exp:* Instr, Dept Math, Univ Tex, Austin, 80-82; asst prof, Fac Admin Studies, York Univ, 82-83; asst prof, Sch Bus, Dalhousie Univ, 83-86, assoc prof, 86-87. *Mem:* Inst Mgt Sci; Asn Comput Mach; Inst Elec & Electronics Engrs. *Res:* Design and analysis of methods for multi-criteria decision making; design and analysis of algorithms for continuous an discrete optimization. *Mailing Add:* Sch Comput Sci Tech Univ NS PO Box 1000 Halifax NS B3J 2X4 Can. *Fax:* 902-492-1517; *E-Mail:* barzilai@tuns.ca

BASAR, RONALD JOHN, RESEARCH ENGINEERING. *Current Pos:* DIR ENG & OPERS, AM MULTI GRAPHICS DIV, AM INT, CHICAGO, 89- *Personal Data:* b Kingston, Pa, Mar 28, 50; div; c Amber L & Kimberly A. *Educ:* Wayne State Univ, BS, 62; Rochester Inst Technol, MS, 76, MBA, 79. *Prof Exp:* Regist prof engr, res engr & mgr, Eastman Kodak Co, Rochester, NY, 72-87; dir strategic mkt develop, BAT Indust, Glassboro, NJ, 87-89. *Concurrent Pos:* Consult, RJB Financial Mkt; mem, Rochester Inst Technol. *Res:* Engineering executive; research engineering; electrical engineering; 4 patents for market introduction of line of Green Chemicals; 2 patents for laser imaging master. *Mailing Add:* 912 Shambliss Lane Buffalo Grove IL 60089

BASART, JOHN PHILIP, RADIO ASTRONOMY, NONDESTRUCTIVE EVALUATION. *Current Pos:* asst prof to assoc prof radio astron & elec eng, 69-80, PROF ELEC ENG, IOWA STATE UNIV, 80- *Personal Data:* b Des Moines, Iowa, Feb 26, 38; m 60; c 2. *Educ:* Iowa State Univ, BS, 62, MS, 63, PhD(elec eng), 67. *Prof Exp:* Instr electronics technol, Iowa State Univ, 64-67; res assoc radio astron, Nat Radio Astron Observ, Va, 67-69. *Concurrent Pos:* Syst scientist, Nat Astron Observ, NMex, 79-81. *Mem:* Am Astron Soc; Inst Elec & Electronics Engrs; Am Geophys Union; Int Astron Union; Royal Astron Soc. *Res:* Nondestructive evaluation; improvement of radio astronomy maps by development of new signal processing procedures; signal processing; radio galaxies; processing x-ray images of materials; eddy-current signal processing. *Mailing Add:* Dept Elec Eng Durham Ctr Iowa State Univ Ames IA 50011

BASAVAIAH, SURYADEVARA, SOLID STATE PHYSICS, ELECTRONICS. *Current Pos:* RES STAFF MEM APPL RES, WATSON RES CTR, IBM CORP, NY, 68- *Personal Data:* b Munnalur, India, Dec 12, 38; m 69; c 1. *Educ:* Madras Univ, BE, 60; Indian Inst Sci, Bangalore, ME, 61; Princeton Univ, MSE, 63; Univ Pa, PhD(elec eng), 68. *Prof Exp:* Sr res fel transistor sect, Nat Phys Lab, India, 61-62; instr elec eng, Drexel Univ, 63-66. *Mem:* Am Phys Soc; Inst Elec & Electronics Engrs. *Res:* Josephson tunnel junctions; superconductivity; thin films; semiconductor devices; active electronic circuits. *Mailing Add:* 92 Austin Rd Mahopac NY 10541

BASBAUM, CAROL BETH, IMMUNOCHEMISTRY MUCINS. *Current Pos:* ASSOC PROF HISTOL, UNIV CALIF, SAN FRANCISCO, 86- *Educ:* Univ Pa, PhD(anat), 72. *Res:* Tracheal secretion regulation. *Mailing Add:* Dept Anat Univ Calif Third St & Parnassus Ave Box 0452 San Francisco CA 94143-0001

BASCH, JAY JUSTIN, biological chemistry, for more information see previous edition

BASCH, PAUL FREDERICK, PUBLIC HEALTH, PARASITOLOGY. *Current Pos:* assoc prof, 70-83, PROF INT HEALTH, STANFORD UNIV, 83-, EMER PROF, 97- *Personal Data:* b Vienna, Austria, Nov 10, 33; nat US; m 66, Maria N Mourao; c Richard J & Daniel D. *Educ:* City Col New York, 54; Univ Mich, MS, 56, PhD(zool), 58; Univ Calif, Berkeley, MPH, 67. *Prof Exp:* Asst prof biol, Kans State Teachers Col, 59-62; from asst res zoologist to assoc res zoologist, Hooper Found, Univ Calif, San Francisco, 62-70. *Concurrent Pos:* Res zoologist, Inst Med Res, Malaysia, 63-65 & 69-70; mem panel parasitic dis, US-Japan Coop Med Sci Prog, NIH, 74-78 & Trop Med & Parasitol Study Sect, 77-81; dep chmn, US Schistosomiasis Deleg to People's Repub China, 76-79, distinguished scholar, 84; consult, WHO, Pan Am Health Orgn, UNICEF, UN Indust Develop Orgn, USAID, Off Technol Assessment & NIH, Kaiser Permanente. *Mem:* Am Soc Parasitol; Am Soc Trop Med & Hyg; Nat Coun Int Health; Royal Soc Trop Med & Hyg; Am Pub Health Asn. *Res:* Epidemiology and control of diseases; international health; planning and evaluating health projects in developing countries. *Mailing Add:* Dept Health Res & Policy Stanford Univ Sch Med Stanford CA 94305-5092. *Fax:* 650-843-1544; *E-Mail:* pbasch@leland.stanford.edu

BASCH, ROSS S, DEVELOPMENTAL IMMUNOLOGY, HEMATOLOGY. *Current Pos:* From asst prof to assoc prof, 66-82, PROF PATH, SCH MED, NY UNIV, 82- *Personal Data:* b Sept 6, 37; m 61; c 3. *Educ:* NY Univ, MD, 61. *Concurrent Pos:* Lab med officer, Dept Immuno Chem, Walter Reed Army Inst Res, US Army, 62-64; guest investr, Biochem Genetics Lab, Rockefeller Univ, 64-66; consult, Ortho Pharmaceut Co, 75-; vis fel, Dept Zool, Univ Col, London, 76-77; asst pathologist, Bellevue Hosp, New York, 77-; dir, Instrumentation Unit, Dept Path, NY Univ Sch Med, 80-, prog dir, Immunol Course, 81-86. *Mem:* Am Asn Immunologists; Am Asn Pathologists; Am Soc Flow Cytometry; Int Soc Develop & Comp Immunol; Soc Develop Biol; NY Acad Sci; Am Soc Microbiol; Soc Anal Cytol. *Res:* Developmental immunology; developmental hematology; maintenance of the differentiated state. *Mailing Add:* Dept Path Sch Med NY Univ 550 First Ave MBS 512 New York NY 10016-6402. *Fax:* 212-263-8211

BASCO, N, PHOTOCHEMISTRY, ATMOSPHERIC CHEMISTRY. *Current Pos:* RETIRED. *Personal Data:* b London, Eng, July 13, 29; m 56; c 2. *Educ:* Univ Birmingham, BSc, 53, PhD(chem), 56; Univ Cambridge, PhD, 66. *Prof Exp:* Sr sci off, Civil Serv, UK, 56-58; Imp Chem Indust fel chem, Univ Cambridge, 58-61; lectr, Univ Sheffield, 61-64; from asst prof to prof chem, Univ BC, 64-91. *Mem:* Royal Soc Chem; Inter-Am Photochem Soc. *Res:* Chemical kinetics studied by flash photolysis and kinetic spectroscopy; electronic absorption spectra of transient species; atmospheric photochemistry. *Mailing Add:* 4706 W Sixth Ave Vancouver BC V6T 1C5 Can

BASCOM, WILLARD, OCEANOGRAPHY, ARCHAEOLOGY. *Current Pos:* PROJ DIR, ANCIENT SHIPS SOC, 85- *Personal Data:* b New York, NY, Nov 7, 16; m 47; c 1. *Hon Degrees:* DSc, Univ Genoa, Italy, 92. *Honors & Awards:* Compass Award for Outstanding Contrib to Oceanog, Marine Technol Soc, 70; Explorers Medal, Explorers Club, 80; Rolex Award, 92. *Prof Exp:* Mining engr, Idaho, Ariz, Colo & NY, 40-45; res engr, waves & beaches, Univ Calif, 45-51 & oceanog instruments, Scripps Inst Oceanog, 51-54; tech dir, Comt Civil Defense, 54-55; exec secy, Meteorol Comt, 56; sabbatical yr study Polynesian hist, Tahiti, 57; exec secy maritime res comt, Nat Res Coun, 58; dir, Mohole Proj, AMSOC Comt, Nat Acad Sci, 59-62; pres, Ocean Sci & Eng, Inc, 62-70; pres, Seafinders, Inc, 71-73; dir, Southern Calif Coastal Water Res Proj, 73-85. *Concurrent Pos:* Consult, Comt Amphibious Opers, 49, Rockefeller Bros spec study group, 56-57 & sci progs, Columbia Broadcasting Syst TV, 58-59; mem panel underwater swimmers, Nat Acad Sci-Nat Res Coun, 50-53, proj Nobska, 56; mem plowshare comn, AEC, 61-69; mem, Naval Res Adv Comt, 70-; mem Lab Bd for Undersea Warfare, 73-; mem ocean sci bd, Nat Acad Sci, 78-84; mem, Coastal Eng Res Bd, US Army Corps Engrs, 78-86; dir expeds, Kelton Found, 91- *Mem:* Fel AAAS; Marine Technol Soc; Int Asn Water Pollution Res. *Res:* Oceanographic engineering and instrumentation; drilling in the deep sea; waves; beaches; science writing; undersea diamond mining; deep water archaeology; marine ecology and environmental studies; search for ancient ships with sonar global positioning satellite remotely operated vehicles in the Black Sea, Sea of Marmara, Algean Sea and find them. *Mailing Add:* 5137 Vista Hermosa Long Beach CA 90815

BASCUNANA, JOSE LUIS, TRANSPORTATION FUEL ECONOMY, INTELLIGENT VEHICLE-HIGHWAY SYSTEMS. *Current Pos:* SR TECH ADV, TECHNOL ASSESSMENT DIV, NAT HWY TRAFFIC & SAFETY ADMIN, DEPT TRANSP, 77- *Personal Data:* b Paris, France, Feb 10, 27; US citizen; m 57, Irene; c Xavier, Alicia, Guillermo, Irene & Enrique.

Educ: Cath Inst Arts & Indust, Spain, BS, 47; Univ Rochester, MS, 61, PhD(mech & aerospace sci), 68; Eastern Mich Univ, MA, 78. *Honors & Awards:* Honor, Res Soc Sigma Xi. *Prof Exp:* Design engr, Ctr Study Tech Automotive, Spain, 47-56, head car sect, 56-58; proj engr, Barreiros Diesel, Spain, 61-63; tech assoc eng res, Univ Rochester, 63-64; sr res engr power train systs res dept, Ford Motor Co, 67-70; chief hwy vehicle sect, Div Emission Control Technol, Environ Protection Agency, 70-77. *Concurrent Pos:* Prof engr. *Mem:* Am Soc Mech Engrs; Soc Automotive Engrs; Air & Waste Mgt Asn; Combustion Inst; Am Soc Testing Mat; Tire Soc. *Res:* Engine design and research; energy conversion and power plants air pollution; tire research; automotive crash avoidance research; published 14 papers in professional journals. *Mailing Add:* 9104 Cranford Dr Potomac MD 20854. *Fax:* 202-366-7237; *E-Mail:* jbascunana@mhtsa.dot.gov

BASDEKAS, NICHOLAS LEONIDAS, engineering mechanics; deceased, see previous edition for last biography

BASDEKIS, COSTAS H, POLYMER CHEMISTRY. *Current Pos:* RETIRED. *Personal Data:* b Manchester, NH, Feb 20, 21; m 45; c 4. *Educ:* Univ NH, BS, 42. *Prof Exp:* Polymer chemist, Plastics Div, Monsanto Plastics & Resins Co, 42-48, fibers chemist, Cent Res Dept, Dayton, Ohio, 48-50, group leader, 50-52, from group leader to sr group leader polymers, Plastics Div, 52-60, asst res dir polystyrene plastics, 60-64, mgr res new polymers, Plastics Div, 64-78, mgr res & develop explor polymers, New Prod, Develop Dept, 78-82. *Concurrent Pos:* Consult, 82-. *Mem:* Am Chem Soc. *Res:* Polystyrene and acrylonitrile-butadiene-styrene copolymer plastics; high nitrile polymers for barrier applications; synthesis and application studies of new types of engineering thermoplastics; process and product development of reinforced thermoplastics; exploratory polymers. *Mailing Add:* 57 Warwick St Longmeadow MA 01106-1046

BASEMAN, JOEL BARRY, MICROBIOLOGY. *Current Pos:* AT DEPT MICROBIOL, UNIV TEX HEALTH SCI CTR. *Personal Data:* b Boston, Mass, Apr 28, 42; m 68; c 3. *Educ:* Tufts Univ, BS, 63; Univ Mass, MS, 65, PhD(microbiol), 68. *Prof Exp:* Asst prof, 71-76, assoc prof microbiol, Sch Med, Univ NC, Chapel Hill, 76- *Concurrent Pos:* NIH fel, Harvard Univ & Harvard Med Sch, 68-71; USPHS grant, Univ NC, Chapel Hill, 75-76 & 78-79; US Army Res & Develop Command grant, 75-76 & 78-79. *Mem:* AAAS; Am Soc Microbiol; Sigma Xi. *Res:* Biochemistry of pathogenesis; regulation of animal cell growth. *Mailing Add:* Dept Microbiol Med Sch Univ Tex 7703 Floyd Curl Dr San Antonio TX 78284-6200

BASERGA, RENATO, PATHOLOGY. *Current Pos:* res prof, Fels Res Inst, 65-68, chmn dept, 68-73, PROF, DEPT PATH, SCH MED, TEMPLE UNIV, 68-, CHMN DEPT, 80-, SR INVESTR, FELS RES INST, 65- *Personal Data:* b Milan, Italy, Apr 11, 25; nat US; m 53, 74; c 2. *Educ:* Univ Milan, MD, 49. *Honors & Awards:* Louis Gross Mem Lectr, 74; Searle Lectr, Brit Soc Cell Biol, 76. *Prof Exp:* Asst path, Univ Milan, 49-51; assoc oncol, Med Sch, Univ Chicago, 53-54; from instr to assoc prof path, Med Sch, Northwestern Univ, 58-65. *Concurrent Pos:* Consult, Argonne Nat Lab, 59; chmn path study sect, NIH, 71-73 & mem cancer spec prog adv comt, 75-; first ann fac res award, Temple Univ, 82; Wellcome vis prof cell biol, 83. *Mem:* AAAS; Am Asn Cancer Res; Am Asn Path & Bact; Am Soc Exp Path; Am Soc Biol Chemists; Am Soc Microbiol. *Res:* Experimental pathology; control of cell division in normal and pathologic tissues; microinjection and hybrid cells to study gene expression during cell proliferation. *Mailing Add:* Jefferson Cancer Inst Bluemle Life Sci Bldg 624 233 S Tenth St Philadelphia PA 19107-5541

BASFORD, ROBERT EUGENE, CELL BIOLOGY. *Current Pos:* RETIRED. *Personal Data:* b Montpelier, NDak, Aug 21, 23; m 65, Carol Phebus; c Lee (Phebus). *Educ:* Univ Wash, BS, 51, PhD(biochem), 54. *Prof Exp:* From asst prof to prof, Univ Pittsburgh, 58-93, emer prof biochem, Sch Med, 93-94. *Concurrent Pos:* Res fel, Inst Enzyme Res, Univ Wis, 54-58. *Mem:* AAAS; Am Soc Cell Biol; Am Thoracic Soc; Reticuloendothelial Soc; Oxygen Soc; Am Soc Biochem & Molecular Biol. *Res:* Terminal electron transport in the mitochondria of heart and brain; energy metabolism of brain; biochemical basis of phagocytosis; neutrophil-endothelial cell interaction. *Mailing Add:* 1814 Murdoch St Pittsburgh PA 15217

BASH, FRANK NESS, RADIO ASTRONOMY. *Current Pos:* univ fel & fac assoc, Univ Tex, Austin, 67-69, from asst prof to prof, 69-85, chmn dept, 82-86, EDMONDS REGENTS PROF ASTRON, UNIV TEX, AUSTIN, 85-, DIR, MCDONALD OBSERV, 91- *Personal Data:* b Medford, Ore, May 3, 37; m 60, Susan M Fay; c Kathryn (Cervenke) & F Lee. *Educ:* Willamette Univ, AB, 59; Harvard Univ, MA, 62; Univ Va, PhD(astron), 67. *Prof Exp:* Assoc astronr, Nat Radio Astron Observ, 62-64, res assoc, 65-67. *Concurrent Pos:* Prin investr, NSF, 72-; Blunk prof, Univ Tex, 82-83. *Mem:* Am Astron Soc; Int Sci Radio Union; Int Astron Union. *Res:* Observational radio astronomy; star formation in spiral galaxies and the dynamics of giant molecular clouds; interpretation of neutral hydrogen and carbon monoxide observations in the galaxy. *Mailing Add:* McDonald Observ Mail Code C1402 Univ Tex Austin TX 78712. *Fax:* 512-471-1635; *E-Mail:* fnb@astro.as.utexas.edu

BASH, PAUL ANTHONY, COMPUTATIONAL CHEMISTRY, ENZYMOLOGY. *Current Pos:* RES BIOPHYS, ARGONNE NAT LAB, 92- *Personal Data:* b Reno, Nev, Sept 27, 52. *Educ:* Univ Calif, Berkeley, AB, 74, PhD(biophys), 86. *Prof Exp:* Fel chem, Harvard Univ, 86-90; asst prof chem & biophys, Fla State Univ, 90-92. *Mem:* Biophys Soc; Am Chem Soc; Am Phys Soc. *Res:* Computational methods to study structure-function relationships in biological macromolecules; theoretical investigations of enzyme reaction mechanisms and the process of protein folding. *Mailing Add:* Biophys Dept Argonne Nat Labs 9700 S Case Ave Argonne IL 60439

BASHAM, CHARLES W, HORTICULTURE, PLANT PHYSIOLOGY. *Current Pos:* asst prof, 65-75, ASSOC PROF HORT, COLO STATE UNIV, 75- *Personal Data:* b Ponca City, Okla, July 25, 34; m 63. *Educ:* Okla State Univ, BS, 56; Univ Md, PhD(hort), 64. *Prof Exp:* Instr hort, Okla State Univ, Contract Imp Ethiopian Agr Col, 59-61; asst prof, Kans State Univ, 64-65. *Mem:* Am Soc Hort Sci; Nat Asn Col & Teachers Agr; Sigma Xi. *Res:* computer applications in agriculture; production of vegetable crops under irrigation. *Mailing Add:* 1221 Green St Ft Collins CO 80524

BASHAM, JACK T, FOREST PATHOLOGY, STEM DECAY. *Current Pos:* RETIRED. *Personal Data:* b Lachine, Que, Nov 2, 26; m 56; c 3. *Educ:* Univ Toronto, BSc, 48, MA, 50; Queen's Univ, Ont, PhD(forest path), 58. *Honors & Awards:* Can Forestry Sci Achievement Award, Can Inst Forestry, 83. *Prof Exp:* Res scientist, Can Dept Agr, 48-60; res scientist, Can Forestry Serv, 60-88, part time res scientist, 88-91. *Mem:* Can Inst Forestry. *Res:* Ecology and succession patterns of fungi in their invasion and destruction of heartwood in living trees and of stem wood in recently killed trees, and their impact on forest management. *Mailing Add:* 2006 Queen St E Sault Ste Marie ON P6A 2H2 Can

BASHAM, JERALD F, SEMICONDUCTOR MANUFACTURING, OPTOELECTRONICS. *Current Pos:* VPRES, OPTOSWITCH INC, 89- *Personal Data:* b Alma, Ark, Apr 2, 42; m 80; c 3. *Educ:* Univ Ark, BSEE, 69; Stanford Univ, MSEE, 70. *Prof Exp:* Tech staff mem, Sandia Nat Labs, 69-75; dir opers, TRW Optoelectronics, 76-88; vpres, Alltest, Inc, 88-89. *Mem:* Inst Elec & Electronics Engrs. *Res:* Technical sales and marketing. *Mailing Add:* 3317 Bandolino Plano TX 75023

BASHAM, JULIA L, MAMMALS OF OHIO, CORAL REED FISH DISTRIBUTION IN CARIBBEAN. *Current Pos:* ASSOC PROF BIOL, SHAWNEE STATE UNIV, 91- *Personal Data:* b Portsmouth, Ohio, Sept 14, 50; m 73, David R; c 2. *Educ:* Univ Cincinnati, BA, 72, BS, 72, MS, 73; Marshall Univ, MA, 89. *Mem:* Nat Marine Educr Asn. *Mailing Add:* 940 Second St Portsmouth OH 45662

BASHAM, SAMUEL JEROME, JR, NUCLEAR ENGINEERING. *Current Pos:* Prin mech engr tribology, Battelle Mem Inst, 53-60, proj leader nuclear mat, 60-66, assoc div chief nuclear eng, Columbus Labs, 66-73, assoc sect mgr, 73-78, dept mgr eng develop, 78-80, mgr, Waste Packaging Prog Off, 80-83, Repository Proj Off, 83-85, asst prog mgr, Off Nuclear Waste Isolation, 85-89, prog mgr, Mich Low-Level Radiation Wasta Proj, 89-91, PROJ MGR, D&D PROG, BATTELLE-LANSING, 91- *Personal Data:* b Adairville, Ky, Feb 25, 27; m 49, Ellen Barnard; c George A & Emily A. *Educ:* Univ Ky, BS, 53; Ohio State Univ, MS, 74. *Concurrent Pos:* Chmn, Nuclear Eng Div, Am Soc Mech Engrs, 90-91. *Mem:* Am Nuclear Soc; fel Am Soc Mech Engrs; Sigma Xi. *Res:* Nuclear fuel materials development; radiation effects on instrumentation and electromechanical devices; nuclear waste isolation; decontamination and decommissioning. *Mailing Add:* 734 Whithorn Ct Westerville OH 43081. *Fax:* 614-424-3954

BASHAM, TERESA, IMMUNOLOGY, CANCER RESEARCH. *Current Pos:* Res assoc, 82-86, SR RES ASSOC, MED RES, STANFORD UNIV MED SCH, DEPT MED, DIV INFECTIOUS DIS, 86- *Personal Data:* b Roanoke, Va, Nov 3, 47; m 80; c 2. *Educ:* Va Commonwealth Univ, BS, 70; George Wash Univ, PhD(immunogenetics), 80. *Mem:* Int Soc Interferon Res; Am Asn Immunologists. *Res:* Possible cures for non-hodgkins lymphoma using natural biological products alone and in combination. *Mailing Add:* Sr Res Assoc Stanford Univ Sch Med Saratoga CA 95070-5809

BASHARA, N(ICOLAS) M, ELECTRICAL ENGINEERING. *Current Pos:* coordr optics res, Elec Mat Lab, 56-81, from assoc prof to prof elec eng, 61-73, res prof eng, 73-81, EMER RES PROF ENG, UNIV NEBR, LINCOLN, 81- *Personal Data:* b Bismarck, NDak, Mar 8, 17; m 41. *Educ:* Univ Nebr, BS, 47, MS, 58. *Prof Exp:* Physicist, Minn Mining & Mfg Co, 47-56. *Concurrent Pos:* NSF grants, 58-81; Off Naval Res grants, 60-71; sr ed Proc 2nd & 3rd Int Conf Ellipsemetry, 69 & 76. *Mem:* Fel Optical Soc Am. *Res:* Co-author one book. *Mailing Add:* 5431 Cloudburst Lane Lincoln NE 68521

BASHAW, ELEXIS COOK, CYTOGENETICS, PLANT BREEDING. *Current Pos:* asst prof, Tex Agr Exp Sta, 52-55, GENETICIST, AGR RES SERV, USDA, TEX A&M UNIV, 55- *Personal Data:* b Mt Juliet, Tenn, July 21, 23; m 45; c 2. *Educ:* Purdue Univ, BS, 47, MS, 48; Tex Agr & Mech Col, PhD(genetics), 54. *Honors & Awards:* Genetics & Plant Breeding Award, Nat Coun Com Plant Breeders, 81; Crop Sci Award, Crop Sci Soc Am, 82. *Prof Exp:* Asst agronomist, La Agr Exp Sta, 48-50. *Mem:* Fel AAAS; fel Am Soc Agron; fel Crop Sci Soc Am. *Res:* Cytogenetics of grasses, especially genetics of apomixis, reproductive systems; radiation breeding and interspecific hybridization. *Mailing Add:* 1208 Ashburn Ave College Station TX 77840

BASHE, WINSLOW JEROME, JR, PEDIATRICS, PREVENTIVE MEDICINE. *Current Pos:* prof, 79-90, EMER PROF COMMUNITY MED, WRIGHT STATE UNIV, 90- *Personal Data:* b Chicago, Ill, Mar 10, 20; m 53; c 3. *Educ:* Seton Hall Col, BS, 42; Loyola Univ, MD, 45; Columbia Univ, MPH, 59. *Prof Exp:* Intern gen med, Gorgas Hosp, CZ, 45-46, resident med, 46-47; resident pediat, Sea View Hosp, NY, 48-49; resident, Children's Hosp Philadelphia, 50, res assoc, 52-53; pvt pract, 53-57; epidemiologist commun dis, Ohio Dept Health, 57-58, chief div, 59-63; assoc clin prof pediat, Col Med, Univ Cincinnati, 63-70; assoc prof prev med & pediat, Ohio State Univ, 71-79. *Concurrent Pos:* Instr, Univ Pa, 51-53; instr & asst prof, Ohio State

Univ, 57-63. *Mem:* AAAS; Am Pub Health Asn; Sigma Xi. *Res:* Virology; mumps and hepatitis; staphylococcal disease; bone maturation of children; influenza; trichinosis; sudden cardiac death; general epidemiology. *Mailing Add:* Sch Med Wright State Univ PO Box 927 Dayton OH 45401

BASHEY, REZA ISMAIL, BIOCHEMISTRY. *Current Pos:* from asst prof to assoc prof med, 77-88, SR INVESTR, PHILADELPHIA GEN HOSP & ASSOC, RHEUMATOLOGY RES LAB, DEPT MED, UNIV PA, 75- *Personal Data:* b Bombay, India, Aug 28, 32; m 61; c 3. *Educ:* Univ Bombay, BSc, 52, MSc, 54; Rutgers Univ, PhD(biochem), 58. *Prof Exp:* Mem fac, Sch Med, Univ Miami, 62-64; res assoc biochem, Albert Einstein Col Med, 64-66, asst prof, 66-70; res asst prof, Hahnemann Med Col & Hosp, 70, res assoc prof med, 71-72, assoc prof med & biochem, 72-75, vis assoc prof biol & chem, 75-77. *Concurrent Pos:* Fel biochem, Univ Southern Calif, 58-60; partic fel, Howard Hughes Med Inst, Fla, 60-62; pool officer med sci, Indian Coun Med Res, Ministry Health, India, 64; assoc prof, Dept Med, Sect Rheumatology, Thomas Jefferson Univ, 88, prof, 90. *Mem:* AAAS; Am Chem Soc; Am Soc Biochem & Molecular Biol. *Res:* Connective tissue; collagen and glycosammoglycans, biosynthesis and involvement in fibrillogenesis; heart valve biochemistry in normal and diseased conditions; scleroderma and other skin diseases; cardiac collagen in hypertrophy and fibrosis. *Mailing Add:* Dept Med Thomas Jefferson Univ 508BLSB 233 Tenth St Philadelphia PA 19107

BASHIRELAHI, NASIR, BIOCHEMISTRY. *Current Pos:* from asst prof to assoc prof, 71-93, ASSOC PROF, DEPT SURG, DIV UROL, SCH MED, UNIV, MD, 77-, PROF BIOCHEM, SCH DENT, 93- *Personal Data:* b Tehran, Iran, Aug 26, 35; US citizen; m 78, Ziba; c Sasha & Nabil. *Educ:* Univ Tehran, BS, 60, Pharm D, 62, Univ Louisville, MS, 65, PhD(biochem), 68. *Prof Exp:* Assoc biochem, Harvard Med Sch, 70-71; asst dept surg, Mass Gen Hosp, 70-71. *Mem:* Endocrine Soc; AAAS; Biophys Soc; Soc Exp Biol & Med; Am Asn Advan Aging Res; Am Soc Biochem & Molecular Biol. *Res:* Mechanism of action and metabolism of steroid hormones; hormones and cancer; aging and differentiation. *Mailing Add:* Dept Biochem Univ Md Sch Dent 666 W Baltimore St Baltimore MD 21201-1586

BASHKIN, STANLEY, ATOMIC PHYSICS, NUCLEAR PHYSICS. *Current Pos:* dir, Van De Graaff Lab, 70-80, assoc dean, Col Liberal Arts, 80-82, PROF PHYSICS, UNIV ARIZ, 62- *Personal Data:* b Brooklyn, NY, June 20, 23; m 57; c 3. *Educ:* Brooklyn Col, BA, 44; Univ Wis, PhD(physics), 50. *Prof Exp:* Asst physics, Manhattan Proj, 44-46; asst prof physics, La State Univ, 50-53; from res assoc to assoc prof, Univ Iowa, 53-62. *Concurrent Pos:* Res fel, Calif Inst Technol, 59; Fulbright res scholar, Australian Nat Univ, 60, res fel, 69; mem comt atomic & molecular physics, Nat Acad Sci-Nat Res Coun; sr vis fel, Nuclear Physics Lab, Oxford Univ, 77-78; sr von Humboldt fel, Univ Bochum, 82. *Mem:* Optical Soc Am; Am Phys Soc; for mem Royal Soc Gothenburg. *Res:* Nuclear energy levels; atomic lifetimes; nuclear astrophysics; structures of highly ionized atoms. *Mailing Add:* Dept Physics Univ Ariz Tucson AZ 85721

BASHKOW, THEODORE R(OBERT), DATA COMMUNICATION, COMPUTER ARCHITECTURE. *Current Pos:* RETIRED. *Personal Data:* b St Louis, Mo, Nov 16, 21; m 60, Delphina Brownlee; c Lynn. *Educ:* Washington Univ, BS, 43; Stanford Univ, MS, 47, PhD(elec eng), 50. *Prof Exp:* Mem tech staff, Radio Corp Am Labs, 50-52 & Bell Tel Labs, 52-58; from assoc prof to prof elec eng, Columbia Univ, 58-79, chmn dept, 68-71, prof comput sci, 79-91. *Concurrent Pos:* Consult, Dewey Electronics, Advan Comput Tech, World Health Orgn & Network Anal Corp, 59-; chmn, Sci Secy Comt, 63-65; partic, Int Fedn Info Processing Socs Cong, 65; corp secy, Sullivan Comput Corp, 79-87, Chopp Comput Co, 87-93. *Mem:* Inst Elec & Electronics Engrs; Asn Comput Mach. *Res:* Digital computer architecture; distributed and parallel processing; data communications. *Mailing Add:* 92 Jay St Katonah NY 10536

BASHOUR, FOUAD A, BIOLOGY & MEDICINE, CARDIOLOGY. *Current Pos:* prof med & physiol, Southwestern Med Ctr, 71-95, EMER PROF PHYSIOG & MED, UNIV TEX, 95- *Personal Data:* b Tripoli, Lebanon, Jan 3, 24; US citizen; m 78, Val Imm. *Educ:* Am Univ Beirut, BA, 44, MD, 49; Univ Minn, PhD(med), 57. *Honors & Awards:* Officer, Order of the Cedar of Lebanon, 71. *Prof Exp:* Intern, Am Univ Beirut, 49-50; med officer, UN Relief & Works Agency, 50-51; resident internal med, Hosps, Univ Minn, 51-54, instr med, 55-57; res assoc, Med Sch, Am Univ Beirut, 57, asst prof med & in chg cardiopulmonary lab sect, 57-59; from instr internal med to assoc prof med, 59-63; prof med, Univ Tex Health Sci Ctr, Dallas, 71-84, emer prof, 95- *Concurrent Pos:* Mem sr med staff, Parkland Mem Hosp, Dallas & Zale Lipshy Univ Hosp; med & cardiac consult, St Paul Hosp, Dallas, John Peter Smith Hosp, Ft Worth, Methodist Hosps, Dallas, Wilford Hall Hosp, USAF Lackland AFB & Tex State Dept Pub Welfare; cardiac consult, Wilford Hall Hosp & Lackland AFB; mem ad hoc comt coronary care unit & coun basic sci, Am Heart Asn; ad hoc proj site visit, Nat Heart Inst, 65; pres, Cardiol Fund; mem, Coun Circulation & Basic Sci, Am Heart Asn, Coun Circulation & Cent Res Rev Comt; Fouad Bashour distinguished chair, Cardiovasc Physiol, 84 & 90, Fouad Bashour prof, 81; dir, Cardiovasc Inst, Methodist Hosp, Dallas, 67-78; consult, Nat Heart & Lung Inst; fel, Circulation Group, Am Physiol Soc, 75; hon adv, Univ Kuwait, 74-84. *Mem:* Am Heart Asn; fel Am Col Chest Physicians; Am Fedn Clin Res; Am Physiol Soc; Cent Soc Clin Res; Sigma Xi; Asn Advan Med Instrumentation; Am Soc Internal Med. *Res:* Cardiovascular physiology and diseases; author of over 200 publications. *Mailing Add:* Univ Tex Southwestern Med Ctr 5323 Harry Hines Blvd L4218 Dallas TX 75235-7297. *Fax:* 214-648-9376

BASILA, MICHAEL ROBERT, PHYSICAL CHEMISTRY. *Current Pos:* CONSULT, 88- *Personal Data:* b Scranton, Pa, June 5, 30; m 54; c 6. *Educ:* Norwich Univ, BS, 52; Rensselaer Polytech Inst, PhD(phys chem), 58. *Prof Exp:* Res chemist, Gulf Res & Develop Co, Pa, 58-61, supvr chem physics sect, 61-64, supvr catalysis sect, 64-67, supvr catalytic mechanisms sect, 67-68; dir res & develop, Howe Baker Eng, Inc, Tex, 68-70; tech dir catalyst, Nalco Chem Co, Chicago, Ill, 70-76; head lab, Katalco Corp, Chicago, 76-80. *Mem:* Catalysis Soc. *Res:* Infrared spectroscopy; molecular complexes; kinetics of catalytic reactions; process and catalyst development. *Mailing Add:* 807 Woodland Hills Dr Tyler TX 75701

BASILE, DOMINICK V, MORPHOLOGY, BRYOLOGY. *Current Pos:* assoc prof, 71-77, PROF BOT, LEHMAN COL, 77- *Personal Data:* b Yonkers, NY, Oct 15, 31; m 59; c 3. *Educ:* Manhattan Col, BS, 58; Columbia Univ, MA, 62, PhD(bot), 64. *Prof Exp:* Teaching asst bot, Columbia Univ, 58-63, preceptor, 63-64; guest investr plant biol, Rockefeller Univ, 64-65, res assoc, 65-66; asst prof bot, Columbia Univ, 66-71. *Concurrent Pos:* NSF fel, 64-65; adj cur, NY Bot Garden, 71- *Mem:* Am Bryol & Lichenological Soc; Torrey Bot Club (vpres, 75, corresp secy, 80-); Am Inst Biol Sci; Sigma Xi; Am Soc Plant Physiol. *Res:* Chemical regulation of morphogenesis and phylogeny of plants, especially the Bryophyta. *Mailing Add:* Biol Sci Dept Lehman Col City Univ New York Bronx NY 10468

BASILE, LOUIS JOSEPH, MOLECULAR SPECTROSCOPY, INORGANIC CHEMISTRY. *Current Pos:* RETIRED. *Personal Data:* b Chicago, Ill, Mar 20, 24; m 53, Catharine F Nelson; c Joseph, Mary & Anne. *Educ:* Univ Chicago, BS, 48, MS, 49; St Louis Univ, PhD(chem), 54. *Honors & Awards:* Meggers Award, Soc Appl Spectros, 75. *Prof Exp:* Assoc chemist, Argonne Nat Lab, 52-84. *Concurrent Pos:* Mem bd, sect comt N15, methods of nuclear mat control, Am Nat Stand Inst; assoc ed, Appl Spectros, 71-84. *Mem:* Fel AAAS; Am Chem Soc; Sigma Xi; Soc Appl Spectros. *Res:* Energy transfer; plastics; hydrides of boron; rare earths; transplutonium chemistry; infrared spectroscopy; high pressure molecular spectroscopy. *Mailing Add:* 9544 S Springfield Evergreen Park IL 60642-2013

BASILE, ROBERT MANLIUS, PHYSICAL GEOGRAPHY, SOIL MORPHOLOGY. *Current Pos:* prof, 69-81, EMER PROF GEOG, UNIV TOLEDO, 81- *Personal Data:* b Youngstown, Ohio, Mar 12, 16; m 45, Anne Webb; c Lorraine B & Karen L. *Educ:* Washington & Lee Univ, BS, 38; Mich State Univ, MS, 40; Ohio State Univ, PhD(geog), 53. *Prof Exp:* Instr soils & geog, Northwestern State Col, Okla, 40-42; from instr to prof geog, Ohio State Univ, 50-69. *Concurrent Pos:* Vis prof, Univ Winnipeg, 62, San Jose State, 66, Nat Defense Educ Act Inst, Univ SC, 67 & Univ Wyo, 81. *Res:* Climatology and the morphology of soils. *Mailing Add:* 5929 Angleview Ct Sylvania OH 43560-1204

BASILEVSKY, ALEXANDER, ECONOMETRICS, ECONOMICS. *Current Pos:* ASSOC PROF STATIST, UNIV WINNIPEG, CAN, 77- *Personal Data:* b USSR, April 11, 43; Can citizen; m 66; c 2. *Educ:* Concordia Univ, Can, BA, 64; Univ Southampton, Eng, MA, 69, PhD(statist), 73. *Prof Exp:* Lectr statist, Univ Kent, Eng, 70-75; sr researcher econ, Man Guaranteed Income Exp, 75-77. *Concurrent Pos:* Consult, Man Guaranteed Income Exp, 77-78; pres-at-large, Statist Asn Man; adj prof, Univ Man, 79-80. *Mem:* Am Statist Asn; Can Statist Asn. *Res:* Linear statistical models and their application; estimation in presence of missing data; analysis of socio-economic experiments. *Mailing Add:* Dept Math Univ Winnipeg 515 Portage Ave Winnipeg MB R3B 2E9 Can

BASILI, VICTOR ROBERT, COMPUTER SCIENCE, SOFTWARE ENGINEERING. *Current Pos:* CONSULT, 88- *Personal Data:* b Brooklyn, NY, Apr 13, 40; m 67, Patricia A D'Amato; c Alexander, Brian & Theodore. *Educ:* Fordham Univ, BS, 61; Syracuse Univ, MS, 63, Univ Tex, Austin, PhD(comput sci), 70. *Honors & Awards:* Meritorious Awards, Inst Elec & Electronics Engrs. *Prof Exp:* Res asst comput ctr, Syracuse Univ, 61-63; from instr to asst prof math & comput sci, Providence Col, 63-67; teaching asst comput sci, Univ Tex, Austin, 67-69, curric coordr, Southwest Region Educ Comput Network, 69-70; from asst prof to prof, Inst Advan Comput Studies, Univ Md, 70-88, chmn, Dept Comput Sci, 82-88. *Concurrent Pos:* Prin investr grants, Off Naval Res, 72-85, NASA Goddard Space Flight Ctr 75-88 & Air Force Off Sci Res, 74-88; comput sci consult, Inst Comput Appln Sci & Eng, NASA-Langley Res, Hampton, Va, 74-; expert comput sci math, Naval Res Lab, Washington, DC, 75-; consult, Naval Surface Weapons Ctr, Dahlgren, Va, 75-77, Comput Sci Corp, Falls Church, Va, 77- & IBM Fed Systs Div, Gaithersburg, Md, 77-; assoc ed, J Systs & Software, 84-; mem, Search Comt Dir, Univ Md Inst Advan Comput Sci, 92-93, chmn, Software Prof Master's Degree Comt; mem, Deans Comt to Eval, Univ Md, Inst Advan Comput Sci; govt consult, Expert Witness, Fed Aviation Admin, IDA, US Army Oper Test & Eval Agency; indust consult, United Technol Corp, IBM, Ericsson Telecom, Andersen & Coopers & Lybrand; ed-in-chief, Trans Software Eng, 88-92; bd mem, Comput Res Asn, 84-93, treas, 89-91. *Mem:* Fel Inst Elec & Electronic Engrs Comput Soc; Asn Comput Mach. *Res:* Research is centered around viewing software engineering as an experimental science; activities include the building of descriptive models of software processes, products and other forms of experience, experimenting with these models in order to build improvement oriented packaged prescriptive models; specific developments include the Quality Improvement Paradigm, the Goal/Question/Metric Factory and the Experience Factor Organization. *Mailing Add:* Dept Comput Sci Univ Md Rm 4111 AV Williams Bldg College Park MD 20742. *Fax:* 301-405-6707; *E-Mail:* basili@cs.umd.edu

BASILICO, CLAUDIO, GROWTH FACTORS, CELL CYCLE. *Current Pos:* res scientist, 67-69, from assoc prof to prof path, 70-90, PROF MICROBIOL & CHMN DEPT, NY UNIV SCH MED, 90- *Personal Data:* b Milan, Italy, Feb 7, 36; US citizen; m 61; c 3. *Educ:* Univ Milan, Italy, MD, 60. *Prof Exp:* Instr, Inst Clin Med, Univ Milan, 61-62; ricercatore qualificato, Int Lab Genetics & Biophys, Naples, Italy, 63-66; res assoc cell biol, Albert Einstein Col Med, 66-67. *Concurrent Pos:* Res fel, Div Biol, Calif Inst Technol, 62; instr animal cell cult, Cold Spring Harbor Lab, 74, mem bd trustees, 81-86; dir, Prog Viral & Molecular Oncol, NY Univ Cancer Ctr, 77-; mem, Adv Comt Virol & Cell Biol, Am Cancer Soc, 78 & Adv Comt Cellular & Develop Biol, 79-82; chmn, Gordon Res Conf, Meriden, NH, 87; prof, Dept Genetics, Univ Milan, 87. *Mem:* Am Soc Microbiol; Am Soc Cell Biol; Am Asn Cancer Res; Am Soc Virol. *Res:* Molecular mechanisms of carcinogenesis; genes and gene-functions involved in regulating the proliferation of normal and cancer cells. *Mailing Add:* Dept Microbiol 550 First Ave NY Univ Sch Med New York NY 10016-6481

BASIN, M(ICHAEL) A(BRAM), ELECTRICAL ENGINEERING. *Current Pos:* RETIRED. *Personal Data:* b Harbin, Manchuria, Apr 13, 29; US citizen; m 54; c 2. *Educ:* Calif Inst Technol, BS, 51, MS, 52, PhD(elec eng & physics), 54. *Prof Exp:* Elec engr, Gen Elec Co, 51; res engr, analog comput & aerodyn, Calif Inst Technol, 51-54, res engr, 54-55; mgr eng serv div, Comput Eng Assocs, 55-58; mgr sonar res & develop, Hughes Aircraft Co, 58-64; sr mem tech staff, Data Systs Div, Litton Industs, Inc, 64-66, tech mgr undersea warfare progs, 66-70, tech dir, Advan Navy Systs, 70-72; founder & pres, SDP Inc, 72-90; mgr, Sherman Oaks Field Off, Orincon-SDP, 90-91. *Concurrent Pos:* Instr eng exten, Univ Calif, Los Angeles, 58; consult, Comput Eng Assocs, 58-59; resident scientist, Tudor Hill Lab, Bermuda under subcontract to Litton Industs, Inc from Hudson Labs, Columbia Univ, 65-66. *Mem:* Inst Elec & Electronics Engrs; Am Inst Aeronaut & Astronaut; Acoustical Soc Am; Sigma Xi. *Res:* Sonar system design; marine technology; signal processing and display studies; direct analog computer technique development and utilization; aeroelastic dynamic and static analyses. *Mailing Add:* 3522 Wrightwood Ct Studio City CA 91604

BASINGER, JAMES FREDERICK, PALEOBOTANY. *Current Pos:* PROF GEOL SCI, UNIV SASK, 81- *Personal Data:* m 92, Elisabeth E McIver; c Claire O. *Educ:* Univ Alta, BSc, 73, MSc, 76, PhD(paleobot), 79. *Prof Exp:* Fel, Ind Univ, 79-80, Univ Adelaide, Australia, 80-81, Univ Calgary, 81. *Concurrent Pos:* Res fel, Natural Sci & Eng Res Coun Can, Univ Sask, 81-91; assoc ed, Can J Bot, 92- *Mem:* Bot Soc Am; Int Orgn Paleobot; Can Bot Asn. *Res:* Evolution of high latitude vegetation; evolution of northern deciduous and mixed evergreen forests; early cretaceous floras of western Canada; devonian floras of the Canadian Arctic Islands; tertiary climate change in the high northern latitudes. *Mailing Add:* Dept Geol Sci Univ Sask Saskatoon SK S7N 5E2 Can. *Fax:* 306-966-8593; *E-Mail:* jim.basinger@sask.usask.ca

BASINGER, RICHARD CRAIG, MATHEMATICS, SYSTEMS ANALYSIS. *Current Pos:* ASSOC DIV LEADER, LAWRENCE LIVERMORE NAT LAB, 79- *Personal Data:* b Kansas City, Kans, Oct 29, 38; m 61; c 2. *Educ:* Univ Mo-Rolla, BS, 60; Univ Kans, MA, 62, PhD(math), 65. *Prof Exp:* Mem tech staff weapon systs anal, Atomic Energy Comn, Sandia Corp, 65-79. *Res:* Mathematical analysis; growth properties of meromorphic functions; weapons systems analysis; operations research; mathematical software. *Mailing Add:* 2712 Superior Dr Livermore CA 94550

BASINSKI, ZBIGNIEW S, METAL PHYSICS, MATERIAL SCIENCE. *Current Pos:* RES PROF, MCMASTER UNIV, 87-, EMER PROF MAT SCI, 93- *Personal Data:* b Wolkowysik, Poland, 28. *Educ:* Univ Oxford, BSc, 52, MA, 55, PhD, 64. *Mem:* Fel Royal Soc London; fel Royal Soc Can. *Res:* Metal Physics; material science. *Mailing Add:* Inst for Mat Res ABB 427 McMaster Univ 1280 Main St W Hamilton ON L8S 4M1 Can

BASKERVILLE, CHARLES ALEXANDER, ENGINEERING GEOLOGY, LANDSLIDE RESEARCH. *Current Pos:* from asst prof to prof eng geol, 65-79, dean, Sch Gen Studies, 70-79, EMER PROF, DEPT EARTH & PLANETARY SCI, CITY COL, CITY UNIV NY, 83-; PROF GEOL, CENT CONN STATE UNIV, 90- *Personal Data:* b New York, NY, Aug 19, 28; m 53, 79, Susan Platt; c Mark D, Shawn A, Charles M & Thomas M. *Educ:* City Col New York, BS, 53; NY Univ, MS, 58, PhD(micropaleont, stratig), 65. *Honors & Awards:* Award Excellence Eng Geol, Nat Consortium Black Prof Develop, 78. *Prof Exp:* Asst civil engr, NY State Dept Transp, 53-65; proj chief & res eng geol, US Geol Surv, 79-90. *Concurrent Pos:* Eng geol consult, Madigan-Hyland-Praeger Cavanaugh-Waterbury Engrs, 68-69, St Raymond's Cemetery, 70-73 & Consol Edison Co NY, 73; mem, Nat Adv Comt Minority Partic in Geosci, Dept Interior, 72-75; panelist & chmn, NSF Grad Fel Prog, 79-80; chmn educ & training subcomt, US Nat Comt Tunnelling Technol, Nat Res Coun, 83-88; commonwealth vis prof geol, George Mason Univ, Fairfax, Va, 87-89; guest lectr, Syracuse Univ, Hofstra Univ, State Univ NY, Binghamton, Lafayette Col, Easton, Pa; prin investr planetary geol, NASA; mem, Adv Comt Earth Sci, Nat Res Coun, 89-92; mem, NY Low Level Radioactive Waste Comt, Nat Acad Sci; prof physics/earth sci, Cent Coun State Univ, 91-95. *Mem:* Fel Geol Soc Am; Am Inst Prof Geologists; Sigma Xi; NY Acad Sci; Asn Eng Geologists; Int Asn Eng Geol. *Res:* Landslide studies, State of Vermont; landslide process research and susceptibility mapping; engineering and geologic mapping of New York; ground failure hazards. *Mailing Add:* Cent Conn State Univ 1615 Stanley St New Britain CT 06050. *Fax:* 860-827-7877; *E-Mail:* smtp%baskerville@ccsu.ctsateu.edu

BASKERVILLE, GORDON LAWSON, FORESTRY, ECOLOGY. *Current Pos:* PROF FORESTRY, UNIV NEW BRUNSWICK, 74- *Personal Data:* b Emerson, Man, Can, Feb 20, 33; m 58; c 4. *Educ:* Univ New Brunswick, BScF, 55; Yale Univ, MF, 57, PhD(forest ecol), 64. *Prof Exp:* Res scientist silvicult, Can Dept Forestry, 55-74. *Concurrent Pos:* Mem Can subcomt terrestial productivity, Int Biol Prog, 65- *Mem:* Ecol Soc Am; Soc Am Foresters; Can Inst Forestry; Can Pulp & Paper Asn. *Res:* Physiological and ecological basis for silviculture; total biomass and productivity in forests. *Mailing Add:* Dept Forestry Univ BC 2329 West Mall Vancouver BC V6T 1W5 Can

BASKES, MICHAEL I, ATOMISTIC CALCULATIONS, INTERATOMIC POTENTIALS. *Current Pos:* Staff mem, Sandia Nat Labs, 69-83, supvr sci comput, 83-84, supvr theoret, 84-89, SUPRVR MAT PROCESSES, SANDIA NAT LABS, 89- *Personal Data:* b Chicago, Ill, June 13, 43; m 68, Carole Dixon; c Michelle & David. *Educ:* Calif Inst Technol, BSc, 65, PhD(mat sci), 70. *Honors & Awards:* Outstanding Res Award, US Dept Energy, 82 & 88. *Concurrent Pos:* Vis scientist, Univ Delft, Neth, 79; detailee, temp asst US Dept Energy, 90-91; ed-in-chief, Modelling & Simulation in Mat Sci & Eng, 92-; mem, Nat Mat Adv Bd, 96- *Mem:* Mat Res Soc; Metals Soc. *Res:* Development of interatomic potentials; atomistic calculations of defects, surfaces, interfaces and dislocations; atomistic and phenomenological calculations of the interaction of hydrogen and helium with metals. *Mailing Add:* Sandia Nat Labs MS 9403 PO Box 969 Livermore CA 94551-0969. *Fax:* 510-294-3410; *E-Mail:* baskes@ca.sandia.gov

BASKETT, THOMAS SEBREE, WILDLIFE BIOLOGY. *Current Pos:* prof, 73-85, EMER PROF WILDLIFE & FISHERIES, UNIV MO, COLUMBIA, 85- *Personal Data:* b Liberty, Mo, Jan 23, 16; m. *Educ:* Cent Methodist Col, Mo, AB, 37; Univ Okla, MS, 39; Iowa State Col, PhD(zool), 42. *Honors & Awards:* Aldo Leopold Award. *Prof Exp:* Res asst, Iowa State Col, 38-41, exten wildlife specialist, USDA, 41, asst prof zool, 46-47; asst prof wildlife mgt, Univ Conn, 47-48; biologist, US Fish & Wildlife Serv, Mo, 48-68; chief, Div Wildlife REs, US Bur Sport Fisheries & Wildlife, Washington, DC, 68-73; biologist & leader, Mo Coop Wildlife Res Unit, US Fish & Wildlife Serv, 73-85. *Concurrent Pos:* Ed, J Wildlife Mgt, 66-68. *Mem:* Wildlife Soc (pres, 71); Am Ornithologists Union. *Res:* Wildlife management; ecology of pheasant, bobwhite, swamp rabbit and bullfrog; effects of timber harvest on deer foods; breeding biology and behavior of mourning dove; terrestrial habitat evaluation. *Mailing Add:* 201 Bittersweet Ct Columbia MO 65203

BASKIN, DENIS GEORGE, PEPTIDES, BRAIN. *Current Pos:* res asst prof, Dept Med & Biol Sci, Univ Wash, 79-85, res assoc prof, Dept Med & Biol Struct, 85-89, DIR CYTOHISTOCHEM LAB, DIABETES RES CTR, SCH MED & DIR CORE HISTOLOGY/EM LAB, UNIV WASH, 79-, RES PROF, DEPTS MED & BIOL STRUCT & VET ADMIN MED CTR, SEATTLE, 89-, ASSOC DIR, DIABETES-ENDOCRINOL RES CTR, 92- *Personal Data:* b Minneapolis, Minn, Feb 7, 41; m 64; c 4. *Educ:* San Francisco State Col, BA, 62; Univ Calif, Berkeley, PhD(zool), 69. *Prof Exp:* NIH fel, Albert Einstein Col Med, 69-71; from asst prof to assoc prof zool, Pomona Col, 77-79. *Concurrent Pos:* NIH & NIMH res fel, Dept Anat, Sch Med, Univ Minn, Minneapolis, 77-78; ed-in-chief, J Histochem-Cytochem, 95-; mem coun, Histochem Soc 86-88. *Mem:* Int Fedn Soc Histochem & Cytochem (secy, 95-); Endocrine Soc; Am Diabetes Asn; Sigma Xi; Soc Neurosci; Histochem Soc (pres-elect & pres, 88-89); Soc Study Ingestive Behav. *Res:* Brain regulation of metabolism; insulin receptors in the brain; leptin receptors in the brain; localization of peptide and neurotransmitter receptors; neuropeptide regulation of body weight and obesity. *Mailing Add:* Res Serv Div Metabolism Mail Stop 151 Dept Vet Affairs Puget Sound Health Care Syst 1660 S Columbian Way Seattle WA 98108-1532. *Fax:* 206-764-2164; *E-Mail:* baskindg@u.washington.edu

BASKIN, JERRY MACK, PLANT ECOLOGY. *Current Pos:* from asst prof to assoc prof, 68-81, PROF BOT, UNIV KY, 81- *Personal Data:* b Covington, Tenn, July 27, 40; m 68. *Educ:* Union Univ, Tenn, BS, 63; Vanderbilt Univ, PhD(biol), 67. *Prof Exp:* Res assoc plant physiol, Univ Fla, 67-68. *Mem:* Ecol Soc Am; Bot Soc Am; Torrey Bot Club. *Res:* Autecology of herbaceous, vascular plants; biology and phytogeography of plant taxa endemic to rock outcrop communition of inglaciated eastern United States; biology of plants rare in Kentucky. *Mailing Add:* Dept Biol Sci Univ Ky 500 S Limestone St Lexington KY 40506-0001

BASKIN, RONALD J, BIOPHYSICS, FORCE GENERATION IN MOTOR PROTEINS. *Current Pos:* from asst prof to assoc prof, Univ Calif, Davis, 64-71, assoc dean, Col Lett & Sci, 67-71, chmn dept, 71-79, PROF MOLECULAR & CELLULAR BIOL, UNIV CALIF, DAVIS, 71- *Personal Data:* b Joliet, Ill, Nov 25, 35; m 58, Lydia Lendl; c James & Thomas. *Educ:* Univ Calif, Los Angeles, AB, 57, MA, 59, PhD(biophys), 60. *Prof Exp:* Fel biophys, Univ Calif, Los Angeles, 60-61; asst prof biol, Rensselaer Polytech Inst, 61-64. *Mem:* AAAS; Biophys Soc Am; Soc Cell Biol; Am Physiol Soc. *Res:* Muscle biophysics; thermodynamics of biological systems; force generation in motor proteins. *Mailing Add:* Dept Molecular & Cellular Biol Univ Calif Davis CA 95616. *E-Mail:* rjbaskin@ucdavis.edu

BASKIN, STEVEN IVAN, PHARMACOLOGY, TOXICOLOGY. *Current Pos:* res assoc, 71-73, res asst prof, 73-74, asst prof, 74-78, ASSOC PROF PHARMACOL, MED COL PA, 78; TEAM LEADER, CARDIAC PATHOPHYSIOL, US ARMY MED RES INST CHEM DEFENSE. *Personal Data:* b Los Angeles, Calif, Nov 14, 42; m 66; c 2. *Educ:* Univ Southern Calif, PharmD, 66; Ohio State Univ, PhD(pharmacol), 71. *Honors & Awards:* Pharmaceut Mfg Asn Award, 75-77; Am Heart Asn Southeastern Pa Award, 75-77. *Prof Exp:* NIH trainee, Ohio State Univ Col Med, 67-71. *Concurrent Pos:* Consult, Minn Mining & Mfg Co, 74-77, NSF, 75-, Syntex

Pharmaceut Co, 77-, Nat Inst Aging, 77 & Dept Pub Welfare, Commonwealth Pa, 78- *Mem:* Am Heart Asn; Int Study Group Res Cardiac Metabolism; AAAS; Am Fedn Clin Res; Gerontol Soc. *Res:* Pharmacology of taurine and related amino acids; digitalis and other inotrophic agents; phenytoin and other antiepileptic drugs; neurotransmitters; mechanisms; kinetics and toxicity; aging and effects of drugs on aging. *Mailing Add:* Biochem Technol Attn: MCMR-UV-PB US Army Med Res Inst 3100 Rickett's Point Rd Aberdeen Proving Ground MD 21010-5425

BASLER, EDDIE, JR, PLANT PHYSIOLOGY. *Current Pos:* assoc prof, 57-67, PROF BOT, OKLA STATE UNIV, 67- *Personal Data:* b Blanchard, Okla, Mar 25, 24; m 56; c 4. *Educ:* Univ Okla, BS, 50, MS, 52; Washington Univ, PhD(bot), 54. *Prof Exp:* Res assoc, Washington Univ, 54-55, asst prof bot, 55-57. *Mem:* Am Soc Plant Physiologists; Bot Soc Am; Weed Sci Soc Am. *Res:* Mechanisms of herbicidal action; translocation of herbicides and auxins; metabolism of herbicides. *Mailing Add:* 1619 E McElroy Pl Stillwater OK 74075

BASLER, ROY PRENTICE, RADIOPHYSICS, IONOSPHERIC PHYSICS. *Current Pos:* SR PHYSICIST, SRI INT, 73- *Personal Data:* b Florence, Ala, Aug 12, 35; m 58; c 5. *Educ:* Hamilton Col, AB, 56; Univ Alaska, MS, 61, PhD(physics), 64. *Prof Exp:* Res assoc, Geophys Inst, Univ Alaska, 58-64; staff physicist, ITT Electro-Physics Labs, 64-73. *Concurrent Pos:* Mem comn III, Int Sci Radio Union. *Mem:* Am Geophys Union; AAAS; Fedn Am Scientists. *Res:* High frequency radio propagation in the ionosphere search for extraterrestrial intelligence; solar-terrestrial relations; solar power satellites; ionospheric radio wave absorption; scintillation of satellite radio signals. *Mailing Add:* 311 Claire Pl Menlo Park CA 94025

BASMADJIAN, DIRAN, CHEMICAL ENGINEERING. *Current Pos:* RETIRED. *Personal Data:* b Dresden, Ger, Mar 4, 29; Can citizen. *Educ:* Swiss Fed Inst Technol, dipl ing chem, 52; Univ Toronto, MASc, 54, PhD(chem eng), 59. *Prof Exp:* Sci officer, Fuels Div, Dept Mines & Tech Survs, Can, 58-59; from asst prof to assoc prof, Univ Toronto, 59-72, prof chem eng, 72- *Concurrent Pos:* Consult, Chem Proj Ltd, Fibreglas Can Ltd, St Lawrence Cement Co, B F Goodrich Can Ltd, Spar Aerospace Ltd & Aerofall Mills Ltd. *Res:* Industrial gas adsorption and drying operations; mathematical analysis and modelling of heat and mass transport phenomena; biophysical studies of kidney function. *Mailing Add:* Dept Chem Eng Univ Toronto 200 Col Toronto ON M5S 3E5 Can

BASMAJIAN, JOHN ARAM, METALLURGY. *Current Pos:* RETIRED. *Personal Data:* b Binghamton, NY, Mar 10, 29; c 1. *Educ:* Purdue Univ, BS, 56; Rensselaer Polytech Inst, MS, 61. *Prof Exp:* Process metallurgist, Knolls Atomic Power Lab, 58-59, irradiations engr, 59-62; staff mem, Los Alamos Sci Lab, Univ Calif, 62-67; sr res scientist, Pac NW Labs, Battelle Mem Inst, 67-70; prin engr, Westinghouse Hanford Co, 70-88; consult, 88-89. *Mem:* Am Inst Mining, Metall & Petrol Engrs; Am Soc Metals; Am Nuclear Soc; NY Acad Sci. *Res:* Irradiation effects in materials; physical metallurgy of ferrous and nonferrous metals; nuclear metallurgy; refractory metal technology; liquid metal technology; plutonium and uranium metallurgy; nuclear ceramic materials. *Mailing Add:* PO Box 445 Richland WA 99352

BASMAJIAN, JOHN V, NEUROSCIENCES. *Current Pos:* prof med & dir rehab progs, 77-86, EMER PROF MED & ANAT, MCMASTER UNIV & CHEDOKE HOSPS, 86-; DIR RES & TRAINING GRANT, EASTER SEAL RES INST, TORONTO, 90- *Personal Data:* b Constantinople, Turkey, June 21, 21; Can citizen; m 47, Dora Lucas; c Haig, Nancy & Sally. *Educ:* Univ Toronto, MD, 45; FRCP(C), FACRM, FRCPS. *Honors & Awards:* Starr Medal, 56; Kabakjian Award, 65; Gold Key Recipient, Am Cong Rehab Med, 77; Henry Gray Laureate Award, Am Asn Anatomists, 91. *Prof Exp:* Demonstr anat, Univ Toronto, 46-47, lectr, 49-51, from asst prof to prof, 51-57; prof & head dept, Queen's Univ, Ont, 57-69; prof anat & phys med & dir, Regional Rehab Ctr, Emory Univ, 69-77. *Concurrent Pos:* Asst resident surg, Hosp Sick Children, 47-48 res assoc, 55-57; clin asst phys med, St Thomas Hosp, London, 53; hon secy, Banting Res Found, 55-57; Nat Res Coun exchange scientist, Soviet Acad Sci, 63; chief, Neurophysiol Lab, Ga Ment Health Inst, 69-77; JCB grant award, 85. *Mem:* AAAS; fel Am Col Angiol; Am Acad Neurol; Am Asn Anat; Can Asn Anat; fel Soc Behav Med; fel Royal Col Physicians. *Res:* Electromyography of normal anatomic and physiologic functions and of diseased muscle; nerve-muscle electrophysiology; studies of normal vascular patterns; biomechanics; bioengineering; psychophysiology. *Mailing Add:* 106 Forsyth N Hamilton ON L8S 4E4 Can. *Fax:* 905-521-7927

BASOLO, FRED, INORGANIC CHEMISTRY. *Current Pos:* from instr to assoc prof, Northwestern Univ, Evanston, Ill, 46-59, chmn dept, 69-72, Morrison prof, 80-90, PROF CHEM, NORTHWESTERN UNIV, EVANSTON, ILL, 59-, MORRISON EMER PROF ORG CHEM, 90- *Personal Data:* b Coello, Ill, Feb 11, 20; m 47; c 4. *Educ:* Southern Ill Norm Univ, BEd, 40; Univ Ill, MS, 42, PhD(chem), 43. *Hon Degrees:* DSC, Southern Ill Univ, Carbondale, 84. *Honors & Awards:* Award in Inorg Chem, Am Chem Soc, 64, Award for Mechanisms of Inorg Reactions, 71, Award for Distinguished Serv in Inorg Chem, 75, George C Pimentel Award Chem Educ, 92; Bailar Medalist, 73; Dwyer Medalist, 77; James Flack Norris Award, 81; Oesper Mem Award; Award Res Inorg Chem, Italian Chem Soc, 88; Harry & Carol Mosher Award, 90; Chinese Chem Soc Medal, 91; Monie A Ferst Medal, Sigma Xi, 92; Chem Pioneer Award, Am Inst Chemists, 92, Gold Medal Award, 93; Numerous Named Lectureships. *Prof Exp:* Res chemist, Rohm & Haas Chem Co, Pa, 43-46. *Concurrent Pos:* Guggenheim fel, Tech Univ Denmark, 54-55; NSF sr fel, Inst Inorg Chem, Univ Rome, 61-62; NATO vis prof, WGer, 69; bd trustees & bd chmn, Gordon Res Conf, 76; chmn, Chem Sect, AAAS, 79; mem, Bd Chem Sci & Technol, Nat Acad Sci-Nat Res Coun, 81-86; hon prof, Lanzhou Univ, 85, Zhongshan Univ, 88; distinguished vis prof, Onio State Univ, 92. *Mem:* Nat Acad Sci; Sigma Xi; Am Chem Soc (pres-elect, 82, pres, 83); fel Japanese Soc Prom Sci; fel AAAS; fel Am Acad Arts & Sci; Ital Acad Sci. *Res:* Coordination compounds; reaction mechanisms of inorganic complex compounds; metal nitrenes; synthetic oxygen-carriers; more than 350 scientific publications. *Mailing Add:* Dept Chem Northwestern Univ Evanston IL 60208

BASOR, ESTELLE, MATHEMATICS. *Current Pos:* PROF MATH, CALIF POLYTECH STATE UNIV, 76- *Educ:* Univ Calif, BA, PhD. *Concurrent Pos:* Vis assoc prof, Univ Calif, Santa Cruz, 82, 85; sabbatical, Bryn Mawr Col, 83-84, Univ Calif, Santa Cruz, 91. *Mem:* Am Math Soc; Asn Women Math. *Mailing Add:* Math Dept Calif Polytech State Univ San Luis Obispo CA 93407

BASORE, B(ENNETT) L(EE), COMMUNICATIONS THEORY, SCIENCE. *Current Pos:* PROF ELEC ENG, OKLA STATE UNIV, 67-, HEAD, GEN ENG, 78- *Personal Data:* b Oklahoma City, Okla, Aug 31, 22; div; c 3. *Educ:* Okla Agr & Mech Col, BS(math), 48; Mass Inst Technol, ScD(elec eng), 52. *Prof Exp:* Asst, Okla Agr & Mech Col, 46-48; asst, Mass Inst Technol, 48-49, res asst, res lab of electronics, 50-52, asst group leader, Lincoln Lab, 52; staff mem, Sandia Corp, 52-57; assoc tech dir, Dikewood Corp, 57-63; phys sci officer, US Arms Control & Disarmament Agency, 63-67. *Concurrent Pos:* Indust electronics fel, 51; interim assoc dean, Okla State Univ, 87-; consult, US Air Force, Jet Propulsion Lab, US Arms Control & Disarmament Agency, Sandia Nat Labs, Battelle-Columbus. *Mem:* Inst Elec & Electronics Engrs; Am Soc Eng Educ; Sigma Xi. *Res:* Communication theory and signal processing; radar systems; stochastic systems. *Mailing Add:* Dept Elec Eng Okla State Univ Stillwater OK 74078-0001

BASOV, NIKOLAI GENNADIEVICH, PHYSICS. *Current Pos:* Staff, P N Lebedev Phys Inst, USSR Acad Sci 48-58, vdir sci work, 58-73, dir, 73-89, HEAD, LAB QUANTUM RADIO PHYSICS, P N LEBEDEV PHYS INST, USSR ACAD SCI, 63-, DIR, 89-; PROF SOLID STATE PHYSICS, MOSCOW INST PHYS ENGRS, 63- *Personal Data:* b Usman, Russia, Dec 14, 22; m 50, Ksenia Tikhonovna; c Gennadiy & Dmitriy. *Educ:* Moscow Mech Inst, D, 56. *Hon Degrees:* LLD, Polish-Mil-Tech Acad, 72, Jena Univ, 74, Prague Poly Inst, 75, Univ Pavia, 77 & Madrid Poly Univ, 85. *Honors & Awards:* Nobel Prize in Quantum Electronics, 64; Lenin Prize, 59; Gold Medal, Czech Acad Sci, 75; A Volta's Gold Medal, 77; E Henkel Gold Medal, Ger Dem Repub, 86; Commodor's Cross Order of Merit, Poland, 86; Kalinga Prize, UNESCO, 86; Gold Medal, Slovakian Acad Sci, 88; M V Lomonosov Gold Medal, USSR Acad Sci, 89; State Prize, USSR, 89; Edward Teller Medal, 91. *Mem:* Fel Optical Soc Am; fel Indian Nat Sci Acad; Europ Acad Sci & Arts; hon mem Int Acad Sci; USSR Acad Sci (pres, 67-90); hon mem Acad Natural Sci Russ Fedn; Acad Sci Ger Dem Rep; Polish & Czech Acad Sci; Ger Acad Natural Sci; Bulgarian Acad Sci; Royal Swed Acad Eng; European Acad Arts, Sci & Humanities. *Res:* Principle of molecular generator, realized molecular generator on molecular beam of ammonia; 3-level system for receiving states with inversal population suggested PN Lebedev Physics Institute; author of over 500 works. *Mailing Add:* 53 Leninsky Prospekt Moscow Russia

BASRI, SAUL ABRAHAM, ELEMENTARY PARTICLE PHYSICS. *Current Pos:* RETIRED. *Personal Data:* b Baghdad, Iraq, Feb 15, 26; nat US; m 50; c 2. *Educ:* Mass Inst Technol, BS, 48; Columbia Univ, PhD(physics), 53. *Prof Exp:* Res asst physics, Columbia Univ, 52-53, res scientist, 53; from asst prof to assoc prof, Colo State Univ, 53-67, prof physics, 67-85. *Concurrent Pos:* Fulbright lectr, Univ Rangoon, Burma, 56 & Univ Ceylon, 65-66; vis prof, Israel Inst Technol, 73-74. *Mem:* Am Phys Soc; Am Asn Physics Teachers. *Res:* Elementary particle theory; algebraic s-matrix theory. *Mailing Add:* 5575 High Country Ct Boulder CO 80301

BASS, ALLAN DELMAGE, PHARMACOLOGY. *Current Pos:* prof & chmn dept, 52-73, dir neurosci prog, 71-73, assoc dean biomed sci, 73-75, actg dean med sch, 73-74, EMER PROF PHARMACOL, VANDERBILT UNIV, 75- *Personal Data:* b Marcus, Iowa, Feb 12, 10; m 44; c 2. *Educ:* Simpson Col, BS, 31; Vanderbilt Univ, MS, 32, MD, 39. *Prof Exp:* Intern, Vanderbilt Hosp, 39-40, asst resident physician, 40-41, resident & instr med, 43-44; instr pharmacol, Yale Univ, 42-43; prof pharmacol & chmn dept,Syracuse Univ, 45-55. *Concurrent Pos:* Mem Gen Med Res Prog Proj Comt, NIH, 64-67; mem, US Food & Drug Admin, 67-70; consult, Div Res Grants, NIH Res Analysis & Eval, 68; mem Res Adv Comt, NIMH, 68-70; chmn bd, Tenn Neuropsychiat Inst, 70-75; Nat Bd Med examr & Ann Rev Pharmacol; mem ed bd, Int Quart Sci Rev J, 73-; mem Drug Res Bd, Nat Acad Sci, 74-76; assoc chief staff educ, Vet Admin Hosp, Nashville, Tenn, 75-81; interim dir, Tenn Neuropsychiat Inst, Nashville, 81-84; consult, Soc Security Disability Serv, 85- *Mem:* AAAS; Am Soc Pharmacol & Exp Therapeut (pres, 67-68); AMA; Am Col Physicians; Fedn Am Socs Exp Biol. *Res:* Autonomic and endocrine pharmacology; neuropsychopharmacology; steroid metabolism; cyanide poisoning; hypnotics; nucleoproteins. *Mailing Add:* Vanderbilt Univ Med Ctr AA-2232 Med Ctr N Nashville TN 37232-0001

BASS, ARTHUR, environmental information management systems, applied remote sensing; deceased, see previous edition for last biography

BASS, DAVID A, MEDICINE. *Current Pos:* from asst prof to assoc prof, Dept Med, 76-83, ASSOC BIOCHEM, BOWMAN GRAY SCH MED, 81-, PROF, DEPT MED, 83-, SECT HEAD, SECT PULMONARY MED, 88- *Personal Data:* b Oklahoma City, Okla, June 10, 41; c 2. *Educ:* Yale Univ, BA,

64; Johns Hopkins Univ, MD, 68; Oxford Univ, Eng, DPhil, 73; Am Bd Internal Med, cert, 74. *Prof Exp:* Intern, Osler Med Serv, Johns Hopkins Hosp, 68-69, jr resident, 69-70, sr resident, 73-74; res fel, Nuffield Dept Med, Oxford Univ, Eng, 70-73, Commonwealth Fund fel, Radcliffe Infirmary, 70-73; from instr to asst prof, Dept Med, Univ Tex Southwestern Med Sch, 74-76. *Concurrent Pos:* NIH res fel infectious dis, Univ Tex Southwestern Med Sch, 74-76, grants, 79-; vis prof, Cambridge, Eng, 80; assoc dir, Oncol Res Ctr, Bowman Gray Sch Med, dir, Cell Biol Prog; affil, NC Bapt Hosp, Winston-Salem. *Mem:* Am Soc Clin Invest; fel Am Col Chest Physicians; fel Am Col Physicians; Am Soc Biol Chemists; Am Asn Immunologists; Am Thoracic Soc; Am Fedn Clin Res; Am Soc Microbiol; Reticuloendothelial Soc. *Res:* Elucidation of mechanisms of priming and stimulation of the bactericidal respiratory burst of human neutrophils. *Mailing Add:* Div Pulmonary & Critical Care Bowman Gray Sch Med Med Ctr Blvd Winston-Salem NC 27157-1054

BASS, EUGENE L, ANIMAL PHYSIOLOGY, ZOOLOGY. *Current Pos:* asst prof, 72-83, ASSOC PROF BIOL, UNIV MD EASTERN SHORE, 83- *Personal Data:* b Brooklyn, NY, Sept 27, 42; m 68, Linda Epstein; c 1. *Educ:* City Univ NY, BS, 64; Univ Mass, PhD(zool), 70. *Prof Exp:* Asst prof biol, Salisbury State Col, 69-72. *Concurrent Pos:* Prin investr, USDA, 73-78, NIH, 81-85. *Mem:* Am Soc Zoologists; Am Inst Biol Sci; Sigma Xi. *Res:* Use of alternatives to vertebrate animals in toxicity testing and risk assessment; carbohydrate utilization in Crustaceans and effects on feeding. *Mailing Add:* Dept Biol Univ Md Princess Anne MD 21853. *E-Mail:* ebass@umes.umd.edu

BASS, GEORGE F, NAUTICAL ARCHAEOLOGY, PRECLASSICAL ARCHAEOLOGY. *Current Pos:* prof, 76-80, DISTINGUISHED PROF ANTHROP, TEX A&M UNIV, 80- *Personal Data:* b Columbia, SC, Dec 9, 32; m 60, Ann; c Gordon & Alan. *Educ:* Johns Hopkins Univ, MA, 55; Univ Pa, PhD(class archaeol), 64. *Hon Degrees:* Dr, Bogazici Univ, Istanbul, 87. *Honors & Awards:* Nogi Award, Underwater Soc Am, 74; LaGorce Medal, Nat Geog Soc, 79; Gold Medal for Distinguished Achievement, Archaeol Inst Am, 86; Centennial Award, Nat Geog Soc, 88. *Prof Exp:* From asst prof to assoc prof class archaeol, Univ Pa, 64-73. *Concurrent Pos:* Geddes-Harrower prof Greek art & archaeol, Univ Aberdeen, Scotland, 84. *Mem:* Inst Nautical Archaeol (pres, 73-82); Archaeol Inst Am; Asn Field Archaeol; Am Orient Soc; Soc Hist Archaeol. *Res:* Excavations of ancient shipwrecks; preclassical eastern Mediterranean cultures. *Mailing Add:* Tex A&M Univ Nautical Archaeol PO Drawer HG College Station TX 77841. *Fax:* 409-845-6399

BASS, HENRY ELLIS, PHYSICAL ACOUSTICS, CHEMICAL PHYSICS. *Current Pos:* From assoc prof to prof, 70-88, DISTINGUISHED PROF PHYSICS, UNIV MISS, 88-, ACTG CHAIR, 92-, DIR, NAT CTR PHYS ACOUST, 92- *Personal Data:* b Tulsa, Okla, Aug 31, 43; m 78, Judy C Sneed; c Belinda S (Heflin), Christine A (Ware), Henry E Jr & John D. *Educ:* Okla State Univ, BS, 65, PhD(physics), 71. *Honors & Awards:* Biennial Award, Acoust Soc Am, 78. *Concurrent Pos:* Mem working group S1-57, Am Nat Standards Inst, 72; pres, Arnold, Bass & Assoc, sci consults, 74-; mem res study group RSG-11, NATO, 82-; assoc ed, J Acoust Soc Am. *Mem:* Fel Acoust Soc Am; Sigma Xi. *Res:* Physical acoustics, especially molecular relaxation in the gas phase and long range sound propagation; chemical kinetics, especially molecular energy transfer. *Mailing Add:* Dept Physics & Astron Univ Miss University MS 38677. *Fax:* 601-232-7494; *E-Mail:* pabass@olemiss.edu

BASS, HYMAN, MATHEMATICS. *Current Pos:* from asst prof to assoc prof, 63-65, chmn dept, 75-78, PROF MATH, COLUMBIA UNIV, 65- *Personal Data:* b Houston, Tex, Oct 5, 32; m 58; c 3. *Educ:* Princeton Univ, BA, 55; Univ Chicago, MS, 56, PhD(math), 59. *Honors & Awards:* Hedrich Lectr, Math Asn Am, 68; Philips Lectr, Haverford Col, 70 & 75; Cole Prize Algebra, Am Math Soc, 75; Barrett Mem Lectr, Univ Tenn, 78; Karcher Lectr, Univ Okla, 79. *Prof Exp:* Ritt instr math, Columbia Univ, 59-62; NSF fel, Col France, 62-63. *Concurrent Pos:* Vis prof & lectr, numerous US & foreign univs, 62-; chmn dept, Barnard Col, Columbia Univ, 64-65; Sloan fel, 64-66; Guggenheim fel, Inst Higher Sci Studies, Paris, 68-69; ed, J Indian Math Soc, 68-70, Cambridge Tracts Pure & Appl Math, 68-, Bull Am Math Soc, 69-72 & 82-86, J Pure & Appl Algebra, 70-86, Am J Math, 71-77, Commun Algebra, 74-85 & Ann Math, 78-84. *Mem:* Nat Acad Sci; Am Math Soc (vpres, 78-80); Math Soc France; London Math Soc; Math Asn Am; fel AAAS; Am Acad Arts & Sci. *Res:* Homological algebra; algebraic number theory; algebraic geometry; algebraic K-theory; group theory; author of 71 technical publications. *Mailing Add:* Dept Math Columbia Univ New York NY 10027

BASS, JACK, METAL PHYSICS, LOW TEMPERATURE PHYSICS. *Current Pos:* From asst prof to assoc prof, 64-73, chmn physics, 83-88, PROF PHYSICS, MICH STATE UNIV, 73- *Personal Data:* b New York, NY, Apr 1, 38; m 59, Joanne Meyers; c Deborah, Sandra & Judith. *Educ:* Calif Inst Technol, BS, 59; Univ Ill, MS, 61, PhD(physics), 64. *Concurrent Pos:* Guest docent, Swiss Fed Inst Technol, 70-71; vis prof, Cath Univ, Nijmegen, Neth, 78-79 & Bar-Ilan Univ, Israel, 79; vis prof, Max-Planck-Inst, Grenoble, France, 88-89. *Mem:* Fel Am Phys Soc; Am Asn Physics Teachers; AAAS; Sigma Xi; Mat Res Soc. *Res:* Electron transport properties of metals; low and ultra-low temperature physics; point defects in metals; artifical metallic superlattices; spin glasses; giant magnetoresistance. *Mailing Add:* Dept Physics Col Natural Sci Mich State Univ East Lansing MI 48824. *Fax:* 517-353-4500

BASS, JAMES W, PEDIATRICS, INFECTIOUS DISEASES. *Current Pos:* CHIEF, DEPT PEDIAT, TRIPLER ARMY MED CTR, HONOLULU, 81- *Personal Data:* b Shreveport, La, May 25, 30; c 2. *Educ:* Tulane Univ, BS, 52, MPH, 68; La State Univ, New Orleans, MD, 57. *Prof Exp:* Researcher infectious dis, US Walter Reed Army Inst Res, Md, 60-63; asst chief pediat, Madigan Gen Hosp, Tacoma, Wash, 63-66; instr pediat, Sch Med, Tulane Univ & vis pediatrician, Charity Hosp La, New Orleans, 66-68; from asst dir to dir intern training, 68-71, asst chief pediat serv, 68, chief dept pediat, Tripler Army Med Ctr, Honolulu, 68-75; from asst clin prof to assoc clin prof pediat, Sch Med, Univ Hawaii, 68-73, clin prof pediat, Sch Med, Univ Hawaii, Manoa, 73-75 & trop med & med microbiol, 74-75; chief, Dept Pediat, Walter Reed Army Med Ctr, 75-81; prof & chmn, Dept Pediat, Sch Med, Uniformed Servs Univ Health Sci, 76-81. *Concurrent Pos:* From asst clin prof to assoc clin prof pediat, Sch Med, Univ Hawaii, 68-73; consult pediat infectious dis, Kauikeolani Childrens Hosp, Honolulu, 70-75; assoc clin prof pediat, Univ Southern Calif, 72-; consult pediat, Surgeon General of US Army, 75-81; clin prof pediat, Sch Med, Georgetown Univ, Washington, DC, 75-78, prof, 78-81. *Mem:* AMA; Soc Pediat; Am Pediat Soc; Infectious Dis Soc Am; fel Am Col Physicians. *Res:* Microbiology; infectious diseases; fel Am Col Physicians. Res: Microbiology. *Mailing Add:* Dept Pediat Tripler Army Med Ctr Honolulu HI 96859-0001

BASS, JON DOLF, PHOTOGRAPHIC CHEMISTRY, PHOTOGRAPHIC PATENTS. *Current Pos:* RETIRED. *Personal Data:* b Saginaw, Mich, Oct 31, 33; m 59, Edith D Kletzien; c Kristin, Margrit, Berit & Erika. *Educ:* Univ Mich, BS, 56; Univ Wis, PhD(org chem), 60. *Prof Exp:* Lab asst, Mellon Inst, 51-52; teaching asst, Univ Wis, 58-59; res chemist, Air Force Cambridge Res Labs, Mass, 60-62; res fel chem, Harvard Univ, 62-63; from res chemist to sr res chemist, Kodak Res Labs, 63-70, res assoc, 70-91. *Mem:* Am Chem Soc; Soc Imaging Sci & Technol. *Res:* organic semiconductors and photoconductors; photochemical organic synthesis; photographic chemistry; physical development; lithographic chemistry; spectral sensitization and image amplification processes; interrelation of patents, innovation, and technology transfer; technology forecasting. *Mailing Add:* 546 Wahlmont Dr Webster NY 14580

BASS, JONATHAN LANGER, PHYSICAL CHEMISTRY. *Current Pos:* supvr mat eval, PQ Corp, 77-85, mgr analysis characterization & testing, 85-90, prin scientist, 90-93, SR RES FEL, PQ CORP, 93- *Personal Data:* b New York, NY, May 12, 38; m 71; c 2. *Educ:* Univ Rochester, BS, 59; Univ Minn, Minneapolis, PhD(phys chem), 65. *Prof Exp:* Chemist, maintenance lab, hq Ogden Air Mat Area, Hill AFB, Utah, 65-66 & weapons lab, Kirtland AFB, NMex, 66-68; chemist, Wash Res Ctr, W R Grace & Co, 68-77. *Mem:* Am Chem Soc; Soc Appl Spectros; Catalysis Soc; Am Soc Testing & Mat. *Res:* Characterization of inorganic oxides by infrared spectroscopy, porosimetry, scanning electron microscopy and x-ray analysis; degradation and tensile properties of polymers; atomic spectroscopy; thermal analysis; wet chemical analysis of inorganics; chemical modification of surfaces, separation and purification. *Mailing Add:* 39 Lee Rd Audubon PA 19403-2003

BASS, LEONARD JOEL, COMPUTER SCIENCES. *Current Pos:* SR MEM TECH STAFF, SOFTWARE ENG INST, CARNEGIE MELLON UNIV, 86- *Personal Data:* b Kalamazoo, Mich, Oct 30, 43; m 67; c 3. *Educ:* Univ Calif, Riverside, BA, 64, MA, 66; Purdue Univ, PhD(comput sci), 70. *Prof Exp:* Prof computer sci, Univ RI, 70-86. *Mem:* Asn Comput Mach; Inst Elec & Electronics Engrs. *Res:* Software engineering; data base management systems; user interfaces. *Mailing Add:* Software Eng Inst Carnegie Mellon Univ Pittsburgh PA 15213

BASS, MARY ANNA, food science, nutrition; deceased, see previous edition for last biography

BASS, MAX H(ERMAN), ENTOMOLOGY. *Current Pos:* PROF & HEAD, DEPT ENTOM, COASTAL PLAIN STA, UNIV GA, 80- *Personal Data:* b Troy, Ala, Dec 27, 34; m 56, E(dna) M Findley; c Susan (Boudman), Nancy (Lundy), Jennifer (Demarta) & Joan C. *Educ:* Troy State Col, BS, 57; Ala Polytech Inst, MS, 59; Auburn Univ, PhD(entom), 64. *Prof Exp:* Instr zool, Auburn Univ, 59-60, res entom, 60-80, from asst prof to prof entom, 63-80. *Mem:* Sigma Xi; Entom Soc Am. *Res:* Bionomics; control of insects affecting soybeans and peanuts. *Mailing Add:* Coastal Plain Sta PO Box 748 Tifton GA 31793-0748. *Fax:* 912-386-3086

BASS, MICHAEL, LASERS & OPTICS. *Current Pos:* vpres res, 88-93, PROF PHYSICS & ELEC ENG, UNIV CENT FLA, 93- *Personal Data:* b New York, NY, Oct 24, 39; m 62; c 2. *Educ:* Carnegie-Mellon Univ, BS, 60; Univ Mich, MS, 62, PhD(physics), 64. *Prof Exp:* Actg asst prof physics, Univ Calif, Berkeley, 64-66; sr res scientist, res div, Raytheon Co, 66-73; from assoc dir to dir, Ctr Laser Studies, Univ Southern Calif, 73-84, prof elec eng, 81-84, chmn dept, 84-89. *Concurrent Pos:* Consult, Aerospace Corp, Exxon Nuclear, McDonnell Douglas, Los Alamos Nat Lab, Rogers Corp & AMP Corp. *Mem:* Fel Inst Elec & Electronics Engrs; fel Optical Soc Am; fel Laser Inst Am; Sigma Xi; AAAS. *Res:* Light-matter interactions; laser damage; optical properties of matter; nonlinear optics; optically pumped solid state lasers. *Mailing Add:* Univ Cent Fla Creol Bldg PO Box 162700 Orlando FL 32816-2700. *Fax:* 407-823-6880; *E-Mail:* bass@mail.creol.ucf.edu

BASS, MICHAEL LAWRENCE, ANIMAL PHYSIOLOGY, ECOLOGY & TOXICOLOGY. *Current Pos:* Instr biol, 68-73, asst prof, 74-77, ASSOC PROF BIOL, MARY WASHINGTON COL, 77-, CHMN BIOL SCI, 88- *Personal Data:* b Eskdale, WVa, Jan 10, 45; m 68; c 2. *Educ:* Va Polytech Inst, BS, 66; Med Col Va, MS, 70; Va Polytech Inst & State Univ, PhD(zool), 75. *Concurrent Pos:* Consult, Southeastern Inst Res, 70-; consult, Sharpley Labs Inc, 75-76, vpres, 76-78. *Mem:* AAAS; Am Soc Zoologists; Am Inst Biol Sci; Sigma Xi. *Res:* Environmental toxicology; aquatic ecology; physiological effects of pollutants on aquatic invertebrates and vertebrates with special interests on the effects of the interaction of temperature and toxicity. *Mailing Add:* Dept Biol Mary Washington Col 1301 College Ave Fredericksburg VA 22401-5300

BASS, NORMAN HERBERT, NEUROCHEMISTRY, NEUROLOGY. *Current Pos:* PROF NEUROL & DEAN, MED COL GA, 85- *Personal Data:* b New York, NY, July 10, 36; m 61; c 3. *Educ:* Swarthmore Col, BA, 58; Yale Univ, MD, 62. *Honors & Awards:* S Weir Mitchell Res Award, Am Acad Neurol, 67. *Prof Exp:* Intern med, Sch Med, Univ Wash, 62-63; resident neurol, Sch Med, Univ Va, 63-65; Nat Inst Neurol & Commun Disorders & Stroke fels neurochem, McLean Hosp Res Lab, Harvard Univ, 65-67; asst prof neurol, Sch Med, Univ Va, 67-70, assoc prof pharmacol, 70-73, prof neurol & dir, Clin Neurosci Res Ctr, 74-79; prof neurol & chmn dept, Univ Ky Med Ctr, 79-85. *Concurrent Pos:* Markle scholar award, 69-74; Nat Inst Neurol & Commun Disorders & Stroke res career develop award, 71-76; vis prof, Inst Pharmacol, Univ Gothenburg, Sweden, 72-73; assoc ed, Neurochem Res, 78. *Mem:* Am Soc Neurochem; Asn Univ Professors Neurol; fel Am Acad Neurol; Am Neurol Asn; Am Asn Anatomists. *Res:* Neurochemistry of developing brain; microchemistry of cerebral cortex maturation; malnutrition and hormonal imbalance during critical periods of brain development; experimental epilepsy; blood-brain-barrier; inborn errors of human brain metabolism; neuropharmacology of morphine abuse. *Mailing Add:* Dept Neurol 30 Warren St Boston MA 02135-3680

BASS, PAUL, PHARMACOLOGY, PHYSIOLOGY. *Current Pos:* PROF PHARMACOL, SCH PHARM & SCH MED, UNIV WIS-MADISON, 70- *Personal Data:* b Winnipeg, Man, Aug 12, 28; m 53; c 2. *Educ:* Univ BC, BSP, 53, MA, 55; McGill Univ, PhD(pharmacol), 57. *Prof Exp:* Asst, Ayerst, McKenna & Harrison, Can, 56; res pharmacologist, Parke Davis & Co, 60-70. *Concurrent Pos:* Fel biochem, McGill Univ, 57-58; fel physiol, Mayo Found, 58-60. *Mem:* Am Soc Pharmacol; Soc Exp Biol & Med; Pharmacol Soc Can; Am Gastroenterol Asn. *Res:* Motility, secretion and absorption of the gastro-intestinal tract; cardiovascular and autonomic nervous system pharmacology. *Mailing Add:* Sch Pharm Univ Wis-Madison Madison WI 53706

BASS, ROBERT GERALD, ORGANIC CHEMISTRY, POLYMER CHEMISTRY. *Current Pos:* assoc prof, 62-72, PROF CHEM, VA COMMONWEALTH UNIV, 72- *Personal Data:* b Durham, NC, May 2, 33; m 59; c 2. *Educ:* Va Polytech Inst, BS, 54; Univ Va, PhD(chem), 61. *Prof Exp:* Res chemist, E I du Pont de Nemours & Co, Inc, 59-62. *Concurrent Pos:* Fel, Univ Va, 62. *Mem:* Am Chem Soc; Sigma Xi; Soc Advan Mat & Process Eng. *Res:* Organic chemistry; thermally stable high performance polyers, synthesis and reactions of heterocyclic compounds; acetylenic compounds, conjugated systems, enol-keto and ring-chain tautomerism; mesoionic compounds; transformation steroids. *Mailing Add:* Dept Chem Va Commonwealth Univ PO Box 842006 Richmond VA 23284-2006. *Fax:* 804-367-8599

BASS, STEVEN CRAIG, COMPUTER ENGINEERING. *Current Pos:* PROF ELEC & COMPUTER ENG, GEORGE MASON UNIV, FAIRFAX, VA, 88- *Personal Data:* b Indianapolis, Ind, July 29, 43; m 65, 89; c 2. *Educ:* Purdue Univ, BSEE, 66, MSEE, PhD(elec eng), 71. *Prof Exp:* From asst prof to prof elec eng, Purdue Univ, West Lafayette, 71-88. *Concurrent Pos:* Prin engr, Mitre Corp, 88. *Mem:* Inst Elec & Electronic Engrs; Audio Eng Soc. *Res:* Digital signal processing; computer-aided circuit design; very large scale integration of circuits; computer architecture. *Mailing Add:* Dept Elec & Comput Eng Univ Notre Dame Notre Dame IN 46556

BASS, THOMAS D, AQUATIC INVERTEBRATE ECOLOGY. *Current Pos:* PROF BIOL, UNIV CENT OKLA, 85- *Personal Data:* b Port Arthur, Tex, June 18, 56; m, Donna Lynn Pace; c Courtney M. *Educ:* Lamar Univ, BSc, 78, MS, 79; Tex A&M Univ, PhD(zool), 85. *Concurrent Pos:* Vis lectr & researcher, Mountain Res Sta, Univ Colo, 87-88; vis asst prof, Univ Okla, 89; Fulbright scholar, Univ WI, Barbados, 95-96; vis res fel, Univ WI, 96. *Mem:* Sigma Xi; NAm Benthological Soc. *Res:* Ecology and distribution of aquatic macroinvertebrates, especially freshwater insects of Oklahoma and on Caribbean islands. *Mailing Add:* Dept Biol Univ Central Okla 100 N University Dr Edmond OK 73034. *Fax:* 405-330-3824; *E-Mail:* dbass@aix1.ucok.edu

BASS, WILLIAM MARVIN, III, PHYSICAL ANTHROPOLOGY, ANTHROPOMETRICS. *Current Pos:* prof, 71-94, EMER PROF ANTHROP & HEAD DEPT, UNIV TENN, KNOXVILLE, 94- *Personal Data:* b Staunton, Va, Aug 30, 28; m 53; c 3. *Educ:* Univ Va, BA, 51; Univ Ky, MS, 56; Univ Pa, PhD(anthrop), 61; Am Bd Forensic Anthrop, dipl, 78. *Prof Exp:* Instr phys anthrop & anat, Grad Sch Med, Univ Pa, 56-60; instr anthrop, Univ Nebr, 60; from instr to prof, Univ Kans, 60-71. *Concurrent Pos:* Res grant, Univ Kans, 61-68; NSF res grants, Smithsonian Inst, 62 & 63; Nat Park Serv grant, 63 & 66; NSF grants, 65, 67 & 69; Nat Geog grant, 68. *Mem:* Am Asn Phys Anthrop; Am Anthrop Asn; Soc Am Archaeol; Am Acad Forensic Sci. *Res:* Identification of human skeletal material. *Mailing Add:* Dept Anthrop 252 S Stadium Hall Univ Tenn Knoxville TN 37996

BASS, WILLIAM THOMAS, SOFTWARE ENGINEERING & DEVELOPMENT. *Current Pos:* RES ENGR, MERCER UNIV, 91- *Personal Data:* b Jefferson City, Tenn, Feb 18, 42; m 64, Mardi Blanchard; c David, Allan & Elizabeth. *Educ:* Carson Newman Col, BS, 64; Univ Tenn, PhD(physics), 70. *Prof Exp:* Assoc prof physics, Macon Jr Col, 70-85; Litton Indust & Applied Technol Div, 86-90. *Concurrent Pos:* Instr, Governor's Hon Prog, Ga; adj prof, Wesleyan Col, 75 & 81. *Mem:* Am Asn Physics Teachers. *Res:* Educational uses of computers & microcomputers; software and systems development; scientific algorithms. *Mailing Add:* 5123 Rivoli Dr Macon GA 31210. *Fax:* 912-929-6406; *E-Mail:* bass_wt@mercer.edu

BASSECHES, HAROLD, PHYSICAL CHEMISTRY. *Current Pos:* Mem tech staff, 52-59, supvr semiconductor mat group, Pa, 59-62, magnetic mat group, 62-67, head Film Technol Dept, 67-70, HEAD THIN FILM MAT & TECHNOL DEPT, BELL TEL LABS, NJ, 70- *Personal Data:* b Brooklyn, NY, Nov 27, 23; m 46; c 3. *Educ:* City Col New York, BS, 43; Ohio State Univ, PhD(phys chem), 51. *Mem:* Am Chem Soc; fel Am Inst Chem; Sigma Xi. *Res:* Preparation and processing of materials whose electric and magnetic properties are of use in modern solid state devices; development of thin film materials and processes for hybrid integrated circuits. *Mailing Add:* 618 N Glenwood St Allentown PA 18104-4943

BASSEL, ROBERT HAROLD, NUCLEAR PHYSICS. *Current Pos:* RETIRED. *Personal Data:* b Johnstown, Pa, Feb 16, 28; c 1. *Educ:* Univ Pittsburgh, BSc, 52, PhD(physics), 58. *Prof Exp:* Physicist, Oak Ridge Nat Lab, 58-66; assoc physicist, Brookhaven Nat Lab, 66-68; assoc prof physics, Univ Pittsburgh, 68-69; res physicist, Naval Res Lab, 64-90. *Mem:* Fel Am Phys Soc; fel AAAS. *Res:* Nuclear and atomic reaction; evaluations of neutron induced reaction on cross sections. *Mailing Add:* 4938 Maple Creek Dr Apt C Trotwood OH 45426

BASSER, PETER J, BIOMEDICAL ENGINEERING, APPLIED MATHEMATICS. *Current Pos:* Staff fel, 86-90, sr staff fel, 90-92, TENURED BIOMED ENGR, MECH ENG SECT, BIOMED ENG & INSTRUMENTATION PROG, NIH, BETHESDA, 92- *Educ:* Harvard Col, AB, 80; Harvard Univ, SM, 82, PhD(eng mech), 86. *Concurrent Pos:* Engr res & develop, Medi-Tech, Inc Watertown, 83; develop engr & syst adminr, Hewlett-Packard Med Instruments, 83-86; biome engr, Dept Anesthesia, Brigham & Women's Hosp, Boston, 85-87; vis scientist, Univ Pisa, Italy, 88, Mech Eng Lab, Agency Indust Sci & Technol, Ministry Int Trade & Indust, 89; guest researcher, Continuum Electromech Group, Dept Comput Sci & Elect Eng, Mass Inst Technol, 89-; guest lectr, Dept Physics, Univ Md, 90-91, Dept Bioeng, Johns Hopkins Univ, 93-94; vis assoc prof, Lady Davis Fel, Technian, Israel, 94- *Mem:* Biomed Eng Soc; Biophys Soc. *Res:* Contributed numerous articles to professional journals; biomedical engineering; biophysical chemistry. *Mailing Add:* NIH Bldg 13 Rm 3N16 Bethesda MD 20892. *E-Mail:* pjbasser@helix.nih.gov

BASSETT, ALTON HERMAN, TEXTILE CHEMISTRY. *Current Pos:* RETIRED. *Personal Data:* b Hartford, Conn, Nov 27, 30; m 57, Joan Tolley; c Linda A & Barbara (Erdman). *Educ:* Middlebury Col, BA, 53. *Prof Exp:* Staff chemist, Am Viscose Corp, 55-58; proj dir sanit & surg prod, Chicopee Mfg Co Div, Johnson & Johnson, 58-60, dir prof develop, 60-69, asst dir res, 74-88, consult, 89-95. *Mem:* AAAS; Am Asn Textile Technologists; Am Chem Soc. *Res:* Concentrated effort in development of new surgical dressings and applications; new textile constructions, nonwovens. *Mailing Add:* 73 Harriet Dr Princeton NJ 08540

BASSETT, ARTHUR L, CARDIOVASCULAR PHYSIOLOGY, PHARMACOLOGY. *Current Pos:* assoc prof pharmacol & surg, Univ Miami, 73-76, dir grad affairs ,comt, dept pharmacol, 75-82, PROF PHARMACOL, MED SCH, UNIV MIAMI, 76-; DIR NIH PHARMACOL TRAINING GRANT 76-82, 85- *Personal Data:* b New York, NY, Feb 26, 35; m 60; c 2. *Educ:* City Col New York, BS, 55; State Univ NY, PhD(physiol), 65. *Prof Exp:* Technician, Med Ctr, NY Univ, 56-58; res asst, State Univ NY Downstate Med Ctr, 58-60, asst physiol, 60-61 & 63- 65; fel pharmacol, Col Physicians & Surgeons, Columbia Univ, 65-67, assoc, 67-68, asst prof pharmacol, 68-73. *Concurrent Pos:* Polachek Found fel med res, 67-; Nat Heart Inst res career develop award, 69-73; grants, AMA, 69-72, Heart Asn Gtr Miami, 73-, Fla Heart Asn, 74- & NIH, 76-; vpres, Heart Asn Greater Miami, 83-; NIH Pharmacol Study Sect, 84-88. *Mem:* Biophys Soc; Am Soc Clin Pharmacol & Therapeut; Am Soc Pharmacol & Exp Therapeut; Am Physiol Soc. *Res:* Excitation and contraction cardiac muscle; cardiac arrhythmias and antiarrhythmic drugs; cardiac hypertrophy. *Mailing Add:* Dept Pharmacol R-189 Univ Miami Med Sch PO Box 016189 Miami FL 33101-6189

BASSETT, CHARLES ANDREW LOOCKERMAN, orthopedic surgery, cell physiology; deceased, see previous edition for last biography

BASSETT, DAVID R, PHYSICAL CHEMISTRY, COLLOID CHEMISTRY. *Current Pos:* Res chemist, Union Carbide Corp, 68-80, sr res chemist, 80-86, corp fel, 86-92, DIR RES, UNION CARBIDE CORP, 92- *Personal Data:* b Winston-Salem, NC, Jan 23, 39; m 61; c 3. *Educ:* Lafayette Col, AB, 61; Lehigh Univ, MS, 63, PhD(phys chem), 68. *Mem:* Am Chem Soc. *Res:* Surface chemistry; polymer colloids; polymers for electronics. *Mailing Add:* Union Carbide Corp Emulsion Systs 410 Gregson Dr Cary NC 27511-6445. *Fax:* 919-469-6797

BASSETT, EMMETT W, MICROBIOLOGY. *Current Pos:* RETIRED. *Personal Data:* b Martinsville, Va, Jan 23, 21; m 50; c 3. *Educ:* Tuskegee Inst, BS, 42; Univ Mass, MS, 50; Ohio State Univ, PhD(dairy technol), 54. *Prof Exp:* Res assoc microbiol, Col Physicians & Surgeons, Columbia Univ, 55-59, asst prof, 59-67; sr scientist, Ortho Res Found, NJ, 67-69; asst prof microbiol, Col Med & Dent NJ, 69-73, assoc prof, 73-87. *Mem:* Am Soc Biol Chemists. *Res:* Aromatic synthesis in molds; studies on the combining region and biosynthesis of antibodies. *Mailing Add:* 286 Grade Hill Rd Grahamsville NY 12740

BASSETT, HENRY GORDON, STRATIGRAPHY. *Current Pos:* RETIRED. *Personal Data:* b Newton, Mass, Nov 12, 24; m 49; c 3. *Educ:* McGill Univ, BSc, 49, MSc, 50; Princeton Univ, AM & PhD(geol), 52. *Honors & Awards:* Pres Gold Medal, Can Inst Mining & Metall, 50. *Prof Exp:* Geologist, Shell Can Ltd, 52-72, head stratig serv group, Shell Develop Co, 72-76, sr staff geologist, Shell Oil Co, 76-80; sr staff geologist & mgr geol technol, Sohio Petrol Co, 80-85. *Mem:* Am Asn Petrol Geol; Can Asn Petrol Geol; fel Geol Asn Can; Asn Prof Engrs. *Res:* Geology of northern and western Canada. *Mailing Add:* 3320 Las Huertas Rd Lafayette CA 94549

BASSETT, JAMES WILBUR, ANIMAL SCIENCE. *Current Pos:* PROF ANIMAL SCI, TEX A&M UNIV, 63- *Personal Data:* b Greenville, Tex, July 22, 23; m 49; c 6. *Educ:* Tex A&M Univ, BS, 48, PhD(animal breeding, 65; Mont State Univ, MS, 57. *Prof Exp:* Asst county agt, Ark Agr Exten Serv, 48-50; asst prof wool technol, Mont State Univ, 51-63. *Mem:* Am Soc Animal Sci. *Res:* Wool and mohair technology, production and marketing. *Mailing Add:* 303 W Dexter Dr College Station TX 77840

BASSETT, JOSEPH YARNALL, JR, ORGANIC CHEMISTRY. *Current Pos:* RETIRED. *Personal Data:* b Asheville, NC, Aug 2, 27; m 53, Lucretia Blankenship; c Mary A & Christine. *Educ:* Univ NC, BS, 51, PhD(chem), 58. *Prof Exp:* Raw mat qual control analyst, Am Enka Corp, 53; lab asst, Univ NC, 53-56; develop chemist, Union Carbide Chem Co, WVa, 57-64; asst prof chem, WVa State Col, 62-64; asst prof, Western Carolina Univ, 64-69, chmn div natural sci & math, 69-76, dept head, 84-87, prof chem, math, 69-91, facil & planning coordr, 77-91. *Mem:* AAAS; Am Chem Soc; Sigma Xi. *Res:* Esterification; plasticizers; telomerization; terpene chemistry. *Mailing Add:* Western Carolina Univ PO Box 1524 Cullowhee NC 28723-1524

BASSETT, MARK JULIAN, PLANT BREEDING. *Current Pos:* from asst prof to assoc prof, 70-84, PROF VEG CROPS, UNIV FLA, 84- *Personal Data:* b Washington, Ind, May 15, 40. *Educ:* Lake Forest Col, BA, 63; Univ Md, MS, 67, PhD(hort), 70. *Mem:* Am Soc Hort Sci; Am Soc Agron. *Res:* Genetic studies and varietal improvement of beans and carrots; special emphasis on induced mutations, linkage studies developing a primary drisomic series, and cytoplamic male sterility in bean. *Mailing Add:* 2900 NW 32nd St Gainesville FL 32605

BASSETT, WILLIAM AKERS, MINERALOGY, GEOPHYSICS. *Current Pos:* PROF GEOL, CORNELL UNIV, 78- *Personal Data:* b Brooklyn, NY, Aug 3, 31; m 62, Jane Kermes; c Kari N, Jeffrey K & Penelope N. *Educ:* Amherst Col, BA, 54; Columbia Univ, MA, 56, PhD(geol), 59. *Honors & Awards:* Roebling Medal, 94; Bridgman Award, 97. *Prof Exp:* Res assoc chem, Brookhaven Nat Lab, 60-61; from asst prof to prof geol, Univ Rochester, 60-78. *Concurrent Pos:* Res collabr, Brookhaven Nat Lab, 58-62; res assoc, Columbia Univ, 59-62; Guggenheim fel, 85. *Mem:* AAAS; Geol Soc Am; Mineral Soc Am; Am Geophys Union; Geochem Soc. *Res:* Structure and chemistry of sheet silicates; radioactive age dating of volcanic rocks and Pre-Cambrian rocks; behavior of solids at pressures and temperatures comparable with the earth's interior. *Mailing Add:* Dept Geol Sci Snee Hall Cornell Univ Ithaca NY 14853

BASSHAM, JAMES ALAN, BIOCHEMISTRY. *Current Pos:* RETIRED. *Personal Data:* b Sacramento, Calif, Nov 26, 22; m 56; c 5. *Educ:* Univ Calif, BS, 45, PhD(chem), 49. *Prof Exp:* Dept head, Chem Bidynamics Div, Lawrence Berkeley Lab, Univ Calif, 76-81, chemist, Bio-org Chem Group, 49-77, sr staff chemist II, 78-85. *Concurrent Pos:* NSF sr fel, Oxford Univ, 56-57; lectr chem, Univ Calif, Berkeley, 57-59, adj prof biochem, 72-80; vis prof, dept biochem & biophys, Univ Hawaii, 68-69; consult, 86-88. *Mem:* Am Chem Soc; AAAS; Am Soc Plant Physiol. *Res:* Regulation of metabolism and gene expression in photosynthetic plant cells and plant cells in tissue culture. *Mailing Add:* 785 Balra Dr El Cerrito CA 94530

BASSI, SUKH D, DEVELOPMENTAL GENETICS. *Current Pos:* PROF & CHIEF MICROBIOLOGIST, MIDWEST SOLVENTS CO, INC, ATCHISON, KANSAS, 81- *Personal Data:* b Kericho, Kenya; US citizen; m 71; c 1. *Educ:* Knox Col, BS, 65; St Louis Univ, Mo, MS, 67, PhD(biol), 70. *Prof Exp:* Prog specialist biol, Clark Col, 70-71; from asst prof to assoc prof biol, Benedictine Col, 71-76. *Concurrent Pos:* Consult, Environ Coun Atchison, Kans, 71- *Mem:* Am Inst Biol Sci; Am Physiol Soc; AAAS; Am Chem Soc; Am Asn Cereal Chemists; Sigma Xi. *Res:* Interaction of juvenile hormone and molting hormone with carrier and receptor proteins in the large milkweed bug, Oncopeltus fasciatus; bioconversion of starch and cellulose into alcohol. *Mailing Add:* 1300 Main St Atchison KS 66002-2666

BASSICHIS, WILLIAM, THEORETICAL NUCLEAR PHYSICS. *Current Pos:* ASSOC PROF PHYSICS, TEX A&M UNIV, 70- *Personal Data:* b Cleveland, Ohio, Aug 9, 37. *Educ:* Mass Inst Technol, BS, 59; Case Inst Technol, MS, 61, PhD(physics), 63. *Prof Exp:* Vis scientist, Weizmann Inst Sci, 63-64 & Saclay Nuclear Res Ctr, France, 64-65; asst prof physics, Mass Inst Technol, 66-70. *Concurrent Pos:* Consult, AEC, Lawrence Radiation Lab, Univ Calif, Livermore, 66- *Res:* Nuclear structure and reactions. *Mailing Add:* 1811 Shadowwood Dr College Station TX 77840

BASSIM, MOHAMAD NABIL, MATERIALS SCIENCE, CHEMICAL ENGINEERING. *Current Pos:* PROF, DEPT MECH ENG, UNIV MAN. *Personal Data:* b Cairo, Egypt, Oct 10, 44; Can citizen; m 75; c 2. *Educ:* Cairo Univ, BSc 65; Univ Va, MSc, 70, PhD(mat sci), 73. *Prof Exp:* Res engr metall, Atomic Energy Estab Egypt, 65-68; sr scientist mat sci, Univ Va, 73; sr res scientist metall, Ecole Polytechnique, Univ Montreal, 73- *Concurrent Pos:* Vpres, Tektrend Int, 78- *Mem:* Am Soc Metals; Can Inst Mining & Metall; Sigma Xi. *Res:* Physical metallurgy; dislocation theory, fracture and nondestructive testing; computer modeling. *Mailing Add:* Dept Mech Eng Univ Man 356 Eng Bldg Rm 348B Winnipeg MB R3T 2N2 Can

BASSIN, ROBERT HARRIS, MICROBIOLOGY. *Current Pos:* staff fel, 68-73, STAFF MICROBIOLOGIST & HEAD VIRAL BIOCHEM SECT, NAT CANCER INST, 73- *Personal Data:* b Washington, DC, May 2, 38; m 61; c 3. *Educ:* Princeton Univ, AB, 59; Rutgers Univ, PhD(microbiol), 65. *Prof Exp:* From res asst to res assoc microbiol, Rutgers Univ, 61-66; Imp Cancer Res Fund fel, London, Eng, 66-68. *Mem:* AAAS; Soc Gen Microbiol; Tissue Cult Asn; Am Soc Microbiol; Am Asn Cancer Res; Sigma Xi. *Res:* RNA tumor virology; replication and transfomation by murine sarcoma and leukemia viruses in cell culture. *Mailing Add:* 7806 Marion Lane Bethesda MD 20814

BASSINGTHWAIGHTE, JAMES B, PHYSIOLOGY, BIOPHYSICS. *Current Pos:* dir, Ctr Bioeng, 75-80, PROF BIOENG, COL ENG & SCH MED, UNIV WASH, 75-, MEM BIOMATH GROUP FAC, 75- *Personal Data:* b Toronto, Ont, Sept 10, 29; m 55, Joan E Graham; c Anne, Mary, Alan, Sarah & Rebecca. *Educ:* Univ Toronto, BA, 51, MD, 55; Univ Minn, PhD(physiol), 64. *Honors & Awards:* Alza Award, Biomed Eng Soc, 86; Lewellen-Thomas Lectr, Univ Toronto, 91. *Prof Exp:* Intern, Toronto Gen Hosp, 55-56; gen practitioner, Ont, 56-57; house physician internal med, Hammersmith Hosp, London, 57-58; fel med & physiol, Mayo Grad Sch Med, Univ Minn, 58-61; teaching asst, Univ Minn, Minneapolis, 61-62; res asst, Mayo Grad Sch Med, Univ Minn, from asst prof to prof physiol, 67-75, assoc prof bioeng, 72-75, prof med, 75. *Concurrent Pos:* Minn Heart Asn fel, 59-62; NIH career develop award, 64-74; vis prof, Pharmacol Inst, Univ Berne, 70-71; mem study sect, Nat Heart & Lung Inst, 70-74; chmn, Biotechnol Resources Adv & Rev Comt, Div Res Resources, NIH, 77-79; mem, US Nat Comn, Int Union Physiol Sci, 78-86, chmn, 83-86 & chmn, Comn Bioeng in Physiol, 86-96. *Mem:* AAAS; Am Heart Asn; Am Physiol Soc; Biophys Soc; Microcirculatory Soc (pres-elect, 89-90, pres, 90-91); Biomed Eng Soc (Pres, 77-78). *Res:* Cardiovascular and transport physiology; internal medicine; biomedical engineering; cardiology; fractols and chios in physiology membrane transport in intact organs; biochemical kinetics modeling in physiology. *Mailing Add:* Dept Bioeng Univ Wash Seattle WA 98195-7962. *Fax:* 206-685-2651; *E-Mail:* jbb@nsr.bioeng.washington.edu

BASSIOUNY, MOHAMED ALI, RESTORATIVE DENTISTRY, PERIODONTICS. *Current Pos:* from asst prof to assoc prof, 78-86, PROF OPER DENT, SCH DENT, TEMPLE UNIV, 86- *Personal Data:* b Dessouk, Egypt, Nov 21, 41. *Educ:* Alexandria Univ, BDS, 65; Manchester Univ, MSc, 74, PhD(biomat), 77; Temple Univ Sch Dent, DMD, 84. *Prof Exp:* Lectr & res assoc appl dent mat, Victoria Univ, UK, 74-77, fel res assoc, 77-78. *Concurrent Pos:* Consult, Imp Chem Indust, 75-, Recket Toiletry Co, 77, Star Dent, Syntex Corp, 78-81, Premier Dent Prod, 81, Johnson & Johnson Dent Prod Co, 81- & Teledyne-Getz, 84-; pres collegial assembly, Sch Dent, Temple Univ, 86-87. *Mem:* Am Asn Dent Res; Int Asn Dent Res. *Res:* Anti-plaque agent; visible light cured composite concept; chemically activated veneer material; cosmetic restorative dentistry; dental adhesives; posterior composites; prosthodontics. *Mailing Add:* 1113 Edann Rd Oreland PA 19075

BASSNER, SHERRI LYNN, MARKET DEVELOPMENT, APPLICATIONS DEVELOPMENT. *Current Pos:* sr res chemist, 88-97, LEAD APPLNS CHEMIST, AIR PROD & CHEM INC, 97- *Personal Data:* b New York, NY, Sept 4, 62. *Educ:* Goucher Univ, BA, 84; Pa State Univ, PhD(chem), 88. *Mem:* Am Chem Soc; Steel Struct Painting Coun. *Res:* Developed the synthesis and studied the reactions of several organometallic complexes; developed new compounds for aluminum vapor deposition; developing new resins for polyurethane coatings. *Mailing Add:* 7201 Hamilton Blvd Allentown PA 18195

BAST, ROBERT CLINTON, JR, TUMOR IMMUNOLOGY, TUMOR BIOLOGY. *Current Pos:* dir clin res progs, Duke Comprehensive Cancer Ctr, 84-87, prof med, 84-92, CO-DIR DIV HEMAT-ONCOL, DUKE UNIV MED CTR, 84-, PROF MICROBIOL & IMMUNOL, 85-, DIR DUKE COMPREHENSIVE CANCER CTR, 87-, WELLCOME CLIN PROF MED, 92- *Personal Data:* b Washington, DC, Dec 8, 43; m 72, Blanche Simpson; c Elizabeth. *Educ:* Wesleyan Univ, BA, 65; Harvard Univ, MD, 71. *Honors & Awards:* Dominus Award, 84; Edward G Waters Mem lectr, 87; Robert C Knapp Award, 90; John Ohtani Mem lectr, Univ Hawaii, 91; D Nelson Henderson lectr Univ Toronto, 91; Stolte Mem lectr, Free Univ Amsterdam, 92; Arnold O Beckman Distinguished lectr, Am Asn Clin Chem, 93. *Prof Exp:* Res assoc biol br, Nat Cancer Inst, 72-74, res scientist, 74-75; from asst prof to assoc prof med, Harvard Med Sch, 77-84. *Concurrent Pos:* Clin fel med, Harvard Med Sch, 75-77; fel med oncol, Sidney Farber Cancer Inst, 76-77; asst med, Peter Beut, Brigham Hosp, 76-77; mem, Numerous Nat Comts, 76-; asst physician, Dana-Farber Cancer Inst, 77-83, assoc physician, 83-84; jr assoc med, Brigham & Women's Hosp, 77-82, assoc physicians, 82-84; consult oncologist, Boston Hosp Women, 78-80; attend physician, Dana Farber Cancer Inst & Brigham & Women's Hosp, 78-84, W Roxbury Vet Adm Hosp, 80, Duke Univ Med Ctr, 85-, Durham Vet Adm Med Ctr, 85-; lectr, Dept Immunol, Harvard Med Sch, 78-84, Dept Path, 80, Dept Microbiol/Immunol, Duke Univ Med Ctr, 85-; instr med, Harvard Med Sch, 79-84; vis prof, Univ Ariz Cancer Ctr, 86, Peking Union Med Col, Beijing, China, 88, Radiumhemmet, Karolinska Inst, Swed, 91; chmn, Immunol Subcomt, Am Asn Cancer Res, 86-87, Immunol, Transplantation & Biomarkers Subcomt, 89-90. *Mem:* Am Asn Immunologists; Am Asn Cancer Res; Am Asn Clin Oncol; Am Soc Clin Invest; fel Am Col Physicians. *Res:* Clinical application of monoclonol antibodies; autologous bone marrow transplantation; development of CA125 and other tests to monitor and detect epithelial ovarian cancer; applied monoclonal antibodies to treat epithelial malignancies and bone marrow; changes in growth factors. *Mailing Add:* Div Res Univ Tex Anderson Cancer Ctr 1515 Holcombe Blvd Box 092 Houston TX 77030

BAST, ROSE ANN, UNDERGRADUATE TEACHING. *Current Pos:* RETIRED. *Personal Data:* Sept 10, 34. *Educ:* Notre Dame col, BS, 60; Univ Okla, MS, 63, PhD(zool), 66. *Prof Exp:* From asst prof to assoc prof biol, Notre Dame Col, 66-77; assoc prof biol & chair, Mount Mary Col, 77-87. *Concurrent Pos:* John D & Catherine T. McArthur Found grant, Am Coun Learned Socs. *Mem:* NY Acad Sci; Am Inst Biol Sci; AAAS. *Res:* Growth factors (proteins) from the salivary glands of mice; writing science on the junior high school and secondary high school levels to promote increased scientific literacy (for Salem Press Publications). *Mailing Add:* Mount Mary Col 2900 N Menomonee River Pkwy Milwaukee WI 53222-4545. *Fax:* 414-256-1205

BASTA, MILAN, IMMUNOLOGY OF GASTRO-INTESTINAL TRACT, COMPLEMENT IN IMMUNOREGULATION AT MUCOSAL SITES. *Current Pos:* vis fel, 85-88, vis assoc, 88-92, RES IMMUNOLOGIST, NIH, BETHESDA, 92- *Personal Data:* b Apatin, Yugoslavia, Oct 5, 51; m 78, 92, Rosario M Lozano; c Izabela & Alexander. *Educ:* Belgrade Univ Sch Med, MD, 77, MS, 80, PhD(immunol & genetics), 85. *Concurrent Pos:* Writer, dir & producer video, Cold Spring Harbor Lab Press, 93- *Mem:* Am Asn Immunologists; Am Soc Human Genetics. *Res:* The mode of beneficial effect of high-dose intravenous immunoglobulins in immune disorders through interface with the complement system; the role of complement in immune response at mucosal sites; the function of normal human appendix; appendicitis as a model for the pathogenesis of infectious diseases; development of the immune system; molecular biology of scar formation; control of fibrosis. *Mailing Add:* 9012 Wandering Trail Dr Potomac MD 20854. *Fax:* 301-402-0672; *E-Mail:* milanb@codon.nih.gov

BASTIAANS, GLENN JOHN, ANALYTICAL CHEMISTRY. *Current Pos:* SR VPRES & CHIEF TECH OFFICER, INTEGRATED CHEM SENSORS, 85- *Personal Data:* b Oak Park, Ill, Oct 25, 47; m 74; c 1. *Educ:* Univ Ill, Urbana, BS, 69; Ind Univ, Bloomington, PhD(chem), 73. *Prof Exp:* Fel chem, Colo State Univ, 73-74; asst prof chem, Georgetown Univ, 75-79; asst prof chem, Tex A&M Univ, 79- *Mem:* Am Chem Soc; Soc Appl Spectros. *Res:* Development of instrumentation for analytical chemistry; development of surface acoustic wave devices as biosensors, chemical sensors, surface coating monitors and surface reaction monitors; atomic and laser spectroscopy for analytical applications. *Mailing Add:* 2506 Ridgetop Rd Ames IA 50014

BASTIAN, JAMES W, ENDOCRINOLOGY. *Current Pos:* CONSULT, 90- *Personal Data:* b Indianapolis, Ind, Apr 17, 26; m 50, Helen M Hawkins; c Thomas, Keith & Karen. *Educ:* Purdue Univ, PhD(biol sci), 54. *Prof Exp:* Pharmacologist, Armour Pharmaceut Co, 54-67, head dept pharmacol, 67-77, mgr tech develop, 77-86, consult, 86-89. *Mem:* Am Soc Pharmacol & Exp Therapeut; Am Soc Bone & Mineral Res. *Res:* Calcium metabolism; calcitonin-pharmacology dosage-form development. *Mailing Add:* 126 Chestnut St Park Forest IL 60466. *E-Mail:* bastian@interaccess.com; Website: http://www.bonepain.com/myviews/

BASTIAN, JOHN F, PEDIATRICS, IMMUNOLOGY ALLERGY. *Current Pos:* DIR IMMUNOL, CHILDRENS HOSP, SAN DIEGO, 81-, DIR, PEDIAT IMMUNOL CLIN, 86-; ASSOC CLIN PROF, MED CTR UNIV CALIF, SAN DIEGO, 88- *Personal Data:* b Nov 12, 51. *Educ:* Univ Ill, BA, 76; Rush Med Col, MD, 77; Am Bd Pediat, cert, 83; Am Bd Allergy & Immunol, cert, 85. *Prof Exp:* Intern, Univ Calif, San Diego, 77-78, resident, 78-80, chief resident, 80-81, fel pediat immunol & allergy, 81-82; fel pediat immunol & allergy, Scripps Clin & Res Found, 82-83. *Concurrent Pos:* Attend physician pediat, Childrens Hosp, San Diego, 84-, Pediat Intensive Care Unit, 84-; chmn, Physicians Emergency Ref Comt Qual Assurance; mem, Calif AIDS Leadership Subcomt, 88- *Mem:* Am Acad Pediat; Am Fedn Clin Res; AAAS; Am Asn Immunologists; Clin Immunol Soc. *Res:* Alternatives of cellular immunity and antibody responses after severe head injury in children; new uses of intravenous immune globulin therapy; post-traumatic meningitis in adolescents and children. *Mailing Add:* Dept Pediat Children's Hosp 3020 Children's Way MC No 5064 San Diego CA 92123

BASTIAN, JOSEPH, NEUROBIOLOGY. *Current Pos:* GEORGE LYNDCROSS PROF, UNIV OKLA, 74- *Personal Data:* b Mare Island, Calif, Feb 13, 44; m 66; c 3. *Educ:* Elmhurst Col, BS, 66; Univ Notre Dame, PhD(biol), 69. *Prof Exp:* Fel neurobiol, Univ Notre Dame, 69-70, Purdue Univ, 70-72; asst res neuroscientist, Sch Med, Univ Calif, San Diego, 72-74. *Concurrent Pos:* Fel, Nat Inst Neurol Dis & Stroke, 70, res grant, 75. *Mem:* AAAS; Soc Neurosci. *Res:* Neurophysiology of the electrosensory system in weakly electric fish and the role of the cerebellum in processing sensory information; mechanisms of the excitation-coupling process in skeletal muscle. *Mailing Add:* Dept Zool Univ Okla 900 Asp Ave Norman OK 73019-4050

BASTRESS, E(RNEST) KARL, engineering; deceased, see previous edition for last biography

BASU, AMIYO K, SOLAR POWER, PHOTOVOLTAIC POWER. *Current Pos:* TEAM LEADER, DELPHI AUTOMOTIVE SYSTS, GEN MOTORS, 96- *Personal Data:* m 78, Malabika; c Ayan. *Educ:* NMex State Univ, BS, 74, MS, 75, PhD(mech eng), 95. *Prof Exp:* Gen mgr, Oxide Indust, 95-96. *Concurrent Pos:* Mem, Solar Heating Comt, Elec Power Res Inst, 79-83; dir, Arienna Solar Energy Soc, 82-84; comt mem, Am Soc Mech Engrs, 86-89. *Mem:* Am Soc Mech Engrs. *Res:* Solar regeneration; laser systems; parameter estimation (statistical). *Mailing Add:* 225 N Mesa Hills Dr No 2112 El Paso TX 79912

BASU, ASIT PRAKAS, RELIABILITY THEORY, APPLIED STATISTICS. *Current Pos:* chmn dept, 76-83, PROF STATIST, UNIV MO, COLUMBIA, 74- *Personal Data:* b Mar 17, 37; US citizen; m 66; c 2. *Educ:* Univ Calcutta, BSc, 56, MSc, 58; Univ Minn, PhD(statist), 66. *Prof Exp:* Assoc lectr statist & math, Indian Inst Technol, Kharagpur, 60-62; asst statist, Rutgers Univ & Univ Minn, 62-66; asst prof, Univ Wis, 66-68; res staff mem, IBM Res Ctr, 68-70; asst prof indust eng, Northwestern Univ, 70-71; assoc prof math, Univ Pittsburgh, 71-74. *Concurrent Pos:* Consult, Statist & Reliability Theory, Survival Anal. *Mem:* Fel Am Statist Asn; fel Inst Math Statist; fel Royal Statist Soc; fel Int Statist Inst; Biomet Soc; Am Soc Qual Control; fel AAAS. *Res:* Nonparametric statistics; life testing and reliability; biomedical applications; parametric and nonparametric inference in reliability; bayesian statistics. *Mailing Add:* Dept Statist Univ Mo Columbia MO 65211

BASU, DEBABRATA, statistics, for more information see previous edition

BASU, MANJU, BIOCHEMISTRY, IMMUNOLOGY. *Current Pos:* res asst chem, 70-74, res assoc chem & biochem, 74-81, asst res prof, 81-85, ASSOC RES PROF CHEM & BIOCHEM, UNIV NOTRE DAME, 85- *Personal Data:* b Calcutta, India, Aug 10, 42; US citizen; m 66; c 2. *Educ:* Univ Calcutta, BSc, 63, MSc, 65, DSc(biochem), 74. *Prof Exp:* Res fel biochem, Bose Res Inst, 65-66; res asst biol, Johns Hopkins Univ, 67-70. *Concurrent Pos:* New Investr Award, Nat Cancer Inst, NIH, Bethesda, Md, 83-86; vis scientist, Indian Inst Chem Biol, Calcutta, 83. *Mem:* Soc Complex Carbohydrates; Am Soc Biol Chemists. *Res:* Biosynthesis of tumor-specific fucose-containing glycosphigolipids; purification and properties of N-Acetylglucosaminyltransferases involved in the synthesis of I/i-antigens. *Mailing Add:* Dept Chem & Biochem Univ Notre Dame Stepan Chem Hall Rm 440 Notre Dame IN 46556-5628

BASU, MITALI, RECEPTOR BIOCHEMISTRY, PROTEIN BIOCHEMISTRY. *Current Pos:* sr scientist biochem, 89-92, ASSOC RES INVESTR, DEPT BRONCOPULMONARY RES, HOFFMANN-LAROCHE, NUTLEY, 92- *Personal Data:* b Calcutta, West Bengal, India, Nov 24, 51; m 82, Dilip K Mitra. *Educ:* Calcutta Univ, India, BS, 73, MS, 75, PhD(biochem), 81. *Prof Exp:* Sr res fel biochem, Dept Biochem, Calcutta Univ, India, 80-82; res assoc biochem, Sloan-Kettering Inst Cancer Res, New York, NY, 82-83, Sch Med, Univ Pa, Philadelphia, Pa, 83-85; postdoctoral res assoc biochem, Sch Med, Univ Pa, Philadelphia, Pa, 83-85; res asst prof biochem, Univ Fla, Gainesville, Fla, 85-88; res asst prof biochem, Univ Kans Med Ctr, Kansas City, Kans, 88-89. *Mem:* Am Soc Cell Biol; Soc Leukocyte Biol; Am Soc Biochem & Molecular Biol. *Res:* Receptor-ligand interactions and signal transduction; growth-factors and immunomodulators expression, purification and characterization of recombinant proteins of pharmaceutical interest; allergy and inflammation. *Mailing Add:* Hoffmann-La Roche 340 Kingsland St Bldg 123-133 Nutley NJ 07110-1199

BASU, PRASANTA KUMAR, PATHOLOGY, IMMUNOLOGY. *Current Pos:* SR OPHTHALMOLOGIST, TORONTO HOSP, 59- *Personal Data:* b Mymensingh, Bangladesh, Apr 1, 22; Can citizen; m 48; c 1. *Educ:* Univ Calcutta, BSc, 41, MB, 46, DOMS, 51. *Hon Degrees:* FRCP(C). *Honors & Awards:* S Biswas Mem Medal, India, 82; S C Dutta Mem Medal, India, 86; Semi-Centennial Award, Can Ophthal Soc, 87 & 90. *Prof Exp:* Head ophthal, Ramakrishna Mission Hosp, Vrindaban, India, 51-59. *Concurrent Pos:* Colombo Plan fel, Univ Toronto, 55-56, res assoc, 57-65, clin teacher, 58-59, assoc prof, 59-70, prof, 70-89, dir ophthal res, 59-, emer prof ophthal, 89-; res assoc, Univ Calif, San Francisco, 57; career investr, Med Res Coun Can, 65-; assoc med dir, Ont Div Eye Bank Can, 68- *Mem:* Asn Res Vision & Ophthal; Can Ophthal Soc; Can Implant Asn (secy, 81-86); Int Med Res Found (vpres, 81-86); Can Fedn Biol Socs; All India Ophthal Soc. *Res:* Corneal transplant immunology; preservation of cornea, sclera and fascia lata; ocular effects of air, water and electromagnetic pollutants; diabetic retinopathy; application of ocular cell and organ cultures in ophthalmic research; third world ophthalmology. *Mailing Add:* 716-701 Esquimalt Rd Victoria BC V9A 3L5 Can

BASU, RAJAT SUBHRA, SOLVENT DEVELOPMENT, CHEMICAL PROCESSES. *Current Pos:* res physicist, Allied Signal Inc, 81-84, sr res physicist, 84-89, group leader, 89-92, prin scientist, 93-97, SR PRIN SCIENTIST, ALLIED SIGNAL INC, 97- *Personal Data:* b Calcutta, India, Oct 26, 45; US citizen; m 73, Chandra Mukherji; c Shome & Sankha. *Educ:* Calcutta Univ, BSc, 65, MSc, 68; Univ Md, College Park, PhD(physics), 77. *Honors & Awards:* Heroes of Chem, Am Chem Soc, 97. *Prof Exp:* Res assoc, Univ Md, College Park, 77-80; sr analyst, SASC, 80-81. *Concurrent Pos:* Chair, Comt Thermophys Properties, Am Soc Mech Engrs, 88-91. *Mem:* Am Phys Soc; Am Soc Mech Engrs; Sigma Xi. *Res:* Development of environmentally safe alternates to chlorofluorocarbons; simulation and modeling of thermophysical properties; theory and experimental research on individual solvents; simulation of chemical processes using aspen. *Mailing Add:* Allied Signal Inc 20 Peabody St Buffalo NY 14210-1523. *Fax:* 716-827-6373; *E-Mail:* rajat.basu@alliedsignal.com

BASU, SUBHASH CHANDRA, GLYCOLIPID & DNA BIOSYNTHESIS. *Current Pos:* from asst prof to assoc prof, 70-82, PROF CHEM, UNIV NOTRE DAME, IND, 83-, CHMN, BIOCHEM, BIOPHYS & MOLECULAR BIOL PROG, 86- *Personal Data:* b Calcutta, India, May 28, 38; US citizen; m 66; c 2. *Educ:* Univ Calcutta, BSc, 58, MSc, 60; Univ Mich, PhD(biochem), 66; Univ Calcutta, DSc(biochem), 76. *Prof Exp:* Lectr chem, Vidyasager Col, Univ Calcutta, 60-61; teaching asst biochem, Univ Mich, 61-64, teaching fel, 64-65, res asst, Rackham Arthritis Res Unit, 65-66; fel, Johns Hopkins Univ, 66-67, res assoc, 67-70. *Concurrent Pos:* Res fel, Helen Hay Whitney Found, NY, 67-70; vis scientist, Gothenburg Univ, 68; Kennedy Found travel fel, Sweden, 68. *Mem:* Am Soc Biol Chemists; Int Soc Neurochem; Soc Complex Carbohydrates; NY Acad Sci; Am Soc Neurochem; Am Soc Cell Biol; Sigma Xi; Soc Cryobiol. *Res:* Biosynthesis of gangliosides and blood group glycosphingolipids; differentiation of tumor cells; control of DNA polymerase activities of neural cells. *Mailing Add:* Dept Chem & Biochem Univ Notre Dame Stepan Chem Hall Rm 443 Notre Dame IN 46556-5601

BASU, SUNANDA, PHYSICS. *Current Pos:* PROG DIR AERONOMY, NSF, 92- *Personal Data:* b Calcutta, India, Dec 9, 40; US citizen; m 61, Santimay; c Susanto. *Educ:* Calcutta Univ, BSc, 60, PhD(radio physics), 72; Boston Univ, AM, 63. *Prof Exp:* Res assoc, Inst Radio Physics, Univ Calcutta, 73-75; resident res assoc, Air Force Geophys Lab, Nat Acad Sci, 75-78; sr physicist, Emmanuel Col, Boston, 78-89; sr res physicist, Inst Space Res, Boston Col, 89-92. *Concurrent Pos:* Mem, US Nat Deleg, Int Sci Radio Union, 81, 84, 87, 90 & 93, Exec Comt, 88-90, vchairperson, 91-93, chairperson, 94-; consult, Ctr Space Res, Mass Inst Technol, 91-92; prin investr, Dept Defense NSF & NASA. *Mem:* Am Geophys Union; AAAS; Int Sci Radio Union; Sigma Xi (pres, 86-87). *Res:* Ionospheric radio wave propagation; equatorial and high latitude plasma structure, their generation and effects; ionospheric modification by high power radio waves. *Mailing Add:* NSF 4201 Wilson Blvd Rm 775 Arlington VA 22230. *Fax:* 703-306-0377; *E-Mail:* sbasu@nsf.gov

BASU, TAPAN KUMAR, VITAMINOLOGY, DRUG-NUTRIENT INTERACTIONS & NUTRITION. *Current Pos:* assoc prof, 81-83, PROF NUTRIT, DEPT AGR FOOD & NUTRIT SCI, UNIV ALTA, CAN, 83-, HON PROF MED, DEPT MED, 84-, MCCALLA PROF, 94-, KILLAM ANNUAL PROF, 96- *Personal Data:* b Burdwan, West Bengal, India, Sutapa Mukhopadhyay; c Anita & Malini. *Educ:* Calcutta Univ, India, BSc, 59, BVSc, 62; London Univ, Eng, MSc, 68; Surrey Univ, PhD(biochem), 71. *Honors & Awards:* Borden Prize, Can Soc Nutrit Sci, 84. *Prof Exp:* Head, Metab Unit, Res Dept, Marie Curie Mem Found, Eng, 71-75; lectr nutrit, Dept Biochem, Univ Surrey, Eng, 75-81. *Concurrent Pos:* McCalla res prof, Univ Alta, 93-94. *Mem:* NY Acad Sci; fel Am Col Nutrit; Am Inst Nutrit; Can Soc Nutrit; Nat Inst Nutrit; Can Dietetic Asn; fel Int Col Nutrit (vpres). *Res:* Bio and metabolic availability of vitamins in the presence of cancer and diabetes; modulation of cholesterol metabolism by dietary fibers; toxicities of mega vitamins. *Mailing Add:* Dept Agr Food & Nutrit Sci Univ Alta 3-18B Agr/ Forestry Edmonton AB T6G 2P5 Can. *Fax:* 403-492-4921; *E-Mail:* tbasu@ afns.ualberta.ca

BATALDEN, PAUL B, AMBULATORY CARE QUALITY ASSURANCE, PEDIATRICS. *Current Pos:* CHMN BD, INST HEALTH CARE IMPROVEMENT BOSTON, MASS, 91-, SR VPRES HEALTH PROF DEVELOP, 96; DIR, HEALTH CARE IMPROVEMENT LEADERSHIP DEVELOP, CTR EVAL CLIN SCI, DARTMOUTH MED SCH, 94- *Personal Data:* b Minneapolis, Minn, Dec 4, 41; m, La Vonne; c Maren & Sonya. *Educ:* Augsburg, Col, Minneapolis, BA, 63; Univ Minn, BS, MD, 67; Am Pd Pediat, cert, 76. *Prof Exp:* Clin assoc, Nat Cancer Inst, NIH, 69-70; med dir, Job Corps Dept Labor, Off Admin, Health Serv & Mental Health Admin Systs, Dept Health Educ & Welfare, 70-72; asst surgeon gen & dir, Bur Community Health Serv, 73-75; dir, Qual Assurance Proj, Interstudy, Minneapolis, 75-76; pediatrician, Park Nicollet Med Ctr, 75-86, dir, Qual Assurance Prog & Health Serv Res Ctr, 76-84, exec vpres, 84-86; vpres med care, Hosp Corp Am, 86-94. *Concurrent Pos:* Pres, St Louis Park Med Ctr Found, 81-84; breech chmn, Dept Health Care Qual Improv, Henry Ford Health Sci Ctr, vpres, Henry Ford Health Syst; bd dirs, Allina, 90-, Health Systs, 95- *Mem:* Inst Med-Nat Acad Sci; Am Pub Health Asn; Ambulatory Pediat Asn. *Res:* Systems for managing improvement of health and value of health care for a panel of patients; systems for assessing the burden of illness in a defined population; system for assessing the degree to which health care workers can learn in their work setting; author of numerous articles in various journals. *Mailing Add:* 55 Eagle Ridge Lebanon NH 03766

BATATA, AL, LYMPHOLOGY & CANCER IMMUNOLOGY. *Current Pos:* PROF & CHMN, DEPT PATH, SCH MED, WRIGHT STATE UNIV, 77- *Personal Data:* b Egypt, Jan 18, 27, US citizen; m 68, Julia Ann Chattan; c Sara & Amber. *Educ:* Cairo Univ, Egypt, MB & BCh, 50, DM, 60, DMSc, 60 & 62; LMSSA, London, Eng, 68. *Prof Exp:* Rotating intern, Bab el Sharia Hosp, Cairo, Egypt, 50-51; family pract, Egypt, 51-56; resident clin Path & Int Med, Cairo Univ Hosps, Egypt, 56-59; anat & clin pathologist, Cent Pub Health Ref Labs, Egypt, 57-64; res asst path, Oxford Med Sch, Radcliffe Hosp, Eng, 64-65; sr registrar & registrar, Post Grad Med Sch London, Nat Hosp Nervous Dis, 65-67; staff pathologist, Children's Cancer Res Found, West Park Hosp Area Lab, Eng, 67-68; res assoc hematopath, Harvard Med Sch, 68-71; asst prof path, Marquette Med Sch, Med Col Wis, 71-77. *Concurrent Pos:* Dir labs, Ahmad Maher Hosp, Cairo, 62-64; dir, Lymphol & Cancer Immunol Lab, Sch Med, Wright State Univ, 77-, prof & dir path teaching prog, 77-; active staff pathologist, Kettering Hosp, 78- *Mem:* AMA; Int Acad Path; Col Am Pathologists; Soc Hematopathologists; Am Soc Clin Pathologists; Asn Path Chmn. *Res:* Hematological leukemia and lymphoma diagnosis and immunphenotyping and immunogenotyping career for DNA and cell cycle analysis; immunodeficiency syndromes for diagnosis. *Mailing Add:* 3525 Southern Blvd Kettering OH 45429. *Fax:* 937-297-8002

BATCHELDER, ARTHUR ROLAND, CHEMICAL SAFETY. *Current Pos:* SAFETY CONSULT, 94- *Personal Data:* b Haverhill, Mass, Apr 17, 32; m 55; c 3. *Educ:* Univ Mass, BS, 54; Va Polytech Inst, MS, 66; Cornell Univ, PhD, 71. *Prof Exp:* Soil scientist agr res, Agr Res Serv, USDA, 57-87; pres, Hazard Training Assoc Inc, 86-94. *Concurrent Pos:* Collateral duty safety officer, 79-87; mem, cert bd hazardous mat technicians & supervisors, World Safety Orgn, 89- *Mem:* Am Soc Agron; World Safety Orgn; Sigma Xi; Soil Sci Soc Am; Am Chem Soc; Nat Fire Protection Asn. *Res:* Chemical safety training. *Mailing Add:* 255 Bogie Ave Red Feather Lakes CO 80545

BATCHELDER, DAVID G(EORGE), AGRICULTURAL ENGINEERING. *Current Pos:* from instr to prof, 55-85, EMER PROF AGR ENG, OKLA STATE UNIV, 85- *Personal Data:* b Hiawatha, Kans, Apr 30, 20; m 44; c 4. *Educ:* Kans State Univ, BS, 55; Okla State Univ, MS, 62. *Prof Exp:* Farmer, 46-53. *Concurrent Pos:* Mem Coop in agr between US & USSR, SEA & State Dept, 77- *Mem:* Am Soc Agr Engrs; Sigma Xi. *Res:* Equipment design and testing of machinery for seed metering; seed bed preparation; planting; weed control; plant preparation for harvest; harvesting for cotton production in Oklahoma; field forage drying. *Mailing Add:* 1102 S Stanley St Stillwater OK 74074

BATCHELDER, GERALD M(ILES), CIVIL ENGINEERING. *Current Pos:* RETIRED. *Personal Data:* b Exeter, NH, June 4, 25; m 49, Elizabeth Barker; c 6. *Educ:* Univ NH, BS, 50; Purdue Univ, MS, 52. *Prof Exp:* Res engr, Mass Inst Technol, 52; engr, NH Dept Pub Works & Hwys, 52-53; res assoc prof, Eng Exp Sta, Univ NH, 53-70, assoc prof math, Div Continuing Educ, 57-73, prof civil technol & adj prof civil eng, 70-90, prof, Sch Life Long Learning, 73-90. *Mem:* Am Soc Testing & Mat; Nat Soc Prof Engrs. *Res:* Physical properties of materials; nondestructive testing of concrete; strength, dynamic properties and durability studies of concrete; materials science; micro-hardness conversion. *Mailing Add:* PO Box 138 Stratham NH 03885

BATCHELDER, WILLIAM HOWARD, MATHEMATICAL PSYCHOLOGY, COGNITIVE SCIENCE. *Current Pos:* assoc prof, 70-75, PROF COGNITIVE SCI, UNIV CALIF, IRVINE, 76- *Personal Data:* b Columbus, Miss, May 29, 40; c Jennifer L & Sarah M. *Educ:* Ind Univ, BA, 62; Stanford Univ, PhD(psychol), 66. *Prof Exp:* Asst prof psychol, Univ Ill, Urbana, 66-70. *Concurrent Pos:* Vis lectr, Univ Wis, 70; prin investr, Nat Res Coun, 71-73, NSF, 89-, co-prin investr, 83-; ed, J Math Psychol, 74-79; panel mem, Measurement, Methodology & Statist, NSF, 93- *Mem:* Soc Math Psychol (pres, 89-90); Am Psychol Soc; Psychomet Soc; Psychosom Soc; Am Statist Asn; Am Math Soc. *Res:* Develop formal models and measurement tools in the social science including cognitive psychology, cultural anthropology and social networks; numerous articles in related journals. *Mailing Add:* Cognitive Studies Univ Calif Irvine Irvine CA 92717-0001. *Fax:* 714-725-2307

BATCHELOR, B(ARRINGTON) D(EVERE), CIVIL ENGINEERING. *Current Pos:* from asst prof to assoc prof, 66-72, PROF CIVIL ENG, QUEEN'S UNIV, 72- *Personal Data:* b Lucea, Jamaica, WI, July 2, 28; m 60; c 3. *Educ:* Univ Edinburgh, BSc, 56; Imp Col, dipl, 61, Univ London, PhD(civil eng), 63. *Prof Exp:* Asst engr, Sir William Halcrow & Partners, Consult Engrs, Eng, 56-58; exec engr, Ministry of Educ, WI, 58-60, sr exec engr, 63-64; dir, Caribbean Consult Engrs, Ltd, 64-66. *Concurrent Pos:* Partner, Franks & Batchelor, Consult Engrs, WI, 64-66; mem task force, Ont Hwy Bridge Design Code, 76-; mem adv comt sci & technol, Can Broadcasting Corp, 84-87; mem, Nat Bldg Code Can; mem task force, new draft Am Asn State Hwy & Transp Off, 89- *Mem:* Am Soc Civil Engrs; Am Concrete Inst; Asn Prof Engrs Ont; Can Soc Eng. *Res:* Engineering structures; concrete bridges. *Mailing Add:* Ellis Hall Queen's Univ Kingston ON K7L 3N6 Can

BATCHELOR, BILL, ENVIRONMENTAL ENGINEERING. *Current Pos:* From asst prof to assoc prof, 76-86, Halliburton prof, 86-87, PROF CIVIL ENG, TEX A&M UNIV, COL STAT, 86-, DIR, INST ENVIRON ENG, 92- *Personal Data:* b Houston, Tex, Feb, 9, 49; m 73, Colleen Jennings; c Brian J & Megan J. *Educ:* Rice Univ BA, 71, MS, 74; Cornell Univ, PhD, 76. *Honors & Awards:* Harrison Prescott Eddy Medal, 83. *Concurrent Pos:* Consult, US Environ Protection Agency, Wash, 85-, Argonne Nat Lab & PRC Environ Mgt, 92-; bd dirs, Inst Environ Eng, Tex A&M Univ Syst. *Mem:* Fel AAAS; Asn Environ Eng Prof (secy & treas, 84-86); Water Environ Fedn; Am Chem Soc; Am Soc Civil Engrs; Am Water Works Asn. *Res:* Development of model and design procedure for single-sludge denitrification; demonstration feasibility of ultra-high lime treatment for recycled cooling water; demonstrated feasibility of autotrophic denitrification using sulfur. *Mailing Add:* Dept Civil Eng Tex A&M Univ College Station TX 77843-3136. *Fax:* 409-862-1542; *E-Mail:* bill_batchelor@tamu.edu

BATCHELOR, JOHN W, ELECTRICAL ENGINEERING. *Current Pos:* RETIRED. *Personal Data:* b Winchester, Ind, Nov 17, 14. *Educ:* Butler Univ, AB, 35; Purdue Univ, BSEE, 37. *Prof Exp:* Asst dept mgr, Westinghouse Elec Co, 37-38. *Mem:* Nat Acad Engrs; Inst Elec & Electronics Engrs; Am Soc Mech Eng. *Mailing Add:* 500 Rte 909 A239 Verona PA 15147-3831

BATCHER, KENNETH EDWARD, PARALLEL PROCESSING. *Current Pos:* PROF ENG, KENT STATE UNIV, 89- *Personal Data:* b St Albans, NY, Dec 27, 35; m 67; c 2. *Educ:* Iowa State Univ, BS, 57; Univ Ill, MS, 62, PhD(elec eng), 64. *Honors & Awards:* Eckert-Mauchly Award, Asn Comput Mach & Inst Elec & Electronics Engrs, 90. *Prof Exp:* Trainee, Goodyear Atomic Corp, 57-58, develop engr, Goodyear Aircraft Corp, 58-60; res & teaching asst elec eng, Univ Ill, 60-64; staff engr comput, Goodyear

Aerospace Corp, Akron, 64-77, prin engr, 77-87; prin engr, Loral Defense Syst, Div, 87-89. *Mem:* Asn Comput Mach; Sigma Xi. *Res:* Digital computers, especially design of parallel networks and parallel processors. *Mailing Add:* 2007 Kingsdale Dr Stow OH 44224. *E-Mail:* batcher@mcs.kent.edu

BATCHMAN, THEODORE EARL, INTEGRATED OPTICAL DEVICES, MICROWAVE MEASUREMENT DEVICES. *Current Pos:* DEAN, COL ENG, UNIV NEV, 95- *Personal Data:* b Great Bend, Kans, Mar 29, 40; m 61, Nancy Leatherman; c Teddie S (Federici), Timothy B & Tracey N (Speed). *Educ:* Univ Kans, BS, 62, MS, 63, PhD(elec eng), 66. *Prof Exp:* Engr sci specialist, LTV Missiles & Space Div, 66-70; sr lectr elec eng, Univ Queensland, Australia, 70-75; vis asst prof, Univ Va, 75-76, from asst prof to prof elec eng, 76-88; dir, Sch Elec Eng & Comput Sci, Univ Okla, 88-92, Sch Elec Eng, 92-95. *Concurrent Pos:* Consult, Laser Electronic Party Ltd, 73-75 & Commonwealth Va, 81-86. *Mem:* Inst Elec & Electronics Engrs; Soc Photo-Optical Instrumentation Engrs; Optical Soc Am; Am Soc Eng Educ. *Res:* Passive and active integrated optical waveguides; miniature implantable electric field probe for radio frequencies; liquid crystal fault detection on integrated circuits; pressure sensor research using fiber sensors and capacitive sensors for biomedical applications. *Mailing Add:* 12500 Fieldcreek Lane Reno NV 89511. *Fax:* 702-784-4466; *E-Mail:* batch_t@unr.edu

BATCHO, ANDREW DAVID, ORGANIC CHEMISTRY. *Current Pos:* sr res chemist, 61-76, res fel, 76-84, RES INVESTR, HOFFMANN-LA ROCHE, INC, 85- *Personal Data:* b Somerville, NJ, July 9, 34; m 70; c 1. *Educ:* Rutgers Univ, BS, 55; Univ Calif, PhD(chem), 59. *Prof Exp:* Sr res chemist, Am Cyanamid Co, 58-61. *Mem:* Am Chem Soc. *Res:* Synthetic organic chemistry; natural products. *Mailing Add:* 19 White Oak Dr Caldwell NJ 07006

BATDORF, ROBERT LUDWIG, SOLID STATE SCIENCE. *Current Pos:* RETIRED. *Personal Data:* b Reading, Pa, Sept 18, 26; m 53, Shirley Johnson; c 2. *Educ:* Albright Col, BS, 50; Univ Minn, PhD(phys chem), 55. *Prof Exp:* Mem tech staff, Bell Labs, 55-65, supvr, Solid State Device Technol Group, 65-68, dept head semiconductor mat & appl chem, 68-73, semiconductor technol, 73-89. *Mem:* AAAS; Am Chem Soc. *Res:* Diode and field effect transistor development; integrated circuit process technology, especially ion implantation techniques, diffusion, and chemical processing; physical diagnostic analytical techniques such as scanning electron microscopy, electron beam and ion beam microprobes; micromachined silicon sensor technology. *Mailing Add:* 707 Warren St Reading PA 19601-1336

BATDORF, SAMUEL BURBRIDGE, COMPOSITES ENGINEERING MECHANICS, FRACTURE. *Current Pos:* RETIRED. *Personal Data:* b China, Mar 31, 14; m 40, Carol Schweiss; c Samuel C & Laura A. *Educ:* Univ Calif, AB, 34, MA, 36, PhD(theoret physics), 38. *Honors & Awards:* Silver Medallion, Am Soc Mech Engrs, 80. *Prof Exp:* Instr physics, Univ Utah, 38; from asst prof to assoc prof, Univ Nev, 38-43; aeronaut res scientist, Langley Lab, Nat Adv Comt Aeronaut, 43-51; adv physicist, Westinghouse Res Labs, 51-52; mgr advan develop, Mat Eng Dept, Westinghouse Elec Corp, 52-55, dir develop, Eng Hq Staff, 55-56; asst dir res & mgr, Electronics Div, Lockheed Missile Syst Div, Lockheed Aircraft Corp, 56-57, tech dir, Weapon Syst Div, 57-58; chmn man-in-space proj, Inst Defense Analyst, 58-59, chmn commun satellite proj, 59-60; mgr prod planning, Aeronutronic Div, Ford Motor Co, 60-61, dir res physics & electronics, 61-62; dir off res, Aerospace Corp, 62-64, dir, Appl Mech & Physics Subdiv, 64-70, group dir appl technol concepts, 70-71, prin staff scientist, 72-77; adj prof, Univ Calif, Los Angeles, 73-85. *Concurrent Pos:* Chmn, Langley Adv Study Comt, Nat Adv Comt Aeronaut, 45-51, Subcomt Aircraft Struct Metals, 45-51, mem, Comt Aircraft Struct Mat, 47-51; mem, Panel Physics Solids, Res & Develop Bd, 49-51 & Adv Comt Solid State Physics, Off Naval Res, 49-52; adv Comt Aeromech, Air Force Off Sci Res, 67-74; distinguished prof, Tsing Hua Univ, Taiwan, 69; adv Comt Solid Mech, NSF, 78-80. *Mem:* Fel Am Phys Soc; fel Am Inst Aeronaut & Astronaut; hon mem Am Soc Mech Engrs; fel Am Acad Mech (past pres). *Res:* Mechanics; elasticity; theory of plates and shells; plasticity; fracture; composites; geophysics. *Mailing Add:* 5536 B Via La Mesa Laguna Hills CA 92653

BATE, GEOFFREY, SOLID STATE PHYSICS. *Current Pos:* vis prof, 86-87, PROF & ASSOC DEAN, SCH ENG, SANTA CLARA UNIV, 87- *Personal Data:* b Sheffield, Eng, Mar 30, 29; m 53; c 4. *Educ:* Univ Sheffield, BSc, 49, PhD(physics), 52. *Honors & Awards:* Centennial Medal, Inst Elect & Electronics Engrs, 84. *Prof Exp:* Sci officer physics, Royal Naval Sci Serv, Eng, 52-56; res assoc, Univ BC, 56-57, asst prof, 57-59; staff physicist, Develop Lab, Data Systs Div, Int Bus Mach Corp, 59-60, adv physicist, 60-65, mgr advan rec technol, 63-65, sr physicist & mgr res physics, IBM Corp, 65-78; vpres, Advan Develop, 78-82, sr vpres eng, Verbatim Corp, 82-86. *Concurrent Pos:* Adj prof, Syracuse Univ, 61-65, Colo State Univ, 72- *Mem:* Am Phys Soc; Sigma Xi; fel Inst Elec & Electronics Engrs. *Res:* Ferromagnetism of high-coercivity materials; semiconductors and infrared photoconductors; physics of magnetic and optical recording; magnetic properties of recording materials; high-frequency properties of soft-magnetic materials. *Mailing Add:* 23344 Camino Hermoso Los Altos Hills CA 94024

BATE, GEORGE LEE, physics, applied mathematics, for more information see previous edition

BATE, ROBERT THOMAS, SEMICONDUCTORS. *Current Pos:* physicist, 64-68, sr scientist, 68-72, BR MGR, CENT RES LABS, TEX INSTRUMENTS INC, DALLAS, 72- *Personal Data:* b Denver, Colo, Apr 1, 31; m 51; c 5. *Educ:* Univ Colo, BS, 55; Ohio State Univ, MS, 57. *Honors & Awards:* Texas Instruments Fel Award, 85. *Prof Exp:* Physicist, Eng Lab, US Bur Standards, 55; res asst, Ohio State Univ, 56-57; physicist, Battelle Mem Inst, 57-64. *Concurrent Pos:* Mem, Solid State Sci Comt, Nat Acad Sci, 81. *Mem:* Fel Am Phys Soc; sr mem Inst Elec & Electronics Engrs. *Res:* Semiconductor device research, nonvolatile semiconductor memory, physical limits on logic devices; electrical properties of semiconductors; quantum devices. *Mailing Add:* 3106 Kristin Ct Garland TX 75044

BATEMAN, ANDREW, STRUCTURAL ANALYSIS, INFLAMMATION. *Current Pos:* Fel peptide biol, 85-90, ASST PROF PEPTIDE BIOL, MCGILL UNIV, 90- *Personal Data:* b London, UK, Dec 12, 59; m 90. *Educ:* Univ London, UK, BSc, 81, PhD(biochem), 85. *Mem:* Am Peptide Soc. *Res:* Isolation, structural analysis and biological activity of peptides involved in inflammation. *Mailing Add:* Endocrine Lab Rm L205 Royal Victoria Hosp 687 Pine Ave W Montreal PQ H3A 1A1 Can

BATEMAN, DURWARD F, PLANT PATHOLOGY. *Current Pos:* assoc dean, Sch Agr & Life Sci & Dir, NC Agr Res Serv, 79-86, DEAN, COL AGR & LIFE SCI, NC STATE UNIV, 86- *Personal Data:* b Tyner, NC, May 28, 34; m 53; c 3. *Educ:* NC State Col, BS, 56; Cornell Univ, MS, 58, PhD(plant path), 60. *Prof Exp:* From asst prof to prof plant path, Cornell Univ, 60-79, chmn dept, 70-79. *Concurrent Pos:* NIH spec fel, Dept Plant Path, Univ Calif, Davis, 67; vis prof plant path, NC State Univ, 74-75; chmn, Southern Agr Exp Sta Dirs Asn, 85; trustee, Charles Valentine Riley Med Found, Wasington, DC, 85-; pres, Southern Asn Agr Scientists, 90; mem bd trustees, Int Potato Ctr, Lima, Peru, 91- *Mem:* AAAS; fel Am Phytopath Soc (vpres, 75, pres-elect, 76, pres, 77, past-pres, 78); Int Soc Plant Path; Sigma Xi. *Res:* Ecology of soil borne pathogens; physiology of parasitism and disease and pathogen physiology; biochemical basis of pathogenic mechanisms and host reactions to infection; enzymatic decomposition of plant cell walls by phytopathogenic organisms. *Mailing Add:* Dean Agr & Life Sci NC State Univ PO Box 7642 Raleigh NC 27695-0001

BATEMAN, FELICE DAVIDSON, MATHEMATICS. *Current Pos:* RETIRED. *Personal Data:* b Springfield, Mass, Sept 2, 22; m 48, Paul T; c Sarah E. *Educ:* Smith Col, AB, 43; Univ Mich, AM, 44, PhD(math), 50. *Prof Exp:* Instr math, NJ Col Women, Rutgers Univ, 47-49; instr math, Univ Ill, Urbana-Champaign, 54-55 & 57-58, asst prof, 58-89. *Concurrent Pos:* Mem sch math, Inst Advan Study, 49-50; vis lectr, Swarthmore Col, 61-62 & Sarah Lawrence Col, 64-65; ed consult, Math Reviews, 80-81. *Mem:* Am Math Soc; Math Asn Am. *Res:* Linear algebras with radical. *Mailing Add:* 108 Meadows Ct Urbana IL 61801

BATEMAN, JOHN LAURENS, RADIOBIOLOGY, ONCOLOGY. *Current Pos:* ASST PROF MED, SCH MED, STATE UNIV NY, STONY BROOK, 74- *Personal Data:* b Washington, DC, Mar 30, 26; m 50, 80; c 5. *Educ:* Mass Inst Technol, SB, 46; Johns Hopkins Univ, MD, 56; Am Bd Nuclear Med, dipl, 74. *Prof Exp:* Intern, Stamford Hosp, 56-57; resident internal med, Greenwich Hosp Asn, 57-58; res assoc, 58-61, res collabr, 61-67, scientist, Med Res Ctr, Brookhaven Nat Lab, 67-71; ASSOC CHIEF NUCLEAR MED, VET ADMIN HOSP, 74- *Mem:* Soc Nuclear Med; Radiation Res Soc; NY Acad Sci. *Res:* Group techniques in cancer patients; medical ethics and quality of terminal care; dynamic and metabolic aspects of nuclear medicine; radiation dose-rate effect. *Mailing Add:* Nuclear Med Serv (115) Vet Admin Med Ctr Northport NY 11768

BATEMAN, JOSEPH R, HEMATOLOGY, ONCOLOGY. *Current Pos:* from instr to assoc prof med, 60-75, prof, 75-82, EMER PROF MED, UNIV SOUTHERN CALIF, 82- *Personal Data:* b Chicago, Ill, Sept 3, 22; m 48; c 2. *Educ:* George Washington Univ, MD, 47; Am Bd Internal Med, dipl, 57. *Prof Exp:* Intern med, Gorgas Hosp, Balboa, CZ, 47-48; fel, Vet Admin Hosp, Grand Junction, Colo, 54-56; resident, Vet Admin Hosps, Albuquerque, NMex, 58-61, hematologist, Oakland, Calif, 56-60. *Concurrent Pos:* Fel hemat, Univ Southern Calif, 60-62; consult, Vet Admin Hosp, 64-; chmn, Western Cancer Study Group; chief med oncol div, Los Angeles County-Univ Southern Calif Med Ctr; dir, Home Care Serv Dept, Los Angeles County-Univ Southern Calif Med Ctr. *Mem:* Am Col Physicians; Am Soc Clin Oncol; Am Asn Cancer Res; Am Asn Cancer Educ; Am Fed Clin Res. *Res:* Clinical research; cancer chemotherapy. *Mailing Add:* 1491 Old CC Rd Colville WA 99114

BATEMAN, LEONARD A, ENGINEERING, HYROELECTRIC DEVELOPMENT & HIGH VOLTAGE DIRECT CURRENT TRANSMISSION. *Current Pos:* PRES & CHIEF EXEC OFFICER, BATEMAN & ASSOCS, WINNIPEG, CAN, 79-, CHAIRMAN & CEO MON-HYDRO, 72-79. *Personal Data:* b Jan 14, 19; wid, Eileen E Campbell (deceased); c 3. *Educ:* BSc, 42, MSc, 48, BSAM, 60. *Honors & Awards:* Gold Medal Award, Can Coun Prof Engrs, 94. *Prof Exp:* Chief engr, Mon-Hydro, 70-72, chmn & chief exec officer, 72-79. *Concurrent Pos:* Mem, Int Conf Large High Voltage Elec Systs. *Mem:* World Energy Coun. *Mailing Add:* Bateman & Assocs 231 Brock St Winnipeg MB R3N 0Y7 Can

BATEMAN, MILDRED MITCHELL, PSYCHIATRY. *Current Pos:* prof & chmn, 77-82, PROF PSYCHIAT, SCH MED, MARSHALL UNIV, 82-; STAFF PSYCHIAT, HUNTINGTON VET ADMIN MED CTR, 86- *Personal Data:* b Cordele, Ga, Mar 22, 22; c 2. *Educ:* J C Smith Univ, BS, 41; Woman's Med Col Pa, MD, 46. *Honors & Awards:* Warren Williams Distinguished Award, Am Psychiat Asn, 91. *Prof Exp:* Staff physician, Larkin State Hosp WVa, 47-48, clin dir, 51-52, 55-58, supt, 58-60; supvr, Dir Prof Servs, WVa Dept Ment Health, 60-62, dir, State Capital, 62-77. *Concurrent Pos:* Mem, Comn Ment Illness & Ment Retardation, Comn Aging, WVa Comn Ment Retardation, Gov WVa Comn Status of Women & Coop Health

Statist Adv Comt, Nat Ctr Health Statist; trustee, Menninger Found; prof psychiat & chmn dept, Marshall Univ. *Mem:* Inst Med-Nat Acad Sci; Am Psychiat Asn (vpres, 73); AMA. *Res:* Published numerous articles in various journals. *Mailing Add:* Dept Psychiat Marshall Univ Sch Med Huntington WV 25701

BATEMAN, PAUL TREVIER, MATHEMATICS, NUMBERTHEORY. *Current Pos:* from asst prof to assoc prof, Univ Ill, Urbana-Champaign, 50-58, head dept, 65-80, prof, 58-89, EMER PROF MATH, UNIV ILL, URBANA-CHAMPAIGN, 89- *Personal Data:* b Philadelphia, Pa, June 6, 19; m 48, Felice Davidson; c Sarah E. *Educ:* Univ Pa, AB, 39, AM, 40, PhD(math), 46. *Prof Exp:* Lectr statist, Bryn Mawr Col, 45-46; instr math, Yale Univ, 46-48; res, Inst Advan Study, 48-50. *Concurrent Pos:* NSF sr fel, Inst Advan Study, 56-57; researcher, Univ Pa, 61-62; mem math adv panel, NSF, 63-66; vis prof, City Univ New York, 64-65; CIC exchange prof, Univ Mich, 80-81. *Mem:* Am Math Soc; Math Asn Am; London Math Soc. *Res:* Number theory and related parts of algebra, analysis, and mathematics of computation. *Mailing Add:* Dept Math Univ Ill Urbana IL 61801. *E-Mail:* bateman@math.uiuc.edu

BATEMAN, ROBERT CAREY, JR, BIOCHEMISTRY, PROTEIN SCIENCE. *Current Pos:* ASSOC PROF BIOCHEM, UNIV SOUTHERN MISS, 88- *Personal Data:* b Franklinton, La, Oct 16, 58. *Educ:* La State Univ, Baton Rouge, BS, 80; Univ NC, Chapel Hill, PhD(biochem), 85. *Prof Exp:* Teaching fel, Univ Tex Southwestern Med Ctr, 85-88. *Mem:* Am Chem Soc; Am Soc Biochem & Molecular Biol; Protein Soc. *Res:* Study of enzymes involved in postranslational processing of biologically active peptides; design of enzyme inhibitors; development of biosensors to be used in seafood quality control. *Mailing Add:* Dept Chem & Biochem Univ Southern Miss Southern Sta Box 5043 Hattiesburg MS 39406-5043

BATES, CARL H, MATERIALS CHARACTERIZATION & FAILURE ANALYSIS, VITICULTURE TRACE ELEMENT ANALYSIS. *Current Pos:* ENVIRON SCIENTIST CONSULT, ESSEX THERMODYNAMICS CORP, 89- *Personal Data:* b Rothwell, Yorkshire, Eng, Jan 1, 39; m 85, Jennifer Evans; c Carla. *Educ:* Sheffield Univ Yorkshire Eng, BSc, 61; Pa State Univ, PhD(geochem), 65. *Prof Exp:* Sr sci officer ceramics, GEC Wembley Eng, 66-68; sr res scientist mat sci, Bell Aerospace Buffalo, 68-71; owner viticulture, Fourthriding Vineyards, 71-77; consult energy, Niagara Co Energy Comt, 77-80; sr process engr refractories, Carborundum Co N Falls, 80-86; sr res engr ceramics, Norton Co, Worcester, 86-89. *Concurrent Pos:* Fulbright Scholar. *Mem:* Am Ceramic Soc; Brit Ceramic Soc. *Res:* Casting of complex shapes of silicon nurde bonded silicon carbide ceramics for abrasion, high temperature and corrosion resistant applications; high purity ceramics; failure analysis and materials characterization; environmental implications of wood gasification, trace elements; analysis & recycling essential nutrients back into the environment. *Mailing Add:* 116 Wildwood Ave Worcester MA 01603

BATES, CHARLES CARPENTER, OCEANOGRAPHY. *Current Pos:* RETIRED. *Personal Data:* b Harrison, Ill, Nov 4, 18; m 42, Pauline Barta; c Nancy (Yanity), Priscilla (Robinson) & Sally J. *Educ:* DePauw Univ, BS, 39; Univ Calif, Los Angeles, MA, 44; Tex A&M Univ, PhD, 53. *Honors & Awards:* Silver Medal, US Dept Transp, 74, Gold Medal, 79; President's Award, Am Asn Petrol Geologists, 53. *Prof Exp:* Geophys trainee, Carter Oil Co, Okla, 39-41; spec asst to pres, Am Meteorol Soc, Ill, 45-46; oceanog technician sci surv, Bikini Atomic Bomb Test, Woods Hole Oceanog Inst, 46; from oceanogr to dep div dir, Div Oceanog, Hydrog Off, Navy Dept, 46-57, tech coordr environ systs, Off Naval Res, 57-59 & Off Dept Chief Naval Opers, 59-60, chief, Vela Uniform Br, Advan Res Proj Agency, Off Secy Defense, 60-64, sci & tech dir, Naval Oceanog Off, 64-68; sci adv to Commandant, HQ, USCG, 68-79; prin assoc, Spectrum Int Assocs, 86-89. *Concurrent Pos:* Consult oceanogr & meteorologist, Bates & Glenn, Washington, DC, 47; consult meteorologist, A H Glenn & Assocs, La, 48-54; mem, Comt Meteorol Uses of Satellites, Space Sci Bd, Nat Acad Sci; State Dept alt observer, Austral Season Inspection by US under Antarctic Treaty, 63-64; mem, Earth Sci Div, Nat Res Coun, 63-66, mem, Maritime Transp Res Bd, 68-71; mem, Merchant Marine Coun, USCG, 68-71; co-chmn panel on marine facil, US-Japan Natural Resources Prog, 69-75. *Mem:* Am Meteorol Soc; Am Asn Petrol Geologists; Soc Explor Geophysicists (vpres, 65-66); fel AAAS; hon mem Soc Explor Geophysicists. *Res:* Forecasting wave and surf conditions; history of geophysics; delta formation; sea-ice; detection underground nuclear explosions; global budget of petroleum hydrocarbon influx into ocean. *Mailing Add:* 136 W La Pintura Green Valley AZ 85614-1927

BATES, CHARLES JOHNSON, FOOD TECHNOLOGY, BIOLOGY. *Current Pos:* RETIRED. *Personal Data:* b Dayton, Ohio, May 4, 30; m 53, Nancy Lindbeck; c Charles J Jr, Richard L & Priscilla B (Crosland). *Educ:* Calif Inst Technol, BS, 51; Mass Inst Technol, PhD(food technol), 57. *Prof Exp:* Develop engr food prod, Procter & Gamble Co, 57-62, technol serv mgr indust food prod, 62-67, mkt mgr indust detergents, 67-72; vpres tech, Am Maize Prod Co, Inc, 72-93. *Mem:* Fel Inst Food Technologists (pres, 85-86); Am Asn Cereal Chemists. *Mailing Add:* 760 Williams Dr Crown Point IN 46307. *Fax:* 219-662-2855; *E-Mail:* batescj@crown.icongrp.com

BATES, CLAYTON WILSON, JR, SOLID STATE PHYSICS. *Current Pos:* assoc prof mat sci, 72-77, PROF MAT SCI, STANFORD UNIV, 77- *Personal Data:* b New York, NY, Sept 5, 32; m 68; c 2. *Educ:* Manhattan Col, BS, 54; Polytech Inst Brooklyn, MEE, 56; Harvard Univ, ME, 60; Washington Univ, PhD(physics), 66. *Prof Exp:* Solid-state physicist, Sylvania Elec Prod, NY, 55-57; sr engr physics, Varian Assoc, 66-72. *Concurrent Pos:* Vis prof reader, Imperial Col Sci & Technol, 68; consult, Varian Assoc, 72-; mem panel optical physics, Nat Acad Sci, 74-; consult & part owner, Diagnostics Info Inc, 75-; consult, Spectra-Physics, Inc, 75-77 & Bell Tel Labs, Murray Hill, 78-79; vis prof, Princeton Univ, 78-79. *Mem:* Fel Am Phys Soc; Optical Soc Am; sr mem Inst Elec & Electronics Engrs; Soc Photo-Optical Instrumentation Engr; Royal Photog Soc Gt Brit. *Res:* Electrical and optical properties of crystalline and amorphous solids and surfaces; photoelectric emission; luminescence phosphors; electronically conducted glasses; interaction of intense radiation with matter. *Mailing Add:* Sch Eng Rm 1124 Howard Univ 2300 Sixth St NW Washington DC 20059

BATES, DAVID JAMES, ELECTRONICS ENGINEERING. *Current Pos:* RETIRED. *Personal Data:* b Portland, Ore, Oct 22, 28; m 49; c 5. *Educ:* Ore State Univ, BS, 51, MS, 53; Stanford Univ, PhD(appl physics), 58. *Honors & Awards:* Technol Medal, Asn Old Crows, 76. *Prof Exp:* Res assoc, W W Hansen Labs, Stanford Univ, 52-57; sect head, Power Tube Dept, Hughes Aircraft Co, 57-62; sect mgr, Phys Electronics Labs, 62-63; sr eng mgr, Wave Tube Dept, Varian Assocs, 63-65; sect head medium power res & develop, Tektronix, Inc, 65-73, mgr, Power Tube Eng Dept, 73-77, chief engr, Tube Div, 77-79, sr eng, 79-82, eng mgr, Display Devices & Components Group, 82-86, mgr technol & instrument group, 86-90; dir indust rels, Col Eng, Ore State Univ, 90-92. *Mem:* Inst Elec & Electronics Engrs; Sigma Xi; Sci Res Soc Asn. *Res:* Microwave amplifiers; electron linear accelerators; electron bombarded semiconductor amplifiers. *Mailing Add:* 6591 Failing St West Linn OR 97068

BATES, DAVID MARTIN, TAXONOMIC BOTANY, ETHNOBOTANY. *Current Pos:* From asst prof to assoc prof, 63-75, dir, L H Bailey Hortorium, 69-83, PROF BOT, CORNELL UNIV, 75- *Personal Data:* b Everett, Mass, May 31, 34; m 56; c 2. *Educ:* Cornell Univ, BS, 59; Univ Calif, Los Angeles, PhD(bot), 63. *Honors & Awards:* Gold Medal, Garden Club Am, 79. *Mem:* Fel AAAS; Soc Econ Botanists (pres, 90); Am Soc Plant Taxonomists (pres, 83); Inst Asn Plant Taxonomists; Bot Soc Am. *Res:* Systematics of family Malvaceae and cultivated plants; ethnobotany; plant resource management. *Mailing Add:* L H Bailey Hortorium Cornell Univ 462 Mann Libr Ithaca NY 14853-4301

BATES, DAVID VINCENT, ATMOSPHERIC SCIENCES, SCIENCE POLICY. *Current Pos:* dean, 72-77, prof, 72-87, EMER PROF MED, UNIV BC, 87- *Personal Data:* b West Malling, Kent, Eng, May 20, 22; Can citizen; wid; c 3. *Educ:* Cambridge Univ, MB Bchir, 45, MD, 54; Royal Col Physicians, London, MRCP, 48. *Honors & Awards:* Robert Cooke Medal, Am Acad Allergy, 66; Ramazzini Medal, Col Ramazzini, 85; Connaught Award, Can Lung Asn, 91; Trudeau Gold Medal, Am Thorac Soc, 93. *Prof Exp:* Physician med, Royal Victoria Hosp, 56-72. *Concurrent Pos:* Chmn physiol, McGill Univ, Montreal, 67-72. *Mem:* Can Thoracic Soc (pres, 64); Am Thoracic Soc; Soc Occup & Environ Health; Am Physiol Soc; Air Pollution Control Asn. *Res:* Health effects due to air pollution; respiratory physiology; occupational lung disease. *Mailing Add:* 4891 College Highroad Vancouver BC V6T 1G6 Can. *Fax:* 604-228-4412; *E-Mail:* dvbates@msn.com

BATES, DONALD GEORGE, HISTORY OF MEDICINE. *Current Pos:* assoc prof hist med, McGill Univ, 66-76, chmn dept, 66-82 & 87-88, assoc prof hist & social aspects med, 71-84, COTTON-HANNAH PROF HIST MED, MCGILL UNIV, 76- *Personal Data:* b Windsor, Ont, March 18, 33; div; c Gregory H & Jennifer A. *Educ:* Univ Western Ont, MD, 58, BA, 60; Johns Hopkins Univ, PhD, 75. *Prof Exp:* From instr to asst prof hist med, Johns Hopkins Univ, 62-66. *Mem:* Am Asn Hist Med; Soc Social Hist Med. *Res:* Medicine and the scientific revolution; nature of scientific knowledge; medical knowledge in cross-cultural perspective. *Mailing Add:* Dept Social Studies Med McGill Univ 3655 Drummond St Montreal PQ H3G 1Y6 Can. *Fax:* 514-398-1498

BATES, DONALD W(ESLEY), agricultural engineering; deceased, see previous edition for last biography

BATES, DOUGLAS MARTIN, STATISTICAL COMPUTING, NONLINEAR REGRESSION. *Current Pos:* PROF STATIST, DEPT STATIST, UNIV WIS-MADISON, 80- *Personal Data:* b Regina, Sask, July 5, 49; m 74; c 2. *Educ:* Queen's Univ, BSc, 71, PhD(statist), 78; Univ Calif, Los Angeles, MA, 73. *Prof Exp:* Asst prof statist, Dept Math, Univ Alta, 78-80. *Concurrent Pos:* Consult, Statist Lab, Univ Wis, Madison, 80-82. *Mem:* Am Statist Asn; Royal Statist Soc; Asn Comput Mach; Statist Soc Can. *Res:* Statistical computing, particularly in the area of nonlinear models and applications of computational linear algebra. *Mailing Add:* Dept Statist Univ Wis 1210 W Dayton St Madison WI 53706-1685

BATES, FRANK S, CHEMICAL ENGINEERING. *Current Pos:* assoc prof, 89-91, PROF, CHEM ENG & MAT SCI, UNIV MINN, 91- *Personal Data:* b Apr 10, 54. *Educ:* State Univ NY, Albany, BS, 76; Mass Inst Technol, SM, 79, ScD(chem eng), 82. *Honors & Awards:* John H Dillon Medal, Am Phys Soc, 89; Presidential Young Investr Award, 89; George Taylor Distinguished Res Award, Univ Minn, 93. *Prof Exp:* Res asst, Mass Inst Technol, 77-82; mem tech staff, AT&T Bell Labs, 82-88, distinguished mem tech staff, 88-89. *Concurrent Pos:* Gen Elec distinguished vis prof, Univ Mass, Amherst, 88. *Mem:* Fel Am Phys Soc; Am Chem Soc; Am Inst Chem Engrs. *Res:* Thermodynamics, dynamics, physics and chemistry of polymers and polyer mixtures. *Mailing Add:* Dept Chem Eng 151 Amundson Hall 421 Washington Ave SE Minneapolis MN 55455-0132

BATES, G WILLIAM, REPRODUCTIVE ENDOCRINOLOGY. *Current Pos:* EXEC VPRES & CHIEF MED OFFICER, PRINCIPALCARE, INC, 96- *Personal Data:* b Durham, NC, Feb 15, 40; m 69; c 3. *Educ:* Univ NC, BS, 62, MD, 65; Mass Inst Technol, SM, 84. *Prof Exp:* Asst prof obstet & gynec, Univ Tenn, Knoxville, 72-76; res fel reprod endocrinol, Univ Tex Southwestern Med Sch, 76-78; prof obstet & gynec, Univ Miss Med Ctr, 78-86; prof obstet & gynec, Med Univ SC, 86-96, dean Col Med, 86-96. *Concurrent Pos:* Chmn Indust Comt, Am Fertility Soc, 87-; consult to surgeon gen, USAF, 87- *Mem:* Am Fertility Soc; Am Col Obstetricians & Gynecologists; Endocrine Soc; Soc Gynec Invest; Soc Gynec Surgeons. *Res:* Elucidated the role of the adipocyte in both thin and obese women on reproductive function; studies include the metabolism of estradiol 17-B and alternatives in the gonadotropin secretory pattern as affected by alterations in body weight. *Mailing Add:* PrincipalCare Inc 109 Westpark Dr Suite 420 Brentwood TN 37027-5032

BATES, GEORGE WINSTON, NUTRITION, BIOAVAILABILITY OF IRON. *Current Pos:* PROF BIOCHEM & NUTRIT, FACIL SCI NUTRIT, TEX A&M UNIV, 69- *Educ:* Univ Southern Calif, PhD(biochem), 66. *Mailing Add:* Dept Biochem & Biophys Tex A&M Univ College Station TX 77843-2128

BATES, GRACE ELIZABETH, MATHEMATICS. *Current Pos:* from instr to prof, 46-79, EMER PROF MATH, MT HOLYOKE, 79- *Personal Data:* b Albany, NY, Aug 13, 14. *Educ:* Middlebury Col, BS, 35; Brown Univ, ScM, 38; Univ Ill, PhD(math), 46. *Hon Degrees:* DSc, Middlebury Col, 72. *Prof Exp:* Teacher high sch, Vt, 35-36 & Pa, 38-43; instr math, Sweet Briar Col, 43-44. *Concurrent Pos:* Trustee, Teachers Ins & Annuity Asn, 65-69; mem, Comn Undergrad Prog Math, 70-74. *Mem:* Am Math Soc; Math Asn Am. *Res:* Modern algebra; free loops and nets and their generalizations; probability; mathematical statistics. *Mailing Add:* Pennswood Village No A109 Newtown PA 18940

BATES, HAROLD BRENNAN, JR, zoology, for more information see previous edition

BATES, HERBERT T(EMPLETON), chemical engineering; deceased, see previous edition for last biography

BATES, J(UNIOR) LAMBERT, MATERIALS SCIENCE. *Current Pos:* CONSULT, 93- *Personal Data:* b Ogden, Utah, Mar 21, 28; m 52, Ala J Odum; c Steven, Debra, Scott, Roger & Holly. *Educ:* Brigham Young Univ, BS, 53; Univ Utah, PhD(metall), 57. *Prof Exp:* Sr res scientist, Hanford Labs, Gen Elec Co, 57-64; res assoc reactor & mat technol, Battelle Mem Inst, 65-69, tech leader thermophys properties & mgr, Phys Ceramics Sect, 69-70, tech leader, Pac Northwest Labs, 70-86, sr staff scientist, 78-86, chief scientist, at Dept, 86-93. *Mem:* Fel Am Ceramic Soc (vpres, 78-79, pres-elect, 82-83, pres, 83-84,). *Res:* High temperature thermal, electrical, physical and electrochemical properties of ceramics; MHD, fuel cells, thermoelectrics, nuclear, solar, fossil and other energy materials; corrosion and electrochemical interactions ceramics; electrolytes; electronically conducting high-temperature ceramics. *Mailing Add:* 1605 S Sunset St Richland WA 99352. *Fax:* 509-375-2186; *E-Mail:* jlbates@aol.com

BATES, JASON H T, RESPIRATORY MECHANICS, PHYSIOLOGICAL SYSTEMS MODELING. *Current Pos:* res fel, 81-83, ASSOC PROF MED & BIOMED ENG, MEAKINS-CHRISTIE LAB, MCGILL UNIV, 83- *Personal Data:* b Surrey, Eng, 56. *Educ:* Canterbury Univ, Christ Church, NZ, BSc (Hons), 78; Otago Univ, Dunedin, NZ, PhD(med), 81. *Mem:* Inst Elec & Electronics Engrs; Am Physiol Soc; Biomed Soc. *Mailing Add:* Meakins-Christie Labs McGill Univ 3626 St Urbain St Montreal PQ H2X 2P2 Can

BATES, JOHN BERTRAM, COLLOID CHEMISTRY. *Current Pos:* RETIRED. *Personal Data:* b Big Flats, NY, Sept 7, 14; m 44; c 2. *Educ:* Clarkson Col Technol, BS, 36; Rice Inst, MA, 39, PhD(colloid chem), 41. *Honors & Awards:* Ault Award, Nat Asn Printing Ink Mfrs, 82. *Prof Exp:* Chemist, Corning Glass Works, NY, 36-37; res chemist, Sun Chem Corp, 41-42; Am Petrol Inst fel, Univ Mich, 42-44; leader, phys chem sect, Sun Chem Corp, 44-50, asst dir graphic arts labs, 50-56; vpres & tech dir, Ho-Par, Inc, 56-60; staff chemist, HRB-Singer, Inc, 60-62; tech dir, Flint Ink Corp, 62-82, vpres res & develop, 82-88. *Concurrent Pos:* Chmn steering comt, ink misting comt & newsink comt, Nat Asn Printing Ink Mfrs Tech Inst, 75-88. *Mem:* AAAS; Am Chem Soc; Soc Rheol; Inter-Soc Color Coun; Soc Coating Technol. *Res:* Pigment and printing ink chemistry; x-ray diffraction; gas adsorption on pigments; rheology of pigment dispersions; iron cyanide chemistry; particle size methods; surface chemistry in pigment dispersions; spectrophotometry and spectrofluorometry. *Mailing Add:* 46701 Betty Hill Lane Plymouth MI 48170-3070

BATES, JOHN BRYANT, SOLID STATE ELECTROCHEMISTRY. *Current Pos:* staff scientist, 69-80, GROUP LEADER, SOLID STATE DIV, OAK RIDGE NAT LAB, 80- *Personal Data:* b Harlan, Ky, Mar 11, 42; m 63, Sharon Craft; c Sean & Erin. *Educ:* Univ Ky, AB, 64, PhD(chem), 68. *Honors & Awards:* Res & Develop 100 Award. *Prof Exp:* Res assoc chem, Univ Md, College Park, 68-69. *Concurrent Pos:* Vis prof, Univ Paris, 84; adj prof, Univ Tenn, 84- *Mem:* Fel Am Physics Soc; Electrochem Soc; Vacuum Soc. *Res:* Impedance spectroscopy; electrical response and microstructure of metal-electrolyte interfaces; solid state lithium batteries; rechargeable, thin film lithium batteries; lithium intercalation compounds; oxynitride ceramic; physical and chemical properties of inorganic thin films. *Mailing Add:* MS 6030 Solid State Div Oak Ridge Nat Lab PO Box 2008 Oak Ridge TN 37830-6030. *Fax:* 423-574-4143; *E-Mail:* joh@ornl.gov

BATES, JOSEPH H, MEDICINE, BACTERIOLOGY. *Current Pos:* From instr to assoc prof med, 61-71, ASST PROF MICROBIOL, SCH MED, UNIV ARK, LITTLE ROCK, 63-, PROF MED, 71-, VCHMN DEPT, 78- *Personal Data:* b Little Rock, Ark, Sept 19, 33; m 55; c 4. *Educ:* Univ Ark, BS & MD, 57, MS, 63. *Honors & Awards:* Abernathy Medal, Internal Med, Am Col Physicians, 81. *Concurrent Pos:* Fel infectious dis, 61-63; clin investr pulmonary dis, Vet Admin Hosp, Little Rock, 63-65, chief pulmonary & infectious dis serv, 65-67, chief med, 67- *Mem:* Am Thoracic Soc; Am Fedn Clin Res; Infectious Dis Soc Am; Am Col Physicians. *Res:* Unclassified mycobacteria, mycobacteriophage and their interrelationships; genetics of atypical mycobacteria. *Mailing Add:* McClellan Med Ctr 4300 W Seventh St Little Rock AR 72205-5411

BATES, LLOYD M, RADIOLOGICAL PHYSICS. *Current Pos:* RETIRED. *Personal Data:* b Westville, NS, Dec 25, 24; m 46; c 2. *Educ:* Univ NB, BSc, 50; Univ Sask, MSc, 52; Johns Hopkins Univ, ScD(radiol physics), 66. *Prof Exp:* Physicist, Prov NB, 52-57; asst prof radiol, Sch Med, Univ Md, 57-59; from instr to assoc prof radiol, Sch Pub Health, Johns Hopkins Univ, 59-75, radiation safety officer, Med Insts, 66-75; sr staff physicist, Am Asn Physicist Med, 74-77, dir coord, CRP Coord Prog, 77-91. *Mem:* Am Asn Physicists in Med; Sigma Xi; Am Col Radiol; Am Pub Health Asn; Health Physics Soc. *Res:* Evaluation of radiological imaging systems; application of radioactive materials to physiological studies; design and development of radiotherapy apparatus; radiation control at medical installations. *Mailing Add:* 7104 Sheffield Rd Baltimore MD 21212

BATES, LYNN SHANNON, MICROSCOPY. *Current Pos:* consult, LSB Prod, 81-86, PRES, ALTECA LTD, 86- *Personal Data:* b Salem, Ohio, May 7, 40; m 66, Gyll C Floding; c Tammy C, Heidi L, Kerri N & Mindy S. *Educ:* Heidelberg Col, BS, 62; Purdue Univ, West Lafayette, MS, 66; Kans State Univ, PhD(grain sci), 72. *Prof Exp:* Biochemist, Rockefeller Found, Int Maize & Wheat Improv Ctr, Mex, 66-68; asst prof, Dept Grain Sci & Indust, Kans State Univ, 72-81. *Concurrent Pos:* Rockefeller Found grant, 73-77; NSF travel grant, barley genetics III, 75, food sci genetics fac, 75-81; prin investr, Am Soybean Asn, 88-89; adj prof, Dept Foods & Nutrit, Kans State Univ, 91. *Mem:* Am Asn Cereal Chemists; Am Chem Soc; Am Asn Feed Microscopists (pres, 87-88); Inst Food Technologists; Asn Off Analytical Chem; Coun Agr Sci & Technol. *Res:* Intergeneric hybridization of cereals and legumes; nutritional improvement of cereal grains and legumes; enzyme-based rapid quality control kits; quality and utilization of roasted/dried feed ingredients and wastes; feed microscopy; forensic food microscopy. *Mailing Add:* 1814 Laramie Manhattan KS 66502

BATES, MARGARET WESTBROOK, BIOCHEMISTRY, NUTRITION. *Current Pos:* RETIRED. *Personal Data:* b Boston, Mass, Oct 5, 26. *Educ:* Wellesley Col, BA, 48; Cornell Univ, MS, 50; Harvard Univ, DSc(nutrit), 54. *Prof Exp:* Fel nutrit, Harvard Univ, 54-55; USPHS fel med res, Univ Toronto, 55-57; from res assoc to res asst prof biochem & nutrit, Univ Pittsburgh, 57-67, from res asst prof to res assoc prof, Lab Clin Sci, 67-73, res assoc prof psychiat, 73-77, res assoc prof epidemiol & head nutrit core lab, 77-89. *Mem:* AAAS; Am Inst Nutrit; Am Chem Soc; Brit Biochem Soc. *Res:* Fat metabolism; ketone body metabolism; plasma transport of fatty acids. *Mailing Add:* 118 Mayflower Dr Pittsburgh PA 15238

BATES, PETER WILLIAM, NONLINEAR PARTIAL DIFFERENTIAL EQUATIONS, DYNAMICAL SYSTEMS. *Current Pos:* assoc prof, 84-88, PROF MATH, BRIGHAM YOUNG UNIV, 88-, CHAIR, DEPT MATH, 92- *Personal Data:* b Manchester, Eng, Dec 27, 47; m 72, Teri Tobler; c 4. *Educ:* Univ London, BSc, 69; Univ Utah, PhD(math), 76. *Prof Exp:* Asst prof math, Pan Am Univ, 76-79; from asst prof to assoc prof, Tex A&M Univ, 78-85. *Concurrent Pos:* Vis asst prof, Univ Tex, Austin, 78-79; res fel math, Heriot-Watt Univ, 82; prog dir appl math, NSF, 87-89; prog dir, Soc Indust & Appl Math, 90-93; vis prof, Univ Utah, 91; vis fel, Isaac Newton Inst, Univ Cambridge, 96. *Mem:* Am Math Soc; Soc Indust & Appl Math. *Res:* Nonlinear partial differential equations and dynamical systems; qualitative behavior of solutions to models of phase transition. *Mailing Add:* 3343 Navajo Lane Provo UT 84604. *Fax:* 801-378-3703; *E-Mail:* peter@math.byu.edu

BATES, RICHARD DOANE, JR, PHYSICAL CHEMISTRY. *Current Pos:* from asst prof to assoc prof, 73-95, PROF CHEM, GEORGETOWN UNIV, 95- *Personal Data:* b Elizabeth, NJ, July 24, 44; m 71; c 2. *Educ:* Cornell Univ, BA, 66; Columbia Univ, MA, 67, PhD(chem), 71. *Prof Exp:* Preceptor chem, Columbia Univ, 67-68. *Concurrent Pos:* Res fel, Northwestern Univ, 81; pres, Univ Fac Senate, Georgetown Univ, 95- *Mem:* Sigma Xi; Am Chem Soc; Am Phys Soc; Am Asn Univ Profs; Laser Inst Am; Royal Soc Chem. *Res:* Molecular dynamics of reacting and non-reacting chemical systems; vibrational energy transfer and the role of vibrational energy in chemical reactions; solvent-solute interactions in solutions by magnetic resonance. *Mailing Add:* Dept Chem Georgetown Univ 606 Reiss Sci Washington DC 20057. *Fax:* 202-687-6209; *E-Mail:* bates@guvax.acc.georgetown.edu

BATES, RICHARD PIERCE, agronomy, plant breeding, for more information see previous edition

BATES, ROBERT BROWN, ORGANIC CHEMISTRY. *Current Pos:* from asst prof to assoc prof , 63-69, PROF ORG CHEM, UNIV ARIZ, 69- *Personal Data:* b Huntington, NY, Dec 16, 33; m 55; c 3. *Educ:* Rutgers Univ, BS, 54; Univ Wis, PhD(org chem), 57. *Prof Exp:* Res fel, Mass Inst Technol, 57-58; from instr to asst prof org chem, Univ Ill, 58-63. *Concurrent Pos:* Sloan Found fel, 67-69. *Mem:* Am Chem Soc; Am Crystallog Asn. *Res:* Natural product structure, synthesis and biogenesis; carbanions. *Mailing Add:* 2212 N Frennea Dr Tucson AZ 85712-2906

BATES, ROBERT CLAIR, VIROLOGY, MICROBIOLOGY. *Current Pos:* From asst prof to assoc prof, 72-85, PROF VIROL, VA POLYTECH INST & STATE UNIV, 85- *Personal Data:* b Portland, Ore, Mar 8, 44; m 69; c 3. *Educ:* Lewis & Clark Col, Ore, BA, 66; Wash State Univ, MS, 68; Colo State Univ, PhD(virol), 72. *Concurrent Pos:* Am Cancer Soc grant, Va Polytech Inst, 76-78; NIH grants, 76-79 & 80-83; consult, Carborundum Co, 76-78; NSF grants, Va Polytech Inst, 78-80 & 81-84, Am Cancer Soc grant, 84- 90. *Mem:* Sigma Xi; AAAS; Am Soc Microbiol; Am Soc Biol Chemists; Am Soc Virol. *Res:* Cellular and molecular aspects of parovirus replication, characterization of viral enzymes and viral replication intermediates, replication of viral DNA and viral morphogenesis. *Mailing Add:* Dept Biol Microbiol Sect Va Polytech Inst & State Univ Blacksburg VA 24061-0406

BATES, ROBERT P(ARKER), FOOD SCIENCE & TECHNOLOGY. *Current Pos:* assoc prof food sci, 67-81, PROF FOOD SCI & HUMAN NUTRIT, INST FOOD & AGR SCI, UNIV FLA, 81- *Personal Data:* b Cambridge, Mass, May 11, 32; m 56, 66; c 5. *Educ:* Mass Inst Technol, BS, 59, PhD(food sci), 66; Univ Hawaii, MS, 63. *Prof Exp:* Res engr, Forte Eng Co, 59-60; fel, Inst Nutrit Cent Am & Panama, 66-67. *Mem:* Inst Food Technol. *Res:* Tropical food processing; appropriate food technology; food processing systems; research and teaching; product development; new food resources. *Mailing Add:* Dept Food Sci & Human Nutrit Univ Fla 329 FSB Bldg Gainesville FL 32611-2002

BATES, ROBERT WESLEY, physiological chemistry; deceased, see previous edition for last biography

BATES, ROGER GORDON, ANALYTICAL CHEMISTRY. *Current Pos:* prof, 69-79, EMER PROF CHEM, UNIV FLA, 79- *Personal Data:* b Cummington, Mass, May 20, 12; m 41, Jo Jones; c May (Daw). *Educ:* Univ Mass, BS, 34; Duke Univ, AM, 36, PhD(phys chem), 37. *Honors & Awards:* Hillebrand Prize, 55; US Dept Com Except Serv Award, 57; Anal Chem Award, Am Chem Soc, 69; Anachem Award, 83. *Prof Exp:* Asst chem, Duke Univ, 34-37; Sterling fel, Yale Univ, 37-39; chemist, Nat Bur Standards, 39-57, chief electrochem anal sect, 57-69, asst chief anal chem div, 58-67. *Concurrent Pos:* Lectr, Trinity Col, DC, 47-49; USPHS fel, Univ Zurich, 53-54; chmn, Comn Electrochem Data, Int Union Pure & Appl Chem, 53-59, mem, US Nat Comt, 59-65, mem, Comn Electrochem, 59-67, mem, Comn Symbols, Terminology & Units, 63-71, chmn, Comn Electroanal Chem, 71-79, mem, Anal Div Comt, 79-83. *Mem:* AAAS; Am Chem Soc. *Res:* Electrode potentials; homogeneous equilibria; thermodynamics of electrolytic solutions; nonaqueous solutions; seawater; standardization of pH measurements, dissociation of weak acids and bases. *Mailing Add:* Dept Chem Univ Fla Gainesville FL 32611. *E-Mail:* rgbates@nervm.nerdc.ufl.edu

BATES, STEPHEN ROGER, CHILD NEUROLOGY. *Current Pos:* ASSOC PROF PEDIAT & NEUROL, UNIV ARK, 88-; DIR, PEDIAT & NEUROL, ARK CHILDREN'S HOSP, 88- *Personal Data:* b London, Eng, Aug 17, 44; US citizen; m 68; c 3. *Educ:* Univ London, MD, 68; Royal Col Obstetricians & Gynecologists, dipl. *Prof Exp:* Rotating intern, St George's Hosp, London, 69-70; resident pediat, Children's Hosp Med Ctr, Cincinnati, Ohio, 71-72, pediat neurol, 72-73, asst to chief-of-staff, 75-82; resident neurol, Med Ctr, Univ Cincinnati, 73-74, chief resident, 74-75, instr pediat & neurol, 75-76, from asst prof to assoc prof clin pediat & clin neurol, Dept Pediat & Neurol, 76-88; asst chief-of-staff, Children's Hosp Med Ctr, 82-88; assoc chief-of-staff, Convalescent Hosp for Children, 84-88. *Concurrent Pos:* Consult child neurologist, Clermont Co Health Serv & Diag Ctr, 74-76, Univ Affil Cincinnati Ctr Develop Dis, 75-, Resident Home for Retarded, Cincinnati, 80-; attend pediatrician, Children's Hosp Med Ctr, 75-, Electroencephalography Lab, 76-83 & Comprehensive Epilepsy Prog, 80-; attend neurologist, Ohio & Holmes Hosp Div, Univ Hosp, Cincinnati, 75-; mem, Cerebral Palsy Sub-Comt, Bur Crippled Children's Serv, Ohio State, 82-; staff consult pediat neurologist, The Christ Hosp, Our Lady of Mercy Hosp, 84-, Good Samaritan Hosp, 85-, Dearborn Co, Ind, 85-, Bethesda Hosps, Ohio, 86-; vis prof child neurol, Sao Paulo, Brazil, 85. *Mem:* Brit Med Asn; Am Acad Neurol; Child Neurol Soc; Am Epilepsy Soc; Am Med EEG Asn; AAAS. *Res:* Clinical pediatric neurology, especially in fields of epilepsy and migraine. *Mailing Add:* Dept Neurol Ark Children's Hosp 800 Marshall St Little Rock AR 72202

BATES, THOMAS EDWARD, SOIL SCIENCE. *Current Pos:* RETIRED. *Personal Data:* b Irricana, Alta, July 13, 26; m 53; c 2. *Educ:* Ont Agr Col, BSA, 55; NC State Col, MS, 54; Iowa State Univ, PhD(soil fertil), 61. *Prof Exp:* Res officer agron, Tobacco Res Bd, Rhodesia & Nyasaland, 51-58; asst soil fertil, Iowa State Univ, 58-61; asst prof soil fertil, Ont Agr Col, 61-65; assoc prof soil fertil, Univ Guelph, 65-68, prof soil sci, 68-92. *Concurrent Pos:* Assoc ed, Soil Sci Soc Am J, J Environ Qual, Fertilizer Res. *Mem:* Am Soc Agron; Agr Inst Can; Can Soil Sci Soc. *Res:* Soil fertility pertaining to fertilizer use and metal toxicities. *Mailing Add:* 303 Edinburgh St S Guelph ON N1G 2K3 Can

BATES, THOMAS FULCHER, MINERALOGY. *Current Pos:* RETIRED. *Personal Data:* b Evanston, Ill, Jan 2, 17; m 42, 76, Gwendolyn Fossum; c 3. *Educ:* Denison Univ, BA, 39; Columbia Univ, MS, 40, PhD(geol), 44. *Hon Degrees:* DSc, Denison Univ, 68. *Prof Exp:* From instr to assoc prof, Pa State Univ, 42-53, asst to vpres for res, 61-65, dir inst sci & eng, 63-65, asst dean grad sch, 64-65, vpres planning, 67-72, prof mineral, 53-77; phys scientist, US Geol Surv, 77-82. *Concurrent Pos:* Sci adv, Secy Interior, Washington, DC, 65-67. *Mem:* AAAS; fel Geol Soc Am. *Res:* X-ray and electron microscopic studies of clay and other minerals; origin of the Edwin clay, Ione, California; mineralogical investigation of fine-grained rocks; uraniferous black shales and lignites; clay minerals of Hawaii; application of earth sciences to land use and energy planning. *Mailing Add:* 903 Outer Dr State College PA 16801-8236

BATES, WILLIAM K, BIOCHEMISTRY, CELL BIOLOGY. *Current Pos:* from asst prof to assoc prof biol, 66-74, head dept, 79-88, PROF BIOL, UNIV NC, GREENSBORO, 88- *Personal Data:* b Houston, Tex, Nov 16, 36; m 59, Wilma Hettler; c Lorie L & Paul W. *Educ:* Rice Univ, BA, 59, PhD(biochem), 63. *Prof Exp:* USPHS trainee biol sci, Stanford Univ, 63-66. *Mem:* AAAS; Am Soc Cell Biol; Am Soc Biochem & Molecular Biol; Sigma Xi. *Res:* Intra-cellular distribution and kinetics of enzymes; cytoplasmic inheritance; radiotracer applications; computer applications in biological studies. *Mailing Add:* Dept Biol Univ NC 1000 Spring Garden Greensboro NC 27412-5001. *Fax:* 910-334-5839

BATESON, MARY CATHERINE, ANTHROPOLOGY. *Current Pos:* CLARENCE ROBINSON PROF ANTHROP & ENG, GEORGE MASON UNIV, 87- *Personal Data:* b New York, NY, Dec 8, 39; m 60, J Barkev Kassarjian; c Sevanne Margaret. *Educ:* Radcliffe Col, BA, 60; Harvard Univ, PhD, 63. *Hon Degrees:* DHL, Fordham Univ, 94 & Univ Redlands, 96. *Prof Exp:* Instr Arabic, Harvard Univ, 63-66; assoc prof anthrop, Ateneo de Manila Univ, 66-68; sr res fel psychol & philos, Brandeis Univ, 68-69; assoc prof anthrop, Northeastern Univ, Boston, 69-71, vis prof, 74-75; researcher, Univ Tehran, 72-74; prof anthrop & dean grad studies, Damavand Col, 75-77; prof anthrop & dean social sci & humanities, Univ NIran, 77-79; vis scholar, Harvard Univ, 79-80; dean fac & prof anthrop, Amherst Col, 80-87. *Concurrent Pos:* Fel, NSF, 68-69, Wenner-Gren Found, 72, Bunting Inst, 83 & 84 & Guggenheim Found, 87-88; pres, Int Intercult Studies, 79- *Mem:* Am Anthrop Asn. *Res:* Individual adaptation to change; women's life histories. *Mailing Add:* 47 Depot Rd Hancock NH 03449-5306

BATESON, ROBERT NEIL, ENGINEERING. *Current Pos:* INSTR ELECTRONIC ENG TECHNOL, ANOKA RAMSEY STATE JR COL, 68-, HEAD DEPT, 69- *Personal Data:* b Hibbing, Minn, Apr 22, 31; m 54; c 3. *Educ:* Univ Minn, BME, 54, MSEE, 68. *Prof Exp:* Staff mem, Sandia Corp, 54-58; res engr, Cent Res Lab, Gen Mills, Inc, 58-66; group leader, 66-68. *Res:* New methods and equipment for processing food; new sensors for food processes; development of effective methods of teaching; development of engineering technology courses. *Mailing Add:* 3301 Poe Rd Minneapolis MN 55429

BATEY, HARRY HALLSTED, JR, INORGANIC CHEMISTRY. *Current Pos:* From instr to prof, 51-96, EMER PROF CHEM, WASH STATE UNIV, 96- *Personal Data:* b Grand Island, Nebr, Feb 1, 23; m 45; c 4. *Educ:* Cornell Col, AB, 46; Ohio State Univ, MSc, 48, PhD(chem), 51. *Concurrent Pos:* UNESCO sci teaching expert, Iran, 68-69. *Mem:* AAAS; Am Chem Soc; Sigma Xi. *Res:* Inorganic nitrogen compounds; oxyhalides; gas chromatography of inorganic substances; non-aqueous solvents; science education. *Mailing Add:* Beaver Creek Nordman ID 83848

BATEY, ROBERT WILLIAM, CHEMICAL ENGINEERING, FOOD ENGINEERING. *Current Pos:* PROP, B80 ENG ASSOCS, 85- *Personal Data:* b Wilsall, Mont, Nov 16, 18; m 44. *Educ:* Univ Minn, BS 47. *Prof Exp:* Proj engr, Gen Mills, Inc, 47-50 & Good Foods, Inc, 50-51; chief process engr, Pillsbury Mills, Inc, 51-55; plant tech dir, Dromedary Co, Nat Biscuit Co, 55-56; head process control sect, Tenco, Inc, 56-58; dir food technol, Foster D Snell, Inc, 58-63; sr res assoc, ITT Continental Baking Co, 63-84. *Mem:* Am Inst Chem Engrs; Am Chem Soc; Inst Food Technol; Sigma Xi. *Res:* Cereal; fats and oils processing; industrial waste disposal; microwave processing; development of new instruments for process analysis and control; uses of new sources of energy; evaluate and develop energy concepts; patents; rheology. *Mailing Add:* 38 Meadowlark Rd Rye Brook NY 10573-1220

BATH, DONALD ALAN, ANALYTICAL CHEMISTRY, ENVIRONMENTAL CHEMISTRY. *Current Pos:* asst prof, 78-84, ASSOC PROF CHEM, WESTERN ILL UNIV, 84- *Personal Data:* b Los Angeles, Calif, May 14, 47. *Educ:* Rose Polytech Inst, BS, 69; Mont State Univ, PhD(chem), 75. *Prof Exp:* Res assoc environ chem, Univ Ill, 76-77; asst prof chem, Ill State Univ, 77-78. *Concurrent Pos:* Vis asst prof, Inst Environ Studies, Univ Ill, 77-78; vis assoc prof chem, Univ Ill, 87-88. *Mem:* Soc Appl Spectros; Am Chem Soc. *Res:* Development of instrumentation and techniques for the analysis of organometallics in the environment and design and theoretical characterization of nonflame atomizers for atomic absorption spectrometry. *Mailing Add:* Dept Chem Western Ill Univ Macomb IL 61455-1396

BATH, JAMES EDMOND, ENTOMOLOGY, PLANT PATHOLOGY. *Current Pos:* RETIRED. *Personal Data:* b Santa Ana, Calif, May 4, 38; m 58; c 3. *Educ:* Univ Calif, Davis, 60; Univ Wis, MS, 62, PhD(entom), 64. *Prof Exp:* From asst prof to prof entom, Mich State Univ, 64-85, chmn dept, 74-85. *Concurrent Pos:* Entomologist, Coop State Res Serv, USDA, 79; coordr integrated pest mgt prog, USDA, Sci Educ Admin, 79-80; chmn, N Cent Integrated Pest Mgt Steering Comn, 80-86. *Mem:* AAAS; Entom Soc Am; Am Phytopath Soc; Soc Nematol. *Res:* Mode of plant virus transmission by insects, especially circulative viruses and aphid vectors; development of interdisciplinary implementation of integrated pest management approach in agriculture. *Mailing Add:* 565 Park Estates Sq Venice FL 34293

BATHA, HOWARD DEAN, PHYSICAL CHEMISTRY. *Current Pos:* MGR RES & ENG, BIDDEFORD, ME, 83- *Personal Data:* b Phillips, Wis, July 3, 25; m 48; c 4. *Educ:* Carroll Col, BA, 50; Univ Rochester, PhD, 54. *Prof Exp:* Group leader chem, Olin-Mathieson Chem Co, 54-56, sr res proj specialist, 56-58; res specialist, Carborundum Co, 58-63, mgr res br, 63-69, assoc dir res & develop, 69-74, dir develop, 74-81; tech asst to pres, Mat Int, Lexington, Mass, 80-83. *Mem:* Am Chem Soc; AAAS; Sigma Xi; Am

Ceramic Soc. *Res:* Free radical reactions; inorganic hydrides; high temperature reactions; mechanisms of crystal growth; silicon carbide; high performance composites; smart materials. *Mailing Add:* Eight Whippoorwill Circle Kennebunk ME 04043-2440

BATHALA, MOHINDER S, ANALYTICAL CHEMISTRY. *Current Pos:* RES REL, BRISTOL-MYERS SQUIBB CO, 84- *Personal Data:* b India, Dec 25, 40; US citizen; m 67; c 3. *Educ:* Panjab Univ, India, BS, 64, MS, 66; Ohio State Univ, PhD(natural prod chem), 73. *Prof Exp:* Sr scientist, Cooper Labs, 76-77, A H Robins Co, 77-80; sr res investr, E R Squibb & Son Inc, 80-83. *Mem:* Am Pharmaceut Asn; Acad Pharmaceut Sci; Am Chem Soc. *Res:* Analyses of various drugs and their metabolites from biological fluid by gas chromatography, liquid chromatography and gas chromatography and mass spectrography methods; isolation and identification of drug metabolites from biological materials. *Mailing Add:* Drug Metab Dept Squibb Inst Med Res PO Box 4000 Princeton NJ 08540

BATHEN, KARL HANS, physical oceanography; deceased, see previous edition for last biography

BATICH, CHRISTOPHER DAVID, PHYSICAL CHEMISTRY, BIOMATERIALS. *Current Pos:* assoc prof, 81-88, PROF, MAT SCI & ENG DEPT, UNIV FLA, 88- *Personal Data:* b Jersey City, NJ, Dec 25, 43; c 3. *Educ:* Pa State Univ, BS, 65; Rutgers Univ, New Brunswick, PhD(org chem), 74. *Prof Exp:* Qual control chemist, White Labs, Kenilworth, NJ, 65-67; staff scientist, Cent Res & Develop Dept, Du Pont Exp Sta, 74-81. *Concurrent Pos:* Assoc dir, Biomed Eng Ctr. *Mem:* Am Chem Soc; Soc Biomat; AAAS. *Res:* Ultraviolet photoelectron and x-ray photoelectron studies of organic molecules; polymer surfaces, x-ray photoelectron, especially biological systems and synthetic polymers which are in contact with living cells; composite interface studies; scaffolds for guided tissue regeneration; controlled drug delivery. *Mailing Add:* 317 Mat Sci & Eng Dept Univ Fla Gainesville FL 32611. *Fax:* 352-392-3771; *E-Mail:* cbati@mse.ufl.edu

BATKIN, STANLEY, NEUROSURGERY, NEUROSCIENCES. *Current Pos:* RETIRED. *Personal Data:* b New York, NY, Nov 23, 12; m 52, Helen Lewinson; c William, Fredric & Maya. *Educ:* NY Univ, BS, 33; Univ Edinburgh, MD, 44; Am Bd Neurol Surg, dipl. *Honors & Awards:* Res Award, Am Cancer Soc, 72. *Prof Exp:* Clin tutor surg neurol, Univ Edinburgh, 44-46; asst prof neurol, Med Sch, Univ Ark, 49-50; asst prof neurol & neurosurg, State Univ NY Upstate Med Ctr, 50-51, asst clin prof neurol & neurosurg & neurologist, Univ Hearing & Speech Ctr, 51-63. *Concurrent Pos:* Chief neurosurg div, Vet Admin Hosp, Little Rock, Ark, 49-50; neurosurgeon, Syracuse Mem Hosp, Syracuse Univ Hosp, Couse-Irving Hosp, Syracuse Gen Hosp, Midtown Hosp & Community Hosp of Syracuse, 51-63; neurol consult, NY State Educ Dept, Div Voc Rehab, 52-63; neurologist, Syracuse Cerebral Palsy Clin, Syracuse Univ Hearing & Speech Ctr, 52-63; lectr, Depts Spec Educ & Audiol, Syracuse Univ, 52-63; chief div neurol & neurosurg, Permanente Med Group, 63-79; neurol consult & mem fac, Rehab Hosp Pac & Hyperbaric Treatment Facil, Univ Hawaii; lectr geront, Sch Public Health, Univ Hawaii; vis prof, Israel Naval Hyperbaric Inst, Haifa, 87; vis neurologist, Dept Health, Scotland, 46-48; vis prof, Dept Anat & Embryol, Hebrew Univ & Hadassah Med Sch, 93. *Mem:* AAAS; Am Acad Neurol; Asn Res Nerv & Ment Dis; Am Asn Neurol Surgeons; Sigma Xi. *Res:* Neurophysiology; oncology; central nervous system regeneration. *Mailing Add:* Univ Hawaii Sch Med-Physiol Honolulu HI 96822. *Fax:* 808-956-5506

BATLOGG, BERTRAM, SUPERCONDUCTIVITY, SOLID STATE PHYSICS. *Current Pos:* DEPT HEAD, SOLID STATE PHYSICS & MAT RES, AT&T BELL LABS, 78-, MEM STAFF, 79- *Personal Data:* Austria citizen. *Educ:* Swiss Fed Inst Technol, dipl, 74, PhD(nat sci), 79. *Concurrent Pos:* Dir, Consortium Superconducting Elec. *Mem:* Fel Am Phys Soc; Mat Res Soc. *Res:* Superconductivity; materials physics; magnetism. *Mailing Add:* Bell Labs Lucent Technologies Rm 1D369 700 Mountain Ave Murray Hill NJ 07974

BATOREWICZ, WADIM, ORGANIC CHEMISTRY. *Current Pos:* SR RES CHEMIST, CHEM DIV, UNIROYAL, INC, 67- *Personal Data:* b Poland, Nov 7, 34; US citizen; m 58. *Educ:* Univ Minn, BCh, 60, PhD(org chem), 67. *Prof Exp:* Chemist, Minn Mining & Mfg Co, 60-62. *Mem:* Am Chem Soc. *Res:* Chemistry of organophosphorus compounds; chemistry of polyurethanes; flame retardants for polymers; flammability of polymers; agriculture and food chemistry. *Mailing Add:* 999 Whalley Ave 1E New Haven CT 06515-1757

BATRA, GOPAL KRISHAN, biotechnology, for more information see previous edition

BATRA, INDER PAUL, SOLID STATE PHYSICS. *Current Pos:* tech staff, San Jose Res Lab, IBM Corp, 79-80, vis scientist, Res Lab, Yorktown Heights, 80-81, mgr, Struct Mech Dept, 90-94, PROF SCIENTIST, SURFACE SCI GROUP, RES LAB, IBM CORP, 69-, PROG DIR, 95- *Personal Data:* b India, June 25, 42; m 70, Uma Leekha; c Puja & Mala. *Educ:* Univ Delhi, BSc, 62, MSc, 64; Simon Fraser Univ, PhD(physics), 68. *Prof Exp:* Nat Res Coun Can fel, Simon Fraser Univ, 68-69. *Concurrent Pos:* Vis scientist, IBM Zurich Res Lab, Switz, 85-86; dir tech staff, IBM Res Lab, San Jose, 79-80. *Mem:* Fel Am Phys Soc; Am Vacuum Soc. *Res:* Interband optical absorption; phonon assisted transitions in semiconductors; photoconductivity; stimulation scattering of laser light; theoretical studies of electronic transport; chemisorption and electronic structure of surfaces, metal semiconductor interfaces and polymers by molecular orbital cluster and band stucture techniques; linear combination of atomic orbital scheme and pseudopotential method for electronic structure of solids; theoretical studies of helium diffraction from surfaces; scanning tunneling microscopy; quantum transport. *Mailing Add:* PHP/802 IBM Almaden Res Ctr 650 Narry Rd San Jose CA 95120. *E-Mail:* ipbatra@almaden.ibm.com

BATRA, KARAM VIR, PHARMACOLOGY, TOXICOLOGY. *Current Pos:* CONSULT, MAT & ENVIRON TOXICOL, BATRA INT, 95- *Personal Data:* b Jhelum, Panjab, India, Jan 3, 32; US citizen; m 63, Helga Meyer; c Peter, Hans, Erich & Ingrid. *Educ:* Panjab Univ, India, BPharm, 52; Univ Minn, MS, 57; Univ Chicago, PhD(pharmacol), 63. *Prof Exp:* Gen trainee res mfg, Glaxo Labs Ltd, India, 52-54; med rep, Alamagamated Chem & Dyestuff Co Ltd, India, 54-55; res fel, Inst Med Res, Chicago Med Sch, 63-64; res biochemist, Vet Admin Hosp, Hines, Ill & Northwestern Univ, 64-66; res pharmacologist, IIT Res Inst, 66-68; from instr to asst prof pharmacol, Chicago Col Osteop Med, 68-73; sr pharmacologist, Haskell Lab Toxicol & Indust Med, E I du Pont de Nemours & Co, Inc, 73-75; sr toxicologist, SRI Int, Arlington, 76-78; sr pharmacologist/toxicologist, Ctr Devices Radiol Health, Food & Drug Admin, US Dept Helath & Human Serv, 78-95. *Concurrent Pos:* Consult tumor res, Vet Hosp, Hines, 70-73; adj asst prof psychopharmacol, Univ Del, 75-77. *Mem:* Am Soc Pharmacol & Exp Therapeut. *Res:* Metabolism and distribution of drugs; effect of drugs on cells in culture; radio-incorporation studies; biochemistry of carcinogenesis; chemical constitution and pharmacological-biological activity; lipoproteins; cellular toxicology; cardiovascular pharmacology; preclinical investigations and screening; behavioral pharmacology and toxicology; factor VIII and prostacyclin in endothelial cells damage. *Mailing Add:* 2252 Senseney Lane Falls Church VA 22043-3105. *E-Mail:* kbatra@worldnet.att.net

BATRA, LEKH RAJ, MYCOLOGY. *Current Pos:* res mycologist, Plant Protection Inst, 67-85, RES MICROBIOLOGIST & SCI ADV BELTSVILLE AREA, SCI & EDUC ADMIN, USDA, 86- *Personal Data:* b Panjab, India, Nov 26, 29; nat US; m 60, Suzanne W Tubby; c Mira K & Persa O. *Educ:* Panjab Univ, India, BSc, 52, MSc, 54; Cornell Univ, PhD(mycol), 58. *Prof Exp:* Res scholar mycol, Govt India, 54-55; lectr biol, Desh Bandhu Col, India, 55; instr plant path, Cornell Univ, 57-58; lectr biol, Swarthmore Col, 58-60; res assoc, Univ Kans, 60-62, from asst prof to assoc prof bot, 62-68. *Concurrent Pos:* Directorate of Plant Quarantine, Govt India, 60; vis res fel, Fed Forest & Timber Mgt Res Ctr, Hamburg, Ger, 62; mem, US Fedn Cult Collection, 81-83, Comt Int Union, Nat Acad Sci & Am Type Cult Collection, 83-89, Int Sci Bd, 89-92; adj prof, Towson State Univ. *Mem:* Mycol Soc Am; Am Soc Microbiol; Microbiol Soc (secy, 81-); Soc Conserv & Field Ecol (secy-treas, 80-84); Int Mycol Asn. *Res:* Morphology and taxonomy Hemiascomycetes and Discomycetes; ambrosia fungi, cereal, cotton diseases; biological control of plant pathogens; fermented foods of the orient; insect-fungus mutualism and mimicry; author, editor and co-editor of several books. *Mailing Add:* 90 Lake St Saranac Lake NY 12983. *Fax:* 301-504-5449

BATRA, NARENDRA K, SOLID STATE PHYSICS, ULTRA SONICS NON-DESTRUCTIVE TESTING. *Current Pos:* RES PHYSICIST, NAVAL RES LAB, 82- *Personal Data:* b India, Sept 15, 43. *Educ:* Columbia Univ, MA, 67; Wayne State Univ, PhD(physics), 72. *Prof Exp:* Fac mem, Va Tech, 74-76; contractor, Wright Air Force Base, 77-82. *Mem:* Inst Elec Electronics Engrs; Am Soc Non-Destructive Testing; Am Phys Soc. *Mailing Add:* Code 6380 Naval Res Lab 4555 Overlook Ave SW Washington DC 20375

BATRA, PREM PARKASH, BIOCHEMISTRY. *Current Pos:* from asst prof to prof biol, 65-74, PROF BIOCHEM & MOLECULAR BIOL, SCH MED, WRIGHT STATE UNIV, 74- *Personal Data:* b Jhang Maghiana, India, Apr 1, 36; US citizen; m 82, Rosemarie Lewandowski; c Madhu (Joni) & Renee. *Educ:* Panjab Univ, India, BS, 55, MS, 58; Univ Ariz, PhD(agr chem), 61. *Prof Exp:* Res assoc biochem, Univ Ariz, 61-63; fels, Univ Utah, 63-64 & Johns Hopkins Univ, 64-65; biochemist, aging res lab & geront br NIH, Vet Admin Hosp, 65. *Concurrent Pos:* NIH spec fel, Univ Ky, 73-74; vis prof, Okayama Univ Sci (Japan), 84 & 88. *Mem:* Am Chem Soc; Am Soc Biochem & Molecular Biol. *Res:* Protein conformation; protein chemistry; circular dichroism; biosynthesis of carotenoids in plants and microorganisms. *Mailing Add:* Dept Biol Chem Sch Med Wright State Univ Dayton OH 45431. *Fax:* 513-873-3731; *E-Mail:* pbatra%desire@wsu.bitnet

BATRA, ROMESH CHANDER, ENGINEERING MECHANICS. *Current Pos:* CLIFTON C GARVIN PROF, VA TECH, 94- *Personal Data:* b Panjab, India, Aug 16, 47; m 72, Manju Dhamija; c Monica R & Meenakshi R. *Educ:* Panjabi Univ, India, BSc, 68; Univ Waterloo, MASc, 69; Johns Hopkins Univ, PhD(mech), 72. *Honors & Awards:* Alexander Von Humboldt Award for Sr Scientists, 92; Jai Krishna Award, Indian Geotech Soc, 88. *Prof Exp:* Postdoc assoc mech, Johns Hopkins Univ, 72-73; res assoc eng mech, McMaster Univ, 73-74; asst prof, Univ Mo, Rolla, 74-76 & Univ Ala, 76-77; from assoc prof to prof, Univ Mo, Rolla, 81-94. *Concurrent Pos:* Univ Mo, Rolla grants, 76, 78, 79 & 81, 82-88; res engr, Athena Eng Co, Ala, 76-77; consult, Xerox Corp, 78-80, Dames & Moore, 80, Army Ballistic Res Lab, 85-88, Hewlett-Packard, 87 & Belloit Manhatten, 87; NSF grant, 80-82 & 87-97; Army grant, 83-; Aro grant, 85- *Mem:* Fel Am Soc Mech Engrs; fel Am Acad Mech; Soc Eng Sci; Soc Rheology; fel Am Soc Eng Educ; Int Asn Comput Mech. *Res:* Adiabatic shear banding; applications of finite element method to solving thermomechanical problems; penetration mechanics, smart materials, metal forming. *Mailing Add:* ESM Dept VA Tech Blacksburg VA 24061-0219. *Fax:* 540-231-4574; *E-Mail:* rbatra@vt.edu

BATRA, SUBHASH KUMAR, FIBER-TEXTILE TECHNOLOGY & ANALYSIS, NON WOVENS TECHNOL & ENGINEERING. *Current Pos:* assoc prof textile mat & mgt, Sch Textiles, 77-84, PROF TEXTILE ENG & SCI, NC STATE UNIV, 84-; DIR, NONWOVENS COOP RES CTR, 91- *Personal Data:* b Bannu, Pakistan, Oct 4, 35; US citizen; m 90, Elizabeth J Mutran. *Educ:* Univ Delhi, BS, 57; Mass Inst Technol, SM, 61, SM, 77; Rensselaer Polytech Inst, PhD(mech), 66. *Honors & Awards:* Harold-Dewitt Smith Medal & Award, Am Soc Testing Mat; E R Schwarz Lectr, 95. *Prof Exp:* Asst, Weaving Dept, Ahmedabad New Cotton Mill, India, 57-58; res engr mech eng, Mass Inst Technol, 61-62; sr scientist lubrication technol & tribology, Battelle Mem Inst, 66-70; res assoc mech eng, Mass Inst Technol, 70-77. *Concurrent Pos:* Vis fel, Sloan Sch Mgt, Mass Inst Technol, 75-76; consult, World Bank, Washington, DC, 76-77, Avtex Fibers Inc, Front Royal, Va, 78 & Monsanto Textile Co, NC, 79-80; secy, Textile Div, Am Soc Mech Engrs, 78-83 & chmn, 83-84; vis scholar, Israel Fiber Inst, 82; chmn, Gordon Res Conf Fiber Sci, 85; Charles A Cannon prof, 96- *Mem:* Fel Am Soc Mech Engrs; Fiber Soc (pres, 87); Am Acad Mech; Sigma Xi; fel Textile Inst. *Res:* Fiber physics; mechanics of nonwovens and textile structures; textile technology; fiber fatigue. *Mailing Add:* Sch Textiles NC State Univ PO Box 8301 Raleigh NC 27695-8301. *Fax:* 919-515-4556; *E-Mail:* subhash_batra@ncsu

BATRA, SUZANNE WELLINGTON TUBBY, ENTOMOLOGY. *Current Pos:* consult, Apicult Res Br, 70-74, RES ENTOMOLOGIST, AGR RES SERV, USDA, 74- *Personal Data:* b New York, NY, Dec 15, 37; m 60, Lekh R; c Mirabai K (Sweeney) & Persaram O. *Educ:* Swarthmore Col, BA, 60; Univ Kans, PhD(entom), 64. *Prof Exp:* Res assoc entom, Univ Kans, 64-67; res, Utah State Univ, 68-69. *Concurrent Pos:* Grantee, Sigma Xi & Am Philos Soc, 64-65; sr res officer, Punjab Agr Univ, 65; ed, J Kans Entom Soc, 66-67; adj prof, Univ Md. *Mem:* AAAS; Sigma Xi. *Res:* Ecology, behavior of insects; evolution of social behavior; management of crop pollinators; insect-fungus symbioses; Apoidea; biological control of weeds. *Mailing Add:* Bee Res Lab Bldg 476 Beltsville Agr Res Ctr USDA Beltsville MD 20705. *Fax:* 301-504-8736

BATRA, TILAK RAJ, MOLECULAR GENETICS, QUANTITATIVE GENETICS. *Current Pos:* RES SCIENTIST, AGR CAN, OTTAWA, 76- *Personal Data:* b Girotte, India, Dec 11, 36; Can citizen; m 62; c 2. *Educ:* Jabalpur Univ, India, BVSc, 59; Univ Hawaii, MS, 66; Univ Ill, PhD(animal breeding), 68. *Honors & Awards:* Excellence in Genetics & Physiol Award, Can Soc Animal Sci, 93. *Prof Exp:* Lectr, Vet Col, India, 62-64; res asst, Univ Ill, 66-68, res assoc, 68-69; res programmer, Univ Guelph, 69-76. *Mem:* Am Dairy Sci Asn; Can Soc Animal Sci; Nat Mastitis Coun; Int Soc Animal Genetics (secy-treas); Can Soc Animal Sci. *Res:* Dairy cattle breeding. *Mailing Add:* Ctr Food & Animal Res Res Br Agr Can Ottawa ON K1A 0C6 Can. *Fax:* 613-759-1355; *E-Mail:* batrat@em.agr.ca

BATRIN, GEORGE LESLIE, ENGINEERING MATHEMATICS, ENGINEERING STATISTICS. *Current Pos:* APP ENGR, GATES RUBBER CO, 88- *Personal Data:* b Detroit, Mich, May 20, 57. *Educ:* Carnegie-Mellon Univ, BS, 85, MA, 86. *Prof Exp:* Safety engr, Carnegie-Mellon Univ, 84-85. *Concurrent Pos:* Engr, US Tank Automotive Command, 87-88; process engr, Turnmatic, Inc, 87-88. *Mem:* Am Math Soc; Math Asn Am; Soc Indust & Appl Math; Soc Automotive Engrs; Soc Mfg Engrs; Indust Math Soc. *Res:* Mathematical investigation into modeling belt slippage during a rapid deceleration internal; reliability equations for machinery and belt mass reduction for power transmission; Department of Energy's testing and evaluation in the automotive industry. *Mailing Add:* 37965 Willowood Ct Harrison Township MI 48045

BATSAKIS, JOHN G, MEDICINE, PATHOLOGY. *Current Pos:* CHMN & PROF, DEPT PATH, UNIV TEX M D ANDERSON HOSP, HOUSTON, 81-, RUTH LEGGET JONES PROF, 82- *Personal Data:* b Petoskey, Mich, Aug 14, 29; m 57, Mary J Savagci; c Laura L (Hansen), Sharon B (Maultsby) & George J. *Educ:* Albion Col, BS, 51; Univ Mich, MD, 54. *Prof Exp:* Intern path, Univ Hosp, George Washington Univ, 54-55; resident, Univ Mich, 55-59; chief clin path, Walter Reed Gen Hosp, Washington, DC, 59-61; assoc pathologist, Bronson Methodist Hosp, Kalamazoo, Mich, 61-; from asst prof to prof path, Univ Mich, Ann Arbor, 62-79, from assoc dir to co-dir clin labs, Univ Hosp, 64-79; chief, Path Dept, Maine Med Ctr, 79-81. *Concurrent Pos:* Consult, Vet Admin Hosp, Ann Arbor, 62- & Armed Forces, 72- *Mem:* Fel Col Am Path; Asn Mil Surg US; fel Am Col Physicians; Am Asn Clin Chemists; fel Am Soc Clin Pathologists. *Res:* Clinical chemistry; head and neck, gastrointestinal and thyroid pathology; clinical enzymology; salivary gland disease. *Mailing Add:* 1701 Hermann Dr Houston TX 77004. *Fax:* 713-794-1695

BATSHAW, MARK LEVITT, DEVELOPMENTAL PEDIATRICS, METABOLISM. *Current Pos:* W T GRANT PROF PEDIAT, UNIV PA SCH MED, 88- *Personal Data:* b Montreal, Que, Sept 19, 45; m 69; c Elissa, Michael & Andrew. *Educ:* Univ Pa, BA, 67; Univ Chicago, MD, 71. *Prof Exp:* Intern pediat, Hosp Sick Children, Toronto, 71-72, resident, 72-73; fel, Johns Hopkins Med Inst, 73-75, instr, 75-76, from asst prof to assoc prof pediat, 76-88. *Concurrent Pos:* Develop pediatrician, John F Kennedy Inst, Baltimore, 75-; physician-in-chief, Children's Seashore House, Philadelphia, 88- *Mem:* Soc Pediat Res; fel Royal Acad Physicians & Surg; Am Acad Pediat; Soc Inherited Metab Dis; Soc Develop Pediat. *Res:* Investigation of genetics, neurochemistry and gene therapy for inborn errors of urea cycle metabolism. *Mailing Add:* Children's Seashore House 3405 Civic Ctr Blvd Philadelphia PA 19104

BATSON, ALAN PERCY, COMPUTER SCIENCE. *Current Pos:* from instr to assoc prof physics, 58-67, dir, Comput-Sci Ctr, 62-72, PROF COMPUT SCI, UNIV VA, 67- *Personal Data:* b Birmingham, Eng, Sept 18, 32; m 57, 68; c 4. *Educ:* Univ Birmingham, BSc, 53, PhD(physics), 56. *Prof Exp:* Fel, Univ Birmingham, 56-58. *Mem:* Inst Elec & Electronics Engrs; Asn Comput Mach. *Res:* Computer systems. *Mailing Add:* Dept Comput Sci Univ Va Thornton Hall Charlottesville VA 22903

BATSON, BLAIR EVERETT, PEDIATRICS. *Current Pos:* chmn dept, 55-88, PROF PEDIAT, SCH MED, UNIV MISS, 55- *Personal Data:* b Hattiesburg, Miss, Oct 24, 20; m 54. *Educ:* Vanderbilt Univ, BS, 41, MD, 44; Johns Hopkins Univ, MPH, 54. *Prof Exp:* Intern pediat, Vanderbilt Univ Hosp, 44-45; asst resident, Johns Hopkins Hosp, 45-46; asst resident, Vanderbilt Univ Hosp, 48-49, instr pediat, Sch Med, Vanderbilt Univ, 49-52; instr pediat, Med Sch & pub health adminr, Div Maternal & Child Health, Sch Hyg & Pub Health, Johns Hopkins Univ, 52-54, asst prof, 54-55. *Concurrent Pos:* Resident pediatrician, Vanderbilt Univ Hosp, 49-50; consult pediat & US Air Force examr, Am Bd Pediat. *Mem:* AMA; Am Acad Pediat; Am Pub Health Asn; Am Pediat Soc. *Res:* Growth and development in children; immunization; handicapped children. *Mailing Add:* Dept Pediats Univ Miss Sch Med 2500 N State St Jackson MS 39216-4505

BATSON, DAVID BANKS, TOXICOLOGY. *Current Pos:* Regulatory scientist, Div Drugs Ruminant Species, 72-80, EXTRAMURAL RES COORDR & HEALTH SCIENTIST ADMIN, CTR VET MED, FOOD & DRUG ADMIN, 80- *Personal Data:* b Tenn, April 14, 44; m 93, Joan Collins. *Educ:* Austin Peay State Univ, BS, 66; Univ Tenn, MS, 68, PhD(animal sci), 72. *Mem:* AAAS; Soc Study Reprod; Am Soc Animal Sci; Asn Gov Toxicologists; Int Soc Study Xenobiotics. *Res:* Pharmacology and toxicology of animal drugs and feed additives; aquaculture research; analytical methods development. *Mailing Add:* 14608 Nadine Dr Rockville MD 20853

BATSON, GORDON B, CIVIL ENGINEERING, STRUCTURAL DESIGN. *Current Pos:* From asst prof to assoc prof civil eng, 61-77, PROF CIVIL & ENVIRON ENG, CLARKSON UNIV, 77- *Personal Data:* b Addison, Maine, Oct 3, 32; m 61, Katharine Wragg; c Andrew A, Nathan A & Alexander W. *Educ:* Univ Maine, BS, 55, MS, 56; Carnegie-Mellon Univ, PhD (civil eng), 62. *Mem:* Am Soc Civil Engrs; fel Am Concrete Inst; Am Soc Testing & Mat; Sigma Xi; Am Soc Eng Educ. *Res:* Fracture mechanics applied to concrete; crack arrest in concrete using fibers. *Mailing Add:* Dept Civil Eng Clarkson Univ Box 5710 Potsdam NY 13699-5710. *Fax:* 315-268-7985; *E-Mail:* gordon@sun.soe.clarkson.edu

BATSON, MARGARET BAILLY, PSYCHIATRY, NEUROLOGY. *Current Pos:* from asst prof to assoc prof pediat, Univ Miss Med Ctr, 55-80, assoc prof psychiat & chief, Div Human Behavior, 59-80, dir, Infant & Child Develop Clin, 65-80, asst prof microbiol & assoc mem grad fac, 67-80, EMER ASSOC PROF, UNIV MISS MED CTR, 80-; MED DIR, HUDSPETH RETARDATION CTR, 80- *Personal Data:* b New York, NY, July 13, 14; div. *Educ:* Manhattanville Col, BA, 37; Columbia Univ, MA, 40, PhD(bact), 49; Univ Rochester, MD, 51. *Prof Exp:* Clin instr bact, Columbia Univ, 39-41; intern pediat, Johns Hopkins Univ Hosp, 51-52, asst resident, 53-54, chief res, 54, instr, Sch Med, Univ & pediatrist-in-chg, Hosp, 54-55; asst resident pediat, Univ Minn, 52-53. *Concurrent Pos:* Consult, Inpatient, Diag & Eval Dept. *Mem:* Sigma Xi. *Res:* Pediatric neurology; microbiology; immunology; human behavior. *Mailing Add:* 52 Eastbrooke Jackson MS 39216-4714

BATSON, OSCAR RANDOLPH, pediatrics, for more information see previous edition

BATSON, RAYMOND MILNER, planetary cartography & digital image processing, for more information see previous edition

BATSON, WILLIAM EDWARD, JR, PLANT PATHOLOGY. *Current Pos:* from asst prof to assoc prof, 71-82, PROF PLANT PATH, MISS STATE UNIV, 82- *Personal Data:* b Taylors, SC, Apr 3, 42; m 65; c 2. *Educ:* Clemson Univ, BS, 65, MS, 66; Tex A&M Univ, PhD(plant path), 71. *Prof Exp:* Res assoc plant path, Tex A&M Univ, 67-71. *Mem:* Am Phytopath Soc. *Res:* Seedling diseases of cotton. *Mailing Add:* Dept Entomol Miss State Univ PO Box EM Mississippi State MS 39762-9999

BATSTONE, JOANNA L, COMPUTER SCIENCE. *Current Pos:* COMPUT SCIENTIST, IBM THOMAS J WATSON RES CTR. *Honors & Awards:* Robert Lansing Hardy Gold Medal Award, Minerals, Metals & Mat Soc, 91; Cosslett Award, Microbeam Analysis Soc, 89; Burton Award, Micros Soc Am, 95. *Mailing Add:* Thomas J Watson Res Ctr IBM 30 Saw Mill Rd Hawthorne NY 10532

BATT, ELLEN RAE, PHYSIOLOGY. *Current Pos:* FAC MEM, SARAH LAWRENCE COL, 87- *Personal Data:* b New York, NY, Sept 24, 34. *Educ:* Barnard Col, AB, 56, Columbia Univ, MA, 59, PhD(zool), 67. *Prof Exp:* NIH fel, 67-70, res assoc, 70-73, asst prof physiol, Columbia Univ, 73-81. *Concurrent Pos:* Consult, Harlem Hosp, 88- *Mem:* Am Soc Zoologists; AAAS; Sigma Xi; Am Physiol Soc; NY Acad Sci. *Res:* Transport through red blood cell, bacterial, and intestinal membranes; neonatal development of rodent intestine with respect to transport. *Mailing Add:* Dept Human Genetics Sarah Lawrence Col Bronxville NY 10708

BATT, RUSSELL HOWARD, PHYSICAL CHEMISTRY. *Current Pos:* asst prof, 68-73, ASSOC PROF CHEM, KENYON COL, 73- *Personal Data:* b Worcester, Mass, July 27, 38; m 60; c 2. *Educ:* Univ Rochester, BS, 60; Univ Calif, Berkeley, PhD(chem), 65. *Prof Exp:* Asst prof chem, Wesleyan Univ, 64-66; res instr, Dartmouth Col, 66-68. *Mem:* Am Chem Soc; Sigma Xi. *Res:* Photoconductivity in molecular crystals; low temperature calorimetry; biology and chemistry of trace heavy metal environmental pollutants. *Mailing Add:* Dept Chem Kenyon Col Gambier OH 43022

BATT, WILLIAM, BIOCHEMISTRY. *Current Pos:* from inst to prof, Manhattan Col, 59-71, head dept, 64-72, dir admis, 72-81, PROF CHEM, MANHATTAN COL, 71- *Personal Data:* b Buffalo, NY, May 25, 31. *Educ:* Cath Univ Am, BA, 54, MS, 56; Georgetown Univ, PhD(biochem), 59. *Prof Exp:* Instr chem, La Salle Acad, RI, 54-55 & De La Salle Col, Washington, DC, 55-59. *Concurrent Pos:* NIH fel, Brookhaven Nat Lab, 63-64. *Mem:* AAAS; NY Acad Sci; Am Chem Soc; Am Inst Chemists. *Res:* Physical aspects of enzyme catalyzed reactions; kinetics and mechanisms of enzyme substrate interaction; thrombin. *Mailing Add:* Dept Acct & Info Syst Manhattan Col 4513 Manhattan Col Bronx NY 10471-4097

BATTAGLIA, FREDERICK CAMILLO, PEDIATRICS, PHYSIOLOGY. *Current Pos:* assoc prof, Dept Pediat & Obstet-Gynec, Univ Colo, 65-69, dir, Div Perinatal Med, 70-74, chmn, Dept Pediat, 74-88, PROF, DEPT PEDIAT & OBSTET-GYNEC, SCH MED, UNIV COLO, 69- *Personal Data:* b Weehawken, NJ, Feb 15, 32; c 2. *Educ:* Cornell Univ, BA, 53; Yale Univ, MD, 57; Am Bd Pediat, cert, 64 & cert, neonatol-perinatol, 75. *Hon Degrees:* DSc, Univ Ind, 90. *Honors & Awards:* E Mead Johnson Award Pediat Res, Am Acad Pediat, 69; Agnes Higgins Award, March of Dimes, 86. *Prof Exp:* Intern, Dept Pediat, Johns Hopkins Hosp, Md, 57-58, resident, 60-62; USPHS fel, Dept Biochem, Univ Cambridge, Eng, 58-59; Josiah Macy Found fel, Dept Physiol, Sch Med, Yale Univ, 59-60; asst prof pediat, Johns Hopkins Univ, 63-65. *Concurrent Pos:* Attend pediatrician, Johns Hopkins Hosp, 62, Union Mem Hosp, Md, 64-65, Children's Hosp, Colo & Denver Gen Hosp, 67- & Fitzsimons Army Med Ctr, 70-; contrib ed, J Pediat, 66-74; co-dir, Newborn Ctr, Colo Gen Hosp, 67-74; assoc ed, Biol Neonate, 79-; mem, Low Birthweight Comt, NIH, 84, Human Embryol & Develop Study Sect, Nat Inst Child Health & Human Develop, 86- *Mem:* Inst Med-Nat Acad Sci; Soc Gynec Invest; Perinatal Res Soc (secy-treas, 70-73, pres, 74-75); Am Acad Pediat; Sigma Xi; AAAS; Am Pediat Soc; Soc Pediat Res (pres, 76-77); Asn Am Physicians. *Res:* Perinatal physiology; intrauterine growth retardation; biochemistry; author and co-author of several books on various aspects of fetal and maternal medicine. *Mailing Add:* Perinatal Pediat Univ Colo Med Ctr 4200 E Ninth Ave Denver CO 80262

BATTAILE, JULIAN, BIOCHEMISTRY. *Current Pos:* RETIRED. *Personal Data:* b Sept 26, 25; US citizen; m 58; c 2. *Educ:* La State Univ, BS, 47; Univ Ill, MS, 48; Ore State Univ, PhD(biochem), 60. *Prof Exp:* Instr chem, Southeast La Col, 47; asst prof, Southwestern La Inst, 48-50; chemist, Ethyl Corp, 51-54; instr chem, Ore State Univ, 57-58; NIH fel, Univ Calif, Davis, 60-62; from asst prof to prof chem, Southern Ore State Col, 62-88. *Mem:* Am Chem Soc; Sigma Xi. *Res:* Biosynthesis of monoterpenes. *Mailing Add:* 1216 Tolman Creek Rd Ashland OR 97520-3653

BATTAN, LOUIS JOSEPH, meteorology; deceased, see previous edition for last biography

BATTARBEE, HAROLD DOUGLAS, ENDOCRINOLOGY, CARDIOVASCULAR PHYSIOLOGY. *Current Pos:* From instr to assoc prof, 71-85, PROF PHYSIOL, SCH MED, LA STATE UNIV, SHREVEPORT, 85- *Personal Data:* b Highlands, Tex, July 25, 40; m 65, 82; c 4. *Educ:* Univ Houston, BS, 66; Baylor Col Med, PhD(physiol), 71. *Concurrent Pos:* Mem, med res & develop adv comt, US Army, 82-87; consult, US Dept Defense, US Army Aeromed Res Lab, 82-; assoc mem,Grad Fac, La State Univ, Shreveport, 73- *Mem:* AAAS; Am Physiol Soc; Am Heart Asn. *Res:* Cardiovascular physiology; stress physiology; role of dietary sodium and potassium in the pathogenesis of hypertension; baroreflex control of heart rate and peripheral resistances in hypertension; endocrine and sympathetic nervous system function changes induced by chemical warfare pretreatment and antidotal drugs; portal venous hypertension and visceral blood flow. *Mailing Add:* Dept Physiol PO Box 33932 La State Univ Sch Med Shreveport LA 71130

BATTE, WILLIAM GRANVILLE, ELECTRICAL ENGINEERING. *Current Pos:* PRES, COMPUT RES INC, 80- *Personal Data:* b Jarratt, Va, Jan 26, 27; m 50; c 2. *Educ:* Va Polytech Inst, BS(elec eng) & BS(indust eng), 50; Case Inst Technol, PhD(elec eng), 65. *Prof Exp:* Scientist, NASA Langley Res Ctr, 54-67; assoc prof elec eng, Univ Va, 67-69; prof sci, Old Dominion Univ, 69-76, adj prof elec eng, 76-80. *Mem:* Inst Elec & Electronics Engrs; Asn Comput Mach. *Res:* Digital computer and control engineering; computer time sharing and control; digital logic. *Mailing Add:* 113 Marvin Dr Hampton VA 23666

BATTEN, ALAN HENRY, ASTRONOMY. *Current Pos:* sci officer, Dom Astrophys Observ, 61-70, assoc res officer, 70-75, sr res officer, 76-91, GUEST WORKER, DOM ASTROPHYS OBSERV, 91- *Personal Data:* b Tankerton, Eng, Jan 21, 33; Can citizen; m 60, Lois E Dewis; c Michael H & Margaret E. *Educ:* Univ St Andrews, BSc, 55, DSc, 74; Univ Manchester, PhD(close binary systs), 58. *Prof Exp:* Res assoc astron, Univ Manchester, 58-61. *Concurrent Pos:* Nat Res Coun Can fel, 59-61; lectr, Univ Victoria, 61-64; Can Nat Comt, 64-70 & 76-82, organizing comts & comns 30-42, 67-, pres, Comn 30, 76-79, mem, Organizing Comt 26, 73-79, pres comn 42, 82-85; on leave, Vatican Observ, Castel Gandolfo, Italy, 70; guest investr, Inst Astron & Space Physics, Buenos Aires, 72, chmn, Can Organizing Comt IAU, XVII Gen Assembly, 75-79; ed, J Royal Astron Soc Can, 80-88; Erskine vis fel, Univ Canterbury, Chris Church, NZ, 95. *Mem:* Fel Royal Soc Can; Am Astron Soc; Royal Astron Soc Can (pres, 74-76, hon pres, 93); Int Astron Union (vpres, 85-91); fel Royal Astron Soc; Can Astron Soc (pres, 71-73). *Res:* Spectroscopic and photometric studies of close binary systems; radial velocities of stars; history of astronomy; assisting astronomers in developing countries science and religion. *Mailing Add:* Dom Astrophys Observ 5071 W Saanich Rd Victoria BC V8X 4M6 Can. *Fax:* 250-363-0045

BATTEN, BRUCE EDGAR, CELLULAR ENDOCRINOLOGY. *Current Pos:* VPRES SALES, CULVEX. *Educ:* Med Col Va, PhD(anat), 77. *Prof Exp:* Assoc prof anat, Sch Med, Tufts Univ, 80- *Mailing Add:* 3711 Lexington Ave N Shoreview MN 55126

BATTEN, CHARLES FRANCIS, PHYSICAL CHEMISTRY. *Current Pos:* res assoc chem, 76-80, SR RES SCIENTIST, UNIV HOUSTON, 80- *Personal Data:* b Manchester, NH, Apr 15, 42. *Educ:* St Anselms Col, AB, 64; Univ Notre Dame, MS, 66, PhD(chem), 71. *Prof Exp:* Fel chem, Univ Houston, 71-72, vis asst prof, 72-73; res fel chem, Univ Nebr-Lincoln, 75-76. *Concurrent Pos:* Anal Lab mgr, NUS Corp. *Mem:* Sigma Xi; Am Chem Soc. *Res:* Atmospheric pressure ionization mass spectrometry; photoionization mass spectrometry; analytic detectors based on ionization and electron capture; kinetics and thermodynamics of negative ion reactions. *Mailing Add:* 7994 Locke Lane Apt 29 Houston TX 77063

BATTEN, GEORGE L, JR, HYDROGEN BONDING IN CELLULOSIC WEBS, LIQUID IMBIBITION IN CELLULOSIC WEBS. *Current Pos:* res & develop mgr, 89-90, TECH SERV MGR, GA-PAC CORP, 90- *Personal Data:* b Smithfield, NC, Oct 31, 52; m 77, Jeanne L Smith; c Brigid C, Kathleen V, Jason M & Reilly N. *Educ:* Wake Forest Univ, BS, 75; Univ NC, Chapel Hill, PhD(chem physics), 78. *Prof Exp:* Res chemist, Westvaco Corp, 78-82, res group leader, 82-89. *Mem:* Am Chem Soc; Tech Asn Pulp & Paper Indust; fel Am Inst Chemists. *Res:* Nature of hydrogen bonding in cellulosic webs; relations between hydrogen bond density and mechanical properties of cellulosic webs; liquid imbibition into capillaries and packed beds; author of 3 electronic books. *Mailing Add:* 1685 Planters Row Stone Mountain GA 30087. *Fax:* 770-322-9773; *E-Mail:* glbatten@gapac.com

BATTEN, GEORGE WASHINGTON, JR, MATHEMATICS. *Current Pos:* asst prof math, 66-81, ASSOC PROF ELEC ENG & MATH, UNIV HOUSTON, 81- *Personal Data:* b Houston, Tex, Sept 4, 37; m 61; c 1. *Educ:* Rice Univ, BA, 59, MA, 61, PhD(math), 63. *Prof Exp:* Res assoc math, Univ Ill, 63-64; asst biomathematician, Univ Tex M D Anderson Hosp & Tumor Inst, 64-65, asst prof biomath, 65-66. *Concurrent Pos:* Vis lectr math, Rice Univ, 66. *Mem:* Soc Indust & Appl Math; Inst Elec & Electronics Engrs. *Res:* Probability theory; partial differential equations; numerical analysis. *Mailing Add:* Advan Imag Measurement Syst 3333 W Alabama Suite 103 Houston TX 77098

BATTEN, LYNN MARGARET, GEOMETRIES OF DIMENSION. *Current Pos:* PROF & HEAD, DEPT MATH & ASTRON, UNIV MAN, 89- *Personal Data:* b Blyth, Eng, Oct 31, 48; Can & Brit citizen. *Educ:* Univ Waterloo, PhD(math), 76. *Prof Exp:* Prof, Univ Winnipeg, 75-89. *Concurrent Pos:* Bd mem, Can Math Soc, 81-83 & 93-, mem res comt, 93- *Mem:* Can Math Soc (vpres, 97-); Am Math Soc; Asn Women Math; Australian Combinational Soc. *Res:* Embedding problems in geometries of dimension greater than or equal to 2; problems in combinatorial geometry and in design theory; cryptography. *Mailing Add:* Dept Math & Astron Univ Man Winnipeg MB R3T 2N2 Can. *Fax:* 204-261-0177; *E-Mail:* batten@ccu.umanitoba.ca

BATTEN, ROGER LYMAN, INVERTEBRATE PALEONTOLOGY. *Current Pos:* RETIRED. *Personal Data:* b Hammond, Ind, June 22, 23. *Educ:* Univ Wyo, BA, 48; Columbia Univ, PhD(geol), 55. *Prof Exp:* Geologist, US Geol Surv, 54-55; from asst prof to assoc prof geol, Univ Wis, 55-62; assoc prof, Columbia Univ, 62-68, prof geol, 68-90; cur, Am Mus Natural Hist, 67-90. *Concurrent Pos:* Assoc cur, Am Mus Natural Hist, 62-67. *Mem:* Paleont Soc; Geol Soc Am. *Res:* Evolution and ecology of the primitive gastropods; Permian stratigraphy; recent marine ecology; population analysis. *Mailing Add:* 77 E Missouri Unit 76 Phoenix AZ 85012

BATTENBURG, JOSEPH R, MECHANICAL ENGINEERING. *Current Pos:* PROF MECH ENG, CALIF STATE UNIV, FRESNO, 81- *Personal Data:* b Chicago, Ill, Jan 16, 34; m 54; c 4. *Educ:* Andrews Univ, BS, 54; Mich Univ, BSE, 56; Univ Southern Calif, MSE, 60; Wis Univ, PhD(mech eng), 67. *Prof Exp:* Instr eng, Walla Walla Col, 56-58; mem tech staff, Hughes Aircraft Co, Inc, 58-60; sr design engr, NAm Aviation, Inc, 60-62; asst prof mech eng, Nev, 62-64; lectr & instr, Wis, 64-67; asst prof, San Jose State Col, 67-68; assoc prof mech eng & chmn eng, Purdue Univ, Calumet Campus, 68-76; exec engr advan technol, Eaton Corp, 76-81. *Concurrent Pos:* NASA fel, Univ Houston, 67 & Stanford, 77; NSF fac res partic, Ford Motor Co, 75; US State Dept prof, Cairo Univ, Egypt, 75-76; tech consult, US State Dept, 81. *Mem:* Am Soc Eng Educ; Sigma Xi; Soc Automotive Engrs. *Res:* Fatigue testing and determination of fatigue properties of engineering materials; educational research in teaching techniques and metallurgical design. *Mailing Add:* Dept Mech Eng Calif State Univ 2220 E San Ramon Fresno CA 93740-8028

BATTER, JOHN F(REDERIC), JR, product management, venture capital investment, for more information see previous edition

BATTERMAN, BORIS WILLIAM, X-RAY PHYSICS, EXPERIMENTAL SOLID STATE PHYSICS. *Current Pos:* assoc prof, 65-68, dir sch appl & eng physics, 74-78, PROF APPL ENG PHYSICS, CORNELL UNIV, 68-, DIR, CORNELL HIGH ENERGY SYNCHROTRON SOURCE LAB, 78-, WALTERS CARPENTER SR PROF ENG, 85- *Personal Data:* b New York, NY, Aug 25, 30; c 3. *Educ:* Mass Inst Technol, BS, 52, PhD(physics), 56. *Prof Exp:* Elec res electrostatic generators, Nat Bur Standards, 51; lab asst soil solidification, Mass Inst Technol, 51-52, asst physics, 52-53; mem tech staff, Bell Tel Labs, 56-65. *Concurrent Pos:* Fulbright Scholar, Technish Hochschule, Stuttgart, Germany, 53; Guggenhein & Fulbright-Hays fels, 71; Alexander von Humbolt fel, Berlin, Germany, 83. *Mem:* Fel AAAS; fel Am Phys Soc; Am Crystallog Asn. *Res:* X-ray, synchrotron radiation and neutron diffraction applied to solid state physics problems; studies of thermal vibrations in crystals. *Mailing Add:* CHESS Wilson Lab Cornell Univ Ithaca NY 14853

BATTERMAN, ROBERT COLEMAN, pharmacology; deceased, see previous edition for last biography

BATTERMAN, STEVEN C(HARLES), APPLIED MECHANICS, BIOMECHANICS. *Current Pos:* asst prof to assoc prof appl mech, Univ Pa, 64-74, assoc prof orthopedic surg res, Sch Med, 72-75, prof appl mech, 74-79, prof biomech in vet med, Sch Vet Med, 75-84, PROF BIOENG, UNIV PA, 74-, PROF BIOENG ORTHO SURG, SCH MED, 75- *Personal Data:* b Brooklyn, NY Aug, 15, 37; m 59, Judith Wilpon; c Scott, Risa & Daniel. *Educ:* Cooper Union, BCE, 59; Brown Univ, ScM, 61, PhD(eng), 64. *Hon Degrees:* MA, Univ Pa, 71. *Honors & Awards:* Robert Ridgway Award, Am Soc Civil Engrs; Founders Award, Am Acad Forensic Sci, 92. *Prof Exp:* Instr eng, Roger Williams Jr Col, 61-62 & Brown Univ, 63-64. *Concurrent Pos:* NSF res grant, 64-70, fel & vis assoc prof, Israel Inst Technol, 70-71; consult, Dept Defense, Advan Res Proj Agency, 68-69 & USN, Naval Air Develop Ctr, 69-70; Nat Inst Dental Res res grant, 73-77; vis prof, Tel-Aviv Univ, 84. *Mem:* Am Soc Civil Engrs; Am Soc Mech Engrs; Am Soc Eng Educ; Am Soc Safety Engrs; Biomed Eng Soc; Am Acad Mech; Soc Expt Mech; Sigma Xi; fel Am Acad Forensic Sci (pres, 94-95); Soc Automotive Engr; Asn Advan Automotive Med. *Res:* Solid and structural mechanics with applications to elasticity, plasticity and viscoelasticity; plates and shells; biomechanics in human and animal systems with applications to orthopedics, dentistry and veterinary medicine; biomechanics of injury. *Mailing Add:* Dept Bioeng Univ Pa Philadelphia PA 19104-6392. *Fax:* 215-573-2071, 609-424-9487; *E-Mail:* batterman@aol.com

BATTERMAN, STUART A, RISK ASSESSMENT, AIR QUALITY. *Current Pos:* PROF, UNIV MICH, 89- *Personal Data:* b Kings City, Md, Feb 26, 56. *Educ:* Rutgers Univ, BS, 79; Mass Inst Technol, MS, 81, PhD(civil & environ eng), 86. *Prof Exp:* Prof, Tex A&M Univ, 86-89. *Concurrent Pos:* Res scientist, NASA, 86- *Mem:* Am Geophys Union; Asn Environ Eng Prof; Automatic Welding Mach Asn; Am Soc Heating Refrig & Air Conditioning Engrs. *Res:* Fate and transport of volatile organic compounds in air, water and soil. *Mailing Add:* SPH Univ Mich Main Campus 109 Observatory Dr Ann Arbor MI 48109-2029

BATTERSHELL, ROBERT DEAN, PESTICIDE CHEMISTRY. *Current Pos:* MGR NEW BUS DEVELOP, ISK BIOTECH CORP, 90- *Personal Data:* b Dover, Ohio, Jan 23, 31; m 58, Thelma Mumby; c Anne, Carol, John & Mary. *Educ:* Bowling Green State Univ, BS, 52; Purdue Univ, PhD, 60. *Honors & Awards:* Outstanding Contrib to Chem Award, Am Chem Soc, 83. *Prof Exp:* Chemist, Callery Chem Co, 52 & 54-55; sr res chemist, Diamond Alkali Co, 59-68; group leader, Diamond Shamrock Corp, 68-78, Licensing & Chem Acquisitions, 78-83; mgr, licensing, SDS Biotech Corp, 83-85; mgr new bus develop, Fermenta Plant Protection Co, 85-90. *Mem:* Am Chem Soc; Chem Soc Japan; Am Phytopath Soc; Int Union Pure & Appl Chem; Licensing Exec Soc. *Res:* Synthesis of organic pesticides; chemistry of aliphatic and aromatic fluorine compounds; structure activity relationships using Hansch & conformational analysis biological plant disease control. *Mailing Add:* Ten Bryn Mawr Dr Painesville OH 44077-5306. *Fax:* 440-354-9506

BATTERSON, STEVEN L, DYNAMICAL SYSTEMS, NUMERICAL ANALYSIS. *Current Pos:* Asst prof, 76-82, ASSOC PROF MATH, EMORY UNIV, 82- *Personal Data:* b Newport News, Va, Nov 21, 50. *Educ:* Col William & Mary, BA, 71; Northwestern Univ, MA, 72, PhD(math), 76. *Concurrent Pos:* Mem, Inst Advan Study, 80-81; vis scholar, Boston Univ, 85; res assoc, Univ Calif, Berkeley, 90. *Mem:* Am Math Soc; Asn Women Math. *Res:* Dynamics of eigenvalve computation. *Mailing Add:* Dept Math Emory Univ Atlanta GA 30322-0001

BATTEY, JAMES F, GENETICS, NEUROCHEMISTRY. *Current Pos:* sr investr, Med Oncol Br, Nat Cancer Inst, 83-88, SECT CHIEF, MOLECULAR NEUROSCI, LAB NEUROCHEM, NAT INST NEUROL DIS & STROKE, NIH, 88- *Personal Data:* b Boston, Mass, Nov 23, 52; m 81; c 2. *Educ:* Stanford Univ, MD & PhD(biophys), 80. *Prof Exp:* Intern pediat, Stanford Univ, 80-81; postdoctoral fel, Dept Genetics, Harvard Univ, 81-83. *Concurrent Pos:* Adj prof genetics, George Washington Univ, 90- *Mem:* Am Soc Biol Chemists; Soc Neurosci. *Res:* Molecular genetic analysis of the structure, function and regulation of genes encoding neuropeptides and their receptors. *Mailing Add:* NIDCD NIH 5 Res Ctr Rm 2B28 Rockville MD 20850

BATTIFORA, HECTOR A, PATHOLOGY. *Current Pos:* PROF PATH, MED SCH, NORTHWESTERN UNIV, CHICAGO, 69-; CHMN & DIR SURG PATH, CITY OF HOPE MED CTR, 87- *Personal Data:* b Peru, Dec 11, 30; US citizen; m 59; c 3. *Educ:* San Marcos Univ, Lima, BS, 50, MD, 57. *Prof Exp:* Assoc pathologist, Presby St Lukes Hosp, Chicago, 64-69. *Mem:* Am Asn Path & Bact; Am Soc Exp Path; Soc Exp Biol & Med; Int Acad Path. *Res:* Experimental oncology; ultrastructure of human tumors; immunohistochemistry in tumor diagnosis. *Mailing Add:* 1752 Wilson Ave Arcadia CA 91006

BATTIGELLI, MARIO C, INDUSTRIAL MEDICINE. *Current Pos:* assoc prof, 66-69, assoc prof med, 69-74, PROF MED & ENVIRON SCI & ASSOC PROF FAMILY MED, SCH MED, UNIV NC, CHAPEL HILL, 74- *Personal Data:* b Florence, Italy, Dec 18, 27; US citizen; m 58; c 4. *Educ:* Univ Florence, MD, 51; Univ Pittsburgh, MPH, 57. *Prof Exp:* Resident instr med, Univ Milan, 52-53, instr, 54-55, assoc, 57-58; res assoc, Univ Pittsburgh, 59-61, asst prof occup med, 62-66. *Mem:* AMA; Am Thoracic Soc; AAAS; Sigma Xi. *Res:* Environmental health; industrial toxicology; chest diseases; pulmonary physiology; inhalation experimental toxicology. *Mailing Add:* 1307 Wildwood Dr Chapel Hill NC 27514

BATTIN, RICHARD H(ORACE), APPLIED MATHEMATICS. *Current Pos:* assoc dir, C S Draper Lab, 58-87, adj prof aeronaut & astronaut, 79-95, SR LECTR, MASS INST TECHNOL, 95- *Personal Data:* b Atlantic City, NJ, Mar 3, 25; m 47; c Thomas, Pamela & Jeffrey. *Educ:* Mass Inst Technol, SB, 45, PhD(appl math), 51. *Honors & Awards:* Louis W Hill Space Transp Award, Am Inst Aeronaut & Astronaut, 72, Mech & Control of Flight Award, 78; Super Achivement Award, Inst Navig, 80; Dirk Brouwer Award, Am Astronaut Soc, 96. *Prof Exp:* Instr math, Mass Inst Technol, 46-52, res mathematician, 51-56; sr staff mem, Arthur D Little, Inc, 56-58. *Mem:* Nat Acad Eng; hon fel Am Inst Aeronaut & Astronaut; Int Astronaut Acad; fel Am Astronaut Soc. *Res:* General circulation of the atmosphere; random processes in automatic control; scientific computation; digital data processing; guidance and control of ballistic missiles and satellites; astrodynamics. *Mailing Add:* 15 Paul Revere Rd Lexington MA 02173

BATTIN, WILLIAM JAMES, thermodynamics, automatic control systems; deceased, see previous edition for last biography

BATTIN, WILLIAM T, ZOOLOGY. *Current Pos:* RETIRED. *Personal Data:* b Hackensack, NJ, Aug 21, 27; div; c 3. *Educ:* Swarthmore Col, BA, 50; Univ Minn, PhD(zool), 56. *Prof Exp:* From instr to asst prof biol, Wesleyan Univ, 55-58; assoc prof, Simpson Col, 58-59; from asst prof to prof, State Univ NY, Binghamton, 59-74, distinguished teaching prof biol, 74-91. *Mem:* AAAS; Am Soc Zool; Am Inst Biol Sci; Nat Asn Biol Teacher; Nat Sci Teachers Asn. *Res:* Physiology of nucleus and nuclear membrane; cytoplasmic DNA of amphibian oocytes; humanistic biology. *Mailing Add:* 156 Fairlawn Ave Albany NY 12203

BATTINO, RUBIN, PHYSICAL CHEMISTRY, THERMODYNAMICS. *Current Pos:* RETIRED. *Personal Data:* b New York, NY, June 22, 31; m 60, Charlotte A Ridinger; c David R & Banjamin S. *Educ:* City Col, NY, BA, 53; Duke Univ, MA, 54, PhD(chem), 57; Wright State Univ, MS, 78. *Prof Exp:* Res chemist, Leeds & Northrup Co, 56-57; from instr to asst prof chem, Ill Inst Technol, 57-66; assoc prof, Wright State Univ, 66-69, prof chem, 69-95. *Concurrent Pos:* Sect ed, Chem Abstr, 63-73; vis prof, Hebrew Univ, 76 & 79, Ben Gurion Univ, 79, Univ New Eng, 79 & Univ Canterbury, 80, 87-88, 96-97, Rhodes Univ, 86 & 91, Okayama Univ Sci, 82 & 90, Univ Turku, 92; Sr Fulbright Scholar, Australia, 79. *Mem:* AAAS; Am Chem Soc; Int Union Pure & Appl Chem; Sigma Xi. *Res:* Thermodynamics of solutions of nonelectrolytes; gas solubilities; solubility of gases in liquids, particularly the high- precision solubility of gases in water; chemical education. *Mailing Add:* Dept Chem Wright State Univ Dayton OH 45435. *Fax:* 937-725-2301; *E-Mail:* rbattino@desire.wright.edu

BATTISTA, ARTHUR FRANCIS, neurosurgery, neurophysiology, for more information see previous edition

BATTISTA, ORLANDO ALOYSIUS, chemistry; deceased, see previous edition for last biography

BATTISTA, SAM P, PHARMACOLOGY, PHYSIOLOGY. *Current Pos:* RETIRED. *Personal Data:* b Orange, NJ, June 22, 24; m 50; c 3. *Educ:* St John's Univ, NY, BS, 50; Univ Wis, MS, 57; Boston Univ, PhD(pharmacol), 68. *Prof Exp:* Res chemist, Merck & Co, Inc, 51-53; consult pharmacologist, Arthur D Little, Inc, 58- *Mem:* Am Soc Pharmacol & Exp Therapeut. *Res:* Inhalation and effects of pharmacological agents on ciliary function. *Mailing Add:* 900 River Reach Dr No 105 Ft Lauderdale FL 33315

BATTISTE, DAVID RAY, ORGANIC CHEMISTRY, POLYMER CHEMISTRY. *Current Pos:* res chemist molecular struct, Phillips Petrol Co, 78-80, corp res, 80-83, sr res chemist, transparent resins & stabilization, 83-91, TECH MGR, POLYMER STABILIZATION, PHILLIPS PETROL CO, 91- *Personal Data:* b Mobile, Ala, Oct 15, 46; m 69; c 2. *Educ:* Univ Fla, BS, 69; La State Univ, PhD(org chem), 74. *Prof Exp:* Sr develop chemist agr chemicals, Ciba-Geigy Corp, 74-75; res assoc alkaloid synthesis, Rice Univ, 75-77; res chemist new prod from terpenes, Glidden-Durkee, 77-78. *Mem:* Am Chem Soc; Sigma Xi; Am Soc Mass Spectrometry; Soc Plastic Engrs. *Res:* Stereochemistry; heterocyclic chemistry; olefin reactions; Fourier transform infrared spectroscopy; reaction mechanisms; pillared clays; mass spectrometry; polymer additives. *Mailing Add:* Phillips Petroleum Co 142 CPL-PRC Bartlesville OK 74004

BATTISTE, MERLE ANDREW, ORGANIC CHEMISTRY. *Current Pos:* from asst prof to assoc prof, 61-70, chmn, Org Div, Chem Dept, 74-84, PROF CHEM, UNIV FLA, 70- *Personal Data:* b Mobile, Ala, July 22, 33; m 90, Janice M Bruce; c John L & Mark A. *Educ:* The Citadel, BS, 54; La State Univ, MS, 56; Columbia Univ, PhD(org chem), 59. *Prof Exp:* Res assoc chem, Univ Calif, Los Angeles, 59-60. *Concurrent Pos:* Alfred P Sloan res fel, 67-69; Fulbright-Hays sr res scholar, Ger, 73-74; Erskine fel, Univ Canterbury, NZ, 87. *Mem:* Am Chem Soc. *Res:* Synthetic and natural products chemistry; small-ring compounds; reaction mechanisms; stereochemistry and rearrangements of bridged polycyclic systems; organometallic chemistry; photochemical transformations. *Mailing Add:* Dept Chem Univ Fla Gainesville FL 32611. *Fax:* 352-392-9131; *E-Mail:* mbattiste@pine.circa.ufl.edu

BATTISTI, ANGELO JAMES, ORGANIC PHOTOCHEMISTRY, METAL FINISHING. *Current Pos:* TECH DIR, J C DOLPH CO, 86- *Personal Data:* b Little Falls, NY, July 26, 45; m 67; c 3. *Educ:* State Univ NY at Albany, BS, 67, at Buffalo, PhD(chem), 71. *Prof Exp:* Vis res assoc, Ohio State Univ, 71-72; res chemist, GAF Corp, Binghamton, NY, 72-74, group leader, 74-76, mgr commercial develop, New York, NY, 76-79; tech mgr, Sel-Rex, Occidental Petrol Corp, 79-83; mgr coating technol, St Regis Corp, 83-84; tech dir, Olin Hunt Corp, 84-86. *Mem:* Am Chem Soc; Nat Elec Mfrs Asn; Am Soc Testing Mat; Int Electrotech Comn. *Res:* Organic photochemistry; photographic science; chemistry of semiconductor and microelectronic materials including photoresists, masking materials, metal finishing chemicals and insulating (dielectric) polymers; electrical and electronic dielectric compounds. *Mailing Add:* 20 Fairway Dr Cranbury NJ 08512-3199

BATTISTO, JACK RICHARD, IMMUNOLOGY, MICROBIOLOGY. *Current Pos:* sci dir, Dept Immunol, 74-81, STAFF MEM, RES INST, CLEVELAND CLIN FOUND, 81- *Personal Data:* b Niagara Falls, NY, Sept 13, 22; m 50, Lillian Mangone; c Scott & Jeth. *Educ:* Cornell Univ, BS, 49; Univ Mich, MS, 50, PhD(bact), 53. *Prof Exp:* Vis investr immunol, Rockefeller Inst Med Res, 53-55; asst prof microbiol, Sch Med, Univ Ark, 55-57; Pop Coun sr fel, Weizmann Inst Sci, Israel, 63-64; from asst prof to prof microbiol & immunol, Albert Einstein Col Med, 57-74. *Concurrent Pos:* NIH fel, 53-55; F G Novy res fel; pop coun res fel; adj prof, Case Western Res Univ, 76- *Mem:* AAAS; Am Asn Immunologists; Harvey Soc; NY Acad Sci; Transplantation Soc; Reticuloendothelial Soc. *Res:* Hypersensitivities to simple chemical compounds; immunological unresponsiveness to haptenes; naturally occurring delayed type iso-hypersensitivity; autologous mixed lymphocyte reaction; splenic influence on lymphoid tissue; regulation of immunological responses; cytolytic T cell reactions. *Mailing Add:* Dept Immunol Res Inst Cleveland Clin Found Cleveland OH 44195. *Fax:* 561-347-0068; *E-Mail:* jackbattisto:72530.443@compuserve.com

BATTLES, JAMES E(VERETT), METALLURGICAL ENGINEERING, CORROSION. *Current Pos:* asst metallurgist, 64-70, metall engr, 70-85, leader, mat group, Chem Eng Div, 72-84, mgr, Electro Magnetic Casting Proj, 85-88, SR METALL ENGR, ARGONNE NAT LAB, 85-, MGR, IFR PYROMETALL PROCESS PROG, 88-, ASSOC DIV DIR, NUCLEAR PROGS, CHEM TECHNOL DIV, 90- *Personal Data:* b Alabama City, Ala, Apr 5, 30; m 51; c 4. *Educ:* Univ Ala, BS, 60; Ohio State Univ, MS, 61, PhD(metall eng), 64. *Prof Exp:* Helper, open hearth, Sheffield Steel Div, Armco Steel Corp, Tex, 48-49, receiving clerk, 50-58, res asst, 60. *Mem:* Am Soc Metals; Am Inst Mining, Metall & Petrol Engrs; Electro Chem Soc; Metall Soc. *Res:* Reactions of tungsten and tungsten oxides with water vapor; mass spectrometic and thermodynamic studies of refractory metal oxides, nuclear metal oxides and nuclear metal carbides; corrosion nuclear fuel element materials; materials development; corrosion studies and failure analysis for high performance lithium/metal sulfide and sodium/sulfur secondary batteries for electric vehicle propulsion; electromagnetic casting process development for steel sheet; development of pyrometallurgical processing of metal and oxide nuclear fuels; nuclear waste treatment. *Mailing Add:* Chem Technol Div Argonne Nat Lab 9700 S Cass Ave Argonne IL 60439

BATTLES, WILLIS RALPH, PETROLEUM CHEMISTRY. *Current Pos:* MGR, W B PROD CO, REDONDO BEACH, CALIF, 82- *Personal Data:* b Erie, Pa, Nov 12, 14; m 41; c 3. *Educ:* Univ Calif, Los Angeles, AB, 36. *Prof Exp:* Inspector, Shell Oil Co, Calif, 36-42; chem operator, Trojan Powder Co, Ohio, 42-43 & Dow Chem Co, Calif, 43-44; res chemist, Union Oil Co, 44-46; bus mgr & partner, Calif Car Bed Co, 46-51; chemist, Fletcher Oil Co, 51-57, chief chemist, 57-59; chemist, Charles Martin & Co, San Pedro, 59-60; chemist, Atlantic Richfield Co, Wilmington, 60; sr anal chemist, Arco-Watson Refinery, 60-82. *Mem:* AAAS; Am Chem Soc; Am Inst Chemists. *Res:* Analytical methods research, especially for trace contaminants in petroleum products. *Mailing Add:* 560 S Helberta Ave Redondo Beach CA 90277-2598

BATTLEY, EDWIN HALL, MICROBIOLOGY, BIOCHEMISTRY. *Current Pos:* ASSOC PROF ECOL & EVOLUTION, STATE UNIV NY, STONY BROOK, 62- *Personal Data:* b Detroit, Mich, Jan 24, 25. *Educ:* Harvard Col, BA, 49; Fla State Univ, MS, 51; Stanford Univ, PhD(biol), 56. *Prof Exp:* Asst, Lab Microbiol, Technol Univ Delft, 55-56 & Sch Med, Wash Univ, 56-57; instr biol chem, Seton Hall Col Med & Dent, 57-60; asst prof biol, Dartmouth Col, 60-62. *Res:* Biochemistry and physiology of microorganisms; thermodynamics of biological processes; general biology. *Mailing Add:* Dept Ecol State Univ NY Stony Brook Main 100 Nicolls Rd Stony Brook NY 11794-0001

BATTOCLETTI, JOSEPH H(ENRY), ELECTRICAL ENGINEERING. *Current Pos:* PROF BIOMED ENG, DEPT NEUROSURG, MED COL WIS, 70- *Personal Data:* b Bridgeport, Ohio, Mar 12, 25; m 51, Rosemary Mashl; c Maryrose, Theresa, Anne, Elizabeth, Mary C, Timothy & James. *Educ:* Univ Detroit, BEE, 47; Northwestern Univ, MSEE, 49; Univ Calif, Los Angeles, PhD, 61. *Honors & Awards:* Centennial Medal, Inst Elec & Electronics Engrs & Mem Award, Milwaukee Sect. *Prof Exp:* Mem staff electronic eng develop, Motorola, Inc, Ill, 49-51; from instr to assoc prof elec eng, Loyola Univ, Los Angeles, 51-62, head dept, 62; Nat Acad Sci-Agency Int Develop electronics consult, Chilean Univs, 62-63; assoc prof elec eng, Marquette Univ, 63-66; res scientist, Badger Meter Mfg Co, 66-68, mgr, Dept Appl Res, 68-70; researcher biomed eng, Res Serv, Vet Admin Ctr, Wood, Wis, 78-95. *Concurrent Pos:* Adj prof, Elec & Biomed Eng Depts, Marquette Univ. *Mem:* Inst Elec & Electronics Engrs; Biomed Eng Soc. *Res:* Electronics; nuclear magnetic resonance flowmeters and imaging; biological effects of electric, magnetic and electromagnetic fields; permanent magnets; finite element analysis; nuclear magnetic resonance measurement of bone mineral content; nerve regeneration. *Mailing Add:* Dept Neurosurg Med Col Wis Clinic Froedtert 9200 W Wisconsin Ave Milwaukee WI 53226

BATTS, BILLY STUART, FISH BIOLOGY, ECOLOGY. *Current Pos:* asst prof, 63-68, ASSOC PROF BIOL, LONGWOOD COL, 68- *Personal Data:* b Raleigh, NC, July 14, 34; m 56; c 2. *Educ:* NC State Univ, BS, 56, PhD, 70; Univ Wash, MS, 60. *Prof Exp:* Fisheries biologist, Univ Wash, 60-62. *Mem:* Am Fisheries Soc; Am Soc Ichthyologists & Herpetologists; fel Am Inst Fishery Res Biologists; Am Inst Biol Sci. *Res:* Lepidology of flounders; life history of skipjack tuna, especially age and growth, food habits, sexual maturity and reproduction. *Mailing Add:* Dept Natural Sci Longwood Col 201 High St Farmville VA 23901-1895

BATTS, HENRY LEWIS, JR, ECOLOGY. *Current Pos:* from instr to prof, 50-78, EMER PROF BIOL, KALAMAZOO COL, 78; EXEC DIR, KALAMAZOO NATURE CTR, 61- *Personal Data:* b Macon, Ga, May 24, 22; m 45; c 3. *Educ:* Kalamazoo Col, AB, 43; Univ Mich, MS, 47, PhD(zool), 55. *Hon Degrees:* ScD, Western Mich Univ, 76. *Prof Exp:* Asst biol & instr ornith, Kalamazoo Col, 40-43; asst zool, Univ Mich, 46-48, teaching fel, 48-50. *Concurrent Pos:* Instr, Exten Serv, Univ Mich, 53; ed, Bull Wilson Ornith Soc, 59-63; founding trustee, Environ Defense Fund, Inc, 67- *Mem:* fel AAAS; Wilson Ornith Soc (2nd vpres, 64-66, 1st vpres, 66-68, pres, 68-69); Am Ornithologists Union; Ecol Soc Am; Nat Audubon Soc. *Res:* Ecology of birds; nest activities of the American Goldfinch; bird nest identification; population and distribution of birds; pesticides; environmental degradation. *Mailing Add:* 2315 Angling Rd Kalamazoo MI 49008

BATTY, JOHN MICHAEL, GEOGRAPHY. *Current Pos:* PROF SPATIAL ANAL & PLANNING & DIR, CTR ADVAN SPATIAL ANAL, UNIV COL LONDON, 95- *Personal Data:* b Liverpool, Eng, Jan 11, 45; m 69, Susan E Howell; c Daniel J. *Educ:* Univ Manchester, BA, 66; Univ Wales, PhD, 83. *Honors & Awards:* Wesley Rougall Prize, 91. *Prof Exp:* Lectr geog, Univ Reading, Eng, 72-76; vis asst prof, Univ Waterloo, Ont, Can, 74-75; reader, Univ Reading, 76-79; prof, Univ Wales, Cardiff, 79-90, dean environ design, 83-86, head dept, 85-89, chmn planning, 87-90; dir, Nat Ctr Geog Info & Analyst & prof geog, State Univ NY, Buffalo, 90-95. *Concurrent Pos:* Adj prof civil eng, Univ Waterloo, 76-78; vis fel, Sch Environ Planning, Univ Melbourne, 82; vis prof, Nat Ctr Supercomput Applns, Univ Ill, 86, Dept Geog, Univ Bristol, UK, 95; Croucher fel, Ctr Urban Studies & Planning, Univ Hong Kong, 86. *Mem:* Royal Soc Arts. *Res:* Geography; environmental design; geographer educator; application of computer-based methods of spatial, geographic and urban problems. *Mailing Add:* Ctr Advan Spatial Anal Univ Col London London WC1E 6BT England. *Fax:* 44-171-813-2843; *E-Mail:* m.batty@ucl.ac.uk

BATTY, JOSEPH CLAIR, THERMODYNAMICS, PHYSICAL CHEMISTRY. *Current Pos:* from asst prof to assoc prof, 63-77, PROF MECH ENG, UTAH STATE UNIV, 78-, DEPT HEAD, 97- *Personal Data:* b Wallsburg, Utah, June 27, 39; m 59; c 3. *Educ:* Utah State Univ, BS, 61, MS, 62; Mass Inst Technol, ScD(mech eng), 69. *Prof Exp:* Proj engr, Nielson & Maxwell Consult Engrs, 62-63. *Concurrent Pos:* NSF fac fel, 67-69. *Mem:* Am Soc Mech Engrs; Am Soc Eng Educ. *Res:* Thermodynamics of gas-solid reactions; ultrafiltration and reverse osmosis applications in food processing; utilization of animal wastes; energy use in irrigation, food systems, and at manmade water recreation areas; use of saline water in energy development, salt gradient solar panels. *Mailing Add:* Dept Mech Eng Utah State Univ Logan UT 84322-4130

BATY, RICHARD SAMUEL, OPTIMAL CONTROL, OPTIMAL FILTERING. *Current Pos:* CHIEF SCIENTIST WEAPON SYSTS MODELING & SIMULATION, BDM INT, INC, 83- *Personal Data:* b Lawrence, Kans, July 13, 37; m 63. *Educ:* Univ NMex, BS, 60; Air Force Inst Technol, MS, 66; Univ Calif Los Angeles, PhD(eng), 70. *Prof Exp:* Officer res & anal, USAF, 60-83. *Concurrent Pos:* Proj engr aerospace ground equip, USAF Manned Orbiting Lab, 67-68 & elec propulsion, Air Force Rocket Propulsion Lab, 71-73; study dir missile intercept effectiveness, Air Force Studies & Anal, 74-80; working group chmn, Mil Opers Res Soc, 78; prog mgr smart weapons, Defense Advan Res Projs Agency, 80-83; Nat Comt mem, Asst Secy Defense-C3I, 86-87. *Mem:* Sigma Xi. *Res:* Methods of implementing advanced missile guidance techniques; improving tracking of new generation penetrator systems. *Mailing Add:* 6620 Vista Del Monte NE Albuquerque NM 87109

BATZAR, KENNETH, FLUOROPOLYMER TECHNOLOGY. *Current Pos:* Sr res chemist, E I Du Pont De Nemours & Co, Newark, 66-77, res assoc, 77-86, mem staff, 80-96, SR RES ASSOC, 86-, DU PONT FLOUROPROD, CHESTNUT RUN PLAZA, 97- *Personal Data:* b Brooklyn, NY, May 30, 38; m 62; c 2. *Educ:* Brooklyn Col, BS, 59, MA, 62; City Univ New York, PhD(inorg chem), 66. *Mem:* Am Chem Soc; Sigma Xi. *Res:* Pigment technology; fluoropolymer technology; high performance coatings; thermally stable polymers. *Mailing Add:* Du Pont Flouroprod Chestnut Run Plaza B711 PO Box 80711 Wilmington DE 19880-0711

BATZEL, ROGER ELWOOD, NUCLEAR CHEMISTRY. *Current Pos:* RETIRED. *Personal Data:* b Idaho, Dec 1, 21; m 46; c 3. *Educ:* Univ Idaho, BS, 47; Univ Calif, PhD, 51. *Prof Exp:* Sr chemist, Calif Res & Develop Co, 51-53; from assoc dir to emer dir, Lawrence Livermore Lab, 53-88. *Mem:* Am Phys Soc. *Res:* High energy nuclear reactions; research and development. *Mailing Add:* 315 Bonanza Way Danville CA 94526

BATZER, HAROLD OTTO, ENTOMOLOGY. *Current Pos:* CONSULT, 88- *Personal Data:* b Gillett, Wis, Jan 22, 28; m 51; c 3. *Educ:* Univ Minn, BS, 52, MS, 55, PhD, 65. *Prof Exp:* Entomologist, NCent Forest Exp Sta, US Forest Serv, 54-64, insect ecologist, 64-70, prin insect ecologist, 70-83. *Concurrent Pos:* Leader subj group S2.06-8, Int Union Forest Res Orgns, 76-86; adj prof, Univ Minn, 76-; pest mgt consult, 83- *Mem:* Entom Soc Am; Soc Am Foresters; Int Soc Arboricult. *Res:* Forest insects, particularly the role of insects in natural forest ecosystems; completing emphasis on insects of aspen forests. *Mailing Add:* 791 Redwood Lane New Brighton MN 55112

BATZING, BARRY LEWIS, MICROBIOLOGY. *Current Pos:* from asst prof to assoc prof, 76-84, chmn, Dept Biol Sci, 91-94, PROF MICROBIOL, STATE UNIV NY COL, CORTLAND, 84- *Personal Data:* b Rochester, NY, May 6, 45; m 68; c 2. *Educ:* Cornell Univ, BS, 67; Pa State Univ, MS, 69, PhD(microbiol), 71. *Concurrent Pos:* Investr, Immunol Carcinogenesis Sect, Biol Div, Oak Ridge Nat Lab-Grad Sch Biomed Sci, Univ Tenn, 71-73; guest scientist, Environ Sci Div, Oak Ridge Nat Lab, 81-82. *Mem:* Am Soc Microbiol; Sigma Xi; AAAS. *Res:* Microbial physiology, ultrastructure, and ecology. *Mailing Add:* Dept Biol Sci State Univ NY Col Cortland PO Box 2000 Cortland NY 13045-0900

BATZLI, GEORGE OLIVER, POPULATION & COMMUNITY ECOLOGY, NUTRITIONAL ECOLOGY. *Current Pos:* from asst prof to assoc prof, 71-80, head dept ecol, 83-88 & 95-97, PROF, UNIV ILL, URBANA-CHAMPAIGN, 81- *Personal Data:* b Minneapolis, Minn, Sept 23, 36; m 59; c 2. *Educ:* Univ Minn, Minneapolis, BA, 59; San Francisco State Univ, MA, 65; Univ Calif, Berkeley, PhD(zool), 69. *Prof Exp:* Res assoc animal sci & nutrit, Univ Calif, Davis, 69-71; lectr biol, Univ Calif, Santa Cruz, 71. *Concurrent Pos:* NIH fel, 69-71; sr scientist, NSF, 76-78; res scientist, ecol div, Dept Sci Indust Res, NZ, 79; res fel, Univ Oslo, 82; ecol panel, NSF, 84-87; vis scholar, Univ Calif, Berkeley, 89. *Mem:* Fel AAAS; Int Asn Ecol; Ecol Soc Am; Am Soc Mammal; Brit Ecol Soc; Am Soc Naturalists. *Res:* Multifactorial approaches to population dynamics, habitat selection, and community organization of voles; herbivore-plant interactions, including the effects of plant quality on herbivores and the impact of herbivores on vegetation. *Mailing Add:* Dept Ecol Ethology & Evolution Univ Ill Shelford Vivarium 606 E Healy St Champaign IL 61820

BAU, HAIM HEINRICH, FLUID MECHANICS, HEAT TRANSFER. *Current Pos:* from asst prof to assoc prof, 80-92, PROF, UNIV PA, 92- *Personal Data:* b Krakow, Poland, Jan 2, 47; US citizen; m 82, Sheryl L Jones; c 2. *Educ:* Technion, Israel, BS, 69, MS, 73; Cornell Univ, PhD(mech eng), 80. *Honors & Awards:* R Teetor Award, Soc Automotive Engrs, 85. *Prof Exp:* Mem res & develop staff, Israeli Defense Force, 69-77. *Concurrent Pos:* NSF presidential young investr, 84; consult, Panametrics Inc, 86-, Hewlett-Packard, Avondale Div, 91-; vis prof, Royal Inst Technol, Sweden, 89. *Mem:* Fel Am Soc Mech Engrs; Soc Indust & Appl Math; Am Phys Soc. *Res:* Active control of convective flows; buoyancy induced flows-transitions, bifurcations and chaos; transport in micro-structures; flow and boiling in porous media; interaction between stress waves transmitted in solid waveguides and adjecent media; mesoscopic machines. *Mailing Add:* Univ Pa 111 Town Bldg-D3 Philadelphia PA 19104-6315. *Fax:* 215-573-2065; *E-Mail:* bau@eniac.seas.upenn.edu

BAU, ROBERT, INORGANIC CHEMISTRY. *Current Pos:* asst prof, 69-74, assoc prof, 74-77, PROF CHEM, UNIV SOUTHERN CALIF, 77- *Personal Data:* b Shanghai, China, Feb 10, 44; m 70; c 3. *Educ:* Univ Hong Kong, BSc, 63; Univ Calif, PhD(chem), 68. *Honors & Awards:* Alexander von Humboldt Sr US Scientist Prize, 85. *Prof Exp:* Res fel chem, Harvard Univ, 68-69. *Concurrent Pos:* Sloan Found res fel, 74-76; NIH res career develop award, 75-80. *Mem:* Am Chem Soc; The Chem Soc; Am Crystallog Asn. *Res:* Structural investigations of transition metal hydride compounds; neutron diffraction analysis of chiral organic compounds. *Mailing Add:* Dept Chem Univ Southern Calif Los Angeles CA 90089. *Fax:* 213-740-0930; *E-Mail:* bau@chem1.usc.edu

BAUBLITZ, MILLARD, JR, QUANTUM MECHANICS, PHYSICS OF SOLIDS AT HIGH PRESSURES. *Current Pos:* ASST PROF, DIV SCI & MATH, COL GEN STUDIES, BOSTON UNIV, 88- *Personal Data:* b Baltimore, Md, Dec 31, 52; m 81, Cathy A; c Paul & John. *Educ:* Univ Md, College Park, BS, 74; Cornell Univ, PhD(physics & mat sci), 82. *Prof Exp:* Res asst, Ctr Theoret Physics, Univ Md, College Park, 72-73; asst scientist, Goddard Space Flight Ctr, NASA, 73-75; teaching asst, Dept Mat Sci & Eng, Cornell Univ, 78, 79; scientist, Polaroid Corp Res Lab, 81-88. *Concurrent Pos:* Mem, Polaroid Microelectronics & Mat Labs, 81-88; vis res assoc physics, Col Liberal Arts, Boston Univ, 87-88. *Mem:* Life mem Am Phys Soc; Sigma Xi. *Res:* Major research interests have been concentrated in the fields of physics and materials science; the properties of solids under very high pressure; certain applied physics problems in imaging; the foundations of quantum mechanics. *Mailing Add:* Boston Univ 871 Commonwealth Ave Boston MA 02215

BAUCHWITZ, PETER S, ORGANIC CHEMISTRY, PHYSICAL & POLYMER CHEMISTRY. *Current Pos:* RETIRED. *Personal Data:* b Ger, 1920; US citizen; m 59; c 4. *Educ:* Univ Chicago, PhD, 56. *Prof Exp:* Develop engr, Govt Labs, Akron, 47-51; res chemist, E I du Pont de Nemours Co, Inc, 56-85. *Mem:* Am Chem Soc; Sigma Xi. *Res:* High polymers; analytical chemistry. *Mailing Add:* 23 Harlech Dr Wilmington DE 19807

BAUDE, FREDERIC JOHN, ANALYTICAL CHEMISTRY, ORGANIC CHEMISTRY. *Current Pos:* SR ANALYTICAL CHEMIST, H B FULLER CO, 80- *Personal Data:* b Milwaukee, Wis, Oct 13, 38; m 63; c 3. *Educ:* Univ Wis, BS, 60; Univ Minn, MS, 63, PhD(org chem), 65. *Prof Exp:* Sr res chemist anal chem, E I du Pont de Nemours & Co, 64-79; chemist anal chem, Iowa Testing Labs Inc, 79-80. *Mem:* Am Chem Soc. *Res:* General agrichemical analysis, especially pesticide residue analysis, environmental chemistry of pesticides, and animal and plant metabolism of pesticides. *Mailing Add:* H B Fuller Co 1200 Walters Blvd Vadnais Heights MN 55110-5146

BAUDER, JAMES WARREN, SOIL PHYSICS, AGRICULTURAL ENGINEERING. *Current Pos:* ASSOC PROF SOIL SCI, MONT STATE UNIV, 80- *Personal Data:* b Gloversville, NY, Apr 22, 47; m 73; c 3. *Educ:* Univ Mass, BS, 69, MS, 71; Utah State Univ, PhD(soil physics), 74. *Prof Exp:* Asst prof soil sci, NDak State Univ, 74-78 & Univ Minn, St Paul, 78-80. *Concurrent Pos:* Consult, Int Joint Comn, 75-77 & NDak Irrig Task Force, 76-78. *Mem:* Soil Sci Soc Am; Am Soc Agron. *Res:* Soil physical properties as they relate to tillage, soil conservation erosion; irrigation return flow, nitrogen leaching and transformation. *Mailing Add:* Dept Plant & Soil Sci Mont State Univ Bozeman MT 59717-0001

BAUE, ARTHUR EDWARD, SURGERY, CARDIOVASCULAR PHYSIOLOGY. *Current Pos:* assoc dean clin affairs, 85-86, vpres, Med Ctr, 86-90, PROF SURG, SCH MED, ST LOUIS UNIV, 85- *Personal Data:* b St Louis, Mo, Oct 7, 29; m 56, Rosemary Dysart; c Patricia (Nizen), Arthur II & William. *Educ:* Westminster Col, AB, 50; Harvard Univ, MD, 54; Am Bd Surg, dipl, 62; Am Bd Thoracic Surg, dipl, 63. *Hon Degrees:* MA, Yale Univ, 75. *Honors & Awards:* James D Rives Lectr, La State Univ, 82; John B Hodgen Lectr, St Louis Surg Soc, 82; Joshua E Jensen Lectr, 84; Charles Puestow Lectr, Loyola-Stritch Sch Med, 85; Arthur Dean Bevan Lectr, Chicago Surg Soc, Univ Chicago, 86; Walkoff Lectr, Case Western Res Univ, 87; Curtis P Artz Mem Lectr, Am Col Surgeons, Univ SC, 88. *Prof Exp:* From intern to chief resident, Mass Gen Hosp, 54-61; fel surg, Harvard Med Sch, 61-62; sr registr thoracic surg, Sch Med, Bristol Univ, 62; asst prof surg, Univ Mo, 62-64; from asst prof to assoc prof, Univ Pa, 64-68; Edison prof surg, Sch Med, Washington Univ, 67-75; Donald Guthrie prof & chmn, Dept Surg, Sch Med, Yale Univ, 75-85. *Concurrent Pos:* Markle scholar acad med, 63; consult, Nat Bd Med Examr, 63-74 & Vet Admin, 64-67; USPHS res career develop award, 65-66; surgeon-in-chief & dir, Jewish Hosp St Louis, 67-75; chief gen & thoracic surg, Yale-New Haven Hosp, 75-85, chief surg, 75-85; vis prof numerous hosps & univs, 75-; chief ed, Archives Surg, 77-88; guest prof, Ludwig Maximillian Univ, Ger, 81-82; lectr, Gordon Conf Multiple Organ Failure, 89. *Mem:* Am Col Surgeons; AMA; Asn Am Med Cols; Am Physiol Soc; Soc Univ Surgeons; AAAS; Shock Soc (pres, 82-83); Am Asn Surg Trauma (vpres, 86-87); Am Asn Thoracic Surg; Am Col Cardiol; Am Heart Asn; Soc Critical Care Med. *Res:* Thoracic and cardiovascular surgery. *Mailing Add:* St Louis Univ Hosp 3635 Vista Ave at Grand Blvd PO Box 15250 St Louis MO 63110. *Fax:* 314-577-8315

BAUER, AARON MATTHEW, ZOOLOGY. *Current Pos:* from asst prof to assoc prof, 88-95, PROF BIOL, VILLANOVA UNIV, 95- *Personal Data:* b New York, NY, June 27, 61; m 95, Monica M Frelow. *Educ:* Mich State Univ, BS, 82; Univ Calif, Berkeley, PhD(zool), 86. *Honors & Awards:* Emerald Award, Can, 95. *Prof Exp:* Univ postdoctoral fel, Univ Calgary, 87-88. *Concurrent Pos:* Marsh Grant Fund, Nat Acad Sci, 83; lectr functional & evolutionary vertebrate morphol, Univ Calif, Berkeley, 87; res assoc, Dept Vert Zool, US Nat Mus Natural Hist, 89-, Dept Herpet, Calif Acad Sci, 87-, Mus Natural Sci, La State Univ, 94-; Am Philos Soc grant, 93; Nat Geographic Soc Res Grant 94-96; Fulbright African regional res grant, 96. *Mem:* Am Inst Biol Sci; Am Soc Ichthyologists & Herpetologists; Brit Herpet Soc; Can Soc Zoologists; Sigma Xi; Australian Herpet Soc; Herpet Asn Africa; Soc Syst Zool; fel Zool Soc SAfrica; Herpetologists' League; Soc Study Amphibians & Reptiles. *Res:* Systematics and evolutionary morphology of geckos; historical zoogeography of southern hemisphere vertebrates; evolution of island herpetofaunas and tail autotomy; ecology of tropical reptiles and causes of extinction in reptiles; specialized integumentary derivatives of lizards; comparative anatomy and evolution of digital patterns in reptiles; history of herpetology; developmental ostcology of reptiles. *Mailing Add:* Biol Dept Villanova Univ Villanova PA 19085. *Fax:* 610-519-7863

BAUER, ARMAND, SOIL SCIENCE, CHEMISTRY. *Current Pos:* SOIL SCIENTIST, AGR RES SERV, USDA, 76- *Personal Data:* b Zeeland, NDak, Nov 29, 24; m 49; c 4. *Educ:* NDak State Univ, BS, 50, MS, 55; Colo State Univ, PhD(soil sci), 63. *Prof Exp:* Soil scientist, US Dept Agr Soil Conserv Serv, 50-54, NDak State Univ, 55-76. *Mem:* Soil Sci Soc Am; fel Soil Conserv Soc Am; Am Soc Agron. *Res:* Soil management and conservation; soil water management for dryland and irrigated agriculture; soil fertility and plant nutrition. *Mailing Add:* 1814 N 20th Bismarck ND 58501

BAUER, BEVERLY ANN, enzyme assisted synthesis, for more information see previous edition

BAUER, C(HARLES) L(LOYD), THIN FILMS, SURFACES & INTERFACES. *Current Pos:* from asst prof to assoc prof, 61-73, Dir, Ctr Joining Mat, 73-79, PROF METALL & MAT SCI, CARNEGIE-MELLON UNIV, 73- *Personal Data:* b Elizabeth, NJ, July 4, 33; m 59; c David W & Lisa A. *Educ:* Rensselaer Polytech Inst, B Met Eng, 55; Yale Univ, MEng, 59, DEng(metall), 61. *Hon Degrees:* DSc, Ecole Polytech Federale de Lausanne, Switz, 84. *Prof Exp:* Res engr, Int Nickel Co, 55; instr, New Haven Col, 58-60. *Concurrent Pos:* NSF res fel, FRG & Japan, 67-68; vis prof, Ecole Polytech Federale de Lausanne, Switz, 70-71, 72, 75 & 84, Univ Bordeaux, France, 91, Ecole Nat Polytech, St Martin d'Heres & SGS Thomson, France, 92, Forschungszentrum, Ger, 92; surv visits USSR, Nat Acad Sci, 73 & 79, vis scientist EGer & France, 83-84. *Mem:* Am Inst Mining, Metall & Petrol Engrs. *Res:* Configurations, thermodynamics and kinetics of lattice imperfections and their interactions, especially related to solid-state phase transformations; structure and properties of grain and interphase boundaries; preparation, characterization and properties of thin films and thin-film couples; tribology of thin-film media, especially for magnetic storage applications. *Mailing Add:* Dept Metall & Mat Carnegie-Mellon Univ 5000 Forbes Ave Pittsburgh PA 15213-3815. *Fax:* 412-268-7596

BAUER, CARL AUGUST, ASTRONOMY. *Current Pos:* RETIRED. *Personal Data:* b Marion Co, Kans, Nov 10, 16; m 41; c 3. *Educ:* Univ Minn, BA, 42; Univ Chicago, MS, 44; Harvard Univ, PhD(astron), 49. *Prof Exp:* Instr, US Army Air Force, Univ Minn, 42; res asst, Yerkes Observ, Univ Chicago, 42-44; instr physics & math, reserve officers training corps, NDak Agr Col, 44; instr astron, Ind Univ, 45; instr & res assoc, observ, Univ Mich, 47-50 & Harvard Univ, 51; asst prof astron, Pa State Univ, 51-56, assoc prof, 56-80. *Mem:* AAAS; Am Astron Soc; Am Meteorol Soc; Int Astron Union; Sigma Xi. *Res:* Stellar and solar spectroscopy; meteoritics; production of helium by cosmic radiation in meteorites and other developments of the parent planet hypothesis; origin of comets. *Mailing Add:* 444 E McCormick Ave State College PA 16801

BAUER, CARL EUGENE, PHOTOSYNTHESIS. *Current Pos:* Asst prof, 88-93, ASSOC PROF, DEPT BIOL, IND UNIV, 94- *Personal Data:* b St Paul, Minn, Feb 1, 56; m 78, Christine G; c Scott, Kevin, & Brian (deceased). *Educ:* Univ Minn, BS, 78; Wash State Univ, MS, 80; Univ Ill, Urbana, PhD(microbiol), 86. *Honors & Awards:* Res Career Develop Award, NIH, 93; Young Investr Award, Am Soc Photobiol, 94. *Concurrent Pos:* Vis scientist, E I Dupont de Nemours & Co, 86-88. *Mem:* Am Soc Microbiol; Genetics Soc Am; Am Soc Biochem & Molecular Biol; Int Soc Plant Molecular Biol. *Res:* Define tran-acting transcription factors involved in controlling photosynthesis gene expression; characterizing chlorophyll biosynthesis genes from bacteria, algae and plants. *Mailing Add:* Jordan Hall Bloomington IN 47405-6800. *Fax:* 812-855-6705; *E-Mail:* cbauer@sunflower.bio.indiana.edu

BAUER, CHARLES EDWARD, HIGH DENSITY HIGH PERFORMANCE ELECTRONICS PACKAGING, MANUFACTURING MATERIALS & PROCESSES. *Current Pos:* PRES, TECHLEAD CORP, 90- *Personal Data:* b Astoria, Ore; m; c 2. *Educ:* Stanford Univ, BS, 72; Ohio State Univ, MS, 75; Ore Grad Ctr, PhD(mat sci & eng), 80; Univ Portland, MBA, 88. *Prof Exp:* Res assoc, Stanford Ctr Mat Res, 74; mat sci engr III, Tektronix Inc, 78-80, eng mgr I, 80-82, eng mgr II, 82-85, mgr, Packaging Unit, 85-86, mgr, Packaging Opers, 86-88; dir, Res & Technol, MicroLithics Corp, 88-90. *Concurrent Pos:* Adj prof mech eng, Univ Portland, 81-82, adj asst prof bus admin, 85-89; vis prof mech eng, Fla Int Univ, 91; adj prof mech eng, elec & comput eng, Univ Colo, Boulder. *Mem:* Int Soc Hybrid Microelectronics; Am Soc Metals Int; Int Electronics Packaging Soc (vpres, 89-90). *Res:* Electronics packaging and interconnection; manufacturing materials and processes; real time manufacturing; process and quality control; design for manufacturability; high speed, high performance electronics; high density surface mount manufacturing and assembly; optoelectronics. *Mailing Add:* 31321 Island Dr Evergreen CO 80439. *E-Mail:* bauerc@boulder.colorado.edu

BAUER, CHRISTIAN SCHMID, JR, COMPUTER ENGINEERING, REAL-TIME SYSTEM SIMULATION. *Current Pos:* From asst prof to assoc prof indust eng, 70-91, PROF & CHMN, DEPT COMPUT ENG, UNIV CENT FLA, 91- *Personal Data:* b Biloxi, Miss, Sept 19, 44. *Educ:* Univ Fla, BSIE, 66, MSE, 67, PhD(civil eng), 75. *Mem:* Nat Soc Prof Engrs; Inst Elec & Electronics Engrs; Asn Comput Mach; AAAS; Inst Indust Engr. *Res:* Real-time systems simulation and modelling research; glass-cockpit displays for light aircraft. *Mailing Add:* Dept Comput Eng Univ Cent Fla Box 25000 Orlando FL 32816-0001

BAUER, DANIEL A, PHYSICS, DETECTOR INSTRUMENTATION. *Current Pos:* RES PHYSICIST, UNIV CALIF, SANTA BARBARA, 84- *Personal Data:* b Vancouver, Wash, Nov 1, 52; m 81, Karen S Stricker; c Rachel A & Jenny M. *Educ:* Lewis & Clark Col, BA, 74; Mich State Univ, PhD(physics), 81. *Prof Exp:* Res assoc, Fermi Nat Accelerator Lab, 79-81; res asst prof, Univ Pa, 81-84. *Mem:* Sigma Xi; Am Phys Soc. *Res:* Colliding beam physics; two-photon interactions; particle detector instrumentation; neutrine oscillations; search for dark matter. *Mailing Add:* SLAC MS 67 PO Box 4349 Stanford CA 94309. *E-Mail:* dan_bauer@slac.stanford.edu

BAUER, DAVID FRANCIS, MATHEMATICAL STATISTICS. *Current Pos:* asst prof, 74-78, ASSOC PROF MATH SCI, VA COMMONWEALTH UNIV, 78-, ASST CHMN, 90- *Personal Data:* b Lehighton, Pa, Apr 13, 40; c Lillian & Sarah. *Educ:* East Stroudsburg State Col, BS, 63; Ohio Univ, MS, 65; Univ Conn, PhD(math statist), 70. *Prof Exp:* Instr math, Denison Univ, 65-66; assoc mem tech staff, Traffic Studies Ctr, Bell Tel Labs, NJ, 66-67; asst prof statist & comput sci, Univ Del, 70-74. *Mem:* Sigma Xi; Math Asn Am; Am Statist Asn; Inst Math Statists. *Res:* Nonparametric methods and applications of statistics. *Mailing Add:* Dept Math Sci Va Commonwealth Univ Richmond VA 23284-2014. *Fax:* 804-828-8785; *E-Mail:* dbauer@gems.vcu.edu

BAUER, DAVID ROBERT, POLYMER DEGRADATION & STABILITY. *Current Pos:* STAFF SCIENTIST, FORD MOTOR CO, 77- *Personal Data:* b Portland, Ore, Aug 20, 49; m 71; c 2. *Educ:* Calif Inst Tech, BS, 71; Stanford Univ, PhD(chem physics), 75. *Prof Exp:* Post doctorate, Univ Ill, 75-77. *Concurrent Pos:* ed, Polymer Degradation & Stabilization. *Mem:* Am Chem Soc; Sigma Xi; Fedn Soc Coatings Technol. *Res:* Chemical and physical characterization of coatings, including crosslinking, corrosion performance, rheology, adhesion, and weathering with emphasis on photodegradation and stabilization. *Mailing Add:* 30102 Lyndon Livonia MI 48154-4465

BAUER, DENNIS PAUL, PHARMACEUTICAL ORGANIC CHEMISTRY, INORGANIC CHEMISTRY. *Current Pos:* DIR, MKT & BUS DEVELOP, SALSBURY CHEM, 95- *Personal Data:* b Pittsburgh, Pa, July 29, 48; m 71. *Educ:* Univ Cincinnati, BS, 71, PhD(org chem), 76; Univ Ga, MS, 73; La State Univ, MBA, 82. *Prof Exp:* Res assoc, Univ Calif, Berkeley, 76-77; from res chemist to sr res chemist, Ethyl Corp, 77-83, sr com develop chemist, 83-85, res supvr, 85-87, prod mgr, Pharmaceut Intermediates, 88-91, dir pharmaceut develop, 91-95. *Concurrent Pos:* NSF grant, Univ Cincinnati, 75-76 & Univ Calif, Berkeley, 76-77. *Mem:* AAAS; Am Chem Soc; The Chem Soc; NY Acad Sci. *Res:* Organic synthesis; drug intermediate synthesis; transition and rare earth organometallic chemistry; alpha-keto carboxylic chemistry; amine and amino acid chemistry; chemistry of thiophene compounds; surfactant chemistry; development of pharmaceutical fine chemicals. *Mailing Add:* Salsbury Chemicals 1205 11th St Charles City IA 50616. *Fax:* 504-388-7599

BAUER, DIETRICH CHARLES, IMMUNOLOGY. *Current Pos:* from asst prof to assoc prof microbiol, 61-69, PROF MICROBIOL & IMMUNOL, IND UNIV, INDIANAPOLIS, 69-, CHMN DEPT, 81- *Personal Data:* b Elgin, Ill, July 1, 31; m 54, Lois Reed. *Educ:* Univ Ill, BS, 54; Mich State Univ, MS, 57, PhD(microbiol), 59. *Prof Exp:* Res asst microbiol, Mich State Univ, 57-59; fel immunol, Case Western Res Univ, 59-61. *Mem:* AAAS; Am Soc Microbiol; Am Asn Immunol. *Res:* Virulence factors of Leptospirae; in vitro antibody synthesis; molecular forms of antibody; comparative reactivity of immunoglobulins; intracellular assembly of gamma globulin; suppression of immune response; immunological tolerance. *Mailing Add:* Dept Microbiol & Immunol Ind Univ Sch Med 635 Barnhill Dr MS 255 Indianapolis IN 46223. *Fax:* 317-274-4090

BAUER, DOUGLAS CLIFFORD, NUCLEAR ENGINEERING, MECHANICAL ENGINEERING. *Current Pos:* CONSULT, 88- *Personal Data:* b Boston, Mass, May 11, 38; m 62; c 2. *Educ:* Cornell Univ, BME, 61, MS, 67; Carnegie-Mellon Univ, PhD(nuclear eng), 72. *Prof Exp:* Tech asst nuclear & coal plants, Am Elec Power Serv Corp, 65; teaching & eng asst thermal power plants, Cornell Univ, 65-67; res assoc spatial nuclear reactor control, Carnegie-Mellon Univ, 71-72; sr engr nuclear thermal res, Bettis Atomic Power Lab, Westinghouse Elec Corp, 67-72; White House fel spec asst to Secy Dept Transp, 72-73; asst dir res & develop energy conserv, Dept Interior, Fed Energy Admin, 73-74; dir res planning, Fed Energy Admin, 74-75, assoc asst admin utility load mgt, 75-76; dir div nuclear & appln res, ERDA, 75-77; asst adminr utility systs regulation, Econ Regulatory Admin, Dept Energy, 77-80. *Mem:* Sigma Xi. *Res:* Utility load management; rate structures; power generation techniques including co-generation; nuclear research including gas cooled reactors; advanced isotope separation; space nuclear systems; economic, environmental assessments; transmission; distribution. *Mailing Add:* 8310 Weller Ave McLean VA 22102

BAUER, ERNEST, ATMOSPHERIC PHYSICS. *Current Pos:* CONSULT, NAVAL RES LAB, 96- *Personal Data:* b Vienna, Austria, Mar 24, 27; US citizen; m 59, Marion Correa; c Eric & Sharon. *Educ:* Cambridge Univ, BA, 47, PhD(theoret physics), 50. *Prof Exp:* Fel physics, Nat Res Coun Can, 50-52; res assoc, Inst Math Sci, NY Univ, 52-54, adj asst prof, Col Eng, 55-56, res assoc, 55-57, instr math, 53-54 & 56-57; asst prof physics, Univ NB, 54-55; prin scientist, Avco Res & Advan Develop, 57-59; staff scientist, Aeronutronic Div, Philco Corp, 59-65; res staff mem, Sci & Technol Div, Inst Defense Anal, 65-95. *Concurrent Pos:* Lectr, Cath Univ Am, 68-69 & City Col NY, 70-71; exhibitioner, scholar & prizeman, Selwyn Col, Cambridge Univ; consult, NASA, 79-81; mem, Air Pollution Indicators Task Force, Great Lakes Sci Adv Bd & US-Can Int Joint Comn, 85-86. *Mem:* Fel Am Phys Soc; Am Geophys Union. *Res:* Atmospheric sciences; stratospheric and tropospheric pollution; cloud and aerosol physics; remote sensing; ionospheric perturbations; nuclear weapons effects. *Mailing Add:* 8109 Fenway Rd Bethesda MD 20817-2762. *Fax:* 703-578-2877; *E-Mail:* ernestbaue@aol.com

BAUER, ERNST GEORG, SURFACE PHYSICS, THIN FILM PHYSICS. *Current Pos:* DISTINGUISHED RES PROF, ARIZ STATE UNIV, TEMPE, 96- *Personal Data:* b Schoenberg, Ger, Feb 27, 28; US citizen; m 55, 83, Anastassia Pavloyska; c Susanne, Michael & Peter. *Educ:* Univ Munich, MS, 53, PhD(physics), 55. *Honors & Awards:* Gaede Prize, Ger Vacuum Soc,

88; Welch Award, Am Vacuum Soc, 92; Niedersachsen Prize, Ger, 94. *Prof Exp:* Asst, Phys Inst, Univ Munich, 54-58; br head, Naval Weapons Ctr, China Lake, Calif, 58-69; prof & dir, Phys Inst Clausthal Tech Univ, 69-96. *Mem:* Fel Am Phys Soc; fel Am Vacuum Soc; Mat Res Soc; Ger Electron Microscope Soc. *Res:* Surface science; electron and crystal physics; surface electron microscopy; invention of LEEM (low energy electron microscope); author of book: Elehtwen beupump, 58 (German); author and co-author, approximately 300 papers. *Mailing Add:* Dept Physics Ariz State Univ Tempe AZ 85287-1504

BAUER, EUGENE ANDREW, BIOLOGY, DERMATOLOGY. *Current Pos:* prof & chmn dermat, 88-95, DEAN, SCH MED, STANFORD UNIV, 95- *Personal Data:* b Mattoon, Ill, Jun 17, 42; m 66; c 4. *Educ:* Northwestern Univ, BS & MD, 67, Nat Bd Med Examrs, dipl, 68, Am Bd Dermat, dipl, 73. *Honors & Awards:* Montagna Award, Soc Invest Dermat, 85; Sulzberger Award, Am Acad Dermat, 89. *Prof Exp:* Instr dermat, Wash Univ Sch Med, 71-72, from asst prof to prof, 74-88. *Concurrent Pos:* Bd dirs, Soc Invest Dermat, 81-86; dir, DEBRA Ctr Res & Ther Epidermolysis Bullosa, 82-88; mem, NIH, 85-88; chmn study sect, Arth Musullosk Skin, 85-88; chmn study sect, Arth Musullosk Skin, 85-88; mem bd sci counselors, Div Cancer Biol, Nat Cancer Inst, 89-93. *Mem:* Inst Med-Nat Acad Sci; Am Acad Dermat; Am Fedn Clin Res; Am Soc Clin Invest; Asn Am Physicians; Am Dermat Asn. *Res:* Collagen biochemistry; degredation of extracellular matrix; collagenases and role in normal and pathologic remodelling in connective tissue; epidermolysis bullosa; tumor invasion. *Mailing Add:* Off Dean Suite M-121 Stanford Univ Sch Med Stanford CA 94305

BAUER, FRANCES BRAND, APPLIED MATHEMATICS. *Current Pos:* res scientist, 61-80, SR RES SCIENTIST ELASTICITY, FLUID DYNAMICS & COMPUT, COURANT INST MATH SCI, NY UNIV, 80- *Personal Data:* b New York, NY, July 5, 23; wid. *Educ:* Brooklyn Col, AB, 43; Brown Univ, MS, 45, PhD(appl math), 48. *Honors & Awards:* Pub Serv Award, NASA, 76, Cert Recognition, 77 & 80. *Prof Exp:* Res assoc appl math, Brown Univ, 45-48; res assoc aero eng structures, Polytech Inst Brooklyn, 49-50; sr mathematician, Reeves Instrument Corp, 50-51 & 51-61; mathematician, Bur Stand, Am Univ, 51-52. *Concurrent Pos:* NASA-Ames Stanford fac fel, 89. *Mem:* Am Math Soc; Sigma Xi. *Res:* Transonic flow; supercritical wing sections I; supercritical wing sections II & III; computational method in plasma physics; magnetohydrodynamic equilibrium and stability of stellarators; the beta equilibrium, stability, and transport codes. *Mailing Add:* 200 East End Ave New York NY 10128. *Fax:* 212-995-4121, 995-4120; *E-Mail:* bauer@scires.acf.nyu.edu

BAUER, FREDERICK WILLIAM, ORGANIC CHEMISTRY, RESEARCH ADMINISTRATION. *Current Pos:* group leader, Cent Res Labs, Allied Corp, 60-62, asst dir res admin to dir res admin, 62-69, asst mgr employee rels, 69-80, MGR ENVIRON SERV, CORP TECHNOL, ALLIED CORP, 80- *Personal Data:* b Wakefield, RI, Oct 22, 22; m 54; c 5. *Educ:* Washington & Lee Univ, BS, 43; Princeton Univ, MA, 50, PhD(org chem), 52. *Prof Exp:* Jr asst res chemist, Tenn Eastman Corp, 43-44, asst res chemist, 46-47; technician, Textile Res Inst, 47, res chemist, 51-52; res chemist, Gen Labs, US Rubber Co, 52-54, org chemist, Textile Div, 54-56 & Res Ctr, 56-60. *Mem:* Am Chem Soc; Sigma Xi. *Res:* Structure of cellulose; rubber and polymers; textile finishing and chemical modifications; scientific personnel administration; polymer characterization; industrial hygiene, safety; product safety; hazardous waste disposal. *Mailing Add:* 19 Geneva Ct Packanack Lake Wayne NJ 07470-4203

BAUER, GUSTAV ERIC, ANATOMY. *Current Pos:* from instr to assoc prof, 63-76, PROF ANAT, UNIV MINN, MINNEAPOLIS, 76- *Personal Data:* b New York, NY, Jan 26, 35; m 71, Jean M Gale; c 5. *Educ:* Queens Col, NY, BS, 57; Western Res Univ, MA, 59; Univ Minn, PhD(anat), 63. *Prof Exp:* Jr chemist, Sperry-Rand Corp, 57. *Concurrent Pos:* USPHS fel, 65-66; mem corp, Marine Biol Lab, Woods Hole. *Mem:* Am Diabetes Asn; Am Soc Cell Biologists; Am Asn Anatomists. *Res:* Topographic organization, growth and regeneration of pancreatic islets of Langerhans; insulin metabolism and clearance by major salivary glands. *Mailing Add:* Dept Cell Biol & Neuroanat Univ Minn 321 Church St SE Minneapolis MN 55455. *Fax:* 612-624-8118; *E-Mail:* bauer@lenti.med.unm.edu

BAUER, HEINZ, PATHOLOGY. *Current Pos:* clin assoc prof to assoc prof, 61-65, PROF PATH, SCH MED, GEORGETOWN UNIV, 65- *Personal Data:* b Vienna, Austria, Nov 28, 14; US citizen; m 39; c 2. *Educ:* Univ Vienna, 33-38; Emory Univ, MD, 51. *Prof Exp:* Nat Cancer Inst trainee, Emory Univ, 54-56, from assoc to assoc prof path, 56-61. *Concurrent Pos:* Res assoc, Mt Sinai Hosp, NY, 61-64. *Mem:* Fel Col Am Path; Am Asn Path & Bact; NY Acad Sci; Am Soc Exp Path; Int Acad Path. *Res:* Infectious diseases; immunopathology; germ-free animal research; rheumatology. *Mailing Add:* 4701 Willard Ave Apt 1510 Chevy Chase MD 20815-4628

BAUER, HENRY HERMANN, CHEMISTRY. *Current Pos:* dean, Col Arts & Sci, 78-86, PROF CHEM & SCI STUDIES, VA POLYTECH INST & STATE UNIV, 86- *Personal Data:* b Vienna, Austria, Nov 16, 31; c Helen & Judith A. *Educ:* Univ Sydney, BSc, 52, MSc, 53, PhD(chem), 56. *Honors & Awards:* Sydney S Negus Lectr, Va Acad Sci, 84. *Prof Exp:* Res assoc chem, Univ Mich, 56-58; from lectr to sr lectr, Univ Sydney, 58-66; from assoc prof to prof, Univ Ky, 66-78. *Concurrent Pos:* Fulbright travel award, 56-58; vis lectr chem & res scientist, Univ Mich, 65-66; vis prof, Univ Southampton, 72-73 & Japan Soc Promotion Sci, 74. *Mem:* Soc Sci Explor. *Res:* Case studies of controversies; distinguishing science and pseudo-science; interactions of science and society. *Mailing Add:* 234 Lane Hall Va Polytech Inst & State Univ Blacksburg VA 24061-0227. *Fax:* 540-231-7013; *E-Mail:* hhbauer@rt.edu

BAUER, HENRY RAYMOND, III, COMPUTER SCIENCE, COMPILER CONSTRUCTION. *Current Pos:* From asst prof to assoc prof, 73-84, chmn, 78-86, PROF COMPUT SCI, UNIV WYO, 84-, CHMN, 93- *Personal Data:* b Meriden, Conn, Jan 16, 43; m 76, Penelope Hanchey. *Educ:* Brown Univ, ScB, 65; Stanford Univ, MS, 67, PhD(comput sci), 73. *Concurrent Pos:* Team chmn, CSAB, 85-92 & 93- *Mem:* Asn Comput Mach; Inst Elec & Electronics Engrs; Comput Soc. *Res:* Programming languages; compilers; parallel computation and compilers. *Mailing Add:* Dept Comput Sci Univ Wyo Box 3682 Laramie WY 82071. *Fax:* 307-766-4036; *E-Mail:* bauer@uwyo.edu

BAUER, JAMES H(ARRY), METALLURGICAL ENGINEERING. *Current Pos:* RETIRED. *Personal Data:* b Valley City, Ohio, June 5, 22; m 48, Grace Jones; c 1. *Educ:* Ohio State Univ, BMetE, 51. *Honors & Awards:* Award of Merit, Am Soc Testing & Mat. *Prof Exp:* Metallurgist, Southwind Div, Stewart-Warner Corp, 51-53, chief metallurgist, 53-56; chief metallurgist, Ohio Injector Co, 56-61, mgr mat control, 61-63; chief metall chemist, Develop & Eng Dept, Am Stand Inc, 63-67, mgr stand & reliability, 67-71, mgr codes dept, 71-88. *Mem:* Am Soc Testing & Mat. *Res:* Codes, standards and federal regulatory agency specifications in all phases of plumbing standards. *Mailing Add:* 3410 Country Club Dr Medina OH 44256-8713. *Fax:* 330-723-9934

BAUER, JERE MARKLEE, MEDICINE. *Current Pos:* from asst resident to instr internal med, 42-46, instr & res asst endocrinol & metab, 46-48, from asst prof to assoc prof, 48-72, PROF INTERNAL MED, UNIV MICH, ANN ARBOR, 72- *Personal Data:* b Ft Worth, Tex, Apr 24, 15; m 61; c 2. *Educ:* Univ Tex, MD, 41, BA, 44. *Prof Exp:* Intern, Med Br, Univ Tex, 41-42. *Mem:* AAAS; AMA; fel Am Col Physicians; Am Diabetes Asn; Am Heart Asn. *Res:* Endocrine and metabolic diseases; metabolic aspects of cancer. *Mailing Add:* 326 Juniper Lane Ann Arbor MI 48105-1051

BAUER, JOEL, GASTROINTESTINAL SURGEON, LAPAROSCOPY. *Current Pos:* From asst prof to assoc prof, 75-89, PROF SURG, MT SINAI SCH MED, 90- *Personal Data:* m, b New York, NY, Aug 16, 42; c 2. *Educ:* Univ Vt, BS, 63; NY Univ, MD 67. *Prof Exp:* Residency surg, Mu Sinai Hosp, 67-73; chief surg, Rickenbacher AFB, 73-75. *Mem:* Am Col Surgeons; Soc Surg Alimentary Tract; Am col Gastroenterol; Am Soc Colorectal Surg; NY Acad Med; Asn Acad Surg. *Res:* Clinical research on topics relating to gastrointestinal surgery and particularly inflammatory bowel disease; clinical and animal studies on use of prosthetic materials for abdominal hernia repair. *Mailing Add:* 25 E 69th St New York NY 10021-4925

BAUER, JOHN HARRY, NEPHROLOGY, HYPERTENSION. *Current Pos:* from asst prof to assoc prof, Univ Mo, 75-87, dir, Clin Res unit, 91-95, assoc chmn, Dept Internal Med, 93-95, PROF MED NEPHROLOGY, MED CTR, UNIV MO-COLUMBIA, 87-, ASSOC DEAN, VET AFFAIRS, 95-; CHIEF OF STAFF, HARRY S TRUMAN MEM VET HOSP, 95- *Personal Data:* b Philadelphia, Pa, Apr 15, 43; m 66; c 2. *Educ:* State Univ NY Buffalo, BA, 65; Jefferson Med Col, MD, 69. *Prof Exp:* Intern, Med Ctr, Ind Univ, 69-70, resident, 70-71; med officer, Lemoore Naval Hosp, Calif, 71-73; fel renal med, Med Ctr, Ind Univ, 73-74 & hypertension, 74-75. *Concurrent Pos:* Staff physician, H S Truman Mem Vet Hosp, 75-85, chief med serv, 93-95; res assoc, Vet Admin, 79-81. *Mem:* Am Soc Hypertension; Am Soc Nephrology; Am Col Physicians; Am Heart Asn; Cent Soc Clin Res; Sigma Xi. *Res:* Hypertension; renal function; drug effects on renal function, body fluid composition and renin-aldosterone system; diabetes and kidney disease; Angiotensin II. *Mailing Add:* Dept Med N 425 Sch Med Univ Mo Columbia MO 65212

BAUER, KURT W, CITY PLANNING & MUNICIPAL ENGINEERING. *Current Pos:* asst dir, 61-62, EXEC DIR, SOUTHEASTERN WIS REGIONAL PLANNING COMN, 62- *Personal Data:* b Milwaukee, Wis, Aug 25, 29; m 55, Arlene V English; c Elizabeth, Caroline & Kurt K. *Educ:* Marquette Univ, BS, 51; Univ Wis, MS, 55, PhD(civil eng), 61. *Honors & Awards:* Harland Bartholomew Award, Am Soc Civil Engrs, 70, Surveying & Mapping Award, 94; Pub Serv Award, US Dept Transp, Fed Hwy Admin, 77. *Prof Exp:* City planner, South Milwaukee, Wis, 53-55; instr civil eng, Univ Wis, 55-56 & 60-61; assoc engr, H C Webster & Sons Consult Engr, 56-59; chief current city planning, Madison, 59-60. *Concurrent Pos:* Lectr civil eng, Marquette Univ, 61-62, adj prof, 68-; lectr, Univ Wis, 62-64; consult, Nat Water Comn, 70-73 & US Housing & Urban Develop & US Dept Interior, 89-90; mem exec comt, Transp Res Bd, 75-79; survr, Milwaukee Co, 84- *Mem:* Am Soc Civil Engrs; Am Inst Cert Planners; hon mem Soil Conserv Soc Am; Am Cong Surveying & Mapping. *Res:* Municipal engineering; city and regional planning. *Mailing Add:* 2515 Broken Hill Ct Waukesha WI 53188. *Fax:* 414-547-1103

BAUER, LUDWIG, SYNTHETIC ORGANIC MEDICINAL CHEMISTRY. *Current Pos:* from asst prof to assoc prof, 55-65, PROF CHEM, UNIV ILL, CHICAGO, 65- *Personal Data:* b Ger, July 27, 26; nat US; m 57, Ella Bamberger; c Phillip M & Alan J. *Educ:* Univ Sydney, BSc, 49, MSc, 50; Northwestern Univ, PhD(chem), 52. *Prof Exp:* Res assoc, Harvard Univ, 52-53, Columbia Univ, 53 & Univ Sydney, 53-54; res chemist, Elkin Chem Co, 55. *Mem:* Am Chem Soc; Int Soc Heterocyclic Chem. *Res:* Synthesis of potential medicinal agents; fundamental chemistry of aromatic heterocyclic compounds. *Mailing Add:* Med Chem M/C 781 Col Pharm Univ Ill Chicago 833 S Wood St Chicago IL 60612-7231

BAUER, MARVIN E, REMOTE SENSING. *Current Pos:* dir, Remote Sensing Lab, 83-91, PROF, UNIV MINN, 83- *Personal Data:* b Valparaiso, Ind, July 24, 43; m 69, Jean Warner. *Educ:* Purdue Univ, BSA, 65, MS, 67; Univ Ill, PhD(agron), 70. *Honors & Awards:* Alan Gordon Mem Award, Am Soc Photogram & Remote Sensing, 95. *Prof Exp:* Res agronomist, Dept Agron & prog leader, Crop Inventory Res, Lab Appln Remote Sensing, Purdue Univ, 70-83. *Concurrent Pos:* Ed, Remote Sensing Environ J, 80- *Mem:* Am Soc Agron; Am Soc Photogram & Remote Sensing; Inst Elec & Electronics Engrs; Sigma Xi; Int Soc Remote Sensing; Soc Am Foresters. *Res:* Remote sensing of agricultural and natural resources; applications of satellite remote sensing and digital image processing to resource inventory and analysis. *Mailing Add:* Forest Resources Univ Minn 115 Green Hall 1530 Cleveland Ave St Paul MN 55108-6112. *Fax:* 612-625-5212; *E-Mail:* mbauer@forestry.umn.edu

BAUER, MICHAEL ANTHONY, DISTRIBUTED COMPUTING, SOFTWARE ENGINEERING. *Current Pos:* ASSOC PROF COMPUT SCI, UNIV WESTERN ONT, 75-, CHMN DEPT, 91- *Personal Data:* b Dayton, Ohio, Feb 18, 48; m 75; c Andrea & Michelle. *Educ:* Univ Dayton, BSc, 70; Univ Toronto, MSc, 71, PhD(computer sci), 78. *Prof Exp:* Researcher artificial intel, Edinburgh Univ, 74-75. *Concurrent Pos:* Consult, Geac Computers Int, 84-88; mem bd, Can Info Processing Soc, 84-88 & Asn Comput Mach, 89-; adv, Int Bus Mach Ctr Advan Studies, 90-91. *Mem:* Asn Comput Mach; Inst Elec & Electronics Engrs. *Res:* Distributed computing, especially distributed algorithms, correctness, languages for distributed computing, verification; software engineering, including methodologies, formal specifications, development environments. *Mailing Add:* Dept Comput Sci Univ Western Ont London ON N6A 5B7 Can. *Fax:* 519-661-3515; *E-Mail:* bauer@csd.uwo.ca

BAUER, PENELOPE HANCHEY, PHYTOPATHOLOGY, CYTOLOGY. *Current Pos:* asst prof, 69-74, assoc prof, 74-80, PROF BOT & PLANT PATH, COLO STATE UNIV, 81- *Personal Data:* b Oberlin, La, Apr 12, 42; m 76, Henry R III. *Educ:* McNeese State Col, BS, 64; La State Univ, MS, 66; Univ Ky, PhD(plant path), 68. *Prof Exp:* Res asst plant path, La State Univ, 64-67; res asst, Univ Ky, 67-68. *Concurrent Pos:* Vis scientist, Univ Calif, Berkeley, 82 & 91. *Mem:* Am Phytopath Soc; Bot Soc Am; Am Soc Plant Physiologists. *Res:* Physiology and ultrastructure of host-plant parasite relations. *Mailing Add:* Dept Plant Path Colo State Univ Ft Collins CO 80523-0001

BAUER, PETER, ELECTRICAL & MECHANICAL ENGINEERING. *Current Pos:* CONSULT & PRES, ACT CO, MD, 76- *Personal Data:* b Reichenberg, Czech, Mar 2, 32; wid; c 2. *Educ:* Fed Tech Col, Vienna, MS(elec eng) & MS(mech eng), 53. *Prof Exp:* Develop engr, Laurence Scott & Electromotors Ltd, Eng, 53-54; sr engr, Pye Ltd, 54-56, dept mgr, 56-60; dept supvr, Univac Div, Remington Rand Group, Sperry Rand Corp, Pa, 60-62; sr eng proj mgr, 62-63, prin engr, 63-69, chief staff consult, 69-71, chief scientist, 71-76. *Mem:* Fel Brit Interplanetary Soc; Asn Austrian Eng & Archit. *Res:* Variable speed alternating current commutator machines; television transmission; digital information recording; fluidics and pure fluid systems. *Mailing Add:* Rte 1 Box 804 Bras d'Or NS B0C 1B0 Can

BAUER, RAYMOND THOMAS, MARINE BIOLOGY, MARINE INVERTEBRATE ZOOLOGY. *Current Pos:* res assoc prof, 86-94, PROF, DEPT BIOL, UNIV SOUTHWESTERN LA, 94- *Personal Data:* b Kansas City, Mo, July 29, 47; m, Lydia Rodriguez. *Educ:* Univ Mo, Kansas City, BS, 69; Univ Calif, San Diego, PhD(marine biol), 76. *Prof Exp:* Lectr invert zool, Calif Polytech State Univ, 76-78; res fel, Nat Mus Natural Hist, Smithsonian Inst, 80-81; from asst prof to assoc prof marine biol, Univ PR, Rio Piedras, 81-85. *Mem:* AAAS; Crustacean Soc; Am Soc Zoologists; Am Micros Soc; Animal Behav Soc; Sigma Xi. *Res:* Biology and ecology of marine invertebrates, especially the Crustacea; numerous articles in scientific journals. *Mailing Add:* Dept Biol Univ Southern La Lafayette LA 70504-2451. *Fax:* 318-231-5834; *E-Mail:* rtbauer@usl.edu

BAUER, RICHARD G, POLYMER CHEMISTRY, ORGANIC CHEMISTRY. *Current Pos:* PRES & OWNER, RGB CONSULT SERV, 96- *Personal Data:* b Kent, Ohio, Dec 9, 35; m 58; c 3. *Educ:* Kent State Univ, BS, 56; Univ Akron, MS, 60, PhD(polymer sci), 66. *Prof Exp:* Res chemist, Gen Tire & Rubber Co, 56-60 & Air Reduction Chem & Carbide Co, 61-63; sect head, Goodyear Tire & Rubber Co, Akron, 63-96. *Mem:* AAAS; Am Chem Soc; Soc Petrol Engrs; Soc Plastics Engrs. *Res:* Preparation and characterization of polymers and organic chemicals related to the polymer field; granted 38 US patents. *Mailing Add:* 1624 Chadwick Dr Kent OH 44240-4410. *Fax:* 330-677-8602; *E-Mail:* rbauer4593@aol.com

BAUER, RICHARD M, TECHNICAL MANAGEMENT. *Current Pos:* CONSULT, 90- *Personal Data:* b Appleton, Wis, Apr 30, 28; m 50; c 5. *Educ:* Lawrence Col, BS, 53. *Prof Exp:* From jr process engr to sr process engr, Marathon Corp, Am Can Co, Wis, 55-58, sr process engr, Marathon Div, 58-60, group leader, 60-65, mgr indust prod develop, 65-67, mgr converting paperboard & spec prod res & develop, 67-68, assoc dir, 68-70, lab dir consumer prod, 70-78, managing dir dry forming tech, 78-82; lab dir Consumer Prods Res & Develop, James River Corp, 82-84; vpres, Neenah Tech Ctr, 84-90. *Concurrent Pos:* Marathon Div consult, Glamakote carton process to US & Europ countries, 61-80. *Res:* Research and development in the field of wood fiber treatments to manufacture soft, absorbent, bulky substrates from wet forming and dry forming processes. *Mailing Add:* 405 South Way Ct Salem SC 29676. *Fax:* 864-944-2385

BAUER, ROBERT, CLINICAL BIOCHEMISTRY. *Current Pos:* assoc res biochemist, 61-71, res scientist, 71-79, SR RES SCIENTIST, DIAG DIV, MILES, INC, 79-, STAFF SCIENTIST, 84- *Personal Data:* b Grand Rapids, Mich, May 5, 26; m 51; c 3. *Educ:* Western Mich Univ, BS, 50, MS, 62. *Prof Exp:* Chemist, Socony Mobil Oil Co, Inc, 51-55; plastics chemist, Dow Chem Co, 55-58; chemist, Upjohn Co, 58-60. *Mem:* AAAS; Am Chem Soc. *Res:* Diagnostic aid and analytical aids for industry. *Mailing Add:* 56180 County Rd 21 Bristol IN 46507-9513

BAUER, ROBERT FOREST, PETROLEUM ENGINEERING, OFFSHORE DRILLING. *Current Pos:* OWNER, BAUER LAND & CATTLE CO, 83- *Personal Data:* b Declo, Idaho, Jan 10, 18; m 40; c 4. *Educ:* Southern Calif Univ, BS, 42. *Prof Exp:* Field res engr, Union Oil Co, Calif, 42-48, prod foreman, 48-50, dist prod foreman, 50-52, chief field engr, 52-54; mgr, Offshore Group, Union, Continental, Shell & Super Oil Co, 54-58; pres, Global Marine Explor Co, 58-66, chmn, Global Marine, Inc, 66-83. *Concurrent Pos:* Mem, UN Econ Comn Asia & Far East, 69; distinguished lectr marine affairs, Ore State Univ, 69. *Mem:* Nat Acad Eng; Am Inst Mining, Metall & Petrol Engrs; Am Petrol Inst. *Res:* Salt water based rotary mud; electromagnetic methods of geophysical exploration; design and fabrication of diving bell for gravimetric surveying of submerged land; extraction of bitumen from bituminous sands; stimulation of well production with salt solutions; use of surfactants to improve operating efficiency of producing wells; technology of drilling from a floating vessel. *Mailing Add:* 8570 Enramada Whittier CA 90605

BAUER, ROBERT STEVEN, EXPERIMENTAL SOLID STATE PHYSICS & CHEMISTRY. *Current Pos:* mem res staff surface & bulk electronic properties of solids, 70-79, SR SCIENTIST, XEROX PALO ALTO RES CTR, 79- *Personal Data:* b Brooklyn, NY, Dec 8, 44; m 67; c 4. *Educ:* Rensselaer Polytech Inst, BEE, 66; Stanford Univ, MS, 67, PhD(elec eng), 71. *Concurrent Pos:* Mem, Tech Comt, Annual Conf on Physics & Chem of Semiconductor Interfaces, 77-; vchmn, Users Orgn, Systs Simulation Res Lab, 80, chmn, 81, chmn, Users Meeting, 79 & 80; chmn, Sixth Annual Conf on Physics of Compound Semiconductor Interfaces, 79; mem tech comt, Int Conf on Physics of Metal-Oxide Semiconductor Insulators, 80; mem adv panel, Dept Defense Workshop on Submicron Devices, 81 & NSF Ctr for Res in Surface Sci, 81; dir, Second Int Union Pure & Appl Physics/UNESCO Semiconductor Symp, 82. *Mem:* Am Phys Soc; Am Vacuum Soc; Inst Elec & Electronics Engrs; Sigma Xi. *Res:* Photoelectron and modulated optical spectroscopy studies of surface, interface and bulk electronic states of crystalline and amorphous semiconductors, insulators and ionic conductors; use of synchrotron radiation for probing properties of solids; chemical bonding, semiconductor interface formation, (schottky barriers and heterostructures) oxidation, reaction, interdiffusion, impurities/defects, and electron/lattice effects; molecular beam epitaxy. *Mailing Add:* Xerox Park 3333 Coyote Hill Rd Palo Alto CA 94304

BAUER, ROGER DUANE, BIOCHEMISTRY. *Current Pos:* From asst prof to assoc prof chem, Calif State Univ, Long Beach, 59-69, chmn dept, 66-75, dean, Sch Natural Sci, 75-88, prof, 69-93, EMER PROF CHEM, CALIF STATE UNIV, LONG BEACH, 93- *Personal Data:* b Oxford, Nebr, Jan 17, 32; m 56; c 3. *Educ:* Beloit Col, BS, 53; Kans State Univ, MS, 57, PhD(biochem), 60. *Concurrent Pos:* Am Coun Educ fel, 70-71. *Mem:* Am Chem Soc; Radiation Res Soc; Sigma Xi. *Res:* Metabolism and structure of nucleoproteins; science education. *Mailing Add:* Sch Natural Sci Calif State Univ Long Beach CA 90840

BAUER, RONALD SHERMAN, ORGANIC CHEMISTRY. *Current Pos:* CHEMIST, SHELL DEVELOP CO, 58- *Personal Data:* b Huntington Park, Calif, Feb 24, 32; m 58; c 1. *Educ:* Univ Calif, BS, 54, PhD(chem), 58. *Mem:* Am Chem Soc. *Res:* Synthesis and polymerization of halogenated allenes; polymerization of epoxides and related materials; process and product development on weatherable and high solids epoxy resins and coating systems. *Mailing Add:* 5427 Crown Colony Houston TX 77069-3309

BAUER, RUDOLF WILHELM, NUCLEAR PHYSICS, ATOMIC & MOLECULAR PHYSICS. *Current Pos:* div leader, 76-83, PHYSICIST, LAWRENCE LIVERMORE LAB, UNIV CALIF, 64-, DEP DIV LEADER, 83- *Personal Data:* b Rothenburg, Ger, Nov 28, 28; US citizen; m 58, Margret Baer; c Peter, Andrew & Barbara. *Educ:* Amherst Col, BA, 52; Mass Inst Technol, PhD(physics), 59. *Prof Exp:* From instr to asst prof physics, Mass Inst Technol, 59-64. *Mem:* Am Phys Soc; Inst Elec & Electronics Engrs. *Res:* Nuclear physics; atomic and molecular physics; gamma and x-ray spectroscopy; neutron physics; plasma physics; diagnostics; accelerators; detectors. *Mailing Add:* L-056 Lawrence Livermore Lab Livermore CA 94550. *Fax:* 510-423-8086; *E-Mail:* bauer2@llnl.gov

BAUER, SIMON HARVEY, CHEMICAL KINETICS, STRUCTURAL CHEMISTRY. *Current Pos:* from instr to prof, 39-77, EMER PROF CHEM, CORNELL UNIV, 77- *Personal Data:* b Kaunas, Lithuania, Oct 12, 11; nat US; m 38, Miriam Rosoff; c Frederick, Deborah & Ross. *Educ:* Univ Chicago, BS, 31, PhD(chem), 35. *Honors & Awards:* Alexander von Humboldt Award, 79. *Prof Exp:* Fel, Calif Inst Technol, 35-37; instr fuel technol, Pa State Col, 37-39. *Concurrent Pos:* Consult, Los Alamos Nat Labs & Argonne Nat Lab; Guggenheim Mem Found fel, 49; NSF sr fel, 62-63; adj prof, Inst Molecular Sci, Japan, 83. *Mem:* Fel AAAS; fel Am Phys Soc; fel Am Inst Chemists; Fedn Am Scientists; Am Chem Soc. *Res:* Electron diffraction; compounds of boron; molecular spectra; rates of energy transfer processes and of very rapid reactions as studied in shock tubes; chemical lasers; laser induced chemical conversions; structural studies with x-ray absorption fine structure; combustion mechanisms of hydrocarbons and boron hydrides. *Mailing Add:* Dept Chem Cornell Univ Ithaca NY 14853. *Fax:* 607-255-4137

BAUER, STEWART THOMAS, organic chemistry; deceased, see previous edition for last biography

BAUER, VICTOR JOHN, PHARMACEUTICAL. *Current Pos:* dir chem res, Hoechst-Roussel Pharmaceut Inc, 71-74, vpres oper, 74-80, exec vpres & chief oper officer, 80-87, pres, 89-92, EXEC VPRES, RES & MFG DIV, HOECHST ROUSSEL PHARMACEUT INC, 87- *Personal Data:* b New York City, NY, May 14, 35; m 57, Sonia Witkowski; c Katherine E & Steven E. *Educ:* Mass Inst Technol, BS, 56; Univ Wis, PhD, 60. *Prof Exp:* Res fel, Harvard Univ, 61 res chemist, Lederle Labs, NY, 61-71. *Mem:* Am Chem Soc. *Res:* Pharmaceutical company executive. *Mailing Add:* 947 Sunset Ridge Bridgewater NJ 08807-1325

BAUER, WALTER, SOLID STATE PHYSICS. *Current Pos:* mem tech staff, 69-74, div supvr, 74-78, DEP MGR, SANDIA LABS, 78- *Personal Data:* b Innsbruck, Austria, Mar 29, 35; US citizen; m 64. *Educ:* Univ Calif, Berkeley, AB, 57; Univ Ill, MS, 59, PhD(physics), 62. *Prof Exp:* Sr physicist, Atomics Int Div, NAm Aviation, Inc, 62-67, res specialist, 67-69. *Concurrent Pos:* Exten instr, Univ Calif, Los Angeles, 63-66. *Mem:* AAAS; Am Phys Soc; Sigma Xi. *Res:* Defects in metals; electron radiation effects; inert gas migration in metals; ion implantation; magnetic fusion energy; science administration. *Mailing Add:* PO Box 969 Sandia Labs Livermore CA 94550

BAUER, WENDY HAGEN, ASTRONOMY. *Current Pos:* asst prof, 79-87, ASSOC PROF, WELLESLEY COL, 87- *Personal Data:* b Aberdeen, Wash, May 11, 50; m 87; c 1. *Educ:* Mt Holyoke Col, BA, 71; Univ Hawaii, MS, 74, PhD(astron), 77. *Prof Exp:* Fel astron, Harvard-Smithsonian Ctr Astrophys, 77-79. *Concurrent Pos:* Vis asst prof, Univ NMex, 84-85. *Mem:* Am Astron Soc; Sigma Xi; Astron Soc Pac; Int Astron Union. *Res:* Optical and infrared observation of mass loss from cool stars; mass loss from late-type stars. *Mailing Add:* Whitin Observ Wellesley Col Wellesley MA 02181

BAUER, WILLIAM, JR, organic chemistry, chemical engineering; deceased, see previous edition for last biography

BAUER, WILLIAM EUGENE, ANALYTICAL CHEMISTRY. *Current Pos:* RETIRED. *Personal Data:* b Greensburg, Pa, Jan 21, 33; m 68; c 3. *Educ:* Miami Univ, BA, 54; Pa State Univ, PhD(chem), 59. *Prof Exp:* Instr chem, Lucknow Christian Col, India, 59-, head dept, 70-96. *Concurrent Pos:* Vis asst prof & asst ed, Newslett, Adv Coun Col Chem, Wabash Col, 64-65. *Mem:* Am Chem Soc; Indian Chem Soc; Sigma Xi. *Res:* Polarography; emission and absorption spectroscopy; instrumentation. *Mailing Add:* 2951 Quincy Lane Lansing MI 48910

BAUER, WILLIAM R, NUCLEIC ACID STRUCTURE, DNA & PROTEIN INTERACTIONS. *Current Pos:* assoc prof microbiol, 73-78, PROF MICROBIOL, STATE UNIV NY HEALTH SCI CTR, STONY BROOK, 78- *Personal Data:* b Friend, Nebr, July 10, 39. *Educ:* Calif Inst Technol, PhD(phys chem), 69. *Honors & Awards:* Am Can Soc Scholar. *Prof Exp:* Asst prof chem, Univ Colo, Boulder, 69-73. *Concurrent Pos:* Guggenheim fel; NIH sr res fel. *Mem:* Am Soc Biol Chemists; Am Soc Virol; Am Soc Microbiol; Biophys Soc; Am Chem Soc. *Res:* Structure and properties of superhelical DNA; DNA-protein interactions. *Mailing Add:* Dept Microbiol Suny Stony Brook Health Sci Ctr Stony Brook NY 11794-5222. *Fax:* 516-632-8891; *E-Mail:* wbauer@sunysb.edu

BAUERLE, RONALD H, MOLECULAR BIOLOGY, ENZYME STRUCTURE & FUNCTION. *Current Pos:* assoc prof, 69-89, PROF BIOL, UNIV VA, 90-, CHMN BIOL, 93- *Personal Data:* b Newport Ky, Dec 16, 37; m 61, Judith Ann Chaffin; c Cynthia & Jennifer. *Educ:* Thomas More Col, AB, 57, Univ Houston, MS, 59, Purdue Univ, PhD(microbiol), 63. *Prof Exp:* Instr microbiol, Purdue Univ, 61-62; res assoc molecular biol, Cold Spring Harbor Lab Quant Biol, 63-66; asst prof, Div Biol, Southwest Ctr Advan Studies, 66-69. *Concurrent Pos:* Fel, NIH, Ctr Advan Studies, Univ Va, 63-66, NIH career develop award, 67-69, 71-76; vis prof, Univ Munster, 75; vis scholar, Stanford Univ, 84. *Mem:* AAAS; Genetics Soc Am; Am Soc Microbiol; Am Soc Biochem & Molecular Biol; Protein Soc. *Res:* Allosteric mechanisms of enzyme control; genetics of bacteria; mechanism of protein synthesis; structure, function, evolution and assembly of complex enzymes; molecular genetics of prokaryotes. *Mailing Add:* Dept Biol Gilmer Hall Univ Va Charlottesville VA 22903-2477. *Fax:* 804-982-5626; *E-Mail:* rhb7g@virginia.edu

BAUERMEISTER, HERMAN OTTO, INDUSTRIAL ORGANIC CHEMISTRY. *Current Pos:* RETIRED. *Personal Data:* b St Louis, Mo, Jan 18, 14; m 84, Emily H Stevens. *Educ:* Armour Inst Technol, BS, 37; Ill Inst Technol, MS, 41; DePaul Univ, JD, 46. *Prof Exp:* Chemist, Commonwealth Edison Co, 37-40; patent examr insecticides & foods, US Patent Off, 40-42; res engr catalysis & synthetic rubber, Sinclair Refining Co, 42-46; patent att inorg chem & electronics, Monsanto Co, 46-82. *Mem:* Am Chem Soc. *Res:* Heat transfer and distillation; catalysis; organic phosphorus chemistry; detergents; electronic devices. *Mailing Add:* 7413 Truelight Ch Rd Charlotte NC 28227

BAUERNFEIND, JACOB (JACK) C(HRISTOPHER), FOOD TECHNOLOGY. *Current Pos:* RETIRED. *Personal Data:* b North Branch, NY, Apr 30, 14; m 39, Lillian Nurmi; c Kathleen, Michael & Edmund. *Educ:* Cornell Univ, BS, 36, MS, 39, PhD(nutrit, biochem & physiol), 40. *Prof Exp:* Asst nutritionist & instr, Cornell Univ, 36-40; nutritionist & res chemist, Hiram Walker & Son, Inc, Peoria, Ill, 40-44; chief appl nutrit, Hoffmann-LaRoche Inc, Nutley, NJ, 44-55, dir, Food & Agr Prod Develop Dept, 55-61, dir, Agr Res Dept, 61-68, dir agrochem & asst to vpres chem res, 68-71, coordr nutrit res, 72-79. *Concurrent Pos:* Consult food technol & nutrit, 79- *Mem:* Am Chem Soc; NY Acad Sci; Poultry Sci Asn; Am Soc Animal Sci; fel Inst Food Technologists; Fedn Am Soc Exp Biol; Am Inst Nutrit; Am Soc Clin Nutrit. *Res:* General nutrition; biochemistry; nutrients in human nutrition; nutrient delivery systems; nutrition of the elderly; prevention of blindness of dietary origin; experimental and practical feeding of animals; vitamins, antioxidants, drugs and carotenoids in human and agricultural applications; animal health and veterinary medicine; agricultural and food chemical research; food technology; food preservation. *Mailing Add:* 3664 NW 12th Ave Gainesville FL 32605-4852

BAUGH, ANN LAWRENCE, HAZARDOUS WASTES, PETROLEUM INDUSTRY. *Current Pos:* ENVIRON CONSULT, 95- *Personal Data:* b Freeport, Tex, Sept 4, 38; div. *Educ:* Southwestern Univ, Tex, BS, 60; Univ Tex, Austin, MA, 63, PhD(chem), 66; Pepperdine Univ, Malibu, Calif, MBA, 82. *Prof Exp:* Asst prof chem, Southwestern Univ, Tex, 64-67; Welch fel, Univ Tex, Austin, 66-69; tech specialist & proj engr, Lockheed Propulsion Co, 69-75; sr res chemist & group leader, Occidental Res Corp, 75-82; prog develop mgr, Rockwell Int, 83-86; consult, Appl Geosci Corp, 87-89; adminr environ progs, Unocal Corp, 89-95. *Mem:* Am Chem Soc; Air Waste Mgt Asn; Am Inst Chem Engrs. *Res:* Microwave spectroscopy and molecular structure; aging studies of solid propellants and composites; instrument automation, computer programming; synthetic fuels; coal conversion, desulfurization, combustion kinetics and liquefaction; geothermal hydrogen sulfide abatement; phosphates research; hazardous materials. *Mailing Add:* PO Box 156 Idyllwild CA 92549-0156. *Fax:* 213-977-6364; *E-Mail:* eslaalb@hes.unocal.com

BAUGH, CHARLES M, BIOCHEMISTRY. *Current Pos:* assoc prof, 67-70, prof, Nutrit Div, Univ SAla, 70-73, prof biochem & chmn dept, 73-81, assoc dean, 76-87, DEAN BASIC MED SCI, COL MED, UNIV SALA, 87- *Personal Data:* b Fayetteville, NC, June 20, 31; m 52; c 4. *Educ:* Univ Chicago, SB, 58; Tulane Univ, PhD(biochem), 62. *Prof Exp:* Fel biochem, Tulane Univ, 62-63, from instr to asst prof, 63-65; asst prof pharmacol med, Wash Univ, 65-67. *Concurrent Pos:* External assessor, Nat Res Coun Australia, 76-81; pres, Ala Acad Sci, 82; mem, bd trustees, Ala Acad Sci, 83-; pres, SAla Med Sci Found, 82- *Mem:* Am Chem Soc; Am Inst Nutrit; Am Soc Biol Chem & Molecular Biol; NY Acad Sci; Soc Exp Biol Med. *Res:* Biosynthesis of the pteridine nucleus, as found in the vitamins, folic acid and riboflavin; antimetabolites in nucleic acids. *Mailing Add:* PO Box 586 Salemburg NC 28385

BAUGHCUM, STEVEN LEE, KINETICS, MOLECULAR PHOTODISSOCIATION. *Current Pos:* res analyst, 88-93, SR PRIN ENGR, BOEING CO, 93- *Personal Data:* b Atlanta, Ga, Dec 18, 50. *Educ:* Emory Univ, BS, 72; Harvard Univ, AM, 73, PhD(chem), 78. *Prof Exp:* Phys chemist, Air Force Cambridge Res Labs, 76; res assoc, Joint Inst Lab Astrophys, Univ Colo & Nat Bur Stand, 78-80; mem staff, Los Alamos Nat Lab, 80-87; prin res scientist & mgr, Chem Physics Prog, Spectra Technol Inc, 87-88. *Concurrent Pos:* Res asst, Emory Univ, 68-72; res asst, Harvard Univ, 72-78 & teaching fel, 73-76. *Mem:* Sigma Xi; Am Chem Soc; Combustion Inst; Am Geophys Union; AAAS; Am Inst Aeronaut & Astronaut. *Res:* Modeling and analysis of combustion chemistry and atmospheric chemistry, with particular emphasis on the possible impact of supersonic aircraft on the stratospheric ozone layer. *Mailing Add:* 2215 185th Pl NE Redmond WA 98052. *Fax:* 425-234-4543; *E-Mail:* baughcum@atc.boeing.com

BAUGHMAN, GEORGE LARKINS, ANALYTICAL CHEMISTRY, ENVIRONMENTAL CHEMISTRY. *Current Pos:* adj res prof, 85-95, SR TEXTILE RES CHEMIST, DEPT TEXTILES, MERCHANDISING & INTERIORS, UNIV GA, 95- *Personal Data:* b Palatka, Fla, June 29, 38; m 58; c 2. *Educ:* Fla State Univ, BS, 60. *Prof Exp:* Mfg engr anal chem, Martin-Marietta Corp, 60-61; chemist, Aero-Chem Res Lab, 61-63; aerospace engr anal chem, J F Kennedy Space Ctr, NASA, 63-70; sr res chemist, Environ Res Lab, US Environ Protection Agency, 70-83, dir res, 83-85. *Mem:* Am Chem Soc; Sigma Xi; Soc Environ Chem Toxicol; Am Asn Textile & Colorists. *Res:* Elucidation of transport and transformation mechanisms of aquatic pollutants; kinetics of environmental processes; environmental behavior and waste treatment of dyes and other textile chemicals. *Mailing Add:* 165 Red Fox Run Athens GA 30605

BAUGHMAN, GLENN LAVERNE, ORGANIC POLYMER CHEMISTRY. *Current Pos:* RETIRED. *Personal Data:* b Dover, Pa, Apr 26, 31; m 56, Madeline L Albright; c Philip H & Stephen N. *Educ:* Gettysburg Col, AB, 53; Pa State Univ, PhD(org chem), 61. *Prof Exp:* Chemist, Armstrong Cork Co, 55-57; res chemist, E I du Pont de Nemours & Co, 61-64; sr res chemist, PPG Industs, Barberton, 64-80, res assoc, Chem Div, 80-89. *Concurrent Pos:* Instr, Barberton Tech Sch, 64-65; instr chem, Univ Akron, 89-91. *Mem:* Am Chem Soc. *Res:* Unsaturated polyesters for thermosetting castings; monomer structure-polymer property correlations; organometallics chemistry; photochemistry; synthesis of agricultural chemical intermediates; theral hazards. *Mailing Add:* 479 Dohner Dr Wadsworth OH 44281-2141

BAUGHMAN, RAY HENRY, ELECTRONIC & OPTICAL MATERIALS, POLYMERS. *Current Pos:* Staff scientist, Allied-Signal, Inc, 70-73, group leader polymer sci, Mat Res Ctr, 74-77, mgr org mat sci, 77-79, specialty polymers, 79-90, res fel, 90-97, AEROSPACE FEL RES & TECHNOL, ALLIEDSIGNAL INC, 97- *Personal Data:* b York, Pa, Jan 14, 43; m 89, Karen McCarthy; c Lara, Heather, Dana, Rebecca & Alexander. *Educ:* Carnegie-Mellon Univ, BS, 64; Harvard Univ, MS, 66, PhD(mat sci), 71. *Honors & Awards:* Chem Pioneer Award, Am Inst Chemists, 95; Coop Res Award Polymer Sci & Eng, Am Chem Soc, 96. *Concurrent Pos:* Mem orgn comt, Int Conferences Synthetic Metals, 81-94, adv groups, NSF, NATO,

Japan Found, Dept Energy & MRC. *Mem:* Fel Am Phys Soc; Am Chem Soc; Mat Res Soc; AAAS; fel Am Inst Chemists. *Res:* Electrical, optical and mechanical properties of materials; solid state reactions; novel forms of carbon; new material sythesis, properties and applications; highly conducting organic polymers; high temperature superconductors; polymer processing; intelligent materials; sensors; actuators. *Mailing Add:* AlliedSignal Res & Technol 101 Columbia Rd Morristown NJ 07962-1021. *Fax:* 973-455-5991

BAUGHMAN, RUSSELL GEORGE, PHYSICAL CHEMISTRY. *Current Pos:* RETIRED. *Personal Data:* b Washington, DC; m 69, Deborah Dye; c Steven. *Educ:* William Jewell Col, BA, 68; Iowa State Univ, PhD(phys chem), 77. *Prof Exp:* Grad asst, Iowa State Univ, 68-69, 73-77; from asst prof to prof phys chem, Truman State Univ, 77-97. *Concurrent Pos:* Med technician, USAF, 69-73. *Mem:* Am Chem Soc; Am Crystallog Asn; Sigma Xi. *Res:* X-ray diffraction studies of pesticides and charge transfer complexes; quantum mechanics. *Mailing Add:* Div Sci Truman State Univ Kirksville MO 63501

BAUGHN, CHARLES (OTTO), JR, BIOLOGY. *Current Pos:* RETIRED. *Personal Data:* b Bicknell, Ind, Feb 25, 21; m 44, Marianna Coffey; c Charles C, David & Lisa. *Educ:* Ind State Teachers Col, BSc, 47; Univ NC, MS, 49, PhD(parasitol, bact), 52. *Prof Exp:* Instr parasitol, Univ NC, 50-52; parasitologist, Stamford Res Labs, Am Cyanamid Co, 52-55, group leader bact, Lederle Labs, 55-61, mgr microbial dis sect, Agr Res Ctr, 61-64; asst dir res, Hess & Clark Div, Richardson-Merrell, Inc, 64-69; sr investr, Squibb Inst Med Res, 69-84. *Mem:* AAAS; Am Soc Microbiol; NY Acad Sci; Sigma Xi. *Res:* Chemotherapy of microbial infections; resistance to infection. *Mailing Add:* 29 Maple Ave Flemington NJ 08822

BAUGHN, ROBERT ELROY, SEXUALLY TRANSMITTED DISEASES. *Current Pos:* from instr to asst prof, 75-83, assoc prof microbiol, immunol & dermat, 83-93, PROF MICROBIOL & IMMUNOL, BAYLOR MED COL, HOUSTON, 93-; DIR MICROBIOL, SYPHILIS RES LAB, VET AFFAIRS MED CTR, HOUSTON, 77-, ASSOC CAREER SCIENTIST, 90- *Personal Data:* b Chanute, Kans, Jan 31, 40; m 65, Myra Phillips; c Heather & Brenna. *Educ:* The Citadel, BS, 63; Univ Tenn, Memphis, MS, 66; Univ Cincinnati, PhD(microbiol & immunol), 75; Houston Baptist Univ, MBA, 80. *Prof Exp:* Chief, Bact Br, Sixth US Army Med Lab, Ft Baker, Calif, 67-68, chief bact, serol & parasitol, 376th Med Detachment, US Army, Thailand, 68-69; microbiologist, John L Hutchenson-Tri-Co Mem Hosp, Ft Oglethorpe, Ga, 69-71. *Concurrent Pos:* Clin assoc prof, med tech & cytogenetics, Sch Allied Health Sci, Univ Tex, Houston, 86- *Mem:* Sigma Xi; Am Soc Microbiol; Am Asn Immunologists; Reticuloendothelial Soc; Undersea Med Soc; Am Venereal Dis Asn; Am Soc Clin Pathologists. *Res:* Induction, regulation and control of immune responses in chronic infections; host-parasite relationships in infectious processes and mechanisms of pathogenesis; the role of immune complexes in pathogenesis and regulation of immune function. *Mailing Add:* Syphilis Res Lab Bldg 109 Rm 234A Vet Admin Med Ctr 2002 Holcombe Blvd Houston TX 77030. *Fax:* 713-790-9141; *E-Mail:* baughn9@idt.net

BAUGUESS, CARL THOMAS, JR, PHARMACEUTICS. *Current Pos:* assoc prof, 70-77, PROF PHARMACEUT, UNIV SC, 77-, DIR GRAD PROG, COL PHARM, 75- *Personal Data:* b Lancaster Co, Pa, Sept 30, 28; m 65. *Educ:* Univ NC, BS, 54, MS, 66; Univ Miss, PhD, 70. *Honors & Awards:* Lederle Award, 75. *Prof Exp:* Pharmacist, Jonesboro's Lee Drug Store, 54-57; instr & dir pharmaceut exten serv, Univ NC, 57-60, part-time instr, 60-64; pharm consult, NC Heart Asn, 64-67; asst prof pharmaceut, Northeast La State Univ, 67-68. *Mem:* Am Pharmaceut Asn; Sigma Xi. *Res:* Investigations of new drugs for antitumor activity in mouse leukemia; pharmacokinetic studies of drug concentration changes after adminstration by various routes in larger animals; microencapsulation of basic drugs by spray dry techniques. *Mailing Add:* 3208 Keenan Dr Columbia SC 29201

BAUKNIGHT, CHARLES WILLIAM, JR, CHEMISTRY. *Current Pos:* MEM STAFF, CHEM DEPT, TOWSON STATE UNIV, 89- *Personal Data:* b Atlanta, Ga, June 29, 59. *Educ:* Duke Univ, BA, 81; Clemson Univ, PhD(org chem), 87. *Prof Exp:* Postdoctoral, Chem Dept, Univ Iowa, 87-89. *Mem:* Sigma Xi. *Res:* Synthesis of precursors to potentially crantioselective fluorinating agents; synthesis and chemistry of perfluorinated nitrites and nitrogen-bromine compounds. *Mailing Add:* 103 Victoria Circle Anderson SC 29621-4058

BAULD, NATHAN LOUIS, ORGANIC CHEMISTRY. *Current Pos:* from instr to assoc prof, 61-73, PROF CHEM, UNIV TEX, AUSTIN, 73- *Personal Data:* b Clarksburg, WVa, Dec 12, 34; m 71; c 2. *Educ:* WVa Univ, BS, 56; Univ Ill, PhD(org chem), 59. *Prof Exp:* NSF fel, Harvard Univ, 59-60; res chemist, Rohm and Haas Co, Pa, 60-61. *Concurrent Pos:* Sloan Found fel, 66-68. *Mem:* Am Chem Soc. *Res:* Physical-organic and stereochemistry; anion radicals; molecular orbital theory; aromatic systems; cation radicals. *Mailing Add:* Dept Chem Univ Tex Austin TX 78712-1167

BAULD, NELSON ROBERT, JR, ENGINEERING MECHANICS. *Current Pos:* assoc prof, 63-77, PROF ENG MECH, CLEMSON UNIV, 77- *Personal Data:* b Clarksburg, WVa, May 18, 31; m 51; c 2. *Educ:* WVa Univ, BSME, 58, MS, 60; Univ Ill, PhD(theoret & appl mech), 63. *Prof Exp:* Instr eng mech, WVa Univ, 58-60; instr, Va Polytech Inst, 60-61. *Mem:* Am Soc Eng Educ. *Res:* Time-dependent studies of engineering members made from materials that creep, including columns, torsion members, plates and shells; applied mathematics. *Mailing Add:* 134 Mountain View Lane Clemson SC 29631

BAULE, GERHARD M, ELECTRICAL ENGINEERING. *Current Pos:* RETIRED. *Personal Data:* b Syracuse, NY, Jan 20, 34; m 55; c 4. *Educ:* Syracuse Univ, BEE, 56, MEE, 58, PhD(elec eng), 63. *Honors & Awards:* Res Award, Sigma Xi, 64. *Prof Exp:* Res asst elec eng, Syracuse Univ, 56-58, from instr to asst prof, 58-69, assoc prof elec eng, 69- & assoc prof comput eng, 77- *Res:* Application of electrical science to medicine. *Mailing Add:* 5302 Onondaga Rd Camillus NY 13031

BAULIEU, ETIENNE-EMILE, ENDOCRINOLOGY. *Current Pos:* SCI DIR, NIH & MED RES, 63- *Personal Data:* b Strasbourg, France, Dec 12, 26; m 47, Yolande Compagnon; c Catherine, Laurent & Frederique. *Hon Degrees:* Dr med & phys sci, Univ Paris, 55; Dr, Univ Gand, 91 & Tufts Univ, 91. *Honors & Awards:* Claude Bernard Lectr; Reichstein Award, Int Soc Endocrinol, 72; Roussel Prize, 76; Pincus Mem Award, 78; First Europ Medal, Eng Soc Endocrinol, 85; Lasker Award, 89. *Prof Exp:* Intern, Hosp Paris, 51; from lectr to prof biol chem, Univ Reims Sch Med, 58, Univ Rouen Sch Med, 60-61, & Fac Med, Univ Paris, 61; vis lectr, Columbia Univ, NY, 61-62. *Concurrent Pos:* Co-founder, Int Soc Res Biol Reproduction, 67; chmn sci coun, Found Res Med Francaise, 73-75, Inst Nat Sante Recherche Medicale 75-79 & Centre Int Recherches Medicales Franceville, Gabon, 78-85. *Mem:* Fr Soc Biochem; Fr Soc Endocrinol; Am Acad Achievement; Royal Soc Med; Endocrine Soc; Fr Acad Sci; NY Acad Sci. *Res:* Secretion, metabolism, physi-pathology and mechanism of action of steroid hormones; biology of reproduction. *Mailing Add:* Unite 33 Inserm Hosp Bicetre 80 Ruedu Gen Leclerc 94276 Bicetre France

BAUM, BERNARD, POLYMER CHEMISTRY. *Current Pos:* CONSULT, 90- *Personal Data:* b Boston, Mass, Sept 21, 24; m 53; c 1. *Educ:* Lowell Technol Inst, BS, 47; Clark Univ, MS, 49, PhD(chem), 50. *Prof Exp:* Chemist, Sherwin-Williams Co, 50-53; develop assoc, Union Carbide Plastics Co, 53-62; group leader, Allied Chem Co, 62-63 & Borden Chem Co, 63-64; mgr prod develop, Cast Nylon Dept, Budd Co, 64-67; mgr, Chem & Mat Develop Lab, Springborn Labs, Inc, 67-69, mgr, Chem & Mat Div, 69-72, vpres & mgr, Mat Res & Develop, 72-90. *Mem:* Am Chem Soc; Air Pollution Control Asn; Soc Plastics Engr. *Res:* Polymer chemistry; synthesis; structure vs properties; coatings; elastomers; permanence properties of materials. *Mailing Add:* 44 Kirkwood Rd Hartford CT 06117

BAUM, BERNARD R, TAXONOMY, BOTANY. *Current Pos:* Res scientist, Plant Res Inst, 67-73, sect chief, 73-87, PRIN RES SCI, BIOSYSTEMATICS RES INST, CAN DEPT AGR, 80- *Personal Data:* b Paris, France, Feb 14, 37; m 61; c 1. *Educ:* Hebrew Univ, Jerusalem, MS, 63, PhD(tamarix taxon), 66. *Honors & Awards:* Lawson Medal, Can Bot Asn. *Concurrent Pos:* Asst ed, Can J Bot, 74-, Euphytica, 87- *Mem:* AAAS; Bot Soc France; Int Asn Plant Taxon; Can Bot Asn; fel Royal Soc Can; Bot Soc Am; Am Soc Plant Taxonomists. *Res:* Monograph of Tamarix, Avena and Hordeum; nomenclature; utilization of computers for taxonomy; taxometrics and statistics; evolution; international registries of cultivars. *Mailing Add:* Res Br ECORC KW Neatby Bldg Cent Exp Farm Agr & Agr Food Ottawa ON K1A 0C6 Can. *Fax:* 613-996-9564

BAUM, BRUCE J, ORAL MEDICINE. *Current Pos:* Sr investr, lab molecular aging, Nat Inst Aging, 78-82, CLIN DIR & CHIEF, CLIN INVEST & PATIENT CARE BR, NAT INST DENT RES, NIH, 82- *Personal Data:* b Lynn, Mass, Oct 28, 45; m; c 2. *Educ:* Univ Va, BA, 67; Tufts Univ, DMD, 71; Boston Univ, PhD(biochem), 74. *Honors & Awards:* Carl A Schlack Award, 87. *Concurrent Pos:* Wellcome vis prof, 88. *Mem:* AAAS; Am Soc Biol Chemists; Int Asn Dent Res; Geront Soc Am; Am Acad Oral Med. *Mailing Add:* Nat Inst Dent Res NIH Bldg 10 Rm 1N-113 Bethesda MD 20892-1190

BAUM, BURTON MURRY, ORGANIC CHEMISTRY, INORGANIC CHEMISTRY. *Current Pos:* MGR, ECOLAB INC, 83- *Personal Data:* b Brooklyn, NY, Dec 6, 34; m 65; c 2. *Educ:* Brooklyn Col, BS, 56; Univ Pittsburgh, PhD(org chem), 62. *Prof Exp:* Res chemist, 62-75, mgr, FMC, 75-83. *Mem:* Am Chem Soc. *Res:* Preparation and bleaching of textiles; flame retardants; detergents; organic synthesis; phosphorus chemistry; pulp and paper chemistry; odor counteractants; cleaners and disinfectants. *Mailing Add:* 1742 Lansford Lane Mendota Heights MN 55118

BAUM, CARL E(DWARD), ELECTROMAGNETICS. *Current Pos:* SR SCIENTIST ELECTROMAGNETICS, PHILLIPS LAB, 71-, FEL, 96- *Personal Data:* b Binghamton, NY, Feb 6, 40. *Educ:* Calif Inst Technol, BS, 62, MS, 63, PhD(elec eng), 69. *Honors & Awards:* Richard R Stoddart Award, Inst Elec & Electronics Engrs, Electromagnetic Compatibility Soc, 84; Harry Diamond Mem Award, Inst Elec & Electronics Engrs, 87. *Prof Exp:* Proj officer, Air Force Weapons Lab, 63-67 & 68-71. *Concurrent Pos:* Mem, comn B US Nat Comt, Int Union Radio Sci, 75-, comn E, 82-, comn A, 90-, US deleg gen assembly, Peru 75, Finland, 78, Washington, DC, 81, Italy, 84, Israel, 87, Czech, 90, Japan, 93, chmn, int comn E Working group, 81-; distinguished lectr, Inst Elec & Electronics Engrs, Antennas & Propagation Soc, 77-78, co-chmn, Joint Comt High-Power Electromagnetics, 78-; adv, numerous US govt agencies. *Mem:* Fel Inst Elec & Electronics Engrs; Int Union Radio Sci; Electromagnetics Soc (pres, 83-85). *Res:* Electromagnetic theory and applications; antennas, propagation, scattering, interaction, protection, and related pulse power for electromagnetic pulse, lightning, high power microwaves, and transient radar (high power electromagnetics); author of one book and numerous publications on electromagnetic theory. *Mailing Add:* 5116 Eastern SE Unit D Albuquerque NM 87108. *Fax:* 505-846-0417

BAUM, DAVID, PEDIATRIC CARDIOLOGY, PHYSIOLOGY. *Current Pos:* PROF PEDIAT & DIR DIV PEDIAT CARDIOL, SCH MED, STANFORD UNIV, 71- *Personal Data:* b Saratoga Springs, NY, Aug 4, 27; m 59; c 4. *Educ:* Dartmouth Col, AB, 51; Cornell Univ, MD, 55. *Prof Exp:* Intern med, Kings County Hosp, NY, 55-56; resident pediat, New York Hosp-Cornell Med Ctr, 56-59; asst pediat cardiol, Johns Hopkins Hosp, 59-60 & Mayo Clin, 60-61; from instr to assoc prof pediat, Sch Med, Univ Wash, 62-71, asst prog dir, Clin Res Ctr, 63-70. *Concurrent Pos:* Fel pediat cardiol, Johns Hopkins Hosp, 59-60 & Mayo Clin, 60-61; consult, Madigan Army Hosp, Ft Lewis & Rainier Sch, Buckley, Wash, 62-71 & Silas Hayes Army Hosp, Ft Ord, Calif; res trainee biochem, Sch Med, Univ Wash, 65-66. *Mem:* Soc Pediat Res; Am Pediat Soc; Soc Exp Biol & Med; Am Heart Asn; Am Physiol Soc; Perinatal Res Soc. *Res:* Metabolic aspects or hypoxia and heart failure as related to thermoregulation, execise and growth in children with cardiovascular disease; adipose tissue development and obesity. *Mailing Add:* Dept Pediat Lucille Salter Packard Children's Hosp Stanford 750 Welch Rd Suite 305 Palo Alto CA 94304

BAUM, DENNIS WILLARD, high energy density systems, for more information see previous edition

BAUM, ELEANOR KUSHEL, ELECTRICAL ENGINEERING, ENGINEERING. *Current Pos:* chmn, 71-84, dean, Sch Eng, 84-87, PROF ELEC ENG, PRATT INST, 65-; SCH ENG, COOPER UNION, NY, 87-, DIR, RES FOUND. *Personal Data:* b Poland; US citizen; m 62; c 2. *Educ:* City Col New York, BEE, 59; Polytech Inst NY, MEE, 61, PhD(elec eng), 64. *Honors & Awards:* Emily Warren Roebling Award, 88; Upward Mobility Award, Soc Women Engrs, 90. *Prof Exp:* Engr, Sperry Corp, 61-63. *Concurrent Pos:* Consult, 75-; prog visitor, Accreditation Bd Eng & Technol, 82-92, dir, 90-92; bd examiners, Grad Rec Exam, 85-90; lectr, var community groups; dir, Alleghany Power Systs Corp, 88-, Am Soc Eng Educ, 89-91. *Mem:* Fel Inst Elec & Electronics Engrs; Am Soc Eng Educ; fel Soc Women Engrs. *Res:* Engineering education; engineering curricula; systems and control; career guidance for women in engineering. *Mailing Add:* Sch Eng Cooper Union 51 Astor Pl New York NY 10003

BAUM, GARY ALLEN, SOLID STATE PHYSICS, RESEARCH ADMINISTRATION. *Current Pos:* VPRES RES & ACAD AFFAIRS, INST PAPER SCI & TECHNOL, 96- *Personal Data:* b New Richmond, Wis, Oct 2, 39; m 64, Paula Vanhooser; c 2. *Educ:* Wis State Univ, River Falls, BS, 61; Okla State Univ, MS, 64, PhD(physics), 69. *Honors & Awards:* Process & Prod Qual Div Award, Tech Asn Pulp & Paper Indust, 87, Res & Develop Div Award, 94. *Prof Exp:* Res engr, Douglas Aircraft Co, Calif, 63-64; physicist, Dow Chem Co, Colo, 64-65, sr physicist, 65-66; from asst prof to assoc prof, Inst Paper Chem, 69-79, prof physics, 79-88, dir, Paper Mat Div, 83-88; JVA fel, James River Corp, 88-89, dir corp res & develop, 89-94; head, Wood & Paper Sci Dept, NC State Univ, 94-96. *Concurrent Pos:* Adj prof, Inst Paper Chem, 88; bd dirs, Tech Asn Pulp & Paper Indust Found. *Mem:* Fel Tech Asn Pulp & Paper Indust; Am Phys Soc; Soc Wood Sci & Technol; fel Int Acad Wood Sci. *Res:* Vapor deposition, sputtering and accelerated ion techniques for thin film preparation; electrical and thermal properties of rutile; electrical properties of polymers; mechanical properties of paper and paperboard; acoustic measurements in plate materials; research management. *Mailing Add:* 500 Tenth St NW Atlanta GA 30318. *Fax:* 404-894-5301; *E-Mail:* gabaum@ipst.edu

BAUM, GEORGE, IMMUNOLOGY. *Current Pos:* ADJ LECTR, PACE UNIV, 88- *Personal Data:* b Hungary, Jan 11, 33; US citizen; m 54; c 3. *Educ:* Case Inst Technol, BS, 54; Ohio State Univ, MS, 60, PhD, 66. *Prof Exp:* Engr solid fuel propellants, Wright Air Develop Command, 54-65; res engr synthetic hydraul fluids, Air Force Mat Lab, 55-65; res chemist, Corning Glass Works, 66-76; staff scientist, Technicon Instrument Corp, 76-88. *Concurrent Pos:* Vis res assoc, Beth Israel Hosp, 75-76; chairperson, Putnam Co, Environ Coun, 97- *Mem:* NY Acad Sci; Am Chem Soc; AAAS. *Res:* Organometallic synthesis; reinforced plastics; peptide chemistry; fluoroaromatic chemistry; ion-selective electrodes; immobilized enzymes; affinity chromatography; hormone secretion by tumor cells; purification and derivatization of antibodies. *Mailing Add:* 63 Rambler Rd RR No 14 Kent Lakes NY 10512-9022

BAUM, GERALD A(LLAN), POLYMER CHEMISTRY, TECHNICAL WRITING. *Current Pos:* prog mgr, Core Technol, 86-89, sr develop chemist, 89-92, SR TECH COMMUN SPECIALIST, PROD TECHNOL, HOECHST CELANESE CORP, 92- *Personal Data:* b New York, NY, June 25, 29; m 54, Joyce Stotter; c Kenneth & Michael. *Educ:* City Col New York, BS, 51; Pa State Univ, PhD(chem), 55. *Prof Exp:* Engr insulation & chem develop sect, Westinghouse Elec Corp, 55-58; sr chemist res & develop, Resin Res Labs, Inc, 58-61; supvr plastics prod, M & T Chem, Inc, 61-67; res assoc, Ciba-Geigy Corp, 67-71, supvr new prod develop, Additives Dept, Plastics & Additives Div, 71-74; supvr tech serv, Tenneco Chem, Inc, 74-76; mgr additives res & develop, Dart Industs, Inc, 76-79, dir, compounded prod res & develop, Dart & Kraft, Inc, 79-85; mgr, plastic applns & develop, GAF Corp, 85-86. *Concurrent Pos:* Guest lectr, NJ Inst Technol, 59-61; pres, Palisades Sect, Soc Plastic Engrs, 72-73. *Mem:* Am Chem Soc; Soc Plastics Engrs; Soc Tech Commun. *Res:* Plastics additives; stabilizers; specialty polymers. *Mailing Add:* 337 McKinley Blvd Paramus NJ 07652. *Fax:* 973-635-4165

BAUM, GERALD L, MEDICINE. *Current Pos:* PROF, 75-93, EMER PROF MED, SCH MED, TELAVIV UNIV, 93-; MED DIR, ISRAEL LUNG ASN, TEL AVIV, 75- *Personal Data:* b Milwaukee, Wis, Dec 19, 24; m 51; c 3. *Educ:* Univ Wis, BS, 45, MD, 47. *Honors & Awards:* Medalist, Am Col Chest Physicians, 89. *Prof Exp:* Intern, Jewish Hosp, Cincinnati, 47-48, resident med, 48 & 49-51; res chest med, Bellevue Hosp, New York, 51-52; fel bronchology, St Luke's Hosp, Chicago, 52; fel med mycol, Jewish Hosp, Cincinnati, 56-58; chief pulmonary sect, Vet Admin Hosp, Cincinnati, 58-65; prof med, Sch Med, Case Western Res Univ, 65-75. *Concurrent Pos:* NIH fel, Tel Hashomer, Israel, 63-64 & Kupat Cholim award, Israel, 63-64; assoc prof, Univ Cincinnati, 64-65; chief pulmonary sect, Vet Admin Hosp, Cleveland, 65-73. *Mem:* Am Thoracic Soc; Am Col Physicians; Am Fedn Clin Res; Am Col Chest Physicians; Int Soc Human & Animal Mycol; Israel Chest Med Soc. *Res:* Pulmonary diseases, particularly fungus infections; rehabilitation of patients with chronic pulmonary insufficiency and tuberculosis; immunologic lung disease; mucociliary clearance. *Mailing Add:* Rechov Hagolan 52 Givat Savyon Israel

BAUM, HARRY, ANALYTICAL CHEMISTRY. *Current Pos:* supvr, Analysis Develop Lab, Rohm and Haas Co, 48-69, supt qual control, 69-78, sr tech assoc, 78-80. *Personal Data:* b New York, NY, Oct 23, 15; m 44, Phyllis E Hague; c Louis J & Rebecca A. *Educ:* City Col New York, BS, 36; NY Univ, MS, 39. *Prof Exp:* Res chemist, Beth Israel Hosp, New York, 36-38; asst microchem, NY Univ, 38-39; res chemist, Gen Cigar Co, Pa, 40-41; supvr & plant chemist, US Rubber Co, Iowa, 41-43; supvr, Anal Res Lab, Publicker Indust, 46-47. *Concurrent Pos:* Referee, Collab Int Pesticide Analytical Coun, 69-79; consult, 81- *Mem:* AAAS; Am Chem Soc; fel Asn Off Anal Chemists. *Res:* Analytical research and development. *Mailing Add:* 8210 Stockton Rd Elkins Park PA 19027

BAUM, HOWARD JAY, FORENSIC MOLECULAR BIOLOGY, CLINICAL LABORATORY ADMINISTRATION. *Current Pos:* ASST DIR FORENSIC BIOL, OFF CHIEF MED EXAMR, 90- *Personal Data:* b New York, NY, May 11, 57. *Educ:* Cornell Univ, BS, 79; Brandeis Univ, PhD(biochem), 86. *Prof Exp:* Res scientist, Life Codes Corp, 85-90. *Concurrent Pos:* Adj asst prof immunol & microbiol, NY Med Col, 87-; clin asst prof forensics, New York Univ, 90- *Mem:* Am Soc Human Genetics; NE Asn Forensic Scientists. *Res:* Investigating and identifying polymorphic human loci to be detected by restriction fragment length polymorphism, PCR and sequence based systems; forensic molecular biology methods development; development of new genomic DNA amplication and non-isotopic detection systems; repeated sequences in the human genome. *Mailing Add:* Off Chief Med Examr 520 First Ave New York NY 10016

BAUM, HOWARD RICHARD, COMBUSTION FLUID MECHANICS, COMPUTATIONAL COMBUSTION. *Current Pos:* FEL, NAT INST STAND & TECHNOL, 83- *Personal Data:* b New York, NY, April 3, 36; m 61, Alice L Prince; c Allen & Sarah. *Educ:* Polytech Inst Brooklyn, BS, 57, MS, 59; Harvard Univ, PhD(appl math), 64. *Honors & Awards:* Silver Medal, US Dept Com, 81, Gold Medal, 83. *Prof Exp:* From lectr to asst prof mech eng, Harvard Univ, 64-71; sr scientist, Aerodyne Res Inc, 71-75; res physicist, Nat Bur Stand, 75-83. *Concurrent Pos:* Springer prof mech eng, Univ Calif, Berkeley, 85; panel nuclear winter res, Nat Acad Sci, 86-; Off Naval Res opportunities panel, Naval Studies Bd, Nat Res Coun, 86-87, 91; invited lectr, Second Int Symp Fire Safety Sci, 88, US/Japan Joint Sem, Comput in Heat Transfer Sci, 91; Japan Soc Prom Sci fel, 94; invited lectr, Sixth Int Symp Numerical Combustion, 96. *Mem:* Int Asn Fire Safety Sci; NY Acad Sci; Sigma Xi; Soc Indust & Appl Math; Combustion Inst. *Res:* Mathematical modeling of fire induced flow phenomena; turbulent combustion processes; ignition and flame spread in microgravity environment; development of computational techniques to study these phenomenas. *Mailing Add:* Nat Inst Stand & Technol Gaithersburg MD 20899. *Fax:* 301-975-4052; *E-Mail:* howard.baum@nist.gov

BAUM, J(AMES) CLAYTON, MOLECULAR SPECTROSCOPY, H-BONDING. *Current Pos:* asst prof, 79-82, ASSOC PROF CHEM, FLA INST TECHNOL, 82- *Personal Data:* b Washington, DC, May 11, 46; m 77, Melissa Powers; c Matthew & Kathryn. *Educ:* Williams Col, BA, 68; Princeton Univ, PhD(chem), 76. *Prof Exp:* Res assoc chem, Fla State Univ, 74-77; vis asst prof, Bowdoin Col, 77-79. *Concurrent Pos:* Lectr, Bowdoin Col, 80-82, vis assoc prof, 89-90. *Mem:* Am Chem Soc. *Res:* Molecular spectroscopy, including the study of photophysical and photochemical problems and energy transfer and relaxation processes; physical chemistry of molecular and aggregate phenomena that serve as prototypes for complex events in molecular biology. *Mailing Add:* Dept Chem Fla Inst Technol Melbourne FL 32901-6988. *Fax:* 407-768-8000 Ext 8951; *E-Mail:* cbaum@fit.edu

BAUM, JOHN, RHEUMATOLOGY, IMMUNOLOGY. *Current Pos:* asst prof med, Univ Rochester, 68-72, assoc prof prev med & community health, 69, assoc prof pediat, 70-72, prof med, 72-93, EMER PROF MED, PREV MED & COMMUNITY HEALTH, SCH MED & DENT, UNIV ROCHESTER, 93-, PROF PED, 95- *Personal Data:* b New York, NY, June 2, 27; m 50, Erna Bailis; c Nina, Jane, Carl, Antonia & Theodore. *Educ:* NY Univ, BA, 49, MD, 54. *Prof Exp:* Instr med, Southwestern Med Sch, Univ Tex, 59-62, asst prof, 62-68. *Concurrent Pos:* Dir arthritis clin, Parkland Mem Hosp, Dallas, Tex, 59-68, dir med clin, 65-67; consult rheumatol & co-dir arthritis clin, Scottish Rite Hosp Crippled Children, Dallas, 60-68; clin scholar, Arthritis Found, 64-69; sr assoc physician, Strong Mem Hosp, Rochester, NY, 68-72, dir pediat arthritis clin, 70-, physician & pediatrician, 72-; mem merit rev bd immunol, Vet Admin, 70-76; mem test comt rheumatol, Am Bd Internal Med, 71-76, consult, 78-79; mem drug efficacy panel, Nat Acad Sci, 60-65 & DMSO panel, 72-74; coordr prob area, Eval Therapeut in Arthritis, US-USSR Coop Pub Health & Med Sci, 74-; mem adv panel clin immunol, US Pharmacopoeia, 75- *Mem:* Am Rheumatism Asn; Am Fedn Clin Res; Am Soc Human Genetics; Am Asn Immunologists; Heberden Soc; hon mem Polish Rheumatism Soc; master Am Col Rheumatology. *Res:*

Clinical studies of delayed hypersensitivity and mechanisms of inflammation in humans; chemotaxis of polymorphonuclear leukocytes in human disease; drug studies in juvenile arthritis; soft-tissue rheumatism; hypermobility. *Mailing Add:* Strong Mem Hosp 601 Elmwood Ave Rochester NY 14642. *Fax:* 716-273-1070; *E-Mail:* nbm@duhura.cc.rochester.edu

BAUM, JOHN W, HEALTH PHYSICS, BIOELECTROMAGNETICS. *Current Pos:* assoc health physicist, 65-68, scientist, 68-75, SR SCIENTIST, BROOKHAVEN NAT LAB, 75-, HEAD, RADIOL SCI DIV, DEPT ADVAN TECHNOL, 90- *Personal Data:* b Clarion, Iowa, Mar 22, 31; m 55, Anne T Baron; c 6. *Educ:* Univ Iowa, BS, 53; Univ Rochester, MS, 54; Univ Mich, PhD(environ health), 64. *Prof Exp:* Engr, Gen Elec Co, Richland, Wash, 54-56; chief health physics, Armour Res Found, Chicago, 56-58; supvr, Allis Chalmers Mfg Co, Milwaukee, 58-61; lectr radiol health, Univ Mich, Ann Arbor, 61-65. *Mem:* Fel Health Physics Soc; Radiation Res Soc; Am Nuclear Soc; Nat Coun Radiation Protection Measurements. *Res:* Radiation protection; dosimetry; radiobiology; mutagenesis; carcinogenesis; bioelectromagnetics. *Mailing Add:* c/o Brookhaven Nat Lab Bldg 703M Upton NY 11973

BAUM, JOHN WILLIAM, ORGANIC CHEMISTRY. *Current Pos:* RETIRED. *Personal Data:* b Highland Park, Ill, Mar 22, 40; m 62, Nancy C Carnahan; c Annaliese M (deceased), Mark A & Rachel. *Educ:* Univ Minn, BA & BChem, 62; Wash Univ, PhD(org chem), 67. *Prof Exp:* Res chemist, MacMillan Bloedel Res Ltd, BC, 67-70; dir chem develop, Sandoz Crop Protection Corp, 71-81, chemist, Zoecon Corp, 81-88, prin scientist, 88-92, prin scientist, Sandoz Agro, Inc, 92-97. *Mem:* AAAS; Am Chem Soc; Sigma Xi. *Res:* Chemical information retrieval. *Mailing Add:* 922 El Cajon Way Palo Alto CA 94303

BAUM, JOSEPH HERMAN, pathology, for more information see previous edition

BAUM, JULES LEONARD, OPHTHALMOLOGY, OCULAR INFECTIONS & CORNEAL DISEASES. *Current Pos:* from asst prof to prof, 65-91, RES PROF OPHTHAL, SCH MED, TUFTS UNIV, 91- *Personal Data:* b New York, NY, Mar 13, 31; m 90, Laura Burde; c Jeffrey & Alison. *Educ:* Dartmouth Col, AB, 52; Tufts Univ, MD, 56; NY Univ, MS, 62; Am Bd Ophthal, dipl, 65. *Honors & Awards:* William Warner Hoppin Award, NY Acad Med, 59; Sr Hon Award, Am Acad Ophthal, 90. *Prof Exp:* Residency ophthal, Bellevue Hosp, NY, 62-64; NIH fel, Corneal Unit, Retina Found & Mass Eye & Ear Infirmary, Boston, 64-65. *Concurrent Pos:* Ed, Invest Ophthal & Visual Sci, 78-82, Am J Ophthal, 85-91, Ophthal Surg, 85-95 & Cornea, 89-; consult, Educ Mat Proj Appraisal Panel, Asn Am Med Col, 79- & Adv Panel Ophthal, US Pharmacopeial Conv, 80-; trustee, Asn Res Vision & Ophthal, 81-86; pres, Ocular Microbiol Immunol Group, 90-91. *Mem:* AAAS; Asn Res Vision & Ophthal (vpres, 86); Am Acad Ophthal; Sigma Xi; Am Ophthal Soc; Castroriy & Corneal Soc (Exec Soc Treas, 79-87, Vpres 87-89, Pres, 89-91). *Res:* Biochemistry of cornea; ocular pharmacology of antibiotics; physiology of tearing; treatment of infectious diseases of the eye; corneal diseases. *Mailing Add:* Boston Eye Assocs 1244 Boylston St Chestnut Hill MA 02167. *Fax:* 617-735-8814

BAUM, LAWRENCE STEPHEN, ONCOLOGY, CELL PHYSIOLOGY. *Current Pos:* asst prof, 66-69, ASSOC PROF BIOL, NORTHEAST LA UNIV, 69-, DIR, CANCER RES CTR, 81- *Personal Data:* b Scranton, Pa, Mar 3, 38; m 57; c 3. *Educ:* Univ Ala, BS, 60, MS, 62, PhD(cell physiol), 65. *Prof Exp:* Asst prof biol, Exten Ctr, Univ Ala, 65-66. *Mem:* Am Physiol Soc; Sigma Xi. *Res:* Angiogenesis during tumor development; scanning electron microscope study of surface morphology of neoplastic urothelium; mode of action of various chemical carcinogens; incidence of cancer in Louisiana. *Mailing Add:* Dept Biol Northeast La Univ 700 University Ave Monroe LA 71209-0001

BAUM, LINDA LOUISE, ACUTE PHASE REACTANTS, NATURAL KILLER CELLS. *Current Pos:* asst prof, 82-85, ASSOC PROF IMMUNOL, CHICAGO MED SCH, 85- *Personal Data:* b 1949; m 73, Robert G; c Jonathan & Emily. *Educ:* Mich State Univ, PhD(microbiol), 76. *Prof Exp:* Asst prof, Rush Univ, 78-82. *Mem:* Am Soc for Microbiol; Am Asn Immunol; Soc Leukocyte Biol. *Res:* Antibody dependent cell-mediated cytotoxicity; cell-mediated response to human immunodeficiency virus. *Mailing Add:* Dept Microbiol Finch Univ Health Sci Chicago Med Sch 3333 Green Bay Rd North Chicago IL 60064-3095. *Fax:* 847-578-3349

BAUM, MARTIN DAVID, PHOTOGRAPHIC SCIENCE, ORGANIC PHOTOCHEMISTRY APPLIED. *Current Pos:* vpres technol, 94-95, SR VPRES, ULANO CORP, 96- *Personal Data:* b New York, NY, Jan 30, 41; m 64, Linda Brunstein; c Allen & Laura. *Educ:* Mass Col Pharm, BS, 62, MS, 64; Univ Ill Med Ctr, PhD(org chem), 68. *Prof Exp:* Res chemist photochem, E I du Pont de Nemours & Co Inc, 68-71, mkt rep, 72-73, sr res chem, 74, res supv, 74-80, res mgr, photog syst, mkt tech mgr, diagnostic imaging, 87-93. *Mem:* Am Chem Soc. *Res:* Synthesis of dyes for use in photographic systems; development of products based on silver and non-silver photography. *Mailing Add:* 255 Butler St Brooklyn NY 11217

BAUM, PARKER BRYANT, PHYSICAL CHEMISTRY, INORGANIC CHEMISTRY. *Current Pos:* RETIRED. *Personal Data:* b Memphis, Tenn, Dec 21, 23; m 54; c 2. *Educ:* Col of William & Mary, BS, 47; Univ Tenn, MS, 52; Univ NC, PhD(phys chem), 62. *Prof Exp:* Instr chem, Old Dominion Col, 47-50, from asst prof to prof, 52-65; from assoc prof to prof chem, Skidmore Col, 67-87. *Mem:* AAAS; Am Chem Soc. *Res:* Thermodynamics; electromotive force measurements; applications of computers to science education. *Mailing Add:* PO Box 265 Ballston Spa NY 12020

BAUM, PAUL FRANK, MATHEMATICS. *Current Pos:* PROF MATH, PENN STATE, 87- *Personal Data:* b New York, NY, July 20, 36; m 61; c 2. *Educ:* Harvard Univ, AB, 58; Princeton Univ, PhD(math), 63. *Prof Exp:* Instr math, Princeton Univ, 62-63; NSF fel, Oxford & Cambridge Univs, 63-64; fel, Inst Advan Study, 64-65; asst prof, Princeton Univ, 65-67; from assoc prof to prof math, Brown Univ, 67-87. *Mem:* Am Math Soc. *Res:* Algebraic topology; lie groups; k-theory; k-homology; operator algebras. *Mailing Add:* Pa State Univ University Park PA 16802-6401

BAUM, PAUL M, experimental physics, for more information see previous edition

BAUM, PETER JOSEPH, PHYSICS. *Current Pos:* PRES, BAUM TECHNOL, 92- *Personal Data:* b Lennox, Calif, June 4, 43; wid; c Maryann. *Educ:* Univ Calif, Santa Barbara, BA, 65; Univ Nev, Reno, MS, 67; Univ Calif, Riverside, PhD(physics), 71. *Prof Exp:* Res engr microelectronics, Autonetics Div, NAm Rockwell Corp, 67-68; physicist comput anal, Corona Lab, Naval Weapons Ctr, 68-70; res assoc solar-plasma physics, Univ Calif, Riverside, 70-74, Air Force Off Sci Res grant, 72-74, res physicist solar-plasma physics, 74-85; mem tech staff, Gen Res Corp, Santa Barbara, Calif, 85-92. *Concurrent Pos:* US deleg, Int Atomic Energy Agency Fourth Conf Plasma Physics & Controlled Nuclear Fusion Res, USAEC, 71; consult, Sandia Labs, Albuquerque, NMex, 73-75; NSF grant, instr astron, Riverside City Col, 75-80; mem tech staff, Energy Sci Prog, Univ Calif, 80-; Calif Space Inst grant, 81. *Mem:* Am Geophys Union; Am Phys Soc; Am Astron Soc; Am Inst Aeronaut & Astronaut. *Res:* Solar flares; laboratory study of magnetic field line reconnection; geomagnetic substorms; magnetic energy conversion; plasma radiation sources; controlled thermonuclear fusion; five-meter terrella experiment; wind energy potential in the San Gorgonio Pass region; space propulsion. *Mailing Add:* 1180 Garden Lane Santa Barbara CA 93108. *Fax:* 805-969-1073; *E-Mail:* pjbemail@gte.net

BAUM, RICHARD T, MECHANICAL ENGINEERING. *Current Pos:* RETIRED. *Personal Data:* b New York, NY, Oct 3, 19. *Educ:* Columbia Univ, BA, 40, BS, 41, MS, 48. *Honors & Awards:* Egleston Medalist Columbia Univ, 85. *Prof Exp:* Engr, Elec Boat Co, Groton, Conn, 41-43; assoc, Jaros, Baum & Bolles, NYC, 46-58, partner, 58-92, emer partner & consult to firm, 86-92. *Mem:* Nat Acad Eng; NY Acad Sci; fel Am Soc Heating, Refrig & Air Conditioning Engrs; fel Am Consult Engrs Coun; Nat Soc Prof Engrs; Nat Soc Energy Engrs; fel Am Soc Mech Engrs. *Mailing Add:* 9 Ivy Hill Rd Chappaqua NY 10514-1805

BAUM, ROBERT HAROLD, ORAL MICROBIOLOGY, ANAEROBIC MICROBIOLOGY. *Current Pos:* asst prof microbiol, Sch Pharm, 71-74, assoc prof, Sch Dent, 74-87, ASSOC PROF MICROBIOL & IMMUNOL, SCH MED, TEMPLE UNIV, 87- *Personal Data:* b New York, NY, June 15, 36; m 57, Barbara I Saul; c Neil B, Steven K & Joanna E. *Educ:* Cornell Univ, BS, 57; Univ Ill, PhD(biochem), 62. *Prof Exp:* Res asst, Univ Ill, 61-62; Am Cancer Soc fel, Oak Ridge Nat Lab, 62-64; asst prof biochem, State Univ NY Col Forestry, Syracuse Univ, 64-71. *Mem:* AAAS; Sigma Xi; Am Soc Microbiol; Am Chem Soc; Am-Int Asn Dent Res. *Res:* Properties related to the adherence of cariogenic streptococci; analysis of nonspecific microbial inhibitors in saliva; metabolism of terpenoids by microorganisms; isolation and study of quinones of lactic acid bacteria; role of anaerobic microorganisms in endodontic infections. *Mailing Add:* Dept Microbiol Sch Med Temple Univ Philadelphia PA 19140-5101. *E-Mail:* baumrh@astro.ocis.temple.edu

BAUM, SANFORD, ENGINEERING ECONOMICS. *Current Pos:* RETIRED. *Personal Data:* b San Francisco, Calif, Oct 22, 24; m 55; c 3. *Educ:* Univ Calif, Berkeley, BS, 51; Stanford Univ, MS, 67, PhD(indust eng), 76. *Prof Exp:* Sr investr, US Naval Radiol Defense Lab, 51-60; design engr, Martin-Marietta Aerospace, 60-64; sr analyst, Stanford Res Inst, 64-75; prof indust eng, Univ Utah, 75- *Mem:* Inst Indust Engrs; Inst Mgt Sci. *Res:* Strategic weapon analysis; civil defense; fall out; advanced space systems; energy conservation; multi-criterion optimization random search approaches to operations research; engineering economics. *Mailing Add:* 4761 Ichabod Dr Salt Lake City UT 84117

BAUM, SIEGMUND JACOB, PHYSIOLOGY, RADIOBIOLOGY. *Current Pos:* RETIRED. *Personal Data:* b Vienna, Austria, Nov 14, 20; nat US; m 47, Arline R Weber; c Jonathan, Andrew, Vicki, Joseph & Anthony. *Educ:* Univ Calif, Los Angeles, BA, 49, MA, 50; Univ Calif, Berkeley, PhD(physiol), 59. *Honors & Awards:* Sci Award, US Naval Radiol Defense Lab, 60; Except Civilian Serv Medal, Defense Nuclear Agency USA, 73. *Prof Exp:* Physiologist, US Naval Radiol Defense Lab, 50-60; group leader physiol & radiobiol, Douglas Missile & Space Systs, 60-62; head cellular radiobiol div, Armed Forces Radiobiol Res Inst, 62-64, chmn exp path dept, 64-76, chmn exp hemat dept, 76-82. *Concurrent Pos:* Adj prof physiol, Uniformed Serv Univ, Sch Med, 78-88, consult radiobiol, 82-; ed, Exp Hemat Today, 77-88. *Mem:* Am Physiol Soc; Radiation Res Soc; Int Soc Exp Hemat (treas, 81-89); Transplantation Soc. *Res:* Endocrinology; biological effects of radiation; erythrocyte precursor system; post-irradiation bone marrow therapy; experimental hematology; space radiobiology. *Mailing Add:* 6600 Greyswood Rd Bethesda MD 20817-1537

BAUM, STANLEY, RADIOLOGY. *Current Pos:* PROF RADIOL & CHMN DEPT, SCH MED, UNIV PA, 75-, CHMN RADIOL, HOSP UNIV PA, 75- *Personal Data:* b New York, NY, Dec 26, 29; m 58; c 3. *Educ:* NY Univ, BA, 51; State Univ Utrecht, MD, 57. *Prof Exp:* Intern, Kings Co Hosp Med Ctr, 57-58; Nat Cancer Inst resident radiol, Grad Hosp, Univ Pa, 58-61; fel cardiovasc radiol, Sch Med, Stanford Univ, 61, instr radiol, 62; from instr to prof, Univ Pa, 62-71; prof radiol, Harvard Med Sch, 71-75. *Concurrent Pos:* Asst radiologist, Grad Hosp, Univ Pa, 62-; consult, Vet Admin Hosp, Wilmington, Del, 63-66 & Vet Admin Hosp, Philadelphia, 65-; asst radiologist, Presby-Univ Pa Med Ctr, 66-71; radiologist, Mass Gen Hosp, 71-75. *Mem:* Inst Med-Nat Acad Sci; Am Col Radiol; Radiol Soc NAm; Am Col Cardiol; Am Gastroenterol Asn; Asn Univ Radiol. *Res:* Cardiovascular radiology; selective arteriography; pharmacologic control of portal hypertension. *Mailing Add:* Univ Hosp 3400 Spruce St Philadelphia PA 19104

BAUM, STEFI ALISON, ASTRONOMY. *Current Pos:* POSTDOCTORAL RESEARCHER, NETH FOUND RES ASTRON, 87- *Personal Data:* b Chicago, Ill, Dec 11, 58; m 85, Christopher Peter O'Dea; c Connor & Kieran Peter. *Educ:* Harvard Univ, BA, 80; Univ Md, PhD(astron), 87. *Honors & Awards:* Annie Jump Cannon Award, Am Astron Soc, 93. *Mem:* Am Astron Soc. *Mailing Add:* Space Telescope & Sci Inst 3700 San Martin Dr Baltimore MD 21218-2410

BAUM, STEPHEN GRAHAM, INTERNAL MEDICINE, INFECTIOUS DISEASES. *Current Pos:* assoc, 68-69, asst prof med, 69-73, assoc prof med & cell biol, 73-78, PROF MED, CELL BIOL, MICROBIOL & IMMUNOL, ALBERT EINSTEIN COL MED, 78-, DIR MD-PHD PROG, 73-, CO-DIR INFECTIOUS DIS DIV, 75-, SCI DIR ANALYSIS ULTRASTRUCTURE CTR & DIR OFF GRAD EDUC, 84- *Personal Data:* b New York, NY, Apr 28, 37; wid; c 1. *Educ:* Cornell Univ, AB, 58; NY Univ, MD, 62. *Prof Exp:* From intern to resident med, Harvard Div, Boston City Hosp, 62-68. *Concurrent Pos:* Nat Inst Allergy & Infectious Dis res assoc virol, 64-66; Med Res Coun spec fel, Nat Inst Med Res, London, 66-67; NY Health Res Coun career scientist, 68-; Am Cancer Soc fac res assoc. *Mem:* Infectious Dis Soc Am; Am Soc Clin Invest; Harvey Soc; Am Soc Microbiol. *Res:* Viral oncology; electron microscopy. *Mailing Add:* Mt Sinai Sch Med Beth Israel Med Ctr First Ave 16th St New York NY 10003-8902

BAUM, STUART J, ORGANIC CHEMISTRY, BIOORGANIC CHEMISTRY. *Current Pos:* RETIRED. *Personal Data:* b Brooklyn, NY, Mar 7, 39; m 64; c 2. *Educ:* Queens Col, BS, 60; Cornell Univ, MS, 63, PhD(molecular biol), 65. *Prof Exp:* From asst prof to prof, State Univ NY Col Plattsburgh, 65-76, prof chem, 65- *Mem:* Am Chem Soc. *Res:* Organic reaction mechanisms; organometallic chemistry; mechanisms of biochemical reactions; structure of coordination complexes; chemical education. *Mailing Add:* 8460-S Southbridge Dr Ft Myers FL 33912

BAUM, WERNER A, METEOROLOGY, CLIMATOLOGY. *Current Pos:* prof & dean, 79-90, EMER PROF METEOROL & DEAN, COL ARTS & SCI, FLA STATE UNIV, 90- *Personal Data:* b Giessen, Ger, Apr 10, 23; nat US; m 45, Shirley Bowman; c Janice & Sandra. *Educ:* Univ Chicago, BS, 43, MS, 44, PhD(meteorol), 48. *Hon Degrees:* ScD, Mt St Joseph Col, RI, 71, Univ RI, 74; DPA, Husson Col, 72. *Honors & Awards:* Spec Citation, Am Meteorol Soc, 62, Charles Franklin Brooks Award, 75, Cleveland Abbe Award, 88; Sci Freedom & Responsibility Award, AAAS, 85. *Prof Exp:* From assoc prof to prof meteorol, Fla State Univ, 49-58, head dept, 49-58, dir univ res, 57-58, dean grad sch & dir res, 58-60, dean fac, 60-63, vpres acad affairs, 63; prof meteorol & vpres acad affairs, Univ Miami, 63-65; prof meteorol & vpres sci affairs, NY Univ, 65-67; dep adminr, Environ Sci Serv Admin, 67-68; prof physics & geog & pres, Univ RI, 68-73; prof geog & univ chancellor, Univ Wis-Milwaukee, 73-79. *Concurrent Pos:* Ed, J Meteorol, Am Meteorol Soc, 49-61; mem, comt climat adv to US Weather Bur, Nat Acad Sci, 55-58, chmn, Panel on Educ, Comt Atmospheric Sci, 62-64; mem coun, Oak Ridge Inst Nuclear Studies, 58-62; mem exec reserve, US Weather Bur, 58-63, chmn adv comt educ & training, 64-66; trustee, Univ Corp Atmospheric Res, 59-63, 65-67 & 80-83, corp secy, 63-67; mem, Adv Panel on Atmospheric Sci Prog, NSF, 63-67, chmn, 65-67; dir, Fund for Overseas Res Grants & Educ, 65-74; mem sci adv coun, Tex Christian Univ Res Found, 67-73, 74 77; US rep, Panel of Experts on Meteorol Educ & Training, World Meteorol Orgn, UN, 71-80; mem, Nat Sea Grant Prog Adv Panel, 74-78; life trustee, Univ RI Found, 75. *Mem:* Fel AAAS; fel & hon mem Am Meteorol Soc (pres, 77-78); fel Am Geog Soc; fel Am Geophys Union. *Res:* Evaluation and analysis of foreign meteorological material; academic and scientific administration; climatology. *Mailing Add:* 4436 Meandering Way Tallahassee FL 32308. *E-Mail:* wabaum@freenet.fsu.edu

BAUM, WILLIAM ALVIN, GALAXIES, PLANETARY SCIENCE & COSMOLOGY. *Current Pos:* PROF, UNIV WASH, 90- *Personal Data:* b Toledo, Ohio, Jan 18, 24; m 61, Ester Bru. *Educ:* Univ Rochester, BA, 43; Calif Inst Technol, MS, 45, PhD(physics), 50. *Honors & Awards:* Shapley lectr, Am Astron Soc, 61-; Asteroid Billbaum named in honor, 91. *Prof Exp:* Physicist, Naval Res Lab, Washington, DC, 46-49; astronr, Mt Wilson & Palomar Observ, 50-65; dir, Planetary Res Ctr, Lowell Observ, 65-90. *Concurrent Pos:* Guggenheim fel, 60-61; adj prof, Ohio State Univ, 69-89 & Northern Ariz Univ, 73-89; consult, Off Space Sci, NASA, 70-, mem bd dirs, Assoc Univ Res Astron, 76-79, Viking Orbiter Imaging Team, 70-79 & Hubble Space Telescope Camera Team, 77-97; chmn, Div Planetary Sci, Am Astron Soc, 76-77. *Mem:* Am Astron Soc; Int Astron Union; Royal Astron Soc Brit; Astron Soc Pac. *Res:* Photoelectric photometry; photoelectric image-receiving systems; optical instrument development; globular star clusters; stellar populations; magnitudes and redshifts of galaxies; planetary science; spacecraft instrumentation; observational cosmology; constancy of physical constants. *Mailing Add:* Univ Wash 2124 NE Park Rd Seattle WA 98105. *E-Mail:* baum@astro.washington.edu

BAUMAL, REUBEN, renal pathology, for more information see previous edition

BAUMAN, BERNARD D, ORGANIC CHEMISTRY. *Current Pos:* PRES, COMPOSITE PARTICLES, INC, 93- *Personal Data:* b Rochester, NY, June 15, 46; m, Anne Bellotti; c Sarah, Brenden & Justin. *Educ:* Eastern Nazarene Col, BA, 68; State Univ NY Albany, PhD(org chem), 73. *Prof Exp:* Scholar org chem, Pa State Univ, 73-74; sr chemist org chem, Rohm & Haas Co, 74-76; mgr, Composite Prod, Air Prod & Chem, Inc, 76-93. *Mem:* Am Chem Soc; Soc Plastic Eng. *Res:* Surface modification of plastics and elastomers; development of novel composite systems. *Mailing Add:* 2715 Acorn Dr Emmaus PA 18049-9802. *Fax:* 610-791-2486

BAUMAN, DALE E, NUTRITIONAL BIOCHEMISTRY. *Current Pos:* PROF NUTRIT BIOCHEM, CORNELL UNIV, 79-, LIBERTY HYDE BAILEY PROF, 87- *Personal Data:* b Dec 26, 42; m 65, L Marie Vinande; c Rebecca, Todd & Jeffrey. *Educ:* Mich State Univ, BS, 64, MS, 68; Univ Ill, PhD(nutrit biochem), 69. *Honors & Awards:* Young Scientist Res Award, Am Soc Animal Sci, 77, Animal Growth & Develop Award, 96; Nutrit Res Award, Am Dairy Sci Asn, 82, Physiol Award, 94; Charles A Black Award, Coun Agr Sci Tech, 95; USDA Super Serv Award, 86; Am Cyanamid Award, Am Dairy Sci Asn, 87; Liberty Hyde Bailey Prof Cornell, 87. *Prof Exp:* From asst prof to assoc prof, Univ Ill, 69-78. *Concurrent Pos:* Mem, US Bd Agr & US Comt Biotechnol, 89-; hon res fel, Hannah Res Inst, Scotland, 89. *Mem:* Nat Acad Sci; Am Inst Nutrit; Am Soc Animal Sci; Am Dairy Sci Asn; AAAS. *Res:* Animal nutrition; physiology. *Mailing Add:* Cornell Univ 262 Morrison Ithaca NY 14853. *Fax:* 607-255-9829; *E-Mail:* deb6@cornell.edu

BAUMAN, HOWARD EUGENE, FOOD SCIENCE. *Current Pos:* RETIRED. *Personal Data:* b Woodworth, Wis, Mar 20, 25; m 48; c 2. *Educ:* Univ Wis, BS, 49, MS, 51, PhD(bact), 53. *Prof Exp:* Head bact sect res & develop, Pillsbury Mills Inc, 53-55, head biol res br, Cent res, Pillsbury Co, 55-60, assoc dir res, 60-67, dir corp res, 67-69, vpres sci & technol, Minneapolis, 69-90. *Mem:* AAAS; Am Soc Microbiol; Soc Indust Microbiol; Am Asn Cereal Chemists; Inst Food Technol. *Res:* Nutrition; microbiology. *Mailing Add:* 4580 Greenwood Dr Minnetonka MN 55343

BAUMAN, JOHN E, JR, INORGANIC CHEMISTRY. *Current Pos:* from asst prof to assoc prof, 61-75, PROF CHEM, UNIV MO, COLUMBIA, 75- *Personal Data:* b Kalamazoo, Mich, Jan 18, 33; m 64, Barbara Curry; c John, Catherine & Amy. *Educ:* Univ Mich, BS, 55, MS, 60, PhD(chem), 61. *Prof Exp:* Res chemist, Midwest Res Inst, 55-58. *Concurrent Pos:* Mem staff, Scripps Inst Oceanog, Univ Calif, 70. *Mem:* Am Chem Soc; Sigma Xi. *Res:* Thermodynamics of inorganic coordination compounds; ionic reactions in solution; calorimetry; corrosion; chemical oceanography; modeling of geologically important aqueous solutions; development of instrumentation labs for secondary science teachers. *Mailing Add:* Dept Chem Univ Mo Columbia MO 65211

BAUMAN, JOHN W, JR, PHYSIOLOGY. *Current Pos:* RETIRED. *Personal Data:* b Stockton, Calif, Dec 17, 18; m 48; c 4. *Educ:* Univ Southern Calif, AB, 48; Univ Calif, Berkeley, PhD(physiol), 55. *Prof Exp:* Instr physiol, Sch Med, NY Univ, 56-58, asst prof, 58-61; res scientist exp med, Bur Res, Princeton, NJ, 61-62, chief group med sect, 62-70; assoc prof physiol, NJ Col Med & Dent, 70-90. *Concurrent Pos:* Fel biol, Princeton Univ, 68-70; adj asst prof, Med Sch, NY Univ, 61-62; vis prof physiol, NJ Col Med & Dent, 68, 69. *Mem:* Am Physiol Soc; Am Soc Nephrol; Endocrine Soc; Brit Soc Endocrinol. *Res:* Endocrine effects on renal function; mechanisms of antidiuresis and water diuresis; proteinuria; sodium and hypertension. *Mailing Add:* 82 Fair Acres Ct Princeton NJ 08540

BAUMAN, NORMAN, PHARMACOLOGY, MEDICINE. *Current Pos:* ASST DIR LICENSING, INNAPHARMA, 93- *Personal Data:* b Brooklyn, NY, Aug 20, 32; m 57, Jean Krause; c Anne (Wightman), Sydney & Ellen. *Educ:* Harvard Univ, AB, 53; NY Univ, MD, 57. *Prof Exp:* Intern, Bronx Munic Hosp, 57-58; fel rheumatology, Duke Univ, 60-61, asst res med, 61-62, fel rheumatology, 62-64, instr med, 62-64; sr scientist, Lederle Labs, Am Cyanamid Co, 64-93. *Concurrent Pos:* Res assoc, Nat Inst Arthritis & Metab Dis, 58-60; consult. *Mem:* Math Asn Am; Am Rheumatism Asn. *Res:* Mechanism of drug action; quantitative structure activity relationships; rheumatology. *Mailing Add:* Innapharma 10 Mountainview Rd Suite 301 Upper Saddle River NJ 07458. *Fax:* 914-368-3180

BAUMAN, RICHARD GILBERT, PHYSICAL CHEMISTRY. *Current Pos:* CONSULT, R&D AUDITS, 89- *Personal Data:* b Warren, Ohio, Sept 14, 24; m 45, Gloria Gordon; c Pamela (Goetsch), Betsy (Snow) & Jennie (Gwilym). *Educ:* Case Inst Technol, BS, 44, MS, 48, PhD(phys chem), 51; Harvard Univ, advan mgt prog, 62. *Prof Exp:* Instr phys chem, Fenn Col, 46-47 & Case Inst Technol, 47-50; res chemist, B F Goodrich Co, 50-58, mgr tire res, 58-64, dir prod res, 64-72, dir tire res, 73-88. *Concurrent Pos:* Chemist, Brookhaven Nat Lab, 53-54. *Mem:* Am Chem Soc; Indust Res Inst; Sigma Xi; Tire Soc. *Res:* Phase equilibria; polymerization reactions; physical properties of high polymers; polyelectrolytes; oxidation of high polymers; nuclear engineering; processing of reactor fuels; research administration; tire materials and construction. *Mailing Add:* 19 Glen Oaks Lane Berea OH 44017. *Fax:* 440-234-1550

BAUMAN, ROBERT ANDREW, ORGANIC CHEMISTRY. *Current Pos:* RETIRED. *Personal Data:* b Rochester, NY, Apr 17, 23. *Educ:* Univ Rochester, BS, 43; Univ Ill, PhD(chem), 46. *Prof Exp:* Spec res asst, Univ Ill, 43-46; res chemist, Gen Aniline & Film Corp, 46-48; asst, Univ Ill, 48-50; res chemist, Gen Aniline & Film Corp, 50-52; res chemist, Colgate-Palmolive-Peet Co, 52-53 & Colgate Palmolive Co, 53-63, res assoc, Colgate-Palmolive Co, 63-68, sr res assoc, 68-78, sr scientist, 78-83. *Mem:* Am Chem Soc. *Res:* Organic synthesis; surfactants; oral chemotherapy; fabric beneficiation. *Mailing Add:* Ten Landing Lane Apt 8C New Brunswick NJ 08901-1047

BAUMAN, ROBERT POE, SCIENCE EDUCATION, THERMODYNAMICS. *Current Pos:* chmn dept, 67-73, prof, 67-92, dir, Proj on Teaching & Learning Univ Col, 75-78, EMER PROF PHYSICS, UNIV ALA, BIRMINGHAM, 92- *Personal Data:* b Jackson, Mich, May 8, 28; m 49, Edith Gerkin; c Katherine, David, Jeffrey & Alice. *Educ:* Purdue Univ, BS, 49, MS, 51; Univ Pittsburgh, PhD(physics), 54. *Prof Exp:* Asst, Purdue Univ, 49-51 & Mellon Inst Indust Res, 51-54; from instr to assoc prof chem, Polytech Inst Brooklyn, 54-67. *Concurrent Pos:* Mem tech staff, Bell Labs, Murray Hill, 66; vis fel, Joint Inst Lab Astrophy, 80-81. *Mem:* Am Asn Physics Teachers (pres, 83); Coblentz Soc (pres, 72-74). *Res:* Vibrational spectra and molecular structure; teaching-learning theory. *Mailing Add:* Dept Physics Univ Ala Birmingham Univ Sta Birmingham AL 35294

BAUMAN, THOMAS TROST, AGRONOMY. *Current Pos:* PROF AGR EXTEN RES & TEACHING, PURDUE UNIV, 76- *Personal Data:* b Lafayette, Ind, Sept 11, 39; m 65; c 3. *Educ:* Purdue Univ, BS, 63, MS, 65, PhD(weed sci), 76. *Concurrent Pos:* Mem Task Force, Coun Agr Sci & Technol, 81-; guest lectr, Ill Spray Sch & Mich Pesticide Training Sch, 81. *Mem:* Weed Sci Soc Am (pres, 94); Am Agron Soc; Soil Sci Soc Am. *Res:* Soybean weed control; tillage systems on soybean weed control; weed competition; corn weed management. *Mailing Add:* Bot & Plant Path Dept 234 Connolly St West Lafayette IN 47906-2724

BAUMANN, ARTHUR NICHOLAS, INORGANIC CHEMISTRY, ANALYTICAL CHEMISTRY. *Current Pos:* res chemist, Fla Exp Sta, 52-59, sr res chemist, tech div, 59-61, supvr tech serv, 61-64, chief chemist, 64-69, sr process engr, 69-74, mgr develop, Agr Prod Div, 74-80, mgr develop eng, New Wales Chem Opers, Int Minerals & Chem Corp, 80-86, PROCESS CONSULT, 86- *Personal Data:* b Bogota, NJ, Dec 15, 22; m 50, Elizabeth McNelis; c 2. *Educ:* Fla Southern Col, BS, 51. *Prof Exp:* Lab technician, phosphate rock div, Int Minerals & Chem Corp, Fla, 49-50; jr process engr, Davison Chem Co, 52. *Concurrent Pos:* Counr, Am Chem Soc, 83; mem, Resource Mgt Comt, Fertilizer Inst; chmn, Tech Adv Comt, Fla Inst Phosphate Res, 81-; vol exec, Int Exec Serv Corps, Egypt, Morrocco & Zimbabwe. *Mem:* Am Chem Soc; Am Inst Chem Engrs. *Res:* Production of alkali polyphosphates; defluorinated phosphate rock; anhydrous hydrogen fluoride; fluoride chemicals; potassium compounds; automation of wet chemical analytical methods for process control; solvent extraction; uranium recovery; phosphate process chemistry. *Mailing Add:* 2329 Rogers Rd Lakeland FL 33813-3139

BAUMANN, CARL AUGUST, NUTRITIONAL BIOCHEMISTRY. *Current Pos:* res fel biochem, 36-38, from instr to prof, 38-76, EMER PROF BIOCHEM, UNIV WIS-MADISON, 76- *Personal Data:* b Milwaukee, Wis, Aug 10, 06. *Educ:* Univ Wis, BS, 29, MS, 31, PhD(biochem), 33. *Prof Exp:* Asst biochem, Univ Wis-Madison, 29-34; Gen Educ Bd fel, Univ Heidelberg, Copenhagen Univ & Cambridge Univ, 34-36. *Concurrent Pos:* Consult, Off Sci Res & Develop, DC, 45-46; mem study sect nutrit, Am Cancer Soc; mem study sect nutrit & metab & nutrit, NIH, 48-60; mem nutrit surv, Interdept Comt Nutrit Nat Defense, NIH, Chile, 60; chief-of-party, Ford Found Basic Sci Proj, Agrarian Univ, Peru, 66-69; AID-Midwestern Univs Consortium Int Activities consult, Agr Univ, Indonesia, 74 & 75. *Mem:* AAAS; Am Chem Soc; Am Soc Biol Chem; fel Am Inst Nutrit. *Res:* Vitamins; nutrition; tumor development; skin and intestinal sterols; selenium metabolism. *Mailing Add:* 1840 N Prospect Ave No 821 Milwaukee WI 53202-1164

BAUMANN, DWIGHT MAYLON BILLY, SYSTEMS DESIGN, SYSTEMS SCIENCE. *Current Pos:* prof, 70-76, PROF ENG DESIGN, CARNEGIE MELLON UNIV, 76- *Personal Data:* b Ashley, NDak, May 12, 33; m 54; c 3. *Educ:* NDak State Univ, BSME, 55; Mass Inst Technol, MSME, 57, ScD, 60. *Honors & Awards:* Chester Carlson Award, Am Soc Eng Educ, 82. *Prof Exp:* Teaching asst physics, NDak State Univ, 54-55; instr eng design, Mass Inst Technol, 56-60, asst prof to assoc prof mech eng, 60-70. *Concurrent Pos:* Pres, Icon Corp, 64-69; dir, Graphic Sci Corp, 67-75; chmn, Eng Design Prog, 70-; pres & dir, Ctr Entrepreneurial Develop, 71-; co-dir, Transp Res Inst, Carnegie-Mellon Univ, 76- *Mem:* Am Soc Mech Engrs; Am Soc Eng Educ; Sigma Xi. *Res:* Development of clinical approaches to engineering education. *Mailing Add:* 1235 Squirrel Hill Ave Pittsburgh PA 15217-1147

BAUMANN, E(DWARD) ROBERT, SANITARY ENGINEERING. *Current Pos:* from assoc prof to prof, 53-72, Anson Morston Distinguished Prof civil eng, 72-91, EMER DISTINGUISHED PROF, CIVIL ENG, IOWA STATE UNIV, 91- *Personal Data:* b Rochester, NY, May 12, 21; m 46; c 2. *Educ:* Univ Mich, BSE, 44; Univ Ill, BS, 45, MS, 47, PhD(sanit eng), 54. *Honors & Awards:* Gascoigne Medal, Water Pollution Control Fedn, 62, A S Bedell Award, 76, Philip F Morgan Award, 86; Pub Award, Am Waters Works Asn, 62 & 80, Purification Div Award, 65, A P Black Res Award, 78; Gold Medal Award, Filtration Soc, 70; Nalco Award, Asn Environ Eng Prof, 80. *Prof Exp:* Instr civil eng, Univ Ill, 47, res assoc sanit eng, 47-53. *Concurrent Pos:* NSF fel, King's Col, Eng, 59-60. *Mem:* Am Soc Civil Engrs; Nat Soc Prof Engrs; Am Soc Eng Educ; Am Inst Chem Engrs; Sigma Xi; Asn Environ Eng Prof; Am Water Works Asn; Water Pollution Control Fedn; Am Acad Environ Engrs. *Res:* Water treatment; sewage treatment; hydraulics. *Mailing Add:* 1627 Crestwood Circle No C Ames IA 50010-5520

BAUMANN, FREDERICK, ANALYTICAL CHEMISTRY. *Current Pos:* TECH CONSULT, 94- *Personal Data:* b Los Angeles, Calif, Nov 26, 30; m 62; c David, Chris & Hilary. *Educ:* Univ Calif, Los Angeles, BS, 52; Univ Wis, PhD(anal chem), 56. *Prof Exp:* Res chemist, Calif Res Corp, 56-65; mgr res, Varian Inst Div, 65-69, mgr res & eng, 70-79, managing dir, Varian Techtron, 80-81, tech dir, 81-82, mgr data syst oper, Varian Inst Group, 82-89, mgr strategic & tech planning, 89-90, tech consult, Varian Assocs, 91-93. *Concurrent Pos:* Instr gas chromatography, Exten, Univ Calif, 64-70; adv bd anal chem, Res & Eng Mgt, 72-74. *Mem:* Am Chem Soc; Sigma Xi. *Res:* Gas chromatography; liquid chromatography; laboratory automation; mass spectrometry; electrochemistry; expertise in development of scientific instruments. *Mailing Add:* 166 Rudgear Dr Walnut Creek CA 94596-6316

BAUMANN, GERHARD, ENDOCRINOLOGY. *Current Pos:* from asst prof to assoc prof, 77-88, PROF MED, SCH MED, NORTHWESTERN UNIV, 88- *Personal Data:* b Basel, Switz, Sept 15, 41; m 72, Mary P; c Catherine. *Educ:* Univ Basel, MD, 67. *Prof Exp:* Vis scientist endocrinol, NIH, 74-77. *Concurrent Pos:* Fel, Peter Bent Brigham Hosp, 69-71. *Mem:* Am Fedn Clin Res; Endocrine Soc; Cent Soc Clin Res; Am Soc Clin Invest; Asn Am Physicians; Sigma Xi. *Res:* Pituitary gland; human growth hormone with its molecular variants; somatomedin; prolactin; insulin receptors; growth hormone receptors; growth hormone binding proteins. *Mailing Add:* Ctr Endocrinol Metab & Molecular Med Northwestern Univ Sch Med Chicago IL 60611

BAUMANN, HANS D, FLUID MECHANICS, VALVE ACOUSTICS. *Current Pos:* CONSULT, 91- *Personal Data:* m, Sigrio Doornkaat; c 2. *Educ:* Metallf Achschule Bielefelp, WGer, BS, 53; Columbia-Pac Univ, PhD(mech eng), 82. *Prof Exp:* Chief engr, Welland S Texhorn Co, 54-58; sr develop engr, Masoneilan Co, 58-63; dir, Cashco, Inc, 63-66; mgr res & develop, Worthington S/A, 66-68; vpres, Masoneilan Int Inc, 68-74; consult mech eng, 74-77; pres, H D Baumann Assoc, 77- *Concurrent Pos:* Dir, H B Serv Inc, 81-, dir StP, Instrument Soc Am, 89-; tech expert, IEC/SC 65B, 86-; guest prof, Kobe Univ, Japan & Korean Inst Advan Technol, 89. *Mem:* Fel Instrument Soc Am; Am Soc Mech Engrs; hon mem Spanish Eng Soc. *Res:* author of 68 publications on valve sizing, cavitation, aerodynamic noise and co-author of four hand books on instrumentation, valves and acoustics; author of one handbook on control valves. *Mailing Add:* 32 Pine Rye NH 03870. *Fax:* 603-436-0996.

BAUMANN, JACOB BRUCE, ORGANIC CHEMISTRY. *Current Pos:* asst prof, 65-71, ASSOC PROF CHEM, PA STATE UNIV, SCHUYLKILL CAMPUS, 71- *Personal Data:* b Fremont, Ohio, Sept 11, 32; m 57; c 3. *Educ:* Amherst Col, BA, 54; Univ Mich, MS, 57, PhD(chem), 61. *Prof Exp:* From instr to asst prof chem, Defiance Col, 60-65. *Mem:* Am Chem Soc. *Res:* Aromatic nucleophilic substitution. *Mailing Add:* Dept Chem Schuylkill Campus Pa State Univ 200 University Dr Schuylkill Haven PA 17972-2202

BAUMANN, NORMAN PAUL, NUCLEAR PHYSICS, ACOUSTIC MEASUREMENTS. *Current Pos:* RETIRED. *Personal Data:* b Sylvan Grove, Kans, Nov 18, 27; m 54; c 1. *Educ:* Univ Kans, BS, 51, MS, 52, PhD(physics), 55. *Prof Exp:* Physicist, Savannah River Lab, E I du Pont de Nemours & Co, 55-93. *Mem:* Am Phys Soc; Am Nuclear Soc. *Res:* Reactor physics and design; acoustic analysis of reactor systems; nondestructive assay of nuclear materials; criticality monitoring; radiation damage reactor materials. *Mailing Add:* 1330 Evans Rd Aiken SC 29803-5336

BAUMANN, PAUL C, ECOTOXICOLOGY, ECOEPIDEMIOLOGY. *Current Pos:* AQUATIC TOXICOLOGIST, BIOL RESOURCES DIV, US GEOL SURV, 97- *Personal Data:* b Aurora, Ill, Oct 6, 46; m 84, Denise Shackelford; c Brendan C. *Educ:* Beloit Col, Wis, BS, 68; Univ Wis-Madison, MS, 72, PhD(zool), 75. *Prof Exp:* Group leader, Ecol Serv Tex Instruments, 76-78; fishery biologist aquatic toxicol, US Fish & Wildlife Serv, 78-93; fishery biologist aquatic toxicol, Nat Biol Surv, 93-96. *Concurrent Pos:* Adj asst prof, Dept Zool, Ohio State Univ, 78-95, Sch Natural Resources, 80-95, Environ Sci, 80-95; adj assoc prof, Dept Zool, Sch Natural Resources, 96- *Mem:* Soc Environ Toxicol & Chem; Am Fisheries Soc; Sigma Xi. *Res:* Neoplasia in fish and carcinogen causes, particularly PAH; teratogenic and other reproductive effects of contaminants on aquatic vertebrates; immunoassays and other biomarkers of toxicant exposure and pathology in fish. *Mailing Add:* Field Res Sta BRD-USGS Ohio State Univ 473 Kottman Hall 2021 Coffey Rd Columbus OH 43210. *Fax:* 614-292-7432; *E-Mail:* baumann@osu.edu

BAUMANN, RICHARD WILLIAM, SYSTEMATIC ENTOMOLOGY, AQUATIC BIOLOGY. *Current Pos:* asst prof, 75-80, ASSOC PROF ENTOM, BRIGHAM YOUNG UNIV, 80- *Personal Data:* b Castle Dale, Utah, July 24, 40; m 64; c 6. *Educ:* Univ Utah, BA, 65, MS, 67, PhD(aquatic entom), 70. *Prof Exp:* Res guest aquatic entom, Max Planck Limnol Inst, 70-71; asst prof limnol, Southwest Mo Univ, 71-72; assoc cur entom, Smithsonian Inst, 72-75. *Concurrent Pos:* Supvr res Moraca River, Yugoslavia, Off Limnol & Oceanog, Smithsonian Inst, 73-75; investr ecol, Bur Land Mgt, 74-75; adj prof, NTex State Univ, 74- *Mem:* Sigma Xi; Entom Soc Am; Am Entom Soc; NAm Benthol Soc. *Res:* Studies on the systematics, phylogeny and ecology of the stoneflies, Insecta Plecoptera, of the northern hemisphere; ecological studies of aquatic insects in western North America. *Mailing Add:* Dept Zool 575 WIDB Brigham Young Univ Provo UT 84602-1049

BAUMANN, ROBERT JAY, CHILD NEUROLOGY, NEUROEPIDEMIOLOGY. *Current Pos:* assoc prof, 78-92, HEAD, CHILD NEUROL SECT, UNIV KY, 78-, PROF NEUROL & PEDIAT, 92- *Personal Data:* b Chicago, Ill, Oct 22, 40; m 64; c 3. *Educ:* Tufts Univ, BS, 61; Western Reserve Univ, MD, 65. *Prof Exp:* Resident pediat, Univ Chicago, 65-67, resident neurol, 67-69; child neurologist, US Air Force, 69-71; resident neurol, Univ Chicago, 71-72. *Concurrent Pos:* Neuroepidemiologist, Nat Inst Neurol Commun Disorders & Stroke, Bethesda, Md, 78-79; mem res comt neuroepidemiol, World Fedn Neurol, 78- *Mem:* Child Neurol Soc; Am Acad Neurol; Soc Epidemiol Res; Am Acad Pediat; Int Child Neurol Soc. *Res:* Epidemiology of neurological disease; neonatal stroke and cerebral palsy. *Mailing Add:* Dept Neurol Univ Ky Med Sch 800 Rose St Lexington KY 40536-0001. *Fax:* 606-323-1040; *E-Mail:* neu101@ukcc.uky.edu

BAUMANN, THIEMA WOLF, NEUROHISTOCHEMISTRY, HISTOLOGY. *Current Pos:* PROF LIFE SCI, LOGAN COL, 77- *Personal Data:* b St Louis, Mo, May 30, 21; m 50, Erwin W; c William T. *Educ:* Harris Col, AB, 42; Washington Univ, AM, 44; St Louis Univ, PhD(neuroanat), 66. *Prof Exp:* Res dir genetics, St Louis Univ, 60-77; prof histol-anat, Southern Ill Sch Dent Med, 80-81. *Concurrent Pos:* Prin investr, Found Orthod Educ & Res, 60-77; vis prof, Southern Ill Sch Dent Med, 80-81. *Mem:* Sigma Xi; AAAS. *Res:* Localization of neurotransmitters visually demonstrated by histochemistry; documentation of genetics and patterns of human skeletal growth; supra segmental inhibition of spinal reflex mechanisms; breathing reflexes; effects of therapeutic ionizing radiation on bone; phylogeny of the central nervous system; cell biology. *Mailing Add:* 6504 Devonshire St St Louis MO 63109. *Fax:* 314-227-9338

BAUMANN, WOLFGANG J, MEMBRANE BIOPHYSICS, LIPID BIOCHEMISTRY. *Current Pos:* res fel, Univ Minn, 63-66, res assoc, 66-67, from asst prof to assoc prof, 67-74, asst to dir, 79-81, PROF, HORMEL INST, UNIV MINN, 74- *Personal Data:* b Crailsheim, Ger, May 26, 36; m 67; c Christoph G & Nikola A. *Educ:* Univ Stuttgart, BS, 57, MS, 61, PhD(org chem), 63. *Prof Exp:* Asst chem, Univ Stuttgart, 61-63. *Concurrent Pos:* Assoc ed, Lipids, 74-84, co-ed, Lipids, 85 & ed-in-chief, 86-, ed, Communications, Lipids, 75-80; consult, NIH, NSF & USDA. *Mem:* Am Chem Soc; AAAS; Am Oil Chemists Soc; Am Soc Biochem Molecular Biol; Am Heart Asn; Biophys Soc. *Res:* Nuclear magnetic resonance spectroscopy on biological and model membranes; membrane regulation by lysophospholipids; lysophospholipid/cholesterol interactions; lip differentiation in gap junetion domains; lipid packing in highly curved memberous systems; liposome/cell interactions. *Mailing Add:* Hormel Inst Univ Minn PO Box 656 Austin MN 55912-0656. *Fax:* 561-437-9699

BAUMBACH, LISA LORRAINE, INHERITED NEUROLOGICAL DISORDERS, INHERITED DISORDERS OF GROWTH. *Current Pos:* geneticist, Muscular Dystrophy Asn Clin, Dept Neurol, co-dir, DNA Diag Lab, Dept Pediat, ASST RES PROF & DIR, NEUROGENETICS LAB, DEPTS PEDIAT, NEUROL & BIOCHEM, UNIV MIAMI SCH MED, 91- *Personal Data:* b May 22, 58. *Educ:* Univ Fla, Gainesville, BA, 80, PhD(biochem & molecular biol), 86; Am Bd Med Genetics, cert Biochem & Molecular Genetics, 93. *Prof Exp:* Assoc, Kleberg DNA Diag Lab, Baylor Col Med, 86-87, fel, Inst Molecular Genetics, 87-89; fel biochem & human genetics, Div Genetics, Univ Colo, Health Sci Ctr, 89-90, res fel, Div Biochem Genetics, 90. *Concurrent Pos:* Fel, Muscular Dystrophy Asn, 88-90, clin fel, 89-90; lectr Univ Miami, 91-93, Miami Children's Hosp, 92; vis prof, Dept Obstet & Gynec, Univ Tenn, 93; co-investr, Nat Inst Child Health & Human Develop, NIH, 93- *Mem:* Am Soc Human Genetics; Asn Clin Lab Dirs; fel Am Col Med Genetics; Am Acad Neurol; AAAS; Int Neurofibromatosis Found; Soc Inherited Metab Dis. *Res:* Author of over 45 publications; human genetics; neurology; biochemistry; metabolic diseases. *Mailing Add:* Dept Pediatrics & Genetics Univ Miami Sch Med 1601 NW 12th Ave Rm 6020 Mailman Ctr Miami FL 33136. *Fax:* 305-547-3919

BAUMBER, JOHN SCOTT, PHYSIOLOGY. *Current Pos:* asst prof, 70-72, ASSOC PROF PHYSIOL, UNIV CALGARY, 72-, ASST DEAN FAC MED, 74- *Personal Data:* b London, Eng, June 4, 37; m 61; c 4. *Educ:* Univ Nottingham, BSc, 58; Queen's Univ, Ont, MSc, 60, PhD(physiol), 63, MD, 66. *Prof Exp:* Mo Heart Asn fel, 67-69; asst prof physiol, Univ Mo-Columbia, 69-70. *Mem:* Can Med Asn; Can Physiol Soc; Am Physiol Soc. *Res:* Cardiovascular, renal and endocrine physiology with emphasis on cardiodynamics, hemodynamics and heart failure; the renin-angiotensin-aldosterone system; hypoxia. *Mailing Add:* Direct of Med Educ Univ Calgary 3330 Hospital Dr NW Calgary AB T2N 4N1 Can

BAUMEISTER, CARL FREDERICK, INTERNAL MEDICINE. *Current Pos:* RETIRED. *Personal Data:* b Dolliver, Iowa, May 15, 07; m 30; c 1. *Educ:* Univ Chicago, BS, 30; Univ Iowa, MD, 33. *Prof Exp:* Intern & resident, Univ Hosps, Ind Univ & Univ Louisville, 33-37; physician, Council Bluffs Clin, 37-43; asst prof clin med, Col Med, Univ Ill, 43-65; clin asst prof med, Stritch Sch Med, Loyola Univ, Chicago, 70-73; asst prof clin med, Col Med, Univ Ill, 73-81. *Concurrent Pos:* Head dept internal med, Suburban Med Ctr, Berwyn, 43; mem, Inst Med Chicago. *Mem:* AMA; Asn Am Med Cols; Am Heart Asn; Am Diabetes Asn; Am Med Writers Asn. *Res:* Role of the computer as a diagnostic aid in the surgical abdomen; mechanisms and prevention of type III sinus block headaches; recognition and prevention of variant vascular headaches. *Mailing Add:* 120 S Delaplaine Rd Riverside IL 60546

BAUMEISTER, PHILIP WERNER, OPTICAL COATING TECHNOLOGY. *Current Pos:* CONSULT, 92- *Personal Data:* b Troy, Ohio, Mar 17, 29; m 52; c 3. *Educ:* Stanford Univ, BS, 50; Univ Calif, Berkeley, PhD(physics), 59. *Prof Exp:* From asst prof to prof optics, Univ Rochester, 59-78; chief scientist, Optical Coating Lab Inc, 79-85; optical coating engr, Coherent Inc, 85-92. *Mem:* Optical Soc Am; Am Vacuum Soc; Soc Vacuum Coaters. *Res:* Optical interference coatings; optical instrumentation; optical properties of thin, solid films; optical filter design. *Mailing Add:* 1050 Sholem Lane Sebastopol CA 95472-4033

BAUMEL, JULIAN JOSEPH, AVIAN & HUMAN ANATOMY, EVOLUTIONARY ZOOLOGY. *Current Pos:* From instr to prof, 53-93, EMER PROF ANAT, CREIGHTON UNIV, 94- *Personal Data:* b Sanford, Fla, July 26, 22; m 45; c Robert, Dinah & Felicia. *Educ:* Univ Fla, BS, 47, MS, 50, PhD, 53. *Concurrent Pos:* Chmn, Int Comt Avian Anat Nomenclature; pres, Nebr State Anat Bd, 70-93; vis scholar, Burke Mus, Univ Wash. *Mem:* Am Asn Anatomists; Am Soc Zoologists; Am Ornith Union; World Asn Vet Anat; Asn Avian Veterinarians. *Mailing Add:* Dept Birds Univ Wash Box 353010 Seattle WA 98195. *Fax:* 206-685-3039; *E-Mail:* jjbaumel@u.washington.edu

BAUMEL, PHILIP, HIGH ENERGY PHYSICS. *Current Pos:* from instr to assoc prof, 61-72, from asst dean to assoc dean, 80-86, PROF PHYSICS, CITY COL NEW YORK, 72-, CHMN, 89- *Personal Data:* b New York, NY, June 12, 32; m 56; c 4. *Educ:* City Col New York, BS, 53; Columbia Univ, PhD(physics), 60. *Prof Exp:* Asst prof physics, Fairleigh Dickinson Univ, 59-61. *Mem:* Am Asn Physics Teachers. *Res:* Particle physics. *Mailing Add:* 51 Chestnut Oval Orangeburg NY 10962

BAUMEYER, JOEL BERNARD, MATHEMATICS. *Current Pos:* ASST PROF MATH, CHRISTIAN BROS COL, MEMPHIS, 79- *Personal Data:* b St Louis, Mo, Nov, 30, 36. *Educ:* St Mary's Col, Minn, BA, 58, MEd, 63; St Louis Univ, MA, 77, PhD(math), 79. *Prof Exp:* Instr math & sci, St George High Sch, Evanston, Bishop Carrol High Sch, Wichita, Kans & Christian Bros High Sch, Peoria, 58-77; asst prin, Bishop Caroll High Sch, Wichita, Kans, 65. *Mem:* Nat Coun Teachers Math; Math Asn Am. *Mailing Add:* Dept Math & Sci Christian Bros Univ 650 E Parkway S Memphis TN 38104-5581

BAUMGARDNER, F WESLEY, ENVIRONMENTAL PHYSIOLOGY. *Current Pos:* CHIEF CHEMICAL DEFENSE BR, USAF SCH AEROSPACE MED, TEX, 71- *Educ:* Univ Buffalo, PhD(physiol), 71. *Res:* Personal protective equipment. *Mailing Add:* AL/CVTS US Air Force 25 Gillingham Dr Suite 25 Brooks AFB TX 78235-5104

BAUMGARDNER, JOHN RUDOLPH, MANTLE DYNAMICS. *Current Pos:* TECH STAFF MEM, LOS ALAMOS NAT LAB, 84- *Personal Data:* b Marshall, Tex, Jan 23, 44; m 79; c 1. *Educ:* Tex Tech Univ, BS, 68; Princeton Univ, MS, 70; Univ Calif, Los Angeles, MS, 81, PhD(geophys & space physics), 83. *Prof Exp:* Officer laser optics, Air Force Weapons Lab, USAF, 71-75; tech staff lasers, Rocketdyne, Rockwell Int, 78-83. *Concurrent Pos:* Consult, Ger Weather Serv, 95-97; prin investr, High Performance Comput & Commun Initiative, NASA, 96- *Mem:* Am Geophys Union. *Res:* Terra code, a three-dimensional spherical finite element code for modeling the dynamics of planetary mantles and lithospheres on large parallel supercomputing platforms. *Mailing Add:* Los Alamos Nat Lab MS B216 Los Alamos NM 87545

BAUMGARDNER, KANDY DIANE, GENETICS. *Current Pos:* From asst prof to assoc prof, 73-86, PROF ZOOL, EASTERN ILL UNIV, 86- *Personal Data:* b Peoria, Ill, Sept 16, 46. *Educ:* Bradley Univ, BS, 68; Utah State Univ, PhD(zool), 74. *Mem:* AAAS; Sigma Xi; Am Genetic Asn. *Res:* The population biology of the lambdoid bacteriophages, particularly competition between lambda, phi-eighty and a hybrid type. *Mailing Add:* Col Sci Utah State Univ Logan UT 84322-4400

BAUMGARDNER, MARION F, AGRONOMY. *Current Pos:* in-chg state soil testing opers, 58-61, from instr to assoc prof agron, 58-73, leader earth sci res progs, Lab Appln Remote Sensing, 72-80, Purdue Univ, PROF AGRON, PURDUE UNIV, WEST LAFAYETTE, 73-, ASSOC DIR, LAB APPL REMOTE SENSING, 80- *Personal Data:* b Wellington, Tex, Feb 7, 26; m 55; c 3. *Educ:* Tex Tech Col, BS, 50; Purdue Univ, MS, 55, PhD(soil fertil, plant nutrit), 64. *Hon Degrees:* DSc, DePauw Univ, 80. *Honors & Awards:* Klinck lectr, Can, 72. *Prof Exp:* Lectr agron, Agr Inst, Allahabad, India, 50-53; admin secy int student conf, Nat Coun Churches, NY, 55-56. *Concurrent Pos:* Purdue Univ rep, Ford Found Agr Develop Prog, Arg, 64-66; consult, Food & Agr Orgn, Arg, 70, Bulgaria, 71, 72 & Sudan, 74, Am Univ, Washington, DC & Lilly Endowment, Niger, 73 & Int Develop Res Centre, Ottawa, to Sudan, 75-77; mem agr panel, Nat Acad Eng, 74; vis scientist, Int Inst Aerial Surv & Earth Sci, Enschede, Neth, 74-75; mem, Int Comt Remote Sensing for Develop, Nat Acad Sci, 75-76; nat bd mem, United Methodist Comt on Relief, 76-; chmn study panel remote sensing, Agr Res Inst. *Mem:* Am Soc Agron; Int Soil Sci Soc; Soil Sci Soc Am; Am Soc Photogram; Int Asn Ecol; Sigma Xi. *Res:* Applications of remote sensing technology; digital analysis of multispectral data for identification, characterization and mapping of earth surface features; relationships between physicochemical and multispectral properties of soils. *Mailing Add:* 239 Timbercrest Rd West Lafayette IN 47906

BAUMGARDNER, RAY K, LIMNOLOGY. *Current Pos:* Asst prof aquatic biol, 65-69, assoc prof biol sci, 69-74, prof biol sci & head dept, 74-83, Univ Registrar, 83-87, DEAN & PROVOST, NORTHWESTERN STATE UNIV, FT POLK, LA, 87- *Personal Data:* b Ridgway, Colo, Dec 26, 33; m 59; c 2. *Educ:* Ft Lewis Col, AB, 59; Adams State Col, BS, 61; Okla State Univ, MS, 62, PhD(zool), 66. *Mem:* Am Soc Limnol & Oceanog. *Res:* Water pollution; primary productivity and its relation to water quality; effect of impoundments on streams. *Mailing Add:* Dept Math & Sci Northwestern State Univ La 350 Sam Sibley Rd Natchitoches LA 71497-0001

BAUMGARDT, BILLY RAY, ANIMAL NUTRITION. *Current Pos:* DIR AGR EXP STA & ASSOC DEAN AGR, PURDUE UNIV, 80- *Personal Data:* b Lafayette, Ind, Jan 17, 33; m 52; c 3. *Educ:* Purdue Univ, BS, 55, MS, 56; Rutgers Univ, PhD(agr biochem), 59. *Honors & Awards:* Nutrit Res Award, Am Dairy Sci Asn, 66, Award of Honor, 93. *Prof Exp:* Instr dairy sci, Rutgers Univ, 56-59; from asst prof to assoc prof, Univ Wis-Madison, 59-67; prof animal nutrit, Pa State Univ, Univ Park, 67-80, head dept, 70-79, assoc dir, Agr Exp Sta, 79-80. *Mem:* Am Dairy Sci Asn (pres, 85); Am Soc Animal Sci; Am Inst Nutrit; fel AAAS; Sigma Xi. *Res:* Rumen physiology and biochemistry; food evaluation; regulation of food intake; relation of nutrition to body composition. *Mailing Add:* 2614 Trace 26 West Lafayette IN 47906-1888. *Fax:* 765-494-0808; *E-Mail:* brb@aes.purdue.edu

BAUMGART, RICHARD, AUTOMOTIVE CHEMICALS. *Current Pos:* SUPVR AUTOMOTIVE CHEM, ASHLAND OIL, KY, 86- *Personal Data:* b Princeton, Ind, Sept 2, 47; m 68; c 3. *Educ:* Murray State Univ, Ky, BS, 70. *Prof Exp:* Chemist, Champion Lab Inc, 72-86. *Mailing Add:* Ashland Oil 22nd & Front Sts Ashland KY 41101

BAUMGARTEN, ALEXANDER, CLINICAL IMMUNOLOGY, LABORATORY MEDICINE. *Current Pos:* from asst prof to assoc prof, 70-81, PROF LAB MED, MED SCH, YALE UNIV, 82-; DIR, PRENATAL LAB, YALE-NEW HAVEN HOSP. *Personal Data:* b Warsaw, Poland, Nov 27, 35; Australian citizen; m 69, Rachel; c Amala & Jason. *Educ:* Sydney Univ, MB, BS, 59; Univ NSW, PhD(immunopath), 69. *Hon Degrees:* MA, Yale Univ. *Prof Exp:* Resident med, Royal Prince Alfred Hosp, Sydney, Australia, 59; resident, Royal Adelaide Hosp, 60; registr, Alfred Hosp, Melbourne, 61. *Concurrent Pos:* Consult & panelist, Food & Drug Admin, 83-86. *Mem:* Am Asn Immunologists; Am Soc Microbiol; Royal Col Pathologists Australasia. *Res:* Clinical and general immunology; protein polymorphism; alpha-fetoprotein in pregnancy. *Mailing Add:* Dept Lab Med Yale New Haven Hosp New Haven CT 06510. *Fax:* 203-795-6266; *E-Mail:* alexander.baumgarten@yale.edu

BAUMGARTEN, HENRY ERNEST, SYNTHETIC ORGANIC CHEMISTRY, COMPUTERS IN CHEMISTRY. *Current Pos:* from instr to prof org chem, Univ Nebr, Lincoln, 49-64, found prof, 64-89, actg chmn dept, 70-71, chmn dept, 71-75, interim assoc vchancellor res, 90-93, EMER PROF ORG CHEM, UNIV NEBR, LINCOLN, 94- *Personal Data:* b Texas City, Tex, Feb 27, 21; m 48, Dorothy Jefferis; c Karl, Eric, Gretchen & Kurt. *Educ:* Rice Univ, BA, 43, MA, 44, PhD(org chem), 48. *Prof Exp:* Lab asst, Rice Univ, 41-43; asst, Off Rubber Res, Univ Ill, 48-49. *Concurrent Pos:* Guggenheim fel & vis assoc, Calif Inst Technol, 62-63; consult, div instnl progs, NSF, 63-67; vis scholar & vis prof, Stanford Univ, 77-78; vis prof, Peking Univ, 85. *Mem:* Fel AAAS; Am Chem Soc. *Res:* Reactions of organic nitrogen compounds; alpha lactams; organic electrochemistry; organometallic chemistry; computers in chemical research. *Mailing Add:* Dept Chem Univ Nebr Lincoln NE 68588-0304. *E-Mail:* heb@unlinfo.unl.edu

BAUMGARTEN, JOSEPH RUSSELL, MECHANICAL ENGINEERING, MACHINE DESIGN. *Current Pos:* prof, 78-92, EMER PROF MECH ENG, IOWA STATE UNIV, 92- *Personal Data:* b Louisville, Ky, July 6, 28; m 53, Martha Blakeney; c Joseph Jr, Jean & David. *Educ:* Univ Dayton, BME, 50; Purdue Univ, MSME, 55, PhD(mech eng), 58. *Prof Exp:* Assoc res engr, Res Labs, Whirlpool Corp, 58-60; eng assoc, Prod Eng Div, Nat Cash Register Co, 60-62, head consult, Serv Dept, 62-65; assoc prof mech eng, Ga Inst Technol, 65-70; prof mech eng, Univ Nebr, Lincoln, 70-78. *Concurrent Pos:* Mem automation comt, Engrs Joint Coun, 64; vis prof, Polytecnica Warsaw, 75-76, Technische Hogeschool Delft, 81-82, & Cath Univ, Leuven, 87-88; fac fel, NASA, 77, Sandia Nat Lab, 86; Fulbright fel, 81, NATO fel, 87. *Mem:* Am Soc Mech Eng. *Res:* Machinery vibrations and dynamics; dynamics of electromechanical design; design automation; vibration damping from viscoelastic coating; robotics; nutation of spin-stabilized satellites; elastic and plastic strain propagation; path and position synthesis; kinematics; tire dynamics. *Mailing Add:* 1404 20th St Ames IA 50010

BAUMGARTEN, REUBEN LAWRENCE, PHYSICAL ORGANIC CHEMISTRY. *Current Pos:* RETIRED. *Personal Data:* b New York, NY, Nov 19, 34; m 63, Iris Lesson; c Lainie & Steven. *Educ:* City Col New York, BS, 56; Univ Mich, MS, 58, PhD(chem), 62. *Prof Exp:* Instr chem, Hunter Col, 62-66, George N Shuster fel grant, 64-65; from asst prof to prof, Lehman Col, 66-77, chmn, Chem Dept, 78-96. *Mem:* Am Chem Soc; Sigma Xi. *Res:* Organic chemistry of nitrogen; reaction of hydroxylamines and derivatives; nuclear magnetic resonance; magnetic isomerism; aromatic ring current; prochirality in nuclear magnetic resonance; qualitative detection of amines, glycoproteins, Rimini-Simon test and mechanism. *Mailing Add:* Dept Chem Herbert H Lehman Col Bedford Park Blvd W Bronx NY 10468

BAUMGARTEN, RONALD J, ORGANIC CHEMISTRY, ENVIRONMENTAL CHEMISTRY. *Current Pos:* ASSOC PROF ORG CHEM, UNIV ILL, CHICAGO CIRCLE, 64- *Personal Data:* b New York, NY, May 7, 35. *Educ:* Brooklyn Col, BS, 56; Johns Hopkins Univ, MA, 58, PhD(org chem), 62. *Prof Exp:* Res assoc, Ind Univ, 61-62; fel, Brandeis Univ, 63-64. *Concurrent Pos:* Vis asst prof, Univ Ill, Urbana, 65-66; NSF fel, 70-72; vis scientist, State Univ Leiden, 71-72; vis prof, Univ Christchurch, NZ, 81. *Res:* New approaches to deamination; photochemical reductions; new synthetic procedures; aldehyde and ketone syntheses. *Mailing Add:* Dept Chem M/C 111 Univ Ill Chicago Chicago IL 60607

BAUMGARTEN, WERNER, BIOCHEMISTRY. *Current Pos:* CONSULT TO THE PHARMACEUT INDUST, 84- *Personal Data:* b Berlin, Ger, Feb 14, 14; nat US; m 48; c 1. *Educ:* Univ Munich, Dipl, 37; Calif Inst Technol, PhD(org chem, biochem), 41. *Prof Exp:* Res chemist, Hiram Walker & Sons, 41-45, J T Baker Chem Co, NJ, 45-48 & Merck & Co, 48-49; res assoc, Sharp & Dohme, 49-56, res assoc, Merck Sharp & Dohme Res Labs, 56-65, sr res fel, 65-69, dir hemat, 69-71; sr info scientist, Res Labs, Hoffman-LaRoche, 71-73; asst dir clin res, Hoechst-Rossel Pharmaceut, 73-75; med writer, ICI United States Inc, 75-77, clin assoc, ICI Americas Inc, 77-84. *Mem:* Am Chem Soc; fel NY Acad Sci; Am Soc Biol Chem; Am Soc Hemat; Int Soc Hemat; Sigma Xi; fel AAAS. *Res:* Sugar chemistry; heat of combustion of organic compounds; microbiological analysis of amino acids; determination of vitamins and carotenoids; isolation of natural products; fermentation; therapeutic enzymes; protein chemistry; blood coagulation; clinical research. *Mailing Add:* Pharmaceut Indust 2420 Oak Circle Huntingdon Valley PA 19006-5622

BAUMGARTNER, GEORGE JULIUS, ORGANIC CHEMISTRY. *Current Pos:* RETIRED. *Personal Data:* b Atchison, Kans, June 27, 24; m 54; c 6. *Educ:* St Benedict's Col, BSc, 45; Univ Notre Dame, PhD, 53. *Prof Exp:* Prof chem, Mt St Scholastica Col, 50-71, dean acad affairs, Benedictine Col, 68-71, prof chem, 71-78, asst dean, 73-78, acad dean, 78-88. *Mem:* Am Chem Soc. *Res:* Reactions of tetrahydrofuryl compounds. *Mailing Add:* 119 E Mound St Atchison KS 66002-2014

BAUMGARTNER, JAMES EARL, MATHEMATICS. *Current Pos:* J W Young res instr, Dartmouth Col, Hanover, NH, 69-71, asst prof, 71-76, assoc prof, 76-80, prof, 80-83, J G KEMENY PROF MATH, DARTMOUTH COL, HANOVER, NH, 83- *Personal Data:* b Wichita, Kans, Mar 23, 43; m 66, Yolanda Yen-Hsu Lou; c Eric J & Jonathan D. *Educ:* Univ Calif, Berkeley, AB, 64, PhD, 70; AM(hon), Dartmouth Col, 81. *Concurrent Pos:* Vis prof, Calif Inst Technol, Pasadena, 71-72; consult ed, J Symbolic Logic, 83-90; consult, Col Bd, 90- *Mem:* Am Math Soc; Math Asn Am; Asn Symbolic Logic. *Res:* Mathematics education. *Mailing Add:* Dartmouth Col Dept Math Hanover NH 03755-1890

BAUMGARTNER, WERNER ANDREAS, DRUG DETECTION BY HAIR ANALYSIS, BIOPHYSICAL CHEMISTRY. *Current Pos:* FOUNDER & CHMN BD, PSYCHEMEDICS CORP, SANTA MONICA, 87- *Personal Data:* b Poertschach, Austria, May 6, 35; m 68; c 2. *Educ:* Univ New South Wales, BSc, 60, PhD(phys chem), 64. *Prof Exp:* Res asst phys chem, Commonwealth Sci & Indust Res Orgn, Australia, 55-56; res asst biophys chem, physics dept, St Vincent Hosp, Australia, 56-60; scholar, Univ New South Wales, 64-66; assoc scientist, Jet Propulsion Lab, Calif Inst Technol, 66; asst prof phys chem, Calif State Col, Long Beach, 67-70; dir biophys chem, Tritium & Dial Lab, Nuclear Dynamics, Inc, 70-71. *Concurrent Pos:* Asst prof, Calif State Col, Long Beach, 67-68; assoc scientist, Scripps Inst Oceanog, 70 & Immunochem Lab, Vet Admin Hosp, Sepulveda, 70-71; res chemist, Vet Admin Hosp, Long Beach, 71-73 & Vet Admin Hosp, Wadsworth, 73- *Mem:* Am Chem Soc. *Res:* Theory of metal and enzyme catalysis; charge-transfer complexes in catalysis; immunochemistry and membrane processes; function of vitamin E and selenium; catalytic labeling of unstable biochemicals; analysis of drugs of abuse in hair. *Mailing Add:* 5832 Uplander Way Culver City CA 90230

BAUMHEFNER, DAVID PAUL, DYNAMICAL METEOROLOGY. *Current Pos:* RES SCIENTIST METEOROL, NAT CTR ATMOSPHERIC RES, 66- *Personal Data:* b Denver, Colo, Nov 18, 41; m 64; c 2. *Educ:* Univ Calif, Los Angeles, BA, 65, MA, 66. *Prof Exp:* Res asst meteorol, Univ Calif, Los Angeles, 63-66. *Mem:* Am Meteorol Soc; Can Meteorol Soc. *Res:* Numerical weather prediction; diagnostic analysis of atmospheric behavior. *Mailing Add:* 878 Pimlico Ct Boulder CO 80303

BAUMILLER, ROBERT C, MEDICAL GENETICS, CLINICAL CYTOGENETICS. *Current Pos:* DEAN & PROF, COL HEALTH SCI, UNIV DETROIT, MERCY, 91- *Personal Data:* b Baltimore, Md, Apr 15, 31. *Educ:* Loyola Col, Md, BS, 53; St Louis Univ, PhL & PhD(biol), 61; Woodstock Col, Md, STB, 65. *Honors & Awards:* Winkler Award, Mercy Hosp, 75; Carroll Medal, Loyola Col, 84; Jordonian Medal, Univ Ammon, 86. *Prof Exp:* Nat Found fel, Univ Wis, 61-62; asst med, Sch Med, Johns Hopkins Univ, 62-67; assoc prof, Sch Med, Georgetown Univ, 67-80, prof obstet, gynec & pediat, 80-91. *Concurrent Pos:* Prin investr, USPHS res grant, 64-67; AEC grant, 67-70; sr res fel, Kennedy Inst Study Reproduction & Bioethics; mem bd dir, Sex Info & Educ Coun US, 70-74; consult, Clin Pharmacol Assocs, 71-73; assoc ed, Linacre Quart, 71-78; mem med adv bd, Hemophilia Soc, Capitol Area, 74- & 76-; consult, Pope John XXIII Med-Moral Res Ctr, 75-; mem med adv bd, Childbirth Educ Asn, 77-; assoc ed, Downs Syndrome, 78-; consult, Nat Clearinghouse for Genetic Disease, Dept Health & Human Serv, 78-82; dir, Nat Ctr Educ Maternal & Child Health, 82-; mem bd trustees, Loyola Col, 90-; consult, Nat Heart, Blood & Lung Inst, NIH, 93- *Mem:* AAAS; fel Am Col Med Genetics; Am Soc Human Genetics; fel Am Bd Med Genetics; Sigma Xi; fel Asn Clin Scientists. *Res:* Basic genetic research through clinical genetic and clinical cytogenetic research; publish in genetic ethics and genetic education. *Mailing Add:* Univ Detroit Mercy Dept Health Sci 8200 W Outer Dr PO Box 96 Detroit MI 48219. *Fax:* 313-993-6175

BAUMMER, J CHARLES, JR, AMMONIA CHEMISTRY & TOXICOLOGY, DREDGING. *Current Pos:* MGR, ENVIRON MGT, EA ENG SCI TECHNOL INC, 76- *Personal Data:* b Baltimore, Md, May 20, 45; m 68; c 4. *Educ:* Loyola Col, BS, 67; Johns Hopkins Univ, MSE, 69, PhD(environ eng sci), 72. *Prof Exp:* Staff officer, Nat Acad Sci, 72-73; staff asst, Nat Comn Water Qual, 73-76. *Concurrent Pos:* Mem State Water Qual Adv Comt, 88. *Res:* Impact of dredging, hazardous waste and wastewater discharges on water quality. *Mailing Add:* EA Eng Sci & Technol Inc 15 Loveton Circle Sparks MD 21152

BAUMRUCKER, CRAIG RICHARD, ENDOCRINOLOGY, GROWTH FACTORS. *Current Pos:* assoc prof, 81-91, PROF NUTRIT & PHYSIOL, PA STATE UNIV, 92- *Personal Data:* b Jan 22, 44; m, Nancy J Gray; c Kara M (Speaker) & C Tate. *Educ:* Purdue Univ, PhD(animal sci), 74. *Prof Exp:* Asst prof dairy sci, Univ Ill, Urbana, 74-81. *Concurrent Pos:* Ed bd, J Dairy Sci; vis assoc prof, Inst Animal Breeding, Univ Bern, Switz, 89-90. *Mem:* Endocrine Soc; Am Soc Cell Biol; Am Dairy Sci Asn; Am Soc Animal Sci. *Res:* Effects of growth factors on bovine mammary and intestinal tissues; synthesis of IGF and IGF-binding proteins by mammary tissue; the assurance of IGF and IGF-binding proteins in mammary secretions; the effects of mammary secretions on the intestinal growth of the neonate. *Mailing Add:* Dept Dairy & Animal Sci 302 Henning Bldg Pa State Univ University Park PA 16802-0001. *Fax:* 814-863-6042; *E-Mail:* crb@psuvm.psu.edu

BAUMSLAG, GILBERT, MATHEMATICS. *Current Pos:* DISTINGUISHED PROF MATH, CITY COL CITY UNIV NEW YORK, 73- *Personal Data:* b Johannesburg, SAfrica, Apr 30, 33; m 59; c 2. *Educ:* Univ Witwatersrand, BS, 53, Hons, 55, DSc, 76; Univ Manchester, PhD(math), 58. *Prof Exp:* Lectr math, Univ Manchester, 58-59; instr, Princeton Univ, 59-60; from asst prof to assoc prof, Courant Inst Math Sci, NY Univ, 62-64; prof, City Univ New York, 64-68; mem, Inst Advan Study, 68-69; prof, Rice Univ, 69-73. *Concurrent Pos:* Sloan fel, Rice Univ. *Mem:* Am Math Soc; London Math Soc. *Res:* Group theory. *Mailing Add:* Dept Math City Univ NY City Col 160 Convent Ave New York NY 10031-9101

BAUMSTARK, BARBARA RUTH, MOLECULAR GENETICS, GENE EXPRESSION. *Current Pos:* PROF & GRAD DIR, DEPT BIOL, GA STATE UNIV, 84- *Personal Data:* b Pasadena, Calif, June 1, 48. *Educ:* Univ Calif, Riverside, BA, 70; Mass Inst Technol, PhD(biochem), 76. *Prof Exp:* Instr biol, Mass Inst Technol, 76; res assoc microbiol, Emory Univ Sch Med, 76-80, asst prof biochem, 80-84. *Res:* Research involves the study of gene expression and its regulation in bacteriophage. *Mailing Add:* Dept Biol Ga State Univ PO Box 4010 Atlanta GA 30302-4010

BAUMSTARK, JOHN SPANN, BIOCHEMISTRY, MICROBIOLOGY. *Current Pos:* assoc prof biol chem, 72-79, PROF & DIR RES OBSTET & GYNEC, SCH MED, CREIGHTON UNIV, 72-, PROF PATH, 74-, PROF BIOL CHEM, 79- *Personal Data:* b Cape Girardeau, Mo, Dec 23, 27; m 52; c 3. *Educ:* Southeast Mo State Col, BS, 51; Univ Mo, AM, 53, PhD(biochem), 57. *Prof Exp:* Instr agr chem, Univ Mo, 55-57; sr scientist biochem microbiol, Res Dept, Mech Div, Gen Mills, Inc, 57-60, prin scientist, 60-61; from instr to asst prof obstet & gynec, Med Sch, Tufts Univ, 63-72. *Concurrent Pos:* Sr biochemist, St Margaret's Hosp, Boston, Mass, 61-72. *Mem:* Am Asn Path; Am Soc Microbiol; Am Soc Biol Chem; Am Chem Soc; Soc Exp Biol Med; Electrophoresis Soc; Asn Prof Gynec Obstet. *Res:* Proteolytic enzymes; proteins; amino acids; chromatography; experimental pathology. *Mailing Add:* Dept Obstet & Gynec Creighton Univ Sch Med 818 S 130th St Omaha NE 68154

BAUR, FREDRIC JOHN, JR, PHYSIOLOGICAL & ORGANIC CHEMISTRY, NUTRITION. *Current Pos:* RETIRED. *Personal Data:* b Toledo, Ohio, July 14, 18; m 43, Elaine McCleery; c Linda L, Lawrence J & Ronald S. *Educ:* Univ Toledo, BS, 39; Ohio State Univ, MS, 41, PhD(physiol chem), 43; cert com, Univ Cincinnati, 56. *Prof Exp:* Instr physiol chem, Ohio State Univ, 43-44; res chemist, Procter & Gamble Co, 46-56, in charge flavor chem, Food Div, 56-60, in charge anal labs, 60-65, in charge factory anal methods-sanit, Food Div, 65-74, in charge good mfg practices/qual assurance, Corp Compliance Rev, 74-78, spec assignment, 78-82, rep asn off anal chemist, 82-89. *Concurrent Pos:* Health lecr, Am Asn Retired Persons. *Mem:* Am Chem Soc; Inst Food Technol; fel Asn Official Anal Chemists; Am Oil Chemists Soc; Am Asn Cereal Chemists. *Res:* Interesterification of fats; synthesis of compounds containing fatty groups; acetin fats; chemistry and utility of flavors; analysis of foods and food raw materials; sanitary design of buildings and equipment; measurement and control of infesting pests; good manufacturing practices for foods; regulatory compliance. *Mailing Add:* 1545 Larry Ave Cincinnati OH 45224

BAUR, JAMES FRANCIS, PLASMA PHYSICS, NUCLEAR RADIATION HARDENING. *Current Pos:* PHYSICS COORDR, FUSION DIV, GEN ATOMICS, 75-; PRIN INVESTR, RADIATION HARDENING PROG, US DEPT ENERGY, 81- *Personal Data:* b McKeesport, Pa, Oct 22, 38; m 60; c 2. *Educ:* Univ Fla, BS, 60, MS, 61; Univ Colo, PhD(physics), 75. *Prof Exp:* Airborne, ranger, command & staff, US Army Corps Eng, 60-68, asst prof, lab dir, physics, US Military Acad, West Point, 65-68; res asst, Joint Inst Lab Astrophysics, 70-75. *Concurrent Pos:* Infrared consult, Atlantic Missile Range, Pan Am World Airways, 60-61; Fusion Core Exp, 83-86, Nat Design Team, Compact Ignition, Off Fusion Energy, 86-; sci fac fel, Nat Sci Found. *Mem:* Am Phys Soc; AAAS; Optical Soc Am; Sigma Xi; Inst Elec & Electronics Engrs. *Res:* Plasma Diagnostics; nuclear radiation hardening; fusion physics; spectroscopy. *Mailing Add:* Sci Solutions Inc 6920 Miramar Rd Suite 201 San Diego CA 92121-2642

BAUR, JOHN M, MICROBIOLOGY. *Current Pos:* Chmn, 70-80, ASST PROF BIOL, BRESCIA COL, OWENSBORO, KY, 67-, CHMN, 82- *Personal Data:* b Owensboro, Ky, Feb 2, 39; m 66. *Educ:* Brescia Col, Owensboro, Ky, BA, 61; Kent State Univ, MA, 63. *Prof Exp:* Instr microbiol, Col St Teresa, Winona, Minn, 63-65, asst prof, 65-67. *Concurrent Pos:* Dir, Med-Tech Prog, Brescia Col, Owensboro, Ky, 70-80, 82-, chief, pre-prof adv, 82- *Res:* Determination of oxygen usage by certain lung parasites; transplantation techniques in mammals; thyroxine uptake by irradiated thyroid gland cells. *Mailing Add:* Dept Math & Sci Brescia Col 717 Frederica St Owensboro KY 42301-3019

BAUR, MARIO ELLIOTT, ENVIRONMENAL PHYSICAL CHEMISTRY, ENVIRONMENTAL & PRODUCT SAFETY. *Current Pos:* from asst prof to assoc prof, 62-79, PROF CHEM, UNIV CALIF, LOS ANGELES, 79- *Personal Data:* b Indianapolis, Ind, Aug 23, 34; m 60, 97, Ida Perry; c Nicolaas, Matthew, Kim, Joshua & Saskia. *Educ:* Univ Chicago, AB, 53, MS, 55; Mass Inst Technol, PhD(chem), 59. *Honors & Awards:* Dow-Hansen Award, 93. *Prof Exp:* Asst chem, Mass Inst Technol, 55-56 & 58-59; NSF fel, State Univ Utrecht, 59-61; res assoc, Univ Calif, San Diego, 61-62. *Concurrent Pos:* Consult, 75- *Mem:* AAAS; Am Phys Soc; Royal Soc Chem; Neth Phys Soc; Am Geophys Union; Soc Environ Toxicol Chem. *Res:* Physical geochemistry; paleochemistry; origin and evolution of the terrestrial atmosphere; chemical effects on evolutionary trends; chemical breakdown of materials in the environment; fire propagation; statistical mechanics and statistical analysis. *Mailing Add:* Dept Chem & Biochem Univ Calif Los Angeles CA 90024. *Fax:* 310-206-4038

BAUR, THOMAS GEORGE, ASTROPHYSICS, SOLAR PHYSICS. *Current Pos:* CHIEF EXEC OFFICER, MEADOWLAND OPTICS, 83- *Personal Data:* b Bad Axe, Mich, Mar 5, 44. *Educ:* Univ Mich, BS, 66; Univ Colo, MS, 69. *Honors & Awards:* Technol Advan Award, Nat Ctr Atmospheric Res, 76. *Prof Exp:* Instr physics & math, St Dominic Col, 69-70; support scientist solar physics, Nat Ctr Atmospheric Res, 70-83. *Mem:* Soc Photo-Optical Instrumentation Engrs; Optical Soc Am (pres, Rocky Mt sect, 88). *Res:* Solar magnetic field measurement; polarimetry; optical design; stellar photometry. *Mailing Add:* Weld County Rd 1 Longmont CO 80504

BAUR, WERNER HEINZ, mineralogy, crystallography, for more information see previous edition

BAURER, THEODORE, ENVIRONMENTAL SCIENCE, ENERGY RESOURCES. *Current Pos:* RETIRED. *Personal Data:* b New York, NY, June 20, 24; m 47; c 2. *Educ:* Queens Col, NY, BS, 45; Syracuse Univ, PhD(chem), 53; Temple Univ, JD, 80. *Prof Exp:* Asst, Syracuse Univ, 47-48 & Atomic Energy Comn, 51-53; res chemist, mineral beneficiation lab, Columbia Univ, 53-56; adv res engr, Sylvania Elec Prod, Inc & Sylvania Corning Nuclear Corp, 56-57; res phys chemist, Grumman Aircraft Eng Corp, 57-63; proj scientist, Gen Appl Sci Labs, Inc, 63-66; sr scientist, Gen Elec Co, Space Sci Lab, 66-80. *Concurrent Pos:* Guest scientist, free radicals res prog, Nat Bur Standards, 58-59; co-ed, Defense Nuclear Agency Reaction Rate Handbk; consult attorney & scientist, 80; attorney at Law, 80- *Mem:* AAAS; Am Chem Soc; Am Phys Soc; NY Acad Sci; Am Bar Asn. *Res:* Gas-phase kinetics; upper and lower atmosphere chemistry; propulsion and combustion chemistry; free radicals chemistry; spacecraft internal and external environmental quality; space experiments definition; chemical systems analyses; environmental science; law. *Mailing Add:* 751 Woodside Rd Jenkintown PA 19046-3331

BAUS, BERNARD V(ILLARS), ENGINEERING, CHEMISTRY. *Current Pos:* PRES, INDUST CHEM CORP, 74- *Personal Data:* b Gramercy, La, Sept 27, 25; m 57, Regine Lagier; c Bernard Andre & James Richard. *Educ:* Tulane Univ, BE, 45; Cornell Univ, PhD(chem eng), 50. *Prof Exp:* Chem engr plants technol sect, E I du Pont de Nemours & Co, 50-55, asst tech supt to tech supt, 55-58, sr supvr res & develop, 58-59, tech investr int dept; mgr spec proj, Commonwealth Oil Refining Co, Inc, 62-65, vpres chem develop, 65-70, pres, 70-71, vpres, Petrochem, Commonwealth Petrochem Co, 70-71; consult, Am-Rican Group, 71-73. *Concurrent Pos:* Dir, SGI Int. *Mem:* AAAS; Am Inst Chem Engrs; Am Chem Soc; Sigma Xi. *Res:* Heat transfer; process development; plastics research; corporate planning and project development. *Mailing Add:* 17 Emajagua St Punta Las Marias Santurce PR 00913. *Fax:* 787-836-1240

BAUSELL, R BARKER, JR, RESEARCH METHODOLOGY. *Personal Data:* m 78, Carole R Vinograd; c Jesse T & Rebecca B. *Educ:* Univ Del, BS, 68, PhD(educ res & eval), 75. *Honors & Awards:* Outstanding Res Award, Nat Wellness Conf, 86 & 87. *Prof Exp:* Res methodologist Med Col Pa, 75-76; prof, coord, fac res, Univ Md, Baltimore, 76-91, dir, Off Res Methodology, 91-94. *Concurrent Pos:* Consult & dir, Prev Res Ctr, Rodale Press Inc. *Res:* Documented effects of class size on student learning; effects of teacher experience on student learning; determinations of health seeking; author of numerous monographs contributed over 100 articles to professional journals; research methodology educator; educational research and evaluation. *Mailing Add:* Univ Md Off Res Methodology 655 W Lombard St Baltimore MD 21201

BAUSHER, LARRY PAUL, SYNTHETIC & ORGANIC CHEMISTRY. *Current Pos:* SYNTHESIS CHEMIST, ACCOSTANDARD INC, 95- *Personal Data:* b Reading, Pa, July 8, 39; m 78, Phyllis Bruskin; c Benjamin. *Educ:* Franklin & Marshall Col, AB, 61; Univ Calif, Los Angeles, PhD(org chem), 67. *Prof Exp:* Res chemist, Hercules, Inc, 67-69; res fel chem, Wesleyan Univ, 69-71; res fel chmn, Yale Univ, 71-83, assoc res scientist, 83-90, res scientist, 90-95. *Mem:* AAAS; Am Chem Soc; Sigma Xi; NY Acad Sci. *Res:* Synthesis and purification of environmental chemicals, PCBs (polychlorinated biphenyls), pesticides, explosives. *Mailing Add:* 75 Forest Ct N Hamden CT 06518

BAUSHER, MICHAEL GEORGE, PLANT PHYSIOLOGY, BIOCHEMISTRY. *Current Pos:* PLANT PHYSIOLOGIST, SCI & EDUC ADMIN-AGR RES, USDA, 75- *Personal Data:* b Philadelphia, Pa, Mar 28, 45. *Educ:* Del Valley Col, BS, 67; Rutgers Univ, MS, 69; Univ Fla, PhD(plant physiol), 74. *Prof Exp:* Res asst hort, Rutgers Univ, 67-69; res asst plant physiol, Univ Fla, 69-74, res assoc, 74-75. *Concurrent Pos:* Adj asst prof, Univ Fla, 75- *Mem:* AAAS; Am Soc Hort Sci; Am Soc Plant Physiol. *Res:* Chemical plant growth regulators; chemistry of disease response in plants. *Mailing Add:* 1404 Palmer Ave Winter Park FL 32789

BAUSSUS VON LUETZOW, HANS GERHARD, MATHEMATICS. *Current Pos:* RETIRED. *Personal Data:* b Nortorf, Ger, Feb 13, 21; US citizen; m 52; c 3. *Educ:* Univ Kiel, BS & MS, 49, DSc(math), 63. *Prof Exp:* Sci asst opers res, State Energy Admin, Ger, 49-51; asst prof math & physics, Zimmermann Col & Com Col, 52-56; unit chief math anal, Aeroballistics Lab, US Army Ballistic Missile Agency, 56-57, dep sect & dep br chief anal invest & aerophys & geophys, 57-58, sci adv math statist, 59-60; sci adv earth & space sci, Aeroballistics Lab, Marshall Space Flight Ctr, 60-62; tech chief systs div, US Army Strategy & Tactics Anal Group, 62-63; prin scientist, Advan Progs, Gen Precision Co, 63-64; referent, Prog Coord Opers Res Budgeting, Off Fed Minister Defense, Ger, 64-66; sr scientist, US Army Topog Labs, 66-88. *Mem:* Am Geophys Union; assoc fel Am Inst Aeronaut & Astronaut; Acad Polit Sci. *Res:* Applied mathematics; dynamic meteorology; geodesy inertial navigation; operations research. *Mailing Add:* 545 Baarson Blvd Helena MT 59601

BAUST, JOHN G, CRYOBIOLOGY, CRYOSURGERY. *Current Pos:* DIR & LEAD PROF CRYOBIOL, CTR CRYOBIOL RES, 86- *Personal Data:* b Flushing, NY, Oct 6, 42. *Educ:* Univ Alaska, PhD(physiol), 70. *Honors & Awards:* Serv Medal, NSF Sci; Outstanding Scientist, Sigma Xi. *Prof Exp:* Dir & Luyet prof, Inst Low Temperature Sci, Univ Houston, 84-86. *Concurrent Pos:* Vpres res & develop, Cryomed Sci Inc; adj prof, Med Col Pa. *Res:* Research and technical expertise in cryomedical sciences especially cryosurgery, cryopreservation and low temperature behavior of cellular systems; physiology; cryogenic engineering. *Mailing Add:* Ctr Cryobiol Res State Univ NY Binghamton NY 13902-6000

BAUSUM, HOWARD THOMAS, MICROBIOLOGY, ENVIRONMENTAL SCIENCES. *Current Pos:* res microbiologist, Biomed Res & Develop Lab, 72-96, CTR HEALTH PROM & PREV MED, DIV TOXICOL, US ARMY, 96- *Personal Data:* b Guilin, China, July 20, 33; US citizen; m 60, Gwendolyn Jordan; c David H, Susan L & Richard J. *Educ:* Carson-Newman Col, BS, 54; Univ Tenn, MS, 56; Univ Tex, PhD(zool, genetics), 64. *Prof Exp:* Biologist, US Army Biol Labs, Ft Detrick, Md, 60-61; asst prof microbiol, Sch Med, Univ Kans, 64-65; asst prof genetics, Iowa State Univ, 65-68; microbiologist, US Army Biol Labs, 68-71; staff assoc, Comn Sci Educ, AAAS, 71-72. *Mem:* Sigma Xi; Am Soc Microbiol; Genetics Soc Am; NY Acad Sci. *Res:* Environmental microbiology; fate of pollutant chemicals; health effects of pollutant chemicals. *Mailing Add:* Ctr Health Prom & Prev Med US Army Aberdeen Proving Ground MD 21010-5422. *Fax:* 410-612-6710; *E-Mail:* howard_bausum@chppm-ccmail.apgea.army.mil

BAUTISTA, ABRAHAM PARANA, EXPERIMENTAL IMMUNOPATHOLOGY, PATHOPHYSIOLOGY. *Current Pos:* asst prof physiol, 89-93, ASSOC PROF PHYSIOL & MED, LA STATE UNIV MED CTR, 94- *Personal Data:* b Davao City, Philippines, Mar 15, 52; US citizen. *Educ:* Far Eastern Univ, Philippines, BS, 72; Univ Tokyo, dipl, 78; Univ Aberdeen, Scotland, MS, 81, PhD(immunol), 84. *Prof Exp:* Microbiol lectr & sr researcher, Univ Santo Tomas, Manila, 76-81; res assoc exp immunopath, ECarolina Univ, 84-89. *Concurrent Pos:* Int fel microbiol, UNESCO, Japan, 77-78; int scholar immunol, Brit Coun, London, 79-80; res scholar immunol & med, Servier Labs, Eng, 81-84; prin investr, USPHS-Nat Inst Alcohol Abuse & Alcoholism, 91-; reviewer, Jefferson Trust VA, 93; mem, Study Sect Spec Prog Proj, NIH, 97 & adhoc mem, Study Sect, Alcohol-Toxicol-2, Nat Inst Alcohol Abuse & Alcoholism, 97. *Mem:* Am Asn Immunol; Res Soc Alcoholism; Soc Leukocyte Biol; Sigma Xi; AAAS; NY Acad Sci; Shock Soc. *Res:* Biological, immunological and molecular mechanisms of macrophage and leukocyte activation during infection, sepsis, endotoxemia, metabolic disorders and alcohol intoxication. *Mailing Add:* Physiol MEB La State Univ Med Ctr 1901 Perdido St New Orleans LA 70112-1328. *Fax:* 504-568-6158

BAUTZ, GORDON T, PHARMACOLOGY. *Current Pos:* RES SCIENTIST, HOFFMAN LAROCHE, INC, 69- *Personal Data:* b June 6, 42; m 65, Delmae Hanneman; c Tracy & Jennifer. *Educ:* Salem Col, WVa, BS, 64. *Mem:* Am Soc Pharm & Exp Therapeut; Drug Info Asn; Pharmaceut Mfg Asn; NY Acad Sci. *Res:* Central nervous system; pharmacology. *Mailing Add:* Dept Preclin Develop Hoffman LaRoche Inc 340 Kingsland Ave Nutley NJ 07110-1150. *Fax:* 973-235-7292; *E-Mail:* bautzg@rnisdo.dnet.roche.com

BAUTZ, LAURA PATRICIA, ASTRONOMY, SCIENCE ADMINISTRATION. *Current Pos:* sr staff assoc, NSF, 76-79, dep dir, Div Physics, 79-82, dir, Div Astron Sci, 82-92, dep dir, Div Physics, 92-93, DEP DIR, INT PROGS, NSF, 94- *Personal Data:* b Washington, DC, Sept 3, 40. *Educ:* Vanderbilt Univ, BA, 61; Univ Wis, PhD(astron), 67. *Prof Exp:* From instr to asst prof astron, Northwestern Univ, Evanston, 65-72; prog dir, NSF, 72-73; assoc prof astron, Northwestern Univ, Evanston, 73-75. *Concurrent Pos:* Trustee, Adler Planetarium, 73-76; vis scientist, Lawrence Berkeley Lab, 90-92. *Mem:* AAAS; Int Astron Union; Am Phys Soc. *Res:* Clusters of galaxies. *Mailing Add:* No 506 1325 18th St Washington DC 20036

BAVELAS, JANET BEAVIN, DISCOURSE ANALYSIS, FACE-TO-FACE DIALOGUE. *Current Pos:* from asst prof to assoc prof, 70-86, PROF PSYCHOL, UNIV VICTORIA, BC, 86- *Personal Data:* b Feb 12, 40. *Educ:* Stanford Univ, AB, 61, AM, 68, PhD(psychol), 70. *Prof Exp:* Res asst, Ment Res Inst, Palo Alto, Calif, 61-66, res assoc, 66-70. *Concurrent Pos:* Assoc dean grad studies & res, Univ Victoria, BC, 83-87. *Mem:* Fel Can Psychol Asn; fel Int Commun Asn; fel Royal Soc Can. *Res:* Natural language in face-to-face dialogue; microanalysis of verbal and nonverbal communication; discourse analysis; research methods; legal discourse. *Mailing Add:* Dept Psychol Univ Victoria PO Box 3050 Victoria BC V8W 3P5 Can. *Fax:* 250-721-8929; *E-Mail:* jbb@uvvm.uvic.ca

BAVISOTTO, VINCENT, BIOCHEMISTRY. *Current Pos:* RETIRED. *Personal Data:* b Buffalo, NY, Jan 21, 25; m 89, Judy A Conklin; c 4. *Educ:* Univ Buffalo, BA, 48; Pa State Univ, MS, 50, PhD(biochem), 52. *Prof Exp:* Sr res chemist, Gen Biochem, Inc, 52-54; dir res, Paul Lewis Labs, Inc, 55-61, dir res & develop, Paul Lewis Labs Div, Chas Pfizer & Co, Inc, 61-67; tech dir, Theodore Hamm Co, 67-72; assoc dir res & develop, Heublein Inc, 72-74; vpres brewing & res, Miller Brewing Co, 74-90. *Mem:* Fel Am Chem Soc; Am Soc Brewing Chemists (pres, 72); Inst Food Technol; Master Brewers Asn Am (pres, 88-89); AAAS. *Res:* Basic and applied research on problems related to brewing, dairy, meat, enzyme, wine, spirited and chemical manufacturing industries. *Mailing Add:* 5780 Mary Lane Oconomowoc WI 53066

BAVISTER, BARRY DOUGLAS, FERTILIZATION, EMBRYOGENESIS. *Current Pos:* asst prof animal physiol, 79-83, assoc prof vet sci, Primate Res Ctr, 83-89, PROF VET SCI & SR SCIENTIST, PRIMATE RES CTR, UNIV WIS-MADISON, 89- *Personal Data:* b Cambridge, Eng, Mar 15, 43; c 3. *Educ:* Univ Cambridge, Eng, BA, 67, PhD(reproductive physiol), 72. *Prof Exp:* Res fel, Med Sch, Univ Hawaii, 74-75; asst res pathologist, Med Sch, Univ Calif, Los Angeles, 76-78; lectr animal physiol, dept animal physiol, Univ Calif, Davis, 78-79. *Mem:* Soc Study Fertil; Soc Study Reproduction; Tissue Culture Asn. *Res:* Physiology, morphology and biochemistry of mammalian gametes, fertilization and embryogenesis, and the development of culture media for study of these processes in vitro. *Mailing Add:* 2120 Keyes Ave Madison WI 53711

BAVLEY, ABRAHAM, CHEMISTRY. *Current Pos:* CONSULT, 83- *Personal Data:* b Boston, Mass, June 3, 15; m 46. *Educ:* Tufts Col, BS, 36; Harvard Univ, MA & PhD(org chem), 40. *Prof Exp:* Chemist, Ansco Div, Gen Aniline & Film Co, Inc, NY, 40-43, leader colorformer group, 43-45; asst prof chem, Xavier Univ, Ohio, 45-46 & Gevaert Photo-Prod, Belg, 46-47; res chemist, Charles Pfizer & Co, Inc, NY, 47-51, res supvr, 51-58, mgr res, Greensborough Sect, 58-59; asst dir res, Gillette Safety Razor Co, Mass, 59-60; mgr res, Philip Morris, Inc, 60-65; vpres & tech dir, Marion Labs, Inc, Mo, 65-69; vpres & sci dir, Knoll Pharmaceut Co, 69-71; assoc, Res Corp, 74-83. *Concurrent Pos:* Consult, 71-74. *Res:* Organic synthesis; medicinal chemistry; chemistry of natural products. *Mailing Add:* 11 Black Watch Trail Morristown NJ 07960

BAW, PHILEMON S H, HEAT TRANSFER, FLUID DYNAMICS. *Current Pos:* MECH ENGR, LEVY ASSOC, INC, 78- *Personal Data:* b Kobe, Japan, May 5, 39; m 63; c 2. *Educ:* Cheng Kung Univ, Taiwan, BS, 59; Rutgers Univ, MS, 66, PhD(mech eng), 68. *Honors & Awards:* Teetor Award, Soc Automotive Engrs, 70. *Prof Exp:* Engr, Yue Loong Motor Co, China, 61-63; res asst, Rutgers Univ, 64-68; asst prof mech, aerospace & indust eng, La State Univ, Baton Rouge, 68-78. *Concurrent Pos:* Vis prof, Cheng Kung Univ, Taiwan, 72-73. *Mem:* Asn Energy Engrs; Am Soc Eng Educ. *Res:* Gas-solid suspension flow; unsteady state heat transfer; energy conservation and management. *Mailing Add:* 17715 Crossing Blvd Baton Rouge LA 70810

BAWA, KAMALJIT S, POPULATION BIOLOGY, TROPICAL ECOLOGY. *Current Pos:* from asst prof to assoc prof, 74-81, prof biol, 81-96, chmn, Biol Dept, 89-92, DISTINGUISHED PROF BIOL, UNIV MASS BOSTON, 96- *Personal Data:* b Kapurthala, India, Apr 7, 39; m 69; c 2. *Educ:* Punjab Univ, India, BS, 58, BS Hons, 60, MS Hons, 62, PhD(bot), 67. *Prof Exp:* Res asst, Bot Dept, Punjab Univ, India, 62-67; res assoc & instr genetics, Col Forest Resources, Univ Wash, Seattle, 67-72; Charles Bullard fel, Harvard Univ, 72. *Concurrent Pos:* Prin investr, NSF grants, 75-; mem, La Selva Adv Comt, Orgn Trop Studies, 78-85 & adv panel, NSF Conserv & Restoration Biol, 91; counr, Asn Trop Biol, 85-86; assoc ed, Conserv Biol, 86-; Guggenheim fel, 87-; res prof, Univ Mass, Boston, 91-94; Pew Scholar in conser & environ, 91-95. *Mem:* Soc Study Evolution; Soc Conserv Biol; Ecol Soc Am; Am Soc Naturalists; Asn Trop Biol; AAAS. *Res:* Conservation of biological diversity, population biology of tropical rain forest trees; conservation and management of tropical forest resources; author of over 100 publications. *Mailing Add:* Dept Biol Univ Mass Boston MA 02125

BAWA, MOHENDRA S, CHEMICAL ENGINEERING, APPLIED CHEMISTRY. *Current Pos:* mem tech staff, 65-80, SR MEM TECH STAFF RES & DEVELOP, TEX INSTRUMENTS, INC, DALLAS, 65- *Personal Data:* b Jagraon, Panjab, India, June 10, 31; m 63, Ofir; c Sandy & Pamela. *Educ:* East Panjab Univ, India, BSc, 49; Calcutta Univ, MSc, 54; Univ Houston, PhD(chem eng), 65. *Honors & Awards:* Gold Medal, Directorate of Educ, Panjab, 45. *Prof Exp:* Asst plant mgr, Assoc Pigments Ltd, Calcutta, 55; sci asst surface coatings, Govt Test House, 55; chem eng asst process design, Kilburn & Co, 55-56; sr sci officer fuel chem, Cent Fuel Res Inst, 56-61; res fel energy conversion, Dept Chem Eng, Univ Houston, 61-65. *Concurrent Pos:* Res engr, Retzloff Chem Co, Tex, 63-64 & Houston Res Inst, 64-65. *Mem:* Am Inst Chem Engrs; Electrochem Soc; Am Asn Crystal Growth. *Res:* Process analysis and development; mass transfer processes; energy conversion processes; kinetics of electrode reactions; silicon and boron chemistry; coal science and fuel technology; new product development; surfactants; ablative heat shields; cermets; molten salt reaction media; single crystal silicon growth; hydrogen storage alloys. *Mailing Add:* 3313 Steven Dr Plano TX 75023. *Fax:* 903-868-7759

BAWDEN, JAMES WYATT, PHYSIOLOGY, TOOTH ENAMEL FORMATION & FLUORIDES. *Current Pos:* from asst prof to assoc prof, Univ NC, Chapel Hill, 61-65, asst dean res, 63-66, prof, 65-77, dean, Sch Dent, 66-74, ALUMNI DISTINGUISHED PROF PEDIAT DENT, UNIV NC, CHAPEL HILL, 77- *Personal Data:* b St Louis, Mo, Apr 23, 30; m 88, Merrie Teat; c 5. *Educ:* Univ Iowa, DDS, 54, MS, 60, PhD(physiol), 61. *Prof Exp:* USN Dent Corps, 54-56, pvt pract, 56-58; fel physiol, Univ Iowa, 58-61. *Concurrent Pos:* NIH grant, 63-; vis prof, Sch Dent, Univ Lund, Sweden, 74-75; prin investr, NIH-Univ NC Dent Res Inst grant, 75-76 & W V Kellogg grant, 76-79 & 92-93; vis prof, Karolinska Inst, Swed. *Mem:* Inst Med-Nat Acad Sci; Int Asn Dent Res; Am Dent Asn; Inst Med; Am Acad Pediat Dent; Am Asn Dental Res (pres, 84-85). *Res:* Pediatric dentistry; signal tranduction during tooth development; the effect of maternal metabolic status on the metabolism of the fetus in utero; development of tooth enamel; trace elements; fluoride uptake in developing enamel; clinical studies on fluorides. *Mailing Add:* Sch Dent Univ NC Chapel Hill NC 27599. *Fax:* 919-966-3683

BAWDEN, MONTE PAUL, PARASITOLOGY, EDUCATIONAL ADMINISTRATION. *Current Pos:* CONSULT, PREPARATION INT BUS & TRAVEL, 93- *Personal Data:* b Salt Lake City, Utah, June 3, 43; m 84; c 6. *Educ:* Univ Calif, Riverside, BA, 65; Rutgers Univ, New Brunswick, PhD(zool), 70. *Prof Exp:* Res asst, Rutgers Univ, 65-66; fel, Dept Trop Pub Health, Sch Pub Health, Harvard Univ, 69-71, res assoc med parasitol, 71-73; scientist, Immuno-Parasitol Dept, Naval Med Res Inst, Bethesda, 73-76, head, Malaria Serol Br, 77-79, asst dir & admin officer, Naval Med Res & Training Unit, Gorgas Mem Lab, Panama, 79-85, mil officer & dep head, Malaria Div, Bethesda, 85-87, adminr malaria prog, 87-88, head, Res Sci Dept, Cairo, Egypt, 88-90, actg exec officer, 88; parasitologist, Med Serv Corps, USN, 73-93; dir, Mil Training Network Resuscitative Med, Mil Med Educ Inst, Uniformed Serv Univ Health Sci, Bethesda, 90-93, asst prof, 90-93. *Concurrent Pos:* Lectr, Health Sci Educ & Training Command, Med Technologists Sch, Bethesda, 74-79, lectr med parasitol, Naval Med Res & Training Unit, Gorgas Lab Panama, 79-85, guest lectr, Naval Sch Health Care Admin, 73-76, Uniformed Serv Univ Health Sci, 78-79 & 90- & lectr clin med parasitol, Infectious Dis & Dermat Res Prog, Naval Hosp, Bethesda, 86-88; adj assoc & head, Photog Support Div, Naval Med Res & Training Unit, Gorgas Mem Lab, Panama, 79-85; consult diagnosis parasitic dis, Santo Tomas Hosp & Gorgas Army Hosp, Panama, 79-85; jungle survivor trainer, Jungle Oper Training Ctr, Ft Sherman,Panama, 80-85; clin asst prof trop med & med parasitol, Med Ctr, La State Univ, 82-85; prog adminr, US AID Proj, Egypt, 88-90. *Mem:* Am Soc Trop Med & Hyg; Royal Soc Trop Med & Hyg. *Res:* Malaria trypanosomiasis, and schistosomiasis; vaccines and diagnostics; intestinal parasites. *Mailing Add:* 522 W Erie St Lewiston MT 59457

BAWDON, ROGER EVERETT, CLINICAL MICROBIOLOGY, MICROBIAL GENETICS. *Current Pos:* DIR CLIN MICROBIOL LAB, DETROIT GEN HOSP, 76- *Personal Data:* b Highmore, SDak, Sept 6, 39; m 61; c 1. *Educ:* SDak State Univ, BS, 61, MS, 63; Kans State Univ, PhD(microbiol), 72. *Prof Exp:* Clin fel microbiol, St Joseph Mercy Hosp, 74-76; ASST PROF MICROBIOL, SCH MED, WAYNE STATE UNIV, 76- *Concurrent Pos:* Fel, Univ Mich & St Joseph Mercy Hosp, 74-76. *Mem:* Sigma Xi; Am Soc Microbiol; Acad Clin Lab Physicians & Scientists. *Res:* Genetics of anaerobic bacteria. *Mailing Add:* 3603 Vinecrest Dr Dallas TX 75229

BAX, AD, NUCLEAR MAGNETIC RESONANCE. *Current Pos:* vis res assoc, 83-85, VIS RES SCIENTIST, NAT INST DIABETES, DIGESTIVE & KIDNEY DIS, NIH, BETHESDA, 85- *Personal Data:* b Zevenbergen, Neth, June 14, 56; m 86, Ingrid Pufahl; c Nicolas & Christina. *Educ:* Delft Univ Technol, PhD(appl physics), 81. *Prof Exp:* Res fel, Delft Univ Technol, Neth & Oxford Univ, Eng, 78-81; assoc, dept chem, Colo State Univ, Ft Collins, 82-83. *Concurrent Pos:* Assoc ed, J Biomolecular NMR, 90- *Res:* Two-dimensional and multiple quantum nuclear magnetic resonance and their applications in chemistry, biochemistry and biology. *Mailing Add:* 5623 Oak Pl Bethesda MD 20817

BAXENDALE, PETER HERBERT, MATHEMATICS. *Current Pos:* PROF, DEPT MATH, UNIV SOUTHERN CALIF, LOS ANGELES, 88- *Personal Data:* b Derby, Eng, May 22, 48. *Educ:* Univ Cambridge, BA, 69; Univ Warwick, MS, 70, PhD(math), 74. *Honors & Awards:* Rollo Davidson Prize, 88. *Prof Exp:* Lectr, Dept Math, Univ Warwick, 72-73; lectr, Dept Math, Univ Aberdeen, Scotland, 73-87; assoc prof, Dept Math, Univ Fla, Gainesville, 87-88. *Concurrent Pos:* Mem, Sch Math, Inst Advan Studies, Princeton, NJ, 76-77; vis assoc prof, Dept Math, Univ Southern Calif, Los Angeles, 82-83; assoc prof, Lab Probabilities, Univ Paris VI, 84; mem, Inst Math & Appln, Univ Minn, Minneapolis, 86; Off Naval Res grant, 91-93. *Mem:* Fel Inst Math Statist. *Res:* Gaussian measures on function spaces. *Mailing Add:* Univ Southern Calif DRB 155 Los Angeles CA 90232-1113

BAXLEY, WILLIAM ALLISON, INTERNAL MEDICINE, CARDIOLOGY. *Current Pos:* assoc prof, 72-76, PROF MED, SCH MED, UNIV ALA, BIRMINGHAM, 76- *Personal Data:* b Washington, DC, May 10, 33; c 3. *Educ:* Duke Univ, BS, 55, MD, 62. *Prof Exp:* Intern med, Duke Hosp, Durham, NC, 62-63; med resident, Univ Wash, 63-64; asst med & res fel, Univ Wash & Vet Admin Hosp, 64-66; from instr to asst prof cardiol, Med Ctr, Univ Ala, 66-70; assoc prof med, Sch Med, Univ NMex, 70-72. *Concurrent Pos:* Mem coun clin cardiol, Am Heart Asn, 67. *Mem:* Am Fedn Clin Res; Am Heart Asn; fel Am Col Cardiol; fel Am Col Physicians; fel Soc Cardiac Angiography & Interventions. *Res:* Intervoutional cardiology and coronary angioplasty. *Mailing Add:* Dept Med Univ Ala Sch Med Birmingham AL 35294. *Fax:* 205-934-0378

BAXMAN, HORACE ROY, CHEMISTRY. *Current Pos:* RETIRED. *Personal Data:* b Lansing, Ill, Jan 27, 21; m 44; c 4. *Educ:* Ind Univ, BS, 43; Cornell Univ, PhD(inorg chem), 47. *Prof Exp:* Chemist, Monsanto Chem Co, Oak Ridge, 47-48; assoc chemist, Argonne Nat Lab, 48-52; mem staff, Los Alamos Nat Lab, 52-73, sect leader, 73-90. *Mem:* Fel Am Inst Chemists; Am Nuclear Soc; Am Chem Soc. *Res:* High Vacuum; boron compounds; spectrophotometry; unsymmetrical organoboron compounds; solvent extraction; fuel processing; uranium chemistry; process research on actinide elements; materials research on pyrolytic carbon. *Mailing Add:* 512 Superstition Dr SE Rio Rancho NM 87124

BAXT, WILLIAM G, MEDICINE. *Current Pos:* PROF & CHAIR, DEPT EMERGENCY MED, UNIV PA MED CTR & CHIEF EMERGENCY MEDICINE SERV, 94- *Personal Data:* b Mar 31, 41. *Educ:* Brown Univ, BA, 63; Yale Univ, MD, 67; Am Bd Internal Med, cert, 72; Am Bd Emergency Med, cert, 87. *Honors & Awards:* Physician's Recognition Award, AMA, 85. *Prof Exp:* Intern, Columbia-Presby Hosp, NY, 67-68, resident, 70-71, fel hemat, 71-73; sr asst surgeon, USPHS, 68-69, surgeon, 69-70; asst prof med, Univ Calif San Diego Sch Med, La Jolla, 73-76, res biologist, Dept Biol, 76-77, asst clin prof med, 76-77; med dir, Life Flight Aeromed Prog, Univ Calif San Diego Med Ctr, 80-89; prof clin med & surg, Univ Calif San Diego Sch Med, 89-94. *Concurrent Pos:* Investr, Nat Heart Inst Lab Biochem Genetics, Bethesda, 68-70; asst adj prof med, Univ Calif San Diego Sch Med, 78-80, assoc prof med, 80-84, adj prof med & surg, 84-89; assoc dir, Div Emergency Med Serv, Univ Calif San Diego Med Ctr, 78-80, dir, 80-94. *Mem:* Inst Med-Nat Acad Sci; Soc Acad Emergency Med. *Res:* Contributor of numerous publications. *Mailing Add:* Dept Emergency Med Univ Pa Med Ctr Ground Silverstein Pavilion 3400 Spruce St Philadelphia PA 19104-4283

BAXTER, ANN WEBSTER, MICROBIAL PHYSIOLOGY. *Current Pos:* RETIRED. *Personal Data:* b Evanston, Ill, July 25, 17; div; c Elizabeth B (Yancey) & Ellen L. *Educ:* Rockford Col, BA, 38; Univ NC, Chapel Hill, PhD(bact immunol), 67. *Honors & Awards:* 75th Anniversary Bronze Medallion, Am Soc Microbiol, 74, Serv Plaque, 75. *Prof Exp:* Res technician physiol, Sch Med, Univ Louisville, 56-57; res technician bact, Am Sterilizer Co, Pa, 58-59; teacher, high sch, NC, 60-63; from asst prof to assoc prof microbiol, Clemson Univ, 67-82. *Concurrent Pos:* Mem, SC Br, Am Soc Microbiol. *Res:* Bacterial growth and metabolism; factors affecting bacterial membrane transport; mechanisms of active transport of amino acids in bacteria; effects of environmental pollutants on survival of bacteria. *Mailing Add:* 209 Wyatt Ave Clemson SC 29631

BAXTER, CHARLES RUFUS, SURGERY. *Current Pos:* From asst prof to assoc prof, 62-71, dir, Wound Ctr, 93-97, PROF SURG, SOUTHWEST MED SCH, UNIV TEX, DALLAS, 71- *Personal Data:* b Paris, Tex, Nov 4, 29; c 3. *Educ:* Univ Tex, BA, 50; Univ Tex Southwest Med Sch Dallas, MD, 54. *Honors & Awards:* H Steward Allen Award, Am Burn Asn, 81; G Whitdrer Int Burn Prize, 83; Curtiss P Artz Nat Trauma Award, 84; Achievement Award, Am Asn Tissue Banks, 88. *Concurrent Pos:* NIH res fel, 59-61; dir, Parkland Hosp Burn Ctr, Dallas, 61-, med dir, 72-; dir, Student Health Servs, Southwest Med Sch, Univ Tex, Dallas, 62-72; chmn, Surg Res Adv Bd Burns & Res, Shriners Hosps Crippled Children, 78-; mem, Surg A Study Sect, NIH, 78-; exec comt, Am Col Surgeons Comt Trauma, 78- *Mem:* Am Surg Soc; Am Col Surgeons; Am Burn Asn (pres, 72-73); Am Asn Surg Trauma; Int Soc Burn Injuries. *Res:* Burns and trauma; electrolyte and fluid balance in burns and trauma; circulatory and fluid volumes changes in burns; leukocyte function in burns; preservation of transplantable human tissues and organs; experimental skin grafting; chronic wound care. *Mailing Add:* Univ Tex Southwest Med Sch Parkland Mem Hosp 5323 Harry Hines Blvd Dallas TX 75235

BAXTER, CLAUDE FREDERICK, PHYSIOLOGY, BIOCHEMISTRY. *Current Pos:* SR RES BIOCHEMIST, DIV NEUROBIOL, CITY OF HOPE MED CTR, DUARTE, CALIF, 56-; CHIEF NEUROCHEM LABS, VET ADMIN HOSP, SEPULVEDA, 63- *Personal Data:* b Hamburg, Ger, July 24, 23; nat US; m 52; c 3. *Educ:* Univ Calif, Davis, PhD, 54. *Prof Exp:* Res physiologist, Univ Calif, Davis, 54; fel, McCollum-Pratt Inst, Johns Hopkins Univ, 54-56. *Concurrent Pos:* Assoc prof physiol, Univ Calif, Los Angeles, 64-74, res prof psychiat, 74- *Mem:* AAAS; Int Soc Neurochem; Am Soc Biol Chemists; Am Chem Soc; NY Acad Sci. *Res:* Milk synthesis; sulfur metabolism; neurochemistry; metabolism and functional aspects of nitrogenous compounds in nervous system; neurotransmitter substances; protein synthesis; osmotic regulation in nervous system; nerve regeneration; aging of nervous system and convulsive disorders. *Mailing Add:* Neurochem Labs Vet Admin Med Ctr 8343 Jamieson Ave Northridge CA 91325-3931

BAXTER, DENVER O(LEN), AGRICULTURAL ENGINEERING. *Current Pos:* ASST PROF AGR ENG, UNIV TENN, KNOXVILLE, 56- *Personal Data:* b Crandall, Ga, June 26, 25. *Educ:* Univ Ga, BS, 50; Univ Mo, MS, 51. *Prof Exp:* Exten agr engr, Univ Ky, 51-54, Univ Ga, 54-56. *Concurrent Pos:* Reviewer, Fed Res Grants, USDA, collabr, functional struct & environ requirements for com animal prod struct; design engr, Animal Prod Facil, Agr Exp Sta, Univ Tenn. *Mem:* Am Soc Agr Engrs; Am Soc Eng Educ. *Res:* Alternate energy systems; earth-tube heat exchangers; solar energy; environmental factors of plant and animal production; application of structural products; functional, structural and environmental design of structures for agriculture; rural housing. *Mailing Add:* Dept Agr Eng Univ Tenn 1345 Circle Park Knoxville TN 37996-0001

BAXTER, DONALD WILLIAM, MEDICINE, NEUROLOGY. *Current Pos:* RETIRED. *Personal Data:* b Brockville, Ont, Aug 24, 26. *Educ:* Queen's Univ, Ont, MD, CM, 51; McGill Univ, MSc, 53; Am Bd Psychiat & Neurol, dipl, 58. *Prof Exp:* From instr to asst prof, Sch Med, Univ Sask, 57-62; prof neurol, Fac Med, McGill Univ, 63- *Concurrent Pos:* Dir, Montreal Neurol Inst, 84-91. *Mem:* Am Acad Neurol; Can Med Asn; Am Neurol Soc; Can Neurol Asn. *Mailing Add:* 1321 Sherbrooke St W No D71 Montreal PQ H3G 1J4 Can. *E-Mail:* 72172.2411@compuserve. com

BAXTER, GENE FRANCIS, POLYMER CHEMISTRY. *Current Pos:* sr develop chemist, 73-77, chief develop chemist, 77-83, sr scientist, 83-85, CONSULT, GA-PAC CORP, 85- *Personal Data:* b Sanish, NDak, July 25, 22; m 49, 70; c 3. *Educ:* Univ Wash, BS, 44. *Honors & Awards:* Distinguished Scientist Award, Georgia-Pacific Corp, 85. *Prof Exp:* Res chemist, Am Marietta Corp, 44-56, res group leader, 56-59, info coordr, 59-61, info coordr, Martin-Marietta Corp, 61-62; sr res scientist, Weyerhaeuser Co, 62-73. *Mem:* Am Chem Soc. *Res:* Polymers; adhesives; thermosetting resins; bonded wood products; plywood; laminated beams; construction materials; formaldehyde polymers; phenolic resins; aromatic amine reactions. *Mailing Add:* 195 Tiburon Dr 2883 Miller Rd Lithonia GA 30038

BAXTER, GEORGE T, FISH BIOLOGY, LIMNOLOGY. *Current Pos:* RETIRED. *Personal Data:* b Grover, Colo, Mar 19, 19; m 42; c 3. *Educ:* Univ Wyo, BS & MS, 46; Univ Mich, PhD(zool), 52. *Prof Exp:* From instr to assoc prof, Univ Wyo, 47-59, actg head dept, 68-70, prof zool, 59-84. *Mem:* Am Fisheries Soc. *Res:* Limnology of alpine lakes; fishery management, primarily salmonids in the Rocky Mountains; ichthyology and herpetology of Wyoming. *Mailing Add:* 1614 Bonneville Laramie WY 82070

BAXTER, JAMES WATSON, industrial minerals, fluorspar deposits; deceased, see previous edition for last biography

BAXTER, JOHN DARLING, BIOCHEMISTRY, ENDOCRINOLOGY. *Current Pos:* sr fel oncol, Dept Biochem & Biophys, Univ Calif, San Francisco, 70-72, from asst prof to prof med & biochem, 72-76, dir, endocrine res div, 76-81, DIR ENDOCRINOL DIV, UNIV CALIF, SAN FRANCISCO, 80-, DIR, METABOLIC RES UNIT, 81- *Personal Data:* b Lexington, Ky, June 11, 40; m 63; c 2. *Educ:* Univ Ky, BS, 62; Yale Univ, MD, 66. *Prof Exp:* Intern internal med, Yale-New Haven Hosp, 66-67, resident, 67-68; res assoc molecular biol, Nat Inst Arthritis & Metab Dis, 68-70. *Concurrent Pos:* Nat Inst Arthritis & Metab Dis res career develop award, 72-75; prin investr, NIH grants, 74-, co-prin investr, 77-; prin investr, Howard Hughes Med Inst, 75-81. *Mem:* Endocrine Soc; Am Fedn Clin Res; Am Soc Clin Invest; Am Thyroid Asn; Asn Am Physicians; Am Chem Soc. *Res:* Molecular biology of the renin-angiotensim system; thyroid hormone action and growth hormone gene expression. *Mailing Add:* Metabolic Res Univ Calif-SF 1141 HSW Box 0540 San Francisco CA 94143

BAXTER, JOHN EDWARDS, PHYSICAL CHEMISTRY, BIOCHEMISTRY. *Current Pos:* from asst to assoc prof, 71-81, dir, comput-based educ, 78-84, PROF BIOCHEM, CTR HEALTH SCI, UNIV TENN, MEMPHIS, 81-, ACTG DIR, HEALTH SCI COMPUT CTR, 81- *Personal Data:* b Meridian, Miss, Aug 29, 37; m 68; c 3. *Educ:* Millsaps Col, BS, 58; Vanderbilt Univ, MS, 60; Duke Univ, PhD(phys chem), 66. *Prof Exp:* Res assoc phys chem, Duke Univ, 66; asst prof physics & chem, NC Wesleyan Col, 66-71. *Mem:* Asn Develop Comput Based Instrnl Systs; Am Chem Soc; Sigma Xi. *Res:* Utilization of self instructional methods in biochemistry education. *Mailing Add:* Rm 789 L/N Bldg Univ Tenn-Memphis Memphis TN 38163

BAXTER, JOHN LEWIS, FISHERIES MANAGEMENT. *Current Pos:* RETIRED. *Personal Data:* b San Diego, Calif, July 31, 25; m 47, Enid Wallin; c Jeffrey L & William E. *Educ:* Univ Calif, Berkeley, AB, 51. *Prof Exp:* Marine biologist, fisheries lab, State Dept Fish & Game, Calif, 51-63, supvr, pelagic fish prog, 63-70, chief marine resources br, 70-71; spec asst to dir, Nat Marine Fisheries Serv, Washington, DC, 71-73; marine sport fish coordr, 73-74, supvr north ocean area, 74-81, regional mgr, Marine Resources Region, Calif Dept Fish & Game, 81-85. *Concurrent Pos:* Res fel, Scripps Inst Oceanog, 66-72; marine ed, Calif Fish & Game, 62-66; ed-in-chief, Fish Bull, 66-70; exec secy, Marine Fisheries Adv Comt, Dept Com, 71-73. *Mem:* Am Inst Fishery Res Biol; Am Fisheries Soc. *Res:* Biology of sport and commercial fishes. *Mailing Add:* 5772 Garden Grove Blvd No 477 Westminster CA 92683-1858

BAXTER, LARRY KINGSBURY, CAPACITIVE SENSORS. *Current Pos:* CONSULT ENGR, PICTURETEL CORP, 93- *Personal Data:* b Boston, Mass, Mar 27, 38; m 81, Carol Marby; c AJ, Shenna & Kathy. *Educ:* Rensselaer Polytech Inst, BS, 61. *Prof Exp:* Vpres eng, Kronos, Inc, 77-79, Echolab Inc, 80-93. *Concurrent Pos:* Lectr senors, 97- *Res:* Capacitive sensors. *Mailing Add:* 73 Eastern Point Blvd Gloucester MA 01930. *E-Mail:* baxterl@pictel.com

BAXTER, LINCOLN, II, APPLIED PHYSICS, OCEAN ACOUSTICS. *Current Pos:* RETIRED. *Personal Data:* b Washington, DC, July 25, 24; m 50, Frances Schulze; c Lincoln A & Eric L. *Educ:* Univ Richmond, BS, 46. *Prof Exp:* Teaching asst physics, Cornell Univ, 46-49; res asst physics, Polaroid Corp, 49-55; res assoc appl physics, 56-61, res specialist appl physics, Woods Hole Oceanog Inst, 61-86. *Mem:* Am Asn Physics Teachers; Acoust Soc Am; Optical Soc Am; Royal Astron Soc Can. *Res:* Ocean acoustics; underwater optics; computer data processing; navigation; optics of polarizers. *Mailing Add:* 53 Emmons Rd Falmouth MA 02540

BAXTER, LUTHER WILLIS, JR, PLANT PATHOLOGY. *Current Pos:* assoc prof, 66-70, PROF PLANT PATH & PHYSIOL, CLEMSON UNIV, 70- *Personal Data:* b Lawrenceburg, Ky, Nov 25, 24; m 48; c 3. *Educ:* Eastern Ky State Col, BS, 50; La State Univ, MS, 52, PhD, 54. *Prof Exp:* Plant pathologist, Kaiser Aluminum & Chem Corp, 54-55; assoc plant pathologist, Clemson Univ, 55-58; prof plant path & head dept agr, Western Ky State Col, 58-66. *Concurrent Pos:* Consult, Kaiser Aluminum & Chem Corp, 56. *Mem:* Am Phytopath Soc. *Res:* Diseases of camellias; physiology of reproduction in fungi. *Mailing Add:* 2927 N Bayshore Dr Seneca SC 29678

BAXTER, NEAL EDWARD, INTERNAL MEDICINE, AEROSPACE MEDICINE. *Current Pos:* MED DIR, WESTINGHOUSE ELEC CORP, 57- *Personal Data:* b Bluffton, Ind, Sept 13, 08; m 52; c 5. *Educ:* Ind Univ, AB, 32, MD, 35. *Honors & Awards:* John A Tamesia Award, Aerospace Med Asn, 65. *Prof Exp:* Intern, Indianapolis City Hosp, 35-36; physician gen pract, 36-54. *Concurrent Pos:* Assoc, Woolery Clin, Bloomington, Ind, 36-37; specialist aerospace & internal med, pvt pract, 54-; dir found, Sch Bus, Ind Univ, 69-; aviation med examr, Fed Aviation Agency. *Mem:* Am Acad Gen Pract; Am Diabetes Asn; fel Am Acad Family Physicians; Aerospace Med Asn (pres, 65-66); Civil Aviation Med Asn (pres, 62). *Res:* Aviation physiology and oxygen equipment; syncopal reactions of anoxic subjects observed in the low pressure chamber; civil aviation medicine; medical aspects of business aviation. *Mailing Add:* 1624 Buffstone Ct Bloomington IN 47401

BAXTER, ROBERT MACCALLUM, BIOCHEMISTRY, LIMNOLOGY. *Current Pos:* RES SCIENTIST LIMNOL, NAT WATER RES INST, CAN, 73- *Personal Data:* b Summerside, PEI, Apr 25, 26; m 53; c 3. *Educ:* Mt Allison Univ, BSc, 47; McGill Univ, PhD(biochem), 52. *Prof Exp:* Res officer chem microbiol, Nat Res Coun, Ottawa, 52-61; prof chem, Haile Sellassie Univ, 61-73. *Concurrent Pos:* Fel, Tech Univ Norway, 59-60. *Mem:* Brit Biochem Soc; Can Biochem Soc; Can Soc Microbiol; Int Asn Theoret & Appl Limnol. *Res:* Physiology of microbial halophilism and psychrophilism; tropical limnology; environmental impacts of dams and impoundments; chemical limnology of humic substances; microbial metabolism of environmental contaminants. *Mailing Add:* 2256-1 Upper Middle Rd Burlington ON L7P 2Z9 Can

BAXTER, ROBERT WILSON, PALEOBOTANY. *Current Pos:* RETIRED. *Personal Data:* b June 7, 14; m 45; c 1. *Educ:* Wash Univ, AB, 37, MS, 47, PhD(paleobot), 49. *Prof Exp:* Asst instr bot, Univ Hawaii, 38-39; from asst prof to prof bot, Univ Kans, 49-83, chmn dept, 53-57, emer prof, 83. *Concurrent Pos:* Fulbright lectr, Univ Col WI, 55-56; NSF res award, 58, 61 & 63. *Mem:* Bot Soc Am; Int Soc Plant Morphol; Int Soc Plant Taxon. *Res:* Carboniferous flora of the central United States; cretaceous Dakota sandstone flora. *Mailing Add:* 1010 Wellington Rd Lawrence KS 66049

BAXTER, RONALD DALE, ELECTRICAL ENGINEERING, SOLID STATE ELECTRONICS. *Current Pos:* prin scientist, 74-83, corp scientist, 83-91, MGR, SOLID STATE TECHNOL, LEEDS & NORTHRUP CO, 91- *Personal Data:* b Pittsburgh, Pa, Oct 17, 34; m 58; c 3. *Educ:* Ohio State Univ, BSEE, 60, MSc, 63. *Prof Exp:* From assoc to assoc mgr & scientist, Battelle Columbus Labs, 60-74. *Mem:* Am Vacuum Soc. *Res:* Electrical properties of semiconductors and other solid state materials; solid state device development; thin film techniques for device fabrication including chemical and physical vapor deposition methods; solid state sensors development; micromachining-microfabrication. *Mailing Add:* 3050 Cloverly Dr Furlong PA 18925

BAXTER, ROSS M, pharmacy, for more information see previous edition

BAXTER, SAMUEL G, electrical engineering, for more information see previous edition

BAXTER, SUSAN MCAFEE, NUCLEAR MAGNETIC RESONANCE SPECTROSCOPY, TRANSCRIPTIONAL REGULATION. *Current Pos:* RES SCIENTIST, WADSWORTH CTR, NY STATE DEPT HEALTH, 94-; ASST PROF BIOMED SCI, STATE UNIV NY, ALBANY, 95- *Personal Data:* m 93, Wade W. *Educ:* Univ Va, BA, 84; Northwestern Univ, MS, 88, PhD(chem), 92. *Prof Exp:* Res scientist, Monsanto Agr Co, 84-87; NIH postdoctoral fel, Univ Ore, 92-94. *Concurrent Pos:* Adj asst prof biol sci, State Univ NY, Albany, 97- *Mem:* AAAS; Am Chem Soc. *Res:* Nuclear magnetic resonance spectroscopic techniques that result in structural information on the atomic scale; elucidate mechanisms underlying recognition and specificity of DNA-binding proteins, including homeodomains and endonucleases. *Mailing Add:* Wadsworth Ctr Empire State Plaza Albany NY 12201-0509. *Fax:* 518-273-2900; *E-Mail:* baxter@wadsworth.org

BAXTER, WILLARD ELLIS, MATHEMATICS. *Current Pos:* from asst prof to prof, 58-94, chmn dept, 70-75, EMER PROF MATH, UNIV DEL, 94- *Personal Data:* b Chester, Pa, Dec 14, 29; m 54; c 3. *Educ:* Ursinus Col, BS, 51; Univ Wis, MS, 52; Univ Pa, PhD, 56. *Prof Exp:* Asst prof math, Ohio Univ, 56-58. *Mem:* Am Math Soc; Math Asn Am; Sigma Xi. *Res:* Structure theory of rings. *Mailing Add:* 405 Apple Rd Newark DE 19711

BAXTER, WILLIAM D, IMMUNOBIOLOGY. *Current Pos:* Asst prof, 66-71, ASSOC PROF BIOL, BOWLING GREEN STATE UNIV, 71- *Personal Data:* b Larned, Kans, Sept 13, 36; m 59; c 3. *Educ:* Phillips Univ, AB, 60; Univ Kans, PhD(zool), 66. *Concurrent Pos:* Adj prof, Med Col Ohio,

Toledo, 68- *Mem:* AAAS; Electron Micros Soc Am; Sigma Xi. *Res:* Immunology, especially early cellular events associated with the establishment of immunity; electron microscopy of animal tissues. *Mailing Add:* Dept Biol Bowling Green State Univ 1001 E Wooster St Bowling Green OH 43403-0001

BAXTER, WILLIAM JOHN, METAL PHYSICS. *Current Pos:* assoc sr res physicist, Gen Motors Corp, 64-66, sr res physicist, 66-78, staff res scientist, 78-82, sr staff res scientist, 82-93, PRIN RES SCIENTIST, RES LABS, GEN MOTORS CORP, 93- *Personal Data:* b Whinburgh, Eng, July 31, 35; US citizen; m 60; c 3. *Educ:* Oxford Univ, BA, 57, DPhil(physics), 61. *Honors & Awards:* Second Prize Photog Exhib, Am Soc Testing & Mat, 73. *Prof Exp:* Res physicist, Fulmer Res Inst, Eng, 60-61; res assoc internal friction, Cornell Univ, 61-63. *Concurrent Pos:* Fel, Cornell Univ, 61-63. *Mem:* Am Soc Testing & Mat; Am Phys Soc; Am Inst Mining, Metall & Petrol Engrs Metall Soc; Am Soc Metals. *Res:* Exoelectron emission and photoelectron microscopy; fatigue and deformation of metals; crack detection; internal friction; metal composites. *Mailing Add:* GMNAO Res & Develop Ctr Dept Physics (32) 30500 Mound Rd PO Box 9055 Warren MI 48090-9055

BAXTER, WILLIAM LEROY, virology, for more information see previous edition

BAY, DARRELL EDWARD, MEDICAL ENTOMOLOGY, VETERINARY ENTOMOLOGY. *Current Pos:* PROF ENTOM, TEX A&M UNIV, 74- *Personal Data:* b Hays, Kans, Dec 22, 42; m 75, Ann Query; c Laura E. *Educ:* Kans State Univ, BS, 64, MS, 67, PhD(entom), 74. *Honors & Awards:* Outstanding Med/Vet Entomol Award, Am Registry Prof Entomologists. *Prof Exp:* Entomologist, Walter Reed Army Inst Res, 68-71. *Mem:* Entom Soc Am. *Res:* Biology, ecology and control of livestock insects. *Mailing Add:* Dept Entom Tex A&M Univ College Station TX 77843

BAY, ERNEST C, MEDICAL ENTOMOLOGY, URBAN ENTOMOLOGY. *Current Pos:* supt, 75-85, PROF ENTOM, WESTERN WASH RES & EXTEN CTR, WASH STATE UNIV, 85- *Personal Data:* b Schenectady, NY, Aug 7, 29; m 63; c 2. *Educ:* Cornell Univ, BS, 53, PhD(entom), 60. *Prof Exp:* Specialist entom, Univ Calif, Riverside, 60-61, asst entomologist biol control, 61-69, head div, 69-71; head dept entom, Univ Md, College Park, 71-75. *Concurrent Pos:* NIH grant, 61-65; WHO consult, Nicaraguan Ministry Health, 64, Far East, 67, Nigeria, 72; secy gen, XV Int Cong Entom, 73-75. *Mem:* Entom Soc Am; Am Mosquito Control Asn. *Res:* Ecology and control of insects of medical and veterinary importance; ecology and control of chironomid midges; biological control of medically important insects. *Mailing Add:* 617 Fifth Ave NW Puyallup WA 98371-4257

BAY, ROGER R(UDOLPH), FORESTRY HYDROLOGY, RESEARCH ADMINISTRATION. *Current Pos:* CONSULT, NATURAL RESOURCES RES & DEVELOP, 88- *Personal Data:* b La Crosse, Wis, Nov 27, 31; m 58, Ruth Buckley; c 2. *Educ:* Univ Idaho, BS, 53; Univ Minn, MF, 54, PhD(forestry), 67. *Prof Exp:* Forester, Forest Serv, USDA, 54, res forester, 56-61, proj leader, NCent Forest Exp Sta, 61-70, from asst chief to chief, Br Watershed & Aquatic Habitat Res, Div Forest Environ Res, 70-73, asst to dep chief res, 73-74, dir, Intermountain Forest & Range Exp Sta, 74-83, dir, Pac Southwest Forest & Range Exp Sta, 83-88. *Concurrent Pos:* Mem, Foreign Agr Orgn Wateshed Cong, Arg, 71; consult gen forestry, Arg, 81-; consult, Col Trop Agr & Human Resources, Univ Hawaii. *Mem:* AAAS; Am Forestry Asn; Soc Am Foresters; Am Geophys Union; Int Soc Trop Forestry; Nitrogen Fixing Tree Asn. *Res:* Watershed management research; forest hydrology; forestry research planning, management and evaluation. *Mailing Add:* 6931 Mogollon Dr Bozeman MT 59715

BAY, THEODOSIOS (TED), CHEMICAL ENGINEERING, SYSTEMS DESIGN. *Current Pos:* RETIRED. *Personal Data:* b Montreal, Que, Apr 22, 31; m 59; c 3. *Educ:* McGill Univ, BEng, 53; Princeton Univ, MSEng, 55. *Prof Exp:* Chem engr, Esso Res & Eng Co, 57-60; assoc scientist, Leeds & Northrup Co, 60-61, res scientist, 61-63, sr scientist systs anal, 63-75, prin scientist, 75-81; assoc engr, Mobil Res & Develop Corp, 81-88, sr assoc engr, 88-96. *Mem:* Am Inst Chem Engrs. *Res:* Automatic control of chemical processes; computer control; systems science. *Mailing Add:* 112 Knollwood Dr Lansdale PA 19446

BAYER, ARTHUR CRAIG, ORGANIC PROCESS RESEARCH, FLAME RETARDANT CHEMISTRY. *Current Pos:* SR GROUP LEADER, CIBA-GEIGY CORP, 88- *Personal Data:* b Brooklyn, NY, Apr 5, 46; m 76, Barbara Dockendorf; c Craig A & Jessica A. *Educ:* Manhattan Col, BS, 67; State Univ NY, Buffalo, PhD(org chem), 72. *Prof Exp:* Res assoc, Univ Ore, 72-74; res chemist, Hooker Chem Corp, 74-78; sr res chemist, Stauffer Chem Co, 78-84; dir res, First Chem Corp, 84-88. *Mem:* AAAS; Am Chem Soc; Am Mgt Asn; Sigma Xi. *Res:* The invention and development of new syntheses of organic molecules as applied to agricultural and pharmaceutical chemical manufacturing processes. *Mailing Add:* 12335 Cardeza Ave Baton Rouge LA 70816. *Fax:* 504-642-1165

BAYER, BARBARA MOORE, PHARMACOLOGY. *Current Pos:* RES ASST PROF PHARMACOL, GEORGETOWN UNIV, 82- *Personal Data:* b Henderson, Tex, Dec 10, 48; m 72; c 1. *Educ:* Univ Tex, El Paso, BS, 72; Ohio State Univ, PhD(pharmacol), 77. *Prof Exp:* Lab instr chem, Univ Tex, El Paso, 70-72; res assoc pharmacol, Toxicol Lab, Ohio State Univ, 72-76, pharmacol fac, 77; res fel, NIH, Bethesda, 77-79, staff fel, 79-81; spec asst sci, Food & Drug Admin, Rockville, 81-83. *Concurrent Pos:* Sci consult to comnr, Food & Drug Admin, 83-; prin investr, Nat Inst Arthritis & Infectious Disease, 83-85. *Mem:* AAAS; Found Advan Educ Sci; Am Soc Pharmacol & Exp Therapeut; Sigma Xi. *Res:* Cellular action of anti-inflammatory drugs, cell cycle analysis and the regulation and metabolism of histamine and polyamines in normal and rapidly growing tissues. *Mailing Add:* Dept Pharmacol Georgetown Med Sch 3900 Reservoir Rd NW Washington DC 20007-2188

BAYER, CHARLENE WARRES, INDOOR AIR RESEARCH, MASS SPECTROMETRY. *Current Pos:* sr res scientist, 83-90, PRIN RES SCIENTIST, GA TECH RES INST, 90- *Personal Data:* b Loredo, Tex, Aug 13, 50; m 75; c 2. *Educ:* Baylor Univ, BS, 72; Emory Univ, MS, 74, PhD(org chem), 81. *Prof Exp:* Chemist, Smith Kline Corp, 74-75, Emory Univ, 75-76 & US Geol Surv, 80-83; consult, Ga Inst Technol, 77-80. *Concurrent Pos:* Consult, S C Johnson, Inc, 88- & DuPont, 91-; mem, Sleep Prods Safety Coun, 93- *Mem:* Am Chem Soc; Am Soc Heating, Refrig & Air Conditioning Engrs; Am Soc Mass Spectrometry; Sigma Xi; Int Soc Indoor Air Qual & Climate. *Res:* Trace analysis and separations sciences and mass spectrometry of environmental samples, particularly of air quality analysis; air quality evaluation by chromatographic and mass spectrometric determination of volatile organic compounds; source characterization using environmental chambers; building policies; trace species detection and identification. *Mailing Add:* 627 Rosecommon Dr Norcross GA 30092-1852

BAYER, DAVID E, PLANT PHYSIOLOGY. *Current Pos:* Assoc agriculturalist, 59-62, from asst botanist to assoc botanist, 62-73, BOTANIST, UNIV CALIF, DAVIS, 73-, PROF, 78- *Personal Data:* b Grass Valley, Ore, Aug 1, 26. *Educ:* Ore State Univ, BS, 51, MS, 53; Univ Wis, PhD(agron), 58. *Mem:* Weed Soc Am. *Res:* Plant physiology, particularly pertaining to herbicides and their effects on plants. *Mailing Add:* Dept Plant Biol Univ Calif Davis CA 95616-5200

BAYER, FREDERICK MERKLE, ZOOLOGY. *Current Pos:* vis cur, 71, CUR, NAT MUS NATURAL HIST, DEPT INVERT ZOOL, SMITHSONIAN INST, 75- *Personal Data:* b Asbury Park, NJ, Oct 31, 21. *Educ:* Univ Miami, BS, 48; George Washington Univ, MS, 54, PhD(zool), 58. *Prof Exp:* Asst dir, State Mus, Fla, 42-46; asst marine invert, Marine Lab, Univ Miami, 46-47; from asst cur to assoc cur, US Nat Mus, 47-61; assoc prof, 62-63, prof, Sch Marine & Atmospheric Sci, Univ Miami, 64-75. *Concurrent Pos:* Mem, Bikini Sci Resurv Exped, USN, 47, Ifaluk Atoll Surv Team, Pac Sci Bd, Nat Res Coun-Nat Acad Sci, 53, Palau Island Exped, Vanderbilt Found, 55 & Gulf of Guinea Exped, Inst Marine Sci, Univ Miami, 64 & 65, Southwestern Caribbean Exped, 66, Hispaniola-Jamaica Exped, 70 & Caribbean Basin Exped, 72; ed, Bull Marine Sci of Gulf & Caribbean, 62-71; mem, Int Comn Zool Nomenclature, 72- *Mem:* Paleont Soc Am; Sigma Xi. *Res:* Taxonomy, zoogeography and ecology of Octocorallia. *Mailing Add:* Dept Invert Zool Smithsonian Inst W323-NHB163 Washington DC 20560

BAYER, GEORGE HERBERT, WEED SCIENCE. *Current Pos:* CONSULT, 88- *Personal Data:* b Woodhaven, NY, Dec 7, 24; m 54. *Educ:* Cornell Univ, BS, 50, MS, 52, PhD(veg crops), 65. *Prof Exp:* Res asst, GLF Soil Bldg, 54-55, tech field rep, 55-61; res asst, Cornell Univ, 61-64; herbicide develop mgr, 64-65, Agway Inc, 64-65, sr staff scientist, 66-85. *Concurrent Pos:* Courtesy prof, Veg Crops Dept, Cornell Univ, 80-91; weed scientist consult, 85- *Mem:* Fel Weed Sci Soc Am (treas, 79-81); Coun Agr Sci & Technol; Sigma Xi. *Res:* Discover and evaluate the activity of the various classes of herbicides on vegetable, forage and tree fruit crops. *Mailing Add:* 216 Forest Home Dr Ithaca NY 14850

BAYER, HORST OTTO, ORGANIC CHEMISTRY. *Personal Data:* b Stuttgart, Ger, Oct 21, 34; US citizen; m 55, Carol J Dresser; c Keith & Kevin. *Educ:* Rochester Inst Technol, BS, 57; Purdue Univ, PhD(org chem), 61. *Prof Exp:* Sr chemist, Pesticide Syntheses Group, Rohm & Haas Co, 62-65, head res lab, 65-73, proj leader, 73-81, sect mgr, Res Lab, 81-85, dept mgr, Herbicides Res Lab, 85-92. *Concurrent Pos:* NSF-NATO fel, Univ Munich, 61-62. *Mem:* Am Chem Soc; Sigma Xi. *Res:* Synthesis, structure and activity studies relating to herbicides, insecticides, fungicides and plant growth regulators; process development and start-up. *Mailing Add:* 186 Red Rose Dr Levittown PA 19056

BAYER, MANFRED ERICH, CELL BIOLOGY, VIROLOGY. *Current Pos:* asst mem molecular biol, 62-67, assoc mem, 67-78, mem, 78-86, SR MEM, INST CANCER RES, 86- *Personal Data:* b Goerlitz, Silesia, Sept 22, 28; WGer citizen; m 58; c 2. *Educ:* Univ Hamburg, Dr med, 56; Inst Trop Med & Parasitol, dipl, 61. *Prof Exp:* Fel neurol, Univ Hosp, Hamburg, 56-58; fel virol, Inst Trop Dis, 58-59, res assoc, 59-60, asst mem, 60-62. *Concurrent Pos:* Vis scientist, Inst Cancer Res, France, 61; prin investr grants, NIH & NSF, 66-; adj prof, Dept Microbiol, Med Sch, Univ Pa, 71-, mem, Grad Group Microbiol, 76-; vis prof, Inst Virol, Kyoto Univ, Japan, 77; NSF panel mem, 82-84; biol instrumentation & study sections, Med Sci Spec Prog, NIH Microbiol Chem, 79-86; vis prof, Biozentrum Univ Basel, Switz, 84, Max Planck Inst for Immunobiol, Freiburg, WGer, 86; hon vis prof, Dept Microbiol, Dalhousie Univ Med Sch, Halifax, Can, 85- *Mem:* Am Soc Microbiol; Biophys Soc Am; Electron Microscope Soc Am; Electron Microscope Soc Can; Am Soc Cell Biol; Am Soc Virol. *Res:* Kinetics and mechanisms of virus infection; cell surface charge, electrophoresis; cell surface structure and function; isolation of receptor domains; metal interactions with membranes. *Mailing Add:* Inst Cancer Res 7701 Burholme Ave Fox Chase Cancer Ctr Philadelphia PA 19111-2412

BAYER, MARGRET H(ELENE) JANSSEN, MEMBRANE PHYSIOLOGY. *Current Pos:* res assoc, Inst Cancer Res, 62-76, SR RES ASSOC BIOL & MICROBIOL, FOX CHASE CANCER CTR, 77- *Personal Data:* b 1931; m 58, Manfred E; c 2. *Educ:* Univ Hamburg, dipl, 58, Dr rer nat, 61, Dr habil(plant physiology), 76. *Prof Exp:* Res assoc biol, Univ Hamburg, 58-61. *Concurrent Pos:* Vis prof, Dept Biol, Univ Hamburg, 75, habilitation, 76; vis lectr, Univ Pa, Philadelphia, 79-80; NSF & NIH Fed grants. *Mem:* Am Soc Microbiol; Am Soc Plant Physiologists; fel Am Acad Microbiol; Fedn Europ Soc PLant Physiol. *Res:* Biology of microorganisms; membrane biology and biochemistry; biology of plant tumors; regulation and control of abnormal growth; comparative oncology. *Mailing Add:* Inst for Cancer Res Fox Chase Cancer Ctr Philadelphia PA 19111-2497. *Fax:* 215-728-2412

BAYER, RAYMOND GEORGE, TRIBOLOGY, FAILURE ANALYSIS. *Current Pos:* INDEPENDENT CONSULT, 92- *Personal Data:* b New York, NY, June 9, 35; m 58, Barbara A Sartini; c Joseph, Matthew, Mary & Karen. *Educ:* St Johns Univ, NY, BS, 56; Brown Univ, RI, MS, 59. *Honors & Awards:* Award of Merit, Am Soc Testing & Mat. *Prof Exp:* Sr eng, IBM Corp, Endicott, NY, 58-91. *Mem:* Fel Am Soc Testing & Mat. *Res:* Tribology with particular emphasis on the development of approaches for predicting wear behavior; stress testing of electronic packages. *Mailing Add:* 4609 Marshall Dr W Vestal NY 13850

BAYER, RICHARD EUGENE, ANALYTICAL CHEMISTRY, INORGANIC CHEMISTRY. *Current Pos:* Assoc prof, 58-66, chmn dept, 67-76, PROF CHEM, CARROLL COL, WIS, 66-,PRES,BIONOMICS CORP,71- *Personal Data:* b Milwaukee, Wis, Jan 11, 32; m 57; c 4. *Educ:* Carroll Col, Wis, BS, 54; Ind Univ, PhD(chem), 59. *Honors & Awards:* Am Chem Soc Award. *Mem:* Am Chem Soc; Sigma Xi. *Res:* Rare earth chelates; atomic absorption; selective ion electrodes; chemical health and safety; solid waste disposal. *Mailing Add:* 1016 E Roberta Ave Waukesha WI 53186-5593

BAYER, ROBERT CLARK, LOBSTER NUTRITION. *Current Pos:* PROF ANIMAL VET & AQUATIC SCI, UNIV MAINE, ORONO, 72-, PROJ DIR, LOBSTER RES PROJ; EXEC DIR, LOBSTER INST. *Personal Data:* b New York, NY, July 4, 44; m 67; c 3. *Educ:* Univ Vt, BS, 66, MS, 68; Mich State Univ, PhD(avian physiol), 72. *Honors & Awards:* Lobster Sci Award, Int Lobster Cong, 93. *Mem:* AAAS; Nat Shellfisheries Asn; World Maricult Soc; Am Inst Nutrit. *Res:* Lobster nutrition, health and behavior. *Mailing Add:* 128 Hitchner Hall Univ Maine Orono ME 04473

BAYER, SHIRLEY ANN, NEUROANATOMY, DEVELOPMENTAL NEUROBIOLOGY. *Current Pos:* PROF BIOL, IND UNIV PURDUE UNIV, INDIANAPOLIS, 81- *Personal Data:* b Evansville, Ind, Aug 20, 40; m 73, Joseph Altman. *Educ:* St Mary-of-the-Woods Col, BA, 63; Calif State Univ, Fullerton, MA, 69; Purdue Univ, PhD(biol), 74. *Prof Exp:* Teacher biol, Guerin High Sch, Ill, 63-65 & Our Lady of Providence High Sch, Ind, 65-66; teacher & chmn sci dept, Marywood Sch, Calif, 66-70; res scientist, Purdue Univ, 73-81. *Mem:* Soc Neurosci. *Res:* Light microscopy studies on the development of the central and peripheral nervous systems in the rat; using x-irradiation and trimated-thymidine autoradiography. *Mailing Add:* Dept Biol Ind Univ Purdue Univ 1100 W Michigan St Indianapolis IN 46202-2880. *Fax:* 317-274-2846

BAYER, THOMAS NORTON, GEOLOGY, PALEONTOLOGY. *Current Pos:* asst prof, 64-68, PROF EARTH SCI, WINONA STATE UNIV, 68- *Personal Data:* b Elyria, Ohio, Dec 23, 34; m 74. *Educ:* Macalester Col, BA, 57; Univ Minn, MS, 60, PhD(geol), 65. *Prof Exp:* Instr geol, Macalester Col, 57-64. *Concurrent Pos:* Lectr, Macalester Col, 61-64; consult classroom prod, KTCA-TV, 62-63. *Mem:* Sigma Xi; Geol Soc Am; Am Asn Petrol Geologists; Paleont Soc; Soc Econ Paleont & Mineral. *Res:* Paleoecology of lower Paleozoic invertebrate faunas. *Mailing Add:* Dept Geol Winona State Univ PO Box 5838 Winona MN 55987-0838

BAYES, KYLE D, CHEMICAL DYNAMICS. *Current Pos:* chmn dept, 87-90, from asst prof to assoc prof, 60-71, PROF CHEM, UNIV CALIF, LOS ANGELES, 71- *Personal Data:* b Colfax, Wash, Mar 3, 35; m 61; c 2. *Educ:* Calif Inst Technol, BS, 56; Harvard Univ, PhD(chem), 59. *Prof Exp:* NSF fel, Univ Bonn, 59-60. *Concurrent Pos:* Sloan vis lectr, Harvard Univ, 66; Erskine fel, Univ Canterbury, NZ, 88. *Mem:* AAAS; Am Phys Soc; Am Chem Soc. *Res:* Chemical kinetics and spectroscopy of gas phase reactions. *Mailing Add:* Dept Chem Univ Calif Los Angeles CA 90024

BAYEV, ALEXANDER A, biotechnology; deceased, see previous edition for last biography

BAYHURST, BARBARA P, NUCLEAR CHEMISTRY, RADIO CHEMISTRY. *Current Pos:* STAFF MEM RADIOCHEM, LOS ALAMOS SCI LAB, UNIV CALIF, 55- *Personal Data:* b Vivian, La, Mar 31, 26; div; c 4. *Educ:* La State Univ, BS, 46. *Mem:* Am Chem Soc; AAAS. *Res:* Absolute counting; cross-section measurements; atomic devices as research tools; nuclear waste disposal. *Mailing Add:* 1201 Sixth St Los Alamos NM 87544

BAYLESS, DAVID LEE, TOTAL QUALITY MANAGEMENT. *Current Pos:* PRES, BAYLESS & ASSOCS, 93- *Personal Data:* b Alliance, Ohio, June 12, 38; m 63; c 3. *Educ:* Muskingum Col, AB, 60; Fla State Univ, MS, 63; Tex A&M Univ, PhD(statist), 68. *Prof Exp:* Asst, Fla State Univ, 61-63; assoc mem staff, Bell Tel Labs, NJ, 63-64; consult, Gen Food Tech Ctr, NY, 64-65; fel, Tex A&M Univ, 65-68; mgr prog develop & sci statist scientist, Res Triangle Inst, 68-83; vpres, Westat, Inc, 83-92. *Concurrent Pos:* Adj assoc prof statist, NC State Univ, 68-; asst to dir res, Nat Assessment Educ Proj, 70. *Mem:* Am Statist Asn. *Res:* Survey research methods and application in education, health and crime; quality management applications to education and business. *Mailing Add:* 105 Dundee Ct Cary NC 27511. *Fax:* 919-380-9575

BAYLESS, LAURENCE EMERY, BIOLOGY. *Current Pos:* From asst prof to assoc prof, 66-77, PROF BIOL, CONCORD COL, 77- *Personal Data:* b Richmond, Va, Aug 27, 38; m 62. *Educ:* Univ Tenn, AB, 61; Tulane Univ, MS, 62, PhD(biol), 66. *Mem:* Am Soc Ichthyol & Herpet; Soc Study Amphibians & Reptiles; Ecol Soc Am; Sigma Xi. *Res:* Population ecology and life history of amphibians. *Mailing Add:* Dept Biol Concord Col PO Box 1000 Athens WV 24712-1000

BAYLESS, PHILIP LEIGHTON, ORGANIC CHEMISTRY. *Current Pos:* prof & chmn dept, 54-88, EMER PROF CHEM, WILMINGTON COL, 88- *Personal Data:* b Indianapolis, Ind, Feb 23, 28; m 49, Barbara Staley; c Margaret, Elaine & Jean. *Educ:* Oberlin Col, AB, 49; Duke Univ, PhD(chem), 54. *Honors & Awards:* Gustav Ohaus-NSTA Award, Nat Sci Teacher's Asn, 75. *Concurrent Pos:* Alexander von Humboldt fel, 63-64; fac fel, Nat Acad Sci, 70-71; assoc prof, Univ Petrol & Minerals, Dhahran, Saudi Arabia, 76-77; ed eng, Gmelin Inst, Frankfurt, Ger, 88-90. *Mem:* Am Chem Soc. *Res:* Mechanisms of chemical reactions; metal-organic compounds. *Mailing Add:* 71 Faculty Pl Wilmington OH 45177

BAYLEY, HENRY SHAW, BIOCHEMISTRY, NUTRITION. *Current Pos:* from asst prof to assoc prof, 65-76, PROF NUTRIT, UNIV GUELPH, 76- *Personal Data:* b Macclesfield, Eng, Aug 21, 38. *Educ:* Univ Reading, BSc, 60; Univ Nottingham, PhD, 63. *Honors & Awards:* Borden Award, Nutrit Soc Can, 77. *Prof Exp:* Asst lectr nutrit, Wye Col, Univ London, 63-65. *Mem:* Am Soc Animal Sci; Am Inst Nutrit; Can Soc Animal Sci; Nutrit Soc Can; Brit Nutrit Soc. *Res:* Energy metabolism: factors influencing digestion and absorption of major energy yielding nutrients, use of respiration calorimeter and substrate turnover rates as indicators of metabolic response to stessors such as cold and exercise. *Mailing Add:* Dept Nutrit Univ Guelph Guelph ON N1G 2W1 Can. *Fax:* 519-763-5902; *E-Mail:* ntrbay@vm.uoguelph.ca

BAYLEY, STANLEY THOMAS, MOLECULAR BIOLOGY OF ONCOGENIC TRANSFORMATION & CELL GROWTH. *Current Pos:* prof, 67-92, chmn dept, 68-74, interim dir, Inst Molecular Biol & Biotechnol, 85-88, EMER PROF BIOL, MCMASTER UNIV, 92- *Personal Data:* b Grays, Essex, Eng, Nov 5, 26; Can citizen; m 50, Betty E Cole; c Elizabeth G & Valerie A. *Educ:* Univ London, BSc, 46, PhD(physics), 50. *Honors & Awards:* Centennial Medal Can, 68, Silver Jubilee Medal, 78. *Prof Exp:* Nuffield res fel biophys, King's Col, Univ London, 50-52; from asst res officer to sr res officer, Nat Res Coun Can, 52-67. *Res:* Molecular biology of DNA tumor viruses, particularly the effect of adenovirus EIA on cell growth. *Mailing Add:* Dept Biol McMaster Univ 1280 Main St W Hamilton ON L8S 4K1 Can. *Fax:* 905-522-6066; *E-Mail:* bayley@mcmaster.ca

BAYLIFF, WILLIAM HENRY, FISHERIES. *Current Pos:* scientist, 58-65, SR SCIENTIST, INTER-AM TROP TUNA COMN, SCRIPPS INST OCEANOG, 65- *Personal Data:* b Annapolis, Md, Aug 29, 28; m 69, Norma J York; c 619-546-7025. *Educ:* Western Md Col, BA, 49; Univ Wash, MS, 54, PhD, 65. *Honors & Awards:* W F Thompson Award, Am Inst Fishery Res Biologists, 69. *Prof Exp:* Biologist, State Dept Fisheries, Wash, 52-54, 57-58. *Concurrent Pos:* Marine fishery biologist, Food & Agr Orgn, UN, 67-68, consult, Develop Prog Fishery Proj, Callao, Peru, 71, convener, working party tuna and billfish tagging, Panel Experts Facilitation Tuna Res, 70-87; mem ed comt, Fishery Bull, Nat Marine Fisheries Serv, 70-78, 87-90; consult, Direccion General de Recursos Marinos, Ministerio de Comercio e Industrias, Republic of Panama, 83. *Mem:* Am Inst Fishery Res Biologists; Am Fisheries Soc. *Res:* Biology and population dynamics of marine fishes. *Mailing Add:* Inter-Am Trop Tuna Comn Scripps Inst Oceanog 8604 La Jolla Shores Dr La Jolla CA 92037-1508. *Fax:* 619-546-7133; *E-Mail:* wbaycliff@iattc.ucsd.edu

BAYLINK, DAVID J, MINERAL METABOLISM. *Current Pos:* CHIEF MINERAL METAB, PETTIS VET HOSP, 81-; PROF MED, LOMA LINDA UNIV, 81- *Personal Data:* b Portland, Ore, May 24, 31. *Educ:* Loma Linda Univ, MD, 57. *Mailing Add:* Jerry Pettis Vet Admin Hosp 11201 Benton St Loma Linda CA 92357-0001

BAYLIS, JEFFREY ROWE, ETHOLOGY, ICHTHYOLOGY. *Current Pos:* asst prof, 76-81, ASSOC PROF ZOOL, UNIV WIS-MADISON, 81- *Personal Data:* b Jackson, Mich, Nov 1, 45. *Educ:* Univ Calif, Santa Barbara, BA, 68; Univ Calif, Berkeley, MA, 72, PhD(zool), 75. *Prof Exp:* Fel zool, Rockefeller Univ, 74-76. *Mem:* Animal Behav Soc; Sigma Xi; Soc Study Evolution; Am Soc Ichthyologists & Herpetologists; AAAS. *Res:* Analysis of the social communicatory signals of animals, with special regard to the evolutionary origins of the signals and the environmental pressures that shaped them; evolution of sexual behavior and parental care; population biology of fishes. *Mailing Add:* 8735 Hidden Valley Rd Cross Plains WI 53528-9441. *E-Mail:* jrbyls@wiscmacc.bitnet

BAYLIS, JOHN ROBERT, JR, GENETICS. *Current Pos:* asst prof, 67-74, ASSOC PROF GENETICS, UNIV W FLA, 74- *Personal Data:* b Chicago, Ill, May 12, 27; m 54; c 2. *Educ:* Utah State Univ, BS, 51; Northwestern Univ, MS, 56; Fla State Univ, PhD(genetics), 66. *Prof Exp:* Biologist, Oak Ridge Nat Lab, 66-67. *Mem:* Genetics Soc Am; Am Inst Biol Sci; Environ Mutagen Soc; Sigma Xi. *Res:* Fungal genetics; environmental mutagenesis. *Mailing Add:* 3660 Maule Rd Pensacola FL 32503

BAYLIS, WILLIAM ERIC, ATOMIC PHYSICS, THEORETICAL PHYSICS. *Current Pos:* asst prof to assoc prof, 69-78, head, Physics Dept, 93-96, PROF PHYSICS, UNIV WINDSOR, 78- *Personal Data:* b Providence, RI, Nov 28, 39; m 61, Bobbye K Whitenton; c Evelyn M (Somer) & Katherine R. *Educ:* Duke Univ, BSc, 61; Univ Ill, MSc, 63; Tech Univ Munich, DSc(physics), 67. *Prof Exp:* Res asst physics, Max Planck Inst Extraterrestrial Physics, Garching, WGer, 63-67; res assoc atomic physics, Joint Inst Lab Astro-Physics, Boulder, Colo, 67-69. *Concurrent Pos:* Vis scientist atomic physics, Max Planck Inst Fluid-dyn, Gottingen, WGer, 76-77; vchmn, Div Atomic & Molecular Physics, Can Asn Physicists, 84-85, chmn, 85-86, vchmn, Div Theoret Physics, 96-97, chmn, 97-99; vis scientist atomic physics, Inst Fundamental Res, CEN-Saclay, France, 85; assoc ed, Advan Appln Clifford Algebras, 94-97, Can J Physics, 96-99. *Mem:* Fel Am Phys Soc; Can Asn Physicists. *Res:* Calculations of atomic and molecular structure; pseudopotential methods; pressure broadening of spectral lines; inelastic atomic collisions at thermal and keV energies; relativistic and correlation effects in electron/positron scattering of atoms; Pauli-algebra approach to relativistic physics; clifford algebras in physics. *Mailing Add:* Dept Physics Univ Windsor Windsor ON N9B 3P4 Can. *Fax:* 519-973-7075; *E-Mail:* baylis@uwindsor.ca

BAYLISS, COLIN EDWARD, CARDIOVASCULAR SURGERY, MEDICAL EDUCATION. *Current Pos:* from asst prof to assoc prof surg, 74-93, from asst prof to assoc prof physiol, 76-93, PROF SURG & PHYSIOL, UNIV TORONTO, 93- *Personal Data:* b Montreal, Que, Aug 13, 36; m 62, Sheila Fosbury; c Melinda, Julie & Peter. *Educ:* Univ Toronto, MD, 61; FRCS(C), 69. *Honors & Awards:* Starr Medal, 78. *Prof Exp:* Resident surg, Univ Toronto, 61-68, Frenchay Hosp, Eng, 68; asst res surgeon, Univ Calif, Los Angeles, 69-71; staff surgeon cardiovasc surg, Toronto Western Hosp, 71-75. *Concurrent Pos:* Med Res Coun Can scholar, 71-76; res surgeon, Clin Sci Div, Univ Toronto, 71-89; Starr Mem Grad Scholar, 76; dir, Med Physiol Teaching Unit, 89- *Mem:* Am Physiol Soc; Soc Thoracic Surgeons; Can Cardiovasc Soc; Am Heart Asn; Can Asn Univ Surgeons; Can Physiol Soc; Can Soc Cardiovasc & Thoracic Surgeons. *Res:* Myocardial function; development of isolated, perfused rabbit heart septum model (parabiotic); coronary microcirculation; cardiomyocyte culture; myocardial ischemia; no reflow phenomenon; myocardial preservation; medical education. *Mailing Add:* Med Sci Bldg Rm 3238 Univ Toronto Toronto ON M5S 1A8 Can. *Fax:* 416-978-4940

BAYLISS, JOHN TEMPLE, PHYSICS. *Current Pos:* CONSULT, 85- *Personal Data:* b Richmond, Va, July 6, 39; m 71, Mary Lynn Skinner; c W Temple, Ann F & A Thompson. *Educ:* Bowdoin Col, BA, 61; Univ Va, PhD(physics), 67. *Prof Exp:* Asst prof physics, Va Commonwealth Univ, 67-73; conserv coordr, Va Energy Off, 75-78; prog develop officer, Va Dept Mines, Minerals & Energy, 78-79, energy div dir, Energy Div, 79-85. *Concurrent Pos:* Consult, energy & pub policy, 85- *Res:* Conservation techniques and state policy; allocation of energy costs among institutional functions. *Mailing Add:* 1114 Dover Rd Manakin-Sabot VA 23103

BAYLISS, PETER, X-RAY POWDER DIFFRACTION. *Current Pos:* From asst prof to prof, 67-92, asst head dept, 80-84, EMER PROF GEOL, UNIV CALGARY, 92- *Personal Data:* b Eng; m 66. *Educ:* Univ NSW, BE, 59, MSc, 62, PhD(geol), 67. *Concurrent Pos:* Abstractor, Mineral Abstr, 69-; chmn, Minerals Comt Powder Diffraction File, 77-91; adv bd, Powder Diffraction, 86-; ed, Can Mineralogist, 87-92; ed, Minerals, Powder Diffraction Stand, 89-92; chmn, Int Mineral Asn Comm Mineral Classification, 90-94. *Mem:* Mineral Asn Can; Mineral Soc Gt Brit; fel Mineral Soc Am. *Res:* Mineral classification; powder x-ray diffraction data. *Mailing Add:* Dept Mineral Australian Mus 6 College St Sydney NSW 2000 Australia

BAYLOR, CHARLES, JR, ORGANIC CHEMISTRY, PHOTOGRAPHIC CHEMISTRY. *Current Pos:* RES ASSOC CHEMIST, E I DU PONT DE NEMOURS & CO, INC, 66- *Personal Data:* b Baltimore, Md, Dec 5, 40; c Tamara & Christopher. *Educ:* Morgan State Col, BS, 62; Utah State Univ, PhD(chem), 67. *Mem:* Am Chem Soc. *Res:* Synthesis, analytical methods and structure determination of organic compounds; surfactant applications, polymers and emulsion polymerization; gel technology and immunoassays; holographic materials. *Mailing Add:* 2720 Grubb Rd Chalfonte II Wilmington DE 19810-2350. *Fax:* 302-695-9631

BAYLOR, DENIS ARISTIDE, NEUROPHYSIOLOGY. *Current Pos:* assoc prof physiol, 74-75, assoc prof, 75-78, PROF NEUROBIOL, SCH MED, STANFORD UNIV, 78-, CHMN, DEPT NEUROBIOL, 92- *Personal Data:* b Oskaloosa, Iowa, Jan 30, 40; m 83, Eileen Vantassel; c Denis & Michael. *Educ:* Knox Col, BA, 61; Yale Univ, MD, 65. *Hon Degrees:* DSc, Knox Col, 89. *Honors & Awards:* Rank Prize Optoelectronics, 80; Proctor Medal, Asn Res Vision & Ophthal, 86; Kayser Int Award Res Vision & Ophthal, 86. *Prof Exp:* Fel neurophysiol, Sch Med, Yale Univ, 65-68; staff fel, Lab Neurophysiol, Nat Inst Neurol & Commun Disorders & Stroke, 68-70; USPHS spec fel, Physiol Lab, Cambridge Univ, 70-72; assoc prof physiol, Univ Colo Med Ctr, Denver, 72-74. *Concurrent Pos:* Ed, J Physiol, 77-84, Neuron, 88-93. *Mem:* Nat Acad Sci; Physiol Soc; Soc Gen Physiologists; Asn Res Vis & Ophthal; Soc Neurosci; Biophys Soc. *Res:* Generation and transmission of neural signals in the vertebrate retina. *Mailing Add:* Dept Neurobiol Stanford Univ Sch Med Stanford CA 94305

BAYLOR, JOHN E, AGRONOMY. *Current Pos:* assoc prof agron & assoc exten specialist, 57-65, prof agron & exten specialist, 65-83, EMER PROF, PA STATE UNIV, UNIVERSITY PARK, 83- *Personal Data:* b Belvidere, NJ, Sept 16, 22; m 50, Mary Henrietta Hauck; c Sue Ann & Martha Ellen. *Educ:* Rutgers Univ, BSc, 47, MSc, 48; Pa State Univ, PhD(agron), 58. *Honors & Awards:* Medallion Award, Am Forage & Grassland Coun, 71; Zur Crain Award, Nat Silo Asn, 71; Gamma Sigma Delta Exten Award, 75; Am Soc Agron Exten-Indust Award, 75; Pa Grassland Coun Bicentennial Award, 76; Agron Exten Educ Award, Am Soc Agron, 80. *Prof Exp:* Asst exten specialist farm crops, Rutgers Univ, 48-49, assoc exten specialist, 49-55. *Concurrent Pos:* Consult, IRI Res Inst, Brazil, 64; chair gov bd XIV, Int Grassland Cong; pres, Forage & Grassland Found. *Mem:* Fel Am Soc Agron; Am Forage & Grassland Coun (pres, 67-70, secy-treas, 73-); Coun Agr Sci & Technol; Am Soc Animal Sci. *Res:* Forage crop production and management. *Mailing Add:* 298 E McCormick Ave State College PA 16801

BAYLOUNY, RAYMOND ANTHONY, ORGANIC CHEMISTRY. *Current Pos:* from asst prof to assoc prof org chem, 63-67, chmn dept, 67-69 & 82-83, PROF CHEM, FAIRLEIGH DICKINSON UNIV, 77- *Personal Data:* b Paterson, NJ, Aug 11, 32; m 59, Kathryn Gerdeman; c Cecilia, James, John & Anne Marie. *Educ:* Seton Hall Univ, BS, 54; Univ Md, MS, 58, PhD(org chem), 60. *Honors & Awards:* E Emmet Reid Award, Am Chem Soc, 94. *Prof Exp:* Instr org chem & biochem, Brooklyn Col, 60-63. *Concurrent Pos:* Sr fel, Princeton Univ, 69-70; vis prof, Columbia Univ, 77 & 83-84 & Univ Med & Dent NJ, 93-94; counr, Am Chem Soc, 86- *Mem:* Am Chem Soc. *Res:* Theoretical organic chemistry; biochemistry; thermal rearrangement of unsaturated esters; synthesis and structure analysis of natural products; newer methods of organic synthesis; mechanistic organic chemistry. *Mailing Add:* Fairleigh Dickinson Univ Madison Campus Madison NJ 07940. *Fax:* 973-443-8766

BAYLY, M BRIAN, STRUCTURAL GEOLOGY. *Current Pos:* From asst prof to assoc prof, 62-74, PROF GEOL, RENSSELAER POLYTECH INST, 74- *Personal Data:* b Northwood, Eng, Apr 16, 29; m 60, Helen Bailey; c 5. *Educ:* Cambridge Univ, BA, 52, MA & MSc, 62; Univ Chicago, PhD(geol), 62. *Res:* Tectonics, structural geology, deformation processes, with emphasis on quantitative mechanical theories. *Mailing Add:* Dept Earth & Environ Sci Rensselaer Polytech Inst Troy NY 12180-3590. *Fax:* 518-276-8627; *E-Mail:* baylym@rpi.edu

BAYM, GORDON A, NUCLEAR, ASTROPHYSICS & CONDENSED MATTER PHYSICS. *Current Pos:* from asst prof to assoc prof, 63-68, prof physics, 60-93, CTR ADVAN STUDY PROF PHYSICS, UNIV ILL, URBANA-CHAMPAIGN, 93- *Personal Data:* b New York, NY, July 1, 35; c 4. *Educ:* Cornell Univ, BA, 56; Harvard Univ, AM, 57, PhD(physics), 60. *Honors & Awards:* Alexander von Humboldt Sr Scientist Award, 83. *Prof Exp:* NSF fel, Inst Theoret Physics, Denmark, 60-62; lectr & asst res physicist, Univ Calif, Berkeley, 62-63. *Concurrent Pos:* A P Sloan Found res fel, 65-68; vis prof, Univ Tokyo, 68, Univ Kyoto, 68, Nordita, Copenhagen, 70, 76, Niels Bohr Inst, 76 & Nagoya Univ, 79; assoc ed, Nuclear Physics, 71-; vis scientist, Acad Sinica, Beijing, 79; Alexander von Humboldt Found Fel, 83-89; NSF vis comt, Kellogg Lab, Caltech, 83-85; corresp, Comments Nuclear & Particle Physics, 86-; trustee, Associated Univs Inc, 86-90; mem, Theoretical Physics, Nat Safety Anal Ctr Subcomt, 86-88; organizer, Quark Matter, 88, Lenox, Mass, 88 & Workshop Ultrarelativistic Heavy Ion Physics, Italy, 88; vchmn, Forum Hist Physics, Am Phys Soc, 94-95, chair elect, 95-96, chair, 96-97; chmn, Physics Sect, Nat Acad Sci, 95-; mem, Comt Nuclear Physics, Nat Res Coun, 96-, Comt Hist Physics, Am Inst Physics, 96- *Mem:* Nat Acad Sci; fel AAAS; fel Am Phys Soc; Am Astron Soc; fel Am Acad Arts & Sci; Int Astron Union. *Res:* Low temperature physics; astrophysics; theory of many body systems; nuclear physics. *Mailing Add:* Loomis Lab Physics Univ Ill 1110 Green St Rm 337D Urbana IL 61801

BAYMAN, BENJAMIN, NUCLEAR PHYSICS. *Current Pos:* assoc prof physics, 65-68, PROF PHYSICS, 68-, Fel, UNIV MINN, MINNEAPOLIS, 75- *Personal Data:* b New York, NY, Dec 12, 30; m 57; c 2. *Educ:* Cooper Union, BChE, 51; Univ Edinburgh, PhD(physics), 55. *Prof Exp:* Asst prof, Princeton Univ, 60-65. *Concurrent Pos:* Res fel, theoret physics, Univ Edinburg, 55-56; Ford Fuond fel, theoret nuclear physics, Inst Theoret Physics, Denmark, 56-60. *Mem:* Am Phys Soc. *Res:* Interpretation of experimental data on atomic nuclei obtained by nuclear reaction and radioactivity studies in terms of nuclear models. *Mailing Add:* Dept Physics Univ Minn Minneapolis MN 55455

BAYNE, CHARLES KENNETH, statistics, for more information see previous edition

BAYNE, CHRISTOPHER JEFFREY, COMPARATIVE IMMUNOBIOLOGY. *Current Pos:* from asst prof to assoc prof, 71-82, chair, 86-89, PROF ZOOL, ORE STATE UNIV, 82- *Personal Data:* b Trinidad, WI, Aug 31, 41; m 63; c 3. *Educ:* Univ Wales, BSc, 63, PhD(zool), 67. *Prof Exp:* Fel, Marine Sci Labs, Menai Bridge, Wales, 66-67; lectr marine zool, Univ Wales, 67-68; res assoc molluscan physiol, Univ Mich, 68-71. *Concurrent Pos:* Investr, Univ Stockholm, 76-77, Univ Tromso, 84, Wageningen Univ, 85; chair, Div Comp Immunol, Am Soc Zool, 88-90; pres-elect, Int Soc Develop & Comp Immunol, 94-97. *Mem:* AAAS; Am Fisheries Soc; Am Soc Zool; Int Soc Develop Comp Immunol; Am Soc Parasitol. *Res:* Comparative immunology; molluscan and trematode cell culture; immuno-parasitology; mechanisms of immunity in deuterostome invertebrates; teleost immunology; mechanisms of natural immunity; phagocytic cells; stress hormones' influence on phagocytes; neuro-immunology, especially catecholamine regulation of defenses; fish and molluscan models incorporating helminth parasites. *Mailing Add:* Dept Zool Ore State Univ Corvallis OR 97331-2914. *Fax:* 541-787-0501

BAYNE, DAVID ROBERGE, LIMNOLOGY, AQUATIC FLORA. *Current Pos:* PROF FISHERIES & ALLIED AQUACULT, AUBURN UNIV, 72- *Personal Data:* b Selma, Ala, Jan 29, 41; m 85, Robin E Pattillo. *Educ:* Tulane Univ, BA, 63; Auburn Univ, MS, 67, PhD(aquatic ecol), 70. *Prof Exp:* Asst prof biol, Ga Col, 70-71. *Concurrent Pos:* Fishery adv, El Salvador, Cent Am, 72-73. *Mem:* Am Fisheries Soc; Am Soc Limnol & Oceanog; Aquatic Plant Mgt Soc; NAm Lake Mgt Soc. *Res:* Limnological studies of large multipurpose reservoirs; fresh water plankton communities; effects of contamination on aquatic communities; limnology of water impoundments of southeast United States with emphasis on plankton communities and primary productivity; plankton management in aquaculture. *Mailing Add:* Dept Fish & Allied Aquacult Auburn Univ Auburn University AL 36849. *Fax:* 334-844-9208; *E-Mail:* dbayne@ag.auburn.edu

BAYNE, ELLEN KAHN, EXTRACELLULAR MATRIX, CYTOKINES. *Current Pos:* Sr res immunologist, 82-88, RES FEL, MERCK SHARP & DOHME RES LAB, 88- *Personal Data:* b Oct 27, 1949; m 74; c 2. *Educ:* Northwestern Univ, PhD(cell biol), 76. *Mem:* Am Soc Cell Biol. *Res:* Use of immunocytechnical techniques to examine metalloproteinases and inhibitors in cartilage and synorial tissue; role of inflammatory mediators in rheumatoid and osteoarthritis. *Mailing Add:* Dept Biochem & Molecular Biol Merck Res Labs Rm 80N-A38 PO Box 2000A Rahway NJ 07065-0900

BAYNE, HENRY GODWIN, BACTERIOLOGY-FOOD. *Current Pos:* RETIRED. *Personal Data:* b New York, NY, Dec 2, 25; m 58; c 3. *Educ:* Brooklyn Col, BA, 49, MA, 54. *Prof Exp:* Sr technician microbiol, Western Reserve Univ, 50-51; health inspector, NY Dept Health, 53-55, jr bacteriologist, 55; microbiologist, Western Utilization Res, USDA, 55-87. *Mem:* Am Soc Microbiol. *Res:* Investigation of biochemical and physiological processes of bacterial and other organisms found in agricultural products. *Mailing Add:* 246 Purdue Ave Berkeley CA 94708. *E-Mail:* hgbayne@aol.com

BAYNE, JAMES WILMER, mechanical engineering; deceased, see previous edition for last biography

BAYNES, JOHN WILLIAM, BIOCHEMISTRY, CLINICAL CHEMISTRY. *Current Pos:* asst prof, 76-86, PROF BIOCHEM, UNIV SC, 86- *Personal Data:* b Baltimore, Md, Dec 30, 40; m 75; c 2. *Educ:* Loyola Col, Md, BS, 62; Marshall Univ, MS, 69; Johns Hopkins Univ, PhD(biochem), 73; Univ Minn, Minneapolis, MS, 76. *Prof Exp:* Fel lab med & biochem, Univ Minn, 73-76. *Mem:* AAAS; Am Chem Soc; Soc Complex Carbohydrates. *Res:* Chemistry-biochemistry of complex carbohydrates; glycoproteins; regulation of plasma protein catabolism; host-pathogen interactions. *Mailing Add:* Dept Chem & Biochem Univ SC Columbia SC 29208-0001. *Fax:* 803-777-9521

BAYNEY, RICHARD MICHAEL, alzheimers disease, gene cloning & expression, for more information see previous edition

BAYNTON, HAROLD WILBERT, METEOROLOGY. *Current Pos:* RETIRED. *Personal Data:* b Brandon, Man, Sept 16, 20; nat US; m 47; c 3. *Educ:* Univ Mich, MS, 57, MA, 59, PhD(diffusion), 63. *Prof Exp:* Weather forecaster, Meteorol Serv Can, 42-52, res meteorologist, 52-55; res assoc meteorol, Univ Mich, 55-58; res meteorologist, Systs Div, Bendix Aviation Corp, 58-63; climatologist, Martin Co, 63-64; meteorologist, Nat Ctr Atmospheric Res, Boulder, 65-85. *Concurrent Pos:* Affil prof, Va Polytech Inst, 67-70. *Mem:* Am Meteorol Soc; Air Pollution Control Asn; fel Royal Meteorol Soc; Can Meteorol & Oceanog Soc. *Res:* Applications of probability and statistical methods to meteorology in the realm of applied pollution; radar, air pollution. *Mailing Add:* 415 Kiowa Pl Boulder CO 80303

BAYRD, EDWIN DORRANCE, MEDICINE, HEMATOLOGY. *Current Pos:* From instr to assoc prof, 47-67, PROF MED, MAYO MED SCH, 67- *Personal Data:* b Chicago, Ill, Nov 12, 17; m 42, Muriel Burns; c 5. *Educ:* Dartmouth Col, AB, 39; Harvard Med Sch, MD, 42; Univ Minn, MS, 47. *Concurrent Pos:* Fel trop med & parasitol, Tulane Univ, 43-44; fel med, Mayo Found, Univ Minn, 47; consult, Mayo Clin, Methodist & St Mary's Hosps, 47-; ed-in-chief, Mayo Clin Proc, 62-; Sir Norman Paul vis prof, Sydney Hosp, Australia, 63; chmn div hemat, Mayo Clin, 67-72, pres staff, 69-70, emer staff, 88- *Mem:* AAAS; AMA; Am Fedn Clin Res; Am Soc Hemat; Int Soc Hemat; Cent Soc Clin Res. *Res:* Clinical and protein aspects of plasma cell disease, especially multiple myeloma macroglobulinemia and systematized amyloidosis. *Mailing Add:* Mayo Med Ctr Rochester MN 55905

BAYS, JAMES PHILIP, ORGANIC CHEMISTRY, COMPUTATIONAL CHEMISTRY. *Current Pos:* from asst prof to assoc prof, 77-87, PROF CHEM, ST MARYS COL, 87- *Personal Data:* b West Frankfort, Ill, Feb 19, 41; m 63, June M Nielsen; c Timothy James & Daniel Mark. *Educ:* Northwestern Univ, BS, 63; Univ Wis, PhD(org chem), 68. *Prof Exp:* NIH fel chem, Yale Univ, 68-70; asst prof, Grinnell Col, 70-77. *Concurrent Pos:* ACM fac fel, Argonne Nat Lab, 71-72; asst prof biochem, Med Sch, Rush Univ, 74-77; res assoc, Univ Notre Dame, 78-86; Lilly Found Open Fac Fel, 90-91. *Mem:* Am Chem Soc; Am Sci Affil; Sigma Xi. *Res:* Reactions of synthetic utility; molecular modeling. *Mailing Add:* Dept Chem & Physics St Mary's Col Notre Dame IN 46556. *E-Mail:* pbays@saintmarys.edu

BAYUZICK, ROBERT J(OHN), PHYSICAL METALLURGY, SURFACE PHYSICS. *Current Pos:* instr phys metall, 69, from asst prof to assoc prof mat sci, 69-77, dir mat sci, 74-75, PROF MAT SCI, VANDERBILT UNIV, 77- *Personal Data:* b Braddock, Pa, Sept 6, 37; m 61; c 2. *Educ:* Univ Pittsburgh, BS, 61; Univ Denver, MS, 63; Vanderbilt Univ, PhD(mat sci), 69. *Prof Exp:* Metall technician radiation damage, Bettis Atomic Power Lab, Westinghouse Elec Corp, 55-56 & 56-60; statist clerk, Fed Bur Invest, 56; metall engr, Bell Aerosysts Co, 61; res asst phase equilibria, Denver Res Inst, 61-63; res metallurgist, Battelle Mem Inst, 64-65. *Mem:* Am Soc Metals; Am Inst Mining, Metall & Petrol Eng; Am Asn Univ Profs; Sigma Xi. *Res:* Atomic structure and topography of grain boundaries; various aspects of problems in thin films; atomic mechanisms of crack initiation. *Mailing Add:* 7902 Highway 100 Nashville TN 37221-4120

BAZ, AMR MAHMOUD SABRY, CONTROLS, PASSIVE & ACTIVE VIBRATION CONTROL. *Current Pos:* assoc prof, 79-86, PROF MECH ENG, CATHOLIC UNIV AM, 86- *Personal Data:* b Cairo, Egypt, Oct 12, 45; m, Maha; c Hisham & Karim. *Educ:* Cairo Univ, Egypt, BSc, 66; Univ Wis-Madison, MSc, 70, PhD(mech eng), 73. *Honors & Awards:* James Lincoln Found Award, 73; Nat Medal Excellence in Arts & Sci, Govt of Egypt, 80; Burno Dimiani Award. *Prof Exp:* Teaching asst, Mech Eng Dept, Cairo Univ, 66-68, asst prof, 75-77, assoc prof, 79-83; res asst, Univ Wis, 68-73, teaching fel, 73-75, res assoc, 77-79. *Concurrent Pos:* Mem res staff, Western Elec Res Lab, 79; prin investr, Naval Sea Command Syst, 84-88, NASA-Goodard, 84-89, army res off, 85- *Mem:* Fel Am Soc Mech Engrs; Am Inst Aeronaut & Astronaut. *Res:* Active control of structure; dynamics and vibration of structures. *Mailing Add:* Dept Mech Eng Cath Univ Am 620 Michigan Ave NE Washington DC 20064

BAZAN, NICOLAS GUILLERMO, NEUROCHEMISTRY & NEUROLOGY, OPHTHALMOLOGY. *Current Pos:* PROF OPHTHAL, NEUROL & BIOCHEM, MED SCH, LA STATE UNIV, NEW ORLEANS, 81-, ERNEST C & YVETTE C VILLERE CHAIR RES RETINAL DEGENERATION, 84-, DIR, NEUROSCI CTR, 88- *Personal Data:* b Los Sarmientos, Arg, May 22, 42; m 65; c 5. *Educ:* Univ Tucuman, Arg, MD, 65, PhD(med sci), 71. *Honors & Awards:* William & Mary Greve Int Award, Res to Prevent Blindness, Inc, 83. *Prof Exp:* Teaching asst biol, Univ Tucuman, Arg, 60-65; fel enzym, Col Physicians & Surgeons, Columbia Univ, 65-66; fel, dept biol chem, Harvard Med Sch, 66-67, res assoc, 67-68; asst prof biochem, fac med, Univ Toronto, 68-70; asst dir, dept neurochem, Clarke Inst Psychiat, Toronto, 68-70; dir, Inst Biochem, UNS-CONICET, Blanca, Arg, 70-81. *Concurrent Pos:* Fel enzym, Inst Biochem, Buenos Aires, 64; prin investr, CONICET, Arg, 76-81; vis prof ophthal, Baylor Col Med, 77; mem, Neurosci Steering Comt, La State Univ Med Ctr, 84-; pres, Brain Chem Tech Corp, 85-; sr ed, Molecular Neurobiol Rev, 86-; Jacob Javits Neurosci investr, 89- *Mem:* Int Soc Neurochem; Am Soc Neurochem; Am Soc Biol Chemists; Soc Neurosci; Am Epilepsy Soc; Brit Soc Nutrit Med. *Res:* Neurochemical research of excitable membranes; synapse; photoreceptors; retinal degeneration; nutrition; essential fatty acids; retinitis pigmentosa; cell biology of metabolism; visual cell renewal; retinal pigment epithelium; epilepsy; arachidonic acid; cell signaling and membrane lipids; inositol lipids and diacylglycerol calcium; eye inflammation; stroke cerebral ischemia and brain damage; prostaglandins and leukotrienes; biotechnology. *Mailing Add:* Eye Ctr La State Sch Med 2020 Gravier St Suite B New Orleans LA 70112-1272

BAZANT, ZDENEK P(AVEL), STRUCTURAL MECHANICS & ENGINEERING. *Current Pos:* assoc prof civil eng, 69-73, dir, Ctr Concrete & Geomat, 81-87, PROF CIVIL ENG, NORTHWESTERN UNIV, 73-, WALTER P MURPHY PROF, ENDOWED CHAIR CIVIL ENG, 90- *Personal Data:* b Prague, Czech, Dec 10, 37; nat US; m 67; c 2. *Educ:* Prague Tech Univ, civil engr, 60, Docent(concrete struct), 67; Czech Acad Sci, PhD(eng mech), 63; Charles Univ, Prague, dipl(theoret physics), 66. *Hon Degrees:* Dr, Czech Tech Univ Prague, CRUT, Czech, 91. *Honors & Awards:* Gold Medal, Int Union Testing Labs in Mat & Struct, 75; W L Huber Civil Eng Res Prize, Am Soc Civil Engrs, 76, T Y Lin Restressed Concrete Award, 77, Newmark Medal, 96; Humboldt Award, 90; Gold Medal Bldg Res, Inst Spain, 90; Govt Lectureship Award, Nat Sci Coun, Rep China, 91; Medal Merit Czech Soc Mech, Prague, 93; Prager Medal, Soc Eng Sci, 96. *Prof Exp:* Bridge engr, Dopravoprojekt Bridge Consult Off, Czech, 61-63; sr res engr, Bldg Res Inst, Prague Tech Univ, 63-67, adj prof, 64-67; vis res fel, Centre d'Etude du Batiment et de Travaux Publics, Paris, France, 66-67; sr res fel civil eng, Univ Toronto, 67-68; vis assoc res engr, Univ Calif, Berkeley, 69. *Concurrent Pos:* French Govt fel, 66; Ford Sci Found fel, 68; dir grants, NSF, Elec Power Res Inst, Nat Res Coun, Defense Nuclear Agency, Dept Energy, 70-; dir, NSF grants, 71-, Air Force Off Sci Res grants, 75-, Dept Energy, 81-89, Off Naval Res, 90-; consult, Sargent & Lundy, Chicago, 73-, Argonne Nat Lab, 74-, Oak Ridge Nat Lab, 75-, Babcock & Wilcox, Ohio, 78-81, Sandia Labs, 79, Ont Hydro, 80, Teng & Assoc, 85- & M&M Engrs, 86-; chmn, Comt Properties Mat, Am Soc Civil Engrs, 75-77 & 81-83, Comt Fracture Mech, Am Concrete Inst, 85-, Comt on Creep, Int Union Testing Labs Mat & Struct, 81-; vis prof, Royal Inst Technol, Stockholm, 77, Politevmico di Milano, 82, Swiss Fed Inst Technol, 83, Ecole Normale Supereur, Paris, 88, Tech Univ, Munich, 90-91, Tech Unvi, Stuttgart, 91-92, Inst Nat Sci Appl, France, 93, Lulea Univ, Sweden, 94, Swiss Fed Inst Technol, Zurich, 95; Guggenheim fel, 78-79, Kajima Found Fel, Tokyo, 87 & NATO fel, sr guest scientist, France, 88; dir, Elec Power Res Inst contract, Los Alamos Sci Lab grant; dir, Ctr Concrete & Geomat, 81-; ed-in-chief J Eng Mech, 89-; fel, Japan Soc Prom Sci, 96. *Mem:* Nat Acad Eng; Fel Am Soc Civil Engrs; fel Am Concrete Inst; fel Am Acad Mech; Int Union Testing Labs Mat & Struct; fel Am Soc Mech Engrs; Am Ceramic Soc; Int Asn Bridge & Struct Eng; Soc Eng Sci (pres, 93); Int Asn Fracture mech (pres, 91-93); fel Int Union Res Labs Mats & Scis Paris. *Res:* Creep; inelasticity and failure of concrete, rocks and soils; moisture and thermal effects in concrete; plasticity and viscoelasticity; structural stability; fracture and continuum mechanics; thin-wall structures; design of nuclear structures, bridges, tall buildings; published over 330 research papers in professional journals and 4 patents. *Mailing Add:* Dept Civil Eng Northwestern Univ 2474 Tech Inst Evanston IL 60201-5506

BAZER, FULLER WARREN, ANIMAL SCIENCE, REPRODUCTIVE PHYSIOLOGY. *Current Pos:* PROF & O D BUTLER CHMN ANIMAL SCI, TEX A&M UNIV, 92-, DIR, CTR ANIMAL BIOTECHNOL, 92- *Personal Data:* b Shreveport, La, Sept 2, 38; m 62, Elmire A Schaaf; c Amy E & Beth A. *Educ:* Centenary Col, BS, 60; La State Univ, Baton Rouge, MS, 63; NC State Univ, PhD(physiol), 69. *Honors & Awards:* Physiol & Endocrinol Res Award, Am Soc Animal Sci, L E Casida Award Grad Educ, 95; Res Award, Sigma Xi, 76; Res Award, Soc Study Reproduction, 90. *Prof Exp:* From asst prof to prof animal sci, Univ Fla, 68-92, DIR, INSTIT BIOSCI & TECHNOL, 94- *Concurrent Pos:* Ed-in-chief, Biol of Reproduction, 89-95. *Mem:* AAAS; Soc Study Reproduction (pres-elect, 95-96, pres, 96-97); Am Soc Animal Sci; Soc Theriogenology; Endocrine Soc. *Res:* Uterine protein secretion of domestic animals as related to embryonic development and corpus luteum function; steroids and proteins secreted by the concepts. *Mailing Add:* Dept Animal Sci Tex A&M Univ College Station TX 77843-2471. *Fax:* 409-862-2660; *E-Mail:* fbazer@uthuax.tamu.edu

BAZER, JACK, MATHEMATICS, PHYSICS. *Current Pos:* Jr res scientist, NY Univ, 51-53, res assoc, 53-58, sr scientist, 58, from asst prof to assoc prof, 58-65, PROF MATH, COURANT INST MATH SCI, NY UNIV, 65- *Personal Data:* b New York, NY, Dec 23, 24; m 51; c 2. *Educ:* Cornell Univ, BA, 47; Columbia Univ, MA, 49; NY Univ, PhD(math), 53. *Concurrent Pos:* Consult, Grumman Aircraft Eng Corp, Long Island, 60; mem, Comn IV, Int Sci Radio Union. *Mem:* Am Math Soc. *Res:* Diffraction theory of scalar and vector fields; magnetogasdynamics; plasma physics; probability theory; partial differential equations. *Mailing Add:* Dept Math NY Univ Courant 251 Mercer St New York NY 10012

BAZETT-JONES, DAVID PAUL, MOLECULAR BIOLOGY. *Current Pos:* fel, 81-84, MOLECULAR BIOLOGIST, SCRIPPS CLIN RES FOUND, 84- *Personal Data:* b Toronto, Ont, Mar 26, 53; m 81. *Educ:* Univ Waterloo, BSc, 75; Univ Toronto, MSc, 78, PhD(biophysics), 81. *Mem:* Can Soc Cell Biol; Micros Soc Can. *Res:* Relationship between structures and composition of euharyotic chromation with transcriptional regulation; developed electron spectroscopic imaging. *Mailing Add:* Dept Med Biochem Univ Calgary 3330 Hospital Dr NW Calgary AB T2N 4N1 Can

BAZINET, GEORGE FREDERICK, BIOCHEMICAL GENETICS. *Current Pos:* PROF BIOL, SIENA COL, 70- *Personal Data:* b Glens Falls, NY, July 16, 37; m 62; c 3. *Educ:* St Michaels Col, BA, 60; St Johns Univ, MS, 63; Hahnemann Med Col, PhD(genetics), 67. *Prof Exp:* Fel, Med Sch, Yale Univ, 69-70. *Res:* Biochemical genetics of Nicrassa; metabolic activites of halobacteria halobium. *Mailing Add:* Dept Biol Siena Col 515 Loudonville Rd Loudonville NY 12211-1459

BAZZARRE, TERRY LEE, NUTRITION, ENDOCRINOLOGY. *Current Pos:* STAFF SCIENTIST, AM HEART ASN, 92- *Personal Data:* b Beckley WVa, May 19, 49; m 71, Christine Lee Hunter; c Lee M. *Educ:* Va Polytech Inst & State Univ, BS, 71, MS, 73, PhD(human nutrit), 75. *Prof Exp:* Asst prof, Univ NC, Chapel Hill, 75-78, assoc prof, Greensboro, 78-92. *Mem:* Am Col Sports Med; Am Col Nutrit; Am Inst Nutrit. *Res:* Interactive effects of diet and exercise on obesity, blood lipids and blood pressure; hormonal regulation; sports nutrition; nutritional assessment of special populations including youth, the elderly, African Americans and athletes. *Mailing Add:* Am Heart Asn 7272 Greeneville Ave Dallas TX 75231-4596

BAZZAZ, FAKHRI AL, PLANT ECOLOGY, ENVIRONMENTAL BIOLOGY. *Current Pos:* PROF BIOL, HARVARD UNIV. *Personal Data:* b Baghdad, Iraq, June 16, 33; US citizen; m 58; c 2. *Educ:* Univ Baghdad, BA, 53; Univ Ill, MS, 60, PhD(bot), 63. *Prof Exp:* Asst prof ecol, Univ Ill, 63-64; lectr bot, Univ Baghdad, 64-66; asst prof ecol, Univ Ill, Urbana, 66-72, assoc prof ecol & forestry, 72-77, prof plant biol & forestry, 77- *Concurrent Pos:* Head, Dept Plant Biol, Univ Ill, 82-84 actg dir, Sch Life Sci, 83-84; Guggenheim fel, 88. *Mem:* Fel AAAS; Ecol Soc Am; Brit Ecol Soc. *Res:* Physiological ecology of successional plants; plant community organization; effects of environmental pollution. *Mailing Add:* Dept Organismic & Evolutionary Biol Harvard Univ 26 Oxford St Cambridge MA 02138-2902

BAZZAZ, MAARIB BAKRI, BIOPHYSICS, MICROBIOLOGY. *Current Pos:* RES ASSOC CELLULAR & DEVELOP BIOL, HARVARD UNIV, CAMBRIDGE, MASS, 84- *Personal Data:* b Baghdad, Iraq, Nov 27, 40; m 58, Fakhri; c 2. *Educ:* Univ Ill, Urbana, BS, 61, MS, 63, PhD(biol), 72. *Prof Exp:* Instr plant physiol, Univ Baghdad, Col Sci, 64-66; res assoc photosynthesis, Inst Environ Studies, Univ Ill, 72-74; res assoc photosynthesis, Dept Hort, Univ Ill, Urbana, 74-78, res scientist, Dept Bot, 78-84. *Mem:* Am Soc Plant Physiologists; Sigma Xi. *Res:* Structural characterization and study of the biosynthetic and photosynthetic aspects of newly discovered chlorophylls isolated from a mutant of zea mays; degradation of chlorosphyll; effect of pollutants on photosynthesis. *Mailing Add:* Biol Lab Harvard Univ 16 Divinity Ave Cambridge MA 02138

BEA, ROBERT G, CIVIL ENGINEERING. *Current Pos:* PROF, DEPT CIVIL ENG & NAVAL ARCH & OFFSHORE ENG, UNIV CALIF, BERKELEY, 88- *Educ:* Univ Fla, BS, 59, MS, 60. *Honors & Awards:* J Hillis Miller Eng Award; Croes Medal, Am Soc Civil Engrs, 59. *Prof Exp:* Sr staff civil engr, Shell Oil Co, 59-76; chief engr & vpres, Ocean Eng Div, Woodward-Clyde Consult, 76-81; vpres, PMB Syst Eng, Inc, 81-88. *Concurrent Pos:* Consult prof civil eng, Stanford Univ, 85-89. *Mem:* Nat Acad Eng. *Res:* Coastal, offshore and ocean engineering; methods to define design criteria for fixed and mobile offshore structures; development of guidelines for the requalifications and rehabilitation of marine structures and ships; evaluation of forces due to waves, currents, earthquakes, ice and sea floor slides; development of technology for evaluation of the dynamic response characteristics of marine foundations and structures. *Mailing Add:* 215 McLaughlin Hall Univ Calif Berkeley Berkeley CA 94720-1712. *Fax:* 510-631-1587; *E-Mail:* rgbea@evker.berkeley.edu

BEACH, BETTY LAURA, FOOD SCIENCE, NUTRITION. *Current Pos:* CHIEF, DIETETIC SERV, DEPT VET AFFAIRS MED CTR, OMAHA, NEBR, 87- *Personal Data:* b Falls City, Nebr. *Educ:* Univ Nebr, Lincoln, BS, 58; Univ Wis-Madison, MS, 67, PhD(food sci & admin), 74. *Prof Exp:* Dietetic intern, USPHS, Staten Island, NY, 58-59, staff dietitian, Detroit, 59-62, clin dietitian, Staten Island, 62-63, chief food procurement & prod, 66-68, asst dir dietetics, 68-69; from asst prof to prof dietetics, Univ Tenn, Knoxville, 69-82; dir, Dietetic Internship, Edward J Hines Jr Vet Admin Hosp, Ill, 82-87. *Concurrent Pos:* Dir coordr diet prog, Nutrit Found Mary Swartz Rose fel, 72-82. *Mem:* Am Dietetic Asn; Inst Food Technologists; Am Hosp Asn Food Serv Adminr. *Res:* Development of quantitative methods to control resources in food service systems; development and evaluation of clinical dietetic staffing guidelines; nutritional care protocols to shorten patient stay. *Mailing Add:* 1408 S 126th St Omaha NE 68144. *Fax:* 402-449-0697

BEACH, DAVID H, LIPID BIOCHEMISTRY, ANALYTICAL CHEMISTRY. *Current Pos:* From res asst to res assoc, 64-75, res asst prof, 75-81, UNIV INSTRNL SPECIALIST, STATE UNIV NY UPSTATE MED CTR, 81-, RES ASSOC PROF, 87- *Personal Data:* b Syracuse, NY, July 4, 39; m 61, Judith A Sherman; c Lisa, Christopher & Scott. *Educ:* Syracuse Univ, BA, 61; State Univ NY Upstate Med Ctr, MS, 69, PhD(microbiol), 73. *Mem:* AAAS; Am Soc Parasitologists; Soc Protozoologists; Sigma Xi; Am Soc Microbiol. *Res:* Lipid biochemistry and metabolic studies of protozoan blood flagellates of the genes Leishmania and Trypanosoma; gas chromatography; mass spectrometry; infrared and nuclear magnetic resonance spectrometry. *Mailing Add:* Dept Microbiol & Immunology State Univ NY Health Sci Ctr Syracuse NY 13210. *Fax:* 315-464-4417; *E-Mail:* beachd@vax.cs.hscsyr.edu

BEACH, DAVID H, MICROBIOLOGY. *Current Pos:* SR STAFF SCIENTIST, COLD SPRING HARBOR LAB, NEW YORK. *Educ:* Univ Cambridge, Eng, BA, 75; Univ Miami, PhD(physiol & biophysics), 77. *Honors & Awards:* Eli Lilly & Co Res Award, Am Soc Microbiol, 95. *Prof Exp:* Investr, Howard Hughes Med Inst. *Concurrent Pos:* Adj assoc prof, State Univ NY, Stony Brook; chair cancer biol, Inst Child Health, London. *Mem:* Am Asn Cancer Res; Am Soc Microbiol; fel Royal Soc. *Res:* Cell cycle control. *Mailing Add:* Cold Spring Harbor Lab One Bungtown Rd Cold Spring Harbor NY 11724

BEACH, EUGENE HUFF, NUCLEAR PHYSICS, ENGINEERING MANAGEMENT. *Current Pos:* SR ENGR, EPOCH ENG, INC, 85- *Personal Data:* b Highland, Mich, Oct 9, 18; m 44, Ruby L Beauchamp; c Eugene H Jr. *Educ:* Univ Mich, BSE, 41, MS, 47, PhD(physics), 53. *Prof Exp:* Elec engr, Naval Ord Lab, 41-46, electronic scientist, Underwater Ord, 53-55, chief weapon mech div, 55-58, proj mgr, 58-59, chief underwater elec engr dept, 59-73, assoc head underwater weapons develop directorate, 73-75; head ord syst develop dept, Naval Surface Weapons Ctr, 75-77, dep tech dir, 77-78, head, Underwater Syst Dept, 78-79, assoc tech dir, 79-80; instr, Mass Inst Technol & Univ Md, 80-85. *Concurrent Pos:* Eng res assoc, Cyclotron Proj, Univ Mich, 50-52. *Mem:* Sigma Xi. *Res:* Angular distribution studies on phosphorous reactions; issued US for Sterling Engine. *Mailing Add:* 12201 Remington Dr Silver Spring MD 20902

BEACH, HARRY LEE, JR, PROPULSION, COMBUSTION. *Current Pos:* Res engr, Langley Res Ctr, NASA, 70-75, head, Combustion Sect, 75-77, leader performance anal group, 77-80, asst, 80-81, head Hypersonic Propulsion BR, 81-89, head Nat Aerospace Plane, 89-92, DEP DIR, LANGLEY RES CTR, NASA, 92- *Personal Data:* b Richmond, Va, Aug 16, 44; m 66; c 3. *Educ:* NC State Univ, BS, 66, MS, 68, PhD(mech eng), 70. *Concurrent Pos:* Asst prof lectr, Joint Inst Advan Flight Sci, George Washington Univ, 77-; adj prof, Christopher Newport Col, 80- *Mem:* Fel Am Inst Aeronaut & Astronaut. *Res:* Direct and conduct research for supersonic combustion ramjet propulsion including combustion fundamentals, computational fluid dynamics, combustion diagnostics, inlet and combustor conceptual design and testing, and inlet-combustor component integration. *Mailing Add:* NASA Langley Res Ctr 11 Langley Blvd MS 102 Hampton VA 23681

BEACH, JAMES M, OPTICAL RECORDING PHYSIOLOGY. *Current Pos:* RES PROF, UNIV VA, 84- *Personal Data:* b Rochester, NY, 49. *Educ:* Univ Mich, EE, 71; Univ Va, PhD(biomed eng), 83. *Mem:* Biomed Eng Soc. *Mailing Add:* Dept Biomed Eng Univ Va 1105 W Main St Charlottesville VA 22903-2821

BEACH, LOUIS ANDREW, EXPERIMENTAL NUCLEAR PHYSICS, NUCLEAR ENGINEERING. *Personal Data:* b Greenville, Ind, June 2, 25; m 56, Virginia McHugh; c Andrew, Ann M, Ruth & Covert. *Educ:* Ind Univ, BS, 44, MS, 47, PhD(physics), 49. *Prof Exp:* Asst physics, Ind Univ, 46-49; res assoc nuclear physics, Cornell Univ, 49-51; nuclear physicist, 51-55, head, Nuclear Reactions Br, 55-65, head, Physics I Sect, 65-71, head, Nuclear Physics Sect, 71-78, head, Mat Sect, 78-80, res physicist, US Naval Res Lab, 80-87; consult physicist, Sachs & Freeman Assoc, 87-91. *Concurrent Pos:* Lectr, Cath Univ Am, 60-66. *Mem:* AAAS; Am Phys Soc; Sigma Xi. *Res:* Disintegration studies of beta decay; interactions of Bremstrahlung radiation with matter; shielding of nuclear radiation; nuclear reactors; nuclear structure; studies with cyclotron beams; radiation damage to metallurgical systems; nuclear detectors and electronics. *Mailing Add:* 1200 Waynewood Blvd Alexandria VA 22308-1842

BEACH, NEIL WILLIAM, ZOOLOGY. *Current Pos:* asst prof, 60-64, ASSOC PROF BIOL, GETTYSBURG COL, 64- *Personal Data:* b Ann Arbor, Mich, Apr 11, 28; div; c 3. *Educ:* Univ Mich, BS, 50, MS, 51, PhD(zool), 56. *Prof Exp:* Instr zool, Univ Mich, 56-57; asst prof biol, Lake Forest Col, 57-60. *Concurrent Pos:* NSF grants, Mich Biol Sta, 55, Duke Marine Lab, 58 & 59; NSF sci fels, 60-62. *Mem:* Am Micros Soc; Sigma Xi; Am Soc Zool. *Res:* Invertebrate zoology and ecology; rotifera; distribution, life history and ecology of the oyster crab, Pinnotheres ostreum and pea crabs of Australia. *Mailing Add:* 172 Gordon Ave Gettysburg PA 17325-3109

BEACH, SHARON SICKEL, computer science, intelligent systems, for more information see previous edition

BEACHAM, TERRY DALE, SALMON STOCK INDENTIFICATION, SALMON DEVELOPMENT MORPHOLOGY & POPULATION DIFFERENTIATION. *Current Pos:* prog head pink & chum salmon, 80-87, sect head salmon dynamics, 87-92, SECT HEAD ASSESSMENT METHODS, PAC BIOL STA, 92- *Personal Data:* b Winnipeg, Man, Nov 19, 52; m 81, Ruth E Withler; c Christopher & Alexander. *Educ:* Univ Man, BSc (Hons), 74; Univ BC, PhD(zool), 79. *Prof Exp:* Res scientist, Bedford Inst Oceanog, 79-80. *Res:* Stock indentification of salmon using genetic and DNA variation; comparative development and morphology of salmon populations; quantitative genetics and disease resistance of salmon, as well as growth and maturity; photoperiod and timing of maturity. *Mailing Add:* Pac Biol Sta Nanaimo BC V9R 5K6 Can. *Fax:* 250-756-7053; *E-Mail:* beachamt@pbs.dfo.ca

BEACHEM, CEDRIC D, PHYSICAL METALLURGICAL ENGINEERING. *Current Pos:* RETIRED. *Personal Data:* b Beaufort, NC, May 2, 32. *Educ:* NC State Univ, BS, 57. *Honors & Awards:* Sam Tour Award, Am Soc Testing & Mat. *Prof Exp:* Metall engr, Naval Res Lab, 57- *Mem:* Fel Am Soc Mat; Am Soc Testing & Mat; Nat Asn Corrosion Engrs. *Mailing Add:* 3600 Spruell Dr Silver Spring MD 20902

BEACHLEY, NORMAN HENRY, MECHANICAL ENGINEERING. *Current Pos:* PROF MECH ENG, UNIV WIS-MADISON, 66- *Personal Data:* b Washington, DC, Jan 13, 33; m 59; c 3. *Educ:* Cornell Univ, BME, 56, PhD(mech eng), 66. *Prof Exp:* Mem tech staff eng, Hughes Aircraft Co, 56-57; mem tech staff eng, Space Technol Labs, 59-63. *Concurrent Pos:* Consult, Lawrence Livermore Lab, 78-81, Nat Bur Stand, 78-; res fel, Sci & Engr Res Coun, 81-82. *Mem:* Am Soc Mech Engrs; Soc Automotive Engrs; Sigma Xi. *Res:* Energy storage powerplant systems for motor vehicles; mechanical design of internal combustion engines; fluid power systems; continously-variable transmissions. *Mailing Add:* 327 Mech Eng Univ Wis 1513 University Ave Madison WI 53706-1512

BEACHLEY, ORVILLE THEODORE, JR, MAIN-GROUP ORGANOMETALLIC CHEMISTRY. *Current Pos:* from asst prof to assoc prof, 66-85, PROF CHEM, STATE UNIV NY BUFFALO, 85-, ASSOC VPRES RES, 94- *Personal Data:* b East Orange, NJ, Nov 8, 37; m 62, Inez Parker; c Andrew & Jennifer. *Educ:* Franklin & Marshall Col, BSc, 59; Cornell Univ, PhD(inorg chem), 62. *Prof Exp:* NIH fel chem, Univ Durham, 63-64; asst prof, Cornell Univ, 64-66. *Mem:* Am Chem Soc; The Chem Soc. *Res:* Preparative and physical inorganic chemistry with emphasis on organometallic, hydride and heterocyclic derivatives of main group and transition elements. *Mailing Add:* Dept Chem State Univ NY Buffalo NY 14260. *Fax:* 716-645-6963; *E-Mail:* beachley@acsu.buffalo.edu

BEACHY, CHRISTOPHER KING, SALAMANDER ECOLOGY & LIFE-HISTORY EVOLUTION. *Current Pos:* ASST PROF BIOL, CLARKE COL, 94- *Personal Data:* b Lemore, Calif, Nov 19, 64; m 91, Connie L Ory. *Educ:* Col Wooster, BA, 86; Western Carolina Univ, MS, 88; Univ Southwestern La, PhD(environ & evolutionary biol), 92. *Prof Exp:* Researcher, Highlands Biol Sta, 92; asst prof biol, Jamestown Col, 93-94. *Concurrent Pos:* Vis instr & adj grad fac, evolutionary processes, Western Carolina Univ, 93- *Mem:* Soc Study Evolution; Am Soc Ichthyologists & Herpetologists; Herpetologists' League; Sigma Xi; Soc Study of Amphibian & Reptile. *Res:* Ecological studies on the lungless salamanders that are designed to elucidate the mechanisms that resulted in their current distribution and unique characteristics. *Mailing Add:* Dept Biol Clarke Col 1550 Clarke Dubuque IA 58401. *E-Mail:* cbeachy@keller.clarke.edu

BEACHY, ROGER NEIL, PLANT VIROLOGY, CELL BIOLOGY. *Current Pos:* MEM, SCRIPPS RES INST, HEAD, DIV PLANT BIOL, SCRIPPS FAMILY CHAIR. *Personal Data:* b Plain City, Ohio, Oct 4, 44; div; c Kathryn C & Kyle A. *Educ:* Goshen Col, BA, 66; Mich State Univ, PhD(plant path), 73. *Honors & Awards:* Ruth Allen Award, Am Phytopath Soc, 90. *Prof Exp:* Res assoc & NIH fel plant virol, Cornell Univ, 73-76; res assoc, US Plant, Soil & Nutrit Lab, Ithaca, NY, 76-78; from asst prof to prof, Dept Biol, Washington Univ, St Louis, 76- *Concurrent Pos:* Adj prof, Dept Plant Path, Univ Calif, Riverside & Dept Biol, Peking Univ, Beijing. *Mem:* Nat Acad Sci; Am Soc Plant Physiologists; fel AAAS; Int Soc Plant Molecular Biol; Am Soc Virol; Am Soc Biol Chem; Am Phytopath Soc. *Res:* Plant viral messenger RNAs; effects of virus gene products on infected host cells; genetic transformation of plants for virus resistance. *Mailing Add:* Div Plant Biol BCC 206 Scripps Res Inst 10550 N Torrey Pines Rd La Jolla CA 92037. *Fax:* 619-784-2994; *E-Mail:* beachy@scripps.edu

BEACOM, STANLEY ERNEST, RUMINANT NUTRITION. *Current Pos:* RETIRED. *Personal Data:* b Ft Macleod, Alta, May 18, 27; m 57, Jean Lonsdale; c Kathryn & Connie. *Educ:* Univ Alta, BSc, 49, MSc, 51; McGill Univ, PhD(ruminant nutrit), 59. *Prof Exp:* Broiler super poultry prod & mgt, Swift Can, Calgary, Alta, 51-52; tech officer poultry & swine nutrit, Agr Can, Res Br, Melfort, 52-53, res officer swine & beef cattle nutrit, 53-61 & animal nutrit & pasture res, 61-66, res dir agr, 66-90. *Mem:* Agr Inst Can; Can Soc Animal Prod (pres, 68). *Res:* Forage crop harvesting and utilization with specialization on improved efficiency of use of forage crops in rations for growing beef heifers and finishing of beef steers. *Mailing Add:* Box 296 Melfort SK S0E 1A0 Can

BEADLE, BUELL WESLEY, CHEMISTRY. *Current Pos:* RETIRED. *Personal Data:* b Port Barre, La, Sept 9, 11; m 34; c 2. *Educ:* Kans State Col, BS, 35, MS, 38; Purdue Univ, PhD(agr biochem), 42. *Prof Exp:* Asst chemist, Exp Sta, Kans State Col, 35-42; res chemist, Am Meat Inst, Chicago, 42-47, chemist in charge phys & analytical chem, Am Meat Inst Found, 47-48; dir & vpres, George W Gooch Labs, 48-50; head tech div & comndr staff, Naval Ord Test Sta, China Lake, 50-51, head staff, 52-54; chmn, Div Chem & Chem Eng, Southwest Res Inst, San Antonio, 55-57, dir chem & chem eng, Midwest Res Inst, Kansas City, Mo, 57-63; exec dir res & develop, Farmland Industs, Inc, 63-68, vpres res & develop, 68-76. *Concurrent Pos:* Asst, Purdue Univ, 40-42; from res assoc to asst prof pharmacol, Univ Chicago, 43-48. *Mem:* AAAS; Am Chem Soc; Am Soc Biol Chem; fel Am Inst Chemists; Am Oil Chemists Soc. *Res:* Physical and analytical methods; stability of vitamins; fat autoxidation, rancidity and antioxidants; spectrophotometric methods; high frequency electronic processing. *Mailing Add:* 9020 Cottonwood Lenexa KS 66215-3263

BEADLE, CHARLES WILSON, MECHANICAL ENGINEERING. *Current Pos:* RETIRED. *Personal Data:* b Beverly, Mass, Jan 24, 30; m 56; c 3. *Educ:* Tufts Univ, BS, 51; Univ Mich, MSE, 54; Cornell Univ, PhD(eng mech), 61. *Prof Exp:* Res engr, Res Lab Div, Gen Motors Corp, 51-53 & RCA Res Lab, 54-57; prof mech eng & chmn dept, Univ Calif, Davis, 61-91. *Concurrent Pos:* Ford Found fel, Advan Testing Dept, Ford Motor Co, 65-66. *Mem:* Fel Am Soc Mech Engrs; Am Soc Eng Educ. *Res:* Machine design; dynamic structural analysis; computer-aided mechanical design. *Mailing Add:* Dept Mech Eng Univ Calif Davis CA 95616

BEADLE, RALPH EUGENE, VETERINARY PHYSIOLOGY. *Current Pos:* from asst prof to assoc prof physiol, 74-81, assoc prof, 81-83, PROF CLIN SCI, SCH VET MED, LA STATE UNIV, 83- *Personal Data:* b Plentywood, Mont, Apr 26, 43; m 68; c 2. *Educ:* Colo State Univ, DVM, 67; Univ Ga, PhD(vet physiol), 73. *Prof Exp:* Instr clins, Sch Vet Med, Univ Ga, 67-68, res assoc physiol, 68-71, asst prof clins, 72; resident, Sch Vet Med, Mich State Univ, 72-73, asst prof anesthesiol, 73-74. *Mem:* Com Resperatory Soc; assoc fel Am Col Vet Pharm & Therapeut; Am Soc Vet Med Asn. *Res:* Comparative aspects of chronic obstructive pulmonary disease and gas transport in the lungs. *Mailing Add:* 12006 Park Meadow Ave Baton Rouge LA 70816. *Fax:* 504-346-3295

BEADLES, JOHN KENNETH, ICHTHYOLOGY, LIMNOLOGY. *Current Pos:* PROF BIOL & CHMN, BIOL SCI DEPT, ARK STATE UNIV, 68- *Personal Data:* b Alva, Okla, Sept 22, 31; m 55; c 2. *Educ:* Northwestern State Col, BS, 57; Okla State Univ, MS, 63, PhD(ichthyol, limnol), 66. *Prof Exp:* High sch teacher, 57-62; res asst, Okla State Univ, 63-64; asst prof biol, Ark State Univ, 65-66; asst prof zool, Haile Selassie Univ, 66-68. *Concurrent Pos:* Proj dir, Environ Inventory & Assessment, US Army Corps Engrs, 72-78 & Environ Inventory, US Soil Conserv Serv, 74-78. *Mem:* Am Soc Ichthyologists & Herpetologists; Sigma Xi; Am Fishery Soc. *Res:* Fishery biology; catfish farming; fish survey. *Mailing Add:* 1111 Thrush Rd Jonesboro AR 72401

BEADLING, LESLIE CRAIG, BIOCHEMISTRY. *Current Pos:* mgr tech servs, Pharmacia Fine Chems, 75-81, tech dir, 81-84, vpres, 84-87, sr vpres, Processs Separation Div, 87-90, VPRES RES & BUS DEVELOP, PHARMACIA FINE CHEMS, 90- *Personal Data:* b Pittsburgh, Pa, Oct 15, 46; c 3. *Educ:* Col William & Mary, BS, 68; Yale Univ, PhD(biochem), 73. *Prof Exp:* Res asst biochem, Health Ctr, Univ Conn, 72-75. *Concurrent Pos:* NIH fel, Health Ctr, Univ Conn, 73-75. *Mem:* Am Chem Soc; AAAS; Am Soc Microbiol. *Res:* Biochemical separations techniques; chromatography, electrophoresis and centrifugation techniques; ultrafiltration, process control. *Mailing Add:* 20 Sturbridge Dr W Piscataway NJ 08854. *Fax:* 732-457-8246

BEAGRIE, GEORGE SIMPSON, dentistry, periodontics, for more information see previous edition

BEAHM, EDWARD CHARLES, PHYSICAL CHEMISTRY, MATERIALS CHEMISTRY. *Current Pos:* MEM RES STAFF NUCLEAR FUEL CHEM, OAK RIDGE NAT LAB, 74- *Personal Data:* b Philadelphia, Pa, July 9, 39; m 67; c 1. *Educ:* Temple Univ, AB, 67; Pa State Univ, PhD(chem), 73. *Prof Exp:* Fel, Mat Res Lab, Pa State Univ, 73-74. *Mem:* Am Nuclear Soc; Am Ceramic Soc; Am Soc Metals; Sigma Xi. *Res:* High temperature chemistry; thermodynamics; materials compatibility. *Mailing Add:* 106 Cooper Circle Oak Ridge TN 37830

BEAK, PETER, ORGANIC CHEMISTRY. *Current Pos:* From instr to assoc prof, 61-70, PROF ORG CHEM, UNIV ILL, URBANA-CHAMPAIGN, 70- *Personal Data:* b Syracuse, NY, Jan 12, 36; m 59, Sandra Burns; c Bryan & Stacia. *Educ:* Harvard Univ, BA, 57; Iowa State Univ, PhD(org chem), 61.

Concurrent Pos: Sloan fel, 67-69; Guggenheim fel, 68-69. *Mem:* Fel AAAS. *Res:* New organic reactions; synthetic, structural and mechanistic organic chemistry. *Mailing Add:* 361 Roger Adams Lab Univ Ill 1209 W California Urbana IL 61801-3731

BEAKLEY, GEORGE CARROLL, JR, MECHANICAL ENGINEERING. *Current Pos:* RETIRED. *Personal Data:* b Marble Falls, Tex, Feb 3, 22; m 44; c 4. *Educ:* Tex Technol Univ, BSME, 47; Univ Tex, MSME, 52; Okla State Univ, PhD(mech eng), 56. *Honors & Awards:* Chester F Carlson Award, Am Soc Eng Educ, 73, Donald E Marlowe Award; Western Electric Award, Am Soc Eng Educ, 77. *Prof Exp:* Assoc prof mech eng, Tarleton State Univ, 47-53; stress analyst, Bell Helicopter Corp, 53-54; prof eng, assoc dean eng & dir, Sch Eng, Ariz State Univ, 56-91, dean, Col Eng & Appl Sci, 87-89. *Concurrent Pos:* Consult, 52-93. *Mem:* Fel Am Soc Eng Educ; fel Am Soc Mech Eng; Nat Soc Prof Engrs; Am Inst Indust Eng; Am Soc Heating Refrig & Air Conditioning Engrs; fel Accreditation Bd Engrs & Technologists. *Res:* Engineering design; engineering administration; author or co-author of 29 engineering textbooks. *Mailing Add:* Col Eng Ariz State Univ Tempe AZ 85287-0001

BEAL, JACK LEWIS, PHARMACOGNOSY. *Current Pos:* RETIRED. *Personal Data:* b Harper, Kans, July 7, 23; m 48, Earlene Maninger; c Linda, Michael & Karen. *Educ:* Univ Kans, BS, 48, MS, 50; Ohio State Univ, PhD(pharmacog), 52. *Honors & Awards:* Edwin L Newcomb Mem Award Pharmacog, 58; Res Achievement Award in Natural Prod Chem, Am Pharmaceut Asn & Acad Pharmaceut Sci, 82. *Prof Exp:* Instr pharmacy & pharmacog, Univ Kans, 49-50; from asst prof to prof pharmacog, Ohio State Univ, 52-78, prof & asst dean, 78-81, prof & assoc dean, 81-86. *Concurrent Pos:* Ed, J Natural Prod, 77-84; NSF fac fel, 58-59; mem rev comt, US Pharmacopoeia, 75-80. *Mem:* Am Asn Cols Pharm; Am Soc Pharmacog (pres, 62-63); fel Acad Pharmaceut Sci; Am Pharmaceut Asn. *Res:* Drugs of biological origin; drug plant research and cultivation; isolation of plant constituents; plant biochemistry; chemical microscopy. *Mailing Add:* 5544 Rockwood Rd Columbus OH 43229

BEAL, JACK W, ACCELERATOR DESIGN, FUSION ENERGY RESEARCH. *Current Pos:* ASSOC PROF PHYSICS & CHAIR DEPT, FAIRFIELD UNIV. *Personal Data:* b Coffeyville, Kans, June 1, 38. *Educ:* Univ Mich, PhD(accelerator design), 64. *Prof Exp:* Staff mem, Lawrence Livermore Nat Lab; br chief, US AEC; consult. *Concurrent Pos:* Fulbright scholar, 94-95. *Mem:* Am Phys Soc; Am Nuclear Soc; Inst Electrical Int Engrs; Sigma Xi. *Res:* Airborne particulates. *Mailing Add:* Dept Physics Fairfield Univ N Benson Rd Fairfield CT 06430. *Fax:* 203-254-4277; *E-Mail:* jwbeal@fair1.fairfield.edu

BEAL, JAMES BURTON, JR, INORGANIC CHEMISTRY. *Current Pos:* PROF CHEM, UNIV MONTEVALLO, 69- *Personal Data:* b Galveston, Tex, Nov 22, 32; m 53; c 4. *Educ:* Baylor Univ, BA, 53; Agr & Mech Col Tex, MS, 59, PhD(chem), 63. *Prof Exp:* Res chemist, Gen Chem Div, Allied Chem Corp, 62-63; assoc res dir, Chem Div, Ozark-Mahoning Co, 64-69. *Mem:* Am Chem Soc; Sigma Xi. *Mailing Add:* PO Box 505 Montevallo AL 35115-0505

BEAL, JIM C(AMPBELL), ELECTRICAL ENGINEERING, ELECTROMAGNETICS. *Current Pos:* ASST SUPV SUPPORT GROUPS, FLA POWER & LIGHT CO. *Personal Data:* b London, Eng, July 15, 33; m 70. *Educ:* Univ London, BSc, 58, PhD(elec eng, microwaves), 64. *Prof Exp:* Res engr, Redifon Ltd, Eng, 62-65; asst prof elec eng, Colo State Univ, 65-67; from asst prof to assoc prof, Queen's Univ, 67-74, prof elec eng, 74-, assoc dean res ser, 76- *Mem:* Inst Elec & Electronics Engrs; Inst Elec Engrs Eng. *Res:* Electromagnetic guided waves in communications systems and guided radar. *Mailing Add:* Dept Elec Eng Queens Univ Kingston ON K7L 3N6 Can

BEAL, JOHN ANTHONY, ANATOMY, NEUROANATOMY. *Current Pos:* ASSOC PROF ANAT, MED CTR, LA STATE UNIV, 78- *Personal Data:* b Cleveland, Ohio, Mar 30, 45; m 69; c 3. *Educ:* Xavier Univ, BS, 67; Univ Cincinnati, PhD(anat), 71. *Prof Exp:* Asst prof, Med Sch, Wayne State Univ, 71-78. *Res:* Fine structure of the nervous system; synaptology; spinal cord. *Mailing Add:* Dept Anat La State Univ Sch Med Shreveport PO Box 33932 Shreveport LA 71130

BEAL, KATHLEEN GRABASKAS, ZOOLOGY. *Current Pos:* instr math & statist, 88-92, STATIST CONSULT, WRIGHT STATE UNIV, 92- *Personal Data:* b Youngstown, Ohio, June 2, 51; m 76; c 1. *Educ:* Ohio Dominican Col, BS, 73; Ohio State Univ, MS, 75, PhD(zool), 78. *Prof Exp:* Instr, Capital Univ, 78-81, asst prof zool, 81-85. *Mem:* AAAS; Am Ornith Soc; Animal Behav Soc; Ecol Soc Am; Am Arachnological Soc. *Res:* Behavioral ecology of birds, jumping spiders (salticidae) and terrestrial isopods. *Mailing Add:* 616 Xenia Ave Yellow Springs OH 45387

BEAL, MYRON CLARENCE, BIOMECHANICS. *Current Pos:* prof biomech, 74-81, prof family med, 81-89, EMER PROF FAMILY MED, MICH STATE UNIV, 89- *Personal Data:* b New York, NY, Dec 4, 20; m 48, Esther N; c Rebeca (Johnson), M Flint, Shelley (Rees), Julie (Wilson) & Christina (Bailey). *Educ:* Univ Rochester, AB, 42, Chicago Col Osteopath Med, DO, 45; Univ Chicago, MS, 49. *Honors & Awards:* Gutensohn/Denslow Award, 88. *Prof Exp:* Asst dir clinics osteopath med, Chicago Col Osteopath Med, 46-49; instr, London Col Osteopath, 49-51; pvt pract, Rochester, NY, 51-74. *Concurrent Pos:* Mem, Nat Bd Examiners Osteopath Physicians & Surgeons, 60-84, NY State Bd Med, 61-73; trustee, Chicago Col Osteop Med, 69-93; actg chmn biomed, Mich State Univ, 75-77; chmn bd dir, Chicago Col Osteop Med, 86-90; ed, Am Acad Osteop, 88- *Mem:* Am Osteop Asn; fel Am Acad Osteop. *Res:* Biomechanics interrater reliability of palpatory examination procedures, and the use of physical tests to determine patient improvement; mechanics of joint motion; clinical management of cervical spine injury; influence of manipulation on static respiratory mechanics and neuroendocrine response. *Mailing Add:* 5873 Seneca Point Rd Naples NY 14512

BEAL, PHILIP FRANKLIN, III, ORGANIC CHEMISTRY. *Current Pos:* RETIRED. *Personal Data:* b Brewster, NY, Oct 2, 22; m 47; c 4. *Educ:* Williams Col, AB, 43; Ohio State Univ, PhD(org chem), 49. *Prof Exp:* Jr chemist, Winthrop Chem Co, 43-44; res assoc, UpJohn Co, 50-66, head chem process res & develop, 66-69, mgr, 69-70, group mgr chem process res & develop, 70-78, dir fine chem specialties prod & support servs, 78-79, dir fine chem prod, 79-80, dir fine chem res & develop, 80-84. *Mem:* Am Chem Soc. *Res:* Aliphatic diazo compounds; diazoketones; partial and total synthetic steroid work; synthetic prostaglandins. *Mailing Add:* 690 W Main St Homer MI 49245

BEAL, RICHARD SIDNEY, JR, SYSTEMATICS. *Current Pos:* RETIRED. *Personal Data:* b Victor, Colo, May 7, 16; m 87, Evorine C Baggett; c Andrew A. *Educ:* Univ Ariz, BS, 38; Univ Calif, PhD(entom), 52. *Prof Exp:* Asst prof biol, Westmont Col, 47-48; instr lib arts, San Francisco Baptist Col, 48-51; prof syst theol, Conservative Baptist Theol Sem, 51-56; entomologist, Agr Res Serv, USDA, 56-58; assoc prof entom, Ariz State Univ, 58-62; assoc dean arts & sci, Northern Ariz Univ, 62-65, dean, Grad Sch, 65-81, prof zool, 81-83, emer prof entom, 84-87,; acad vpres, Colo Christian Univ, 87-89, prof biol & emer prof entom, 89-94. *Mem:* Coleopterists Soc; Am Entom Soc; Soc Syst Zool; Am Sci Affiliation. *Res:* Biology and systematics of coleopterous family Dermestidae. *Mailing Add:* 1094 Pine Country Ct 180 S Garrison St Prescott AZ 86303. *E-Mail:* rsbeal@northlink.com

BEAL, ROBERT CARL, GEOLOGY, PHYSICS. *Current Pos:* PRIN PHYSICIST, JOHNS HOPKINS APPL PHYSICS LAB, 73- *Personal Data:* b Boston, Mass, Dec 28, 40; m 62; c 1. *Educ:* Mass Inst Technol, BS, 61; Univ Md, MS, 68. *Prof Exp:* Design engr, Johns Hopkins Appl Physics Lab, 61-68; syst engr, Itek Corp, 68-72. *Concurrent Pos:* Consult, EG&G, Bedford, Mass, 72-73; vis scientist, Jet Propulsion Lab, 77-78; prin investr, Johns Hopkins Appl Physics Lab, 78-81; ed, Spaceborne Synthetic Aperture Radar Oceanog, 80-81. *Mem:* Am Geophys Union; Union Radio Scientists Int. *Res:* Interpretation and analysis of oceanographic data from satellite sensors, particularly microwave sensors such as the synthetic aperture radar; ocean wave generation and propagation; spatial evolution of ocean wave spectra. *Mailing Add:* 12222 Carrol Mill Rd Ellicot City MD 21042

BEAL, STUART KIRKHAM, MECHANICAL & CHEMICAL ENGINEERING. *Current Pos:* sr fel, Adv Comt Reactor Safeguards, 80-82, PRIN SCIENTIST, SC&A INC, 82- *Personal Data:* b New York, NY, Nov 20, 32; m 54, Elizabeth Neale; c Anne & Laura. *Educ:* Va Polytech Inst, BS, 54; Univ Pittsburgh, MS, 63. *Prof Exp:* Jr engr nuclear systs design, Westinghouse Elec Corp, 54-55, assoc engr, 58-60, engr nuclear systs design & analysis, 60-66, sr engr corrosion-prod res, 66-72, fel engr corrosion-prod res, environ modelling and analysis, 72-75, adv engr math modelling corrosion-prod res, aerosol physics, Bettis Atomic Power Lab 75-80. *Mem:* Am Nuclear Soc; Inst Elec & Electronics Engrs. *Res:* Mathematical modelling; environmental modelling; aerosol physics. *Mailing Add:* 3708 Camelot Dr Annandale VA 22003

BEAL, THOMAS R, engineering mechanics, engineering, for more information see previous edition

BEAL, VIRGINIA ASTA, NUTRITION. *Current Pos:* RETIRED. *Personal Data:* b Hull, Mass, Oct 31, 18. *Educ:* Simmons Col, BS, 39; Harvard Univ, MPH, 45. *Honors & Awards:* Medallion Award, Am Dietetic Asn. *Prof Exp:* Nutritionist, Maternal & Child Health, Sch Pub Health, Harvard Univ, 39-46; instr physiol growth, Sch Med, Univ Colo, 48-54, asst prof human growth, 54-59, asst clin prof pediat, 59-71, nutritionist, Child Res Coun, 46-71; from assoc prof to prof nutrit, Univ Mass, Amherst, 71-86, emer prof, 86. *Mem:* Fel Am Pub Health Asn; Am Inst Nutrit; Am Dietetic Asn; Soc Nutrit Educ; NY Acad Sci; Sigma Xi. *Res:* Nutritional intake during pregnancy and childhood and its relationship to physical and physiological growth and development; education. *Mailing Add:* Applewood One Spencer Dr Apt 339 Amherst MA 01002-3367

BEALE, ALBERTO JORGE, agronomy, for more information see previous edition

BEALE, ELMUS G, TISSUE-SPECIFIC GENE EXPRESSION, P-ENDPYRUVATE CARBOXYKINASE FUNCTION & REGULATION. *Current Pos:* asst prof, 84-93, ASSOC PROF, TEX TECH UNIV HEALTH SCI CTR, 93- *Personal Data:* b Paris, Tenn, Jan 4, 48; m 70, Elaine Fuksa; c Emily L & Julia A. *Educ:* Okla State Univ, BS, 70; Baylor Col Med, PhD(cell biol), 77. *Prof Exp:* Fel, Univ Iowa, 77-80, res scientist, 80-84. *Concurrent Pos:* Prin investr, NIH/NIGMS grant, 88-, Tex Advan Res Prog, 94- *Mem:* AAAS; Am Diabetes Asn; Am Soc Cell Biol; Endocrine Soc. *Res:* The mechanisms of regulation and the function of the phosphoenolpyruvate carboxykinase gene in fat cells; glucagon; insulin. *Mailing Add:* Dept Cell Biol & Anat Tex Tech Univ Health Sci Ctr Sch Med Lubbock TX 79430-0001. *E-Mail:* beale@tthsc4.hsc.ttu.edu

BEALE, GUY OTIS, AUTOMATIC CONTROLS, DIGITAL SIMULATION. *Current Pos:* ASSOC PROF ELEC & COMPUT ENG, GEORGE MASON UNIV, 86- *Personal Data:* b Cleveland, Ohio, June 16, 44; m 67; c 1. *Educ:* Va Polytech Inst, BS, 67; Lynchburg Col, MS, 74; Univ Va, PhD(elec eng), 77. *Prof Exp:* Electronic engr, Babcock & Wilcox, 71-78, chief electronic engr, 78-81, eng prod mgr, 81; asst prof elec eng, Vanderbilt Univ, 81-86. *Concurrent Pos:* Consult, Babcock & Wilcox & Sverdrup Technol, Inc, 82-, Merrick Eng, 84, Vanderbilt Univ Med Ctr, 84-85 & David Taylor Res Ctr, 88-93. *Mem:* Inst Elec & Electronics Engrs; Sigma Xi. *Res:* Modern control and estimation theory; intelligent systems for design; optimal digital simulation; microprocessor-based industrial automation. *Mailing Add:* Elec & Comput Eng George Mason Univ 4400 University Dr Fairfax VA 22030. *Fax:* 703-993-1601; *E-Mail:* gbeale@bass.gmu.edu

BEALE, LUTHER A(LTON), STRUCTURAL ANALYSIS. *Current Pos:* RETIRED. *Personal Data:* b Jacksonville, Fla, July 30, 23; m 58; c 3. *Educ:* Ga Inst Technol, BS, 48, MS, 54; Univ Tex, PhD, 67. *Prof Exp:* Design engr, Robert & Co Assocs, 48-49; instr math, Ga Inst Tech, 49-50, asst prof eng mech, 54-55; expressway engr, McDougald Construct Co, 50-51; contractor, 51-52; opers engr, US Army Corps Engrs, 52-54; prof civil eng & head dept, Lamar Univ, 55-84. *Mem:* Am Soc Civil Engrs; Nat Soc Prof Engrs. *Res:* Structural analysis directed toward improvement of present design techniques and methods. *Mailing Add:* 261 Berry Rd Beaumont TX 77706

BEALE, PAUL DREW, CRITICAL PHENOMENA, STATISTICAL MECHANICS. *Current Pos:* ASST PROF PHYSICS, DEPT PHYSICS, UNIV COLO, BOULDER, 84- *Personal Data:* b Wilmington, NC, Feb 20, 55; m 80. *Educ:* Univ NC, Chapel Hill, BS, 77; Cornell Univ, PhD(physics), 82. *Prof Exp:* Res fel physics, Dept Theoret Physics, Oxford Univ, 82-84. *Concurrent Pos:* Vis researcher, Los Alamos Nat Lab, 84-; consult, Electromagnetic Applns, Denver, 85. *Mem:* Am Phys Soc. *Res:* Theoretical critical phenomena; critical and multicritical phenomena in pure and random systems; phenomenological finite-size scaling; statistical mechanics of model systems; theory of failure in random systems; ferroelectrics. *Mailing Add:* 371 N Cedar Brook Rd Boulder CO 80304

BEALE, SAMUEL I, CHLOROPLAST DEVELOPMENT, TETRAPYRROLE BIOSYNTHESIS. *Current Pos:* from asst prof to assoc prof, 79-86, PROF BIOL, BROWN UNIV, 86- *Personal Data:* b Los Angeles, Calif, June 25, 42. *Educ:* Univ Calif, Los Angeles, BS, 64, MS, 66, PhD(bot), 70. *Prof Exp:* Res assoc, Brookhaven Nat Lab, 70-72; res botanist, Univ Calif, Davis, 72-73, res biochemist, 73-74; res fel, Rockefeller Univ, 74-76, asst prof, 76-77; lectr bot, Univ Calif, Davis, 77-78, asst res biochemist, Sch Med, 78-79. *Concurrent Pos:* Jr investr, Summer Res Prog, Marine Biol Lab, Woods Hole, Mass, 74, assoc investr, 75, guest investr, 76-; mem adv panel, Cell Biol Prog, NSF, 83-84, Metab Biol Prog, 84-86 & cell biol Sci, 90- *Mem:* AAAS; Am Soc Biol Chemists; Am Soc Plant Physiologists; Int Soc Plant Molecular Biol; Sigma Xi; NY Acad Sci. *Res:* Biosynthesis of photosynthetic and respiratory pigments and related products; expression of photosynthetic competence; regulation of chloroplast development. *Mailing Add:* Div Biol & Med Brown Univ Providence RI 02912-0001

BEALE, WILLIAM TAYLOR, ENGINEERING. *Current Pos:* PRES, SUNPOWER INC, ATHENS, 74- *Personal Data:* b Cattanooga, Tenn, Apr 17, 28; m 59, Carol P Brand; c Faith, Daniel & John. *Educ:* Wash State Col, BSME, 50; Calif Inst Technol, MSME, 53. *Prof Exp:* Res engr, Wash State Col, Pullman, 50-52; engr, NACA, Cleveland, 53-56; res engr, Mass Inst Technol, Cambridge, 57-58; asst prof, Boston Univ, 58-59; assoc prof, Ohio Univ, Athens, 59-74. *Res:* Invention of free piston stirling engine; cooled variable expansion ratio diesel free piston; engineering company executive. *Mailing Add:* Sunpower Inc 182 Mill St South Athens OH 45701-2625

BEALER, STEVEN LEE, CARDIOVASCULAR PHYSIOLOGY. *Current Pos:* from asst prof to assoc prof, 79-89, PROF PHYSIOL, UNIV TENN, 89- *Personal Data:* b Evansville, Ind, July 10, 49. *Educ:* Univ Wyo, BS, 71, MS, 73, PhD(psychol), 76. *Prof Exp:* Fel, Univ Iowa, 76-79. *Mem:* Am Physiol Soc; Soc Neurosci. *Res:* Central nervous system control of cardiovascular regulation and fluid-electrolyte balance, including plasma volume regulation; hypertension, diabetes, vascular responses to hemorrhage and control of blood flow. *Mailing Add:* 1661 Hayne Rd Memphis TN 38119

BEALES, FRANCIS WILLIAM, GEOLOGY. *Current Pos:* assoc prof, 51-74, PROF GEOL, UNIV TORONTO, 74- *Personal Data:* b Bristol, Eng, Feb 7, 19; Can citizen; m 54; c 5. *Educ:* Cambridge Univ, BA, 46; Univ Toronto, PhD(geol), 52. *Prof Exp:* Lectr geol, McMaster Univ, 47-51. *Mem:* Am Asn Petrol Geol; hon mem Soc Econ Paleont & Mineral; Geol Soc Am; Geol Asn Can; Int Asn Sedimentol; hon mem Can Asn Petrol Geol. *Res:* Stratigraphy with special interest in limestones as petroleum reservoirs or metallic mineral host rock. *Mailing Add:* Dept Geol Sci Univ Toronto Toronto ON M5S 1A1 Can

BEALL, ARTHUR CHARLES, JR, MEDICINE. *Current Pos:* resident surg affil hosps, Baylor Col Med, 55-60, resident thoracic surg, 60-61, from instr to assoc prof, 59-71, PROF SURG, BAYLOR COL MED, 71- *Personal Data:* b Atlanta, Ga, Aug 17, 29; m 49; c 2. *Educ:* Emory Univ, BS, 50, MD, 53. *Prof Exp:* Intern surg, Barnes Hosp, St Louis, Mo, 53-54; resident, Methodist Hosp, Houston, Tex, 54-55. *Mem:* Am Asn Thoracic Surg; Am Col Cardiol; Am Col Chest Physicians; Am Col Surgeons; Soc Thoracic Surg. *Res:* Cardiovascular surgery, especially open heart surgery; techniques of extracorporeal circulation; pulmonary embolectomy; development of artificial heart valves; management cardiovascular trauma. *Mailing Add:* Dept Surg Baylor Col Med One Baylor Plz Houston TX 77030-3411

BEALL, CHARLES EDWARD, ANALYTICAL CHEMISTRY, PHYSICS. *Current Pos:* sr res chemist, 88-95, RES SCIENTIST, VISTA CHEM CO, AUSTIN, 95- *Personal Data:* b Texarkana, Tex, 1961; m 85, Lee Ann Brixey; c Audrey G & Spencer W. *Educ:* Midwestern State Univ, BS, 83; Univ Wis, PhD(anal chem), 88. *Mem:* Am Inst Chemists; Am Soc Mass Spectrometry. *Res:* Gas chromatography; gas chromatography/mass spectroscopy analysis of surfactants and surfactant interdiates. *Mailing Add:* Vista Chem Co PO Box 200135 Austin TX 78720. *Fax:* 512-331-2594; *E-Mail:* cbeall@cvcnet.com

BEALL, CYNTHIA M, ANTHROPOLOGY. *Current Pos:* From asst prof to assoc prof, 76-87, PROF ANTHROP, CASE WESTERN RES UNIV, 87- *Personal Data:* b Urbana, Ill, Aug 21, 49. *Educ:* Univ Pa, BA, 70; Pa State Univ, MA, 72, PhD(anthrop), 76. *Concurrent Pos:* Res grantee, NSF, 81, 83, 86, 87 & 93-95, Am Fedn Aging Res, 83 & 86, Nat Geog Soc, 83, 86-87, 93 & 95; fel, Nat Prog Advan Study & Res China, Nat Acad Sci, 86-87; co-ed, J Crosscult Geront, 86-95; pres, Human Biol Coun, 92-94. *Mem:* Nat Acad Sci; AAAS; Am Anthrop Asn; Am Asn Phys Anthrop; Soc Study Human Biol; Asn Anthrop & Geront. *Res:* Contributed many articles to professional journals; field research in Peru, Bolivia, Nepal, Tibet, Mongolia and Ethiopia. *Mailing Add:* Case Western Res Univ 10900 Euclid Ave Cleveland OH 44106

BEALL, FRANK CARROLL, WOOD SCIENCE. *Current Pos:* PROF & DIR, FOREST PROD LAB, 88- *Personal Data:* b Baltimore, Md, Oct 3, 33; m 63, Holmes; c Amanda J (Cysewski), Mark W & Alyssa J. *Educ:* Pa State Univ, BS, 64; State Univ NY Col Forestry, Syracuse Univ, MS, 66, PhD(wood physics), 68. *Prof Exp:* Res technologist, US Forest Prod Lab, 66-68; asst prof wood sci & technol, Pa State Univ, University Park, 68-73, assoc prof, 73-75; assoc prof wood sci, Univ Toronto, 75-77; sr sci spec, Weyerhaeuser Co, 77-88. *Concurrent Pos:* Western rep, Nat Planning Comt Forest Prod Res; assoc ed, J Acoust Emission. *Mem:* Soc Wood Sci & Technol (pres, 91-92); Forest Prod Soc; Am Soc Testing & Mat; Am Soc Non-Destructive Testing; fel Acoust Emissions Working Group (secy-treas, 91-). *Res:* Nondestructive evaluation; adhesion and adhesives; thermal degradation; moisture measurement and control; over 80 papers and patents in wood science and technology. *Mailing Add:* Dept Environ Sci Univ Calif Berkeley CA 94720-0001. *Fax:* 510-215-4299; *E-Mail:* beallfc@nature.berkeley.edu

BEALL, GARY WAYNE, physical chemistry, inorganic chemistry, for more information see previous edition

BEALL, GEORGE HALSEY, GEOCHEMISTRY, CERAMICS. *Current Pos:* From sr geologist to res geologist, Corning Glass Works, 62-65, res assoc geol, 65-66, mgr glass-ceramic res dept, 66-77, RES FEL, CORNING GLASS WORKS, 77- *Personal Data:* b Montreal, Que, Oct 14, 35; m 62, 76; c 4. *Educ:* McGill Univ, BSc, 56, MSc, 58; Mass Inst Technol, PhD(geol), 62. *Mem:* AAAS; Mineral Soc Am; fel Am Inst Chemists; fel Am Ceramic Soc; Am Chem Soc. *Res:* Nucleation and growth of crystals in glass; glass-ceramics; synthetic mica; silica polymorph solid solutions; phase equilibria; petrology of basalt. *Mailing Add:* 16 Woodland Dr Big Flats NY 14814

BEALL, GILDON NOEL, ALLERGY, IMMUNOLOGY. *Current Pos:* instr, 60-61, from asst prof to assoc prof, 61-70, PROF MED, SCH MED, UNIV CALIF, LOS ANGELES, 70-, CHIEF ALLERGY & CLIN IMMUNOL & DIR MED CLIN, HARBOR-UCLA MED CTR, 68- *Personal Data:* b Raymond, Wash, Sept 11, 28; m 51; c 4. *Educ:* Univ Wash, BS, 50, MD, 53. *Prof Exp:* Asst med, Sch Med, Univ Wash, 57-60. *Mem:* Am Soc Clin Invest; Sigma Xi; fel Am Col Physicians; fel Am Acad Allergy. *Res:* Application of immunology to clinical medicine and allergy; mechanism of asthma pathogenesis; autoimmune thyroid disease; clinical trials for AIDS/HIV infection. *Mailing Add:* 2716 Via Anita Palos Verdes Estates CA 90274

BEALL, HERBERT, INORGANIC CHEMISTRY, CHEMICAL EDUCATION. *Current Pos:* asst prof, 68-73, assoc prof chem, 73-89, PROF CHEM, WORCESTER POLYTECH INST, 89- *Personal Data:* b Chatham, Ont, Aug 26, 39; US citizen; m 77, Barbara A Slovinsky; c Anne, Katherine & Nicole. *Educ:* Univ Wis, BS, 61; Harvard Univ, PhD(chem), 67. *Prof Exp:* Sr res chemist, Olin Res Ctr, 67-68. *Concurrent Pos:* Vis lectr, Univ Canterbury, 74-75. *Mem:* Am Chem Soc. *Res:* Inorganic chemistry of coal and carbon; chemical education. *Mailing Add:* Dept Chem Worcester Polytech Inst Worcester MA 01609

BEALL, JAMES HOWARD, ACTIVE GALACTIC NUCLEI, RELATIVISTIC PARTICLE BEAMS. *Current Pos:* PROF PHYSICS, ST JOHNS COL, ANNAPOLIS, MD, 82-; SR CONSULT PHYSICS, NAVAL RES LAB, 83- *Personal Data:* b Grantsville, WVa, May 12, 45; m 66; c Tara S & Aaron J. *Educ:* Univ Colo, BA, 72; Univ Md, MS, 75, PhD(physics), 79. *Prof Exp:* Teaching asst physics, Univ Md, 72-75; res asst physics, Lab Astro & Solar Physics, Goddard Space Flight Ctr, 75-78; cong sci fel pub policy, Off Tech Assessment, US Cong, 78-79; proj scientist pub policy, Sci & Anal BKO, 79-81; resident assoc physics, Naval Res Lab, Nat Acad Sci, 81-83. *Concurrent Pos:* Bd dirs, Word Works Inc, Washington, DC, 75-; prin investr, Astron Liberal Arts, NSF grant, 91-; prof, Space Sci Inst, George Mason Univ, 91-; sci & eng adv bd, High Frontier, Arlington, Va, 91- *Mem:* Am Phys Soc; Am Astron Soc; AAAS; Sci Res Soc NAm; Am Astronaut Soc. *Res:* Theoretical and observational astrophysics and public policy; develop models for the energy loss mechanism of a beam of relativistic particles propagating through the ambient medium of an active galaxy; time variability of active galactic nuclei and quasars; emission mechanisms for the x-ray radiation observed in these objects; responsible for first report of concurrent radio and x-ray variability of an active galaxy; export control policy; first prediction of inverse compton x-ray emission from supernovac; first prediction of detectable infrared and optical emission from binary x-ray stars; accretion disks. *Mailing Add:* Code 7620 Naval Res Lab Washington DC 20375

BEALL, JAMES ROBERT, PHYSIOLOGY, BIOCHEMISTRY. *Current Pos:* TOXICOL PROG MGR, US DEPT ENERGY, 81- *Personal Data:* b Stillwater, Okla, June 29, 40. *Educ:* Okla State Univ, BS, 63; Univ Okla, MS, 65, PhD(physiol), 69. *Prof Exp:* Res asst physiol, Med Ctr, Univ Okla, 63-66; res asst reproductive physiol, Inst Health Sci, Brown Univ, 66-69; prin toxicologist, Dept Toxicol & Path, Schering Corp, 69-77; sr toxicologist & biol sci adminr toxic substances, Off Toxic Substance, Environ Protection Agency, 77-79; spec asst occup health, Directorate Tech Support, Occup Safety & Health Admin, 79-81. *Concurrent Pos:* Environ Protection Agency rep, Toxic Substances Control Act, Interagency Testing Comt, 77-78; chmn interagency regulatory liaison group, Work Group on Testing Guidelines, Environ Protection Agency, 77-79; US rep, Expert Work Group Orgn Econ Coop & Develop, 78-; consult toxicol, 78-; mem bd dir, Am Bd Toxicol Inc, 81-85, Toxicol Lab Accreditation Inc, 84-; mem bd dir, Asn Govt Toxicologists, 83-86, pres, 83-86. *Mem:* Soc Toxicol; Am Col Toxicol; Am Teratology Soc; Sigma Xi; Asn Govt Toxicologists. *Res:* Biochemistry of reproduction and teratology; indoor air pollution; toxicology; manage health effects research involving the interaction of exogenous chemicals with living systems. *Mailing Add:* 4804 Old Middletown Rd Jefferson MD 21755

BEALL, PAULA THORNTON, BIOPHYSICS, CELL BIOLOGY. *Current Pos:* Instr, 74-77, ASST PROF BIOPHYS, BAYLOR COL MED, 77- *Personal Data:* b Cameron, Tex, July 22, 46. *Educ:* Rice Univ, BA, 68; Univ Tex, MS, 70, PhD(biophys), 76. *Concurrent Pos:* Group leader, Ciba Geigy Pharmaceut Co, 83-86; dir prod develop, Tanox Biosysts, 86-91; pres, Robesco Eng, 91-93, Beall & Assocs Tech Consults, 94- *Mem:* Am Physiol Soc; Sigma Xi; AAAS. *Res:* Role of water in physiological events; water-macromolecular interactions on the cellular level in growth, development and disease; cytoskeletal structure and cytoplasmic ground substance, nutritional requirements of cells; magnetic resonance imaging; scientific administration. *Mailing Add:* 3007 Conway Houston TX 77025-2609

BEALL, ROBERT ALLAN, PHYSICS, PHYSICAL METALLURGY. *Current Pos:* RETIRED. *Personal Data:* b Seattle, Wash, Mar 15, 20; m 42, Junanne Sexsmith; c Jane (deceased), Magruder & Robert. *Educ:* Univ Wash, BS, 41. *Honors & Awards:* H R Russ Ogden Award, Am Soc Testing & Mat, 86; Spec Melting Technol Award, Int Conf Vacuum Metall, 88. *Prof Exp:* Res supvr phys metall, Bur Mines, 49-78; consult reactive metals melting & casting, 78-97. *Concurrent Pos:* Mem subcomt, Mat Adv Bd Refractory Metals, Nat Acad Sci, 64 & Mat Adv Bd High Performance Steel & Ti Castings, 68; mem US working group electrometall, US-USSR, 73-77; consult, Union Carbide Nuclear Co, Oak Ridge, 74-76; mem expert melting zirconium, Int Atomic Energy Agency, Arg, 78-80. *Mem:* Sigma Xi. *Res:* Melting and casting reactive and refractory metals. *Mailing Add:* PO Box 446 Lincoln City OR 97367

BEALL, ROBERT JOSEPH, BIOCHEMISTRY. *Current Pos:* med dir, Cystic Fibrosis Found, Bethesda, Md, 80-84, nat dir, 81-84, exec vpres, 84-93, PRES & CHIEF EXEC OFFICER, CYSTIC FIBROSIS FOUND, 94- *Personal Data:* b Washington, DC, May 19, 43; m 67; c 2. *Educ:* Albright Col, BS, 65; State Univ NY Buffalo, MA, 70, PhD(biol), 70. *Honors & Awards:* NIH Merit Award, 80. *Prof Exp:* Asst biol, State Univ NY, Buffalo, 65-70; from instr to asst prof physiol, Sch Med, Case Western Reserve Univ, 70-74, from instr to asst prof, Sch Dent, 71-74; grants assoc, NIH, 74-75, chief, Endocrinol & Metab Dis Br, 78-79; Dir, Metab Dis Prog, Extramural Progs, Nat Inst Arthritis, Metab & Digestive Dis, 75-78. *Mem:* AAAS; Am Soc Human Genetics; NY Acad Sci; Am Soc Microbiol; Sigma Xi. *Res:* Molecular endocrinology, mechanism of action of adrenocorticotropic hormone; cyclic nucleotide synthesis and action, steriodogenesis, assay of adrenocorticotropic hormone in plasma, neoplastic endocrine tissue, genetic diseases, metabolic control; cystic fibrosis. *Mailing Add:* 5 Aqueduct Ct Potomac MD 20854

BEALL, S(AMUEL) E, JR, CHEMICAL ENGINEERING, NUCLEAR ENGINEERING. *Current Pos:* RETIRED. *Personal Data:* b Richland, Ga, May 16, 19; m 48; c 5. *Educ:* Univ Tenn, BS, 43. *Prof Exp:* Chem engr smokeless powder process develop, E I du Pont de Nemours & Co, 43-45; with Oak Ridge Nat Lab, 45-63, dir, Reactor Div, 63-75, dir, Energy Div, 75-77, dir, Planning-Energy Div, 77-79, consult energy & environ progs, 79-, dir, Tenn Energy Authority, 79-88. *Mem:* Fel Am Nuclear Soc; AAAS. *Res:* Smokeless powders; nuclear reactor development and operation; energy systems; environmental effects; solar technology. *Mailing Add:* 1032 Craigland Ct Knoxville TN 37919

BEALMEAR, PATRICIA MARIA, EXPERIMENTAL PATHOLOGY. *Current Pos:* ASSOC CANCER RES SCIENTIST, DEPT DERMAT, ROSWELL PARK MEM INST, 76- *Personal Data:* b Dodge City, Kans, Oct 23, 29. *Educ:* Mt St Scholastica Col, BS, 49; Univ Notre Dame, PhD(biol), 65. *Prof Exp:* Chmn sci dept, high schs, Kans, 52-62, Mo, 62-63; asst prof biol, Mt St Scholastica Col, 65-66; res scientist microbiol, Univ Notre Dame, 66-71; from asst prof to assoc prof exp biol, Baylor Col Med, 71-76. *Concurrent Pos:* Bd trustees, Int Soc Exp Hemat, 75-77; exec secy, Int Asn Gnotobiology, 81- *Mem:* Am Asn Immunologists; Asn Gnotobiotics (exec secy, 75-); Int Soc Exp Hemat; Am Soc Exp Path; Soc Exp Biol & Med; AAAS; Am Asn Lab Animal Sci; Am Asn Pathologists; NY Acad Sci; Sigma Xi. *Res:* Bone marrow transplantation; cellular immunology; radiation pathology and treatment; application of germfree research to the clinical situation. *Mailing Add:* 65 Brooklyn Dr East Aurora NY 14052

BEALOR, MARK DABNEY, ORGANIC CHEMISTRY. *Current Pos:* RETIRED. *Personal Data:* b Shamokin, Pa, Sept 27, 21; m 51, Margaret Helmetag; c John S. *Educ:* Univ Pa, BS, 49; Univ Ore, MA, 54, PhD(chem), 56. *Prof Exp:* Chemist, Sharp & Dohme Inc, 49-51; sr chemist, Niagara Div, Food Mach & Chem Co, Inc, 55-57; sr chemist, S C Johnson & Son, Inc, 57-68, res supvr, 68-77, technol invest & licensing, 78-85. *Mem:* Am Chem Soc; Soc Cosmetic Chem; Sigma Xi. *Res:* Chemical structure versus biological activity; carbonyl condensations; product development. *Mailing Add:* 42 Pier Pointe New Bern NC 28562-8857

BEALS, EDWARD WESLEY, MATHEMATICAL ECOLOGY, NATURAL HISTORY. *Current Pos:* asst prof bot, Univ Wis, 66-67, lectr zool, 67-68, asst prof, 68-69, from assoc prof to prof zool & bot, 69-92, EMER PROF ZOOL, UNIV WIS-MADISON, 92; PROF ENVIRON SCI, UNITY COL, 92- *Personal Data:* b Wichita, Kans, July 1, 33; div; c Monica. *Educ:* Earlham Col, BA, 56; Univ Wis-Madison, MS, 58, PhD(bot), 61. *Prof Exp:* Instr biol, Am Univ Beirut, 61-62; from asst prof to assoc prof, Haile Selassie Univ, 62-65; asst prof bot & zool, Univ Wis Ctr Syst, 65-66. *Mem:* Ecol Soc Am; Am Ornithologists Union; Am Soc Naturalists; Soc Study Evolution; Cooper Ornith Soc; Sigma Xi. *Res:* Mathematical analysis of ecological communities; interrelations between vegetation and animals, especially birds and mammals; factors in species diversity and niche specialization; allelopathy in plant communities. *Mailing Add:* Environ Sci Bldg Unity Col Unity ME 04988. *Fax:* 207-948-6277

BEALS, HAROLD OLIVER, WOOD TECHNOLOGY, PALEOBOTANY. *Personal Data:* b Mishawauka, Ind, July 4, 31; m 59, 82; c 1. *Educ:* Purdue Univ, BSF, 55, MS, 57, PhD(bot), 60. *Prof Exp:* Secy, Evans Prod Inc, Kans, 58-59; from asst prof to prof forestry, Auburn Univ, 60-96. *Concurrent Pos:* Consult; mem & housing rehab inspector, Southern Bldg Code Cong Int Inc. *Mem:* AAAS; Forest Prod Res Soc (secy-treas, 62-64). *Res:* Plant anatomy. *Mailing Add:* 9955 US Hwy 280W Waverly AL 36879

BEALS, R MICHAEL, MATHEMATICS. *Current Pos:* ASSOC PROF MATH, RUTGERS UNIV, 81- *Personal Data:* b Erie, Pa, July 28, 54. *Educ:* Univ Chicago, BA & MS, 76; Princeton Univ, PhD(math), 80. *Mem:* Am Math Soc; Math Asn Am. *Mailing Add:* Dept Math Rutgers Univ New Brunswick NJ 08903-2101

BEALS, RICHARD WILLIAM, PARTIAL DIFFERENTIAL EQUATIONS, FUNCTIONAL ANALYSIS. *Current Pos:* PROF MATH, YALE UNIV, 77- *Personal Data:* b Erie, Pa, May 28, 38; m 62; c 3. *Educ:* Yale Univ, BA, 60, MA, 62, PhD(math), 64. *Prof Exp:* Instr math, Yale Univ, 64-65; vis asst prof, Univ Chicago, 65-66, from asst prof to prof, 66-77. *Mem:* Am Math Soc; Math Asn Am. *Res:* Inverse scattering; pseudodifferential operators; complex analysis; global analysis; transport theory. *Mailing Add:* Yale Univ 10 Hillhouse PO Box 208283 New Haven CT 06520-8283

BEALS, ROBERT J(ENNINGS), CERAMIC ENGINEERING, ANALYTICAL CHEMISTRY. *Current Pos:* DIR RES & DEVELOP, THE HALL CHINA CO, 72- *Personal Data:* b Decatur, Ill, Nov 12, 23; m 52; c 3. *Educ:* Univ Ill, BS, 47, MS, 50, PhD(ceramic eng), 55. *Prof Exp:* Asst ceramic eng, Univ Ill, 47-52, from instr to assoc prof, 52-62; assoc ceramic engr, Argonne Nat Lab, 62-69; asst tech dir, Charles Taylor Sons Co, 69-70, tech dir, 70-71. *Concurrent Pos:* Comnr, Eng Manpower Comn, Engrs Joint Coun, 70-; consult, E R Advan Ceramics; pres, Eng Acreditation Comn of Accreditation Bd, Eng & Technol. *Mem:* Fel Am Ceramic Soc (treas, 78-80, pres, 81-82); Nat Inst Ceramic Engrs. *Res:* Nuclear ceramic materials; ceramic chemistry; high temperature materials; high temperature x-ray analysis; manufacture of refractories; ceramic whitewares; electrical ceramics. *Mailing Add:* 438 Smithfield St East Liverpool OH 43920

BEALS, RODNEY K, ORTHOPEDIC SURGERY. *Current Pos:* From instr to assoc prof, 61-80, PROF ORTHOP SURG, MED SCH, UNIV ORE, 80- *Personal Data:* b Portland, Ore, Jan 4, 31; m 56; c 3. *Educ:* Willamette Univ, BA, 53; Univ Ore, MD, 56; Am Bd Orthop Surg, dipl, 64. *Mem:* Am Acad Orthop Surg. *Res:* Clinical orthopedics. *Mailing Add:* Div Orthop Rehab Univ Ore Med Sch Portland OR 97201

BEAM, CARL ADAMS, MICROBIAL GENETICS, RADIOBIOLOGY. *Current Pos:* assoc prof biol, 63-75, PROF BIOL, BROOKLYN COL, 75- *Personal Data:* b Olympia, Wash, July 5, 20; m 52. *Educ:* Brown Univ, BA, 42; Yale Univ, MS, 47, PhD(microbiol), 50. *Prof Exp:* Res assoc biophysics, Univ Calif, Berkeley, 50-56; asst prof, Yale Univ, 56-63. *Concurrent Pos:* NIH fel, 50-51, res grants & sr investr, 56-63. *Mem:* Phycol Soc Am; Radiation Res Soc; Biophys Soc; Genetics Soc Am; Soc Protozoologists. *Res:* Biological factors affecting radiation sensitivity; dinoflagellate genetics and diversification. *Mailing Add:* 202 Marlborough Rd Brooklyn NY 11226

BEAM, CHARLES FITZHUGH, JR, ORGANIC CHEMISTRY, POLYMER CHEMISTRY. *Current Pos:* DEPT CHEM, COL CHARLESTON, 82- *Personal Data:* b New York, NY, Sept 24, 40; m 83; c 2. *Educ:* City Col New York, BS, 63; Univ Md, College Park, PhD(org chem), 70. *Prof Exp:* Asst gen & phys chem, Univ Md, 63-65, org polymer chem, 65-68; res assoc, P M Gross Chem Lab, Duke Univ, 68-71 & Lehigh Univ, 71-72; assoc prof chem, dir sci res & title III coordr, Newberry Col, 73-82. *Concurrent Pos:* Prin investr, numerous chem res grants, 72- *Mem:* Am Chem Soc; fel Am Inst Chemists; fel The Royal Chem Soc. *Res:* Preparation of new heterocyclic compounds with potential biological activity via strong-base multiple anion synthesis methods and techniques; organic synthesis with multiple anions; medicinal syntheses; pyrolysis studies; organic chemistry of high polymers. *Mailing Add:* Dept Chem Col Charleston Charleston SC 29424-0002

BEAM, EDWARD ANTHONY, III, MOLECULAR BEAM EPITAXY, METALORGANIC CHEMICAL VAPOR DEPOSITION. *Current Pos:* BR MGR III-V MAT, RAYTHEON TI SYSTS, 97. *Personal Data:* b Greensburg, Pa, Oct 4, 62; m 91, Maureen Burbey; c Erin, Jennifer & Rachel. *Educ:* Carnegie-Mellon Univ, BS, 84, MS, 86, PhD(metal & mat sci), 89. *Prof Exp:* Mem tech staff, Tex Instruments Inc, 89-97. *Mem:* Am Asn Crystal Growth; Inst Elec & Electronics Engrs; Mat Res Soc. *Res:* Advanced epitaxial growth procedures of III-V compound semi-conductor materials for application to electronic devices. *Mailing Add:* PO Box 655936 MS-134 Dallas TX 75243. *E-Mail:* beam@resbld.csc.ti.com

BEAM, JOHN E, FOOD SCIENCE, DAIRY SCIENCE. *Current Pos:* MEM STAFF, LIFESAVER INC, 78- *Personal Data:* b Honesdale, Pa, Oct 27, 31; m 61; c 3. *Educ:* Pa State Univ, BS, 57; Univ Mass, MS, 59, PhD(food sci), 62. *Prof Exp:* Instr dairy mfg, Univ Mass, 57-59, res, 59-62; proj leader res & develop, Ross Labs, Abbott Labs, 62-64; in charge spec projs food res & develop, Beech-Nut, Inc, 64-67, mgr processed food res, 67-68, food res, 68, mgr prod develop, 68-78. *Concurrent Pos:* Mem lab comt, Wash Lab, Nat Canners Asn. *Mem:* AAAS; Inst Food Technol; Am Dairy Sci Asn; Sci Res Soc Am; Sigma Xi. *Res:* Dairy chemistry; gelling agents; infant nutrition; food product development; confections development; candy and chewing gum; cough and cold products; beverages. *Mailing Add:* 5140 River Chase Ridge Winston-Salem NC 27104

BEAM, KURT GEORGE, JR, ELECTROPHYSIOLOGY, NEUROBIOLOGY. *Current Pos:* assoc prof, 86-, PROF, COLO STATE UNIV. *Personal Data:* b Chicago, Ill, Aug 13, 45; m 70; c 2. *Educ:* Pomona Col, BA, 67; Univ Wash, PhD(physiol), 74. *Prof Exp:* Fel, Dept Pharmacol, Yale Univ, 74-77; asst prof, Dept Physiol, Univ Iowa, 77-86. *Concurrent Pos:* Res career develop award, NIH. *Mem:* Biophys Soc; Fedn Am Soc Exp Biol; Soc Neurosci; Soc Gen Physiologists; AAAS. *Res:* Voltage clamp techniques to characterize the electrical excitability of normal and denervated mammalian skeletal muscle, to understand developmental, hormonal, neurotrophic regulation of the physiology of electrically excitable cells; electrophysiological cell biological and molecular biological studies of nerve and muscle development; excitation-contraction coupling; calcium channels in nerve and muscle. *Mailing Add:* Dept Physiol Colo State Univ Ft Collins CO 80523-0001. *Fax:* 970-491-7569

BEAM, WALTER R(ALEIGH), SYSTEMS ARCHITECTURE, MANUFACTURING SYSTEMS. *Current Pos:* CONSULT, 89- *Personal Data:* b Richmond, Va, Aug 27, 28; c David & James. *Educ:* Univ Md, BS, 47, MS, 50, PhD(elec eng), 53. *Honors & Awards:* Except Civilian Serv Decoration, USAF. *Prof Exp:* Instr elec eng, Univ Md, 47-51; res engr, RCA Labs, 52-56, mgr microwave appl res, 56-59; prof elec eng, Rensselaer Polytech Inst, 59-64, head dept, 59-62; mem res staff, IBM Corp, 64-67, dir eng technol, IBM Syst Develop Div, 67-69; tech & mgt consult, 70-74; dep advan technol, Off Asst Secy USAF, 74-81; vpres res & develop, Sperry Div, 81-83, consult, 83-85; prof systs eng, George Mason Univ, 85-89. *Mem:* Fel Inst Elec & Electronics Engrs. *Res:* Computer technology and systems; electronic materials and devices; microwave electronics; application of computers in management; author of 3 books. *Mailing Add:* 3824 Ft Worth Ave Alexandria VA 22304. *E-Mail:* wrbeam@aol.com

BEAMAN, BLAINE LEE, MICROBIOLOGY. *Current Pos:* from asst prof to assoc prof, 75-82, PROF MED MICROBIOL, SCH MED, UNIV CALIF, DAVIS, 82- *Personal Data:* b Portland, Ore, July 28, 42; m 65; c 1. *Educ:* Utah State Univ, BS, 64; Univ Kans, PhD(microbiol), 68. *Prof Exp:* Asst prof med microbiol, Sch Med & Dent, Georgetown Univ, 70-75. *Concurrent Pos:* Fel, Sch Med, NY Univ, 68-70; Latin Am vis prof, Venezuela, 80. *Mem:* Am Soc Microbiol; AAAS; NY Acad Sci; fel, Am Acad Microbiol; Reticuloendothelial Soc. *Res:* Mechanisms of nocardial pathogenesis; induction, pathogenicity and biology of bacterial L-forms; the role of the alveolar macrophage in lung defense; infectious diseases of the lungs; bacterial cell wall biochemistry and bacterial ultrastructure. *Mailing Add:* Dept Med Microbiol Univ Calif Davis Sch Med Davis CA 95616

BEAMAN, DONALD ROBERT, ELECTRON SPECTROSCOPY, METALLURGY. *Current Pos:* SR RES SPECIALIST X-RAY & ELECTRON SPECTROS, DOW CHEM CO, 65- *Personal Data:* b Chicago, Ill, Apr 2, 33; m 69; c 3. *Educ:* Univ Ill, BS, 58, MS, 61, PhD(metall), 63. *Honors & Awards:* Environ Qual Award, US Environ Protection Agency, 76; 1978 Presidential Award, Microbeam Anal Soc, 78. *Prof Exp:* Metallurgist alloy steel develop, Inland Steel Co, 58-59; res asst physics, Univ Ill, 62-63, asst prof metall, 63-64; res metallurgist electron probe, Int Nickel Co, 64-65. *Concurrent Pos:* US deleg water qual comt, Int Standards Orgn, 77-; mem water qual comt, Am Nat Standards Inst, 77- *Mem:* Microbeam Anal Soc (treas, 70-71, 75-76, pres elect, 72, pres, 73); Am Soc Metals; Am Soc Testing & Mat. *Res:* X-ray and electron spectroscopy of materials using electron probe analysis, scanning and transmission electron microscopy, Auger electron spectroscopy and analytical transmission electron microscopy. *Mailing Add:* 930 Balfour Midland MI 48640

BEAMAN, JOHN HOMER, SYSTEMATIC BOTANY. *Current Pos:* From asst prof to assoc prof, 56-68, PROF BOT, MICH STATE UNIV, 68-, CUR, BEAL-DARLINGTON HERBARIUM, 56- *Personal Data:* b Marion, NC, June 20, 29; m 58; c 2. *Educ:* NC State Col, BS, 51; State Col Wash, MS, 53; Harvard Univ, PhD, 57. *Concurrent Pos:* Nat Acad Sci-Nat Res Coun sr vis res assoc, Smithsonian Inst, 65-66; mem ed comt, Flora NAm Prog, 66-73; mem bd dirs, Orgn Trop Studies, 72-79; prog dir syst biol, NSF, 79-81. *Mem:* Bot Soc Am; Am Soc Plant Taxon (pres, 80); Int Asn Plant Taxon; Soc Econ Bot (pres, 80-81); Ecol Soc Am; Sigma Xi. *Res:* Biosystematic studies in alpine flora of Mexico and Central America; monographic studies in Asteraceae; Compositae of Mexico; computer applications in systematic biology. *Mailing Add:* 1565 Woodside Dr East Lansing MI 48823

BEAMER, PAUL DONALD, VETERINARY PATHOLOGY. *Current Pos:* PROF VET PATH & HYG, UNIV ILL, URBANA-CHAMPAIGN, 64-, ASST TO DEAN, COL VET MED, 77- *Personal Data:* b Avonmore, Pa, Sept 21, 14; m 36; c 1. *Educ:* Ohio State Univ, DVM, 41; Univ Ill, MS, 45, PhD, 51. *Prof Exp:* Asst bacteriologist & pathologist, State Dept Agr, Ohio, 41-42; asst vet path & hyg, State Dept Agr, Ill, 42-44; war food asst, Univ Ill, 44-46, from asst prof to prof vet path & hyg, 46-60; adv to dean col vet med, Uttar Pradesh Agr Univ, India, 60-64. *Mem:* Fel Am Vet Med Asn; Am Col Vet Path; Int Acad Path; Sigma Xi. *Res:* Infectious diseases of livestock; bovine tuberculosis; brucellosis; swine enteritis; Newcastle disease of poultry; lead poisoning in wild ducks. *Mailing Add:* 71 Greencroft Dr Champaign IL 61821

BEAMER, ROBERT LEWIS, PHARMACY, BIOCHEMISTRY. *Current Pos:* from asst prof to assoc prof pharmaceut chem, 59-69, assoc dean col pharm, 72-75, PROF MED CHEM, UNIV SC, 69-, CHMN, DEPT BASIC PHARMACEUT SCIS, COL PHARM, 92- *Personal Data:* b Pulaski, Va, June 9, 33; m 59, Joan Fanning; c Janelle E. *Educ:* Med Col Va, BS, 55, MS, 57, PhD(chem), 59. *Prof Exp:* Asst chem, Med Col Va, 55-58, NIH fel, 58-59. *Concurrent Pos:* Mead Johnson res grant, 62-63; NIH res grant, 64-; vis prof, Cornell Univ Med Col, 77-78. *Mem:* Am Chem Soc; Am Pharmaceut Asn; Sigma Xi; Am Asn Pharmaceut Scientists. *Res:* Synthetic estrogenic agents; antimetabolites in cancer chemotherapy; catalytic hydrogenation; asymmetric synthesis; enzyme inhibition; computer modeling of drugs; antiestrogens and breast cancer. *Mailing Add:* Col Pharm Univ SC Columbia SC 29208. *Fax:* 803-777-2775; *E-Mail:* n490045@univscvm.csd.scarolina.edu

BEAMES, CALVIN G, JR, PHYSIOLOGY. *Current Pos:* from asst prof to assoc prof, 62-70, prof, 70-, EMER PROF PHYSIOL, OKLA STATE UNIV. *Personal Data:* b Kingston, Okla, Oct 29, 30; m 52; c 3. *Educ:* NMex Highlands Univ, AB, 55, MS, 56; Univ Okla, PhD(physiol, biochem), 61. *Prof Exp:* Asst physiol, Univ Okla, 55-56; teacher biol, Santa Fe High Sch, 56-57; asst physiol, Univ Okla, 57-60; trainee, Rice Univ, 60-61, NIH fel, 61-62. *Mem:* Am Physiol Soc. *Res:* Carbohydrate and lipid metabolism and transport mechanisms. *Mailing Add:* 2222 N Glenwood Dr Stillwater OK 74075

BEAMES, R M, ANIMAL NUTRITION, PIGS FISH & HORSES. *Current Pos:* from asst prof to assoc prof, 69-88, PROF ANIMAL SCI, FAC AGR SCI, UNIV BC, 88- *Personal Data:* b Brisbane, Australia, Oct 12, 31; m 56, Lilian Pope; c 4. *Educ:* Univ Queensland, BAgrSc, 54, MAgrSc, 62; McGill Univ, PhD(nutrit), 65. *Prof Exp:* Husb officer, Animal Res Inst Yeerongpilly, Queensland Dept Primary Industs, 54-65, sr husb officer, 65-68. *Mem:* Can Soc Animal Sci; Brit Nutrit Soc; Australian Soc Animal Prod. *Res:* Nutritive value of grains for pigs; use of amino acids in pig rations; value of grain screenings for pigs; the use of the rat for a model for pig nutrition; digestibility measurements with fish. *Mailing Add:* Dept Animal Sci Suite 208 2357 Main Mall Vancouver BC V6T 1Z4 Can. *Fax:* 604-822-4400

BEAMISH, FREDERICK WILLIAM HENRY, ECOLOGY, HYDROBIOLOGY. *Current Pos:* from asst prof to assoc prof, 65-72, dept chmn, 74-79, PROF ZOOL, UNIV GUELPH, 72- *Personal Data:* b Toronto, Ont, July 31, 35; m 58; c 3. *Educ:* Univ Toronto, BA, 58, PhD(zool), 62. *Prof Exp:* Assoc scientist behav & physiol biol, Biol Sta, Fisheries Res Bd Can, 62-65. *Mem:* Am Fisheries Soc; Am Soc Ichthyol & Herpet. *Res:* Physiology and ecology of cyclostome and teleost fishes; fish energetics and nutrition; fish toxicology. *Mailing Add:* Dept Zool Univ Guelph Guelph ON N1G 2W1 Can

BEAMISH, ROBERT EARL, CARDIOLOGY. *Current Pos:* CONSULT, DIV CARDIOVASC SCI, ST BONIFACE RES CTR, 87- *Personal Data:* b Shoal Lake, Man, Sept 9, 16; m 43; c 3. *Educ:* Brandon Col, BA, 37; Univ Man, MD, 42, BSc, 44; FRCP(C), 50. *Hon Degrees:* DSc, Brandon Univ, 88, Univ Man, 89. *Honors & Awards:* Medal Serv, Can Med Asn, 92; Ann Achievement Award, Can Cardiovasc Soc, 93. *Prof Exp:* Demonstr med, Fac Med, Univ Man, 46-49, from lectr to prof, 49-81; med dir, Great-West Life Assurance Co, 70-81; emer prof, Univ Man, 81- *Concurrent Pos:* Cardiologist, Manitoba Clin, 46-70; Nuffield Dom traveling fel, Gt Brit, 47-48; asst physician, Winnipeg Gen Hosp, 47-57, assoc physician, 57-; mem bd dir, Can Heart Found, 63-75; regional rep, Coun Clin Cardiol, Am Heart Asn, Can, 63-; ed-in-chief, Can J Cardiol, 84-96. *Mem:* Fel Am Col Cardiol; fel Am Col Physicians; Can Cardiovasc Soc (hon secy & treas, 57-, pres, 69-70); Inter-Am Soc Cardiol; Can Med Asn. *Res:* Clinical and laboratory research in ischemic heart disease with special reference to the therapeutic use of anticoagulants and stress-induced heart disease. *Mailing Add:* St Boniface Res Ctr 351 Tache Winnipeg MB R2H 2A6 Can

BEAN, BARBARA LOUISE, CARDIOVASCULAR PHARMACOLOGY, CARDIOVASCULAR PHYSIOLOGY. *Current Pos:* PVT PRACT, 93- *Personal Data:* b Doddington, Eng, Sept 20, 48; m 78; c 1. *Educ:* Univ Surrey, BSc, 70; Univ London, PhD(physiol), 76. *Prof Exp:* Res asst hypertension, London Hosp Med Col, 70-75; res fel, Med Res Coun Blood Pressure Unit, Western Infirmary, Glasgow, Scotland, 75-76 & NIH, Bethesda, Md, 77-78; asst prof cardiovasc pharmacol, Med Ctr, George Washington Univ, 78-93. *Concurrent Pos:* Res fel, Ciba-Geigy Corp, Gt Brit, 75-76. *Mem:* Med Res Soc; Fedn Am Soc Exp Biol. *Res:* Mechanisms in the development and maintenance of renal hypertension; antihypertensive factors in the renal medulla; central actions of angiotensins; mechanism of action of vasodilator drugs. *Mailing Add:* 505 Epping Forest Rd Annapolis MD 21401-6562

BEAN, BARRY, CELLULAR MOTILITY, REPRODUCTIVE CELL BIOLOGY. *Current Pos:* asst prof, 73-79, chmn dept, 83-85, ASSOC PROF BIOL, LEHIGH UNIV, BETHLEHEM, PA, 79- *Personal Data:* b Framingham, Mass, Nov 2, 42. *Educ:* Tufts Univ, BS, 64; Rockefeller Univ, PhD(life sci), 70. *Honors & Awards:* Woodrow Wilson hon fel, 64. *Prof Exp:* Fel microbiol, Rockefeller Univ, 64-70; res assoc biochem, Indian Inst Sci, Bangalore, 70-71; res fel USPHS, Rockefeller Univ, NY, 71-73. *Mem:* Am Soc Cell Biol; Am Fertil Soc; Am Soc Androl; NY Acad Sci; Am Soc Human Genetics; Europ Soc Human Reproduction & Embryol. *Res:* Sperm function and the events surrounding fertilization and gene transmission; cellular motility and behavior; fertility and diseases involving infertility. *Mailing Add:* Dept Biol & Cellular Molecular Biol Lehigh Univ 111 Research Dr Iacocca Hall Bethlehem PA 18015-4791

BEAN, BRENT LEROY, LASERS, QUANTUM OPTICS. *Current Pos:* PHYSICIST, OPTIMETRICS INC, 79- *Personal Data:* b Rexburg, Idaho, June 13, 41; m 65; c 6. *Educ:* Brigham Young Univ, BS, 66, MS, 68; NMex State Univ, PhD(physics), 72. *Prof Exp:* Res asst laser physics, Univ Laval, Quebec, 72-74; vis asst prof physics, Emory Univ, 74-78; physicist, Sci Appln, Inc, 78-79. *Concurrent Pos:* Consult physics, Eng Exp Sta, Ga Inst Technol, 75-78. *Mem:* Optical Soc Am. *Res:* Development of the far infrared laser; use of the far infrared laser for water vapor continuum measurements; atmospheric transmission measurements in natural and obscured environments. *Mailing Add:* Watson Lane Las Cruces NM 88047

BEAN, C THOMAS, JR, POLYMER CHEMISTRY. *Current Pos:* RETIRED. *Personal Data:* b Winchester, Ill, May 14, 20; m 44; c 2. *Educ:* Western Ill State Col, BEd, 42; Univ Kans, MA, 46, PhD(org chem), 49. *Prof Exp:* Anal control chemist, Hiram Walker & Sons, Inc, Ill, 42; asst instr chem, Univ Kans, 42-44; analysis lab foreman, Tenn Eastman Corp & Clinton Eng Works, Tenn, 44-46; supvr asst instr Qual Analysis, Univ Kans, 46-49; res chemist, J T Baker Co, 49-50; res chemist, Hooker Chem Corp, 50-56, res supvr, 56-62, mgr proj eval, 74-78, res sect mgr, plastics sect existing prod res, 62-; dir admin & tech serv, Ashland Oil Inc, Ashland Petrol Co, 81-85. *Concurrent Pos:* Mgr res planning & eng, Ashland Petrol Co, 79-81. *Mem:* Am Chem Soc; Am Inst Chem Engrs. *Res:* Vapor phase chlorination of hydrocarbons; insecticides; polyester resins; high temperature elastomers; corrosion control; epoxy resins; fire hazard reduction. *Mailing Add:* 2716 Auburn Ave Ashland KY 41102-6170

BEAN, CHARLES PALMER, physics, biophysics; deceased, see previous edition for last biography

BEAN, DANIEL JOSEPH, LIMNOLOGY. *Current Pos:* RETIRED. *Personal Data:* b Enosburg Falls, Vt, June 12, 34; m 58, Joanne Egan; c Jonathan, Jason & David. *Educ:* Univ Vt, BA, 60, MS, 62; Univ RI, PhD(biol sci), 69. *Prof Exp:* Instr biol, Marist Col, 64-68; from asst prof to prof biol, St Michael's Col, Vt, 68-97, chmn biol dept, 74-84, chmn dept, 89-96. *Concurrent Pos:* Pres, Vt Acad Arts & Sci. *Mem:* AAAS; Am Soc Limnol & Oceanog; Am Inst Biol Sci; Sigma Xi. *Res:* River zooplankton and benthic fauna; lake zooplankton. *Mailing Add:* 163 Lyman Ave Burlington VT 05401. *E-Mail:* dbean@smcvt.edu

BEAN, GEORGE A, PLANT PATHOLOGY. *Current Pos:* assoc prof bot, 66-72, assoc prof plant path, 72-76, assoc prof bot, 76-80, PROF BOT, UNIV MD, COLLEGE PARK, 80- *Personal Data:* b Hempstead, NY, Apr 3, 33; m 57; c 2. *Educ:* Cornell Univ, BS, 58; Univ Minn, MS, 60, PhD(plant path), 63. *Prof Exp:* Plant pathologist, Nat Capitol Region, US Dept Interior, 63-66. *Mem:* Am Phytopath Soc. *Res:* Physiology and chemistry of plant disease causing fungi. *Mailing Add:* HJ Paterson Hall Univ Md College Park MD 20742-0001

BEAN, GERRITT POST, ORGANIC CHEMISTRY. *Current Pos:* from assoc prof to prof, 67-87, EMER PROF CHEM, WESTERN ILL UNIV, 87-; VIS FEL, UNIV COLO, BOULDER, 87- *Personal Data:* b Amsterdam, NY, Apr 29, 29; m 93, Maria T Rauasio. *Educ:* Northeastern Univ, BS, 52; Pa State Univ, PhD(org chem), 56. *Prof Exp:* Process develop chemist, Merck & Co, Inc, 56-57; res chemist, Althouse Chem Co, Inc, 57-60; asst prof chem, Douglass Col, Rutgers Univ, 60-66; vis prof, Univ East Anglia, 66-67. *Mem:* AAAS; Am Chem Soc; The Chem Soc; fel Am Inst Chem. *Res:* Reactions and properties of 5-membered heterocycles; effect of substituents on reactions and properties of heterocycles; molecular orbital calculations. *Mailing Add:* 1140 Portland Pl Apt 105 Boulder CO 80304. *E-Mail:* gpbean@cechem.colorado.edu

BEAN, JOHN CONDON, SYNTHESIS & CHARACTERIZATION OF ELECTRONIC MATERIALS. *Current Pos:* JOHN MARSHALL MONEY PROF ELEC ENG, UNIV VA, 97- *Personal Data:* b Seattle, Wash, Sept 1, 50; m 71, Kristine M Jordan; c Emily K & Jeffrey C. *Educ:* Calif Inst Technol, BS, 72; Stanford Univ, MS, 74, PhD(appl physics), 76. *Prof Exp:* Mem tech staff solid state electronics, AT&T Bell Labs 76-85, distinguished mem tech staff, 85-86, head, Mat Sci Dept, 86-97. *Mem:* Am Phys Soc; fel Inst Elec & Electronics Engrs; Bohmische Phys Soc; Am Vacuum Soc; Electrochem Soc; Mat Res Soc. *Res:* Extension of conventional silicon technology through the addition of heterostructure physics and devices based on novel epitaxial materials. *Mailing Add:* Univ Va Thorton Hall Charlottesville VA 22903-2442. *Fax:* 908-582-3901; *E-Mail:* jcb@physics.att.com

BEAN, MICHAEL ARTHUR, PATHOLOGY, IMMUNOLOGY. *Current Pos:* MEM, PAC NORTHWEST RES FOUND, 88- *Personal Data:* b Alliance, Nebr, Sept 18, 40. *Educ:* Univ Colo, BA, 62, MD, 67. *Prof Exp:* Pathologist, Registry of Radiation Path, Armed Forces Inst Path, Washington, DC, 69; pathologist, Atomic Bomb Casualty Comn, Hiroshima, Japan, 69-70; assoc immunol, Sloan-Kettering Inst Cancer Res, 72-75, lab head tumor-host immunol, 74-75; sr investr, Va Mason Res Ctr, 75-77, assoc dir, 80-83, mem, 77-88. *Concurrent Pos:* Asst attend path, Mem Hosp, New York, 73-75; asst prof biol, Sloan-Kettering Div, Grad Sch, Cornell Univ, 74-75; affil investr, Fred Hutchinson Cancer Ctr, Seattle, 75-; affil assoc prof micro-immunology, Sch Med, Univ Wash, 76- *Mem:* AAAS; Am Asn Cancer Res; Am Asn Immunologists. *Res:* Tumor-host immunology; transplantation immunology. *Mailing Add:* Pac Northwest Res Found 720 Broadway Seattle WA 98122-4327

BEAN, RALPH J, MATHEMATICS. *Current Pos:* PROF MATH, STOCKTON STATE COL, 71- *Personal Data:* b Atlantic City, NJ, Aug 13, 33; m 59; c 3. *Educ:* Univ Pittsburgh, BS, 57, MA, 60; Univ Md, PhD(math), 62. *Prof Exp:* Res scientist, Lewis Lab, NASA, 57-58; from instr to asst prof math, Univ Wis, 62-67; assoc prof, Univ Tenn, 67-71. *Concurrent Pos:* Math Asn Am vis lectr, 63-; NSF res grants, 65-71; vis prof math, Univ Houston, 81-82. *Mem:* Am Math Soc; Math Asn Am; Nat Coun Teachers Math; Am Fedn Teachers. *Res:* Point set topology; Euclidian spaces and manifolds. *Mailing Add:* Stockton State Col Pomona NJ 08240-9999

BEAN, ROBERT JAY, GEOPHYSICS. *Current Pos:* CONSULT, 90- *Personal Data:* b Dallas, Tex, Aug 9, 24. *Educ:* Southern Methodist Univ, BS, 48; Harvard Univ, AM, 50, PhD(geophys), 51. *Prof Exp:* Geophysicist, Shell Oil Co, 51-89, geophys adv, 83-89. *Mem:* Soc Explor Geophys; Europ Soc Explor Geophys. *Res:* Gravity and magnetic interpretation. *Mailing Add:* 1108 W Tri Oaks Lane No 147 Houston TX 77043

BEAN, ROBERT TAYLOR, HYDROGEOLOGY, ENGINEERING GEOLOGY. *Current Pos:* CONSULT GEOLOGIST, 71- *Personal Data:* b Cherokee, Iowa, Feb 8, 13; m 53, Lois McAlister; c Donna E. *Educ:* Col Wooster, AB, 34; Ohio State Univ, MA, 42. *Prof Exp:* Asst geol, Stanford Univ, 46; geologist, US Geol Surv, 47; from jr to sr eng geologist, Calif Dept Water Resources, 47-56, supv eng geologist, 56-66; tech adv hydrogeol, UN, 66-71. *Concurrent Pos:* Consult, Chile-Calif Prog, 64; lectr, Calif State Univ, Northridge, 72-78; lectr, Calif State Univ, Los Angeles, 74-89; vis prof, Univ Calif, Los Angeles, 89-90. *Mem:* Fedn Am Sci; Asn Eng Geologists (pres, 60-61); fel Geol Soc Am; Am Geophys Union; Asn Ground Water Scientists & Engrs. *Res:* Water resources evaluation; international peace. *Mailing Add:* 650 W Harrison Ave Claremont CA 91711

BEAN, ROSS COLEMAN, biochemistry, for more information see previous edition

BEAN, VERN ELLIS, HIGH PRESSURE PHYSICS, PRESSURE METROLOGY. *Current Pos:* physicist, Nat Bur Stand, 72-88, PHYSICIST, NAT INST STAND & TECHNOL, 88- *Personal Data:* b La Grande, Ore, Jan 19, 37; m 61, Carol Allred; c Gregory, Scot, Charis & Laura. *Educ:* Brigham Young Univ, BS, 62, MS, 64, PhD(physics), 73. *Honors & Awards:* Bronze Medal, US Dept Comm, 81. *Prof Exp:* Physicist, Lawrence Radiation Lab, Univ Calif, Livermore, 64-67. *Concurrent Pos:* Consult, Egyptian Orgn Standardization, 81 & 85; consult, Nat Phys Lab, New Delhi, India, 83; vis prof, Inst Metrol, "G Colonnetti", Italy, 88. *Res:* Development of techniques for the accurate measurement of static and dynamic pressure; development of techniques for precise measurements at high pressure. *Mailing Add:* 9420 Gas House Pike Frederick MD 21701. *Fax:* 301-869-5924

BEAN, WENDELL CLEBERN, ELECTRICAL ENGINEERING. *Current Pos:* PROF ELEC ENG, LAMAR UNIV, 68- *Personal Data:* b Port Arthur, Tex, Apr 28, 34; m 61. *Educ:* Lamar State Col, BA & BS, 55; Univ Pittsburgh, MS, 58, PhD(elec eng), 61. *Prof Exp:* Jr engr, Westinghouse Elec Corp, 55; sr engr, Bettis Atomic Power Lab, 55-67; USPHS spec res fel, 67-68. *Mem:* Inst Elec & Electronics Engrs. *Res:* Signal processing, biological systems modeling. *Mailing Add:* Dept Elec Eng Lamar Univ PO Box 10029 Beaumont TX 77710

BEAN, WILLIAM CLIFTON, MATHEMATICS, AEROSPACE ENGINEERING. *Current Pos:* aerospace technologist flight simulator software design, Flight Crew Support Div, 63-66, aerospace technologist, Mission Planning & Anal Div, 66-71, AEROSPACE ENG, MISSION PLANNING & ANALYSIS DIV, NASA-JOHNSON SPACECRAFT CTR, 71- *Personal Data:* b Paris, Tex, Sept 10, 38. *Educ:* Univ Tex, Austin, BA, 59, MA, 60, PhD(math), 71. *Honors & Awards:* Apollo Achievement Award, NASA, 69. *Prof Exp:* Spec instr math, Univ Tex, Austin, 60-63. *Concurrent Pos:* Asst instr, Univ Tex, Austin, 70-71. *Mem:* Am Inst Aeronaut & Astronaut; Math Asn Am; Tensor Soc; NY Acad Sci. *Res:* Optimum interplanetary trajectory design; studies on extensor structures in the calculus of variations; space shuttle communication and data handling. *Mailing Add:* PO Box 58454 Houston TX 77258

BEAN, WILLIAM J, JR, VIROLOGY. *Current Pos:* res assoc, 75-77, asst mem virol, 77-82, ASSOC MEM, VIROL & MOLECULAR BIOL DIV, ST JUDE CHILDREN'S RES HOSP, 82- *Personal Data:* b Mar 16, 45; US citizen; div; c 1. *Educ:* Univ Maine, BS, 67, MS, 69; Rutgers Univ, PhD(microbiol), 74. *Prof Exp:* Fel virol, Waksman Inst Microbiol, Rutgers Univ, 74-75. *Concurrent Pos:* Asst prof microbiol, Ctr Health Sci, Univ Tenn, 81-85. *Mem:* Am Soc Microbiol; Int Soc Antiviral Res; Am Soc Virol. *Res:* Genetics and molecular biology of influenza virus. *Mailing Add:* 1755 Forrest Ave Memphis TN 38112

BEANE, DONALD GENE, MATHEMATICS, DISCRETE MATHEMATICS. *Current Pos:* from asst prof to prof, 66-94, EMER PROF MATH, COL WOOSTER, 94- *Personal Data:* b Aurora, Ill, Aug 25, 29; m 52, Marjorie Pixley; c David, John & Linda. *Educ:* Iowa Wesleyan Col, AB, 51; Univ Ill, MA, 58, PhD(math ed), 62; Ohio State Univ, MSc, 66. *Prof Exp:* Asst prof educ, 62-65. *Concurrent Pos:* Teaching fel, Great Lakes Cols Asn, 75-76. *Mem:* Math Asn Am; Nat Coun Teachers Math. *Res:* Mathematical education; discrete mathematics; combinatorics. *Mailing Add:* Dept Math Col Wooster Wooster OH 44691. *E-Mail:* beane@acs.wooster.edu

BEANS, ELROY WILLIAM, MECHANICAL ENGINEERING. *Current Pos:* from asst prof to assoc prof, 73-88, prof 88-, EMER PROF MECH ENG, UNIV TOLEDO, ASST CHMN, 89- *Personal Data:* b Toledo, Ohio, Dec 25, 31; m 54. *Educ:* Ohio State Univ, BME & MSc, 53; Pa State Univ, PhD(mech eng), 61. *Prof Exp:* Design engr, NAm Aviation, Inc, 54-56; instr mech eng, Pa State Univ, 56-58, res asst 58-59, instr aeronaut eng, 60-61; sr engr, Battelle Mem Inst, 61-64; group leader, NAm Aviation, Inc, 64-65, proj engr, 65-66; asst prof mech eng, Ohio State Univ, 66-70; tech specialist, Rockwell Int, 70-73. *Mem:* Am Soc Mech Engrs; Combustion Inst. *Res:* Propulsion; IC engines; combustion; gas dynamics; therymodynamics. *Mailing Add:* 3719 Fairwood Dr Sylvania OH 43560

BEAR, CHRISTINE ELEANOR, EPITHELIAL CELL ION TRANSPORT, CHLORIDA CHANNELS. *Current Pos:* asst prof, 88-93, ASSOC PROF PHYSIOL, UNIV TORONTO, 93-; SCIENTIST, RES INST, HOSP SICK CHILDREN, 93- *Personal Data:* b Toronto, Ont, May 29, 57; m, Kevin Graham; c Caitlin. *Educ:* Univ Toronto, BSc, 78, PhD(physiol), 84; McGill Univ, MSc, 81. *Honors & Awards:* Scientist Award, Med Res Coun, Can. *Concurrent Pos:* Scientist, Res Inst Hosp Sick Children, 87- *Res:* Study of epithelial cell ion transport processes; assessing the role of chloride channels in glandular cell secretion and volume regulation; study of cystic fibrosis transmembrane-conductance regulator a chloride channel and the protein product of the cystic fibrosis gene; use electrophysiology to study chloride channels; examination of ATPuse activity of cystic fibrosis transmembrane-conductance regulator; structural biology of cystic fibrosis transmembrane-conductive regulator; expression of circulating immune complex family of chloride channels; purification of circulating immune complex family of chloride channels. *Mailing Add:* Res Inst Hosp Sick Children 555 University Ave Toronto ON M5C 1X8 Can. *Fax:* 416-813-5028

BEAR, DAVID GEORGE, MECHANISMS OF GENE EXPRESSION. *Current Pos:* asst prof cell biol, 82-88, ASSOC PROF CELL BIOL, SCH MED, UNIV NMEX, 88-, DIR GRAD STUDIES, 89- *Personal Data:* b 1950. *Educ:* Univ Ariz, BS, 72; Univ Calif, Santa Cruz, PhD(chem), 78. *Prof Exp:* Res assoc, Univ Ore, 78-82. *Concurrent Pos:* NIH fel, 78-81. *Mem:* Elec Micros Soc Am. *Res:* Structure and function of transcriptional apparatus; mechanisms of polyadenylation and transcription termination. *Mailing Add:* Dept Cell Biol Sch Med Univ NMex Albuquerque NM 87131-5226

BEAR, HERBERT S, JR, ANALYSIS & FUNCTIONAL ANALYSIS. *Current Pos:* chmn dept, 69-74, grad chmn, 80-83, PROF MATH, UNIV HAWAII, MANOA, 69- *Personal Data:* b Philadelphia, Pa, Mar 13, 29; m 51, 84; c 2. *Educ:* Univ Calif, Berkeley, BA, 50, PhD(math), 57. *Prof Exp:* Instr math, Univ Ore, 55-56; assoc, Univ Calif, Berkeley, 56-57; from instr to asst prof, Univ Wash, 57-62; assoc prof, Univ Calif, Santa Barbara, 62-67; prof, NMex State Univ, 67-69. *Concurrent Pos:* Vis asst prof, Princeton Univ, 59-60; vis assoc prof, Univ Calif, San Diego, 65-66; trustee, Berkeley Math Sci Res Inst, 81-91. *Mem:* Am Math Soc; Math Asn Am. *Res:* Functional analysis. *Mailing Add:* Dept Math Univ Hawaii at Manoa Honolulu HI 96822

BEAR, JOHN L, INORGANIC CHEMISTRY. *Current Pos:* assoc prof, 63-72, PROF CHEM, UNIV HOUSTON, 72-, CHMN CHEM, 75- *Personal Data:* b Lampasas, Tex, Mar 6, 34; m 60; c 3. *Educ:* Southwest Tex State Col, BS, 55, MA, 56; Tex Tech Col, PhD(inorg chem), 60. *Prof Exp:* Fel inorg chem, Fla State Univ, 60-62, asst prof, 62-63. *Mem:* Am Chem Soc. *Res:* Fast reactions in solution; thermodynamics of metal ion complex formation in solution; dimeric metal complexes. *Mailing Add:* Col Nat Sci & Math Univ Houston Houston TX 77204-5502

BEAR, PHYLLIS DOROTHY, MICROBIAL GENETICS, MOLECULAR BIOLOGY. *Current Pos:* assoc prof, 68-74, PROF MOLECULAR BIOL, UNIV WYO, 74- *Personal Data:* b New York, NY, Aug 7, 31. *Educ:* San Diego State Col, BS, 56; Univ Calif, Los Angeles, PhD(microbiol), 66. *Prof Exp:* Res technician marine genetics, Scripps Inst, Univ Calif, 56-62. *Concurrent Pos:* Carnegie fel, Carnegie Inst, 66-68. *Mem:* AAAS; Am Soc Microbiol. *Res:* Structure and function of microbial nucleic acid; regulation of gene expression in bacterial viruses; pathogenesis of Anaplasma marginale. *Mailing Add:* 2626 Wyandotte St San Diego CA 92117

BEAR, RICHARD SCOTT, molecular biology, biophysics; deceased, see previous edition for last biography

BEARCE, DENNY N, GEOLOGY. *Current Pos:* MEM FAC, UNIV ALA, BIRMINGHAM, 77-, CHMN DEPT GEOL 77- & PROF GEOL, 81- *Personal Data:* b Pittsburgh, Pa, Nov 1, 34; m 57; c 2. *Educ:* Brown Univ, BA, 56; Mo Sch Mines, BS, 62, MS, 63; Univ Tenn, PhD(geol), 66. *Prof Exp:* Geologist, Mobile Oil Co, 63-64; asst prof geol, Eastern Ky Univ, 66-67; from asst prof to assoc prof geol, Birmingham-Southern Col, 67-73, chmn dept, 70-73. *Mem:* Am Asn Petrol Geol; fel Geol Soc Am. *Res:* Mapping and describing structure and stratigraphy of lower Cambrian and Precambrian rocks in Blue Ridge province of eastern Tennessee; structure and stratigraphy of Talladega Metamorphic Belt of east Alabama. *Mailing Add:* Dept Geol Univ Ala Univ Sta 1717 Seventh Ave S Birmingham AL 35294-0001

BEARCE, WINFIELD HUTCHINSON, ORGANIC CHEMISTRY. *Current Pos:* PROF, CENT COL, 87- *Personal Data:* b Lewiston, Maine, Oct 20, 37; m 61; c 2. *Educ:* Bowdoin Col, AB, 59; Lawrence Col, MS, 61, PhD, 64. *Prof Exp:* Sr res chemist, St Regis Paper Co, 64-66; assoc prof chem, Mo Valley Col, 66-80, prof chem & acad dean, 80-87; High Point Col, 83-87. *Mem:* Am Chem Soc. *Res:* Carbohydrate chemistry, particularly the stability, with respect to acid, of the glycosidic linkage in carbohydrate polymers; essential oils as a source of substrate for mechanistic studies. *Mailing Add:* 1113 Bruce Lane Pella IA 50219-1999

BEARD, BENJAMIN H, PLANT BREEDING & GENETICS. *Current Pos:* RETIRED. *Personal Data:* b Blair, Nebr, Jan 12, 18; m 45; c 1. *Educ:* Univ Mo, BS, 50, MS, 52; Univ Nebr, PhD(agron), 55. *Prof Exp:* Instr field crops, Univ Mo, 51-52; res geneticist, Sci & Educ Admin, Agr Res, USDA, Univ Minn, 55-60; res geneticist, Sci & Educ Admin, Agr Res, USDA, Univ Calif, 60-82. *Concurrent Pos:* Res assoc agron, Univ Nebr, 51-53; lectr, Univ Calif, 74-82. *Mem:* Am Genetic Asn; Crop Sci Soc; Sigma Xi; Am Soc Agron. *Res:* Radiation genetics; cytogenetics; breeding and genetics of oilseed crops; horticulture. *Mailing Add:* 6929 Radiance Circle Citrus Heights CA 95621

BEARD, CHARLES IRVIN, radiophysics, remote sensing, for more information see previous edition

BEARD, CHARLES NOBLE, GEOLOGY. *Current Pos:* EMER PROF GEOL, CALIF STATE UNIV, 70- *Personal Data:* b India, Dec 27, 06; m 33; c 1. *Educ:* Ind Univ, BA, 35, MA, 36; Univ Ill, PhD(geol), 41. *Concurrent Pos:* Cartographer, USAF, 42-46. *Mem:* Fel Geol Asn Am. *Res:* Columnar jointing of lava in California, Washington and Devil's Tower, Wyoming. *Mailing Add:* Calif State Univ 5241 N Maple Ave Fresno CA 93740-0001

BEARD, CHARLES WALTER, VETERINARY VIROLOGY. *Current Pos:* VPRES RES & TECHNOL, US POULTRY & EGG ASN, TUCKER, GA, 93- *Personal Data:* b Tifton, Ga, Nov 16, 32; m 60; c 4. *Educ:* Univ Ga, DVM, 55; Univ Wis, MS, 64, PhD(vet sci), 65. *Prof Exp:* Mem staff, USDA, 65-72, dir, Southeast Poultry Res Lab, Agr Res Serv, 72-93. *Mem:* Am Vet Med Asn; Am Asn Avian Path. *Res:* Aerobiology; respiratory diseases; viruses; techniques of aerosol exposure; influence of route of administration on host response. *Mailing Add:* 130 Red Fox Run Athens GA 30605

BEARD, DAVID BREED, theoretical physics, for more information see previous edition

BEARD, ELIZABETH L, PHYSIOLOGY-BLOOD FLUIDITY & ATHEROGENESIS. *Current Pos:* From instr to assoc prof, 55-68, PROF BIOL SCI, LOYOLA UNIV, LA, 68- *Personal Data:* b New Orleans, La, Apr 2, 32. *Educ:* Tex Christian Univ, BA, 52, BS, 53, MS, 55; Tulane Univ, PhD(physiol), 61. *Concurrent Pos:* Res assoc, Dept Physiol, Sch Med, Tulane Univ, 60-63; prof biol sci, Med Reinforcement & Enrichment Prog, Sch Med, Tulane Univ, 68-; vis prof, Dept Physiol, Harvard Med Sch, 83-84 & Mont State Univ, 94. *Mem:* AAAS; NY Acad Sci; Am Asn Univ Prof; Am Physiol Soc; Soc Exp Biol & Med. *Res:* Blood proteolytic activity, particularly as related to stress in mammals and to atherosclerosis. *Mailing Add:* 6127 Garfield New Orleans LA 70118. *Fax:* 504-865-2288

BEARD, GEORGE B, EXPERIMENTAL NUCLEAR PHYSICS. *Current Pos:* assoc prof, 60-65, chmn, Dept Physics, 73-77 & 80-81, actg chmn, Dept Comput Sci, 84-85, assoc dean, Col Lib Arts, 86, PROF PHYSICS, WAYNE STATE UNIV, 65- *Personal Data:* b Marblehead, Mass, Feb 22, 24; m 55; c 5. *Educ:* Harvard Univ, AB, 47; Univ Mich, MS, 48, PhD(physics), 55. *Prof Exp:* Asst, Univ Mich, 50-51; from instr to asst prof physics, Mich State Univ, 54-60. *Concurrent Pos:* Res prof, Dept Nuclear Eng, Univ Mich, 61; resident res assoc, Argonne Nat Lab, 63-65, resident assoc, 69-70; vis prof, Univ Melbourne, Australia, 81-82. *Mem:* Fel Am Phys Soc; Am Asn Physics Teachers. *Res:* Low energy nuclear spectroscopy; lifetimes of lowlying excited states; Mossbauer effect studies. *Mailing Add:* Dept Physics Wayne State Univ Detroit MI 48202

BEARD, JAMES B, STRESS PHYSIOLOGY, TURFGRASS CULTURE. *Current Pos:* PRES, INT SPORTS TURF INST INC, 92- *Personal Data:* b Piqua, Ohio, Sept 24, 35; m 55, Harriet J; c James C & John W. *Educ:* Ohio State Univ, BS, 57; Purdue Univ, MS, 59, PhD(environ plant physiol), 61. *Honors & Awards:* Hon Serv Award, Int Turfgrass Soc, 73; Service Recognition Award, Am Sod Producers Asn, 75; Oberly Award, Am Libr Asn, 78; Turfgrass Sci Award, Crop Sci Soc Am, 88, Crop Sci Res Award, 91. *Prof Exp:* From asst prof to prof environ physiol grasses, Mich State Univ, 61-75; prof environ physiol grasses, Tex A&M Univ, 75-92, interim head soil & crop sci, 80. *Concurrent Pos:* NSF Post-doctoral fel, 69-70. *Mem:* Int Turfgrass Soc (pres, 69); fel Am Soc Agron; fel Crop Sci Soc Am (pres, 86); Am Soc Hort Sci; Coun Agr Sci & Technol; fel AAAS. *Res:* Microenvironment and physiology of heat, cold, drought and wear stresses in perennial turf grasses; shade adaptation; rooting; turfgrass culture; sod production and utilization; sports field and golf course turfgrass culture; root zone stabilization. *Mailing Add:* Int Sports Turf Inst 1812 Shadowood Dr College Station TX 77840. *Fax:* 409-693-4787

BEARD, JAMES DAVID, MEDICAL PHYSIOLOGY, PHARMACOLOGY. *Current Pos:* from instr to assoc prof physiol & biophys, 65-93, assoc prof psychiat, 74-82, DIR, ALCOHOL RES CTR, UNIV TENN, MEMPHIS, 67-, PROF PSYCHIAT, COL MED, 82-, PROF

PHYSIOL & BIOPHYSICS, 93- *Personal Data:* b Dayton, Ohio, July 21, 37; m 59, Patricia A Brown; c James G & Christopher P. *Educ:* DePauw Univ, BA, 59; Univ Tenn, PhD(physiol), 63. *Honors & Awards:* James H Tharp Award Alcohol Res, 74. *Prof Exp:* Instr & fel physiol, Sch Med, Marquette Univ, 63-65. *Concurrent Pos:* Physiologist, Res Serv, Vet Admin Hosp, Wood, Wis, 63-65; Nat Acad Sci-Nat Comn Int Unit Physiol Sci travel grant, Tokyo, 65; dir, Alcohol & Drug Res Ctr & Clin Labs, Memphis Ment Health Inst, 67-, dir res, 72-; mem bd, Nat Coun Alcoholism; mem res initial rev group, Study Sect, Nat Inst Alcohol Abuse & Alcoholism, 76-79, chairperson, 77-78, chairperson, Biomed Sect, 79; mem, bd dirs, Res Soc Alcoholism, 87-91. *Mem:* Sigma Xi; Res Soc Alcoholism (treas, 93-); AAAS; Soc Neurosci; Int Soc Biomed Res Alcoholism. *Res:* Pathophysiology of acute and chronic alcoholism; cardiovascular dynamics; fluid and electrolyte metabolism including trace metals; renal physiology; genetics and ethanol metabolism. *Mailing Add:* Univ Tenn PO Box 40966 Memphis TN 38174-0966

BEARD, JAMES TAYLOR, HEAT TRANSFER, THERMAL SYSTEMS DESIGN & ANALYSIS. *Current Pos:* asst prof, 65-69, asst provost, Acad Space Admin, 72-77, ASSOC PROF ENG, UNIV VA, 69- *Personal Data:* b Birmingham, Ala, Oct 1, 39; m 65; c 2. *Educ:* Auburn Univ, BME, 61; Okla State Univ, MS, 63, PhD(mech eng), 65. *Prof Exp:* Res asst eng, Okla State Univ, 64-65. *Concurrent Pos:* Partner, Assoc Environ Consults, 71-; lectr solar energy & energy policy, Pakistan & Cyprus, US Info Angecy, 78; mem, Tech Adv Comt, Va Air Pollution Control Bd, 78-87. *Mem:* Am Soc Mech Engrs; Am Soc Heating, Refrig & Air-Conditioning Engrs; Air Pollution Control Asn. *Res:* Convective heat and mass transfer; solar energy; combustion; thermal sciences; radiation heat transfer. *Mailing Add:* JT Beard Inc 2 James St No 3A Frederick MD 21701

BEARD, JEAN, SCIENCE EDUCATION. *Current Pos:* assoc prof, 69-80, PROF NATURAL SCI & DIR SCI EDUC, SAN JOSE STATE UNIV, 80- *Personal Data:* b Cedar Falls, Iowa, Apr 12, 34. *Educ:* State Univ Iowa, BA, 56; Univ Northern Iowa, MA, 60; Ore State Univ, PhD(sci educ), 69. *Prof Exp:* Teacher jr high sch, Minn, 56-59 & 60-61; instr prof educ & sci supvr, Mankato State Col, Wilson Campus Sch, 61-65; part-time instr sci educ, Ore State Univ, 65-68. *Mem:* Nat Asn Biol Teachers; Nat Sci Teachers Asn; Nat Asn Res Sci Teaching. *Res:* Assessment of science achievements by students in general education science, kindergarten-14th grade, including science processes, science knowledge and attitudes about natural phenomena and organisms; rational general education about energy alternatives. *Mailing Add:* Dept Biol Sci San Jose State Univ One Washington Sq San Jose CA 95192-0001

BEARD, KENNETH VAN KIRKE, ATMOSPHERIC SCIENCE, PHYSICS. *Current Pos:* PROF & PRIN SCIENTIST, DEPT ATMOSPHERIC SCI, ILL STATE WATER SURV, UNIV ILL, 74- *Personal Data:* b Cheyenne, Wyo, Apr 9, 37; m 63, Lynn J Grenwalt; c 3. *Educ:* Calif State Univ, Los Angeles, BSc, 66; Univ Calif, Los Angeles, MSc, 68, PhD(meteorol), 70. *Prof Exp:* Res meteorologist, Univ Calif, Los Angeles, 68-70 & 71-74; vis scientist, Nat Ctr Atmospheric Res, 70-71. *Concurrent Pos:* Environ Protection grant, 72-75; NSF grants, 75-95. *Mem:* Fel Am Meteorol Soc; Am Geophys Union; AAAS; Am Asn Aerosol Res; Sigma Xi. *Res:* Cloud and precipitation physics; aerosol physics; atmospheric scavenging; radar meterology; drop dynamics and interactions. *Mailing Add:* Dept Atmospheric Sci Univ Ill 105 S Gregory Dr Urbana IL 61801

BEARD, LEO ROY, WATER RESOURCES ENGINEERING, HYDROLOGY. *Current Pos:* SR STAFF ENGR, ESPEY HUSTON & ASSOC, 80- *Personal Data:* b West Baden, Ind, Apr 6, 17; m 39, 74, Marjorie P Wood; c Patricia M (Huntzicker), Thomas E & James R. *Educ:* Calif Inst Technol, BS, 39. *Honors & Awards:* Hunter Rouse Award; Julian Hinds Award, Am Soc Civil Engrs. *Prof Exp:* Engr, Corps Engrs, Los Angeles, 39-49, Off, Chief of Engrs, 49-52 & Corps Engrs, Sacramento, 52-64, dir hydrol eng ctr, 64-72; prof civil eng & dir, Ctr Res Water Resources, Univ Tex, Austin, 72-80. *Concurrent Pos:* US Navy, 45-46; vis lectr, Univ Calif, 66-67, Utah State Univ, 67 & Univ Calif, Davis, 70-72; consult, H G Acres Ltd, Can, Tex Water Develop Bd, Calif Dept Water Resources, Sask-Nelson Basin Bd, Can, Aleyeska Pipeline Co, Electrobras of Brazil & others. *Mem:* Nat Acad Eng; Am Geophys Union; hon mem Am Soc Civil Engrs; hon mem Am Water Resources Asn; fel Int Water Resources Asn; fel AAAS. *Res:* Analysis of water resource systems; simulation of stochastic processes in hydrology. *Mailing Add:* 606 Laurel Valley Rd Austin TX 78746

BEARD, LUTHER STANFORD, SYSTEMATIC BOTANY. *Current Pos:* assoc prof, Campbell Univ, NC, 61-67, chmn, Biol Dept, 63-76, prof, 67-94, EMER PROF BIOL, CAMPBELL UNIV, NC, 94- *Personal Data:* b Langley, SC, Feb 21, 29; m 52; c 2. *Educ:* Furman Univ, BS, 50; Univ NC, MA, 59, PhD(bot), 64. *Prof Exp:* Teacher high sch, SC, 55-58; instr biol, Furman Univ, 58-59. *Mem:* Am Soc Plant Taxon; Soc Study Evolution; Sigma Xi. *Res:* Taxonomy of the genus Schrankia and its relation to the genus Mimosa. *Mailing Add:* 502 Gregory Circle Buies Creek NC 27506

BEARD, MARGARET ELZADA, CELL BIOLOGY. *Current Pos:* SR SCIENTIST & LECTR, DEPT BIOL, COLUMBIA UNIV, 82-; SR SCIENTIST, NATHAN KLINE INST PSYCHIAT RES, 88- *Personal Data:* b Washington, DC, Oct 17, 41. *Educ:* Wellesley Col, BA, 63; Univ Mich, MS, 65, PhD(zool), 67. *Prof Exp:* Fel path, Albert Einstein Col Med, 67-69, asst prof, 69-70; asst prof res ophthal, Sch Med, Univ Ore, 72-75; asst prof biol, 75-81, sr res biologist & dir micros, Reed Col, 81-82. *Concurrent Pos:* Horace H Rackham fel; NIH fel. *Mem:* Am Soc Cell Biol; NY Acad Sci; AAAS; Histochem Soc; Sigma Xi. *Res:* Investigations of the structure and function of peroxisomes; role of endocytosis in Alzheimer's disease; interrelation of nitric oxide and peroxisomes. *Mailing Add:* NK1 Bldg 37 Rockland City Psychiat Ctr Orangeburg NY 10962

BEARD, OWEN WAYNE, INTERNAL MEDICINE, CARDIOLOGY. *Current Pos:* CHIEF GERIAT, SCH MED SCI, UNIV ARK, LITTLE ROCK, 75-, EMER PROF MED, 84- *Personal Data:* b Wattensaw, Ark, Nov 15, 16; wid; c Margaret (Miller), William K & BarbaraJo (Pierce). *Educ:* Okla State Univ, 37-39; Univ Ark, BSM & MD, 43; Am Bd Internal Med, dipl, 50. *Prof Exp:* Instr med, Med Br, Univ Tex, 45-47; from asst prof to prof med, Sch Med, Univ Ark, Little Rock, 47-84; chief geriat, Vet Admin Hosp, Little Rock, 75-84. *Concurrent Pos:* Asst chief med, Vet Admin Hosp, Little Rock, 55-75. *Mem:* Am Heart Asn; Am Col Physicians; fel Am Col Cardiol; Geront Soc; fel Am Geriat Soc. *Res:* Cardiovascular disease. *Mailing Add:* 7008 Rockwood Rd Little Rock AR 72207

BEARD, RICHARD B, ELECTRICAL & BIOMEDICAL ENGINEERING. *Current Pos:* assoc prof, 65-72, dir, Biomed Eng & Sci Inst, 74-78, PROF ELEC ENG, DREXEL UNIV, 72-, LESTER A KRAUS PROF, ELEC CHEM ENG DEPT. *Personal Data:* b Boston, Mass, Dec 17, 22; m 48; c 3. *Educ:* Northeastern Univ, BS, 47; Lowell Technol Inst, cert, 48; Harvard Univ, SMEE, 50; Univ Pa, PhD(elec eng), 65. *Prof Exp:* Chemist, Weymouth Artificial Leather Co, 47-48; appln engr, Minneapolis-Honeywell Regulator Co, 50-54, res engr, 54-57; instr elec eng, Drexel Univ, 58-60; res assoc, Univ Pa, 60-65. *Concurrent Pos:* Consult, Johnson & Johnson, 77- & Stand Pressed Steel, 78- *Mem:* Acoust Soc Am; Inst Elec & Electronics Engrs; Am Chem Soc; Soc Biomat; NY Acad Sci. *Res:* Biomaterials; bioelectrochemistry; biophysics; dielectric and ultrasonic measurements on macro molecules; polyelectrolytes and tissue; correlation of biocompatability and electrode impedance for stimulating electrodes; integrity of Latex & Plastic barriers. *Mailing Add:* 21 Willow Way Atco NJ 08004-1339

BEARD, RODNEY RAU, PREVENTIVE MEDICINE, ENVIRONMENTAL HEALTH. *Current Pos:* from instr to prof pub health & prev med, Stanford Univ, 40-69, exec, 49-69, dir rehab, 55-60, prof family, community & prev med, 69-77, EMER PROF PREV MED, SCH MED, STANFORD UNIV, 77- *Personal Data:* b Guinda, Calif, Dec 27, 11; m 38, Marion L Harper; c Julie A, Philip, Marian & Edin. *Educ:* Stanford Univ, AB, 32, MD, 38; Harvard Univ, MPH, 40; Am Bd Prev Med, dipl, 49. *Prof Exp:* Clin lab technician, French Hosp, San Francisco, 33-37; intern, Gorgas Hosp, CZ, 37-38; asst resident pub health & prev med, Hosps & instr, Nursing Sch, Stanford Univ, 38-39; Rockefeller fel med sci, Sch Pub Health, Harvard Univ, 39-40. *Concurrent Pos:* Med dir, Pac Div, Pan Am Airways, 40-49; mem comn A, Comt Aviation Med, Nat Res Coun, 41-47, mem comt effects of atmospheric contaminants on human health & welfare, 68-70; clin prof, Sch Pub Health, Univ Calif, 52-64, lectr, 64-72; dept dir comn environ hyg, Armed Forces Epidemiol Bd, 54-56, dir, 56-66, mem, 66-73; consult indust med, US Vet Admin, 54-67; consult, Off Surgeon Gen, US Dept Army, 54-73; mem, Nat Adv Heart Coun, NIH, 57-61, mem, Nat Adv Coun Environ Health Sci, 71-74, consult to dir, Nat Inst Environ Health Sci, 74-75; vis prof, Univ Milan, 60-61; trustee, Am Bd Prev Med, 61-70; mem, Nat Adv Coun Pub Health Training, 65-69; consult, Surgeon Gen, USAF, 66-69; mem tech adv comt, Calif Air Resources Bd, 69-72; mem subcomt atherosclerosis, Intersoc Comn Heart Dis Resources, 69-71; consult, Calif Dept Health Servs, 52-; vis prof, Univ Occup & Environ Health, Kitakyushu, Japan, 80; mem, Biomet & Epidemiol Contract Rev Comt, Nat Cancer Inst, NIH, HEW, 82-85. *Mem:* Fel Am Pub Health Asn; fel Am Acad Occup Med; Soc Occup & Environ Health; Asn Teachers Prev Med (pres, 58-59); fel Am Col Prev Med; fel AAAS. *Res:* Occupational medicine; air pollution; epidemiology; behavior toxicology. *Mailing Add:* Stanford Med Ctr Stanford CA 94305-5092. *E-Mail:* rbeard@leland.stanford.edu

BEARD, WILLIAM CLARENCE, MINERALOGY. *Current Pos:* asst prof, 67-69, ASSOC PROF GEOL, CLEVELAND STATE UNIV, 69- *Personal Data:* b Gallipolis, Ohio, June 9, 34; m 60. *Educ:* Ohio State Univ, BSc, 60, PhD(mineral), 65. *Prof Exp:* Res chemist, Linde Div, Union Carbide Corp, 65-67. *Mem:* Mineral Soc Am; Nat Asn Geol Teachers. *Res:* High temperature phase equilibrium of minerals and ceramics; crystal chemistry; hydrothermal synthesis; crystal growth; thermal analysis of minerals and ceramics. *Mailing Add:* 166 Carman Dr Apt 101 Gallipolis OH 45631

BEARD, WILLIAM QUINBY, JR, INDUSTRIAL CHEMISTRY. *Current Pos:* SR RES CHEMIST, RES & DEVELOP LAB, CHEM DIV, VULCAN MAT CO, 68- *Personal Data:* b Beaufort, SC, Apr 10, 32; m 57; c 2. *Educ:* Univ NC, BS, 54; Duke Univ, PhD(org chem), 59. *Prof Exp:* Res fel chem, Duke Univ, 59-60; res chemist, Ethyl Corp, La, 60-68. *Mem:* Am Chem Soc. *Res:* Chlorinated hydrocarbons. *Mailing Add:* 9328 Briarwood Ct Wichita KS 67212-4275

BEARDALL, JOHN SMITH, PHYSICS, ASTRONOMY. *Current Pos:* TECH STAFF, ANALYTICAL SCIS CORP, 87- *Personal Data:* b Springville, Utah, Feb 4, 39; m 68; c 5. *Educ:* Brigham Young Univ, BA, 60, MS, 68. *Prof Exp:* Develop engr, Hercules Inc, 61-67; staff mem physics, Los Alamos Nat Lab, Univ Calif, 69-87. *Mem:* Optical Soc Am. *Res:* Remote sensing, arms control verification, sensors. *Mailing Add:* 9802 Meadow Knoll Ct Vienna VA 22181

BEARDEN, ALAN JOYCE, BIOPHYSICS. *Current Pos:* res biophysicist & lectr, 69-72, res biophysicist & adj assoc prof biophysics, Donner Lab & Div Med Physics, 73-76, chmn dept, 78-84, prof 76-93, EMER PROF BIOPHYSICS, DONNER LAB, UNIV CALIF, BERKELEY, 93- *Personal Data:* b Baltimore, Md, Nov 23, 31. *Educ:* Johns Hopkins Univ, AB, 50, PhD(physics), 59. *Honors & Awards:* Teaching Apparatus Award, Am Asn Physics Teachers, 62. *Prof Exp:* Instr physics, Univ Wis-Madison, 59-60; asst prof, Cornell Univ, 60-64; NIH spec fel biophysics, Univ Calif, San Diego, 64-66, asst prof chem, 66-68. *Concurrent Pos:* USPHS res career develop award, 70-75; fac sr scientist, Lawrence Berkeley Lab. *Mem:* Fel Am Phys Soc; Biophys Soc; AAAS. *Res:* Auditory transduction, cochlear dynamics; physics of energy transduction processes in biology; applications of electron spin resonance and lasers to biophysics; laser-feedback microscopy. *Mailing Add:* 1322 Queens Rd Univ Calif Berkeley CA 94708-2114. *Fax:* 510-549-2240; *E-Mail:* healey@garnet.berkely.edu

BEARDEN, HENRY JOE, REPRODUCTIVE PHYSIOLOGY. *Current Pos:* RETIRED. *Personal Data:* b Starkville, Miss, May 12, 26; m 46; c 3. *Educ:* Miss State Univ, BS, 50; Univ Tenn, MS, 51; Cornell Univ, PhD(animal breeding), 54. *Prof Exp:* Instr dairy, Univ Tenn, 51; asst prof dairy exten & res, Cornell Univ, 54-60; prof dairy sci & head dept, Miss State Univ, 60-90. *Mem:* Am Dairy Sci Asn; Soc Study Reproduction; US Animal Health Asn; Sigma Xi. *Res:* Animal physiology; dairy cattle genetics. *Mailing Add:* 1892 Hickory Dr Starkville MS 39759

BEARDEN, WILLIAM HARLIE, PHYSICAL ORGANIC CHEMISTRY. *Current Pos:* app chemist, 84-87, NMR PROD MGR, JEOL, 87-, MGR, ANAL INSTRUMENTS DIV, JEOL, 90- *Personal Data:* b Kileen, Tex, Aug 18, 49; m 70; c 3. *Educ:* Centenary Col, BS, 71; Univ Houston, PhD(chem), 75. *Prof Exp:* NSF res asst chem, Calif Inst Technol, 75-77; asst prof chem, Jackson State Univ, 77-84. *Mem:* Am Chem Soc; Am Soc Testing & Mat. *Res:* Structure determinations of organic compounds using nuclear magnetic resonance via nonclassical methods, solid state NMR. *Mailing Add:* JEOL 11 Dearborn Rd Peabody MA 01960-3823

BEARDMORE, PETER, PHYSICAL METALLURGY. *Current Pos:* MGR, DEPT MAT SCI, SCI RES STAFF, FORD MOTOR CO, 66-, DIR, CHEM & PHYSICS SCI LABS, 92- *Personal Data:* b Stoke-on-Trent, Eng, Aug 5, 35; m 58; c 1. *Educ:* Univ Sheffield, BMet, 58; Univ Liverpool, PhD(metall), 66. *Prof Exp:* Res metallurgist, English Elec Co, 58-60; mem res staff metall, Mass Inst Technol, 60-63; res fel, Univ Liverpool, 63-66. *Mem:* Am Inst Mining, Metall & Petrol Eng; Am Soc Metals. *Res:* Deformation and fracture of materials; mechanical properties of body centered cubic metals and of polymeric materials, including fatigue behavior. *Mailing Add:* Dept Chem & Physics Sci Res Staff Ford Motor Co PO Box 2053 Dearborn MI 48121

BEARDMORE, WILLIAM BOONE, MICROBIOLOGY. *Current Pos:* MGR, CELL & TISSUE CULT RES DEPT, WARNER LAMBERT DIAG, 81- *Personal Data:* b Salem, Ohio, Aug 14, 25; m 48; c 2. *Educ:* Ohio State Univ, BSc, 48, MSc, 50, PhD(bact), 53. *Prof Exp:* From asst to asst instr bact, Ohio State Univ, 48-53; assoc res microbiologist virol, Parke, Davis & Co, 53-56, mgr biol control dept, 56-63, from res virologist to sr res virologist, 63-67, lab dir, 67-81. *Mem:* AAAS; Am Soc Microbiol; Sigma Xi. *Res:* Viruses and tissue cultures. *Mailing Add:* 213 Nesbit Lane Rochester MI 48309-2174

BEARDSLEE, RONALD ALLEN, CLINICAL CHEMISTRY. *Current Pos:* res scientist clin chem, 74-79, ASST DIR, RES DEPT, BIO-SCI LABS, 79- *Personal Data:* b Asheville, NC, Feb 1, 46; m 70. *Educ:* Univ Calif, Santa Barbara, BS, 68, PhD(chem), 72. *Prof Exp:* Presidential intern protein res, Western Regional Res Ctr, USDA, 72-73. *Mem:* Am Chem Soc; Am Asn Clin Chem. *Res:* Development of new chemical and physical methods for the analysis of materials of clinical significance. *Mailing Add:* Smith Kline Beecham 6511 Golden Gate Dr Dublin CA 94568-2907

BEARDSLEY, GEORGE PETER, BIO-ORGANIC CHEMISTRY. *Current Pos:* res fel pediat hemat, 76-79, instr pediat, 79-81, ASST PROF PEDIAT, MED SCH, HARVARD UNIV, 81-; PROF PEDIAT & PHARMACOL, YALE UNIV, 85-, CHIEF, PEDIAT HEMAT/ONCOL. *Personal Data:* b New York, NY, Dec 29, 40; m 72; c 1. *Educ:* Mass Inst Technol, BS, 67; Princeton Univ, PhD(chem), 71; Duke Univ, MD, 74. *Honors & Awards:* Fac Res Award, Am Cancer Soc. *Prof Exp:* Resident physician pediat, Yale New Haven Hosp, Yale Univ, 74-76. *Concurrent Pos:* Dir, Pediat Oncol Prog, Yale Comprehensive Cancer Ctr. *Mem:* Am Asn Cancer Res; Am Chem Soc; Am Soc Hemat; Soc Pediat Res. *Res:* Bio-organic chemistry of purines and pteridinos; mechanisms of drug action; pediatric hematology and oncology. *Mailing Add:* Dept Pediat Yale Univ 333 Cedar St New Haven CT 06510

BEARDSLEY, IRENE ADELAIDE, MAGNETIC RECORDING, MAGNETISM & MAGNETIC MATERIALS. *Personal Data:* b San Diego, Calif, Aug 18, 35; m 86, Dan S Bloomberg; c Carolyn D Ortenburger & Teresa A Ortenburger. *Educ:* Stanford Univ, BS, 57, MS, 58, PhD(physics), 65. *Prof Exp:* Scientist, Space Physics Dept, Lockheed Missiles & Space Co, 58-62, res scientist, Mat Sci Lab, Calif, 66-69; consult, Almaden Res Ctr, IBM Corp, San Jose, Calif, 69-76, res staff mem, 76-93. *Mem:* Am Phys Soc; Sigma Xi; sr mem Inst Elec & Electronics Engrs; Magnetics Soc. *Res:* Theoretical studies of magnetic recording. *Mailing Add:* 1013 Paradise Way Palo Alto CA 94306. *E-Mail:* ireneab@aol.com

BEARDSLEY, JOHN WYMAN, JR, ENTOMOLOGY. *Current Pos:* from assoc prof entom & assoc entomologist to prof entom & entomologist, 68-92, EMER PROF ENTOM & ENTOMOLOGIST, UNIV HAWAII, 92- *Personal Data:* b Los Angeles, Calif, Mar 25, 26; m 48, 83; c Steven, Laurel, John R & Claire. *Educ:* Univ Calif, BS, 50; Univ Hawaii, MS & PhD, 63. *Prof Exp:* Asst entomologist, US Trust Territory Pac Islands, 52-54; from asst to assoc entomologist, Exp Sta, Hawaiian Sugar Planters Asn, 54-72; assoc prof entom, Univ Hawaii, 63-66; assoc res entomologist, Univ Calif, Berkeley, 66-68. *Concurrent Pos:* Chmn, Dept Entom, Univ Hawaii, 81-; consult entomologist, ABA Int, Bangladesh, 84; Fulbright sr res scholar, La Trobe Univ, Melbourne Inst, 71-72. *Mem:* Am Entom Soc; Int Org Biol Control. *Res:* Taxonomy of scale insects and parasitic wasps; insect biology; biological control; sugar cane and pineapple entomology. *Mailing Add:* Dept Entom Univ Hawaii Manoa Honolulu HI 96822

BEARDSLEY, ROBERT CRUCE, PHYSICAL OCEANOGRAPHY. *Current Pos:* assoc scientist, 75-81, dept chmn, 85-90, SR SCIENTIST, WOODS HOLE OCEANOG INST, 81-, DIR, COASTAL RES CTR, 92- *Personal Data:* b Jacksonville, Fla, Jan 28, 42; m 66, Susan Keller; c Elizabeth & Jean. *Educ:* Mass Inst Technol, BS, 64, PhD(oceanog), 68. *Prof Exp:* From asst prof to assoc prof oceanog, Mass Inst Technol, 67-75. *Mem:* Fel AAAS; Am Geophys Union; Am Meteorol Soc. *Res:* Geophysical fluid dynamics; coastal oceanography. *Mailing Add:* 38 Mares Pond Dr East Falmouth MA 02536. *E-Mail:* rbeardsley@whoi.edu

BEARDSLEY, ROBERT EUGENE, MICROBIOLOGY, GENETICS. *Current Pos:* dean, Sch Arts & Sci, 77-83, prof, 77-97, EMER PROF BIOL, IONA COL, 97- *Personal Data:* b Walton, NY, June 11, 23; m 48; c 3. *Educ:* Manhattan Col, BS, 50; Columbia Univ, AM, 51, PhD(zool), 60. *Prof Exp:* From instr to assoc prof, Manhattan Col, 51-68, dir, Lab Plant Morphogenesis, 62-69, prof biol, 68-77, head dept, 69-77, vis prof biol, 77-80. *Concurrent Pos:* Guggenheim fel, 66; vis investr, Inst Paris, 66-67 & Univ Paris, 75. *Mem:* Am Pub Health Asn; Sigma Xi; Am Soc Microbiol. *Res:* Mechanisms of tumor induction in crown gall. *Mailing Add:* 242 Mountaindale Rd Yonkers NY 10710-3512

BEARE, STEVEN DOUGLAS, ORGANIC CHEMISTRY, PHYSICAL CHEMISTRY. *Current Pos:* SR RES ASSOC, E I DU PONT DE NEMOURS & CO, 69- *Personal Data:* b Detroit, Mich, May 31, 44; m 65; c 2. *Educ:* Oakland Univ, BA, 65; Univ Ill, Urbana-Champaign, MS, 67, PhD(org chem), 69. *Prof Exp:* Teaching asst chem, Univ Ill, 65-67, res asst org chem, 67-69. *Mem:* Am Chem Soc; Am Inst Aeronaut & Astronaut. *Res:* Determinations of optical purities and correlations of absolute configurations of alcohols, hydroxy acids, amino acids, amines, sulfoxides and phosphine oxides by nuclear magnetic resonance spectroscopy in chiral solvents. *Mailing Add:* 7 Brookland Ave Wilmington DE 19805

BEARER, ELAINE L, ANATOMIC PATHOLOGY. *Current Pos:* ASST PROF, BROWN UNIV, 91- *Personal Data:* c 2. *Educ:* NY Univ, MA, 73; Univ Calif, San Francisco, PhD(exp path), 82, MD, 83. *Prof Exp:* Fel biochem path, Univ Calif, San Francisco, 86-91. *Mem:* Am Soc Cell Biol. *Res:* Transformation of the radially symmetric egg into a complex life-form; shape-changes and migrations of specific populations of cells. *Mailing Add:* Div Biol & Med Brown Univ Box G BMC 502 Providence RI 02912

BEARE-ROGERS, JOYCE LOUISE, BIOCHEMISTRY, NUTRITION. *Current Pos:* RETIRED. *Personal Data:* b Ont, Sept 8, 27; m 61, Charles G Rogers; c Anne C. *Educ:* Univ Toronto, BA, 51, MA, 52; Carleton Univ, Ont, PhD(biochem), 66. *Hon Degrees:* DSc, Univ Man, 85; DSC Univ Guelph, 93. *Honors & Awards:* Borden Award, Nutrit Soc Can, 72; Queen's Silver Jubilee Medal, 77; Medaille Chevreul, 84; Normann Medal, 87; Earle Willard McHenry Award, Can Soc, 93. *Prof Exp:* Instr physiol, Vassar Col, 54-56; res scientist, Bur Nutrit Sci, Food Directorate, Ottawa, 56-75, chief, nutrit res, 75-91; consult, Food & Agr Orgn UN, Rome, Italy, 92-93. *Concurrent Pos:* Non-resident prof, Dept Biochem, Univ Ottawa; mem, Order of Can, 92. *Mem:* Am Inst Nutrit; Am Oil Chemists Soc; Can Biochem Soc; Can Soc Nutrit Sci; Can Athero Soc; fel Royal Soc Can. *Res:* Effects of dietary components on tissue phospholipids; nutritional aspects of oils and fats. *Mailing Add:* 41 Okanagan Dr Nepean ON K1A 0L2 Can

BEARMAN, RICHARD JOHN, PHYSICAL CHEMISTRY, CHEMICAL PHYSICS. *Current Pos:* prof, 72-97, EMER PROF CHEM, UNIV NSW, 97- *Personal Data:* b New York, NY, June 23, 29; m 61, Mirion Yang; c 2. *Educ:* Cornell Univ, AB, 51; Stanford Univ, PhD(chem), 56. *Prof Exp:* Asst, Yale Univ, 56-57; from asst prof to prof chem, Univ Kans, 57-71. *Concurrent Pos:* Guggenheim fel, 62-63; vis reader, Univ New Eng, Australia, 68-69; hon fel, Res Sch Phys Sci, Australian Nat Univ, 68-69. *Mem:* Am Chem Soc; Am Phys Soc; fel Am Inst Chemists; fel Royal Australian Chem Inst. *Res:* Statistical mechanics and thermodynamics of irreversible processes; membrane permeation; thermal diffusion in liquids; equilibrium theory of fluids; P-V-T measurements. *Mailing Add:* Dept Chem Univ New South Wales ADFA Univ Col Northcutt Dr Canberra ACT 2600 Australia

BEARN, ALEXANDER GORDON, PHARMACEUTICAL ADMINISTRATION, GENETICS. *Current Pos:* ADJ PROF, ROCKEFELLER UNIV, 66- *Personal Data:* b Cheam, Eng, Mar 29, 23; US citizen; m 52, Slocom; c Helen E & Gordon C F. *Educ:* Univ London, MB & BS, 46, MD, 51; FRCP(E), 68; FRCP, 70. *Hon Degrees:* MD, Cath Univ, Korea, 68; Dr, Univ Rene Descartes, Paris, 75. *Honors & Awards:* Lowell Lectr, Harvard Univ, 58; Murray Gordon Lectr, Downstate Med Ctr, 62; Augustus B Wadsworth Lectr, NY State Dept Health, 62; Stevenson Mem Lectr, Presby Hosp, 63; Louis Gross Mem Lectr, NY Univ, 69; Lilly Lectr, Royal Col Physicians, 73; Harvey Lectr, 75; Mary H Edens Lectr, Univ Tex, 75; Lettsomian Lectr, Med Soc London, 76; Abernethian Lectr, St Bartholomew's Hosp, 77; Rufus Cole Lectr, Rockefeller Univ, 80. *Prof Exp:* Intern, Guy's Hosp, London, 46-47, serv, 47-49; intern & resident, Post-Grad Med Sch, Univ London, 49-51; from asst to assoc, Rockefeller Univ, 51-57, from asst physician to sr physician, 51-66, from assoc prof to prof, 57-66,; prof med & chem dept, Med Col, Cornell Univ, 66-77, Stanton Griffis distinguished med prof, 76-79; sr vpres, Med & Sci Affairs, Merck Sharp & Dohme Int, 79-88. *Concurrent Pos:* Mem, Genetics Training Comt, USPHS,

61-65, Genetics Study Sect, 66-70, Comn Human Health Resources, Nat Acad Sci, 73-78, Adv Comt Radiation Effects, 75-81 & 82-87; physician-in-chief, NY Hosp, 66-77; vis prof, var US & foreign univs, 71-81; trustee, Harold Hughes Med Inst. *Mem:* Nat Acad Sci; fel AAAS; Am Philos Soc; Harvey Soc (pres, 72); Am Soc Human Genetics (pres, 71); Sigma Xi. *Res:* Human genetics; internal medicine. *Mailing Add:* Rockefeller Univ 1230 York Ave New York NY 10021-6399

BEARSE, GORDON EVERETT, poultry science; deceased, see previous edition for last biography

BEARSE, ROBERT CARLETON, APPLIED PHYSICS. *Current Pos:* from asst prof to assoc prof, 69-75, assoc dean res admin, 75-78, PROF PHYSICS, UNIV KANS, 75-, ASSOC VCHANCELLOR RES GRAD STUDIES & PUB SERV, 78- *Personal Data:* b Hartford, Conn, May 22, 38; m 63; c George C & James E. *Educ:* Rice Univ, MA, 62, PhD(physics), 64. *Prof Exp:* Res assoc physics, Argonne Nat Lab, 66-68, asst physicist, 68-69. *Concurrent Pos:* Vis staff mem, Los Alamos Sci Lab, NMex, 72-93. *Mem:* Sigma Xi; AAAS; Am Phys Soc. *Res:* Applications of nuclear physics in other disciplines. *Mailing Add:* 1215 W 28th Ct Lawrence KS 66046. *Fax:* 785-864-5272; *E-Mail:* bbearse@research.rgsps.ukans.edu

BEASLEY, ANDREW BOWIE, ANATOMY, GENETICS. *Current Pos:* instr, Med Col Pa, 61-63, from asst prof to assoc prof anat, 63-84, actg chmn dept, 71-73, asst dean student affairs, 75-77, ASSOC DEAN STUDENT AFFAIRS, MED COL PA, 77-, PROF ANAT NEUROBIOL, 84- *Personal Data:* b Upper Zion, Va, Sept 7, 31; div; c Eliza & Julie. *Educ:* Va Polytech Inst, BS, 52, MS, 56; Med Col Pa, ScD(anat & genetics), 61. *Prof Exp:* Asst zool, Va Polytech Inst, 54-55; res asst genetics, Columbia Univ, 55-58. *Concurrent Pos:* Vis prof anat, Fac Libr Med, Lille, France, 78-79. *Mem:* Asn Am Med Cols. *Res:* Developmental genetics and anatomy of central nervous system. *Mailing Add:* Off Student Affairs MCP Hahnemann Sch Med Allegheny Univ Health Sci 2900 Queen Lane Philadelphia PA 19129

BEASLEY, CLARK WAYNE, INVERTEBRATE ZOOLOGY. *Current Pos:* from asst prof to assoc prof, 69-77, CHMN DEPT, MCMURRY COL, 72-, PROF BIOL, 73- *Personal Data:* b Pittsburg, Kans, June 6, 42; m 65, Barbara Allman; c Craig & Stacy. *Educ:* Kans State Col Pittsburg, BS, 64; Univ Okla, PhD(zool), 68. *Prof Exp:* Instr biol, Mo Southern State Col, 68-69. *Mem:* AAAS; Am Inst Biol Sci; Am Micros Soc. *Res:* Invertebrate taxonomy, especially Tardigrada. *Mailing Add:* Dept Biol McMurry Univ Abilene TX 79697-0368. *E-Mail:* c_beasley@mcm.acu.edu

BEASLEY, CLOYD O, JR, PLASMA PHYSICS. *Current Pos:* SR RES SCIENTIST, FUSION ENERGY DIV, OAKRIDGE NAT LAB, 62- *Personal Data:* b Florence, Ala, July 9, 33. *Educ:* Vanderbilt Univ, BA, 55, MA, 57; Univ Wis, PhD(physics), 62. *Prof Exp:* Appl sci rep physics, Int Bus Mach Corp, 57-58. *Concurrent Pos:* Res assoc, Culham Lab, UK, 66-67 & Max-Planck Inst for Plasmaphysik, Fed Repub Ger, 77-78; consult, Div Magnetic Fusion Energy, US Dept Energy, 81-84. *Mem:* Am Phys Soc. *Res:* Plasma micro-instability theory; micro-instabilities in mirror-confined plasmas; combined numerical-analytical approach to investigation of equilibria and stability on Tokamaks; neoclassical transport in stellaratus and finite-aspect-ratio Tokamaks. *Mailing Add:* 119 Clemson Dr Oak Ridge TN 37830-7665

BEASLEY, DEBBIE SUE, SALT & WATER METABOLISM, RENAL BLOOD FLOW. *Current Pos:* ASST RES PROF PHYSIOL & MED, UNIV HOSP, 84- *Educ:* Univ Mich, PhD(physiol), 82. *Mailing Add:* Dept Med New Eng Med Ctr 750 Washington St Boston MA 02111

BEASLEY, EDWARD EVANS, PHYSICS. *Current Pos:* chmn dept, 60-72, PROF PHYSICS, GALLAUDET UNIV, 65- *Personal Data:* b Oakland, Calif, Mar 19, 24; m 49, Nelle C Sloan; c Anne. *Educ:* US Naval Acad, BS, 44; Univ Md, MS, 57, PhD(physics), 63. *Prof Exp:* Asst physics, Univ Md, 56-60. *Concurrent Pos:* Dir, NSF Summer Sci Inst, Gallaudet Univ, 65-66. *Mem:* Am Phys Soc; Am Asn Physics Teachers. *Res:* Electron spin resonance in ultraviolet-irradiated aliphatic hydrocarbon glasses at liquid nitrogen temperature. *Mailing Add:* Dept Physics Math & Comput Sci Gallaudet Univ 800 Florida Ave NE Bldg HMB Rm 344D Washington DC 20002

BEASLEY, JAMES GORDON, ORGANIC CHEMISTRY, MEDICINAL CHEMISTRY. *Current Pos:* PROF MED CHEM, SAMFORD UNIV, 82- *Personal Data:* b Tela, Honduras, Nov 13, 28; US citizen; m 63, Lola M Russell; c Cecilee R. *Educ:* Auburn Univ, BS, 51, MS, 55; Univ Va, PhD(org chem), 62. *Prof Exp:* Asst gen chem, Auburn Univ, 53-55; assoc prof chem, Memphis State Univ, 59-62; res assoc pharmaceut chem, Col Pharm, Univ Tenn, 62-63, asst prof pharmaceut & med chem, 63-65, assoc prof med chem, 65-71, dir chem enzym lab, 68-71; prof chem, Lambuth Col, 71-82. *Concurrent Pos:* Asst, Univ Va, 59; co-investr, NSF grant, 64-66, co-prin investr, NSF res grant, 66-72; res grants, Marion Labs, 66-72 & A H Robins, 70-73. *Mem:* Am Chem Soc; Am Asn Col Pharm; Sigma Xi; AAAS. *Res:* Organic synthesis and biochemical evaluation of compounds with pharmacodynamic potential; correlation of molecular constitution and biochemical response. *Mailing Add:* 1613 Forest Ridge Rd Homewood AL 35226-3229

BEASLEY, JOSEPH NOBLE, VETERINARY PATHOLOGY. *Current Pos:* PROF ANIMAL SCI, UNIV ARK, FAYETTEVILLE, 65- *Personal Data:* b Centerton, Ark, Mar 11, 24; m 56; c 1. *Educ:* Tex A&M Univ, DVM, 49, MS, 56; Univ Okla, PhD(med sci), 64. *Prof Exp:* Instr vet sci, Univ Ark, 49-51; instr vet med & surg, Tex A&M Univ, 51-52; pathologist, Ark Livestock Sanit Bd, 52-55; from asst prof to assoc prof vet path, Tex A&M Univ, 56-65. *Mem:* Am Vet Med Asn; Am Col Vet Path; Int Acad Path; Conf Res Workers Animal Dis; Am Asn Avian Path. *Res:* Comparative pathology of psittacosis ornithosis; canine dirofilariasis, Maren's disease. *Mailing Add:* Dept Animal Sci Univ Ark ANSC 103e Fayetteville AR 72701-1202

BEASLEY, LEROY B, MATHEMATICS. *Current Pos:* from asst prof to assoc prof, 81-91, PROF MATH, UTAH STATE UNIV, 91- *Personal Data:* b Shelley, Idaho, July 31, 42; m 75, Debra A Schaeter; c Mia (Crosthwaite) & Lisa. *Educ:* Idaho State Univ, BS, 64, MS, 66; Univ BC, PhD(math), 69. *Prof Exp:* Teacher & head math, Middleton Sch Dist, Idaho, 72-81. *Concurrent Pos:* Prin investr, NSF, 78-80; vis prof, Univ Col, Dublin, 87-88 & 95, Technion Inst Technol, Israel, 94-95, Univ de Lisboa, 95; consult patent, Ken J Peterson, PLLC, 96- *Mem:* Math Asn Am; fel Inst Combinatorics & Appln; Int Linear Algebra Soc; Irish Math Soc; Korean Math Soc. *Res:* Combinational matrix theory; published over 75 research articles in US and 7 foreign countries. *Mailing Add:* Dept Math & Statist Utah State Univ Logan UT 84322-3900. *Fax:* 435-797-1822; *E-Mail:* lbeasley@usu.edu

BEASLEY, MALCOLM ROY, MATERIALS PHYSICS. *Current Pos:* assoc prof, 74-80, PROF APPL PHYSICS & ELEC ENG, STANFORD UNIV, 80- *Personal Data:* b San Francisco, Calif, Jan 4, 40; m 62, JoAnne Horstall; c Michael, Matthew & Claire. *Educ:* Cornell Univ, BS, 62, PhD(physics), 68. *Prof Exp:* Res fel eng & appl physics, Harvard Univ, 67-69, from asst prof to assoc prof, 69-74. *Mem:* Nat Acad Sci; fel Am Phys Soc; fel Acad Arts & Sci; Mat Res Soc; Inst Elec & Electronics Engrs; fel AAAS. *Res:* Basic and applied superconductivity. *Mailing Add:* 125 Bryant St Palo Alto CA 94301-1103

BEASLEY, PHILIP GENE, ANIMAL PHYSIOLOGY, PLANT PHYSIOLOGY. *Current Pos:* from asst prof to prof, 66-87, EMER PROF BIOL & CHMN DEPT, UNIV MONTEVALLO, 87- *Personal Data:* b Harrisburg, Ill, Dec 22, 27; m 52. *Educ:* Wash Univ, AB, 49; Auburn Univ, MS, 62, PhD(zool), 67. *Prof Exp:* With Fed Bur Invest, 50-59; instr fisheries, Auburn Univ, 60-66. *Concurrent Pos:* Pres, Ala Acad Sci, 86-87. *Mem:* AAAS; Sigma Xi. *Mailing Add:* 501 Shoshone Dr Montevallo AL 35115

BEASLEY, WAYNE M(ACHON), PHYSICAL CERAMICS, CRYSTALLOGRAPHY. *Current Pos:* res asst prof x-ray diffraction, Dept Mech Eng, 57-66, res assoc prof & adj assoc prof mat sci, 66-72, assoc prof mat sci, Mat Sci Div, 72-84, grad prog cord, 82-84, CONSULT, MAT SCI DIV, 84- *Personal Data:* b Everett, Mass, May 23, 22; m 45; c 1. *Educ:* Harvard Univ, SB, 46; Mass Inst Technol, SM, 65. *Prof Exp:* Physicist optics, R L Evans Assocs, 46-47; instr NH pub sch, 47-48; physicist optics, C P Shillaber, 48-51; engr corrosion films, Clarostat Mfg Co, 51-55; phys metallurgist nuclear fuel & instr physics, Metals & Controls Corp, 55-57. *Concurrent Pos:* Dir X-ray diffraction lab, Eng Exp Sta, Univ NH, 63-72; vis scientist, Mass Inst Technol, 78. *Mem:* Am Phys Soc; European Phys Soc; Int Soc Stereology. *Res:* X-ray diffraction; microstructures; structure determinations of sulfosalts; characterization of particle compacts of ceramic materials; characterization of ferromagnetic materials; x-ray diffraction studies of refractory, composite materials. *Mailing Add:* 22 Weeks Lane Rochester NH 03867-8017

BEASLEY, WILLIAM HAROLD, LIGHTNING, ATMOSPHERIC PHYSICS. *Current Pos:* dep dir, Ctr Anal & Prediction Storms, 89-91, dir, 91-96, ASSOC PROF, SCH METEOROL, UNIV OKLA, 90- *Personal Data:* b Dallas, Tex, Oct 23, 44; m 67, 83; c 2. *Educ:* Rice Univ, BA, 67, MS, 69; Univ Tex, Dallas, PhD(physics), 74. *Prof Exp:* Res & develop engr antennas, Collins Radio Co, 68-70; physicist, Environ Res Lab & Wave Propagation Lab, Nat Oceanic & Atmospheric Admin, 72-73; asst prof physics, WTex State Univ, 74-75; assoc, Univ Fla, 75-79, vis asst prof electromagnetics, 79-83; assoc prog dir meteorol, NSF, 83-86; sr staff officer, Nat Acad Sci/Nat Res Coun, 86-87; prog mgr, Ctr & Facil, Div Atmospheric Sci, NSF, 87-89. *Concurrent Pos:* Prin investr, NSF grants, WTex State Univ, 75-76, Univ Fla, 79-81 & 81-83, Univ Okla, 91; consult, Lightning Location & Protection, Inc, 77-81; assoc ed, US Nat Report, Int Union Geodesy & Geophys, 87; secy, Sect W, AAAS, 87- & Atmospheric Sci Sect, Am Geophys Union, 88-90. *Mem:* Am Asn Physics Teachers; Am Geophys Union; Am Meteorol Soc; Sigma Xi; AAAS. *Res:* Observations of lightning electromagnetic fields and optical emissions; thunderstorms; infrasound from severe storms; antennas. *Mailing Add:* Sch Meteorol Univ Okla 100 E Boyd Rm 1310 Norman OK 73019

BEASON, ROBERT CURTIS, MAGNETIC SENSORY PERCEPTION, ANIMAL ORIENTATION. *Current Pos:* from asst prof to assoc prof behav ecol, 78-90, PROF BIOL, STATE UNIV NY, GENESEO, 90- *Personal Data:* b Ft Scott, Kans, May 12, 46; div; c Zachary A. *Educ:* Bethany Nazarene Col, AB, 68; Western Ill Univ, MS, 70; Clemson Univ, PhD(zool), 76. *Prof Exp:* Teaching asst, gen biol, Western Ill Univ, 68-70; res scientist, USAF, 70-74; res asst, Clemson Univ, 74-76; res scientist, US Forest Serv, 76; vis lectr behav ecol, Univ Calif, Irvine, 77; vis asst prof, Western Ill Univ, 77-78. *Concurrent Pos:* Prin investr, Clemson Univ & US Dept Interior, 74-76, Res Found, State Univ NY, 79-80, NSF, 81 & 87-88, NIH, 88-90, NSF, 90-94 & Whitehall Found, 91-95. *Mem:* Soc Neurosci; elective mem Am Ornithologists Union; Animal Behav Soc; Int Soc Behav Ecol; Am Soc Naturalists; Int Soc Neuroethology. *Res:* Environmental and sensory cues used by migratory birds for migration, orientation and navigation and how each cue is utilized for migratory orientation; sensory basis of magnetic perception. *Mailing Add:* Biol Dept State Univ NY One College Circle Geneseo NY 14454. *Fax:* 716-245-5007; *E-Mail:* beason@uno.cc.geneseo.edu

BEATON, ALBERT E, STATISTICS. *Current Pos:* PROF, BOSTON COL, 90- *Personal Data:* b Boston, Mass, Aug 9, 31; m 59, Joan G; c Albert E III & Douglas L. *Educ:* State Teachers Col Boston, BS, 55; Harvard Univ, MEd, 56, EdD, 64. *Honors & Awards:* Wilcoxon Award, Am Soc Qual Control, 77; Award Tech Contrib, Nat Coun Measurement Educ. *Prof Exp:* Res asst, Harvard Univ, 56-57, managing dir, Littauer Statist Lab, 57-59, dir, Harvard Statist Lab, 59-62, actg mgr, Harvard Comput Ctr, 62, res assoc educ & IBM res fel, 62-64; adv statist & data analysis, Nat Assessment Educ Progress, 64-70, dir, Off Data Anal Res, Educ Testing Serv, 70-81, dir data analysis & res, 83-90. *Concurrent Pos:* Res assoc, Educ Res Corp, 56-57; vis lectr, Sch Educ & Grad Sch, Boston Col, 60-61; pres, Albert E Beaton Assocs, Inc; consult, Cabot Corp, Ceir, Inc, Cides, Dominican Repub, Gen Elec Corp, Gillette Safety Razor Corp, Infrared Industs, Can Ministry of Youth, Nat Bur Econ Res, Prudential Life Ins Co, RCA Corp, S C Johnson & Co, Union Carbide Corp, US Res Corp, US Off Educ & US Off Econ Opportunity; vis res statistician & vis lectr statist, Princeton Univ, 66-78; vis res scientist, Patricks Col, Dublin, 79-80; vis lectr, Trinity Col, Dublin, 80; dir, Ctr Study Testing & Eval & Educ Policy Boston Col, 93-, Int Study dir, Third Int Math & Sci Study, 93- *Mem:* Am Educ Res Asn; Am Psychol Asn; Am Statist Asn; Asn Comput Mach; Psychomet Soc. *Res:* Design and analysis of national and international surveys of educational attainment and general statistical computer methods. *Mailing Add:* Boston Col Ctr Testing Campion Hall Rm 323 Chestnut Hill MA 02167. *Fax:* 617-552-8419; *E-Mail:* beatonal@bc.edu

BEATON, DANIEL H(ARPER), CHEMICAL ENGINEERING. *Current Pos:* RETIRED. *Personal Data:* b Paisley, Scotland, Aug 14, 10; US citizen; wid; c Ronald J. *Educ:* Cooper Union, BS, 33. *Prof Exp:* Chem engr, Plastics Dept, E I du Pont de Nemours & Co, 33-36, control & develop engr, 36-43, process control supvr, 41-43, chem supvr, 43-45, develop engr, 45-48, tech sect engr, 48-58, res engr, 58-67, sr res engr, 67-74. *Mem:* Am Chem Soc. *Res:* Improved compositions for high polymers; reaction kinetics; rheology; degradation mechanisms. *Mailing Add:* 1505 14th St Parkersburg WV 26101

BEATON, GEORGE HECTOR, NUTRITION, BIOCHEMISTRY. *Current Pos:* From asst prof to assoc prof nutrit, Sch Hyg, Univ Toronto, 55-63, prof & head dept, 63-75, actg dir, Sch Hyg, 74-75, actg dean fac food sci, 75-81, prof nutrit & food sci & chmn dept, 75-81, PROF, NUTRIT SCI, FAC MED, UNIV TORONTO, 81- *Personal Data:* b Oshawa, Ont, Dec 20, 29; m 53; c 3. *Educ:* Univ Toronto, BA, 52, MA, 53, PhD(nutrit), 55. *Honors & Awards:* Borden Award, Nutrit Soc Can, 68; E W McHenry Award, 84. *Concurrent Pos:* WHO fel, Inst Nutrit Cent Am & Panama, 61; mem expert adv comt nutrit in pregnancy & lactation & expert adv panel nutrit, WHO, 64, mem expert group in vitamin requirements, Food & Agr Orgn-WHO, 67, mem expert group vitamin & mineral requirements, 69, mem expert comt nutrit, 70, protein & energy requirements, 71 & 81; mem, diet & non-communicable dis comt, 89, trace element requirements comt, 90. *Mem:* Am Inst Nutrit; Nutrit Soc Can (secy, 57-60, vpres, 64-65, pres, 65-66). *Res:* Nutrition in pregnancy; biochemical assessment of nutritional status; intermediary metabolism and essential nutrients; public health applications of nutrition information; interpretation of nutrient requirements. *Mailing Add:* Dept Nutrit Sci Univ Toronto Fac Med Toronto ON M5S 1A8 Can

BEATON, JAMES DUNCAN, SOIL FERTILITY. *Current Pos:* CONSULT. *Personal Data:* b Vancouver, BC, Aug 28, 30; m 52; c 3. *Educ:* Univ BC, BSA, 51, MSA, 53; Utah State Univ, PhD(soils), 57. *Prof Exp:* Lab asst soil bact, Univ BC, 51-53, spec lectr, Dept Soil Sci, 56, instr, 57-59; phys chemist, Soil Sect, Exp Farm, Can Dept Agr, 59-61; soil scientist, Res & Develop Div, Consol Mining & Smelting Co Can, Ltd, 61-64, head soil sci res, Res & Corp Develop, 64-67; sr agronomist, Cominco Ltd, BC, 67-68; dir agr res, Sulphur Inst, 68-73; chief agronomist, Cominco Ltd, Alta, 73-78; western dir, Potash & Phosphate Inst, Alta, 78-86, vpres, 86-88, sr vpres, Int Progs, Potash & Phosphate Inst, Atlanta, Ga, 88-92, pres, Potash & Phosphate Inst Can, Saskatoon, 88-92. *Mem:* Fel Soil Sci Soc Am; fel Can Soc Soil Sci; Brit Soc Soil Sci; Int Soc Soil Sci; fel Am Soc Agron; hon mem Nat Fertilizer Solutions Asn. *Res:* Soil fertility and reactions of fertilizers in soils; forest fertilization. *Mailing Add:* 3934 Gallagher's Circle Kelowna BC V1W 1Z9 Can

BEATON, JOHN MCCALL, PSYCHOPHARMACOLOGY. *Current Pos:* from res assoc to instr, 71-74, from asst prof to assoc prof psychiat, 74-84, assoc prof psychol, 78-84, ASST PROF PHARMACOL, UNIV ALA, BIRMINGHAM, 75-, PROF PSYCHIAT & PSYCHOL 84- *Personal Data:* b Huntly, Scotland, June 21, 44; m 68; c 2. *Educ:* Univ Aberdeen, BSc, 66, MSc, 69; Univ Ala, Birmingham, PhD(physiol), 73. *Prof Exp:* Sr res assoc psychol, Addiction Res Found, Toronto, 69-71. *Mem:* Brit Psychol Soc; Soc Neurosci; Am Soc Pharmacol & Exp Therapeut; Collegium Internationale Neuro-Psychopharmacologicum. *Res:* Psychopharmacological study of hallucinogenic agents using operant conditioning tecniques; animal models of psychoses especially with relationship to schizophrenia; the effects of amino acid loadings on behavior. *Mailing Add:* Dept Psychiat Univ Ala Birmingham Sta Birmingham AL 35294-0001

BEATON, JOHN ROGERSON, NUTRITION. *Current Pos:* RETIRED. *Personal Data:* b Oshawa, Ont, Sept 7, 25; m 48; c 4. *Educ:* Univ Toronto, BA, 49, MA, 50, PhD(nutrit), 52. *Prof Exp:* Res fel nutrit, Univ Toronto, 49-51, res assoc, 51-52, asst prof, 52-55,; defense sci serv officer, Defence Res Bd, Can, 55-59, sect head, Defence Res Med Labs, 59-63; prof physiol, Univ Western Ont, 63-67; prof nutrit & chmn div, Univ Hawaii, 67-69; dean col human biol, Univ Wis-Green Bay, 69-70, dean cols, 70-75; dean col human ecol, Univ Md, College Park, 75- *Concurrent Pos:* Lectr food chem, Univ Toronto, 50-55. *Mem:* Soc Exp Biol & Med; Am Soc Biol Chemists; Am Inst Nutrit; Nutrit Soc Can; Soc Nutrit Educ; Can Physiol Soc. *Res:* Vitamin B-6; metabolic functions; amino acid metabolism in pregnancy and malignancy; physiology of cold exposure and hypothermia; metabolic effects of hormones; effects of exercise; fat mobilizing substances in urine; regulation of food intake; physiology and biochemistry of hyperphagia. *Mailing Add:* 9211 Montpiler Dr Laurel MD 20708-2551

BEATON, ROY HOWARD, CHEMICAL ENGINEERING. *Current Pos:* RETIRED. *Personal Data:* b Boston, Mass, Sept 1, 16; m 39, 78, 82, Leora Schier; c Constance (Fegley) & Roy H Jr. *Educ:* Northeastern Univ, BS, 39; Yale Univ, DEng, 42. *Hon Degrees:* DSc, Northeastern Univ, 67. *Prof Exp:* Res chem engr, E I du Pont de Nemours & Co, Inc, Va, 42-43; group leader, Metall Lab, Ill, 43 & Clinton Lab, Tenn, 44; sr supvr, Tech Div, Hanford Eng Works, Wash, 45-46; from chief supvr, Tech Div, to div engr, Design Div, Hanford Works, Gen Elec Co, 46-48, head separations, Tech Div, 48-51, asst mgr, Tech Div & chief process engr, 51, mgr design, 52-56, construct eng, 56-57, gen mgr, X-ray Dept Defense Prod, 57-62, Spacecraft Dept, 63-64 & Apollo Systs Dept, 64-67, vpres & gen mgr, Electronic Systs Div, 68-74, Energy Systs & Technol Div, 74-75 & Nuclear Energy Systs Div, 75-77, sr vpres & group exec, Nuclear Energy Group, 77-81. *Mem:* Nat Acad Eng; Am Inst Chem Engrs; fel Am Inst Chemists; Am Inst Aeronaut & Astronaut; sr mem Inst Elec & Electronics Engrs; Am Nuclear Soc. *Res:* Nuclear engineering; spacecraft design and manufacturing; manned space flight checkout; radar, sonar and weapon control systems design and manufacturing; nuclear reactors and fuel design and manufacturing. *Mailing Add:* 12 Fawn Lane Sequim WA 98382

BEATTIE, ALAN GILBERT, SOLID STATE PHYSICS. *Current Pos:* MEM STAFF, SANDIA NAT LAB, 65- *Personal Data:* b Oakland, Calif, Apr 2, 34; m 61; c 3. *Educ:* Univ Calif, Berkeley, BA, 59; Univ Wash, MS, 60, PhD(physics), 65. *Prof Exp:* Res engr, Algae Res Proj, Univ Calif, Berkeley, 59-60. *Concurrent Pos:* Assoc ed, J of Acoustic Emissions, 81. *Mem:* Inst Elec & Electronics Engrs; Am Soc Testing & Mat; Acoustic Emission Working Group; Am Phys Soc; Sigma Xi. *Res:* Ultrasonics; acoustic emission. *Mailing Add:* Orgn 9742 Sandia Nat Labs Albuquerque NM 87185

BEATTIE, CRAIG W, ONCOLOGY, CELLULAR ENDOCRINOLOGY. *Current Pos:* PROF PHARMACOL, SURG & PHARM, SCH MED, UNIV ILL, CHICAGO, 83- *Personal Data:* b Elizabeth, NJ, Oct 26, 43. *Educ:* Univ Del, PhD(biol), 71. *Mailing Add:* USDA Agr Res Serv MARC PO Box 166 State Spur 18D Clay Center NE 68933-0166

BEATTIE, DIANA SCOTT, BIOCHEMISTRY, BIOENERGETICS & METABOLISM. *Current Pos:* PROF BIOCHEM & CHMN DEPT, SCH MED, WVA UNIV, 85- *Personal Data:* b Cranston, RI, Aug 11, 34; m 56; c Elizabeth, Sara J, Rachel & Ruth. *Educ:* Swarthmore Col, BA, 56; Univ Pittsburgh, MS, 58, PhD(biochem), 61. *Prof Exp:* Res assoc biochem, Univ Pittsburgh, 61-68; from asst prof to prof biochem, Mt Sinai Sch Med, 68-85. *Concurrent Pos:* Mem, Phys Biochem Study Sect, NIH, 79-85; mem, Grad Fac PhD Prog Biochem, Biol & Biomed Sci, City Univ NY, 69-85; vis prof, Univ Louvain, Lovain-la-Neuve, Belg, 82; Fogarty Int fel, 82; mem, Metab Biol Rev Panel, NSF, 86-89, mem Basic Sci Merit Review Bd, Vet Admin, 88-92; mem grad fac, WVa Univ, 85-; vis prof, Univ Nairobi, Kenya, 93; Fulbright res fel, 93. *Mem:* Asn Med & Grad Depts Biochem (pres, 97); Am Soc Biol Chemists; Am Soc Cell Biologists; Biophys Soc; Coun Acad Soc Asn Am Med Col. *Res:* Mitochondrial biogenesis, including various aspects of protein synthesis, enzymology and its regulation; bioenergetics and protein chemistry of electron transport chain; intracellular targeting of proteins. *Mailing Add:* Dept Biochem WVa Univ Sch Med PO Box 9142 Morgantown WV 26506-9142. *Fax:* 304-293-6846; *E-Mail:* dbeattie@wvuhscl.hsc.wvu.edu

BEATTIE, DONALD A, ENERGY, SPACE TECHNOLOGY. *Current Pos:* CONSULT, 84- *Personal Data:* b New York, NY, Oct 30, 29; m 72, Ann Kean; c Thomas J & Bruce A. *Educ:* Columbia Univ, AB, 51; Colo Sch Mines, MS, 58. *Prof Exp:* Officer & aviator, US Navy, 51-56; regional geol, Mobil Oil Co, 58-63; aerospace tech, Nat Aeronaut & Space Admin, 63-72; div dir, Res & Develop, NSF, 73-75; asst admin, Energy Res & Develop Admin, 75-77; asst secy, Dept Energy, 77-78; div dir, res & develop, NASA, 78-82; vpres, BDM Corp, 83-84. *Concurrent Pos:* Solar energy coordr, US & USSR Coop Sci & Tech, 74-76 & Vienna Inst Comp Econ Studies, 79; advisor, Montgomery Col, 78-81; US rep, Vienna Inst Comp Econ Studies, 79; vis lectr, Georgetown Univ, 82, Nat Space Club, Youth Educ, 84-88; mem adv comt, NASA, 88-92. *Mem:* Geol Soc Am; fel AAAS; Nat Space Club. *Res:* Study of lunar surface phenomena leading to the design and development of geological and geophysical experiments for the Apollo Program; renewable energy technologies; systems engineering; author of one book. *Mailing Add:* 13831 Dowlais Dr Rockville MD 20853. *Fax:* 904-287-6322

BEATTIE, EDWARD J, SURGERY, THORACIC SURGERY. *Current Pos:* chief thoracic surgeon & dir, Kriser Lung Cancer Ctr & dir Clin Cancer Progs, 85-95, MED DIR, CANCER CTR, BETH ISRAEL MED CTR, 95-; PROF SURG, ALBERT EINSTEIN SCH MED, NY, 94- *Personal Data:* b Philadelphia, Pa, June 30, 18; m 77, Nicole Grove; c Bruce S. *Educ:* Princeton Univ, BA, 39; Harvard Univ, MD, 43; Am Bd Surg, dipl, 49; Am Bd Thoracic Surg, dipl, 51. *Hon Degrees:* LLD, Hampden-Sydney Col, 78. *Prof Exp:* Resident surg, Peter Bent Brigham Hosp, Boston, 42-43, from asst resident surgeon to resident surgeon, 44-45, jr assoc surg, 45-47; fel, George Washington Univ, 47-48, asst prof & Markle scholar, 48-52; from asst prof to prof, Univ Ill, 52-65; chief thoracic surgeon, Mem Hosp, New York, 65-75, chmn, Dept Surg, 66-78, chief med officer, 66-83, gen dir & chief operating officer, 74-83; prof surg, Cornell Univ, 65-83, emer prof, 83; prof surg & oncol, Univ Miami, 83-85; prof surg, Mt Sinai Sch Med, NY, 85-94. *Concurrent Pos:* Instr, Harvard Univ, 45-47; Moseley travel fel from Harvard Univ, Postgrad Med Sch, Univ London, 46-47; consult, Gallinger Munic Hosp, Washington, DC, Walter Reed Army Hosp, Newton D Baker & Mt Alto Vet Admin Hosps, 48-52; consult, Chicago State Tuberc Sanitorium, Univ Ill Hosps & Hines Vet Admin Hosp, 52-65 & Rockefeller Univ, 77-92; thoracic surgeon, Presby-St Luke's Hosp, Chicago, 54-65; mem bd, Am Bd Thoracic Surg, 60-65, from vchmn to chmn, 65-69; mem, Sloan Kettering Inst, 66-83. *Mem:* Am Asn Thoracic Surg; Am Col Surg; Soc Vascular Surg; Soc Clin Surg; Am Surg Asn; Am Radiol Soc. *Res:* Thoracic surgery; multidisciplinary approach, including early detection, surgery, internal and external radiotherapy and medical oncology, to decrease present high mortality from lung cancer. *Mailing Add:* Cancer Ctr 10 Union Sq E New York NY 10003. *Fax:* 212-844-8299

BEATTIE, JAMES MONROE, HORTICULTURE. *Current Pos:* RETIRED. *Personal Data:* b Washington, DC, Feb 14, 21; m 42; c 2. *Educ:* Univ Md, BS, 41; Cornell Univ, PhD(pomol), 48. *Prof Exp:* From asst prof to prof hort, Ohio Agr Exp Sta, 48-63, from asst dir to assoc dir, Ohio Agr Res & Develop Ctr, 63-73; dean, Col Agr, dir Agr Exp Sta & dir Coop Exten Serv, Pa State Univ, University Park, 73-81. *Mem:* fel Am Soc Hort Sci (pres, 69-70); Am Inst Biol Sci. *Res:* Nitrogen and mineral nutrition of fruit crops; reclamation of strip mine spoils; culture and management of fruit plantings. *Mailing Add:* 1244 Westerly Pkwy Apt 32 State College PA 16801-4171

BEATTIE, RANDALL CHESTER, AUDIOLOGY. *Current Pos:* asst prof, 72-77, ASSOC PROF AUDIOL, CALIF STATE UNIV, LONG BEACH, 77- *Personal Data:* b Orlando, Fla, June 12, 45; m 67; c 1. *Educ:* Northern Ill Univ, BS, 67; Univ Ill, MS, 69; Univ Southern Calif, PhD(audiol), 72. *Prof Exp:* Speech & hearing specialist, Georgetown, Ill, 67-69; audiologist, Los Angeles Outpatient Clin, Vet Admin, 69-72; educ audiologist, Alhambra Sch Dist, 72. *Mem:* Am Speech & Hearing Asn. *Res:* Speech audiometry; hearing aids. *Mailing Add:* Dept Commun Dis Calif State Univ Long Beach 2501 Csulb Long Beach CA 90840-0004

BEATTIE, THOMAS ROBERT, MEDICINAL & SYNTHETIC ORGANIC CHEMISTRY, COMBINATORIAL CHEMISTRY. *Current Pos:* assoc dir med chem, 93-96, SCI ADV, AMYLIN PHARMACEUT, INC, 96- *Personal Data:* b Philadelphia, Pa, Aug 31, 40; m 61, Mary A McClellan; c Patricia, Kathleen & Thomas. *Educ:* Univ Pa, BS, 61; Univ Wis, PhD(org chem), 65. *Prof Exp:* Postdoctoral fel, Mass Inst Technol, 65-66; sr res chemist, Merck & Co, Inc, 66-73, from res fel to sr res fel, 73-93. *Concurrent Pos:* Mem, Atlanta Univ Ctr, Inc Chancellor's Circle, 81-; mem, Med Chem Adv Comt, Dept Chem, San Diego Univ, 94- *Mem:* Am Chem Soc. *Res:* Medicinal and synthetic organic chemistry; immunoregulants; diabetes. *Mailing Add:* Amylin Pharmaceut Inc 9373 Towne Ctr Dr San Diego CA 92121. *Fax:* 619-554-1474; *E-Mail:* tbeattie@amylin.com

BEATTIE, WILLARD HORATIO, PHYSICAL CHEMISTRY. *Current Pos:* RETIRED. *Personal Data:* b Oak Park, Ill, Mar 3, 27; m 54; c 3. *Educ:* Univ Chicago, BA, 51, MS, 54; Univ Minn, PhD(analytical chem), 58. *Prof Exp:* Res chemist, Shell Chem Co, 58-62; sr res chemist, Beckman Instruments, Inc, 62; asst prof chem, Calif State Col, Long Beach, 62-67; mem staff, Los Alamos Sci Lab, 67-90. *Concurrent Pos:* Res prof, Univ Calif, Santa Barbara, 75-76. *Res:* Light scattering; chemical laser development; laser isotope separation; radiation chemistry of gases; analytical chemical instrumentation; fuels from coal and natural gas; inorganic fluorine chemistry. *Mailing Add:* 4045 Pamela Pl Las Cruces NM 88005-5641

BEATTY, CHARLES LEE, MATERIALS SCIENCE ENGINEERING. *Current Pos:* PROF, DEPT MAT SCI & ENG, UNIV FLA, 79- *Personal Data:* b Kempton, Ind, Nov 7, 39; m 72; c 3. *Educ:* Purdue Univ, BS, 65; Case Western Reserve Univ, MS, 68; Univ Mass, MS, 71, PhD(polymer sci & eng), 72. *Concurrent Pos:* Researcher, Xerox, 72-79; assoc prof polymer sci, Univ Rochester, 76-77, assoc prof mech & aerospace sci, 76-78; chmn-elect, Eng Properties & Struct Div, Soc Plastics Engrs; coun mem, Soc Plastics Engrs, 88-91. *Mem:* Am Inst Chem Engrs; Nat Asn Corrosion Engrs; Am Chem Soc; Am Phys Soc; Soc Plastics Engrs; Soc Biomaterials; Am Soc Testing & Mat. *Res:* Solid-state properties of polymers ranging from diffusion to calorimetry; mechanical properties in the linear and non-linear viscoelastic region. *Mailing Add:* Dept Mat Sci & Eng Univ Fla 132 Rhines Hall Gainesville FL 32611-2066

BEATTY, CLARISSA HAGER, biochemistry; deceased, see previous edition for last biography

BEATTY, DAVID DELMAR, comparative physiology, for more information see previous edition

BEATTY, JAMES WAYNE, JR, PHYSICAL CHEMISTRY. *Current Pos:* from asst prof to assoc prof chem, 63-74, chmn, dept chem, 81-87, PROF CHEM, RIPON COL, 74- *Personal Data:* b Fargo, NDak, Sept 9, 34; wid; c 3. *Educ:* NDak State Univ, BSc, 56; Mass Inst Technol, PhD(phys chem), 60. *Prof Exp:* From instr to asst prof physics, Colby Col, 60-63. *Concurrent Pos:* Consult-evaluator, NCent Asn Cols & Schs, 73-; deleg, Wis Gov Conf Libr & Info Serv, 78. *Mem:* Am Chem Soc; Am Phys Soc; Am Asn Univ Professors. *Res:* Measurement of transport properties of gases, particularly diffusion coefficients; determination of force law constants from this data; computer assisted instruction in chemistry. *Mailing Add:* Dept Chem Ripon Col 511 Griswold #1 Ripon WI 54971

BEATTY, JOHN C, COMPUTER SCIENCE, COMPUTER GRAPHICS. *Current Pos:* Asst prof, 78-84, ASSOC PROF COMPUTER SCI, UNIV WATERLOO, 84- *Personal Data:* b New York, NY, Nov 27, 47. *Educ:* Princeton Univ, BS, 69; Univ Calif, Berkeley, PhD(computer sci), 78. *Concurrent Pos:* Vis scientist, Xerox Palo Alto Res Ctr, 85-86. *Mem:* Asn Comput Mach; Inst Elec & Electronics Engrs; Sigma Xi. *Mailing Add:* 228 Herbert St Waterloo ON N2J 1T9 Can

BEATTY, JOSEPH JOHN, ECOLOGY, BIOMETRICS. *Current Pos:* Instr biol, Dept Zool, 79-90, dir, Biol Prog, 90, SR INSTR, BIOL PROG, OREGON STATE UNIV, 93- *Personal Data:* b Detroit, Mich, Feb 19, 47; m 88, Anita L Upenicks. *Educ:* Univ Mo, Columbia, BS, 70, AM, 73; Ore State Univ, PhD(zool), 79. *Mem:* Am Soc Ichthyologists & Herpetologists; Herpetologists League; Soc Study Amphibians & Reptiles; AAAS; Am Inst Biol Sci. *Res:* Ecology and evolutionary biology of amphibians, primarily northwestern plethodontid salamanders. *Mailing Add:* Ore State Univ Biol 2042 Cordley Hall Corvallis OR 97331-2908

BEATTY, K(ENNETH) O(RION), JR, BIOMEDICAL ENGINEERING, FIRES & ARSON. *Current Pos:* prof chem eng, NC State Univ, 46-61, actg head dept, 59-60, Reynolds Prof, 61-79, EMER REYNOLDS PROF ENG, NC STATE UNIV, 79- *Personal Data:* b East Lansdowne, Pa, Dec 18, 13; m 36, Mary C Carter; c Susan J (Jolly/Woodruff), Prudence C (Abram) & Lucy. *Educ:* Lehigh Univ, BS, 35, MS, 37; Univ Mich, PhD(chem eng), 46. *Prof Exp:* Chem engr, Dow Chem Co, 37-39; from instr to asst prof, Univ RI, 39-44; res assoc engr, Univ Mich, 44-46. *Concurrent Pos:* Eng consult, 49-; proj engr, Pratt & Whitney, 57; consult, 61-; US del, Assembly Int Heat Transfer Conf, 67-72; mem sci coun, Int Ctr Heat & Mass Transfer, Yugoslavia, 68-82; legal expert, 75- *Mem:* Fel Am Inst Chem Engrs; Am Chem Soc; Int Asn Arson Investr; Sigma Xi; Nat Fire Protection Asn. *Res:* Heat transfer; infrared thermography; fluid dynamics; devices for braille readers; biomedical engineering; legal expert in fires and arson; legal expert in slips, trips and falls. *Mailing Add:* 323 Shepherd St Raleigh NC 27607-4031

BEATTY, KENNETH WILSON, ZOOLOGY, LIMNOLOGY. *Current Pos:* INSTR BIOL, COL SISKIYOUS, 60- *Personal Data:* b Oklahoma City, Okla, Feb 22, 29; m 65; c 3. *Educ:* Univ Calif, Davis, BS, 52, MA, 60, PhD(limnol), 68. *Prof Exp:* Lab technician animal husb, Univ Calif, Davis, 54-60. *Concurrent Pos:* Biologist, US Geol Surv, 71-73. *Mem:* Am Soc Limnol & Oceanog; Ecol Soc Am; Am Inst Biol Sci; Nat Asn Biol Teachers; Am Nature Study Soc. *Res:* Ecology of new reservoirs; benthic ecology of alpine lakes; behavior and reproductive cycles of woodpeckers; mastitis studies under controlled management practices. *Mailing Add:* Dept Natural Sci Col Siskiyous 800 College Ave Weed CA 96094-2806

BEATTY, MARVIN THEODORE, SOILS, RESOURCE MANAGEMENT. *Current Pos:* RETIRED. *Personal Data:* b Bozeman, Mont, Mar 13, 28; m 56, Ellouise Skimmer; c 4. *Educ:* Mont State Col, BS, 50; Univ Wis, PhD(soils), 55. *Prof Exp:* Soil scientist, Soil Conserv Serv, 50-56; from asst prof to prof soils, Univ Wis-Madison, 56-88, chmn environ resources unit, 70-72, chmn, Natural & Environ Resources, 72-77, dean commun progs, 77-83, assoc dean & dir, Coop Exten Serv, 83-88. *Mem:* Am Soc Agron; Soil Conserv Soc Am; Nat Univs Exten Asn; fel AAAS. *Res:* Soil surveys and the interpretation of physical and chemical properties of soils as they affect sustained use of soils for agriculture; engineering; urban development; soil conservation; natural resource and environmental education programs; soil sci applies to archaeology. *Mailing Add:* 4702 Waukesha St Madison WI 53705. *E-Mail:* mtbeatty@facstaff.wisc.edu

BEATTY, MILLARD F, NONLINEAR ELASTICITY, CONTINUUM MECHANICS. *Current Pos:* PROF & CHMN ENG MECH, UNIV NEBR, LINCOLN, 90- *Personal Data:* b Baltimore, Md, Nov 13, 30; m 51, Nadine Chumley; c Scott M, Laura M (Allen) & Ann N (Lassetter). *Educ:* Johns Hopkins Univ, BES, 59, PhD(mech), 64. *Prof Exp:* Instr eng physics, Loyola Col, Md, 59-60; instr mech, Johns Hopkins Univ, 60-63; asst prof mech eng, Univ Del, 63-67; from assoc prof to prof eng mech, Univ Ky, 67-90. *Concurrent Pos:* Vis res scientist, Johns Hopkins Univ, 73-74; res adv group, Inst Paper Chem, 79-82; sr fel, Inst Math & Its Applns, Univ Minn, 84-85; ed, Math & Mech Solids. *Mem:* Soc Natural Philos; fel Am Acad Mech; Am Asn Physics Teachers; fel Am Soc Mech Engrs; Soc Eng Sci; Math Asn Am. *Res:* Nonlinear elasticity applied to study the Mullins (stress softening) effect in rubberlike materials; nonlinear oscillations of rubber suspension systems; theory of Bell constrained materials. *Mailing Add:* Univ Nebr Lincoln NE 68588-0347. *Fax:* 402-472-8292; *E-Mail:* mbeatty@unlinfo.unl.edu

BEATTY, OREN ALEXANDER, FOREST SCIENCE, TREE FARMER. *Current Pos:* RETIRED. *Personal Data:* b Nobob, Ky, July 3, 01; m 33; c 9. *Educ:* Univ Louisville, MD, 30. *Prof Exp:* Med dir & supt, Richland Hosp, Mansfield, Ohio, 42-51, Hazelwood Sanatorium, Louisville, Ky, 51-62 & Richland Hosp, 62-72. *Concurrent Pos:* Asst prof, Sch Med, Univ Louisville, 52-62; tuberc controller, Lorain Co Tuberc Clin, 65-72; consult, 72-81. *Mem:* AMA; fel Am Col Chest Physicians; Am Lung Asn. *Res:* Diseases of the chest; undulant fever in relation to chest involvement; tuberculosis cavities. *Mailing Add:* 3717 Hanover Rd Louisville KY 40207

BEATTY, PATRICK GIBSON, MEDICAL ONCOLOGY, BONE MARROW TRANSPLANT. *Current Pos:* PROF MED, UNIV UTAH, 90- *Personal Data:* b Salisbury, Md, Nov 3, 48; m 73; c 2. *Educ:* Univ Chicago, PhD(path & immunol), 75, MD, 76. *Prof Exp:* from fel to assoc prof, Univ Wash, 79-90. *Mem:* Am Soc Histocompatibility & Immunogenetics (pres elect, 96-97); Nat Marrow Donor Prog; Am Asn Immunol; Am Soc Hemat. *Res:* Immunogenetics of bone marrow transplantation. *Mailing Add:* Div Hematol Oncol Univ Utah 50 N Medical Dr Salt Lake City UT 84132

BEATY, DAVID WAYNE, ECONOMIC GEOLOGY, STABLE ISOTOPE GEOCHEMISTRY. *Current Pos:* GEOLOGIST, CHEVRON OIL FIELD RES CO, 86- *Personal Data:* b St Louis, Mo, Nov 12, 53; m 78; c 2. *Educ:* Dartmouth Col, AB, 75; Calif Inst Technol, PhD(geol), 80. *Prof Exp:* Geologist, Noranda Explor, Inc, 80-86. *Mem:* Soc Econ Geologists; Am Geophys Union; Mineral Soc Am; Geochem Soc. *Res:* Mineral exploration; hydrothermal processes; igneous and ore petrology. *Mailing Add:* Chevron Petroleum Technol Co PO Box 446 La Habra CA 90633-0446

BEATY, EARL CLAUDE, PHYSICS. *Current Pos:* FEL, JOINT INST LAB ASTROPHYS, UNIV COLO, BOULDER, 62- *Personal Data:* b Zeigler, Ill, Nov 6, 30; m 52; c 3. *Educ:* Murray State Col, AB, 52; Washington Univ, PhD, 56. *Prof Exp:* physicist, Nat Bur Stand, 56-77 & 78- *Concurrent Pos:* Nat Res Coun fel, 56-57; consult, Int Atomic Energy Agency, 77-78. *Mem:* Am Phys Soc. *Res:* Atomic physics. *Mailing Add:* 3005 Stanford Ave Univ Colo Boulder CO 80303

BEATY, MYRON HOLMES, FRESHWATER LIMNOLOGICAL ECOLOGY, FRESHWATER PHYCOLOGY. *Current Pos:* ASST PROF BOT & ECOL, MERRIMACK COL, 95- *Personal Data:* b Media, Pa, Oct 18, 63; m 90, Alisa Ann Windley. *Educ:* NC State Univ, BS, 89; Va Polytech Inst & State Univ, MS, 91, PhD(biol), 95. *Concurrent Pos:* Core fac, Wetlands Resources, Isle Schools Manne Labs, 96- *Mem:* Phycol Soc Am; Sigma Xi. *Res:* Investigations of lentic freshwater ecosystems; nutrient dynamics; phytoplankton community structure and function; taste and odor problems in drinking water supplies caused by compounds produced (or breakdown products of those produced) by the phytoplankton community. *Mailing Add:* Merrimack Col 315 Turnpike St North Andover MA 01845. *E-Mail:* mbeaty@merrimack.edu

BEATY, ORREN, III, CARDIOVASCULAR PHYSIOLOGY, ADRENERGIC MECHANISMS. *Current Pos:* PEDIAT, HEMAT & ONCOL FEL, ST JUDES CHILDRENS RES HOSP, 92- *Personal Data:* b Las Cruces, NMex, Nov 13, 45; m 71; c 3. *Educ:* Richmond Col, BS, 68; Wake Forest Univ, PhD(physiol), 74; Kirksville Col Osteop Med, DO, 88. *Prof Exp:* Teaching asst chem, Richmond Col, 68-69; fel physiol, Sch Med, Mayo Grad Sch, Mayo Clin, 74-76, vis scientist, 77-79; asst prof, Kirksville Col Osteop Med, 79-84, vis asst prof physiol; resident med & pediat, ECarolina Univ Sch Med, 88-92. *Mem:* Sigma Xi; Am Physiol Soc. *Res:* Regulation of arterial blood pressure and peripheral circulation through both local and reflex mechanisms as well as the control of peripheral adrenergic neurotransmission. *Mailing Add:* St Judes Childrens Res Hosp 332 N Lauderdale PO Box 318 Memphis TN 38101-0318

BEAUBIEN, STEWART JAMES, lubrication, energy analysis, for more information see previous edition

BEAUCHAMP, EDWIN KNIGHT, BRITTLE FRACTURE, HIGH TEMPERATURE DEFORMATION. *Current Pos:* RETIRED. *Personal Data:* b Ely, Nev, July 16, 30; m 54; c 6. *Educ:* Univ Nev, Reno, BS, 52; Northwestern Univ, Evanston, MS, 54; Univ Utah, Salt Lake City, PhD(physics), 61. *Prof Exp:* Res asst, Northwestern Univ, 52-53; jr engr develop, Boeing Aricraft Corp, 53; res engr, Lockheed Aircraft, 56-57; asst res & teaching, Univ Utah, 57-61; res scientist, Glass Res, Corning Glass Works, 61-64; distinguished mem tech staff mat & res, Sandia Nat Labs, 64-95. *Mem:* Am Ceramic Soc; Mat Res Soc. *Res:* Brittle fracture of ceramics and glasses; subcritical crack growth in glasses and glass-ceramics; internal friction in glasses; dielectric breakdown in ceramics; sintering of explosively shocked ceramics. *Mailing Add:* 7509 Harwood Ave NE Albuquerque NM 87110

BEAUCHAMP, ERIC G, SOIL FERTILITY & SOIL NITROGEN, PLANT NUTRITION. *Current Pos:* from asst prof to assoc prof, 67-79, PROF SOIL SCI, UNIV GUELPH, 79- *Personal Data:* b Grenville, Que, Jan 6, 36; m 58; c 3. *Educ:* McGill Univ, BScAgr, 60, MSc, 62; Cornell Univ, PhD(soil sci), 65. *Prof Exp:* Res scientist, Res Br, Can Dept Agr, 65-67. *Mem:* Am Soc Agron; Agr Inst Can; Can Soc Soil Sci; Int Soc Soil Sci. *Res:* Response of field crops to nitrogen fertilizers; soil nitrogen transformations. *Mailing Add:* Dept Land Resource Sci Univ Guelph Guelph ON N1G 2W1 Can

BEAUCHAMP, GARY KEITH, ANIMAL BEHAVIOR. *Current Pos:* ASSOC MEM, MONELL CHEM SENSES CTR, 73-, DIR, 90- *Personal Data:* b Belvidere, Ill, Apr 5, 43; m 67; c 2. *Educ:* Carleton Col, BA, 65; Univ Chicago, PhD(biopsychol), 71. *Prof Exp:* Fel chemosensation, Univ Pa, 71-73, asst prof psychol, Dept Otorhinolaryngol & Human Commun, Med Sch, 74- *Mem:* AAAS; Asn Chemoreception Soc. *Res:* Investigation of the role of the chemical senses in regulating behavior and physiology in a variety of animal species, including humans. *Mailing Add:* Monell Chem Senses Ctr 3500 Market St Philadelphia PA 19104-3308

BEAUCHAMP, JESSE LEE, PHYSICAL CHEMISTRY. *Current Pos:* Noyes instr, 67-69, from asst prof to assoc prof, 69-74, PROF CHEM, CALIF INST TECHNOL, 74- *Personal Data:* b Glendale, Calif, Nov 1, 42; m 82, Patricia Dummer; c 4. *Educ:* Calif Inst Technol, BS, 64; Harvard Univ, PhD(chem), 67. *Honors & Awards:* Pure Chem Award, Am Chem Soc, 78. *Concurrent Pos:* Alfred P Sloan Found fel, 68-70; John Simon Guggenheim Mem fel, 76-77; mem, Comt Critical Technol, Nat Res Coun, 91-92, chmn, Comt Com Aviation Security, 93-; cominsioner, White House Comn Safety & Security, 96- *Mem:* Nat Acad Sci; Am Chem Soc; fel AAAS. *Res:* Gas phase ion chemistry; structures, properties and reactions of organic ions; chemical applications of ion cyclotron resonance spectroscopy; biomolecule structure determination; explosives detection and aviation security; chemical imaging of surfaces. *Mailing Add:* A A Noyes Lab 127-72 Calif Inst Technol Pasadena CA 91125

BEAUCHAMP, JOHN J, APPLIED STATISTICS, DATA ANALYSIS. *Current Pos:* RES STATISTICIAN, ENG, PHYSICS & MATH DIV, OAK RIDGE NAT LAB, 84-, SR RES STAFF MEM, COMPUT SCI & MATH DIV, 84- *Personal Data:* b Nashville, Tenn, Sept 17, 37; m 72, Betty J Balls; c John & Karen. *Educ:* Vanderbilt Univ, BA, 59, MAT, 60; Fla State Univ, MS, 63, PhD(statist), 66. *Prof Exp:* Asst prof math, Birmingham-Southern Col, 60-61; biomet trainee statist, Vanderbilt Univ, 61-62; statistician, Math Div, Oak Ridge Nat Lab, 67-73; statistician, Comput Sci Div, Nuclear Div, Union Carbide Corp, 73-84. *Concurrent Pos:* Instr math & sci, Roane St Community Col, 76-79; instr biomed sci, Univ Tenn, 80, 86 & 88-90. *Mem:* Am Statist Asn. *Res:* Nonlinear estimation; model building; multivariate analysis; applied statistics; regression, design and analysis of experiments. *Mailing Add:* Oak Ridge Nat Lab PO Box 2008 Oak Ridge TN 37831-6367

BEAUCHAMP, LILIA MARIE, MEDICINAL CHEMISTRY, ANTIVIRAL CHEMOTHERAPY. *Current Pos:* SR RES CHEMIST, BURROUGHS WELLCOME CO, 57- *Personal Data:* b New York, NY. *Educ:* St John's Univ, BS, 53; Fordham Univ, MS, 55. *Prof Exp:* Analytical chemist, Colgate Palmolive Co, 55-57. *Mem:* Am Chem Soc. *Res:* Synthesis of new drugs for biological testing; antiviral agents; acyclic nucleosides. *Mailing Add:* 3003 Wycliff Rd Raleigh NC 27607-3038

BEAUCHENE, ROY E, NUTRITION, GERIATRICS. *Current Pos:* assoc prof, 68-72, head, Dept Food Sci, Nutrit & Food Syst Admin, 77-81, PROF NUTRIT, UNIV TENN, KNOXVILLE, 72- *Personal Data:* b Sioux City, Iowa, Sept 4, 25; m 52; c 4. *Educ:* Morningside Col, BS, 51; Kans State Univ, MS, 52, PhD, 56. *Prof Exp:* Asst chem, Kans State Univ, 51-56; from asst prof to assoc prof human nutrit res, Tex Woman's Univ, 56-58, prof nutrit & biochem res, 58-63; NIH res scientist, Geront Br, Baltimore City Hosps, 63-68. *Concurrent Pos:* Guest scholar, Kans State Univ, 73; pres, Univ Tenn, Knoxville Chap Sigma Xi, 90-91. *Mem:* Am Chem Soc; fel Geront Soc; Am Inst Nutrit; Sigma Xi; fel Am Col Nutrit. *Res:* Nutrition and aging; bone density. *Mailing Add:* 9020 Bluegrass Rd Knoxville TN 37922-5924

BEAUDET, ARTHUR L, HUMAN GENETICS,. *Current Pos:* from asst prof to assoc prof, 71-82, PROF GENETICS & PEDIAT, BAYLOR COL MED, HOUSTON, 82- *Personal Data:* b Woonsocket, RI, July 4, 42; m 67, Marjorie Miller; c Nicole & Alissa. *Educ:* Col Holy Cross, BS, 63; Yale Univ, MD, 67. *Prof Exp:* Intern & resident pediat, Johns Hopkins Hosp, 67-69; res assoc biochem, NIH, Bethesda, 69-71. *Concurrent Pos:* Investr, Howard Hughes Med Inst, 73-80, 85-; mem, Genetic Basis Dis Rev Comt, 80-84 & Biochem II Study Sect, NIH, 85-89. *Mem:* Inst Med-Nat Acad Sci; Soc Pediat Res; Fedn Am Soc Biol Chemists; Am Soc Human Genetics; Genetics Soc Am; Asn Am Physicians. *Res:* Molecular human genetics; human genetic diseases, inborn errors of metabolism; inborn errors of metabolism; cystic fibrosis; gene therapy. *Mailing Add:* Inst Molecular Genetics Baylor Col Med Howard Hughes Med Inst 1 Baylor Plaza Houston TX 77030. *Fax:* 713-797-6718

BEAUDET, ROBERT A, CHEMICAL PHYSICS, PHYSICAL CHEMISTRY. *Current Pos:* from asst prof to assoc prof, 63-71, chmn dept, 74-76, PROF CHEM, UNIV SOUTHERN CALIF, 71- *Personal Data:* b Woonsocket, RI, Aug 18, 35; m 57; c 7. *Educ:* Worcester Polytech Inst, BS, 57; Harvard Univ, AM & PhD(phys chem), 62. *Honors & Awards:* Alexander von Humboldt Award, 74-75. *Prof Exp:* Res scientist, Jet Propulsion Lab, Calif Inst Technol, 61-63. *Concurrent Pos:* Consult, Jet Propulsion Lab, Calif Inst Technol, 63-; NIH grant, Univ Southern Calif, 64; A P Sloan Found res fel, 67-71; consult, Army Sci Adv Panel, 68-75, mem, 75-77, assoc mem, Army Sci Bd, 78-79. *Mem:* Am Chem Soc; Am Phys Soc. *Res:* Microwave spectroscopy; rotational spectra; molecular structure; intra molecular interactions; laser spectroscopy; boron hydrides; carboranes. *Mailing Add:* 887 Vallombrosa Dr Pasadena CA 91107-5642

BEAUDOIN, ADRIEN ROBERT, CELL MORPHOLOGY, MEMBRANE FUNCTIONS. *Current Pos:* from asst prof to prof, 72-81, FULL PROF, UNIV SHERBROOKE, 81- *Personal Data:* b Bury, Que, Sept 3, 40; m 64, Lorraine Langlois; c Luc, Chantal & Claude. *Educ:* Univ Sherbrooke, BSc, 66; Univ Laval, DSc, 70. *Honors & Awards:* Diatome Prize, Am Soc Micros, 85. *Prof Exp:* Res assoc, Duke Univ, 70-71, Univ Laval, 71-72; dir, Ctr Res Mechanisms Secretion, 82-88. *Mem:* Am Soc Cell Biol; Micros Soc Can; Can Biochem Soc; Can-French Asn Advan Sci. *Res:* Cell secretory mechanisms; intracellular route and processing of the secretory proteins of pancreas; characterization of adenosine triphosphate-diphosphohydrolase in eukaryotic cells; membrane shedding mechanisms and cancer; microvisicular secretion. *Mailing Add:* Bept Biol Univ Sherbrooke 2500 Univ Blvd Sherbrooke PQ J1K 2R1 Can. *Fax:* 819-821-8049

BEAUDOIN, ALLAN ROGER, TERATOLOGY, DEVELOPMENTAL TOXICOLOGY. *Current Pos:* from asst prof to prof, 61-93, EMER PROF ANAT & CELL BIOL, MED SCH, UNIV MICH, ANN ARBOR, 93- *Personal Data:* b New Britain, Conn, Aug 25, 27; m 50, Dorothy Jones; c Sandra, Arthur, Bruce & Craig. *Educ:* Univ Conn, BS, MS, 51; Univ Iowa, PhD(zool), 54. *Prof Exp:* Instr zool, Univ Iowa, 53-54; instr zool, Vassar Col, 54-55, instr physiol, 55-56; from instr to asst prof anat, Col Med, Univ Fla, 56-61. *Concurrent Pos:* Vis res assoc prof, Karolinska Inst, Sweden, 67-68; consult, Parke-Davis, 84-92. *Mem:* AAAS; Am Soc Zoologists; Am Asn Anatomists; Teratology Soc (pres, 78-79); Soc Develop Biol. *Res:* Teratology. *Mailing Add:* Dept Anat & Cell Biol Univ Mich Med Sci II Bldg Ann Arbor MI 48109

BEAUDREAU, GEORGE STANLEY, BIOCHEMISTRY. *Current Pos:* assoc prof, 63-77, PROF CHEM & AGR CHEM, ORE STATE UNIV, 63- *Personal Data:* b Ferndale, Wash, Dec 2, 25; m 46; c 4. *Educ:* Wash State Col, BS, 49; Ore State Col, MS, 52, PhD, 54. *Prof Exp:* Fel biol sci, Purdue Univ, 54-56; res assoc, Duke Univ, 56-63. *Mem:* Am Chem Soc; Am Asn Cancer Res. *Res:* Intermediary metabolism and enzymology; antibiotics; tumor virus; tissue culture. *Mailing Add:* 1511 SW Park Ave Portland OR 97201

BEAUDRY, BERNARD JOSEPH, metallurgy, material science, for more information see previous edition

BEAUFAIT, FREDERICK W, ENGINEERING ADMINISTRATION. *Current Pos:* dean eng, 86-95, PROF CIVIL ENG, COL ENG, WAYNE STATE UNIV, 95- *Personal Data:* b Vicksburg, Miss, Nov 28, 36; m 64, Lois Erdman; c Paul & Nicole. *Educ:* Miss State Univ, BS, 58; Univ Ky, MS, 61; Va Polytech Inst, PhD (structural eng), 65. *Prof Exp:* Structural eng, US Army Engrs, Vicksburg, 58-59; eng, L E Gregg & Assoc, Lexington, Ky, 59-60; vis lectr, Univ Liverpool, 60-61; instr, Va Polytech Inst, 61-65; prof civil eng, Vanderbilt Univ, 65-79; prof & chmn, Dept Civil Eng, WVa Univ, 83-86, assoc dean, Col Eng, 83-86. *Concurrent Pos:* Instr, Dept Civil Eng, Univ Ky, 59-60; structural eng, US Army Corps Engrs, 66 & 77; vis prof, Dept Civil & Structural Eng, Univ Wales, 75-76; vis prof, Div Basic Sci & Eng, Univ Autonoms Metropolitana, Mex, 83; dir, NSF Eng Educ, Greenfield Coalition, 95- *Mem:* Am Soc Civil Engrs; Am Soc Eng Educ; Nat Soc Prof Engrs. *Res:* The behavior of reinforced concrete and the nonlinear response and analysis of structural systems. *Mailing Add:* Col Eng Wayne State Univ Detroit MI 48202. *Fax:* 313-577-5300

BEAULIEU, J A, bacteriology, immunology, for more information see previous edition

BEAULIEU, JACQUES ALEXANDRE, APPLIED PHYSICS. *Current Pos:* PRES, BEAULIEU CONSULTS INC, 91- *Personal Data:* b St Jean, Que, Apr 15, 32; m 55, Fleur-Ange Tardif; c Jacqueline & Pierre. *Educ:* McGill Univ, BSc, 53, MSc, 54; Univ London, PhD, 69. *Hon Degrees:* PhD, Univ Moncton, 72. *Honors & Awards:* Armchambeault Medal, Can-Fr Asn Advan Sci, 71, J A Bombardier Medal, 80; T Eady Medal, Royal Soc Can, 78; Dennis Gabor Award, Soc Photo-Instrumentation Engrs, 86; Can Asn Physicists Medal for Achievements in Indust & Appl Physics, 93. *Prof Exp:* Res scientist, Dept Nat Defense, Valcartier, 54-71, sr systs officer, 74-91; dir res & develop, Gentec Co, Que, 71-74. *Mem:* Fel Royal Soc Can; Can Asn Physicists; Can-Fr Asn Advan Sci; Optical Asn Am. *Res:* Industrial and applied physics; contributed numerous articles to professional journals and patents in field. *Mailing Add:* 2526 Chasse St Ste-Foy PQ G1W 1L9 Can

BEAULIEU, JOHN DAVID, SCIENTIFIC TEAM CONSTRUCTION & OVERSIGHT. *Current Pos:* geologist, 70-77, DEP STATE GEOLOGIST, ORE DEPT GEOL & MINERAL INDUSTS, 77- *Personal Data:* b Hanford, Wash, July 22, 44; m 67, Kathleen; c Michael, Patrick & Matthew. *Educ:* Univ Wash, BS, 66; Stanford Univ, PhD(geol), 71. *Prof Exp:* Prof geol, Univ Ore, 69-70. *Concurrent Pos:* Fel, NSF, 67-69. *Res:* Cenozoic behavior of the San Andreas Fault in the Santa Cruz Mountains, California; structure and stratigraphy of Oregon; geologic history and hazards of Oregon; plate tectonics; geothermal potential and mineral potential of Oregon; reactor siting with respect to geology; science in natural resource management; resource management with supervisory regulatory responsibilities for oil, gas, geothermal, metals and non metals; attention to emerging science with challenges of exploration, production, and reclamation. *Mailing Add:* Dept Geol & Mineral Industs 965 State Off Bldg 800 Oregon St NE Portland OR 97201

BEAUMARIAGE, D(ONALD) C(URTIS), ELECTRICAL ENGINEERING, SYSTEMS MANAGEMENT. *Current Pos:* CHIEF, OCEAN & LAKES LEVELS DIV, NAT OCEAN SERV, 91- *Personal Data:* b Bridgeville, Pa, Aug 12, 25; m 47, Alma Lewandowsky; c Linda L. *Educ:* Cornell Univ, BEE, 46; Carnegie Inst Tech, MSEE, 48, DSc, 50; Mass Inst Technol, SMIM, 60. *Prof Exp:* Res engr, Carnegie Inst Tech, 48-49, instr elec eng, 49-50; group leader systs anal, Air Armamant Div, Sperry Gyroscope Co, 50-54; from mgr systs proj & electronic syst design to mgr data syst ctr, RCA, 54-64; dir info sci, Defense Systs Div, Bunker-Ramo Corp, Calif, 64-68, Eastern Tech Ctr, Md, 68-69; pres, Universal Info Technologies, Inc, 69-71; dir, Man Undersea Sci & Technol Prog, Nat Oceanic & Atomospheric Admin, 71-80, chief, Ocean Systs Div, 81-90. *Concurrent Pos:* Sloan fel, Sch Indust Mgt, Mass Inst Technol, 59-60; mem, Prog Sr Govt Mgrs, Harvard Bus Sch, 81; regist prof engr, Mass. *Mem:* Inst Elec & Electronics Engrs; Sigma Xi. *Res:* Electronic control systems; information sciences and systems; technical direction; management; ocean engineering; environmental measurement systems. *Mailing Add:* Ocean & Lake Levels Div Nat Ocean Serv 6001 Executive Blvd Bldg 1 Rockville MD 20852. *Fax:* 301-713-4437; *E-Mail:* Omnet: d.beaumariage

BEAUMARIAGE, TERRENCE GILBERT, COMPUTER SIMULATION, OBJECT ORIENTED DESIGN. *Current Pos:* ASST PROF INDUST ENG, DEPT INDUST & MGT SYSTS ENG, ARIZ STATE UNIV, 89-, ASSOC DIR RES, SYSTS SIMULATION LAB, 90- *Personal Data:* b Washington, Pa, July 10, 61; m 86. *Educ:* Rochester Inst Technol, BS, 84; Okla State Univ, MS, 87, PhD(indust eng), 90. *Prof Exp:* Teaching asst indust eng, Dept Indust Eng & Mech, Okla State Univ, 84-85; mat handler engr, Telex Comput Prod, 87; res asst, Okla State Univ Ctr Comput Int Mfg, 85-89. *Concurrent Pos:* Asst engr, Rochester Prod Div Gen Motors, 81-82, O'Donnell & Assocs, Inc, 82; cost engr, IBM Fed Systs Div, 82-83, mfg eng, 83-84; mfg engr, IBM Entry Systs Div, 85. *Mem:* Inst Indust Engrs; Am Soc Eng Educ; Am Soc Qual Control; Soc Comput Simulation. *Res:* Implementation of a comprehensive manufacturing systems engineering workbench within an object oriented programming environment; workbench will support object oriented simulation modeling; manufacturing system data management; shop floor control and manufacturing data analysis. *Mailing Add:* Dept Indust Eng Ore State Univ 118 Covell Hall Corvallis OR 97331-2407

BEAUMONT, RALPH HARRISON, JR, CHEMISTRY. *Current Pos:* PRES & DIR RES, CATALYST SOUTH, INC, 91-; PRES, SEDGEFIELD CONSULT, INC, 91- *Personal Data:* b Roxbury, NY, Nov 10, 23; m 50; c 6. *Educ:* Colgate Univ, BA, 43; Rutgers Univ, PhD(chem), 53. *Prof Exp:* Asst, Rutgers Univ, 43-44, 46-59 & 51; res chemist spec prob sect, NB Lab, AEC, 49-51 & Allied Chem, 51-52; asst dir res, Huyck Corp, 52-57, dir chem res, 57-63; tech dir, W F Fancourt & Co, 64-66, vpres res & develop, 66-70; pres & dir res, Brin Mont Corp, 68-91. *Mem:* Am Chem Soc; Sigma Xi. *Res:* Analytical chemistry; inorganic chemistry; physical chemistry; kinetics and mechanism of reactions; textile chemistry; general textile auxiliaries; surfactants and rubber chemicals; urethane systems, acrylic monomers. *Mailing Add:* 5314 Dorchester Rd Greensboro NC 27407-7306

BEAUMONT, RANDOLPH CAMPBELL, INORGANIC CHEMISTRY. *Current Pos:* AT BEAUMONT CHEM CO, 89- *Personal Data:* b Los Angeles, Calif, Oct 15, 41; m 66; c 3. *Educ:* Whitman Col, BA, 63; Univ Idaho, PhD(inorg chem), 67. *Prof Exp:* Asst prof chem, Alma Col, Mich, 67-83. *Concurrent Pos:* Postdoctoral work, McMaster Univ, Ont, 73-74. *Mem:* Am Chem Soc; Sigma Xi. *Res:* Inorganic, physical and analytical chemistry; nitriles of period 2 elements; peroxo and superoxo complexes of transition metals; carbonoanions (synthesis and properties). *Mailing Add:* 3085 W Brenda Loop Flagstaff AZ 86001-0917

BEAUMONT, ROSS ALLEN, mathematics; deceased, see previous edition for last biography

BEAUREGARD, MARC DANIEL, PROTEIN STRUCTURE & STABILITY, DE NOVO PROTEIN DESIGN. *Current Pos:* asst prof biochem & protein eng, 92-96, ASSOC PROF BIOCHEM, UNIV PEI, 96- *Personal Data:* b Drummondville, Que, Dec 14, 62; m, Christine Lacrosse; c Vincent & Julie. *Educ:* Univ Que, Trois-Rivieres, BSc, 85, PhD(biophys), 89. *Prof Exp:* Natural Sci & Eng Res Coun fel, Max-Planck-Inst, Strahlenchemie, Ger, 89, Univ De Liege, Belg, 90, J Wise fel, Agr Can, 90-92. *Concurrent Pos:* Adj prof, Atlantic Vet Col, 92- *Mem:* Protein Soc; Fed Am Soc Exp Biol. *Res:* Modification and study of synthetic, mutant and natural proteins. *Mailing Add:* Chem Dept Univ PEI Charlottetown PE C1A 4P3 Can. *Fax:* 902-566-0632; *E-Mail:* mbeauregard@upei.ca

BEAUREGARD, RAYMOND A, RING THEORY. *Current Pos:* From asst prof to assoc prof, 68-82, PROF MATH, UNIV RI, 82- *Personal Data:* b New Bedford, Mass, Feb 10, 43; m 64; c 3. *Educ:* Providence Col, AB, 64; Univ NH, MS, 66, PhD(algebra), 68. *Mem:* Am Math Soc; Math Asn Am. *Res:* Noncommutative rings; noncommutative integral domains, unique factorization; right LCM domains; principal right ideal domains; ring theory; author of linear algebra text book. *Mailing Add:* Dept Math Univ RI Kingston RI 02881

BEAVEN, MICHAEL ANTHONY, PHARMACOLOGY & IMMUNOPHARMACOLOGY, BIOCHEMISTRY. *Current Pos:* vis fel, Lab Chem Pharmacol, Nat Heart Lung & Blood Inst, NIH, 62-66, res pharmacologist, 66-68, sr investr, Exp Therapeut Br, 68-74, sr investr, Pulmonary Br, 74-77, chief, Sect Cellular Pharmacol, Lab Cellular Metab, 77-82, DEP CHIEF, LAB CHEM PHARMACOL, NAT HEART LUNG & BLOOD INST, NIH, 82- *Personal Data:* b London, Eng, Dec 4, 36; US citizen; m 64. *Educ:* Chelsea Col Sci & Technol, Univ London, London, BPharm, 59, PhD(med), 62. *Honors & Awards:* Dirs Award, NIH, 89. *Prof Exp:* Demonstr, Chelsea Col Sci & Technol, London, 59-62. *Concurrent Pos:* USPHS vis fel, Nat Heart Inst, 62-63, vis assoc, 64; assoc mem, Darwin Col, Cambridge Univ, Eng, 82-83; fel, Japanese Soc Prom Sci, 89. *Mem:* Am Asn Immunologist; Pharmaceut Soc Gt Brit; Am Soc Pharmacol & Exp Therapeut. *Res:* Mechanisms of mast cell degranulation; mechanisms of cell activation; role of histamine in pathological and physiological reactions; author of over 150 scientific articles. *Mailing Add:* Lab Pharmacol Nat Heart Lung & Blood Inst NIH Bldg 10 Rm 8N109 Bethesda MD 20892-1760

BEAVEN, VIDA HELMS, HEALTH SCIENCE ADMINISTRATION. *Current Pos:* spec asst to dir, Nat Heart, Lung & Blood Inst, 76-77, actg dir, Fogarty Int Ctr, 80-81, spec asst to dep dir, 77-86, ASST DIR PROG COORD, NIH, 86- *Personal Data:* b Bluefield, WVa, June 2, 39; m 64. *Educ:* Ind Univ, BA, 61, MA, 62; George Wash Univ, PhD (biochem),68. *Prof Exp:* Staff fel, Nat Heart Inst, NIH, 68-71, grants assoc, Div Res Grants, 71-72, spec asst to assoc dir, Extramural Progs, Nat Inst Arthritis, Metab & Digestive Dis, 72-73; Biomed Health Progs adv, Off Asst Secy Health, Dept Health & Human Serv, 73-76. *Mailing Add:* 10810 Kenilworth Ave Garrett Park MD 20896

BEAVER, BONNIE VERYLE, VETERINARY ANIMAL BEHAVIOR. *Current Pos:* instr vet anat, 69-72, from asst prof to prof vet anat, 72-86, PROF & CHIEF MED, SMALL ANIMAL MED & SURG, TEX A&M UNIV, 86- *Personal Data:* b Minneapolis, Minn; wid. *Educ:* Univ Minn, BS, 66, DVM, 68; Tex A&M Univ, MS, 72. *Honors & Awards:* Animal Welfare Award, Am Vet Med Asn, 96. *Prof Exp:* Instr vet surg & radiol, Univ Minn,

68-69. *Concurrent Pos:* Mem, Vet Med Adv Comt, Dept Health, Educ & Welfare, 72-74, Nat adv Food & Drug Comt, 75; mem, Comt Animal Models & Genetic Stocks, Nat Acad Sci, 84-89; mem, Panel on Microlivestock, Nat Res Coun, 86-87, Adv Comt Pew Nat Vet Educ Prog, Pew Charitable Trusts, 87-92; distinguished practr, Nat Acad Prac Vet Med; charter dipl, Am Col Vet Behaviorists. *Mem:* Am Vet Med Asn; Am Animal Hosp Asn; Am Soc Vet Animal Behav; Am Asn Equine Practitioners; Animal Behav Soc; AAAS. *Res:* Domestic animal behavior; specific projects which evaluate behavior and examine problem behaviors and how they develop. *Mailing Add:* Dept Small Animal Med & Surg Tex A&M Univ College Station TX 77843-4474

BEAVER, DONALD LOYD, VERTEBRATE ECOLOGY. *Current Pos:* asst prof, 72-77, ASSOC PROF ZOOL, MICH STATE UNIV, 77- *Personal Data:* b Hayden, Colo, Sept 16, 43; m 66; c 1. *Educ:* Colo State Univ, BS, 65, MS, 67; Univ Calif, Berkeley, PhD(zool), 72. *Mem:* Am Ornithologists Union; Wilson Ornith Soc; Sigma Xi. *Res:* Ecological and behavioral aspects of foraging in birds, including selection of foraging patch, optimal food choice and time and energy spent foraging. *Mailing Add:* Dept Zool Mich State Univ 203 Natural Sci East Lansing MI 48824-1115

BEAVER, EARL RICHARD, PHYSICAL CHEMISTRY. *Current Pos:* Sr chemist, Monsanto Co, 69-73, process specialist, 73-74, group supvr, 74-77, mgr results mgt, 77-79, mgr process tech, 79-83, DIR BUS DEVELOP & TECHNOL, MONSANTO CO, 83- *Personal Data:* b Newburgh, NY, Mar 2, 45; m 66. *Educ:* McMurry Col, BA, 66; Tex Tech Univ, 66-69, PhD(phys chem), 70. *Concurrent Pos:* Welsh Found fel. *Mem:* Am Chem Soc; Am Inst Chem Engrs. *Res:* Application of differential thermal analysis, thermogravimetric analysis and adsorption measurements to the solution of process problems in heterogeneous catalysis. *Mailing Add:* Monsanto Co MZ A3NB 800 N Lindbergh Blvd St Louis MO 63141-7843

BEAVER, H H, PETROLEUM. *Current Pos:* Asst prof, 53-59, CHMN GEOL, BAYLOR UNIV, 76- *Personal Data:* b Steubenville, Ohio, July 24, 25. *Educ:* Univ Wis-Madison, PhD(geol), 54. *Mem:* Fel Geol Soc Am. *Mailing Add:* Dept Geol Baylor Univ PO Box 97354 Waco TX 76798

BEAVER, PAUL CHESTER, parasitology, tropical medicine; deceased, see previous edition for last biography

BEAVER, ROBERT JOHN, STATISTICAL MODELING, EXPERIMENTAL DESIGN. *Current Pos:* PROF STATIST & STATISTICIAN, UNIV CALIF, RIVERSIDE, 70- *Personal Data:* b Mt Carmel, Pa, Mar 27, 37; m 70, Barbara Mattick; c Krista Ann & David Carleton. *Educ:* Bloomsburg State Univ, BS, 59; Bucknell Univ, MS, 64; Univ Fla, MStat, 66, PhD(statist), 70. *Prof Exp:* Statist consult, Teacher Eval Proj, Univ Fla, 66, dir, Comput-Assisted Instr Proj, 66-67, instr statist, 67-68; med statistician, Med Div, Oak Ridge Assoc Univs, 68. *Mem:* Am Statis Asn; Int Biometric Soc. *Res:* Model building as applied to problems of choice; paired comparisons; experimental design; statistical modeling in the biosciences; agricultural design of experiments. *Mailing Add:* Dept Statist Univ Calif 900 University Ave Riverside CA 92521-0138. *Fax:* 909-787-3286; *E-Mail:* beaver@mail.ucr.edu

BEAVER, W DON, CHEMISTRY. *Current Pos:* RETIRED. *Personal Data:* b Elkhart, Kans, May 7, 24; m 46; c 2. *Educ:* Bethany Nazarene Col, AB, 46; Okla State Univ, MS, 53, PhD(chem), 55. *Prof Exp:* Teacher pub schs, Okla, 47-48; instr math & chem, Bethany Nazarene Col, 48-51; asst chem, Okla State Univ, 52-55; prof, Southern Nazarene Univ, 55-91, chmn, Div Natural Sci, 68-91, vpres acad affairs, 82-91. *Concurrent Pos:* Assoc dean, Inst Res, Southern Nazarene Univ, 76-, acad dean, 78- *Mem:* Am Chem Soc; Sigma Xi. *Res:* Use of borohydrides as reducing agents and coordination complexes of the transition metals in aqueous and non-aqueous solvents. *Mailing Add:* Dept Chem Southern Nazarene Univ 4509 N Peniel Bethany OK 73008

BEAVER, W(ILLIAM) L(AWRENCE), EXERCISE PHYSIOLOGY, MEDICAL COMPUTER SYSTEMS. *Current Pos:* CONSULT, EXCERCISE PHYSIOL, 78- *Personal Data:* b Yucaipa, Calif, Oct 9, 20; m 44, May Merit; c Judith E (Rock) & Robert A. *Educ:* Univ Calif, BS, 44, PhD(elec eng), 51. *Prof Exp:* Res engr, Univ Calif, 47-51; sr scientist, Varian Assoc, 51-74; adj prof, Stanford Univ, 74-78. *Mem:* Sigma Xi; Am Physiol Soc; Inst Elec & Electronics Engrs. *Res:* Computer analysis in physiology and medicine; exercise and respiratory physiology; on-line computer systems for gas exchange and cardio-respiratory analysis; ultra-sonic imaging. *Mailing Add:* PO Box 390157 Mountain View CA 94039

BEAVER, WILLIAM THOMAS, CLINICAL PHARMACOLOGY, ANALGESIOLOGY. *Current Pos:* assoc prof, 68-79, PROF PHARMACOL & ANESTHESIOL, SCHS MED & DENT, GEORGETOWN UNIV, 79-, MEM GEN STAFF, DEPT ANESTHESIOL, UNIV HOSP, 69- *Personal Data:* b Albany, NY, Jan 27, 33; m 61; c 3. *Educ:* Princeton Univ, AB, 54; Cornell Univ, MD, 58. *Prof Exp:* Intern surg-med, Roosevelt Hosp, New York, 58-59; USPHS fel pharmacol, Med Col, Cornell Univ, 59-61, from instr to asst prof, 61-68. *Concurrent Pos:* Clin asst, Mem Hosp, NY, 61-68; asst vis physician, Dept Med, James Ewing Hosp, 62-68; res assoc, Sloan-Kettering Inst Cancer Res, 63-68; attend physician, Calvary Hosp, 64-68; consult, Food & Drug Admin, 69-76, Fed Trade Comn, 70-75 & AMA Drug Eval, 71-; mem, Adv Panel Analgesics, Sedatives & Anti-inflammatory Agts, US Pharmacopoeia, 71-75, chmn, 76-80, mem, Comt Revision, 75-80. *Mem:* AAAS; Am Soc Clin Pharmacol & Therapeut; Int Asn Study Pain; Am Soc Pharmacol & Exp Therapeut. *Res:* Clinical pharmacology of analgesic drugs; controlled clinical trials of analgesic efficacy. *Mailing Add:* Dept Pharmacol Georgetown Univ Sch Med Washington DC 20007-2195. *Fax:* 202-687-5015

BEAVERS, DOROTHY (ANNE) JOHNSON, ORGANIC CHEMISTRY. *Current Pos:* RETIRED. *Personal Data:* b Worcester, Mass, July 11, 27; wid; c Leo II. *Educ:* Clark Univ, BA, 49; Duke Univ, PhD(org chem), 55. *Prof Exp:* Res chemist, Am Cyanamid Co, 49-51; asst gen & org chem, Duke Univ, 51-54; sr res chemist, Eastman Kodak Co, 54-61, res assoc, 61-90. *Concurrent Pos:* USPHS grant, 53-54. *Mem:* AAAS; Am Chem Soc; Soc Photog Scientists & Engrs. *Res:* Synthetic organic chemistry; surface active agents; aromatic cyclodehydration; chemical transfer; rapid processing of photographic emulsions; photographic paper products; biochemistry of mental illness and retardation; emulsion addenda; biochemistry and clinical chemistry; sensitization of emulsions; color reversal systems; high speed photographic films; granted over 40 US patents & over 100 foreign patents. *Mailing Add:* 70 Rainbow Dr Rochester NY 14622. *E-Mail:* dbeavers@monroe.edu

BEAVERS, ELLINGTON MCHENRY, CHEMISTRY. *Current Pos:* PRES, BEACON RES, INC, 81-; CHAIR, BIOCOAT, INC, 91- *Personal Data:* b Atlanta, Ga; m 57; c 1. *Educ:* Emory Univ, BS, 38, MS, 39; Univ NC, PhD(chem), 41. *Hon Degrees:* DSc, Beaver Col, 93. *Prof Exp:* Res chem, Rohm & Haas Co, 41-47, lab head, 47-55, res supvr, 55-59, assoc dir res, 60-69, dir, Res & Develop, 69-73, vpres, 70-73, mem, Bd Dirs, 71-81, sr vpres, 73-75, group vpres, 75-81. *Mem:* Am Chem Soc (treas); Am Inst Chemists; Am Inst Chem Engrs. *Res:* Research and discovery with the objective of improving the biocompatibility of implantable medical devices. *Mailing Add:* 931 Coates Rd Meadowbrook PA 19046. *Fax:* 215-572-7595

BEAVERS, GORDON STANLEY, FLUID MECHANICS, ENGINEERING MECHANICS. *Current Pos:* From asst prof to assoc prof, Univ Minn, Minneapolis, 63-74, assoc head dept, 72-83, assoc dean, 83-91, actg dean, 91-93, PROF AEROSPACE ENG, UNIV MINN, MINNEAPOLIS, 74- *Personal Data:* b Doncaster, Eng, Oct 16, 36; nat US; m 66, Janet Christianson; c Michael. *Educ:* Cambridge Univ, BA, 59, PhD(mech eng), 63; Harvard Univ, SM, 60. *Mem:* Am Inst Aeronaut & Astronaut; Am Soc Mech Engrs; Soc Rheology. *Res:* Flows through porous media; fluid mechanics; gas dynamics; rheological fluid mechanics. *Mailing Add:* Dept Aerospace Eng & Mech Univ Minn 110 Union St Minneapolis MN 55455. *E-Mail:* beavers@aem.umn.edu

BEAVO, JOSEPH A, CYCLINUCLEOTIDES. *Current Pos:* PROF PHARMACOL, UNIV WASH, 77- *Educ:* Vanderbilt Col, PhD(physiol), 70. *Mem:* Nat Acad Sci. *Mailing Add:* Dept Pharmacol SJ-30 Univ Wash Seattle WA 98195-0001

BEBB, HERBERT BARRINGTON, SOLID STATE PHYSICS. *Current Pos:* OWNER, BARY BEGG & ASSOC, 90- *Personal Data:* b Wichita Falls, Tex, June 22, 35; m 58; c 2. *Educ:* Univ Okla, BS, 59; Syracuse Univ, MS, 64; Univ Rochester, PhD(optics), 65. *Prof Exp:* Assoc physicist, Fed Systs Div, Int Bus Mach Corp, 59-61, mem res staff, Res Lab, 61-62; res assoc, Inst Optics, Univ Rochester, 65-66; theoret physicist, Tex Instruments Inc, 66-69, mgr appl optics br, 69, dir advan technol lab, 69-74; mgr, Prod Develop Dept, Xerox Corp, 74-80, mgr, Advan Prod & Technol, 80-90. *Concurrent Pos:* Consult, Int Bus Mach Corp, 65. *Mem:* Am Phys Soc; Optical Soc Am; Math Asn Am. *Res:* Theoretical study of optical properties of solids; ultrasonic surface waves; liquid crystal phenomena; infrared sensors; semiconductor technology; systems engineering. *Mailing Add:* Bary Bebb & Assoc 2129 Monarch Ridge Circle El Cajon CA 92019

BEBBINGTON, W(ILLIAM) P(EARSON), CHEMICAL ENGINEERING. *Current Pos:* RETIRED. *Personal Data:* b Painted Post, NY, Sept 10, 15; m 40; c 3. *Educ:* Cornell Univ, BChem, 36, PhD(chem eng), 40. *Honors & Awards:* Robert E Wilson Award, Am Inst Chem Engrs. *Prof Exp:* Chem engr, Ammonia & Polychem Dept, E I du Pont de Nemours & Co, 40-50, chem engr explosives dept, Atomic Energy Div, 50-52, supt heavy water tech sect, Savannah River Plant, 52-55, asst sect dir, Savannah River Lab, 55-59, supt separations tech sect, Savannah River Plant, 59-62, gen supt, Works Tech Dept, 62-74. *Mem:* Fel Am Inst Chem Engrs. *Res:* Heavy water technology; chemical separations of nuclear fuels; environmental effects of nuclear industry. *Mailing Add:* 4275 Owens Rd Apt No 2307 Evans GA 30809

BEBERNES, JERROLD WILLIAM, APPLIED MATHEMATICS. *Current Pos:* from asst prof to assoc prof, 62-71, PROF MATH, UNIV COLO, BOULDER, 71- *Personal Data:* b Cotesfield, Nebr, Apr 7, 35; m 56; c 3. *Educ:* Univ Nebr, BS, 57, MA, 59, PhD(math), 62. *Prof Exp:* Mathematician, US Naval Ord Lab, Calif, 57; instr math, Univ Nebr, 59-60. *Mem:* Am Math Soc; Math Asn Am; Soc Indust & Appl Math. *Res:* Functional analysis, differential equations, reaction diffusion equations, combustion problems, nonlocal problems and shear banding phenomena. *Mailing Add:* Dept Appl Math Univ Colo Boulder Box 526 Boulder CO 80309-0526. *E-Mail:* bebernes@newton.colorado.edu

BEBOUT, DON GRAY, SEDIMENTOLOGY. *Current Pos:* RETIRED. *Personal Data:* b Moneson, Pa, Jan 23, 31; m 52; c 3. *Educ:* Mt Union Col, BS, 52; Univ Wis, MS, 54; Univ Kans, PhD(geol), 61. *Prof Exp:* Asst micropaleont, Univ Kans, 56-57 & 59-60; sr res specialist geol, Exxon Prod Res Co, Tex, 60-72; res scientist geol, Bur Econ Geol, Univ Tex, Austin, 72-79; prof dept geol & dir, La Geol Surv, La State Univ, 79-81; sr res scientist, Bur Econ Geol, Univ Tex, 81-94. *Concurrent Pos:* Lectr, Dept Geol Sci, Univ Tex, Austin, 75-79; distinguished lectr, Am Asn Petrol Geologists. *Mem:* Fel Geol Soc Am; Am Asn Petrol Geologists; hon mem Soc Econ Paleontologists & Mineralogists. *Res:* Subsurface distribution of sedimentary facies along the Texas gulf coast; evaluating the potential of producing geothermal energy from Texas gulf coast geopressured reservoirs; characterization of carbonate reservoir. *Mailing Add:* 3304 Bridle Path Austin TX 78703

BECCHETTI, FREDERICK DANIEL, PHYSICS. *Current Pos:* from asst prof to assoc prof, 73-82, PROF PHYSICS, UNIV MICH, ANN ARBOR, 83- *Personal Data:* b Minneapolis, Minn, Mar 3, 43; c 2. *Educ:* Univ Minn, BS, 65, MS, 68, PhD(physics), 69. *Prof Exp:* Vis asst prof physics, Niels Bohr Inst, 69-71; res assoc, Lawrence Berkeley Lab, 71-73. *Concurrent Pos:* NSF fel, Niels Bohr Inst, 70-71. *Mem:* Fel Am Physics Soc; Am Asn Physics Teachers; Inst Elec & Electronics Engrs; Am Asn Physics Med. *Res:* Experimental nuclear physics; nuclear radiation detectors. *Mailing Add:* Dept Physics Univ Mich Ann Arbor MI 48109

BECHARA, IBRAHIM, POLYMER CHEMISTRY. *Current Pos:* mgr polymer res, 88-93, GROUP MGR, WATER-BORNE TECHNOL, WITCO CORP, 93- *Personal Data:* b Bazzak, Syria, Jan 16, 43; US citizen; m 71, Huda I Masso; c 3. *Educ:* Hobart Col, BS, 63; Univ Del, PhD(chem), 67. *Prof Exp:* Res chemist, Air Prod & Chem, 67-80, sr prin res chemist, 80-84; mgr, urethane res, Polyvinyl Chem, 85-86. *Mem:* Am Chem Soc. *Res:* Synthesis of organic chemicals via liquid and gas phase methods; homogenous catalysis of organic reactions, mainly isocyanate reactions and structures and properties of polyurethanes; reaction injection molding and thermal and spectroscopic analysis of polymeric materials; water borne polyurethanes; chemistry and technology. *Mailing Add:* 241 Covington Ct Naperville IL 60565-3341. *Fax:* 708-458-1599

BECHER, PAUL, PHYSICAL CHEMISTRY. *Current Pos:* PRES, PAUL BECHER ASSOCS, LTD, 81- *Personal Data:* b Brooklyn, NY, Mar 24, 18; m 45; c 2. *Educ:* Polytech Inst Brooklyn, BS, 40, MS, 42, PhD(chem), 49. *Honors & Awards:* Langmuir lectr, Div Colloid & Surface Chem, Am Chem Soc, 83. *Prof Exp:* Assoc prof chem, NGa Col, 48-51; sr proj chemist, Colgate-Palmolive Co, 51-57; res assoc, Atlas Chem Industs, Inc, 57-67, prin scientist, ICI Americas Inc, 67-70, mgr, Phys Chem Sect, Chem Res Dept, 70, dir, Specialty Chem Res Dept, 75-79, assoc dir, Corp Res Dept, 80-81. *Mem:* fel Soc Cosmetic Chemists; Sigma Xi; Am Chem Soc; fel Am Inst Chemists. *Res:* Emulsions; surface chemistry. *Mailing Add:* 520 Windley Rd Wilmington DE 19803-5244. *Fax:* 302-477-1577

BECHER, WILLIAM D(ON), COMPUTER ENGINEERING, COMPUTER EDUCATION. *Current Pos:* ENGR CONSULT, WIDBEC ENG, 76- *Personal Data:* b Bolivar, Ohio, Nov 26, 29; m 50, Helen Hager; c Eric & Patricia. *Educ:* Tri-State Col, BS, 50; Univ Mich, MS, 61, PhD(elec eng), 68. *Prof Exp:* Proj engr, Bogue Elec Co, 50-53; sr develop engr, Goodyear Aircraft Corp, 53 & 55-57; sr systs engr, Beckman Instruments, Inc, 57-58; staff engr, Bendix Systs Div, Bendix Corp, 58-60, sect supvr, 60-63; res engr, Willow Run Lab, 63-68; from asst prof to prof elec eng, Univ Mich, Dearborn, 68-78, chmn dept, 71-76; dept mgr, Environ Res Inst Mich, 77-79; dean, Col Eng, NJ Inst Technol, 79-81; assoc dir, Infrared & Optical Div, Environ Res Inst Mich, 81-88 & 89-91; chmn & prof elec eng, Calif State Univ, Fresno, 88; adj prof elec eng & comput sci, Univ Mich, Ann Arbor, 78-79 & 81-95. *Concurrent Pos:* Lectr elec eng, Univ Mich, Dearborn, 64-66. *Mem:* Sr mem Inst Elec & Electronics Engrs; Am Soc Eng Educ. *Res:* Computer aided design and instruction; digital computer design; switching theory; image processing; radar systems design; electronic circuits and systems; digital instrumentation systems. *Mailing Add:* 691 Spring Valley Dr Ann Arbor MI 48105. *E-Mail:* becher@eecs.umich.edu

BECHHOEFER, JOHN, SOFT-CONDENSED MATTER, PATTERN FORMATION & NONLINEAR PHYSICS. *Current Pos:* ASST PROF, DEPT PHYSICS, SIMON FRASER UNIV, 91- *Personal Data:* b Washington, DC, 1961. *Educ:* Harvard Col, BA, 82; Univ Chicago, MS, 85, Phd(physics), 88. *Prof Exp:* Res assoc.Univ.DeParis-Syd, 88-89, Ecole Narmale Superievre De Lyon, 89-91. *Mem:* Am Phys Soc; Can Asn Physicists; Int Liquid Crystal Soc. *Res:* Experimental pattern formation in soft-condensed matter systems; application of atomic force microscopy to soft materials; liquid crystals; dynamics of first-order phase transitions. *Mailing Add:* Dept Physics Simon Fraser Univ Burnaby BC V5A 1S6 Can. *Fax:* 604-291-3592

BECHHOFER, ROBERT E(RIC), mathematical & engineering statistics, for more information see previous edition

BECHIS, DENNIS JOHN, CRT DESIGN, COMPUTER SIMULATION. *Current Pos:* mem tech staff, 80-89, GROUP HEAD, DAVID SARNOFF RES CTR, RCA LABS, PRINCETON, 89- *Personal Data:* b Boston, Mass, Aug 10, 51; m 85, Maria Harris; c Christopher, Margarite & Dennison. *Educ:* Harvard Col, BA, 73; Univ Md, MS, 76, PhD(physics), 78. *Honors & Awards:* David Sarnoff Award, 83. *Prof Exp:* Res asst high energy physics, Univ Md, 75-78; res assoc, Rutgers Univ, 78-80. *Mem:* Am Phys Soc; Soc Info Display. *Res:* Computer experiments and theoretical analyses in electron optics and heat transfer to aid in the understanding and design of cathode ray tube display devices; development of computer models of electron beams and heat transfer. *Mailing Add:* David Sarnoff Res Ctr CN5300 Princeton NJ 08543-5300. *Fax:* 609-734-2049

BECHIS, KENNETH PAUL, ELECTRO-OPTIC SENSORS, SPACE TECHNOLOGY. *Current Pos:* mem tech staff, TASC, 79-80, sect mgr, 80-82, DEPT MGR, TASC, 82-, MSI GROUP MGR, 93- *Personal Data:* b Boston, Mass, July 22, 49; m 76, Donna Friedman; c Seth & Bret. *Educ:* Harvard Col, AB, 70; Mass Inst Technol, SM, 73; Univ Mass, Amherst, PhD(astrophys), 76. *Prof Exp:* Res asst, Res Lab Electronics, Mass Inst Technol, 71-74; res physicist, Radiometric Technol, Inc, 74-75; res asst, Dept Physics & Astron, Univ Mass, Amherst, 74-76, res assoc & lectr astron, 76-79; site mgr, Five Col Radio Astron Observ, 76-79. *Concurrent Pos:* Consult, TASC, 78-79; payload specialist, Starlab Space Shuttle Mission, 87-90. *Mem:* Am Astron Soc; Inst Elec & Electronics Engrs; Sigma Xi; Soc Photo-Optical Instrumentation Engrs; Int Union Radio Sci. *Res:* New space technology; advanced optics and detectors for remote sensing, phenomenology, surveillance, reconnaissance, and guidance systems. *Mailing Add:* TASC 55 Walkers Brook Dr Reading MA 01867. *Fax:* 781-942-7100; *E-Mail:* hpbechis@tasc.com

BECHT, CHARLES, IV, PROCESS EQUIPMENT, ELEVATED TEMPERATURE DESIGN. *Current Pos:* PRIN, BECHT ENG CO, 86- *Personal Data:* b Newark, NJ, Oct 5, 54; m 81, Mary K Barnwell; c George, Charles, Derek, John & Kristen. *Educ:* Union Col, Schenectady, BS, 76; Stanford Univ, MS, 77. *Prof Exp:* Lead engr, Energy Systs Group, Rockwell Int, 77-80; staff engr, Exxon Res & Engr Co, 80-86. *Concurrent Pos:* Mem, Design & Anal Comt Pressure Vessel & Piping Div, Am Soc Mech Engrs, 88- *Mem:* Fel Am Soc Mech Engrs; Am Soc Civil Eng. *Res:* Design rules and analysis methods for high temperature equipment, piping and expansion joints; new equipment for synfuels and other severe service processes. *Mailing Add:* Shalebrook Dr Harding Township NJ 07960-6638. *E-Mail:* chuck@becht.com

BECHTEL, DONALD BRUCE, ELECTRON MICROSCOPY, DIGITAL IMAGE ANALYSIS. *Current Pos:* Chemist, 74-77, RES CHEMIST, US GRAIN MKT RES LAB, 77- *Personal Data:* b Paterson, NJ, Aug 1, 49; m 71, Kathleen A Barnwell; c Michael & Ryan. *Educ:* Iowa State Univ, BS, 71, MS, 74; Kans State Univ, PhD(microbiol), 82. *Concurrent Pos:* Adj asst prof, Kans State Univ, 83-; assoc ed, Am Asn Cereal Chemists, 85-89. *Mem:* Am Asn Cereal Chemists; Bot Soc Am; Sigma Xi. *Res:* Mechanisms of storage protein synthesis and deposition in wheat; post-translational modifications in developing kernels; improvement of methods for the identification and characterization of specific wheat storage proteins. *Mailing Add:* US Grain Mkt Res Lab 1515 College Ave Manhattan KS 66502-2736

BECHTEL, JAMES HARVEY, PHYSICS. *Current Pos:* RES SCIENTIST PHYSICS, GEN MOTORS RES LABS, 76- *Personal Data:* b Bellefontaine, Ohio, Mar 25, 45. *Educ:* Miami Univ, BS, 67; Univ Mich, Ann Arbor, MS, 68, PhD(physics), 73. *Prof Exp:* Teaching asst physics, Univ Mich, 68-69; physicist, Night Vision Lab, US Army, 69-71; res asst physics, Univ Mich, 71-73; res fel, Harvard Univ, 73-76. *Mem:* AAAS; Am Phys Soc; Optical Soc Am; Am Chem Soc. *Res:* Quantum electronics; nonlinear optics; Raman spectroscopy; damage in laser materials; combustion diagnostics; flame structure; flame quenching; ignition. *Mailing Add:* 2640 Del Mar Heights Rd Suite 207 Del Mar CA 92014-3110

BECHTEL, PETER JOHN, AGRICULTURAL BIOCHEMISTRY. *Current Pos:* dept head food sci & human nutrit, 90-95, PROF DEPT FOOD SCI & HUMAN NUTRIT, COLO STATE UNIV, 90- *Personal Data:* b Minneapolis, Minn, Apr 9, 43; m 63; c 2. *Educ:* Parsons Col, BS, 66; Mich State Univ, PhD(food sci), 71. *Prof Exp:* Chemist prod develop, Res Group, Quaker Oats Co, 66-67; biologist human nutrit, Human Nutrit Div, USDA, 70-71; scholar biochem, Univ Calif, Davis, 71-76; expert molecular biol, Nat Cancer Inst, NIH, 76-77; asst prof animal sci, Biochem & Food Technol, Iowa State Univ, 77-80; from assoc prof to prof, Dept Animal Sci, Food Sci & Physiol, Univ Ill, 80-90. *Concurrent Pos:* Fel, Muscular Dystrophy Asn Am, 72-75; vis scientist, Sabbatical, Dept Cell Genetics, Nobel Inst & Karolinska Inst, Stockholm Sweden, 88-89; adj, Dept Pediat, Univ Colo Med Sch. *Mem:* Inst Food Technologists; Am Soc Animal Sci; Am Inst Nutrit. *Res:* Biochemical regulatory mechanisms; muscle growth and development; unimional quality of food. *Mailing Add:* Dept Food Sci & Human Nutrit Colo State Univ Ft Collins CO 80523-0001. *Fax:* 970-491-7252; *E-Mail:* bechtel@cahs.colostate.edu

BECHTEL, ROBERT D, MATHEMATICS. *Current Pos:* RETIRED. *Personal Data:* b Chicago, Ill, Apr 2, 31; m 52; c 3. *Educ:* McPherson Col, BS, 53; Kans State Univ, MS, 59; Purdue Univ, PhD(math educ), 63. *Prof Exp:* Teacher high schs, Kans, 55-58; asst prof math, Kans State Univ, 63-66; assoc prof, Purdue Univ, 66-71, prof math educ, 71-92. *Mem:* Math Asn Am; Am Math Soc; Sigma Xi. *Res:* Mathematics education. *Mailing Add:* 3798 S Elati St Englewood CO 80110

BECHTEL, STEPHEN D, JR, CIVIL ENGINEERING. *Current Pos:* pres, 60-73, chmn, 73-90, ENGR, BECHTEL CORP, 41-, EMER CHMN, 90-; EMER CHMN, FREMONT GROUP INC & SEQUOIA VENTURES INC, 95- *Personal Data:* b Oakland, Calif, May 10, 25; m 46, Elizabeth M Hogan; c 5. *Educ:* Purdue Univ, BS, 46; Stanford Univ, MBA, 48. *Hon Degrees:* DEng, Purdue Univ, 72; DSc, Colo Univ, 81. *Honors & Awards:* Herbert Hoover Medal, 80; Nat Medal of Technol, 91. *Prof Exp:* Dir, IBM, Gen Motors, Tenneco; former chmn, Nat Acad Eng; chmn, Fremont Group Inc & Sequoia Ventures Inc, 80-95. *Concurrent Pos:* Life trustee, Calif Inst Technol; hon trustee, Calif Acad Sci. *Mem:* Nat Acad Eng; fel Am Soc Civil Engrs; Am Inst Metall Eng; AAAS; Am Acad Arts & Sci; Royal Acad Eng. *Mailing Add:* Bechtel Group Inc PO Box 19365 San Francisco CA 94119-3965

BECHTEL, STEPHEN E, MECHANICAL ENGINEERING. *Current Pos:* ASSOC PROF, DEPT ENG MECH, OHIO STATE UNIV, 86- *Educ:* Univ Mich, BS, 79; Univ Calif, Berkeley, PhD(eng), 83. *Prof Exp:* Res asst, Univ Calif, Berkeley, 79-83. *Concurrent Pos:* Mem, Grad Studies Com, Dept Eng Mech, Ohio State Univ, 86-, Dept Eng Mech Rep Col, Eng Undergrad Hon Com, 87-, Undergrad Com Dept Eng Mech, 88-; Consult, Hoechst Celanese Corp, Rockwell Int & Los Alamos Nat Lab. *Mem:* Am Soc Mech Engrs; Am Acad Mech; Soc Rheology. *Res:* Modeling of industrial polymer processing and fiber spinning; viscoelastic fluid flows; free surface flows; instability mechanisms; material characterizations, transducer-characterization in non-destructive evaluation. *Mailing Add:* Ohio State Univ Dept Eng Mech 155 W Woodruff Ave Columbus OH 43210

BECHTLE, DANIEL WAYNE, OPTICS, ELECTRONICS. *Current Pos:* MEM TECH STAFF OPTICS, DAVID SARNOFF RES CTR, 78- *Personal Data:* b Myrtle Creek, Ore, May 18, 49; m 74. *Educ:* Univ Ore, BA(physics) & BA(math), 71; Univ Colo, PhD(physics), 77. *Concurrent Pos:* Consult, Burleigh Instruments, 75- *Mem:* Inst Elec & Electronic Engrs. *Res:* Optics, electronics and microwaves; Brilloun spectroscopy; fiber-optics communication. *Mailing Add:* 23 Whitehall Rd Trenton NJ 08690

BECHTLE, GERALD FRANCIS, ORGANIC CHEMISTRY. *Current Pos:* RETIRED. *Personal Data:* b Ottawa, Kans, Nov 4, 21. *Educ:* Ottawa Univ, Kans, BS, 43; Univ Kans, MS, 50. *Prof Exp:* Sr chemist, Sherwin-Williams Co, 47-54; assoc chemist, Midwest Res Inst, 55-67; chemist, Cook Paint & Varnish Co, 67-89. *Res:* Resin; paint; oils and fats. *Mailing Add:* 4516 Broadway Apt 31 Kansas City MO 64111

BECHTOL, KATHLEEN B, IMMUNOLOGY. *Current Pos:* RETIRED. *Personal Data:* b Oakland, Calif, July 13, 45. *Educ:* Stanford Univ, PhD(biol), 73. *Prof Exp:* Assoc prof, Wistar Inst, 83-85; sr scientist, Genentech Inc, 85-89. *Mem:* Am Soc Cell Biol. *Mailing Add:* 928 E Arques Ave Sunnyvale CA 94086-4520

BECHTOLD, MAX FREDERICK, PHYSICAL CHEMISTRY. *Current Pos:* RETIRED. *Personal Data:* b North Manchester, Ind, Jan 3, 15; m 37; c 4. *Educ:* Manchester Col, BS, 35; Purdue Univ, PhD(phys chem), 39. *Prof Exp:* Chemist, E I Du Pont De Nemours & Co, Inc, 39-67, res supvr, Cent Res Dept, Exp Sta, 67-80. *Mem:* AAAS; Sigma Xi; Am Chem Soc. *Res:* Inorganic polymerization kinetics; colloid chemistry of organic polymers; thin film techniques; solid state reactions in ceramics and metallic high temperature materials; refractory and magnetic powders; batteries, Rankine cycle engines and their fluids; solar energy conversion; scratch-resistant coatings; polysilicic acid chemistry; films and fibers from polymer dispersions. *Mailing Add:* 491 Bayard Rd Kennett Square PA 19348

BECHTOLD, WILLIAM ERIC, METABOLISM, HUMAN DOSIMETRY. *Current Pos:* Postdoctoral fel, 81-83, STAFF SCIENTIST, INHALATION TOXICOL RES INST, 83- *Personal Data:* b New Orleans, La, Oct 10, 52; m 85. *Educ:* Emory Univ, BS, 75; PhD(phys chem), 81. *Mem:* Am Chem Soc. *Res:* Metabolism and disposition of inhalted xenobiotics; trace analysis of organic compounds in biological and environmental matricies; determination of human dosimetry to organic toxicants using biological monitoring. *Mailing Add:* PO Box 5890 Albuquerque NM 87185

BECK, AARON TEMKIN, PSYCHIATRY. *Current Pos:* instr, Univ Pa, 54-57, assoc, 57-58, from asst prof to prof psychiat, 58-83, univ prof, 83-, EMER UNIV PROF PSYCHIAT, UNIV PA. *Personal Data:* b Providence, RI, July 18, 21; m 50; c 4. *Educ:* Brown Univ, BA, 42; Yale Univ, MD, 46. *Hon Degrees:* MA, Univ Pa, 70; DMS, Brown Univ, 82. *Honors & Awards:* Found fund prize res psychiat, Am Psychiat Asn, 79; Paul Hoch Award, Am Psychopath Asn, 83; Distinguished Sci Award, Am Psychol Asn, 89. *Prof Exp:* Asst chief dept neuro-psychiat, Valley Forge Army Hosp, Va, 52-54. *Concurrent Pos:* Sect chief, Philadelphia Gen Hosp, 58-; consult, Vet Admin Hosp, Philadelphia, 67-; spec consult, Ctr Studies Suicide Prev, NIMH, 69-72, chmn, Task Force Suicide Prev in 70's, 69-70; trustee, Am Acad Psychoanal, 70-74. *Mem:* Inst Med-Nat Acad Sci; Am Psychopath Asn; Am Psychiat Soc; Asn Advan Behav Ther; Am Psychol Asn; Psychiat Res Soc. *Res:* Depression; suicide; cognitive aspects of psychopathology; cognitive therapy; anxiety and panic disorders. *Mailing Add:* Ctr Cognitive Ther Rm 754 The Sci Ctr 3600 Market St Philadelphia PA 19104-2648

BECK, ALAN EDWARD, GEOPHYSICS. *Current Pos:* from asst prof to prof, Univ Western Ont, 58-93, actg head dept, 61-63, head dept, 63-93, EMER PROF, DEPT EARTH SCIS, UNIV WESTERN ONT, 93- *Personal Data:* Can citizen; m 55, Julia M Langley; c J Helen, James R A & Graham J. *Educ:* Univ London, BSc & BSc(physics), 51; Australian Nat Univ, PhD(geophys), 57. *Honors & Awards:* Wilson Medal, Can Geophys Union. *Prof Exp:* Physicist, instruments develop sect, Brit Oxygen Co, Ltd, 51-52; scientist II, Nat Coal Bd Mining Res Estab, 56-57; Nat Res Coun Can fel, 57-58, sr fel, 65-66. *Concurrent Pos:* H C Webster fel, Univ Queensland, 74-75; chmn, Can Nat Comt, Int Union Geo & Geophys, 80-84; mem, Comt on Data for Sci & Technol Task Group on Transp Properties, 78-84; chmn, Earth Sci Grants Selection Comt, Nat Sci & Eng Res Coun, 83-84, coun chmn Can Earth Sci Dept, 85-87, & 91-93; pres, Int Heat Flow Comn, 83-87; mem, exec comt IASPEI, 87-95; mem, Environ Protection Agency Panel Physics & Chem Water; exec secy, Coun Chairs Can Earth Sci Dept, 93- *Mem:* Am Geophys Union; Soc Explor Geophys; Geol Asn Can; Can Geophys Union; Can Soc Explor Geophysicists; Can Asn Physicists. *Res:* Terrestrial heat flow; energy balance of the earth; exploration methods. *Mailing Add:* Dept Earth Sci Univ Western Ont London ON N6A 5B8 Can. *E-Mail:* abeck@julian.uwo.ca

BECK, ALBERT J, ZOOLOGY. *Current Pos:* PRIN & SR ANALYST, ECO-ANALYSTS, 73- *Personal Data:* b Nyack, NY, Aug 13, 35; m 59. *Educ:* Univ Calif, Davis, AB, 57, MA, 61, PhD(zool), 66. *Prof Exp:* Assoc zool, Univ Calif, Davis, 63-64; asst res parasitologist, G W Hooper Found, Univ Calif, ICMRT, Malaysia, 65-69; asst res zoologist, Sch Pub Health, Univ Calif, Berkeley, 69-73. *Concurrent Pos:* Med zoologist, Inst Med Res, Malaysia, 66-68; trustee, Butte County Mosquito Abatement Dist, 73-; lectr geog, Calif State Univ, Chico, 75-; mem, Planning Comn, City of Chico, 75-79; pres, Calif Mosq Vector Control Asn Bd trustees, 86-87. *Mem:* AAAS; Am Soc Mammal; Wildlife Dis Asn; Soc Vector Ecologists; Asn Environ Prof; Am Planning Asn; Am Water Works Asn; Sigma Xi; Acoust Soc Am. *Res:* Ecology of ectoparasites; epidemiology of zoonotic diseases; biological indicators; host-parasite relationships. *Mailing Add:* 36 Dean Way Chico CA 95926

BECK, ANATOLE, MATHEMATICS. *Current Pos:* from asst prof to assoc prof, 58-66, PROF MATH, UNIV WIS-MADISON, 66- *Personal Data:* b New York, NY, Mar 19, 30; div; c Nina R & Mical D. *Educ:* Brooklyn Col, BA, 51; Yale Univ, MA, 53, PhD(math), 56. *Prof Exp:* Ford instr math, Williams Col, 55-56; res assoc, Tulane Univ, 56-57; traveling fel, Yale Univ, 57-58. *Concurrent Pos:* Vis scholar, Hebrew Univ, Israel & Univ Gottingen, Ger, 64-65, London Sch Econ, 85 & Univ Col, London, 91-92; NSF sr fel, Univ Warwick, Univ London, Univ Erlangen & Hebrew Univ, 68-69; vis prof, Univ Md, 71 & Technische Univ Munich, 73; chair math, London Sch Econ, Univ London, 73-75. *Mem:* Sigma Xi; Math Asn Am. *Res:* Probability of Banach spaces; topological dynamics; ergodic theory; measure theory; mathematics for the social sciences; search theory. *Mailing Add:* Dept Math Univ Wis Madison WI 53706. *Fax:* 608-263-8891; *E-Mail:* beck@math.wisc.edu

BECK, BARBARA NORTH, immunogenetics, t-cell activation, for more information see previous edition

BECK, BENNY LEE, ENVIRONMENTAL SCIENCES. *Current Pos:* RETIRED. *Personal Data:* b Burlington, Ind, June 13, 32; m 56; c 3. *Educ:* Univ Wis, BS, 53, MS, 56, PhD(anal chem), 57. *Prof Exp:* From res chemist to sr res chemist, Humble Oil & Refining Co, 57-64; supv chemist, Anvil Points Oil Shale Res Ctr, Colo, 64-65; staff chemist, Chem Plant Lab, Exxon Chem Co, 65-77, sr sect supvr, 77-81, environ coordr, 81-84, lab head, Baytown Olefins Plant, 84-88, environ mgr, 88-90, sr staff environ engr, 90- *Mem:* Am Soc Testing & Mat; Air & Waste Mgt Asn. *Res:* General petrochemical analysis. *Mailing Add:* 20611 Apache Trail Baytown TX 77532

BECK, CHARLES BEVERLEY, plant morphology, for more information see previous edition

BECK, CHARLES I, ARTIFICIAL SWEETENERS, OTHER FOOD INGREDIENTS. *Current Pos:* PRIN, STRATECON, 88- *Personal Data:* b Newark, NJ, Apr 13, 37; m 64, Lorna Intorf; c Earl D & Debra L. *Educ:* Cornell Univ, BS, 60, MS, 61; Univ Calif, Davis, PhD(agr chem), 67. *Prof Exp:* Spec 4th class, Armed Forces Food & Container Inst, 61-63; sr chem engr, Gen Mills Inc, 67-70; mgr food res, Searle Biochemics, 70-76; mgr advan food res, Kitchens Sara Lee, 76-81; pres, RJR Tech Co, 81-87. *Concurrent Pos:* Instr food sci, Ill Inst Technol, 74-77. *Mem:* Inst Food Technologists; Am Asn Cereal Chemists; Am Chem Soc; Am Oil Chem Soc; Licensing Exec Soc; Res & Develop Asn. *Res:* Enzymes, freeze drying, textured vegetable proteins, artificial sweeteners, frozen bakery goods, special dietary foods, and other food technologies; technical and marketing issues for food ingredients. *Mailing Add:* Stratecon 5215 Mountain View Rd Winston-Salem NC 27104-5117. *Fax:* 910-765-5149; *E-Mail:* beck_stratecon@compuserve.com

BECK, CURT B(UXTON), CHEMICAL ENGINEERING. *Current Pos:* CONSULT ENGR, 84- *Personal Data:* b Dallas, Tex, Aug 6, 24; m 57; c 3. *Educ:* Mass Inst Technol, BS, 45, MS, 52; Environ Engrs Intersoc, dipl; Am Acad Environ Eng, dipl. *Prof Exp:* Admin asst dir res, Cabot Corp, 45-66, assoc dir res, 66-95, corp energy utilization officer, 70-84. *Concurrent Pos:* Consult engr environ & energy use, 84-; ed, Environ Newsletter. *Mem:* Am Chem Soc; Air & Waste Mgt Asn; fel Am Inst Chem Engrs; Am Acad Environ Engrs. *Res:* Combustion; heat transfer; fluid flow; air and water ecology. *Mailing Add:* 1940 Fir St Pampa TX 79065. *E-Mail:* Internet Home Page: http://www.n-tex.net/usr/b/beck

BECK, CURT WERNER, ORGANIC CHEMISTRY, ARCHAEOLOGICAL CHEMISTRY. *Current Pos:* from lectr to assoc prof, 57-66, PROF CHEM, VASSAR COL, 66-, MATTHEW VASSAR JR PROF, 70- *Personal Data:* b Halle, Ger, Sept 10, 27; nat US; m 53, Lily Yallourakis; c Curt P & Christopher P. *Educ:* Tufts Univ, BS, 51; Mass Inst Technol, PhD(org chem), 55. *Honors & Awards:* Res Award, Mid-Hudson Sect, Am Chem Soc. *Prof Exp:* Instr, Franklin Technol Inst, 51-56; asst prof, Robert Col, Istanbul, 56-57. *Concurrent Pos:* Ed, Art & Archaeol Tech Abstracts; sect ed, Chem Abstracts. *Mem:* Am Chem Soc; Archaeol Inst Am; Royal Soc Chem; fel Royal Soc Arts; fel Int Inst Conserv Hist & Artistic Works. *Res:* Application of chemistry to archaeology; composition of resinous materials, tar and pitch. *Mailing Add:* Dept Chem Vassar Col Poughkeepsie NY 12601-6198. *Fax:* 914-437-5732

BECK, DAVID PAUL, BIOCHEMISTRY, MOLECULAR GENETICS. *Current Pos:* PRES, CORIELL INST MED RES, 91- *Personal Data:* b Wilmington, Del, Aug 3, 44; m 66, Jeanne Crawford; c 2. *Educ:* Princeton Univ, AB, 66; Johns Hopkins Univ, PhD(biochem), 71. *Prof Exp:* Helen Hay Whitney fel, 71; fel biochem, Harvard Univ, 71-74; res assoc neurochem, Md Psychiat Res Ctr, Baltimore, 74-77; grants assoc, Nat Inst Gen Med Sci, Bethesda, Md, 77-78, adminr Genetics Prog, 78-81, chief, Molecular & Med Genetics Sect, Genetics Prog, 81-84; assoc dir admin, Pub Health Res Inst, NY, 84-91. *Concurrent Pos:* Adj prof, Univ Med & Dent, NJ. *Mem:* Am Soc Cell Biol; AAAS; Am Soc Human Genetics. *Res:* Membrane structure and function; role of membranes in regulating cellular metabolism; substrate translocation processes; oxidative phosphorylation. *Mailing Add:* Coriell Inst Med Rsch 401 Haddon Ave Camden NJ 08057. *E-Mail:* dabeck@umdnj.edu

BECK, DONALD EDWARD, SURFACE PHYSICS. *Current Pos:* RETIRED. *Personal Data:* b Logan, Iowa, June 12, 34. *Educ:* Univ Calif, Berkeley, BS, 56, MA, 58, PhD(physics), 65. *Prof Exp:* Vis lectr physics, St Andrews Univ, 66-67; asst prof, Univ Va, 67-72; from asst prof to assoc prof physics, Univ Wis-Milwaukee, 72-96. *Mem:* AAAS; Am Phys Soc; Sigma Xi. *Res:* Theoretical studies of the electronic properties of metal and semiconductor surfaces. *Mailing Add:* 1928 McKinley St Honolulu HI 96822

BECK, DONALD RICHARDSON, ATOMIC & MOLECULAR THEORY. *Current Pos:* asst dept head, Physics, 85-88, dir, Ctr Exp Comput, 88-91, PROF PHYSICS, MICH TECHNOL UNIV, 80- *Personal Data:* b Paterson, NJ, Mar 31, 40; m 68, Susan Gilbert; c Richard. *Educ:* Dickinson Col, BS, 62; Lehigh Univ, MS, 64, PhD(physics), 68. *Prof Exp:* Jr vis scientist physics, Jt Inst Lab Astrophys, Univ Colo, 68-69; res assoc chem, Yale Univ, 69-73, res assoc eng & appl sci, 73-74; asst prof chem, Belfer Grad Sch Sci, Yeshiva Univ, 74-76. *Concurrent Pos:* Vis prof, Nat Hellenic Res Found, Athens, Greece, 76-78; vis res assoc prof, Physics Dept, Univ Ill, Urbana, 78-80. *Mem:* Am Phys Soc; Sigma Xi. *Res:* Quantum theory of atoms, molecules and solids, including relativistic and correlation effects, with application to transition metal and rare earth atoms, alkane potential energy surfaces; properties; term, fine and hyperfine structure; transition probabilities; binding and Auger energies; autoionizing states; electron affinities. *Mailing Add:* Physics Dept Mich Technol Univ Houghton MI 49931. *Fax:* 906-487-2933; *E-Mail:* donald@phy.mtu.edu

BECK, DORIS JEAN, MICROBIAL GENETICS. *Current Pos:* asst prof, 74-81, ASSOC PROF MICROBIOL, BOWLING GREEN STATE UNIV, 81- *Personal Data:* b Blissfield, Mich. *Educ:* Bowling Green State Univ, BS, 60; Mich State Univ, MS, 71, PhD(microbiol), 74. *Prof Exp:* Teacher sec educ chem, DeWitt Pub Schs, 61-63 & Holt Pub Schs, 63-68; asst microbiol, Mich State Univ, 68-71. *Concurrent Pos:* Adj prof, Med Col Ohio, Toledo, 80-91; res assoc, Yale Univ Sch Med, 81-82. *Mem:* AAAS; Am Soc Microbiol; Sigma Xi. *Res:* Studies of platinum antitumor agents which cause mutations and induce filament formation in cells of Escherichia coli; mutagenesis and DNA repair. *Mailing Add:* 1879 Mercer Bowling Green OH 43402. *E-Mail:* dbeck@bgnet.bgsu.edu

BECK, FRANKLIN H(ORNE), METALLURGICAL ENGINEERING. *Current Pos:* RETIRED. *Personal Data:* b Bethlehem, Pa, Apr 5, 20; m 44; c 3. *Educ:* Pa State Univ, BS, 43; Ohio State Univ, MS, 47, PhD(metall eng), 49. *Prof Exp:* Metall engr, E I du Pont de Nemours & Co, 43-46; res assoc metall eng, Ohio State Univ, 46-49, res asst prof, 49-54, supvr, 54-59, from asst prof to prof metall eng, 52-82, dir metals res eng exp sta, 58-82. *Concurrent Pos:* Co-ed, Corrosion J. *Mem:* Am Soc Metals; Nat Asn Corrosion Engrs. *Res:* Determination of corrosion mechanisms; effects of metallurgy of materials on corrosion. *Mailing Add:* 2191 Haverford Rd Columbus OH 43220

BECK, GAIL EDWIN, FLORICULTURE, PLANT PHYSIOLOGY. *Current Pos:* instr & exten specialist com floricult, 49-52, from instr to prof, 52-85,EMER PROF FLORICULT, UNIV WIS-MADISON, 85- *Personal Data:* b Dunn Co, Wis, July 25, 23; m 50, Lois K Heasley; c Paul L, Juelene K & Genevieve E (Magnuson). *Educ:* Mich State Univ, BS, 48, MS, 49; Univ Wis, PhD(floricult, plant physiol), 56. *Honors & Awards:* Alex Laurie Award for Floricult Educ & Res, Soc Am Florists, 83. *Prof Exp:* Instr, Dept Hort, Mich State Univ, 48-49. *Concurrent Pos:* Vis prof & actg head, Dept Biol, Eastern Nazarene Col, Mass, 67-68. *Mem:* Am Soc Hort Sci; Am Asn Arboreta & Botanic Gardens. *Res:* Physiology of floriculture crops; florist crop production. *Mailing Add:* 5860 Wild Fig Lane Ft Myers FL 33919-3452

BECK, HAROLD LAWRENCE, RADIATION PHYSICS, ENVIRONMENTAL HEALTH & SAFETY. *Current Pos:* physicist, Environ Measurements Lab, US Dept Energy, 63-88, dir, Instrumetation, Environ Measurements Lab, 88-96, ACTG DEP DIR, US DEPT ENERGY, 92-, DIR, ENVIRON SCI DIV, 96- *Personal Data:* b Detroit, Mich, Jan 7, 38. *Educ:* Univ Miami, BS, 60. *Prof Exp:* Tech intern, AEC, NY, 62-63. *Concurrent Pos:* Tech rep, Div Biomed & Environ Res, Washington, DC, US Energy Res & Develop Admin, 77-78; US deleg, Int Electrotech Comn SC 45, 88-; mem, Nat Coun Radiation Protection & Measurements, 92-; sci vpres, Nat Coun Radiation Protection & Measurement, 95- *Mem:* AAAS; Am Nuclear Soc; fel Health Physics Soc; Inst Elec & Electronics Engrs. *Res:* Environmental pollutant instrumentation; environmental radioactivity; radiation measurement techniques; radiation transport; naturally occurring radioactivity. *Mailing Add:* USDOE Environ Measurements Lab 201 Varick St New York NY 10014. *Fax:* 212-620-3600; *E-Mail:* hbeck@eml.doe.gov

BECK, IVAN THOMAS, GASTROENTEROLOGY. *Current Pos:* assoc prof, Queens Univ, 66-73, prof med, 73-89, prof physiol, 77-89, EMER PROF MED & PHYSIOL, QUEENS UNIV, ONT, 89- *Personal Data:* b Budapest, Hungary, May 22, 24; nat Can; m 49; c 1. *Educ:* Univ Geneva, MD, 49; McGill Univ, dipl, 55, PhD(invest med), 63; FRCP(C). *Honors & Awards:* Gastroenterol Unit, Queen's Univ named in Honor, 89; Distinguished Serv Award, Can Asn Gastroenterol, 91. *Prof Exp:* Lectr pharmacol, McGill Univ, 49-52; actg head pharmacol, Univ Montreal, 54-56; res assoc, Royal Victoria Hosp, McGill Univ, 58-66, lectr, Dept Invest Med, 58-66, dir, gastrointestinal lab, 60-66. *Concurrent Pos:* Assoc physician & gastroenterologist in chg, St Mary's Hosp, 60-66; chmn, Med Adv Bd, Can Found Ileitis & Colitis, 85-89; chmn bd, Can Digestive Dis Found, 94- *Mem:* Fel Am Col Physicians; master Am Col Gastroenterol; Am Soc Pharmacol; Can Physiol Soc; Can Asn Gastroenterol (secy, 60, pres, 67). *Res:* Pharmacology; physiopathology and therapy of the gastrointestinal tract; effect of alcohol on small intestine; intestinal inflammation and inflammatory medication; intestinal blood flow; esophageal disorders. *Mailing Add:* Div Gastroenterol Hotel Dieu Hosp 166 Brock St Kingston ON K7L 5G2 Can. *Fax:* 613-544-3114

BECK, JAMES DONALD, INORGANIC CHEMISTRY. *Current Pos:* from asst prof to assoc prof, 68-78, head dept, 71-72, PROF CHEM, VA STATE UNIV, 78- *Personal Data:* b York Co, Pa, Dec 24, 40; m 62, Gale Kramer; c Andrew E & Kristine R. *Educ:* Kutztown State Col, BS, 62; Univ Del, PhD(chem), 69. *Prof Exp:* Teacher chem, Piscataway Twp High Sch, NJ, 62-64; asst, Univ Del, 64-68. *Mem:* Sigma Xi; Am Chem Soc; Nat Sci Teachers Asn; Am Asn Univ Prof. *Res:* Antioxidants in fats and oils; computers in chemical education. *Mailing Add:* Dept Chem Va State Univ Box 9174 Petersburg VA 23806-0001. *Fax:* 804-524-6801

BECK, JAMES RICHARD, ORGANIC CHEMISTRY. *Current Pos:* RETIRED. *Personal Data:* b Paris, Ill, Aug 17, 31. *Educ:* Univ Calif, Berkeley, BS, 57; Univ Ill, PhD(org chem), 61. *Prof Exp:* NSF res fel, Swiss Fed Inst, Zurich, 61-62; res chemist, Eli Lilly & Co, 62-88. *Mem:* Am Chem Soc; Swiss Chem Soc; Sigma Xi; Int Soc Heterocyclic Chem. *Res:* Synthetic organic chemistry; herbicides; plant growth regulators; chemical hybridizing agents; heterocyclic chemistry; nonaqueous diazotization; aromatic nitro displacement. *Mailing Add:* 10023 Penrith Dr Indianapolis IN 46229-1342

BECK, JAMES S, CELL BIOLOGY, SIMULATION. *Current Pos:* from assoc prof to prof med biophys, 69-78, EMER PROF MED, UNIV CALGARY, 78- *Personal Data:* b Dallas, Tex, Dec 8, 31; wid; c 3. *Educ:* Wash Univ, MD, 57; Univ Calif, Berkeley, PhD(biophys), 62. *Prof Exp:* Intern, Mt Zion Hosp & Med Ctr, San Francisco, 57-58; Nat Cancer Inst fel, Univ Calif, Berkeley, 58-62, assoc res biophysicist, Lawrence Radiation Lab, 62; asst prof physiol & lectr physics, Univ Minn, Minneapolis, 62-69. *Concurrent Pos:* Dir, Bragg Creek Inst Nat Philos, 74- *Mem:* Soc Math Biol; Biophys Soc; AAAS. *Res:* Mechanisms of cellular responses to liquid binding by receptors; physical properties of erythrocytes. *Mailing Add:* 4959 Vantage Cresent NW Calgary AB T3A 1X6 Can

BECK, JAMES V(ERE), MECHANICAL ENGINEERING, HEAT TRANSFER. *Current Pos:* from instr to assoc prof, 62-71, PROF MECH ENG, MICH STATE UNIV, 71- *Personal Data:* b Cambridge, Mass, May 18, 30; m 60, Barbara Rettie; c Sharon & Douglas. *Educ:* Tufts Univ, BS, 56; Mass Inst Technol, SM, 57; Mich State Univ, PhD(mech eng), 64. *Prof Exp:* Jr design engr, Pratt & Whitney Aircraft, Mass, 56-57; sr scientist, Res & Adv Develop Div, Avco Corp, 57-60, sr staff scientist, 60-62. *Concurrent Pos:* Consult, Res & Adv Develop Div, Avco Corp, Mass, 62-64, Instrument Div, Lear Siegler, Inc, 64-68, Sandia Nat Labs, 77-79 & Oak Ridge Nat Labs, 66, 82- *Mem:* Am Soc Mech Eng. *Res:* Numerical methods in transient heat conduction; transient determination of thermal properties and parameters; nonlinear estimation of parameters; inverse heat conduction; author of three books and 100 papers. *Mailing Add:* Dept Mech Eng Mich State Univ East Lansing MI 48824. *Fax:* 517-353-1750; *E-Mail:* beck@egr.msu.edu

BECK, JAY VERN, BIOCHEMISTRY, MICROBIOLOGY. *Current Pos:* prof, 51-77, EMER PROF BACT, BRIGHAM YOUNG UNIV, 77- *Personal Data:* b American Fork, Utah, Jan 15, 12; m 31; c 6. *Educ:* Brigham Young Univ, AB, 33, AM, 36; Univ Calif, PhD(soil microbiol), 40. *Prof Exp:* Instr chem & math, High Sch, Utah, 35-36 & Dixie Jr Col, 36; technician plant nutrit, Univ Calif, 36-39; from jr chemist to assoc chemist, Food & Drug Admin, Fed Security Agency, 39-44; asst prof chem, Univ Idaho, 44-46; microbiologist, Pa Grade Crude Oil Asn, 46-47; from asst prof to assoc prof bact, Pa State Col, 47-51. *Concurrent Pos:* Spec instr, Univ San Francisco, 38; Guggenheim Found fel, Univ Sheffield, 57-58; spec fel, NIH, 65-; mem, Nat Sci Bd, 82-86. *Mem:* AAAS; Am Chem Soc; Am Soc Microbiol. *Res:* Uric acid as an index of filth in foods; minor element deficiency in plants; Utah sorgo syrup; purine fermentation by bacteria; purine determinations; microbial oxidation of sulfide minerals. *Mailing Add:* 4914 W Mountain View Circle Highland UT 84003-9557

BECK, JEANNE CRAWFORD, BIOCHEMISTRY, MOLECULAR GENETICS. *Current Pos:* asst dir, 94-96, DEPUTY DIR, CORIELL CELL REPOSITORIES, CAMDEN, NJ, 96- *Personal Data:* b Mt Pleasant, Pa, Mar 18, 43; m 66, David P Beck; c Jennifer J & David A. *Educ:* Wilson Col, AB, 65; Johns Hopkins Univ, PhD(biochem), 69. *Prof Exp:* USPHS-Nat Cancer Inst fel, Sch Med, Johns Hopkins Univ, 69-71 & Biol Labs, Harvard Univ, 71-74; sr staff fel, Geront Res Ctr, Nat Inst Aging, 74-80; mem fac, Dept Obstet & Gynec, Sch Med, Johns Hopkins Univ, 80-84 & Dept Med, Mt Sinai Sch Med, NY, 85-93; res dir, Nat Dis Res Interchange, 93-94. *Concurrent Pos:* Mem Nat Action Plan on Breast Cancer; mem, Biol Res Bank Working Group, 95-; mem, NJ Com on Cancer Res, Breast Cancer Adv Group, 95-

Mem: Am Soc Human Genetics; Am Soc Cell Biol; Am Soc Nephrol; Sigma Xi. *Res:* Role of membrane components in membrane structure and function; mechanism of transport of inorganic ions, amino acids, and sugars in kidney brush border; alteration of membrane function in aging tissues. *Mailing Add:* Coriell Inst Med Res 401 Haddon Ave Camden NJ 08103. *Fax:* 609-964-0254; *E-Mail:* jbeck@umdnj.edu

BECK, JOHN CHRISTIAN, INTERNAL MEDICINE, GERIATRICS. *Current Pos:* prof med, 79-93, dir, Acad Geriat Resources Ctr, 84-90, EMER PROF MED, UNIV CALIF, LOS ANGELES, 93- *Personal Data:* b Audubon, Iowa, Jan 4, 24; Can citizen; c 1. *Educ:* McGill Univ, BSc, 44, MD, CM, 47, MSc, 51, dipl, 52; FRCP (C), 51; FRCP(L), 71;. *Hon Degrees:* PhD, Ben-Gurion Univ Negev, 81; DSc, McGill Univ, 94. *Honors & Awards:* Simeone Lectr, Brown Univ, 77; John McCreary Mem Lectr, Univ BC, 85; Ronald V Christie Award, Can Asn Prof Med, 87; Milo D Leavitt Mem Award, Am Geriatrics Soc, 88; Bruce Hall Mem Lectr, Univ NSW, 89; Allen T Bailey Mem Lectr, Univ Sask, 89; Duncan Graham Award, Royal Col Physicians & Surgeons, 90; Joseph T Freeman Award, Geront Soc Am, 90; Irving S Wright Award, Am Fedn Aging Res, 91. *Prof Exp:* Res asst, Royal Victoria Hosp, 49-53; res assoc & lectr med & clin med, McGill Univ, 54-55, res fel, Univ Clin, 55-57, from asst prof to assoc prof med, 55-64, chmn, Dept Med & dir, Univ Clin, 64-74, prof, Dept Med, 64-75; prof med, Univ Calif, San Francisco, 74-79, dir, Univ Calif, Los Angeles & Univ Southern Calif, Long Term Care Geront Ctr, 80-85. *Concurrent Pos:* Res asst, Cleveland Clin, Ohio, NEng Med Ctr, Boston, Righosp, Copenhagen & Univ Col Hosp, Eng, 49-53; clin asst, Royal Victoria Hosp, 52-54, chief, Endocrine-Metab Unit, 54-64, dir, Div Endocrine-Metab & asst physician, 55-57, assoc physician, 57-60, physician, Dept Med & dir, 60-64, physician-in-chief, 64-74, sr physician, 74-81; Markel Scholar, 54-59; consult, var hosps, 64-88; dir, Que Camp for Diabetic Children; dir & chmn, Am Bd Int Med; pres, Am Bd Med Spec, Inst Med; dir, Robert Wood Johnson Clin Scholar Prog & sr consult, Robert Wood Johnson Found, 73-78; attend staff, Univ Calif Med Ctr, 79-, Jewish Homes Aging, Los Angeles, 82-; dir, Calif Geriat Educ Ctr, 87-, Long-Term Care, Nat Resource Ctr, Univ Calif Los Angeles USC, 88-94; consult, Rand Corp, Koret Found, Delta Airlines, Bur Health Prof; mem, Sub-Comt Aging, Am Col Physicians, 87-, Pub Policy Comt, Asn Geront in Higher Educ, 90-91; sr natural scientist, Rand Corp, 90- *Mem:* Inst Med-Nat Acad Sci; Can Soc Clin Invest (pres); Am Fedn Clin Res; fel Am Col Physicians; Int Soc Endocrinol (secy-gen); fel Royal Soc Can; hon fel Royal Soc Physicians; Endocrine Soc (vpres); Am Diabetes Asn; fel AAAS; Am Clin & Climat Asn; Am Geriat Soc; Am Physiol Soc; Am Soc Clin Invest; Asn Am Med Cols. *Res:* Cinical and health services research in geriatrics; author of numerous publications. *Mailing Add:* 32-144CHS Box 951687 Univ Calif Sch Med 10833 Le Conte Ave Los Angeles CA 90024-1687. *Fax:* 310-312-0546

BECK, JOHN LOUIS, quality affairs, analytical chemistry, for more information see previous edition

BECK, JOHN R(OLAND), VERTEBRATE ECOLOGY, ECONOMIC BIOLOGY. *Current Pos:* PRIN CONSULT, BIOL ENVIRON CONSULT SERV, PHOENIX, 78- *Personal Data:* b Las Vegas, NMex, Feb 26, 29; m 51, Doris Olson; c Elizabeth (Aguiar), Thomas, Patricia (Carter) & J William. *Educ:* Okla A&M Col, BS, 50; Okla State Univ, MS, 57. *Prof Exp:* Wildlife asst, King Ranch, Tex, 50-51; asst instr zool, Okla State Univ, 51-53; control agt, US Fish & Wildlife Serv, 53-54, res biologist, 55-57, control biologist, 57-65; instr physiol, Univ Tenn, 54-55; dir, Treasure Lake Job Corps Conserv Ctr, US Dept Interior, 65-67, state supvr, Div Wildlife Serv, Bur Sport Fisheries & Wildlife, 67-69; dir qual control, Bio-Serv Corp, 69-78, vpres, 70-78. *Concurrent Pos:* Lectr, Ohio State Univ, 59-65; grain sanit consult, 59-79; guest lectr, Bowling Green State Univ, 60-79; adv bd, Sch Allied Health, Ferris State Col, 73-79; fac, Agr Div, Ariz State Univ, 80-90; chmn pesticides, Am Soc Testing & Mat, 80-82; spec asst dept adminr, Animal Plant Health Inspection Serv, USDA, 86-87; expert witness, pesticides/hazardous chem, 87-96. *Mem:* Wildlife Soc; fel Royal Soc Health; Am Soc Testing & Mat; Sci Writers Soc; Sigma Xi. *Res:* Vertebrate pest control; development of avicides and control methods; zoonoses control; grain sanitation and quality control; desert crop research; pest management. *Mailing Add:* PO Box 25824 Prescott Valley AZ 86312. *Fax:* 520-772-1069

BECK, JOHN ROBERT, MEDICAL DECISION MAKING, MEDICAL INFORMATICS. *Current Pos:* PROF PATH MED INFORMATICS, BAYLOR COL MED, 92- *Personal Data:* b Cleveland, Ohio, Sept 8, 53; m 75, Sharon Dombkowski; c Ben, Stefan & Meredith. *Educ:* Dartmouth Col, AB, 74; Johns Hopkins Univ, MD, 78. *Honors & Awards:* Young Investr Awards, Acad Clin Lab Physicians & Scientists, 79, 80 & 81. *Prof Exp:* Resident path, Dartmouth-Hitchcock Med Ctr, 78-80; clin fel med, Div Clin Decision Making, New Eng Med Ctr, 81; instr path, Sch Med, Tufts Univ, 81; asst prof path, Dartmouth Med Sch, 82-87, dir, Prog Med Info Sci, 84-89, asst prof community & family med, 85-87, assoc prof path & community med, 87-89; prof path med & pub health, Ore Health Sci Univ, 89-92. *Concurrent Pos:* Consult, Nat Libr Med, 85-86, WHO, 85-87; res career develop award, Nat Libr Med, 86-91, Biomed Libr Rev Comt, 88-92; ed-in-chief, Med Desision Making, 89- *Mem:* Am Med Informatics Asn; Soc Med Decision Making (secy-treas, 85-87, vpres, 87-88); Am Fedn Clin Res; Col Am Pathologists; Acad Clin Lab Physicians & Scientists; Am Col Med Informatics. *Res:* Theory of medical decision making; mathematical analysis of diagnostic tests; application of stochastic models to decision analysis; information technology in academic health science centers. *Mailing Add:* One Baylor Plaza IREL 405 Houston TX 77030. *Fax:* 713-798-3729; *E-Mail:* jrbeck@6cm.tnc.edu

BECK, KARL MAURICE, ORGANIC CHEMISTRY. *Current Pos:* CONSULT, 84- *Personal Data:* b Belleville, Ill, June 16, 22; m 45, Ann Werner; c Susan, Allen & Laura. *Educ:* Monmouth Col, BS, 43; Univ Ill, PhD(org chem), 48. *Hon Degrees:* LLD, Monmouth Col, 93. *Prof Exp:* Asst chem, Univ Ill, 43, mem, Nat Defense Res Comt, Off Sci Res & Develop, 44-45, mem, Comt Med Res, 45-46; res chemist, Abbott Labs, 48-53, tech serv rep, 53-56, head tech serv, Chem Mkt Div, 57-62, sci employ, 62-64; vpres, Cyclamate Corp Am, 64-66; mgr prod planning & serv, Abbott Labs, 67-70, mgr chem div, new prod res, 70-71, mgr mkt res & develop, chem & agr prod, 71-84. *Concurrent Pos:* Tech ed, Food Prod Develop, 67-79. *Mem:* Am Chem Soc; Inst Food Technologists; Com Develop Asn. *Res:* Synthetic organic chemistry; chemical warfare with poison gases; reduction of nitro carboxylic esters; piperazines; diuretics; phenolic Mannich bases; sweetening agents; food and beverage technology; food chemicals; plastics additives; chemical antimicrobial agents; paint technology. *Mailing Add:* 2923 Belle Glade Dr Toledo OH 43617-2313

BECK, KEITH RUSSELL, TEXTILE CHEMISTRY. *Current Pos:* PROF TEXTILE CHEM, NC STATE UNIV, 86- *Personal Data:* b Hudson, Mich, Apr 25, 44; m 68, Beverly Seiser; c Brady, Kelli & Kerri. *Educ:* Adrian Col, BS, 65; Purdue Univ, PhD(chem), 70. *Prof Exp:* Vis asst prof & res assoc, Purdue Univ, 69-70; asst prof chem, Elmhurst Col, 70-77; assoc prof textile sci, Purdue Univ, 77-86. *Concurrent Pos:* Consult. *Mem:* Am Asn Textile Chemists & Colorists; Am Chem Soc; Soc Appl Spectros. *Res:* Synthesis and high-performance liquid chromatographic analysis of textile finishes; near infrared analysis of textile substrates; non-formaldehyde crosslinkers for cellulose; real-time data acquisition in batch dyeing; supercritical fluid extractions, dyeing and cleaning. *Mailing Add:* 5909 Countryview Lane Raleigh NC 27606-9464. *E-Mail:* keith_beck@ncsu.edu

BECK, KENNETH CHARLES, RESPIRATORY PHYSIOLOGY, PULMONARY VASCULAR MECHANICS. *Current Pos:* ASST PROF PHYSIOL, MAYO CLIN & FOUND, 80- *Educ:* Univ Wash, Seattle, PhD(physiol & biophys), 80. *Res:* Pulmonary function. *Mailing Add:* 821 1/2 St SW Apt 10 Rochester MN 55902-6355

BECK, LLOYD WILLARD, CHEMISTRY. *Current Pos:* RETIRED. *Personal Data:* b Batesville, Ind, Aug 10, 19; m 45; c 3. *Educ:* DePauw Univ, AB, 41; Univ Wis, PhD(org chem), 44. *Prof Exp:* Res chemist, Procter & Gamble Co, 44-55, assoc dir, Res Div, 55-71, assoc dir, Prof & Regulatory Serv Div, 71-81; exec vpres, Hilltop Res, Inc, 81-84. *Mem:* AAAS; Am Chem Soc; Soc Invest Dermat; Am Inst Nutrit; Soc Toxicol. *Res:* Synthesis of compounds related to female sex hormones; synthetic lubricants; food chemistry; nutrition; metabolism; hazard assessments; toxicology; clinical research. *Mailing Add:* 401 Wells Lane Versailles KY 40383-1546

BECK, LOIS GRANT, ANTHROPOLOGY, MIDDLE EAST STUDIES. *Current Pos:* from asst prof to assoc prof, 80-92, PROF, WASH UNIV, ST LOUIS, 92- *Personal Data:* b Bogota, Colombia, Nov 5, 44; m, Henry Huang; c Julia. *Educ:* Portland State Univ, BA, 67; Univ Chicago, MA, 69, PhD, 77. *Prof Exp:* Asst prof, Amherst Col, Mass, 73-76 & Univ Utah, Salt Lake City, 76-80. *Concurrent Pos:* Bd dirs, Middle East Studies Asn, 82-91; res grants, Fulbright Found, Nat Endowment for Humanities & Soc Sci Res Coun. *Mem:* Middle East Studies Asn; Soc Iranian Studies (exec secy, 79-82); Am Anthrop Asn; Sigma Xi. *Res:* Anthropology; nature of relationships between tribes and states in the Middle East; political anthropological research on tribes in Iran, 20th century and in the post-revolutionary period. *Mailing Add:* Dept Anthrop Wash Univ One Brookings Dr Campus Box 1114 St Louis MO 63130

BECK, LUCILLE BLUSO, AUDIOLOGY. *Current Pos:* INSTR AUDIOL, BIOCOMMUN LAB, DEPT HEARING & SPEECH SCI, UNIV MD, 73-; ASSOC CHIEF AUDIOL & SPEECH PATH, VET ADMIN MED CTR. *Personal Data:* b Baltimore, Md, July 21, 49; m 73. *Educ:* Adelphi Univ, BA, 71; Univ Md, MA, 73, PhD(hearing & speech sci), 78. *Prof Exp:* Supvry audiologist, Cent Audiol & Speech Path & Nat Hearing Aid Prog, Vet Admin Med Ctr, 77-81. *Concurrent Pos:* Prof lectr, George Washington Univ; mem, Ear, Nose & Throat Devices Panel, FDA & Working Group Hearing Aids, Am Nat Standard Inst S3 48. *Mem:* Sigma Xi; Acoust Soc Am; Am Speech & Hearing Asn; Am Auditory Soc. *Res:* Auditory habilitation; auditory prosthetic devices; hearing aids. *Mailing Add:* Dept Speech & Hearing Sci George Washington Univ 2035 H St NW Washington DC 20052-0001

BECK, MAE LUCILLE, ORGANIC CHEMISTRY. *Current Pos:* from asst prof to assoc prof, 60-83, EMER PROF CHEM, SIMMONS COL, 84- *Personal Data:* b Buffalo, NY, Mar 27, 30. *Educ:* Mich State Univ, BS, 51; Smith Col, AM, 55; Univ Pa, PhD(org chem), 60. *Prof Exp:* Polymer chemist, E I du Pont de Nemours & Co, 51-53; instr chem, Smith Col, 55-56. *Concurrent Pos:* NIH grant, 62-64; res fel, Harvard Univ, 66-67; artist, Boston Sch. *Mem:* Am Chem Soc; Sigma Xi. *Res:* Organic sulfur chemistry; antimetabolites; organic natural products and drugs; environmental health. *Mailing Add:* RFD Marlborough NH 03455

BECK, MYRL EMIL, JR, PALEOMAGNETISM, TECTONICS. *Current Pos:* assoc prof geol, 69-73, PROF GEOL, WESTERN WASH UNIV, 73- *Personal Data:* b Redlands, Calif, May 13, 33; m 83, Linda Joyce; c 3. *Educ:* Stanford Univ, BA, 55, MS, 60; Univ Calif, Riverside, PhD(geol), 68. *Prof Exp:* Asst paleomagnetism, Dept Geophys, Stanford Univ, 61-62; geologist, Standard Oil Co Calif, 62 & US Geol Surv, 62-66. *Concurrent Pos:* Res assoc, Univ Puget Sound, 72-; vis prof, Geophys Inst, Swiss Fed Inst Technol, Zurich, 73, Northwestern Univ & Univ Ariz, 84-85. *Mem:* Fel Am Geophys

Union; Fel Geol Soc Am; Geol Soc Chile. *Res:* Application of paleomagnetism and other techniques to study of tectonic processes; regional tectonics of western North America, the Andes and the Aegean. *Mailing Add:* Dept Geol Western Wash Univ Bellingham WA 98225

BECK, PAUL ADAMS, physical metallurgy, magnetism in alloys; deceased, see previous edition for last biography

BECK, PAUL EDWARD, ORGANIC CHEMISTRY. *Current Pos:* assoc prof, 66-74, chmn dept, 75-84, PROF CHEM, CLARION UNIV, 74- *Personal Data:* b Lancaster, Pa, Jan 14, 37. *Educ:* Franklin & Marshall Col, BS, 58; Duquesne Univ, PhD(org chem), 63. *Prof Exp:* Res chemist, E I du Pont de Nemours & Co, Inc, 63-66. *Mem:* AAAS; Am Chem Soc; Am Inst Chemists; NY Acad Sci; Controlled Release Soc. *Res:* New synthetic methods; new polymers and polymer reactions; polymeric drug delivery systems. *Mailing Add:* Dept Chem Clarion Univ Clarion PA 16214

BECK, PAUL W, physical chemistry, for more information see previous edition

BECK, RAYMOND WARREN, microbiology, for more information see previous edition

BECK, ROBERT EDWARD, COMPUTATIONAL ALGEBRA. *Current Pos:* From instr to assoc prof, 66-78, PROF MATH, VILLANOVA UNIV, 78- *Personal Data:* b Denver, Colo, June 7, 41; m 65; c 3. *Educ:* Harvey Mudd Col, BS, 63; Univ Pa, MA, 65, PhD(math), 69. *Concurrent Pos:* Chmn, Dept Math, Villanova Univ, 78-81 & dir comput sci prog, 85-; Fulbright exchange, 81-82. *Mem:* Asn Comput Mach; Am Math Soc; Sigma Xi. *Res:* Computational methods in nonassociative algebras; algorithms for operations research models; user/system interface design. *Mailing Add:* Dept Comput Sci Villanova Univ Villanova PA 19085-1699

BECK, ROBERT FREDERICK, HYDRODYNAMICS, NAVAL ARCHITECTURE. *Current Pos:* from asst prof to prof, Univ Mich, Ann Arbor, 72-91, actg dir, Ship Hydrodynamics Lab, 87-88, dir, 88-91, chair, Dept Naval Archit & Marine Eng, 91-94, PROF, DEPT NAVAL ARCHIT & MARINE ENG, UNIV MICH, ANN ARBOR, 94- *Personal Data:* b Flushing, NY, June 11, 43; m 71; c 2. *Educ:* Univ Mich, BSE, 65; Mass Inst Technol, MS, 67, Naval Arch, 68, PhD(naval archit), 70. *Prof Exp:* Res fel appl math, Univ Adelaide, 71-72. *Concurrent Pos:* Vis assoc prof, Dept Ocean Eng, Mass Inst Technol, 72-73, vis prof, 86-87, Fac Math & Comput Sci, Univ Adelaide, Australia, 95; mem, Long Range Ship Res Adv Comt, Nat Res Coun, 78-80, Comn Liquid Slosh Loading Cargo Tanks, 83-85, Loads Adv Group, 83-; chmn, Analytic Ship Wave Rel Panel H-5, Soc Naval Archit & Marine Engrs, 78-95; consult, Marine Eng Sect, Exxon Prod Res Inc, Tex, 79-80; mem, Transp Res Inst Exec Comt, Univ Mich, 92- *Mem:* Fel Soc Naval Archit & Marine Engrs. *Res:* Ship hydrodynamics, particularly ship wave resistance, ship maneuvering, ship motions and seakeeping. *Mailing Add:* Dept Naval Archit & Marine Eng Univ Mich Main Campus 2600 Draper Rd Ann Arbor MI 48109-2145

BECK, ROBERT NASON, PHYSICS OF NUCLEAR MEDICINE. *Current Pos:* PROF RADIOL SCI, UNIV CHICAGO, 76-, DIR, FRANKLIN MCLEAN INST, 77-, DIR, CTR IMAGING SCI, 86- *Personal Data:* b San Angelo, Tex, Mar 26, 28; m 58. *Educ:* Univ Chicago, AB, 54, BS, 55. *Honors & Awards:* Aebersold Award, Soc Nuclear Med, 91. *Prof Exp:* Chief scientist, Argonne Cancer Res Hosp, 57-67. *Concurrent Pos:* Mem, Int Comn on Radiation Units, 68-; mem, Nat Coun on Radiation, Protection & Measurements, 70- *Mem:* Soc Nuclear Med; Am Asn Physicists Med; Inst Elec & Electronics Engrs Nuclear & Plasma Sci Soc; Soc Magnetic Resonance Imaging. *Res:* Development of a theory of the process by which images can be formed of the distribution of radioactive material in a patient, in order to diagnose his/her disease. *Mailing Add:* Dept Radiol Univ Chicago Pritzker Sch Med 5841 Maryland Ave Chicago IL 60637-1463

BECK, ROLAND ARTHUR, inorganic & physical chemistry, chemical engineering, for more information see previous edition

BECK, RONALD RICHARD, PHYSIOLOGY, ENDOCRINOLOGY. *Current Pos:* ASSOC PROF PHYSIOL, SCH MED, UNIV SC, 75-, ASST DEAN GRAD SCH, 81- *Personal Data:* b Tiltonsville, Ohio, Oct 8, 34; m 61; c 3. *Educ:* Univ Ohio, BS, 61; Ohio State Univ, MS, 67, PhD(physiol), 68. *Prof Exp:* From asst prof to assoc prof physiol, Sch Med, Ind Univ, Indianapolis, 68-75. *Concurrent Pos:* NIH grant, 72-74, 78-81. *Mem:* Am Physiol Soc; Endocrine Soc. *Res:* Effects of endotoxin on metabolism and metabolic regulation. *Mailing Add:* Dept Physiol Univ SC Sch Med Columbia SC 29208

BECK, SIDNEY L, DEVELOPMENTAL TOXICOLOGY, DEVELOPMENTAL GENETICS. *Current Pos:* PROF BIOL & CHMN, DEPAUL UNIV, 87- *Personal Data:* b New York, NY, Mar 28, 35; m 55; c 2. *Educ:* City Col New York, BS, 55; Univ Kans, MA, 57; Brown Univ, PhD(biol), 60. *Prof Exp:* Instr zool, Univ Mich, 60-61, USPHS fel, 61-64; NIH spec fel, Univ Col, London, 64-65, res assoc genetics, 65; from asst prof to assoc prof biol, Univ Toledo, 65-69; prof biol, Wheaton Col, Mass, 69-85, chmn dept, 69-83; prof biol, Ball State Univ, 85-87, chmn dept, 85-86. *Concurrent Pos:* Mem, Inst Lab Animal Resources Comt Genetic Standards, Nat Acad Sci, 66-69; biologist, US Environ Protection Agency, 75-76, prin investr, 77-80; sr fel path, Univ Wash, Seattle, 83-84; consult teratology, Mass Gen Hosp, 85-87; vis prof, Harvard Univ, 85-87. *Mem:* AAAS; Am Soc Zoologists; Teratology Soc; Soc Develop Biol; Am Genetic Asn; Sigma Xi. *Res:* Developmental toxicology; mammalian genetics and development; postnatal teratology; role of genotype in susceptibility to teratogens. *Mailing Add:* Dept Biol DePaul Univ Chicago IL 60614. *Fax:* 773-325-7596; *E-Mail:* sbeck@condor.depaul.edu

BECK, SIDNEY M, BACTERIOLOGY, MICROBIOLOGY & MEDICAL DIAGNOSTICS. *Current Pos:* RETIRED. *Personal Data:* b Pleasant Grove, Utah, Mar 10, 19; m 48, Bessie R Bjarnson; c Mark, Eric, Claudia & Wendy. *Educ:* Brigham Young Univ, AB, 41, MA, 48; Pa State Univ, PhD(bact), 51. *Prof Exp:* Chemist, US Bur Mines, 42-44; from asst prof to prof bact, Univ Idaho, 51-91. *Mem:* Am Chem Soc. *Res:* Soil organic matter turnover; plant root exudates; bacterial nitrogen fixation; bacterial purine metabolism and nutrition; production of alternate fuels (biodiesel) from plant oils (rapeseed). *Mailing Add:* 1205 Kouse St Moscow ID 83843-3827

BECK, STANLEY DWIGHT, ZOOLOGY, INSECT PHYSIOLOGY. *Current Pos:* From instr to prof, 48-69, W A HENRY PROF, 69-88, EMER PROF ENTOM, UNIV WIS-MADISON, 89- *Personal Data:* b Portland, Ore, Oct 17, 19; m 43, Isabel H Stalker; c Bruce D, Diana H & Marianne E. *Educ:* State Col Wash, BS, 42; Univ Wis, MS, 47, PhD(zool), 50. *Hon Degrees:* DSc, Luther Col Iowa, 72. *Honors & Awards:* Founders Mem Award, Entomological Soc Am. *Mem:* Nat Acad Sci; AAAS; Entom Soc Am (pres, 82). *Res:* Insect nutrition; metabolism and endocrinology; photoperiodism; insect disease, seasonal development plus plant resistance. *Mailing Add:* 6100 Gateway Green Madison WI 53716-3916

BECK, STEPHEN D, NUMERICAL. *Current Pos:* PROF MATH, BLOOMSBURG UNIV, PA, 71- *Personal Data:* b Brooklyn, NY, Mar 29, 30. *Educ:* Tufts Univ, BS, 51; Iowa State Univ, MS, 55; Rensselaer Polytech Inst, PhD(mech), 69. *Mem:* Math Asn Am; Soc Indust & Appl Math. *Mailing Add:* 220 W First St Bloomsburg PA 17815-1109

BECK, STEVEN MICHAEL, PHYSICAL CHEMISTRY. *Current Pos:* mem tech staff, 83-90, RES SCI, ELEC TECHNOL CTR, AEROSPACE CORP, 90- *Personal Data:* b Oakland, Calif, Jan 11, 54. *Educ:* Univ Calif, Santa Barbara, BS, 76; Rice Univ, PhD(phys chem), 80. *Prof Exp:* Fel, Bell Tel Labs, 80-82, Occidental Res Corp, 83. *Mem:* Am Phys Soc. *Res:* Laser spectroscopy; solid state physics; molecular beams; clusters. *Mailing Add:* Aerospace Corp M2/253 PO Box 92957 Los Angeles CA 90009

BECK, STEVEN R, ENZYME IMMOBILIZATION, PROCESS DEVELOPMENT. *Current Pos:* sr biochem engr, 88-91, MGR PROCESS ENG DEVELOP, SYNTEX CHEM, 91- *Personal Data:* b Manhattan, Kans, Jan 26, 47; m 69, Candace Unruh; c Jim, Stephanie & Sarah. *Educ:* Kans State Univ, BSChe, 69; Univ Tex, Austin, PhD(chem eng), 72. *Prof Exp:* Sr res engr, Atlantic Richfield Co, 72-77; from asst prof to prof chem eng, Tex Tech Univ, 77-88, chmn dept, 81-88. *Mem:* Am Inst Chem Engrs; Am Chem Soc; Am Soc Eng Educ; Sigma Xi. *Res:* Development of novel manufacturing processes for bulk pharmaceutical chemicals; reactor design and simulation; bioreactor design. *Mailing Add:* 5040 Ingersoll Pl Boulder CO 80303-1220. *Fax:* 303-938-6590

BECK, SUSAN L, ONCOLOGY. *Current Pos:* oncol clin nurse specialist, Health Sci Ctr, 86-90, from asst prof res to assoc prof res, 88-96, ASSOC PROF, UNIV UTAH COL NURSING, 96- *Personal Data:* b Sept 12, 52; m 73, Howard; c Karl. *Educ:* Duquesne Univ, BS, 74; Univ Pittsburgh, MN, 78; Univ Utah, PhD(nursing), 88. *Prof Exp:* Staff nurse, Allegheny Gen Hosp, 74-76, team leader, Oncol Unit, 77-78; clin nurse specialist oncol, St Francis Gen Hosp, 78-82 & Southeastern Utah Dist Health Dept, 82-84; clin supvr, Castleview Hosp, 82; nurse researcher, Dept Nursing Pract, Univ Utah Hosp, 88-95, proj dir, Prog Improve Patient Care, 89-95. *Concurrent Pos:* Grantee, Univ Utah Col Nursing, 88-91, Robert Wood Johnson Found, 89-90, 90-92 & 92-95, Asn Operating Rm, 89-90, Delores Dore Eccles Found, 91-93 & Utah Dept Health, 93-94; J William Fulbright scholar, 96; vis prof, Univ Pretoria Fac Med, 96. *Mem:* Asn Health Serv Res; Am Nurses Asn; Oncol Nursing Soc; Am Pain Soc; Int Soc Oral Oncol; Int Asn Study Pain; Int Soc Nurses Cancer Care. *Res:* Therapeutic use of music on cancer-related pain; the impact of a systematic oral care protocol on stomatitis after chemotherapy; health services research on organizational change. *Mailing Add:* Col Nursing Univ Utah 10 S 2000 E Front St Salt Lake City UT 84112-5880. *Fax:* 801-581-4642; *E-Mail:* susan.beck@nurs.utah.edu

BECK, THEODORE R(ICHARD), CHEMICAL ENGINEERING, ELECTROCHEMISTRY. *Current Pos:* PRES, ELECTROCHEM TECHNOL CORP, 75- *Personal Data:* b Seattle, Wash, Apr 11, 26; m 51, Ruth E Schaumberger; c Randi M & Maren L. *Educ:* Univ Wash, BS, 49, MS, 50, PhD(chem eng), 52. *Honors & Awards:* Outstanding Achievement Award, Electrochem Soc, 81, Acheson Medal, 90. *Prof Exp:* Res engr process develop, E I du Pont de Nemours & Co, 52-54; group leader reduction res, Kaiser Aluminum & Chem Corp, 54-59; sect head electrochem, Am Potash & Chem Corp, Nev, 59-61; res specialist electrochem & energy conversion, Aero-space Div, Boeing Co, 61-65, sr basic res scientist, Boeing Sci Res Labs, 65-72; div mgr, Flow Res, Inc, 72-75. *Concurrent Pos:* Res prof, Dept Chem Eng, Univ Wash, 72-80; mem, Panel Electrochem Corrosion, Nat Mat Adv Bd, 85-86. *Mem:* AAAS; Am Chem Soc; fel Electrochem Soc (pres, 75-76); Nat Asn Corrosion Eng; fel Am Inst Chem Engrs. *Res:* Fused salt and aqueous electrolysis; process development; batteries; fuel cells; energy conversion; corrosion; wear; electrokinetic phenomena. *Mailing Add:* 10035 31st Ave NE Seattle WA 98125-7705

BECK, THOMAS W, MUSCLE PHYSIOLOGY, ENDOCRINOLOGY. *Current Pos:* res technologist ophthal, 87-89, RES TECHNOLOGIST RADIOL, UNIV WASH, SEATTLE, 89- *Personal Data:* b Spokane, Wash, Apr 20, 48. *Educ:* Wash State Univ, BS, 70, MS, 72; Mich State Univ, PhD(dairy sci), 76. *Prof Exp:* Res assoc, Okla State Univ, 76-78; asst prof reproduction, Ohio State Univ, 78-84; prin res scientist cellular & molecular biol, Battelle Mem Inst, Columbus, Ohio, 84-86. *Concurrent Pos:* Consult, Cellular & Molecular Biol Sect, Battelle Mem Inst, Columbus, Ohio, 83-84. *Res:* Understanding the process of muscle contraction at the level of the interaction between the molecules of actin and myosin. *Mailing Add:* 20800 SW Wright St Aloha OR 97007-1001

BECK, WARREN FINDLAY, PHOTOSYNTHESIS. *Current Pos:* ASST PROF CHEM, VANDERBILT UNIV, 91- *Personal Data:* b Knoxville, Tenn, Dec 15, 60; m, Lynmarie A Posey. *Educ:* Davidson Col, NC, BS, 82; Yale Univ, PhD(biophys & physchem), 88. *Prof Exp:* Postdoctoral associateship, Dept Chem, Yale Univ, 88-89; Miller postdoctoral fel, Dept Chem, Univ Calif, Berkeley, 89-91. *Concurrent Pos:* Searle scholar, 92-95; Lilly endowment teaching fel, 93-94; lectr, Murray State Univ, Univ Ala, Tuscaloosa & Birmingham, 95, Yale Univ, 96. *Mem:* Am Chem Soc; Biophys Soc; Am Soc Photobiol; AAAS. *Res:* Author of numerous published articles. *Mailing Add:* Dept Chem Vanderbilt Univ PO Box 1822 Sta B Nashville TN 37235

BECK, WARREN R(ANDALL), CERAMICS SCIENCE & TECHNOLOGY, GLASS SCIENCE. *Current Pos:* RETIRED. *Personal Data:* b Bethlehem, Pa, Feb 14, 18; m 39, 70, Carol Anderson; c Dianne E (Blankenship), Kathryn L (Thostenson), Vicki A (Martin) & Constance R (Stiles). *Educ:* Pa State Col, BS, 42; Univ Minn, MS, 47. *Honors & Awards:* IR-100 Award; Gjeisbeek Ceramic Soc Award, 95. *Prof Exp:* Res asst ceramics, Pa State Col, 42-43; ceramist, Cent Res Lab, 43-47, sect leader inorg res, 48-55, mgr res & develop, Inorg Dept, 55-67 & Glass Bubble Proj, 67-74; corp scientist, Minn Mining & Mfg Co, 74-89. *Concurrent Pos:* Adj prof, Univ Wis, Menomonie, 87- *Mem:* Fel Am Ceramic Soc; Brit Soc Glass Technol. *Res:* Glass technology, unusual optical glasses; crystallographic inversions; polymorphism; solid state ceramics; ion exchange; glass microbubbles; foam composites. *Mailing Add:* 2700 Bayshore Blvd No 9203 Dunedin FL 34698

BECK, WILLIAM CARL, surgery; deceased, see previous edition for last biography

BECK, WILLIAM F(RANK), CHEMICAL ENGINEERING. *Current Pos:* Res engr, 64-66, res supvr process eng, 66-68, ASST DIR PROD RES, FMC CORP, 68-, EXEC VPRES, CHICAGO, 94- *Personal Data:* b Lansing, Mich, Aug 4, 38; m 60; c 3. *Educ:* Univ Mich, BS(chem eng) & BS(mat eng), 60; Mass Inst Technol, ScD(chem eng), 64. *Mem:* Am Inst Chem Engrs; Am Inst Chem. *Res:* Crystallization from solutions; applied surface chemistry; engineering kinetics; chlorinated hydrocarbons; soda ash. *Mailing Add:* FMC Corp 200 E Randolph Dr Chicago IL 60601

BECK, WILLIAM J, ENVIRONMENTAL HEALTH, BACTERIOLOGY. *Current Pos:* RETIRED. *Personal Data:* b Fredericktown, Mo, Aug 2, 21; m 47; c 2. *Educ:* Southeast Mo State Col, BS, 47; Univ Mo, Columbia, MA, 50; Univ Mich, MPH, 59, PhD(environ health), 70. *Prof Exp:* Chief lab technician bacteriol, Vet Admin Hosp, 47-49; environ bacteriologist, Mo Div Health Labs, 50-58; food technologist, Washington, DC Health Dept, 60-61; chief, Northwest Water Hyg Lab, USPHS, 61-69, chief, Health Res Ctr, 69-71; asst regional health admin, Boston, Mass, 71-74; USPH Serv, 75-82; dep dir, Environ Control & Opidemol, 83-84; consult, Environ Control, 84-90. *Concurrent Pos:* Lectr, Sch Fisheries, Univ Wash, 65-69. *Mem:* Am Pub Health Asn; Nat Shellfisheries Asn; Conf State & Prov Pub Health Lab Dirs; Sigma Xi. *Res:* Public health aspects of milk, food, fresh and estuarine water; environmental effects of man's health and well being in the Arctic and sub-Arctic. *Mailing Add:* 1610 Green Berry Rd Jefferson City MO 65101

BECK, WILLIAM SAMSON, BIOCHEMISTRY, HEMATOLOGY. *Current Pos:* from asst prof to assoc prof, 57-79, TUTOR BIOCHEM SCI, HARVARD UNIV, 57-, PROF MED, 79-; PROF HEALTH SCI & TECHNOL, MASS INST TECHNOL, 71- *Personal Data:* b Reading, Pa, Nov 7, 23; m 64, Hanne Troedsson; c Thomas R, Peter D, John C & Paul B. *Educ:* Univ Mich, BS, 43, MD, 46. *Hon Degrees:* AM, Harvard Univ, 70. *Honors & Awards:* Wenner-Gren Prize, 55. *Prof Exp:* Clin instr, Med Sch, Univ Calif, Los Angeles, 50-53, instr, 53-55, asst prof med, 55-57. *Concurrent Pos:* Fel biochem, NY Univ, 55-57; chief hemat & med sects, Atomic Energy Proj, Univ Calif, Los Angeles, 51-57; estab investr, Am Heart Asn, 55-60; chief hemat unit, 57-76, dir hemat res lab, Mass Gen Hosp, Boston, 57-; mem hemat study sect, NIH, 67-71; mem adv coun, Nat Inst Arthritis, Metab & Digestive Dis, 72-75; dir admis, Harvard Med Sch, 75-88. *Mem:* AAAS; Asn Am Physicians; Am Soc Biol Chem & Molecular Biol; Am Soc Clin Invest; Am Asn Cancer Res; Am Soc Hematol. *Res:* Vitamin B12, folic acid; nucleic acid and bacterial metabolism; enzymology; blood cell biochemistry. *Mailing Add:* Dept Med Harvard Univ & Mass Gen Hosp Fruit St Boston MA 02114. *Fax:* 617-726-3760; *E-Mail:* wsbeck@warren.med.harvard.edu

BECKEL, CHARLES LEROY, THEORETICAL PHYSICS. *Current Pos:* from assoc prof to prof, Univ NMex, 66-94, asst dean grad sch, 71-72, actg dir, Inst Social Res & Develop, 72, actg vpres res, 72-73, EMER PROF PHYSICS, UNIV NMEX, 95- *Personal Data:* b Philadelphia, Pa, Feb 7, 28; m 58, Josephine Ann Beck; c Amanda S, Sarah K, Timothy C & Andrea C. *Educ:* Univ Scranton, BS, 48; Johns Hopkins Univ, PhD(physics), 54. *Honors & Awards:* Award in Solid State Physics & Mat Sci, US Dept Energy, 88. *Prof Exp:* Asst, Johns Hopkins Univ, 49; asst, Sch Pharm, Univ Md, 49-53; from asst prof to assoc prof physics, Georgetown Univ, 53-64; mem res staff, Inst Defense Analysis, 64-66. *Concurrent Pos:* Consult, Ballistics Res Lab, Aberdeen Proving Ground, Md, 55-57, Inst Defense Analysis, 62-64 & 66-69, Dikewood Corp, 67-72 & 74-80, Albuquerque Urban Observ, 69-71, Los Alamos Nat Lab, 79-80, US Army Control & Disarm Agency, 81-84; Fulbright lectr, Univ Peshawar, 57-58 & Cheng Kung Univ, Taiwan, 63-64; vis prof theoret chem, Univ Oxford, 73; phys sci officer, US Arms Control & Disarm Agency, 80-81; vis prof chem & molecular sci, Univ Sussex, UK, 87; vis prof physics, Univ Scranton, 95. *Mem:* Am Phys Soc; Bioelectromagnetics Soc. *Res:* Electronic and vibrational struct of solids (theory), molecules (theory); quantum mechanics; operations research; study of biomolecule conformation; electric field effects on biological cells. *Mailing Add:* Dept Physics & Astron Univ NMex Albuquerque NM 87131-1156. *Fax:* 505-277-1520; *E-Mail:* clbeckel@unm.edu

BECKEMEYER, ELIZABETH FRANCES, insect oogenesis, for more information see previous edition

BECKEN, BRADFORD ALBERT, ELECTRONICS ENGINEERING. *Current Pos:* mgr syst eng lab, Raytheon Co, 67-68, prog mgr, 68-69, mgr eng, Submarine Signal Div, 70-83, dir technol, 83-94, CONSULT, RAYTHEON CO, 94- *Personal Data:* b Providence, RI, Oct 5, 24; m 46, Gaynelle M Lane; c Bradford A Jr, Brian A, Christian L & Anne Tracey. *Educ:* US Naval Acad, BS, 46; US Naval Postgrad Sch, BS, 52; Univ Calif, Los Angeles, MS, 53, PhD(physics), 61. *Honors & Awards:* Silver Medal, Am Defense Preparedness Asn, 87, Gold Medal, 95. *Prof Exp:* Sonar prof officer, Oper Test & Eval Force, US Navy, 53-56, head, Surface Ship Sonar Design Br, Bur Ships, 56-58, sonar prog officer, US Navy Electronics Lab, 60-63, mgr, Ship Sonar Prog, Bur Ships, 63-65, head, Sonar Adv Develop Br, Submarine Warfare Proj Off, 65-67. *Concurrent Pos:* Consult, Airtronics Inc, Dulles Int Airport, DC, 67- *Mem:* Fel Acoust Soc Am. *Res:* Directional distribution of ambient noise in the ocean; all aspects of the design, development, test, evaluation and operation of sonar systems for the detection of submarines. *Mailing Add:* 260 Fischer Circle Portsmouth RI 02871. *E-Mail:* bbecken@ccmail.ssd.ray.com

BECKEN, EUGENE D, COMMUNICATIONS. *Current Pos:* RETIRED. *Personal Data:* b Thief River Falls, Minn, Apr 29, 11; m 38; c 2. *Educ:* Univ NDak, BSEE, 32; Univ Minn, MSEE, 33; Mass Inst Technol, MS, 52. *Prof Exp:* RCA Commun, Inc, 35, transmitting shift engr, 35-36, eng asst, 36-42, asst to station plant supt, 42-48, supt tech opers & maintenance & plant opers engr, 53-59, vpres opers eng, 59-60, vpres & chief engr, 60-68, vpres syst oper, 68-70, exec vpres opers, RCA Global Commun, Inc, 70-72, pres, 72-75, chmn exec comt bd dir, 75-76. *Concurrent Pos:* Mem, Nat Indust Adv Comt, Fed Commun Comn, 59-; Independent res, astro & energy physics, 76- *Mem:* Fel Inst Elec & Electronics Engrs; AAAS; NY Acad Sci; Sigma Xi. *Res:* International radio cable and satellite communications; energy transfers in atmospheric sciences and in astrophysics. *Mailing Add:* 52 Rutland Rd Glen Rock NJ 07452-1221

BECKENDORF, STEVEN K, DEVELOPMENTAL BIOLOGY, GENETICS. *Current Pos:* Asst prof, 76-84, ASSOC PROF MOLECULAR BIOL, UNIV CALIF, BERKELEY, 84- *Personal Data:* b Portland, Ore, Jan 17, 44; m 68. *Educ:* Univ Calif, Los Angeles, AB, 66; Calif Inst Technol, PhD(biochem), 72. *Mem:* Genetics Soc Am; Soc Develop Biol. *Res:* Eukaryotic gene expression; glue protein genes of drosophila melanogaster; mechanisms of pattern formation in early development; salivary gland development in diosophila melanogaster. *Mailing Add:* Dept Molecular & Cell Biol Univ Calif Berkeley CA 94720-4759. *Fax:* 510-642-7000; *E-Mail:* beckendo@mendel_berkeley.edu

BECKENSTEIN, EDWARD, MATHEMATICAL ANALYSIS. *Current Pos:* assoc prof, 72-77, chmn dept, 77-81, PROF MATH, ST JOHN'S UNIV, NY, 81- *Personal Data:* b New York, NY, Oct 21, 40; m; c 1. *Educ:* Polytech Inst, Brooklyn, BS, 62, MS, 64, PhD(math), 66. *Prof Exp:* From instr to asst prof math, Polytech Inst, Brooklyn, 65-67; asst prof, St John's Univ, NY, 67-68; from asst prof to assoc prof, Polytech Inst, Brooklyn, 68-72. *Mem:* Am Math Soc. *Res:* Abstract algebra; topology; functional analysis; theory of commutative Banach algebras. *Mailing Add:* 5 Flora Dr Holmdel NJ 07733-2005

BECKER, AARON JAY, HIGH TEMPERATURE CHEMISTRY, MOLTEN SALT CHEMISTRY. *Current Pos:* RES ASSOC, EI DU PONT, WILMINGTON, 90- *Personal Data:* b Brooklyn, NY, Apr 28, 40; div; c 2. *Educ:* Brooklyn Col, BS, 61; Univ Wash, MS, 64; Ill Inst Technol, PhD(chem), 71. *Prof Exp:* Scientist chem, Ill Inst Technol Res Inst, 65-68; resident assoc, Argonne Nat Labs, 68-71; fel, McMaster Univ, 71-73; scientist, Alcoa Labs, 73-76, sr scientist, 76-78, staff scientist, 78-83, tech specialist chem, 83-91. *Concurrent Pos:* Vis scientist & lectr, Tech Univ, Norway, 88. *Mem:* Am Chem Soc; Sigma Xi; Am Inst Mining Engrs. *Res:* Production of metals from ores; fused salt chemistry; utilization of natural resources; production of chemicals from coal; electrochemistry; aluminum smelting; ceramic powder synthesis; plasmas. *Mailing Add:* 1218 Evergreen Rd Wilmington DE 19803

BECKER, ALEX, MINERAL EXPLORATION, INSTRUMENTATION. *Current Pos:* PROF APPL GEOPHYSICS, UNIV CALIF, 81- *Personal Data:* b Bialystok, Poland, July 27, 35; US citizen; m 60; c 3. *Educ:* McGill Univ, BEng, 58, MSc, 61, PhD(physics), 64. *Honors & Awards:* Cimm Bell

Medal. *Prof Exp:* Res scientist geophys, Geol Surv, Can, 65-69; prof appl geophy, Ecole Polytech Montreal, 69-80; dir res, Questor Surv, 80-81. *Mem:* Soc Exp Geophys. *Res:* Airborne geophysical instrumentation; data acquisition and interpretation; subsurface electromagnetic imaging. *Mailing Add:* Dept Mat Sci & Mineral Eng Univ Calif Berkeley CA 94720-1760

BECKER, ANTHONY J, JR, physiology, immunology, for more information see previous edition

BECKER, BARBARA, biochemistry, for more information see previous edition

BECKER, BENJAMIN, MICROBIOLOGY, BIOCHEMISTRY. *Current Pos:* assoc prof cell biol, to prof cell biol, 69-77, prof, 77-81, EMER PROF BIOL SCI, PURDUE UNIV, 81- *Personal Data:* b New York, NY, Apr 22, 16; m 51; c 2. *Educ:* Rutgers Univ, BS, 37, MS, 62, PhD(microbiol), 65. *Prof Exp:* Asst prof microbiol, biochem & gen biol, Hamilton Col, 65-69. *Concurrent Pos:* Consult, indoor environ microbiol. *Mem:* Am Soc Microbiol; Am Chem Soc; Am Inst Biol Sci. *Res:* Actinomycetes; cell wall analyses; microbial transformations; asparaginase in leukemia; leprosy immunogens; new antifungal agents; antibiotics; nonspecific immunostimulaters; lures and traps for cat and dog fleas; alternatives to pesticides; soil screening for actinomycetes and drugs. *Mailing Add:* 5126 Fairfield Ave Ft Wayne IN 46807-3219

BECKER, BRUCE CLARE, CLINICAL PSYCHOLOGY, CLINICAL NEUROPSYCHOLOGY. *Current Pos:* PRES, NEUROPSYCHOL ASSOCS LTD, 84- *Personal Data:* b Seattle, Wash, Dec 9, 29; m 55, Carol Peddle; c Cheryl, Cecilia, Bruce, Gregory, Kurt, Christopher & Lisa. *Educ:* St Ambrose Col, BA, 50; St Louis Univ, MA, 54; Loyola Univ, PhD(psychol), 62. *Prof Exp:* Clin psychologist, US Naval Training Ctr, Great Lakes, Ill, 55-58 & Naval Hosp, 58-65; clin neuropsychologist, Vet Admin Hosp, Downey Ill, 65-68, chief, Psychol Serv, 68-69; dir, Psychol Training & Res, Naval Hosp Bethesda, Md, 69-84. *Concurrent Pos:* Assoc neurology & psychiat, Med Sch, Northwestern Univ, 67-69; assoc clin prof psychol, George Washington Univ Med Sch, 70-75; clin assoc, Cath Univ Am, 73-75; clin assoc prof psychiat, Georgetown Univ Med Sch, 74-, clin assoc prof neurol, 78-; adj prof med psychol, Uniformed Servs Univ Health Sci, 78- *Mem:* Fel Am Psychol Asn; Int Neuropsychol Soc; Undersea Med Soc. *Res:* Interest in brain, behavior relationships with an emphasis on brain damage due to head injury, toxic exposure, and prolonged or repeated undersea diving. *Mailing Add:* 9508 Newbold Pl Bethesda MD 20817

BECKER, CARL GEORGE, PATHOLOGY. *Current Pos:* assoc prof path & assoc pathologist, 70-76, PROF PATH & ATTENDING PATHOLOGIST, NEW YORK HOSP-CORNELL MED CTR, 76- *Personal Data:* b Philadelphia, Pa, Mar 18, 36; m 61; c 3. *Educ:* Yale Univ, BS, 57; Cornell Univ, MD, 61. *Prof Exp:* From intern to resident path, New York Hosp-Cornell Med Ctr, 61-66, asst prof, 66-68; pathologist, Naval Hosp, St Albans, 68-70. *Concurrent Pos:* USPHS trainee path, Med Col, Cornell Univ, 62-66; mem, Thrombosis Coun, Am Heart Asn. *Mem:* Am Asn Path (pres, 85-86); Harvey Soc; Int Acad Path; Sigma Xi. *Res:* Arteriosclerosis; rheumatic heart disease; renal disease; immunopathology; hemostasis and thrombosis; microbiology. *Mailing Add:* Dept Path Med Col Wis 8700 W Wisconsin Ave Milwaukee WI 53226-3512

BECKER, CARTER MILES, PATHOLOGY, BIOPHYSICS. *Current Pos:* ASST PROF PATH & LAB MED & DIR, DIV LAB HEMAT, UNIV CINCINNATI MED CTR, 82- *Personal Data:* b Allentown, Pa, Mar 6, 40; c 2. *Educ:* Pa State Univ, BA, 62; Jefferson Med Col, MD, 66. *Prof Exp:* Intern path, Yale New Haven Med Ctr, 66-67; postdoc fel biophys, Mass Inst Technol, 67-70, res assoc, 70-77; c1 & res fel hemat, Mass Gen Hosp, 75-78; resident path, Worcester Mem Hosp, 78-81, attending pathologist, 81-82. *Concurrent Pos:* Mem, Coun Thrombosis, Am Heart Asn; res fel med, Harvard Med Sch, 75-78. *Mem:* Am Asn Pathologists; Col Am Pathologists; Int Acad Path; Am Heart Asn; Int Soc Thrombosis & Haemostasis; AAAS. *Res:* Investigations of molecular mechanisms involved in blood coagulation, hemostasis and thrombosis, especially the structure and function of fibrinogen association products and the effect of soluble fibrinogen-fibrin complexes on platelet function. *Mailing Add:* 4303 Autumn Ridge Lane Sandusky OH 44870-7028

BECKER, CLARENCE DALE, FISHERIES. *Current Pos:* RETIRED. *Personal Data:* b Albany, Ore, Aug 17, 30; m 62; c Terren Dale, Kendal Scott, Susan Carol & Sarah Marie. *Educ:* Ore State Univ, BS, 53, MS, 55; Univ Wash, PhD(fisheries), 64. *Honors & Awards:* Dis Serv Award, Am Fisheries Soc, 80. *Prof Exp:* Fisheries biologist, Fisheries Res Inst, Univ Wash, 55-59, res asst, 59-63, res assoc Col Fisheries, 63-67; res scientist, Pac Northwest Labs, Battelle Mem Inst, 67-70, sr res scientist, 70-93. *Concurrent Pos:* Fel, Am Inst Fisheries Res Biologists, 85. *Mem:* Pac Fisheries Biologists; Am Fisheries Soc; fel Am Inst Fisheries Res Biologists. *Res:* Fisheries biology; aquatic toxicology; freshwater ecology; environmental assessments; impact of human populations. *Mailing Add:* 702 S 48th West Richland WA 99353

BECKER, CLARENCE F(REDERICK), AGRICULTURAL ENGINEERING. *Current Pos:* RETIRED. *Personal Data:* b Dazey, NDak, Mar 27, 20; m 44; c 2. *Educ:* NDak Agr Col, BS, 43, MS, 49; Mich State Univ, PhD(agr eng), 56. *Prof Exp:* Dist rep, Food Mach & Chem Co, 47-49; agr engr & head div, Univ Wyo, 49-83; sci coop, State Res Serv, USDA, 83-88. *Concurrent Pos:* Consult, Food & Agr Orgn UN, 64, 66; chief of party, Univ Wyo team, Kabul Univ, Afghanistan, 68-70. *Mem:* Am Soc Agr Eng. *Res:* Agricultural mechanization. *Mailing Add:* 2453 Leisure World Mesa AZ 85206

BECKER, DAVID STEWART, BIOPHYSICS, ARTIFICIAL INTELLIGENCE. *Current Pos:* RES SCIENTIST, ILL INST TECHNOL RES INST, 72- *Personal Data:* b Chicago, Ill, Aug 28, 45. *Educ:* Stanford Univ, BS, 67; Univ Wis, Madison, MS, 69; Ill Inst Tech, PhD(physics), 77. *Prof Exp:* Scientist, Hallicrafters, Northrop Corp, 69-71; lectr, North Park Col, 71. *Res:* Toxic chemical risk analysis; artificial intelligence; natural language processing; decision theory; mathematical modeling. *Mailing Add:* 18 Augustus Rd Lexington MA 02173-4332

BECKER, DAVID VICTOR, NUCLEAR MEDICINE, THYROID DISEASE. *Current Pos:* assoc prof med, 61-75, PROF RADIOL, COL MED, CORNELL UNIV, 61-, PROF MED, 75-, DIR DIV NUCLEAR MED, NEW YORK HOSP-CORNELL MED CTR, 55- *Personal Data:* b New York, NY, May 24, 23; wid; c Daniel & Susan. *Educ:* Columbia Univ, AB, 43, MA, 44; NY Univ, MD, 48. *Honors & Awards:* Hon mem Med Acad Sr Croatia, 88- *Prof Exp:* Rotating intern, Sinai Hosp, Baltimore, Md, 48-49; med intern, Maimonides Hosp, Brooklyn, 49-50; Runyan fel, Dept Clin Invest & Biophys, Sloan-Kettering Inst, New York, 50-52; chief radioisotope unit, Surg Res Unit, Brooke Army Med Ctr, Ft Sam Houston, Tex, 52-54; asst resident med serv, New York Hosp-Cornell Med Ctr, 54-55; from instr med & radiol to asst prof med, 57-61. *Concurrent Pos:* Asst attend physician, New York Hosp-Cornell Med Ctr, 57-62, assoc attend physician, 62-74, attend radiologist, 71-, attend physician, 75-; mem, Mayor's Tech Adv Comt Radiation, New York, 73-89; mem med adv comt, NY State Dept Health, 73; mem task force short lived radionuclides, Bur Radiol Health, Food & Drug Admin, 75-85, consult, 76; mem, Nat Coun Radiation Protection & Measurement Sci Comt, Nat Coop Thyroid Can Treat Study Group, 78 & NY State Dept Health Radiol Adv Comt, 87-; mem tech adv comt, Radiation to the Health Comnr NY City; NY Health Comnr Ad Study Comt for Disposal of Low-Level Radioactive Wastes, NY, 78-84; mem med radiation adv comt, FDA, 82-86, consult, Nat Ctr Devices & Radiol Health, Nat Can Inst Thyroid & Iodine 131 Assessment Comt; chmn, Working Group Fallout Effects Chernobyl Accident, Nat Cancer Inst. *Mem:* Fel Am Col Physicians; Am Thyroid Asn (1st vpres, 76, pres-elect, 81, pres); Soc Nuclear Med (trustee); Endocrine Soc; Am Fedn Clin Res; mem Publ & Radiation Effects Comt. *Res:* Endocrinology and radiation effects; clinical thyroid physiology and disease; nuclear medicine; treatment of typhoid cancer hyperthyroidism with radioidine. *Mailing Add:* Div Nuclear Med 525 E 68th St New York NY 10021. *Fax:* 212-746-8873

BECKER, DONALD A, BOTANY, PLANT ECOLOGY. *Current Pos:* ECOLOGIST, US ARMY CORPS ENGRS, OMAHA, 85- *Personal Data:* b Valley City, NDak, July 27, 38; m 60; c 3. *Educ:* Valley City State Col, BS, 60; Univ NDak, MS, 65, PhD(ecol), 68. *Prof Exp:* High sch teacher, Wyo, 60-62; instr biol, Univ NDak, 67-68; from asst prof to assoc prof biol, Midland Lutheran Col, 68-75; environ specialist, Mo Basin States Asn, Omaha, 75-81. *Concurrent Pos:* NSF res fel, Okla State Univ, 70-71; Cottrell res grant, 75; study mgr, Mo River Floodplain Study, 80-81; veg res grant, US Nat Park Serv, 82-85. *Mem:* Ecol Soc Am. *Res:* Dispersal ecology; plant autecology; senescence abscission in plants; nitrogen fixation in legumes; environmental planning and assessment; ecology of great plains rivers; floodplain management studies, prairie management planning. *Mailing Add:* 21706 Edgevale Pl Elkhorn NE 68022

BECKER, DONALD ARTHUR, NEUTRON ACTIVATION ANALYSIS, TRACE ELEMENT ANALYSIS. *Current Pos:* Res chemist textile sect, Org & Fibrous Mat Div, Nat Bur Stand, 61-62, res chemist photochem sect, Phys Chem Div, 62-64, res chemist, Analytical Chem Div, 64-73, chief activation analytical sect, 73-75, asst chief, Analytical Chem Div, 75-76, sci asst to dir, Inst Mat Res, 76, mgr recycled oil prog, 76-82, spec asst to dir, 82-84, SR RES CHEMIST, CTR ANALYTICAL CHEM, NAT BUR STAND, 85- *Personal Data:* b Detroit, Mich, Feb 14, 38; m 60, Linda Knorr; c Steven & Tracy. *Educ:* Valparaiso Univ, BS, 59; Fla State Univ, MS, 61. *Honors & Awards:* Silver Medal Award, US Dept Com, 82; Award of Merit, Am Soc Testing & Mat, 91. *Concurrent Pos:* Chmn, Nuclear Methods Task Group, Am Soc Testing & Mat; chair, Biol & Med Div, Am Nuclear Soc; fel, Wash Acad Sci, 87. *Mem:* Am Chem Soc; Am Soc Testing & Mat; fel Am Nuclear Soc. *Res:* Trace elemental analysis using neutron activation, including radiochemical separations, improvement of accuracy and precision, and evaluation of reactor neutron irradiation facilities; characterization of recycled oils by research on test procedures. *Mailing Add:* Analytical Chem Div Chem Sci & Technol Lab Nat Inst Stand & Technol Gaithersburg MD 20899-0001

BECKER, DONALD EUGENE, ANIMAL NUTRITION, ANIMAL PHYSIOLOGY. *Current Pos:* PRES, OXFORD FEEDERS, INC, 89- *Personal Data:* b Delavan, Ill, Feb 2, 23; m 49, Elsie J Hendrickson; c Esther B (Gasser), Phyllis B (Boreman), Donald E Jr, William E & Beth B (Kasper). *Educ:* Univ Ill, BS, 45, MS, 47; Cornell Univ, PhD(nutrit), 49. *Honors & Awards:* Am Feed Mfrs Award, 57; Morrison Award, 77. *Prof Exp:* Asst animal sci, Univ Ill, 45-47; assoc prof animal nutrit, Univ Tenn, 49-50; from asst prof to prof, Univ Ill, Urbana-Champaign, 58-84, head, Dept Animal Sci, 67-84; chmn, Dept Animal Sci, Ohio State Univ, Columbus, 84-87; pvt indust consult, 87- *Concurrent Pos:* Mem, Subcomt Nutrient Requirements of Swine, Nat Res Coun; ed, J Animal Sci, 66-69. *Mem:* Fel AAAS; Am Soc Animal Sci (pres, 70-71); Animal Nutrit Res Coun; Poultry Sci Asn; Am Inst Nutrit; Sigma Xi. *Res:* Metabolic function of cobalt in ruminant nutrition; chemistry and morphology of bovine blood; protein and amino acid nutrition for pregnancy, lactation, growth and fattening; antibiotics and nonruminant nutrition; comparative value of carbohydrates and available energy values of feeds. *Mailing Add:* 2209 Combes St Urbana IL 61801. *Fax:* 217-367-2360

BECKER, EDWARD BROOKS, GENERAL MANAGEMENT, ENVIRONMENTAL MANAGEMENT. *Current Pos:* MGT & ENVIRON CONSULT, 90- *Personal Data:* b Emporia, Kans, Aug 12, 31; m 59; c 3. *Educ:* Kans State Teachers Col, AB, 53; Univ Kans, PhD(inorg chem), 59. *Prof Exp:* Sr res chemist, Chem Div, PPG Industs, 60-61; proj mgr, Alexandria Div, AMF, 61-63; res chemist, Gulf Res & Develop Co, 64-70; dir bur air pollution control & solid & hazardous waste mgt, State of Wis, 70-78; pres, RMT, Inc, 78-90; pres, Becker & Assocs, consults to mgt. *Concurrent Pos:* Chmn, State & Territorial Air Pollution Prog Admin, 74. *Mem:* AAAS; Am Chem Soc; fel Am Inst Chemists. *Res:* High temperature plasma chemistry; air pollution control; solid waste management; nitrogen-phosphorus-potassium fertilizer chemistry; management of consulting firms. *Mailing Add:* 1132 Univ Bay Dr Madison WI 53705

BECKER, EDWARD SAMUEL, PULP TECHNOLOGY, POLLUTION CONTROL. *Current Pos:* PRES, ECONOTECH SERV LTD, 72- *Personal Data:* b Bisbee, Ariz, Sept 8, 29; m 51, Norma Kloster; c Keith & Kathy. *Educ:* Ore State Col, BS, 51, MS, 53, PhD(forest prod chem), 57. *Prof Exp:* Sect leader develop pulping, Rayonier, Inc, 57-64 & G L Pulp & Papermaking Union Camp, 64-65; dept mgr, Columbia Cellulose Co, Ltd, 66-68, mgr tech develop, 69-71, dir tech & environ control, 72. *Mem:* Tech Asn Pulp & Paper Indust; Can Pulp & Paper Asn; fel Chem Inst Can. *Res:* Technical consulting; research and development management; technical service; pulp and paper; pilot plant operation; management consulting; pulp bleaching. *Mailing Add:* Econotech Serv Ltd 852 Derwent Way Annacis Island New Westminster BC V3M 5R1 Can. *Fax:* 604-526-1898

BECKER, EDWIN DEMUTH, PHYSICAL CHEMISTRY. *Current Pos:* phys chemist, NIH, 55-68, chief sect molecular biophys, 62-80, mem fac grad prog, 63, asst chief, Lab Phys Biol, 64-72, chief, Lab Chem Physics, Nat Inst Arthritis, Metab & Digestive Dis, 72-81, actg dir, Fogarty Int Ctr, 79-80, assoc dir, NIH, 80-88, CHIEF NMR SECT, NAT INST DIABETES & DIGESTIVE & KIDNEY DIS, NIH, 88- *Personal Data:* b Columbia, Pa, May 3, 30; m 53; c 2. *Educ:* Univ Rochester, BS, 52; Univ Calif, PhD(chem), 55. *Honors & Awards:* Coblentz Mem Prize Chem Spectros, 66; Dept Health, Educ & Welfare Superior Serv Award, 74; NIH Dir Award, 89. *Prof Exp:* Asst chem, Univ Calif, 53-54, instr, 55. *Concurrent Pos:* Sr asst scientist, USPHS, 55-58; prof lectr, Georgetown Univ, 58-; mem adv bd, Off Critical Tables, 67-69; mem, Joint Comt Atomic & Molecular Data, 67-89, chmn comt, 78-81; mem prog comt, Exp NMR Conf, 68-70, chmn, 69; mem comn molecular structure & spectros, Int Union Pure & Appl Chem, 73-81, chmn comn, 75-81; mem bd dirs, Found Advan Educ Sci, 76-79; mem, US Nat Comt, 79-86, secy, Phys Chem Div, Int Union Pure & Appl Chem, 81-85, chmn, 85-86, chmn publ comt, 86-94, secy gen, 96-; mem, Int Activ Comn, Am Chem Soc, 87-, chmn, 93-95; mem coun, Int Soc Magnetic Resonance, 90- *Mem:* AAAS; Coblentz Soc; Am Soc Appl Spectros; Am Chem Soc; fel AAAS; foreign fel, Nat Acad Sci India. *Res:* Molecular structure; infrared spectroscopy; nuclear magnetic resonance; hydrogen bonding. *Mailing Add:* Bldg 5 Rm 124 NIH Bethesda MD 20892-0520. *Fax:* 301-435-2413; *E-Mail:* tbecker@nih.gov

BECKER, ELIZABETH ANN (WHITE), ENVIRONMENTAL ANALYSIS, PHARMACEUTICAL ANALYSIS. *Current Pos:* ENVIRON SPECIALIST, MEAD JOHNSON NUTRIT GROUP, EVANSVILLE, 89- *Personal Data:* b Cincinnati, Ohio, Sept 2, 50; div. *Educ:* Miami Univ, BA, 72; Univ Cincinnati, MS, 74, PhD(chem), 80. *Prof Exp:* Scientist, Mead Johnson & Co, Div Bristol Myers, 80-87; group leader, Bristol-Myers US Pharmaceut & Nutrit Group, Evansville, 87-89. *Concurrent Pos:* Ind cert wastewater treatment plant operator, Indust Class D, 89- *Mem:* Am Chem Soc. *Res:* Synthesis of analogs of natural products; analysis and stability determination of pharmaceutical compounds; compliance specialist, environmental with an emphasis in water & wastewater. *Mailing Add:* Bristol Myers Squibb B414 2400 W Lloyd Expressway Evansville IN 47721-0002

BECKER, ELMER LEWIS, IMMUNOLOGY. *Current Pos:* prof path, Health Ctr, 70-80, Boehringer Ingelheim, prof immunol, 84-89, EMER PROF, UNIV CONN, FARMINGTON, 89- *Personal Data:* b Chicago, Ill, Feb 17, 18; m 46; c 3. *Educ:* Univ Ill, MD, 45, PhD(biochem), 47. *Honors & Awards:* Rouse-Whipple Award, Am Asn Pathol. *Prof Exp:* Asst prof biochem, Col Med, Univ Ill, 47-49, asst prof bact, 50-51; chief dept immunochem, Walter Reed Army Inst Res, Washington, DC, 52-69. *Concurrent Pos:* John Simon Guggenheim Mem Found fel, 69-70. *Mem:* AAAS; hon fel Am Acad Allergy; Am Asn Immunol; emer mem Am Asn Path. *Res:* Antigen-activated enzyme systems; chemotaxis; lysosomal enzyme release; neutrophil responses. *Mailing Add:* Dept Path Univ Conn Farmington CT 06032. *Fax:* 860-679-2936

BECKER, ERNEST I, CHEMISTRY. *Current Pos:* RETIRED. *Personal Data:* b Cleveland, Ohio, Aug 18, 18; m 47, Marion Ferris; c Jonathan D, Kenneth A, Mark E, Robert N & Paula S. *Educ:* Case Western Reserve Univ, BS, 41, MS, 43, PhD(chem), 46. *Prof Exp:* Instr, Polytech Univ, 46, from asst prof to prof chem, 47-56; prof chem, Univ Mass, 65-88, chmn dept, 65-67 & 68-72. *Concurrent Pos:* Chmn, Div Nat Sci, Univ Mass, Boston, 65-70; indust consult, acad & govt; Fulbright prof, Ankara Univ, Turkey, 87-88; expert witness. *Mem:* Fel AAAS; Am Chem Soc; fel NY Acad Sci; Royal Soc Chem; Am Inst Chemists. *Res:* Synthesis reactions and spectra of tetracyclones; synthesis and properties of monomeric and polymeric fluors; organotin compounds; mechanism of organomagnesium reactions; oxazoles base condensations of active methylene compounds. *Mailing Add:* 32 Oxford Rd Newton MA 02159-2405

BECKER, F(LOYD) K(ENNETH), ELECTRONICS ENGINEERING. *Current Pos:* dir, 80-90, EMER DIR, TELECOMMUN SYSTS LAB, UNIV COLO, 90- *Personal Data:* b Denver, Colo, June 10, 24; m 45; c 3. *Educ:* Univ Colo, BS, 45; Calif Inst Technol, MS, 47. *Prof Exp:* Dial equip engr, Mt States Tel & Tel Co, 47-51; mem tech staff, Bell Tel Labs, 51-66, head dept, Customer Switching Lab, 66-80. *Concurrent Pos:* Spec probs engr, Off Naval Res, 52-53. *Mem:* Sr mem Inst Elec & Electronics Engrs; Sigma Xi. *Res:* Data communication; discrete systems theory; switching theory. *Mailing Add:* 5118 N 109th St Longmont CO 80501-8408

BECKER, FREDERICK F, PATHOLOGY, ONCOLOGY. *Current Pos:* chmn, Dept Anat & Res Path, 76-79, VPRES RES, M D ANDERSON HOSP, HOUSTON, 79- *Personal Data:* b New York, NY, July 23, 31; m 71. *Educ:* Columbia Univ, BA, 52; NY Univ, MD, 56. *Prof Exp:* Intern, Boston City Hosp, 56-57; asst & actg dir exp path, US Naval Med Res Inst, 60-61; from asst prof to prof path, Sch Med, NY Univ, 62-70; dir path, Bellevue Hosp, 70-76. *Concurrent Pos:* Univ fel path, Sch Med, NY Univ, 57-60; career investr, NY Health Res Coun, 62-; consult, US Naval Hosp, St Albans, NY, 62- *Res:* Carcinogenesis. *Mailing Add:* Univ Tex MD Anderson Cancer Ctr 1515 Holcombe Blvd Box 101 Houston TX 77030-4095

BECKER, GARY STANLEY, ECONOMICS. *Current Pos:* asst prof, Univ Chicago, 54-57, Ford Found vis prof econ, 69-70, univ prof, 70-83, chmn, Dept Econs, 84-85, UNIV PROF ECON & SOCIOL, UNIV CHICAGO, 83- *Personal Data:* b Pottsville, Pa, Dec 2, 30; m 79, Guity Nashat; c Judith S & Catherine J. *Educ:* Princeton Univ, AB, 51; Univ Chicago, AM, 53, PhD, 55; Hebrew Univ, Jerusalem, PhD(hon), 85. *Honors & Awards:* Nobel Prize in Econ Scis, 92; John Bates Clark Medal, Am Econ Asn, 67; Frank E Seldman Distinguished Award Polit Econ, 85, John R Commons Award, Omicron Delta Epsilon, 87. *Prof Exp:* From asst prof to assoc prof, Columbia Univ, New York City, 57-60, prof econ, 60-68 & Arthur Lehman prof, 68-70. *Concurrent Pos:* Mem & sr res assoc, Ctr Econ Anal Human Behav, Nat Bur Econ Res, 57-79, res policy adv, 72-78; assoc, Econ Res Ctr, Nat Opinion Res Ctr, Chicago, 80-; assoc mem, Inst Fiscal & Monetary Policy, Ministry Japan, 88- *Mem:* Nat Acad Sci; Am Acad Arts & Scis; Am Econ Asn (vpres, 74, pres, 87); Am Philos Soc; fel Am Statis Asn; Nat Acad Educ; Econometric Soc; Mont Pelerin Soc (vpres, 89-90, pres, 90-92). *Mailing Add:* Dept Econ Univ Chicago 1126 E 59th St Chicago IL 60637-1539

BECKER, GEORGE CHARLES, FOREST ENTOMOLOGY, URBAN ECOLOGY. *Current Pos:* assoc prof, 66-69, PROF BIOL, METRO STATE COL, 69-, CHMN DEPT BIOL, 71- *Personal Data:* b Stevens Point, Wis, July 21, 35; m 64, Irene Colvin; c Lisa A, Julie R & Grant C. *Educ:* Univ Minn, BS, 60; Univ Wis, MS, 62, PhD(entomol), 65. *Prof Exp:* Asst prof, Univ Wis-Whitewater, 64-66. *Mem:* Sigma Xi. *Res:* Diprionidae. *Mailing Add:* Dept Biol Metro State Col Denver Campus Box 53 PO Box 173362 Denver CO 80217-3362. *Fax:* 303-556-4941; *E-Mail:* beckerg@mscd.edu

BECKER, GERALD ANTHONY, mathematics, for more information see previous edition

BECKER, GERALD LEONARD, biochemistry, for more information see previous edition

BECKER, GORDON EDWARD, SURFACE PHYSICS. *Current Pos:* MEM TECH STAFF, BELL TEL LABS, 53- *Personal Data:* b St Louis, Mo, Sept 27, 20; m 56; c 2. *Educ:* Columbia Univ, BA, 42, AM, 43, PhD(physics), 46. *Prof Exp:* Asst physics, Columbia Univ, 42-44, res assoc, Radiation Lab, 43-46, instr physics, 46-47 & Stanford Univ, 47-51; sci staff, Hudson Labs, Columbia Univ, 51-53. *Mem:* Am Phys Soc; Inst Elec & Electronics Engrs. *Res:* Molecular beams. *Mailing Add:* 2872 Village Dr Marietta GA 30062

BECKER, HARRY CARROLL, ANALYTICAL CHEMISTRY. *Current Pos:* RETIRED. *Personal Data:* b Bisbee, Ariz, Oct 31, 13; m 40; c Gregory S. *Educ:* Univ Ill, BS, 36, MS, 37, PhD(analytical chem), 40. *Prof Exp:* Analytical res, Texaco Inc, 40-43, supvr, 44-62, res assoc, 62-78. *Mem:* AAAS; Am Chem Soc; Sigma Xi. *Res:* Radiation chemistry; analysis of petroleum products; analytical studies with neutrons and energetic charged particles; scanning electron microscopy and electron microprobe. *Mailing Add:* 18 Nutting Rd Westford MA 01886

BECKER, HENRY A, CHEMICAL ENGINEERING. *Current Pos:* from asst prof to assoc prof, 63-68, head dept, 76-87, PROF CHEM ENG, QUEEN'S UNIV, 68-; PROF GAS COMBUSTION ENG, BRIT GAS, CONSUMERS GAS, NAT SCI ENG RES COUN, 92- *Personal Data:* b Castor, Alta, Apr 15, 29; m 57; c 3. *Educ:* Univ Sask, BChE, 52, MSc, 55; Mass Inst Technol, ScD(chem eng), 61. *Honors & Awards:* Eng Medal, Asn Prof Engrs, Ont, 90; Izack Walton Killam Prize, Can Coun, 91. *Prof Exp:* Jr res officer, Div Appl Biol, Nat Res Coun Can, 52-57, asst res officer, 57-61; asst prof chem eng, Mass Inst Technol, 61-63. *Concurrent Pos:* Ford Found fel, Mass Inst Technol, 61-63; SRC sr res fel, Univ Sheffield, 73. *Mem:* Am Inst Chem Engrs; Combustion Inst; fel Chem Inst Can; Can Inst Energy; Am Soc Eng Educ; AAAS. *Res:* Diffusion in polymers; sedimentation; fluidization; drying; turbulence; jets and boundary layers; combustion; radiation; biochemical engineering; forest fire research. *Mailing Add:* Dept Chem Eng Queen's Univ Kingston ON K7L 3N6 Can

BECKER, JEFFREY MARVIN, MOLECULAR BIOLOGY. *Current Pos:* from asst prof to assoc prof, 72-78, PROF MICROBIOL, UNIV TENN, KNOXVILLE, 78-, DIR, GRAD PROG CELLUAR, MOLECULAR & DEVELOP BIOL. *Personal Data:* b Baltimore, Md, July 13, 43; m 82, Nancy Ring; c Rachel, Benjamin & Sarah. *Educ:* Emory Univ, BA, 65; Ga State Univ, MS, 67; Univ Cincinnati, PhD(microbiol), 70. *Prof Exp:* Weizmann fel biophys, Weizmann Inst, Rehovot, Israel, 70-71, NATO-NSF fel, 71-72. *Concurrent Pos:* Consult, Oak Ridge Nat Lab, 74-; NIH res career develop award, 75-80; Fogarty sr int fel, 85-86. *Mem:* Am Soc Microbiol; AAAS; Am Asn Univ Prof; Am Soc Biochem & Molecular Biol. *Res:* Membrane transport; peptide transport and utilization in microorganisms; development of antifungal drugs. *Mailing Add:* Dept Microbiol Univ Tenn Walters Life Sci Bldg Knoxville TN 37996-0845. *Fax:* 423-974-4007; *E-Mail:* becker@utkvs.utk.edu

BECKER, JERRY PAGE, MATHEMATICS. *Current Pos:* assoc prof, 79-83, PROF, COL EDUC, SOUTHERN ILL UNIV, 83- *Personal Data:* b North Redwood, Minn, Mar 1, 37; m 59, Tedda Matson; c Alison, Jeffrey & Brian. *Educ:* Univ Minn, Minneapolis, BS, 59; Univ Notre Dame, MS, 61; Stanford Univ, PhD(math educ), 67. *Honors & Awards:* Serv Award, Sch Sci & Math Asns, 90. *Prof Exp:* Pub sch teacher, Minn, 59-60 & 61-63; res asst math educ, Sch Educ, Stanford Univ, 63-64, res asst, Sch Math Study Group, 64-67; from asst prof to assoc prof, Grad Sch Educ, Rutgers Univ, 67-75; vis assoc prof math sci, Northern Ill Univ, 75-76; math teacher, Clinton Rosette Mid Sch, DeKalb, Ill, 77-78. *Concurrent Pos:* Instr, NSF Inst, Univ San Francisco, 65-67 & Rutgers Univ, 67-68; consult, NSF Sci Educ Improv Prog, India, 67 & 68, supvr, 69 & 70, staff scientist math, Sci Liaison Staff, New Delhi, 71-72; mem, US Comn Math Instr, Nat Acad Sci, 73-77, co-chmn, Panel US Arrangements Third Cong Math Educ, 74-76; consult, UN Develop Prog, 75; head deleg, Am Math Educ, Peoples Repub China, 77, 80, 84 & 87, Japan, 77, 88; co-prin investr integrating prob solving into math teaching, 83-84, 87-89, prin investr, cross-cultural study prob solving behav maths, 85-86, 89-90, co-prin investr intensive study prob solving, 88-89, prin investr cross-nat prob solving res, 90-95, investr develop middle sch math profs, 90-92; pres, Sch Sci & Math Asn, 92-94; mem, US Nat Comn Math Instr, 94-97; bd dirs, Nat Coun Teachers Math, 95-98. *Mem:* Math Asn Am; Nat Coun Teachers Math; Int Org Women & Maths Educ; Sch Sci & Math Asns; Nat Coun Supvrs Math. *Res:* Mathematics curriculum development; teacher training; psychology of learning; achievement testing in mathematics; evaluation of mathematics education programs; applications of microcomputers in mathematics teaching; international mathematics education; open-ended problem solving in maths; research, psychology, and women in math education. *Mailing Add:* Curr Inst Southern Ill Univ Carbondale IL 62901-4610

BECKER, JOHN ANGUS, EXPERIMENTAL NUCLEAR PHYSICS. *Current Pos:* SR PHYSICIST, LAWRENCE LIVERMORE NAT LAB, LIVERMORE, CALIF, 78- *Personal Data:* b New York, NY, Nov 25, 36; m 79, Elsie Lengyel. *Educ:* Queens Col (NY), BS, 57; Fla State Univ, PhD(physics), 62. *Prof Exp:* Asst physics, Fla State Univ, 58-62, res assoc, 62; res assoc, Brookhaven Nat Lab, 62-64; res scientist, Lockheed Palo Alto Res Labs, 64-78. *Concurrent Pos:* Sr fel, Oxford Univ, 71-72; assoc prof, Univ Minn, 74-75. *Mem:* Fel Am Phys Soc; AAAS. *Res:* Experimental, low-energy nuclear physics; nuclear reactions initiated by accelerator beams; gamma-ray and particle detectors and instrumentation. *Mailing Add:* Lawrence Livermore Nat Lab Livermore CA 94550. *E-Mail:* becker@lll_winken.llnl.gov

BECKER, JOHN HENRY, ION TRANSPORT, HIBERNATION. *Current Pos:* ASSOC PROF PHYSIOL, DR WILLIAM M SCHOLL COL PODIATRIC MED, 86- *Personal Data:* b Denver, Colo, Mar 29, 48; m 72; c 1. *Educ:* Loyola Univ, BS, 70; Univ Ill, MS, 73, PhD(physiol), 78. *Prof Exp:* Investr cell biol, Oak Ridge Nat Lab, 77-79; asst prof biol, Knox Col, 79-86. *Concurrent Pos:* Vis prof, Univ Ill, Urbana, 81; actg assoc dean, Dr William M Scholl Col Podiatric Med, 90- *Mem:* Sigma Xi; Am Physiol Soc. *Res:* Measurement of adaptations of membrane transport systems to various stresses: temperature, carcinogens, cell culture conditions. *Mailing Add:* Dr William M Scholl Col Podiatric Med 1001 N Dearborn St Chicago IL 60610-2890

BECKER, JOSEPH F, chemistry, biochemistry, for more information see previous edition

BECKER, JOSEPH WHITNEY, BIOCHEMISTRY, STRUCTURAL CHEMISTRY. *Current Pos:* sr res fel, 90-96, SR INVESTR, MERCK RES LABS, MERCK & CO, INC, 96- *Personal Data:* b New London, Conn, Apr 17, 43; m 76, Betsy A Stern; c Rachel E (Becker). *Educ:* Yale Univ, BA, 64; Stanford Univ, PhD(phys chem), 70. *Prof Exp:* Postdoctoral fel develop & molecular biol, Rockefeller Univ, 70-71, res assoc, 71-72, from asst prof to assoc prof, 72-90. *Mem:* Am Soc Biochem & Molecular Biol; Am Crystallog Asn; AAAS; Sigma Xi. *Res:* Macromolecular crystallography. *Mailing Add:* R50-105 Merck & Co Inc PO Box 2000 Rahway NJ 07065-0900. *Fax:* 732-594-5042; *E-Mail:* beckerj@merck.com

BECKER, JOSHUA A, MEDICINE, RADIOLOGY. *Current Pos:* PROF RADIOL, CHMN DEPT & DIR, STATE UNIV NY DOWNSTATE MED CTR, 70- *Personal Data:* b Philadelphia, Pa, Nov 28, 32; m 59; c 2. *Educ:* Temple Univ, AB, 53, MD, 57, MS, 61. *Prof Exp:* Intern, Philadelphia Gen Hosp, 58; resident radiol, Univ Hosp, Temple Univ, 61, instr, Sch Med, 63-65; from asst prof to assoc prof, Col Physicians & Surgeons, Columbia Univ, 65-70. *Concurrent Pos:* James Picker Found scholar radiol res, 64-65; from asst attend physician to assoc attend physician, Presby Hosp, 65-70; consult, Bronx Vet Admin Hosp, 67-70 & Brooklyn Vet Admin Hosp, 70- *Mem:* Am Col Radiol; Asn Univ Radiol. *Mailing Add:* Dept Biol SUNY Health Sci Ctr Brooklyn Box 1198 Brooklyn NY 11203

BECKER, KENNETH LOUIS, INTERNAL MEDICINE, ENDOCRINOLOGY. *Current Pos:* clin investr med & endocrinol, 64-65, CHIEF SECT METAB, VET ADMIN HOSP, WASHINGTON, DC, 65-, DIR ENDOCRINOL, 74-; PROF MED, GEORGE WASHINGTON UNIV, 74- *Personal Data:* b New York, NY, Mar 11, 31; m 54; c 2. *Educ:* Univ Mich, BA, 52; NY Med Col, MD, 56; Univ Minn, PhD(med, physiol), 64; Am Bd Internal Med, dipl, 66 & cert endocrinol & metab, 73. *Honors & Awards:* Meritorious Res Award, Mayo Clin, 63; Outstanding Sci Presentation, Am Col Physicians, 74; Res Award, Am Col Chest Physicians, 79. *Prof Exp:* Intern, Mt Sinai Hosp, NY, 56-57; resident internal med, Mayo Clin, 59-64; from asst prof to assoc prof med, George Washington Univ, 64-74. *Concurrent Pos:* Consult, Wash Hosp Ctr, 64- *Mem:* Fel Am Col Physicians; Am Fedn Clin Res; Am Soc Clin Pharmacol & Therapeut; Endocrine Soc; Am Diabeties Asn. *Res:* Endocrinology of cancer; endocrine function of the lungs. *Mailing Add:* Vet Affairs Hosp 50 Irving St NW 151-J Washington DC 20422

BECKER, KURT HEINRICH, PHYSICS. *Current Pos:* assoc prof, 88-92, PROF PHYSICS, CITY COL NEW YORK, 92- *Personal Data:* b Zweibrucken, Ger, Mar 24, 53. *Educ:* Univ Saarbrucken, dipl physics, 78, DrRerNat(physics), 81. *Prof Exp:* Postdoctoral physics res, Univ Windsor, Can, 82-84; vis asst prof physics, Lehigh Univ, Bethlehem, Pa, 84-86, asst prof, 86-88. *Mem:* Am Phys Soc; Can Asn Physicists; Geo Phys Soc; NY Acad Sci; AAAS; Sigma Xi; German Phys Soc. *Res:* Electron collision processes with atoms and molecules from fundamental to applied aspects, three-body problems, precision measurements of fundamental constants. *Mailing Add:* Physics Dept City Col NY Convent Ave at 138th St New York NY 10031

BECKER, LAWRENCE CHARLES, COMPUTER INTERFACING, DATA ACQUISITION. *Current Pos:* From asst prof to assoc prof, 63-81, PROF PHYSICS, HIRAM COL, 81- *Personal Data:* b Schenectady, NY, Aug 1, 34; m 57, Mary Larsen; c David A & Jonathan K. *Educ:* Carleton Col, BA, 56; Yale Univ, BD, 59, MS, 60, PhD(physics), 64. *Concurrent Pos:* Res physicist, NASA Lewis Res Ctr, 69-70; tech writer, Ohio Scientific, 80-83; res scientist, 84-85, syst engr, Geocomp Corp, 87- *Mem:* AAAS; Am Phys Soc; Am Asn Physics Teachers. *Res:* Hardware & software development for a remote data acquisition system; electronic development for computer automated equipment for performing mechanical tests on soil samples. *Mailing Add:* Dept Physics Box 1778 Hiram Col Hiram OH 44234-1778

BECKER, LEWIS CHARLES, HEART IMAGING, MYOCARDIAL PROTECTION. *Current Pos:* PROF MED, DIV CARDIOL, SCH MED, JOHNS HOPKINS UNIV, 72- *Educ:* Johns Hopkins Univ, MD, 66. *Res:* Nuclear cardiology. *Mailing Add:* Dept Med Sch Med Johns Hopkins Univ 500 Halsted Baltimore MD 21287

BECKER, MARTIN, NUCLEAR ENGINEERING. *Current Pos:* PROF MAT SCI TECHNOL, ORE GRAD INST SCI TECHNOL, 96- *Personal Data:* b New York, NY, May 11, 40; m 61; c 6. *Educ:* NY Univ, BS, 60; Mass Inst Technol, SM, 62, PhD(nuclear eng), 64. *Honors & Awards:* Glenn Murphy Award, Am Soc Elec Eng. *Prof Exp:* Theoret physicist advan develop activity, Knolls Atomic Power Lab, Gen Elec Co, 64-65, supv physicist, 65-66; from assoc prof to prof nuclear eng, Rensselaer Polytech Inst, 66-90, assoc dean, 86-90, adj prof nuclear eng & eng physics, 90-96. *Concurrent Pos:* Consult, Savannah River Lab, E I du Pont de Nemours & Co, Inc, 68, United Nuclear Corp, Gen Elec, Los Alamos Nat Lab, NY Pub Serv Comn & others; Victor P Clarke prof eng, Univ Miami, Coral Gables, 90-; Victor P Clarke prof eng, Univ Miami, Coral Gables, 90- *Mem:* Fel Am Nuclear Soc; sr mem Inst Elec & Electronics Engrs; Am Soc Eng Educ. *Res:* Nuclear reactor physics; reactor dynamics and control; mathematical methods; calculus of variations; nuclear rocket propulsion; nuclear fuel management; optimization; radiation effects in electronics; energy modeling. *Mailing Add:* Dept Mat Sci & Eng Ore Grad Inst Sci Technol PO Box 91000 Portland OR 97291-1000

BECKER, MARTIN JOSEPH, cell marker analysis, for more information see previous edition

BECKER, MICHAEL ALLEN, RHEUMATOLOGY. *Current Pos:* PROF MED, UNIV CHICAGO, 80- *Personal Data:* b New York, NY, Oct 3, 40; m 80; c 4. *Educ:* Univ Pa, BA, 61, MD, 65. *Prof Exp:* From intern & resident int med, Barnes Hosp, Wash Univ, 65-70; res assoc biochem, NIH, 66-69; fel rheumatol, 70-72, Univ Calif, San Diego, 70-72, from asst prof to assoc prof med, 72-79. *Concurrent Pos:* Clin investr, US Vet Admin, 74-77; prin investr, NIH res grants, 75-; vis investr, Imp Cancer Res Fund, 79-80; Guggenheim Found Fel, 79; sr res investr, Univ Mich, Ann Arbor, 87-88. *Mem:* Asn Am Physicians; Am Col Physicians; Am Fedn Clin Res; AAAS; Am Soc Clin Invest; Am Col Rheumatology. *Res:* Regulation of human biosynthetic process; investigation of inherited defects in purine metabolism. *Mailing Add:* Dept Med Rheumatol Sect Univ Chicago Pritzker Sch Med 5841 S Maryland Ave MC 0930 Chicago IL 60637. *Fax:* 773-702-3467

BECKER, MICHAEL FRANKLIN, ELECTRICAL ENGINEERING, LASER APPLICATIONS. *Current Pos:* ASST PROF ELEC ENG, UNIV TEX, AUSTIN, 73- *Personal Data:* b Cheverly, Md, Nov 3, 47; m 70. *Educ:* Johns Hopkins Univ, BES, 69; Stanford Univ, MS, 70, PhD(elec eng), 73. *Prof Exp:* Res engr microwave develop, US Naval Res Lab, 66-69, res engr solid state develop, 69-71; res asst laser appln, Microwave Lab, Stanford Univ, 71-73. *Mem:* Inst Elec & Electronics Engrs; Optical Soc Am; Am Inst Physics; AAAS; Nat Soc Prof Engrs; Sigma Xi. *Res:* Nonlinear optics; multiphoton excitation; picosecond laser applications to semiconductor materials; optical processing. *Mailing Add:* Dept Elec & Comput Eng Univ Tex MC R8625 PRC-MER Austin TX 78712

BECKER, MILTON, SOLID STATE PHYSICS. *Current Pos:* PHYSICIST, SEMICONDUCTORS, CONTINENTAL DEVICE CORP, 58-, VPRES RELIABILITY, 61- *Personal Data:* b Chicago, Ill, July 13, 20; m 53; c 1. *Educ:* Univ Chicago, BS, 41; Purdue Univ, PhD(physics), 51. *Prof Exp:* Physicist, Electronics, Naval Res Labs, 42-47; physicist, semiconductors, Hughes Semiconductors, 51-58. *Concurrent Pos:* Consult, AEC Proj, 56-57; tech dir, Epidyne, Inc, 73-74. *Mem:* Am Phys Soc; Sigma Xi. *Res:* Microwave propagation in ionized media; optical properties of silicon and germanium in the infrared; electrical properties of semiconductor junctions. *Mailing Add:* 3100 Corda Dr Los Angeles CA 90049-1104

BECKER, NORWIN HOWARD, PATHOLOGY, HISTOCHEMISTRY. *Current Pos:* ATTEND PATHOLOGIST, MONTEFIORE HOSP, 67- *Personal Data:* b New York, NY, Apr 23, 30; m 51; c 3. *Educ:* Cornell Univ, AB, 50, MNS, 52; State Univ NY, MD, 55. *Prof Exp:* Intern med, Montefiore Hosp, NY, 55-56; asst resident path, Long Island Jewish Hosp, 56-57; asst resident, Montefiore Hosp, 57-58, Nat Cancer Inst trainee, 58-59, from asst pathologist to assoc pathologist, 59-67; from asst prof to assoc prof, 64-74, prof path, Albert Einstein Col Med, 74- *Mem:* Am Col Path; Am Soc Exp Path; Am Soc Hemat; Am Soc Clin Pathologists. *Res:* Histochemistry and electron microscopy of the central nervous system; choroid plexus function; surgical pathology; hematopathology. *Mailing Add:* Dir Anat Path Two Squirrel Wood Ct New City NY 10956-7611. *Fax:* 718-920-7611

BECKER, RALPH SHERMAN, MOLECULAR SPECTROSCOPY, PHOTOPHYSICS. *Current Pos:* PROF, INST CHEM & BIOL, NEW UNIV LISBON, 92- *Personal Data:* b Benton Harbor, Mich, Mar 14, 25; c 3. *Educ:* Univ Vt, BS, 49; Univ NH, MS, 50; Fla State Univ, PhD(chem), 55. *Honors & Awards:* Japanese Soc Promotion Sci Award, 71; Southwest Regional Award, Am Chem Soc, 81; Southeast Tex Sect Award, Am Chem Soc, 80, Esther Farfel Res Award, 79; Fulbright vis prof, Lisbon, 88. *Prof Exp:* Dir phys & inorg res, Frederick S Bacon Labs, 52; from asst prof to prof chem, Univ Houston, 63-92. *Concurrent Pos:* Fulbright vis prof, Univ Barcelona, 62-63; vis prof, Weizmann Inst, 63 & 79, Univ Tubingen, Ger, 73 & 75, Univ Kyushu, 71, Univ Zurich, 71, Univ Paris, 76 & 78, Univ Wyo, 75, Univ Tokyo, 80, Inst Solid State Physics, 80, Univ Quebec, 89, Univ Coimbra, 90, Univ Perugia, Italy, 90, Univ Dublin, Ireland, 91; electronic transition in molecules, NSF, 64; consult, Phillips Petrol Co & others; sr fel, Sci Res Coun Eng, 81-83; vis, Soviet Union, Byelorussian Acad Sci, 85; vis prof, Inst Chem & Biol, Lisbon, Portugal, 92-; dept chem, Univ Ark. *Res:* Intercombinations of electronic states; photochemistry; visual pigments; photoisomerization; laser flash photolysis; photophysics; photochromism; photosensitizers; non-linear optics. *Mailing Add:* 211 Spring St Eureka Springs AR 72632. *Fax:* 501-253-6234; *E-Mail:* raphael@ipa.net

BECKER, RANDOLPH ARMIN, OPTICS, INSTRUMENTATION. *Current Pos:* RETIRED. *Personal Data:* b Bowler, Wis, Dec 29, 24; m 56, Fern L Lugenheim; c Christy, Holly & Heidi. *Educ:* Tex Col Arts & Indust, BS, 49, MS, 53. *Prof Exp:* Observing asst astron, Univ Chicago MacDonald Observ, Tex, 50; physicist, White Sands Missile Range, 50-57, chief optical res sect, Range Instrumentation Develop Div, 57-61; sr res engr space optics, Jet Propulsion Lab, Calif Inst Technol, 61-63, res specialist, 63-70, staff scientist, Space Photog Sect, 70-73; sr scientist, Xerox Electro-Optical Systs, 73-84. *Res:* Optical instrumentation; materials suitable for optical systems in interplanetary space; design and execution of television experiments on planetary space missions; deep-space mission design. *Mailing Add:* 616 E Mendocino Altadena CA 91001

BECKER, RICHARD ALAN, STATISTICAL COMPUTING, DATA ANALYSIS. *Current Pos:* MEM TECH STAFF, AT&T BELL LABS, 74- *Personal Data:* b Cincinnati, Ohio, Nov 20, 49; m 79. *Educ:* Harvard Univ, AB, 72. *Honors & Awards:* Youden Prize, Technometrics, 87. *Prof Exp:* Engr, Procter & Gamble, 72-73; programmer, Nat Bur Econ Res, 73-74. *Concurrent Pos:* Consult, New Eng Med Ctr, 73; adv bd mem, Comput Res Lab, NMex State Univ, 86-; mem, Mgt Comt, J Computational & Graphical Statist, 90-93; prog chair graphics, Am Statist Asn, 90-91 & 93. *Mem:* Fel Am Statist Asn; Asn Comput Mach; Inst Math Statist; Inst Elec & Electronics Engrs Comput Soc. *Res:* Computer graphics; statistical computing and data analysis; created S language; auditing of data analyses; brushing scatterplots; dynamic graphics for statistics. *Mailing Add:* AT&T Bell Labs Rm 2C-259 600 Mountain Ave Murray Hill NJ 07974. *E-Mail:* rab@research.att.com

BECKER, RICHARD LOGAN, THEORETICAL NUCLEAR PHYSICS, ATOMIC PHYSICS. *Current Pos:* PHYSICIST, OAK RIDGE NAT LAB, 57- *Personal Data:* b Dayton, Ohio, Dec 29, 29; m 54; c 2. *Educ:* Harvard Univ, BA, 52; Yale Univ, MS, 53, PhD(physics), 57. *Concurrent Pos:* Vis fel, Princeton Univ, 59-60; lectr & prof, Univ Tenn, 61- *Mem:* Fel Am Phys Soc. *Res:* Theoretical many-body physics; nuclear self-consistent field theory; nuclear structure theory; nuclear scattering theory; ion atom collision. *Mailing Add:* 2780 Oak Ridge Turnpike Oak Ridge TN 37830

BECKER, ROBERT ADOLPH, PLANETARY SCIENCE. *Current Pos:* RETIRED. *Personal Data:* b Tacoma, Wash, Feb 10, 13; m 44; c 5. *Educ:* Col Puget Sound, BS, 35; Calif Inst Technol, MS, 37, PhD(physics), 41. *Prof Exp:* Asst physics, Col Puget Sound, 33-35; asst fel & asst nuclear physics, Calif Inst Technol, 35-41; asst physicist, Dept Terrestrial Magnetism, Carnegie Inst, 41; from asst physicist to physicist, Nat Bur Standards, 41-43; physicist, Radiation Lab, Univ Calif, 43; mem staff appl physics lab, Univ Wash, 43-45, sr physicist, 45; from asst prof to prof physics, Univ Ill, 46-60; dir Space Physics Lab, 60-68, assoc gen mgr lab opers, 68-73, consult physicist, Aerospace Corp, 73-75. *Concurrent Pos:* Guggenheim fel, 58-59. *Mem:* Fel AAAS; NY Acad Sci; fel Am Phys Soc; Am Astron Soc; fel Explorers Club. *Res:* Nuclear, space and atmospheric physics; astrophysics; proton and deuteron induced nuclear reactions; radioactive decay schemes from betatron produced radioactivities; element synthesis in the stars; structure of the upper atmosphere; planetary science. *Mailing Add:* 8133 Ellen Bogen Sunland CA 91040

BECKER, ROBERT HUGH, ANALYTICAL CHEMISTRY, CATALYSIS. *Current Pos:* SR RES CHEMIST, CALSICAT DIV, MALLINCKRODT INC, 75- *Personal Data:* b Greenville, Pa, July 19, 34; m 63; c 7. *Educ:* St Bonaventure Univ, BS, 56; Univ Notre Dame, PhD(org chem), 60. *Prof Exp:* NIH res assoc org chem, NMex Highlands Univ, 59-61; instr chem, Lawrence Col, 61-63; from asst prof to assoc prof, Gannon Col, 63-75, dir, Sci Res Prog, 69-75. *Concurrent Pos:* Petrol Res Fund res grant, 63-65; consult, Calsicat Div, Mallinckrodt Inc, 67-75. *Mem:* Am Chem Soc; Am Oil Chem Soc. *Res:* Instrumental and qualitative organic analysis; spectroscopy; chromatography; catalysis. *Mailing Add:* 6812 Old Ridge Rd Fairview PA 16415

BECKER, ROBERT O, ORTHOPEDIC SURGERY, BIOPHYSICS. *Current Pos:* from instr to assoc prof, 56-66, PROF ORTHOP SURG, STATE UNIV NY UPSTATE MED CTR, 66- *Personal Data:* b River Edge, NJ, May 31, 23; m 46, Lillian Moller; c Lisa, Michael & Adam. *Educ:* Gettysburg Col, BA, 46; NY Univ, MD, 48. *Honors & Awards:* William S Middleton Award, 64; Nicholas Andre Award, 78. *Prof Exp:* Chief, Orthop Sect, Vet Admin Hosp, Syracuse, 56-80, med investr, 72-80. *Concurrent Pos:* Mem, Spec Study Sect Biomed Eng, NIH & Sanguine Study Comt, USN; mem, Sanguine Study Comt, USN; assoc chief of staff for res, Vet Admin Hosp, Syracuse, 65-72; consult biomed effects electromagnetic environ factors, 80-; vpres, Res Berbeu Biomagnetics, Lowville, NY. *Mem:* NY Acad Sci; Int Soc Bioelec; Bioelectromagnetics Soc; AAAS. *Res:* Biological solid state; organic semiconductors; biological control systems as applied to growth control; regenerative mechanisms and relationship to central nervous system to physical factors of environment; bioeffects of electromagnetic fields; therapeutic effects electromagnetic fields; therapeutic actions; electrochemical techniques. *Mailing Add:* Star Route Lowville NY 13367

BECKER, ROBERT PAUL, ENDOTHELIAL CELLS, CYTOCHEMISTRY. *Current Pos:* asst prof anat, 78-83, ASSOC PROF ANAT & CELL BIOL, COL MED, UNIV ILL, CHICAGO, 83- *Personal Data:* b Murphysboro, Ill, Oct 15, 42; m 64; c 2. *Educ:* Univ Chicago, PhD(anat), 73. *Prof Exp:* Res assoc cell biol, Univ Chicago, 73-77; instr anat, 77-78. *Mem:* Am Soc Cell Biol; Histochem Soc; Am Asn Anatomists; Sigma Xi. *Res:* Cell surface structure and function; endocytosis; exocytosis; cell recognition; endothelial cell biology. *Mailing Add:* Dept Anat & Cell Biol MC 512 Univ Ill Col Med 808 S Wood St Chicago IL 60612-7308

BECKER, ROBERT RICHARD, BIOCHEMISTRY. *Current Pos:* RETIRED. *Personal Data:* b Aitkin, Minn, Feb 16, 23; m 56; c 2. *Educ:* Univ NDak, BS, 48; Univ Wis, MS, 51, PhD(biochem), 52. *Prof Exp:* From instr to asst prof chem, Columbia Univ, 52-60; biochemist, Oak Ridge Nat Labs, 60-62; assoc prof chem, Ore State Univ, 62-67, prof biochem, 67-90, chmn, Biol Prog, 78-86. *Concurrent Pos:* Vis scientist, Dept Biol, Brookhaven Nat Labs, 68-69; mem, NIH Pathobiol Chem Study Sect, 75-77, Biomed Sci Study Sect, 81-83, chmn, 83; vis scholar oceanog, Univ Wash, 86. *Mem:* AAAS; Am Soc Biol Chemists; Am Chem Soc. *Res:* Protein chemistry; polypeptides; thermophilic enzymes. *Mailing Add:* Dept Biochem Ore State Univ Corvallis OR 97331-6503. *Fax:* 541-737-0481

BECKER, ROBERT S, IMMUNOLOGY, MICROBIOLOGY. *Current Pos:* RES MGR, CONNAUGHT LABS INC, 88- *Personal Data:* b Kansas City, Mo, Dec 12, 56. *Educ:* Univ Kans, BA, 79, PhD(microbiol), 84. *Prof Exp:* Res asst prof, Loyola Univ, 86-88. *Mem:* NY Acad Sci; Am Asn Immunol. *Mailing Add:* Dept Res Connaught Labs Inc Rte 611 PO Box 187 Swiftwater PA 18370-0187

BECKER, ROGER JACKSON, SOLID STATE PHYSICS, RAMAN SPECTROSCOPY. *Current Pos:* RES PHYSICIST, UNIV DAYTON, 77- *Personal Data:* b Findlay, Ohio, June 9, 44; c 1. *Educ:* Lake Forest Col, BA, 67; Mass Inst Technol, MS, 72; Thomas Jefferson Univ, PhD(solid state physics), 77. *Prof Exp:* Fel, Univ Guelph, 76-77. *Mem:* Am Inst Physics; Am Phys Soc. *Res:* Raman spectroscopy, surface chemistry and surface Raman, layered compound, turbulent flow and laser diagnostics in combustion; lattice dynamics; fluid dynamics. *Mailing Add:* Res Inst Appl Phys Div Univ Dayton Dayton OH 45469

BECKER, ROLAND FREDERICK, ANATOMY & GROSS ANATOMY, ENTERYOLOGY & NEURANATOMY. *Current Pos:* RETIRED. *Personal Data:* b Methuen, Mass, Aug 12, 12; m 36; c 2. *Educ:* Mass State Col, BS, 35, MS, 37; Northwestern Univ, PhD(anat), 40. *Prof Exp:* Asst psychol, Mass State Col, 35-37; asst anat, Med Sch, Northwestern Univ, 38-40, instr, 40-44, assoc, 44-45, asst prof, 45-46; assoc prof, Sch Med, Univ Wash, 46, chmn dept, 46-48; dir neurol div, Daniel Baugh Inst Anat, Jefferson Med Col, 49-52; assoc prof anat & dir lab neonatal sci, Duke Univ, 52-69; prof anat, Col Osteop Med, Mich State Univ, 69-71, prof biomechanics & coordr res prog, 71-75, coordr educ prog, 75-76; prof anat, Sch Med, ECarolina Univ, 76-79, emer prof, 79-87. *Concurrent Pos:* Consult, Eng Corps, US Army, 52-54, NIH, 57-59 & Greenbrier Col Osteop Med, 74; AID med educr, Thailand, 61-63; deans consult, Sch Med, Carolina Univ, 78-87. *Mem:* Am Asn Anatomists; Soc Reproduction; Soc Exp Biol & Med; Am Psychol Asn; Southern Soc Anatomists. *Res:* Neuroanatomy and fetal physiology; behavioral development; neuro-musculo-skeletal system; high altitude research; olfactory discrimination. *Mailing Add:* 102 Heartwood Dr Grimesland NC 27837

BECKER, SHELDON THEODORE, ELECTRICAL ENGINEERING. *Current Pos:* mem tech staff, Bell Labs, 67-83, MEM TECH STAFF, BELL COMMUN RES, 83- *Personal Data:* b Chicago, Ill, Sept 26, 38; m 74, Leslie J Burg; c Barrie L Harper. *Educ:* Univ Ill, BS, 60, MS, 61; Ill Inst Technol, PhD(elec eng), 67. *Prof Exp:* Teaching asst, Ill Inst Technol, 62-63, instr elec eng, 63-67. *Mem:* Inst Elec & Electronics Engrs; Asn Comput Mach. *Res:* Computer systems, performance and evaluation, expert systems; Operations research. *Mailing Add:* Bellcore 444 Hoes Lane Rrc 1N323 Piscataway NJ 08854

BECKER, STANLEY J, STRUCTURAL DYNAMICS, APPLIED MATHEMATICS. *Current Pos:* RETIRED. *Personal Data:* b New York, NY, Oct 21, 21; m 53; c 3. *Educ:* Cooper Union, BME, 48; Polytech Inst, Brooklyn, MS, 53; Univ Pittsburgh, PhD(math), 64. *Prof Exp:* Jr engr, NYC Dept Pub Works, 48-51; stress analyst, Heavy Press Prog, Loewy-Hydropress Div, Baldwin-Lima-Hamilton Corp, 51-57, consult stress anal, 68-69; sr engr, Bettis Atomic Power Lab, Westinghouse Elec Corp, 57-62; engr, Re-entry Systs Dept, Gen Elec Co, 62-68, specialist comput sci, Space Systs Div, 69; res engr, Gilbert Assocs Inc, 69-76; sr engr, Nuclear Components Div, Allis-Chalmers Corp, 77. *Concurrent Pos:* Instr elec eng, Mass Inst Technol & King of Prussia Grad Ctr, Pa State Univ; sr eng fel, Villanova Univ, 90- *Mem:* Am Soc Mech Eng; Am Math Soc; Am Inst Physics; Am Acad Mech. *Res:* Pressure vessels; power piping. *Mailing Add:* 474 Regimental Rd King of Prussia PA 19406-1564

BECKER, STANLEY LEONARD, SCIENCE EDUCATION, HISTORY OF SCIENCE. *Current Pos:* asst prof physics, 68-71, prof philos & comput sci, 83-88, ASSOC PROF SCI, BETHANY COL, WVA, 71-, PROF PHILOS & GEO SCI , 88- *Personal Data:* b Syracuse, NY, June 19, 29; m 52, Saundra Rosenthal; c Jonathan & Carol. *Educ:* NY State Col Environ Sci & Forestry, BS, 53; Univ Wis-Madison, PhD(hist sci), 68. *Prof Exp:* Chemist, Bristol Labs, Bristol-Myers Co, 52-60; asst prof gen sci, Univ Hawaii, 67-68. *Concurrent Pos:* Vis prof hist sci, Conn Agr Exp Sta, 75-76; vis prof geog, Westminster Col, 75, 77, 79, 81 & 83. *Mem:* Hist Sci Soc; NY Acad Sci. *Res:* History of agriculture, biochemistry and vitamins; hybrid corn; agriculture and patents; economic geography. *Mailing Add:* Philos & Gen Sci Bethany Col PO Box 526 Bethany WV 26032. *E-Mail:* s.becker@mail.bethanywv.edu

BECKER, STEPHEN FRALEY, THEORETICAL PHYSICS, COMPUTER SCIENCE. *Current Pos:* Asst prof, 69-80, ASSOC PROF PHYSICS & HEAD DEPT, BUCKNELL UNIV, 80- *Personal Data:* b Toledo, Ohio, Aug 13, 42; m 64. *Educ:* Miami Univ, AB, 65; Rutgers Univ, MS, 66, PhD(physics), 69. *Concurrent Pos:* Instr, Lewisburg Fed Penitentiary, 71. *Mem:* Am Inst Physics; Am Phys Soc; Am Math Soc. *Res:* Three body problem; scattering theory; theoretical particle physics; complexity theory. *Mailing Add:* Dept Physics Bucknell Univ Lewisburg PA 17837-2005

BECKER, STEVEN ALLAN, PLANT ANATOMY, MORPHOLOGY. *Current Pos:* Asst prof, 68-74, assoc prof bot, 74-, PROF BOT, EASTERN ILL UNIV. *Personal Data:* b Anamosa, Iowa, Nov 23, 38; m 61; c 2. *Educ:* Cornell Col, BA, 60; Univ Iowa, MS, 66, PhD(bot), 68. *Mem:* Bot Soc Am; Am Inst Biol Sci. *Res:* Developmental plant anatomy-morphology. *Mailing Add:* Dept Bot Eastern Ill Univ 600 Lincoln Ave Charleston IL 61920-3011

BECKER, ULRICH J, HIGH ENERGY PHYSICS. *Current Pos:* res assoc high energy physics, 68-70, from asst prof to assoc prof, 70-78, PROF PHYSICS, MASS INST TECHNOL, 78- *Personal Data:* b Dortmund, Ger, Dec 17, 38; m 66, Gerda Barthel; c Katharina, Peter & Robert. *Educ:* Univ Marburg, Vordiplom, 60; Univ Hamburg, Diplom, 64, PhD(physics), 68. *Hon Degrees:* DSc, Univ Hamburg, 76. *Honors & Awards:* Award, Europ Phys Soc, 95. *Prof Exp:* Sci employee exp physics, Deutsches Elektronen-Synchrotron, Hamburg, 64-68. *Concurrent Pos:* Res coun mem, Deutsches Elektronen-Synchrotron, Hamburg, 70-71 & 80-82; mem, LEP Sci Coun, Nuclear Res Coun Europ, Geneva, Switz, 86-90, staff mem, 79-80; prof, Fed Tech Univ, Zuerich, Switz, 91-92. *Mem:* Am Phys Soc; Ger Phys Soc. *Res:* High energy particle physics; co-discoverer of the new meson J (3.1); experimental study of vector mesons; measurements of constants of electro weak theory, Z, search for new particle. *Mailing Add:* Dept Physics Mass Inst Technol 77 Massachusetts Ave Cambridge MA 02139. *Fax:* 617-253-4100

BECKER, WALTER ALVIN, GENETICS. *Current Pos:* asst prof poultry sci & asst poultry scientist, Wash State Univ, Pullman, 60-62, assoc poultry scientist, 62-68, from assoc prof to prof genetics, 62-82, actg chmn, Prog Genetics, 67-68, poultry scientist, 68-82, chmn, Prog Genetics & Cell Biol, 79-82, EMER CHMN GENETICS & EMER POULTRY SCIENTIST, WASH STATE UNIV, 82-;. *Personal Data:* b Pittsburgh, Pa, Dec 1, 20; m 52, Mary Jane Bar; c Sandra G & Bruce D. *Educ:* Stanford Univ, AB, 52; Univ Calif, Berkeley, MS, 55, PhD(genetics), 56. *Prof Exp:* Res asst genetics, Univ Calif, 53-56; asst poultry scientist, Western Wash Exp Sta, Wash State Col, Puyallup, 56-60. *Concurrent Pos:* Consult, US Forest Serv, 63-83 & Wash State Univ, 83-85; vis researcher, Inst Animal Genetics, Univ Edinburgh, 64-65; self publ, 83-; pres, Acad Enterprises, 83- *Mem:* Fel AAAS. *Res:* Quantitative genetics. *Mailing Add:* 320 SE Nebraska St Pullman WA 99163-2240. *E-Mail:* beckerwa@wsu.edu

BECKER, WAYNE MARVIN, PLANT PHYSIOLOGY, BIOCHEMISTRY & MOLECULAR BIOLOGY. *Current Pos:* from asst prof to assoc prof bot, 69-75, PROF BOT, UNIV WIS-MADISON, 75- *Personal Data:* b Waukesha, Wis, May 29, 40; m 63, Patricia Mickel; c Lisa (Smit) & Heather (Flemming). *Educ:* Univ Wis-Madison, BS, 63, MS, 65, PhD(biochem), 67. *Prof Exp:* NATO fel molecular biol, Beatson Inst Cancer Res, Scotland, 67-68, NIH fel, 68-69. *Concurrent Pos:* Guggenheim res fel, Univ Edinburgh, 75-76; Midwest Univs Consortium Int Activ consult, chem, Univ Indonesia, 86; Erskine teaching fel, Canterbury Univ, NZ, 95. *Mem:* AAAS; Am Soc Plant Physiol; Int Soc Plant Molecular Biol; Am Sci Affil; Am Soc Bioethics. *Res:* Plant molecular biology; light-regulated expression of genes encoding enzymes of the photorespiratory pathway; nucleic acid metabolism in plants. *Mailing Add:* Dept Bot Birge Hall Univ Wis Madison WI 53706. *Fax:* 608-262-7509; *E-Mail:* wbecker@facstaff.wisc.edu

BECKER, WILHELM, FREE ELECTRON DEVICES, MULTIPHOTON PROCESSES. *Current Pos:* vis scientist physics, Inst Mod Optics, 81-84, assoc prof, 86-91, RES ASSOC PROF, DEPT PHYSICS & ASTRON, UNIV NMEX, 84-86 & 92- *Personal Data:* b Konigsberg, Ger, Feb 17, 42. *Educ:* Tech Univ, Munich, dipl, 67, Drrernat, 69, Drhabil, 76. *Prof Exp:* Asst prof, Univ Tubingen, 70-79; vis scientist, Max-Planck Inst, Quantum Optics, 80. *Concurrent Pos:* Privatdozent, Univ Tubingen, 76-86; vis scientist, Tech Univ, Munich, 93- *Mem:* Am Phys Soc; Sigma Xi. *Res:* Interaction of matter with intense electromagnetic fields; multiphoton ionization, free-electron lasers, laser induced damage to thin films, quantum optics, quantum electrodynamics. *Mailing Add:* Dept Phys T30 Tech Univ Munich 85748 Garching Germany

BECKERLE, JOHN C, PHYSICAL OCEANOGRAPHY, ATMOSPHERIC TURBULENCE. *Current Pos:* MEM STAFF, SCI APPLN RES ASSOC U SCI APPLN RES CORP AM, 80- *Personal Data:* b Mt Vernon, NY, Feb 14, 23; div; c John D & Michael J. *Educ:* Manhattan Col, BS, 48; Cath Univ Am, PhD(physics), 53. *Honors & Awards:* Radford Gold Medal Physics. *Prof Exp:* Asst physics, Cath Univ Am, 48-51; physicist, Electronic Comput, Appl Physics Labs, Johns Hopkins Univ, 50; res assoc chem, Naval Ord Contract, Cath Univ Am, 51-53; mem tech staff, Bell Tel Labs, 53-60; mgr sonics res, Schlumberger Well Surv Corp, 60-64; assoc scientist, Woods Hole Oceanog Inst, 64-80. *Mem:* Am Meteorol Soc. *Res:* Mathematical physics; electromagnetic and acoustic wave propagation; underwater sound; heat conduction in solids; sonic well logging; optical signal processing; internal gravity waves in the ocean; Rossby waves in the Sargasso Sea; geophysics; atmospheric sciences; earth sciences (seismology); dynamics of severe storms. *Mailing Add:* 38 Two Ponds Rd Falmouth MA 02540

BECKERMAN, BARRY LEE, OPHTHALMOLOGY. *Current Pos:* ASST CLIN PROF OPHTHAL, ALBERT EINSTEIN COL MED, BRONX, NY, 73- *Personal Data:* b New York, NY, Jan 12, 41; m 65, Nancy Greyson; c Ellen & Sara. *Educ:* Cornell Univ, AB, 61; NY Univ, MD, 65. *Prof Exp:* Intern surg, Tufts New Eng Med Ctr, 65-66; lt comdr surg, USPHS, 66-68; from resident to chief resident ophthal, NY Univ-Bellevue Med Ctr, 68-72; instr, Albert Einstein Col Med, 72-73; dir electrophysiol, Retina Serv, Montefiore Hosp, Bronx, NY, 73-86. *Concurrent Pos:* Adj attend ophthal, Northern Westchester Hosp, Mt Kisco, NY, 73-81, chief ophthal, 81-; assoc attend, Westchester County Med Ctr, 79-97. *Mem:* Asn Res Vision & Ophthal; NY Acad Sci. *Res:* Clinical research in the diagnosis of ocular and especially retinal disorders, particularly development of diagnostic techniques and application to clinical disease; clinical practice. *Mailing Add:* 344 Main St Mt Kisco NY 10549

BECKERMAN, ROBERT CY, PEDIATRICS. *Current Pos:* dir, Pediat Pulmonary & Sleep Lab, 80-90, PROF PHYSIOL & CHIEF PEDIAT PULMONOLOGY, UNIV TULANE SCH MED, 78-, DIR, FEL PROG PEDIAT PULMONARY SECT, 83- *Personal Data:* b Brooklyn, NY, Oct 29, 46; c Sarah, Ashley & Molly. *Educ:* Dickinson Col, BS, 68, Jefferson Med Col, MD, 72. *Concurrent Pos:* Dir & chief pediat pulmonary, CF Ctr, La, New Orleans, 87-; dir, Pulmonary Ctr, SLa, New Orleans & Pediat Pulmonary Outreach Prog, Lafayette, La, 88-; chief med consult, Audubon Zoo. *Mem:* Am Acad Pediat; Soc Pediat Res; Spinal Muscular Atrophy Asn. *Res:* Pediatrician; pulmonology. *Mailing Add:* Tulane Univ Sch Med 1430 Tulane Ave New Orleans LA 70112-2699

BECKERMANN, CHRISTOPH, THERMAL SCIENCES, MATERIALS PROCESSING. *Current Pos:* from asst prof to assoc prof, 87-96, PROF MECH ENG, UNIV IOWA, 96- *Personal Data:* b Hildesheim, Ger, July 24, 60; m 86; c 2. *Educ:* Purdue Univ, MS, 84, PhD(mech eng), 87. *Concurrent Pos:* NSF presidential young investr award, 89-94. *Mem:* Am Soc Mech Engrs; Am Soc Eng Educ; Minerals Metals Mining Soc. *Res:* Heat transfer and fluid mechanics; transport phenomena in materials processing; solidification and welding; porous media; natural and double-diffusive convection; electronic cooling. *Mailing Add:* Dept Mech Eng Univ Iowa Iowa City IA 52242. *Fax:* 319-335-5669; *E-Mail:* becker@icaen.uiowa.edu

BECKETT, JACK BROWN, PLANT GENETICS. *Current Pos:* RETIRED. *Personal Data:* b Hutsonville, Ill, Aug 10, 25; m 70, Dorothy E Burchett; c John C. *Educ:* Univ Wash, BS, 50; Univ Wis, MS, 52; PhD(hort genetics), 54. *Prof Exp:* Asst hort, Univ Wis, 50-54; plant geneticist, USDA, Univ Ill, 54-63; plant geneticist, USDA, Univ Mo, Columbia, 63-90, asst prof genetics, 67-70, asst prof agron, 70-91. *Concurrent Pos:* Consult, 91- *Mem:* Am Soc Agron; Genetics Soc Am; Am Genetic Asn. *Res:* Genetics and cytogenetics of maize, with particular emphasis on development and use of B-A translocations. *Mailing Add:* 607 Longfellow Lane Columbia MO 65203

BECKETT, JAMES REID, ANALYTICAL CHEMISTRY, ORGANIC CHEMISTRY. *Current Pos:* EOR supvr, 87-89, mgr spec proj & financial consult, 90-91, DIR COALBED METHANE, OXY USA INC, 91- *Personal Data:* b Los Angeles, Calif, Apr 27, 46; m 85, Sandy Hardin; c Sean M. *Educ:*

Ft Hays State Univ, BS, 72; Univ Wyo, PhD(chem), 78. *Prof Exp:* Sr lab technician chem, Chemagro Agr Div, Mobay Chem Corp, Kansas City, 67-71; consult chem, Wyo Anal Labs Inc, Laramie, 77-78; res chemist, Cities Serv Co, 78-81, region petrol engr, 81-86. *Concurrent Pos:* Res assoc, Univ Wyo, 78; chmn & pres, Oxy Pipeline Inc, 88-90; vpres, Oakwood Gathering Inc, 90-93. *Mem:* Am Chem Soc; Soc Petrol Engrs. *Mailing Add:* 10808 S Eric Tulsa OK 74137

BECKETT, ROYCE E(LLIOTT), ENGINEERING MECHANICS. *Current Pos:* prof, 77-93, EMER PROF MECH ENG & HEAD DEPT, AUBURN UNIV, 93- *Personal Data:* b Hinch, Mo, May 31, 23; m 54; c 3. *Educ:* Univ Ill, BS, 44, MS, 49; Wash Univ, DSc(appl mech), 53. *Prof Exp:* From asst prof to prof mech, Univ Iowa, 53-68; dir, Res & Eng Lab, Army Weapons Command, 68-77. *Mem:* Am Soc Mech Engrs; Soc Indust & Appl Math; Sigma Xi. *Res:* Response of structures to dynamic loads; thermal stresses; numerical solutions. *Mailing Add:* 1235 Hickory Lane Auburn AL 36830-2545

BECKETT, SIDNEY D, CARDIOVASCULAR PHYSIOLOGY. *Current Pos:* ASSOC DEAN RES & GRAD STUDIES, COL VET MED, AUBURN UNIV, 81- *Personal Data:* b Bruce, Mich, Feb 11, 32. *Educ:* Univ Mo, PhD(physiol), 66. *Mem:* Am Physiol Soc; Am Vet Asn. *Mailing Add:* Col Vet Med Green Hall Rm 106 Auburn AL 36849-5517

BECKHAM, ROBERT R(OUND), CHEMICAL ENGINEERING. *Current Pos:* CONSULT MECH ENG, 80- *Personal Data:* b Toledo, Ohio, May 8, 15; m 45, Rosemary Wernert; c Robert Jr, Carol & James. *Educ:* Univ Mich, BS, 42. *Prof Exp:* Lab asst, Libbey-Owens-Ford Glass Co, 34-37, 38-40 & Univ Mich, 40-41; asst prod supt, Dow Chem Co, 42-47; res chem engr, Libbey-Owens-Ford Glass Co, 47-59, res specialist, 59-64, asst dir res, 64-67, sr scientist-consult, 67-80. *Res:* Organic glass substitutes; laminated glass; plastic dyeing; films on glass; vacuum equipment; special machines. *Mailing Add:* 2553 Charlestown Ave Toledo OH 43613-4327

BECKHOFF, GERHARD FRANZ, ELECTRICAL ENGINEERING, COMPUTER SCIENCE. *Current Pos:* lectr, 65-66, asst prof, 66-69, actg chmn dept, 70-77, ASSOC PROF COMPUT SCI, UNIV WESTERN ONT, 69-; VIS PROF, DEPT ELEC ENG, UNIV PETROL & MINERALS. *Personal Data:* b Ger, Oct 13, 29; m 63; c 2. *Educ:* Inst Technol Ger, Dipl Ing, 56; Southern Methodist Univ, MS, 60; Laval Univ, DSc(elec eng), 66. *Prof Exp:* Engr, Continental Electronics Mfg Co, Tex, 57-59; instr elec eng & res asst, Laval Univ, 60-65. *Concurrent Pos:* Fel, Inst Prog, Fac Sci, Univ Paris, 69-70. *Mem:* Inst Elec & Electronics Engrs. *Res:* Network synthesis; computer-assisted circuit design of analog and digital filters; sequential machine theory; theory of algebraic languages and codes. *Mailing Add:* 407 Fox Ave London ON N6G 1H7 Can

BECKHORN, EDWARD JOHN, INDUSTRIAL ENZYMES, FERMENTATION. *Current Pos:* CONSULT, 86- *Personal Data:* b Ithaca, NY; m 44, Verna Eaton; c Marilyn. *Educ:* Cornell Univ, BS, 47, MS, 48, PhD(microbiol, genetics), 50. *Prof Exp:* Res assoc, Dept Genetics, Carnegie Inst Wash, 50-52; dir microbiol res, Wallerstein Co Div, Baxter Labs, 52-57, from asst dir res to dir res, 57-70; mgr sci serv, Lehn & Fink Prod Co Div, Sterling Drug Co, 71-73; dir sci serv, Cunningham & Walsh Inc, 74-, vpres, 80-86. *Mem:* Am Soc Microbiol; Soc Indust Microbiol. *Res:* Production and industrial or pharmaceutical applications of fermentation products, enzymes, antibiotics, organic acids; formulation, efficacy and toxicology of disinfectants, antimicrobials and consumer household chemical specialties; food processing with enzymes; regulatory affairs; advertising claim substantiation. *Mailing Add:* 435 Nassau Ct Marco Island FL 34145-4014

BECKING, RUDOLF (WILLEM), ENVIRONMENTAL SCIENCES, NATURAL RESOURCES. *Current Pos:* from assoc prof to prof forestry & tropical forestry, 60-83, PROF NATURAL RESOURCES, HUMBOLDT STATE UNIV, 83- *Personal Data:* b Blora, Java, Indonesia, Oct 19, 22; m 52, H Louise Scheltema; c 3. *Educ:* Agr Univ Wageningen, MF temperate forestry & MF trop forestry, 52; Univ Wash, PhD(forest mgt), 54. *Prof Exp:* Forest officer, Dutch Forest Serv, 54-56; asst prof, Univ NH, 56-57 & Pa State Univ, 57-58; assoc prof forestry, Auburn Univ, 58-60. *Concurrent Pos:* Mem, Sta Int Geobot Mediterranean & Alpine, France, 47-; forest inventory expert, Foreign Agr Orgn, Indonesia, 80-81. *Mem:* Am Inst Biol Sci; Ecol Soc Am; Int Asn Veg Sci; Cooper Ornithol Soc. *Res:* Phytosociology; forest ecology; photo interpretation; tropical rain forest dynamics; sustainable forest growth and yield studies; planetary applications. *Mailing Add:* 1415 Virginia Way Arcata CA 95521-6855

BECKINGHAM, KATHLEEN MARY, DEVELOPMENTAL MOLECULAR BIOLOGY. *Current Pos:* from asst prof to assoc prof, 80-92, PROF BIOCHEM & CELL BIOL, RICE UNIV, HOUSTON, TEX, 92- *Personal Data:* b Sheffield, UK, May 8, 46; m 86, Robert B Weisman; c Caroline M. *Educ:* Cambridge Univ, BA, 67, MA, 68, PhD(biochem), 72. *Prof Exp:* Fel, Inst Molecular Biol, Denmark, 70-72; Nat Inst Med Res, Mill Hill, London, Eng, 72-74, staff mem, 74-76; res assoc biochem, Dept Microbiol, Med Sch, Univ Mass, Worcester, 76-78, instr, 78-80. *Mem:* Am Soc Biol Chemists; Am Soc Cell Biol; Soc Develop Biol; Genetic Soc Am. *Res:* In vivo and in vitro studies of calmodulin function in drosophila, genetic, molecular and biochemical studies; studies of two naturally exposed genes of drosphila-bicaudal and ME31B. *Mailing Add:* Dept Biochem & Cell Biol Rice Univ PO Box 1892 Houston TX 77251-1892. *Fax:* 713-285-5154; *E-Mail:* kate@rice.edu

BECKJORD, ERIC STEPHEN, ENERGY, NUCLEAR ENGINEERING. *Current Pos:* DIR RES, US NUCLEAR REGULATORY COMN, 86- *Personal Data:* b Evanston, Ill, Feb 17, 29; m 53, Caroline W Gardner; c Eric H, Amy W, Charles A & Sarah H. *Educ:* Harvard Univ, AB, 51; Mass Inst Technol, MS, 56; Univ Chicago, MBA, 84. *Prof Exp:* Develop engr, Gen Elec, San Jose, Calif, 56-60, proj engr, Pleasanton, Calif, 60-63; eng mgr, Westinghouse Elec Corp, Pittsburgh, 63-70, vpres, Westinghouse Nuclear Europ, Brussels, 70-73, proj dir & mgr strategic planning-nuclear, Westinghouse Elec Corp, Pittsburgh, 73-75; dep dir, Fed Energy Admin, 75; dir, Div Reactor Develop & Demonstration, Energy Res & Develop Admin, 76-77; dir nuclear power develop, Dept Energy, 77-78, coordr int nuclear study, 78-80; dep dir, Argonne Nat Lab, 80-84; vis prof nuclear eng, Mass Inst Technol, 84-86. *Mem:* Fel Am Nuclear Soc; sr mem Inst Elec & Electronics Engrs; Sigma Xi. *Res:* Boiling water reactor design. *Mailing Add:* Nuclear Regulatory Comn-Nuclear Regulatory Res Mail Stop NL-007 Washington DC 20555

BECKLAKE, MARGARET RIGSBY, OCCUPATIONAL LUNG DISEASE, RESPIRATORY DISEASE EPIDEMIOLOGY. *Current Pos:* from asst prof to assoc prof exp med, McGill Univ, 61-71, assoc prof epidemiol, 67-72, PROF MED & EPIDEMIOL, MCGILL UNIV, 72-73; SR PHYSICIAN, ROYAL VICTORIA HOSP, MONTREAL, 74-, EMER PROF MED & EPIDEMIO, MCGILL UNIV, 73- *Personal Data:* b London, Eng, May 27, 22; Can citizen; m 48, Maurice McGregor; c James & Margaret. *Educ:* Univ Witwatersrand, SAfrica, MB, BCh, 44, MD, 51; MRCP, 46; FRCP, 72. *Hon Degrees:* MD, Univ Witwatersrand, 74. *Honors & Awards:* Louis Mark Mem lectr, Am Col Chest Physicians, 82. *Prof Exp:* Lectr med, Univ Witwatersrand, 50-54; physiologist, Med Bur Occup Dis, SAfrica, 54-57; asst physician, Royal Victoria Hosp, Montreal, 64-66, assoc physician, 66-73. *Concurrent Pos:* Hon prof community health, Univ Witwatersrand, 84-85. *Mem:* Am Thoracic Soc; Can Thoracic Soc (pres, 78-79); Med Res Coun Can; fel Royal Soc Can. *Res:* Cardiac output responses to exercise in athletes; the effects of pneumocomiosis on lung function; the natural history of asbestos related pulmonary fibrosis and other asbestos related disease; lung disease in occupationally exposed workers; environmental lung disease; respiratory disease; epidemiology of asthma and airway disease in adults and children. *Mailing Add:* Joint Depts Epivomiol & Brostats & Occup Health McGill Univ 1110 Pine Ave W Montreal PQ H3A 1A3 Can. *Fax:* 514-398-8981; *E-Mail:* becklake@meakins.lan.mcgill.ca

BECKLEY, RONALD SCOTT, EMULSION POLYMERIZATION. *Current Pos:* RES CHEMIST, ROHM & HAAS CO INC, 73- *Personal Data:* b Lebanon, Pa, Feb 23, 44:; m 67, Bonnie L Moyer; c Stacie M & Steven R. *Educ:* Lebanon Valley Col, BS, 66; Univ Colo, PhD(chem), 70. *Prof Exp:* Fel chem, Ohio State Univ, 70-72; vis lectr, Univ Colo, 72-73. *Mem:* Am Chem Soc; Sigma Xi. *Res:* Polymer chemistry including coating, emulsion polymerization and polymer synthesis. *Mailing Add:* 513 Kleman Rd Gilbertsville PA 19525-9752

BECKMAN, ALEXANDER LYNN, NEUROPHYSIOLOGY, NEUROPHARMACOLOGY. *Current Pos:* PROF PSYCHOL, CALIF STATE UNIV, LONG BEACH, 86- *Personal Data:* b Los Angeles, Calif, June 9, 41; m 62, 83; c 2. *Educ:* Univ Calif, Los Angeles, BA, 64; Univ Calif, Santa Barbara, PhD(psychol), 68. *Prof Exp:* USPHS fel, Inst Neurol Sci, Univ Pa, 68-70, asst prof physiol, Sch Med, 71-78; mem staff, Alfred I DuPont Inst, 78-86, sr res scientist, 78-86. *Concurrent Pos:* Univ Pa Plan to Develop Scientists in Med Res fel, 70-73. *Mem:* Soc Neurosci; Am Physiol Soc; Int Hibernation Soc. *Res:* Central nervous system mechanisms controlling body temperature; changes in central nervous system function during hibernation; actions of endogenous opioid peptides in central nervous system. *Mailing Add:* Dept Psychol Calif State Univ 1250 Bellflower Blvd Long Beach CA 90840-0901. *Fax:* 562-985-8004

BECKMAN, ARNOLD ORVILLE, CHEMISTRY. *Current Pos:* vpres, Nat Tech Labs, Beckman Instruments, Inc, 37-39, pres, 39-50, Arnold O Beckman, Inc, 42-57, pres, 50-65, EMER FOUNDER & CHMN, BECKMAN INSTRUMENTS, INC, 50- *Personal Data:* b Cullom, Ill, Apr 10, 00; m 25; c 2. *Educ:* Univ Ill, BS, 22, MS, 23; Calif Inst Technol, PhD(photochem), 28. *Hon Degrees:* LLD, Univ Calif, Riverside, 66, Loyola Univ, 69, Pepperdine Univ, 77 & Ill Wesleyan Univ, 91; DSc, Chapman Col, 65, Whittier Col, Univ Ill, 82, Clarkson Univ, 89 & Rockefeller Univ, 92; DHL, Calif State Univ, Fullerton, 84 & Ill State Univ, 90. *Honors & Awards:* Hoover Medal, Am Asn Eng Socs, 81; Millikan Award, Calif Inst Technol, 85; Gold Medal, Am Inst Chemists, 87; Vermilye Medal, 87; Nat Medal of Technol, 88; Nat Medal of Sci, 89; Henry Townley Heald Award, Ill Inst Technol, 89; Charles Lathrop Parsons Award, Am Chem Soc, 89; Bower Award, Franklin Inst, 92; Van Slyke Award, Am Asn Clin Chem, 93. *Prof Exp:* Res engr, Bell Tel Labs, 24-26; instr chem, Calif Inst Technol, 26-29, asst prof, 29-40. *Concurrent Pos:* Pres, Helipot Corp, 44-58; trustee, Calif Inst Res Found & Calif Mus Found; chmn bd trustees, Syst Develop Found; dir, Scripps Clin & Res Found & Ear Res Found; chmn emer bd, Calif Inst Technol. *Mem:* Nat Acad Eng; hon fel Am Acad Arts & Sci; Instrument Soc Am (pres, 52); fel AAAS; hon fel Am Inst Chem; fel Asn Clin Scientists; fel Royal Soc Arts; Am Chem Soc; Newcomen Soc; hon mem Am Asn Clin Chem. *Res:* Applied chemistry; development of scientific instruments; photochemistry. *Mailing Add:* Beckman Instruments Inc 2500 Harbor Blvd Fullerton CA 92634-3100

BECKMAN, BARBARA STUCKEY, ERYTHROLEUKEMIA, HEMATOPHARMACOLOGY. *Current Pos:* ASSOC PROF PHARMACOL, SCH MED, TULANE UNIV, 78- *Educ:* Johns Hopkins Univ, PhD(pharmacol), 78. *Res:* Arachidonic acid metabolism; cyclic nucleotides. *Mailing Add:* Dept Pharmacol Sch Med Tulane Univ 1430 Tulane Ave New Orleans LA 70112-2699

BECKMAN, CARL HARRY, plant pathology, histopathology, for more information see previous edition

BECKMAN, DAVID ALLEN, TERATOLOGY, FETAL PHYSIOLOGY. *Current Pos:* RES DEPT DIV DEVELOP BIOL, ALFRED I DUPONT INST. *Personal Data:* b 1950; m 82; c 2. *Educ:* Univ Calif, Davis, BS, 72, MS, 74, PhD(physiol), 79. *Prof Exp:* Asst prof pediat, Dept Post-Grad Develop Biol, Jefferson Med Col, Thomas Jefferson Univ, 80- *Mem:* Sigma Xi; Am Physiol Soc; Teratology Soc; Radiation Res Soc. *Res:* Developmental biochemistry; placental transport. *Mailing Add:* Dept Pediat Thomas Jefferson Univ 16 S Stuyvesant Dr Wilmington DE 19809

BECKMAN, DAVID LEE, PULMONARY PHYSIOLOGY. *Current Pos:* PROF PHYSIOL, EAST CAROLINA UNIV, 76- *Personal Data:* b Dayton, Ohio, May 11, 39; m 69. *Educ:* Ohio State Univ, BS, 62, MS, 64, PhD(physiol), 67. *Prof Exp:* Res assoc physiol, Ohio State Univ, 64-65; res assoc biosci, Univ Mich, 67-69, res physiologist, 70-71; asst prof anesthesiol & physiol, Wayne State Univ, 71-73; Hill prof physiol, Univ NDak, 73-76. *Concurrent Pos:* Partic, Biospace Training Prog, NASA & Univ Va, 67. *Mem:* AAAS; Am Physiol Soc; Soc Exp Biol & Med; Undersea Med Soc; Aerospace Med Asn. *Res:* Respiratory physiology; biomechanics; environmental physiology; lung mechanics; hyperbaric medicine; cardiovascular physiology; autonomic pharmacology. *Mailing Add:* Dept Physiol East Carolina Univ Sch Med Brody Med Sci Bldg Greenville NC 27858-4354

BECKMAN, FRANK SAMUEL, MATHEMATICS, COMPUTER SCIENCE. *Current Pos:* exec officer, PhD Comput Sci Prog, 85-88, prof, Grad Ctr, 89-93, EMER PROF GRAD CTR, CITY UNIV NEW YORK, 93- *Personal Data:* b New York, NY, Apr 10, 21; m 51, Shirley C Blum; c Susan, Denise & Jonathan. *Educ:* City Col New York, BS, 40; Columbia Univ, AM, 47, PhD(math), 65. *Prof Exp:* Civilian instr aircraft eng, US Army Air Corps, 41-44; asst prof math, Pratt Inst, 47-51; asst to mgr, Sci Comput Ctr, IBM Corp, 51-56, prod planning rep, 56-57, mgr, Appl Prog Systs, 57-59, mgr, Educ & Data Processing, Watson Sci Comput Lab, 59-60, from asst to assoc dir, Comput Sci & Educ Systs Res Inst, 60-66, res mgr spec projs, 66-71; prof comput & info sci & chmn dept, Brooklyn Col, 71-85. *Concurrent Pos:* Ed, Soc Indust & Appl Math Rev, 60-64; adj assoc prof, Columbia Univ, 65-71. *Mem:* Am Math Soc; Asn Comput Mach; Math Asn Am; Soc Indust & Appl Math. *Res:* Elliptic partial differential equations; education in computer-allied subjects; automata theory. *Mailing Add:* 16 Garwood Rd Fair Lawn NJ 07410-4522. *E-Mail:* bckgc@cunyvm

BECKMAN, JEAN CATHERINE, ORGANIC CHEMISTRY. *Current Pos:* asst prof, 78-84, ASSOC PROF CHEM, UNIV EVANSVILLE, 84- *Personal Data:* b Detroit, Mich, Sept 25, 51. *Educ:* Colby Col, AB, 73; Ind Univ, PhD(chem), 77. *Prof Exp:* Res asst, Purdue Univ, 77-78. *Mem:* Am Chem Soc; AAAS; Sigma Xi. *Mailing Add:* Dept Chem Univ Evansville 1800 Lincoln Ave Evansville IN 47722-0002

BECKMAN, JOSEPH ALFRED, POLYMER CHEMISTRY. *Current Pos:* Res org chemist, 64-69, mgr org chem res, 69-71, asst dir res, 80-87, MGR ELASTOMER SYNTHESIS RES, CENT RES LABS, FIRESTONE TIRE & RUBBER CO, 71; VPRES RES & DEVELOP, DSM COPOLYMER INC, 87- *Personal Data:* b Macomb, Ill, Oct 30, 37; m 59, Peggy; c Bruce & Jill. *Educ:* Western Ill Univ, AB, 60; Iowa State Univ, PhD(org chem), 65. *Concurrent Pos:* Mem, Polymer, Org & Rubber Divisions, Am Chem Soc, Akron Rubber Group. *Mem:* Am Chem Soc. *Res:* Synthesis, characterization, evaluation and application of organic and inorganic polymers. *Mailing Add:* DSM Copolymer Inc Res & Develop PO Box 291 Baton Rouge LA 70821-2591. *Fax:* 504-356-7929

BECKMAN, WILLIAM A, MECHANICAL ENGINEERING. *Current Pos:* from asst prof to assoc prof, 63-77, PROF MECH ENG, UNIV WIS-MADISON, 77- *Personal Data:* b Detroit, Mich, Nov 11, 35; m 57; c 3. *Educ:* Univ Mich, BSE, 58, MSE, 60, PhD(mech eng), 64. *Honors & Awards:* Centennial Medal, Am Soc Mech Engrs, 81; Abbot Award, Am Sect Int Solar Energy Soc, 79. *Prof Exp:* Engr missile div, Chrysler Corp, 58-59. *Mem:* Am Soc Mech Engrs; Solar Energy Soc; Sigma Xi. *Res:* Radiation heat transfer; boiling heat transfer; solar energy utilization. *Mailing Add:* 4406 Fox Bluff Rd Middleton WI 53562-2334

BECKMANN, PETR, radiophysics; deceased, see previous edition for last biography

BECKMANN, ROBERT B(ADER), CHEMICAL ENGINEERING. *Current Pos:* head dept, Univ Md, 61-66, prof, 61-88, dean eng, 66-77, EMER PROF CHEM ENG, UNIV MD, COLLEGE PARK, 88- *Personal Data:* b St Louis, Mo, Sept 15, 18; m 42, 57, 81, Jean L Bourque; c 2. *Educ:* Univ Ill, BS, 40; Univ Wis, PhD(chem eng), 44. *Prof Exp:* Engr, State Hwy Dept, Colo, 36; lab analyst, Merchants Exchange Lab, Mo, 40; instr chem eng, Univ Wis, 42-44; res chemist, Humble Oil & Ref Co, Texas, 44-46; from asst prof to prof chem eng, Carnegie Inst Tech, 46-61. *Concurrent Pos:* Consult chem engr, 46- *Mem:* AAAS; Am Soc Eng Educ; Am Chem Soc; Am Inst Chem Engrs; Sigma Xi. *Res:* Solvent extraction; kinetics and catalysis; process engineering and design; heat and mass transfer in agitated systems. *Mailing Add:* 10218 Democracy Lane Potomac MD 20854-4032

BECKNER, EVERET HESS, PLASMA PHYSICS, NUCLEAR PHYSICS. *Current Pos:* VPRES, LOCKHEED MARTIN CORP, 96- *Personal Data:* b Clayton, NMex, Feb 24, 35; m 84, Mary Caroline Allen; c Gregory, Lee Elizabeth & Matthew. *Educ:* Baylor Univ, BS, 56; Rice Univ, MA, 59, PhD(physics), 61. *Prof Exp:* Staff scientist, Lockheed Missiles & Space Co, 56-57; staff mem, Sandia Nat Labs, 61-66, div supvr, 66-69, dept mgr, 69-74, dir, 74-83, vpres, 83-91; prin dep asst secy, US Dept Energy, 91-96. *Mem:* Fel Am Phys Soc; AAAS. *Res:* Plasma physics and magnetohydrodynamics; plasma spectroscopy; pulsed electron accelerators; beam-plasma interactions; electron beam fusion; laser fusion; nuclear waste management. *Mailing Add:* 3100 Calle de Alamo NW Albuquerque NM 87104

BECKNER, SUZANNE K, CLINICAL TRIALS, CELLULAR IMMUNOLOGY. *Current Pos:* SR STUDY DIR, WESTAT, 95- *Personal Data:* b Hagertown, Md, July 30, 50; m 71, William. *Educ:* Hood Col, BS, 71, Georgetown Univ, PhD(biochem), 80. *Prof Exp:* Staff fel, Nat Inst Arthritis, Diabetes & Digestive & Kidney Dis, NIH, 80-85, head immunotherapy sect, Nat Cancer Inst, 85-88; dir, Cell Biochem Business, LTI, 89-92; vpres, Clinical Develop, Cal-Sci Corp, 93-95. *Mem:* AAAS; Am Soc Biochem & Molecular Biol. *Res:* Initiate, manage and analyze clinical trials, identify new business opportunities, analyze and report clinical data, design new strategies for design and analysis of human clinical trials. *Mailing Add:* Sr Study Dir Westat 1650 Research Blvd Rockville MD 20850. *Fax:* 301-738-8379; *E-Mail:* becknes1@westat.com

BECKSTEAD, JAY H, HEMATOPATHOLOGY. *Current Pos:* PROF, DEPT PATH, VET ADMIN ORE HEALTH SCI UNIV, 89- *Personal Data:* b Pocatello, Idaho, Mar 4, 48. *Educ:* Univ Utah, BA, 70, MD, 74. *Prof Exp:* Prof, Dept Path, Univ Calif, 78-89. *Mailing Add:* Dept Path L113 Ore Health Sci Univ Portland OR 97201-3098

BECKSTEAD, LEO WILLIAM, ENGINEERING, EXTRACTIVE METALLURGY. *Current Pos:* CONSULT, 90- *Personal Data:* b Salt Lake City, Utah, Feb 9, 49; m 72; c 4. *Educ:* Univ Utah, BS, 71, MS, 73, PhD(metall), 75. *Honors & Awards:* Marcus A Grossmann Award, Am Soc Metals, 74. *Prof Exp:* Res engr extractive metall, Occidental Res Corp, 75-77; res metallurgist, Amax, 77-80, sr metall engr, 80-90. *Mem:* Am Soc Mining Engrs; Am Inst Mining, Metall & Petrol Engrs; Am Inst Chem Engrs. *Res:* Metallurgical treatment of ores and concentrates; unit processes such as leaching, solution purification, precipitation and roasting are optimized and integrated to develop an overall method of treatment; methods applied on a bench, pilot or full size plant scale. *Mailing Add:* 869 Estates Los Alamos NM 87544

BECKWITH, JOHN BRUCE, PATHOLOGY. *Current Pos:* from instr to assoc prof path, 64-74, PROF PATH & PEDIAT, SCH MED, UNIV WASH, 74-; CHMN DEPT PATH, DENVER CHILDREN'S HOSP, 85- *Personal Data:* b Spokane, Wash, Sept 18, 33; m 54; c 3. *Educ:* Whitman Col, BA, 54; Univ Wash, MD, 58. *Hon Degrees:* DSc, Whitman Col, 80. *Prof Exp:* Resident pediat path, Children's Hosp, Los Angeles, Calif, 59-60, resident path, Cedars of Lebanon Hosp, Los Angeles, 60-62; chief resident, Children's Hosp, Los Angeles, Calif, 62-64; pathologist, Children's Orthop Hosp & Med Ctr, 64-84; from instr to assoc prof path, 64-74, prof path & pediat, Sch Med, Univ Wash, 74- *Concurrent Pos:* NIH res grant, 66- *Mem:* AMA; Col Am Pathologists; Int Soc Pediat Oncol; Int Pediat Asn; Soc Pediat Path. *Res:* Sudden death in infancy; pathogenesis of tumors in children. *Mailing Add:* Sair Hosp/Clin 25673 Lawton Ave Loma Linda CA 92354-3731

BECKWITH, JONATHAN ROGER, GENETICS, BACTERIAL GENETICS. *Current Pos:* assoc, 65-66, from asst prof to prof, Dept Bact & Immunol, 66-69, PROF GENETICS, MED SCH, HARVARD UNIV, 69-, AM CANCER SOC RES PROF, 80- *Personal Data:* b Cambridge, Mass, Dec 25, 35; m 60; c 2. *Educ:* Harvard Univ, BA, 57, PhD, 61. *Honors & Awards:* Eli Lilly Award, 70; Jacques Monod Mem Lectr, Inst Pasteur, 88; Medal, Genetic Soc Am, 93. *Prof Exp:* NIH fel, 61-65. *Concurrent Pos:* Guggenheim fel, 70; chmn, Dept Microbiol & Molecular Genetics, Med Sch, Harvard Univ, 71-73, dir, Genetics Training Grant, 75-; vis prof, Univ Calif, Berkeley, 85; mem, Adv Bd, Coun Responsible Genetics & Eritrean Relief Comt, 85-, Sci Adv Bd, Int Inst Genetics & Biophys, 86- & Ethics Working Group Off Human Genome Res, NIH, 89- *Mem:* Nat Acad Sci; Am Soc Exp Biologists; Am Soc Microbiol; AAAS; fel Am Acad Arts & Sci; assoc mem Europ Molecular Biol Orgn. *Res:* Use of bacterial genetics to study various problems of membrane biology, including protein secretion across membranes, the mechanism of cell division and membrane protein topology. *Mailing Add:* Dept Microbiol Med Sch Harvard Univ 25 Shattuck St Boston MA 02115

BECKWITH, RICHARD EDWARD, STATISTICS, OPERATIONS RESEARCH. *Current Pos:* PROF MGT INFO SCI, SCH BUS & PUB ADMIN, CALIF STATE UNIV, SACRAMENTO, 81- *Personal Data:* b San Jose, Calif, July 21, 27; m 82; c 3. *Educ:* Stanford Univ, BS, 49, MS, 54; Purdue Univ, PhD, 59. *Prof Exp:* Statistician, US Fish & Wildlife Serv, 51-52; asst statist, Stanford Univ, 52-53; opers res, Case Inst Technol, 54-55; instr math, Purdue Univ, 55-58; sr res engr, Jet Propulsion Lab, Calif Inst Technol, 58-59; supvr opers res sect, Aeronutronic Div, Ford Motor Co, 59-62; assoc prof, Grad Sch Bus Admin, Univ Southern Calif, 62-68; prof quant methods & assoc dean, Sch Bus Admin, Ga State Univ, 68-69; prof mgt sci, Grad Sch Bus Admin, Tulane Univ, 69-81. *Concurrent Pos:* Lectr univ exten, Univ Calif, 59-63. *Mem:* Am Statist Asn; Opers Res Soc Am; Inst Mgt Sci; Decision Sci Inst. *Res:* Industrial operations research; applied statistics; mathematical programming; Monte Carlo method; queuing; reliability; management control systems; weapon systems analysis; scientific programming in statistics, probability, management science and applied mathematics. *Mailing Add:* 3798 Sheridan Rd Cameron Park CA 95682-8930

BECKWITH, STERLING, electrical engineering, physics; deceased, see previous edition for last biography

BECKWITH, STEVEN VAN WALTER, ASTRONOMY. *Current Pos:* MANAGING DIR, MAX PLANCK INST, 93- *Personal Data:* b Madison, Wis, Nov 20, 51; c 2. *Educ:* Cornell Univ, BS, 73; Calif Inst Technol, PhD(physics), 78. *Honors & Awards:* Fullam Award, Dudley Observ. *Prof Exp:* From assoc prof to prof astron, Cornell Univ, 84-93,. *Mem:* Am Astron Soc; Int Astron Union; AAAS; APS. *Res:* Observational programs using both ground-based and airborne astronomical telescopes for studies of star formation, stellar evolution and the interstellar medium; instrumentation for infrared astronomy; infrared imaging techniques including speckle interferometry. *Mailing Add:* Max Planck Inst Fur Astron Konigstuhl 17 69117 Heidelberg Germany

BECKWITH, WILLIAM FREDERICK, CHEMICAL ENGINEERING. *Current Pos:* From asst prof to prof chem eng, 63-89, DIR GEN ENG & ENG GRAPHICS, CLEMSON UNIV, 89- *Personal Data:* b Marshalltown, Iowa, Oct 4, 34; m 59; c 4. *Educ:* Iowa State Univ, BS, 57, MS, 61, PhD(chem eng), 63. *Concurrent Pos:* Sabbatical leave, Univ Maine, 79. *Mem:* Am Inst Chem Eng; Am Soc Eng Educ; Sigma Xi; Tech Asn Pulp & Paper Indust. *Res:* Chemical engineering transport phenomena and heat transfer; nonwoven fabric formation by wet-lay process; wet end chemistry of paper making. *Mailing Add:* 110 Jones Ct Central SC 29630-9094

BECKWITT, RICHARD DAVID, MOLECULAR EVOLUTION, POPULATION GENETICS. *Current Pos:* asst prof, 85-90, assoc prof biol, 90-93, PROF BIOL, FRAMINGHAM STATE COL, 93-, DEPT CHAIR, 96- *Personal Data:* b Detroit, Mich, Apr 25, 49; m 74, Gloria Kaminski; c Katherine & Emily. *Educ:* Univ Calif, Berkeley, BA, 70; Univ Southern Calif, PhD(biol), 79. *Prof Exp:* Res assoc, Vantuna Res Group, Occidental Col, 80-85; molecular biol, Univ Southern Calif, 81-83. *Concurrent Pos:* Consult, Biotechnol Group, US Army Natick Res, Develop & Eng Ctr, 89-96. *Mem:* AAAS; Am Soc Zoologists. *Res:* Molecular evolution and population genetics of invertebrates; genetic engineering of spider silk. *Mailing Add:* Dept Biol Framingham State Col Framingham MA 01701-2471. *Fax:* 508-626-4794; *E-Mail:* rbeckwi@fre.mass.edu

BECRAFT, LLOYD G(RAINGER), chemical engineering, for more information see previous edition

BECVAR, JAMES EDGAR, BIOCHEMISTRY. *Current Pos:* ASSOC PROF BIOCHEM, UNIV TEX, EL PASO. *Educ:* Univ Mich, PhD(biochem & biophys), 73. *Mailing Add:* Dept Chem Univ Tex El Paso TX 79968-0001

BEDAIR, SALAH M, ELECTRICAL ENGINEERING. *Current Pos:* PROF ELEC & COMPUT ENG, MAT SCI & ENG, NC STATE UNIV, 82- *Personal Data:* c 2. *Educ:* Alexandria Univ, Egypt, BS, 60; Univ Calif, Berkeley, PhD(eng sci), 69. *Honors & Awards:* Dept Energy Award. *Concurrent Pos:* Fulbright fel. *Mem:* Fel Inst Elec & Electronics Engrs. *Res:* Optical and microwave devices; quantum devices; photovoltaic and solar energy; thin film technology, molecular beam epitaxy, chemical vapor deposition, atomic layer epitaxy, laser assisted epitaxy; laser interactions with surfaces; interface properties and defects; phase equilibrium; author of 200 publications. *Mailing Add:* Dept Elec & Comput Eng NC State Univ Box 7911 Raleigh NC 27695-7911

BEDARD, DONNA LEE, BIODEGRADATION OF HALOGENATED AROMATICS, MOLECULAR GENETICS. *Current Pos:* molecular biologist, 81-90, MICROBIOLOGIST, GROUP LEADER, GEN ELEC RES & DEVELOP CTR, 90- *Personal Data:* b Adams, Mass, May 5, 47; m 77; c 2. *Educ:* Tufts Univ, BS, 69; Univ Chicago, PhD(biol), 73. *Prof Exp:* Res assoc, Univ Rochester, 74-75; fel res assoc, Johns Hopkins Univ, 75-78; prof biol, Bennington Col, 78-80; res scientist, NY State Dept Health, 80-81. *Mem:* Am Soc Microbiol. *Res:* Biochemical and genetic basis for bacterial oxidation of polychlorinated biphenyls; congener specificity; degradative pathways; reductive dechlorination of polychlorinated biphenyls by anaerobic bacteria; microbial transformation of halogenated aromatic compounds. *Mailing Add:* Gen Elec Res & Develop Ctr Bldg K-1 PO Box 8 Rm 3B 12 Schenectady NY 12301

BEDARD, RONALD LEO, ENVIRONMENTAL REGULATORY COMPLIANCE, ENVIRONMENTAL RECORDS & REPORTING. *Current Pos:* PRES, AIR RESOURCES INC, 91- *Personal Data:* b Moosup, Conn, Dec 29, 33; m 56,82, Marlene Brown; c Majorie, Vincent, David, Sandra, Jeffrey & Thomas. *Educ:* Univ RI, BS, 56; Univ Calif, Berkeley, PhD(org chem), 62. *Prof Exp:* Chemist, Res & Develop Labs, Uniroyal Corp, 61-66; sect leader, Pack Lab, Flex Pack Div, Crown-Zellerbach Corp, 66-71; tech dir, Chemelex Div, Raychem Corp, 71-74; tech mgr, St. Louis Plant, Flex Pack Div, Crown-Zellerbach Corp, 74-83; prod mgr, ESL Div, Int Paper Co, 83-87; tech dir, Princeton Packaging Inc, 87-91; corp dir tech servs, Bagcraft Corp Am, 91-95. *Concurrent Pos:* Adj prof, Triton Col, 95-96. *Mailing Add:* 2443 Courtyard Circle No 6 Aurora IL 60506-6618

BEDDOES, M(ICHAEL) P(ETER), ELECTRICAL ENGINEERING. *Current Pos:* from asst prof to prof, 56-89, EMER PROF ELEC ENG, UNIV BC, 89- *Personal Data:* b London, Eng, Feb 22, 24; m 48, Maureen Kelly; c 3. *Educ:* Glasgow Univ, BSc, 45; Univ London, PhD(elec eng), 58. *Prof Exp:* Apprentice, Gen Elec Corp, Coventry, Eng, 45-48; sr engr, Plessey Corp, Ilford, 48-52; asst chief engr, McMichael Radio, Slough, 52-53. *Mem:* Assoc mem Brit Inst Elec Eng; sr mem Inst Elec & Electronics Engrs. *Res:* Aids for disabled people including the blind and for recent immigrants; neural networks in speech research and in a model of the jaw. *Mailing Add:* Dept Elec Eng Univ BC 2075 Westbrook Pl Vancouver BC V6T 1W5 Can. *E-Mail:* mikeb@ee.ubc.ca

BEDELL, GEORGE NOBLE, INTERNAL MEDICINE. *Current Pos:* from asst prof to assoc prof, 54-68, PROF INTERNAL MED & DIR PULMONARY DIS DIV, UNIV IOWA, 68- *Personal Data:* b Harrisburg, Pa, May 1, 22; m 50, 70; c 9. *Educ:* DePauw Univ, BA, 44; Univ Cincinnati, MD, 46. *Prof Exp:* Nat Heart Inst fel, 52-54. *Concurrent Pos:* Nat Heart Inst spec fel, Univ Pa, 54-55; USPHS career develop award, 62; vis prof, Post-grad Sch Med, Univ London, 65-66. *Mem:* AAAS; Am Soc Clin Invest; Am Thoracic Soc; Am Col Chest Physicians; Am Fed Clin Res; Fedn Am Soc Exp Biol. *Res:* Pulmonary disease; clinical, cardiovascular and respiratory physiology. *Mailing Add:* Dept Internal Med Univ Iowa Col Med Iowa City IA 52242-0001

BEDELL, GLENN WESLEY, DISCOVERY & DEVELOPMENT OF SPECIAL ANALYTICAL REDUCING AGENTS. *Current Pos:* sr res scientist, 92-94, DIR SPEC ANALYTICAL REDUCING AGENTS PROD & SR RES SCI, GLOBAL ADVAN TECHNOL, 94- *Personal Data:* b Shelbyville, Ill, June 4, 38. *Educ:* Greenville Col, BA, 60; Univ Ill, Urbana-Champaign, MEd, 65, PhD, 72. *Prof Exp:* Teacher, Elgin Pub Sch, 60-64; postdoctoral instr, Univ Ill, 72-73; asst prof microbiol & plant physiol, Cornell Col, 73-77; NIH postdoctoral fel, Univ Iowa Col Med, 77-80; asst prof, Univ Nev, Reno, 80-86; sr res assoc chem, NMex State Univ, 86-88, col assoc prof toxicol & sr res specialist, 90-92. *Concurrent Pos:* Res biologist, Reno Res Ctr, US Bur Mines, 85-86; sr res assoc chem, Bio-Recovery Systs, 86-88, sr res scientist, 90-92; co-prin investr & res specialist, NMex State Univ, 90-92. *Mem:* Sigma Xi; Am Soc Microbiol. *Res:* Discovered, developed and in charge of producing special analytical reducing agents; cell extracts that reduce certain metal ions to metal crystals; recipient of 2 US patents. *Mailing Add:* 3145 Las Placitas Rd Las Cruces NM 88011. *Fax:* 505-646-6613

BEDELL, KEVIN SHAWN, FERMI LIQUID THEORY, MANY BODY THEORY OF STRONGLY CORRELATED MATERIALS. *Current Pos:* STAFF MEM, THEORET CONDENSED MATTER & STATIST PHYSICS GROUP, LOS ALAMOS NAT LAB, 86-, DIR CORRELATED ELECTRON THEORY PROG, THEORET DIV, 91- *Personal Data:* b Flushing, NY, July 7, 48; m 70, Carmen E Uriarte; c Christopher M. *Educ:* Dowling Col, BS, 71; State Univ NY, Stony Brook, MS, 72, PhD(physics), 79. *Prof Exp:* Res assoc, Univ Ill, Urbana, 79-82; res assoc, State Univ NY, Stony Brook, 82, res fel, Inst Theoret Physics, 82-85; vis prof, Kamerlingh Onnes Lab, Leiden, 85-86. *Concurrent Pos:* Vis scientist, Nordic Inst Theoret Atomic Physics, 81 & 83, Inst Laue-Langevin, France, 83, Kamerlingh Onnes Lab & Lorentz Inst, 87 & Nat Inst Nuclear Physics, Univ Trnto, 88; dep dir, Advan Studies Prog High Temperature Superconductivity, Los Alamos Nat Lab, 89-91; adj prof physics, Univ Fla, 91- & Fla State Univ, 91- *Mem:* Fel Am Phys Soc. *Res:* Many-body theory of strongly correlated electronic materials with a recent emphasis on the metal-insulator transition due to correlations; properties of fermi liquids and fermi liquid theory. *Mailing Add:* Los Alamos Nat Lab PO Box 1663 Los Alamos NM 87545. *Fax:* 505-665-3003; *E-Mail:* ksb@viking.lanl.gov

BEDELL, LOUIS ROBERT, SURFACE PHYSICS, ELECTRONICS. *Current Pos:* ASST PROF PHYSICS, NORTHEAST LA UNIV, 70- *Personal Data:* b Niagara Falls, NY, Nov 14, 39; m 64; c 5. *Educ:* Auburn Univ, BS, 63; Brown Univ, MS, 68, PhD(physics), 71. *Prof Exp:* Res asst surface physics, Field Res Lab, Mobil Oil Co, 63-65. *Mem:* Am Phys Soc; Am Vacuum Soc. *Res:* Gas adsorption and absorption on clean metal surfaces using low energy electron diffraction and Auger electron spectroscopy. *Mailing Add:* Dept Physics Northeast La Univ Monroe LA 71209-0001

BEDELL, THOMAS ERWIN, ANIMAL SCIENCE & NUTRITION, RESOURCE MANAGEMENT. *Current Pos:* assoc prof agr, Exten & Area Livestock Exten Agt, 73-76, prof, Exten Range Land Resources Spec, 76-92, EMER PROF, ORE STATE UNIV, 92- *Personal Data:* b Santa Cruz, Calif, Dec 21, 31; m 83, Gretchen Bencene; c Shelley (Stiles), Kristin & Robin (McWalters). *Educ:* Calif State Polytech Col, BS, 53; Univ Calif, MS, 57; Ore State Univ, PhD, 66. *Prof Exp:* Jr specialist range mgt, Univ Calif, 57, asst agriculturist, Agr Exten, 57-63; from instr to asst prof range mgt, Ore State Univ, 66-70; exten range mgt specialist & assoc prof range mgt, Univ Wyo, 70-73. *Concurrent Pos:* Cert range mgt consult. *Mem:* Soc Range Mgt (pres, 89). *Res:* Range management and improvement. *Mailing Add:* 25488 Wonderly Lane Philomath OR 97370. *Fax:* 541-737-0504

BEDENBAUGH, ANGELA LEA OWEN, CHEMISTRY. *Current Pos:* res assoc, 66-80, RES ASSOC PROF CHEM, UNIV SOUTHERN MISS, 80- *Personal Data:* b Seguin, Tex, Oct 6, 39; m 61, John H; c Melanie C. *Educ:* Univ Tex, BS, 61; Univ SC, PhD(chem), 67. *Prof Exp:* Geol mapping asst, Univ Tex, 58-59, lab instr, 60-61. *Concurrent Pos:* Statewide Workshops Cross-over High Sch Chem Teachers, NSF, Sec Sci In-Serv Workshops. *Mem:* Am Chem Soc; Nat Sci Teachers Asn; Sigma Xi. *Res:* Dissolving metal reductions; development of new syntheses; developing new general chemistry experiments. *Mailing Add:* 63 Suggs Rd Hattiesburg MS 39402-9642. *Fax:* 601-266-4712; *E-Mail:* abeden@whale.st.usm.edu

BEDENBAUGH, JOHN HOLCOMBE, ORGANIC CHEMISTRY. *Current Pos:* assoc prof, 68-74, PROF CHEM, UNIV SOUTHERN MISS, 74-, CHMN DEPT, 70- *Personal Data:* b Newberry, SC, Apr 9, 31; m 61. *Educ:* Newberry Col, BS, 53; Univ NC, MA, 57; Univ Tex, PhD(chem), 62. *Prof Exp:* Instr chem, Randolph-Macon Woman's Col, 56-58; assoc prof, Columbia Col, SC, 61-68. *Mem:* AAAS; Am Chem Soc; Nat Sci Teachers Asn; Sigma Xi. *Res:* Synthesis of heterocyclic compounds; chemical education; dissolving metal reductions; organic reagents for inorganic analysis. *Mailing Add:* 63 Suggs Rd Hattiesburg MS 39402-9642

BEDERSON, BENJAMIN, EXPERIMENTAL ATOMIC MOLECULAR & OPTICAL PHYSICS. *Current Pos:* from asst prof to prof, NY Univ, 52-92, chmn dept, 73-76, dean grad sch Arts & Sci, 86-89, EMER PROF PHYSICS, NY UNIV, 92- *Personal Data:* b New York, NY, Nov 15, 21; m 56, Betty E Weintraub; c Joshua, Geoffrey, Aron & Benjamin. *Educ:* City Col New York, BSc, 46; Columbia Univ, MA, 48; NY Univ, PhD(physics), 50. *Prof Exp:* Res worker, Los Alamos Sci Lab, 44-45; mem staff, Res Lab Electronics, Mass Inst Technol, 50-51. *Concurrent Pos:* Chmn Int Conf Physics of Electronic & Atomic Collisions, 58, 61 & 85; vis fel, Joint Inst Lab Astrophys, Nat Bur Stand, Univ Colo, 68-69; sci consult, Acad Press, NY; mem organizing comt, Int Conf Atomic Physics, 68; chmn atomic & molecular physics comt, Nat Acad Sci-Nat Res Coun, 70-; mem adv comt, Physics Div, Nat Sci Found, 72-75; ed, Phys Rev A, 78-; co-ed Advan in Atomic, Molecular & Optical Physics, 78; ed-in-chief, Am Phys Soc, 92-96, emer ed-in-chief, 96- *Mem:* Fel Am Phys Soc; fel AAAS. *Res:* Atomic collisions and structure; polarized and laser excited beams; atomic and molecular clusters. *Mailing Add:* Dept Physics NY Univ Four Washington Pl New York NY 10003. *E-Mail:* bederson@acf2.nyu.edu

BEDFORD, ANTHONY, CONTINUUM MECHANICS. *Current Pos:* from asst prof to assoc prof, 75-81, PROF MECH, UNIV TEX, AUSTIN, 81- *Personal Data:* b Baton Rouge, La, Oct 7, 38; m 61; c 2. *Educ:* Univ Tex, Austin, BS, 61; Calif Inst Technol, MS, 62; Rice Univ, PhD(mech), 67. *Prof Exp:* Engr res & develop, Douglas Aircraft Co, 62-64; mem tech staff res & develop, TRW Systs, 66-68. *Concurrent Pos:* NSF grants, 69-70, 72-74 & 75-77, ONR grants, 86, 87 & 88; consult, Tracor Inc, 73-74 & Sandia Labs, 73-83; tech ed, Appl Mech Rev, 74-83. *Mem:* Soc Natural Philos; Soc Eng Sci; Am Acad Mech. *Res:* Constitutive theories for mixtures; wave propagation; ocean sediment acoustics. *Mailing Add:* 3510 Highland View Dr Austin TX 78731

BEDFORD, BARBARA LYNN, ECOSYSTEM SCIENCE, WETLAND ECOLOGY. *Current Pos:* asst prof ecol & systs, 80-89, assoc dir, 80-90, ASST PROF, DEPT NATURAL RESOURCES, ECOSYSTEMS RES CTR, 89-, DIR, 91- *Personal Data:* b Odessa, Tex, Mar 24, 46; m 82; c 1. *Educ:* Marquette Univ, AB, 68; Univ Wis-Madison, MS, 77, PhD(environ sci land resources), 80. *Concurrent Pos:* Consult, Am Soc Planning Officials, 74, Ga Dept Natural Resources, 76, Environ Law Inst, 76-78, Ill Natural Areas Inventory, 77, Wis Dept Justice, 77-80 & Nature Conservancy, Wis, 80; guest lectr, Sch Pub & Environ Affairs, Ind Univ, 77, 80 & Rocky Mtn Biol Lab, 79; pres-elect, Asn Ecosystem Res Ctrs, 90-91. *Mem:* Sigma Xi; Ecol Soc Am; Am Inst Biol Sci. *Res:* Responses of wetland ecosystems to natural and human induced stress; attempts to identify the appropriate and minimum set of system components and interactions necessary to predicting those responses. *Mailing Add:* Dept Natural Res-Fernow Hall Cornell Univ Ithaca NY 14853-8101

BEDFORD, JAMES WILLIAM, WATER CHEMISTRY, RISK ASSESSMENT & COMMUNICATION. *Current Pos:* OMBUDSMAN, ENVIRON HEALTH, MICH DEPT PUB HEALTH, 90- *Personal Data:* b Colfax, Wash, Dec 3, 42; m 65, Kathel Kirkpatrick; c 2. *Educ:* Mich State Univ, BS, 65, MS, 67, PhD(entom), 70. *Prof Exp:* Chemist, Dept Natural Resources, Mich Environ Lab, 70-84, asst dir, 73-84; sr toxicologist, Toxic Substance Control Comn, 84-89. *Concurrent Pos:* Instr, Lansing Community Col, 80- *Mem:* Am Fisheries Soc; Sigma Xi; Soc Toxicol. *Res:* Biological monitoring of pesticides; pesticide residue analysis; pesticide and heavy metal pollution; lamellibranch physiology; environmental toxicology; risk communication. *Mailing Add:* Mich Dept Pub Health PO Box 30195 Lansing MI 48909. *Fax:* 517-335-9775; *E-Mail:* bedfords@state.mi.us

BEDFORD, JOEL S, RADIOBIOLOGY, CYTOGENETICS. *Current Pos:* PROF RADIOL & RADIATION BIOL, COLO STATE UNIV, 75- *Personal Data:* b Denver, Colo, Feb 14, 38; m 62; c 3. *Educ:* Univ Colo, BA, 61, MS, 64; Oxford Univ, DPhil, 66. *Prof Exp:* Instr, 66-67, James Picker Found res fel, 67-68, from asst prof to assoc prof radiobiol, Col Med, Vanderbilt Univ, 68-75. *Concurrent Pos:* NIH radiation study sect, 84-88, chmn, 86-88, assoc ed radiation res, 87- *Mem:* Radiation Res Soc. *Res:* Genetics control of cellular radiosensitivity; radiation genetics and cytogenetics; radiation effects on the cell cycle; cellular responses to hyperthermia; mechanisms of thermotolerance development in mammalian cells. *Mailing Add:* Dept Radiol Technol Colo State Univ Ft Collins CO 80523-0001

BEDFORD, JOHN MICHAEL, ANATOMY, PHYSIOLOGY. *Current Pos:* PROF REPRODUCTIVE BIOL & ANAT, MED COL, CORNELL UNIV, 72- *Personal Data:* b Sheffield, Eng, May 21, 32. *Educ:* Cambridge Univ, BA, 55, MA & VetMB, 58; Univ London, PhD, 65. *Prof Exp:* Jr fel surg, Vet Sch, Bristol Univ, 58-59; res assoc physiol, Worcester Found, Mass, 59-61; asst prof, Royal Vet Col, Univ London, 61-66; scientist, Worcester Found, Mass, 66-67; from asst prof to assoc prof anat, Columbia Univ, 70-72. *Mem:* Soc Study Reproduction; Am Asn Anatomists; Endocrine Soc; Brit Soc Study Fertil. *Res:* Reproductive physiology; sperm maturation in the male; capacitation of sperm in the female; fertilization; physiology of the ovum. *Mailing Add:* Dept Reproductive Biol Cornell Univ Med Col 1300 York Ave New York NY 10021

BEDFORD, RONALD ERNEST, TEMPERATURE STANDARDS, RADIOMETRY. *Current Pos:* Asst res officer, Nat Res Coun Can, 55-61, assoc res officer, 61-70, sr res officer, Div Physics, 70-89, head, Heat Thermometry Sect, 80-87, head, Photom Radiometry Sect, 87-91, prin res officer, Div Physics, 90-92, dir, Inst Nat Measurements Stand, 92-95, GUEST WORKER, NAT RES COUN CAN, 95- *Personal Data:* b Manitoba, Can, June 26, 30; m 55, Gertrude Cole; c Michael, Dianne & Susan. *Educ:* Univ Man, BSc Hons, 52; Univ BC, MA, 53, PhD(physics), 55. *Concurrent Pos:* Can deleg, Consultative Comt Thermometry, 71-, mem, Working Group 2, 71-, chmn, 78-; adv prof physics, Inst Technol, Harbin, China. *Mem:* Optical Soc Am. *Res:* Primary temperature standards; thermocouple and optical thermometry; radiometry. *Mailing Add:* Inst Nat Measurements Stand Nat Res Coun Can Ottawa ON K1A 0R6 Can. *Fax:* 613-952-1394; *E-Mail:* ron.bedford@nrc.ca

BEDGOOD, DALE RAY, MATHEMATICS, STATISTICS. *Current Pos:* PROF MATH & HEAD DEPT, ETEX STATE UNIV, 67- *Personal Data:* b Saltillo, Tex, Aug 10, 32; m 59; c 2. *Educ:* ETex State Univ, BS, 54; Univ Ark, MA, 59; Okla State Univ, EdD(math), 64. *Prof Exp:* Asst math, Univ Ark, 58-59; instr, Northeast La State Col, 59-62, asst prof, 64-65, assoc prof & head dept, 65-67. *Concurrent Pos:* Asst, Okla State Univ, 62-64; consult, NASA, Ala, 64-65, Cambridge Res Assoc, Mass, 66-67. *Mem:* Am Math Soc; Math Asn Am; Nat Coun Teachers Math. *Res:* Point-set topology; general analysis; teacher education and training at the elementary and secondary levels. *Mailing Add:* Dept Math ETex State Univ ETex Sta Commerce TX 75428

BEDIENT, JACK DEWITT, MATHEMATICS. *Current Pos:* asst prof math, 63-71, ASSOC PROF MATH, ARIZ STATE UNIV, 71- *Personal Data:* b Ithaca, NY, Jan 30, 26; m 49; c 4. *Educ:* Albion Col, BA, 48; Univ Colo, MS, 60, EdD(math educ), 66. *Prof Exp:* High sch teacher, Wash, 50-59. *Mem:* Math Asn Am. *Res:* Mathematics education; training secondary school mathematics teachers. *Mailing Add:* 8021 E Osborn No 213A Scottsdale AZ 85251

BEDIENT, PHILLIP E, MATHEMATICS. *Current Pos:* from asst prof to assoc prof, 59-68, chmn, Dept Math & Astron, 72-81, prof, 68-87, EMER PROF MATH, FRANKLIN & MARSHALL COL, 87- *Personal Data:* b Foochow, China, Oct 15, 22; US citizen; m 43, Marie Pangborn; c Richard E & Mary Jane (Wood). *Educ:* Park Col, AB, 43; Univ Mich, MA, 46, PhD(math), 59. *Prof Exp:* From instr to assoc prof math, Juniata Col, 50-55; instr, Univ Mich, 56-59. *Mem:* Am Math Soc; Math Asn Am. *Res:* Special functions; partial differential equations. *Mailing Add:* Dept Math & Astron Franklin & Marshall Col Lancaster PA 17604-3003

BEDINGER, CHARLES ARTHUR, JR, zoology, for more information see previous edition

BEDINGFIELD, CHARLES H(OSMER), chemical engineering; deceased, see previous edition for last biography

BEDNAR, JONNIE BEE, mathematics, computer science, for more information see previous edition

BEDNAR, RODNEY ALLAN, ENZYMOLOGY, REACTION MECHANISMS. *Current Pos:* ASST PROF PHARMACOL SCI & CHEM, STATE UNIV NY, STONY BROOK, 85- *Personal Data:* b Norristown, Pa, Nov 6, 55. *Educ:* Juniata Col, BS, 77; Univ Del, PhD(chem), 81. *Prof Exp:* Chemist, E I Du Pont de Nemours & Co, 77; NIH fel, Brandeis Univ, 82-85. *Mem:* Am Chem Soc; Sigma Xi; AAAS; Biophys Soc. *Res:* Mechanisms of enzyme action; general acid-base catalysis; chemical modification and site-directed mutagenesis of chalcane isomerase; mechanisms of proton transfer; structure-function relationship in enzyme catalysis. *Mailing Add:* 213 Musket Circle Lansdale PA 19446-4052

BEDNARCYK, NORMAN EARLE, NUTRITIAN, REGULATORY AFFAIRS. *Current Pos:* head lipid chem, Nabisco Brands, Inc, 67-72, head nutrit serv, 72-74, mgr sci serv, 75-81, mgr tech reg affairs, 82-89, mgr nutrient & formula data resources, 89-95, scientist nutrit info, 95-96, CONSULT, NABISCO BRANDS, INC, 96- *Personal Data:* b Buffalo, NY, Oct 12, 38; m 63, Elizabeth Kloeblen; c 3. *Educ:* Mass Inst Technol, BS, 60, MS, 62; Rutgers Univ, PhD(food sci), 67. *Prof Exp:* Res chemist, Lever Bros Co, 62-64; sr res chemist mix develop, Gen Mills, Inc, 67. *Mem:* Inst Food Technologists. *Res:* Nutritional composition of foods; food regulations. *Mailing Add:* 416 Patton Pl Wyckoff NJ 07481-1512. *Fax:* 201-236-9319; *E-Mail:* nbednarcyk@aol.com

BEDNAREK, ALEXANDER R, MATHEMATICS. *Current Pos:* RETIRED. *Personal Data:* b Buffalo, NY, July 15, 33; m 54; c 4. *Educ:* State Univ NY, Albany, BS, 57; Univ Buffalo, MA, 59, PhD(math), 61. *Prof Exp:* Instr math, Univ Buffalo, 58-60; mathematician, Goodyear Aerospace Corp, Ohio, 61-62; asst prof, Univ Akron, 62-63; from asst prof to prof, Univ Fla, 63-95, chmn dept, 69-95, co-dir, Ctr Appl Math, 76-95. *Concurrent Pos:* Vis staff mem, Los Alamos Sci Lab, 76- *Mem:* Am Math Soc; Math Asn Am; Polish Math Soc. *Res:* Topological algebra and the theory of relations, their applications to theoretical computer science. *Mailing Add:* 530 NE Seventh Ave Gainesville FL 32611-2082

BEDNAREK, JANA MARIE, MOLECULAR BIOLOGY, PROTEIN CHEMISTRY. *Current Pos:* RES CHEMIST, HEMAT-ONCOL SERV, DEPT HEMAT, MOLECULAR BIOL LAB, DEPT CLIN INVEST, WALTER REED ARMY MED CTR, 81- *Personal Data:* b Bratislava, Czech; US citizen; m 66; c 1. *Educ:* Charles Univ, Master's, 59; Univ Va, Charlottesville, PhD(biochem), 73. *Prof Exp:* NIH postdoctoral fel, Dept Biochem, Med Sch, Univ Va, Charlottesville, 73-75; postdoctoral fel phys chem, Dept Chem, Univ SC, Columbia, 75-76, res fel & res asst prof biochem, 76-79; res assoc, Dept Biochem, Med Univ SC, Charleston, 79-80. *Concurrent Pos:* Guest researcher, Dept Biochem, Nat Cancer Inst, NIH, Bethesda, Md, 81-90; prin investr, grant, Univ SC, Columbia, 78-79, ten approved protocols, Walter Reed Army Med Ctr, 81- *Mem:* Sigma Xi; NY Acad Sci; assoc mem Am Soc Biochem & Molecular Biol. *Res:* Protein chemistry; biochemistry; molecular biology of human neutrophils and their precursors in human bone marrow; study of hepatitis C virus. *Mailing Add:* Dept Clin Invest Walter Reed Army Med Ctr Georgia Ave Washington DC 20307. *Fax:* 202-782-3881

BEDNARZ, JAMES C, WILDLIFE ECOLOGY. *Current Pos:* ASST PROF WILDLIFE ECOL, ARK STATE UNIV, 93- *Educ:* NMex State Univ, BS, 76, PhD(biol), 86; Iowa State Univ, MS, 79. *Prof Exp:* Wildlife biologist, US Fish & Wildlife Serv, 77-78; res assoc, Univ NMex, 85-91; dir higher educ & res, Hawk Mountain Sanctuary Asn, 87-90; prin investr, Greenfalk consult, 90-91. *Concurrent Pos:* Wildlife consult, 79-80 & 91-; invited mem, Eastside Forests Sci Panel. *Mem:* Am Ornithologists Union; Animal Behav Soc; Wildlife Soc; Cooper Ornith Soc; Wilson Ornith Soc; Raptor Res Found; Sigma Xi. *Res:* Conservation biology; influence of human disturbance on wildlife populations; effects on habitat alterations on wildlife populations; social behavior of birds and mammals; evolution of mating systems; influence of ecology on animal social systems; migratory strategies of birds; evolutionary principles to conservation and wildlife management. *Mailing Add:* Dept Biol Sci Ark State Univ Main Campus PO Box 599 State University AR 72467-0599

BEDNEKOFF, ALEXANDER G, BIOCHEMISTRY. *Current Pos:* from asst prof to assoc prof, 66-73, PROF CHEM, PITTSBURG STATE UNIV, 73- *Personal Data:* b Seattle, Wash, June 13, 32; m 58, Lucy Winslow; c George, Peter & Katherine. *Educ:* Univ Wash, BS, 54; Univ Wis, MS, 61, PhD(biochem), 62. *Prof Exp:* Asst prof biochem, SDak State Univ, 62-66. *Mem:* Am Chem Soc; Sigma Xi. *Res:* Blood group substances of cattle and sheep; urinary calculi. *Mailing Add:* Dept Chem Pittsburg State Univ Pittsburg KS 66762

BEDNORZ, JOHANNES GEORG, CERAMIC PHYSICS. *Current Pos:* SR RES STAFF MEM, IBM ZURICH RES LAB, SWITZ, 82- *Personal Data:* b May 16, 50. *Educ:* Univ Munster, BS, 76; Swiss Fed Inst Technol, PhD, 82. *Honors & Awards:* Nobel Prize in Physics, 87; Marcel-Benoist Prize, 86; Victor Moritz Goldschmidt Prize, Ger Mineral Soc, 87; Robert Wichard Pohl Prize, Ger Physics Soc, 87; Thirteenth Fritz London Mem Award, 87; Dannie Heineman Prize, Repub Ger, 87; Otto-Klung Prize, 87; Int Prize, Am Phys Soc, 88; Hewlett-Packard Europhys Prize, 88. *Concurrent Pos:* Lectr, Swiss Fed Inst Technol, Zurich & Univ Zurich, 87- *Res:* Preparation, crystal growth and characterization of high refractive oxide materials (phase transition, quantum ferroelectricity); oxides with metallic conductivity and superconductivity. *Mailing Add:* IBM Zurich Res Lab Saemerstrasse Four 8803 Rueschlikon Zurich Switzerland

BEDNOWITZ, ALLAN LLOYD, X-RAY CRYSTALLOGRAPHY. *Current Pos:* res staff mem x-ray crystallog, 67-70, mgr, Lab Automation Appln, 71-77, mgr consult, educ & comput serv anal, 78-80, WITH COMPUT GRAPHICS SUBSYST, THOMAS J WATSON RES CTR, IBM CORP, 80- *Personal Data:* b New York, NY, Oct 7, 39; m 84, Penelle Paderewski; c Jared, Noah & Mia. *Educ:* Cooper Union, BChE, 60; Polytech Inst Brooklyn, MS, 63, PhD(chem physics), 66. *Prof Exp:* Fel x-ray crystallog, Brookhaven Nat Lab, 65-67. *Concurrent Pos:* Mem tech planning staff, Thomas J Watson Res Ctr, IBM Corp, 83-84. *Mem:* Am Crystallog Asn; Am Phys Soc; Sigma Xi; Asn Comput Machines; NY Acad Sci. *Res:* Crystal structure analysis by direct methods; computer control of experiments in research laboratories; computer programming for problems in x-ray crystallography; laboratory automation; computer graphics and multimedia. *Mailing Add:* PO Box 537 Millwood NY 10546. *Fax:* 914-945-2141; *E-Mail:* benwitz@watson.ibm.com

BEDO, DONALD ELRO, PHYSICS. *Current Pos:* RES PHYSICIST, USAF CAMBRIDGE RES LABS, CRUU, 62- *Personal Data:* b Erie, Pa, Dec 25, 29. *Educ:* Pa State Univ, BS, 51; Cornell Univ, PhD, 57. *Prof Exp:* Corning Glass Found fel, Cornell Univ, 56-58, res assoc physics, 58-60. *Mem:* Am Phys Soc. *Res:* Soft x-ray and extreme ultraviolet spectroscopy; photoemission; electromagnetic theory. *Mailing Add:* 43 Temple St Arlington MA 02174

BEDOIT, WILLIAM CLARENCE, JR, ORGANIC CHEMISTRY, PHYSICAL ORGANIC CHEMISTRY. *Current Pos:* RETIRED. *Personal Data:* b Chattanooga, Tenn, Apr 20, 22; m 43, Rebecca I Miller; c William C III & Thomas M. *Educ:* Univ Tenn, BS, 47, MS, 48, PhD(phys org chem), 50. *Prof Exp:* Res chemist, Carbide & Carbon Chem Corp, 50-52 & Mallinckrodt Chem Works, 52-54; sr res chemist, Jefferson Chem Co, 54-57, mgr market develop, 57-70, mgr urethane mkt develop, 70-71; mkt mgr, Martin Sweets Co, 71-73, vpres, 73; pres, UCT Inc, 73-84; consult, Union Carbide Corp, 84-85. *Concurrent Pos:* Instr, Morris Harvey Col, 51-52. *Mem:* Am Chem Soc; Soc Plastics Indust; fel Am Inst Chemists; Com Develop Asn. *Res:* Catalytic hydrogenation; chemical kinetics; distillation; organic preparations; market development; organic chemistry; petrochemicals; catalysis; all aspects of new urethane technology. *Mailing Add:* 8618 Brow Lake Rd Soddy Daisy TN 37379-4500

BEDROSIAN, E(DWARD), ELECTRONICS ENGINEERING. *Current Pos:* SR STAFF, RAND CORP, 57- *Personal Data:* b Chicago, Ill, May 22, 22; m 45, 71, Patricia Gardner; c William C, Barbara A, Charles E, Edward G & Victoria G. *Educ:* Northwestern Univ, BS, 49, MS, 50, PhD(elec eng), 53. *Prof Exp:* Sr engr, Motorola, Inc, 53-57. *Concurrent Pos:* Adj prof elec eng, Univ Southern Calif, 68-71. *Mem:* Inst Elec & Electronics Engrs; Am Inst Aeronaut & Astronaut; Inst Advan Engrs. *Res:* Radio and radar systems analysis; communication theory; conduct technical system analysis of military and civilian communicaton satellite systems. *Mailing Add:* Rand Corp 1700 Main St Santa Monica CA 90407-2138. *Fax:* 310-393-4818; *E-Mail:* edward_bedrosian@rand.org

BEDROSIAN, KARAKIAN, FOOD TECHNOLOGY. *Current Pos:* PRES, NAT PAK SYSTS, 78-, CHMN, NATURAL PAK PRODUCE, 88- *Personal Data:* b Milford, Mass, June 29, 33; m 54; c Mardenos, Edward & Taniel. *Educ:* Univ Mass, BS, 54; Cornell Univ, MS, 56; Univ Ill, PhD(food technol), 58; Mich State Univ, MBA, 62. *Honors & Awards:* Inst Food Technol Indust Achievement Award, 64. *Prof Exp:* Assoc res food technologist, Whirlpool Corp, 58-61, mgr food sci & technol, 61-62, dir res & develop, Tectrol Div, 62-63, dir res & develop, St Joseph Opers, 63-65; mgr new prod lab, Lever Bros Co, 65-66, tech mgr new prod & opers anal, 66-67; vpres res, DCA Food Indust, Inc, 67-71; pres, Bedrosian & Assocs, 71- *Concurrent Pos:* Chmn bd, Natural Pak Produce. *Mem:* AAAS; Inst Food Technol; Am Soc Heating, Refrig & Air-Conditioning Engrs; Asn Res Dirs. *Res:* New product development; microwave processing; extruded foods; fruit and vegetable storage and distribution. *Mailing Add:* Sherwood Ct Alpine NJ 07620

BEDROSIAN, SAMUEL D, systems engineering, communications; deceased, see previous edition for last biography

BEDROSSIAN, CARLOS WANES MENINO, PULMONARY PATHOLOGY, CYTOPATHOLOGY OF SEROUS EFFUSIONS. *Current Pos:* PROF PATH, WAYNE STATE UNIV, 91-; CHIEF CYTOPATH, DETROIT MED CTR, 91- *Personal Data:* b Uberaba, Minas Gerais, Brazil, May 1, 44; US citizen; m 70, Ursula Kennedy; c Richard, Vanessa & Robert. *Educ:* Col Moura Lacerda, Brazil, BS, 61; Univ Sao Paulo Med Sch, Brazil, MD, 67. *Honors & Awards:* Commissioner's Medal, Am Soc Clin Path, 90. *Prof Exp:* Chief labs, Brazilian Air Force, 68-69; dir cytopath, Vet Admin Hosp, Okla Children's Mem Hosp & Univ Okla Health Sci Ctr, 73-75, Hermann Hosp, Tex Med Ctr, 75-81 & Vanderbilt Univ Hosp, Tenn, 81-84; staff pathologist & chief lab serv, Vet Admin Med Ctr, Tenn, 84; attend pathologist, Bethesda Gen Hosp, St Louis, Mo, 85-89; dir, Cytopath Lab, Univ Iowa, Hosps & Clins, 89-91. *Concurrent Pos:* Dir, Immunocytochem Lab, St Louis Univ Sch Med, Mo, 84-89, Cytopath Lab, St Louis Univ Hosp, Mo, 84-89 & Electron Micros Lab, Vet Admin Med Ctr, St Louis, 86-87; ed-in-chief, Diag Cytopath, 85-; consult pathologist, Cardinal Glennon Mem Hosp, St Louis, 86-88; mem, Cytopath Educ Consortium, Am Soc Cytol, Am Soc Clin Path & Am Soc Cytotechnol, 90-92. *Mem:* Am Soc Clin Path; Col Am Pathologists; Int Acad Path; Am Soc Cytol; Soc Ultrastruct Path. *Res:* Pulmonary pathology; cytopathology of serous fluids; author of one publication. *Mailing Add:* Cytol Dept Detroit Med Ctr 4707 St Antoine Blvd Detroit MI 48201

BEDWELL, THOMAS HOWARD, PHYSICS. *Current Pos:* RETIRED. *Personal Data:* b Forest, Idaho, Feb 17, 15; m 56. *Educ:* Univ SDak, AB, 43, AM, 47, ME, 58; Univ Nebr, PhD(physics, educ), 66; Univ Okla, MS, 74, MNSc, 78. *Prof Exp:* Instr physics, Univ SDak, 44-48; asst prof, Fla State Univ, 48-50; plant engr, Freeman Co, SDak, 50-53; chmn elec div, Southern State Col (SDak), 53-57; assoc prof physics, Univ SDak, 58-64; from assoc prof to prof physics, Northern Ariz Univ, 64-81. *Concurrent Pos:* Fel, Univ Okla, 70-71; chmn, Am Physics Teachers Lect Series, 63-64; judge, Future Scientists of Am Found, Region VI, 58; environ monitoring consult, East SDak, Northern States Power, 63-64. *Mem:* Fel AAAS; Am Phys Soc; Inst Elec & Electronics Engrs; Sigma Xi; Am Meteorol Soc; Am Geophys Union. *Res:* Environmental science; radio physics; atmospheric science. *Mailing Add:* 2030 S Glenrose Dr Camp Verde AZ 86322

BEDWORTH, DAVID D, PRODUCTION CONTROL, COMPUTER-AIDED MANUFACTURING. *Current Pos:* fac assoc, Ariz State Univ, 62-63, from asst prof to assoc prof, 63-69, prof indust eng, 74-94, chair, Dept Indust Engrs, 76-80, EMER PROF, INDUST ENG, ARIZ STATE UNIV, 94- *Personal Data:* b Manchester, Eng, Nov 29, 32; US citizen; m 61; c 2. *Educ:* Lamar State Col, BSIE, 55; Purdue Univ, MSIE, 59, PhD(indust eng), 61. *Honors & Awards:* Wickenden Award Am, Soc Eng Educ. *Prof Exp:* Methods engr indust eng, Boeing Airplane Co, Kans, 55; instr, Purdue Univ, 58-60, res asst, 60-61; sr systs analyst, Process Comput Sect, Gen Elec Co, Ariz, 61-62, consult analyst, 62-63. *Mem:* Am Inst Indust Engrs; Am Soc Eng Educ; Soc Mfg Engrs. *Res:* Time-series analysis and forecasting; industrial engineering computer application; scheduling activities; computer aided manufacturing. *Mailing Add:* Dept Indust & Mgt Syst Eng Ariz State Univ Tempe AZ 85287-5906. *Fax:* 602-965-8692; *E-Mail:* icddb@asuvm.inre.asu.edu

BEDZYK, MICHAEL J, CRYSTALLOGRAPHY. *Current Pos:* PROF, DEPT MAT SCI, NORHTWESTERN UNIV; STAFF, ARGONNE NAT LAB. *Honors & Awards:* Bertram Eugene Warren Diffraction Physics Award, Am Crystallog Asn, 94. *Mailing Add:* Dept Mat Sci Northwestern Univ 1031 Tech Inst Evanston IL 60201-5506

BEEBE, GEORGE WARREN, PHOTOGRAPHIC CHEMISTRY. *Personal Data:* b Eau Claire, Wis, Sept 9, 36; m 59, Donna R Nelson; c Karin, Eric & Scott. *Educ:* Wis State Univ-Eau Claire, BS, 58; Mich State Univ, PhD(tertrazoles), 64. *Prof Exp:* Sr res specialist, Photo Prod Lab, 3M Co, 63-96. *Res:* Nitrogen heterocycles; condensed ring hydrocarbons; fluorescence, tetrazole synthesis; chemiluminescence; organic dyes; polyurethanes; aliphatic epoxides; resin curing systems; color photographic chemistry; photographic emulsion making, digestion and coating. *Mailing Add:* 2435 Arona St St Paul MN 55113. *E-Mail:* gwbeebe@ix.netcom.com

BEEBE, GILBERT WHEELER, RADIATION EPIDEMIOLOGY. *Current Pos:* EPIDEMIOLOGIST, RADIATION EPIDEMIOL BR, NAT CANCER INST, NIH, 77- *Personal Data:* b Mahwah, NJ, Apr 3, 12; m 33, Ruth Lillian White; c Alfred, Beatrice, Brian & Christopher. *Educ:* Dartmouth Col, AB, 33; Columbia Univ, MA, 38, PhD(sociol, statist), 42. *Honors & Awards:* Cutter lectr prev med, Harvard Sch Pub Health, 79; Wade Hampton Frost lectr, Am Pub Health Asn, 80; Director's Award, NIH, 85; Special Recognition Award, PHS, 83. *Prof Exp:* Statistician, Nat Comt Maternal Health, 34-41; mem tech staff, Milbank Mem Fund, 41-46; statistician, Div Med Sci, Nat Acad Sci-Nat Res Coun, 46-77, dir, Follow-Up Agency, 57-77. *Concurrent Pos:* Res assoc, Milbank Mem Fund, 39-41; chief, Reports & Analysis Br, Control Div, Off Surgeon Gen, US Army, 43-46, consult, 46-50; consult, Comn Reorgn Exec Br, Hoover Comn, 48; chief epidemiol & statist dept, Atomic Bomb Casualty Comn, Japan, 58-60, 66-68 & 73-75, mem bd dirs & chief scientist, Radiation Effects Res Found, Japan, 75; mem subcomt somatic effects, Nat Acad Sci Adv Comt Biol Effects of Ionizing Radiation, 69-72 & 77-80; mem res training comt, Nat Inst Environ Sci, 70-73; mem, Comt Biol Effects Ionizing Radiations, Nat Acad Sci, 77-80; mem sci panel, Comt Interagency Radiation Res & Policy coord, Off Sci & Technol Policy, Exec Off Pres, 84-95. *Mem:* Fel AAAS; Am Epidemiol Soc (vpres, 78-79); Soc Epidemiol Res; fel Am Statist Asn; Int Epidemiol Asn; Radiation Res Soc; Health Physics Soc. *Res:* Application of statistical methods to research in clinical medicine and epidemiology; estimation of the risks associated with exposure to ionizing radiation. *Mailing Add:* Radiation Epidemiol Br Exec Plaza N Suite 400 Nat Cancer Inst Bethesda MD 20892. *Fax:* 301-496-1854; *E-Mail:* gilbert_beebe@nih.gov

BEEBE, RICHARD TOWNSEND, INTERNAL MEDICINE. *Current Pos:* assoc, 32-37, from assoc prof to prof, 37-67, head dept, 48, DISTINGUISHED PROF MED, ALBANY MED COL, 67- *Personal Data:* b Great Barrington, Mass, Jan 22, 02; m 32; c 3. *Educ:* Princeton Univ, BS, 24; Johns Hopkins Univ, MD, 28; Am Bd Internal Med, dipl. *Hon Degrees:* ScD, Albany Med Col, 82. *Prof Exp:* Res fel, Thorndike Mem Lab, 29-30; asst resident med, Johns Hopkins Univ, 30-32. *Concurrent Pos:* Physician-in-chief, Albany Hosp, 48-67, sr physician, 67- *Mem:* Assoc AMA; Am Soc Clin Invest; Am Clin & Climat Asn; fel & master Am Col Physicians. *Mailing Add:* Albany Med Ctr Albany NY 12208

BEEBE, ROBERT RAY, EXTRACTIVE METALLURGY OF GOLD & BASE METALS. *Current Pos:* CONSULT, MINERAL INDUST, 91- *Personal Data:* b Butte, Mont, Apr 21, 28; m 56; c 1. *Educ:* Mont Sch Mines, BS, 53, MS, 54. *Honors & Awards:* Krumb Lectr, Am Inst Mining Metall & Petrol Engrs, 90. *Prof Exp:* Dir res, Carpco Res & Eng, 65-67, pres, 72-73; gen mgr proj develop, Marcona Corp, 67-73, vpres, 73-76; sr metall engr, Newmont Mining Corp, 76-80, vpres, 80-86; vpres, Homestake Mining Co, 86-88, sr vpres, 88-91. *Concurrent Pos:* Vchmn, Comt Competitiveness, US Minerals & Metals Indust, 87-89; mem, Nat Mat Adv Bd, 90-92. *Mem:* Nat Acad Eng; Soc Mining Minerals & Explor; Mining & Metall Soc Am (pres, 87-89); AAAS; Minerals Metals & Mat Soc. *Res:* Mining and mineral project development and administration; mineral processing and extractive metallurgical research; mineral economics and public policy. *Mailing Add:* PO Box 32048 Tucson AZ 85151. *Fax:* 520-529-1813; *E-Mail:* raybeebe@aol.com

BEEBEE, JOHN CHRISTOPHER, ENGINEERING PHYSICS. *Current Pos:* prof, 84-86, PROF MATH, UNIV ALASKA, ANCHORAGE, 87- *Personal Data:* b Glendale, Calif, Mar 7, 41; m 69, Karen Willmore; c Adrian & Robin. *Educ:* Pomona Col, BA, 63; Univ Calif, Riverside, MA, 65; Univ Wash, PhD(math), 72. *Prof Exp:* Asst prof math, Alaska Methodist Univ, 71-74; researcher, Alaska Res Assoc, 74-75; teacher, East High Sch, 75-78; researcher, Energy Syst, Inc, 78-84; prof, Calif State Col, Bakersfield, 87. *Mem:* Am Math Soc; Math Asn Am. *Res:* Cost and scientific feasibility of various energy supply or conversion projects or concepts; properties of cyclic sequences and exact covering systems. *Mailing Add:* 9571 Midden Way Anchorage AK 99507. *E-Mail:* afjcb@alaska.edu

BEECHAN, CURTIS MICHAEL, TEACHING. *Current Pos:* asst prof, 86-95, ASSOC PROF CHEM, STERLING COL, 95- *Personal Data:* b Loma Linda, Calif, Sept 19, 47. *Educ:* Univ Calif, Riverside, BS, 70; Stanford Univ, PhD(org chem), 78. *Prof Exp:* Res chemist, Univ Calif, Riverside, 78-79, San Diego, 82-84; org chemist & supvr, Rachelle Labs, Inc, 79-80; org chemist, Ultrasystems, Inc, 81-82; asst prof chem, Mt St Mary's Col, 84-86. *Mem:* Am Chem Soc. *Res:* Marine natural products chemistry. *Mailing Add:* 714 N Broadway Sterling KS 67579. *Fax:* 316-278-2775

BEECHER, CHRISTOPHER W W, BIOSYNTHESIS, PLANT TISSUE CULTURE. *Current Pos:* vis asst prof, 85-89, asst prof, 89-93, ASSOC PROF, COL PHARM, UNIV ILL, CHICAGO, 93- *Personal Data:* b New York, NY, Aug 20, 48; m 81; c Francis & William. *Educ:* NY Univ, BA, 74, MS, 80; Univ Conn, PhD(pharmacog), 86. *Prof Exp:* Res asst, Univ Conn, 78-84. *Concurrent Pos:* Dir, Metmap Database, 87-; mgr & assoc dir, Napralert Database, 90- *Mem:* Am Soc Pharmacog; Am Soc Plant Physiol; Sigma Xi. *Res:* Information management techniques in biological studies; computer assisted drug discovery methodology; control of biosynthetic capacity in plant tissue cultures. *Mailing Add:* 915 S Clinton Ave Oak Park IL 60304-1821

BEECHER, GARY RICHARD, NUTRITIONAL BIOCHEMISTRY. *Current Pos:* biochemist, Protein Nutrit Lab, Nutrit Inst, 71-82, RES LEADER, NUTRIENT COMPOS LAB, BELTSVILLE HUMAN NUTRIENT RES CTR, AGR RES SERV, USDA, 82- *Personal Data:* b Wilton, Wis, May 25, 39; m 62, Sigrid C Pierce; c Julie, Jennifer & Jody. *Educ:* Univ Wis-Madison, BS, 61, MS, 63, PhD(biochem), 66. *Prof Exp:* Biochemist, US Army Med Res & Nutrit Lab, 66-68; asst prof biochem, Kans State Univ, 68-71. *Concurrent Pos:* Collab scientist, Carolina Univ, Med Sch 74-82; consult, Am Res Prod Corp, 80-82, Anal Proc Inc, 82-88. *Mem:* AAAS; Am Inst Nutrit; Sigma Xi; Inst Food Technol. *Res:* Analytical chemistry in biological and food systems. *Mailing Add:* Food Composition Lab Rm 202 Bldg 161E 10300 Baltimore Ave Beltsville MD 20705. *Fax:* 301-504-8314; *E-Mail:* beecher@bhnrc.usda.gov

BEECHER, WILLIAM JOHN, ORNITHOLOGY. *Current Pos:* RES ASSOC, BIRD DIV, FIELD MUS NAT HIST, 87- *Personal Data:* b Chicago, Ill, May 23, 14. *Educ:* Univ Chicago, BS, 47, MS, 49, PhD, 54. *Honors & Awards:* Nat Asn Biol Teachers Award; US Environ Protection Agency Environ Qual Award, 76; Cyrus Mark Award. *Prof Exp:* Asst zool, Chicago Natural Hist Mus, 37-42, asst zool, Educ Dept, 46-54; asst zool, Conserv Dept, Cook County Forest Preserve Dist, 54-57; dir, Chicago Acad Sci, 58-83; pres, Beecher Res Co, 83- *Concurrent Pos:* Mem biol comt, Ill Bd Higher Educ; vchmn, Ill Chap Nature Conserv; mem environ comt, Northeastern Ill Plan Comn; mem open lands proj; mem, Wetlands Comt, Biol Comn, Univ Chicago, Adventurers Club, 67-, Explorers Club, 88- *Mem:* AAAS; Am Ornith Union; Wilson Ornith Soc; Cooper Ornith Soc; Soc Study Evolution; fel Royal Soc Arts. *Res:* Birds, anatomy and classification, ecology and migration; other vertebrates, comparative anatomy of the ear, migration and homing; inventor of high-tech spectacle binoculars; convertible to stereomicroscope and benefit to victims of macular degeneration. *Mailing Add:* 1960 N Lincoln Park W Chicago IL 60614-5456

BEECHLER, BARBARA JEAN, MATHEMATICS. *Current Pos:* from assoc prof to prof, 67-89, EMER PROF MATH, PITZER COL, 89- *Personal Data:* b Rockford, Ill, Dec 13, 28. *Educ:* Univ Iowa, BA, 49, MS, 51, PhD(math), 55. *Prof Exp:* Instr math, Smith Col, 52-54; asst prof, Wilson Col, 55-58, assoc prof & chmn dept, 58-60; assoc prof, Wheaton Col, Mass, 60-67. *Mem:* Math Asn Am; Am Math Soc. *Res:* Arithmetic properties of integral domains; local rings. *Mailing Add:* Dept Math Pitzer Col 1050 N Mills Ave Claremont CA 91711-6110

BEECKMANS, JAN MARIA, CHEMICAL ENGINEERING. *Current Pos:* PROF CHEM ENG, UNIV WESTERN ONT, 66- *Personal Data:* b Antwerp, Belg, June 17, 30; Can citizen; m 57, 70; c 3. *Educ:* Univ London, BSc, 53; Univ Toronto, MASc, 54, PhD(phys chem), 58. *Prof Exp:* Res assoc chem eng, Imp Oil, Ltd, 58-59; chemist, Ont Res Found, 59-61; asst prof indust hyg, Univ Toronto, 61-66. *Mem:* Chem Inst Can. *Res:* Fluidization; solids separation. *Mailing Add:* Dept Chem Eng Univ Western Ont 1151 Richmond St London ON N6A 3K7 Can

BEEDE, CHARLES HERBERT, ORGANIC CHEMISTRY. *Current Pos:* res chemist, 64-80, res assoc, 80-84, SR SCIENTIST, JOHNSON & JOHNSON, 85- *Personal Data:* b Chelsea, Mass, Dec 4, 34; m 57; c 1. *Educ:* Northeastern Univ, BS, 57; Mass Inst Technol, PhD(org chem), 62. *Prof Exp:* Res chemist, Org & Polymer Chem, Hercules Powder Co, 61-63. *Mem:* NY Acad Sci; AAAS; Am Chem Soc; Sigma Xi. *Res:* Polymer synthesis, particularly vinyl, emulsion, stereoregular and condensation; organic synthesis; chemistry of small-ring compounds; pressure-sensitive adhesives; controlled release-transdermal delivery; absorbable polymers; hydrophilic polymers. *Mailing Add:* 6102 Tiffany Park Ct Arlington TX 76016-2037

BEEDLE, LYNN SIMPSON, CIVIL ENGINEERING, TALL BUILDINGS. *Current Pos:* DIR, COUN TALL BLDG & URBAN HABITATION, 76- *Personal Data:* b Orland, Calif, Dec 7, 17; m 46, Ella M Grimes; c Lynn S Jr, Helen E, Jonathan P, David J & Edward (Grimes). *Educ:* Univ Calif, BS, 41; Lehigh Univ, MS, 49, PhD(civil eng), 52. *Honors & Awards:* A F Davis Silver Medal, Am Welding Soc, 57; E E Howard Award, Am Soc Civil Engrs, 63, Hadesty Award, 93; T R Higgins lectr, Am Inst Steel Construct, 73; John Fritz Medal, 94. *Prof Exp:* Prog eng, Todd Calif Shipbldg Corp, 41; officer in charge underwater exp, US Navy, Norfolk Naval Shipyard, 42-47; dep officer in charge inst group, Oper Crossroads, US Navy Bur, 46-47; from asst prof to distinguished prof, Lehigh Univ, 52-60, dir, High-Rise Inst, 83-88. *Concurrent Pos:* Student Naval archit, US Navy Postgrad Sch, Naval Acad, 41-42, instr, 42; consult, Indian Stand Inst, 57-58; dir, Fritz Eng Lab, 60-84; chmn, Struct Stability Res Coun, 66-70, dir, 70-93; chmn, Coun Tall Bldg & Urban Habitat, 70-76, dir, 76-; ed, Costruzioni Metalliche Mag, 80; consult, Freeman, Fox & Partners, 81. *Mem:* Nat Acad Eng; hon mem Am Soc Civil Engrs; Am Inst Steel Construct; hon mem Int Asn Bridge & Struct Eng; Am Welding Soc. *Res:* Research in plastic design and steel, large bolted joints, column stability, planning and design of tall buildings. *Mailing Add:* 102 Cedar Rd Hellertown PA 18055. *Fax:* 610-758-4522; *E-Mail:* lsb0@lehigh.edu

BEEHLER, BRUCE MCPHERSON, CONSERVATION BIOLOGY, TROPICAL ECOLOGY. *Current Pos:* NATURAL RESOURCE MGT OFFICER, US DEPT STATE, 95- *Personal Data:* b Baltimore, Md, Oct 11, 51; m 82, Carol Elizabeth Hare; c Grace, Andrew & Cary. *Educ:* Williams Col, BA, 74; Princeton Univ, MA, 78, PhD(biol), 83. *Prof Exp:* Sci asst to secy & secy emer, Smithsonian Inst, 81-89, zoologist, Nat Mus Natural Hist, 89-91; assoc res zoologist, Wildlife Conserv Soc & Conserv Int, 91-93; sr ecologist, Conserv Int, 93-95. *Concurrent Pos:* Res assoc, Dept Vert Zool, Nat Mus Natural Hist, Smithsonian Inst, 85-; adj prof, Clemson Univ, 89-91; assoc ed, The Auk, 89-92. *Mem:* Fel Am Ornithologists Union; AAAS; Wilsa Ornith Soc; Royal Australian Ornith Univ. *Res:* Ornithology of New Guinea and India, with specializations on the birds of paradise and on the ecology of tropical rain forest; conservation biology. *Mailing Add:* OES/ETC Rm 4333 US Dept State Washington DC 20520. *Fax:* 202-647-5247; *E-Mail:* bbeehler@state.gov

BEEHLER, JERRY R, MATHEMATICS. *Current Pos:* PROF MATH & DEAN ARTS & SCI, TRI-STATE UNIV, 69- *Personal Data:* b Lekhart, Ind, Jan 16, 43. *Educ:* Univ Toronto, PhD(math), 73. *Mem:* Math Asn Am. *Mailing Add:* 3040 S Old 27 Angola IN 46703

BEEHLER, ROGER EARL, PHYSICS. *Current Pos:* from asst chief to assoc chief time & frequency div, 68-75, CHIEF TIME & FREQUENCY SERV, NIST, 75- *Personal Data:* b Rochester, Ind, May 8, 34; m 56; c 3. *Educ:* Purdue Univ, BS, 56. *Honors & Awards:* US Dept Com Silver Medal, 64. *Prof Exp:* Physicist, Allison Div, Gen Motors Corp, Ind, 56-57; physicist, Nat Bur Stand, 57-60, proj leader atomic frequency stand, 60-65, asst sect chief, Atomic Time & Frequency Stand Sect, 65-66; physicist, Frequency & Time Div, Hewlett-Packard Co, 66-68. *Res:* Atomic beam frequency standards; time; frequency. *Mailing Add:* 203 Springs Dr Louisville CO 80027-3201

BEEK, JOHN, chemical engineering; deceased, see previous edition for last biography

BEEKMAN, BRUCE EDWARD, COMPARATIVE PHYSIOLOGY. *Current Pos:* From asst prof to assoc prof physiol, 58-71, chmn dept biol, 72-75, PROF PHYSIOL, CALIF STATE UNIV, LONG BEACH, 71- *Personal Data:* b Upland, Calif, Apr 18, 30; c 4. *Educ:* San Diego State Col, BA, 52; Ind Univ, PhD, 65. *Mem:* Am Soc Zoologists. *Res:* Comparative physiology and biochemistry of oxygen carriers. *Mailing Add:* 400 S Flower #56 Orange CA 92668-3460

BEEKMAN, JOHN ALFRED, MATHEMATICS, ACTUARIAL SCIENCE. *Current Pos:* From asst prof to prof, 63-89, Lincoln Nat Corp prof actuarial sci, 89-96, EMER LINCOLN NAT CORP PROF ACTUARIAL SCI, BALL STATE UNIV, 96- *Personal Data:* b LaCrosse, Wis, July 14, 31; m 55, Jane Kyhl; c Karen & Ann. *Educ:* Univ Iowa, BA, 53, MS, 57; Univ Minn, Minneapolis, PhD(math), 63. *Concurrent Pos:* Vis prof statist, Univ Iowa, 69-70. *Mem:* Am Math Soc; Soc Actuaries; Am Acad Actuaries; Math Asn Am; Sigma Xi. *Res:* Probability theory; Gaussian Markov and collective risk stochastic processes; mathematical demography including population projection techniques; actuarial applications of mathematical risk theory. *Mailing Add:* Dept Math Sci Ball State Univ Muncie IN 47306-0490. *Fax:* 765-285-1797; *E-Mail:* oojabeekman@suvc.bsu.edu

BEEL, JOHN ADDIS, ORGANIC CHEMISTRY. *Current Pos:* from asst prof to prof chem, 49-84, head dept, 49-52, actg chmn sci div, 57, 64 & 68, actg assoc dean, 69, assoc dean, Arts & Sci, 71-, EMER PROF CHEM, UNIV NORTHERN COLO, 84- *Personal Data:* b Butte, Mont, Sept 20, 21; m 44; c 2. *Educ:* Mont State Col, BSc, 42; Iowa State Univ, PhD(org chem), 49. *Honors & Awards:* Meritorious Serv Award, Am Chem Soc, 69. *Prof Exp:* Instr chem, Iowa State Univ, 45-49. *Mem:* Sigma Xi; Am Chem Soc. *Res:* Organometallic compounds; chemotherapy. *Mailing Add:* Dept Chem Univ Northern Colo Greeley CO 80631

BEELER, BYRON, AGRICULTURE. *Current Pos:* FEL, AGR INST CAN, 95. *Mailing Add:* Ciba Geigy Can Ltd 6860 Century Ave Mississauga ON L5N 2S5 Can

BEELER, DONALD A, BIOCHEMISTRY. *Current Pos:* instr, 63-64, from asst prof to assoc prof, 64-75, PROF BIOCHEM, ALBANY MED COL, 75- *Personal Data:* b Elmwood, NS, Aug 16, 31; m 53; c 4. *Educ:* McGill Univ, BSc, 53; Purdue Univ, MS, 59, PhD(biochem), 62. *Prof Exp:* Fel biochem, Univ Wis, 61-63. *Mem:* Fedn Am Soc Exp Biol. *Res:* Hepatic, biliary and lung phospholipid metabolism. *Mailing Add:* Dept Biochem Albany Med Col A-10 Albany NY 12208

BEELER, GEORGE W, JR, INFORMATION SCIENCE & SYSTEMS. *Current Pos:* Assoc consult, Mayo Clin & instr, Mayo Med Sch, 67-68, head sect info processing & systs, 80-86, head sect info systs technol, 87-90, CONSULT PHYSIOL & BIOPHYS, MAYO CLIN & ASST PROF, MAYO MED SCH, 69-, CHMN DIV INFO ARCH & TECHNOL, 90- *Personal Data:* b West Point, NY, Oct 5, 38; m 65; c 2. *Educ:* Princeton Univ, BSE, 60; Calif Inst Technol, MS, 61, PhD(elec eng), 65. *Mem:* Inst Elec & Electronics Engr; Am Med Informatics Asn. *Res:* Analysis of biological systems; excitation-contraction coupling in cardiac muscle; application of computers to biomedical research and practice. *Mailing Add:* Mayo Clinic 200 SW First St Rochester MN 55905

BEELER, JOE R, JR, solid state physics; deceased, see previous edition for last biography

BEELER, MYRTON FREEMAN, CLINICAL PATHOLOGY, CLINICAL CHEMISTRY. *Current Pos:* assoc prof to prof, 87-87, dir grad prog clin chem, 70-87 EMER PROF PATH, LA STATE UNIV, MED CTR, NEW ORLEANS, 87- *Personal Data:* b Winthrop, Mass, Apr 27, 22. *Educ:* Harvard Univ, AB, 45; NY Med Col, MD, 49. *Prof Exp:* Resident path, Worcester City Hosp, Mass, 52-54; resident path, New Eng Deaconess Hosp, Boston, 54-56, asst pathologist, 56-58; dir labs, Ochsner Clin & Ochsner Found Hosp, 58-67. *Concurrent Pos:* Assoc pathologist, Charity Hosp of La, New Orleans, 67-, dir clin chem, 75-81; consult clin path, Vet Admin Hosp, 71- & USPHS Hosp, 74-79; ed-in-chief, Am J Clin Path, 80- *Mem:* Am Soc Clin Path; Col Am Path Physicians & Scientists; AOA. *Res:* Medical decision making. *Mailing Add:* LSU Med Ctr Path Dept Suite 5103 1901 Perdido St New Orleans LA 70112-1328

BEELER, TROY JAMES, MUSCLE & MEMBRANE BIOCHEMISTRY. *Current Pos:* ASSOC PROF MED BIOCHEM, UNIFORMED SERV UNIV HEALTH SCI, 80- *Educ:* Univ Tenn, PhD(biochem), 78. *Mailing Add:* Dept Biochem Uniformed Serv Univ Health Sci 4301 Jones Bridge Rd Bethesda MD 20804-4799

BEELIK, ANDREW, SYNTHETIC ORGANIC & NATURAL PRODUCTS CHEMISTRY. *Current Pos:* RETIRED. *Personal Data:* b Nizne Valice, Czech, Dec 12, 24; US citizen; m 51, Shirley J Kennedy. *Educ:* Univ Agrarian Sci, Hungary, dipl, 47; Univ Toronto, MSA, 52; McGill Univ, PhD(chem), 54. *Prof Exp:* Lectr org chem, Royal Mil Col, Can, 54-55; from res chemist to sr res chemist, ITT Rayonier Inc, 55-62, res group leader, 62-72, res supvr, 72-78, mgr lab serv, Rayonier Res Ctr, 78-82. *Mem:* Am Chem Soc; Sigma Xi. *Res:* Chemistry of wood constituents; cellulose acetate and viscose processes; instrumental analysis. *Mailing Add:* 2012 Walker Park Rd Shelton WA 98584

BEELMAN, ROBERT B, FOOD SCIENCE, ENOLOGY. *Current Pos:* Asst prof, 70-75, ASSOC PROF FOOD SCI, PA STATE UNIV, UNIVERSITY PARK, 75- *Personal Data:* b Elyria, Ohio, May 16, 44; m 68. *Educ:* Capital Univ, BS, 66; Ohio State Univ, MS, 67, PhD(food sci), 70. *Mem:* Am Soc Microbiol; Inst Food Technologists; Am Soc Enol. *Res:* Effects of processing on the quality of fruits, vegetables and mushrooms; evaluation of vinification practices on eastern United States table wines; stimulation of malo-lactic fermentation in table wines; food microbiology. *Mailing Add:* Dept Food Sci 111 Borland Lab Pa State Univ University Park PA 16802-2504

BEEM, JOHN KELLY, GEOMETRY, APPLIED MATH. *Current Pos:* from asst prof to assoc prof, 68-79, PROF MATH, UNIV MO, COLUMBIA, 79- *Personal Data:* b Detroit, Mich, Jan 24, 42; m 64, Eloise Yamamoto; c Thomas. *Educ:* Univ Southern Calif, AB, 63, MA, 65, PhD(math), 68. *Concurrent Pos:* Grantee, NSF, 69-71 & NSF, 89-91. *Mem:* Am Math Soc; Math Asn Am; Gen Relativity & Gravitation Soc; Sigma Xi. *Res:* Geometry of Lorentzian manifolds and general relativity. *Mailing Add:* 5204 E Tayside Circle Columbia MO 65203-5191

BEEM, MARC O, MEDICINE. *Current Pos:* RETIRED. *Personal Data:* b Chicago, Ill, June 25, 23; m 46; c 4. *Educ:* Williams Col, BA, 45; Univ Chicago, MD, 48. *Prof Exp:* From asst prof to assoc prof, Univ Chicago, 54-64, prof pediat, 64- *Res:* Infectious diseases; virology. *Mailing Add:* 327 E Third St Hillsdale IL 60521

BEEMAN, CURT PLETCHER, ANALYTICAL CHEMISTRY. *Current Pos:* from res assoc to sr res assoc, 79-90, SR RES SCIENTIST, INT PAPER CO, 90- *Personal Data:* b Mt Vernon, Ohio, May 30, 44; m 66, Elisabeth Bartlett; c Anne E & Christopher P. *Educ:* Univ Fla, BS, 67; Auburn Univ, MS, 69, PhD(chem), 71. *Prof Exp:* Res asst chem, Univ Alta, 71-73; res assoc, Mt Holyoke Col, 73-77; res assoc, Drinking Water Qual Res Ctr, Fla Int Univ, 77-79. *Mem:* Am Chem Soc; Sigma Xi. *Res:* Gas chromatography and gas chromatography/mass spectrometry; instrumental analysis of wood, paper products and process components; inductively coupled plasma spectroscopy. *Mailing Add:* 6658 Hounds Run N Mobile AL 36608-5421

BEEMAN, DAVID EDMUND, JR, THEORETICAL PHYSICS. *Current Pos:* asst prof physics, 69-74, assoc prof, 69-, ADJ PROF ELEC & COMPUT ENG, HARVEY MUDD COL, 90- *Personal Data:* b Sacramento, Calif, Dec 12, 38; m 65; c 2. *Educ:* Stanford Univ, BS, 61; Univ Calif, Los Angeles, MA, 63, PhD(physics), 67. *Prof Exp:* Res assoc theoret physics, Atomic Energy Res Estab, Eng, 67-69. *Mem:* AAAS; Am Phys Soc. *Res:* Theoretical solid state physics; amorphous materials. *Mailing Add:* Dept Elec & Comput Eng Univ Colo CB425 Boulder CO 80309

BEEMON, KAREN LOUISE, MOLECULAR BIOLOGY, VIROLOGY. *Current Pos:* from asst prof to assoc prof, 81-91, PROF BIOL, JOHNS HOPKINS UNIV, 91- *Personal Data:* b Jackson, Mich, Apr 11, 47; m 74; c Nicole A & Claire E. *Educ:* Univ Mich, BS, 69; Univ Calif, Berkeley, MA, 72, PhD(molecular biol), 74. *Honors & Awards:* Fac Res Award, Am Cancer Soc. *Prof Exp:* NIH fel molecular biol, Univ Calif, Berkeley, 74-76, lectr, 75; NIH fel tumor virol, Salk Inst, 76-78, sr res assoc tumor virol, 78-81. *Concurrent Pos:* Mem, NIH Study Sect Immunol, Virol & Path, 90-94. *Mem:* Am Soc Microbiol; Am Soc Virol; Asn Women Sci; AAAS. *Res:* Animal virology; retrovirus genome structure and gene expression at the post-transcriptional level. *Mailing Add:* Biol Dept Johns Hopkins Univ 3400 N Charles St Baltimore MD 21218-2608. *Fax:* 410-516-7292

BEENE, JAMES ROBERT, HEAVY ION NUCLEAR PHYSICS & REACTIONS, HYPERFINE INTERACTIONS PHYSICS. *Current Pos:* res staff mem, Oak Ridge Nat Lab, 76-87, sr res staff mem, 87, group leader, 87-93, head, Nuclear Physics Res Sect, 93-95, DIR HOLIFIELD HEAVY ION RES FACIL, OAK RIDGE NAT LAB, 95- *Personal Data:* b Chattanooga, Tenn, Sept 29, 47; m 70, Elaine M Lehr; c Sarah E, Charles S & Philip A. *Educ:* Univ of South, BA, 69; Oxford Univ, PhD(physics), 74. *Prof Exp:* Nat Res Coun postdoctoral fel, Chalk River Nuclear Lab, Atomic Energy Can Ltd, 74-76. *Mem:* Fel Am Phys Soc; Nat Asn Advan Sci. *Res:* The study of the spectroscopic properties of highly excited collective nuclear states and the dynamics of intermediate and high energy heavy ion nuclear reactions. *Mailing Add:* 128 Oklahoma Ave Oak Ridge TN 37830. *Fax:* 423-574-1268; *E-Mail:* beenejr@ornl.gov

BEER, ALAN E, OBSTETRICS & GYNECOLOGY, TRANSPLANTATION BIOLOGY. *Current Pos:* PROF OBSTET & GYNEC, CHICAGO MED SCH, 87-, PROF MICROBIOL & IMMUNOL, 87- *Personal Data:* b Milford, Ind, Apr 14, 37; m 59; c 4. *Educ:* Ind Univ, BS, 59, MD, 62. *Honors & Awards:* Carl Hartman Award, Am Fertil Soc, 70. *Prof Exp:* Intern, Methodist Grad Med Ctr, Ind, 62-63; surgeon, USPHS Div Indian Health, USPHS Indian Hosp, Tuba City, Ariz, 63-65; from resident to chief resident obstet & gynec, Hosp Univ Pa, 65-69; fel med genetics & obstet & gynec, Sch Med, Univ Pa, 68-70, asst prof, 70-71; from asst prof to assoc prof cell biol & obstet & gynec, Univ Tex Health Sci Ctr, Dallas, 71-77, prof, 77-79; prof gynec, Women's Hosp, Univ Mich, 79-87, chmn dept, 79-87. *Concurrent Pos:* Smith Kline & French foreign fel, Nigeria, 62-63. *Mem:* AAAS; Transplantation Soc; Soc Study Reprod; Am Col Obstet & Gynec; Soc Gynec Invest. *Res:* Immunobiology of mammalian reproduction; immunological significance of the mammary gland; elicitation and expression of immunity in the uterus; transplantation immunobiology. *Mailing Add:* Reprod Immunol Clin Univ Health Sci Chicago Med Sch 3333 Green Bay Rd North Chicago IL 60064-3095

BEER, ALBERT CARL, physics; deceased, see previous edition for last biography

BEER, BERNARD, behavioral pharmacology, for more information see previous edition

BEER, CHARLES, AGRICULTURAL ECONOMICS. *Current Pos:* RETIRED. *Personal Data:* b Le Sueur Co, Minn, Dec 18, 23. *Educ:* Univ Minn, St Paul, BS, 48; Mich State Univ, MS, 55, PhD(agr econ), 57. *Prof Exp:* Exten agent, Univ Minn, Anoka County, 49-53; asst prof agr econ, Mich State Univ, 57-62; prof, Univ Mo, Columbia, 62-64; specialist farm mgt, Exten Serv, USDA, 64-66, asst dir, 66-68, dir agr prod, Exten Serv, 68-74, dir independent family owned farm prog, 74-78, chief, Current & Future Priorities Staff, Sci & Educ Admin, 78-80, dep adminr, 81-85. *Mem:* Am Soc Farm Mgr & Rural Appraisers; Am Agr Econ Asn; Am Soc Agr Consult; World Futures Soc. *Mailing Add:* 490 M St SW Washington DC 20024

BEER, COLIN GORDON, HISTORY & PHILOSOPHY OF ETHOLOGY. *Current Pos:* assoc prof, 64-69, prof, 69-80, PROF II PSYCHOL, RUTGERS UNIV, 80- *Personal Data:* b Waipukurau, NZ, Mar 13, 33; m 59, Jeanette Scott; c Stephen & Jeremy. *Educ:* Univ Otago, NZ, BSc, 54, MSc, 56; Oxford Univ, DPhil, 60. *Hon Degrees:* MA, Oxford Univ, 70. *Prof Exp:* Jr lectr zool, Univ Otago, 56; sci officer, Ministry of Aviation, UK, 59-60; lectr, Univ Otago, 62-64. *Concurrent Pos:* Fel, Inst Animal Behav, Rutgers Univ, 60-61; co-ed, Animal Behav Monographs, 67-73; mem, Psychobiol Adv Panel, NSF, 68-69 & 70-72; lectr & tutorial fel zool, Oxford Univ, 69-70; consult ed, J Comp & Physiol Psychol, 69-80; assoc ed, Advan Study Behav, 73-92, Animal Learning & Behav, 76-77; mem, Int Ethological Comt, 74-81. *Mem:* Am Ornithologists Union; Animal Behav Soc; Soc Philos & Psychol. *Res:* Breeding biology and social behavior of birds, concentrating on aspects of communication and social development in gulls; conceptual and historical aspects of ethology. *Mailing Add:* Dept Psychol Rutgers Univ Newark Campus Newark NJ 07102. *Fax:* 973-648-1102; *E-Mail:* beer@andromeda.rutgers.edu

BEER, FERDINAND P(IERRE), MECHANICS. *Current Pos:* EMER UNIV DISTINGUISHED PROF, LEHIGH UNIV, 84- *Personal Data:* b Binic, France, Aug 8, 15; nat US; m 40; c 2. *Educ:* Col Geneva, BachD, 33; Univ Geneva, licence, 35, PhD(potential theory), 37; Univ Paris, licence, 38. *Prof Exp:* Instr math, Goddard Col, 41-42 & Univ Kansas City, 42-43; asst prof physics, Williams Col, Mass, 43-46, asst prof math, 46-47; from asst prof to assoc prof, 47-51, head dept mech, Lehigh, Univ, 57-68, prof mech, 51-68, chmn dept mech & mech eng, 68-84. *Concurrent Pos:* Consult, Sprauge Elec Co, 45-47, Fed Civil Defense Admin, 51-52 & Boeing Airplane Co, 56-57. *Mem:* Am Math Soc; Am Soc Eng Educ; Am Soc Mech Engrs; Sigma Xi. *Res:* Potential theory; mechanics; vibrations; stochastic processes. *Mailing Add:* 2485 Hickory Lane Coopersburg PA 18036

BEER, GEORGE ATHERLEY, NUCLEAR PHYSICS, INTERMEDIATE ENERGY PHYSICS. *Current Pos:* from asst prof to assoc prof, 69-84, PROF NUCLEAR PHYSICS, UNIV VICTORIA, 85- *Personal Data:* b Salmon Arm, BC, Jan 3, 35; m 94, Helen Tuele; c Theresa. *Educ:* Univ BC, BASc, 57, MSc, 59; Univ Sask, PhD(nuclear physics), 66. *Prof Exp:* Res officer reactor physics, Atomic Energy Can Ltd, 59-61; Nat Res Coun fel nuclear physics, Inst Nuclear Physics, Darmstadt Tech Univ, 67-69. *Concurrent Pos:* Vis scientist, Europ Orgn Nuclear Res, 75-76. *Mem:* Can Asn Physicists. *Res:* Neutron gas scintillation spectroscopy; low-power reactor; nuclear structure investigations using inelastic electron scattering; intermediate energy physics and accelerator design. *Mailing Add:* Dept Physics Univ Victoria Box 1700 Victoria BC V8W 2Y2 Can. *Fax:* 250-721-7715

BEER, JANOS MIKLOS, COMBUSTION SCIENCE & TECHNOLOGY, POWER GENERATION TECHNOLOGY. *Current Pos:* prof, 76-93, dir, Combustion Res Facil, 79-93, EMER PROF CHEM & FUEL ENG, DEPT CHEM ENG, MASS INST TECHNOL, 93- *Personal Data:* m 44, Marta Csato. *Educ:* Budapest Tech Univ, BEng, 50; Sheffield Univ, PhD(chem eng & fuel technol), 60, DSc, 68. *Hon Degrees:* Dr, Univ Miskolc, 87; Budapest Tech Univ, 97. *Honors & Awards:* Moody Award, Am Soc Mech Engrs, 65, Percy Nicholls Gold Medal, 88; Melchett Medal, Inst Energy, London, 85; Alfred Egerton Gold Medal, Combustioin Inst, 86; Coal Sci Gold Medal, Brit Coal Utilization Res Asn, 86; Axel Axelson Johnson Medal, Royal Swed Acad Eng Sci, 95. *Prof Exp:* Head, Res Sta, Int Flame Res Found, Ijmuiden, Holland, 60-63; prof fuel sci, Pa State Univ, 63-65; prof & head, Dept Chem Eng, Univ Sheffield, Eng, 65-76. *Concurrent Pos:* Supt res, Int Flame Res Found, Ijmuiden, Holland, 72-89; chmn, Clean Coal Utilization China Proj, Nat Acad Eng, 87-88; mem, Nat Coal Coun, 93- *Mem:* Fel Royal Acad Eng; fel Am Soc Mech Eng; sr fel Inst Energy Eng; foreign mem Finnish Acad Eng; hon mem Hungarian Acad Sci; hon mem Hungarian Acad Eng. *Res:* Reduction of combustion generated pollution; reduction of nitrogen oxides emission from flames by combustion process modification; energy conservation by improved efficiency of electric power generation. *Mailing Add:* Mass Inst Technol 66-548 77 Massachusetts Ave Cambridge MA 02139

BEER, JOHN JOSEPH, HISTORY OF CHEMISTRY. *Current Pos:* asst prof, 61-63, ASSOC PROF HIST, UNIV DEL, 63- *Personal Data:* b Saarbrucken, Germany, July 17, 27;US citizen; m 51; c 4. *Educ:* Earlham Col, AB, 50; Univ Ill, MS, 52, MA, 54, PhD(hist), 56. *Prof Exp:* Asst prof hist, Hanover Col, 56-57; asst prof chem, E Ill Univ, 57-58; asst prof hist, Okla State Univ, 58-61. *Concurrent Pos:* Fulbright fel, 54- *Mem:* AAAS; Am Hist Asn; Hist Sci Soc; Soc Hist Technol; Soc Hist Alchemy & Chem. *Res:* History of chemistry and the chemical industry; history of appropriate technology. *Mailing Add:* 308 Apple Rd Newark DE 19711

BEER, MICHAEL, MOLECULAR BIOLOGY. *Current Pos:* from asst prof to assoc prof, 58-63, chmn dept, 74-79, PROF BIOPHYS, JOHNS HOPKINS UNIV, 63- *Personal Data:* b Budapest, Hungary, Feb 20, 26; m 54; c 3. *Educ:* Univ Toronto, BA, 49, MA, 50; Univ Manchester, PhD(phys chem), 53. *Prof Exp:* Instr physics, Univ Mich, 53-56; fel biophys, Nat Res Coun Can, 56-58. *Concurrent Pos:* NIH spec fel & chmn biophys training comt & sr fel, 67-68; mem, US Nat Comt of Int Union Pure & Appl Biophys, 74-; NATO fel, 75. *Mem:* Biophys Soc (pres, 75-76); Electron Micros Soc Am (pres, 80); AAAS; Sigma Xi. *Res:* Structure of biological macromolecules using optical methods; fine structure of cells; viruses and macromolecules as revealed by electron microscope. *Mailing Add:* Arts & Sci Johns Hopkins Univ 34th & Charles St Baltimore MD 21218

BEER, REINHARD, INFRARED SPECTROSCOPY. *Current Pos:* sr scientist, Jet Propulsion Lab, Calif Inst Technol, 63-67, group leader, 67-68, mem tech staff, 68-71, mgr atmospheric & oceanog sci, 90-92, GROUP SUPVR TROPOSPHERIC SCI, JET PROPULSION LAB, CALIF INST TECHNOL, 71-, SR RES SCIENTIST, 85- *Personal Data:* b Berlin, Ger, Nov 5, 35; m 60, Margaret A Taylor. *Educ:* Univ Manchester, BSc, 56, PhD(physics), 60. *Honors & Awards:* Except Sci Achievement Medal, NASA, 74, Group Achievement Award, 80 & 86. *Prof Exp:* Res asst physics, Univ Manchester, 56-60, sr res asst astron, 60-63. *Concurrent Pos:* Vis assoc prof astron, Univ Tex, Austin, 74. *Mem:* Optical Soc Am; Int Astron Union; Am Astron Soc; AAAS. *Res:* Application of infrared interference spectroscopy to physics and astronomy; Fourier spectroscopy of atmospheres. *Mailing Add:* Jet Propulsion Lab Space Sci Div 183/301 4800 Oak Grove Dr Pasadena CA 91109

BEER, ROBERT EDWARD, ENTOMOLOGY. *Current Pos:* from instr to prof, 50-88, chmn dept, 61-68 & 75-84, EMER PROF ENTON, UNIV KANS, 88- *Personal Data:* b Los Angeles, Calif, Apr 28, 18; m 41, Margaret Robey; c Kathleen. *Educ:* Univ Calif, BS, 47, MS, 48, PhD(entom), 50. *Prof Exp:* Res asst entom, Univ Calif, 47-49. *Concurrent Pos:* From assoc state entomologist to state entomologist, Kans, 53-63; from assoc prof to prof, Biol Sta, Univ Mich, 57-69; prof, Biol Sta, Univ Minn, 71-73 & 76, Eastern Mich Univ, 81. *Mem:* AAAS; Entom Soc Am; Soc Study Evolution (treas); Sigma Xi; Acarol Soc Am. *Res:* Biology and taxonomy of mites and sawflies; agricultural entomology. *Mailing Add:* Dept Entom Univ Kans Lawrence KS 66045

BEER, STEVEN VINCENT, PLANT PATHOLOGY. *Current Pos:* Asst prof, 69-77, ASSOC PROF PLANT PATH, CORNELL UNIV, 77- *Personal Data:* b Boston, Mass, July 19, 41; m 63; c 3. *Educ:* Cornell Univ, BS, 65; Univ Calif, Davis, PhD(plant path), 69. *Mem:* Am Phytopath Soc; AAAS; Am Soc Microbiol. *Res:* Epidemiology, physiology and control of plant diseases caused by bacteria with emphasis on fire blight; molecular genetics, physiology and ecology of phytopathogenic bacteria; biological control of phytopathogenic bacteria; biotechnology. *Mailing Add:* Dept Plant Path 334 Plant Sci Bldg Cornell Univ Ithaca NY 14853-0001

BEER, SYLVAN ZAVI, PHYSICAL CHEMISTRY. *Current Pos:* CONSULT, 88- *Personal Data:* b New York, NY, Feb 5, 29; m 52; c 2. *Educ:* Brooklyn Col, BS, 51; Polytech Inst Brooklyn, PhD(phys chem), 58. *Prof Exp:* Chemist, Hexagon Labs, 51-52; instr chem, New York Community Col, 55-57; Crucible Steel Co fel high temperature chem, Mellon Inst, 57-60 & 76-88; staff scientist, Crucible Steel Co Am, 60-62; sr engr, Dept Chem, Westinghouse Elec Corp, 62-64 & Solid State Phenomena Dept, 64-67; mgr res & develop, Special Metals Corp, 67-70; vpres technol, Technostruct Corp, 70-72; consult, 72-76; vpres to pres, Niagara Scientific, 76-88. *Concurrent Pos:* Dir, Mfr Assistance Ctr, Syracuse Univ. *Mem:* AAAS; Am Chem Soc;

Electrochem Soc; Am Soc Metals; Fedn Am Scientists; Sigma Xi. *Res:* High temperature chemistry; electrochemistry; air and water pollution; sensors/ monitors development, instrumentation, superionic conductors, energy storage; new product development. *Mailing Add:* 315 Scott Ave Syracuse NY 13224-1725. *Fax:* 315-446-7612; *E-Mail:* Bitnet: szbeer@suvm.acs.syr.edu

BEERBOWER, JAMES RICHARD, PALEONTOLOGY. *Current Pos:* chmn, 69-75 & 84-86, prof, 69-91, EMER PROF GEOL, STATE UNIV NY, BINGHAMPTON, 91- *Personal Data:* b Ft Wayne, Ind, Apr 5, 27; c 4. *Educ:* Univ Colo, BA, 49; Univ Chicago, PhD(paleozool), 54. *Prof Exp:* From instr to assoc prof geol, Lafayette Col, 53-64; prof, McMaster Univ, 64-69. *Mem:* Soc Econ Paleont & Mineral; Soc Vert Paleont; fel Geol Soc Am; Paleontologic Soc; Palaeontologic Asn. *Res:* Physiological paleoecology; paleoecology and evolution of terrestrial ecosystems; sedimentology of alluvial deposits and marine shales. *Mailing Add:* Dept Geol State Univ NY Binghamton NY 13902-6000. *Fax:* 607-777-2288

BEEREL, PETER ANTHONY, COMPUTER-AIDED DESIGN, ASYNCHRONOUS VERY LARGE SCALE INTEGRATION DESIGN. *Current Pos:* ASST PROF ELEC ENG, UNIV SOUTHERN CALIF, 94- *Personal Data:* b Buffalo, NY, June 13, 67. *Educ:* Princeton Univ, BSE, 89; Stanford Univ, MSE, 92, PhD(elec eng), 94. *Honors & Awards:* Cancer Award, NSF, 95; Charles E Molnar Award, Phillips & Sun Microsysts, 97. *Concurrent Pos:* Zumberge fel, Univ Southern Calif, 95; consult, Intel Corp, 95-; prin investr, NSF, 95-; co-prin investr, Semiconductor Res Asn, 97. *Mem:* Inst Elec & Electronics Engrs; Asn Comput Mach. *Res:* Very large scale integration design and computer-aided design of mixed asynchronous and synchronous circuits. *Mailing Add:* EEB 350 Elec Eng Systs Univ Southern Calif Los Angeles CA 90089-8001

BEERING, STEVEN CLAUS, EDUCATION ADMINISTRATION, MEDICINE. *Current Pos:* PRES, PURDUE UNIV, 83- *Personal Data:* b Berlin, Germany, Aug 20, 32; US citizen; m 56, Jane Pickering; c Peter, David & John. *Educ:* Univ Pittsburgh, BS, 54, MD, 58. *Hon Degrees:* DSc, Ind Cent Univ, 83, Univ Evansville, 84, Hanover Col, 86, Ramapo Col, 86, Anderson Col, 87 & Ind Univ, 88. *Honors & Awards:* Convocation Medal, Am Col Cardiol, 83. *Prof Exp:* Asst dean, Sch Med, Ind Univ, 69-70, assoc dean, 70-74, dir, Med Ctr, 74-83, dean, Sch Med, 74-83. *Concurrent Pos:* Consult, Indianapolis Vet Admin Hosp, St Vincent Hosp, Indianapolis; chmn, Ind Med Educ Bd, 74-83, Coun Deans, Asn Am Med Cols, 80-81, Asn Am Med Cols, 82-83. *Mem:* Nat Acad Sci Inst Med. *Mailing Add:* Off Pres Purdue Univ West Lafayette IN 47907-1031

BEERMAN, HERMAN, dermatology; deceased, see previous edition for last biography

BEERMANN, DONALD HAROLD, MEAT SCIENCE, PHYSIOLOGY. *Current Pos:* Asst prof, 78-84, ASSOC PROF ANIMAL SCI & FOOD SCI, CORNELL UNIV, 85- *Personal Data:* b Denison, Iowa, Oct 4, 49; m 75. *Educ:* Iowa State Univ, BS, 71; Univ Wis-Madison, MS, 74, PhD(muscle biol & human physiol), 76. *Concurrent Pos:* Wis Heart Asn fel, Muscle Biol Lab, Univ Wis, 76-77, fel neurophysiol, Sch Med, 77-78. *Mem:* Am Soc Animal Sci; Am Meat Sci Asn; Inst Food Technologists; AAAS; Am Inst Nutrit. *Res:* Meats processing; muscle physiology; muscle biochemistry; muscle growth and development; animal physiology and metabolism. *Mailing Add:* Dept Animal Sci B-53 Morrison Hall Cornell Univ Ithaca NY 14853-0001

BEERS, THOMAS WESLEY, FOREST MENSURATION. *Current Pos:* RETIRED. *Personal Data:* b Greensburg, Pa, Oct 23, 30; m 53; c 4. *Educ:* Pa State Univ, BS, 55, MS, 56; Purdue Univ, PhD(forest mgt), 60. *Prof Exp:* From instr to assoc prof, Purdue Univ, West Lafayette, 56-69, prof forestry, 69-91. *Mem:* Soc Am Foresters. *Res:* Forest mensuration techniques and instruments; inventory procedures and data processing methods, especially timber stand estimates by point sampling; forest management site productivity studies; computer programming of forestry problems. *Mailing Add:* 1134 Williams St State College PA 16801

BEERS, WILLIAM HOWARD, REPRODUCTIVE BIOLOGY, CELL BIOLOGY. *Current Pos:* chmn dept, 78-80, PROF, DEPT BIOL, NY UNIV, 78- *Personal Data:* b Panama City, Panama, June 19, 43; US citizen; div; c 1. *Educ:* Harvard Univ, AB, 65; Rockefeller Univ, PhD(life sci), 71. *Prof Exp:* Rockefeller Found fel, reproductive biol, Univ Ill, 71-73; from asst prof to assoc prof cell biol, Rockefeller Univ, 73-78. *Concurrent Pos:* Res career develop award, USPHS, Nat Inst Child Health & Human Develop, 77-78. *Res:* Mechanisms of ovarian function. *Mailing Add:* 10550 N Torrey Pine Rd BCC-506 La Jolla CA 92037

BEERS, YARDLEY, MOLECULAR SPECTROSCOPY, ATOMIC & MOLECULAR PHYSICS. *Current Pos:* RETIRED. *Personal Data:* b Philadelphia, Pa, Apr 2, 13; m 45, Dorothy N Sands; c G Jerome & Deborah Y (Jones). *Educ:* Yale Univ, BS, 34; Princeton Univ, MA, 37, PhD(physics), 41; Univ Colo, BA, 86. *Prof Exp:* Asst physics, Princeton Univ, 40; instr, NY Univ, 40-41 & Smith Col, 41-42; staff mem radiation lab, Mass Inst Technol, 42-45, res assoc, 46; from asst prof to prof physics, NY Univ, 46-61; chief millimeter wave res sect, Nat Bur Stand, 61-62, chief radio standards physics div, 62-68, consult, 68-79. *Concurrent Pos:* Consult, Brookhaven Nat Lab, 47-58; Fulbright grant, Nat Stand Lab, Australia & vis lectr, Univ Sydney, 56; vis lectr, Univ Colo, Boulder, 63-64 & 75; adj prof, Univ Denver, 65-67; vis prof, Colo State Univ, 67-68 & Univ Colo, Denver, 69; archeol vol, Peel Castle, Isle of Man, 85, 87. *Mem:* Inst Elec & Electronics Engrs; Sigma Xi; Am Asn Physics Teachers; fel Am Phys Soc; fel Explorers Club. *Res:* Direct determination of the charge of the beta particle; microwave and millimeter wave spectra of gases; stark effect; laser power and energy measurements; theory of radiation; double resonant antennas; classical radiation. *Mailing Add:* 740 Willowbrook Rd Boulder CO 80302-7437

BEERSTECHER, ERNEST, JR, biochemistry; deceased, see previous edition for last biography

BEERY, DWIGHT BEECHER, PHYSICS. *Current Pos:* from asst prof to assoc prof, 69-79, PROF PHYSICS, 79-, CHAIR, MANCHESTER COL, 86- *Personal Data:* b Troy, Ohio, Dec 5, 37; m 62; c 3. *Educ:* Manchester Col, BA, 59; Ind Univ, Bloomington, MS, 62; Mich State Univ, PhD(physics), 69. *Prof Exp:* Teaching asst physics, Ind Univ, Bloomington, 60-62; instr, Manchester Col, 62-64; teaching asst, Mich State Univ, 64-65, res asst, 65-69. *Mem:* Am Asn Physics Teachers; Am Phys Soc. *Res:* Nuclear physics gamma ray spectroscopy in the neutron deficient region. *Mailing Add:* Dept Physics Manchester Col North Manchester IN 46962

BEESE, RONALD ELROY, PHYSICAL CHEMISTRY, INORGANIC CHEMISTRY. *Current Pos:* From res chemist to sr res chemist, 51-67, res assoc, 67-78, SR RES ASSOC, BARRINGTON TECH CTR, AM CAN CO, 78- *Personal Data:* b Milwaukee, Wis, May 19, 29; m 54; c 2. *Educ:* Lawrence Col, BS, 51. *Mem:* Am Chem Soc; Nat Asn Corrosion Eng; Electrochem Soc. *Res:* Electrochemical corrosion research involving the evaluation of corrosion mechanisms related to products packaged in metallic containers. *Mailing Add:* 618 Concord Pl Barrington IL 60010

BEESLEY, EDWARD MAURICE, mathematics; deceased, see previous edition for last biography

BEESLEY, ROBERT CHARLES, INTESTINAL TRANSPORT, MEMBRANE TRANSPORT. *Current Pos:* ASSOC PROF GASTROINTESTINAL PHYSIOL, DEPT PHYSIOL & BIOPHYS, HEALTH SCI CTR, UNIV OKLA, 81- *Educ:* Univ Calif, Berkeley, PhD(physiol), 74. *Mailing Add:* Dept Physiol Univ Okla Health Sci Ctr PO Box 26901 Oklahoma City OK 73190-0001

BEESON, EDWARD LEE, JR, MOLECULAR SPECTROSCOPY. *Current Pos:* oceanogr, 84-94,PHYS SCIENTIST, NAVAL OCEANOG OFF, 94- *Personal Data:* b Bartow, Fla, Mar 9, 28; m 59, Louise Colledge; c Benjamin, Bradley & Matthew. *Educ:* Emory Univ, BA, 49, MS, 50; Ga Inst Technol, PhD(physics), 60. *Prof Exp:* Instr physics, Chattanooga Univ, 50-51 & Ga Inst Technol, 54-59; from asst prof to prof physics, Univ New Orleans, 60-83. *Concurrent Pos:* NIH res grant, 61-66. *Res:* Microwave spectroscopy. *Mailing Add:* 7222 Claridge Ct New Orleans LA 70127

BEESON, JUSTIN LEO, FUEL CHEMISTRY, SYNTHETIC FUELS. *Current Pos:* HEAD ENERGY SYSTS, MIDWEST RES INST, 81- *Personal Data:* b Des Moines, Iowa, Sept 6, 30. *Educ:* Iowa State Univ, BS, 54, MS, 69, PhD(chem eng), 73. *Prof Exp:* Develop chemist, Goodyear Tire & Rubber Co, 59-66; res assoc, Iowa State Univ, 73-75; eng supvr, Inst Gas Technol, 75-81. *Mem:* Am Chem Soc; Am Inst Chem Engrs; Sigma Xi; Nat Soc Prof Engrs. *Res:* Synthetic fuels from coal, oil shale and biomass; hydrocarbon processing; coal beneficiation. *Mailing Add:* 2107 Peach St Morgantown WV 26505-2921

BEESON, PAUL BRUCE, MEDICINE, INFECTIOUS DISEASES. *Current Pos:* prof, 74-81, EMER PROF MED, UNIV WASH, 81- *Personal Data:* b Livingston, Mont, Oct 18, 08; m 42, Barbara Neal; c John, Peter & Judy. *Educ:* McGill Univ, MDCM, 33. *Hon Degrees:* DSc, Emory Univ, 68, McGill Univ, 71, Albany Med Col, 75 & Yale Univ, 75. *Prof Exp:* Intern, Univ Pa Hosp, 33-35; from asst resident to resident, Rockefeller Inst Hosp, 37-39; resident med, Peter Bent Brigham Hosp, Boston, 39-40; chief physician, Harvard Univ Field Hosp, Unit, Eng, 41-42; from asst prof to prof med, Med Sch, Emory Univ, 42-52, chmn dept, 46-52; prof & chmn dept, Med Sch, Yale Univ, 52-65; Nuffield prof clin med, Oxford Univ, 65-74; distinguished physician, US Vet Admin, 74-81. *Mem:* Nat Acad Sci; Am Soc Clin Invest; Soc Exp Biol & Med; Asn Am Physicians. *Res:* Infectious diseases; immunology; clinical medicine. *Mailing Add:* 21013 NE 122nd St Redmond WA 98053

BEESTMAN, GEORGE BERNARD, AGRICULTURAL CHEMISTRY, WEED SCIENCE. *Current Pos:* SR RES ASSOC, DUPONT, 90- *Personal Data:* b Hammond, Wis, July 17, 39; m 65; c 2. *Educ:* Wis State Univ, River Falls, BS, 61; Univ Wis, MS, 67, PhD(soil chem), 69. *Prof Exp:* Sr res chemist, Monsanto Agr Prod Co, 68-73, from res specialist to sr res specialist, 73-89; dir, Res & Develop, United Indust, 89-90. *Concurrent Pos:* Mem, Comt Publs, Am Soc Testing & Mat. *Mem:* Am Soc Agron; Soil Sci Soc Am; Sigma Xi; AAAS; Weed Sci Soc Am; Am Chem Soc; Am Soc Testing & Mat. *Res:* Fertilizer nutrient imbalance effects on crop quality; influence of soil properties on insecticide uptake and translocation by plants; herbicide dissipation modes in soils; pesticide formulation; pesticides suspension formulations; dry flowable pesticide formulations; microencapsulation; granted 5 US and over 140 foreign patents. *Mailing Add:* DuPont Exp Sta Bldg 402 Rm 2108 Wilmington DE 19880. *Fax:* 302-695-7804

BEETON, ALFRED MERLE, LIMNOLOGY OF GREATLAKES. *Current Pos:* dir, Great Lakes & Marine Waters Ctr, 76-86, PROF ATMOSPHERIC & OCEANIC SCI, COL ENG & PROF NATURAL RESOURCES, UNIV MICH, ANN ARBOR, 76-; ACT CHIEF SCIENTIST, NAT OCEANIC & ATMOSPHERIC ADMIN, 96- *Personal Data:* b Denver, Colo, Aug 15, 27; m 45, 66, Ruth E Holland; c Maureen A, Heather A, Celeste N, Jonathan E & Daniel P. *Educ:* Univ Mich, BS, 52, MS, 54, PhD(zool), 58. *Hon Degrees:* DSc, Univ Wis, 96. *Honors & Awards:* James W Moffett Publ Award, US Bur Com Fisheries Lab, Mich, 67. *Prof Exp:* Instr biol, Wayne State Univ, 56-57; chief environ res prog, US Bur Com Fisheries, 57-66; prof zool & asst dir, Ctr Great Lakes Studies, Univ Wis-Milwaukee, 66-76, assoc dean grad sch, 73-76. *Concurrent Pos:* Lectr civil eng, Univ Mich, 62-66; mem planning comt, Int Symp on Eutrophication, Nat Acad Sci, 65-68 & chmn panel on freshwater life & wildlife, Comt Water Qual Criteria, 70-72, chmn, Int Environ Prog Comm, 80-83; consult, US Army CEngrs & Metrop Sanit Dist Greater Chicago, 68-79, Greater Cleveland Growth Asn, 70 & US Environ Protection Agency, 72-76; dir, Great Lakes Environ Res Lab, 86-96; comnr, Toxic Substances Control Comn, Mich, 87-89. *Mem:* Am Soc Limnol & Oceanog (treas, 62-81); Am Soc Zool; Int Soc Limnol; Int Asn Great Lakes Res. *Res:* Limnology of the Great Lakes; vertical migration and related behavior of planktonic Crustacea; limnology of man-made tropical lakes. *Mailing Add:* Great Lakes Environ Res Lab 2205 Commonwealth Blvd Ann Arbor MI 48105. *E-Mail:* al.beeton@noaa.gov

BEEVERS, HARRY, BIOCHEMISTRY. *Current Pos:* PROF BIOL, UNIV CALIF, SANTA CRUZ, 69- *Personal Data:* b Durham, Eng, Jan 10, 24; nat US; m 49, Jean Sykes; c Michael. *Educ:* Univ Durham, BSc, 44, PhD, 47. *Hon Degrees:* DSc, Purdue Univ, 71, Univ Newcastle, Eng, 74 & Nagoya Univ, Japan, 86. *Honors & Awards:* Fulbright lectr, Australia, 62; Stephen Hales Award, Am Soc Plant Physiol, 70; Von Humboldt Preistrager, 87. *Prof Exp:* Asst plant physiol, Oxford Univ, 46-48, chief res asst, 48-50; vis prof, Purdue Univ, 50, from asst prof to prof, 51-69. *Concurrent Pos:* Demonstr & tutor, Oxford Univ, 46-50; NSF sr fel, 63-64. *Mem:* Nat Acad Sci; Am Soc Biol Chemists; Am Soc Plant Physiol (pres, 62); hon mem Ger Bot Soc; fel Am Acad Arts & Sci; Nat Acad Lincei; Acad Europ. *Res:* Plant metabolism. *Mailing Add:* Biol Dept Univ Calif Santa Cruz CA 95060

BEEVERS, LEONARD, PLANT PHYSIOLOGY. *Current Pos:* PROF BOT, UNIV OKLA, 71-, CHMN DEPT, 81- *Personal Data:* b Co Durham, Eng, Aug 7, 34; m 60, Patricia Owen; c Richard N & Kevin J. *Educ:* Univ Durham, BSc, 58; Univ Wales, PhD(agr bot), 61. *Prof Exp:* Res assoc agron, Univ Ill, Urbana-Champaign, 61-63, from asst prof to assoc prof hort, 63-71. *Mem:* Am Soc Plant Physiol (secy, 77-81, pres-elect, 81, pres, 82). *Res:* Intermediary nitrogen metabolism with specific reference to reserve protein accumulation; glycoprotein biosynthesis and post translational modification and intracellular transport of proteins, general plant physiology; nitrate assimilation. *Mailing Add:* Dept Bot & Microbiol Univ Okla Norman OK 73019. *Fax:* 405-325-7619; *E-Mail:* lbeevers@ou.edu

BEEVIS, DAVID, HUMAN FACTORS. *Current Pos:* tech officer, 81-83, DEFENCE SCIENTIST, DEFENCE & CIVIL INST ENVIRON MED, CAN, 83- *Personal Data:* b Surrey, UK, July 19, 40; Can citizen; m 61; c 2. *Educ:* Royal Aircraft Estab, Tech Col Farnborough, Eng, cert, 61, 62; Col Aeronaut Cranfield, Eng, MSc, 64. *Prof Exp:* Sci asst ergonomics, Royal Aircraft Establishment, UK, 73; ergonomist, Ergonomics Lab, EMI Electronics Ltd, 74-76 & 78-81; human eng specialist, Canadair Ltd, 77-78. *Concurrent Pos:* Vis scientist, TNO Inst fur Zintuigsfhysiologie, The Netherlands, 80-81; consult, Ergonomics Soc, UK, 79, soc rep, Comt Conf City in the year 2000, 69-70, asst ed, Newslett, 69-71; Can rep, NATO AC243, Workshop on Applications Systs, Ergonomics to Weapons Systs Dept & RMC Shrivenham, 84; mem, Defense & Civil Inst Environ Med, univ grants comt human eng, 73-76. *Mem:* Human Factors Soc; Ergonomics Soc UK; Human Factors Asn Can (secy, 79-80). *Res:* Study of human performance as it affects the design of modern systems, and the study of the most effective means of incorporating human performance data into systems design. *Mailing Add:* 140 Newton Dr Willowdale ON M2M 2N3 Can

BEEZHOLD, DONALD H, CELLULAR IMMUNOLOGY. *Current Pos:* asst res scientist & dir, 88-92, assoc res scientist & dir, 92- 96, SR RES SCIENTIST & DIR, LAB MICROPHAGE BIOL, GUTHRIE RES INST, 96- *Personal Data:* b Chicago, Ill, Oct 17, 55; m 77, Elizabeth W Verwoerd; c Brain, Eric & Kevin. *Educ:* Trinity Christian Col, BA, 77; Univ Ill Med Ctr, MS, 79, PhD(anat & cell biol), 81. *Prof Exp:* Instr anat, Med Col Ga, 82-84, asst prof, Dept Anat, 84-88. *Concurrent Pos:* Consult, Regent Hosp Prod Ltd, London Int Group, Habash, Habash & Davis. *Mem:* Am Asn Immunologists; Int Endotoxin Soc; NY Acad Sci; Soc Leukocyte Biol; Am Col Allergy Asthma & Immunol; Clin Immunol Soc. *Res:* Signal transduction mechanisms involved in monocyte tumor neurosis factor secretion and allergen identification in latex allergy. *Mailing Add:* Lab Macrophage Biol Guthrie Res Inst Guthrie Found One Guthrie Sq Sayre PA 18840. *Fax:* 717-882-4666; *E-Mail:* dbeezhol@inet.guthrie.org

BEFELER, BENJAMIN, CARDIOVASCULAR DISEASE. *Current Pos:* from instr to asst prof, 69-74, ASSOC PROF MED, SCH MED, UNIV MIAMI, 74- *Personal Data:* b San Jose, Costa Rica, Dec 8, 39; US citizen; m 65; c 3. *Educ:* Nat Univ Mex, MD, 63, Univ Miami, MBA, 93; Am Bd Internal Med, dipl, 74, cert cardiovasc dis, 75. *Prof Exp:* Intern, Span Hosp & Nat Univ Mex, 62; intern med, Mt Sinai Hosp, Cleveland, Ohio, 64, asst resident, 65; resident med, Vet Admin Hosp & Case Western Reserve Univ Hosp, 66-67, resident cardiol, 67-68; USPHS fel med, Med Sch, Univ Calif, San Francisco, 68-69; chief cardiocasc lab, Vet Admin Hosp, Miami, 71-78. *Concurrent Pos:* Preceptor clin diag, Med Sch, Case Western Reserve Univ, 66-68; staff cardiologist, Mt Sinai Hosp, Miami Beach, 69-71; staff physician, Cardiopulmonary Lab, Div Cardiol, Dept Internal Med, Mt Sinai Hosp Greater Miami, 69-71; attend physician, Univ Miami Hosps & Clins, 71- & Univ Miami Jackson Mem Hosp, 71-; civilian consult cardiol, USAF Hosp, Homestead, Fla, 72-; ed consult, Chest, 74; mem res & educ comt, Vet Admin Hosp, Miami, 74-76; fel clin coun, Am Heart Asn; chief cardiol, Cedars Med Ctr, Miami, 86-88, chief staff, 89-90, mem, bd dirs, 89-91. *Mem:* Fel Am Col Physicians; fel Am Col Chest Physicians; fel Am Col Cardiol; fel Am Col Angiol; Am Heart Asn. *Res:* Mechanism of antiarrhythmias in patients with coronary artery disease; Wolff-Parkinson-White syndrome and the role of arrhythmias in determining patient prognosis; natural course of coronary artery disease. *Mailing Add:* 1321 NW 14th St No 202 Miami FL 33125

BEFUS, A(LBERT) DEAN, MUCOSAL IMMUNOPARASITOLOGY, MAST CELL BIOLOGY. *Current Pos:* DIR PULMONARY RES & ASTRA CHAIR ASTHMA, UNIV ALTA. *Personal Data:* b Edmonton, Alta, Oct 8, 48; m 70; c 2. *Educ:* Univ Alta, Can, BSc, 70; Univ Toronto, MSc, 72; Univ Glasgow, PhD(immunoparasitol), 75. *Honors & Awards:* Young Canadian Res Award, Int Develop Res Ctr, 83; Henry Baldwin Ward Medal, Am Soc Parasitol, 88. *Prof Exp:* Asst prof mucosal immunol, Dept Path, McMaster Univ, 78-82, assoc prof immunol & parasitol, dept path, 82-85; from assoc prof to prof microbiol & infectious dis, Univ Calgary, Alta, 86- *Concurrent Pos:* Univ Toronto, Open fel, 70-71; Ontario Grad Scholar, 71-72, Commonwealth Scholar, 74-75; Med Res Coun Can, fel, 75-78; Rockefeller Fel Trop & Geog Med, 80-84; vis scientist, Med Res Coun Lab, The Gambia, WAfrica, 83; Alta Heritage Found, Med Res Scholar, 85- *Mem:* Am Asn Immunologists; Can Soc Immunol; Brit Soc Parasitol; Am Soc Trop Med Hyg; Am Soc Parasitol; Soc Muscosal Immunol. *Res:* Mechanisms of host resistance at lung and intestine; ontogeny, molecular differentiation and functional heterogeneity of mast cells during neuroimmunology. *Mailing Add:* Dept Med Rm 574 HMRC Univ Alta Edmonton AB T6G 2S2 Can. *Fax:* 403-492-5329

BEGA, ROBERT V, PLANT PATHOLOGY, PHYTOPATHOLOGY. *Current Pos:* RETIRED. *Personal Data:* b Milford, Mass, Aug 17, 28; m 72, Joan Fisher; c Cyrise. *Educ:* Univ Calif, BS, 53, PhD(path), 57. *Prof Exp:* Plant path, Univ Calif, Berkeley, 55-85, lectr, 56-85, assoc, Exp Sta, 57-85. *Concurrent Pos:* Plant pathologist, Pac Southwest Forest & Range Exp Sta, USDA, 56-88; consult, Hawaii Dept Agr, 62-73, Environ Protection Agency, 68-76, NASA, 70-85, Univ Hawaii, 72-73, USDA, 73, Europ Common Mkt, 84 & private consult 85-; adj prof, Univ Hawaii, 72-73. *Mem:* Am Phytopath Soc; Am Forestry Asn; Sigma Xi; Int Soc Plant Path. *Res:* Biology of rust fungi; root disease fungi; mycorrhiza; physiology of host-parasite relationship; aerobiology, microclimatology; biological control; air pollution. *Mailing Add:* 21275 Clydesdale Rd Grass Valley CA 95949. *E-Mail:* bega@netshel.net

BEGALA, ARTHUR JAMES, PHYSICAL CHEMISTRY. *Current Pos:* CHEMIST, NALCO CHEM CO, 84- *Personal Data:* b Newark, NJ, Sept 10, 40; m 66; c 2. *Educ:* Lehigh Univ, BS, 62; Rutgers Univ, PhD(chem), 71. *Prof Exp:* Chemist, E I du Pont de Nemours & Co, 62-63; res asst chem, Rutgers Univ, 64-68; sr res chemist, Am Cyanamid Co, 68-84. *Mem:* Am Chem Soc; Sigma Xi. *Res:* Synthesis and characterization of polyelectrolytes and investigation of various polymer interactions with specific metallic and oxide substrates. *Mailing Add:* 833 Thornapple Dr Naperville IL 60540-6346

BEGAY, FREDERICK, PHYSICS. *Current Pos:* staff mem x-ray spectros, 71-72, STAFF MEM LASER FUSION, LOS ALAMOS SCI LAB, UNIV CALIF, 72- *Personal Data:* b Towaco, Colo, July 2, 32; m 52; c 7. *Educ:* Univ NMex, BS, 61, MS, 63, PhD(physics), 72. *Prof Exp:* Res physicist, Air Force Weapons Lab, Kirtland AFB, NMex, 63-65; res assoc high energy neutron physics, Univ NMex, 65-71. *Concurrent Pos:* Mem, Nat Res Coun, 72- *Mem:* Am Phys Soc. *Res:* High energy gamma ray physics; solar wind physics; high energy neutron physics; plasma physics in exploding wire systems and other high energy pulsed power systems; satellite instrumentation; design and physics of high energy vacuum systems. *Mailing Add:* 2480 36th St Los Alamos NM 87544

BEGELL, WILLIAM, TWO PHASE HEAT TRANSFER, THERMODYNAMIC PROPERTIES. *Current Pos:* PRES, BEGELL HOUSE, INC PUBL, 91- *Personal Data:* b Wilno, Poland, May 18, 28; US citizen; m 48, Esther Kessler; c Frederick P (deceased) & Alissa M. *Educ:* City Col New York, BChE, 53; Polytech Inst Brooklyn, MChE, 58. *Hon Degrees:* DSc, Acad Sci BSSR, Minsk, 84. *Honors & Awards:* Distinguished Serv Award, Am Soc Mech Engrs, 92. *Prof Exp:* Dir, Heat Transfer Res Facil, Columbia Univ, 55-59; exec pres, Scripta technica, 59-73; pres, Hemisphere Publ, 74-91. *Concurrent Pos:* Ed & publ, Hemisphere Publ Corp, 74-; vis prof, George Washington Univ, 76-77; mem, Bd Commun, Am Soc Mech Engrs, 80-, bd Asn Am Publ, 80-88 & Eng Libr, 88-; chmn, Publ Develop Bd, NY Acad Sci, 90-; pres & chief scientist, Byelocorp Sci, Inc. *Mem:* Fel Am Soc Mech Engrs; Am Inst Chem Engrs; Am Chem Soc; Am Astronaut Soc. *Res:* Heat transfer in two phase systems, specifically in nuclear reactors; safety in thermal hydraulic systems; measurements in high temperature and high pressure power and chemical systems. *Mailing Add:* 46 E 91st St Apt 6A New York NY 10128

BEGELMAN, MITCHELL CRAIG, HIGH ENERGY ASTROPHYSICS, ASTROPHYSICAL GAS DYNAMICS & PLASMA ASTROPHYSICS. *Current Pos:* from asst prof to assoc prof, 82-91, PROF ASTROPHYS, UNIV COLO, BOULDER, 91-, FEL, JOINT INST LAB ASTROPHYS, 84- *Personal Data:* b New York, NY, Mar 14, 53; m 87, Claire M Hay. *Educ:* Harvard Univ, AB & AM, 74; Univ Cambridge, Eng, PhD(astrophys), 78. *Honors & Awards:* Presidential Young Investr Award, NSF, 84; Helen B Warner Prize, Am Astron Soc, 88. *Prof Exp:* Sci & Eng Res Coun fel, Univ

Cambridge, Eng, 78-79 & 81-82; res astronr, Univ Calif, Berkeley, 79-82. *Concurrent Pos:* Vis scientist, N Copernicus Astron Ctr, Warsaw, Poland, 80. *Mem:* Am Astron Soc; Int Astron Union; fel Royal Astron Soc. *Res:* Theoretical research on a wide range of topics in astrophysics. *Mailing Add:* Joint Inst Lab Astrophys Univ Colo Boulder CO 80309-0440. *Fax:* 303-492-5235; *E-Mail:* mitch@jila.colorado.edu

BEGG, DAVID A, CELL BIOLOGY, CELL MOTILITY. *Current Pos:* asst prof anat, 79-85, ASSOC PROF ANAT & CELL BIOL, MED SCH, HARVARD UNIV, 85- *Personal Data:* b Lawrence, Mass, Dec 16, 43; m 68; c 2. *Educ:* Colby Col, AB, 65; Univ Pa, MS, 68, PhD(cell biol), 75. *Prof Exp:* Fel, Univ Va, 76-79. *Mem:* Develop Biol Soc; Am Soc Cell Biol; Am Asn Anatomists; AAAS; NY Acad Sci. *Res:* Control of the organization of actin in the egg cortex; mechanism of fertilization; mechanism of cell division; actomyosin-based aspects of cell locomotion. *Mailing Add:* Univ Alberta Fac Med 5-25 Med Sci Bldg Edmonton AB T6G 2H7 Can

BEGGS, ALAN H, III, HUMAN MOLECULAR GENETICS. *Current Pos:* fel pediat, Harvard Med Sch, Childrens Hosp, 88-92, instr, Med Sch, 92-93, RES ASSOC MED, CHILDRENS HOSP, 92-, ASST PROF PEDIAT, HARVARD MED SCH, 93- *Personal Data:* b New York, NY, Sept 1, 60. *Educ:* Cornell Univ, AB, 82; Johns Hopkins Univ, PhD(human genetics), 87; Am Board Med Genetics, Cert, 93. *Prof Exp:* Fel pediat genetics, Johns Hopkins Sch Med, 87-88. *Mem:* Am Soc Human Genetics; Am Soc Microbiol; AAAS. *Res:* Understanding the molecular basis for human genetic diseases and developing improved diagnostic and therapeutic methods; neuromuscular, neurologic and opthamologic diseases. *Mailing Add:* 126 Langdon St Newton MA 02158. *Fax:* 617-735-7588; *E-Mail:* beggs@rascal.harvard.edu

BEGGS, WILLIAM H, ANTIFUNGAL DRUGS. *Current Pos:* RES MICROBIOLOGIST, GEN MED RES SERV, VET AFFAIRS MED CTR, 65- *Personal Data:* b Ft Dodge, Iowa, Feb 19, 35; m 57, Nancy F Ost; c John & Margaret. *Educ:* Univ Minn, BA, 56; Kans State Univ, MS, 59; Univ Cincinnati, PhD(microbiol), 64. *Prof Exp:* Jr scientist, Univ Minn, 59-61. *Mem:* Fel Am Inst Chemists; Am Soc Microbiol; Am Chem Soc. *Res:* Biological activities; modes of action; chemical properties and chemotherapeutic potentials of antifungal drugs. *Mailing Add:* Gen Med Res Serv 151 Vet Affairs Med Ctr Minneapolis MN 55417-2300

BEGGS, WILLIAM JOHN, DESIGN OF EXPERIMENTS, REGRESSION ANALYSIS. *Current Pos:* sr mathematician, 70-82, FEL MATHEMATICIAN, BETTIS ATOMIC POWER LAB, WESTINGHOUSE ELEC CORP, 82-, ADV SCIENTIST, 96- *Personal Data:* b Pittsburgh, Pa, Apr 9, 42; m 65; c 3. *Educ:* Allegheny Col, BS, 64; Univ Wis, MS, 66, PhD(statist), 69. *Honors & Awards:* George Westinghouse Signature Award of Excellence, 89. *Prof Exp:* Res statistician, Chem Div, Am Cyanamid Co, 69-70. *Concurrent Pos:* Lectr, Bettis Reactor Eng Sch. *Mem:* Am Statist Asn. *Res:* Application of Kalman filter to engineering problems; design and analysis of accelerated test data. *Mailing Add:* 933 Bridgewater Dr Pittsburgh PA 15216

BEGIN-HEICK, NICOLE, CELL BIOLOGY, METABOLISM. *Current Pos:* assoc prof, Univ Ottawa, 72-80, prof, 80-94, vpres res, Sch Med, 87-89, dean grad studies res, 89-94, EXEC DIR, ONT COUN GRAD STUDIES & ONT COUN UNIV RES, DEPT BIOCHEM, FAC MED, UNIV OTTAWA, 96- *Personal Data:* b Que, Can, Oct, 30, 37; m 65, Hans Heick; c Caroline & Christopher. *Educ:* Laval Univ, BScD, 57; Cornell Univ, MS, 60; McGill Univ, PhD(biochem), 65. *Honors & Awards:* Jeanne Manery-Fisher Award, Can Soc Biochem & Cellular & Molecular Biol, 96. *Prof Exp:* Fel biochem, Univ Toronto, 64-65; fel physiol, Duke Univ, 65-67; from asst prof to assoc prof biochem, Laval Univ, 67-72. *Concurrent Pos:* Mem, Med Res Coun Can, 77-84; coordr, Nutrit Prog, Dept Biochem, Univ Ottawa, 77-84; Nat Sci Eng Res Coun Can, 87-92; vpres, Can Fedn Biol Soc, 91-92, pres, 92-93; vchair, Ont Coun Grad Studies, 92-93, chair, 93-94. *Mem:* Am Inst Nutrit; Can Soc Biochem Molecular & Cell Biol; Can Soc Nutrit Sci. *Res:* Metabolic aberations in experimental obesity; mechanisms of regulation of Adipocyte Adenylate Cyclase; mechanisms of insulin secretion; adipocyte growth and differentiation. *Mailing Add:* Dept Biochem Fac Med Univ Ottawa 451 Smyth Rd Ottawa ON K1N 6N5 Can. *Fax:* 613-562-5440

BEGLAU, DAVID ALAN, AMORPHOUS SILICON THIN FILM DEVICES, MATERIALS SCIENCE & DEPOSITION TECHNIQUES. *Current Pos:* Scientist, 81-85, SR SCIENTIST, ENERGY CONVERSION DEVICES, INC, 85- *Personal Data:* b Detroit, Mich, Jan 11, 58; m 84; c 2. *Educ:* Mich Technol Univ, BS, 81. *Res:* Solid-state physics; novel solid-state devices; silicon photovoltaics; chalcogenide thermoelectric devices; chalcogenide threshold switching devices; memory devices; liquid crystal displays; silicon transistors and diodes. *Mailing Add:* 47 Mechanic St Oxford MI 48371

BEGLEITER, HENRI, PSYCHOPHYSIOLOGY, NEUROPHYSIOLOGY. *Current Pos:* Res assoc neurophysiol, State Univ NY, 64-66, asst prof psychiat & psychophysiol, 67-72, assoc prof psychiat, 72-75, DIR, NEURODYNAMICS LAB, 66-, PROF PSYCHIAT & NEUROSCI, SCH MED, STATE UNIV NY, DOWNSTATE MED CTR, 75- *Personal Data:* b Nimes, France, Sept 11, 35; US citizen; m 63; c 2. *Educ:* New Sch Social Res, PhD(psychophysiol), 67. *Honors & Awards:* Thorp Award; Isaacson Prize. *Mem:* Fel AAAS; Am Psychol Asn; Soc Psychophysiol Res; NY Acad Sci; fel Am Electroencephalogram Soc; Am Col Neurosychopharmacol. *Res:* Neurophysiological correlates of brain dysfunction. *Mailing Add:* Dept Psychiat State Univ NY Health Sci Ctr 450 Clarkson Ave Box 1203 Brooklyn NY 11203-2012

BEGLEY, JAMES ANDREW, metallurgical engineering, mechanical engineering, for more information see previous edition

BEGLEY, R T, NUCLEAR SCIENCE. *Current Pos:* CONSULT, SAVANNAH RIVER LAB, AIKEN, SC. *Mailing Add:* 101 Red Oak Lane Aiken SC 29803

BEGOVAC, PAUL C, CELLULAR BIOLOGY, CELLULAR INTERACTIONS. *Current Pos:* proj mgr med devices, 78-82, RES SCIENTIST, W L GORE & ASSOC, INC, 93- *Personal Data:* b Marquette, Mich, Mar 10, 56. *Educ:* Northern Ariz Univ, BSc, 78; Univ Fla, PhD(anat & cell biol), 88. *Prof Exp:* Fel cellular biochem, M D Anderson Cancer Ctr, Univ Tex, 88-90; asst prof cell biol, Univ Okla, 90-93. *Concurrent Pos:* Prin investr, Okla Ctr Advan Sci & Technol, 91-93. *Mem:* Am Soc Cell Biol; AAAS. *Res:* Cellular and molecular basis of cell-cell and cell-extracellular matrix interactions; cell migration of neurite processes and capillary endothelial cells; cell surface receptor function. *Mailing Add:* Sci Ctr W L Gore & Assoc Inc PO Box 1980 Flagstaff AZ 86002-1980

BEGOVICH, NICHOLAS A(NTHONY), ELECTRONICS. *Current Pos:* MGT & TECH CONSULT, 75- *Personal Data:* b Oakland, Calif, Nov 29, 21; wid. *Educ:* Calif Inst Technol, BS, 43, MS, 44, PhD(elec eng), 48. *Prof Exp:* Asst & res engr, Calif Inst Technol, 44-46, instr elec eng, 47-48; res physicist, Hughes Aircraft Co, 48-51, staff consult, 51-52, dir eng, Ground Systs Group, 51-61, vpres, 61-70, asst group exec, 61-66, group exec, 66-69, vpres corp hq, 70; corp vpres, Litton Industs & pres, Data Systs Div, 70-74. *Concurrent Pos:* Consult, Off Secy Defense, 51-57 & 76, Appl Physics Lab, Johns Hopkins Univ, 77-, Off Secy Army, 83-; mem, Army Sci Bd, 83-89. *Mem:* Am Phys Soc; Opers Res Soc Am; fel Inst Elec & Electronics Engrs; Soc Automotive Engrs; AAAS; Sigma Xi. *Res:* Theory of high frequency vacuum tubes; electro-magnetic field; radar detection theory and air defense system analysis. *Mailing Add:* 136 N Miramonte Dr Fullerton CA 92635-3608. *Fax:* 714-526-5724

BEGUE, WILLIAM JOSEPH, MICROBIAL PHYSIOLOGY, ANALYTICAL BIOCHEMISTRY, ANIMAL PHYSIOLOGY & DEVELOPMENT. *Current Pos:* RETIRED. *Personal Data:* b Chicago, Ill, June 15, 31; m 52, Jane Curtis; c Jane, William & Catherine. *Educ:* Col St Thomas, BS, 53; Univ Minn, MS, 60, PhD(microbiol), 63. *Prof Exp:* From instr to asst prof microbiol, Univ Ky Med Ctr, 63-67; sr scientist, Lilly Res Labs, Div Eli Lilly & Co, 67-74, res scientist analytical microbiol, 74-86, animal physiol & develop, 86-93. *Mem:* Am Soc Microbiol; Sigma Xi. *Res:* Development of analytical methods for new compounds, mostly antibiotics as found in animal feed and tissues; microbial nutrition, physiology and metabolism; biochemistry; enzymology; animal nutrition; environmental issues in agriculture; animal physiology and development. *Mailing Add:* 2739 Saturn Dr Indianapolis IN 46229-1163

BEGUIN , FRED P, ACOUSTICS, PHYSICS. *Current Pos:* RETIRED. *Personal Data:* b Brussels, Belg, Oct 13, 09; US citizen; m 34; c 1. *Educ:* State Tech Col Brussels, BS, 31; State Sch Cinematography, Paris, BSc, 33; Univ City Paris, prof radio commun, 33; Nat Radio Electronics Inst, Brussels, lic prof physics, 44; Colby Col, cert engr noise control, 71. *Honors & Awards:* Nat Sci Achievement Award, Audio Eng Soc, 70; Nat Safety Coun Award, 77; Silver Cert Award, Acoust Soc Am, 85. *Prof Exp:* Patent analyst, French Thomson-CSF Co, Paris, France, 31-34; high tech proj engr, Philips Res Labs, Holland, 34-44; tech dir recording & mfg, Decca Records Belg & France, 44-46; Europ dir, Motorola Corp Chicago, 46-50; audio consult, Electronics Div, Gen Elec Co, Syracuse, NY, 50-59; chief scientist electroacoust res & develop, Am Optical Corp, 59-72; dir, Hearing & Noise Control Ctr, Harrington Mem Hosp, Southbridge, 72-77; consult environ acoust physicist, Port Charlotte, Fla, 83-86. *Concurrent Pos:* Chmn, TV Stand Comn Belg Eng Soc & Ministry Commun, Brussels, 44-46; tech consult to Belg embassy in US, Belg Ministry Foreign Trade Econ Affairs, 51-53; safety equip indust rep & mem, Noise & Bioacoust Comts, Accoust Soc Am, Am Stand Inst, 63-72; acoust consult, Worcester Mem Auditorium, Environ Protect Agency, Occup Safety Health Admin & Pub Health Serv, Mass, 65-67. *Mem:* Inst Elec & Electronics Engrs; fel Audio Eng Soc; emer mem Acoust Soc Am; emer mem NY Acad Sci; emer mem Am Inst Physics; hon mem Indust Safety Equip Asn. *Res:* Engineering; architectural acoustics; sound recording and reproduction; psychological and physiological acoustics; bioacoustics; noise; shock; vibration; hearing; audiology; audiometry; noise-abatement; speech communications in noise; environmental acoustics; measurement instrumentation. *Mailing Add:* Acoust Physicist PO Box 2750 Port Charlotte FL 33949

BEGUN, DAVID RENE, PALEOANTHROPOLOGY, PALEOPRIMATOLOGY. *Current Pos:* ASSOC PROF ANTHROP, UNIV TORONTO, 89- *Personal Data:* b Croix-Chapeax, Charente-Maritime, France, Sept 24, 59; US & French citizen; m 82, Dana L Bovee; c Andre D Bovee-Begun, Alyx E Bovee-Begun & Mara R Bovee-Begun. *Educ:* Univ Pa, BA, 81, MA, 84, PhD(anthrop), 87. *Prof Exp:* Res fel, Smithsonian Inst, 86-87; asst prof lectr anthrop, George Wash Univ, 87-89. *Concurrent Pos:* Res assoc, Smithsonian Inst, 87-91, res consult, 87-89; instr anat, Georgetown Univ, 87-88, Johns Hopkins Univ, 88-89; fel, Johns Hopkins Univ Sch Med, 88-89; vis assoc prof, Univ Calif, Berkeley, 93. *Mem:* Am Asn Phys Anthropologists; Can Asn Phys Anthropologists. *Res:* Paleobiology of fossil apes of the Miocene epoch; evolutionary relations among the great apes and humans; functional anatomy and behavioral reconstruction of fossil primates. *Mailing Add:* Dept Anthrop Univ Toronto Toronto ON M5S 1A1 Can. *Fax:* 416-978-8850; *E-Mail:* begun@epas.u.toronto.ca

BEGUN, GEORGE MURRAY, physical inorganic chemistry, chemical physics; deceased, see previous edition for last biography

BEHAL, FRANCIS JOSEPH, BIOCHEMISTRY. *Current Pos:* PROF BIOCHEM & CHMN DEPT, SCH MED, TEX TECH UNIV, 71- *Personal Data:* b Yoakum, Tex, Oct 10, 31; m 55; c 2. *Educ:* St Edward's Univ, BS, 53; Univ Tex, MA, 56, PhD(chem), 58. *Prof Exp:* From asst prof to assoc prof biochem, Med Col Ga, 58-68, dir grad div, 64-66, dir sch grad studies, 66-68, prof biochem & microbiol & dean sch grad studies, 68-71. *Concurrent Pos:* Mem, Tenth Int Cancer Cong. *Mem:* Am Soc Biol Chemists; fel Am Acad Microbiol; fel Am Inst Chem; Soc Exp Biol & Med. *Res:* Comparative enzymology of mammalian and microbial peptidases. *Mailing Add:* Dept Biochem & Surg Tex Tech Univ Health Sci Ctr Lubbock TX 79430-0001

BEHAN, MARK JOSEPH, PHYSIOLOGICAL ECOLOGY. *Current Pos:* Chmn, Wildlife Biol Degree Progs, 70-74, PROF BOT, UNIV MONT, 61- *Personal Data:* b Denver, Colo, Jan 17, 31; c 3. *Educ:* Univ Denver, BA, 53; Univ Wyo, MS, 58; Univ Wash, PhD(plant physiol), 63. *Concurrent Pos:* Fulbright lectr, Nepal, 82-83; consult, USAID, Nepal, 84-85 & 86-87 & US Fish & Wildlife Serv, India, 90- *Mem:* Ecol Soc Am; Int Mountain Soc. *Res:* Forest tree physiology; ecology. *Mailing Add:* Div Biol Sci Univ Mont Missoula MT 59612

BEHAN-PELLETIER, VALERIE MARY, SOIL ZOOLOGY. *Current Pos:* RES SCIENTIST, BIOL RESOURCES DIV, AGR CAN, 81- *Personal Data:* b Drogheda, Ireland, Feb 15, 48; Can citizen; m 77, Guy Pelletier. *Educ:* Univ Col, Dublin, Ireland, BSc, 68; McGill Univ, Montreal, Can, MSc, 72, PhD(soil zool), 78. *Prof Exp:* Res asst soil zool, Univ Col, Dublin, Ireland, 68-69, Trinity Col, Dublin, 72-73 & Univ Alaska, Fairbanks, 75; lectr biol, John Abbott Col, Ste Anne de Bellevue, 78-81. *Concurrent Pos:* Chair, Can Nat Collection Curatorial Comt, Biosysts Res Ctr, Ottawa, 82-86; mem, Sci Comt, Biol Surv Can, 83-; assoc ed, Can Entomologist, 86-91; adj prof, McGill Univ, Montreal, 88-; sci ed, Mem Entom Soc Can, 91-; mem, Scope Comt Soils & Sediments, 96-; JSPS fel, 97. *Mem:* Entom Soc Can; Soil Ecol Soc; Acarol Soc Am. *Res:* Systematics and ecology of oribatida especially of North America; biodiversity of oribita in arctic or tropical ecosystems. *Mailing Add:* Biol Resourses Div ECORC Agr Can K W Neatby Bldg C E F Ottawa ON K1A 0C6 Can. *Fax:* 613-759-1927; *E-Mail:* behanpv@em.agr.ca

BEHAR, MARJAM GOJCHLERNER, ANALYTICAL BIOCHEMISTRY. *Current Pos:* health scientist admin & exec secy metallobiochem study sect, 80-84, health scientist adminr & exec secy spec rev sect, div res grants, 84-95, HEALTH SCIENTIST ADMINR & SCIENTIFIC REV ADMINR, BIOCHEM SCI REV SECT, NIV, MD, 95- *Personal Data:* b Luck, Poland, Dec 8, 25; US citizen; m 51; c 3. *Educ:* Univ Havana, DSc, 50. *Prof Exp:* Res chemist, Va Smelting Co, Cuba, 50-53; control res chemist, Lab Geol, 53-54; instr high sch, Cuba, 54-55; chemist, Garden State Tanning Corp, Pa, 55-57; jr prod engr, Lansdale Div, Philco Corp, 58-61; res assoc anesthesiol, 62-70, res specialist anesthesiol, Univ Hosp, Univ Pa, 70-79. *Mem:* Am Soc Anesthesiologists; Am Chem Soc; NY Acad Sci; Soc Appl Spectros; fel Am Inst Chemists. *Res:* Anesthesia research; effect of anesthetic agents on blood flows, metabolism and blood viscosity; radioimmuno assay; health science administration. *Mailing Add:* NIH Rm 5218 Rocklege Bldg MSC 7852 6701 Rocklege Dr Bethesda MD 20892-7852. *Fax:* 301-480-2241; *E-Mail:* bpm@drgpo.drg.nih.gov

BEHBEHANI, ABBAS M, CLINICAL VIROLOGY. *Current Pos:* asst prof, Univ Kans, 64-66, sr res assoc pediat, Sect Virus Res, 66-67, from assoc prof to prof path, Sch Med, 67-90, EMER PROF PATH, SCH MED, UNIV KANS, 90- *Personal Data:* b Iran, July 27, 25; US citizen; m 58; c Ray, Allen & Bita. *Educ:* Ind Univ, AB, 49; Univ Chicago, MS, 51; Southwestern Med Sch Univ Tex, PhD(virol), 55. *Prof Exp:* Assoc prof microbiol, Univ Tehran, 56-60; virologist, Med Ctr, Baylor Univ, 60-63, res asst prof virol, Col Med, 63-64. *Concurrent Pos:* Dir cent state health labs, Ministry Health, Tehran, 56-59; clin asst prof, Univ Tex Southwestern Med Sch Dallas, 61-64. *Mem:* AAAS; Am Soc Microbiol; Soc Exp Biol & Med; fel Am Acad Microbiol. *Res:* Properties and characteristics of enteroviruses; use of cell and organ culture for pathological studies of human disease; development of more rapid procedures in diagnostic virology, evaluation of anti-viral drugs in vitro; history of smallpox and yellow fever; Persian founders of Islamic medicine; over 72 articles and 3 books. *Mailing Add:* Dept Path & Lab Med Univ Kans Sch Med Kansas City KS 66160. *Fax:* 913-588-7073

BEHE, MICHAEL JOSEPH, DNA STRUCTURE STUDIES, CHROMATIN STRUCTURE STUDIES. *Current Pos:* ASSOC PROF CHEM, LEHIGH UNIV, 85- *Personal Data:* b Altoona, Pa, Jan 18, 52; m 84; c 5. *Educ:* Drexel Univ, BS, 74; Univ Pa, PhD(biochem), 78. *Prof Exp:* Assoc, NIH, 78-82; asst prof chem, Queens Col, 82-85. *Concurrent Pos:* Assoc prof biochem, Hershey Med Ctr, Pa State Univ, 89. *Mem:* Am Soc Biochem & Molecular Biol; Biophys Soc. *Res:* Sequence dependence of DNA structure and its effects on interactions with DNA binding proteins. *Mailing Add:* Dept Biol Sci Lehigh Univ 111 Research Dr Bethlehem PA 18015. *Fax:* 610-758-5851; *E-Mail:* mjb1@lehigh.edu

BEHER, WILLIAM TYERS, BIOCHEMISTRY. *Current Pos:* Res asst, 50-52, sr res assoc biochem, Edsel B Ford Inst Med Res, 52-77, sr staff investr biochem, 77-80, DIR, GASTROENTEROL RES LAB, HENRY FORD HOSP, 80- *Personal Data:* b Aurora, Ill, Dec 14, 22; m; c 5. *Educ:* NCent Col, BA, 44; Wayne State Univ, PhD(biochem), 50. *Concurrent Pos:* Instr, Wayne State Univ, 52-60. *Mem:* AAAS; Am Chem Soc; Am Soc Biol Chem; Soc Exp Biol & Med; Am Heart Asn. *Res:* Steroid and bile acid metabolism and nutrition; steroid x-ray diffraction. *Mailing Add:* 2025 Laudrome Dr Royal Oak MI 48073-3957

BEHFOROOZ, ALI, COMPUTER SCIENCE, EDUCATION PROGRAMMING LANGUAGES. *Current Pos:* PROF & DIR, GRAD PROG COMP SCI, TOWSON STATE UNIV, 87- *Personal Data:* b May 24, 42; Iranian citizen; m 71, Fariden Ari; c Amir. *Educ:* Univ Tehran, BS, 65, MS, 66; Mich State Univ, MS, 72, MS, 73, PhD(comput sci), 75. *Prof Exp:* Instr math, Univ Tehran & Nat Univ Iran, 65-70; res asst comput, Mich State Univ, 72-74; dir, Inst Res & asst prof comput, Moorhead State Univ, 74-76, from assoc prof to prof comput sci, 76-86, chmn, 84-86; funding chair, Comput Sci Dept, Calif State Univ, Bakersfield, Calif, 86-87. *Concurrent Pos:* Grant, Educ Radio & TV of Iran, 75; NSF grant, 78-80; res consult, Gen Nutrit Corp, 79-86; vis prof, Univ Calif, Santa Barbara, 81-82; adj prof, Johns Hopkins Univ. *Mem:* Asn Comput Mach; Inst Elec & Electronics Engrs Comput Soc. *Res:* Formal languages, compiler design, software engineering, computer application in education and programming languages; publications: seven text books in computer science and over 20 papers in computer science education and related topics. *Mailing Add:* Dept Comput & Info Sci Towson State Univ Towson MD 21204-7097. *Fax:* 410-830-3868; *E-Mail:* behforoozt-a@toe.towson.edu

BEHKI, RAM M, MOLECULAR BIOLOGY. *Current Pos:* res officer, Microbiol Res Inst, 65-67, res scientist, Cell Biol Res Inst, 67-72, SR RES SCIENTIST, CHEM & BIOL RES INST, CAN DEPT AGR, 73- *Personal Data:* b Nawashahr, India, Mar 31, 32; m 60; c 3. *Educ:* Panjab Univ, India, BSc, 52; Univ Nagpur, MSc, 54, PhD(biochem), 59. *Prof Exp:* Sr sci asst biochem, Nat Chem Lab, Coun Sci & Indust Res, India, 57-59; res fel, Stritch Med Sch, Loyola Univ, Ill, 59-60, instr, 60-61; Jane Coffin Childs Mem Fund fel, Nat Cancer Inst, Md, 61-62; res fel, Mass Gen Hosp, Boston, 62-63 & Western Res Univ, 63-65. *Concurrent Pos:* Vis scientist, Ctr Study Nuclear Energy, Mol, Belg, 73-74. *Mem:* Am Chem Soc; Am Soc Plant Physiologists. *Res:* Nucleic acids and protein metabolism in normal and abnormal growth; plant cell culture; protoplast technology; genetic modification of plant cells by molecular biology techniques; nucleic acid isolation and characterization; molecular biology nitrogen fixation; rhizobium genetics. *Mailing Add:* 31 Trimble Crescent Nepean ON K2H 7M9 Can

BEHL, WISHVENDER K, PHYSICAL CHEMISTRY, ELECTROCHEMISTRY. *Current Pos:* RES CHEMIST, US ARMY RES LAB, FT MONMOUTH, 67- *Personal Data:* b Dhariwal, India, Dec 26, 35; m 77, Ravi K Sharma; c Vikas & Renuka. *Educ:* Univ Delhi, BSc Hons, 55, MSc, 57, PhD(phys chem), 62. *Honors & Awards:* Jr Sci Exhib Prize, Univ Delhi, 55. *Prof Exp:* Res assoc, NY Univ, 62-64 & Brookhaven Nat Lab, NY, 64-67. *Mem:* Fel Am Inst Chemists; Am Chem Soc; Electrochem Soc. *Res:* Chemistry of molten salts, potential measurements polarography, chronopotentiometry, linear sweep voltammetry, thermodynamics, transference numbers and ionic mobilities measurements; diffusion coefficients; molten salt batteries; solid state galvanic cells; electroanalytical chemistry; lithium-inorganic electrolyte cells; holder of 29 patents, published 43 research papers in international parofessional journals. *Mailing Add:* Sensors & Electronic Devices Directorate US Army Res Lab ATTN: AMSRL-SE-DC Ft Monmouth NJ 07703. *Fax:* 732-427-3665; *E-Mail:* wbehl@arl.mil

BEHLE, WILLIAM HARROUN, ORNITHOLOGY. *Current Pos:* from instr to assoc prof biol, 37-50, head dept gen biol, 48-54, dir biol gen educ, 54-63, prof, 50-77, EMER PROF BIOL, UNIV UTAH, 77- *Personal Data:* b Salt Lake City, Utah, May 13, 09; m 34, Dorothy Davis; c Howard W & Raymond D. *Educ:* Univ Utah, AB, 32, AM, 33; Univ Calif, PhD(zool), 37. *Prof Exp:* Asst mus vert zool, Univ Calif, 33-37. *Mem:* Am Ornithologists Union; Cooper Ornith Soc; Wilson Ornith Soc. *Res:* Geographic variation and distribution of birds; birds of Utah; systematic ornithology. *Mailing Add:* Dept Biol Univ Utah Salt Lake City UT 84112

BEHLING, ROBERT EDWARD, GEOLOGY. *Current Pos:* asst prof, 71-76, ASSOC PROF GEOL, 76-, ASST VPRES, ACAD AFFAIRS ADMIN, WEST VA UNIV, 78- *Personal Data:* b Milwaukee, Wis, Sept 11, 41; m 70; c 1. *Educ:* Univ Wis-Milwaukee, BS, 63; Miami Univ, Oxford, Ohio, MS, 65; Ohio State Univ, PhD(geol), 71. *Prof Exp:* Res assoc geol, Inst Polar Studies, Ohio State Univ, 65-70. *Concurrent Pos:* Co-prin investr, NSF grant, Off Polar Prog, 66-75; geol coordr, Argonne Nat Lab grant, 76-78; co-prin investr, Nat Park Serv grant, Nat Landmark Prog, 73-; consult, Quaternary Mapping Proj, US Geol Surv, 77-79; co-prin investr, Wetlands Study, US Army Corps Engrs, 81- *Mem:* Geol Soc Am; Glaciol Soc; Am Quaternary Asn; Clay Minerals Soc; Nat Asn Geol Teachers; Sigma Xi. *Res:* Physical and chemical weathering in ice-free areas of Antarctica; physical-chemical weathering and landform development in humid, temperate climates. *Mailing Add:* 416 Devon Rd Morgantown WV 26505-2206

BEHLOW, ROBERT FRANK, ANIMAL PARASITOLOGY. *Current Pos:* RETIRED. *Personal Data:* b Cleveland, Ohio, Mar 16, 26; m 54; c 3. *Educ:* Ohio State Univ, DVM, 53. *Prof Exp:* Prof animal path & head state diag lab, Univ Ky, 54-64; gen mgr, Blue Chip Mills, Ill, 64; prof animal sci & exten vet, NC State Univ, 64-86. *Concurrent Pos:* Pres, NC Qual Enterprises Inc. *Mem:* Am Vet Med Asn. *Res:* Isolation of Histoplasma capsulatum from a calf and a pig; swine parasite control. *Mailing Add:* 121 Calibre Chase Dr Raleigh NC 27609

BEHM, ROY, analytical chemistry, for more information see previous edition

BEHME, RONALD JOHN, GENETICS, MICROBIOLOGY. *Current Pos:* asst prof, 73-79, ASSOC PROF MICROBIOL & IMMUNOL, UNIV WESTERN ONT, 79- *Personal Data:* b Evansville, Ind, Apr 12, 38; m 63; c 2. *Educ:* Univ Evansville, AB, 60; Ind Univ, PhD(genetics), 69. *Prof Exp:* Lectr zool & genetics, Ind Univ, 65-67; res assoc genetics, Univ Waterloo, 67-69; Can Med Res Coun fel, Univ Western Ont, 69-72; vis prof genetics, Univ Waterloo, 72-73. *Concurrent Pos:* Owner, Microsystems Res. *Mem:* Sigma Xi; Am Soc Microbiol; Can Soc Microbiol; Can Col Microbiologists. *Res:* Genetics of antibiotic resistance in bacteria; plasmids; anaerobic bacteriology; automation in clinical microbiology. *Mailing Add:* 51 Brentwood Crescent London ON N6G 1X4 Can

BEHMER, DAVID J, FISHERIES. *Current Pos:* from asst prof to assoc prof, 67-81, PROF BIOL, LAKE SUPERIOR STATE UNIV, 81- *Personal Data:* b Milwaukee, Wis, May 29, 41; m 63; c 3. *Educ:* Wis State Col, Stevens Point, BS, 63; Iowa State Univ, MS, 65, PhD(fisheries biol), 66. *Prof Exp:* Lectr fisheries, Humboldt State Col, 66-67. *Mem:* Am Fisheries Soc. *Res:* Statistics; fishes or fisheries; genetics. *Mailing Add:* Dept Biol Lake Superior State Univ 1000 College Dr Sault Ste Marie MI 49783-1637

BEHNKE, JAMES RALPH, FOOD SCIENCE. *Current Pos:* sect mgr, 73-74, mgr prod develop, 74-77, dir frozen foods, 77-78, refrig & frozen foods dir, 78-79, corp vpres, 79-80, sr vpres, opers & technol, 81-86, corp sr vpres, growth , 86-88, CORP SR VPRES GROWTH & TECHNOL, PILLSBURY CO, 86- *Personal Data:* b Milwaukee, Wis, May 2, 43; m 66; c 2. *Educ:* Univ Wis-Madison, BS, 66, MS, 68, PhD(food sci), 71. *Prof Exp:* From group leader to sr group leader prod develop, Quaker Oats Co, 71-74. *Mem:* Inst Food Technologists; Am Asn Cereal Chemists. *Res:* Identification, development and process engineering of consumer marketed and packaged food products. *Mailing Add:* Pillsbury co 330 University Ave Minneapolis MN 55414

BEHNKE, ROY HERBERT, INTERNAL MEDICINE. *Current Pos:* prof internal med & chmn dept, 72-94, PROF MED & EMER CHMN, UNIV SFLA, TAMPA, 94- *Personal Data:* b Chicago, Ill, Feb 24, 21; m 44, Ruth Zinszek; c Roy Jr, Donald, Michael & Elise. *Educ:* Hanover Col, AB, 43; Ind Univ, MD, 46; Am Bd Internal Med, dipl, 56. *Hon Degrees:* ScD, Hanover Col, 72. *Prof Exp:* Markle scholar, Sch Med, Ind Univ, Indianapolis, 52-57, from instr to prof med, 52-72. *Concurrent Pos:* Chief med, Indianapolis Vet Admin Hosp, 57-72; chmn, Vet Admin Pulmonary Dis Res Comt, 62-68, mem, Vet Admin Coop Studies Res Comt, 66-70; chmn, Inter-Soc Comn Heart Dis Res, 69-77; mem residency rev comt, Internal Med, 70-75, chmn, 73-75; mem, Vet Admin Res Develop Career Comt, 79-, chmn, 81-83; mem res coord comt, Am Lung Asn, 83-85, bd dirs, 83-87, chmn res comt, 85-87. *Mem:* Am Fedn Clin Res; Am Thoracic Soc/Am Lung Asn; Southern Soc Clin Res; AMA; fel master Am Col Physicians; Cent Soc Clin Res; Am Col Chest Physicians. *Res:* Cardiopulmonary disease. *Mailing Add:* 5111 Rolling Hill Ct Tampa FL 33617-1024. *Fax:* 813-971-4375

BEHNKE, WALLACE B, JR, ELECTRICAL ENGINEERING, NUCLEAR ENGINEERING. *Current Pos:* CONSULT ENGR, 89- *Personal Data:* b Evanston, Ill, Feb 5, 26; m 49, Joan Murphy; c Susan (Jones), Ann (Engeli) & Thomas Behnke. *Educ:* Northwestern Univ, BS, 45, BSEE, 47. *Honors & Awards:* James N Landis Medal, Am Soc Mech Engrs, 89; Outstanding Contrib Award, Inst Elec & Electronics Engrs, 92. *Prof Exp:* Mem staff, Commonwealth Edison, Chicago, 47-69, vpres, 69-73, exec vpres, 73-80, vchmn, 80-89, mem, bd dirs & trustee, 77-91. *Concurrent Pos:* Vchmn, Tech Activ Bd, Inst Elec & Electronics Engrs, chmn, Periodicals Coun; mem bd dirs, Ravenswood Hosp, 63-71, La Salle Bank Lake View, 70-89, Northwestern Mem Hosp, 71-88, Stand Am Life Ins Co, 78-82, United Way Chicago, 78-82, Ill Inst Technol, 79-89, Paxall Group Inc, 83-85, Tuthill Pump Co, 83-89, Calunet Indust, 87-89 & Arch Develop Corp, 88-90; mem, Adv Comt, Idaho Nat Eng Lab, 86-93; dir & chmn, Atomic Indust Forum; chmn, Univ Chicago Sci Tech Adv Comt, Argonne Nat Lab, 91-95. *Mem:* Nat Acad Eng; fel Inst Elec & Electronics Engrs; Am Nuclear Soc; Power Eng Soc (pres, 88-89); Western Soc Engrs (pres, 75-76). *Mailing Add:* 323 Glen Eagle Ct Kiawah Island SC 29455-5728. *Fax:* 802-768-2063; *E-Mail:* w.behnke@ieee.org or 105366.3543@compuserve.com

BEHNKE, WILLIAM DAVID, BIOLOGICAL CHEMISTRY, BIOPHYSICS. *Current Pos:* ASSOC PROF BIOCHEM, COL MED, UNIV CINCINNATI, 74- *Personal Data:* b Pasadena, Calif, Jan 15, 41; m 62; c 3. *Educ:* Univ Calif, Berkeley, AB, 63; Univ Wash, PhD(biochem), 68. *Prof Exp:* Fel, Harvard Med Sch, 68-72; asst prof chem, Univ SC, 72-74. *Mem:* Biophys Soc; Am Soc Biol Chemists; NY Acad Sci. *Res:* Molecular interaction of colipase with an artificial interface; metalloprotein structure and function. *Mailing Add:* Dept Molecular Genetics Biochem & Microbiol Univ Cincinnati Col Med 231 Bethesda Ave Cincinnati OH 45267-0524

BEHOF, ANTHONY F, JR, PHYSICS. *Current Pos:* ASST PROF PHYSICS, DEPAUL UNIV, 67- *Personal Data:* b Chicago, Ill, Apr 30, 37. *Educ:* DePaul Univ, BS, 59; Univ Notre Dame, PhD(nuclear physics), 65. *Prof Exp:* Instr physics, Univ Notre Dame, 65; res physicist & Nat Res Coun-Naval Res Lab fel, US Naval Res Lab, 65-67. *Mem:* AAAS; Am Phys Soc; Am Asn Physics Teachers; Sigma Xi. *Res:* Experimental nuclear physics, especially low energy nuclear reactions; nuclear structure physics. *Mailing Add:* Dept Physics DePaul Univ 2219 N Kenmore Ave Chicago IL 60614-3504

BEHR, ELDON AUGUST, WOOD SCIENCE, WOOD TECHNOLOGY. *Current Pos:* RETIRED. *Personal Data:* b Minneapolis, Minn, July 29, 18; m 50; c 2. *Educ:* Univ Minn, BS, 40, PhD(agr biochem), 48. *Prof Exp:* Asst chemist, Am Creosoting Co, Ky, 40-42; wood technologist, Air Forces, US Army, NJ, 42-43; tech dir res, Chapman Chem Co, 47-50, vpres & mgr tech dept, 50-59; from assoc prof to prof forestry, Mich State Univ, 59-80. *Mem:* Am Wood Preserver's Asn; Railway Tie Asn; Railway & Locomotive Hist Soc. *Res:* Evaluation of wood preservatives; fibre preservatives; natural durability of wood; termite resistance of wood; test methods for decay of wood products. *Mailing Add:* 1802 Estate Lane Northfield MN 55057

BEHR, INGA, CHEMISTRY. *Current Pos:* RETIRED. *Personal Data:* b Plovdiv, Bulgaria, Sept 8, 23; US citizen; m 51; c 2. *Educ:* Univ Geneva, MS, 47, PhD(analytical chem), 50. *Prof Exp:* Asst, Univ Geneva, 48-50; chemist, Weizmann Inst, 50-51; res chemist, Israel AEC, 52-58; res chemist, Bio-Sci Lab, Calif, 59; NIH grant, City of Hope, 60-62; from instr to assoc prof, Pasedena City Col, 62-76, prof gen chem & qual analysis, 76-86. *Concurrent Pos:* Asst prof, Los Angeles State Col, 63-64. *Mem:* Sr mem Am Chem Soc. *Res:* Clinical biochemistry; nature of urochrome pigments; marine biology. *Mailing Add:* 395 S Oakland Ave Pasadena CA 91101

BEHR, LYELL CHRISTIAN, ORGANIC CHEMISTRY. *Current Pos:* from asst prof to assoc prof chem, 47-54, head dept, 63-64, dean, Col Arts & Sci, 64-80, PROF CHEM, 54-, EMER DEAN COL ARTS & SCI, MISS STATE UNIV, 80- *Personal Data:* b Minneapolis, Minn, May 4, 16; m 54; c 4. *Educ:* Univ Minn, BChem, 37; Univ Ill, PhD(org chem), 41. *Prof Exp:* Lab asst chem, Univ Ill, 37-40; Hormel fel, Univ Minn, 41-42; chemist, Chem Warfare Serv, Columbia Univ, 42-43; res chemist, E I du Pont de Nemours & Co, Del, 43-47. *Mem:* AAAS; Am Chem Soc; The Chem Soc. *Res:* Heterocyclic and synthetic organic chemistry; azoxy compounds. *Mailing Add:* Dept Chem Box CH Miss State Univ Mississippi State MS 39762-5613

BEHR, STEPHEN RICHARD, NUTRITION, PHYSIOLOGY. *Current Pos:* clin res assoc, Abbott Int, 87-90, sr clin res assoc, 90-91, CLIN RES SCIENTIST, ROSS LABS, 91- *Personal Data:* b Portland, Ore, Jan 1, 52; c 2. *Educ:* Whitman Col, BA, 74; Columbia Univ, MS, 77; Cornell Univ, PhD(nutrit biochem), 83. *Prof Exp:* Postdoctoral fel, Cornell Univ, 83-84; postdoctoral fel, Sch Med, Stanford Univ, 84-85, Am Heart Asn Calif Affil res fel, 85-87. *Concurrent Pos:* Am Inst Nutrit; Am Oil Chemists Soc. *Res:* Nutrition and cardiovascular disease: effects of dietary fats and fiber on blood lipids, lipoproteins and platelet composition and function; effect of antioxidants on lipoprotein metabolism; lipids and energy metabolism. *Mailing Add:* Ross Prod Div/Abbott Med Nutrit Res & Develop 625 Cleveland Ave Columbus OH 43215-1724

BEHRAVESH, MOHAMAD MARTIN, PHYSICS, ULTRASONICS. *Current Pos:* mgr, Nondestructive Eval Prog, 84-88, Corrosion Control Prog, 88-90, mgr, qual assurance prog, 91-92, MGR STEAM GENERATOR NDE, ELEC POWER RES INST, 92- *Personal Data:* b Tehran, Iran, Mar 21, 45; m 77. *Educ:* Univ Kans, BS, 68; Iowa State Univ, MS, 70; Georgetown Univ, PhD(physics), 74. *Prof Exp:* Asst prof physics, Abadan Inst Technol, Iran, 74-78; group leader ultrasonil nondestructive eval, Battelle Mem Inst, 78-80; dep div mgr, Elec Power Res Inst, NDE Ctr, Charlotte, NC, 80-84. *Concurrent Pos:* Vis scholar, Georgetown Univ, 76-77; guest scientist, Nat Bur Stand, 77. *Mem:* Acoust Soc Am; Am Soc Mech Eng; Am Soc Qual Control. *Res:* Physical acoustics and nondestructive evaluation and testing; corrosion. *Mailing Add:* Nuclear Power Div Elec Power Res Inst 3412 Hillview Ave Palo Alto CA 94303

BEHREND, DONALD FRASER, WILDLIFE MANAGEMENT, ENVIRONMENTAL SCIENCES. *Current Pos:* provost, Univ Alaska, Anchorage, 85-88, vpres acad affairs, 85-87, exec vpres, 87-88, chancellor, 88-, EMER CHANCELLOR, UNIV ALASKA, ANCHORAGE. *Personal Data:* b Manchester, Conn, Aug 30, 31; m 57; c 3. *Educ:* Univ Conn, BS, 58, MS, 60; State Univ NY, PhD(forest zool), 66. *Prof Exp:* Asst forestry & wildlife mgt, Univ Conn, 58-60; forest game mgt specialist, Ohio Div Wildlife, 60; from res asst to res assoc forest zool, Col Forestry, State Univ NY, Syracuse, 60-67; asst prof wildlife resources, Univ Maine, 67-68; dir wildlife res, Archer & Anna Huntington Wildlife Forest Sta, Col Environ Sci & Forestry, State Univ NY, Syracuse, 68-73, actg dean grad studies, 73, exec dir, Inst Environ Prog Affairs & asst vpres res, 73-79, vpres acad affairs & prof, Col Environ Sci & Forestry, State Univ NY, Syracuse, 79-85. *Concurrent Pos:* Leader deer res, Maine Dept Inland Fisheries & Game, 67-68. *Mem:* Soc Am Foresters; Wildlife Soc; Sigma Xi. *Res:* Ecology, behavior and management of forest wildlife with emphasis on snowshoe hares, white-tailed deer and songbirds; environmental research administration. *Mailing Add:* 333 M St Apt 403 Anchorage AK 99501-1902

BEHRENDT, JOHN CHARLES, MARINE GEOPHYSICS, ANTARCTIC GEOPHYSICS. *Current Pos:* res geophysicist, 77-95, EMER SCIENTIST, US GEOL SURV, COLO, 95-; FEL, INST ARCTIC & ALPINE RES, UNIV COLO, BOULDER, 95- *Personal Data:* b Stevens Point, Wis, May 18, 32; div; c Kurt A & Marc R. *Educ:* Univ Wis, BS, 54, MS, 56, PhD(geophys), 61. *Honors & Awards:* Explorers Club; Antarctia Serv Medal, NSF. *Prof Exp:* Asst seismologist, Ellsworth Sta Antarctica, 56-58; proj assoc, Univ Wis, 58-64; geophysicist, Colo, 64-68 & 70-72, Geol Liberia, 68-70, geologist in charge, Off Marine Geol, Woods Hole Off, 72-74, chief br Atlantic-Gulf of Mex Geol, Off Marine Geol, US Geol Surv, Woods Hole, Mass 74-77. *Concurrent Pos:* Coord, Antarctic Res, 77; mem US deleg, Antarctic Treaty Meeting, 77-; coord, Charleston Earthwake Res, 78-83; proj chief & prin investr Antarctic res, NSF grants, US Geol Surv. *Mem:* Am Geophys Union; Soc Explor Geophys; fel Geol Soc Am; AAAS. *Res:* Aeromagnetic aeroradioactivity, gravity and seismic investigations on West African continental margin, Antarctica and western United States; aeromagnetic, multichannel seismic and gravity research of the transition North America to the Atlantic Ocean; midcontinent rift system; West Antarctica rift system; lithospheric controls on the behavior of the West Antarctic ice sheet. *Mailing Add:* INSTAAR Univ Colo Boulder CO 80309-0450. *Fax:* 303-236-1425

BEHRENS, EARL WILLIAM, MARINE GEOLOGY. *Current Pos:* RETIRED. *Personal Data:* b Albany, NY, Nov 4, 35; m 66, Barbara M Mayer; c Mikael A & Amy M. *Educ:* Cornell Univ, BA, 56; Univ Mich, MS, 58; Rice Univ, PhD(geol), 63. *Prof Exp:* Res scientist assoc, Inst Marine Sci, Univ Tex, 61-74, asst prof to assoc prof geol, 65-74; assoc prof marine sci, Univ Tex, 74-96. *Concurrent Pos:* Panelist, Shoreline Erosion Adv Panel, US Army Corps Engrs, 74-80. *Mem:* AAAS; Am Geophys Union; fel Geol Soc Am; Soc Sedimentary Geol; Int Asn Sedimentologists; Am Asn Univ Profs. *Res:* Continental slope sedimentation and seismic stratigraphy; high resolution seismic profiling and data processing; quaternary stratigraphy and sedimentation; sea level fluctuations; sedimentary textures. *Mailing Add:* Marine Sci Dept Univ Tex Austin TX 78712-1162. *Fax:* 512-471-6732

BEHRENS, ERNST WILHELM, POLYMER PHYSICS. *Current Pos:* RETIRED. *Personal Data:* b Piraeus, Greece, Nov 10, 31; div; c 2. *Educ:* Univ Gottingen, BS, 54, teacher's dipl & MS, 57, PhD(solid state physics), 61. *Prof Exp:* Physicist, Siemens Co, Ger, 61-66; scientist, Lockheed-Ga Co, 66-69; Physicist & Res Fel, Armstrong World Industs, 69-94. *Concurrent Pos:* Europ AEC res fel, Magnetic Resonance Br, Grenoble Nuclear Res Ctr, France, 61. *Mem:* Am Phys Soc. *Res:* Mathematical modeling; astronomy; cosmology. *Mailing Add:* PO Box 5361 Lancaster PA 17606-5361

BEHRENS, H WILHELM, AERONAUTICS, FLUID MECHANICS & LASERS. *Current Pos:* sr staff scientist, 73-76, mgr, Appl Physics Dept, 76-85, MGR FLUID & THERMO PHYSICS DEPT, TRW SPACE & TECHNOL GROUP, TRW SYSTS INC, 85- *Personal Data:* b Zeven, Ger, July 16, 35; m 64, Sondra L Rogers; c Christine & Bill. *Educ:* Munich Tech Univ, Dipl Ing, 60; Von Karman Inst Fluid Mech, Belg, Dipl, 61; Calif Inst Technol, PhD(aeronaut), 66. *Prof Exp:* Res fel aeronaut, Calif Inst Technol, 66-67, asst prof, 67-73. *Concurrent Pos:* Tech fel, TRW, 91-; assoc ed, Am Inst Aeronaut Astronaut, 92-94. *Mem:* Am Inst Aeronaut & Astronaut; Sigma Xi; Am Soc Mech Engrs. *Res:* Supersonic and hypersonic aerodynamics; hypersonic wakes; flow separation; viscous and turbulent flows; chemical laser fluid mechanics; pulsed laser acoustics; aero-optics; dusty flows. *Mailing Add:* 4821 Falcon Rock Pl Palos Verdes Peninsula CA 90274

BEHRENS, HERBERT CHARLES, OPHTHALMOLOGY. *Current Pos:* from assoc prof to prof, 57-71, EMER PROF OPHTHAL, UNIV SOUTHERN CALIF, 71- *Personal Data:* b Cedarburg, Wis, Dec 16, 04; m 30; c 3. *Educ:* Univ Wis, BA, 27; Northwestern Univ, MD, 31; Univ Pa, MSc, 35. *Prof Exp:* Asst clin prof ophthal, Loma Linda Univ, 41, 48-52, assoc prof, 52-57. *Mem:* Am Acad Ophthal & Otolaryngol. *Mailing Add:* 5810 S Friends Ave Whittier CA 90601

BEHRENS, HERBERT ERNEST, PHYSICS, PHOTOGRAPHY. *Current Pos:* RETIRED. *Personal Data:* b Milwaukee, Wis, Nov 9, 15; m 41; c 5. *Educ:* Ill State Univ, BS, 37; Univ Wis, MS, 47. *Prof Exp:* Teacher high sch, Ill, 37-41; res physicist, Photo-Prod Dept, E I du Pont de Nemours & Co, Parlin, NJ, 47-80. *Mem:* Soc Photog Sci & Eng. *Res:* Photographic materials and processes. *Mailing Add:* PO Box 128 Metuchen NJ 08840

BEHRENS, MILDRED ESTHER, ZOOLOGY. *Current Pos:* RETIRED. *Personal Data:* b Geneva, NY, Apr 26, 22. *Educ:* Univ Rochester, BS, 50; Syracuse Univ, PhD(zool), 63. *Prof Exp:* Res scientist, Masonic Med Res Lab, 63-84. *Res:* Electrophysiology of the planarian photoreceptor and the Limulus lateral eye. *Mailing Add:* 5 Terrace Hill Dr New Hartford NY 13413

BEHRENS, RICHARD, WEED SCIENCE. *Current Pos:* assoc prof agron, 58-63, chmn plant physiol fac, 68-71, PROF AGRON, UNIV MINN, MINNEAPOLIS, 63- *Personal Data:* b Zenda, Wis, Nov 14, 21; m 50; c 2. *Educ:* Univ Wis, BS, 49, MS, 50, PhD(agron), 52. *Honors & Awards:* Publ Award, Weed Sci Soc Am, 62. *Prof Exp:* Plant physiologist agr res serv, USDA, 52-58. *Mem:* Am Soc Plant Physiol; fel Weed Sci Soc Am (pres, 67). *Res:* Basic and applied aspects of weed control research; absorption, translocation and mode of action of herbicides; effect of environment on herbicidal action; effect of environment on weed competition. *Mailing Add:* 1490 Country Rd C2 W St Paul MN 55113

BEHRENS, ROBERT GEORGE, PHYSICAL CHEMISTRY. *Current Pos:* staff mem, 76-86, assoc group leader, Mat Chem Group, 86-87, PROJ LEADER, ADV RECOVERY PROCESSES, LOS ALAMOS NAT LAB, 88- *Personal Data:* b Mineola, NY, Mar 6, 43; m 70; c 1. *Educ:* Hartwick Col, BA, 65; Pa State Univ, PhD(chem), 71. *Prof Exp:* Fel, Dept Chem, Univ Kans, 71-74; adj asst prof & assoc prof dir, dept chem, Col of City Univ New York, 74-76. *Concurrent Pos:* Mem, Tech Comt Space Mat Processing, Am Inst Aeronaut & Astronaut. *Mem:* Am Inst Aeronaut & Astronaut; Am Ceramic Soc. *Res:* High temperature chemistry and thermodynamics of nuclear and weapon related materials; plutonium and tritium technology; space materials processing; novel high temperature techniques for the synthesis of ceramics and alloys. *Mailing Add:* 1049 Cedro Ct Los Alamos NM 87544

BEHRENS, WILLY A, VITAMINS. *Current Pos:* RETIRED. *Personal Data:* b Santiago, Chile, Aug 19, 38. *Educ:* Univ Santiago, BA; Ottawa Univ, PhD(biochem), 73. *Prof Exp:* Postdoctoral fel, Ottawa Univ, 73-77; res scientist, Nutrit Res Div Nat Health & Welfare, Can, 77-94. *Mem:* Am Inst Nutrit. *Res:* Metabolic role of vitamin E and C. *Mailing Add:* 176 Woodridge Crescent Unit 17 Nepean ON K2B 7S9 Can

BEHRENTS, ROLF GORDON, ORTHODONTICS, CRANIOFACIAL BIOLOGY. *Current Pos:* PROF ORTHOD & CHMN, UNIV TENN, 84- *Personal Data:* b Galesburg, Ill, July 21, 47; m 78, Eileen Starkman; c Nathaniel & Jenna. *Educ:* St Olaf Col, BA, 69; Meharry Med Col, DDS, 73; Case Western Reserve Univ, MS, 75; Univ Mich, PHD(human growth), 84. *Honors & Awards:* Hellman Res Award, Am Asn Orthodontists, 76 & 85. *Prof Exp:* Fel human growth, Univ Mich, 75-78. *Concurrent Pos:* Res assoc, Bolton-Bush Growth Study Ctr, 84. *Mem:* Am Asn Orthodontists. *Res:* Human craniofacial growth in childhood, adolescence and adulthood. *Mailing Add:* 875 Union Ave Memphis TN 38163

BEHRINGER, ROBERT ERNEST, LASERS. *Current Pos:* CONSULT, 91- *Personal Data:* b Springfield, Mass, May 18, 31; m 56, Fe Clara Paez; c Richard, Patricia, Jacqueline, Karen & Ernest. *Educ:* Worcester Polytech Inst, BS, 53; Univ Calif, MA, 55, PhD(physics), 58. *Prof Exp:* Physicist, Gen Elec Co, 53; asst physics, Univ Calif, 53-58; assoc physicist, Int Bus Mach Corp, 58-60; consult, Atomics Int Div, NAm Aviation, Inc, 60-63; physicist, US Off Naval Res, 63-88; vpres, Ballena Systs Corp, 88-91. *Concurrent Pos:* From asst prof to assoc prof physics, San Fernando Valley State Col, 60-65; consult, Marquardt Corp, 61-63. *Mem:* Am Phys Soc; Sigma Xi. *Res:* Theoretical investigation in the field of ferro-magnetism; nuclear resonance; metallic conductivity; electrooptics; laser physics; free electron lasers. *Mailing Add:* 3475 Rhododendron Dr Florence OR 97439

BEHRLE, FRANKLIN C, PEDIATRICS, NEONATAL & PERINATAL MEDICINE. *Current Pos:* prof, NJ Med Sch, 61-92, chmn dept, 64-85, asst dean, 67-73, EMER PROF PEDIAT, NJ MED SCH, 92- *Personal Data:* b Ansonia, Conn, June 4, 22; m 45; c 5. *Educ:* Dartmouth Col, AB, 44; Yale Univ, MD, 46. *Prof Exp:* From instr to assoc prof pediat, Sch Med, Univ Kans, 51-61. *Mem:* Soc Pediat Res; fel Am Acad Pediat. *Res:* Respiratory problems of newborn. *Mailing Add:* PO Box 437 Grantham NH 03753

BEHRMAN, EDWARD JOSEPH, BIOCHEMISTRY. *Current Pos:* from asst prof to assoc prof, 65-69, PROF BIOCHEM, OHIO STATE UNIV, 69- *Personal Data:* b New York, NY, Dec 13, 30; m 53; c 3. *Educ:* Yale Univ, BS, 52; Univ Calif, PhD(biochem), 57. *Prof Exp:* Fel biochem, Cancer Res Inst, Nat Cancer Inst, 57-60, res assoc, 60-64; asst prof res, Brown Univ, 64-65. *Concurrent Pos:* Res fel biochem, Harvard Med Sch, 59-61, res assoc, 61-64, tutor, Harvard Col, 61-64. *Mem:* Royal Soc Chem; Am Chem Soc. *Res:* Peroxydisulfate oxidations; osmium chemistry; nucleic acid chemistry; sugar phosphates. *Mailing Add:* Dept Biochem Ohio State Univ Columbus OH 43210

BEHRMAN, HAROLD R, PHYSIOLOGY, BIOCHEMISTRY. *Current Pos:* assoc prof, 76-81, DIR, REPROD BIOL SECT, 76-, PROF OBSTET, GYNEC & PHARMACOL, SCH MED, YALE UNIV, 81- *Personal Data:* b Vidora, Sask, Nov 26, 39; m 81; c 3. *Educ:* Univ Man, BSc, 62, MSc, 65; NC State Univ, PhD(physiol), 67. *Honors & Awards:* Lalor Award, 71. *Prof Exp:* Res asst sensory & digestive physiol, NC State Univ, 64-67; Can Med Res Coun res fel reprod endocrinol, Harvard Med Sch, 67-70, assoc, 70-71, asst prof physiol, 71-72; dir, Dept Reprod Biol, Merck Inst Therapeut Res, NJ, 72-75. *Concurrent Pos:* Lalor fel, Harvard Med Sch, 71-73; Fulbright-Hays distinguished prof award, 79; Alta Heritage vis prof, 83; vis scientist award, Alta Heritage Found, 83-84. *Mem:* Endocrine Soc; Can Physiol Soc; Soc Study Reproduction; AAAS; Am Physiol Soc; Soc Gynec Invest. *Res:* Polypeptide and peptide hormone interrelationships; prostaglandins; purines, oxygen radicals. *Mailing Add:* Dept Obstet & Gynec Sch Med Yale Univ 333 Cedar St PO Box 208063 New Haven CT 06520-8063. *E-Mail:* harold.behtman@yale.edu

BEHRMAN, RICHARD ELLIOT, PEDIATRICS, NEONATOLOGY. *Current Pos:* Gertrude C Tucker prof & chmn, Dept Pediat, Sch Med, 76-82, DEAN, SCH MED, 80-, VPRES MED AFFAIRS, CASE WESTERN RES UNIV, 87- *Personal Data:* b Philadelphia, Pa, Dec 13, 31; m 54; c 4. *Educ:* Amherst Col, BA, 53; Harvard Univ, JD, 56; Univ Rochester, MD, 60. *Prof Exp:* Intern pediat, Johns Hopkins Hosp, 60-61, resident pediat & mem staff, Lab Obstet Physiol, 63-65; scientist, Lab Perinatal Physiol, Nat Inst Neurol Dis & Blindness, 61-63, sect chief physiol & biochem & actg lab chief, 62-63; from asst prof to assoc prof pediat, Med Sch, Univ Ore & from assoc scientist to scientist, Ore Regional Primate Res Ctr, 65-68, physician in-chg nursery serv, Med Sch & chmn, Dept Perinatal Physiol, Res Ctr, 65-68; prof pediat, Col Med, Univ Ill, 68-71; prof, Col Physicians & Surgeons, Columbia Univ, 71-74, chmn dept, 71-76, Carpentier prof pediat, 74-76; dir, Pediat Serv, Babies Hosp, 71-76 & Dept Pediat, Rainbow Babies & Children's Hosp, Univ Hosps, Cleveland, 76-82. *Concurrent Pos:* Whipple scholar, Univ Rochester & Johns Hopkins Hosp, 60-61; Wyeth fel pediat, 63-65; grants, Med Res Found, Ore, 65-66, United Health Found, 66-67, Nat Inst Child Health & Human Develop, 66-69, Pharmaceut Mfrs Asn Found, 70-72 & Robert Wood Johnson Found, 73-76; examr, Am Bd Pediat, 74-77, mem sub-bd neonatal-perinatal med, 75-77; mem bd maternal, child & family health res, Nat Res Coun, 74-; dir, Stanford Health Serv, 97-, Stanford Health Ctr, Univ Calif, San Francisco, 97-; dir & chmn bd, Lucila Puckance Found for Children, 97- *Mem:* Inst Med-Nat Acad Sci; fel Am Acad Pediat; Am Pediat Soc; Perinatal Res Soc; Sigma Xi; Soc Gynec Invest; Soc Pediat Res (vpres, 76-77). *Res:* Fetal, newborn and placental physiology; transfers of gases and solutes across the placenta; reproductive physiology; water and electrolyte balance; acid-base adjustments; membrane transport; bilirubin metabolism; protein binding. *Mailing Add:* David & Lucille Packard FD Ctr Future of Children 300 Second St Los Altos CA 94022

BEHRMAN, RICHARD H, MEDICAL IMAGING. *Current Pos:* ASST PROF RADIATION ONCOL & RADIOL, SCH MED, TUFTS UNIV, BOSTON, 88- *Personal Data:* b New York, NY, May 2, 44; m 78; c 2. *Educ:* Lehigh Univ, BA, 66; McGill Univ, MSc, 68, PhD(physics), 71. *Prof Exp:* Fel, McGill Univ, 72-73; prof physics, Dawson Col, Montreal, 73-85; assoc prof physics, Simmons Col, Boston, 85-87. *Concurrent Pos:* Vis res assoc, McGill Univ & Univ Paris, 76-78; vis assoc prof, Swarthmore Col, 81-82. *Mem:* Am Phys Soc; Am Asn Physicists Med; Am Col Med Physics. *Res:* Diagnostic x-ray and nuclear medicine imaging. *Mailing Add:* New Eng Med Ctr 750 Washington St Boston MA 02111. *Fax:* 617-636-0041; *E-Mail:* richard. behrman@es.nemc.org

BEHRMAN, SAMUEL J, OBSTETRICS & GYNECOLOGY. *Current Pos:* PROF OBSTET & GYNEC, UNIV S FLA, 92- *Personal Data:* b Worcester, SAfrica, Sept 10, 20; US citizen; m 56; c 2. *Educ:* Univ Cape Town, MB, ChB, 44; Univ Mich, MS, 49; FRCOG, 60. *Prof Exp:* From instr to assoc prof obstet & gynec, Univ Mich Ann Arbor, 48-56, prof obstet & gynec, coordr postgrad med & res lectr pub health, 56-77, lectr family planning & dir, Ctr Reproductive Biol, 66-77; prof obstet & gynec, Wayne State Univ, 77-; dir & chmn obstet & gynec, William Beaumont Hosp, 77-92. *Concurrent Pos:* Res grants, Macy Found, 48-62 & NIH, 64-67; consult, Ypsilanti State Hosp, Wayne Co Gen Hosp & Sinai Hosp, 56-; ed, Int J Fertil, 58-76 & J Int Fertil Asn, 62; guest prof, Univ London, 64; consult, Maternal Health Comt, AMA, 64-; mem, Sci Adv Bd, Human Life Found; consult, US AID; pres, Int Fedn Fertil Socs, 71-74; mem, Task Force Immunol, WHO, 72-; mem, Adv Bd, Food & Drug Admin, 73- *Mem:* Fel Am Asn Obstet & Gynec; Am Fertil Soc (pres, 78-79); fel Am Col Surgeons; Am Col Obstet & Gynec; Royal Soc Med. *Res:* Reproductive physiology. *Mailing Add:* 4405 W Beach Park Rd Tampa FL 33609

BEHRMANN, ELEANOR MITTS, CHEMISTRY, ORGANIC BIOCHEMISTRY. *Current Pos:* RETIRED. *Personal Data:* b Williamstown, Ky, May 24, 17; m 46; c 2. *Educ:* Univ Ky, BS, 38, MS, 39; Iowa State Univ, PhD, 43. *Prof Exp:* Chemist, Shell Develop Co, 43-46; instr chem, Harvard Univ, 46-48; from instr to assoc prof chem, Univ Cincinnati, 57-79. *Mem:* Am Chem Soc. *Res:* Glucose amine chemistry; phenolic resins; organic synthesis. *Mailing Add:* 5897 Crittenden Dr Cincinnati OH 45244-3827

BEHROOZI, FEREDOON, SUPERCONDUCTIVITY & MAGNETISM, MONOMOLECULAR FILMS. *Current Pos:* PROF PHYSICS & HEAD DEPT, UNIV NORTHERN IOWA, 92- *Personal Data:* b Tehran, Iran, Jan 8, 41, US citizen; m 69, Mary Spalding; c Farzi, Cyrus, David & Peter. *Educ:* Univ Wash, BS, 64; Univ Pittsburgh, PhD(physics), 69. *Prof Exp:* Asst prof physics, Pahlavi Univ, Shiraz, Iran, 69-74; res assoc optics, Naval Res Lab, 74-75; from asst prof to prof physics, Univ Wis-Parkside, 75-92, chmn dept, 83-92. *Concurrent Pos:* Resident scientist, Argonne Nat Lab, 82-83; vis scientist, Naval Res Lab, 87-88; vis scholar, Northwestern Univ, 86- *Mem:* Am Phys Soc; Am Asn Physics Teachers; Sigma Xi. *Res:* Electromagnetic properties of superconductors; anisostropy and critical phenomena in magnetic systems; 2D phase transitions; mathematical modeling of many-body systems; light scattering; lattice dynamics of rare gas solids; monolayers and LB films. *Mailing Add:* Dept Physics Univ Northern Iowa Cedar Falls IA 50614-0150. *E-Mail:* behroozi@cobra.uni.edu

BEICHL, GEORGE JOHN, PHYSICAL CHEMISTRY, INORGANIC CHEMISTRY. *Current Pos:* instr, St Joseph's Col, 40-44, from asst prof to prof, 47-89, chmn dept, 66-89, EMER PROF CHEM, ST JOSEPH'S COL, 89- *Personal Data:* b Philadelphia, Pa, Aug 20, 18; m 51, Isabella Lass; c Isabel, Karen, Christine & Lisa. *Educ:* St Joseph's Col, BS, 39; Univ Pa, MS, 42, PhD, 53. *Hon Degrees:* ScD, St Josephs Univ, 89. *Prof Exp:* Asst, AEC, Los Alamos, 46. *Concurrent Pos:* Sr res investr, Univ Pa, 53-54; NSF fel, Munich, Ger, 58-59. *Mem:* Am Chem Soc. *Res:* Boron and copper compounds. *Mailing Add:* 6387 Drexel Rd Philadelphia PA 19151-2511

BEIDLEMAN, JAMES C, ALGEBRA. *Current Pos:* From asst prof to assoc prof, 64-83, PROF MATH, UNIV KY, 83- *Personal Data:* b Wilkes-Barre, Pa, Nov 13, 36; c 2. *Educ:* Bucknell Univ, BA, 58, MS, 59; Pa State Univ, PhD(math), 64. *Concurrent Pos:* NSF grant on near-rings, 66-68, grant on groups & near-rings, 68-70; Ger acad exchange grant, 82. *Mem:* Am Math Soc; London Math Soc. *Res:* Fitting funetors of finite solvable groups; infinite solvable groups. *Mailing Add:* Dept Math Univ Ky Lexington KY 40506-0027

BEIDLEMAN, RICHARD GOOCH, ECOLOGY, HISTORY OF SCIENCE. *Current Pos:* from asst prof to prof, 57-92, chmn dept, 68-71, EMER PROF BIOL, COLO COL, 88- *Personal Data:* b Grand Forks, NDak, June 3, 23; 46, 91, Linda G Havighurst; c Sterling K, Janet G (Robson) & Carol A (Tiemeyer). *Educ:* Univ Colo, BA, 47, MA, 48, PhD(zool), 54. *Hon Degrees:* DS, Colo Col, 89. *Honors & Awards:* Romco Environ Award, 71. *Prof Exp:* Asst univ mus, Univ Colo, 46-48; asst prof zool, Colo State Univ, 48-56; asst prof biol, Univ Colo, 56-57. *Concurrent Pos:* Ford Found Fund Adv Ed grant, 54-55; Am Inst Biol Sci vis biologist prog comnr, Comn Undergrad Educ Biol Sci, NSF; mem consult bur steering comt, Biol Sci Curric Study; Hulbert endowed chair, Southwestern Studies, Colo Col, 92. *Mem:* Fel AAAS; Hist Sci Soc; Ecol Soc Am; Am Soc Mammal; Sigma Xi; Am Behav Soc; Soc Range Mgt. *Res:* Species association groups among birds; vertebrate ecology of Western biotic communities; winter bird population studies; small mammal population studies; significance of the American frontier on natural science; history of American biology. *Mailing Add:* 766 Bayview Ave Pacific Grove CA 93950-2509

BEIDLER, LLOYD M, PHYSIOLOGY, BIOPHYSICS. *Current Pos:* from asst prof to prof physiol, 50-56, prof biol sci, 56-93, EMER PROF BIOL SCI, FLA STATE UNIV, 93- *Personal Data:* b Allentown Pa, Jan 17, 22; m 46; c 6. *Educ:* Muhlenberg Col, BS, 43; Johns Hopkins Univ, PhD(biophys), 51. *Hon Degrees:* LLD, Muhlenberg Col, 69. *Honors & Awards:* Bowditch lectr, 59; Tanner lectr, Inst Food Technol Sci, 68. *Prof Exp:* Physicist, Radiation Lab, Johns Hopkins Univ, 44-45. *Concurrent Pos:* Nat lectr, Sigma Xi, 61. *Mem:* Nat Acad Sci; Am Physiol Soc; AAAS; Am Acad Arts & Sci. *Res:* Biophysical properties of chemoreceptors; mechanisms of taste stimulation; olfaction. *Mailing Add:* Dept Biol Sci Fla State Univ Tallahassee FL 32306

BEIER, EUGENE WILLIAM, ELEMENTARY PARTICLE PHYSICS. *Current Pos:* from asst prof to assoc prof, 67-79, PROF PHYSICS, UNIV PA, 79- *Personal Data:* b Harvey, Ill, Jan 30, 40; m 74; c 1. *Educ:* Stanford Univ, BS, 61; Univ Ill, MS, 63, PhD(physics), 66. *Honors & Awards:* Rossi Prize, Am Astron Soc, 89. *Prof Exp:* Res assoc physics, Univ Ill, 66-67. *Concurrent Pos:* Mem comt, Brookhaven Nat Lab High Energy Physics, 80-82, Prog Adv Comt, 89-92; prin investr res contract, Dept Energy, 81-90; consult, Univ Chicago, Argonne Nat Labs, 88-93. *Mem:* Fel Am Phys Soc; Sigma Xi; Am Asn Univ Professors. *Res:* Experimental research in elementary particle physics; nuclear astrophysics. *Mailing Add:* Dept Physics Univ Pa Philadelphia PA 19104-6396

BEIER, ROSS CARLTON, IMMUNOCHEMISTRY & MOLECULAR MODELING CHROMATOGRAPHY. *Current Pos:* Res chem, Nat Cotton Path Res Lab, USDA, College Station, Tex, 79-80, res chem, Vet Toxicol & Entom Res Lab, Food Animal Protection Res Lab, 80-90, proj leader, Food & Feed Safety Res Unit, 90-91, RES CHEMIST, FOOD ANIMAL PROTECTION RES LAB, AGR RES SERV, USDA, COLLEGE STATION, TEX, 91- *Personal Data:* b Portage, Wis, Dec 27, 46; m 74, Janet M Bauknecht; c Joshua Carlton, Samuel Robert & Jordan Ross. *Educ:* Univ Wis-Stevens Pt, BS, 69; Mont State Univ, PhD(org chem), 80. *Concurrent Pos:* Mem, Grad Fac, Tex A&M Univ, 82-96; ed, Sect Natural Prod Toxicol, J Quintessence; Dept Vet Anat & Pub Health, 96- *Mem:* Am Chem Soc; Phytochem Soc Nam; fel Am Inst Chemists. *Res:* Hapten chemistry conversions and protein conjugations in the development of nonochonal antibodies; molecular design and modeling of small molecules with the use of computer aided chemistry. *Mailing Add:* USDA ARS FAPRL 2881 F & B Rd College Station TX 77845-4998. *Fax:* 409-260-9332; *E-Mail:* rcbeier@ usda.tamu.edu

BEIERWAITES, WILLIAM HENRY, MEDICINE. *Current Pos:* AT DEPT MED, HYPERTENSION RES LAB, HENRY FORD HOSP, DETROIT. *Personal Data:* b Saginaw, Mich, Nov 23, 16; m 42; c 3. *Educ:* Univ Mich, AB, 36, MD, 41; Am Bd Internal Med, dipl. *Prof Exp:* From intern to asst resident med, Cleveland City Hosp, 41-43; resident, 44, from instr to assoc prof, 45-59, prof med, Univ Hosp, 59-, dir nuclear med, Univ Mich, Ann Arbor, 52- *Concurrent Pos:* Guggenheim Found fel & Commonwealth Found fel, 66-67; mem adv comt, IAE Comn, 74- *Mem:* Fel Am Col Physicians; Am Thyroid Asn (vpres, 64); Am Fedn Clin Res (pres, 54); Soc Nuclear Med (pres-elect, 64, pres, 65); Am Cancer Soc. *Res:* Internal nuclear medicine; diagnosis and treatment of cancer, hypertension, thyroid and heart disease using radionuclide labeled compounds. *Mailing Add:* Hypertension Res Henry Ford Hosp E&R 7123 2799 W Grand Blvd Detroit MI 48202-2689

BEIGEL, ALLAN, psychiatry; deceased, see previous edition for last biography

BEIGELMAN, PAUL MAURICE, medicine, for more information see previous edition

BEIGHLEY, CLAIR M(YRON), mechanical engineering, aerospace engineering, for more information see previous edition

BEIGHTLER, CHARLES SPRAGUE, INDUSTRIAL ENGINEERING, OPERATIONS RESEARCH. *Current Pos:* RETIRED. *Personal Data:* b Cincinnati, Ohio, Mar 18, 24; m 57; c 4. *Educ:* Univ Mich, BS, 50, MS, 54; Northwestern Univ, PhD(indust eng), 61. *Honors & Awards:* Lanchester Prize, Opers Res Soc Am. 67. *Prof Exp:* Aeronaut eng designer, Aeronca Mfg Co, 50-51; engr res labs, Gen Motors Corp, 54-55; opers res analyst, Arthur Anderson & Co, 55-56, Caywood-Schiller, Assocs, 56-57 & Ernst & Ernst, 57-58; from asst prof to prof mech eng, Univ Tex, Austin, 61-97. *Concurrent Pos:* Fulbright lectr, Univ Freiburg, 71-72. *Mem:* Opers Res Soc Am; Am Inst Indust Engrs; Inst Mgt Sci; Sigma Xi; Am Statist Asn. *Res:* Optimization theory; optimal design. *Mailing Add:* 7007 Edgefield Dr Austin TX 78731

BEIL, RALPH GREGORY, APPLICATIONS OF FINSLER GEOMETRY TO MICROPHYSICS, CLASSICAL ELECTROMAGNETIC THEORIES OF PARTICLES. *Current Pos:* ADJ PROF PHYSICS, E TEX BAPTIST UNIV, 83- *Personal Data:* b Oklahoma City, Okla, Sept 21, 38; m 60, Gail Kimes; c Thomas, Laura & Angelique. *Educ:* Okla State Univ, BS, 60, MS, 64; Johannes Gutenberg Univ, Dr rerum nat (theoret physics), 67. *Prof Exp:* Res engr, Lockheed Calif Co, 60-63; res asst, Max Planck Inst, 65-67; sect head nuclear eng, Schlumberger, Houston, 68-71; prof physics, Wiley Col, Tex, 71-74. *Mem:* Am Phys Soc; Am Asn Physics Teachers; Am Math Soc;

Tensor Soc; Balkan Soc Geometers. *Res:* Finsler extensions of general relativity; applications of differential geometry in classical field theory. *Mailing Add:* 313 S Washington Marshall TX 75670-4157. *E-Mail:* rbeil@etbu.edu

BEIL, ROBERT J(UNIOR), ENGINEERING SCIENCE, APPLIED MATHEMATICS. *Current Pos:* Assoc prof, 48-88, chmn dept, 68-71, EMER PROF ENG MECH, VANDERBILT UNIV, 71- *Personal Data:* b Lima, Ohio, Jan 15, 24; m 44, Mary M Stuart; c Mary S. *Educ:* ETenn State Univ, BS, 47; Okla Agr & Mech Col, MS, 49; Vanderbilt Univ, BE, 60; Purdue Univ, PhD(eng sci), 66. *Res:* Engineering mechanics. *Mailing Add:* 621 Laurel Lake Rd Apt B-120 Palm Coast NC 28722-7436

BEILBY, ALVIN LESTER, ELECTROANALYTICAL CHEMISTRY, CHEMICAL EDUCATION. *Current Pos:* Instr chem, 58-60, from asst prof to assoc prof, 60-72, chmn dept, 72-85, PROF CHEM, POMONA COL, 72- *Personal Data:* b Watsonville, Calif, Sept 17, 32; m 58, Ruby Irene Nelson; c Mark Alfred & Lorene Sigrid. *Educ:* San Jose State Col, BA, 54; Univ Wash, PhD(chem), 58. *Concurrent Pos:* Petrol Res Fund fac award, Univ Ill, 64-65; guest worker & res chemist, Nat Bur Standards, 71-72; NSF sci fac prof develop award, Lockheed Palo Alto Res Lab, 79-80; guest prof, Uppsala Univ, Sweden, 86-87. *Mem:* Am Chem Soc; Sigma Xi; AAAS; Soc Electroanal Chem. *Res:* Use and nature of carbon as an electrode material for electro-analytical methods; chemical education; environmental chemistry; archaeological chemistry. *Mailing Add:* Seaver Chem Lab Pomona Col 645 N College Ave Claremont CA 91711. *Fax:* 909-624-5509; *E-Mail:* abeilby@pomona.edu

BEILBY, MARK ALFRED, EXPERIMENTAL GRAVITATIONAL PHYSICS. *Current Pos:* RES ASSOC, SYRACUSE UNIV, 95- *Personal Data:* m 90, Pamela James; c Jared. *Educ:* Occidental Col, BA, 82; Univ Calif, Los Angeles, MS, 85; Univ Calif, Irvine, PhD(physics), 95. *Prof Exp:* Systs anal engr, Honeywell, 82-84. *Mem:* Am Asn Physics Teachers; Am Phys Soc. *Res:* Development of laser interferometer gravitational-wave observatory. *Mailing Add:* Dept Physics Syracuse Univ Syracuse NY 13244

BEILER, THEODORE WISEMAN, ORGANIC CHEMISTRY. *Current Pos:* RETIRED. *Personal Data:* b Meadville, Pa, Apr 29, 24; m 51, Dorthea A Brush; c Theodore D. *Educ:* Allegheny Col, BS, 48; Harvard Univ, MA, 50, PhD(chem), 52. *Prof Exp:* Sr asst scientist, USPHS, 51-53; from asst prof to prof, Stetson Univ, 53-68, chmn dept chem, 63-89, William Kenan prof chem, 68-89; Fulbright lectr, Univ Panjam, WPakistan, 62-63. *Concurrent Pos:* Vis scientist, NIH, 58; vis prof, Duke Univ, 79-80. *Mem:* Am Chem Soc; Sigma Xi; Am Asn Univ Professors. *Res:* Syntheses of alicyclic systems; transformations of amino acids. *Mailing Add:* 813 Oak Tree Terr DeLand FL 32724-3610

BEILSTEIN, HENRY RICHARD, MICROBIOLOGY, PUBLIC HEALTH. *Current Pos:* ADJ ASSOC PROF MICROBIOL & IMMUNOL, DEPT BIOMED SCI, ALLEGHENY SCH HEALTH SCI & DEPT MICROBIOL & IMMUNOL, MCP/HAHNEMANN SCH MED, 70-; ASSOC PROF MICROBIOL & IMMUNOL, PA COL PODIATRIC MED, 74-; INSTR, OGONTZ CAMPUS, PA STATE UNIV, 90- *Personal Data:* b Philadelphia, Pa, Dec 2, 20; m 46, Grace A Marple; c Janet L (Bittner), Richard A (deceased) & David R. *Educ:* Philadelphia Col Pharm & Sci, BSc, 43, MSc, 61, PhD(microbiol), 70. *Prof Exp:* Anal chemist immunochem & org chem, Merck, Sharpe & Dohme, 43-45; sr microbiologist, Dept Pub Health, City Philadelphia, 45-61, asst dir, Pub Health Labs, 61-70, dir, 70-78; educ coordr instr microbiol & med lab technol, 78-79, dir & chmn, Dept Med Lab Technol, Manor Col, 79-86. *Concurrent Pos:* Bacteriologist & consult, N Broad & Cherry Hill Clin Labs, 47-73; prof microbiol & med technol, Franklin Sch Sci & Arts, Philadelphia, 56-71; adj asst prof microbiol & immunol, Sch Med, Temple Univ, 69-82; vis assoc prof, Dept Microbiol & Immunol, Hahnemann Med Col & Hosp, 70-; consult, Smith Kline Labs, Pa, 71-78; assoc prof microbiol, Pa Col Podiatric Med, 74-82 & 86-; pres, Eastern Pa Br, Am Soc Microbiol, 81-83, Del Valley Chap, Christian Med & Dent Soc, 82-84; adj prof biol, Beaver Col, Glenside, Pa, 86-88; adj instr, Montgomery Co Community Col. *Mem:* Am Soc Microbiol; fel Am Pub Health Asn; Am Sci Affil; fel Am Acad Microbiol. *Res:* Clinical and laboratory aspects of sexually transmitted disease; immunofluorescence. *Mailing Add:* 1032 E Mt Pleasant Ave Philadelphia PA 19150-3421. *E-Mail:* beilstein@allegheny.edu

BEIM, HOWARD, ENVIRONMENTAL SCIENCE, HAZARDOUS MATERIALS. *Current Pos:* PROF CHEM, US MERCHANT MARINE ACAD, 80- *Personal Data:* b New York City, NY, Dec 6, 40. *Educ:* Univ Pa, PhD(org chem), 69. *Res:* Environmental science; hazardous materials. *Mailing Add:* Dept Math & Sci US Merchant Marine Acad Kings Point NY 11024-0169

BEIN, DONALD, MATHEMATICS. *Current Pos:* From asst prof to assoc prof, 64-74, PROF MATH, FAIRLEIGH DICKINSON UNIV, 74- *Personal Data:* b New York, NY, Dec 13, 34; m 60; c 2. *Educ:* Brooklyn Col, BS, 57; NY Univ, PhD(math), 64. *Mem:* Am Math Soc; Math Asn Am; Soc Indust & Appl Math. *Res:* Parabolic partial differential equations. *Mailing Add:* Dept Math Fairleigh Dickinson Univ Teaneck NJ 07666

BEINDORFF, ARTHUR BAKER, POLYMER CHEMISTRY. *Current Pos:* RETIRED. *Personal Data:* b Omaha, Nebr, Apr 16, 25; m 46, Doris Easterbrook; c Nancy L (Richbourg), Michael A & Robert A. *Educ:* Univ Nebr, BS, 47, MA, 49, PhD(biochem), 52. *Prof Exp:* From chemist to sr chemist, Chemstrand Corp, Monsanto Co, Ala, 52-58, group leader nylon polymer res, 58-59, head personnel sect Res Ctr, NC, 59-62, mgr patent liaison, 62-66, assoc dir patent liaison, Textiles Div, NY, 66-67, tech dir polyester, Ala, 67-70, dir tire technol, 70-74, dir apparel fibers technol, Monsanto Textiles Co, Fla, 74-75, dir, acrylic fiber technol, 75-84, dir, Decatur Ala Tech Ctr, 75-84, dir, technol exchange, 84-85. *Concurrent Pos:* Prof & chmn, Dept Chem, Athens Col, 52-55; prof & chmn, St Bernard Col, 54-56. *Mem:* Am Chem Soc; Soc Automotive Eng; Am Asn Textiles Technol; Sigma Xi. *Res:* Exploratory organic polymer chemistry; nylon; polyester; acrylic; synthetic fiber research and development. *Mailing Add:* 2812 Burningtree Mt Rd SE Decatur AL 35603

BEINEKE, LOWELL WAYNE, MATHEMATICS, GRAPH THEORY. *Current Pos:* from asst prof to assoc prof, 65-71, prof math, 71-86, JACK W SCHREY PROF MATH, PURDUE UNIV, FT WAYNE, 86- *Personal Data:* b Decatur, Ind, Nov 20, 39; m 67; c 2. *Educ:* Purdue Univ, BS, 61; Univ Mich, MA, 62, PhD(math), 65. *Prof Exp:* Res asst math inst soc res, Univ Mich, 62-63. *Concurrent Pos:* Res asst, Univ Col, Univ London, 66-67; consult inst soc res, Univ Mich, 65; tutor, Oxford Univ, 73-74; vis lectr, Polytechnic, North London, 80-81; assoc ed, J Graph Theory; bd gov, Math Asn Am, 90- *Mem:* Am Math Soc; Math Asn Am; Am Asn Univ Professors; Sigma Xi; London Math Soc. *Res:* Graph theory; network theory; mathematical models in the social sciences; combinatorial analysis; research and writing the theory and application of graphs; embedding and drawings of graph on surfaces, round-robin and bipartite tournaments, line graphs and line digraphs, multi-dimensional trees, and vulnerability of graphs. *Mailing Add:* Ind Univ Ft Wayne IN 46805. *Fax:* 219-481-6880; *E-Mail:* beineke@cvax.ipfw.indiana.edu

BEINEKE, WALTER FRANK, FOREST GENETICS. *Current Pos:* ASSOC PROF FORESTRY, PURDUE UNIV, 64- *Personal Data:* b Indianapolis, Ind, Mar 7, 38; m 61; c 2. *Educ:* Purdue Univ, BS, 60; Duke Univ, MF, 61; NC State Univ, PhD(forest genetics), 66. *Concurrent Pos:* Consult blackwalnut mgt & genetic improv, 90- *Mem:* Soc Am Foresters; Sigma Xi; Int Union Forestry Res Orgn. *Res:* Genetic improvement of black walnut, Juglans nigra, including selection, vegetative propagation, progeny testing, flowering and breeding; clones; tissue culture of hardwood trees. *Mailing Add:* Dept Forestry Purdue Univ West Lafayette IN 47907-1968

BEINERT, HELMUT, BIOINORGANIC CHEMISTRY, ENZYMOLOGY. *Current Pos:* res assoc, Inst Enzyme Res, 51-52, from asst prof to prof enzyme chem, 52-84, chmn sect III, 58-84, prof biochem, 67-84, EMER PROF ENZYME CHEM, INST ENZYME RES & EMER PROF BIOCHEM, UNIV WIS-MADISON, 84- *Personal Data:* b Lahr, Ger, Nov 17, 13; nat US; m 44, Elisabeth Meyhoefer; c 4. *Educ:* Univ Leipzig, Dr rer nat(chem), 43. *Hon Degrees:* DSc, Univ Wis Milwaukee, 87, Univ Konstane, Ger, 94. *Honors & Awards:* Res Career Award, NIH 63; Sr Scientist Award, Alexander von Humboldt Found, 81; Keilin Medal, 85; Sir Hans Krebs Medal, 89; Lipmann Lect & Plaque, 93; Warburg Medal 94. *Prof Exp:* Res assoc biol chem, Kaiser Wilhelm Inst Med Res, Ger, 43-45; biochemist, Air Force Aeromed Ctr, Ger, 46 & USAF Sch Aviation Med, 47-50; prof biochem & distinguished scholar residence, Med Col Wis, 85-94. *Concurrent Pos:* Permanent guest prof, Univ Konstanz, Ger, 67. *Mem:* Nat Acad Sci; Am Chem Soc; Am Soc Biol Chem & Molecular Biol; fel Am Acad Arts & Sci; Soc Biol Inorg Chem. *Res:* Structure and function of iron-sulfur proteins. *Mailing Add:* Inst Enzyme Res Univ Wis 1710 University Ave Madison WI 53705-4098. *Fax:* 608-265-2904

BEINFELD, MARGERY COHEN, PEPTIDE BIOSYNTHESIS & PROCESSING , CHOLECYSTOKININ. *Current Pos:* PROF, DEPT PHARM EXP THER, SCH MED, TUFTS UNIV, 95- *Personal Data:* b Washington, DC, Oct 21, 45; m 70, Solon; c Benjamin E & Molly T. *Educ:* Wash Univ, St Louis, BS, 68, PhD(biol), 73. *Prof Exp:* Fel biochem, Med Ctr, St Louis Univ, 73-75; fel psychiat, Med Ctr, Wash Univ, 75-79; guest worker, NIMH-NIH, 79-81; staff fel, Nat Inst Arthritis, Metab & Digestive Dis-NIH, 80-81; from asst prof to prof pharmacol, Med Ctr, St Louis Univ, 81-95, PROF PHARMACOL & PHYSIOL, 90-95. *Concurrent Pos:* Vis assoc prof biochem, Paris Six, Paris, France, 87-88, vis prof biochem, 90. *Mem:* Soc Neurosci; AAAS. *Res:* Biosynthesis, processing and regulation of release of neuropeptides with a focus on cholecystokinin; molecular cloning of monobasic pro-hormone cleaving enzymes; production of prohormones and processing enzymes by recombinant DNA methods. *Mailing Add:* Dept Pharm Exp Ther Tufts Univ Sch Med 136 Harrison Ave Boston MA 02111

BEINFEST, SIDNEY, ORGANIC CHEMISTRY, CHEMICAL ENGINEERING. *Current Pos:* RETIRED. *Personal Data:* b Brooklyn, NY, Oct 29, 17; m 42, Eleanor Kligfield; c Bennett & Elliot. *Educ:* Brooklyn Col, BA, 38; Univ Ark, MS, 39; Polytech Inst Brooklyn, PhD(chem), 49. *Prof Exp:* Dir res & develop, Premo Pharmaceut Labs, Inc, 41-45; vpres in charge opers, Berkeley Chem Corp, 46-63; tech vpres, Millmaster Chem Corp, 63-64, vpres technol, Millmaster Onyx Chem Corp, Jersey City, 64-74, vpres corp tech, Millmaster Onyx Corp, NY, 74-86. *Mem:* AAAS; NY Acad Sci; Am Chem Soc; Sci Res Soc Am; Sigma Xi. *Res:* Cyanine dyes; pyrazine derivatives; barbiturates; anti-malarial drugs; muscle relaxant; tranquillizing drugs. *Mailing Add:* 248 Emerson Lane Berkeley Heights NJ 07922

BEINFIELD, WILLIAM HARVEY, INTERNAL MEDICINE, PHARMACOLOGY. *Current Pos:* from asst instr to instr med, NY Med Col, 50-54, instr physiol, 50-52, assoc, 52-54, from assoc prof to prof, 56-64, from assoc to prof pharmacol, 56-90, asst prof med, 56-90, EMER PROF PHARMACOL & MED, NY MED COL, 91- *Personal Data:* b St Louis, Mo, Apr 8, 18; m 50; c 2. *Educ:* Univ Wis, BA, 40; Columbia Univ, MD, 43; Am

Bd Internal Med, dipl, 52. *Concurrent Pos:* Adv drug & formulary comt, Dept Hosp, NY; pres, Corlette Glorney Found Med Res, 81- *Mem:* Fel Am Col Physicians; Am Heart Asn; Am Thoracic Soc; fel NY Acad Med; fel NY Acad Sci. *Res:* Cardiopulmonary physiology and pharmacology; studies of spontaneous mechanical activity of airway smooth muscle in vivo and its modulation by endogenous mediator substances and drugs. *Mailing Add:* 150 E 69th Apt 16G New York NY 10021

BEINING, PAUL R, MICROBIOLOGY, BIOCHEMISTRY & IMMUNOLOGY. *Current Pos:* instr, 49-51, assoc prof, 67-75, PROF BIOL, UNIV SCRANTON, 75- *Personal Data:* b Pittsburgh, Pa, Feb 2, 23. *Educ:* Spring Hill Col, BS, 49; Cath Univ Am, MS, 52, PhD(microbiol), 62. *Prof Exp:* Instr, St Joseph's Col, Pa, 62-63, asst prof, 63-66; assoc prof & chmn dept, Wheeling Col, 66-67. *Concurrent Pos:* Researcher, Georgetown Univ, 69-71; guest researcher, NIH, 71-80, Food & Drug Admin, 81-91. *Mem:* AAAS; Am Soc Microbiol. *Res:* Biochemical and serological characteristics of in-vivo and in-vitro cultivated Staphyloccus aureus; increased protection with active immunization with influenza virus; polyphasic taxonomy of marine and non-marine Micrococci; ultrastructure and biochemical analysis of staphylococcal membrane systems; immune response in mice to staphylococcal lipo teichoilacid; enhanced immune response in mice to type VI capsular polysaccharide; antibody induced immunosuppression; immune response to conserved areas of the human immunodeficiency virus. *Mailing Add:* Univ Scranton Campion Hall Scranton PA 18510-4623

BEIQUE, RENE ALEXANDRE, RADIATION PHYSICS. *Current Pos:* RETIRED. *Personal Data:* b Cornerbrook, Nfld, Nov 29, 25; m 51; c 3. *Educ:* Univ Montreal, BA, 47, BSc, 50, MSc, 51; Mass Inst Technol, PhD(physics), 58. *Prof Exp:* Jr physicist, High Voltage Lab, Mass Inst Technol, 52-53; physicist, Montreal Gen Hosp, 58-68 & Notre Dame Hosp, 68-91; assoc prof radiol, Univ Montreal, 69-71, prof, 71- *Concurrent Pos:* Lectr, McGill Univ, 60-69, asst prof, 69-; consult, Montreal Children's Hosp, 60- *Mem:* Soc Nuclear Med; Can Asn Physicists; Can Asn Radiol. *Res:* Physics of radiology, especially diagnostic radiology. *Mailing Add:* 405 Bienville Longueuil PQ J4H 2E8 Can

BEIRNE, BRYAN PATRICK, ECONOMIC ENTOMOLOGY. *Current Pos:* dir, Pestology Ctr, Simon Fraser Univ, 67-79, prof, 67-93, dean grad studies, 79-83, EMER PROF PEST MGT, SIMON FRASER UNIV, 83- *Personal Data:* b Wexford, Ireland, Jan 22, 18; m 48; c Patrick & Anne. *Educ:* Univ Dublin, PhD(entom), 40, MSc, 41, MA, 42. *Honors & Awards:* Gold Medal, Entom Soc Can. *Prof Exp:* Asst lectr zool, Univ Dublin, 42-43, asst dir mus zool & comp anat, 42-49, lectr entom, 43-49; sr entomologist, Res Br, Can Dept Agr, 49-55, dir, Res Inst, Belleville, Ont, 55-67. *Mem:* Am Entom Soc; Entom Soc Can; Royal Irish Acad. *Res:* Biological control; pest management; ecology of agricultural insects; insect taxonomy; history of Irish entomology. *Mailing Add:* Dept Biol Sci Simon Fraser Univ Burnaby BC V5A 1S6 Can

BEISEL, WILLIAM R, INFECTIOUS DISEASES, METABOLISM & NUTRITION. *Current Pos:* ADJ PROF, JOHNS HOPKINS SCH HYG & PUB HEALTH, 85- *Personal Data:* b Philadelphia, Pa, Apr 8, 23; m 49, Betty Lois Figg; c Kirk W, Daniel S, Carl J, Beth A & Ruth E. *Educ:* Muhlenberg Col, BA, 46; Ind Univ, Indianapolis, MD, 48; Am Bd Internal Med, dipl, 55. *Honors & Awards:* Hoff Gold Medal, Walter Reed Army Inst Res, 57; Award & Commendation, Army Sci Conf, 66; Stitt Award, Asn Mil Surgeons, 68; B L Cohen Award, Am Soc Microbiol, 82; Robert Herman Award, Am Soc Clin Nutrit, 95. *Prof Exp:* Intern, Fitsimmons Army Hosp, Denver, Colo, US Army, 48-49, resident med, Letterman Gen Hosp, San Francisco, 49-52, asst chief dept med, 21st Army Sta Hosp, Korea, 53-54, chief dept med, US Army Hosp, Ft Leonard Wood, Mo, 54-56, basic sci yr, Walter Reed Army Inst Res, DC, 56-57, chief dept metab, 57-60, chief phys sci div, Walter Reed Med Unit, Ft Detrick, Md, 62-68, sci adv, 69-80, dep scientist, 80-84, spec asst surgeon gen biotechnol, 84-85. *Concurrent Pos:* Fel metab, Sch Med, Univ Calif, San Francisco, 61-62; chief med sect 4, Walter Reed Army Hosp, Washington, DC & asst prof, Sch Med, Georgetown Univ, 57-60; mem, study sect pharmacol & exp therapeut, NIH, 59-60, study sect endocrinol, 64-68; consult metab dis to Surgeon Gen, US Army, 66-76; assoc prof, Sch Med, Univ Md, 67-77; mem, infective agents res eval comt, Vet Admin, 69-71; mem, Grad Sch Adv Coun, Hood Col, 75-; chmn subcomt nutrit & infection, Nat Res Coun, 76-77; consult, Div Polar Progs, NSF, 76-80; Dept Defense rep, NIH Interagency Comt Recombinant DNA Res, 76-85; chmn, Nutrit Adv Group, AMA, 77-80; chmn, Life Sci Res Off Adv Coun, Fed Am Soc Exp Biol, 77-; chmn, Subcomt Nutrit & Infection, Int Union Nutrit Sci, 78-; assoc ed, J Nutrit Immunol, 92-; mem, Comt Mil Nurit, Nat Acad Sci, 93- *Mem:* Fel Am Col Physicians; Am Inst Nutrit; Infectious Dis Soc Am; Am Soc Clin Nutrit. *Res:* Broad aspects of endocrinology, metabolism, nutrition and immunology, especially as they pertain to and help regulate the responses of a host to the stress of infectious illness and malnutrition on the immune system. *Mailing Add:* 2108 Harlans Run Naples FL 34105

BEISER, CARL A(DOLPH), PHYSICAL METALLURGY. *Current Pos:* supvr phys metall, 60-64, asst div chief, Res & Develop Dept, 64-67, div chief mat res, 67-78, DIR RES, NAT STEEL CORP, 78- *Personal Data:* b Cleveland, Ohio, Apr 28, 29; m 50; c 2. *Educ:* Case Inst Technol, BS, 51, MS, 53, PhD(phys metall), 57. *Prof Exp:* Res asst metall, Case Inst Technol, 51-57; metall engr, Union Carbide Metals Co, 57-60. *Mem:* Am Soc Metals; Sigma Xi. *Res:* Ferrous materials. *Mailing Add:* 6108G Graygate Lane Charlotte NC 28210-4030

BEISER, HELEN R, PSYCHOANALYSIS, CHILD PSYCHIATRY. *Current Pos:* From instr to assoc prof psychiat, 52-76, chmn child analysis training, Inst Psychoanalysis, 69-78, clin prof, 76-79, EMER PROF PSYCHIAT, UNIV ILL COL MED, 79- *Personal Data:* b Chicago, Ill, Nov 15, 14. *Educ:* Univ Ariz, BS, 35; Univ Ill, MS & MD, 41. *Honors & Awards:* Friend of Children, Ill Child Care Asn, 86. *Concurrent Pos:* Fel staff & consult, Inst Juv Res, 48-80; med dir, North Shore Ment Health Clin, 53-54. *Mem:* Am Psychoanalysis Asn; Am Acad Child Psychiat; Am Psychiat Asn. *Res:* Evaluation and measurement in child diagnosis and treatment; personality and achievement in medical students; process of supervision in psychotherapy; psychological meaning of games. *Mailing Add:* 5333 N Sheridan Rd 18C Chicago IL 60640

BEISHLINE, ROBERT RAYMOND, PHYSICAL ORGANIC CHEMISTRY. *Current Pos:* assoc prof, 66-74, PROF CHEM, WEBER STATE UNIV, 74- *Personal Data:* b Ogden, Utah, Nov 28, 30; m 59, Audrey Andelin; c Erin, Ben, Megan & Rob. *Educ:* Brigham Young Univ, BS, 55, MS, 57; Pa State Univ, PhD(chem), 62. *Prof Exp:* Res chemist, Am Cyanamid Co, 62-63; asst prof chem, State Univ NY Albany, 63, Res Found fac res fel, 64. *Mem:* Am Chem Soc; Sigma Xi. *Res:* Chemical kinetics of organic reactions; reaction mechanisms; mechanism of coal hydrogenation by hydrogen donor solvents; pyrolysis of coal-related model compounds. *Mailing Add:* 1769 Oak St Ogden UT 84401-2106. *Fax:* 801-626-7445

BEISLER, JOHN ALBERT, MEDICINAL CHEMISTRY. *Current Pos:* HEALTH SCIENTIST ADMIN, DIV RES GRANTS, NIH, 81- *Personal Data:* b Hackensack, NJ, May 18, 37; m 68, Sabine Schmidt; c Katarina & Joshua. *Educ:* Fairleigh Dickinson Univ, BS, 60; Rutgers Univ, PhD(org chem), 64. *Prof Exp:* Fel, Cambridge Univ, Eng, 64-66; staff fel steroid chem, Nat Inst Arthritis & Metab Dis, 66-71; sr investr med chem, Microbiol Assoc Whittaker Corp, 71-74; res chemist med chem, Nat Cancer Inst, 74-81. *Concurrent Pos:* Lectr, Am Univ, Washington, DC, 73. *Mem:* Am Chem Soc; Royal Soc Chem; AAAS; Biophys Soc. *Res:* Rational design and synthesis of drug molecules having a potential chemotherapeutic value in the treatment of cancer in humans. *Mailing Add:* Biophys Study Sect NIH Westwood Bldg Rm 334 Bethesda MD 20892. *Fax:* 301-594-7043; *E-Mail:* bbe@cu.nih.gov

BEISPIEL, MYRON, ORGANIC CHEMISTRY. *Current Pos:* CHMN SCI DEPT, RANNEY SCH, 63- *Personal Data:* b New York, NY, Nov 21, 31; m 54; c 3. *Educ:* Brooklyn Col, BS, 53; NY Univ, PhD(chem), 59. *Prof Exp:* Instr chem, NY Univ, 57-59; with Nuodex Prod Co, Div Heyden Newport Chem Co, 59-61; with Sci Design Co, Inc, 61-63. *Concurrent Pos:* Dir environ health lab, Woodbridge Twp, NJ; consult, Cent Jersey Regional Air Pollution Control Agency, NJ, 73-; asst dir, Middlesex County Pub Health Lab, 78- *Mem:* Am Chem Soc; Am Analytical Chem Soc; Sigma Xi. *Res:* Organic and inorganic synthesis; analysis techniques, especially gas chromatography; photo chemistry; auto and catalytic oxidation; air and water pollution problems; analytical microscopy; environmental health and impact studies; public health. *Mailing Add:* 11 Gayle St New Monmouth NJ 07748-1419

BEISSER, ARNOLD RAY, psychiatry; deceased, see previous edition for last biography

BEISSNER, ROBERT EDWARD, THEORETICAL SOLID STATE PHYSICS. *Current Pos:* PHYSICIST, SOUTHWEST RES INST, 69- *Personal Data:* b San Antonio, Tex, Oct 27, 33; m 54; c 6. *Educ:* St Mary's Univ, BS, 55; Tex Christian Univ, MA, 60, PhD(physics), 65. *Prof Exp:* Nuclear engr, Westinghouse Elec Corp, 55-56 & Gen Dynamics Corp, 56-69. *Mem:* Am Phys Soc; AAAS. *Res:* Theory of defects in metals; applications of scattering theory in nondestructive evaluation. *Mailing Add:* Southwest Res Inst PO Drawer 28510 San Antonio TX 78228

BEISTEL, DONALD W, PHYSICAL CHEMISTRY. *Current Pos:* asst prof, 68-69, ASSOC PROF CHEM, UNIV MO-ROLLA, 69- *Personal Data:* b Sunbury, Pa, Feb 29, 36; m 63; c 1. *Educ:* Bucknell Univ, BS, 58; Univ Del, PhD(chem), 63. *Prof Exp:* Mem tech staff, Directorate Res & Develop, US Army Missile Command, Redstone Arsenal, Ala, 63-64; asst prof chem, Franklin & Marshall Col, 64-66 & Marshall Univ, 66-68. *Mem:* AAAS; Am Chem Soc; Soc Appl Spectros. *Res:* Elucidation of molecular structure and electronic configurations of polynuclear aromatic compounds by application of nuclear magnetic resonance; applications of computer methods to chemistry; molecular orbital calculations on chemical carcinogens. *Mailing Add:* Dept Chem Univ Mo 1101 McCutcheon Rd Rolla MO 65401-2631

BEITCH, IRWIN, EMBRYOLOGY, CYTOLOGY. *Current Pos:* from asst prof to assoc prof, 69-76, PROF BIOL, QUINNIPIAC COL, 76- *Personal Data:* b Brooklyn, NY, Nov 28, 37; m 63; c 2. *Educ:* Univ Richmond, BS, 60, MS, 62; Univ Va, PhD(biol), 68. *Prof Exp:* NIH trainee ophthal res, Col Physicians & Surgeons, Columbia Univ, 67-69. *Mem:* AAAS; Am Soc Zool; Am Inst Biol Sci; NY Acad Sci. *Res:* Electron microscopy of keratinization and feather development; electron microscopy of eye tissues; histology; histochemistry and electron microscopy of endorphin secretion in earthworms. *Mailing Add:* Dept Med Lab Sci Quinnipiac Col Hamden CT 06518-9987

BEITCHMAN, BURTON DAVID, PROCESS DEVELOPMENT, ANALYTICAL DEVELOPMENT. *Current Pos:* RETIRED. *Personal Data:* b Philadelphia, Pa, May 1, 26; m 56, Irma Shavelson; c Mark I & Ruth S (Krass). *Educ:* Temple Univ, BA, 48; Rutgers Univ, MS, 52, PhD(org chem), 54; Widener Col, MBA, 73. *Prof Exp:* Chemist, Publicker Industs, Inc, 48-49;

asst res specialist, Rutgers Univ, 54-56; chemist, Nat Bur Stand, 57-60; chemist, Air Prod & Chem Inc, 60-66, sr res chemist, 66-80, sr prin res chemist, 66-82; supvr chem develop Lab, Allied Corp, 84-94. *Mem:* Am Chem Soc. *Res:* Organic synthesis; isocyanates; polyurethanes; chemical additives; amine catalysts and curing agents; peroxide decomposition accelerators; new products and process research and development; fluorochemicals; oxidation reactions, homogeneous and heterogeneous catalysis; process safety, process development, analytical methods development; cumene to phenol-acetone process. *Mailing Add:* 134 Parkview Dr Springfield PA 19064-1735

BEITINGER, THOMAS LEE, PHYSIOLOGICAL ECOLOGY, BIOSTATISTICS. *Current Pos:* asst prof, 76-82, assoc prof, 82-90, PROF, DEPT BIOL SCI, UNIV NORTH TEX, 90- *Personal Data:* b Prairie du Chein, Wis, Mar 4, 45; m 67, Claudia Tesch; c Thane S & Grant T. *Educ:* Hamline Univ, BS, 67; Univ RI, MS, 69; Univ Wis-Madison, PhD(zool), 74. *Prof Exp:* Ecologist, Great Lakes Thermal Effects Prog, Argonne Nat Lab, 74-76. *Mem:* Am Fisheries Soc; Sigma Xi. *Res:* Behavioral and physiological responses of animals to environmental variables; temperature preference, avoidance and regulation of ectothermic organisms; aquatic toxicology; biostatistics. *Mailing Add:* Dept Biol Sci Univ North Tex Denton TX 76203. *Fax:* 817-565-3821

BEITINS, INESE ZINTA, PEDIATRIC ENDOCRINOLOGY. *Current Pos:* AT DEPT PEDIAT, UNIV MICH, ANN ARBOR. *Personal Data:* b Riga, Latvia. *Educ:* Univ Toronto, MD, 62; FRCP(C), 67. *Prof Exp:* Rotating intern med & surg, Toronto Western Hosp, 62-63; resident pediat, Hosp Sick Children, Toronto, 63-65; fel pediat, Johns Hopkins Hosp, 65-66; resident path & med, Hosp Sick Children & Toronto Gen Hosp, 66-67; staff physician pediat, Hosp Sick Children, 67-68; fel pediat endocrinol, Johns Hopkins Hosp, 68-71; Busswell fel & res asst prof pediat, State Univ NY Buffalo, 72-73; asst prof pediat, Harvard Med Sch, 73-79, assoc prof, 79-; asst gynec, Mass Gen Hosp, 77- *Mem:* Lawson Wilkins Pediat Endocrine Soc; Am Fedn Clin Res; Endocrine Soc; NY Acad Sci; Royal Col Med London. *Res:* Adrenal steroid measurement and their role in hypertension, maternal fetal interrelationships and disorders such as congenital virilizing adrenal hyperplasia; Gonadotropin heterogeneity, subunits and biological versus immunological activity; effects of nutrition and exercise on reproduction. *Mailing Add:* Dept Pediat Med Prof Bldg Univ Mich 1522 Simpson Rd E Ann Arbor MI 48109-0600

BEITZ, ALVIN JAMES, NEUROCYTOLOGY, NEUROCHEMISTRY. *Current Pos:* from asst prof to assoc prof, 82-88, PROF VET BIOL & NEUROSCI, UNIV MINN, 88- *Personal Data:* b Meadville, PA, Feb 16, 49; US citizen; m 71; c 7. *Educ:* Gannon Univ, BS, 71; Univ Minn, PhD(anat), 76. *Prof Exp:* Fel neuroanat, Harvard Med Sch, 76-78; asst prof anat, Univ SC, 78-82. *Concurrent Pos:* Review ed, J Synapse, 87-; mem NIH study sect, 87. *Mem:* Soc Neurosci; Int Brain Res Orgn; AAAS; Am Asn Anatomists; Am Pain Soc. *Res:* Elucidate chemical framework of key brain regions involved in pain, pain modulation, motor coordination, learning and memory; aging and alzheimers disease; mechanics underlying epilepsy. *Mailing Add:* 8060 Groveland Rd St Paul MN 55112

BEITZ, DONALD CLARENCE, NUTRITIONAL BIOCHEMISTRY. *Current Pos:* from asst prof to assoc prof, 67-77, PROF ANIMAL SCI & BIOCHEM, IOWA STATE UNIV, 77-, DISTINGUISHED PROF AGR, 89- *Personal Data:* b Stewardson, Ill, Mar 30, 40; m 63; c David & Jennifer. *Educ:* Univ Ill, BS, 62, MS, 63; Mich State Univ, PhD(biochem, dairy sci), 67. *Honors & Awards:* Nutrit Res Award, Am Feed Indust Asn & Am Dairy Sci Asn; Am Cyanamid Award, Am Dairy Sci. *Prof Exp:* Ralston Purina fel, 62-65; NIH fel, 65-67. *Mem:* AAAS; Am Dairy Sci Asn; Am Soc Animal Sci; Am Inst Nutrit; Sigma Xi; Am Soc Biochem & Molecular Biol. *Res:* Lipid metabolism in farm animals; ketosis in dairy cattle; catecholamine metabolism in pigs; etiology of milk fever in dairy cattle; mitochondrial DNA and milk production. *Mailing Add:* Dept Animal Sci Iowa State Univ 313 Kildee Hall Ames IA 50011-3150. *Fax:* 515-294-6445

BEIZER, BORIS, COMPUTER & INFORMATION SCIENCE. *Current Pos:* CONSULT, SOFTWARE TESTING & QUAL ASSURANCE, 83- *Personal Data:* b Brussels, Belg, June 25, 34; US citizen; m 55; c 2. *Educ:* City Col NY, BS, 56; Univ Pa, MS, 62, PhD(comput sci), 66. *Prof Exp:* Technician med instrumentation, Columbia-Presby Med Ctr, 54-56; sr engr, Repub Aviation Corp, NY, 56-58; prin engr, Airborne Instrument Labs, 58-59; proj engr, Comput Div, Philco Corp, Pa, 59-61; chief logic design, Navig Comput Corp, 61-63; sr staff scientist, Pa Res Assocs, 63-66; chief scientist, Data Systs Analysts, Inc, Pennsauken, 66-87. *Mem:* Inst Elec & Electronics Engrs; Asn Comput Mach; Asn Software Test Eng. *Res:* Computer system architecture; performance analysis and modeling; computer controlled communications; testing and quality assurance. *Mailing Add:* 1232 Glenbrook Rd Huntingdon Valley PA 19006

BEIZER, LAWRENCE H, INTERNAL MEDICINE, HEMATOLOGY. *Current Pos:* instr med, Univ Pa, Sch Med, 46-49, assoc, 49-50, from asst prof to prof, 50-77, dir, Div Hemat, 50-70 & Div Oncol, 70-75, co-dir, Div Hemat & Oncol, Grad Hosp, 75-79, EMER PROF CLIN MED, SCH MED, UNIV PA, 77-, CONSULT, DIV HEMAT & ONCOL, GRAD HOSP, 79- *Personal Data:* b Scranton, Pa, Feb 17, 09; m 51; c 3. *Educ:* Univ Pa, BS, 30; Harvard Med Sch, MD, 34; Univ Minn, MS, 42. *Prof Exp:* Intern, Philadelphia Gen Hosp, 34-36; resident clin path, Hosp Univ Pa, 36-37; fel, Mayo Clin, 37-43. *Concurrent Pos:* Assoc med, Woman's Med Col, 46-48, from clin asst prof to clin assoc prof, 48-56, consult, Hosp, 47-56; consult, Valley Forge Army Hosp, Phoenixville, 47-74, Vet Hosp, Philadelphia, 53-56, Walson Army Hosp, Ft Dix, NJ, 60-63 & Vet Hosp, Wilmington, Del, 62-66; physician, Presby-Univ Pa Med Ctr, 70- *Mem:* Fel Am Col Physicians; Am Soc Hemat; Am Soc Clin Oncol; Sigma Xi. *Res:* Clinical hematology, especially bone marrow aspiration biopsy and mutiple myeloma; oncology. *Mailing Add:* 1408 Augusta Circle Mt Laurel NJ 08054-2760

BEJAN, ADRIAN, MECHANICAL ENGINEERING, MATERIALS SCIENCE. *Current Pos:* prof, Dept Mech Eng & Mat Sci, 84-89, J A JONES PROF, DEPT MECH ENG, DUKE UNIV, 89- *Personal Data:* b Sept 24, 48; c 3. *Educ:* Mass Inst Technol, SB & SM, 72, PhD(mech eng), 75. *Hon Degrees:* PhD, Univ Bucharest, 92. *Honors & Awards:* Ralph R Teetor Award, Soc Automotive Engrs, 80; Gustus L Larson Award, Am Soc Mech Engrs, 88, James Harry Potter Gold Medal, 90. *Prof Exp:* Res asst, Dept Mech Eng, Mass Inst Technol, 71-74, lectr & res assoc, 75-76; fel, Miller Inst Basic Res Sci, Univ Calif, Berkeley, 76-78; asst prof, Dept Mech Eng, Univ Colo, Boulder, 78-81, Croft prof, Col Eng, 81-82, assoc prof, Dept Mech Eng, 81-84. *Concurrent Pos:* Consult, Dept Energy, NSF, Solar Energy Res Inst, Procter & Gamble, Lord Corp, John Wiley & Sons, McGraw Hill, Harper & Row, Hemisphere Pub Corp, Rolscreen Co & ENI Inc; fac fel, Univ Colo, 84-85; F Mosey vis scholar, Univ Western Australia. *Mem:* Fel Am Soc Mech Engrs; Am Acad Mech. *Res:* Entropy generation through heat and fluid flow; convection heat transfer; advanced engineering thermodynamics, heat transfer; convection in porous media. *Mailing Add:* Dept Mech Eng Duke Univ Durham NC 27706-8001

BEJAR, EZRA, CARDIOVASCULAR PHARMACOLOGY, CELL & MOLECULAR CARDIOLOGY. *Current Pos:* LAB DIR, REES-STEALY RES FOUND, 92- *Personal Data:* b Mexico City, Mex, Sept 2, 58; m 82, Veronica Angeles; c Ezra A & Paula C. *Educ:* Autonomous Metrop Univ, BS, 81, MS, 85; Univ Pac, PhD(pharmacol), 91. *Honors & Awards:* Carl C Riedesel Award, 88; Travel Award, Am Soc Pharmacog, 89. *Prof Exp:* Grad res fel, Mex Med Inst, 82-85, assoc scientist, 85-87; teaching asst, Univ Pac, 87-91; res scientist, Univ Miss, 91-92. *Concurrent Pos:* Instr biophys, Simon Bolivar Univ, 85-86, animal physiol, 85-86; nat investr, Mex Govt, 86; adj prof biol, San Diego State Univ, 92-; peer reviewer, J Natural Prod, 93-; res grantee, Sharp Found, 94-, Calif Metab Res Found, 94-, Fogarty Int, NIH, 96- & Mus Man, 95; res assoc, San Diego Mus Man, 95- *Mem:* Soc Advan Chicanos & Native Am Sci; Am Soc Pharmacog; Am Soc Pharmacol & Exp Therapeut. *Res:* Cardiac mechanics, assessment of myocyte contractility by video microscopy and digital image processing; cardiovascular pharmacology; pharmacodynamics of naturally-occurring compounds; antioxidants and reperfusion-induced injury. *Mailing Add:* 2001 Fourth Ave San Diego CA 92101-2303. *Fax:* 619-235-8745; *E-Mail:* ebejar@sunstroke.sdsu.edu

BEJNAR, WALDEMERE, GEOLOGY. *Current Pos:* CONSULT GEOLOGIST, 58-; PRES, WALDMERE BEJNAR & ASSOCS INC, 59- *Personal Data:* b Hamtramck, Mich, Feb 7, 20; m 46, Katherine Marble; c Thaddeus, Craig, Diana (Russell), Tarn (Stevens) & Tor (John). *Educ:* Univ Mich, BS, 43, MA, 47; Univ Ariz, PhD(geol), 50; Univ NMex, MS, 65. *Prof Exp:* Geologist, US Dept Reclamation, 50 & Foreign Sect, US Geol Surv, Nigeria, 50-52; asst prof geol, NMex Inst Mining & Technol, 52-55; consult geologist, 55-58; assoc sponsor, Dale Carnegie & Assocs, 58-63. *Concurrent Pos:* prof geol & geog, New Mex Highlands Univ, 65-80. *Mem:* Am Inst Prof Geol; Sigma Xi. *Res:* Ore deposition; ground water; landslides. *Mailing Add:* Hope Farm Rd Socorro NM 87801

BEKEFI, GEORGE, physics; deceased, see previous edition for last biography

BEKENSTEIN, JACOB DAVID, RELATIVITY, ASTROPHYSICS. *Current Pos:* PROF, RACAH INST PHYSICS, HEBREW UNIV, ISRAEL, 90-POLAK CHAIR, THEORET PHYSICS, 93- *Personal Data:* b Mexico City, Mex, May 1, 47; US & Israeli citizen; m 78, Bilha Sorek; c Yehonadav, Uriah & Rivka. *Educ:* Polytech Inst Brooklyn, BS & MS, 69; Princeton Univ, PhD(physics), 72. *Honors & Awards:* Bergmann Prize Sci, Israel, 77; Landau Prize Res, Israel, 81; Gravity Res Found First Prize, 81; Rothschild Prize Physics, Israel, 88. *Prof Exp:* Res assoc, Ctr Relativity Theory, Dept Physics, Univ Tex, Austin, 72-74; sr lectr, Dept Physics, Ben-Gurion Univ Negev, Israel, 74-76, from assoc prof to prof, 76-92, Arnow chair astrophys, 83-92. *Concurrent Pos:* Vis prof, Univ Calif, Santa Barbara, 80&92-93, Princeton Univ, 80, Univ Tex, Austin 86 & Univ Toronto, 87; steering comt, Jerusalem Winter Sch Theoret Physics; mem, Int Comt Gen Relativity. *Mem:* Israeli Phys Soc; Int Astron Union; Soc Gen Relativity. *Res:* Physical properties of collapsed stars; thermodynamics of black holes; variability of particle properties; relativistic magnetohydrodynamics; gravitational effects on quantum processes; formation of galaxies, cosmology information theory. *Mailing Add:* Racah Inst Physics Hebrew Univ Givat Ran Jerusalem 91904 Israel

BEKERSKY, IHOR, BIOCHEMISTRY. *Current Pos:* DIR PHARMCEUT, FUJISAWA USA INC, 91- *Personal Data:* b USSR, Oct 25, 40; US citizen; m 65; c 3. *Educ:* Hunter Col, BA, 61; NY Univ, MS, 71, PhD(biochem), 78. *Prof Exp:* Res technician, Dept Environ Med, NY Univ, 61-64; res assoc, Pub Health Res Inst, 68-71; asst scientist drug metab, Dept Pharmacokinetics, Hoffman La Roche, Inc, 71-72, assoc scientist, 72-75, scientist, 75-78, sr scientist biopharmaceuts, 78-81, asst res group chief biopharmaceut, 81-87; dir pharmaceut chem, Hazelton Labs, 87-91. *Mem:* Acad Pharmaceut Sci; Am Soc Pharmacol & Exp Therapeut; Sigma Xi. *Res:* Renal drug disposition and factors affecting the mechanisms of drug elimination; preclinical animal models to study drug disposition and pharmacokinetics. *Mailing Add:* Fujisawa USA Inc 3 Pkwy N Deerfield IL 60015

BEKEY, GEORGE A(LBERT), ROBOTICS, INTELLIGENT MANUFACTURING. *Current Pos:* from asst prof to assoc prof, Univ Southern Calif, 62-68, chmn, Elec Eng Systs Dept, 78-82, dir, Robotics Inst, 83-86, chmn, Comput Sci Dept, 84-89, PROF COMPUT SCI, ELEC ENG & BIOMED ENG, UNIV SOUTHERN CALIF, 68-, ASSOC DEAN RES, 96- *Personal Data:* b Czech, June 19, 28; US citizen; m 51, Shirley White; c Ronald & Michelle. *Educ:* Univ Calif, BS, 50; Univ Calif, Los Angeles, MS, 52, PhD(eng), 62. *Prof Exp:* Tech asst & res engr, Sch Eng, Univ Calif, Los Angeles, 50-54; mgr, Comput Ctr, Beckman Instruments, Los Angeles, 56-58; group leader, sect head & sr staff engr, TRW Systs, Los Angeles, 58-62. *Concurrent Pos:* Nat lectr, Sigma Xi, 76-77; ed, Trans Robotics & Automation, Inst Elec & Electronics Engrs, 85-; assoc ed, Math & Comput Simulation & Trans Soc Comput Simulation; grants, NSF, 87-89, 87- & 90-, NASA-Jet Propulsion Lab, 83-89, Kaprielian Res Innovation Fund, 89-92; dir, Robotics Res Lab, Univ Southern Calif, 90-; ed, Autonomous Robots, 93- *Mem:* Nat Acad Eng; fel Inst Elec & Electronics Engrs; fel AAAS; Asn Comput Mach; Am Asn Artificial Intel; Soc Comput Simulation; Int Neural Network Soc; Robotics & Automation Soc (pres, 96-97). *Res:* Intelligent robotic systems; artificial intelligence and robotics in medicine; biological signal processing; autonomous, intelligent robots equipped with sensory feedback which are capable of adaption to environmental change. *Mailing Add:* Dept Comput Sci Univ Southern Calif 941 W 37th Pl Los Angeles CA 90089-0781. *E-Mail:* bekey@robotics.usc.edu

BEKHOR, ISAAC, in situ hybridization, dna cloning; deceased, see previous edition for last biography

BEKOFF, ANNE C, DEVELOPMENTAL NEUROBIOLOGY, NEUROETHOLOGY. *Current Pos:* Res assoc neurophysiol, 75-76, asst prof, 76-82, assoc prof, 82-89, PROF, DEPT ENVIRON POP & ORGANISMIC BIOL, UNIV COLO, 89- *Personal Data:* b Denver, Colo, May 19, 47; m 70. *Educ:* Smith Col, BA, 69; Wash Univ, St Louis, Mo, PhD(neurobiol & develop), 74. *Concurrent Pos:* Alfred P Sloan Found res fel, 79-81; John Simon Guggenheim res fel, 83-84; mem coun, Int Soc Neuroethol, 90-95. *Mem:* Soc Neurosci; fel AAAS; Int Brain Res Orgn; Animal Behav Soc; Int Soc Neuroethol. *Res:* Studies of the ontogeny of the motor control mechanisms underlying the production of coordinated behaviors in embryonic and posthatching chicks using neurophysiological, kinematic and behavioral techniques. *Mailing Add:* Dept Environ Pop & Organismic Biol Univ Colo Boulder Campus Box B-334 Boulder CO 80309-0334

BEKOFF, MARC, ANIMAL BEHAVIOR. *Current Pos:* asst prof, 74-80, PROF BIOL, UNIV COLO, BOULDER, 80- *Personal Data:* b Brooklyn, NY, Sept 6, 45; m 70. *Educ:* Washington Univ, AB, 67, PhD(animal behav), 72; Hofstra Univ, MA, 68. *Prof Exp:* Asst prof biol, Univ Mo, St Louis, 73-74. *Concurrent Pos:* Guggenheim Mem Found fel, 81. *Mem:* Animal Behav Soc; Am Soc Zoologists; Am Soc Mammalogists; US Antarctic Res Prog; Sigma Xi. *Res:* Social ecology of mammals, especially canids; mathematical models of social interaction; animal social development; communication processes. *Mailing Add:* Dept Environ Pop & Org Biol Univ Colo Boulder PO Box 334 Boulder CO 80309

BELADY, LASZLO ANTAL, SOFTWARE SYSTEMS, COMPUTER SCIENCES. *Current Pos:* CHMN & DIR, MITSUBISHI ELEC RES LABS, INC, 91- *Personal Data:* b Budapest, Hungary, Apr 29, 28; m 59; c 2. *Educ:* Tech Univ, Budapest, BS, 49, MS, 50. *Honors & Awards:* Warnier Prize, 90. *Prof Exp:* Mem res staff comput sci, IBM, T J Watson Res Ctr, Yorktown, NY, 61-84; vpres software eng, Microelectronics & Comput Technol Corp, Austin, Tex, 84-91. *Concurrent Pos:* Vis prof, Univ Calif, Berkeley, 71-72, Imp Col, London Univ, 74; adj prof, NY Polytech Univ, 81-83. *Mem:* Fel Inst Elec & Electronics Engrs; Asn Comput Mach. *Res:* Design of complex systems, particularly software systems which are controlling distributed, real time processes. *Mailing Add:* Mitsubishi Elec Res Labs 201 Broadway 8th Fl Cambridge MA 02139

BELAGAJE, RAMA M, ORGANIC CHEMISTRY, BIOCHEMISTRY. *Current Pos:* SR RES SCIENTIST, ELI LILLY & CO, 79- *Personal Data:* b Belagaje, Karnataka State, India, May 9, 42; US citizen; m 73, K S Nalini; c Samir & Sudhir. *Educ:* Mysore Univ, India, BSc, 62; Banaras Hindu Univ, India, MSc, 65; NY Univ, MS, 70, PhD(org chem), 71. *Prof Exp:* Instr chem, St Philomena's Col, India, 62-63; res fel, Indian Inst Sci, India, 65-67; teaching fel, NY Univ, 71-72; sr res assoc, Mass Inst Technol, 72-79. *Concurrent Pos:* Chmn & adminr, India Community Ctr, 88-90. *Mem:* Am Chem Soc; NY Acad Sci; hon mem Acad Gen Educ. *Res:* Protein engineering by recombinant DNA technology, DNA systhesis and bacterial expression of foreign proteins. *Mailing Add:* Eli Lilly & Co Dept MC 625 Bldg 98/2 Indianapolis IN 46285-0002. *Fax:* 317-276-9086

BELAND, GARY LAVERN, ECONOMIC ENTOMOLOGY. *Current Pos:* RES ENTOMOLOGIST, CIBA GEIGY SEED DIV, 89- *Personal Data:* b Los Angeles, Calif, May 18, 42; m 85; c 3. *Educ:* Kearney State Col, BA, 65; Univ Nebr, Lincoln, MS, 68, PhD(entom), 72. *Prof Exp:* Instr entom, Univ Nebr, Lincoln, 69-72; res entomologist, USDA Sci & Educ Admin-Agr Res, 72-79; res entomologist, Funk Seeds Int, 79-84, mgr entom-path res, 84-87, mgr res support technol, 88. *Mem:* Entom Soc Am; Am Registry Prof Entomologists; Sigma Xi. *Res:* Host plant resistance; biology and ecology of insect pests of corn, soybeans, sorghum and cotton. *Mailing Add:* 205 Felmley Dr Normal IL 61761

BELAND, PIERRE, ECOLOGY, MARINE SCIENCES. *Current Pos:* SCI DIR, ST LAWRENCE INST ECOTOXICOL, MONTREAL, 87- *Personal Data:* b Quebec, Que, Oct 4, 47; div; c 2. *Educ:* Laval Univ, BA, 67, BSc, 71; Dalhousie Univ, PhD(pop biol), 74. *Prof Exp:* Consult ecologist, Nat Mus Natural Sci, Ottawa, 76-77, paleocologist, 77-80; ecologist, Can Dept Fisheries & Oceans, Rimouski, Que, 81-82, chief, Fisheries Ecol Res Ctr, 82-87. *Concurrent Pos:* Fel, Ctr Overseas Off Sci & Tech Res, New Caledonia, 74-75 & Dept Zool, Univ Queensland, 75; assoc prof, Univ Que Rimouski; invited prof, Nat Inst Sci Res-Oceanol, Rimouski; adj prof, Univ Montreal, 93-; comnr, Int Joint Comn, 95- *Res:* Marine ecosystems: population dynamics, predation, food chains; contamination of marine mammals and effects on stocks; organic contaminants flow. *Mailing Add:* St Lawrence Inst Ecotoxicol 460 Champ de Mars Suite 504 Montreal PQ H2Y 1B4 Can

BELANGER, ALAIN, endocrinology, chemistry, for more information see previous edition

BELANGER, BRIAN CHARLES, INSTRUMENTATION, ELECTRICAL ENGINEERING. *Current Pos:* DEP DIR, ADVAN TECHNOL PROG, NAT INST STAND & TECHNOL, 90- *Personal Data:* b Eveleth, Minn, Feb 2, 41; m 62, Dian Olson; c Marcel & Lia. *Educ:* Calif Inst Technol, BS, 63; Univ Southern Calif, PhD(elec eng), 68. *Honors & Awards:* Bronze Medal, US Dept Com, 80, Silver Medal, 95. *Prof Exp:* Res staff mem, Gen Elec Res & Develop Ctr, 68-72; chief, Advan Energy Delivery Systs Br, US Energy Res Develop Admin, 72-76; chief, Off Measurement Serv, US Nat Bur Standards, 77-83, liaison, Dept Defense, 83-86, assoc dir prog develop, Ctr Electronics & Elec Eng, 86-90. *Concurrent Pos:* Fel, US Com Dept Sci & Technol, 83-84. *Mem:* Inst Elec & Electronics Engrs. *Res:* Technology policy; general advanced technology; standards. *Mailing Add:* 5730 Avery Park Dr Rockville MD 20855-1738

BELANGER, DAVID GERALD, SOFTWARE ENGINEERING RESEARCH. *Current Pos:* researcher, 79-82, supvr, 82-85, HEAD, SOFTWARE ENG RES DEPT, AT&T BELL LABS, 85- *Personal Data:* b Rockville, Conn, Dec 8, 44; m 71, Maryann McBride; c John & Erin. *Educ:* Union Col, BS, 66; Case Western Reserve Univ, MS, 68, PhD(math), 71. *Prof Exp:* From asst prof to assoc prof, Univ SAla, 71-79. *Concurrent Pos:* Mathematician, US Army CEngr, 73-79; vpres, Gulf Coast Data Systs, 77-79. *Mem:* Soc Indust & Appl Math; Asn Comput Mach; Inst Elec & Electronics Engrs Comput Soc. *Res:* Concepts, technology and frameworks to improve the creation of software systems; transfer of that technology to practice; emphasis on system, software, data and process architectures. *Mailing Add:* 20 Royce Brook Rd Belle Mead NJ 08502. *Fax:* 908-582-3063; *E-Mail:* dgb@research.att.com

BELANGER, JACQUELINE M R, EXTRACTION CHEMISTRY. *Current Pos:* SR RES SCIENTIST & ACTG HEAD ANALYTICAL PROGS, ENVIRON CAN, 93- *Personal Data:* b Mont-Joli, Que, Jan 8, 54. *Educ:* Univ Moncton, BSc, 76, BEd, 77, MSc, 78; Carleton Univ, PhD(chem), 84. *Honors & Awards:* Gold Medal, Soc Chem Indust, 76. *Prof Exp:* Res scientist, Drug Id Div, Health & Welfare Can, 84-85; res scientist, Agr Can, 85-89, asst dep dir, Land Resource Res Ctr, 90-91, res scientist & team leader, Ctr Food & Animal Res, 91-93; sci adv mgt, Indust, Sci & Technol CDN, 89-90. *Concurrent Pos:* Managing ed, Spectros: An Int J, 81-91; teaching master, Algonquin Col, Ottawa, 85, sci prog adv, 85; mem, Nat Adv Comt Agr & Natural Resources, Can Broadcasting Corp, 88-90; res assoc, Fac Grad Studies, Univ Moncton, 89-; mem, Food Conserv & Innocuity Eval Comt, Corpaq, 90; mem, Alt Selection Comt Indust Fel Grants, Nat Sci & Eng Res Coun, 93- *Mem:* Chem Inst Can; Can Soc Chem; Am Chem Soc; Am Soc Mass Spectrometry; Int Union Pure & Appl Chem; Am Inst Chemist Inc. *Res:* Extraction, isolation, purification and structure elucidation of natural compounds of biological interest from various sources; spectroscopy; chromatography; development of the microwave-assited process for environmental applications and other extraction/analytical techniques for emergency response. *Mailing Add:* Environ Can 3439 River Rd Ottawa ON K1A 0H3 Can. *Fax:* 613-990-2855; *E-Mail:* belanger.jacqueline@etc.ec.gc.ca

BELANGER, LUC, ONCOLOGY, DEVELOPMENTAL BIOLOGY. *Current Pos:* from asst prof to assoc prof, 78-88, PROF & MOLECULAR BIOL, LAVAL UNIV 88-, DIR ONCOL, CANCER RES CTR, 84-; DIR ONCOL, L'HOTEL-DIEU QUE RES CTR, 91- *Personal Data:* b Montreal, Que, July 2, 48. *Educ:* Petit Seminaire Chicoutimi, BA, 67; Laval Univ, MD, 71, PhD(biochem), 75. *Prof Exp:* Fel, biochem & molecular biol, Med Res Coun-Univ Calif, San Diego, Salk Inst, Vanderbilt Univ, 75-78. *Concurrent Pos:* Scholar molecular biol, Med Res Coun Can, 78-83; mem bd, Int Soc Oncodevelop Biol & Med, 80-90; mem, cancer grants panel, Med Res Coun, 80-83, scholar panel, Nat Cancer Inst, 80-82, fac med coun Laval Univ, 81-87, adv comt cancer, Que Ministry Health, 90-91; mem coun, Med Res Coun Can, 88-, Nat Cancer Inst Can, 88-; pres, scholar bd, Fonds Recherche Sante Que (FRSQ), 88-91, Meed Res Coun Bd Eval Grants Progs Performances, 90-93. *Mem:* Can Soc Cellular & Molecular Biol; Am Soc Cell Biol. *Res:* Cellular and molecular mechanisms underlying differentiation and transformation of hepatocytes; hereditary tyrosinemia; breast cancer; gene regulation albumin/AFP locus; cancer gene therapy. *Mailing Add:* L'Hotel-Dieu de Que Res Ctr Quebec PQ G1R 2J6 Can

BELANGER, PATRICE CHARLES, ANALYTICAL CHEMISTRY, MEDICINAL CHEMISTRY. *Current Pos:* RETIRED. *Personal Data:* b Montreal, Que, Dec 31, 40; m 64; c 3. *Educ:* Univ Montreal, BSc, 62, MSc, 63, PhD(org chem), 66. *Prof Exp:* Sr res chemist, Merck Frosst, 66-77, res fel, 77-81, sr res fel, dir qual assurance, 87-96. *Mem:* Chem Inst Can; Am Chem Soc; Ordre des Chimistes du Quebec. *Res:* Allergic asthma; muscle relaxants and analgesics; anti-inflammatories. *Mailing Add:* 419 Davignon Dr Montreal PQ H9B 1Y4 Can

BELANGER, PIERRE ROLLAND, ELECTRICAL ENGINEERING. *Current Pos:* assoc prof, 67-77, chmn, 78-84, PROF ELEC ENG, MCGILL UNIV, 77-, DEAN FAC, GRAD STUDIES & RES, 84- *Personal Data:* b Montreal, Que, Aug 18, 37; m 63, Margaret Clark; c Mark, Suzanne & David. *Educ:* McGill Univ, BEng, 59; Mass Inst Technol, SM, 61, EE, 62, PhD(elec eng), 64. *Honors & Awards:* Centennial Medal, Inst Elec & Electronics Engrs, 84. *Prof Exp:* From instr to asst prof elec eng, Mass Inst Technol, 63-65; systs analyst, Foxboro Co, 65-67. *Concurrent Pos:* Mem, Adv Comt Eng, Natural Sci & Eng Res Coun Can, 83-87; mem, Nat Adv Bd Sci & Technol, 87-90. *Mem:* Inst Elec & Electronics Engrs. *Res:* Control engineering. *Mailing Add:* 59 Somerville St Westmount PQ H3Z 1J4 Can. *Fax:* 514-398-7379; *E-Mail:* pierce@eng1.lan.mcgill.ca

BELANGER, THOMAS V, LIMNOLOGY. *Current Pos:* asst prof, 78-79, ASSOC PROF ENVIRON SCI, FLA INST TECHNOL, 82- *Personal Data:* b Carrington, NDak, May 25, 48; m. *Educ:* Ill State Univ, BS, 71; Univ Fla, MS, 74, PhD(environ eng sci), 79. *Prof Exp:* Aquatic biologist, Environ Sci & Eng, Inc, 71-74. *Concurrent Pos:* Prin investr, Lake Washington Water Qual Study, Dept Environ Regulation, 78- & Upper St John's Diag Study, Environ Protection Agency, 81-82; consult groundwater seepage, E Lake Tohopekaliga & oxygen budgets, Everglades Water Conserv Areas, SFla Water Mgt Dist. *Mem:* Am Water Resources Asn; Am Soc Limnol & Oceanog; Sigma Xi. *Res:* Limnology; aquatic ecology; groundwater/surface water interaction; gas transfer at water surfaces. *Mailing Add:* Dept Oceanog Fla Inst Technol 150 W University Blvd Melbourne FL 32901-6967

BELARDINELLI, LUIZ, CARDIOLOGY, ELECTROPHYSIOLOGY. *Current Pos:* CHMN, CARDIOL DEPT, UNIV FLA, 88- *Educ:* Med Cath Fac Found, Brazil, MD, 75. *Prof Exp:* Assoc prof med & physiol, Med Ctr, Univ Va, 76-88. *Mailing Add:* Univ Fla PO Box 100277 Gainesville FL 32610-0277

BELBECK, L W, VETERINARY MEDICINE. *Current Pos:* VET, HEALTH ANIMALS BR, CAN DEPT AGR, 66- *Personal Data:* b London, Ont, Aug 24, 43; c 2. *Educ:* Ont Vet Col, DVM, 66. *Prof Exp:* Vet, Oakridge Animal Clin, 66-67. *Mem:* Can Coun Animal Care; Can Asn Lab Animal Sci; Can Asn Lab Sci; Can Fedn Humane Soc; Can Vet Med Asn. *Mailing Add:* 7 Delbrook Ct Hamilton ON L8S 2B9 Can

BEL BRUNO, JOSEPH JAMES, REACTION DYNAMICS, LASER PHOTOCHEMISTRY. *Current Pos:* from asst prof to assoc prof, 82-94, PROF CHEM, DARTMOUTH COL, 94- *Personal Data:* b Passaic, NJ, June 30, 52; m 80, Kathleen Cassidy; c Joseph H & Elizabeth K. *Educ:* Seton Hall Univ, BS, 74; Rutgers Univ, PhD(phys chem), 80. *Hon Degrees:* MS, Dartmouth Col, 96. *Prof Exp:* Res chemist, Am Cyanamid Co, 74-76; res assoc, Princeton Univ, 80-82. *Concurrent Pos:* Alexander Von Humboldt Fel, 88. *Mem:* Sigma Xi; Am Chem Soc; Am Phys Soc. *Res:* Laser photochemistry and spectroscopy of small organic molecules; reactions in intense, non-resonant laser fields; chemical dynamics of gas phase reactions; time-of-flight mass spectrometry; far-infrared spectroscopy; formation dynamics of films on surfaces. *Mailing Add:* Dept Chem Dartmouth Col Hanover NH 03755. *Fax:* 603-646-3946; *E-Mail:* jjb@dartmouth.edu

BELCASTRO, PATRICK FRANK, PHARMACY. *Current Pos:* asst prof pharm, 54-76, prof indust pharm, 76-90, EMER PROF INDUST PHARM, PURDUE UNIV, WEST LAFAYETTE, 90- *Personal Data:* b 1920; US citizen; m 63, Hanna Jensen; c Paul & Helen. *Educ:* Duquesne Univ, BS, 42; Purdue Univ, MS, 51, PhD(pharm), 53. *Prof Exp:* Instr pharm & chem, Duquesne Univ, 46-49; asst prof pharm, Ohio State Univ, 53-54. *Concurrent Pos:* Contrib ed, Int Pharmaceut Abstr, Pharmaceut Technol. *Mem:* Am Pharmaceut Asn; Am Inst Hist Pharm; Am Asn Univ Profs. *Res:* Effects of x-irradiation on pharmacological action of certain drugs. *Mailing Add:* Sch Pharm & Pharmacal Sci Purdue Univ West Lafayette IN 47907

BELCHER, MELVIN B, ELECTRICAL ENGINEERING. *Current Pos:* RETIRED. *Personal Data:* b Shawnee, Okla, Sept 4, 25; m 48, Barbara Nesslage; c 3. *Educ:* Univ Calif, Berkeley, BS, 51; Univ Southern Calif, MS, 69. *Prof Exp:* Test engr, Gen Elec Co, NY, 51-52, anal engr, 52-54, engr, 54-55, sales engr, Calif, 55-58; asst prof elec eng, Calif State Polytech Univ, Pomona, 58-59; mgr sales, Gen Elec Co, Nev, 59-61; from asst prof to assoc prof, Calif State Polytech Univ, Pomona, 61-69, prof elec eng, 69-85, assoc dean eng, 75-80, dir, Int Prog, 80-85, emer prof, 85. *Concurrent Pos:* Mem, Calif State Polytech Univ, Pomona, Tech Col Prog, Dar es Salaam, Tanzania, Africa, 65-67 & 70-72; consult & lectr, Univ Technol Malaysia, 95-96. *Mem:* Am Soc Eng Educ; Inst Elec & Electronics Engrs; Inst Advan Eng; Nat Soc Prof Engrs. *Res:* Network analysis and synthesis; electrical machines; precision measurements, power system analysis. *Mailing Add:* Elec & Comput Eng Dept Calif Polytech Univ Pomona CA 91768. *E-Mail:* mbb@gte.com

BELCHER, ROBERT ORANGE, BOTANY. *Current Pos:* RETIRED. *Personal Data:* b Williamsburg, Ky, June 29, 18; m 38; c 2. *Educ:* Berea Col, AB, 38; Univ Mich, MS, 47, PhD(bot), 55; Mich Tech Univ, MS, 82. *Honors & Awards:* US Typhus Comn medal, 46. *Prof Exp:* Asst biol, Purdue Univ, 38-40; fel bot, Univ Mich, 46; from asst prof to prof biol, Eastern Mich Univ, 46-80, head dept, 58-66. *Concurrent Pos:* Staff scientist, Legis Office Sci Adv, Lansing, Mich, 81; curric consult, Fac Sci & Educ, Sana'a Univ, North Yemen, 80. *Mem:* AAAS; Int Asn Plant Taxon; Am Soc Plant Taxon. *Res:* Systematic botany of pantropical composite weeds; all species of Senecio in Australasia; utilization of fuel wood. *Mailing Add:* PO Box 242 1206 Elbridge Ypsilanti MI 48198

BELDEN, DAVID LEIGH, MECHANICAL ENGINEERING. *Current Pos:* EXEC DIR, AM SOC MECH ENGRS, 87- *Personal Data:* b Minneapolis, Minn, Jan 9, 35; m 56, Lois M Lind; c Richard A & Grant D. *Educ:* Univ Omaha, BS, 61; Stanford Univ, MS, 63, PhD, 69. *Hon Degrees:* DSc, Manhattan Col, 92. *Prof Exp:* Exec dir, Inst Indust Engrs, 76-87. *Concurrent Pos:* Adj prof, Far East Div, Univ Md, 70; assoc prof, George Washington Univ, 74. *Mem:* Fel Am Inst Indust Engrs; fel Inst Prod Engrs; Am Soc Mech Engrs; Am Asn Eng Socs; Coun Eng & Sci Soc Execs (pres, 84-85); Am Soc Eng Educ; hon mem Australian Inst Indust Engrs; assoc mem Japan Mgt Asn. *Res:* Engineering administration. *Mailing Add:* Am Soc Mech Engrs 345 E 47th St New York NY 10017-2330

BELDEN, DON ALEXANDER, JR, ZOOPHYSIOLOGY. *Current Pos:* asst prof, 56-65, ASSOC PROF ZOOL, UNIV DENVER, 65- *Personal Data:* b Akron, Ohio, July 13, 26; m 52; c 2. *Educ:* Middlebury Col, BA, 50; Williams Col, MA, 52; Wash State Univ, PhD(zool), 58. *Prof Exp:* Asst zool, Middlebury Col, 49-50; asst biol, Williams Col, 50-52; res fel zool, Wash State Univ, 52-56. *Mem:* Sigma Xi. *Res:* Cellular biology. *Mailing Add:* 2060 E Amherst Ave Denver CO 80210

BELDEN, EVERETT LEE, VETERINARY IMMUNOLOGY, VETERINARY MICROBIOLOGY. *Current Pos:* Instr microbiol, 62-65, from asst prof to assoc prof, 70-82, PROF IMMUNOL, UNIV WYO, 82- *Personal Data:* b Bridgeport, Nebr, Aug 14, 38; m 61, 81; c 3. *Educ:* Univ Wyo, BS, 60, MS, 62; Univ Calif, Davis, PhD(microbiol), 71. *Mem:* Am Soc Microbiol; Am Asn Vet Immunologists. *Res:* Humoral and cellular immune response in the bovine; infectious reproductive diseases in cattle and sheep; chlamydial diseases in domestic animals; monoclonal antibodies; reproductive immunology. *Mailing Add:* 1314 Renshaw St Laramie WY 82070

BELEW, JOHN SEYMOUR, ORGANIC CHEMISTRY. *Current Pos:* from asst prof to assoc prof, Baylor Univ, 56-63, dean, Col Arts & Sci, 74-79, asst vpres undergrad affairs, 78-79, vpres acad affairs, 79-83, provost, 83-87, exec vpres acad affairs, 87- 89, vpres & provost, 90-91, PROF CHEM, BAYLOR UNIV, 63-, EMER PROVOST, 91- *Personal Data:* b Waco, Tex, Nov 3, 20; m 44, Ruth McAtee; c Jay & Janet. *Educ:* Baylor Univ, BS, 41; Univ Wichita, MS, 47; Univ Wis, PhD(chem), 51. *Hon Degrees:* LLD, Hong Kong Baptist Univ, 95. *Prof Exp:* Res assoc org chem, Brown Univ, 51-53; actg asst prof chem, Univ Va, 53-56. *Mem:* AAAS; Am Chem Soc; Royal Soc Chem. *Res:* Reactions of ozone; heterocycle and o-quinone syntheses; oxidations with transition metal oxides. *Mailing Add:* Provost Emer Baylor Univ Waco TX 76798. *Fax:* 254-848-4155; *E-Mail:* john_belew@baylor.edu

BELEW-NOAH, PATRICIA W, PATHOLOGY, MICROBIOLOGY. *Current Pos:* res technician, Div Infectious Dis, 69-74, Div Dermat, 74-78, INSTR MICROBIOL, DIV DERMAT, UNIV TENN, MEMPHIS, 78- *Personal Data:* b Memphis, Tenn, June 12, 40; m 59, 84; c 2. *Educ:* Univ Tenn, BS, 61, PhD(path), 78. *Prof Exp:* Med technologist microbiol, City Memphis Hosp, Tenn, 61-69. *Concurrent Pos:* Dermat Found grant, 78-79. *Mem:* Soc Invest Dermat. *Res:* Activation of alternative complement pathway; normal cutaneous microflora; psoriasis and streptococcal associated psoriasis, seborrheic dermatitis. *Mailing Add:* Dept Path Univ Tenn Col Med 800 Madison Ave Memphis TN 38163-0001

BELFORD, GENEVA GROSZ, DISTRIBUTED SYSTEMS, DATABASES. *Current Pos:* res assoc chem, Univ Ill, Urbana-Champaign, 59-61, asst prof math, 64-72, res asst prof, Ctr Advan Comput, 72-77, assoc prof computer sci, 77-82, PROF COMPUTER SCI, UNIV ILL, URBANA-CHAMPAIGN, 82- *Personal Data:* b Washington, DC, May 18, 32; m 54, R Linn. *Educ:* Univ Pa, BA, 53; Univ Calif, Berkeley, MA, 54; Univ Ill, PhD(comput theory), 60. *Prof Exp:* NIH fel, 61-64. *Mem:* Inst Elec & Electronics Engrs; Asn Comput Mach. *Res:* Analysis of computer systems, especially data management systems and distributed systems. *Mailing Add:* 2318 DCL Dept Comput Sci Univ Ill 1304 W Springfield Ave Urbana IL 61801. *E-Mail:* belford@cs.uiuc.edu

BELFORD, JULIUS, PHARMACOLOGY, BIOCHEMICAL. *Current Pos:* RETIRED. *Personal Data:* b Brooklyn, NY, Feb 3, 20; m 55, Marilyn Esbin; c Frances, Morris E & Martin H. *Educ:* Brooklyn Col, BA, 40; Long Island Univ, BS, 43; Yale Univ, PhD(pharm), 49. *Prof Exp:* From asst prof to prof pharm, State Univ NY Downstate Med Ctr, 49-84, asst to dean, 58-61, actg chmn, Dept Pharmacol, 71-72, assoc dean opers, 77-84, emer prof, 84. *Concurrent Pos:* Exchange prof, St Mary's Hosp Med Sch, London, 52-53; USPHS spec fel, Mario Negri Inst Pharmacol Res, Milan, Italy, 65. *Mem:* Fel AAAS; Am Soc Pharmacol; NY Acad Sci. *Res:* Pharmacology of drugs affecting the cardiovascular and respiratory systems; experimental epilepsy and anticonvulsants; medical education. *Mailing Add:* 543 South St Chenango Forks NY 13746-9734

BELFORD, R LINN, ELECTRON MAGNETIC RESONANCE, DISORDERED SOLIDS. *Current Pos:* from instr to assoc prof, 55-81, PROF PHYS CHEM, UNIV ILL, URBANA, 81-; DIR, ILL EPR RES CTR, 91- *Personal Data:* b St Louis, Mo, Dec 13, 31; m 54, Geneva Grosz. *Educ:* Univ Ill, BS, 53; Univ Calif, Berkeley, PhD(chem), 55. *Honors & Awards:* John Kuebler Award. *Prof Exp:* Chemist, Univ Ill, 52; asst, Univ Calif, 53, chemist radiation lab, 53-54. *Concurrent Pos:* Sloan fel, 61-63; mem biophys & biophys chem fel comt, NIH, 65-69, sr fel, 66-67; prin investr, NSF, 58-86, Dept Energy, 85- & NIH, 85-; co-dir, Ill Electron Paramagnetic Resonance Res Ctr, 85-90. *Mem:* AAAS; Am Phys Soc; Am Chem Soc; Soc Appl Spectros; Sigma Xi; Int Electron Paramagnetic Resonance Soc. *Res:* Physical, inorganic and biomolecular chemistry; spectra and bonding of transition-metal chelate compounds; electron paramagnetic resonance and nuclear quadrupole coupling; structure and dynamics of radical species; disordered solids; surface species; radicals and ions in biology. *Mailing Add:* 1208 Lakeside Lane Mahomet IL 61853-9767. *Fax:* 217-244-3186; *E-Mail:* rbelford@uiuc.edu

BELFORT, GEORGES, SEPARATIONS TECHNOLOGY. *Current Pos:* assoc prof chem eng, 78-81, PROF CHEM ENG, RENSSELAER POLYTECH INST, 81- *Personal Data:* b Johannesburg, SAfrica, May 8, 40; US citizen; m 67; c 3. *Educ:* Univ Cape Town, BSc, 63; Univ Calif, Irvine, MS, 69, PhD(eng), 72. *Honors & Awards:* Plenary Lectr, NAm Membrane Soc, 88. *Prof Exp:* Res engr, chem engr separations, Astropower Labs, McDouglas Corp, 64-70; vis sr lectr separations & desalination, Univ Cape Town, 72; sr lectr environ & separations eng, Sch Appl Sci & Technol, Hebrew Univ Jerusalem, 73-78. *Concurrent Pos:* Mem bd adv, Nat Coun Res & Develop, Israel, 76-78; assoc prof civil eng, Northwestern Univ, 77-78; consult membranes, Amicon Corp, Mass, 78-; reviewer proposals, NSF, Dept Energy & NIH; consult, Danish Sugar Co, Denmark, 80-, water comnr, SAfrica, 82-, W R Grace & Co & Lyonnaise de Eaux, France, Air Prod & Chem Inc, 88-, Dow Chem Co, 90- *Mem:* Am Inst Chem Engrs; Am Chem Soc; NAm Membrane Soc. *Res:* Separations technology including cross-flow membrane processes (ultrafiltration and reverse osmosis); biochemical engineering; animal cell culture; thermodynamics and measurement of activated carbon absorption from aqueous phase; molecular surface force measurements; continuous bioreactor development; fluid mechanics. *Mailing Add:* Chem Eng Rensselaer Polytech Inst 110 Eighth St Troy NY 12180-3522

BELFORT, MARLENE, BIOCHEMISTRY. *Current Pos:* RES SCIENTIST, WADSWORTH LABS, NY STATE DEPT HEALTH, ALBANY, 78-, DIR, DIV GENETIC DIS, 93- *Personal Data:* b Cape Town, SAfrica, July 26, 45; US citizen; m 67, Georges; c David, Gabriel & Jonathan. *Educ:* Univ Cape Town, BS, 66; Univ Calif, Irvine, PhD(microbiol genetics), 72. *Prof Exp:* Res assoc & teaching fel microbiol & chem, Hebrew Univ, Hadassah Med Sch, Israel, 73-77; res assoc molecular biol, Biochem Dept, Northwestern Univ, Evanston, Ill, 77-78. *Concurrent Pos:* Assoc prof, Sch Pub Health Sci, State Univ, NY, 85-91, prof, 91-; adj assoc prof microbiol, Albany Med Col, NY, 84-94; chairperson, Microbial Genetics Study Sect, NIH; ed, J Gene, RNA & Nucleic Acids Res. *Mem:* Am Soc Microbiol; Am Soc Biochemists; fel Am Acad Arts & Sci. *Res:* Regulation of gene expression in pro and eukaryotes; mobile DNA (DNA rearrangements); RNA splicing; DNA-protein interactions. *Mailing Add:* Wadsworth Ctr NY State Dept Health PO Box 22002 Albany NY 12201-2002

BELFORTE, DAVID ARTHUR, OPTICS, LASERS. *Current Pos:* PRES, BELFORTE ASSOCS, 82- *Personal Data:* b Framingham, Mass, Oct 25, 32; m 58, Virginia Elizabeth Crowley; c Steven. *Educ:* Northeastern Univ, BS, 63, MS, 70. *Honors & Awards:* Pres Award, Laser Inst Am, 88, Arthur L Schawlow Award, 95. *Prof Exp:* Staff scientist, Raytheon Co, 51-65; vpres, Thomson Gen Corp, 65-70; dir mkt, Am Optical Corp, 70-73; mgr, Ferranti Elec Inc, 73-76; dir mkt, Avco Everett Metal Working Lasers, 76-81. *Mem:* Fel Laser Inst Am; Am Welding Soc; Soc Mfg Engrs; Ukranian Acad Eng Sci. *Mailing Add:* Belforte Assoc PO Box 245 Sturbridge MA 01566-0245. *Fax:* 508-347-7737; *E-Mail:* dave8@hey.net

BELIAN, RICHARD DUANE, SPACE & MAGNETOSPHERIC PHYSICS, SATELLITE PARTICLE INSTRUMENTATION. *Current Pos:* energetic particle sect leader, 92-93, STAFF MEM SPACE PHYSICS, LOS ALAMOS NAT LAB, 67-, ENERGETIC PARTICLE TEAM LEADER, UNIV CALIF, 93- *Personal Data:* b Santa Fe, NMex, Feb 23, 38; m 32, Mary Romero; c Richard M, Raymon D & Anthony P. *Educ:* Univ NMex, BS, 65, MS, 67. *Mem:* Am Astron Soc; Am Geophys Union. *Res:* Magnetospheric physics, substorm related particle events; solar energetic particle events; new energetic particle instruments. *Mailing Add:* Los Alamos Nat Lab Group NIS-2 MS D436 Los Alamos NM 87545. *Fax:* 505-665-4414; *E-Mail:* rdbelian@lanl.gov

BELINFANTE, JOHAN G F, AUTOMATED THEOREM PROVING. *Current Pos:* assoc prof, 73-79, PROF MATH, GA INST TECHNOL, 79- *Personal Data:* b Leiden, Neth, Feb 2, 40; US citizen; m 69, Irene Ann Vahanian. *Educ:* Purdue Univ, BS, 58; Princeton Univ, PhD(physics), 61. *Prof Exp:* NSF fel physics, Calif Inst Technol, 61-62; res asst, Univ Pa, 62-64; from asst prof to assoc prof, Carnegie-Mellon Univ, 64-73. *Mem:* Am Math Soc; Am Phys Soc; Math Asn Am; Soc Natural Philos. *Res:* Lie algebras; computers in algebra; computer assisted proofs in set theory. *Mailing Add:* Dept Math Ga Inst Technol Atlanta GA 30332-0160. *E-Mail:* belinfan@math.gatech.edu

BELINSKY, STEVEN ALAN, DNA METHYLATION, ONCOGENE & SUPPRESSOR GENES. *Current Pos:* MOLECULAR BIOLOGIST, INHALATION TOXICOL RES INST, 90- *Personal Data:* b High Point, NC, Mar 22, 56; m 89. *Educ:* Univ NC, Chapel Hill, BS, 78, PhD(toxicol), 84. *Prof Exp:* Sr staff fel, Nat Inst Environ Health Sci, 84-90. *Concurrent Pos:* Postdoctoral fel, Nat Res Serv Award, Nat Inst Environ Health Sci, 84-86; clin assoc prof, Col Pharm, Univ NMex, 91- *Mem:* Am Asn Cancer Res. *Res:* Identification of critical target genes involved in the development and progression of lung cancer. *Mailing Add:* 13604 Crested Botte Dr NE Albuquerque NM 87112

BELISLE, BARBARA WOLFANGER, cell biology, insect cell culture, for more information see previous edition

BELITSKUS, DAVID, PHYSICAL INORGANIC CHEMISTRY. *Current Pos:* Res engr, Aluminum Co Am, 64-67, sr res scientist, 67-75, sci assoc, 75-78, sect head, 78-81, FEL, ALCOA LABS, ALUMINUM CO AM, 81- *Personal Data:* b Cuddy, Pa, Dec 24, 38; m 68; c 4. *Educ:* Duquesne Univ, BS, 61; Univ Pittsburgh, PhD(phys chem), 64. *Mem:* Am Ceramic Soc; Sigma Xi; Metall Soc. *Res:* X-ray crystal structure analyses; oxidation of light metal alloys; batteries and fuel cells; properties of lubricants and corrosion inhibitors; metallothermic reductions; metal matrix composites; carbon properties; ceramic matrix composites. *Mailing Add:* 2361 Meadow Rd New Kensington PA 15068

BELJAN, JOHN RICHARD, AEROSPACE MEDICINE, BIOMEDICAL ENGINEERING. *Current Pos:* pres, 91-93, EMER PRES, NORTHROP UNIV, LOS ANGELES, CALIF, 93- *Personal Data:* b Detroit, Mich, May 26, 30; m 52, Bernadette M Marenda; c John R, Paul E & Ann M. *Educ:* Univ Mich, BS, 51, MD, 54. *Honors & Awards:* Bauer Lectr, Aerospace Med Asn, 79. *Prof Exp:* Clin instr surg, Sch Med, Univ Mich, 56-59; dir med serv, Stuart Co, Calif, 65; from asst prof to assoc prof surg, Sch Med, Univ Calif, Davis, 66-74, asst to dean, 70-71, asst dean, 71-74, from asst prof to assoc prof eng, Col Eng, 68-74; dean, Sch Med, Wright State Univ, 74-80, prof surg & biomed eng, 74-83, vprovost, 74-78, vpres health affairs, 78-80, provost & sr vpres, 81-83; provost & vpres acad affairs, Hahnemann Univ, 83-85, prof surg & biomed eng, 83-86, spec adv to pres, 85-86; vpres acad affairs, Calif State Univ, Long Beach, 86-89, prof anat, physiol & biomed eng, 86-92. *Concurrent Pos:* Consult, HEW, 72-86, Vet Admin, 75-93, Booz-Allen & Hamilton, 79-85 & AT Kearney, 85- *Mem:* Am Col Surgeons; AMA. *Res:* General surgery; aerospace medicine; biomedical engineering; telemetry. *Mailing Add:* 6490 Saddle Dr Long Beach CA 90815-4740

BELK, GENE DENTON, ANIMAL HUSBANDRY. *Current Pos:* PRES, BRACKENRIDGE STABLES, INC, 75-; ADJ PROF, OUR LADY OF THE LAKE UNIV, SAN ANTONIO, 78- *Personal Data:* b Dallas, Tex, Dec 27, 38; m 63, Mary Schug. *Educ:* Univ Tex, Austin, BSEd, 66, MA, 69; Ariz State Univ, PhD(zool), 74. *Honors & Awards:* Wilks Award, 68; R M Harris Award, 77. *Prof Exp:* Vis asst prof invert zool, Ariz State Univ, 74-75. *Concurrent Pos:* Chair, Inland Water Specialist Group, Species Survival Comn, Int Union Conserv Nature & Natural Resources; res assoc, Smithsonian Inst. *Mem:* Crustacean Soc (treas, 86-); Sigma Xi; AAAS; Southwestern Asn Naturalists; Soc Conserv Biol. *Res:* Systematics and distribution of the crustacean orders Anostraca, Spinicaudata and Laevicaudata; study of all aspects of their natural history, systematics and behavior. *Mailing Add:* 840 E Mulberry San Antonio TX 78212-3194. *Fax:* 210-732-3943; *E-Mail:* dbelk@texas.net

BELKER, ARNOLD M, VASECTOMY REVERSAL, MICROSURGICAL RECONSTRUCTION OF MALE REPRODUCTION SYSTEM. *Current Pos:* from clin instr to clin assoc prof, 66-83, CLIN PROF SURG-UROL, UNIV LOUISVILLE SCH MED, 83- *Personal Data:* b Louisville, Ky, Feb 27, 34; m 58, Terry Marks; c Paul & Jill. *Educ:* Univ Louisville Sch Med, BS, 54, MD, 58. *Concurrent Pos:* Sci comt mem, Asn Vol Surg Contraception, 88-; Chmn, Male Reproduction - Urol Comt, Am Fertil Soc, 92-94; mem, Concept Clearance Funding for Vasectomy Reversal Res, NIH, 89, partic, Policy Conf on Vasectomy & Prostate Cancer, 93. *Mem:* Am Soc Andrology (pres, 96-97); Am Urol Asn; Soc Reproductive Surgeons (pres, 92-93); Am Soc Reprod Med; Soc Study Male Reproduction (pres, 95-96). *Res:* Clinical research regarding vasectomy reversal and microsurgical corrections of obstruction of male reproductive system. *Mailing Add:* 250 E Liberty St Suite 602 Louisville KY 40202-1576

BELKIN, BARRY, OPERATIONS RESEARCH. *Current Pos:* V PRES OPERS RES & MATH, DANIEL H WAGNER, ASSOCS, 67- *Personal Data:* b Philadelphia, Pa, May 4, 40; m 64; c 2. *Educ:* Mass Inst Technol, BS, 62; Univ Pa, MA, 64; Cornell Univ, PhD(math), 68. *Honors & Awards:* Rist Prize, Mil Opers Res Soc, 75. *Mem:* Inst Math Statist; Soc Indust & Appl Math. *Res:* First passage problems; tracking algorithms; theory of random walk. *Mailing Add:* 1229 Waterford Rd West Chester PA 19380

BELKNAP, JOHN KENNETH, PSYCHOPHARMACOLOGY, DRUG ABUSE. *Current Pos:* PROF PHARMACOL, VA MED CTR, 90- *Personal Data:* b Wilmington, NC, Jan 14, 43. *Educ:* Univ Colo, Boulder, BA, 66, PhD(psychol), 71. *Prof Exp:* Asst prof psychol, Univ Tex, Austin, 72-78; assoc prof pharmacol, Sch Med, Univ NDak, 78-85, prof, 85-90. *Concurrent Pos:* Fel, Univ Tex, Austin, 71-72; prin investr, Nat Inst Drug Abuse grant, 75- *Mem:* Behav Genetics Asn; Am Soc Pharmacol & Exp Therapeut; Soc Neurosci. *Res:* Drug dependence; alcohol and barbiturates; pharmacogenetics of opioid analgesia. *Mailing Add:* Res Serv 151 Vet Admin Med Ctr Portland OR 97201-2964

BELKNAP, ROBERT WAYNE, PHYSIOLOGY. *Current Pos:* from asst prof to assoc prof, 60-76, PROF BIOL, CREIGHTON UNIV, 76- *Personal Data:* b Omaha, Nebr, Jan 13, 24; m 53; c 2. *Educ:* Creighton Univ, BS, 49, MS, 51; Univ Calif, PhD, 58. *Prof Exp:* Jr res physiologist, Univ Calif, 58-60. *Concurrent Pos:* Instr, Vet Admin Hosp, Omaha, 62- *Mem:* AAAS; NY Acad Sci; Am Soc Zool; Soc Nuclear Med; Am Statist Asn; Sigma Xi. *Res:* Mammalian physiology and environmental physiology; tissue metabolism; heat and cold exposure; hypothermia. *Mailing Add:* 3366 S 112th St Omaha NE 68144-4630

BELL, A(UDRA) EARL, GENETICS. *Current Pos:* from asst prof to prof, 48-88, EMER PROF ANIMAL SCI, PURDUE UNIV, WEST LAFAYETTE, 88- *Personal Data:* b Providence, Ky, May 9, 18; m 41, Floris S Thorning; c Robert E, Donald W & Diane L (Blindbury). *Educ:* Univ Ky, BS, 39; La State Univ, MS, 41; Iowa State Col, PhD(genetics), 48. *Prof Exp:* Asst genetics, Iowa State Col, 41-42, 46-48; genetics consult, Farm Bur Coop, 65-80; chmn, Pop Genetics Inst, 65-85. *Concurrent Pos:* Guggenheim fel, 64-65; Japan SPS fel, Kyoto Univ, 87-88. *Mem:* Fel AAAS; Am Genetics Asn; Am Soc Animal Sci; Genetics Soc Am; Am Soc Naturalists. *Res:* Population genetics in poultry, drosophilia and tribolium; genetics of disease resistance. *Mailing Add:* 3913 Calle Real San Clemente CA 92673

BELL, ALAN EDWARD, PHYSICS. *Current Pos:* MEM TECH STAFF, IBM RES LABS, ALMEDEN RES CTR. *Personal Data:* b London, Eng, July 1, 48; m 72. *Educ:* Univ London, BSc, 69, PhD(metal physics) & DIC, 73; Royal Col Sci, ARCS, 69. *Prof Exp:* Res asst metal physics, Imp Col, Univ London, 72-74; mem tech staff optical rec, David Sarnoff Res Ctr, RCA Corp, 74- *Concurrent Pos:* Vis res fel, David Sarnoff Res Ctr, RCA Corp, 73-74. *Mem:* Optical Soc Am; Inst Elec & Electronics Engrs. *Res:* High density optical recording of video and digital signals; and digital optics of thin films; thermal analysis applied to silicon crystal growth and laser annealing. *Mailing Add:* Almeden Res Ctr 650 Harry Rd San Jose CA 95120-6099

BELL, ALEXIS T, CHEMICAL ENGINEERING. *Current Pos:* From asst prof to assoc prof, Univ Calif, Berkeley, 67-76, asst dean, Col Chem, 79-81, chmn, Dept Chem Eng, 81-91, PRIN INVESTR, MAT & MOLECULAR RES DIV, LAWRENCE BERKELY LAB, UNIV CALIF, BERKELY, 75-, PROF CHEM ENG, 76-, DEAN, COL CHEM, 94- *Personal Data:* b New York, NY, Oct 16, 42. *Educ:* Mass Inst Technol, BS, 64, ScD(chem eng), 67. *Honors & Awards:* R A Glenn Award, Am Chem Soc, 78; Curtis W McGraw Res Award, Am Soc Eng Educ, 81; Donald L Katz Lectr, Univ Mich, 84; Paul E Emmett Award, Catalysis Soc, 85; B F Dodge Lectr, Yale Univ, 88; R H Wilhelm Award, Am Inst Chem Engrs, 92; Langmuir lectr, Am Chem Soc, 92. *Concurrent Pos:* Consult, Tracer Labs, Calif, 67-69, Int Plasma Corp, 69-, Tegal Corp & Lockheed Space & Missile Co; fac sr scientist, Lawrence Berkeley Nat Lab. *Mem:* Nat Acad Eng; Am Inst Chem Engrs; Electrochem Soc; Sigma Xi; Am Chem Soc; fel AAAS. *Res:* Heterogeneous catalysis; synthesis hydrocarbons and oxygenated compounds; spectroscopic techniques and isotopic tracer techniques for study of catalyzed reactions; theoretical techniques for predicting dynamics of surface reactions on metals; sorption and diffusion of molecules in zeolites. *Mailing Add:* Dept Chem Eng Univ Calif 107 Gilman Hall Berkeley CA 94720-9989

BELL, ALFRED LEE LOOMIS, JR, medicine; deceased, see previous edition for last biography

BELL, ALLEN L, ELECTRON MICROSCOPY, HISTOLOGY. *Current Pos:* ASSOC PROF ANAT, NEW ENG COL OSTEOP MED, 78- *Personal Data:* b Bangor, Maine, Apr 13, 37; m 60; c 2. *Educ:* Univ Mich, BA, 59; State Univ NY, PhD(anat), 66. *Prof Exp:* Instr anat, Upstate Med Ctr, State Univ NY, 66-67; asst prof, Univ Colo Med Ctr, 67-72. *Concurrent Pos:* Dir, Electron Micros Lab, Marine Biol Lab, Mass, 63-72. *Res:* Fine structure of photoreceptors of vertebrate and invertebrates; mammalian kidney disorders; fine structure of virus; spider silk spinning gland. *Mailing Add:* Anat Dept New Eng Col Osteop Med 605 Pool Rd Biddeford ME 04005-9524

BELL, ALOIS ADRIAN, BIOCHEMISTRY, MICROBIOLOGY. *Current Pos:* res plant pathologist plant indust sta, USDA, 65-70, dir nat cotton path res lab, 70-77, res leader, supvr res plant path, Crops Res Div, 77-87, RES PLANT PATHOLOGIST, AGR RES SERV, USDA, COLLEGE STATION, TX, 87- *Personal Data:* b Bloomfield, Nebr, Jan 25, 34; m 58; c 2. *Educ:* Univ Nebr, BSc, 55, MSc, 58, PhD(bot), 61. *Prof Exp:* Asst prof bot, Univ Md, 61-65. *Concurrent Pos:* Grad Sch Res Coun grant, Univ Md, 62, USPHS res grant, 63-66; Competitive res grant, USDA, 72-75. *Mem:* Fel Am Phytopath Soc. *Res:* Biochemistry of virulence and natural products in phytopathogenic fungi; biochemistry and physiology of disease resistance and fungal pathogenesis of cotton; development of biocontrol agents and beneficial microorganisms for cotton; synthetic organic and natural products chemistry. *Mailing Add:* 3503 Spring Lane Bryan TX 77802

BELL, ANTHONY E, SURFACE PHYSICS. *Current Pos:* staff scientist, 76-85, ASSOC RES PROF PHYSICS, ORE GRAD CTR, 85- *Personal Data:* b Ramsgate, Eng, Aug 23, 37; m 63; c 1. *Educ:* Univ London, BS, 59, PhD(phys chem), 62. *Prof Exp:* Res assoc, Univ Chicago, 63-65; physicist, Field Emission Corp, 65-69; assoc prof chem, Linfield Col, 69-76. *Concurrent Pos:* NSF grants, 70-71, 80-82, 82-85 & 86-89. *Mem:* Am Chem Soc. *Res:* Field emission of electrons for application in scanning electron microscopes; electron beam lithography liquid metal field ion source development and characterization. *Mailing Add:* Dept Physics & Elec Ore Grad Ctr 19600 NW Von Neuman Beaverton OR 97006-6904

BELL, BARBARA, SOLAR PHYSICS, CLIMATOLOGY. *Current Pos:* Res asst, Harvard Observ, 48-57, sci asst to dir, 57-71, astronr, Harvard Col Observ, 71-73, ASTRONR, CTR ASTROPHYS, 73- *Personal Data:* b Evanston, Ill, Apr 1, 22. *Educ:* Radcliffe Col, AB, 44, MA, 49, PhD(astron), 51. *Mem:* Am Astron Soc; Am Res Ctr Egypt; Int Astron Union; Archaeol Inst Am. *Res:* Spectroscopy and the solar spectrum; solar-geomagnetic correlations; modern climatology, post-glacial climate fluctuations and their possible role in ancient history, especially of Egypt and the Nile. *Mailing Add:* Ctr Astrophys 60 Garden St Cambridge MA 02138. *E-Mail:* bbell@cfa.harvard.edu

BELL, CARL F, PLANT PATHOLOGY. *Current Pos:* Assoc prof, 61-69, PROF BIOL, SHEPHERD COL, 69- *Personal Data:* b Otsego, Ohio, Nov 24, 33; m 61. *Educ:* Muskingum Col, BS, 55; Miami Univ, MS, 58; Ohio State Univ, PhD(plant path), 61. *Mem:* Am Phytopath Soc. *Res:* Physiology of fungus parasitism. *Mailing Add:* Dept Biol Shepherd Col Shepherdstown WV 25443

BELL, CHARLES BERNARD, JR, MATHEMATICS, STATISTICS. *Current Pos:* PROF BIOSTATIST, SAN DIEGO STATE UNIV, 81- *Personal Data:* b New Orleans, La, Aug 20, 28; m 53; c 4. *Educ:* Xavier Univ, La, BS, 47; Univ Notre Dame, MS, 48, PhD, 53. *Prof Exp:* Asst math, Univ Notre Dame, 49-51; res engr, Douglas Aircraft Co, 51-55; asst prof math & physics, Xavier Univ, La, 55-57; instr math & res assoc statist, Stanford Univ, 57-58; from asst prof to prof math, San Diego State Col, 58-66; prof, Case Western Res Univ, 66-68; prof math & statist, Univ Mich, Ann Arbor, 68-71; prof math, Tulane Univ, 74-78; prof biostatist, Univ Wash, 78-81. *Mem:* Fel Inst Math Statist; fel Am Statist Asn; Am Math Soc; Soc Espanola Inv Oper. *Res:* Nonparametric statistics and applications of stochastic processes; biostatistics and signal detection. *Mailing Add:* Math Dept San Diego State Univ San Diego CA 92182-0002

BELL, CHARLES E, JR, PHYSICAL ORGANIC CHEMISTRY. *Current Pos:* from asst prof to assoc prof chem, 62-67, asst dean grad studies, 72-75, PROF CHEM, 67-, ASSOC DEAN GRAD STUDIES, OLD DOMINION UNIV, 75- *Personal Data:* b Norwood, Mass, Aug 8, 31; m 55; c 4. *Educ:* Univ Va, BS, 54, MS, 55, PhD(chem), 61. *Prof Exp:* Chemist, Prod Res Div, Esso Res & Eng Co, Standard Oil, NJ, 60-62. *Mem:* Sigma Xi; Am Chem Soc. *Res:* Kinetics and mechanisms of organic reactions; analysis of chemical composition of jellyfish; organic pollutants in drinking water. *Mailing Add:* 6150 Eastwood Terr Norfolk VA 23508-1113

BELL, CHARLES EUGENE, JR, FACILITIES PLANNING. *Current Pos:* Indust engr, Signode Industs, 57-61, asst plant mgr, 61-64, div indust engr, 64-69, asst div mgr, 69-76, eng mgr, 76-93, CONSULT ENG, SIGNODE INDUSTS, 93- *Personal Data:* b New York, NY, Dec 13, 32; m 67, Doris R Clifton; c Scott. *Educ:* Johns Hopkins Univ, BE, 54, MSE, 59. *Concurrent Pos:* Mem, Int Indust Eng Conf Comt, 84 & 92. *Mem:* Nat Soc Prof Engrs; Inst Indust Engrs; Soc Plastics Engrs. *Mailing Add:* 1021 W Old Mill Rd Lake Forest IL 60045

BELL, CHARLES VESTER, ELECTRICAL ENGINEERING. *Current Pos:* ACAD VPRES, PAC UNION COL, 84- *Personal Data:* b Starkville, Miss, Mar 19, 34; m 54; c 3. *Educ:* Miss State Univ, BS, 56; Stanford Univ, MS, 57, PhD(elec eng), 60. *Prof Exp:* Asst prof physics, Walla Walla Col, 60-62; sect head, Hughes Aircraft Co, 62-72; assoc prof physics, 72-74, dean eng, Walla Walla Col, 74-84. *Mem:* Sigma Xi; Inst Elec & Electronics Engrs; Am Soc Eng Educ. *Res:* Microwave electronics; biological effects of microwave radiation. *Mailing Add:* 175 Edgewood Pl Angwin CA 94508-9750

BELL, CHARLES W, plant physiology, for more information see previous edition

BELL, CHESTER GORDON, COMPUTER SCIENCE, ELECTRICAL ENGINEERING. *Current Pos:* from assoc prof to prof comput sci, 66-78, PROF ELEC ENG & COMPUT SCI, CARNEGIE-MELLON UNIV, 78-; BD DIRS & TRUSTEE, COMPUT MUS, 82- *Personal Data:* b Kirksville, Mo, Aug 19, 34; m 59, Gwendolyn K Druyor; c Brigham R & Laura L. *Educ:* Mass Inst Technol, BS, 56, MS, 57. *Hon Degrees:* DEng, Worcester Polytech Inst, 92. *Honors & Awards:* Nat Medal Technol, 91; McDowell Award; Eckert-Mauchly Award; Von Neumann Medal, Inst Elec & Electronics Engrs, 92. *Prof Exp:* Res engr, Res Lab Electronics, Mass Inst Technol, 59-61; mgr comput design, Digital Equip Corp, 61-66. *Concurrent Pos:* Consult, Digital Equip Corp, 66-, vpres, 72-83; vchmn technol, Encore, 83-85; vpres, Ardent Comput, 85-89; consult, Kubota Pac, Santa Clara; asst dir, Comput & Info Sci & Eng, NSF, 86-87. *Mem:* Nat Acad Eng; fel Inst Elec & Electronics Engrs; fel Asn Comput Mach; fel AAAS. *Res:* Design of digital computers; computer and information processing; startup companies. *Mailing Add:* 450 Old Oak Ct Los Altos CA 94022. *E-Mail:* gbell@mojave.stanford.edu

BELL, CLARA G, IMMUNOLOGY, IMMUNOGENETICS. *Current Pos:* USPHS res assoc immunol, 69-70, asst prof, 70-73, ASSOC PROF IMMUNOL, UNIV ILL MED CTR, CHICAGO, 73- *Personal Data:* b Romania, Oct 16, 37; US citizen; m 64; c 3. *Educ:* Hebrew Univ Jerusalem, BSc, 59, MSc, 60, PhD(immunol), 64. *Honors & Awards:* Boris Pragel Gold Medal, NY Acad Sci, 72. *Prof Exp:* Fel immunol, Univ Sydney, 64, res fel immunochem, 66-68. *Concurrent Pos:* On leave, NIH career develop award & assoc prof, Karolinska Inst Tumor Biol, Stockholm, Sweden, 75-77. *Mem:* Am Asn Immunologists; AAAS; NY Acad Sci; Sigma Xi; Brit Biochem Soc. *Res:* Functional analysis of lymphocyte sub-populations in terms of membrane markers and specificities, DNA, immunoglobulin, antibody and lymphokine synthesis, secretion and cellular responsiveness in immunity and surveillance; immune repertoire to self-non-self, autoimmune mechanisms vaccination. *Mailing Add:* Dept Micro Biol Univ Ill 835 S Wolcott Ave M/C 790 Chicago IL 60612-7344

BELL, CLYDE RITCHIE, BOTANY. *Current Pos:* from asst prof to prof, 55-86, EMER PROF BOT, UNIV NC, CHAPEL HILL, 86- *Personal Data:* b Cincinnati, Ohio, Apr 10, 21; m 43. *Educ:* Univ NC, AB, 47, MA, 49; Univ Calif, Berkeley, PhD(bot), 53. *Prof Exp:* Instr bot, Univ Ill, 53-55. *Concurrent*

Pos: Dir, NC Bot Garden, 66- *Mem:* Bot Soc Am (treas, 72-76, vpres, 78); Am Inst Biol Sci; Am Soc Plant Taxonomists (secy, 59-62, pres, 76); Int Asn Plant Taxonomists; fel AAAS. *Res:* Systematic botany; plant evolution; pollination biology; flora of the Southeastern United States. *Mailing Add:* 5000 Walnut Cove Rd Chapel Hill NC 27516

BELL, CURTIS CALVIN, SENSORY PHYSIOLOGY, SENSORY MOTOR. *Current Pos:* SR SCIENTIST, NEUROL SCI INST, GOOD SAMARITAN HOSP & MED CTR, 65- *Educ:* Univ Calif, Los Angeles, PhD(anat), 64. *Mailing Add:* Robert S Dow Neurol Sci Inst Legacy Health Sys 1120 NW 20th St Portland OR 97209-1539

BELL, CURTIS PORTER, MATHEMATICS. *Current Pos:* asst prof, 63-67, ASSOC PROF MATH, WOFFORD COL, 67- *Personal Data:* b Augusta, Ga, July 26, 34; m 61; c 1. *Educ:* Wofford Col, BS, 55; Univ Ga, MA, 60, PhD(math), 63. *Prof Exp:* Instr math & physics, Limestone Col, 55-56; asst math, Univ Ga, 62-63. *Mem:* Am Math Soc; Math Asn Am. *Res:* Point set topology. *Mailing Add:* Dept Math Wofford Col 429 N Church St Spartanburg SC 29303-3612

BELL, DUNCAN HADLEY, INSTRUMENTATION, AUTOMATION. *Current Pos:* sr res biochemist, 85-91, SR BIOMED ENGR, LEDERLE LABS, AM CYANAMID CO, 91- *Personal Data:* b Stamford, Conn, June 23, 52; m 78; c 4. *Educ:* Col Wooster, BA, 74; Mich State Univ, PhD(biochem), 79. *Prof Exp:* Res asst, Dept Bot & Plant Path, Mich State Univ, 74-79; res assoc, Radiation Lab, Univ Notre Dame, 79-82; res fel, Univ Glasgow, 82-85. *Mem:* Inst Elec & Electronics Engrs; NY Acad Sci. *Res:* Instrumentation; computers, robotics and equipment design; radiation chemistry, enzyme inactivation, kinetics and pH gradients; fluorescent pH indicating probes. *Mailing Add:* Dept 948 Med Res Div Am Cyanamid Co B175 Rm 145 Pearl River NY 10965. *Fax:* 914-732-5581

BELL, EDWARD FRANK, PEDIATRICS, NEONATOLOGY. *Current Pos:* from asst prof to assoc prof, 79-88, PROF PEDIAT, 88-, DIR NEONATOLOGY, UNIV IOWA, 88- *Personal Data:* b Washington, Pa, Apr 15, 48. *Educ:* Washington & Jefferson Col, BA, 69; Columbia Univ, MD, 73. *Prof Exp:* Residency pediat, Columbia-Presby Med Ctr, 73-76; fel neonatology, McMaster Univ Med Ctr, 76-77, Women & Infants Hosp RI, 77-79. *Mem:* Soc Pediat Res; Am Pediat Soc; Am Inst Nutrit. *Res:* Thermal physiology; nutrition and body composition of premature infants; anemia of prematurity. *Mailing Add:* Dept Pediat Univ Iowa Iowa City IA 52242

BELL, EDWIN LEWIS, II, HERPETOLOGY. *Current Pos:* from asst prof to prof biol, Albright Col, 54-91, preprof adv health sci, 61-87, chmn dept, 65-84, EMER PROF BIOL, ALBRIGHT COL, 91- *Personal Data:* b Danville, Pa, May 13, 26; m 50, Frances L Reichard; c Ernest M, Stephen T & Eric L. *Educ:* Bucknell Univ, BS, 48; Pa State Univ, MS, 50; Univ Ill, PhD(zool), 54. *Prof Exp:* Asst prof biol, Moravian Col, 52-54. *Concurrent Pos:* Dir biol sci curric study teachers inserv inst, NSF, 66-67; spec collections asst archivist, Libr, Albright Col. *Mem:* Am Soc Ichthyol & Herpet; Herpetologists League; Soc Study Amphibians & Reptiles. *Res:* Herpetology of Huntingdon County, Pennsylvania; study of lizard Sceloporus occidentalis; sexing of Drosophila larvae; dorman panther legend. *Mailing Add:* 1454 Oak Lane Reading PA 19604. *Fax:* 610-921-7509

BELL, ELDON E, PREVENTIVE MEDICINE, AEROSPACE MEDICINE. *Current Pos:* DIR, DOMESTIC PROGS, DEPT STATE, WASHINGTON, DC, 95- *Personal Data:* b Portland, Ore, Oct 12, 34. *Educ:* UNIV WASH, BS, 56, MD, 60; HARVARD UNIV, MPH, 63. *Prof Exp:* Flight surgeon, USAF, 59-69; country doctor, Day Country Med Ctr, SDak, 69-84. *Concurrent Pos:* Master flight surgeon, Nat Guard, SDak, 71-85. *Mem:* AMA. *Mailing Add:* Dept State Domestic Prog Washington DC 20520

BELL, EUGENE, CELLMATIC INTERACTION. *Current Pos:* SR SCIENTIST, MARINE BIOL LAB, 91-, PRES & CHIEF EXEC OFFICER, TISSUE ENG INC, 93- *Personal Data:* b New York, NY, Oct 28, 18. *Educ:* Brown Univ, PhD(biol), 54. *Prof Exp:* Prof biol, Mass Inst Technol, 57-86, emer prof, 86, sci organagenesis, 86-91. *Mailing Add:* Tissue Eng Inc 451 D St Box 199 Boston MA 02210

BELL, FRANK F, AGRONOMY. *Current Pos:* RETIRED. *Personal Data:* b Savannah, Tenn, Nov 6, 15; m 40; c 3. *Educ:* Univ Tenn, BS, 37, MS, 49; Iowa State Univ, PhD(agron), 56. *Prof Exp:* From instr to prof agron, Univ Tenn, Knoxville, 46-81. *Concurrent Pos:* Vis prof, Iowa State Univ, 61, NC State Univ, 67 & Univ Ky, 71; US rep, Int Soil Cong, Adelaide, Australia, 68; agron consult, US AID Prog, India, 70. *Mem:* AAAS; Am Soc Agron; Soil Sci Soc Am; Int Soc Soil Sci. *Res:* Soil productivity; management research. *Mailing Add:* 135 Judith Dr Knoxville TN 37920

BELL, FRED E, biochemistry; deceased, see previous edition for last biography

BELL, GEORGE IRVING, THEORETICAL BIOLOGY. *Current Pos:* mem staff, Los Alamos Nat Lab, 51-69, alt div leader, Theoret Div, 70-80, group leader theoret biol & biophys, 74-90, div leader, 80-89, actg dir, Ctr Human Genome Studies, 88-89, SR FEL, LOS ALAMOS NAT LAB, 89- *Personal Data:* b Ill, Aug 4, 26; m 56, Virginia Lotz; c Carolyn & George. *Educ:* Harvard Univ, AB, 47; Cornell Univ, PhD(physics), 51. *Honors & Awards:* Sowles Medal, 80. *Prof Exp:* Asst, Cornell Univ, 47-49. *Concurrent Pos:* Vis lectr, Harvard Univ, 62-63; vis prof, Med Ctr, Univ Colo, 70-84; scholar human biol, Eleanor Roosevelt Cancer Res Ctr, Denver, 77-88, Nat Cancer Inst, Div Cancer Biol & Diag; mem, Basel Inst Immunol, Switz, 79-80, bd, Sci Counr, 85-89; consult, Nat Cancer Inst Div Cancer Biol & Diag, 84-92; mem sci bd, Santa Fe Inst, 86-; chmn, oversight Group Supercomput, 87-; adv coun, Nat Ctr Res Resources, NIH, 91-94. *Mem:* Fel AAAS; fel Am Phys Soc; Biophys Soc. *Res:* Theoretical physics theory of cell adhesion; nuclear reactor theory; theoretical immunology, mathematical models in biophysics; sequencing the human genome; analyzing repetitive DNA. *Mailing Add:* T Div MS K710 Los Alamos Nat Lab Los Alamos NM 87545. *Fax:* 505-665-3493; *E-Mail:* gib@lanl.gov

BELL, GORDON M(ORETON), MINERAL ENGINEERING, EXTRACTIVE METALLURGY. *Current Pos:* RETIRED. *Personal Data:* b Liverpool, Eng, Oct 17, 20; wid; c Barbara (Carman). *Educ:* Univ BC, BASc, 42; Mass Inst Technol, DSc, 53. *Prof Exp:* Plant asst, Falconbridge Nickel Mines, Ltd, 42-44; metallurgist, Aluminum Co Can, Ltd, 44-47; asst prof metall, Univ BC, 47-49; instr, Mass Inst Technol, 49-53; res engr, Extractive Metall Div, Alcoa Labs, Aluminum Co Am, 53-57, sr res engr, 57-65, sci assoc, 65-71, sect head, Geol & Raw Mat Res, 71-73, eng assoc, 73-85. *Mem:* Am Inst Mining, Metall & Petrol Eng; Sigma Xi. *Res:* Beneficiation of coal, clay, fluorspar, copper and aluminum ores; extraction of aluminum from ores; ore sampling, phases and properties of aluminas. *Mailing Add:* 825 Morewood Ave Condo G-8 Pittsburgh PA 15213-2923

BELL, GRAHAM ARTHUR CHARLTON, ECOLOGY. *Current Pos:* ASST PROF ECOL, MCGILL UNIV, 76- *Personal Data:* b Leicester, Eng, Mar 3, 49; m 71; c 3. *Educ:* Oxford Univ, BA, 70, DPhil(ecol), 74. *Prof Exp:* Fel ecol, Univ York, 74-75. *Mem:* Soc Study Evolution; Ecol Soc Am; Brit Ecol Soc; Am Soc Naturalists. *Res:* Evolution of genetic systems and sexuality; life histories; sexual selection; population dynamics. *Mailing Add:* Dept Biol McGill Univ Sherbrooke St W Montreal PQ H3A 2M5 Can

BELL, GRAYDON DEE, PHYSICS, ASTROPHYSICS. *Current Pos:* from asst prof to assoc prof, 57-65, chmn dept, 71-81, PROF PHYSICS, HARVEY MUDD COL, 65- *Personal Data:* b Paducah, Ky, May 5, 23; m 54; c 3. *Educ:* Univ Ky, BS, 49; Calif Inst Technol, MS, 51, PhD(physics), 57. *Prof Exp:* Asst prof physics, Robert Col, Istanbul, 51-54; res asst, Calif Inst Technol, 54-56, res fel, 56-57. *Concurrent Pos:* NSF res grants, 60-70, fac fel, Nat Res Coun Can, 70-71; physicist, Nat Bur Standards, 63-64; vis scientist, Australia, 78-79; consult, GTE Labs, 79, 80 & 81. *Mem:* AAAS; Am Phys Soc; Am Astron Soc; Am Asn Physics Teachers. *Res:* Experimental measurement of f-values for spectral lines of heavy elements. *Mailing Add:* Dept Physics Harvey Mudd Col Claremont CA 91711

BELL, H(ARRY) R(ICH), civil engineering, surveying engineering, for more information see previous edition

BELL, HAROLD, MATHEMATICS. *Current Pos:* From asst prof to assoc prof, 64-74, PROF MATH, UNIV CINCINNATI, 74- *Personal Data:* b New York, NY, June 25, 32; m 56; c 4. *Educ:* Univ Miami, BS, 58, MS, 59; Tulane Univ, PhD(math), 64. *Mailing Add:* 3511 Cornell Pl Cincinnati OH 45220-1503

BELL, HAROLD E, clinical pathology; deceased, see previous edition for last biography

BELL, HAROLD MORTON, ANALYTICAL CHEMISTRY. *Current Pos:* Asst prof, 66-75, ASSOC PROF CHEM, VA POLYTECH INST & STATE UNIV, 75- *Personal Data:* b Monticello, Ky, May 7, 40; m 60; c 2. *Educ:* Eastern Ky Univ, BBS, 60; Purdue Univ, PhD(chem), 64. *Mem:* Am Chem Soc. *Res:* Nuclear magnetic resonance; computers in chemistry. *Mailing Add:* 708 Circle Dr NW Blacksburg VA 24060-3208

BELL, HELEN, BIOCHEMISTRY, INSTRUMENTAL ANALYSIS. *Current Pos:* PROF CHEM, DYERSBURG STATE COMMUNITY COL, 83- *Personal Data:* b Halls, Tenn, June 4, 37. *Educ:* Univ Tenn, BS, 59, BA, 59, PhD(biochem), 75. *Prof Exp:* Teacher chem & biochem, Dyersburg High Sch, 59-69; supvr inst, Dyersburg City Sch Syst, 69-83. *Mem:* Am Chem Soc; AAAS; Nat Sci Teachers Asn. *Mailing Add:* Dept Arts & Sci Dyersburg State Community Col 1510 Lake Rd Dyersburg TN 38024-2450

BELL, HOWARD E, RINGS, NEAR-RINGS. *Current Pos:* assoc prof, 67-76, chmn dept, 75-78 & 95-98, PROF MATH, BROCK UNIV, 76- *Personal Data:* b Albany, NY, Jan 20, 37; m 61, Mary Frazier; c Katherine & Colin. *Educ:* Union Univ, NY, BS, 58; Univ Wis, MS, 59, PhD(math), 61. *Prof Exp:* Asst prof math, Union Univ, NY, 61-63 & State Univ NY, Binghamton, 63-66; assoc prof, Union Univ, NY, 66-67. *Concurrent Pos:* Vis prof, Mount Holyoke Col, 79; bd gov, Math Asn Am, 88-91. *Mem:* Am Math Soc; Math Asn Am; Can Math Soc. *Res:* Algebra, especially rings and near-rings. *Mailing Add:* Dept Math Brock Univ St Catharines ON L2S 3A1 Can. *Fax:* 905-682-9020; *E-Mail:* hbell@spartan.ac.brocku.ca

BELL, IAN, INDUSTRIAL ORGANIC CHEMISTRY. *Current Pos:* VPRES RES & DEVELOP, RUETGERS-NEASE CHEM CO, INC, 68- *Personal Data:* b Chorley, Eng, Sept 29, 32; m 56; c 3. *Educ:* Univ Manchester, BSc, 53, PhD(org chem), 56; Penn State, MBA, 79. *Prof Exp:* Tech officer org chem, Imp Chem Indust, Ltd, Eng, 58-60; from res chemist to dir res, Nease

Chem Co, Inc, 60-67; chemist, Winthrop Labs, Eng, 67-68. *Mem:* Am Chem Soc. *Res:* Acetylenic chemistry; steroid structure determination; oxo process; aromatic and aliphatic intermediates; hydrotropes. *Mailing Add:* 2138 N Oak Lane State College PA 16803-1124

BELL, J(OHN) M, CIVIL & SANITARY ENGINEERING. *Current Pos:* NIH res proj asst, 58-62, asst prof sanit eng, 62-68, ASSOC PROF ENVIRON ENG, PURDUE UNIV, WEST LAFAYETTE, 69- *Personal Data:* b Tappan, NY, Oct 8, 35; m 60; c 4. *Educ:* Clarkson Col Technol, BSCE, 57; Purdue Univ, MSCE, 59, PhD(refuse analysis), 63. *Prof Exp:* Civil engr, Civil Aeronaut Admin, Idlewild Airport, NY, 57. *Mem:* Am Soc Civil Engrs; Water Pollution Control Fedn; Am Water Works Asn; Sigma Xi. *Res:* Collection and disposal of municipal refuse; statistical design and analysis of field and laboratory experiments; industrial wastes treatment; water supply and treatment; sludge concentration; waste treatment in lagoons; stream sampling; stream biology. *Mailing Add:* 828 Bur Oak Ct E Lafayette IN 47905

BELL, JACK PERKINS, BIOCHEMISTRY, BIOLOGY. *Current Pos:* CONSULT, SEPARATION SCI, 93- *Personal Data:* b San Francisco, Calif, Jan 24, 40; m 65; c 2. *Educ:* Univ Wash, BS, 62; Univ Wis-Madison, PhD(org chem), 67. *Prof Exp:* Biochemist, Stanford Res Inst, 67-69 & Syntex Res Div, 69-78; mem staff, Waters Assocs, 78-80; regional sales mgr, Appl Analytical Indust, 80-81; prod line mgr, High Performance Liquid Chromatography, Varian Assocs, 81-89; western regional mkt, SFE/SFC, Suprex Corp, 90-91; bioseparation develop, HPLC/CE, Beckman Instruments, 92-93. *Concurrent Pos:* Lectr, High Tech Product Mkt. *Mem:* AAAS; Am Chem Soc; Sigma Xi. *Res:* RNA and DNA polymerases; nucleotides as probes of biochemical mechanisms and as drugs; synthesis and biological properties of polynucleotides; development of new drugs and immunoassays; identification of drug metabolites; development and marketing of high performance liquid chromatography; automated sample handling products; supercritical fluid extraction and chromatography; capillary electrophoresis. *Mailing Add:* 2950 Windtree Ct Lafayette CA 94549-4824

BELL, JAMES F(REDERICK), solid mechanics, continuum physics; deceased, see previous edition for last biography

BELL, JAMES MILTON, CHILD & ADOLESCENT PSYCHIATRY. *Current Pos:* from clin asst prof to clin assoc prof, 59-80, CLIN PROF PSYCHIAT, ALBANY MED COL, 80-; SR CHILD ADOLESCENT PSYCHIATRIST, BERKSHIRE FARM CTR & SERV FOR YOUTH, 86- *Personal Data:* b Portsmouth, Va, Nov 5, 21. *Educ:* NC Col, Durham, BS, 43; Meharry Med Col, MD, 47; Am Bd Psychiat & Neurol, dipl, cert psychiat, 56, child psychiat, 60. *Honors & Awards:* Pres Award, Meharry Med Col, 72. *Prof Exp:* Intern, Harlem Hosp, NY, 47-48; from asst physician to clin dir, Lakin State Hosp, WVa, 48-51; fel psychiat, Menninger Sch Psychiat, 53-56; asst sect chief, Childrens Unit, Topeka State Hosp, Kans, 56-58; clin dir & psychiatrist, Bershire Farm Ctr & Serv Youth, 59-86. *Concurrent Pos:* Resident psychiat, Winter Vet Admin Hosp, 53-56; civilian consult, Irvin Army Hosp, Kans, 57-58; fel child psychiat, Menninger Found, 57-58; chief consult psychiatrist, Parsons Child & Family Ctr, NY, 59-77 & staff psychiatrist, 77-; asst to dispensary psychiatrist, Albany Med Ctr Clin, 60-; trainee consult, Albany Child Guide Ctr, 60-; mem instrnl staff, Frederick A Moran Inst Delinq & Crime, St Lawrence Univ, 65-70; consult on adolescence & mem med adv bd, NY State Div Youth, 65-76; mem & vchmn subcomt returning vet, NY State Post Vietnam Planning Comt, 68-; consult, Astor Home for Children, NY; mem, Gov State Wide Comt for 1970, White House Conf Children & Youth; mem bd dirs & exec comt, Guild Farm, Mass; deleg, White House Conf Children & Youth; chmn, Comt & Adolescent on Psychiat Facil Children & Adolescents, Am Acad Child Psychiat, 73-75; chmn, Coun Nat Affairs & Comt Psychiat Facil Affairs, Am Psychiat Asn, 73-75; consult, West Point Mil Acad Hosp, NY, 77; consult, 85- *Mem:* Fel NY Acad Sci; Group Advan Psychiat; fel Am Psychopath Asn; fel Am Soc Adolescent Psychiat; fel Am Psychiat Asn; Am Acad Child & Adolescent Psychiat; fel Am Col Psychiat; fel AAAS; Black Psychiatrists Am; AMA. *Res:* Child psychiatry; delinquency. *Mailing Add:* Hudsonview 175 Old Post Rd Croton-on-Hudson NY 10520

BELL, JAMES PAUL, CHEMICAL ENGINEERING, POLYMER SCIENCE. *Current Pos:* assoc prof, 69-75, PROF CHEM ENG, INST MAT SCI, UNIV CONN, 75-, ASSOC DIR, 95- *Personal Data:* b Pulaski, Tenn, Nov 4, 34; m 55; c Kenneth, Virginia, David & Linda. *Educ:* Lehigh Univ, BSc, 56; Mass Inst Technol, DSc(chem eng), 66. *Prof Exp:* Sr res engr polymer res, Res & Develop Div, plastics dept, E I du Pont de Nemours, 56-62; res specialist, Textile Fibers Div & New Enterprise Div, Monsanto Co, 66-69. *Concurrent Pos:* Fulbright-Hays sr lectr, Coun Int Exchange Scholars, Univ Freiburg, Ger, 75-76; vis prof & Lady Davis fel, Israel Inst Technol & vis prof, Univ Naples, 83, Univ Trento, 97; dir, Polymer Prog, Univ Conn, 92-94. *Mem:* Am Inst Chem Engrs; Am Phys Soc; Am Chem Soc; Adhesion Soc. *Res:* Mechanical properties of polymers; structure and properties of epoxy resins; adhesion of polymers to metals; electropolymerization; coatings by spontaneous polymerization. *Mailing Add:* Dept Chem Eng Box U-222 Univ Conn Storrs CT 06268. *Fax:* 860-486-4745; *E-Mail:* jbell@maic.ims.uconn.edu

BELL, JEFFREY, immunology, for more information see previous edition

BELL, JERRY ALAN, PHYSICAL CHEMISTRY. *Current Pos:* PROG DIR, SCI MATH & TECHNOL EDUC PROG, AAAS, 92- *Personal Data:* b Davenport, Iowa, June 28, 36; m 61, 84, Mary Ann Stepp; c Allan, John, Christina & Allison. *Educ:* Harvard Univ, AB, 58, PhD(chem), 62. *Honors & Awards:* Catalyst Award, Mfg Chemists Asn, 77. *Prof Exp:* Res assoc chem, Brandeis Univ, 61-62; asst prof, Univ Calif, Riverside, 62-67; from assoc prof to prof, Simmons Col, 67-93. *Concurrent Pos:* Vis res prof, Brandeis Univ, 80-81; vis prof, Harvard Univ, 87-88; div dir, directorate Sci & Engr Educ, NSF, 84-86. *Mem:* Fel AAAS; Am Chem Soc; Nat Sci Teachers Asn; Nat Coun Teachers Math. *Res:* Kinetics of fast reactions; methylene reactions; flash photolysis; photochemistry; enzyme kinetics and mechanism; chemical education. *Mailing Add:* AAAS 1200 New York Ave NW Washington DC 20005-3920. *Fax:* 202-371-9849; *E-Mail:* jbell@aaas.org

BELL, JIMMY HOLT, ANALYTICAL CHEMISTRY. *Current Pos:* Chemist, 57-60, res chemist, 60-72, assoc scientist, 72-80, SCIENTIST, LORILLARD, INC, 80- *Personal Data:* b Burlington, NC, Jan 26, 35; m 61; c 3. *Educ:* Elon Col, BS, 56. *Mem:* Am Chem Soc. *Res:* Analysis of the chemical composition of tobacco from harvest to curing; chemical changes during manufacturing processes; isolation and identification of the components of tobacco combustion. *Mailing Add:* 1826 New Garden Rd Greensboro NC 27410-2006

BELL, JIMMY TODD, PHYSICAL CHEMISTRY. *Current Pos:* Res chemist chem technol div, 63-74, group leader, 74-80, MGR FUEL CYCLE CHEM, OAK RIDGE NAT LAB, 80- *Personal Data:* b Hazlehurst, Ga, Dec 17, 38; m 61; c 2. *Educ:* Berry Col, AB, 60; Univ Miss, PhD(phys chem), 63. *Mem:* AAAS; Am Chem Soc; Am Nuclear Soc. *Res:* High temperature and pressure spectroscopy of transuranium element aqueous solutions; photochemistry of actinides; tritium equilibrias; tritium permeation; high temperature materials chemistry; fuel cycle chemistry. *Mailing Add:* 137 Bowsprit Lane Kingston TN 37763-9648

BELL, JOHN FREDERICK, FOREST MENSURATION, FOREST MANAGEMENT. *Current Pos:* RETIRED. *Personal Data:* b Ashland, Ore, Jan 7, 24; m 50; c 4. *Educ:* Ore State Univ, BS, 49; Duke Univ, MF, 51; Univ Mich, PhD, 70. *Prof Exp:* Tech asst, Ore State Forestry Dept, 49-50, inventory forester, 51-53, unit forester, 53-55, supvr forest inventory, 55-59; from asst prof to assoc prof, Col Forestry, Ore State Univ, 59-72, prof forest mensuration, 72-85. *Concurrent Pos:* Chmn, Forest Inventory Working Group, Soc Am Foresters. *Mem:* Soc Am Foresters. *Res:* Forest measurements and sampling. *Mailing Add:* 465 NW Elizabeth Dr Corvallis OR 97330

BELL, JOHN MILTON, ANIMAL NUTRITION. *Current Pos:* From asst prof to assoc prof animal husb, Univ Sask, 48-54, prof & head dept, 54-75, assoc dean, 75-80, Burford Hooke prof, 80-84, prof animal sci, Res Col Agr, 84-89, EMER PROF ANIMAL SCI, UNIV SASK, 89- *Personal Data:* b Islay, Alta, Jan 16, 22; m 44; c 5. *Educ:* Univ Alta, BScA, 43; McGill Univ, MSc, 45; Cornell Univ, PhD, 48. *Hon Degrees:* DSc, McGill, 86. *Honors & Awards:* Borden Award, 62; Order of Can, 73; Canola Res Award, 81; Jas McAnsh Award, 88. *Concurrent Pos:* Chmn, Comt Animal Nutrit, Sask Adv Coun Animal Prod; mem bd gov, Univ Sask, 77-83. *Mem:* Am Soc Animal Sci; Am Inst Nutrit; Can Soc Animal Sci (pres, 52); fel Agr Inst Can; fel Royal Soc Can. *Res:* Swine nutrition; dairy calf nutrition; toxic factors in rapeseed; environmental temperature effects on animals. *Mailing Add:* Animal Sci Bldg Rm 112 Univ Sask Saskatoon SK S7N 0W0 Can

BELL, JONATHAN GEORGE, MATHEMATICS, BIOMATHEMATICS. *Current Pos:* AT DEPT MATH, HEALTH SCI CTR, STATE UNIV NY. *Personal Data:* b Spokane, Wash. *Educ:* San Diego State Univ, BA, 69, MS, 71; Univ Calif, Los Angeles, PhD(appl math), 77. *Prof Exp:* Mathematician acoust, Naval Undersea Ctr, 74; programmer, Logicon, Inc, 75; asst prof appl math, Tex A&M Univ, 77- *Mem:* Soc Indust & Appl Math; Am Math Soc; Sigma Xi. *Res:* Mathematical modeling of the nerve conduction process, analyzing the models for solution behavior; models of nerve bundles and flow of nutrients in trees. *Mailing Add:* State Univ NY Buffalo 106 Diefendorf Hall Buffalo NY 14214-3093

BELL, JULIETTE B, MOLECULAR GENETICS. *Current Pos:* STAFF FEL, NAT INST ENVIRON HEALTH SCI, RESEARCH TRIANGLE PARK, NC, 90- *Personal Data:* b Apr 15, 55. *Educ:* Talladega Col, BA, 77; Atlanta Univ, PhD(chem, biochem), 87. *Prof Exp:* Asst chemist, Southern Res Inst, Birmingham, Ala, 77-78; Carolina minority postdoctoral scholar, Univ NC, Chapel Hill, 87-87, postdoctoral fel, 89-90. *Concurrent Pos:* Sub teacher, SC Pub Sch, 78-79; teaching asst, Clark Col, Atlanta, 82. *Mem:* Asn Women in Sci (co-pres, 91-92); AAAS; Am Soc Biochem & Molecular Biol. *Res:* Molecular genetic and biochemical studies of protein structure/function relationships in nucleotide biosynthesis and metabolism. *Mailing Add:* Dept Nat Sci Fayetteville State Univ 1200 Murchison Rd Fayetteville NC 28301-4298

BELL, KENNETH J(OHN), CHEMICAL ENGINEERING. *Current Pos:* from assoc prof to prof, 61-76, REGENTS PROF CHEM ENG, 76-, KERR-MCGEE CHAIR CHEM ENG, OKLA STATE UNIV, 90- *Personal Data:* b Cleveland, Ohio, Mar 1, 30; m 56; c 4. *Educ:* Case Inst Technol, BSChE, 51; Univ Del, MChE, 53, PhD (chem eng), 55. *Honors & Awards:* Don Q Kern Award, Am Inst Chem Engrs, 78. *Prof Exp:* Engr heat transfer, Hanford Oper, Gen Elec Co, 55-56; asst prof chem eng, Case Inst Technol, 56-61. *Concurrent Pos:* Mem vis fac, Oak Ridge Sch Reactor Technol, 58; consult numerous indust & govt agencies; sr res engr, Heat Transfer Res, Inc,

68-69; sr chem engr, Argonne Nat Lab, 85- *Mem:* Fel Am Inst Chem Engrs; Am Soc Eng Educ; Nat Soc Prof Engrs. *Res:* Design of heat transfer equipment. *Mailing Add:* Sch Chem Eng 401 Eng N Okla State Univ Stillwater OK 74078

BELL, M(ARION) W(ETHERBEE) JACK, NAVAL SCIENCE. *Current Pos:* RETIRED. *Personal Data:* b Wichita Falls, Tex, Aug 17, 27; wid; c 6. *Educ:* US Merchant Marine Acad, BS, 49. *Prof Exp:* propulsion engr, Columbus Div, NAm Aviation Inc, 54-57, proj engr missile preliminary design, 57-61, chief sci space systs, Space & Info Systs Div, 62-63, dir, lunar & planetary systs, 63-66, mgr, advan systs, 66-69, chief prog eng, Space Div, NAm Rockwell Corp, 69-71, proj mgr, Advan Shuttle Proj, 72-77, dir advan syst, Shuttle Orbiter Div, 77-81, asst chief engr, preliminary design & mission analysis, Space Group, Rockwell Int Corp, 81-84; sr systs engr, TRW, 85-94. *Mem:* Am Inst Aeronaut & Astronaut; Brit Interplanetary Soc. *Res:* Design and development of advanced space vehicle systems; synthesis and analysis of advanced spacecraft and launch vehicle system concepts; synthesis, analysis, design and test of rocket propulsion systems. *Mailing Add:* 3332 Corinna Dr Rancho Palos Verdes CA 90274

BELL, MALCOLM RICE, ORGANIC CHEMISTRY. *Current Pos:* res assoc, 55-61, res chemist-group leader, 61-65, SECT HEAD, STERLING-WINTHROP RES INST, 65- *Personal Data:* b New Britain, Conn, Aug 22, 28; m 60; c 3. *Educ:* Rensselaer Polytech Inst, BS, 50; Cornell Univ, PhD(chem), 55. *Prof Exp:* Develop chemist, Allied Chem & Dye Corp, 50-51; asst, Cornell Univ, 51-55. *Mem:* Am Chem Soc. *Res:* Gliotoxin; synthetic analgesic agents; synthetic therapeutic agents. *Mailing Add:* Rd 1 box 156A East Greenbush NY 12061-9731

BELL, MARCUS ARTHUR MONEY, PLANT ECOLOGY, ETHNOBOTANY. *Current Pos:* RETIRED. *Personal Data:* b Victoria, BC, Mar 1, 35; m 59; c 3. *Educ:* Univ BC, BSF, 57, PhD(plant ecol), 64; Yale Univ, MF, 58. *Prof Exp:* Lectr plant & human ecol, bot, morphol & taxon, Univ Victoria, 61-63, instr, 63-64, cur, herbarium hot collections, 63-, asst prof bot, 64-70, assoc prof biol, 70- *Concurrent Pos:* Nat Res Coun Can res grants, 65-, travel grant, Van Dusen fel & Ger Acad Exchange Serv grant, 65; Neth Educ Dept grant & Brit Coun grant, 66. *Mem:* AAAS; Ecol Soc Am; Can Bot Asn; Int Asn Plant Taxon; Int Asn Plant Ecol. *Res:* Forest ecology; classification and analysis of plant communities and environments; forest productivity, environmental information; ecological aspects of waste disposal; ethnobotany of British Columbia native groups. *Mailing Add:* Dept Biol Sci Univ Victoria Box 1700 Victoria BC V8W 2Y2 Can

BELL, MARVIN CARL, ANIMAL NUTRITION. *Current Pos:* assoc prof animal husb & assoc animal husbandman, 51-65, PROF ANIMAL SCI, UNIV TENN, KNOXVILLE, 65- *Personal Data:* b Centertown, Ky, Nov 24, 21; m 48; c 2. *Educ:* Univ Ky, BS, 47, MS, 49; Okla Agr & Mech Col, PhD(animal nutrit), 52. *Prof Exp:* Res asst animal husb, Univ Ky, 47-48; asst, Okla Agr & Mech Col, 48-51; from assoc scientist to scientist, AEC, 58-74. *Concurrent Pos:* Mem staff, Travel Lect Prog, Oak Ridge Inst Nuclear Studies, 59-; mem protection & measures sci comt, Nat Coun Radiation, 63. *Mem:* Fel AAAS; Am Inst Nutrit; fel Am Soc Animal Sci; Nutrit Today Soc; fel Nat Feed Ingredients Asn. *Res:* Metabolism studies with cattle and sheep; urea and stilbestrol feeding to ruminants; fescue poisoning investigations; feeding value of wood molasses; radioisotope tracers in nutrition studies; irradiation effects on metabolism in large animals; mineral metabolism; hypomagnesemia tetany; vitamin injections. *Mailing Add:* 4608 Hill Top Rd Knoxville TN 37920-2917

BELL, MARVIN DRAKE, SOLID STATE PHYSICS. *Current Pos:* RETIRED. *Personal Data:* b Tulsa, Okla, Jan 14, 29; m 50; c 4. *Educ:* Okla State Univ, BS, 55, MS, 56, PhD(physics), 64. *Prof Exp:* Asst chemist, Phillips Petrol Co, 52-54, res physicist, 56-58; res assoc physics, Okla State Univ, 64-65; assoc prof, Western Ky Univ, 65-67; chmn dept, Cent Mo State Univ, 67-81, prof physics, 67-93. *Concurrent Pos:* Fac fel, Solar Energy Res Inst, 80. *Mem:* Am Phys Soc; Optical Soc Am; Am Asn Physics Teachers; Solar Energy Soc; Laser Inst Am. *Res:* Electron spin resonance in semiconducting diamonds; photoconductivity; photovoltaic effect; electrical properties of diamonds; holography; coherent optics; solar energy materials research. *Mailing Add:* 521 SW 301st Rd Warrensburg MO 64093

BELL, MARY, CELL BIOLOGY, HUMAN ANATOMY. *Current Pos:* HEALTH SCIENTIST ADMIN, NIH, 89- *Personal Data:* b Providence, RI, May 21, 37. *Educ:* Brown Univ, AB, 58; Yale Univ, PhD(anat), 65. *Prof Exp:* Asst scientist, Dept Cutaneous Biol & Electron Micros, Ore Regional Primate Res Ctr, 64-71, assoc scientist, 71-74; asst prof, Dept Environ Health & Dept Anat, Col Med, Univ Cincinnati, 74-81, assoc prof, Dept Anat, Cell Biol & Dermat, 81- 84; prin scientist, Gillette Res Inst, 85-89. *Concurrent Pos:* Assoc prof, Div Dermat, Sch Med, Univ Ore, 70-74. *Mem:* Am Soc Cell Biol; Am Asn Anatomists; Electron Micros Soc Am; Soc Investigative Dermat. *Res:* Ultrastructure of skin; effects of topical agents in epithelia. *Mailing Add:* c/o NIH-NCI-DEA-GRB 6130 Executive Blvd Rm 611A Bethesda MD 20892-0001

BELL, MAURICE EVAN, OPERATIONS RESEARCH. *Current Pos:* asst dean res, Col Earth & Mineral Sci, Pa State Univ, 56-72, prof, 56-76, assoc dean, 72-76, EMER PROF GEOPHYS & ASSOC DEAN, PA STATE UNIV, UNIVERSITY PARK, 76- *Personal Data:* b New Castle, Ohio, Sept 10, 10; wid; c 1. *Educ:* Kenyon Col, ScB, 32; Mass Inst Technol, PhD(physics), 37. *Prof Exp:* Res engr, Westinghouse Elec & Mfg Co, 37-41; res assoc underwater sound, Harvard Univ, 41-42; res assoc opers res, Nat Defense Res Comt, Off Sci Res & Develop & US Navy, 42-47; sci liaison officer, Off Naval Res, London, 48, dep sci dir, 49-50, sci dir, 51-53; eng mgr, Sylvania Missile Systs Lab, Sylvania Elec Prod, Inc, 54, mgr solid state br, Physics Lab, 54-56. *Res:* Ionization probabilities; dielectric properties of solids; high vacuum lubricants; operations research; missile systems; semiconductor physics. *Mailing Add:* 1008 Glenn Circle N State College PA 16803-3464

BELL, MAX EWART, plant morphology, for more information see previous edition

BELL, MICHAEL ALLEN, EVOLUTION, PALEOBIOLOGY. *Current Pos:* asst prof, 78-84, ASSOC PROF ECOL & EVOLUTION, STATE UNIV NY, STONY BROOK, 84- *Personal Data:* b Brooklyn, NY, Sept 17, 47; div; c David B, Sam R & Madeline R. *Educ:* Univ Calif, Los Angeles, BA, 70, MA, 75, PhD(biol), 76. *Prof Exp:* Lectr biol, Univ Calif, Los Angeles, 78. *Concurrent Pos:* Res assoc ichthyol, Natural Hist Mus Los Angeles County, 76-; James Chair prof pure & appl sci, St Francis Xavier Univ, Antigonish, NS, 92. *Mem:* AAAS; Am Soc Ichthyologists & Herpetologists; Soc Study Evolution (secy, 88-90); Soc Syst Zool. *Res:* Evolutionary biology of stickleback fish; roles of natural selection and gene flow in formation of patterns of spatial differentiation and variation within populations; patterns and rates of evolution in fossils; mechanisms of morphological change in evolution. *Mailing Add:* Dept Ecol & Evolution State Univ NY Stony Brook NY 11794-5245. *Fax:* 516-689-6682; *E-Mail:* mabell@life.bio.sunysb.edu

BELL, MILO C, FISHERIES, ENGINEERING. *Current Pos:* from instr to prof, 40-75, EMER PROF FISHERIES, UNIV WASH, 75-; PRES, MILO BELL CONSULT, 90- *Personal Data:* b 1905; US citizen. *Educ:* Univ Wash, BS, 23. *Prof Exp:* Mem staff, Wash Dept Fisheries, 30-33, 35-43. *Concurrent Pos:* Mem, Int Pac Salmon Fisheries Comn, 43-51; consult, Wash Dept Fisheries, 51-57, var US power co, 57- & Wash Water Res Ctr, 68-69. *Mem:* Nat Acad Eng. *Mailing Add:* PO Box 23 Mukilteo WA 98275

BELL, NORMAN H, ENDOCRINOLOGY, METABOLISM. *Current Pos:* dir, Gen Clin Res Ctr, 79-91, PROF MED PHARMACOL & DIR, DIV BONE & MINERAL METAB, MED UNIV SC, CHARLESTON, 79- *Personal Data:* b Gainesville, Ga, Feb 11, 31; m 59, 68, 72, Ledlie Dinsmore; c Douglas H, Julianne (Rankin) & Bayard G. *Educ:* Emory Univ, AB, 51; Duke Univ, MD, 55. *Honors & Awards:* Frederic C Bartter Award, Am Soc Bone & Mineral Res, 92. *Prof Exp:* From intern to asst resident med, Duke Univ Med Ctr, 55-57; clin assoc, Nat Inst Allergy & Infectious Dis, 57-59; staff investr endocrinol, Nat Heart Inst, 59-63; assoc med, Med Sch, Northwestern Univ, 63-65, asst prof, 65-68; assoc prof, Sch Med, Ind Univ, Indianapolis, 68-71, prof med pharmacol & dir, Clin Res Ctr, 71-79. *Concurrent Pos:* Attend physician, Res Vet Admin Hosp, 64-68; career develop award, USPHS, 65-68; chief, Sect Metab, Indianapolis Vet Admin Hosp, 68-74, assoc chief staff, 71-78; med investr, Vet Admin Hosp, Charleston, 81-87; mem, Gen Med B Study Sect, NIH, 82-86, chmn, 85-86. *Mem:* AAAS; Asn Am Physicians; Am Soc Bone & Mineral Res (secy-treas, 77-85, pres, 86-87); Am Soc Nephrol; Am Soc Clin Invest; Am Soc Pharm Exp Therapeut. *Res:* Bone and mineral metabolism. *Mailing Add:* Vet Admin Med Ctr 109 Bee St Charleston SC 29401-5703. *Fax:* 803-577-4318

BELL, NORMAN R(OBERT), engineering consulting; deceased, see previous edition for last biography

BELL, PAUL BURTON, JR, ELECTRON MICROSCOPY, CELL MOTILITY. *Current Pos:* from asst prof to assoc prof biol, 79-93, ASSOC PROVOST, 92-, PROF BIOL, DEPT ZOOL, UNIV OKLA, NORMAN, 93- *Personal Data:* b Memphis, Tenn, June 24, 46; m 79, Terry Carrel; c Peter E & Heather M. *Educ:* Wash Univ, St Louis, AB, 68; Yale Univ, PhD(biol), 75. *Prof Exp:* Fel cell biol, Wallenberg Lab, Uppsala Univ, Sweden, 74; fel biol, div biol, Calif Inst Tech, 74-76, res fel, 76-79; vis lectr, Cell Biol Inst, Linkoping Univ, Sweden, 89-90. *Concurrent Pos:* Actg asst prof biol, dept biol, Univ Calif, Los Angeles, 76-78, adj asst prof, 78-79; vis researcher, dept path, Linkoping Univ, Sweden, 84-88. *Mem:* AAAS; Am Soc Cell Biol; Am Soc Zool; Soc Develop Biol; Electron Micros Soc Am; Scand Soc Electron Micros. *Res:* Mechanism of cell motility and contact inhibition of movement; tumor invasion and metastasis; structure and function of the cytoskeleton; electron microscopic and immunoelectron microscopic methods; quantitative immunofluorescence light microscopy. *Mailing Add:* Off Registr Univ Okla Main Campus 900 Asp Ave Norman OK 73019-4050. *Fax:* 405-325-7383; *E-Mail:* pbell@uoknor.edu

BELL, PAUL HADLEY, biochemistry; deceased, see previous edition for last biography

BELL, PERSA RAYMOND, NUCLEAR MEDICINE, CLIMATOLOGY. *Current Pos:* RETIRED. *Personal Data:* b Ft Wayne, Ind, Apr 24, 13; m 41, 67, Mozelle Rankin; c Raymond Thomas. *Educ:* Howard Col, BSc, 36, DSc, 54. *Hon Degrees:* DSc, Howard Col, 54. *Honors & Awards:* Longstreth Medal, Franklin Inst, 64. *Prof Exp:* Mem staff, Nat Defense Res Comt Proj, Univ Chicago, 40-41; mem staff radiation lab, Mass Inst Technol, 41-46; physicist, Oak Ridge Nat Lab, 46-67 & 70-78; chief, Lunar & Earth Si Div, Manned Spacecraft Ctr, Houston, NASA, 67-70; staff mem, Inst Energy Anal, Oak Ridge Assoc Univs, 79-86. *Mem:* Am Phys Soc; Am Geophys Union; Sigma Xi; Soc Nuclear Med. *Res:* Electronic and physics instrumentation; nuclear physics; plasma physics; nuclear medical instrumentation; planetary research; hemispheric studies of carbon dioxide concentration. *Mailing Add:* 132 Westlook Circle Oak Ridge TN 37830

BELL, PETER M, GEOCHEMISTRY, GEOPHYSICS. *Current Pos:* GEOPHYSICIST, CARNEGIE INST, 64- *Personal Data:* b New York, NY, Jan 3, 34; m 59; c 4. *Educ:* St Lawrence Univ, BS, 56; Univ Cincinnati, MS, 59; Harvard Univ, PhD(geophys sci), 63. *Prof Exp:* Fel, Carnegie Inst, 63-64; corp technologist, Solid State Sci, 83-84, vpres sci & technol, Norton Christenson, 84-86, Norton Co, 86-90, vpres corp res & chief scientist, Norton Co,90- *Concurrent Pos:* Mat Adv Bd, Nat Res Coun, Mass Inst Technol, bd gov, Assoc Inst Physics. *Mem:* Geol Soc Am; fel Mineral Soc Am; fel Am Geophys Union. *Res:* High pressure-temperature experimental geochemistry and geophysics. *Mailing Add:* Box 195 Galesville MD 20765

BELL, RAYMOND MARTIN, ASTRONOMY. *Current Pos:* from instr to assoc prof, 37-46, prof & chmn dept, 46-75, EMER PROF PHYSICS, WASHINGTON & JEFFERSON COL, 75- *Personal Data:* b Weatherly, Pa, Mar 21, 07; m 42, Lillian M Kelly; c Carol A (Macomber), Martha J (Butler) & Edward F. *Educ:* Dickinson Col, AB, 28; Syracuse Univ, AM, 30; Pa State Univ, PhD(physics), 37. *Hon Degrees:* ScD, Washington & Jefferson Col, 76. *Prof Exp:* Asst physics, Syracuse Univ, 28-30 & Pa State Univ, 30-37. *Mem:* Am Asn Physics Teachers; Am Inst Physics. *Res:* Raman spectra; propagation of radio waves; Allison magnetooptic effect; dielectric measurements of porous materials; barium titanate. *Mailing Add:* 1506 First Ave N Apt 2 Coralville IA 52241

BELL, RICHARD DENNIS, PHYSIOLOGY. *Current Pos:* MEM STAFF, CHICAGO COL OSTEOP MED, 80- *Personal Data:* b Prague, Okla, Apr 21, 37; m 61. *Educ:* Univ Okla, BS, 60, MS, 65, PhD(physiol), 68; Okla State Univ, BS, 61. *Prof Exp:* Res asst prof urol & asst prof physiol, biophys & allied health educ, Health Sci Ctr, Univ Okla, 68-80. *Concurrent Pos:* USPHS res grant, 69-71. *Mem:* NY Acad Sci; Am Physiol Soc; Sigma Xi. *Res:* Renal physiology; body fluids and electrolytes; blood and lymph vascular systems of the kidney and their relationships to renal function. *Mailing Add:* 1018 Meadow Crest La Grange Park IL 60526

BELL, RICHARD OMAN, SOLID STATE PHYSICS, PHOTOVOLTAICS. *Current Pos:* res assoc, 75-93, CONSULT, MOBIL SOLAR ENERGY CORP, 93- *Personal Data:* b Havre, Mont, Feb 16, 33; m 57, Virginia Miller; c David, Margaret, Katherine & Edward. *Educ:* Mont State Univ, BS, 55; Univ Calif, Los Angeles, MS, 58; Boston Univ, PhD(physics), 68. *Prof Exp:* Mem tech staff, Hughes Res Labs, Calif, 56-58; staff scientist, Raytheon Co, Mass, 60-62; sr scientist, 62-66, group leader electronic mat, Tyco Labs, Waltham, 67-74. *Mem:* Am Phys Soc; Inst Elec & Electronics Engrs; Sigma Xi. *Res:* Electronic materials and devices for solar energy applications; evaluation of physical and electronic properties of semiconductor, ferroelectric and ferromagnetic materials. *Mailing Add:* 24 Austin Rd Sudbury MA 01776

BELL, RICHARD THOMAS, URANIUM RESOURCE ASSESSMENT, URANIUM METALLURGY. *Current Pos:* RETIRED. *Personal Data:* b Haileybury, Ont, May 1, 37; m 62; c 3. *Educ:* Univ Toronto, BA, 60, MA, 62, Princeton Univ, PhD(geol), 66. *Prof Exp:* Tech officer, Geol Surv Can, 62-63, res scientist, 66-69; from asst prof to assoc prof sedimentology & struct, Brock Univ, 69-75; res scientist, Geol Surv Can, 75-93. *Mem:* Fel Geol Soc Am. *Res:* Metallurgy research & regional assessment of uranium in Western Canada & northern Quebec; regional geological studies in precambrian rocks in western Canada, Central Keewatin. *Mailing Add:* 146 Elmer Ave Toronto ON M4L 3R8 Can

BELL, ROBERT EDWARD, nuclear physics; deceased, see previous edition for last biography

BELL, ROBERT EUGENE, ARCHAEOLOGY, PHYSICAL ANTHROPOLOGY. *Current Pos:* RETIRED. *Personal Data:* b Marion, Ohio, June 16, 14; m 38; c 2. *Educ:* Univ NMex, BA, 40; Univ Chicago, MA, 43, PhD(anthrop), 47. *Honors & Awards:* Clarence H Webb Award, 85; Shirk Mem Award, 87; Distinguished Serv Award, Plains Anthrop Soc, 94. *Prof Exp:* From asst prof to prof anthrop, Univ Okla, 47-67, chmn dept, 47-55, head cur, Social Sci Div, 47-80, George Lynn Cross Res prof anthrop, 67-80. *Concurrent Pos:* Wenner-Gren Found res grant, 55-56; ed elect, Soc Am Archaeol, 65-66. *Mem:* AAAS; Soc Am Archaeol; fel Am Anthrop Asn; Am Asn Phys Anthrop; Sigma Xi. *Res:* Archaeology of Southern Plains; early man in the new world. *Mailing Add:* 1120 Berry Circle Norman OK 73072

BELL, ROBERT JOHN, spectroscopy, solid state physics, for more information see previous edition

BELL, ROBERT LLOYD, MEDICINE, NEUROSURGERY. *Current Pos:* chief neurosurg, 64-69, CHIEF NUCLEAR MED, VET ADMIN HOSP, 69-; CHIEF NEUROSURG, CHESTER COUNTY HOSP, 70- *Personal Data:* b McKeesport, Pa, Sept 3, 23; m 51; c 2. *Educ:* Washington & Jefferson Col, BS, 43; Univ Pittsburgh, MD, 47. *Prof Exp:* Asst instr neurosurg, State Univ NY Downstate Med Ctr, 54-55, from instr to assoc prof, 55-61. *Mem:* Am Col Nuclear Med (pres, 81-); Am Bd Nuclear Med; Am Bd Neurol Surg Soc Nuclear Med; fel Am Col Surg; Cong Neurol Surg. *Res:* Nuclear instrumentation; brain tumor localization. *Mailing Add:* Sair Hosp/Clin 51 S 12th Ave Coatesville PA 19320-3529

BELL, ROBERT MAURICE, BIOCHEMISTRY, MOLECULAR BIOLOGY. *Current Pos:* from asst prof to prof, Duke Univ, 72-87, head, Sect Cell Growth, Regulation & Oncogenesis, 87-93, JAMES B DUKE PROF BIOCHEM, MED CTR, 87-, DEP DIR, DUKE COMPREHENSIVE CANCER CTR, 87-, CHMN, MOLECULAR CANCER BIOL DEPT, DUKE UNIV, 93- *Personal Data:* b Lincoln, Nebr, Mar 24, 44; m 66; c 2. *Educ:* Univ Nebr, Lincoln, BS, 66; Univ Calif, Berkeley, PhD(biochem), 70. *Prof Exp:* NSF fel, Wash Univ, 70-72. *Concurrent Pos:* NSF grant, Med Ctr, Duke Univ, 73-74, NIH grant, 74-, Nat Found-March of Dimes grant, 74-76; estab investr, Am Heart Asn, 74-79, grant, 76-78; Macy fac scholar, Med Res Coun Lab Molecular Biol, Cambridge, Eng; assoc ed, J Biol Chem, Duke Univ Med Ctr, 87-; chmn, Basic Sci Planning Comt, Duke Univ Comprehensive Cancer Ctr, 88-, mem, numerous comts, 84-; sci adv comt, Gallo Res Clin, Univ Calif, San Francisco, 88- *Mem:* Am Soc Biol; Am Soc Microbiol; Am Asn Cancer Researchers; Nat Acad Sci Spain; Am Soc Biol Chem & Molecular Biol. *Res:* Regulation of enzymes of phospholipid and triacylglycerol synthesis; membrane biogenesis; diacylglycerols function as intracellular regulators, second messengers, of protein kinases; phospholipid bilayer assembly; transbilayer movement of phospholipids; mechanism of oncogene action in cellular transformation; signal transduction mechanisms; regulation of diacylglycerol second messenger generation and attenuation; diacylglycerol metabolism; diacylglycerols as intracellular regulators of protein kinase C; diacylglycerol protein kinase C structure-function relationships; sphingosine/lysosphingolipid second messengers and signal transduction; sphingosine-protein kinase C structure activity relationships; biological activities and function of sphingoglycolipids, sphingolipid cycles; mechanism of negative growth factors action; regulation of sphingosine/lysosphingosine production & metabolism; structure and function of protein kinase C; structure and function of enzymes of lipid metabolism; role of sphingolipid breakdown production cellular regulation. *Mailing Add:* Dept Biochem Duke Univ Med Sch Duke Univ Med Ctr Durham NC 27710-7599

BELL, ROBIN GRAHAM, RESISTANCE TO HELMINTHS LGE, IMMUNOGENETICS. *Current Pos:* res officer, 76-79, from asst prof to prof immunol, 79-95, DIR IMMUNOL UNIT, DEPT MICROBIOL & IMMUNOL, J A BAKER INST ANIMAL HEALTH, NY STATE COL VET MED, CORNELL UNIV, 95- *Personal Data:* b Canberra, Australia, July 12, 42; div; c 3. *Educ:* Australian Nat Univ, BSc, 68, PhD(immunol), 71. *Prof Exp:* Med res fel microbiol, Univ Western Australia, 71-73, res officer immunol & microbiol, Princess Margaret Hosp, 73-76. *Concurrent Pos:* Mem, Trop Med & Parasitol Study Sect, Nat Inst Allergy & Infectious Dis, 87-91. *Mem:* Am Asn Immunologists; Am Soc Trop Med & Hyg. *Res:* Immunity at mucosal surfaces, mechanisms of anti-parasite immunity, genetics of resistance and susceptibility to parasites in mammalian species; role of effects of IgE in protection. *Mailing Add:* J A Baker Inst NY State Col Vet Med Ithaca NY 14853

BELL, ROGER ALISTAIR, ASTROPHYSICS. *Current Pos:* from asst prof to assoc prof, 63-76, dir, 87-91, PROF ASTRON, UNIV MD, 76- *Personal Data:* b Walton-on-Thames, Eng, Sept 16, 35; m 60, Sylvia A Gandine-Stanton; c Alistair M & Andrew C. *Educ:* Univ Melbourne, BSc, 57; Australian Nat Univ, PhD(astron), 62. *Hon Degrees:* Dr, Uppsala Univ, Sweden, 82. *Prof Exp:* Lectr physics, Univ Adelaide, 62-63. *Concurrent Pos:* Prin res fel, Royal Greenwich Observ, 69-70; vis prof, Copenhagen, 74; sr res assoc, Nat Res Coun, 78-79, 93; prog dir, Div Astron Sci, NSF, 81-84; vis scientist, Space Telescope Sci Inst, 92-93; secy, US Nat Comt, Int Astron Union; gov bd, Am Inst Physics, 90-96. *Mem:* Am Astron Soc (secy, 89-95); Royal Astron Soc; Int Astron Union. *Res:* Stellar atmospheres, spectroscopy and photometry. *Mailing Add:* Astron Dept Univ Md College Park MD 20742. *Fax:* 301-314-9067

BELL, ROMA RAINES, NUTRITION. *Current Pos:* lectr nutrit, 78-80, HEAD, DEPT NUTRIT & DIETETICS, CURTIN UNIV TECHNOL, 81- *Personal Data:* b Clark, SDak, July 21, 44; m 71. *Educ:* SDak State Univ, BS, 66; Univ Calif, PhD(nutrit), 70. *Prof Exp:* Res assoc nutrit, Univ Ill, Urbana-Champaign, 70-71, asst prof nutrit, 74-77. *Mem:* Am Inst Nutrit; Nutrit Soc Australia. *Res:* Nutritional surveys; mineral metabolism; calcium, phosphorus and selenium; energy utilization and energy balance. *Mailing Add:* Sch Pub Health Curtin Univ Technol PO Box U1987 Perth WA 6001 Australia

BELL, RONDAL E, CELL PHYSIOLOGY. *Current Pos:* DEAN COL, CENT METHODIST COL, 78- *Personal Data:* b Kennett, Mo, Dec 29, 33; m 54; c 2. *Educ:* William Jewell Col, BA, 55; Univ NMex, MS, 60; Univ Miss, PhD(immunol, path), 71. *Prof Exp:* Asst biol, Univ NMex, 57-60; prof biol, Millsaps Col, 60-78. *Concurrent Pos:* Dir, NSF grants, Univ Colo, 64-66. *Mem:* AAAS; Am Soc Microbiol; Sigma Xi; NY Acad Sci. *Res:* Biochemical and immunological aspects of hormonally induced polyarteritis nodosa. *Mailing Add:* 2008 Timberview Dr Edmond OK 73013

BELL, ROSS TAYLOR, SYSTEMATIC ZOOLOGY. *Current Pos:* Instr, 55-58, from asst prof to assoc prof, 58-72, PROF ZOOL, UNIV VT, 73- *Personal Data:* b Apr 23, 29; m 57. *Educ:* Univ Ill, BA, 49, MS, 50, PhD(entom), 53. *Mem:* Soc Study Evolution. *Res:* Systematics morphology and zoogeography of the carabid beetles, especially rhysodine beetles. *Mailing Add:* Dept Zool Univ Vt Marsh Life Sci Burlington VT 05405-0001

BELL, RUSSELL A, ORGANIC CHEMISTRY. *Current Pos:* from asst prof to assoc prof, 64-73, PROF ORG CHEM, MCMASTER UNIV, 73- *Personal Data:* b Christchurch, NZ, Feb 3, 35; m 62; c 2. *Educ:* Univ Victoria, NZ, MSc, 58; Univ Wis, MS, 60; Stanford Univ, PhD(chem), 63. *Prof Exp:* Res assoc org chem, Univ Mich, 62-63; fel, Nat Res Coun Can, 63-64. *Mem:* Am

Chem Soc; Royal Soc Chem. *Res:* Total synthesis of organic natural products related to macrolide antibiotics; nuclear magnetic resonance; nuclear overhauser effect. *Mailing Add:* Dept Chem McMaster Univ Hamilton ON L8S 4L8 Can

BELL, SANDRA LUCILLE, BOTANY, CYTOGENETICS. *Current Pos:* From instr to assoc prof bot, Univ Tenn, 60-80. *Personal Data:* b Dupo, Ill, Dec 20, 35. *Educ:* Eastern Ill Univ, BS, 57; Univ Chicago, PhD(bot), 60. *Concurrent Pos:* Consult biol div, Oak Ridge Nat Lab, 62-69; res assoc, Nat Inst Agron, Paris, France, 66-67. *Mem:* AAAS; Am Soc Plant Physiol; Am Soc Cell Biol. *Res:* Chromosome cytology of higher plants; chemical effects on chromosomes. *Mailing Add:* 9408 Sarasota Dr Knoxville TN 37923

BELL, STANLEY C, ORGANIC CHEMISTRY, MEDICINAL CHEMISTRY. *Current Pos:* dir, 82-90, SR DIR, MED CHEM, WORLDWIDE, R W JOHNSON PHARMACEUT RES INST, RARITAN, NJ, 90- *Personal Data:* b Philadelphia, Pa, June 23, 31; m 67; c 2. *Educ:* Univ Pa, BA, 52; Temple Univ, MA, 54, PhD(org chem), 59. *Prof Exp:* Res assoc med chem, Merck Sharp & Dohme, 54-59; sr res chemist, Wyeth Labs Div, Am Home Prod Corp, 59-63, group leader, 63-68, mgr, Med Chem Sect, 68-82. *Concurrent Pos:* Former secy, chmn, Div Med Chem, Am Chem Soc; vis lectr, PMA; book reviewer, J Med Chem; med chem rep, Int Union Pure & Appl Chem; consult ed, Bioorg & Med Chem Lett; coun, Am Chem Soc. *Mem:* Am Chem Soc; NY Acad Sci; AAAS; Sigma Xi; Int Union Pure & Appl Chem. *Res:* Synthesis of new organic compounds as potential medicinal products; central nervous system; allergy; gastrointestinal immunomodulators; cardiovascular; B-lactam antibiotics; 210 patents and publications; endocrine inflammation. *Mailing Add:* 732 Braeburn Lane Narberth PA 19072-1507

BELL, STOUGHTON, MATHEMATICS, COMPUTER SCIENCE. *Current Pos:* assoc prof math, 67-71, dir, Comput Ctr, 67-79, PROF MATH & COMPUT SCI, UNIV NMEX, 71- *Personal Data:* b Waltham, Mass, Dec 20, 23; m 49; c 4. *Educ:* Univ Calif, AB, 50, MA, 53, PhD, 55. *Prof Exp:* Researcher math, Univ Calif, 52-55; staff mem, Math Res Dept, Sandia Corp, 55-64, supvr, Systs Anal Div, 64-66. *Concurrent Pos:* Vis lectr, Univ NMex, 56-66; nat lectr, Asn Comput Mach, Inc, 73-74. *Mem:* AAAS; Soc Indust & Appl Math; Am Statist Asn; Am Math Soc; Math Asn Am. *Res:* Rarefied gas dynamics; ordinary differential equations; operations research; weapons systems analysis; computing systems. *Mailing Add:* Comput Sci Dept Univ NMex Main Campus Albuquerque NM 87131-1386

BELL, THADDEUS GIBSON, ELECTRONICS ENGINEERING. *Current Pos:* CONSULT, 85- *Personal Data:* b Leominster, Mass, Feb 6, 23; m 50, Charlotte Ann Groh; c Theodore & Susan (Wurtz). *Educ:* Yale Univ, BS, 45. *Honors & Awards:* Solberg Award, Am Soc Naval Engrs, 68; Bushnell Award, Am Defense Preparedness Asn, 86. *Prof Exp:* Physicist acoust, US Naval Underwater Systs Ctr, 47-85. *Mem:* Fel Acoust Soc Am; Am Soc Naval Engrs. *Res:* Sonar design and analysis; underwater sound propagation; operations research; military oceanography. *Mailing Add:* 9 Colonial Dr Waterford CT 06385. *E-Mail:* 74067.3335@compuserve.com

BELL, THOMAS NORMAN, KINETICS, CATALYSIS. *Current Pos:* assoc prof, 67-75, chmn dept, 70-75, PROF CHEM, SIMON FRASER UNIV, 75- *Personal Data:* b Runcorn, Eng, Apr 18, 32. *Educ:* Univ Durham, BSc, 53, PhD(kinetics), 56. *Prof Exp:* Fel, Cambridge Univ, 56-57 & Univ Manchester, 57-58; sr lectr chem, Univ Adelaide, 58-67. *Concurrent Pos:* Nat Res Coun Can fel, 63-64. *Mem:* Fel Chem Inst Can. *Res:* Free radical reactions in gas phase; reaction mechanisms; catalytic hydrogenolysis of halocarbons. *Mailing Add:* Dept Chem Simon Fraser Univ Vancouver BC V5A 1S6 Can. *Fax:* 604-291-3765; *E-Mail:* tbell@sfu.ca

BELL, THOMAS WAYNE, MOLECULAR RECOGNITION, MOLECULAR ARCHITECTURE. *Current Pos:* PROF CHEM, UNIV NEV, RENO, 95- *Personal Data:* b Indianapolis, Ind, Jan 12, 51. *Educ:* Calif Inst Technol, BS, 74; Univ Col London, PhD(organic chem), 80. *Prof Exp:* NIH postdoctoral, Cornell Univ, 80-82; asst prof chem, State Univ NY, Stony Brook, 82-87; from asst prof to prof chem, State Univ NY, Stony Brook, 82-95. *Concurrent Pos:* Vis prof, Univ Louis Pasteur de Strasbourg, France, 90 & ECPM, Strasbourg, France, 96. *Mem:* Am Chem Soc; AAAS; Sigma Xi; Int Soc Antiviral Res. *Res:* Synthesis of heterocycles, artificial receptors, designed analytical reagents, chemical sensors, biocompatible materials, artificial ion channels, ionophores and antiviral drugs. *Mailing Add:* Univ Nev MS 216 Reno NV 89557-0020

BELL, VERNON LEE, JR, POLYMER CHEMISTRY, ORGANIC CHEMISTRY. *Current Pos:* RETIRED. *Personal Data:* b Omaha, Nebr, June 2, 27; m 49; c 2. *Educ:* Doane Col, AB, 50; Ala Polytech Inst, MS, 53; Univ Nebr, Lincoln, PhD(chem), 58. *Prof Exp:* Water analysis chemist, US Geol Surv, 51; fiber res chemist, Chemstrand Corp, Ala, 53-55; water analysis chemist, US Geol Surv, 55-56; res chemist, Film Dept, Exp Sta, E I du Pont de Nemours & Co, Inc, Del, 58-61 & Mylar Res Lab, Ohio, 62-63; polymer chemist, Langley Res Ctr, NASA, 63-68, head polymeric mat sect, 68-70, head nonmetallic mat br, 70-74, staff chemist, 74-80, sr scientist, 80-85. *Concurrent Pos:* Liaison mem comt aerospace struct adhesives, Nat Mat Adv Bd, 72-74; chief scientist, Graphite Fiber Risk Analysis Prog, 78-80; adv coun, Col Sci & Math, Auburn Univ, 86-90. *Mem:* Am Chem Soc. *Res:* Aromatic organophosphorus chemistry; benzacridines; Zeigler catalysis; polyhydrocarbons; polytrienes and Diels-Alder adducts; aromatic polyesters, synthesis and radiation effects; synthesis and properties of thermostable aromatic-heterocyclic polymers; polyimides; polyimidazopyrrolones; adhesives; composites; carbon fibers. *Mailing Add:* 7840 Sunset Dr Hayes VA 23072-3625

BELL, WALTER E, EPILEPSY. *Current Pos:* CHIEF, TECH INFO SECT, EPILEPSY BR, NAT INST NEUROL DIS & STROKE, NIH, 92- *Personal Data:* B Boise, Idaho, Feb 26, 36. *Educ:* Portland State Univ, BS, 61; NC State Univ, PhD(biomath), 72. *Prof Exp:* Statistician & clin proj mgr, Pharmaceut Indust, 72-92. *Mem:* Am Statist Asn. *Mailing Add:* Epilepsy Br NIH Fed Bldg Rm 516 7550 Wisconsin Ave Bethesda MD 20892-9020. *Fax:* 301-402-2157; *E-Mail:* wb22g@nih.gov

BELL, WARREN NAPIER, HEMATOLOGY. *Current Pos:* RETIRED. *Personal Data:* b Winnipeg, Man, May 8, 21; m 50; c 3. *Educ:* Univ Man, MD, LM, CC, 44; Univ Pa, MSc, 52, DSc, 55; FRCP(C), 53. *Honors & Awards:* Chown Prize, Univ Man, 44. *Prof Exp:* Assoc med, Univ Pa, 41-53, Damon Runyan scholar, 52-53, mem hemat staff, Hosp, 51-53; Storey Fund fel, Cambridge Univ, 53-54; assoc prof med & prof clin lab sci, Univ Miss & dir labs, Univ Hosp, 54-88. *Mem:* AMA; Sigma Xi. *Res:* Mechanisms of coagulation and hemolysis. *Mailing Add:* 3928 Eastwood Dr Jackson MS 39211

BELL, WILLIAM AVERILL, PATHOLOGY, ORAL PATHOLOGY. *Current Pos:* HEAD, PATH DIV, SCH DENT, MARQUETTE UNIV, 74- *Personal Data:* b Havre, Mont, Nov 29, 34; m 61; c 3. *Educ:* Mont State Univ, BS, 57; Wash Univ, DDS, 61. *Prof Exp:* Res path, Nat Inst Dent Res, 67-69; res assoc embryol, Nat Inst Child Health & Human Develop, 69-70. *Concurrent Pos:* Consult oral path, Vet Admin, San Francisco, 69-70; NIH Spec fel, Scripps Inst Oceanog, Univ Calif, San Diego, 70-72; consult oral path, Vet Admin, Wood, Wis, 74-; consult duel speciality, Am Dent Asn, 75-76. *Mem:* Am Acad Oral Path. *Res:* Dentistry; pulp pathology; embryology; the effect of current on sea urchin embryos. *Mailing Add:* 120 Lakeview Ave NE Atlanta GA 30305-3725

BELL, WILLIAM E, PEDIATRIC NEUROLOGY. *Current Pos:* from asst prof to assoc prof, 65-72, PROF PEDIAT & NEUROL, UNIV IOWA, 72- *Personal Data:* b Fairmont, WVa, July 31, 29; m 58; c 2. *Educ:* Univ WVa, AB, 51, BS & MS, 53; Med Col Va, MD, 55; Am Bd Psychiat & Neurol, dipl neurol, 63; Am Bd Pediat, dipl, 69. *Prof Exp:* Instr neurol, Univ Iowa, 62-64, asst prof pediat & neurol, 64; asst prof pediat, Univ Tex, 64-65. *Mem:* Fel Am Acad Neurol; fel Am Acad Pediat. *Res:* Infections and metabolic disorders of the nervous system in childhood. *Mailing Add:* Dept Pediat Univ Iowa Col Med Iowa City IA 52242-1000

BELL, WILLIAM HARRISON, ORAL SURGERY. *Current Pos:* assoc prof, 72-79, PROF ORAL SURG, SOUTHWESTERN MED SCH, UNIV TEX HEALTH SCI CTR DALLAS, 79- *Personal Data:* b St Louis, Mo, Mar 28, 27; m 65; c 4. *Educ:* St Louis Univ, BS, 50, DDS, 54; Am Bd Oral Surg, dipl. *Honors & Awards:* Res Recognition Award, Am Soc Oral Surgeons, 77; John J Geis Oral Surg Award, 84. *Prof Exp:* Intern oral surg, Metrop Hosp, New York, 54-55; resident, Univ Tex M D Anderson Hosp & Tumor Inst, Houston, 55-56; teaching fel, Univ Tex Dent Br Houston, 56-57, asst prof, Dent Sci Inst, 57-66, asst mem inst, 66-72. *Concurrent Pos:* Consult, Vet Admin Hosp, Dallas, 61-; pvt pract, 61- *Mem:* Am Dent Asn; Am Soc Oral Surg; Am Equilibration Soc; Int Asn Dent Res. *Res:* Bone graft and bone graft substitutes; developmental and acquired jaw deformities; surgical-orthodontics and bone healing; bone physiology; neuro-musculo-skeletal adaptation to surgical repositioning of the jaws; orthognathic surgery. *Mailing Add:* Coastal Surg Specialists 800 Hospital Dr New Bern NC 28560-3452

BELL, WILLIAM ROBERT, JR, INTERNAL MEDICINE, HEMATOLOGY. *Current Pos:* from asst prof to assoc prof, 70-80, PROF MED RADIOL & NUCLEAR MED, JOHNS HOPKINS UNIV, 81- *Personal Data:* b Greece, NY; m 66; c William R III, George H & Elizabeth E. *Educ:* Univ Notre Dame, BS, 57; George Washington Univ, MS, 60, PhD(pharmacol), 61; Harvard Med Sch, MD, 63; Univ London, HRA, 68. *Hon Degrees:* HRA, Univ London, 70. *Honors & Awards:* C V Mosby Award; Physician Scientist Award, Am Col Physicians, 96. *Prof Exp:* Consult, Lab Physiol, Nat Cancer Inst, 59-61; intern med, Johns Hopkins Hosp, 63-64, asst resident, 66-67; clin assoc, NIH, 64-66; vis scientist, Royal Postgrad Med Sch London, Hammersmith Hosp, 67-68; sr resident med, Harvard Med Ctr-Peter Bent Brigham Hosp, 68-69. *Concurrent Pos:* Admin officer, Nat Cancer Inst, 65-66, exec co-dir lymphoma task force, 64-66; consult, Twyford Labs, London, 67-68, Walter Reed Army Hosp, NIH & Food & Drug Admin; mem, Coun Thrombosis, Am Heart Asn. *Mem:* Am Fedn Clin Res; Am Soc Hemat; Am Heart Asn. *Res:* Blood coagulation; thrombotic disorders; fibrinogen biosynthesis. *Mailing Add:* Dept Hemat Johns Hopkins Hosp Baltimore MD 21287-4928. *Fax:* 410-614-9782; *E-Mail:* wrsb@welchlink.welch.jhu.edu

BELL, ZANE W, IMAGE PROCESSING, RADIATION GAUGING. *Current Pos:* Res staff, Oak Ridge Electron Linear Accelerator, 79-83, COMPUT & TELECOMMUNICATIONS SERVS DIV, MARTIN-MARIETTA ENERGY SYSTS, 83- *Personal Data:* b New York, NY, Aug 15, 52; m 77, Linda Weitz; c Noah & Kira. *Educ:* Rensselaer Polytech, BS, MS, 73; Univ Ill, PhD(nuclear physics) 79; Univ Tenn, MS, 86. *Concurrent Pos:* Pvt consult. *Mem:* Am Phys Soc; Inst Elec & Electronics Engrs; Sigma Xi. *Res:* Image processing; ultrasonics; radiography; radiation gauging; radiation detector development. *Mailing Add:* Y12 Plant Bldg 9103 MS 8141 PO Box 2009 Oak Ridge TN 37831-8141. *Fax:* 423-576-2782; *E-Mail:* bellzw@ornl.gov

BELLA, IMRE E, FOREST MENSURATION & MANAGEMENT. *Current Pos:* Res forester, 64-70, RES SCIENTIST GROWTH & YIELD, 71-, PROJ LEADER, CAN FORESTRY SERV, 78- *Personal Data:* b Hungary; Can citizen; c 1. *Educ:* Univ BC, BSF, 58, PhD(forest mgt), 70; Univ Wash, MF, 64. *Mem:* Can Inst Forestry. *Res:* Forest stand growth and yield simulation modeling (individual tree distance dependent); growth and yield research on thinning, spacing, general stocking-density-growth relationships and yield prediction and modeling. *Mailing Add:* 4803 154th St Edmonton AB T6H 5K6 Can

BELLABARBA, DIEGO, ENDOCRINOLOGY. *Current Pos:* asst to assoc prof med, 68-79, PROF MED, MED SCH, UNIV SHERBROOKE, 79- *Personal Data:* b Rome, Italy, Aug 13, 35; Can citizen; m 63; c 3. *Educ:* Univ Rome, MD, 59. *Prof Exp:* Asst physician, Univ Hosp, Rome, Italy, 60-64; clin res fel med, Mass Gen Hosp, Boston, 64-65; res assoc, Bronx Vet Admin Hosp, NY, 66-68. *Concurrent Pos:* Fulbright scholar, 64-65; Med Res Coun Can scholar, 69-74; Que Health Res Coun res scholar, 75-81; mem, endocrine Comt, Med Res Coun Can, 79-81. *Mem:* AAAS; Am Fedn Clin Res; Endocrine Soc; Am Thyroid Asn; Can Soc Clin Invest. *Res:* Ontogeny of hormone receptors; metabolism of triiodothyronine in health and disease. *Mailing Add:* Dept Endocrinol Univ Sherbrooke Fac Med Sherbrooke PQ J1H 5N4 Can

BELLACK, JACK H, SUBSTATION DESIGN & APPLICATION, BATTER STANDARDS. *Current Pos:* CONSULT BATTERY STAND, INST ELEC & ELECTRONICS ENGRS, 87- *Personal Data:* b Newberry, Mich, Mar 1, 26; m 48; c 3. *Educ:* Mich Technol Univ, BSEE, 49; Case Western Reserve Univ, MSEA, 63. *Prof Exp:* Engr, US Bur Reclamation, 49-53 & AEC, 53-54; instr, Fenn Col Eng, 56-66; engr, Cleveland Elec Illum Co, 54-70, gen supv engr, 70-87. *Concurrent Pos:* Co-chmn, Working Group Auxiliaries, Inst Elec & Electronics Engrs, 67-70, chmn, Working Group Batteries, 69-87, mem, Substas Comt, 70-78. *Mem:* Fel Inst Elec & Electronics Engrs. *Res:* Battery standards for use in the industry and for nuclear plants; battery standards for all photovoltaic, UPS systems and new battery types. *Mailing Add:* 3825 Deer Run Denver NC 28037

BELLAH, ROBERT GLENN, ENVIRONMENTAL BIOLOGY. *Current Pos:* from instr to prof, Bethany Col, Kans, 57-90, chmn, Div Natural Sci & Math, 71-85, Milfred Riddle McKeown distinguished prof sci, 80-90, prof & head dept biol, 80-90, EMER PROF, BETHANY COL, KANS, 90- *Personal Data:* b Nocona, Tex, June 21, 27; m 57, Patricia Ann McClelland; c Karil, Robi, Richard & John. *Educ:* McPherson Col, BS, 54; Kans State Univ, MS, 57, PhD(bot), 69. *Prof Exp:* Teacher pub sch, Kans, 55. *Mem:* Sigma Xi; Am Inst Biol Sci. *Res:* Social behavior of vertebrates, especially domestic chickens; plant ecology; forest successions on flood plains of rivers; floristics. *Mailing Add:* 319 S Third Lindsborg KS 67456

BELLAK, LEOPOLD, PSYCHIATRY, PSYCHOANALYSIS. *Current Pos:* from vis clin prof to clin prof, 75-87, EMER PROF PSYCHIAT, ALBERT EINSTEIN COL MED, NY UNIV & CLIN PROF PSYCHOL, FEL PROG PSYCHOTHER, 87- *Personal Data:* b Vienna, Austria, June 22, 16; nat US; div; c Kerin (Adams) & Katrina (Bronfman). *Educ:* Hamerling Gym, Vienna, Matura, 35; Boston Univ, MA, 39; Harvard Univ, MA, 41; NY Med Col, MD, 44. *Honors & Awards:* Frieda Fromm Reichmann Award, Am Acad Psychoanal, 81; Bruno Klopfer Award, Soc Personality Assessment, 91; Award for Distinguished Prof Contrib to Knowledge, Am Psychol Asn, 92. *Prof Exp:* Instr psychol, Boston Ctr Adult Educ, 39-42; instr, City Col New York, 42-44; from intern to med officer, St Elizabeths Hosp, DC, 44-46; instr psychol, George Washington Univ & USDA Grad Sch, 45-46; assoc psychiat, NY Med Col, 46-50, clin asst prof, 50-56. *Concurrent Pos:* Dir, Dept Psychiat, City Hosp, Elmhurst, 58-64; NIMH grant proj dir trouble shooting clin, Elmhurst Hosp & prin investr, Schizophrenia Res Proj; chief psychiat consult, Altro Health & Rehab Serv, Inc, 47-58; vis prof psychiat & behav sci, Sch Med, George Wash Univ, 75-79. *Mem:* Fel Am Psychiat Asn; Am Psychoanal Asn; fel Am Psychol Asn; Am Psychol Asn. *Res:* Projective techniques; manic-depressive psychosis; schizophrenia; ego function assessment; geriatric psychiatry; author 35 books, 300 articles; brief therapy; attention deficit disorder in adults. *Mailing Add:* 15 Shadow Lane Larchmont NY 10538. *Fax:* 914-833-1633

BELLAMY, DAVID, PLASTICS. *Current Pos:* vpres tech admin, 75-84, VPRES VENTORE TECHNOL, BAXTER HEALTH CARE CORP, 84- *Personal Data:* b Rochester, NY, July 17, 26; m 58; c 4. *Educ:* Yale Univ, BS, 49; Univ Chicago, MBA, 69. *Prof Exp:* Chief engr, Fenwal Labs, Inc; biomed engr, Baxter Health Care Corp, 60-65, dir biomed eng, 65-75. *Mem:* Soc Cryobiol; NY Acad Sci; Am Asn Blood Banks. *Res:* Blood processing equipment; hospital devices. *Mailing Add:* 92 Robsart Rd Kenilworth IL 60043

BELLAMY, DAVID P, TOPOLOGY, CONTINUUM THEORY. *Current Pos:* From asst prof to assoc prof math, 68-79, PROF MATH SCI, UNIV DEL, 79- *Personal Data:* b Bristol, Va, Apr 25, 44; div; c Lori M. *Educ:* King Col, AB, 64; Mich State Univ, MS, PhD(math), 68. *Mem:* Am Math Soc. *Res:* Point set topology; continua theory. *Mailing Add:* Dept Math Univ Del Newark DE 19716. *E-Mail:* bellamy@math.udel.edu

BELLAMY, JOHN C, CIVIL ENGINEERING. *Current Pos:* RETIRED. *Personal Data:* b Cheyenne, Wyo, Apr 18, 15; m 40; c 5. *Educ:* Univ Wyo, BS, 36; Univ Wis, PhM, 38; Univ Chicago, PhD(meteorol), 46. *Honors & Awards:* Losey Award, Inst Aeronaut Sci, 44; Thurlow Award, Am Inst Navig, 46; Medal of Freedom, Pres US, 46. *Prof Exp:* Partner, Bellamy & Sons, Engrs, Wyo, 38-42; asst prof meteorol, Univ Chicago, 42-47; assoc dir, Cook Res Labs, Ill, 47-60; prof res engr, 60; prof civil eng, dir res & dir, Nat Resources Res Inst, Univ Wyo, 60-81. *Concurrent Pos:* Dir inst trop meteorol, Univ PR, 43-44; mem, World Meteorol Orgn, 46-47, US Data Processing Comt, Int Geophys Yr, 55-57, US Meteorol Panel, 56-58 & Gov Adv Comt Indust Develop, 66-67; mem, Western Interstate Nuclear Bd, 67-80. *Mem:* Am Meteorol Soc; Am Inst Navig (pres, 62-63); Geophys Union; Am Soc Eng Educ; Sigma Xi. *Res:* Operational engineering; navigation; meteorology. *Mailing Add:* 2308 Holliday Dr Laramie WY 82070-4847

BELLAMY, RONALD FRANK, CORONARY PHYSIOLOGY. *Current Pos:* Vchmn dept mil med, 85-88, STAFF THORACIC SURG SERV, UNIFORMED SERV UNIV HEALTH SCI, 88- *Educ:* State Univ NY, Buffalo, MD, 61. *Res:* Thoracic surgery. *Mailing Add:* Borden Inst Walter Reed Army Med Ctr Washington DC 20307-0001

BELLAMY, WINTHROP DEXTER, MICROBIOLOGY, WASTE RECYCLING. *Current Pos:* CONSULT WASTE RECYCLING, 78- *Personal Data:* b Philadelphia, Pa, Oct 7, 15; m 47, Dorothy Landry; c Henry D & Janet A. *Educ:* Cornell Univ, BS, 38, PhD(biochem & microbiol), 45. *Prof Exp:* Teaching asst bact, Cornell Univ, 41-43, instr, 43-45; res assoc microbiol, Sterling Winthrop Chem Co; res biochemist, Res & Develop Ctr, Gen Elec Co, 49-78. *Concurrent Pos:* Adj prof food sci dept, Cornell Univ, Ithaca, NY, 78-84. *Mem:* Fel AAAS; fel NY Acad Sci; Am Soc Microbiol; fel Am Acad Microbiol; Am Chem Soc; Sigma Xi. *Res:* Microbial degradation of organic wastes; single cell protein production from cellulosic wastes; use of thermophilic microorganisms for waste conversion; biological effects of ionizing radiation. *Mailing Add:* 5548 Hamlet Lane Ft Myers FL 33919-2713

BELLAN, PAUL MURRAY, PLASMA PHYSICS. *Current Pos:* Assoc prof, 77-90, PROF PHYSICS, CALIF INST TECHNOL, 90- *Personal Data:* b Winnepeg, Can, Apr 18, 48. *Educ:* Univ Man, BS, 70; Princeton Univ, PhD(physics), 76. *Mem:* Am Phys Soc. *Res:* Current drive laser induced-flourescent physics; anomalous current diffusion; spheromak injection into tokamales. *Mailing Add:* 128-95 Calif Inst Technol-Watson Pasadena CA 91125

BELLAND, RENE JEAN, MOLECULAR BIOLOGY. *Current Pos:* RES ASSOC, UNIV ALTA, 93- *Personal Data:* b Edmonton, Alta, June 23, 54; m 81; c 2. *Educ:* Univ Alta, BSc, 78; Mem Univ Nfld, MSc, 81, PhD(biol), 85. *Prof Exp:* Fel bryol, Univ BC, 86-88, res scientist, 88-93. *Mem:* Can Bot Asn; Am Bryological & Lichenological Soc. *Res:* Bryophytes of the national parks of eastern Canada; relationship of bryophytic distribution to environmental factors in Canada; ecology of peatlands in Alberta. *Mailing Add:* Dept Biol Sci CW 405 Univ Alta Edmonton AB T6G 1E9 Can. *Fax:* 403-492-1899

BELLANGER, MAURICE G, COMMUNICATION SYSTEMS, SIGNAL PROCESSING. *Current Pos:* res & develop engr, 67-74, dept head, 75-84, SCI DIR TELECOMMUN, TRT-PHILIPS CO, FRANCE, 88- *Personal Data:* b France, June 21, 41; m 65; c 2. *Educ:* ENST, Paris, Engr, 65; Univ Paris, DSc, 81. *Honors & Awards:* Centennial Medal, Inst Elec & Electronics Engrs, 84. *Prof Exp:* Prof automatic control & signal processing, Univ Paris, 84-87. *Concurrent Pos:* Vis prof, Univ Calif, Santa Barbara, 87; adj prof, Ecole Superieure D'Electricite, France, 87-; chmn, Tech Prog, Inst Elec & Electronics Engrs, 88. *Mem:* Inst Elec & Electronics Engrs; Europ Asn Signal Processing (pres, 88-92). *Res:* Signal processing mainly for application in communication; digital signal processing; adaptive digital filter and signal analysis; theory, algorithms, structures for implementation and integrated circuits for realization. *Mailing Add:* Cnam 292 Rue St Martin 75141 Paris Cedex 03 France

BELLANTI, JOSEPH A, PEDIATRICS, MICROBIOLOGY. *Current Pos:* from asst prof to assoc prof, 63-70, PROF PEDIAT & MICROBIOL, SCH MED, 70-, DIR CTR INTERDISCIPLINARY STUDIES IMMUNOL, GEORGETOWN UNIV, 75- *Personal Data:* b Buffalo, NY, Nov 21, 34; m 58; c 7. *Educ:* Univ Buffalo, MD, 58; Am Bd Pediat, cert, 64; Am Bd Allergy & Immunol, dipl, 74. *Honors & Awards:* William Peck Sci Res Award, 66; Sci Exhibit Award, Am Acad Clin Pathologists & Col Am Path, 66; E Mead Johnson Award, Am Acad Pediat, 70. *Prof Exp:* Intern, Millard Fillmore Hosp, Buffalo, 58-59; resident pediat, Children's Hosp Buffalo, 59-61; NIH spec trainee immunol, J Hillis Miller Health Ctr, Univ Fla, 61-62; res virologist, Dept Virus Dis, Walter Reed Army Inst Res, Washington, DC, 62-64. *Concurrent Pos:* Mead Johnson grant pediat res, 64; mem growth & develop comt, NIH, 70-75; mem, med adv comt, Nat Kidney Found, 71-; chmn, Infectious Dis Comt, 72; dir, Am Bd Allergy & Immunol, 75- *Mem:* AMA; fel Am Acad Pediat; fel Am Acad Allergy; fel Am Acad Allergists; fel Am Asn Clin Immunol & Allergy. *Res:* Immunologic aspects of facultatively slow virus infections; biochemical changes in human polymorphonuclear leukocytes during maturation. *Mailing Add:* Dept Pediat & Microbiol Sch Med Immunol Ctr Georgetown Univ G1034 Gorman Bldg Washington DC 20007-2197

BELLAVANCE, DAVID WALTER, CHEMICAL VAPOR DEPOSITION, SEMICONDUCTOR PROCESSING. *Current Pos:* mem tech staff mat growth, 73-86, semiconductor process eng mgr, 87-89, SR MEM TECH STAFF, TEX INSTRUMENTS INC, 87- *Personal Data:* b Attleboro, Mass, Aug 30, 43; m 69, Maria Garcia; c Angela. *Educ:* Tufts Univ, BS, 65; Brown Univ, PhD(chem), 70. *Prof Exp:* Mem tech staff mat growth, Allied Chem Corp, 70-73. *Mem:* Electrochem Soc; Am Vacuum Soc. *Res:* Crystal growth and thin film epitaxy of silicon, III-V compounds, magnetic garnets, infrared materials, laser materials, and opto-electronic materials; semiconductor chemical vapor deposition and plasma etch processes; semiconductor equipment design; thin film epitaxy of silicon, III-V and IV-VI compounds; crystal growth. *Mailing Add:* 7410 La Cosa Dr Dallas TX 75248

BELL BURNELL, S JOCELYN, PUBLIC UNDERSTANDING OF SCIENCE, POSITION OF WOMEN IN SCIENCE. *Current Pos:* PROF PHYSICS & CHAIR DEPT, OPEN UNIV, 91- *Personal Data:* b UK, July 15, 43; div; c 1. *Educ:* Univ Glasow, BSc, 65; Univ Cambridge, PhD(radio astron), 69. *Hon Degrees:* DSc, Heriot-Watt Univ, 93, Cambridge, 96, DUniv, York, 94, Warwick, 95, Newcastle, 95. *Honors & Awards:* Michelson Medal, Franklin Inst, Philadelphia, 73; J Robert Oppenheimer Mem Prize, Ctr Theoret Studies, Miami, 78; Beatrice M Tinsley Prize, Am Astron Soc, 87; Herschel Medal, Royal Astron Soc, London, 89. *Prof Exp:* Fel, Univ Southhampton, Eng, 68-70, teaching fel, physics, 70-73; grad programmer, 74-76, assoc res fel, Mullard Space Sci Lab, Univ Col, London, 76-82; sr res fel, Royal Observ, Edinburgh, Scotland, 82-86, sr sci officer, 86-89, grade 7, 89-91. *Concurrent Pos:* Tutor, consult, examr, lectr, Open Univ, UK, 73-87; ed, The Observ, 73-76; chair, Europ Comn, Training & Mobility Res, Physics Panel, 96-; foreign mem Onsala Telescope Bd, Swed, 95-; hon fel, New Hall Cambridge, 96. *Mem:* Royal Astron Soc (vpres, 95); Int Astron Union; fel Inst Physics; Am Astron Soc. *Res:* Research in astronomy at many wavelengths - radio to gamma rays; neutron stars. *Mailing Add:* Dept Physics Open Univ Walton Hall Milton Keynes MK7 6AA England. *Fax:* 44-1908-654192

BELLENOT, STEVEN F, MATHEMATICAL ANALYSIS, COMPUTER SCIENCE. *Current Pos:* From asst prof to assoc prof, 74-84, PROF MATH, FLA STATE UNIV, 84- *Personal Data:* b Glendale, Calif, Aug 4, 48; m 75, Ellen Rumsey; c Cassandra & Elizabeth. *Educ:* Harvey Mudd Col, BS, 70; Claremont Grad Sch, PhD(math), 74. *Concurrent Pos:* Vis assoc prof math & comput sci, Clarkson Col, 80-81; tech staff, Jet Propulsion Labs, 85-91; vis prof math, Univ Tex, Austin, 87-88. *Mem:* Am Math Soc; Math Asn Am; AAAS; Asn Comput Mach. *Res:* Functional analysis, especially banach spaces; parallel and distributed simulations, especially time warp. *Mailing Add:* Dept Math Fla State Univ Tallahassee FL 32306-3027

BELLER, BARRY M, CARDIOLOGY. *Current Pos:* MEM STAFF, CARDIOVASC ASSOCS, 72- *Personal Data:* b New York, NY, Dec 12, 35; m 58; c 2. *Educ:* Columbia Univ, AB, 56, MD, 60. *Prof Exp:* Intern, Univ Chicago Hosps, 60-61, from asst resident to sr resident internal med, 61-64, USPHS res trainee cardiol, 63-64; assoc med, Albert Einstein Col Med, 66-67, asst prof, 67-68; assoc prof med & head sect cardiovasc dis, Med Sch, Univ Tex, San Antonio, 68-72. *Concurrent Pos:* Consult, USPHS Surv, 62; consult tech rev comt artificial heart prog, Nat Heart Inst-NIH, 69; mem coun clin cardiol, Am Heart Asn, 69. *Mem:* AAAS; Am Fedn Clin Res; Fel Am Heart Asn; fel Am Col Cardiol; fel Am Col Physicians. *Res:* Myocardial protein synthesis; hemodynamics; electrocardiography. *Mailing Add:* Humana Hosp Metro GL 72 Metro Prof Bldg San Antonio TX 78212

BELLER, FRITZ K, OBSTETRICS & GYNECOLOGY. *Current Pos:* PROF OBSTET & GYNEC, UNIV IOWA, 88- *Personal Data:* b Munich, Ger, May 17, 24; US citizen; m 48; c 2. *Educ:* Univ Berlin, Dr med, 48; Univ Giessen, MedSciD, 55. *Hon Degrees:* Dr, Univ Akita, Japan. *Prof Exp:* Docent obstet & gynec, Univ Giessen, 52-56; docent, Univ Tubingen, 56-58, head dept, 58-61, prof, 61; vis assoc prof, Sch Med, NY Univ, 61-63, from assoc prof to prof, 63-72; prof obstet & gynec & chmn dept, Univ Munster, 72-88. *Concurrent Pos:* Vis fac, Ben Gurion Univ. *Mem:* Fel Am Col Obstet & Gynec; Am Col Surg; Am Soc Exp Path; Soc Gynec Invest; fel Royal Soc Med; hon fel Polish Soc Obstet Gynec; fel Am Gynec Soc; fel Am Asn Obstet Gynec; fel Am Gynec Obstet Soc. *Res:* Hematological problems in obstetrics; intravascular coagulation and proteolysis; gynecological oncology. *Mailing Add:* Dept Obstet-Gynec Univ Iowa Hosp & Clin 200 Hawkins Dr Iowa City IA 52242-1087

BELLER, GEORGE ALLAN, NUCLEAR CARDIOLOGY. *Current Pos:* PROF MED & HEAD DIV CARDIOL, UNIV VA SCH MED, 77- *Personal Data:* b New York, NY, Dec 23, 40. *Educ:* Dartmouth Col, AB, 62; Univ Va, MD, 66. *Honors & Awards:* William S Middleton Lectr, Wis Med Soc, 68. *Prof Exp:* Med intern, Univ Wis Hosp, 66-67, asst resident, 67-68; sr asst resident, Boston City Hosp, 68-69; clin & res fel cardiol, Mass Gen Hosp, 73-74; from instr to asst prof med, Harvard Med Sch, 74-77. *Concurrent Pos:* Estab investr, Am Heart Asn, 77; mem, Cardiovasc & Pulmonary Study Sect, Nat Heart, Lung & Blood Inst, 87-91; chmn bd govs, Am Col Cardiol, 94-95; pres, Am Prof Cardiol, 95. *Mem:* Am Heart Asn; Am Fedn Clin Res; Am Soc Clin Investr; Am Physiol Soc; fel Am Col Physicians; fel Am Col Cardiol. *Res:* Development of nuclear cardiology techniques for assessing regional myocardial blood flow, function and viability; determination of noninvasive strategies for risk stratification in patients with coronary artery disease. *Mailing Add:* Div Cardiol Univ Va Med Sch Box 158 Charlottesville VA 22908-0158

BELLER, MARTIN LEONARD, ORTHOPEDIC SURGERY. *Current Pos:* assoc prof, 72-77, CLIN PROF ORTHOP SURG, SCH MED, UNIV PA, 77- *Personal Data:* b New York, NY, Apr 30, 24; m 47, Wilma Kjelgaard; c Alan Lewis, Beatrice A (Foreman) & Peter J. *Educ:* Columbia Univ, AB, 44, MD, 46; Am Bd Orthop Surg, dipl, 55. *Prof Exp:* Intern, Mt Sinai Hosp, New York, 46-47; resident orthop surg, Hosp Joint Dis, 49-52. *Concurrent Pos:* Attend orthop surgeon, Albert Einstein Med Ctr, 60-70, chmn dept orthop surg, Daroff Div, 70-79, emer chmn, 79-; attend orthop surgeon, Hosp Univ Pa, 63-; travelling fel, Am Orthop Asn, 63. *Mem:* Fel Am Acad Orthop Surgeons; fel Int Soc Orthop Surg & Traumatol; AMA; fel Am Col Surgeons; fel Am Orthop Asn. *Res:* Radioactive phosphorus and other isotopes in evaluating circulation of bone; x-ray densitometry of bone with aluminum step wedge; bone metabolism; osteoporosis; Paget's disease; total joints; spine survey. *Mailing Add:* RR 1 Box 256B Gaines PA 16921-9768

BELLES, FRANK EDWARD, COMBUSTION SCIENCE. *Current Pos:* CONSULT, COMBUSTION & ENERGY UTILIZATION TECHNOL, 82- *Personal Data:* b Cleveland, Ohio, Feb 28, 23; m 46; c 3. *Educ:* Western Res Univ, BS, 47; Case Inst Technol, MS, 52. *Prof Exp:* Aeronaut res scientist, NASA Lewis Res Ctr, 47-57, head, Gas Dynamics Sect, 57-64, head, Kinetics Sect, 64-71, chief, Propulsion Chem Br, 71-72, dir, Aerospace Safety Res & Data Inst, 72-74; dir, Labs Res & Develop, Am Gas Asn, 74-82. *Mem:* Am Chem Soc; Combustion Inst; Am Soc Gas Engrs; AAAS; Sigma Xi. *Res:* Flame quenching and fire extinguishing; high-temperature reactions; gaseous detonations; rocket propellant safety; combustion research and development. *Mailing Add:* 26376 John Rd Apt 316 Olmsted Fallas OH 44138-1269

BELLET, EUGENE MARSHALL, PESTICIDE CHEMISTRY. *Current Pos:* DIR RES & DEVELOP, KALO LAB, 76- *Personal Data:* b Hollywood, Calif, July 3, 40; m 68; c 5. *Educ:* Univ Calif, Riverside, BS, 63, MS, 69, PhD(chem & entom), 71. *Prof Exp:* Staff physicist residue chem, Univ Calif, Riverside, 65-68, environ sci fel, 69-71; res fel, Univ Calif, Berkeley, 71-73; chemist, Off Pesticide Prog, Environ Protection Agency, 73-74; mgr prod regist div, Weslaco Tech Ctr, Ansul Co, 74-76. *Mem:* Am Chem Soc; Entom Soc Am; Sigma Xi. *Res:* Synthesis, chemistry and toxicology of organophosphorus compounds and bicyclic phosphates; chemistry of organoarsenicals; synthesis and development of new pesticides. *Mailing Add:* Chem Consults Int Inc 7270 W 98th Terr Suite 100 Overland Park KS 66212-6166

BELLETIRE, JOHN LEWIS, SYNTHETIC ORGANIC & NATURAL PRODUCTS CHEMISTRY. *Current Pos:* asst prof chem, 81-86, ASSOC PROF CHEM, UNIV CINCINNATI, 86- *Personal Data:* b Chicago, Ill, Aug 23, 43; m 75. *Educ:* Univ Chicago, SB, 65; Northwestern Univ, PhD(org chem), 72. *Prof Exp:* Res scientist med chem, Pfizer Inc, 74-78; res fel, Dept Chem, Univ Wis, 78-81. *Mem:* Am Chem Soc; The Chem Soc; Sigma Xi. *Res:* Medicinal chemistry of diabetes; organic synthesis of novel heterocycles; anthracyclinones; heterolytic fragmentation reactions; photochemistry; oxidative coupling of electron-rich intermediates. *Mailing Add:* 7260 Auburn Rd Concord OH 44077-9724

BELLHORN, MARGARET BURNS, BIOCHEMISTRY. *Current Pos:* PROF OPHTHAL, UNIV CALIF, DAVIS, 85- *Personal Data:* b Sharon, Pa, Nov 26, 39. *Educ:* Allegheny Col, BS, 61; Yale Univ, MS, 62; Albert Einstein Col Med, PhD(biochem), 71. *Prof Exp:* From instr ophthal to instr biochem, Albert Einstein Col Med, 72-75, asst prof ophthal, 73-85, asst prof biochem, 75-85. *Mem:* Am Chem Soc; Asn Res Vision Ophthal. *Res:* Biochemical and morphological analysis of spontaneous and induced retinal degenerations and transport of substances through the retinal vessels; secondary ion mass spectrometry as a tool for chemical analysis of biological systems. *Mailing Add:* 28500 Alta Vis Winters CA 95694

BELLINA, JOSEPH HENRY, OBSTETRICS & GYNECOLOGY, BIOENGINEERING. *Current Pos:* clin instr to clin asst prof, 69-78, clin assoc prof, 78-80, CLIN PROF, SCH MED, LA STATE UNIV, 80-; RES ASSOC, ELECTROSCI & BIOPHYS RES LAB, TULANE UNIV, 78- *Personal Data:* b New Orleans, La, Jan 30, 42; c 2. *Educ:* La State Univ, MD, 65; Am Bd Obstet & Gynec, dipl, 73; Century Univ, Calif, PhD(Engr); Am Bd Laser Surg, 85. *Honors & Awards:* William B Mark Award, 85; Sigma Xi, 88. *Prof Exp:* Lectr, Univ Southwestern La, 68-69. *Concurrent Pos:* Vis surgeon, Charity Hosp, 69-; co-dir, Ultra-sound Diagnostic Sect & Ctr Reproductive Biol, Jo Ellen Smith-F Edward Hebert Mem Hosp, dir, Laser Sect; chmn, Laser Res Found; laser consult, Sch Med, Johns Hopkins Univ & Baylor Col Med; carbon dioxide laser res award, Cavitron Corp, 76-, Cooper Corp, 79, Laser Indust Israel, 79, Hamilton Pierce Co, 79 & Advan Surg Techol, Inc, 80; laser res award, Coherent Radiation, 76-; A Ward Ford Mem Inst grant, 79; Nat Cancer Inst grant, 80; nat adv, Nat Inst Child Health & Human Develop, NIH. *Mem:* Fel Am Col Obstet & Gynec; Am Asn Gynec Laparoscopists; Am Soc Colposcopy & Colpomicros; Int Soc Study Vulva Dis; Am Inst Ultrasound Med; Fallopine Int Soc. *Res:* Cervical intraepithelia neoplasia biomolecular structure responses to carbon dioxide laser, and other neoplastic processes and their relationship to molecular engineering; reproductive microsurgery. *Mailing Add:* One Galleria Blvd No 810 Metairie LA 70001-2082

BELLINA, JOSEPH JAMES, JR, SURFACE PHYSICS, INTERFACE PHYSICS. *Current Pos:* asst prof, 75-76, ASSOC PROF PHYSICS, ST MARY'S COL, 76-; NSF COL PROF, DEPT METALL ENG & MAT SCI, NOTRE DAME UNIV, IND, 76- *Personal Data:* b Orange, NJ, Mar 27, 40; div; c 5. *Educ:* Univ Notre Dame, BS, 61, PhD(physics), 66. *Prof Exp:* Res assoc physics, Barus Surface Physics Lab, Brown Univ, 66-68; res scientist, McDonnell Douglas Corp, 68-74; vis asst prof, Southern Ill Univ-Edwardsville, 74-75. *Mem:* Am Phys Soc; Am Asn Physics Teachers; Sigma Xi; Mat Res Soc; Am Vacuum Soc. *Res:* Low energy electron diffraction; ellipsometry; corrosion; stress-corrosion cracking; vacuum technology; auger spectroscopy; surface chemistry; affect of hydrogen on bonding at surfaces and interfaces of high strength isothermal remanent magnetization and nickel based alloys; metal reactions with silicon carbide; surface chemistry polymers. *Mailing Add:* Dept Chem & Physics St Mary's Col Notre Dame IN 46556. *E-Mail:* JBellina@saintmarys.edu

BELLINA, RUSSELL FRANK, ORGANIC CHEMISTRY. *Current Pos:* Res chemist, 68-73, res supvr synthesis chem, 73-74, lab adminr, 74-76, area supvr-tech, 76, chief chemist, Control Lab, Belle WVa Plant, 76-78, res mgr synthesis, Biochem Dept, 78-80, prin consult life sci res planning, Cent Res & Develop Dept, 80-81 & Corp Plans Dept, 81, MGR, AGRICHEMICALS DEVELOP, AGR PRODS DEPT, E I DU PONT DE NEMOURS & CO, INC, 81- *Personal Data:* b Newark, NJ, June 24, 42; m 66; c 2. *Educ:* Fairleigh

Dickinson Univ, BS, 64; Seton Hall Univ, MS, 66, PhD(org chem), 68. *Mem:* Am Chem Soc. *Res:* Agricultural chemistry, synthesis and market development of biologically active chemicals designed for use as insecticides, fungicides, bactericides, herbicides, and plant growth modifiers. *Mailing Add:* 708 Westcliff Rd Edenridge III Wilmington DE 19803-1712

BELLINGER, LARRY LEE, PHYSIOLOGY. *Current Pos:* from asst prof to assoc prof, 76-85, PROF PHYSIOL, BAYLOR COL DENT, DALLAS, GRAD SCH, BAYLOR UNIV, WACO TEX, 85- *Personal Data:* b Oakland, Calif, May 12, 47; m 73; c 3. *Educ:* Univ Calif, Davis, BS, 69, PhD(physiol), 74. *Prof Exp:* NIH fel physiol, State Univ NY, Buffalo, 74-76. *Mem:* Endocrine Soc; Am Physiol Soc; Soc Neurosci; Soc Exp Biol Med; Am Inst Nutrit; Soc Study Ingestive Behav. *Res:* The study of neurophysiological and neuroendocrine parameters involved in food intake and body weight control. *Mailing Add:* Dept Biomed Sci Baylor Col Dent 3302 Gaston Ave Dallas TX 75266-0677

BELLINGER, PETER F, ENTOMOLOGY. *Current Pos:* from asst prof to assoc prof, 58-65, PROF BIOL, CALIF STATE UNIV, NORTHRIDGE, 65- *Personal Data:* b New Haven, Conn, June 15, 21; m 53. *Educ:* Yale Univ, BA, 42, PhD, 52. *Prof Exp:* Lectr zool, Univ Col WI, 52-56; instr, Yale Univ, 56-58. *Mem:* Entom Soc Am; Lepidopterists Soc. *Res:* Collembola. *Mailing Add:* Dept Biol Calif State Univ Northridge 18111 Nordoff State Northridge CA 91330-8303

BELLINO, FRANCIS LEONARD, BIOCHEMICAL ENDOCRINOLOGY, ENDOCRINOLOGY OF AGING. *Current Pos:* ENDOCRIN PROG ADMIN, NAT INST AGING, NIH, 91- *Personal Data:* b Elizabeth, NJ, Dec 7, 38; m 63; c 11. *Educ:* St Francis Col, Pa, BA, 60; Univ Notre Dame, BS, 61; Univ Pittsburgh, MS, 65; State Univ NY Buffalo, PhD(biophys sci), 71. *Prof Exp:* Assoc engr, Westinghouse Elec Corp, 61-65; instr physics, St Francis Col, Pa, 65-67; assoc res scientist, Med Found Buffalo, 71-81; from res asst prof to res assoc prof, State Univ NY, Buffalo, 81-90; grants assoc, NIH, 90-91. *Concurrent Pos:* Prin investr, NIH grant, 77-90. *Mem:* Inst Elec & Electronics Engrs; Endocrine Soc; Am Soc Biochem & Molecular Biol. *Res:* Purification and characterization of estrogen synthetase from human placenta; mechanism of physiological regulation of estrogen synthetase in normal and malignant human trophoblast in culture. *Mailing Add:* Nat Inst Aging NIH Gateway Bldg Suite 2C231 Bethesda MD 20892-9205. *Fax:* 301-402-0010; *E-Mail:* bellinof@qw.nia.nih.gov

BELLION, EDWARD, MEMBRANES, PROTEINS. *Current Pos:* from asst prof to assoc prof, 70-90, PROF CHEM, UNIV TEX, ARLINGTON, 90- *Personal Data:* b Liverpool, Eng, Sept 6, 44; US citizen; m 84; c 3. *Educ:* Univ Leeds, Eng, BSc, 65, PhD(biochem), 68. *Prof Exp:* Res fel chem, Univ Minn, 68-70. *Concurrent Pos:* Adj assoc prof, dept biochem, Health Sci Ctr Dallas, Univ Tex, 70-86, vis assoc prof, dept pharmacol, 84-85. *Mem:* Am Chem Soc; Am Soc Microbiol; Am Soc Biol Chem & Molecular Biol. *Res:* Biochemistry of microbial growth on one-carbon compounds, including enzymology, transport, membrane studies and assembly of penoxisomes. *Mailing Add:* Dept Chem & Biochem Univ Tex Box 19065 Arlington TX 76019-0001

BELLIS, EDWARD DAVID, zoology, for more information see previous edition

BELLIS, VINCENT J, JR, AQUATIC ECOLOGY. *Current Pos:* PROF BIOL, E CAROLINA UNIV, 66- *Personal Data:* b Penn Yan, NY, Jan 18, 38; m 58; c 2. *Educ:* NC State Col, BS, 60, MS, 63; Univ Western Ont, PhD(bot), 66. *Mem:* AAAS; Phycol Soc Am; Am Inst Biol Sci; Brit Phycol Soc; Int Phycol Soc. *Res:* General estuarine and coastal ecology; effects of development on natural ecosystems of eastern North Carolina. *Mailing Add:* Dept Biol E Carolina Univ Greenville NC 27834

BELLIVEAU, LOUIS J, PHYSICS, APPLIED MATHEMATICS. *Current Pos:* RETIRED. *Personal Data:* b Boston, Mass, Nov 18, 26; m 52, Mary G Williams; c Jeanette, Maureen, Sharon, Carol, James & Paul. *Educ:* Boston Col, BS, 51, MS, 52. *Prof Exp:* Physicist explosions, Naval Ship Res & Develop Ctr, Md, 52-54, naval architect submarines, 54-57; physicist explosions, Naval Surface Weapons Ctr, Naval Ord Lab White Oak, 57-63; br chief explosives, Navy Dept, 63-67; physicist fluids, Defense Nuclear Agency, 67-72; supvry physicist, Harry Diamond Labs, US Army Lab Command, 72-92. *Concurrent Pos:* Contractor, Army Res Lab, 96- *Mem:* Am Phys Soc. *Res:* Explosives; explosions, chemical and nuclear; vulnerability of military equipment to blast and shock. *Mailing Add:* 1132 Parrish Dr Rockville MD 20851

BELLMER, ELIZABETH HENRY, BOTANY, ZOOLOGY. *Current Pos:* RETIRED. *Personal Data:* b New York, Sept 30, 27. *Educ:* Trinity Col (DC), AB, 59; Cath Univ Am, MS, 62, PhD(bot), 68. *Prof Exp:* From instr to assoc prof, Trinity Col, DC, 59-84, prof biol, 84- *Mem:* AAAS; Am Genetic Asn; Am Inst Biol Sci; Sigma Xi. *Res:* Time of embryonic fusion of the malleus and incus of the guinea pig; distribution, variation and chromosome number in the Appalachian shale barren endemic Eriogonum Allenii Watson. *Mailing Add:* Dept Biol Trinity Col Washington DC 20017

BELLMORE, MANDELL, ELECTRICAL ENGINEERING, OPERATIONS RESEARCH. *Current Pos:* MEM STAFF, BLOCK MCGIBONY & ASSOCS, 72- *Personal Data:* b Washington, DC, May 22, 35; m 57; c 2. *Educ:* Univ Md, BS, 57; Cath Univ Am, MEE, 61; Johns Hopkins Univ, PhD(opers res), 65. *Prof Exp:* Sr design engr, Electronics Div, Am Car Foundry, Md, 60-62; eng specialist, Martin-Marietta Corp, 62-64; mem tech staff, Mitre Corp, Va, 64-65; from asst prof to assoc prof opers res, Johns Hopkins Univ, 65-72. *Concurrent Pos:* Consult, Task Force Sci & Technol, President's Comn Law Enforcement & Criminal Justice, 66; adv, Law Enforcement Assistance Agency, US Dept Justice, 68; mem adv comt, Secy Health & Ment Hyg, State of Md, 70. *Mem:* Opers Res Soc Am; Inst Elec & Electronics Engrs; Inst Mgt Sci. *Res:* Graph and network theory; theory of optimization; mathematical programming; computers. *Mailing Add:* 3609 Woodvalley Dr Baltimore MD 21208

BELLO, JAKE, PHYSICAL BIOCHEMISTRY. *Current Pos:* assoc scientist, 60-67, dir grad studies chem, Roswell Park Div, 73-80, PRIN SCIENTIST, 67-, CHMN, CHEM DEPT, ROSWELL PARK MEM INST, 80- *Personal Data:* b Detroit, Mich, Feb 22, 28; m 57. *Educ:* Wayne Univ, BS, 48, PhD(chem), 52. *Prof Exp:* Fel org chem, Purdue Univ, 52-53; fel protein chem, Calif Inst Technol, 53-56; chemist, Eastman Kodak Co, NY, 56-58; sr res assoc protein chem, Polytech Inst Brooklyn, 58-59. *Concurrent Pos:* Mem comt biophys training, NIH. *Mem:* AAAS; Am Chem Soc; NY Acad Sci. *Res:* Protein and nucleic acid chemistry and structure; mechanism of gelation of gelatin; polymers; interferon inducers. *Mailing Add:* 1088 Delaware Ave Buffalo NY 14209

BELLO, P(HILLIP), ELECTRICAL ENGINEERING. *Current Pos:* PRES, BELLO, INC, 94- *Personal Data:* b Lynn, Mass, Oct 22, 29; m 52; c 2. *Educ:* Northeastern Univ, BS, 53; Mass Inst Technol, SM, 55, ScD(elec eng), 59. *Prof Exp:* Asst, Mass Inst Technol, 53-55; res assoc, Northeastern Univ, 55-56, asst prof commun, 56-57; eng specialist, Sylvania Appl Res Lab, 59-61; sr scientist, Adcom, Inc, 61-65; dir commun res & vpres, Signatron, Inc, 65-72; pres, CNR, Inc, 72-82 & Milcom, Inc, 82-88; consult engr, Mitre, 88-94. *Mem:* Fel Inst Elec & Electronics Engrs. *Res:* Communications; administrations research and development. *Mailing Add:* 80 Gary Rd Needham MA 02194

BELLOLI, ROBERT CHARLES, ORGANIC CHEMISTRY. *Current Pos:* from asst prof to assoc prof, 68, dept chair, 83-89, PROF CHEM, 76-, COORDR UNDERGRAD STUDIES, CALIF STATE UNIV, FULLERTON, 89- *Personal Data:* b St Louis, Mo, Nov 3, 42; m 68, Shirley M Packard; c Christopher & Jeffrey. *Educ:* St Louis Univ, BS in Chem, 64; Univ Calif, Berkeley, PhD(org chem), 68. *Prof Exp:* Teaching asst chem, Univ Calif, Berkeley, 64-65. *Concurrent Pos:* Res Corp grant, 69-70; Petrol Res Fund grant, Am Chem Soc, 72-74; NSF-SOS grant, 78; Instrumentation grant HPLC, NSF, 84. *Mem:* Am Chem Soc; AAAS. *Res:* Physical-organic chemistry; organic analytical problems; chemical education. *Mailing Add:* Dept Chem & Biochem Calif State Univ Fullerton CA 92634

BELLONCIK, SERGE, AGRICULTURE, VIROLOGY. *Current Pos:* PROF MICROBIOL, UNIV QUE, TROIS RIVIERES, 72-; PROF VIROL, INST ARMAND FRAPPIER, UNIV QUE, LAVAL, 78- *Personal Data:* b Aleppo, Syria, Feb 19, 44; Can citizen. *Educ:* Univ Montpellier, France, Agr Eng, 67, DEA, 68, Dr(biol sci), 69. *Concurrent Pos:* Fel, Univ Montreal, 69-72; examr grant, Dept Educ, Que, 77-; head grad students comt, Univ Que, 77-78. *Mem:* Am Mosquito Control Asn; Can Micros Soc; Can Soc Microbiologists; Am Soc Microbiologists. *Res:* Invertebrate virology; biological control of insects; virus transmitted by arthropods (arbovirus); epidemiological survey by virus isolation and serology; insect tissue culture. *Mailing Add:* Inst Armand Frappier PO Box 100 Station LDR Laval PQ H7N 4Z3 Can

BELLONE, CLIFFORD JOHN, MOLECULAR IMMUNOLOGY. *Current Pos:* from asst prof to assoc prof, 74-84, PROF IMMUNOL, SCH MED, ST LOUIS UNIV, 84- *Personal Data:* b San Francisco, Calif, Feb 9, 41; m 63; c 5. *Educ:* Univ Notre Dame, BS, 63, PhD(microbiol), 71. *Prof Exp:* Fel immunol, Univ Calif, San Francisco, 71-74. *Mem:* Am Asn Immunologists. *Res:* Regulation of cytorine gene expression. *Mailing Add:* Dept Microbiol-Path Sch Med St Louis Univ 1402 S Grand Blvd St Louis MO 63104-1079

BELLOW, ALEXANDRA, MATHEMATICS. *Current Pos:* prof, 67-96, EMER PROF MATH, NORTHWESTERN UNIV, 96- *Personal Data:* b Bucharest, Rumania, Aug 30, 35; m, Alberto P Calderon. *Educ:* Univ Bucharest, MS, 57; Yale Univ, PhD(math), 59. *Honors & Awards:* Sr Distinguished Scientist Award, Humboldt Found, 87. *Prof Exp:* Res assoc math, Yale Univ, 59-61; res assoc, Univ Pa, 61-62, asst prof, 62-64; assoc prof, Univ Ill, Urbana, 64-67. *Concurrent Pos:* Ed, Transactions Am Math Soc, 74-77; Fairchild distinguished scholar, Calif Inst Technol, 80. *Mem:* Am Math Soc; Sigma Xi. *Mailing Add:* Dept Math Northwestern Univ Evanston IL 60208-2730

BELLOW, DONALD GRANT, MECHANICAL ENGINEERING, APPLIED MECHANICS. *Current Pos:* sessional lectr mech eng, 58-63, from asst prof to assoc prof, 63-70, prof mech eng, 70-96, chmn dept, 75-84, assoc vpres facil, 89-94, EMER PROF, UNIV ALTA, 96- *Personal Data:* b Winnipeg, Man, Aug 5, 31; m 56, Jean Daye; c Jonathan M & Denise (Bellow-Jackson). *Educ:* Univ BC, BASc, 56; Univ Alta, MSc, 60, PhD(mech eng), 63. *Honors & Awards:* L C Charlesworth Award, Asn Prof Eng Geologists & Geophys Alta. *Prof Exp:* Design engr, Can Industs Ltd, 56-57; proj engr, Gen Motors Diesel Ltd, 57-58. *Mem:* Am Soc Mech Engrs; Soc Exp Mech; fel Can Soc Mech Engrs; Asn Prof Eng Geologists & Geophysicists Alta; fel Can Acad Eng. *Res:* Static and dynamic analyses of machine elements; problems related to metal fatigue and brittle fracture as applied to the petroleum industry and steel industry; wear of metals and non-metallics. *Mailing Add:* 4915-115A St Edmonton AB T6H 3P7 Can. *Fax:* 403-492-1439

BELLUM, JOHN CURTIS, ADAPTIVE OPTICS, NON-LINEAR OPTICS. *Current Pos:* SR STAFF ENGR, HUGHES AIRCRAFT CO, 87- *Personal Data:* b Lakeland, Fla, Aug 2, 45; m 77; c 3. *Educ:* Ga Inst Technol, BS, 68; Univ Fla, PhD(physics), 76. *Prof Exp:* Fel, Dept Chem, Univ Rochester, 76-78; sci assoc, Dept Physics, Univ Kaiserslautern, Fed Repub Ger, 78-80; vis asst prof, Dept Physics, Univ SFla, 80-81; res assoc, Quantum Theory Proj, Dept Chem, Univ Fla, 81; asst prof, Dept Physics & Astron, Inst Modern Optics, Univ NMex, 81-85; prin scientist, Litton Laser Systs (Albuquerque Opers), 85-87. *Concurrent Pos:* Lectr physics, Univ Md, Europ Div, Fed Repub Ger, 80; guest scientist, Max-Planck-Inst Quantum Optics, Fed Repub Germany, 82. *Mem:* Am Phys Soc; Sigma Xi. *Res:* Molecular collision theory; laser-induced molecular rate processes; electronic-vibrational-rotational energy transfer in molecular collisions; nonlinear optical wavefront control; optical phase conjugation; laser radar; nonconventional adaptive imaging. *Mailing Add:* 8505 Cherry Hills Dr NE Albuquerque NM 87111

BELLVE, ANTHONY REX, MAMMALIAN REPRODUCTION, SPERMATOGENESIS. *Current Pos:* PROF, COL PHYSICIANS & SURGEONS, COLUMBIA UNIV, 85- *Personal Data:* b Wanganui, NZ, July 16, 40; m 61, 83, Renate Wack; c Stephen, Karl, Shanley, Marcel & Andre. *Educ:* Massey Col, BAgSc, 64, MAgSc, 67; NC State Univ, PhD(biochem & reproduction), 70. *Honors & Awards:* Am Soc Animal Sci Award; Goding Res Award. *Prof Exp:* Agr adv officer, NZ Dept Agr, 64-66; staff scientist reproduction, Ruakura Agr Res Ctr, 67-68; res fel, NC State Univ, 68-70 & Johns Hopkins Univ, 70-71; res assoc, Harvard Med Sch, 71-72, from asst prof to assoc prof physiol, 72-85. *Concurrent Pos:* mem, Lab Human Reprod & Biol, Harvard Med Sch, 71-85, dep chmn, Div Med Sci, 79-81, assoc chmn, Div Med Sci, 81-82; consult, Ctr Pop Res, Nat Inst Child Health & Human Develop, 77-88. *Mem:* Am Soc Cell Biol; Am Soc Develop Biol; Am Soc Andrology; Soc Study Reproduction; Soc Study Fertil; Endocrine Soc. *Res:* Regulation of mammalian spermatogenesis, including biochemical processes controlling the proliferation of stem cells, purification and characterization of a spermatogenic growth factor, and the molecular events involved in biogenesis, assembly and reorganization of the developing germ cell; endocrinology. *Mailing Add:* Dept Anat & Cell Biol Columbia Univ 650 W 168th St New York NY 10032-3702. *Fax:* 212-305-3970; *E-Mail:* abellve@ix.netcom.com

BELLWARD, GAIL DIANNE, BIOCHEMICAL PHARMACOLOGY, CYTOCHROMES. *Current Pos:* Lectr pharmacol, Univ BC, 66-67, from asst prof to prof, 67-85, chmn dept, 81-85, asst dean, Grad Studies & Res, Fac Pharmaceut Sci, 85-89, ASSOC DEAN, UNIV BC, 97- *Personal Data:* b Brock, Sask, May 27, 39; div. *Educ:* Univ BC, BSP, 60, MSP, 63, PhD(pharmacol), 66. *Concurrent Pos:* Fel med, Sch Med, Emory Univ, 68-69; mem, pharm sci grants comt, Med Res Coun Can, 70-74; vis prof, Univ Toronto, 71-72, Univ Sask & Dalhousie Univ, 75-76 & Royal Postgrad Med Sch, London, 75; mem, Pharm Exam Bd Can, 76-79; mem subcomt women pharmacol, Am Soc Pharmacol & Exp Therapeut, 80-85; mem expert adv comt dioxins, Dept Nat Health, Welfare Environ Can, 82-83; mem expert adv comt, Can Drug Scheduling Study Group, 85-86; Killam sr fel, 89-90. *Mem:* Sox Toxicol Can (vpres, 93-95, pres, 95-97); Am Soc Biochem & Molecular Biol; Int Soc Study Xenobiotics; Am Soc Pharmacol & Exp Therapeut; Pharmacol Soc Can (secy, 77-80, vpres, 85-87, pres, 87-89). *Res:* Pharmacology; drug metabolism and interactions; toxicology; enzymology; cytochromes P-450; inhibitors of cytochromes P-450; effects of sex hormones on P-450; dioxin toxicity. *Mailing Add:* Fac Pharm Sci Univ BC Vancouver BC V6T 1Z3 Can. *Fax:* 604-822-3035; *E-Mail:* gailbe@unixg.ubc.ca

BELLY, ROBERT T, MICROBIOLOGY, CELL BIOLOGY. *Current Pos:* SR RES BIOLOGIST, EASTMAN KODAK CO, 73- *Personal Data:* b Trenton, NJ, Feb 19, 45; m; c 1. *Educ:* Rutgers Univ, AB, 66; Pa State Univ, PhD(microbiol), 70. *Prof Exp:* Res assoc microbiol, Ind Univ, 70-71 & Univ Wis, 71-73. *Concurrent Pos:* NIH fel, Univ Wis, 72-73. *Mem:* Am Soc Microbiol; Soc Indust Microbiol (pres, 88); AAAS; Sigma Xi. *Res:* Microbial degradation; cell biology; cellular diagnostics; digital microscopy. *Mailing Add:* 736 Blue Creek Dr Webster NY 14580

BELMAKER, ROBERT HENRY, BIOLOGICAL PSYCHIATRY. *Current Pos:* PROF PSYCHIAT, BEN GURION UNIV, 85- *Personal Data:* b Los Angeles, Calif, July 8, 47; m 67, Elaine Zarembka; c Miriam, Johathan, Reuren, Amos, Aaron & Gideon. *Educ:* Harvard Univ, BA, 67; Duke Med School, MD, 71. *Honors & Awards:* Bennett Award, Soc Biological Psychiatry, 80; Anna Monika Prize, 83; Ziskind-Somerfeld Prize, Soc Biol Psychiat, 93; Lilly Prize, Evrop Col Neuropsychopharmacol, 96. *Prof Exp:* Clin assoc, NIMH, 72-74; dir res, Jerusalem Ment Health Ctr, 74-85. *Concurrent Pos:* Assoc dir, Beersheva ment Health Ctr. *Mem:* Corresp fel Am Psychiat Asn; corresp mem Am Col Neuropsychopharmacol; Evrop coll neuropsychopharmacol. *Res:* second messenger function in the brain, especially camp and indsitol; trancranial magnetic stimulation of the brain in depression. *Mailing Add:* PO Box 481 Omer Israel. *Fax:* 972-7-6401621; *E-Mail:* belmaker@bgvmail.bgu.ac.il

BELMAN, SIDNEY, BIOCHEMISTRY. *Current Pos:* Instr indust med, NY Univ, 58-61, asst prof environ med, 61-67, assoc prof, 67-76, PROF ENVIRON MED, NY UNIV, 76- *Personal Data:* b New York, NY, 1926; m 51, Hilda Lieblein; c Sherry & Vickie. *Educ:* City Col New York, BS, 48; Polytech Inst Brooklyn, MS, 52; NY Univ, PhD(biochem), 58. *Mem:* AAAS; NY Acad Sci; Am Chem Soc; Am Asn Cancer Res. *Res:* Cancer. *Mailing Add:* NY Univ Dept Environ Med 550 First Ave New York NY 10016

BELMARES, HECTOR, POLYMER ENGINEERING, COMPUTATIONAL CHEMISTRY. *Current Pos:* CHIEF CHEMIST, SOLA OPTICAL USA, INC, 84- *Personal Data:* b Monclova, Mex, Feb 21, 38; m, Eleanor J Wold; c Michelle A, Michael P, Elizabeth M & Mary E. *Educ:* Mex Technol Inst, Monterrey, BSc, 60; Cornell Univ, PhD(phys org chem), 63. *Prof Exp:* Fel, Calif Inst Technol, 63-65; sr res chemist, Rohm & Haas Co, 66-72; res & technol vpres, Akzo Group, Monterrey, Mex 73-77. *Concurrent Pos:* Res & technol 3rd World, Mex, UN Indust Develop Orgn, 78-85. *Mem:* Am Chem Soc; Sigma Xi; NY Acad Sci; AAAS; Soc Plastics Engrs. *Res:* By computation and experimentation obtain new materials and technologies for the opthalmic lens industry; silicon, radiation curing, thermosett, thermoplastic, coating, and surface chemistry. *Mailing Add:* Santa Rosa CA 95404. *Fax:* 707-765-1378; *E-Mail:* 73361.125@compuserve.com

BELMONT, DANIEL THOMAS, CHEMICAL PROCESS DEVELOPMENT. *Current Pos:* RES ASSOC, WARNER-LAMBERT/PARKE-DAVIS, 85- *Personal Data:* b Ft Thomas, Ky, Feb 2, 57; m 80; c 2. *Educ:* Northern Ky Univ, BS, 80; Ohio State Univ, PhD(org chem), 85. *Mem:* Am Chem Soc; AAAS. *Res:* Investigate and develop chemical processes for the synthesis of bulk pharmaceuticals; manage compliance with cGmP, safety and environmental regulations. *Mailing Add:* Parke-Davis Pharmaceut Res & Develop 188 Howard Ave Holland MI 49424-6517

BELMONT, HERMAN S, PSYCHIATRY, PSYCHOANALYSIS. *Current Pos:* SUPVR & TRAINING ANALYST CHILD & ADULT PSYCHOANAL, INST PHILADELPHIA ASN PSYCHOANALYSIS, 56- *Personal Data:* b Philadelphia, Pa, Mar 13, 20; m 46, Lorraine; c Eileen, Janet & Donald. *Educ:* Univ Pa, AB, 40, MD, 43. *Prof Exp:* Rockefeller fel psychiat, Pa Hosp Ment & Nerv Dis, Inst Pa Hosp, 44, 46 & 47; instr sch med, Univ Pa, 47-48, assoc, 48-52; dir child analysis training, Inst Philadelphia Asn Psychoanal, 57-63; assoc prof & sr attend child psychiat, Hahnemann Med Col & Hosp, 52-60, clin prof, 60-63, prof ment health sci & dir div child psychiat, 63-87, dept chmn, 72-87, emer prof Ment Health Sci, Hahnemann Med Col & Hosp, 88- *Concurrent Pos:* Mem, Govt Comprehensive Ment Health Planning Adv Comt, 64-66; mem adv comt child psychiat planning, Comnr Ment Health, State of Pa, 64; mem task force II, Joint Comn Ment Health Children, 67. *Mem:* Am Psychoanal Asn; Int Psychoanal Asn; Am Orthopsychiat Asn; Am Psychiat Asn; Am Acad Child Psychiat. *Res:* Undergraduate and graduate training; administration of a program in child psychiatry integrating individual psychodynamics and social applications; application of individual psychodynamic knowledge to preventive work with children. *Mailing Add:* 3472 NE Causeway Blvd No 3-401 Jensen Beach FL 34957-4251. *E-Mail:* hsblsb@juno.com

BELMONTE, ALBERT ANTHONY, PHARMACEUTICS. *Current Pos:* assoc dean, 81-88, DEAN & PROF, COL PHARM, ST JOHN'S UNIV, 88- *Personal Data:* b Lynn, Mass, July 17, 44; m 67; c 3. *Educ:* Northeastern Univ, BS, 67, MS, 69; Univ Conn, PhD(pharmaceut), 72. *Honors & Awards:* Award, McKesson & Robbins, 67; Lederle Pharm Fac Award, 76. *Prof Exp:* Res asst pharm, Univ Conn, 70-72; asst prof pharmaceut, Sch Pharm, Auburn Univ, 72-78, assoc prof, 78-81. *Concurrent Pos:* Consult, Natchaug Hosp, 70-72 & Bur Drugs, Food & Drug Admin, 77-; Auburn Univ Res Found fel, 73-74. *Mem:* AAAS; Am Pharmaceut Asn; Am Asn Pharmaceut Sci; Am Asn Cols Pharm; Am Soc Hosp Pharmacists; Nat Asn Retail Druggists. *Res:* Membrane phenomena and model systems; surface chemistry of carcinogens; electrical phenomena at interfaces; dosage form design and their parameters. *Mailing Add:* Dean Col Pharm St John's Univ 8150 Utopia Pkwy Jamaica NY 11439-0001

BELNAP, JAYNE, MICROBIOLOGY, BOTANY-PHYTOPATHOLOGY. *Current Pos:* BIOLOGIST RES, NAT PARK SERV, 86- *Educ:* Univ Calif, Santa Cruz, BA(biol) & BA(environ studies), 80; Stanford Univ, MS, 84; Brigham Young Univ, PhD(bot), 90. *Mem:* Ecol Soc Am; Am Soc Biologists & Lichenologists. *Res:* Ecology of cold-desert organisms, specifically cyanobacterial soil crusts; role of soil crusts in community dynamics, plant nutrition and soil stability; use of cyanobactrim and soil lichens as biomonitors for air and soil pollution. *Mailing Add:* Box 50 Moab UT 84532-0050

BELOHOUBEK, ERWIN F, MICROWAVES, ELECTRONICS. *Current Pos:* RETIRED. *Personal Data:* b Vienna, Austria, May 7, 29; US citizen; m 54; c 2. *Educ:* Vienna Tech Univ, dipl ing, 53, Dr Tech(microwaves), 55. *Honors & Awards:* Microwave Appln Award, Inst Elec & Electronics Engrs, 80. *Prof Exp:* Proj engr, RCA Tube Div, David Sarnoff Res Ctr, 56-57, mem tech staff, Microwave Advan Develop Lab, 57-65, group leader, 65-69, head microwave circuits technol, Microwave Technol Ctr, 69-87, head microwave circuits res, Microwave & Design Automation Lab, 87-89, consult, 89-94. *Mem:* Fel Inst Elec & Electronics Engrs. *Res:* Slow wave circuits for traveling wave tubes and magnetrons; crossed-field microwave delay tubes; solid state amplifiers, oscillators and multipliers; hybrid integrated microwave circuits; solid state radar systems; microwave superconductor applications. *Mailing Add:* 729 N 26th St Philadelphia PA 19130

BELON, ALBERT EDWARD, AERONOMY, REMOTE SENSING. *Current Pos:* RETIRED. *Personal Data:* b Gap, Hautes Alpes, France, May 2, 30; US citizen; m 55; c 3. *Educ:* Univ Alaska, BS, 52; Univ Calif, Los Angeles, MA, 54. *Honors & Awards:* Meritorious Serv Award, NSF, 70; Except Sci Achievement Medal, NASA, 74. *Prof Exp:* Physicist geophys, Int Geophys Inc, 53-54; res geophysicist, Univ Calif, Los Angeles, 54-56; instr, Geophys Inst, Univ Alaska, 56-61, assoc prof physics, 61-69; prog dir solar-terrestrial res, NSF, 68-70; prof physics, Geophys Inst, Univ Alaska, 69-86, assoc dir, 76-86. *Concurrent Pos:* Consult, Los Alamos Sci Lab, 67-77;

mem, Inter-Union Comn Solar-Terrestrial Physics, 68-70 & Comt Polar Res, Panel on Upper Atmospheric Physics, Nat 73-76. Sci, 73- *Mem:* Am Geophys Union; Int Union Geod & Geophys. *Res:* Spectrophotometry of upper atmospheric phenomena; auroral morphology and magnetospheric convection; applications of satellite and aircraft imagery to Alaskan resources surveys. *Mailing Add:* PO Box 163 Ester AK 99725

BELSER, WILLIAM LUTHER, JR, GENETICS. *Current Pos:* asst res biologist, 57-61, from asst prof to prof, 61-92, EMER PROF MICROBIOL, UNIV CALIF, RIVERSIDE, 92- *Personal Data:* b Hershey, Pa, May 28, 25; m 53, Nao Okuda. *Educ:* Lafayette Col, BA, 48; Yale Univ, PhD(microbiol), 55. *Prof Exp:* USPHS fel, marine genetics, Scripps Inst, 55-57. *Mem:* Am Soc Microbiol; Brit Soc Gen Microbiol; Sigma Xi. *Res:* Regulation of metabolic flow in bacteria with emphasis on tryptophan and pyrimidine biosynthesis; comparative biochemistry in the Enterobacteriaceae; enzyme formation and function. *Mailing Add:* 4730 Riverview Dr Riverside CA 92509

BELSERENE, EMILIA PISANI, ASTRONOMY. *Current Pos:* RETIRED. *Personal Data:* b New Rochelle, NY, Dec 12, 22; wid; c 2. *Educ:* Smith Col, AB, 43; Columbia Univ, AM, 47, PhD(astron), 52. *Prof Exp:* Asst, Lick Observ, 43-44; assoc in astron, Columbia Univ, 54-73; mem fac physics & astron, Hunter Col, 52 & 56-71, Lehman Col, 71-78; dir, Maria Mitchell Observ, 78-90. *Concurrent Pos:* Vis lectr, Pa State Univ, 78-79; res assoc, Harvard Col Observ, 79-83; lectr, Univ Mass, Boston, 85, adj assoc prof, 87. *Mem:* Am Astron Soc; Sigma Xi. *Res:* Photographic photometry; variable stars. *Mailing Add:* 421 E Ahlvers Port Angeles WA 98362

BELSHE, JOHN FRANCIS, ZOOLOGY, ECOLOGY. *Current Pos:* from asst prof to assoc prof, 64-74, PROF BIOL, CENT MO STATE UNIV, 74- *Personal Data:* b Marshall, Mo, Feb 6, 35; m 57; c 2. *Educ:* Cent Mo State Col, BS, 57; Univ Miami, MS, 61, PhD(zool), 67. *Prof Exp:* Instr biol, Miami-Dade Jr Col, 61-63, asst prof, 63-64. *Concurrent Pos:* Lic Designated Qualified Person (DQP), Horse Protection Act. *Mem:* AAAS; Am Fisheries Soc; Am Soc Zool; Nat Asn Biol Teachers; Sigma Xi. *Res:* Aquatic ecology; aquatic entomology; population studies of Tribolium; environmental education; odonata of Missouri and the Ozark Plateau. *Mailing Add:* Dept Biol Cent Mo State Univ Warrensburg MO 64093

BELSHEIM, ROBERT OSCAR, RESEARCH ADMINISTRATION. *Current Pos:* RETIRED. *Personal Data:* b Leland, Iowa, Aug 26, 24. *Educ:* Iowa State Col, BS, 44; Purdue Univ, MS, 48, PhD(eng mech), 53. *Prof Exp:* Mech engr, Naval Res Lab, 44-47, chief specialist, 44-45, res engr, 50-58, head, Struct Br, 58-70, consult, 70-77; res asst, Purdue Univ, 47-48, instr, 48-50; consult, NKF Eng Assoc, Inc, 77-85. *Mem:* Am Soc Mech Engrs; Sigma Xi. *Res:* Structural dynamics; shock and vibration; mechanical properties of materials; underwater technology; stress analysis; engineering mechanics. *Mailing Add:* 2475 Virginia Ave NW Apt 514 Washington DC 20037-2639

BELSKY, MELVIN MYRON, BIOLOGY. *Current Pos:* From asst prof to prof, 62-91, EMER PROF BIOL, BROOKLYN COL, 91- *Personal Data:* b Brooklyn, NY, Apr 26, 26; m 52, Charlotte Miller. *Educ:* Brooklyn Col, BS, 49, MA, 51; Univ Pa, PhD(bot), 55. *Concurrent Pos:* Res assoc, Queens Univ, Can, 55, Univ Calif, Berkeley, 63-64. *Mem:* NY Acad Sci; Am Soc Microbiol; AAAS; Sigma Xi. *Res:* Intermediary metabolism; marine mycology; hormone action; enzymology; membrane transport. *Mailing Add:* Dept Biol Brooklyn Col Brooklyn NY 11210

BELSKY, THEODORE, HAZARDOUS WASTE, INDUSTRIAL HYGIENE. *Current Pos:* pub health chemist, 69-86, environ biochemist, 86-94, RES CHEMIST, CALIF STATE DEPT TOXIC SUBSTANCES CONTROL, 94- *Personal Data:* b New Brunswick, NJ, Dec 24, 30; m 52, Gloria A England; c Elena. *Educ:* Univ Calif, Berkeley, BS, 60, PhD(biophys), 66. *Prof Exp:* Biophysicist, Space Sci Lab, Univ Calif, Berkeley, 63-66; asst res geochemist, Space Sci Lab, Univ Calif, Los Angeles, 66-68; asst chemist, Western Regional Lab, USDA, Calif, 69. *Concurrent Pos:* Intersoc comt mem, 71-78. *Mem:* AAAS; Am Chem Soc. *Res:* Organic microanalysis of air pollutants and occupational and environmental contaminants, including dioxins. *Mailing Add:* Calif State Dept Health Serv 2151 Berkeley Way Berkeley CA 94704

BELT, CHARLES BANKS, JR, economic geology; deceased, see previous edition for last biography

BELT, EDWARD SCUDDER, SEDIMENTOLOGY. *Current Pos:* DIR, PRATT GEOL MUSEUM, 87- *Personal Data:* b New York, NY, Aug 4, 33; m 61; c 4. *Educ:* Williams Col, BA, 55; Harvard Univ, AM, 57; Yale Univ, MA, 59, PhD(geol), 63, Amherst Col, MA, 78. *Prof Exp:* Asst prof geol, Villanova Univ, 62-66; from asst prof to assoc prof, 66-78, chmn dept, 71-76, prof Geol, Amherst Col, 78- *Concurrent Pos:* NSF grant, 64-67 & 85-88; Am Philos Soc & Nat Geog Soc grant, 72-73; Quebec grant, 70-79; NRC grant, UK, 77; vis prof, Colo State Univ, 79-80; geologist, Coal Br, US Geol Surv, 80-83, 86-88, NDak Geol Surv, 83 & Earth Sci & Res Inst, Univ SC, 83-84; ROA NSF grant, 84-86, 88-90. *Mem:* Am Inst Mining, Metall & Petrol Eng; Am Asn Petrol Geol; Soc Econ Paleont & Mineral; Geol Soc Am; Int Asn Sedimentology. *Res:* Stratigraphic relationships of facies, depositional environments and regional tectonics of Carboniferous strata in eastern Canada, Scotland and Appalachian Basin USA; Ordovician strata in Quebec; Pleistocene sediments in North Carolina; Paleocene sediments in North Dakota; Karoo and younger strata in Madagascar; sedimentology of fluvial, lacustrine, estuarine, deltaic, and deep-sea paleoenvironments. *Mailing Add:* Dept Geol Amherst Col Amherst MA 01002

BELT, ROGER FRANCIS, CRYSTALLOGRAPHY. *Current Pos:* staff scientist, 64-71, RES DIR, AIRTRON DIV, LITTON INDUSTS, INC, 71- *Personal Data:* b Springfield, Ohio, Mar 20, 29; m 56; c 3. *Educ:* Ohio State Univ, BS, 50; Duquesne Univ, MS, 52; Univ Iowa, PhD(chem), 56. *Prof Exp:* Chemist, E I du Pont de Nemours & Co, 53; sr chemist, B F Goodrich Co, 56-61; sr scientist, Harshaw Chem Co, 61-64. *Mem:* AAAS; Am Chem Soc; Am Crystallog Asn; fel Am Inst Chem; Am Inst Physics; Am Phys Soc. *Res:* Solid state physics; x-ray crystallography, crystal growth; morphology; physical properties; perfection. *Mailing Add:* 2 Buckley Hill Rd Morristown NJ 07960

BELT, WARNER DUANE, ANATOMY, CYTOLOGY. *Current Pos:* assoc prof, 67-69, chmn, 73-77, PROF ANAT, SCH MED, TUFTS UNIV, 67- *Personal Data:* b Bellaire, Ohio, Dec 29, 25; m 50; c 4. *Educ:* Bethany Col, BS, 48; Ohio State Univ, MSc, 50, PhD(anat), 55. *Prof Exp:* Asst instr anat, Ohio State Univ, 51-53, instr, 53-55; res assoc, Univ Calif, Los Angeles, 55-56; asst prof, Emory Univ, 56-59; from asst prof to assoc prof, Med Col Va, 59-64. *Mem:* Am Asn Anat. *Res:* Fine structural cytology; structure of endocrine and exocrine secretory cells; fine structure of steroids secretory organs; cytoplasmic interrelationships. *Mailing Add:* Dept Anat Tufts Univ Sch Med 136 Harrison Ave Boston MA 02111-1800

BELTON, MICHAEL J S, ASTRONOMY. *Current Pos:* ASTRONR, KITT PEAK NAT OBSERV, 64- *Personal Data:* b Bognor Regis, Eng, Sept 29, 34; m 61; c 2. *Educ:* Univ St Andrews, BSc, 59; Univ Calif, Berkeley, PhD(astron), 64. *Mem:* AAAS; Am Meteorol Soc; Am Astron Soc. *Res:* Planetary atmospheres and spectroscopy; space photography. *Mailing Add:* Kitt Peak Nat Observ 950 N Cherry Ave Tucson AZ 85719

BELTON, PETER, BIOLOGY, PEST-MANAGEMENT. *Current Pos:* assoc prof biol & pest mgt, 67-96, ADJ PROF, SIMON FRASER UNIV, 96- *Personal Data:* Driffield, UK, Sept 6, 30; Can citizen; m 57, Elizabeth M Cawthra; c Jill, Jim & Owen. *Educ:* Univ London, BSc, 55; Univ Glasgow, PhD(insect physiol), 70. *Prof Exp:* Asst zool, Univ Glasgow, 57-60; res assoc, Col Physicians & Surgeons, Columbia Univ, 60-61; res officer, Res Inst, Can Agr, 61-67. *Concurrent Pos:* Mem, Pest Mgt Adv Comt, Dept Nat Defense, Can, 75-; mem, BC Plant Protection Adv Comt, 91-96; ed, J Entom Soc BC, 93- *Mem:* Am Mosquito Control Asn; BC Entom Soc. *Res:* Analysis of the sensory physiology and behavior of pests, particularly insects; mosquito biology and behavior; bioacoustics. *Mailing Add:* Dept Biol Sci Simon Fraser Univ Burnaby BC V5A 1S6 Can. *E-Mail:* belton@sfu.ca

BELTRAMI, EDWARD J, MATHEMATICS. *Current Pos:* CONSULT, 80- *Personal Data:* b New York, NY, Apr 21, 34; m 62. *Educ:* Polytech Inst, Brooklyn, BS, 56; NY Univ, MS, 59; Adelphi Univ, PhD(math), 62. *Prof Exp:* Res mathematician, Grumman Aircraft Eng Corp, 56-62; res mathematician, Saclant Anti-Submarine Warfare Res Ctr, 62-63 & Grumman Aircraft Eng Corp, 63-66; prof appl math & urban sci, State Univ NY, Stony Brook, 60-80. *Mem:* Opers Res Soc; Soc Indust & Appl Math; Math Asn Am. *Res:* Mathematical optimization techniques and abstract analysis, with emphasis on optical resource allocation. *Mailing Add:* 9 S Gate Rd East Setauket NY 11733

BELTZ, CHARLES R(OBERT), AERONAUTICS, REFRIGERATION. *Current Pos:* RETIRED. *Personal Data:* b Pittsburgh, Pa, Feb 23, 13; m 35; c 6. *Educ:* Cornell Univ, ME, 35; Univ Pittsburgh, AE, 37. *Prof Exp:* Proj engr, Skycar, Stout Eng Labs, 39-42; aeronaut engr cycle-weld aeronaut, Chrysler Corp, 42-46; proj mgr exp flight controls, Fairchild Eng & Airplane Corp, 46-48; pres, Aeronaut & Refrig Beltz Eng Labs, 50-93. *Concurrent Pos:* Designer, Beltemp Ice Skating Rinks. *Mem:* Am Soc Heating, Refrig & Air Conditioning Engrs; Am Inst Aeronaut & Astronaut. *Res:* Aeronautical experimental research and design of simplified control systems; refrigeration and low temperature development and designs. *Mailing Add:* 500 Lakeland St Grosse Point MI 48230

BELTZ, RICHARD EDWARD, BIOCHEMISTRY. *Current Pos:* From instr to assoc prof, 56-70, PROF BIOCHEM, SCH MED, LOMA LINDA UNIV, 70- *Personal Data:* b Loma Linda, Calif, June 20, 29; m 51; c 2. *Educ:* Walla Walla Col, BS, 50; Univ Southern Calif, MA, 51, PhD(biochem, nutrit), 56. *Concurrent Pos:* USPHS sr res fel & career develop award, 60-64. *Mem:* AAAS; Am Chem Soc; Sigma Xi. *Res:* Nucleic acids; control of DNA biosynthesis; metabolism of deoxynucleotides and deoxynucleosides; liver regeneration. *Mailing Add:* Dept Biochem Loma Linda Univ Sch Med 25027 Mound St Loma Linda CA 92350-0001

BELYEA, GLENN YOUNG, WILDLIFE ECOLOGY. *Current Pos:* WILDLIFE RES BIOLOGIST, MICH DEPT NAT RESOURCES, EAST LANSING, 72- *Personal Data:* b Portland, Maine, Apr 3, 43; m 65; c 2. *Educ:* Univ Maine, BA, 65, MS, 67; Mich State Univ, PhD(wildlife ecol), 76. *Prof Exp:* Entomologist vector control, US Army 67-69. *Mem:* Wildlife Soc; Raptor Res Found; Lepidopterist's Soc. *Res:* Management and population status of raptors and sandhill cranes in Michigan; hunting and non-hunting recreational uses of public and private lands in Southern Michigan. *Mailing Add:* 8051 Clark Rd Bath MI 48808

BELZER, FOLKERT O, surgery; deceased, see previous edition for last biography

BELZILE, RENE, ANIMAL NUTRITION. *Current Pos:* RETIRED. *Personal Data:* b Kapuskasing, Ont, Mar 6, 30; m 57; c 3. *Educ:* Univ Ottawa, BA, 51; McGill Univ, BScAgr, 55; Purdue Univ, MSc, 57; Univ Sask, PhD(animal nutrit), 63. *Prof Exp:* Lectr biochem, Ont Agr Col, 57-60; from asst prof to assoc prof, Laval Univ, 63-72, prof animal nutrit, 72-95, chmn dept, 74-77. *Concurrent Pos:* Feedstuffs Act Can res grant, 65-67; asst ed, Can J Animal Sci, 75-77; chmn, Fur Bearing Animal Comt, Que Coun Animal Prod, 77-84; prof & chmn, Dept Animal Soc, Nat Univ Rwanda, 88-90. *Mem:* Nutrit Soc Can; Can Soc Animal Sci. *Res:* plant proteins for mink; evaluation of new feeding programs for foxes and mink; energy & protein requirements of mink; mycotoxins and swine nutrition. *Mailing Add:* 1141 Lombard Ste-Foy PQ G1W 4J3 Can

BEMENT, A(RDEN) L(EE), JR, MATERIALS SCIENCE, NUCLEAR ENGINEERING. *Current Pos:* BASIL S TURNER DISTINGUISHED PROF ENG, PURDUE UNIV, 93- *Personal Data:* b Pittsburgh, Pa, May 22, 32; wid; c Kristine, Kenneth, Cynthia, Mark, David, Paul, Mary & Loretta. *Educ:* Colo Sch Mines, EMet, 54; Univ Idaho, MS, 59; Univ Mich, PhD(metall eng), 63. *Hon Degrees:* PhD, Cleveland State Univ, 90. *Honors & Awards:* Distinguished Civilian Serv Medal, US Dept Defense, 80. *Prof Exp:* Metall engr, Hanford Labs, Gen Elec Co, 54-59, sr engr, 59-65; mgr reactor metals res, Pac Northwest Lab, Battelle Mem Inst, 65-66, mgr metall res, 66-68, mgr fuels & mat dept, 68-70; prof nuclear mat, Mass Inst Technol, 70-76; dir, Off Mat Sci, Defense Advan Res Projs Agency, Dept Defense, 76-79, dep undersecy defense, Res & Eng, 79-81; vpres tech resources, TRW Inc, 81-89, vpres sci & technol, 89-92. *Concurrent Pos:* Lectr, Ctr Grad Studies, Univ Wash, Richland, 63-70; adj assoc prof, metall dept, Ore State Univ, 68-70; prof, dept nuclear eng & dept metall & mat sci, Mass Inst Technol, 70-76; adj prof, metall & mat sci dept, Case Western Reserve Univ, 83-; numerous comts, govt, nat & int. *Mem:* Nat Acad Eng; fel Am Soc Metals; fel Am Nuclear Soc; fel Am Inst Chem; Sigma Xi. *Res:* Irradiation effects; deformation and fracture; energy materials technology; defense materials technology; materials science administration. *Mailing Add:* Sch Mat Eng 1289 MSEE Bldg Purdue Univ West Lafayette IN 47907-1289. *Fax:* 765-494-1204; *E-Mail:* bement@ecu.purdue.edu

BEMENT, ROBERT EARL, RANGE SCIENCE. *Current Pos:* CONSULT, 73- *Personal Data:* b Denver, Colo, Jan 24, 18; m 39, Thelma Frances Johnson; c Thomas Robert & Robert Edward. *Educ:* Colo State Univ, BS, 40, MF, 47, PhD, 68; US Army Command & Gen Staff Col, dipl, 62. *Honors & Awards:* Trail Boss Award, Soc Range Mgt, 84. *Prof Exp:* Instr range forage plants, Colo State Univ, 47-48; range conservationist soil conserv serv, USDA, 48, soil conservationist, 48-55, res range conservationist cent plains exp range, 55-61, res range conservationist in charge, 61-65, res range scientist in charge, 65-73, range scientist agr res serv, 66-69, range scientist in charge forage & range res br crops res lab, Colo State Univ, 69-73. *Concurrent Pos:* Spec lectr col forestry, Colo State Univ, 59-; agr res serv rep, Tech Comt Seedling Estab Range Plants, Great Plains Coun, 60-, comt chmn, 62-63, agr res serv rep, Range & Livestock Mgt Comt, 70-, consult, Food & Agr Orgn, UN, Iceland, 73-78; consult, Int Prog Ecol Mgt of Arid and Semi-arid Rangelands in Africa and Near East, 74-75 & USAID on grazing management in eleven african countries, 77-; expert witness, Colorado Water Courts, 77-78; sr range adv to Niger Range & Livestock Proj; dir, City of Aurora Range Reseeding, 87-96; range witness, Navajo Nation, 90-93. *Mem:* Am Soc Range Mgt; Sigma Xi; Am Soc Animal Sci. *Res:* Relationship of season and degree of grazing to vegetation, gains per animal and animal gain per acre; artificial range revegetation, including role of temperature and moisture as modified by mulches. *Mailing Add:* 41300 County Rd K-6 Mancos CO 81328. *E-Mail:* 75753.605@compuserve.com

BEMENT, SPENCER L, BIOENGINEERING, ROBOTICS. *Current Pos:* From instr to assoc prof, 63-77, PROF ELEC ENG & COMP SCI, UNIV MICH, 77- *Personal Data:* b Detroit, Mich, Apr 1, 37; m 62; c 3. *Educ:* Univ Mich, BSE, 60, MSE, 62, PhD(bioeng), 67. *Concurrent Pos:* Vis assoc prof, Med Sch, Univ Vt, 76. *Mem:* AAAS; Inst Elec & Electronics Engrs; Soc Neurosci; Biomed Eng Soc; Sigma Xi. *Res:* Communications and systems theory applied to neural information coding and transmission; passive and active electrical properties of biological neural tissue; digital signal processing; bioinstrumentation. *Mailing Add:* Dept Elec Eng & Comp Sci Univ Mich Ann Arbor MI 48109

BEMILLER, JAMES NOBLE, CARBOHYDRATE CHEMISTRY, ORGANIC & NATURAL PRODUCTS CHEMISTRY. *Current Pos:* PROF FOOD SCI & DIR, WHISTLER CTR FOR CARBOHYDRATE RES, PURDUE UNIV, WEST LAFAYETTE, IND, 86- *Personal Data:* b Evansville, Ind, Apr 7, 33; m 60; c 2. *Educ:* Purdue Univ, BS, 54, MS, 56, PhD(biochem), 59. *Prof Exp:* Asst biochem, Purdue Univ, 54-59, asst prof, 59-61; from asst prof to prof chem & biochem, Southern Ill Univ, Carbondale, 61-85, actg chmn dept, 66-67, prof, Sch Med, 71-85, actg dean, Col Sci, 76-77, asst dean curric, 77-79, chmn, Dept Med Biochem, 80-83. *Concurrent Pos:* Chmn, Div Carbohydrate Chem, Am Chem Soc, 65-66. *Mem:* Fel AAAS; Am Chem Soc; Am Asn Cereal Chem; fel Am Inst Chem (secy, 85, pres, 88); Am Soc Biochem & Molecular Biol. *Res:* Carbohydrate chemistry; poly saccharides chemistry; industrial uses of carbohydrates. *Mailing Add:* Ctr Carbohydrate Res Dept Food Sci Purdue Univ 1160 Smith Hall West Lafayette IN 47907-1160

BEMILLER, PARASKEVI MAVRIDIS, HUMAN DEVELOPMENT, CELLULAR AGING. *Current Pos:* ASSOC PROF ANAT, PURDUE UNIV, 86- *Personal Data:* US citizen. *Educ:* Am Univ Beirut, BA, 53, MS, 55; Purdue Univ, PhD(physiol biochem), 61. *Prof Exp:* Instr biol, Am Univ Beirut, 55-58; researcher, Marine Biol Lab, Woods Hole, Mass, 59; res assoc physiol, Purdue Univ, 61; res assoc, Sch Med, Southern Ill Univ, 66-68, teaching assoc, 68-71, asst prof biol, 72-79, assoc prof embryol, 79-86. *Mem:* Am Soc Cell Biol; Am Asn Anatomists; Am Aging Asn; Sigma Xi; Tissue Cult Asn. *Res:* Study of changes which occur in cells during aging; use of human diploid fibroblasts to study morphological and biochemical changes which occur as cells age in vitro; nucleolar changes and ribosomal RNA processing. *Mailing Add:* 2829 Bentbrook Lane West Lafayette IN 47906-5275

BEMIS, CURTIS ELLIOT, JR, NUCLEAR PHYSICS, NUCLEAR CHEMISTRY. *Current Pos:* researcher, 65-66, res mem staff, Nuclear Spectros, 66-79, SR STAFF, PHYSICS DIV, OAK RIDGE NAT LAB, 79- *Personal Data:* b Boston, Mass, Feb 18, 40; m 62; c 3. *Educ:* Univ NH, BS, 61; Mass Inst Technol, PhD(nuclear chem), 65. *Prof Exp:* Res asst nuclear chem, Mass Inst Technol, 61-64; Sweden-Am Found & Fulbright-Hayes fels nuclear spectros, Nobel Inst Physics, Stockholm, Sweden, 64-65. *Mem:* AAAS; fel Am Phys Soc; Sigma Xi. *Res:* Nuclear spectroscopy and low energy nuclear physics; heavy ion physics; transuranium element nuclear and atomic structure physics and health physics; production and identification of new transuranium elements and isotopes; laser spectroscopy and lasers in nuclear physics. *Mailing Add:* 509 Clearview Dr Los Gatos CA 95030

BEMPONG, MAXWELL ALEXANDER, GENETIC TOXICOLOGY. *Current Pos:* from asst prof to assoc prof, 67-74, PROF BIOL, NORFOLK STATE UNIV, 74- *Personal Data:* b Akim-Oda, Ghana, Sept 14, 38; m 68; c 2. *Educ:* Lincoln Univ, Mo, BSc, 64; Tenn State Univ, MS, 65; Mich State Univ, PhD(cytogenetics), 67. *Prof Exp:* Teaching fel, Univ Nev, 69-70; fel, Johns Hopkins Univ, 75-77. *Concurrent Pos:* Dir, Biomed Res Norfolk State Univ, 75-; ed, J Basic Appl Sci, 81-; ed, J Toxicol & Biomed Sci & Trans Nat Inst Sci. *Mem:* Environ Mutagen Soc; Nat Inst Sci; Tissue Cult Asn; Am Col Toxicol; NY Acad Sci; Sigma Xi; Europ Acad Sci; Europ Soc Arts & Lett. *Res:* Genetic toxicological analysis of anti-neoplastic drugs and industrial toxicants; in vivo and in vitro estimation of mutagenesis and carcinogenesis in laboratory rodents; chemical-induced morphological modulation in malignant cells in vitro and examination of the comparative in vivo tumorigenicity of the revertant and parental cell types. *Mailing Add:* Dept Biol Norfolk State Univ 2401 Corprew Ave Norfolk VA 23504-3907

BEMRICK, WILLIAM JOSEPH, PARASITOLOGY. *Current Pos:* RETIRED. *Personal Data:* b Superior, Wis, Jan 19, 27; m 67; c 6. *Educ:* Superior State Col, BS, 50; Univ Wis, MS, 55, PhD(zool), 57. *Prof Exp:* Res asst zool & parasitol, Univ Wis, 53-57, teaching asst, 57; from asst prof to prof vet med parasitol, Univ Minn, St Paul, 57-90. *Concurrent Pos:* Presiding officer, Annual Midwestern Conf Parasitologists, 74. *Mem:* Am Soc Parasitol. *Res:* Host parasite relationships; parasitic immunology; electron microscopy of parasites; Coccidia and coccidiosis morphology and epidemiology of Giardia species. *Mailing Add:* 2217 Scudder St St Paul MN 55108

BEN, MANUEL, TECHNICAL MANAGEMENT, WATER POLLUTION. *Current Pos:* RETIRED. *Personal Data:* b Syracuse, NY, July 30, 16; wid; c Allan W & Francine A (Savin). *Educ:* Univ Mich, BS, 39. *Honors & Awards:* C H Proctor Mem Award, 64. *Prof Exp:* Asst bearing metallurgist, AC Spark Plug Div, Gen Motors Corp, Flint, Mich, 40-41, bearing chemist supvr, 41-45, sr res chemist & supvr, 45-53, sr res chemist, Gen Motors Res Labs, Warren, Mich, 53-54, supvr, 54-66, supvr mfg staff, Mfg Develop, 66-72, sr design engr, Chevrolet Motor Co Div, 72-74, eng supvr & staff develop engr, Gen Motors Mfg Develop, 74-76, Plant Eng Develop, 76-81. *Concurrent Pos:* Consult & teacher, 81- *Mem:* Am Electroplaters Soc (vpres, 59-62, pres, 62-63, past pres, 63-64); Electrochem Soc; Brit Inst Metal Finishing. *Res:* Decorative, corrosion protection, and engineering electroplating (electrochemistry); anodizing and electroless plating (electrochemistry); strategies and equipment technology and systems to control water pollution and air emissions. *Mailing Add:* 5734 Templar Crossing West Bloomfield MI 48322-1367

BEN, MAX, PHARMACOLOGY, PHYSIOLOGY. *Current Pos:* CONSULT CLIN STUDIES, FOOD & DRUG ADMIN, 89- *Personal Data:* b Utica, NY, Oct 12, 26; m 52, Dorene E; c Lisa A (Leard), Edward H, Ellen S (Cutler) & Jennifer R (Pecor). *Educ:* Syracuse Univ, BA, 51; Princeton Univ, MA, 53, PhD(physiol), 54. *Prof Exp:* Lab asst gen biol, Utica Col, 50-51; asst biol & biochem, Princeton Univ, 51-53, asst endocrinol to Prof Swingel, 53-54; assoc surg res, Harrison, Dept Surg Res, Med Sch, Univ Pa, 54-56 & Merck, Sharp & Dohme, 56-58; sect head, Endocrine Res & Eval, Squibb Inst, 58; sr scientist, Warner-Lambert Res Inst, 58-62; sci dir pharmacol & co-dir mkt, Hazelton Labs, Inc, 62-64, sr pharmacologist & sci dir develop, 64-65; UN tech assistance expert pharmacol & adv to Nat Coun Res & Develop, Prime Minister's Off, Israel, 65-68; exec secy, Nat Biol Cong, 69-70; exec vpres & dir, Health Sci Assocs, Bethesda, Md, 70-74; pres, Mediserv Int, 74-77; dir corp res, Dept Toxicol & Biochem Pharmacol, Miles Labs, Inc, 77-79; med dir, Med Prod Div, US Packaging Corp, 79-81; vpres & sci dir, Life Sci, Inc, 81-83; vpres & med dir, Belmac Corp, 83-86; pres & dir, Valcor Sci Ltd, 86-89. *Concurrent Pos:* Consult pharmacol & toxicol, NIH contract, 58. *Mem:* Soc Toxicol; Am Physiol Soc; fel NY Acad Sci; Am Soc Clin Pharmacol & Therapeut; Am Soc Pharmacol & Exp Therapeut; AAAS; Sigma Xi; Am Inst Biol Sci; Am Acad Clin Toxicol; Am Asn Poison Control Ctrs; Genetic Toxicol Asn. *Res:* Over 90 publications in endocrinology, shock, pharmacology and toxicology; investigation of cancer chemotherapeutic agents; cardiovascular and endocrine pharmacology and physiology; studies of drug abuse in man. *Mailing Add:* 812 Amelia Court NE St Petersburg FL 33702-2784. *Fax:* 813-525-8071

BENACERRAF, BARUJ, IMMUNOLOGY, EXPERIMENTAL PATHOLOGY. *Current Pos:* FABYAN EMER PROF COMP PATH, MED SCH, HARVARD UNIV, 91- *Personal Data:* b Caracas, Venezuela, Oct 29, 20; US citizen; m 43, Annette Dreyfus; c Beryl. *Educ:* Univ Paris, Lic es lett, 40; Columbia Univ, BS, 42; Med Col Va, MD, 45. *Hon Degrees:* MD, Univ Geneva, 80; DSc, NY Univ & Va Commonwealth Univ, 81, Yeshiva Univ & Univ Aix-Marseille, 82, Columbia Univ, 85, Adelphi Univ, 88; PhD, Weizmann Inst Sci, 89, Bordeaux II, 91, Harvard Univ, 92. *Honors & Awards:* Nobel Prize Physiol of Med, 80; R E Dyer lectr, NIH, 69; Harvey lectr, 71; Rabbi Shai Shacknai lectr & Prize Immunol & Cancer Res, Hebrew Univ Jerusalem, 74; T Duckett Jones Mem Award, Helen Hay Whitney Found, 76; J S Blumenthal lectr Allergy & Immunol, 80; Waterford Biomed Sci Award, 80; Rous-Whipple Award, Am Asn Pathologists, 85; Margaret Byrd Rawson Award, Am Dyslexia Soc, 88; Distinguished Investr Award, Am Rheumatism Asn, 88; Nat Medal of Sci, 90; Charles Dana Award, 96. *Prof Exp:* Intern, Queens Gen Hosp, NY, 45-46 & US Army, 46-48; res fel, Dept Microbiol, Col Physicians & Surgeons, Columbia Univ, 48-50; sr researcher, Nat Ctr Sci Res, Hosp Broussais, Paris, 50-56; from asst prof to prof path, Sch Med, NY Univ, 56-68; chief, Lab Immunol, Nat Inst Allergy & Infectious Dis, NIH, 68-70; Fabyan prof comp path & chmn, Dept Path, Harvard Univ, 70-91; pres & chief exec officer, Dana-Farber Cancer Inst, Boston, 80-92, pres, 91-95. *Concurrent Pos:* Mem, immunol study sect, NIH, 65-69; sci adv immunol, WHO, 65-; trustee & mem, sci adv bd, Trudeau Found, 70-76; mem, sci adv bd, Mass Gen Hosp, 71-74; assoc ed, Am J Path, Lab Invest, J Exp Med, J Immunol, J Exp Path & Immunol Commun; mem bd gov, Weizmann Inst Sci, 76; mem & chmn, sci adv comt, Ctr Immunol Marseille, Nat Ctr Sci Res-Nat Inst Health & Med Res, France, 78-84; mem, adv coun, Nat Inst Allergy & Infectious Dis & adv comt, Basel Inst Immunol, 85. *Mem:* Nat Acad Sci; Inst Med-Nat Acad Sci; Am Asn Immunologists (pres, 73-74); Am Asn Pathologists & Bacteriologists; fel Am Acad Arts & Sci; Soc Exp Biol & Med; NY Acad Sci; Am Soc Exp Path; Fedn Am Soc Exp Biol (pres, 74-75); Int Immunol Soc (pres, 80-83). *Res:* Antibody synthesis and structure; hypersensitivity; immunopathology; immunogenetics. *Mailing Add:* 111 Perkins St Jamaica Plain MA 02130-4313

BENACH, JORGE L, MEDICAL ENTOMOLOGY. *Current Pos:* Med entomologist, Bur Acute Commun Dis Control, Albany, 71-72, SR MED ENTOMOLOGIST, WHITE PLAINS REGIONAL OFF, NY STATE DEPT HEALTH, 72- *Personal Data:* b Havana, Cuba, June 27, 45; US citizen; m 68; c 2. *Educ:* Upsala Col, BA, 66; Seton Hall Univ, MS, 68; Rutgers Univ, PhD(entom), 71. *Mem:* AAAS; Am Asn Trop Med & Hyg; NY Acad Sci; Am Mosquito Control Asn. *Res:* Characterization and identification of Rickettsial pathogens and the epidemiology of Rickettsial diseases in New York. *Mailing Add:* 8 Patriot Ct Stony Brook NY 11790

BEN-AKIVA, MOSHE E, ECONOMETRICS, INTELLIGENT VEHICLE-HIGHWAY SYSTEMS. *Current Pos:* Res asst, 68-73, PROF TRANSP, MASS INST TECHNOL, 73- *Personal Data:* b Tel Aviv, Israel, June 11, 44; c Ori, Lea, Danna & Elana. *Educ:* Technion-Israel Inst Technol, BSc, 68; Mass Inst Technol, SM 71, PhD(transp), 73. *Hon Degrees:* Dr, Univ Lumiere Lyon, Lyon, France, 92. *Concurrent Pos:* Prin, Cambridge Syst, Inc, 72-; vis prof, Technion-Israel Inst Technol, 78-79 & 81-82; dir, Hague Consult Group, 85-; mem, Transp Res Bd, Tech Panel IVHS-Idea, Transp Demand Forecasting Comt, Telecommunications & Travel Behav Comt, Transp Res Forum, Regional Sci Asn, Opers Res Soc Am. *Res:* Intelligent vehicle-highway systems; transportation systems analysis; demand modeling; econometrics; infrastructure management. *Mailing Add:* Dept Civil Eng Mass Inst Technol Rm 1-181 Cambridge MA 02139

BENARD, BERNARD, ENDOCRINOLOGY, MEDICINE. *Current Pos:* vdean res, 79-81, vrector res, 81-89, PROF MED, MED SCH, UNIV SHERBROOKE, 67- *Personal Data:* b Dorval, Que, Oct 16, 33; Can citizen; m 62; c 4. *Educ:* Univ Montreal, BA, 55, MD, 60; McGill Univ, MSc, 65. *Prof Exp:* Resident med, Notre-Dame Hosp, Montreal, 60-63; res fel, Dept Anat, McGill Univ, Montreal, 63-65, Thyroid Unit, Mass Gen Hosp, Boston, 65-66 & Food & Nutrit Sci, Mass Inst Technol, 66-67. *Concurrent Pos:* Res fel, Med Res Coun Can, 63-67; coun mem, Can Soc Clin Invest, 68-71; consult & mem, MRC Comt Clin Res, 71-75; consult, Que Ministry Educ, 73-77 & Que Ministry Social Affairs, 76- *Mem:* Endocrine Soc; Am Thyroid Asn; Can Soc Clin Res; Royal Col Physicians Can; Can Soc Endocrinol. *Res:* Studies on thyroid tumors; studies on viral transformation of thyroid cells; studies of steroid receptors. *Mailing Add:* Dept Med Endocrinol Univ Sherbrooke Fac Med 3001 12th Ave N Sherbrooke PQ J1H 5N4 Can

BENARD, MARK, ANALYSIS OF ALGORITHMS, SOFTWARE ENGINEERING. *Current Pos:* asst prof, 70-75, assoc prof math, 75-80, ASSOC PROF COMPUTER SCI, TULANE UNIV, 80- *Personal Data:* b Pittsburgh, Pa, Jan 4, 44; m 73. *Educ:* Tulane Univ, BA, 65; Yale Univ, MPhil, 67, PhD(math), 69. *Prof Exp:* Instr math, Yale Univ, 69-70. *Mem:* Am Math Soc; Computer Soc; Inst Elec & Electronics Engrs; Sigma Xi. *Res:* Design and analysis of algorithms; distributed processing; software engineering. *Mailing Add:* Computer Sci Dept Tulane Univ New Orleans LA 70118

BENARDE, MELVIN ALBERT, EPIDEMIOLOGY, PUBLIC HEALTH. *Current Pos:* assoc prof, 67-74, prof community med, 74-, ACTG CHMN, COMMUNITY MED & ENVIRON HEALTH, HAHNEMANN MED COL, 81-; DIR, ASBESTOS/LEAD CTR & PROF EPIDEMIOLOGY & PUB HEALTH, TEMPLE UNIV, 87. *Personal Data:* b Brooklyn, NY, June 15, 23; m 51; c Scott, Andrea & Dana. *Educ:* St John's Univ, NY, BS, 48; Univ Mo, MS, 50; Mich State Univ, PhD(bact), 54. *Prof Exp:* Res asst virus res, Pub Health Res Inst, NY, 50-51; food specialist, Off Naval Res, Naval Supply Depot, Bayonne, 54-55; asst prof, Seafood Processing Lab, Univ Md, 55-61; assoc prof, Bioeng Lab, Dept Civil Eng, Rutgers Univ, 61-67. *Concurrent Pos:* WHO fel, Sch Hyg & Trop Med, Univ London, 63; mem bd dirs, Am Coun Sci & Health. *Mem:* Fel Am Pub Health Asn; Sigma Xi; Asn Teachers Prev Med; fel Royal Soc Health. *Res:* Nosocomial infections; microbial metabolism of synthetic detergents; effects of synthetic chemicals on tissue cultures; germicidal effects of chlorine compounds; evaluation of medical care delivery; environmental factors in pancreatic cancer. *Mailing Add:* Asbestos/Lead Ctr, Temple Univ 1616 Walnut St Philadelphia PA 19103. *Fax:* 609-951-9745

BENAROYA, HAYM, SPACE BUSINESS, PROMOTION LUNAR INDUSTRIALIZATION. *Current Pos:* PROF MECH & AEROSPACE ENG, RUTGERS UNIV, 89- *Personal Data:* b 1954; US citizen; m 83, Shelley K Deutsch; c Ana F & Adam N. *Educ:* Cooper Union, BECE, 76; Univ Pa, MS, 77, PhD(eng), 81. *Prof Exp:* Sr res engr, Weidlinger Assocs, 81-89. *Concurrent Pos:* Adj prof eng, Cooper Union, 81-89; founder & dir, Lab Extraterrestrial Struct Res, Rutgers Univ; tech ed, Appl Mech Reviews. *Mem:* Am Acad Mech; Am Inst Aeronaut & Astronaut; Am Soc Mech Eng; Brit Interplanetary Soc. *Res:* Probabilistic methods in mechanics; space and lunar structures; structural and random vibrations. *Mailing Add:* Dept Mech & Aerospace Eng Rutgers Univ PO Box 909 Piscataway NJ 08855-0909. *Fax:* 732-445-5313; *E-Mail:* benaroya@rci.rutgers.edu

BENATAR, SOLOMON ROBERT, MEDICAL SCHOOL ADMINISTRATION, MEDICAL ETHICS. *Current Pos:* chmn, Dept Med, 80-91, vpres, 86-95, PROF UNIV CAPE TOWN, 80-, DIR, BIOETHICS CTR, 92- *Personal Data:* b Selukwe, South Rhodesia, Feb 6, 42; m 65, Evelyn M Goldberg; c David, Michael & Brian. *Educ:* Univ Cape Town, MBChB, 65; Col Med SAfrica, FFA(SA), 71, MRCP, 72, FRCP, 81; FACP, 93. *Honors & Awards:* African Oxygen Gold Medal, Col Med SAfrica, 71; Hamilton Maynard Mem Medal, SAfrican Med J, 77. *Prof Exp:* Intern med & obstet gynecol, Groote Schuur Hosp, Cape Town, 66, res anesthesiol, 68-70, res internal med, 70-71, physician internal med & chest dis, 74-80; family doctor, primary health care, pvt pract, 67-68; res fel anesthesiol, Northwick Park Hosp, London, 72; res fel chest dis, Brompton Hosp, London, 72, res, 73. *Concurrent Pos:* Res fel, Imp Chem Industs, 72; chmn fac med, Col Med SAfrica, 80-, vpres, 89-92; physician-in-chief, Dept Med, Groote Schuur Hosp, 80-; int adv respiratory med, 87-; vis prof, several univs, US & UK; vpres, Col Med SAfrica, 89-; fel prog ethics & professions, Harvard Univ, 94-95, vis prof, Med Sch, 94-95. *Mem:* Foreign assoc Inst Med-Nat Acad Sci; Med Asn SAfrica; Royal Col Physicians; Col Med SAfrica; Acad Sci SAfrica. *Res:* Clinical and epidemiological aspects of asthma, tuberculosis, venous thromboembolism and sarcoidosis; health economics and health services research; medical ethics and philosophy of medicine; national health service; author of over 200 publications. *Mailing Add:* 41 Willow Rd Newlands Cape Town 7700 South Africa. *Fax:* 27-21-448-6815

BENBOW, ROBERT MICHAEL, DNA REPLICATION, GENETIC TRANSFORMATION. *Current Pos:* RETIRED. *Personal Data:* b San Pedro, Calif, Nov 10, 43; m 75; c 7. *Educ:* Yale Univ, BS, 67; Calif Inst Technol, PhD(biophysics), 72. *Prof Exp:* Helen Hay Whitney res fel, Med Res Coun, Lab Molecular Biol, 72-75; from asst prof to assoc prof biol, Johns Hopkins Univ, 75-85; prof, Iowa State Univ, 85-97, dir, Nucleic Acid Fac, 86-97. *Concurrent Pos:* Mem cell biol panel, NSF, 80-84; biotechnol Coun, Iowa State Univ, 87-90. *Mem:* Am Soc Biochem & Molecular Biol. *Res:* Molecular mechanisms of DNA replication and genetic transformation in early embryos of the frog, Xenopus laevis; soybean Glycine max. *Mailing Add:* 7420 Lakeview Dr Bethesda MD 20817

BENBROOK, CHARLES M, AGRICULTURAL TECHNOLOGY RISK ASSESSMENT. *Current Pos:* BENBROOK CONSULT SERV, 91- *Personal Data:* b Los Angeles, Calif, Nov 26, 49; m 73; c 3. *Educ:* Harvard Univ, BA, 71; Univ Wis-Madison, MS, 80, PhD(agr econ), 81. *Prof Exp:* Policy analyst, Coun Environ Qual, 80-82; staff dir, Subcomt on Dept Opers Res & Foreign Agr, Comt Agr, US House Rep, 82-84; exec dir, Bd Agr, Nat Res Coun, 84-90. *Mem:* Am Agr Econ Asn; Soil Conserv Soc Am. *Res:* Agricultural policy analysis, particularly food safety and natural resource use issues; international competitiveness and development. *Mailing Add:* Benbrook Consult Serv 409 First St SE Washington DC 20003. *Fax:* 202-546-5028; *E-Mail:* benbrook@hillnet.com

BENCALA, KENNETH EDWARD, GEOCHEMISTRY, HYDROBIOLOGY. *Current Pos:* CHEM ENGR, WATER RESOURCES DIV, US GEOL SURV, 78- *Personal Data:* b Detroit, Mich, 1951. *Educ:* Harvey Mudd Col, BS, 73; Calif Inst Technol, MS, 75, PhD(chem eng), 79. *Mem:* Am Geophys Union; Sigma Xi; Am Chem Soc. *Res:* Develop quantitative formulations of the processes determining the rate and extent of the reactions of stream solutes with sediments. *Mailing Add:* 20170 Kilbride Dr Saratoga CA 95070-4337

BENCE, ALFRED EDWARD, ELECTRON MICROPROBE THEORY & APPLICATIONS. *Current Pos:* res assoc, Exxon Prof Res, 80-82, sr res assoc, Exxon Minerals, Exxon Prod Res Co, 82-89, EXXON VALDEZ, NRDA LITIGATION SUPPORT, EXXON USA, 89- *Personal Data:* b Saskatoon, Sask, Aug 30, 40; m 88, Lillian J Breton; c Carolyn E. *Educ:* Univ Sask, BEng, 62; Univ Tex, Austin, MA, 64; Mass Inst Technol, PhD(geochem), 66. *Prof Exp:* Res fel, Calif Inst Technol, 66-68; from asst prof to prof petrol, State Univ NY, 68-80. *Concurrent Pos:* Vis fel, Australian Nat Univ, 74-75 & 79; expert, Fac Subcomt of Lunar & Planetary Sample Planning Team, Johnson Space Ctr, NASA, 76-79, prin investr, 76-80, prin investr, Spec Recognition Lunar Prog, 79; assoc ed, J Geophys Res, 78-81; counr, Geochem Soc, 83-86. *Mem:* Am Geophys Union; Geochem Soc; Microbeam Anal Soc; Am Asn Petrol Geologists. *Res:* Chemical and mineralogical study of terrestrial and extraterrestrial basaltic systems; the genesis of volcanogenic massive sulfide deposits with an emphasis on rock-water interactions; geochemistry of petroleum source rocks; hydrocarbon geochemistry of subtidal sediments; degradation of petroleum hydrocarbons in the marine environment. *Mailing Add:* Exxon Prod Res Co PO Box 2189 Houston TX 77252. *Fax:* 713-656-1794

BENCOMO, JOSE A, JR, THERAPEUTIC RADIOLOGIC PHYSICS & DIAGNOSTIC RADIOLOGIC PHYSICS. *Current Pos:* res asst diag imaging, M D Anderson Cancer Ctr, Grad Sch Biomed Sci, Univ Tex, 77-82, asst physicist diag imaging, 83-85, assoc physicist diag radiation physics, 90-93, ASST PROF PHYSICS DIAG IMAGING, M D ANDERSON CANCER CTR, GRAD SCH BIOMED SCI, UNIV TEX, 86-; ASSOC PHYSICIST & ASST PROF RADIATION PHYSICS, RADIOL PHYSICS CTR, 93- *Personal Data:* b Caracas, Venezuela, Nov 27, 46; US citizen; m 76, Blanca Dehoyos; c Jose A III & Aaron E. *Educ:* Cent Univ, Caracas, Venezuela, BS, 74; Univ Tex Houston, MS, 78, PhD(biophys), 82. *Honors & Awards:* Itek Award, Soc Photog Scientists & Engrs, 84. *Prof Exp:* Instr physics, Univ Simon, Bolivar, Venezuela, 74-75, assoc prof, 82-83. *Concurrent Pos:* Prin investr, Advan Technol & Advan Res Prog, Tex Higher Educ Coord Bd Grant, 88-90; qual assurance physicist, MD Anderson Cancer Ctr, Houston, 90-; chmn, Specialized Master Comt, Grad Sch Biomed Sci & Exec Comt, 90-91 & Radiol Physics Ctr, 93- *Mem:* Am Asn Physicist Med; Am Col Med Physics; Am Col Radiol; Mat Res Soc; Am Soc Therapet Radiol & Oncol. *Res:* Quantitative medical imaging; digital radiography; associated image processing for application in diagnostic radiology; development of x-ray receptors and image processing techniques related to specific diagnostic tools; evaluation of display and viewing requirements; stereotretic radiosurgery quality assurance; radiation therapy 3D treatment planning and diemetry qualty assurance. *Mailing Add:* M D Anderson Cancer Ctr Univ Tex RPC Box 547 Houston TX 77030. *Fax:* 713-794-1364; *E-Mail:* josebencomo@isqm.mda.uth.tmc.,edu

BENCOSME, SERGIO ARTURO, BIOPATHOLOGY RESEARCH & EDUCATION IN POSTGRADUATE MEDICINE. *Current Pos:* assoc prof, Queen's Univ, Ont, 53-57, from assoc prof to prof path, 59-77, sesional prof, 78-95 EMER PROF PATH, QUEENS UNIV ONT, 96- *Personal Data:* b Montecristi, Dominican Repub, Apr 27, 20; Can citizen;; m 47, Betha Rojas; c Rasanna, Yolanda, Violeta, Rolando & Humberto. *Educ:* Univ Montreal, MD, 47; McGill Univ, MSc, 48, PhD(path), 50. *Honors & Awards:* Medal Duarte, Sanchez y Mella, Knighthood, Govt Dominican Repub, 68; An Prize, Dominican Acad Sci, 87; Laudacio Academico Acad Sci, Dominican Repub, 94. *Prof Exp:* Asst prosector, Royal Victoria Hosp, Montreal, 50-51; asst prof path, Univ Ottawa, 51-53; asst res pathologist, Univ Calif, Los Angeles, 57-59. *Concurrent Pos:* Can Life Ins Officer's Asn fel, 53-56; assoc prof, Queen's Univ, Ont, 53-57; Can Cancer Soc traveling fel, US, 54; Ont Cancer Treatment & Res Found traveling fel, Univ Calif, Los Angeles, 56, lectr, 57; actg dir, Hotel Dieu Hosp, Ont, 57; pres, Burton Soc Electron Micros, 59; assoc prof path, Queens Univ, Ont, 59-65, prof, 65-85; mem coun basic sci, Am Heart Asn, 62-; dir inst biomed, Univ Pedro Henriquez Urena, Santo Domingo, 73; adv & dir, Med Sch, Pontifica Universidad Catolica Madre y Maestra, Santiago Dominican Repub, 77, founder & dir, Ctr Human & Exp Biol, 77, dir MSc prog res biomed scis, 77; dir, Dept Clin Res, Hosp Regional Universitano, 79, exec dir Hosp Libr, 79. *Mem:* Nat Acad Sci; Am Asn Anat; Am Asn Path & Bact; Am Soc Exp Path; Soc Exp Biol & Med; Am Asn Inv Path; Can Asn Path; Am Soc Cell Biol. *Res:* Pancreatic islets; kidney pathology; myocardium pathology; cancer of the breast; transfer of science and technology from developed to underdeveloped countries. *Mailing Add:* Calle 30 No 11 La Zurza Santiago Dominican Republic. *Fax:* 809-241-5888; *E-Mail:* h.jmcabral@codetel.net.do

BENCSATH, KATALIN A, COMBINATORIAL GROUP THEORY, DISCRETE MATHEMATICS. *Current Pos:* instr, 81-83, asst prof, 83-88, ASSOC PROF MATH & COMPUT SCI, MANHATTAN COL, 88- *Personal Data:* b Szeged, Hungary, 1945; US citizen; m 70, Mihaly Mezei. *Educ:* Eotvos Lorand Univ, Budapest, Cert(math), 68; Queens Col City Univ NY, MA, 76; Grad Sch City Univ NY, PhD(math), 83. *Prof Exp:* Mathematician, Kozti, Inst Archit, Budapest, 68-69; mathematician & appln programmer, opers res, Infelor Systs Eng Inst, Budapest, 69-72. *Concurrent Pos:* Consult, Futi Data Processing Inst, Budapest, 68-69; adj lectr math, Hunter Col City Univ New York, 76-81; Univ assoc, NY Univ, 86-; vis scholar, Fac Resource Network, Courant Inst Math Sci, NY Univ, 89 & scholar-in-residence, 93. *Mem:* Am Math Soc; Math Asn Am; NY Acad Sci; Sigma Xi. *Res:* The structural and residual properties of one-relator groups and their generalization; problems concerning the existence of certain algorithms in various classes of infinite discrete groups. *Mailing Add:* Dept Math & Comput Sci Manhattan Col Riverdale NY 10471. *E-Mail:* kbencsat@manvax.cc.mancol.edu

BEND, JOHN RICHARD, COMPARATIVE PHARMACOLOGY, BIOCHEMICAL TOXICOLOGY. *Current Pos:* CHMN DEPT PHARM & TOXICOL, UNIV WESTERN ONT. *Personal Data:* b Teulon, Can, Aug 10, 42; m 67; c 2. *Educ:* Univ Manitoba, BSc, 64, MSc, 67; Univ Sydney, PhD(pharm & chem), 71. *Prof Exp:* Asst lectr pharm, Univ Manitoba, 66-67; vis assoc, Nat Inst Environ Health Sci, NIH, 70-76, sect head, 76-78, actg chief, 78-79, res chemist, Lab Pharmacol, 80-, chief, 80- *Concurrent Pos:* Vis scientist, C V Whitney Marine Lab, Univ Fla, 76-; mem, Comt Environ Pharmacol, Am Soc Pharmacol Exp Therapeut, 76-; adj assoc prof, NC State Univ, 78-; assoc ed, Metab Basis Detoxification, 80-81, Reviews Biochem Toxicol, 77-; ed, Chemico-Biol Interactions, 78-; adj assoc prof, Univ NC, 80- *Mem:* Am Soc Pharmacol & Exp Therapeut; AAAS. *Res:* Relationships between xenobiotic metabolism and target organ and cell toxicity in mammalian and aquatic species; characteristics of the enzyme systems responsible for the metabolic activation and detoxication of chemicals. *Mailing Add:* Dept Pharmacol & Toxicol Univ Western Ont Med Sci Bldg London ON N6A 5C1 Can

BENDA, EVELYN JENENNE, NURSING ADMINISTRATION, REPRODUCTIVE NURSING. *Current Pos:* PROF NURSING & REGISTRAR, COE COL, 83- *Personal Data:* b Elbader, Iowa, Apr 21, 47; div; c Gary, Erin & Kelly. *Educ:* Univ Iowa, BS, 73, MA, 75, PhD(educ admin), 89. *Prof Exp:* Staff nurse, Univ Iowa Hosps, 73-75, Supvr, 81-83; asst prof, Univ Iowa, 75-81. *Res:* Factors associated with retention of nursing students; correlates of fetal well-being following labor amnioinfusions. *Mailing Add:* Coe Col 1220 First Ave NE Cedar Rapids IA 52402

BENDA, GERD THOMAS ALFRED, PLANT PHYSIOLOGY. *Current Pos:* RETIRED. *Personal Data:* b Berlin, Ger, Nov 19, 27; nat US; m 56, Donna Hoaglin; c Maximilian & Jonathan. *Educ:* Princeton Univ, AB, 46; Yale Univ, MS, 49, PhD(bot), 51. *Prof Exp:* Instr plant physiol, Yale Univ, 52-53; vol worker dept plant path, Rothamsted Exp Sta, 53-54; USPHS res fel virus lab, Univ Calif, 54-56, jr res biologist, 56-57; from asst prof to assoc prof biol, Univ Notre Dame, 57-64; Rockefeller Found grant virol sect, Inst Agron, Brazil, 64-65; plant physiologist, Agr Res Serv, USDA, 66-87. *Mem:* Bot Soc Am; Am Soc Sugar Cane Technol. *Res:* Physiology of plant virus diseases. *Mailing Add:* 118 Fahey St Houma LA 70360-7598

BENDA, MIROSLAV, MATHEMATICS, COMPUTER SCIENCE. *Current Pos:* MODELING ANALYST, BOEING COMPUT SERV, 80- *Personal Data:* b Czech, Oct 28, 44; US citizen. *Educ:* Univ Warsaw, MSc, 68; Univ Wis, MA, 69, PhD(math), 70; Univ Wash, MSc, 81. *Prof Exp:* Lectr math, Univ Calif, Berkeley, 70-72; asst prof math, Univ Wash, 72-80. *Concurrent Pos:* Prof, Inst Math, Sao Paulo, Brazil, 76. *Mem:* Am Math Soc; Asn Comput Mach; Soc Comput Simulation. *Res:* Theory of models; optimization; computer simulation. *Mailing Add:* 7301 34th Ave NW Seattle WA 98117

BENDALL, VICTOR IVOR, ORGANIC CHEMISTRY. *Current Pos:* assoc prof, 66-69, PROF CHEM, EASTERN KY UNIV, 69- *Personal Data:* b London, Eng, Dec 14, 35; m 66; c 2. *Educ:* Univ London, BSc, 57; Bucknell Univ, MS, 60; Brown Univ, PhD(chem), 64. *Prof Exp:* Res chemist, Brit-Thompson-Houston Co, Eng, 57-58; res assoc, Univ Chicago, 63-64; asst prof chem, George Peabody Col, 64-66. *Concurrent Pos:* Res grant, Sch Pharm, Univ London, 77-78. *Mem:* Am Chem Soc; Royal Soc Chem. *Res:* Small and medium alicyclic compounds; carbenes and reactive intermediates. *Mailing Add:* 105 Hammons Richmond KY 40475-2307

BENDAPUDI, KASI VISWESWARARAO, STRUCTURAL ENGINEERING, ANALYSIS & DESIGN OF STRUCTURES. *Current Pos:* Struct engr, 73-85, asst mgr struct eng, 85-88, MGR STRUCT ENG, LOCKWOOD GREENE ENGRS, INC, 88- *Personal Data:* b Eluru, India, July 28, 46; US citizen; m 77; c 2. *Educ:* Andhra Univ, India, BE, 68; Univ Mo-Rolla, MS, 71. *Prof Exp:* Struct engr, bridge design, Wilbur Smith & Assocs, 71-73. *Concurrent Pos:* Mem, Standards Subcomt Perm Railing, Am Soc Civil Engrs, 87-, Task Comt Design of D L Grids, 88-, Comt Spec Structures, 88- & Standards Subcomt Seismic Rehab of Buildings, 90-; off evaluator, Accreditation Bd Eng & Technol, 90- *Mem:* Am Soc Civil Engrs; Am Inst Steel Construct; Am Concrete Inst; Am Asn Artificial Intel. *Res:* Design of industrial structures; vibration control; seismic design of structures; industrial floors; artificial intelligence in structural engineering; analysis and design of special structures. *Mailing Add:* 14034 Prestwick Dr Dallas TX 75234

BENDAT, JULIUS SAMUEL, RANDOM DATA ANALYSIS, APPLIED MATHEMATICS. *Current Pos:* CONSULT, 70- *Personal Data:* b Chicago, Ill, Oct 26, 23; m 47; c 2. *Educ:* Univ Calif, AB, 44; Calif Inst Technol, MS, 48; Univ Southern Calif, PhD(math), 53. *Prof Exp:* Res asst physics radiation lab, Univ Calif, 42-45; asst appl mech, Calif Inst Technol, 46-48; asst prof aeronaut eng col aeronaut, Univ Southern Calif, 48-49, lectr math, 49-58; res engr, Northrop Aircraft, Inc, 53-55; mem sr staff, Thompson-Ramo-Wooldridge, Inc, 55-62; pres, Measurement Anal Corp, 62-70. *Concurrent Pos:* Asst, Univ Calif, 44-46; res physicist, Calif Inst Technol, 47-48. *Mem:* Am Math Soc; Math Asn Am; Soc Indust & Appl Math; Sigma Xi. *Res:* Abstract analysis; prediction and filter theory; system engineering; mathematical physics; information theory and circuit theory; random noise theory; vibration and acoustics research. *Mailing Add:* J S Bendat Co 833 Moraga Dr-10 Los Angeles CA 90049-1634

BENDAYAN, MOISE, HISTOLOGY, ELECTRON MICROSCOPY. *Current Pos:* from asst prof to assoc prof, 79-88, PROF ANAT, UNIV MONTREAL, 88-, CHMN ANAT, 90- *Personal Data:* b Tanger, Morocco, June 21, 49; m 76, Alice; c Rachel & Naomi. *Educ:* Univ Bordeaux, BS, 68; Univ Montreal, BSc, 72, MSc, 74, PhD(anat), 76. *Honors & Awards:* Vector Award, Am Soc Histochem, 83; Robert Feulgen Award, Soc Histochem, 84; Murray L Barr Award, Can Asn Anat, 82. *Prof Exp:* Fel histol, Univ Geneva, 76-79. *Concurrent Pos:* Scholar, Med Res Coun Can, 80-85, scientist, 85-90; vis prof, Inst Sci Res Cancer, France, 81 & 82, Univ Western Ont, 84, Weizmann Inst Sci, Israel, 86, Mich State Univ, 87, Hebrew Univ, Jerusalem, 87, Univ Minn, 88, Univ Ill, 90, Univ Reims, France, 91, Queen's Univ, Kingston, Ont, 93. *Mem:* Histochem Soc (pres, 89-90); Can Soc Electron Micros; Can Asn Anatomists (vpres, 93-94); Que Diabetes Asn; Can Fedn Biol Soc. *Res:* Perform cytochemistry at the electron microscope level; introduced the colloidal gold techniques in cytochemistry; studies of diabetes complications, such as pancreas alterations in diabetes and modifications of the vascular walls during microangiopathy; protein secretion. *Mailing Add:* Dept Anat Univ Montreal CP 6128 Succursale Centreville Montreal PQ H3C 3J7 Can. *Fax:* 514-343-2459

BENDEL, WARREN LEE, NUCLEAR PHYSICS. *Current Pos:* RETIRED. *Personal Data:* b Ravenna, Ohio, Jan 19, 25; m 56, Adele Slama; c Kathleen. *Educ:* Kent State Univ, BS, 46; Univ Ill, MS, 47, PhD(physics), 53. *Prof Exp:* Lab asst physics, Kent State Univ, 46; asst, Univ Ill, 46-50; res asst, Los Alamos Sci Lab, 49; res asst, Univ Ill, 50-53; physicist, US Naval Res Lab, 53-84. *Concurrent Pos:* Vis fac mem, Univ Md, 71-72. *Mem:* Am Phys Soc. *Res:* Nuclear spectroscopy; photonuclear reactions; electron accelerators; electron scattering; radiation effects on spacecraft. *Mailing Add:* 2714 Stone Edge San Antonio TX 78232-4218

BENDER, CARL MARTIN, HIGH ENERGY PHYSICS, MATHEMATICAL PHYSICS. *Current Pos:* PROF PHYSICS, WASHINGTON UNIV, 77- *Personal Data:* b Brooklyn, NY, Jan 18, 43; m 66, Jessica Waldbaum; c Michael & Daniel. *Educ:* Cornell Univ, AB, 64; Harvard Univ, AM, 65, PhD(theoret physics), 69. *Honors & Awards:* Burlington Northern Fac Achievement Award, 85. *Prof Exp:* Mem physics res, Inst Advan Study, 69-70; from asst prof to assoc prof math, Mass Inst Technol, 70-77. *Concurrent Pos:* Woodrow Wilson fel, 64-65, NSF fel, 64-69, Sloan Found fel, 72-77; vis scientist, Imp Col, London, 74 & 86-87; sci consult, Los Alamos Nat Lab, 79-; ed, Comput & Math Physics, Am Inst Physics; Fulbright fel; Lady Davis fel. *Mem:* Fel Am Physics Soc. *Res:* Quantum field theory; perturbation theory; group theory; applied mathematics. *Mailing Add:* Dept Physics Wash Univ St Louis MO 63130. *Fax:* 314-935-6219; *E-Mail:* cmb@howdy.wustl.edu

BENDER, DANIEL FRANK, PHYSICAL ORGANIC CHEMISTRY, ANALYTICAL CHEMISTRY. *Current Pos:* RES CHEMIST WATER POLLUTION, ENVIRON PROTECTION AGENCY, 73- *Personal Data:* b Cincinnati, Ohio, Mar 22, 36; m 59, Mary Grace Haeufle; c Pete, Tim, Greg, Mary, Sue, Jenny & Jill. *Educ:* Xavier Univ, Ohio, BS, 59, MS, 63; Univ Cincinnati, PhD(phys org chem), 67. *Prof Exp:* Chemist, Nat Air Pollution Control Admin, USPHS, US Dept Health, Educ & Welfare, 60-61, res chemist, 61-67, res chemist environ control admin, Bur Solid Waste Mgt, 67-69, supvr res chemist, Res Serv, Chem Studies Group, 69-73. *Concurrent Pos:* Pyrolysis session moderator, Nat Indust Solid Wastes Mgt Conf, 70, pyrolysis session chmn, Am Chem Soc Solid Waste Chem Symp, 70; adj asst prof chem, Raymond Walters Br, Univ Cincinnati, 73-77; part-time fac, dept phys sci, N Ky Univ, 83-86; adj asst prof chem, Univ Col, Univ Cincinnati, 87- *Mem:* Am Chem Soc; Chem Soc; Sigma Xi. *Res:* Structure-activity relationships; reaction mechanisms; organic molecular orbital theory; absorption and fluorescence spectroscopy; column and thin-layer chromatography; ultramicroorganic analysis of environmental pollutants; pyrolytic synthesis; water pollution; analytical methodology research; environmental research; quality assurance management. *Mailing Add:* 9536 Lansford Dr Cincinnati OH 45242. *Fax:* 513-569-7115; *E-Mail:* bender.dan@epamail.epa.gov

BENDER, DAVID BOWMAN, NEUROPHYSIOLOGY, NEUROBIOLOGY. *Current Pos:* asst prof, 76-82, ASSOC PROF, PHYSIOL DEPT, STATE UNIV NY, 82- *Personal Data:* b Boston, Mass, Aug 7, 42. *Educ:* Harvard Col, BA, 64; Princeton Univ, MA, 72, PhD(psychol), 74. *Prof Exp:* Res assoc, Psychol Dept, Princeton Univ, 74-76. *Concurrent Pos:* Proj dir, Nat Eye Inst grant, 78-94; guest researcher, NIMH, 90-91, Lab Neurophychol, 91-92. *Mem:* Asn Res Vision & Opthalmol; AAAS; NY Acad Sci. *Res:* Neurobiol of the central nervous system; neurophysiology of vision. *Mailing Add:* 329 Cary Hall Buffalo NY 14214. *E-Mail:* pgybendr@ubvms.bitnet, david@bender.med.buffalo.edu

BENDER, DONALD LEE, CIVIL ENGINEERING, HYDROLOGY. *Current Pos:* RETIRED. *Personal Data:* b Powell, Wyo, Sept 7, 31; m 54; c 5. *Educ:* Univ Wyo, BS, 53; Colo State Univ, MS, 55; Univ Wis, PhD(hydrol), 63. *Prof Exp:* Hydraul res engr, Colo State Univ, 55-56; from instr to assoc prof civil eng, 56-71, prof civil eng, Wash State Univ, 71-73, assoc dean eng, 73-86; at Dept Civil Eng, Gonzaga Univ, 86- *Concurrent Pos:* Prog intern, Am Coun Educ Acad Admin, 70-71. *Mem:* Am Soc Civil Engrs; Am Geophys Union; Am Soc Eng Educ; Nat Soc Prof Engrs. *Res:* Water resources development, particularly surface hydrology; dimensionless unit hydrograph and the prediction of flood peaks and flood flows in rivers; mechanics of infiltration. *Mailing Add:* 1532 E Pinecrest Rd Spokane WA 99203

BENDER, EDWARD ANTON, MATHEMATICS. *Current Pos:* assoc prof, 74-77, PROF MATH, UNIV CALIF, SAN DIEGO, 78- *Personal Data:* b Brooklyn, NY, Feb 7, 42; m; c 3. *Educ:* Calif Inst Technol, BS, 63, PhD(math), 66. *Prof Exp:* Instr math, Harvard Univ, 66-68; res mathematician, Inst Defense Analysis, 68-74. *Res:* Combinatorics. *Mailing Add:* Dept Math Univ Calif San Diego La Jolla CA 92093-0001

BENDER, HARVEY ALAN, GENETICS, BIOMEDICAL LEGAL ETHICS. *Current Pos:* DIR, NORTH CENT IND REGIONAL GENETICS CTR, 79- *Personal Data:* b Cleveland, Ohio, June 5, 33; m 56; c 3. *Educ:* Case Western Reserve Univ, AB, 54; Northwestern Univ, MS, 57, PhD(biol sci), 59, Am Bd Med Genetics, dipl, 82. *Prof Exp:* USPHS fel, Univ Calif, 59-60; from asst prof to assoc prof, 60-69, prof biol, Univ Notre Dame, 69-, mem Sr Staff, Radiation Lab, 64- *Concurrent Pos:* Vis prof in-serv inst, Purdue Univ, 62; Gosney fel & USPHS spec fel, Calif Inst Technol, 65-66; vis prof human genetics, Yale Univ Sch Med & res assoc, Sch Law, 73-74; exec dir, Nat Ctr Law & Handicapped; at-large mem, Yale Univ Task Force Genetics & Reproduction, 73-; consult ed, Mental Retardation; consult, President's Comt Ment Retardation, Nat Comn Protection Human Subjects of Biomed & Behav Res; adj prof med genetics, Sch Med, Ind Univ, 78- *Mem:* Fel AAAS; Am Genetic Asn; Am Soc Zoologists; Am Soc Human Genetics; Radiation Res Soc; Soc Develop Biol. *Res:* Developmental genetics; human genetics; biomedical legal ethics; histochemistry. *Mailing Add:* PO Box 369 Notre Dame IN 46556-0369

BENDER, HOWARD L, PLASTICS CHEMISTRY. *Current Pos:* INDEPENDENT CONSULT PLASTICS, 66- *Personal Data:* b Williamstown, WVa, Sept 14, 1893; m 18; c 2. *Educ:* Marietta Col, AB, 17, AM, 18; Case Inst, BS, 19; Columbia Univ, PhD(chem), 25. *Hon Degrees:* DSc, Marietta Col, 53. *Honors & Awards:* Hyatt Award, 53. *Prof Exp:* Res chemist, Dow Chem Co, 19-21; instr chem, Marietta Col, 21; res chemist, Union Carbide Plastics Co, 22-51, asst dir res, 51-58, consult, 58-66. *Mem:* Am Chem Soc. *Res:* Thermosetting resins and plastics; synthetic resins; acetylene gas reactions; polymers; phenolformaldehyde resins. *Mailing Add:* 32 Sylvan Morris Plains NJ 07950-2193

BENDER, HOWARD SANFORD, POLYMER CHEMISTRY, ORGANIC CHEMISTRY. *Current Pos:* DIR RES & DEVELOP, SANNCOR INDUSTS INC, 87- *Personal Data:* b Brooklyn, NY, Aug 19, 35; m 61; c 2. *Educ:* State Univ NY Buffalo, BS, 57; Bucknell Univ, MS, 60; Univ Del, PhD(org chem), 62. *Honors & Awards:* Roon Award, 70. *Prof Exp:* Res chemist cent res labs, Interchem Corp, 62-65; from assoc sr res chemist to sr res chemist, Gen Motors Corp, 65-71, supvr coatings, Res Lab, 71-75, dept res scientist, 75-84; dept head coatings res, Masonite Corp, 84-87. *Mem:* Am Chem Soc; Fedn Socs Paint Technol; Sigma Xi. *Res:* Surface coatings; paint; organic synthesis; adhesives; urethanes. *Mailing Add:* B F Goodrich Co 9921 Brecksville Rd Brecksville OH 44141

BENDER, JAMES GREGG, HEMATOLOGY, FLOW CYTOMETRY. *Current Pos:* res scientist, Baxter Healthcare Corp, 88-90, sr res scientist, 90-93, Baxter scientist, 93-94, MGR, FLOW CYTOMETRY FACIL, BAXTER HEALTHCARE CORP, 88-, PROJ LEADER, IMMUNOTHERAPY DIV, 93-, DIR RES, 94- *Personal Data:* b Denver, Colo, Oct 23, 49; m 73, Carol Schreiner; c 2. *Educ:* Colo State Univ, BS, 71 & 72; Univ Mich, MPH, 75; Univ NMex, PhD(immunol), 83. *Honors & Awards:* Outstanding Sci Contrib, Baxter Int, 90; Triumphs through Technol Award, Leukemia Soc Am, 93. *Prof Exp:* Res asst med, Univ NMex, 80-82, fel, 83-85, res asst prof path, 85-88. *Mem:* Soc Leukocyte Biol; Am Asn Immunologists; Am Soc Hemat; Int Soc Anal Cytol; Int Soc Exp Hemat. *Res:* Characterizing hematopoietic stem cells using flow cytometry and the development of purification and culture systems to provide therapeutic cell populations for the treatment of cancer. *Mailing Add:* Immunotherapy Div Baxter Healthcare Corp Baxter Technol Park Round Lake IL 60073-9799. *Fax:* 847-270-5406; *E-Mail:* bender@apollo.roundlake.baxter.com

BENDER, LEONARD FRANKLIN, medicine; deceased, see previous edition for last biography

BENDER, MARGARET MCLEAN, ORGANIC CHEMISTRY. *Current Pos:* RETIRED. *Personal Data:* b Easthampton, Mass, May 14, 16; m 43, Paul. *Educ:* Mt Holyoke Col, BA, 37, MA, 39; Yale Univ, PhD(org chem), 41. *Prof Exp:* Instr chem, Conn Col, 41-42; proj assoc, Yale Univ, 42-43; proj assoc, Chem Dept, Univ Wis-Madison, 43-45, lectr, Exten Div, 51-69, proj assoc radiocarbon dating, Ctr for Climatic Res, 63-73, assoc scientist, 73-77, sr scientist, 77-81. *Res:* Radiocarbon dating; carbon isotope ratios of plants. *Mailing Add:* 3305 Kingston Dr Madison WI 53713

BENDER, MAX, PHYSICAL CHEMISTRY, COLLOID CHEMISTRY. *Current Pos:* from asst prof to prof, 61-85, EMER PROF CHEM, FAIRLEIGH DICKINSON UNIV, 85- *Personal Data:* b Boston, Mass, Oct 23, 14; m 47, May; c Sanford R & Leslie M. *Educ:* Northeastern Univ, SB, 36; Mass Inst Technol, SM, 37; NY Univ, PhD(chem), 50. *Prof Exp:* Charge of lab, Manton-Gaulin Mfg Co, Inc, 38-40; sr res chemist & group leader colloid & phys chem, Interchem Corp, 41-48; sr res chemist, Am Cyanamid Co, 50-61. *Concurrent Pos:* Consult. *Mem:* AAAS; fel NY Acad Sci; Am Chem Soc; Am Inst Chem; Sigma Xi. *Res:* Electrokinetics; dispersions; emulsions; rheology; interfactial chemistry; sorption; diffusion; gelation; membranes; biophysics-living systems interfacial dynamics. *Mailing Add:* 16 S Woodland Ave East Brunswick NJ 08816-1631

BENDER, MICHAEL A, CYTOGENETICS, ENVIRONMENTAL HEALTH. *Current Pos:* SR SCIENTIST, BROOKHAVEN NAT LAB, 75- *Personal Data:* b New York, NY, July 25, 29; m 50, 69, 79, Belinda S Gilmer; c Michele (Myers), Leslie, Sabina (Millbank) & William. *Educ:* Univ Wash, BS, 52; Johns Hopkins Univ, PhD(biol), 56. *Prof Exp:* Nat Cancer Inst fel biol, Johns Hopkins Univ, 56-58; biologist, Oak Ridge Nat Lab, 58-69; assoc prof radiol, Sch Med, Vanderbilt Univ, 69-71; geneticist, US AEC, 71-73; vis prof, Sch Med, Johns Hopkins Univ, 73-75. *Mem:* Fel AAAS; Am Soc Cell Biol; Radiation Res Soc; Am Soc Photobiol; Nat Coun Radiation Protection & Measurement. *Res:* Eukaryotic chromosome structure; mechanisms of mutagenesis; environmental mutagenesis and oncogenesis. *Mailing Add:* Med Dept Brookhaven Nat Lab Upton NY 11973. *Fax:* 516-282-5311

BENDER, MICHAEL E, pollution biology, aquatic toxicology; deceased, see previous edition for last biography

BENDER, PATRICK KEVIN, CALCIUM CALMADULIN REGULATION, GENETICS OF PHOSPHORYLASE KINASE. *Current Pos:* ASST PROF BIOCHEM, VA POLYTECH INST, 89- *Personal Data:* b Cleveland, Ohio, Apr 8, 53; m 85; c 2. *Educ:* Kent State Univ, BS, 75; Univ Va, PhD(biol), 82. *Prof Exp:* Postdoctoral res, Univ Tex Med Sch, Houston, 81-83; postdoctoral res, Univ Va, 83-84, res asst prof biol, 84-89. *Mem:* Am Soc Cell Biologists; AAAS. *Res:* Calcium/calmodulin regulation of metabolic processes with particular efforts in the calmodulin regulation of the phosphorylase kinase enzyme; additional investigations of the regulation of calmodulin gene(s) expression in cultured muscle cells. *Mailing Add:* Dept Biochem 124 Va Polytech Inst W Campus Dr Blacksburg VA 24061-0001

BENDER, PAUL ELLIOT, MEDICINAL CHEMISTRY. *Current Pos:* SR INVESTR MED CHEM, SMITH KLINE & FR LABS, 69- *Personal Data:* b Long Beach, NY, Dec 11, 42; m 65, Daryl J Meltzer; c Michael & Becky. *Educ:* State Univ NY, Stony Brook, BS, 63; Univ Ill, Urbana, MS, 66, PhD(org chem), 69. *Mem:* Am Chem Soc; NY Acad Sci. *Res:* Design and synthesis of leukotrienes, cannabinoids, peptides, conjugated proteins and various heterocyclic compounds to investigate their potential for medicinal use; the design of novel bioactive molecules and the application of modern synthetic organic chemistry to the synthesis of a wide group of heterocycles, leukofrienes, cannabinoids, peptides, etc for medicinal research and development. *Mailing Add:* 504 Lilac Lane Cherry Hill NJ 08003

BENDER, PAUL J, PHYSICAL CHEMISTRY. *Current Pos:* RETIRED. *Personal Data:* b Mansfield, Ohio, Nov 20, 17; m 43. *Educ:* Yale Univ, BS, 39, PhD(phys chem), 42. *Prof Exp:* Phys chemist, Off Sci Res & Develop proj, Yale Univ, 42; instr phys chem, Univ Wis-Madison, 42-45, from asst prof to prof, 45-79, emer prof chem, 79-80. *Res:* Thermodynamic properties of solutions; Raman spectroscopy; vapor pressures for liquids; nuclear magnetic resonance spectroscopy. *Mailing Add:* 3305 Kingston Dr Madison WI 53713

BENDER, PETER LEOPOLD, PHYSICS. *Current Pos:* PHYSICIST, NAT BUR STANDARD, 56- *Personal Data:* b New York, NY, Oct 18, 30; m 53; c 3. *Educ:* Rutgers Univ, BS, 51; Princeton Univ, PhD(physics), 56, MA, 57. *Honors & Awards:* Gold Medal, US Dept Com, 59; Samuel Wesley Stratton award, Nat Bur Stand, 62. *Concurrent Pos:* Fulbright grant, Leiden Univ, 51-52; mem, Joint Inst Lab Astrophys, Nat Bur Stand & Univ Colo, 62-, chmn, 69-70; adj prof, Univ Colo, 64-; NSF adv panel for physics, 72-75; NASA lunar adv comn, 73-75, sub-panel on Relativity & Gravity, 74-76; Nat Acad Sci comn on planet explor, 76-77, comn on geod, 76-79, chmn comn earth sci in space, 77-, space sci bd, 77- & comn gravitational physics, 78- *Mem:* Fel AAAS; Am Astron Soc; Am Geophys Union; fel Optical Soc Am; fel Am Phys Soc. *Res:* Atomic physics; geophysics; astronomy. *Mailing Add:* Univ Colo CB 440 Boulder CO 80309

BENDER, PHILLIP R, MATHEMATICS. *Current Pos:* instr, 60-63, asst prof, 66-74, ASSOC PROF & ASST CHMN DEPT, MARQUETTE UNIV, 74- *Personal Data:* b Milwaukee, Wis, Sept 20, 27; m 56; c 5. *Educ:* Purdue Univ, BS, 51; Marquette Univ, MS, 59; Iowa State Univ, PhD(math), 66. *Prof Exp:* Qual control engr, A-P Controls Corp, 51-55; instr math, Milwaukee Sch Eng, 50-60. *Mem:* Math Asn Am; Soc Indust & Appl Math. *Res:* Differential equations; asymptotic behavior of solutions; numberical solutions. *Mailing Add:* 1929 N 71st St Milwaukee WI 53213

BENDER, ROBERT ALGERD, MICROBIOLOGY, MOLECULAR BIOLOGY. *Current Pos:* ASST PROF MICROBIOL, DIV BIOL SCI, UNIV MICH, 78- *Personal Data:* b Bethlehem, Pa, Apr 17, 46. *Educ:* Mass Inst Technol, BS, 68, PhD(microbiol), 76; Univ Southern Maine, MS, 72. *Prof Exp:* Fel molecular biol, Albert Einstein Col Med, 76-78. *Concurrent Pos:* Jr fac res award, Am Cancer Soc, 78-81. *Mem:* Am Soc Microbiol; Genetics Soc Am. *Res:* Microbiol regulation: nitrogen metabolism in the bacterium Klebsiella and regulation of the cell cycle in the bacterium Caulobacter. *Mailing Add:* Dept Biol 4013 Nat Sci Bldg Univ Mich 830 N University Ave Ann Arbor MI 48109-1048

BENDER, WELCOME W(ILLIAM), AERONAUTICAL ENGINEERING. *Current Pos:* AT DEPT BIOL CHEM, HARVARD MED SCH. *Personal Data:* b Elizabeth, NJ, Nov 30, 15; m 46; c 7. *Educ:* Mass Inst Technol, BS, 38, MS, 39. *Prof Exp:* Tech dir, Pilotless Aircraft Sect, Martin Co Div, Martin Marietta Corp, 39-48, mgr, Electromech Dept, 49-51, chief electronics engr, 52-55, dir, Res Inst Advan Studies, 55-62, co dir res, 62-66, dir, Space Explor Group, 64-66, Voyager prog scientist, 66-67, prog scientist, Planetary Systs, 67-69, proj scientist, Viking Proj, 69- *Concurrent Pos:* Vpres, J R Nelson & Assoc, Inc, Consult Engrs, 72-; pres, Custom Eng, Inc, 75-81. *Mem:* AAAS; assoc fel Am Inst Aeronaut & Astronaut; Am Astronaut Soc; fel Inst Elec & Electronics Engrs. *Res:* Research management in the aerospace industry. *Mailing Add:* Dept Biochem Harvard Univ Med Sch 25 Shattuck St Boston MA 02115-6027

BENDERSKY, MARTIN, TOPOLOGY. *Current Pos:* AT DEPT MATH, RIDER COL. *Personal Data:* b New York, NY, Apr 15, 45; m 71; c 1. *Educ:* City Col New York, BS, 66; Univ Calif, Berkeley, PhD(math), 71. *Prof Exp:* Asst math, Aarhus, Denmark, 71-72; vis lectr, Univ Wash, 72-73, asst prof math, 73- *Res:* Study of the Adams-Novikov spectral sequence, particularly the description of an unstable version and an appropriate Curtis-Kan algebra. *Mailing Add:* Dept Math City Univ NY-Hunter Col 695 Park Ave New York NY 10021

BENDICH, ADRIANNE, VITAMINS RESEARCH, ANTIOXIDANTS. *Current Pos:* Sr scientist, Hoffmann-La Roche, 81-88, sr clin res coordr, 88-93, clin res sci, 93-95, ASST DIR, HOFFMANN-LA ROCHE INC, 95- *Personal Data:* b New York, NY; m 84, David Kafkewitz; c Jorden & Debra. *Educ:* City Col NY, BS, 65; Iowa State Univ, MS, 66; Rutgers Univ, PhD(immunol), 81. *Honors & Awards:* Roche Res & Develop Prize, 92; Tribute to Women in Indust Award, 95. *Concurrent Pos:* Ed, J Nutrit Immunol, 90-; mem adv bd, Fedn Am Soc Exp Biol; ed, J Nutrit & Free Radicals Biol & Med. *Mem:* Am Asn Immunologists; NY Acad Sci; Am Inst Nutrit; Am Soc Clin Nutrit; Inst Food Technologists; Sigma Xi; Oxygen Soc. *Res:* Beneficial effects of supplemental vitamins on immune function; over 60 publications; maternal and optimal pregnancy outcomes. *Mailing Add:* Hoffmann-La Roche Inc 340 Kingsland St Bldg 787/5 Nutley NJ 07110-1199. *Fax:* 201-909-8479

BENDICH, ARNOLD JAY, MOLECULAR BIOLOGY, BIOCHEMISTRY. *Current Pos:* assoc prof, 70-83, PROF BOT & GENETICS, UNIV WASH, 83- *Personal Data:* b New York, NY, May 5, 42. *Educ:* Univ Vt, BA, 62; Univ Wash, PhD(microbiol), 69. *Prof Exp:* Res assoc molecular biol, Dept Terrestrial Magnetism, Carnegie Inst, Wash, 64-65. *Concurrent Pos:* Mem, Genetic Biol Panel, NSF. *Mem:* Int Soc Plant Molecular Biol; fel AAAS; Genetics Soc Am. *Res:* Mitochondrial genome structure. *Mailing Add:* Dept Bot Univ Wash Box 35-5325 Seattle WA 98195. *Fax:* 206-685-1728; *E-Mail:* bendich@u.washington.edu

BENDISZ, KAZIMIERZ, STRESS ANALYSIS, NUMERICAL METHODS. *Current Pos:* WRITER, TECH BOOKS, 80- *Personal Data:* b Warsaw, Poland, Feb 11, 14; US citizen; m 50; c Anna & Zofia. *Educ:* Univ Warsaw, Poland, BS, 39; Univ Munich, Ger, MS, 47. *Prof Exp:* Supvr mach design, Power Press Design Bur, Warsaw, Poland, 48-53; consult engr mach design, diverse institutions, 54-63; sr asst numerical methods, Dept Mach Design, Warsaw Univ, 63-65; researcher seals, Univ Stuttgart, Ger, 65-68; design engr valves, Anchor Valve Co, Hayward, Calif, 68-69 & piping, Pac Gas & Elec Co, Calif, 70-79. *Concurrent Pos:* Teacher mech, Radio a Telecom Technicum, Warsaw, Poland, 53-63; design engr, Inst Heat Engines, Univ Warsaw, Poland, 57-60, supvr & design engr, Inst Astron, 60-63; instr mach design & mech, Heald Eng Col, Calif, 70-79. *Mem:* Am Soc Mech Engrs. *Res:* Separation of liquids of different viscosities by mechanical means; rotary shaft seals for chemical industry; stress analysis in mechanical elements. *Mailing Add:* 1442 Sanchez St San Francisco CA 94131-2024

BENDITT, EARL PHILIP, pathology; deceased, see previous edition for last biography

BENDIX, SELINA (WEINBAUM), environmental management; deceased, see previous edition for last biography

BENDIXEN, HENRIK H, ANESTHESIOLOGY. *Current Pos:* prof, Columbia Univ, 73-94, actg provost & vpres health sci, 80-81, alumni prof, 84, vpres health sci & dean fac med, 84-89, E M Papper prof anesthesiol, 85-86, sr assoc vpres health sci & sr assoc dean fac med, 89-94, EMER PROF ANESTHESIOL, COL PHYSICIANS & SURGEONS, COLUMBIA UNIV, 94- *Personal Data:* b Fredriksberg, Denmark, Dec 2, 23. *Educ:* Univ Copenhagen, MD, 51. *Hon Degrees:* Dr, Jagiellonian Univ, Krakow, Poland, 85, Univ Copenhagen, 87. *Honors & Awards:* Wesley Bourne Lectr, McGill Univ, 69; Husfeldt Lectr, Danish Soc Anesthesiol, 74; Benjamin Howard Robbins Mem Lectr, Vanderbilt Univ, 75; John J Bonica Lectr, Univ Wash, 82; Ralph Waters Award, 85. *Prof Exp:* Med dir, Univ Hosp, San Diego, 71-72. *Concurrent Pos:* Dir, Anesthesiol Serv, Presby Hosp, 73-85; consult, Dept Anesthesia, Vassar Brothers Hosp, Poughkeepsie, NY, 77-; chmn, Comt Prof Safety & Liability, Presbyn Hosp, NY, 82-83; chmn, Postgrad Assembly in Anesthesiology; chmn, Policy Comt Sci & Technol & Orthop Search Comt, Columbia Univ, NY, 82- *Mem:* Inst Med-Nat Acad Sci; fel AAAS; fel Am Col Anesthesiol; AMA; NY Acad Sci; Am Soc Pharmacol & Exp Therapeut; Am Soc Anesthesiologists; Int Anesthesia Res Soc; Asn Am Med Col; Am Heart Asn. *Res:* Critical, intensive and respiratory care; respirators and resuscitation; hypoxia; catecholamines; monitoring; cost effectiveness of care; epidemiology and statistics in clinical medicine; published numerous articles in various journals. *Mailing Add:* 129 Columbia Ave Rancho Mirage CA 92270

BENDIXEN, LEO E, PLANT PHYSIOLOGY. *Current Pos:* RETIRED. *Personal Data:* b Mills, Utah, Oct 21, 23; m 49; c 4. *Educ:* Utah State Univ, BS, 53; Univ Calif, Davis, MS, 56, PhD(plant physiol), 60. *Prof Exp:* Sr lab technician agron, Univ Calif, Davis, 55-61; from asst prof to assoc prof, Ohio State Univ, 61-70, prof agron, 70-89. *Concurrent Pos:* Sr fel, East-West Ctr, 75-76. *Mem:* Int Weed Sci Soc; Weed Sci Soc Am; Coun Agr Sci & Technol. *Res:* Physiological and biochemical aspects of herbicides; physiological and ecological aspects of plant reproduction and growth; physiological and anatomical aspects of plagiotropic growth; weed hosts as pest reservoirs of organisms affecting crops. *Mailing Add:* 793 Island Ct Columbus OH 43214

BENDLER, JOHN THOMAS, POLYMER PHYSICS, STATISTICAL MECHANICS. *Current Pos:* ASSOC PROF CHEM, SDAK SCH MINES & TECHNOL. *Personal Data:* b Derby, Conn, Oct 5, 44; m, Julie Radlund. *Educ:* Holy Cross Univ, AB, 66; Yale Univ, PhD, 74. *Honors & Awards:* Woodrow Wilson fel, Yale Univ, 67. *Prof Exp:* Instr chem, Northern Ill Univ, 72-75; res assoc, Midland Macro Molecular Inst, 75-77; polymer physicist, Gen Elec Co, 78- *Concurrent Pos:* Postdoctoral res, Wash Univ, 77; vis prof, Colo State Univ, 90; G E Coolidge fel. *Mem:* Fel Am Phys Soc; Am Chem Soc. *Mailing Add:* Dept Chem & Chem Eng SDak Sch Mines & Technol 501 E St Joseph St Rapid City SD 57701-3995. *Fax:* 518-387-5812; *E-Mail:* bendler@crd.ge.com

BENDT, PHILIP JOSEPH, CRYOGENICS, EXPERIMENTAL NUCLEAR PHYSICS. *Current Pos:* RETIRED. *Personal Data:* b Syracuse, NY, Dec 21, 19. *Educ:* Mass Inst Technol, BS, 42; Columbia Univ, PhD(physics), 51. *Prof Exp:* Staff mem, Los Alamos Nat Lab, 51-80; consult, 80-91. *Mem:* Am Phys Soc. *Res:* Superfluid hydrodynamics; electron-electron paramagnetic resonance; neutron capture gamma spectroscopy. *Mailing Add:* 350 Camino Encantado Los Alamos NM 87544

BENDURE, ROBERT J, INORGANIC CHEMISTRY, POLLUTION CHEMISTRY. *Current Pos:* RETIRED. *Personal Data:* b Steubenville, Ohio, May 2, 20; m 42; c 2. *Educ:* Miami Univ, BA, 42. *Honors & Awards:* Lundell Bright Mem Award, Am Soc Testing & Mat, 72. *Prof Exp:* Chem analyst, Armco Inc, 42-44 & 46-47, sr analyst, 47-49, from chemist to sr chemist, 49-61, supv chemist, 61-68, mgr chem labs, 68-70, dir chem res, 70-80, corp dir res & technol, 80-83. *Mem:* AAAS; Am Chem Soc; fel Am Soc Testing & Mat. *Res:* Inorganic analytical chemistry using both classical and instrumental methods; ferrous and nonferrous metals analysis; inclusions; intermetallic compounds and dissolved gases in steel; air and water pollution control; industrial hygiene; corrosion. *Mailing Add:* 825 W Lane Lebanon OH 45036

BENEDEK, ANDREW, CHEMICAL & ENVIRONMENTAL ENGINEERING. *Current Pos:* CHMN & CHIEF EXEC OFFICER, ZERON ENVIRON INC, 87- *Personal Data:* b Budapest, Hungary, May 29, 43; Can citizen; m 66. *Educ:* McGill Univ, BEng, 66; Univ Wash, PhD(chem eng), 70. *Honors & Awards:* L K Cecil Award, Am Inst Chem Eng, 82. *Prof Exp:* Asst prof, 70-76, assoc prof chem eng, McMaster Univ, 76-86. *Concurrent Pos:* Consult govt & chem indust, 75-; coordr water res group, 76- *Mem:* Am Inst Chem Engrs; Chem Inst Can; Can Soc Chem Engrs. *Res:* Mass transfer in gas-liquid dispersions; polarographic oxygen probe response; water treatment processes such as coagulation; activitated carbon adsorption and ozonation. *Mailing Add:* Zenon Environ Inc 845 Harrington Court Burlington ON L7N 3P3 Can

BENEDEK, GEORGE BERNARD, PHYSICS. *Current Pos:* from assoc prof to prof physics, 61-79, ALFRED H CASPARY PROF PHYSICS & BIOL PHYSICS, MASS INST TECHNOL, 79- *Personal Data:* b New York, NY, Dec 1, 28; m 55; c 2. *Educ:* Rensselaer Polytech Inst, BS, 49; Harvard Univ, MA, 52, PhD(physics), 53. *Honors & Awards:* Debye Lectr chem, Cornell Univ, 72; Recognition Award, Alcon Res Inst, 87; Irving Langnuir Prize in Chem Physics, Am Physc Soc, 95; Science poor l'art award-LVMH Moet Hennessey, Louis Vuitton Co, 95; Proctor Medal Award, Asn Res Vision & Ophthal, 97. *Prof Exp:* Mem staff, Lincoln Lab, Mass Inst Technol, 53-55; res fel, Harvard Univ, 55-57, lectr solid state physics, 57-58, asst prof appl physics, 58-61; prof physics, Div Health Sci & Technol, Harvard-Mass Inst Technol. *Concurrent Pos:* Guggenheim fel, Stanford Univ, 60; prof fel, Atomic Energy Res Estab, Harwell, Eng, 67; consult physics, Retina Found, Boston, 68-91; lectr physics, Harvard Univ, 75-85; mem vision res prog comt, Nat Eye Inst, 83-87; Walker-Ames prof, Univ Wash, Seattle, 84. *Mem:* Nat Acad Sci; Inst Med-Nat Acad Sci; fel Am Phys Soc; fel Am Acad Arts & Sci. *Res:* Magnetic resonance; high pressure physics; solid state physics; critical phenomena and light scattering with lasers; biological physics. *Mailing Add:* Dept Physics Rm 13-2005 Mass Inst Technol Cambridge MA 02139-4307

BENEDEK, GIORGIO, PHYSICS. *Current Pos:* from asst to assoc prof, 65-85, PROF, UNIV MILAN, 85- *Personal Data:* b Bologna, Italy, Feb 4, 41; m 69, Carmen Lavarini; c Stefania C. *Educ:* Univ Milan, DPhysics, 65; cert, 71. *Honors & Awards:* Int Chair Franqui Found, 85; Alexander von Humboldt Found Award, 90; Max Planck Award, 92. *Prof Exp:* Researcher, Nat Res Coun, Milan, 67-74, head researcher, 74-82. *Concurrent Pos:* Consult, UNESCO-Roste, Venice, Italy, 89- & FNRS, Brussels, 90-; permanent dir, Int Sch Solid State Physics, Erice, Italy, 90- *Mem:* Am Phys Soc; Europ Phys Soc; Ital Phys Soc; Mat Res Soc; NY Acad Sci. *Res:* Theory of surfce phonous; theoretical foundations of surface phousu spectroscopy with atom scattering; new carbon structures and cluster-assembled materials; author of numerous books and articles in professional journals. *Mailing Add:* Via don Minzoni 48 Poasco San Donato Milan I-20097 Italy. *Fax:* 39-2-2392414; *E-Mail:* benedek@axpmi.mi.infn.it

BENEDEK, ROY, THEORETICAL PHYSICS. *Current Pos:* PHYSICIST, ARGONNE NAT LAB, 74- *Personal Data:* b New York, NY, July 2, 45. *Educ:* Cornell Univ, BS, 66, MS, 67; Brown Univ, PhD(physics), 72. *Prof Exp:* Res assoc, physics, Cornell Univ, 71-74. *Mem:* Am Phys Soc; AAAS. *Mailing Add:* Mat Sci Div Bldg 223 Argonne Nat Lab 9700 S Cass Ave Argonne IL 60439

BENEDETTI, JACQUELINE KAY, BIOSTATISTICS. *Current Pos:* ASSOC PROF, UNIV WASH. *Personal Data:* b Chicago, Ill, July 22, 48. *Educ:* Univ Calif, Los Angeles, BA, 70; Univ Wash, PhD(biomath), 74. *Prof Exp:* NIH gen med sci fel, Sch Med, Univ Calif, Los Angeles, 74-76, asst prof in residence biomath, 76-80. *Mem:* Inst Math Statist; Am Statist Asn; Biomet Soc. *Res:* Analysis of categorical data, including multidimensional contingency table analysis, and measures of association for two-way tables; clinical trials statistics. *Mailing Add:* Dept Biostatist Box 357232 Univ Wash Seattle WA 98195-0001

BENEDETTO, JOHN JOSEPH, HARMONIC ANALYSIS, WAVELETS. *Current Pos:* res assoc, Inst Fluid Dynamics & Appl Math, 65-66, from asst prof to assoc prof, 66-72, PROF MATH, UNIV MD, COLLEGE PARK, 72- *Personal Data:* b Melrose, Mass, July 16, 39; m 68, Catherine Hausler; c John, Robert & Gary. *Educ:* Boston Col, BA, 60; Harvard Univ, MA, 62; Univ Toronto, PhD(math), 64. *Prof Exp:* Assoc mem tech staff, Radio Corp Am, Burlington, 61-62, mem tech staff, 62-64; teaching fel math, Univ Toronto, 62-64; asst prof, NY Univ, 64-65. *Concurrent Pos:* Assoc mathematician, Int Bus Mach Corp, Mass, 64-; vis prof, Scuola Normale Superiore, Pisa, 70-71, 74, Mass Inst Technol, 73 & 80-81; consult, Prometheus Inc, 86-, Mitre Corp, 87- *Mem:* Am Math Soc; Math Asn Am; Inst Elec & Electronics Engrs; Soc Indust & Appl Math. *Res:* Wavelet/Gabor decompositions, irregular sampling, filter design; signal processing. *Mailing Add:* Dept Math Univ Md College Park MD 20742-4015. *E-Mail:* jjb@math.umd.edu

BENEDICT, ALBERT ALFRED, IMMUNOLOGY. *Current Pos:* PROF MICROBIOL & CHMN DEPT, UNIV HAWAII, 63- *Personal Data:* b Pasadena, Calif, Nov 26, 21; m 47; c 1. *Educ:* Univ Calif, AB, 48, MA, 50, PhD(bact), 52. *Prof Exp:* Res assoc, Univ Calif, 49-52; res assoc virol med br, Univ Tex, 52-53, asst prof prev med & pub health, 53-57; assoc prof bact, Univ Kans, 57-63. *Concurrent Pos:* WHO consult, 71. *Mem:* AAAS; Am Soc Microbiol; Soc Exp Biol & Med; Am Asn Immunol. *Res:* Avian immunoglobulins; structure, genetics and synthesis of immunoglobulins. *Mailing Add:* 5607 Halekawani St Honolulu HI 96821

BENEDICT, BARRY ARDEN, HYDRAULIC ENGINEERING. *Current Pos:* prof & dept head, 86-88, DEAN & JACK THIGPEN PROF CIVIL ENG, LA TECH UNIV, 88- *Personal Data:* b Wauchula, Fla, Feb 7, 42; m 75, Sharon Parker; c Mark, Erin, Beau & Brooke. *Educ:* Univ Fla, BCE, 65, MSE, 67, PhD(civil eng), 68. *Prof Exp:* Res assoc, Coastal & Oceanog Eng Dept, Univ Fla, 68-69; from asst prof to assoc prof hydraulic & water resources eng & prog dir, Vanderbilt Univ, 69-75; assoc prof civil eng, Tulane Univ, 75-77; assoc prof civil eng, Univ SC, 78-80; prof, Dept Civil Eng, Univ Fla, Gainesville, 80-86. *Mem:* Am Soc Eng Educ; Am Soc Civil Engrs. *Res:* Mechanics of heated discharges into water bodies; modeling thermal stratification in reservoirs; water quality modeling and spill modeling; groundwater modeling; diffuser discharge modeling; saltwater intrusion, upcoming; storm drain design. *Mailing Add:* Col Eng La Tech Univ 305 Wisteria St Ruston LA 71272-0001. *Fax:* 318-257-2562; *E-Mail:* benedict@engr.latech.edu

BENEDICT, C R, PLANT BIOCHEMISTRY, PLANT PHYSIOLOGY. *Current Pos:* prof plant biochem, Tex A&M Univ, 69-79, interim head dept, 79-81, asst head, Dept Plant Biochem, 81-83, PROF BIOCHEM, TEX A&M UNIV, 83- *Personal Data:* b Lake Placid, NY, June 26, 30; m 54; c 2. *Educ:* Cornell Univ, BS, 54, MS, 56; Purdue Univ, PhD(plant biochem), 60. *Prof Exp:* Asst prof biochem, Wayne State Univ, 62-66; sr plant physiologist, USDA, 66-69. *Mem:* Am Chem Soc; Am Soc Biochem & Molecular Biol; Am Soc Plant Physiologists; Am Soc Agron. *Res:* Enzymology and biochemistry of natural products including the regulation of carotenes, polyisoprenoid and the anti-ovarian cancer drug taxol. *Mailing Add:* Dept Biochem & Biophys Tex A&M Univ College Station TX 77843-2128

BENEDICT, CHAUNCEY, PLANT BIOCHEMISTRY. *Current Pos:* sr scientist, USDA, 66-69, PROF PLANT PHYSIOL, TEX A&M UNIV, 69- *Personal Data:* b Lake Placid, NY, June 10, 30; m 54; c 1. *Educ:* Cornell Univ, BS, 54, MS, 56; Purdue Univ, PhD(plant biochem), 60. *Prof Exp:* Res assoc biochem, Brookhaven Nat Lab, 60-61; fel & asst prof biol, Dartmouth Med Sch, 61-62; asst prof biochem, Wayne State Univ, 62-66. *Concurrent Pos:* Mem subcomt biol chem, Nat Res Coun, 64-67. *Mem:* Am Soc Plant Physiol. *Res:* Plant metabolism and carotene synthesis; stable carbon isotopes; enzymes; terpene synthesis; crop science. *Mailing Add:* Dept Biochem & Biophysics Tex A&M Univ College Station TX 77843-5000

BENEDICT, ELLEN MARING, BIOLOGY, SPELEOLOGY. *Current Pos:* RES & WRITING, 78- *Personal Data:* b Eugene, Ore, Aug 28, 31; m 51; c 5. *Educ:* Portland State Univ, BS, 65, MS, 69, PhD(environ sci biol), 78. *Prof Exp:* Instr gen sci biol, Portland State Univ, 69-72; chief investr, Nat Speleological Soc Res Adv grant, 74-75. *Concurrent Pos:* Res assoc biol, Portland State Univ, 78; mem, Int Ctr Arachnology Doc; instr, Malheur Field Sta, 74-, adj prof biol, 88-; proj dir, Diamond Craters Geol Area, Bur Land Mgt, 79; adj prof biol, Pac Univ, 79-88. *Mem:* Am Arachnological Soc; Brit Arachnological Soc; fel Nat Speleological Soc; Sigma Xi. *Res:* Ecology and systematics of pseudoscorpions; soil arthropod population densities and monitoring techniques; biota of caves; cave microclimates. *Mailing Add:* 8106 SE Carlton Portland OR 97206-6327

BENEDICT, GEORGE FREDERICK, ASTROMETRY, IMAGE PROCESSING. *Current Pos:* Astron, 72-, fac mgr astron data reduction & anal syst, 81-87, RES SCIENTIST, UNIV TEX, AUSTIN, 87- *Personal Data:* b Los Angeles, Calif, Mar 17, 45; m 67; c 2. *Educ:* Univ Mich, BS & BS, 67; Northwestern Univ, MS, 69, PhD(astron), 72. *Concurrent Pos:* Consult, Boller & Chivens Div, Perkin Elmer Corp, 73-76 & Monsanto Mound Res Facil, 78-81; mem, NASA Space Telescope Astrometry Team, 77- *Mem:* Am Astron Soc; Int Astron Union. *Res:* Astrometry; space astronomy; galaxy photometry; digital image processing and analysis. *Mailing Add:* McDonald Observ Univ Tex Austin TX 78712

BENEDICT, JAMES HAROLD, BIOCHEMISTRY. *Current Pos:* RETIRED. *Personal Data:* b Floral Park, NY, Mar 9, 22; m 48, Elaine W Engerer; c 4. *Educ:* NY Univ, AB, 44; Univ Pittsburgh, PhD(chem), 50. *Prof Exp:* Asst chem, Univ Pittsburgh, 46-47; chemist, Procter & Gamble Co, 49-73, toxicologist, 73-83. *Mem:* Fel AAAS; Am Chem Soc; Am Acad Clin Toxicol; fel Am Soc Testing & Mat. *Res:* Fat metabolism; trace analyses; toxicology. *Mailing Add:* 5583 Jessup Rd Cincinnati OH 45247

BENEDICT, JOHN HOWARD, JR, BEHAVIOR, ECOLOGY. *Current Pos:* PROF ENTOM, AGR EXP STA, TEX A&M UNIV, CORPUS CHRISTI, 88- *Personal Data:* b San Antonio, Tex, Mar 31, 44; m 65; c 2. *Educ:* Calif State Univ, Los Angeles, BA, 69; Univ Calif, Davis, PhD(entom), 75. *Prof Exp:* Res entomologist VI, Rockefeller Found-Univ Calif, Davis, 75-76; asst prof, 77-81, assoc prof, 82-88. *Concurrent Pos:* Consult Hopkins Agr Serv & Agr Chem Indust; vis prof, Dept Biol, Tex A&I Univ, 88-90, teacher, 88-; consult, Monsanto Co, 90-; adj prof, Dept Biol, Tex A&M Univ, Corpus Christi, 90-, Kingsville, 92- *Mem:* AAAS; Entom Soc Am. *Res:* Pest management and evaluation genetically engineered plants and host plant resistance throughout the US; to identify and utilize sources of resistance in cotton to plant bugs, bollweevil and heliothis; behavioral and semichemical mechanisms of insect-plant interactions; mechanistic modeling insect-plant-environment crop systems. *Mailing Add:* Tex A&M Univ Dept Entomol Rte 2 Box 589 Corpus Christi TX 78406. *Fax:* 512-265-9201

BENEDICT, JOSEPH T, inorganic chemistry, academic administration; deceased, see previous edition for last biography

BENEDICT, MANSON, CHEMICAL & NUCLEAR ENGINEERING. *Current Pos:* from prof to inst prof nuclear eng, 51-73, head dept, 58-71, EMER INST PROF NUCLEAR ENG, MASS INST TECHNOL, 73- *Personal Data:* b Lake Linden, Mich, Oct 9, 07; wid, Marjorie O Allen; c Mary (Sauer) & Marjorie (Cohn). *Educ:* Cornell Univ, BChem, 28; Mass Inst Technol, MS, 32, PhD (phys chem), 35. *Honors & Awards:* Nat Medal of Sci; Walker Award, Wilson Award, Fritz Medal & Founders Award, Am Inst Chem Engrs; Compton Award, Am Nuclear Soc, Seaborg Medal; Perkin Medal, Soc Chem Indust; Founders Award, Nat Acad Engrs; Fermi Award, Atomic Energy Comn, 72. *Prof Exp:* Res chemist, Nat Aniline & Chem Co, 29-30 & 37-38 & Nat Res Coun fel, 35-36; res assoc geophys, Harvard Univ, 36-37; res chemist, M W Kellogg Co, NJ, 38-42; head process develop, Kellex Corp, NY, 42-46; dir process develop, Hydrocarbon Res, Inc, 46-51; chief opers anal staff, Atomic Energy Comn, 51-52; sci dir, Nat Res Corp, 51-57. *Concurrent Pos:* Mem gen adv comt, Atomic Energy Comn, 58-68, chmn, 62-64; dir, Burns & Roe, Inc, 78-87. *Mem:* Nat Acad Sci; Nat Acad Eng; Am Inst Chem Engrs; Am Nuclear Soc (vpres, 61-62, pres, 62-63); Am Chem Soc; Am Philos Soc. *Res:* Isotope separation; nuclear chemical technology. *Mailing Add:* 108 Moorings Park Dr Naples FL 34105-2155

BENEDICT, ROBERT CURTIS, BIOCHEMISTRY. *Current Pos:* RES CHEMIST, EASTERN REGIONAL RES CTR, USDA, WYNDMOOR, 66- *Personal Data:* b Bridgeport, Conn, May 17, 32; m 58; c 3. *Educ:* Univ Conn, BS, 53; Cornell Univ, MS, 55; Univ Pa, PhD(biochem), 65. *Prof Exp:* Pa Plan Med Res fel, 64-66. *Mem:* AAAS; Am Chem Soc; Am Soc Microbiol; Inst Food Technologists; Am Meat Sci Assoc. *Res:* Biochemistry of meat and muscle; molecular biology of pathogenic bacteria. *Mailing Add:* 1915 Huntingdon Rd Huntingdon Valley PA 19006-4301

BENEDICT, SUSAN, HIV-AIDS NURSING, ANESTHESIOLOGY. *Current Pos:* asst dean grad progs & prof, Col Nursing, 91-94, assoc dean res, 94-96, PROF ANESTHESIA, MED UNIV SC, 92-, PROF NURSING, 94-, CHAIRPERSON, DEPT HEALTH PATTERNS & SYMPTOM MGT, 96- *Educ:* Villa Maria Col, BS, 72; Univ Ala, MS, 79, DSc(nursing), 83. *Prof Exp:* Nurse, Mem Sloan Kettering Cancer Ctr & Clin Res Ctr, NY Hosp, Cornell Med Ctr, 64; nurse anesthetist, Mercy Hosp, New Orleans, 66-67, Charlotte, 68-70; instr anesthesia, Charity Hosp, Xavier Univ, 67-68, Hamot Hosp/Gannon Univ, 71-73; nurse anesthetist, Pvt Pract, 73-82; dir, Pain Mgt Ctr NAla, 82-84; asst prof nursing, Univ Ala, 84-89; assoc, HIV Ctr Clin & Behav Studies, Columbia Univ Presby Med Ctr, 89-91, asst dean prog planning, Sch Nursing, 89-91. *Concurrent Pos:* Ruding postdoctoral res fel, Columbia Univ, 90-91; J William Fulbright scholar, Univ Iceland, 96; vis prof, Univ Tenn, 96. *Mem:* Am Asn Nurse Anesthetists; Am Nurses Asn; Oncol Nursing Soc; Am Pain Soc; Int Asn Study Pain; Asn Nurses AIDS Care; fel Am Acad Nursing; Sigma Xi. *Res:* Ethical and legal aspects of assisted suicide; health care needs and resources for people with AIDS; breast biopsy and cancer detection practices; published 20 articles. *Mailing Add:* Col Nursing Med Univ SC 171 Ashley Ave Charleston SC 29425

BENEDICT, WINFRED GERALD, PLANT PATHOLOGY. *Current Pos:* from assoc prof to prof, 57-84, EMER PROF BIOL, UNIV WINDSOR, 86- *Personal Data:* b Wallaceburg, Ont, Mar 18, 19; m 43; c Ruth, Joan, Anne & Grace. *Educ:* Ont Agr Col, BSA, 49; Univ Toronto, PhD(plant path & mycol), 52; Univ Leeds, MPhil, 71; Univ Windsor, BA, 81. *Prof Exp:* Asst-assoc plant pathologist, Can Dept Agr, 52-57. *Concurrent Pos:* Vis prof, Univ Leeds, 69-70. *Mem:* Am Phytopath Soc; Can Phytopath Soc; fel Linnean Soc London. *Res:* Diseases of forage and field crops; physiology of plant infection; mycology, myxomycetes; effect of light intensity and wavelength on early stages of leaf spot infections. *Mailing Add:* 3276 Bruce Ave Windsor ON N9E 1W7 Can

BENEDICTY, MARIO, GEOMETRY, MATH EDUCATION. *Current Pos:* from assoc prof to prof, Univ Pittsburgh, 57-92, chmn dept, 63-69, actg chmn, 78-79, EMER PROF MATH, UNIV PITTSBURGH, 92- *Personal Data:* b Trieste, Italy, July 16, 22; m 47, Alfonsina Mucciante; c Gustavo & Franca. *Educ:* Univ Rome, MathD, 46, Libera Docenza, 52. *Prof Exp:* Asst prof analytical geom, Univ Rome, 48-51, assoc prof algebraic geom, 51-58. *Concurrent Pos:* Co-worker math, Dizionario Enciclopedico dell Enciclopedia Italiana, 54-56, ed, 56-57, contribr, 60; vis prof, Univ BC, 60-62 & Colo State Univ, 76. *Mem:* AAAS; Am Math Soc; Math Asn Am; NY Acad Sci. *Res:* Algebraic geometry and related fields; projective geometries; math education; co-authored a book in discrete mathematics. *Mailing Add:* 101 Alma St No 508 Palo Alto CA 94301

BENEDIK, MICHAEL JOSEPH, PROTEIN SECRETION IN BACTERIA. *Current Pos:* asst prof, 89-91, ASSOC PROF, UNIV HOUSTON, 91- *Personal Data:* b Indianapolis, Ind, Jan 29, 55; m 82, Kathryn Kotrla; c Christopher & Jeremy. *Educ:* Univ Chicago, BA, 76; Stanford Univ, PhD(biol), 82. *Prof Exp:* Staff scientist, DWAX Res Inst, 82-84; asst prof, Tex A&M Univ, 85-89. *Concurrent Pos:* Vis scientist, NIH, 93-94. *Mem:* Am Soc Microbiol; AAAS. *Res:* Molecular genetic analysis of protein secretion by bacteria, techniques in molecular biology. *Mailing Add:* Dept Biophysics Univ Houston Houston TX 77204-0001. *Fax:* 713-743-8351; *E-Mail:* benedik@uh.edu

BENEKE, EVERETT SMITH, BOTANY, MICROBIOLOGY. *Current Pos:* From asst prof to prof, Dept Bot & Microbiol, 58-67, prof, 67-88, EMER PROF BOT & MICROBIOL, DEPT MICROBIOL & PUB HEALTH, MICH STATE UNIV, 88- *Personal Data:* b Greensboro, NC, July 6, 18. *Educ:* Miami Univ, AB, 40; Ohio State Univ, MS, 41; Univ Ill, PhD(bot), 48. *Honors & Awards:* Sigma Xi Jr Award, 58; William A Western Award, Mycol Soc Am, 84; Rhods Benham Award, Med Mycol Soc Am, 86; Plaque Award, Int Union Microbiol Soc, 87. *Concurrent Pos:* Tech consult, Pan Am Union, San Paulo, Brazil, 60; WHO fel, Indonesia, 69; chmn, Mycol Sect, Int Union Microbiol Socs, 71-78. *Mem:* Am Soc Microbiol; Med Mycol Soc Am (secy-treas, 76-79, pres, 81); Int Union Microbiol Soc; hon mem Mycol Soc Am (actg secy-treas, 54, secy-treas, 56-59, vpres, 60, pres, 62); fel AAAS. *Res:* Saprolegniales and other related water molds; mycology, medical mycology; industrial mycology. *Mailing Add:* 1208 Georgetown Dr Safety Harbor FL 34695-4429

BENEMANN, JOHN RUDIGER, BIOCHEMISTRY, SOLAR ENERGY. *Current Pos:* CONSULT, 88- *Personal Data:* b Ger, Oct 18, 43; US citizen; m 65; c 2. *Educ:* Univ Calif, Berkeley, BS, 65, PhD(biochem), 70. *Prof Exp:* Res chemist biochem, Univ Calif, San Diego, 70-74; res biochem solar energy, Lawrence Berkeley Lab, Univ Calif, 75-76, assoc res biochem waste water treat, Sanit Eng Res Lab, 76-80; mem staff, Ecoenergetics Inc, 80-84; assoc prof, Ga Inst Technol, 84-88. *Concurrent Pos:* Consult, Off Technol Assessment, US Congress, 78-, State Water Resources Control Bd, Calif, 78-, Off Appropriate Technol, Calif, 78-, Nat Bur Stand, 80-88, Dupont Co, 3MG, Kimberly Clark, US Dept Energy. *Mem:* AAAS; Am Soc Microbiol; Sigma Xi; World Agr Soc. *Res:* Biological solar energy; nitrogen fixation; microalgae mass culture; blue green algae; aquatic plants; waste water aquaculture; toxicology; biofuels; biophotolysis. *Mailing Add:* 343 Carravelle Dr Walnut Creek CA 94598-7932

BENENATI, R(OBERT) F(RANCIS), NUCLEAR ENGINEERING, COMPUTER SCIENCE. *Current Pos:* RETIRED. *Personal Data:* b Brooklyn, NY, Jan 28, 21; m 44; c 5. *Educ:* Polytech Inst Brooklyn, BChE, 42, MChE, 47, DChE, 59. *Prof Exp:* Head, Operating Dept, Kellex Corp, 44-46; design engr, Hydrocarbon Res Co, 46-49; from instr to prof chem eng, Polytech Inst Brooklyn, 49-91, dir, Comput Ctr, 65-70, head, Chem Eng Dept, 72-74 & 83-85, head, Nuclear Eng Dept, 83-85. *Concurrent Pos:* Consult, H K Ferguson Co, 51-52, Walter Kidde Nuclear Labs, 52-54, Sanderson & Porter, 54-67 & Brookhaven Nat Labs, 71- *Mem:* Am Chem Soc; Am Nuclear Soc; Am Inst Chem Engrs; Sigma Xi. *Res:* Nuclear engineering; nuclear reactor design; heat transfer operations; mass transfer operations; water desalination; computer simulation systems. *Mailing Add:* 75 Deepdale Dr Manhasset NY 11030

BENENSON, ABRAM SALMON, MEDICAL RESEARCH, MICROBIOLOGY. *Current Pos:* prof & head div, 82-92, EMER PROF EPIDEMIOL & BIOSTATIST RES, GRAD SCH PUB HEALTH, SAN DIEGO STATE UNIV, 92- *Personal Data:* b Napanoch, NY, Jan 22, 14; m 39, Regina Van Aalten; c Michael W, Tom, James & Sonia. *Educ:* Cornell Univ, AB, 33, MD, 37; Am Bd Path, Am Bd Prev Med & Am Bd Med Microbiol, dipl. *Honors & Awards:* First Award, Army Sci Conf, 57; Award for Excellence, Am Pub Health Asn, 91, John Snow Award, 92. *Prof Exp:* Rotating intern, Queens Gen Hosp, New York, 37-39; pschiatric intern, Bellevue Hosp, 39; asst & chief lab serv, Tripler Gen Hosp, Honolulu, 41-42; asst virus lab, Army Med Dept Res & Grad Sch, US Dept Army, Washington, DC, 46-47, instr path & bact, Med Sch Tufts Col, 47-49, prof mil sci & tactic, 47-49, dir, Second Army Area Med Lab, Ft George G Meade, Md, 49-52, dir, Trop Res Med Lab, San Juan, PR, 52-54, dir exp med, Camp Detrick, Md, 54-55, dir div immunol, Walter Reed Army Inst Res, 56-60, dir div commun dis & immunol, 60-62; dir, Pakistan-SEATO Cholera Res Lab, 62-66; prof prev med & microbiol, Jefferson Med Col, 66-69; prof community med & chmn dept, Col Med, Univ Ky, 69-77; dir, Gorgas Mem Lab, 77-81. *Concurrent Pos:* From assoc mem to mem comn immunization, Armed Forces Epidemiol Bd, 56-72, dir, 67-72, mem, 77-83, 85-93, dir, Subcomt Dis Control, 77-93; mem study group on typhoid vaccines, WHO & expert comt on cholera, 62-73, mem expert adv panel comt bact dis, 73-84, consult, Expert Comt Biol Stand, 58 & Expert Comt on Smallpox, 64, 67; mem bd sci counsr, Div Biol Stand, NIH, 67-71, chmn, 69-71, mem cholera adv comt, 68-72; ed, Control Commun Dis of Man, Am Pub Health Asn, 70, 75, 80, 85, 90 & 95; mem, Cholera Panel, US-Japan Coop Sci Prog, 73-77; res fel, Sch Microbiol, Univ Melbourne, 76-77; adj prof, Dept Prev & Community Med, Univ Calif, San Diego, 82- *Mem:* AAAS; Am Pub Health Asn; Am Epidemiol Soc (secy-treas, 73-77); Am Asn Immunol; Am Soc Trop Med & Hyg; Infectious Dis Soc Am. *Res:* Immunology; virology; epidemiology; clinical pathology; infectious diseases; diseases of the tropics. *Mailing Add:* Grad Sch Pub Health San Diego State Univ San Diego CA 92182. *Fax:* 619-594-6112

BENENSON, DAVID MAURICE, PLASMA PHYSICS, PLASMA CHEMISTRY. *Current Pos:* assoc prof, State Univ NY, 63-67, dir, Lab Power & Environ Studies, 77-78, assoc chmn, Dept Elec & Comput Eng, 78-83, chmn, 83-89, PROF, PLASMA & GAS DYNAMICS, STATE UNIV NY, BUFFALO, 67- *Personal Data:* b Brooklyn, NY, Jan 22, 27; m 55, Lydia K Chapman; c Kathleen & Patricia. *Educ:* Mass Inst Technol, BS, 50; Calif Inst Technol, MS, 53, PhD(aeronaut), 57. *Prof Exp:* Proj engr, Calif Inst Technol, 50-53; res engr, Res Labs, Westinghouse Elec Corp, 57-63. *Concurrent Pos:* Instr, Carnegie Inst Technol, 58-62; investr, NSF, 64-85; consult, Gen Elec Co, 74-86. *Mem:* Inst Elec & Electronics Engrs. *Res:* Plasma and gas dynamics; turbomachinery; boundary layer analysis; flow problem; heat transfer; aerodynamic noise; energy conversion; power distribution; plasma processing; plasma chemistry; materials processing. *Mailing Add:* 53 Andover Lane Williamsville NY 14221. *Fax:* 716-645-5964

BENENSON, RAYMOND ELLIOTT, PARTICLE-SOLID INTERACTIONS, PHYSICS EDUCATION. *Current Pos:* assoc prof, 67-70, PROF PHYSICS, STATE UNIV NY, ALBANY, 70- *Personal Data:* b New York, NY, Dec 12, 25; m 56; c 3. *Educ:* Mass Inst Technol, BS, 46; Univ Chicago, MS, 49; Univ Wis, PhD(physics), 55. *Prof Exp:* Assoc physicist, Brookhaven Nat Lab, 54-56; physicist, Wright Air Develop Ctr, Brookhaven, 56; instr physics, City Col New York, 56-60, from asst prof to assoc prof, 60-67. *Concurrent Pos:* Res assoc, Pegram Lab, Columbia Univ, 56-; co-worker, Phys Inst Basel, 62-63; resident visitor, Bell Labs, Murray Hill, NJ, 78-79; collabr, Chem Eng, Grenoble, France, 85-86; guest scientist, Nat Inst Stand & Technol, 92-93. *Mem:* Am Phys Soc; Am Asn Physics Teachers; Mat Res Soc. *Res:* Fast neutron and gamma ray spectroscopy in conjunction with Van de Graaff accelerators; hydrogen profiling in solids, nuclear reaction and back scattering analysis; channeling; teaching experiments. *Mailing Add:* State Univ NY Dept Physics 1400 Washington Ave Albany NY 12222

BENENSON, WALTER, NUCLEAR PHYSICS. *Current Pos:* from asst prof to prof physics, 63-97, assoc dir, Nat Superconducting Cyclotron Lab, 80-82 & 89-95, PROF NUCLEAR PHYSICS, MICH STATE UNIV, 72-, UNIV DISTINGUISHED PROF, 97- *Personal Data:* b New York, NY, Apr 27, 36; m 69, Autje Semmsrott; c Arleigh & Tanya. *Educ:* Yale Univ, BS, 57; Univ Wis, MS, 59, PhD(physics), 62. *Honors & Awards:* A V Humboldt Sr Scientist Award, 89. *Prof Exp:* Res assoc nuclear physics, Nuclear Res Inst, Strasbourg, 62-63. *Concurrent Pos:* Vis fel, Australian Nat Univ, 68; vis prof, Univ Grenoble, 70; Nat Acad Sci fel, Poland & Czech, 74; mem, Int Union Pure & Appl Physics on Atomic Masses & Fundamental Constants, 76-; vis consult, Lawrence Berkeley Lab, 78-79. *Mem:* Fel Am Phys Soc. *Res:* Nuclear temperature measurements; heavy ion gamma production; mass measurements of nuclei far from stability; direct nuclear reactions; heavy ion pion production; radioactive beams. *Mailing Add:* Cyclotron Lab Mich State Univ East Lansing MI 48824. *E-Mail:* benenson@nscl.msu.edu

BENEPAL, PARSHOTAM S, PLANT GENETICS, PLANT PHYSIOLOGY. *Current Pos:* PROF LIFE SCI & CHMN DEPT, VA STATE COL, 67- *Personal Data:* b Bhagomajra-Punjab, India, Feb 25, 33; m 54; c 3. *Educ:* Punjab, India, BS, 53, MS, 58; Kans State Univ, PhD(plant genetics, hort), 67. *Prof Exp:* Res asst, Regional Res Lab, USDA, Kans State Univ, 62-65. *Concurrent Pos:* USDA Agr Res Serv grant, 68-75. *Mem:* AAAS; Am Genetic Asn; fel Royal Hort Soc. *Res:* Plant sciences; genetics and biochemistry of insect and disease resistance; breeding for quality and agronomic and physiological research on crop plants. *Mailing Add:* 4708 Ridgecrest Lane Colonial Heights VA 23834

BENERITO, RUTH ROGAN, PHYSICAL CHEMISTRY. *Current Pos:* RETIRED. *Personal Data:* b New Orleans, La, Jan 12, 16; m 50, Frank Henshaw. *Educ:* Sophie Newcomb Mem Col, BS, 35; Tulane Univ, MS, 38; Univ Chicago, PhD(chem), 48. *Hon Degrees:* DSc, Tulane Univ, 81. *Honors & Awards:* Fed Woman Award, 68, Southern Chemist Award, 68; Garvan Medalist, 70; Southwest Regional Award, Am Chem Soc, 72. *Prof Exp:* Instr chem, Randolph-Macon Women's Col, 40-43; asst prof, Tulane Univ, 43-53; phys chemist, Southern Regional Res Ctr, USDA, 53-58, head colloidal chem invest, Cotton Chem Lab, 58-61, head Phys Chem Group, Natural Polymers Lab, 61-86. *Concurrent Pos:* Adj prof, Med Sch & Grad Sch, Tulane Univ, 53-86, Univ New Orleans, 81-96. *Mem:* AAAS; Am Chem Soc; Sigma Xi; fel Am Inst Chemists; Am Asn Textile Chem Colorists. *Res:* Thermodynamics of electrolytic solutions; kinetics and reaction mechanisms; cellulose reactions; surface phenomena; equilibrium; x-ray diffraction. *Mailing Add:* 4733 Marigny St New Orleans LA 70122

BENES, ELINOR SIMSON, MICROSCOPIC ANATOMY, HERPETOLOGY. *Current Pos:* RETIRED. *Personal Data:* b Yreka, Calif, Oct 5, 24; m 45, 76, Norman S; c Gregory, Heather, Michelle & Francine. *Educ:* San Jose State Col, AB, 45; Ariz State Univ, MS, 60; Univ Calif, Davis, PhD(zool), 66. *Prof Exp:* NIH fel, Univ Calif, Davis, 66-67; from instr to prof biol sci, Calif State Univ, Sacramento, 67-89. *Concurrent Pos:* Res assoc, Dept Herpet, Calif Acad Sci & Nat Hist Dept, Nev State Mus. *Mem:* Soc Study Amphibians & Reptiles; Am Soc Ichthyol & Herpet; Orgn Trop Studies. *Res:* Behavioral response to color; microanatomy; growth and natural history of lizards. *Mailing Add:* 2617 Michael Dr Carson City NV 89703-1513

BENES, VACLAV EDVARD, MATHEMATICS. *Current Pos:* STAFF MEM, NJ INST TECHNOL, 75- *Personal Data:* b Brussels, Belgium, July 24, 30; nat US; m 51; c 2. *Educ:* Harvard Univ, BA, 50; Princeton Univ, PhD(logic), 53. *Prof Exp:* Instr logic & philos, Princeton Univ, 52-53; mem tech staff, Bell Tel Labs, Inc, 53-75. *Mem:* Am Math Soc; Math Asn Am; Soc Indust & Appl Math; Inst Math Statist. *Res:* Probability; stochastic processes; logic; set theory; linear systems; circuit theory; functional equations; information theory; theory of queues and congestion. *Mailing Add:* 26 Taylor St Millburn NJ 07041

BENESCH, JAY F, APPLIED SUPERCONDUCTIVITY, FREE ELECTRON LASER COMPONENT DESIGN. *Current Pos:* SR STAFF SCIENTIST, CONTINUOUS ELECTRON BEAM ACCELERATOR FACIL, 91- *Personal Data:* b New York, NY, Mar 22, 52. *Educ:* Mass Inst Tech, SB, 73; Yale, MS, 75; Univ Tex, Austin, PhD(physics), 81. *Prof Exp:* Res assoc III, Fusion Res Ctr, Univ Tex, Austin, 81-83; systs integration mgr, Gen Elec Magnet Systs, 83-87, staff scientist, Gen Elec Corp Res & Develop, 88-89; mgr, SSC Magnet Prog, US Dept Energy, 89-91. *Mem:* Am Phys Soc; AAAS; Am Vacuum Soc; Am Statist Asn. *Res:* Design, build and debug machines for others to do research on or provide medical diagnostics with; applied plasma physics; applied superconductivity. *Mailing Add:* PO Box 2755 Newport News VA 23609-0755. *E-Mail:* benesch@cebaf.gov

BENESCH, RUTH ERICA, BIOCHEMISTRY. *Current Pos:* res assoc, 60-64, from asst prof to assoc prof, 64-80, PROF BIOCHEM, COL PHYSICIANS & SURGEONS, COLUMBIA UNIV, 80- *Personal Data:* b Paris, France, Feb 25, 25; US citizen; m 46; c 2. *Educ:* Univ London, BS, 46; Northwestern Univ, PhD(biochem), 51. *Prof Exp:* Demonstr chem, Univ Reading, 46-47; res assoc biochem, Johns Hopkins Univ, 47-48; fel, State Univ Iowa, 52; fel, Enzyme Inst, Univ Wis, 55; independent investr, Marine Biol Lab, Woods Hole, 56-60. *Mem:* Am Chem Soc; Am Soc Biol Chemists; Biophys Soc; Am Soc Hemat. *Res:* Physical biochemistry; protein chemistry; enzymology; structure-function relationships in hemoglobin; sickle cell anemia; hematology. *Mailing Add:* Dept Biochem & Molecular Biophys Col Physicians & Surgeons Columbia Univ 630 W 168th St New York NY 10032-3702

BENESCH, SAMUEL ELI, SYSTEMS THEORY. *Current Pos:* RETIRED. *Personal Data:* b Baltimore, Md, Aug 19, 24; m 54; c 2. *Educ:* Johns Hopkins Univ, BA, 50; Univ Ill, MA, 51, PhD(math), 53. *Prof Exp:* Res supvr exterior ballistics, Calif Inst Technol, 53-62; staff lab dept mgr space systs, TRW Systs Group, 62-70; exec dir psychol, Los Angeles Ctr Group Psychother, 70-71; dir training crisis intervention, Childrens Hosp, Los Angeles, 71-72; staff scientist defense systs, TRW Systs Group, Redondo Beach, 72-76, dept mgr, 77-92. *Mem:* AAAS; Am Math Soc; Am Soc Psychical Res; Sigma Xi. *Res:* Systems models of consciousness. *Mailing Add:* 5155 1/2 Village Green Los Angeles CA 90016

BENESCH, WILLIAM MILTON, MOLECULAR PHYSICS, MOLECULAR SPECTROSCOPY. *Current Pos:* from assoc prof to prof, 62-92, EMER PROF PHYSICS, UNIV MD, COLLEGE PARK, 92- *Personal Data:* b Baltimore, Md, Apr 22, 22; m 46, Joan Sagner; c Amy, Sarah & Jane. *Educ:* Lehigh Univ, BA, 42; Johns Hopkins Univ, MA, 49, PhD(physics), 52. *Prof Exp:* Jr instr physics, Johns Hopkins Univ, 42-44; Comn Relief Belg fel, Univ Liege, 52-53; asst prof, Univ Pittsburgh, 53-60; res fel, Weizmann Inst Sci, 60. *Concurrent Pos:* Dir inst molecular physics, Univ Md, College Park, 73-76; consult, Argonne Nat Lab, 74-77; fel, Dept Physics, Johns Hopkins Univ, 77-; assoc ed, J Optical Soc Am, 77-84. *Mem:* Fel Am Phys Soc; fel Optical Soc Am; Soc Appl Spectros; Sigma Xi. *Res:* Infrared spectroscopy; solar and atmospheric spectroscopy; molecular interactions; atomic and molecular structure; recent publications have been on the spectrum of the aurora borealis and the underlying atomic and molecular processes which give rise to its excitation and development. *Mailing Add:* Inst Molecular Physics Univ Md College Park MD 20742. *E-Mail:* wb@umd5.umd.edu

BENET, LESLIE Z, PHARMACOKINETICS. *Current Pos:* from asst prof to assoc prof, 69-76, vchmn dept, 73-78, dir, Drug Studies Unit, Drug Kinetics & Dynamics Ctr, 78-96, PROF BIOPHARMACEUT SCI & PHARMACEUT CHEM SCH PHARM, UNIV CALIF, SAN FRANCISCO, 76-, CHMN, DEPT PHARM, 78-, CHMN, DEPT BIOPHARM SCI, 96. *Personal Data:* b Cincinnati, Ohio, May 17, 37; m 60, Carol Ann Levin; c Reed M & Gillian V. *Educ:* Univ Mich, AB, 59, BS, 60, MS, 62; Univ Calif, PhD(pharmaceut chem), 65. *Hon Degrees:* PharmD, Uppsala Univ, Sweden, 87; PhD, Leiden Univ, Neth, 95, Univ Ill, 97. *Honors & Awards:* Res Achievement Award Pharmaceut, Acad Pharmaceut Sci, 82; Pfizer Lectr, La State Univ Med Ctr, 85; Edward R Garrett Lectr, Univ Fla, 87; Varro E Tyler Distinguished Lectr, Purdue Univ, 88; Distinguished Serv Award, Am Col Clin Pharmacol, 88; Volwiler Distinguished Res Achievement Award, Am Asn Cols Pharm, 91; Rawls-Palmer Award & Lectureship, Am Soc Clin Pharmacol & Therapeut, 95. *Prof Exp:* Asst prof pharm, Wash State Univ, 65-69. *Concurrent Pos:* Assoc ed, J Pharmacokinetics & Biopharmaceut, 72-75, ed, 76-; chmn, Pharmacol Study Sect, NIH, 79-81; mem bd dirs, Am Found Pharmaceut Educ, 87-; mem sci adv bd, Smithkline Beecham Pharmaceut, 89-92; mem, Generic Drugs Adv Comt, Food & Drug Admin, 90-94; bd dirs, Am Asn Pharmaceut Scientists, 88-93 & Medication Mgt Techs Inc; bd pharm Sci, Int Pharm Fedn, 88, chair, 96-; chmn bd, AvMax Inc, 94-; chmn, AAAS, 96. *Mem:* Inst Med-Nat Acad Sci; fel Acad Pharmaceut Res & Sci; fel AAAS; fel Am Asn Pharmaceut Scientists (pres, 86, treas, 87); Am Asn Cols Pharm; Am Asn Univ Professors; Am Col Clin Pharmacol; Am Pharmaceut Asn; Am Soc Clin Pharmacol & Therapeut; Am Soc Pharmacol & Exp Therapeut; Sigma Xi. *Res:* Development of the correlation of pharmacokinetics and pharmacodynamics for drugs in various patient populations with specific study areas of immunosuppressive agents; nitroglycerin and its dinatrate metabolites; nonsteroidal anti-inflammatory agents and anti-hypertensive agents. *Mailing Add:* 53 Beach Rd Belvedere CA 94920-2364. *Fax:* 415-476-8887; *E-Mail:* benet@itsa.ucsf.edu

BENEVENGA, NORLIN JAY, BIOCHEMISTRY, NUTRITION. *Current Pos:* proj assoc, 65-66, from asst prof to assoc prof, 66-74, PROF MEAT & ANIMAL SCI & NUTRIT SCI, UNIV WIS-MADISON, 74- *Personal Data:* b San Francisco, Calif, Feb 16, 34; m 56; c 3. *Educ:* Univ Calif, Davis, BS, 59, EE & MS, 60, PhD(nutrit), 65. *Prof Exp:* Res assoc amino acid metab, Mass Inst Technol, 65. *Concurrent Pos:* Mem, Nat Res Coun Sub-Comt Lab Animal Nutrit, 74. *Mem:* AAAS; Am Nutrit Soc; Am Inst Nutrit; Am Soc Animal Sci; Brit Biochem Soc. *Res:* Nutritional and metabolic effects of amino acid excesses and imbalances and digestion and metabolism of lactose. *Mailing Add:* Dept Meat & Animal Sci Univ Wis 1675 Observatory Dr Madison WI 53706-1284

BENEVENTO, LOUIS ANTHONY, NEUROPHYSIOLOGY, NEUROANATOMY. *Current Pos:* PROF & HEAD ANAT, UNIV MD, 89- *Personal Data:* b Waterbury, Conn, Nov 17, 40. *Educ:* Rensselaer Polytech Inst, BS, 62, MS, 64; Univ Md, PhD(physiol), 68; Brown Univ, MD, 70. *Prof Exp:* Nat Inst Neurol Dis & Stroke res fel neurosci, Brown Univ, 68-70; spec fel neurophysiol, Max Planck Inst Psychiat, Ger, 70-71; asst prof physiol, Sch Med, Univ Va, 71-72; from assoc prof to prof anat & ophthal, Col Med, Univ Ill Med Ctr, 76-89. *Concurrent Pos:* Vis scientist, John Curtin Sch Med, Australia, 75-76; vis prof, Johns Hopkins Univ Sch Med, 87- *Mem:* AAAS; NY Acad Sci; Am Asn Univ Prof; Am Acad Arts & Sci; Am Anat Asn; Soc Neurosci. *Res:* Anatomical and physiological correlates of the non-primary visual pathways-visuomotor, multimodal and associational systems. *Mailing Add:* Anat Dept Univ Md Sch Dent 666 W Baltimore St Baltimore MD 21201

BENFEY, BRUNO GEORG, PHARMACOLOGY, THERAPEUTICS. *Current Pos:* lectr, 52-54, asst prof, 54-60, assoc prof pharmacol, 60-75, PROF PHARMACOL & THERAPEUT, MCGILL UNIV, 75- *Personal Data:* b Dusseldorf, Ger, Oct 9, 17; m 49; c 3. *Educ:* Univ Hamburg, Md, 48; Univ Gottingen, dipl chem, 50. *Prof Exp:* Asst org chem, Univ Gottingen, 48-50; asst, Second Clin Internal Med, Univ Hamburg, 50-51; sci asst, Inst Physiol Chem, Univ Gottingen, 51; USPHS fel physiol chem, Yale Univ, 51-52. *Mem:* Am Soc Pharmacol & Exp Therapeut; Pharmacol Soc Can; Can Physiol Soc. *Res:* Molecular weight of heparin; isolation of pikromycin from actinomycetes; enzymatic studies with amino acids and peptides; chemistry of pituitary hormones; pharmacology and biochemistry of sympathomimetic and adrenergic blocking agents. *Mailing Add:* Dept Pharmacol & Therapeut McGill Univ Montreal PQ H3G 1Y6 Can

BENFEY, OTTO THEODOR, ORGANIC CHEMISTRY, HISTORY & PHILOSOPHY OF SCIENCE. *Current Pos:* Dana prof, 73-88, EMER PROF CHEM & HIST SCI, GUILFORD COL, 89-; ED, CHEM HERITAGE, CHEM HERITAGE FOUND, 89- *Personal Data:* b Berlin, Ger, Oct 31, 25; nat US; m 49, Rachel Thomas; c Stephen A, Philip N & Christopher E. *Educ:* Univ London, BSc, 45, PhD(org chem), 47. *Prof Exp:* From asst prof to assoc prof chem, Haverford Col, 48-56; from assoc prof to prof, Earlham Col, 56-73. *Concurrent Pos:* Res fel, Columbia Univ, 47-48 & Harvard Univ, 55-56; lectr, Univ Dublin, 61, Univ Sao Paulo, 63 & Univ Santiago, Chile, 66; ed chem, Am Chem Soc, 63-78, chmn, Div Hist Chem, 66; mem, Adv Coun Col Chem, 65-68; Danforth Found E Harris Harbison fel, 67-68; Fulbright-Hays res & study award, Kwansei-Gakuin Univ, Japan, 70-71; vis prof, Int Christian Univ Tokyo, Japan, 85-86; ed, Chem Hertiage, 89-96, ed at large, Chem Heritage Found, 96; adj prof, Dept Hist & Sociol Sci, Univ Pa, 90-96; sr res fel, Edelstein Ctr Hist & Sci, Hebrew Univ, Jerusalem, 91. *Mem:* Am Chem Soc; Hist Sci Soc; Sigma Xi; Soc Social Responsibility Sci (pres, 51-53). *Res:* Mechanism of organic reactions; solvent and salt effects in unimolecular solvolysis; history of chemistry; Oriental science; chemical education. *Mailing Add:* 909 Woodbrook Dr Greensboro NC 27410. *E-Mail:* benfeyot@rascal.guilford.edu

BENFIELD, CHARLES W(ILLIAM), ELECTRONICS, NAVIGATION. *Current Pos:* CONSULT, 82- *Personal Data:* b Crossnore, NC, Aug 2, 21; wid. *Educ:* Univ Fla, BEE, 48. *Hon Degrees:* PhD, Fla Res Inst, 72. *Honors & Awards:* Burka Award, Inst Navig, 66. *Prof Exp:* Electronics technician, Flagler Radio Corp & Miami Army Air Field, 45; electronic scientist, US Naval Res Lab, Washington, DC, 48-50; radio engr, Isle of Dreams Broadcasting Corp, Fla, 50-51; electronics engr, Develop Lab, Bendix Pac Div, Calif, 51-52; electronic scientist, USN Underwater Sound Ref Lab, 53-59; sr develop engr, Aeronaut Div, Honeywell, Inc, St Petersburg, 59-65, staff engr advan planning, 65-66; sr engr marine systs anal, RCA Missile Test Proj, 66-74; staff engr, Electronics Br, Tech & Logistics Serv Div, US Army Aeromed Res Lab, Ala, 74-76, chief engr, 76-78, chief engr, Data Systs & Instrumentation Br, Res Systs Div, US Army Aviation Develop Test Activ, Ala, 78-79, chief, Instrumentation Lab, 79-82. *Concurrent Pos:* Prin instr, Orange Co Adult & Vet Inst, Orlando, 56-59; guest lectr, Univ SFla, 61-62 & Long Beach Col Res Unit, 62; lectr, Fla Vis Sci Prog, 63-66; consult, Inventrex Corp & Stratum Corp, 80-, Nicoa Corp, Neo-Dyne Res Corp & Aim Mfg Co, 82-; pres, Kosmon Publ Inc, 85- *Mem:* Am Inst Navig; sr mem Inst Elec & Electronics Engrs; assoc fel Am Inst Aeronaut & Astronaut. *Res:* Astronautics; gravity; parapsychology; oceanography; geodetic survey of undersea transponders; biomedical instrumentation; data acquisition systems; development of systems and procedures for precision location of target areas in deep ocean; granted 2 patents. *Mailing Add:* Kosmon Publ Inc PO Drawer 4670 Hualapai AZ 86412-4670

BENFIELD, ERNEST FREDERICK, STREAM ECOLOGY. *Current Pos:* res assoc, 70-71, from asst prof to assoc prof, 71-83, PROF, VA POLYTECH INST & STATE UNIV, 83- *Personal Data:* b Bangor, Maine, Feb 1, 42; m 63; c 3. *Educ:* Appalachian State Univ, BS, 64, MA, 65; Va Polytech Inst & State Univ, PhD(zool), 71. *Prof Exp:* Instr biol, Gordon Mil Col, 65-67. *Concurrent Pos:* Am Elec Power Serv Corp grant, 70-77; FMC Corp grant, 73-76; USERDA grants, 74-77; USDA Forest Serv grant, 76-81; Va Comn Game Inland Fisheries grant, 77-80; Va State Water Control Bd, 78-80; consult, Merck & Co, E I du Pont de Nemours & Co, Inc, Tenn Valley Authority, US Army Corps Engrs, 70-78; NSF grants, 79-88 & 91-; US Environ Protection Agency grant, 80-82 & 89-91; assoc ed, Am Midland Naturalist, 82-85, J NAm Benthological Soc, 85-88, 93-96; interim managing ed, J NAm Benthological Soc, 89-91, pres 94-95. *Mem:* Ecol Soc Am; NAm Benthological Soc; Sigma Xi; Int Soc Theoret & Appl Limnol. *Res:* Organic matter dynamics in streams; ecology of aquatic macroinvertebrates; pollution ecology of lakes and streams. *Mailing Add:* Dept Biol Va Polytech Inst & State Univ Blacksburg VA 24061. *E-Mail:* benfield@ut.edu

BENFIELD, JOHN R, THORACIC SURGERY, SURGICAL ONCOLOGY. *Current Pos:* PROF & CHIEF CARDIOTHORACIC SURG, UNIV CALIF, DAVIS, 88- *Personal Data:* b Vienna, Austria, June 24, 31; US citizen; m 63; c 3. *Educ:* Columbia Univ, AB, 52; Univ Chicago, MD, 55; Am Bd Surg, dipl, 63; Am Bd Thoracic Surg, dipl, 65. *Prof Exp:* Instr surg, Sch Med, Univ Chicago, 61-64; asst prof, Univ Wis, 64-67; assoc prof surg, Sch Med, Univ Calif-Harbor Gen Hosp, 67-71; prof surg, Univ Calif, Los Angeles, 72-76; Jame Utley prof & chmn surg, Univ Hosp, Boston, 77; chmn surg, City of Hope Med Ctr, 78-87. *Concurrent Pos:* Consult, US Naval Hosp, San Diego & US Naval Hosp, Camp Pendelton, Calif; dir, Am Bd Thoracic Surg; gov, Am Col Surgeons. *Mem:* Am Surg Asn; fel Am Col Surg; Soc Univ Surg; Am Asn Thoracic Surg; Soc Thoracic Surgeons. *Res:* Lung cancer; lung transplantation; carcinogenesis. *Mailing Add:* 2010 Maple Glen Rd Sacramento CA 95864

BENFORADO, JOSEPH MARK, CLINICAL PHARMACOLOGY. *Current Pos:* EMER PROF MED, SCH MED, UNIV WIS-MADISON, 67- *Personal Data:* b New York, NY, June 20, 21; m 48; c 6. *Educ:* City Col New York, BS, 41; Columbia Univ, MA, 42; State Univ NY, MD, 51. *Prof Exp:* Intern, Boston City Hosp, 51-52; res fel pharmacol, Harvard Med Sch, 52-53, instr, 53-57, assoc, 57-58; Life Ins med res fel, Oxford Univ, 57-58; assoc prof pharmacol, Sch Med, State Univ NY Buffalo, 58-67. *Mem:* Am Soc Pharmacol; Sigma Xi. *Res:* Clinical medicine; drug abuse. *Mailing Add:* 4034 Mandan Circle Madison WI 53711-3005

BENFORD, ARTHUR E, plastics chemistry & engineering; deceased, see previous edition for last biography

BENFORD, GREGORY A, PLASMA PHYSICS, ASTROPHYSICS. *Current Pos:* PROF PHYSICS, UNIV CALIF, IRVINE, 71- *Personal Data:* b Mobile, Ala, Jan 30, 41; m 67, Joan Abbe; c Mark & Alyson. *Educ:* Univ Okla, BS, 63; Univ Calif, San Diego, MS, 65, PhD(physics), 67. *Honors & Awards:* Lord Found Award, 95. *Prof Exp:* Res physicist, Lawrence Radiation Lab, 67-71. *Concurrent Pos:* Woodrow Wilson fel; fel, Cambridge Univ. *Mem:* Am Phys Soc; Royal Astron Soc; Soc Scientific Exploration. *Res:* Extremeley strong plasma turbulence; high energy astrophysics. *Mailing Add:* Dept Phys Univ Calif Irvine CA 92717. *E-Mail:* gbenford@uci.edu

BENFORD, HARRY (BELL), NAVAL ARCHITECTURE, MARINE ENGINEERING. *Current Pos:* from asst prof to prof naval archit & marine eng, 48-82, chmn dept, 67-72, EMER PROF NAVAL ARCHIT & MARINE ENG, UNIV MICH, 82- *Personal Data:* b Schenectady, NY, Aug 7, 17; m 41, Elizabeth Smallman; c Howard L, Frank A & Robert J. *Educ:* Univ Mich, BSE, 40. *Honors & Awards:* Linnard Prize, Soc Naval Architects & Marine Engrs, 63, David W Taylor Medal, 76. *Prof Exp:* Staff supvr, ship repair cost estimator & other positions, Newport News Shipbldg & Dry Dock Co, 40-48. *Concurrent Pos:* Exec dir maritime res adv comt, Nat Acad Sci-Nat Res Coun, 59-60; mem at large maritime res, Nat Res Coun, 64-69. *Mem:* fel Soc Naval Archit & Marine Engrs; fel Royal Inst Naval Archit. *Res:* Preliminary design of ships; shipbuilding cost and weight analysis; engineering economy in ship design and operation. *Mailing Add:* 6 Westbury Ct Ann Arbor MI 48105

BENGELE, HOWARD HENRY, PHARMACOKINETICS, PHARMACOLOGY. *Current Pos:* assoc prof med & physiol, 73-97, SR SCIENTIEST, BOSTON UNIV, 97- *Personal Data:* b Sewickley, Pa, Sept 17, 37. *Educ:* Blackburn Col, Carlinville, Ill, AB, 63; Univ Iowa, PhD(physiol & biophys), 69. *Prof Exp:* Fel physiol, Univ Toronto, 69-71; res assoc, Univ NMex, Albuquerque, 71-73. *Mem:* Am Physiol Soc; Soc Magnetic Resonance Med; NY Acad Sci. *Res:* Pharmacology and pharmacokinetics of new MRI contrast agents and target organ nucleosides. *Mailing Add:* Res & Develop Dept Advan Magnetics Inc 61 Mooney St Cambridge MA 02138-1038

BENGELSDORF, IRVING SWEM, SCIENCE WRITING. *Current Pos:* lectr sci commun & dir, Inst, 71-80, tech writer specialist, 81-88, CONSULT, JET PROPULSION LAB, CALIF INST TECHNOL, 88- *Personal Data:* b Chicago, Ill, Oct 23, 22; m 49, Beverly Knapp; c Ruth (LeGue), Lea (Bengelsdorf) & Judith (Stickel). *Educ:* Univ Ill, BS, 43; Univ Chicago, MS, 48, PhD(chem), 51. *Honors & Awards:* Jean M Kline Mem Award, Am Cancer Soc, 65; James T Grady Award, Am Chem Soc, 67; Westinghouse Writing Award, AAAS, 67, 69; Claude Bernard Sci Jour Award, Nat Soc Med Res, 68. *Prof Exp:* Res fel chem, Calif Inst Technol, 51-52; instr, Univ Calif, Los Angeles, 52-54 & Gen Elec Res Lab, 54-59; group leader org chem res, Texus Res Ctr, 59-60; sr scientist, US Borax Res Corp, 60-63; sci ed, Los Angeles Times, 63-70. *Concurrent Pos:* Sr lectr, Sch Jour, Univ Southern Calif, 66, 68 & Dept Chem, 71, 73, 74; sr lectr, Dept Chem, Univ Calif, Los Angeles, 67, 68, 71; sci columnist & contrib ed, Enterprise Sci Serv, Newspaper Enterprise Asn, 71-74; distinguished vis prof sci, Whittier Col, 74; vis distinguished prof chem, Univ Southern Calif, 77-85; contrib sci columnist, Los Angeles Herald Examr, 78-86; hon fel award, Soc Tech Commun, 79; mem tech staff, Aerospace Corp, 81. *Mem:* AAAS; Am Chem Soc; Chem Soc London; NY Acad Sci; hon fel Soc Tech Commun. *Res:* Explanation of principles and philosophy of science and technology to nonscientists. *Mailing Add:* 3778 Via Las Villas Oceanside CA 92056-7258

BENGSTON, JOEL, TRANSPORT THEORY, SYSTEMS ANALYSIS & TECHNOLOGY ASSESSMENT. *Current Pos:* SR SCIENTIST, SCI APPLN INT CORP, 83- *Personal Data:* b Cleveland, Ohio, Dec 17, 26; m 50; c 4. *Educ:* Trinity Col, Conn, BS, 47; Yale Univ, MS, 49, PhD(physics), 52. *Prof Exp:* Instr physics, Worcester Polytechnic Inst, 47-48; physicist, Oak Ridge Nat Lab, 52-55, Radiation Lab, Univ Calif, 55-58; div mgr, Aerojet Gen Nucleonics, 58-60; mgr physics theory & math, Combustion Eng Nuclear Div, 60-62; res staff mem, Inst Defense Analysis, 62-69 & 73-79, asst to pres, 69-73; sr staff mem, R&D Assocs, Va, 79-83. *Concurrent Pos:* Lectr nuclear eng, Univ Calif, Berkeley, 56-60; consult, Off Dir Defense Res & Eng, 67-72 & 78-79, US Army, 74, SRI Int, 77-80, Ballistic Missile Defense Prog

Off, 79-80 & 82-83, Mitre Corp, 82. *Mem:* Am Phys Soc. *Res:* Technical assessment of foreign research and development activities; analysis of US emerging technologies; analysis of US space and missile systems. *Mailing Add:* MS C-6 SAIC 10260 Campus Pt Dr San Diego CA 92121

BENGTSON, GEORGE WESLEY, FOREST BIOLOGY, FOREST ECOLOGY. *Current Pos:* CONSULT, INT FERTILIZER DEVELOP CTR, 91- *Personal Data:* b Sealy, Tex, Nov 3, 30; m 59; c 3. *Educ:* La State Univ, BS, 52; Duke Univ, MF, 55; Yale Univ, PhD(plant physiol, soils), 61. *Honors & Awards:* John Beale Mem Award, Soc Am Foresters, 91. *Prof Exp:* Res forester physiol, soils, Forest Serv, USDA, 55-65 & Nat Fertilizer Develop Ctr, US Tenn Valley Authority, 65-79; assoc dean, Col Forestry, Ore State Univ, 79-89; dir, Ctr Forested Wetlands Res, Forest Serv, USDA, 89-91. *Mem:* Fel Soc Am Foresters; Soil Sci Soc Am; Int Union Forest Res Orgn. *Res:* Forest tree nutrition with emphasis on fertilizer; utilization of wastes as soil amendments, ecological implications of intensive silviculture; forest wetland ecology. *Mailing Add:* 618 Cary Dr Auburn AL 36830

BENGTSON, HARLAN HOLGER, MUNICIPAL WASTEWATER TREATMENT, FLUID MECHANICS. *Current Pos:* dir, Environ Resources Training Ctr, 84-88, PROF CIVIL ENG, SOUTHERN ILL UNIV, EDWARDSVILLE, 75-, ASST DEAN, SCH ENG, 88- *Personal Data:* b Maquokata, Iowa, Oct 4, 41; m 65, Kathryn E Hotovec; c LaVay, Dyann, Craig & Joseph. *Educ:* Iowa State Univ, BS, 63, MS, 65; Univ Colo, PhD(chem eng), 71. *Prof Exp:* Process develop engr, E I du Pont de Nemours & Co, 63; prod develop engr, Minn Mining & Mfg, 64-65; asst prof eng sci, Rockhurst Col, 71-75. *Concurrent Pos:* Consult, Panhandle Eastern Pipeline Co, 71, Am Steel Foundries, 77 & Geo Environ Serv, 92- *Mem:* Nat Soc Prof Engrs; Am Soc Eng Educ; Water Environ Fedn. *Res:* Energy production from wastes by anaerobic digestion; mathematical modeling of biological wastes treatment. *Mailing Add:* Sch Eng Southern Ill Univ 6 Hairpin Dr Edwardsville IL 62026-0001

BENGTSON, ROGER D, PLASMA PHYSICS, ATOMIC PHYSICS. *Current Pos:* Fac assoc, Univ Tex, 68-70, from asst prof to assoc prof, 70-81, chmn dept, 83-88, PROF PHYSICS, UNIV TEX, AUSTIN, 81- *Personal Data:* b Wausa, Nebr, Apr 29, 41; m 63; c 2. *Educ:* Univ Nebr, BS, 62; Va Polytech Inst, MS, 64; Univ Md, PhD, 68. *Mem:* Am Phys Soc; Sigma Xi. *Res:* Plasma spectroscopy; experimental plasma physics. *Mailing Add:* Dept Physics Univ Tex Austin TX 78712

BENHAM, CRAIG JOHN, PHYSICAL CHEMISTRY, MOLECULAR BIOLOGY. *Current Pos:* PROF BIOMATH SCI, MT SINAI SCH MED, 88- *Personal Data:* b Chicago, Ill, Sept 1, 46; m 75, Marcia Benham; c Allana & Ashley. *Educ:* Swarthmore Col, AB, 68; Princeton Univ, MA, 71, PhD(math), 72. *Prof Exp:* Asst prof math, Univ Notre Dame, 72-76, Lawrence Univ, 77-78, Univ Ky, 78-81; res fel biol, Calif Inst Technol, 76-77; assoc prof math, Univ Ky, 81-88. *Concurrent Pos:* Vis res scientist, NY State Dept Health, 78, Cancer Res Inst, 79; fel, Alfred P Sloan Found, 82. *Mem:* AAAS. *Res:* Theoretical calculations of the equilibria and kinetics of DNA conformations; superhelically stressed molecules, including mechanical equilibria, conformational transitions and superhelical regulation of DNA activities. *Mailing Add:* 24 Mohawk Trail Katonah NY 10536. *Fax:* 212-860-4630; *E-Mail:* benham@msvax.mssm.edu

BENHAM, JUDITH LAUREEN, ADHESIVES RELEASE MATERIALS, POLYMER CHEMISTRY. *Current Pos:* Res specialist, 3M, 81-82, res supvr, 82-83, res mgr, 83-88, lab mgr, Specialty Chem Div, 88-90, tech dir, Indust Tape Div, 90-92, TECH DIR, MASKING & PACKAGING SYSTS DIV, 3M, 92- *Personal Data:* m 89, Richard Pyle; c Blair. *Educ:* Univ Rochester, BA, 69; Univ Wis, Madison, PhD(org chem), 78. *Concurrent Pos:* Bd mem & chmn, Polymer Chem Div, Am Chem Soc, 90. *Mem:* Am Chem Soc; Sigma Xi. *Res:* Production of chemicals; high performance polymers; adhesives; release materials; radiation curable materials and electronically active materials. *Mailing Add:* 9317 Wedgewood Dr Woodbury MN 55125-9303

BENI, GERARDO, THEORETICAL ROBOTICS. *Current Pos:* PROF ELEC ENG, UNIV CALIF, RIVERSIDE, 91- *Personal Data:* b Florence, Italy, Feb 21, 46; US citizen; m, Susan Hackwood; c Catherine & Juliet. *Educ:* Univ Florence, Laurea in physics, 70; Univ Calif, Los Angeles, PhD(physics), 74. *Prof Exp:* Res physicist, Scattering & Low Energy Physics Dept, AT&T Bell Labs, Murray Hill, 74-76, Theoret Physics Dept, 76, mem tech staff, Solid State Physics Res Dept, Holmdel, 77-81, Robotic Systs & Robotic Technol Res Dept, 82-84; prof elec & comput eng, Univ Calif, Santa Barbara, 84-91, dir, Ctr Robotic Systs in Microelectronics, 85-91. *Concurrent Pos:* Mem, Comn Eng & Tech Systs, Mfg Studies Bd, Nat Res Coun; ed & founder, J Robotic Systs, 83- *Mem:* Fel Am Phys Soc; Robot Soc Japan; AAAS. *Res:* Theoretical robotics; swarm intelligence; distributed autonomous robotic systems; intelligent multimedia systems; solid state physics and devices; theories of one dimensional systems. *Mailing Add:* Univ Calif Bourns Hall 3A325 Riverside CA 92521-4009. *E-Mail:* beni@engr.ucr.edu

BENICEWICZ, BRIAN CHESTER, POLYMER CHEMISTRY, ORGANIC CHEMISTRY. *Current Pos:* staff mem, 85-91, sect leader, Polymers Sect, 91-93, DEP GROUP LEADER, POLYMERS & COATING GROUP, LOS ALAMOS NAT LAB, 93- *Personal Data:* b Danbury, Conn, June 1, 54; m 84, Pamela King; c Derek & Leigh A. *Educ:* Fla Inst Technol, BS, 76; Univ Conn, MS, 78, PhD(polymer chem), 80. *Prof Exp:* Res chemist, Celanese Res Co, 80-82; sr scientist, Ethicon, Inc, 82-85. *Mem:* Am Chem Soc; Mat Res Soc; Soc Advan Mat & Plastics Eng. *Res:* Chemistry of high polymers; high temperature polymers; liquid crystal polymers; high performance polymers; piezoelectric and conducting polymers; biomedical polymers; polymer synthesis. *Mailing Add:* PO Box 1663 MS E549 Los Alamos NM 87545. *E-Mail:* benicewicz_bc@lanl.gov

BENIN, DAVID B, CONDENSED MATTER PHYSICS, PHOTOPHYSICS OF ORGANIC MOLECULES. *Current Pos:* asst prof, 70-76, ASSOC PROF PHYSICS, ARIZ STATE UNIV, 76- *Personal Data:* b Chicago, Ill, May 19, 41; m 83; c 1. *Educ:* Cornell Univ, BA, 63; Univ Rochester, MS, 66, PhD(physics), 68. *Prof Exp:* Res assoc physics, Cornell Univ, 67-69 & Univ Ore, 69-70. *Concurrent Pos:* Vis assoc prof, Brown Univ, 76-77. *Mem:* Am Phys Soc. *Res:* Condensed matter physics theory; lattice dynamics and transport properties of phonon systems; theory and transport properties of superfluid helium; photophysical properties of organic molecules. *Mailing Add:* 2101 E Vaughn St Tempe AZ 85283

BENINGER, PETER GERARD, FEEDING & DIGESTION IN MOLLUSCS & CRUSTACEANS, REPRODUCTION IN MOLLUSCS & CRUSTACEANS. *Current Pos:* from asst prof to assoc prof, 82-90, PROF INVERT & MARINE BIOL, UNIV MONCTON, 90- *Personal Data:* b Nicaragua, Oct 31, 53; Can citizen; m 82, Sylvie Argouarch. *Educ:* Univ Western Ont, BA, 75; Dalhousie Univ, BSc(Hon), 77; Univ Western Brittany, DEA, 78, doctorate, 81 & 87, habilitation, 92. *Prof Exp:* Asst prof, Univ Western Brittany, 81-82. *Concurrent Pos:* Assoc researcher, Univ Western Brittany, 89-, prof biol, 92; vis scientist, Dept Fisheries & Oceans, 91-92; hon res assoc, Univ NB, 93- *Mem:* Nat Shellfisheries Asn; Crustacean Soc; Micros Soc Can. *Res:* Feeding and reproductive mechanisms and strategies of molluscs and decapods; digestion physiology. *Mailing Add:* Dept Biol Fac Sci Univ Moncton Moncton NB E1A 3E9 Can. *Fax:* 506-858-4541; *E-Mail:* beningp@bosoleil.ci.umoncton.ca

BENINGER, RICHARD J, BIOLOGICAL PSYCHOLOGY, PSYCHOPHARMACOLOGY. *Current Pos:* from asst prof to assoc prof, 80-88, PROF PSYCHOL & PSYCHIAT, QUEENS UNIV, CAN, 88- *Personal Data:* b Walkerton, Ont, Feb 11, 50; m 89, Lynne Hanson; c Max & Mariah. *Educ:* Univ Western Ont, BA, 73; McGill Univ, MA, 74, PhD(psychol), 77. *Prof Exp:* Fel psychopharmacol, Univ BC, 77-80. *Concurrent Pos:* Career scientist res award, Ministry Health, Ont, 82-92; asst prof psychiat, Queens Univ, 83-95; vis scientist, Dept Pharmacol Pitie Salp trie re, Paris, 87-88. *Mem:* Fel AAAS; Can Col Neuropsychopharmacol; Europ Behav Pharmacol Soc; Soc Neurosci; Am Psychol Soc; Can Soc Brain, Behav & Cognitive Sci. *Res:* Central nervous system transmitter substances in behavior; the role of dopamine in the control of locomotor activity and learning; the role of acetylcholine in memory. *Mailing Add:* Dept Psychol Queens Univ Kingston ON K7L 3N6 Can. *Fax:* 613-545-2499; *E-Mail:* beninger@paulov.psyc.queensu.ca

BENINGTON, FREDERICK, ORGANIC CHEMISTRY, MATHEMATICS. *Current Pos:* assoc prof, 62-71, prof med chem, 71-79, PROF PSYCHIAT, MED CTR, UNIV ALA, 78- *Personal Data:* b Chelsea, Mass; m 40, Helen J Pelham; c Michael & Phyllis. *Educ:* Tufts Univ, BSc, 39. *Hon Degrees:* PhD, Univ Wis, 68. *Prof Exp:* Res chemist, Innis Speiden Co, 39-41 & Niacet Chem Corp, 41-45; physicist, Corning Glass Works, 45-47; res engr, Battelle Mem Inst, 47-49, sr res assoc, 49-52. *Concurrent Pos:* Instr, Niagara Univ, 42-44; consult chemist, 49- *Mem:* Am Chem Soc; Nat Speleological Soc; Sigma Xi; Cave Res Found; Explorer's Club. *Res:* Thermodynamics and kinetics of gas reactions; free radical reactions; organometallic reactions; syntehsis of psychotomimetic compounds; author or co-author of numerous publications. *Mailing Add:* Sch Neurosci Res Prog CDLD Bldg 9th Floor Univ Ala Med Ctr Birmingham AL 35233

BENIOFF, PAUL, QUANTUM COMPUTATION. *Current Pos:* nuclear theoret chemist, 61-78, environ scientist, 78-94, STAFF MEM, PHYSICS DIV, ARGONNE NAT LAB, 95- *Personal Data:* b Pasadena, Calif, May 1, 30; m 59, Hanna Leshner; c Leora, Ron & Ilana. *Educ:* Univ Calif, Berkeley, PhD(chem), 59. *Prof Exp:* Nuclear chemist, Lab Electronics, Tracerlab, Inc, 52-54; Weizmann fel, Weizmann Inst, Israel, 60-61; Ford grant, Inst Theoret Physics, Copenhagen Univ, 61. *Concurrent Pos:* Vis prof, Dept Hist & Philos Sci, Tel Aviv Univ, 80, CNRS, Univ Marseille, Luminy France, 80. *Mem:* AAAS; Am Phys Soc. *Res:* Molecular structure; relationship between foundations of physics and mathematics; quantum mechanical models of computers. *Mailing Add:* Argonne Nat Lab 9700 S Cass Ave Argonne IL 60439. *Fax:* 630-252-6008; *E-Mail:* pbenioff@anl.gov

BENIRSCHKE, KURT, PATHOLOGY. *Current Pos:* PROF REPRODUCTIVE MED & PATH, UNIV CALIF, SAN DIEGO, 70- *Personal Data:* b Gluckstadt, Ger, May 26, 24; nat US; m 52; c 3. *Educ:* Univ Hamburg, MD, 48. *Honors & Awards:* Presidential Medal, NY Acad Sci, 84. *Prof Exp:* Assoc path, Harvard Med Sch, 57-60; prof & chmn dept, Dartmouth Med Sch, 60-70; dir res, San Diego Zoo, 75-86. *Mem:* Col Am Path; Am Asn Path & Bact; Sigma Xi. *Res:* Placental pathology; developmental anomalies and twinning processes; comparative mammalian cytogenetics; cause of sterility in hybrids; pathology of human fetus and placenta; gemellology; mammalian hybrids. *Mailing Add:* Dept Path 8321 Univ Calif Med Ctr 224 Dickinson St San Diego CA 92103-8321

BENISEK, WILLIAM FRANK, BIOCHEMISTRY. *Current Pos:* asst prof, 69-75, ASSOC PROF BIOCHEM, SCH MED, UNIV CALIF, DAVIS, 75- *Personal Data:* b Los Angeles, Calif, Oct 12, 38; m 60; c 2. *Educ:* Calif Inst Technol, BS, 60; Columbia Univ, MA, 61; Univ Calif, Berkeley, PhD(biochem), 66. *Prof Exp:* USPHS fel biophys, Yale Univ, 66-68; biochemist, Sch Med, Stanford Univ, 68-69. *Mem:* Am Soc Biol Chem; Am Chem Soc. *Res:* Protein chemistry; structures and conformations of protein molecules; chemical mechanisms of enzyme-catalyzed reactions. *Mailing Add:* Dept Biol Chem Univ Calif Davis CA 95616-5224

BENISON, BETTY BRYANT, HEALTH EDUCATION. *Current Pos:* PROF BIOMECH & PHYSIOL, TEX CHRISTIAN UNIV, 69- *Personal Data:* b Irvine, Ky, Aug 25, 39; wid; c 1. *Educ:* La State Univ, Baton Rouge, BS, 55; Univ Mich, Ann Arbor, MA, 58; Univ NMex, PhD(health, phys educ), 68; Tex Woman's Univ, MS, 90. *Prof Exp:* Instr phys educ, C E Byrd High Sch, Shreveport, La, 55-56 & Miss State Col Women, 56-57; asst, Univ Mich, Ann Arbor, 57-58; asst prof, Stephen F Austin Univ, 58-59, NTex State Univ, 59-64 & Univ NMex, 64-69. *Concurrent Pos:* Mem, Nat Coun Outdoor Educ, Am Alliance Health, Phys Educ & Recreation, 73-; consult, Col Educ Adv Bd, Am Heart Asn, 74-75 & Adapted & Corrective Ther, Standford Convalescent Ctrs, 74-; grant, Tex Christian Univ, 74-75, Am Heart Asn, 75 & NIH-NASA, SW Med Sch, Dallas, 76; Tex Christian Univ fel, Cooper Aerobics Ctr, Dallas, 75-76; sabbatical mem staff, Aerobics Ctr, Dallas, 76. *Mem:* Am Pub Health Asn; Am Col Sports Med; Int Soc Sports Psychol; Soc Behav Kinesiology; Am Heart Asn; Am Asn Sex Educrs, Counrs & Therapists. *Res:* Proper electrode placement in stress testing; comparative studies of cardiac impairments; development and evaluation of high-level physical fitness programs. *Mailing Add:* Phys Educ Tex Christian Univ 2800 S University Dr Ft Worth TX 76129-0001

BEN-ISRAEL, ADI, OPTIMIZATION, LINEAR ALGEBRA. *Current Pos:* chmn, Opers Res Prog, 76-80, H FLETCHER BROWN PROF MATH, UNIV DEL, 76- *Personal Data:* b Rio de Janeiro, Brazil, Nov 6, 33; m 64; c 2. *Educ:* Israel Inst Technol, BSc, 55, Dipl Ing, 56, MSc, 59; Northwestern Univ, PhD(eng sci), 62. *Prof Exp:* Vis asst prof statist, Carnegie Inst Technol, 62-63; sr lectr math, Israel Inst Technol, 63-65; assoc prof systs eng, Univ Ill, Chicago Circle, 65-66; from assoc prof to prof eng sci, Northwestern Univ, 66-70; prof appl math & chmn dept, Technion-Israel Inst Technol, 70-75; prof, Indust Eng Dept, Northwestern Univ, 75-76. *Mem:* Oper Res Soc Am; Am Math Soc; Soc Indust Appl Math; Math Prog Soc. *Res:* Matrix theory; mathematical programming; operations research; fishery management; natural resource and environmental management; optimal engineering design; numerical analysis. *Mailing Add:* Rutgers Univ RUTCOR PO Box 5062 New Brunswick NJ 08903-5062

BENITEZ, FRANCISCO MANUEL, ORGANIC SYNTHETIC CHEMISTRY, POLYMER CHEMISTRY. *Current Pos:* res chemist, 77-93, LATIN AM INTERMEDIATE MKT MGR, EXXON CHEM CO, 93- *Personal Data:* b Cuba, Apr 12, 50; US citizen; m 77. *Educ:* Wilmington Col, BA, 72; Miami Univ, PhD(chem), 77. *Mem:* Am Chem Soc; Sigma Xi. *Res:* Synthetic and mechanistic aspects of sulfur chemistry; synthetic organic acids; hydrocarbon resins. *Mailing Add:* Exxon Chem Interam Inc PO Box 4693 Houston TX 77210-4693

BENJAMIN, ARLIN JAMES, NUCLEAR WEAPON EFFECTS ON MILITARY SYSTEMS. *Current Pos:* PRIN ENGR, NORTHROP GRUMMAN CORP, 86- *Personal Data:* b Guthrie, Okla, Oct 9, 33; m 64, Patricia A Crabb; c Arlin J, Cynthia D & Deborah D. *Educ:* Sam Houston State Univ, BS, 55; Okla State Univ, MS, 57. *Prof Exp:* Res engr, Boeing Co, 57-63; lead nuclear engr, LTV Corp, 63-64; oper res analyst, Res Triangle Inst, 64-66; sr oper res analyst, Gen Dynamics Corp, 66-68; tech mgr, Control Data Corp, 68-70, BDM Corp, 81-86; sr scientist, Southwest Res Inst, 70-78; prin scientist, Hittman Assocs, Inc, 78-81. *Mem:* Am Geophys Union; Am Nuclear Soc; Am Phys Soc; fel Phys Soc London; Europ Phys Soc; fel Inst Physics; AAAS. *Res:* Determine nuclear radiation suseptibility of electronic circuits and components contained in strategic military systems; peer publication evaluation; electronic circuit analyses; specifying nuclear radiation testing. *Mailing Add:* 5600 Liberty Pkwy Suite 100 Oklahoma City OK 73110-2856. *Fax:* 405-732-8726

BENJAMIN, BEN MONTE, ORGANIC CHEMISTRY, FUEL CHEMISTRY. *Current Pos:* Org chemist, 52-80, GROUP LEADER CHEM & SR SCIENTIST, COAL CONVERSION, OAK RIDGE NAT LAB, 80- *Personal Data:* b St Petersburg, Fla, Feb 16, 23; m 48; c 3. *Educ:* Univ Fla, BS, 48, MS, 49, PhD(org chem), 52. *Mem:* Am Chem Soc. *Res:* Organic reaction mechanisms; isotopic tracer studies; nuclear magnetic resonance; coal chemistry. *Mailing Add:* 848 W Outer Dr Oak Ridge TN 37830

BENJAMIN, CHESTER RAY, MYCOLOGY. *Current Pos:* RETIRED. *Personal Data:* b Alliance, Ohio, Jan 23, 23; m 47, Margaret E Hart; c Karen S (Paris). *Educ:* Mt Union Col, BS, 48; Univ Iowa, MS, 54, PhD(bot), 55. *Honors & Awards:* Plaque Award, Japanese Toxic Micro-Organisms Panel, US-Japan Coop Natural Resources Prog, 69. *Prof Exp:* Chemist res & develop div, Babcock-Wilcox Co, 48-51; asst bot, Univ Iowa, 51-53, asst mycol, 53-55; mycologist cult collection invest, Fermentation Lab, Northern Utilization Res & Develop Div, Agr Res Serv, USDA, 55-60, prin mycologist, cur nat fungus collections & leader mycol invests, Crops Protection Res Br, Plant Sci Res Div, 60-71, liaison officer assigned to Dept of State, Int Progs Div, 71-74, asst dir int progs staff, Sci & Educ Admin, 75-78, actg dir, 79, assoc coordr, Int Orgn Affairs, Off Int Coop & Develop, 80-84. *Concurrent Pos:* Mem, Nat Res Coun, 61-67, hon res assoc, Smithsonian Inst, 61-68; chmn toxic micro-organisms panel, Joint US-Japan Coop Develop Natural Resources Prog, 64-69, collabr, 69-75; mem, US Nat Comt, Int Union Biol Sci, 65-71, secy, 69-71; mem spec comt fungi & lichens, Tenth & 11th Int Bot Cong, 64-72; chmn US deleg, US-Japan Joint Panel Conf Toxic Micro-Organisms, 66-68; alt US deleg, 17th Gen Assembly, Int Union Biol Sci, 70; mem, US deleg to 16th-21st sessions conf & numerous sessions coun, Food & Agr Orgn UN, 71-81, alt US deleg regional conf Latin Am, 72, conf mem, Staff Pension comt, 71-73; US coordr, Joint US-Japan Coop Develop Natural Resources Prog, 76-80. *Mem:* Fel AAAS; Mycol Soc Am (pres, 66-67). *Res:* Classification of the ascomycetes and mucorales; nomenclature of fungi; international agriculture and organization affairs related to agriculture. *Mailing Add:* 315 Timberwood Ave Silver Spring MD 20901

BENJAMIN, DAVID CHARLES, PROTEIN FOLDING, MICROBIOLOGY. *Current Pos:* From asst prof to assoc prof, 71-80, PROF MICROBIOL, SCH MED, UNIV VA, 80- *Personal Data:* b Aug 19, 36. *Educ:* Univ Calif, Los Angeles, BS, 65, PhD(biol), 69. *Concurrent Pos:* Consult, Regulatory Biol Panel & Cell Biol Panel, NSF, 74-77, ad hoc reviewer, 77-, Immunol Sci Study Sect, NIH, 81-85; vis prof, Transplantation Biol Unit, Clin Res Ctr, Harrow, Eng, 77-78, Univ Sydney, Australia, 87-88; assoc provost res, Univ Va, 84-87, dir, Commonwealth Protein & Nucleic Acid Sequencing Ctr, actg dir, Beirne B Carter Ctr Immunol Res, Provosts Acad Adv Comt. *Mem:* Sigma Xi. *Res:* Cellular immunology; protein folding; structural immunology; numerous technical publications. *Mailing Add:* Beirne Carter Ctr Immunol Res Health Sci Ctr Univ Va MR4 Box 4012 Charlottesville VA 22908-0001

BENJAMIN, DAVID MARSHALL, CLINICAL PHARMACOLOGY. *Current Pos:* CONSULT, CLIN PHARMACOL & TOXICOL, 86- *Personal Data:* b Boston, Mass, July 16, 46. *Educ:* Boston Univ, AB, 68; Univ Vt, MS, 70, PhD(pharmacol), 73. *Prof Exp:* Asst dir sci affairs, Pfizer Pharmaceut, 73-74; clin res scientist Clin Pharmacol, Hoffman La Roche, 74-86. *Concurrent Pos:* Asst adj prof pharmacol, Col Med, Cornell Univ, 76- *Mem:* Am Soc Clin Pharmacol & Therapeut; Am Col Clin Pharmacol; Acad Pharmaceut Sci; Am Acad Clin Toxicol; Sigma Xi. *Res:* Clinical pharmacology and pharmacokinetics of drugs; correlations between pharmacokinetics and pharmacodynamics of drugs; early development of new drug entities; drug interactions; clinical toxicology. *Mailing Add:* Two Hammond Pond Pkwy Apt 605 Chestnut Hill MA 02167-2121

BENJAMIN, FRED BERTHOLD, PHYSIOLOGY. *Current Pos:* RETIRED. *Personal Data:* b Darmstadt, Ger, Oct 24, 12; nat US. *Educ:* Bonn Univ, DMD, 35; Univ Ill, MS, 49; Loyola Univ, PhD(physiol), 53. *Prof Exp:* Pvt pract dent, Kashmir, India, 36-46; res assoc physiol, Univ Ill, 49-53; asst prof, Univ Pa, 53-60; sr res coordr, Life Sci Lab, Repub Aviation Corp, 60-64; chief eval br, Off Space Med, NASA, 64-66, staff asst, Apollo Med Support, 66-70; sr res physiologist, Res Inst, Nat Hwy Traffic Safety Admin, 70-79. *Concurrent Pos:* Prof lectr, Sch Med, George Washington Univ, 64-66. *Mem:* AAAS; Soc Exp Biol & Med; Am Physiol Soc; Aerospace Med Asn. *Res:* Pain sensation; reaction to heat; effects of alcohol and narcotic drugs. *Mailing Add:* 15300 Beaverbrook Ct Silver Spring MD 20906-1355

BENJAMIN, PHILIP PALAMOOTTIL, NUCLEAR CHEMISTRY, NUCLEAR MEDICINE. *Current Pos:* PROF CHEM, MO BAPTIST COL, 90- *Personal Data:* b Eraviperur, India, Sept 5, 32; m 60, Ivy; c Ivan, Evan, Bevan & Cyril. *Educ:* Univ Madras, BSc, 52; St John's Col, India, MSc, 55; McGill Univ, PhD(radiochem), 65. *Prof Exp:* Lectr chem, Ewing Christian Col, Univ Allahabad, 55-60, asst prof, 65-66; asst prof radiol & radiochem, Case Western Res Univ, 66-75; dir, Medi-Nuclear Inst, 75-89. *Concurrent Pos:* Res grants, Squibb Inst Med Sci, 68-69; Am Cancer Soc res grant, 69-; consult, Squibb Inst Med Res & Abbott Labs. *Mem:* AAAS; Soc Nuclear Med; fel Am Inst Chem; NY Acad Sci; Chem Inst Can. *Res:* Radiochemical investigations of nuclear fission products; distribution of nuclear charge in fission; applications of radiochemistry to nuclear medicine. *Mailing Add:* 1109 Orchard Lakes Dr St Louis MO 63146

BENJAMIN, REGINA M, RURAL HEALTH CARE. *Current Pos:* OWNER & ADMINR, BAYOU LA BATRE RURAL HEALTH CLIN INC, 90- *Personal Data:* b Mobile, Ala, 1956. *Educ:* Xavier Univ, New Orleans, BS, 79; Univ Ala, Birmingham, MD, 84; Tulane Univ, MBA, 92; Am Bd Family Pract, dipl. *Concurrent Pos:* Bd trustees, AMA, 95-; mem, Clin Lab Improvement Act Comt, Dept Health & Human Servs; vpres, Gov's Comn Aging; mem, Gov's Health Care Reform Task Force; clin prof, Univ Ala, Birmingham & Univ SAla. *Mem:* Inst Med-Nat Acad Sci; fel Am Col Family Surgeons. *Mailing Add:* 13823 Shell Belt Rd Bayou La Batre AL 36509-2301

BENJAMIN, RICHARD KEITH, MYCOLOGY. *Current Pos:* from asst prof to assoc prof, 52-62, PROF BOT, CLAREMONT GRAD SCH, 62; MYCOLOGIST, RANCHO SANTA ANA BOT GARDEN, 52- *Personal Data:* b Argenta, Ill, Apr 9, 22; m 46; c 2. *Educ:* Univ Ill, BS, 47, MS, 49, PhD(bot), 51. *Prof Exp:* Nat Res Coun fel bot, Harvard Univ, 51-52. *Concurrent Pos:* Ed-in-chief, Mycol Soc Am, 71-75, Aliso, 58- *Mem:* Bot Soc Am; Mycol Soc Am (secy-treas, 60-62, vpres, 63, pres, 65); Brit Mycol Soc. *Res:* Laboulbeniales; Mucorales. *Mailing Add:* 1542 Bates Pl Claremont CA 91711-3107

BENJAMIN, RICHARD WALTER, NUCLEAR PHYSICS, NUCLEAR ENGINEERING. *Current Pos:* mgr advan planning & anal, 88-94, SR ADV SCIENTIST, ACCELERATOR PROD TRITIUM WESTINGHOUSE SAVANNAH RIVER CO, 94- *Personal Data:* b Albany, NY, Dec 8, 35; m 61, Sally Chenault; c Andrew H. *Educ:* Lamar State Col, BS, 58; Southern Methodist Univ, MS, 61; Univ Tex, Austin, PhD(physics), 65. *Prof Exp:* Design engr, Los Alamos Sci Lab, 58-59; res scientist physics, Tex Nuclear Corp, 61-66; res assoc, Swiss Fed Inst Technol, 66-68; staff physicist, Savannah River Lab, E I du Pont, 68-83; tech adv, Off Nuclear Mat Prod, US Dept Energy, 83-84; res supvr, Environ Transp, Savannah River Lab, E I du Pont de Nemours & Co, 84-88. *Concurrent Pos:* Lectr, Paine Col, 69-73. *Mem:* Am Phys Soc; Am Nuclear Soc; AAAS; Swiss Phys Soc; Europ Phys Soc. *Res:* Nuclear fuel cycle studies and planning, radioactive waste management; neutron cross section measurement, evaluation and testing, particularly of the actinide nuclides; environmental transport, aqueous and atmospheric; technical planning; accelerator production of radiosotopes. *Mailing Add:* Westinghouse Savannah River Co Savannah River Site Aiken SC 29808. *Fax:* 803-725-0632; *E-Mail:* richard.benjamin@srs.gov

BENJAMIN, ROBERT FREDRIC, EXPERIMENTAL PHYSICS. *Current Pos:* STAFF PHYSICIST, LOS ALAMOS NAT LAB, 73- *Personal Data:* b Washington, DC, Jan 19, 45; m 68; c 2. *Educ:* Cornell Univ, BS, 67; Mass Inst Technol, PhD(physics), 73. *Concurrent Pos:* Vis scientist, Maxwell Labs, 80, 86. *Mem:* Am Phys Soc. *Res:* Laser-plasma interactions, x-ray and optical diagnostics and short pulse phenomena; high energy density phenomena; fluid instabilities. *Mailing Add:* 315 Rover Blvd Los Alamos NM 87544

BENJAMIN, ROBERT MYLES, NEUROPHYSIOLOGY. *Current Pos:* USPHS fel, Univ Wis-Madison, 54-56, from instr to assoc prof physiol, 56-65, prof neurophysiol & physiol, 65-87, EMER PROF NEUROPHYSIOL & PHYSIOL, SCH MED, UNIV WIS-MADISON, 87- *Personal Data:* b Bronxville, NY, Aug 13, 27; m 60; c 4. *Educ:* St Lawrence Univ, BS, 49; Brown Univ, MS, 51, PhD(psychol), 53. *Concurrent Pos:* Mem neurol study sect, NIH, 67-71. *Mem:* Am Physiol Soc; Am Asn Anatomists; Soc Neurosci. *Res:* Sensory neurophysiology. *Mailing Add:* Dept Neurophysiol 283 Med Sci Bldg Madison WI 53706

BENJAMIN, ROBERT STEPHEN, MEDICAL ONCOLOGY, CLINICAL PHARMACOLOGY. *Current Pos:* asst internist & asst prof clin pharmacol, M D Anderson Hosp & Tumor Inst, Univ Tex Syst Cancer Ctr, 74-77, assoc internist, 77-81, prof clin pharmacol, chief, Sect Clin Pharmacol & assoc prof med, Dept Develop Therapeut, Univ Tex Syst Cancer Ctr, 77-81, INTERNIST, M D ANDERSON CANCER CTR, UNIV TEX, 81-, ASHBEL SMITH PROF MED, CHMN DEPT, DEPT MELANOMA/ SARCOMA MED ONCOL, 93-, MED DIR, MULTI DISP SARCOMA CTR, 93- *Personal Data:* b Brooklyn, NY, Apr 20, 43; m 65; c 2. *Educ:* Williams Col, AB, 64; NY Univ, MD, 68. *Honors & Awards:* J D Lane Award, USPHS, 73; Jeffrey A Gottlieb Mem Award, 88. *Prof Exp:* Sr clin assoc, Baltimore Cancer Res Ctr, Nat Cancer Inst, 72-73; from asst prof med to physician specialist, Los Angeles Co Univ Southern Calif Med Ctr, 73-74. *Concurrent Pos:* Clin assoc, Nat Cancer Inst, Baltimore Cancer Res Ctr, 70-72; mem, NIH, Nat Cancer Inst Clin Trials Comt, 75-, Am Cancer Soc jr fac clin fel, 75. *Mem:* Am Fedn Clin Res; Am Soc Clin Oncol; Am Asn Cancer Res; AMA. *Res:* Clinical trials in medical oncology; clinical pharmacology of chemotherapeutic agents; particular interest in clinical and pharmacologic studies of anthracycline antibiotics. *Mailing Add:* Univ Tex M D Anderson Cancer Ctr 1515 Holcombe Blvd Box No 77 Houston TX 77030

BENJAMIN, STEPHEN ALFRED, RADIATION BIOLOGY, TOXICOLOGY. *Current Pos:* assoc prof, Col Vet Med & Biomed Sci, Colo State Univ, 77-81, dir, Radiol Health Lab, 77-91, assoc dean, Grad Sch, 86-94, PROF PATH & RADIATION BIOL & ENVIRON HEALTH, COL VET MED & BIOMED SCI, COLO STATE UNIV, 81-, CO-DIR, CTR ENVIRON TOXICOL, 92- *Personal Data:* b New York, NY, Mar 27, 39; c 4. *Educ:* Brandeis Univ, AB, 60; Cornell Univ, DVM, 64, PhD(path), 68; Am Col Vet Path, dipl, 69. *Prof Exp:* Instr comp path & pathologist, Col Med, Pa State Univ, 67-68, asst prof, 68-70; exp path, Inhalation Toxicol Res Inst, Lovelace Found, 70-77. *Concurrent Pos:* Vis fel comp path, Dept Path, Sch Med, Johns Hopkins Univ, 66-67; clin assoc path, Dept Path, Univ NMex, Sch Med, 71-77. *Mem:* Am Col Vet Pathologists; US & Can Acad Pathologists; Radiation Res Soc; Am Vet Med Asn; AAAS. *Res:* Effects of radiation and other toxic agents on mammalian systems with emphasis on immunologic effects and carcinogenesis; effects of injurious agents on the developing prenatal and early postnatal mammal. *Mailing Add:* Dept Path Col Vet Med & Biomed Sci Colo State Univ Ft Collins CO 80523. *Fax:* 970-491-8304; *E-Mail:* sbenjamin@vines.colostate.edu

BENJAMIN, WILLIAM B, MOLECULAR BIOLOGY, ENDOCRINOLOGY. *Current Pos:* PROF, DEPT PHYSIOL & BIOPHYS, SCH MED, STATE UNIV NY, 82- *Personal Data:* b Brooklyn, NY, Jan 28, 34; m 83, Carol Eisenberg; c Jeremy. *Educ:* Columbia Col, BA, 51; Col Physicians & Surgeons, MD, 59. *Mem:* Am Soc Biochem & Molecular Biol; Fedn Am Socs Exp Biol. *Mailing Add:* Dept Physiol & Biophys Sch Med State Univ NY Stony Brook NY 11794-8661

BENJAMINI, ELIEZER, IMMUNOLOGY. *Current Pos:* PROF IMMUNOL, SCH MED, UNIV CALIF, DAVIS, 70- *Personal Data:* b Tel-Aviv, Israel, Feb 8, 29; US citizen; m 53; c 2. *Educ:* Univ Calif, Berkeley, BS, 52, MS, 54, PhD(insect toxicol), 58. *Honors & Awards:* Fac Res Award, Sch Med, Univ Calif Davis, 77. *Prof Exp:* Toxicologist, Nat Canners Res Asn Lab, Calif, 54-57; jr specialist, Citrus Exp Sta, Univ Calif, Riverside, 57-58; from asst res scientist to assoc res scientist, Kaiser Found Res Inst, San Francisco, 59-66, res scientist & asst dir lab med entom, 66-70. *Concurrent Pos:* Prin investr, var res grants, 61-; mem, Calif Cancer Res Coord Comt, 76-; mem adv panel, NSF, 77-80. *Mem:* Am Chem Soc; Am Asn Immunol; Sigma Xi. *Res:* Immune response to antigenic determinants and its manipulation; characterization and synthesis of antigenic determinants of proteins with particular emphasis on the relationship between structure and immunological activity; regulation of the immune response; immunochemical and immunobiologic studies of retroviruses. *Mailing Add:* 3506 Bravat Dr Huntington Beach CA 92649

BENJAMINOV, BENJAMIN S, ORGANIC CHEMISTRY. *Current Pos:* assoc prof org chem, 59-66, PROF CHEM, ROSE-HULMAN INST TECHNOL, 66- *Personal Data:* b Sofia, Bulgaria, Mar 21, 23; US citizen; m 47. *Educ:* Univ Kans, BA, 52; Allegheny Col, MS, 58; Weizmann Inst, PhD(org chem), 64. *Prof Exp:* Instr chem, Univ Mass, 53-54 & Rockford Col, 54-56; assoc prof & head dept, Alliance Col, 56-59. *Concurrent Pos:* Nat Cancer Inst fel, 62-64; Fulbright grant & vis prof, Univ Strasbourg, 70-71. *Mem:* AAAS; Am Chem Soc; The Chem Soc; Sigma Xi; Israel Chem Soc. *Res:* Chemistry of natural products, especially terpenes and steroids; reaction mechanisms; stereochemical, elucidative and structural problems; coordination compounds; bicyclic and small ring compounds; biosynthetic and synthetic investigations; lipid chemistry. *Mailing Add:* 267 E Vista Dr Terre Haute IN 47803

BENJAMINS, JOYCE ANN, NEUROCHEMISTRY. *Current Pos:* from asst prof to assoc prof, 75-85, PROF NEUROL, SCH MED, WAYNE STATE UNIV, 85- *Personal Data:* b Bay City, Mich, June 1, 41; m 65, David; c 2. *Educ:* Albion Col, BA, 63; Univ Mich, PhD(biochem), 67. *Prof Exp:* Fel pediat & genetics, Sch Med, Stanford Univ, 67-68; res assoc neurol, Sch Med, Johns Hopkins Univ, 68-69, from instr to asst prof, 69-73; asst prof biochem & res scientist, Biol Sci Res Ctr, Sch Med, Univ NC, Chapel Hill, 73-75. *Concurrent Pos:* Mem, Neurol B Study Sect, Nat Inst Neurol & Commun Disorders & Stroke, 78-82; mem, Sci Review Comt, Amyotrophic Lateral Sclerosis Soc Am, 81-84, Adv Comt Res, Nat Multiple Sclerosis Soc, 85-855; Javitz neuroscience res award, 87-94. *Mem:* Soc Neurosci; Am Soc Neurochem. *Res:* Developmental neurochemistry; lipid and protein synthesis assembly of membranes in developing nervous system especially myelination; glial cultures and cytoskeleton; glycolipid antibodies. *Mailing Add:* Dept Neurol 6E UHC Wayne State Univ Sch Med 540 E Canfield Ave Detroit MI 48201-1928. *Fax:* 313-577-7552

BENJAMINSON, MORRIS AARON, MICROBIOLOGY, DEVELOPMENTAL GENETICS. *Current Pos:* DIR, NSTAR RES INC, 75-; PRES, ZYMOTECH ENTERPRISES, LTD, 92-; CHMN, DEPT INSTRNL DEVELOP & APPL BIOSCI, SCH HEALTH SCI, TOURO COL, 93- *Personal Data:* b Bronx, NY, Aug 6, 30; div; c Brina M & Ari J. *Educ:* Long Island Univ, BS, 51; NY Univ, MS, 61, PhD(biol), 67. *Prof Exp:* Med technician, First Med Field Lab, US Army, 52-54; sr biol technician, Sloan-Kettering Inst Cancer Res, 54-55; med technician microbiol, Vet Admin Hosp, New York, 56-59; res asst, Margaret M Caspary Inst Vet Res, 59-61; res assoc, Bronx-Lebanon Hosp Ctr, 61-64; sr task leader, Naval Appl Sci Lab, 64-69; asst prof, Dent Sch, NY Univ, 69-74; assoc prof allied health & coordr med technol, York Col, NY, 74-75; assoc prof microbiol, NY Col Osteop Med, 84-90; dir, Res & Develop, Ctr Practical Solutions, 91-93. *Concurrent Pos:* Grant, Am Cancer Soc, NY Univ, 65, Navy Independent Explor Res, 66, Lehn & Fink Prod Group of Sterling Drug Co, 80, Sci & Technol Found, State NY, 88; US Navy contract, NY Univ, 69-71, NSF grant, 74-75; adj asst prof, City Col New York, 69-75; consult, Dept Air Resources, New York, 71-; mem, Environ Rev Comt, Continuing Educ Units, Am Soc Microbiol, 77; USDA coop agreement, 78-; vis res scientist, Dent Res Inst, NY Univ, 78-; treas/exec vpres & dir res & develop, BioDor Chem Prods Ltd, Bridgeport, Conn, 78-80; assoc prof pub health, Arnold & Marie Schwartz Col Pharm Health Sci, Long Island Univ, 79-83; expert witness, Microbiol Drift Panel, Pub Serv Comn, State NY, 81; consult, biogenetic toxicity testing, Electro-Optics Devices Corp; reviewer, J Histochem & Cytochem, 90 & Ctr Indoor Air Res, 93; dir, Inst Econ Growth, Local Develop Corp. *Mem:* AAAS; Am Soc Microbiol; NY Acad Sci; Sigma Xi; Histochem Soc; Am Inst Biol Sci; Int Asn Comp Res Leukemia & Related Dis; Am Soc Gravitational & Space Biol. *Res:* Clinical and industrial microbiology; cytochemistry; automation; aerobiology; public health; developmental genetics; gravitational biology. *Mailing Add:* Church St Sta PO Box 1212 New York NY 10007. *Fax:* 516-736-6812

BEN-JONATHAN, NIRA, NEUROENDOCRINOLOGY, REPRODUCTIVE PHYSIOLOGY. *Current Pos:* PROF CELL BIOL, UNIV CINCINNATI. *Personal Data:* b Holon, Israel, Nov 23, 40. *Educ:* Univ Tel-Aviv, BSc, 67; Univ Ill, Urbana, MSc, 69, PhD(physiol), 72. *Prof Exp:* Teacher chem, Alpha High Sch, Tel-Aviv, 66-67; from teaching asst to res asst physiol, Univ Ill, Urbana, 68-71; fel endocrinol, Univ Tex Southwestern Med Sch, 72-74, asst prof physiol, 74-75; from asst prof to assoc prof, Sch Med, Ind Univ, 76-83, prof physiol, 83- *Concurrent Pos:* Fel, Pop Coun, 72-73; res career develop award, NIH, 78-82, Endocrinol Study Sect, 84-87, chmn, 87-88. *Mem:* Am Endocrine Soc; Am Physiol Soc; Soc Neurosci; Int Soc Neuroendocrinol; Soc Study Reproduction. *Res:* Neuronal-endocrine interrelations; hypothalamic catecholamines and releasing hormones and the control of tropic hormones secretion by the anterior pituitary gland; catecholamines and ovarian function; catecholamines during fetal development. *Mailing Add:* Dept Anat & Cell Biol Univ Cincinnati Cincinnati OH 45264-0521

BENKENDORF, CAROL ANN, INDUSTRIAL TOXICOLOGY, CHEMICAL CARCINOGENESIS. *Current Pos:* PRES, TOXICOL DATA SERV INC, 83-, TOXDATA SYSTS INC, 86- *Personal Data:* b Indianapolis, Ind, Feb 8, 40; m 60; c 9. *Educ:* St Mary's Col, BS, 61; Univ Mich, MS, 75, PhD(toxicol), 78; Am Bd Toxicol, dipl, 81. *Prof Exp:* Lab asst, Northern Regional Lab, USDA, 61-62; consult, Clement Assocs, 77-78; asst toxicologist, Ford Motor Co, 78-82. *Concurrent Pos:* Mem, Am Conf Chem Labeling; Secy-treas, Hazard Commun Resources, Inc, 86- *Mem:* Am Chem Soc; Am Indust Hyg Asn; Genetic Toxicol Asn; AAAS; Nat Safety Coun. *Res:* Consulting. *Mailing Add:* 380 Sutton Rd Barrington IL 60010-4210

BENKESER, ROBERT ANTHONY, ORGANIC CHEMISTRY. *Current Pos:* From asst prof to assoc prof, 46-54, head dept, 74-78, PROF CHEM, PURDUE UNIV, WEST LAFAYETTE, 54- *Personal Data:* b Cincinnati, Ohio, Feb 16, 20; m 46; c 5. *Educ:* Xavier Univ, Ohio, BS, 42; Univ Detroit, MS, 44; Iowa State Col, PhD(org chem), 47. *Honors & Awards:* F S Kipping Award, Am Chem Soc, 69. *Mem:* Am Chem Soc. *Res:* Organometallics and synthetic organic chemistry; reactions of organosilicon compounds; reductions in amine solvents; metallations and reactions of benzylic Grignard systems. *Mailing Add:* 2113 Fairway Lane Lafayette IN 47906-4942

BENKOVIC, STEPHEN J, ORGANIC CHEMISTRY, PHYSICAL CHEMISTRY. *Current Pos:* from asst prof to assoc prof, 65-70, PROF CHEM, PA STATE UNIV, 70-, EVAN PUGH PROF, 77-, UNIV CHAIR BIOL SCI, 84-, EBERLY CHAIR CHEM, 86- *Personal Data:* b Orange, NJ, Apr 20, 38. *Educ:* Lehigh Univ, AB & BS, 60; Cornell Univ, PhD(org chem), 63. *Honors & Awards:* Pfizer Enzyme Award, Am Chem Soc, 77. *Prof Exp:* Res assoc, Univ Calif, Santa Barbara, 64-65. *Concurrent Pos:* Alfred P Sloan fel, Pa State Univ, 68-70, NIH career develop award, 69-74, Guggenheim fel, 76; co-chmn, Third Biannual Conf Biochem Mech, Los Angeles, 72, NATO Conf Catalysis, Sardinia, 72 & Gordon Conf, 73 & 76; mem, NIH Med Chem Panel, 72-76; mem med chem, NIH Physiol Chem Study Sect, 78-; mem, NJ Comm Molecular Biol, 84, externa adv group, Geisinger Hosp, 84, Sci Adv Bd Pa State Biotechnol Inst, 85 & Searle Scholars Prog, Chicago Community Trust, 85. *Mem:* Nat Acad Sci; Inst Med-Nat Acad Sci; Fedn Am Biologists; Sigma Xi; Royal Soc Chem; Am Acad Arts & Sci; Am Chem Soc. *Res:* Mechanisms of enzymatic reactions. *Mailing Add:* Dept Chem Pa State Univ University Park PA 16802

BENMAMAN, JOSEPH DAVID, PHARMACOKINETICS. *Current Pos:* from asst prof to assoc prof phys chem, 68-74, PROF PHARMACOKINETICS, COL PHARM, MED UNIV SC, 74- *Personal Data:* b Tetuan, Morocco, Dec 12, 24; US citizen; m 60; c 2. *Educ:* Univ Madrid, Lic pharm, 54, PhD(pharmaceut chem), 60. *Prof Exp:* Asst prof phys chem, Univ Madrid, 54-60; prof phys chem & chmn dept, Univ Oriente, Venezuela, 60-63; res chemist, Sch Pharm, Univ Calif, San Francisco, 63-65, res chemist, Sch Med, 65-68. *Mem:* Am Chem Soc; Am Pharmaceut Asn; Acad Pharmaceut Sci; Pan-Am Fedn Pharm & Biochem (secy, Sci Div, 72-75). *Res:* Methods of separation and analysis of biological materials; kinetics and mechanisms of reactions; drug stability; kinetics of absorption, distribution, metabolism and excretion of drugs; clinical pharmacokinetics; drug design. *Mailing Add:* 22 Charlestowne Rd Med Univ SC Charleston SC 29407

BENMARK, LESLIE ANN, CHEMICAL ENGINEERING. *Current Pos:* systs analyst, E I du Pont de Nemours & Co, Old Hickory, 68-70, syst analyst supvr, 70-75, design supvr, 75-76, planning & indust eng supvr, 76-79, bus anal mgr, 79-87, bus strategy mgr, 87-90, mgt systs consult, 90-93, SR CONSULT INFO SYSTS, E I DUPONT DE NEMOURS & CO, WILMINGTON, 93- *Personal Data:* m 69, Gary N. *Educ:* Univ Tenn, BS, 67, MS, 70; Vanderbilt Univ, PhD, 76; Univ Del, JD, 84. *Prof Exp:* Systs analyst, Monsanto Co, St Louis, 67-68. *Concurrent Pos:* Comput sci instr, Univ Tenn, Nashville, 73-75; asst to dean eng & dir women eng prog, Vanderbilt Univ, 75-79; chair, Total Qual Eng Comt, Union Pan-Am Asns Eng; mem bd dirs mfg studies, Nat Res Coun, 93- *Mem:* Nat Acad Eng; fel Inst Indust Engrs; fel Inst Indust Engrs Ireland; Nat Soc Prof Engrs; Am Soc Eng Educ; Union Pan-Am Asns Eng. *Mailing Add:* E I du Pont de Nemours & Co Inc 3524A Nemours Bldg Wilmington DE 19898

BENNER, BLAIR RICHARD, CHEMICAL METALLURGY, MINERAL BENEFICIATION. *Current Pos:* scientist, 86-91, sr scientist, 91-94, RES FEL, NATURAL RESOURCES RES INST, UNIV MINN, DULUTH, 94- *Personal Data:* b Braddock, Pa, Mar 29, 47; m 74; c 3. *Educ:* Pa State Univ, BS, 69; Stanford Univ, MS, 71. *Prof Exp:* Jr metallurgist, NMex State Bur Mines & Mineral Resources, 71-73; res metallurgist extractive metall, Deepsea Ventures Inc, Tenneco Co, 73-76; res engr, US Steel Res Lab, 76-80, sr res engr, 80-86. *Mem:* Am Inst Mining, Metall & Petrol Engr. *Res:* Extraction of uranium from phosphoric acid; hydrometallurgical processing of deep ocean nodules; restoration of in-situ uranium mines; gravity concentration of iron ore; by product recovery from in-situ uranium leaching; computer modeling of grinding circuits; iron ore flotation; process control. *Mailing Add:* Coleraine Res Lab Coleraine MN 55722. *Fax:* 218-245-4219; *E-Mail:* bbenner@d.umn.edu

BENNER, GERELD STOKES, CATALYSIS, INORGANIC CHEMISTRY. *Current Pos:* CONSULT, 87-; CHEMIST TECH DEVELOP, MPR SERVS INC, DICKINSON, TEX, 89- *Personal Data:* b Waukeegan, Ill, July 27, 33; m 76, Carole Gall; c Lori (Balkum). *Educ:* Univ NC, Chapel Hill, BS, 61; Ohio State Univ, MS, 63, PhD(inorg chem), 66. *Prof Exp:* Sr res chemist, Goodyear Tire & Rubber Co, 66-74; res chemist catalysis, MW Kellogg, Houston, 74-87. *Mem:* Am Chem Soc; Sigma Xi; Catalysis Soc Am. *Res:* Development and improvement of catalysis and catalytic processes in the fields of petroleum refineries, petrochemicals and ammonia synthesis. *Mailing Add:* 22707 Goldstone Katy TX 77450-1617

BENNER, ROBERT E, OPTICS, MATERIALS SCIENCE. *Current Pos:* MEM STAFF, APPL PHYSICS DIV, SANDIA LABS, LIVERMORE, CALIF, 80-; AT DEPT ELEC ENG, UNIV UTAH. *Personal Data:* b Lock Haven, Pa. *Educ:* Lehigh Univ, BS, 71; Univ Rochester, PhD(mat sci), 78. *Prof Exp:* Vis instr physics, Univ Toledo, 77; mem res staff, Yale Univ, 77-78, asst prof appl sci, 78-80. *Mem:* Am Phys Soc. *Res:* Brillouin and Raman scattering; nonlinear optics; Raman monitoring of aerosols; evanescent wave spectroscopy. *Mailing Add:* 3355 E Edward Circle Salt Lake City UT 84124

BENNER, RUSSELL EDWARD, MECHANICAL ENGINEERING. *Current Pos:* RETIRED. *Personal Data:* b Quakertown, Pa, Dec 19, 25; m 54; c 2. *Educ:* Cornell Univ, BME, 47; Lehigh Univ, MSME, 51, PhD(mech eng), 59. *Prof Exp:* Designer, Yale & Towne Mfg Co, Pa, 47-49; instr mech eng, Lehigh Univ, 49-59; res eng, E I Du Pont de Nemours & Co, 59-62; prof, Lehigh Univ, 62-93. *Concurrent Pos:* Consult, Fuller Co Div, Gen Am Transp Corp, 62-67. *Mem:* Am Soc Mech Engrs; Soc Exp Stress Anal; Am Soc Eng Educ. *Res:* Machine design; stress analysis; system dynamics; structural and systems reliability. *Mailing Add:* 705 Lehigh Dr Quakertown PA 18951

BENNET, ARCHIE WAYNE, EDUCATIONAL ADMINISTRATION. *Current Pos:* DEAN ENG, MISS STATE UNIV, 96- *Personal Data:* b Rocky Mount, Va, May 5, 37; m 58, Shirley Turner; c Elizabeth (Varnes) & David W. *Educ:* Va Polytech Inst & State Univ, BS, 60, MS, 63; Univ Fla, PhD(elec eng), 66. *Honors & Awards:* Outstanding Serv Award, Am Soc Eng Educ, 75. *Prof Exp:* Systs engr, Gen Elec, 60-61; from instr to assoc prof elec eng, Va Tech, 61-74, chmn, Comput Eng Group, 72-81, prof elec eng & comput sci, 74-81; head elec & comput eng, Clemson Univ, 81-88, assoc dean & spec asst to pres, 86-93, sr vprovost & dean, Grad Sch, 93-96. *Concurrent Pos:* Eng consult, Litton Industs, 68-81, Babcock & Wilcox, 77; bd dirs, Am Soc Eng Educ, 76-78; comput systs consult, IBM, 85; educ consult, State of Fla, 88; mgt consult, Pryor Resources, 89-; vchmn & chmn, Nat Asn Elec Eng Dept Heads. *Mem:* Am Soc Eng Educ; Inst Elec & Electronics Engrs; Int Asn Math & Comput in Simulation (vpres, 79-85); Nat Asn Elec Eng Dept Heads; Asn Comput Mach. *Res:* Continuous and discrete control theory; telecommunication and systems networking; system simulation; optimal and adaptive control. *Mailing Add:* 900 Yorkshire Rd Starkville MS 39759

BENNET, GEORGE KEMBLE, JR, OPERATIONS RESEARCH, INDUSTRIAL ENGINEERING. *Current Pos:* dept head indust eng, Tex A&M Univ, 86-91, assoc dean eng, 91-92, asst dir res, Tex Eng Exp Sta, 91-92, DIR & ASSOC VCHANCELLOR ENG, TEX A&M UNIV, 92- *Personal Data:* b Jacksonville, Fla, Apr 2, 40; m 66; c 2. *Educ:* Fla State Univ, BS, 62; San Jose State Col, MS, 68; Tex Tech Univ, PhD(indust eng), 70. *Prof Exp:* Assoc engr, Martin Marietta Co, 62-63; math analyst, Lockheed Missiles & Space Co, 63-66; asst dir comput ctr, Tex Tech Univ, 66-69; asst prof indust eng & opers res, Va Polytech Inst & State Univ, 70-74; prof & head indust syst eng, Univ SFla, 74-86. *Concurrent Pos:* Ed, Logistics Sprectrum, 84-88. *Mem:* Am Inst Indust Engrs; Soc Logistics Engrs; Am Soc Eng Educ. *Res:* Development of smooth empirical Bayes estimation techniques; design and development of consumer commodity regulatory systems; design of cost based quality control systems. *Mailing Add:* Tex Eng Exten Serv Tex A&M Univ College Station TX 77843-8000

BENNETT, A(RTHUR) D(AVID), mechanical engineering; deceased, see previous edition for last biography

BENNETT, ALAN JEROME, SEMICONDUCTOR PHYSICS, DEVICE PHYSICS. *Current Pos:* mgr prog develop, 92-93, mgr indust partnerships, 94-96, MGR PROG DEVELOP, FISSION ENERGY SYSTS SAFETY PROGS, LIVERMORE NAT LABS, 97- *Personal Data:* b Philadelphia, Pa, June 13, 41; m 63; c 3. *Educ:* Univ Pa, BA, 62; Univ Chicago, MS, 63, PhD(physics), 65. *Prof Exp:* Physicist, Phys Sci Br, Res & Develop Ctr, Gen Elec, 66-74, mgr, Solid State Common Br, 75-77, mgr, Rel Ultrasonic Imager Prog, 77-78, mgr planning & resources, electronics sci & eng, 78-79; dir, Gould Electronics Lab, 79-84; vpres res, Varian Assoc, 84-91. *Concurrent Pos:* Fel, NSF, Cambridge Univ, 66; vis assoc prof, Cornell Univ, 70, Technion,72. *Mem:* Am Phys Soc; Inst Elec & Electronics Engrs; Indust Res Inst; AAAS; Am Mgt Asn. *Res:* Solid state communications; ultrasonic imaging; semiconductor fabrication equipment; computer systems; laboratory instrumentation; medical therapeutics. *Mailing Add:* Lawrence Livermore Nat Lab PO Box 808 L638 Livermore CA 94550. *Fax:* 510-423-2157

BENNETT, ALBERT FARRELL, COMPARATIVE PHYSIOLOGY, PHYSIOLOGICAL ECOLOGY. *Current Pos:* from asst prof to assoc prof, 74-83, actg dean, 86-87, PROF BIOL SCI, UNIV CALIF, IRVINE, 83-, CHAIR, DEVELOP & CELL BIOL, 84- *Personal Data:* b Whittier, Calif, July 18, 44; m 77; c 4. *Educ:* Univ Calif, Riverside, AB, 66; Univ Mich, PhD(zool), 71. *Prof Exp:* Lectr zool, Univ Mich, 70-71; Miller fel, Univ Calif, Berkeley, 71-73, actg asst prof, 73-74. *Concurrent Pos:* Prin investr, NSF grants, 75-; NIH Career Develop Award, 78-83; vis res assoc, Univ Chicago, 81-82; vis res fel, Univ Adelaide, SAustralia, 83-84. *Mem:* Am Physiol Soc; Am Soc Naturalists; Am Soc Zoologists; Ecol Soc Am; Soc Exp Biol. *Res:* Activity and exercise physiology of vertebrates; comparative respiratory and muscle physiology; physiological ecology; ecological energetics. *Mailing Add:* Dept Ecol & Evolutionary Biol Univ Calif Sch Biol Sci Irvine CA 92717-0001

BENNETT, ALBERT GEORGE, JR, COMPOSITE AIRCRAFT DEVELOPMENT, AUTOMATED COMPOSITE MANUFACTURING. *Current Pos:* assoc prof, 69-76, PROF AERONAUT ENG, MISS STATE UNIV, MISS, 76-, DIR, RASPET FLIGHT RES LAB, 79- *Personal Data:* b Booneville, Miss, Aug 8, 37; m 60; c 2. *Educ:* Miss State Univ, BS, 59; Univ Ill, MS, 64, PhD(aeronaut & astronaut eng), 70. *Prof Exp:* Aerodynamicist, Douglas Aircraft Co, Santa Monica, Calif, 59-62; asst prof aeronaut eng, Miss State Univ, Miss, 63-66; instr aeronaut & astronaut eng, Univ Ill, 66-76. *Concurrent Pos:* Fac fel, NASA-Am Soc Eng Educ, summer fac fel res, Langley, 70-75; mem, Commun & Instrumention Support Serv, Miss State Univ, 81-, Strategic Defens Initiative Orgn Tech Appl Adv Comt, Dept Defense, 86-89; consult, Lockheed-Ga, co-chmn, Safety Rev Bd, 84-87, Aero Corp, 85, Aerovironment Inc, 85; chmn, Power Generation Subcomt, 86-89. *Mem:* Sigma Xi; Soc Aeronaut Eng; Am Inst Aeronaut & Astronaut. *Res:* Prototype composite aircraft development; parameter identification of aircraft performance; automation of composite fabrication; ultrasonic imaging of composite. *Mailing Add:* Blackjack Rd Starkville MS 39759

BENNETT, ARCHIE WAYNE, ELECTRICAL ENGINEERING, COMPUTER SCIENCE. *Current Pos:* PROF ELEC ENG & COMPUT ENG & HEAD DEPT, CLEMSON UNIV, 81- *Personal Data:* b Rocky Mount, Va, May 5, 37; m 58; c 2. *Educ:* Va Polytech Inst, BSEE, 60, MSEE, 63; Univ Fla, PhD(elec eng), 66. *Prof Exp:* Systs engr, Gen Elec Co, 60-61; from instr to assoc prof elec eng, Va Polytech Inst & State Univ, 61-72, prof elec eng & comput sci, 72-81. *Mem:* Inst Elec & Electronics Engrs; Am Soc Eng Educ; Asn Comput Mach; Int Asn Math & Comput Simulation. *Res:* Digital computer design; computer graphics; digital simulation. *Mailing Add:* Dean Grad Sch Clemson Univ Clemson SC 29632-0001

BENNETT, BASIL TAYLOR, LABORATORY ANIMAL MEDICINE, EXPERIMENTAL PATHOLOGY. *Current Pos:* dir prof serv, 74-76, asst admin, 76-78, DIR, BIOL RESOURCES LAB, UNIV ILL, 78-, ASSOC VCHANCELLOR RES RESOURCES, 96- *Personal Data:* b Durham, NC, July 20, 44; m 64, Elizabeth Booth; c Michael & Raleigh. *Educ:* Auburn Univ, DVM, 69; Univ Ill, PhD(path), 74. *Honors & Awards:* Flynn Award, 79. *Prof Exp:* Resident investr, Hines Vet Admin Hosp, Ill, 69-74. *Concurrent Pos:* Chief, Res Lab Animal Med Sci & Technol, 72-79; bd dir, Am Col Lab Animal Md, 87-89, Am Soc Lab Animal Practrs, 89-91; mem, Nat Asn Biomed Res, 84-87. *Mem:* Am Vet Med Asn; Am Soc Lab Animal Practr; Am Col Lab Animal Med; Am Asn Lab Animal Sci (pres, 85); Am Soc Primatology; Asn Primate Vet (pres, 82-83). *Res:* Laboratory animal medicine and technology as they apply to improving the experimental models that are available. *Mailing Add:* Biol Resources Lab 1840 W Taylor St Chicago IL 60612. *Fax:* 312-996-8065; *E-Mail:* b.taylor.bennett@uic.edu

BENNETT, BYRON J(IRDEN), ELECTRICAL ENGINEERING. *Current Pos:* prof elec eng & head dept, 60-63, DEAN, COL ENG & DIR, ENG EXP STA, MONT STATE UNIV, 63- *Personal Data:* b Loraine, Tex, Oct 4, 20; m 47; c 7. *Educ:* Tex Technol Col, BS, 43; Stanford Univ, MS, 49, PhD(elec eng), 52. *Prof Exp:* Test engr, Gen Elec Co, 40-41; radio engr, Philco Co, 42-43; instr elec eng, Tex Technol Col, 43-44, assoc prof, 46-52; mgr, Comput Lab, Stanford Res Inst, 52-58; mgr advan technol, Int Bus Mach Corp, 58-60. *Concurrent Pos:* Instr, Temple Univ, 42-43; lectr, Stanford Univ, 56-60; asst prof, San Jose State Col, 59-60; consult, Electronics Res Lab, Endowment & Res Found, 60-; Westinghouse fel; tech prog dir, Navy Res & Develop Clin, 63-64; mem bd dirs, Montronics, Inc, Fluke Mfg Co, Inc, 63-; mem bd dirs, Develop Technol, Inc, 70- *Mem:* Sigma Xi; Inst Elec & Electronics Engrs. *Res:* Transistors; magnetics; electroluminescence; photoconductors. *Mailing Add:* Elec Eng Mont State Univ Bozeman MT 59717

BENNETT, C FRANK, IMMUNOLOGY, MOLECULAR PHARMACOLOGY. *Current Pos:* sr scientist, ISIS Pharmaceut, 89-90, group leader, 90-92, assoc dir, 92-93, DIR, ISIS PHARMACEUT, 93- *Personal Data:* b Farmington, NMex, Nov 1, 56; m 86, Paula Chamberland; c Christopher, Nicholas & Alexander. *Educ:* Univ NMex, BS, 80; Baylor Col Med, PhD(pharmacol), 85. *Prof Exp:* Fel, Smithkline & French Labs, 85-87, assoc sr investr, 87-89. *Mem:* Am Soc Cell Biol; AAAS. *Res:* Rationale drug discovery in areas of inflammation, cardiovascular and oncology; mechanisms of cellular communication and signal transduction pathways. *Mailing Add:* ISIS Pharmaceut 2280 Faraday Ave Carlsbad CA 92008-7208. *Fax:* 760-931-0209

BENNETT, C LEONARD, SATELLITE COMMUNICATIONS, ANTENNAS & PROPAGATION. *Current Pos:* prin engr commun, 83-86, CONSULT ENGR COMMUN SYST, RAYTHEON CO, 86- *Personal Data:* b Lowell, Mass, Oct 5, 39; m 66, Patricia; c Craig & Dawn. *Educ:* Lowell Technol Inst, BS, 61; NC State Univ, MS, 64; Purdue Univ, PhD(elec eng), 68. *Prof Exp:* Mem tech staff, electromagnetic res, Sperry Res Ctr, 68-73, mgr syst appln, Radar Target Class, 73-83. *Concurrent Pos:* Lectr, Advan Study Inst, N Atlantic Treaty Orgn, 79, Short Courses Comput Methods Electromagnetics, 80-84; adj prof, Univ Man, 76-77 & Northeastern Univ, 82-83; assoc ed, Trans, Antennas & Propagation, Inst Elec & Electronics Engrs, 82- *Mem:* Fel Inst Elec & Electronics Engrs; Inst Elec & Electronics Engrs Antenna Propagation Soc; Union Radio Sci Int. *Res:* Development and applications of computational methods in electromagnetics, transient electromagnetic and radar target classification; design and development of satellite communication systems. *Mailing Add:* 304 Reedy Meadow Rd Groton MA 01450

BENNETT, CARL ALLEN, STATISTICS. *Current Pos:* mgr, Appl Math Dept, Battelle Mem Inst, 65-68, mgr, Systs & Electronics Div, 68-70, sr staff scientist, 70-71, STAFF SCIENTIST, HUMAN AFFAIRS RES CENTERS, BATTELLE MEM INST, 71- *Personal Data:* b Winfield, Pa, Nov 22, 21; m 44; c 2. *Educ:* Bucknell Univ, AB, 40, MA, 41; Univ Mich, AM, 42, PhD(math), 52. *Hon Degrees:* DSc, Bucknell Univ, 72. *Prof Exp:* Jr chemist, Chem & Metall Lab, Univ Chicago, 44; sr chemist & qual control supvr, Tenn Eastman Corp, 44-46; from chief statist & head appl math to mgr appl math dept, Hanford Labs, Gen Elec Co, 47-65. *Concurrent Pos:* Res assoc math, Princeton Univ, 50; vis prof statist, Stanford Univ, 64. *Mem:* Fel AAAS; fel Am Statist Asn; fel Am Soc Qual Control; fel Inst Nuclear Mat Mgt; Biomet Soc. *Res:* Application of statistical and mathematical techniques to industrial problems; order statistics; nonparametric methods; variance component analysis. *Mailing Add:* 11121 SE 59th St Bellevue WA 98006

BENNETT, CARL LEROY, WILDLIFE RESEARCH, BIOMETRY. *Current Pos:* RETIRED. *Personal Data:* b Stambaugh, Mich, May 22, 35; m 56; c 4. *Educ:* Mich State Univ, BS, 60, MS, 65. *Prof Exp:* Res biologist waterfowl, Erie Fishing & Shooting Club, 61; biometrician, Wildlife Div & Res & Develop, Mich Dept Natural Resources, Lansing, 61-70, supvr forest wildlife res, 70-81, sect head wildlife res, wildlife div, 81-95. *Concurrent Pos:* Instr wildlife biomet, Mich State Univ, 77 & 81. *Mem:* Wildlife Soc; Sigma Xi. *Res:* Interactive dynamics of animals and their habitats, especially white-tailed deer in its northern environment. *Mailing Add:* 6467 Shoeman Rd Haslett MI 48840

BENNETT, CARROLL G, DENTISTRY. *Current Pos:* prof pedodontics & chmn div, Univ Fla, 73-74, prof pediat dent & chmn dept, 74-84, dir admissions & student financial aid, 85, ASSOC DEAN, ADMIS & STUD AFFAIRS, UNIV FLA, 95-; CONSULT, 84- *Personal Data:* b Richmond, Va, Dec 8, 33; m 56, Sue Hunter; c Susan (Najjar) & Elizabeth (Eifert). *Educ:* Randolph-Macon Col, BS, 55; Med Col Va, DDS, 59, MS, 62; Am Bd Pedodont, dipl, 67. *Prof Exp:* Instr dent anat & pedodontics, Sch Dent, WVa Univ, 62-63, from asst prof to prof pedodontics & chmn dept, 63-73, asst dean student affairs, 72-73. *Concurrent Pos:* Chmn, Am Bd Pedodontics, 78. *Mem:* Am Dent Asn; Am Soc Dent for Children; Int Asn Dent Res; Am Acad Pediat Dent. *Res:* Pedodontics; growth, development and clinical research in children's dentistry. *Mailing Add:* Col Dent Univ Fla Box J100445 Gainesville FL 32610-0445

BENNETT, CARROLL O(SBORN), CHEMICAL ENGINEERING. *Current Pos:* PROF CHEM ENG, UNIV CONN, STORRS, 64- *Personal Data:* b New Britain, Conn, Apr 1, 21; m 49; c 3. *Educ:* Worcester Polytech Inst, BS, 43; Yale Univ, DEng(chem eng), 50. *Honors & Awards:* Fulbright lectr, Nancy Univ, 52-53; Warren K Lewis Award, Am Inst Chem Engrs. *Prof Exp:* From asst prof to prof chem eng, Purdue Univ, 49-59; mgr process res & develop, Lummus Co, 59-64. *Concurrent Pos:* Nat Ctr Sci Res, Ministry Educ, France, 57-58; AID prof, Univ Santa Maria, Chile, 64; vis lectr, Yale Univ, 66-70; vis prof, Univ Lyon, France, 77-78, Univ Paris, 84- *Mem:* Am Chem Soc; Am Inst Chem Engrs. *Res:* High pressure; thermodynamics; heat and mass transfer; heterogeneous catalysis. *Mailing Add:* Dept Chem Eng Univ Conn Storrs CT 06269-3222

BENNETT, CECIL JACKSON, ANIMAL GENETICS, BEHAVIORAL GENETICS. *Current Pos:* from asst prof to prof, 57-90, EMER PROF BIOL, NORTHERN ILL UNIV, 90- *Personal Data:* b Eau Claire, Wis, Oct 4, 27; m 51, Donna I Campbell; c Scott J & Carroll A. *Educ:* Univ Wis, BS, 49, PhD(zool & genetics), 59; Wash Univ, MA, 53. *Prof Exp:* Lab maintenance man zool, Univ Okla, 53-55; res asst genetics, Univ Wis, 55-57. *Mem:* AAAS; Soc Study Evolution; Genetics Soc Am; Am Genetics Asn; Am Inst Biol Sci. *Res:* Population genetics; gene action; behavior in Drosophila. *Mailing Add:* Dept Biol Northern Ill Univ De Kalb IL 60115-2861. *E-Mail:* 105035.1264@compuserve.com

BENNETT, CHARLES FRANKLIN, BIOGEOGRAPHY, ECOLOGY. *Current Pos:* From instr to assoc prof geog, 59-69, chmn dept, 83-87, prof biogeog, 69-93, EMER PROF BIOGEOG, UNIV CALIF, LOS ANGELES, 93- *Personal Data:* b Oakland, Calif, Apr 10, 26; m 47; c 1. *Educ:* Univ Calif, Los Angeles, BA, 55, PhD(geog), 60. *Concurrent Pos:* Consult, Tex Instruments Corp, 63-64 & AEC, 65-67; Off Naval Res fel res in Panama, Univ Calif, Los Angeles, 63; res assoc, Smithsonian Trop Res Inst, 66-; directorate 1 trop forests, Man & the Biosphere, Dept State-UNESCO, 78-; Guggenheim fel, 70-71. *Mem:* Fel AAAS; Ecol Soc Am; Brit Ecol Soc; Am Geog Soc; Asn Trop Biol; Soc Conserv Biol; Sigma Xi. *Res:* Ecology of human modified ecosystems; ecology of the humid tropics; ecology of tropical agricultural systems; conservation of biotic resources in underdeveloped countries. *Mailing Add:* Dept Geog Univ Calif Los Angeles CA 90095-1430. *E-Mail:* chasben@ucla.edu

BENNETT, CHARLES H, QUANTUM MATHEMATICS. *Current Pos:* IBM RES FEL, IBM, 95- *Personal Data:* b July, 1943. *Mem:* Nat Acad Sci. *Mailing Add:* IBM T J Watson Res Ctr Yorktown Heights NY 10598

BENNETT, CHARLES L, RADIO ASTRONOMY, COSMOLOGY. *Current Pos:* ASTROPHYSICIST, GODDARD SPACE FLIGHT CTR, NASA, 84- *Personal Data:* b New Brunswick, NJ, Nov 16, 56; m 84; c 1. *Educ:* Univ Md, BS, 78; Mass Inst Technol, PhD(physics), 84. *Prof Exp:* Res asst radio astron, res lab electronics, Mass Inst Technol, 78-84. *Mem:* Am Astron Soc; Am Inst Physics; Int Astron Union; Am Phys Soc; Sigma Xi. *Res:* Radio astronomy; submillimeter wave astronomy; cosmology; instrumentation for astronomy. *Mailing Add:* NASA/Goddard Space Flight Ctr Code 685 Greenbelt MD 20771-0001

BENNETT, CHARLES LOUGHEED, NUCLEAR PHYSICS. *Current Pos:* PHYSICIST, LAWRENCE LIVERMORE NAT LABS, 84- *Personal Data:* b Duluth Minn, Dec 27, 49. *Educ:* Univ Minn, BA, 72; Univ Rochester, MA, 75, PhD(physics), 77. *Prof Exp:* Res asst to res assoc physics, Univ Rochester, 72-78; asst prof physics, Princeton Univ, 78-84. *Mem:* AAAS; Am Phys Soc. *Res:* Nuclear reactions and nuclear structure, especially multi-nucleon transfer spectroscopy; radiocarbon and other radioisotope dating; solar neutrino physics. *Mailing Add:* Lawrence Livermore Nat Labs L-43 PO Box 808 Livermore CA 94550

BENNETT, CLEAVES M, PREVENTIVE MEDICINE, HYPERTENSION. *Current Pos:* assoc chief, div nephrology, Harbor-UCLA Med Ctr, 70-76, assoc clin prof med, 77-83, CLIN PROF MED, 83-, DIR, RENAL HYPERTENSION CLIN, 78- *Personal Data:* b Champaign, Ill, July 9, 34; m 85; c 3. *Educ:* Carleton Col, BA,55;Univ Rochester, MD, 60; Am Bd Internal Med, dipl, 70;dipl, nephrology, 74. *Prof Exp:* Fel, dept biochem, Univ Rochester, 57-58, 79-; intern, dept med, UCLA Med Ctr, 60-61, jr resident, 61-62; sr resident, dept med, Albert Einstein Col Med, 62-63, chief resident, 63-64; fel, Lab Kidney & Electrolyte Metab, Nat Heart Inst, NIH, 64-65, investr, USPHS, 65-67; clin investr, Vet Admin Hosp, Durham, NC, 67-69. *Concurrent Pos:* Dir, Renal Hypertension Clin,Harbor-UCLA Med Ctr, 70-76,from asst prof to assoc prof med, 69-76; med dir, Biomed Applns Dialysis Ctr, 72-75; chief, div nephrology, King Faisal Specialist Hosp, 76-77; dir,Hypertension Clin, Vet Admin Wadsworth Hosp Ctr, 77-78; med dir, Pritkin Longevity Ctr, 78-80; med dir, Innerhealth Progs, 80- *Mem:* Am Physiol Soc; Am Soc Nephrology; Int Soc Nephrology; Am Fedn Clin Res; fel Am Col Physicians. *Res:* Kidney physiology; hypertension; renal disease and dialysis; nutrition and exercise physiology. *Mailing Add:* Inner Health 1000 W Ninth St Los Angeles CA 90015

BENNETT, CLIFTON FRANCIS, WOOD CHEMISTRY, SPECIALTY PRODUCTS CHEMISTRY. *Current Pos:* PRIN CHEMIST, PACE INT LTD PARTNERSHIP, 85- *Personal Data:* b Tillamook, Ore, July 27, 25; m 56, Marvilena Anderson; c Genevieve, Gretchen & Michelle. *Educ:* Lewis & Clark Col, 49; Ore State Univ, MS, 52; McGill Univ, PhD(wood chem), 56. *Prof Exp:* Res chemist, Weyerhaeuser Co, 51-53; res chemist, Crown Zellerbach Corp, 55-81; prin chemist, Container Corp Am, 81-84. *Concurrent Pos:* Nat dir, US Jr Chamber of Com, 58-59; instr, Portland Continuation Ctr, Ore State Syst Higher Educ, 63-65; adv, Chem Explorer Post 404, 67-77; Nat Acad Sci exchange scientist, Czech & Romania, 72-73 & 79, Poland, 84 & Romania, 91. *Mem:* Am Chem Soc; Tech Asn Pulp & Paper Indust. *Res:* Cellulose reactions; substitutions and fractionations; organic sulfur compounds; lignin; organic chemical synthesis; pulp and paper chemistry; specialty chemicals; aircraft cleaners; granted US patents and one Czech patent. *Mailing Add:* 5661 Branch Rd Wapato WA 98951

BENNETT, COLIN, MATHEMATICS. *Current Pos:* assoc prof, 79-82, PROF MATH, UNIV SC, 82-, CHMN, DEPT MATH, 85- *Personal Data:* b Newcastle upon Tyne, Eng, Jan 16, 46; m 67; c 2. *Educ:* Univ Newcastle, BSc, 67, PhD(math), 71. *Prof Exp:* Harry Bateman res instr math, Calif Inst Technol, 71-73, asst prof, 73-76; assoc prof math, McMaster Univ, 76-79. *Concurrent Pos:* NSF res grants, 74-76 & 80-82; Nat Sci & Eng Res Coun Can res grant, 77-80. *Mem:* Am Math Soc; Math Asn Am; Can Math Soc. *Res:* Harmonic analysis; approximation theory; interpolation of operators. *Mailing Add:* Dept Math Univ SC Columbia SC 29208-0001

BENNETT, DAVID ARTHUR, BIOINORGANIC CHEMISTRY. *Current Pos:* asst prof chem, Middlebury Col, 74-80. *Personal Data:* b Cleveland, Ohio, Dec 9, 42; c 2. *Educ:* Muskingum Col, BS, 64; Northwestern Univ, MAT, 65; Cornell Univ, PhD(chem), 73. *Prof Exp:* Instr sci, Am Sch, Switz, 65-67; res assoc chem, Purdue Univ, 72-74. *Mem:* AAAS; Am Chem Soc. *Res:* Chemical and biochemical studies of porphyrins and porphyrin containing biological molecules. *Mailing Add:* 7820 Overhill Rd Bethesda MD 20814-1115

BENNETT, DEBRA A, NEUROSCIENCES. *Current Pos:* ASSOC DIR CLIN DEVELOP, CIBA-GEIGY CORP, 81- *Personal Data:* b Boundbrook, NJ. *Educ:* Drew Univ, BA, 76; Fairleigh-Dickinson Univ, MA, 78; Univ RI, PhD, 81. *Mem:* Am Psychol Asn; Neurosci Soc; Am Soc Pharmacol & Exp Therapeut; Am Psychol Soc; NY Acad Sci. *Mailing Add:* Ciba-Geigy Corp 556 Morris Ave Summit NJ 07901-1398

BENNETT, DONALD RAYMOND, PHARMACOLOGY. *Current Pos:* sr scientist, Dept Drugs, 76-80, assoc dir, 80-85, DIR, DIV DRUGS & TOXICOL, AMA, 85- *Personal Data:* b Mishawaka, Ind, Feb 16, 26; m 47; c 2. *Educ:* Univ Mich, BS, 49, MS, 51, MD, 55, PhD, 58; Am Bd Family Pract, cert, 76, 83 & 90. *Prof Exp:* From asst prof to assoc prof pharmacol, Univ Mich, 57-65; mgr, Biosci Res Lab, Dow Corning Corp, 65-74. *Mem:* Am Soc Pharmacol & Exp Therapeut; Soc Toxicol; Am Acad Family Physicians; Am Soc Clin Pharmacol & Therapeut. *Mailing Add:* USP Convention Inc 515 N State St Rm 8273 Chicago IL 60610-4312

BENNETT, DWIGHT G, JR, VETERINARY MEDICINE. *Current Pos:* PROF CLIN SCI, COLO STATE UNIV, 75- *Personal Data:* b Pittsburgh, Pa, Aug 27, 35; m 59; c 2. *Educ:* Univ Ill, BS, 57, DVM, 59; Univ Wis, MS, 63, PhD(vet sci), 64. *Prof Exp:* Private practice, 59; asst vet sci, Univ Wis, 62-63, USPHS fel, 63-64; from asst prof to assoc prof vet parasitol, Purdue Univ, 64-73, prof vet parasitol & large animal clin, 73-75. *Concurrent Pos:* Mem, Nat Bd Vet Med Examrs, 71- *Mem:* Am Vet Med Asn; Am Asn Vet Parasitol; World Asn Advan Vet Parasitol; Am Asn Equine Practitioners; Sigma Xi. *Res:* Chemotherapy and immunology of nematode parasites of ruminants; chemotherapy of parasites of horses. *Mailing Add:* 2307 Tanglewood Dr Ft Collins CO 80525-1952

BENNETT, EDGAR F, REACTOR PHYSICS. *Current Pos:* RETIRED. *Personal Data:* b Colebrook, NH, July 29, 29; m 70. *Educ:* Univ NH, BS, 51, MS, 53; Princeton Univ, PhD(physics), 57. *Prof Exp:* Physicist, Div Reactor Physics, Argonne Nat Lab, 57-93. *Mem:* Am Nuclear Soc; Sigma Xi. *Res:* Radiation detection; radiation instrumentation. *Mailing Add:* 913 Clyde Dr Downers Grove IL 60515

BENNETT, EDWARD OWEN, BACTERIOLOGY. *Current Pos:* RETIRED. *Personal Data:* b St Louis, Mo, Mar 16, 26; m 47; c 2. *Educ:* Univ Houston, BS, 49; Univ Iowa, MS, 51; Baylor Univ, PhD, 58. *Prof Exp:* From asst prof to assoc prof, Univ Houston, 51-63, chmn dept bact, 64-67, 79-81, assoc dean col arts & sci, 67-73, prof bact, 63-93. *Concurrent Pos:* Consult, various co. *Mem:* Am Soc Microbiol; Soc Indust Microbiol; fel Am Acad Microbiol; fel Soc Tribology & Lubrication Engrs. *Res:* Antimicrobial agents. *Mailing Add:* 834 Country Club Dr La Grange TX 78945

BENNETT, ELBERT WHITE, experimental nuclear physics; deceased, see previous edition for last biography

BENNETT, F LAWRENCE, COLD REGIONS CONSTRUCTION, PROJECT MANAGEMENT. *Current Pos:* from assoc prof to prof eng mgt, Univ Alaska, Fairbanks, 68-74, asst to chancellor, 77-79, vchancellor acad affairs, 79-82, dept head, 69-78, PROF, UNIV ALASKA, FAIRBANKS, 74-, DEPT HEAD ENG MGT, 83- *Personal Data:* b Troy, NY, Apr 4, 39; m 62, Margaret A Musgrave; c 2. *Educ:* Rensselaer Polytechnic Inst, BcE, 61; Cornell Univ, MS, 63, PhD(civil eng), 66. *Honors & Awards:* Peyton Cold Regions Eng Award, Am Soc Civil Engrs, 96- *Prof Exp:* Planning engr, United Engrs & Constructors Inc, 65-68; vis assoc prof civil eng, NC State Univ, 74-75; actg vpres acad; vis res prof, Lulea Univ, Sweden, 92 affairs, Alaska Pac Univ, 82-83. *Concurrent Pos:* Eng & mgt consult, 69-; prin investr, Sch Eng, Univ Alaska, 70- *Mem:* Am Soc Civil Engrs; Nat Soc Prof Engrs; Am Soc Eng Educ; Sigma Xi. *Res:* Cold regions construction techniques and management; construction productivity; project management; network scheduling; computer applications; engineering economy. *Mailing Add:* Dept Eng Mgt Univ Alaska Fairbanks AK 99775. *Fax:* 907-474-6087; *E-Mail:* ffflb@aurora.alaska.edu

BENNETT, FOSTER CLYDE, ENGINEERING PHYSICS. *Current Pos:* RETIRED. *Personal Data:* b Wilmette, Ill, Oct 14, 14; m 40, Mary L MacPhail; c Donald, William, Tom, James, George, Elizabeth & Karen. *Educ:* Univ Ill, BS, 36; Calif Inst Technol, MS, 37. *Honors & Awards:* Doehler Award, Am Die Casting Inst, 64. *Prof Exp:* Engr res & develop, Dow Chem Co, 37-40, supt electrothermal magnesium plant, 40-43, supt sodium prod plant, 44-49, supt pressure die casting, 49-61, supvr, Metals Lab, 61-70, assoc scientist, Inorganic Chem Dept, 70-72; sr res scientist, Battelle Columbus Labs, 72-82; pres, Die Casting Consult, Inc, 72-90, vpres, 90-93. *Res:* Pressure and gravity casting techniques, nonferrous alloys; molten metal handling; heat transfer and process analysis. *Mailing Add:* 4590 Knightsbridge Blvd Apt 201 Columbus OH 43214

BENNETT, FREDERICK DEWEY, FLUID MECHANICS. *Current Pos:* CONSULT, 70- *Personal Data:* b Miles City, Mont, June 2, 17; m 39, 80; c 6. *Educ:* Oberlin Col, AB, 37; Pa State Col, MS, 39, PhD(physics), 41. *Prof Exp:* Asst physics, Pa State Col, 38-41; from instr to asst prof, Univ NH, 41-43; physicist, Spec Projs Lab, AMC, Wright Field, Ohio, 43-46; from asst prof to assoc prof elec eng, Univ Ill, 46-48; physicist, Ballistics Res Lab, Aberdeen Proving Ground, 48-63, chief exterior ballistics div, 62-70. *Concurrent Pos:* Fel, Dept Mech & Mat Sci, Johns Hopkins Univ, 71-80, Dept Chem Eng, 81- *Mem:* AAAS; fel Am Phys Soc; Am Geophys Union. *Res:* Physics of hydrogen palladium system; aircraft antennas; diffusion of hydrogen through metals; optical methods in analysis of airflow; exploding wires; volcanic ash formation. *Mailing Add:* 314 Fox Rd Havre de Grace MD 21078

BENNETT, G(ARY) F, BIOCHEMICAL, CHEMICAL & ENVIRONMENTAL ENGINEERING. *Current Pos:* From asst prof to prof, 63-92, EMER PROF BIOCHEM ENG, UNIV TOLEDO, 92- *Personal Data:* b Windsor, Ont, July 22, 35; m 63, Judith Connarbe; c Ritchie B & Allison J. *Educ:* Queen's Univ, Ont, BSc, 57; Univ Mich, MSE, 60, PhD(chem eng), 63. *Honors & Awards:* Environ Award Chem Eng, Am Inst Chem Engrs, 75, Serv to Soc Award, 82. *Concurrent Pos:* Consult, Great Lakes Container Corp, 76-84 & Assoc Chem & Environ Serv, 79-84, Envirosafe, 84-; ed, J Hazardous Mat, 80-, Environ Progress, 82- *Mem:* Am Inst Chem Engrs; Am Acad Environ Engrs. *Res:* Oxygen transfer; industrial waste water treatment; hazardous chemical spills; air flotation. *Mailing Add:* Col Eng Univ Toledo Toledo OH 43606. *Fax:* 419-530-8086

BENNETT, GARY COLIN, CELL BIOLOGY. *Current Pos:* From lectr to assoc prof, 70-82, PROF ANAT, McGILL UNIV, 82- *Personal Data:* b Montreal, Que, Oct 18, 39; m 67. *Educ:* Sir George Williams Univ, BA & BSc, 64; McGill Univ, MSc, 67, PhD(anat & cell biol), 71. *Concurrent Pos:* Fel, Ctr Nuclear Study, Saclay, France, 71-72. *Mem:* Am Asn Anatomists; Am Asn Cell Biol. *Res:* Synthesis and fate of glycoproteins in various cell types as studied by autoradiography; membrane biogenesis. *Mailing Add:* Dept Anat & Cell Biol McGill Univ 3640 University St Montreal PQ H3A 2B2 Can

BENNETT, GARY L, NUCLEAR PROPULSION FOR SPACECRAFT SYSTEMS. *Current Pos:* PROG MGR SPACE POWER & PROPULSION, NASA HQ, 88- *Personal Data:* b Twin Falls, Idaho, Jan 17, 40; m 61; c 1. *Educ:* Univ Idaho, BS, 62, MNS, 66; Wash State Univ, PhD(physics), 70. *Prof Exp:* Physicist, Idaho Nat Eng Lab, 62-66, Space Nuclear Propulsion Off, Lewis Res Ctr, 70-71; flight safety officer, Space Nuclear Systems Off, US AEC, 71-74; tech asst & br chief, US Nuclear Regulatory Comn, 74-79; div dir, Space Nuclear Power Prog, US Dept Energy, 80-88. *Mem:* Fel Am Phys Soc; Sigma Xi; Planetary Soc; fel Brit Interplanetary Soc; assoc fel Am Inst Aeronaut & Astronaut; Am Astronaut Soc; Am Asn Physics Teachers. *Res:* Technical program management of spacecraft propulsion technology including electric propulsion, high performance chemical thrusters and advanced concepts. *Mailing Add:* NASA-Advanced Space Power Syst Code Ct Trans Div Washington DC 20546

BENNETT, GARY LEE, PRODUCTION SYSTEMS. *Current Pos:* RES GENETICIST, MEAT ANIMAL RES CTR, AGR RES SERV, USDA, 85- *Personal Data:* b Sioux City, Iowa, Mar 5, 51; m 75, Betsy Blake; c Emily & Andrew. *Educ:* Iowa State Univ, BS, 73; Ohio State Univ, MS, 75, PhD, 77. *Prof Exp:* Fel, Univ Nebr, 77-81; scientist, NZ Min Agr Fish, 81-85. *Concurrent Pos:* Adj assoc prof, Univ Nebr, 86- *Mem:* Am Soc Animal Sci; Sigma Xi. *Res:* Modeling and simulation of livestock systems; livestock genetics; statistical methods. *Mailing Add:* US Meat Animal Res Ctr PO Box 166 Clay Center NE 68933-0166

BENNETT, GEORGE KEMBLE, QUALITY ENGINEERING, RELIABILITY & MAINTAINABILITY. *Current Pos:* head indust eng, 86-91, HALLIBURTON PROF, TEX A&M UNIV, 86- *Personal Data:* b Jacksonville, Fla, Apr 2, 40; m 82; c 4. *Educ:* Fla State Univ, BS, 62; San Jose State Univ, MS, 68; Texas Tech Univ, PhD(indust eng), 70. *Honors &*

Awards: Pres Award Merit, Soc Logistics Engrs, 87; Award of Excellence, Qual & Reliability Eng, Inst Indust Eng, 92; Centennial Cert, Am Soc Eng Educ, 93. *Prof Exp:* Assoc engr, Martin Co, 62-63; sr engr, Lockheed Missiles & Space Co, 63-66; vis scientist, NASA, 69-70; asst prof indust eng, Va Tech, 70-73; staff engr, Honeywell Avionics, 79-86; prof indust eng, 73-79, chmn dept, Univ SFla, 79-86. *Concurrent Pos:* Asst dir, Tex Eng Exp Sta, 91-92; assoc dean eng, Tex A&M Univ, 91-; dir, Tex Eng Exten Serv, 92-; assoc vice chancellor eng, Tex A&M Univ Syst, 92- *Mem:* Fel Inst Indust Engrs; fel Soc Logistics Engrs; Am Soc Eng Educ. *Res:* Development of cost based sampling plans and procedures; the effect of inspection error in sampling plan design; empirical Bayes parameter estimation procedures for reliability engineering. *Mailing Add:* Indust Eng Texas A&M Univ College Station TX 77843-0100. *Fax:* 409-862-2888; *E-Mail:* gkb1344@zeus.tamu.edu

BENNETT, GEORGE NELSON, REGULATION, TRANSCRIPTION. *Current Pos:* From asst prof to assoc prof, 78-92, PROF BIOCHEM, RICE UNIV, 92- *Personal Data:* m 83, Lolin Wang; c Alan & Neal. *Educ:* Purdue Univ, PhD(biol sci), 74. *Mem:* Am Chem Soc; Am Soc Biochem & Molecular Biol. *Res:* Prokaryotic molecular biology; clostridial biotechnology; bacterial response to acids; genetic engineering and metabolic engineering. *Mailing Add:* Dept Biochem Rice Univ 6100 Main St PO Box 1892 Houston TX 77251-1892

BENNETT, GERALD WILLIAM, RADIATION PHYSICS, MEDICAL PHYSICS. *Current Pos:* CONSULT, DIAG MED PHYSICS, 93- *Personal Data:* b Hempstead, NY, June 15, 33; m 55; c 6. *Educ:* Brooklyn Polytech Inst, BME, 55; Hofstra Univ, MA, 62; State Univ NY, Stony Brook, PhD(physics), 68; Am Bd Nuclear Med, dipl. *Prof Exp:* Jr engr, NY Naval Shipyard, 56; mech engr, Fairchild Engine Div, NY, 56-59; physicist, Ger Electron Synchrotron, Hamburg, 68-69; oper engr, Cosmotron Div, Brookhaven Nat Lab, 59-64, develop engr, 64-68, physicist, Accelerator Dept, 69-76, physicist, Med Dept, 76-88, physicist, Ags Dept, 88-93. *Concurrent Pos:* Prin invest, Nat Cancer Inst Res Grant, 75-78; prof, Clin Campus, State Univ NY, Stony Brook, 75-; consult nuclear med, Northport Vet Admin Hosp, 76- *Mem:* Inst Elec & Electronics Engrs; Am Col Nuclear Med; Soc Nuclear Med; Am Col Med Physics. *Res:* Radiation physics; instrumentation; medical applications of protons, anti-protons and heavy ions. *Mailing Add:* 21 Watchogue East Moriches NY 11940

BENNETT, GLENN ALLEN, ORGANIC CHEMISTRY, BIOCHEMISTRY. *Current Pos:* Chemist biol insecticides, 62-72, RES CHEMIST MYCOTOXINS, SCI & EDUC ADMIN-AGR RES, USDA, PEORIA, ILL, 72- *Personal Data:* b La Follette, Tenn, Nov 18, 38; m 71; c 2. *Educ:* Bradley Univ, BA, 62; Iowa State Univ, MS, 66. *Mem:* Am Chem Soc; Sigma Xi; Am Oil Chemists Soc; Asn Off Anal Chemists. *Res:* Analysis of agricultural commodities for fungal metabolites, specifically mycotoxins, by high-pressure liquid chromatography, gas chromatography, gas chromatography-mass spectrometry and thin layer chromatography; development of methods to detoxify contaminated grains. *Mailing Add:* 111 High St Metamora IL 61548

BENNETT, GLENN TAYLOR, novel laser & nonlinear optic systems, ultrafast diagnostics, for more information see previous edition

BENNETT, GORDON DANIEL, WELL HYDRAULICS, REGIONAL FLOW SYSTEM ANALYSIS. *Current Pos:* SR ASSOC, S S PAPADOPULOS & ASSOC, INC, 87- *Personal Data:* b Elmira, NY, Oct 5, 31; m 58; c 3. *Educ:* Univ Notre Dame, BS, 56; Pa State Univ, MS, 61. *Honors & Awards:* O E Meinzer Award, Geol Soc Am, 81; Distinguished Serv Award, US Dept Interior, 86. *Prof Exp:* Geophysicist, US Geol Surv, 56-61, tech adv, USAID, 62-66, hydrologist, US Geol Surv, 66-81, chief ground water br, 81-82, asst chief, water resources dir, 82-85, res hydrologist, 85-86; mgr, Kearney Inc, 86-87. *Mem:* Fel Geol Soc Am; Am Geophys Union; Asn Ground Water Scientists & Engrs. *Res:* Effects of wellbores on regional flow; well hydraulics; movement of contaminants; freshwater-saltwater relationships; characterization of regional flow systems. *Mailing Add:* 5402 Water Crest Ct Fairfax VA 22032

BENNETT, GORDON FRASER, entomology, protozoology; deceased, see previous edition for last biography

BENNETT, GUDRUN STAUB, CELL BIOLOGY, NEUROBIOLOGY. *Current Pos:* RES SCIENTIST, DEPT ZOOL & ASSOC PROF, DEPT ANAT & CELL BIOL & DEPT NEUROSCI, UNIV FLA, 86-, RES PROF, 93- *Personal Data:* b New York, NY, Nov 13, 40; m 62; c 2. *Educ:* Vassar Col, AB, 61; Rockefeller Univ, PhD(life sci), 68. *Prof Exp:* Instr, Dept Path, Univ Ky, 71-72; res assoc, Fla State Univ, 72-76; res assoc, Dept Anat, Univ Pa, 76-79, from res asst prof to res assoc prof, 79-86. *Mem:* AAAS; Am Soc Cell Biol; Soc Neurosci. *Res:* Neuronal cytoskeletons; function and metabolism of neurofilaments; neuronal differentiation; cell differentiation. *Mailing Add:* Dept Anat & Cell Biol Univ Fla Health Ctr PO Box 100235 Gainesville FL 32610-0235

BENNETT, HAROLD EARL, OPTICAL PHYSICS, OPTICAL TESTING. *Current Pos:* head phys optics br, 60-78, PHYSICIST, NAVAL WEAPONS CTR, 56-, ASSOC HEAD PHYS DIV, 71- *Personal Data:* b Missoula, Mont, Feb 25, 29; m 52, 84; c 2. *Educ:* Univ Mont, BA, 51; Pa State Univ, MS, 53, PhD(physics), 55. *Honors & Awards:* L T E Thompson Award, Naval Weapons Ctr, 74; Captain Robert Dexter Conrad Award, US Navy, 79; Technol Achievement Award, Int Soc Optical Eng, 83. *Prof Exp:* Physicist, Nat Bur Standards, 53 & Wright Air Develop Ctr, 55-56. *Concurrent Pos:* Fel Ord Sci, Naval Weapons Ctr, 72. *Mem:* Fel Optical Soc Am; Am Phys Soc; fel Int Soc Optical Eng (pres, 88). *Res:* Optical properties of solids; solid state physics; optical instrumentation; thin films; laser components; large optics. *Mailing Add:* Bennett Optical Res Inc 201 S Sandes Ridgecrest CA 93555

BENNETT, HOLLY VANDER LAAN, CELL BIOLOGY, ACTIN-MEMBRANE INTERACTION. *Current Pos:* FEL, WHITEHEAD INST, 86- *Personal Data:* b Alexandria, Va, Feb 13, 57; m 88. *Educ:* Wheaton Col, BA, 78; Albert Einstein Col Med, PhD(anat & struct biol), 86. *Mem:* NY Acad Sci; Am Soc Cell Biol; Electron Micros Soc; Biophys Soc. *Res:* Intestinal epithelial ankyrin. *Mailing Add:* 112 Nonantum St Newton MA 02158

BENNETT, HUGH DEEVEREAUX, MEDICINE. *Current Pos:* PROF MED & ASSOC DEAN, HAHNEMANN MED COL, 62- *Personal Data:* b Brooklyn, NY, Jan 19, 18; m 41. *Educ:* Univ Chicago, BS, 40, MD, 42. *Prof Exp:* Instr med, Med Sch, Northwestern Univ, 51-53; from asst prof to assoc prof, Col Med, Baylor Univ, 53-62. *Concurrent Pos:* Asst chief med serv, Vet Admin Hosp, Ill, 51-53, chief med serv, Houston, 53-62; attend physician, Philadelphia Gen Hosp, 62-; vis prof, Free Univ Lille, France, 75- *Mem:* Fel Am Col Physicians; AMA. *Res:* Hepatic and gastrointestinal diseases. *Mailing Add:* Hahnemann Univ Sch Med Univ Hosp 235 N 15th St Philadelphia PA 19102-1178

BENNETT, IAN CECIL, dentistry, for more information see previous edition

BENNETT, IVAN FRANK, psychiatry, for more information see previous edition

BENNETT, JAMES ANTHONY, CANCER. *Current Pos:* ASST PROF IMMUNOL, ALBANY MED COL UNION UNIV, 79- *Personal Data:* b Buffalo, NY, Jan 9, 48; m 75. *Educ:* Univ Notre Dame, BA, 69; State Univ NY, Buffalo, MS, 72, PhD(pharmacol), 76. *Prof Exp:* From res asst to res assoc, Yale Univ, 76-78, res fel, 78-79. *Mem:* Am Asn Cancer Res; Am Asn Immunologists. *Res:* Investigation of immunological changes during preclinical and clinical chemoimmunotheraphy. *Mailing Add:* Dept Pharm & Ther Albany Med Col 47 New Scotland Ave Albany NY 12208-3412

BENNETT, JAMES AUSTIN, ANIMAL BREEDING. *Current Pos:* RETIRED. *Personal Data:* b Taber, Alta, Jan 29, 15; nat US; m 40; c 5. *Educ:* Utah State Univ, BS, 40, MS, 41; Univ Minn, PhD(animal breeding), 57. *Prof Exp:* Livestock asst, Dom Dept Agr Can, 41-45; from asst prof to prof animal sci, Utah State Univ, 45-93, head dept, 50-76. *Mem:* AAAS; Am Soc Animal Sci; Sigma Xi; Am Genetics Asn. *Res:* Breeding phases of beef cattle and sheep. *Mailing Add:* 307 E 500 N Logan UT 84321

BENNETT, JAMES GORDY, JR, POLYMER CHEMISTRY. *Current Pos:* RETIRED. *Personal Data:* b Washington, DC, Aug 29, 32; m 56; c 2. *Educ:* NY State Col Teachers, Albany, BS, 54; Rensselaer Polytech Inst, PhD(chem), 59. *Prof Exp:* Assoc res chemist, Parke Davis & Co, Mich, 59-60; sr res chemist, Huyck Felt Co, NY, 60-63; res chemist, Gen Elec Co, 63-72, plant chemist, 72-79, mgr, Process Technol Plastics Div, 79-96. *Mem:* Am Chem Soc. *Res:* Organic and polymer synthesis; oxidative coupling chemistry; homogeneous and heterogeneous catalysis. *Mailing Add:* 610 Cortland St Albany NY 12208

BENNETT, JAMES PETER, AIR POLLUTION ECOLOGY. *Current Pos:* ADJ PROF, UNIV WIS-MADISON, 93 *Personal Data:* b Chicago, Ill, Aug 25, 44. *Educ:* Wash Univ, BA, 66; Univ Mich, Ann Arbor, MA, 69; Univ BC, PhD(plant sci), 75. *Prof Exp:* Sr scientist ecol, Hudson River Valley Comn, Tarrytown, NY, 69-70; instr, Pratt Inst, 70-71; asst prof & olericult crop ecol, Dept Veg Crops, Univ Calif, Davis, 75-80; res ecologist, Air Qual Div, Nat Park Serv, US Dept Interior, 80-93. *Mem:* AAAS; Am Inst Biol Sci; Am Soc Hort Sci; Crop Sci Soc Am. *Res:* Plant competition, density, spacing, productivity; whole plant development and growth analysis; allometry; yield component compensation; experimental design; air pollution effects on native vegetation; plant ecology. *Mailing Add:* Inst Environ Studies Univ Wis-Madison 610 Walnut St Madison WI 53705

BENNETT, JEAN MCPHERSON, OPTICAL PHYSICS. *Current Pos:* RETIRED. *Personal Data:* b Kensington, Md, May 9, 30; div. *Educ:* Mt Holyoke Col, BA, 51; Pa State Univ, MS, 53, PhD(physics), 55. *Hon Degrees:* DSc, Mt Holyoke Col, 92. *Honors & Awards:* Woman Scientist of the Year, Naval Weapons Ctr, 79, LTE Thompson Award, 88; David Richardson Medal, Optical Soc Am, 90; Lifetime Achievement Award, Women Sci & Eng, 93. *Prof Exp:* Physicist, Nat Bur Stand, 51, 53 & Wright Air Develop Ctr, 55-56; res scientist, Naval Weapons Ctr, 60-85, sr res scientist, 87-95, physicist, 56-95. *Concurrent Pos:* Vis prof, Univ Ala, Huntsville, 86-87 & Mt Holyoke Col, 94-95; vis scientist, Uppsala Univ Uppsala, Inst Optical Res, Stockholm, Sweden, 88; sr fel, Naval Weapons Ctr, 89; distinguished fel, Naval Air Warfare Ctr, 94. *Mem:* Fel Optical Soc Am (vpres, 84, pres elect, 85, pres, 86-87). *Res:* Optical properties of solids; solid state physics; interferometry; thin films; characterization of optical surfaces. *Mailing Add:* Code 4B1A00D Michelson Lab Naval Air Warfare Ctr China Lake CA 93555. *Fax:* 760-939-1409; *E-Mail:* jbennett@peewee.chinalake.navy.mil

BENNETT, JESSE HARLAND, AGRICULTURE, FORESTRY. *Current Pos:* plant physiologist, Plant Stress Lab, Plant Physiol Inst, Agr Res Serv Sci & Educ, 74-84, PLANT PHYSIOLOGIST, AGR RES STA, USDA, LOGAN, UTAH, 84- *Personal Data:* b Lehi, Utah, June 21, 36; m 58; c 3. *Educ:* Utah State Univ, BS, 61; Univ Utah, PhD(bot) & cert environ toxicol, 69. *Honors & Awards:* Res Excellence Award, Environ Protection Agency, 87. *Prof Exp:* USPHS trainee environ toxicol, Ctr Environ Biol, Univ Utah, 65-68; NIH fel & res assoc biophys, Ctr Biol Natural Syst, Wash Univ, 69-70; res assoc, Dept Biol, Univ Utah, 70-74. *Concurrent Pos:* Air pollution consult & researcher, Ajax Presses, Utah Power & Light Co, 71-73; sci reviewer, J Environ Qual Sci, Nat Acad Sci, Coun Environ Qual, NSF, Energy Res & Develop Admin, Dept Energy, Environ Protection Agency & USDA, 74-81. *Mem:* AAAS; Am Soc Plant Physiologists; Ezra Taft Benson Agr & Food Inst; Bot Soc Am. *Res:* Physiology, metabolism and control of plant growth; environmental pollution and stress. *Mailing Add:* 2030 N 1400 E Logan UT 84321

BENNETT, JOAN WENNSTROM, GENETICS, MYCOLOGY. *Current Pos:* from asst prof to prof biol, 70-91, PROF CELLULAR & MOLECULAR BIOL, TULANE UNIV, 91- *Personal Data:* b Brooklyn, NY, Sept 15, 42; m 66, David Peterson; c John, Daniel & Mark. *Educ:* Upsala Col, BS, 63; Univ Chicago, MS, 64, PhD(bot), 67. *Hon Degrees:* DLitt, Upsala Col, 90. *Prof Exp:* Res assoc, NSF fel, Univ Chicago, 67-68; Nat Res Coun fel, 68-70. *Concurrent Pos:* NSF fel, 70-71; collabr, Southern Regional Res Ctr, 71-; lectr, Am Soc Microbiol Found, 81; chmn, Fermentation & Biotech Div, Am Soc Microbiol, 85-86; bd, Soc Indust Microbiol, 87; vis scientist, Leiden Univ, 91-92. *Mem:* Fel AAAS; fel Soc Indust Microbiol; Brit Mycol Soc (vpres, 89-90); Genetics Soc Am; fel Am Soc Microbiol (pres, 90-91); Mycol Soc Am; Soc Gen Microbiol; hon mem Czech Soc Microbiol. *Res:* Aflatoxin biosynthesis; genetics of secondary metabolism; biotechnology. *Mailing Add:* Dept Cell & Molecular Biol Tulane Univ New Orleans LA 70118

BENNETT, JOE CLAUDE, RHEUMATOLOGY. *Current Pos:* PRES & CHIEF EXEC OFFICER, BIOCRYST PHARMACEUT, 96- *Personal Data:* b Birmingham, Ala, Dec 12, 33; m 58; c 3. *Educ:* Howard Col, AB, 54; Harvard Med Sch, MD, 58. *Hon Degrees:* DSc, Univ Ala, Birmingham, 92. *Prof Exp:* Intern med, Med Ctr, Univ Ala, 58-59, asst resident, 59-60; Arthritis & Rheumatism Found fel, 60-62; res assoc molecular biol, NIH, 62-64; sr res fel biol chem, Calif Inst Technol, 64-65; asst prof med, Univ Ala, Birmingham, 65-66, assoc prof med & microbiol & asst dir div clin immunol & rheumatology, 66-70, prof & chmn microbiol, 70-82, prof, Dept Med & dir, Div Clin Immunol & Rheumatology, 70-83, prof & chmn, Dept Med, 82-93, 93-96. *Concurrent Pos:* Clin fel rheumatology, Mass Gen Hosp, Harvard Med Sch, 60-61, res fel, 61-62; Markle scholar acad med, 65-70; Nat Inst Gen Med Sci res career develop award, 65-75; mem study sect for training in rheumatology, NIH, 69-72, chmn, 70-72, mem & chmn study sect for allergy & immunol, 75-78; mem, Comt Eval Clin Competance, Am Bd Internal Med, 87-, chmn, Subcomt Methods, 90, Comt Res & Develop, 87-, mem gov bd, 87-; mem sci adv comt, Biocryst, Inc, Merck, Genentech, Warren Alpert Found, Harvard Med Sch, Charles E Culpeper Found, Inc, 89-; mem prog comt, Inst Med-Nat Acad Sci, 90-, chair, Health Scis Policy Bd; numerous lectrs & vis professorships. *Mem:* Inst Med-Nat Acad Sci; Genetics Soc Am; Am Asn Immunologists; Am Soc Clin Invest; Am Asn Physicians; fel AAAS; master Am Col Physicians; Am Acad Allergy & Immunol; Am Acad Microbiol; Soc Exp Biol & Med; Protein Soc (pres, 81-82); Am Col Rheumatology (pres, 81-82). *Res:* Genetic determinants of protein structure; structural aspects of immunoglobulins; molecular basis of disease states; immunochemistry; cell surface structure. *Mailing Add:* Univ Ala Birmingham 1070 Admin Bldg 701 20th St S Birmingham AL 35244

BENNETT, JOHN E, INFECTIOUS DISEASES. *Current Pos:* clin assoc, Nat Inst Allergy & Infectious Dis, NIH, 61-64, actg head, Infectious Dis Sect, 65-66, head, 66-71, HEAD, CLIN MYCOL SECT, LCI, NAT INST ALLERGY & INFECTIOUS DIS, NIH, 71- *Personal Data:* b El Centro, Calif, Mar 6, 33; m 58; c 2. *Educ:* Stanford Univ, Calif, BS, 55; Johns Hopkins Univ, MD, 59. *Honors & Awards:* R R Hawkins Award, 79. *Prof Exp:* Intern, Johns Hopkins, 59-60; asst resident med, Univ Wash, Seattle,, 60-61 & Washington Univ, St Louis, 64-65. *Concurrent Pos:* Prof med, Dept Med, Uniformed Serv Univ Health Sci, 76-; lectr, Dept Micros & Med, Sch Med, Johns Hopkins Univ, 76- *Mem:* Master Am Col Physicians; Asn Am Physicians; Am Soc Clin Invest; Infectious Dis Soc. *Res:* Host defense, chemotherapy and mechanisms of drug resistance; infectious diseases. *Mailing Add:* Clin Mycol Sect Bldg 10 Rm 11C304 LCI, NIAID, NIH 9000 Rockville Pike Bethesda MD 20892

BENNETT, JOHN FRANCIS, HISTORY & PHILOSOPHY OF SCIENCE, ABSOLUTE YLEMICS. *Current Pos:* RETIRED. *Personal Data:* b Palo Alto, Calif, Jan 13, 25; div; c Erica (Leary). *Educ:* Stanford Univ, AB, 46, PhD(biol), 62. *Prof Exp:* Physicist, US Navy Electronics Lab, 50-51; asst biol, Hopkins Marine Sta, Calif, 53-54; asst, Stanford Univ, 54-56, actg instr, 57-60; NIH fel microbiol, 61-63; asst prof hist & philos sci, Univ Pa, 63-69; vis scholar biol sci, Stanford Univ, 69-71; proj dir natural sci, Sullivan Assocs, 71-74; staff mem, Encycl Britannica, 75; lectr embryol, human ecol & grad biol, San Jose State Univ, 76-78; lectr on Cosmos Earth & Life & Interdisciplinary Sci, San Francisco State Univ, 78-82, instr physics, Castilleja Sch, 83-84; res assoc, Univ Calif, Berkeley, 84-87; substitute teacher, Tricity (Fremont Network, Union City), 85-87. *Concurrent Pos:* Fulbright guest prof, Inst Statist, Univ Vienna, 67-68. *Mem:* AAAS; Sigma Xi. *Res:* Macroevolution theory; energetics; working on absolute Ylemics, the upshot of energetics, provisional titles, the Love of God and its applications. *Mailing Add:* 659 Univ Ave #H402 Palo Alto CA 94301. *E-Mail:* ylemguru@aol.com

BENNETT, JOHN M, INTERNAL MEDICINE, HEMATOLOGY. *Current Pos:* asst prof to assoc prof med, 69-76, PROF ONCOL MED, SCH MED, UNIV ROCHESTER, 76- ASSOC DIR CLIN ONCOL, UNIV ROCHESTER CANCER CTR, 74- *Personal Data:* b Boston, Mass, Apr 24, 33; m 57; c 3. *Educ:* Harvard Univ, AB, 55; Boston Univ, MD, 59. *Prof Exp:* Instr med, Harvard Med Sch, 65-66; head morphol & histochem sect, Clin Path Dept, NIH, 66-68; asst prof med, Sch Med, Tufts Univ, 68-69. *Concurrent Pos:* Dir outpatient labs, Boston City Hosp, 68-69; mem lymphoma task force, Nat Cancer Inst, 68-74; dir hemat & med oncol, Highland Hosp, Rochester, 69-74; head med oncol unit, Strong Mem Hosp, 74- *Mem:* AAAS; Am Soc Hemat; Am Fedn Clin Res; Am Soc Clin Oncol; Am Col Physicians. *Res:* Diagnosis by cyctochemical techniques and treatment of malignant disorders of the hematopoietic system. *Mailing Add:* Univ Rochester Cancer Ctr 601 Elmwood Ave Rochester NY 14642-0001

BENNETT, KENNETH A, BIOLOGICAL & FORENSIC ANTHROPOLOGY, HUMAN GENETICS. *Current Pos:* assoc prof, 70-75, PROF ANTHROP, UNIV WIS-MADISON, 75- *Personal Data:* b Butler, Okla, Oct 3, 35; m 59, Helen Maze; c Letitia A & Cheri L. *Educ:* Univ Tex, BA, 61; Univ Ariz, MA, 66, PhD(anthrop), 67. *Prof Exp:* Asst prof anthrop, Univ Ore, 67-70. *Concurrent Pos:* Ed, Yrbk Phys Anthrop, 76-81; rev article ed, Human Biol, 81-87; burial sites preserv bd, State Wis, 87-89. *Mem:* Human Biol Coun; Am Asn Phys Anthrop; Soc Study Evolution; Soc Study Human Biol; Soc Syst Zool; Am Soc Nat; Am Acad Forensic Sci. *Res:* Human skeletal anatomy; human genetics; forensic anthrop. *Mailing Add:* Dept Anthrop 5240 Soc Sci Bldg Univ Wis 1180 Observatory Dr Madison WI 53706-1393

BENNETT, LARRY E, INORGANIC CHEMISTRY. *Current Pos:* assoc prof, 70-74, PROF CHEM, SAN DIEGO STATE UNIV, 74- *Personal Data:* b San Diego, Calif, Feb 29, 40. *Educ:* San Diego State Univ, BS, 62; Stanford Univ, PhD(chem), 65. *Prof Exp:* NSF fel chem, Columbia Univ, 65-66; asst prof, Univ Fla, 66-70. *Concurrent Pos:* Vis prof, Stanford Univ, 77. *Res:* Coordination complexes of transition metals; mechanisms of electron transfer and substitution processes; design and synthesis of complexes for investigation of mechanism and possible new modes of reaction; bioinorganic redox processes. *Mailing Add:* Dept Chem San Diego State Univ San Diego CA 92182-1030

BENNETT, LAWRENCE HERMAN, PHYSICS, MATERIALS SCIENCE. *Current Pos:* LEADER MAGNETIC MAT GROUP, NAT INST STANDARDS & TECHNOL, 83- *Personal Data:* b Brooklyn, NY, Oct 17, 30; m 53; c 3. *Educ:* Brooklyn Col, BA, 51; Univ Md, MS, 55; Rutgers Univ, PhD(physics), 58. *Honors & Awards:* Gold Medal, Dept of Commerce, 71; Burgess Mem Award, Am Soc Metals, 75. *Prof Exp:* Physicist, US Naval Ord Lab, 51-53; physicist, Metal Physics Sect, Nat Bur Standards, 58-63, chief, Alloy Physics Sect, 63-81, div scientist, Metall Div, 81-83. *Concurrent Pos:* Letr, Grad Sch, Univ Md, 58-61, assoc prof, 61-76, prof, 76- *Mem:* Fel Am Phys Soc; fel Am Soc Metals; Am Inst Mining, Metall & Petrol Eng; Am Soc Test & Mat; Mat Res Soc. *Res:* Magnetic properties of materials; nuclear magnetic resonance; Mossbauer effect; alloy theory; superconductivity. *Mailing Add:* Mag Mater Group Nat Inst Stand Technol Rte 270 & Quince Orchard Rd Gaithersburg MD 20899

BENNETT, LEE COTTON, JR, MARINE GEOPHYSICS. *Current Pos:* ASST DIR, ENROLLMENT MGT, DREXEL UNIV, PHILADELPHIA, 96- *Personal Data:* b Philadelphia, Pa, Mar 14, 33; m 53, Asia Alderson; c Brooks, Bruce & Miriam. *Educ:* Haverford Col, BA, 55; Temple Univ, MS, 58; Bryn Mawr Col, PhD, 66. *Prof Exp:* Res asst solid state physics, Franklin Inst Labs, Pa, 55-58, res physicist, 58-59; res asst geophys, Woods Hole Oceanog Inst, 63-66; asst prof oceanog, Univ Wash, 66-73, asst prof geophys, 68-73; geophysicist, L C B Consults, 73-82; sr instr, Franklin Inst Sci Mus, 82-96, sr mus educr, 86-96. *Concurrent Pos:* Actg asst prof, Univ Wash, 64; instr, Shoreline Community Col, 75-76; vol instr, Franklin Inst Mus, 79-82; asst dir, Del Valley Sci Fairs, Inc, 88- *Mem:* Am Geophys Union; AAAS; Sigma Xi. *Res:* Continuous seismic profiling; seismic absorption in unconsolidated sediments; shoreline processes; experiential education in science museums. *Mailing Add:* 224 Haverford Ave Swarthmore PA 19081

BENNETT, LEONARD LEE, JR, BIOCHEMICAL PHARMACOLOGY. *Current Pos:* RETIRED. *Personal Data:* b Savannah, Ga, Nov 10, 20; m 49, Martha C Davis; c Walter Lee, Deborah Ann & Brian Whitley. *Educ:* Vanderbilt Univ, AB, 42, MS, 43; Univ NC, PhD(org chem), 49. *Prof Exp:* Asst, Vanderbilt Univ, 42-43; instr, Univ Ga, 43-44; asst & fel, Univ NC, 45-47; res assoc, Southern Res Inst, 45, res chemist, 48-56, head biochem div, 56-64, dir biochem res, 64-85. *Concurrent Pos:* Mem adv comt res ther cancer, Am Cancer Soc, 56-58 & 60-63; mem chemother study sect, NIH, 64-68; assoc ed, Cancer Res, 77-86. *Mem:* Am Asn Cancer Res; Am Soc Biol Chemists; Am Soc Pharmacol & Exp Therapeut. *Res:* Biochemistry of cancer; mechanisms of drug action; biochemistry of purines and pyrimidines. *Mailing Add:* Southern Res Inst PO Box 55305 Birmingham AL 35255-5305

BENNETT, LESLIE L, anatomy; deceased, see previous edition for last biography

BENNETT, LESLIE R, RADIOLOGY. *Current Pos:* asst clin prof radiol, 49-52, actg chief div radiobiol, Atomic Energy Proj, 50-52, from asst prof to assoc prof radiol, 52-60, PROF RADIOL, SCH MED, UNIV CALIF, LOS ANGELES, 60-, CHIEF CLIN RADIOISOTOPE SERV, 52- *Personal Data:* b Denver, Colo, Feb 13, 18; m 48; c 4. *Educ:* Univ Calif, AB, 40; Univ Rochester, MD, 43. *Prof Exp:* Intern, Strong Mem Hosp, Rochester, NY, 44;

asst radiation biol & pediat, Univ Rochester, 46-49. *Mem:* Am Roentgen Ray Soc; Am Soc Exp Path; Radiation Res Soc; Soc Nuclear Med. *Res:* Radiobiology. *Mailing Add:* Dept Radiol Sci Univ Calif Los Angeles Med Ctr 10833 LeConte Ave Los Angeles CA 90024-1721

BENNETT, LLOYD M, SCIENCE EDUCATION. *Current Pos:* asst prof educ & sci educ, 63-66, assoc prof sci educ, 66-71, Univ grants, 63-70, PROF SCI EDUC, TEX WOMAN'S UNIV, 71- *Personal Data:* b Columbus, Ind, Nov 22, 28; m 56; c 2. *Educ:* Ball State Teachers Col, AB, 50; Butler Univ, MS, 52; Univ Tex, MA, 58; Fla State Univ, PhD(marine biol, sci educ), 63. *Prof Exp:* Elem sch teacher, Ind, 50-51; res chemist, Firestone Tire & Rubber Co, Ind, 51-53; high sch teacher, Ind, 53-55; instr & asst biol, Univ Tex, 55-57; teacher & chmn, Dept Sci, Tex, 57-59; assoc prof biol, Amarillo Col, 59-60; prof biol & chem & dir, Eve Div, Indian River Jr Col, 60-61; asst physiol, Fla State Univ, 61-63. *Concurrent Pos:* Hogg Found ment health grant, Univ Tex & Hogg Found, 64; co-researcher, Hogg Found grant, 65-66; UNESCO consult elem sci & math educ, Govt Philippines, 74. *Mem:* AAAS; Nat Asn Res Sci Teaching; Nat Asn Biol Teachers; Nat Sci Teachers Asn; Sch Sci & Math Asn. *Res:* Devising, writing, standardizing and implementing the new Twupps curricular program in science for early childhood, including hands-on experiences; research in science for preschool level; preschool curricular developmental research in science. *Mailing Add:* PO Box 23029 Curriculum Tex Woman's Univ Sta Denton TX 76204-1029

BENNETT, LONNIE TRUMAN, MATHEMATICS, STATISTICS. *Current Pos:* asst prof, 66-69, ASSOC PROF MATH, NORTHEAST LA STATE UNIV, 69- *Personal Data:* b Gorum, La, June 9, 33; m 55; c 4. *Educ:* Northwest State Col (La), BS, 55; La State Univ, MA, 60; Okla State Univ, PhD(statist), 66. *Prof Exp:* Mathematician, Western Geophys Co Am, 55; teacher pub sch, 57-59; instr math, La State Univ, 60-62. *Concurrent Pos:* Consult, Marshall Space Flight Ctr, NASA, Ala, 66-67. *Mem:* Math Asn Am; Am Statist Asn. *Res:* Experimental design. *Mailing Add:* Dir Acad Comput Northeast La Univ 700 University Ave Monroe LA 71209-0001

BENNETT, MARTIN ARTHUR, CHEMISTRY. *Current Pos:* sr fel, 70-79, prof fel, 79-92, PROF, AUSTRALIAN NAT UNIV, 92- *Personal Data:* b Harrow, UK, Aug 11, 35; m 64, Rae E Mathews; c Simon & Andrew. *Educ:* Imp Col Sci, BS, 57, PhD, 60; Univ London, DSc, 74. *Honors & Awards:* H G Smith Medal, Royal Australian Chem Inst, 77, G J Burrows Award, 87; Nyholm Medal, Royal Soc Chem, 91; Max Planck Res Prize, Alexander von Humboldt Found, 94. *Prof Exp:* Turner & Newall fel, Univ Col, London, 61-63 & lectr chem, 63-67; fel, Res Sch Chem, Canberra, Australia, 67-70. *Mem:* Fel Australian Acad Sci; Am Chem Soc; Royal Soc Chem; Royal Australian Chem Inst. *Res:* Discovery of formation of transition metal to carbon bonds in cyclometallated complexes; stabilization of short-lived organic molecules, such as benzyne and cyclohexyne in form of transition metal complexes; authored 200 articles to professional journals. *Mailing Add:* Res Sch Chem Australian Nat Univ Canberra ACT 0200 Australia

BENNETT, MARY KATHERINE, MATHEMATICS. *Current Pos:* from asst to assoc prof math, 70-72, PROF MATH, UNIV MASS, AMHERST, 79- *Personal Data:* b Waterbury, Conn, Jan 30, 40. *Educ:* Albertus Magnus Col, BS, 61; Univ Mass, MA, 65, PhD(math), 66. *Prof Exp:* Teacher high sch, Conn, 61-63; asst prof math, Univ Mass, Amherst, 66-68; John Wesley Young res instr, Dartmouth Col, 68-70. *Mem:* Am Math Soc; Math Asn Am. *Res:* Lattice theory, particularly lattices of convex geometries and geometric lattices. *Mailing Add:* Dept Math Univ Mass Amherst MA 01003-0113

BENNETT, MICHAEL, EXPERIMENTAL PATHOLOGY, HEMATOLOGY. *Current Pos:* PROF PATH, SOUTHWESTERN MED SCH, 81- *Personal Data:* b Goose Creek, Tex, Feb 11, 36; m 60; c 4. *Educ:* Baylor Univ, MD, 61. *Prof Exp:* Intern, Cleveland Metrop Gen Hosp, Ohio, 62; resident path, Philadelphia Gen Hosp, Pa, 63; biologist, Oak Ridge Nat Labs, 63-65; mem staff, Roswell Park Mem Inst, 65-68, assoc cancer res scientist, 68-72; assoc prof path, Sch Med, Boston Univ, 72-78, prof path & micro, 78-81. *Concurrent Pos:* Resident path, Buffalo Gen Hosp, 69-71. *Mem:* Am Soc Exp Path; Am Asn Immunol; Int Asn Hemat; Reticuloendo Soc. *Res:* Function of hemopoietic stem cells; cellular immunology; bone marrow transplantation; immunogenetics. *Mailing Add:* Dept Path Univ Tex Southwestern Med Sch 5323 Harry Hines Blvd Dallas TX 75235-9072

BENNETT, MICHAEL VANDER LAAN, CELLULAR & MOLECULAR NEUROSCIENCE. *Current Pos:* prof anat, 67-74, chmn neurosci, 82-96, PROF NEUROSCI & DIR DIV CELLULAR NEUROBIOL, ALBERT EINSTEIN COL MED, 74-, SYLVIA & ROBERT S OLNICK PROF, 86- *Personal Data:* b Madison, Wis, Jan 7, 31; div; c Nicholas Toscan & Elena Paula. *Educ:* Yale Univ, BS, 52; Oxford Univ, DPhil(physiol), 57. *Prof Exp:* Res worker, Dept Neurol, Col Physician & Surgeons, Columbia Univ, 57-58, res assoc, 58-59, from asst prof to assoc prof neurol, 59-66. *Concurrent Pos:* Rhodes scholar, 52; Grass fel, 58; sr res fel, NIH, 60-62; co dir neurobiol course, Marine Biol Lab, 70-74; adv group, comt teaching & res basic neurol & commun sci, Nat Acad Sci, 73-74, proj rev & comt, Neurol Disorders Prog, 77-81, sci adv comt, Irma T Hirschl Trust, 77-81, comt models biomed res, NAS, 83-85, US Nat Comt, Int Union Physiol Sci, 83-85; mem coun, Soc Neurosci, 76-80 & prog comt, 80-83; chmn, Biol Sci Sect, NY Acad Sci, 78 & bd gov, 80-82; ed, Brain Res, 75-, J Cell Biol, 83-85, J Neurobiol, 69-95, & asssoc ed, 79-85, J Neurocytol, 80-82 & J Neurosci, 81-85. *Mem:* Nat Acad Sci; fel AAAS; Am Asn Anatomists; Am Physiol Soc; Am Soc Cell Biol; Biophys Soc; fel NY Acad Sci. *Res:* Author of over 250 publications in structure and physiology of gap junctions and glutamate receptors. *Mailing Add:* Albert Einstein Col Med Yeshiva Univ Bronx NY 10461. *Fax:* 718-430-8944; *E-Mail:* mbennett@aecom.yu.edu

BENNETT, MIRIAM FRANCES, BIOLOGICAL RHYTHMS, COMPARATIVE PHYSIOLOGY. *Current Pos:* Dana prof, Colby Col, 73-80, chmn Dept Biol, 73-88, Kenan Prof, 80-93, EMER KENAN PROF, COLBY COL, 93- *Personal Data:* b Milwaukee, Wis, May 17, 28. *Educ:* Carleton Col, BA, 50; Mt Holyoke Col, MA, 52; Northwestern Univ, PhD(biol), 54. *Hon Degrees:* MA, Colby Col, 73. *Prof Exp:* Asst zool, Mt Holyoke Col, 50-52; asst biol, Northwestern Univ, 52-53; from instr to prof, Sweet Briar Col, 54-73, chmn dept, 64-73. *Concurrent Pos:* Guest investr, Inst Zool, Univ Munich, 60-61 & 68; NSF fel, 61; mem, Marine Biol Lab, Woods Hole. *Mem:* Fel AAAS; Animal Behav Soc; Am Zool Soc; NY Acad Sci; Am Micros Soc; Int Soc Chronobiol. *Res:* Biological rhythmicity; invertebrate and amphibian hormones, regeneration. *Mailing Add:* 95 Ten Lots Rd Fairfield ME 04937-3000

BENNETT, OVELL FRANCIS, organic chemistry, for more information see previous edition

BENNETT, PETER A, PHYSICS. *Current Pos:* res specialist, 83-84, asst prof, 84-90, ASSOC PROF PHYSICS, ARIZ STATE UNIV, 90- *Educ:* Univ Minn, BA, 74; Univ Wis, PhD(physics), 80. *Prof Exp:* Fel, KFA-Julich, 80-81; fel, AT&T Bell Labs, 81-83. *Concurrent Pos:* Sabbattical, IBM Watson & AT&T Bell Labs. *Mem:* Am Phys Soc; Am Vacuum Soc; Mat Res Soc. *Res:* Surface phase transitions and critical phenomena; electronic structure of metallic alloys; surface reconstruction, unit cell geometry, especially of semiconductors; silicide thin films in UHV. *Mailing Add:* Dept Physics & Astron Ariz State Univ PO Box 871504 Tempe AZ 85287-1504

BENNETT, PETER BRIAN, ANESTHESIOLOGY, PHYSIOLOGY. *Current Pos:* prof biomed eng, Duke Univ, 72-75, dir res anesthesiol, 73-84, co-dir, F G Hall Environ Res Lab, 74-77, dir, F G Hall Environ Res Lab, 77-88, PROF ANESTHESIOL, MED CTR, DUKE UNIV, 72-, ASSOC PROF PHYSIOL, 75-, SR DIR, HYPERBARIC CTR, 88- *Personal Data:* b Portsmouth, Eng, June 12, 31; m 56, Margaret Warren; c Caroline & Christopher. *Educ:* Univ London, BSc, 51; Univ Southampton, PhD(physiol, biochem), 64, DSc(physiol, biochem), 84. *Honors & Awards:* Oceaneering Int Award, Undersea Med Soc, 75; Sci Award, Underwater Soc Am, 80; Albert Behnke Award, Undersea Med Soc, 83; Greenstone Award, Nat Asn Underwater Instrs, 85; Prince Tomahito of Mikasa Award, 90. *Prof Exp:* Asst head, Surg Sect, Royal Navy Physiol Lab, Alverstoke, Eng, 53-56, head, Inert Gas Narcosis Sect, 56-66; head pressure physiol, Can Defense & Civil Inst Environ Res, 66-68; head pressure physiol, Royal Navy Physiol Lab, 68-72. *Concurrent Pos:* Exec dir, Divers Alert Network, 81- *Mem:* AAAS; NY Acad Sci; Undersea Med Soc (pres, 75-76); Soc Neurosci; Aerospace Med Asn; foreign mem, Russ Acad Sci. *Res:* Inert gas narcosis; mechanisms of anesthesia; high pressure nervous syndrome; decompression sickness; oxygen toxicity; hyperbaric physiology and medicine. *Mailing Add:* Duke Univ Med Ctr FG Hall Lab PO Box 3823 Durham NC 27702-3823. *Fax:* 919-684-6002

BENNETT, PETER HOWARD, EPIDEMIOLOGY, MEDICINE. *Current Pos:* vis assoc arthritis, NIH, 64-68, assoc chief epidemiol, Clin Field Studies Unit, 68-70, chief epidemiol & field studies br, 70-85, CHIEF PHOENIX EPIDEMIOL & CLIN RES BR, NAT INST DIABETES, DIGESTIVE & KIDNEY DIS, PHOENIX, ARIZ, 85- *Personal Data:* b Farnworth, Eng, June 21, 37; c 1. *Educ:* Univ Manchester, BSc, 58, MB, ChB, 61, FFCM, 73, FRCP, 79. *Honors & Awards:* Lilly Award, Am Diabetes Asn, 77; Luther Terry Award, USPHS, 79; Claude Bernard Award, Europ Asn Study Diabetes, 92. *Prof Exp:* House physician, Royal Infirmary, Manchester, Eng, 62, house surgeon, 62-63; house phsyician, Postgrad Med Sch, London, Eng, 63-64; house physician, Nat Hosp Nerv Dis, Queen Square, 64. *Concurrent Pos:* Vis fel arthritis, NIH, 63; res fel, Postgrad Med Sch, London, 64; assoc, Col Med, Univ Ariz, 68-; epidemiologist, SPac Comn, 80-81; consult, WHO. *Mem:* Am Rheumatism Asn; Am Diabetes Asn; fel Am Epidemiol Soc; Soc Epidemiol Res; Am Diabetes Asn. *Res:* Clinical rheumatology; epidemiologic studies of arthritis and diabetes; clinical research in diabetes. *Mailing Add:* 298 W Georgia Ave Phoenix AZ 85013. *Fax:* 602-263-1669; *E-Mail:* phb@cu.nih.gov

BENNETT, RAYMOND DUDLEY, AGRICULTURAL BIOCHEMISTRY, NATURAL PRODUCTS CHEMISTRY. *Current Pos:* res chemist, Calif Inst Technol, 64-69, res chemist, 69-93, ACTG RES LEADER, FRUIT & VEG CHEM LAB, AGR RES SERV, US DEPT AGR, 93- *Personal Data:* b Meriden, Conn, May 9, 31; m 61, Larita Sayre; c Laura & Miles. *Educ:* Univ Conn, BS, 53; Purdue Univ, MS, 55, PhD(pharm chem), 58. *Prof Exp:* Fel org chem, Univ Va, 58-60; res chemist, Nat Insts Health, 60-63. *Mem:* Am Chem Soc; AAAS; Phytochem Soc NAm. *Res:* Structure determination of citrus constituents; nuclear magnetic resonance; biochemistry of citrus fruits. *Mailing Add:* 827 N Altadena Dr Pasadena CA 91107-1850

BENNETT, RICHARD BOND, ORGANIC CHEMISTRY. *Current Pos:* from asst prof to assoc prof, 67-74, chmn dept, 69-71 & 80-86, PROF CHEM, THIEL COL, 74- *Personal Data:* b Grove City, Pa, Nov 28, 32; m 61, Jacqueline Gorun; c David & George. *Educ:* Grove City Col, BS, 54; Ohio State Univ, MSc, 55, PhD(carbohydrate chem), 64. *Prof Exp:* Res chemist, Gulf Res & Develop Co, 58; asst prof chem, Millikin Univ, 61-63. *Mem:* Am Chem Soc; Sigma Xi. *Res:* Aldonamide hydrolysis; ketose synthesis. *Mailing Add:* Dept Chem Thiel Col Greenville PA 16125-2182

BENNETT, RICHARD HAROLD, MARINE GEOLOGY, GEOTECHNIQUE. *Current Pos:* cartogr, Environ Sci Serv Admin, Dept Com, 65-66, res oceanogr, Nat Oceanic & Atmospheric Admin-Atlantic Oceanog & Meteorol Labs-Dept Com, 66-, MGR, MARINE

GEOTECH-RATIONAL USE OF SEA FLOOR PROG, NAT OCEANIC & ATMOSPHERIC ADMIN, 76-, CHIEF SCI, SEAFLOOR DIV, NORDA, US NAVY. *Personal Data:* b Washington, DC, July 27, 39; m 65; c 3. *Educ:* Am Univ, BS, 67; Tex A&M Univ, PhD(oceanog), 76. *Prof Exp:* Geol asst, US Geol Surv, Dept Interior, 58-64; field crew chief surv, Gravity Meter Explor Co, 64-65. *Concurrent Pos:* Adv, Deep Sea Drilling Prog, Int Phase Ocean Drilling; USSAC adj prof, Oceanic Eng Div, Univ Miami & Texas A&M Univ; pres, Sea Probe, 95. *Mem:* Soc Econ Paleontologists & Mineralogists; Asn Int L'Etude Argiles; Am Soc Civil Engrs. *Res:* Marine geotechnique; sedimentology; clay fabric of submarine sediments; seafloor stability studies of continental margins; in situ measurement of submarine sediment properties; pore pressures in surficial sediments; geophysical and hydrographic surveys, mapping, sediment & transport processes, seafloor stability. *Mailing Add:* 156 Donley Burks Rd Carriere MS 39426

BENNETT, RICHARD HENRY, ORGANIC CHEMISTRY. *Current Pos:* sr staff chemist, Texaco Chem Co, 80-82, prod mgr, 82-90, sr coordr prod safety, 90-93, MGR ENVIRON, HEALTH & SAFETY, TEXACO CHEM CO, 93- *Personal Data:* b Hart Co, Ky, Mar 4, 44; m 94, Joyce E Murphy; c Phil, Paul & Dawn. *Educ:* Western Ky Univ, BS, 65; Vanderbilt Univ, PhD(org chem), 69. *Prof Exp:* Res chemist petrol chem, Texaco Res Lab, 69-75; res chemist liquid chromatography, Jefferson Chem Co, 75-80. *Mem:* Am Chem Soc. *Res:* Improvement of refinery processes; isolation and identification of trace organics present in refinery waste water streams; high pressure liquid chromatography. *Mailing Add:* 6315 Clairmont Dr Austin TX 78749

BENNETT, ROBERT BOWEN, physics, for more information see previous edition

BENNETT, ROBERT M, RHEUMATOLOGY, IMMUNOLOGY. *Current Pos:* assoc prof, 76-81, PROF MED, ORE HEALTH SCI UNIV, 81-, HEAD DIV ARTHRITIS & RHEUMATIC DIS, 85- *Personal Data:* b Berkhamsted, Eng, Nov 30, 40; US citizen; m 65; c 3. *Educ:* Univ London, MB & BS, 64, MD, 78; FRCP, 85. *Prof Exp:* House surgeon, Middlesex Hosp, London, 64; house physician, Taplow Hosp, Maidenhead, UK, 65; med officer, RAF, 65-70; registr rheumatology, Hammersmith Hosp, London, 70-72; asst prof med, Univ Chicago, 72-76. *Concurrent Pos:* Consult, Vet Admin Hosp, Portland, Ore, 76-; mem med bd, Am Lupus Soc & Am Fibromyalgia Syndrome Asn. *Mem:* Am Rheumatism Asn; Am Asn Immunologists; Brit Soc Rheumatology; Med Res Soc Gt Brit; Am Psychosom Soc; AAAS; fel Am Col Physicians. *Res:* Arthritis and rheumatic diseases; biological role of lactoferrin; DNA receptors, basic pathophysiology and abnormalities of receptor function in systemic lupus erythematosus and allied disorders; fibromyalgia, clinical and basic studies; adult growth hormone deficiency in fibromyalgia. *Mailing Add:* Div Rheumat Ore Health Sci Univ 3181 SW Sam Jackson Park Rd Portland OR 97201-3098

BENNETT, ROBERT PUTNAM, ORGANIC CHEMISTRY, FUEL TECHNOLOGY. *Current Pos:* SELF EMPLOYED CONSULT, 93- *Personal Data:* b Hartford, Conn, Dec 11, 32; div; c 4. *Educ:* Trinity Col, Conn, BS, 55, MS, 57; Case Inst Technol, PhD(org chem), 60. *Prof Exp:* Fel chem, Pa State Univ, 60-61; res chemist, Am Cyanamid Co, 61-66, sr res chemist, 66-69; lab dir, 69-74, dir chem res & develop, 74, asst vpres res & develop, 75-78, vpres & tech dir, Apollo Technologies Inc, 78-83; vpres, GUS Inc, 83-88; dir process develop & eng, Natec Res Inc, 88-93. *Mem:* Am Chem Soc. *Res:* Catalytic reactions; combustion reactions; catalysis petroleum chemistry; air pollution chemistry and control; coal chemistry. *Mailing Add:* 6601 Sands Point Dr No 13 Houston TX 77074-3732. *Fax:* 713-773-3534

BENNETT, SARA NEVILLE, FUNGAL GENETICS. *Current Pos:* From instr to prof biol, Ga Southern Col, 66-90, PROF BIOL, GA SOUTHERN UNIV, 90- *Personal Data:* b Bulloch Co, Ga, Mar 8, 31; m 48, Lovett; c Sara C (Broucek), Barbara (Leapard) & Lovett Jr. *Educ:* Ga Southern Col, BS & BSEd, 64, MS, 67; Univ Ga, PhD(microbiol), 75. *Mem:* Genetics Soc Am; AAAS; Sigma Xi; Am Inst Biol Studies. *Res:* Genetics of osmotic-sensitive and morphological mutants of the fungus Neurospora. *Mailing Add:* Dept Biol Ga Southern Univ 8042 Landrum Box Statesboro GA 30458-8100. *Fax:* 912-681-0845; *E-Mail:* sbennett@gsvms2.cc.gasou.edu

BENNETT, STEPHEN LAWRENCE, CEMENTED CARBIDES. *Current Pos:* RES ENGR, GTE VALENITE CORP, TROY, MICH, 86- *Personal Data:* b Winnipeg, Man, Oct 14, 38; US citizen; m 70; c 2. *Educ:* Univ Man, BSc, 60, MSc, 61; Queen's Univ, Ont, PhD(solid state chem), 66. *Prof Exp:* Res officer solid state chem, Div Appl Chem, Nat Res Coun, 61-62; res assoc high temperature chem, Univ Kans, 66-68; assoc physicist, Math & Physics Div, Midwest Res Inst, Kansas City, Mo, 68-70; res assoc, Rockefeller Univ, New York, 70-72 & Rice Univ, Houston, Tex, 72-74; res staff mem, Metals & Ceramics Div, Oak Ridge Nat Lab, 74-78; mat scientist, Kennametal Inc, Greensburg, Pa, 78-86. *Mem:* Sigma Xi; Am Chem Soc; Am Ceramic Soc. *Res:* Electrical and magnetic properties of solids; single crystal growth; high temperature mass spectrometry; thermodynamic properties of solids; vaporization phenomena; chemical ionization mass spectrometry; negative ionization mass spectrometry; electron affinities; directional solidification; carbon control in cemented carbides; advanced cutting tool materials; modifications to surface microstructure of cemented carbides. *Mailing Add:* Valenite Inc 1711 Thunderbird Dr Troy MI 48084-5465

BENNETT, STEWART, POLARIZATION OF LIGHT. *Current Pos:* PRES, ANOTHER LEAF INC, 96- *Personal Data:* b New York, NY, Feb 14, 33. *Educ:* Cornell Univ, AB, 53, PhD(nuclear physics), 61. *Prof Exp:* Res physicist anti-submarine warfare, Opers Res Inc, 60-61; staff scientist plasma physics, Res & Adv Develop Div, Avco Corp, 61-63, chief sect, 63-69; mgr, Polaroid Corp, 69-79, gen mgr, Polarizer Div, 79-95. *Mem:* Am Phys Soc. *Res:* Plasma and discharge physics; cosmic rays; light polarization. *Mailing Add:* 133 Annursnac Hill Rd Concord MA 01742

BENNETT, THOMAS EDWARD, PHYSIOLOGY, BIOLOGY. *Current Pos:* MEM FAC, DEPT BIOL, BELLARMINE COL, 80-, CHMN, DEPT BIOL, 85- *Personal Data:* b Norristown, Pa, Mar 14, 50; m 75; c 3. *Educ:* Pa State Univ, BS, 72, MS, 75, PhD(physiol), 79. *Prof Exp:* Lab instr biol, Pa State Univ, 72-77, asst, 74-77; instr anat & physiol, Sch Nursing, Philipsburg State Gen Hosp, 73-80. *Concurrent Pos:* Histologist, Depts Poultry Sci & Food Sci, Pa State Univ, 72-74. *Res:* Sensory, neural and endocrine responses to environmental stressors; auditory physiology; effects of gravity on cardiovascular system; space physiology. *Mailing Add:* Dept Biol Bellarmine Col 2001 Newburg Rd Louisville KY 40205-1863

BENNETT, THOMAS P(ETER), EXPERIMENTAL BIOLOGY. *Current Pos:* PRES, SCI SERVS INC, 96- *Personal Data:* b Lakeland, Fla, Oct 8, 37. *Prof Exp:* Dir biol, Fla Mus Natural Hist, Univ Fla, 86-96. *Mailing Add:* Sci Servs Inc 1719 N St NW Washington DC 20036

BENNETT, W DONALD, PHYSICS, METALLURGY. *Current Pos:* sr sci adv, 75-78, dir prog eval, 78-88, MINES & RESOURCES, MGT CONSULT, 88- *Personal Data:* b Sheffield, Eng, May 2, 24; Can citizen; m 57; c 4. *Educ:* Univ Sheffield, BSc, 43, PhD(physics), 49. *Prof Exp:* Nat Res Coun Can fel physics, 49-51; res scientist metall, Dept Mines & Technol Survs, Ont, 51-55, sr sci officer, 55; design specialist physics, Canadair, Ltd, Que, 55-57; adv engr metall, Can Westinghouse Co, Ltd, 57-62; head phys metall res, Falconbridge Nickel Mines, Ltd, 62-68; sci adv, Sci Coun Can, 68-72, Sci Coun Can Embassy, Washington, DC, 72-75. *Mem:* Am Soc Metals; Am Inst Mining, Metall & Petrol Engrs; fel Brit Inst Physics & Phys Soc. *Res:* Order-disorder in binary alloy systems; metallurgy of titanium, beryllium, zironium and uranium; nickel alloy development; high purity metals; science policy. *Mailing Add:* 17 Borduas Ct Kanata ON K2K 1K9 Can

BENNETT, W SCOTT, ELECTROMAGNETIC COMPATIBILITY ENGINEERING. *Current Pos:* CONSULT ELECTROMAGNETIC COMPATIBILITY ENG, 90- *Personal Data:* b Wash, DC, Nov 29, 29. *Educ:* Syracuse Univ, BEE, 63, MSEE, 65, PhD(elec eng), 67. *Prof Exp:* Instr elec eng, Syracuse Univ, 65-67; asst prof, Va Polytech Inst & State Univ, 67-70; staff engr, Burroughs Corp, 70-74; mem tech staff, Hewlett-Packard Co, 74-90. *Concurrent Pos:* Distinguished lectr, Inst Elec & Electronics Engrs, Electromagnetic Compatibility Soc, 88-90; assoc ed, Inst Elec & Electronics Engrs, Electromagnetic Compatibility Soc Trans, 89- *Mem:* Inst Elec & Electronics Engrs; Inst Elec & Electronics Engrs Electromagnetic Compatibility Soc. *Res:* Incorporation of electromagnetic compatibility into the initial design of electronic equipment; measurement of unintentional radiated electromagnetic emissions. *Mailing Add:* 1324 Meadow Ridge Ct Loveland CO 80537

BENNETT, WILLIAM D, LUNG BIOLOGY. *Current Pos:* res asst prof, Pulmonary Med & Ctr Environ Med & Lung Biol, 88-95, RES ASSOC PROF, UNIV NC, CHAPEL HILL, 95- *Personal Data:* b July 18, 52; c 2. *Educ:* USAF Acad, BA, 74; Johns Hopkins Univ, PhD(health sci), 83. *Honors & Awards:* New Investr Award, NIH, 86. *Prof Exp:* Physicist, Electronic Syst Div, Hanscom AFB, USAF, 74-79; fel, Pulmonary Dis Div, Dept Med, State Univ NY, Stony Brook, 83-85, instr, 85-86, res asst prof, 86-88. *Mem:* Am Physiol Soc; Am Thoracic Soc; Int Soc Aerosols Med. *Mailing Add:* Ctr Environ Med & Lung Biol 104 Mason Farm Rd CB No 7310 Univ NC Chapel Hill NC 27599-7310. *Fax:* 919-966-9863; *E-Mail:* bennett.william@epamail.epa.gov

BENNETT, WILLIAM EARL, INORGANIC CHEMISTRY. *Current Pos:* RETIRED. *Personal Data:* b Eskridge, Kans, Dec 29, 23; m 52. *Educ:* Sterling Col, BS, 47, Univ Kans, PhD(chem), 51. *Prof Exp:* Res assoc chem, Univ Chicago, 51-52 & Mass Inst Technol, 52-53; from asst prof to assoc prof inorg chem, Univ Iowa, 59-94. *Mem:* Am Chem Soc. *Res:* Coordination compounds; ion exchange. *Mailing Add:* Dept Chem Univ Iowa Iowa City IA 52242

BENNETT, WILLIAM FRANKLIN, thrombolytic drugs, for more information see previous edition

BENNETT, WILLIAM FREDERICK, SOIL & SOIL SCIENCE, AGRONOMY. *Current Pos:* RETIRED. *Personal Data:* b Plainview, Ark, Jan 23, 27; m, Audrey N Binkley; c Linda, Fred & Jackie. *Educ:* Okla State Univ, BS, 50; Iowa State Univ, MS, 52, PhD, 58. *Prof Exp:* Exten area agronomist, Iowa State Univ, 51-54, exten agronomist, 54-57; exten soil chemist, Tex A&M Univ, 57-63; chief agronomist, Elcor Chem Corp, 63-68; prof agron, Tex Tech Univ, 68-93, assoc dean agr sci, 70-93, dir develop, 93-97. *Mem:* Am Soc Agron; Soil Sci Soc Am. *Res:* Soil fertility and fertilizer use on agronomic and vegetable crops; plant analysis and soil testing; developing diagnostic tools. *Mailing Add:* Agr Sci Tex Tech Univ Lubbock TX 79409-2123. *Fax:* 806-742-2836

BENNETT, WILLIAM M, INTERNAL MEDICINE, NEPHROLOGY. *Current Pos:* asst prof, 70-74, assoc prof, 74-78, PROF MED, ORE HEALTH SCI UNIV, 78-, PROF PHARMACOL, 81- *Personal Data:* b Chicago, Ill, May 6, 38; m 77, Sandra Silen; c Andy, Jean, Garrett (deceased), Grant &

Gray. *Educ:* Northwestern Univ, BS, 60, Md, 63. *Honors & Awards:* Discovery Award, Med Res Found, 91. *Prof Exp:* Instr med, Harvard Med Sch, 69-70. *Concurrent Pos:* Chmn, Nephrology Subspecialty Bd, Am Bd Internal Med. *Mem:* Am Soc Nephrol; Int Soc Nephrol; Am Soc Pharmacol & Exp Therapeut; Am Fedn Clin Res; fel Am Col Physicians. *Res:* Investigations into the mechanisms of drug nephrotoxicity and the proper prescribing of drugs to patients with renal failure. *Mailing Add:* Div Nephrol Dept Med Ore Health Sci Univ 3181 SW Sam Jackson Park Rd Portland OR 97201

BENNETT, WILLIAM PATRICK, MUTATION SPECTRUM ANALYSIS, MOLECULAR CARCINOGENESIS. *Current Pos:* med staff fel, 89-94, SR STAFF FEL, NAT CANCER INST, NIH, 94- *Personal Data:* b Winston-Salem, NC, Feb 19, 56. *Educ:* Duke Univ, AB, 78; Univ NC, Chapel Hill, MS, 81; Rowman Gray Sch Med, MD, 85. *Prof Exp:* Intern path, Mass Gen Hosp, Boston, 85-86, resident, 86-87, res fel, 87-89. *Mem:* AAAS; Am Asn Cancer Res; Am Soc Investigative Path. *Res:* Mutation spectrum analysis of iamogenic and tobacco-associated cancers; molecular pathogenesis and epidemiology of human lung and esophageal cancer. *Mailing Add:* 37 Convent Dr MSC 4255 Bldg 37 Rm 2C25 Bethesda MD 20892. *Fax:* 301-496-0497

BENNETT, WILLIAM RALPH, JR, PHYSICS. *Current Pos:* instr, Yale Univ, 57-59, res assoc, 59, from assoc prof to prof physics & appl sci, 62-70, master, Stillman Col, 81-87, CHARLES BALDWIN SAWYER PROF ENG & APPL SCI & PROF PHYSICS, YALE UNIV, 70- *Personal Data:* b NJ, Jan 30, 30; m 52, Frances Commins; c Jean, William R & Nancy. *Educ:* Princeton Univ, BA, 51; Columbia Univ, PhD(physics), 57. *Hon Degrees:* MA, Yale Univ, 65; Dsc, Univ New Haven, 74. *Honors & Awards:* Morris N Liebmann Award, Inst Elec & Electronics Eng, 65; Western Elec Fund Award, Am Soc Eng Educr, 77. *Prof Exp:* Asst physics, Radiation Lab, Columbia Univ, 52-54, asst, Cyclotron Group, 54-57; instr, Yale Univ, 57-59, res assoc, 59; mem tech staff, Bell Tel Labs, 59-62. *Concurrent Pos:* Consult, Tech Res Group, Inc, 62-67, Inst Defense Anal, 63-70, Army Res Off, Durham, 65-, CBS Labs, 66-68, Madrigal Audio Labs, 87-88, Kahn Commun, 88-89, Reeves Sci, 89-90, MCG Int, 92 & Oak Ridge Assoc Univs, 91-92; vis scientist, Am Inst Physics Prog, 63-64; Sloan Found fel, 63-65; mem adv panel, Nat Acad Sci to Nat Bur Stand, 63-69, chmn, 66; John S Guggenheim Found fel, 67; guest of Soviet Acad Sci, 67, 69 & 79; consult & mem bd dirs, Laser Sci Corp, 68-69; mem lab adv bd for res, Naval Res Adv Comt, 68-76 & Avco Corp, 78. *Mem:* Fel Am Phys Soc; fel Optical Soc Am; fel Inst Elec & Electronics Engrs. *Res:* Atomic and molecular physics; positronium; optical pumping; inelastic collisions; radiative lifetimes; excitation processes; optical and rf spectroscopy; gas lasers; lasers, medical diagnostics with computers, biophysics and acoustics; physics of musical instruments. *Mailing Add:* Dunham Lab Yale Univ New Haven CT 06520. *Fax:* 203-624-6678; *E-Mail:* ap207@biomed.med.yale.edu

BENNETT, WORD BROWN, JR, NATURAL PRODUCTS CHEMISTRY. *Current Pos:* RETIRED. *Personal Data:* b Nashville, Tenn, Oct 24, 15; m 39; c 4. *Educ:* Vanderbilt Univ, MS, 40. *Prof Exp:* Chief chemist, US Tobacco Co, 40-56, res dir, 56-66, vpres res & develop, 66-80. *Mem:* Am Chem Soc. *Res:* Dark tobacco. *Mailing Add:* 2700 Overhill Dr Nashville TN 37214-1298

BENNETTE, JERRY MAC, IRRIGATION MANAGEMENT. *Current Pos:* from asst prof to assoc prof, 79-90, PROF, UNIV FLA, 90-, DEPT CHMN, 93- *Personal Data:* b Abilene, Tex, July 16, 52; m 74; c 1. *Educ:* Tex Tech Univ, BS, 74, MS, 76; Univ Nebr, PhD(agron), 79. *Prof Exp:* Res asst agron, Tex Tech Univ, 74-76 & Univ Nebr, 76-79. *Mem:* Crop Sci Soc Am; Soil Sci Soc Am; Am Soc Agron. *Res:* Physiological and morphological factors which are related to heat and drought resistance of agronomic crops; efficient irrigation scheduling techiques; environmental effects of crop growth, physiology and yield. *Mailing Add:* Agron Dept Box 110500 Univ Fla Gainesville FL 32611

BENNETZEN, JEFFREY LYNN, BIOTIC STRESS RESISTANCE IN PLANTS, PLANT GENOME ORGANIZATION. *Current Pos:* from asst prof to assoc prof, 83-91, PROF BIOL, PURDUE UNIV, 91- *Personal Data:* b Dayton, Ohio, May 22, 52; m 76, Rebecca L Wong; c Michael A & Daniel A. *Educ:* Univ Calif, San Diego, BA, 74; Univ Wash, PhD(biochem), 80. *Honors & Awards:* Pres Young Investr Award, NSF, 86; Fulbright Award, Fulbright Found, 90. *Prof Exp:* Fel, Wash Univ, 80-81, Stanford Univ, 80-81; Monsanto fel, Univ Calif, Berkeley, 80-81; res scientist, Int Plant Res Inst, 81-83. *Concurrent Pos:* Consult var cos & orgns, 83-; vis scholar, John Innes Inst, 90-91. *Mem:* AAAS; Am Phytopath Soc; Genetics Soc Am. *Res:* Molecular and genetic studies of stress resistance and genome organization in plants; disease resistance genes, transposable elements, gene regulation, cereal genome mapping, genome evolution. *Mailing Add:* Dept Biol Sci Purdue Univ West Lafayette IN 47907-1968

BENNICK, ANDERS, SALIVARY PROTEIN, PROTEIN STRUCTURE. *Current Pos:* PROF BIOCHEM & CHMN, GRAD DEPT DENT, UNIV TORONTO, 72- *Educ:* Univ Toronto, PhD(biochem), 70. *Mailing Add:* Dept Biochem Univ Toronto Toronto ON M5S 1A8 Can

BENNIGHOF, R(AYMOND) H(OWARD), electronics engineering; deceased, see previous edition for last biography

BENNING, CARL J, JR, ELECTRICAL ENGINEERING. *Current Pos:* RETIRED. *Personal Data:* b Springfield, Mo, Dec 4, 30; m 55; c 1. *Educ:* US Naval Acad, BS, 53; Univ NMex, MS, 64. *Prof Exp:* Staff mem systs eng, Sandia Corp, 57-62, reliability eng, 63-64; res asst, Univ NMex, 62-63; sr engr, Braddock-Dunn-McDonald, 64-65 & Tracor, Inc, 65-67; sr mem tech staff, Tex Instruments, Inc, 67-90. *Mem:* Inst Elec & Electronics Engrs. *Res:* Submarine antenna design; microwave breakdown in wave guides; reliability analysis; moving target indicator radar design; deceptive electronic counter measures systems; signal processing; IR image processing for target detection; system analysis. *Mailing Add:* 6522 Redpine Dallas TX 75248

BENNINGTON, JAMES LYNNE, PATHOLOGY. *Current Pos:* CLIN PROF PATH, STANFORD MED SCH, CHMN DEPT PATH & CLIN LAB, CHILDRENS HOSP SAN FRANCISCO & ADULT MED CTR, SAN FRANCISCO, 70- *Personal Data:* b Evanston, Ill, Apr 29, 35; m 59; c 2. *Educ:* Univ Chicago, MD, 59, MS, 62. *Prof Exp:* Intern, Presby-St Lukes Hosp, Chicago, 59-60; trainee path, USPHS, 60-62; resident, Kaiser Found Hosp, Oakland, Calif, 62-64; assoc prof, Sch Med, Univ Wash, 64-69. *Concurrent Pos:* Chief & dir labs, King County Hosp, Wash, 66-69. *Mem:* Am Soc Clin Path; Col Am Path; Int Acad Path. *Res:* Oncology; cellular kinetics of normal and neoplastic tissue; cytomorphometry of neoplastic cells. *Mailing Add:* 1998 Broadway Apt 1207 San Francisco CA 94109-2206

BENNINK, MAURICE RAY, HUMAN NUTRITION, NUTRITIONAL BIOCHEMISTRY. *Current Pos:* asst prof, 73-78, ASSOC PROF FOOD SCI & HUMAN NUTRIT, MICH STATE UNIV, 78- *Personal Data:* b Coopersville, Mich, May 31, 44; m 68; c 2. *Educ:* Mich State Univ, BS, 66; Colo State Univ, MS, 68; Univ Ill, PhD(nutrit sci), 73. *Prof Exp:* Lab technician clin biochem, Blodgett Mem Hosp, Grand Rapids, Mich, 68-70. *Mem:* Inst Food Technol; Am Inst Nutrit. *Res:* Interactions of diet and colon cancer; diet and lipid metabolism. *Mailing Add:* Dept Food Sci & Human Nutrit Mich State Univ 106 Food Sci Bldg East Lansing MI 48824-1224

BENNION, DOUGLAS NOEL, chemical engineering, electrochemistry; deceased, see previous edition for last biography

BENNION, DOUGLAS WILFORD, PETROLEUM ENGINEERING, COMPUTER SCIENCE. *Current Pos:* from asst prof to assoc prof chem eng, 65-72, PROF CHEM & PETROL ENG, UNIV CALGARY, 72- *Personal Data:* b Cardston, Alta, June 2, 31; m 57; c 3. *Educ:* Univ Okla, BS, 56; Pa State Univ, MS, 62, PhD(petrol eng), 65. *Prof Exp:* Trainee engr, Mobil Oil Can Ltd, 56, jr engr, 57-60, prod engr, 60-61. *Mem:* Can Inst Mining & Metall; Am Inst Mining, Metall & Petrol Engrs; Can Inst Chem Engrs. *Res:* Flow of fluid in heterogeneous porous media; use of numerical models to simulate fluid flow behavior. *Mailing Add:* 118 Country Club Lane Calgary AB T2M 4L4 Can

BENNISON, ALLAN P, GEOLOGY. *Current Pos:* GEOL CONSULT, 68- *Personal Data:* b Stockton, Calif, Mar 8, 18; m 41; c 3. *Educ:* Univ Calif, Berkeley, AB, 40. *Honors & Awards:* Distinguished Serv Award, Am Asn Petrol Geol, 86; Distinguished Serv Award, Soc Econ Paleont & Mineral, 90. *Prof Exp:* Fel geol, Antioch Col, 40-42; photogrammet engr, US Geol Surv, 42-45; asst chief geologist, Tri-Pet Corp, Columbia, 45-49; staff stratigrapher, Sinclair Oil & Gas Co, Okla, 49-68. *Concurrent Pos:* Lectr, Univ Tulsa, 64; deleg, Int Geol Cong, Prague, Czech, 68-; compiler geol hwy map ser, Am Asn Petrol Geol, 72- *Mem:* AAAS; Am Asn Petrol Geol; Soc Econ Paleont & Mineral; Am Asn Petrol Geologists; Geol Soc Am; Explorers Club. *Res:* Cretaceous stratigraphy of California; stratigraphy of Oklahoma, Kansas, Colombia, Somalia and Mexico; tectonics of Alaska, California, Wyoming and Utah. *Mailing Add:* 1410 Terrace Dr Tulsa OK 74104-4626

BENNISON, BERTRAND EARL, MEDICINE. *Current Pos:* RETIRED. *Personal Data:* b Boston, Mass, Apr 18, 15; m 43, Lella Brice; c 4. *Educ:* Mass Inst Technol, SB, 37; Harvard Univ, MD, 41; Univ Pittsburgh, MPH, 54. *Prof Exp:* Med intern, US Marine Hosp, NY, 41-42; med officer, USPHS, 42-54; asst dir med res div, Esso Res & Eng Co, 54-59, asst dir res, Ortho Pharmaceut Corp, NJ, 60-66; prof biol sci & head dept, Drexel Univ, 66-71; dir, Leon County Health Dept, Fla, 71-76; health prog supvr, Fla Dept Health & Rehab Serv, 77-78. *Concurrent Pos:* Adj prof, Div Reproductive Biol, Hahnemann Med Col; vis prof, Dept Urban & Regional Planning, Fla State Univ, 72-75; clinician, 78-81. *Mem:* AAAS; Am Pub Health Asn. *Res:* Preventive medicine. *Mailing Add:* PO Box 224 Eastham MA 02642-0224

BENNUN, ALFRED, BIOCHEMISTRY, BIOPHYSICS. *Current Pos:* RETIRED. *Personal Data:* b Buenos Aires, Arg, July 9, 34; m 61; c 1. *Educ:* Nat Univ Cordoba, BS, 54, MS, 57, PhD(biochem, pharm), 63. *Prof Exp:* Lab instr, Dept Psychiat, Sch Med, Nat Univ Cordoba, 56-57, instr histol & embryol, 57-59; instr biol chem, Univ Buenos Aires, 62-63; fel biochem, Weizmann Inst, 63-64; res assoc, Duke Univ, 64-65; NIH fel, NY, 65-66 & spec fel, Cornell Univ, 66-67; lectr prof, Univ PR, 67-68, asst prof, 68-69; assoc prof biochem, Newark Col Arts & Sci, Rutgers Univ, 69-95. *Concurrent Pos:* Resident, Clin Path Lab, Ment Health Hosp of State Inst Health, Cordoba, Arg, 56-57; fel, Arg Coun Sci Res, 61 & 63; res grants, NIH, 68-70, Res Corp, 69-72, Rutgers Res Fund, 69-73 & Charles & Johanna Busch Mem Fund, 74-76; mem, Comt Bioenergetics, Int Union Pure & Appl Biophys. *Mem:* Am Chem Soc; Am Soc Plant Physiol; Fedn Am Soc Exp Biol; Biophys Soc; NY Acad Sci. *Res:* Phosphorus metabolism; enzymology; cellular respiration; oxidative and photophosphorylation; hormone receptors and enzymatic regulation; theoretical bioenergetics. *Mailing Add:* Dept Biol Sci Rutgers State Univ 195 University Ave Newark NJ 07102-1814

BENOIT, GUY J C, biology, microbiology; deceased, see previous edition for last biography

BENOIT, PETER WELLS, DENTISTRY, ANATOMY. *Current Pos:* PVT PRACT, ORAL/FACIAL PAIN, 89- *Personal Data:* b Boston, Mass, Dec 9, 39; m 65; c 2. *Educ:* Tufts Univ, BS, 61, DMD, 65, MS, 67, PhD(anat), 71. *Prof Exp:* Consult pharmacol, Astra Pharmaceut Prod Inc, Mass, 71-72; assoc prof oral biol, Sch Dent, Emory Univ, 72-88. *Concurrent Pos:* USPHS fel oral path, Tufts Univ, Boston, 65-67, instnl training grant anat, 67-71; residency, Facial Pain Ctr, Univ Fla, 88-89. *Mem:* Int Asn Den Res; Am Acad Oral Path; Sigma Xi. *Res:* Dental research. *Mailing Add:* 3364 Thornwood Dr Atlanta GA 30340

BENOIT, RICHARD J, LIMNOLOGY. *Current Pos:* prof, 72-84, EMER PROF NATURAL SCI, MOHEGAN COMMUNITY COL, 84-, DIR, ECOSCI LAB, NORWICH, CONN, 70- *Personal Data:* b Chicopee Falls, Mass, July 10, 22. *Educ:* Yale Univ, BS, 48, PhD(zool), 57. *Prof Exp:* Supvr biochem processes & chief marine sci, Gen Dynamics, 59-70. *Concurrent Pos:* Adj assoc prof bot, Conn Col, New London, 84- *Mem:* Sigma Xi; Int Soc Limnol. *Res:* Ecological value scales; aquatic geochemistry; natural purification in aquatic ecosystems. *Mailing Add:* 162 Beach St Westerly RI 02891

BENOITON, NORMAND LEO, AMINO ACID & PEPTIDE CHEMISTRY. *Current Pos:* from asst prof to prof, 61-97, EMER PROF BIOCHEM, UNIV OTTAWA, 97- *Personal Data:* b Somerset, Man, Sept 30, 32; m 73, Ljuba Dojcinovic. *Educ:* Loyola Col, Can, BSc, 53; Univ Montreal, MSc, 55, PhD(biochem), 56. *Prof Exp:* Vis scientist, Nat Insts Health, 56-58; Imp Chem Industs res fel, Univ Exeter, 58-60; assoc res officer, Nat Res Coun Can, 60-61. *Concurrent Pos:* Career investr, Med Res Coun Can, 61-95; consult, Abbott, 90-92. *Mem:* Am Chem Soc; Am Peptide Soc; Eur Peptide Soc. *Res:* Chemistry of peptide synthesis. *Mailing Add:* Dept Biochem Univ Ottawa Ottawa ON K1H 8M5 Can. *E-Mail:* benoiton@aixl.uottawa.ca

BENOKRAITIS, VITALIUS, NUMERICAL ANALYSIS, GRAPHICS APPLICATIONS. *Current Pos:* DESIGN ANALYST, AAI CORP, 81- *Personal Data:* b Keturkaimis, Lithuania, July 25, 41; m 67; c 1. *Educ:* Kent State Univ, BS, 64; Univ Ill, MS, 66; Univ Tex, PhD(comput sci), 74. *Prof Exp:* Asst prof comput sci, Va Commonwealth Univ, 74-75; mathematician, Ballistic Res Labs, US Army, 75-81. *Mem:* Soc Indust & Appl Math; Asn Comput Mach; Am Math Soc. *Res:* Iterative solution of large linear systems; numerical solution of partial differential equations; mathematical modeling; real time simulation; computer natural language processing. *Mailing Add:* 206 Fairway Circle Cross Junction VA 22625

BENOLKEN, ROBERT MARSHALL, CELL PHYSIOLOGY. *Current Pos:* RETIRED. *Personal Data:* b St Paul, Minn, May 11, 32; m 57; c 6. *Educ:* Marquette Univ, BS, 54; Johns Hopkins Univ, PhD(biophys), 59. *Prof Exp:* Asst physics, Marquette Univ, 53-54; asst biophys, Johns Hopkins Univ, 54-56, res assoc, 56-59; from asst prof to assoc prof, Univ Minn, Minneapolis, 59-68; prof neural sci, Grad Sch Biomed Sci, Univ Tex, 68-80; instr physics, Chemeketa Community Col, 80-91. *Mem:* Soc Gen Physiologists; Biophys Soc. *Res:* Cellular physiology; physiology of visual sense cells; electrophysiology. *Mailing Add:* 23870 Summerhaven Dr Lyons OR 97358

BENOS, DALE JOHN, PHYSIOLOGY, BIOPHYSICS. *Current Pos:* assoc prof, 85-87, RES SCIENTIST, CF RES CTR, UNIV ALA, BIRMINGHAM, 85-, PROF PHYSIOL-BIOPHYS, 87- *Personal Data:* b Cleveland, Ohio, Sept 30, 50. *Educ:* Case Western Reserve Univ, BA, 72; Duke Univ, PhD(physiol & pharmacol), 76. *Prof Exp:* Postdoctoral physiol, Med Ctr, Duke Univ, 76-78; from asst prof to assoc prof physiol-biophys, Harvard Med Sch, 78-85. *Concurrent Pos:* Nat Res Serv Award, Nat Inst Arthritis, Metabolism & Digestive Dis, NIH, 76-78; prin investr, NIH, 79-, Off Naval Res; mem, Cellular Biol & Physiol Study Sect, NIH, 85-89. *Mem:* Am Physiol Soc; Am Soc Cell Biol; Biophys Soc; Soc Gen Physiologists; Soc Study Reproduction; NY Acad Sci. *Res:* Mechanisms of cation transport across epithelial and cellular membranes; development aspects of ionic transport and metabolic function in preimplantation mammalian embryos and cultured neural and epithelial cell lines. *Mailing Add:* Dept Physiol & Biophys Univ Ala 1918 University Blvd BH5B 706 VAB Birmingham AL 35294-0005

BENRUD, CHARLES HARRIS, STATISTICS, AGRICULTURAL ECONOMICS. *Current Pos:* RETIRED. *Personal Data:* b Goodhue, Minn, Apr 30, 21; m 49, Audrey Anderson; c Edith (Roberts), Kurt M & Erik C. *Educ:* Univ Minn, BS, 48, MS, 49, PhD(agr econ), 63. *Prof Exp:* Asst agr agent, Agr Exten Serv, Faribault Co, Minn, 49-50, 4H Club agent, Hennepin Co, 50-53 & agr agent, Ramsey Co, 53-55; asst prof econ & statist & asst economist, SDak State Col, 55-58, assoc prof & assoc economist, 58-63; sr statistician, Res Triangle Inst, 63-83, res statistician, 83-93. *Res:* Sampling; variances of estimates; population projection; farm management. *Mailing Add:* 118 Amesbury Lane Cary NC 27511

BENS, FREDERICK PETER, MARKET DEVELOPMENT REFRACTORY METALS, MOLTEN SALT BATH TECHNOLOGY. *Current Pos:* mgr mkt develop, 74-89, MGR, CORP DEVELOP & CONSULT, KOLENE CORP, 89- *Personal Data:* b Detroit, Mich, Oct 20, 13. *Educ:* Wayne State Univ, BS, 36. *Honors & Awards:* Cert of Appreciation, Soc Automotive Engrs, 75; Allan Ray Putnam Serv Award, Am Soc Metals Int, 91. *Prof Exp:* Anal chemist to res supvr, Climax Molybdenum Co, 36-57, asst mgr, 57-59, mgr, Automotive Dept, 74. *Mem:* Am Foundrymen's Soc; Am Soc Metals Int; Am Inst Mining & Metall Engrs; fel Soc Automotive Engrs; Am Soc Testing & Mat; Soc Mfg Engrs; Am Ord Asn; Nat Asn Corrosion Engrs. *Res:* Chromium-base alloys for high velocity machine gun liners; super-charger buckets for gas turbines; Nine United States patents and one British patent. *Mailing Add:* 51 Claireview Rd Grosse Pointe MI 48236

BENSADOUN, ANDRE, NUTRITION, PHYSIOLOGY. *Current Pos:* assoc prof physiol, 67-76, PROF NUTRIT BIOCHEM, CORNELL UNIV, 76- *Personal Data:* b Fes, Morocco, Nov 10, 31; US citizen; m 59; c 3. *Educ:* Univ Bordeaux, BS, 51; Nat Sch Advan Agron, France, BSEng, 56; Univ Toulouse, MS, 56; Cornell Univ, PhD(nutrit), 60. *Prof Exp:* Res nutritionist, Cornell Univ, 59-65; asst prof nutrit, Univ Ill, Urbana, 65-67. *Mem:* Am Inst Nutrit; Soc Exp Biol & Med; Am Soc Biochem & Molecular Biol; Am Soc Cell Biol. *Res:* Lipid metabolism; lipid transport; lipoproteins; lipases; molecular biology of lipases. *Mailing Add:* Div Nutrit Sci 321 Savage Hall Cornell Univ Ithaca NY 14853-0001

BENSCH, KLAUS GEORGE, HUMAN PATHOLOGY. *Current Pos:* prof & actg chmn path, 68-84, PROF & CHMN PATH, SCH MED, STANFORD UNIV, 84- *Personal Data:* b Miedar, Ger, Sept 1, 28; nat US; m 55; c 3. *Educ:* Univ Erlangen, MD, 53; Am Bd Path, dipl, 59. *Prof Exp:* From instr to assoc prof path, Sch Med, Yale Univ, 58-68. *Mem:* Am Soc Invest Path. *Res:* Cellular pathology and its underlying molecular mechanisms. *Mailing Add:* Dept Path Stanford Univ Med Ctr L-235 Stanford CA 94305-5324

BENSCHOTER, REBA ANN, BIOMEDICAL COMMUNICATIONS, ALLIED HEALTH PROFESSIONS ADMINISTRATION. *Current Pos:* assoc prof, 69-70, DIR BIOMED COMMUN, UNIV NEBR MED CTR, 70-, ASSOC PROF BIOMED EDUC, 78-, ASSOC PROF COL NURSING, 79-, ASSOC PROF DEPT ADULT & CONTINUING EDUC, 84-, ASSOC DEAN ALLIED HEALTH, 85-, PROF ALLIED HEALTH, 88- *Personal Data:* b Smithland, Iowa, June 14, 30; m 56, Leon G; c Brooke (Mowitz), Mary L (Miller), Brian & Annmarie (Rollag). *Educ:* Briar Cliff Col, BA, 52; Iowa State Univ, MS, 56; Univ Nebr, Lincoln, PhD(adult educ), 78. *Honors & Awards:* Golden Raster Award, Health Sci Commun Asn, 81. *Prof Exp:* Dir AV Aids Sect, Nebr Psychiat Inst, 60-62, from instr to asst prof med teaching aids, 62-69. *Concurrent Pos:* Dir Commun Sect, Nebr Psychiat Inst, 62-88; consult, Nat Libr Med, 72-86, Vet Admin, 74-76, Nat Heart, Lung & Blood Inst, 76-; reader-consult, Pub Health Serv Health Manpower Progs, Dallas region, 74-76; mem, Nat Res & Demonstration Rev Comn, 74-76, consult for rev, Nat Heart Lung & Blood Inst, NIH, 76-; consult, Proj Hope, Zhejiang Med Univ, China, 87, Univ Mich, 87, George Washington Univ, 90- & Univ SFla, 93. *Mem:* Health Sci Commun Asn (pres, 76-77); Asn Biomed Commun Dirs (pres, 93-94); Asn Allied Health Professions; Asn Med Illustrators; Asn Educ & Commun Technol. *Res:* Use of two-way television systems in education and psychiatric care; training biomedical communications specialists; computer applications in health sciences administration; education of allied health personnel for rural practice; distance learning; communication systems; telemediums. *Mailing Add:* 2528 S 40th St Omaha NE 68105. *Fax:* 402-559-7103; *E-Mail:* rbenscho@unmc.edu

BENSEL, JOHN PHILLIP, SOLID STATE PHYSICS. *Current Pos:* mem staff, 76-80, RES ENGR, DEPT PHYSICS, COL WILLIAM & MARY, 80- *Personal Data:* b Glen Ridge, NJ, Oct 30, 45; m 70. *Educ:* Stevens Inst Technol, BS, 67; Univ Pa, PhD(physics), 73. *Prof Exp:* Res assoc physics, Univ Ill, Urbana, 73-76. *Mem:* Am Phys Soc. *Res:* Instrumentation and fabrication techniques; production of custom made instruments with special expertise in scintilants and light guides, vacuum systems, crygenics; general mechanical fabrication as applied to all fields of physics. *Mailing Add:* Dept Physics Col William & Mary Williamsburg VA 23185

BENSELER, ROLF WILHELM, DENDROLOGY, FOREST BIOLOGY. *Current Pos:* from asst prof to assoc prof, 68-75, PROF BIOL SCI, CALIF STATE UNIV, HAYWARD, 75- *Personal Data:* b San Jose, Calif, Sept 24, 32; m 61; c 2. *Educ:* Univ Calif, Berkeley, BS, 57, PhD(bot), 68; Yale Univ, MF, 58. *Prof Exp:* Jr specialist, Sch Forestry, Univ Calif, 58-60; instr biol, Modesto Jr Col, 61-63; lectr, San Jose State Univ, 67. *Mem:* Am Inst Biol Scientists; Bot Soc Am; Am Soc Plant Taxonomists. *Res:* Reproductive biology and biosystematics of woody plants. *Mailing Add:* Dept Biol Sci Calif State Univ 25800 Carlos Bee Blvd Hayward CA 94542-3000

BENSEN, DAVID WARREN, SOIL CHEMISTRY. *Current Pos:* RETIRED. *Personal Data:* b Paterson, NJ, Feb 6, 28; m 54, H Evelyn Streicher; c Douglas, Debra, Clark & Michelle. *Educ:* Rutgers Univ, BSA, 54, MS, 55, PhD(soil chem), 58. *Prof Exp:* Chemist, Hanford Atomic Prod Oper, 58-63; sr res scientist, Isotopes, Inc, 63-66; tech mgr gov contracts, US Naval Radiol Defense Lab, 66-67; res analyst, Res & Eng Off, Civil Defense, Off Secy Army, 67-73, dep dir hazard eval & vulnerability reduction div, Defense Civil Preparedness Agency, 73-78, prog mgr nuclear hazards, Off Res, 78-81, sr scientist, Fed Emergency Mgt Agency, 81-86; sr staff officer & prog adminr, Nat Acad Sci/Nat Res Coun, 86-92. *Mem:* Sigma Xi; Health Physics Soc. *Res:* Soil chemistry; soil-plant relationships; soil fertility; plant nutrition; radioactive waste disposal; radionuclide reactions with soils and minerals; fallout contamination in the food chain; fallout phenomenology; radiological hazard assessment; radiological countermeasures and protection; civil defense. *Mailing Add:* 4624 Sunflower Dr Rockville MD 20853

BENSEN, JACK F, speech & hearing sciences, for more information see previous edition

BENSINGER, DAVID AUGUST, DENTISTRY, PERIODONTOLOGY. *Current Pos:* RETIRED. *Personal Data:* b St Louis, Mo, May 14, 26; div; c 2. *Educ:* Wash Univ, BA, 44; St Louis Univ, DDS, 48. *Prof Exp:* From instr to asst prof, 49-55, Wash Univ, 49-55, asst dean, 69-71, assoc prof dent med, Sch Dent, 55-, assoc dean, 71- *Concurrent Pos:* Consult, US Air Force, 59- *Mem:* Fel Am Col Dent; Am Acad Periodont; Am Soc Periodont; Int Asn Dent Res. *Res:* Oral diagnosis; time-lapse alterations in periodontal disease. *Mailing Add:* 4501 Lindell Blvd No 96 St Louis MO 63108

BENSINGER, JAMES ROBERT, ELEMENTARY PARTICLE PHYSICS. *Current Pos:* from asst prof to assoc prof, 74-89, PROF PHYSICS, BRANDEIS UNIV, 89- *Personal Data:* b Washington, DC, Aug 20, 41; m 66, Carolyn Kopperl; c Jenifer & David G. *Educ:* Bucknell Univ, BS, 63; Univ Wis, PhD(physics), 70. *Prof Exp:* Asst prof physics, Univ Pa, 73-74. *Mem:* Am Phys Soc. *Res:* Superconducting super collider physics. *Mailing Add:* Dept Physics Brandeis Univ Waltham MA 02254-9110. *Fax:* 781-736-2915; *E-Mail:* bensinger@binah.cc.brandeis.edu

BENSON, ALVIN K, SEISMIC INVERSION IMAGING & MODELING, ENVIRONMENTAL & ENGINEERING GEOPHYSICS. *Current Pos:* PROF GEOPHYS, BRIGHAM YOUNG UNIV, 86- *Personal Data:* b Payson, Utah, Jan 25, 44; m 66, Connie L Perry; c Alauna M, Alisa M & Alaura D. *Educ:* Brigham Young Univ, BS, 66, PhD(theoret physics), 72. *Honors & Awards:* Citation of Meritorious Achievement, Inter Biographical Ctr, 94; Distinguished Leadership Award, Am Biog Inst, 94. *Prof Exp:* Assoc prof physics, Ind Univ, 72-78, head dept, 76-78; res physicist, Conoco Inc, 78-80, sr res geophysicist, 80-81, supvr geophys res, 81-84; res assoc, Dupont, 84-86. *Concurrent Pos:* Lectr astron, Jefferson Community Col, 77-78; consult, City of New Albany, Ind, 77-78, City of Provo, Utah, 88-92, Kuwait Univ, 89-90, Certified Environ Inc, 90- & Govt Guatemala, 91-92; vis prof geophys, Brigham Young Univ, 84-85; prin investr, Provo, Rotary Club, 87-88, Geol Soc Am, 88-90 & Am Asn Petrol Geologists, 88-89; dist rep, Soc Explo Geophysicists. *Mem:* Am Phys Soc; Soc Explor Geophysicists; Am Geophys Union; Environ & Eng Geophys Soc; Soc Eng & Mineral Explor Geophysicists. *Res:* Modeling and imaging of geophysical data sets; seismic to delineate subsurface geology and conditions; equations for porous rock systems; environmental applications; author of four books on geophysics. *Mailing Add:* 249 W 1100 S Orem UT 84058. *E-Mail:* al_benson@byu.edu

BENSON, ANDREW ALM, BIOCHEMISTRY, PLANT PHYSIOLOGY. *Current Pos:* chmn, Dept Marine Biol, Scripps Inst Oceanog, 65-70, assoc dir inst, 66-70, chmn, Marine Biol Res Div, 67-70, actg chmn, 70-71, dir, Physiol Res Lab, 70-77, prof, 62-88, EMER PROF BIOL, SCRIPPS INST OCEANOG, UNIV CALIF, SAN DIEGO, 88- *Personal Data:* b Modesto, Calif, Sept 24, 17; m 42, 71, Dorothy Dorgan; c Linnea (Benson) & Claudia (Matthews). *Educ:* Univ Calif, Berkeley, BS, 39; Calif Inst Technol, PhD(org chem), 42. *Hon Degrees:* DPhil, Univ Oslo, 65; Dr, Univ Pierre et Marie Curie, Paris, 86. *Honors & Awards:* Sugar Res Found Award, 50; Lawrence Mem Award, US Atomic Energy Comn, 62; Stephen Hales Award, Am Soc Plant Physiol, 72; Supelco Sci Award, Am Oil Chemists Soc, 87. *Prof Exp:* Instr chem, Univ Calif, Berkeley, 42-43, asst dir, Bio-Org Group, Radiation Lab, 46-55; res assoc, Stanford Univ, 44-45; asst, Calif Inst Technol, 45-46; from assoc prof to prof agr & biol chem, Pa State Univ, 55-61; prof in residence physiol chem & biophys & res biochemist, Lab Nuclear Med, Univ Calif, Los Angeles, 61-62. *Concurrent Pos:* Fulbright lectr, Agr Col Norway, 51-52; consult, Molecular Biol Prog, NSF, 61-63 & Space Biol Panel, Am Inst Biol Sci/NASA, 81-87; adv coun, Cousteau Soc, 77-; mem, adv bd, Australian Inst Marine Sci, 75 & Marine Biotechnol Inst, Co, Tokyo, 90-; sr Queens fel, Australia, 79. *Mem:* Nat Acad Sci; Am Soc Biol Chem; Am Chem Soc; Am Soc Plant Physiol; Royal Norweg Soc Sci & Lett; Am Acad Arts Sci. *Res:* Photosynthesis metabolism after mathanol treatment; salmon metabolism; arsenic metabolism; mangrove physiology; radiochromatography; hot-atom chemistry; lipid biochemistry; biological membrane surfactants; phosonic and sulfonic acid metabolism; arsenic metabolism; coral metabolism; wax ester metabolism; radioisotope applications. *Mailing Add:* Scripps Inst Oceanog Univ Calif San Diego La Jolla CA 92093-0202. *Fax:* 619-534-7313; *E-Mail:* abenson@ucsd.edu

BENSON, ANN MARIE, DETOXIFICATION ENZYMES, CANCER CHEMOPREVENTION MECHANISMS. *Current Pos:* asst prof, 84-90, ASSOC PROF BIOCHEM, UNIV ARK MED SCI, 91- *Personal Data:* b NY, Jan 16, 36. *Educ:* City Col NY, BS, 57, Univ Hawaii, PhD(biochem), 69. *Prof Exp:* Fel biochem, Univ Hawaii, 69-70 & pharmacol, Johns Hopkins Med Sch, 70-72; res assoc pharmacol, Johns Hopkins Med Sch, 72-84. *Mem:* Am Soc Biol & Molecular Biol; Am Soc Pharmacol & Exp Therapeut; AAAS. *Res:* Biochemical mechanisms of protection against chemical carcinogenesis and toxicity. *Mailing Add:* Slot 516 Univ Ark Med Sci 4301 W Markham St Little Rock AR 72205-7199. *Fax:* 501-686-8169

BENSON, BARRETT WENDELL, ORGANIC CHEMISTRY. *Current Pos:* assoc prof, 67-72, chem dept, 72-77, PROF CHEM, BLOOMSBURG STATE COL, 72- *Personal Data:* b Brattleboro, Vt, Sept 4, 39; m 57; c 4. *Educ:* Middlebury Col, AB, 61; Univ Vt, PhD(org chem), 65. *Prof Exp:* Asst prof chem, Fresno State Col, 65-67. *Concurrent Pos:* NSF res grants, 68-; vis prof, Dartmouth Col, 74. *Mem:* Am Chem Soc. *Res:* Organic structure determination; organic reaction mechanisms. *Mailing Add:* 807 Country Club Dr Bloomsburg PA 17815

BENSON, BRENT W, BIOPHYSICS, RADIATION CHEMISTRY. *Current Pos:* ASSOC PROF PHYSICS, LEHIGH UNIV, 72- *Personal Data:* b Chicago, Ill, Apr 10, 41; m 62; c 2. *Educ:* Knox Col, Ill, BA, 63; Pa State Univ, MS, 65, PhD(biophys), 69. *Prof Exp:* Asst prof physics, Southern Ill Univ, 69-72. *Concurrent Pos:* Consult, Bell Tel Labs, 80-83; res scientist, Max Planck Inst, Stuttgart, 87. *Mem:* AAAS; Biophys Soc; Am Phys Soc; Radiation Res Soc. *Res:* Electron spin resonance studies of radiation induced free radicals in important biological molecules; biological and molecular effects due to decay of incorporated radioisotopes; reactions of microcircuit materials with atomic oxygen and other species produced by electrical discharge of gas mixtures; point defects in semiconductors. *Mailing Add:* Physics Bldg 16 Lehigh Univ 27 Memorial Dr W Bethleham PA 18015-3044

BENSON, CARL SIDNEY, GLACIOLOGY. *Current Pos:* asst prof geophys res, Univ Alaska, 60-61, assoc res geophysicist, 61-62, assoc prof, 62-69, chmn, Dept Geol, 69-73, prof, 69-87, EMER PROF GEOPHYS INST, UNIV ALASKA, 87-; HYDROLOGIST, US GEOL SURV, 90- *Personal Data:* b Minneapolis, Minn, June 23, 27; m 55, Ruth Gronlid; c 3. *Educ:* Univ Minn, BA, 50, MS, 56; Calif Inst Technol, PhD(geol), 60. *Prof Exp:* Physicist, Snow, Ice & Permafrost Res Estab, 52-56. *Concurrent Pos:* Glaciol panel, Comt Polar Res, Nat Res Coun-Nat Acad Sci, 64-67; mem, Gov Environ Adv Bd Alaska, 75- *Mem:* Fel AAAS; fel Am Geophys Union; Meteorol Soc; fel Arctic Inst NAm; Int Glaciol Soc; Geol Soc Am. *Res:* Glacier-volcano interactions; freezing processes; physical processes in seasonal snow cover; low temperature air pollution. *Mailing Add:* Geophys Inst Univ Alaska Fairbanks AK 99775-0800

BENSON, CHARLES EVERETT, BIOCHEMICAL GENETICS, INFECTIOUS DISEASES. *Current Pos:* trainee, Univ Pa, 69-71, scholar, Pa Plan Develop Scientists Med Res, 71-74, res assoc biochem genetics, 73-75, asst prof, Sch Allied Med Prof & Sch Med, 75-79, assoc prof, 79-80, assoc prof microbiol & dir clin microbiol, Large Animals Sch Vet Med, 80-88, chmn clin studies, New Bolton Ctr, 89-94, PROF MICROBIOL, LARGE ANIMALS SCH VET MED, UNIV PA, 88- *Personal Data:* b Dayton, Ohio, Dec 15, 37; m 60, Gail E Smith; c Deborah E & Charles N. *Educ:* Franklin Col, AB, 60; Miami Univ, MS, 64; Wake Forest Univ, PhD(microbiol), 69, Univ Pa, MA. *Hon Degrees:* MA, Univ Pa. *Honors & Awards:* President's Award, Am Soc Microbiol, 69. *Prof Exp:* Teacher gen sci, Cornell Heights Elem Sch, 60-61; res asst cardiac physiol, Dept Res, Miami Valley Hosp, 63-65. *Mem:* Am Soc Microbiol; NY Acad Sci; Soc Gen Microbiol; Sigma Xi; Am Asn Vet Lab Diagnosticians; AAAS. *Res:* Interrelationship of gene and enzyme function in purine metabolism of enteric bacteria the mechanism of salmonella pathogenesis; mechanism of host bacteria interaction in the disease process; Potomac Horse Fever-isolation of the etiological agent and characterization of the disease; salmonella enteritidis in poultry; food safety. *Mailing Add:* 123 Hawthorne Ave Haddonfield NJ 08033. *Fax:* 215-444-9564; *E-Mail:* cebenson@vet.upenn.edu

BENSON, DALE B(ULEN), CHEMICAL ENGINEERING. *Current Pos:* RETIRED. *Personal Data:* b Madison, Wis, Aug 21, 30; m 59, Maria A Sautner; c Linda, Sonya & Roland. *Educ:* Mont State Univ, BA, 52, MS, 55, PhD(chem eng), 59. *Prof Exp:* Res engr chem, Calif Res Corp, 58-59; sr res engr, Chevron Res Co, Stand Oil Co Calif, 59-85. *Mem:* Am Inst Indust Engrs; Am Inst Chem Engrs. *Res:* Catalytic hydrotreating of shale oil; petroleum process development; process planning. *Mailing Add:* 2808 Appaloosa Ct Pinole CA 94564

BENSON, DAVID BERNARD, APPLICATIONS OF CATEGORY THEORY IN COMPUTER SCIENCE. *Current Pos:* from asst prof to assoc prof comput sci, PROF, WASH STATE UNIV 70- *Personal Data:* b Seattle, Wash, Nov 18, 40. *Educ:* Calif Inst Technol, BS, 62, MS, 63, PhD(eng sci & math), 68. *Prof Exp:* Asst prof comput sci, Univ NC, Chapel Hill, 67-70. *Concurrent Pos:* Vis assoc prof comput sci, Univ Colo, Boulder, 75-76; vis comput scientist, Univ Edinburgh, Scotland, 83, Univ Sydney, Australia, 90. *Mem:* Asn Comput Mach; Am Math Soc; AAAS; Sigma Xi. *Res:* Applications of accessible categories in the theory of programming and to hardware specification; geometric logic; higher-dimensional categories. *Mailing Add:* 725 NE Illinois Ave Pullman WA 99163-3920. *E-Mail:* dbenson@eecs.wsu.edu

BENSON, DAVID MICHAEL, PLANT PATHOLOGY. *Current Pos:* from asst prof to assoc prof, 74-84, PROF PLANT PATH, NC STATE UNIV, 84- *Personal Data:* b Dayton, Ohio, Aug 28, 45; m 67, Patricia Miller; c 3. *Educ:* Earlham Col, BS, 67; Colo State Univ, MS, 68, PhD(plant path), 73. *Prof Exp:* Fel plant path, Univ Calif, Berkeley, 73-74. *Concurrent Pos:* Ed Phytopath, 87-90 & Crop Prolechans, 94-96; sect ed, Can J Microbiol, 94-96. *Mem:* Fel Am Phytopath Soc; Sigma Xi. *Res:* Ecology of soil-borne plant pathogens; phytophthora diseases; ornamental diseases; biocontrol. *Mailing Add:* Dept Plant Path NC State Univ Box 7629 Raleigh NC 27695-7629

BENSON, DEAN CLIFTON, MATHEMATICS. *Current Pos:* RETIRED. *Personal Data:* b Hazelton, NDak, Oct 25, 18; m 43; c 2. *Educ:* Sioux Falls Col, BA, 41; Iowa State Col, MS, 47, PhD(math), 54. *Prof Exp:* Aeronaut res photogr, Nat Adv Comt Aeronaut, Langley Field, 44-45; asst prof math, Sioux Falls Col, 47-50; instr, Iowa State Col, 50-54; asst prof, SDak Sch Mines & Tech, 54-56; asst prof, Chico State Col, 56-60; prof math, SDak Sch Mines & Technol, 60-81, chmn dept, 65-81. *Mem:* Am Math Soc; Math Asn Am. *Res:* Analysis; differential equations; complex variables; vector analysis. *Mailing Add:* 1425 Linwood Dr Hayden ID 83835-8807

BENSON, DENNIS ALAN, NEUROPHYSIOLOGY, PHYSIOLOGICAL PSYCHOLOGY. *Current Pos:* COMPUT SCIENTIST, NIH, 87- *Personal Data:* b New York, NY, Apr 8, 44; m 69; c 1. *Educ:* Univ Fla, BS, 69, PhD(physiol psychol), 73. *Prof Exp:* Fel, Sch Med, Johns Hopkins Univ, 74-77, res scientist neurosci, Dept Biomed Eng, 77-81. *Concurrent Pos:* NIH fel, 74-76; NATO travel grant, Conf Animal Behav, Ulm, Ger, 77; Comput Res Specialist, Nat Libr Med, 80-81. *Mem:* Acoust Soc Am; Soc Neurosci; AAAS. *Res:* Neurophysiology of auditory system; electrophysiological correlates of behavior; lateralization of function. *Mailing Add:* 3921 49th St NW Washington DC 20016

BENSON, DONALD CHARLES, DIFFERENTIAL EQUATIONS, SOFTWARE SYSTEMS. *Current Pos:* from asst prof to assoc prof, 57-68, prof, 68-83, EMER PROF MATH, UNIV CALIF, DAVIS, 83- *Personal Data:* b Modesto, Calif, June 6, 27; m 54; c 2. *Educ:* Pomona Col, BA, 50; Stanford Univ, MS, 52, PhD(math), 54. *Prof Exp:* Instr math, Princeton Univ, 54-55; asst prof, Carnegie Inst Technol, 55-57. *Concurrent Pos:* Freelance, Software Develop, 83- *Mem:* Am Math Soc; Math Asn Am. *Res:* Analysis; inequalities; nonlinear ordinary differential equations. *Mailing Add:* 215 Aguirre Way Cotati CA 94931

BENSON, EDMUND WALTER, INORGANIC CHEMISTRY, ANALYTICAL CHEMISTRY. *Current Pos:* asst prof, 67-72, ASSOC PROF CHEM, CENT MICH UNIV, 72- *Personal Data:* b Woburn, Mass, July 27, 38; m 73; c 2. *Educ:* Univ NH, BS, 61; Univ Tenn, MS, 63, PhD(chem), 67. *Prof Exp:* Res assoc chem, Univ Ill, 66-67. *Mem:* Am Chem Soc; Sigma Xi. *Res:* Water analysis and quality. *Mailing Add:* Dept Chem Cent Mich Univ 338 Dow Mt Pleasant MI 48859

BENSON, ELLIS STARBRANCH, PATHOLOGY. *Current Pos:* From instr to asst prof lab med, 50-53, asst prof, lab med, 53-57, from asst dir to dir clin labs, 53-66, assoc prof path, lab med, 57-61, head lab med, 66-73, PROF LAB MED & BIOCHEM, UNIV MINN, 61-, HEAD LAB MED & PATH, 73- *Personal Data:* b Xuchang, China, Oct 28, 19; m 47; c 3. *Educ:* Augustana Col, BA, 41; Univ Minn, MD, 45. *Hon Degrees:* DSc, Midland Lutheran Col, Fremont, NE, 86. *Honors & Awards:* G T Evans Award, Acad Clin Lab Physicians & Scientists, 72; George H Whipple lectr, Univ Rochester, 77; Ward Burdick Award, Am Soc Clin Path, 78. *Concurrent Pos:* USPHS sr res fel, 57-63; trustee, Am Bd Path, 71-83. *Mem:* Am Soc Clin Path; Am Soc Biol Chemists; Am Asn Path & Bact; Biophys Soc; Am Soc Cell Biol; Am Soc Hemat. *Res:* Muscle structure and function; hemoglobin and red blood cell structure and function. *Mailing Add:* Dept Lab Med & Path Univ Minn Box 609 Minneapolis MN 55455-0392

BENSON, ERNEST PHILLIP, JR, INORGANIC CHEMISTRY. *Current Pos:* asst prof, 66-74, ASSOC PROF CHEM, IDAHO STATE UNIV, 74- *Personal Data:* b New Castle, Pa, Feb 21, 36; m 60. *Educ:* Geneva Col, BS, 58; Mich State Univ, PhD(inorg chem), 63. *Prof Exp:* Res fel, Pa State Univ, 63-64; asst prof chem, Fairleigh Dickinson, Florham-Madison Campus, 64-66. *Mem:* Am Chem Soc; Sigma Xi. *Res:* Electron transfer reactions; preparation of coordination compounds; reactions of oxyanions. *Mailing Add:* Dept Chem Box 8160 Idaho State Univ Pocatello ID 83209-8160

BENSON, FRANK ATKINSON, MICROWAVES, TRANSMISSION LINES. *Current Pos:* lectr elec eng, Univ Sheffield, 49-59, sr lectr, 59-61, reader electronics, 61-67 prof & depth head, 67-87, EMER PROF ELECTRONIC & ELEC ENG, UNIV SHEFFIELD, 87- *Personal Data:* b Grange-over-Sands, Eng, Nov 21, 21; m 50, Kathleen M Paskell; c Peter J & Trevor M. *Educ:* Univ Liverpool, BEng, 42, MEng, 45; Univ Sheffield, PhD(elec eng), 52, DEng, 57. *Honors & Awards:* Order Brit Empire, 88. *Prof Exp:* Res officer, Admiralty Signal Estab, 43-46; asst lectr elec eng, Univ Liverpool, 46-49. *Concurrent Pos:* Pro vice chancellor, Univ Sheffield, 72-76, dean, 78-81; hon fel, Sheffield Hallam Univ, 79. *Mem:* fel Inst Elec Engrs; fel Inst Elec & Electronics Engrs. *Res:* Published about 200 papers on microwaves, transmission lines, gas discharges and electrical engineering education; author of books on voltage stabilization and microwaves and textbook for undergraduate engineers. *Mailing Add:* 64 Grove Rd Sheffield S7 2GZ England

BENSON, FRED J(ACOB), CIVIL ENGINEERING. *Current Pos:* RETIRED. *Personal Data:* b Grainfield, Kans, Sept 27, 14; m 37; c 3. *Educ:* Kans State Univ, BS, 35; Agr & Mech Col Tex, MS, 36. *Hon Degrees:* Dr Eng, Kans State Univ, 80. *Honors & Awards:* Edmund Friedman Prof Recognition Award, Am Soc Civil Engrs, 73. *Prof Exp:* Draftsman, Kans Hwy Comn, 35; instr, Purdue Univ, 36-37; draftsman, Int Boundary Comn, Tex, 37; from instr to assoc prof civil eng, Tex A&M Univ, 37-47, prof, 47-80, dean eng, 57-78, vpres & dir res found, 63-80, vpres eng & non-renewable resources, 78-79, vchancellor, 79-80, pres, Tex A&M Res Found, 80- *Concurrent Pos:* Asst city engr, Wichita Falls, 38; city engr, College Station, 47-63; exec officer, Tex Transp Inst, 55-62; vdir, Tex Eng Exp Sta, 56-57, dir, 62-78; eng consult. *Mem:* Soc Civil Engrs; Am Road Builders Asn; Sigma Xi; hom mem Am Soc Civil Engrs. *Res:* Highway and airfield pavements; aggregates; bituminous materials; concrete. *Mailing Add:* 817 Rosemary Dr Bryan TX 77802

BENSON, FREDERIC RUPERT, organic chemistry, information science; deceased, see previous edition for last biography

BENSON, GEORGE CAMPBELL, THERMODYNAMICS. *Current Pos:* HON SR SCIENTIST, DEPT CHEM ENG, UNIV OTTAWA, 84- *Personal Data:* b Toronto, Ont, July 25, 19; m 46; c 2. *Educ:* Univ Toronto, BA, 42, MA, 43, PhD(chem), 45. *Honors & Awards:* Bronze Medal, Brit Asn, 42. *Prof Exp:* Res chemist, Chem Div, Nat Res Coun Can, 45-49; mem solid state physics group, Bristol Univ, 49-50; res chemist, chem div, Nat Res Coun Can, 51-84. *Mem:* Am Phys Soc; Am Chem Soc; Royal Soc Can; Chem Inst Can. *Res:* Thermodynamic studies of mixtures of nonelectrolytes. *Mailing Add:* 210 Sandridge Rd 770 King Edward Ave Ottawa ON K1L 5A2 Can

BENSON, GILBERT THOMAS, GEOLOGY. *Current Pos:* asst prof geol, 68-74, ASSOC PROF EARTH SCI, PORTLAND STATE UNIV, 74- *Personal Data:* b Los Angeles, Calif, Oct 3, 29; m 57; c 1. *Educ:* Stanford Univ, BS, 52, MS, 53; Yale Univ, PhD(geol), 63. *Prof Exp:* Geologist, Texaco, Inc, 53-58; asst prof geol, Univ Ore, 62-68. *Mem:* Geol Soc Am; Am Asn Petrol Geologists; Sigma Xi. *Res:* Structural, areal and petroleum geology. *Mailing Add:* 2705 Glen Eagles Rd Lake Oswego OR 97034

BENSON, HARRIET, ORGANIC CHEMISTRY, PHARMACEUTICAL REGULATIONS. *Current Pos:* Consult, 95- *Personal Data:* b Kansas City, Mo, May 17, 41. *Educ:* Wellesley Col, BA, 63; Univ Kans, PhD(org chem), 67. *Prof Exp:* Lit specialist, Shell Develop Co, 63-64; fel, State Univ Groningen, 68-69; mem staff tech info & regulatory affairs, Alza Corp, 69-87, vpres regulatory affairs & tech publ, 87-95. *Concurrent Pos:* Workshop facilitator, Am Med Writer Asn, 76- *Mem:* AAAS; Am Chem Soc; fel Am Med Writers Asn; Drug Info Asn; Am Asn Pharmaceut Scientists. *Res:* Conformational factors in free radical and photochemical reactions; scientific literature related to pharmaceutical sciences including medicinal, pharmaceutical, organic, physical and polymer chemistry, clinical and veterinary medicine and toxicology; technical writing and editing. *Mailing Add:* 2825 Ramona Palo Alto CA 94306

BENSON, HERBERT, CARDIOLOGY. *Current Pos:* CHIEF, DIV BEHAV MED, NEW ENG DEACONESS HOSP, 87-, PRES, MIND/BODY INST, 88- *Personal Data:* b Yonkers, NY, Apr 24, 35; m 62; c 2. *Educ:* Wesleyan Univ, BA, 57; Harvard Med Sch, MD, 61. *Prof Exp:* Assoc physician med & dir Hypertension Sect, Beth Israel Hosp, 74-87, dir, Div Behav Med, 78-87. *Concurrent Pos:* USPHS fel cardiol, Thorndike Mem Lab, Harvard Med Sch, 65-67, Med Found grant behav physiol, 67-69; prog dir, Gen Clin Res Ctr, Boston City Hosp, 72-74 & Gen Clin Res Ctr, Beth Israel Hosp, 74-78; expert consult, Spec Action Off Drug Abuse Prev, Exec Off of Pres, Washington, DC, 74; mem, Med Adv Bd, Coun High Blood Pressure Res, 76-; mem, Acad Behav Med Res, 78- *Mem:* AAAS; Am Fedn Clin Res; Am Physiol Soc; Am Psychosom Soc; fel Am Col Cardiol. *Res:* Behavioral aspects of cardiovascular disease and other diseases related to so-called stress; the counterpart of the fight or flight response-the relaxation response. *Mailing Add:* Div Behav Med & the Mind Body Inst 185 Pilgrim Rd Boston MA 02215

BENSON, JAMES R, LIQUID CHROMATOGRAPHY, BIOCHEMISTRY. *Current Pos:* PRES, SUNSTROM RES CORP, 91- *Personal Data:* b NJ, 42; m 84; c 1. *Educ:* Stanford Univ, PhD(med microbiol), 74. *Prof Exp:* Pres, Interaction Chem, Inc, 79-90. *Mem:* Am Soc Biochem & Molecular Biol; Am Soc Microbiol. *Mailing Add:* Sunstorm Res Corp 15143 Kennedy Rd Los Gatos CA 95032-6518

BENSON, JOHN ALEXANDER, JR, GASTROENTEROLOGY. *Current Pos:* from assoc prof to prof med, 59-93, head, Div Gastroenterol, 59-75, interim dean, Sch Med, 91-93, DEAN & EMER PROF MED, SCH MED, ORE HEALTH SCI, UNIV ORE, 93- *Personal Data:* b Manchester, Conn, July 23, 21; m 47; c 4. *Educ:* Wesleyan Univ, BA, 43; Harvard Med Sch, MD, 46. *Prof Exp:* Instr med, Harvard Med Sch, 56-59. *Concurrent Pos:* Attend in med, Vet Admin Hosps, Boston, 58-59 & Portland, Ore, 60-75; consult gastroenterol, Vancouver, Wash, 60-75; mem, Sub Specialty Gastroenterol Bd, Am Bd Internal Med, 61-66, chmn, 61-66, mem, 69-91, secy-treas, 72-75, pres, 75-91, emer pres, 91-; consult, Madigan Gen Army Hosp. *Mem:* Inst Med-Nat Acad Sci; master Am Col Physicians; AMA; Am Asn Study Liver Diseases; Am Soc Internal Med; Am Clin & Climat Asn (vpres); Am Fedn Clin Res; Am Gastroenterol Asn (secy, 70-73, vpres, 75-76, pres-elect, 76-77, pres, 77-78); Sigma Xi. *Res:* Normal and abnormal intestinal absorption. *Mailing Add:* Sch Med Ore Health Sci Univ 3181 SW San Jackson Park Rd (L102) Portland OR 97201. *Fax:* 503-494-3400; *E-Mail:* bensonj@ohsu.edu

BENSON, KATHERINE ALICE, DEVELOPMENTAL PHYSIOLOGY. *Current Pos:* CONSULT, 75- *Personal Data:* b Roanoke, Va, June 29, 38; m 62; c 2. *Educ:* Col William & Mary, BS, 60; Univ Va, PhD(biol), 65. *Prof Exp:* Asst prof zool, La State Univ, 65-67; assoc prof biol, Radford Col, 67-75. *Mem:* Am Soc Zool. *Res:* Mechanisms of histolysis of insect tissues during metamorphosis; reorientation of physiological mechanisms in developing cells of insects and the lower vertebrates. *Mailing Add:* Psychol Dept Div Soc Sci Univ Minn Morris MN 56267

BENSON, KEITH RODNEY, HISTORY OF BIOLOGY, HISTORY OF MEDICINE. *Current Pos:* from asst prof to assoc prof, 81-94, PROF HIST BIOL, UNIV WASH, 94- *Personal Data:* b Portland, Ore, July 22, 48. *Educ:* Whitworth Col, BA, 70; Ore State Univ, MA, 73, PhD(hist sci & gen sci), 79. *Honors & Awards:* NSF Scholar's Award, 89. *Prof Exp:* Asst prof biol/hist sci, Pac Lutheran Univ, 79-81. *Concurrent Pos:* Adj prof, Hist Dept, Univ Wash, 85-; book rev ed, J Hist Biol, 85-; mem, Forum Hist Sci Am. *Mem:* Sigma Xi; Hist Sci Soc; Am Soc Zoologists; Int Soc Hist Philos & Soc Social Studies Biol. *Res:* History of American biology; role of biological institutions in growth of American biology; nineteenth century morphology, European and American; history of ethics in science. *Mailing Add:* Dept Med Hist & Ethics Box 357120 Univ Wash Seattle WA 98195

BENSON, LARRY V, PALEOCLIMATE RESEARCH, ISOTOPIC & CHEMICAL BEHAVIOR OF LAKES. *Current Pos:* RES HYDROLOGIST-PROJ CHIEF, US GEOL SURV, 81- *Personal Data:* b Pontiac, Mich, Feb 6, 44. *Educ:* Wheaton Col, BS, 66; Brown Univ, PhD(earth sci), 74. *Prof Exp:* Asst prof geol, Univ Nebr, Lincoln, 73-74; prin investr, Desert Res Inst, 74-76; staff scientist, Earth Sci Div, Lawrence Berkeley Lab, 77-82. *Concurrent Pos:* Res affil, Nat Ctr Atmospheric Res, 88-, Inst Arctic & Alpine Res, 89-; adj prof, Univ Nev Reno, 93- *Mem:* Am Quaternary Asn; Am Geophys Union. *Res:* Chemical (inorganic and isotopic) and physical behavior of arid surface-water systems. *Mailing Add:* US Geol Surv 3215 Marine St Boulder CO 80303. *Fax:* 303-447-2505

BENSON, LOREN ALLEN, PHYSICAL CHEMISTRY. *Current Pos:* CHIEF SCIENTIST, DATRAN CORP, 70- *Personal Data:* b St Louis, Mo, Mar 19, 32; m 58; c 3. *Educ:* Wash Univ, AB, 52; St Louis Univ, PhD, 59. *Prof Exp:* Oper analyst, Inst Defense Analysis, 58-65; mem staff, Lambda Corp, 65-67; chief scientist, Keystone Comput Assocs, 67-70. *Mem:* AAAS; Asn Comput Mach. *Res:* Computer science; operations research; communications analysis. *Mailing Add:* 40 Autumn Ridge Rd Trumbull CT 06611

BENSON, NORMAN G, BIOLOGY, LIMNOLOGY. *Current Pos:* Fishery res biologist, US Fish & Wildlife Serv, 57-61, chief, N Cent Res Invest, US Bur Sport Fisheries & Wildlife, 61-75, fish & wildlife adminr & team leader nat stream alteration team, US Fish & Wildlife Serv, 75-78, fishery biologist, nat coastal ecosyst team, 78-84. *Personal Data:* b Berlin, Conn, May 7, 23; m 51; c 5. *Educ:* Univ Maine, BS, 48; Univ Mich, MA, 51, PhD(fisheries), 53. *Concurrent Pos:* Consult, James Bay Energy Co, Montreal, 76-85. *Mem:* Am Fisheries Soc; Ecol Soc Am; fel Am Inst Fishery Res Biol. *Res:* Trout stream ecology; fish population dynamics; large reservoir limnology and fish populations; water management. *Mailing Add:* 1330 Northface Ct Colorado Springs CO 80919-1507

BENSON, RALPH C, JR, SURGERY. *Current Pos:* PROF UROL, MAYO MED SCH & CHMN, DEPT UROL, MAYO CLIN, JACKSONVILLE, FLA, 86- *Personal Data:* b Birmingham, Ala, Jan 16, 42; c 2. *Educ:* Stanford Univ, BS, 63; Johns Hopkins Med Sch, MD, 67. *Prof Exp:* Intern, Univ Ore, 67-68; resident, Mayo Grad Sch, 70-75; asst prof urol, Univ Wis Med Sch, 76-79; from instr to asst prof urol, Mayo Med Sch, 80-81; consult, dept urol, Mayo Clin, 80-86. *Concurrent Pos:* Consult, div urol, Univ Wis Hosps & Clins, 76-79. *Mem:* Sigma Xi; Am Med Asn; Am Urol Asn; Am Col Surgeons; Am Soc Laser Med & Surgery; Int Soc Urol. *Res:* Phenochromocytoma of the bladder. *Mailing Add:* 2400 Patterson St No 101 Nashville TN 37203-1562

BENSON, RICHARD C, MICROELECTRONIC MATERIALS, SURFACE SCIENCE. *Current Pos:* sr chemist, 72-80, PRIN PROF STAFF, APPL PHYSICS LAB, JOHNS HOPKINS UNIV, 80-, GROUP SUPVR, 90- *Personal Data:* b Kalamazoo, Mich, Jan 23, 44; m 72, Jill Robinson; c Michelle & Ross. *Educ:* Mich State Univ, BS, 66; Univ Ill, PhD(phys chem), 72. *Prof Exp:* Res assoc, Univ Ill, 71-72. *Mem:* Am Phys Soc; Am Vacuum Soc; Inst Elec & Electronic Engrs; Mat Res Soc. *Res:* Sensor and surface science; properties of microelectronic materials; stability of spacecraft materials; molecular spectroscopy; mass spectrometry; gas chromatography; application of optical techniques to surface science. *Mailing Add:* Appl Physics Lab Johns Hopkins Univ Laurel MD 20723. *E-Mail:* richard.benson@jhuapl.edu

BENSON, RICHARD CARTER, OPTIMAL DESIGN. *Current Pos:* asst prof, 80-83, ASSOC PROF MECH ENG, UNIV ROCHESTER, 83- *Personal Data:* b Newport News, Va, July 29, 51; m 76; c 1. *Educ:* Princeton Univ, BSE, 73; Univ Va, MS, 74; Univ Calif, Berkeley, PhD(mech eng), 77. *Honors & Awards:* Henry Hess Award, Am Soc Mech Engrs, 84. *Prof Exp:* Tech specialist & proj mgr, Xerox Corp, 77-80. *Concurrent Pos:* Consult, 80-; assoc ed, Appl Mech Rev, 85- *Mem:* Am Soc Mech Engrs; Am Soc Eng Educ; Soc Tribiologists & Lubrication Engrs; Am Acad Mech. *Res:* Nonlinear plate and shell theory, structural mechanics, and machine dynamics; applications to very flexible structures such as paper sheets, computer floppy disks, and collapsible shells; stability and control of mechanical structures. *Mailing Add:* Dept Mech Eng Univ Rochester 500 Joseph C Wilson Rochester NY 14627-9000

BENSON, RICHARD EDWARD, analytical chemistry; deceased, see previous edition for last biography

BENSON, RICHARD HALL, PALEONTOLOGY, OCEANOGRAPHY. *Current Pos:* res paleobiologist & cur, 64-84, SR SCIENTIST, SMITHSONIAN INST, 84- *Personal Data:* b Huntington, WVa, May 19, 29; m 57. *Educ:* Marshall Col, BS, 51; Univ Ill, MS, 53, PhD(geol), 55; Univ Leicester, MSc, 71, DSc, 83. *Honors & Awards:* Nat Mus Nat Hist Dirs Award, Smithsonian Inst, 74. *Prof Exp:* Asst, State Geol Surv, Ill, 51-53, asst geologist, 55-56; from asst prof to prof geol, Univ Kans, 55-82. *Concurrent Pos:* Vis scientist, Soc Nat Elf-Aquitain, Pau, France, 76-77. *Mem:* Paleont Soc; Soc Syst Zool; Paleont Asn Gt Brit; fel AAAS; Int Paleont Asn (treas). *Res:* Micropaleontology; Recent and Cenozoic Ostracoda; deep-sea environmental studies; paleoecology; Cenozoic stratigraphy; analysis of morphological change through computer simulation; studies in North African geology and the origin of the Mediterranean. *Mailing Add:* Dept Paleobiol MRC NHB 121 Smithsonian Inst Mus Natural Hist Washington DC 20560

BENSON, RICHARD NORMAN, PETROLEUM GEOLOGY & GEOLOGY, MICROPALEONTOLOGY. *Current Pos:* scientist, 75-81, SR SCIENTIST, DEL GEOL SURV, 81-, JOINT APPOINTMENT ASSOC PROF, DEPT GEOL, UNIV DEL, 85- *Personal Data:* b Sioux City, Iowa, Nov 11, 35; m 59, Deanna Dovre; c Amy Christine. *Educ:* Augustana Col, Ill, BA, 58; Univ Minn, Minneapolis, PhD(geol), 66. *Prof Exp:* Geologist, Exxon, 66-69; asst prof geol, Augustana Col, Ill, 69-75. *Concurrent Pos:* Shipboard scientist, Deep Sea Drilling Proj, Legs 12, 65; geologist, Water Resources Div, US Geol Surv, 74-79; alt Del rep, Mid-Atlantic Regional Tech Working Group, & OCS Policy Com, Outer Continental Shelf Adv Bd, US Dept Interior, 79-; ed, Del Geol Surv publ; prin investr, res contracts, Continental Margins Prog Minerals Mgt Serv, Asn Am State Geologists, 83- *Mem:* AAAS; Am Asn Petrol Geol; Sigma Xi; NAm Microplant Sect, Soc Econ Paleontologists & Mineralogist; Geol Soc Am. *Res:* Geological history stratigraphy and hydrocarbon resources of the Atlantic continental margin of North America; radiolarian and foraminiferal biostratigraphy and paleoecology; paleoenvironmental interpretation of marine sedimentary rocks; petroleum geology; interpretation of seismic reflection profiles; seismic stratigraphy. *Mailing Add:* Del Geol Surv Univ Del Newark DE 19716. *Fax:* 302-831-3579; *E-Mail:* rnbenson@udel.edu

BENSON, ROBERT FRANKLIN, EXPERIMENTAL DESIGN, LIQUID CHROMATOGRAPHY. *Current Pos:* mfg eng mgr, 91-97, STAFF SCIENTIST, BIO-RAD, 97- *Personal Data:* b Cumberland, Md, Jan 22, 41; m 63, Linda Phillips; c Miles D. *Educ:* WVa Univ, BS, 63; Univ SC, MS, 65; Rensselaer Polytech Inst, PhD(org chem), 74. *Prof Exp:* Asst res chemist, Sterling-Winthrop Res Inst, 65-73; sr res chemist, GAF Res Lab, 75-77; sr scientist, Waters Assocs, 77-85; chief chemist & res & develop mgr, Rainin Instrument Co, 85-91. *Concurrent Pos:* Assoc, Rensselaer Polytech Inst, 73-75. *Mem:* Am Chem Soc. *Res:* Development & manufacturing of clinical methods; experimental design of methods. *Mailing Add:* Bio-Rad Labs Inc 4000 Afred Nobel Dr Hercules CA 94547

BENSON, ROBERT FREDERICK, SPACE PHYSICS, IONOSPHERIC PHYSICS. *Current Pos:* GEOPHYSICIST, GODDARD SPACE FLIGHT CTR, NASA, 65- *Personal Data:* b Minneapolis, Minn, Mar 16, 35; m 58, Marilyn J Evers; c Maia, Susan & Gregory. *Educ:* Univ Minn, BS, 56, MS, 59; Univ Alaska, PhD(geophys), 63. *Prof Exp:* Int Geophys Year scientist, Arctic Inst NAm, 56-58; asst geophysicist, Geophys Inst, Univ Alaska, 59-63; asst prof astron, Univ Minn, 63-64. *Concurrent Pos:* Nat Acad Sci-Nat Res Coun resident res assoc, 64-65. *Mem:* Am Polar Soc; Am Geophys Union; Int Union Radio Sci; Antarctican Soc. *Res:* Radio star scintillations; ionospheric cross modulation; plasma waves, stimulated instabilities and non-linear phenomena in the topside ionosphere; ionospheric electron temperature; equatorial ionospheric plasma bubbles; planetary radio emissions. *Mailing Add:* Code 692 NASA/Goddard Space Flight Ctr Greenbelt MD 20771. *Fax:* 301-286-1683; *E-Mail:* u2rfb@lepvax.gsfc.nasa.gov

BENSON, ROBERT HAYNES, ANIMAL BREEDING. *Current Pos:* RETIRED. *Personal Data:* b Hanover, NH, 24; m 50; c 3. *Educ:* Univ NH, BS, 49; WVa Univ, MS, 51; Univ Wis, PhD, 55. *Prof Exp:* Dairy husbandman, Univ Wis, 53-55; exten dairyman, Univ Conn, 55-86. *Concurrent Pos:* Mem coord group, Nat Dairy Herd Improv Asn Prog, 68-71, policy bd, 83-85 & rules comt, 83-; chmn, New Eng Green Pastures Dairymen of Year Comt, 83- & Conn Mastitis Coun, 82- *Mem:* Am Dairy Sci Asn. *Res:* Type classification of dairy cattle; environmental influences and their effect on milk production; dairy cattle breeding. *Mailing Add:* 1440 Ashley Dr Virginia Beach VA 23454

BENSON, ROBERT JOHN, COMPUTER SCIENCE. *Current Pos:* AFFIL ASSOC PROF COMPUT SCI, WASH UNIV, 68-, DIR COMPUT FACIL, 73-, ASSOC VCHANCELLOR, 75- *Personal Data:* b Michigan City, Ind, Sept 2, 43; m 66, Nancy L White; c John R & David P. *Educ:* Wash Univ, St Louis, BS, 65, JD, 68. *Concurrent Pos:* Consult, 68-; dir, Ctr Study Data Processing, 80-; pres, Regional Consortium Educ & Technol, St Louis, 84- *Mem:* Data Processing Mgt Asn; Asn Comput Mach; Asn Systs Mgt. *Res:* Data processing and computer systems. *Mailing Add:* Wash Univ PO Box 1106 St Louis MO 63188-1106

BENSON, ROBERT LELAND, ENTOMOLOGY, ENZYMOLOGY. *Current Pos:* mem staff biochem & biophys, Univ Calif, 76-80. *Personal Data:* b Tucson, Ariz, Oct 27, 41; m 66. *Educ:* Pomona Col, BA, 63; Univ Ill, Urbana-Champaign, PhD(entom), 69. *Prof Exp:* Staff fel, Geront Res Ctr, NIH, Md, 68-70; asst prof entom, Wash State Univ, 70-76. *Mem:* AAAS; Sigma Xi. *Res:* Synthesis of aminosugars and chitin in insects; properties of enzymes involved in aminosugar metabolism; hormonal control metabolic processes; ultrastructural localization of disaccharidases in mammalian intestine. *Mailing Add:* 5120 Cowell Blvd Davis CA 95616-4409

BENSON, ROBERT WILMER, ELECTRICAL ENGINEERING, PHYSICS. *Current Pos:* PRES, BONITRON, INC, 62- *Personal Data:* b Grand Island, Nebr, Jan 21, 24; m 52; c 3. *Educ:* Wash Univ, BSEE, 48, MSEE, 49, PhD(elec eng), 51. *Prof Exp:* Res assoc physics, Cent Inst Deaf, St Louis, 49-54; asst dir, Armour Res Found, Chicago, 54-60; prof elec eng, Vanderbilt Univ, 60-62. *Concurrent Pos:* Consult, Am Acad Ophthal & Otolaryngol, 52-; mem hearing & bioacoust comt, Nat Res Coun, 56-63, chmn helmets comt, 68-73; mem exec bd dirs, Wilkerson Hearing & Speech Ctr, 68- & Am Red Cross, Nashville, 74- *Mem:* Fel Acoust Soc Am; Inst Elec & Electronics Engrs. *Res:* Acoustics and electronic instrumentation. *Mailing Add:* Bonitron Inc 521 Fairground Ct Nashville TN 37211

BENSON, ROYAL H, organic chemistry, analytical chemistry; deceased, see previous edition for last biography

BENSON, SIDNEY WILLIAM, PHYSICAL CHEMISTRY. *Current Pos:* distinguished prof, 76-91, sci co-dir, 78-91, EMER DISTINGUISHED PROF CHEM, UNIV SOUTHERN CALIF, 91-, EMER SCI CO-DIR, HYDROCARBON RES INST, 91- *Personal Data:* b New York, NY, Sept 26, 18; m 86, Anna Bruni; c Nicholas & Jeannette. *Educ:* Columbia Univ, BA, 38; Harvard Univ, MA & PhD(phys chem), 41. *Hon Degrees:* Dr, Univ Nancy, France, 89. *Honors & Awards:* Glidden Lectr, Purdue Univ, 61; Petrol Chem Award, Am Chem Soc, 77, Tolman Award, 78 & Langmuir Award, 86; Frank Gucker Mem Lectr, Indiana Univ, 84; Polanyi Medal, Royal Soc Eng, 86; G N Lewis Lectr, Univ Calif, Berkeley, 89; Kapitza Medal Sci, Russia, 97. *Prof Exp:* Res assoc, Harvard Univ, 41; instr chem, City Col New York,

42-43; res chemist, Manhattan Proj, Kellex Corp, 43; from asst prof to prof chem, Univ Southern Calif, 43-63, dir, Chem Physics Prog, 62-63; chmn, Dept Kinetics & Thermochem, Stanford Res Inst, 63-76. *Concurrent Pos:* Consult, Goodyear Tire & Rubber Co, 57-62 & 70-75, Douglas Aircraft Co, 58-70, Jet Propulsion Labs, 61-65 & Aerospace Labs, 61-91; ed-in-chief, Int J Chem Kinetics, 67-83; mem adv coun, Gordon Res Conf, 68-71, 78-81; mem comt selection postdoctoral res fels, NSF, 69; mem org solvents adv comt, Nat Air Pollution Control Admin, 69-72; chem eval panel phys chem, Nat Bur Stand, 69-72; mem Comt on Data for Sci & Technol & chmn task group chem kinetics, Int Coun Sci Unions, 69-74; mem, Comn Motor Vehicle Exhausts, Nat Acad Sci, 71-74 & Sci Adv Panel, State of Calif Air Resources Bd, 72-76, chmn, 75-76; vis prof, Univ Utah, 71, Univ Paris, 50, 71-72 & 79, Tex A&M Univ, 78 & Univ Lausanne, 79; hon vis prof, Univ St Andrews, Scotland, 73, Univ Guelph & Waterloo, Can, 81 & hon Brotherton prof, Univ Leeds, Eng, 84; adv panel, Biol & Climate Effects, US Environ Protection Agency, 77; consult, Occidential Res Corp, 78, TRW, 78-79, Seoul Nat Univ, 79-80 & Gas Res Inst, 79-80, Panel Fossil Energy Res, Dept Energy, 81-82; mem bd dirs, Pyrotech, KTI, 80-84; assoc mem, Comm Chem Kinetics, Int Union Pure & Appl Chem. *Mem:* Nat Acad Sci; fel AAAS; fel Am Phys Soc; Am Chem Soc; fel Japan Soc Advan Sci; assoc mem Int Union Pure & Appl Chem; Nat Acad Sci India; Indian Acad Sci. *Res:* Photochemistry; kinetics; theory of liquid structure; catalysis adsorption; statistical mechanics; free radicals; thermochemistry; quantum mechanics. *Mailing Add:* Dept Chem Univ Southern Calif Los Angeles CA 90089-1661. *E-Mail:* benson@mizar.usc.edu

BENSON, SPENCER ALAN, GENETICS, MEMBRANES. *Current Pos:* asst prof, 89-93, ASSOC PROF MICROBIOL, UNIV MD, COLLEGE PARK, 93- *Personal Data:* b St Albans, Vt, Nov 2, 51; m, Lynne M Davidson. *Educ:* Univ Vt, BA, 73; Univ Chicago, PhD(genetics), 78. *Prof Exp:* Fel petrol res fund, Univ Chicago, 78-79; Nat Cancer Inst fel, Frederick Cancer Res Facil, 79-83, scientist, 83-84; res molecular biologist, Princeton Univ, 84-87. *Concurrent Pos:* Lectr, Princeton Univ, 86-88. *Mem:* AAAS; Genetics Soc Am; Am Soc Microbiol. *Res:* Roles outer membranes play in cell permeability and the genetics of long term non-lethal selections for enhanced growth characteristics. *Mailing Add:* Dept Microbiol Univ Md College Park MD 20742-0001. *Fax:* 301-314-9489; *E-Mail:* sb77@umail.umd.edu

BENSON, WALTER RODERICK, PHARMACEUTICAL CHEMISTRY, ANALYTICAL CHEMISTRY. *Current Pos:* PRES, BENSON & ASSOC, 91- *Personal Data:* b Chicago, Ill, Oct 16, 29; m 57, Ellen; c 3. *Educ:* Univ Ill, BS, 51; Univ Colo, PhD(chem), 58. *Prof Exp:* Chemist, Griffith Labs, Ill, 53-54; asst, Univ Colo, 54-57; fel, Purdue Univ, 58-59; asst prof chem, Colo State Univ, 59-63; sect head, Pesticides Br, Div Food Chem, Food & Drug Admin, 63-69, br chief, Instrumental Appln Res Br, 69-77, dir, Div Drug Chem, Bur Drugs, 77-85; WHO/Stc, Zimbabwe, 87-90; Unicef, Tanzania, 91. *Concurrent Pos:* Prof lectr, USDA Grad Sch, 65-71 & Am Univ, 67; consult chemist, 86-; Int Orgn Chem Sci Develop, 91-; mem, Phoenix Regulatory Assocs, 93-; chmn, Joint Working Party Environ Anal Chem Develop Countries, Int Orgn Chem Sci Develop & Int Union Pure & Appl Chem, 94- *Mem:* Asn Off Anal Chemists; Am Chem Soc; Sigma Xi; Int Union Pure & Appl Chem; Int Orgn Chem Sci Develop. *Res:* Electron spin immunoassay; radioactive drug analysis; synthetic organic chemistry; bridgehead rearrangements; organic mechanisms; carbamate pesticides; oximes; agricultural and pharmaceutical chemistry; photochemistry; drug analysis; environmental analysis of chemistry in developing countries. *Mailing Add:* Benson & Assoc 6209 Crathie Lane Bethesda MD 20816-1003. *Fax:* 301-229-3913; *E-Mail:* wbenson270@aol.com

BENSON, WALTER RUSSELL, PATHOLOGY, MEDICINE. *Current Pos:* from asst prof to assoc prof, 56-67, PROF PATH, MED SCH, UNIV NC, CHAPEL HILL, 67- *Personal Data:* b Tamaqua, Pa, July 27, 20; m 50; c 4. *Educ:* Duke Univ, MD, 44. *Prof Exp:* Instr path, Sch Med, Duke Univ, 52-54, assoc, 54-55; asst prof, Sch Med, Univ Louisville, 55-56. *Mem:* Am Asn Path; Am Soc Exp Path; Int Acad Path. *Res:* Cardiovascular pulmonary diseases; protein metabolism; neoplasia. *Mailing Add:* 310 Cedar St Chapel Hill NC 27514

BENSON, WILLIAM EDWARD BARNES, GEOLOGY. *Current Pos:* SR STAFF OFFICER, NAT ACAD SCI, 80- *Personal Data:* b West Haven, Conn, May 15, 19; m 44, Freda Hill; c Sharon (Rachel), M Lynn (Walker) & William E Jr. *Educ:* Yale Univ, BA, 40, MS, 42, PhD(geol), 52. *Honors & Awards:* Penfield Prize; Hurlbut-Runk Prize; Distinguished Serv Award, NSF. *Prof Exp:* Geologist, Conn State Geol & Nat Hist Surv, 40-41, US Geol Surv, 42-54, actg chief, Gen Geol Br, 53-54; exec secy, Div Earth Sci, Nat Res Coun, 54-55; chief geologist, Manidon Mining Inc, 55-56; mem staff, NSF, 56-79, from prog dir to head earth sci sect, 57-75, chief scientist, Earth Sci Div, 75-79. *Concurrent Pos:* Adv, Pres Off Sci & Technol Policy, 76-77; vis prof, Univ Hawaii, 80; consult, Environ Geol & Nuclear Waste Mgt, 80- *Mem:* AAAS; fel Am Geophys Union; fel Geol Soc Am. *Res:* Marine geology; geomorphology; glacial geology; tertiary stratigraphy; economic geology. *Mailing Add:* 7531 Parish Lane Falls Church VA 22042. *Fax:* 202-334-1377; *E-Mail:* bilfre@aol.com

BENSON, WILLIAM HAZLEHURST, AQUATIC TOXICOLOGY, ENVIRONMENTAL TOXICOLOGY. *Current Pos:* assoc prof, 88-94, PROF TOXICOL, UNIV MISS, 94-, DIR, RES INST PHARMACEUT SCI, 96- *Personal Data:* b Philadelphia, Pa, Nov 21, 54; US & Brit citizen; m 77, Mary T; c Ian H & William O. *Educ:* Fla Inst Technol, BS, 76; Univ Ky, MS, 80, PhD(toxicol), 84. *Honors & Awards:* Cert Merit, Environ Chem Div, Am Chem Soc, 88; Dow-Dow Corning Distinguished Lect in Environmental Toxicology, Mich State Univ, 89. *Prof Exp:* Sr scientist toxicol, Cannon Labs, Inc, 76-78; from asst prof to assoc prof toxicol, Northeast La Univ, 84-88. *Concurrent Pos:* Dir, Toxicol Prog, Northeast La Univ, 87-88; coordr, Environ Toxicol Res Prog, Univ Miss, 89- *Mem:* Am Chem Soc; Soc Environ Toxicol & Chem; Soc Toxicol; Am Asn Col Pharm. *Res:* Assessment of the acute and chronic health effects of environmental contaminants; research areas also include reproduction studies in aquatic animals; use of biomarkers in environmental monitoring; residue health effects; pesticide toxicology; rural health endocrine effects. *Mailing Add:* 440 Cherokee Dr Oxford MS 38655. *Fax:* 601-232-5118; *E-Mail:* flbenson@umsvh

BENT, BRIAN E, PHYSICAL CHEMISTRY, SURFACE CHEMISTRY. *Current Pos:* PROF CHEM, COLUMBIA UNIV, 88- *Personal Data:* b Minneapolis, Minn, Oct 18, 60; m 91. *Educ:* Carleton Col, BA, 82; Univ Calif, Berkeley, PhD(chem), 86. *Prof Exp:* Postdoctoral, AT&T Bell, 86-88. *Concurrent Pos:* Nat Sci found fel; presidential young investr, 89- *Mem:* AAAS; Am Vacuum Soc; Am Chem Soc; Am Phys Soc; Mat Res Soc. *Res:* Surface chemistry, heterogeneous catalysis, materials deposition and growth. *Mailing Add:* Dept Chem Columbia Univ 116th St & Broadway New York NY 10027

BENT, DONALD FREDERICK, MICROBIOLOGY. *Current Pos:* CONSULT. *Personal Data:* b Clinton, Mass, Nov, 16, 25; m 51; c 3. *Educ:* Univ NH, BS, 48, MS, 53; Univ Md, PhD(microbiol), 57. *Prof Exp:* Spec staff asst, Am Coun Ed, 56; instr bact & immunol, Harvard Med Sch, 56-59; owner & dir, Health Serv Lab, 60-78; vpres, Biospheric Consult Int, Inc, 74-77; dir, NH Water Supply & Pollution Control Comn Lab, Concord, 77-90. *Concurrent Pos:* Div dir, Biol Labs, Mass Dept Pub Health, 56-59; mem fac, Colby Jr Col Women, 56-69; vpres, Bio-tronics Res, Inc, 61-66; Fulbright lectr, Med Fac, Univ Malaya, 66-67; dir, Clin Microbiol Div, Metpath Lab, Inc, NJ, 69-71; bd, State Health Officer Biosphenic; consult, Corp BCI; dir, Libratary State NH Environ Serv; found & vpres, Water Test Corp, 82-85. *Mem:* Am Soc Microbiol; Nat Environ Health Asn. *Res:* Clinical and environmental microbiology; bacterial toxins; immunology; diagnostic and automated microbiology; water quality; environmental health laboratory management. *Mailing Add:* 31 Lamson Lane PO Box 32 New London NH 03257-0032

BENT, HENRY ALBERT, PHYSICAL CHEMISTRY. *Current Pos:* RETIRED. *Personal Data:* b Cambridge, Mass, Dec 21, 26; m 59; c 2. *Educ:* Oberlin Col, AB, 49; Univ Calif, PhD(chem), 52. *Honors & Awards:* Award, Am Chem Soc, 80; James Flack Norris Award Chem Educ, 84. *Prof Exp:* Asst, Univ Calif, 49-51; instr phys chem, Univ Conn, 52-55; res fel, Univ Minn, Minneapolis, 55-57, from asst prof to prof inorg chem, 57-69; prof chem, NC State Univ, 69-89; prof chem, Univ Pittsburgh, 89-91. *Concurrent Pos:* Lectr, Gulbenkian Inst Advan Study, Portugal, 70, 71 & 72; Chautauqua course dir, AAAS, 72-74, 77, 82, 84 & 85; chmn, Div Chem Educ, Am Chem Soc, 78; job lectr, Mem Univ Nfld, 81; vis prof, Willimas Col, 81. *Mem:* Fel AAAS; Am Chem Soc; Am Phys Soc. *Res:* Thermodynamics; molecular structure; intermolecular interactions; localized molecular orbitals; history of chemistry; philosophy of science; chemical education. *Mailing Add:* 5816 Solway St Pittsburgh PA 15217-1229

BENT, RICHARD LINCOLN, ORGANIC CHEMISTRY. *Current Pos:* RETIRED. *Personal Data:* b Rochester, NY, Oct 25, 17. *Educ:* Cambridge Univ, BA, 39. *Prof Exp:* Chemist, Eastman Kodak Co, 41-48, res chemist, 48-71, res assoc, Color Photog Div, 71-79. *Mem:* Am Chem Soc; Soc Photog Sci & Eng. *Res:* Synthesis of photographic developing agents. *Mailing Add:* PO Box 25506 Rochester NY 14625-0506

BENT, ROBERT DEMO, PHYSICS. *Current Pos:* from asst prof to assoc prof, 58-66, PROF PHYSICS, IND UNIV, BLOOMINGTON, 66- *Personal Data:* b Cambridge, Mass, Dec 22, 28; m 56; c 3. *Educ:* Oberlin Col, AB, 50; Rice Inst, AM, 52, PhD(physics), 54. *Prof Exp:* Res assoc physics, Rice Inst, 54-55; res assoc, Columbia Univ, 55-58. *Concurrent Pos:* Guggenheim fel, Oxford & Atomic Energy Authority Res Estab, Harwell, Eng, 62-63. *Mem:* Fel Am Phys Soc. *Res:* Intermediate energy nuclear physics. *Mailing Add:* Dept Physics Ind Univ Bloomington IN 47405

BENT, SAMUEL W, analysis of algorithms, for more information see previous edition

BENTALL, RAY, GEOLOGY. *Current Pos:* HYDROLOGIST, CONSERV & SURV DIV, INST AGR & NATURAL RESOURCES, UNIV NEBR, LINCOLN, 74- *Personal Data:* b Grand Rapids, Mich, June 28, 17; m 38, 81; c 2. *Educ:* Univ Mich, BS, 38; Univ Tenn, MS, 40. *Prof Exp:* Geologist, State Div Geol, Tenn, 40-43; geologist, US Geol Surv, Tenn, 43-45 & Nebr, 45-67, hydrologist, Nebr, 67-73. *Mem:* Sigma Xi. *Res:* Hydrology. *Mailing Add:* 5432 Sea Mountain Rd Lincoln NE 68521

BENTLEY, BARBARA LEE, ECOLOGY OF NITROGEN FIXATION, PLANT & HERIVORE INTERACTIONS. *Current Pos:* DIR ENVIRON PROG, RED BUTTE GARDEN & ARBORETUM, PROF BIOL, UNIV UTAH, 96- *Personal Data:* b Los Angeles, Calif, Dec 14, 42; m 80, Glenn Prestwich; c Steven & Jocelyn. *Educ:* Willamette Univ, BA, 64; Univ Calif, Los Angeles, MA, 66; Univ Kans, PhD(ecol), 74. *Prof Exp:* From asst prof to prof ecol, State Univ NY, 73-96, dean grad sch, 83-87. *Concurrent Pos:* Instr, Cuttington Col, WAfrica, 66-68, Johnson Co Community Col, 69-70 & Biol Sta, Univ Mich, 74; coordr, Orgn Trop Studies, 72-. vpres. 79-82; vis scientist, Inst Nac de Pesquises da Amazonia, Brazil, 74; consult, Brookhaven Nat Lab, 78-85; Fulbright fel, 87; NSF vis prof, 88-89; bd dir, Am Inst Biol Sci, 91-94. *Mem:* Am Soc Naturalists (secy, 88-91); Ecol Soc Am (vpres,

89-90); Brit Ecol Soc; Asn Trop Biol; Bot Soc Am; NY Acad Sci; AAAS. *Res:* Nitrogen fixation in tropical environments; plant and insect interactions; geographic variation in termite populations; plant/herbivore interactions in Lupinus; effects of global environmental change on plants in their natural environments. *Mailing Add:* Dept Biol Univ Utah Salt Lake City UT 84112. *E-Mail:* bbentley@biology.utah.edu

BENTLEY, C FRED, AGRICULTURAL EDUCATION & RESEARCH, SOIL SCIENCE. *Current Pos:* from asst prof to prof, 46-79, dean, Fac Agr, 58-68, EMER PROF SOIL SCI, UNIV ALTA, 79-; CONSULT AGROLOGIST, 79- *Personal Data:* b Cambridge, Mass, Mar 14, 14; Can citizen; m, Helen Signe. *Educ:* Univ Alta, BS, 39, MS, 42; Univ Minn, PhD(soil sci), 45. *Hon Degrees:* DSc, Univ Guelph, 84. *Honors & Awards:* H H Bennett Award, Soil & Water Conserv Soc, 89. *Prof Exp:* Instr soil sci, Univ Minn, 42-43; instr & asst prof soil sci, Univ Sask, 43-46. *Mem:* Fel, Agr Inst Can (past pres); fel, Soil Sci Soc Am; fel, AAAS; fel, Can Soil Sci Soc (past pres); fel, Am Soc Agron; Int Soil Sci Soc (past pres); fel, Roy Soc Can; hon mem Soil & Water Conserv Soc; Soil Conserv Can (hon vpres). *Mailing Add:* 13103 66th Ave Edmonton AB T6H 1Y6 Can

BENTLEY, CHARLES RAYMOND, ANTARCTIC GEOPHYSICS, ANTARCTIC GLACIOLOGY. *Current Pos:* proj assoc geophys, Univ Wis-Madison, 59-61, from asst prof to assoc prof, 61-68, prof geophys, 67-87, A P CRARY PROF GEOPHYS, UNIV WIS-MADISON, 87- *Personal Data:* b Rochester, NY, Dec 23, 29; m 64, Marybelle; c Molly & Alexander. *Educ:* Yale Univ, BS, 50; Columbia Univ, PhD(geophys), 59. *Honors & Awards:* Bellingshausen-Lazarev Medal, Acad Sci, USS; Seligman Crystal, Int Glaciol Soc, 90. *Prof Exp:* Asst, Columbia Univ, 52-55, geophysicist, 55-56; traverse co-leader seismologist, Int Geophys Year, Antarctic Prog, Arctic Inst NAm, 56-58, traverse leader, 58-59. *Concurrent Pos:* NSF sr fel, Mass Inst Technol, 68-69; alt US deleg, Sci Comt Antarctic Res, 81-, vpres, 90-94; chmn, Bd Assoc Ed, Antarctic Res Series, Am Geophys Union, 74-90; secy chmn, Working Group Solid Earth Geophys, Sci Comt Antarctic Res, 76-82; mem, Polar Res Bd, 78-, chmn, 82-86, chmn, Comt Glaciol, 78-81; vpres, Int Glaciological Soc, 78-81; mem, Bd of Arctic Inst NAm, 87-; vpres, Int Comn on Snow Ice, 87-95; chmn, group specialists on global change & the Antarctic, Sci Comt Antarctic Res, 92- *Mem:* Fel AAAS; Am Quaternary Asn; fel Am Geophys Union; Geol Soc Am; Int Glaciological Soc; Seismol Soc Am; Sigma Xi; Soc Explor Geophys; fel Arctic Inst NAm. *Res:* Geophysical studies on polar ice sheets and glaciological applications of geophysical methods. *Mailing Add:* Geophys & Polar Res Ctr 1215 W Dayton St Madison WI 53706. *Fax:* 608-262-0693; *E-Mail:* bentley@geology.wisc.edu

BENTLEY, DAVID R, NEUROBIOLOGY, DEVELOPMENTAL BIOLOGY. *Current Pos:* asst prof, 68-73, assoc prof, 73-78, PROF NEUROBIOL, ZOOL DEPT, UNIV CALIF, BERKELEY, 78-, CHAIRPERSON DEPT, 82- *Personal Data:* b Lansing, Mich, June 18, 40; c 2. *Educ:* Williams Col, AB, 62; Univ Mich, MS, 64, PhD(zool), 66. *Prof Exp:* Fel, Inst fur Vergleichende Tierphysiologie, 66-67 & Stanford Univ, 67-68. *Concurrent Pos:* Prin investr, NIH, 69-; Alexander von Humboldt Sr Scientist Award, WGer Govt, 74. *Mem:* Soc Neurosci. *Res:* Long-distance pathfinding by nerve cell growth coneso, the establishment of nerve trunks and neural differentiation during embryonic development of the grasshopper. *Mailing Add:* Dept Molecular & Cell Biol Univ Calif 142 LSA 3200 Berkeley CA 94720-3200

BENTLEY, DONALD LYON, MATHEMATICAL STATISTICS. *Current Pos:* from asst prof to assoc prof, 64-74, PROF MATH, POMONA COL, 74-, LINGURN H BURKHEAD CHAIR MATH, 82- *Personal Data:* b Los Angeles, Calif, Apr 25, 35; m 57, Anne Alexander; c James, Jillene & Janet. *Educ:* Stanford Univ, BS, 57, MS, 58, PhD(statist), 61. *Prof Exp:* Asst prof math statist, Colo State Univ, 61-64. *Concurrent Pos:* Prin investr, NSF grant, 62-64; NIH grant, 68-70; NSF fac fel, 70-71; consult, 65- *Mem:* Inst Math Statist; fel Am Statist Asn; Biomet Soc; Royal Statist Soc; Soc Epidemiol Res. *Res:* Mathematical statistics and stochastic processes and their application to biomedical phenomena. *Mailing Add:* Dept Math Pomona Col Claremont CA 91711. *E-Mail:* dbentley@pomona.claremont.edu

BENTLEY, GEOFFREY KINGSLEY, BUSINESS ADMINISTRATION. *Current Pos:* MGR BUS RES, TEXTRON DEFENSE SYSTS, 84- *Personal Data:* b Glastonbury, Conn, Dec 16, 35; m 60, Martha Wentworth Smith; c Nigel, Amy & Rory. *Educ:* Wesleyan Univ, BA, 57; Mass Inst Technol, SB, 58, SM, 60; Northeastern Univ, MBA, 71. *Honors & Awards:* Aerospace Contrib to Soc Award, Am Inst Aeronaut & Astronaut, 95. *Prof Exp:* Aerodyn engr, Douglas Aircraft Co, 60-63; group leader, Avco Systs Div, 63-74, prog mgr transp systs, 74-77, mgr bus res, 80-82; cong fel, New Eng Cong Caucus, 78-79; fel, Ctr Advan Study, Mass Inst Technol, 83. *Concurrent Pos:* Assoc tech comt, Am Inst Aeronaut & Astronaut, 83-; chmn, Forecast Comt, Electronics Indust Asn, 89- *Mem:* Fel Am Inst Aeronaut & Astronaut; fel Electronics Indust Asn; fel Sigma Xi. *Res:* Contributed articles to professional journals. *Mailing Add:* 282 Autumn Lane Carlisle MA 01741-1736

BENTLEY, GLENN E, ANALYTICAL CHEMISTRY, RADIOCHEMISTRY. *Current Pos:* MEM STAFF RADIO-ANALYTICAL CHEM, LOS ALAMOS SCI LAB, 76- *Personal Data:* b Los Alamos, NMex, Oct 25, 46; m 73; c 2. *Educ:* NMex Inst Mining & Technol, BS, 69; Ariz State Univ, PhD(analytical chem), 76. *Prof Exp:* Res assoc analytical chem, Univ Colo, 75-76. *Mem:* Am Chem Soc; Soc Appl Spectros; Sigma Xi. *Res:* Development of separation methods for novel radioisotopes; hot cell process development; trace element determinations and methods development for many elements from many materials. *Mailing Add:* 412 Cheryl Ave Los Alamos NM 87544

BENTLEY, HARRY THOMAS, III, PHYSICS, ELECTROOPTICS. *Current Pos:* Engr physics, Sverdrup AEDC, Inc, 66-74, sr res engr physics & sr proj mgr, 74-81, mgr, Adv Propulsion diag group, 81-85, ENG SPECIALIST, SVERDRUP AEDC, INC, 85-; SYSTS ENGR, LEWIS SPACE SHUTTLE MAIN HEALTH MONITORING PROG, NASA. *Personal Data:* b Oak Park, Ill, Jan 30, 42; m 77; c 4. *Educ:* NC State Univ, BS, 64, MS, 66; Univ Tenn Space Inst, MS, 87. *Concurrent Pos:* Consult, Indust Nucleonics Corp, 64-66, Sci Appl, Inc, 74-76 & Sci Metrics, Inc, 74-76; vpres, Home Plans Referral Inc, 88- *Mem:* Soc Photo-Optical Instrument Eng; Nat Mgt Asn; sr mem Am Inst Aeronauts & Astronauts; Sigma Xi. *Res:* Electro-optical instrumentation; laser velocimetry, particle sizing, combustion gas analysis and plasma physics; the measurement and modeling of the radiative transfer process associated with turbine engine propulsion systems; advanced electro-optical techniques for gas species identification; developed techniques for assessing propulsion related observables and countermeasures; over 30 papers published. *Mailing Add:* 208 Jamestown Rd Tullahoma TN 37388. *E-Mail:* bentley@edge.net

BENTLEY, HERSCHEL LAMAR, EXTENSIONS OF TOPOLIGICAL SPACES. *Current Pos:* assoc prof, 71-75, PROF MATH, UNIV TOLEDO, 75- *Personal Data:* b Sylacauga, Ala, July 14, 39; m 59, Georgina Miranda; c Herschel, Daniel, Timothy & Jeanie. *Educ:* Univ Ariz, BS, 61, MS, 63; Rensselaer Polytech Inst, PhD(math), 65. *Prof Exp:* Eng trainee, Hughes Aircraft Co, 59-60; grad asst, Univ Ariz, 61-63; mathematician, Gulf Res Develop, 63; asst prof math, Rensselaer Polytech Inst, 65-66, Univ NMex, 66-69 & Bucknell Univ, 69-71. *Concurrent Pos:* Doctoral fel, NDEA, 63-65. *Res:* General topology; categorical topology; nearness spaces extensions of topological spaces. *Mailing Add:* Dept Math Univ Toledo Toledo OH 43606

BENTLEY, J PETER, BIOCHEMISTRY. *Current Pos:* res asst, 59-62, res assoc, 62-64, instr exp biol, 64-65, asst prof exp biol & biochem, 65-68, assoc prof biochem, 68-76, PROF BIOCHEM, SCH MED, ORE HEALTH SCI UNIV, 76- *Personal Data:* b Oldham, Eng, Sept 15, 31; US citizen; m 57; c 3. *Educ:* Univ Ore, MS, 61, PhD(biochem, physiol), 63. *Prof Exp:* Res asst, Harvard Med Sch, 57-59. *Mem:* Am Soc Biol Chem; Soc Complex Carbohydrates. *Res:* Biosynthesis of connective tissue components; collagen and proteoglycans. *Mailing Add:* Ore Health Sci Univ Sch Med L349 3181 SW Sam Jackson Park Rd Portland OR 97201-3098

BENTLEY, JOHN JOSEPH, RADICAL STRUCTURE & REACTIVITY CALCULATIONS. *Current Pos:* res assoc, Radiation Lab, Univ Notre Dame, 75-78, scientist, 78-82, consult & analyst, Comput Ctr, 82-84, ASSOC SCIENTIST & ASST DIR, RADIATION LAB, UNIV NOTRE DAME, 84. *Personal Data:* b Washington, DC, Nov 13,46; m 71, Alice Hoffer; c Stephen. *Educ:* Col Holy Cross, BS, 67; Carnegie-Mellon Univ, MS, 70, PhD(phys chem), 75. *Prof Exp:* Res assoc, Chem Dept, Carnegie-Mellon Univ, 75. *Mem:* Am Chem Soc. *Res:* Theoretical study of structure and reactivity of transient radical species in gas phase and solution. *Mailing Add:* 1342 Longfellow Ave South Bend IN 46615-1122. *E-Mail:* john.bentley@nd.edu

BENTLEY, KENNETH CHESSAR, ORAL SURGERY. *Current Pos:* from asst prof to assoc prof, 66-75, PROF ORAL SURG, McGILL UNIV, 75-, CHMN DEPT ORAL SURG & DIR DIV SURG & ORAL MED, 68-; DENT SURGEON-IN-CHIEF, MONTREAL GEN HOSP, 70- *Personal Data:* b Montreal, Que, Sept 22, 35; m 61; c 2. *Educ:* McGill Univ, DDS, 58, MD, CM, 62. *Prof Exp:* Jr rotating intern, Montreal Gen Hosp, 62-63, jr asst resident, 63-64; partic prog oral surg, Bellevue Hosp, New York, 64-66, chief resident, 65-66. *Concurrent Pos:* Dean fac dent, McGill Univ, 77-87. *Mailing Add:* Montreal Gen Hosp 1650 Cedar Ave Montreal PQ H3G 1A4 Can

BENTLEY, KENTON EARL, analytical chemistry, remote sensing, for more information see previous edition

BENTLEY, MICHAEL DAVID, ORGANIC CHEMISTRY. *Current Pos:* asst prof, 69-74, assoc prof, 74-81, PROF CHEM, UNIV MAINE, 81- *Personal Data:* b Jacksonville, Fla, Feb 7, 39; m 63, Ruth Coulter; c Heidi & Elizabeth. *Educ:* Auburn Univ, BSChem, 63, MS, 65; Univ Tex, Austin, PhD(org chem), 69. *Prof Exp:* NIH fel, Univ Calif, Berkeley, 68-69. *Concurrent Pos:* Foreign specialist, Japan Agency Sci & Technol, 82; Fulbright sr res scholar, Int Ctr Insect Physiol & Ecol, Nairobi, Kenya, 83. *Mem:* Am Soc Pharmacol; Int Soc Chem Ecol; Sigma Xi; Am Chem Soc. *Res:* Plant chemistry; polymer chemistry; medicinal chemistry. *Mailing Add:* Dept Chem Univ Maine Orono ME 04473

BENTLEY, MICHAEL MARTIN, SIGNAL TRANSDUCTION, GENE EXPRESSION. *Current Pos:* fel, 76-81, ASSOC PROF GENETICS, UNIV CALGARY, 81- *Personal Data:* b Detroit, Mich, Nov 2, 47; Can citizen; m 69, Laura S; c Mark, Christopher & Joseph. *Educ:* Col Wooster, BA, 69; McMaster Univ, PhD(genetics), 77. *Prof Exp:* Asst prof, Alta Heritage Found Med Res Scholar, 81. *Concurrent Pos:* Adj mem, Cancer Biol Res Group, Univ Calgary, 91- *Mem:* Genetics Soc Can; Genetics Soc Am; Sigma Xi. *Res:* Understanding the function of protein kinase-c and the regulation of its gene expression in the drosophila melanogaster model system. *Mailing Add:* Dept Biol Sci Univ Calgary Calgary AB T2N 1N4 Can. *Fax:* 403-289-9311; *E-Mail:* bentley@acs.ucalgary.ca

BENTLEY, ORVILLE GEORGE, ANIMAL SCIENCE & NUTRITION, NUTRITION. *Current Pos:* dean agr, 65-82, EMER DEAN AGR, COL AGR, UNIV ILL, URBANA-CHAMPAIGN, 89- *Personal Data:* b Midland, SDak, Mar 6, 18; m 42, Enolia Anderson; c Peter T & Craig E. *Educ:* SDak

State Col, BS, 42; Univ Wis, MS, 47, PhD(biochem), 50. *Hon Degrees:* DSc, SDak State Univ, 74 & Univ Wis, 84. *Prof Exp:* From asst prof to prof animal sci, Ohio Agr Exp Sta & Dept Animal Sci, Ohio State Univ, 50-58; dean & dir agr, Col Agr & Agr Exp Sta, SDak State Univ, 58-65; asst secy agr, sci & educ, USDA, Washington, DC, 82-89. *Concurrent Pos:* Res award, Animal Nutrit, Am Soc Animal Sci, 58; mem, Bd Trustees, Univ Beirut, 73-91, Bd Int Food & Agr, USAID, 76-79, Sci Forum, Helsinki Accord, Hamburg, 80, Nat Res Councils Govt-Univ-Indust Roundtable, 84-89 & President's Adv Panel for US-Japan Joint High-Level Sci & Tech Agreement, 89-; mem & leader, Indo-Am Sub-comn on Agr, 80, 84 & 87; co-chair, Venezuela-US Agr Comn, 90-; emer trustee, Univ Beirut, 91- *Mem:* AAAS; Am Inst Nutrit; Am Soc Animal Sci. *Res:* Ruminant nutrition, especially on microbial breakdown of cellulose; academic administration coordinating teaching, research and extension education in agriculture, home economics and agricultural economics. *Mailing Add:* 2030 Bentbrook Dr Champaign IL 61821-9221

BENTLEY, RONALD, BIOCHEMISTRY. *Current Pos:* from asst prof to prof biochem, 53-92, chmn dept, 72-76, EMER PROF BIOCHEM, UNIV PITTSBURGH, 92- *Personal Data:* b Derby, Eng, Mar 10, 22; US citizen; wid, Marian Blanchard; c Colin & Peter. *Educ:* Univ London, BSc, 43, PhD(org chem), 45. *Hon Degrees:* DSc, Univ London, 65. *Honors & Awards:* Pittsburgh Award, Am Chem Soc, 79. *Prof Exp:* Commonwealth Fund fel, Col Physicians & Surgeons, Columbia Univ, 46-47, res assoc biochem, 51-52; mem sci staff, Nat Inst Med Res, London, 48-51. *Concurrent Pos:* Guggenheim fel, Inst Biochem, Univ Lund, 64; mem microbial chem study sect, NIH, 72-76. *Mem:* AAAS; Am Soc Microbiol; Am Soc Biochem & Molecular Biol; Am Soc Chem; Royal Soc Chem; Biochem Soc. *Res:* Biochemistry of microorganisms; carbohydrate biochemistry; biosynthesis of aromatic compounds; stereochemical implications in biology. *Mailing Add:* Dept Biol Sci Univ Pittsburgh Pittsburgh PA 15260

BENTLEY, WILLIAM ROSS, FOREST MANAGEMENT, FOREST POLICY. *Current Pos:* PRES, SALMON BROOK ASSOCS, 94- *Personal Data:* b Oakland, Calif, Jan 29, 38; m 90, Ann Wilhelm; c Michael, Annie, Andrew, Russell & Frederick. *Educ:* Univ Calif, BS, 60, PhD(agrecon), 65, Univ Mich, MF, 61. *Prof Exp:* Asst specialist forestry, Calif Agr Exp Sta, 62-63; asst prof forestry, Iowa State Univ, 63-66; assoc prof forestry & agri econ, Univ Wis, 66-69; prof NR mgt, Univ Mich, 69-76; mgr forestry res, Crown Zellerbach Corp, 76-80; prof resource mgt, Conn, 80-83; prog officer, Ford Found, New Delhi, 83-85; sr prog officer, Windrock Int, 85-94. *Concurrent Pos:* Bullard fel forestry, Harvard Univ, 75-76; lectr & res scientist forest mgt, Yale Univ, 90-95, sr res scholar, 95-97; sr Fulbright res scientist, Univ Canterbury & Lincoln Univ, NZ, 91-94; exec dir, 7th Am Forest Cong, 95-96. *Mem:* Soc Am Foresters; Indian Soc Tree Scientists; Int Asn Study Common Property Resources. *Res:* Forest management strategies that increase productivity, sustainability, and equity for the rural poor; long term price trends and investment analysis; small and large-scale processes for public participation in forest management and policy. *Mailing Add:* 83 Day St Granby CT 06035. *E-Mail:* b.bentley@cgnet.com

BENTON, ALLEN HAYDON, ZOOLOGY, ENTOMOLOGY. *Current Pos:* prof, 62-73, chmn dept, 66-69, DISTINGUISHED TEACHING PROF BIOL, 73-, FAC EXHANG PROF, 78-, EMER PROF BIOL, STATE UNIV NY COL FREDONIA, 84- *Personal Data:* b Ira, NY, Sept 4, 21; m 47, Marjorie Hall; c Thomas, Christopher & Holly. *Educ:* Cornell Univ, BS, 48, MS, 49, PhD(vert zool), 52. *Honors & Awards:* Kasling Lectr, State Univ NY Col Fredonia, 79. *Prof Exp:* From instr to assoc prof biol, State Univ NY, Albany, 49-62, fac exchange prof, 74-84. *Concurrent Pos:* Vis prof biol, Concord Col, 69-70; vis prof, Univ Minn, 70; freelance writer sci & nature columnist, Dunkirk NY Evening Observer, 86- *Mem:* Am Ornith Union; Am Soc Mammal. *Res:* Bird distribution in New York State; life histories of small mammals; taxonomy, distribution and host relationships of American Siphonaptera. *Mailing Add:* 292 Water St Fredonia NY 14063

BENTON, ALLEN WILLIAM, BIOCHEMISTRY, PHYSIOLOGY. *Current Pos:* asst prof, 66-69, assoc prof, 69-77, PROF ENTOM, PA STATE UNIV, 77- *Personal Data:* b Greenwich, Conn, June 8, 31; m 54; c 3. *Educ:* Univ Conn, BS, 58, MS, 62; Cornell Univ, PhD(entom), 65. *Prof Exp:* Soil scientist, Soil Conserv Serv, USDA, 54-62; asst prof entom & apicult, Rutgers Univ, 65-66. *Concurrent Pos:* Consult, Center Labs, 65-, Pharmacia, 75-, Good Samaritan Hosp, Johns Hopkins Univ, 75- & Buffalo Gen Hosp, 74-; owner, Vespid Labs, mfr Vespid venoms. *Mem:* Entom Soc Am; Bee Res Asn. *Res:* Venoms, biochemistry and physiological effects upon animals; biochemistry of allergens. *Mailing Add:* 771 Linden Hall Rd Boalsburg PA 16827-1048

BENTON, ARTHUR LESTER, NEUROPSYCHOLOGY, NEUROSCIENCES. *Current Pos:* PROF NEUROL & PSYCHOL, UNIV IOWA, 48- *Personal Data:* b New York, NY, Oct 16, 09; m 39; c 3. *Educ:* Oberlin Col, AB, 31, AM, 33; Columbia Univ, PhD, 35. *Hon Degrees:* DSc, Cornell Col, 78; PscholD, Univ Rome, 90. *Prof Exp:* Assoc prof med psychol, Sch Med, Univ Louisville, 46-48. *Concurrent Pos:* USPHS res grant, Univ Iowa, 54-82, USPHS spec fel neuropsychol, 58-59; consult, NIH, 61-; vis prof, Fac Med, Univ Milan, 64, Free Univ, Amsterdam, 71, Dept Neurol, Univ Helsinki, 74 & Tokyo Metrop Inst Geront, 74; dir studies, Sch Higher Studies, Paris, 79; Lansdowne Scholar, Univ Victoria (Can), 80; vis lectr, Univ Mich, 86. *Mem:* Am Psychol Asn; Am Neurol Asn; Am Acad Neurol; Int Neuropsychol Soc (pres, 70-72); Am Orthopsychiat Asn (pres, 64-65). *Res:* Behavioral disabilities associated with brain disease. *Mailing Add:* 504 Manor Dr Iowa City IA 52246. *Fax:* 319-356-4505

BENTON, CHARLES HERBERT, RESEARCH MANAGEMENT, PRODUCT DEVELOPMENT. *Current Pos:* RETIRED. *Personal Data:* b Kansas City, Mo, Nov 16, 25; m 50, Betty L Richardson; c 2. *Educ:* Univ Kans, BS, 48; Univ Ill, PhD(org chem), 51. *Prof Exp:* Res chemist, Eastman Chem Div, 51, sr res chemist, 52-59, sales supvr, 60-64, head prod develop, 65-69, res assoc, 70, sr res assoc, 71, mgr sales develop & tech serv, 72, dir, Health & Nutrit Res Div, Eastman Chem Div, 73-87. *Concurrent Pos:* Consult, 88- *Mem:* Am Chem Soc. *Res:* Consultation on research and development related to products for human and animal health and nutrition. *Mailing Add:* 4308 Gray Fox Dr Kingsport TN 37664-4417

BENTON, DUANE ALLEN, BIOCHEMISTRY. *Current Pos:* DIR NUTRIT RES, ROSS LABS, 70- *Personal Data:* b Waterloo, Iowa, June 1, 31; m 68, Norma Magnus; c Allen, Paul & Rachel. *Educ:* Mich State Univ, BS, 52; Univ Wis, MS, 54, PhD(biochem), 56. *Prof Exp:* Asst prof biochem, Okla State Univ, 56-59; cancer res scientist, Roswell Park Mem Inst, 59-63; assoc prof animal nutrit, Cornell Univ, 63-66; head biochem invest, USDA, 66-70. *Mem:* AAAS; Fedn Am Soc Exp Biol; Am Inst Nutrit; Am Chem Soc. *Res:* Amino acid interrelationships in the nutrition of animals; dietary interrelations and their effects on metabolism; infant nutrition. *Mailing Add:* 1515 Carriage Rd Dowell OH 43065

BENTON, DUANE MARSHALL, ENVIRONMENTAL EDUCATOR, ENVIRONMENTAL AUDIT & NOISE SPECIALIST. *Personal Data:* b Savannah, Ohio, Nov 1, 33; m 60, Kay Hutchison; c Mary K (Cochran), Kristyanne (Maldonado) & Michael D. *Educ:* Ashland Col, AB, 55; Univ Utah, BS, 58; Ohio State Univ, MS, 64; George Washington Univ, MS, 67. *Honors & Awards:* Nat Guard Minuteman Award, 83. *Prof Exp:* Asst chem, Ohio State Univ, 55-57; asst anal res chemist, Hess & Clark Div, Richardson-Merrell Inc, 58-59; instr physics, meteorol, math & chem, Ashland Col, 59-60 & 62-64, from asst prof to assoc prof phys sci, 64-73; environ phys scientist, Dept Army Hq, Environ Off, Washington, DC, 73-78, environ protection specialist, Army Mat Command Environ Div & chief, Pollution Abatement Opers Ctr, Alexandria, Va, 78-95. *Concurrent Pos:* Colonel, Ohio Air Nat Guard, NJ Air Nat Guard & USAFR, 52-86; AEC res grant, 64-67; comdr, 164 Weaflt, 71-76 & 204 Weaflt, 78-80; consult, Army Environ Educ & Training, 75-95; weather & civil eng staff officer, State Hq, NJ Air Nat Guard, 76-78, dir plans & progs, 82-85; lectr chem, physics & meteorol, Northern Va Community Col, 76-86; consult & planner, Army Environ Noise & Audit, 84-95; planner radio activ, hazardous & multihazardous mats, Fed Emer Mgt Agency, 85-87. *Mem:* Nat Asn Environ Prof; Am Meterol Soc; Environ Auditing Roundtable; Air & Waste Mgt Asn. *Res:* Photosynthesis; C-14 uptake in algae of Lake Erie; spectrophotometric detn of mixtures phenylmercuric acetate and iron; ANG weather flights in total force concept. *Mailing Add:* 1706 Briery Rd Farmville VA 23901-2556

BENTON, EUGENE VLADIMIR, RADIOLOGICAL PHYSICS. *Current Pos:* res prof, 69-73, PROF PHYSICS, UNIV SAN FRANCISCO, 73- *Personal Data:* b Russia, July 23, 37; US citizen; m 61; c 2. *Educ:* San Jose State Col, BA, 58, MA, 60; Stanford Univ, PhD(physics), 68. *Honors & Awards:* Gold Medal Sci Achievement, Naval Radiol Defense Lab, 69; Komos Achievement Award, NASA, 75, 78 & 81; Alexander von Humboldt Prize, 79. *Prof Exp:* Instr physics, San Jose State Col, 58-60; from jr investr to investr, US Naval Radiol Defense Lab, 61-69. *Concurrent Pos:* Consult, Lawrence Berkeley Lab, Univ Calif, 69-; mem adv sci comt, 75, Nat Coun Radiation Protection & Measurements, 84-; mem, Comt Space Res, 85- *Mem:* AAAS; Am Phys Soc. *Res:* Medical physics; nuclear photographic emulsions; radiation dosimetry; materials science; solid state physics; radiation effects in solids; nuclear particle track detectors. *Mailing Add:* Dept Physics & Eng Univ San Francisco Ignatian Heights San Francisco CA 94117

BENTON, FRANCIS LEE, ORGANIC CHEMISTRY. *Current Pos:* assoc prof chem, 59-62, prof, 62-77, EMER PROF CHEM, ST MARY'S COL, IND, 77- *Personal Data:* b Moxahala, Ohio, Feb 12, 12; m 40; c 3. *Educ:* Ohio State Univ, BChE, 35, MS, 36, PhD(chem), 40. *Prof Exp:* Instr chem, Univ Notre Dame, 40-42, from asst prof to assoc prof, 42-52; res chemist, Armour Lab, 52-59. *Mem:* Am Chem Soc. *Res:* General organic synthesis; isolation of naturally occurring substances of biological origin and investigation of their molecular structure. *Mailing Add:* 1714 E Cedar St South Bend IN 46617

BENTON, GEORGE STOCK, METEOROLOGY, SCIENCE POLICY. *Current Pos:* civil engr, Johns Hopkins Univ, 48-52, assoc prof, 52-57, actg chmn, Dept Civil Eng, 58-60, chmn, Dept Mech, 60-66, chmn, Dept Earth & Planetary Sci,69-70, dean fac arts & sci, 70-72, PROF METEOROL, JOHNS HOPKINS UNIV, 57- *Personal Data:* b Oak Park, Ill, Sept 24, 17; m 45; c 4. *Educ:* Univ Chicago, SB, 42, PhD(meteorol), 47. *Prof Exp:* From asst to asst prof meteorol, Univ Chicago, 42-48. *Concurrent Pos:* Dir, Insts Environ Res, Environ Sci Serv Admin, Boulder, Colo, 66-69; vpres, Homewood Divs, Johns Hopkins Univ, 72-76; assoc admr, Nat Oceanic & Atmospheric Admin, 77-81; US rep, World Met Org, 77-81. *Mem:* Fel Am Meteorol Soc (pres, 69-70); fel Am Geophys Union; fel Am Acad Arts & Sci. *Res:* Flow of stratified and rotating fluid; general circulation of the atmosphere; mesoscale meteorology. *Mailing Add:* Dept Earth & Planetary Sci Johns Hopkins Univ 34th & Charles Sts Baltimore MD 21218

BENTON, JOHN WILLIAM, JR, PEDIATRICS, NEUROLOGY. *Current Pos:* from instr to asst prof pediat & neurol, Univ Ala, 60-66, dir, Ctr Develop & Learning Disorders, 62-68, assoc prof pediat & assoc prof Div Neurol, 66-69, interim chmn dept, & dir, Children's Hosp, 69-83, PROF PEDIAT & NEUROL, SCH MED, UNIV ALA, BIRMINGHAM, 69- *Personal Data:* b Enterprise, Ala, July 3, 30; m 55; c 3. *Educ:* Univ Ala, BS, 51; Med Col Ala, MD, 55; Am Bd Pediat, dipl, 62; Am Bd Psychiat & Neurol, dipl, 69. *Prof*

Exp: Intern pediat, Univ Ala Hosp, Birmingham, 55-56; resident, Univ Utah, 56-57 & Univ Minn, Minneapolis, 59-60. *Concurrent Pos:* NIH trainee neurol, Med Col, Univ Ala, 60-62; fel, Mass Gen Hosp, Harvard Med Sch, 64-66. *Mem:* Am Pediat Soc; Am Acad Neurol; Am Acad Pediat. *Res:* Acute ataxia; acute encephalopathy of undetermined origin; convulsive disorders. *Mailing Add:* Univ Ala Children's Hosp 1600 Seventh Ave Suite 554 Birmingham AL 35233-1786

BENTON, KENNETH CURTIS, POLYMER CHEMISTRY. *Current Pos:* SR RES ASSOC, PENFORD PROD CO, CEDAR RAPIDS, IA, 93- *Personal Data:* b Whitinsville, Mass, Sept 15, 41. *Educ:* Worcester Polytech Inst, BS, 63; Univ Akron, PhD(polymer chem), 69. *Prof Exp:* Sr res chemist, Copolymer Rubber & Chem Corp, 67-70, group leader polymers, CPC Int, Inc, 70-74; sr res chemist, Stand Oil Co, Ohio, 74-93. *Mem:* Am Chem Soc; Soc Plastics Engrs. *Res:* Synthesis of acrylonitrile barrier resins for packaging applications; synthesis of starch derivations. *Mailing Add:* 1957 Mt Vernon Rd SE Cedar Rapids IA 52403

BENTON, STEPHEN ANTHONY, IMAGING PHYSICS. *Current Pos:* PROF MEDIA TECHNOL, MASS INST TECHNOL, 82- *Personal Data:* b San Francisco, Calif, Dec 1, 41; m 64; c 2. *Educ:* Mass Inst Technol, BS, 63; Harvard Univ, MS, 65, PhD(appl physics), 68. *Prof Exp:* Asst prof appl physics, Div Eng & Appl Physics, Harvard Univ, 68-73; sr scientist, res labs, Polaroid Corp, 61-85. *Concurrent Pos:* Vis prof physics, Univ Reading, Eng, 72-73; vis scientist, Harrison Spectros Lab, Mass Inst Technol, 81-82; chmn, US Nat Comn, Int Comn for Optics, 82-84; gov, Soc Photo-optical Instrumentation Engrs; trustee, Mus Holography. *Mem:* Fel Optical Soc Am; fel Soc Photographic Scientists & Engrs; Inst Elec & Electronic Engrs; Soc Photo-optical Instrumentation Engrs. *Res:* Image communication systems, holography. *Mailing Add:* Mass Inst Tech Media Lab 20 Ames St E 15-418 Cambridge MA 02139

BENTON, WILLIAM J, VETERINARY VIROLOGY. *Current Pos:* Res assoc poultry path & virol, Univ Del, 56-66, asst prof, 66-67, actg chmn dept animal sci & agr biochem, 67-68, prof & chmn dept, 68-71, asst dean, Col Agr Sci & asst dir, Agr Exp Sta, 71-74, assoc dean, Col Agr Sci & assoc dir, Agr Exp Sta, 74-94, PROF ANIMAL SCI, UNIV DEL 71- *Personal Data:* b Franklin, Va, June 28, 33; m 55; c 2. *Educ:* Univ Ga, DVM, 56; Univ Del, MS, 59, PhD(biol sci), 66. *Mem:* Am Vet Med Asn; Am Asn Avian Path. *Res:* Application of pathology, serology, immunology and virology in the study of avian diseases such as infectious laryngotracheitis, infectious synovitus, avian leukosis, mycoplasma gallisepticum infection, Newcastle disease, infectious bronchitis and infectious bursal disease. *Mailing Add:* 101 Brandon Lane Franklin VA 23851-2301

BENTRUDE, WESLEY GEORGE, ORGANIC CHEMISTRY, ORGANOPHOSPHORUS CHEMISTRY. *Current Pos:* from asst prof to assoc prof, 64-72, PROF CHEM, UNIV UTAH, 72- *Personal Data:* b Waterloo, Iowa, Mar 13, 35; m 55, Marilyn M Murphy; c Brenda & Brian. *Educ:* Iowa State Univ, BS, 57; Univ Ill, PhD(org chem), 61. *Prof Exp:* Res chemist, Celanese Chem Co, 61-63; res assoc, Univ Pittsburgh, 63-64. *Concurrent Pos:* Vis scholar, Univ Calif, Los Angeles, 75-76; Humboldt fel, 77 & 81; vis prof, Univ Marseille, France, 83. *Mem:* Am Chem Soc; Am Sci Affiliation; Int Soc Antiviral Res; Interam Photochem Soc. *Res:* Organophosphorus chemistry; mechanisms of free-radical reactions; physical organic chemistry; bio-organic chemistry; photochemistry; exploring photorearrangements and free radical chemistry of organophosphorus compound; use NMR methods to probe conformational properties of molecules structurally analogous to the anticancer agent cyclophospharnide and the bioregulator cAMP. *Mailing Add:* Dept Chem Univ Utah Salt Lake City UT 84112. *Fax:* 801-581-8433; *E-Mail:* bentrude@chemistry.utah.edu

BENTZ, ALAN P(AUL), AIR POLLUTION, DIESEL EXHAUST EMISSIONS. *Current Pos:* CONSULT, JBL ASSOC, INC, 96- *Personal Data:* b Minneapolis, Minn, Apr 1, 27; m 47, Anne H Siebrecht; c Brooks A, Drew A & Bryan A. *Educ:* Pa State Univ, BS, 47; Univ Minn, MS, 49; Rutgers Univ, PhD, 58. *Honors & Awards:* Secretary's Merit Award, Dept Transp. *Prof Exp:* Asst, Univ Minn, 47-49; asst prof, US Naval Acad, 49-51; pharmaceut develop chemist, Am Cyanamid Co, 51-56, polymer res chemist, 57-63; flavor chemist, Gen Foods Corp, 63-73; sr res chemist, Res & Develop Ctr, USCG, 73-80, chief, Chem Br, 80-81, proj mgr chem protective clothing, 82-90, Mat Sci Marine Eng Br, 91-96. *Concurrent Pos:* Adj prof org chem, Univ Conn, 77- *Mem:* Am Chem Soc; Am Soc for Testing & Mat. *Res:* Management; marine diesel exhaust emissions, marine corrosion of aircraft, chemical permeation of protective clothing materials, forensic oil spill identification; hazardous chemical pollution; Fourier transform infrared spectroscopy; gas chromatography; calorimetry; patents in pharmaceutical processing and food flavor compositions. *Mailing Add:* 52 Cove Rd Stonington CT 06378-2300. *Fax:* 860-441-2792

BENTZ, BRYAN LLOYD, SURFACE ANALYSIS USING STATIC SIMS, PORTABLE MASS SPECTROMETER SENSORS. *Current Pos:* MEM TECH STAFF, DAVID SARNOFF RES CTR, 87- *Personal Data:* b York, Pa, June 6, 53; m 85, Paula Jane Gale; c Elizabeth W (Gale-Bentz). *Educ:* Univ Va, BS, 75, PhD(chem), 80. *Prof Exp:* Guest scientist, Max Planck Inst Plasmaphys, 79-81; mem tech staff, RCA Labs, Princeton, 82-87. *Concurrent Pos:* Prin investr, Advan Res Proj Agency, 91-92. *Mem:* Am Soc Mass Spectrometry; Sigma Xi; Am Chem Soc; Am Vacuum Soc; Bohmische Phys Soc. *Res:* Organic mass spectrometry; ion optics; surface analysis using static secondary ion mass spectrometry; trace element analysis and atomic beams; developed first quadrupole glow-discharge mass spectroscopy instrument; development of portable mass spectrometer sensors. *Mailing Add:* David Sarnoff Res Ctr CN 5300 Princeton NJ 08543-5300. *E-Mail:* bbentz@sarnoff.com

BENTZ, GREGORY DEAN, BIOLOGY. *Current Pos:* PVT PRACT, 91- *Personal Data:* b Cleveland, Ohio, Nov 6, 45; m 88; c 3. *Educ:* Allegheny Col, BS, 67; Kent State Univ, MA, 69; Univ Pittsburgh, PhD(biol), 76; Autonomous Univ City Juarez, Mexico, MD, 88. *Prof Exp:* Postdoctoral fel, Smithsonian Inst, 76-77, res assoc, 77-85; from asst prof to assoc prof biol, Mt Vernon Col, 78-85, chmn, Dept Math & Sci, 84-85; chief resident, Dept Family Med, Eastern Va Grad Sch Med, 88-91. *Mem:* Am Acad Family Physicians. *Res:* Processes of evolution of structural adaptations in vertebrates; anatomical descriptions of structural variations and determining how such structures may have evolved; medical essays; vertebrate morphology; family medicine; biosystematics. *Mailing Add:* 444 Walker Rd Great Falls VA 22066

BENTZ, RALPH WAGNER, physical chemistry, organic chemistry; deceased, see previous edition for last biography

BENTZEL, CARL JOHAN, EPITHELIAL PHYSIOLOGY, NEPHROLOGY. *Current Pos:* PROF, DEPT MED, ECAROLINA UNIV, 84- *Personal Data:* b Vicksburg, Miss, June 29, 34; m 62, Sara Baker; c 4. *Educ:* Univ Ala, BS, 54, MD, 58. *Prof Exp:* Intern Med, Presbyterian Hosp Col Physicians & Surgeons, 58-59, resident, 59-61; clin assoc, Nat Cancer Inst, NIH, 61-63; res fel, biophysics, Biophys Lab, Med Sch, Harvard Univ, 64-66; from asst prof to prof med, State Univ NY, Buffalo, 66-84. *Concurrent Pos:* Buswell fel, State Univ NY, Buffalo, 68-71; clin investr, Vet Admin Hosp, 71-73; estab investr, Am Heart Asn, 74-79 & Am Soc Clin Invest. *Mem:* Am Soc Clin Invest; Am Physiol Soc; Am Soc Nephrology; Am Bd Internal Med & Nephrology; Int Soc Nephrology. *Res:* Epithelial transport with particular reference to the role of the paracellular pathway and cytoplasmic mechanisms for control of tight junction permeability. *Mailing Add:* Dept Med E Carolina Univ Sch Med Brody Bldg Greenville NC 27858

BENUCK, MYRON, NEUROCHEMISTRY. *Current Pos:* SR RES SCIENTIST BIOCHEM, CTR NEUROCHEM, N S KLINE INST, 67- *Personal Data:* b Chicago, Ill, July 7, 34; m 68; c 2. *Educ:* Univ Chicago, BA & BS, 57, MS, 62; Univ Ill, PhD(physiol), 66. *Prof Exp:* Fel neurochem, Albert Einstein Col Med, 65-67. *Mem:* Am Soc Neurochem; Am Soc Biol Chemists; Int Soc Neurochem; Soc Neurosci. *Res:* Brain metabolism. *Mailing Add:* Ctr Neurochem N S Kline Inst Orangeburg NY 10962

BENUMOF, REUBEN, ENGINEERING PHYSICS. *Current Pos:* prof physics & head dept, 56-77, PROF APPL SCI, COL STATEN ISLAND, 77- *Personal Data:* b New York, NY, Nov 30, 12; m 36, Gertrude Cohen; c Natalie & Jonathan. *Educ:* City Col New York, BS, 33, MS, 37; NY Univ, PhD(physics), 45. *Prof Exp:* Elec engr, Fed Power Comn, 37-38; lectr physics, City Col New York, 45-56; assoc prof, Stevens Inst Technol, 51-56; consult, Jet Propulsion Lab, 85-88. *Concurrent Pos:* Res partic, Oak Ridge Nat Lab, 56-58; fel, NSF, 59-61, dir optical pumping equip proj, 63-65; dir, nuclear reactor kinetics res proj, 65-70, physics eng, 71-; fel, State Univ NY, 67, 69, 72; vis prof, Univ Zambia, 73; fel, NASA-Am Soc Eng Educ, 77; mem staff hazardous waste mgt, Argonne Nat Lab, 81; fel, Jet Propulsion Lab, 83 & 85; fel, Naval Ocean Systs Ctr, 84; fel, Naval Res Lab, 86-87, Air Force Geophysics Lab, 88-90; sr fel, Naval Air Warfare Ctr, 93-95. *Mem:* AAAS; Am Phys Soc; Am Asn Physics Teachers; Am Soc Eng Educ; Inst Elec & Electronic Engrs. *Res:* Astronomical theory of climate; mathematical modeling of microelectronic devices, and heflex bioengineering test and high electron mobility transistors. *Mailing Add:* 21-15 34th Ave Long Island City NY 11106

BENVENISTE, JACOB, NUCLEAR PHYSICS, ATOMIC & MOLECULAR PHYSICS. *Current Pos:* RETIRED. *Personal Data:* b Portland, Ore, Dec 21, 21; m 44, Lucie Almeleh; c Richard N, David M & Daniel S. *Educ:* Reed Col, BA, 43; Univ Calif, PhD(physics), 52. *Prof Exp:* Radio engr, Naval Res Lab, 43-46; asst physics, Reed Col, 46; asst physics, Univ Calif, 47-50, physicist, Lawrence Radiation Lab, 50-63; physicist, Aerospace Corp, 63-65, sr staff scientist advan concepts, 65, dir, Nuclear Effects Subdiv, 65-68; dir res, Physics Int Co, 68-72, vpres, 69-72; sr staff scientist, Aerospace Corp, 72-82; chief scientist, Northrup Res & Tech Ctr, 82-88. *Concurrent Pos:* Mem, Nuclear Cross Sect Adv Group, 56-63; deleg, Geneva Conf, 58; mem, Defense Nuclear Agency Adv Panels, 65-68. *Mem:* AAAS; Am Phys Soc; Sigma Xi. *Res:* Solid state physics; radiation damage and effects; instrumentation; energy sources; laser gyroscopes; elementary particle physics; nuclear structure. *Mailing Add:* 4458 170th Ave SE Bellevue WA 98006

BENYAJATI, SIRIBHINYA, RENAL PHYSIOLOGY, COMPARATIVE PHYSIOLOGY. *Current Pos:* ASST PROF PHYSIOL, COL MED, UNIV OKLA, 87- *Educ:* Brown Univ, PhD(physiol), 77. *Prof Exp:* Res assoc physiol, Col Med, Univ Ariz, 78-87. *Mailing Add:* Dept Physiol Col Med Univ Okla Health Sci Ctr Oklahoma City OK 73190-0001

BEN-YOSEPH, YOAV, BIOCHEMICAL GENETICS, IMMUNOCHEMISTRY. *Current Pos:* assoc prof, 81-88, PROF PEDIAT, BIOCHEM, OBSTET & GYNEC, WAYNE STATE UNIV, SCH MED, 88- *Personal Data:* b Petah-Tikva, Israel, Jan 8, 41; m 74, Miriam; c Roey & Gilad. *Educ:* Hebrew Univ, Israel, BS, 65, MS, 68, PhD(immunol), 73. *Prof Exp:* Lectr immunochem, Weizmann Inst Sci, 73-75; res assoc genetics, Children's Mem Hosp, 75-81; asst prof pediat, Northwestern Univ, Sch Med, Chicago, 75-79, assoc prof, 79-81. *Concurrent Pos:* Res fel, Med-Chem Inst, Berne Univ, Switz, 74. *Mem:* Am Soc Human Genetics; Soc Pediat Res; Soc Inherited Metabolic Dis; NY Acad Sci. *Res:* Lysosomal enzymes deficiencies; cystic fibrosis; post-translational process in glycoprotein synthesis; autoimmune diseases. *Mailing Add:* Pediat Childrens Hosp Mich 3901 Beaubien Detroit MI 48201-2119

BENYSHEK, LARRY L, ANIMAL BREEDING. *Current Pos:* from asst prof to prof, 76-88, PROF & HEAD, DEPT ANIMAL & DAIRY SCI, UNIV GA, 93- *Personal Data:* b Concordia, Kans, Feb 26, 47; m 66; c 2. *Educ:* Kans State Univ, BS, 69; Va Polytech Inst & State Univ, MS, 71, PhD(animal breeding), 73. *Prof Exp:* Dir res & educ beef cattle performance prog, NAm Limousin Found, 73-74; asst prof agr, Ft Hays Kans State Col, 74-76. *Mem:* Am Soc Animal Sci. *Res:* Selection response using National Sire Evaluation in beef cattle; development of national and international beef cattle genetic evaluation program; development of carcass trait genetic values for beef cattle. *Mailing Add:* Dept Animal Sci Univ Ga 1180 E Broad St Athens GA 30601-3040. *Fax:* 706-542-0399; *E-Mail:* qllb@uga.cc.uga.edu

BENZ, EDMUND WOODWARD, SURGERY. *Current Pos:* Res asst physiol, Sch Med, Vanderbilt Univ, 38-40, surg training, Hosp, 40-45, resident surgeon, 44-45, from asst prof to assoc prof, 52-83, EMER CLIN PROF SURG, VANDERBILT UNIV, 83- *Personal Data:* b Nashville, Tenn, May 8, 11; m 45; c 4. *Educ:* Vanderbilt Univ, AB, 37, MD, 40. *Concurrent Pos:* Pvt pract, 45-; mem surg staff, Hosps; chmn cancer study group, Tenn/Mid-South Regional Med Prog, 68-72; consult, Disability Determination Serv Social Security Agency, 83- *Mem:* AAAS; AMA; Am Col Surg. *Res:* Traumatic shock; wound healing and temperature; control of respiration; action potentials in peripheral nerve, splenectomy in hemophilia. *Mailing Add:* 3704 M Estes Rd Nashville TN 37215

BENZ, EDWARD JOHN, CLINICAL PATHOLOGY, MICROBIOLOGY. *Current Pos:* VPRES, UTILIZATION REV, SACRED HEART HOSP, BETHLEHEM, PA, 89- *Personal Data:* b Pittsburgh, Pa, June 11, 23; m 45, Verna Cuddyre; c Edward J Jr, Thomas J, Gregory P & Mary L. *Educ:* Univ Pittsburgh, MD, 46; Univ Minn, MS, 52. *Prof Exp:* Dir labs & pathologist, St Luke's Hosp, 53-84, dir, Lab Clin Path, 58-90, vpres, Med Affairs, 84-89. *Concurrent Pos:* Consult, Palmerton Hosp; adj prof microbiol, Lehigh Univ, 65-74; chmn med adv comt labs, Pa Dept Health, 74-76. *Mem:* Am Asn Path & Bact; Int Acad Path; Col Am Pathologists; Am Soc Clin Pathologists; Am Col Physician Execs. *Mailing Add:* 1564 Saucon Valley Rd Bethlehem PA 18015

BENZ, FREDERICK W, PHARMACOLOGY, BIOCHEMISTRY. *Current Pos:* ASSOC PROF PHARMACOL, COL MED, UNIV LOUISVILLE, 78- *Personal Data:* b White Plains, NY, June 5, 44; m 69; c 2. *Educ:* Manhattan Col, BS, 66; Univ Iowa, MS, 68, PhD(pharmacol), 70. *Prof Exp:* NIH fel, Molecular Pharmacol Unit, Med Res Coun, Cambridge, Eng, 70-72; sr sci staff, Nat Inst Med Res, Mill Hill, London, Eng, 72-73; asst prof pharmacol, Univ Wis-Madison, 73-78. *Mem:* AAAS; Am Chem Soc; Protein Soc; Sigma Xi. *Res:* Biological applications of magnetic resonance; protein structure and folding; drug-protein interactions; sulfhydryl-disulfide biochemistry and pharmacology. *Mailing Add:* Dept Pharmacol Univ Louisville Louisville KY 40292-0001

BENZ, GEORGE WILLIAM, ORGANIC CHEMISTRY. *Current Pos:* RETIRED. *Personal Data:* b Ulm, Ger, June 26, 22; US citizen; m 47; c 5. *Educ:* Dartmouth Col, AB, 43; Univ Tex, MA, 46, PhD(org chem), 50. *Prof Exp:* Chemist, Winthrop Chem Co, 43-44, Heyden Chem Co, 49-52, Callery Chem Co, 52 & Polak's Frutal Works, 52-55; pres, Ulbeco, Inc, 55-87. *Concurrent Pos:* Prof, Ulster County Community Col, Stone Ridge, NY, 69-, chmn Dept Phys Sci, 71- *Mem:* Am Chem Soc. *Res:* Organic synthesis; organometallic compounds; perfume and flavor chemicals. *Mailing Add:* 33 Ocean Ave Palm Beach Shores FL 33404

BENZ, GEORGE WILLIAM, PARASITIC COPEPODS OF FISHES, HOST-PARASITE INTERACTIONS IN FISH SYSTEMS. *Current Pos:* Supvr, Lab & Biol Servs, 91-92, CUR FISHES, TENN AQUARIUM, 92- *Personal Data:* b New Haven, Conn, Jan 1, 54; m, Judith Dwyer. *Educ:* Univ Conn, BS, 76, MS, 79; Univ BC, PhD(parasitol), 93. *Prof Exp:* Fisheries biologist, Conn Dept Environ Protection, 80-85. *Concurrent Pos:* Res assoc, Nat Marine Fisheries Serv, 78-; co-prin investr, Tenn Wildlife Resources Agency, 93-, NSF, 93- *Mem:* Sigma Xi; World Asn Copedologists; Am Elasmobranch Soc; Am Soc Parisitologists; Am Asn 2001 Parks & Aquariums. *Res:* Historical ecology studies of siphonostome copepods infecting fishes using phylogenetic methods to retrieve historical patterns and mapping techniques to understand evolution of ecological life history traits. *Mailing Add:* One Broad St Tennessee Aquarium PO Box 11048 Chattanooga TN 37401-2048. *Fax:* 423-267-3561

BENZ, M G, METALLURGY. *Current Pos:* Metallurgist, 61-80, MGR, PHYS METALL BRANCH, GEN ELEC RES & DEVELOP CTR, 80- *Personal Data:* b New York, NY, June 23, 35; m 59; c 4. *Educ:* Middlebury Col, BA, 56; Mass Inst Technol, MS, 59, ScD(metall), 61. *Honors & Awards:* Geisler Award, Am Soc Metals, 70. *Mem:* Am Inst Mining, Metall & Petrol Engrs; Am Soc Metals; Inst Elec & Electronics Engrs. *Res:* Process and physical metallurgy; iron carbon phase diagram; high temperature calorimetry; continuous casting of metals; process thermodynamics and kinetics; superconducting materials; permanent magnet materials; superalloys; oxidation and hot corrosion. *Mailing Add:* 11 Parkwood Dr Burnt Hills NY 12027

BENZ, SAMUEL P, SUPERCONDUCTOVE ELECTRONICS. *Current Pos:* Nat Res Coun fel, 90-92, PHYSICIST, NAT INST STANDARDS & TECHNOL, 92- *Educ:* Luther Col, BA, 85; Harvard Univ, PhD(physics), 90. *Prof Exp:* Res asst, Harvard Univ, 85-90. *Res:* Digital superconducting electronics; programmable voltage standards; two-dimensional array coherent oscillators. *Mailing Add:* Div 814-03 Nat Inst Standards & Technol 325 Broadway Boulder CO 80303-3328. *E-Mail:* benz@cmg.eeel.nist.gov

BEN-ZE'EV, AVRI, MOLECULAR BIOLOGY OF THE CYTOSKELETON. *Current Pos:* res assoc, 79-81, sr scientist, 81-84, PROF CELL BIOL, WEIZMANN INST SCI, 85- *Personal Data:* b Tirgu-Mures, Romania, Feb 11, 47; Israeli citizen; m 75; c 2. *Educ:* Hebrew Univ, Jerusalem, Israel, BSc, 70, MSc, 72, PhD(virol), 77. *Prof Exp:* Postdoctoral cell biol, Mass Inst Technol, 77-79. *Concurrent Pos:* Vis prof, Dept Surg Children's Hosp, Harvard Med Sch, Boston, Mass & Dept Biochem, Med Sch, Boston Univ, Mass, 86-87, La Jolla Cancer Res Ctr, Calif, 92-93. *Mem:* Am Soc Cell Biol; Israeli Soc Cell Biol (treas, 91-); Israeli Soc Biochem; Israeli Soc Electronmicros. *Res:* Cytoskeletal proteins at areas of cell-cell and cell-matrix contact in the regulation of cell growth, differentiation and tumor invasion. *Mailing Add:* Dept Molecular Genetics & Virol Weizmann Inst Sci Rehovot 76100 Israel. *Fax:* 972-8-342422; *E-Mail:* lgbenzev@weizmann.weizmann.ac.il

BENZER, SEYMOUR, MOLECULAR NEUROGENETICS. *Current Pos:* prof biol, 67-75, BOSWELL PROF NEUROSCI, CALIF INST TECHNOL, 75- *Personal Data:* b New York, NY, Oct 15, 21; m 42, 80, Carol A Miller; c Barbara A (Freidin), Martha J (Goldberg) & Alexander R. *Educ:* Brooklyn Col, BA, 42; Purdue Univ, MS, 43, PhD(physics), 47. *Hon Degrees:* DSc, Purdue Univ, 68, Columbia Univ, 74, Yale Univ, 77, Brandeis Univ & City Univ New York, 78, Univ Paris, 83, Rockefeller Univ, 93. *Honors & Awards:* Sigma Xi Award; Howard Taylor Ricketts Award; Gairdner Award, Can, 64; McCoy Award, 65; Lasker Award, 71; T Duckett Jones Award & Prix Charles-Leopold Mayer, French Acad Sci, 75; Louisa Gross Horwitz Prize, Columbia Univ, 76; Harvey Prize, Technion, Israel & Warren Triennial Prize, 77; Dickson Award, 78; Nat Medal Sci, 83; Rosentiel Award, 86; Thomas Hunt Morgan Medal, Genetics Soc Am , 86; Karl Spencer Lashley Award, Am Philos Soc, 88; Ralph W Gerard Medal, Soc Neurosci, 89; Helmerick Award, Retina Res Found, 90; Wolf Prize for Med, Israel, 91, Crafoord Prize, Royal Swed Acad Sci, 93. *Prof Exp:* From instr to asst prof physics, Purdue Univ, 45-48; biophysicist, Oak Ridge Nat Lab, 48-49; res fel biophys, Calif Inst Technol, 49-51; Fulbright res scholar, Pasteur Inst, Paris, 51-52; from asst prof to Stuart distinguished prof biophys, Purdue Univ, 53-67. *Concurrent Pos:* NSF sr res fel, Cambridge Univ, 57-58. *Mem:* Nat Acad Sci; Am Acad Arts & Sci; Am Philos Soc; Biophys Soc Am; Soc Neurosci; Indian Acad Sci; Genetics Soc Am. *Res:* Behavioral and developmental genetics and neurophysiology of Drosophila; molecular genetics; genetics and physiology of the nervous system and behavior; behavioral and developmental genetics and neurophysiology of Drosophila; author of numerous publications and articles. *Mailing Add:* 2075 Robin Rd San Marino CA 91108-2831

BENZIGER, THEODORE MICHELL, CHEMICAL ENGINEERING. *Current Pos:* CONSULT, CHEM PROCESS DEVELOP, 82- *Personal Data:* b Waterloo, Iowa, Nov 14, 22; m 43; c 3. *Educ:* Iowa State Univ, BS, 44. *Honors & Awards:* Crozier Prize, Am Defense Preparedness Asn, 78. *Prof Exp:* Res engr chem eng, Union Carbide Corp, 46-52; asst group leader, Explosives Res & Dev, Los Alamos Nat Lab, Univ Calif, 52-82. *Res:* Explosives-organic synthesis, process development and design, formulation, fabrication and materials evaluation; manufacture of insensitive, thermally-stable explosives; explosives manufacturing processes; plastic-bonded explosives. *Mailing Add:* 1122 Taos Hwy Santa Fe NM 87501

BENZING, DAVID H, BIOLOGY. *Current Pos:* Assoc prof, 65-77, chmn dept biol, 81-82 & 83-88, PROF BIOL, OBERLIN COL, 77- *Personal Data:* b Chicago, Ill, Oct 13, 37. *Educ:* Miami Univ, BA, 59; Univ Mich, MS, 62, PhD(bot), 65. *Concurrent Pos:* Robert S Danforth prof biol, Oberlin Col. *Mem:* NSF sci fac fel, Univ SFla, 71-72; Bot Soc Am; Sigma Xi; Asn Trop Biol. *Res:* Adaptive biology of vascular epiphytes; demography, nutrition, water balance, and interaction with host vegetation, with major emphasis on Bromeliaceae and Orchidaceae. *Mailing Add:* Dept Biol Oberlin Col Oberlin OH 44074. *E-Mail:* david_benzing@qmgate.cc.oberlin.edu

BENZING, GEORGE, III, PEDIATRIC CARDIOLOGY, PHYSIOLOGY. *Current Pos:* From asst to assoc prof, 64-72, PROF PEDIAT, COL MED, UNIV CINCINNATI, 72-; ATTEND CARDIOLOGIST, CHILDREN'S HOSP, 70- *Personal Data:* b Hamilton, Ohio, Nov 18, 26. *Educ:* Univ Cincinnati, BS, 51, MD, 58; Am Bd Pediat, dipl, 63, cert pediat cardiol, 64. *Concurrent Pos:* Assoc attend cardiologist, Children's Hosp, 66-70. *Mem:* Am Heart Asn; Sigma Xi. *Res:* Myocardial performance as evaluated by ventricular function curves and cardiopulmonary bypass. *Mailing Add:* Div Cardiol Children's Hosp Cincinnati OH 45229

BENZINGER, JAMES ROBERT, ELECTRICAL INSULATION, SUPERCONDUCTIVITY. *Current Pos:* CONSULT, SPAULDING COMPOSITE CO, 90- *Personal Data:* b Buffalo, NY, Nov 26, 22; wid; c Barbara A (Larsen), Suzy & Judith (Gibson). *Educ:* Canisius Col, BS, 48, MS, 54. *Prof Exp:* Plant chemist, Spaulding Fibre Co, Inc, 48-53, res chemist, 53-56, group leader, 56-58, mgr plastics res & develop, 58-67, mgr advan develop, 67-76, mgr corp prod develop, 76-86, tech dir, 86-90. *Concurrent Pos:* Consult, 90- *Mem:* Am Chem Soc; Soc Plastics Eng. *Res:* Product and process development of thermosetting composites and filament wound structures for electrical insulation; industrial thermosetting laminates; chemistry of high polymers and adhesives, including phenolics, epoxies, melamines, polymides and polyesters. *Mailing Add:* 135 Hillside Dr Orchard Park NY 14127-1995

BENZINGER, ROLF HANS, BIOCHEMICAL GENETICS. *Current Pos:* asst prof biol, 67-70, ASSOC PROF BIOL, UNIV VA, 70- *Personal Data:* b Rostock, Ger, Dec 4, 35; div; c Elinor & Philip. *Educ:* Johns Hopkins Univ, BA, 56, PhD(biochem genetics), 61. *Prof Exp:* Ger Res Asn fel, Max Planck Inst Biochem, 61-65; State of Geneva assistantship, Lab Biochem Genetics,

Geneva, 65-67. *Concurrent Pos:* Ctr Advan Studies res grant, Univ Va, 67-68; NIH res grants, 68-76; NIH res career develop award, 71-76; prog assoc prokaryotic genetics, NSF, 84-85; instr DNA forensics, FBI Acad, 88 & 91; mem, Ctr Bioprocess Develop, Univ Va, 90- *Mem:* Fel AAAS; Am Soc Microbiol. *Res:* Plasmid instability in B subtilis; injection of T5 phage DNA and control of membrane structure; DNA forensics. *Mailing Add:* Dept Biol Gilmer Hall Univ Va Charlottesville VA 22901. *E-Mail:* rhb@fvirginia.edu

BENZINGER, WILLIAM DONALD, INDUSTRIAL CHEMISTRY, MEMBRANE TECHNOLOGY. *Current Pos:* DIR, MFG DEVELOP, PALL CORP, 88- *Personal Data:* b Pittsburgh, Pa, Feb 6, 40; m 62; c 2. *Educ:* Univ Notre Dame, BS, 61; Pa State Univ, PhD(inorg chem), 67. *Prof Exp:* Res chemist, Res Labs, US Army Edgewood Arsenal, Md, 67-68; sr res chemist, Penwalt Corp, 69-75, proj leader, 76-83; mgr membrane technol, Culligan Int Co, 83-87 & sheet membrane prod, Sepracor Inc, 87-88. *Mem:* Am Chem Soc; NAm Membrane Soc. *Res:* Coordination chemistry; inorganic polymers; fiber reinforced composites; coatings; electrochemistry; industrial processes; membrane technology; ultrafiltration; waste treatment; polymer properties; reverse osmosis; water treatment; ultrapure water. *Mailing Add:* 44 Burham Dr Smithtown NY 11787-1033

BENZO, CAMILLO ANTHONY, DEVELOPMENTAL ENDOCRINOLOGY, EXPERIMENTAL DIABETES. *Current Pos:* asst prof, 70-75, ASSOC PROF GROSS ANAT, STATE UNIV NY UPSTATE MED CTR, 75- *Personal Data:* b Utica, NY, Dec 31, 42. *Educ:* Syracuse Univ, BA, 64; Univ Pa, PhD(anat), 69. *Prof Exp:* Fel gross anat, Univ Pa, Med Sch, 69-70. *Concurrent Pos:* Dir, Cent New York Cadaver Donor Prog, State Univ NY, Upstate Med Ctr, 71-; adj assoc prof biol, Sch Environ Sci & Forestry, State Univ NY, 75- *Mem:* Am Asn Anatomists; Am Soc Zoologists. *Res:* Problems in embryonic development and in biochemical events during cellular differentiation; problems in the development and regulation of glycogen metabolism in avian and in diabetic mammalian systems. *Mailing Add:* Dept Anat State Univ NY Health Sci Col Med 750 E Adams St Syracuse NY 13210-2306

BEN-ZVI, ILAN, HIGH BRIGHTNESS ELECTRON LINACS, SHORT WAVELENGTH FREE-ELECTRON LASERS. *Current Pos:* SR PHYSICIST & HEAD, ACCELERATOR TEST FACIL, BROOKHAVEN NAT LAB, 89- *Personal Data:* b Tel-Aviv, Israel, Apr 13, 41; m 66, Ruth Yakhin; c David & Anat. *Educ:* Hebrew Univ, Jerusalem, BSc, 65; Weizmann Inst Sci, MSc, 67, PhD(physics), 70. *Prof Exp:* Vis res assoc, Physics Dept, Stanford Univ, 70-75; sr res fel, Weizmann Inst Sci, 75-89. *Concurrent Pos:* Vis assoc prof, State Univ NY, Stony Brook, 80-87, vis prof, 88-89, adj prof physics, 89- *Mem:* Fel Am Phys Soc; Int Soc Optical Eng; NY Acad Sci. *Res:* Generation and measurement of high-brightness electron-beams, short wavelength free-electron lasers and advanced accelerator concepts; superconducting radiofrequency accelerators. *Mailing Add:* 74 Christian Ave Setauket NY 11733. *Fax:* 516-344-3029; *E-Mail:* ilan@bnl.gov

BEOUGHER, ELTON EARL, MATHEMATICS. *Current Pos:* from asst prof to assoc prof, 68-76, chmn dept, 73-82, PROF MATH, FT HAYS STATE UNIV, 76- *Personal Data:* b Gove, Kans, Mar 22, 40; m 60; c 2. *Educ:* Ft Hays State Univ, BS, 61, MA, 64; Univ Mich, PhD(math educ), 68. *Prof Exp:* Teacher, Winona Consol Schs, Kans, 61-64 & Garden City Schs, 64-65. *Mem:* Math Asn Am; Nat Coun Teachers Math. *Res:* Mathematical education and curriculum; psychology of learning mathematics. *Mailing Add:* Dept Math Ft Hays State Univ 600 Park Hays KS 67601

BEQUETTE, B WAYNE, PROCESS CONTROL, PROCESS DESIGN. *Current Pos:* ASSOC PROF CHEM ENG, RENSSELAER POLYTECH INST, 88- *Personal Data:* b Fayetteville, Ark, July 13, 57. *Educ:* Univ Ark, BS, 80; Univ Tex, MSE, 85, PhD(chem eng), 86. *Prof Exp:* Fel chem eng, Univ Tex, 86-87; vis lectr chem eng, Univ Calif-Davis, 87-88. *Concurrent Pos:* Assoc ed, Automatica; publicity chair, Am Corp Conf, 90. *Mem:* Am Inst Chem Engrs. *Res:* Nonlinear control of chemical processes; nonlinear dynamics; data reconciliation; multi-rate sampled data control; control of drug delivery systems. *Mailing Add:* Dept Chem Eng Rensselaer Polytech Inst Troy NY 12180-3590. *Fax:* 518-276-4030; *E-Mail:* bequette@rpi.edu

BERAN, DONALD WILMER, OBSERVING SYSTEMS. *Current Pos:* res meteorologist, Nat Oceanic & Atmospheric Admin, 70-75, supvry res meteorologist, 75-78, chief, Remote Sensor Appln, Wave Propagation Lab, 79-83, dir prof prog, 83-85, chief, Remote Profiler Prog, 86-90, dir, Wind Profiler Prog, 90-93, CHIEF ADVAN PROGS, NAT OCEANIC & ATMOSPHERIC ADMIN, 93- *Personal Data:* b Wheatland, Wyo, Aug 15, 35; m 56, Marilyn Cole; c David D. *Educ:* Utah State Univ, BSc, 58; Colo State Univ, MSc, 66; Univ Melbourne, PhD(meteorol), 70. *Honors & Awards:* Gold Medal Award, Dept Com, 85 & 93, Tech Transfer Award, 93. *Prof Exp:* Engr-meteorologist, Martin Co, 62-64; res asst meteorol, Colo State Univ, 64-66; sr meteorologist, Allied Res Assocs, 66-67; res fel, Univ Melbourne, Australia, 67-70. *Mem:* Am Meteorol Soc; Am Geophys Union. *Res:* Satellite meteorology; satellite based lidar for global wind measurements; development of prototype regional observing and forecasting service program for improving local weather services; wind profiler demonstration network-strategy for coastal forecast systems; development of acoustic sounding methods for remote sensing of boundary layer phenomena. *Mailing Add:* Nat Oceanic & Atmospheric Admin Environ Technol Lab R/E/ET 325 Broadway Boulder CO 80303-3328

BERAN, GEORGE WESLEY, VETERINARY PUBLIC HEALTH & FOOD SAFETY. *Current Pos:* prof vet microbiol, 73-93, DISTINGUISHED PROF VET MED, COL VET MED, IOWA STATE UNIV, 93- *Personal Data:* b Riceville, Iowa, May 22, 28; m 54, Janice A Van Zomeren Beran; c Bruce, Anne & George Jr. *Educ:* Iowa State Univ, DVM, 54; Kans Univ, PhD(med microbiol), 59; Am Col Vet Prev Med, dipl, Am Col Epidemiol, dipl. *Hon Degrees:* LHD, Silliman Univ, Philippines, 73. *Honors & Awards:* James H Steele Award, World Vet Epidemiol Soc, 79; Gold Head Cane Award, Am Vet Epidemiol Soc, 93. *Prof Exp:* Epidemic intel serv officer, USPHS, 54-56; prof microbiol, Silliman Univ, Philippines, 60-73, dir, Van Houweling Lab, 61-73. *Concurrent Pos:* Consult, WHO and/or Pan Am Health Orgn, India, 71, Malaysia, 71, Laos, 72, Philippines, 73, 74, 76 & 78, Jamaica, 79, Ecuador, 84, 85, 86 & 89, Mexico, 85, 87, 88, 89, 90 & 97, Surinam, 85 & Belize, 93 & Jamaica, 95 & 96; Fulbright prof, Ahmadu Bello Univ, Zaria, Nigeria, 80; vis lectr, Chuinan & Taipei, Taiwan, 83 & 96, Loja & Guayaquil, Ecuador, 83, Beijing & Wuhan, China, 88, Budapest, Hungary, 88 & 90; exchange deleg, Mexico, 87, 88, 89, 90, USSR, 89 & 90, Costa Rica, 90, Latvia, 93 & Ukraine, 96. *Mem:* Am Vet Med Asn; Conf Pub Health Veterinarians; Asn Teachers Vet Pub Health; Am Col Vet Prev Med; Am Asn Food Hyg Veterinarians; US Animal Health Asn; fel Royal Soc Health; Sigma Xi. *Res:* Epidemiology and immunology of rabies; epidemiology of pseudorabies; food virology; food safety; drug use in animals. *Mailing Add:* Microbiol Immunol & Prev Med Iowa State Univ Col Vet Med Ames IA 50011. *Fax:* 515-294-8500; *E-Mail:* gberan@iastate.edu

BERAN, JO ALLAN, ENVIRONMENTAL & INORGANIC CHEMISTRY. *Current Pos:* from asst prof to assoc prof, 68-76, chmn dept, 75-81, PROF CHEM, TEX A&M UNIV, 76- *Personal Data:* b Odell, Nebr, Aug 24, 42; m 64; c Kyle & Greg. *Educ:* Hastings Col, BA, 64; Univ Kans, PhD(chem), 68. *Concurrent Pos:* Vis prof, Univ Tex, Austin, 88-89, Univ Calif, San Diego, 91-92; res & develop chemist, Naval Air Warfare Ctr, Weapons Div, China Lake, Calif, 96. *Mem:* Am Chem Soc. *Res:* Gas phase studies of ions produced by photoionization; investigations in chemical education; environmental chemistry. *Mailing Add:* Dept Chem Texas A&M Univ PO Box 161 Kingsville TX 78363

BERAN, MARK JAY, PHYSICS, ENGINEERING SCIENCE. *Current Pos:* prof eng, 74-, ADJ PROF, TEL-AVIV UNIV. *Personal Data:* b New York, NY, Aug 19, 30; m 53; c 3. *Educ:* Mass Inst Technol, SB, 52; Harvard Univ, SM, 53, PhD, 55. *Prof Exp:* Hydrodynamicist, Hydrodyn Lab, Mass Inst Technol, 51-55; group leader math, Waltham Airborne Systs Lab, Radio Corp Am, 55-56; res physicist, Air Force Cambridge Res Ctr, 56-59 & Tech Opers, 59-61; from assoc prof to prof mech eng, Univ Pa, 61-74. *Concurrent Pos:* Fulbright scholar, Dept Electronics, Weizmann Inst Sci, Israel, 67-68. *Mem:* Fel Optical Soc Am; fel Acoust Soc Am; Am Phys Soc. *Res:* Underwater acoustics; applied physics; fluid mechanics; electromagnetic theory; plasma physics; statistical continuum theory; coherence theory. *Mailing Add:* Elec Eng Cath Univ Amer Washington DC 20064 Israel

BERAN, ROBERT LYNN, PROCESS & PRODUCT OPTIMIZATION. *Current Pos:* res engr, 72-77, sr res engr, 77-79, group leader, 79-81, RES DIR, WESTVACO CORP, 81- *Personal Data:* b Eau Claire, Wis, Oct 1, 43; m 71; c 2. *Educ:* Univ Wis-Madison, BS, 67, PhD(mech eng), 71. *Honors & Awards:* George Olmsted Award, Am Paper Inst, 78. *Prof Exp:* Design engr, Monitor Data Systs, Inc, 71-72. *Mem:* Tech Asn Pulp & Paper Indust; AAAS. *Res:* Theoretical and experimental investigations of papermaking processes satisfying technical needs and business goals of manufacturing, converting, and product development groups; physics of paper and papermaking. *Mailing Add:* 110 Parkview Ave Covington VA 24426

BERANBAUM, SAMUEL LOUIS, RADIOLOGY. *Current Pos:* from asst clin prof to assoc clin prof, 48-60, CLIN PROF RADIOL, NY UNIV, 60-, ATTEND RADIOLOGIST, UNIV HOSP, BELLEVUE MED CTR, 55- *Personal Data:* b Toronto, Ont, Can, Apr 20, 15; US citizen; m 49; c 3. *Educ:* Univ Toronto, BA, 37, MD, 40. *Prof Exp:* Intern, Mt Sinai Hosp, Cleveland, 40-42; resident radiol, Postgrad Hosp, New York, 42-45; instr, Columbia Univ, 45-48. *Concurrent Pos:* Assoc attend radiologist, Postgrad Hosp, New York, 45-48; dir radiol, St Barnabas Hosp, 45-70; consult, St Lukes Hosp, 70-; consult radiology, Vet Admin Hosp & Lenox Hill Hosp, 75- *Mem:* Fel Am Col Gastroenterol; fel Am Col Radiol; Radiol Soc NAm; Am Roentgen Ray Soc; Asn Gastro-Intestinal Radiologists. *Res:* Special procedures in roentgen diagnostics; fluoroscopy and radiography of the gastro-intestinal tract; right side diverticular disease; gastric volvulus; elusive abdominal tumors. *Mailing Add:* 121 E 60th St New York NY 10022-1109

BERANEK, DAVID T, MUTAGENESIS, CARCINOGENESIS. *Current Pos:* res chemist, 77-91, PROG ANALYST RES CHEM, NAT CTR TOXICOL RES, 91- *Personal Data:* b LaCrosse, Wis, Jan 31, 44; m 68, Barbara J Schlicht; c Peter, Susanne, Daniel & Michael. *Educ:* Univ Wis-LaCrosse, BA, 68, MA, 76; Univ Ark, PhD, 89. *Prof Exp:* Med res technician, Med Sch, Wash Univ, 76-77. *Mem:* Am Chem Soc; AAAS. *Res:* Biochemical mechanisms of mutagenesis and carcinogenesis caused by alkylating agents and aromatic amines and amides; site specific mutagenesis of aromatic amines in eucaryotic organisms. *Mailing Add:* Nat Ctr Toxicol Res HFT-321 N Ctr Dr Jefferson AR 72079-9502

BERANEK, LEO LEROY, ACOUSTICS, COMMUNICATIONS. *Current Pos:* CONSULT, ACOUSTICS, 87- *Personal Data:* b Solon, Iowa, Sept 15, 14; m 41, 85, Gabriella Sohn; c James & Thomas. *Educ:* Cornell Col, AB,36; Harvard Univ, MS, 37, ScD(physics), 40. *Hon Degrees:* ScD, Cornell Col, 46; DEng, Worcester Polytech Inst, 71; DCS, Suffolk Univ, 79; LLD, Emerson Col, 82; DPS, Northeastern Univ, 84. *Honors & Awards:* Biennial Award,

Acoust Soc Am, 44; Wallace Clement Sabine Award, Acoust Soc Am, 61; Gold Medal, Audio Eng Soc, 71; Gold Medal, Acoust Soc Am, 75; Abe Lincoln TV Award, 76. *Prof Exp:* From instr to asst prof physics & communication eng, Harvard Univ, 40-43, dir electro-acoustic lab, 43-46 & systs res lab, 45-46; Guggenheim Mem Found fel, Harvard Univ & Mass Inst Technol, 46-47; assoc prof commun eng, Mass Inst Technol, 47-58, tech dir, Acoustics Lab, 47-53, lectr, 58-80; pres & chief exec officer, Bolt, Beranek & Newman Inc, 53-69, dir, 53-83, chief scientist, 69-71; pres, elec off, 71-79, chmn bd, Boston Broadcasters Inc, 83-87. *Concurrent Pos:* Pres, elec off, Bolt, Beranek & Newman, Inc, 53-69, dir, 53-83, chief scientist, 69-71; trustee, Cornell Col, 56-71 & Emerson Col, 74-79; chmn bd, Mueller-BBN GmbH, Munich, 62-86; mem, Aeronaut & Space Eng Bd, Nat Acad Eng, 65-76, comn pub eng policy, 66-71, marine bd, 67-71, coun, 69-71; vchmn, Mass Comn Ocean Mgt, 68-71; mem vis comt, Dept Soc Rels & Psychol, Harvard Univ, 64-70, dept biol, 71-77, 86-, mem adv comt mgt develop progs, Grad Sch Bus Admin, 65-71, mem advan mgt prog, 65-71, vis comt, 87-90; bd overseers, Harvard Univ, 84-90. *Mem:* Nat Acad Eng; fel AAAS; hon mem Acoust Soc Am (vpres, 49-50, pres, 54-55); hon mem Audio Eng Soc (pres, 67-68); fel Am Acad Arts & Sci (pres, 89-92); fel Inst Elec & Electronic Engrs; fel Am Inst Phys. *Res:* Architectural acoustics; electromechanico-acoustical devices; acoustic measurements; noise control techniques. *Mailing Add:* 975 Memorial Dr Suite 804 Cambridge MA 02138-5755. *Fax:* 617-492-7816

BERANEK, WILLIAM, JR, BIOCHEMISTRY. *Current Pos:* PRES, IND ENVIRON INST, 90- *Personal Data:* b Chicago, Ill, Jan 8, 46. *Educ:* Univ Wis, BS, 67; Calif Inst Technol, PhD(chem), 73. *Prof Exp:* Res assoc biochem, Med Ctr, Duke Univ, 73-75, res fel, 75-77; asst dir, Holcombe Res Inst, Butler Univ, 77-78, assoc dir, 78-90. *Concurrent Pos:* Consult prog planning, WNET-TV, New York, 76-; adj assoc prof chem, Butler Univ, 77- *Mem:* AAAS; Am Chem Soc; NY Acad Sci. *Res:* Protein-sugar interactions; biochemical aspects of ecological and environmental issues; public policy issues involving chemistry and biochemistry. *Mailing Add:* Ind Environ Inst 4834 N Illinois St Indianapolis IN 46208-3526

BERARD, ANTHONY D, JR, TOPOLOGY, COMPUTER SCIENCES. *Current Pos:* from assoc prof to prof math, 72-87, PROF MATH & COMPUT SCI, KING'S COL, 87- *Personal Data:* b Lynn, Mass, Sept 23, 42; m 80, Louise McNertney. *Educ:* The Citadel, BS, 64; Case Western Res Univ, MA, 67, PhD(math), 68. *Prof Exp:* Asst prof math, USAF Inst Technol, 68-72. *Mem:* Am Math Soc; Math Asn Am; Asn Comput Mach; Inst Elec & Electronics Engrs; Nat Comput Graphics Asn. *Res:* Characterization of metric spaces by the use of their midsets; computer graphics; modeling; simulation. *Mailing Add:* 7 Twain Circle Conyngham PA 18219-9999

BERARD, COSTAN WILLIAM, MEDICINE, PATHOLOGY. *Current Pos:* PATHOLOGIST, ST JUDE CHILDREN'S RES HOSP, MEMPHIS, 80- *Personal Data:* b Cranford, NJ, Dec 23, 32; m 58; c 2. *Educ:* Princeton Univ, AB, 55; Harvard Univ, MD, 59. *Prof Exp:* Intern surg, Univ Rochester, 59-60; res assoc, Walter Reed Inst Res, 60-62, dept chief, 62-63; resident, Nat Cancer Inst, 63-66, staff pathologist, 66-80, head, Hematopath Sect, 70-80. *Mem:* AMA; Fedn Am Soc Exp Biol; Am Soc Exp Path. *Res:* Metabolic response to cancer with particular reference to immunology; metabolic response to trauma with particular reference to wound healing. *Mailing Add:* 4576 Park Ave Memphis TN 38117-4714

BERARD, MICHAEL F, CERAMICS ENGINEERING. *Current Pos:* instr, Dept Ceramic Eng & jr engr, Ames Lab, Atomic Energy Comn, 64-67, asst prof, Dept Ceramic Eng & assoc engr, 67-71, assoc prof, Dept Ceramic Eng & engr, 71-77, PROF, DEPT MAT SCI & ENG & SR ENGR, AMES LAB, IOWA STATE UNIV, 77- *Personal Data:* b Des Moines, Iowa, Aug 9, 38. *Educ:* Iowa State Univ, BS, 60, MS, 62, PhD(ceramic eng), 68. *Prof Exp:* Develop engr, Aerojet-Gen Corp, 62-64. *Mem:* Am Ceramic Soc; Nat Inst Ceramic Engrs; Am Soc Eng Educ. *Res:* Diffusion, defect structure and electrical conductivity in ceramic materials; properties of rare earth oxides. *Mailing Add:* Dept Eng Iowa State Univ Ames IA 50011-2010

BERARDINELLI, FRANK MICHAEL, POLYMER CHEMISTRY. *Current Pos:* Chemist to,sr res chemist, 43-60, group leader polyacetal res & develop, 60-74, RES SUPVR, CELANESE RES CO, 74- *Personal Data:* b Newark, NJ, June 6, 20; m 57; c 2. *Educ:* Seton Hall Univ, BS, 43. *Mem:* Am Chem Soc; Sigma Xi. *Res:* Synthesis and processing of cellulosic plastics; textile finishes and plasticizer synthesis and evaluation; polyethylene film studies; emulsion, condensation and ionic polymerization of polymers; polyacetals; composites; high temperature polymers. *Mailing Add:* Four Garland Dr Brick NJ 08723-7827

BERARDO, PETER ANTONIO, PARTICLE PHYSICS, COMPUTER MODELS. *Current Pos:* PHYSICIST TREAT PLANNING DEVELOP, LOS ALAMOS NAT LAB, 75-; PRIN INVESTR, PROG MGR, MGR, LOCKHEED MARTIN, 85- *Personal Data:* b Los Angeles, Calif, Apr 25, 39; m 63, Barbara Cady; c Alan & Ryan. *Educ:* Univ Calif, Los Angeles, BS, 64, MS, 65, PhD(physics), 71. *Honors & Awards:* Joint Serv Commendation Medal, Defense Nuclear Agency, 73. *Prof Exp:* Physicist dosimetry, Armed Forces Radiobiol Res DNA Inst, 70-73; physicist strategic planning, Joint Strategic Target Planning Staff, Joint Chiefs Staff, 73-75. *Concurrent Pos:* Adj prof physics, Univ NMex, 79-85. *Mem:* Am Phys Soc; Am Asn Physicists Med; Inst Elec & Electronics Engrs; Aerospace Indus Assoc Am. *Res:* Practical applications of physics; optimized planning; machine intelligence; robotics. *Mailing Add:* 0/H123 B/250 Lockheed MSC 3251 Hanover St Palo Alto CA 94304

BERBARI, EDWARD J, MEDICAL INSTRUMENTATION, CARDIAC ELECTROPHYSIOLOGY. *Current Pos:* PROF, UNIV OKLA HEALTH SCIS CTR, 80- *Personal Data:* b Massillon, Ohio, May 6, 49; m 77; c 4. *Educ:* Carnegie-Mellon Univ, BS, 71; Univ Miami, MS, 73; Univ Iowa, PhD(elec eng), 80. *Mem:* Fel Inst Elec & Electronics Engrs; Int Soc Comput Electrocardiography; NAm Soc Pacing & Electrophysiol. *Res:* High resolution computer techniques for recording electrical activity of the heart to identify individuals at risk for sudden cardiac death due to arrhythmias. *Mailing Add:* Vet Admin Med Ctr 921 NE 13th St Oklahoma City OK 73104-5028

BERBEE, JOHN GERARD, PLANT PATHOLOGY, FORESTRY. *Current Pos:* assoc prof plant path, 57-69, PROF PLANT PATH & FORESTRY, UNIV WIS-MADISON, 69- *Personal Data:* b Hamilton, Can, Oct 12, 25; m 50; c 3. *Educ:* Univ Toronto, BScF, 49; Yale Univ, MF, 50; Univ Wis, PhD(plant path), 54. *Prof Exp:* Asst forest biologist, Can Dept Agr Sci Serv, 54-57. *Concurrent Pos:* Sr lectr plant sci, Univ Ife, Nigeria, 64-67. *Mem:* Am Phytopath Soc; Soc Am Foresters. *Res:* Disease of forest trees and breeding for disease resistance; forest tree virology; tropical plant pathology. *Mailing Add:* 5114 Tomahawk Trail Madison WI 53705

BERBERIAN, PAUL ANTHONY, arterial wall metabolism, pathobiology of arteriosclerosis, for more information see previous edition

BERBERIAN, STERLING KHAZAG, MATHEMATICAL ANALYSIS, ALGEBRA. *Current Pos:* prof, 68-91, EMER PROF MATH, UNIV TEX, AUSTIN, 91- *Personal Data:* b Waukegan, Ill, Jan 15, 26; m 61, Carol A Restemyer; c James G & Susan D. *Educ:* Mich State Univ, BS, 48, MS, 50; Univ Chicago, PhD(math), 55. *Prof Exp:* Instr math, Fisk Univ, 50, Southern Ill Univ, 51-52 & Univ Ill, 52-53; from instr to asst prof, Mich State Univ, 55-57; from asst prof to prof, Univ Iowa, 57-66; ed, Math Rev, Ann Arbor, Mich, 66-68. *Concurrent Pos:* Vis prof, Ind Univ, Bloomington, 70-71, Univ Reading & Univ Poitiers, 81-82; lectr, Int Ctr Pure & Appl Math, France, 86. *Mem:* French Math Soc; Math Asn Am. *Res:* Hilbert space; integration theory; operator algebras; regular rings; Baer rings. *Mailing Add:* Dept Math Univ Tex Austin TX 78712

BERCAW, JAMES ROBERT, textile products, for more information see previous edition

BERCAW, JOHN EDWARD, ORGANOMETALLIC CHEMISTRY. *Current Pos:* Arthur Amos Noyes res fel chem, 72-74, from asst prof to prof, 77-93, CENTENNIAL PROF CHEM, CALIF INST TECHNOL, 93- *Personal Data:* b Cincinnati, Ohio, Dec 3, 44; m 65, Diane Ingram; c 2. *Educ:* NC State Univ, BS, 67; Univ Mich, Ann Arbor, PhD(chem), 71. *Honors & Awards:* Award in Pure Chem, Am Chem Soc, 80, Award in Organometall Chem, 90, Award for Distinguished Serv in Advan Inorg Chem, 97; Sir Edward Frankland Prize Lectr, Royal Soc Chem, 92; Baker Lectr, Cornell Univ, 93; Wynberg Lectr, Univ Groningen, Neth, 95. *Concurrent Pos:* Alfred P Sloan res fel, Calif Inst Technol, 76-78, Dreyfus teacher scholar, 77-82; consult, Exxon Res & Eng Co, 79-, Lawrence Berkeley Lab, Mat & Chem Sci Div Rev Panel, 84; Shell distinguished prof, 85-90; chmn-elect, Div Inorg Chem, 87, chmn, 88; mem adv bd, Inorganica Chemica Acta, 88-, sci rev comt, OER/Basic Chem Sci, Solar Energy Res Inst, 90-; vchmn, Gordon Res Conf Organometall Chem, 90. *Mem:* Nat Acad Sci; Am Chem Soc; fel AAAS; fel Am Acad Arts & Sci. *Res:* Synthetic and mechanistic organotransition metal chemistry with special emphasis on activation of small molecules at early transition metal centers; model catalysts for Ziegler-Nalta polymenzation of olefins, hydrocarbon oxidation with transition metal complexes. *Mailing Add:* 1455 Afton St Pasadena CA 91103. *Fax:* 626-585-0147

BERCH, JULIAN, CHEMISTRY. *Current Pos:* RES SUPVR, GILLETTE RES INST, 67- *Personal Data:* b Winnipeg, Man, Oct 13, 16; nat US; m 44; c 4. *Educ:* Univ Wash, BS, 38. *Prof Exp:* Chemist, Fish & Wildlife Serv, 39-40; chemist, Nat Bur Standards, 42-43; res assoc, Textile Res Found, 43-44 & Harris Res Labs, 45-67. *Mem:* AAAS; Am Chem Soc; Am Asn Textile Chem & Colorists. *Res:* Surface active agents and detergents; technology of non-woven fabrics; mechanism of wool felting and shrinkage control; wool chemistry; textile application of rubber latices and permanent-press finishes; water pollution. *Mailing Add:* 2100 Washington Ave Silver Spring MD 20910

BERCHTOLD, GLENN ALLEN, ORGANIC CHEMISTRY. *Current Pos:* From instr to assoc prof, 60-69, PROF CHEM, MASS INST TECHNOL, 69- *Personal Data:* b Pekin, Ill, July 1, 32; m 59; c 3. *Educ:* Univ Ill, BS, 54; Univ Ind, PhD(org chem), 59. *Mem:* Am Chem Soc. *Res:* Organic synthesis. *Mailing Add:* PO Box 248 Eastham MA 02642-0248

BERCOV, RONALD DAVID, ALGEBRA. *Current Pos:* from asst prof to assoc prof, 63-74, PROF MATH, UNIV ALTA, 74- *Personal Data:* b Edmonton, Alta, Dec 14, 37; m 65; c 2. *Educ:* Univ Alta, BSc, 59; Calif Inst Technol, PhD(math), 62. *Prof Exp:* Res assoc math, Cornell Univ, 62-63. *Concurrent Pos:* Vis assoc prof, Univ Wash, 69; ed, Can Math Bull, 70. *Mem:* Am Math Soc; Math Asn Am; Can Math Cong. *Res:* Group theory, primarily in the field of permutation groups. *Mailing Add:* Dept Math Univ Alta 632 Cent Acad Bldg Edmonton AB T6G 2G1 Can

BERCOVICI, DAVID ANTHONY LEONARDO, GEOPHYSICAL FLUID DYNAMICS, NONLINEAR & COMPLEX SYSTEMS. *Current Pos:* asst prof, 90-95, ASSOC PROF, DEPT GEOL & GEOPHYS, UNIV HAWAII, MANOA, 95- *Personal Data:* b Rome, Italy, Sept 18, 60; US citizen; m 83. *Educ:* Harvey Mudd Col, BS, 82; Univ Calif, Los Angeles, MS, 87, PhD(geophys & space physics), 89. *Honors & Awards:* Presidential Young Investr, NSF, 94; James B Macelwane Medal, Am Geophys Union, 96. *Prof Exp:* W M Keck postdoctoral res fel, Woods Hole Oceanog Inst, 89-90. *Concurrent Pos:* Panel mem, NSF, 92-93, Venus Data Anal Prog, NASA, 93-94; prin investr, NSF & NASA. *Mem:* Fel Am Geophys Union. *Res:* Thermal convection and fluid flow in the earth's mantle; origin of plate tectonics; cause for hotspots (volcanic) and mantle plumes. *Mailing Add:* Dept Geol & Geophys Univ HI Honolulu HI 96822. *Fax:* 808-956-2538; *E-Mail:* dberco@soest.hawaii.edu

BERCOVITZ, ARDEN BRYAN, REPRODUCTIVE ENDOCRINOLOGY. *Current Pos:* REPRODUCTIVE ENDOCRINOLOGIST, CTR REPRODUCTION ENDANGERED SPECIES, ZOOL SOC SAN DIEGO, 88- *Personal Data:* b Los Angeles, Calif, Oct 18, 45; c 1. *Educ:* Calif State Polytech Univ, Pomona, BS, 68; Wash State Univ, MS, 70; Univ Mo, Columbia, PhD(physiol), 76. *Prof Exp:* Fel environ physiol, Univ Mo, 70-73; res assoc animal sci, La State Univ, 73-75; res fel, San Diego Zoo, 77-78; instr human physiol, San Diego City Col, 77; avian reproductive physiologist, res & ornith depts, San Diego Zoo, 78-88; RES ASSOC, HUBB/SEA WORLD RES INST, 77- *Concurrent Pos:* Fel, USPS, 70-73; res fel, Scripps Found, 77; NSF grant, 78-80; spec educ consult, San Diego Unified Sch Dist, 83-; adj fac, San Diego State Univ, 84-; Inst Mus Serv grant, 85-86; spec educ consult, San Diego Univ Sch Dist, 85-; lectr, animal metaphores, wild side res & intuitive prob solving. *Mem:* Am Asn Zool Parks & Aquaria; Sigma Xi; Am Soc Zool. *Res:* Reproductive endocrinology of endangered species; non invasive methodologies, neonatal sex steroids and paleo- endocrinology. *Mailing Add:* 10565 Caminito Banyon San Diego CA 92131

BERCZI, ISTVAN, IMMUNOLOGY. *Current Pos:* from asst prof to assoc prof, 74-91, PROF IMMUNOL, UNIV MAN, 91- *Personal Data:* b Bekes, Hungary, Nov 12, 38; Can citizen; m 67, Anna Kovacs; c Stephen G, Anthony W & Anna H. *Educ:* Budapest Vet Sch, Hungary, DVM, 62; Univ Man, PhD(immunol), 72. *Prof Exp:* Res scientist microbiol, Vet Med Res Inst, Hungarian Acad Sci, Budapest, 62-67. *Mem:* Am Asn Immunologists; Can Soc Immunol; Int Soc Neuroimmunomodulation; AAAS; Endocrine Soc. *Res:* Cancer immunology; regulation of the immune response; function and the pituitary gland; prolactins importance as an immunoregulatory hormone; neuroendocrine immunoregulation. *Mailing Add:* Dept Immunol Univ Man Fac Med Winnipeg MB R3E 0W3 Can

BERDAHL, DONALD RICHARD, organic chemistry, polymer chemistry, for more information see previous edition

BERDAHL, PAUL HILLAND, INFRARED PHYSICS, LIGHT SCATTERING. *Current Pos:* STAFF SCIENTIST, ENERGY & ENVIRON DIV, LAWRENCE BERKELEY LAB, UNIV CALIF, 76- *Personal Data:* b Washington, DC, Aug 1, 45; m, Jane Upson; c Edgar J & Carl T. *Educ:* Rice Univ, BA, 67; Stanford Univ, MS, 68, PhD (theoret physics), 72. *Prof Exp:* Res assoc, Dept Physics, Stanford Univ, 72-73 & Univ Wash, Seattle, 73-75. *Concurrent Pos:* Chmn, Solar Radiation Div, Am Solar Energy Soc, 82. *Mem:* Am Phys Soc; Mat Res Soc. *Res:* Infrared radiative properties of narrow-band gap semiconductors and other materials; transport properties of superconductors and theory of superfluidity; radiation transfer in atmosphere; magnetochemistry. *Mailing Add:* 3905 Lyman Rd Oakland CA 94602. *Fax:* 510-486-5530; *E-Mail:* phberdahl@lbl.gov

BERDAN, JEAN MILTON, INVERTEBRATE PALEONTOLOGY. *Current Pos:* RETIRED. *Personal Data:* b New Haven, Conn, May 9, 16. *Educ:* Vassar Col, AB, 37; Yale Univ, MS, 43, PhD(geol), 49. *Prof Exp:* Geologist, Ground Water, US Geol Surv, 42-46, geologist, paleont & stratig, 49-85. *Mem:* Geol Soc Am; Am Paleont Soc; Brit Paleont Asn; Am Paleont Res Inst; Int Paleont Asn; Sigma Xi. *Res:* Lower Paleozoic ostracode faunas. *Mailing Add:* 510 21st NW No 408 Washington DC 20006

BERDANIER, CAROLYN DAWSON, NUTRITIONAL BIOCHEMISTRY. *Current Pos:* prof foods & nutrit & head dept, 77-88, PROF NUTRIT, UNIV GA, 77- *Personal Data:* b East Brunswick, NJ, Nov 14, 36; m 57; c 3. *Educ:* Pa State Univ, BS, 58; Rutgers Univ, MS, 63, PhD(nutrit), 66. *Honors & Awards:* Lamar Dodd Award, 84; Geo Nutrit Coun Award, 82; Borden Award, Am Home Econ Asn, 92. *Prof Exp:* Res asst nutrit, Douglass Col, 62-63; NIH fel, Rutgers Univ, 66-67; res nutritionist, Human Nutrit Res Div, Agr Res Serv, USDA, 68-75; from res asst prof to res assoc prof, Depts Med & Biochem, Col Med, Univ Nebr, 75-77. *Concurrent Pos:* Asst prof nutrit, Univ Md, 70-75. *Mem:* Am Inst Nutrit; Am Soc Clin Nutrit; Soc Exp Biol & Med; NAm Soc Study Obesity; Sigma Xi Am Diabetes Asn; Am Diabetes Asn. *Res:* Hormones and metabolic control mechanisms; nutrient-genetic interactions; carbohydrate nutrition; diet-drug interactions; obesity; diabetes; lipemia. *Mailing Add:* Dept Nutrit Univ Ga Athens GA 30602. *Fax:* 706-542-5059; *E-Mail:* cberdani@hestia.fcs.uga.edu

BERDICHEVSKY, ALEXANDER, MECHANICS OF HYPERELASTIC MATERIALS, COMPOSITE MATERIALS PROCESSING. *Current Pos:* SR SCIENTIST, CHICAGO RAWHIDE MFG CO, SKF, 92- *Personal Data:* b Moscow, USSR, Oct 26, 50; US citizen; m 73, Irene M. *Educ:* Moscow Univ, BS & MS, 72, PhD(mech), 82. *Prof Exp:* Sr res scientist, Waters Div, Millipore, 87-90; staff scientist, Mat Div, Lord Corp, 90-92. *Mem:* Soc Mech Engrs. *Res:* Computation of effective properties of inhomogenious media, composite processing; resin transfer molding and similar processes, mechanics of elastomers; computational aspects, modeling, etc. *Mailing Add:* 964 Shambliss Lane Buffalo Grove IL 60089. *Fax:* 847-742-7845

BERDICK, MURRAY, PHARMACEUTICAL PRODUCTS, CONSUMER PRODUCT INTEGRITY. *Current Pos:* CONSULT, 80- *Personal Data:* b New Rochelle, NY, June 27, 20; m 47, Joan Jacobstein; c Dena A (Cosgrove). *Educ:* George Washington Univ, BS, 42; Polytech Inst Brooklyn, MS, 49, PhD(polymer chem), 54. *Honors & Awards:* Cosmetic Sci & Indust Award, Cosmetic, Toiletry & Fragrance Asn, 71; Soc Cosmetic Chemists Medal Award, 75. *Prof Exp:* Asst, Am Electroplaters Soc, Bur Stand, Washington, DC, 40-42; test engr, Gen Elec Co, NY, 42-43, chemist, 43-46; proj leader, Evans Res & Develop Corp, 46-51, coord res, 53-60, vpres & dir res, 60-61; res mgr, Chesebrough-Pond's Inc, 62-64, dir, Clinton Labs, 64-69, dir, Res Labs, 69-70, dir appl res, 71-75, dir regulatory affairs, 75-80. *Concurrent Pos:* Chmn, Food & Drug Admin-Toilet Goods Asn Sci Liaison Comt, 69-71; chmn, Inter-Indust Color Comt, 71-76; lectr, Yale Univ, 80-82. *Mem:* Am Chem Soc; Am Inst Chemists; NY Acad Sci; Asn Res Dirs; AAAS; Sigma Xi. *Res:* Interaction of proteins and polyelectrolytes; sustained release drugs; transepidermal moisture loss; food, drug and cosmetic color safety; polymerization; unsaturated polyesters; fiber physics; properties of high polymers; cosmetic and pharmaceutical products. *Mailing Add:* PO Box 836 68 Turtle Bay Dr Branford CT 06405-0836. *Fax:* 203-488-3438

BERDJIS, FAZLOLLAH, REPRESENTATIONS OF GROUPS & ALGEBRAS, HIGH ENERGY PHYSICS. *Current Pos:* PROF PHYSICS & MATH, ORANGE COAST COL, COSTA MESA, 90- *Personal Data:* b Soleymanieh, Ira, Feb 4, 43; div; c Vahid & Monireh. *Educ:* Univ Munich, Ger, Vordipl physics, 67, dipl phys, 72, Dr, 78. *Prof Exp:* Asst, Math & Physics, Univ Munich, Ger, 67-77; sci co-worker, Max Planck Inst, Stanberg, Ger, 78-81; asst prof elem particle physics, Univ Ill, Chicago, 82-85; instr math, Valley Col, La, 89-90. *Concurrent Pos:* instr elem particle physics, Univ Munich, 78-81. *Mem:* Am Math Soc; Am Phys Soc. *Res:* Investigation and classification of the invariants of real and complex lie algebras. *Mailing Add:* 2781 Bluebird Circle Costa Mesa CA 92626. *Fax:* 714-556-7921

BERECEK, KATHLEEN HELEN, CARDIOVASCULAR PHYSIOLOGY, HYPERTENSION RESEARCH. *Current Pos:* ASSOC PROF PHYSIOL & BIOPHYSICS, UNIV ALA, BIRMINGHAM, 81- *Personal Data:* b Chicago, Ill. *Educ:* St Xavier Col, BS, 68; Univ Mich, Ann Arbor, MS, 71, PhD(physiol), 76. *Honors & Awards:* Marion Young Scholars Award, Am Soc Hypertension, 88. *Prof Exp:* Scholar, Dept Physiol, Univ Mich, 76-77; res assoc, Dept Pharmacol, Univ Heidelberg, 78-79; res fel, Cardiovasc Ctr, Univ Iowa, 79-81. *Concurrent Pos:* Assoc scientist, Hypertension Prog, Univ Ala, Birmingham, 81; estab investr, Am Heart Asn, 82, mem high blood pressure res coun, basic sci circulation. *Mem:* Am Physiol Soc; Soc Exp Biol & Med; Am Heart Asn; Sigma Xi; AAAS; Am Fed Clin Res; Soc Neurosci; Am Soc Hypertension. *Res:* Role of the central nervous system and angiotensin II in arterial pressure regulation and the pathogenesis of hypertension; exploration of the role of vasopressin in arterial pressure regulation and hypertension. *Mailing Add:* Dept Physiol & Biophys Univ Ala 988 Basic Health Sci Ctr Birmingham AL 35294-0005

BEREK, JONATHAN S, GYNECOLOGIC ONCOLOGY. *Current Pos:* oncol fel, Univ Calif, Los Angeles, Sch Med, 79-81, from asst prof to assoc prof, gynec & oncol, 84-86, PROF & DIR, DIV GYNEC ONCOL, VCHMN, DEPT OBSTET GYNEC & CHIEF GYNEC, SCH MED, UNIV CALIF, LOS ANGELES, 86-, CHIEF STAFF, MED CTR, 96- *Personal Data:* b Fremont, Nebr, Apr 21, 48; m 70, Deborah L Jones; c Johathan M, James S & Jessica E. *Educ:* Brown Univ, BA, 70, MMSc, 73; Johns Hopkins Univ, MD, 75. *Prof Exp:* Intern & resident, obstet & gynec, Brigham Women's Hosp, Harvard Med Sch, 75-79. *Mem:* Soc Gynec Oncologists; Am Soc Clin Oncologists; Am Radium Soc; Soc Surg Oncologists; Am Assoc Cancer Res. *Res:* Clinical gynecologic oncology, ovarian cancer, tumor biology and genetics, gynecologic surgery. *Mailing Add:* Div Gynec Oncol Univ Calif Los Angeles Sch Med Rm 24-127 CHS Los Angeles CA 90095-1740. *Fax:* 310-206-3670

BEREMAN, ROBERT DEANE, INORGANIC CHEMISTRY, BIOINORGANIC CHEMISTRY. *Current Pos:* assoc dean phys & math sci, 82-93, PROF CHEM, NC STATE UNIV, 79-, ENVIRON SCI FAC, MAT SCI FAC, 88-, ASSOC DEAN UNDERGRAD STUDIES, DIR FIRST YR COL, 94- *Personal Data:* b Clinton, Ind, Oct 2, 43; m 65, Barbara Melbourne; c Matthew & Michael. *Educ:* Butler Univ, BS, 65; Mich State Univ, PhD(inorg chem), 69. *Prof Exp:* Res asst chem, Butler Univ, 61-65; asst inorg chem, Mich State Univ, 65-69; NSF fel phys-inorg chem, Univ Ill, Urbana, 69-70; from asst prof to assoc prof inorg chem, State Univ NY, Buffalo, 70-79. *Concurrent Pos:* Dreyfus Found fel, 75- *Mem:* Am Chem Soc; Sigma Xi. *Res:* Preparation and characterization of innorganic comlexes whih of metalloenty surface studies; new organo sulfur complexes, characterization; serv as model anters nanophase syntheses; copper enzymes. *Mailing Add:* First Yr Col NC State Univ Box 7925 Nelson Hall 5BD Raleigh NC 27695-7925

BEREN, SHELDON KUCIEL, CHEMISTRY. *Current Pos:* CHMN, BEREN CORP, 70-, PRES, BERENERGY CORP, 81- *Personal Data:* b Marietta, Ohio, Oct 7, 22; m 46, 68; c 7. *Educ:* Harvard Univ, BS, 44. *Prof Exp:* Chem engr, AEC, 44-46; dir res & prod, Marco Chem Co, Tex, 46-47; mem staff, Okmar Oil Co, 48-70. *Res:* Crude oil production. *Mailing Add:* 1635 Tennyson St Denver CO 80204

BERENBAUM, MAY ROBERTA, CHEMICAL ECOLOGY. *Current Pos:* From asst prof to assoc prof, 80-90, PROF ENTOM, UNIV ILL, URBANA-CHAMPAIGN, 90-, DEPT HEAD, 92- *Personal Data:* b Trenton, NJ, July 22, 53; m 88, Richard J Leskosky; c Hannah Antonia Leskosky. *Educ:* Yale Univ, BS, 75; Cornell Univ, PhD(ecol & syst), 80. *Honors & Awards:* George Mercer Award, Ecol Soc Am, 88; Founders Mem Award, Entom Soc Am, 94; fel Am Assoc Adv Sci. *Concurrent Pos:* Assoc ed entom, Am Midland Naturalist, 82-85; Presidental Young Investr award, NSF, 84-89; univ scholar, Univ Ill, Urbana-Champaign, 85-88; assoc ed, Evolution, 90-95; assoc ed, Chemoecology, 90-97; bd agr, Nat Res Coun, 95-98. *Mem:* Nat Acad Sci; fel AAAS; Entom Soc Am; Ecol Soc Am; Phytochem Soc Am; Int Soc Chem Ecol; fel Am Acad Arts & Sci; Sigma Xi; Soc Stud & Evolutron; Am Soc Naturalists. *Res:* Chemical aspects of insect-plant interaction; evolutionary ecology of insects; phototoxicity of plant products; host-plant resistance. *Mailing Add:* Dept Entom 320 Morrill Hall Univ Ill 505 S Goodwin Urbana IL 61801-3795. *Fax:* 217-244-3490; *E-Mail:* maybe@uiuc.edu

BERENBAUM, MORRIS BENJAMIN, POLYMER CHEMISTRY, ORGANIC CHEMISTRY. *Current Pos:* tech dir, 69-71, vpres res & develop, 71-79, dir res, Specialty Chem Div, 79-84, CHIEF SCIENTIST, CHEM SECT, ALLIED SIGNAL CORP, 84- *Personal Data:* b Chicago, Ill, Dec 19, 24; m 46; c 3. *Educ:* City Col New York, BChE, 44; Polytech Inst Brooklyn, PhD(org chem), 51. *Prof Exp:* Res engr, Stand Brands, Inc, 44, jr engr, Process Res on Food Prods, 44-45; chemist, Stauffer Chem Corp, 45-48, res chemist, 51-55; supvr res sect, Thiokol Chem Co, 55-58, mgr res dept, 58-60, dir res dept, 60-62, tech dir, 62-69. *Concurrent Pos:* Mem bd dirs, Frontier Sci & Technol Res Found. *Mem:* Am Chem Soc; Sigma Xi; Soc Plastics Eng; NY Acad Sci. *Res:* fluorocarbons; fluorochemicals; specialty chemicals; fibers and fiber finishes. *Mailing Add:* 59 Crest Dr Summit NJ 07901-4179

BERENBERG, WILLIAM, CHILDREN WITH HANDICAPS, PEDIATRICS. *Current Pos:* Assoc prof, 53-70, PROF PEDIAT, HARVARD MED SCH, 70-; ASSOC PHYSICIAN IN CHIEF, CHILDRENS HOSP BOSTON, 70- *Personal Data:* b Haverhill, Mass, Oct 29, 15; wid; c 2. *Educ:* Harvard Univ, AB, 36; Boston Univ, MD, 40. *Honors & Awards:* Jacobi Award, 49; Weinstein Award, United Cerebral Palsy, 69; Presidential Medal Merit, Ecuador, 70. *Concurrent Pos:* Consult, Mass Gen Hosp, 50-; chief med serv, Childrens Hosp Boston, 53-70; mem, Mass Cerebral Palsy Comn; chmn res coun, Nat United Cerebral Palsy. *Mem:* Soc Pediat Res; Am Pediat Soc; Am Acad Pediat; Am Acad Cerebral Palsy; Am Acad Neurol. *Res:* Handicapped children; pulmonary disease. *Mailing Add:* Childrens Hosp 300 Longwood Ave Boston MA 02115-5737

BERENBOM, MAX, BIOCHEMISTRY. *Current Pos:* RETIRED. *Personal Data:* b Saskatoon, Sask, Sept 4, 19; nat US; m 47; c 2. *Educ:* Univ Sask, BA, 41, MA, 43; Univ Toronto, PhD(biochem), 47. *Prof Exp:* Sr res fel, Nat Cancer Inst, 47-49, spec res fel, 49-50, vis scientist, 50-51; assoc oncol, Med Ctr, Univ Kans, 51-54, asst prof oncol & biochem, 54-57; dir biochem, Menorah Med Ctr, 57-89. *Mem:* Am Chem Soc; fel AAAS; Am Asn Clin Chem. *Res:* Intermediary metabolism; enzymes and tissue components in normal and abnormal states; radiation effects; carcinogenesis. *Mailing Add:* 10750 Bridlespur Terr Kansas City MO 64114-5047

BERENDES, HEINZ WERNER, PUBLIC HEALTH, EPIDEMIOLOGY. *Current Pos:* asst dir, Collab Res, Nat Inst Neurol Dis & Blindness, NIH, 60, chief, Perinatal Res Br, 60-73, chief, Contraceptive Eval Br, 74-79, dir res prog, 79-86, DIR RES PROG, NAT INST CHILD HEALTH & HUMAN DEVELOP & DIR DIV PREV RES, 90- *Personal Data:* b Dortmund, Ger, May 1, 25; US citizen; m 84; c 3. *Educ:* Univ Goettingen, Ger, MD, 49; Univ Munich, MD, 52; Johns Hopkins Univ, MHS, 72. *Prof Exp:* From instr to asst prof, dept pediat, Univ Minn Hosp, 54-60. *Concurrent Pos:* Clin prof pediat, Howard Univ, 61-; temporary adv, expert comt prevention perinatal mortality & morbidity, WHO, 69 & Sci Group Steroid Contraception & Risk Neoplasia, 77; mem, Sci Adv Group, Special Prog Res & Training Human Reproduction, WHO, 79, chmn, 79; consult, fertility & maternal health drug adv comt, Food & Drug Admin, 79-, Environ Protection Agency, 80-; sr assoc, Dept Epidemiol, Johns Hopkins Univ, 81-; bd dirs, Better Babies Proj, Inc. *Mem:* Soc Epidemiol Res; Am Col Epidemiol; Am Pub Health Asn; Int Epidemiol Soc; Soc Pediat Epidemiol. *Res:* Perinatal factors in child development including developmental disorders of infancy and childhood, epidemiology of high-risk pregnancies, and adverse medical effects of contraceptive methods currently in use. *Mailing Add:* 7020 Barkwater Ct Bethesda MD 20817

BERENDSEN, PETER BARNEY, ANATOMY, CELL BIOLOGY. *Current Pos:* instr anat, 72-73, asst prof, 73-81, ASSOC PROF ANAT, UNIV MED & DENT NJ, 81-, ASST DEAN, 90- *Personal Data:* b Los Angeles, Calif, July 14, 37; m 62, Sallyann Lawrence; c Thomas, Margaret & Raymond. *Educ:* St Marys Col, Calif, BS, 60; George Washington Univ, MS, 65, PhD(anat), 72. *Prof Exp:* Res asst hemat, Armed Forces Inst Path, 60-65; res assoc path, Univ Mich, 65-67; guest worker physiol, NIH, 70-72, res physiologist, 72. *Mem:* Micros Soc Am; Am Asn Anat; Sigma Xi; Microcirculatory Soc; Am Soc Cell Biol. *Res:* Intestinal absorption; lipid metabolism; reticuloendothelial and endothelial function; pulmonary ultrastructure. *Mailing Add:* Univ Med & Dent NJ 185 S Orange Ave Newark NJ 07103. *Fax:* 973-982-4630

BERENDZEN, RICHARD, ASTRONOMY, HISTORY OF SCIENCE. *Current Pos:* dean, Col Arts & Sci, Am Univ, Washington, DC, 74-76, provost, 76-79, pres, 80-90, PROF PHYSICS, AM UNIV, WASHINGTON, DC, 74- *Personal Data:* b Walters, Okla, Sept 6, 38; m 64, Gail Edgar; c Deborah & Natasha. *Educ:* Mass Inst Technol, BS, 61; Harvard Univ, MA, 67, PhD, 69. *Hon Degrees:* DSc, Univ Colombo; LHD, Bridgewater Col; LLD, Univ Charlestown, Kean Col NJ, Seton Hall Univ, WVa Weylayan Col. *Prof Exp:* Res scientist, Geophys Corp Am, 59-64; fel, Harvard Univ, 61-64; from lectr to prof astron, Boston Univ, 65-73, actg chmn dept, 71-72. *Concurrent Pos:* Res scientist, Astronaut Div, Ling-Temco-Vought Corp, 62-63; staff mem astron ed, Proj Physics, Harvard Univ, 65-66; mem comn teaching astron & comn hist sci of Int Astron Union; consult, Educ Coop, Natick, Mass; adv, NAm Fedn Planetarium Educators; ed, J Col Sci Teaching, Nat Sci Teachers Asn & Cosmic Search; mem Astron Surv Comt, Nat Acad Sci; astron adv bd, Ctr Hist & Philos Physics, Am Inst Physics; invited partic sem, Int Union Pure & Appl Physics, 70; arranger & chmn, Int Conf Educ & Hist Mod Astron, Am Astron Soc-NY Acad Sci; dir, Nat Sci Found prog, Case Studies Proj Develop Mod Astron; arranger & chmn, Conf Life Beyond Earth & Mind of Man, NASA, Boston, 72; consult, Off Acad Affairs, Am Coun Educ & Space Sci Bd, Nat Acad Sci, 73-74; mem energy task force, Wash Bd Trade, 74-75 & comts col sci teaching & publ of Nat Sci Teachers Asn, 74-80; consult or adv, Am Inst Physics, NASA, US State Dept, US Info Agency, Smithsonian Inst, UNESCO & US House Rep; educ & astron expert, WUSA-TV & WTOP Newsradio, Washington, DC, 84-90. *Mem:* Fel AAAS; Am Astron Soc; Hist Sci Soc; Int Astron Union; AAAS. *Res:* Astronomy education; cosmology; search for extraterrestrial intelligence; sociology of science; science education and planning; American higher education; international education; academic administration. *Mailing Add:* Physics Dept AM Univ Washington DC 20016-8058. *Fax:* 703-416-0378

BERENJI, HAMID R, FUZZY LOGIC, NEURAL NETWORKS. *Current Pos:* SR RES SCIENTIST, NASA AMES RES CTR, 86- *Personal Data:* b Kermanshah, Iran, May 26, 58. *Educ:* Iran Univ Sci & Technol, BS, 78; Univ Southern Calif, MS, 80, PhD(systs eng), 86. *Concurrent Pos:* Adj prof, Santa Clara Univ, 86-; pres & chief exec officer, Intelligent Inference Systs Corp, 93-; distinguished lectr, Asn Comput Mach, 93. *Mem:* Am Asn Artificial Intel; sr mem Inst Elec & Electronics Engrs; Asn Comput Mach. *Res:* Development of machine learning methods for applying in knowledge-based (fuzzy logic) systems; adaptive fuzzy systems; neural networks and artificial intelligence. *Mailing Add:* NASA Ames Res Ctr MS-262-2 Moffett Field CA 94035. *Fax:* 650-604-3594

BERENS, ALAN PAUL, MATHEMATICAL STATISTICS. *Current Pos:* res statistician, 69-80, SR RES STATISTICIAN, UNIV DAYTON RES INST, 80- *Personal Data:* b Cincinnati, Ohio, June 15, 34; m 57, Lydia Powers; c Alan Jr, Timothy, Rebecca, Kathleen & Daniel. *Educ:* Univ Dayton, BS, 55; Purdue Univ, MS, 57, PhD(math statist), 63. *Prof Exp:* Instr math, Purdue Univ, 58-62; head statist dept, Technol Inc, Ohio, 62-68; vpres, Beta Industs, 68-69. *Mem:* Am Statist Asn. *Res:* Application of mathematical statistics and probability to physical science research; NDI reliability, structural integrity. *Mailing Add:* 4940 James Hill Rd Kettering OH 45429. *E-Mail:* berensap@udri.udayton.edu

BERENS, ALAN ROBERT, POLYVINYL CHLORIDE, DIFFUSION IN POLYMERS. *Current Pos:* RETIRED. *Personal Data:* b Oak Park, Ill, Sept 28, 25; m 49; c 2. *Educ:* Harvard Univ, AB, 47; Case Western Reserve Univ, MS, 49, PhD(chem), 51. *Prof Exp:* Res chemist, B F Goodrich Co, 50-60, from res assoc to sr res assoc, 60-71, res fel, 71-78, sr res fel polymerization, 78-87, consult, 88-92. *Mem:* Am Chem Soc; Am Inst Chem Engrs; fel Am Inst Chemists. *Res:* Vinyl polymerization; polyvinyl chloride structure, rheology, stability and morphology; diffusion of small molecules in polymers and polymer relaxations; appoximately fifty scientific publications. *Mailing Add:* RD 2 Box 3510 Middlebury VT 05753-8904

BERENS, MICHAEL E, BRAIN TUMOR BIOLOGY. *Current Pos:* STAFF SCIENTIST BIOL, BARROW NEUROL INST, 90- *Personal Data:* b Rochester, Minn, June 25, 53. *Educ:* Ariz State Univ, BS, 76, PhD(biol), 82. *Prof Exp:* Asst prof biol, Univ Calif, San Diego, 84-90. *Mem:* Am Asn Cancer Res; Am Soc Cell Biol; AAAS. *Mailing Add:* Dept Neurol & Oncol Barrow Neurol Inst 350 W Thomas Rd Phoenix AZ 85013-4496

BERENS, RANDOLPH LEE, CELL BIOLOGY, PROTOZOOLOGY. *Current Pos:* ASST PROF PHYSIOL, SCH MED, ST LOUIS UNIV, 78-; ASST PROF MED & MICROBIOL, UNIV COLO HEALTH SCI CTR. *Personal Data:* b Los Angeles, Calif, June 13, 43; m 68; c 1. *Educ:* Univ Calif, Irvine, BS, 67, PhD(cell biol), 75. *Prof Exp:* Res asst cell biol, Univ Calif, Irvine, 71-75; fel, Sch Med, Washington Univ, 75-78 *Concurrent Pos:* Instr physiol, Cerritos Col, 74-75; prin investr grants, WHO, 79-82, NIH, 81- *Mem:* Am Soc Protozoologists; Am Soc Microbiologists; AAAS; NY Acad Sci; Am Soc Parasitologists. *Res:* Various intermediate metabolic pathways in pathogenic protozoans with the primary goal of finding metabolic differences between these organisms and their mammalian hosts. *Mailing Add:* Dept Infectious Dis Univ Colo Health Sci Ctr Box B168 4200 E Ninth Ave Denver CO 80262-0001

BERENSON, GERALD SANDERS, INTERNAL MEDICINE, CARDIOLOGY. *Current Pos:* PROF MED & PEDIAT, TULANE MED CTR, 92- *Personal Data:* b Bogalusa, La, Sept 19, 22; m 51, Joan Seidenbach; c Leslie, Ann, Robert & Laurie. *Educ:* Tulane Univ, BS, 43, MD, 45. *Honors & Awards:* Searle Distinguished Award for Res on Hypertension in Blacks; Lydia J Roberts Mem Lectureship. *Prof Exp:* Asst med, Sch Med, Tulane Univ, 48-49, instr, 49-52; USPHS fel pediat, Univ Chicago, 52-54; from asst prof to prof, Sch Med, La State Univ Med Ctr, New Orleans, 54-91, dir, Specialized Ctr Res Arteriosclerosis, 72- 87, head sect cardiol, 75. *Concurrent Pos:* Dir Nat Res & Demonstration Ctr Arteriosclerosis, NIH, Nat Heart, Lung & Blood Inst, 85-87, Tulane Nat Ctr Cardiovasc Health, 92-; Boyd prof,

La State Univ. *Mem:* Soc Exp Biochem & Med Biol; Am Soc Bio Chem & Molecular Biol; fel Am Col Physicians; fel Am Col Cardiol. *Res:* Cardiology; atherosclerosis; biochemistry of connective tissues; cardio-vascular connective tissue in arteriosclerosis; epidemiology of cardio-vascular disease; studying a total community of children, greater than five thousand, for the natural history of cardio-vascular disease and essential hypertension (Bogalusa Heart Study); cardio-vascular health education and health promotion for children from kindergarten through sixth grade (Heart Smart program). *Mailing Add:* Cardiovasc Health Ctr Tulane Univ 1501 Canal St New Orleans LA 70112. *Fax:* 504-585-7194

BERENSON, JAMES R, HEMATOLOGY & ONCOLOGY, CANCER GENETICS. *Current Pos:* fel hemat & oncol, Univ Calif, Los Angeles, 80-83, adj prof med, 82-83, from asst prof to assoc prof, WLos Angeles Vet Admin Med Ctr, 83-92, CHIEF MED ONCOL & ASSOC PROF MED, W LOS ANGELES VET ADMIN MED CTR, UNIV CALIF, 92- *Personal Data:* b Portland, Ore, Aug 13, 52; m, Debra Marsha Arnovitz; c Shira & Ariana. *Educ:* Stanford Univ, BS, 73; Univ Calif, San Diego, MD, 77. *Prof Exp:* Intern internal med, Med Ctr, Univ Utah, 77-80. *Concurrent Pos:* March of Dimes spec fel, 82; Damon Runyon-Walter Winchell fel, 82-84; Ralph Goldman Res Award, 89-91. *Mem:* Am Soc Clin Oncol; Am Asn Cancer Res; Am Soc Hemat. *Res:* Lymphoid malignancies; multiple myeloma; bone metastases. *Mailing Add:* 11301 Wilshire Blvd 111H Los Angeles CA 90073. *Fax:* 310-268-4908; *E-Mail:* berenson.james@west_la.va.gov

BERENSON, MALCOLM MARK, GASTROENTEROLOGY, HEPATOLOGY. *Current Pos:* ASSOC PROF GASTROENTEROL, SCH MED, UNIV UTAH, 71- *Educ:* Univ Pittsburgh, MD, 63. *Res:* Nutrition. *Mailing Add:* Sch Med Univ Utah Med Ctr Salt Lake City UT 84132-0001

BERENT, STANLEY, CLINICAL PSYCHOLOGY, NEUROPSYCHOLOGY. *Current Pos:* assoc prof & dir, Neuropsychol Div, 79-88, PROF, UNIV MICH, 88-, CHIEF, PSYCHOL DIV & DIR NEUROPSYCHOL, 93-, DIR, NEUROBEHAV TOXICOL PROG, 97- *Personal Data:* b Norfolk, Va, Mar 10, 41; m 74, Joy Mckeever; c V Melissa, Alison & Rachel. *Educ:* Old Dom Univ, BS, 66; Va Commonwealth Univ, MS, 68; Rutgers Univ, PhD(clin psychol), 72; Am Bd Prof Psychol, dipl. *Prof Exp:* Instr psychol, Va Commonwealth Univ, 67-68; res asst psychiat, Rutgers Med Sch, 68-71; intern psychol, NIHM, St Elizabeths Hosp, 71-72; asst prof psychiat, Med Sch, Univ Va, 72-77, asst prof psychol, 75-77, assoc prof psychiat & psychol, 77-79; chief psychol, Vet Admin Med Ctr, Ann Arbor, 79-85. *Concurrent Pos:* Consult, NIMH, St Elizabeths Hosp, 72-75 & Univ Va, 79-81, Vet Admin, NIH & var others; vis prof, Univ London, 88-89. *Mem:* Fel Am Psychol Asn; Soc Neurosci; Int Soc Neuropsychol; Am Acad Neurol; Am Epilepsy Soc; AAAS; Sigma Xi. *Res:* Behavioral and electrophysiological studies of epilepsy and other neurological disorders, lateralization and other functional organization of brain in normal and pathological conditions and implications of disordered cognition for psycho-social functioning and behavior; pet and other imaging techniques for the study of brain-behavior relationships; effects of environmental toxins on the central nervous system and behavior; neurobehavioral toxicology. *Mailing Add:* Med Ctr Univ Mich Box 0840 480 Med Inn Ann Arbor MI 48109-0840. *Fax:* 313-936-9262

BERERA, GEETHA POONACHA, materials research, electro-optics, for more information see previous edition

BERES, JOHN JOSEPH, PHYSICAL POLYMER CHEMISTRY. *Current Pos:* sr res chemist, Gen Corp, 77, group leader polymer characterization, 80, sect head polymer structure, 81, mgr anal res & servs, 88, POLYMER CHARACTERIZATION, GEN CORP, 77- *Personal Data:* b Beaver Falls, Pa, May 1, 47; m 75. *Educ:* Geneva Col, BS, 69; Carnegie-Mellon Univ, MS, 73, PhD(phys chem), 75. *Prof Exp:* Fel polymers, Univ Mass, 75-77. *Mem:* Am Crystallog Asn; Sigma Xi; Am Chem Soc; Soc Appl Spectroscopy. *Res:* X-ray structural investigations of polymers; structure-property relationships in polymers, especially polyurethanes and polyphosphazenes; solution characterization of elastomers, spectroscopy, thermal analysis, lims, microscopy. *Mailing Add:* 6014 Echodell NW North Canton OH 44720-7218

BERES, WILLIAM PHILIP, NUCLEAR PHYSICS. *Current Pos:* assoc prof, 69-75, PROF PHYSICS, WAYNE STATE UNIV, 75- *Personal Data:* b Peabody, Mass, Jan 8, 36; m 66; c 3. *Educ:* Mass Inst Technol, BS, 59, PhD(physics), 64. *Prof Exp:* Asst physics, Mass Inst Technol, 60-64; res physicist, GCA Corp, 64; res assoc physics, Univ Md, 64-66; asst prof, Duke Univ, 66-69. *Concurrent Pos:* Fulbright lectr sci educ, Hebrew Univ, Jerusalem, 77-78. *Mem:* Am Phys Soc; Am Asn Physics Teachers. *Res:* Theory of nuclear structure and reactions; microscopic nuclear calculations; quasiparticles; local and non-local potentials; photonuclear reactions; heavy ion reactions; nuclear processes in stars. *Mailing Add:* Dept Physics Wayne State Univ Detroit MI 48202

BERESFORD, WILLIAM ANTHONY, HISTOLOGY, NEUROANATOMY. *Current Pos:* from asst prof to assoc prof, 68-76, PROF ANAT, WVA UNIV, 76- *Personal Data:* b London, Eng, Aug 13, 36; m 57; c 3. *Educ:* Oxford Univ, BA, 59, DPhil (histol), 64. *Prof Exp:* Lectr histol, Univ Liverpool, 63-65; asst prof anat, Am Univ Beirut, 65-68. *Mem:* Bone & Tooth Soc; Anat Soc Gt Brit & Ireland; Ger Anat Soc; Int Soc Differentiation; Am Soc Zoologists. *Res:* Metaplasia; ectopic bone and cartilage; bone induction; reptilian liver histology. *Mailing Add:* Dept Anat WVa Univ Sch Med Morgantown WV 26506-0002

BERESNIEWICZ, ALEKSANDER, PHYSICAL CHEMISTRY. *Current Pos:* res chemist, 54-68, RES ASSOC, E I DU PONT DE NEMOURS & CO, INC, 68-, RES FEL, 78- *Personal Data:* b Lithuania, Apr 5, 27; nat US; m 54, Irene Corcoran; c John M, Edward C, Alexander, Richard L & Mark D. *Educ:* Marquette Univ, BS, 51; Univ Ill, PhD(chem), 54. *Prof Exp:* Asst, Univ Ill, 51-53. *Mem:* Am Chem Soc; Sigma Xi; NY Acad Sci. *Res:* Physical chemistry of high polymers; relation between the structure of polymers and their physical properties; development of different fluoropolymers. *Mailing Add:* 2501 Elmdale Lane Wilmington DE 19810-3418

BERESTON, EUGENE SYDNEY, DERMATOLOGY, MYCOLOGY. *Current Pos:* RETIRED. *Personal Data:* b Baltimore, Md, Feb 21, 14; m 42, 80, Betty Gundersheimer; c Linda, David & Michael. *Educ:* Johns Hopkins Univ, AB, 33; Univ Md, MD, 37; Univ Pa, MSc, 45, DSc, 55; Am Bd Dermat, dipl. *Prof Exp:* Intern, Conemaugh Valley Mem Hosp, Johnstown, Pa, 37-38 & Mercy Hosp, Baltimore, 38-39, grad student, Dermat Univ Pa, 39-40; asst dermat, Skin & Cancer Unit, NY Postgrad Hosp, Columbia Univ, 40-41; resident, Montefiore Hosp, NY, 40-41; asst dermatologist, Outpatient Dept, Univ Hosp, 46-50, Univ Md, Baltimore City, instr, Sch Med, 46-47, assoc, 47-52, from asst prof to assoc prof dermat, 52-95, dermatologist, Univ Hosp, 50-95. *Concurrent Pos:* Asst, Sch Med, Johns Hopkins Univ, 46-50, instr, 50-60, chief, Fungus Lab, Hosp, 46-51, dermatologist, 50-60; attend dermatologist, Sinai Hosp, 47-80, consult staff, 80-; dermatologist, Mercy Hosp, 50-67, chief dermatologist, 67-; asst investr, US Dept Army Fungus Res Proj, 51-57; consult dermatologist, US Vet Admin Hosp, Baltimore & Ft Howard, 46-77 & Spring Grove State Hosp, 47-82; mem dermat staff, US Vet Admin Hosp, Washington, DC, 77-83. *Mem:* Fel AMA; fel Am Col Physicians; Am Acad Dermat; fel Royal Soc Health; Royal Soc Med Affil. *Res:* Aspergillus infection of nails; nutritional requirements of microsporum group of fungi and Trichophyton Tonsurans; fluorescent compound in fungus infected hairs; fungal antibiotics. *Mailing Add:* 7 Slade Ave Baltimore MD 21208

BERETS, DONALD JOSEPH, CATALYSIS, HETEROGENEOUS. *Current Pos:* PRES, CHEMISTS GROUP, INC, STAMFORD, CONN, 86- *Personal Data:* b New York, NY, July 6, 26; m 56, Eileen Tolkowsky; c James & Susan (Connell). *Educ:* Harvard Univ, AB, 46, MA, 47, PhD(chem), 49. *Prof Exp:* Res chemist, Am Cyanamid Co, 49-54, group leader, 54-60, sect mgr, Energy Conversion Res, 60-67, mgr, Mat Sci, 67-73, mgr catalyst res, Chem Res Div, 73-86. *Concurrent Pos:* Assoc, Mass Inst Technol, 49. *Mem:* Am Chem Soc; AAAS. *Res:* New product development; catalysis; surface chemistry; pigments; solid state physics and chemistry. *Mailing Add:* 47 E Ridge Rd Stamford CT 06903-4337. *Fax:* 203-329-2377

BEREZIN, ALEXANDER A, THEORETICAL SOLID STATE PHYSICS, ELECTROSTATICS. *Current Pos:* assoc prof eng physics, 80-86, PROF ENG PHYSICS, MCMASTER UNIV, HAMILTON, ONT, 96- *Personal Data:* b Sverdlovsk, USSR, Apr 26, 44; Can citizen; m 67, Irene Semenova; c Maria & Peter. *Educ:* Leningrad State Univ, MSc, 66, PhD(theor physics), 70. *Prof Exp:* Assoc prof physics, Higher Naval Eng Col, Leningrad, 74-77; res assoc solid state physics, Univ Alta, Edmonton, 78-80. *Concurrent Pos:* Vis prof, Tokyo Denki Univ, Japan, 87. *Mem:* Am Phys Soc; Can Asn Physicists. *Res:* Electronic processes in semiconductors and microelectronic devices; effects of stable isotopes; non-linear physics and chaos; plasma physics and electronics; philosophical problems of physics; social aspects of science and engineering. *Mailing Add:* Dept Eng Physics McMaster Univ Hamilton ON L8S 4L7 Can. *E-Mail:* berezin@mcmaster.ca

BEREZNEY, RONALD, CELL BIOLOGY, BIOCHEMISTRY. *Current Pos:* from asst prof to assoc prof, 75-85, PROF CELL & MOLECULAR BIOL, STATE UNIV NY BUFFALO, 86- *Personal Data:* b New York, NY, Dec 25, 43; c 2. *Educ:* Fairleigh Dickinson Univ, BS, 66; Purdue Univ, PhD(membrane biochem), 71. *Prof Exp:* Res asst molecular biol, Inst Cancer Res, Col Physician & Surgeons, Columbia Univ, 65-66; fel cell biol, Univ Freiburg, Ger, 71-72; res assoc pharmacol, Sch Med, Johns Hopkins Univ, 72-75. *Mem:* Am Soc Cell Biol; Am Chem Soc; AAAS; Am Soc Biochem & Molecular Biol. *Res:* Molecular biology of the eucaryotic nucleus; nuclear matrix organization and function in normal and cancer cells; DNA replication; molecular properties and topography of nuclear proteins. *Mailing Add:* Dept Biol Sci State Univ NY PO Box 601300 Buffalo NY 14260-1300

BERG, ALFRED OREN, CLINICAL PRACTICE GUIDELINES, CLINICAL EPIDEMIOLOGY. *Current Pos:* PROF & ASSOC CHAIR, UNIV WASH, 79- *Personal Data:* b Wichita, Kans, July 3, 49. *Educ:* Tabor Col, BA, 70; Wash Univ, MD, 74; Univ Wash, MPH, 79. *Concurrent Pos:* Assoc ed, J Am Bd Family Pract, 91- *Mem:* Inst Med-Nat Acad Sci; Am Col Prev Med; Am Acad Family Physicians; Soc Teachers Family Med. *Res:* Evidence based medical practice; developing and implementing clinical practice guidelines. *Mailing Add:* Box 356390 Seattle WA 98195

BERG, BENJAMIN NATHAN, NUTRITION. *Current Pos:* RETIRED. *Personal Data:* b New York City, NY, Dec 8, 97; m 24; c 1. *Educ:* Columbia Univ, MD, 20. *Prof Exp:* Dept path, Columbia Presby Hosp, NY. *Mem:* Am Soc Exp Path; Soc Exp Biol & Med; Harvey Soc; Teratology Soc; AAAS. *Res:* Relation of nutrition to reproduction and aging; endocrine factors in reproduction; teratology; nephrosis; muscular dystrophy; spontaneous diseases of lab animals; physiology of stomach, gall bladder, liver and pancreas; mechanisms of fetal resorptions and malformations. *Mailing Add:* 40 E 88th St New York NY 10128-1176

BERG, CARL JOHN, JR, MARINE BIOLOGY, AQUACULTURE & FISHERIES MANAGEMENT. *Current Pos:* PVT CONSULT, 90- *Personal Data:* b Bridgeport, Conn, June 6, 44; m 85; c 2. *Educ:* Univ Conn, BA, 66; Univ Pac, MS, 68; Univ Hawaii, PhD(zool), 71. *Prof Exp:* Asst prof biol, City Univ New York, 71-76; res assoc mollusks, Harvard Univ, 76-80; assoc scientist marine biol, Marine Biol Lab, 79-86; biol scientist, Fla Marine Res Inst, 86-90. *Concurrent Pos:* Adj asst prof, Pace Univ & Univ Southern Calif, 72; assoc, Am Mus Natural Hist, 72-78; investr & instr, Marine Biol Lab, 74-79; res assoc, Columbia Univ, 78-81; intermittent fac, US Nat Marine Fisheries Serv, 80-82. *Mem:* Sigma Xi; Explorers Club; Ecol Soc Am; AAAS; World Aquacult Soc. *Res:* Aquaculture development and fisheries management; marine invertebrates; larval dispersion around islands. *Mailing Add:* PO Box 681 Kilauea HI 96754

BERG, CLAIRE M, BACTERIAL GENETICS, DNA SEQUENCING STRATEGIES. *Current Pos:* from asst prof to assoc prof, 68-82, PROF BIOL, UNIV CONN, 82- *Personal Data:* b Mt Vernon, NY, Apr 24, 37. *Educ:* Cornell Univ, BS, 59; Univ Chicago, MS, 62; Columbia Univ, PhD(genetics), 66. *Prof Exp:* NATO fel, Med Res Coun-Microbiol Gen Res Unit, Hammersmith Hosp, London, Eng, 66-67; Jane Coffin Childs fel, Molecular Biol Lab, Univ Geneva, Switz, 67-68. *Mem:* Genetics Soc Am; Am Soc Microbiol; Fedn Am Scientists; AAAS; Am Women Sci. *Res:* Uses of transposable elements in genetic analysis and DNA sequencing; molecular genetics. *Mailing Add:* U-131 Molecular Cell Biol Dept Univ Conn 354 Mansfield Rd Storrs CT 06269-0001. *Fax:* 860-486-1936; *E-Mail:* berg@uconnvm.uconn.edu

BERG, CLYDE C, PLANT BREEDING, PLANT GENETICS. *Current Pos:* res geneticist, 66-79, RES AGRONOMIST, AGR RES SERV, USDA, 79- *Personal Data:* b Meriden, Kans, Nov 2, 36; m 58, Rebecca M Hoskinson; c Judy E (West), Karen L (Duncan) & Larry K. *Educ:* Kans State Univ, BS, 58; Okla State Univ, MS, 61; Wash State Univ, PhD(genetics), 65. *Prof Exp:* Asst prof agron & genetics & asst agronomist, Wash State Univ, 65-66. *Mem:* Am Genetic Asn; Am Forage & Grassland Coun; Crop Sci Soc Am; Genetics Soc Can; Am Soc Agron. *Res:* Genetics, cytogenetics and breeding Festuca arundinacea, Festuca pratnesis, Lolium perenne, Lolium multiforum, Dactylis glomerata, Bromus inermis, Phleum pratense (cool season perennial forage grasses) for improved forage quality and resistance to diseases. *Mailing Add:* 272 Bradley Ave State College PA 16801-6318

BERG, DANA B, SCIENCE WRITING. *Current Pos:* RETIRED. *Personal Data:* b Chicago, Ill, July 8, 21; m 52; c 1. *Educ:* Ill Inst Technol, BS, 43. *Prof Exp:* Res & develop engr, Linde Air Prods Lab, NY, 43-48; from asst ed to ed, Putman Pub Co, 48-66, chmn ed bd, 66-67, staff consult, 67-68; sr tech ed, Argonne Nat Lab, 68-85. *Res:* Technical writing; editing; staff administration. *Mailing Add:* 1629 77th Ave Elmwood Park IL 60707

BERG, DANIEL, SCIENCE POLICY, TECHNICAL MANAGEMENT. *Current Pos:* vpres acad affairs & provost, Rensselaer Polytech Inst, 83-84, actg pres, 84-85, pres, 85-87, INST PROF SCI & TECHNOL, RENSSELAER POLYTECH INST, 83- *Personal Data:* b New York, NY, June 1, 29; m 56; c 3. *Educ:* City Col New York, BS, 50; Yale Univ, MS, 51, PhD(phys chem), 53. *Honors & Awards:* Belden Prize; Wilbur Cross Medal; Townsend Harris Medal. *Prof Exp:* Res phys chemist, Insulation Dept, Westinghouse Res Labs, 53-60, mgr, Phys & Inorg Chem Sect, 60-65, mgr inorg mat sci & technol res & develop, 65-67, mgr insulation & chem technol, 67-69, dir energy systs res, 69-76; tech dir uranium resources, Westinghouse Elec, 76-77; prof sci & technol & dean, Col Sci, Carnegie-Mellon Univ, 77-81, provost, 81-83. *Concurrent Pos:* Mem, Conf Elec Insulation, Nat Acad Sci-Nat Res Coun, 66, chmn, Conf Elec Insulation & Dielectric Phenomena; mem bd dirs, Duquesne Light, Hy-tech, Perfect-A-Tec, Inc; mem bd trustees, Argonne Univ Assoc, 78-; mem mfg bd, Dielectrics & Dielectric Phenomena, Nat Res Coun, Nat Acad Sci; mem, Rev Comt, Nat Bur Stand Exp Technol Incentives Prog; chmn, Educ Adv Bd, Nat Acad Eng. *Mem:* Nat Acad Eng; Am Chem Soc; fel Inst Elec & Electronics Engrs; fel Am Inst Chemists; fel AAAS; Am Phys Soc; Technol & Serv Soc. *Res:* Dielectrics; electrical breakdown; energy conversion. *Mailing Add:* Rensselaer Polytech Inst 5015 CII 110 Eighth St Troy NY 12180. *E-Mail:* bergd@rpi.edu

BERG, EDUARD, GEOPHYSICS, INVERSE THEORY. *Current Pos:* GEOPHYSICIST, HAWAII INST GEOPHYS, 72- *Personal Data:* b Trier, Ger, Nov 9, 28; m 55, Francoise Lyssens. *Educ:* Univ Saarlandes, dipl phys, 53, Dr rer nat(physics), 55. *Honors & Awards:* Harry Wood Oscar Award, Carnegie Inst Wash, 63. *Prof Exp:* Mem, Inst Sci Res Cent Africa, Congo, 55-63; from assoc prof to prof geophys, Univ Alaska, 63-72, dir seismol prog, 63-72. *Concurrent Pos:* Res mem fac, Univ Bonn, 57 & Univ Calif, Berkeley, 61; seismol consult, Mining Union Upper Katanga, 60-61; head seismic & volcanic depts & time serv, Inst Sci Res Cent Africa, 59-63; vis prof, Hawaii Inst Geophys, 71-72; chmn, Dept Geol & Geophys, Univ Hawaii, 81-84. *Mem:* Seismol Soc Am; Am Geophys Union; Soc Explor Geophysicists. *Res:* Seismology; geodesy; volcanology; inverse theory. *Mailing Add:* Hawaii Inst Geophys Univ Hawaii Manoa Honolulu HI 96822-2270

BERG, EUGENE WALTER, ANALYTICAL CHEMISTRY. *Current Pos:* RETIRED. *Personal Data:* b Dade City, Fla, Nov 10, 26; m 81, Thelma Pampel; c Robert E, Lisa B (Granzin) & John G (deceased). *Educ:* Miss Col, BS, 49; Univ Tex, PhD(chem), 52. *Prof Exp:* From asst prof to prof chem, La State Univ, 52-83, chmn dept, 73-76. *Mem:* Am Chem Soc; assoc Int Union Pure & Appl Chem. *Res:* Ion exchange; chromatography; separation techniques; solvent extraction; beta-dikotane chelates. *Mailing Add:* 425 Nelson Dr La State Univ Baton Rouge LA 70808

BERG, GEORGE G, TOXICOLOGY, CYTOCHEMISTRY. *Current Pos:* lectr gen biol & embryol, Univ Sch, 55-63, instr pharmacol, 56-64, asst prof, 60-64, assoc prof radiation biol biophys, 64-88, EMER PROF ENVIRON MED, SCH MED, UNIV ROCHESTER, 88- *Personal Data:* b Warsaw, Poland, May 27, 19; nat US; m 91, Rae Bolgla; c Peggy, Carl & Lora B (Chaibi). *Educ:* Temple Univ, BA, 42; Columbia Univ, MS, 47, PhD(zool), 54. *Honors & Awards:* Sol Feinstone Environ Award, 87. *Prof Exp:* Res assoc, Sch Med, Georgetown Univ, 49-51; res collabr, Dept Biol, Brookhaven Nat Lab, 54-55. *Concurrent Pos:* Vis prof environ sci, Zhejiang Univ, China, 89. *Mem:* Fedn Am Sci; Sigma Xi; AAAS; Soc Toxicol; Soc Risk Anal; NY Acad Sci. *Res:* Histochemical localization of polyphosphate hydrolases by chelate removal; inhibitor partition equations for toxicokinetics of mercuric and methylmercuric salts; environmental toxicity. *Mailing Add:* 1242 Wildcliff Pkwy Atlanta GA 30329. *Fax:* 404-872-4103; *E-Mail:* george_berg@compuserve.com

BERG, GERALD, VIROLOGY, MICROBIOLOGY. *Current Pos:* res prof, 83-91, EMER RES PROF, DEPT CIVIL & ENVIRON ENG, UNIV CINCINNATI, 91- *Personal Data:* b New York, NY, Nov 3, 28; m 55; c 3. *Educ:* Syracuse Univ, AB, 51, MS, 52, PhD(bact), 55. *Prof Exp:* Asst, Upstate Med Ctr, State Univ NY, 53-54; res fel virol, Children's Hosp Res Found, Cincinnati, Ohio, 55; researcher, USPHS, 55-64, chief virus dis studies, 64-67, chief virol, Fed Water Qual Admin, 67-74; chief biol methods br, Environ Monitoring & Support Lab, US Environ Protection Agency, 74-81, tech adv, Dir Off, 81-83. *Concurrent Pos:* Adj prof, Univ Cincinnati, 69-83. *Mem:* Fel Am Acad Microbiol; Am Soc Microbiol; Am Pub Health Asn; Am Water Works Asn. *Res:* Kinetic virucidal and bactericidal studies in disinfection; molecular basis, indicators of fecal pollution, methods for detecting viruses in drinking, renovated, waste and other waters; viruses in sludges and in solids associated with various waters; virus multiplication, isolation and identification; epidemiology of virus dissemination. *Mailing Add:* Dept Civil & Environ Eng Mail Stop 0071 Univ Cincinnati Cincinnati OH 45221-0071

BERG, GUNNAR JOHANNES, ELECTRICAL ENGINEERING. *Current Pos:* from asst prof to assoc prof, 64-74, prof, 74-88, EMER PROF ELEC ENG, UNIV CALGARY, 88- *Personal Data:* b Ullsfjord, Norway, Mar 1, 30; m 62, Norma H Cann; c 4. *Educ:* Tech Univ Norway, Siving, 57; Univ BC, MASc, 60. *Prof Exp:* Instr elec eng, Tech Univ Norway, 57-58; res asst, Univ BC, 58-59, instr, 59-60, 62-64; staff engr, BC Energy Bd, 60-64. *Concurrent Pos:* Proj mgr, Univ Calgary, 89-97. *Mem:* Inst Elec & Electronics Engrs; Can Elec Asn. *Res:* Induction motor modeling and performance analysis; power system load behavior and representation; power system planning. *Mailing Add:* Dept Elec Eng Univ Calgary Calgary AB T2N 1N4 Can. *Fax:* 403-289-0717

BERG, HENRY CLAY, GEOLOGY. *Current Pos:* CONSULT GEOLOGIST, 84- *Personal Data:* b Brooklyn, NY, Apr 23, 29; m 82, Judith Graham; c Jadine. *Educ:* Brooklyn Col, BA, 51; Harvard Univ, AM, 56. *Prof Exp:* Geologist US Geol Surv, 56-84, chief, Menlo Tech Report Unit, 65-67, mgr, Alaskan Mineral Resources Assessment Prog, 74-80, geologist in charge, Alaskan Geol Br, 80-82. *Mem:* Fel Geol Soc Am. *Res:* Areal geology tectonics and mineral resources of southeastern Alaska. *Mailing Add:* 115 Malvern Ave Fullerton CA 92832

BERG, HOWARD CURTIS, BIOPHYSICS. *Current Pos:* PROF BIOL, HARVARD UNIV, 86- *Personal Data:* b Iowa City, Iowa, Mar 16, 34; m 64, Mary E Guyer; c Henry G, Alexander H & Elena C. *Educ:* Calif Inst Technol, BS, 56; Harvard Univ, AM, 60, PhD(chem physics), 64. *Honors & Awards:* Biol Physics Prize, Am Phys Soc, 84. *Prof Exp:* Jr fel, Harvard Univ, 63-66, from asst prof biol to assoc prof biochem, 66-70, chmn, Bd Tutors Biochem Sci, 66-70; assoc prof to prof molecullar, cellular & develop biol, Univ Colo, Boulder, 74-79, chmn dept, 76-77; prof biol, Calif Inst Technol, 79-86. *Concurrent Pos:* Mem, Rowland Inst Sci, 86- *Mem:* Nat Acad Sci; fel AAAS; fel Am Phys Soc; Am Soc Biol Chemists; fel Am Acad Microbiol; Am Acad Arts & Sci. *Res:* Chemical structure of cell membranes; motility and chemotaxis of bacteria. *Mailing Add:* Molecular & Cellular Biol Harvard Univ 16 Divinity Ave Cambridge MA 02138. *Fax:* 617-496-1114; *E-Mail:* hberg@biosun.harvard.edu

BERG, HOWARD MARTIN, MATERIALS SCIENCE. *Current Pos:* STAFF SCIENTIST SEMICONDUCTOR GROUP, MOTOROLA, INC, 71- *Personal Data:* b Chicago, Ill, Aug 31, 42; m; c 3. *Educ:* Univ Ill, BS, 65; Northwestern Univ, PhD(mat sci), 71. *Prof Exp:* Metallurgist, Pratt & Whitney Aircraft, 65-67. *Mem:* Am Soc Metals; Inst Elec & Electronics Engrs; Int Soc Hybrid Microelectronics. *Res:* Assembly and packaging of semiconductor devices; x-ray diffraction; field ion microscopy. *Mailing Add:* Motorola Inc 2100 E Elliot Rd Tempe AZ 85284

BERG, IRA DAVID, MATHEMATICS. *Current Pos:* assoc prof, 71-74, PROF MATH, UNIV ILL, URBANA, 74- *Personal Data:* b New York, NY, Nov 27, 31; m 62; c 3. *Educ:* Univ Pa, BS, 53; Lehigh Univ, MS, 59, PhD(math), 62. *Prof Exp:* Lectr math, Yale Univ, 62-64; from asst prof to assoc prof, Univ Ill, Urbana, 64-70; assoc prof, Queen's Univ, Ont, 70-71. *Mem:* Am Math Soc; Sigma Xi. *Res:* Functional and harmonic analysis; differential geometry. *Mailing Add:* 401 Eliot Dr Urbana IL 61801-6725

BERG, J(OHN) ROBERT, GEOLOGY, CHEMISTRY. *Current Pos:* from assoc prof to prof geol, Wichita State Univ, 46-81, head dept, 53-63, dean Univ col, 62-69, chmn dept, 76-81, EMER PROF GEOL, WICHITA STATE UNIV, 81- *Personal Data:* b Chicago, Ill, Feb 18, 15; m 40; c 1. *Educ:* Augustana Col, AB, 38; Univ Iowa, MS, 40, PhD(geol), 42. *Prof Exp:* Asst mineral, petrol & econ geol, Univ Iowa, 39-42; supvr mil explosives, E I Du Pont de Nemours & Co, Inc, 42-44; sub-surface geologist, Shell Oil Co, Kans, 44-46. *Concurrent Pos:* Mem bd dirs & secy-treas, Petrol Resources Fund, Inc, 69-; ed, Trans, Kans Acad Sci, 85- *Mem:* Am Chem Soc; Geol Soc Am; Am Asn Petrol Geologists; Nat Asn Geol Teachers (pres, 56-58). *Res:* Petrology of alkaline igneous rocks; pre-Cambrian stratigraphy and petrology; petroleum exploratory statistics; geological education. *Mailing Add:* Dept Geol Wichita State Univ Wichita KS 67260-0001

BERG, JAMES IRVING, GLASS SCIENCE, FOUNDATION OF PHYSICS. *Current Pos:* CONSULT, 94- *Personal Data:* b Minneapolis, Minn, May 5, 40; m 66; c 2. *Educ:* Univ Minn, BS, 62; Ohio State Univ, PhD(physics), 69. *Prof Exp:* Prin res scientist physics, Honeywell Corp Res Ctr, 69-71; sr physicist, Graphics Res & Develop Ctr, Addressograph Multigraph Corp, 72-74; res assoc mat sci, Case Western Res Univ, 74-76; sr scientist, Owens-Corning Fiberglas Corp, 76-81, res assoc, Tech Ctr, 81-85. *Mem:* Am Phys Soc; Am Ceramic Soc; Sigma Xi. *Res:* Research to revise the foundations of physics to eliminate dilemmas created a casual model of the universe. *Mailing Add:* 11185 Anerson Lakes Pkwy Apt 226 Eden Prairie MN 55344-7400

BERG, JEFFREY HOWARD, ORGANIC CHEMISTRY. *Current Pos:* SR GROUP LEADER, ORTHO PHARMACEUT CORP, 78- *Personal Data:* b New York, NY, Feb 6, 43; m 66; c 2. *Educ:* Yeshiva Col, BA, 64; NY Univ, PhD(org chem), 69, MBA, 73. *Prof Exp:* Teaching asst chem, NY Univ, 64-69; sr chemist, Gen Foods Corp, 69-73; qual control supvr & chief chemist, I Rokeach & Sons, Inc, 73-74; sr group leader, Johnson & Johnson, 74-78. *Mem:* Am Chem Soc; Inst Food Technologists; Am Asn Med Instrumentation. *Res:* Chlorinated anthraquinodimethanes and related compounds; crowded anthracenes; food chemistry with emphasis on flavors and carbohydrates; orthopaedic and textile new product development; medical electrodes; contraceptive devices. *Mailing Add:* Three Fairhill Rd Edison NJ 08817-2927

BERG, JEREMY M, BIOPHYSICS. *Current Pos:* PROF & DIR, DEPT BIOPHYS, JOHNS HOPKINS UNIV. *Honors & Awards:* Pure Chem Award, Am Chem Soc, 93. *Res:* Chemistry. *Mailing Add:* Dept Biophys Johns Hopkins Univ WBSB 713A 725 N Wolfe St Baltimore MD 21205

BERG, JOHN CALVIN, CHEMICAL ENGINEERING. *Current Pos:* From asst prof to assoc prof, 64-73, PROF CHEM ENG, UNIV WASH, 73- *Personal Data:* b Minneapolis, Minn, Nov 18, 37. *Educ:* Carnegie Inst Technol, BS, 60; Univ Calif, Berkeley, PhD (chem eng), 64. *Mem:* Am Inst Chem Engrs; Am Chem Soc. *Res:* Interfacial phenomena; thermodynamics. *Mailing Add:* Dept Chem Eng Univ Wash PO Box 351750 Seattle WA 98195

BERG, JOHN RICHARD, PHYSICAL CHEMISTRY, INORGANIC CHEMISTRY. *Current Pos:* CONSULT, 90-; BD DIRS, COLUMBIA RES CORP, 92- *Personal Data:* b Chippewa Falls, Wis, Apr 24, 32; m 56; c 4. *Educ:* Col St Thomas, BS, 54; Iowa State Univ, PhD(phys chem, physics), 61. *Prof Exp:* Asst chem, Iowa State Univ, 54-61; sr chemist, Minn Mining & Mfg Co, 61-66, supvr, 66-69, mgr, 69-83, govt serv mgr, 83-86; prin dept asst sec conserv & renewable energy, US Dept Energy, 86-88, asst sec, 88-90. *Concurrent Pos:* Arlington Co Four Mile Run Watershed Joint Planning Comn, 94-, Environ & Energy Conserv Comn, 97- *Mem:* Am Chem Soc; AAAS; Am Inst Chemists; Sigma Xi. *Res:* Photoconductivity; solid state chemistry; preparative inorganic chemistry; imaging chemistry; optics; data processing; new product development, technical service and sales/marketing. *Mailing Add:* 3202 N Tacoma St Arlington VA 22213-1340. *Fax:* 703-642-1538

BERG, JONATHAN H, IGNEOUS *Current Pos:* PROF GEOL, NORTHERN ILL UNIV, 77- *Personal Data:* b Milaca, Minn, Apr 10, 47. *Educ:* Univ Minn, BA, 69; Franklin & Marshall Col, MS, 71; Univ Mass, PhD(geol), 76. *Prof Exp:* Res assoc, Univ Mass, 76-77. *Concurrent Pos:* Vis fel, Australian Nat Univ, 90; assoc ed, Am Mineralogist, 94-96. *Mem:* Fel Geol Soc Am; Mineral Soc Am; Mineral Soc Can; Am Geophys Union. *Res:* Composition and evolution of granulites and the lower crust; geochemistry and origin of flood basalts and ocean-island basalts; origin of anorthosites; geology of Antarctica. *Mailing Add:* Dept Geol Northern Ill Univ De Kalb IL 60115. *Fax:* 815-753-1945; *E-Mail:* jon@geol.niu.edu

BERG, JOSEPH WILBUR, JR, GEOPHYSICS. *Current Pos:* CONSULT, 87- *Personal Data:* b Essington, Pa, Oct 6, 20; m 50, Lillian Douglas; c Anne L (Jenkins), Joseph W & Frederick D. *Educ:* Univ Ga, BS, 47; Pa State Univ, MS, 52, PhD(geophys), 54. *Prof Exp:* Instr, Armstrong Col, Ga, 47-48; asst prof, Univ Tulsa, 54-55; assoc prof geophys, Univ Utah, 55-60; prof, Ore State Univ, 60-66; exec secy, Off Earth Sci, Nat Acad Sci, 66-87. *Concurrent Pos:* Geophysicist, Inst Defense Analysis, 60-61; vis prof, Cornell Univ, 69-70; mem bd dirs, Sci Serv, 75- *Mem:* Soc Explor Geophys (vpres, 75); Seismol Soc Am (pres, 68); Am Geophys Union; Earthquake Eng Res Inst; Geol Soc Am; Sigma Xi. *Res:* Earth structure as determined by seismic, gravitational and magnetic methods; heat flow. *Mailing Add:* 3319 Dauphine Dr Falls Church VA 22042

BERG, LLOYD, CHEMICAL ENGINEERING. *Current Pos:* prof chem eng & head dept, 46-79, PROF CHEM ENG, MONT STATE UNIV, 80- *Personal Data:* b Paterson, NJ, Aug 8, 14. *Educ:* Lehigh Univ, BS, 36; Purdue Univ, PhD(chem eng), 42. *Prof Exp:* Lacquer formulator, Pittsburgh Plate Glass Co, NJ, 36; tech salesman, Sherwin-Williams Co, 36-39; instr powder & explosives, Purdue Univ, 41-42; res chem engr & group leader, Gulf Res & Develop Co, Pa, 42-46; assoc prof chem eng, Univ Kans, 46. *Mem:* Fel Am Inst Chem Engrs; Am Chem Soc; Am Soc Eng Educ. *Res:* Desulfurization of petroleum; battery active manganese dioxide; fuels from shale oil; coal liquefaction; azeotropic and extractive distillation. *Mailing Add:* Dept Chem Eng Mont State Univ Bozeman MT 59717-0001

BERG, M(ORRIS), CERAMICS. *Current Pos:* ADJ PROF, CERAMIC DIV, DEPT MAT SCI, UNIV ILL, 82- *Personal Data:* b Columbus, Ohio, June 9, 21; m 56; c 2. *Educ:* Ohio State Univ, BCerE, 42; Mass Inst Technol, ScD(ceramics), 53. *Honors & Awards:* Ferro Award, 52; David Sarnoff Award, 62. *Prof Exp:* Process engr, AC Spark Plug Div, Gen Motors Corp, 42-44, ceramic res engr, 46-48; res asst, Mass Inst Technol, 49-53; ceramic proj engr, Bur Mines, 53-54; sr engr, RCA, 54-63; staff res scientist, Gen Motors Corp, 63-76, staff engr inorg mat, AC Spark Plug Div, 76-82. *Mem:* Am Ceramic Soc; Am Soc Metals; Soc Automotive Engrs. *Res:* Electronic ceramics; microelectronics; catalysts; metallurgy; physics. *Mailing Add:* 12 Fields E Champaign IL 61821

BERG, MARIE HIRSCH, BIOCHEMISTRY. *Current Pos:* RETIRED. *Personal Data:* b Mannheim, Ger, Mar 20, 09; nat US; wid; c Michael C. *Educ:* Univ Heidelberg, PhD(chem), 34. *Prof Exp:* Prod chemist, Fat & Oil Indust, Ger, 34-36; asst to Prof G Bredig, Univ Karlsruhe, 36-37; Lambert Pharmacol Co Fel, Colgate-Palmolive-Peet Col fel & res assoc, Northwestern Univ, 41-47; chief chemist, Dept Path, St Luke's Hosp, Chicago, Ill, 47-48; biochemist, Dept Dermat, Univ Mich, 48-51; mem staff, Wayne Co Gen Hosp, Eloise, Mich, 51-52; mem, Dept Biol, Hamline Univ, 52-59 & Dept Chem, 55-59; res assoc, Sch Med, Univ Minn, 53-59 & Dept Agr Biochem, 59-60; prof chem & chmn, Div Natural Sci & Math, Northwestern Col, Minn, 60-67, lectr sci, 67-76, adv fire protection prog, Metrop Community Col, 76-87. *Concurrent Pos:* Fire protection instr, Suburban Hennepin Voc Tech Schs; adj prof, Fire Protection, Univ Minn, 75-87; lectr, Div Fire Protection & Hazardous Mat, Univ Minn Exten, 76-88. *Mem:* Fel AAAS; fel Am Sci Affil; Int Fire Serv Instr; Am Chem Soc; Am Asn Univ Women; Sigma Xi. *Res:* Science education; pyorhea dental research porphyrines, lead poisoning; fire science. *Mailing Add:* 121 Washington Ave S Apt 1917 Minneapolis MN 55401-2135

BERG, MARK ALAN, ULTRAFAST SPECTROSCOPY. *Current Pos:* ASST PROF CHEM, UNIV TEX, 87- *Personal Data:* b Dec 1, 58. *Educ:* Univ Minn, BS, 79; Univ Calif, Berkeley, PhD(chem), 85. *Prof Exp:* Assoc chem, Stanford Univ, 85-87. *Concurrent Pos:* Dreyfus distinguished young fac award, Dreyfus Found, 87; NSF presidential young investr, 90; Alfred P Sloan Found res fel, 92. *Mem:* Am Phys Soc; Am Chem Soc. *Res:* Using time-resolved non-linear spectroscopies and ultrafast laser techniques to study the molecular motions in liquids and the resulting solvent effects on chemical reactions. *Mailing Add:* Chem Dept Univ SC 730 S Main Columbia SC 29208. *Fax:* 512-471-8696

BERG, MYLES RENVER, ELECTRICAL ENGINEERING. *Current Pos:* CONSULT, 92- *Personal Data:* b Riverside, Calif, Sept 6, 32; m 59; c 4. *Educ:* Stanford Univ, BS, 55, MS, 56. *Prof Exp:* Res engr radio physics lab, SRI Int, 55-65; mem tech staff, Aerospace Corp, 66-72; group dir advan systs, Lincoln Lab, Mass Inst Technol, 72-73; mgr strategic systs, Technol Serv Corp, 73-74, sr res specialist probe systs, 75-77; sr staff engr signal processing syst, Space Syst Div, Lockheed Missiles & Space Co, 77-92. *Concurrent Pos:* Mem reentry physics panel, Nat Acad Sci, 64-67; dir, Big Ten Oil Co, 76-88, vpres, 77-88; dir, Eagle Creek Mining & Drilling Co, 88-, Suprise Oil Co, 89- *Mem:* Inst Elec & Electronics Engrs; Sigma Xi. *Res:* Signal processing; satellite systems; communication systems; oil production; computer sciences; radio propagation; radar systems; counter measures; reentry physics. *Mailing Add:* 52 Marianna Lane Atherton CA 94027

BERG, NORMAN J, solid state physics; deceased, see previous edition for last biography

BERG, PAUL, BIOCHEMISTRY, MOLECULAR GENETICS OF EUKARYOTES. *Current Pos:* from assoc prof to prof, Stanford Univ, 59-69, chmn dept, 69-74, Willson prof biochem, Med Ctr, 70-94, DIR, BECKMAN CTR MOLECULAR & GENETIC MED, MED CTR, STANFORD UNIV, 85-, VIVIAN K & ROBERT W CAHILL PROF, CANCER RES, 94- *Personal Data:* b New York, NY, June 30, 26; m 47, Mildred Levy; c John. *Educ:* Pa State Univ, BS, 48; Western Res Univ, PhD, 52. *Hon Degrees:* DSc, Univ Rochester, Yale Univ, 78, Wash Univ, 86, Ore State Univ, 89 & Pa State Univ, 95. *Honors & Awards:* Nobel Prize Chem, 80; Sarasota Med Award, 79; NY Acad Sci Award, 80; Albert Lasker Award, 80; Sci Freedom & Responsibility Award, AAAS, 82; Nat Medal of Sci, 83; Nat Libr Med Medal, 86. *Prof Exp:* From asst to assoc prof microbiol, Sch Med, Wash Univ, 55-59. *Concurrent Pos:* Am Cancer Soc res fel, Inst Cytophysiol, Copenhagen & Sch Med, Wash Univ, 52-54 & scholar, 54-57; ed, Biochem & Biophys Res Commun, 59-68; mem, Study Sect Physiol Chem, NIH, 62-66; chmn, Gordon Conf Nucleic Acids, 66-75; mem, Gen Med Basic Sci Comt & Biochem Comt, Nat Bd Med Examr, 68-69; mem adv bd, Jane Coffin Childs Found, 71; Salk Inst fel, 73-; mem adv bd, NIH, 75. *Mem:* Nat Acad Sci; Inst Med-Nat Acad Sci; Am Acad Arts & Sci; Am Soc Biol Chem (pres, 75); Am Chem Soc; fel AAAS; Philos Soc; hon mem Acad Natural Sci Russ Fed Repub; foreign mem Royal Soc; fel Am Acad Microbiol; Pontifical Acad Sci. *Res:* Mechanism of gene expression in higher organisms, particularly the interplay of viral and cellular genes in regulating growth and division. *Mailing Add:* Sch Med Stanford Univ Stanford CA 94305. *Fax:* 650-725-4951

BERG, RICHARD A, TISSUE ENGINEERING, BIOMATERIALS & WOUND HEALING. *Current Pos:* PROF BIOCHEM, UNIV MED & DENT NJ, 86- *Personal Data:* b Spokane, Wash, Apr 27, 45. *Educ:* Univ Chicago, BS, 67; Univ Pa, PhD, 72. *Honors & Awards:* Sinsheimer Award, 76. *Prof Exp:* From asst prof to assoc prof biochem, Col Med & Dent, NJ, 72-80. *Concurrent Pos:* Pulmonary Br, NIH, 78-80. *Mem:* Am Soc Biochem & Molecular Biol; Am Chem Soc; Inst Elec & Electronics Engrs; Am Mgt Asn. *Res:* Connective tissue biochemistry; skin, bone and cartilage; regulation of gene expression of macromolecules; tissue engineering. *Mailing Add:* Collagen Corp 2500 Faber Pl Palo Alto CA 94303

BERG, RICHARD ALLEN, ASTRONOMY. *Current Pos:* CONSULT, RAND CORP, 71- *Personal Data:* b Chicago, Ill, June 12, 42; m 68. *Educ:* Univ Ill, Urbana, BSc, 64; Univ Va, MA, 66, PhD(astron), 70. *Prof Exp:* Phys scientist astron & cartog, Aeronaut Chart & Info Ctr, St Louis, Mo, 64-70; fel, Dept Physics, Univ Del, 70-72, asst prof astron, 72-73; asst prof astron, Univ Rochester, 73-78; phys scientist, DMA Aerospace Ctr, St Louis, 78-80. *Mem:* Am Astron Soc; Int Astron Union; Sigma Xi. *Res:* Spectroscopy and photometry of spectrum variable stars; high-speed photometry of transient events in cataclysmic variables; computer applications in astronomical observing; image processing. *Mailing Add:* 3327 Quesada St NW Washington DC 20015-1664

BERG, RICHARD BLAKE, GEOLOGY OF INDUSTRIAL MINERALS. *Current Pos:* ECON GEOLOGIST & CUR, MINERAL MUS, MONT BUR MINES & GEOL, MONT COL MINERAL SCI & TECHNOL, 66- *Personal Data:* b Portland, Ore, Mar 7, 37; m 65, Betty L Huddleston; c Eric & Cathy. *Educ:* Beloit Col, BS, 59; Univ Mont, PhD(geol), 64. *Prof Exp:* Instr geol, State Univ NY Col Plattsburgh, 64-66. *Mem:* Geol Soc Am; Soc Econ Geol; Soc Mining, Metall & Explor. *Res:* Mineralogy; zeolites, vermiculite, talc and chlorite; geology of industrial minerals in Montana. *Mailing Add:* Mont Bur Mines & Geol Mont Tech 1300 W Park St Butte MT 59701. *Fax:* 406-496-4451; *E-Mail:* dick@mbmgsun.mtech.edu

BERG, RICHARD CARL, GROUNDWATER RESOURCE ASSESSMENT VIA AQUIFER MAPPING & GEOLOGIC FRAMEWORK DEVELOPMENT, AQUIFER SENSITIVITY & VULNERABILITY ASSESSMENTS. *Current Pos:* from res asst to res assoc, Ill State Geol Surv, 74-79, asst geologist, Groundwater Sect, 80-82, assoc geologist, 82-86, geologist, 86-88, geologist & head, Groundwater Protection Sect, 88-89, sr geologist & head, 89-92, SR GEOLOGIST & HEAD, GEOL MAPPING SECT & QUATERNARY GEOL SECT, ILL STATE GEOL SURV, 92- *Personal Data:* b Worcester, Mass, Apr 24, 49; m 73, Robbie Cessna; c Ryan, Robyn & Renee. *Educ:* Ind State Univ, BS, 71; Eastern Mich Univ, MA, 74; Univ Ill, PhD(soil geomorphol), 79. *Honors & Awards:* John C Fry Mem Award in Environ Geol, Geol Soc Am & Asn Am State Geologists, 91. *Prof Exp:* Teaching asst/fel earth sci, Eastern Mich Univ, 71-73; teaching asst weather/climate, Univ Ill, 73-74. *Concurrent Pos:* Adj prof, Univ SC, Earth Sci & Resources Inst. *Mem:* Geol Soc Am; Am Inst Prof Geologists; Am Quaternary Asn. *Res:* Development of methodologies to portray variable sequences of geologic materials in three-dimensions and then to interpret sequences according to groundwater contamination potentials. *Mailing Add:* Ill State Geol Surv Champaign IL 61820. *Fax:* 217-244-7004; *E-Mail:* berg@geoserv.isgs.uiuc.edu

BERG, RICHARD HAROLD, SANITARY ENGINEERING, ENVIRONMENTAL ENGINEERING. *Current Pos:* ASSOC PROF CIVIL ENG, WESTERN WASH UNIV, 71- *Personal Data:* b Seattle, Wash, Aug 6, 37; m 60; c 2. *Educ:* Univ Wash, BS, 59, MS, 61; Ore State Univ, PhD(civil eng), 66. *Prof Exp:* Instr eng, Skagit Valley Col, 61-62 & Univ Wash, 62-63; assoc prof civil eng, Seattle Univ, 68-71. *Concurrent Pos:* Sr scientist, Dept Interior res grant, 69-70. *Mem:* Water Pollution Control Fedn; Asn Environ Eng Prof; Am Asn Univ Prof. *Res:* Liquid waste treatment; biological environmental control; environmental systems analysis; mathematical modeling. *Mailing Add:* Dept Geog Western Wash Univ MS 9080 Bellingham WA 98225-9080

BERG, ROBERT FRANK, CONDENSED MATTER PHYSICS. *Current Pos:* Nat Res Coun assoc, 83-85, PHYSICIST, THERMOPHYS DIV, NAT INST STAND & TECHNOL, 85- *Personal Data:* b Birmingham, Ala, Aug 7, 55; m 79, Carol K Emerson; c 3. *Educ:* Univ Va, BS, 77; Duke Univ, MA, 79; Univ Fla, PhD, 83. *Honors & Awards:* Technol Achievement Award (co-winner), Ctr Chem Technol, 90. *Mem:* Am Physics Soc; Sigma Xi; Am Inst Aeronaut & Astronaut. *Res:* Development of a space shuttle experiment to measure the viscosity near the critical point of xenon; analysis in support of the critical point equilibration experiment flown on the IML-Z space shuttle flight in 1994. *Mailing Add:* Div 838 Nat Inst Stand & Technol Gaithersburg MD 20899. *E-Mail:* robert.berg@nist.gov

BERG, ROBERT R, PETROLEUM GEOLOGY, SEDIMENTOLOGY & STRATIGRAPHY. *Current Pos:* prof & head, Tex A&M Univ, 67-72, assoc dean geosci, 72, dir, Off Univ Res, 72-82, PROF GEOL, TEX A&M UNIV, 72-, MICHEL T HALBOUTY CHAIR GEOL, 82- *Personal Data:* b St Paul, Minn, May 28, 24; m 46; c 3. *Educ:* Univ Minn, BA, 48, PhD(geol), 51. *Honors & Awards:* Ben H Parker Mem Medal, Am Inst Prof Geologists, 81; Sidney Powers Mem Award, Am Asn Petrol Geologists, 93. *Prof Exp:* Geologist, oil & gas explor, Calif Co, 51-56; div geologist, Cosden Petrol Corp, 57-58; gen partner, Embar Oil Co, 59-63; partner, Berg & Wasson Consult, 63-66. *Concurrent Pos:* Vpres, Rock Mountain Asn Geologists, 63, pres, 66; assoc ed, Geol Soc Am, 65-66; assoc ed, Am Asn Petrol Geologist, 66, mem, Res Comt, 73. *Mem:* Nat Acad Eng; fel Geol Soc Am; hon mem Am Asn Petrol Geologists (pres-elect, 83); hon mem Am Inst Prof Geologists (secy-treas, 69, pres, 71); Sigma Xi; Soc Econ Palentologists & Mineralogists. *Res:* Stratigraphy; geology of petroleum; origin and properties of sandstones that are reservoirs for oil and gas; hydrostatic and hydrodynamic trapping of oil and gas; prediction of reservoir properties for enhanced recovery of oil. *Mailing Add:* Dept Geol Tex A&M Univ College Station TX 77843-3115

BERG, ROBERT W, POULTRY GENETICS. *Current Pos:* poultry exten specialist, Inst Agr, 58-84, EMER PROF, UNIV MINN, ST PAUL, 84- *Personal Data:* b Welch, Minn, Apr 9, 17; m 44; c 3. *Educ:* Univ Minn, BS, 41, MS, 50, PhD(poultry husb, animal breeding), 53. *Prof Exp:* Inspector, Minn Poultry Improve Bd, 45-48; asst geneticist, Western Coop Hatcheries, 53; geneticist & hatchery mgr, Jerome Turkey Hatchery, Inc, 53-58. *Mem:* Poultry Sci Asn; World Poultry Sci Asn; Sigma Xi. *Res:* Poultry husbandry and genetics; effects of light intensity on growth of turkeys in a total confinement program. *Mailing Add:* 2925 Lincoln Dr No 406 Roseville MN 55113

BERG, ROY TORGNY, ANIMAL GENETICS. *Current Pos:* Lectr animal husb, Univ Alta, 50-52, from asst prof to prof, 55-89, dept chmn, 77-82, dean fac agr forestry, 83-88, EMER PROF ANIMAL SCI, UNIV ALTA, 89- *Personal Data:* b Millicent, Alta, Apr 8, 27; m 51, Margaret V Barnes; c Ruth E, Paula M, Kevin J & Nora W. *Educ:* Univ Alta, BSc, 50; Univ Minn, MS, 54, PhD(animal breeding), 55. *Hon Degrees:* DSc, Univ Guelph, 91. *Honors & Awards:* Genetic & Physiol Medal, Can Soc Animal Sci, 81, Cert Merit, 82; Sir Frederick Haultain Prize in Sci, 89; Sci & Technol Award, Can Meat Coun, 89. *Concurrent Pos:* Nat Res Coun sr res fel, 64-65; vis prof, Edinburgh, 72, Copenhagen, 74 & 77, Cairo, 80; consult. *Mem:* Fel Agr Inst Can; Am Soc Animal Sci; Am Meat Sci Asn; Genetics Soc Can; Agr Inst Can; Am Genetics Asn; Brit Soc Animal Prod. *Res:* Animal breeding; genetics; developed breeding and selection systems for beef cattle production; elucidated the growth and development of carcass components (muscle, bone and fat) in cattle and other ungulates. *Mailing Add:* Fac Agr Forestry Univ Alta Edmonton AB T6G 2P5 Can

BERG, STEVEN PAUL, BIOCHEMISTRY. *Current Pos:* ASST PROF BIOL, UNIV DENVER, 77- *Personal Data:* b Minneapolis, Minn, Dec 28, 48; m 70; c 2. *Educ:* Pac Lutheran Univ, BS, 70; Purdue Univ, PhD(biochem), 75. *Prof Exp:* Res assoc photosynthesis, Dept Biol, Wayne State Univ, 75-76, NSF fel, 76-77. *Concurrent Pos:* Prin investr, USDA grant, 77- *Mem:* Am Soc Plant Physiologists; Am Soc Biol Chemists. *Res:* Photosynthetic electron transport and photophosphorylation; chloroplast membrane proteins and membrane structure. *Mailing Add:* Sci & Eng Dept Winona State Univ 201 Stark Hall Winona MN 55987

BERG, VIRGINIA SEYMOUR, PLANT PHYSIOLOGY. *Current Pos:* asst prof, 84-88, ASSOC PROF, DEPT BIOL, UNIV NORTHERN IOWA, CEDAR FALLS, 88- *Personal Data:* b Mass, July 30, 48. *Educ:* Tufts Univ, BS, 72; Univ Wash, MS, 75, PhD(plant physiol), 80. *Prof Exp:* Fel, Dept Land, Air & Water Resources, Univ Calif, Davis, 81-84. *Concurrent Pos:* Vis prof, Plant Ecol Group, Univ Andes, Venezuela, 82; vis prof, Fitotechnia Inst, Cordoba, Spain; vis scientist, Int Ctr Trop Agr, Cali, Columbia. *Mem:* AAAS; Am Soc Plant Physiologists; Sigma Xi. *Res:* Plant water relations; energy budgets; effects of acidity on plant surfaces. *Mailing Add:* Dept Biol Univ Northern Iowa Cedar Falls IA 50614-0001

BERG, WILLIAM ALBERT, SOIL CONSERVATION. *Current Pos:* RETIRED. *Personal Data:* b Sterling, Colo, Jan 12, 30; m 60, Dorcas Hill; c Jeffrey, Rodger, Michael & David. *Educ:* Colo State Univ, BS, 53, MS, 57; NC State Univ, PhD(soils), 60. *Prof Exp:* Soil scientist, US Forest Serv, 60-68; from asst prof to prof agron, Colo State Univ, 68-80; soil scientist, Agr Res Serv, USDA, 80-96. *Mem:* Am Soc Agron; Soc Range Mgt; Soil & Water Conserv Soc; Soil Sci Soc Am. *Res:* Application of soils information in range management; vegetation establishment and grazing management on marginal farmland and drastically disturbed land. *Mailing Add:* 2496 W Old Hwy 64 Lexington NC 22295

BERG, WILLIAM EUGENE, BIOLOGY. *Current Pos:* from instr to prof biol, Univ Calif, Berkeley, 47-70, prof zool, 70-80, vchmn dept, 73-77, EMER PROF ZOOL, UNIV CALIF, BERKELEY, 80- *Personal Data:* b Round Mountain, Nev, Dec 6, 18; m 47. *Educ:* Calif Inst Technol, BS, 39, MS, 40; Stanford Univ, PhD(biol), 46. *Prof Exp:* Asst biol, Stanford Univ, 41-43, res assoc, 43; res assoc, Univ South Calif, 43. *Mem:* Am Soc Zoologists; Sigma Xi. *Res:* Physiological embryology; aviation physiology; human exercise physiology. *Mailing Add:* PO Box 1810 Pollock Pines CA 95726-1810

BERG, WILLIAM KEITH, PSYCHOLOGY, DEVELOPMENTAL PSYCHOPHYSIOLOGY. *Current Pos:* asst prof, 73-77, PROF PSYCHOL, UNIV FLA, 77- *Personal Data:* b Cloquet, Minn, July 20, 43; m 67; c 1. *Educ:* Univ Minn, Duluth, BA, 65; Univ Wis, MA, 68, PhD(psychophys), 71. *Prof Exp:* Asst prof child behav & develop, Univ Iowa, 70-73. *Concurrent Pos:* Grant reviewer, NSF, NIH, NIMH, March of Dimes. *Mem:* Soc Res Child Develop; Soc Psychophysiol Res; Am Psychol Asn; fel AAAS; fel Am Psychol Asoc; Int Soc Develop Psychobiol. *Res:* Habituation, attention, and learning behavior in young infants assessed with physiological response systems; physiological evaluation of visual stress during video display viewing. *Mailing Add:* Dept Psychol Univ Fla 114 Psychol Bldg Gainesville FL 32611-2065

BERGBREITER, DAVID EDWARD, POLYMER SURFACE CHEMISTRY, HOMOGENEOUS CATALYSIS. *Current Pos:* chmn, Org Div, 83-87, PROF ORG CHEM, TEX A&M UNIV, 74- *Personal Data:* b Chicago, Ill, Nov 10, 48; m 71, Lynne Baumgardner; c Sarah & Amy. *Educ:* Mich State Univ, BS, 70; Mass Inst Technol, PhD(chem), 74. *Prof Exp:* Texaco fel, Mass Inst Technol, 71-73. *Mem:* Am Chem Soc; AAAS. *Res:* Organic, organometallic and polymer chemistry; new catalysts, new methods for synthesis and mechanistic studies in organometallic chemistry, asymmetric synthesis and polymer modification. *Mailing Add:* Dept Chem Tex A&M Univ College Station TX 77843-3255

BERGDOLL, MERLIN SCOTT, BIOCHEMISTRY. *Current Pos:* prof, Dept Foods & Nutrit, 66-68, prof, Food Res Inst & Dept Food Sci, 68-88, EMER PROF, UNIV WIS-MADISON, 88- *Personal Data:* b Petersburg, WVa, Sept 23, 16; div; c 3. *Educ:* WVa Univ, BS, 40; Purdue Univ, PhD(agr biochem), 46. *Hon Degrees:* Dr, Univ Madrid, Spain, 89. *Honors & Awards:* Ray A Kroc Prof Award for Res on Food Toxicol. *Prof Exp:* Asst chemist, Purdue Univ, 42-46; instr, Biochem & Food Res Inst, Univ Chicago, 46-50, from asst prof to assoc prof, Food Res Inst, 50-66. *Mem:* Am Chem Soc; Am Soc Microbiol; Inst Food Technol; Am Soc Biol Chem. *Res:* Production, purification, physico-chemical properties, structure, immunology and analysis of the staphylococcal enterotoxins; toxic shock syndrome toxin-1 purification and characterization. *Mailing Add:* Food Res Inst Univ Wis Madison WI 53706

BERGDOLT, VOLLMAR EDGAR, MECHANICAL ENGINEERING. *Current Pos:* res asst mech eng, 53-56, asst prof mech & nuclear eng, 56-58, from assoc prof to prof, 58-64, asst dean grad sch, 64-69, prof mech eng, 69-84, EMER PROF MECH ENG, PURDUE UNIV, 84- *Personal Data:* b Evansville, Ind, Dec 29, 18; m 45; c 4. *Educ:* Purdue Univ, BSME, 39, MSME, 46, PhD(heat transfer), 56. *Prof Exp:* Asst engr, Am Creosoting Co, Ky, 39-40; mech engr, Ballistic Res Labs, Aberdeen Proving Ground, Md, 46-53. *Concurrent Pos:* Vis prof, Indian Inst Technol, Kanpur, 63-64; prof mech eng, Univ Zambia, Lusaka, 71-73. *Mem:* Am Soc Eng Educ; Am Soc Mech Engrs. *Res:* Energy conversion in mechanical systems; kinematics and mechanical design. *Mailing Add:* 1209 Sunset Lane West Lafayette IN 47906

BERGE, DOUGLAS G, ANALYTICAL CHEMISTRY. *Current Pos:* from asst prof to assoc prof, 66-82, PROF CHEM, UNIV WIS-OSHKOSH, 82- *Personal Data:* b Montevideo, Minn, Sept 19, 38; m 66, Ruth Ertz; c Sonya. *Educ:* Mankato State Col, BS & BA, 61; Univ Iowa, PhD(analy chem), 65. *Prof Exp:* Asst prof chem, Adrian Col, 65-66. *Mem:* Am Chem Soc. *Res:* Equilibrium studies; separations. *Mailing Add:* Dept Chem Univ Wis Oshkosh WI 54901-8645

BERGE, JON PETER, EXPERIMENTAL HIGH ENERGY PHYSICS. *Current Pos:* PHYSICIST, FERMI NAT ACCELERATOR LAB, 74- *Personal Data:* b Madison, Wis, Feb 4, 35; m 59; c 2. *Educ:* Univ Calif, BA, 56, MA, 58, PhD(physics), 63. *Prof Exp:* Res assoc physics, Lawrence Radiation Lab, Univ Calif, Berkeley, 56-67; res officer, Univ Oxford, 67-70; physicist, Ctr Europ Nuclear Res, Geneva, 70-74. *Mem:* Am Phys Soc; AAAS. *Res:* Bubble chamber data analysis computer programming. *Mailing Add:* Fermilab PO Box 500 Batavia IL 60510

BERGE, KENNETH G, INTERNAL MEDICINE. *Current Pos:* from instr to assoc prof, Mayo Grad Sch Med, 57-74, PROF MED, MAYO MED SCH, 74- *Personal Data:* b Wahkon, Minn, Feb 9, 26; m 48, Aline Hoyt; c Elizabeth A (Devine), William H & Keith H. *Educ:* Univ Minn, BA, 48, BS, 49, BMed, 51, DMed, 52, MS, 55. *Honors & Awards:* Billings Silver Medal, AMA, 57. *Prof Exp:* Asst med, Mayo Clin, 55, consult, 55-88; NW area found prof community health, 77-84. *Concurrent Pos:* Consult & vchmn steering comt coronary drug proj, Nat Heart & Lung Inst, 62-87, mem epidemiol & biomet adv comt, 70-72, mem policy adv bd, Hypertension Detection & Followup Prog, 71-87, mem policy bd, Aspirin Myocardial Infarction Study, 75-80; fel coun arteriosclerosis & epidemiol, Am Heart Asn; mem sect arteriosclerosis & ischaemic heart dis, Int Soc Cardiol; mem bd dir, Rochester Methodist Hosp, 70-84; head sect med, 70-80, Mayo Clin, pres voting staff, 76; mem, Olmsted County Bd Health, 75-81, chmn, 77; State Health Adv Coun, 80-82; chmn steering comt, systolic hypertension in the elderly prog, NIH, 84- *Mem:* Fel Am Col Physicians; AMA; Am Fedn Clin Res. *Res:* Cardiovascular research, especially epidemiology, atherosclerosis and hypertension. *Mailing Add:* Mayo Clin Rochester MN 55905

BERGE, TRYGVE O, virology, immunology; deceased, see previous edition for last biography

BERGELIN, OLAF P(REYSZ), CHEMICAL ENGINEERING. *Current Pos:* assoc dean col grad studies & coord res, 68-77, EMER PROF CHEM ENG, UNIV DEL, 77- *Personal Data:* b Big Rapids, Mich, Nov 8, 11; m 42; c 3. *Educ:* Univ Mich, BSE, 35, MS, 36, ScD(chem eng), 42. *Honors & Awards:* Medal, Govt of Afghanistan, 68. *Prof Exp:* Asst eng res, Univ Mich, 35-37; student engr, Union Oil Co, Calif, 39; chem engr, Hercules Powder Co, Wilmington, 41-42; from assoc prof to prof chem eng, Univ Del, 46-56; educ consult, Tex Agr & Mech Col Pakistan Proj, Dacca, E Pakistan, 56-62; proj dir, Kabul Afghan-Am Prog, Educ Serv, Inc, Afghanistan, 63-68. *Concurrent Pos:* Res Corp grant, Fulbright res fel, NZ Geothermal Power Proj, 51; technol transfer consult, Univ Del, 77- *Mem:* Am Chem Soc; Am Inst Chem Engrs; Am Soc Eng Educ; Am Soc Mech Engrs; Am Numis Soc. *Res:* Heat transfer in tubular heat exchangers; two phase fluid flow; boiling. *Mailing Add:* 1410 SW 20th St Cape Coral FL 33991-3265

BERGEMAN, THOMAS H, atoms in external fields, diatomic spectroscopy, for more information see previous edition

BERGEN, CATHARINE MARY, SCIENCE EDUCATION. *Current Pos:* from assoc prof to prof, 41-72, EMER PROF SCI, JERSEY CITY STATE COL, 72- *Personal Data:* b Garden City, NY, Jan 16, 12. *Educ:* Wellesley Col, AB, 33; Columbia Univ, AM, 35, PhD(sci educ), 42. *Prof Exp:* Sci consult pub sch, Garden City, NY, 34-37; asst physics, Hofstra Col, 39-40; teacher elem sci, Lincoln Sch, Teachers Col, Columbia Univ, 40-43. *Mem:* AAAS; Am Phys Soc; Am Asn Physics Teachers. *Res:* Sources of science information used by children; analysis of science material published for laymen; use of mathematics in science. *Mailing Add:* 83 Bentley Ave Jersey City NJ 07304

BERGEN, DONNA CATHERINE, NEUROLOGY. *Current Pos:* resident neurol, 72-75, staff neurologist, 75-80, ASSOC PROF NEUROL, MED COL, RUSH UNIV, 80-, SR ATTEND NEUROLOGIST, 80- *Personal Data:* b Crawfordsville, Ind, Mar 17, 45; m 78, Tom Madden. *Educ:* Vassar Col, BA, 67; Univ Ill, MD, 71. *Prof Exp:* Intern med, Evanston Hosp, Ill, 71-72. *Concurrent Pos:* Consult neurologist, Cook Co Hosp, Chicago, Ill. *Mem:* Am Acad Neurol; Am Epilepsy Soc; Am EEG Soc; Am Bd Qualification EEG. *Res:* Clinical electroencephalography; clinical neuropharmacology; epilepsy. *Mailing Add:* Rush Med Col Rush Presby St Lukes Hosp 1753 W Congress Pkwy Chicago IL 60612

BERGEN, JAMES DAVID, METEOROLOGY, AIR POLLUTION. *Current Pos:* AIR QUAL RES SPECIALIST, PIMA CO DEPT ENVIRON QUAL, 86- *Personal Data:* b Spokane, Wash, May 29, 32; m 74; c 1. *Educ:* Univ Wash, BS, 55; Colo State Univ, MS, 64, PhD(atmospheric sci), 67. *Prof Exp:* Res aeronaut engr, Space Task Group, NASA, 59-61; climatologist, US Navy Hydrographic Off, 61-62; res meteorologist, Rocky Mountain Sta, Subalpine Hydrol Res Unit, 62-74, Mountain & Forest Meteorol Proj, 74-78; res meteorologist, Snow Zone Hydrol Proj, Pac Southwest Forest & Range Exp Sta, 78-82, meteorologist, Forest Fire Meteorol Proj, 82-86. *Concurrent Pos:* Consult, Task Force Aerial Applications, 78; mem spec grad affil fac, Dept Watershed Mgt, Colo State Univ, 67-70; vis scientist, Dept Watershed Mgt, Univ Ariz, 81-82; mem, Canopy & Diffusion Comts, Coop Field Exp, US Army-US Forest Serv, 83-86; prin investr, mesometeorol study, DPG, US Army-US Forest Serv, 85-86; vol scientist, Forest Fire Meteorol Proj, Pac Southwest Forest Range Exp Sta, 86-90. *Mem:* Am Meteorol Soc; Sigma Xi. *Res:* Forest meteorology; boundary layer in mountain terrain; snow physics; analysis of airflow and turbulence in and near forest stands; modeling and measurement of airflow in complex terrain for input into pollution transport models. *Mailing Add:* 1031 W Safari Dr Tucson AZ 85704-2841

BERGEN, ROBERT LUDLUM, JR, POLYMER CHEMISTRY, MATERIALS SCIENCE. *Current Pos:* CONSULT, 86- *Personal Data:* b Islip, NY, Oct 29, 29; m 51, Grace-Elizabeth Field; c Beryl F, Alice D, Robert L III & Jennifer U. *Educ:* Williams Col, AB, 51; Cornell Univ, MS, 53, PhD(phys chem), 55. *Prof Exp:* Sr res chemist chem div, US Rubber Co, 55-60, sr res specialist, 60-69; mgr textile & plastic res, Res Ctr, Uniroyal Inc, 69-72, mgr Paracril res & develop, 72-74, mgr synthetic rubber res & develop, Chem Div, 74-77, group mgr chem & polymers res & develop, 77-79, mgr corp res & dev 79-81, dir res & develop, Uniroyal Eng Prod Co, 81-85, dir corp eng, Uniroyal Inc, 85. *Concurrent Pos:* Instr, New Haven Col, 64-67, adj prof, 67-69; adj prof math, Univ New Haven, 86-93. *Mem:* Fel AAAS; Am Chem Soc; Sigma Xi. *Res:* Physical chemistry and physics of polymers; rheology; statistical experimentation; physics of polymer blends; environmental stress cracking of plastics; fiber spinning; fibers for pollution control; polymer flammability; rubber chemistry; synthetic elastomers for specialty applications; chemicals for specialty applications; thermoplastic elastomers; synthetic lubricants. *Mailing Add:* 79 Lebanon Rd Bethany CT 06524-3033

BERGEN, STANLEY S, JR, INTERNAL MEDICINE. *Current Pos:* PROF INTERNAL MED, RUTGERS MED SCH & NJ MED SCH & PRES, COL MED & DENT NJ, 71- *Personal Data:* b Princeton, NJ, May 2, 29; m 65; c 5. *Educ:* Princeton Univ, AB, 51; Columbia Univ, MD, 55. *Prof Exp:* Med dir, St Luke's Hosp, Greenwich, Conn, 62-64; actg chief med serv, Ft Jay Army Hosp, New York, NY, 60-62; dir med, Cumberland Hosp, 64-68; chief commun med, Brooklyn-Cumberland Med Ctr, 68-70; sr vpres, New York City Health & Hosps Corp, 70-71. *Concurrent Pos:* Zabriskie fel, St Luke's Hosp, New York, 58-59; Hartford Found grant, 63-65; assoc prof med, State Univ NY Downstate Med Ctr, 64-71. *Mem:* NY Acad Sci; fel Am Col Physicians; fel Am Soc Clin Nutrit; AMA; Sigma Xi. *Res:* Carbohydrate and hepatic metabolism; endocrinology; development of new health care delivery system. *Mailing Add:* Univ Med-Dent NJ 30 Bergen St Newark NJ 07107-3000

BERGEN, WERNER GERHARD, ANIMAL NUTRITION, GROWTH BIOLOGY. *Current Pos:* PROF & HEAD, DEPT ANIMAL & DAIRY SCI, AUBURN UNIV, AL, 95- *Personal Data:* b Warstade, Ger, Apr 23, 43; US citizen; m 66, Anita Lynn Reuter; c 1. *Educ:* Ohio State Univ, BSc, 64, MSc, 66, PhD(protein nutrit), 67. *Honors & Awards:* Nutrit Res Award, Am Soc Animal Sci, 79; Animal Growth & Develop Award, Am Soc Animal Sci, 91. *Prof Exp:* From asst prof to prof growth biol & nutrit, Mich State Univ, 67-95. *Mem:* Am Soc Animal Sci; Am Soc Nutrit Sci; Am Soc Exp Biol; Soc Exp Biol & Med; Nutrit Soc UK. *Res:* Nutritional biochemistry; genome regulation of animal growth; protein turnover in animals; muscle biology; regulation of lipid deposition in animals. *Mailing Add:* Dept Animal & Dairy Sci Col Agr Auburn Univ Auburn AL 36849-5415. *E-Mail:* wbergen@acesag.auburn.edu

BERGENBACK, RICHARD EDWARD, GEOLOGY. *Current Pos:* assoc prof, 68-80, PROF GEOL, UNIV TENN, CHATTANOOGA, 80- *Personal Data:* b Allentown, Pa, Oct 23, 26; m 47, Audrey L Lothrop; c 3. *Educ:* Lafayette Col, AB, 48; Lehigh Univ, MS, 50; Pa State Univ, PhD, 64. *Prof Exp:* Asst, Lehigh Univ, 48-50; geologist, Cities Serv Res & Develop Co, 57-58; geologist-in-chg fuels br, Tenn Valley Authority, 58-60; teacher, Baltimore County, Md, 60-61; asst, Pa State Univ, 61-64, res assoc, 64-65; asst prof geol, Southern Conn State Col, 65-66; assoc prof geol & geog & chmn dept, Howard Univ, 66-68. *Concurrent Pos:* Instr eve col, Univ Chattanooga, 58-59. *Mem:* Geol Soc Am; Am Asn Petrol Geologists. *Res:* Petrology and geochemistry of sedimentary rocks, especially carbonate rocks; regional stratigraphy, especially coal-bearing rocks. *Mailing Add:* 2242 Peterson Dr Chattanooga TN 37421

BERGENDAHL, MAXIMILIAN HILMAR, ECONOMIC GEOLOGY, MINERAL EXPLORATION. *Current Pos:* CONSULT. 83- *Personal Data:* b Reading, Pa, Apr 24, 21; m 45, 78, Mildred J Stripling; c Mark. *Educ:* Brown Univ, AB, 50. *Prof Exp:* Geologist, US Geol Surv, 51-67; sr geologist, Amax Explor Inc, 67-81; explor supvr, Phillips Petrol Co, 82. *Mem:* Fel Explorers Club; Am Inst Prof Geologists. *Res:* Geology and stratigraphy of Florida phosphate deposits; late Cenozoic stratigraphy of south-central Florida; uranium deposits of Wyoming; stratigraphy of northeastern Wyoming; pre-Cambrian geology; ore deposits of central Colorado; gold deposits of the United States; metals exploration of western United States, Middle Eastern countries and South America. *Mailing Add:* 2209 Queensbury Way Bella Vista AR 72719

BERGER, ALAN ERIC, NUMERICAL ANALYSIS, APPLIED MATH. *Current Pos:* MATHEMATICIAN, NAVAL SURFACE WARFARE CTR, 72- *Personal Data:* b Plainfield, NJ, Sept 4, 46. *Educ:* Rutgers Univ, AB, 68; Mass Inst Technol, MS, 69, PhD(math), 72. *Mem:* Am Math Soc; Soc Indust & Appl Math; AAAS; Am Phys Soc; Am Chem Soc; Protein Soc. *Res:* Numerical solution of partial differential equations; numerical analysis of physical models; interdisciplinary collaboration. *Mailing Add:* Naval Surface Warfare Ctr Code B40 Dahlgren VA 22448-5100. *E-Mail:* aberger@nswc.navy.mil

BERGER, ALBERT JEFFREY, NEUROPHYSIOLOGY, RESPIRATORY PHYSIOLOGY. *Current Pos:* from asst prof to assoc prof, 78-85, PROF PHYSIOL, UNIV WASH, 85- *Personal Data:* b New York, NY, Jan 7, 43; m 65; c 1. *Educ:* Cornell Univ, BChE, 64; Princeton Univ, MA, 65, PhD(chem eng), 67; Univ Calif, San Francisco, PhD(physiol), 76. *Prof Exp:* Res engr, Shell Develop Co, 67-70; asst prof chem eng, Rensselaer Polytech Inst, 70-72; adj asst prof physiol, Univ Calif, San Francisco, 76-78. *Concurrent Pos:* Spec fel, NIH, USPHS, 72-76, Res Career Develop Award, 77-82, Jacob Javits Neurosci Invest Award, 85-; assoc staff mem, Cardiovasc Res Inst, Univ Calif, San Francisco, 77-78; Guggenheim fel, 81-82, Fogarty Sr Int fel, NIH, 88-89; vis scientist, Inst Neurol, London, Eng, 81-82; vis prof, Dept Physiol, Kyoto Univ, Kyoto, Japan. *Mem:* Am Physiol Soc; Soc Neurosci; AAAS. *Res:* Neural regulation of respiration; neuronal connectivity; neuroanatomy. *Mailing Add:* Dept Physiol & Biophys Univ Wash Med Sch Box 357290 Seattle WA 98195-0001

BERGER, ALFRED H, PISTON ENGINE ENGINEERING, PRINTED CIRCUIT ENGINEERING. *Current Pos:* SR DESIGN ENGR, CONVAIR, 56- *Personal Data:* b New York, NY, Feb 17, 34; m 66, Louise; c Karen & Paul. *Concurrent Pos:* Eng designer, Cubic Corp, 69-83, 87-90 & Squire Whitehouse, 83-87. *Res:* Inventor and patentee of electric screwdriver, electric wrench and of rocking ball I.C. engine. *Mailing Add:* 3324 Cowley Way Apt 2 San Diego CA 92117-6311

BERGER, ANDREW JOHN, anatomy, ornithology; deceased, see previous edition for last biography

BERGER, ANN ELIZABETH, LYMPHOCYTE ACTIVATION, HYBRIDOMAS. *Current Pos:* RES SCIENTIST, UPJOHN CO, 81- *Educ:* Duke Univ, PhD(immunol), 78. *Mailing Add:* Dept Cell Biol Pharmacia & Upjohn Inc 301 Henrietta St 7239-209-230 Kalamazoo MI 49007-4940

BERGER, BERNARD BEN, WATER SUPPLY, WASTEWATER TREATMENT. *Current Pos:* RETIRED. *Personal Data:* b New York, NY, Aug 21, 12. *Educ:* Mass Inst Technol, BS, 35; Harvard Univ, MS, 48. *Prof Exp:* Sanit engr, Kent Co, Mich, 39-41; prof, Univ Mass, 66-78, emer prof civil eng, 78-96. *Mem:* Nat Acad Eng; Am Water Works Asn; Am Acad Environ Eng; Water Pollution Control Fedn; hon fel Inst Water Pollution Control UK; Int Water Resources Asn. *Mailing Add:* Dept Civil Eng Univ Mass Amherst MA 01003

BERGER, BEVERLY JANE, RISK ANALYSIS. *Current Pos:* REP, FED LAB CONSORTIUM TECHNOL TRANSFER, WASHINGTON, DC, 90- *Personal Data:* b Morristown, NJ, Apr 28, 39. *Educ:* Univ NMex, BA, 61, MEdSci, 65, MS, 67; Univ Calif, Davis, PhD(genetics), 71. *Prof Exp:* NIH fel biostatist, Sch Pub Health, Univ Calif, Berkeley, 71-73; math biologist, Lawrence Livermore Lab, Univ Calif, 73-76; prog mgr chem hydrogen storage systs, US Dept Energy, 76-79, prog mgr biomass energy systs, 79, dir, Biomass Energy Technol Div, 79-86; asst dir life sci, Off Sci & Technol Policy, Exec Off Pres, 87-89. *Concurrent Pos:* Mem, Domestic Policy Coun Working Groups on Health Policy, Agent Orange, Energy, Environ & Natural Resources, 87-89; chmn, Fed Coord Coun Sci, Eng & Technol, Comt Life Sci, 87-89; mem, Fed Coord Coun Sci, Eng & Technol Comts, Biotechnol Sci Coord Comt, Comt Interagency Radiation Res & Policy Coord & Comt Earth Sci, 87-89. *Mem:* Genetics Soc Am; AAAS; Sigma Xi; Soc Risk Anal. *Res:* Liaison between consortium and Washington based organizations including federal government; policy formulation related to health, biological, physical sciences. *Mailing Add:* 1601 N Randolph St Arlington VA 22207

BERGER, BEVERLY KOBRE, GENERAL RELATIVITY. *Current Pos:* from asst prof to prof physics, 77-96, PROF & CHAIR PHYSICS, OAKLAND UNIV, ROCHESTER, MICH, 96- *Personal Data:* b Passaic, NJ, May 22, 46; m 70, Richard L. *Educ:* Univ Rochester, BS, 67; Univ Md, PhD(physics), 72. *Prof Exp:* Res assoc, Joint Inst Lab Astrophys, Univ Colo & Nat Bur Stand, 72-74; res staff physicist & lectr, Yale Univ, 74-77. *Concurrent Pos:* Res assoc, Enrico Fermi Inst, Univ Chicago, 80; vis asst physicist, Inst Theoret Physics, Univ Calif, Santa Barbara, 81, vis assoc physicist, 86, vis physicist, 93; vis asst prof, Dept Physics & Astron, Univ Md, 82; vis assoc prof, Astron Dept, Univ Mich, 83-84; physicist, Lawrence Livermore Nat Lab, 86; founding chair, Topical Group Gravitation, Am Phys Soc, 96-97. *Mem:* Am Phys Soc; Sigma Xi; Int Soc Gen Relativity & Gravitation. *Res:* Classical general relativity; cosmological models; quantum gravity; quantum field theory in curved spacetime; astrophysics; numerical relativity. *Mailing Add:* Physics Dept Oakland Univ Rochester MI 48309. *Fax:* 313-370-3408; *E-Mail:* berger@oakland.edu

BERGER, BRUCE S, ENGINEERING MECHANICS. *Current Pos:* assoc prof mech eng, 63-69, PROF MECH ENG, UNIV MD, COLLEGE PARK, 69- *Personal Data:* b Philadelphia, Pa, May 23, 32; m 58, Fredericka J Nolde; c Eric & Conrad. *Educ:* Univ Pa, BSc, 54, MSc, 58, PhD(eng mech), 62. *Prof Exp:* Math analyst, Gen Elec Co, 55-56; instr eng, Univ Pa, 56-60; asst prof appl math, Vanderbilt Univ, 61-63. *Concurrent Pos:* Naval Res & Develop Ctr grant, 68-70; Off Naval Res grant, 71-76; Dept Energy res grant, 81-85; vis prof, Imp Col Sci & Tech, London, 83-84, 91; Dept Energy res grant, 93-96. *Mem:* Am Soc Mech Engrs; Soc Indust & Appl Math; Sigma Xi. *Res:* Continuum mechanics; dynamical systems and chaos; machine tool dynamics. *Mailing Add:* Dept Mech Eng Univ Md College Park MD 20742. *Fax:* 301-314-9477

BERGER, BYRON ROLAND, ECONOMIC GEOLOGY, GEOCHEMISTRY. *Current Pos:* GEOLOGIST, US GEOL SURV, 77- *Personal Data:* b Seattle, Wash, Mar 27, 44; m 65; c 2. *Educ:* Occidental Col, BA, 66; Univ Calif, Los Angeles, MS, 75. *Prof Exp:* Geologist, Continental Oil Co, 71-77, res scientist geol, 77. *Mem:* Geol Soc Am; Am Geophys Union. *Res:* Geochemistry of mineral deposits; exploration geochemistry; geochemistry of supergene processes. *Mailing Add:* Federal Ctr MS 973 Denver CO 80225

BERGER, DANIEL RICHARD, ORGANIC CHEMISTRY. *Current Pos:* sect head, 84-90, TECH SERV MGR, AKZO CHEM INC, 90- *Personal Data:* b Oakland, Calif, Nov 3, 33; m 58. *Educ:* Stanford Univ, BS, 54; Northwestern Univ, PhD(chem), 58. *Prof Exp:* Instr chem, Northwestern Univ, 57-58; chemist, Am Cyanamid Co, 58-59; chemist, Richards Co, 59-64, tech serv mgr, Org Chem Div, 64-74, prod develop mgr, 74-78, tech dir, Org Chem Div, 78-82; chief chemist, Far Best Co, 82-84. *Concurrent Pos:* Lectr eve div, Northwestern Univ, 59-68. *Mem:* Am Oil Chem Soc; Am Chem Soc. *Res:* Rearrangements of alpha-halogenated ethers; mechanism; ethers; surfactant chemistry. *Mailing Add:* 1324 Allison Lane Schaumburg IL 60194-2722

BERGER, DANIEL S, ELECTRICAL ENGINEERING, BIOPHYSICS. *Current Pos:* RETIRED. *Personal Data:* b Brooklyn, NY, Aug 11, 23; m 50; c 2. *Educ:* Cooper Union, BEE, 48; Ill Inst Technol, MSEE, 54. *Honors & Awards:* Award Estab Global UVB Network, NATO Advan Res Workshop Ozone Depletion, 93. *Prof Exp:* Jr engr cent sta develop, Western Union, 48-50; sr engr flow meter develop, Mittelman Electronics, Chicago, 50-52; chief engr component res, Sci Specialties, Inc, 52-56; proj engr med electronics, Bionics, Inc, Philadelphia, 56-60; asst prof med physics, Sch Med, Temple Univ, 60-85, sr assoc prof. *Concurrent Pos:* Instr electronics, Pa State Univ, 59-61. *Mem:* Inst Elec & Electronics Engrs; Optical Soc Am; Illum Eng Soc; AAAS. *Res:* Developed diagnostic and therapeutic light sources; meters of effective light intensity for various biological systems; tissue oxygen electrodes and pulsing circuits; blind guidance devices; phonocardiography apparatus. *Mailing Add:* 6655 Lawnton Ave Philadelphia PA 19126

BERGER, EDMOND LOUIS, ELEMENTARY PARTICLE, THEORETICAL PHYSICS. *Current Pos:* asst physicist, 69-70, assoc physicist, 70-76, HIGH ENERGY THEORY GROUP LEADER, ARGONNE NAT LAB, 74-, SR PHYSICIST, 76- *Personal Data:* b Salem, Mass, Dec 5, 39; m 64, Susan Teffner; c Bruce, Catherine & Stephen. *Educ:* Mass Inst Technol, BS, 61; Princeton Univ, PhD(physics), 65. *Prof Exp:* Asst prof physics, Dartmouth Col, 65-68; res physicist, Lawrence Radiation Lab, 68-69. *Concurrent Pos:* Vis scientist, Theory Div, CERN, Geneva, Switz, 72-74, 83-84 & 92-93; vis scientist, Theory Group, Stanford Linear Accelerator Ctr, 78-79; mem, Physics Adv Comt, Fermi Nat Accelerator Lab, 80-83, Dept Energy Revs High Energy Physics Progs, Brookhaven Nat Lab, 85, Stanford Linear Accelerator Ctr, 85, Lawrence Berkeley Lab, 86 & 89, Sci Prog Comt, Rencontres de Moriond, Les Arcs, France, 88-97, Nat Comt Particle Theory, 89-90, High Energy Physics Adv Comt, 91-94, Subpanel on US High Energy Physics Res Prog, 90; fel comt chmn, Div Particles & Fields, Am Phys Soc, 90 & 91; chmn, Organizing Comt, 1990 Summer Study High Energy Physics, Res Directions for the Decade, Snowmass, Colo, 90; mem, strategic planning team for sci & technol, US Dept Energy, 93-94; High Energy & Nuclear Physics Adv Comt, Brookhaven Nat Lab, 95- *Mem:* Fel Am Phys Soc. *Res:* Quantum chromodynamics; gauge theories; strong interactions of elementary particles; phenomenological models of quasi-two-body and multiparticle production; nuclear dependence of short distance processes. *Mailing Add:* High Energy Physics Bldg 362 Argonne Nat Lab Argonne IL 60439. *Fax:* 630-252-5047; *E-Mail:* elb@hep.anl.gov

BERGER, EDWARD ALAN, BIOCHEMISTRY, DEVELOPMENTAL BIOLOGY. *Current Pos:* SCIENTIST, NIH. *Personal Data:* b Bronx, NY, Mar 25, 48. *Educ:* City Col New York, BS, 68; Cornell Univ, PhD(biochem), 72. *Honors & Awards:* Merck Award, NSF. *Prof Exp:* Fel biochem, Cornell Univ, 72-73, neurobiol, Sch Med, Stanford Univ, 73-76 & cell & develop biol, Scripps Clin & Res Found & Univ Calif, San Diego, 76-77; staff scientist cell, Worcester Found Exp Biol, 77- *Concurrent Pos:* Lt Joseph P Kennedy Jr fel neurosci, Sch Med, Stanford Univ, 73-75; staff scientist res grants, Am Cancer Soc, NIH, March Dimes Birth Defects Found, Worcester Found, 78-; mem, biomed sci study sect, NIH. *Mem:* Am Soc Cell Biol; Nat Soc Autistic Children; Am Soc Biol Chemists; AAAS; Soc Develop Biol. *Res:* Structure and function of biological membranes; cell surface interactions during development; molecular basis of cell-cell recognition; control of cell differentiation by cell-cell contact. *Mailing Add:* Lab Viral Dis NIAID NIH Bldg 4 Rm 236 Bethesda MD 20892-0445

BERGER, EDWARD MICHAEL, GENETICS. *Current Pos:* from asst prof to assoc prof, 75-84, PROF BIOL, DARTMOUTH COL, 84- *Personal Data:* b New York, NY, May 2, 44; m 67; c 4. *Educ:* Hunter Col, BA, 65; Syracuse Univ, MS, 67, PhD(genetics), 69. *Prof Exp:* NIH fel develop biol, Harvard Univ, 69-70, Univ Chicago, 70-71 & State Univ NY Albany, 71-75. *Concurrent Pos:* Prog dir cellbiol, NSF, 86-87. *Mem:* AAAS; Genetics Soc Am; Soc Zool; Am Soc Naturalists. *Res:* Molecular genetics. *Mailing Add:* Dept Biol Dartmouth Col Hanover NH 03755-1893

BERGER, FRANK MILAN, MEDICAL RESEARCH, PHARMACOLOGY. *Current Pos:* RETIRED. *Personal Data:* b Pilsen, Czech, June 25, 13; nat US; m 75, A Christine Spadi; c Franklin M & Thomas J. *Educ:* Prague Univ, MD, 37. *Hon Degrees:* DSc, Philadelphia Col Pharm & Sci, 66. *Honors & Awards:* Czechoslovak Nat Prize Sci Res, 38; P K Smith Mem lectr, 69; Taylor Manor Psychiat Award, 70. *Prof Exp:* Chief res, Monsall Hosp, Manchester, 41-43; chief bacteriologist, W Riding of Yorkshire, 43-45; head pharm & bact, British Drug House, 45-47; asst prof pediat, Univ Rochester, 47-49; dir res, Wallace Labs, 49-58, pres, 58-73; prof psychiat & co-dir psychopharmacol doctoral prog, Univ Louisville Sch Med, 74-90. *Concurrent Pos:* Mem adv coun biol, Princeton Univ, prof lectr, 69-76; chmn ad hoc study group clin pharmacol, Walter Reed Army Med Ctr, Washington, DC, 74-80; hon prof microbiol, Waksman Inst, Rutgers Univ, 82. *Mem:* Fel AAAS; fel NY Acad Sci; Am Soc Pharmacol & Exp Therapeut; Am Soc Microbiol; fel Am Col Neuropsychopharmacol. *Res:* Muscle relaxants mephenesin, carisoprodol; tranquilizers; meprobamate; non-specific immunity, protodyne, adjuvants; antiepileptic felbamate. *Mailing Add:* 190 E 72nd St Suite 32B New York NY 10021-4520. *Fax:* 212-737-7510

BERGER, FRANKLIN GORDON, BIOCHEMISTRY, MOLECULAR BIOLOGY. *Current Pos:* DEPT BIOL, UNIV SC. *Personal Data:* b Providence, RI, Sept 26, 47. *Educ:* State Univ NY, Buffalo, BA, 69; Purdue Univ, PhD(biochem), 74. *Prof Exp:* Res asst biochem, Purdue Univ, 69-74; res assoc, Cornell Univ, 74-76; res fel biochem, Roswell Park Mem Inst, 76-79, cancer res scientist, 79- *Concurrent Pos:* NIH fel, Cornell Univ, 75-76. *Res:* Biochemical genetics; hormonal and developmental regulation of mammalian gene expression. *Mailing Add:* Dept Biol Univ SC Columbia SC 29208-0001

BERGER, HAROLD, parasitology, for more information see previous edition

BERGER, HAROLD, NONDESTRUCTIVE TESTING, RADIOLOGICAL PHYSICS. *Current Pos:* PRES, INDUST QUAL, INC, 81- *Personal Data:* b Syracuse, NY, Oct 7, 26; m 52, Dawn Beranek; c Susan, Margaret, Thomas, Joseph & Daniel. *Educ:* Syracuse Univ, BS, 49, MS, 51. *Honors & Awards:* Achievement Award, Am Soc Nondestructive Test, 67, Pres Honour Lect, 71, Gold Medal, 82; Radiation Indust Award, Am Nuclear Soc, 74; Silver Medal, US Dept Com, 79; Award of Merit, Am Soc Testing & Mat, 88; C W Briggs Award, 94. *Prof Exp:* Physicist x-ray dept advan develop lab, Gen Elec Co, 50-59; sr physicist solid state devices div, Battelle Mem Inst, 59-60; assoc physicist metall div, Argonne Nat Lab, 60-70, group leader, Nondestructive Testing Mat Sci Div, 65-73, sr physicist, 70-73; physicist, Reactor Radiation Div, Nat Bur Stand, 73-76, prog mgr nondestructive eval, 75-78, chief, Off Nondestructive Eval, 78-81. *Concurrent Pos:* Vis scientist, Ctr Nuclear Studies, Grenoble, 68-69; tech ed, Mat Eval, Am Soc Nondestructive Testing, 69-87, fel, 73, Mehl hon lectr, 75; chmn, Tech Comt 135, Subcomt 3, acoust methods, Int Standardization Orgn, 83-86; chmn, Isotopes & Radiation Div, Am Nuclear Soc, 76-77; Am Soc Testing & Mats comn, chmn subcomt, E-7, 79-84, 91, chmn subcomt, E-7.05, 84-92; fel-by-courtesy, Johns Hopkins Univ, 86- *Mem:* hon mem & fel Am Soc Nondestructive Testing; Sigma Xi; fel Am Nuclear Soc; fel Am Soc Testing & Mat; Am Soc Metals; fel Brit Inst Nondestructive Testing. *Res:* X-ray and light detection techniques; ultrasonic imaging methods for nondestructive evaluation; x-radiography & proton radiography; neutron radiography; development of nondestructive testing techniques; infrared imaging. *Mailing Add:* 9832 Canal Rd Gaithersburg MD 20879. *Fax:* 301-948-9037

BERGER, HARVEY J, NUCLEAR MEDICINE. *Current Pos:* sr vpres, Med Affairs, 86-87, sr vpres, Res & Develop, 87-89, EXEC VPRES & PRES, RES & DEVELOP DIV, CENTOCOR, INC, 89- *Personal Data:* b New York, NY, June 6, 50; m 76; c 2. *Educ:* Colgate Univ, AB, 72; Yale Univ, MD, 77. *Honors & Awards:* Mem Medal Award, Asn Univ Radiologists, 79; Marc Tetalman Award, Soc Nuclear Med, 81; Cline Fixott Mem Lectr, Am Acad Dent Radiol, 84. *Prof Exp:* Dir cardiovasc imaging, Yale-New Haven Hosp, 81-84; from asst prof to assoc prof radiol & med, Yale Univ, 83-84; prof radiol & med & dir, Div Nuclear Med, Emory Univ, 84-86. *Concurrent Pos:* Estab investr, Am Heart Asn, 81-84; mem, Nat Bd Trustees, Soc Nuclear Med, 83-85; mem task force nuclear cardiol, Int Soc & Fedn Cardiol & WHO, 83-84; NHLBI site visitor, NIH & Veteran's Admin Study Sects, 84-; US ed-in-chief, Nuclear Med Commun, 85-87; assoc ed, Am J Cardiac Imaging, 85-88; adj prof, Univ Pa, 86-; mem sci affairs & drug regulatory affairs comn, Indust Biotechnol Asn, 87-; mem bd dirs, Centocor Develop Corp, 89-; mem, US-Japan Dialogue on Working Environ for Res, Nat Res Coun, 90-, Panel Govt Role Civilian Technol, Comn on Sci, Eng & Public Policy, 90-; mem biotechnol adv comt, Univ Pa, 90- *Mem:* Fel Am Col Cardiol; fel Am Col Physicians; Soc Nuclear Med; Soc Exp Biol & Med; Fel Am Heart Asn Coun Cardiovasc Radiol & Circulation; Am Physiol Soc; NY Acad Sci; AAAS; Sigma Xi; Am Fedn Clin Res. *Res:* Cardiovascular biology; biotechnology; clinical trial design and clinical epidemiology; development and validation of cardiovascular imaging techniques; discovery and development of monoclonal antibodies, proteins and small molecules as pharmaceutical products; technology transfer between academia, government and the private sector. *Mailing Add:* Ariad Pharmaceut 26 Landsdowne St Cambridge MA 02139

BERGER, JACQUES, protozoology, history of biology & ecotoxicology; deceased, see previous edition for last biography

BERGER, JAMES DENNIS, cell biology, for more information see previous edition

BERGER, JAMES EDWARD, PHARMACOLOGY. *Current Pos:* from asst prof to assoc prof, 67-80, PROF PHARMACOL, COL PHARM, BUTLER UNIV, 80- *Personal Data:* b Pinson Fork, Ky, Sept 10, 35; m 56; c 4. *Educ:* Univ Cincinnati, BS, 59, MS, 61; Univ Fla, PhD(pharmacol), 67. *Honors & Awards:* Meritorious Serv Medal, Am Heart Asn, 86. *Prof Exp:* Res asst bact, Surg Bact Res Lab, Cincinnati Gen Hosp, Ohio, 60-62, res assoc, 62-64. *Concurrent Pos:* Mead-Johnson grant, 70-71; consult pharmacologist, Vet Admin Hosp, 69-73, Wishard Mem Hosp, 71-75 & St Vincent Hosp, 75-; consult several legal firms in Indiana. *Mem:* Sigma Xi; Am Heart Asn; AAAS; Am Pharmaceut Asn; Am Hosp Asn. *Res:* Staphylococcal toxin purification and production; action of quinidine on the heart as related to alpha and beta adrenergic receptors in the tissue; calcium antagonist in smooth and myocardial tissue; morphine addiction and alpha and beta adrenergic antagonist. *Mailing Add:* Dept Pharmacol Butler Univ 4600 Sunset Ave Indianapolis IN 46208

BERGER, JAY MANTON, THEORETICAL PHYSICS, COMPUTER SCIENCE. *Current Pos:* sr engr, Adv Systs Develop Div, 56-71, prod assurance adv, Data Processing Group, 71-72, adv litigation anal, 72-80, PROG MGR, DATA PROCESSING GROUP, IBM CORP, 81- *Personal Data:* b New York, NY, Oct 29, 27; m 48; c 3. *Educ:* Univ Mich, BS, 47; Columbia Univ, AM, 48; Case Inst Technol, PhD(physics), 53. *Prof Exp:* Instr physics, Fenn Col, 48-51; res assoc, Princeton Univ, 52-56. *Concurrent Pos:* Consult, Radiation Lab, Univ Calif, 54 & Lockheed Missile Systems, 55; vis prof math, physics, & comput sci, Savannah State Col, 80-81. *Mem:* Am Phys Soc. *Res:* Noise and information theory; applied mathematics; theoretical nuclear physics; plasma physics; astrophysics; field theory; systems design. *Mailing Add:* 57 Fuller Rd Briarcliff Manor NY 10510

BERGER, JERRY EUGENE, atmospheric chemistry, for more information see previous edition

BERGER, JOEL GILBERT, MEDICINAL CHEMISTRY. *Current Pos:* SECT HEAD CENT NERVOUS SYST, SCHERING CORP, 76- *Personal Data:* b Brooklyn, NY, June 2, 37; m 62; c 1. *Educ:* City Col New York, BS, 57; NY Univ, MS, 60, PhD(org chem), 62. *Prof Exp:* Chemist, Esso Res & Eng Co, 62-64 & Wallace & Tiernan, Inc, 64-65; res assoc, Princeton Univ, 65-66; sr med chemist, Endo Labs Inc, 66-73, group leader, 73-76. *Mem:* Am Chem Soc; NY Acad Sci. *Res:* Reaction mechanisms; chemistry of pyrroles and indoles; synthesis of drugs affecting the central nervous system. *Mailing Add:* 50-54 W Lindsley Rd Cedar Grove NJ 07009

BERGER, JOSEF, PHYSICAL ELECTRONICS, SEMICONDUCTOR TECHNOLOGY & INSTRUMENTATION. *Current Pos:* VPRES, TENCOR INSTRUMENTS, ADVAN DEVELOP, 90- *Personal Data:* b Hradec Kralove, Czech, Oct 30, 40; US citizen; m 63; c 2. *Educ:* Czech Inst Technol, Prague, MSc, 63; Czech Acad Sci, PhD(phys electronics), 68. *Prof Exp:* Proj leader phys electronics, Inst Radio Eng & Electronics, Czech Acad Sci, 63-68; res assoc silicon integrated circuits, Stanford Univ, 68-72; mem tech staff, Solid State Lab, Hewlett-Packard Co, 72-74, lab proj mgr, 74-75, res & develop prog mgr, Silicon Integrated Circuit Lab, 77-80; founder & pres, Very Large-Scale Intergratation Stand, 84-90. *Mem:* Sr mem Inst Elec & Electronics Engrs; Sigma Xi. *Res:* Integrated circuits for biomedical applications; metal-oxide-silicon integrated circuits; charge coupled devices; semiconductor memories; silicon integrated circuit technology; metrology for semiconductor processes. *Mailing Add:* 1460 Topar Ave Los Altos CA 94024-5943

BERGER, KENNETH WALTER, audiology; deceased, see previous edition for last biography

BERGER, LAWRENCE, MEDICINE, NEPHROLOGY. *Current Pos:* clin asst physician, Mt Sinai Hosp, 57-63, asst attend physician, 63-72, res assoc med, 69-79, assoc attend, 72-79, assoc clin prof med, 72-79, ATTEND PHYSICIAN, MT SINAI HOSP, 79-, CLIN PROF MED, 79- *Personal Data:* b New York, NY, Apr 6, 26; m 50, Beatrice Neuringer; c 4. *Educ:* NY Univ, BA, 47; Chicago Med Sch, MD & MB, 51; Am Bd Internal Med, dipl in Nephrology. *Prof Exp:* Intern, Mt Sinai Hosp, 51-52, resident med, 54-56; resident, Montefiore Hosp, 52-53; NIH res fel, Med Col, Cornell Univ, 53-54; asst, Goldwater Mem Hosp, 56-57, asst attend, 56-58; res fel, 57-69. *Mem:* AAAS; AMA; Am Fedn Clin Res; fel Am Col Physicians; fel NY Acad Med; Am Soc Nephrology. *Res:* Renal function; physiology; renal uric acid excretion. *Mailing Add:* 119 E 84th St New York NY 10028

BERGER, LESLIE RALPH, MICROBIAL PHYSIOLOGY, ENVIRONMENTAL SCIENCES. *Current Pos:* from asst prof to prof microbiol, 60-93, chmn, 78-85 & 91-93, EMER PROF MICROBIOL, UNIV HAWAII, 93- *Personal Data:* b London, Eng, Dec 18, 28; nat citizen; m 54; c 2. *Educ:* Univ Cincinnati, BS, 50; Univ Wash, MS, 53; Univ Calif, PhD(microbiol), 57. *Prof Exp:* Res microbiologist, Scripps Inst Oceanog, 57-59; asst biochemist, Univ Calif, Davis, 59-60. *Mem:* Am Soc Microbiol; UK Soc Gen Microbiol; Soc Appl Microbiol. *Res:* Physiology of growth at increased hydrostatic pressure; cytology and physiology of photosynthetic organisms at increased hydrostatic pressure; kinetics of allosteric enzymes at extreme physical environments; corrosion of heat exchangers in nuclear reactors and OTEC systems. *Mailing Add:* Dept Microbiol 2538 Mall Univ Hawaii Honolulu HI 96822. *Fax:* 808-988-4593; *E-Mail:* leslie@hawaii.edu

BERGER, LUC, MAGNETISM. *Current Pos:* Swiss Nat Sci Found fel physics, 60-61, from instr to assoc prof, 61-74, PROF PHYSICS, CARNEGIE-MELLON UNIV, 74- *Personal Data:* b Morges, Switz, May 2, 33. *Educ:* Univ Lausanne, BS, 55, PhD(physics), 60. *Mem:* Am Phys Soc; Inst Elec & Electronics Engrs. *Res:* Electronic structure of transition metals; ferromagnetism; transport processes in ferromagnets. *Mailing Add:* Dept Physics Carnegie-Mellon Univ 5000 Forbes Ave Pittsburgh PA 15213

BERGER, MARTIN, PHYSICS. *Current Pos:* PRES, OCCIDENTAL RES CORP & SR VPRES RES & DEVELOP, OCCIDENTAL PETROL CORP, 77- *Personal Data:* b New York, NY, May 23, 26; m 47; c 3. *Educ:* Columbia Univ, BS, 49. *Prof Exp:* Physicist, Tire Div, US Rubber Co, 50-55; engr, Res Labs, Chrysler Corp, 55-56; physicist, Chem Res Div, Esso Res & Eng Co, 56-60, sr physicist, Ctr Basic Res, 60-62, res assoc polymers, 62-64, sect head elastomer res, Enjay Polymer Lab, Exxon Res & Eng Co, 64-68, dir phys & eng sci, Corp Res Lab, 68-75, dir, Govt Res Labs, 75-76. *Res:* Polymer structure and properties, their relationship and methods of changing structure to improve properties; separations, electrochemistry and materials. *Mailing Add:* Invention Submission Corp 217 Ninth St Pittsburgh PA 15222

BERGER, MARTIN JACOB, MATHEMATICAL PHYSICS. *Current Pos:* PHYSICIST, NAT BUR STAND, 52- *Personal Data:* b Vienna, Austria, July 12, 22; nat US; c 3. *Educ:* Univ Chicago, PhD, 51. *Prof Exp:* Fel statist, Univ Chicago, 51-52. *Concurrent Pos:* Mem, Comt Nuclear Sci, Nat Acad Sci-Nat Res Coun. *Mem:* Am Phys Soc; Radiation Res Soc. *Res:* Radiation transport theory; Monte Carlo methods; atmospheric and auroral physics; nuclear medicine; shielding. *Mailing Add:* 5011 Elm St Bethesda MD 20814

BERGER, MELVIN, IMMUNOLOGY. *Current Pos:* chief, Allergy-Immunol Div, Dept Pediat, 84-87, CHIEF, SECT IMMUNOL & INFECTIOUS DIS, DEPT PEDIAT, SCH MED, CASE WESTERN RES UNIV, 87- *Personal Data:* b Philadelphia, Pa, Mar 7, 50; div; c 2. *Educ:* Western Res Univ, BA, 70; Case Western Res Univ, MD & PhD(biochem), 76. *Prof Exp:* Resident pediat, Childrens Hosp Med Ctr, Boston, 76-78; clin assoc allergy & immunol, Nat Inst Allergy & Infectious Dis, NIH, 78-81; asst chief, Allergy-Immunol Serv, Walter Reed Army Med Ctr, Washington, DC, 81-84. *Concurrent Pos:* Clin fel pediat, Harvard Med Sch, 76-78; asst prof pediat & med, Uniformed Serv Univ Health Sci, 81-84; clin care consult, Nat Inst Health Clin Ctr, 81-84; assoc prof pediat & path, Sch Med, Case Western Res Univ, 84-93, prof pediat & gen med sci, 93- *Mem:* Soc Pediat Res; Am Acad Allergy & Immunol; Am Asn Immunologists; Am Acad Pediat; Am Soc Clin Invest. *Res:* Host defense mechanisms and their defects; role of infection and the immune response in cystic fibrosis. *Mailing Add:* Dept Pediat Case Western Res Univ Sch Med Rainbow Babies & Children's Hosp 2101 Adelbert Rd Cleveland OH 44106-2624. *Fax:* 216-844-3757

BERGER, MELVYN STUART, MATHEMATICS. *Current Pos:* dir, Ctr Appl Math & Math Sci, 80-82 & 85, PROF MATH, UNIV MASS, AMHERST, 78-, DIR CTR APPL MATH, NONLINEAR SCI & MATH COMPUT, 89- *Personal Data:* b Brooklyn, NY, Aug 23, 39; m 77; c 2. *Educ:* Univ Toronto, BA, 61; Yale Univ, MA, 63, PhD(math), 64. *Prof Exp:* From asst prof to assoc prof math, Univ Minn, Minneapolis, 64-69; from assoc prof to prof math, Belfer Grad Sch, Yeshiva Univ, 69-78. *Concurrent Pos:* Vis mem, Courant Inst, 66-68; vis mem, Inst Advan Study, Princeton, 72-73, mem, 77-79; invited prof, Univ Paris, 81, 83 & 84, Princeton Univ, 83, Mass Inst Technol, 85, Oxford Univ, Eng, 85. *Mem:* Am Math Soc; Soc Indust & Appl Math; AAAS. *Res:* Nonlinear analysis; partial differential equations, mathematical physics and differential geometry; functional analysis; applied mathematics; nonlinear aspects of high technology; computer graphics. *Mailing Add:* Dept Math 1464 Beacon St Newton MA 02159

BERGER, MITCHELL HARVEY, ORGANIC CHEMISTRY, POLYMER CHEMISTRY. *Current Pos:* proj scientist, Coatings Mat Div, 80-81, SR CHEMIST, COATED FILMS DIV, SEALED AIR CORP, 81- *Personal Data:* b Miami Beach, Fla, Mar 19, 49; m 72; c 1. *Educ:* City Col New York, BS, 70; Univ Rochester, MS, 73, PhD(chem), 75. *Prof Exp:* Res assoc org chem, Cornell Univ, 74-76; chemist, Chem & Plastics Div, Union Carbide Corp, 76-80. *Mem:* Am Chem Soc; Sigma Xi. *Mailing Add:* HenKel Surface Technol 12801 Newburgh Rd Livonia MI 48150

BERGER, NEIL EVERETT, APPLIED MATHEMATICS. *Current Pos:* Asst prof, 68-75, ASSOC PROF MATH, UNIV ILL CHICAGO, 75- *Personal Data:* b New York, NY, Oct 8, 42; div; c 1. *Educ:* Columbia Univ, BS, 63; NY Univ, MS, 65, PhD(appl math), 68. *Honors & Awards:* Monroe Martin Prize, Inst Fluid Dynamics & Appl Math, Univ Md, 74. *Mem:* Soc Indust & Appl Math; AAAS; Am Math Soc; Math Asn Am. *Res:* Partial differential equations of elasticity; fluid dynamics; asymptotic expansions. *Mailing Add:* Dept Math Univ Ill Chicago 851 S Morgan Chicago IL 60607-7045. *Fax:* 312-996-1491; *E-Mail:* berger@uic.edu

BERGER, PAUL RAYMOND, SEMICONDUCTOR MATERIALS & DEVICES. *Current Pos:* ASST PROF ELEC ENG, UNIV DEL, 92- *Personal Data:* b Lafayette, Ind, May 8, 63; m 89, Rita J Szokowski; c Janine K & Maria K. *Educ:* Univ Mich, Ann Arbor, BSE, 85, MSE, 87, PhD(elec eng), 90. *Prof Exp:* Mem tech staff, AT&T Bell Labs, 90-92. *Concurrent Pos:* Fac early career develop award, NSF, 96. *Mem:* Inst Elec & Electronics Engrs; Optical Soc Am; Mat Res Soc. *Res:* Growth and materials characterization of III-V compound and Group V semiconductor materials; fabrication of high-speed optical and electronic devices; optoelectronic integrated circuits. *Mailing Add:* Univ Del 140 Evans Hall Newark DE 19716. *Fax:* 302-831-4316; *E-Mail:* pberger@ee.udel.edu

BERGER, PHILIP JEFFREY, ANIMAL BREEDING, STATISTICAL ANALYSIS. *Current Pos:* asst prof, Iowa State Univ, 72-78, assoc mem grad fac, 74-79, assoc prof animal breeding, 78-81, MEM GRAD FAC, IOWA STATE UNIV, 79-, PROF ANIMAL SCI, 82- *Personal Data:* b Newark, NJ, June 28, 43; m 65, Frances Williams; c Sarah & Philip. *Educ:* Del Valley Col, BS, 65; Ohio State Univ, MS, 67, PhD(animal breeding), 70. *Prof Exp:* Res & teaching asst animal breeding, Ohio State Univ, 65-70, fel, 71. *Mem:* Am Soc Animal Sci; Am Dairy Sci Asn; Biomet Soc; Sigma Xi. *Res:* Development of computing procedures for best linear unbiased prediction of breeding values, predictability of correlated responses in breeding populations, economic evaluation of productive traits and recovery of selection response; development of high performance scientific computing techniques; genetic prediction of animal merit in populations under selection. *Mailing Add:* 2518 Kellogg Ames IA 50010-4863. *Fax:* 515-294-2401; *E-Mail:* pjberger@iastate.edu

BERGER, RALPH JACOB, SLEEP THERMOREGULATION. *Current Pos:* from asst prof to prof psychol & biol, 68-94, EMER PROF BIOL, UNIV CALIF, SANTA CRUZ, 74- *Personal Data:* b Vienna, Austria, Sept 16, 37; m 63; c 2. *Educ:* Cambridge Univ, BA, 60, MA, 64; Univ Edinburgh, PhD(psychol), 63. *Prof Exp:* Res asst, Dept Psychol Med, Univ Edinburgh, 60-63; res psychologist, Lab Paranatal Physiol, Nat Inst Neurol Dis & Blindness, NIH, San Juan, PR, 63-65; asst res anatomist, Univ Calif, Los Angeles, 65-68. *Concurrent Pos:* Vis asst prof, Univ PR, 63-64; vis res fel, Univ Tasmania, 95- *Mem:* AAAS; Soc Neurosci; Sleep Res Soc; Europ Sleep Res Soc. *Res:* Sleep; thermoregulation; metabolism; hibernation; epistemological implications of neurobiological research. *Mailing Add:* Sinsheimer Labs Univ Calif Santa Cruz CA 95064

BERGER, RICHARD DONALD, PLANT PATHOLOGY. *Current Pos:* PROF PLANT PATH, UNIV FLA, 66- *Personal Data:* b Macungie, Pa, Jan 15, 34; m 62; c 2. *Educ:* Kutztown State Col, 55; Univ Wis, PhD(plant path), 62. *Honors & Awards:* Campbell Award, Am Phytopath Soc & Campbell Soup Co, 74. *Prof Exp:* Res fel, Univ Wis, 62-63; plant pathologist, Pa State Univ, 63-66. *Concurrent Pos:* Res award, Fla Fruit & Veg Asn, 72; assoc ed, J Am Phytopath Soc, 76- *Mem:* Fel Am Phytopath Soc. *Res:* Epidemiology of vegetable and field crop diseases; Cercospora taxonomy; disease modeling; computer simulation of epidemics. *Mailing Add:* Dept Plant Pathol Univ Fla Gainesville FL 32611-2002

BERGER, RICHARD LEE, civil engineering, ceramics engineering, for more information see previous edition

BERGER, RICHARD LEO, PLASMA PHYSICS. *Current Pos:* RES SCIENTIST, PLASMA PHYSICS, LAWRENCE LIVERMORE NAT LAB, 91- *Personal Data:* b Salem, Mass, May 13, 44; m 70. *Educ:* Princeton Univ, AB, 66; Univ Md, PhD(physics), 72. *Prof Exp:* Res assoc physics, Dept Astro-Geophys, Univ Colo, 72-74; res assoc plasma physics, Plasma Physics Lab, Princeton Univ, 74-77; res scientist, plasma physics, KMS Fusion Inc, 77-90. *Mem:* Am Phys Soc. *Res:* Theoretical plasma physics: parametric instabilities; large-amplitude nonlinear waves; plasma kinetic theory. *Mailing Add:* L-472 Lawrence Livermore Nat Lab PO Box 808 Livermore CA 94550. *E-Mail:* berger5@iini.gov

BERGER, RICHARD S, ORGANIC POLYMER CHEMISTRY. *Current Pos:* RETIRED. *Personal Data:* b Brooklyn, NY, Apr 28, 29; m 54; c 2. *Educ:* Stanford Univ, BS, 50; Univ Wis, PhD(org chem), 54. *Prof Exp:* Fel, Univ Minn, 54; chemist, Shell Develop Co, 56-65; mgr, Fiber Chem Br, Res Div, Phillips Petrol Co, 65-70, dir res proj, 70-73 & strategic planning, 73-91. *Res:* Synthetic polymer chemistry; polymer and fiber stabilization; chemical modification of polyamide, polyester and polyolefin polymers and fibers. *Mailing Add:* 344 Pimlico Rd Greenville SC 29607

BERGER, ROBERT, ELECTRICAL ENGINEERING. *Current Pos:* STAFF MEM, LINCOLN LAB, MASS INST TECHNOL, 64- *Personal Data:* b New York, NY, July 10, 38; m 67; c 3. *Educ:* Rensselaer Polytech Inst, BEE, 60; Harvard Univ, MS, 61, PhD(appl math), 65. *Mem:* Inst Elec & Electronics Engrs. *Res:* Wafer-scale integrated circuits; computer architecture. *Mailing Add:* Lincoln Lab Rm L300 Mass Inst Technol 244 Wood St Lexington MA 02173

BERGER, ROBERT ELLIOTT, TECHNOLOGICAL INNOVATION ASSESSMENT. *Current Pos:* mech engr, Prod Safety Technol Div, 75-79, prog analyst off dir, 79-81, gen phys scientist, Ctr Chem Eng, 81-82, dir tech assessment, Off Naval Res, 82-83, DIR INNOVATION & TECHNOL DIV, SMALL BUS ADMIN, 83- *Personal Data:* b Baltimore, Md, July 22, 47; m 69; c 2. *Educ:* Case Western Res Univ, BS, 68; Johns Hopkins Univ, PhD(biomech), 73. *Prof Exp:* Assoc, US Nat Bur Standards, 73-74; res assoc, Optical Mfrs Asn, 74-75. *Mem:* Am Soc Mech Engrs; Am Soc Testing & Mat; Am Nat Standards Inst. *Res:* Measurements and modelling of solid fluid flows with industrial applications; identification of injury mechanisms associated with products; development of human injury tolerance criteria and product safety test methods. *Mailing Add:* US Dept Energy Off Energy Res ER 32 19901 Germantown Rd Germantown MD 20874-9918

BERGER, ROBERT LEWIS, THERMOMETRY, INSTRUMENTATION. *Current Pos:* mem staff, Lab Tech Develop, 67-77, chief, Sect Biophys Instrumentation, Lab Tech Develop, 77-89, CHIEF, SECT BIOPHYS INSTRUMENTATION, LAB BIOPHYS CHEM, NAT HEART, LUNG & BLOOD INST, 89- *Personal Data:* b Omaha, Nebr, Sept 2, 25; m 50, 81, Victoria A Harden; c David, Karen, Christine & Kathryn (dec). *Educ:* Colo Agr & Mech Col, BS, 50; Pa State Univ, MS, 53, PhD(physics), 56. *Prof Exp:* Instr physics, Park Col, 50-51; fel, Brit-Am Exchange, Am Cancer Soc, Cambridge Univ, 56; asst prof physics, Utah State Univ, 57-60, assoc prof, 60-62. *Concurrent Pos:* Vis scientist, Dept Chem, Univ Calif, San Diego, 69-71; ed, Nat Bur Stand publ, 70-72. *Mem:* Fel AAAS; fel Am Phys Soc; Soc Gen Physiol; Biophys Soc; Am Soc Biochem & Molecular Biol; Sigma Xi. *Res:* Enzyme kinetics and mechanisms; spectroscopy, fluid dynamics and computers; microcalorimetry; dye laser spectroscopy; Mossbauer spectroscopy; near ir and roman spectroscopy. *Mailing Add:* Nat Heart Lung & Blood Inst Bldg 10 Rm 7N321 4503 Anamere St Bethesda MD 20819-3930. *Fax:* 301-295-4628; *E-Mail:* rlberger@aol.com

BERGER, ROBERT S, insect toxicology, for more information see previous edition

BERGER, S EDMUND, ORGANIC CHEMISTRY. *Current Pos:* RETIRED. *Personal Data:* b Osijek, Yugoslavia, Nov 13, 22; nat US; m 47; c 2. *Educ:* Univ Rome, ChD(org chem), 48. *Prof Exp:* Asst org chem, Univ Rome, 48-49; res chemist, Dept Legal Med, Harvard Med Sch, 49-51; res chemist, 51-63, res supvr, 63-80, group leader, 80-82, tech supvr, Allied Corp, 82-87. *Mem:* Am Chem Soc; Am Translr Asn. *Res:* Polyurethane chemistry; polyesters; diisocyanates; food acidulants; surfactants; liquid ion exchange; exploratory organic synthesis; catalysis; fluorocarbon solvents; precision cleaning. *Mailing Add:* 298 Grayton Rd Tonawanda NY 14150-8622

BERGER, SELMAN A, ANALYTICAL CHEMISTRY, ENVIRONMENTAL CHEMISTRY. *Current Pos:* from asst prof to assoc prof, 71-80, dep dept chmn, 72-82, PROF CHEM, JOHN JAY COL, CITY UNIV NEW YORK, 81-, DEPT CHMN, 82- *Personal Data:* b Brooklyn, NY, Aug 31, 42; wid; c Mark & Eric. *Educ:* Brooklyn Col, BS, 64; Univ Conn, MS, 67, PhD(analytical chem), 69. *Prof Exp:* Teaching asst chem, Univ Conn, 64-69; fel, Dalhousie Univ, Halifax, NS, 69-70; sr chemist, Toxicol Lab, Bur Labs, NYC Dept Health, 70-71. *Concurrent Pos:* Doctoral fac chem, City Univ New York, Grad Ctr, 73- *Mem:* Am Chem Soc; Sigma Xi. *Res:* Spectroscopic methods for trace analysis; flame methods; complexation and solvent extraction methods; mathematical modeling of solvent extraction equilibria. *Mailing Add:* Dept Sci John Jay Col Criminal Justice City Univ NY 445 W 59th St New York NY 10019. *Fax:* 212-237-8742

BERGER, SHELBY LOUISE, BIOCHEMISTRY, CELL & MOLECULAR BIOLOGY. *Current Pos:* Fel biochem, Nat Inst Arthritis & Metab Dis, 68-70, staff fel, 70-71, sr staff fel biochem & cell biol, Nat Inst Dent Res, 72-74 & Nat Cancer Inst, 74-76, RES CHEMIST BIOCHEM & CELL BIOL, NAT CANCER INST, NIH, 76- *Personal Data:* b New York, NY, Jan 5, 41; m 73. *Educ:* Bryn Mawr Col, AB, 62; Harvard Univ, PhD(biophys), 68. *Mem:* Am Soc Biol Chemists. *Res:* Control of the metabolism of messenger ribonucleic acid and heterogeneous nuclear ribonucleic acid in physiologically resting, growing and malignant human lymphocytes; interferon. *Mailing Add:* Nat Cancer Inst NIH Bldg 10 Rm B109 Bethesda MD 20892-0001

BERGER, SHELDON, MEDICINE, ENDOCRINOLOGY. *Current Pos:* from asst prof to assoc prof, 65-76, ASSOC PROF MED, NORTHWESTERN UNIV, CHICAGO, 76- *Personal Data:* b Chicago, Ill, Nov 12, 28; m 50; c 4. *Educ:* Univ Ill, BA, 49, BS, 51, MD, 53. *Prof Exp:* Physician in charge, Radioisotope Lab, 59-63, asst dir dept metab & endocrine res, 60-63; assoc dir dept res & educ, Evanston Hosp, 63-65, coordr res labs, 65-69. *Concurrent Pos:* NIH trainee metab & endocrine, Michael Reese Hosp, Chicago, 58-59; NIH trainee thyroid res methods, Beth Israel Hosp, Boston, 59. *Mem:* Am Col Physicians; Endocrine Soc. *Res:* Diabetes; general metabolism; thyroid physiology; internal medicine. *Mailing Add:* Northwestern Univ Med Sch Northwestern Mem Hosp 211 E Chicago Ave Suite 930 Chicago IL 60611-2616

BERGER, STANLEY A(LLAN), FLUID MECHANICS, BIOENGINEERING. *Current Pos:* lectr aeronaut sci, 61, from asst prof to assoc prof, 61-70, PROF ENG SCI, UNIV CALIF, BERKELEY, 70- *Personal Data:* b Brooklyn, NY, Aug 9, 34; c Shoshana & Maya. *Educ:* Brooklyn Col, BS, 55; Brown Univ, PhD(appl math), 59. *Prof Exp:* Res assoc aeronaut eng, Princeton Univ, 59-60. *Concurrent Pos:* Consult, Rand Corp, Lockheed Space & Missile Co, Sci Appln, Inc, Flow Res, Inc, IBM & Alcoa Res Lab; vchair, Appl Mech Div, Am Soc Mech Engrs, 96- *Mem:* Fel Am Physics Soc; Soc Indust & Appl Math; fel Am Soc Mech Engrs; fel AAAS; fel Am Inst Aeronaut & Astronaut. *Res:* Fluid mechanics; explosions; wake flows; viscous flows; physiological fluid mechanics; vortex breakdown; flow in curved tubes; numerical methods in fluid mechanics. *Mailing Add:* Dept Mech Eng Univ Calif Berkeley CA 94720-1740. *Fax:* 510-642-6163; *E-Mail:* saberger@me.berkeley.edu

BERGER, STEVEN BARRY, APPLIED MATHEMATICS. *Current Pos:* mem staff, Dept Elec Eng & Comput Sci, George Washington Univ, 80-; DIR & PROF COMPUT SCI & MATH DEPT, LEWIS UNIV. *Personal Data:* b New York, NY, Dec 29, 46. *Educ:* Mass Inst Technol, SB, 67, PhD(physics), 73. *Prof Exp:* Res assoc physics, Boston Univ, 73-74; fel physics, Mass Inst Technol, 74-78; mem staff, TRW Systs Group, 78-80. *Concurrent Pos:* Fight-for-Sight fel, NY, 74-76; asst ed, Am J Physics, 75-78; sr scientist, Itek Corp, 76-77. *Mem:* Sigma Xi; Am Phys Soc; Am Optical Soc; NY Acad Sci; Math Asn Am. *Mailing Add:* Math & Comput Sci Dept Lewis Univ 500 S Independence B Romeoville IL 60441-2298

BERGER, TOBY, INFORMATION THEORY, COMMUNICATIONS. *Current Pos:* from asst prof to assoc prof, 68-77, prof elec eng, 77-87, J PRESTON LEVIS PROF ENG, CORNELL UNIV, 87- *Personal Data:* b Sept 4, 40; US citizen; m 61; c Elizabeth & Lawrence. *Educ:* Yale Univ, BE, 62; Harvard Univ, MS, 64, PhD(appl math), 66. *Honors & Awards:* Frederick E Terman Award, ASEE, 82. *Prof Exp:* Assoc scientist, Raytheon Co, 62-66, sr scientist, 66-68. *Concurrent Pos:* Consult, Raytheon Co, 68-, IBM Fed Systs Div, 75-, Schlumberger, 81-, TCSI, 86-, AT&T Bell Labs, 87-; Guggenheim fel, 75-76, fel Japan Soc Prom Sci, 80-81, fel Ministry Educ People's Repub China, 81-; ed-in-chief, Inst Elec & Electronics Engrs Trans Info Theory, 87- *Mem:* AAAS; Sigma Xi; Inst Elec & Electronics Engrs. *Res:* Information theory and communication theory, especially source encoding; video compression. *Mailing Add:* 422 Highland Rd Ithaca NY 14850. *Fax:* 607-255-9072

BERGER, WOLFGANG HELMUT, MICROPALEONTOLOGY, OCEAN HISTORY. *Current Pos:* from asst prof to assoc prof, 71-81, PROF OCEANOG, SCRIPPS INST OCEANOG, 81- *Personal Data:* b Erlangen, Ger, 1937; m 66; c 2. *Educ:* Univ Erlangen, cand geol, 61; Univ Colo, Boulder, MSc, 63; Univ Calif, San Diego, PhD(oceanog), 68. *Honors & Awards:* Bigelow Medal, Woods Hole Oceanog Inst, 79; Huntsman Medal, Bedford, 84; Humboldt Award, Bonn, 86; Ewing Medal, Am Geophys Union, 89; Prince Albert I Medal, 91; Balzan Prize, 93. *Prof Exp:* Asst res oceanogr, Scripps Inst Oceanog, 68-70; asst geol, Univ Kiel, 70-71. *Concurrent Pos:* Consult, Oceanog Div, NSF, 73-75 & Deep Sea Drilling Proj, Joint Oceanog Inst Deep Earth Sampling, 74-; guest prof, Univ Kiel, 77 & 80; res assoc, Univ Bremen, 87-; interim dir, Scripps Inst Oceanog, 96-97. *Mem:* AAAS; Geol Soc Am; Am Geophys Union; Am Soc Limnol Oceanogr. *Res:* Ecology and paleoecology of planktonic foraminifera; biogenous sedimentation in the deep ocean; paleo-oceanography; history of the carbon cycle and climate. *Mailing Add:* Scripps Inst Oceanog Univ Calif San Diego La Jolla CA 92093

BERGERON, CLIFTON GEORGE, CERAMIC ENGINEERING. *Current Pos:* res assoc ceramic eng, Univ Ill, 57-61, from asst prof to prof ceramic eng, 61-88, head dept, 79-86, EMER PROF, UNIV ILL, 88- *Personal Data:* b Los Angeles, Calif, Jan 5, 25; m 50, Laura Kaario; c Ann & Louis. *Educ:* Univ Ill, BS, 50, MS, 59, PhD(ceramic eng), 61. *Honors & Awards:* Friedberg Lectr, Nat Inst Ceramic Engrs, 85; Outstanding Educr Award, Am Ceramic Soc, 87. *Prof Exp:* Ceramic res engr, A O Smith Corp, 50-53, sr res engr, 53-55; staff engr res & develop labs, Whirlpool Corp, 55-57. *Mem:* AAAS; fel Am Ceramic Soc; Nat Inst Ceramic Engrs; Am Soc Testing & Mat; Am Soc Eng Educ; Am Asn Univ Prof. *Res:* Nucleation and crystal growth in glasses; dielectric properties of ceramic coating; high temperature chemical reactions and coatings for metals; electrical conduction in ceramic materials. *Mailing Add:* 208 W Michigan Urbana IL 61801

BERGERON, CLYDE J, JR, PHYSICS. *Current Pos:* asst, 55-60, from asst prof to assoc prof, 60-68, PROF PHYSICS, UNIV NEW ORLEANS, 68-, CHMN DEPT, 74- *Personal Data:* b New Orleans, La, July 2, 32; m 56; c 3. *Educ:* Loyola Univ, BS, 55; La State Univ, PhD, 59. *Prof Exp:* Res asst, Loyola Univ, 54-55. *Concurrent Pos:* Consult, Electronuclear Dov, Oak Ridge Nat Lab, 61 & 62-66; Equip subcontract, Oak Ridge Nat Lab, 63-; Res Corp grant, 67-68. *Mem:* Am Phys Soc; Sigma Xi; Am Asn Physics Teachers. *Res:* Solid state low temperature physics; physics of metals, especially superconductivity. *Mailing Add:* Dept Physics Univ New Orleans New Orleans LA 70148

BERGERON, GEORGES ALBERT, physiology; deceased, see previous edition for last biography

BERGERON, JOHN ALBERT, CYTOLOGY. *Current Pos:* MEM STAFF, GEN ELEC RES LAB, 64-, RES SCIENTIST, RES & DEVELOP CTR, 64-, MGR DIAGNOSTIC PROJS, CORP RES & DEVELOP, 70- *Personal Data:* b Cumberland, RI, June 13, 29; m 52; c 3. *Educ:* Brown Univ, BA, 51; Cornell Univ, PhD(zool), 56. *Prof Exp:* Asst hist embryol, Cornell Univ, 51-55; assoc physiologist, Brookhaven Nat Lab, 55-61, physiologist, 61-64. *Concurrent Pos:* Mem, Biol Stain Comn. *Mem:* Soc Gen Physiol; Am Soc Microbiol; Am Soc Cell Biol; Fedn Am Soc Exp Biol; Soc Cryobiol. *Res:* Electromicroscopy; sub-cellular fractions; physicochemical aspects of the behavior of dyes and photosynthetic pigments; hemostatic mechanisms. *Mailing Add:* Gen Elec Co Res & Develop Ctr PO Box 8 Bldg K1, Rm 3B14 Schenectady NY 12301

BERGERON, JOHN JOSEPH MARCEL, CELL BIOLOGY. *Current Pos:* from asst prof to assoc prof, 74-82, PROF ANAT, MCGILL UNIV, 82-, CHAIR ANAT & CELL BIOL, 96- *Personal Data:* b Belleville, Ont, Dec 22, 46; m 71; c 2. *Educ:* McGill Univ, BSc, 66; Oxford Univ, DPhil(biochem), 69. *Honors & Awards:* Murray J Barr Award, Can Asn Anatomists. *Prof Exp:* Res assoc cell biol, Rockefeller Univ, 69-71; scientist, Nat Inst Med Res, 71-74. *Mem:* Biochem Soc; Am Soc Cell Biol; Am Soc Biol Chem; Endocrine Soc; fel Royal Soc Can. *Res:* Membrane biogenesis; hormone action; glycosylation. *Mailing Add:* Dept Anat & Cell Biol McGill Univ 3640 Univ St Montreal PQ H3A 2B2 Can. *E-Mail:* enix@musica.mcgill.ca

BERGERON, KENNETH DONALD, NUCLEAR ENGINEERING, SOFTWARE SYSTEMS. *Current Pos:* Physicist, Plasma Theory Div, 74-78, syst analyst, Solar Energy Dept, 78-81, TECH SUPVR, REACTOR SAFETY ANALYSIS, SANDIA NAT LABS, 81- *Personal Data:* b Jacksonville, Fla, May 20, 46; div. *Educ:* Brown Univ, ScB, 68; Brandeis Univ, MS, 69, PhD(physics), 75. *Res:* Ion emission in diodes; magnetic insulation; insulator flashover; sheaths in plasma; solar industrial process heat; energy economics; nuclear reactor severe accident analysis; computer code development. *Mailing Add:* Sandia Nat Labs MS 0739 PO Box 5800 Albuquerque NM 87185-0739

BERGERON, MICHEL, PHYSIOLOGY, NEPHROLOGY. *Current Pos:* from asst prof to assoc prof physiol, 67-75, chmn dept, 86-93, PROF PHYSIOL, UNIV MONTREAL, 75- *Personal Data:* b Alma, Que. *Educ:* Laval Univ, BA, 53, MD, 59; McGill Univ, MSc, 64. *Prof Exp:* Intern internal med, Huntington Mem Hosp, 59-60; resident, Lahey Clin, 61-62; Med Res Coun Can res fel, Nuclear Res Ctr, France, 64-67, scholar, 67-72. *Concurrent Pos:* Ed-in-chief, Med Sci, Paris, Montreal. *Mem:* AAAS; Am Soc Nephrology; Can Soc Physiol (pres, 86-); Can Soc Nephrology; Asn Sci, Eng & Technol Community Can (pres, 78). *Res:* Amino acid transport; micropuncture techniques; electron microscopy; radioautography, renal physiology; membrane transport. *Mailing Add:* Dept Physiol Univ Montreal Montreal PQ H3C 3T8 Can

BERGERON, ROBERT F(RANCIS) (TERRY), JR, applied mathematics, computer science, for more information see previous edition

BERGES, DAVID ALAN, ORGANIC CHEMISTRY, MEDICINAL CHEMISTRY. *Current Pos:* SR INVESTR, SMITH KLINE BEECHAM PHARMACEUT, 68- *Personal Data:* b Evansville, Ind, Aug 5, 41; m 65, Gayle S Grote; c Heather E (Pepor), Grant S, Bradford K & Christopher T. *Educ:* Evansville Col, BA, 63; Ind Univ, PhD(chem), 67. *Prof Exp:* Assoc org chem, Nat Ctr Sci Res, Inst Chem Natural Substances, France, 67-68. *Mem:* Am Chem Soc; AAAS. *Res:* Isolation, structure elucidation and synthesis of natural products; development of new organo-chemical synthetic methods; conformational analysis; biological properties, chemistry and synthesis of betalactam antibiotics; synthesis of enzyme inhibitors; synthesis of antiviral agents. *Mailing Add:* 18 Buckwalter Rd Phoenixville PA 19460

BERGESON, HAVEN ELDRED, HIGH ENERGY PHYSICS. *Current Pos:* asst prof physics, 63-64, asst res prof, 64-68, assoc prof, 68-75, chmn, Physics Dept, 76-80, PROF PHYSICS, UNIV UTAH, 75- *Personal Data:* b Logan, Utah, Dec 22, 33; m 57; c 8. *Educ:* Univ Utah, BS, 58, PhD(physics), 62. *Prof Exp:* Physicist, Space Sci Lab, Gen Elec Co, 61-63. *Mem:* Am Phys Soc; Am Asn Physics Teachers. *Res:* Cosmic ray physics; cosmic ray anisotropies; high energy neutrino interactions; muon production; ultra high energy collisions; extensive air showers; air scintillation. *Mailing Add:* Dept Physics Univ Utah 201b J Fletcher Bldg Salt Lake City UT 84112

BERGEY, GREGORY KENT, NEUROLOGY, NEUROPHYSIOLOGY. *Current Pos:* asst prof neurol & physiol, 83-89, assoc prof neurol, 89-, PROF NEUROL & PHYSIOL, 89-96, 96- SCH MED, UNIV MD, 89-; DIR, MD EPILEPSY CTR, 87- *Personal Data:* b Bryn Mawr, Pa, Nov 9, 49; m 72, Stefanie Antonaicos; c 2. *Educ:* Princeton Univ, AB, 71; Univ Pa, MD, 75. *Prof Exp:* From intern to resident internal med, Yale-New Haven Hosp, 75-77; res assoc neurobiol, Lab Develop Neurobiol, NICHD, NIH, 77-81; resident neurol, Johns Hopkins Hosp, 79-83. *Mem:* Soc Neurosci; Am Acad Neurol; Am Epilepsy Soc; Am Neurol Asn. *Res:* Mechanisms of action of convulsants and anticonvulsants; actions of clostridial neurotoxins; intractable seizures; seizure propagation; computer analysis of seizure onset and propagation. *Mailing Add:* Dept Neurol Sch Med Univ Md 22 S Greene St Baltimore MD 21201. *Fax:* 410-328-0697; *E-Mail:* gbergey@umabnet.ab.umd.edu

BERGEY, JAMES L, CARDIOVASCULAR PHARMACOLOGY. *Current Pos:* sr res fel, Squibb Inst Med Res, Princeton, NJ, 82-89, assoc dir licensing, 89-92, DIR LICENSING, BRISTOL-MYERS SQUIBB, 92- *Personal Data:* b Allentown, Pa, May 22, 45; div; c Kristie L & Susanne J. *Educ:* Temple Univ, BS, 68, PhD(cardiovasc pharmacol), 76. *Prof Exp:* Res assoc electrophysiol, Sch Med, Temple Univ, 75-76; sr res pharmacologist, Res Div, Wyeth Labs Inc, 76-81; sr pharmacologist, Pharm Div, Ciba-Geigy Corp, 81-82. *Mem:* Sigma Xi; NY Acad Sci; Am Heart Asn. *Res:* Enzymatic regulation of ionic permeability in biological membranes; role of calcium in pathological processes, including hypertension and cardiac arrhythmias; cardiac cellular electrophysiology. *Mailing Add:* 117 Shady Lane Lansdale PA 19446-1414. *Fax:* 609-252-6148

BERGGREN, GERARD THOMAS, JR, PLANT PATHOLOGY. *Current Pos:* ASST SPECIALIST PLANT PATH, COOP EXTEN, LA STATE UNIV, BATON ROUGE, 77- *Personal Data:* b New Orleans, La, Dec 8, 46; m 67; c 2. *Educ:* Southeastern La Univ, BS, 69; La State Univ, MS, 71, PhD(plant path), 74. *Prof Exp:* Res plant pathologist, Ansul Co, 74-75; mgr prod develop, Kalo Lab, Marion Labs, 75-76, mgr field res, 76-77. *Mem:* Am Phytopath Soc. *Res:* Applied plant pathology in the areas of cotton, soybean, sugarcane, fruits, nuts and small grain. *Mailing Add:* 2324 Ben Hur Rd Baton Rouge LA 70820

BERGGREN, MICHAEL J, INVERSE SCATTERING, ULTRASOUND IMAGING. *Current Pos:* res asst prof 78-84, RES ASSOC PROF BIOENG, UNIV UTAH, 85- *Personal Data:* b Menominee, Mich, Feb 22, 39. *Educ:* Univ Mich, BS, 61; Stanford Univ, PhD(physics), 69. *Prof Exp:* Teaching asst physics, Stanford Univ, 61-63, res asst, 63-69; asst prof, Mankato State Col, 69-73; vis scientist, Mayo Found, Mayo Clin, 74-75, res fel, Biophys Sci Unit, 75-78. *Concurrent Pos:* Res asst, Kaman Nuclear, Colo, 62. *Mem:* Am Asn Physicists in Med; Sigma Xi; Am Phys Soc; Inst Elec & Electronics Engrs. *Res:* Medical imaging techniques with emphasis on computerized tomography from ultrasonic, x-ray and radioisotope sources. *Mailing Add:* Univ Utah Merrill Eng Bldg Salt Lake City UT 84112. *Fax:* 801-585-5361; *E-Mail:* berggren@ee.utah.edu

BERGGREN, RONALD B, SURGERY. *Current Pos:* from asst prof to prof, 65-86, dir plastic surg, Col Med, Univ Hosps & Childrens Hosp, Columbus, 65-85, EMER PROF SURG, OHIO STATE UNIV, 86- *Personal Data:* b Staten Island, NY, June 13, 31; m 54, Mary Beth Griffith; c Karen B (Murray) & Eric G. *Educ:* Johns Hopkins Univ, AB, 53; Univ Pa, MD, 57; Am Bd Surg, dipl, 64; Am Bd Plastic Surg, dipl, 67. *Prof Exp:* From asst instr to instr, Univ Pa, 58-65. *Concurrent Pos:* Pres, Plastic Surg Educ Found, 86-87; chmn, Am Bd Plastic Surg, 87-88; chmn, Accreditation Coun Grad Med Educ, 89 & 94. *Mem:* AAAS; fel Am Col Surg; Am Soc Plastic & Reconstruct Surg; Am Soc Surg Trauma; Am Asn Plastic Surg (vpres, 88-89, pres, 90-91); Med Spec Soc (pres, 94-); Plastic Surg Educ Found (pres, 86-87). *Res:* Low temperature preservation of tissues and organs; clinical problems in reconstruction of traumatic deformities of the face. *Mailing Add:* 9787 Windale Farms Circle Galena OH 43021-9609. *Fax:* 614-965-5379

BERGGREN, THAGE, AUTOMOTIVE ENGINEERING. *Current Pos:* Mfg engr & head truck opers, A B Volvo, Sweden, 60, prod coordr, Truck Div, 66, chief engr, Volvo Trucks Corp, 78-79, managing dir, Volvo Europe, 79, pres, Volvo White Trucks Corp, 79-81, PRES, CHIEF EXEC OFFICER & DIR, VOLVO GM HEAVY TRUCKS CORP, 87- *Honors & Awards:* Eli Whitney Productivity Award, Soc Mfg Engrs, 90. *Mailing Add:* Volvo GM Heavy Truck Corp PO Box 26115 7825 Nat Serv Rd Greensboro NC 27409-9667

BERGGREN, WILLIAM ALFRED, GEOLOGY, MICROPALEONTOLOGY. *Current Pos:* SR SCIENTIST, WOODS HOLE OCEANOG INST, 65- *Personal Data:* b New York, NY, Jan 15, 31; m 54, 82, Marie-Pierre Aubry; c Erik, Anna L, Anders & Sara M. *Educ:* Dickinson Col, BA, 52; Univ Houston, MSc, 57; Univ Stockholm, PhD(geol), 60, DSc(geol), 62. *Honors & Awards:* Mary Clark Thompson Medal Paleont, Nat Acad Sci, 82. *Prof Exp:* Micropaleontologist, Shell Oil Co, 55-57; res assoc micropaleont, Univ Stockholm, 57-62, Doktorand stipendiat, 60-62; res paleontologist, Oasis Oil Co, Libya, 62-65. *Concurrent Pos:* Fel, Princeton Univ, 60-61; Am Asn Petrol Geol grant-in-aid, 61-62; Sigma Xi grant-in-aid, 62; exchange student, Soviet-Am Cult Exchange Prog, 62; Rumanian-Am Acad Sci Exchange Prog, 69; mem adv panel, Joint Oceanog Deep Earth Sampling Prog Atlantic, Inst Comn Deep Sea Stratig, 67-68; working group on biostratig zonation of Cretaceous & Cenozoic for correlation in marine geol, Comn Stratig, Int Union Geol Sci, 68-; co-ed, J Paleont. *Mem:* Nat Acad Sci; Am Asn Petrol Geol; hon mem Soc Explor Paleont & Mineral; Am Geophys Union; Sigma Xi; fel Geol Soc Am; Paleont Soc. *Res:* Studies in Mesozoic and Cenozoic planktonic Foraminifera, including their evolutionary development and world-wide stratigraphic correlation based on their occurrence; integration of data from micropaleontology, biostratigraphy, seismic stratigraphy, radioisotopic measurements in preparation of integrated time scales for Cenozoic era. *Mailing Add:* Dept Geol & Geophys Woods Hole Oceanog Inst Woods Hole MA 02543. *Fax:* 508-457-2187; *E-Mail:* wberggren@whol.edu

BERGH, ARPAD A, PHYSICAL CHEMISTRY. *Current Pos:* mem tech staff, Bell Tel Labs, 59-63, supvr planar transistor tech, 64-69, head, Lightwave Devices Dept, 69-86, DIV MGR, BELL COMMUN RES, BELL LABS, 86- *Personal Data:* b Hungary, Apr 26, 30; US citizen; m 56; c 4. *Educ:* Univ Szeged, MS, 52; Univ Pa, PhD(phys chem), 59. *Prof Exp:* Res assoc, Geophys Inst, Hungary, 52-56. *Mem:* Fel Inst Elec & Electronics Engrs. *Res:* Reaction kinetics; homogeneous reactions and catalysis in gases and aqueous solutions; physical chemistry of electron devices; processing, operation and failure mechanisms of semiconductor devices; opto-electronic devices including III-V semiconductor materials and the physics and fabrication of LED displays and opto-isolators. *Mailing Add:* 3917 Highwood Ct NW Washington DC 20007

BERGH, BERTHOLD ORPHIE, AVOCADO, EVOLUTION. *Current Pos:* asst, Genetics Dept, Univ Calif, Riverside 52-56, asst geneticist, Citrus Exp Sta, 56-67, genetics specialist, Citrus Exp Stat, 67-, EMER GENETICS SPECIALIST, UNIV CALIF, RIVERSIDE. *Personal Data:* b Sask, Jan 30, 25; m 48; c 2. *Educ:* Univ Sask, BS, 50; Ohio State Univ, MSc, 51; Univ Calif, PhD(genetics), 56. *Prof Exp:* Res officer, Fruit Breeding, Can Dept Agr, 51-52. *Concurrent Pos:* Consult, UN Foreign Agr Orgn, Kenya, 80; avocado consult var countries. *Mem:* AAAS; Bot Soc Am; Am Genetic Asn; Am Soc Hort Sci; Sigma Xi; Am Inst Biol Sci. *Res:* Basic genetic studies of the tomato and the pepper; commercial improvement of the avocado. *Mailing Add:* Bot & Plant Sci Dept Univ Calif Batchelor Hall Riverside CA 92521

BERGHEL, HAL L, COMPUTATIONAL LOGIC & LINGUISTICS, INTELLIGENT SYSTEMS. *Current Pos:* assoc prof, 86-89, PROF COMPUT SCI, UNIV ARK, 89- *Personal Data:* b Minneapolis, Minn, May 10, 46; m 83, Margi; c David, Steven & Kevin. *Educ:* Univ Nebr, BA, 71, MA, 73, MA, 76, PhD(philos), 77. *Honors & Awards:* Distinguished Serv Award, Asn Comput Mach, 96, Outstanding lect, 96. *Prof Exp:* Asst prof mgt, Univ Nebr, 79-80, asst prof comput sci, 80-86. *Concurrent Pos:* Consult, Berghel & Assocs, 82-; adj res fel, Nat Ctr Toxicol Res, 88-91; chair, Spec Interest Group on Appl Comput, Asn Comput Mach, 90-93, nat lectr, 91 & 93- & dir, Technol Outreach Prog, 93-; distinguished vis, Inst Elec & Electronics Engrs, 93-; chmn bd dir, Ark Soc Comput & Info Technol. *Mem:* Asn Comput Mach; Inst Elec & Electronics Engrs Comput Soc. *Res:* Projects and publications in internet and world wide web technology development/software architecture; approximate string matching and information retrieval with incomplete specifications; non-resolution based inferencing and information customization. *Mailing Add:* Dept Comput Sci Univ Ark Fayetteville AR 72701. *E-Mail:* hlb@acm.org

BERGHOEFER, FRED G, OPERATIONS RESEARCH. *Current Pos:* RETIRED. *Personal Data:* b Chicago, Ill, June 7, 21; m 50; c 3. *Educ:* Rose Polytech, BS, 43; Univ Chicago, SM, 49. *Prof Exp:* Radar engr, Naval Res Lab, 43-45, analyst, Opers Eval Group, 50-66, study dir, Ctr Naval Anal, 66-84. *Mem:* AAAS; Opers Res Soc Am; Inst Elec & Electronics Engrs. *Res:* Operations analysis of naval operations, especially antisubmarine warfare, air warfare, and guided missiles. *Mailing Add:* 2720 N Fillmore St Alexandria VA 22207

BERGIN, MARION JOSEPH, GEOLOGY. *Current Pos:* RETIRED. *Personal Data:* b Lavoye, Wyo, May 2, 27; m 58; c 3. *Educ:* Univ Wyo, BS, 51. *Prof Exp:* Geologist, US Geol Surv, 51-92. *Res:* Geology of mineral fuels. *Mailing Add:* 100 Yeonas Dr SW Vienna VA 22180

BERGLES, ARTHUR E(DWARD), MECHANICAL ENGINEERING. *Current Pos:* CLARKE & CROSSAN PROF ENG & DIR, HEAT TRANSFER LAB, RENSSELAER POLYTECH INST, 86-, DEAN ENG, 89- *Personal Data:* b New York, NY, Aug 9, 35; m 60; c 2. *Educ:* Mass Inst Technol, SB & SM, 58, PhD(mech eng), 62. *Honors & Awards:* Heat Transfer Mem Award, Am Soc Mech Engrs, Dedicated Serv Award; US Sr Scientist Award, Alexander von Humboldt Found, Ger; Fel Award, Int Centre Heat & Mass Transfer; Lamme Award, Am Soc Eng Educ; Teetor Award, Soc Automotive Engrs; Kern Award, Am Inst Chem Engrs. *Prof Exp:* Engr, US Steel Corp, 55, Stone & Webster Eng Corp, 57 & Joseph Kaye & Co, 58; res asst mech eng, Mass Inst Technol, 59-62, fel & asst prof, 63-68, chmn, Eng Proj Lab, 67-68, assoc dir, Heat Transfer Lab, 66-69, assoc prof, 68-69, vis prof, 70, lectr, 71; prof mech eng, Ga Inst Technol, 70-72; prof & chmn dept, Iowa State Univ, 72-83, distinguished prof eng & prof mech eng, 83-86. *Concurrent Pos:* Consult numerous indust. *Mem:* Am Soc Heating, Refrig & Air Conditioning Engrs; fel Am Soc Eng Educ; fel Am Soc Mech Engrs (vpres, 81-85, bd gov, 85-89, pres, 90-91); Am Inst Chem Engrs; fel AAAS; Soc Automotive Engrs. *Res:* Augmentation of convective heat transfer; two-phase gas-liquid flow and heat transfer; heat transfer to laminar internal flows; cooling of electronic equipment; heat recovery systems. *Mailing Add:* Dept Mech Eng Rensselaer Polytech Inst 110 Eighth St Troy NY 12180-3590

BERGLUND, CARL NEIL, electrical engineering, for more information see previous edition

BERGLUND, LARRY GLENN, MECHANICAL ENGINEERING, BIOENGINEERING. *Current Pos:* PROF, TOHOKU UNIV, SENDAI, JAPAN, 96- *Personal Data:* b Minneapolis, Minn, Oct 17, 38; m 62; c 2. *Educ:* Univ Minn, Minneapolis, BME, 62, MSME, 65; Kans State Univ, PhD(mech eng), 71. *Honors & Awards:* Teetor Award, Soc Automotive Engrs, 74; Nevins Award, Am Soc Heating, Refrig & Air Conditioning Engrs, 79. *Prof Exp:* Develop engr absorption refrig, The Trane Co, Wis, 65-68; USPHS bioenviron eng trainee mech eng, Kans State Univ, 68-71; asst prof mech eng, Mich Technol Univ, 72-75; from asst fel to assoc fel, John B Pierce Found Lab, 75-96. *Concurrent Pos:* Lectr environ technol, Col Archit, Yale Univ, 75- *Mem:* Am Soc Heating, Refrig & Air Conditioning Engrs; Am Soc Mech Engrs. *Res:* Biothermal engineering; thermal physiology; physiological modeling; ventilation; thermal comfort; clothing; energy utilization in buildings; heating and air conditioning systems; air quality. *Mailing Add:* 27 Applewood Rd Branford CT 06405

BERGMAN, ABRAHAM, MEDICINE, PEDIATRICS. *Current Pos:* PROF PEDIAT, SCH MED & PROF HEALTH SERV, SCH PUB HEALTH & COMMUNITY MED, UNIV WASH, 64-; DIR DEPT PEDIAT, HARBORVIEW MED CTR, 83- *Personal Data:* b Seattle, Wash, May 11, 32; c 5. *Educ:* Reed Col, BA, 54; Western Reserve Univ, MD, 58; Am Bd Pediat, dipl, 63. *Prof Exp:* Intern, Children's Hosp Med Ctr, Boston, 58-59, jr asst resident, 59-60; exchange registr, Pediat Unit, St Mary's Hosp, London, Eng, 60-61; res fel pediat, State Univ NY Upstate Med Ctr, 61-63. *Mem:* Fel Am Acad Pediat; Ambulatory Pediat Asn; Am Pediat Soc. *Res:* Epidemiology; public policy in health; medical care; injury prevention. *Mailing Add:* Univ Wash Harborview Med Ctr Pediat ZA53 Ninth Ave Seattle WA 98104-2499

BERGMAN, ELLIOT, ORGANIC CHEMISTRY. *Current Pos:* DIR RES, GRIFFIN CORP, VALDOSTA, GA, 86- *Personal Data:* b Brooklyn, NY, Feb 2, 30; m 52; c 3. *Educ:* Brooklyn Col, BS, 51; Cornell Univ, PhD(org chem), 55. *Prof Exp:* Instr org chem, Univ Calif, 55-56; chemist, Shell Develop Co, Emeryville, Calif, 56-64, group leader, 64, supvr org chem, Agr Res Labs, Modesto, Calif, 65-67, head org chem div, Woodstock Agr Res Ctr, Shell Res Ltd, Eng, 67-70, asst to mgr res & develop, Agr Div, Shell Chem Co, 70-71, proj mgr consumer prod, 71-74; vpres res & develop, Liquid Crystal Technol Inc, 74-76, vpres original equip mfr & int mkt, 75-76; mgr, crop chem res & develop, Mobil Chem Co, 76-80, planning mgr, 81; asst dir, Stauffer Chem Co, Western Res Ctr, Richmond, Calif, 81-86. *Concurrent Pos:* Off Naval Res asst, Cornell Univ, 51-53; Proctor & Gamble Fel; mem, Dirs Comt Nat Agr Chems Asn; chmn-elect, Gordon Res Conf, 81-83, chmn, 84-85; mem res dirs comt, Nat Agr Chemicals Asn. *Mem:* Am Chem Soc; Plant Growth Regulator Soc Am. *Res:* Fluorine, organometallic, organophosphorus, polymer and agricultural chemistry; consumer products; cholesteric liquid crystal materials for consumer, industrial and medical products (visual displays); biotechnology and genetic engineering. *Mailing Add:* 1201 Cloverhill Rd Valdosta GA 31602-1265

BERGMAN, ERNEST L, HORTICULTURE, PLANT NUTRITION. *Current Pos:* from asst prof to prof, 58-87, EMER PROF PLANT NUTRIT, PA STATE UNIV, 87- *Personal Data:* b Munich, Ger, July 12, 22; nat US; m 48, Alice Adler. *Educ:* Kanton Landwirtsch, Schwand, Switz, dipl landwirt, 41; Ore State Col, BS, 55; Mich State Univ, MS, 56, PhD(hort), 58. *Honors & Awards:* Kenneth Post Award, Am Soc Hort Sci, 68. *Prof Exp:* Res asst veg crops, Kanton Gartenbau Schule, Oeschberg, Switz, 45; pomologist, Schweizerisch Obstbauzentrale, 46; pvt enterprise, 47-53. *Concurrent Pos:* Var int assignments Arg, Uruguay, People's Repub China, Senegal & Mali; vpres int affairs, Am Soc Hort Sci, 86-87. *Mem:* Fel AAAS; fel Am Soc Hort Sci; Am Soc Plant Physiol; Am Soc Agron; Int Soc Hort Sci. *Res:* Mineral nutrition of horticultural plants, vegetables and fruits; plant nutrition and agriculture on international level. *Mailing Add:* 1421 Harris St State College PA 16803-3024

BERGMAN, GEORGE MARK, NONCOMMUTATIVE RING THEORY, UNIVERSAL ALGEBRA. *Current Pos:* Asst prof, 67-78, PROF MATH, UNIV CALIF, BERKELEY, 78- *Personal Data:* b Brooklyn, NY, July 22, 43; m 81, Mary F Anderson; c Rebecca N Anderson-Bergman, Clifford I Anderson-Bergman, Jeffrey E Watson & Michael L Anderson-Bergman. *Educ:* Univ Calif, Berkeley, BA, 63; Harvard Univ, PhD(math), 68. *Mem:* Am Math Soc. *Res:* Study of non-commutative rings, especially those characterized by universal properties; free ideal rings and related classes of rings; representable functions among varieties of algebras; construction of counterexamples. *Mailing Add:* Dept Math Univ Calif Berkeley CA 94720-3840. *E-Mail:* gbergman@math.berkeley.edu

BERGMAN, HAROLD LEE, AQUATIC TOXICOLOGY, FISH PHYSIOLOGY. *Current Pos:* from asst prof to assoc prof, 75-84, PROF ZOOL & PHYSIOL, UNIV WYO, 84-, J E WARREN DISTINGUISHED PROF ENERGY & ENVIRON, 95- *Personal Data:* b Sault St Marie, Mich, July 8, 41; m 68; c 2. *Educ:* Eastern Mich Univ, BA, 68, MS, 71; Mich State Univ, PhD(fisheries biol), 73. *Prof Exp:* Fishery biologist, Great Lakes Fishery Lab, US Fish & Wildlife Serv, Ann Arbor, Mich, 68-71; res asst fishery biol, Dept Fisheries & Wildlife, Mich State Univ, East Lansing, 71-73, res assoc environ physiol, Dept Physiol, 74; res assoc environ impact, Environ Sci Div, Oak Ridge Nat Lab, Oak Ridge, Tenn, 74-75. *Concurrent Pos:* Dir, Red Buttes Environ Biol Lab, Univ Wyo, 84-,actg dir, Wyo Water Res Ctr,86-87; vis prof, Dept Physiol, Univ Nairobi, 88; vis scientist, Environ Res Lab, US Environ Protection Agency, 88; adj prof marine biomed & environ sci, Med Univ SC, 93- *Mem:* Sigma Xi; Am Fisheries Soc; fel AAAS; NAm Benthological Soc; Soc Environ Toxicol & Chem (pres,84-85). *Res:* Fish physiology and toxicology; energy-related water quality problems; national and international environmental policy; public education on environmental issues. *Mailing Add:* Dept Zool & Physiol Univ Wyo Univ Sta Box 3166 Laramie WY 82071. *Fax:* 307-766-5625; *E-Mail:* bergman@uwyo.edu

BERGMAN, HYMAN CHAIM, pharmacology, for more information see previous edition

BERGMAN, KENNETH DAVID, BIOLOGY. *Current Pos:* assoc prof, 79-93, PROF BIOL, CELL BIOL & GENETICS, KEENE STATE COL, NH, 93-, DEPT CHAIR, 93- *Personal Data:* b Shafter, Calif, Mar 24, 49; m 78; c Erica & Deborah. *Educ:* Univ Calif, Berkeley, AB, 71; Harvard Univ, PhD(cell biol), 77. *Prof Exp:* Fel, Dept Biol, Harvard Univ, 77-78. *Mem:* AAAS; Am Pub Health Asn; Am Genetics Asn. *Mailing Add:* 14 Blackberry Lane Keene NH 03431-2117. *E-Mail:* kbergman@keene.edu

BERGMAN, KENNETH HARRIS, ATMOSPHERIC SCIENCES & CLIMATE. *Current Pos:* MGR GLOBAL MODELING & ANALYSIS SCI DIV OFF, MISSION TO PLANET EARTH, NASA, 90- *Personal Data:* b Plainfield, NJ, Dec 11, 35; m 78, Mary A Luster. *Educ:* Rutgers Univ, BS, 58; Univ Wash, PhD(atmospheric sci), 69. *Prof Exp:* Design engr, Semiconductor Div, Radio Corp Am, 58-59; asst, dept atmospheric sci, Univ

Wash, 60-65; asst prof meteorol, San Jose State Col, 65-70; fel, Tex A&M Univ, 70-71; res meteorologist, Nat Hurricane Res Lab, Nat Weather Serv, Nat Oceanic & Atmospheric Agency, 71-73 & Nat Meteorol Ctr, 73-79; assoc prog dir, Climate Dynamics Prog, NSF, 79-82, actg prog dir, 82-83; meteorologist, Climate Analysis Ctr, Nat Weather Serv, Nat Oceanic & Atmospheric Admin, 83-87; sr prog officer, Bd Atmospheric Sci & Climate, Nat Res Coun, Nat Acad Sci, 87-90. *Concurrent Pos:* Ed, J Climate Appl Meteorol, Am Meteorol Soc, 82-84. *Mem:* Am Meteorol Soc; Sigma Xi. *Res:* Mass exchange between stratosphere and troposphere; dynamics and dynamic stability of convective atmospheric vortices; atmospheric transport and diffusion in the 100 meter boundary layer; dynamic meteorology, numerical modeling and weather prediction; numerical objective analysis of synoptic data; climate change and prediction; climate monitoring and information services; atmospheric and climate research program management. *Mailing Add:* NASA Hq Code YS 300 E St Washington DC 20546. *Fax:* 202-358-2770; *E-Mail:* kbergman@mtpe.hq.nasa.gov

BERGMAN, MOE, EDUCATIONAL ADMINISTRATION, MEDICAL & HEALTH SCIENCES. *Current Pos:* prof, 75-85, EMER PROF, SACKLER SCH MED, TEL-AVIV UNIV, ISRAEL, 85-; EMER PROF, HUNTER COL, NY, 75- *Personal Data:* b Brooklyn, NY, Mar 28, 16; m 38, Hannah Goodelman; c Jay. *Educ:* Univ Ill, AB, 37; Columbia Univ, MA, 39, EdD(audiol), 49. *Honors & Awards:* Carhart Mem lectr, Am Auditory Soc, 94; Aram Glorig Award, 19th Int Cong Audiol, Jerusalem, 88. *Prof Exp:* Dir spec educ, Peekskill Union Free Schs, 38-43; chief audiologist, NY Regional Off, Vet Admin, 46-53; prof lect audiol, Col Physicians & Surgeons & Teachers Col, Columbia Univ, 48-58; dir, Speech & Hearing Ctr, Hunter Col, NY, 53-69. *Concurrent Pos:* Consult, Indust Home for Blind, 59-64 & NY Dept Health, 60-75; exec officer, PhD Prog Speech, City Univ New York, 65-69; vis prof, Med Sci, Tel-Aviv Univ, 68-69 & 71; hon pres, Israeli Speech & Hearing Asn. *Mem:* AAAS; fel Am Speech & Hearing Asn; Acoust Soc Am; Israel Speech & Hearing Asn (hon pres); hon mem Israeli Med Asn Otolaryngolog; Am Inst Physics; Acad Rehab Audiol. *Res:* Binaural and stereophonic hearing; audiology in audiosurgery; auditory perception in blind persons; development of audiology services; hearing in primitive peoples; presbycucis; aging speech perception; hearing and aging; central auditory dysfunction in brain pathology; noise-induced changes in cochlear function. *Mailing Add:* 10 Wissotzky St Tel-Aviv Israel

BERGMAN, NORMAN, ANESTHESIOLOGY. *Current Pos:* PROF ANESTHESIOL, MED SCH, UNIV ORE & DIR ANESTHESIA SERV, MED SCH HOSPS, 70- *Personal Data:* b Seattle, Wash, Oct 14, 26; m 52; c 2. *Educ:* Reed Col, BA, 49; Univ Ore, MD, 51. *Prof Exp:* Assoc anesthesiol, Columbia Univ, 54-58; asst attend, Presby Hosp, New York, 54-58; from asst prof to prof, Col Med, Univ Utah, 58-70; chief anesthesiol serv, Vet Admin Hosp, 58-70. *Concurrent Pos:* Vis res assoc, Royal Col Surgeons & Post-Grad Med Sch, Univ London & Hammersmith Hosp, 63-64; Nat Heart Inst spec fel, 63-64. *Mem:* Am Soc Anesthesiol; AMA; Fedn Am Soc Exp Biol. *Res:* Respiratory changes during anesthesia; physiology of artificial respiration. *Mailing Add:* Ore Health Sci Univ Univ Hosp 3181 SW Sam Jackson Park Rd Portland OR 97201-3011

BERGMAN, R A, ADMINISTRATION. *Current Pos:* COMNR, ROYAL CAN MOUNTED POLICE. *Honors & Awards:* H T Airey Award, Can Inst Mining, Metall & Petrol, 94. *Mailing Add:* Royal Can Mounted Police 1200 Vanier Pkwy Ottawa ON K1A 0R2 Can

BERGMAN, RAY E(LDON), APPLIED MATHEMATICS, OPERATIONS RESEARCH. *Current Pos:* RETIRED. *Personal Data:* b Drumright, Okla, Nov 6, 28; m 59, Helen Clark; c Yvonne & Erik. *Educ:* Okla State Univ, BS, 50; Univ Denver, MA, 58. *Prof Exp:* Res engr, Physics Div, Denver Res Inst, 53-54; petrol engr, reservoir analist, Creole Petrol Corp, 54-56; instr math, Univ Denver, 58-59; opers res analyst, develop dept, Syst Develop Corp, 59-61; mathematician, Test Data Div, Pac Missile Range, 61-68; opers res analyst, Naval Civil Eng Lab, 68-88; instr math, Moorpark Col, 89-93. *Concurrent Pos:* Pac Missile Range scholar, Univ Calif, Los Angeles, 65-66. *Mem:* Sigma Xi. *Res:* Management and operational systems analysis; instrumentation analysis; celestial mechanics of near-earth satellites. *Mailing Add:* 9950 E Sandshell Ct Tucson AZ 85748-2124. *E-Mail:* rayberg@azstarnet.com

BERGMAN, RICHARD N, METABOLIC RESEARCH. *Current Pos:* PROF PHYSIOL, SCH MED, UNIV SOUTHERN CALIF, 80-, HEAD, METABOLIC UNIT. *Personal Data:* b Chicago, Ill, Nov 7, 44; c 2. *Educ:* Univ Pittsburgh, PhD(physiol), 71. *Mem:* Am Physiol Soc; Am Fedn Clin Res; Endocrine Soc; AAAS. *Mailing Add:* Dept Physiol & Biophys Sch Med Univ Southern Calif 1333 San Pablo St MMR-630 Los Angeles CA 90033

BERGMAN, ROBERT, MECHANICAL ENGINEERING & TELECOMMUNICATIONS. *Current Pos:* SYST ENG & PROJ MGR, AT&T BELL LAB, 87- *Personal Data:* b New York, NY, Sept 2, 31; c 2. *Educ:* NY Univ, BME, 54; City Univ NY, MME, 62. *Prof Exp:* Engr aircraft radar, Gen Precision Lab, 58-63; lead engr satellites, Radio Corp Am, 63-68; bus planning reentry vehicles, Gen Elec Co, 68-74; asst prog mgr, Princeton Univ, 74-81, head proj safety, Fusion Energy, 81-83, head safety training, 83-86; syst safety mgr satellites, Sci Appln Int Corp, 86-87. *Concurrent Pos:* Serv develop mgr telecommunications, AT&T, 87-97. *Mailing Add:* 300 Dodds Lane Princeton NJ 08540

BERGMAN, ROBERT GEORGE, ORGANOMETALLIC CHEMISTRY, INORGANIC CHEMISTRY. *Current Pos:* PROF CHEM, UNIV CALIF, BERKELEY, 77- *Personal Data:* b Chicago, Ill, May 23, 42; m 65, Wendy Street; c 2. *Educ:* Carleton Col, BA, 63; Univ Wis, PhD(chem), 66. *Honors & Awards:* Award Organometallic Chem, Am Chem Soc, 86, Cope Scholar Award, 87, Arthur C Cope Award, 96; E O Lawrence Award Chem, US Dept Energy, 94. *Prof Exp:* Arthur Amos Noyes instr chem, Calif Inst Technol, 67-69, from asst prof to prof chem, 69-77. *Concurrent Pos:* NATO fel chem, Columbia Univ, 66-67; Alfred P Sloan Found fel, 70-72; NIH & NSF grants; sr scientist, Lawrence Berkeley Nat Lab, Calif; Fairchild distinguished scholar, Calif Inst Technol, 84. *Mem:* Nat Acad Sci; Am Chem Soc; Am Acad Arts & Sci. *Res:* Synthesis and reaction mechanisms of organic and transition metal organometallic compounds; catalysis. *Mailing Add:* 501 Coventry Rd Kensington CA 94707-1316. *E-Mail:* rgberg@violet.berkeley.edu

BERGMAN, ROBERT K, MEDICAL RESEARCH. *Current Pos:* RETIRED. *Personal Data:* b Great Falls, Mont, Apr 5, 34; m 57; c 6. *Educ:* Mont State Univ, Bozeman, BS, 56, MS, 57; Univ Mo, Columbia, PhD, 63. *Honors & Awards:* Commendation Medal, USPHS, 88. *Prof Exp:* Res asst, Dairy Indust Dept, Mont State Univ, Bozeman, 56-57, instr, 58-60; res asst, Dairy Husb Dept, Univ Mo, Columbia, 60-63; staff fel, Lab Microbial Struct & Function, Rocky Mountain Labs, Hamilton, Mont, Nat Inst Allergy & Infectious Dis, NIH, 63-66, sr scientist, 66-74, scientist dir, 74-81, asst to chief, 81-85, chief, Opers Br, 85-96. *Concurrent Pos:* Ralston Purina fel, 60-61, NSF fel, 61-62 & 62-63. *Res:* Phenomena related to hypersensitivity in mice; experimental allergic encephalomyelitis in rats. *Mailing Add:* NIH Nat Inst Allergy & Infectious Dis Rocky Mountain Opers Br Rocky Mountain Labs 903 S Fourth St Hamilton MT 59840

BERGMAN, RONALD ARLY, ANATOMY, PHYSIOLOGY. *Current Pos:* PROF ANAT, COL MED, UNIV IOWA, 80- *Personal Data:* b Chicago, Ill, June 21, 27; m 54, Phyllis Stephenson; c Christopher, Peter, David & Matthew. *Educ:* Univ Ill, BS, 50, MS, 53, PhD(physiol, zool & chem), 55. *Honors & Awards:* The Order of Merit, Repub Lebanon. *Prof Exp:* Nat Found Infantile Paralysis fel, Karolinska Inst, Sweden, 55-56; instr epidemiol, Sch Hyg & Pub Health, Johns Hopkins Univ, 56-57, res assoc anat, Sch Med, 57-59, from asst prof to assoc prof, 68-74; prof human morphol, Sch Med, Am Univ Beirut, 74-80. *Concurrent Pos:* Vis assoc prof anat, Am Univ Beirut, 69. *Mem:* Am Asn Anatomists; Am Soc Cell Biol; Electron Micros Soc Am. *Res:* Human anatomic variation in muscles, organs, vascular system and nerve; co-author of 10 books on human variation, histology, neuroscience, sectional anatomy and MR of head and neck and body. *Mailing Add:* 618 Brookland Park Dr Iowa City IA 52246. *Fax:* 319-335-7198

BERGMAN, THEODORE L, HEAT TRANSFER, FLUID DYNAMICS. *Current Pos:* ASST PROF MECH ENG, UNIV TEX, AUSTIN, 85- *Personal Data:* b Seneca, Kans, Oct 12, 56. *Educ:* Univ Kans, BSME, 78; Purdue Univ, MSME, 81, PhD(mech eng), 85. *Prof Exp:* Mech engr, Black & Veatch Consult Engrs, 78-80. *Mem:* Am Soc Mech Engrs; Sigma Xi. *Res:* Basic and applied heat transfer and fluid dynamics; natural convection; double-diffusive convection. *Mailing Add:* Dept Mech Eng Univ Tex Austin TX 78712

BERGMANN, DIETRICH R(UDOLF), URBAN TRANSPORTATION SYSTEMS ENGINEERING, HIGHWAY SAFETY ENGINEERING. *Current Pos:* PRES & DIR ENG, RAILWAY SYSTS ENG CORP, 81- *Personal Data:* b Detroit, Mich, Aug 12, 38; c Liisa L & Erich G. *Educ:* Univ Mich, BS, 61; Stanford Univ, MS, 64, PhD(civil eng), 69. *Prof Exp:* Res civil engr, Syst Anal Div, Battelle Mem Inst, 64-65; asst prof civil eng, Wayne State Univ, 69-70, asst prof indust eng & opers res, 70-72; sr res engr, Gen Motors Res Labs, 72-74; eng projs mgr, Gen Motors Transp Systs Div Ctr, 74-78, mgr technol assessment, 78-80. *Concurrent Pos:* Consult, West Bay Rapid Transit Authority, Calif, 66, DeLeuw, Cather & Co, Calif, 66-67, Automotive Safety Found, Washington, DC, 67 & Transp Technol Inc, Colo, 70; mem, Transp Res Bd, Nat Res Coun, Nat Acad Sci & Nat Acad Eng, 63, chmn, Comt Comput Graphics & Interactive Tech, 79-82. *Mem:* Nat Soc Prof Engrs; Am Rwy Eng Asn; Am Soc Civil Engrs. *Res:* Analysis, design, and management of urban public transportation system operations; economic evaluation and cost-effectiveness analysis of governmental investments in transportation systems and other types of public works; freight railroad systems engineering analysis and design; highway safety engineering. *Mailing Add:* PO Box 351 St Clair Shores MI 48080-0351

BERGMANN, ERNEST EISENHARDT, LASERS, FIBER OPTICS. *Current Pos:* mem tech staff, 84-88, DISTINGUISHED MEM TECH STAFF, AT&T BELL LABS, 88- *Personal Data:* b New York, Nov 2, 42; m 67, Marianne deGraaf; c Dominique, Gabrielle & Marcel. *Educ:* Columbia Univ, AB, 64; Princeton Univ, MA, 66, PhD(physics), 69. *Prof Exp:* From asst prof to prof physics, Lehigh Univ, 69-85. *Concurrent Pos:* Vis staff mem, Los Alamos Sci Lab, 77-78; Consult, Bell Labs, Allentown, 81-84. *Mem:* Am Phys Soc; Optical Soc Am. *Res:* Fiber-optic communication; theory and experiment in lasers and optical resonators; quantum mechanics. *Mailing Add:* AT&T Bell Labs 9999 Hamilton Blvd Breinigsville PA 18031

BERGMANN, FRED HEINZ, GENETICS. *Current Pos:* RETIRED. *Personal Data:* b Feuchtwagen, Ger, Jan 26, 28; nat US; m 66, Barbara R; c David M & Sarah N. *Educ:* Mass Inst Technol, BS, 50, MS, 51; Univ Wis, PhD(biochem), 57. *Honors & Awards:* USPHS Superior Serv Award, 74. *Prof Exp:* Jr res chemist, Ethicon Suture Labs, 51-53; USPHS fel, Microbiol Dept, Med Sch, Washington Univ, 57-59; fel biol, Brandeis Univ, 59-61; res biochemist, NIH, 61-66; sci adminr, Res Grants Br, 66-72; dir genetics prog, nat Inst Gen Med Sci, 72-88. *Mem:* Am Soc Human Genetics; Genetics Soc Am. *Res:* Carboxyl activation of amino acids; protein synthesis; science policy. *Mailing Add:* 5430 41 Pl NW Washington DC 20015

BERGMANN, OTTO, THEORETICAL PHYSICS. *Current Pos:* assoc prof, 62-67, PROF PHYSICS, GEORGE WASHINGTON UNIV, 67- *Personal Data:* b Vienna, Austria, Feb 7, 25; m 57; c 2. *Educ:* Univ Vienna, PhD(physics), 49. *Prof Exp:* Scholar, Dublin Inst Adv Studies, 51-52; sr res fel, Dept Math Physics, Univ Adelaide, 52-55; sr res fel physics, Univ New Eng, Australia, 56-58; res physicist, Res Inst Advan Study, Univ Baltimore, 58-60; assoc prof, Univ Ala, 60-62. *Concurrent Pos:* Vis prof, Univ Ala, 58-59; vis prof, Inst Theoret Physics, Univ Vienna, Austria, 73-74. *Mem:* Am Phys Soc; Sigma Xi. *Res:* Classical and quantized field theories; theory of relativity. *Mailing Add:* Samson Hall Rm 209 2036 H St NW Washington DC 20052. *E-Mail:* ottobe@gwis.circ.gwu.edu

BERGMANN, PETER GABRIEL, THEORETICAL PHYSICS. *Current Pos:* from assoc prof to prof, 47-82, EMER PROF PHYSICS, SYRACUSE UNIV, 82-, RES PROF, 82-; RES PROF, NY UNIV, 83- *Personal Data:* b Berlin, Ger, Mar 24, 15; US citizen; m 36, Margot Eisenhardt; c Ernest & John. *Educ:* Prague Univ, PhD(theoret physics), 36. *Hon Degrees:* Tech Univ, Dresden, 79. *Honors & Awards:* Boris Pregel Award, NY Acad Sci, 70; Albert Einstein Medal, Berne, Switz, 92. *Prof Exp:* Mem & asst, Sch Math, Inst Adv Study, 36-41; asst prof physics, Black Mountain Col, 41-42 & Lehigh Univ, 42-44; staff mem & asst dir sonar anal group, Div War Res, Columbia Oceanog Inst, Woods Hole, 44-47. *Concurrent Pos:* Adj prof, Polytech Inst Brooklyn, 47-57; lectr, Marburg Univ, 55, Univ Stockholm, 58 & Int Sch Cosmology & Gravitation & Int Sch Astrophysics D Chalonge, Int Ctr Sci Culture, Erice, Italy, 75, 77, 81, 83, 87-93, course dir, 79, 85 & 95; vis prof, Brandeis Univ, 57 & King's Col, Univ London, 58, Queens Col, 87; vis prof, Yeshiva Univ, 59-63, prof & chmn dept, 63-64 & vis prof, Belfer Grad Sch Sci; mem, Int Soc Gen Relativity & Gravitation , pres, 77-80,. *Mem:* Fel AAAS; Fedn Am Sci; fel Am Phys Soc; Am Math Soc; Europ Phys Soc; Sigma Xi; Int Soc Gen Relativity & Gravvitation (pres, 77-80). *Res:* Relativistic field theories, including quantization; wave propagation and scattering; electron optics; tactosols; stochastic problems; irreversible processes; author of several books. *Mailing Add:* Dept Physics NY Univ 4 Washington Pl New York NY 10003

BERGMANN, STEVEN R, CARDIOVASCULAR DISEASE, NUCLEAR CARDIOLOGY. *Current Pos:* PROF & DIR, NUCLEAR CARDIOVASC COL PHYSICIANS & SURGEONS, COLUMBIA UNIV, 96- *Personal Data:* b New York, NY, Feb 4, 51; m 75, Joanne L Rubin. *Educ:* George Wash Univ, BA, 72; Wash Univ, St Louis, Mo, MD, 85; Hahnemann Med Col, PhD(physiol & biophys), 78. *Prof Exp:* Fel cardiovasc dis, Washington Univ, St Louis, 77-80, from instr to prof, Cardiovasc Div, 79-96. *Concurrent Pos:* Mem, Basic Sci Coun, Am Heart Asn. *Mem:* Am Physiol Soc; Am Heart Asn; Soc Nuclear Med; AAAS; fel Am Col Cardiol; Am Soc Clin Invest. *Res:* Positron emission tomography for measurement of myocardial blood flow and metabolism; thrombolytic therapy for salvage of ischemic myocardium. *Mailing Add:* Cardiol-Col Physicians & Surgeons Columbia Univ 630 W 168th St New York NY 10032

BERGMARK, WILLIAM R, ORGANIC CHEMISTRY. *Current Pos:* asst prof, 68-73, PROF ORG CHEM, ITHACA COL, 73- *Personal Data:* b Mankato, Minn, Oct 28, 40; m 63. *Educ:* St Olaf Col, BA, 62; Mass Inst Technol, PhD(org chem), 66. *Prof Exp:* Res chemist, Am Cyanamid Co, 66-67; res assoc org chem, State Univ NY Buffalo, 67-68. *Concurrent Pos:* Res grants, Petrol Res Fund & Res Corp, 69- *Mem:* Am Chem Soc. *Res:* Photochemistry; small ring compounds; electron transfer reactions. *Mailing Add:* 7 Hickory Trail Ithaca NY 14850-9660

BERGNA, HORACIO ENRIQUE, COLLOID CHEMISTRY, SURFACE CHEMISTRY. *Current Pos:* sr res chemist, 56-74, staff chemist, 74-78, res assoc, 78-88, SR RES ASSOC, E I DU PONT DE NEMOURS & CO, 88- *Personal Data:* b La Plata, Arg, Feb 11, 24; nat US; m 51; c 1. *Educ:* La Plata Nat Univ, Lic, 48, Dr Chem, 50. *Honors & Awards:* Croix de Chevalier dans l'ordre des Palmes Academiques, French Govt, 70. *Prof Exp:* Chemist colloid sci, Lab Testing Mat & Tech Res, 44-50; Fr Govt fel, Univ Paris, 51; US Govt & Orgn Am States fels, Mass Inst Technol, 52, mem staff surface chem, 52-56. *Concurrent Pos:* Asst anal chem, La Plata Nat Univ, 44-46. *Mem:* AAAS; Am Chem Soc; Sigma Xi; Kolloid Gesellschaft; Arg Chem Asn. *Res:* Surface and colloid chemistry of silica, other oxides and aluminosilicates. *Mailing Add:* 34 Vining Lane Westhaven Wilmington DE 19807-3128

BERGO, CONRAD HUNTER, ORGANIC CHEMISTRY, PHYSICAL CHEMISTRY. *Current Pos:* PROF, E STROUDSBURG UNIV, 80- *Personal Data:* b Evanston, Ill, Jan 5, 43; m 77, Nancy Wallace; c 2. *Educ:* St Olaf Col, BA, 65; Univ Minn, Minneapolis, PhD(org chem), 72. *Prof Exp:* Lectr org chem, Chiengmai Univ, US Peace Corps, 72-75; res assoc pharmacol, Col Med, Univ Ky, 75-77; asst prof chem, Alliance Col, 77-80. *Mem:* Am Chem Soc; Sigma Xi. *Res:* Laser measurements of reaction kinetics; study of carbonyl frequencies in aromatic systems; laser based experiments in physical chemistry. *Mailing Add:* 204 Analomink St East Stroudsburg PA 18301-2604. *E-Mail:* cbergo@esu.edu

BERGOMI, ANGELO, ORGANIC CHEMISTRY. *Current Pos:* SR RES CHEMIST ORG CHEM, GOODYEAR TIRE & RUBBER CO, 69- *Personal Data:* b Milan, Italy, Oct 22, 33; US citizen. *Educ:* Univ Milan, Dr(org chem), 60; Univ Birmingham, MSc, 65. *Prof Exp:* Chemist org chem, Montecatini-Edison, 61-69. *Res:* Catalytic isomerization of hydrocarbons; preparation of hydrocarbon resins; synthesis of rubber chemicals; fluorocarbon chemistry. *Mailing Add:* 1485 E Archwood Ave Chem Res & Develop Akron OH 44306

BERGOUGNOU, MAURICE A(MEDEE), CHEMICAL ENGINEERING. *Current Pos:* PROF CHEM ENG, UNIV WESTERN ONT, CAN, 67- *Personal Data:* b Bach, France, Sept 7, 28; m 55; c 2. *Educ:* Univ Nancy, MS, 53; Univ Minn, PhD(chem eng), 58. *Prof Exp:* Asst chem eng, Univ Minn, 54-58; sr engr petrol develop, Exxon Res & Eng Co, Standard Oil Co, 58-62, eng res, 62-67. *Concurrent Pos:* Pvt consult fluidized reactors. *Mem:* AAAS; Am Chem Soc; Am Inst Chem Engrs; fel Chem Inst Can; Can Soc Chem Eng. *Res:* Chemical reactor technology; fluidization; chemical process development; fluidized reactor design; application of fluidization to chemical and energy processes; design and scale-up of conventional industrial fluidized reactors; development of the ultra-rapid fluidized reactor and of ultra rapid fluidized crackers and pyrolyzers for all kinds of hydrocarbon and carbonaceous feedstocks. *Mailing Add:* 24 Foxchapel Rd London ON N6G 1Z2 Can

BERGQUIST, JAMES WILLIAM, computer sciences, applied mathematics, for more information see previous edition

BERGS, VICTOR VISVALDIS, virology; deceased, see previous edition for last biography

BERGSAGEL, DANIEL EGIL, INTERNAL MEDICINE, ONCOLOGY. *Current Pos:* RETIRED. *Personal Data:* b Outlook, Sask, Apr 25, 25; m 50; c 4. *Educ:* Univ Man, MD, 49; Oxford Univ, DPhil, 55; Am Bd Internal Med, dipl, 59; FRCP(C), 68. *Prof Exp:* Asst resident, Winnipeg Gen Hosp, 50-51 & Salt Lake Co Gen Hosp, Utah, 51-52; assoc internist, Univ Tex M D Anderson Hosp, 55-65; chief med, Princess Margaret Hosp, 65-90. *Concurrent Pos:* Prof med, Univ Toronto, 65- *Mem:* AMA; Am Fedn Clin Res; Int Soc Hemat. *Res:* Tumor growth; cancer chemotherapy. *Mailing Add:* 20 Highland Crescent Toronto ON M4W 2S7 Can

BERGSTEIN, JERRY MICHAEL, PEDIATRICS, NEPHROLOGY. *Current Pos:* PROF PEDIAT & HEAD PEDIAT NEPHROLOGY, SCH MED, IND UNIV, 77- *Personal Data:* b June 26, 39; m 63, Renee Hillman; c Stephanie, Michael & Jeffrey. *Educ:* Univ Minn, MD, 65. *Prof Exp:* Head, Pediat Nephrol, Sch Med, Univ Calif, Los Angeles, 73-77. *Mem:* Am Soc Nephrol; Am Soc Pediat Nephrol; Soc Pediat Res; Soc Exp Biol & Med; Int Soc Nephrol. *Res:* Hemolytic-uremic syndrome; pathogenesis of glanerular diseases. *Mailing Add:* James Whitcomb Riley Hosp Children Univ Ind Sch Med Indianapolis IN 46202

BERGSTEN, JANE WILLIAMS, SURVEY SAMPLE DESIGN. *Current Pos:* RETIRED. *Personal Data:* b Detroit, Mich, June 25, 27; m 56; c 3. *Educ:* Univ Mich, BA, 49, MA, 51; Univ Iowa, PhD(appl statist), 72. *Prof Exp:* Sampling statistician, Surv Res Ctr, Univ Mich, 49-56; statistician, Nat Ctr Health Statist, 56-60; sr statistician, Res Triangle Inst, 73-97. *Concurrent Pos:* Res psychologist, Am Col Testing, 73. *Mem:* Am Statist Asn; Int Asn Surv Statisticians; Am Educ Res Asn. *Res:* Survey design and implementation; sample design and selection; data analysis and statistical report writing; project management and direction; methodological research. *Mailing Add:* 631 Kensington Dr Chapel Hill NC 27514

BERGSTRALH, JAY THOR, planetary science; deceased, see previous edition for last biography

BERGSTRESSER, KENNETH A, BIOLOGY, ZOOLOGY. *Current Pos:* assoc prof biol, 58-71, prof, 71-77, EMER PROF BIOL, MORAVIAN COL, 77- *Personal Data:* b Lower Saucon Township, Pa, May 25, 12; m 39; c 3. *Educ:* Albright Col, BS, 34; Univ Pittsburgh, MS, 37; Lehigh Univ, PhD(cell biol), 74. *Prof Exp:* Asst prof biol, Beaver Col, 37-41; field dir, Am Red Cross, 43-45; assoc prof biol, Moravian Col, 46-52; chief bacteriologist, R K Laros Co, 52-58. *Concurrent Pos:* Northhampton County Comm Col, 77-82. *Mem:* AAAS; Am Soc Microbiol; Sigma Xi; Am Soc Zoologists. *Res:* Bacteriology; industrial fermentations; cytology; cell biology. *Mailing Add:* 3020 Applehill Dr Cornwall PA 17016-0125

BERGSTRESSER, PAUL RICHARD, DERMATOLOGY. *Current Pos:* from asst prof to assoc prof, 76-86, PROF INTERNAL MED & CHMN, HEALTH SCI CTR, UNIV TEX, DALLAS, 86- *Personal Data:* b Ottawa, Kans, Aug 24, 41; m 69; c 2. *Educ:* Sch Med, Stanford Univ, MD, 68; Am Bd Dermat, cert, 76. *Prof Exp:* Intern med, Sch Med, Univ NMex, 68-69; resident dermatol, Sch Med, Stanford Univ, 69-70; resident, Sch Med, Univ Miami, 72-74, res assoc, 74-75, asst prof dermatol, 75-76. *Mem:* Soc Invest Dermat; fel Am Col Physicians; Am Acad Dermat; Am Fedn Clin Res; AAAS. *Res:* Immunology in dermatology, control mechanisms in epidermal proliferation. *Mailing Add:* Dept Dermat Univ Tex Southwestern Med Ctr 5323 Harry Hines Blvd Dallas TX 75235-9069. *Fax:* 214-648-9292

BERGSTROM, CLARENCE GEORGE, ORGANIC CHEMISTRY. *Current Pos:* RETIRED. *Personal Data:* b Chicago, Ill, Oct 23, 25; m 48; c 3. *Educ:* Ill Inst Technol, PhD(chem), 51. *Prof Exp:* res chemist, G D Searle & Co, 50-77, head, Stability Lab, 80-86, consult, 86-89. *Mem:* Am Chem Soc. *Res:* Steroids; synthetic organic chemistry; medicinal chemistry; stability testing; pharmaceutical products. *Mailing Add:* 101 Summit Ave Apt 614 Park Ridge IL 60068-4194

BERGSTROM, DONALD EUGENE, NUCLEIC ACID CHEMISTRY. *Current Pos:* assoc prof, 80-85, PROF ORG CHEM, UNIV NDAK, 86- *Personal Data:* b Tacoma, Wash, Oct 9, 43; m 70; c 3. *Educ:* Univ Wash, BS, 65; Univ Calif, Berkeley, PhD(chem), 70. *Honors & Awards:* Sci Res Soc Fac Award Outstanding Res, Sigma Xi, 85. *Prof Exp:* Res assoc, Univ Ill, 70-72; asst prof org chem, Rockefeller Univ, 72-74 & Univ Calif, Davis, 74-80. *Concurrent Pos:* Consult, Riker Labs, 3M, St Paul, Minn, 82-; mem, bio-organic & natural prods study sect, Nat Inst Health, 88-91. *Mem:* Am Chem Soc; AAAS; NY Acad Sci; Sigma Xi. *Res:* Synthetic, organic and bioorganic chemistry; synthesis and reactions of nucleosides; nucleotides and nucleic acids; organopalladium chemistry; synthesis of fluorinated bioactive compounds; design and synthesis of antiviral agents. *Mailing Add:* Dept Med Chem & Pharm Purdue Univ West Lafayette IN 47907-2902

BERGSTROM, GARY CARLTON, DISEASES OF FIELD CROPS, PHYSIOLOGY OF PARASITISM. *Current Pos:* asst prof, 81-87, ASSOC PROF PLANT PATH, CORNELL UNIV, 87- *Personal Data:* b Chicago, Ill, May 12, 53; m 83, Frances Brach; c Walter C & Helen K. *Educ:* Purdue Univ, BS, 75, MS, 78; Univ Ky, PhD(plant path), 81. *Prof Exp:* Teaching asst biol, Purdue Univ, 75-76, res asst plant path, 76-77; res asst plant path, Univ Ky, 78-81. *Concurrent Pos:* Co-chmn, NY State Pest Control Conf, 84; pres, Northeast Corn Improv Conf, 87-; team leader, Field Crops, Fungicide Assessment Proj, Nat Agr Pesticide Impact Assessment Prog-USDA, 89-91, chair, NCent Regional Corn & Sorghum Dis, 91. *Mem:* Am Phytopath Soc; Am Soc Agron; Crop Sci Soc Am; Int Soc Plant Path; Can Soc Plant Path. *Res:* Biology, epidemiology and management of leaf and stem diseases of corn, small grain cereals, and forage legumes of importance in New York State. *Mailing Add:* 113 Birchwood Dr Ithaca NY 14850. *E-Mail:* gcb3@cornell.edu

BERGSTROM, K SUNE D, CHEMISTRY. *Current Pos:* prof chem, Karolinska Inst, 58-80, dean med fac, 63-66, rector, 69-77, PROF, DEPT BIOCHEM, KAROLINSKA INST, SWEDEN, 90- *Personal Data:* b Stockholm, Sweden, Jan 10, 16; m 43. *Educ:* Karolinska Inst, MD & DMedSci, 44. *Hon Degrees:* Dr, Univ Basel, 60, Univ Chicago, 60, Harvard Univ, 76, Mt Sinai Med Sch, 76, Med Acad Wroclaw, 76; DSc, McMaster Univ, 88. *Honors & Awards:* Nobel Prize in Physiol or Med, 82; Dohme Lectr, Johns Hopkins Univ, 73; Merrimon Lectr, Univ NC, 73; V D Mattia Lectr, Roche Inst, 74; Harvey Lectr, Harvey Soc, 74; Francis Amory Prize, Am Acad Arts & Sci, 75; Benjamin Franklin Medal, Am Philos Soc, 88. *Prof Exp:* Asst, Biochem Dept, Med Nobel Inst, Karolinska Inst, Stockholm, 44-47; prof physiol chem, Univ Lund, 47-58. *Concurrent Pos:* Res fel, Basel Univ, 46-47; chmn bd dirs, Nobel Found, 75-87; Albert Lasker Basic Med Res Award, 77; chmn, Adv Comt Med Res, WHO, 77-82; chmn, Sci & Tech Adv Group Human Reproduction, WHO, Geneva, 85-90. *Mem:* Inst Med-Nat Acad Sci; Royal Swed Acad Sci (pres, 65); Am Acad Arts & Sci; Am Soc Biol Chemists; Am Philos Soc. *Res:* Biochemistry; physiology. *Mailing Add:* Karolinska Inst Nobel Forum Box 270 Stockholm 171 77 Sweden

BERGSTROM, ROBERT CHARLES, VETERINARY PARASITOLOGY. *Current Pos:* RETIRED. *Personal Data:* b Newcastle, Wyo, Mar 23, 22; m 48; c 2. *Educ:* Colo State Univ, BS, 50; Univ Wyo, MS, 56, PhD(zool), 64. *Prof Exp:* Surv supvr, Bur Entom & Plant Quarantine, USDA, 50-51; instr high sch, Wyo & Mont, 51-57; technologist, Dept Entom & Parasitol, Univ Wyo, 57-58; instr high sch, Wyo, 58-61; teaching asst zool, Univ Wyo, 61-62, parasitologist, Div Microbiol & Vet Med, 62-87. *Concurrent Pos:* NIH fel, Med Sch, Mex, 66; res vet micro & pathol, Wash State Univ, 81. *Mem:* Am Soc Parasitologists; World Asn Advan Vet Parasitol; Am Asn Vet Parasitol; NY Acad Sci; Sigma Xi. *Res:* Helminths of domestic animals, especially research physiological responses of the host animal to nematode parasite infections; dual infections; domestic ruminants. *Mailing Add:* 1757 N Heights Circle Sheridan WY 82801

BERGSTROM, ROBERT EDWARD, GEOLOGY. *Current Pos:* geologist & head groundwater geol & geophys explor sect, 63-74, prin geologist, 74-81, chief, 81-83, EMER CHIEF, ILL GEOL SURV, 83- *Personal Data:* b Rock Island, Ill, Mar 27, 23; m 46, Margaret Carlson; c Elizabeth (Selander), Joan (Kemna) & John. *Educ:* Augustana Col (Ill), AB, 47; Univ Wis, MS, 50, PhD(geol), 53. *Prof Exp:* Instr geol, Beloit Col, 50-51; integrated lib studies, Univ Wis, 52-53; asst geologist, Ill Geol Surv, 53-55, assoc geologist, 55-59, geologist, 59-61; proj geologist, Kuwait, Parsons Corp, 61-63. *Concurrent Pos:* Mem comt geol sci, Nat Acad Sci, 69-71; mem comt surface mining & reclamation, Nat Res Coun, 78-80. *Mem:* Geol Soc Am; Am Inst Prof Geol; Asn Groundwater Scientists & Engrs. *Res:* Ground water geology; geology of Kuwait; geology of waste disposal. *Mailing Add:* 2004 Galen Dr Champaign IL 61821

BERGSTROM, STIG MAGNUS, GEOLOGY, INVERTEBRATE PALEONTOLOGY. *Current Pos:* from asst prof & cur to assoc prof & cur, 68-72, PROF GEOL, OHIO STATE UNIV, 72- *Personal Data:* b Skovde, Sweden, June 12, 35; m 82, Birgitta Malmsten. *Educ:* Lund Univ, Sweden, Fil Kand, 59, PhD(geol), 61. *Hon Degrees:* Dr Lund Univ, 87. *Honors & Awards:* Assar Hadding Prize, 95. *Prof Exp:* Amanuensis geol, Lund Univ, 58-60; res asst, Ohio State Univ, 60-61; lectr, Lund Univ, 62-68. *Concurrent Pos:* Fulbright scholar, 60; fel, Scand-Am Found, 64. *Mem:* Geol Soc Am; Paleont Soc; Paleont Asn; Am Asn Petrol Geologists; Royal Physiog Soc. *Res:* Stratigraphy, fossils and geologic history of the lower Paleozoic of North America, Northwestern Europe, South America and China. *Mailing Add:* Dept Geol Sci Ohio State Univ 125 S Oval Mall Columbus OH 43210

BERGSTROM, WILLIAM H, PEDIATRICS. *Current Pos:* From assoc prof to prof, 55-77, EMER PROF PEDIAT, STATE UNIV NY MED CTR, 85- *Personal Data:* b Bay City, Mich, Jan 1, 21; m 44, Charlotte Stuart; c 4. *Educ:* Amherst Col, BA, 42; Univ Rochester, MD, 45. *Concurrent Pos:* Adj prof biochem, 76-85. *Mem:* AAAS; Am Pediat Soc; Soc Pediat Res; Soc Exp Biol & Med; Am Soc Bone & Mineral Res. *Res:* Electrolyte metabolism; blood-bone equilibria. *Mailing Add:* 750 E Adams St Syracuse NY 13210-2306

BERGTROM, GERALD, MOLECULAR BIOLOGY & EVOLUTION, INSECT PHYSIOLOGY. *Current Pos:* from asst prof to assoc prof, 78-87, PROF BIOL SCI, UNIV WIS-MILWAUKEE, 88- *Personal Data:* b New York, NY, Feb 14, 45. *Educ:* City Col New York, BSc, 67; Brandeis Univ, PhD(biol), 74. *Prof Exp:* Fel insect develop, Univ Conn, 73-75; asst prof biol, Vanderbilt Univ, 75-78. *Mem:* AAAS; Am Soc Cell Biol. *Res:* Hemoglobin synthesis during insect development and in response to insect growth homones; molecular biology of hemoglobin synthesis, assembly and secretion; insect globin gene structure, evolution and regulation; regulation of hemostasis. *Mailing Add:* Dept Biol Sci Univ Wis-Milwaukee Milwaukee WI 53201. *Fax:* 414-229-3926; *E-Mail:* bergtrom@csd.uwm.edu

BERHANU, PAULOS, METABOLISM, DIABETES. *Current Pos:* res assoc, Dept Med, Div Endocrinol, 79-81, asst prof med, 81-87, ASSOC PROF MED, DIV ENDOCRINOL & ASSOC PROF BIOCHEM, BIOPHYSICS & GENETICS, UNIV COLO HEALTH SCIS CTR, 87- *Educ:* Haile Selassie I Univ, BSc, 68; Univ Mich, MS, 69; Loma Linda Univ, MD, 73; Nat Bd Med Examrs, dipl, 74; Am Bd Internal Med, cert, 77. *Honors & Awards:* Getachew Boladia Mem Lectr, Fac Sci, Addis Ababa Univ, 94. *Prof Exp:* Intern internal med, Univ Southern Calif Med Ctr, 73-74; resident internal med, Loma Linda Univ Med Ctr, 74-76, clin fel endocrinol, metab & diabetes, 76-77; fel endocrinol, metabol & diabetes, Johns Hopkins Univ Sch Med, 77-79. *Concurrent Pos:* Grantee, NIH, 81-84, 83-87, 89-92 & 92-96, Nat Res Soc Am, 84-86, Diabetes Res & Educ Found, 85-86, 87-88; new investr res award, NIH, 81-84; Roerig vis prof diabetes mgt, Harvard Med Sch-Joslin Diabetes Ctr, 90; prin investr, Hoechst-Roussel Pharmaceut, 92; Pfizer vis prof diabetes mgt, Vanderbilt Univ Med Ctr, 93; Am Cancer Soc postdoctoral fel award, 93-94; J William Fulbright sr scholar, Addis Ababa Univ Sch Med, Ethiopia, 94-95. *Mem:* Am Diabetes Asn; Am Fedn Clin Res; Endocrine Soc; AAAS; Am Soc Cell Biol; Int Diabetes Fedn. *Res:* Regulation of insulin receptors; mechanism of insulin action; mechanisms of insulin resistance; pathophysiology of the insulin resistance of obesity and diabetes mellitus. *Mailing Add:* Div Endocrinol Metab & Diabetes Univ Colo Health Sci Ctr B151 4200 E Ninth Ave Denver CO 80262

BERHOW, MARK ALAN, NATURAL PRODUCTS ANALYSIS, PLANT ENZYMOLOGY. *Current Pos:* Res assoc, 83-85, RES CHEMIST, AGR RES SERV, USDA, 85- *Personal Data:* b Iowa City, Iowa, Nov 20, 54. *Educ:* Univ Portland, BS 77; Wash State Univ, PhD(biochem), 84. *Concurrent Pos:* Japan Sci & Technol Agency fel, 91. *Mem:* Am Soc Plant Physiol. *Res:* Citrus quality factors, especially the secondary metabolites, flavonoids and limonoids; biochemistry of the accumulation and metabolism of these compounds in citrus and citrus relatives. *Mailing Add:* USDA Agr Res Serv NCAUR 1815 N University St Peoria IL 61604. *Fax:* 626-449-3059; *E-Mail:* mark@ucrvms.bitnet

BERI, AVINASH CHANDRA, hyperfine interactions, surface chemical physics, for more information see previous edition

BERI, RAJESH GAJANAN, CELL CULTURE, MEMBRANE RECOVERY. *Current Pos:* RES ASSOC, LONZA BIOLOGICS INC, 96- *Personal Data:* b Mumbai, India, Dec 4, 65. *Educ:* Indian Inst Technol, BTech, 87; Worcester Polytech Inst, MS, 90, PhD(chem eng), 94. *Concurrent Pos:* Postdoctoral res fel, Alpha-Beta Technol, 94; postdoctoral res assoc, T Breeders Inc, 95; vis adj fac, Worcester Polytech Inst, 95-96. *Mem:* Am Chem Soc; Am Inst Chem Engrs. *Res:* Develop, optimize and scale up cell culture and membrane recovery processes for production of monoclonal antibodies and therapeutic proteins; fluid mixing momentum, heat and mass transfer analysis in large scale bioreactors. *Mailing Add:* 101 International Dr Portsmouth NH 03801. *E-Mail:* rberi@tellink.net

BERING, CHARLES LAWRENCE, BIOCHEMISTRY, MICROBIOLOGY. *Current Pos:* ASSOC PROF CHEM, CLARION UNIV PA, 88- *Personal Data:* b Houston, Tex, July 29, 47. *Educ:* Univ Houston, BS, 70; Purdue Univ, PhD(biochem), 75. *Prof Exp:* Res assoc & lectr biochem, Northwestern Univ, 75-78; chmn dept nat sci, 80-84, assoc prof chem, State Univ NY, Col Technol, 78-88. *Concurrent Pos:* Workshop dir, Monroe County Community Col, 84; sci adv, Cobleskill Agr & Technol Col, 84-87; vis prof, Imperial Col, London, 85; vis res assoc, Univ Col-Cardiff. *Mem:* AAAS; Am Chem Soc; Am Soc Biochem & Molecular Biol; Am Soc Microbiol. *Res:* Microbial degradation of aromatic compounds; microbial synthesis of rare intermediates in path of degradation. *Mailing Add:* Dept Chem Clarion Univ Pa Clarion PA 16214

BERING, EDGAR ANDREW, JR, medicine, neurosurgery; deceased, see previous edition for last biography

BERING, EDGAR ANDREW, III, MAGNETOSPHERIC PHYSICS, SPACE PLASMA PHYSICS. *Current Pos:* Res sci, 74, from vis asst prof to assoc prof, 75-89, PROF PHYSICS, UNIV HOUSTON, 89- *Personal Data:* b New York, NY, Jan 9, 46; m 85, Barbara A Clark; c Edgar A IV & Janet

I. *Educ:* Harvard Col, BA, 67; Univ Calif, Berkeley, PhD(physics), 74. *Concurrent Pos:* Partner, 84-87, vpres, IF&G Tech Consults Inc, 87- *Mem:* Am Geophys Union; Am Astron Soc; Sigma Xi; AAAS; NY Acad Sci. *Res:* Study of the earth's magnetosphere and ionosphere; electrodynamics of the polar cusp; development of an x-ray camera for auroral studies. *Mailing Add:* Dept Physics Univ Houston Houston TX 77204-5504. *Fax:* 713-743-3589; *E-Mail:* bering@space.phys.uh.edu

BERINGER, ROBERT, PHYSICS. *Current Pos:* RETIRED. *Personal Data:* b Pittsburgh, Pa, Oct 14, 17; m 42; c 3. *Educ:* Washington & Jefferson Col, BS, 39; Yale Univ, PhD(physics), 42. *Prof Exp:* Asst radiation lab, Mass Inst Technol, 42-46; asst prof physics, 46-50, from assoc prof to prof physics, Yale Univ, 50-, dir heavy ion accelerator lab, 88. *Mem:* Am Phys Soc. *Res:* Counting techniques; microwave physics; electronics; nuclear particle accelerators. *Mailing Add:* 3997 Whitney Ave New Haven CT 06517

BERINGER, THEODORE MICHAEL, CELL BIOLOGY, CELLULAR ULTRASTRUCTURE. *Current Pos:* ASSOC PROF HISTOL & CELL BIOL, UNIV MO, 80- *Personal Data:* b May 1, 44. *Educ:* Regis Col, BSc, 66: Loyola Univ, PhD(anat), 72. *Prof Exp:* Nat Inst Neurol Dis & Stroke postdoctoral fel physiol, State Univ NY, 72-73; asst prof Histol, Tufts Med Sch, 73-80. *Mem:* Am Soc Cell Biol. *Res:* Liposome mediated chemotherapy; renal membrane transport mechanisms and ultrastructure of cell membrane macromolecules. *Mailing Add:* Univ Mo 2411 Holmes Kansas City MO 64108. *Fax:* 816-235-5218; *E-Mail:* tberinger@vaxl.umkc.edu

BERK, ARISTID D, ELECTRICAL ENGINEERING, ELECTROMAGNETISM. *Current Pos:* RETIRED. *Personal Data:* b Istanbul, Apr 28, 25; m 48, Hope Semon; c Dimitri James & Deon Despina. *Educ:* Robert Col, Istanbul, BS, 47; Rensselaer Polytech Inst, MS, 51; Mass Inst Technol, ScD(elec eng), 54. *Prof Exp:* Mem tech staff, Hughes Aircraft Co, 54-55, group head, 55-56, asst sect head & sr mem tech staff, 56-58, sect head solid state sect, 58-60; exec vpres, Micromega Corp, 60-75; vpres eng, Electronic Systs Div, Sams Bunker Ramo Corp, 76-77, pres, Amphenol Div, 77-82. *Concurrent Pos:* Lectr, Univ Calif, Los Angeles, 55-58. *Mem:* Inst Elec & Electronics Engrs; Am Phys Soc; Sigma Xi. *Res:* Electromagnetic theory; ferromagnetism at microwave frequencies; author of several papers. *Mailing Add:* 24603 Skyline View Dr Malibu CA 90265

BERK, ARNOLD J, MICROBIOLOGY. *Current Pos:* from asst prof to assoc prof microbiol, 79-86, chmn dept, 88-92, PROF MICROBIOL & MOLECULAR GENETICS, UNIV CALIF, LOS ANGELES, 86- *Personal Data:* b Los Angeles, Calif, Dec 23, 49; m 71, Juzette Cleson; c Benjamin & Anna. *Educ:* Univ Calif, Berkeley, BA, 71; Stanford Univ, MD, 76. *Honors & Awards:* Trygve Tuve Lectr, NIH, 79, Merit Award, 87. *Prof Exp:* Res assoc molecular biol, Mass Inst Technol, 76-79. *Concurrent Pos:* Mem, Sci Adv Bd, Amgen, Inc, Thousand Oaks, Calif, 80- & Genetics Panel, NSF, 84-88; ed, Virol, 85-92; chmn, Gordon Conf Animal Cells & Viruses, 86. *Mem:* Am Soc Microbiol; Fedn Am Socs Exp Biol. *Res:* Biochemistry of transcription initiation by RNA polymerases II and III; transformation by adenovirus EIB proteins. *Mailing Add:* Molecular Biol Inst Univ Calif Los Angeles CA 90024-1570

BERK, BERNARD, CHEMISTRY. *Current Pos:* res & develop chemist & head dept, Tech Serv Lab ER Squibb & Sons, 46-66, mgr mfg, Overseas Plants, 53-55, assoc tech dir, Overseas Div, 55-58, dir, Steroid Prep Lab, Squibb Inst Med Res, 58-66, dir, Res Prod Lab, 66-70, MGR, ANTIBIOTIC MFG PLANNING, E R SQUIBB & SONS, 70-, DIR CHEM DEVELOP, 79- *Personal Data:* b Brooklyn, NY, Dec 23, 15; m 40; c 1. *Educ:* Ind Univ, BA, 37, MA, 38, PhD(org chem), 41; NY Univ, MChE, 47. *Prof Exp:* Jr chemist, Ind Ord Works, 41-42; res chemist, Lawrence Richard Bruce, Conn, 42-46. *Mem:* Assoc Am Chem Soc; Am Inst Chem Eng; assoc NY Acad Sci. *Res:* Organic synthesis; antibiotics; wool dyeing processes; vapor phase catalytic reduction over intermetallic catalysts; crystallization of penicillin salts. *Mailing Add:* 45 Ocean Ave No 5H Monmouth Beach NJ 07750-1312

BERK, HERBERT L, PLASMA PHYSICS. *Current Pos:* PHYSICIST (RES SCIENTIST) & PROF PHYSICS, INST FUSION STUDIES, UNIV TEX, AUSTIN, 90- *Personal Data:* b New York, NY, Sept 29, 38. *Educ:* NY Univ, BS, 60; Princeton Univ, MA, 62, PhD(plasma physics), 64. *Prof Exp:* NSF fel, Culham Lab, Abingdon, Eng, 64-65; res asst, Univ Calif, San Diego, 65-67; physicist, Lawrence Livermore Nat Lab, 67-73, 74-77 & 78-80; assoc res physicist, Princeton Plasma Physics Lab, 73-74; physicist (regents scientist), Lawrence Berkeley Lab, 77-78. *Concurrent Pos:* Instr basic physics, Univ Calif, San Diego, 66-67; lectr, advan plasma physics, Dept Appl Sci, Univ Calif, Davis, 70-72 & 74; guest lectr microinstability & Tokamak confinement, Dept Elec Eng, Univ Calif, Berkeley, 70-72, guest lectr elec eng, 69-80; chmn human rights comt, Plasma Physics Sect, Am Phys Soc, 89-92, Comt Int Freedom Scientists, 91-93; mem spec task force, Aid to Former Soviet Union, 92-93. *Mem:* Fel Am Phys Soc. *Res:* Plasma physics; author of 145 publications. *Mailing Add:* Inst Fusion Studies Univ Texas RLM Hal 11 218 Austin TX 78712

BERK, JACK EDWARD, GASTROENTEROLOGY. *Current Pos:* prof med & chmn dept, Univ Calif, Irvine, 63-73, head, Div Gastroenterol, 63-79, asst dean, 79-90, DISTINGUISHED PROF, COL MED, UNIV CALIF, IRVINE, 79- *Personal Data:* b Philadelphia, Pa, Nov 24, 11; m 37, Adeline Alberts; c Phillip H (deceased) & Richard H. *Educ:* Univ Pa, BA, 32, MSc, 39, DSc(med), 43; Jefferson Med Col, MD, 36; Am Bd Internal Med & Am Bd Gastroenterol, dipl, 43. *Honors & Awards:* Schindler Award, Am Soc Gastrointestinal Endoscopy, 66; Rorer Award, Am Col Gastroenterol, 70, 74, 78 & 79; Distinguished Physician Award, Nat Found for Ileitis & Colitis, 80; Distinguished Sci Achievement Award, Am Col Gastroenterol, 82; Clin Achievement Award, Am Col Gastroenterol, 88; Laureate Award, Am Col Physicians, 90-; Backus Medal, World Orgn Gastroenterol. *Prof Exp:* Instr gastroenterol, Grad Sch Med, Univ Pa, 41-46; asst prof, Med Sch, Temple Univ, 46-54, asst dir, Fels Res Inst, 46-54; assoc prof clin med, Wayne State Univ, 54-62, prof clin med, 62-63. *Concurrent Pos:* Consult, Surgeon Gen, US Army, 47-, Cedars Sinai & White Mem Hosps, Los Angeles, Mem Hosp, Long Beach, 63-, Long Beach Vet Admin Hosp, 63- & Sinai Hosp Detroit, 63- dir dept med, Sinai Hosp, Detroit, Mich, 54-63; mem, Gastroenterol Soc, Columbia, Brazil, Venezuela, Ecuador & Peru; mem, Acad Med, Ecuador. *Mem:* Am Soc Gastrointestinal Endoscopy (pres, 58); Bockus Int Soc Gastroenterol (pres, 67-71); master Am Col Physicians; Am Gastroenterol Asn; master Am Col Gastroenterol (pres, 75-76); Inter-Am Gastroenterol Asn (pres, 81-). *Res:* Characterization of serum amylase; acidity of the first part of duodenum in ulcer; tetracycline fluorescence in gastric lesions. *Mailing Add:* 894 Ronda Sevilla Laguna Hills CA 92653

BERK, KENNETH N, STATISTICS, STATISTICAL COMPUTING. *Current Pos:* assoc prof, 69-78, PROF MATH, ILL STATE UNIV, 78- *Personal Data:* b Takoma Park, Md, Sept 24, 38; m 68, Laura Eisenberg; c David & Peter. *Educ:* Carnegie Inst Technol, BS, 60; Univ Minn, PhD(math), 65. *Honors & Awards:* Youden Prize, Am Soc Qual Control, 78. *Prof Exp:* Asst prof math, Northwestern Univ, 65-68; asst prof, Northeastern Ill State Col, 68-69. *Concurrent Pos:* Chair, Am Statist Asn, Statist Comput Sect, 89. *Mem:* Inst Math Statist; fel Am Statist Asn; Int Asn Statist Comput. *Res:* Statistical computing; regression analysis; time series. *Mailing Add:* Dept Math Ill State Univ Normal IL 61761. *Fax:* 309-438-5866; *E-Mail:* kberk@math.ilstu.edu

BERK, RICHARD SAMUEL, microbiology, biochemistry, for more information see previous edition

BERK, ROBERT NORTON, RADIOLOGY. *Current Pos:* PROF RADIOL & CHMN DEPT, UNIV CALIF, SAN DIEGO, 77- *Personal Data:* b Pittsburgh, Pa, Sept 3, 30; m 56; c 3. *Educ:* Univ Pittsburgh, BS, 51, MD, 55. *Prof Exp:* From instr to asst prof radiol, Sch Med, Univ Pittsburgh, 61-65; chief radiol, Passavant Hosp, Pittsburgh, 66-68; assoc prof, Sch Med, Univ Calif, San Diego, 68-74; prof radiol & chmn dept, Univ Tex Health Sci Ctr, Dallas, 74-77. *Concurrent Pos:* Consult radiol, Balboa Naval Hosp, San Diego & Vet Admin Hosp, La Jolla, 70-74; dir radiol, Parkland Mem Hosp, Dallas, 74-77; consult radiol, Vet Admin Hosp, Dallas, 74-77 & Baylor Univ Med Ctr, 74-77; chief radiol serv, Children's Med Ctr, Dallas, 74-77. *Mem:* Asn Univ Radiologists; Am Col Radiol; Radiol Soc NAm; Am Roentgen Ray Soc; Soc Gastrointestinal Radiologists. *Res:* Pharmacokinetics of radiographic contrast materials for cholangiography and cholecystography. *Mailing Add:* 225 W Dickinson St San Diego CA 92103-1910

BERK, TOBY STEVEN, COMPUTER SCIENCES. *Current Pos:* DIR UNDERGRAD PROGS SCH COMPUTER SCI, FLA INT UNIV, 91- *Personal Data:* b Chicago, Ill, Jan 15, 44; m 65, Lynn Lipphare. *Educ:* Univ Mich, BSE, 65; Purdue Univ, MS, 68, PhD(comput sci), 72. *Prof Exp:* Instr comput sci, Ind Univ-Purdue Univ, Indianapolis, 70-72; from asst prof to assoc prof, 72-86, chmn, math sci dept, 81-85, prof comput sci, Fla Int Univ, 87. *Concurrent Pos:* Vis assoc prof, Ohio State Univ, 80-81; vis prof, Univ Colo, 89-90. *Mem:* Asn Comput Mach; Inst Elec & Electronics Engrs. *Res:* Computer graphics; distributed processing; computer education. *Mailing Add:* Sch Comput Sci Fla Int Univ Miami FL 33199. *Fax:* 305-348-3549; *E-Mail:* berke@fiu.edu

BERKA, LADISLAV HENRY, INORGANIC CHEMISTRY. *Current Pos:* from asst prof to assoc prof, 65-69, PROF CHEM, WORCESTER POLYTECH INST, 79- *Personal Data:* b Bay Shore, NY, July 16, 36; m 59; c 2. *Educ:* Union Col, NY, BS, 57; Univ Calif, Berkeley, MS, 60; Univ Conn, Storrs, PhD(chem), 65. *Honors & Awards:* Gustav Ohaus Award, Nat Sci Teachers Asn, 77. *Prof Exp:* Teacher chem, Mineola High Sch, 59-61; instr, Univ Conn, 64-65. *Concurrent Pos:* Consult, Sherman Assocs, 76-; prog dir, Cent Maine Metric Consortium, 77- *Mem:* Am Chem Soc; Sigma Xi. *Res:* Synthesis and characterization of coordination compounds; protonated organic bases; anomalous liquids. *Mailing Add:* 14 Walbridge Rd Paxton MA 01612-1402

BERKEBILE, CHARLES ALAN, GROUNDWATER, COMPUTER MODELING. *Current Pos:* PROF GEOL, DIV SCI, COL SCI & TECHNOL, CORPUS CHRISTI STATE UNIV, 81-, CHAIRPERSON, 90- *Personal Data:* b Jamaica, NY, Mar 4, 38; m 79; c 1. *Educ:* Allegheny Col, BS, 60; Boston Univ, AM, 61, PhD(geol), 64. *Prof Exp:* Mem staff crystal growth, Lab Insulation Res, Crystal Physics Sect, Mass Inst Technol, 63-64; asst prof earth sci, Southampton Col, Long Island, 64-67; mem res staff, Tech Staffs Div, Corning Glass Works, 67-69; assoc prof geol & chmn dept, Southampton Col, Long Island Univ, 69-75, prof geol & marine sci, 75-79 & 80-81. *Concurrent Pos:* Vis assoc scientist & res collab, Crystal Struct Anal Group, Chem Dept, Brookhaven Nat Lab, 66-67; environ consult; vis sr res geologist, Dept Geol & Geophys Sci, Princeton Univ, 79-80. *Mem:* Fel Geol Soc Am; Nat Water Well Asn; Nat Asn Geol Teachers; Asn Ground Water Scientists & Engrs. *Res:* Ground-water resources; field geology. *Mailing Add:* Dept Sci Tex A&M Corpus Christi State Univ 6300 Ocean Dr Corpus Christi TX 78412-5503

BERKELHAMER, LOUIS H(ARRY), CERAMICS, MINERAL TECHNOLOGY. *Current Pos:* RETIRED. *Personal Data:* b Chicago, Ill, Apr 23, 12; m 38; c 2. *Educ:* Univ Ill, BS, 33; Univ Wash, MS, 36. *Prof Exp:* Res ceramic eng, Ill State Geol Surv, 34; res engr ceramic div, Battelle Mem Inst, 36-38; res engr & petrographer, Saranac Lab, Trudeau Found, NY, 38-41; mineral technologist, US Bur Mines, 41-45; ceramic engr, Ohmite Mfg Co, 45-50, dir res & chief ceramics engr, 50-64, dir res & develop eng, 64-68, vpres res & develop eng, 68-71, vpres eng, 71-78, consult eng, 78-81. *Concurrent Pos:* Tech ed, Ceramic Catalogs & Cyclopedia, 34. *Mem:* Am Ceramic Soc; Nat Inst Ceramic Eng; Sigma Xi. *Res:* Properties of clays and non-metallic minerals; mineralogical aspects of silicosis and pneumoconiosis problems; differential thermal analysis studies of non-metallic minerals; properties and composition of molding sands; study of domestic talcs; coatings and composition for electrical resistors and rheostats; new electronic components. *Mailing Add:* 777 Purdy St Birmingham MI 48009-1739

BERKELHAMMER, GERALD, ORGANIC CHEMISTRY, AGROCHEMICAL SYNTHESIS. *Current Pos:* Res chemist, 57-60, group leader, 60-70, mgr org synthesis, 70-85, dir chem discovery, 85-91, EXEC DIR CHEM DISCOVERY AGR RES DIV, AM CYANAMID CO, 91- *Personal Data:* b Newark, NJ, Feb 3, 31; m 54, Sheila Rosenson; c Jill B, Frederick A & Paul D. *Educ:* Brown Univ, AB, 52; Univ Wash, PhD(org chem), 57. *Mem:* Am Chem Soc; AAAS. *Res:* Agricultural and medicinal chemistry; synthesis of agrochemicals and animal health agents. *Mailing Add:* 58 Allison Rd Princeton NJ 08540

BERKELMAN, KARL, EXPERIMENTAL HIGH ENERGY PHYSICS. *Current Pos:* Instr & res assoc physics, 59-60, from asst prof, 61-67, PROF PHYSICS, CORNELL UNIV, 67-, DIR LAB NUCLEAR STUDIES, 85- *Personal Data:* b Lewiston, Maine, June 7, 33; m 59, Mary Hobbie; c 3. *Educ:* Univ Rochester, BS, 55; Cornell Univ, PhD(physics), 59. *Concurrent Pos:* NSF fels, Ital Nat Synchrotron Lab, Frascati, 60-61; European Orgn Nuclear Res, Geneva, Switz, 67-68, 81-82 & 91-92; sci staff mem, Ger Electron Synchrotron, Hamburg, 74-75. *Mem:* Am Phys Soc. *Res:* Meson photoproduction experiments; high energy electron scattering experiments; phenomenological theory of high energy particle reactions; electron-positron colliding beam experiments. *Mailing Add:* Newman Lab Cornell Univ Ithaca NY 14853

BERKER, AHMET NIHAT, CONDENSED MATTER THEORY. *Current Pos:* from asst prof to assoc prof, 79-88, PROF PHYSICS, MASS INST TECHNOL, 88- *Personal Data:* b Istanbul, Turkey, Sept 20, 49; div; c 1. *Educ:* Mass Inst Technol, BS(chem) & BS(physics), 71; Univ Ill, Urbana, MS, 72, PhD(physics), 77. *Honors & Awards:* Sci Award, Turkish Sci & Tech Res Found, 88. *Prof Exp:* Res fel physics, Harvard Univ, 77-79. *Mem:* Fel Am Phys Soc; Am Asn Univ Professors. *Res:* Statistical physics; theory of phase transitions and critical phenomena in condensed matter systems. *Mailing Add:* Dept Physics 12-135 Mass Inst Technol Cambridge MA 02139

BERKES, JOHN STEPHAN, XEROGRAPHIC MATERIALS & PROCESS. *Current Pos:* Scientist mat sci, 68-73, mgr, 73-82, SR MEM RES STAFF, XEROX CORP, 82- *Personal Data:* b Buzias, Rumania, Sept 5, 40; US citizen; m 69; c 4. *Educ:* Mich Technol Univ, BS, 62; Pa State Univ, MS, 64, PhD(solid state sci), 68. *Mem:* Soc Imaging Sci & Technol; Am Vacuum Soc; Sigma Xi. *Res:* Structure, thermal properties, viscous flow, bulk and surface stability of amorphous chalcogenide photoconducting materials; thin films technology; xerographic materials and process. *Mailing Add:* 1137 Hidden Valley Trail Webster NY 14580-9175

BERKEY, DENNIS DALE, DIFFERENTIAL EQUATIONS, APPLIED ANALYSIS. *Current Pos:* from asst prof to assoc prof math, Boston Univ, 74-93, chmn dept, 79-83, assoc vpres acad affairs, 83-85, vice provost, 85-87, provost, 87-91, PROF MATH, BOSTON UNIV, 93-, DEAN LIB ARTS & GRAD SCH, 87- *Personal Data:* b Wooster, Ohio, May 27, 47; m 74, Catherine Grooms; c Cristin, Aaron & Jessica. *Educ:* Muskingum Col, BA, 69; Miami Univ, MA, 71; Univ Cincinnati, PhD(math), 74. *Prof Exp:* Instr math, Miami Univ, 73-74. *Concurrent Pos:* Danforth Assoc, 79. *Mem:* Am Math Soc; Math Asn Am; Soc Indust & Appl Math; Asn Comput Mach. *Res:* Qualitative theory for linear systems; periodic and almost periodic solution of differential systems; perturbation methods; bifurcation problems; optimal control theory. *Mailing Add:* Boston Univ Rm CAS 106 725 Commonwealth Ave Boston MA 02215

BERKEY, DONALD C, ENGINEERING. *Current Pos:* RETIRED. *Mem:* Nat Acad Eng. *Mailing Add:* 2171 Gulf Shore Blvd N Apt 304 Naples FL 33940

BERKEY, GORDON BRUCE, ASTROPHYSICS, PHYSICS. *Current Pos:* From asst prof to assoc prof, 69-82, PROF PHYSICS, MINOT STATE COL, 82- *Personal Data:* b DuBois, Pa, June 1, 42; m 64, Judy Kirkwood; c Joyce (Schmeichel) & Jennifer (Kouba). *Educ:* Cornell Univ, AB, 64; Purdue Univ, MS, 67, PhD(physics), 69. *Mem:* Sigma Xi; Am Asn Phys Teachers. *Res:* Propagation of galactic cosmic-ray electrons; production of x-rays and gamma rays by cosmic-ray electrons. *Mailing Add:* 2305 19th Ave NW Minot ND 58703-1649

BERKHEIMER, HENRY EDWARD, AQUEOUS POLYMER SYSTEMS. *Current Pos:* ASST PROF, LYCOMING COL, WILLIAMSPORT, PA, 88- *Personal Data:* b Williamsport, Pa, Oct 13, 29; m 81, Nancy Kalemba; c Karen, Charles & David. *Educ:* Dickinson Col, AB, 51; Bucknell Univ, MS, 53; Pa State Univ, PhD(org chem), 58. *Prof Exp:* Res fel, Harvard Univ, 58-59; res chemist, Jackson Lab, E I du Pont de Nemours & Co, Inc, NJ, 59-62; sr res chemist, A E Staley Mfg Co, 62-63; res chemist, Elastomer Chem Dept, Exp Sta, E I du Pont de Nemours & Co Inc, Chestnut Run, 63-69, res chemist, 69-79, sr res chemist, 79-80, res assoc, 80-84, tech consult, Elastomer Lab, 84-88. *Concurrent Pos:* Lectr chem, Glassboro State Col, 77 & Widener Univ, 77-81, Pa State Univ, Del Co Campus, 87. *Mem:* Am Chem Soc. *Res:* Polymer synthesis and mechanisms of polymerization; latex technology; formation and properties of films from polymer solutions and dispersions. *Mailing Add:* 2035 N Konkle Rd Montoursville PA 17754-9607

BERKHEISER, SAMUEL WILLIAM, CLINICAL PATHOLOGY. *Current Pos:* RETIRED. *Personal Data:* b Ashland, Pa, July 29, 22; m 46, Harriet Hoover; c Samuel W Jr. *Educ:* Western Res Univ, BS, 43, MD, 46. *Prof Exp:* Intern, Geisinger Mem Hosp, Danville, Pa, 46-47; res path & bact, Albany Hosp & Med Sch, NY, 49-50; path & clin path, Youngstown Hosp Asn, Ohio, 50-52, asst pathologist, 52; from asst pathologist to assoc pathologist, Guthrie Clin, Robert Packer Hosp, Sayre, 52-55; assoc pathologist, Harrisburg Polyclin Hosp, Pa, 55-69, dir labs, 69-79. *Concurrent Pos:* Spec study, Armed Forces Inst Path, 52; consult, Vet Admin Hosp, Lebanon, Pa. *Mem:* Col Am Pathologists; Am Soc Clin Pathologists; AMA; Aerospace Med Asn. *Res:* Nevi and malignant melanomas of skin; tumors of thyroid and parotid gland; cysts of mediastinum and diaphragm; hypothyroidism; metabolic craniopathy; problems in diagnosis of skin lesions; epithelial hyperplasia of lung associated with cortisone and thromboembolism. *Mailing Add:* Dept Labs Harrisburg Polyclin Med Ctr Harrisburg PA 17110

BERKHOLTZ, NICHOLAS EVALD, ORDNANCE ENGINEERING, TECHNOLOGY TRANSFER PROJECT ENGINEERING. *Current Pos:* CONSULT, 92- *Personal Data:* b Majori, Latvia, Apr 19, 28; US citizen; m 57, Elga O Martinsons; c Karin R & Ingrid M. *Educ:* Iowa State Univ, BS, 56; Univ Minn, MS, 63. *Honors & Awards:* Life Prof Engr, Nat Soc Prof Engrs, 93; Quarter Century Award, Am Soc Mech Engrs, 95, Distinguished Serv Award, 97. *Prof Exp:* Prin develop engr, Minneapolis-Honeywell Reg Co, 56-71, proj engr, Honeywell Inc, 71-72, prin systs engr, 73-75, proj engr, 77-79, transl mgr, 79-80, mgr mfg methods & technol, 80-81, supvr, Honeywell Proving Ground, 81-84, prog mgr, Honeywell Inc, 84-87; dir opers, Valtest Inc, 72-73; consult engr, Stetter Assocs Inc, 75-77; eng mgr, Alliant Techsysts Inc, 87-92. *Concurrent Pos:* Expert consult, TEI/TECH Resources Network Corp, 95- *Mem:* US Naval Inst; Nat Soc Prof Engrs; fel Am Soc Mech Engrs; Nat Inst Eng Ethics. *Res:* Metal-explosive interactions; directed-energy devices. *Mailing Add:* 18225 Hermitage Way Minnetonka MN 55345-3210. *E-Mail:* berkh001@tc.umn.edu

BERKHOUT, AART W J, GEOPHYSICS, GEOLOGY. *Current Pos:* assoc geophysicist, Mobil Oil Co, Dallas, Tex, 71-74, geophys specialist, 74-79, supvr gravity magnetic appln, 79-82, coordr seismic interpretation, 82-89, GEOPHYS INTERPRETATION COORDR, NEW EXPLOR VENTURES, MOBIL OIL, CO, DALLAS, TEX, 89-, ASSOC GEOPHYS ADV, MNBD, EXPLOR SAM. *Personal Data:* b Dinteloord, Netherlands, June 13, 39; m 66, Janet Wood; c Kevin & Kathryn. *Educ:* Technol Univ Delft, MSc, 64; Queen's Univ (Ont), PhD(geol, geophys), 68. *Prof Exp:* Res scientist, Tulsa Res Ctr, Sinclair Oil Corp, 67-69; res geophysicist, Prod Res Lab, Atlantic Richfield Co, 69-71. *Concurrent Pos:* Polar Continental Shelf Proj, Can govt acquisition of gravity data in the Arctic. *Mem:* Soc Explor Geophysicists; Royal Netherlands Geol & Mining Soc; Netherlands Royal Inst Engrs. *Res:* Interpretation of potential field data, especially gravity and magnetic observations, in terms of geological prospects for oil or mineral accumulation; regional gravity field of the Canadian Arctic; special seismic studies; amplitude-hydrocarbon relationships; amplitude with offset related to lithology; seismic sequence stratigraphy. *Mailing Add:* 15706 Nedra Way Dallas TX 75248

BERKLAND, JAMES OMER, EARTHQUAKE HISTORY & PREDICTION. *Current Pos:* RETIRED. *Personal Data:* b Glendale, CA, July 31, 30; m 66; c 2. *Educ:* Univ Calif, Berkeley, BS, 58; San Jose State Univ, MS, 69. *Prof Exp:* Geol asst, US Geol Surv, 58-64, eng geologist, US Bur Reclamation, 64-69; consult, 69-72; asst prof geol, Appalachian State Univ, 72-73; co geologist, Santa Clara County, 73-94. *Concurrent Pos:* Adj prof, San Jose State Univ, 74-76. *Mem:* Fel Geol Soc Am; Asn Eng Geologists; AAAS; Ctr Study Early Man; Seismol Soc Am; Earthquake Eng Res Asn. *Res:* Coined the term 'seismic window'; extinct Miocene shrew named for him; over 50 scientific publications. *Mailing Add:* 14927 E Hills Dr San Jose CA 95127

BERKLAND, TERRILL RAYMOND, SCIENCE EDUCATION. *Current Pos:* Instr gen sci, 66-70, from asst prof to assoc prof, 72-90, PROF EARTH SCI & EDUC, CENT MO STATE UNIV, 90- *Personal Data:* b Mason City, Iowa, Oct 17, 41; m 67. *Educ:* Loras Col, BS, 64; Drake Univ, MA, 66; Univ Iowa, PhD(sci educ), 73. *Res:* Understanding of science process and interest in science teaching among prospective elementary teachers. *Mailing Add:* Dept Earth Sci Cent Mo State Univ Warrensburg MO 64093

BERKLEY, DAVID A, SPEECH. *Current Pos:* supvr, 80-90, head, acoust res dept, 90-95, DIV MGR SPEECH PROCESSING HARDWARE & SOFTWARE RES, AT&T LABS, 96- *Personal Data:* b Brooklyn, NY, Apr 28, 40; m 73; c 3. *Educ:* Cornell Univ, BEE, 61, PhD(appl physics), 66. *Prof Exp:* Res assoc electron & med physics, Chalmers Tech Sweden, 66-80; mem tech staff acoust res, Bell Tel Labs, 68-80, supvr, 80-90, head acoust res dept, 90-95. *Mem:* Acoust Soc Am; NY Acad Sci. *Res:* Acoustics signal processing and electroacoustics; speech and hearing; speaker recognition, large vocabulary speech recognition and language translation. *Mailing Add:* AT&T Lab Res Rm 2D537 Murray Hill NJ 07974. *E-Mail:* dab@research.att.com

BERKLEY, JOHN LEE, GEOLOGY, IGNEOUS PETROLOGY. *Current Pos:* asst dean, State Univ NY, Fredonia, 90-91, assoc dean 91-92, dean 92-93, ASSOC PROF IGNEOUS-METAMORPHIC PETROL, STATE UNIV NY, FREDONIA, 82- *Personal Data:* b Lawrence, Kans, May 17, 48; m 77, Mira Tetkowski; c 2. *Educ:* Univ Minn, Duluth, BS, 70; Univ Mo, Columbia, MS, 72; Univ NMex, PhD(geol), 77. *Prof Exp:* Engr aid defense contracts, M B Assocs, San Ramon, Calif, 73; meteorites & ocean basalts, Inst Meteoritics, Univ NMex, 77-79; res assoc, Lunar Planetary Lab, Univ Ariz, 79-82. *Mem:* Geol Soc Am; Mineral Soc Am; Am Geophys Union; Meteoritical Soc; Sigma Xi. *Res:* Achondrite meteorites; petrology and geochemistry of Ureilite and HED achondrite meteorites (NASA grant NAG9-82); petrology and geochemistry of volcanic ash beds, Mohawk Valley, New York. *Mailing Add:* Geosci Dept State Col Fredonia NY 14063. *E-Mail:* Bitnet: berkley@fredonia

BERKLEY, KAREN J, PAIN, INNERVATION OF FEMALE REPRODUCTIVE ORGANS. *Current Pos:* res assoc, 68-80, from assoc prof to prof, 80-89, MCKENZIE PROF, FLA STATE UNIV, 89- *Personal Data:* b New York, NY, Apr 27, 42; wid; c Lara & Tamara. *Educ:* Brown Univ, BA, 63; Univ Wash, PhD(physiol & biophys), 68. *Concurrent Pos:* Mem study sect, NIH, 78-82, 89-91; vis prof, Univ Kiel, Ger, 82, & int fel, Japanese Soc Prom Sci, 87; counr, Soc Neurosci, 82-86, Int Asn Study Pain, 93-96. *Mem:* Fel Am Psychol Asn; Int Asn Study Pain; Am Physiol Soc; fel Royal Soc Med; Soc Study of Reproduction; Am Asn Anatomists; Am Pain Asn; Int Brain Res Org; Sigma Xi; fel Japan Soc Prom Sci; Soc Neurosci. *Res:* Neural mechanisms of visceral pain, specifically pelvic and gynecological pain; sex differences in pain. *Mailing Add:* Dept Psychol Fla State Univ Tallahassee FL 32306-1051. *Fax:* 850-644-9874; *E-Mail:* kberkley@psy.fsu.edu

BERKMAN, JAMES ISRAEL, medicine, pathology; deceased, see previous edition for last biography

BERKMAN, MICHAEL G, CHEMISTRY, PATENT LAW. *Current Pos:* PATENT ATTY, MICHAEL G BERKMAN & ASSOC, 91- *Personal Data:* b Poland, Apr 4, 17; nat US; m 41; c 2. *Educ:* Univ Chicago, BS, 37, PhD(org chem), 41; De Paul Univ, JD, 58; John Marshall Law Sch, LLM, 62. *Prof Exp:* Res chemist, Deavitt Labs, Univ Chicago, 39-41, Am Can Co, Ill, 41-42 & Argonne Nat Lab, 46-51; chief chemist, Colburn Labs, Inc, 51-59; patent atty, Mann, Brown & McWilliams, 59-63, Kegan, Kegan & Berkman, 63-84, Trexler, Bushnell, Giangiorgi & Blackstone, 84-91. *Mem:* Am Chem Soc; Sigma Xi; Am Bar Asn. *Res:* Industrial research and development; synthetic coatings; halogenation; atomic energy; heavy metal complexes; chlorination of hydrocarbons; food technology; federal food and drug laws. *Mailing Add:* 939 Glenview Rd Glenview IL 60025-3172

BERKMAN, SAMUEL, CHEMICAL VAPOR DEPOSITION, SHAPED CRYSTAL GROWTH. *Current Pos:* VPRES, NU-TEC CORP, 90- *Personal Data:* b Bronx, NY, July 6, 35; m 64; c 2. *Educ:* Fairleigh Dickinson Univ, BS, 65. *Honors & Awards:* Recognition Award, NASA, 79 & 80. *Prof Exp:* Mem tech staff, RCA/GE/SRI/David Sarnoff Res Ctr, 66-90. *Concurrent Pos:* Consult, David Sarnoff Res Ctr. *Mem:* Am Asn Crystal Growth. *Res:* High temperature materials processing, including semiconductors, optical crystals, and ceramics; analyzed the dynamics of heat, fluid, and mass transport while designing various equipment and processes for crystal growth; fifteen US patents; eight publications including principal co-author of a chapter of one technical book. *Mailing Add:* 1818 Boat Point Dr Point Pleasant NJ 08742

BERKNER, KLAUS HANS, TECHNICAL MANAGEMENT, ACCELERATOR DEVELOPMENT. *Current Pos:* Physicist, Lawrence Berkeley Nat Lab, Univ Calif, 61-78, dep div dir, 82-84, actg div dir, 84-85, div dir accelerator & fusion res, 85-91, assoc lab dir opers, 91-94, SR PHYSICIST, LAWRENCE BERKELEY NAT LAB, 79-, DEP DIR OPERS, 94- *Personal Data:* b Dessau, Ger, Mar 2, 38; US citizen; div; c 2. *Educ:* Mass Inst Technol, SB, 60; Univ Calif, Berkeley, PhD(physics), 64. *Concurrent Pos:* NSF fel, UK Atomic Energy Authority, Culham Lab, Eng, 65-66; mem, Basic Energy Scis adv comt, 91-96, co-chair, 93-96; mem, Fusion Energy adv comt, 91-93. *Mem:* Fel Am Phys Soc. *Res:* Accelerator development; high power neutral beams for heating fusion plasmas; measurement of atomic collision cross sections; electron capture and loss; inner shell excitation. *Mailing Add:* Lawrence Berkeley Nat Lab Univ Calif Berkeley CA 94720. *Fax:* 510-486-6498; *E-Mail:* khberkner@lbl.gov

BERKOF, RICHARD STANLEY, MECHANICAL ENGINEERING. *Current Pos:* MGR ADVAN MFG & SYSTS INTEGRATION, RAYTHEON ENG & CONST, 89- *Personal Data:* b Brooklyn, NY, Mar 2, 41; m 62; c 3. *Educ:* City Col New York, BME, 62; Columbia Univ, MSME, 63; City Univ New York, PhD(eng mech), 69. *Prof Exp:* Engr, Syska & Hennessy, Inc, 62; design engr, Gibbs & Cox, Inc, 63-64; res asst, City Col New York, 64-65, lectr, 65-67, res asst, 67-68; res assoc, Princeton Lab, Am Can Co, 68-73; mgr advan technol, Wickes Gulf & Western Advan Develop & Eng Ctr, 73-79, mgr proposals & planning, 79-84, mgr planning & tech serv, 84-89. *Concurrent Pos:* Consult, Bright Lithographing Corp, 63; ed dynamics, Mechanism & Mach Theory, 75-85; ed spec features, Transactions Am Soc Mech Engrs: J Mech Design, 77-79, tech ed pro tem, 79-80. *Mem:* Soc Mfg Engrs; Am Soc Eng Educ; Am Soc Mech Engrs; Am Nuclear Soc; US Comt Theory Mach & Mechanisms. *Res:* Dynamics and kinematics of machines. *Mailing Add:* PO Box 55 Cresco PA 18326

BERKOFF, CHARLES EDWARD, drug discovery & development, licensing, for more information see previous edition

BERKOVITS, SHIMSHON, CRYPTOGRAPHY, SECURITY. *Current Pos:* asst prof math, 74-80, chmn, Dept Comput Sci, 79-82, assoc prof comput sci, 80-86, ASSOC PROF MATH, UNIV LOWELL, 86-; MEM TECH STAFF, MITRE CORP, 76- *Personal Data:* b Berlin, Ger, Oct 5, 36; US citizen; m 63; c 7. *Educ:* Mass Inst Technol, SB, 57; Univ Chicago, MS, 60; Northeastern Univ, PhD(math), 73. *Prof Exp:* Mem tech staff, Mitre Corp, 63-70; asst prof math, Boston Univ, 68-74. *Mem:* Asn Comput Mach. *Res:* Modern uses of cryptography in communications and computer security; design and implementation of public key systems; appropriate system parameter selection; potential attack avoidance. *Mailing Add:* Dept Math Univ Mass One University Ave Lowell MA 01854-2881. *Fax:* 617-271-3598; *E-Mail:* shim@mailia.mitre.org

BERKOVITZ, LEONARD DAVID, MATHEMATICS. *Current Pos:* head dept, 75-80, PROF MATH, PURDUE UNIV, 62- *Personal Data:* b Chicago, Ill, Jan 24, 24; m 53, Anna Whitehouse; c Dan M & Kenneth E. *Educ:* Univ Chicago, PhD(math), 51. *Prof Exp:* AEC fel, Stanford Univ, 51-52; res fel, Calif Inst Technol, 52-54; mathematician, Rand Corp, 54-62. *Concurrent Pos:* Assoc ed, J Optimization Theory & Appln, J Math Anal & Appln; ed, Soc Indust & Appl Math J Control, 70-81 & 86-89, managing ed, 82-85. *Mem:* Am Math Soc; Math Asn Am; Soc Indust & Appl Math. *Res:* Calculus of variations; optimal control; game theory. *Mailing Add:* Dept Math Purdue Univ West Lafayette IN 47907. *E-Mail:* brkld@math.purdue.edu

BERKOW, SUSAN E, EPIDEMIOLOGY. *Current Pos:* DIR, FROZEN FOOD TECHNOL CTR, NAT FOOD PROCESSORS ASN, 93-; ADJ ASSOC PROF EPIDEMIOL, GEORGE MASON UNIV, 94- *Personal Data:* b Brooklyn, NY, Sept 19, 49; m, Charles S Cox Jr. *Educ:* Univ Md, BS, 70, PhD(nutrit sci), 82; Johns Hopkins Univ, cert epidemiol, 85. *Honors & Awards:* Grad Stud Award, Int Union Nutrit Scientists, 80. *Prof Exp:* Fel, Georgetown Univ Med Sch, 82-84; prog officer, Food & Nutrit Bd, Inst Med, Nat Acad Sci, 84-90; vpres, Sci & Regulatory Affairs, Am Frozen Food Inst, 91-92. *Concurrent Pos:* Nutrit consult, Georgetown Diet Mgt & Eating Dis Clin, Georgetown Univ Med Ctr, 84-90; lectr, George Washington Med Sch, 86; mem exec comt, Refrigerated & Frozen Food Div, Inst Food Technologist, 93- *Mem:* Am Inst Nutrit; Am Soc Clin Nutrit; Inst Food Technologists; Am Dietetic Asn; NAm Soc Study Obesity. *Res:* Effect of cleaners and sanitizers on biofilms found in frozen food processing environments; ice crystallization kinetics. *Mailing Add:* 1211 Tatum Dr Alexandria VA 22307. *Fax:* 202-639-5991

BERKOWER, IRA, VIRAL IMMUNITY, ANTIGEN PROCESSING. *Current Pos:* sr investr, Molecular Immunol Lab, Div Biochem & Biophys, 83-92, LAB CHIEF, LAB IMMUNOREGULATION, DIV ALLERGENIC PROD & PARASITOL, CTR BIOLOGICS, FOOD & DRUG ADMIN, 93- *Personal Data:* b New York, NY, Aug 15, 48; m 72; c 3. *Educ:* Yale Univ, BS & MS, 69; Albert Einstein Col Med, PhD(molecular biol), 74, MD, 75. *Prof Exp:* Intern & resident, Columbia Presby Med Ctr, 75-78; res fel rheumatology, Kunkel Lab, Rockefeller Univ, 78-79; res assoc immunol, Nat Cancer Inst, NIH, 79-82, cancer expert, 82-83. *Concurrent Pos:* Lectr, Found Advan Educ Sci, NIH, 87-88, Univ Nebr & Mass Inst Technol, 89, Univ Tex & Downstate Med Ctr, 90; mem, Ad Hoc Study Sect Cancer AIDS, NIH, 89-90; guest lectr, Dept Biochem, George Washington Univ, 90-91. *Mem:* Am Asn Immunol; Am Fedn Clin Res; Am Col Physicians. *Res:* Immunity to viral protein antigens; mapping sites on viral proteins which are targets of neutralizing antibodies and soluble receptor proteins and the mechanism of inactivation; pathways of antigen processing leading to T cell recognition of viral antigens, including the signals for entry into each processing pathway; vaccine design to improve potency. *Mailing Add:* Ctr Biologics Food & Drug Admin 8800 Rockville Pike Bldg 29 Rm 523 Bethesda MD 20892

BERKOWITZ, BARRY ALAN, PHARMACOLOGY. *Current Pos:* PRES & CHIEF EXEC OFFICER, CHEMGENICS PHARMACEUT INC, 92- *Personal Data:* b Brookline, Mass, Dec 29, 42; m 63; c 2. *Educ:* Northeastern Univ, BS, 64; Univ Calif, PhD(pharmacol), 68. *Prof Exp:* Fel, Roche Inst Molecular Biol, 68-70, res assoc, 70-71, assoc mem pharmacol, 71-80; mem staff, Smith Kline & French Labs, Philadelphia, 80-83, vpres biol sci & biopharmaceut res & develop, 83-88; pres & chief exec officer, Magainin Sci Inc, 88-92. *Concurrent Pos:* Vis assoc prof pharmacol, Med Col, Cornell Univ, 71- *Mem:* AAAS; NY Acad Sci; Am Soc Pharmacol & Exp Therapeut. *Res:* Neurochemistry and pharmacology of blood vessels; pharmacology of narcotics and narcotic antagonist analgesics; biogenic amines; cardiovascular disease. *Mailing Add:* Chem Genics Pharmaceut Inc One Kendall Sq Bldg 300 Cambridge MA 02139

BERKOWITZ, CAROL DIANE, CHILD ABUSE, FAILURE TO THRIVE. *Current Pos:* assoc chair pediat dept, 87-89, actg chair, 89-92, DIR PEDIAT CLIN, HARBOR-UNIV CALIF, LOS ANGELES MED CTR, 78-, DIR PEDIAT RESIDENCY TRAINING, 80- ASSOC CHAIR PEDIAT DEPT, 92- *Personal Data:* b New York, NY, Oct 17, 44; m 67, David; c Nicole A & Ellie P. *Educ:* Barnard Col, AB, 65; Columbia Univ, MD, 69. *Prof Exp:* Pediatrician, HEW, 72-74, DePaulo Med Group, 74-76, Torres Med Ctr, 76-78. *Concurrent Pos:* Physician, Los Angeles Co Health Dept, 74, 76; co-dir, Craniofacial Clin, Harbor-Univ Calif, Los Angeles Med Ctr, 78-, dir, Behavioral Pediat, 80-; consult, Los Angeles Super Ct, Los Angeles Sheriff Dept, US Postal Serv, US Customs Serv, Los Angeles Co Pub Defender, 84- *Mem:* Am Acad Pediat; Ambulatory Pediat Asn (pres, 80-91); Am Bd Pediat; Soc Behav Pediat; Asn Pediat Prog Dirs; Am Pediat Soc. *Res:* Primary care pediatrics; child abuse; child sexual abuse and relationship to Human Immunodeficiency Virus. *Mailing Add:* 1000 W Carson St BIN 437 Torrance CA 90509

BERKOWITZ, DAVID ANDREW, BIOMEDICAL ENGINEERING, TECHNOLOGY ASSESSMENT. *Current Pos:* NAT ACCT MGR, VARIAN ONCOL SYST, 95- *Personal Data:* b Brooklyn, NY, Mar 21, 52; m 75, Amy Silverman; c Aaron, Leah & Daniel. *Educ:* Rensselaer Polytech Inst, BS, 74, ME, 75, cert clin eng, 75. *Honors & Awards:* Eng Design Award, Am Soc Eng Educ, 74. *Prof Exp:* Proj engr mech design & develop, Automatech Indust, 75-77; proj officer biomed eng, Emergency Care Res Inst, 77-79, sr proj engr & consult, 80-86, vpres, Health Systs Group, 86-95. *Concurrent Pos:* Instr biomed eng, Bridgeport Eng Inst, 77; consult biomed technol, Park City Hosp, 77. *Mem:* Am Soc Mech Engrs; Asn Advan Med Instrumentation; Nat Soc Prof Engrs; Am Col Health Care Execs; Am Col Clin Engrs. *Res:* Medical devices their impact on health care; technology assessment, planning, evaluation and acquisition; accident investigation; teaching; consulting on medical equipment, systems and facilities; special interest in medical equipment assessment and acquisition. *Mailing Add:* Varian Oncol Syst 2250 Newmarket Pkwy Suite 120 Marrieta GA 30067. *Fax:* 610-353-9506

BERKOWITZ, HARRY LEO, radiation physics, theoretical physics, for more information see previous edition

BERKOWITZ, JEROME, MATHEMATICS. *Current Pos:* res asst, 50-56, from asst prof to assoc prof math, 56-65, PROF, COURANT INST MATH SCI, NY UNIV, 65- *Personal Data:* b Brooklyn, NY, Oct 2, 28; m 54; c 2. *Educ:* NY Univ, PhD(math), 53. *Prof Exp:* Mathematician, Reeves Instrument Corp, 48. *Mem:* Am Math Soc; Math Asn Am; Sigma Xi. *Res:* Functional analysis; magnetohydrodynamics. *Mailing Add:* 170 Second Ave New York NY 10003-5779

BERKOWITZ, JESSE M, gastroenterology, medical science, for more information see previous edition

BERKOWITZ, JOAN B, PHYSICAL CHEMISTRY. *Current Pos:* phys chemist, 57-80, VPRES, ARTHUR D LITTLE, INC, 80-, SECT MGR, 81- *Personal Data:* b Brooklyn, NY, Mar 13, 31; m 59; c 1. *Educ:* Swarthmore Col, BA, 52; Univ Ill, PhD(phys chem), 55. *Prof Exp:* NSF fel, Yale Univ, 55-57. *Mem:* Am Chem Soc; Electrochem Soc; Am Phys Soc. *Res:* Thermodynamics of inorganic systems at high temperatures; oxidation of refractory metals and alloys; electrochemistry in flames; mass spectrometry; solid-gas interactions; inorganic coating technology; heterogeneous catalytic recombination; high temperature vaporization; hazardous waste management. *Mailing Add:* 1940 35th St NW Washington DC 20007-2213

BERKOWITZ, JOSEPH, CHEMICAL PHYSICS. *Current Pos:* physicist, 57-73, SR PHYSICIST, ARGONNE NAT LAB, 73- *Personal Data:* b Czech, Apr 22, 30; US citizen; m 58; c 2. *Educ:* NY Univ, BE, 51; Harvard Univ, PhD(phys chem), 55. *Honors & Awards:* Alexander von Humboldt Award, 88. *Prof Exp:* Jr chem engr, Brookhaven Nat Lab, 51-52; res assoc physics, Univ Chicago, 55-57. *Concurrent Pos:* Vis asst prof, Univ Ill, 59-60; Guggenheim Found fel phys inst, Univ Freiburg, 65-66; vis prof, Northwestern Univ, 73. *Mem:* Am Chem Soc; Am Phys Soc; Am Soc Mass Spectrometry. *Res:* Molecular structure; chemical kinetics; high temperature thermodynamics; mass spectrometry; photoionization; photoelectron spectroscopy. *Mailing Add:* Chem Div Bldg 203 Argonne Nat Lab 9700 S Cass Ave Argonne IL 60439

BERKOWITZ, LEWIS MAURICE, ORGANIC CHEMISTRY. *Current Pos:* CHEMIST, US ARMY, EDGEWOOD ARSENAL, 63- *Personal Data:* b New York, NY, Apr 12, 31; m 68; c 1. *Educ:* City Col New York, BS, 52; Columbia Univ, AM, 53, PhD(chem), 57. *Prof Exp:* Chemist, Engelhard Indust Inc, 57-58, US Vitamin & Pharmaceut Indust Corp, 59-60 & Gen Foods Corp, 60-63. *Mem:* Am Chem Soc; Sigma Xi. *Res:* Structure-activity relationship of chemotherapeutic and physiologically active compounds; organic synthesis; enzyme immobilization. *Mailing Add:* 627 Leafydale Terr Baltimore MD 21208

BERKOWITZ, RAYMOND S, RADAR SYSTEMS. *Current Pos:* from res asst to assoc prof, 47-77, PROF ELEC ENG, UNIV PA, 77- *Personal Data:* b Philadelphia, Pa, Feb 21, 23; m 46; c 3. *Educ:* Univ Pa, BSEE, 43, MSEE, 48, PhD, 51. *Prof Exp:* Engr, Radio Corp Am, 43-44. *Concurrent Pos:* Consult, Radio Corp Am, 59- *Mem:* AAAS; Am Soc Eng Educ; Inst Elec & Electronics Engrs; Soc Indust & Appl Math; Sigma Xi. *Res:* Radar; general systems engineering; statistical communication theory. *Mailing Add:* 511 Woodbrook Lane Philadelphia PA 19119-1041

BERKOWITZ, SIDNEY, INDUSTRIAL ORGANIC CHEMISTRY. *Current Pos:* Res chemist, 58-70, sr res chemist, 70-76, res assoc, 76-80, SR RES ASSOC, FMC CORP, PRINCETON, 80- *Personal Data:* b Perth Amboy, NJ, Aug 1, 21; m 45; c 2. *Educ:* Rutgers Univ, BA, 65. *Mem:* Catalyst Soc; fel Am Inst Chemists. *Res:* Heterocyclic chemistry with emphasis on the reactions of isocyanic acid and many of its polymeric derivatives, both linear and cyclic; high temperature catalytic and hot tube oxidations. *Mailing Add:* 6101 Wirt Ave Baltimore MD 21215-3737

BERKSON, DAVID M, MEDICINE. *Current Pos:* PROF COMMUNITY HEALTH, PREV MED & MED, SCH MED, NORTHWESTERN UNIV, 82- *Personal Data:* b Chicago, Ill, Oct 16, 28; m 73; c 3. *Educ:* Univ Ill, BS, 49; Northwestern Univ, Chicago, MD, 53. *Prof Exp:* Assoc prof community health & prev med, Sch Med, Northwestern Univ, Chicago, 72-82; heart dis control officer, Chicago Bd Health, 73-90. *Concurrent Pos:* Assoc attend physician, Michael Reese Hosp, Chicago, 61-80; head sect cardiovasc dis, St Joseph Hosp, Chicago, 63- *Mem:* AAAS; Am Heart Asn; AMA; fel Am Col Physicians; fel Am Col Cardiol. *Res:* Cardiovascular diseases; epidemiology of hypertensive and atherosclerotic coronary heart disease. *Mailing Add:* 2800 N Sheridan Rd No 500 Chicago IL 60657-6156

BERKSON, EARL ROBERT, MATHEMATICS. *Current Pos:* assoc prof, 64-67, PROF MATH, UNIV ILL, URBANA, 73- *Personal Data:* b Chicago, Ill, June 6, 34; m 60; c 3. *Educ:* Univ Calif, Los Angeles, BS, 56, MA, 57; Univ Chicago, PhD(math), 60. *Prof Exp:* From instr to asst prof math, Univ Calif, Los Angeles, 60-64. *Concurrent Pos:* Vis asst prof, Univ Calif, Berkeley, 64-65. *Mem:* Am Math Soc. *Res:* Operator theory; spectral theory; complex analysis. *Mailing Add:* Dept Math Univ Ill 1409 W Green St Urbana IL 61801-2917

BERKSON, HAROLD, ENVIRONMENTAL BIOLOGY. *Current Pos:* RETIRED. *Personal Data:* b Easton, Pa, Oct 30, 29; m 58, Helen Paders; c Deborah & Joan. *Educ:* Rutgers Univ, BA, 51; Amherst Col, MA, 53; Univ Calif, San Diego, PhD(environ physiol), 63. *Prof Exp:* Asst comp anat, Amherst Col, 51-53; asst eng scientist, NY Univ, 54-55; biochem technician, M D Anderson Hosp & Tumor Inst, Univ Tex, 55-56; asst biol oceanogr, Narragansett Marine Lab, Univ RI, 56-58; asst physiol & ecol, Scripps Inst, Univ Calif, 58-63; marine biologist, Fed Water Pollution Control Admin, 63-68; chief biol & ecol sci sect, Estuarine & Oceanog Progs Br, 68-70; specialist environ policy, Cong Res Serv, Libr of Cong, 70-72; sr environ specialist, Nuclear Regulatory Comn, 72-80, sr prog & planning analyst, 80-83, chief, Planning & Resources Anal Br, 83-84, spec asst environ policy, 84-85, sr proj mgr, 85-88. *Mem:* Sigma Xi; Am Inst Fishery Res Biologists. *Res:* Estuarine ecology; adaptation to the environment; prolonged and deep-diving by air-breathing vertebrates; environmental management; environmental impact assessment. *Mailing Add:* Marine Biol 12001 Whippoorwill Lane Rockville MD 20852

BERKSON, JONATHAN MILTON, MARINE GEOPHYSICS, UNDERWATER ACOUSTICS. *Current Pos:* GEOPHYSICIST, NAVAL RES LAB, 86- *Personal Data:* b Chicago, Ill, Feb 23, 41; m 75; c 3. *Educ:* Univ Ill, BS, 63; Univ Wis, MS, 69, PhD(geophys), 72. *Prof Exp:* Res asst, Geophys & Polar Res Ctr, Univ Wis, 66-72, fel, 72-73; geophysicist, US Naval Oceanog Off, 73-76; geophysicist, Naval Oceanog & Atmospheric Res Lab, 76-83; sr scientist, Saclant Undersea Res Ctr, 83-86. *Mem:* Acoust Soc Am; Soc Explor Geophysicists; Am Geophys Union; Sigma Xi. *Res:* Marine geophysics; underwater acoustics. *Mailing Add:* Code 7120 Naval Res Lab Washington DC 20375-5350

BERKUT, MICHAEL KALEN, BIOLOGICAL CHEMISTRY. *Current Pos:* RETIRED. *Personal Data:* b NY, June 30, 15; m 38, Cora L Mills; c Jack C & Nancy K. *Educ:* NC State Col, BS, 41; Univ NC, PhD(biol chem), 53. *Prof Exp:* Chemist, NC State Lab Hyg, 41; instr chem, NC State Col, 42; from instr to assoc prof biol chem, Univ NC, Chapel Hill, 47-74, assoc prof biochem, nutrit & physiol, 74-77, assoc prof physiol & prof biochem, 77-80; vis prof, NC Health Manpower Prog, 80-91. *Concurrent Pos:* Res biochemist, US AEC, 62-64; dir, Erythropoietin Lab, Univ NC Hosps. *Mem:* AAAS; Am Chem Soc; Am Asn Clin Chemists. *Res:* Mineral metabolism; mechanism of biological calcification; neural and humoral influences on hematopoiesis. *Mailing Add:* 807 Old Mill Rd Chapel Hill NC 27514

BERKY, JOHN JAMES, LABORATORY SAFETY, BIOLOGY PROGRAM MANAGEMENT. *Current Pos:* RETIRED. *Personal Data:* b Billings, Mont, Nov 19, 24; m 50; c 3. *Educ:* NDak State Univ, BS, 49; Pa State Univ, MS, 51, PhD(microbial physiol), 54; Nat Registry Microbiol, registered, 63; Am Acad Microbiol, cert specialist microbiol, Pub Health & Medical Lab Microbiol, 70, Food, Dairy & Sanit Microbiol, 75. *Honors & Awards:* Award of Merit, Food & Drug Admin, 78. *Prof Exp:* Food res microbiologist, Armour Res Div, Chicago, 54-56, asst sect chief bacteriol, 56-58; asst chief, Lab Div, US Army Biol Opers, Pine Bluff, Ark, 58-59, chief, Biol Lab Div, 59-71; sr investr, Virol & Cell Cult Lab, 71-77, dir, Div Analytical Serv, Microbiol & Immunol Div, 77-79, dir, qual assurance & safety staff, Nat Ctr for Toxicol Res, 79-86. *Mem:* NY Acad Sci; Sigma Xi. *Res:* Cell culture systems in toxicology, toxicity testing, carcinogenesis; virus-chemical interactions; microbial metabolism, food research microbiology, microbial processes fermentations by-products purification and assay; contract administration and laboratory management. *Mailing Add:* 724 Weston Rd P-4 Hot Springs AR 71913

BERL, SOLL, BIOCHEMISTRY, NEUROCHEMISTRY. *Current Pos:* res prof, 73-88, EMER RES PROF NEUROL, MT SINAI SCH MED, 88- *Personal Data:* b New York, NY, June 12, 18; m 56, Theresa Beshi; c Katherine, Elizabeth, David & Erica. *Educ:* St John's Univ, BS, 40; Univ Wis, MS, 43; Western Res Univ, MD, 50. *Honors & Awards:* Lucy G Moses Prize, 70. *Prof Exp:* Intern, Long Island Col Hosp, 50-51; resident psychiat, Bellevue Med Ctr, NY Univ, 51-54; NIH fel, 56; sr res scientist neurochem, NY Psychiat Inst, 57-61, assoc res scientist, 61-62; res assoc, Col Physicians & Surgeons, Columbia Univ, 62-64, from asst prof to assoc prof neurochem, 64-73. *Concurrent Pos:* Vet Admin training fel, 51-54; asst attend, Vanderbilt Clin, Columbia-Presby Med Ctr, 57-64; NIH res career develop award, 62. *Mem:* AAAS; Am Psychiat Asn; Am Soc Neurochem; Am Soc Biol Chemists; Am Chem Soc; Int Soc Neurochem. *Res:* Amino acid and protein metabolism of the central nervous system in relation to structure and function; psychiatry. *Mailing Add:* 857 Rte 23 Craryville NY 12521-9774

BERL, WALTER G(EORGE), COMBUSTION, FIRE RESEARCH. *Current Pos:* group supvr, Fire Probs Group, 77-80, PRIN STAFF CHEMIST, APPL PHYSICS LAB, JOHNS HOPKINS UNIV, 45- *Personal Data:* b Vienna, Austria, July 3, 17; nat US; m 52, 89, Shirley A Foynes; c Kathleen M (Victorino). *Educ:* Carnegie Inst Technol, BS, 37, PhD(phys chem), 41; Harvard Univ, MS, 39. *Honors & Awards:* Foster Mem lectr, State Univ NY, Buffalo, 48. *Prof Exp:* Res fel & instr, Carnegie Inst Technol, 42-45. *Concurrent Pos:* Ed, Fire Res Abstr & Rev, 58-64; assoc ed, Am Rocket Soc J, 60-62 & Am Inst Aeronaut & Astronaut J, 63-64; mem comt fire res, Nat Acad Sci-Nat Res Coun, 65-68; US ed, Combustion & Flame, 66-71; mem adv comt, NSF-Res Appl Nat Needs, 72; consult, Nuclear Regulatory Comn, 76-80; ed-in-chief, Johns Hopkins Appl Tech Digest, 80-88, ed, Appl Tech Rev, 88-90. *Mem:* Sigma Xi; fel AAAS; fel NY Acad Sci; Am Chem Soc; Am Inst Aeronaut & Astronaut. *Res:* Combustion; propulsion; fuels; propellants; instrumental analysis; origin of petroleum; fuel cells. *Mailing Add:* 4928 Sentinel Dr Apt 206 Bethesda MD 20816

BERLAD, ABRAHAM LEON, CHEMICAL PHYSICS, MECHANICAL ENGINEERING. *Current Pos:* chmn, Mech Eng Dept, 66-69, prof, 66-84, EMER PROF ENG, STATE UNIV NY, STONY BROOK, 84-; EMER PROF, UNIV CALIF, SAN DIEGO, 95- *Personal Data:* b New York, NY, Sept 20, 21; m 49, Alice M Halber; c Glenda, Edward & Nancy. *Educ:* Brooklyn Col, BA, 43; Ohio State Univ, PhD(physics), 50. *Prof Exp:* Aeronaut res scientist, Nat Adv Comt Aeronaut, 51-54, head, Combustion Fundamentals Sect, 54-56; sr staff scientist, Convair Sci Res Lab, 56-63; vis prof, Dept Aeronaut Sci, Univ Calif, Berkeley, 63-64; mem staff, Physics Dept, Gen Res Corp, 64-66. *Concurrent Pos:* Consult, AEC, 73-75, Energy Res & Develop Agency, US Dept Energy, NASA & Nat Res Coun; vis prof, Univ Calif, San Diego & Hebrew Univ Jerusalem, 74; vis sr scientist, Brookhaven Nat Lab, 75; fel, E I Du Pont Co; adj prof combustion sci, Energy Ct, Univ Calif, San Diego, 84-95. *Mem:* Am Phys Soc; Combustion Inst; Int Astronaut Fedn. *Res:* Irreversible processes; unstable media; crystallization and combustion theory; radiation phenomena; stability of reaction processes; atmospheric and environmental rate processes; thermokinetic systems; nuclear containment safety. *Mailing Add:* PO Box 2008 Rancho Santa Fe CA 92067

BERLANDI, FRANCIS JOSEPH, INDUSTRIAL HYGIENE, CHEMISTRY. *Current Pos:* CERTIFIED INDUST HYGIENIST, TOUCHSTONE ENVIRON CONSULTS, 80- *Personal Data:* b Boston, Mass, Mar 23, 41. *Educ:* Mass Inst Technol, BS, 62; Univ Mich, MS, 64, PhD(analytical-nuclear chem), 66. *Prof Exp:* Mgr, Geonuclear Dept, Teledyne Isotopes, 68-73; mgr anal serv indust hyg & chem, Environ Res & Technol, Inc, 73-76; mgr environ serv indust hyg, Environ Sci Assocs, Inc, 76-80. *Mem:* Am Indust Hyg Asn; Sigma Xi. *Res:* Physical-chemical in situ measurements; design, management and interpretation of large scale environmental field studies. *Mailing Add:* Touchstone Environ Consult 33 Thompson St Winchester MA 01890

BERLE, PETER ADOLF AUGUSTUS, ENVIRONMENTAL SCIENCES, FORESTRY. *Current Pos:* DIR & HOST THE ENVIRONMENT SHOW, NAT PUB RADIO, 95- *Personal Data:* b New York, NY, Dec 8, 37; m 60, Lila Sloane Wilde; c Adolf Augustus, Mary Alice, Beatrice Lila & Robert Thomas. *Educ:* Harvard Univ, BA, 58, LLB, 64. *Hon Degrees:* LLD, Hobart Smith Col, 77, Long Island Univ, 93, S Vt Col, 96; LLB, N Adams Teachers Col, 88. *Prof Exp:* Assoc, Paul, Weiss, Rifkind, Wharton & Garrison, NY, 64-71; partner, Berle Butzel & Kass, NY, 71-76 & 79-85; NY State comnr environ conserv, 76-79; pres & chief exec officer, Nat Audobon Soc, 85-95. *Concurrent Pos:* Teaching fel econs, Harvard Col, 63-64; assoc adj prof, Sch Urban Affairs Hunter Col, 74-84; chmn, NY Gov's Transition Task Force Environ, 74-75; comnr, NY State Moreland Act Comn Nursing Homes, 75-77; vis prof environ sci & forestry, State Univ NY, 80; bd dirs, Clean Site Inc, 86-93; chmn, Comn Adirondacks 21st Century, 89-90; mem, Nat Comt Environ, 91-92 & Comn Int Environ Law, World Conserv Union. *Res:* Energy policy; international human rights; international environmental law. *Mailing Add:* Box 881 Stockbridge MA 01262

BERLEKAMP, ELWYN R(ALPH), MATHEMATICS, ELECTRICAL ENGINEERING. *Current Pos:* PRES, HAZELNUT FUTURES, 90- *Personal Data:* b Dover, Ohio, Sept 6, 40; m 66; c 3. *Educ:* Mass Inst Technol, BS & MS, 62, PhD(elec eng), 64. *Honors & Awards:* Centennial Medal, Inst Elec & Electronics Engrs, 84, Koji Kobayashi Computers & Commun Award, 90, Richard W Hamming Medal, 91, Shannon Lectr, Inst Elec & Electronics Engrs, 93. *Prof Exp:* Asst prof elec eng, Univ Calif, Berkeley, 64-67; consult, Bell Tel Labs, 67-71; prof math, elec eng & comput sci, Univ Calif, Berkeley, 71-83; pres, Cyclotomics, Eastman Kodak, 83-89. *Mem:* Nat Acad Eng; Am Math Soc; fel Inst Elec & Electronics Engrs. *Res:* Information theory, coding and related problems in combinatorial mathematics and computer science; recent extensions of game theory; use of statistical information theory to forecast stock and commodity prices. *Mailing Add:* 64 Shattuck Sq Ste 101 Berkeley CA 94704. *Fax:* 510-849-0376

BERLEY, DAVID, ELEMENTARY PARTICLE PHYSICS, ASTROPHYSICS. *Current Pos:* prog dir elec particle physics, 80-92, PROG MGR, LASER INTERFEROMETRY GRAVITATIONAL WAVE OBSERV, NSF, 93- *Personal Data:* b Brooklyn, NY, Mar 25, 30; m 62, Estelle Radbill; c 2. *Educ:* Union Col, NY, BS, 51; Cornell Univ, PhD(physics), 57. *Prof Exp:* Res assoc, Columbia Univ, 57-59 & 62; Louis de Broglie fel, Col de France, 59-61; physicist, Brookhaven Nat Lab, 62-74, head, Exp Div, Accelerator Dept, 69-74; prog dir, NSF, 74-77; actg head, Accelerator Opers Br, Div High Energy Physics, US Dept Energy, 77-80. *Concurrent Pos:* Fulbright fel, 59 & 60; vis prof physics, Univ Md, 88-89. *Mem:* AAAS; fel Am Phys Soc; Sigma Xi. *Res:* Elementary particle physics; weak interactions; decay of muons, hyperons and kaons; strong interactions; cosmic rays; administration of elementary particle physics programs. *Mailing Add:* 3535 Chesapeake St NW Washington DC 20008

BERLIN, BYRON SANFORD, VIROLOGY. *Current Pos:* RETIRED. *Personal Data:* b Detroit, Mich, Mar 19, 21; m 46; c 6. *Educ:* Wayne State Univ, BA, 42, MD, 45; Am Bd Med Microbiol, dipl, 68. *Prof Exp:* Coman fel, Univ Chicago, 50-52, resident med, 52-54; res assoc, Sch Pub Health, Univ Mich, 54-59, asst prof, 59-67; assoc prof med & path, Med Sch, Northwestern Univ, Chicago, 67-94; coordr phys, Bur Lab & Epidemiol Serv, Mich Dept Pub Health. *Concurrent Pos:* Mem, Am Bd Med Microbiol. *Mem:* Am Asn Immunologists; Soc Exp Biol & Med. *Res:* Immunology; infection; vaccinology. *Mailing Add:* 940 Longfellow East Lansing MI 48823

BERLIN, CHARLES I, AUDIOLOGY. *Current Pos:* assoc prof, 67-70, PROF OTOLARYNGOL, MED SCH, LA STATE UNIV MED CTR, NEW ORLEANS, 70-, DIR, KRESGE HEARING RES LAB OF THE SOUTH, 68- *Personal Data:* b New York, NY, Dec 26, 33; m 58; c 4. *Educ:* NY Univ, BS, 53; Univ Wis, MA, 54; Univ Pittsburgh, PhD(hearing & speech), 58. *Honors & Awards:* Nat Inst Neurol Dis & Blindness res career develop award, 63-67. *Prof Exp:* Audiologist & speech pathologist, US Vet Admin Hosp, Calif, 59-61; asst prof otolaryngol, Johns Hopkins Hosp, 63-67. *Concurrent Pos:* Fel med audiol, Johns Hopkins Hosp, 62-63. *Mem:* AAAS; fel Acoust Soc Am; fel Am Speech & Hearing Asn; Sigma Xi; Am Acad Audiol. *Res:* Hearing and speech sciences; evoked potentials; speech perception; communication in pathological states in humans and animals; otoacoustic emissions; hearing disorders and hearing aids. *Mailing Add:* 6001 Pratt Dr New Orleans LA 70122-2751

BERLIN, CHESTON MILTON, PEDIATRICS. *Current Pos:* assoc prof pediat & pharmacol, 71-75, asst dean student affairs, 72-87, PROF PEDIAT & PHARMACOL, PA STATE UNIV, 75-, UNIV PROF, COL MED, 86- *Personal Data:* b Pittsburgh, Pa, Mar 28, 36; m 60, Anne Risher; c Jean, Douglas, Alexander & Gordon. *Educ:* Haverford Col, BA, 58, Harvard Med Sch, MD, 62. *Prof Exp:* Asst prof pediat, Sch Med, Univ Ala, 67-68 & George Washington Univ, 68-71. *Concurrent Pos:* Markle scholar acad med, 69-74. *Mem:* Am Soc Exp Pharmacol & Therapeut; Am Soc Clin Pharmacol & Therapeut; Am Pediat Soc; Am Acad Pediat; Am Inst Nutrit. *Res:* Excretion of drugs and chemicals in human milk; antibody formation in lupus; salt excretion in hypertension; pharmacology of movement disorders in children. *Mailing Add:* Dept Pediat Hershey Med Ctr PO Box 850 Hershey PA 17033. *Fax:* 717-531-8985; *E-Mail:* cmb6@psu.edu

BERLIN, ELLIOTT, BIOCHEMISTRY, NUTRITION. *Current Pos:* RETIRED. *Personal Data:* b Baltimore, Md, Jan 4, 34; m 56; c 5. *Educ:* Johns Hopkins Univ, BS, 57, MA, 59; Univ Md, College Park, PhD(biochem), 66. *Prof Exp:* Res chemist, Agr Res Serv, USDA, 62-96. *Concurrent Pos:* Lectr, Catonsville Community Col, 65-68; lectr, Univ Md, College Park, 69-70 & 80-; instr, Bowie State Col, 71-72; adj prof, Southeastern Univ, 73-74. *Mem:* AAAS; Biophys Soc; Am Chem Soc; Am Inst Nutrit; Am Oil Chemists Soc; NY Acad Sci. *Res:* Nutritional factors affecting physical chemical properties and biological function of biomembranes; membrane fluidity; lipoprotein chemistry; water binding by proteins and other membranes. *Mailing Add:* 5807 Narcissus Ave Baltimore MD 21215-3546

BERLIN, FRED S, PSYCHIATRY. *Current Pos:* ASSOC PROF, SCH MED, JOHNS HOPKINS UNIV, 78- *Personal Data:* b Pittsburgh, Pa, July 27, 41; m 70; c 4. *Educ:* Univ Pittsburgh, BA, 64; Fordham Univ, MA, 66; Dalhousie Univ, MD & PhD(psychol), 74. *Res:* Biological determinants of sexual phenomology relations between biological factors and states of mind. *Mailing Add:* 101 Meyer Bldg Johns Hopkins Hosp 600 N Wolfe St Baltimore MD 21205-2104

BERLIN, GRAYDON LENNIS, PHYSICAL GEOGRAPHY. *Current Pos:* asst prof, 69-80, ASSOC PROF GEOG, NORTHERN ARIZ UNIV, 80- *Personal Data:* b St Petersburg, Pa, May 21, 43; m 64; c 1. *Educ:* Clarion State Col, BS, 65; Ariz State Univ, MA, 67; Univ Tenn, PhD(geog), 70. *Prof Exp:* Asst prof & res assoc geog, Fla Atlantic Univ, 68-69. *Concurrent Pos:* Res assoc, US Geol Surv, 70- *Mem:* Am Soc Photogram; Asn Am Geogr; Nat Res Soc NAm; Sigma Xi. *Res:* Environmental impacts and modifications; remote sensing of natural resources; fossil landscapes; urban climatology; land use. *Mailing Add:* 1180 Rockridge Rd Flagstaff AZ 86001

BERLIN, IRVING NORMAN, CHILD & ADOLESCENT PSYCHIATRY. *Current Pos:* MED DIR, NAMASTE CHILD & FAMILY DEVELOP CTR, 91- *Personal Data:* b Chicago, Ill, May 31, 17; m 43; c 3. *Educ:* Univ Calif, Los Angeles, BA, 39; Univ Calif, San Francisco, MD, 43. *Honors & Awards:* McGrath Award, Asn Suicidology; Irving Philips Mem Award, Am Acad Child & Adolescent Psychiat, 96. *Prof Exp:* Lectr psychiat, Sch Med, Univ Calif, San Francisco, 50-52, clin instr, 52-54, asst res psychiatrist, 55-56, asst clin prof psychiat, 56-60, assoc clin prof, 60-65; prof psychiat & pediat & head div child psychiat, Sch Med, Univ Wash, 65-75; prof psychiat & pediat & head child psychiat, Univ Calif, Davis, 75-78; prof psychiat & pediat, Sch Med, Univ NMex, 78-93. *Concurrent Pos:* Fel child psychiat, Langley Porter Inst, 46-50; consult, McAuley Neuropsychiat Inst, Calif, 60-, Ctr Training Community Psychiat, 61- & Training Br, NIMH, 74-; Grant Found grant, 73-75; Robert Wood Johnson grant, 87-89; sr consult, Ment Health Indian Health Serv. *Mem:* Fel Am Orthopsychiat Asn; fel Am Psychiat Asn; fel Am Acad Child Psychiat (pres, 75); fel Am Soc Adolescent Psychiat. *Res:* Childhood psychosis; mental health consultation and community psychiatry; training in mental health specialties; early intervention and prevention child mental illness; prevention adolescent Indian suicide and Indian pregnancy and alcoholism. *Mailing Add:* 1400 Carlisle Blvd NE Suite B Albuquerque NM 87110-5667

BERLIN, JERRY D, CELL BIOLOGY. *Current Pos:* PROF BIOL & DEAN SCI & MATH, SOUTHWEST MO STATE UNIV, 88- *Personal Data:* b Trenton, Mo, Aug 28, 34; m 58; c 3. *Educ:* Univ Mo, BS, 60, MA, 61; Iowa State Univ, PhD(cell biol), 64. *Prof Exp:* Fel, Iowa State Univ, 64; biol scientist, Gen Elec Co, 64-65; sr res scientist, Pac Northwest Lab, Battelle Mem Inst, 65-68; assoc prof, 68-73, prof biol & chmn dept biol sci, Tex Tech Univ, 73-87, adj prof anat, Sch Med, 74-87. *Concurrent Pos:* Grants, AEC, Cotton Producers Inst & Cotton Inc, 73- *Mem:* AAAS; Am Micros Soc; Am Soc Cell Biol; Bot Soc Am; Electron Micros Soc Am; NSF. *Res:* Cotton fiber initiation and development; effect of water stress on plants, especially at the cellular and subcellular level. *Mailing Add:* 2913 S Glendale Ave Springfield MO 65804-0094

BERLIN, KENNETH DARRELL, NUCLEAR MAGNETIC RESONANCE, SPECTROSCOPY. *Current Pos:* from asst prof to prof, 60-71, REGENTS PROF CHEM, OKLA STATE UNIV, 71- *Personal Data:* b Quincy, Ill, June 12, 33; m 58, Grace F Smith; c Grace E & James D. *Educ:* NCent Col, Ill, BA, 55; Univ Ill, PhD(org chem), 58. *Honors & Awards:* Award in Res, Sigma Xi, 69. *Prof Exp:* Fel chem, Univ Fla, 58-60. *Concurrent Pos:* App mem, Res Rev Panel, NSF fac fels, 69 & 70; mem, Med Chem Study Sect B, NIH, 69-73; develop therapeut rev comt, Nat Cancer Inst, 83-87; mem, Okla affil, Am Heart Asn Comt, 83-86. *Mem:* Sr mem Am Chem Soc; The Chem Soc; Int Soc Heterocyclic Chemists. *Res:* Organophosphorus chemistry; heterocyclic medicinal compounds; nuclear magnetic resonance spectroscopy; organometallics; synthetic organic chemistry; antiarrhythmic agents; anticancer agents. *Mailing Add:* Dept Chem Okla State Univ Stillwater OK 74078-0447

BERLIN, NATHANIEL ISAAC, MEDICAL RESEARCH. *Current Pos:* RETIRED. *Personal Data:* b New York, NY, July 4, 20; m 53; c 2. *Educ:* Western Res Univ, BS, 42; Long Island Col Med, MD, 45; Univ Calif, PhD(med physics), 49. *Honors & Awards:* Superior Serv Award, Dept Health, Educ & Welfare. *Prof Exp:* Intern, Kings Co Hosp, Brooklyn, 45-46, res pathologist, 46-47; fel, Univ Calif, 49-50, res assoc, 50-51, instr, 51, lectr & res assoc, 51-52, lectr & assoc res med physicist, 52-53; Nat Heart Inst spec res fel, Nat Inst Med Res, London, 53-54; med officer, Anal Br, Effects Div, Hqs Armed Forces Spec Weapons Proj, 54-56; head metab serv, Gen Med Br, NIH, 56-59, chief, 59-61, clin dir, 61-71, sci dir gen labs & clin, Nat Cancer Inst, 69-72, dir, Div Cancer Biol & Diag, 72-75; Genevieve B Teuton Prof Med & Dir, Cancer Ctr, Northwestern Univ, Chicago, 75-87; prof oncol, dep dir, Sylvester Comprehensive Cancer Ctr, Miami, 87-93. *Concurrent Pos:* Mem med staff, Highland-Alameda Co Hosp, Calif, 49-54; consult, US Naval Hosp, 55-65, Radiation Lab, Univ Calif, 55-57 & Defense Atomic Support Agency, Dept Defense, 57-59; assoc ed, Cancer Res; mem, Adv Comt Blood Dis & Resources, Nat Heart & Lung Inst, 76-80, rev comt, Cancer Pre-Clin Prog Proj, Nat Cancer Inst, 81-85; alumni lectr, State Univ NY. *Mem:* AAAS; Am Soc Clin Invest; Soc Exp Biol & Med; Am Physiol Soc; Am Asn Cancer Res; Asn Am Physicians; Am Clin & Climat Asn. *Res:* Erythropoiesis; use of radioactive isotopes in biological and medical research; cancer research. *Mailing Add:* 19355 Turnberry Way Apt 5J North Miami Beach FL 33180

BERLINCOURT, TED GIBBS, PHYSICS. *Current Pos:* RETIRED. *Personal Data:* b Fremont, Ohio, Oct 29, 25; m 53, Marjorie Alkins; c Leslie Ellen (Berlincourt Yale). *Educ:* Case Inst Technol, BS, 49; Yale Univ, MS, 50, PhD(physics), 53. *Prof Exp:* Lab asst, Yale Univ, 49-50, res asst, 50-51; proj physicist, Naval Res Lab, 52-55; supvr electronic properties unit, Atomics Int Div, NAm Aviation, Inc, 55-64, group leader electronic properties, NAm Rockwell Sci Ctr, 64-65, assoc dir, 65-70, chief scientist, NAm Rockwell Microelectronics Co, 69-70; prof physics & chmn dept, Colo State Univ, 70-72; dir, Phys Sci Div, 72-81, dir math & phys sci, Off Naval Res, 81-86; dir res & lab mgt, Off Defense Dir Res Eng, 86-92. *Concurrent Pos:* Mem Instrumentation Panel, Nat Acad Sci-Nat Res Coun Physics Surv, 71 & Interface & Applns Panel, 84; Navy liaison rep, Div Phys Sci, Nat Res Coun, 72-76; orgn comt, Appl Superconductivity Confs, 66-72. *Mem:* Fel AAAS; fel Am Phys Soc; Sigma Xi; Inst Elec & Electronics Engrs. *Res:* Superconductivity; Fermi surfaces; de Haas-van Alphen effect; galvano-magnetic effects; magnetism; cryogenics; pulsed magnetic fields; metal-oxide-semiconductor large-scale-integration technology; scintillation counters; x-ray diffraction; research and development management and policy. *Mailing Add:* 7844 Langley Ridge Rd McLean VA 22102

BERLIND, ALLAN, NEUROSCIENCES. *Current Pos:* from asst prof to assoc prof, 71-83, PROF BIOL, WESLEYAN UNIV, 83- *Personal Data:* b New York, NY, Dec 24, 42; m 68; c 2. *Educ:* Swarthmore Col, BA, 64; Harvard Univ, MA, 65, PhD(biol), 69. *Prof Exp:* NIH fel, Univ Calif, Berkeley, 69-71. *Concurrent Pos:* Vis assoc prof zool, Univ Hawaii, Manoa, 80-81. *Mem:* Soc Neurosci. *Res:* Neurophysiology; neuroendocrinology. *Mailing Add:* Dept Biol Wesleyan Univ Middletown CT 06459

BERLINER, ERNST, ORGANIC CHEMISTRY. *Current Pos:* RETIRED. *Personal Data:* b Katowice, Ger, Feb 18, 15; nat US; m 47, Frances Bondhus; c Susan L. *Educ:* Harvard Univ, MA, 40, PhD(org chem), 43. *Honors & Awards:* Award, Am Chem Soc, 71. *Prof Exp:* Pvt asst antimalarials, Harvard Univ, 43-44; lectr, Bryn Mawr Col, 44-45, from asst prof to prof org chem, 45-85. *Concurrent Pos:* Guggenheim fel, 62. *Mem:* Fel AAAS; Am Chem Soc; Royal Soc Chem; Sigma Xi. *Res:* Physical-organic aspects of aromatic chemistry; hyperconjugation; aromatic substitution; isotope effects; polynuclear aromatic reactivities; halogenation of acetylenes. *Mailing Add:* Dept Chem Bryn Mawr Col Bryn Mawr PA 19010

BERLINER, FRANCES (BONDHUS), ORGANIC CHEMISTRY. *Current Pos:* RETIRED. *Personal Data:* b Oskaloosa, Iowa, Nov 21, 21; m 47, Ernst; c Susan L. *Educ:* William Penn Col, BA, 43; Bryn Mawr Col, MA, 44, PhD(org chem), 47. *Prof Exp:* Demonstr, Bryn Mawr Col, 46-50, from instr to asst prof chem, 50-57, lectr, 57-71, assoc prof, 71-85. *Mem:* Am Chem Soc; Sigma Xi. *Res:* Aromatic chemistry. *Mailing Add:* Dept Chem Bryn Mawr Col Bryn Mawr PA 19010

BERLINER, HANS JACK, COMPUTER SCIENCE, ARTIFICIAL INTELLIGENCE. *Current Pos:* SR PRIN SCIENTIST COMPUT SCI, CARNEGIE-MELLON UNIV, 69- *Personal Data:* b Berlin, Ger, Jan 27, 29; US citizen; wid. *Educ:* George Washington Univ, BA, 54; Carnegie-Mellon Univ, PhD(comput sci), 75. *Prof Exp:* Develop syst analyst, IBM, 61-69. *Mem:* Fel Am Asn Artificial Intel; Asn Comput Mach; Int Joint Conf Artificial Intel. *Res:* Construction of intelligent systems, specializing in game playing and search; developed the B* tree search algorithm and the SNAC method of doing polynomial evaluation. *Mailing Add:* Comput Sci Dept Carnegie-Mellon Univ Pittsburgh PA 15213

BERLINER, JUDITH A, BLOOD VESSEL DISEASES. *Current Pos:* ASSOC PROF PATH, SCH MED, UNIV CALIF, LOS ANGELES, 81- *Personal Data:* b Cincinnati, Ohio, Sept 9, 39. *Educ:* Brown Univ, PhD(biol), 68. *Mem:* Am Soc Cell Biol; Am Heart Asn; Am Diabetes Asn. *Mailing Add:* Dept Path Univ Calif Los Angeles Sch Med Ctr Health Sci Los Angeles CA 90024-1732

BERLINER, LAWRENCE J, BIOPHYSICAL CHEMISTRY. *Current Pos:* from asst prof to assoc prof, 69-82, PROF CHEM, OHIO STATE UNIV, 82- *Personal Data:* b Los Angeles, Calif, Sept 18, 41; m 79; c 3. *Educ:* Univ Calif, Los Angeles, BS, 63; Stanford Univ, PhD(phys chem), 67. *Prof Exp:* Res chemist, Sun Oil Co, 62 & Chevron Res Corp, Stand Oil Co, Calif, 63; Brit Heart Found-Am Heart Asn fel molecular biophysics, Oxford Univ, 67-68; Am Heart Asn fel phys chem, Stanford Univ, 68-69. *Concurrent Pos:* Estab investr, Am Heart Asn, 75-80; exchange vis to Bulgaria & Hungary, Nat Acad Sci, 79; UNESCO-Orgn Am States lectr, Chile, 79 & NSF-Nat Coun Sci & Technol lectr, US-Romania, 81; Lady Davis vis prof, Technion, 81; vis prof, Ministry Sci, Japan, 89; assoc ed, J Protein Chem; Fogarty int fel, Biomolecular Res Inst, Australia, 92-94. *Mem:* Am Chem Soc; Am Soc Biol & Molecular Biol; Soc Magnetic Resonance Med; Int Soc Magnetic Resonance; NY Acad Sci; fel AAAS. *Res:* Structure-function relations in biomolecules by magnetic resonance methods; small molecule binding; conformational changes; x-ray structural investigations; applications of magnetic resonance to biology; electron magnetic resonance imaging; in-vivo ESR. *Mailing Add:* Dept Chem Ohio State Univ 120 W 18th Ave Columbus OH 43210-1173

BERLINER, MARTHA D, MICROBIOLOGY, MYCOLOGY. *Current Pos:* ADJ PROF MICROBIOL, EASTERN VA MED SCH, NORFOLK, 87- *Personal Data:* b Antwerp, Belg, Nov 18, 28; US citizen; m 52; c 2. *Educ:* Hunter Col, BA, 49; Univ Mich, MS, 50; Columbia Univ, PhD(mycol), 53. *Prof Exp:* Jr scientist cytol, Sloan Kettering Inst, 50-51; sr scientist microbiol, Res & Advan Develop Div, Med Sci Dept, Avco Corp, 60-62, sr staff scientist space microbiol, 62-65; PROF BIOL, VA COMMONWEALTH UNIV, 78-87; from instr to assoc prof, 65-78, PROF BIOL, SIMMONS COL, 78- *Concurrent Pos:* Instr, Lynn Hosp, Mass, 53-62; sr res assoc, Dept Microbiol, Sch Pub Health, Harvard Univ, 65-74; ed consult, Charles River Breeding Labs, 75-; prog assoc, NSF, 81-82. *Mem:* Am Mycol Soc; Am Soc Microbiol; NY Acad Sci; Int Soc Human & Animal Mycol; Med Mycol Soc Americas. *Res:* Medical mycology; microscopy; biological rhythms; radiation and environmental effects; protoplasts and wall deficient variants; biological parameter of pathogenicity in fungi; protoplasts of fungi and algae. *Mailing Add:* 2224 Bayville Rd Virginia Beach VA 23455-2861

BERLINER, ROBERT WILLIAM, PHYSIOLOGY, INTERNAL MEDICINE. *Current Pos:* prof, 73-85, dean, 73-84, EMER PROF & EMER DEAN, SCH MED, YALE UNIV, 85- *Personal Data:* b New York, NY, Mar 10, 15; m 41, Leah Silver; c Robert, Alice, Nancy & Henry. *Educ:* Yale Univ, BS, 36; Columbia Univ, MD, 39. *Hon Degrees:* DSc, Med Col Wis & Yale Univ, 73. *Honors & Awards:* Homer W Smith Award, 65; Res Achievement Award, Am Heart Asn, 70; A Ross McIntyre Award, 70; J M Smith Prize, 78; R G Daggs Award, 82; D M Hume Mem Award, Nat Kidney Found, 83; G M Kober Medal, Asn Am Physicians, 84. *Prof Exp:* Intern, Presby Hosp, NY, 39-41; resident physician, Goldwater Mem Hosp, 42-43; asst med, Col Med, NY Univ, 43-44, instr, 44-47; asst prof med, Columbia Univ, 47-50; chief, Lab Kidney & Electrolyte Metab, Nat Heart Inst, 50-62, dir intramural res, 54-68; dir labs & clins, NIH, 68-69, dep dir for sci, 69-73. *Concurrent Pos:* Res fel, Goldwater Mem Hosp, NY, 43-44, res asst, 44-47; res assoc, Dept Hosps, NY, 47-50; lectr, Sch Med, George Washington Univ, 51-73; Am Soc Clin Invest rep, Nat Res Coun, 57-60; prof lectr, Sch Med & Dent, Georgetown Univ, 64-73; coun, Nat Acad Sci, 78-81; mem, Bd Dirs, AAAS, 83-87; dir, Pew Scholars Prog, Yale Univ, 84-91. *Mem:* Nat Acad Sci; Am Acad Arts & Sci; AAAS (vpres, 72); Am Physiol Soc (pres, 67); Soc Exp Biol & Med (pres, 81-82); Am Asn Physicians; Sigma Xi. *Res:* Physiology of kidney; electrolyte transport. *Mailing Add:* Sch Med Yale Univ 333 Cedar St New Haven CT 06510

BERLINGHIERI, JOEL CARL, SPECTROSCOPIC INSTRUMENTATION DESIGN. *Current Pos:* from asst prof to assoc prof, 71-81, PROF PHYSICS, THE CITADEL, 81- *Personal Data:* b Boston, Mass, Dec 18, 42; m 71; c 1. *Educ:* Boston Col, BS, 64; Univ Rochester, MS, 66, PhD(physics), 70. *Prof Exp:* Asst prof physics, Colgate Univ, 69-71. *Concurrent Pos:* Res assoc, Univ Houston, 73-75. *Mem:* Inst Elec &

Electronics Engrs; Am Asn Physics Teachers; Acoust Soc Am; Optical Soc Am. *Res:* Design and development of novel optical instruments including interferometer based spectrometers. *Mailing Add:* The Citadel Charleston SC 29403

BERLINGUET, LOUIS, BIOCHEMISTRY. *Current Pos:* PRES, COUN SCI & TECHNOL QUE, 90- *Personal Data:* b Trois-Rivers, Que, Jun 20, 26. *Educ:* Univ Montreal, BS, 47; Laval Univ, PhD(chem), 50, FRSC(C). *Hon Degrees:* DSc, Univ Laval, 50. *Honors & Awards:* Jacques Rousseau Prize, 81. *Prof Exp:* Prof biochem, head dept & assoc dean, Fac Med, Laval Univ, 50-69; vpres res, Univ Que, 69-72, actg pres, 73; vchmn, Bd Gov & chmn, Exec Comt, Int Develop Res Ctr, Ottawa, 70-76, sr vpres, 76-80; sci adv, Can Embassy, Paris, 80-83; secy sci & technol, Ministry State & chief sci adv, Govt Can, 83-85; gen dir, Inst Res Occup Health & Safety Can, 85-90. *Concurrent Pos:* Vpres, Appln Sci & Technol Adv Comt, UN, 78; expert adv, Nat Res Coun, Fisheries Res Bd & Defense Res Bd. *Mem:* Royal Soc Can; fel Chem Inst Can; Can Biochem Soc (pres, 64); Asn Can-French Advan Sci (pres, 69); Asn Sci Eng & Technol Community Can (pres, 71). *Res:* Cancer biochemistry; antimetabolites; amino acids; published approximately 100 scientific papers. *Mailing Add:* Sci & Technol Coun Que 2050 Rene-Levesque Blvd E 5th Floor Ste Foy PQ G1V 2K8 Can

BERLINROOD, MARTIN, DEVELOPMENTAL BIOLOGY. *Current Pos:* ASST DEAN, SCHOOL HUMAN & SCI, ITHACA COL, ITHACA, 88- *Personal Data:* b New York, NY, Aug 20, 43; m 86; c 2. *Educ:* City Col NY, BS, 64; Univ Tex, Austin, PhD(zool), 69. *Prof Exp:* Res assoc biol sci, State Univ NY Albany, 68-70; from asst prof to assoc prof biol sci, Goucher Col, 70-88. *Concurrent Pos:* Registr, Goucher Col, 81-84, asst dean, 82-84, actg dean, 84-85, assoc dean, 85-88; asst dean, Sch Humanities, Ithaca Col, 88- *Res:* Axoplasmic transport in embryonic nerve fibers; axonal outgrowth and guidance in amphibian embryos. *Mailing Add:* 294 Enfield Main Rd Ithaca NY 14850

BERLOW, STANLEY, PEDIATRICS. *Current Pos:* ASSOC PROF PEDIAT, MED SCH, UNIV WIS-MADISON, 71- *Personal Data:* b New York, NY, June 16, 21; m 47; c 6. *Educ:* Univ Mich, BA, 40; Harvard Univ, MA, 41, MD, 50. *Prof Exp:* Intern pediat, Mass Gen Hosp, 50-51, chief resident, 53-54; resident, Babies Hosp, NY, 51-53; from instr to asst prof, Med Sch, Marquette Univ, 54-65; assoc prof pediat, Chicago Med Sch & med dir dysfunctioning child prog, Michael Reese Hosp & Med Ctr, Chicago, 65-69. *Res:* Biochemistry of mental retardation. *Mailing Add:* 3100 Lake Mendota Dr Madison WI 53705

BERLOWITZ TARRANT, LAURENCE, developmental biology, biomaterials, for more information see previous edition

BERLYN, GRAEME PIERCE, PLANT ANATOMY, TREE PHYSIOLOGY. *Current Pos:* From instr to assoc prof wood anat, 60-78, PROF ANAT & PHYSIOL, SCH FORESTRY & ENVIRON STUDIES, YALE UNIV, 78- *Personal Data:* b Chicago, Ill, Sept 6, 33; m 58; c 2. *Educ:* Iowa State Univ, BS, 56, PhD(anat), 60. *Hon Degrees:* MA, Yale Univ, 78. *Concurrent Pos:* Res collabr, Brookhaven Nat Lab, 63-66; ed, J Sustainable Forestry. *Mem:* Soc Wood Sci & Technol; Am Soc Plant Physiol; Int Asn Wood Anatomists; Bot Soc Am; fel Int Acad Wood Sci. *Res:* Quantitative cytochemistry; electron microscopy; reaction wood; developmental and experimental anatomy of pine embryos and seedlings; cell wall structure; microtechnical methods; effect of enzymatic hydrolysis on cell wall structure and free space; variation in DNA content of nuclei from populations of Pinus rigida; biotechnology of temperate and tropical trees; alpine ecophysiology. *Mailing Add:* Yale Univ 370 Prospect New Haven CT 06511

BERLYN, MARY K BERRY, GENETICS. *Current Pos:* res scientist, Dept Biol, 88-94, SR RES SCI, DEPT BIOL, SCH FORESTRY, YALE UNIV, 94- *Personal Data:* b Iowa Co, Iowa, Dec 28, 38; m 58; c 2. *Educ:* Iowa State Univ, BS, 59; Yale Univ, PhD(genetics), 66. *Prof Exp:* Res staff biologist, Yale Univ, 67-71, res assoc, 71-73; staff scientist, Conn Agr Exp Sta, 74-82; assoc prof, Lehman Col & Grad Ctr, City Univ New York, 82-88. *Concurrent Pos:* Dir, Ecoli Genetic Stock Ctr. *Mem:* AAAS; Genetics Soc Am; Am Soc Microbiol. *Res:* Somatic cell genetics of plants; RNA polymerase mutants of E coli; histidine and polyaromatic biosynthetic pathways in prokaryotes and eukaryotes; genetic database development. *Mailing Add:* Dept Biol & Sch Forestry Yale Univ PO Box 6666 New Haven CT 06511. *Fax:* 203-432-3854; *E-Mail:* berlyn@cgsc.giology.yale.edu

BERLYN, ROBIN WILFRID, MECHANICAL ENGINEERING. *Current Pos:* sr res asst woodlands res, 60, assoc engr, 61-66, mech engr, 66-75, sr scientist, Forest Eng Res Inst Can, 75-79, sr scientist, 79-85, SR RES ENGR, PULP & PAPER RES INST CAN, 85- *Personal Data:* b Montreal, Que, Dec 3, 34; m 59; c 3. *Educ:* McGill Univ, BEng, 58; Univ London, DIC, 61. *Prof Exp:* Prod develop engr, Can Ingersoll-Rand Co Ltd, Que, 58-60. *Mem:* Tech Asn Pulp & Paper Indust; Can Pulp & Paper Asn. *Res:* Removal of bark from wood; off-road mobility of logging vehicles; measurement of forest environmental factors and their effect on the productivity of logging machines; upgrading wood chips for use in pulp and paper manufacture. *Mailing Add:* 381 Elm Ave Westmount PQ H3Z 1Z4 Can

BERLYNE, GEOFFREY MERTON, NEPHROLOGY, RENAL PHYSIOLOGY. *Current Pos:* PROF MED, STATE UNIV NY, BROOKLYN, 76- *Personal Data:* b Britain, May 11, 31; US citizen; m 59; c 3. *Educ:* Univ Manchester, MBChB, 54, MD, 66; MRCP, 56; FRCP, 69. *Prof Exp:* Reader med, Univ Manchester, 68-70; prof life sci & med, Univ Negev, Israel, 70-80. *Concurrent Pos:* Ed, Nephron, 71-, Contrib to Physiol, 75- & Renal Physiol, 78-; vis prof, Univ Otago, 80. *Mem:* Am Soc Nephrol; Am Soc Artificial Internal Organs; Am Col Nutrit; NY Acad Sci; Am Col Physicians; Am Soc Trace Element Res. *Res:* Trace elements in renal disease; electrolyte physiology; nutrition in renal disease. *Mailing Add:* 800 Poly Pl Brooklyn NY 11209

BERMAN, ALAN, PHYSICS, PHYSICAL OCEANOGRAPHY. *Current Pos:* AT ROSENSTIEL SCH MARINE & ATMOSPHERIC SCI; DIR RES, US NAVAL RES LAB, 67- *Personal Data:* b Brooklyn, NY, Nov 2, 25; m 62; c 5. *Educ:* Columbia Univ, AB, 47, PhD(physics), 52. *Prof Exp:* Res physicist, Hudson Labs, Columbia Univ, 52-57, assoc dir, 57-63, dir, 63-67. *Mem:* Fel Am Phys Soc; fel Acoust Soc Am. *Res:* Atomic beams. *Mailing Add:* 5300 Holmes Run Pkwy Apt 214 Alexandria VA 22304

BERMAN, ALEX, HISTORY OF PHARMACY. *Current Pos:* prof hist & soc studies in pharm, 68-74, EMER PROF HIST & HIST STUDIES IN PHARM, COL PHARM, UNIV CINCINNATI, 75- *Personal Data:* b New York, NY, Feb 7, 14; m 43, Hortense Behr. *Educ:* Fordham Univ, BS, 47; Univ Wis, MS, 51, PhD(hist of pharm & sci), 54. *Honors & Awards:* Kremers Award, Am Inst Hist Pharm, 63. *Prof Exp:* Pharmacist, Vet Admin, 48-49; asst hist of pharm, Alumni Res Found, Univ Wis, 50-53; staff assoc, Am Pharmaceut Asn, 53-54; pharmacist, Univ Mich Hosp, 54-55; asst prof hist of pharm, Univ Wis, 55-56; asst prof pharm, Univ Mich, 56-61; assoc prof, Univ Tex, 61-68. *Concurrent Pos:* Guggenheim Mem Found fel, 58-59; NSF grant, 62-64; hon pres, Am Inst Hist Pharm, 85-87. *Mem:* Am Pharmaceut Asn; hon mem Am Soc Hosp Pharmacists; Am Asn Hist Med; Am Inst Hist Pharm (pres, 67-69); Int Acad Hist Pharm. *Res:* Nineteenth century pharmaceutical and medical Americana and French pharmacy; history of hospital pharmacy. *Mailing Add:* 310 Bryant Cincinnati OH 45220

BERMAN, BARRY L, PHOTONUCLEAR REACTIONS, ELECTROMAGNETIC INTERACTIONS. *Current Pos:* PROF PHYSICS, GEORGE WASHINGTON UNIV, 85-, DEPT CHMN, 93- *Personal Data:* b Chicago, Ill, Mar 8, 36; m 63, Ruth Decker; c 2. *Educ:* Harvard Univ, BA, 57; Univ Ill, MS, 59, PhD(physics), 63. *Prof Exp:* Nuclear physicist, Lawrence Livermore Lab, 63-85. *Concurrent Pos:* Vis prof, Yale Univ, 69-70, Univ Toronto, 70 & 75, Univ Sao Paulo, 77, Mass Inst Technol, 82; guest prof, Univ Frankfurt, 74; Sir Thomas Lyle fel, Univ Melbourne, 78, mem subcomt photonuclear reactions, US Nuclear Data Comt, 73, mem subcomt basic sci, 73-75; vis scientist, Ctr d'Etudes Nucleaires, Saclay, France, 80-81; guest scientist, Lawrence Berkeley Lab, 86, Los Alamos Nat Lab, 85, 88, 89, 91 & 92, Continuous Electron Beam Accelerator Facil, 91-92. *Mem:* Fel Am Phys Soc. *Res:* Photonuclear reactions, electron and proton scattering, pion physics; neutron physics; nuclear astrophysics; applications; channeling and transition radiation. *Mailing Add:* Dept Physics George Washington Univ Washington DC 20052. *Fax:* 202-994-3001; *E-Mail:* berman@gwuvm.gwu.edu

BERMAN, CAROL MAY, PARENT-OFFSPRING RELATIONS, SOCIAL BEHAVIOR & ORGANIZATION AMONG NON-HUMAN PRIMATES. *Current Pos:* from asst prof to assoc prof, 79-92, PROF ANTHROP, STATE UNIV NY, BUFFALO, 92- *Personal Data:* b San Francisco, Calif, Apr 11, 49; m 83, Edward Cooper; c Samuel R Berman-Cooper. *Educ:* Brandies Univ, BA, 71; Univ Cambridge, UK, PhD(animal behav), 79. *Prof Exp:* Psychologist, Environ Protection Agency, 71-72; res psychologist, Food & Drug Admin, 72-73; asst prof anthrop, State Univ NY, Buffalo, 79-85. *Concurrent Pos:* Vis scientist, Caribbean Primate Res Ctr, 73-75, collaborating scientist, 88-; animal behav consult, New Scientist Mag, 77-78; vis scholar, Univ Cambridge UK, 85; co-dir grad group evolutionary biol & ecol, State Univ NY, Buffalo, 90- *Mem:* Animal Behav Soc; Am Primatological soc; Soc Behav Ecol. *Res:* Long term, longitudinal research into the possible social and biological causes and consequences of inter-individual variation in maternal care patterns among free-ranging non-human primates. *Mailing Add:* Dept Anthrop State Univ NY Buffalo NY 14261

BERMAN, DAVID ALBERT, PHARMACOLOGY. *Current Pos:* from instr to assoc prof, 52-63, PROF PHARMACOL & TOXICOL, UNIV SOUTHERN CALIF, 63- *Personal Data:* b Rochester, NY, Nov 4, 17; m 45, Miriam; c Shelley (Stone) & Judy (McCleese). *Educ:* Univ Southern Calif, BS, 40, MS, 48, PhD(pharmacol), 51. *Prof Exp:* Life Ins Med res fel, 51-52. *Concurrent Pos:* USPHS spec fel, 60-61. *Mem:* Am Soc Pharmacol & Exp Therapeut. *Res:* Cardiac metabolism in relation to drug action. *Mailing Add:* 3304 Scadlock Lane Sherman Oaks CA 91403. *Fax:* 213-342-2709

BERMAN, DAVID ALVIN, INORGANIC CHEMISTRY, CORROSION. *Current Pos:* RETIRED. *Personal Data:* b Milwaukee, Wis, Apr 13, 24; m 70. *Educ:* Univ Wis, BS, 48; Univ Mich, MS, 50, PhD(inorg chem), 57. *Prof Exp:* Instr, Wis State Teachers Col, Oshkosh, 50; asst prof chem, Exten Div, Univ Wis, 55-63 & Carroll Col, Wis, 64-65; chemist, Naval Air Eng Ctr, Naval Air Develop Ctr, 67-86. *Mem:* AAAS; Am Chem Soc; Sigma Xi. *Res:* Corrosion; electrochemistry; hydrogen embrittlement. *Mailing Add:* 173 Deerfield Dr Souderton PA 18964-1933

BERMAN, DAVID MICHAEL, MATHEMATICS. *Current Pos:* from instr to assoc prof, 74-90, PROF MATH, UNIV NEW ORLEANS, 90- *Personal Data:* b Boston, Mass, May 14, 46. *Educ:* Dartmouth Col, AB, 67; Univ Pa, PhD(appl math), 73. *Prof Exp:* Vis instr math, Franklin & Marshall Col, 73-74. *Concurrent Pos:* Vis scholar, Smith Col, 87. *Mem:* Soc Indust Appl & Math. *Res:* Graph theory. *Mailing Add:* Dept Math Univ New Orleans New Orleans LA 70148-0001

BERMAN, DAVID S, VERTEBRATE PALEONTOLOGY. *Current Pos:* Asst cur vert paleont, 70-78, assoc cur, 79-89, CUR, CARNEGIE MUS NATURAL HIST, 89- *Personal Data:* b Los Angeles, Calif, Jan 10, 40; div. *Educ:* Univ Calif, Los Angeles, BA, 62, MA, 65, PhD(zool), 69. *Mem:* Paleont Soc; Am Soc Ichthyologists & Herpetologists; Soc Study Evolution. *Res:* Paleontology of late Paleozoic vertebrates. *Mailing Add:* Carnegie Mus Natural Hist 4400 Forbes Ave Pittsburgh PA 15213

BERMAN, DAVID THEODORE, VETERINARY SCIENCE. *Current Pos:* Res asst, 44-46, from instr to assoc prof, 46-57, chmn dept, 64-68, assoc dean grad sch, 69-75, PROF VET SCI & BACT, UNIV WIS-MADISON, 57- *Personal Data:* b Brooklyn, NY, June 14, 20; m 44; c 2. *Educ:* Brooklyn Col, BA, 41; Cornell Univ, DVM, 44; Univ Wis, MS, 46, PhD, 49. *Honors & Awards:* Animal Health Award, USDA, 80. *Concurrent Pos:* Coop agent, USDA, 46-57; mem, Conf Res Workers Animal Dis NAm, 47-; consult, Nat Brucellosis Comt, 58-; grad sch G I Haight traveling fel, State Serum Inst, Copenhagen, Denmark & Vet Lab, Weybridge, Eng, 63; expert comt brucellosis, WHO, 63-70, mem, 70-85; mem bd sci counr, Nat Inst Allergy & Infectious Dis, 74-78, chmn, 78, chmn, Nat Brucellosis Tech Comn, 76-79; chmn, Div Microbial Pathogenesis, Am Soc Microbiol, 85. *Mem:* AAAS; Am Soc Microbiol; Am Vet Med Asn; US Animal Health Asn; Am Asn Immunol. *Res:* Immunology and bacteriology of brucellosis; microbial variation; staphylococcal infection; hypersensitivity in experimental arthritis; antigenic analysis mycobacteria; chlamydia; immune response mucosae. *Mailing Add:* Dept Vet Sci & Bacteriol Univ Wis 1655 Linden Dr Madison WI 53706

BERMAN, ELEANOR, PHARMACOLOGY, BIOCHEMISTRY. *Current Pos:* RETIRED. *Personal Data:* b Duluth, Minn, Oct 5, 21. *Educ:* Wis State Col, Superior, BS, 42; Univ Minn, Minneapolis, MS, 50, PhD(pharmacol), 57. *Prof Exp:* Teacher pub schs, Mich, 42-45 & Wis, 45-46; med technologist, St Mary's Hosp, Duluth, Minn, 46-48; clin biochemist, Ill Masonic Hosp, Chicago, 53-66; toxicologist, Hektoen Inst, 66-71 & Div Biochem, Cook County Hosp, 71-93. *Mem:* Am Asn Clin Chem; fel Am Acad Forensic Sci; Am Chem Soc; Soc Appl Spectros. *Res:* Clinical toxicology; lead poisoning and trace metals in clinical chemistry. *Mailing Add:* 2500 Lakeview Chicago IL 60614-1836

BERMAN, ELIZABETH FAITH, PHARMACOLOGY. *Current Pos:* RES SCIENTIST, PROCTER & GAMBLE CO, 84- *Personal Data:* b Schenectady, NY, May 31, 54. *Educ:* Washington Univ, St Louis, BS, 76; Temple Univ, PhD(pharmacol), 82. *Mem:* Am Soc Pharmacol & Exp Therapeut; Sigma Xi; Inflammation Res Soc; AAAS. *Mailing Add:* 3522A Brookstone Dr PO Box 398707 Cincinnati OH 45209

BERMAN, ELLIOT, PHOTOCHEMISTRY. *Current Pos:* PRES, PHOTOX CORP, 93-; VPRES, ZENTOX CORP, 96- *Personal Data:* b Quincy, Mass, Jan 13, 30; m 53, Charlotte Tannen; c Laurance, Judd M & Douglas I. *Educ:* Brown Univ, ScB, 51; Boston Univ, PhD(org chem), 56. *Prof Exp:* Sr chemist, Fundamental Res Dept, Nat Cash Register Co, 55-57, head, Org Sect, 57-59; head, Chem Sect, Res Div, Itek Corp, 59-61, mgr, Chem Dept, 61-64, tech dir res, 64-65, dir, Lexington Res Labs, 65-67, dir photosensitive mat, 67-69; consult, 69-73; pres & chmn, Solar Power Corp, 73-75; dir, Ctr Energy Studies, Boston Univ, 75-78, res prof appl sci, 78-79; chief scientist, Arco Solar Inc, 79-89; pres, Proj Sunrise, Inc, 90-93. *Concurrent Pos:* Instr, Univ Dayton, 56-57; asst prof, Univ Cincinnati, 56-58; pres, Sun Systs, Inc, 78- *Mem:* AAAS; Am Chem Soc; Solar Energy Soc; Royal Soc Chem. *Res:* Reversible photochemical systems; kinetics and mechanisms of reactions at solid interfaces; photochemistry; photophysics; solar energy utilization; photography; pollution control. *Mailing Add:* PO Box 15717 Boston MA 02215. *Fax:* 617-353-6466

BERMAN, GERALD, MATHEMATICS. *Current Pos:* RETIRED. *Personal Data:* b Can, Nov 12, 24; US citizen; m 48; c 4. *Educ:* Univ Toronto, BA, 47, MA, 48, PhD(math), 50. *Prof Exp:* From instr to assoc prof math, Ill Inst Technol, 50-59; chmn, Dept Combinatorics & Optimization, Univ Waterloo, 66-78, prof math, 59-89. *Concurrent Pos:* Consult, Inst Air Weapons Res, Chicago, 57-59, Martin-Marietta Corp, Colo, 59-63 & Defense Res Bd Can, 64-68. *Mem:* Am Math Soc; Math Asn Am; Soc Indust & Appl Math; Opers Res Soc Am; Can Math Cong. *Res:* Applied mathematics; combinatorics; optimization. *Mailing Add:* 4 Atlantis Unionville ON L3P 7B5 Can

BERMAN, GERALD ADRIAN, ELECTRICAL ENGINEERING. *Current Pos:* CHIEF, TECHNOL ASSESSMENT & PLANNING, VOICE AM, 83- *Personal Data:* b Bridgeport, Conn, Dec 26, 34; m 60; c 2. *Educ:* Univ Miami, BS, 55; La State Univ, MS, 57; Univ Detroit, DrEng(elec eng), 68. *Prof Exp:* Instr elec eng, La State Univ, 56-57; from instr to asst prof, Univ Miami, 57-66; from instr to assoc prof & chmn elec eng, Univ Detroit, 66-77; proj mgr & group leader, Nat Inst Standards & Technol, 77-83. *Concurrent Pos:* Res consult, Detroit Edison Power Co, 70-; res consult, Ford Motor Co, 73-74; res consult, Bendix Res Labs, 76; res consult, US Army, 75; NASA fac fel, 72. *Mem:* Am Soc Testing & Mat; Inst Elec & Electronics Engrs; Broadcast Technol Soc (pres). *Res:* Oceanographic engineering; underwater acoustics and instrumentation; information display systems; environmental engineering; electrostatic precipators; biological effects of magnetic fields; automotive instrumentation; radio propogation; broadcast system engineering; computer graphics. *Mailing Add:* Voice Am Cohen Bldg Rm 4242 330 Independence Ave SW Washington DC 20547

BERMAN, HELEN MIRIAM, STRUCTURAL BIOLOGY. *Current Pos:* PROF II, RUTGERS UNIV, 89- *Personal Data:* b Chicago, Ill, May 19, 43; m 76, Peter Young; c Jason A. *Educ:* Barnard Col, AB, 64; Univ Pittsburgh, PhD(crystallog), 67. *Prof Exp:* NIH traineeship biochem crystallog, Univ Pittsburgh, 67-69; res assoc molecular struct, Inst Cancer Res, Fox Chase Cancer Ctr, 69-73, from asst mem to sr mem, 73-89. *Concurrent Pos:* Dir, Res Comput Facil FCCC; mem, NIH Study Sect, 80-84, US Nat Comt Crystallog, 80-93; mem, Biol Adv Comt, NSF, 92-96; mem, Nat Needs Biomed Res Personnel, 93. *Mem:* Fel AAAS; Am Crystallog Asn (pres, 88); Biophys Soc; Am Chem Soc; Am Soc Biol Chem & Molecular Biol. *Res:* Crystal structures of nucleic acid components and proteins; structural interactions between nucleic acids and proteins; structural database development. *Mailing Add:* Dept Chem Rutgers Univ PO Box 939 Piscataway NJ 08855-0939. *Fax:* 732-932-5958; *E-Mail:* bermanl@adenine.rutgers.edu

BERMAN, HERBERT JOSHUA, physiology; deceased, see previous edition for last biography

BERMAN, HOWARD MITCHELL, BIOCHEMISTRY, MOLECULAR IMMUNOLOGY. *Current Pos:* RETIRED. *Personal Data:* b Pittsburgh, Pa, May 1, 36; m 58, Zenita Miller; c Amy B & Ellen R. *Educ:* Univ Pittsburgh, BS, 57. *Prof Exp:* Res chemist, Vet Admin Med Ctr, Pittsburgh, 60-72; health sci adminr, Vet Admin Cent Off, Washington, DC, 72-79, chief prog rev div, 79-87; health sci adminr, Nat Inst Allergy & Infectious Dis, NIH, 87-89, Div Res Grants, 89-95. *Concurrent Pos:* Vet Admin rep, Fed Interagency Recombinant DNA Comt, 79-87; consult peer review. *Mem:* Fel Am Inst Chemists; AAAS. *Res:* Biochemical pharmacology and use of gas chromatography and mass spectrometry for analysis; enzyme purification; cell membrane ATPase and structure-function relationships; cell membrane aging; immunogenetics. *Mailing Add:* 3225 Birchtree Lane Silver Spring MD 20906. *Fax:* 301-460-9022; *E-Mail:* hberman@ix.netcom.com

BERMAN, IRWIN, ANATOMY, HEMATOLOGY. *Current Pos:* asst prof, 59-62, ASSOC PROF ANAT, SCH MED, UNIV MIAMI, 62- *Personal Data:* b New York, NY, Dec 4, 24; m 51; c 2. *Educ:* Seton Hall Univ, BS, 49; NY Univ, MS, 51, PhD(physiol), 55. *Prof Exp:* Asst radiobiol, Brookhaven Nat Lab, 55-56; res assoc, Sch Med, Stanford Univ, 56-59. *Concurrent Pos:* Am Cancer Soc fel, Brookhaven Nat Lab, 55-56 & Sch Med, Stanford Univ, 56-57; NIH res fel, 57-58; USPHS spec res fel, Harvard Med Sch, 63-64. *Mem:* AAAS; Am Soc Cell Biologists; Am Asn Anat; Radiation Res Soc; Sigma Xi. *Res:* Electron microscopy; radiation biology; oncology. *Mailing Add:* Univ Miami Sch Med PO Box 016960 Miami FL 33101

BERMAN, JEROME RICHARD, INTERNAL MEDICINE, GASTROENTEROLOGY. *Current Pos:* fel, Univ Cincinnati, 47-50, from instr to assoc prof med, 48-67, clin prof, 67-74, prof med, 74-87, EMER PROF MED, UNIV CINCINNATI, 87-; ATTEND PHYSICIAN, UNIV CINCINNATI HOSP, 74- *Personal Data:* b New York, NY, Aug 7, 20; m 46, Estelle Brown; c Arthur E. *Educ:* Univ Cincinnati, BA, 41, MD, 44. *Concurrent Pos:* Med consult, Integrated Acad Info Mgt Syst, 87-89, Med Info, 87-89, consult, Time Proj, NLM-NIH. *Mem:* AAAS; Am Fedn Clin Res; Am Asn Study Liver Dis; fel Am Col Physicians; fel Am Col Gastroenterol; Sigma Xi; Am Gastroenterol Asn; Am Soc Gastrointestinal Endoscopy. *Res:* Gastroenterology. *Mailing Add:* 3904 Wess Park Dr Cincinnati OH 45217. *Fax:* 513-221-0336; *E-Mail:* jrberman@pol.net

BERMAN, JOEL DAVID, MATHEMATICS. *Current Pos:* From asst prof to assoc prof, 70-82, PROF MATH, UNIV ILL, CHICAGO, 82- *Personal Data:* b Minneapolis, Minn, Jan 1, 43. *Educ:* Univ Minn, Minneapolis, BA, 65; Univ Wash, PhD(math), 70. *Mem:* Am Math Soc; Math Asn Am. *Res:* Lattice theory and universal algebra. *Mailing Add:* Dept Math Univ Ill Chicago M/C 249 851 S Morgan St Chicago IL 60607-7045

BERMAN, JOSEPH MICHAEL, CALCULUS, DIFFERENTIAL EQUATIONS. *Current Pos:* asst prof, 87-92, ASSOC PROF MATH, HAMPDEN-SIDNEY COL, 92- *Personal Data:* b Gainesville Fla, Sept 30, 39; m 80, Joan Benfield; c Karl, Laura (Studdard) & Alysia. *Educ:* Univ Fla, BS, 61; Brown Univ, MS, 70; Univ RI, PhD(math), 80. *Prof Exp:* Inst math, Salve Regina Col, 65-67, asst prof math, 67-70, chmn, Math Dept, 68-70; asst prof math, George Mason Univ, 72-74, Va State Univ, 74-83 & James Madison Univ, 83-87. *Concurrent Pos:* J William Fulbright teaching fel, Univ Malawi-The Polytech, 94-95. *Mem:* Math Asn Am; Am Asn Univ Profs. *Res:* Asymptotic behavior of an S-I-R-S model for the spread of disease; results on stability of generalized control systems. *Mailing Add:* Dept Math & Comput Sci Box 121 Hampden-Sydney Col Hampden-Sydney VA 23943. *Fax:* 804-223-6347; *E-Mail:* mikeb@mail.hsc.edu

BERMAN, JULIAN, AERONAUTICAL ENGINEERING. *Current Pos:* RETIRED. *Personal Data:* b New York, NY, Oct 4, 24; m 48; c 3. *Educ:* City Col New York, BS, 44; NY Univ, MS, 48. *Prof Exp:* Mathematician aerial survs, Fairchild Aerial Surv Inc, 47-48, engr, Fairchild Aircraft Co, 48-50; res scientist, Nat Adv Comt Aeronaut, 50-56; engr, Repub Aviation Corp, 56-64; engr, Grumman Aircraft & Eng Corp, Bethpage, 64-73; chief flutter & vibration engr, Fairchild Repub Co, 73-90. *Concurrent Pos:* Exten instr, George Washington Univ, 54-55. *Mem:* Assoc fel Am Inst Aeronaut & Astronaut. *Res:* Aeroelasticity; vibrations; flutter; structural mechanics; oscillatory aerodynamics. *Mailing Add:* 27 Oriel Way Marlboro NJ 07746

BERMAN, LAWRENCE URETZ, POLYMER CHEMISTRY, ENVIRONMENTAL SCIENCE. *Current Pos:* PRES, BERMAN ASSOC, 95- *Personal Data:* b Chicago, Ill, Aug 4, 19; m 50, Evelyn Berger; c Mary. *Educ:* Univ Ill, Urbana, BS, 41; Northwestern Univ, MS, 47. *Prof Exp:* Asst chem org chem dept, IIT Res Inst, 48-56, assoc chemist, 56, res chemist, 56-65; res chemist bus equip group, Explor Res Dept, Bell & Howell Co, 65-68; res chemist, Res & Develop Div, Kraft Inc, 68-82; consult, Hazardous Mat Mgt Syst, Inc, 82-86. *Concurrent Pos:* Elem chem teacher, 93- *Mem:* Fel AAAS; Am Chem Soc; fel Am Inst Chem. *Res:* Synthesis of new organic compounds, including monomers and polymers; development of organic reaction processes by new techniques and commercial scale-up. *Mailing Add:* 8025 N Hamlin Ave Skokie IL 60076-3403

BERMAN, LONNY E, PHYSICS. *Current Pos:* asst scientist, 87-89, assoc scientist, 89-91, SCIENTIST, NAT SYNCHROTRON LIGHT SOURCE, BROOKHAVEN NAT LAB, 91- *Personal Data:* b Sept 5, 60. *Educ:* Cornell Univ, BA, 81, MS, 83, PhD(physics), 88. *Prof Exp:* Teaching asst, School Appl & Eng Physics, Cornell Univ, 82- 84, res asst, 81-87. *Mailing Add:* Nat Synchrotron Light Source Brookhaven Nat Lab Bldg 725D Upton NY 11973

BERMAN, LOUIS, astronomy; deceased, see previous edition for last biography

BERMAN, M LAWRENCE, ANESTHESIOLOGY, CLINICAL PHARMACOLOGY. *Current Pos:* PROF ANESTHESIA, SCH MED, VANDERBILT UNIV, 74-, ASSOC PROF PHARMACOL, 76- *Personal Data:* b Stanford, Conn, July 13, 29; m; m; c 2. *Educ:* Univ Conn, BS, 51; Univ Wash, MS, 54, PhD, 56; Univ NC, MD, 64. *Prof Exp:* Toxicologist & asst chief environ health lab, Air Materiel Command, Wright-Patterson AFB, 56-57, prin investr pharmacol-biochem, Aerospace Med Lab, Wright Air Develop Ctr, 57-60; resident anesthesia, Sch Med, Univ NC, Chapel Hill, 65-67; from asst prof to assoc prof, Sch Med, Northwestern Univ, 67-74. *Mem:* Am Soc Clin & Exp Pharmacol; Int Anesthesia Res Soc; Am Soc Clin Res; Am Soc Anesthesiol; Asn Univ Anesthetists. *Res:* Man in space program; humoral response to stress; catabolism of catechol amines; psychotropic drugs; drug metabolism. *Mailing Add:* 3255 New Med Ctr Vanderbilt Hosp Nashville TN 37232

BERMAN, MARLENE OSCAR, NEUROPSYCHOLOGY, PHYSIOLOGICAL PSYCHOLOGY. *Current Pos:* res assoc, 71-72, from asst prof to assoc prof, 72-81, PROF NEUROL & PROF PSYCHIAT, SCH MED, BOSTON UNIV, 82-; RES PSYCHOLOGIST, DEPT VET AFFAIRS MED CTR HOSP, 73- *Personal Data:* b Philadelphia, Pa, Nov 21, 39; div; c Jesse M. *Educ:* Univ Pa, BA, 61; Bryn Mawr Col, MA, 64; Univ Conn, PhD(psychol), 68. *Prof Exp:* Instr psychol, Univ Conn, 66-68; USPHS fel, Harvard Univ, 68-70, instr, 70. *Concurrent Pos:* Res assoc psychol, Vet Admin Hosp, Boston, 70-73, med clin investr award, 73-76; instr psychol, Exten Sch, Harvard Univ, 70-76; Nat Inst Neurol & Commun Dis & Stroke res grant, 72-76, res career develop award, 76-81; affil prof psychol, Clark Univ, 72-; mem ment health small grant comt, NIMH, 74-78; Sigma Xi Nat lectr, 80-81; res sci develop award, Nat Inst Alcohol Abuse & Alcoholism, 81-86, mem biomed res rev comt, 87-91, chmn, 90-91; Fulbright sr scholar award, 91-; merit award & sr scientist award, Nat Inst Alcohol Abuse & Alcoholism, 96- *Mem:* Sigma Xi; fel Am Psychol Asn; Soc Neurosci; Psychonomic Soc; Int Neuropsychol Soc. *Res:* Normal and pathological brain function, including mechanisms of cerebral specialization, Korsakoff's syndrome, aphasia, Huntington's disease, Parkinsonism and dementia; emphasis on understanding mechanisms of disordered memory, perception and cognition. *Mailing Add:* 115 Cotton St Newton MA 02158-2639

BERMAN, MICHAEL ROY, CROSSBRIDGE KINETICS. *Current Pos:* ASST PROF, DEPT ANAT, JOHNS HOPKINS UNIV, 85- *Personal Data:* b Brooklyn, NY, Jan 22, 47; m 72; c 2. *Educ:* City Col, City Univ New York, BS, 69; Ohio State Univ, MS, 77, PhD(physiol), 79. *Prof Exp:* Assoc, Univ Vt, 79-81, fel, 81-82, res assoc physiol & biophysics, 82-85. *Res:* Chemical and geometrical factors which modulate crossbridge kinetics in striated muscle. *Mailing Add:* 9076 Meadow Heights Randallstown MD 21133

BERMAN, NANCY ELIZABETH JOHNSON, CEREBRAL CORTICAL DEVELOPMENT, NEUROAIDS. *Current Pos:* PROF ANAT, UNIV KANS MED CTR, 87- *Personal Data:* b Paducah, Ky, Aug 14, 46; m 70; c 3. *Educ:* Lawrence Univ, BA, 68; Mass Inst Technol, PhD(psychol & brain sci), 72. *Prof Exp:* Res asst brain sci, Mass Inst Technol, 68-72; fel anat, Sch Med, Univ Pa, 72-74; res assoc neuroanat & neurophysiol, Sch Med, Wash Univ, 74-76; asst prof physiol, Med Col Pa, 76-80, asst prof anat, 77-80, assoc prof physiol & anat, 81-87. *Concurrent Pos:* Mem neurobehav sect, NIMH, 83-87. *Mem:* Soc Neurosci; Asn Res Vision & Ophthal. *Res:* Anatomy, physiology and development of the visual system; brain development, cytokine expression in the brain; aquired immunodeficiency syndrome neuropathology. *Mailing Add:* Dept Anat Univ Kans Med Ctr 3901 Rainbow Blvd Kansas City KS 66160-7400. *Fax:* 913-588-2710

BERMAN, NEIL SHELDON, CHEMICAL ENGINEERING. *Current Pos:* from asst to assoc prof, 64-70, PROF ENG, ARIZ STATE UNIV, 70- *Personal Data:* b Milwaukee, Wis, Sept 21, 33; m 62, Sarah Ayres; c Jenny & Daniel. *Educ:* Univ Wis, BS, 55; Univ Tex, MS, 61, MA & PhD(chem eng), 62. *Prof Exp:* Designs engr, Stand Oil Co Calif, 55-56; res scientist, E I Du Pont de Nemours & Co, 62-64. *Concurrent Pos:* Prin investr grants, NSF, Petrol Res Fund & US Dept Transp; vis prof, Pa State Univ, 72-73 & Univ Tex, Austin, 80 & 83; grad col distinguished res prof, 84-85. *Mem:* Fel AAAS; fel Am Inst Chem Engrs; Am Chem Soc; Am Soc Mech Engrs; Am Phys Soc. *Res:* Thermodynamics; applied mathematics and numerical analysis; fluid dynamics and transport processes related to small particles and polymers; air pollution modeling; laser doppler anemometry; particle counting methods in fluid mechanics. *Mailing Add:* Dept Chem Biol & MHS Eng Ariz State Univ Tempe AZ 85287-6006. *Fax:* 602-965-0037; *E-Mail:* icnsb@asuvm.inre.asu.edu

BERMAN, PAUL RONALD, ATOMIC PHYSICS, LASERS. *Current Pos:* from asst prof to assoc prof, 71-82, PROF PHYSICS, NY UNIV, 82- *Personal Data:* b New York, NY, Feb 5, 45; m 87; c 1. *Educ:* Rensselaer Polytech Inst, BS, 65; Yale Univ, MS, 66, PhD(physics), 69. *Prof Exp:* Instr physics, Yale Univ, 69-71. *Mem:* Fel Am Phys Soc. *Res:* Theoretical atomic and laser physics with special emphasis on collision effects. *Mailing Add:* Dept Physics Univ Mich Ann Arbor MI 48109

BERMAN, REUBEN, CARDIOLOGY. *Current Pos:* RETIRED. *Personal Data:* b Minneapolis, Minn, Feb 8, 08; m 31; c 6. *Educ:* Univ Minn, Minneapolis, BA, 29, MD, 33. *Prof Exp:* Clin prof med, Univ Minn, Minneapolis, 63-77, emer prof, 77-85. *Concurrent Pos:* Prin investr, Coronary Drug Proj, Mt Sinai Hosp, Minneapolis; pvt pract med, 37- *Mem:* Am Col Physicians; Am Col Cardiol; Am Heart Asn. *Mailing Add:* 2809 Drew Ave Minneapolis MN 55416

BERMAN, ROBERT HIRAM, APPLIED MATHEMATICS, PLASMA PHYSICS. *Current Pos:* res assoc, Mass Inst Technol, 78-86. *Personal Data:* b New York, NY, Apr 1, 48; m 86. *Educ:* Mass Inst Technol, BS, 70, PhD(appl math), 75. *Prof Exp:* Res fel, Univ Reading, 75-78. *Mem:* Soc Indust & Appl Math; Royal Astron Soc; Am Astron Soc; Am Phys Soc; Sigma Xi. *Res:* Computational physics; large scale numerical simulations of plasma turbulence, using supercomputers for scientific computing applications and using computer algebra for applications in artificial intelligence. *Mailing Add:* 50 Richfield Rd Arlington MA 02174

BERMAN, SAM MORRIS, THEORETICAL PHYSICS. *Current Pos:* assoc prof, 64-69, PROF, LINEAR ACCELERATOR CTR, STANFORD UNIV, 69- *Personal Data:* b Worcester, Mass, Feb 4, 33; m 57. *Educ:* Univ Miami, Fla, BS, 54, MS, 55; Calif Inst Technol, PhD(physics), 59. *Prof Exp:* Instr, Calif Inst Technol, 55-59; NSF fel, Univ Copenhagen & Bohr Inst, Denmark, 59-64. *Concurrent Pos:* Consult, IBM, 58-59 & Space Tech Labs, 59- *Res:* Quantum theory of fields; quantum electrodynamics and related high energy physics; plasma physics and hydromagnetics. *Mailing Add:* Lawrence Berkeley Labs 1 Cyclotron Rd MS 46-125 Berkeley CA 94720

BERMAN, SHIER, ANALYTICAL CHEMISTRY. *Current Pos:* From asst res officer to prin res officer, anal chem, Chem Div, 57-90, head anal chem, 81-90, DIR MEASUREMENT SCI, INST ENVIRON CHEM, NAT RES COUN CAN, 90- *Personal Data:* b Toronto, Ont, Oct 4, 29; m 51, Shirley Hettler; c Reva, Elliott & David. *Educ:* Univ Toronto, BA, 52, MA, 55, PhD(anal chem), 57. *Honors & Awards:* Fisher Sci Lectr Award, 85. *Concurrent Pos:* Vis scientist, Hebrew Univ Jerusalem, Israel, 65-66 & vis lectr, 70; vis lectr, Queen's Univ, Ont, 75; vis fel, Western Australia Inst Technol, Perth, 85; Can deleg, Int Coun Explor Sea Working Groups, Marine Chem & Marine Sediments, 81-, Count Int Prog Mat working group on metrology in chem analysis; chmn, XXV Colloquium Spectroscopicum Int, 87. *Mem:* Fel Chem Inst Can; Spectros Soc Can (pres, 62-63). *Res:* Inorganic analytical chemistry; trace analysis; optical emission spectroscopy; xray fluorescence spectroscopy; atomic absorption; inductively coupled plasma; photon activation analysis; trace metals in seawater and marine samples; marine reference materials for trace metals. *Mailing Add:* Inst Environ Chem Nat Res Coun Montreal Rd Ottawa ON K1A 0R6 Can. *Fax:* 613-993-2451

BERMAN, SIMEON MOSES, STOCHASTIC PROCESSES. *Current Pos:* assoc prof, 65-77, PROF MATH, COURANT INST MATH SCI, NY UNIV, 77- *Personal Data:* b Rochester, NY, Mar 28, 35; m 55, Iona T Grossman; c 6. *Educ:* City Col New York, BA, 56; Columbia Univ, MA, 58, PhD(math statist), 61. *Prof Exp:* Lectr math, City Col New York, 57-60; res assoc math statist, Columbia Univ, 60-61, asst prof, 61-65. *Concurrent Pos:* Prin investr, NSF Res Grant Stochastic Processes, NY Univ, 66-74 & 96-91; assoc ed, Annal Probability, 79-85; statist consult, EPA Acid Rain res grant, NY Univ 79-83; prin investr short term res 85 & contract, US Army Res Off, NY Univ, 86-92; prin investr NIH res contract, HIV Math Res, NY Univ, 89-92; Guggenheim Mem fel, 92-93. *Mem:* Fel Inst Math Statist; Sigma Xi. *Res:* Probability theory, especially stochastic processes; stochastic models in medicine. *Mailing Add:* Courant Inst Math Sci NY Univ 251 Mercer St New York NY 10012

BERMES, BORIS JOHN, GEOHYDROLOGY. *Current Pos:* RETIRED. *Personal Data:* b Merchantville, NJ, Mar 2, 26; c 3. *Educ:* Colo Sch Mines, Geol Eng, 50; Univ Utah, MS, 54. *Prof Exp:* Geologist, US Geol Surv, 50-54; exploitation engr, Shell Oil Co, 54-56; hydraulic engr, US Dept Interior, 56-73; sr scientist water resources, Geraghty & Miller Inc, West Palm Beach, Fla, 73-85; chief hydrogeologist, Cayman Islands Govt, 85-87. *Concurrent Pos:* Model specialist and drainage adv, UN Develop Prog, 69 & 77; tech officer, Food & Agr Orgn UN, 69-71; consult, World Bank, 78. *Res:* Application of electronic technology to resource appraisal and management for purposes of exploitation and/or environmental protection. *Mailing Add:* PO Box 302 Dunnellon FL 34430

BERMES, EDWARD WILLIAM, JR, CLINICAL CHEMISTRY. *Current Pos:* clin instr, 59-65, from asst prof to assoc prof, 66-74, assoc dir, Clin Labs, 78-81, PROF BIOCHEM & PATH, STRITCH SCH MED, LOYOLA UNIV, CHICAGO, 74-, DIR CLIN CHEM, HOSP, 69-, ASSOC DIR, SCH MED TECHNOL, 70-, DIR, CLIN LABS, 81- *Personal Data:* b Chicago, Ill, Aug 20, 32; m 57; c 5. *Educ:* St Mary's Col, Minn, BS, 54; Loyola Univ Ill, MS, 56, PhD(biochem), 59. *Prof Exp:* Asst biochem, Loyola Univ, Ill, 54-56; chief biochemist, Hektoen Inst Med Res, Cook Co Hosp, Chicago, 58-60. *Concurrent Pos:* Chief biochemist, W Suburban Hosp, Chicago, 60-62; dir biochem, St Francis Hosp, 62-68; ed, Chicago Clin Chemist, 69- *Mem:* AAAS; Am Chem Soc; Am Asn Clin Chem (secy, 78-80); Am Asn Clin Path; Asn Clin Scientists; Sigma Xi. *Res:* Method development in clinical chemistry; test interference in clinical laboratory testing. *Mailing Add:* Dept Path Loyola Univ Med Ctr 2160 S First Ave Maywood IL 60153-5594

BERMON, STUART, SOLID STATE PHYSICS. *Current Pos:* RES STAFF MEM, IBM WATSON RES CTR, 78- *Personal Data:* b Philadelphia, Pa, Dec 2, 36; m 61; c 1. *Educ:* Univ Pa, BA, 58; Univ Ill, MS, 59, PhD(physics), 64. *Prof Exp:* Staff mem physics, Lincoln Lab, Mass Inst Technol, 64-66; asst prof eng, Brown Univ, 66-73; assoc prof physics, City Col New York, 73-78. *Mem:* Am Phys Soc. *Res:* Electron tunneling; superconductivity; properties of thin films; transport in amorphous semiconductors; cyclotron resonance in semiconductors and metals. *Mailing Add:* 7 Z Carpenter Ave Mt Kisco NY 10549

BERMUDEZ, VICTOR MANUEL, SOLID STATE SCIENCE. *Current Pos:* RES PHYSICIST, NAVAL RES LAB, 72- *Personal Data:* b New York, NY, Jan 24, 47. *Educ:* Mass Inst Technol, BS, 67; Princeton Univ, MA, 69, PhD(phys chem), 76. *Mem:* Sigma Xi; Am Phys Soc; Am Vacuum Soc. *Res:* Surface chemistry and surface physics of materials. *Mailing Add:* Code 6863 Naval Res Lab 4555 Overlook Ave SW Washington DC 20375

BERN, HOWARD ALAN, ENDOCRINOLOGY, TUMOR BIOLOGY. *Current Pos:* from instr to prof zool, 48-90, prof zool & res endocrinologist, 61-90, chair, Group Endocrinol, 62-90, RES ENDOCRINOLOGIST, CANCER RES LAB, UNIV CALIF, BERKELEY, 60-, EMER PROF INTEGRATIVE BIOL, 90- *Personal Data:* b Montreal, Que, Jan 30, 20; US citizen; m 46, Estelle Bruck; c Alan & Lauren. *Educ:* Univ Calif, Los Angeles, AB, 41, MA, 42, PhD(zool), 48. *Hon Degrees:* Dr, Univ Rouen, 92; LLD, Hokkaido Univ, 94. *Honors & Awards:* Nieuwland lectr, Univ Notre Dame, 72; Eli Lilly lectr, Endocrine Soc, 75; Geschwind Mem lectr, Univ Calif, Davis, 84; Cowper Distinguished vis lectr, State Univ NY, Buffalo, 84; Huang-Chan Mem lectr, Univ Hong Kong, 85; David Tyler Mem lectr, Univ SFla, 88; Scharrer-Bargmann lectr, Malaga, Spain, 89; Distinguished Serv Award, Soc Advan Chicanos & Native Ams in Sci, 90; C H Li Mem lectr, Nat Univ Taiwan, 91; Meites Lectr endocrin, Mich State Univ, 95; Award Excellence, Physiol Sect, Am Fisheries Soc, 96. *Prof Exp:* Nat Res Coun fel, 46-48. *Concurrent Pos:* Guggenheim fel, 51-52; NSF sr fel, 58-59, 65-66; fel, Ctr Adv Study Behav Sci, Stanford Univ, 60; res prof, Miller Inst Basic Res Sci, 61; vis prof, Bristol Univ, 65-66, Univ Kerala, Trivandrum, India, 67, Univ Tokyo, 71, 86, Univ PR, 73 & 74, Nat Mus Natural Hist, Paris, 81, Toho Univ, Funabashi, Japan, 82-84, 86-89, Watkins vis prof, Wichita State Univ, 84, James vis prof, Xavier Univ, Antigonish, NS, 86, Meiji Univ, 86, Univ Hawaii, 86, 91-93, Yokohama City Univ, Japan, 88 & 95, Univ Fla, 92, Univ Hokkaido, 92; mem, US Deleg to Indo-Am Scholars Conf, Delhi, 74; mem coun, Int Soc Neuroendocrinol, 77-80; Walker-Ames prof, Univ Wash, 77; mem, Adv Comt, NIH Eval Res Needs Endocrin Metab, 78-79; mem, Comt Basic Res, US-France Agreement Cancer Res, Nat Cancer Inst, 79-82; transatlantic lectr, British Soc Endocrinol, 80; distinguished vis, Univ Alta, 81; mem, Comt Int Human Res, Nat Res coun, 81-82, Comt Hormonally Active Agents Environ, 93-95; plenary lectr, Am Soc Zoologists, 84, Centennial plenary lectr, Boston, 89; mem Sloan Medal Selection Comt, Gen Motors Cancer Res Found, 84-85; fac res lectr, Univ Calif, Berkeley, 88; plenary lectr, Japan Zool Soc, 92, Ger Zool Soc, 94; res fel, Japan Soc Prom Sci, Toyama Univ, 93. *Mem:* Nat Acad Sci; Am Soc Zool (pres, 67); Am Physiol Soc; Am Asn Cancer Res; fel AAAS; foreign fel Indian Nat Sci Acad; Am Acad Arts & Sci; foreign fel Nat Acad Lincei Italy; Soc Integrated Comp Biol; Endocrine Soc. *Res:* Comparative endocrinology, especially of prolactin; perinatal hormonal carcinogenesis; hormones and normal and abnormal genital tract and mammary gland growth; neurosecretion and comparative neuroendocrinology; caudal neurosecretory system of fishes; endocrinology of salmon smoltification, hormones and early development of fish; cell culture of genital epithelia; hormonal control of fish growth and osmoregulation. *Mailing Add:* Dept Integrative Biol Univ Calif Berkeley CA 94720-3140. *Fax:* 510-643-6264; *E-Mail:* bern@garnet.berkeley.edu

BERNABEI, STEFANO, PLASMA PHYSICS. *Current Pos:* res assoc, 71-74, res staff mem, 74-85, PRIN RES PHYSICIST, PLASMA PHYSICS LAB, PRINCETON UNIV, 85- *Personal Data:* b San Martino in Rio, Italy, Feb 29, 44. *Educ:* Univ Milan, PhD(physics), 69. *Honors & Awards:* Award Plasma Physics Res, Am Phys Soc, 84. *Prof Exp:* Res asst physics, Univ Milan, 69-71. *Concurrent Pos:* Nat Coun Res Italy fel, Plasma Physics Lab, Princeton Univ, 70-71. *Mem:* Fel Am Phys Soc. *Res:* Plasma heating with radio frequency waves; particularly heating at the lower hybrid frequency in toroidal machines. *Mailing Add:* Plasma Physics Lab Forrestal Campus Princeton Univ PO Box 451 Princeton NJ 08544

BERNACKI, RALPH J, CANCER RESEARCH, CELL BIOLOGY. *Current Pos:* Cancer res scientist I-V, 72-93, CANCER RES VI, DEPT EXP THERAPEUT, ROSWELL PARK CANCER INST, 93- *Personal Data:* b Buffalo, NY, Oct 9, 46; m 69, Celeste Wojtkowski; c Rachelle & Gwen. *Educ:* Rensselear Polytech Inst, BS, 68; Univ Rochester, PhD(pharmacol), 72. *Concurrent Pos:* Prin investr, USPHS-Nat Cancer Inst Grants, 73-; res prof pharmacol, State Univ NY, Buffalo, 82-, dir, Pharmol Prog, Roswell Park Grad Div, 82-85; consult, Nat Cancer Inst-DCT, 85- & Am Cancer Soc, 90-; US Army Med Res & Mat Command DOD Breast Cancer Res Prog, 95. *Mem:* Am Asn Cancer Res; Am Soc Pharmacol & Exp Therapeut; NY Acad Sci; Sigma Xi; Metastasis Soc. *Res:* Design and development of new antitumor agents; tumor cell growth and metastasis; tumor cell surface glycoproteins as a target for chemotherapy. *Mailing Add:* Roswell Park Cancer Inst Buffalo NY 14263. *Fax:* 716-845-8857; *E-Mail:* bernacki@sc3103.med.buffalo.edu

BERNADY, KAREL FRANCIS, PHARMACEUTICAL CHEMISTRY. *Current Pos:* Res chemist org chem, Lederle Labs, Am Cyanamid Corp, 67-75, group leader, 75-81, mgr pharmaceut bulk mfg, 81-83, prod supt, 83-85, mgr chem prod, Lederle Labs, 85-86, PLANT MGR, BOUND BROOK PLANT, AM CYANAMID CO, 86- *Personal Data:* b Baltimore, Md, Feb 1, 41; m 64; c 2. *Educ:* Loyola Col, Md, BS, 63; Fordham Univ, PhD(org chem), 68. *Mem:* Am Chem Soc; NY Acad Sci; AAAS. *Res:* Chemistry of natural products; process research on pharmaceuticals and fine chemicals. *Mailing Add:* 2 St Anthony Lane Chester Springs PA 19425

BERNAL, IVAN, CHEMISTRY. *Current Pos:* assoc prof, 73-75, PROF CHEM, UNIV HOUSTON, 75- *Personal Data:* b Barranquilla, Colombia, Mar 28, 31; m 57, Constance Craytor; c Susan S. *Educ:* Clarkson Col, BS, 54; Univ Va, MS, 56; Columbia Univ, PhD(chem), 63. *Honors & Awards:* US Sr Scientist Award, Alexander von Humboldt Found, 75, 83 & 91; Am Chem Soc Award, 85. *Prof Exp:* Staff mem chem, RCA Labs, NJ, 56-59; Harvard Corp fel, 63-64; asst prof chem, State Univ NY Stony Brook, 64-67; chemist, Brookhaven Nat Lab, 67-73. *Concurrent Pos:* Vis fel, Australian Nat Univ, 80, 86 & 93; ed, Elsevier Series, Stereochem of Organometallic & Inorg Compounds; vis fel, Oriel Co, Oxford Univ, 91. *Mem:* Am Chem Soc; fel NY Acad Sci; Am Crystallog Asn. *Res:* Problems of valence states and of stereochemistry of transition metal ions; spectroscopic and x-ray crystallographic work; absolute configurations of organometallics having metals as chiral centers; structures and absolute configurations of organosulfur compounds, particularly those containing disulfide linkages; the molecular nature of the phenomenon of conglomerate crystallization. *Mailing Add:* Dept Chem Univ Houston Houston TX 77204-5641. *Fax:* 713-743-2709; *E-Mail:* ibernal@uh.edu

BERNAL G, ENRIQUE, OPTICAL PHYSICS, LASERS. *Current Pos:* DIR, CORP PROD DEVELOP, 95- *Personal Data:* b Barranquilla, Colombia, July 30, 38; US citizen; m 61; c 2. *Educ:* Col St Thomas, BS, 60; Univ Minn, MS, 63. *Prof Exp:* Res asst & res scientist, Honeywell Inc, 63-66, prin res scientist, 66-71, sr prin res scientist, 71-75, staff scientist, 75-76, prog mgr, 76, dept mgr, Electro-optics Dept, 77-80, assoc dir, 80-81, dir, Phys Sci Ctr, 81-85, dir eng, Electro-optics Div, 85-90; vpres CVD mat, Morton Int, 90-92; vpres res & develop, Intrasonix, 92. *Mem:* Inst Elec & Electronics Engrs; Optical Soc Am; Soc Photo-Optical & Instrument Engrs; Am Soc Testing & Mat. *Res:* Properties of transparent infrared materials and the effect of laser irradiation on optical properties; optical materials, interferometry and effects of laser irradiation of opaque solids. *Mailing Add:* 19 Wachusett View Dr Westborough MA 01581. *Fax:* 508-347-3849

BERNARD, BERNIE BOYD, ORGANIC GEOCHEMISTRY, EXPLORATION GEOCHEMISTRY. *Current Pos:* VPRES, RES & DEVELOP, O I CORP. *Personal Data:* b Bryan, Tex, Sept 1, 52; m 74; c 2. *Educ:* Abilene Christian Univ, BS, 74; Tex A&M Univ, PhD(oceanog), 78. *Prof Exp:* Asst prof geol, Univ Okla, 78-80. *Concurrent Pos:* Design consult, Oceanog Int Corp, 78- *Mem:* AAAS; Am Chem Soc; Am Geophys Union; Sigma Xi. *Res:* Stable carbon isotope geochemistry; organic diagenesis; geochemical hydrocarbon exploration; microbial methane generation. *Mailing Add:* 1200 Carmel Ct College Station TX 77845

BERNARD, DANE THOMAS, FOOD MICROBIOLOGY. *Current Pos:* microbiologist, 73-77, head microbiol, 77-84, dir, microbiol packaging & processing, 84-, VPRES, EASTERN RES, NAT FOOD PROCESSORS ASN. *Personal Data:* b Evansville, Ind, Dec 29, 48; m 78; c 2. *Educ:* Purdue Univ, BS, 70; Univ Md, MS, 79. *Prof Exp:* Specialist, food inspection, US Army, 70-73. *Mem:* Inst Food Technologists; Am Soc Microbiol; Int Asn Milk Food & Environ Sanitarians. *Res:* Food safety research, mostly dealing with Clostridium botulinum; heat resistance; growth characteristics in various classes of food products; effects of inhibitory substances on growth or toxin production; process establishment for thermally processed foods. *Mailing Add:* 8793 Cardinal Forest Circle Laurel MD 20723

BERNARD, DAVY LEE, NUCLEAR PHYSICS. *Current Pos:* assoc prof, 68-74, PROF PHYSICS, UNIV SOUTHWESTERN LA, 74- *Personal Data:* b Vermillion Parish, La, July 16, 36; m 60; c 3. *Educ:* Univ Southwestern La, BS, 58; Rice Univ, MA, 60, PhD(physics), 65. *Prof Exp:* Asst prof physics, Univ Va, 65-68. *Concurrent Pos:* Res Corp grant, 70; pres, La Acad Sci, 82-83. *Mem:* Am Phys Soc. *Res:* Atomic physics, especially energy loss and charge exchange of ions passing through matter; neutron physics, particularly measurement of neutron scattering cross sections. *Mailing Add:* 218 Sunny Lane Lafayette LA 70506-6339

BERNARD, DOUGLAS ALAN, COMPUTER SIMULATION, POLYMER PHYSICS. *Current Pos:* SR MEM TECH STAFF, TECHNOL MODELING ASSOCS, INC, SUNNYVALE, CALIF, 90- *Personal Data:* b Barrie, Ont, Feb 1, 53. *Educ:* Univ Sask, BSc, 75; Princeton Univ, PhD(physics), 80. *Prof Exp:* Mem res staff, Xerox Res Ctr Can, Xerox Corp, 80-83; sr mem tech staff, Philips Res Labs Sunnyvale, Signetics Corp, 83-90. *Concurrent Pos:* Instr, DeAnza Col, 89-95. *Mem:* Am Phys Soc. *Res:* Process simulation-microelectronics. *Mailing Add:* 5714 McKellar Dr San Jose CA 95129-4125

BERNARD, EDDIE NOLAN, TSUNAMIS. *Current Pos:* mem staff, Geophys Off, Nat Oceanic & Atmospheric Admin, 70-72, res oceanogr, Joint Tsunami Res Effort, 72-77, dir, Nat Tsunami Warning Ctr, 77-80, DIR, PAC MARINE ENVIRON LAB, NAT OCEANIC & ATMOSPHERIC ADMIN, 80- *Personal Data:* b Houston, Tex, Nov 23, 46; m 70; c 1. *Educ:* Lamar Univ, BS, 69; Tex A&M Univ, MS, 70, PhD(phys oceanog), 76. *Prof Exp:* Geophysicist, Pan Am Petrol Co, 69; res oceanogr, Tex A&M Univ, 69-70. *Concurrent Pos:* Dir, Nat Oceanog & Atmospheric Admin, Hydrothermal Vents Prog & Fisheries Oceanog Prog; mem exec comt, Coop Inst Marine Resource Studies, Ore State Univ; mem admin bd, Joint Inst Marine & Atmospheric Res, Univ Hawaii; mem, Panel Wind & Seismic Effects, US-Japan Coop Prog Natural Resources, 81-; mem, Int Recruitment Invests Subarctic Coun, 82-, sci coun, Joint Inst Marine Observation, Scripps Inst Oceanog, 92-, exec comt, Coop Inst Arctic Res, Univ Alaska; bd dirs, Pac Northwest Reg Marine Res Prog, 92- *Mem:* Am Geophys Union; Int Union Geodesy & Geophysics. *Res:* Science administration; tsuhami hazard reduction; contributed articles to professional journals. *Mailing Add:* Pac Marine Environ Lab Nat Oceanog & Atomspheric Admin 7600 Sand Pt Way NE Seattle WA 98115

BERNARD, ERNEST CHARLES, NEMATOLOGY, SOIL ZOOLOGY. *Current Pos:* From asst prof to assoc prof, 77-86, PROF NEMATOL, UNIV TENN, KNOXVILLE, 86- *Personal Data:* b Detroit, Mich, Aug 20, 50; m 74; c 2. *Educ:* Mich State Univ, BS, 72, MS, 74; Univ Ga, PhD(nematol), 77. *Mem:* Soc Nematologists; Am Micros Soc; Sigma Xi. *Res:* Population dynamics and pathogenicity of plant-parasitic nematodes; taxonomy and biology of protura. *Mailing Add:* 205 Plant Sci Bldg Univ Tenn Knoxville TN 37996-4500

BERNARD, GARY DALE, MANUFACTURING SIGNAL-PROCESSING, SENSOR RESEARCH & DEVELOPMENT. *Current Pos:* sr specialist engr, 89-92, OPERS TECHNOL, BOEING COM AIRPLANE GROUP, 89-, LEAD, ADVAN SENSORS LAB, 90-, SR PRIN ENGR, 92- *Personal Data:* b Everett, Wash, Feb 19, 38; m 64, Patricia Walsh; c Lucy, Joann, Susan & Paul. *Educ:* Univ Wash, BSEE, 59, MSEE, 60, PhD(elec eng), 64. *Prof Exp:* Actg instr, Dept Elec Eng, Univ Wash, 60-64; from instr to asst prof elec eng, Mass Inst Technol, 65-68; asst prof ophthal & vis sci, Sch Med, Yale Univ, 68-71, asst prof eng & appl sci, 68-71, assoc prof ophthal & visual sci & eng & appl sci, 71-76, assoc prof ophthal & visual sci, 71-79, sr res scientist, 79-89. *Concurrent Pos:* Ford Found fel, Mass Inst Technol, 65-66,; consult, USN Electronics Lab, 65, Lincoln Lab, 66-68 & Gen Tel & Electronics Corp, 81-86; NIH res career develop award, 71-75, prin investr grant, Nat Eye Inst, 73-86; vis prof, Dept Zool, Univ Zurich, 78, 83 & 89 & Dept Biophys, Univ, Groningen, 82; prin investr, Army Res Off, 86-88, NSF, 88-90 & Nat Geog Soc, 88. *Mem:* Inst Elec & Electronics Engrs. *Res:* Advanced sensor systems for control of aircraft fabrication and assembly processes; sensory information processing by photo-receptor arrays; physiology, photochemistry, and waveguide optics of insect photoreceptors; insect vision. *Mailing Add:* 30714 19th Ave S Federal Way WA 98003. *E-Mail:* gary.d.bernard@boeing.com

BERNARD, GEORGE W, ELECTRON MICROSCOPY, CELL-TISSUE CULTURE. *Current Pos:* PROF ANAT & ORAL BIOL, UNIV CALIF, LOS ANGELES, 67-, CHAIRPERSON ORAL BIOL, 92-, PROF NEUROBIOL, 95- *Personal Data:* b New York, NY, Aug 22, 25; m 86, Ellie Bragg; c Claudia & Nancy. *Educ:* Washington Univ, St Louis, DDS, 47; Univ Calif, Los Angeles, BS, 63, PhD(anat), 67. *Concurrent Pos:* Vis prof, Inst Sci Res on Cancer, France, 70-71, Cordeliers Inst Sch Med, Paris, 80-81; site vis mem, NIH, 72-, NSF, 83-; mem, Oral Med Study Sect, NIH, 77-80; consult, Vet Admin, Long Beach, 79-; NIH fel oral biol; dir, Fac Group Dent Prac, 71-80 & 88-94. *Mem:* Sigma Xi; fel AAAS; Am Asn Anatomists; Int Asn Dent Res; Electron Micros Soc Am; Am Soc Bone & Mineral Res. *Res:* Bone and bone marrow seeking elements of the calcification mechanism; the origin of various bone cells and osteogenic enhancing factors; substrates, carriers and cell interactions to heal bone defects. *Mailing Add:* Dept Neurobiol Sch Med Univ Calif Los Angeles CA 90024. *Fax:* 310-206-5539; *E-Mail:* georgeb@dent.ucla.edu

BERNARD, JOHN MILFORD, PLANT ECOLOGY. *Current Pos:* from asst prof to assoc prof, 64-72, chmn dept, 73-82, PROF BIOL, ITHACA COL, 72- *Personal Data:* b Duluth, Minn, May 22, 33; m 63, Florence Mensorio; c John, Charles & Bernard. *Educ:* Univ Minn, Duluth, BS, 58; Rutgers Univ, MS, 60, PhD(plant ecol), 63. *Prof Exp:* Tech asst biol, Rutgers Univ, 58-62; instr, Franklin & Marshall Col, 62-64. *Concurrent Pos:* Fel, Univ London, 84-85. *Mem:* Torrey Bot Club; Sigma Xi. *Res:* Structure and function of wetland ecosystems. *Mailing Add:* Dept Biol Ithaca Col Ithaca NY 14850-7000. *Fax:* 607-274-1131

BERNARD, JOHN WILFRID, CHEMICAL ENGINEERING, INSTRUMENTATION. *Current Pos:* PRES, BERNARD AUTOMAT CONSULT, 86- *Personal Data:* b Canton, Ohio, Jan 26, 28; m 51; c 3. *Educ:* Case Inst Technol, BS, 52, MS, 61. *Prof Exp:* Instr engr, Dow Chem Co, Midland, Mich, 52-60; systs engr, Indust Nucleonics, Midland, Mich & Ohio State Univ Systs Res Group, Columbus, Ohio, 60; res engr, Foxboro Co, 61-66, mgr syst technol & simulation, 66-70, mgr systs res, 70-71, dir corp res, 71-80, dir Europ technol, 81-85. *Concurrent Pos:* Found Instrumentation Educ & Res fel, 60-61; co-rep, Indust Res Inst, Inc, 71-85 & chmn rules comt, 77-79; treas, Am Automatic Control Coun, 74-80; mem, Am Automatic Control Coun Technol Comt, Automation Res Coun & NSF Indust Panel Sci & Technol. *Mem:* Instrument Soc Am; Nat Soc Prof Engrs; Sigma Xi; Soc Mech Engrs; Soc Mach Intel. *Res:* Systems research in the application of process management and control systems for fluid process industries. *Mailing Add:* 3520 Rocky Point Rd Springfield OH 45502

BERNARD, NICOLE F, IMMUNOLOGY. *Current Pos:* RES MGR IMMUNOL, MONTREAL GEN HOSP, 87- *Personal Data:* b Montreal, Que, May 3, 54. *Educ:* McGill Univ, BS, 76; Duke Univ, PhD(immunol), 82. *Prof Exp:* Fel, Univ NC, Chapel Hill, 82-84, Univ Toronto, 84-87. *Mem:* Am Can Soc Immunol; Can Asn Cancer; Am Asn Immunol. *Mailing Add:* Dept Med Montreal Gen Hosp Res Inst 1650 Cedar Ave Rm C10160 Montreal PQ H3G 1A4 Can

BERNARD, PETER SIMON, FLUID DYNAMICS, TURBULENCE. *Current Pos:* vis asst prof, Inst Phys Sci Technol, 77-79, from asst prof to assoc prof, 79-93, PROF MECH ENG, UNIV MD, 94- *Personal Data:* b New York, NY, Jan 14, 50; m 79; c 3. *Educ:* City Univ NY, BE, 72; Univ Calif, Berkeley, MS, 73, PhD(mech eng), 77. *Prof Exp:* Fel, Lawrence Berkeley Lab, 77. *Concurrent Pos:* Assoc prof, Univ Claude Bernard, Lyon, France, 86; vis prof, Dept Math, Univ Calif, Berkeley, 92-93. *Mem:* Soc Indust & Appl Math; Am Soc Mech Engrs; Am Phys Soc. *Res:* Methods of predicting the mean properties of turbulent flows; analysis of turbulent transport phenomena. *Mailing Add:* Dept Mech Eng Univ Md College Park MD 20742-0001. *E-Mail:* bernard@eng.umd.edu

BERNARD, RICHARD FERNAND, ZOOLOGY. *Current Pos:* assoc prof biol, 69-73, PROF BIOL, QUINNIPIAC COL, 73- *Personal Data:* b Lewiston, Maine, Aug 19, 34; m 59. *Educ:* Univ Maine, BA, 56; Mich State Univ, MS, 59, PhD(zool), 62. *Prof Exp:* Assoc prof zool, Wis State Univ, Superior, 62-69. *Concurrent Pos:* Bd Regents Instnl study grant, 63-64. *Mem:* Am Ornith Union; Am Soc Mammalogists; Nat Audubon Soc. *Res:* Effects of insecticides on wildlife. *Mailing Add:* Dept Biol Box 84 Quinnipiac Col 275 Mt Carmel Ave Hamden CT 06518

BERNARD, RICHARD LAWSON, PLANT BREEDING. *Current Pos:* res agronomist, 54-61, res geneticist, USDA, 61-88, EMER PROF, DEPT CROP SCI, UNIV ILL, URBANA-CHAMPAIGN, 89- *Personal Data:* b Detroit, Mich, Aug 12, 26; div; c Betty R(Marnell), Richard T, Alice J (Woodley) & Daniel L. *Educ:* Ohio State Univ, BS, 49, MS, 50; NC State Col, PhD(field crops), 60. *Honors & Awards:* Genetics & Plant Breeding Award, Nat Coun Com Plant Breeders, 78. *Prof Exp:* Res instr agron, NC State Col, 54. *Concurrent Pos:* Cur, USDA Soybean Germplasm Collection, 54-88. *Mem:* Fel Am Soc Agron; Am Genetic Asn; Crop Sci Soc Am; Sigma Xi. *Res:* Qualitative genetics, germplasm and breeding of soybeans. *Mailing Add:* Univ Ill Dept Crop Sci 1101 Peabody Urbana IL 61801

BERNARD, RICHARD RYERSON, mathematics; deceased, see previous edition for last biography

BERNARD, ROBERT SCALES, SOLID MECHANICS, FLUID MECHANICS. *Current Pos:* RES PHYSICIST MECH, US ARMY ENGR WATERWAYS EXP STA, 73- *Personal Data:* b Conway, SC, Mar 5, 46. *Educ:* Miss State Univ, BS(aero eng) & BS(appl physics), 69, PhD(gen eng), 81; Stanford Univ, MS, 71. *Prof Exp:* Tech staff mem mechanics, Sandia Labs, 69-73. *Mem:* Am Phys Soc. *Res:* Terradynamics; impact phenomena; computational fluid dynamics. *Mailing Add:* 3 Lakewood Lane Vicksburg MS 39180

BERNARD, RUDY ANDREW, NEUROPHYSIOLOGY, BEHAVIOR. *Current Pos:* assoc prof, 69-75, PROF PHYSIOL, MICH STATE UNIV, 75- *Personal Data:* b New York, NY, May 31, 30; m 60; c 3. *Educ:* Univ Montreal, BA, 53; Cornell Univ, MNS, 60, PhD(animal physiol), 62. *Prof Exp:* Asst nutrit, Cornell Univ, 58-60; fel neurophysiol, Univ Wis, 62-64; asst prof physiol, State Univ NY Downstate Med Ctr, 64-66 & Rockefeller Univ, 66-69. *Mem:* AAAS; Am Physiol Soc; Soc Neurosci. *Res:* Anatomy of central taste pathways; electrophysiology of peripheral and central taste mechanisms; behavioral studies of taste preferences; stress hormones, taste, salt intake and hypertension. *Mailing Add:* 111 Giltner Hall Mich State Univ East Lansing MI 48824-1101

BERNARD, SELDEN ROBERT, MATHEMATICAL BIOLOGY. *Current Pos:* res health physicist, 54-57, MEM RES STAFF, OAK RIDGE NAT LAB, 60- *Personal Data:* b Scobey, Mont, Nov 10, 25; c 3. *Educ:* Univ Denver, BS, 48; Univ Chicago, PhD(math biol), 60. *Prof Exp:* Asst chemist, Kaiser Aluminum & Chem Co, 49; fel radiol physics, Oak Ridge Nat Lab, 49-50; health physicist, Union Carbide Nuclear Co, 50-54. *Mem:* AAAS; Health Physics Soc. *Res:* Mathematical biology and health physics; mathematical studies of biological phenomena, especially blood-gas equilibria and compartmental models for metabolism of inorganic ions and molecules; estimation of radiation exposure to organs and tissues from internally contained radionuclides. *Mailing Add:* 109 Packer Rd Oak Ridge TN 37830

BERNARD, WALTER JOSEPH, PHYSICAL CHEMISTRY. *Current Pos:* Assoc dir eng, 64-68, dir res & develop, 68-71, SR SCIENTIST, SPRAGUE ELEC CO, 71- *Personal Data:* b Manchester, NH, Dec 25, 23; m 48; c 4. *Educ:* Univ NH, BS, 50, MS, 51; Mass Inst Technol, PhD(chem), 54. *Concurrent Pos:* Pvt consult, 87- *Mem:* Electrochem Soc; Am Chem Soc. *Res:* Inorganic fluorides; silicon chemistry; oxide films on metals; dielectrics. *Mailing Add:* 206 Bee Hill Rd Williamstown MA 01267

BERNARD, WILLIAM, PHYSICS. *Current Pos:* RETIRED. *Personal Data:* b Philadelphia, Pa, Dec 22, 27; m 53, Geraldine Cox; c William Jr, Julia & Edward. *Educ:* Univ Pa, AB, 49, MS, 53, PhD(physics), 59; George Wash Univ, MA, 88. *Prof Exp:* From sr scientist to prin scientist, Raytheon Res Div,

Waltham, Ma, 59-65; from sr scientist to chief, Advan Res Br, Electronic Components Lab, Electronics Res Ctr, NASA, 65-70; staff assoc, Mat Res Labs Sect, Div Mat Res, NSF, 72-78, sr staff assoc, Directorate Math & Phys Sci, 78-90, sr educ policy adv, directorate educ & human resources, 90-91, sr staff scientist, Div Mat Res, 91-93. *Concurrent Pos:* Actg dep asst dir, Math & Phys Sci, NSF, 80-81 & 82-83, sr policy adv, Assoc Nat Sci Bd, 87-89. *Res:* Condensed matter theory; irreversible thermodynamics; science and science education policy. *Mailing Add:* 8606 Hidden Hill Lane Potomac MD 20854

BERNARD, WILLIAM HICKMAN, physics, for more information see previous edition

BERNARDEZ, TERESA, PSYCHIATRY, PSYCHOANALYSIS. *Current Pos:* CONSULT, 89- *Personal Data:* b Buenos Aires, Arg, June 11, 31; US citizen; c Diego B. *Educ:* Liceo N 1 de Senoritas, Arg, BA, 48; Univ Arg, MD, 56; Am Bd Psychiat & Neurol, cert, 63. *Honors & Awards:* Peace Award, Pawlowski Found, 74. *Prof Exp:* Staff psychiatrist, C F Menninger Mem Hosp, 62-65, Menninger Found, 65-71; from asst prof to assoc prof, Mich State Univ, 71-79, prof, Dept Psychiat, 79-89. *Concurrent Pos:* Fel, Menninger Found, 60-62, Bunting Inst, Harvard Univ, 84-85; clin assoc, Tavistock Clin, London, 77-78; vis prof, Dept Psychol, Univ Bergen, Norway, 77-78; consult, NIMH, 81, Am Psychol Asn, 79; mem, Mich Psychoanal Coun; training analyst, Mich Psychoanal Coun, 89-; priv pract psychoanal, 89-96; scholar, Beatrice M Bain's Res Group, Univ Calif, Berkeley, 96-97. *Mem:* Fel Am Psychiat Asn; Am Orthopsychiat Asn; fel Am Acad Psychoanal. *Res:* Sex-role socialization of women and men and its impact on health; conflicts of contemporary women; gynecological disorders of women and their psychological import. *Mailing Add:* 78 El Camino Real Berkeley CA 94705. *Fax:* 510-643-7288; *E-Mail:* teber@uclink4.berkeley.edu

BERNARDIN, JOHN EMILE, PHYSICAL BIOCHEMISTRY. *Current Pos:* Chemist, 63-70, asst dir, 82-84, RES CHEMIST, WESTERN REGIONAL RES CTR, AGR RES SERV, USDA, 70-82, 84- *Personal Data:* b Santa Monica, Calif, Feb 28, 37; m 58; c 2. *Educ:* Univ Calif, Riverside, BA, 63; Univ Ore, PhD(phys biochem), 70. *Mem:* Int Soc Plant Molecular Biol; Am Asn Cereal Chemists. *Res:* Chromosomal nonhistone proteins. *Mailing Add:* 16 Greenbrae Ct El Sobrante CA 94803

BERNARDIN, LEO J, PAPER CHEMISTRY. *Current Pos:* RETIRED. *Personal Data:* b Lawrence, Mass, June 4, 30; m 56, Joan B Fischer; c 4. *Educ:* Tufts Univ, BS, 52; Inst Paper Chem, MS, 54, PhD(wood chem), 58. *Prof Exp:* Res scientist, Marathon Div, Am Can Co, 57-59; res scientist, Kimberly-Clark Corp, 59-66, sr res scientist, 66-73, res mgr, Res & Eng, 73-81, res assoc, 81-86, sr res fel, 86-92. *Mem:* Am Chem Soc. *Res:* Wood and cellulose chemistry; prehydrolysis of wood; hemicellulose chemistry; synthetic fiber paper; chemical modification of cellulose; absorbent product research and development. *Mailing Add:* 1012 E Lindbergh St Appleton WI 54911

BERNARDIS, LEE L, NEUROVISCERAL PHYSIOLOGY, NEUROENDOCRINOLOGY. *Current Pos:* RES PHYSIOLOGIST & DIR NEUROSCI, VET ADMIN MED CTR, BUFFALO, 78-, RES PROF MED, 80-, ASSOC RES CAREER SCIENTIST, DEPT VET AFFAIRS, 89- *Personal Data:* b Graz, Austria, Sept 18, 26; US citizen; m 58; c 1. *Educ:* Graz Univ, DrPhil, 49; Univ Western Ont, PhD(physiol, biochem), 61. *Prof Exp:* Res tech liver dis, Hosp for Sick Children, Toronto, Ont, 53-56; res mem meat processing & diet res, Can Packers, Ltd, 56-57; res asst physiol, Univ Western Ont, 57-61; res assoc exp path, State Univ NY Buffalo, 61-63, from res assoc prof to res prof surg, 63-80. *Concurrent Pos:* NIH, NSF, & VA grants, 68-; Proj & dir neuroendocrine-neurovisceral res unit, Dept Surg, State Univ NY Buffalo, 73-78, res prof med, 81. *Mem:* Am Asn Univ Prof; Fedn Am Scientists; Am Inst Nutrit; Int Brain Res Orgn; Int Soc Neuroendocrinol; Am Physiol Soc; Int Soc Psychoneuroendocrinol; Endocrine Soc; Can Physiol Soc. *Res:* Hypothalamic regulation of growth, endocrines and metabolism; regulation of body weight and fat; set point regulation; hypothalmic regulation of food intake. *Mailing Add:* Div Endocrinol Vet Admin Med Ctr 3495 Bailey Ave Buffalo NY 14215

BERNARDO, REX NOVERO, UTILIZATION OF MOLECULAR MARKERS IN APPLIED BREEDING, PREDICTION OF HYBRID PERFORMANCE. *Current Pos:* CORN RES SCIENTIST, LIMAGRAIN GENETICS 88- *Personal Data:* b Los Banos, Laguna, Philippines, Mar 22, 65; m 88, Maria C Legaspi; c Alyssa G, Jessica N, Michael R & Matthew R. *Educ:* Visayas State Col Agr; BS, 84; Univ Ill, PhD(agron), 88. *Prof Exp:* Inst plant breeding & genetics, Visayas State Col Agr, 83-85; res & teaching asst statist & genetics, Univ Ill, 85-88. *Mem:* Crop Sci Soc Am; Am Soc Agron. *Res:* Improving the efficiency of breeding methods for hybrid corn development; selection indices and methods for parent selecton in breeding program; prediction of hybrid performance using information from related hybrids. *Mailing Add:* 4805 W Old Church Rd Champaign IL 61821. *Fax:* 217-359-8976

BERNASCONI, CLAUDE FRANCOIS, PHYSICAL ORGANIC CHEMISTRY. *Current Pos:* from asst prof to assoc prof, 67-77, PROF CHEM, UNIV CALIF, SANTA CRUZ, 77- *Personal Data:* b Zurich, Switz, Feb 17, 39; m 63; c 3. *Educ:* Swiss Fed Inst Technol, dipl, 63, PhD(chem), 65. *Prof Exp:* Res asst chem, Swiss Fed Inst Technol, 65-66 & Max Planck Inst Phys Chem, 66-67. *Concurrent Pos:* Res grants, Petrol Res Fund, 69-71, 72-74, 75-77, 86-88, 89-90 & 93-, Res Corp, 70, Alfred P Sloan Found, 71-73 & NSF, 71- *Mem:* Fel AAAS; Am Chem Soc; Chem Soc. *Res:* Mechanisms of nucleophilic aromatic and vinylic substitution reactions; acid-base catalysis; fast reaction kinetics; proton transfer; nucleophilic addition to olefins; physical organic chemistry of transition metal carbene complexes; ab initio calculations. *Mailing Add:* Dept Chem Univ Calif Santa Cruz CA 95064. *Fax:* 408-459-2935; *E-Mail:* bernasconi@chemistry.ucsc.edu

BERNASEK, STEVEN LYNN, SURFACE CHEMICAL PHYSICS. *Current Pos:* From asst prof to assoc prof, 75-86, PROF CHEM, PRINCETON UNIV, 86- *Personal Data:* b Holton, Kans, Dec 14, 49; m 71, Sandra Taylor; c Lisa M & Eric D. *Educ:* Kans State Univ, BS, 71; Univ Calif, Berkeley, PhD(phys chem), 75. *Honors & Awards:* Exxon Solid State Chem Prize, Am Chem Soc, 81; Alexander von Humboldt Award, 86. *Concurrent Pos:* Vis scientist, Chem Div, NSF, 91-92. *Mem:* Am Chem Soc; fel AAAS; Am Vacuum Soc; Am Phys Soc. *Res:* Gas-solid interactions; dynamics of reactions occurring on well characterized transition metal and transition metal compound surfaces. *Mailing Add:* Dept Chem Princeton Univ Princeton NJ 08544. *Fax:* 609-258-1593; *E-Mail:* sberna@pucc.princeton.edu

BERNATH, L(OUIS), CHEMICAL ENGINEERING. *Current Pos:* RETIRED. *Personal Data:* b New York, NY, Dec 31, 21; m 44; c 3. *Educ:* City Col New York, BChE, 43; Univ Del, PhD(chem eng), 50. *Prof Exp:* Asst, City Col New York, 42-43; develop engr, Schenley Res Inst, Inc, 43-45; staff engr, Schenley Labs, Inc, 46-47; Off Naval Res fel, Proj Squid, Univ Del, 47-50; sr engr, E I du Pont de Nemours & Co, Inc, 50-61; chief proj engr, Atomics Int, NAm Aviation, Inc, 61-66, tech adv, 66-69, proj mgr, NAm Rockwell Corp, 69-73; mgr breeder reactor design, Gen Atomic, 73-74; chief nuclear eng, San Diego Gas & Elec, 85-86, mgr generation eng & res & develop, 78-82, mgr nuclear, 82-85, prin scientist energy technols, 85-86. *Mem:* Am Inst Chem Engrs; Am Soc Mech Engrs; Am Nuclear Soc; Nat Soc Prof Engrs; Sigma Xi; fel Inst Advan Eng. *Res:* Boiling heat transfer; reactor technology; energy technology. *Mailing Add:* San Diego Gas & Elec 8043 Hemingway Ave San Diego CA 92120-1715

BERNATH, PETER FRANCIS, PHYSICAL CHEMISTRY, MOLECULAR ASTRONOMY. *Current Pos:* PROF CHEM, UNIV WATERLOO, 91- *Personal Data:* b Ottawa, Can, Dec 7, 53; m 78, Robin Franklin; c Elizabeth & Victoria. *Educ:* Univ Waterloo, BS, 76; Mass Inst Technol, PhD(chem), 80. *Prof Exp:* Res assoc, Herzberg Inst Astrophysics, Nat Res Coun Can, 80-82; from asst prof to assoc prof chem, Univ Ariz, 82-90. *Concurrent Pos:* Sr res scientist, Dept Chem, Univ Ariz, 92- *Mem:* Am Phys Soc; Am Chem Soc; Optical Soc Am. *Res:* Laser and Fourier transform spectroscopy of transient molecules such as free radicals, ions and high temperature molecules; infrared and microwave molecular astronomy. *Mailing Add:* Dept Chem Univ Waterloo Waterloo ON N2L 3G1 Can. *Fax:* 519-746-0435; *E-Mail:* bernath@watsci.uwaterloo.ca

BERNATH, TIBOR, ENVIRONMENT & TOXICOLOGY. *Current Pos:* CONSULT, 86- *Personal Data:* b Bucharest, Romania, Feb 26, 34; US citizen; m 79; c 1. *Educ:* Hebrew Univ, BSc, 63, MSc, 65; Univ Paris, France, DSc, 70; Harvard Sch Pub Health, Boston, MSc, 80. *Prof Exp:* Res assoc, Dept Chem, Ind Univ, Bloomington, 70-71; sr res assoc, Brandeis Univ, 71-75; sr lectr environ sci, Ctr Occup Health, Tel Aviv Univ, Israel, 75-77; res assoc, Harvard Sch Pub Health, Boston, 77-79; sr indust hygienist petrochem, Med Dept, Exxon Corp, NJ, 79-85. *Concurrent Pos:* Mem staff, Develop Toxicol Sect, Smith-Kline Leary Lab, Boston, 72; consult environ health serv, ABT Assoc, Cambridge, 77; lectr, Harvard Col, Cambridge, 78; consult prog toxicol, Mass Col Pharm, Boston, 78. *Mem:* Am Chem Soc; Am Bd Indust Hyg; Brit Occup Health Soc; Europ Soc Toxicol; Am Soc Toxicol. *Res:* Aerometric (aerosols and vapors) and biological methods development in environmental health; health hazard assessments; risk assessments. *Mailing Add:* 1560 N Sandburg Terr Chicago IL 60610-0696

BERNAU, SIMON J, MATHEMATICS. *Current Pos:* DEAN, COL SCI & PROF MATH, CALIF STATE POLYTECHNIC UNIV, POMONA, 95- *Personal Data:* b Wanganui, NZ, June 12, 37; m 59; c 2. *Educ:* Univ Canterbury, BSc, 58, MS, 59; Cambridge Univ, BA, 61, PhD(math), 64. *Prof Exp:* Lectr math, Univ Canterbury, 64-65, sr lectr, 65-66; prof, Univ Otago, NZ, 66-69; prof math, Univ Tex, Austin, 69-85; prof & head dept, Southwest Mo State Univ, Springfield, 86-88; prof & chair dept, Univ Tex, El Paso, 88-95. *Mem:* Am Math Soc; Math Asn Am. *Res:* Lattice ordered algebraic systems; operator theory; functional analysis. *Mailing Add:* Col Sci Calif State Polytechnic Univ, 3801 W Temple Ave Pomona CA 91768. *E-Mail:* simon@math.ep.utexas.edu

BERNAUER, EDMUND MICHAEL, EXERCISE PHYSIOLOGY. *Current Pos:* PROF EXERCISE SCI, UNIV CALIF, DAVIS, 62-, CHAIR DEPT EXERCISE SCI. *Personal Data:* b Chicago, Ill, Sept 27, 26. *Educ:* Ind Univ, BS, 50; Univ Ill, MS, 51 & 59, PhD(physiol), 62. *Concurrent Pos:* Adj prof phys med & rehab, Sch Med, Univ Calif, Davis. *Mem:* Am Col Sports Med; Am Physiol Soc; NY Acad Sci. *Mailing Add:* Dept Exercise Sci Univ Calif Davis CA 95616-5224

BERNAYS, ELIZABETH ANNA, PHYSIOLOGICAL BASIS OF BEHAVIOR, PHYSIOLOGICAL ECOLOGY. *Current Pos:* PROF ENTOM & PROF ECOL & EVOLUTIONARY BIOL & HEAD DEPT ENTOM, UNIV ARIZ, 89- *Personal Data:* b Chihchilla, Queensland, Australia, Dec 31, 40; Brit citizen; m 83. *Educ:* Univ Queensland, BSc, 62; Univ London, MSc, 67, PhD(entom), 70. *Honors & Awards:* Gold Medal, Pontifical Acad Sci, 86. *Prof Exp:* From sr scientist to prin scientist, Ctr Overseas Pest Res, UK, 70-83; prof entom, Univ Calif, Berkeley, 83-90, prof zool, 86-89. *Concurrent Pos:* Ed, Exp & Appl Entom, 78-, CRC Series Plant-Insect Interactions, 87- *Mem:* Int Soc Chem Ecol; Am Soc Zoologists; Entom Soc Am. *Res:* Physiological basis of behavior and ecology of plant-feeding insects; evolutionary and adaptive relationships of plants and insects. *Mailing Add:* Dept Entom Univ Ariz Tucson AZ 85721

BERNAYS, PETER MICHAEL, PHYSICAL INORGANIC CHEMISTRY, INFORMATION SCIENCE. *Current Pos:* RETIRED. *Personal Data:* b New York, NY, July 19, 18; m 47, Marie Rasmusson; c Lynda, Michael & Sally. *Educ:* Mass Inst Technol, BS, 39; Univ Ill, MS, 40, PhD(analytical chem), 42. *Prof Exp:* From instr to asst prof chem, Ill Inst Technol, 46-50; assoc prof, Southwestern La Inst, 50-54; asst ed, Chem Abstr, 54-57, assoc ed, 58, head assignment dept, 59-61, asst to dir res & develop, 61-65, personnel asst, 65-66, sr assoc ed, 66-69, sr ed, 69-71, asst mgr, Phys, Analytic & Inorg Dept, 71-88. *Concurrent Pos:* Res Corp Cotrell grant, 48-50. *Mem:* AAAS; Am Chem Soc. *Res:* X-ray diffraction; inorganic compounds; chemistry of scandium; structural properties of lime; chemical documentation. *Mailing Add:* 2391 Eastcleft Dr Columbus OH 43221-1851

BERNDT, BRUCE CARL, MATHEMATICS. *Current Pos:* from asst prof to assoc prof, 67-75, PROF MATH, UNIV ILL, URBANA-CHAMPAIGN, 75- *Personal Data:* b St Joseph, Mich, Mar 13, 39; m 63, Helen; c Kristin, Sonja & Brooks. *Educ:* Albion Col, AB, 61; Univ Wis-Madison, MS, 63, PhD(math), 66. *Honors & Awards:* Allendorfer Award, 79; Ford Award, 89. *Prof Exp:* Asst lectr math, Glasgow Univ, 66-67. *Concurrent Pos:* Mem, Inst Advan Study, Princeton, NJ, 73-74. *Mem:* Am Math Soc; Math Asn Am. *Res:* Analytic number theory; classical analysis; Ramanujan's notebooks. *Mailing Add:* Dept Math Univ Ill 1409 W Green St Urbana IL 61801-2917. *E-Mail:* berndt@math.uiuc.edu

BERNDT, CHRISTOPHER CHARLES, SURFACE COATINGS & PROTECTION, THERMAL SPRAY TECHNOLOGY. *Current Pos:* assoc prof, 90-93, PROF MAT SCI, STATE UNIV NY, STONY BROOK, 94- *Personal Data:* b Adelaide, Australia. *Educ:* Univ S Australia, BS, 77; Monash Univ, PhD(mat ing), 80. *Honors & Awards:* DuPont Award, 94. *Prof Exp:* Res fel, State Univ Ny, Stony Brook, 80-83; Sr res fel, NASA, Lewis Res Ctr, 83-85; lectr-sr lectr, Monash Univ, 85-90. *Concurrent Pos:* Ed, J Thermal Spray Technol, 90-; res collabr, Brookhaven Nat Lab, 91-; mem, Exec Comt, Thermal Spray Soc. *Mem:* Am Ceramic Soc; Nat Inst Ceramic Eng; Inst Mat UK; Am Soc Metals; Am Soc Testing & Mat; Australian Ceramic Soc; Australian Inst Engrs. *Res:* Thermal spray coatings, in particular examining crack mechanisms and structure property relationships. *Mailing Add:* Dept Mat Sci State Univ NY 100 Nicholls Rd Stony Brook NY 11794-0001. *Fax:* 516-632-8052

BERNDT, DONALD CARL, PHYSICAL ORGANIC CHEMISTRY. *Current Pos:* from asst prof to assoc prof, 62-74, PROF CHEM, WESTERN MICH UNIV, 74- *Personal Data:* b Toledo, Ohio, Apr 11, 35; m 60; c 2. *Educ:* Ohio State Univ, BSc, 57, PhD(org chem), 61. *Prof Exp:* NSF fel org chem, Ohio State Univ, 62. *Mem:* Am Chem Soc. *Res:* Elucidation of reaction mechanisms in organic chemistry, including the study of medium, catalytic, micellar and structural influences. *Mailing Add:* 5248 Green Meadow Kalamazoo MI 49009

BERNDT, NORBERT, PEDIATRICS. *Current Pos:* ASST PROF PEDIAT, CHILDRENS HOSP LOS ANGELES, 89- *Personal Data:* b Dusseldorf, Ger, Dec 22, 53; m, Ingrid Bahner. *Educ:* Heinrich Heine Univ Dusseldorf, dipl biol, 81, MS, 82, PhD(biochem), 86. *Prof Exp:* Res asst, Univ Dundee, 86-89. *Concurrent Pos:* Prin investr, NIH, 89-90. *Mem:* Biochem Soc London. *Res:* Hormonal regulation of cellular activity and protein phosphorylation; diabetes research, insulin action; regulation of gene expression; control of cell growth and oncogenes; growth factor/receptor interactions and protein tyrosine kinases and phosphatases; site directed muta genesis-protein design; author of 7 publications. *Mailing Add:* Children's Hosp Los Angeles 4650 Sunset Blvd Los Angeles CA 90027-6089

BERNDT, WILLIAM O, RENAL TOXICOLOGY & PHARMACOLOGY, GENERAL TOXICOLOGY. *Current Pos:* interim chancellor, Univ Nebr Med Ctr, 91-92, prof pharmacol & Dean Grad Studies & Res, 82-96, vchancellor acad affairs, 85-96, CHANCELLOR, UNIV NEBR MED CTR, 96- *Personal Data:* b St Joseph, Mo, May 33; m 54, Bonnie Lampe; c Barbara, Carol, David, Mary & Paul. *Educ:* Creighton Univ, BS, 54; State Univ NY, Buffalo, PhD(pharmacol), 59. *Prof Exp:* Fel pharmacol, Sch Med, Univ Buffalo, 59; from instr to prof, Dartmouth Med Sch, 59-74; prof pharmacol & toxicol & chmn dept, Med Ctr, Univ Miss, 74-82. *Concurrent Pos:* Estab investr, Am Heart Asn, 64-69; consult, US Environ Protection Agency, Miss State Univ Epilemiol Studies, 78-81; mem, Pharmacol Study Sect, NIH, 80-84; mem, Adv Panel Electrolytes, large vol parenterals & renal drugs, US Pharmacopeial Conv, 80-85 & Cosmetic Ingredient Rev Expert Panel, Cosmetic Toiletry & Fragrance Asn, 83-86, chmn, 86-91; bd sci counrs, DHHS Agency for Toxic Substance & Dis, 88-91; mem, Am Bd Toxicol, 88-92, pres, 92; Secy, Sect Toxicol 90-; mem Subcomt Biol Markers Urinary Toxicol, Nat Res Coun, 91-94; bd publ trustees, Am Soc Pharmacol & Exp Therapeut, 93- *Mem:* Am Chem Soc; Soc Toxicol; Am Soc Pharmacol & Exp Therapeut; Am Soc Nephrol; AAAS; fel Am Acad Toxicol Sci. *Res:* Electrolyte and organic acid transport; renal physiology, pharmacology and toxicology; metabolic aspects of transport processes; diffusion processes; nephrotoxicity studies; effects of mycotoxins; teratogenicity studies. *Mailing Add:* Univ Nebr Med Ctr 600 S 42nd St Omaha NE 68198-6605

BERNDTSON, WILLIAM EVERETT, REPRODUCTIVE PHYSIOLOGY. *Current Pos:* res assoc, 72-75, asst prof reproduction, 76-80, PROF REPRODUCTION, COLO STATE UNIV, 84- *Personal Data:* b Middletown, Conn, Oct 1, 44; m 69; c 3. *Educ:* Univ Conn, BS, 66; Cornell Univ, PhD(reprod physiol), 71. *Prof Exp:* Trainee reproduction, Okla State Univ, 71-72. *Mem:* Soc Study Reproduction; Am Soc Animal Sci; Sigma Xi. *Res:* Cryopreservation of mammalian spermatozoa for artificial insemination; influence of hormones, drugs and exteroceptive stimuli on quantitative aspects of spermatogenesis. *Mailing Add:* Kendall Hall Univ NH Durham NH 03824

BERNE, BERNARD H, IMMUNOLOGY, RHEUMATOLOGY. *Current Pos:* MICROBIOLOGIST & MED OFFICER (REVIEWER), OFF DEVICE EVAL, CTR DEVICES & RADIOL HEALTH, FOOD & DRUG ADMIN, SILVER SPRING, MD, 87- *Personal Data:* b New York, NY, Sept 26, 38. *Educ:* Johns Hopkins Univ, AB, 60; NY Univ Sch Med, MD, 64; Univ Ill, PhD(immunol & microbiol), 72. *Prof Exp:* Intern surg, NY Hosp, Cornell Med Ctr, 64-65; fel, Mayo Grad Sch Med, Univ Minn, 65-66; sr asst surg resident, Univ Chicago Hosp & Clin, 66-67; NIH trainee microbiol & immunol, Univ Ill Med Ctr, 67-68, Schweppe Found fel, 68-71; asst prof path, Med Sci Prog, Ind Univ, 71-74; prin investr immunol, Meloy Labs, Inc, Springfield, Va, 74-75; res med officer immunol & rheumatol, Rheumatol Serv, Walter Reed Army Med Ctr, Washington, DC, 76-84, microbiologist & immunologist, Allergy & Immunol Serv, 84-87. *Mem:* Am Asn Immunologists; Fedn Am Soc Exp Biol. *Res:* Immunochemistry and genetics of rabbit allotypes; immunological relationships of serum macroglobulins; radioimmunoassay and immunodiffusion techniques; characterization and clinical significance of pregnancy proteins; autoimmunity; immune complex assays; anti-DNA antibodies; rheumatology; collagen. *Mailing Add:* Div Gen & Restorative Devices Off Device Eval CDRH FDA HFZ-410 9200 Corporate Blvd Rm 350 Rockville MD 20850-3229

BERNE, BRUCE J, STATISTICAL MECHANICS, COMPUTER SIMULATION. *Current Pos:* mem chem fac, 66-69, assoc prof chem, 69-72, PROF CHEM, COLUMBIA UNIV, 72- *Personal Data:* b New York, NY, Mar 8, 40; m 61. *Educ:* Brooklyn Col, BS, 61; Univ Chicago, PhD(chem physics), 64. *Honors & Awards:* Sackler Distinguished Lectr, Univ Tel Aviv; Von Humboldt Sr Scientist Award. *Prof Exp:* NATO fel, 66. *Concurrent Pos:* Alfred P Sloan Found fel, 67-70; Guggenheim fel, 71-72; chmn, adv panel, Div Chem, NSF; vis prof, Univ Tel Aviv, 72-73 & 78-80; mem, Policy Bd, Nat Resource Comput Chem, Lawrence Berkeley Lab, 80-82; comt Chem Sci, NAS-NRC, 76-78; chmn, Subdiv of Theoret Chem of Am Chem Soc, 88-89; Miller res prof, Univ Calif, Berkeley, 94. *Mem:* Fel Am Phys Soc; AAAS; Am Chem Soc. *Res:* Equilibrium and non-equilibrium statistical mechanics, structure and dynamics of the condensed phases of matter, computer simulation of chemical and biophysical properties; new algorithms in computational chemistry; theoretical chemistry. *Mailing Add:* Dept Chem Havermeyer Hall Columbia Univ PO Box 755 New York NY 10027

BERNE, ROBERT MATTHEW, MEDICAL PHYSIOLOGY, CARDIOVASCULAR PHYSIOLOGY. *Current Pos:* Charles Slaughter prof & chmn dept, 66-88, alumni prof, 88-94, EMER PROF PHYSIOL, UNIV VA MED CTR, 94- *Personal Data:* b Yonkers, NY, Apr 22, 18; m 44, Beth Goldberg; c Julie (Speasmaker) Amy (Kaminshine), Gordon & Michael. *Educ:* Univ NC, AB, 39; Harvard Med Sch, MD, 43. *Hon Degrees:* DSc, Med Col Ohio, 73. *Honors & Awards:* Carl J Wiggers Award, Am Physiol Soc, 75, Ray G Daggs Award, 90, Berne Lectr, 94; Res Achievement Award & Award of Merit, Am Heart Asn, 79, Gold Heart Award, 85; Jacobi Medallion Award, Nat Acad Sci, 86. *Prof Exp:* From asst prof to prof physiol, Case Western Res Univ, 52-66, asst prof med, 57-66. *Concurrent Pos:* Ed, Circulation Res, 70-75; mem panel, Heart & Blood Vessel Dis Task Force, Nat Heart & Lung Inst, 72-, mem proj comt, Heart & Lung Prog, 75-77; mem panel, Heart & Vascular Dis Nat Res & Demonstration Rev Comt, NIH, 73-74; mem, Selection Comt, Ciba Found Award Hypertension, 75-77; mem, Med Adv Bd, Coun High Blood Pressure Res, Am Heart Asn, 76-80, Coun Subcomt Pub Policy, 77-78; chmn-elect, Coun Acad Socs, Am Asn Med Cols, 76-77 & 77-78; mem, Sci Adv Bd, Alfred I Dupont Inst, 78-82, bd dir, Am Heart Asn, 79-80 & 83-85, Pub Comt, 81-85, bd, Nat Med Exam Study Comt, 83-84, Inst Med Mem Comt, 84-85, bd, Inst Med Mem Comt, 84-85, bd, Inst Med Health Sci Policy, 84-85, Award Comt, Lita A Hazen Awards, 84- & Nat Adv Coun, Pew Scholars Prog, 84-89; chmn, Long Range Planning Comt, Am Physiol Soc, 80-84; ed, Ann Rev Physiol, 82-88, field ed, Pflugers Arch, 81-84; pres, Va Affil, Am Heart Asn, 86. *Mem:* Inst Med-Nat Acad Sci; Am Physiol Soc (pres, 72-73); Asn Chmn Depts Physiol (pres, 70-71); Am Soc Clin Invest; Am Heart Asn; fel AAAS; hon fel Am Col Cardiol. *Res:* Cardiovascular physiology, particularly the chemical factors involved in the local regulation of organ blood flow. *Mailing Add:* Dept Physiol MR4-Rm 6032 Univ Va Med Ctr 300 Park Pl Charlottesville VA 22908. *Fax:* 804-982-1631; *E-Mail:* rmb9a@virginia.edu

BERNECKER, RICHARD RUDOLPH, PHYSICAL CHEMISTRY. *Current Pos:* SR SCIENTIST, ENERGETIC MAT DIV, NAVAL SURFACE WARFARE CTR, WHITE OAK LAB, MD, 69- *Personal Data:* b Allentown, Pa, Feb 23, 36; m 59; c 4. *Educ:* Muhlenberg Col, BS, 57; Cornell Univ, PhD(phys chem), 62. *Prof Exp:* Res chemist, Standard Oil, Ind, 61-64, Los Alamos Sci Lab, Univ Calif, 64-69. *Mem:* Combustion Inst; Am Phys Soc; Am Chem Soc; Sigma Xi. *Res:* Sensitivity and detonability of explosives and propellants; mechanism of transition from deflagration to detonation in explosives and propellants. *Mailing Add:* 204 Pewter Lane Silver Spring MD 20905

BERNER, LEO DEWITTE, JR, BIOLOGICAL OCEANOGRAPHY. *Current Pos:* res scientist, 65-66, from assoc prof to prof, 66-87, from asst dean to assoc dean, 67-84, DEAN GRAD COL, TEX A&M UNIV, 84-, EMER PROF OCEANOG, 87- *Personal Data:* b Pasadena, Calif, Feb 11, 22; m 47; c 2. *Educ:* Pomona Col, BA, 43; Scripps Inst Oceanog, Univ Calif, MS, 52; Univ Calif, PhD(oceanog), 57. *Prof Exp:* Asst, Pomona Col, 48-49; res biologist, Scripps Inst Oceanog, Univ Calif, 52-56, jr res biologist, 58-61; fisheries res biologist, US Fish & Wildlife Serv, 57-58; assoc prog dir div sci personnel & educ, NSF, 61-65. *Concurrent Pos:* Biologist, US Navy Oper Wigwam, 55. *Mem:* Fel AAAS; Am Soc Limnol & Oceanog; Sigma Xi. *Res:* Plankton zeography and ecology; pelagic tunicates; taxonomy of tunicata. *Mailing Add:* 1108 Neal Pickett Dr College Station TX 77840

BERNER, LEWIS, ZOOLOGY. *Current Pos:* From asst prof to assoc prof biol, 46-54, actg dir div biol sci, 70-73, dir, 73-75, head biol sci, 59-75, PROF BIOL, UNIV FLA, 54- *Personal Data:* b Savannah, Ga, Sept 30, 15; m 45; c 2. *Educ:* Univ Fla, BS, 37, MS, 39, PhD(zool), 41. *Concurrent Pos:* NIH grant, 53-60; consult entomologist, Gold Coast, Brit WAfrica, 50 & Nyasaland, Brit Cent Africa, 52; ed, Fla Entomologist, 50-63; prof entom, Lake Itasca Biol Sta, Univ Minn, 58-62, 68-69, 73, 75 & 77; USPHS grant, 63-66. *Mem:* Fel Entom Soc; Sigma Xi. *Res:* Ecology and taxonomy of Ephemeroptera; biology; parasitology; mayflies of Southeast. *Mailing Add:* 7081 NW 23rd Ave Gainesville FL 32606

BERNER, ROBERT A, SEDIMENTARY GEOCHEMISTRY. *Current Pos:* from assoc prof to prof, 65-87, ALAN M BATEMAN PROF GEOL & GEOPHYS, YALE UNIV, 87- *Personal Data:* b Erie, Pa, Nov 25, 35; m 59; c John M, Susan E & James C. *Educ:* Univ Mich, BS, 57, MS, 58; Harvard Univ, PhD(geol), 62. *Hon Degrees:* Dr, Univ Aix-Marseille III, France, 91. *Honors & Awards:* Award, Mineral Soc Am, 71. *Prof Exp:* Sverdup fel oceanog, Scripps Inst, 62-63; from asst prof to assoc prof geophys sci, Univ Chicago, 63-65. *Concurrent Pos:* Alfred P Sloan Found fel phys sci, 68-72; assoc ed, Am J Sci, 68-80, 90-, ed, 80-90; Guggenheim Found fel, Swiss Fed Inst Technol, 72; mem, US Nat Comt Geochem, 78-81; NATO vis scientist, Univ Paris, 81 & 84; distinguished vis scientist, State Univ NY, Stony Brook, 85, Nat Ctr, Atmospheric Res, 87, Univ Ctr Ga, 90, Univ NC, 93, Univ Hawaii, 94; chmn, Gordon Conf Chem Oceanog, 86, Nat Res Coun Panel Geochem Cycles, Nat Acad Sci, 88-90; mem, Adv Comt, Earth Sci, NSF, 90-93, Nat Res Coun Comm, Oceanic Carbon, 92-, Ocean Studies Bd, 94- *Mem:* Nat Acad Sci; Geochem Soc (vpres, 82, pres, 83); fel Mineral Soc Am; fel Geol Soc Am; Sigma Xi; fel Am Acad Arts Sci. *Res:* Kinetics of geochemical processes, chemical diagenesis and weathering; biogeochemistry; computer modeling of geochemical cycles; evolution of atmospheric and oceanic composition. *Mailing Add:* Dept Geol & Geophys Yale Univ New Haven CT 06511

BERNERS, EDGAR DAVIS, ACCELERATOR PHYSICS. *Current Pos:* from asst fac fel to fac fel, 67-94, EMER FAC FEL, UNIV NOTRE DAME, 94- *Personal Data:* b Milwaukee, Wis, Aug 22, 27; m 60, Joan McHale; c John, Ann, Catherine & David. *Educ:* Col Holy Cross, BS, 49; Univ Wis, PhD(physics), 57. *Prof Exp:* From instr to asst prof physics, Marquette Univ, 57-67. *Res:* Electrostatic accelerators. *Mailing Add:* Dept Physics Univ Notre Dame Notre Dame IN 46556. *E-Mail:* eberners@nd.edu

BERNETTI, RAFFAELE, ORGANIC CHEMISTRY, ANALYTICAL CHEMISTRY. *Current Pos:* DIR, ANAL & QUAL SUPPORT, CORN PROD TECH CTR, CPC INT, 87- *Personal Data:* b Florence, Italy, Aug 24, 32; m 60, Paola Cioni; c 4. *Educ:* Univ Pisa, MS, 55; Univ Pa, PhD(org chem), 59; Univ Chicago, MBA, 70. *Prof Exp:* Lab dir, Milan Lab, CPC Int, 60-65, sect head org chem, Moffett Tech Ctr, Argo, 65-67, asst dir prod methodology, 67-72, dir com develop, Corp Hq, Englewood Cliffs, NJ, 72-74, dir res & develop, Anal Dept, Moffet Tech Ctr, CPC Int, 75-87. *Concurrent Pos:* Instr, DePaul Univ, 70-72; chmn & ed chief, J Int Asn Off Analytical Chemists, 87-89. *Mem:* Am Chem Soc; Am Asn Cereal Chemists; fel Int Asn Off Analytical Chemists. *Res:* Heterocyclic chemistry; carbohydrate chemistry; starch and dextrose production; dextrose, levulose sweeteners; analytical methods for carbohydrate and food products; project management; agricultural food chemistry. *Mailing Add:* 234 W Grant Village Hinsdale IL 60521-4985. *Fax:* 708-563-6728

BERNEY, CHARLES V, NEUTRON SCATTERING, MOLECULAR SPECTROSCOPY. *Current Pos:* sr res assoc, Nuclear Eng Dept, 73-80, SR RES ASSOC, CHEM ENG DEPT, MASS INST TECHNOL, 80- *Personal Data:* b Walla Walla, Wash, July 11, 31; m 56, 76; c 5. *Educ:* Whitman Col, BA, 53; Univ Wash, PhD(phys chem), 62. *Prof Exp:* Res fel, Mellon Inst, 62-65; asst prof chem, Univ NH, 65-72; sr res assoc, Air Force Rocket Propulsion Lab, 72-73. *Concurrent Pos:* Prin investr, NSF grants, 73, 76, 80 & 83; supvr, Polymer Cent Fac, Mass Inst Technol, 83- *Mem:* AAAS; Am Phys Soc; Sigma Xi. *Res:* Molecular structure; spectroscopy; application of neutron scattering to polymer structure. *Mailing Add:* 91 Standish Rd Watertown MA 02172

BERNEY, REX LEROY, SOLID STATE PHYSICS. *Current Pos:* Asst prof, 78-85, ASSOC PROF PHYSICS, UNIV DAYTON, 85- *Personal Data:* b St Paul, Nebr, Sept 25, 50; m 74, 89. *Educ:* Univ Mo-Columbia, BS, 71, MS, 73, PhD(physics), 78. *Mem:* Am Phys Soc; Sigma Xi. *Res:* Photochromic materials; microcomputers in the laboratory. *Mailing Add:* Dept Physics Univ Dayton Dayton OH 45469-2314

BERNEY, STEVEN, RHEUMATOLOGY, IMMUNOLOGY. *Current Pos:* from asst prof to assoc prof, 71-92, PROF MED & MICROBIOL, HEALTH SCI CTR, TEMPLE UNIV, 92- *Personal Data:* b Germany, Dec 31, 35; US citizen; m 61, Hollis Bruunstein; c Seth, Laura & David. *Educ:* Rutgers Univ, BA, 58; State Univ NY Upstate Med Ctr, MD, 62. *Prof Exp:* Intern & resident internal med, Ohio State Univ Hosp, 62-63 & 65-67; USPHS fel rheumatic dis & immunol, NY Univ, 67-71, Arthritis Found fel, 70-71. *Mem:* fel Am Col Rheumatology; Reticuloendothelial Soc; Am Fedn Clin Res; Am Col Physicians. *Res:* Lymphocyte physiology and immunology; isolation and purification of membrane antigen receptors; circulatory behavior of lymphocytes; mechanism of immunologic depression in aging. *Mailing Add:* Dept Med-Temple Univ Health Sci Ctr 3401 N Broad St Philadelphia PA 19140

BERNEY, STUART ALAN, biochemical psychopharmacology, pharmacokinetics, for more information see previous edition

BERNFELD, PETER, ENZYMOLOGY, BIOCHEMISTRY. *Current Pos:* RETIRED. *Personal Data:* b Leipzig, Ger, June 1, 12; nat US; m 40, Helen C Kroch; c Michele M & Mark R. *Educ:* Univ Leipzig, MS, 35; Univ Geneva, PhD(chem), 37. *Honors & Awards:* Werner Medal, Swiss Chem Soc, 48. *Prof Exp:* From res fel to chief chemist org chem, Univ Geneva, 37-49, privat docent, 47-49; from asst prof to assoc prof biochem & nutrit & biochemist, Cancer Res Control Unit, Tufts Univ, 49-57; sr vpres & dir res, Bio-Res Inst & Bio-Res Consults, 57-88. *Mem:* AAAS; Am Chem Soc; Am Soc Biol Chem; Soc Exp Biol & Med; Am Inst Chemists; Am Asn Cancer Res; Am Col Toxicol. *Res:* Proteins; enzymes; polysaccharides; immobilized enzymes and antigens; studies on serum glycoproteins; humoral antigens prognosticating susceptibility to mammary cancer in women and mice; inhalation toxicity of smoke including tobacco smoke. *Mailing Add:* 247 Farm Lane Westwood MA 02090-1111. *Fax:* 781-320-0312; *E-Mail:* hcbphwb@aol.com

BERNFIELD, MERTON RONALD, CELL BIOLOGY, PEDIATRICS. *Current Pos:* DIR, JOINT PROG NEONATOL, HARVARD MED SCH, 89-, CLEMENT A SMITH PROF PEDIAT, 89-, PROF CELL BIOL, 89- *Personal Data:* b Chicago, Ill, Apr 9, 38; m 59, Audrey Rivkin; c Susan, James & Mark. *Educ:* Univ Ill, Urbana, BS, 59, Chicago, MS & MD, 61. *Prof Exp:* Intern, Res & Educ Hosp, Univ Ill, Chicago, 61-62; asst resident pediat, NY Hosp, Cornel Med Ctr, 62-63; res assoc, Lab Biochem Genetics, Nat Heart Inst, NIH, 63-65; res investr, Nat Inst Child Health & Human Develop, Univ Calif, San Diego, 65-66; chief resident, Med Ctr, from asst prof to prof, Sch Med, Stanford Univ, 67-89, Josephine K Knowles prof human biol, 77-89. *Concurrent Pos:* Guggenheim fel, 72-73; dir, Med Scientist Training Prog, Stanford Univ, 74-77 & Fel Prog Molecular Path Cell Membranes, 76-85, chmn, Prog Human Biol, 77-80; Macy fac scholar, 80-81; chmn, Gordon Res Conf on Basement Membranes, 86-; assoc ed, Develop Biol; dir, Neonatal Develop Biol Training Prog, Stanford Univ. *Mem:* Inst Med- Nat Acad Sci; Am Soc Cell Biol; Am Pediat Soc (treas, 89-); Soc Develop Biol (pres, 91-92); Soc Pediat Res; Asn Am Physicians; Am Soc Biochem & Molecular Biol. *Res:* Determine the chemical events which control cellular behavior during their formation of specific organs and structures during development; how cells interact with each other and with extracellular matrix molecules. *Mailing Add:* Joint Prog Neonatol Harvard Med Sch Enders Nine 300 Longwood Ave Boston MA 02115. *Fax:* 781-335-7677

BERNHAGEN, RALPH JOHN, GEOLOGY. *Current Pos:* chief water planning sect, 68-72, adminr shoreland mgt sect, 72-74, GEOL PROG SUPVR, DIV WATER, OHIO DEPT NATURAL RESOURCES, 74- *Personal Data:* b Toledo, Ohio, Aug 2, 10; m 40; c 2. *Educ:* Ohio State Univ, BA, 37, MA, 39. *Prof Exp:* Jr paleontologist, Shell Oil Co, Tex, 39-41; eng geologist, Lockwood, Andrews & Duller Eng Co, 41; chief geologist, Ohio Water Resources Bd, 41-52; asst chief, Ohio Div, Geol Surv, 52-57; div chief & state geologist, Ohio Geol Surv, 57-68. *Concurrent Pos:* Bd Counr, Dept Geol, Wright State Univ; mem adv comt, Dept Geol & Minerol, Ohio State Univ. *Mem:* Fel Geol Soc Am; Am Asn Petrol Geologists; Asn Am State Geologists; Am Inst Prof Geologists; Sigma Xi. *Res:* Stratigraphy of Ohio and the Appalachian Basin; ground water and petroleum geology. *Mailing Add:* 5916 Linworth Rd Worthington OH 43085

BERNHARD, JEFFREY DAVID, PSORIASIS, PRURITUS. *Current Pos:* fel, Univ Mass, 82-83, from asst prof to assoc prof, 83-92, assoc dean admis, 89-95, PROF MED, UNIV MASS MED SCH, 92- *Personal Data:* b Buffalo, NY, Oct 31, 51. *Educ:* Harvard Col, BA, 73; Harvard Med Sch, MD, 78. *Prof Exp:* Intern med, Beth Israel Hosp, Boston, 78-79; res dermat, Mass Gen Hosp, 79-81, chief resident, 81-82, res fel, 82-83. *Concurrent Pos:* Dir, Div Dermat, Univ Mass Med, 86; asst ed, J Am Acad Dermat. *Mem:* Soc Investigative Dermat; Am Acad Dermat; Sigma Xi; Royal Soc Med. *Res:* Itching; psoriasis; phototherapy; dermatology. *Mailing Add:* Div Dermat Univ Mass Med Ctr Worcester MA 01655-0307

BERNHARD, RICHARD ALLAN, ORGANIC CHEMISTRY. *Current Pos:* from asst prof to assoc prof food sci & technol, 57-70, PROF FOOD SCI & TECHNOL, UNIV CALIF, DAVIS, 70- *Personal Data:* b Pittsburgh, Pa, Oct 29, 23; m 53; c 2. *Educ:* Stanford Univ, BS, 50; Calif Inst Technol, PhD(chem), 55. *Prof Exp:* Res chemist, Lemon Prods, Adv Bd, Calif, 55-57. *Mem:* Am Chem Soc; Inst Food Technol; Sigma Xi. *Res:* Analytical methods for determination of micro-constituents in materials of biological origin; flavor chemistry; theory of chromatographic processes; mode and mechanism of pyrazine formation in model systems. *Mailing Add:* Dept Food Sci & Technol Univ Calif Davis CA 95616

BERNHARD, RICHARD HAROLD, ENGINEERING ECONOMIC ANALYSIS, DECISION ANALYSIS. *Current Pos:* assoc prof, 69-80, PROF INDUST ENG, NC STATE UNIV, 80- *Personal Data:* b New York, NY, Dec 11, 33; m 69, Cynthia A Petersen; c Barbara (Windom), Harold C II & Hans P. *Educ:* Cornell Univ, BME, 56, PhD(opers res), 61; Mass Inst Technol, SM, 58. *Honors & Awards:* Eugene L Grant Award, Am Soc Eng Educ, 84; Wellington Award, Inst Indust Engrs, 95. *Prof Exp:* Asst prof indust eng, Cornell Univ, 61-69. *Concurrent Pos:* Consult, Arthur D Little Inc, 57-59; NSF sci fac fel, Univ NC, Chapel Hill, 71-72; vis prof, Norweg Sch Econ & Bus Admin, 77-78 & Norweg Inst Technol, 88-89, Am Univ Armenia, 93 & 94; vis lectr, Univ Canterbury, NZ, 81-82; Fulbright scholar, Fed Univ Santa Catarina, Brazil, 86. *Mem:* Inst Indust Engrs; Am Soc Eng Educ; Financial Mgt Asn. *Res:* Engineering and managerial economies and decision analysis; mathematical modeling, especially in the presence of constraints and uncertainty, for capital investment planning, finance, production management, cost analysis and cost control. *Mailing Add:* Dept Indust Eng NC State Univ Box 7906 Raleigh NC 27695-7906. *Fax:* 919-515-5281; *E-Mail:* bernhar@eos.ncsu.edu

BERNHARD, ROBERT J, NOISE & VIBRATION CONTROL. *Current Pos:* from asst prof to assoc prof, 82-91, PROF, SCH MECH ENG, PURDUE UNIV, WEST LAFAYETTE, 91-, DIR, RAY W HERRICK LAB, 94- *Personal Data:* b Algona, Iowa, July 28, 52; m 79, Deborah S Kell; c Jay D, Jacqueline E, Jonathan C & Justin B. *Educ:* Iowa State Univ, BS, 73, PhD(mech eng), 82; Univ Md, MS, 76. *Honors & Awards:* Dow Outstanding Young Fac Award, Am Soc Eng Educrs, 87; Prof Progress Engr Award, Iowa State Univ, 91. *Prof Exp:* Engr, Westinghouse Elec, Inc, Baltimore, 73-77; asst prof, Iowa State Univ, Ames, 77-82. *Concurrent Pos:* Consult, Gen Motors, Electricite de France, Automated Anal Corp & Others; prin investr, NASA, Ford, Goodyear, Cummins, Digisonix, NSF & Others; mem, Bd Dir, Inst Noise Control Eng, 88-91; lectr, Tech Ctr Mech Industs, Univ Wis. *Mem:* Am Soc Mech Engrs; Inst Noise Control Eng (vpres, 90-93, pres, 94); Am Soc Eng Educrs; Acoust Soc Am; Am Inst Aeronaut & Astronaut; Soc Automotive Engrs. *Res:* Machinery noise and vibration control; active noise control; acoustical prediction methods; experimental diagnostic methods; noise source identification. *Mailing Add:* Purdue Univ West Lafayette IN 47907-1968. *Fax:* 765-494-0787

BERNHARD, VICTOR MONTWID, MEDICINE. *Current Pos:* VPRES MED AFFAIRS, ENDOVASCULAR TECH INC. *Personal Data:* b Milwaukee, Wis, June 29, 27; m 71, Suzan Baskin; c David M, Todd J & Jon N. *Educ:* Northwestern Univ, BS, 47, MD, 51. *Prof Exp:* From clin instr to clin asst prof surg, Med Col Wis, 59-64; NIH fel cardiovasc surg, Col Med, Baylor Univ, 65; from assoc prof to prof surg, Med Col Wis, 74-84; prof surg & chief, Sect Vascular Surg, Ariz Health Sci Ctr, 84- *Concurrent Pos:* Mem, Coun Cardiovasc Surg, Am Heart Asn. *Mem:* Soc Vascular Surg; fel Am Heart Asn; AMA; Am Col Surg; Int Cardiovasc Soc; Am Surg Soc. *Res:* Vascular diseases; vascular surgery; vascular prostheses; surgery for stroke. *Mailing Add:* Endovascular Tech Inc 1360 O'Brien Dr Menlo Park CA 94025-1436. *Fax:* 520-626-2890

BERNHARD, WILLIAM ALLEN, RADIATION CHEMISTRY. *Current Pos:* asst prof, 70-76, assoc prof radiation biol & biophysics, 76-85, PROF BIOPHYSICS, UNIV ROCHESTER, 85- *Personal Data:* b Philadelphia, Pa, Oct 9, 42; m 65; c 2. *Educ:* Union Col, BS, 64; Pa State Univ, MS, 66, PhD(biophysics), 68. *Honors & Awards:* Merit Award, NIH, 91. *Prof Exp:* Asst biophysics, Pa State Univ, 64-68; res fel biol & med, Argonne Nat Lab, 68-70. *Concurrent Pos:* Career develop award, NIH, 72, res grant awards, 75 & 78; vis prof biol, Univ Regensburg, 75-76; assoc ed, Radiation Res, 75-78; NSF res grant awards, 78 & 80. *Mem:* Biophys Soc; Radiation Res Soc; Am Phys Soc. *Res:* Effects of ionizing radiation on the primary structure of nucleic acids; electron spin resonance spectroscopy. *Mailing Add:* Dept Biophysics Univ Rochester Rochester NY 14642-8408

BERNHARDT, ANTHONY F, APPLIED PHYSICS. *Current Pos:* QUANTA-RAY, 80- *Personal Data:* b Los Angeles, Calif, Apr 16, 45. *Educ:* Univ Calif, Los Angeles, AB, 67; Univ Calif, Davis, MEng, 73, PhD(appl sci), 75. *Prof Exp:* Staff scientist physics, Lawrence Livermore Lab, Univ Calif, 68-72; fel appl sci, Fannie & John Hertz Found, 73-75; staff scientist physics, Lawrence Livermore Nat Lab, Univ Calif, 76-80. *Concurrent Pos:* Consult, W G Reynolds Sr, 75-76. *Mem:* Am Phys Soc. *Res:* Laser isotope separation; atomic and molecular structure and spectroscopy; photochemistry; atomic interactions in strong resonant optical fields. *Mailing Add:* Four the Uplands Berkeley CA 94705

BERNHARDT, ERNEST C(ARL), engineering, for more information see previous edition

BERNHARDT, RANDAL JAY, SURFACTANT CHEMISTRY. *Current Pos:* res chemist, 84-87, group leader, 87-88, MGR RES, STEPAN CO, 88- *Personal Data:* b Quincy, Ill, Nov 25, 56; m 81; c 4. *Educ:* Quincy Col, BS, 78; Univ Iowa, PhD(chem), 84. *Prof Exp:* Teaching asst chem, Univ Iowa, 78-84. *Mem:* Am Chem Soc; Am Oil Chemists Soc. *Res:* Synthesis, characterization and application of organic and organometallic chemicals for the surfactant and specialty chemical industries. *Mailing Add:* 39771 N Wittenburg Antioch IL 60002-9349

BERNHARDT, RICHARD CHARLES, PERSONAL COMMUNICATIONS SYSTEMS, CELLULAR RADIO SYSTEMS & WIRELESS MESSAGING. *Current Pos:* PRIN STAFF ENGR, MOTOROLA, 92- *Personal Data:* b New York, NY, Sept 29, 54; m 79, Michele Sher; c Michael & Victoria. *Educ:* Cooper Union, BE, 76, Manhattan Col, ME, 79. *Prof Exp:* Engr, Singer-Kearfott Div, 76-77; syst analyst, ADT Security Systs, 77-79; mem tech staff, AT&T Bell Labs, 79-83, Bell Communications Res, 84-92. *Mem:* Sr mem Inst Elec & Electonics Engrs. *Res:* Applied research in wireless data messaging, personal communications, and cellular radio systems; architecture, design, performance analysis and simulation of communication systems. *Mailing Add:* 1461 Hideaway Bend Wellington FL 33414. *Fax:* 561-739-2519

BERNHARDT, ROBERT L, III, MODULE & RING THEORY, TORSION THEORY. *Current Pos:* CHMN MATH DEPT, E CAROLINA UNIV, 83- *Personal Data:* b Salisbury, NC, Apr 28, 39; m 75, Judy Hayes; c Lydian. *Educ:* Univ NC, Chapel Hill, BS, 61, MA, 64; Univ Ore, PhD(math), 68. *Prof Exp:* Asst prof math, Univ NC, Greensboro, 68-74; assoc prof math, Chicago State Univ, 74-83, chairperson dept, 77-83. *Mem:* Am Math Soc; Math Asn Am; Sigma Xi; Nat Coun Teachers Math. *Res:* Torsion theory of modules; splitting properties of torsion theories. *Mailing Add:* Dept Math E Carolina Univ E Fifth St Greenville NC 27858. *Fax:* 919-328-6414; *E-Mail:* mabernha@ecuvm.cis.ecu.edu

BERNHEIM, ROBERT A, LASER SPECTROSCOPY. *Current Pos:* from asst prof to assoc prof, 61-69, PROF CHEM, PA STATE UNIV, UNIVERSITY PARK, 69- *Personal Data:* b Hackensack, NJ, June 8, 33; m 75, Marguerite Yevitz; c Britt & Kyle. *Educ:* Brown Univ, BS, 55; Harvard Univ, MA, 57; Univ Ill, PhD(chem), 59. *Honors & Awards:* Alexander von Humboldt Sr Scientist Award, 89. *Prof Exp:* Res fel chem, Columbia Univ, 59-61. *Concurrent Pos:* NSF sr fel, 67-68; Guggenheim fel, 74-75; vis fel, J Inst for Lab Astrophys, 82-83; Fulbright fac scholar, 88-89. *Mem:* Fel Optical Soc Am; Am Chem Soc; fel Am Phys Soc. *Res:* Optical pumping; laser spectroscopy; molecular structure and dynamics. *Mailing Add:* 152 Davey Lab Pa State Univ University Park PA 16802. *Fax:* 814-865-3314

BERNHEIMER, ALAN WEYL, MICROBIOLOGY, TOXINOLOGY. *Current Pos:* chmn basic med sci, 69-74, from instr to prof bact, 41-58, prof, 58-84, EMER PROF MICROBIOL, SCH MED, NY UNIV, 84- *Personal Data:* b Philadelphia, Pa, Dec 9, 13; m 42; c 1. *Educ:* Temple Univ, BS, 35, AM, 37; Univ Pa, PhD(med sci), 42. *Honors & Awards:* Lily Award, 48. *Prof Exp:* Asst biol, Temple Univ, 35-37; instr bact, Pa State Col Optom, 37-39. *Concurrent Pos:* Mem, Marine Biol Lab; consult, Surgeon Gen, 57-; NIH res career award, 62-84; trustee, Cold Spring Harbor Lab Quant Biol, 63-68. *Mem:* Am Soc Microbiol; fel Am Acad Microbiol; Am Micros Soc; Mineral Soc Am; Am Asn Immunol. *Res:* Extracellular toxins and enzymes of bacteria; streptococci and staphylococci; cell membranes; toxins of various invertebrates. *Mailing Add:* Dept Microbiol NY Univ Sch Med New York NY 10016

BERNHEIMER, HARRIET P, MICROBIAL GENETICS. *Current Pos:* from instr to prof, 58-85, EMER PROF MED, STATE UNIV NY DOWNSTATE MED CTR, 85- *Personal Data:* b New York, NY, May 27, 19; m 42, Alan W; c Alan W Jr. *Educ:* Hunter Col, BA, 39; NY Univ, MS, 41, PhD(microbiol), 50. *Prof Exp:* Asst biochem, Col Physicians & Surgeons, Columbia Univ, 50-53. *Concurrent Pos:* NIH grant, 63-70; Health Res Coun NY career scientist award, 64-70; Irma T Hirschl trust career scientist award, 73-77; dir, Med PhD prog, 78- *Mem:* AAAS; Genetics Soc Am; Am Soc Microbiol; Harvey Soc; Sigma Xi. *Res:* Genetic control of capsule production, studied through the bacterial transformation system; biosynthesis of capsular polysaccharide in pneumococcus; pneumococcus bacteriophages. *Mailing Add:* 51 Fifth Ave Apt 2E New York NY 10003-4324

BERNHOLC, JERZY, SEMICONDUCTORS, IMPURITIES. *Current Pos:* assoc prof, 86-90, PROF PHYSICS, NC STATE UNIV, 90- *Personal Data:* b Szczecin, Poland, Feb 12, 52; US citizen; m 82, Alissa Seligman; c Stuart J & Judith I. *Educ:* Univ Lund, Sweden, BSc, 73, PhD(physics), 77. *Prof Exp:* Fel, J T Watson Res Ctr, IBM, 78-80; sr physicist, Exxon Res & Engr Co, 80-86. *Concurrent Pos:* Vis scientist, Dept Theoret Physics, Univ Lund, Sweden, 78 & Calif Inst Technol, Pasadena, 82. *Mem:* Fel Am Phys Soc; Mat Res Soc; Sigma Xi. *Res:* Theoretical condensed matter physics and chemistry and theoretical materials science, impurities in semiconductors, surfaces and interfaces, fullerenes, clusters, surface reactions, supercomputing, parallel computations. *Mailing Add:* Phys Dept NC State Univ Box 8202 Raleigh NC 27695. *Fax:* 919-515-7331; *E-Mail:* bernholc@ncsu.edu

BERNI, RALPH JOHN, ANALYTICAL CHEMISTRY. *Current Pos:* CHEMIST & CONSULT, ENVIRON ANALYSIS INC, 89- *Personal Data:* b New Orleans, La, Nov 1, 31; m 57, 87; c 6. *Educ:* La State Univ, BS, 54; Tulane Univ, MS, 61, PhD(inorg chem), 66. *Prof Exp:* Res assoc chemist, Southern Regional Res Ctr, Agr Res Serv, USDA, 55-65, res chemist, 65-74, res leader, 75-77, lab chief, 77-85, res leader, Compos & Properties Res Unit, 85-88. *Concurrent Pos:* Instr chem, Univ New Orleans, 87- *Mem:* Am Chem Soc; Am Inst Chemists; Sigma Xi. *Res:* Etherification and esterification of cellulose, including reaction mechanisms; metal ion complexes of urea derivatives; transition elements; instrumental analysis. *Mailing Add:* 3117 Clifford Dr 3117 Vlifford Dr Metairie LA 70002-5039

BERNIER, CLAUDE, PHYTOPATHOLOGY. *Current Pos:* from asst prof to assoc prof phytopath, 65-74, PROF PHYTOPATH, UNIV MAN, 74- *Personal Data:* b St Boniface, Man, June 18, 31; m 58; c 3. *Educ:* Univ Man, BA, 53, BSA, 57, MSc, 61; Univ Minn, PhD(plant path), 64. *Prof Exp:* Res officer veg crops, Can Dept Agr, 57-61. *Mem:* Am Phytopath Soc; Can Phytopath Soc. *Res:* Resistance to tan spot of wheat; biology and genetics of the tan spot fungus; diseases of lentil; biological control of take-all. *Mailing Add:* Dept Plant Sci Univ Man Winnipeg MB R3T 2N2 Can

BERNIER, PAUL EMILE, POULTRY GENETICS. *Current Pos:* from assoc prof to prof, 47-77, EMER PROF POULTRY GENETICS, ORE STATE UNIV, 77- *Personal Data:* b St Michel, Que, Oct 22, 11; US citizen; m 40, Isabelle Siracusa. *Educ:* Laval, BSA, 32; Univ Calif, PhD(genetics), 47. *Honors & Awards:* Res Prize, Poultry Sci Asn, 52. *Prof Exp:* Poultry husbandman, Ecole Superieure d'Agr, Que, 28-45, lectr poultry husb, 32-45, lectr genetics, 39-45; chief inspector, Nat Poultry Breeding Prog, Can Dept Agr, 45-47. *Mem:* Fel AAAS; Biomet Soc; Poultry Sci Asn; Genetics Soc Am; Teratology Soc; World's Poultry Sci Asn. *Res:* Genetics of domestic fowl and teratology. *Mailing Add:* 635 NW 34th St Ore State Univ Corvallis OR 97330-5049

BERNIERI, FRANK JOHN, PSYCHOLOGY. *Current Pos:* ASSOC PROF PSYCHOL, UNIV TOLEDO, 94- *Personal Data:* b Brooklyn, NY, May 2, 61; c Jennifer. *Educ:* Univ Rochester, BA; Harvard Univ, PhD(psychol), 87. *Prof Exp:* Asst prof psychol, Ore State Univ, 87-93, assoc prof, 93-94. *Concurrent Pos:* Young investr award, NSF, 92; area consult psychol, NIH, 94, NSF, 94, McArthur Found, 95. *Mem:* Am Psychol Soc; AAAS; Am Psychol Asn; Soc Exp Social Psychol. *Res:* Social perception and interpersonal behavior. *Mailing Add:* Dept Psychol Univ Toledo Toledo OH 43606. *Fax:* 419-530-8479

BERNING, WARREN WALT, PHYSICS, METEOROLOGY. *Current Pos:* SR SCIENTIST, PHYS SCI LAB, NMEX STATE UNIV, 77- *Personal Data:* b Cincinnati, Ohio, July 29, 20; m 46; c 2. *Educ:* Univ Cincinnati, BA, 42; Calif Inst Technol, MS, 46. *Prof Exp:* Aerodynamicist, McDonnell Corp, St Louis, 46 & Curtiss-Wright Corp, Columbus, 46-47; meteorologist, Ballistic Res Lab, Aberdeen Proving Ground, 47-50, physicist, 50-67; dep chief radiation directorate, Defense Atomic Support Agency, 67-71, asst to dep dir theoret res, Defense Nuclear Agency, 71-76; sr oper analyst, SRI Int, 76-77. *Mem:* AAAS; assoc fel Am Inst Aeronaut & Astronaut; Am Meteorol Soc; Am Geophys Union; fel Am Phys Soc. *Res:* Electromagnetic propagation through atmosphere; lower level meteorology; upper atmosphere physics. *Mailing Add:* 11007 Candelight Lane Potomac MD 20854

BERNIUS, MARK THOMAS, ELECTRON & ION OPTICS, MICROSCOPY. *Current Pos:* SR RES PHYSICIST PHYSICS, DOW CHEM CO, 92- *Personal Data:* b Brooklyn, NY, Oct 24, 57. *Educ:* Polytech Inst, BSc, 79; State Univ NY, MSc, 81; Cornell Univ, PhD(nuclear sci & appl physics), 87. *Honors & Awards:* Achievement Awards, NASA, 89. *Prof Exp:* Postdoctoral physics, Jet Propulsion Lab, 87-89; sr res fel geol & planetary sci, Calif Inst Technol, 89-91. *Concurrent Pos:* Consult space sci, Jet Propulsion Lab, 89- *Mem:* Am Phys Soc; Europ Phys Soc; Am Chem Soc. *Res:* Experimental materials research utilizing electron, ion and light microscopies; physics of ion formation and electron-molecule reactions at threshold; theoretical and experimental charged-particle optics; high-precision mass spectrometry. *Mailing Add:* Cent Mat Res Bldg No 1712 Dow Chem Co Midland MI 48674

BERNKOPF, MICHAEL, mathematics, for more information see previous edition

BERNLOHR, ROBERT WILLIAM, MICROBIAL, PHYSIOLOGY. *Current Pos:* prof microbiol & head dept, Pa State Univ, 74-75, prof biochem & biophys & head dept, 75-79, prof biochem & head dept microbiol, cell biol, biochem & biophys, 79-84, PROF BIOCHEM, DEPT BIOCHEM & MOLECULAR BIOL, PA STATE UNIV, 84- *Personal Data:* b Columbus, Ohio, Apr 20, 33; m 55, Carol J Smiley; c David, Timothy, Mark & James. *Educ:* Capital Univ, BS, 55; Ohio State Univ, PhD(biochem), 58. *Hon Degrees:* DSc, Capital Univ, 80. *Prof Exp:* Fel biol, Oak Ridge Nat Lab, 58-60; asst prof biochem, Ohio State Univ, 60-62; from asst prof to prof microbiol & biochem, Univ Minn, 63-74. *Concurrent Pos:* USPHS res career develop award, 62-72; mem adv panel metab biol prog, NSF, 68-71. *Mem:* fel AAAS; Am Soc Biochem & Molecular Biol; Sigma Xi; Am Soc Microbiol. *Res:* Bacterial metabolism; enzymology; regulation of growth; spore formation; bacterial sensing. *Mailing Add:* 208 Althouse Lab Pa State Univ University Park PA 16802-4501. *Fax:* 814-863-7024; *E-Mail:* mullen@math.psu.edu

BERNOCO, DOMENICO, IMMUNOLOGY, VETERINARY GENETICS. *Current Pos:* assoc res immunologist, Tissue Typing Lab, Dept Surg, Univ Calif, Los Angeles, 77-81, res fel, Dept Vet Microbiol, Davis, 67-68, assoc res immunologist, 79-81, ASSOC PROF, DEPT VET MED REPRODUCTION, UNIV CALIF, DAVIS, 79- *Personal Data:* b Cherasco, Italy, Apr 6, 35; m 72. *Educ:* Univ Torino, Italy, DVM, 59; Ministry Pub Inst, Rome, Italy, liberadocenza, 71. *Prof Exp:* Asst prof, Observ Animal Genetics, Torino, Italy, 61-62 & 64-67; asst prof, Inst Med Genetics, Univ Torino, 62-64 & 69-70; mem BII, Basel Inst Immunol, Switz, 70-76. *Concurrent Pos:* Coun-at-large, Am Asn Clin Histocompatibility Testing, 80-83; mem adv bd, J Animal Genetics, 86- *Mem:* Am Asn Immunologists; Int Soc Animal Genetics; Am Soc Histocompatibility & Immunogenetics. *Res:* Histocompatibility complex and blood groups; use of genetic markers for individual identification; pedigree analysis; matching for organ transplantation and identification of animals with superior genetic resistance to disease to improve quantity and quality of food animal products. *Mailing Add:* 1002 Deodara Ct Davis CA 95616-5037. *E-Mail:* dbernoco@ucdavis.ucdavis.edu

BERNOFSKY, CARL, FREE RADICALS & INFLAMMATORY DISEASE, TOXICOLOGY & CARCINOGENESIS. *Current Pos:* BIOCHEM RES CONSULT, 95- *Personal Data:* b Brooklyn, NY, Nov 22, 33; m 57, Shirley Goodman; c Susan & Lauren. *Educ:* Brooklyn Col, BS, 55; Univ Kans, PhD(biochem), 63. *Prof Exp:* Res asst biochem, Am Meat Inst Found, 56-58; res fel, Case Western Res Univ, 62-67; asst prof biochem, Mayo Grad Sch Med, Univ Minn, 67-73, assoc prof biochem, Mayo Med Sch, 73-75; vis assoc prof, Sch Med, Tulane Univ, 75-80, res assoc prof, 80-83, res prof, 83-95. *Concurrent Pos:* Consult, Mayo Clin & Found, 67-74; prin investr, NSF, 71-73, 74-76, 78-81, 83-85 & 90-94, NIH, 73-76, 79-82 & 86-89, Am Cancer Soc, 84-86, Am Inst Cancer Res, 84-86 & Dept Defense, 89-91, 90-94 & 95-97. *Mem:* AAAS; Am Chem Soc; NY Acad Sci; Am Soc Biochem & Molecular Biol; Oxygen Soc; Int EPR Soc. *Res:* Pyridine nucleotide chemistry and metabolism; free radical mechanisms of inflammatory tissue damage; molecular toxicology; carcinogenesis. *Mailing Add:* 6478 General Diaz St New Orleans LA 70124. *E-Mail:* cbernof@aol.com

BERNOR, RAYMOND LOUIS, PALEOBIOLOGY. *Current Pos:* res fel, 80-81, ASSOC PROF ANAT, COL MED, HOWARD UNIV, 81- *Personal Data:* b Los Angeles, Calif, Feb 15, 49. *Educ:* Univ Calif, Los Angeles, BA, 71, MA, 73, PhD(anthrop), 78. *Prof Exp:* Res assoc, Dept Earth Sci, Univ Calif, Riverside, 78-80, curator vertebrate paleontol, 79-81. *Concurrent Pos:* Lectr anthrop, Univ Calif, Los Angeles, 71-79, ed, Anthrop, 78-80; chief vertebrate paleontologist, Archaeol Resource Mgt Corp, Garden Grove, Calif, 78-80; prin proj dir, Paleontol & Multidisciplinary Studies, Environ Res Archaeologists Corp, Los Angeles, Calif, 80; NSF fel; Alexander von Humboldt fel. *Mem:* AAAS; Soc Vertebrate Paleontol; Am Asn Phys Anthropologists; Soc Syst Zool. *Res:* Evolution of Miocene Age mammalian zoogeographic provinces of Eurasia and Africa, and its pertinence to early hominid and pongid evolution and environments; complete mammal faunas and specialization in hipparionine horses and primates. *Mailing Add:* 2415 20th St NW Washington DC 20009

BERNS, DONALD SHELDON, PHYSICAL CHEMISTRY, BIOPHYSICS. *Current Pos:* DIR MED RES ORG, MINISTRY HEALTH ISRAEL. *Personal Data:* b Bronx, NY, June 27, 34; m 56, Sylvia Schleicher; c Brian, Neil & Amy. *Educ:* Wilkes Col, BS, 55; Univ Pa, PhD(phys chem), 59. *Prof Exp:* Calif Res Corp grant chem, Yale Univ, 59-60 & Rockefeller Found grant, 60-61; resident res assoc chem, Argonne Nat Lab, 61-62; sr res scientist phys chem, Div Labs & Res, NY State Dept Health, Albany, 62-67, assoc res scientist, 67-71, dir phys chem labs, 68-74, prin res scientist phys chem, WadsWorth Ctr Labs & Res, 71-77, lab chief molecular biol, 82-83, lab chief biophys, 83-86, sci admin, New Scotland Ave Infectious Dis Labs, 83-86, dir div clin sci, 86-89. *Concurrent Pos:* NSF grant, Div Labs & Res, NY State Dept Health, 62-75; from asst prof to assoc prof biochem, Albany Med Col, 62-76; adj prof chem, Rensselaer Polytech Inst, 71-; Environ Protection Agency spec sr fel & vis prof physiol & microbiol chem, Hadassah Med Sch, Hebrew Univ, Israel, 72-73; NIH grant, 75-; Lady Davis vis prof, Hebrew Univ, Israel, 85. *Mem:* Am Chem Soc; Am Soc Biol Chem; AAAS. *Res:* Energy transduction and transfer in model membrane systems; protein structure and function, particularly algal biliproteins, protein-lipid interaction and membrane assembly; physical chemical properties of biological macromolecules; monolayer studies of lipids and proteins; serology of HIV infection; staging of HIV infection. *Mailing Add:* 47 Hizkiyahu Hamelech Jerusalem Israel. *Fax:* 972-2-6725833; *E-Mail:* berns@yam.suff.cc.huje.ac.il

BERNS, KENNETH, VIROLOGY. *Current Pos:* R A REES PRITCHETT PROF & CHMN, DEPT MICROBIOL, MED COL, CORNELL UNIV, 84-, PROF PEDIAT, 84- *Personal Data:* b Cleveland, Ohio, June 14, 38; m 64, Laura Lawless; c Jonathan & Deborah. *Educ:* Johns Hopkins Univ, AB, 60, PhD(biol), 64, MD, 66. *Prof Exp:* Mem house staff, Johns Hopkins Univ Hosp, 66-67; staff assoc, Nat Inst Arthritis & Metab Dis, 67-68, staff assoc, Nat Inst Allergy & Infectious Dis, 68-70; from asst prof to assoc prof microbiol, 70-76, asst prof pediat, 70-76, dir, Yr One Prog, Sch Med, Johns Hopkins Univ, 73-76; prof & chmn dept immunol & med microbiol, Col Med, Univ Fla, Gainesville, 76-84. *Concurrent Pos:* Shell Oil fel, 63-64; sr asst surgeon, USPHS, 66-67, surgeon, 67-70, sr surgeon, 70-; fel pediat, Johns Hopkins Univ, 66-67; Howard Hughes Med Investr, 70-75; fac res award, Am Cancer Soc, 75-80; consult, Vet Admin Hosp, Gainesville, Fla, 78-84, Bd Army Sci & Technol, Nat Acad Sci-Nat Res Coun, CRDEC, 88-90; chmn, Basic Sci Bd, 79-82, mem exec comt, Col Med, Univ Fla; mem exec comt, Grad Sch Med Sci, Med Col, Cornell Univ; mem, Recombinant DNA Adv Comt, NIH, 80-83, chmn, 83; mem, Genetic Biol Panel, NSF, 81-85; mem, Int Comt Taxon Viruses (Parvoviruses), 81-; Guggenheim hon fel, 82-83; Fogarty Sr Int fel, Weizmann Inst Sci, Israel, 82-83; sci adv, Showa Univ Res Inst Biomedicine in Fla, 83-85; virol study sect, NIH, 85-89; mem, Rev Panel Virol & Microbiol, Am Cancer Soc, 86-89; mem exec bd, Nat Bd Med Examrs, 87-95; chmn, Pub Sci Affil Bd, Am Soc Microbiol, 89-95; chmn, Coun Acad Soc, Asn Am Med Col, 90-91, chmn elect, 93-94, chmn, 94-95; pres, Asn Med Sch, Microbiol & Immunol Chrs, 86; mem bd sci counr, Nat Inst Allergy & Infectious Dis, 92-96. *Mem:* Nat Acad Sci; AAAS; Am Soc Microbiol (pres, 96-97); Am Soc Virol (pres elect, 87, pres, 88-89); Am Soc Biol Chemists; Soc Gen Microbiol; Soc Pediat Res; Harvey Soc; NY Acad Sci (vpres, 90-91, pres, 91-92); Asn Am Med Col; Sigma Xi; fel Am Acad Microbiol. *Res:* DNA structure; structure and replication of animal virus chromosomes; latent infection. *Mailing Add:* 50 Sutton Pl S 6C New York NY 10022

BERNS, MICHAEL W, DEVELOPMENTAL BIOLOGY, CELL BIOLOGY. *Current Pos:* chmn, Gordon Conf, lasers in med & biol, 78. *Personal Data:* b Burlington, Vt, Dec 1, 42; m 63; c 2. *Educ:* Cornell Univ, BS, 64, MS, 66, PhD(biol), 68. *Prof Exp:* Assoc dir laser biol, Pasadena Found Med Res Calif, 69-70; asst prof zool, Univ Mich, 70-72; assoc prof develop biol & cell biol, 72-75, PROF DEVELOP BIOL & CELL BIOL, UNIV CALIF, IRVINE, 75- CHMN DEPT, 75- Concurrent NIH GMS res grants grant laser microbeam effects on chromosomes & mitosis, 70, 72 & 80; NIH-Heart & Lung Inst grant, 71-80; co-prin investr laser microbeam studies on mitosis, NSF, 73-75; co-dir carcinogenesis training grant, NIH-Nat Cancer Inst, 75-80; NSF equip grant, 75; US Air Force grant effects of pollutants on cells, 77-79; Nat Acad Sci ad hoc comt mem, lasers in biomed res, 77; Int Union Against Cancer ICRETT award, US-USSR Joint Prog Estab, 77-80. *Mem:* AAAS; Tissue Cult Asn; Am Soc Cell Biol; Am Soc Photobiol; Soc Develop Biol. *Res:* Laser microbeam studies on chromosomes; nucleoli and mitochondria of tissue culture cells; studies on mitosis of cells; laser instrumentation for biomedical research; cellular and embryonic development. *Mailing Add:* Beckman Laser Inst Med Ctr Univ Calif 1002 Health Science Rd E Irvine CA 92715

BERNSTEIN, ABRAM BERNARD, ENVIRONMENTAL MANAGEMENT, NATURAL & TECHNOLOGICAL HAZARDS. *Current Pos:* ADMIN DIR, RESOURCE MGT PROG, DEPT ENVIRON STUDIES, ANTIOCH NEW ENG GRAD SCH, 90- *Personal Data:* b New York, NY, July 11, 35; div; c 2. *Educ:* City Col NY, BS, 56; Pa State Univ, MS, 59; Univ Wash, PhD(atmos sci), 73. *Prof Exp:* Res meteorologist, Nat Oceanic & Atmospheric Admin, 58-73; staff scientist, Nat Adv Comt Oceans & Atmosphere, 73-78; sr prog officer, Nat Res Coun, Nat Acad Sci, 78-87; vis assoc prof, Dept Technol & Soc, State Univ NY, Stony Brook, 87-90. *Mem:* Am Meteorol Soc; AAAS; Sigma Xi; Am Geophys Union; Soc Risk Anal. *Res:* Atmospheric and oceanic science; natural, technological and environmental hazards; application of new technology to buildings and cities; science, technology and public policy; interdisciplinary communication. *Mailing Add:* PO Box 1178 Keene NH 03431

BERNSTEIN, ALAN, VIROLOGY. *Current Pos:* RETIRED. *Personal Data:* b Brooklyn, NY, Nov 21, 26; m 48, Doris; c David, Saul & Miriam. *Educ:* Philadelphia Col Pharm, BS, 51; Univ Pa, PhD(med microbiol), 54. *Prof Exp:* Bacteriologist, Philadelphia Childrens Hosp, 48-51, res asst, 51-53; bacteriologist, Virus & Rickettsia Sect, Communicable Dis Ctr, USPHS, 53-58; bacteriologist, Wyeth Labs, Marietta, 58-68, managing dir, 68-87. *Concurrent Pos:* Consult, 87- *Res:* Production of bacterial and viral vaccines; control testing of biologicals; serology; epidemiology; production of parenteral pharmaceutical products; diagnostic virology. *Mailing Add:* 24 Bentley Summit Lancaster PA 17603

BERNSTEIN, ALAN, BIOPHYSICS, GENETICS. *Current Pos:* from asst prof to assoc prof, 74-84, PROF, DEPT MED BIOPHYS, UNIV TORONTO, 84-, PROF, DEPT MOLECULAR & MEDICAL GENETICS, 86-; HEAD, DIV MOLECULAR & DEVELOP BIOL, SAMUEL LUNENFELD RES INST, MT SINAI HOSP, 85-, DIR, 94- *Personal Data:* b Toronto, Can, Jun 25, 47. *Educ:* Univ Toronto, BS, 68, PhD(med biophysics), 72. *Honors & Awards:* James Loudon Gold Medal, AAAS, 68; 2nd Allan J Erslev Distinguished lectr, Thomas Jefferson Univ, 92; McLaughlin Medal, Royal Soc Can, 96. *Prof Exp:* Staff mem, Div Biol Res, Ont Cancer Inst, Toronto, 74-85; assoc dir, Samuel Lunenfeld Res Inst Mt Sinai Hosp, 88-94. *Concurrent Pos:* King George V Cancer Res fel, Nat Cancer Inst Can, 72-73; vis prof, Queen's Univ, Kingston, 87; mem, Grad Fac, Inst Med Sci, 87-; int res scholar, Howard Hughes Med Inst, 91-; chair, Int Sci Coun, Israel Cancer Res Fund, 94- *Mem:* Am Soc Microbiol; Can Soc Cell Biol; Genetics Soc Can; fel Royal Soc Can. *Mailing Add:* Samuel Lunenfeld Res Inst Mt Sinai Hosp 600 University Ave Toronto ON M5G 1X5 Can. *Fax:* 416-586-8857; *E-Mail:* bernstein@mshri.on.ca

BERNSTEIN, ALAN D, CARDIAC PACING, CARDIAC ELECTROPHYSIOLOGY. *Current Pos:* res assoc surg, 79-80, sr res assoc, 80-83, DIR TECH RES SURG & TECH DIR PACEMAKER CTR, NEWARK BETH ISRAEL MED CTR, 83- *Personal Data:* b New York, NY, Jan 31, 38; wid. *Educ:* NJ Inst Technol, MS, 75, PhD(elec eng), 79. *Prof Exp:* Instr physics & dir gen physics labs, Rutgers Univ, Newark, 70-78, res specialist physics, 78-79. *Concurrent Pos:* Adj assoc prof surg, Univ Med & Dent NJ, 90-; chmn, Mode Code Comt, NAm Soc Pacing & Electrophysiol, 91- *Mem:* Fel Am Col Cardiol; Biomed Eng Soc; Inst Elec & Electronics Engrs; Asn Advan Med Instrumentation; NAm Soc Pacing & Electrophysiol. *Res:* Cardiac pacing and electrophysiology; cardiac-vibration analysis; biomedical signal processing; computer applications in medicine. *Mailing Add:* Dept Surg Newark Beth Israel Med Ctr 201 Lyons Ave Newark NJ 07112. *Fax:* 973-926-7874

BERNSTEIN, ALLEN RICHARD, NON-STANDARD ANALYSIS. *Current Pos:* PRES, ACAD INFO SERV, INC, 83- *Personal Data:* b Chicago, Ill, Feb 14, 41; m 72, Barbara Rottenberg; c Howard, David & Michael. *Educ:* Calif Inst Technol, BS, 62; Univ Calif, Los Angeles, MA, 64, PhD(math), 65. *Prof Exp:* Asst prof math, Univ Wis-Madison, 65-68; from assoc prof to prof math, Univ Md, College Park, 68-83. *Mem:* Am Math Soc; Asn Symbolic Logic. *Res:* Mathematical logic and its applications; analysis. *Mailing Add:* 7809 Chestnut Ave Bowie MD 20715

BERNSTEIN, ALVIN STANLEY, PSYCHIATRY. *Current Pos:* RETIRED. *Personal Data:* b New York, NY, Nov 2, 29; m 68; c 1. *Educ:* NY Univ, BA, 50; Univ Buffalo, PhD(psychol), 58. *Prof Exp:* Ward psychologist, Vet Admin Hosp, Montrose, NY, 58-61, res psychologist, 61-66; assoc prof psychiat, Col Med, Downstate Med Ctr, State Univ NY, 66-95, assoc prof progs psychiat & biol psychol, Grad Sch, 70-95. *Concurrent Pos:* Lectr psychol, Queens Col, City Univ NY, 60-65; from res asst to asst prof psychiat, Sch Med, Cornell Univ, 65-66; NIMH spec res fel, Downstate Med Ctr, State Univ NY, Downstate Med Ctr, NIMH, 66-68; vis prof, Dept Psychol, Univ York, Eng, 76; mem, Res Rev Comt Psychopath & Clin Biol, NIMH, 79-81; consult, Natural Sci & Rec Coun Can, 82; assoc ed, Psychophysiol, 87-; bd dirs, Soc Psychophysiol Res, 89-92. *Mem:* Soc Psychophysiol Res; fel Int Orgn Psychophysiol; Am Psychol Asn; AAAS. *Res:* Psychophysiological studies of attentional processes in the normal population; specific dysfunctions in schizophrenia and in depression. *Mailing Add:* 43 Wilmington Dr Melville NY 11747

BERNSTEIN, ARON, NUCLEAR PHYSICS. *Current Pos:* PROF PHYSICS, MASS INST TECHNOL, 61- *Personal Data:* b New York, NY, Apr 6, 31. *Educ:* Union Col, BA, 52; Univ Pa, PhD(physics), 57. *Honors & Awards:* Homboldt Award, 93. *Prof Exp:* Res fel & asst prof, Princeton Univ, 57-61. *Concurrent Pos:* Guggenheim Fel, 68. *Mem:* Fel Am Phys Soc; fel AAAS. *Res:* Exploring the basic structure of the nucleon and nuclei using electro magnetic interactions. *Mailing Add:* Mass Inst Technol Bldg 26 419 Cambridge MA 02139. *Fax:* 617-258-5440; *E-Mail:* bernstein@mitlns.mit.edu

BERNSTEIN, BARBARA ELAINE, mathematics, educational psychology, for more information see previous edition

BERNSTEIN, BARRY, APPLIED MATHEMATICS. *Current Pos:* PROF MATH, ILL INST TECHNOL, 66-, ACTG DIR CTR APPL MATH, 70- *Personal Data:* b New York, NY, Nov 20, 30; m 54; c 2. *Educ:* City Col, BS, 51; Ind Univ, MA, 54, PhD(math), 56. *Prof Exp:* Mathematician, US Naval Res Lab, 51-53, 56-61 & Nat Bur Stand, 61-66. *Concurrent Pos:* Lectr, Univ Md, 56-57, 64- & Catholic Univ, 58-64; consult, Nat Bur Stand, 68- *Mem:* Am Math Soc; Soc Rheology; Soc Indust & Appl Math. *Res:* Rheology; continuum mechanics; thermodynamics; mathematical analysis; gas dynamics; biomechanics. *Mailing Add:* Dept Math Ill Inst Technol 3300 S Federal St Chicago IL 60616-3732

BERNSTEIN, BRADLEY ALAN, FOOD SCIENCE, BIOCHEMISTRY. *Current Pos:* PRES, SCHULTZ BERNSTEIN & ASSOC INC, 83- *Personal Data:* b Madison, Wis, May 18, 51; m 82, Kathy Howard. *Educ:* Univ Wis, BS, 73, MS, 74, PhD(food sci), 77. *Honors & Awards:* Steinbock-Borden Award, Univ Wis & S-B Awards Comt, 73. *Prof Exp:* Staff mem, 77-80, dir res & develop food chem, Amber Labs Div, Milbrew, Inc, 80-83. *Mem:* Sigma Xi; Am Chem Soc; Inst Food Technologists; Am Dairy Sci Asn. *Res:* Investigation of the inhibition of cholesterol biosynthesis by orotic acid; isolation and characterization of cytochromes P-450 and P-420 in mammary tissues; development of methods for the utilization of dairy by-products via fermentation. *Mailing Add:* 270 Nob Hill E Colgate WI 53017-9306

BERNSTEIN, BRUCE S, CABLE TECHNOLOGY, POLYMER MEMBRANE TECHNOLOGY TO MEET UTILITY NEEDS. *Current Pos:* from proj mgr to sr proj mgr, 77-91, TECH ADV, ELEC POWER RES INST, 91- *Personal Data:* b Brooklyn, NY, May 19, 31; m 62, Valerie; c Neil & Mark. *Educ:* City Univ NY, BS, 53; Iowa State Univ, MS, 55. *Prof Exp:* Sr res chemist, RAI Res Corp, 61-65; tech dir, Herculite Prod Inc, 65-66; supvr, Polymer Sect Cent Res, Riegel Paper Corp, 66-69; mgr radiation & polymer chem, Radiation Technol Inc, 69-72; adv, Mat Sect, Phelps Dodge Cable & Wire Co, 72-73, asst dir res & develop mat, 74-75; mgr res & develop, Sun Chem Corp, 76-77. *Concurrent Pos:* Vis instr, Cable Eng Clin, Univ Wis, 88-; US rep, Int Conf Large High Voltage Elec Systs, 89-96, convener, WG 15-09 Advan Mat. *Mem:* Am Chem Soc; fel Inst Elec & Electronics Engrs; Soc Plastics Engrs. *Res:* Polymeric materials employed as electrical insulation and structural materials for equipment used in generation, transmission and distribution of electric energy. *Mailing Add:* 1433 Longhill Dr Rockville MD 20854-2603. *Fax:* 301-424-5509

BERNSTEIN, BURTON, LASERS, OPTICAL PHYSICS. *Current Pos:* RETIRED. *Personal Data:* b Brooklyn, NY, Dec 11, 20; m 61, Helen; c Pamela & Ronna. *Educ:* Brooklyn Col, BA, 42; Columbia Univ, MA, 49; Mass Inst Technol, PhD(physics), 54. *Prof Exp:* Res scientist res lab, Philco Corp, 54-57; staff scientist, United Nuclear Corp, 57-58; res physicist, Gen Precision Labs, 58-61; staff physicist, Loral Electronics Corp, 61-62; sr staff scientist, Repub Aviation Corp, 62-64; mgr, Crystal Physics & Laser Develop Lab, Airtron Div Litton Industs, 64-66; from assoc prof to prof physics, Col New Paltz, State Univ NY, 66-95. *Mem:* Am Phys Soc; Sigma Xi. *Res:* Semiconductor surface physics; solid state laser materials. *Mailing Add:* 51 Timberline Dr Poughkeepsie NY 12603

BERNSTEIN, CAROL, MOLECULAR BIOLOGY, GENETICS. *Current Pos:* res assoc microbiol, 68-77, adj asst prof, 77-81, RES ASSOC PROF, COL MED, UNIV ARIZ, 81- *Personal Data:* b Paterson, NJ, Mar 20, 41; m 62, Harris; c Beryl, Golda & Benjamin. *Educ:* Univ Chicago, BS, 61; Yale Univ, MS, 64; Univ Calif, Davis, PhD(genetics), 67. *Prof Exp:* NIH fel zool, Univ Calif, Davis, 67-68. *Concurrent Pos:* Mem, panel grad fels, NSF, 84-86; mem, Nat Coun, Am Asn Univ Professors, 86-89; treas, Nat Assembly State Conferences, Am Asn Univ Professors, 86-89; mem, panel grad fels, NSF, 91-93 & 94; pres, Am Asn Univ Prof, Ariz Conf, 84-90 & 91- *Mem:* Genetics Soc Am; Am Soc Microbiol; Am Asn Univ Professors. *Res:* DNA repair; structure and replication of DNA of microorganisms; mechanisms of chemical mutagenesis; molecular basis of aging; the sexual cycle; etiology of colon cancer. *Mailing Add:* Dept Microbiol & Immunol Col Med Univ Ariz Tucson AZ 85724. *Fax:* 520-626-2100; *E-Mail:* carol@ccit.arizona.edu

BERNSTEIN, DAVID MAIER, inhalation & fiber toxicology, regulatory affairs & pharmaceutical registration, for more information see previous edition

BERNSTEIN, ELAINE KATZ, BIOCHEMISTRY, SCIENCE WRITING. *Current Pos:* SCI WRITER & ED, 74- *Personal Data:* b Baltimore, Md, May 14, 22; m 55; c 2. *Educ:* Goucher Col, BA, 41; Oberlin Col, MA, 42. *Prof Exp:* Asst scientist, Metall Lab, Univ Chicago, 43-46; assoc scientist, Argonne Nat Lab, 46-58, consult clin chem, 58-60; sci info specialist, John Crerar Libr, Chicago, 63-70; writer & ed med & clin chem, 70-74. *Mem:* AAAS; Sigma Xi; Fedn Am Scientists; Scientists in Pub Interest; Radiation Res Soc. *Res:* Clinical chemistry; liver function; toxicology; radiation-induced biochemical changes; leukemia. *Mailing Add:* 1480 Concorde Circle Highland Park IL 60035-3928

BERNSTEIN, ELLIOT R, CHEMICAL PHYSICS, SPECTROSCOPY. *Current Pos:* assoc prof, 75-79, PROF CHEM, COLO STATE UNIV, 79-, ASSOC CHMN, DEPT CHEM, 92- *Personal Data:* b New York, NY, Apr 14, 41; m 65, Barbara Wyman; c Rebecca Ann & Jephta Robin. *Educ:* Princeton Univ, BA, 63; Calif Inst Technol, PhD(chem physics), 67. *Prof Exp:* Res assoc paramagnetic resonance, Univ Chicago, 67-69; asst prof chem, Princeton Univ, 69-75. *Concurrent Pos:* Consult, Los Alamos Nat Lab, 75-, Philip Morris, 84-, Du Pont, 85- *Mem:* Am Chem Soc; fel Am Phys Soc. *Res:* Spectroscopy of inorganic and organic molecular crystals; exchange interactions, magnetic ordering and exciton structure in molecular solids; light scattering studies of phase transition in molecular solids and liquid crystals; spectroscopy of cryogenic liquid solutions and molecular clusters; structure of non rigid molecules; chemical reactions in clusters. *Mailing Add:* Dept Chem Colo State Univ Ft Collins CO 80523. *Fax:* 970-491-1801; *E-Mail:* erb@lamar.colostate.edu

BERNSTEIN, EMIL OSCAR, CELL BIOLOGY. *Current Pos:* MEM STAFF, DEPT BIOL, ALLEGHENY COL, 80- *Personal Data:* b New York, NY, Dec 16, 29; m 51; c 2. *Educ:* Syracuse Univ, AB, 51, MS, 53; Univ Calif, Los Angeles, PhD(zool), 56. *Prof Exp:* Am Cancer Soc fel, Univ Calif, Los

Angeles, 56-57; from instr to assoc prof zool, Univ Conn, 57-65; assoc prof, Univ Md, 65-68; sr res assoc, Gillette Res Inst, 68-73, prin res assoc, 73-80. *Concurrent Pos:* NSF grant, 59-, fel biol inst, Carsberg Found, Copenhagen, 63-64. *Mem:* AAAS; Am Soc Cell Biol; Soc Gen Physiol; Electron Micros Soc Am; Sigma Xi. *Res:* Cell physiology; growth and division of cells; metabolic problems; problem of obligate autotrophy; scanning electron microscopy; skin morphology and physiology; ultrastructure; cell biology and cell physiology. *Mailing Add:* 23 Waterglen Circle Sacramento CA 95826

BERNSTEIN, EUGENE F, surgery; deceased, see previous edition for last biography

BERNSTEIN, EUGENE H, BIOCHEMISTRY, VIRAL ONCOLOGY. *Current Pos:* CONSULT, 89- *Personal Data:* b New York, NY; m 52, Bernice A Frant; c Andrew M, Robert S & Jill T. *Educ:* US Merchant Marine Acad, BS, 47; Rutgers Univ, BS, 51, MS, 52, PhD(biochem, microbiol), 55. *Prof Exp:* USPHS fel, Sloan-Kettering Inst Cancer Res, New York, 55-56; biochemist, Colgate-Palmolive Co Dent Res, NJ, 56-58, sect head, 58-59; owner & dir, Univ Labs, Inc, 59-92. *Concurrent Pos:* Vis investr, Inst Microbiol, Rutgers Univ, 59-68; vis prof, Waksman Inst Microbiol, 82-86 & Robert Wood Johnson Med Sch, Rutgers Univ, 86-89. *Mem:* AAAS; Am Chem Soc; NY Acad Sci; Am Soc Microbiologists; Int Leukemia Soc; Am Acad Microbiologist. *Res:* Enzymology; virology, especially avian and mammalian tumor and leukemia viruses; toxicology; microbiology; nutrition; carcinogenesis; cancer chemotherapy. *Mailing Add:* 901 S Park Ave Highland Park NJ 08904

BERNSTEIN, EUGENE MERLE, atomic & nuclear physics, for more information see previous edition

BERNSTEIN, GERALD SANFORD, reproductive biology, obstetrics & gynecology, for more information see previous edition

BERNSTEIN, HARRIS, GENETICS. *Current Pos:* assoc prof, 68-74, PROF MICROBIOL, COL MED, UNIV ARIZ, 74- *Personal Data:* b Brooklyn, NY, Dec 12, 34; m 62, Carol Adelberg; c Beryl, Golda & Benjamin. *Educ:* Purdue Univ, BS, 56; Calif Inst Technol, PhD(genetics), 61. *Prof Exp:* USPHS res fel genetics, Yale Univ, 61-63; asst prof, Univ Calif, Davis, 63-68. *Concurrent Pos:* Grantee, NSF, 64-79, NIH, 79-87, Am Chem Soc, 76-95. *Mem:* Genetics Soc Am; Am Soc Microbiol; Am Soc Biochem & Molecular Biol; Sigma Xi; fel Am Acad Microbiol. *Res:* Evolution of sexual reproduction; DNA damage as the basis of aging; DNA damage and programmed cell death in relation to colon cancer. *Mailing Add:* Dept Microbiol & Immunol Univ Ariz Med Col Tucson AZ 85724. *Fax:* 520-626-2100; *E-Mail:* carol@ccit.arizona.edu

BERNSTEIN, HERBERT J, RECONSTRUCTIVE KNOWLEDGE, SCIENCE POLICY. *Current Pos:* from asst prof to assoc prof, 71-83, PROF PHYSICS, HAMPSHIRE COL, 71-; MASS INST TECHNOL, 80-; PRES, INST SCI & INTERDISCIPLINARY STUDIES, AMHERST, 92- *Personal Data:* b Washington, DC, Apr 21, 43; m 71, Mary Mayers; c Carolyn J & Laila J. *Educ:* Columbia Univ, BS, 63; Univ Calif, MS, 65, PhD(theoret physics), 67. *Honors & Awards:* Proctor Prize, Sigma Xi, 87. *Prof Exp:* Mem, Inst Advan Studies, Princeton, 67-69. *Concurrent Pos:* Tech Dir, Econ Develop Agency; consult World Bank, Dept Energy; Pres Sci Adv, AAAS; vis scientist, Technion, Haifa, Israel, SLAC, Palo Alto, Calif, ITP, Santa Barbara. *Mem:* Am Phys Soc. *Res:* Quantum interferometry and its implications; quantum computation and teleportation; science policy, especially energy and international science; reconstructive science for social benefit by including its moral and cultural concommittants, assumptions, and effects; multi-particle interferometry. *Mailing Add:* 266 Shays St Amherst MA 01002. *E-Mail:* hbernstein@hamp.hampshire.edu

BERNSTEIN, HERBERT JACOB, BIOINFORMATICS, REAL-TIME INSTRUMENT CONTROL & DATA ACQUISITION. *Current Pos:* CONSULT, BERNSTEIN & SONS, 82- *Personal Data:* b Brooklyn, NY, Sept 26, 44; m 68, Frances C Turnheim; c Michael E & Daniel J. *Educ:* NY Univ, BA, 64, MS, 65, PhD(math), 68. *Prof Exp:* Assoc res scientist, AEC Comput & Appl Math Ctr, Courant Inst Math Sci, NY Univ, 68-70; sci programmer analyst II, Appl Math Dept, Brookhaven Nat Lab, 70-71, sr comput sci analyst, 71-74, assoc scientist, Chem Dept, 74-78, scientist, 78-83. *Concurrent Pos:* Opers mgr, Chem Info Syst, NIH/Environ Protection Agency, 78-79; vis mem, Courant Inst Math Sci, NY Univ, 82-83, dir admin comput, 89-90; res collabr, Brookhaven Nat Lab, 83-93, sr comput analyst, 93-; trustee, Consortium Sci Comput, 84-91; dir, Nysernet, Inc, 86-89, vchmn, 87-89. *Mem:* Am Math Soc; Am Crystallog Asn; Soc Indust & Appl Math; Math Asn Am; Math Asn UK; Brit Crystallog Asn. *Res:* Applied computer science; high speed parallel processing; robotics; data communications; numerical linear algebra; evaluation of computer related technology. *Mailing Add:* PO Box 177 Bellport NY 11713-0177. *Fax:* 516-286-1999; *E-Mail:* yaya@bernstein-plus-sons.com

BERNSTEIN, I LEONARD, CLINICAL IMMUNOLOGY ALLERGY, PULMONARY DISEASES. *Current Pos:* intern, 49-50, CLIN PROF MED & ATTEND PHYSICIAN, CINCINNATI GEN HOSP, 56- *Personal Data:* b Jersey City, NJ, Feb 17, 24; m 48, Miriam; c David, Susan, Ellen & Jonathan. *Educ:* Univ Cincinnati, MD, 49; Am Bd Internal Med, dipl, 58; Am Bd Allergy, dipl, 77; Am Bd Diag Immunol, dipl, 89. *Prof Exp:* Resident, Jewish Hosp, Cincinnati, 50-51; med officer, USAF, 51-53; resident, Bellevue Hosp, 53-55; fel, Northwestern Univ, Chicago, 55-56. *Concurrent Pos:* Co-dir, Allergy Res Lab & Allergy Training Prog, Univ Cincinnati Med Ctr, 58-; consult, Vet Admin, Cincinnati, 64-; chmn, Antigistamine Panel Drug Interaction Proj, Am Pgarmaceut Asn, 75-; chmn educ coun & past pres, Am Acad Allergy, 78-; dir, Am Bd Allery & Immunol, 84-90; gov, Am Bd Internal Med, 86-89; mem, Pulmonary/Allergy Adv Comt, Food & Drug Admin, 88-92. *Mem:* Fel Am Acad Allergy; fel Am Col Physicians; Am Asn Immunologists; Am Thoracic Soc; AAAS; Cent Soc Clin Res. *Res:* Immediate hypersensitivity; regulation of the IgE type of immune response; industrial allergens; platelet function in allergic individuals; clinical investigation of various new drugs and procedures; reproductive immunology; occupational asthma. *Mailing Add:* 8464 Winton Rd Cincinnati OH 45231. *Fax:* 513-931-0779; *E-Mail:* bernstja@mcbeh.san.uc.edu

BERNSTEIN, IRA BORAH, THEORETICAL PHYSICS. *Current Pos:* prof appl physics, 64-88, Carl A Morse prof appl physics, 88-94, CARL A MORSE PROF MECH ENG & APPL PHYSICS, YALE UNIV, 94- *Personal Data:* b Bronx, NY, Nov 8, 24; m 55; c 2. *Educ:* City Col New York, BChE, 44; NY Univ, PhD(physics), 50. *Honors & Awards:* Maxwell Prize, Am Phys Soc. *Prof Exp:* Res physicist, Westinghouse Res Labs, 50-54; sr res physicist, Plasma Physics Lab, Princeton Univ, 54-64. *Concurrent Pos:* Fulbright scholar, 62-63; Guggenheim fel, 69. *Mem:* Nat Acad Sci; fel Am Phys Soc. *Res:* Theoretical plasma physics. *Mailing Add:* Dept Appl Physics Yale Univ New Haven CT 06520-2159

BERNSTEIN, IRWIN SAMUEL, PRIMATOLOGY. *Current Pos:* RES PROF PSYCHOL & ZOOL, UNIV GA, 68- *Personal Data:* b Brooklyn, NY, July 11, 33; m 92, Genie S Smith; c Celeste, Brad, Tao & Evan. *Educ:* Cornell Univ, BA, 54; Univ Chicago, MA, 55, PhD(psychol), 59. *Prof Exp:* Res fel & res assoc psychobiol, Yerkes Regional Primate Res Ctr, 60-67, 67-91. *Concurrent Pos:* Grantee, NSF, NIH, NIMH, Walter Reed Army Inst Res & Wenner Gren Found Arthrop Res. *Mem:* Am Soc Primatologists (pres, 80-82); fel Animal Behav Soc; Int Primatol Soc; Int Ethological Cong. *Res:* Primate social behavior; principles of group organization; communication and comparative patterns of activities in both field and captive group studies; control of aggression; endocrine correlates of sex, stress and aggression; adolescent socialization; dominance. *Mailing Add:* Dept Psychol Univ Ga Athens GA 30602. *E-Mail:* isbern@uga.cc.uga.edu

BERNSTEIN, ISADORE A, BIOCHEMISTRY, TOXICOLOGY. *Current Pos:* res assoc, Inst Indust Health, Univ Mich, 53-56 & 59-70, from instr to assoc prof biol chem, 54-61, from assoc prof to prof indust health, 61-67, prof biol chem, 68-90, prof environ & indust health, 70-90, EMER PROF BIOL CHEM & ENVIRON & INDUST HEALTH, UNIV MICH, ANN ARBOR, 90- *Personal Data:* b Clarksburg, WVa, Dec 23, 19; m 42, Claire Bernstein; c Lynne & Amy. *Educ:* Johns Hopkins Univ, AB, 41; Western Res Univ, PhD(biochem), 52. *Honors & Awards:* Stephan Rothman Mem Award, Soc Invest Dermatol, 81; Order Rising Sun, Japan, 89. *Prof Exp:* Res assoc biochem, Western Res Univ, 51-52, sr instr, 52-53. *Concurrent Pos:* Consult, Vet Admin Hosp, Allen Park, Mich, 61-70 & 72-; USPHS spec fel & vis prof, Inst Protein Res, Osaka Univ, 63-64; WHO travel fel, Western Europe, 72 & China, 86; vis prof, Rockefeller Univ, 77-78; vis scientist, Hebrew Univ, 78; assoc dir res, Inst Environ & Indust Health, Univ Mich, Ann Arbor, 78-89; dir, Toxicol Prog, Univ Mich, Ann Arbor, 83-87; vis scientist, NIH, 88; hon prof, Kunming Med Col, 88- *Mem:* Fel AAAS; Am Soc Biochem & Molecular Biol; Am Soc Microbiol; Am Soc Cell Biol; hon Soc Invest Dermat (vpres, 73-74); Am Chem Soc; Soc Toxicol; Am Col Toxicol; Am Inst Biol Sci; Sigma Xi. *Res:* Cutaneous metabolism, keratinization, neoplasia and differentiation; biochemical mechanisms of accommodation. *Mailing Add:* Sch Pub Health Rm 1528 Univ Mich Ann Arbor MI 48109-2029. *Fax:* 313-764-9424; *E-Mail:* lsabern@sph.umich.edu

BERNSTEIN, JAY, PEDIATRIC PATHOLOGY, RENAL PATHOLOGY. *Current Pos:* dir anat path, William Beaumont Hosp, 69-90, DIR, WILLIAM BEAUMONT HOSP RES INST, 84-, ASSOC MED DIR RES, 90- *Personal Data:* b New York, NY, May 14, 27; m 57, Carol Kritchman; c John & Michael. *Educ:* Columbia Univ, BA, 48; State Univ NY, MD, 52. *Honors & Awards:* Farber Lectr, Soc Pediat Path, 82; Barnett Award, Am Acad Pediat, 97; Pioneer Renal Patr Award, Renal Path Soc, 97. *Prof Exp:* Instr path, Sch Med, Wayne State Univ, 58-60, asst prof pediat, 60-62; from asst prof to assoc prof path, Albert Einstein Col Med, 62-69. *Concurrent Pos:* Attend pathologist, Children's Hosp Mich, Detroit, 57-62; sr res assoc, Child Res Ctr, Wayne State Univ, 60-62; contrib ed path, J Pediat, 68-84; partic pathologist, Int Study Kidney Dis Childhood, 68-86; vis assoc prof path, Albert Einstein Col Med, 69-74, vis prof, 74-; mem, Sci Adv Bd, Mich Kidney Dis Found, 72-89, chmn, 86-88; mem, Comt Classification & Nomenclature Renal Diseases, WHO, 75-77 & 81-95; consult pathologist, Children's Hosp of Mich, 75-; mem sci adv bd, Nat Kidney Found, 76-82; clin prof health sci, Ctr Health Sci, Oakland Univ, Rochester, Mich, 77-90; clin prof path, Sch Med, Wayne State Univ, 77-; co-ed, Perspective in Pediat Path, 78- *Mem:* Am Soc Invest Path; Int Acad Path; Am Soc Nephrology; Am Pediat Soc; Soc Pediat Path (pres, 69); Renal Path Soc (pres, 90-92). *Res:* Congenital renal abnormalities; renal disease-pathogenesis and ultrastructure; publications on pediatric renal pathology. *Mailing Add:* William Beaumont Hosp Res Inst 3601 W 13 Mile Rd Royal Oak MI 48073-6769. *Fax:* 248-551-5069; *E-Mail:* bexnstein@beaumont.edu

BERNSTEIN, JERALD JACK, NEUROANATOMY, NEUROSCIENCE. *Current Pos:* RES PROF NEUROSURG & PHYSIOL, COL MED, GEORGE WASHINGTON UNIV, 80-; CHIEF & CAREER RES SCIENTIST, LAB CENT NERVOUS SYST INJURY & REGENERATION, VET AFFAIRS MED CTR, 80- *Personal Data:* b Brooklyn, NY, Mar 30, 34; m 57, 86; c 2. *Educ:* Hunter Col, BA, 55; Univ Mich, MS, 57, PhD, 59. *Prof Exp:* Asst fisheries, Univ Mich, 56-58, asst zool, Mus Zool, 58-59, asst psychol, 58-59; assoc prof biol, Clarion State Col,

59-60; res biologist, Lab Neuroanat Sci, NIH, 60-65; asst prof anat, Ctr Neurobiol Sci, Col Med, Univ Fla, 65-73, prof neurosci & ophthal, Ctr Neurobiol Sci & Ctr Human Prosthetic Res, 69-81. *Concurrent Pos:* Res prof anat, Hadassah Med Sch, Jerusalem, Israel, 74 - *Mem:* AAAS; Soc Neurosci; Am Asn Pathologists; Am Asn Anat; Am Physiol Soc. *Res:* Morphological and neurochemical basis of spinal cord regeneration; neuro-oncology. *Mailing Add:* Vet Admin Med Ctr 151Q 50 Irving St NW Washington DC 20422

BERNSTEIN, JEREMY, THEORETICAL PHYSICS. *Current Pos:* PROF PHYSICS, STEVENS INST TECHNOL, 67- *Personal Data:* b Rochester, NY, Dec 31, 29. *Educ:* Harvard Univ, BA, 51, MA, 53, PhD(physics), 55. *Honors & Awards:* Westinghouse-AAAS Writing Prize, 64; Am Inst Physics-US Steel Found Sci Writing Prize, 70; Brandeis Award, 79; Brittanica Award, 87. *Prof Exp:* Res assoc physics, Cyclotron Lab, Harvard Univ, 55-57; mem, Inst Advan Study, 57-59; assoc, Brookhaven Nat Lab, 60-62; assoc prof, NY Univ, 62-67. *Concurrent Pos:* NSF fel, 59-61; Ferris prof, Princeton Univ, 80-82; Rabi vis prof, Columbia Univ, 83-84. *Mem:* Fel Am Phys Soc; Franklin Fel Royal Soc Arts. *Res:* Elementary particles weak interactions, and cosmology. *Mailing Add:* Dept Physics Stevens Inst Technol Castle Pt Sta Hoboken NJ 07030

BERNSTEIN, JOEL EDWARD, DERMATOPHARMACOLOGY, NEUROPHARMACOLOGY. *Current Pos:* PRES, GENDERM CORP, 83- *Personal Data:* b Chicago, Ill, Apr 8, 43; m 64; c 3. *Educ:* Carleton Col, BA, 64; Univ Chicago, MD, 69. *Prof Exp:* Res medicine, Univ Chicago, 70-73, clin pharm fel, 76-78, sr med fel, 77-79, asst prof, 79-82; vpres med affiliate, Schering-Plough Corp, 73-75; assoc dir clin res , Abbott Lab, 75-76; assoc prof, Northwestern Univ, 82-83. *Concurrent Pos:* Clin instr, Univ Tenn, 74-75. *Mem:* Am Acad Dermat; Am Soc Clin Pharmacol & Ther; Soc Investigative Dermat. *Res:* Dermato-pharmacology with a special interest in the role of neuropeptides and the skin; published over 100 research papers and textbook chapters. *Mailing Add:* 600 Knights Bridge Pkwy Lincolnshire IL 60069

BERNSTEIN, JOSEPH N, representation theory, differential equations, for more information see previous edition

BERNSTEIN, LAWRENCE, SOFTWARE PROJECT MANAGEMENT, SOFTWARE ARCHITECTURE. *Current Pos:* dir res & develop, AT&T, Bell Labs, 79-84 & 85-86, exec dir systs anal, 86-89, vpres prod mgt, Computer Systs, 89-90, vpres prod mgr, 90-92, CHIEF TECH OFF, AT&T, NETWORK SYSTS, 92- *Personal Data:* b New York, NY, Jan 20, 40; m 75, Christina Yulez; c Michael, Leon & David. *Educ:* Rensselaer Polytech Inst, BEE, 61; NY Univ, MEE, 63. *Prof Exp:* Asst vpres res & develop, Bellcore, 84-85. *Mem:* Fel Inst Elec & Electronics Engrs; Asn Comput Mach. *Res:* Software management including design development and deployment with a special emphasis of software for telecommunication management; network management. *Mailing Add:* AT&T Bell Labs 184 Liberty Corner Rd Rm 4W D12C Warren NJ 07059

BERNSTEIN, LAWRENCE RICHARD, PHARMACEUTICALS, MINERALOGY. *Current Pos:* FOUNDER & RES DIR, GEO MED INC, 95- *Personal Data:* b Los Angeles, Calif, Dec 23, 55; m 84, Pamela M Bain; c Aaron A & Hannah L. *Educ:* Harvard Univ, BA, 77, MA, 78; Stanford Univ, PhD(geol), 85. *Prof Exp:* Geologist, Brit Petroleum, 79-81, US Geol Surv, 82-86; pres & res dir, Amrita Corp, 93-95. *Concurrent Pos:* Consult geol, Mineral Search 86-92; minerals ed, Int Ctr for Diffraction Data, 92- *Mem:* Mineral Soc Am; Am Geophys Union; Sigma Xi. *Res:* Oral pharmaceutical formulation of gallium to treat osteoporosis, hypercalcemia, cancer; crystal chemistry of minor and trace elements in minerals and biologic materials; sulfide mineralogy; exploration and process mineralogy and geochemistry. *Mailing Add:* 380 Willow Rd Menlo Park CA 94025. *Fax:* 650-324-2603; *E-Mail:* larry.b@ix.netcom.com

BERNSTEIN, LESLIE, OTOLARYNGOLOGY, MAXILLOFACIAL SURGERY. *Current Pos:* CONSULT, 86- *Personal Data:* b Poland, Apr 26, 24; US citizen; m 57. *Educ:* Univ Witwatersrand, BDS, 47, MB, BCh, 54; Royal Col Physicians & Surgeons, Eng, dipl laryngol & otol, 59; Am Bd Otolaryngol, dipl, 63. *Honors & Awards:* Harris P Mosher Award, 68; Award of Merit, Am Acad Ophthal & Otolaryngol, 70; Ira Tresley Res Award, 72. *Prof Exp:* From asst prof to assoc prof otolaryngol, Col Med, Univ Iowa, 60-69, chmn sect maxillofacial-plastic surg, 69, prof otolaryngol & maxillofacial surg, 69-72; prof otorhinolaryngolog & chmn dept, Med Sch, Univ Calif, Davis, 72-86. *Mem:* Am Broncho-Esophagol Asn; fel Am Acad Ophthal & Otolaryngol; fel Am Acad Facial Plastic & Reconstruct Surg; fel Am Laryngol, Rhinol & Otol Soc; Int Asn Maxillofacial Surg (vpres). *Res:* Ear; Larynx; broncho-esophagology; cleft palate. *Mailing Add:* 77 Scripts Dr Suite 105 Sacramento CA 95825

BERNSTEIN, LESLIE, EPIDEMIOLOGY OF HORMONE DEPENDENT TUMORS. *Current Pos:* Res assoc biometry & epidemiol, Univ Southern Calif, 81-82, res asst prof, 82-85, from asst prof to assoc prof, 85-91, PROF BIOSTATIST & EPIDEMIOL, UNIV SOUTHERN CALIF, 91-, SR ASSOC DEAN, 96- *Personal Data:* b Los Angeles, Calif, Oct 9, 39; m 58; c 3. *Educ:* Univ Calif, Los Angeles, BA, 64; Univ Southern Calif, MS, 78, PhD(biometry), 81. *Concurrent Pos:* Consult, div geriatric med, Univ Calif Los Angeles, 81-84, Res Triangle Inst, 85-86, Nat Inst Child Abuse & Human Develop, 86, Lawrence Berkely Labs, 80- & Nat Inst Justice, 88; ad hoc reviewer, NIH, 84; prin investr epidemiol studies, Nat Cancer Inst, 85- *Mem:* Fel Am Col Epidemiol; Soc Epidemiol Res; Am Asn Cancer Res; NAm Asn Cent Cancer Registries; Biometrics Soc. *Res:* Evaluation of risk factors for hormone dependent tumors (breast, testis, prostate & thyroid cancer); evaluation of risk factors for multiple primary cancers, particularly the potential of cancer treatment induced second primary tumors; the development of methods for and analysis of animal carcinogenesis bioassays to generate data for human risk evaluation. *Mailing Add:* Dept Prev Med Pub Health Univ Southern Calif Sch Med 1441 Eastlake Ave MS 44 Los Angeles CA 90033-0800

BERNSTEIN, LIONEL M, INFORMATION SCIENCE, GASTROENTEROLOGY. *Current Pos:* prof health professions educ, Univ Ill, 85-88, actg head, Dept Med Educ, 88-90, prof med educ, 88-95, PROF BIOMED COMMUN, UNIV ILL, 88-, ADJ PROF MED EDUC, COL MED, 95- *Personal Data:* b Chicago, Ill, Sept 10, 23; m 52; c 3. *Educ:* Univ Ill, BS, 44, MD, 45, MS, 51, PhD(physiol), 54; Am Bd Internal Med, cert, 54. *Prof Exp:* Res assoc med & clin sci, Univ Ill, 52-53, instr med & physiol, 53-54; chief, Metab Res Div, Med Nutrit Lab, Fitzsimons Army Hosp, Denver, Colo, 54-55; physician sr grade, Vet Admin Hosp, Sepulveda, Calif, 55-56; chief, Gastroenterol Sect, Vet Admin Hosp, Hines, Ill, 56-57, assoc chief staff, 57-62; chief med serv, Vet Admin W Side Hosp, Chicago, 62-67; dir res serv, Vet Admin Cent Off, 67-70; assoc dir extramural progs, Nat Inst Arthritis & Metab Dis, 70-73; dir off prog opers, Dept HEW, 73-74, spec asst, Off Asst Secy Health, 75-77; asst dep dir res & educ, Lister Hill Nat Ctr Biomed Commun, Nat Libr Med, 77-78, dir, 78-83. *Concurrent Pos:* Vet admin mem, Gen Med Study Sect, NIH, 62-67; clin prof med, George Washington Univ, 82-; adj prof med, Sch Med, George Washington Univ, 82; pres, Knowledge Systs, Inc, 83- *Mem:* Inst Med-Nat Acad Sci; AMA; Am Gastroenterol Asn; Am Fedn Clin Res; fel Am Col Physicians; AAAS. *Res:* Renal physiology of clinical disease states; gastroenterology; author or co-author of over 70 publications. *Mailing Add:* Ctr Educ Develop 1802 Kolonama Sq NW Washington DC 20008

BERNSTEIN, MARVIN HARRY, COMPARATIVE PHYSIOLOGY. *Current Pos:* from asst prof to assoc prof, 73-82, head, 90-93, PROF BIOL, NMEX STATE UNIV, 82- *Personal Data:* b Los Angeles, Calif, Dec 30, 43; m 66; c 2. *Educ:* Univ Calif, Los Angeles, BA, 65, MA, 66, PhD(zool), 70. *Prof Exp:* NIH trainee neurophysiol, Univ Calif, Los Angeles, 70-71; from temp instr to temp asst prof zool, Duke Univ, 71-73. *Concurrent Pos:* Fulbright-Hayes Int Travel Award, Israel, 80; prin investr, Minority Biomed Res Support Prog, NMex State Univ, 75-, dir, Minority Access Res Careers Prog, 77-87. *Mem:* Am Physiol Soc; Soc Integrative & Comp Biol; Sigma Xi; fel AAAS. *Res:* Respiration, gas transport, cardiovascular function and temperature compensation in vertebrates during rest and locomotion, growth and adulthood, at sea level and high altitude. *Mailing Add:* Dept Biol NMex State Univ Las Cruces NM 88003. *Fax:* 505-646-5665; *E-Mail:* mbernste@nmsu.edu

BERNSTEIN, MAURICE H(ARRY), ANATOMY, CELL BIOLOGY. *Current Pos:* from asst prof to prof, 58-88, EMER PROF ANAT, SCH MED, WAYNE STATE UNIV, 88- *Personal Data:* b St Louis, Mo, Apr 3, 23; m 67, Harriet Hiester. *Educ:* Wash Univ, AB, 47, PhD(zool), 50. *Prof Exp:* Am Cancer Soc-Nat Res Coun fels, Univ Mo-Columbia, 50-51 & Univ Calif, Berkeley, 51-52; jr staff mem genetics, Carnegie Inst Wash, 52-54; asst res biologist, Virus Lab, Univ Calif, Berkeley, 54-56; res physiologist, Res Inst, Mt Sinai Hosp, Los Angeles, Calif, 56-57; asst res anatomist, Sch Med, Univ Calif, Los Angeles, 57-58. *Concurrent Pos:* Lalor Found fel, Marine Biol Lab, Woods Hole, Mass, 59; consult, Vet Admin, 65-70 & NIH, 67; vis prof anat & reprod biol, Univ Hawaii, 71-72; consult, cell biol; fel, AAAS, 78; Vis Prof anat, Univ Toronto. *Mem:* Emer mem AAAS; emer mem Am Asn Anat; emer mem Am Soc Cell Biol; emer mem Asn Res Vision & Ophthal; Soc Study Reprod; emer mem Micros Soc Am. *Res:* Role of retinal pigment epithelium organelles in visual function; lysosomes and receptor-mediated endocytosis in photoreceptor disk shedding and phagocytosis; regulatory cell interactions, lysosomes, and receptor-mediated endocytosis in testis. *Mailing Add:* 2674 Pine Ridge Dr Lillian AL 36549-5240

BERNSTEIN, RALPH, LIGHTENING SCIENCE RESEARCH & DEVELOPMENT. *Current Pos:* PROJ MGR, EPRI, 92- *Personal Data:* b Zweibrucken, Ger, Feb 20, 33; US citizen; m 59; c 3. *Educ:* Univ Conn, BSEE, 56; Syracuse Univ, MSEE, 60. *Honors & Awards:* Except Sci Achievement Medal, NASA, 74; Cert of Appreciation-Outstanding Serv, Nat Res Coun, 87. *Prof Exp:* Engr & scientist, Palo Alto Sci Ctr, IBM Corp, 56-60, assoc engr, 60-62, staff engr, 62-68, sr engr & mgr, Syst Design Dept, 68-71, sr engr, scientist & mgr, Adv Image Processing Anal Develop Dept, NY, 71-79, staff mem, 79-85, sr tech staff mem & mgr, Image Sci & Applns Dept, 85-92. *Concurrent Pos:* Mem space sci bd, Nat Res Coun-Nat Acad Sci, 77-82, chmn, Comt Data Mgt & Comput, 78-81, mem space appln bd, 82-; consult, NASA Space Appln Adv Comt, 82-85; adj prof, Univ Calif, San Francisco, 83- *Mem:* Fel Inst Elec & Electronics Engrs; Am Soc Photogram. *Res:* Digital image science and research studies for Earth observation sensor data and medical image science; image system research and development; earth resources technology Landsat satellite studies; navigation systems and positioning devices; oceanographic and geophysical computer system development; automatic control systems analysis and development. *Mailing Add:* 1201 Woodview Terr Los Altos CA 94024

BERNSTEIN, ROBERT LEE, PHYSICAL OCEANOGRAPHY, REMOTE SENSING. *Current Pos:* ASST RES OCEANOGR, SCRIPPS INST OCEANOG, UNIV CALIF, SAN DIEGO, 72- *Personal Data:* b Rochester, NY, Nov 6, 44; m 68; c 2. *Educ:* Calif Inst Technol, BS, 66; Columbia Univ, MS, 69, PhD(oceanog), 71. *Concurrent Pos:* Mem, NPac Exp Exec Comt, NSF, 75-; consult, World Meteorol Orgn, 76-77; mem, Sea Satellite Altimeter Exp Team, NASA, 77- *Mem:* Am Geophys Union; AAAS. *Res:* Ocean circulation; mesoscale eddy dynamics; large scale air-sea interaction; methods of satellite oceanography. *Mailing Add:* 9240 Trade Pl Apt 100 San Diego CA 92126

BERNSTEIN, ROBERT STEVEN, EPIDEMIOLOGY. *Current Pos:* epidemic intel serv officer, 79-81, MED EPIDEMIOLOGIST, CTR ENVIRON HEALTH, CTR DIS CONTROL, 81- *Personal Data:* b New York, NY, Aug 11, 43; m 88, Widya Astutie; c Lynn & Aaron. *Educ:* Univ Pa, AB, 65; Pa State Univ, PhD(biochem), 71; Univ Conn, MD, 77; Johns Hopkins Univ, MPH, 79. *Honors & Awards:* Presidential Citation, 80. *Prof Exp:* Fel neuropharmacol, Sch Med, Yale Univ, 71-73; intern med & surg, USPHS Hosp, San Francisco, 77-78. *Concurrent Pos:* Adj asst prof, Sch Med, WVa Univ, 79-81; med epidemiologist, WHO, Indonesia, 85-90 & USAID Div, Human Immunodeficiency virus, Acquired Immunodeficiency Syndrome, 91-92; vis prof, Dept Community Med, Emory Univ, 87-91. *Mem:* AAAS; NY Acad Sci; Am Pub Health Asn; Am Thoracic Soc; Soc Epidemiol Res. *Res:* Epidemiology of acute and chronic diseases in environmental and occupational health; basic science research in enzyme structure and function and in neurochemistry. *Mailing Add:* USAID/AFR/SD/HRD 1111 N 19th St Suite 300 Rosslyn VA 22209

BERNSTEIN, SANFORD IRWIN, DEVELOPMENTAL GENETICS. *Current Pos:* from asst prof to assoc prof, San Diego State Univ, 83-88, assoc dir, 87-92, dir, 92-95, PROF BIOL, SAN DIEGO STATE UNIV, 88-, CHAIR BIOL, 95- *Personal Data:* b Brooklyn, NY, June 10, 53; m 83, Laurel Spear. *Educ:* State Univ, NY, Stony Brook, BS, 74; Wesleyan Univ, PhD(biol), 79. *Prof Exp:* Fel molecular biol, Univ Va, 79-82. *Concurrent Pos:* Co-dir, Recombinant DNA Cert Prog, 83-; estab investr, Am Heart Asn, 89-94; assoc ed, Develop Biol, 91-95; grant rev panel, NIH, Am Heart Asn. *Mem:* AAAS; Genetics Soc Am; Sigma Xi; Am Soc Cell Biol; Am Soc Biochem & Molecular Biol; Soc Develop Biol. *Res:* Molecular structure of Drosophila muscle genes; analysis of genetic defects in muscle genes; mechanism of alternative RNA splicing; function of contractile protein. *Mailing Add:* Dept Biol Molecular Biol Inst San Diego State Univ San Diego CA 92182-4614. *Fax:* 619-594-5676; *E-Mail:* sbernst@sunstroke.sdsu.edu

BERNSTEIN, SELDON EDWIN, MEDICAL GENETICS, HEMATOLOGY. *Current Pos:* assoc staff scientist, Jackson Lab, 56-58, staff scientist, 58-67, asst dir, 64-72, sr staff scientist, 67-87, EMER SR STAFF SCIENTIST, JACKSON LAB, 87- *Personal Data:* b Bangor, Maine, Jan 3, 26; m 50, 59; c 4. *Educ:* Univ Maine, BA, 49, MA, 52; Brown Univ, PhD(biol), 56. *Prof Exp:* Asst, Univ Maine, 49-52; asst, Brown Univ, 52-54. *Concurrent Pos:* Mem bd dirs, Col of the Atlantic, 69-79, chmn, 72-79; lectr zool, Univ Maine, 71-86. *Mem:* Int Soc Exp Hemat; Am Genetic Asn; Am Soc Hemat; NY Acad Sci. *Res:* Normal and pathological gene-environment interactions in the development and regulation of mammalian red cell function; experimental hematology. *Mailing Add:* Jackson Lab 600 Main St Bar Harbor ME 04609

BERNSTEIN, SHELDON, PHYSIOLOGICAL CHEMISTRY. *Current Pos:* PRES, BERNSTEIN ASSOCS, INC, 90- *Personal Data:* b Milwaukee, Wis, Mar 23, 27; m 48, Estelle Katz; c Bradley A, Richard N & Jodi Lynn (Orshan). *Educ:* Univ Wis, BS, 49, PhD(physiol chem), 52. *Honors & Awards:* Van Lanen Award, Am Chem Soc. *Prof Exp:* Asst physiol chem, Univ Wis, 50-52; res biochemist, Upjohn Co, 52-53; vpres & dir res, 53-65, pres & dir res, Milbrew Inc, 65-83; dir tech develop, Univ Foods Corp, 83-89. *Concurrent Pos:* Pres, Bader & Bernstein, Inc, 61-83. *Mem:* AAAS; Am Chem Soc; Am Soc Microbiol; fel Am Inst Chemists; Inst Food Technologists; Sigma Xi. *Res:* Yeast and yeast products; enzymes; microbiological nutrients; nucleic acids; amino acids; vitamins; custom fermentations and fermentation research; food supplements; dairy products; whey fractionation; alcohol fermentation and production. *Mailing Add:* 3600 Mystic Pointe Dr No 913 Aventura FL 33180. *E-Mail:* shelalivai@aul.com

BERNSTEIN, SOL, INTERNAL MEDICINE, CARDIOLOGY. *Current Pos:* MED DIR, HEALTH RES ASN, 54- *Personal Data:* b West New York, NJ, Feb 3, 27; wid; c Paul. *Educ:* Univ Southern Calif, AB, 52, MD, 56. *Hon Degrees:* ScD, Calif Col Podiatry, 78. *Prof Exp:* Resident internal med, Los Angeles County Hosp, Calif, 57-60; from asst prof to prof med, Univ Southern Calif, 63-94, assoc dean, 86-94. *Concurrent Pos:* Fel cardiol, St Vincents Hosp, Los Angeles, 58-59; asst dir, Dept Med, Los Angeles Co-Univ Southern Calif Med Ctr, 66-72, chief prof serv, Gen Hosp, 72-74. *Mem:* Fel Am Col Cardiol; Am Heart Asn; fel Am Col Physicians; Am Diabetes Asn; Am Fedn Clin Res; Sigma Xi. *Res:* Hypertension; hyper cholesterolemia; endocarditis; health care delivery, student health and resident training. *Mailing Add:* 1640 Marengo St Los Angeles CA 90033

BERNSTEIN, STANLEY CARL, PHYSICAL ORGANIC CHEMISTRY. *Current Pos:* from asst prof to assoc prof, 70-84, chmn dept, 79-93, PROF CHEM, ANTIOCH COL, 84- *Personal Data:* b New York, NY, May 19, 37; m 60, Barbara Gilbert; c Lynn & Peter. *Educ:* Queens Col, NY, BS, 58; Univ Mich, MS, 61, PhD(chem), 63. *Prof Exp:* Res assoc chem, Ohio State Univ, 62-64, instr, 63-64; asst prof, Wright State Univ, 64-70. *Mem:* Am Chem Soc; AAAS; Nat Sci Teachers Asn. *Res:* The synthesis of potential fluorogenic pre-column HPLC derivatizing reagents for primary and secondary ammines; science and society. *Mailing Add:* Dept Chem Antioch Col Yellow Springs OH 45387-1697. *Fax:* 937-767-1891; *E-Mail:* sbernstein@antioc.antioch.edu

BERNSTEIN, STANLEY H, INTERNAL MEDICINE, CARDIOLOGY. *Current Pos:* ASSOC PROF CLIN MED, UNIV MIAMI, SCH MED, 74- *Personal Data:* b Brooklyn, NY, Sept 10, 24. *Educ:* Col William & Mary, BS, 45; NY Univ, MD, 48. *Prof Exp:* Vis prof, All India Med Inst, 64; assoc prof med, Univ Conn, 68-74. *Concurrent Pos:* Dir med serv, Mt Sinai Hosp, 68-74. *Mem:* Am Fedn Clin Res; fel Am Col Physicians; Am Heart Asn; AMA; fel NY Acad Med; fel Am Col Cardiol. *Res:* Pathogenesis of rheumatic fever and acute glomerulonephritis following streptococcal infection; the relation of streptococci to pharyngeal infections; myoglobin-antimyoglobin reactions in cardiac muscle after various injuries and its determination by immunofluorescent techniques. *Mailing Add:* 2500 E Hallandale Beach Blvd Hallandale FL 33009

BERNSTEIN, STEPHEN, NEUROPSYCHOLOGY. *Current Pos:* RES ASSOC, E P O BIOL, UNIV COLO, BOULDER, 76- *Personal Data:* b Rochester, NY, Nov 14, 33; m 60. *Educ:* Princeton Univ, AB, 55; Univ Wis, MA, 59, PhD(psychol), 62. *Prof Exp:* NIMH fels, Zurich, Switz, 62-64 & Paris, France, 64-65; trainee, Ment Health Training Prog, Brain Res Inst, Univ Calif, Los Angeles, 65-66, asst prof psychiat, 66-76. *Concurrent Pos:* NIMH career develop award, 66-76. *Mem:* AAAS; Sigma Xi. *Res:* Brain research; emotional development and complex learning in rhesus monkeys; neural mechanisms of behavior in ants, bees and wasps. *Mailing Add:* Dept E P O Biol Univ Colo Boulder CO 80309-0334

BERNSTEIN, THEODORE, ELECTRICAL ENGINEERING. *Current Pos:* PROF ELEC & COMPUTER ENG, UNIV WIS, MADISON, 62- *Personal Data:* b Milwaukee, Wis, Dec 1, 26; m 61; c 2. *Educ:* Univ Wis, BS, 49, MS, 55, PhD(elec eng), 59. *Prof Exp:* Eng designer, Boeing Airplane Co, Wash, 49-52; sr proj engr, AC Electronics, Wis, 52-56; instr elec eng, Univ Wis, 56-59; mem tech staff, TRW Systs Group, Calif, 59-62. *Mem:* Inst Elec & Electronics Engrs; Sigma Xi. *Res:* Magnetic materials and devices; electrical and lightning safety. *Mailing Add:* 5105 Regent St Madison WI 53705-4747

BERNSTEIN, URI, THERMODYNAMIC PROPERTIES. *Current Pos:* DEPT MGR, TECHNOL SERV CORP, 78- *Educ:* Mass Inst Technol, BS, 63; Calif Inst Technol, MS, 68; Univ Calif, PhD(physics), 74. *Prof Exp:* Mem tech staff, Logicon Inc, 69-74, 76-78; instr, Fla Atlantic Univ, 75-76. *Concurrent Pos:* Res fel, Univ Miami, 74-76. *Mem:* Am Phys Soc; Inst Elec & Electronics Engrs; Int Soc Optical Eng. *Res:* Contributed numerous articles to publications. *Mailing Add:* Technol Serv Corp 2950 31st St Santa Monica CA 90405. *Fax:* 310-452-3175; *E-Mail:* uri@tsc.com

BERNSTORF, EARL CRANSTON, ANATOMY. *Current Pos:* assoc prof, 64-80, PROF ANAT, MEHARRY MED COL, 80- *Personal Data:* b Judsonia, Ark, June 17, 21; m 44, Eileen Carpenter; c Robert C, Linda (Sullivan), Steven W & James R. *Educ:* Taylor Univ, BS, 44; Ind Univ, MA, 48, PhD(human anat), 50. *Prof Exp:* Teacher high schs, Ind, 44-46; from instr to asst prof anat, Hahnemann Med Col, 50-58; Ind Univ-AID contract prof, Postgrad Med Ctr, Karachi, Pakistan, 58-63; vis assoc prof, Med Ctr, Ind Univ, 63-64. *Mem:* Endocrine Soc; Am Asn Anat; Pakistan Asn Advan Sci. *Res:* Histology; neuroanatomy; endocrinology. *Mailing Add:* Dept Anat & Cell Biol Meharry Med Col 1005 18th Ave Nashville TN 37220

BERNTHAL, FREDERICK MICHAEL, NUCLEAR CHEMISTRY, NUCLEAR PHYSICS. *Current Pos:* DEP DIR, NSF, 90- *Personal Data:* b Sheridan, Wyo, Jan 10, 43; c 1. *Educ:* Valparaiso Univ, BS, 64; Univ Calif, Berkeley, PhD(chem), 69. *Prof Exp:* Res staff chemist, Heavy Ion Accelerator Lab, Yale Univ, 69-70; asst prof chem & physics, Mich State Univ, 70-75, assoc prof, 75-80; legis asst, 78-80, chief legis asst to US Sen Howard Baker, 80-83; comnr, US Nuclear Regulatory Comn, 83-88; asst secy state, Oceans & Int Environ & Sci Affairs, 88-90. *Concurrent Pos:* Vis scientist, Niels Bohr Inst, Univ Copenhagen, 76-77; NATO sr scientist fel, 77; Cong sci fel, Am Phys Soc, 78-79. *Mem:* AAAS; Am Chem Soc; Am Phys Soc; Sigma Xi. *Res:* Nuclear spectroscopy and structure; behavior of nuclei at very high spin; nuclear decay; applications of nuclear technology. *Mailing Add:* 4936 30th Pl Washington DC 20008

BERNTHAL, HAROLD GEORGE, CHEMISTRY. *Current Pos:* CHMN, COBERN INC, LAKE FOREST, ILL, 86- *Personal Data:* b Frankenmuth, Mich, June 11, 28; m 58, Margaret Hrebek; c Barbara Anne, Karen Elizabeth & James Willard. *Educ:* Mich State Univ, BS, 50. *Prof Exp:* Pres, Am Hosp Supply Corp, Ill, 74-85. *Concurrent Pos:* Bd dirs, Nat Stand Corp, Nalco Chem Co & Butler Mfg Co; trustee, Northwestern Mem Hosp, Vaparaiso Univ & Wheat Ridge Found. *Mem:* Health Industs Asn; Health Indust Mfr Asn; Pharmaceut Mfr Asn. *Mailing Add:* 545 Circle Lane Lake Forest IL 60045-3334

BERNTHAL, JOHN E(RWIN), SPEECH PATHOLOGY. *Current Pos:* DIR BARKLEY MEM CTR, UNIV NEBR, LINCOLN. *Personal Data:* b Sheridan, Wyo, July 18, 40; m 66; c 2. *Educ:* Wayne State Col, BA, 62; Univ Kans, MA, 64; Univ Wis, PhD(commun disorders), 71. *Prof Exp:* Assoc prof speech path, Mankato State Univ, 70-73; asst prof speech path & dir, Speech Clin, Univ Md, 73-79. *Concurrent Pos:* head & prof speech path, Univ Northern Iowa, 79- *Mem:* Fel Am Speech Hearing Lang Asn, 79. *Res:* Child phonology and management of individuals with articulation disorders. *Mailing Add:* 7611 Wren Ct Lincoln NE 68506

BERNTSEN, ROBERT ANDYV, INORGANIC CHEMISTRY. *Current Pos:* from asst prof to assoc prof, 48-57, head dept, 68-80, PROF CHEM, AUGUSTANA COL, 57- *Personal Data:* b Northfield, Minn, Feb 22, 17; m 43; c 2. *Educ:* St Olaf Col, BA, 39; NY Univ, MS, 41; Purdue Univ, PhD(chem), 49. *Prof Exp:* Instr chem, St Olaf Col, 41-43; head dept, Minot State Teachers Col, 43-46. *Mem:* Am Chem Soc. *Res:* Oxidation of carbohydrates with oxides of nitrogen. *Mailing Add:* 4536 25th Ave Rock Island IL 61201-5710

BERNTSON, GARY GLEN, PSYCHIATRY, PEDIATRICS. *Current Pos:* from asst prof to assoc prof, 73-81, PROF, DEPT PSYCHOL, OHIO STATE UNIV, COLUMBUS, 81-, PROF, DEPT PEDIAT, 83-, PROF, DEPT PSYCHIAT, 88- *Personal Data:* b Minneapolis, Minn, June 16, 45; m 84, Sarah T Boysen. *Educ:* Univ Minn, BA, 68, PhD, 71. *Prof Exp:* Fel, Rockefeller Univ, 71-73. *Concurrent Pos:* Fel, USPHS, 72; affil scientist, Yerkes Regional Primate Res Ctr, Emory Univ, 84- *Mem:* Soc Neurosci; Int Soc Develop Psychobiol; Soc Psychophysiol Res. *Res:* Discovery of methods of studying cognition in chimpanzees; novel concepts of control of the autonomic nervous system. *Mailing Add:* 048B Townshend Hall Ohio State Univ 1885 Neil Ave Columbus OH 43210-1281

BERON, PATRICK, URBAN HYDROLOGY, WATER & WASTE TREATMENT. *Current Pos:* ASST PROF WATER RESOURCES, UNIV QUE, MONTREAL, 83- *Personal Data:* b France, Mar 8, 52; Can citizen; m 76; c 2. *Educ:* Nat Inst Appl Sci, Toulouse, France, BEng, 74; Montreal Polytech, MASc, 76, PhD(civil eng), 83. *Prof Exp:* Teacher phys sci, Nat Ministry Educ, Tunisia, 76-78; res assoc, Montreal Polytech, 78-79 & 82, lectr, 80-83, fel, 83. *Mem:* Am Water Resources Asn; Int Asn Water Pollution Res & Control; Int Ozone Asn. *Res:* Improvement of urban drainage techniques; use of ozone as an alternative wastewater treatment; water management. *Mailing Add:* Chem Dept Succurscle Ctr Ville Univ Que PO Box 8888 Montreal PQ H3C 3P8 Can

BEROZA, MORTON, ANALYTICAL, ENVIRONMENTAL & PESTICIDE CHEMISTRY. *Current Pos:* CONSULT, 75- *Personal Data:* b New Haven, Conn, Mar 7, 17; m 46, Hannah Hurwitz; c Robert J & Rosalyn J. *Educ:* George Washington Univ, BS, 43; Georgetown Univ, MS, 46, PhD(org chem, biochem), 50. *Honors & Awards:* Hillebrand Prize, 63; Award in Chromatography & Electrophoresis, Am Chem Soc, 69; Harvey W Wiley Award, 70; Gold Medal Award, Synthetic Org Chem Mfrs Asn, 73; Int Award in Pesticide Chem, Am Chem Soc, 77; Distinguished Scientist Award, Friends Agr Res, 93. *Prof Exp:* Sci asst drugs, Food & Drug Admin, 39-42; chemist & chem engr plastics, US Naval Ord Lab, 46-48; res chemist, USDA, Beltsville, 48-74; sci coordr, Asn Off Anal Chemists, 75-81. *Mem:* AAAS; Am Chem Soc; Entom Soc Am; Soc Exp Biol & Med; Am Inst Chemists. *Res:* Insecticidal alkaloids of plants, isolation and chemical structure; insecticidal synergists of natural origin; synthesis of insect repellents, attractants and insecticides; spectroscopy; chromatography; pesticide residue analysis; analytical micromethodology; pheromones. *Mailing Add:* 821 Malta Lane Silver Spring MD 20901

BERRA, TIM MARTIN, ICHTHYOLOGY, ZOOGEOGRAPHY. *Current Pos:* from asst prof to prof, 72-95, EMER PROF ZOOL, OHIO STATE UNIV, MANSFIELD, 95- *Personal Data:* b St Louis, Mo, Aug 31, 43; m 67, Rita M Flynn. *Educ:* St Louis Univ, BS, 65; Tulane Univ, MS, 67, PhD(biol), 69. *Prof Exp:* NIH trainee environ biol, Tulane Univ, 66-69; Fulbright postdoctoral scholar zool, Australian Nat Univ, 69-70, demonstr, 70; sr tutor biol, Univ Papua New Guinea, 70-71. *Concurrent Pos:* Fulbright sr res scholar zool, Monash Univ, Melbourne, Australia, 79; ed, Ohio J Sci, 81-85; res assoc, Western Australian Mus, Perth, 86 & 88-89; board gov, Am Soc Ichthyologists & Herpetologists, 89-93; vis prof zool, Univ Concepcion, Chile, 92, Univ Otago, Dunedin, NZ, 96; bd trustees, Columbus Zoo, 92- *Mem:* Am Soc Ichthyologists & Herpetologists; Am Fisheries Soc; Soc Syst Biol; Australian Soc Limnol; Australian Soc Fish Biol; AAAS; hon fel Gilbert Ichthyol Soc. *Res:* Ecology, taxonomy, evolution and zoogeography of freshwater fishes; bibliography of naturalists, history of biology, natural history of Australia and New Guinea, and human evolution. *Mailing Add:* Dept Zool Ohio State Univ Mansfield OH 44906. *Fax:* 419-755-4241; *E-Mail:* berra.1@osu.edu

BERREND, ROBERT E, INVERTEBRATE ZOOLOGY. *Current Pos:* asst prof biol, 60-64, ASSOC PROF BIOL, SAN FRANCISCO STATE UNIV, 64- *Personal Data:* b Wausau, Wis, July 12, 25; m 57; c 2. *Educ:* Univ Wis, BA, 49, MA, 52, PhD(protozool), 58. *Prof Exp:* Instr zool, Mont State Univ, 58-60. *Mem:* AAAS; Sigma Xi. *Res:* Distribution of and locomotion in testaceans; estuarine ecology. *Mailing Add:* 529 Cortesi Ave South San Francisco CA 94080

BERRESFORD, GEOFFREY CASE, STOCHASTIC PROCESSES. *Current Pos:* from asst prof to assoc prof, 75-85, PROF MATH, C W POST CAMPUS, LONG ISLAND UNIV, 85- *Personal Data:* b New York, NY, May 25, 44; m 70, Barbara Oppenheim; c Lee & Chris. *Educ:* Lawrence Univ, BA, 67; New York Univ, MS, 71, PhD(math), 74. *Prof Exp:* Lectr natural sci, State Univ NY, Purchase, 73-74, asst prof math, 74-75. *Concurrent Pos:* Chmn speakers bur, Math Asn Am, 85- *Mem:* Math Asn Am; Am Math Soc; Soc Indust & Appl Math; Sigma Xi; NY Acad Sci. *Res:* Probability and partial differential equation; author of technical articles on algorithms, ordinary differential equations, logic, complex analysis; author of 3 textbooks. *Mailing Add:* Dept Math C W Post Campus-Long Island Univ Brookville NY 11548. *E-Mail:* berresfrd@aurora.liunet.edu

BERRETH, JULIUS R, NUCLEAR CHEMISTRY, NUCLEAR WASTE MANAGEMENT. *Current Pos:* MGR, WASTE MGT RES, WESTINGHOUSE IDAHO NUCLEAR. *Personal Data:* b Artas, SDak, Aug 15, 29; m 58; c 3. *Educ:* Cent Wash Col, BA, 52; Wash State Univ, MS, 59. *Prof Exp:* Chemist, Scott Paper Co, 56-57; chemist, Phillips Petrol Co, 57-59, res chemist, Atomic Energy Div, 59-68; res chemist & group leader nuclear chem, Aerojet Nuclear Co, 68-73; group leader, Allied Chem Corp, 73-80; mgr advan process develop, Exxon Nuclear Idaho Co, 80-85. *Mem:* Am Chem Soc; Am Nuclear Soc. *Res:* Preparations and separations of radioactive elements and determination of integral and differential cross-sections; neutron activation analysis on biological and inorganic samples; nuclear waste management; high-level waste immobilization, waste form and process development. *Mailing Add:* 780 S Bellin Rd Idaho Falls ID 83402

BERRETT, DELWYN GREEN, ORNITHOLOGY. *Current Pos:* RICKS COL, 82- *Personal Data:* b Menan, Idaho, July 27, 35; m 63, Francine D Lamph; c Ross F, William J, Leilani, Laura & John L. *Educ:* Brigham Young Univ, BS, 57, MS, 58; La State Univ, PhD(ornith), 62. *Prof Exp:* Mem staff zool, Ricks Col, 62-64; assoc prof zool, Brigham Young Univ, Hawaii Campus, 64-78. *Mem:* Wilson Ornith Soc. *Res:* Taxonomy, classification and distribution of birds. *Mailing Add:* Div Natural Sci Ricks Col Rexburg ID 83440. *E-Mail:* berretd@ricks.edu

BERRETT, PAUL O(RIN), ELECTRICAL ENGINEERING, PHYSICS. *Current Pos:* RETIRED. *Personal Data:* b Riverton, Utah, Mar 1, 28; m 52, Lillian Gerber; c Shaunna (Cuevas), Cynthia (Boyle), Roger, Leon, Bruce, Karen (Cleveland), Mark & Douglas. *Educ:* Univ Utah, BS, 53, PhD(elec eng, physics), 65; Univ Southern Calif, MS, 55. *Prof Exp:* Res engr, Hughes Aircraft Co, 53-56; instr elec eng, Univ Utah, 57-62, res fel, microwave devices lab, 62-64; from asst prof to prof elec eng, 64-71, Brigham Young Univ, 64-96. *Concurrent Pos:* Res engr, Upper Air Res Labs, Univ Utah, 59-61; res engr, Battelle Northwest Labs, 65; workshop, Goddard Space Flight Ctr, NASA, 67; sabbatical leave, Naval Weapons Ctr, China Lake, Calif, 70-71; consult, Eyring Res Inst, Provo, Utah, 82-96. *Mem:* Sr mem Inst Elec & Electronics Engrs; Am Inst Physics. *Res:* Microwaves; field theory; antennas; upper atmosphere measurements; electromagnetic waves in plasmas and plasma diagnostics; rocket plume-electromagnetic wave interactions; microwave systems; active antennas; ground interactive antennas. *Mailing Add:* 643 S 400 E Orem UT 84097

BERRETTINI, WADE HAYHURST, PSYCHIATRY, MOLECULAR BIOLOGY. *Current Pos:* STAFF PSYCHIATRIST, CLIN NEUROGENETICS BR, NIMH, 81-; ADJ ASST PROF DEPTS PHARMACOL & PSYCHIAT, JEFFERSON MED COL, 82- *Personal Data:* b Wilkes-Barre, Pa, July 22, 51; m 86; c 1. *Educ:* Dickinson Col, BS, 73; Jefferson Med Col, MD, 77, PhD (pharm), 79. *Mem:* Am Psychopath Asn; Am Psychiat Asn; Soc Biol Psychiat. *Mailing Add:* 224 Booth Lane Haverford PA 19041-1717

BERRIDGE, MICHAEL JOHN, BIOLOGY, ZOOLOGY. *Current Pos:* PROF, DEPT ZOOL, UNIV CAMBRIDGE, 69-; DEP CHIEF SCI OFFICER, BABRAHAM INST, CAMBRIDGE, 87- *Personal Data:* b Oct 22, 38; m 65, Susan G Winter; c 2. *Educ:* Univ Col, Rhodesia & Nyasaland, BSc; Univ Cambridge, Eng, PhD. *Honors & Awards:* Wolf Med Prize, Wolf Found, 94; H P Heineken Prize, Royal Neth Acad Arts & Sci, 94. *Prof Exp:* Fel, Univ Va, 65-66 & Case Western Res Univ, Cleveland, 66-69. *Res:* Contributed articles to professional journals. *Mailing Add:* Babraham Inst PO Box 158 Cambridge CB4 3ES England

BERRIER, HARRY HILBOURN, VETERINARY PATHOLOGY. *Current Pos:* RETIRED. *Personal Data:* b Norborne, Mo, July 6, 17; m 50. *Educ:* Univ Mo, BSc, 41, MSc, 60; Kans State Univ, DVM, 45. *Prof Exp:* Instr pub schs, Mo, 41-42; practicing veterinarian, Mo, 45-46; from assoc prof to emer prof, Col Vet Med, Univ Mo-Columbia, 85-88. *Concurrent Pos:* NSF fel, Vet Path Div, US Armed Forces Inst Path, 63-64. *Mem:* Am Vet Med Asn; Am Soc Vet Clin Path; fel Am Col Vet Toxicol. *Res:* Ovine pregnancy diseases; veterinary medicine diagnostic aids; canine surgical mouth speculum. *Mailing Add:* 1250 S Cedar Grove Blvd Columbia MO 65201

BERRILL, MICHAEL, ANIMAL BEHAVIOR. *Current Pos:* Asst prof biol, 68-74, ASSOC PROF BIOL, TRENT UNIV, 74-, CHMN, DEPT BIOL, 77- *Personal Data:* b Montreal, Que, Apr 18, 44; m 69. *Educ:* McGill Univ, BSc, 64; Univ Hawaii, MS, 65; Princeton Univ, PhD(animal behav), 68. *Res:* Behavioral ecology and development of behavior of marine and freshwater crustaceans, and of lower vertebrates. *Mailing Add:* Dept Biol Trent Univ Symons Bldg 1600 W Bank Dr Peterborough ON K9J 7B8 Can

BERRIMAN, LESTER P, CHEMICAL ENGINEERING. *Current Pos:* CONSULT ENGR TECHNOL, 87- *Personal Data:* b Berkeley, Calif, Feb 5, 25; m 56, Dorothy Reboly; c 1. *Educ:* Univ Calif, Berkeley, BS, 50. *Prof Exp:* Jr chem engr, Stanford Res Inst, 50-52, assoc chem engr, 52-56, sr chem engr, 56-62, asst mgr agr sci res, 62-64, mgr process eng res, 64-68, mgr chem & mech eng labs, 68-70; dir, Eng Advan Technol Ctr Dresser Industs, 70-85; dir, Advan Tech Ctr presverand, 85-87. *Mem:* Am Chem Soc; Am Inst Chem Engrs; Sigma Xi. *Res:* Automotive air pollution and control; water pollution control; reverse osmosis; solid waste collection, transportation and reclamation; energy conversion and recovery processes; fluid dynamic systems; fluid machinery; materials. *Mailing Add:* 18871 Portofino Dr Irvine CA 92612

BERRY, B(RIAN) S(HEPHERD), MATERIALS SCIENCE, SOLID-STATE PHYSICS. *Current Pos:* RETIRED. *Personal Data:* b Manchester, Eng, Feb 27, 29; nat US; m 52, Maureen S M Keen; c Alison C & Christopher J. *Educ:* Univ Manchester, BSc, 49, MSc, 51, PhD(metall), 54. *Prof Exp:* Asst lectr metall, Univ Manchester, 50-54; asst, Yale Univ, 54-56; investr phys metall, Fulmer Res Inst, Eng, 56-58; mat scientist, Thomas J Watson Res Ctr, IBM, 58-91. *Mem:* Fel Am Phys Soc; Mats Res Soc. *Res:* Anelastic behavior of solids; imperfections in crystals; diffusion; magnetic properties; thin films; amorphous materials; hydrogen in metals. *Mailing Add:* 215 Lakeside Dr Edenton NC 27932

BERRY, BRADFORD WILLIAM, SENSORY EVALUATION. *Current Pos:* RES FOOD TECHNOLOGIST MEAT SCI, USDA, 77- *Personal Data:* b Washington, DC, May 2, 41; m 63; c 3. *Educ:* Wash State Univ, BS, 63; NMex State Univ, MS, 65; Texas A&M Univ, PhD(meat sci). *Prof Exp:* Inst & scientist meat sci, Wash State Univ, 65-70; assoc prof meat sci, Colo State Univ, 72-77. *Mem:* Am Meat Sci Asn; Inst Food Technologists; Am Soc Animal Sci; Food Distrib Res Soc; Am Soc Testing & mats. *Res:* The effects of production, processing and cooking on sensory, instrumental texture, chemical, storage life and microbiological properties of meat products. *Mailing Add:* Meat Sci Res Lab Bldg 201 BARC-E 10300 Baltimore Ave Beltsville MD 20705-2350

BERRY, CHARLES ARTHUR, PHARMACOLOGY. *Current Pos:* asst prof, 64-68, ASSOC PROF PHARMACOL, NORTHWESTERN UNIV, 68- *Personal Data:* b Ketchum, Idaho, Aug 19, 29; m 54; c 1. *Educ:* Univ Idaho, BS, 51; Idaho State Univ, BS, 54; Univ Iowa, MS, 59, PhD(pharmacol), 61. *Prof Exp:* Instr pharmacol, Univ Iowa, 61-62; fel, Stanford Univ, 62-64. *Mem:* AAAS; Am Soc Pharmacol & Exp Therapeut; Soc Neurosci. *Res:* Problems of attention, learning, memory, motivation and animal behavior; investigation of drugs and neural systems interactions; definition of cortical-subcortical relationships. *Mailing Add:* Dept Pharmacol Northwestern Univ Med Sch Chicago IL 60611-3072

BERRY, CHARLES DENNIS, research management, plant physiology, for more information see previous edition

BERRY, CHARLES RICHARD, PLANT PATHOLOGY. *Current Pos:* Plant pathologist, Div Forest Dis Res, 57-62, PLANT PATHOLOGIST, DIV FOREST PROTECTION RES, SOUTHEASTERN FOREST EXP STA, USDA, 66-, PROJ LEADER AIR POLLUTION, 62- *Personal Data:* b Morgantown, WVa, Mar 8, 27; m 48; c 2. *Educ:* Glenville State Col, AB, 49; WVa Univ, MS, 55, PhD(plant path), 58. *Mem:* Soil Sci Soc Am; Am Phytopath Soc. *Res:* Reclamation; air pollution; forest disease. *Mailing Add:* 179 Tara Way Athens GA 30606

BERRY, CHARLES RICHARD, JR, FISH & WILDLIFE SCIENCES. *Current Pos:* assoc prof, 85-91, PROF LEADER AQUATIC ECOL & FISH BIOL, US GEOL SURV, SDAK STATE UNIV, 91- *Personal Data:* b Salisbury, Md, May 11, 45; m 72; c 2. *Educ:* Randolph-Macon Col, BS, 67; Fordham Univ, MS, 70; Va Polytech Inst & State Univ, PhD(fisheries), 76. *Honors & Awards:* Chief's Award Outstanding Sci, Div Coop Res, Nat Biol Serv, 95. *Prof Exp:* Biologist, Va Water Control Bd, 68-72; res asst, Va Comn Game & Inland Fisheries, 72-75; asst leader pollution & fish biol, US Fish & Wildlife Serv, Utah State Univ, 76-85. *Concurrent Pos:* Asst prof, Interdept Prog, Utah State Univ, 79-85; assoc ed, Am Fisheries Soc, 84-87. *Mem:* Am Fisheries Soc; Am Inst Fishery Res Biologists; Am Inst Biol Sci. *Res:* Effects of water pollution and habitat alteration on fish; fishery management in wetlands; endangered fish biology; fish health. *Mailing Add:* SDak Coop Unit Dept Wildlife/Fish Sci SDak State Univ Brookings SD 57007. *Fax:* 605-688-4515

BERRY, CHRISTINE ALBACHTEN, PHYSIOLOGY, BIOPHYSICS. *Current Pos:* Fel renal physiol, 76, lectr physiol, 76-77, ADJ ASST PROF PHYSIOL, UNIV CALIF, SAN FRANCISCO, 77- *Personal Data:* b San Diego, Calif, Nov 27, 46; m 69. *Educ:* Stanford Univ, BA, 68; Yale Univ, PhD(physiol), 74. *Concurrent Pos:* Asst res physiologist, Clinical Res Inst, San Francisco, 76-77. *Mem:* Am Soc Nephrology; Int Soc Nephrology; AAAS; Sigma Xi; Am Physiol Soc. *Res:* Salt and water transport across proximal convoluted tubule of mammalian nephron. *Mailing Add:* Dept Physiol Nephrol 111J Med Sch Univ Calif 4150 Clement St San Francisco CA 94121

BERRY, CLARK GREEN, CHEMISTRY. *Current Pos:* RETIRED. *Personal Data:* b Ilion, NY, Sept 28, 08; m 36; c 2. *Educ:* Clarkson Col Technol, BS, 30. *Prof Exp:* Chemist, Atmospheric Nitrogen Corp, 30-31 & Skenandoa Rayon Corp, 33-37, control supvr, 37-38; res chemist, Inst Paper Chem, 38-42 & Skenandoa Rayon Corp, 42-46; chief chemist, Del Rayon Co, 46-52; lab dir, New Bedford Rayon Co, 52-53, chief chemist & dir res, 53-66; supvry chemist & br head, Bur Engraving & Printing, US Treas Dept, 66-77. *Mem:* Am Chem Soc; Tech Asn Pulp & Paper Indust. *Res:* Viscose rayon; cellulose; synthetic fibers. *Mailing Add:* 16 Briarwood Circle Worcester MA 01606

BERRY, DAISILEE H, PEDIATRICS, HEMATOLOGY. *Current Pos:* from asst prof to assoc prof, 69-76, PROF PEDIAT HEMAT ONCOL, UNIV ARK, LITTLE ROCK, 76- *Personal Data:* b Honolulu, Hawaii. *Educ:* Univ Ark, BS, 49, MD, 59; Western Res Univ, MN, 52. *Prof Exp:* Intern resident pediat, Univ Ark, 59-61; resident fel, Washington Univ, 61-63; fel hemat oncol, Univ Ark, 63-64, asst prof pediat hemat oncol, 64-67; fel hemat, Duke Univ, 67-69. *Mem:* Am Soc Hemat; Am Soc Clin Oncol; Acad Pediat; Am Asn Cancer Educ. *Res:* Pediatric oncology; clinical manifestations of sickle cell anemia. *Mailing Add:* Ark Childrens Hosp 800 Marshall St Little Rock AR 72202-3591

BERRY, DONALD S(TILWELL), CIVIL ENGINEERING. *Current Pos:* RETIRED. *Personal Data:* b Vale, SDak, Jan 1, 11; m 37; c 2. *Educ:* SDak Sch Mines & Technol, BS, 31; Iowa State Col, MS, 33; Univ Mich, PhD(civil eng), 36. *Hon Degrees:* DEng, SDak Sch Mines & Technol, 64. *Prof Exp:* Traffic engr, Nat Safety Coun, 36-43, dir, Traffic & Transp Div, 43-48; prof transp eng, Univ Calif, 48-55 & Purdue Univ, 55-56; prof civil eng, Northwestern Univ, Evanston, 56-77, chmn dept, 62-69, Walter P Murphy prof, 67-78, emer prof civil eng, 78-80. *Concurrent Pos:* With Fed Bur Invest & Off Civilian Defense, 44; chmn, Hwy Res Bd, Nat Acad Sci-Nat Res Coun, 65- *Mem:* Nat Acad Eng; Am Soc Civil Engrs; Inst Traffic Eng. *Res:* Skidding of vehicles on road surfaces; causes of traffic accidents; methods for evaluating the stability of macroscopic materials; vehicle speeds, travel times and intersection delays; capacity of arterial streets. *Mailing Add:* 2520 Park Pl Evanston IL 60201

BERRY, E JANET, ORGANIC CHEMISTRY, CHEMICAL ENGINEERING. *Current Pos:* PATENT ATTY, 63- *Personal Data:* b Wheatland, Ind, May 28, 17; m 69. *Educ:* Purdue Univ, BS, 42, PhD, 46; NY Univ, JD, 52. *Prof Exp:* Res chemist & patent asst, Am Cyanamid Co, 46-48; patent atty, Esso Res & Eng, 48-53; patent atty & dept mgr, Nat Distillers & Chem Corp, 53-63. *Concurrent Pos:* Trustee, Carnegie-Mellon Univ, 86- & Animal Med Ctr, 80-; nat dir, Am Inst Chemists, 86-94. *Mem:* Am Inst Chemists (pres, 80-82); Asn Consult Chemist & Chem Engrs (pres, 76-78); Am Chem Soc; Chem Indust Asn; Soc Chem Indust. *Res:* Chemistry; pharmaceutical chemistry; inventions; patents; innovation; research administration; technology transfer licensing. *Mailing Add:* Two Horatio St Apt 5M New York NY 10014

BERRY, EDWARD ALAN, HEME PROTEIN BIOCHEMISTRY, MEMBRANE PROTEIN PURIFICATION. *Current Pos:* STAFF SCIENTIST, LAWRENCE BERKELEY LAB, 87- *Personal Data:* b Ft Carson, Colo, July 14, 52; m, Li-Shar Huang; c Sharon E. *Educ:* Cornell Univ, PhD(biochem), 81. *Prof Exp:* Res assoc, Biochem Dept, Dartmouth Med Sch, 81-84 & Physiol & Biophys Dept, Univ Ill, Urbana-Champaign, 84-87. *Mem:* Biophys Soc. *Res:* Function and structure of membrane proteins involved in energy conservation; techniques of purification, enzymology, reconstitution, crystallization. *Mailing Add:* Calvin Lab Univ Calif Berkeley CA 94720-9998. *Fax:* 510-486-5342; *E-Mail:* eaberry@lbl.gov

BERRY, EDWIN X, ATMOSPHERIC PHYSICS. *Current Pos:* PRES, EDWIN X BERRY & ASSOC, 87- *Personal Data:* b San Francisco, Calif, June 20, 35; m 57, 73; c 3. *Educ:* Calif Inst Technol, BS, 57; Dartmouth Col, MS, 60; Univ Nev, PhD(physics), 65. *Prof Exp:* Res asst ionospheric physics, Thayer Sch Eng, Dartmouth Col, 59-60; radio propagation engr, Advan Commun Eng Div, Cook Elec Co, 60-61; from res asst to res assoc atmospheric physics, Desert Res Inst, Univ Nev, Reno, 62-72; prog mgr weather modification, NSF, 73-74, phys scientist, 74-76; pres, Atmospheric Res & Technol Inc, 76-87. *Concurrent Pos:* Mem comt on land use planning, 72; chmn comt weather modification, Am Meterol Soc, 74. *Mem:* Am Meteorol Soc. *Res:* Physics; wind energy; numerical models using windows. *Mailing Add:* Edwin X Berry & Assocs 6040 Verner Ave Sacramento CA 95841. *Fax:* 916-344-7243; *E-Mail:* 76260.2307@compuserve.com

BERRY, GAIL W(RUBLE), PSYCHIATRY, PSYCHOANALYSIS. *Current Pos:* ASST CLIN PROF PSYCHIAT, MT SINAI SCH MED, NY, 75-, ASSOC ATTEND PSYCHOANALYST, MT SINAI HOSP, 83- *Personal Data:* b Kalamazoo, Mich, Nov 7, 39. *Educ:* Kalamazoo Col, AB, 60; NY Univ Sch Med, MD, 64. *Prof Exp:* Intern pediat, Kings Co Hosp, Brooklyn, NY, 64-65; resident psychiat, NY Med Col, Metrop Hosp, NY, 65-68; staff psychiatrist, Beth Israel Med Ctr, NY, 68-74; from clin instr psychiat to clin assoc, Mt Sinai Sch Med, NY, 68-75. *Concurrent Pos:* Assoc ed, Acad, Am Acad Psychoanal, 76-83; training & supvry psychoanalyst, NY Med Col, 80-; asst ed, J Am Acad Psychoanal, 84- *Mem:* Am Psychiat Asn; Am Acad Psychoanalysis. *Res:* Psychoanalytic research on incest. *Mailing Add:* 1474 Third Ave New York NY 10028-1981

BERRY, GEORGE WILLARD, GEOLOGY. *Current Pos:* CONSULT GEOLOGIST, 72- *Personal Data:* b Poolville, NY, Feb 22, 15; m 46; c 2. *Educ:* Colgate Univ, AB, 36; Cornell Univ, MS, 38, PhD(struct geol), 41. *Prof Exp:* From asst to sr asst geol, Cornell Univ, 36-38, instr, 38-41; geol scout, Texas Co, Tex, 41-42; geologist, Fla, 46 & Wyo, 46-48; dist geologist, Sun Oil Co, Wyo, 48-52, asst div geologist, Colo, 52-61; sr geologist, Tex, 61-64 & Colo, 64-70; sr res geologist, Cordero Mining Co, 70-72. *Mem:* Am Asn Petrol Geologists; Am Inst Mining, Metall & Petrol Engrs; Geol Soc Am. *Res:* Rocky Mountain geology; geothermal energy. *Mailing Add:* 600 Spruce St Boulder CO 80302

BERRY, GEORGE WILLIAM, CHEMISTRY. *Current Pos:* SR ASSOC, ROBT M STAFFORD INC, 72- *Personal Data:* b Parker, Colo, Feb 6, 07; m 30; c 5. *Educ:* Colo State Col, BSc, 30; Univ Nebr, MSc, 32, PhD(phys chem), 34. *Prof Exp:* Instr org chem, Univ Nebr, 34-35; res chemist, Socony-Vacuum Oil Co, Kans, 35-45; res chemist, Flintkote Co, 45-56, mgr built-up roofing dept, 56-63, tech mgr, Archit Prod Div, 63-66; sr res assoc, Johns-Manville Corp, 66-72. *Concurrent Pos:* Fac mem, Roofing Indust Educ Inst, 80-86. *Mem:* Am Chem Soc; fel Am Inst Chem. *Res:* Utilization of asphalt in building materials; petroleum refining; surface tension of dilute solutions of sodium palmitate. *Mailing Add:* 4363 Woodlark Lane Charlotte NC 28211

BERRY, GREGORY FRANKLIN, magnetohydrodynamics, for more information see previous edition

BERRY, GUY C, POLYMER CHEMISTRY. *Current Pos:* sr fel & assoc prof chem & polymer sci, Carnegie Mellon Univ, 67-73, actg dean, Col Sci, 81-82, actg head chem, 83-84, PROF CHEM & POLYMER SCI, CARNEGIE MELLON UNIV, 73-, HEAD CHEM, 90- *Personal Data:* b Greene Co, Ill, May 11, 35; m 57; c 3. *Educ:* Univ Mich, BS, 57, MS, 58, PhD(chem eng),

60. *Honors & Awards:* Bingham Medal, Soc Rheology, 90. *Prof Exp:* Fel polymer sci, Mellon Inst, 60-67. *Concurrent Pos:* Vis prof, Univ Tokyo, 73, Colo State Univ, 79 & Univ Kyoto, 84; adj prof metall & mat eng, Univ Pittsburgh, 77- *Mem:* Am Chem Soc; Soc Rheology; Japan Soc Rheology. *Res:* Physical chemistry of polymers; solution viscosity; static and dynamic light scattering; rheology; liquid crystalline polymers, glassy polymers. *Mailing Add:* Dept Chem Carnegie Mellon Univ 4400 Fifth Ave Pittsburgh PA 15213. *Fax:* 412-268-1061; *E-Mail:* gcberry@andrew.cmu.edu

BERRY, HENRY GORDON, atomic physics, science education, for more information see previous edition

BERRY, HERBERT WEAVER, PHYSICS. *Current Pos:* RETIRED. *Personal Data:* b Syracuse, NY, Dec 17, 13; m 42; c 2. *Educ:* Syracuse Univ, AB, 37, AM, 39; Washington Univ, PhD(physics), 42. *Prof Exp:* Instr, Case Inst Technol, 42-43; res physicist, Radiation Lab, Univ Calif, 43-45; asst prof physics, Univ Okla, 46; from asst prof to assoc prof physics, Syracuse Univ, 46-54, prof, 54-80. *Mem:* Am Phys Soc; Am Asn Physics Teachers. *Res:* Plasma physics; ionization of gases; scattering in gases. *Mailing Add:* 2649 E Genesee St Syracuse NY 13224

BERRY, IVAN LEROY, AGRICULTURAL ENGINEERING. *Current Pos:* PROF, UNIV ARK, 85- *Personal Data:* b Mt Vernon, Mo, Sept 9, 37; m 59; c 3. *Educ:* Univ Mo, BS, 60, MS, 61; Tex A&M Univ, PhD(agr eng), 69. *Prof Exp:* Agr engr, Agr Res Serv, USDA, 60-65, supvry agr engr, 65-73, res leader, 73-85. *Mem:* Am Soc Agr Engrs; Entom Soc Am; Int Soc Biometeorol. *Res:* Environmental physiology of livestock; livestock shelter design; livestock sprayer design; insect attractants; livestock insect physiology and ecology; integrated pest management. *Mailing Add:* Dept Agr Eng 203 Eng Hall Univ Ark Fayetteville AR 72701-1202

BERRY, JAMES FREDERICK, HERPETOLOGY, CONSERVATION BIOLOGY. *Current Pos:* from asst prof to assoc prof, 78-91, PROF BIOL, ELHERST COL, 91- *Personal Data:* b Washington, DC, Dec 22, 47; c 2. *Educ:* Fla State Univ, BS, 70, MS, 73; Univ Utah PhD(biol), 78, JD, 90. *Prof Exp:* Chemist biochem, Fla Dept Agr, 73. *Concurrent Pos:* Res assoc, Carnegie Mus Nat Hist, Pittsburgh, Pa; atty Burke, Basselman & Weaver, 90-93. *Mem:* Am Soc Zoologists; Soc Study Evolution; Soc Syst Zool; Am Soc Ichthyologists & Herpetologists. *Res:* Evolutionary biology, ecology, and systematics of North and Central American reptiles; ecomorphology in modern turtles; conservation biology. *Mailing Add:* Dept Biol Elmhurst Col Elmhurst IL 60126-3271

BERRY, JAMES FREDERICK, BIOCHEMISTRY, NEUROSCIENCE. *Current Pos:* assoc prof, 61-66, prof, 66-92, EMER PROF NEUROL, MED SCH, UNIV MINN, MINNEAPOLIS, 92- *Personal Data:* b Baltimore, Md, Nov 11, 27; m 52, Ann Smith; c Barbara, Bonnie, Sarah & Catherine. *Educ:* Johns Hopkins Univ, BA, 49; Univ Rochester, PhD(biochem), 53. *Prof Exp:* USPHS fel biochem, Univ Western Ont, 53-55, sr res fel, 53-56, lectr, 55-56; mult sclerosis fel, Agr Res Coun Inst Animal Physiol, Babraham, Eng, 56-57; fel physiol chem, Johns Hopkins Univ, 58-59, instr, 59-61; assoc prof, Med Sch, Univ Minn, Minneapolis, 61-66, prof neurol, 66-86. *Concurrent Pos:* Assoc dir biochem res, Sinai Hosp, Baltimore, 57-61. *Mem:* Fel AAAS; Am Soc Biol Chemists; Am Oil Chemists' Soc; Int Soc Neurochem; Am Soc Neurochem. *Res:* Biochemistry of degenerating and regenerating nerve; lipid and fatty acid composition and biosynthesis in nervous tissue; biosynthesis of choline esters; alcohol and acetaldehyde metabolism. *Mailing Add:* 1059 Woodhill Dr Roseville MN 55113-2017

BERRY, JAMES G(ILBERT), INFORMATION RESOURCE MANAGEMENT. *Current Pos:* RETIRED. *Personal Data:* b Brooklyn, NY, Mar 16, 25; wid; c Thomas J, Patricia S, Kathy A & Daniel R. *Educ:* Univ Mich, BS, 49, MS, 50, PhD(eng mech), 54. *Prof Exp:* Instr eng mech, Univ Mich, 50-55; mem sr tech staff, Space Technol Labs, Calif, 55-63, dir, Titan Prog Off, 63-64; dir, Washington Opers, TRW Systs, 64-71; sr staff specialist, Off Secy Defense, 71-95. *Mem:* Am Soc Mech Engrs; Am Inst Aeronaut & Astronaut. *Res:* Elasticity; shell theory; structural dynamics; stochastic process theory. *Mailing Add:* 1407 Cola Dr McLean VA 22101

BERRY, JAMES WESLEY, ORGANIC CHEMISTRY. *Current Pos:* RETIRED. *Personal Data:* b Rankin, Ill, Mar 23, 26; m 47; c 5. *Educ:* Augustana Col, AB, 49; Univ Ill, PhD(org chem), 53. *Prof Exp:* Res chemist, Rayonier, Inc, 53-55; asst prof chem, Whitworth Col, Wash, 55-56; prof nutrit & food sci & dept head, Univ Ariz, 56-90. *Mem:* Am Chem Soc; Inst Food Technologists. *Res:* Polysaccharides; arid land plants as food sources. *Mailing Add:* 8871 Driftwood Trail Tucson AZ 85749-9656

BERRY, JAMES WILLIAM, SPIDER ECOLOGY. *Current Pos:* From instr to assoc prof, 65-77, PROF ZOOL, BUTLER UNIV, 77- *Personal Data:* b Bristol, Va, Dec 7, 35; m 70; c 1. *Educ:* ETenn State Univ, BS, 57; Va Polytech Inst, MS, 58; Duke Univ, PhD(zool), 66. *Concurrent Pos:* USPHS fel, 66-67; ed, J Arachnology, 91- *Mem:* Am Arachnological Soc (secy, 87-91); Brit Arachnological Soc. *Res:* Spider ecology in North Carolina piedmont; spiders of the Florida Everglades; spider distribution on Pacific Islands; ecology of intertidal spiders. *Mailing Add:* 326 Buckingham Dr Indianapolis IN 46208. *E-Mail:* berry@butleru.edu

BERRY, JOE GENE, FOOD SCIENCE, POULTRY SCIENCE. *Current Pos:* DEPT ANIMAL SCI, OKLA STATE UNIV, STILLWATER. *Personal Data:* b Sayre, Okla, Feb 19, 44; m 65; c 3. *Educ:* Okla State Univ, BS, 65, MS, 67; Kans State Univ, PhD(food sci), 70. *Prof Exp:* ASSOC PROF ANIMAL SCI, PURDUE UNIV, 70- *Mem:* Am Registry Prof Animal Scientists; Poultry Sci Asn. *Res:* Prevention of egg shell damage in production, processing and retailing; poultry products technology. *Mailing Add:* 2108 Country Side Dr Stillwater OK 74074

BERRY, KEITH O, inorganic chemistry, chemical education; deceased, see previous edition for last biography

BERRY, KENNETH J, SOCIOLOGY. *Current Pos:* PROF DEPT SOCIOL, COLO STATE UNIV. *Honors & Awards:* Banner I Miller Award, Am Meteorol Asn, 94. *Mailing Add:* Dept Sociol Colo State Univ Ft Collins CO 80523

BERRY, LEE ALLEN, PHYSICS, PLASMA PHYSICS. *Current Pos:* Res staff mem, Oak Ridge Nat Lab, 70-73, group leader, Tokamak Opers Group, 73-74, sect head, Tokamak Exp, 74-77, prog dir fusion develop, 77-80, mgr, EBT Prog, 80-84, assoc dir, Div Develop & Technol, 84-89, RES STAFF MEM, OAK RIDGE NAT LAB, 89- *Personal Data:* b La Junta, Colo, Mar 18, 45; m 66; c 2. *Educ:* Univ Calif, Riverside, BA, 66, MA, 69, PhD(physics), 70. *Mem:* Fel Am Phys Soc; Am Vacuum Soc. *Res:* Experimental plasma physics; emphasis has been on materials processes and process equipment. *Mailing Add:* Oak Ridge Nat Lab PO Box 2009 MS8071 Oak Ridge TN 37831-8071

BERRY, LEONARD, PHYSICAL GEOGRAPHY, RESOURCE MANAGEMENT. *Current Pos:* actg dir, Grad Sch Geog, 71-72 & 78-79, dir, Int Develop Prog, 74-78, dean, Grad Sch, 75-78, dir, ID prog, 76-83, dir, Grad Sch Geog, 79-83, PROF GEOG, CLARK UNIV, 69-, PROVOST, 83- *Personal Data:* b Malmesbury, Eng, June 5, 30; m 66; c 4. *Educ:* Bristol Univ, BSc, 51, MSc, 56, PhD(geog), 69. *Prof Exp:* Asst lectr geog, Univ Hong Kong, 54-57; from lectr to sr lectr, Univ Khartoum, 57-65; prof, Univ Col, Dar es Salaam, 65-69, dean fac arts & soc sci, 67-69; dir resource mgt, Univ Dar es Salaam, 69-71. *Concurrent Pos:* Consult, Int Develop Res Ctr, Ottawa, 72; mem, comt to Indonesia on natural resources planning, Nat Acad Sci, 72, comt environ implications of US mat policy, 72-73, comt on remote sensing for develop, 75, chmn, OTA comt trop forests, 82-83 & comt Sahel, 82-84. *Mem:* Royal Geog Soc; Inst Brit Geogr; Asn Am Geogr. *Res:* Tropical geomorphology; rural water development; regional planning; natural resource planning; environmental problems and development; rural development Africa. *Mailing Add:* 777 Glades Rd PO Box 3091 Fla Atlantic Univ Boca Raton FL 33431-0991

BERRY, LEONIDAS HARRIS, medicine, gastroenterology-gastroscopy; deceased, see previous edition for last biography

BERRY, MAXWELL (RUFUS), INTERNAL MEDICINE. *Current Pos:* RETIRED. *Personal Data:* b Atlanta, Ga, June 7, 10; m 34; c 4. *Educ:* Cornell Univ, AB, 31, MD, 35; Univ Minn, PhD(med), 42. *Prof Exp:* Bursar, Knickerbocker Fund, Cornell Univ, 33-35; intern med, Bellevue Hosp, NY, 35-37; res physicians, Mayo Clinic, 37-42; assoc med, Hosp Med Col Va, 42, asst prof, 43-44; assoc, Sch Med, Emory Univ, 44-49; dir cancer clin, St Joseph's Infirmary, 47-88, dir Berry Clin, 48-88. *Concurrent Pos:* Consult, Grady Hosp, 44-49; pres, Northwest Hosp Corp, 66-70; chmn bd dirs, West Paces Ferry Hosp, 66-70; chmn bd trustees, Annandale at Suwanee, Inc, 66-73, pres, 73 - *Mem:* Fel Am Col Physicians; fel Am Col Gastroenterol (pres, 65-66); Sigma Xi. *Res:* Tomac oxygen nebulizer; plethysmograph; physiology of circulation and respiration; studies on etiology of duodenal ulcer; clinical gastroenterology. *Mailing Add:* One Magnolia Point Panama City Beach FL 32408

BERRY, MICHAEL JAMES, OPHTHALMOLOGY, LASER THERMAL KERATOPLASTY CORNEAL SHAPING. *Current Pos:* PRES, ANTROPIX CORP, 82-; DIR, CORNEA PROG, SUNRISE TECHNOL, 92- *Personal Data:* b Chicago, Ill, July 17, 47; m 67, 84, Patricia Hackerman; c Michael J II & Jennifer A. *Educ:* Univ Mich, BS, 67; Univ Calif, Berkeley, PhD(chem), 70. *Honors & Awards:* Award Pure Chem, Am Chem Soc, 83; Robert G Denkewalter lectr, 84. *Prof Exp:* From asst prof to assoc prof chem, Univ Wis-Madison, 70-76; mgr photon chem, Allied Chem Corp, 76-79; dir, Rice Quantum Inst, Rice Univ, 79-86; dir, Laser Applns Res Ctr, HARC, 84-90; Robert A Welsh prof chem, Rice Univ, 79-92. *Concurrent Pos:* Alfred P Sloan res fel, 75-76; Camille & Henry Dreyfus found teacher-scholar, 75-76; John Simon Guggenheim Mem Found fel, 81-82; consult, Dow Chem, USA, Mar Chem, Tex Eastern, Dresser, Houston Area Res Ctr, AMOCO; chief scientist, Emmetropix Corp, 91-92. *Mem:* Am Phys Soc; Am Chem Soc; Am Soc Photobiol; fel AAAS; Am Soc Laser Med & Surg; Asn Res Vision & Opthalmol. *Res:* Laser thermal keratoplasty; use of laser light to heat the cornea selectively to modify collagen and produce shape changes that correct ocular refractive errors such as myopia, hyperopia and astigmatism. *Mailing Add:* PO Box 1421 Pebble Beach CA 93953-1421. *E-Mail:* mberry@compuserve.com

BERRY, MICHAEL JOHN, SEISMOLOGY. *Current Pos:* CONSULT, 95- *Personal Data:* b Southport, Eng, Oct 5, 40; Can citizen; m; c 2. *Educ:* Univ Toronto, BSc, 61, MA, 62, PhD(seismol), 65. *Prof Exp:* Res asst inst geophys & planetary sci, Univ Calif, Los Angeles, 65-66; res scientist, Seismol Div, Earth Physics Br, Gov Can, 67-74, dir, Div Seismol & Geothermal Studies,

74-82 & dir, Div Seismol & Geomagnatism, 82-86; dir, Geophys Div, Geol Surv Can, 86-93, dir gen, Minerals & Continental Geosci Br, 93-95. *Concurrent Pos:* Assoc ed, Geosci Can, 74-79, Can Earth Sci, 74-84; mem, Can Nat Comt Earthquake Eng; chmn, Gov Coun Int Seismol Ctr, 83-87; chmn, Coord Comt, Nat Rep, Int Union Comn Lithosphere, 85-89, secy-gen Comn, 90- *Mem:* Seismol Soc Am; Am Geophys Union; Can Geophys Union; Int Union Geodesy & Geophys; Fedn Global Digital Seismograph Networks (pres, 86-89). *Res:* Studies of the Earth's crust and upper mantle using reflection and refraction seismology; seismicity and seismic risk and hazard. *Mailing Add:* RR 2 Woodlawn ON K0A 3M0 Can

BERRY, MICHAEL VICTOR, THEORETICAL PHYSICS. *Current Pos:* from physics lectr to reader, 67-79, prof, 79-88, ROYAL SOC RES PROF, BRISTOL UNIV, 88- *Personal Data:* b Surrey, UK, Mar 14, 41. *Educ:* St Andrews Univ, PhD(theoret physics), 65. *Hon Degrees:* DSc, Exeter Univ, 91. *Honors & Awards:* Maxwell Medal & Prize, Inst Phys, 78; Elliot Montroll Mem Lectr, Leiden, 88; Loeb Lectr Harvard, 89; Racah Mem Lectr, DeShalit Mem Lectr, Weizmann Inst, 89 & 91; Julius Edgar Lilienfeld Prize, Am Phys Soc, 90; Paul Dirac Medal & Prize, Inst Phys, 90; Segre Mem Lectr, Berkeley, 91; Feshbach Lectr, Mass Inst Technol, 92; Walker-Ames Lectr,Seattle, 93; S Town Stephenson Distinguished Lectr, Pullman, 93; Schrodinger Lectr, Imperial Col, 93; Wood Mem Lectr, Newcastle, 93; Racah Mem Lectr, Jerusalem, 94; Dirac Medal & Prize, Int Ctr Theoret Phys, Trieste, 95. *Concurrent Pos:* Kramers prof phys, Univ Utrecht, Neth, 80-81; A D White visiting prof, Cornell Univ, 94- *Mem:* Foreign mem, Nat Acad Sci; Indian Acad Sci. *Res:* Contributed numerous articles to professional publications. *Mailing Add:* H H Wills Physics Lab Univ Bristol Royal Fort Tyndall Ave Bristol BS8 1TL England

BERRY, MYRON GARLAND, PHYSICAL CHEMISTRY. *Current Pos:* from asst prof to assoc prof, 55-62, admin asst, 62-69, prof chem, 62-84, EMER PROF CHEM, MICH TECHNOL UNIV, 84- *Personal Data:* b Franklin, NH, May 24, 19; m 48; c 3. *Educ:* Colby Col, BA, 40; Harvard Univ, MA, 42; Syracuse Univ, PhD(phys chem), 51. *Prof Exp:* Teacher, Dept Phys Sci, Urbana Jr Col, 46-49; asst prof chem, Ohio Wesleyan, 51-55. *Mem:* Am Chem Soc; Sigma Xi. *Res:* Surface chemistry; photochemistry. *Mailing Add:* PO Box 25 Copper Harbor MI 49918-0025

BERRY, RALPH EUGENE, ENTOMOLOGY, INSECT PEST MANAGEMENT. *Current Pos:* from asst prof to assoc prof entom, 68-81, PROF & CHMN ENTOM, ORE STATE UNIV, 81- *Personal Data:* b Gering, Nebr, June 14, 40; m 66; c 4. *Educ:* Colo State Univ, BS, 63, MS, 65; Kans State Univ, PhD(entom), 68. *Prof Exp:* Entomologist, Pesticide Regulation Div, Agr Res Serv, USDA, 65. *Concurrent Pos:* Actg assoc dir, Agr Exp Sta, Ore State Univ, 85-86. *Mem:* Entom Soc Am. *Res:* Applied entomology; biology and control of soil arthropods; ecology of soil insects; investigations of non-insecticidal control of insect pests; pest population ecology; insect-plant interactions; insect pest management. *Mailing Add:* Dept Entom Ore State Univ Corvallis OR 97331-1801

BERRY, RICHARD C(HISHOLM), chemical engineering, polymer chemistry; deceased, see previous edition for last biography

BERRY, RICHARD EMERSON, OCEANOGRAPHY, OPTICS. *Current Pos:* PROF PHYSICS, ST VINCENT COL, 92- *Personal Data:* b Washington, NJ, Nov 11, 33; m 54, Ruth H Enger; c Dirk, Arthur, Richard, Marilyn & Robert. *Educ:* Lafayette Col, BS, 54; Princeton Univ, MA, 56, PhD(physics), 58. *Prof Exp:* Researcher, Gen Elec Co, 57-58; asst prof physics, Lafayette Col, 58-62; assoc prof, Tex Technol Col, 62-65; chmn dept, Indiana Univ Pa, 65-74, prof physics, 74-91; consult laser applns, NASA, 82-97. *Mem:* Am Phys Soc; Sigma Xi; Am Asn Physics Teachers. *Res:* Electron spin resonance in solid state; theory of electricity and magnetism; electromagnetic theory and unidentified flying objects effects; oceanography; LIDAR; semiconductor devices. *Mailing Add:* 340 College Lodge Rd Indiana PA 15701

BERRY, RICHARD G, NEUROPATHOLOGY. *Current Pos:* from assoc prof to prof, 54-84, dir neuropath lab, 54-84, EMER PROF NEUROL, JEFFERSON MED COL, 84- *Personal Data:* b Bethel, Conn, Jan 29, 16; m 42; c 5. *Educ:* Wesleyan Univ, BA, 37; Albany Med Col, MD, 42. *Prof Exp:* Asst psychol, Wesleyan Univ, 38; intern, US Naval Hosp, Newport, RI, 42-43; res neurol, Jefferson Hosp, Philadelphia, 46-47; staff neurologist, US Naval Hosp, 47-50; instr, US Naval Med Sch, 50-53. *Concurrent Pos:* Fel neuropath, US Armed Forces Inst Path, 53-54; clin asst prof, Sch Med & staff neurologist, Univ Hosp, Georgetown Univ, 50-54; consult, Vet Admin Hosps, Coatesville, 58- & Germantown Hosp, Philadelphia, 87- *Mem:* AAAS; Am Neurol Asn; Am Acad Neurol; Am Asn Neuropath; Asn Res Nerv & Ment Dis; Sigma Xi. *Res:* Cerebral vascular disease. *Mailing Add:* 108 N Rolling Rd Springfield PA 19064-1413

BERRY, RICHARD LEE, MEDICAL ENTOMOLOGY, INSECT TAXONOMY. *Current Pos:* MED ENTOMOLOGIST, OHIO DEPT HEALTH, VECTOR BORNE DIS UNIT, 70- *Personal Data:* b Shelby, Ohio, July 28, 42; m 64; c 2. *Educ:* Univ Notre Dame, BS, 64; Tulane Univ, MS, 67; Ohio State Univ, PhD(entom), 70. *Mem:* Entom Soc Am; Am Mosquito Control Asn; Am Soc Trop Med & Hyg; Sigma Xi. *Res:* Epidemiology of mosquito borne encephalitis viruses; arbovirus vector potential of mosquitoes; biology and ecology of mosquitoes; biological control of mosquitoes; taxonomy of Tenebrionidae. *Mailing Add:* 899 Bricker Blvd Columbus OH 43221-1683

BERRY, RICHARD STEPHEN, PHYSICAL CHEMISTRY. *Current Pos:* assoc prof, 64-67, PROF, DEPT CHEM & JAMES FRANCK INST, UNIV CHICAGO, 67-, PROF, COMT PUB POLICY STUDIES, 75-, JAMES FRANCK DISTINGUISHED SERV PROF, 89- *Personal Data:* b Denver, Colo, Apr 9, 31; m 55; c 3. *Educ:* Harvard Univ, AB, 52, AM, 54, PhD(chem), 56. *Honors & Awards:* Seydel-Woolley Lectr, Ga Inst Technol, 71-73; Snider Lectr, Univ Toronto, 79; Hinshelwood Lectr, Oxford Univ, 80; Walter Kaskan Mem Lectr, State Univ NY, 82; Lowdin lectr, Uppsala Univ, 89; Phillips Lectr, Haverford Col, 90; Frederick Kaufaman Lectr Univ Pittsburgh, 96; J Heyrousky Award, Czech Acad Sci, 96. *Prof Exp:* Instr chem, Harvard Univ, 56-57 & Univ Mich, 57-60; asst prof, Yale Univ, 60-64. *Concurrent Pos:* Alfred P Sloan fel, 62-66; guest prof, Copenhagen Univ, 67 & 79; Arthur D Little prof, Mass Inst Technol, 68; lectr, Int Sch Physics, Varenna, 68 & 88 & Int Union Pure & Appl Chem Cong, Sydney, 69; chmn, Subpanel Physics Chem, Physics Surv Comt, Nat Acad Sci, 70-73; assoc ed, J Chem Physics, 72-74 & Reviews Mod Physics, 83-; Guggenheim fel, 73; dir, Bull Atomic Scientists, 75-81; trustee, Aspen Ctr Physics, 76-82; mem numerous sci comts, var socs & govt agencies, 72-; chmn, National Research Council Numerical Data Adv Bd, 81-86; Newton Abraham Prof, 86-87; sr adv & consult, Defense Sci Study Group, Inst Defense Anal, 85-; MacArthur fel, 83; Alexander Von Huboldt, sr scientist award, 93; Noyes lectr, Univ Tex, Austin, 93; Welch Symposium lectr, 98; chair, Nat Res Corn Comt Int Exchange Sci Info, 95-97. *Mem:* Nat Acad Sci; fel Am Acad Art & Sci (vpres, 95-); Am Chem Soc; Royal Danish Acad Sci; fel Am Phys Soc; fel Japan Soc Prom Sci; fel AAAS. *Res:* Atomic-molecular processes; spectroscopy; thermodynamics; Clusters; protein folding. *Mailing Add:* Dept Chem Searle 101 Univ Chicago 5735 S Ellis Ave Chicago IL 60637. *Fax:* 773-702-0805; *E-Mail:* berry@rainbow.uchicago.edu

BERRY, RICHARD WARREN, MARINE GEOLOGY, MARINE GEOCHEMISTRY. *Current Pos:* from asst prof to assoc prof, San Diego State Univ, 61-71, assoc dir, Ctr Marine Studies, 75-77, chmn, Dept Geol Sci, 76-80, PROF GEOL, SAN DIEGO STATE UNIV, 71-, DIR, CLAY MINERALS ANALYSIS LAB, 80- *Personal Data:* b Quincy, Mass, June 21, 33; c 3. *Educ:* Lafayette Col, BS, 55; Wash Univ, MA, 57, PhD(geochem), 63. *Prof Exp:* Instr geol, Trinity Col, Conn, 59-61. *Concurrent Pos:* Fulbright prof, Univ Baghdad, 65-66; Royal Norweg Coun Indust & Sci Res fel, Univ Oslo, 68-69; consult, Nat Coun Educ Geol Sci, various mining & petrol indust co. *Mem:* Mineral Soc Am; fel Geol Soc Am; Soc Sedimentary Geol; Clay Minerals Soc; fel Am Inst Chemists. *Res:* Mineralogy and geochemistry of clay sized ocean bottom sediments and their relationship to cationic concentrations in sea water; distribution of unconsolidated Quaternary sediments on the continental shelf; diagenesis and clay mineralogy. *Mailing Add:* Dept Geol Sci San Diego State Univ San Diego CA 92182-1020

BERRY, ROBERT EDDY, subtropical foods, for more information see previous edition

BERRY, ROBERT WADE, PLANT PATHOLOGY. *Current Pos:* RETIRED. *Personal Data:* b Granbury, Tex, July 21, 30; m 55; c 3. *Educ:* Tex A&M Univ, 52, MS, 60; Univ Wis, PhD(plant path), 63. *Prof Exp:* County agr agent, Tex Agr Exten Serv 54-58, plant pathologist, 63-86. *Mem:* Am Phytopath Soc. *Res:* Disease control in plants. *Mailing Add:* 513 E Kent St Lubbock TX 79403

BERRY, ROBERT WALTER, INORGANIC CHEMISTRY, PHYSICAL CHEMISTRY. *Current Pos:* RETIRED. *Personal Data:* b Atlanta, Ga, Oct 27, 28; m 54, Colleen Rudd; c Robert W Jr & Elizabeth A. *Educ:* Clemson Agr Col, BS, 50; Mich State Univ, PhD(chem), 56. *Prof Exp:* Mem tech staff, Bell Tel Labs, 56-67, head, thin film technol dept, 67-77; head, components & mat dept, AT&T Bell Labs, 77-87. *Mem:* Am Vacuum Soc; Inst Elec & Electronics Engrs; Sigma Xi; Optical Soc Am. *Res:* Electro-optic and dielectric materials and thin metallic and dielectric films as applied to electrical and optical components. *Mailing Add:* 425 Rockhill Circle Bethlehem PA 18017

BERRY, ROBERT WAYNE, NEUROBIOLOGY, PEPTIDES. *Current Pos:* from asst prof to assoc prof cell biol & anat, 73-90, PROF CELL & MOLLECULAR BIOL, SCH MED, NORTHWESTERN UNIV, CHICAGO, 90- *Personal Data:* b Gilmer, Tex, Sept 14, 44; div; c Robert Sydney & Kevin Lee. *Educ:* Calif Tech Inst, BS, 67; Univ Ore, MS, 68, PhD(biol), 70. *Concurrent Pos:* USPHS fel neuropath, Albert Einstein Col Med, 70-71; Nat Inst Neurol Dis & Stroke fel, Calif Inst Technol, 71-72; vis scientist, Alberta Heritage Found, Univ Calgary, 81. *Mem:* Am Soc Neurochem; Soc Neurosci; AAAS; Am Soc Cell Biol. *Res:* Structure and function of neural peptides. *Mailing Add:* Dept Cell & Molecular Biol Northwestern Univ Med Sch 303 E Chicago Ave Chicago IL 60611. *E-Mail:* r-berry@nwu.edu

BERRY, ROY ALFRED, JR, ORGANIC CHEMISTRY. *Current Pos:* asst prof, 62-69, prof, 69-77, J B PRICE PROF CHEM, MILLSAPS COL, 77- *Personal Data:* b New Hebron, Miss, Dec 11, 33; m 57; c 2. *Educ:* Miss Col, BS, 56; Univ NC, PhD(org chem), 62. *Prof Exp:* NSF res fel org chem, Univ Fla, 61-62. *Concurrent Pos:* R J Reynolds res fel, 59-60; Petrol Res Fund asst, 60-61. *Mem:* Am Chem Soc. *Res:* The basicities of the ferrocenylazobenzenes halogenation decarboxylation. *Mailing Add:* Dept Chem Millsaps Col Jackson MS 39210-0001

BERRY, SPENCER JULIAN, INSECT PHYSIOLOGY. *Current Pos:* from asst to assoc prof biol, 64-77, PROF BIOL, WESLEYAN UNIV, 77- *Personal Data:* b Quincy, Mass, May 25, 33; m 57; c 3. *Educ:* Williams Col, BA, 55; Wesleyan Univ, MA, 57; Western Res Univ, PhD(biol), 65. *Prof Exp:* Technician biochem, Harvard Univ Huntington Labs, Mass Gen Hosp, 57-58. *Mem:* Soc Develop Biol; AAAS; Int Soc Develop Biol. *Res:* Physiology of insect development, particularly at the cellular and molecular level. *Mailing Add:* Dept Biol Atwater Sci Ctr Wesleyan Univ Middletown CT 06459-0260. *Fax:* 860-685-2141; *E-Mail:* sberry@wesleyan.edu

BERRY, STANLEY Z, PLANT BREEDING. *Current Pos:* from assoc prof to prof, 67-95, EMER PROF HORT, OHIO STATE UNIV & OHIO AGR RES & DEVELOP CTR, 95- *Personal Data:* b NY, May 10, 30; m 59; c 2. *Educ:* Cornell Univ, BS, 52; Univ NH, MS, 53; Univ Calif, PhD(plant path), 56. *Prof Exp:* Plant scientist, USDA, 56-60; plant breeder, Campbell Soup Co, 60-67. *Mem:* Am Phytopath Soc; Am Soc Hort Sci. *Res:* Plant breeding and the utilization of disease resistance; tomato and vegetable breeding; processing tomato quality. *Mailing Add:* 1043 Buchholz Dr Wooster OH 44691

BERRY, STEPHEN J, MODELING OF PHYSIOLOGICAL SYSTEMS. *Current Pos:* ASST PROF & DIR INFO SYSTS, UNIV CALIF, SAN FRANCISCO, 94- *Personal Data:* b Philadelphia, Pa, 56. *Educ:* West Chester Univ, BA, 56; Johns Hopkins Univ, PhD, 85. *Prof Exp:* Asst prof & dir info systs, Dept Med, Univ Calif, Los Angeles, 91-93. *Mem:* Inst Elec & Electronics Engrs; Am Med Informatics Asn. *Mailing Add:* Univ Calif Sch Med S-224 513 Parnassus San Francisco CA 94143-0410

BERRY, VERN VINCENT, chromotography, separations; deceased, see previous edition for last biography

BERRY, VINOD K, MATERIALS SCIENCE, ELECTRON MICROSCOPY. *Current Pos:* TECH MGR, ELEC DEPT, GEN ELEC PLASTICS, 89- *Personal Data:* b Lahore, India, Nov 30, 36; m 69; c 2. *Educ:* Agra Univ, BSc, 57; Eastern NMex Univ, MS, 76; NMex Inst Mining & Technol, PhD(metall), 77. *Prof Exp:* Sci asst electron micros, Electron Micros Div, Defence Sci Lab, Delhi, India, 60-72; res assoc metall, NMex Inst Mining & Technol, 77; asst prof, Health Sci Ctr, Univ Tex, San Antonio, 78-80; res leader, Dow Chem, 82-89. *Mem:* Mat Res Soc; Am Inst Mining, Metall & Petrol Engrs; Am Soc Cell Biol; Electron Micros Soc Am; Microbeam Analytical Soc. *Res:* Bulk and surface studies of materials using transmission and scanning electron microscopy and various analytical electron optical techniques; morphological and ultrastructural studies of biological tissues and microbiological specimens. *Mailing Add:* 104 Brentwood Heights Parkersburg WV 26101

BERRY, WILLIAM B(ERNARD), ELECTRICAL ENGINEERING, ELECTRONICS. *Current Pos:* from asst prof to assoc prof, 63-70, asst dean res, 74-85, prof elec eng, 70-, prog mgr, cold weather transit technol, 79-93, ACTG DEPT CHMN, UNIV NOTRE DAME, 88-, ASSOC CHAIR, 88-98. *Personal Data:* b Shelby, Ohio, July 23, 31; m 55, Lois G Langford; c Elizabeth, William, M Suzanne & Thomas. *Educ:* Univ Notre Dame, BS, 53, MS, 57; Purdue Univ, PhD(elec eng), 64. *Prof Exp:* From instr to asst prof elec eng, Marquette Univ, 57-61. *Concurrent Pos:* Sr res assoc, Nat Res Coun, 72-73; vis prof, SERI, 86-87; Eng Res Coun; fac adv, Irish Racing Team, 93- *Mem:* Sigma Xi; Electrochem Soc; Am Soc Eng Educ; Inst Elec & Electronics Engrs; Mat Res Soc. *Res:* Solid state energy conversion including thermoelectric phenomena; photovoltaic and thin film electronic phenomena; electric vehicles. *Mailing Add:* Dept Elec Eng 402 Pokagon South Bend IN 46617. *Fax:* 219-631-4393; *E-Mail:* berry.1@nd.edu

BERRY, WILLIAM BENJAMIN NEWELL, PALEOOCEANOGRAPHY, PALEONTOLOGY. *Current Pos:* vis asst prof paleont, Univ Calif, Berkeley, 58-60, from asst prof to assoc prof, 60-68, assoc dir mus paleont, 63-69, vchmn dept paleont, 67-69, dir mus paleont & chmn dept, 75-87, prof paleont, 68-91, CUR PALEOZOIC INVERT, MUS PALEONT, UNIV CALIF, BERKELEY, 60-, PROF GEOL, 91- *Personal Data:* b Boston, Mass, Sept 1, 31; m 61, Suzanne Spaulding; c Bradford. *Educ:* Harvard Univ, AB, 53, AM, 55; Yale Univ, PhD(geol), 57. *Prof Exp:* Asst prof geol, Univ Houston, 57-58. *Concurrent Pos:* Guggenheim fel, 66-67. *Mem:* Paleont Soc; Norweg Geol Soc; Explorers Club. *Res:* Graptolites; paleozoic biostratigraphy; paleo-oceanography; environmental science. *Mailing Add:* Dept Geol Univ Calif Berkeley CA 94720-0001. *Fax:* 510-643-9980; *E-Mail:* bberry@uclinku.berkeley.edu

BERRY, WILLIAM LEE, ORGANIC CHEMISTRY. *Current Pos:* Res chemist, 55-57, group leader, 57-60, dir org pigments res & develop, 60-63, prod mgr, Pigments Div, 63-67, from asst tech dir to tech dir, 67-71, dept mgr color pigments, 71-73, dept mgr, Inorg Chem Div, 73-78, vpres, 78-80, pres, Formica Div, 80-81, PRES, ORG CHEM DIV, AM CYANAMID CO, 81- *Personal Data:* b Auburn, NY, Sept 1, 27; m 50; c 2. *Educ:* Cornell Univ, BA, 51; Univ Mich, PhD(chem), 56. *Mem:* Am Chem Soc; Sigma Xi. *Res:* Synthetic organic chemistry; colored hetero and carbocyclic systems and their utilization; high performance thermoplastic and thermoset resins. *Mailing Add:* 545 Steel Gap Rd Bridgewater NJ 08807-2338

BERRYHILL, DAVID LEE, BACTERIOLOGY. *Current Pos:* Asst prof, 71-75, ASSOC PROF BACT, NDAK STATE UNIV, 75- *Personal Data:* b Council Bluffs, Iowa, Mar 9, 44; m 68. *Educ:* Simpson Col, BA, 66; Iowa State Univ, MS, 69, PhD(bact), 71. *Mem:* Am Soc Microbiol; Int Soc Plant Molecular Biol; Genetics Soc Am; Sigma Xi. *Res:* Bacterial genetics. *Mailing Add:* Dept Vet & Micro Sci NDak State Univ 150 Van Es Fargo ND 58105

BERRYMAN, ALAN ANDREW, ENTOMOLOGY. *Current Pos:* From asst prof to assoc prof, 64-74, PROF ENTOM, WASH STATE UNIV, 74- *Personal Data:* b Tanzania, Africa, Jan 5, 37; div; c Rachael Jean, Ashley Andrea & Annie Augusta. *Educ:* Univ London, BSc, 59; Univ Calif, Berkeley, MS, 61, PhD(entom), 64. *Mem:* Entom Soc Am; Ecol Soc Am; Royal Entom Soc. *Res:* Population dynamics of forest insects; mathematical and computer models of population dynamics; resistance of conifers to insect and fungus invasion; theoretical ecology. *Mailing Add:* Dept Entom Wash State Univ Pullman WA 99164. *E-Mail:* berryman@mail.wsu.edu

BERRYMAN, GEORGE HUGH, NUTRITION, ALLERGY & IMMUNOLOGY. *Current Pos:* assoc prof med, 53-62, EMER PROF MED, STANFORD UNIV, 85- *Personal Data:* b South Shields, Eng, Apr 3, 14; nat US; m 39; c 3. *Educ:* Univ Scranton, BS, 35; Pa State Col, MS, 36; Univ Minn, PhD(biochem, human nutrit), 41; Univ Chicago, MD, 50. *Prof Exp:* Asst animal nutrit, Univ Ill, 37-38; chief, Div Food & Nutrit, Army Med Sch, Washington, DC, 41-44; commanding officer & dir res, Med Nutrit Lab, Chicago, 44-46; head, Nutrit Br, Qm Food & Container Inst, Chicago, 48-49; rotating intern, USPHS Hosp, Staten Island, 50-51; assoc, Abbot Labs, 51-54, head clin invest, 54-58, dir med sci proj, 58-60, dir clin develop, 60-64, med dir, 65-70, vpres med affairs, Dept Med, 70-73. *Concurrent Pos:* From clin asst prof to clin assoc prof med, Univ Ill, 53-77. *Mem:* AAAS; Am Med Asn; Am Soc Clin Nutrit; Am Acad Allergy; fel Am Col Physicians; Am Asn Cert Allergists. *Res:* Nutritional status; appraisal; relation of food; food composition; military nutrition; metabolic disease; allergy; drug reactions. *Mailing Add:* 110 Wood Rd Apt J203 Los Gatos CA 95030

BERRYMAN, JACK HOLMES, RESOURCE MANAGEMENT, FISH & WILDLIFE MANAGEMENT. *Current Pos:* exec vpres, 78-88, EMER COUNR, INT ASN FISH & WILDLIFE AGENCIES, 88- *Personal Data:* b Salt Lake City, Utah, July 28, 21; m 41, 82, June Featherstone; c Marjorie (Porter) & Richard. *Educ:* Westminster Col, AA, 40; Univ Utah, BS, 47, MS, 48. *Honors & Awards:* Am Motors Conserv Prof Award, 76; Distinguished Serv Award, US Dept Interior, 79; Seth Gordon Award, 85; Inst Wildlife Damage Mgt, Utah State Univ, 93. *Prof Exp:* Proj leader big game, Utah State Dept Fish & Game, 47-48, actg coordr wildlife, 48-50; asst regional supvr, US Fish & Wildlife Serv, NMex, 50-53, Minn, 53-59; assoc prof wildlife, Utah State Univ, 59-65; chief div wildlife serv, Bur Sport Fisheries & Wildlife, US Dept Interior, 65-74; actg dep assoc dir, US Fish & Wildlife Serv, 74, chief, Div Tech Assistance, 74-76, chief, Off Exten Educ, 76-78. *Concurrent Pos:* Consult, Off Secy Interior, 62-64 & Gov Comt State Recreation Plan, 64-; deleg, White House Conf Conserv, 62; secy, Int Task Force Wetlands, 82-84; chmn, conserv comt, Boy Scouts Am, 84-; secy, Agr Adv Comt Animal Damage, 88- *Mem:* Wildlife Soc (vpres, 60-62, pres, 64); NY Acad Sci; Am Fisheries Soc; Sigma Xi; Am Forestry Asn; hon mem Can Wildlife Fedn; hon mem Int Asn Fish & Wildlife Agencies. *Res:* Relationships of land and resource use; energy developments; population requirements to fish and wildlife resource management and use. *Mailing Add:* 2082 Steeple Pl Woodbridge VA 22192

BERRYMAN, JAMES GARLAND, APPLIED MATHEMATICAL PHYSICS. *Current Pos:* physicist, Earth Sci Dept, 81-85, physicist & group leader electronics eng, 85-90, PHYSICIST & GROUP LEADER, EARTH SCI, ENVIRON PROGS, LAWRENCE LIVERMORE NAT LAB, 90- *Personal Data:* b Hutchinson, Kans, June 26, 47; m 73, Marcia Ann Griffin; c Rachel Lynne & Martin Andrew. *Educ:* Univ Kans, BA & BS, 69; Univ Wis-Madison, MS, 70, PhD(physics), 75. *Prof Exp:* Asst scientist, Math Res Ctr, Univ Wis, 75-76; res physicist, Explor Res Div, Conoco, 76-77; vis mem, Courant Inst, NY Univ, 77-78 & 87-88; mem tech staff, Ocean Syst, Bell Labs, 78-81. *Concurrent Pos:* Woodrow Wilson fel, 69; NSF fel, 77-78; assoc ed, J Math Physics, 79-81; consult prof, Dept Geophys, Stanford Univ, 92-; assoc tech ed, Inverse Probs Eng, 93-96; vis prof, Inst Earth Physics, Paris, France, 95; sabbatical, Dept Math, Stanford Univ, 95-96. *Mem:* Am Phys Soc; Am Geophys Union; Soc Explor Geophysics. *Res:* Applied mathematical physics; wave propagation in porous materials and composites; fluid flow through porous media; nonlinear waves; nonlinear diffusion; tomography and inverse problems in geophysics; materials science/engineering. *Mailing Add:* Lawrence Livermore Nat Lab PO Box 808 L-202 Livermore CA 94551-9900. *Fax:* 510-422-1002; *E-Mail:* berryman@si23.es.llnl.gov

BERS, ABRAHAM, ELECTRICAL ENGINEERING, PLASMA PHYSICS. *Current Pos:* Res asst elec eng, 53-58, from instr to asst prof, 58-63, assoc prof elec commun, 63-71, PROF ELEC ENG, MASS INST TECHNOL, 71- *Personal Data:* b Cernauti, Romania, May 28, 30; US citizen; m 66; c 2. *Educ:* Univ Calif, Berkeley, BS, 53; Mass Inst Technol, SM, 55, ScD(elec eng), 59. *Concurrent Pos:* Consult sci & eng, various orgns; Ford Found fac exchange fel, Tech Univ, Berlin, 66; John Simon Guggenheim Mem fel, 68-69; assoc prof, Univ Paris, 68-69 & 79-80; dir res, Physics Lab, Polytech Sch, Paris, 79-80, vis prof, Univ Paris, Orsay, 81-88; prin investr grants, Nat Sci Found & Dept Energy, 71- *Mem:* AAAS; Am Phys Soc; Inst Elec & Electronics Engrs. *Res:* Microwave electron beam devices; network and field theory; acoustic surface waves; plasmas; fusion; plasma electrodynamics for fusion energy generation; plasma heating with electromagnetic power sources; surface acoustoelectronic devices; surface wave convolvers; memory correlators. *Mailing Add:* 38-260 Mass Inst Tech Cambridge MA 02139

BERS, DONALD M, CARDIAC PHYSIOLOGY. *Current Pos:* PROF & CHMN PHYSIOL, LOYOLA UNIV, 92- *Personal Data:* b New York, NY, Dec 13, 53; m 76, Kathryn E Hammond; c Brian & Rebecca. *Educ:* Univ Colo, BA, 74; Univ Calif, Los Angeles, PhD(physiol), 78. *Prof Exp:* Teaching asst, Univ Colo, 73-74, Univ Calif, Los Angeles, 75-78; res fel, Univ Calif, Los Angeles, 78-79, Edinburgh Univ, Scotland, 79-80; asst res physiologist, Univ Calif, Los Angeles, 80-82; asst prof, Univ Calif, Riverside, 82-86, assoc prof,

86-89, prof, 89-92, interim div dean, 91-92. *Concurrent Pos:* Teaching asst, Sch Nursing, Univ Calif, Los Angeles, 76-77, teaching assoc, 77-78, adj asst prof, 81-86; res career develop award, NIH, 85-90; Wellcome vis prof, NY Univ, 97. *Mem:* Am Physiol Soc; Biophys Soc; AAAS; Am Heart Asn; Soc Gen Physiologists. *Res:* Regulation of cardiac muscle contraction, particularly with the respect to cellular calcium transport systems such as calcium current and sodium/calcium exchange. *Mailing Add:* Loyola Univ Stritch Sch Med 2160 S First Ave Maywood IL 60153-5500

BERSCH, CHARLES FRANK, MATERIALS ENGINEERING, AERONAUTICAL & ASTRONAUTICAL ENGINEERING. *Current Pos:* RETIRED. *Personal Data:* b Sheboygan, Wis, Jan 23, 27; m 50, 72, Rosemary W Schlesinger; c Tom S & Kathy (Lewis). *Educ:* St Norbert Col, BS, 51. *Prof Exp:* Chemist polymers, Nat Bur Stand, 51-58, phys chemist, 58-59; mat engr nonmetals, Bur Aeronaut, US Navy, 59 & Bur Naval Weapons, 59-66, mat engr, 66-73, supvy mat engr nonmetals, Naval Air Systs Command, 73-79, head, Mat Br, Naval Air Systs Command, 79-80; mgr composites prog, NASA, 80-84, actg mgr, Mat & Struct Off, 82-84; consult, Inst Defense Analyses, 84-88, res staff, 88-96. *Concurrent Pos:* Navy liaison mem, Nat Mat Adv Bd, Nat Acad Sci-Nat Acad Eng, 65-79; US Nat Leader & Navy rep, Tech Coop Prog Polymeric Mat, 73-80; chmn, Naval Adv Coun Mat, 76-78; consult, Dept Energy, 79-83. *Mem:* Fel Am Ceramic Soc; Am Chem Soc; AAAS; Am Inst Aeronaut & Astronaut. *Res:* Composite, particularly property relationships of polymers and ceramics; interface phenomena of composites and adhesives; ceramic bearings; properties and design of transparents; processing and application of advanced composites. *Mailing Add:* 4986 Sentinel Dr Bethesda MD 20816-3518. *Fax:* 703-578-2877; *E-Mail:* cbersch@ida.org

BERSHAD, NEIL JEREMY, COMMUNICATION THEORY, SIGNAL PROCESSING. *Current Pos:* PROF COMMUN INFO THEORY, UNIV CALIF, IRVINE, 66- *Personal Data:* b Brooklyn, NY, Oct 20, 37; c 2. *Educ:* Rensselaer Polytech Inst, BEE, 58, PhD(elec eng), 62; Univ Southern Calif, MS, 60. *Prof Exp:* Staff engr radar signal processing, Hughes Aircraft Co, 58-62; lectr network theory, Northeastern Univ, 62-65; staff engr radar signal processing, Hughes Aircraft Co, 65-69. *Concurrent Pos:* Consult underwater acoustic signal processing, 66-; assoc ed, Transactions Communs, Inst Elec & Electronics Engrs, 74-80, Transaction Acoust, Speech & Signal Processing, 88-90. *Mem:* Fel Inst Elec & Electronics Engrs; Sigma Xi. *Res:* Communication theory; stochastic signal processing; acoustic array processing. *Mailing Add:* 1621 Santiago Dr Newport Beach CA 92660

BERSHADER, DANIEL, aerophysics; deceased, see previous edition for last biography

BERSOHN, MALCOLM, COMPUTATIONAL LINGUISTICS, ARTIFICIAL INTELLIGENCE. *Current Pos:* asst prof, 62-66, PROF CHEM, UNIV TORONTO, 66- *Personal Data:* b New York, NY, May 13, 25; m 64, Joanne Scott; c Diana. *Educ:* Harvard Univ, BS, 43; Columbia Univ, MA, 57, PhD(chem), 60. *Prof Exp:* Res scientist, Calif Res Corp, 60-62. *Concurrent Pos:* Guggenheim fel, Comput Sci Dept, Stanford Univ, 69-71; vis prof, Univ Tokyo, 78. *Mem:* Am Chem Soc; Am Asn Artificial Intel. *Res:* Natural language processing of documents concerned with synthetic organic chemistry; organic synthesis design executed by a computer. *Mailing Add:* Dept Chem Univ Toronto Toronto ON M5S 3H6 Can. *Fax:* 416-964-2041; *E-Mail:* mbersohn@alchemy.chem.utoronto.ca

BERSOHN, RICHARD, CHEMICAL DYNAMICS. *Current Pos:* assoc prof, 59-62, chmn dept, 90-96, HIGGINS PROF CHEM, COLUMBIA UNIV, 62- *Personal Data:* b New York, NY, May 13, 25; c 4. *Educ:* Mass Inst Technol, BS, 44; Harvard Univ, MA, 47, PhD(chem physics), 50. *Honors & Awards:* Herbert Broida Prize, Am Phys Soc, 85. *Prof Exp:* From asst prof to assoc prof chem, Cornell Univ, 51-59. *Concurrent Pos:* NSF fel, Univ Paris, 58; head, Div Chem Physics, Am Phys Soc, 71; Guggenheim fel, Univ Tel Aviv, 72; chmn, Adv Comt Chem Dept, Brookhaven Nat Lab, 81-84; mem, Comt Atomic & Molecular Sci, Nat Res Coun, 84-87. *Mem:* Nat Acad Sci; Am Acad Arts & Sci. *Res:* Dynamics of chemical reactions and photodissociation; state distributions of reaction products. *Mailing Add:* 959 Havemeyer Hall Columbia Univ PO Box 959 New York NY 10027

BERSON, ALAN, CARDIOVASCULAR INSTRUMENTATION. *Current Pos:* DEP CHIEF, DEVICES & TECHNOL BR, NAT HEART, LUNG & BLOOD INST, 78- *Personal Data:* b New York, NY. *Educ:* City Col New York, BEE, 50; George Washington Univ, MSE, 65, PhD(physiol & biophysics), 72. *Prof Exp:* Sect chief comput, Litton, College Park, Md, 54-58; proj engr, Melpar, Arlington, Va, 58-60; chief data processing & instrument cardiovasc res, Vet Admin Med Ctr, Washington, 60-78. *Concurrent Pos:* Mem, stroke coun, Am Heart Asn, electrocardiograph comt, 62-78 & comput subcomt, 85-; res assoc, Georgetown Univ, 66-71; asst res prof, George Washington Univ, 71-78; chmn, electrocardiographs, cardiac monitors & sphygmomanometers subcomts & bd dirs mem, Asn Advan Med Instrumentation; mem, Bd Dirs, Int Soc Computerized Electrocardiology. *Mem:* Inst Elec & Electronics Engrs; AMA; Am Advan Med Instrumentation; Am Heart Asn. *Res:* Cardiovascular instrumentation including electrocardiography, phonocardiography, ultrasound and computers in biological and medical research. *Mailing Add:* 1755 Glastonberry Rd Potomac MD 20854

BERSON, ELIOT LAWRENCE, OPHTHALMOLOGY. *Current Pos:* from instr to assoc prof, 68-82, CHATLOS PROF OPHTHAL, HARVARD UNIV SCH MED, 82-, DIR, BERMAN-GUND LAB STUDY RETINAL DEGENERATIONS, HARVARD MED SCH, 74- *Personal Data:* b Boston, Mass, 1937. *Educ:* Harvard Univ, MD, 62. *Prof Exp:* Intern, Calif Hosp, San Francisco, 62-63; resident ophthal, Barnes & McMillan Hosps, St Louis, 63-66; clin assoc ophthalmologist, Nat Inst Neurol Dis & Blindness, 66-68. *Concurrent Pos:* Surgeon, USPHS, 66-68; asst, Mass Eye & Ear Infirmary, Boston, 68-73, asst surgeon, 74-78; assoc surgeon ophthal, Harvard Med Sch, 79-84, surgeon, 84- *Mem:* AMA; Asn Res Vision & Ophthal; Am Acad Ophthal. *Res:* Retinal degeneration. *Mailing Add:* Berman-Gund Lab Mass Eye & Ear Infirmary 243 Charles St Boston MA 02114-3004

BERSON, JEROME ABRAHAM, ORGANIC CHEMISTRY. *Current Pos:* chmn dept, Yale Univ, 71-74, prof chem, 69-79, Irene E DuPont prof, 79-92, dir phys sci & eng, 83-90, sterling prof, 92-94, STERLING EMER PROF CHEM, YALE UNIV, 94- *Personal Data:* b Sanford, Fla, May 10, 24; m 46, Bella Zevitovsky; c Ruth, David & Jonathan. *Educ:* City Col New York, BS, 44; Columbia Univ, AM, 47, PhD(chem), 49. *Honors & Awards:* James Flack Norris Award, Am Chem Soc, 78, Roger Adams Award, 87, Arthur C Cope Scholar Award, 92. *Prof Exp:* Asst chemist, Hoffmann-La Roche, Inc, 44; lab asst, Columbia Univ, 46-49; fel, Nat Res Coun, Harvard Univ, 49-50; from asst prof to prof chem, Univ Southern Calif, 50-63; prof, Univ Wis, 63-69. *Concurrent Pos:* Sloan fel, 57-61; NSF sr fel, 59-60; vis prof, Univ Calif, Los Angeles, 62, Univ Cologne, 65, Univ Western Ont, 67, Univ Karlsruhe, 81 & Univ Lausanne, 91; mem, Adv Panel Chem, NSF, 64-68; consult, Goodyear Tire & Rubber Co, 65-74, IBM Corp, B F Goodrich Corp, Cord Lab, Am Cyanamid Co & Lubrizol Corp; mem, Med Chem Study Sect, NIH, 69-73; chmn, Div Org Chem, Am Chem Soc, 71; Sherman Fairchild distinguished scholar, Calif Inst Technol, 74-75; mem, Adv Comt, Assembly Math & Phys Sci, Nat Res Coun, 75-77; Alexander von Humboldt sr US scientist award, 80. *Mem:* Nat Acad Sci; Am Chem Soc; Royal Soc Chem; Am Acad Arts & Sci. *Res:* Synthetic and theoretical organic chemistry; mechanisms of organic reactions. *Mailing Add:* Dept Chem Box 6666 Yale Univ 225 Prospect St New Haven CT 06511

BERSTED, BRUCE HOWARD, POLYMER PHYSICS. *Current Pos:* Sr res chemist, 69-81, RES ASSOC, AMOCO CHEM CORP, 81- *Personal Data:* b Chicago, Ill, Sept 25, 40; m 68; c 2. *Educ:* Beloit Col, BA, 63; Univ Ill, MS, 65, PhD(phys chem), 69. *Concurrent Pos:* App to write test procedure vapor pressure osmometry, Am Soc Testing & Mat, 75- *Mem:* Am Phys Soc; Soc Rheology. *Res:* Methods of molecular weight determination; polymer rheology and its relation to molecular weight distribution; dynamic mechanical properties of polymers and composites; dependence of polymer toughness and impact resistance on molecular structure. *Mailing Add:* 880 Ramsden Run Alpharetta GA 30022

BERSU, EDWARD THORWALD, ANATOMY, CYTOGENETICS. *Current Pos:* Asst prof, 76-82, ASSOC PROF ANAT, UNIV WIS-MADISON, 82- *Personal Data:* b Duluth, Minn, May 6, 46. *Educ:* Univ Minn, Duluth, BA, 68; Univ Wis-Madison, PhD(anat), 76. *Mem:* AAAS; Teratology Soc; Am Soc Human Genetics; Am Asn Cin Anatomists. *Res:* Detailed anatomical studies of human, genetically determined multiple congenital malformation syndromes; development analysis of trisomy syndromes in the mouse. *Mailing Add:* Med Sci Ctr Dept Anat Univ Wis 1300 University Ave Madison WI 53706

BERT, CHARLES WESLEY, ENGINEERING MECHANICS, MECHANICAL ENGINEERING. *Current Pos:* from assoc prof to prof, 63-66, dir, Sch Aerospace, 72-77, BENJAMIN H PERKINSON PROF ENG, UNIV OKLA, 78-, GEORGE L CROSS RES PROF, 81-, DIR, SCH AEROSPACE, MECH & NUCLEAR ENG, 90- *Personal Data:* b Chambersburg, Pa, Nov 11, 29; m 57, Charlotte Davis; c Charles & David. *Educ:* Pa State Univ, BS, 51, MS, 56; Ohio State Univ, PhD(eng mech), 61. *Honors & Awards:* Pressure Vessel & Piping Lit Award for 1975, Am Soc Mech Engrs, 76. *Prof Exp:* Aeronaut design engr, Fairchild Aircraft Div, Fairchild Engine & Airplane Corp, Md, 54-56; prin mech engr, Appl Mech Div, Battelle Mem Inst, 56-59, sr engr, 61-62, prog dir, 62-63; instr eng mech, Ohio State Univ, 59-61. *Concurrent Pos:* Prin mech engr, Battelle Mem Inst, 59-61, consult, 63-65; consult, Inst Defense Anal & Univ Engrs, Inc, 64-66, Sandia Labs, 69-76, Firestone Tire & Rubber Co, 76-80 & Univ Technologists, Inc, 77-80; assoc ed, Exp Mech, 82-87 & Appl Mech Rev, 84-87; mem ed bd, Composite Structures, 82- & J Sound & Vibration, 88- *Mem:* Fel Am Soc Mech Engrs; fel Am Acad Mech; Am Soc Eng Educ; Nat Soc Prof Engrs; fel AAAS; Soc Eng Sci; fel Soc Exp Mech; fel Am Inst Aeronaut & Astronaut. *Res:* Composite-material structures; mechanical behavior of materials; structural dynamics; shell structures; thermal stress analysis. *Mailing Add:* Univ Okla Aerospace & Mech Eng 865 Asp Ave Norman OK 73069-4848

BERT, MARK HENRY, NUTRITIONAL BIOCHEMISTRY, STATISTICS. *Current Pos:* asst prof nutrit biochem, 65-68, asst prof nutrit & food & head dept, 68-70, assoc prof, 70-80, PROF NUTRIT & FOOD, UNIV MASS, AMHERST, 80- *Personal Data:* b Lima, Peru, May 1, 16; US citizen; m 60; c 2. *Educ:* Nat Col Agr & Vet Sci, Lima, BS, 39; Univ Ill, Urbana, MS, 48, PhD(nutrit biochem), 55. *Prof Exp:* Specialist in flax fiber processing, Dept Agr, Peru, 40-41; tech dir, Desfibradora de Lino, SA, 41-43; Inter-Am Trade scholar flax fiber processing firms, Ore, 44-46; consult var indust firms & Dept Agr, Peru, 46-47; res biochemist lab, Corn Prod Co, Mass, 55-58, dir res lab, 58-63, biochemist in-chg biochem sect, NJ, 63-65. *Concurrent Pos:* Univ Mass res grant, 66-68. *Mem:* Animal Nutrit Res Coun; Am Chem Soc; Am Statist Asn; Inst Food Technologists; fel Am Inst Chemists. *Res:* Amino acid metabolism; food irradiation effects on protein quality, vitamins, enzyme activity, lipids; nutritive value of algae; vitamin metabolism; statistical design and analysis; computer applications to nutrition; atherosclerosis; radioisotopic techniques. *Mailing Add:* 63 Tracy Circle Amherst MA 01002

BERTALANFFY, FELIX D, anatomy, histology, for more information see previous edition

BERTANI, GIUSEPPE, MOLECULAR GENETICS, BIOTECHNOLOGY. *Current Pos:* sr scientist, 81-91, RES AFFIL, JET PROPULSION LAB, CALIF INST TECHNOL, PASADENA, 91- *Personal Data:* b Como, Italy, Oct 23, 23; nat US; m 54, L Elizabeth Teegarden; c Christopher & Niklas. *Educ:* Univ Milan, DrNatSc, 45. *Hon Degrees:* Dr, Univ Uppsala, 83. *Prof Exp:* Res fel biol, Zool Sta, Naples, 45-46; asst zool, Univ Milan, 46-47 & Univ Zurich, 47-48; res fel genetics, Carnegie Inst, Cold Spring Harbor, NY, 48-49; res assoc bact, Ind Univ, 49-50 & Univ Ill, 50-54; sr res fel biol, Calif Inst Technol, 54-57; assoc prof med microbiol, Med Sch, Univ Southern Calif, 57-60; vis prof microbial genetics, Karolinska Inst, Sweden, 60-64, prof, 64-83. *Mem:* AAAS; Genetics Soc Am; Am Soc Microbiol; Brit Soc Gen Microbiol; Europ Molecular Biol Orgn. *Res:* Genetics of bacteria and bacterial viruses; applied genetics; methanogenic bacteria. *Mailing Add:* 975 Dale St Pasadena CA 91106-4018. *Fax:* 818-393-4057

BERTANI, LILLIAN ELIZABETH, GENETICS, MOLECULAR BIOLOGY. *Current Pos:* SR RES BIOLOGIST, CALIF INST TECHNOL, PASADENA, 85-, LECTR BIOL, 93- *Personal Data:* b Ind, July 9, 31; m 54, Giuseppe; c Christofer & Niklas. *Educ:* Univ Mich, BS, 53; Calif Inst Technol, PhD(virol), 57. *Prof Exp:* Res assoc med microbiol, Univ Southern Calif, 57-60; res assoc microbial genetics, Karolinska Inst, Sweden, 61-65; Med Res Coun fel, Swedish Med Res Coun, 66-75; docent med microbiol, Karolinska Inst, 75-84. *Concurrent Pos:* USPHS fel, 60-61; docent microbiol, Univ Stockholm, 65; vis assoc biol, Calif Inst Technol, Pasadena, 81-84. *Mem:* Am Soc Microbiol; Genetics Soc Am. *Res:* Gene amplification; biomineralization of magnetite. *Mailing Add:* Biol Div Calif Inst Technol Pasadena CA 91125. *Fax:* 626-405-9452; *E-Mail:* lebert@cco.caltech.edu

BERTAUT, EDGARD FRANCIS, COMPUTER SCIENCE. *Personal Data:* b Chicago, Ill, May 23, 31; m 57; c 5. *Educ:* Loyola Univ, Ill, BSc, 53; Carnegie Inst Technol, MS, 56, PhD(inorg chem), 58. *Prof Exp:* Instr chem, Carnegie Inst Technol, 57-58; asst prof, Pa State Univ, 58-60, fel mineral sci, 60-62; asst prof chem, Univ Detroit, 62-68; assoc prof natural sco, Univ DC, 68-70, prof & chem div, 70-71, prof comput sci & chmn prog, 74-80. *Mem:* Am Chem Soc; Nat Sci Teachers Asn; Asn Comput Mach; AAAS. *Res:* High temperature spectra; televised instruction; application of computers to chemistry; computer graphics; operating systems. *Mailing Add:* 6635 Western Ave NW Washington DC 20015

BERTELL, ROSALIE, BIOMATHEMATICS. *Current Pos:* CONSULT, 80- *Personal Data:* b Buffalo, NY, Apr 4, 29. *Educ:* D'Youville Col, BA, 51; Cath Univ Am, MA, 59, PhD(math), 66. *Hon Degrees:* Dr, Mt St Vincent Univ, 85. *Honors & Awards:* Hans Adalbert Schweigart Medal, 83. *Prof Exp:* Teacher Bishop O'Hern High Sch, NY, 56-57; asst math, Cath Univ Am, 57-58; instr, Sacred Heart Jr Col, Pa, 58-62, assoc prof, 65-68; coordr & teacher, D'Youville Acad, Diocese Atlanta, 68-69; assoc prof math, D'Youville Col, 69-73; asst res prof, Grad Sch, State Univ NY Buffalo, 74-80. *Concurrent Pos:* Sr cancer res scientist, Roswell Park Mem Inst, 70-78; cancer res grant, Cancer Res scientist & cancer res consult, 75-; staff expert for Pub Health & Energy Concern, Global Educ Assocs; found & pres bd dir, Ministry of Concern Pub Health, Buffalo & Int Inst of Concern Pub Health, Toronto; ed, Int Perspectives Pub Health. *Mem:* Sigma Xi; Health Phys Soc; Am Acad Polit & Soc Sci; Am Pub Health Asn; Int Biometric Soc; NY Acad Soc. *Res:* Mathematical statistics; analysis; measure theory; aging effect in humans associated with exposure to ionizing radiation; updating relative risk methodology for biomedical applications; life-style and chronic diseases. *Mailing Add:* Int Inst Concern Health 710-264 Queens Quay W Toronto ON M5J 1B5 Can

BERTELO, CHRISTOPHER ANTHONY, PLASTICS ADDITIVES, IMPACT MODIFICATION. *Current Pos:* prin scientist, 90-95, MGR PLASTICS ADDITIVES RES & DEVELOP, ELF-ATOCHEM, KING OF PRUSSIA, PA, 95- *Personal Data:* b Orange, NJ, Apr 22, 47; m 73; c David. *Educ:* Bates Col, BS, 69; Princeton Univ, MS, 73, PhD(chem), 75. *Prof Exp:* Res assoc chem, Univ Iowa, 75-77; vis asst prof, Grinnell Col, 77; sr chemist, Tenneco Chem, Inc, 78-82, Tenneco Polymers, 82-85; sr proj chemist, Met Chem, Rahway, NJ, 85-90. *Mem:* Am Chem Soc; Soc Plastics Indust. *Res:* Plastic additives; polymer stabilizers; catalysts and impact modifiers. *Mailing Add:* 2694 Crest Lane Scotch Plains NJ 07076-1299

BERTELSEN, BRUCE I(RVING), PHYSICS, SURFACE & TRACE ANALYSIS. *Current Pos:* RETIRED. *Personal Data:* b Portland, Maine, Sept 11, 26; m 51; c 3. *Educ:* Univ Maine, BS, 54. *Prof Exp:* From physicist to adv physicist vacuum deposition, xerography & magnetic thin films, Gen Prod Div, IBM Corp, NY, 54-60, res staff mem thin magnetic film memory device process res, Res Lab, Switz, 60-61, from group mgr to sr physicist thin magnetic film process develop, Components Div, 61-68, dept mgr magnetic film device & process develop, Systs Develop Div, 65-68, mgr, Device Thin Film Prod Eng, 68-70, mgr, Tooling & Process Control, Integrated Circuit Prod Eng, 70-71, proj mgr process & mat develop, 71-73, dept mgr int circuit process line automation, 73-76, dept mgr surface & trace anal, 76-81, sr physicist, 80-83, consult tech writer, Patent Dept, 83-84. *Mem:* Sr mem Inst Elec & Electronics Engrs; Am Vacuum Soc. *Res:* Vacuum techniques; electrical and magnetic properties as function of deposition process parameters; computer applications for thin film components; magnetic thin film memory devices; surface and trace analysis, Auger, ESCA, SIMS, ISS, EDX, WDX, radioisotopes; materials and technology for very large scale integrated circuits; granted 17 US patents and over 40 foreign patents. *Mailing Add:* 27 Thayer Beach Rd Colchester VT 05446

BERTELSON, ROBERT CALVIN, ORGANIC PHOTOCHEMISTRY, PHOTOCHROMIC DYESTUFFS. *Current Pos:* CHMN & PRES, CHROMA CHEM INC, 74- *Personal Data:* b Milwaukee, Wis, Nov 5, 31; m 60, Mary L Johnson; c Thomas & Kenneth. *Educ:* Univ Wis, BS, 52; Mass Inst Technol, PhD(org chem), 57. *Prof Exp:* Sr res chemist, Nat Cash Register Co, 57-61, group leader, 61-74. *Concurrent Pos:* Sr res assoc, Nat Acad Sci-Nat Res Coun, 72-74. *Mem:* NY Acad Sci; Am Chem Soc; Soc Photog Scientists & Engrs; Sigma Xi; Am Inst Chemists; Interamerican Photochem Asn. *Res:* Photochromic and photosensitive dyestuffs for optical information storage, exposure indicators and selectively absorbing filters. *Mailing Add:* 5312 Bliss Pl Dayton OH 45440

BERTERA, JAMES H, VISION RESEARCH. *Current Pos:* RES ASSOC VISION, PSYCHOL DEPT, UNIV MASS, 78-, STAFF ASSOC, VISION, EYE RES INST, 86-, ASSOC SCIENTIST, 90- *Personal Data:* b Springfield, Mass, March 18, 48. *Educ:* Fairfield Univ, Conn, BA, 70; Hollins Col, Va, MA, 72, Univ Okla Med Ctr, PhD(biopsychol), 77. *Prof Exp:* Res assoc comput learning, NC State Univ, 71-72; mgr, Neuropsychol Lab, Univ Okla Health Sci, 72-77; res scientist vision, Systs Res Labs, Inc, 77-78. *Res:* Human visual information processing investigated using eye-controlled display techniques; visual disease simulation with artificial scotoma on computer display; eye controlled typewriter. *Mailing Add:* 4 Longfellow Pl Suite 3011 Boston MA 02114

BERTHOLD, JOHN WILLIAM, III, FIBER OPTIC SENSORS, INDUSTRIAL APPLICATIONS OF LASERS. *Current Pos:* sr res physicist, Babcock & Wilcox Co, 79-83, group supvr, 83-84, sect mgr, 84-85, tech adv, 85-90, scientist, 90-94, SR CONSULT ENGR, MCDERMOTT/BABCOCK & WILCOX, 94- *Personal Data:* b York, Pa, May 24, 45; m 74, Jacqueline Reed; c John W IV & Margaret H. *Educ:* Gettysburg Col, BA, 67; Univ Ariz, MS, 74, PhD(optical sci), 76. *Honors & Awards:* Tech Brief Award, NASA, 77. *Prof Exp:* Sr tech aid, Bell Tel Labs Inc, 67-69; from res asst to res assoc, Optical Sci Ctr, Univ Ariz, 69-76; physicist, US Dept Defense, 76-79. *Concurrent Pos:* Consult, Iota Eng Inc, 73-76. *Mem:* Optical Soc Am; fel Soc Photo-Optical Instrumentation Engrs; Inst Elec & Electronics Engrs; Instrument Soc Am. *Res:* Fiber optic intensity sensors for measurement of pressure, acceleration, temperature, strain, flow rate, liquid level, gas concentration, and process chemistry. *Mailing Add:* Babcock & Wilcox 1562 Beeson St Alliance OH 44601. *Fax:* 330-829-7832; *E-Mail:* john.w.berthold@mcdermott.com

BERTHOLD, JOSEPH ERNEST, PHYSICS, ELECTRONICS ENGINEERING. *Current Pos:* mem tech staff integrated circuits, 77-80, supvr, High Voltage Integrated Circuits, Bell Labs, 80-83, EXEC DIR, NETWORK CONTROL RES, BELL CORE, 90- *Personal Data:* b Paterson, NJ, Sept 30, 47; m 69; c 2. *Educ:* Seton Hall Univ, BS, 69; Brown Univ, MS, 73, PhD(physics), 76. *Prof Exp:* Res assoc physics, Lab Atomic & Solid State Physics, Cornell Univ, 75-77. *Mem:* Electrochem Soc; Inst Elec & Electronics Engrs. *Res:* Semiconductor devices, integrated circuits; development of high voltage integrated circuit technology. *Mailing Add:* 640 Johnston Dr Plainfield NJ 07060

BERTHOLD, ROBERT, JR, APICULTURE, ENTOMOLOGY. *Current Pos:* asst prof, 68-76, asst chmn biol, 79-80, assoc dean sci, 87-89, AT DEPT BIOL, DELAWARE VALLEY COL, 89- *Personal Data:* b Paterson, NJ, Aug 2, 41; m 66, Marren Cummings; c Heather & Robert A. *Educ:* Juniata Col, BS, 63; Rutgers Univ, MS, 65; Pa State Univ, PhD(entom), 68. *Prof Exp:* Res asst entom, Rutgers Univ, 63-66 & Pa State Univ, 66-68; asst prof, Delaware Valley Col, 68-76, asst chmn biol, 79-80, assoc dean sci, 87-89. *Mem:* Entom Soc Am; Am Entom Soc; Sigma Xi. *Res:* Insect behavior; German cockroach; honey bee; development of new honey products including marketing studies; uses of beeswax. *Mailing Add:* Dept Biol Delaware Valley Col Doylestown PA 18901

BERTHOLF, DENNIS E, MATHEMATICS. *Current Pos:* Asst prof math, 68-74, ASSOC PROF MATH, OKLA STATE UNIV, 74- *Personal Data:* b Harper, Kans, Aug 19, 41; m 62; c 3. *Educ:* Univ Kans, BS, 63; NMex State Univ, MA, 65, PhD(math), 68. *Mem:* Math Asn Am. *Res:* Abelian group theory; homological algebra. *Mailing Add:* Dept Math Okla State Univ Stillwater OK 74078-0001

BERTHOLF, ROGER L, BIOCHEMISTRY. *Current Pos:* asst prof, 88-93, ASSOC PROF, DEPT PATH & LAB MED, UNIV FLA COL MED, 93- *Personal Data:* b Roanoke, Va, Aug 21, 55; m 85, Marsha G Frazelle; c Aaron L & Abby G. *Educ:* James Madison Univ, BS, 77; Univ Va, MS, 81, PhD(biochem), 85. *Prof Exp:* Res fel neuropath, Dept Path, Univ Va Sch Med, 85-86, res assoc, 86-88. *Concurrent Pos:* Prin investr, Univ Fla, 88-89 & 90, Am Health Asst Found, 89-91, Abbott Labs, 90-91, PB Diag, 90, NIH, 91-, Beckman Instruments, 92, Boehringer Mannheim Diag, 93; dir toxicol & therapeut drug monitoring, Shands Hosp Clin Labs, 88-, pharm & therapeut comt, 89-, chmn med technol prog, 93-; dir forensic & environ toxicol, Univ Fla Diag Referral Labs, 88-, oper comt, 91-; res fac, Univ Fla, Grad Sch, 89-; fac, Ctr Environ & Human Toxicol, 90-, interdisciplinary grad toxicol prog comt, 90-; inspector, Clin Lab Accreditation Prog, Col Am Pathologists. *Mem:* Am Chem Soc; Am Asn Clin Chem; AAAS; fel Am Inst Chemists; fel Asn Clin Scientists. *Res:* Biochemistry; author of over 44 publications. *Mailing Add:* Dept Path Univ Med Ctr 655 W Eighth St Jacksonville FL 32209

BERTHOUEX, PAUL MAC, WATER SUPPLY & POLLUTION CONTROL, ENVIRONMENTAL STATISTICS. *Current Pos:* from asst prof to assoc prof, 71-76, PROF ENVIRON ENG, UNIV WIS-MADISON, 76- *Personal Data:* b Delwein, Iowa, Aug 15, 40. *Educ:* Univ Iowa, BS, 63, MS, 64; Univ Wis-Madison, PhD(civil eng), 69. *Honors & Awards:* Eddy Medal, Water Pollution Control Fedn, 71, Radebaugh Award, 80 & 82; Rudolph Hering Medal, Am Soc Civil Engrs, 75 & 92. *Prof Exp:* Instr prev med, Univ Iowa, 64-65; asst prof civil eng, Univ Conn, 65-67; chief res engr, GKW Consult, Manheim, WGer, 69-71. *Concurrent Pos:* Consult, Tenn Valley Authority, 72-77, Asian Develop Bank, 75-81, 85 & 89-90, WHO, 78-; mem, Comt Nat Statist, Nat Res Coun, 75-76, UNESCO, 93. *Mem:* Am Soc Civil Engrs; Int Asn Water Pollution Res & Control; Water Pollution Control Fedn; AAAS; Am Water Works Asn. *Res:* Drinking water supply and water pollution control, including toxic and hazardous waste treatment, with special interests in optimal process design and environmental statistics. *Mailing Add:* 2205 Eng Bldg Univ Wis 1415 Johnson Dr Madison WI 53706-1691

BERTHRONG, MORGAN, RADIATION INJURY. *Current Pos:* prof & chmn, Univ Colo, 59-61, clin prof, 61-81, EMER CLIN PROF PATH, COLO MED SCH, 89- *Personal Data:* b Aurora Hills, Va, July 17, 18; m 43, 72; c 9. *Educ:* Harvard Med Sch, MD, 43. *Prof Exp:* Resident path, Johns Hopkins Univ & Hosp, 46-50, from instr to assoc prof, 49-53; pathologist, Penrose Hosp, 54-91, dir labs, 67-79. *Concurrent Pos:* Vis prof path & actg chair path, Sch Med, Stanford Univ, 66-67; adj prof path, Univ NMex, 73-; sci adv bd, Armed Forces Inst Path, 82-88. *Mem:* Am Asn Path; Am Soc Clin Path; Int Acad Path; Col Am Path. *Res:* General anatomic pathology, especially diseases of lungs, liver, kidneys and congenital heart; experiments with tuberculosis, hypersensitivity and so-called collagen vascular diseases; radiation injury of all types; radiation injury. *Mailing Add:* Dept Path Penrose Hosp Colorado Springs CO 80907

BERTI, ARTURO LUIS, SANITARY ENGINEERING. *Current Pos:* PRES, ASN MUNDIAL VIVIENDA RURAL, CARACAS, 74- *Personal Data:* b Bocono, Venezuela, Aug 5, 12; m 42, Olga C; c Elena, Arturo, Beatriz & Margarita. *Educ:* Liceo Andres Bello, Caracas, B, 36; Cent Univ, Caracas, PhD, 36; Tex A&M Univ, MS, 39. *Prof Exp:* Chief zona, Malariology Min Sanidad, Maracay, Venezuela, 36-40, chief antimalaria engr, 41-50, chief div, 50-60; dir, Bur Malariology, Maracay, Venezuela, 60-70; pres, Acad Ciencias, Fisicas, Mat y Nat, Caracas, 89-91. *Concurrent Pos:* Field engr, Malariology Min Sanidad, Pto Cabello, Venezuela, 36-37. *Mailing Add:* Calle 14 Urb La Boyera Caracas 1081 Venezuela

BERTIE, JOHN E, PHYSICAL CHEMISTRY, CHEMICAL PHYSICS. *Current Pos:* assoc prof, 67-75, PROF CHEM, UNIV ALTA, 75- *Personal Data:* b London, Eng, Mar 24, 36; Can citizen. *Educ:* Univ London, PhD(phys chem), 60. *Prof Exp:* Fel chem, Div Appl Chem, Nat Res Coun Can, 60-62, asst res officer, 62-65, assoc res officer, 65-67. *Concurrent Pos:* Pres, Asn Acad Staff, Univ Alta, 78-79, gov, 89-92; chmn, Comn I-5, Int Union Pure & Appl Chem, 94-; pres, Coblentz Soc, 95- *Mem:* Am Phys Soc; Chem Inst Can; Soc Appl Spectros. *Res:* Infrared absolute absorption intensities of liquids, optical and dielectric constants; emphasis on hydrogen-bonded systems. *Mailing Add:* Dept Chem Univ Alta Edmonton AB T6G 2G2 Can. *Fax:* 403-492-8231; *E-Mail:* john_bertie@dept.chem.ualberta.ca

BERTIN, JOHN JOSEPH, aerodynamics, for more information see previous edition

BERTIN, MICHAEL C, DESIGN & CONSTRUCTION OF ON-LINE MEASUREMENT SYSTEMS, QUALITY CONTROL SYSTEMS. *Current Pos:* PRES, QUALITY PROFILES, INC, 90- *Personal Data:* b Bronx, NY, Sept 25, 42; m 64; c 2. *Educ:* Mass Inst Technol, BS, 63; Rutgers Univ, MS, 65, PhD(physics), 68. *Prof Exp:* Res assoc, Physics Dept, Stanford Univ, 68-71; sr scientist, Nucleonic Data Systs, Div Sentrol Systs Inc, 71-74, dir, Eng, 74-79, dir, Res & Develop, 79-81; pres, Gamma Instruments Inc, Subsid Sensor Control Corp, 81-88, consult, 88-89. *Concurrent Pos:* Res assoc, Physics Dept, Rutgers Univ, 68; lectr physics, San Jose Univ, 71; assoc prof, Calif State Univ, 81-82. *Mem:* Am Phys Soc. *Res:* Application of measurement and analysis technology to on-line industrial processing; industrial gauging of thickness, width, length, density and other physical properties, and analysis and quality control for these processes; developed gauges and on-line computer systems for use in the metals, rubber, plastics and paper industries; on-line quality control and SPC data gathering and reporting systems. *Mailing Add:* 22 Gillman St Irvine CA 92715

BERTIN, RICHARD J, PHARMACY ADMINISTRATION, PUBLIC HEALTH. *Current Pos:* reviewing pharmacist, 88-90, DIR, ORPHAN PROD GRANTS PROG, OFF ORPHAN PROD DEVELOP, FOOD & DRUG ADMIN, MD, 96- *Personal Data:* b Apr 25, 42; m, Catherine E; c 2. *Educ:* Univ Pittsburgh, BS, 65; Univ Minn, MS, 67, PhD(pharm admin), 76. *Honors & Awards:* Andrew Craigie Award, Asn Military Surgeons US, 95. *Prof Exp:* Pharm resident, Vet Admin Hosp, Pa, 65-66; dep chief pharmacist, Clin Res Ctr, NIMH, Tex, 67-69; asst chief pharmacist, US Pub Health Serv Hosp, NY, 69-71, dep chief pharmacist, 73-74; asst chief pharm br, Bur Med Servs, HSA/PHS, MD, 74-75, chief pharm staff, 75-80, chief prof discipline sect & chief pharm staff, 80-81; spec asst chief Manpower Develop Br, Comn Personnel Opers Div, USPHS, 81-83, chief, Officer Servs Br, Div Comn Personnel, Off Surgeon Gen, 83-88, dir, Dir Comn Personnel, 90-92, chief pharmacist officer, 92-96. *Concurrent Pos:* Consult pharmacist, Fed Bur Prisons Med Prog, US Dept Justice, 75-85 & Fed Emergency Mgt Admin Progs, 75-92; nat bd dirs, Comn Officers Asn, USPHS, 78-84; actg dir, Off Health Prof Servs, 80-81; pharm prog comt, Food & Drug Law Inst, 93-; consult, Dept Educ Re-Recognition Process Am Coun Pharmaceut Educ, 95. *Mem:* Am Soc Health Syst Pharmacists; Am Pharmaceut Asn; Am Asn Cols Pharm; Asn Military Surgeons US. *Res:* Pharmacists role in the control of institutional drug costs; pharmacy professional organization management; development and evaluation of drug distribution systems; drug development and regulation particularly orphan drugs; financing mechanisms for drug programs. *Mailing Add:* Off Orphan Prods Develop Food & Drug Admin 5600 Fishers Ln, Parklawn Bldg Rm 8-73(HR-35) Rockville MD 20857

BERTIN, ROBERT IAN, PLANT REPRODUCTIVE ECOLOGY. *Current Pos:* from asst prof to assoc prof, 84-95, PROF, COL HOLY CROSS, 95- *Personal Data:* b Shreveport, La, Aug 4, 52. *Educ:* Hobart Col, BS, 73; Univ Conn, MS, 76; Univ Ill, PhD(biol), 80. *Prof Exp:* Vis asst prof biol, Bucknell Univ, 80-81, 83-84, Miami Univ, 81-83. *Mem:* Ecol Soc Am; Bot Soc Am; Soc Study Evolution; Am Soc Naturalists. *Res:* Plant reproductive ecology; plant-animal interactions; campsis radicans; effects of pollination on fruit production and seed number and quality. *Mailing Add:* Biol Dept Holy Cross Col 1 College St Worcester MA 01610

BERTINI, HUGO W, PHYSICS. *Current Pos:* PHYSICIST, OAK RIDGE NAT LAB, 53- *Personal Data:* b Chicago, Ill, Dec 12, 26; m 54; c 3. *Educ:* Northwestern Univ, MS, 51; Univ Tenn, PhD(physics), 62. *Mem:* Am Phys Soc; Sigma Xi. *Res:* Nuclear reactor physics; high energy nuclear reactions. *Mailing Add:* 915 W Outer Dr Oak Ridge TN 37830

BERTINO, JOSEPH R, PHARMACOLOGY, MEDICINE. *Current Pos:* HEAD, PROG MOLECULAR PHARMACOL & THERAPEUT, SLOAN-KETTERING CANCER CTR, 87- *Personal Data:* b Port Chester, NY, Aug 16, 30; m 56, M Patricia Hagemeyer; c Fred, Amy, Tom & Paul. *Educ:* State Univ NY Downstate Med Ctr, MD, 54. *Hon Degrees:* MA, Yale Univ, 69. *Honors & Awards:* Exp Therapeut Award, Am Soc Pharmacol, 70; Richard & Hilda Rosenthal Award, Am Asn Cancer Res, 78; Medal, Am Cancer Soc, 93. *Prof Exp:* Intern, Grad Hosp, Univ Pa, 54-55; resident internal med, Vet Admin Hosp, Philadelphia, 55-56; asst prof pharmacol, 61-64, assoc prof, 64-69, prof med & pharmacol, Sch Med, Yale Univ, 69-86. *Concurrent Pos:* USPHS res fel hemat & biochem, Sch Med, Univ Wash, 58-61, career develop award, Nat Cancer Inst, 64-74; consult, Nat Serv Ctr, 64-; Am Cancer Soc prof, 76- *Mem:* Am Soc Hemat; Am Asn Cancer Res; Am Fedn Clin Res; Am Soc Clin Invest; Am Soc Biol Chemists. *Res:* Folic acid and vitamin B12 metabolism; cancer chemotherapy; drug resistance; gene amplification; gene transfer. *Mailing Add:* 117 Sunset Hill Rd Branford CT 06405-6419. *Fax:* 212-639-2767

BERTLES, JOHN F, INTERNAL MEDICINE, HEMATOLOGY. *Current Pos:* PROF MED, COL PHYSICIANS & SURGEONS, COLUMBIA UNIV, 74- *Personal Data:* b Spokane, Wash, June 8, 25; m 48, 81; c 3. *Educ:* Yale Univ, BS, 45; Harvard Med Sch, MD, 52; Am Bd Internal Med, dipl, 61. *Prof Exp:* Intern & asst resident med, Presby Hosp, New York, 52-55; instr, Harvard Med Sch, 59-61; chief, hemat oncol div, St Luke's-Roosevelt's Hosp Ctr, 62-, Dir, Transfusion Serv. *Concurrent Pos:* USPHS res fel, Sch Med & Dent, Univ Rochester, 55-56; USPHS res fel, Harvard Med Sch, 56-57 & res fel, 56-59; from asst attend physician to attend physician, St Luke's Hosp Ctr, 62- *Mem:* Am Soc Clin Invest; Am Physiol Soc; fel Am Col Physicians; Am Soc Hemat; Am Fedn Clin Res. *Res:* Human hemoglobinopathies. *Mailing Add:* 67 Jared Dr White Plains NY 10605

BERTNESS, MARK DAVID, ECOLOGY. *Current Pos:* PROF BIOL, BROWN UNIV, 80- *Personal Data:* b July 13, 1949; m 83, Janette A Bertero; c Sarah. *Educ:* Univ Md, PhD(zool), 79. *Mem:* Ecol Soc Am. *Res:* Organization and dynamics of natural communities; rocky intertidal marine and salt marsh plant communities. *Mailing Add:* Brown Univ Box GW201 Providence RI 02806. *Fax:* 401-863-2166

BERTNOLLI, EDWARD CLARENCE, ELECTRICAL ENGINEERING. *Current Pos:* assoc prof, 65-68, PROF ELEC ENG, UNIV MO-ROLLA, 68- *Personal Data:* b Kansas City, Mo, Aug 8, 35; m 56; c 4. *Educ:* Kansas State Univ, BS, 58, MS, 61, PhD(elec eng), 66. *Prof Exp:* Instr elec eng, Kansas State Univ, 58-65. *Concurrent Pos:* NSF res grant, 66-67; eng prog evaluator, Accreditation Bd Eng & Technol, 88. *Mem:* Inst Elec & Electronics Engrs; Am Soc Eng Educ. *Res:* System theory and design. *Mailing Add:* Elec Eng Dept Univ NFla 4567 St Johns Bluff Rd S Jacksonville FL 32224-2645

BERTOCCI, UGO, ELECTROCHEMISTRY, CORROSION. *Current Pos:* RES CHEMIST, NAT INST STANDARDS & TECHNOL, 71- *Personal Data:* Derna, Libya, Jan 31, 26; US citizen. *Educ:* Univ Milan, Italy, Dr (chem), 50. *Honors & Awards:* Silver Medal, Dept of Com. *Prof Exp:* Asst prof phys chem, Milan Polytech Inst, 50-57; group leader, Italian Comt Nuclear Res, 58-61; chemist, Oak Ridge Nat Lab, 61-71. *Mem:* Int Soc Electrochem; Electrochem Soc; Am Chem Soc; AAAS. *Res:* Electrodeposition; electrochemical properties of metal single crystals; computer simulation of crystal growth; effects of alternating current on corrosion; electrochemical methods for corrosion studies; electrochemical noise measurements; stress corrosion cracking. *Mailing Add:* 5010 Barkwood Pl Rockville MD 20853-2319

BERTOLACINI, RALPH JAMES, INORGANIC CHEMISTRY. *Current Pos:* RETIRED. *Personal Data:* b Pawtucket, RI, Aug 8, 25; m 53, Dorothy Thompsom; c Tom, Joyce & James. *Educ:* Univ RI, BS, 49; Mich State Univ, MS, 51. *Honors & Awards:* Eugene Houdry Award, NAm Catalysis Soc, 87; Ernest W Thiele Award, Chicago Sect, Am Inst Chem Engrs, 93. *Prof Exp:* Asst, Univ RI, 48-49 & Mich State Univ, 49-51; sr res scientist, Am Oil Co,

51-68, proj mgr & res assoc, Amoco Oil, 68-76, proj mgr & sr res assoc, 76-79, dir catalysis res, Res & Develop Div, 79-90, mgr explor & catalysis res & develop, 82- *Concurrent Pos:* Adj prof chem eng, Dept Chem Eng, Univ Del, 91-; sci adv, Argonne Nat Lab, 94- *Mem:* Am Chem Soc; Sigma Xi; Am Inst Chem Engrs; Am Soc Testing & Mat; Catalysis Soc. *Res:* Catalysis; analytical chemistry. *Mailing Add:* 6S572 Millcreek Lane Naperville IL 60540

BERTOLAMI, CHARLES NICHOLAS, ORAL BIOLOGY, ORAL & MAXILLOFACIAL SURGERY. *Current Pos:* PROF, DEPT DENT, UNIV CALIF, LOS ANGELES, 89- *Personal Data:* b Lorain, Ohio, Dec 31, 49; m 77; c 2. *Educ:* Ohio State Univ, DDS, 74; Harvard Univ, DMedSc, 79. *Prof Exp:* Intern oral surg, Mass Gen Hosp, 75-76, asst resident, 78-79, chief resident, 79-80; asst prof oral & maxillofacial surg, Univ Conn, 80-89, asst prof surg, 80-89. *Concurrent Pos:* Clin fel, Harvard Sch Dent Med, 80- *Mem:* Int Asn Dent Res; Am Asn Dent Res; Am Dent Asn; Sigma Xi. *Res:* Wound healing as a developmental phenomenon; role of glycosaminoglycans in tissue repair; experimental animal model systems for hypertrophic scarring; phenomenon of wound contraction. *Mailing Add:* Univ Calif P505 Parnassus Ave PO Box 0430 San Francisco CA 94133-0430

BERTOLDI, GILBERT LEROY, HYDROLOGY, HYDROGEOLOGY. *Current Pos:* Hydrologist/geologist, US Geol Surv, Calif, 65-75, chief proj sect, 75-79, chief, Cent Valley Aquifer Proj, 79-81, regional groundwater specialist, Western Region, 81-85, chief, Calif Dist, 85-87, sr staff scientist, 88-95, EMER SCIENTIST, US GEOL SURV, 95- *Personal Data:* b Fresno, Calif, Mar 10, 38; m 58, Deanna D Lipari; c Christopher B, Anthony A & Alicia C. *Educ:* Calif State Univ, Fresno, BS, 60. *Concurrent Pos:* Instr, Calif State Univ, Fresno, 64-65, Sacramento, 70-71 & Cosumnes River Col, 79-80; appointee, Cosumnes River Col Curriculum Comt, 76- *Mem:* Geol Soc Am; Am Soc Advan Sci; Asn Eng Geologists. *Res:* Methodology and evaluation of hydraulic properties of alluvial systems, flow modeling, land subsidence, and water-mineral phase equilibrium; developed open-channel hydraulic analysis models; author or coauthor of 39 publications. *Mailing Add:* 8490 Berry Rd Wilton CA 95693. *Fax:* 916-978-5529

BERTOLETTE, W(ILLIAM) DEB(ENNEVILLE), chemical engineering; deceased, see previous edition for last biography

BERTOLINI, DONALD R, CELL BIOLOGY, BONE BIOLOGY. *Current Pos:* SR INVESTR, SMITH KLINE BEECHAM, 90- *Personal Data:* b New York, NY, Nov 28, 49; m 73; c 2. *Educ:* Ithaca Col, BA, 71; C W Post Col, MS, 73; Wesleyan Univ, PhD(biol), 83. *Honors & Awards:* Norwich Eaton Res Award, 86. *Prof Exp:* Res assoc, Health Sci Ctr, Univ Tex, 82-86; res scientist, Otsuka Pharmaceut Co Ltd, 86-90. *Mem:* AAAS; Am Soc Cell Biol; Am Soc Bone & Mineral Res. *Res:* Cellular communications through cell contact or specfic molecules; bone cell biology. *Mailing Add:* 109 Trowbridge Lane Downingtown PA 19335

BERTON, JOHN ANDREW, GEOMETRY. *Current Pos:* chmn dept, 67-75, PROF MATH, OHIO NORTHERN UNIV, 67- *Personal Data:* b Villa Park, Ill, June 22, 30; m 52; c 5. *Educ:* Univ Ill, AB, 55, MA, 57, PhD(geom), 64. *Prof Exp:* From instr to asst prof math, Ind State Col, 59-64; assoc prof, Ripon Col, 64-67. *Mem:* AAAS; Am Math Soc; Math Asn Am; Soc Indust & Appl Math; Asn Comput Mach. *Res:* Differential geometry. *Mailing Add:* Dept Math 324 Willeke Ave Ada OH 45810-1644

BERTON, WILLIAM MORRIS, PATHOLOGY. *Current Pos:* prof, 69-86, EMER PROF PATH & MICROBIOL, UNIV NEBR MED CTR, OMAHA, 86- *Personal Data:* b Fresno, Calif, Feb 8, 24; m 49; c 3. *Educ:* Univ Calif, MD, 49. *Prof Exp:* Intern, US Naval Hosp, Mass, 49-50, res path, Methodist Hosp, Ind, 50-51; from intern to resident, Duke Univ Hosp, 51-54, instr, Sch Med, Duke Univ, 52-54; head lab serv & chief res, US Naval Hosp, Camp Pendleton, 55-56; from asst prof to prof, Univ Tenn, 56-68. *Mem:* Asn Am Med Cols; Col Am Path; Am Soc Clin Path; NY Acad Sci; AMA; Sigma Xi. *Res:* Chromatographic methods as applied to pathology and bacteriology. *Mailing Add:* 13136 Mason St Omaha NE 68154-2952

BERTONCINI, PETER JOSEPH, COMPUTER SCIENCE. *Current Pos:* fel quantum chem, 73-74, asst computer scientist reactor physics, 74-80, ASST COMPUTER SCIENTIST, COMPUTER SERV, ARGONNE NAT LAB, 80- *Personal Data:* b Chicago, Ill, Nov 29, 39; m 66, Linda; c Mark & David. *Educ:* Univ Ill, BS, 61; Univ Wis, PhD(phys chem), 68. *Prof Exp:* Fel quantum chem, Argonne Nat Lab, 68-71; fel quantum chem, Fac for Physics, Univ Freiburg, WGermany, 71-73. *Mem:* Am Phys Soc. *Mailing Add:* 335 S Lombard Oak Park IL 60302. *E-Mail:* pjb@anl.gov

BERTONI, HENRY LOUIS, WIRELESS. *Current Pos:* From instr to assoc prof, 66-75, PROF ELECTROPHYS, POLYTECH UNIV 75-, HEAD DEPT ELEC ENG, 90- *Personal Data:* b Chicago, Ill, Nov 15, 38; m 90, Helene Ebenstein; c Elliot & Rachel. *Educ:* Northwestern Univ, BS, 60; Polytech Inst Brooklyn, MS, 62, PhD(electrophys), 67. *Concurrent Pos:* Guest res fel, Univ Col, London, 82-83; summer res fel, Hanscom AFB, Mass, 83. *Mem:* Fel Inst Elec & Electronics Engrs; Int Sci Radio Union; Sigma Xi. *Res:* Ultrahigh-frequency radio propagation in urban environments for application to wireless systems. *Mailing Add:* Polytech Univ 6 Metro Tech Ctr Brooklyn NY 11201. *E-Mail:* hbertoni@prism.poly.edy

BERTONIERE, NOELIE RITA, ORGANIC CHEMISTRY. *Current Pos:* RES CHEMIST TEXTILES & FOOD, SOUTHERN REGIONAL RES CTR, AGR RES SERV, USDA, 60- *Personal Data:* b New Orleans, La, Oct 17, 36. *Educ:* St Mary's Dominican Col, BS, 59; Univ New Orleans, PhD(org chem), 71. *Mem:* Am Chem Soc; Am Asn Textile Chemists & Colorists; Sigma Xi; Fiber Soc; AAAS. *Res:* Cellulose chemistry; durable press cotton fabric; permeation chromatography; supramolecular structure of cellulose; photochemistry of small ring heterocycles and carbenes. *Mailing Add:* 818 Louque Pl New Orleans LA 70124-1734

BERTOSSA, ROBERT C, metallurgy, for more information see previous edition

BERTOZZI, EUGENE R, POLYMER CHEMISTRY. *Current Pos:* CONSULT, 82- *Personal Data:* b Lowell, Mass, Sept 26, 15; m 43; c 3. *Educ:* Worcester Polytech Inst, BS, 38; Brooklyn Polytech Inst, MS, 50. *Prof Exp:* Chemist res & develop, Benzol Prod Co, 38-42; mgr develop, Dept Res & Develop, Thiokol Corp, 42-64, asst tech dir res & develop, 64-68, dir advan technol, 68-72, prin scientist, Chem Div, 72-82. *Mem:* Am Chem Soc; Sigma Xi. *Res:* Process development of organic polysulfide polymers; new polymer products development in condensation and hydrocarbon polymers. *Mailing Add:* Kendall at Hanover 80 Lyme Rd Apt 350 Hanover NH 03755-1234

BERTOZZI, WILLIAM, PHYSICS. *Current Pos:* Staff mem, Div Sponsored Res, Lab Nuclear Sci, 57-58, from instr to assoc prof, 58-68, PROF PHYSICS, MASS INST TECHNOL, 68- *Personal Data:* b Framingham, Mass, June 9, 31; m 56; c 3. *Educ:* Mass Inst Technol, SB, 53, PhD(physics), 58. *Mem:* Am Phys Soc; Am Asn Physics Teachers; AAAS. *Res:* Nuclear physics. *Mailing Add:* 8 Castle Rd Lexington MA 02173

BERTRAM, ROBERT WILLIAM, thin film physics, optical coatings, for more information see previous edition

BERTRAM, SIDNEY, SYSTEMS ENGINEERING, ELECTROMAGNETIC THEORY. *Current Pos:* RETIRED. *Personal Data:* b Winnipeg, Man, July 7, 13; US nat; m 44, Esther Varon; c Irving, Henry, Robert & Suzanne (Scott). *Educ:* Calif Inst Technol, BS, 38; Ohio State Univ, MS, 41, PhD(physics), 51. *Honors & Awards:* Fairchild Photogram Award, Am Soc Photogram, 69. *Prof Exp:* Instr radio & math, Radio Inst Calif, 34-36; res engr, Int Geophys Co, 38-39, Res Found, Ohio State Univ, 41-42, Div War Res, Univ Calif, 42-45 & Boeing Aircraft Co, Wash, 45-46; asst prof commun eng, Ohio State Univ, 46-51; engr, Rand Corp, 51-53 & Syst Develop Corp, 53-57; sr staff scientist, Bunker Ramo Corp, 57-71; sr staff engr, Missile Systs Div, Hughes Aircraft Co, 71-80; lectr, Calif Polytech State Univ, 80-86. *Mem:* Fel Inst Elec & Electronics Engrs. *Res:* Automation of photogrammetric instruments; sonar; radar; simulators; field theory; applied mathematics; missile image matching and infrared seekers. *Mailing Add:* 1210 Oceanaire Dr San Luis Obispo CA 93405

BERTRAM, TIMOTHY ALLYN, IMMUNOPATHOLOGY. *Current Pos:* SECT HEAD DIGESTIVE & NUTRIT TOXICOL, PROCTER & GAMBLE CO, 89- *Personal Data:* b Le Mars, Iowa, Aug 26, 55; m 78; c 3. *Educ:* Iowa State Univ, DVM, 79, PhD(path), 83. *Honors & Awards:* Cert Merit, USDA, 84. *Prof Exp:* Resident toxicol, Iowa Vet Diag Lab, 79-80; res assoc path, Nat Animal Dis Ctr, 80-83, assoc cellular path, 83-85; assoc prof path, Univ Ill, 85-89, adj prof, 93. *Concurrent Pos:* Prin investr, Am Lung Asn, 86-88, USDA, 87-89, NSF, Nat Supercomput Ctr, 88-89; vis scientist biochem path, Nat Inst Environ Health Sci, 87-88; scholar chmn, Am Col Vet Pathologists. *Mem:* Am Vet Med Asn; Am Col Vet Pathologists; Soc Toxicol Path. *Res:* Cellular and biochemical mechanisms of injury induced by infectious/or toxic agents; organ systems include reproductive, respiratory and gastrointestinal. *Mailing Add:* 1596 Congress Hill Lane Fairfield OH 45014

BERTRAMSON, BERTRAM RODNEY, AGRONOMY. *Current Pos:* CONSULT AGRONOMIST, 82- *Personal Data:* b Potter, Nebr, Jan 25, 14; m 38; c 3. *Educ:* Univ Nebr, BS, 37, MS, 38; Ore State Univ, PhD(soils), 41. *Hon Degrees:* DAgr, Univ Nebr, 78. *Prof Exp:* From asst soil physics to asst instr soils, Univ Nebr, 37-38; asst soil fertil, Ore State Col, 38-41; instr soils, Soil Lab, Colo State Col, 41-42; asst prof soil chem, Univ Wis, 46; assoc soil chemist, Dept Agron, Purdue Univ, 46-49; chmn, Dept Agron, Col Agr, Wash State Univ, 49-67, dir resident instr, 67-79; party chief, Morocco Proj, Univ Nebr, 81-82. *Mem:* Fel AAAS; fel Am Soc Agron (vpres, 60, pres, 61); Crop Sci Soc Am; Soil Sci Soc Am; Soil Conserv Soc Am. *Res:* Soil physics; physical properties of the soil as affected by manuring and fertilizers; irrigation efficiency; phosphorus analyses; soil fertility; comparative efficiency of organic phosphorus and of superphosphate; research on potash, manganese, boron, sulfur and magnesium. *Mailing Add:* SE 720 Carolstar Dr Pullman WA 99163-6404

BERTRAND, FOREST, AGRICULTURE. *Current Pos:* RETIRED. *Personal Data:* b St Pie-de-Guire, Que, May 31, 18; m 45, Madeleine Normand; c Jean-Pierre, Louise, Gabriel & Claire. *Educ:* Laval Univ, BA, 39, BSc, 43; McGill Univ, MSc, 45; Cornell Univ, PhD, 56. *Hon Degrees:* DSc, McGill Univ, 77. *Honors & Awards:* Silver Merit Medal, Diocesan of Pocatiere, 61; Govt Can Centenary Medal, 67; Comdr Agron Merit Order, 76. *Prof Exp:* Res officer, Can Dept Agr, 45-60; tech adv, Que Dept Agr, 60-62, head res div, 62-67, dir res & educ, 67-73, dir gen res & educ, 73-79; consult agrologist, 79. *Concurrent Pos:* Secy, Que Agr Res Coun, 60-63, chmn, 63-72, mem, 72- *Mem:* Hon life mem Potato Asn Am. *Mailing Add:* 1570 Chemin Ste Foy Quebec PQ G1S 2P3 Can

BERTRAND, FRED EDMOND, NUCLEAR REACTION MECHANISM. *Current Pos:* staff mem, 70-78, group leader, 78-86, SECT HEAD, PHYSICS DIV, OAK RIDGE NAT LAB, 86- *Personal Data:* b New Orleans, La, Sept 27, 38; m 65; c 2. *Educ:* Southwestern Memphis, BS, 60; La State Univ, MS, 62, PhD(physics), 68. *Prof Exp:* Res assoc, Univ Southern Calif, 68-70. *Mem:* Fel Am Phys Soc. *Res:* Experimental studies of the excitation and decay of nuclear giant resonances following excitation in medium energy hadronic reactions; studies of direct reactions with medium energy nuclear probes; nuclear spectroscopy using direct reactions. *Mailing Add:* Bldg 6000 MS 6368 Oak Ridge Nat Lab PO Box 2008 Oak Ridge TN 37830

BERTRAND, GARY LANE, PHYSICAL CHEMISTRY. *Current Pos:* From asst prof to assoc prof, 66-75, PROF CHEM, UNIV MO-ROLLA, 75- *Personal Data:* b Lake Charles, La, Sept 25, 35; m 64; c 2. *Educ:* McNeese State Col, BS, 57; Tulane Univ, PhD(phys chem), 64. *Prof Exp:* Fel chem, Carnegie Inst Technol, 64-65, asst prof, 65-66. *Mem:* Calorimetry Conf (chmn-elect, 82); Am Chem Soc; Am Soc Enologists. *Res:* Investigations of solvent effects and deuterium isotope effects on the thermodynamic properties of dissolved species; solution calorimetry and dilatometry; physical chemistry of wine. *Mailing Add:* Chem Dept 142 Schrenk Hall Univ Mo-Rolla Rolla MO 65401

BERTRAND, HELEN ANNE, GERONTOLOGY. *Current Pos:* asst prof, 75-81, ASSOC PROF PHYSIOL, UNIV TEX HEALTH SCI CTR, SAN ANTONIO, 81- *Personal Data:* b Wilmington, Del, Nov 24, 39. *Educ:* Univ Del, BA, 61; NC State Univ, PhD(biochem), 70. *Prof Exp:* Res assoc biol, Univ Del, 61-63; res technician plant biol, Rockefeller Univ, 63-64; from instr to asst prof biochem, Med Col Pa, 71-75. *Concurrent Pos:* NIH training grant, Med Col Pa, 70-71. *Mem:* Am Chem Soc; Am Phys Soc; Geront Soc; Sigma Xi. *Res:* Aging; mechanism of life-prolonging action of restricted food intake; adipocyte lipolysis. *Mailing Add:* Dept Physiol Univ Tex Health Sci Ctr 7703 Floyd Curl Dr San Antonio TX 78284-7756. *Fax:* 210-567-4410

BERTRAND, HELMUT, MOLECULAR GENETICS. *Current Pos:* PROF MICROBIOL, MICH STATE UNIV, 92- *Personal Data:* b Asuncion, Paraguay, Dec 29, 37; US citizen; c 2. *Educ:* Bethel Col, Kans, BA, 63; Kans State Univ, MSc, 67, PhD(molecular genetics), 69. *Prof Exp:* NIH fel biochem, Albert Einstein Col Med, 69-70; from asst prof to prof biol, Univ Regina, 70-88; prof & chmn microbiol, Univ Guelph, 88-92. *Concurrent Pos:* Vis scientist physiol chem, Univ Munich, 76-77; vis scientist biochem, Sch Med, St Louis Univ, 80. *Mem:* Genetics Soc Am; AAAS; Am Soc Microbiol; Am Genetics Soc. *Res:* Genetic control of the formation and function of the mitochondrial electron-transport system in Neurospora crassa; cyanide-sensitive and cyanide-insensitive respiratory systems; senescence-inducing plasmids in Neurospora; cytoplasmic hypovirilence in cryphonectria parasitica. *Mailing Add:* Dept Microbiol 318 Giltner Hall Mich State Univ East Lansing MI 48824-1101. *E-Mail:* mhelmut@msu.edu

BERTRAND, JOSEPH AARON, INORGANIC CHEMISTRY. *Current Pos:* from asst prof to assoc prof, 62-70, dir chem, 74-81, PROF CHEM, GA INST TECHNOL, 70- *Personal Data:* b Lake Charles, La, Mar 20, 33; m 57; c 4. *Educ:* McNeese State Col, BS, 55; Tulane Univ, MS, 56, PhD(inorg chem), 61. *Prof Exp:* Instr chem, McNeese State Col, 56-59; res assoc, Mass Inst Technol, 61-62. *Concurrent Pos:* Alfred P Sloan res fel, 66-68; vis prof, Univ Kans, 68. *Mem:* Am Chem Soc; Am Crystallog Asn. *Res:* Structure of transition metal complexes. *Mailing Add:* 1671 Homestead Ave NE Atlanta GA 30306-3131

BERTRAND, JOSEPH E, ANIMAL NUTRITION. *Current Pos:* assoc prof, 66-77, PROF ANIMAL SCI, AGR RES CTR, UNIV FLA, 77- *Personal Data:* b Kaplan, La, June 20, 24; m 61; c 4. *Educ:* Southwestern La Inst, BS, 48; La State Univ, MS, 52, PhD(ruminant nutrition), 60. *Prof Exp:* Res assoc animal indust, La State Univ, 52-56; asst prof, Ark State Col, 56-58; ruminant nutritionist, Com Solvents Corp, New York, 60-66. *Mem:* Am Soc Animal Sci; Poultry Sci Asn; Am Dairy Sci Asn. *Res:* Ruminant nutrition; beef cattle production, especially growing and developing light-weight calves to desired feedlot weights and finishing cattle for market, emphasizing maximum use of locally grown roughages and concentrates. *Mailing Add:* 18 Happy Lane Milton FL 32570

BERTRAND, WILLIAM ELLIS, PUBLIC HEALTH. *Current Pos:* fel, 72-75, chmn dept, 81-86, from instr to PROF, DEPT BIOSTATIST & EPIDEMIOL, TULANE UNIV, 74-, WISNER PROF PUB HEALTH, 86- *Personal Data:* b Midland, Tex, May 24, 44; m, Jane Trowbridge; c Katherine & Jacob. *Educ:* La State Univ, BA, 66; Tulane Univ, PhD, 72. *Prof Exp:* From instr to assoc prof, Delgado Community Col, New Orleans, 66-70. *Concurrent Pos:* Vis lectr, Univ del Valle, Colombia, 69-71 & 73, Sch Social Work, 77-80; adj asst prof & adj prof sociol, Tulane Univ, 74-78, dir, Tulane Int Develop Ctr & Tulane Ctr Int Resource Develop, 88-; dir, Inst Study Change in Americas, New Orleans, 84-86; co-dir & prin investr, Zaire Sch Pub Health, Univ Kinshasa, 85-; grantee, USAID, Zaire, 85, Kenya, 88, Niger, 88 & Sudan, 88; co-prin investr, Kenya Ministry Health, Nairobi, 88-, Niger Ministry Health, Niamey, 88-; prin investr, Famine Early Warning Syst, Africa, 88- *Mem:* Am Col Epidemiol; Am Pub Health Asn; Appl Anthrop Asn; Pan Am Health & Educ Found. *Res:* Famine. *Mailing Add:* 570 Walnut St New Orleans LA 70118

BERTSCH, CHARLES RUDOLPH, PUBLISHING CHEMICAL JOURNALS. *Current Pos:* sr prod ed, 61-69, mgr ed prod, 69-73, HEAD, JOURNALS DEPT, AM CHEM SOC, 73- *Personal Data:* b Long Island, NY, June 13, 31; m 66; c 2. *Educ:* Syracuse Univ, BS, 52; Pa State Univ, PhD(chem), 55. *Prof Exp:* Res chemist, US Naval Propellants Plant, 55-56, Olin Mathieson Chem Corp, 57-58 & Pennsalt Chem Corp, 58-61. *Mem:* Am Chem Soc; Coun Biol Ed; Soc Scholarly Publ. *Mailing Add:* 14012 Manchester Rd Upper Marlboro MD 20774

BERTSCH, GEORGE FREDERICK, NUCLEAR PHYSICS. *Current Pos:* asst prof, 70-74, PROF PHYSICS, MICH STATE UNIV, 74- *Personal Data:* b Oswego, NY, Nov 5, 42; m 64; c 2. *Educ:* Swarthmore Col, BA, 62; Princeton Univ, PhD(physics), 65. *Prof Exp:* Fel physics, Niels Bohr Inst, Copenhagen, Denmark, 65-66; from instr to asst prof, Princeton Univ, 66-69; asst prof, Mass Inst Technol, 69-70. *Concurrent Pos:* Alfred P Sloan Found fel, 69-71; Humbolt fel, 86. *Mem:* AAAS; Am Phys Soc. *Res:* Theoretical studies of nuclear structure based on shell model; qualitative and quantitative understanding of experimental results. *Mailing Add:* Dept Physics FM 15 Univ Wash Seattle WA 98195

BERTSCH, HANS, INVERTEBRATE ZOOLOGY, MALACOLOGY. *Current Pos:* adj fac, 83-93, chair, Dept Math & Natural Sci, 93-95, ASSOC PROF, NAT UNIV, 93- *Personal Data:* b St Louis, Mo, Nov 2, 44; m 93, Suzanne L O'Bourke. *Educ:* San Luis Rey Col, BA, 67; Franciscan Sch Theol, BTh, 71; Univ Calif, Berkeley, PhD(zool), 76. *Prof Exp:* Asst prof biol, Chaminade Univ Honolulu, 76-78; cur marine invert, San Diego Nat Hist Mus, 78-80; prof marine sci, Univ Autonoma de Baja Calif, Ensenada, 81-83. *Concurrent Pos:* Prin investr, Ctr Field Res, 78-80; Nat Teaching fel, Chaminade Univ Honolulu, 76-78; res & tech consult, Mex Nat Fisheries, 84-85; res assoc, Los Angeles Co Mus Nat Hist, 77- & Calif Acad Sci, 72-; bd dirs, SW Wetlands Int Asn, 94- *Mem:* AAAS; Sigma Xi; Malacol Soc Japan; Western Soc Malacologists (pres, 89-). *Res:* Opisthobranch taxonomy; functional morphology; intertidal and subtidal ecology of benthic marine invertebrates; marine zoogeography. *Mailing Add:* Nat Univ 11255 N Torrey Pines Rd La Jolla CA 92037. *Fax:* 619-423-9118; *E-Mail:* hbertsch@nunic.nu.edu

BERTSCH, ROBERT JOSEPH, FREE RADICAL & EMULSION POLYMERIZATION, THERMOSET RESINS. *Current Pos:* SR RES & DEVELOP ASSOC, POLYMER SYNTHESIS, B F GOODRICH CO, 75- *Personal Data:* b Philadelphia, Pa, May 6, 48; m 70, Pamela P Smith; c Denise N & Kirsten E. *Educ:* Drexel Univ, BS, 70; Ohio State Univ, PhD(chem), 75. *Prof Exp:* Undergrad trainee/researcher, Eastern Regional Lab, USDA, 66-71. *Mem:* Am Chem Soc. *Res:* Free radical polymerization, thermoset resin chemistry, synthesis of new organic monomers and polymers and the characterization of polymeric species; development of new emulsion polymers. *Mailing Add:* B F Goodrich Co 9921 Brecksville Rd Brecksville OH 44141. *Fax:* 216-447-5575; *E-Mail:* bertsch@brk.bfg.com

BERTSCH, WOLFGANG, ANALYTICAL CHEMISTRY, ENVIRONMENTAL CHEMISTRY. *Current Pos:* Asst prof, 74-78, ASSOC PROF ANALYTICAL CHEM, DEPT CHEM, UNIV ALA, 78- *Personal Data:* b Ludwigsburg, Ger, Mar 17, 40; c 1. *Educ:* Tech Acad, Isny, Ger, BS, 68; Univ Houston, PhD(chem), 73. *Concurrent Pos:* Environ Protection Agency grant, 76-78; consult, Ionics Res, Houston, 77-78; Off Water Resources Res & Develop grant, 77-78; mem organizing comt, Int Symp on Glass Capillary Columns, Hindelang, Ger, 77-78; ed, J of High Resolution Chromatography & Chromatography Commun, Ger, 78- *Mem:* Am Chem Soc. *Res:* High performance gas chromatography and gas chromatography/mass spectrometry; development of glass capillary columns, environmental and medicinal applications. *Mailing Add:* Univ Ala Box 870336 Tuscaloosa AL 35487-0336

BERTSCHINGER, EDMUND, COSMOLOGY, THEORETICAL ASTROPHYSICS. *Current Pos:* from asst prof to assoc prof, 86-96, PROF PHYSICS, MASS INST TECHNOL, 96- *Personal Data:* b Oakland, Calif, July 24, 58; m 83, Beverly E Hjorth; c Thomas A H. *Educ:* Calif Inst Technol, BS, 79; Princeton Univ, PhD(astrophys sci), 84. *Honors & Awards:* Helen B Warner Prize, Am Astron Soc, 92. *Prof Exp:* Res assoc Univ Va, 83-85; Miller res fel, Univ Calif, Berkeley, 85-86. *Concurrent Pos:* Alfred P Sloan fel, 88-90; Vis physicist, Inst Theoret Physics, 88; mem, Inst Advan Study, 93. *Mem:* Am Astron Soc; fel Am Phys Soc; Int Astron Union; AAAS. *Res:* Theoretical astrophysics; cosmology; galaxy formation; gas dynamics; general relativity; Supercomputer simulations. *Mailing Add:* Mass Inst Technol Room 6-207 Cambridge MA 02139. *E-Mail:* bertschinger@mit.edu

BERTY, JOZSEF M, CHEMICAL ENGINEERING. *Current Pos:* PRES, BERTY REACTION ENGRS, LTD, 78- *Personal Data:* b Budapest, Hungary, Oct 25, 22; US citizen; m 45; c 6. *Educ:* Budapest Tech Univ, dipl chem eng, 44, DSc, 50. *Hon Degrees:* Dr, Veszprem Univ, 88. *Honors & Awards:* Sr Fulbright Lectr, T U Munchen, 73-74. *Prof Exp:* Engr, Nitrochem Works, Ltd, Hungary, 44-45 & Agr & Chem Works, Ltd, 45-46; asst prof, Budapest Tech Univ, 46-50; head dept petrochem, Hungarian Oil & Gas Res Inst, 50-56; vis prof, Inst Chem Technol, Ger, 56-57; engr chem div, Union Carbide Corp, 57-60, group leader res & develop, 60-68, tech mgr, 68-69, asst dir, 69-72; vpres, Autoclave Engrs, Inc, 77-78. *Concurrent Pos:* Assoc prof, Inst Chem Technol, Hungary, 52-54, head dept, 54-56; sr Fulbright scholar, Tech Univ, Munich, Ger, 73-74; adj prof, Univ Akron, 79-82, prof chem eng, 82-89. *Mem:* Am Chem Soc; fel Am Inst Chem Engrs. *Res:* Chemical reaction engineering; chemical reactor design and stability problems; development of basic petrochemical processes; computer simulation experiments; Rotoberty laboratory recycle reactor for catalysis; Oxitox activated sodium carbonate for pollution control. *Mailing Add:* 1806 Bent Pine Hill Fogelsville PA 18051-1501

BERTZ, STEVEN HOWARD, MECHANISTIC CHEMISTRY, THEORETICAL CHEMISTRY. *Current Pos:* RES ASSOC, LONZA INC, 93- *Personal Data:* b Fond du Lac, Wis, Dec 24, 50; m 74; c 2. *Educ:* Univ Wis-Madison, BS, 73; Harvard Univ, AM, 75, PhD(chem), 78. *Prof Exp:* NSF fel, 73-76; mem tech staff, Bell Labs, 78-85, distinguished mem tech staff, 85-91. *Concurrent Pos:* Vis prof, Univ Wis-Madison, 85. *Mem:* Am Chem Soc. *Res:* Chemistry of organocopper reagents; arenesulfonylhydrazones; metal-carbene complexes; glyoxal and malondialdehyde; organotitanium reagents; study of chemical topology, molecular complexity and chemical applications of graph theory and information theory. *Mailing Add:* 88 E Main St No 220 Mendham NJ 07945

BERU, NEGA, MOLECULAR BIOLOGY, BIOCHEMISTRY. *Current Pos:* postdoctoral res assoc & instr, Dept Biochem & Molecular Biol, 84-88, instr, 88-90, ASST PROF, DEPT MED, SECT HEMAT/ONCOL, UNIV CHICAGO, 90- *Personal Data:* b Maichew, Ethiopia, Aug 22, 51. *Educ:* Univ Chicago, BA, 74, PhD(biochem), 83. *Prof Exp:* Writer, Sci Curric Develop Ctr, Ministry Educ, Addis Ababa, Ethiopia, 74-76; lectr, Dept Biol, Addis Ababa Univ, Ethiopia, 76-78. *Mem:* Am Soc Biochem & Molecular Biol; Int Soc Exp Hemat; Sigma Xi. *Res:* Regulation of growth factor gene expression both in normal as well as in leukemic cells at the molecular level; hematopoietic differentiation including signal transduction; study of the second messengers and transcription factors involved in the process. *Mailing Add:* Biotechnol Policy Br Food & Drug Admin CFSAN 200 C St SW HFS-206 Washington DC 20204-0001

BERUBE, ROBERT, STERILIZATION, MICROBIAL CONTROL. *Current Pos:* specialist, Prod Develop, Infection Control, 3M, 77-83, microbiol qual assurance, Med Div, 83-86, Med-Surg Div, 86-88, SPECIALIST, HEALTH CARE & STERILIZATION, MICROBIOL SERV, 3M, 88- *Personal Data:* b Boston, Mass, Apr 23, 35; m 65; c 2. *Educ:* Boston Col, BS, 57; Univ Mass, MS, 59; Kans State Univ, PhD(bact), 67. *Prof Exp:* Asst prof, McNeese State Univ, Lake Charles, La, 67-71; actg br chief, microbiol qual assurance, Becton, Dickinson & Co, 71-73, br chief, 73-75, mgr, 75-77. *Concurrent Pos:* Instr, Kans State Univ, Manhattan, Kans, 65-67. *Mem:* Soc Indust Microbiol; Am Soc Qual Control. *Res:* Develop and validate sterilization cycles (E&O, steam, radiation, dry heat) for medical-surgical devices; develop and validate microbial control systems (sanitization, disinfection); bioburden assessment and validation; microbiological control of water. *Mailing Add:* 211 Maryknoll Dr Stillwater MN 55082

BERVEN, BARRY ALLEN, ENVIRONMENTAL HEALTH PHYSICS & BIOMEDICAL TECHNOLOGY. *Current Pos:* Res staff, Oak Ridge Nat Lab, 79-83, group leader, 83-87, sect head, 88-90, assoc div dir, 91-92, DIR HEALTH SCI RES DIV, OAK RIDGE NAT LAB, 93- *Personal Data:* b Lansing, Mich, Nov 9, 49; m, Ella Stutler; c Kate & Matt. *Educ:* Colo State Univ, BS, 71, MS, 74, PhD(radiol & radiation biol), 79. *Mem:* Sigma Xi; Health Physics Soc. *Res:* Manage a large multidisciplinary scientific staff which conduct basic and applied research in areas impacting human health. *Mailing Add:* 111 Monticello Rd Oak Ridge TN 37830. *Fax:* 423-574-3036

BERWICK, DONALD M, HEALTHCARE QUALITY. *Current Pos:* PRES & CHIEF EXEC OFFICER, INST HEALTHCARE IMPROVEMENT, 91-; ASSOC CLIN PROF PEDIAT, HARVARD MED SCH. *Personal Data:* m, Ann; c Ben, Dan, Jessica & Rebecca. *Educ:* Harvard Univ, BS, MD, MPP. *Prof Exp:* Head qual assurance, Harvard Community Health Plan, 79. *Concurrent Pos:* Prin investr, Nat Demonstration Proj Qual Improvement in Healthcare, 89-91; adj prof mgt, Sch Pub Health, Harvard Univ; mem, Comt Future Patient Record, Inst Med-Nat Acad Sci; vchair, Prev Servs Task Force, Dept Health & Human Servs; assoc pediat, Childrens Hosp, Boston; mem bd trustees, Am Hosp Asn, 96; consult pediat, Mass Gen Hosp; mem, Pres Adv Comn Consumer protection & Qual in Health Care Industry, 97; bd mem, Nat Patient Safety Found. *Mem:* Inst Med-Nat Acad Sci. *Res:* Children's healthcare; healthcare quality management; decision analysis; technology assessment; health policy. *Mailing Add:* Inst Healthcare Improvement 135 Francis St Boston MA 02115

BERY, MAHENDERA K, BIOCHEMICAL ENGINEERING, FERMENTATION ENGINEERING. *Current Pos:* SR RES SCI, E&J GALLOWINERY, 82- *Personal Data:* b Bombay, India; US citizen; m 74; c 2. *Educ:* Birkenheed Technol, Eng, dipl, 68; Univ Birmingham, Eng, MSc, 69; Univ Aston, Eng, PhD(chem eng), 73. *Prof Exp:* Lectr chem eng, Univ Aston, Eng, 70-72; chem engr process develop, Tech Ctr, Gen Foods, 74-77; sr res engr bioenergy, Georgian Technol, Atlanta, 77-82. *Concurrent Pos:* Develop engr prod develop, Barrier Chem Inc, 74-77; process engr pet food, Ralston Purina, St Louis, 77. *Mem:* Am Inst Chem Engrs; Am Chem Soc. *Res:* Production of substitute natural gas from poultry and dairy cow manure and agricultural residues; production of ethanol from cellulosic biomass; extraction and fractionation of chemicals from wood; process design and economic feasibility study of various fermentation plants; biological treatment of waste. *Mailing Add:* E&J Gallo-Winery PO Box 1130 Modesto CA 95353

BERZOFSKY, JAY ARTHUR, IMMUNOGENETICS, ANTIGENIC STRUCTURE. *Current Pos:* res assoc biochem, Nat Inst Arthritis, Metab & Digestive Dis, 74-76, investr immunol, Nat Cancer Inst, 76-79, sr investr immunol, 79-87, CHIEF MOLECULAR IMMUNOGENETICS & VACCINE RES SECT, NAT CANCER INST, NIH, 87- *Personal Data:* b Baltimore, Md, Apr 13, 46; m 69; c 2. *Educ:* Harvard Univ, BA, 67; Albert Einstein Col Med, PhD(molecular biol), 71, MD, 73. *Honors & Awards:* Sophia Freund Prize, Harvard Univ, 67. *Prof Exp:* Resident internal med, Mass Gen Hosp, 73-74. *Concurrent Pos:* Assoc ed, J Immunol, 80-84; fac mem, Found Advan Educ in Sci, 84-; adv ed, Molecular Immunol J, 85- *Mem:* NY Acad Sci; Am Asn Immunologists; Am Fedn Clin Res; Am Soc Biol Chemists; Am Soc Clin Investr (secy-treas, 89-92). *Res:* Antigen-specific genetic, cellular and biochemical regulation of the immune response; mechanism of T-lymphocyte activation by antigen and antigen presentation; antigenic structure of proteins; vaccine development; idiotype interactions. *Mailing Add:* Bldg 10 Rm 6B12 NIH Nat Cancer Inst Bethesda MD 20892-1578

BESCH, EMERSON LOUIS, ENVIRONMENTAL PHYSIOLOGY. *Current Pos:* RETIRED. *Personal Data:* b Hammond, Ind, June 9, 28; m 55; c Karen, Kevin, Kathleen & Kristine. *Educ:* SW Tex State Col, BS, 52, MA, 55; Univ Calif, Davis, PhD(physiol), 64. *Honors & Awards:* Res Award, Am Asn Lab Animal Sci, 75; Cert Aerospace Physiologist, Aerospace Physiologist Soc, 79; Prof Excellence Award, Life Sci & Biomed Eng Br, Aerospace Med Asn, 87. *Prof Exp:* Instr biol, SW Tex State Col, 54-55; res asst animal physiol, Univ Calif, Davis, 60-64, res physiologist & lectr animal physiol, 64-67; from assoc prof to prof physiol & mech eng, Kans State Univ, 67-74; assoc dean, Univ Fla, 74-80 & 81-87, actg dean, 80-81, exec assoc dean, 87-88, prof, 74-93, emer prof, Col Vet Med, 93. *Concurrent Pos:* NIH trainee, 61-64; chmn, Comt Lab Animal Housing, Inst Lab Animal Resources, Nat Acad Sci, 75-77; assoc ed, Lab Animal Sci, 77-82; mem, Ilar Coun, Nat Res Coun, 78-83; chmn, Comt Environ Conditions Lab Animal Rooms, Inst Lab Animal Resources, Nat Acad Sci/Nat Res Coun, 82-84, Comt Lab Animal Housing, 75-78, Environ Health Comt, Am Soc Heating, Refrig & Air Conditioning Eng, 86- *Mem:* Fel Aerospace Med Asn; Am Physiol Soc; Am Asn Lab Animal Sci; Am Soc Heating Refrig & Air-Conditioning Engrs; Soc Exp Biol Med. *Res:* Aviation physiology; effects of mechanical forces on biological systems; definition of environmental requirements for lab animals; adaptation to high altitude; comparative physiology of environmental stresses. *Mailing Add:* 15207 Rompel Trail Dr San Antonio TX 78232-4255

BESCH, EVERETT DICKMAN, VETERINARY SCIENCE. *Current Pos:* RETIRED. *Personal Data:* b Hammond, Ind, May 4, 24; m 46, Mellie D Brockman; c Carolyn D, Ceryl L, Cynthia L, Charlotte A & Everett D. *Educ:* Tex A&M Univ, DVM, 54; Univ Minn, MPH, 56; Okla State Univ, PhD, 63. *Prof Exp:* Instr, Univ Minn, 54-56; asst prof, Okla State Univ, 56-64, prof & head, Dept Vet Parasitol & Pub Health, 64-68; dean, Sch Vet Med, La State Univ, 68-88, prof, 88-89. *Concurrent Pos:* Mem, Nat Adv Coun Health Profs Educ, 82-86. *Mem:* Asn Am Vet Med Cols (secy-treas, 74-78); Am Vet Med Asn (treas, 91-93, vpres, 93-); Asn Teachers Vet Pub Health & Prev Med (pres, 68); Am Soc Parasitologists; Conf Pub Health Vets (pres, 71-72); Am Asn Food Hyg Vets (pres, 76-77); Am Asn Vet Parasitologists (pres, 64-65). *Res:* Arthropod vectors of disease; internal parasites of ruminants. *Mailing Add:* 1453 Ashland Dr Baton Rouge LA 70806-7838

BESCH, GORDON OTTO CARL, PHYSICS EDUCATION, PUBLIC PHYSICS. *Current Pos:* PROF PHYSICS, UNIV WIS-SUPERIOR, 69- *Personal Data:* b Lacrosse, Wis, March 16, 22; m 49; c 4. *Educ:* Univ Wis, Lacrosse, BS, 51; US Merchant Marine Acad, BS, 47; Harvard Univ, Ed Med, 54; Ohio State Univ, PhD(sci ed & physics), 69. *Prof Exp:* Radio officer, marine radiotelegraphy, Am South-African Co, 43-44; third officer, marine sciences, Lykes Steamship Lines, 47-78; div chmn, sci & math, Concordia Teachers Col, 58-68. *Concurrent Pos:* Consult, Dept Agr, State Wis, 72-77; lectr physics, N Park Col, 61-68; univ dir, Nat Sci Found Grants Physics Educ, 72-77. *Mem:* Am Asn Physics Teachers; Am Radio Relay League. *Res:* Public lecture demonstrations on theories in physics such as special theory of relativity and neutron activation analysis of crude protein in grain. *Mailing Add:* 631 N 23rd St Superior WI 54880

BESCH, HENRY ROLAND, JR, CARDIAC PHARMACOLOGY, ALCOHOL TOXICOLOGY. *Current Pos:* asst prof pharmacol, Ind Univ, 71-73, asst prof med biophys, 72-73, assoc prof pharmacol & med, 73-77, SHOWALTER PROF PHARMACOL & CHMN DEPT, SCH MED, IND UNIV, INDIANAPOLIS, 77-; EMER DIR, STATE DEPT TOXICOL, 96- *Personal Data:* b San Antonio, Tex, Sept 12, 42; m 86; c Kurt. *Educ:* Ohio State Univ, BSc, 64, PhD(pharmacol, biophys), 67. *Prof Exp:* Instr steroid biochem, Ohio State Univ, 67-68; dir, State Dept Toxicol, 89-96. *Concurrent Pos:* USPHS fel, Baylor Col Med, 68-70; Med Res Coun fel, Royal Free Hosp Sch Med, London, Eng, 71-72, vis sr lectr, 73-74; sr res assoc, Krannert Inst Cardiol, 74-; Showalter awardee, 75-; mem bd dirs, Watson Pharmaceut, 91-; vis prof, Swiss Fed Inst Technol, 95-96. *Mem:* Am Soc Pharmacol & Exp Therapeut; Am Soc Biol Chem & Molecular Biol; NY Acad Sci; Int Study Group Res Cardiac Metab; Am Heart Asn; Asn Med Sch Pharmacol. *Res:* Cardiac pharmacology; subcellular mechanisms of inotropic and chronotropic drugs; ryanodine structure-activity relationships; alcohol and analytic toxicology. *Mailing Add:* 7555 Terrace Beach Indianapolis IN 46240-3169. *E-Mail:* besch@indiana.edu

BESCH, PAIGE KEITH, BIOCHEMICAL PHARMACOLOGY. *Current Pos:* assoc prof to prof, 68-83, DISTINGUISHED PROF OBSTET & GYNEC, BAYLOR COL MED, 83- *Personal Data:* b San Antonio, Tex, June 23, 31; m 57; c 2. *Educ:* Trinity Univ, BS, 54, MS, 55; Ohio State Univ, PhD(physiol, pharmacol), 60. *Honors & Awards:* Smith Kline Award, Am Asn Clin Chem, 79. *Prof Exp:* Biochemist-in-chg metab sect, Surg Res Unit, Brooke Army Med Ctr, Ft Sam Houston, Tex, 53-54; sr biochemist, Clin Lab, Robert B Green Mem Hosp, San Antonio, 54-55; sr res asst to chmn dept endocrinol, Southwest Found Res & Educ, 55-58; asst, Dept Physiol, Col Med, Ohio State Univ, 58-60, res assoc, Steroid Res Lab, 60, instr pharmacol, Univ, 60-62, co-dir med sch & dir hosp, 60-66, asst prof physiol, obstet & gynec, Med Sch, 62-66, asst prof pharmacol, 63-66, assoc prof obstet & gynec, Univ Hosp, 66-68. *Concurrent Pos:* Res assoc, Columbus Psychiat Inst & Hosp, Ohio, 58-59; dir steroid res lab, Grant Hosp Res & Educ Found, 61-; dir labs, Midwest Found Res & Educ, 64-68; sr consult, Med Res Consult, Inc,

62-68; mem, med lab sci rev comt, USPHS, NIH, 74-77. *Mem:* AAAS; Am Asn Clin Chemists (pres, 81); Sigma Xi; sr mem Am Chem Soc; Soc Exp Biol & Med; fel Nat Acad Clin Biochem. *Res:* Steroid metabolism; pharmacological effects of drugs; ability to alter steroids; fertility and sterility; chemical contraception. *Mailing Add:* Dept Obstet & Gynec Baylor Col Med One Baylor Plaza Houston TX 77030-3498

BESCHORNER, W E, TRANSPLANT IMMUNOLOGY. *Current Pos:* Resident path, 76-80, asst prof, 80-91, ASSOC PROF, DEPT PATH, JOHNS HOPKINS HOSP, 91- *Personal Data:* b Aurora, Ill, June 4, 47. *Educ:* Augustana Col, AB, 68; St Louis Univ, MS, 72; Univ Ill, MD, 76. *Concurrent Pos:* Adj prof, Johns Hopkins Hosp. *Mem:* Am Asn Pathologists; Int Asn Pathologists. *Res:* Mechanisms of tolerance to transplant allografps-proposed a novel approach to inducing specific immune tolerance; immunopathology of AIDS myocarditis and enteropathy. *Mailing Add:* 4310 Farmfield Ct Baldwin MD 21013-9638

BESHARSE, JOSEPH CULP, CELL & MOLECULAR BIOLOGY, POLARITY IN NEURONS. *Current Pos:* PROF & CHMN, DEPT CELLULAR BIOL & ANAT, MED COL WIS, 97- *Personal Data:* b Hickman, Ky, Jan 21, 44; m 66, Janie Robinson; c Kari E & Joseph G. *Educ:* Hendrix Col, BA, 66; Southern Ill Univ, MA, 69, PhD(zool & physiol), 73. *Honors & Awards:* Recognition Award Vision Sci, Alcon Res Inst, 93. *Prof Exp:* Asst prof biol, Old Dominion Univ, 72-75; NIH fel, Col Physicians & Surgeons, Columbia Univ, 75-77; from asst prof to assoc prof cell biol, Sch Med, Emory Univ, 77-84, prof anat, cell biol & ophthal, 84-89; prof & chmn anat & cell biol, Sch Med, Univ Kans, Kansas City, 89-97. *Concurrent Pos:* NIH Res Career Develop Award, 79-84; mem, Vision Res Review Comt, Nat Eye Inst, 82-86 & Visual Sci, C Study Sect, NIH, 92-96; prin investr, NIH, 78- *Mem:* AAAS; Am Soc Cell Biol; Am Soc Zoologists; Asn Res Vision & Ophthal; Soc Neurosci; Am Asn Anatomists. *Res:* Cell biology with emphasis on cell-cell interaction and membrane turnover in retinal tissue; photosensitive membrane turnover in retinal photoreceptors; interactions of photoreceptors with support cells; role of neurons in control circadian rhythmicity. *Mailing Add:* Dept Cellular Biol Med Col Wis 8701 Watertown Plank Rd Milwaukee WI 53226. *Fax:* 414-266-8496; *E-Mail:* jbeshars@post.its.mcw.edu

BESHERS, DANIEL N(EWSON), MECHANICAL PROPERTIES OF MATERIALS. *Current Pos:* from asst prof to assoc prof, 57-69, PROF METALL, HENRY KRUMB SCH MINES, COLUMBIA UNIV, 69- *Personal Data:* b Chicago, Ill, Aug 13, 28; m 53, Maxine McArthur; c George M, Samuel N, Robert N & Clifford M. *Educ:* Swarthmore Col, BA, 49; Univ Ill, MS, 51, PhD(physics), 56. *Prof Exp:* Physicist, Metall Div, US Naval Res Lab, Washington, DC, 55-57. *Concurrent Pos:* Vchmn, Gordon Conf Phys Metall, 64, chmn, 65; vis prof, Univ Poitiers, 79-80. *Mem:* Am Phys Soc; Minerals Metals & Mat Soc; Am Soc Metals Int. *Res:* Elastic constants, anelasticity, nonlinear internal friction, hysteresis, and acoustic harmonic generation; acoustic emission; internal stress; motion of dislocations, domain walls and point defects. *Mailing Add:* 1105 SW Mudd Bldg Columbia Univ New York NY 10027. *E-Mail:* dnb4@columbia.edu

BESKID, GEORGE, BACTERIOLOGY. *Current Pos:* sr bacteriologist, 63-71, res group chief, 71-78, sr res group chief, 78-84, RES INVESTR, HOFFMANN-LA ROCHE, INC, 84- *Personal Data:* b Erie, Pa, Mar 20, 29; m 54; c 3. *Educ:* Univ Buffalo, BA, 50; Syracuse Univ, MS, 54, PhD(bact), 59. *Prof Exp:* Asst bact, Syracuse Univ, 57-59; res assoc microbiol, Hahnemann Med Col & Hosp, 59-61, instr microbiol & surg, 61-63. *Mem:* AAAS; Am Soc Microbiol; Sigma Xi. *Res:* Bacterial sporulation; endotoxin shock; surgical infections; amylase producing bacteria; chemotherapy. *Mailing Add:* 93 Rolling Hills Rd Clifton NJ 07013

BESMANN, THEODORE MARTIN, NUCLEAR ENGINEERING, MATERIALS SCIENCE. *Current Pos:* MEM RES STAFF HIGH TEMPERATURE CHEM NUCLEAR MAT, OAK RIDGE NAT LAB, 75-, GROUP LEADER; ADJ PROF, NUCLEAR ENG DEPT, UNIV TENN, 80- *Personal Data:* b New York, NY, Feb 18, 49. *Educ:* NY Univ, BE, 70; Iowa State Univ, MS, 71; Pa State Univ, PhD(nuclear eng), 76. *Concurrent Pos:* Instr, Roane State Commun Col, 77- *Mem:* Am Nuclear Soc; Sigma Xi; Am Ceramic Soc; AAAS. *Res:* High temperature chemistry of materials for energy systems; national energy policy issues. *Mailing Add:* MS 6063 PO Box 2008 Oak Ridge TN 37831

BESOZZI, ALFIO JOSEPH, ORGANIC CHEMISTRY. *Current Pos:* sr res chemist, 56-67, res group head, 67-74, INDUST HYG CORRDR, PETRO-TEX CHEM CORP, 74- *Personal Data:* b New York, NY, Dec 2, 21; m; c 4. *Educ:* NY Univ, AB, 43, PhD(org chem), 51. *Prof Exp:* Jr pharmaceut chemist, Winthrop Chem Co Div, Sterling Drug, Inc, 43-44; proj leader & consult chem, Evans Res & Develop Corp, 51-56. *Mem:* Am Chem Soc; Catalysis Soc. *Res:* Petrochemical research including heterogeneous catalysis, polymerization and synthesis; pharmaceutical chemistry. *Mailing Add:* 5534 Dumfries Houston TX 77096-4004

BESS, ROBERT CARL, ANALYTICAL CHEMISTRY, ELECTROCHEMISTRY. *Current Pos:* RES CONSULT, TEXACO EPTD, 96- *Personal Data:* b Houston, Tex, Sept 24, 44; m 70; c 2. *Educ:* Tex A&M Univ, BS, 73, PhD(anal chem), 76; Sussex (England), MBA, 88. *Prof Exp:* Lab technician eng, Spencer Buchanan & Assoc, 67; lab technician chem, Nalco Chem Co, 68-72; res chem & res fel, Tex A&M Res Found, 77; sr chemist, Texaco, Inc, 77-79; supvr, Arabian Am Oil Co, 79-90; chief chem engr, Caltex Indonesia, 91-96. *Concurrent Pos:* Tech reviewer, corrosion journals. *Mem:* Am Chem Soc; Electrochem Soc; Nat Asn Chem Engrs; Res Soc NAm; Soc Petrol Engrs; Soc Electroanalytical Chem. *Res:* Inorganic and organic electrochemistry; enhanced oil recovery; corrosion science; reverse osmosis; water treatment; oilfield chemical treatment; scaling in the petroleum industry; geothermal oil recovery; oilfield facilities engineering. *Mailing Add:* Texaco EPTD 3901 Briar Park Houston TX 77042

BESSE, JOHN C, PHARMACOLOGY, PHYSIOLOGY. *Current Pos:* asst prof, 67-76, ASSOC PROF PHARMACOL, MED CTR, UNIV ALA, BIRMINGHAM, 76- *Personal Data:* b Rayne, La, June 23, 33; m 62; c 3. *Educ:* Univ Southwestern La, BSc, 56; Vanderbilt Univ, PhD(pharmacol), 66. *Prof Exp:* Fel pharmacol, State Univ NY Downstate Med Ctr, 65-67. *Mem:* Fedn Am Soc Exp Biol. *Res:* Autonomics and cardiovascular pharmacology; mechanism of action of drugs and hormones in smooth muscle at the level of receptors and membranes; cardiovascular physiology; biophysics of circulation and its correlation to drug activity on the circulation. *Mailing Add:* Dept Pharmacol Univ Ala Med Ctr Univ Ala Birmingham Sta Birmingham AL 35294-0001

BESSER, JOHN EDWIN, THERMODYNAMICS & MATERIAL PROPERTIES, TECHNICAL MANAGEMENT. *Current Pos:* assoc dir chem res, 81-82, tech dir, 82-93, DIR RES & DEVELOP, ALADDIN INDUSTS INC, 93- *Personal Data:* b Louisville, Ky, Jan 25, 47; US citizen; m 69; c 2. *Educ:* Univ Louisville, BS, 69; Mid Tenn State Univ, MBA, 90. *Prof Exp:* Develop chemist, Eastman Chem Prods Inc, 69-72; qual control supvr, Celotex Corp, Div Jim Walter Corp, 72-74, mgr qual, 74-76, mgr tech plant, 76-78; lab mgr, Aladdin Synergetics Inc, 78-81. *Mem:* Am Chem Soc; Am Soc Qual Control; Soc Plastic Engrs. *Res:* Polymeric failure modes in products; relationships between neat polymer characteristics and performance in molded products; balance of economic factors and product performance for cost/performance relationships; polyurethane rigid foam chemistry and application; insulation materials and vacuum technology; granted over 25 patents. *Mailing Add:* 703 Murfreesboro Rd Nashville TN 37210-4521. *Fax:* 615-748-3474; *E-Mail:* jebesser@aladdin-inc.com

BESSETTE, FRANCE MARIE, MOLECULAR BIOPHYSICS. *Current Pos:* ASSOC PROF BIOPHYS, UNIV SHERBROOKE, 71- *Personal Data:* b Magog, Que, Can, June 26, 44. *Educ:* Univ Sherbrooke, BSc, 66, PhD(phys chem), 69. *Prof Exp:* Phys sci specialist, Ministry Health, Que, 70; prof phys chem, Col Gen & Voc Educ, Prov Que, Can, Lionel-Groulx, 71. *Mem:* Biophys Soc; Spectros Soc Can. *Res:* Mathematical characterization of the ECG using spline functions and correlation with numerical elements symptomatic for certain heart diseases in view of diagnostic support; fluorescence properties of grape anthoryanins and of their polymerization with catechins in wine; analytical method of distinguishing between mono and diglucorides; stability-coloration relationship of dimus and trimus for their use as food dyes. *Mailing Add:* Dept Biophys Fac Med Univ Sherbrooke Sherbrooke PQ J1H 5N4 Can

BESSETTE, RUSSELL R, ANALYTICAL ELECTROCHEMISTRY, CHEMICAL INSTRUMENTATION. *Current Pos:* from asst prof to assoc prof, 68-76, chmn, Dept Chem, 86-90, PROF CHEM, UNIV MASS DARTMOUTH, 76- *Personal Data:* b New Bedford, Mass, July 21, 40; m 64; c 2. *Educ:* Univ RI, BS, 62; Univ Mass, Amherst, MS, 65, PhD, 67. *Prof Exp:* Res asst Air Force Off Sci Res, Univ Mass, Amherst, 65-67; sr res chemist, Res Ctr, Olin Corp, 67-68. *Concurrent Pos:* Chem consult, USN; reviewer, Anal Grants Div, NSF; sr res chemist, Alcan Int Ltd, 91. *Mem:* Am Chem Soc; Sigma Xi. *Res:* Electrochemistry of copper lithium and zirconium in non aqueous media; anode-cathode studies for high energy density battery systems; use of new materials as indicating electrodes; determination of dissolved oxygen utilizing a pulsed technique with an electrochemical oxygen sensor. *Mailing Add:* Chem Dept Univ Mass-Dartmouth North Dartmouth MA 02747

BESSEY, PAUL MACK, HORTICULTURE. *Current Pos:* RETIRED. *Personal Data:* b Cudahy, Wis, Mar 23, 25; m 47; c 5. *Educ:* Univ Wis, BS, 49, MS, 51; Mich State Univ, PhD(hort), 57. *Prof Exp:* Asst veg crops & hort, Univ Wis, 49-51; instr & asst hort, Univ Maine, 51-54; asst hort, Mich State Univ, 54-57; asst hort, 57-65, assoc prof hort, 65-78, assoc prof plant sci & assoc res spec hort, Exten Spec Hort, Univ Ariz, 78-86; Pima County Urban Hort Agt, 86-91. *Concurrent Pos:* Landscape consult, 91- *Mem:* Am Soc Hort Sci; Inst Food Technologists. *Res:* Postharvest physiology of fruits and vegetables, potato breeding, vegetable flavor in relation to market quality standards, controlled environments, vegetable adaptation. *Mailing Add:* 2602 E Arroyo Chico Tucson AZ 85716

BESSEY, WILLIAM HIGGINS, SOLID STATE PHYSICS. *Current Pos:* RETIRED. *Personal Data:* b East Lansing, Mich, Mar 18, 13; m 45, Thelma Shelly; c Barbara L & Karen E. *Educ:* Univ Chicago, BS, 34; Carnegie Inst Technol, MS, 35, DSc, 40. *Prof Exp:* Asst, Carnegie Inst Technol, 35-39; instr physics, SDak Sch Mines, 39-40 & NC State Col, 40-42; from instr to asst prof, Carnegie Inst Technol, 42-52; assoc prof, Sch Mines & Metal, Univ Mo, 52-56; prof physics & head dept, Butler Univ, 56-80. *Mem:* Am Phys Soc; Am Asn Physics Teachers; Sigma Xi. *Res:* Diffraction of molecular rays; high speed testing of metals; shaped charges; electrical properties of evaporated metal films; thermal conductivity of ionic crystals. *Mailing Add:* 6421 Peace Pl Indianapolis IN 46268

BESSMAN, ALICE NEUMAN, INTERNAL MEDICINE. *Current Pos:* CHIEF DIABETES SERV, RANCHO LOS AMIGOS HOSP, 68- *Personal Data:* b Washington, DC, Nov 7, 22; m 45; c 2. *Educ:* Smith Col, BA, 43; George Washington Univ, MD, 49; Am Bd Internal Med, dipl, 59. *Prof Exp:* Fel med, DC Gen Hosp, George Washington Univ, 51-52; Nat Found Infantile Paralysis fel pediat, Mass Gen Hosp, 52-53; fel med, DC Gen Hosp, George Washington Univ, 53-54; staff physician, Group Health Asn, Inc, Washington, DC, 54-56; vis physician, Dept Med, Baltimore City Hosps, Johns Hopkins Univ, 56-62, hosp physician, 62-67, asst chief chronic & community med, 67-68; assoc prof, 68-78, prof, Med Sch, Univ Southern Calif, 78- *Concurrent Pos:* Dept Health, Educ & Welfare Social Rehab Serv grant, 65- *Mem:* Am Fedn Clin Res; AMA; Am Col Physicians; Am Diabetes Asn. *Res:* Significance of elevated serum ammonia levels in gastrointestinal bleeding and hepatic failure; ketone and lactate metabolism in diabetes mellitus; delivery of out-patient care via nurse practitioners; microbiology of infected diabetic gangrene. *Mailing Add:* Dept Med Sch Med Univ Southern Calif Los Angeles CA 90033

BESSMAN, JOEL DAVID, HEMATOLOGY, ANEMIA. *Current Pos:* from asst prof to assoc prof med, 79-84, PROF MED & PATH, UNIV TEX MED BR, 81-, ASSOC DIR HEMATOPATH, 93- *Personal Data:* b Norfolk, Va. *Educ:* Columbia Univ, BA, 67, MD, 72. *Honors & Awards:* Benno Schmidt Award for Cancer Research. *Prof Exp:* Intern internal med, Univ Southern Calif, 72-73; res fel drug develop, Nat Cancer Inst, 73-75; resident internal med, Univ Southern Calif, 75-77; fel internal med, Johns Hopkins Med Inst, 77-79. *Concurrent Pos:* Mem adv learning res comt, Am Soc Hemat, 87-90, mem clin lab hemat comt, 85-88, 92-94, chair, 92-94; pres, Island Analysis, Inc, 86- *Mem:* Am Soc Hemat; Am Soc Clin Path; Soc Analytical Cytol; Am Col Physicians. *Res:* Biologic significance of non-discrete hererogenity; new methods for well subject cancer screening; physiology of platelet function; interactive computer education. *Mailing Add:* John Sealy Hosp Univ Tex Med Br Galveston TX 77550. *Fax:* 409-772-3533

BESSMAN, MAURICE JULES, BIOCHEMISTRY. *Current Pos:* from asst prof to assoc prof, 58-66, PROF BIOL, MCCOLLUM-PRATT INST, JOHNS HOPKINS UNIV, 66- *Personal Data:* b Newark, NJ, July 31, 28; m 52; c 4. *Educ:* Harvard Univ, AB, 49; Tufts Univ, MS, 52, PhD(biochem), 56. *Prof Exp:* Fel, Nat Cancer Inst, USPHS, 56-58; instr, Sch Med, Wash Univ, 58. *Mem:* AAAS; Am Soc Biol Chem; Am Chem Soc. *Res:* Enzymology of nucleic acid metabolism. *Mailing Add:* Dept Biol Johns Hopkins Univ Baltimore MD 21218-2680

BESSMAN, SAMUEL PAUL, PEDIATRICS, BIOCHEMISTRY. *Current Pos:* RETIRED. *Personal Data:* b NJ, Feb 3, 21; m 45, Alice Newman; c David, Ellen, Matthew, Libby & Daniel. *Educ:* Washington Univ, MD, 44; Am Bd Pediat, dipl. *Honors & Awards:* Aaron Brown Lectr, Baylor Col Med, 79. *Prof Exp:* Intern, St Louis Children's Hosp, 44-46; pathologist, USPHS, US Marine Hosp, Va, 46-47; fel biochem, Children's Hosp, Washington, DC, 47-48, dir biochem res, 48-54; from assoc prof to prof pediat, Sch Med, Univ Md, 54-68, from assoc prof to prof biochem, 58-68; prof pharmacol & chmn dept, Sch Med, Univ Southern Calif, 68-93, prof pediat, 69-93. *Concurrent Pos:* Fel, Psychiat Inst, NY, 48; assoc prof clin pediat, Sch Med, George Washington Univ, 52; fel, Harvard Univ, 52-53; ed, Biochem Med; assoc ed, Anal Biochem; sr attend physician, Cedars-Sinai Med Ctr, Los Angeles, 72-79, hon attend physician, 80-; founding ed, Biochem Med. *Mem:* Soc Pediat Res; Am Chem Soc; Am Soc Pharmacol & Exp Therapeut; Am Inst Nutrit; Am Soc Biol Chemists; fel AAAS. *Res:* Biochemistry of disease; mechanism of mental symptoms; carbohydrate diseases; artificial pancreas; mechanism of insulin action; stress and diabetes; creating phosphate shutter; introduced treatment or lead poisoning; control of hemoglobin synthesis. *Mailing Add:* Dept Pharmacol Univ Southern Calif 2025 Zonal Ave Los Angeles CA 90033-1089

BESSO, MICHAEL M, NEW TECHNOLOGY, SPECIALTY CHEMICALS. *Current Pos:* VPRES RES & DEVELOP, ATOCHEM NAM, 89- *Personal Data:* b Brooklyn, NY, Mar 30, 30; m 55, Eva Cikvesvili; c Marc & Michelle. *Educ:* Lowell Technol Inst, BSc, 50; Lehigh Univ, MS, 57, PhD(org chem), 59. *Prof Exp:* Chemist, Pinatel Piece Dye Works, Can, 50-51 & Nat Lead Co, 53-55; res chemist, Chas Pfizer & Co, 59-65; sr res chemist, Celanese Corp, 65-68, group leader fibers, plastics & coatings, 69-74, mgr polymer chem, 74-78, mgr explor res, 78-84; vpres res & develop, M&T Chemicals, 84-89. *Mem:* Am Chem Soc; NY Acad Sci; Am Inst Chemists; AAAS. *Res:* Polymer flammability; plastics, and polyester fiber technology; polymer synthesis; increasing productivity of research; polymer stabilization; fermentation chemicals, membrane fabrication and applications; electrochemistry; materials science; research and technology management; international research and development. *Mailing Add:* 74 Crestmont Rd West Orange NJ 07052. *E-Mail:* mmbesso@aol

BEST, CECIL H(AMILTON), ENGINEERING MATERIALS. *Current Pos:* from assoc prof to prof appl mech, 61-75, assoc dean col eng, 68-74, PROF CIVIL ENG, KANS STATE UNIV, 75- *Personal Data:* b Tillsonburg, Ont, Oct 3, 28; US citizen; m 53; c 2. *Educ:* Univ Calif, Berkeley, BS, 55, MS, 56, PhD(eng sci), 60. *Prof Exp:* From res engr to asst specialist, Forest Prod Lab, Univ Calif, Berkeley, 55-60. *Concurrent Pos:* Royal Norweg Coun Sci & Indust res fel, Norweg Inst Technol, 60-61; vis scholar, Univ Calif, Berkeley, 80; res civ engr, US Army Engr, Waterwasy Exp Sta, 85. *Mem:* Fel Am Concrete Inst; fel Am Soc Civil Engrs; Am Soc Testing & Mat; Nat Soc Prof Engrs. *Res:* Structure and properties of engineering materials, primarily cement and concrete. *Mailing Add:* 2709 Aspen Way Manhattan KS 66503

BEST, DAVID MALCOLM, GEOPHYSICS, MATHEMATICS. *Current Pos:* From asst prof to assoc prof, 78-93, interim chair, 84-86, PROF GEOL, NORTHERN ARIZ UNIV, 93-, ASSOC DEAN, ARTS & SCIS, 95- *Personal Data:* b Cardiff, Wales, UK, July 12, 45; US citizen. *Educ:* Univ NC, BS, 67, MS, 70, PhD(geol), 77. *Mem:* Geol Soc Am; Sigma Xi; Am Geophys Union. *Res:* Geophysics of Proterozoic boundaries in Arizona; modelling Cenozoic basins in central Arizona; quantitative geomorphology. *Mailing Add:* Dept Geol Northern Ariz Univ PO Box 4099 Flagstaff AZ 86011-4099. *E-Mail:* david.best@nau.edu

BEST, EDGAR ALLAN, MARINE BIOLOGY. *Current Pos:* RETIRED. *Personal Data:* b Enumclaw, Wash, Aug 17, 25; m 50; c 1. *Educ:* Univ Wash, BS, 53. *Prof Exp:* Fishery biologist, Ore Fish Comn, 53; marine biologist, Calif Dept Fish & Game, 54-57, proj leader, 57-64, supvr, Point Arguello Surv, 64-65; supvr small fish investr, Univ Wash, 65-78, supvr age invest, Int Pac Halibut Comn, 78-86. *Concurrent Pos:* Mem, Int Trawl Fisheries Comt, US State Dept, 59-65; res assoc ichthyol, Santa Barbara Mus Natural Hist, 65-68. *Mem:* Am Inst Fishery Res Biologists (secy, 75-81); Pac Fish Biologists. *Res:* Marine biology and ecology; ecology; life history of marine fishes. *Mailing Add:* 7316 50th Ave NE Seattle WA 98115

BEST, GARY KEITH, MICROBIOLOGY. *Current Pos:* from asst prof to assoc prof, 68-80, PROF MICROBIOL, MED COL GA, 80- *Personal Data:* b Weatherford, Okla, Oct 8, 38; m 62; c 2. *Educ:* Southwestern State Col, Okla, BS, 60; Okla State Univ, PhD(microbiol), 65. *Prof Exp:* Res microbiologist, Agr Res Serv, USDA, 65-68. *Mem:* Am Soc Microbiol. *Res:* Bacterial cell wall synthesis; effect of antibiotics on microorganisms; bacterial virulence mechanisms. *Mailing Add:* Dept Cell & Molecular Biol Med Col Sch Med 1120 15th St Augusta GA 30912-1003

BEST, GEORGE HAROLD, PHYSICS. *Current Pos:* CONSULT, 83- *Personal Data:* b Chicago, Ill, Aug 4, 20; m 44, Elizabeth Fish; c 3. *Educ:* Purdue Univ, BS, 42; Northwestern Univ, MS, 48, PhD(physics), 49. *Prof Exp:* Mem staff, Los Alamos Nat Lab, Univ Calif, 49-83. *Mem:* Am Phys Soc. *Res:* Nuclear physics; nuclear weapons effects; nuclear reactors; directed energy. *Mailing Add:* 332 Manhattan Loop Los Alamos NM 87544. *Fax:* 505-662-4075; *E-Mail:* 104602.216@compuserve.com

BEST, JAY BOYD, PHYSIOLOGY, BIOPHYSICS. *Current Pos:* prof physiol & biophys, 63-87, prof environ health & physiol, 87-88, EMER PROF ENVIRON HEALTH, COLO STATE UNIV, 88- *Personal Data:* US Citizen; m 83; c 1. *Educ:* Univ Tex, AB, 47; Univ Chicago, PhD(physiol), 53. *Prof Exp:* Res assoc psychol, Univ Chicago, 53-55; biomathematics, Walter Reed Army Inst Res, 55-60; assoc prof physiol, Col Med, Univ Ill, 60-63. *Concurrent Pos:* Res fel, Univ Chicago, 53-55; NIH grant, 61-72, NASA grants, 64-69, USDA grants, 79-81 & NSF grant, 85-90; vis scientist, Argonne Lab, 77-78. *Mem:* Fel AAAS; Soc Math Biol; Sigma Xi; Soc Neurosci; Soc Environ Toxicol & Chem. *Res:* Transphyletic animal similarities and predictive toxicology; invertebrate metazoa as models for assessing toxic hazards for higher animals and humans; comparative regulatory biology between flatworms and higher animals; developmental neuroscience; aging. *Mailing Add:* 3521 Centennial Dr Ft Collins CO 80526. *Fax:* 970-491-8304

BEST, LAVAR, BIOACOUSTICS. *Current Pos:* DIR, NEUROSCI LAB, CRAIG HOSP, ENGLEWOOD, COLO, 85- *Personal Data:* b Salt Lake City, Utah, Mar 28, 31; m 54, Elizabeth Hagerstrom; c Cory, Cim, Michele & Lance. *Educ:* Univ Utah, BS, 53, MS, 57, PhD(audiol), 64. *Prof Exp:* Instr res, Med Ctr, Univ Colo, 64-66; asst prof speech & hearing sci, 67-71, assoc prof speech & hearing sci, Univ Denver, 71-78; dir, Neurosensory Diag Ctr, Swed Med Ctr, Colo, 78-85. *Mem:* Fel Am Soc Evoked Potential Monitoring; fel Am Soc Neurophysiol Monitoring. *Res:* Cortical processing of auditory stimuli. *Mailing Add:* Craig Hosp 3425 S Clarkson Englewood CO 80110

BEST, LOUIS BROWN, AVIAN ECOLOGY. *Current Pos:* From asst to assoc prof, 74-79, PROF ECOL, DEPT ANIMAL ECOL, IOWA STATE UNIV, 79- *Personal Data:* b Ogden, Utah, May 7, 44; m 68; c 4. *Educ:* Weber State Col, BS, 68; Mont State Univ, MS, 70; Univ Ill, Urbana-Champaign, PhD(zool), 74. *Mem:* Ecol Soc Am; Am Ornithologists Union; Cooper Ornith Soc; Wilson Ornith Soc. *Res:* Vertebrate ecology, with particular emphasis on various aspects of avian ecology, including breeding biology, feeding behavior, social organization and habitat selection. *Mailing Add:* Dept Animal Ecol Iowa State Univ 124 Sci II Ames IA 50011-3201

BEST, MELVYN EDWARD, MINERAL & PETROLEUM EXPLORATION & PRODUCTION, HYDROGEOLOGY & GROUND-WATER. *Current Pos:* BEMEX CONSULT INT, VICTORIA, BC, 97- *Personal Data:* b Victoria, BC, Mar 8, 41; m 70, Virginia M Pignato; c Lisette A & Aaron M. *Educ:* Univ BC, BSc, 65, MSc, 66; Mass Inst Technol, PhD, 70. *Honors & Awards:* Meritorious Serv Award, Can Soc Explor Geophysicists. *Prof Exp:* Res assoc, Dept Physics, McGill Univ, 70-72; geophysicist minerals, Shell Can Ltd, Alta, 72-78, head nonseismic res, Royal Dutch Shell Explor & Prod Lab, Neth, 78-80, div geophysicist minerals, Shell Can Ltd, Calgary, 80-82, mgr petrol eng res, 82-85; geophys adv, Teknica Resource Develop Ltd, 85-86; head, Basin Anal Subdiv, Atlantic Geosci Ctr, NS, Geol Surv Can, BC, 86-90, dir, Pac Geosci Ctr, 90-94, sr scientist, 94-97. *Concurrent Pos:* Comt mem, Resource Assessment Panel, Jeanne d'Arc Basin, Ottawa, 80-90, Panel Energy, Res & Develop, Calgary, 87-92; mem oil & gas comt, Can-Nfld Offshore Petrol Bd, Calgary, 90-93; ed, Can J Explor Geophys, 93-95, assoc ed, 95-; assoc ed, J Environ & Eng Geophys, 96- *Mem:* Can Soc Explor Geophysicists; Soc Explor Geophysicists. *Res:* Resistivity mapping and electromagnetic imaging; development of sweepem airborne system; Basin analysis and modelling; ground water and contaminant modelling; seismic lithology mapping; reservoir definition and monitoring. *Mailing Add:* 5288 Cordova Bay Rd Victoria BC V8Y 2L4 Can. *Fax:* 250-658-0791; *E-Mail:* best@islandnet.com

BEST, PHILIP ERNEST, SECONDARY ELECTRON EMISSION, SURFACE PHYSICS. *Current Pos:* fel, Inst Mat Sci, 70-71, assoc prof, 71-79, PROF PHYSICS, UNIV CONN, 79- *Personal Data:* b Perth, Australia, July 28, 38; m 60; c 3. *Educ:* Univ Western Australia, BSc, 59, PhD(physics), 63. *Prof Exp:* Instr & res assoc physics, Lab Atomic & Solid State Physics, Cornell Univ, 63-65; exp physicist, Res Labs, United Aircraft Corp, 65-70. *Mem:* Am Phys Soc; Inst Elec & Electronics Engrs; Brit Inst Physics & Phys Soc. *Res:* Interaction of slow electrons and x-rays with matter; electronic excitations at surfaces and in the bulk of solids; electronic properties of small molecules. *Mailing Add:* Dept Physics & Inst Mat Sci Univ Conn 2152 Hillside Rd Storrs CT 06269-3046

BEST, ROBERT GLEN, MEDICAL GENETIC, CLINICAL CYTOGENETICS. *Current Pos:* Fel, 86-89, DIR CLIN GENETICS & ASST PROF MED GENETICS, UNIV, SC, SCH MED, 89- *Personal Data:* b Springfield, Ohio, Jan 27, 58; m 84, Felicia Newton; c Cami, Heidi, Adrian & Joshua. *Educ:* Lehigh Univ, BS, 84; NC State Univ, MS, 83, PhD(genetics/toxicol), 87. *Concurrent Pos:* Consult, Hybritech Inc, 88-91. *Mem:* Am Soc Human Genetics; Am Col Med Genetics; Environ Mutagen Soc; Genetoxicity & Environ Mutagenesis Soc. *Res:* Serum screening during pregnancy to detect birth defects and adverse pregnancy out comes; issues in genetic counseling, clinical genetics and cytogenetics. *Mailing Add:* Dept Obstet & Gynec Univ SC 2 Medical Pk No 301 Columbia SC 29205. *Fax:* 803-434-7756; *E-Mail:* best@.cs.scarolina.edu

BEST, STANLEY GORDON, MECHANICAL ENGINEERING, ELECTRONICS ENGINEERING. *Current Pos:* RETIRED. *Personal Data:* b Chicago, Ill, July 10, 18; m 41; c 4. *Educ:* Purdue Univ, BSME, 40. *Prof Exp:* Anal engr, Hamilton Standard Div, United Aircraft Corp, 40-45, proj engr, 45-55, chief anal, 55-59, chief tech staff, 59-62, chief res, 62-63; tech consult, Hamilton Stand Div, United Technol, 63-81; eng consult, Best Eng, Inc, 81-86. *Res:* Vibration and structural analysis; aerodynamics; stability; control dynamics; thermodynamics; heat transfer; electronic circuitry; computer programming; finite element method development for structures; vibrations; heat transfer; fluid flow; circuit analysis; controls. *Mailing Add:* 53 Coburn Rd Manchester CT 06040

BEST, TROY LEE, VERTEBRATE ECOLOGY, ECOSYSTEM DYNAMICS. *Current Pos:* ASSOC PROF, DEPT ZOOL & WILDLIFE SCI, AUBURN UNIV, 88- *Personal Data:* b Ft Sumner, NMex, Aug 30, 45; c 2. *Educ:* Eastern NMex Univ, BS, 67; Univ Okla, MS, 71, PhD(zool), 76. *Prof Exp:* Preparator zool, Stovall Mus Sci & Hist, Univ Okla, 68-71, res & teaching asst, dept zool, 71-74; asst prof biol, Dept Biol, Northeastern Univ, 74-76; res prof, Llano Estacado Ctr for Advan Prof Studies Res, 76-81; asst prof, Dept Biol, Univ NMex, 83-88. *Concurrent Pos:* Index ed, Syst Zool, 72-; prin consult, US Bur Reclamation, US Fish & Wildlife Serv, USAF, US Army Corp Eng, Sandia Nat Labs, Westinghouse Elec Corp, 81- *Mem:* Am Soc Mammalogists; Ecol Soc Am; Soc Syst Zool; Am Ornithologists Union; AAAS; Sigma Xi. *Res:* Assessment of interrelationships between variation in ecological and morphological characteristics of vertebrates; mammalian systematics utilizing univariate and multivariate statistical techniques; effect of character selection on data analyses; vertebrate feeding ecology. *Mailing Add:* Dept Zool & Wildlife Sci Auburn Univ 331 Funchess Hall Auburn AL 36849-5414

BEST, WILLIAM ROBERT, HEMATOLOGY, BIOSTATISTICS. *Current Pos:* chief staff, 81-92, sr investr health servs res & develop, 92-96, CONSULT, HINES VET ADMIN HOSP, 96- *Personal Data:* b Chicago, Ill, July 14, 22; m 44, Ruth J Stuchlik; c Barbara A (Mulch) & Patrica M (Williams). *Educ:* Univ Ill, BS, 45, MD, 47, MS, 51; Am Bd Internal Med, dipl, 57, cert hemat, 72. *Prof Exp:* From clin asst to assoc prof med, Univ Ill Med Ctr, 48-70, asst dir, Aeromed Lab, 64-67, prof, 70-81, assoc dean, Abraham Lincoln Sch Med, 72-81, chief staff, Univ Ill Hosp, 75-81; prof med & assoc dean, Stritch Sch Med, Loyola Univ Chicago Med Ctr, Hines, 81-92. *Concurrent Pos:* Attend physician, Ill Res & Educ Hosp, 53-81; consult, Vet Admin Hosp, Hines, 53-81, chief midwest res support ctr, 67-72; consult, Grant Hosp, 54-67. *Mem:* AAAS; Am Fedn Clin Res; Am Soc Hemat; Int Soc Hemat; Am Statist Asn; Sigma Xi. *Res:* Statistical methods; cooperative clinical trials; computers in medicine; leukemia and pernicious anemia; Crohn's disease; sickle-cell trait. *Mailing Add:* 367 Blythe Rd Riverside IL 60546

BESTE, CHARLES EDWARD, WEED SCIENCE, HORTICULTURE SCIENCE. *Current Pos:* asst prof, 71-76, ASSOC PROF HORT, UNIV MD, 76- *Personal Data:* b Evansville, Ind, Sept 3, 39; m 94, Anna M Legates; c Lori B (Wickless) & Linda B (Dixon). *Educ:* Purdue Univ, BS, 61, MS, 69, PhD(weed sci), 71. *Honors & Awards:* Past-pres award, Northeastern Weed Sci Soc, 78; IR-4 Meritorious Serv Award, 90. *Prof Exp:* Develop engr, Gen Elec Co, Ind, 61-67. *Concurrent Pos:* Mem, Integrated Pest Mgt Report Comt, Coun Agr Sci & Technol, 78-81; consult, numerous corp, 80-94; Sabbatical, Univ Calif, Davis, 86. *Mem:* Weed Sci Soc Am; Am Soc Hort Sci; Sigma Xi; Int Weed Sci Soc. *Res:* Weed control and sustainable agriculture; studies for horticultural crops and conduct GLP certified field studies with agro-chemicals. *Mailing Add:* Salisbury Facil LESREC Univ Md 27664 Nanticoke Rd Salisbury MD 21801. *Fax:* 410-742-1922; *E-Mail:* cb20@umail.umd.edu

BESTUL, ALDEN BEECHER, PHYSICAL CHEMISTRY. *Current Pos:* RETIRED. *Personal Data:* b Forestburg, SDak, Sept 1, 21; m 47; c 4. *Educ:* St Olaf Col, BA, 42; Pa State Col, MS, 44; Univ Md, PhD(chem), 53. *Prof Exp:* Res asst cryogen, Pa State Col, 44-45; res thermochemist, Stamford Res Labs, Am Cyanamid Co, 46-48; res physicist, Nat Bur Standards, 48-70; gen phys scientist, Off Spec Studies, Nat Oceanic & Atmospheric Admin, 70-85. *Concurrent Pos:* Com Sci & Technol fel, 69-70. *Mem:* AAAS; Am Chem Soc; Am Phys Soc. *Res:* Molecular structure in the vitreous state; rheology of polymers; thermochemistry of organic compounds; research and development evaluation; environmental policy analysis; vitreous state; polymer rheology; thermodynamics and thermochemistry. *Mailing Add:* 9400 Overlea Dr Rockville MD 20850

BETANCOURT, JULIO L, BIOLOGICAL SCIENCE. *Current Pos:* PHYS SCIENTIST & PROJ CHIEF, DESERT LAB, WATER RESOURCES DIV, US GEOL SURV. *Res:* A 40,000 year history of vegetation and climate in Western Argentina; discovery and development of fossil deposits analogous to North American Packrat Middens. *Mailing Add:* US Geol Surv Desert Lab Water Resources Div Tucson AZ 85745

BETH, ERIC WALTER, THEORETICAL PHYSICS. *Current Pos:* asst prof, 62-82, EMER ASST PROF PHYSICS, STATE UNIV NY, BUFFALO, 82- *Personal Data:* b Vienna, Austria, June 7, 12; nat US. *Educ:* Univ Vienna, PhD(physics), 34. *Prof Exp:* Asst physics, Univ Vienna, 36-37; res fel, Univ Calif, 37-38, asst, 38; asst physics, Reed Col, 39-40; vis instr physics & math, Mills Col, 40-41; instr physics, Ill Inst Technol, 41-42; spec consult, Electronic Res Labs, Mass, 46-53; mem sci staff, Melpar, Inc, 53-54; physicist, Union Switch & Signal Div, Westinghouse Air Brake Co, 54-62. *Mem:* NY Acad Sci; Sigma Xi; Am Phys Soc. *Res:* Wave mechanics; quantum theory of the non-idea gas; upper air properties. *Mailing Add:* Dept Physics State Univ NY Buffalo NY 14260

BETHE, HANS ALBRECHT, NUCLEAR PHYSICS, ASTROPHYSICS. *Current Pos:* from asst prof to John Wendell Anderson prof, 35-75, EMER PROF PHYSICS, CORNELL UNIV, 75- *Personal Data:* b Strasbourg, Ger, July 2, 06; nat US; m 39; c 2. *Educ:* Univ Munich, PhD(physics), 28. *Hon Degrees:* DSc, Polytech Inst Brooklyn, 50, Univ Denver, 52, Univ Chicago, 53, Univ Birmingham, Eng, 56, Harvard Univ, 58, Univ Munich & Tech Univ Munich, 68, Univ Seoul & Univ Delhi, 69 & Univ Tubingen & Weizmann Inst, 78. *Honors & Awards:* Nobel Prize in Physics, 67; Morrison Prize, NY Acad Sci, 38 & 40; US Medal Merit, 46; Draper Medal, Nat Acad Sci, 48; Planck Medal, 55; Enrico Fermi Prize, US AEC, 61; Nat Medal Sci, 76. *Prof Exp:* Instr physics, Univ Frankfurt, 28-29 & Univ Stuttgart, 29; lectr, Univ Munich & Univ Tubingen, 30-33 & Univ Manchester, Eng, 33-34; fel, Univ Bristol, 34-35. *Concurrent Pos:* Rockefeller Found Int Educ Bd fel, Cambridge Univ & Univ Rome, 30-32; staff mem, Radiation Lab, Mass Inst Technol, 42-43; chief, Theoret Physics Div, Los Alamos Sci Lab, NMex, 43-46; vis prof, Columbia Univ, 41 & 48; consult, Los Alamos Sci Lab, 47-, Atomic Power Develop Assocs, 53-63 & Avco Everett Res Lab, 55-87; vis prof, Univ Wash, 50, 60, 67, 73 & 76 & Cambridge Univ, 55-56; mem, President's Sci Adv Comt, 56-59; mem, US Delegation to Discussions on Discontinuance of Nuclear Weapons Tests, Geneva, 58-59; vis prof, Calif Inst Technol, 64, 82, 85 & 87, Nordita, Copenhagen, Denmark, 64, 70, 74, 78, 81 & 84 & Mass Inst Technol, 75 & 77 & Harvard Univ, 82. *Mem:* Nat Acad Sci; fel Am Phys Soc (pres, 54); Am Astron Soc; Am Philos Soc. *Res:* Quantum theory of atoms; theory of metals; quantum theory of collisions; theory of atomic nuclei; meson theory; energy production in stars; neutron stars and their formation; quantum electrodynamics; shock wave theory; theory of supernovae. *Mailing Add:* 320 Newman Lab Cornell Univ Ithaca NY 14853

BETHEA, CYNTHIA LOUISE, ENDOCRINOLOGY, REPRODUCTION. *Current Pos:* ASST SCIENTIST, ORE REGIONAL PRIMATE RES CTR, 81- *Personal Data:* b Mobile, Ala, Nov 12, 52. *Educ:* Winthrop Col, BA, 72; Clemson Univ, MS, 74; Emory Univ, PhD(physiol), 78. *Concurrent Pos:* Fel endocrinol, Univ Calif, San Francisco, 81. *Mem:* Soc Neurosci; Fedn Am Soc Exp Biol. *Res:* Examination of the cellular regulation of prolactin and luteinizing hormone secretion and the hypothalamic factors which modify the production of these hormones. *Mailing Add:* Dept Reproductive Physiol Ore Regional Primate Res Ctr 505 NW 185th Ave Beaverton OR 97006-3448

BETHEA, ROBERT MORRISON, CHEMICAL ENGINEERING, AIR POLLUTION. *Current Pos:* from asst prof to assoc prof, 66-74, PROF CHEM ENG, TEX TECH UNIV, 75- *Personal Data:* b Raleigh, NC, Dec 12, 35; m 61, Nancy J Jensen. *Educ:* Va Polytech Inst, BS, 57; Iowa State Univ, MS, 59, PhD(chem eng), 64. *Prof Exp:* Instr chem eng, Iowa State Univ, 59-64; aerospace technologist environ monitoring & control, Langley Res Ctr, NASA, 64-66. *Concurrent Pos:* Res assoc, Iowa Eng Res Inst, Iowa State Univ, 59-64; consult atmosphere control systs, Collins Radio Co, 63-64; chem engr, Indust Environ Res Lab, US Environ Protection Agency, NC, 72; consult, numerous co & agencies; dipl, Am Acad Environ Engrs, Cert Air Pollution Control. *Mem:* Am Inst Chem Engrs; Am Indust Hyg Asn; Air & Waste Mgt Asn. *Res:* Air pollution control system evaluation and design; instrumental methods for air quality control and measurement; applications of engineering control methods to industrial hygiene problems. *Mailing Add:* Dept Chem Eng Texas Tech Univ PO Box 43121 Lubbock TX 79409. *Fax:* 806-742-3552

BETHEA, TRISTRAM WALKER, III, ORGANIC CHEMISTRY, POLYMER CHEMISTRY. *Current Pos:* Res scientist elastomer synthesis, Firestone Tire & Rubber Co, 67-69, sr res scientist elastomer synthesis & polymer physics, 69-78, assoc scientist mat sci, 79-85, RES ASSOC POLYMER SCI, BRIDGESTONE/FIRESTONE RES INC, 85- *Personal*

Data: b Lancaster, SC, July 29, 38; m 70; c 4. *Educ:* Davidson Col, BS, 60; Clemson Univ, MS, 62, PhD(org chem), 65. *Concurrent Pos:* Res assoc, Case Inst Technol, 64-66. *Mem:* Am Chem Soc. *Res:* Polymer chemistry; polymer synthesis; elastomers; structure-property relationships. *Mailing Add:* PO Box 203 Bath OH 44210-0203

BETHEIL, JOSEPH JAY, BIOCHEMISTRY. *Current Pos:* RETIRED. *Personal Data:* b New York, NY, Apr 16, 24; m 84, Esther Apple; c Richard & James. *Educ:* City Col New York, BS, 44; Univ Wis, MS, 47, PhD(biochem), 49. *Prof Exp:* Res asst, Dept Chem, Off Sci Res & Develop Proj, Columbia Univ, 44-45; USPHS fel, Inst Enzyme Res, Univ Wis, 49-50; from instr to asst prof biochem, Sch Med & Dent, Univ Rochester, 50-55; from asst prof to assoc prof biochem, Albert Einstein Col Med, Yeshiva Univ, 55-89. *Concurrent Pos:* USPHS spec fel, Nat Inst Med Res, London, 64-65. *Mem:* AAAS; Am Soc Biol Chemists; Am Inst Nutrit; Harvey Soc; Am Chem Soc. *Res:* Protein chemistry and structure; intermediary metabolism; study of cellular aging; regulation of protein biosynthesis; nutrition. *Mailing Add:* 92 Shoreview Dr Apt 2 Yonkers NY 10710-1351

BETHEL, JAMES SAMUEL, WOOD TECHNOLOGY. *Current Pos:* assoc dean, Grad Sch & Col Forest Res, Univ Washington, 62-64, prof forestry, 62-85, dean, 64-81, emer dean, Col Forest Res, 81-85, EMER PROF FORESTRY, UNIV WASHINGTON, 85- *Personal Data:* b New Westminster, BC, Aug 13, 15; wid; c Ruth Anne (Andersen), James S Jr & John. *Educ:* Univ Wash, BSF, 37; Duke Univ, MF, 39, DF, 47. *Prof Exp:* Instr forestry, Pa State Col, 39-41; asst prof, Va Polytech Inst, 41-42; asst mgr, Tidewater Plywood Co, Ga, 46-48, prod mgr, 48-49; assoc prof wood technol, NC State Col, 49-50, prof & dir, Wood Prod Lab, 50-58, head, Wood Prod Dept & actg dean, Grad Sch, 58-59; head spec proj, Sci Educ Sect, NSF, 59-62. *Concurrent Pos:* UN consult, Yugoslavia, 52; adv, Econ Develop Admin, PR, 56; consult, HEW, 56-, Gov Res Triangle Comt, NC, 57-59 & NSF, 62-; dir, Orgn Trop Studies, 63-; vpres, 64-65, pres, 66-67; ed, J Soc Am Foresters; consult, President's Coun Environ Qual; treas & bd mem, Int Bot Cong, 69; mem, Comt Effects Herbicides Vietnam, Nat Acad Sci; consult, Comt Eng Policy, Nat Acad Eng, 72-73; mem bd agr & renewable res, Nat Acad Sci, 73-75, chmn, Task Force on Educ Agr & Renewable Res & Comt on Renewable for Indust Mat, 74-75, mem, Firewood Crop Panel Task Force & Panel Rev US/USSR Agreement Coop Fields Sci & Technol, Bd Int Sci Exchange, 77; mem, Prog Comt, Int Mat Cong, 77-78; mem, Nat Forest Systs Adv Comt, US Forest Serv, USDA, 78-79; pres, Univ Int Forestry, 79-80, bd mem, 79-81; dir, Ctr Int Forestry, 81-85; consult, UN Food & Agr Orgn, 82-87, US Agency Int Develop, 84-88 & World Bank, 90-94. *Mem:* Fel AAAS; fel Soc Am Foresters; fel Int Acad Wood Sci; Soc Wood Sci & Technol (pres, 58-59, 60-61); fel Inst Wood Sci; Forest Prod Res Soc. *Res:* Wood science, especially anatomy and morphology; relationship of environment to structure of wood in forest trees; wood moisture relationships; tropical forest utilization. *Mailing Add:* Col Forest Resources AR-10 Univ Washington Seattle WA 98195. *E-Mail:* bethel@u.washington.edu

BETHKE, BRUCE DONALD, MOLECULAR GENETICS. *Current Pos:* ASST PROF BIOL, ST VINCENT COL, 95- *Personal Data:* b Rolla, Mo, Dec 22, 58. *Educ:* Col Wooster, BA, 81, Cath Univ Am, MS, 89, PhD(molecular genetics), 91. *Prof Exp:* Int Reciprocal Trade Asn fel, Lab Biochem Genetics, NIH, 91-94, fel, Lab Biochem & Metab, Nat Inst Diabetes, Digestive & Kidney Dis, 94-95. *Mem:* Genetics Soc Am; AAAS. *Res:* Hemologous recombination, both procaryotic and eucaryotic; development of gene delivery systems and analysis of mammalian chromosome position effects; investigations of the molecular basis of development. *Mailing Add:* Dept Biol St Vincent Col 300 Fraser Purchase Rd Latrobe PA 15650-2690. *Fax:* 301-496-0839

BETHKE, PHILIP MARTIN, GEOLOGY. *Current Pos:* geologist, 57-95, chief, Br Exp Geochem & Minerol, 80-83, EMER SCIENTIST, US GEOL SURV, 95- *Personal Data:* b Chicago, Ill, Mar 22, 30; m 55; c 7. *Educ:* Amherst Col, BA, 52, Columbia Univ, MA, 54, PhD(geol), 57. *Prof Exp:* Asst geol, Columbia Univ, 52-53, res asst, 53-54; asst prof, Mo Sch Mines, 55-59. *Mem:* Geol Soc Am; Geochem Soc; Mineral Soc Am (treas, 73-74); Soc Econ Geol (vpres, 92), pres elect, 96, Pres, 97; Am Geophys Union. *Res:* Chemistry of ore deposition; mineralogy of ore minerals; time-space relations in ore deposits; phase equilibria of ore minerals. *Mailing Add:* US Geol Surv Nat Ctr MS 954 Reston VA 20192. *Fax:* 73-648-6383; *E-Mail:* pbethke@usgs.gov

BETHLAHMY, NEDAVIA, FOREST HYDROLOGY. *Current Pos:* CONSULT, 80- *Personal Data:* b Tel-Aviv, Palestine, July 23, 18; US citizen; m 43, Evelyn Nathan; c David & Aliza (Debert). *Educ:* Pa State Col, BS, 39; Yale Univ, MF, 40; Cornell Univ, PhD, 56. *Honors & Awards:* Nat Res, Sigma Xi. *Prof Exp:* Forester Northeastern Forest Exp Sta, US Forest Serv, 46-55, res forester, Pac Northwest Forest & Range Exp Sta, 56-63, proj leader, Intermountain Forest & Range Exp Sta, 63-66; watershed mgr expert, Food & Agr Orgn, UN, Taiwan, 66-68; res forester, 68-69, prin forest hydrologist, Intermountain Forest & Range Exp Sta, US Forest Serv, 69-76. *Concurrent Pos:* Adj prof forest hydrol, Univ Idaho, 69-76; UN Develop Prog, Food & Agr Orgn, Tehran, Iran, 78-79. *Mem:* Soc Am Foresters; Am Geophys Union. *Res:* Hydrology of wildlands, with special emphasis on effects of major wild fires; watershed management. *Mailing Add:* 4043 First Ave NE Seattle WA 98105

BETHUNE, DONALD STIMSON, NONLINEAR OPTICS, LASER PHYSICS. *Current Pos:* Scientist, 77-82, RES STAFF MEM, WATSON RES CTR, IBM RES LAB, IBM CORP, SAN JOSE, CALIF, 82- *Personal Data:* b Philadelphia, Pa, July 2, 48; m 76; c 5. *Educ:* Stanford Univ, BS, 70; Univ Calif, Berkeley, PhD(physics), 77. *Mem:* Am Phys Soc; Optical Soc Am. *Res:* Nonlinear optics; dipole forbidden nonlinear susceptibilities and processes; nonlinear optical method for capturing broadband infared spectra on a nanosecond time scale; time resolved studies of chemical processes. *Mailing Add:* Dept K13-D1 IBM Almoden Resource Ctr 650 Harry Rd San Jose CA 95120-6099

BETHUNE, JOHN EDMUND, endocrinology, for more information see previous edition

BETOWSKI, LEON DONNELLY, JR, MASS SPECTROMETRY, ANALYTICAL CHEMISTRY OF DYES. *Current Pos:* RES CHEMIST, US ENVIRON PROTECTION AGENCY, 79- *Personal Data:* b New York, NY, Aug 10, 44; m 74, Ruth Gavino; c David J. *Educ:* Georgetown Univ, BS, 66; Cornell Univ, PhD(phys chem), 74. *Prof Exp:* Fel, York Univ, Toronto, 74-76; res assoc, Univ Calif, Santa Barbara, 76-79. *Mem:* Am Soc Mass Spectrometry. *Res:* Methods development for the detection of environmental pollutants; computational chemistry. *Mailing Add:* US Environ Protection Agency PO Box 93478 Las Vegas NV 89193-3478. *Fax:* 702-798-2142; *E-Mail:* betowski.don@epamail.epa.gov

BETSCHART, ANTOINETTE, NUTRITIONAL QUALITY OF FOOD, CEREAL SCIENCE. *Current Pos:* RES FOOD TECHNOLOGIST, WESTERN REGIONAL RES CTR, AGR RES SERV, USDA, 71-, RES LEADER & DIR, 91- *Personal Data:* b Manteca, Calif, Apr 12, 39. *Educ:* Univ Calif, Davis, BS, 60, Ore State Univ, MS, 66, Cornell Univ, PhD(food sci & nutrit), 71. *Honors & Awards:* Women Sci & Eng Award, 94. *Prof Exp:* Asst prof food & nutrit, Univ Nev, Reno, 66-68. *Concurrent Pos:* Adj fac, Univ Calif, Berkeley, 73-74, San Jose State Univ, 77-79, San Francisco State Univ, 78-80. *Mem:* Fel Am Asn Cereal Chem (pres, 92-93); Inst Food Technologists. *Res:* Nutritional quality/functions of protein and fiber in ceral grains and oil seeds; development of nutritionally improved, health promoting foods; implement nutrition intervention program in Bolivia. *Mailing Add:* Western Regional Res Ctr ARS USDA 800 Buchanan St Albany CA 94710

BETSO, STEPHEN RICHARD, ANALYTICAL CHEMISTRY, POLYMER CHEMISTRY. *Current Pos:* analytical chemist, 73-77, plastics engr, 77-80, chelation chemist, 80-85, POLYMER CHEMIST, DOW CHEM CO, 85- *Personal Data:* b Brooklyn, NY, May 28, 45; m 68. *Educ:* St Johns Univ, NY, BS, 66; Ohio State Univ, MS, 70, PhD(chem), 71. *Prof Exp:* Res fel analytical chem, Univ Ga, 71-73. *Mem:* Am Chem Soc; Sigma Xi. *Res:* New polymer development. *Mailing Add:* PO Box 1965 Midland MI 48641-1965

BETTEGA, RICHARD, CHEMISTRY, CHEMISTRY ADMINISTRATION. *Current Pos:* DIR FACIL, LEWIS & CLARK COL, 87- *Personal Data:* b San Francisco, Calif, Aug 1, 48. *Educ:* Sonoma State Univ, BS, 72; Univ Ore, PhD(chem), 78. *Prof Exp:* Asst prof chem, Reid Col, 81-87. *Mem:* Am Chem Soc. *Mailing Add:* 1615 VanBuren Oregon City OR 97045-1090

BETTELHEIM, FREDERICK A, PHYSICAL CHEMISTRY. *Current Pos:* chmn dept, 85-91, from asst prof to prof phys chem, 57-93, DISTINGUISHED UNIV RES PROF NATURAL SCI, ADELPHI UNIV, 93- *Personal Data:* b Gyor, Hungary, June 3, 23; nat US; m 47, 89, Vera Deutsch; c Adriel A. *Educ:* Cornell Univ, BS, 53; Univ Calif, MS, 54, PhD(phys chem), 56. *Prof Exp:* Asst chemist, Agr Exp Sta, Israel, 47-51; analyst, NY Agr Exp Sta, 52-53; asst, Univ Calif, Davis, 53-56; instr, Univ Mass, 56-57. *Concurrent Pos:* Lalor Found fel, 58; vis prof, Uppsala Univ, Sweden, 65, Technion, Israel, 65, Weizmann Inst, Israel, 73 & Univ Fla, 81; mem, Adv Bd Mil Personnel Supplies, Nat Acad Sci, 67-71; mem study sects, Nat Eye Inst, NIH, 78-, vis scientist, 85-93; Fulbright prof, Weizman Inst, Israel, 84; ed, Exp Eye Res, 84-92. *Mem:* Am Chem Soc; NY Acad Sci; Fedn Am Socs Exp Biol; Asn Res Vision & Ophthal; Int Soc Eye Res (treas, 84-89). *Res:* Physical chemistry of high polymers; mucopolysaccharides; glycoproteins; lens proteins; x-ray diffraction, birefringence; light scattering high vacuum vapor sorption; infra-red dichroism; molecular, supermolecular structures in cornea, lens, vitreous of the eye; textbook writer: general, organic, and biochemistry. *Mailing Add:* Dept Chem Adelphi Univ Garden City NY 11530. *Fax:* 516-877-4191; *E-Mail:* bettelhe@adlibv.adelphi.edu

BETTEN, J ROBERT, COMMUNICATIONS. *Current Pos:* assoc prof, 62-64, PROF ELEC ENG, UNIV MO-ROLLA, 64-, CHMN DEPT, 67- *Personal Data:* b Omaha, Nebr, Nov 10, 32; m; c 2. *Educ:* Iowa State Univ, BS, 55, MS, 59, PhD(elec eng), 62. *Prof Exp:* Res asst elec eng, Iowa State Univ, 54-55, asst & instr, 58-62; sr elec engr, Gen Dynamics/Convair, 57-58. *Concurrent Pos:* Res & teaching consult, Continental Oil Co, 66- *Mem:* Inst Elec & Electronics Engrs; Am Soc Eng Educ; Sigma Xi. *Res:* Electrical communications, including statistical detection, statistical filtering, information theory, signal analysis and modulation systems. *Mailing Add:* 10501 Co Rd 3010 Rolla MO 65401-9311

BETTEN, PAUL R, SOFTWARE LICENSING, TECHNOLOGY ASSESSMENT & LICENSING. *Current Pos:* sr mech engr, EBR-II Div, 77-89, dir, Off Res & Assessment, Tech Transfer Ctr, 89-94, SR PROG COORDR, TECH TRANSFER CTR, ARGONNE NAT LAB, 94- *Personal Data:* b Pittsburgh, Pa, Oct 31, 46; m, Gayle; c Elizabeth, Samantha & Jonathan. *Educ:* Carnegie Inst Technol, BS, 69; Carnegie Mellon Univ, MS, 70, PhD(mech eng), 73. *Prof Exp:* Sr engr, Combustion Eng, 73-77. *Mem:* Am Soc Mech Engrs; Asn Univ Tech Mgrs; Licensing Exec Soc. *Res:* Technology assessments; technology and software licensing and marketing; strategic planning. *Mailing Add:* Argonne Nat Lab 9700 S Cass Ave Argonne IL 60439-4820. *E-Mail:* betten@anl.gov

BETTENCOURT, JOSEPH S, JR, PARASITOLOGY. *Current Pos:* Instr, 65-67, asst prof, 69-77, ASSOC PROF BIOL, MARIST COL, 78- *Personal Data:* b Cambridge, Mass, Mar 5, 40; m 63; c 3. *Educ:* Suffolk Univ, AB, 62; Univ NH, MS, 65, PhD(zool), 76. *Concurrent Pos:* Dir, Physically Handicapped Sci Prog, NSF, 79-81. *Mem:* Am Soc Parasitologists; AAAS; Sigma Xi. *Res:* Marine fish and fresh water fish hematozoa; life cycles of Trypanoplasmea, host specificity and vector transmission. *Mailing Add:* Div Sci Marist Col Poughkeepsie NY 12601-1387

BETTGER, WILLIAM JOSEPH, TRACE MINERALS, MEMBRANE BIOCHEMISTRY. *Current Pos:* asst prof, 82-88, ASSOC PROF, DEPT NUTRIT SCI, UNIV GUELPH, 88- *Personal Data:* b St Louis, Mo, Sept 10, 53. *Educ:* Univ Mo, BSA, 75, PhD(biochem), 79. *Prof Exp:* Res assoc, dept molecular, cellular & develop biol, Univ Colo, Boulder, 79-80 & dept biochem, Sch Med, St Louis Univ, 80-82. *Mem:* Am Inst Nutrit; Can Soc Nutrit Sci; Tissue Cult Asn. *Res:* Effect of trace minerals on membrane structure and function; nutritional requirements of cells in culture. *Mailing Add:* Dept Nutrit Sci Univ Guelph Guelph ON N1G 2W1 Can

BETTI, JOHN A, AUTOMOTIVE ENGINEERING. *Current Pos:* PVT INVESTOR & CONSULT, 91- *Personal Data:* b Ottawa, Ill, Jan 6, 31; m 53, Joan Doyle; c Diane, Denise, Donna(deceased) & Joan. *Educ:* Ill Inst Technol, BS, 52; Chrysler Inst Eng, MAutomotive Eng, 54. *Prof Exp:* Chassis engr, Chrysler Corp, 52-57, asst managing engr chassis prod planning, 57, exec asst to elec eng chassis & truck design, 57-58, managing engr, Valiant Prog, 58-59, asst chief engr chassis design, 59-60 & elec design, 60-62; exec engr body eng, Ford Motor Co, 62-67, chief elec systs eng, 68, light truck eng, 68-72, chief engine engr, 72-74, chief car planning mgr, 74-75, chief car eng NAm, 75, vpres truck & recreation vehicles, Ford NAm, 75-76, vpres prod develop, Ford Europe, 76-79, vpres power train & chassis, 79-83, vpres mfg & bus develop, Ford NAm, 83-84, exec vpres tech affairs & operating staffs, 84-88 & diversified prods, 88-89; undersecy acquisitions, Dept Defense, 89-91. *Concurrent Pos:* Chmn bd trustees, Gen Motors Eng & Mgt Inst; mem bd dirs, Ford Motor Co, 85-90. *Mem:* Nat Acad Eng. *Mailing Add:* 11964 Lost Tree Way North Palm Beach FL 33408. *E-Mail:* jbetti@concentric.net

BETTI, RAIMONDO, EARTHQUAKE ENGINEERING. *Current Pos:* ASST PROF STRUCT, COLUMBIA UNIV, 91- *Personal Data:* b Rome, Italy, Oct 22, 59; m 91, Lisa Whale. *Educ:* Univ di Roma, Italy, Laurea, 85; Univ Southern Calif, MS, 88, PhD(civil eng), 91. *Prof Exp:* Res assoc, Univ di Roma, Italy, 85-86. *Mem:* Am Soc Civil Engrs; Sigma Xi; Am Acad Mech; Int Soc Boundary Elements; Earthquake Eng Res Inst. *Res:* Focus on earthquake engineering with emphasis on active control of structure and dynamic soil-structure interaction; other interests are in bridge retrofitting and non-destructive evaluation. *Mailing Add:* Columbia Univ 610 SW Mudd Bldg Columbia Univ New York NY 10027. *Fax:* 212-854-6267; *E-Mail:* betti@cucersl.civil.columbia.eng

BETTICE, JOHN ALLEN, MAMMALIAN PHYSIOLOGY. *Current Pos:* ASST PROF PHYSIOL, SCH MED, CASE WESTERN RESERVE UNIV, 74- *Personal Data:* b Columbus, Ind, Nov 27, 42; m 67. *Educ:* Univ Dayton, BS, 65; Johns Hopkins Univ, PhD(physiol), 72. *Concurrent Pos:* fel Sch Med, Johns Hopkins Univ, 72-73; fel, Univ Kans Med Ctr, 73-74. *Mem:* AAAS; Am Physiol Soc. *Res:* Mechanisms of the physiological reactions which buffer changes in acid-base balance of the body and the effects of such inbalances on body functions and cellular metabolism. *Mailing Add:* Dept Basic Med Sci Univ Ill Col Med 1601 Parkview Rockford IL 61107

BETTINGER, DONALD JOHN, INORGANIC CHEMISTRY, CHEMICAL EDUCATION. *Current Pos:* RETIRED. *Personal Data:* b Cincinnati, Ohio, Aug 20, 27; m 51, Coralen Becker; c 4. *Educ:* Miami Univ, BS, 47; Univ Cincinnati, MS, 50; Univ NC, PhD(chem), 55. *Prof Exp:* Asst prof chem, Davidson Col, 50-51 & WVa Univ, 54-58; from asst prof to assoc prof, Denison Univ, 58-63; prof chem, Ohio Northern Univ, 63-79, chmn dept, 63-74, head, Div Math & Natural Sci, 67-74; prof chem, Alice Lloyd Col, 79-89, asst to dean col, 89-91. *Concurrent Pos:* Mem, Comt Chem Educ, Am Chem Soc, chmn, NW Ohio Sect. *Mem:* Am Chem Soc; Sigma Xi. *Res:* Chemical education; preparative inorganic chemistry; inorganic aggregation and polymerization phenomena; structure and stereochemistry of coordination compounds; chemical education. *Mailing Add:* 26915 Bella Vista Dr Howey in the Hills FL 34737-3052

BETTINGER, GEORGE E, PROJECT MANAGEMENT, MANUFACTURING MANAGEMENT. *Current Pos:* dir res & develop, Cardiol Div, 91-93, DIR SITE OPERS, MALLINCKRODT MED INC, 93- *Personal Data:* b Newark, NJ, Apr 26, 45; m 68, Anne M Hausl; c Daniel, Matthew & Christopher. *Educ:* Col Holy Cross, BS, 67; Seton Hall Univ, MS, 69; Rutgers Univ, PhD(microbiol), 72. *Prof Exp:* Res assoc, Univ Rochester Med Sch, 72-74, A I DuPont Inst, 74-77; res mgr, E I Du Pont de Nemours & Co, 77-89; dir res & develop, Cardiopulmonary Div, C R Bard, 89-91. *Mem:* AAAS; Am Soc Microbiol; Regulatory Affairs Prof Soc. *Res:* Microbial physiology, environmental microbiology, mammalian toxicology and medical immunology. *Mailing Add:* Mallinckrodt Inc 1111 S Velasco Angleton TX 77515. *Fax:* 409-848-5054; *E-Mail:* gebetti@mkg.com

BETTINGER, RICHARD THOMAS, SPACE PHYSICS. *Current Pos:* PROG MGR, WEBS SYSTS PROJ STAFF, US TREASURY, 86- *Personal Data:* b Dayton, Ohio, Aug 3, 31; m 52; c 7. *Educ:* Syracuse Univ, BS, 55; Univ Md, PhD(physics), 64. *Prof Exp:* Asst prof physics, Univ Md, College Park, 64-74; mem staff, Betco Electronics, 74-85. *Res:* In situ probe systems for the measurement of ionospheric parameters; vertical ozone distribution measured from satellites. *Mailing Add:* 15000 Donna Dr Silver Spring MD 20905

BETTMAN, JEROME WOLF, MEDICINE, OPHTHALMOLOGY & MEDICOLEGAL ETHICS. *Current Pos:* EXEC DIR BASIC SCI COURSE IN OPHTHAL & UPDATE COURSE, MED SCH, STANFORD UNIV, 70-, EMER CLIN PROF SURG, 74-; EMER CLIN PROF OPHTHAL, MED SCH, UNIV CALIF, SAN FRANCISCO, 76- *Personal Data:* b San Francisco, Calif, June 22, 09; m 35; c 2. *Educ:* Univ Calif, AB, 31, MD, 35. *Honors & Awards:* Award of Honor, Am Acad Ophthal & Otolaryngol, 58; Sr Honor Award, Am Acad Ophthal, 85; Edward Jackson lectr, Univ Colo, 52. *Prof Exp:* From asst resident to resident ophthal, Stanford Univ, 35-37, from assoc instr to assoc clin prof, 37-57, clin prof surg, Med Sch, 57-74. *Concurrent Pos:* consult, Marine Hosp, USPHS & San Francisco Hosp, 57-59; chief ophthal, Presby Med Ctr, 59-66; mem, Comt Sci Assemblies, NIH-Calif Med Asn Sci Bd; chmn, Ethics Comt, Am Acad Ophthal; clin prof ophthal, Med Sch, Univ Calif, San Francisco, 64-76. *Mem:* Asn Res Vision & Ophthal; Am Acad Ophthal (first vpres); Am Col Surgeons; fel Royal Soc Med. *Res:* Factors influencing the blood volume of the choroid and the retina; toxic cataracts; malpractice in ophthalmology. *Mailing Add:* 3910 Sand Hill Rd Woodside CA 94062

BETTMAN, MAX, PHYSICAL CHEMISTRY. *Current Pos:* RETIRED. *Personal Data:* b Ger, Nov 15, 25; nat US; m 57; c 1. *Educ:* Reed Col, BA, 49; Calif Inst Technol, PhD(chem), 52. *Prof Exp:* Res chemist, Calif Res & Develop Co, 52-53 & Union Carbide Corp, 53-64; res chemist, Sci Lab, Ford Motor Co, 64-87. *Mem:* Am Chem Soc; Sigma Xi. *Res:* Materials research for solid state devices; automobile exhaust catalysis; x-ray crystallography. *Mailing Add:* 28328 E Kalong Circle Southfield MI 48034-5640

BETTONVILLE, PAUL JOHN, PHARMACOLOGY. *Current Pos:* Resident internal med, Univ Hosps, 46-48, instr pharmacol & internal med, Sch Med, 48-59, asst prof clin med, 59-72, EMER PROF, SCH MED, ST LOUIS UNIV, 72- *Personal Data:* b St Louis, Mo, July 19, 18; m 50; c 2. *Educ:* St Louis Univ, MD, 42. *Mem:* AAAS; AMA. *Res:* Chemical carcinogenesis. *Mailing Add:* 58 Berrywood Dr St Louis MO 63122

BETTS, ATTIE L(ESTER), ELECTRICAL ENGINEERING. *Current Pos:* prof, 55-78, head dept, 55-70, EMER PROF ELEC ENG, WASH STATE UNIV, 78- *Personal Data:* b Fairy, Tex, July 30, 16; m 40; c 2. *Educ:* Agr & Mech Col Tex, BS, 38, MS, 39; Univ Tex, PhD(elec eng), 52. *Prof Exp:* Asst elec eng, Agr & Mech Col Tex, 38-39; engr, Gulf States Utilities, 39-41; instr elec eng, Okla State Univ, 41-42 & 46, from asst prof to prof, 46-55. *Mem:* Sr mem Inst Elec & Electronics Engrs; Am Soc Eng Educ. *Res:* Electrical power needs and the alternatives. *Mailing Add:* 1927 Jungo Ct Gardnerville NV 89410-7910

BETTS, AUSTIN WORTHAM, CIVIL ENGINEERING, NUCLEAR ENERGY. *Current Pos:* RETIRED. *Personal Data:* b Westwood, NJ, Nov 22, 12; m 34, 92, Roberta Brungardt; c Jerry W, Lee W & Lynn P. *Educ:* US Mil Acad, BS, 34; Mass Inst Technol, MS, 38. *Prof Exp:* Assoc dir nuclear weapons, Los Alamos Sci Lab, 46-48; chief, Atomic Energy Br, US Army Gen Staff, 49-54; dep dir guided missiles, Off Secy Defense, 57-60; dir, Advan Res Proj Agency, Off Defense, 60-61; dir mil appln nuclear weapons, Atomic Energy Chmn Staff, 61-63; chief res & develop multi-discipline, US Army Gen Staff, 66-70; sr vpres multi-discipline, Southwest Res Inst, 71-83. *Concurrent Pos:* Mem, Army Sci Adv Panel, 71-74, consult, 74-79; chmn, Sci Adv Coun, Ballistic Res Lab, 72-77; consult, Energy Res & Develop Admin, 76-77; mem, Army Sci Bd, 78-83; consult, 83-; exec secy, Nat Conf Advan Res, 87- *Mem:* Am Inst Aeronaut & Astronaut; fel Soc Am Mil Engrs; fel Inst Environ Sci; AAAS. *Res:* Competitive interrelationship among available sources of energy. *Mailing Add:* 6414 View Pt San Antonio TX 78229

BETTS, BURR JOSEPH, ANIMAL BEHAVIOR, ECOLOGY. *Current Pos:* from asst prof to assoc prof, 75-87, interim dean, Sch Arts & Sci, 95-96, PROF BIOL, EASTERN ORE STATE COL, 87- *Personal Data:* b Denver, Colo, May 5, 45; m 68, Donna Palmer; c Amy & Erika. *Educ:* Purdue Univ, BS, 67; Univ Mont, PhD(zool), 73. *Prof Exp:* Res assoc, Univ Mont, 73-75. *Concurrent Pos:* Dir, George Ott Wildlife Res Area, 83- *Mem:* Animal Behav Soc; Am Soc Mammalogists; Sigma Xi. *Res:* Social behavior and organizations; time and energy budgets; feeding strategies of birds and mammals; bats. *Mailing Add:* Eastern Ore State Col 1410 L Ave La Grande OR 97850-2899. *Fax:* 541-962-3873; *E-Mail:* bbetts@eosc.osshe.edu

BETTS, DONALD DRYSDALE, THEORETICAL CONDENSED MATTER PHYSICS. *Current Pos:* dean arts & sci, 80-88, dean sci, 88-90, PROF PHYSICS, DALHOUSIE UNIV, 80- *Personal Data:* b Montreal, Que, May 16, 29; m 86, Patricia M Giles; c Malcolm R, Sylvia M, Eric K, Douglas R, Stewart (McWilliams) & Andrew R (McWilliams). *Educ:* Dalhousie Univ, BSc, 50, MSc, 52; McGill Univ, PhD(math physics), 55. *Honors & Awards:* Peter Kirkby Medal, Can Asn Physicists, 96. *Prof Exp:* Nat Res Coun Can fel, Univ Alta, 55-56, from asst prof to prof physics, 56-80, dir, Theoret Physics Inst, 72-78. *Concurrent Pos:* NATO sci fel, King's Col, London, 63-64, Nuffield fel, 70-71; mem, Int Comn Thermodyn & Statist Mech; chmn comn thermodyn & statist mech, Int Union Pure & Appl Physics, 72-75; vis prof chem & physics, Cornell Univ, 75; res fel, Japan Soc Prom Sci, 82; vis prof, Univ New South Wales, 91 & 93; ed, Can J Physics, 92-97; Gordon Godfrey hon vis prof physics, Univ NSW, 96-; mem, Working Group Commun in Physics, Int Union Pure & Appl Physics, 96- *Mem:* Fel Royal Soc Can; Can Asn Physicists (vpres, 68-69, pres, 69-70). *Res:* Theory of phase transitions and critical phenomena especially via high temperature series expansions; theory of quantum spin systems at zero temperature especially via exact solutions on finite lattices. *Mailing Add:* Dept Physics Dalhousie Univ Halifax NS B3H 3J5 Can. *Fax:* 902-494-2835; *E-Mail:* jphysics@adm.dal.ca

BETTS, HENRY BROGNARD, REHABILITATION MEDICINE. *Current Pos:* Staff psychiatrist phys med & rehab, 63-64, assoc med dir, 64-65, MED DIR, REHAB INST CHICAGO, 65-, EXEC VPRES, 69-; PROF REHAB MED & CHMN DEPT, MED SCH, NORTHWESTERN UNIV, CHICAGO, 69- *Personal Data:* b New Rochelle, NY, May 25, 28; m 70. *Educ:* Princeton Univ, BA, 50; Univ Va, MD, 54. *Honors & Awards:* Meritorious Serv Citation, US Pres Comt Employ of Handicapped, 65. *Concurrent Pos:* Consult staff mem, Northwestern Mem Hosp, 67-; dir, Res & Training Ctr 20; mem gov comt, Employ of Handicapped. *Mem:* Am Cong Rehab Med (vpres, 71-, pres, 75-76); Am Acad Phys Med & Rehab. *Res:* Research of prosthetics and orthotics; neuromuscular studies; sociological research. *Mailing Add:* 1727 N Orleans Chicago IL 60614-5719

BETTS, RICHARD RUSSELL, PHYSICS OF STRONG FIELDS, CLUSTERING IN NUCLEI. *Current Pos:* physicist, 79-87, SR PHYSICIST, ARGONNE NAT LAB, 87-; PROF PHYSICS, UNIV ILL, CHICAGO, 94- *Personal Data:* b Yorkshire, Eng, May 21, 47; m 76, Katherine A Puusti; c Nicholas & Alison. *Educ:* Oxford Univ, BA, 68, MA, 84; Univ Pa, MS, 69, PhD(physics), 72. *Prof Exp:* Postdoctoral fel, Univ Pa, 72-73; vis scientist, Niels Bohr Inst, Copenhagen, 73-75; asst prof physics, Yale Univ, 75-79. *Concurrent Pos:* Univ lectr nuclear physics & fel Lady Margaret Hall, Oxford Univ, 84-86; consult & series ed, Inst Physics, 89-; adj prof physics, Univ Ill, Chicago, 93-94. *Mem:* Fel Am Phys Soc. *Res:* Nuclear physics; relativistic heavy ion physics; physics of strong fields and clustering phenomena in nuclei. *Mailing Add:* Phys Dept MC 273 Univ Ill Chicago IL 60607. *E-Mail:* betts@anl.gov, betts@uic.edu

BETZ, A LORRIS, PEDIATRICS. *Current Pos:* from asst prof to assoc prof neurol & pediat, 79-87, PROF PEDIAT, SURG & NEUROL, UNIV MICH, 87-, DIR, NEUROSURG RES, 87- *Personal Data:* b La Crosse, Wis, Feb 9, 47. *Educ:* Univ Wis, BS, 69, MD & PhD(biochem & physiol), 75. *Prof Exp:* Intern pediat, Univ Calif, San Francisco, 75-76, resident, 76-77, postdoctoral fel neurol & pediat, 77-79. *Concurrent Pos:* Estab investr award, Am Heart Asn, 81; assoc chair, Dept Pediat, Univ Mich, 89-; mem bd dirs, Int Soc Cerebral Blood Flow & Metab, 91- *Mem:* Soc Pediat Res; Am Physiol Soc; Int Soc Cerebral Blood Flow & Metab. *Mailing Add:* Dept Pediat Surg & Neurol Univ Mich 5605 Kresge Res Box 0532 1500 E Medical Center Dr Ann Arbor MI 48109-0532

BETZ, EBON ELBERT, MATHEMATICS. *Current Pos:* RETIRED. *Personal Data:* b Springport, Mich, Sept 3, 14; m 43, Ethel Rochlitz; c George Christian, Ralph Ebon, Paul Conrad & Eleanor Lurah (Hess). *Educ:* Albion Col, AB, 34; Univ Mich, AM, 35; Univ Pa, PhD(math), 39. *Prof Exp:* Asst instr math, Univ Pa, 35-38; instr, Haverford Col, 39-41; from instr to prof math, US Naval Acad, 57-91. *Mem:* Am Math Soc. *Res:* Accessibility and separation by simple closed curves; topology. *Mailing Add:* 5 Carvel Rd Annapolis MD 21402

BETZ, GEORGE, OBSTETRICS & GYNECOLOGY, ENDOCRINOLOGY. *Current Pos:* HEAD REPRODUCTIVE ENDOCRINOL, KAISER FOUND, 88- *Personal Data:* b Asherville, Kans, Apr 27, 34; m 83, Trish Wilson; c George, Carter, Virginia & Michael. *Educ:* Kans State Col, BS, 56; Univ Kans, MD, 60, PhD(biochem), 68. *Prof Exp:* Resident gen surg, Denver Gen Hosp, 61-62; resident obstet & gynec, Univ Kans, 62-65, instr, 65-68; from asst prof to assoc prof, 68-77, from res assoc to assoc prof biochem, 71-77, prof obstet & gynec, Univ Colo, Denver, 77- *Concurrent Pos:* Sr fel, NIH, 81-82. *Mem:* Am Soc Biol Chemists; Am Gynec & Obstet Soc; Soc Gynec Invest. *Res:* Biochemistry of reproduction with primary emphasis on steroid converting enzymes; clinical infertility. *Mailing Add:* 2045 Franklin Denver CO 80205

BETZ, JOHN VIANNEY, BACTERIOLOGY, VIROLOGY. *Current Pos:* asst prof, 63-69, ASSOC PROF BOT & BACT, UNIV SFLA, 69- *Personal Data:* b Philadelphia, Pa, Apr 5, 37; m 62; c 2. *Educ:* St Joseph's Col, Pa, BSc, 58; St Bonaventure Univ, PhD(microbiol), 63. *Prof Exp:* Fel microbiol, Ind Univ, 62-63, instr bact, 63. *Mem:* Am Soc Microbiol. *Res:* Interactions of host bacteria and bacteriophages; nature of lysogeny; genetic factors affecting lysogenesis; mechanism of flagellar movement. *Mailing Add:* 14910 Fisher Rd Tampa FL 33613

BETZ, MATHEW J(OSEPH), CIVIL ENGINEERING. *Current Pos:* INDEPENDENT CONSULT, 94- *Personal Data:* b Chicago, Ill, Jan 27, 32; m 63; c 1. *Educ:* Northwestern Univ, BS, 55, MS, 56, PhD(civil eng), 61. *Prof Exp:* Asst prof civil eng, Univ Khartoum, 56-57; instr, Northwestern Univ, 58-59; from asst prof to prof, Ariz State Univ, 61-76, asst dean, 69-70, assoc dean, Grad Col, 70-76, asst acad vpres, 76-83, dir, Ctr Advan Res Transp, 83-88, vprovost planning, 83-93. *Concurrent Pos:* Civil engr, Brookings Inst, DC, 63; consult, Valley Area Transp Study, Ariz, 66-80 & Off Educ, 70-71; mem, Nat Coop Hwy Res Adv Panel, Nat Acad Eng-Nat Acad Sci, 70-74; NSF SEED grant, Kenya, 73; mem, Hwy Res Bd, Nat Res Coun, Nat Acad Sci; consult, World Bank, 77-, US Dept Com, 84. *Mem:* Am Soc Civil Engrs; Inst Transp Engrs; Am Planning Asn; African Studies Asn. *Res:* Transportation engineering and planning; city planning; urban transport planning; transport in developing areas. *Mailing Add:* 6816 E Easle Feather Rd Scottsdale AZ 85262-7184. *E-Mail:* mjbetz@msn.com

BETZ, NORMAN LEO, BEHAVIORAL PHYSIOLOGY, FOOD SCIENCE. *Current Pos:* CHAIR EXCELLENCE, UNIV TENN, MARTIN. *Personal Data:* b Baton Rouge, La, Jan 23, 38; m 60; c 5. *Educ:* La State Univ, BA, 61, MS, 63, PhD(food sci), 66. *Honors & Awards:* Geddes Memorial Award, Am Asn Cereal Chemists, 80. *Prof Exp:* Res assoc, Agr Res Serv, Entom Res Div, USDA, 62-66; chief field messing br/instr, US Army Quartermaster Sch, 66-68; assoc sr scientist, Mallinckrodt Chem Works, 68-72; scientist, Ralston Purina, 72-79, sr scientist, 79-81, dir res & develop planning, 81-82 & dir palatability res, Corp Res & Develop, 82-85; pres, Technol Resources, Ltd, 85- *Concurrent Pos:* Exec ed, Cereal Foods World, Am Asn Cereal Chemists, 74-80; chmn, Am Asn Cereal Chemists, 83. *Mem:* Inst Food Technologists; Am Asn Cereal Chemists (pres-elect, 81, pres, 82); European Chemoreception Res Orgn; Asn Chemoreception Sci. *Res:* Short and long range plans for corporate research and development; identification of appropriate technologies necessary for successful implementation; food technology. *Mailing Add:* Captain Dr Dresden TN 38225

BETZ, ROBERT F, biochemistry, ecology, for more information see previous edition

BETZ, WILLIAM J, NEUROPHYSIOLOGY. *Current Pos:* from asst prof to assoc prof, 71-84, PROF, DEPT PHYSIOL, SCH MED, UNIV COLO, 84- *Personal Data:* b Berwyn, Ill, Feb 3, 43. *Educ:* Wash Univ, BS, 65; Yale Univ, PhD(physiol), 69. *Prof Exp:* Postdoctoral fel, Dept Biophys, Univ Col, London, 69-71. *Mem:* AAAS; Soc Neurosci. *Mailing Add:* Dept Physiol Box C-240 Sch Med Univ Colo 4200 E Ninth Denver CO 80262

BETZER, PETER ROBIN, GEOCHEMISTRY, ANALYTICAL CHEMISTRY. *Current Pos:* From asst prof to prof teaching res, 71-82, PROF ADMIN RES & CHMN DEPT, UNIV SFLA, 82- *Personal Data:* b Delavan, Wis, May 14, 42; m 65, Susan Beers; c Sarah & Katherine. *Educ:* Lawrence Col, BA, 64; Univ RI, PhD(oceanog), 71. *Honors & Awards:* Distinguished Authorship Award, Nat Oceanic & Atmospheric Admin, 85; Plenary Lectr, Australian Marine Sci Meetings, 87. *Concurrent Pos:* Vis prof oceanog, Dept Oceanog, Univ Hawaii & Hawaii Inst Geophys, 81-82; mem, Ocean Chem Panel, NSF, 87, Spec Emphasis Panel Geosci, NSF, 95; vchair, Univ Nat Oceanog Lab Syst, 92-96; invited lectr, Ocean Univ Qingdao, Peoples Repub China, 96. *Mem:* AAAS; Am Geophys Union; Am Inst Chemist; Am Chem Soc; Oceanog Soc. *Res:* Chemical, physical and biological processes influencing the delivery and flux of inorganic and organic materials in the ocean; application of chemical tracers and computer-controlled analytical systems to oceanographic problems. *Mailing Add:* Dept Marine Sci 1830 Seventh St N St Petersburg FL 33704-3322. *Fax:* 813-553-3968; *E-Mail:* prb@marine.usf.edu

BEUCHAT, CAROL ANN, ECOLOGICAL PHYSIOLOGY, COMPARATIVE PHYSIOLOGY. *Current Pos:* RES ASSOC, HUBBS-SEA WORLD RES INST, 90-; ASSOC PROF BIOL, SAN DIEGO STATE UNIV, 90- *Personal Data:* b Calif, June 16, 55. *Educ:* Occidental Col, AB, 76, MA, 77; Cornell Univ, PhD(physiol), 82. *Prof Exp:* NIH fel, Univ Ariz, 82-85, res asst prof, 89-90; asst prof biol, Colgate Univ, 85-88. *Mem:* AAAS; Am Physiol Soc; Am Soc Zoologists; Ecol Soc Am; Am Soc Ichthyologists & Herpetologists; Am Ornith Union. *Res:* Comparative integrative and ecological physiology of vertebrates, especially osmoregulatory physiology, allometry of form and function, animal energetics and thermal biology. *Mailing Add:* Dept Biol San Diego State Univ San Diego CA 92182-0057. *E-Mail:* cbeuchat@sunstroke.sdsu.edu

BEUCHAT, LARRY RAY, FOOD MICROBIOLOGY. *Current Pos:* asst prof, 72-76, assoc prof, 76-81, PROF FOOD MICROBIOL, UNIV GA, 81- *Personal Data:* b Meadville, Pa, July 23, 43. *Educ:* Pa State Univ, BS, 65; Mich State Univ, MS, 67, PhD(food sci), 70. *Honors & Awards:* Samuel Cate Prescott Award, Inst Food Technol, 77. *Prof Exp:* Group leader res & develop, Quaker Oats Co, 70-72. *Mem:* Inst Food Technologists; Am Soc Microbiol; Soc Appl Bact; Int Asn Milk, Food & Environ Sanitarians. *Res:* Environmental factors affecting growth and death of food bore pathogens; chemical changes occurring in peanuts fermented or infected with fungi; conditions for growth of microbial pathogens on nuts and fruits. *Mailing Add:* 2035 Tallwood Pl Griffin GA 30223

BEUERMAN, ROGER WILMER, NEUROSCIENCES, NEUROPHYSIOLOGY. *Current Pos:* ASSOC PROF OPHTHAL, LA STATE UNIV MED SCH, 81- *Personal Data:* b Washington, DC, Oct 3, 43; m 65; c 2. *Educ:* Hood Col, BS, 65; Fla State Univ, PhD(sensory physiol), 73. *Prof Exp:* Sr res fel neurophysiol, Univ Wash, 73-75; res assoc, Div Ophthal, Stanford Univ Med Ctr, 75-81. *Mem:* Int Asn Study Pain; Soc Neurosci; Asn Res Vision Ophthal; Sigma Xi. *Res:* Sensory function and pain in the trigeminal system. *Mailing Add:* La State Univ Eye Ctr 2020 Gravier St-B New Orleans LA 70112-2272

BEUG, MICHAEL WILLIAM, ORGANIC CHEMISTRY, ENVIRONMENTAL CHEMISTRY. *Current Pos:* sr acad dean, 86-92, MEM FAC CHEM, EVERGREEN STATE COL, 72- *Personal Data:* b Austin, Tex, May 18, 44; m 68, Frances A Gresham; c Christopher & Benjamin. *Educ:* Harvey Mudd Col, BS, 66; Univ Wash, PhD(chem), 71. *Prof Exp:* Asst prof chem, Harvey Mudd Col, 71-72. *Mem:* AAAS. *Res:* The effects of pesticides, polychlorinated biphenyls, heavy metals and petroleum on terrestrial and aquatic ecosystems; the detection of pollutants by chromatography and gas chromatography; fungal natural products; agricultural ecology. *Mailing Add:* Evergreen State Col Olympia WA 98505

BEUHLER, ROBERT JAMES, JR, PHYSICAL CHEMISTRY. *Current Pos:* res assoc, 70-72, asst chemist, 72-75, CHEMIST, BROOKHAVEN NAT LAB, 75- *Personal Data:* b Lake Charles, La, Feb 21, 42; m 65, Lois; c Michael, Christopher & John-David. *Educ:* Univ Mich, BS, 63; Univ Wis,

Madison, PhD(phys chem), 68. *Prof Exp:* Res assoc, Argonne Nat Lab, 68-70. *Mem:* Am Soc Mass Spectros; Am Chem Soc. *Res:* Focusing and orientation of molecules in molecular beams; ion-molecule reactions; cluster ion impact phenomena; biological mass spectrometry; cluster ion mass spectroscopy; photon induced desorption phenomina. *Mailing Add:* Chem Dept Brookhaven Nat Lab Upton NY 11973. *Fax:* 516-344-5815

BEUKENS, ROELF PIETER, NUCLEAR PHYSICS, MASS SPECTROMETRY. *Current Pos:* res assoc 76-80, ASSOC PROF PHYSICS, UNIV TORONTO, 80- *Personal Data:* b Venlo, Neth, May 4, 43. *Educ:* State Univ Groningen, Drs, 71; Univ Toronto, PhD(nuclear physics), 76. *Prof Exp:* Fel, 76. *Concurrent Pos:* Consult, Watts, Griffis & McOuat Ltd, 77-78 & Interex Comput Systs Ltd, 77-; Killam fel, 78-79. *Mem:* Can Archaeol Asn. *Res:* Development of ultrasensitive radio isotope dating techniques and ultrasensitive mass spectroscopy using electrostatic accelerators. *Mailing Add:* 60 St George St Univ Toronto Toronto ON M5S 1A7 Can

BEUS, STANLEY S, INVERTEBRATE PALEONTOLOGY, STRATIGRAPHY. *Current Pos:* From asst prof to prof geol, 62-89, chmn, Dept Geol & Geog, 66-69, REGENTS PROF, NORTHERN ARIZ UNIV, 89- *Personal Data:* b Salt Lake City, Utah, July 31, 30; m 53; c 5. *Educ:* Utah State Univ, BS, 57, MS, 58; Univ Calif, Los Angeles, PhD(geol), 63. *Concurrent Pos:* Paleontologist, Mus Northern Ariz, 63-; co-ed, J Paleont, 75-80; consult, Bendix Corp, May Oil Co & US Forest Serv, Grand Canyon Nat Park; secy, Rocky Mountain Sect, Geol Soc Am, 76-84. *Mem:* Geol Soc Am; Paleont Soc; Soc Econ Paleont & Mineral; Am Asn Petrol Geol. *Res:* Paleozoic stratigraphy and paleontology with emphasis on the Grand Canyon area of northern Arizona; invertebrate paleontology; paleoecology. *Mailing Add:* 125 Broken Arrow Way S Sedona AZ 86351

BEUSCH, JOHN U, ELECTRICAL ENGINEERING, APPLIED MATHEMATICS. *Current Pos:* staff mem, Lincoln Lab, Mass Inst Technol, 64, consult, Lincoln Lab & res asst, Opers Res Ctr, 64-65, staff mem, 65-71, GROUP LEADER, LINCOLN LAB, MASS INST TECHNOL, 71-, ASST DIV HEAD, ARROW SPACE DIV. *Personal Data:* b Erie, Pa, Apr 22, 38; m 61, Donna Williams; c Cheryl & Laura. *Educ:* Rochester Inst Technol, BS(mech eng) & BS(elec eng), 61; Mass Inst Technol, SM, 62, PhD(elec eng), 65. *Prof Exp:* Coop student employee, Gen Elec Co, Pa, 57 & Gen Signal Co, NY, 57-61. *Mem:* Inst Elec & Electronics Engrs; Am Inst Aeronaut & Astronaut; Opers Res Soc Am. *Res:* Control systems; control of complex systems; communications theory; operations research; queueing theory; communications satellite planning and preliminary design; air traffic control systems design; tactical communications systems; radar systems. *Mailing Add:* 416 Taylor Rd Stow MA 01775. *Fax:* 781-981-0993; *E-Mail:* beusch@ 11.mit.edu

BEUTE, MARVIN KENNETH, PLANT PATHOLOGY. *Current Pos:* PROF PLANT PATH, NC STATE UNIV, 68- *Personal Data:* b Jenison, Mich, Mar 3, 35; m 55; c 2. *Educ:* Calvin Col, BA, 63; Mich State Univ, PhD(plant path), 68. *Mem:* AAAS; Am Phytopath Soc. *Res:* Ecology of soil borne pathogens; disease complexes; diseases of the peanut. *Mailing Add:* 4104 Picaroy Dr Raleigh NC 27612

BEUTER, JOHN H, FOREST ECONOMICS, FOREST MANAGEMENT. *Current Pos:* CONSULT FORESTER/PRIN, DUCK CREEK ASSOCS, INC, 93- *Personal Data:* b Chicago, Ill, Dec 24, 35; m 60, Jill M Hanson; c J Kurt & Karena M. *Educ:* Mich State Univ, BS, 57, MS, 58; Iowa State Univ, PhD(forestry econ), 66. *Prof Exp:* Resource analyst, US Forest Serv, 61-63, economist & proj leader, 65-68; economist, Mason, Bruce & Girard Consult Foresters, 68-70; from assoc prof to prof forest mgt, Ore State Univ, 76-87, head dept, 76-84, assoc dean, 84-87; consult forester/prin, Mason Bruce & Girard, 88-90; dep asst secy, Nat Res & Environ, USDA, 91-93. *Concurrent Pos:* Courtesy prof, forest resources, Ore State Univ. *Mem:* Soc Am Foresters; Am Forestry Asn. *Res:* Economics of forest management and forest products marketing and utilization; general resource economics; operations research. *Mailing Add:* Duck Creek Assocs Inc 530 NW Oak Ave Corvallis OR 97330. *Fax:* 541-753-9450

BEUTHER, HAROLD, chemical engineering; deceased, see previous edition for last biography

BEUTLER, ERNEST, MEDICINE. *Current Pos:* head, Div Hemat-Oncol, 78-87, chmn, Dept Clin Res, 79-82, CHMN, DEPT MOLECULAR & EXP MED, SCRIPPS CLIN & RES FOUND, 82- *Personal Data:* b Berlin, Ger, Sept 30, 28; US citizen; m 50; c 4. *Educ:* Univ Chicago, PhB, 46, BS, 48, MD, 50. *Hon Degrees:* Dr Philosophiae Honoris Causa, Tel Aviv Univ, 93. *Honors & Awards:* Gairdner Found Award, 75; James Blundell Prize, 85; Nat Heart, Lung & Blood Inst Merit Award, NIH, 87; Acad Clin Biochem Lectureship Award, Kodak Instruments, 90; May Soley Award, Western Soc Clin Invest, 92; Med Achievement Award, Nat Gaucher Found, 92; Fifth Ann Award Excellence Clin Res, NIH Gen Clin Res Centers Prog, 93. *Prof Exp:* From instr to asst prof med, Univ Chicago, 55-59, attend physician, Univ Clins, 55-59; chmn, Div Med, City of Hope Med Ctr, 59-78. *Concurrent Pos:* Assoc clin prof med, Univ Southern Calif, 60-64, clin prof, 64-65 & 67-79; clin prof, Univ Calif-Calif Col Med, 65-67; mem hemat study sect, NIH, 70-74; clin prof, Univ Calif, San Diego, 80- *Mem:* Nat Acad Sci; Am Acad Arts & Sci; Asn Am Physicians; Am Soc Human Genetics; Am Soc Hemat (pres, 78-79); Am Soc Clin Invest. *Res:* Red cell biochemistry and physiology; biochemical genetics; hematology; molecular and population genetics of human diseases. *Mailing Add:* Dept Molecular & Exp Med Scripps Res Inst 10550 N Torrey Pines Rd La Jolla CA 92037

BEUTLER, FREDERICK J(OSEPH), STOCHASTIC OPTIMIZATION, OPTIMIZATION OF QUEUEING SYSTEMS. *Current Pos:* from asst prof to assoc prof aeronaut eng, Univ Mich, 57-63, prof instrumentation, 63-67, prof info & control eng, 67-89, chmn, Comput, Info & Control Eng Prog, 70 & 76-89, chmn, Elec Eng Systs Grad Prog, 84-89, EMER PROF ELEC ENG & COMPUT SCI, UNIV MICH, 90- *Personal Data:* b Berlin, Ger, Oct 3, 26; nat US; m 50, Suzanne Armstrong; c Arthur D, Kathryn R (Peterson) & Michael E. *Educ:* Mass Inst Technol, SB, 49, SM, 51; Calif Inst Technol, PhD(eng sci & math), 57. *Prof Exp:* Jr engr, AC Spark Plug Div, Gen Motors Corp, 49-50; staff mem, Instrumentation Lab, Mass Inst Technol, 50-51, asst, 55-56; res engr, Autonetics Div, NAm Aviation, Inc, 51-54; tech engr, Ramo-Woolridge Corp, 56-57. *Concurrent Pos:* Vis scholar, Univ Calif, Berkeley, 64-65; vis prof, Calif Inst Technol, 67-68; managing ed, Soc Indust & Appl Math J Appl Math, 70-75, ed, 84-90. *Mem:* Am Math Soc; fel Inst Elec & Electronics Engrs; Inst Math Statist. *Res:* Stochastic optimization; applications of functional analysis to systems theory; probability theory and functional analysis applied to communication and large scale systems; queueing networks; operations research; analysis and functional analysis. *Mailing Add:* Elec Eng & Comput Sci Univ Mich Elec Eng & Comput Sci Bldg Ann Arbor MI 48109-2122. *Fax:* 313-763-8041; *E-Mail:* fjb@eecs. umich.edu

BEUTLER, LARRY EDWARD, CLINICAL PSYCHOLOGY. *Current Pos:* PROF PSYCHOL, UNIV CALIF, SANTA BARBARA, 90- *Personal Data:* b Logan, Utah, Feb 14, 41; c Jana, Kelly, Ian D & Gail. *Educ:* Utah State Univ, BS, 65, MS, 66; Univ Nebr, PhD, 70; Am Bd Clin Psychol, dipl. *Prof Exp:* Asst prof psychol, Duke Univ, 70-71, Stephen F Austin State Univ, 71-73; assoc prof, Baylor Col Med, 73-79; prof, Univ Ariz, Tucson, 79-90. *Concurrent Pos:* Ed, J Clin Psychol, 96- *Mem:* Fel Am Psychol Asn; fel Int Acad Eclectic Psychother; Soc Psychother Res (pres, 86-88). *Res:* Eclectic psychotherapy; psychotherapy process and outcome. *Mailing Add:* GSE Univ Calif Santa Barbara CA 93106

BEUTNER, EDWARD C, STRUCTURAL GEOLOGY. *Current Pos:* PROF GEOL, FRANKLIN & MARSHALL COL, 70- *Personal Data:* b Tucson, Ariz, May 22, 39. *Educ:* Penn State Univ, PhD(geol), 68. *Prof Exp:* Res structural geol, Shell Oil Co, 68-70. *Mem:* Fel Geol Soc Am. *Mailing Add:* 1331 Deer Lane Lancaster PA 17601

BEUTNER, ERNST HERMAN, MICROBIOLOGY. *Current Pos:* asst prof bact & immunol, 62-68, PROF MICROBIOL & DERMAT, STATE UNIV NY BUFFALO, 68- *Personal Data:* b Berlin, Ger, Aug 27, 23; nat US; m 49; c 3. *Educ:* Univ Pa, PhD, 51, Am Bd Med Microbiol, dipl; Am Bd Med Lab Immunol, dipl. *Honors & Awards:* Rocha Lima Award, 68; Vincenzo Chiarugi Award, 89. *Prof Exp:* Res supvr, Sias Res Labs, Brooks Hosp, 51-55; res assoc, Harvard Sch Dent Med, 55-56. *Concurrent Pos:* Dir diag; pres, Int Serv for Immunol Labs; fel, Philadelphia Col Physicians. *Mem:* Am Acad Dermat; Soc Investigative Dermat; Am Soc Immunol; NY Acad Sci. *Res:* Quantitation of immunofluorescence staining techniques; tissue immunology of pituitary and salivary glands; thyroiditis; systemic lupus erythematosus; myasthenia gravis; pemphigus bullous pemphigold, psoriasis, dermatitis herpetiformis, celiac disease; immunopathology of the skin. *Mailing Add:* 22 Brantwood Rd Buffalo NY 14226

BEVAK, JOSEPH PERRY, PHYSICAL CHEMISTRY. *Current Pos:* From instr to prof, 56-96, from actg head dept to head dept, 58-69, EMER PROF CHEM, SIENA COL, 96- *Personal Data:* b Detroit, Mich, Mar 8, 29. *Educ:* Wayne State Univ, BS, 50; Mass Inst Technol, PhD(chem), 55. *Mem:* Am Chem Soc; Sigma Xi. *Res:* Thermodynamics of solutions. *Mailing Add:* Dept Chem Siena Col 515 Loudon Rd Loudonville NY 12211-1462. *E-Mail:* bevak@siena.edu

BEVAN, DONALD EDWARD, fish biology; deceased, see previous edition for last biography

BEVAN, JOHN ACTON, PHARMACOLOGY. *Current Pos:* prof & chmn, 83-95, PROF, COL MED, UNIV VT, 95- *Personal Data:* b London, Eng, Apr 24, 30; m 56; c 4. *Educ:* Univ London, BSc, 50, MB & BS, 53. *Prof Exp:* Demonstr pharmacol, St Bartholemew's Med Col, 50-52; actg chmn, Dept Pharmacol, Univ Calif, Los Angeles, 65-66, from asst prof to assoc prof, 57-67, prof, 67-83. *Concurrent Pos:* Mem cardiovasc & renal ad hoc study sect, Nat Heart & Lung Inst, 78-; mem exp cardiovasc sci study sect, NIH, 81-84. *Mem:* Am Soc Pharmacol & Exp Therapeut; Am Physiol Soc. *Res:* Pharmacology of the cardiovascular system. *Mailing Add:* Dept Pharmacol Col Med Univ Vt Burlington VT 05405-0068

BEVAN, ROSEMARY D, VASCULAR DEVELOPMENT. *Current Pos:* ASSOC PROF PHARMACOL, COL MED, UNIV VT, 84- *Educ:* Univ London, MBBS, 53. *Res:* Neural control of vasculature. *Mailing Add:* Dept Pharmacol Univ VT Col Med Given Med Bldg Burlington VT 05405-0068

BEVAN, WILLIAM, BEHAVIOR. *Current Pos:* RETIRED. *Personal Data:* b Plains, Pa, May 16, 22; m 45; c 3. *Educ:* Franklin & Marshall Col, AB, 42; Duke Univ, MA, 43, PhD(exp psychol), 48. *Hon Degrees:* ScD, Fla Atlantic Univ, 68, Emory Univ, 74, Franklin & Marshall Col, 79, Univ Md, 81, Kansas State Univ, 87; LLD, Duke Univ, 72; DHL, Southern Ill Univ, 89. *Honors & Awards:* Sandia Lectr, Univ NMex, 81. *Prof Exp:* Asst, Duke Univ, 42-43, res asst, Frangible Bullet Proj, 43-44, instr psychol, 47; from instr to asst prof, Heidelberg Col, 46-48; from asst prof to prof, Emory Univ, 48-59; prof & chmn dept, Kans State Univ, 59-62, dean, Sch Arts & Sci, 62-63, vpres acad affairs, 63-66; vpres & provost, Johns Hopkins Univ, 66-70, prof, 66-74; dir sci & pub affairs, Duke Univ, 74-83, William Preston Few prof psychol, 74-92, chmn dept, 77-78, provost, 79-82; vpres, John D & Catherine T Macarthur Found, 82-92. *Concurrent Pos:* Res psychologist, Equip Acceptability Proj, US Army, 52; Fulbright res scholar & guest prof, Univ Oslo, Norway, 52-53; opers res specialist, Lockheed Aircraft Corp, 55, staff scientist, 56 & 57; consult, Lockheed Aircraft Corp, 55-59, Baylor Univ, 57-62, Emory Univ, 58-59, Midwest Res Inst, 59-61, Menninger Found, 60-66 & Univ Md, 77-; NSF sr fel & fel, Ctr Advan Study Behav Sci, Stanford, Calif, 65-66; mem, Sci Info Coun, Nat Acad Sci, 66-70; exec officer, AAAS, 70-74; publ, Sci, 70-74; assoc ed, Am Psychologist, 76-85; univ lectr, Brown Univ, 84. *Mem:* Inst Med-Nat Acad Sci; Soc Exp Psychologists; Am Psychol Asn (pres-elect, 81, pres, 82); assoc Am Ecol Soc; fel AAAS; Psychonomic Soc; Soc Social Study Sci; Acad Behav Med Res; Sigma Xi; Hist Sci Soc. *Res:* Perception and other cognitive processes; vision and other sensory processes; human engineering and human factors; public policy; experimental psychology. *Mailing Add:* John D & Catherine T MacArthur Found Human Resources 140 S Dearborn St Suite 1100 Chicago IL 60603

BEVANS, ROWLAND S(COTT), CHEMICAL ENGINEERING. *Current Pos:* RETIRED. *Personal Data:* b Elizabeth, NJ, Apr 7, 19; m 50; c 4. *Educ:* Yale Univ, BE, 40; Carnegie Inst Technol, MS, 41. *Hon Degrees:* ScD, Mass Inst Technol,46. *Prof Exp:* Staff mem, Div Indust Coop, Mass Inst Technol, 42-49, indust liaison officer, 49-52; mem res planning staff, Ethyl Corp, 52-54, prod develop staff, 54-56; mgr appl mech, Res & Develop Lab, Am Stardard, Inc, 57-75; sr process engr, Chem-Pro Equip Corp, 75-84. *Concurrent Pos:* Chem engr, Standard Oil Develop Co, NJ, 46. *Mem:* AAAS; Am Chem Soc; Am Inst Chem Engrs; Am Soc Heating, Air Conditioning & Refrig Engrs. *Res:* High output combustion of volatile liquid fuels. *Mailing Add:* Glen Alpine Rd Morristown NJ 07960-6724

BEVC, DIMITRI, computational seismology, reflections seismology, for more information see previous edition

BEVC, VLADISLAV, ELECTROMAGNETICS THEORY, PLASMA PHYSICS. *Current Pos:* PRES, BEVC ENG INC, 73- *Personal Data:* b Ljubljana, Slovenia, Apr 9, 32; US citizen; m 61, Nada Jarosin; c Dimitri & Rayka. *Educ:* Univ Calif, Berkeley, BSc, 57, MSc, 58, PhD(microwave electronics), 61. *Prof Exp:* Nat Acad Sci-Nat Res Coun & Air Force Off Sci Res res fel, Univ Eng Lab & St Catherine's Col, Oxford Univ, 62-63; assoc prof elec eng, Naval Postgrad Sch, 63-66; mem tech staff, Aerospace Corp, 65-69; physicist, Lawrence Livermore Lab, Univ Calif, 69-73. *Concurrent Pos:* Lectr & sr lectr, Univ Col, Univ Exten & Community Serv Div, Univ Southern Calif, 67-70 & San Francisco State Univ, 77-78; fel, Synergy Res Inst, San Roman, Calif, 94- *Mem:* Am Phys Soc; sr mem Inst Elec & Electronics Engrs; Sigma Xi. *Res:* High energy particle beam transport and dynamics, controlled thermonuclear fusion; electromagnetic theory; wave propagation in plasmas; electron optics. *Mailing Add:* Bevc Eng Inc 51 Hardester Ct Danville CA 94526. *Fax:* 510-837-7612; *E-Mail:* ako@alumni.eecs.berkeley.edu, ako@crl.com

BEVELACQUA, JOSEPH JOHN, NUCLEAR THEORY, HEALTH PHYSICS. *Current Pos:* SR TECH RADIOL CONTROLS ADV, US DEPT ENERGY, WA, 96- *Personal Data:* b Waynesburg, Pa, Mar 17, 49; m 71, Terry Sunders; c Anthony, Jeffrey, Megan, Peter, Michael & Karen. *Educ:* Calif State Col, BS, 70; Fla State Univ, MS, 74, PhD, 76; Am Bd Health Physics, cert comprehensive, 85, cert power reactor, 87. *Honors & Awards:* Von Humboldt Fellowship, 76, US DOE Outstanding Performance Award, 82. *Prof Exp:* Teaching asst physics, Univ Maine, Orono, 70-72, res asst, 72; radiol engr, Bettis Atomic Power Lab, 73, sr radiol engr, 76-78; teaching asst, Fla State Univ, 73-74, from res asst to res assoc, 74-76; nuclear physicist, US Dept Energy, 78-83; sr nuclear engr, Three Mile Island, GPU Nuclear Corp, 83-84, mgr emergency preparedness, 84-86, mgr safety RE group, 86-89, radiol controls dir, 89; supt health physics, Point Beach Nuclear Plant, Wis Elec Power Co, 89-95, prod planning mgr, 95-96. *Concurrent Pos:* Consult, Advan Isotope Separation Selection Bd, US Dept Energy, 81-82; mem nuclear utility coord group, KMC, Inc, 84-88; mem, Babcock & Wilcox Owners Group, 84-86; von Humboldt fel, Univ Hamburg, 76-79; Pres chief exec officer, Bevelacqva Resources, 95- *Mem:* Am Phys Soc; Am Nuclear Soc; Health Physics Soc; NY Acad Sci; Am Acad Health Physics; Soc Nuclear Med; Am Bd Health Physics. *Res:* Low energy nuclear theory involving structure and reaction properties in light nuclei; internal and external dosimetry; emergency preparedness; health physics; nuclear reactor safety; author of 65 publications in nuclear physics including physical review letters covering low energy nuclear theory with a focus upon the structure and reaction properties of light nuclei. *Mailing Add:* 343 Adair Dr Richland WA 99352-8563

BEVELANDER, GERRIT, HISTOLOGY, ANATOMY. *Current Pos:* CONSULT, MONTEREY ABALONE FARMS, 73- *Personal Data:* b West Sayville, NY, Apr 6, 05; m 35; c 1. *Educ:* Hope Col, AB, 26; Univ Mich, AM, 28; Johns Hopkins Univ, PhD(zool), 32. *Honors & Awards:* Res Basic Biomineralization Award, Int Asn Dent Res, 88. *Prof Exp:* Assoc, US Bur Fisheries, 28-29; instr biol, Union Univ, NY, 31-33; res assoc, Col Dent, NY Univ, 33-34, from instr to assoc prof anat, Univ, 34-47, prof histol, 47-62; prof, 62-72, emer prof histol, Univ Tex Dent Br Houston, 72- *Concurrent Pos:* Consult, USPHS, 57-61 & 63-67; mem staff, Marine Biol Lab, Woods Hole & Bermuda Biol Sta. *Mem:* Am Soc Zoologists; Soc Exp Biol & Med; Am Asn Anatomists; fel NY Acad Sci; Int Asn Dent Res (pres). *Res:* Comparative histology of fishes; experimental approach to problems in calcification; histochemistry; integumentary derivatives; dynamic aspects of calcification; marine biology; electron microscope studies relating to mineralization. *Mailing Add:* PO Box 2656 Carmel CA 93921

BEVER, CHRISTOPHER THEODORE, PSYCHIATRY. *Current Pos:* mem bd dirs, 74-77, MEM FAC, WASHINGTON SCH PSYCHIAT, 56-, CHMN PSYCHOTHER PRECEPTORSHIP & SEM PROG, 66- *Personal Data:* b Munich, Ger, Mar 12, 19; nat US; m 44; c 4. *Educ:* Harvard Univ, BA, 40, MD, 43. *Prof Exp:* Intern, Hartford Hosp, Conn, 44; resident psychiat, St Elizabeths Hosp, Washington, DC, 47-48, psychiatrist, 48-50; psychiatrist, Washington Inst Ment Hyg, 50-51; dir, Montgomery Co Ment Hyg Clin, 51-54; assoc prof psychiat, Sch Med, Univ NC, 54-56. *Concurrent Pos:* Clin instr, Sch Med, Georgetown Univ, 49-51; instr, Washington Psychoanalysis Inst, 54-61, teaching analyst, 61-; dir psychiat outpatient ctr, NC Mem Hosp, 54-56; consult, Family Serv Agency, 56-58, St Elizabeths Hosp, Washington, DC, 59-61 & 73-74 & Walter Reed Army Hosp, 71-75; assoc psychiat, Med Sch, George Washington Univ, 57-60, from asst clin prof to assoc clin prof, 60-74, clin prof, 74-; pres, DC Inst Ment Hyg, 66-68, consult, 66-72; pres, Community Psychiat Clin, 73-75; trustee, William Alanson White Psychiat Found, 75- *Mem:* AMA; fel Am Psychiat Asn; Am Psychoanalysis Asn; Am Orthopsychiat Asn; fel Acad Psychoanalysis. *Res:* Continuing education in psychotherapy. *Mailing Add:* 6812 Connecticut Ave Chevy Chase MD 20815-4938

BEVER, JAMES EDWARD, GEOLOGY. *Current Pos:* from asst prof to prof, 54-85, EMER PROF GEOL, MIAMI UNIV, 85- *Personal Data:* b Bellingham, Wash, July 7, 20; m 46, Anne Ruder; c Ernst J. *Educ:* Wash State Univ, BS, 42; Univ Mich, MS, 49, PhD(mineral), 54. *Prof Exp:* Asst purchasing agent, Traub Mfg Co, 47-48; instr mineral, Univ Mich, 50-54, instr conserv & acad counr, 52-54. *Concurrent Pos:* Consult, Oliver Mining Co, 53-54, Encyclop Americana, 56-57, Nat Res Coun, 57-58 & Gen Elec Co, 65-; vpres & dir, Timberline Minerals, Inc, 71-76. *Mem:* AAAS; Geol Soc Am; Mineral Soc Am; Mineral Asn Can. *Res:* Field geology; petrography and petrology; mineral resources; gems. *Mailing Add:* Dept Geol Miami Univ Oxford OH 45056

BEVER, MICHAEL B(ERLINER), materials policy, resource management; deceased, see previous edition for last biography

BEVERIDGE, DAVID L, THEORETICAL CHEMISTRY, MOLECULAR BIOPHYSICS. *Current Pos:* PROF CHEM, WESLEYAN UNIV, 86-, UNIV PROF NATURAL SCI & MATH, 91-, DEAN, 93- *Personal Data:* b Coshocton, Ohio, Jan 29, 38; m 64, Phyllis Cook; c Laura, Andrew & David. *Educ:* Col Wooster, BA, 59; Univ Cincinnati, PhD(phys chem), 65. *Prof Exp:* Asst operating chemist, Monsanto Res Corp, Ohio, 60-62; USPHS fel, Ctr Appl Wave Mech, Paris, 65-66 & Carnegie-Mellon Univ, 66-68; asst prof pharmacol, Mt Sinai Sch Med, 68-70; from assoc prof to prof chem, Hunter Col, 74-86, Thomas Hunter distinguished prof, 84-86. *Concurrent Pos:* NIH res career develop award, 72-77; mem, BBCA Study Sect, NIH, 78-82 & 96-; merit award, NIH, 89- *Mem:* AAAS; Am Chem Soc; Biophys Soc. *Res:* Theoretical chemistry and computational molecular biophysics; statistical thermodynamics and computer simulation of biological molecules; hydration and ion atmosphere of nucleic acids; organization of water in nucleic acid hydrates; solvent effects on conformational stability; dynamical structure of proteins and DNA. *Mailing Add:* Dept Chem Wesleyan Univ Hall-Atwater & Shanklin Labs Middletown CT 06459-0280. *E-Mail:* dbeveridge@wesleyan.edu

BEVERIDGE, JAMES MACDONALD RICHARDSON, BIOCHEMISTRY. *Current Pos:* RETIRED. *Personal Data:* b Dunfermline, Scotland, Aug 17, 12; nat Can; m 40; c 7. *Educ:* Acadia Univ, BSc, 37; Univ Toronto, PhD(biochem), 40; Univ Western Ont, MD, 50. *Hon Degrees:* DSc, Acadia Univ, 62; LLD, Mt Allison Univ, 66 & Queen's Univ, 78. *Prof Exp:* Asst, Dept Med Res, Banting Inst, 40; assoc biochemist, Pac Fisheries Exp Sta, 44-46; lectr path chem, Univ Western Ont, 46-50; Craine prof biochem & head dept, Queen's Univ, Ont, 50-64, dean sch grad studies, 60-64; pres, Acadia Univ, 64 78. *Concurrent Pos:* Officer, Order Can, 77. *Mem:* Royal Soc Can. *Res:* Analysis of protein hydrolysates; choline and fatty liver problem; dietary liver necrosis and lipid and bile acid metabolism; effect of dietary changes on plasma cholesterol levels in human subjects using homogenized rations. *Mailing Add:* RR-1 Canning NS B0P 1H0 Can

BEVERIDGE, TERRANCE JAMES, MICROBIAL ULTRASTRUCTURE, MICROBIAL BIOGEOCHEMISTRY & FINE-GRAINED SOIL DEVELOPMENT. *Current Pos:* asst prof, 78-83, assoc prof, 83-86, PROF MICROBIOL, UNIV GUELPH, 86- *Personal Data:* b Toronto, Ont, Apr 29, 45; m 70, Janice E Barnett; c Braden C & J Bree. *Educ:* Univ Toronto, BSc, 68, dipl bact, 69, MSc, 70; Univ Western Ont, PhD, 74. *Honors & Awards:* Steacie Award for Can Outstanding Young Scientist, 84; Can Soc Microbiol Award, 94. *Concurrent Pos:* Dir, Guelph Region, Nat Sci Eng Res Coun, 81-, Life Sci, Acad III, Royal Soc Can, 92-95; vis prof, Zentrum fur Ultrastrukturforschung, Vienna, 87-, Biozentrum, Switz, 87-; ed, J Bact, 88-96; adj prof, Dept Geol, Univ Western Ont, 89-; Killam Res Fel, 95-97. *Mem:* Can Soc Microbiol; Am Soc Microbiol; fel Royal Soc Can; Soc Gen Microbiol; Royal Soc Can; fel Am Acad Microbiol; fel Can Inst Advan Res; Sigma Xi. *Res:* Molecular ordering of bacterial surfaces so that an understanding of their interaction with the environment can be obtained; electron microscopy, atomic force microscopy and scanning tunneling microscopy. *Mailing Add:* Col Biol Sci Dept Microbiol Univ Guelph Guelph ON N1G 2W1 Can. *Fax:* 519-837-1802; *E-Mail:* tjb@uoguelph.ca

BEVERLEY-BURTON, MARY, zoology, for more information see previous edition

BEVERLY, ROBERT EDWARD, III, GAS LASER DEVELOPMENT. *Current Pos:* SR SCIENTIST, R E BEVERLY III & ASSOCS, 78- *Personal Data:* b Atlanta, Ga, Mar 13, 48. *Educ:* Ga Inst Technol, BS, 69; Univ Cincinnati, PhD(nuc eng), 73. *Prof Exp:* Prin physicist, Phys Sci Sect, Battelle Columbus Labs, 73-78. *Mem:* Asn Comput Mach. *Res:* Development and applications of high-energy and high-power lasers including the aspects of gas-discharge physics; kinetic modeling, optics design, laser propagation and laser-target interactions; laser interaction phenomena. *Mailing Add:* 854 Pipestone Dr Worthington OH 43235-1752. *E-Mail:* reb3@grdata.com

BEVERUNG, WARREN NEIL, JR, MEDICINAL CHEMISTRY, CHEMICAL SEPARATIONS. *Current Pos:* tech rep org synthesis div, 77-80, SE REGIONAL MGR, WATERS ASSOCS, 80- *Personal Data:* b New Orleans, La, Sept 3, 41; m 64; c 2. *Educ:* La State Univ, New Orleans, BS, 64, PhD(org chem), 68. *Prof Exp:* Asst org chem, La State Univ, New Orleans, 64-68; instr & fel, Univ Ill, Chicago Circle, 68-69; sr res chemist, Med Chem Div, Bristol Labs, 69-77. *Mem:* Am Chem Soc. *Res:* Total synthesis of 9-azasteroids; general photochemical processes; synthesis of new biologically active heterocyclic systems. *Mailing Add:* 104 Amesbury Lane Cary NC 27511-5505

BEVIER, MARY LOU, RADIOGENIC ISOTOPIC STUDIES, URANIUM-LEAD GEOCHRONOLOGY. *Current Pos:* postdoctoral geochronology, 85-87, CONTRACT RES GEOLOGIST RADIOGENIC ISOTOPES & GEOCHRONOLOGY, GEOL SURV CAN, 87- *Personal Data:* b Chicago, Ill, Mar 3, 53; m 85. *Educ:* Univ Calif Santa Cruz, BS, 75; Univ BC, MSc, 78; Univ Calif Santa Barbara, PhD(geol sci), 82. *Prof Exp:* Res asst geol earth sci, Los Alamos Nat Lab, 77 & 78; teaching assoc geol, Univ Calif, Santa Barbara, 78-82; asst prof geol, Western State Col, Colo, 82-85. *Concurrent Pos:* Vis prof, Dept Geol Sci, Univ Ore, 84. *Mem:* Geol Soc Am; fel Geol Asn Can; Am Geophys Union; Sigma Xi. *Res:* Radiogenic isotope geology; uranium-lead geochronology; lead-neodymium-strontium tracer studies. *Mailing Add:* Dept Earth/Geo Sci Univ BC 6339 Stores Rd Vancouver BC V6T 1Z4 Can

BEVILL, RICHARD F, JR, VETERINARY PHARMACOLOGY. *Current Pos:* Asst prof, 72-79, PROF PHARMACOL, COL VET MED, UNIV ILL, URBANA, 79- *Personal Data:* b Christopher, Ill, May 18, 34; m 53; c 2. *Educ:* Univ Ill, DVM, 64, PhD(pharmacol), 72. *Mem:* Am Soc Pharmacol & Exp Therapeut; Am Vet Med Asn. *Res:* Pharmacokinetics of antibacterial drugs following their administration to domestic animals; relationships between plasma, urine and tissue residues are stressed. *Mailing Add:* Rte 2 Box 26A Oakland IL 61943-9408

BEVILL, VINCENT (DARELL), MECHANICAL ENGINEERING. *Current Pos:* RETIRED. *Personal Data:* b San Diego, Calif, Mar 31, 28; m 48; c 3. *Educ:* Fresno State Col, BS, 52; Univ Calif, MSc, 65. *Prof Exp:* Chief engr, Griffith-Dyer Co, 52-58; from assoc prof to prof mech eng, Fresno State Col, 64-80. *Concurrent Pos:* Consult mech engr, 58- *Mem:* Nat Soc Prof Engrs; Solar Energy Soc; Am Soc Heat, Refrig & Air-Conditioning Eng. *Res:* Solar energy, environmental control for poultry houses and computer programs for total energy and air conditioning load calculations. *Mailing Add:* 7265 N Doolittle Dr Fresno CA 93722

BEVIN, A GRISWOLD, PLASTIC SURGERY, RECONSTRUCTIVE SURGERY. *Current Pos:* From asst prof to assoc prof plastic surg, 69-79, chief, Div Plastic & Reconstruct Surg, 73-79, PROF PLASTIC SURG, SCH MED, UNIV NC, CHAPEL HILL, 79- *Personal Data:* b New Haven, Conn, Dec 7, 35; m 58; c 5. *Educ:* Wesleyan Univ, AB, 56; Yale Univ, MD, 60; Am Bd Surg, dipl, 67; Am Bd Plastic Surg, dipl, 71. *Prof Exp:* Instr surg, Sch Med, Yale Univ, 66-68. *Concurrent Pos:* Consult, Watts Hosp, Durham, NC, 69-78. *Mem:* Am Asn Univ Prof; Am Col Surgeons; Am Asn Surg Trauma; Am Soc Surg Hand; Am Soc Plastic & Reconstruct Surgeons. *Res:* Wound healing; surgery of the hand; maxillofacial trauma. *Mailing Add:* Div Plastic & Reconstruct Surg Univ NC Med Sch 208H CB No 7195 Chapel Hill NC 27599-7195

BEVIS, HERBERT A(NDERSON), ENVIRONMENTAL ENGINEERING, RADIOLOGICAL HEALTH. *Current Pos:* teaching assoc environ eng, Univ Fla, 61-63, assoc prof, 64-74, vchmn dept, 74-77, asst dean, Col Eng, 78-79, assoc dean, Col Eng, 81-92, PROF ENVIRON ENG, UNIV FLA, 74-, EMER PROF & ASSOC CHMN, DEPT CIVIL ENG. *Personal Data:* b Perry, Fla, Sept 28, 29; m 52, Cotella Ingle; c John H & Gerald C. *Educ:* Univ Fla, BCE, 51, MSE, 52, PhD(sanit eng), 63; US Naval Postgrad Sch, MS, 58. *Prof Exp:* Sanit engr, USPHS, NY, 52-53, DC, 53-54, sanit engr radiol health prog, Wash, 54-55, sanit engr, R A Taft Sanit Eng Ctr, Ohio, 55-56; chief ionizing radiation prog, Tex State Dept Health, 58-61. *Mem:* Nat Soc Prof Engrs; Am Soc Civil Engrs; Am Soc Eng Educ; Asn Environ Eng Profs; Health Physics Soc; Am Acad Environ Engrs. *Res:* Radiological health; environmental radiation surveillance; application of radiological techniques in environmental engineering. *Mailing Add:* 3414 NW Seventh Pl Gainesville FL 32607

BEVIS, JEAN HARWELL, ALGEBRA, SYSTEMS THEORY. *Current Pos:* assoc prof, 69-73, PROF MATH, GA STATE UNIV, 73- *Personal Data:* b Miami, Fla, Dec 6, 39; m 60; c 2. *Educ:* Univ Fla, BS, 61, MS, 62, PhD(math), 65. *Prof Exp:* Asst prof math, Va Polytech Inst, 65-69. *Mem:* Am Math Soc; Math Asn Am. *Res:* Lattices; adjacency matrices; graphs; algebraic representation of properties of graphs. *Mailing Add:* Dept Math & Comput Sci Ga State Univ Atlanta GA 30303-3038

BEVK, JOZE, MICRO-COMPOSITE MATERIALS, SOLID STATE PHYSICS. *Current Pos:* MEM TECH STAFF, BELL LABS, MURRAY HILL, NJ, 81- *Personal Data:* b Ljubljana, Yugoslavia, April 1, 43; US citizen; m 77; c 1. *Educ:* Univ Ljubljana, Yugoslavia, BS, 65; Univ Wis-Madison, MS, 68, PhD(metall eng), 70. *Prof Exp:* Res fel metal physics, Mellon Inst Sci, Carnegie-Mellon Univ, Pittsburgh, 70-72, asst prof, 72-73; from asst prof to assoc prof appld physics, Harvard Univ, 73-80. *Concurrent Pos:* Prin Investgr, Prep & Characterization Improv Superconducting Mats, NSF, 74-80; vis prof appl physics, Stanford Univ, 80; assoc ed, Mats Letters, 81- *Mem:* Am Physi Soc; Am Soc Metals; Am Inst Mining, Metall & Petrol Engrs; Mat Res Soc. *Res:* Superconductivity; composite materials; effect of microstructure on physical properties of materials; electronic structure and stability of metals and alloys; artificially layered materials; metallic glasses; physical properties of micro-composite materials. *Mailing Add:* AT&T Bell Labs 600 Mountain Ave Murray Hill NJ 07974

BEVOLO, ALBERT JOSEPH, SOLID STATE PHYSICS. *Current Pos:* presidential intern, US AEC, 72-73, asst physicist, Ames Lab, Energy Resource & Develop Admin, 73-88, SR PHYSICIST, AMES LAB, USDOE, 88- *Personal Data:* b St Louis, Mo, Oct 20, 40; m 66; c 2. *Educ:* St Louis Univ, BS, 62; MS, 64, PhD(physics), 70. *Prof Exp:* Fel physics, St Louis Univ, 70-72. *Mem:* Am Phys Soc. *Res:* Low temperature specific heat of tungsten bronzes; IV-VI semicomputers and soft mode superconductors; electrochemical energy conversion. *Mailing Add:* Ames Lab Iowa State Univ 125 Spedding Hall Ames IA 50011

BEWLEY, JOHN DEREK, SEED BIOLOGY, DESICCATION-TOLERANCE. *Current Pos:* chmn, Dept Bot, 85-90, PROF BOT, UNIV GUELPH, 85- *Personal Data:* b Preston, Eng, Dec 11, 43; m 66, Christine Kite; c Alexander & Janette. *Educ:* Queen Elizabeth Col, Univ London, BSc, 65, PhD(plant physiol), 68, DSc, 83. *Honors & Awards:* C D Nelson Award, Can Soc Plant Physiol, 78, Gold Metal, 92. *Prof Exp:* Fel plant biochem, Inst Cancer Res, 68-70; from asst prof to prof biol, Univ Calgary, 70-85. *Concurrent Pos:* E W R Steacie Mem fel, Nat Sci & Eng Res Coun, Can, 79-81; vis prof, McGill Univ, 81; mem, Can Strategic Grants Panel Environ & Toxicol, Nat Sci & Eng Res Coun, 81-82, mem & chmn, Plant Biol Grants Selection Panel, 86-90; mem, Seed Storage Adv Panel, Int Bd Genetic Resources, 81-87; rapporteur & convener, Plant Biol Div, Sci Acad, Royal Soc Can, 84-87. *Mem:* Am Soc Plant Physiol; Can Soc Plant Physiol (secy, 83-85, vpres, 87-88, pres, 88-89); fel Royal Soc Can. *Res:* Dormancy and survival mechanisms in plants, molecular, biochemical and physiological aspects; desiccation tolerance in plants, mosses and ferns; weed root biology; development, germination and growth physiology of seeds. *Mailing Add:* Dept Bot Univ Guelph Guelph ON N1G 2W1 Can. *Fax:* 519-767-1991; *E-Mail:* dbewley@uoguelph.ca

BEWTRA, JATINDER KUMAR, ENVIRONMENTAL & BIOCHEMICAL ENGINEERING. *Current Pos:* PROF CIVIL & ENVIRON ENG, UNIV WINDSOR, 68- *Personal Data:* b Nawabshah, India, May 1, 35; m 63, Subash; c Naveen & Monika. *Educ:* Univ Roorkee, BE, 55; Univ Iowa, MS, 60, PhD(sanit eng), 62. *Honors & Awards:* Keefer Medal. *Prof Exp:* Asst engr, Local Self Govt Eng Dept, India, 55-58; scientist in charge, Nat Environ Eng Res Inst, Delhi, India, 62-66; vis assoc prof sanit eng, Shiraz Univ, Iran, 66-68. *Concurrent Pos:* Consult engr. *Mem:* Am Soc Civil Engrs; Am Water Works Asn; Water Environ Fedn; Int Asn Water Qual; Can Soc Civil Eng. *Res:* Physical, chemical and biological aspects of water purification and waste-water treatment; hazardous waste disposal; contaminated sediment-soil remediation. *Mailing Add:* Dept Civil & Environ Eng Univ Windsor Windsor ON N9B 3P4 Can. *Fax:* 519-971-3686; *E-Mail:* bewtra@server.uwindsor.ca

BEX, FREDERICK JAMES, BONE METABOLISM, REPRODUCTIVE PHYSIOLOGY. *Current Pos:* group leader, 77-85, mgr Endocrinol Sect, 85-88, ASSOC DIR PHARM, WYETH LABS, INC, 88- *Personal Data:* b Syracuse, NY, Nov 1, 47; m 72; c 3. *Educ:* Cornell Univ, BA, 69; Univ Conn, MS, 74, PhD(endocrinol), 76. *Prof Exp:* Res asst, Univ Conn, 71-75; res assoc, Worcester Found Exp Biol, 75-77. *Mem:* Endocrine Soc; Soc Study Reprod; Am Soc Andrology; Am Soc Bone Mineral Res. *Res:* Neuroendocrinology of mammalian reproduction, specifically the development of hypothalamic releasing hormone derived and gonadal peptides as fertility regulating agents and as therapy for reproductive pathologies; contraceptive research and general endocrine evaluation of drugs; bone metabolism and calciotropic hormone regulation. *Mailing Add:* Wyeth-Ayerst Res PO Box 8299 Philadelphia PA 19101. *Fax:* 610-489-9839; *E-Mail:* bexf@war.wyeth.com

BEYAD, MOHAMMED HOSSAIN, CHEMISTRY. *Current Pos:* RES CHEMIST, MOBIL CHEM CO, 80-; ALBRIGHT & WILSON, INC. *Personal Data:* b Iran, Nov 28, 50; m 76. *Educ:* Indian Inst Technol, BS, 71, MS, 73; Kans State Univ, PhD(chem), 78. *Prof Exp:* Asst prof chem, Kans State Univ, 79-80. *Concurrent Pos:* Consult, DOM Assocs Int, 79- *Mem:* Am Chem Soc. *Res:* Analytical methods to support programs in polymer res and develop industrial chemicals and chemical coatings; specialize in areas of spectroscopy: fourier transform nuclear magnetic resonance, fourier transform infrared and gas chromatography-mass spectrometry. *Mailing Add:* 12008 Reeds Bluff Lane Midlothian VA 23113

BEYEA, JAN EDGAR, NUCLEAR ACCIDENT ASSESSMENT. *Current Pos:* CHIEF SCIENTIST, CONSULT IN PUB INTEREST, 96- *Personal Data:* b Englewood, NJ, Dec 16, 39; div; c 2. *Educ:* Amherst Col, BA, 62; Columbia Univ, PhD(physics), 70. *Prof Exp:* Res assoc physics, Columbia Univ, 68-70; asst prof physics, Holy Cross Col, 70-76; mem res staff, Ctr Energy & Environ Studies, Princeton Univ, 76-80; sr staff scientist, Nat

Audubon Soc, 80-91, chief scientist & vpres, 92-95. *Concurrent Pos:* Consult, US Coun Environ Qual, 80, Mass Atty Gen, 88 & Nat Res Coun, 89; adv, Off Technol Assessment, 84-88; mem, Comn Alternative Energy Res & Develop Strategies, Nat Res Coun, 90-91; mem, Task Force Econ Modeling, Secy Energy, 91; bd mem, Recycling Adv Coun, Environ Protection Agency, 94-96. *Mem:* Am Phys Soc; AAAS; Health Physics Soc. *Res:* Risk assessment of energy sources; solid waste management; United States energy policy. *Mailing Add:* 53 Clinton St Lambertville NJ 08530

BEYENBACH, KLAUS WERNER, PHYSIOLOGY. *Current Pos:* from asst prof to assoc prof, 78-88, PROF PHYSIOL, CORNELL UNIV, 88- *Personal Data:* b Mainz, WGer, Mar 19, 43; US citizen; m 79, Christa-Maria Kuhn; c Thomas. *Educ:* St Mary's Univ, Tex, BA, 68; Southwest Tex State Univ, MA, 70; Wash State Univ, PhD(physiol), 74. *Honors & Awards:* Alexander Von-Humboldt Preis, 91. *Prof Exp:* Teaching asst, Southwest Tex State Univ, 68-70; NIH trainee, Wash State Univ, 70-74; NIH res fel, Col Med, Univ Ariz, 75-78. *Concurrent Pos:* Nat Kidney Found fel, Dept Physiol, Col Med, Univ Ariz, 74-75; Fogarty sr int fel, 85; vis res prof, Max Planck Inst Molecular Physiol, Dortmund, Ger, 91-92; vpres, Alexander von Humboldt Asn Am, 94-97, pres, 97. *Mem:* Am Soc Physiologists; Am Soc Nephrology; Biophys Soc; Am Soc Zoologists; AAAS; Soc Exp Biol. *Res:* Renal electrolyte transport and electrophysiology; epithelial transport mechanism; comparative epithelial transport physiology. *Mailing Add:* Sect Physiol VRT G26 Cornell Univ Ithaca NY 14853. *Fax:* 607-253-3851; *E-Mail:* kwb1@cornell.edu

BEYER, ANN L, RNA PROCESSING. *Current Pos:* Asst Prof,82-88, ASSOC PROF DEPT MICROBIOL, UNIV VA, 88- *Personal Data:* b Louisville, Ky, Feb 12, 51; m; c 2. *Educ:* Ctr ColKy, BS, 73; Vanderbilt Univ, PhD(molecular biol), 77. *Mem:* Am Soc Cell Biol; Sigma Xi; Am Soc Microbiol. *Res:* Ultrastructural analysis of RNA splicing and ribonucleo protein formation. *Mailing Add:* Dept Microbiol Univ Va Sch Med HSC Box 441 Charlottesville VA 22908

BEYER, ARTHUR FREDERICK, PALEOBOTANY. *Current Pos:* assoc prof, Midwestern State Univ, 50, chmn, Dept Biol, 60-81, prof, 51-92, EMER PROF BOT, MIDWESTERN STATE UNIV, 92- *Personal Data:* b Toledo, Ohio; m 43, Ruth Long; c Bradley A. *Educ:* Ohio Univ, BSc, 43; Ohio State Univ, MSc, 45; Univ Cincinnati, PhD(bot), 50. *Prof Exp:* Instr bot, Western Reserve Univ, 47-50. *Concurrent Pos:* Bd mem, Tex Syst Natural Labs. *Mem:* Bot Soc Am; Sigma Xi. *Res:* Tamarix gallica morphology; ecology; paleoxylotomy. *Mailing Add:* 3208 Milby Ave Wichita Falls TX 76308

BEYER, CARL FREDRICK, CELL BIOLOGY, NEUROBIOLOGY. *Current Pos:* SR RES SCIENTIST, MED RES DIV, AM CYANAMID CO, 85- *Personal Data:* b Louisville, Ky, July 22, 47; m 80; c 1. *Educ:* Bellarmine Col, BA, 69; Rockefeller Univ, PhD(biochem), 74. *Prof Exp:* USPHS postdoctoral fel cell biol & immunol, Rockefeller Univ, 74-77, asst prof, 77-85. *Concurrent Pos:* Vis fel, Int Inst Cellular & Molecular Path, Brussels, Belg, 78-79. *Mem:* AAAS; Am Chem Soc; Am Soc Cell Biol; NY Acad Sci; Sigma Xi. *Res:* New approaches to anti-cancer therapy, especially monoclonal antibody-directed drug delivery. *Mailing Add:* Wyeth-Ayerst Res 200/4601 Pearl River NY 10965

BEYER, EDGAR HERMAN, PLANT BREEDING, PLANT GENETICS. *Current Pos:* PROF CROP SCI, CALIF POLYTECH STATE UNIV, SAN LUIS OBISPO, 81- *Personal Data:* b Melrose Park, Ill, Apr 27, 31; m 54, Carol Lambeth; c Cynthia, Jeanne & Reid. *Educ:* Univ Ill, BS, 58; Purdue Univ, MS, 62, PhD(plant breeding & genetics), 64. *Prof Exp:* Asst prof forage breeding, Univ Md, College Park, 63-66; res dir, Farm Seed Res Corp, 66-74; veg & flower seed prod mgr, Ferry-Morse Seed Co, 74-80; res dir, Growers Seed Asn, Lubbock, Tex, 80-81. *Mem:* Am Soc Agron; Crop Sci Soc Am; Sigma Xi; Nat Asn Col Teachers Agr. *Res:* Testing performance of forage crop varieties; combining ability studies with alfalfa single crosses; improvement of Trifolium pratense by interspecific hybridization; alfalfa breeding and development; cauliflower improvement through selection. *Mailing Add:* Crop Sci Dept Calif Polytech State Univ San Luis Obispo CA 93407. *Fax:* 805-756-6504

BEYER, ELMO MONROE, JR, PLANT BIOCHEMISTRY, CHEMISTRY. *Current Pos:* Res biologist, Ctr Res Dept, E I du Pont de Nemours & Co, Inc, 69-74, res supvr, 74-79, res mgr, Agr Prod Dept, 79-88, DIR DISCOVERY RES, AGR PROD DEPT, E I DU PONT DE NEMOURS & CO, INC, 88- *Personal Data:* b Corpus Christi, Tex, Mar 22, 41; m 64; c 2. *Educ:* Tex Technol Col, BS, 63; Tex A&M Univ, PhD(plant physiol), 69. *Mem:* Am Soc Plant Physiologists; Plant Growth Regulator Soc; Coun Agr Sci & Technol. *Res:* Phytohormones, especially mechanism of ethylene action; effect of ethylene on translocation; plant and cell biology; plant growth regulators, utility and mechanism of action; herbicides; insecticides and fungicides; agrichemicals. *Mailing Add:* 4005 Valley Green RD Wilmington DE 19807

BEYER, GEORGE LEIDY, POLYMER CHEMISTRY. *Current Pos:* RETIRED. *Personal Data:* b Philadelphia, Pa, Jan 12, 19; m 46, Gertrude Thannhauser; c Margaret, Joe & Lance. *Educ:* Juniata Col, BS, 41; Rutgers Univ, PhD(anal chem), 45. *Prof Exp:* Lab asst, Rutgers Univ, 41-43, instr chem, 43-44; phys chemist, 45-55, res assoc res labs, Eastman Kodak Co, 55-83. *Mem:* Am Chem Soc. *Res:* Polymer molecular characterization; light-scattering; exclusion chromatography. *Mailing Add:* 674 Lake Rd Webster NY 14580

BEYER, GERHARD H(AROLD), chemical engineering; deceased, see previous edition for last biography

BEYER, JAMES B, ELECTRICAL ENGINEERING. *Current Pos:* From asst prof to assoc prof, 61-69, PROF ELEC ENG, UNIV WIS-MADISON, 69-, ASSOC CHMN DEPT, 78- *Personal Data:* b Horicon, Wis, July 7, 31; m 55; c 4. *Educ:* Univ Wis, BS, 57, MS, 59, PhD(elec eng), 61. *Concurrent Pos:* Vis prof, Tech Univ Braunschweig, 68-69. *Mem:* Inst Elec & Electronics Engrs; Sigma Xi. *Res:* Microwaves, especially interaction of microwaves with plasmas and semiconductors. *Mailing Add:* 6213 Countryside Lane Madison WI 53705-1025

BEYER, KARL HENRY, JR, clinical pharmacology; deceased, see previous edition for last biography

BEYER, LOUIS MARTIN, NUCLEAR PHYSICS. *Current Pos:* SPARTA INC, HUNTSVILLE. *Personal Data:* b Paducah, Ky, Nov 7, 39; m 59; c 2. *Educ:* Murray State Univ, BS, 62; Mich State Univ, MS, 63, PhD(nuclear physics), 67. *Prof Exp:* From asst prof to assoc prof, 67-75, prof physics, Murry State Col, 75- *Concurrent Pos:* Vis staff mem, Los Alamos Sci Lab, 77- *Mem:* Am Asn Physics Teachers. *Res:* Low energy nuclear structure by methods of beta and gamma ray spectroscopy; atomic structure and lifetime by beam-foil spectroscopic means; x-ray produced by heavy charged particle reactions; two-dimensional image processing; small computer applications in education. *Mailing Add:* Dept Physics & Astron Murray State Univ One Murray St Murray KY 42071-3310

BEYER, ROBERT EDWARD, BIOCHEMISTRY. *Current Pos:* from assoc prof to prof zool, 65-76, PROF BIOL SCI, UNIV MICH, ANN ARBOR, 76- *Personal Data:* b Englewood, NJ, Feb 20, 28; div; c 3. *Educ:* Univ Conn, AB, 50, MSc, 52; Brown Univ, PhD(biol), 54. *Prof Exp:* Asst biol, Brown Univ, 51-53; USPHS fel, Wenner-Gren Inst, Stockholm, 54-56; instr physiol, Sch Med, Tufts Univ, 56-58, asst prof, 58-62; asst prof enzyme chem, Enzyme Inst, Univ Wis-Madison, 62-65. *Concurrent Pos:* USPHS sr res fel, Sch Med, Tufts Univ, 58-59, vis prof biochem, 75-76, NIH Fogarty sr fel, Univ Stockholm, 85-86; NIH res career develop award, Tufts Univ, 59-62 & Univ Wis, 62-65. *Mem:* AAAS; Am Soc Biol Chemists; Biophys Soc; Geront Soc Am. *Res:* Hormonal control of metabolic systems; biochemistry of aging; anticancer enzymes and loenzyme Q function. *Mailing Add:* 1615 Traver Rd Ann Arbor MI 48105-1737

BEYER, ROBERT THOMAS, ACOUSTICS. *Current Pos:* from instr to assoc prof, Brown Univ, 45-58, exec officer, 66-68, 81-85, chmn dept, 58-74, prof, 58-85, EMER PROF PHYSICS, BROWN UNIV, 85- *Personal Data:* b Harrisburg, Pa, Jan 27, 20; m 44, Ellen Fletcher; c Catherine, Margaret, Richard & Mary. *Educ:* Hofstra Univ, AB, 42; Cornell Univ, PhD, 45. *Hon Degrees:* DSc, Hofstra Univ, 85. *Honors & Awards:* Gold Medal, Acoust Soc Am, 84. *Prof Exp:* Asst physics, Cornell Univ, 42-45. *Concurrent Pos:* Advan Educ Fund fel, Univ Calif, Los Angeles, 53-54; consult Russian trans, Am Inst Physics, 55-, Raytheon, 61-71 & Off Naval Res, 74-75; mem, Int Comn Acoust, 75-78, chmn, 78-84; ed, Book Series, Modern Acoust & Signal Processing. *Mem:* Fel Am Phys Soc; fel Acoust Soc Am (vpres, 61-62, pres, 68-69); fel Inst Elec & Electronics Engrs; fel AAAS; Am Asn Physics Teachers. *Res:* Underwater sound; acoustic relaxation times; ultrasonic absorption in liquids and solids; nonlinear acoustics; liquid state; physics in the Soviet Union. *Mailing Add:* Dept Physics Brown Univ Box 1843 Providence RI 02912. *Fax:* 401-863-2024

BEYER, TERRY, COMPUTER SCIENCE. *Current Pos:* MEM TECH STAFF, MENTOR GRAPHICS CORP, 89- *Personal Data:* b Van Nuys, Calif, Nov 26, 39; div. *Educ:* Univ Ore, BA, 62, MA, 64; Mass Inst Technol, PhD(math), 69. *Prof Exp:* Mem tech staff, Bell Tel Labs, 64-65; asst prof comput sci, Univ Ore, 69-74 & 80-83, sr systs programmer, 74-80; software engr, Methus-Computervision, 83-86; prin engr, Rosetta Technols, 86-89. *Concurrent Pos:* Independent software contractor; adj asst prof fine arts, Univ Ore, 82-83. *Res:* Computer science. *Mailing Add:* 7930 SE 30th Ave Portland OR 97202. *E-Mail:* terry_beyer@mentorg.com

BEYER, W NELSON, ENVIRONMENTAL TOXICOLOGY, SOIL ORGANISMS. *Current Pos:* RES ZOOLOGIST, PATUXENT WILDLIFE RES CTR, 77- *Personal Data:* b New York, NY, Jan 14, 50; m 72; c 2. *Educ:* Columbia Univ, BA, 71; Cornell Univ, PhD(ecol), 75. *Mem:* Soc Environ Toxicol & Chem; Soil Sci Soc Am. *Res:* Movement of environmental contaminants into wildlife food chains; soil ingestion by wildlife; concentrations of environmental; contaminants in earthworms; mercury in wildlife. *Mailing Add:* Patuxent Wildlife Res Ctr Laurel MD 20708. *Fax:* 301-497-5675; *E-Mail:* nelson_beyer@nbs.gov

BEYER, WILLIAM A, MATHEMATICS. *Current Pos:* STAFF MEM, LOS ALAMOS NAT LAB, 60- *Personal Data:* b Tyrone, Pa, Nov 9, 24; m 55; c 2. *Educ:* Pa State Univ, BS, 49, PhD(math), 59; Univ Ill, Urbana, MS, 50. *Prof Exp:* Teaching asst math, Pa State Univ, 52-53, instr, 54-55 & 57-59; teaching asst, Queen's Univ, Ont, 53-54; mathematician, Gen Elec Co, Ohio, 55-57. *Concurrent Pos:* Adj prof, Univ NMex, 59-93. *Mem:* Am Math Soc; Math Asn Am; Sigma Xi. *Res:* Mathematical biology; probability; dynamic systems; fractional dimension theory; geometry; optimization. *Mailing Add:* 343 Rim Rd Los Alamos NM 87544. *Fax:* 505-665-5757; *E-Mail:* beyer@lanl.gov

BEYER, WILLIAM HYMAN, MATHEMATICAL STATISTICS, MATHEMATICS. *Current Pos:* from asst prof to assoc prof, Univ Akron, 61-66, head, Dept Math Sci, 69-90, assoc dean, Col Arts & Sci, 90-93, PROF MATH & STATIST, UNIV AKRON, 66- *Personal Data:* b Akron, Ohio, Mar 8, 30; m 59; c 3. *Educ:* Univ Akron, BS, 52; Va Polytech Inst, MS, 54,

PhD(statist), 61. *Prof Exp:* Group leader reliability & qual control, Goodyear Aerospace Corp, 53-57; corp staff statistician, Gen Tire & Rubber Co, 57-58; asst prof math, Va Polytech Inst, 58-61. *Concurrent Pos:* Instr, Univ Akron, 54-56; partic, NSF In-Serv Inst Sec Sch Teachers Math & lectr, Univ Akron, 63-66; ed statist, CRC Press, Inc, Ohio, 66-95, ed math, 75-95; assoc vpres, Admin Support Serv, Univ Akron, 93-96, actg vpres bus & finance, 96, assoc vpres, 96- *Mem:* Am Statist Asn; Math Asn Am; Sigma Xi. *Res:* Experimental design; analysis of variance. *Mailing Add:* Buchtel Hall Univ Akron 302 E Buchtel Ave Akron OH 44325. *Fax:* 330-972-6293

BEYERLEIN, FLOYD HILBERT, ANALYTICAL CHEMISTRY. *Current Pos:* RESEARCH ASSOC ANALYTICAL CHEM, S C JOHNSON & SON, INC, 70- *Personal Data:* b Frankenmuth, Mich, Apr 15, 42; m 65, Sandra Marie Dykhuis; c David, Monica, Elizabeth, Joshua, Thomas & Nathan. *Educ:* Mich State Univ, BS, 64, MS, 67, PhD(analytical chem), 70. *Mem:* Am Chem Soc. *Res:* Methods development in support of product research; update analysis techniques already available in the areas of gas and liquid chromatography; performing research employing super critical fluid chromatography and ion chromatography. *Mailing Add:* S C Johnson & Son Inc 1525 Howe St Racine WI 53403-5011

BEYER-MEARS, ANNETTE, DIABETIC CATARACT & NEPHROPATHY, ALDOSE REDUCTASE INHIBITORS. *Current Pos:* teacher asst, Univ Med & Dent NJ, 74-77, NIH fel ophthal, 78-80, asst prof ophthal, 79-85, asst prof physiol, 80-85, ASSOC PROF OPHTHAL, UNIV MED & DENT NJ, 86- *Personal Data:* b Madison, Wis, May 26, 41. *Educ:* Vassar Col, BA, 63; Fairleigh Dickinson Univ, MS, 73; Univ Med & Dent NJ, PhD, 77. *Prof Exp:* Instr physiol, Springside Sch, Philadelphia, 67-71. *Concurrent Pos:* NIH res award, Nat Eye Inst-NIH, 78-95; Pfizer res award, Pfizer Inc, 85, 87 & 93- *Mem:* Fel Am Physiol Soc; fel NY Acad Sci; fel Soc Neurosci; fel Am Soc Pharmacol & Exp Therapeut; fel Royal Soc Med; fel Sigma Xi; Asn Res Vision & Ophthal; Int Soc Eye Res; AAAS; Am Diabetes Asn; Am Aircraft Owners & Pilots Asn. *Res:* Contributor of articles in the field of diabetic lens and kidney therapy to professional journals. *Mailing Add:* Univ Med & Dent NJ Med Sch 185 S Orange Ave Newark NJ 07103-2714. *Fax:* 973-982-7950

BEYERS, ROBERT JOHN, ECOLOGY, AQUATIC BIOLOGY. *Current Pos:* chmn dept, 74-92, PROF BIOL SCI, UNIV S ALA, 74- *Personal Data:* b Long Beach, Calif, Sept 13, 33; m 54; c Barbara, Robert, Ann-Marie & Angelique. *Educ:* Univ Miami, BS, 54; Univ Tex, PhD(zool), 62. *Prof Exp:* NSF fel ecol, Inst Marine Sci, Univ Tex, 61-62, res assoc scientist, 62-64, head ecol prog, 63-64; from asst prof to assoc prof zool, Lab Radiation Ecol, Univ Ga, 64-74; dir, Savannah River Ecol Lab, 67-74. *Concurrent Pos:* Co-prin investr, AEC contract, 67-74; Fed Water Qual Admin grant, 70-74; vpres, Echo Environ Consults, Inc, 75-77; chmn, Environ Biol Rev Panel, Environ Protection Agency, 81-85; co-prin investr, TVA-AUTRC Contract, 89-91. *Mem:* Fel AAAS; Am Soc Limnol & Oceanog; Ecol Soc Am; Inst Soc Limnol. *Res:* Limnology; marine science; microcosm techniques; measurement of carbon dioxide metabolism in aquatic organisms and ecosystems; effects of radiation and pollution on aquatic ecosystems; fish behavior; microcosms. *Mailing Add:* Dept Biol Sci Univ SAla Mobile AL 36688. *Fax:* 334-414-8220; *E-Mail:* bbeyers@usamail.usouthal.edu

BEYLER, ROGER ELDON, ORGANIC CHEMISTRY. *Current Pos:* RETIRED. *Personal Data:* b Nappanee, Ind, May 20, 22; m 44, 89, Dorothy Brand; c Keith, Eric & Jane. *Educ:* NCent Col, BA, 44; Univ Ill, MS, 47, PhD(chem), 49. *Prof Exp:* Res chemist, Merck & Co, Inc, 49-59; dean, Col Lib Arts & Sci, Southern Ill Univ, Carbondale, 66-74, prof chem, 59-87. *Concurrent Pos:* Orgn Econ Coop & Develop sci fel, Univ Strasbourg, 64. *Mem:* Am Chem Soc; AAAS. *Res:* Synthesis of the alkaloid sparteine; adrenal steroid total synthesis; steroid synthesis; teratogens. *Mailing Add:* 32 Pinewood Carbondale IL 62901-5219

BEYLERIAN, NUREL, STRUCTURAL ENGINEERING, COMPUTER SCIENCE. *Current Pos:* PRES, BOMAR MKT, INC, 95- *Personal Data:* b Istanbul, Turkey, May 8, 37; m 75, Lena Tashjian; c Maral, Talar, & Haig-Ashod. *Educ:* Robert Col, Istanbul, BS, 59, MS, 60; Mich State Univ, PhD(civil eng), 65. *Prof Exp:* Asst prof civil eng, Univ PR, 65-68; instr comput sci, Inst Advan Technol, 68-69, educ mgr, 69-76, dir, 77-95. *Res:* Computer sciences, especially software; peaceful uses of nuclear devices; structural reliability and dynamics. *Mailing Add:* 91 Edmonton Dr Willowdale ON M2J 3W9 Can. *Fax:* 416-494-8093; *E-Mail:* bomarms@msn.com

BEYLKIN, GREGORY, MATHEMATICS. *Current Pos:* PROF APPL MATH, UNIV COLO, BOULDER, 91- *Personal Data:* b St Petersburg, USSR, Mar 16, 53; US citizen; m 74, Helen Simontov; c Michael & Daniel. *Educ:* Univ St Petersburg, Leningrad, dipl math, 75; NY Univ, PhD(math), 82. *Prof Exp:* Assoc res scientist, NY Univ, 82-83; mem prof staff, Schlumberger-Doll Res, Ridgefield, 83-91. *Mem:* Am Math Soc; Soc Indust & Appl Math; Soc Exp Geophysicists. *Res:* Applied mathematics; contributed articles to professional journals. *Mailing Add:* Prog Appl Math Univ Colo Boulder CO 80309-0526

BEYROUTY, CRAIG A, AGRONOMY. *Current Pos:* PROF, DEPT AGRON, UNIV ARK, FAYETTEVILLE. *Honors & Awards:* Ciba-Geigy Agron Award, Am Soc Agron, 91. *Res:* Agronomy. *Mailing Add:* Dept Agron Univ Ark 115 Plant Sci Fayetteville AR 72701-1202

BEYSTER, J ROBERT, SYSTEMS SCIENCE. *Current Pos:* FOUNDER, CHIEF EXEC OFFICER & CHMN BD, SCI APPLNS INT CORP, 69- *Educ:* Univ Mich, BSE, 45, MS, 47, PhD (physics), 50. *Prof Exp:* Sr scientist, Nuclear Submarine Prog, Atomic Power Div, Westinghouse; staff mem, Los Alamos Sci Lab, 51-56; estab & mgr, Gen Atomic 100-million volt Traveling Wave Linear Accelerator Fac. *Concurrent Pos:* Chmn, Reactor Physics Div & Shielding Div, Am Nuclear Soc. *Mem:* Nat Acad Eng; fel Am Nuclear Soc; fel Am Phys Soc. *Res:* Neutron thermalization; co-authored approximately 60 publications and reports. *Mailing Add:* Sci Applns Int Corp 10260 Campus Point Dr San Diego CA 92121

BEZDEK, HUGO FRANK, OCEANOGRAPHY. *Current Pos:* DIR, ATLANTIC OCEANOG & METEOROL LABS, MIAMI, 80- *Personal Data:* b Wash, Feb 28, 36. *Educ:* NMEX State Univ, BS, 65; Univ Colo, PhD, 70. *Prof Exp:* Res scientist, Scripps Inst Oceanog, La Jolla, Calif, 70-74; dep dir, Ocean Sci Res Off Develop, Arlington, Va, 74-80. *Mem:* Acoust Soc Am; Am Geophys Union. *Res:* Ocean sciences. *Mailing Add:* Atlantic Oceanog & Meteorol Labs 4301 Rickenbacker Causeway Va Key Miami FL 33149

BEZDEK, JAMES CHRISTIAN, APPLIED MATHEMATICS. *Current Pos:* MGR, INFO PROC LAB, BOEING, 87- *Personal Data:* b Harrisburg, Pa, Oct 22, 39; m 63; c 4. *Educ:* Univ Nev, Reno, BSCE, 69; Cornell Univ, PhD(appl math), 73. *Prof Exp:* Instr eng mech, Cornell Univ, 72; asst prof math, State Univ NY Col Oneonta, 73-74; asst prof, Marquette Univ, 74-76; assoc prof, Utah State Univ, 76-83; prof & chmn comput sci, Univ SC, 83-87. *Concurrent Pos:* Pres, Int Fuzzy Systs Asn; ed, IJAR, 87-; eminent scholar, Div Comput Sci, Univ WFla. *Mem:* Classification Soc; Soc Indust & Appl Math; Pattern Recognition Soc; Inst Elec & Electronics Engrs; Comput Soc. *Res:* Pattern recognition, cluster analysis and unsupervised learning using fuzzy sets and graphs; applied probability and statistics; numerical fluid mechanics. *Mailing Add:* Comput Sci Dept Univ WFla Pensacola FL 32514

BEZDICEK, DAVID FRED, SOIL MICROBIOLOGY. *Current Pos:* assoc prof, 74-79, PROF SOILS, WASH STATE UNIV, 79- *Personal Data:* b Jackson, Minn, Sept 18, 38; m 62; c 2. *Educ:* SDak State Univ, BS, 60; Univ Minn, MS, 64, PhD(soil sci), 67. *Prof Exp:* Field supvr, Calif Packing Corp, 60-61; asst prof agron, Univ Md, College Park, 67-74. *Concurrent Pos:* Vis scientist, Battelle Pacific Northwest Lab, Richland, Wash, 85-86. *Mem:* Fel Am Soc Agron; Am Soc Microbiol; fel Soil Sci Soc Am. *Res:* Microbial ecology; symbiotic nitrogen fixation; molecular biology. *Mailing Add:* RR 1 Pullman WA 99163

BEZELLA, WINFRED AUGUST, NUCLEAR ENGINEERING, CHEMICAL ENGINEERING. *Current Pos:* NUCLEAR ENGR, ARGONNE NAT LAB, 71- *Personal Data:* b Milwaukee, Wis, Mar 1, 35; m 68; c 2. *Educ:* Univ Wis, BS, 57; Univ Mich, MS, 59; Purdue Univ, PhD(nuclear eng), 72. *Prof Exp:* Engr nuclear eng, Allis Chalmers Mfg Co, 59-64; sr engr nuclear eng, Westinghouse Elec Corp, 64-68. *Mem:* Am Nuclear Soc. *Res:* Thermal and hydraulic design of nuclear reactors; breeder reactor safety analysis and design of in-reactor safety experiments; reactor engineering, reactor physics and reactor kinetic problems associated with reactor development. *Mailing Add:* 4123 W End Rd Downers Grove IL 60515

BEZKOROVAINY, ANATOLY, BIOCHEMISTRY. *Current Pos:* from asst to assoc biochemist, 62-70, assoc prof, 70-73, PROF BIOCHEM & SR BIOCHEMIST, RUSH-PRESBY-ST LUKE'S MED CTR, 73-, DIR EDUC PROGS, 80- & ASSOC CHMN, BIOCHEM DEPT, 83- *Personal Data:* b Riga, Latvia, Feb 11, 35; US citizen; m 64, Marilyn Grib; c Gregory & Alexander. *Educ:* Univ Chicago, BS, 56; Univ Ill, MS, 58, PhD(biochem), 60; Ill Inst Technol, JD, 77. *Prof Exp:* Res assoc biochem, Oak Ridge Nat Lab, 60-61; res chemist, Nat Animal Dis Lab, USDA, Iowa, 61-62. *Concurrent Pos:* From asst prof to assoc prof biochem, Univ Ill Col Med, 62-70, res prof, Dept Path, 74-80; mem bd dirs, Nat Acad Clin Biochemists, 84-86. *Mem:* Am Soc Biol Chemists; Am Chem Soc; Am Inst Nutrit; Am Dairy Sci Asn; Inst Food Technologists. *Res:* Iron metabolism; biochemistry of milk; microbiological iron metabolism; probiotics. *Mailing Add:* Dept Biochem Rush-Presby-St Luke's Med Ctr Chicago IL 60612. *Fax:* 312-942-3053

BEZMAN, RICHARD DAVID, PHYSICAL CHEMISTRY. *Current Pos:* MEM STAFF, CHEVRON RES CO, 80- *Personal Data:* b Pittsburgh, Pa, Oct 2, 46; m 68. *Educ:* Pa State Univ, BSc, 67; Harvard Univ, PhD(chem), 72. *Prof Exp:* Mem tech staff, GTE Lab, Inc, 73-75; sr staff chemist, Linde Div, Union Carbide Corp, 75-80. *Mem:* Am Chem Soc. *Res:* Heterogeneous catalysis; electrochemistry; solid state chemistry. *Mailing Add:* Chevron Res Co 100 Chevron Way Richmond CA 94801-2021

BEZRUKOV, SERGEY MICHAEL, PHYSICS OF ION CHANNELS & SIGNAL TRANSDUCTION IN BIOLOGICAL SYSTEMS. *Current Pos:* Researcher, St Petersburg Nuclear Physics Inst, 73-75, asst res scientist, 75-81, res scientist, 81-87, SR RES SCIENTIST, ST PETERSBURG NUCLEAR PHYSICS INST, 87-; VIS SCIENTIST, NIH, 92- *Personal Data:* b St Petersburg, Russia, June 7, 49; m 77, Ludmilla Balikina; c Semion S & Anna. *Educ:* St Petersburg Polytech Univ, BS, 71, MS, 73; Moscow State Univ, PhD(physics & math), 81. *Concurrent Pos:* Mem, Coun Biol Membranes, Russ Acad Sci, 81-91; vis assoc prof, Univ Md, 90-92. *Mem:* Biophys Soc. *Res:* Physics of charge and matter transport across biological membranes; watching single-molecular transport events; physics of signal transduction in biological systems; noise facilitated signal transmission in ion channels; stochastic resonance at molecular level. *Mailing Add:* NIH Bldg 5 Rm 405 Bethesda MD 20892-0580. *Fax:* 301-496-0201; *E-Mail:* bezrukov@helix.nih.gov

BEZUSZKA, STANLEY JOHN, MATHEMATICAL PHYSICS. *Current Pos:* from asst prof to assoc prof, 53-69, chmn dept, 53-67, PROF MATH, BOSTON COL, 69-, DIR MATH INST, 57- *Personal Data:* b Wilna, Poland, Jan 26, 14; nat US. *Educ:* Boston Col, AB, 39, AM, 40, MS, 42; Weston Col, STL, 47; Brown Univ, PhD(physics), 53. *Prof Exp:* From instr to asst prof physics, Boston Col, 41-43; instr math, Weston Col, 43-45. *Mem:* AAAS; Am Math Soc; Math Asn Am; Acoust Soc Am; Am Phys Soc; Sigma Xi; Nat Coun Teachers Math. *Res:* Theoretical physics; scattering of ultrasonic waves; matrix theory; vector analysis and mathematical physics; mathematics education. *Mailing Add:* Mat Inst Boston Col Chestnut Hill MA 02167-3809

BEZWADA, RAO SRINIVASA, POLYMER CHEMISTRY. *Current Pos:* AT ETHICON, INC. *Personal Data:* b Jammulapalem, India, July 5, 45; US citizen; m 61; c 2. *Educ:* Univ Madras, India, BTech, 68; Stevens Inst Technol, MS, 73, PhD(chem), 81. *Prof Exp:* Chemist, A J & J O Pilar Inc, Newark, NJ, 69-73; supvr Rubber Testing Lab, 74-76, scientist, 77-79, res scientist, chem res div, Am Cyanamid Co, 81- *Mem:* Am Chem Soc; Sigma Xi. *Res:* Synthesis and solution properties of polyurethanes; polyurethane castable elastomers and thermoplastic elastomers; polyurethane coatings; structure-property relations in polyurethanes; adhesion promoters for bonding steel cords to rubber; solution properties of model comb-branched polyurethanes. *Mailing Add:* Ethicon Inc Rte 22 Somerville NJ 08876

BHADA, ROHINTON(RON) K, WASTE MANAGEMENT, ENVIRONMENTAL RESTORATION. *Current Pos:* dept head & prof chem engr, 88-90, ASSOC DEAN & DIR ENG, NMEX STATE UNIV, 90- *Personal Data:* b Bombay, India, Mar 23, 35; US citizen; m 59, Patricia Bergman; c John, James, Sarah, Naomi, Jenny, Nikki & Cindy. *Educ:* Univ Mich, BS, 55, MS, 57, PhD(chem eng), 68; Univ Akron, MBA, 74. *Honors & Awards:* Outstanding Eng Achievement Award, Nat Soc Prof Engrs; Diplomate Award, Am Acad Environ Engrs. *Prof Exp:* Res engr, Babcock & Wilcox Co, 59-72, sect mgr, 72-78, dept mgr, 78-88. *Concurrent Pos:* Adj prof, Youngstown State Univ, 78-88; dir, Waste Mgt Educ & Res Consortium, 89- *Mem:* Am Inst Chem Engrs; Nat Soc Prof Engrs; Am Soc Eng Educ; Coun Chem Res. *Res:* Waste-management and environmental restoration. *Mailing Add:* Dept WERC Col Eng NMex State Univ PO Box 30001 Las Cruces NM 88003-0001. *Fax:* 505-646-4149; *E-Mail:* rbhada@nmsu.edu

BHADURI, SAUMYA, MOLECULAR VIROLOGY, RECOMBINANT DNA TECHNOLOGY. *Current Pos:* MICROBIOLOGIST MOLECULAR BIOL, USDA, 81- *Personal Data:* b Calcutta, India, Sept 9, 42; US citizen; m 74; c 1. *Educ:* Calcutta Univ, India, BSc, 63, MSc, 65, PhD(biochem), 70. *Prof Exp:* Fel molecular biol & biochem, Chem Dept, Nebr Univ, 70; res assoc molecular virol, Inst Molecular Virol, 71-74, instr, 74-76; trainee molecular biol, Dept Path, Med Sch, Washington Univ, 76-77, res instr molecular biol & virol, 77-81. *Mem:* Am Soc Microbiol; Genetic Toxicol Asn; Soc Indust Microbiol. *Res:* Initiation of protein synthesis and coding properties of transfer RNA; transcription mapping of tumor viruses; mapping of phage DNA; characterization of the clustridium botalinum by microbial finger printing; identification and characterization of virulence gene in yesinia enderocolitica to establish key determinants for virulence in Y enderocolitica. *Mailing Add:* Eastern Regional Res Ctr Agr Res Serv USDA 600 E Mermaid Lane Philadelphia PA 19118-2551

BHAGAT, HITESH RAMESHCHANDRA, PREPARATION & EVALUATION OF DRUG DELIVERY SYSTEMS, BIODEGRADABLE VACCINE DELIVERY SYSTEMS. *Current Pos:* dept head, Formulations Develop, 92-96, DIR PHARM DEVELOP, ORAVAX, 96- *Personal Data:* Indian citizen; m 88; c 1. *Educ:* Bombay Univ, BS, 81; Mass Col Pharm, MS, 84, PhD(pharmaceut), 88. *Prof Exp:* Res pharmacist, Hoechst Pharmaceut Ltd, 81-82, Pfeiffer Pharmaceut Sci Lab, 83-88; res affil, Mass Inst Technol, 87-88; asst prof, Univ Md, Baltimore, 88-92. *Mem:* Am Asn Pharmaceut Scientists; Controlled Release Soc. *Res:* Pharmaceutical research and development related to oral and parenteral controlled drug delivery systems of biodegradable polymeric microspheres and implants containing antigens, biotechnology products and conventional drugs. *Mailing Add:* 29 Three Ponds Rd Wayland MA 01778

BHAGAT, PHIROZ MANECK, ARTIFICIAL INTELLIGENCE, THERMAL SCIENCES. *Current Pos:* staff engr, 81-83, SR STAFF ENGR, EXXON RES & ENG CO, 83- *Personal Data:* b Poona, India, Oct 28, 48; m 79, Patricia Steckler; c Kay & Sarah. *Educ:* Indian Inst Tech, BTech, 70; Univ Mich, MSE, 71, PhD(mech eng), 75. *Prof Exp:* Res fel, Harvard Univ, 75-77; asst prof, Columbia Univ, 77-81. *Concurrent Pos:* Adj asst prof, Columbia Univ, 81-84; managing dir, Janus Enterprise Int, 92- *Mem:* NY Acad Sci; Am Soc Mech Engrs; Am Inst Chem Engrs; Sigma Xi; Int Neural Networks Soc. *Res:* Neural nets and scientific computing; thermal sciences; genetic algorithms; artificial intelligence in technical & business applications. *Mailing Add:* 519 Alden Ave Westfield NJ 07090-3040

BHAGAT, PRAMODE KUMAR, NONDESTRUCTIVE EVALUATION, BIOMEDICAL ENGINEERING. *Current Pos:* SUPVRY AEROSPACE ENGR, FAA TECH CTR, ATLANTIC CITY INT AIRPORT, 92- *Personal Data:* b Ranchi, India, Oct 7, 44; US citizen; m 73, Asha; c Rahul. *Educ:* Indian Inst Technol, Madras, BTech, 65; Univ Cincinnati, MS, 69; Ohio State Univ, Columbus, PhD(elec eng), 72. *Prof Exp:* Proj elec eng, Systs Res Labs, Dayton, Ohio, 66-67; res assoc ultrasonics, Ohio State Univ, Columbus, 72-73; res assoc, Univ Ky, 73-74, from asst prof to assoc prof mech eng, 74-86, assoc prof biomed eng, 86-89; mat res engr, Wright-Patterson AFB, 89-92. *Concurrent Pos:* Consult elec eng, Vet Admin Hosp, Lexington, Ky, 75- *Mem:* Inst Elec & Electronics Engrs; Am Soc Nondestructive Testing. *Res:* Biomedical engineering; ultrasonics; microwave spectroscopy; control theory; instrumentation; digital signal processing. *Mailing Add:* FAA Tech Ctr AAR-420 Atlantic City Int Airport NJ 08405

BHAGAT, SATINDAR M, PHYSICS. *Current Pos:* from asst prof to assoc prof, 62-73, PROF PHYSICS, UNIV MD, COLLEGE PARK, 73- *Personal Data:* b Jammu, India, July 19, 33; m 64. *Educ:* Univ Jammu & Kashmir, India, BS, 50; Univ Delhi, MSc, 53, PhD(physics), 56. *Prof Exp:* Lectr physics, Univ Delhi, 55-57; Govt of India res fel, Clarendon Lab, Oxford Univ, 57-60; res assoc, Carnegie Inst Technol, 60-62, instr, 61-62. *Concurrent Pos:* Vis prof, Indian Inst Technol, Kanpur, India, 68-69 & Uppsala Univ, Sweden, 75. *Res:* Thermodynamic and hydrodynamic properties of liquid helium; properties of magnetic systems at low temperatures and other problems in solid state physics; high temperature superconductivity. *Mailing Add:* Dept Physics Univ Md College Park MD 20742

BHAGAT, SURINDER KUMAR, ACADEMIC ADMINISTRATION, ENGINEERING EDUCATION. *Current Pos:* Asst prof sanit eng, Wash State Univ, 65-69, asst prof civil eng & asst sanit engr, Col Eng Res Div, 69-71, asst head sanit eng, 71-72, assoc prof, 71-77, head environ eng, 72-80, actg dir, Water Res Ctr, 77-78, PROF CIVIL & ENVIRON ENG, WASH STATE UNIV, 77-, CHMN DEPT, 80- *Personal Data:* b Sargodha, Pakistan, May 14, 35; m 63; c 1. *Educ:* Univ Panjab, India, BSc, 54; Univ Tex, BS, 61, MS, 62, PhD(environ health eng), 66. *Honors & Awards:* Arthur Sidney Bedell Award, Water Pollution Control Fedn, 80- *Concurrent Pos:* Chmn, Environ Eng Div, Am Soc Eng Educ. *Mem:* Water Pollution Control Fedn; Am Soc Civil Engrs; Am Soc Eng Educ; Asn Environ Eng Prof; Sigma Xi. *Res:* Transport and behavior of radio-nuclides and other materials in an aquatic environment; industrial waste treatment; water quality problems of lakes and rivers. *Mailing Add:* 3355 E Kelton Lane Phoenix AZ 85032

BHAGAVAN, HEMMIGE, NUTRITION, BIOCHEMISTRY. *Current Pos:* NUTRIT COORDR, DEPT CLIN NUTRIT, HOFFMANN-LA ROCHE INC, 80- *Personal Data:* b Hemmige, India, Oct 23, 34. *Educ:* Univ Mysore, BS, 53; Indian Inst Sci, Bangalore, MS, 58; Univ Ill, Urbana-Champaign, PhD(nutrit, biochem), 63. *Prof Exp:* Res asst biochem & nutrit, Cent Food Tech Res Inst, Univ Mysore, India, 57-58, jr sci asst biochem, 58-59; res assoc biol sci, Purdue Univ, 63-64; chief biochem lab, Res Inst, St Joseph Hosp, 64-76; chief, Biochem Lab & dir, Div Nutrit Sci, North Nassau Ment Health Ctr, 76-79; asst dir, Clin Pharmacol & res assoc prof, Dept Med, Thomas Jefferson Univ Med Col, 79-80. *Mem:* Am Inst Nutrit; Am Col Nutrit; NY Acad Sci; Brit Biochem Soc; Soc Exp Biol Med; Am Asn Clin Chem; Soc Biol Psychiat. *Res:* Metabolism and function of vitamins; biochemical effects of vitamin deficiencies; central nervous system function. *Mailing Add:* Dept Clin Nutrit Bldg 42 1st Floor Hoffmann-La Roche Inc Nutley NJ 07110

BHAGAVAN, NADHIPURAM V, CLINICAL BIOCHEMISTRY. *Current Pos:* asst biochemist, 65-70, asst prof anat, 66-70, from assoc prof to prof biochem & med technol, 70-82, PROF & CHMN BIOCHEM & BIOPHYSICS, MED SCH, UNIV HAWAII, MANOA, 82- *Personal Data:* b Mysore, India, Oct 5, 31; m 62; c 2. *Educ:* Univ Mysore, BSc, 51; Univ Bombay, MSc, 55; Univ Calif, PhD(pharmaceut chem), 60. *Prof Exp:* Asst res biochemist, Med Ctr, Univ Calif, San Francisco, 61-65. *Concurrent Pos:* Assoc prof biol & chem, Hawaii Loa Col, 69-70; consult biochemist, Kaiser Found Hosp, Honolulu, 72- *Mem:* Am Chem Soc. *Res:* Immunochemistry; biochemical and immunochemical studies on normal and malignant cell nuclei. *Mailing Add:* 2655 Peter St Honolulu HI 96816

BHAGAVATULA, VIJAYAKUMAR, PATTERN RECOGNITION, SIGNAL PROCESSING FOR DATA STORAGE. *Current Pos:* From res asst to res assoc, Carnegie Mellon Univ, 77-82, from asst prof to assoc prof, 82-91, PROF ELEC ENG, CARNEGIE MELLON UNIV, 91-, ASSOC DEPT HEAD, 94-96. *Personal Data:* b Porumamilla, India, Aug 15, 53; m 82, Latha Bayya; c Ramu, Madhu & Sekhar. *Educ:* Indian Inst Technol, BTech, 75 & MTech, 77; Carnegie Mellon Univ, PhD(elec eng), 80. *Concurrent Pos:* Consult, Westinghouse Elec, 85-88 & Two-Six, Inc, Pittsburgh, 87-88, Teledyne Brown Eng, Huntsville, Ala, 89-92; prin investr pattern recognition algorithms, Sandia Labs, Albuquerque, 87-90, correlators automatic target recognition, Litton Data Syst, 90-92, Advan Res Proj Agency, Holographic Data Storage Systs, 95-, Nat Inst Stand & Technol, Ultrahigh Capacity Optical Disk Proj, 96- & Hughes Aircraft Com 95-; chmn, Max Born Award Comt, Optical Soc Am, 87-89, conf session, Soc Photo-Optical Instrumentation Engrs. *Mem:* Fel Optical Soc Am; fel Soc Photo-Optical Instrumentation Engrs; sr mem Inst Elec & Electronics Engrs; Sigma Xi. *Res:* Published over 200 research papers in areas of optical processing, pattern recognition, signal and image processing, coding theory and signal processing for data storage. *Mailing Add:* Dept Elec & Comput Eng Carnegie Mellon Univ Pittsburgh PA 15213. *E-Mail:* kumar@ece.cmu.edu

BHAGIA, GOBIND SHEWAKRAM, AGRICULTURAL ECONOMICS, STATISTICS. *Current Pos:* PROF & CHMN, DIV BUS & ECON, VOORHEES COL, 81- *Personal Data:* b Karachi, Pakistan, Dec 7, 35; US citizen; m 72; c 1. *Educ:* Univ Rajasthan, BA, 62; Tex A&M Univ, MS, 67; Ore State Univ, PhD(agr econ), 71. *Prof Exp:* Res assoc agr econ, Ore State Univ, 71-75 & Wash State Univ, 75-76; asst prof bus & coordr finance, Prairie View A&M Univ, 76-81. *Concurrent Pos:* Consult local econ develop community, Howard Univ, 77- *Mem:* Am Agr Econ Asn. *Res:* Health economics; environmental economics; microeconomic theory; financial management; investment securities. *Mailing Add:* Dept Bus Paine Col 1235 15th St Augusta GA 30910-2799

BHAKAR, BALRAM SINGH, THEORETICAL NUCLEAR PHYSICS. *Current Pos:* ASSOC PROF PHYSICS, UNIV MANITOBA, 69- *Personal Data:* b Wardha, India, Jan 1, 37; m 68; c 1. *Educ:* Agra Univ, BSc, 57; Aligarh Muslim Univ, India, MSc, 60; Univ Delhi, PhD(physics), 65. *Prof Exp:* Res assoc physics, Bonner Nuclear Lab, Rice Univ, 66-68 & Univ Sussex, 68-69. *Mem:* Am Phys Soc. *Res:* 3-nucleon system using separable potential and Faddeev theory and study of nuclear matter; 4-nucleon system. *Mailing Add:* Physics Dept Univ Man Winnipeg MB R3T 2N2 Can

BHALLA, AMAR S, MATERIALS SCIENCE. *Current Pos:* fac res assoc, 75-81, sr fac res assoc, Mat Res Lab & assoc prof solid state sci, 81-86, SR SCIENTIST & PROF SOLID STATE SCI, PA STATE UNIV, 86- *Personal Data:* b Panjab, India. *Educ:* Rajasthan Univ, India, BS, 61, MS, 63; Pa State Univ, PhD(solid state sci), 71. *Prof Exp:* Lectr physics, Rajasthan Univ, 63-64; res scholar, Banaras Univ, India, 65; res scientist, Nat Phys Lab, India, 66-67; res fel, Pa State Univ, 67-71, fel, 72; res assoc, NASA, 73-75. *Concurrent Pos:* Vis scientist, Univ Turku, 71 & Nat Phys Lab, 71-72; chair prof, Univ Tokyo, 90-91; prog dir, NSF, Washington, DC, 93-96. *Mem:* Fel Am Ceramic Soc; fel Optical Soc Am; Mat Res Soc; Soc Metals; Inst Elec & Electronics Engrs. *Res:* Ferroelectric, pyroelectric and piezoelectric properties of materials; x-ray and electron microscopic studies of materials; crystal growth and characterization; glass ceramics and electronic devices; macro, micro and nano composites; superconductivity; optoelectronics. *Mailing Add:* 253 Mat Res Lab Pa State Univ University Park PA 16802. *E-Mail:* asb2@psuvm.psu.edu

BHALLA, CHANDER P, ATOMIC PHYSICS. *Current Pos:* assoc prof, 66-72, head, Dept Physics, 82-87, PROF PHYSICS, KANS STATE UNIV, 72- *Personal Data:* b Hariana, India, Sept 15, 32; US citizen; m 62; c Anil, Sunit & Neera. *Educ:* Punjab Univ, India, BS, 52, Hons, 54, MS, 55; Univ Tenn, PhD(physics), 60. *Prof Exp:* Asst physics, Univ Tenn, 56-60; sr scientist, Westinghouse Elec Corp, Pa, 60-64; from asst prof to assoc prof physics, Univ Ala, 64-66. *Concurrent Pos:* Consult, Oak Ridge Nat Lab, 58-60, Nat Bur Stand, DC, 62-64, space div, Northrop Corp, Ala, 65-69 & Argonne Nat Lab, 66-69; vis prof, FOM Inst Atomic & Molecular Physics, Amsterdam, Netherlands, 73-74; sr vis fel, Plasma Physics Lab, Univ Princeton, 87. *Mem:* Am Nuclear Soc; fel Am Phys Soc. *Res:* Heavy ion interactions; Auger effect; radiative transitions; internal conversion processes; inelastic and elastic energy loss of heavy ions; atomic structure. *Mailing Add:* Dept Physics Cardwell Hall Kans State Univ Manhattan KS 66506. *Fax:* 785-532-6806; *E-Mail:* bhalla@phys.ksu.edu

BHALLA, RAMESH C, ANATOMY, CELL STRUCTURE. *Current Pos:* asst prof, 73-76, assoc prof, 76-82, PROF ANAT & CELL STRUCTURE, UNIV IOWA MED CTR, 82- *Personal Data:* b Jullundur, India, June 7, 35; US citizen; m 62; c 2. *Educ:* Panjab Univ, India, DVM, 57; Univ Wis-Madison, PhD(physiol), 70. *Prof Exp:* Asst prof vet med, U P Agr Univ, 60-66. *Mem:* Am Physiol Soc; Am Soc Biol Chemists; Am Asn Anatomists. *Res:* Subcellular mechanisms of cardiovascular dysfunction in the hypertensive state; role of cyclic adenylic acid and calcium 2 in the regulation of cardiac and vascular smooth muscle function. *Mailing Add:* Dept Anat Col Med 1-611 Basic Sci Bldg Univ Iowa Iowa City IA 52242

BHALLA, RANBIR J R SINGH, SOLID STATE SCIENCE. *Current Pos:* PRES, BHALLA LIGHTNING INC, 83- *Personal Data:* b Anandpur, India, July 24, 43; m 68; c 2. *Educ:* Univ Jabalpur, BS, 61, MS, 63, PhD(appl physics), 69; Pa State Univ, PhD(solid state sci), 70; Fairleigh Dickonson Univ, MBA, 76. *Prof Exp:* Lectr physics, Govt Sci Col, Univ Jabalpur, 64-66; res physicist inorg mats sci, Cent Res Lab, Am Cyanamid Co, 70-72; sr res engr, inorg mat sci, 72-78, fel res engr, High Intensity Discharge, 78-79, mgr, High Pressure Sodium Discharge Develop, Lamp Div, Westinghouse Elec Corp, 79-83. *Mem:* Illum Eng Soc. *Res:* Preparation, properties and characterization of inorganic materials; display materials, including cathodo and photochromics and phosphors; high intensity discharge. *Mailing Add:* 29 Sylvan Dr Pine Brook NJ 07058

BHALLA, SUSHIL K, CHEMICAL ENGINEERING, TECHNOLOGY MANAGEMENT. *Current Pos:* technol dir, 89-91, VPRES QUAL, CHEM DIV, J M HUBER CORP, 91- *Personal Data:* b Ghaziabad, India, Jan 7, 39; US citizen; m 87, Mary M Lutz; c Michelle L. *Educ:* Kanpur Univ, India, BChe, 61; Indian Inst Technol, Kharagpur, MS, 63; Ohio State Univ, PhD(chem eng), 68. *Prof Exp:* Res engr, FMC Corp, 69-71, prin res engr, 71-74, mgr process eng, 74-76, mgr eng develop, 76-78, dir eng develop, 78-83, mgr technol eval, 83-87. *Mem:* Am Inst Chem Engrs; Comm Develop Asn; Am Prod & Inventory Control Soc. *Res:* Peroxide and peroxide chemicals; development of new methods for manufacturing cyanuric acid; emerging technology evaluation and development; ISO-9000 total quality management. *Mailing Add:* J M Huber Corp 333 Thornall St Edison NJ 08818

BHALLA, VINOD KUMAR, ENDOCRINOLOGY. *Current Pos:* from asst prof to assoc prof, 74-82, PROF ENDOCRINOL, MED COL GA, 82- *Personal Data:* b Lahore, India, Aug 4, 40; m 66, Sarin; c Niti, Jyoti & Varun K. *Educ:* Agra Univ, BS, 62, MS, 64, PhD(natural prod), 68. *Prof Exp:* Fel org chem, Univ Ga, 68-69, res assoc biochem & reproductive physiol, 69-72; res assoc biochem & endocrinol, Emory Univ, 72-74. *Concurrent Pos:* Mem, Endocrine Study Sect, 84-87; reviewer several prof journals. *Mem:* Endocrine Soc; Soc Study Reproduction; Am Soc Biol Chemists; Soc Complex Carbohydrates; NY Acad Sci; Am Fertility Soc. *Res:* Mechanism of action of gonadotropin in testicular functions. *Mailing Add:* Dept Physiol & Endocrinol Med Col Ga Laney Walker Blvd Augusta GA 30912-0001. *Fax:* 706-721-7299

BHANDARKAR, DILEEP PANDURANG, computer science, for more information see previous edition

BHANDARKAR, MANGALORE DILIP, FAILURE ANALYSIS, MATERIALS EVALUATION. *Current Pos:* PRIN QUAL & RELIABILITY ENGR, SEAGATE TECHNOL, 95- *Personal Data:* b Mangalore, India, Mar 12, 46; US citizen; m 76, Jayanthi Shendy; c Naveen & Nithin. *Educ:* Indian Inst Technol, BTech, 68; Univ Calif, Berkeley, MS, 70, DEng, 73. *Prof Exp:* Res metallurgist, Lawrence Berkeley Lab, 73-74; Nat Res Coun res assoc failure anal, Langley Res Ctr, NASA, 74-76; assoc develop engr res & proj mgt, Dept Mat Sci & Eng, Univ Calif, Berkeley, 76-77; prin metallurgist & mgr spec proj, Anamet Labs, 77-95. *Mem:* Am Soc Metals; Am Soc Testing & Mat; Metall Soc Am; Inst Mining & Metall Engrs; Am Soc Mech Engrs. *Res:* Strain-induced transformations in austenitic steels; microstructure and elevated temperature mechanical properties of ferritic alloys containing Laves phases; microstructure and fracture behavior of aluminum alloys and metal-matrix composites; design of abrasion resistant steels; development of improved high-speed tool steels; failure analysis. *Mailing Add:* Seagate Technol 2911 Zanker Rd San Jose CA 95134. *Fax:* 408-456-3078

BHANDARKAR, SUHAS D, MATERIALS SCIENCE, CHEMICAL ENGINEERING. *Current Pos:* Postdoctoral fel mat, AT&T Bell Labs, Murray Hill, NJ, 90-, MEM TECH STAFF, LUCENT TECHNOL. *Personal Data:* b India, Oct 8, 64. *Educ:* Mangalore Univ, India, BS, 86; Univ RI, MS, 88, PhD(chem eng), 90. *Mem:* Am Inst Chem Engrs. *Res:* Topics of ultrafine materials; investigation has ranged from the synthesis, using novel techniques the characterization and their application; application has involved optical and electronic materials and films. *Mailing Add:* Lucent Technol 600-700 Mountain Ave New Providence NJ 07882

BHANU, BIR, INTELLIGENT SYSTEMS, MACHINE INTELLIGENCE. *Current Pos:* prog leader elec eng, 91-94, PROF ELEC ENG & COMPUT SCI, DIR VISUALIZATION & INTEL SYSTS LAB, UNIV CALIF, RIVERSIDE. *Personal Data:* b Etah, UP, India, Jan 8, 51; US citizen; m 82, Archana Bhatnagar; c Shiv B & Ish B. *Educ:* Banaras Hindu Univ, India, BS, 72; Birla Inst Technol & Sci, Pilani, India, ME, 74; Mass Inst Technol, Cambridge, SM & EE, 77; Univ Southern Calif, Los Angeles, Phd(elec eng), 81; Univ Calif, Irvine, MBA, 84. *Prof Exp:* Lectr electronics eng, Birla Inst Technol & Sci, Pilani, India, 74-75; acad assoc res, Comput Sci Dept, IBM Res Lab, San Jose, Calif, 78; res fel, Nat Inst Res Informatics & Automation, France, 80-81; eng specialist res & develop, Ford Aerospace & Commun Corp, 81-84; from asst to assoc prof comput sci, Univ Utah, 84-87, dir, Grad Admin, 85-86; staff scientist & Honeywell Fel & sr Honeywell fel, Honeywell Systs & Res Ctr, 86-91. *Concurrent Pos:* Consult, Evolving Technol Inst, San Diego, 83-85, Sch Med, Univ Calif, Irvine, 83-84 & Bonneville Sci, Salt Lake City, 85-86; prin investr, Dept Defense, NASA, NSF, ARO, AFOSR, DARPA, TRW, LA, 91-, Ford, Rockwell & var other agencies. *Mem:* Fel Inst Elec & Electronics Engrs; AAAS; Am Asn Artificial Intel; Asn Comput Mach; Soc Photo-Optical & Instrumentation Engrs; Int Asn Pattern Recognition. *Res:* Scientific visualization; navigation; outdoor robotics; computer vision; machine learning; signal and image processing; computer graphics; obstacle detection and avoidance; multisensor integration; photointerpretation; automatic target recognition and machine learning in computer vision. *Mailing Add:* Col Eng Univ Calif Riverside CA 92521-0425

BHAPKAR, VASANT PRABHAKAR, MATHEMATICAL STATISTICS. *Current Pos:* assoc prof, 69-73, interim chmn dept, 79-81, PROF STATIST, UNIV KY, 73- *Personal Data:* b India, Apr 8, 31; m 61; c 3. *Educ:* Univ Bombay, BSc, 51, MSc, 53; Univ NC, PhD(math statist), 59. *Prof Exp:* Lectr statist, Univ Poona, 54-60, reader, 60-68, prof, 68-72. *Concurrent Pos:* Vis assoc prof statist, Univ NC, 64-66; vis sr prin res sci, Commonwealth Sci & Indust Res Orgn, Australia, 78; vis prof, Dept Biostatist, Univ Mich, 84-85. *Mem:* Inst Math Statist; fel Am Statist Asn; Int Statist Inst. *Res:* Categorical data, non-parametric methods in statistics; multivariate analysis; statistical inference. *Mailing Add:* Dept Statist Univ Ky 500 S Limestone St Lexington KY 40506-0001

BHAPPU, ROSHAN B, METALLURGICAL ENGINEERING. *Current Pos:* GEN MGR & VPRES, 72-, PRES, MOUNTAIN STATES RES & DEVELOP. *Personal Data:* b Karachi, Pakistan, Sept 14, 26; nat US; m 52; c 3. *Educ:* Colo Sch Mines, ME & MS, 50, DSc, 53. *Prof Exp:* Proj engr, Colo Sch Mines Res Found, 53-55; metallurgist, Miami Copper Co, Ariz, 55-59; sr metallurgist, Bur Mines & Mineral Resources, NMex Inst Mining & Technol, 59-72, res prof metall & mat eng, 67-72, actg chmn dept, 71-72. *Concurrent Pos:* Consult, Pakistan Industs, Ltd, 50 & 54; tech expert, UNESCO, Turkey, 69-70; vpres res, NMex Inst Mining & Technol Res Found, 71- *Mem:* Am Chem Soc; Am Inst Mining, Metall & Petrol Engrs. *Res:* Extractive metallurgy and mineral beneficiation plant design and construction. *Mailing Add:* 2125 N Donner Ave Tucson AZ 85749

BHARADVAJ, BALA KRISHNAN, AEROLASTICITY & COMPUTATIONAL FLUID DYNAMICS, AIRCRAFT DESIGN & MULTIDISCIPLINARY DESIGN OPTIMIZATION. *Current Pos:* prin eng scientist, McDonnell Douglas, 87-91, sr prin eng scientist, 91-93, proj leader & courdr supersonic laminar flow control, 92-97, DYN PROJ MGR, HSR AERO, MCDONNELL DOUGLAS, 92-, PROJ LEADER ACETEAM HIGH SPEED RES PROG, 94- *Personal Data:* b Cuddalore, Tamil Nadu, Dec 22, 52; m 78, Ramaa; c Swetha & Siva. *Educ:* Indian Inst Technol, Madras, BTech, 74; Ga Inst Technol, Atlanta, MS, 75, PhD(aerospace eng), 79. *Honors & Awards:* Monie A Ferst Award, Sigma Xi, 80. *Prof Exp:* Res asst fluid mech, Sch Aerospace Eng, Ga Inst Technol, Atlanta, 74-79, post-doctoral res fel fluid mech, 79-80; asst prof mech & aero eng, Fluid Mech, Instrumentation, Propulsion, Rotor Aerodyn, Col Eng, Boston Univ, 80-87. *Concurrent Pos:* Co-prin investr grant, NIH, 81-83; vis prof, Univ Rome, Italy, 83; consult, Inst Comput Appln Res & Utilization Sci Inc, Lincoln, Mass, 83-87; adj, prof, Calif Polytechnic, Pomona, 90- *Mem:* Fel Am Inst Aeronaut & Astronaut; Soc Automotive Engrs. *Res:* Computational fluid dynamics applied to airplanes; computational methods and design for airplanes with laminar flow control; aerodynamics for high speed civil transport; multidisciplinary methods for airplane design. *Mailing Add:* 5535 Via Verano Yorba Linda CA 92887

BHARADWAJ, PREM DATTA, NUCLEAR PHYSICS. *Current Pos:* from asst prof to assoc prof, 62-66, chmn dept, 76-86, PROF PHYSICS, NIAGARA UNIV, 66- *Personal Data:* b Gorakhpur, India, May 20, 31; m 49, Vidya Sharma; c Rakesh, Rajnesh, Vidhu & Sudhakar. *Educ:* NREC Col, India, BSc, 50; Agra Univ, MSc, 52; State Univ NY Buffalo, PhD, 64. *Honors & Awards:* Hind Rattan Award, Non-Resident Indian Welfare Soc India, 94; Rajiv Gandhi Nat Unity Award, Govt India, 95. *Prof Exp:* Asst prof physics, BR Col, India, 52-54; lectr, GPI Col, 54-56 & Govt Col, Meerut, 56-59; asst prof, BR Col, 59-60. *Mem:* Am Phys Soc. *Res:* High energy physics; theoretical physics. *Mailing Add:* Dept Physics Niagara Univ Niagara Falls NY 14109

BHARAT, RAMASESHA, PHOTODETECTORS, MICROMACHINED DEVICES. *Current Pos:* RETIRED. *Educ:* Saugor Univ, India, BEngg, 53; Stanford Univ, MS, 57, PhD(elec eng), 60. *Prof Exp:* Assoc prof elec eng, Brooklyn Polytech Inst, 66-69; prof, Univ Denver, 69-73; mem tech staff, Rockwell Int, 74-79, mgr, 79-84, dir silicon devices, 84- *Res:* Silicon and germanium devices and materials; photodetectors; focal plane electronics; radiation hardening; cryogenic electronics; micromachined devices; display electronics; integrated circuits. *Mailing Add:* Rockwell Int MS 031 BC 16 3370 Miraloma Ave Orange CA 92667

BHARATH, RAMACHANDRAN, INTELLIGENT & FUZZY SYSTEMS, NEURAL NETWORKS. *Current Pos:* RETIRED. *Personal Data:* b Chennai, India, Jan 7, 35; US citizen. *Educ:* Madras Univ, India, BSc, 54; London Sch Econs, MSc, 67; Simon Fraser Univ, PhD(econs), 76. *Prof Exp:* Mem, Indian Admin Serv, Govt India, 57-76; prof decision sci, col bus, Northern Mich Univ, 82-97. *Concurrent Pos:* Fulbright scholar, Coun Int Exchange Scholars, 88-89. *Mem:* Asn Comput Mach; Brit Comput Soc; Int Neural Networks Soc; Am Asn Artificial Intel; Opers Res Soc; Inst Opers Res & Mgt Sci. *Res:* Logic programming and neural networks. *Mailing Add:* 305 Beech Ave Toronto ON M4E 3J1 Can

BHARATI, SAROJA, CARDIAE PATHOLOGY. *Current Pos:* DIR, MAURICE LEV CONGENITAL HEART & CONDUCTION SYST CTR, HEART INST CHILDREN, CHRIST HOSP & MED CTR, 88-; PROF PATH, RUSH MED COL, CHICAGO, ILL, 89- *Personal Data:* Nat US. *Educ:* Univ Madras, MB & BS, 66. *Prof Exp:* Assoc dir, Congenital Heart Dis Res & Training Ctr, Hektoen Inst Med Res, 76-82; res prof med, Abraham Lincoln Sch Med, Univ Ill, 82-87; clin prof path, Milton S Hershey Med Ctr, Penn State Univ Med Sch, 83-88, Temple Univ, 83-88, Univ Med & Dent NJ-Robert Wood Johnson Med Sch, 86-88. *Concurrent Pos:* Consult, JACC, chest circulation & Am J Cardiol, 77-; chair, Dept Path, Deborah Heart & Lung Ctr, Browns Mills NJ, 82-88; clin prof path, Finch Univ Health Scis, Chicago Med Sch, N Chicago, Il. *Mem:* Am Heart Asn; AMA; fel Am Col Cardiol; fel Am Col Chest Physicians; Am Med Women's Asn; NY Acad Scis. *Res:* Pathology of congenital heart disease; conduction system of the heart; published more than 340 articles in pathology of congenital heart disease and the conduction system of the heart, including the senior author for more than 3 books. *Mailing Add:* Congenital Heart & Conduction Syst Ctr 11745 Southwest Hwy Palos Heights IL 60463

BHARGAVA, HEMENDRA NATH, PHARMACOLOGY. *Current Pos:* from asst prof to assoc prof, 75-81, PROF PHARMACOL, UNIV ILL MED CTR, 81-, AFFIL MED CHEM, 80- *Personal Data:* b Delhi, India, Sept 30, 42; m, Shakti. *Educ:* Banaras Hindu Univ, India, BPharm, 63, MPharm, 65; Univ Calif, San Francisco, PhD(pharm chem), 69. *Honors & Awards:* Madan Mohan Malviya Prize, Banaras Hindu Univ, 63, Univ Gold Medal, 65; Sr Neurosci Achievement Award, Assoc Scientists Indian Origin Am, 91. *Prof Exp:* Fel pharmacol, Univ Calif, San Francisco, 69-72, res pharmacologist, 72-75, lectr, 74-75. *Concurrent Pos:* Res grants, Ill Dept Ment Health & Develop Disabilities & Nat Inst Drug Abuse, Am Heart Asn; univ grants comn fel, Govt India, 63-65; travel award, Am Soc Pharmacol & Exp Therapeut, 78 & 90, NSF, 81; Int Narcotic Res Conf, 83-89; res scientist develop award, Nat Inst Drug Abuse, 92- *Mem:* Am Soc Pharmacol & Exp Therapeut; Soc Neurosci; Int Narcotic Res Club; Indian Soc Neurosci; Am Asn Col Pharm. *Res:* Mechanisms in narcotic tolerance and physical dependence, endorphins and other opiate peptides, drug metabolism, drug effects in disease states, neuropharmacology; treatment of parkinsonism, hypertension and tardive dyskinesias; pharmacology of hypothalamic peptide hormones; aging; receptors. *Mailing Add:* Univ Ill Dept Pharmaceut & Pharmacodynamics Health Sci Ctr 833 S Wood St Rm 310 Chicago IL 60612

BHARGAVA, HRIDAYA NATH, PHARMACEUTICAL & FOOD PROCESSING. *Current Pos:* PROF INDUST PHARM, MASS COL PHARM, 79- *Personal Data:* b Jodhpur, India, Dec 24, 35; US citizen; m 65; c 2. *Educ:* Saugor Univ, India, BS, 58; NDak State Univ, PhD(med chem), 65. *Prof Exp:* Group leader prod & process develop, Revlon Inc, NY, 70-72; res fel prod develop, Merck & Co, Inc, Rahway, NJ, 72-79. *Concurrent Pos:* Consult, Pfeiffer Pharmacuet Sci Labs, 79-, Stiefel Res Labs, 80-, Repub Surinam & World Health Orgn, 81-& Agency Int Develop, 85; prin investr, res grants, NIH, 81- *Mem:* Am Pharmaceut Asn; Acad Pharmaceut Sci; Soc Cosmetic Chemists. *Res:* Pharmaceutical dosage form design and development; application of surfactants in solubilization of drugs; pharmaceutical process evaluation; hydrocolloids in emulsions and suspensions; evaluation of excipeints in solid pharmaceuticals. *Mailing Add:* 21 Sherwood Circle Sharon MA 02067

BHARGAVA, RAMESHWAR NATH, PHYSICS, SOLID STATE PHYSICS. *Current Pos:* PRES, NANOCRYSTALS TECHNOL LTD, 93- *Personal Data:* b Allahabad, India, Dec 25, 39; m 65, Veena; c Sidharth & Amitabh. *Educ:* Univ Allahabad, BS, 57, MS, 59; Columbia Univ, PhD(physics), 66. *Prof Exp:* Res asst physics, Watson Labs, Int Bus Mach Corp, 62-66, consult, Watson Res Ctr, 66-67; mem tech staff, Bell Tel Labs, 67-70; mem tech staff, Philips Labs Div, NAm Philips Corp, 70-74, sr prog leader, 74-78, dept head, 78-88, assoc dir, 88-93. *Concurrent Pos:* Adj prof, Columbia Univ, 93. *Mem:* Fel Inst Elec & Electronics Engrs; fel Am Phys Soc. *Res:* Galvanomagnetic properties of semimetals and semiconductors; optical properties of semiconductors primarily in gallium arsenide, gallium phosphide and II-VI semiconductors; device work in gallium phosphide and zinc selenide diodes; deep states and nonradiative processes in semiconductors; non-linear optics; superconductivity; nanocomposites. *Mailing Add:* 5 Morningside Ct Ossining NY 10562. *Fax:* 914-923-1274

BHARGAVA, TRILOKI NATH, APPLIED STATISTICS. *Current Pos:* from asst prof to assoc prof, Kent State Univ, 62-67, PROF MATH & STATIST, KENT STATE UNIV, 67- *Personal Data:* b Lucknow, India, Aug 21, 33; US citizen; c 5. *Educ:* Lucknow Univ, BSc, 52, MSc, 54; Mich State Univ, PhD(math & statist), 62. *Prof Exp:* Lectr math & statist, Khalsa Col, India, 54-55; lectr, Gujerat Univ, India, 55-57; asst prof, Agra Univ, 57-58; res asst statist, Mich State Univ, 59-61. *Concurrent Pos:* NASA grant, Kent State Univ, 63-67, NSF grant, 64, Environ Protection Agency res grant, 71-; res assoc, Ctr Urban Regionalism, Kent State Univ, 70- *Mem:* Fel Royal Statist Soc; Am Math Soc; Am Statist Soc; Inst Math Statist; Math Asn Am. *Res:* Applied probability and statistics; graph theory; binary systems; ecological systems. *Mailing Add:* Dept Math Kent State Univ Kent OH 44242-0001

BHARJ, SARJIT SINGH, MONOLITHIC MICROWAVE INTEGRATED CIRCUITS, MICROWAVE ENGINEERING. *Current Pos:* MEM TECH STAFF RES, DAVID SARNOFF RES CTR, 89- *Personal Data:* b Kitale, Kenya, Mar 31, 50; US citizen; m; c Havminder, Jasmine, Balunder & Deep-Paul. *Educ:* King's Col, London, BSc, 73; Univ Col, London, MSc, 74, dipl, 74. *Prof Exp:* Appln engr components, Microwave Assocs, 73-76; chief engr systs, Vega Cantley Instruments, 76-78; group leader res, Marconi Space & Defense Ltd, 78-82; proj mgr amplifiers, Microwave Semiconductor Corp, 82-85; mgr, MMIC's Anadigics Inc, 85-89. *Concurrent Pos:* Prin investr, Small Bus Innovation Res Prog contracts, 85-89; proj mgr, govt contracts, 85-; vchmn, Packaging Panel, Microwave Theory & Technique, 88, chmn, Spread Spectrum Panel, 89, Spread Spectrum Workshop, 90; reviewer, Microwave Theory & Technique Publ. *Mem:* Inst Elec Eng; sr mem Inst Elec & Electronics Engrs. *Res:* Monolithic microwave integrated circuit design; development of novel planar components; advancement of evanescent mode waveguide components. *Mailing Add:* 118 Robin Dr Trenton NJ 08619

BHARTENDU, SRIVASTAVA, METEOROLOGY, ATMOSPHERIC PHYSICS. *Current Pos:* RETIRED. *Personal Data:* b Banda, India, Dec 15, 35; Can citizen; m 64, Uma Kumari; c Artee & Rajendu. *Educ:* Univ Allahabad, BSc, 55, MSc, 58; Univ Sask, PhD(atmospheric physics), 64. *Prof Exp:* Res asst physics, Univ Sask, 60-64; fel, NMex Inst Mining & Technol, 65-66; res scientist, Atmospheric Environ Serv, Dept Environ, Can, 66-82, meteorologist, 82-97. *Concurrent Pos:* Fel, Univ Sask, 66; mem working group, Joint Comt Atmospheric Elec, Int Asn Meteorol & Atmospheric Physics & Int Asn Geomagnetism & Aeronomy, 67-71; mem, Subcomn II, Int Comn Atmospheric Elec, Int Asn Meteorol & Atmospheric Physics, 71-; mem, Can Comt Atmospheric Elec, 72-75, chmn, 75-77; mem, Can Nat Comt, Int Union Radio Sci, 74-80; vis scientist, Nat Phys Lab, New Delhi, India, 77-78; vis prof, Merut Univ, Meerut, India, 80; co-chmn, Worging Group Air, Phase Two, Environ Audit East Bayfront/Port Indust Area, Royal Comn Future Toronto Waterfront, 90-91. *Mem:* Am Geophys Union; Am Meteorol Soc; Can Meteorol Soc; Can Soc Agrometeorol (pres, 92-93). *Res:* Atmospheric electricity including its relationship with meteorology, fair weather atmospheric electricity, biological effects of atmospheric electricity; atmospheric acoustics, including thunder, gravity and pressure waves from nuclear and chemical explosions; applied climatology, including socioeconomic impacts; carbon dioxide induced climate change impacts; agrometeorology; air pollution meteorology, biometerology, long range transport of air pollutant (acid rain). *Mailing Add:* 64 Longwood Dr Scarborough ON M1V 3A3 Can

BHARTIA, PRAKASH, MICROSTRIP ANTENNAS, MICROWAVE & MILLIMETER WAVE CIRCUITS. *Current Pos:* scientist, Defence Res Estab Atlantic, Ottawa, 77-82, head, Electromagnetics Sect, 82-85, dir, Aerospace Res & Develop, Nat Defence Hq, 85-86, dir, Res & Develop Commun & Space, 86-89, dir, Sonar Div, 89-91, dir, Radar Div, 91-92, CHIEF DEFENCE RES ESTAB ATLANTIC, OTTAWA, 92- *Personal Data:* b Calcutta, India, Jan 6, 44; Can citizen; m 71, Savitri Kanhai; c Sanjay M & Anil M. *Educ:* Indian Inst Technol, Bombay, BTech Hons, 66; Univ Man, Winnipeg, MSc, 68, PhD(elec eng), 71. *Prof Exp:* Spec lectr & asst prof elec eng, Univ Regina, 73-75, asst dean & assoc prof, 75-77. *Concurrent Pos:* Consult, Winter Haven Indust, Gerling Moore Inc & Lockheed Aircraft & Missiles, 71-; mem, Bd Gov, Int Microwave Power Inst, 75-77 & Can-US Defense Develop & Prod Sharing, 86-89; adj prof elec eng, Univ Ottawa, 77-; Can deleg, Various Comts, NATO, 78-; nat leader, Panel 3 Physics & Electronics, NATO, 86-92; chmn, Sci Comt Nat Indust, Saclantcen, LaSpezia, Italy; dir, Can Ctr Marine Comt, 92-, Tradex Mutual Funds, 91, 92; mem, NS Premiers Coun Appl Sci & Technol. *Mem:* Fel Inst Elec & Electronics Engrs; fel Inst Elec & Telecommun Engrs; Electromagnetics Acad; Int Union Radio Scientists; Int Microwave Power Inst; Inst Elec & Electronics Engrs Microwave Theory & Tech Soc; Inst Elec & Electronics Engrs Antennas & Propagation Soc. *Res:* Millimeter wave technology and microstrip antennas; millimeter wave and microwave circuits; microwave, millimeter wave monolithic integrated circuits, devices, components and systems; author of over 100 publications and co-author of 5 books. *Mailing Add:* Chief Defence Res Estab Atlantic Dartmouth NS B2Y 3Z7 Can. *Fax:* 902-426-9650; *E-Mail:* bhartia@drea.dnd.ca

BHARUCHA, KEKI RUSTOMJI, ORGANIC CHEMISTRY. *Current Pos:* sr res chemist, sr scientist, group leader & res mgr, Can Packers, Ltd, 53-92, CONSULT, RES LABS, MAPLE LEAF FOODS INC, 92- *Personal Data:* b Bombay, India, Feb 4, 28. *Educ:* Univ Bombay, BSc, 46, MSc, 49; Univ London, PhD(org chem) & DIC, 52. *Prof Exp:* Res assoc, Univ Toronto, 52-53. *Res:* Synthetic organic chemistry. *Mailing Add:* 236 Lonsmount Dr Toronto ON M5P 2Z1 Can

BHARUCHA, NANA R, ELECTROCHEMISTRY, SURFACE CHEMISTRY. *Current Pos:* CONSULT, 85- *Personal Data:* b Bombay, India, Oct 20, 26; m 76, Audrey; c Eric, Christopher & David. *Educ:* Univ Bombay, BSc, 46, MSc, 48, PhD(chem), 50; Univ Manchester, PhD(chem technol), 53. *Honors & Awards:* Gold Medal Award, Am Electroplaters Soc, 73; Dr D J I Evans Award, Am Inst Mining, Metall & Petrol Eng, 83. *Prof Exp:* Res chemist, Paint Res Sta, Eng, 54-60; sr investr chem, Brit Non-Ferrous Metals Res Asn, 60-66, head appl chem div, 66-68; group leader, Noranda Res Ctr, 68-69, head Electrochem & Corrosion Dept, 69-70, mgr, Res Div, 70-85; res assoc, McGill Univ, 81-84. *Res:* Corrosion; chemical metallurgy; metal finishing. *Mailing Add:* 376 Princess Louise Dr Orleans ON K4A 1W7 Can

BHASIN, MADAN M, PHYSICAL CHEMISTRY, SURFACE CHEMISTRY. *Current Pos:* proj chemist, Union Carbide Corp, 63-69, proj scientist, 69-77, res scientist, 77-81, sr res sci & group supvr, 81-88, CORP FEL & GROUP SUPVR, UNION CARBIDE CORP, 88- *Personal Data:* b Lahore, India, June 23, 38; US citizen; m 61, Anand Kumri Chugha; c Madhu Singh & Anoop. *Educ:* Univ Delhi, BSc, 58; Notre Dame Univ, PhD(phys chem), 64. *Honors & Awards:* Tech Achievement Award, Union Carbide Corp, 85; Eugene J Houdry Award, NAm Catalysis Soc, 95; Sci Achievement Award, Am Chem Soc, 95. *Prof Exp:* Teaching asst phys chem, Ind Univ, 59-60; res fel, Univ Notre Dame, 60-63. *Concurrent Pos:* Atomic energy estab of India, 58-59. *Mem:* Am Chem Soc; NAm Catalysis Soc. *Res:* Heterogenous catalysis; selective oxidation of olefins and paraffins; selective hydrogenations & hydrocracking; oxidative coupling of methane to ethylene; AUGER; ion-scattering spectrometry; secondary ion mass spectrometry; diffusion in porous catalysts; automotive pollution control. *Mailing Add:* Indust Chem Group Res & Develop Union Carbide Corp Bldg 770 PO Box 8361 South Charleston WV 25303. *Fax:* 304-747-5430

BHASKAR, RAGULA, RESPIRABLE DUST STUDIES, MINE VENTILATION. *Current Pos:* asst prof, 88-94, ASSOC PROF, DEPT MINING ENG, UNIV UTAH, 94- *Personal Data:* b Madras, India, Dec 2, 59; US citizen; m 90, Sanchaita Datta. *Educ:* Indian Sch Mines, BS, 81; Pa State Univ, MS, 84, MS, 87, PhD(mining eng), 87. *Prof Exp:* Res assoc, Pa State Univ, 87-88. *Concurrent Pos:* Chmn student relations comt, Soc Mining Metall & Explor, Am Inst Mining Engrs, 88-93, Publ Comt & Health & Safety Comt, 92; mem, Underground Mine Vent Comt, Soc Metall & Explor, Inst Mining Engrs, 93- *Mem:* Am Inst Mining Engrs; Sigma Xi. *Res:* Expertise research in respirable dust characterization and control and related mathematical modeling; mine ventilation systems design. *Mailing Add:* Dept Mining Eng Univ Utah 313 Browning Salt Lake City UT 84112-1118. *Fax:* 801-585-5410

BHASKAR, SURINDAR NATH, PATHOLOGY, PERIODONTICS. *Current Pos:* PVT PRACT PERIDONT, 78- *Personal Data:* b Rasul, India, Jan 7, 23; nat US; m 50; c William C, Philip B & Thomas A. *Educ:* Punjab Univ, BDS, 42; Northwestern Univ, DDS, 46; Univ Ill, MS, 48, PhD(anat), 51; Am Bd Oral Path & Am Bd Oral Med, dipl. *Honors & Awards:* Henry Spenadel Award, 71; Founders Medal, Asn Mil Surgeons US, 73; Albert L Borish Mem Award, Acad Gen Dent, 79. *Prof Exp:* Instr oral path & histol, Col Dent, Univ Ill, 51-52, assoc prof path, 52-55; chief, Oral Tumors Br, Armed Forces Inst Path, US Army, 55-60, chief, Dept Oral Path, 60-70, dir, Army Inst Dent Res, Walter Reed Army Med Ctr, 70-73, dir personnel, Off Surgeon Gen, 73-75, asst surgeon gen & chief dent corps, 75-78. *Concurrent Pos:* Prof, Sch Dent & Med, Georgetown Univ. *Mem:* Fel AAAS; fel Am Acad Oral Path; Am Acad Oral Med; Am Dent Asn; Int Acad Oral Path; Am Acad Periodont; Int Asn Dent Res; Sigma Xi; Asn Mil Surgeons. *Res:* General and oral pathology; human and experimental tumors of salivary glands; oral tumors and oral diseases; author of 4 text books on histology, pathology, radiology. *Mailing Add:* 333 El Dorado Monterey CA 93940. *Fax:* 408-648-5334, 422-9130

BHASKARAN, GOVINDAN, INSECT ENDOCRINOLOGY, DEVELOPMENTAL BIOLOGY. *Current Pos:* sr scientist, Inst Develop Biol, 73-85, assoc prof biol, 75-81, interim dir, 83-85, PROF BIOL, TEX A&M UNIV, 82- *Personal Data:* b Mavelikara, India, Feb 12, 35; m 62; c 2. *Educ:* Univ Kerala, BSc, 55, MSc, 57; Univ Bombay, PhD(zool), 62. *Prof Exp:* Asst res officer, Indian Coun Med Res, Haffkine Inst, Bombay, 61; sci officer, Bhabha Atomic Res Ctr, Trombay, 61-68; res assoc entom, Univ Ill, Urbana-Champaign, 68-70; sr scientist, Biol Dept, Zoecon Corp, 70-73. *Mem:* AAAS; Soc Develop Biol; Am Soc Zoologists; Entom Soc Am. *Res:* Insect hormones and development; regulation of juvenile hormone biosynthesis. *Mailing Add:* 2005 Langford St College Station TX 77840

BHAT, GOPAL KRISHNA, METALLURGICAL ENGINEERING, MATERIALS SCIENCE. *Current Pos:* fel & head Scaife fellowship metals technol, 58-65, sr fel & head missile mfg eng & technol, 65-72, sr fel & mgr mat process eng, 72-76, DIR METALL & MAT TECHNOL, CARNEGIE-MELLON INST RES, 76- *Personal Data:* b India, Dec 31, 25; US citizen; m 50; c 3. *Educ:* Banaras Hindu Univ, India, BSc, 48; Lehigh Univ, MS, 51, PhD(metall eng), 55. *Prof Exp:* Staff metallurgist high strength steels, Crucible Steel Res Div, Colt Industs, 55-58. *Concurrent Pos:* Spec adv, US Navy Spec Proj Off, 60-62; tech consult, Titan Proj, Lockheed Aircraft Corp, 62-66 & Fast Deployment Logistics Ships Proj, 66-68; mfg tech consult, Air Force Mat Lab, Dayton, 66-74; mat consult, Space Shuttle & Lunar Explorer Projs, NASA, 68-71; vpres & tech dir, Electroslag Inst, 68-71; tech dir, Nutek Mat Inc, 71-76; mem ad hoc comt, Nat Mat Adv Bd, 73-74. *Mem:* Fel Am Soc Metals; Am Vacuum Soc; The Metals Soc; Am Welding Soc; Sigma Xi. *Res:* Plasma heat application technology; electroslag melting, welding, casting technology; materials fabrication and manufacturing technology. *Mailing Add:* 172 Boxfield Rd Pittsburgh PA 15241

BHAT, MULKI RADHAKRISHNA, NUCLEAR PHYSICS. *Current Pos:* res assoc neutron physics, 64-66, from asst physicist to assoc physicist, 66-73, physicist, 73-78, SR PHYSICIST, BROOKHAVEN NAT LAB, 78- *Personal Data:* b Mulki, India, May 7, 30; m 67; c 1. *Educ:* Univ Bombay, BSc, 51; Univ Poona, MSc, 54; Ohio State Univ, PhD(nuclear physics), 61. *Prof Exp:* Nat Res Coun Can fel, 61-63. *Mem:* AAAS; Am Phys Soc. *Res:* Neutron physics; measurement of resonance parameters and neutron capture gamma rays; nuclear spectroscopy; neutron cross-section evaluation; nuclear structure and decay data evaluation. *Mailing Add:* Brookhaven Nat Lab, PO Box 5000 Bldg 197D Upton NY 11973-5000

BHAT, RAMA B, ROTOR DYNAMICS, VIBRATIONS OF STRUCTURES. *Current Pos:* from asst prof to assoc prof, 79-88, PROF MECH ENG, CONCORDIA UNIV, 88- *Personal Data:* b Badur, Kerala, India, Oct 2, 43; Can citizen; m 74, Parvathi; c Mamatha & Aparna. *Educ:* Mysore Univ, BE, 66; Indian Inst Technol, MTech, 68, PhD(mech eng), 73. *Honors & Awards:* Tech Innovation Award, NASA, 83. *Prof Exp:* Scientist, Indian Space Res Orgn, 72-76; res assoc, Langley Res Ctr, NASA, Hampton, Va, 76-79. *Mem:* Fel Am Soc Mech Engrs; fel Inst Engrs India; fel Acoust Soc India; Can Soc Mech Eng; Am Acad Mech. *Res:* Dynamic behavior of rotors supported on fluid film bearings; geared rotors, vibration of plates and beams using beam characteristic orthogonal polynomials; response of structures to random excitations; model testing and analysis; structural acoustics; micromechatronics. *Mailing Add:* Mech Eng Concordia Univ 1455 De Maisonneuve Blvd W Montreal PQ H3G 1M8 Can. *Fax:* 514-848-3175; *E-Mail:* rbhat@vax2.concordia.ca

BHAT, UGGAPPAKODI NARAYAN, APPLIED PROBABILITY, STATISTICS. *Current Pos:* from assoc prof to prof opers res & statist, Southern Methodist Univ, 69-79, head dept, 75-79, assoc dean, 76-79, chmn, Div Math Sci, 79-80, vprovost & dean grad studies, 80-82, chmn, dept statist sci, 87-89, PROF STATIST, SOUTHERN METHODIST UNIV, 79-; DEAN RES & GRAD STUDIES, DEDMAN COL, 92-, INTERIM DEAN, 96- *Personal Data:* b Vittal, India, Nov 17, 33; m 59, Girija Maliye; c Girish & Gouri. *Educ:* Univ Madras, BA, 53, BT, 54; Karnatak Univ, India, MA, 58; Univ Western Australia, PhD(math statist), 64. *Prof Exp:* Teacher high sch, India, 54-56; lectr statist, Karnatak Univ, India, 58-61; asst math, Univ Western Australia, 61-64, temp lectr, 64-65; asst prof statist, Mich State Univ, 65-66; from asst prof to assoc prof opers res, Case Western Reserve Univ, 66-69; assoc dean, Dedman Col, 89-92. *Concurrent Pos:* Assoc ed, Opsearch, 68-, Opers Res, 68-75 & Mgt Sci, 69-74, queueing systems, 86- *Mem:* Fel Am Statist Asn; Inst Math Statist; Opers Res Soc Am; Inst Mgt Sci; Int Statist Inst. *Res:* Queueing theory; probabilistic models for computer and communication systems; applied probability; stochastic processes. *Mailing Add:* Dept Statist Sci Southern Methodist Univ Dallas TX 75275. *Fax:* 214-768-4235; *E-Mail:* nbhat@mail.smu.edu

BHAT, VENKATRAMANA KAKEKOCHI, PHARMACEUTICAL CHEMISTRY, MEDICINAL CHEMISTRY. *Current Pos:* CONSULT CHEMIST, 71- *Personal Data:* b Padre, India, July 26, 33; US citizen; m 67, Clarita Csaky; c Saraswaty D & Tara K. *Educ:* Univ Madras, BSc, 55, BPharm, 58; Univ Wash, PhD(pharmaceut chem), 63. *Prof Exp:* Res assoc carbohydrate chem, Georgetown Univ, 63-67; pharmaceut chemist, Gulf South Res Inst, 67-71. *Mem:* AAAS; Am Chem Soc; Am Inst Chemists; NY Acad Sci; Sigma Xi. *Res:* Synthesis of sulfur containing compounds related to Ephedrine; synthesis of nucleosides, carbohydrates and antimalarials; analytical biochemistry, especially analysis of drugs, herbicides and pesticides using gas chromatography. *Mailing Add:* 8002 53rd Ave W Mukilteo WA 98275-2630

BHATHENA, SAM JEHANGIRJI, ENDOCRINOLOGY, HUMAN NUTRITION. *Current Pos:* res chemist, Carbohydrate Nutrit Lab, 83-96, RES CHEMIST, PHYTONUTRIENT LAB, BELTSVILLE HUMAN NUTRIT LAB, MD, 97- *Personal Data:* b Bombay, India, Sept 18, 36; US citizen; m 75, Pauruchisty K Kias. *Educ:* Univ Bombay, BSc, 61, MSc, 64, PhD(biochem), 70. *Prof Exp:* Vis fel biochem, NIH, 71-73, vis assoc, 74; res biochemist, Diabetes Res Lab, Vet Admin Med Ctr, Washington, DC, 75-82. *Concurrent Pos:* Res instr, Dept Med, Georgetown Univ, Washington, DC, 79-80, res asst prof, 81-83, adj asst prof, 83-90; assoc prof, Dept Human Nutrit & Food Syst, College Park, Md, 90-94. *Mem:* Am Diabetes Asn; Soc Exp Biol & Med; Am Soc Clin Nutrit; Int Neuropeptide Soc; Am Chem Soc; Am Soc Nutrit Sci; Asn Sci Indian Origin Am (secy/treas, 90-91, pres, 97-98). *Res:* Study of dietary regulation of peptide hormones, neuropeptides, opioid peptides and their receptors; endocrine aspects of nutritional disorders; interactions between dietary carbohydrates and trace metals; phytonutrients and human health. *Mailing Add:* Phytonutrient Lab Beltsville Human Nutrit Res Ctr Bldg 307 Rm 315 Beltsville MD 20705-2350. *Fax:* 301-504-9456; *E-Mail:* bhattena@307.bhnrc.usda.gov

BHATIA, ANAND K, ATOMIC PHYSICS. *Current Pos:* AEROSPACE TECHNOLOGIST, GODDARD SPACE FLIGHT CTR, NASA, 65- *Personal Data:* b W Pakistan, Jan 26, 34; m 63; c 1. *Educ:* Univ Delhi, BSc, 53, MSc, 55; Univ Md, PhD(physics), 62. *Prof Exp:* Asst prof physics, Wesleyan Univ, 62-63; res assoc, Nat Acad Sci, 63-65. *Res:* High energy physics; molecular physics. *Mailing Add:* Goddard Space Flight Ctr NASA Code 681 Greenbelt MD 20771

BHATIA, DARSHAN SINGH, FOOD TECHNOLOGY, NUTRITION. *Current Pos:* DIR RES & DEVELOP, COCA-COLA CO, 72- *Personal Data:* b Lahore, India, Apr 12, 23; m 45; c 3. *Educ:* Punjab Univ, BSc, 43, MSc, 45; Mass Inst Technol, ScD, 50. *Prof Exp:* Asst dir, Cent Food Technol Res Inst, Mysore, India, 50-64; chmn, Training Prog, FAO Ctr, Mysore, 64-65; tech mgr, Coca-Cola Export Corp, New Delhi, 65-72. *Concurrent Pos:* Mem panel experts, Adv Comt Appl Sci & Technol to Develop, UN, 67; mem, vis comt, Dept Nutrit & Food Sci, Mass Inst Technol, 75-78. *Mem:* Inst Food Technologists; Am Inst Nutrit; NY Acad Sci. *Res:* Food science and technology; process development, nutrition, management of research and development in food and allied fields. *Mailing Add:* 2290 Bohler Rd Atlanta GA 30327-1104

BHATIA, KISHAN, ORGANIC CHEMISTRY, ANALYTICAL CHEMISTRY. *Current Pos:* DEVELOP SCIENTIST, N L TREATING CHEM, EXXON CHEM CO, 81- *Personal Data:* b Poona, India, Mar 23, 36; c 2. *Educ:* Univ Poona, BSc, 58, MSc, 60; Univ Ark, PhD(org chem), 65. *Prof Exp:* Demonstr chem, Fergusson Col, Univ Poona, 59-60; jr res fel org chem, Nat Chem Lab, India, 60-61; asst, Univ Ark, 61-65; sr res chemist, US Steel Corp, 65-70; fel chem, Mellon Inst, Carnegie-Mellon Univ, 71-75; chromatography sect leader, Allied Chem Corp, 75-76; sr scientist, Pullman Kellogg, Pullman Inc, 76-80. *Mem:* Am Chem Soc; Sigma Xi; Nat Asn Corrosion Engrs; Soc Petrol Engrs. *Res:* Feedstock characterization technology; advanced process instrumentation technology; petroleum and solid fuel chemistry, radiation chemistry, organic chemistry; design and development of chrometographic instrumentations, sectrometry, isotope techniques; computerization and automation technology; corrosion engineering; gas processing technology; corrosion inhibitors and other chemicals for treatment of produced gas and fluids; refinery and petro chemicals; synthetic fuels. *Mailing Add:* 20222 Lavereton Katy TX 77450-2106

BHATIA, NAM PARSHAD, MATHEMATICS. *Current Pos:* vis assoc prof, Dept Math & Inst Fluid Dynamics & Appl Math, College Park, 68-69, dir, Math Grad Prog, Baltimore Co, 71-83, PROF MATH, UNIV MD, BALTIMORE CO, 69- *Personal Data:* b Lahore, India, Aug 24, 32; wid; c Wizie, Rizie & Rajani. *Educ:* Agra Univ, BSc, 52, MSc, 54 & 56; Dresden Tech Univ, Dr rer nat(math), 61. *Prof Exp:* Lectr math, REI Degree Col, Agra Univ, 55-56; asst prof, Birla Col, India, 56-58; aspirant, Dresden Tech Univ, 58-61; asst prof, Birla Col, India, 61-62; vis mathematician, Res Inst Advan Studies, Div Martin Co, Md, 62-63; from asst prof to assoc prof, Case Western Res Univ, 63-68. *Concurrent Pos:* NSF res grant, 64-73; ed, Math Systs Theory, 68-72. *Res:* Dynamical and semi-dynamical systems; theory and application of ordinary differential equations; control theory; stability theory; chaos theory. *Mailing Add:* Dept Math & Statist Univ Md Baltimore Co 5401 Wilkens Ave Catonsville MD 21228-5329. *E-Mail:* bhatia@umbc.umbc-math.edu

BHATIA, SHYAM SUNDER, POPULATION GEOGRAPHY,. *Current Pos:* RETIRED. *Personal Data:* b Rawalpindi, India, July 7, 24; US citizen; m 50; c 2. *Educ:* Univ Panjab, BSc, 43, MA, 47; Univ Kans, PhD(geog), 59. *Prof Exp:* Lectr geog, Univ Col Panjab, New Delhi, 48-56; reader, Univ Delhi, 59-66; from assoc prof to prof geog, Univ Wis-Oshkosh, 66-91. *Concurrent Pos:* Reader, Indian Sch Int Studies, 60-64; exchange vis prof, San Diego State Univ, 75-76. *Mem:* Asn Am Geogr; Sigma Xi. *Res:* Population; agricultural geography; geography of South Asia. *Mailing Add:* 1518 Steinbeck Dr Roseville CA 95747

BHATLA, MANMOHAN N (BART), ENGINEERING. *Current Pos:* Proj mgr, Proj Eng Lab Dir, 64-70, tech mgr, Weston-Europe, 70-78, VPRES, INDUST WASTE MGT, WESTON, 78- *Personal Data:* b India. *Educ:* Punjab Eng Col, India, BSc, 60, Univ Roorkee, India, ME, 61, Okla State Univ, PhD(sanitary & pub health), 64. *Honors & Awards:* George Bradley Gascoigne Medal, Water Pollution Control Fedn, 76. *Mem:* Am Acad Environ Engrs. *Res:* Management and supervision of environmental projects in solid waste and hazardous waste management and water pollution control field; author or coauthor of over 25 publications. *Mailing Add:* 706 Apricot Lane West Chester PA 19380

BHATNAGAR, AJAY SAHAI, ORGANIC CHEMISTRY, REPRODUCTIVE ENDOCRINOLOGY. *Current Pos:* Res assoc physiol, 68-70, ASST PROF OBSTET & GYNEC, MED COL VA, 70-, ASST PROF BIOCHEM, 73- *Personal Data:* b Muree, India, Sept 26, 42; m 70. *Educ:* Cambridge Univ, BA, 63, MA, 67; Univ Basel, PhD(org chem), 67. *Concurrent Pos:* Fel org chem, Univ Basel, 67. *Mem:* AAAS; NY Acad Sci; Am Chem Soc; Swiss Chem Soc; Endocrine Soc. *Res:* Analytical methodology for the estimation of steroids; steroid metabolism in the female; endocrinology of pregnancy. *Mailing Add:* Endocrine Res Ciba-Geigy Ltd K-12515-16 Basel 4002 Switzerland

BHATNAGAR, DEEPAK, PLANT PHYSIOLOGY. *Current Pos:* GENETICIST, SOUTHERN REGIONAL RES CTR, USDA AGR RES SERV, NEW ORLEANS, 85-, ADJ PROF, TULANE UNIV, 91- *Personal Data:* b India, Aug 5, 49; US citizen; m 78, Madhu Kohli; c Deepa. *Educ:* Univ Udaipur, India, BSc Hons, 72; Indian Agr Res Inst, New Delhi, MSc, 74, PhD(agr physics), 77. *Prof Exp:* ICAR jr res fel, Indian Agr Res Inst, New Delhi, 72-74, sr res fel, 74-77; officer, Dept Biophys, All India Inst Med Sci, New Delhi, 77-78; res fel, Dept Biol, Purdue Univ, West Lafayette, Ind, 79-81; sr res assoc, Dept Biochem, Sch Med, La State Univ, 81-85. *Concurrent Pos:* Grants, Dr George S Bell Mem Res Award, Am Heart Asn, 82-83 & 83-84, US Dept Agr, Agr Res Serv Res Assoc Prog, 89-91, 93-95; tech reviewer, J Exp Mycol. *Mem:* Am Soc Biochem & Molecular Biol; Am Chem Soc; Am Soc Plant Physiologists; Am Soc Microbiol; AAAS; Sigma Xi; NY Acad Sci. *Res:* Genetic manipulation of the pertinent fungal genome for the development of the long term procedures for control of the aflatoxin contamination process; utilization of natural products in control of aflatoxin biosynthesis by the fungus. *Mailing Add:* USDA Agr Res Ctr Southern Regional Res Ctr 1100 Robert E Lee Blvd Box 19687 New Orleans LA 70124-4305

BHATNAGAR, DINESH C, INORGANIC CHEMISTRY, ANALYTICAL CHEMISTRY. *Current Pos:* PROF CHEM, ALGONQUIN COL APPL ARTS & TECHNOL, 68- *Personal Data:* b Lahore, WPakistan, Apr 14, 34; m 62; c 2. *Educ:* Univ Delhi, BSc, 53, MSc, 55; Wayne State Univ, PhD(chem), 63. *Prof Exp:* Res asst chem, Nat Chem Lab, India, 56-59; instr, Detroit Inst Technol, 62-63; fel, Univ Ariz, 63-65; asst prof, La Verne Col, 65-67; master, Sch Mines, Haileybury, Ont, Can, 67-68. *Concurrent Pos:* Consult, Garett Res Corp, Calif, 65. *Mem:* Am Chem Soc; Chem Inst Can; Sigma Xi. *Res:* Optical rotary dispersion of inorganic complex ions; luminescence of metal complexes. *Mailing Add:* Dept Chem Algonquin Col 1385 Woodroffe Ave Nepean ON K2G 1V8 CAN

BHATNAGAR, GOPAL MOHAN, MOLECULAR BIOLOGY. *Current Pos:* SCI REV ADMINR, NAT INT CHILD HEALTH & HUMAN DEVELOP. *Personal Data:* b Lucknow, India, July 15, 37; US citizen. *Educ:* Lucknow Univ, India, BSc, 55, MSc, 57, PhD(biochem), 61. *Prof Exp:* Res assoc biochem, Chicago Med Sch, 63-65; res scientist protein chem, Commonwealth Sci & Indust Res Orgn, Melbourne, Australia, 65-69; staff scientist muscle proteins, Boston Biomed Res Inst, 69-72; assoc prof, Lucknow Univ, India, 73-74; prin assoc epidermal proteins, Sch Med, Harvard Univ, 74-77; assoc prof dermat, Sch Med, Johns Hopkins Univ, 77-87; sr chemist, Food & Drug Admin, Rockville, Md, 87- *Concurrent Pos:* Vis scientist, Univ Montreal, 73-; prin investr, res grant, NIH, 76-86; consult, Food & Drug admin, 80-85; guest res scientist, Nat Inst Aging, NIH, 80-88. *Mem:* Am Soc Biol Chemists. *Res:* Molecular changes involved in cellular aging; epithelial differentiation and keratinization; biochemistry and physiology of cardiac muscle; molecular biology of epidermal proteins; regulation of wound healing devices. *Mailing Add:* Div Sci Rev Rm 5E01 NICHD-NIH 6100 Executive Blvd Rockville MD 20852-4910. *Fax:* 301-402-4104

BHATNAGAR, KUNWAR PRASAD, NEUROANATOMY, BIOLOGY OF BATS. *Current Pos:* from asst prof to assoc prof, 72-85, PROF ANAT, SCH MED, UNIV LOUISVILLE, 85- *Personal Data:* b Gwalior, India, Mar 21, 34; US citizen; m 61, Indu; c Divya (Rouben) & Jyoti (Burruss). *Educ:* Agra Univ, BSc, 56; Vikram Univ, India, MSc, 58; State Univ NY, Buffalo, PhD(anat), 72. *Prof Exp:* From lectr to asst prof zool, Madhya Pradesh Educ Serv, India, 58-67; teaching asst anat, State Univ NY, Buffalo, 68-72. *Concurrent Pos:* Sabbatical leave, Max Planck Inst Brain Res, Frankfurt & Inst Anat, Essen, WGer, 78-79 & 86-87; ed, Bat Res News, 82-86; guest ed, J Electron Micros Tech, 92. *Mem:* Am Soc Mammal; Am Asn Anatomists; Sigma Xi. *Res:* Mammalian olfaction; rhinencephalon in Chiroptera; biology of bats; pineal ultrastructure; human development. *Mailing Add:* Health Sci Ctr Dept Anat Scis & Neurobiol Sch Med Univ Louisville Louisville KY 40292-0001. *E-Mail:* kpbhat01@ulkyvm.louisville.edu

BHATNAGAR, LAKSHMI, APPLIED MICROBIOLOGY, ENVIRONMENTAL BIOLOGY. *Current Pos:* SR SCIENTIST, MICH BIOTECHNOL INST, 85- *Personal Data:* b New Delhi, India, Oct 25, 51; m 80, Rita; c Gaurav C & Tushar C. *Educ:* Panjab Univ, BSc(Hon), 71, MSc(Hon), 73; Inst Pasteur, Univ Paris, PhD(microbiol), 85. *Prof Exp:* Scientist in-chg, Biol Evans Ltd, 73-76; scientist, Indian Coun Agr Res, 76-85. *Concurrent Pos:* Vis scientist, Inst Pasteur, 81-85; adj asst prof, Mich State Univ, 89-; prin investr, Great Lakes Protection Fund 91-94. *Mem:* Am Soc Microbiol; Am Chem Soc. *Res:* Applied and environmental microbiology; methanogens, cloning and expression of industrial enzymes, biodegradation of toxic chemicals, development of biocatalysts. *Mailing Add:* 1722 Country View Dr Okemos MI 48864

BHATNAGAR, RAJENDRA SAHAI, BIOCHEMISTRY, BIOPHYSICS. *Current Pos:* assoc prof, 68-74, PROF BIOCHEM, SCH DENT, UNIV CALIF, SAN FRANCISCO, 74- *Personal Data:* b Lucknow, India, Mar 10, 36; m 66; c 2. *Educ:* Agra Univ, BS, 54, MS, 56; Duke Univ, MS, 63, PhD(biochem), 64. *Prof Exp:* Lectr, Govt Col, Rupar, 57-58; tech asst, Tech Develop Dept, Ministry Indust, 58-60; asst instr med & biochem, Sch Med, Univ Pa & Philadelphia Gen Hosp, 65-67; sr res assoc biochem, Med Sch, Northwestern Univ, 67-68. *Concurrent Pos:* Fel, Vet Admin Hosp, Hines, Ill, 64-65 & Sch Med, Univ Pa & Philadelphia Gen Hosp, 65-67; res career develop award, 69; vis prof biophys & biochem, Indian Inst Sci, Bangalore, India, 72-73. *Mem:* AAAS; Am Chem Soc; Am Soc Biol Chemists; NY Acad Sci; fel Am Inst Chemists. *Res:* Biology of connective tissue, especially the biosynthesis and regulation of collagen; structure and interactions of collagen. *Mailing Add:* Sch Dent 661 HSW Univ Calif Box 0424 San Francisco CA 94143-0424

BHATNAGAR, RANBIR KRISHNA, PHARMACOLOGY. *Current Pos:* res assoc, 71-72, from asst prof to assoc prof, 72-81, PROF PHARMACOL, UNIV IOWA, 81- *Personal Data:* b India; US citizen. *Educ:* Univ Lucknow, BSc, 54; Agra Univ, BVSc, 58; Mich State Univ, MS, 63, PhD(pharmacol), 71. *Prof Exp:* Veterinarian, Govt Uttar Pradesh, India, 58-59; res assoc physiol, Col Vet Sci, Mathura, India, 59-61; res assoc pharmacol, Univ Chicago, 65-67. *Concurrent Pos:* Assoc ed, J Pharmacol Methods. *Mem:* Am Soc Pharmacol & Exp Therapeut; Am Soc Neurochem; Soc Neurosci; Int Soc Neurochem. *Res:* Neurochemistry and neuropharmacology with particular emphasis on central nervous system neurotransmitters; factors which influence the growth and differentiation of neurons in central nervous system. *Mailing Add:* Dept Pharmacol Univ Iowa 2471 Bowen Sci Bldg Iowa City IA 52242

BHATNAGAR, YASHRAJ KISHORE, thin films, materials & devices, for more information see previous edition

BHATNAGAR, YOGENDRA MOHAN, MOLECULAR BIOLOGY, EMBRYOLOGY. *Current Pos:* asst prof pediat, 79-80, asst prof anat, 80-84, ASSOC PROF STRUCT & CELLBIOL, UNIV SALA, MOBILE, 84-, ASSOC PROF MED GENETICS, 90-, ASSOC PROF MARINE SCI, 93- *Personal Data:* b Gorakhpur, UP, India, Feb 5, 45; m 74, Sheela P Shah; c Pooja. *Educ:* Univ Lucknow, India, BSc, 62, MSc, 64; Boston Col, PhD(biol), 74. *Prof Exp:* Instr biol, Boston Col, 73-74; res fel physiol, Med Sch, Harvard Univ, 74-76, res assoc, 76-77; sr scientist, EIC Corp, Newton, Mass, 77-79. *Concurrent Pos:* Res fel, Pop Coun, NY, 74-76; adj lectr, Northeastern Univ, Boston, Mass, 77-79; prin investr, NIH, 80-, res career develop award, 85-90. *Mem:* AAAS; Am Soc Biochem & Molecular Biol; Soc Study Reprod. *Res:* Molecular genetics; chromosomes; reproduction. *Mailing Add:* Depts Struct & Cell Biol Col Med 2042 MSB Univ SAla Mobile AL 36688. *Fax:* 334-460-6771

BHATT, GIRISH M, TEXTILE TECHNOLOGY, SYNTHETIC FIBER ENGINEERING. *Current Pos:* TECH DIR, JOHNSON FILAMENTS, INC, 78- *Personal Data:* b Coimbatore, India, June 21, 46; US citizen; m 75, Chhaya; c Deepa & Arti. *Educ:* Univ Madras, India, BS, 68; Univ Conn, Storrs, MS, 70, PhD(chem eng & polymer sci), 74. *Prof Exp:* Res engr, Mill Spinning Dept, Am Enka, 70-71; asst prof man made fibers, Textile Tech Dept, Grad Sch, PSG Col Technol, India, 75-76; asst prof, Chem Eng Dept, Caimbatore Inst Technol, India, 77; vis prof, Dept Chem Eng, Univ Conn, 78; asst prof, Home Econ Dept, Univ Vt, 79-80. *Concurrent Pos:* Lectr textile sci, Univ Vt, 79-80. *Mem:* Am Inst Chem Engrs; Soc Plastic Engrs. *Res:* Processing techniques and formulating polymer blends and alloys to yield high performance fibers and monofilaments. *Mailing Add:* 15 Brownell Way South Burlington VT 05403

BHATT, JAGDISH J, MARINE GEOLOGY. *Current Pos:* assoc prof, 74-84, PROF GEOL & OCEANOG, COMMUNITY COL RI, WARWICK, 84- *Personal Data:* b Umreth, India, Feb 17, 39; US citizen; m 71; c 2. *Educ:* Univ Baroda, BSc Hons, 61; Univ Wis-Madison, MS, 63; Univ Wales, PhD(marine geol), 72. *Prof Exp:* Instr chem & phys sci, Jackson Community Col, Mich, 64-65; instr phys sci & geol, Okla Panhandle State Univ, 65-66; res scientist geol, Stanford Univ, 71-72; asst prof environ sci & oceanog, Rachel Carson Col, Univ Buffalo, 72-74. *Concurrent Pos:* Mem exec comt, Gov Ocean Tech Task Force, RI, 75-76; co-chmn comt on joint offshore tech prog, Univ RI & RI Jr Col, 75-76; chmn comt ocean training prog, RI Jr Col, 77-78; mem sci adv comt, Pac Marine Tech, 90 & 92. *Res:* Geological and geochemical studies of marine sediments, notably carbonates; education techniques and programs for improving undergraduate training in marine, earth and environmental sciences; author of 50 articles including 5 books. *Mailing Add:* Dept Physics Community Col RI 400 East Ave Warwick RI 02886-1805

BHATT, PADMAMABH P, transdermal drug delivery, physical pharmacy, for more information see previous edition

BHATT, PRAVIN NANABHAI, BIOLOGY, HOST RESPONSES. *Current Pos:* SR RES SCIENTIST, VIROL & MICROBIOL, SCH MED, YALE UNIV, 68- *Educ:* Banaras Hindu Univ, India, AMS, 48; Tulane Univ, MD, 64. *Mailing Add:* Sect-Comp-Med Yale Univ PO Box 208016 New Haven CT 06520-8016

BHATT, RAVINDRA NAUTAM, THEORETICAL PHYSICS, ENGINEERING PHYSICS. *Current Pos:* PROF ELEC ENG & PHYSICS, PRINCETON UNIV, 90- *Personal Data:* b New Delhi, India, Jan 20, 52; m 80; c 1. *Educ:* Univ Delhi, BSc, 71; Univ Ill, MS, 74, PhD(physics), 76. *Prof Exp:* Mem tech staff, AT&T Bell Labs, 76-89, dept head, Theoret Physics Res Dept, 89-90. *Concurrent Pos:* Fel, CNRS, Ecole Normale Superieure, Paris, 83; sr vis fel, Imp Col, London, Sci & Eng Res Coun, 84; vis, Inst Theoret Physics, Santa Barbara, 86; trustee, Aspen Ctr Physics; mem, Supercomputer Allocations Comt, Cornell Theory Ctr. *Mem:* Fel Am Phys Soc. *Res:* Metal insulator transitions; disordered systems; spin glasses; quantum fluids and solids; superfluid helium; high temperature superconductivity; charge density waves; structural phase transitions; doped semiconductors; expanded metals; correlated and magnetic systems. *Mailing Add:* Dept Elec Eng Princeton Univ Princeton NJ 08544

BHATTACHARJEE, HIMANGSHU RANJAN, MATERIALS RESEARCH, APPLIED CHEMISTRY. *Current Pos:* SR SCIENTIST & LAB MGR, TEXWIPE CO, UPPER SADDLE RIVER, NJ, 90- *Personal Data:* b Comilla, Bangladesh, Mar 21, 42; US citizen; m 72, Kalpana; c Neeladri & Sandip. *Educ:* Univ Dacca, BSc, 64; Univ Col Sci & Technol, Calcutta, MSc, 67; Wayne State Univ, PhD(chem), 73. *Prof Exp:* Postdoctoral res fel laser chem, Radiation Lab, Univ Notre Dame, 73-74; postdoctoral res fel laser spectros, Univ NB, Can, 74-75; res assoc & chem lectr, Univ Toronto, Can, 75-77; res assoc laser spectros, Univ Calif, Santa Cruz, 77-78; sr res chemist, Allied Signal, Inc, Morristown, NJ, 78-90. *Concurrent Pos:* Prin investr several indust res & develop progs; working group adv, Inst Environ Sci. *Mem:* Am Chem Soc; AAAS; NY Acad Sci; Fine Particle Soc; Inst Environ Sci; Tech Asn Pulp & Paper Indust. *Res:* Laser spectroscopy; printing plates; coatings; photochemistry; clean room and office cleaning products; indicators-time-temperature; lithium dosage; radiation monitoring; polymer modifications; polypeptides; biopolymers electron microscopy; author of 21 publications and 15 US patents. *Mailing Add:* Texwipe Co 650 E Crescent Ave Upper Saddle River NJ 07458-1827. *Fax:* 201-327-5945

BHATTACHARJEE, JNANENDRA K, MICROBIAL GENETICS. *Current Pos:* assoc prof, 68-73, PROF MICROBIOL, MIAMI UNIV, 73- *Personal Data:* b Sylhet, Bangladesh, Feb 1, 36; m; c 2. *Educ:* MC Col, Sylhet, BS, 57; Univ Dacca, MS, 59; Southern Ill Univ, PhD(microbiol), 66. *Honors & Awards:* President's Award, President of Pakistan, 60. *Prof Exp:* Res assoc microbiol, Albert Einstein Med Ctr, Pa, 65-66, asst mem, 66-68. *Concurrent Pos:* NSF res grants, 69, 71, 75, 78 & 79; Lilly Res Found grant, 70, 72; S & H Found res grant, 74; NIH res grant, 85, NSF, 88. *Mem:* AAAS; Genetics Soc Am; Am Soc Microbiol; fel Am Acad Microbiol. *Res:* Genetics of yeast; biosynthetic mechanism of lysine and other related amino acids in yeast; regulation of gene action in eucaryotic organisms; cloning molecular studies and evolutionary diversity of lysine genes of yeast. *Mailing Add:* 454 Emerald Woods Dr Oxford OH 45056

BHATTACHARJI, SOMDEV, structural geology, for more information see previous edition

BHATTACHARYA, AMAR NATH, PHARMACOLOGY, PHYSIOLOGY. *Current Pos:* asst prof, 70-73, ASSOC PROF PHARMACOL, OHIO NORTHERN UNIV, 74- *Personal Data:* b Calcutta, India, Oct 1, 34; m 66; c 1. *Educ:* Bengal Vet Col, India, BVetS, 57; Ohio State Univ, MS, 63, PhD(pharmacol), 67. *Prof Exp:* State vet, Directorate Vet Serv, Govt WBengal, India, 57-59; demonstr, Dept Clin Vet Med & Pharmacol, Bengal Vet Col, 59-61; res asst pharmacol, Col Med, Ohio State Univ, 62-67, res assoc pharmacol & med, 68. *Concurrent Pos:* Ford Found fel physiol, Sch Med, Univ Pittsburgh, 68-70. *Mem:* Soc Study Reprod; Brit Soc Study Fertil; Indian Sci Cong Asn. *Res:* Neuroendocrine control mechanisms of corticotropin and gonadotropins, role of central catecholamines and serotonin; gonad-anterior pituitary feedback interrelationship in subhuman primates, studies with castration, steroids and psychotropic drugs; prostaglandins. *Mailing Add:* RAABC Col Pharm Ada OH 45810

BHATTACHARYA, AMIT, EFFECT OF ENVIRONMENTAL CHEMICALS ON POSTURAL STABILITY, ERGONOMIC RISK FACTORS FOR FALLS IN THE WORKPLACE. *Current Pos:* PROF ENVIRON HEALTH INDUST ENG, UNIV CINCINNATI, 80- *Personal Data:* b Calcutta, India, July 9, 46; US citizen. *Educ:* Birla Eng Col, India, BE, 69; Univ Ky, ME, 71, PhD(mech eng-biomed), 75. *Prof Exp:* Res assoc, Univ Ky, 77-79, biomed res scientist, 79-80. *Concurrent Pos:* Vis prof, Chinese Acad Prev Med, Beijing, 91. *Mem:* Sr mem Biomed Eng Soc; Am Indust Hyg Asn; Am Soc Biomech; Sigma Xi. *Res:* Identification, characterization and prevention of ergonomic risk factors; quantitative posturography for detecting neurotoxicity of chemical exposure; assessing fall potential of a workplace, multiple risk factors effect. *Mailing Add:* Inst Environ Health Univ Cincinnati ML-056 Cincinnati OH 45267

BHATTACHARYA, ASHOK KUMAR, NUCLEAR ENGINEERING, PHYSICS. *Current Pos:* RES PHYSICIST, GEN ELEC CO, 67- *Personal Data:* b Allahabad, India, Oct 14, 35; m 64. *Educ:* Univ Lucknow, BSc, 54, MSc, 56; Univ Ill, Urbana-Champaign, PhD(nuclear eng), 66. *Prof Exp:* Res assoc gas electronics, Univ Ill, Urbana-Champaign, 66-67. *Res:* Gaseous discharge; electronic atomic and molecular processes in a gaseous plasma. *Mailing Add:* 1168 Ford Rd Cleveland OH 44124

BHATTACHARYA, DEBANSHU, METALLURGY, MATERIALS SCIENCE. *Current Pos:* res engr, 76-79, SR RES ENGR, INLAND STEEL RES LABS, 79- *Personal Data:* b Uttarpara, India, June 26, 47. *Educ:* Regional Eng Col, Durgapur, India, BE, 69; Wash State Univ, MS, 71, PhD(eng sci), 75. *Honors & Awards:* Chipman Award, Iron & Steel Soc, 88. *Prof Exp:* Res assoc geosci, Pa State Univ, 75-76. *Concurrent Pos:* Res & teaching asst, Wash State Univ, 60-75. *Mem:* Am Soc Metals; Am Inst Metall Engrs. *Res:* Thermodynamics of alloys; machinability of materials; high temperature mechanical properties of metals; phase transformations in metals. *Mailing Add:* 3018 Elliot Lane Homewood IL 60430

BHATTACHARYA, JAHAR, RESPIRATORY PHYSIOLOGY, MICROCIRCULATORY PHYSIOLOGY. *Current Pos:* fel physiol, 77-80, ASST PROF, DEPT PHYSIOL & MED, UNIV CALIF, SAN FRANCISCO, 85- *Personal Data:* b Calcutta, India, Mar 12, 46; m 72; c 2. *Educ:* All-India Inst Med Sci, MBBS, 69; Oxford Univ, MSc, 72, DPhil, 76. *Honors & Awards:* Res Career Develop Award, 85. *Prof Exp:* Schorstein lectr, Regius Dept Med, Oxford Univ, 73-76; Neizer fel, Div Nephrology, Stanford Univ, 76-77. *Mem:* Am Physiol Soc; Am Microcirculatory Soc. *Res:* Lung microcirculation to determine mechanisms of microvascular fluid flux by a new micropunctive technique. *Mailing Add:* Col P & S Columbia Univ St Luke's-Roosevelt Hosp Ctr 1000 Tenth Ave New York NY 10019-1192

BHATTACHARYA, MALAYA, IMMUNOLOGY, BIOCHEMISTRY. *Current Pos:* Fel, Immunol & Immunochem, 69-71, sr cancer res scientist, 71-78, CANCER RES SCIENTIST IV, ROSWELL PARK MEM INST, 79- *Personal Data:* b Cooch-behar, India, Jan 16, 46; m 72; c 2. *Educ:* Presidency Col, Calcutta, India, BS, 63; Univ Col Sci, Calcutta, MS, 65, PhD(biochem), 69. *Concurrent Pos:* Nat Cancer Inst res grants, 76-79; NSF res grant, 80-81; Am Cancer Soc res grants, 83-86; NIH res grant, 89-92. *Mem:* Am Asn Cancer Res; Am Asn Immunologists. *Res:* Immunobiology of human tumors; immunodiagnosis and immunotherapy of cancer; biological response modifiers. *Mailing Add:* Dept Int Med Univ Ky 207 Combs CRB 800 Rose St Lexington KY 40536-0096. *Fax:* 606-257-8940

BHATTACHARYA, PALLAB KUMAR, COMPOUND SEMICONDUCTOR SYNTHESIS, OPTOELECTRONICS & INTEGRATED OPTICS. *Current Pos:* assoc prof, 84-87, PROF, UNIV MICH, ANN ARBOR, 87- *Personal Data:* b Calcutta, India, Dec 6, 49; m 75; c 2. *Educ:* Univ Calcutta, BS, 68, BTech, 70, MTech, 71, MEng, 76, PhD(elec eng), 78. *Prof Exp:* Sr res asst microwaves, Radar & Communication Ctr, Ind Inst Technol, 72-73, com exec, Hindustan Steel Ltd, Rourkela, India, 73-75; from asst prof to assoc prof elec & comput eng, Ore State Univ, 78-83. *Concurrent Pos:* Consult, Tektronix Inc, Beavertown, Ore, 80-83, prin investr, grants & contracts from NSFS, Dept Eng & NASA, 80-, invited prof microelectron, Swiss Federal Inst Technol, 81-83, consult, Int Tel & Tel, Roanoke, Va, 83-85; Army Res Orgn & Dow Chem, 85-87, Hughes Res Labs, 85-86, Ford Sci Labs, 86-, Rockwell Int, 87; vis prof, Aachen Tech Univ, WGer, 88. *Mem:* Am Phys Soc; sr mem Inst Elec & Electronics Engrs. *Res:* Molecular beam epitaxy of III-V compound semiconductor heterostructures and superlattices and strained-layer heterostructures, their electrical and optical properties and their use in high-speed electronic and opto-electronic devices; optical detectors and modulators, non-linear optical phenomena and integrated optics; over 150 contributed and invited papers. *Mailing Add:* Dept Elec Eng 3316-EECS Univ Mich Main Campus 1301 Beal Ave Ann Arbor MI 48109-2122

BHATTACHARYA, PRABIR, BIOCHEMISTRY, CELL BIOLOGY. *Current Pos:* sr prin scientist, 87-90, DIR RES & DEVELOP, ALPHA THERAPEUT CORP, 90- *Personal Data:* b Gaya, Bihar, India, Jan 24, 48; US citizen; m 75; c 2. *Educ:* Univ Calcutta, India, BS, 67, MS, 69, PhD(biochem), 74. *Prof Exp:* Scientist, Am Red Cross, Bethesda, Md, 84-87. *Concurrent Pos:* Mem, Thrombosis Coun, Am Heart Asn. *Mem:* Am Heart Asn; Am Soc Biol & Molecular Biol. *Res:* Developing therapeutic agents from human plasma. *Mailing Add:* Alpha Therapeut Corp 1213 John Reed Ct City of Industry CA 91745-2455. *Fax:* 402-472-7767

BHATTACHARYA, PRADEEP KUMAR, PLANT PHYSIOLOGY, PLANT PATHOLOGY. *Current Pos:* chmn dept, 73-83 ASSOC PROF BIOL, IND UNIV NORTHWEST, 73-,. *Personal Data:* b Dacca, Brit India, Jan 12, 40. *Educ:* Banaras Hindu Univ, BSc, 57, MSc, 59; Univ Sask, PhD(biol), 66. *Prof Exp:* Lectr bot, MLK Degree Col, Gorakhpur Univ, India, 59-61; res assoc biol & plant physiol, Univ Sask, 66-67; fel bot, Univ Western Ont, 67-69; fel plant path, Univ Wis-Madison, 69-70; asst prof biol, Rockford Col, 70-73. *Concurrent Pos:* Nat Res Coun Can assoc, Dept Biol, Univ Sask, 66-67; Nat Res Coun Can fel, Dept Bot, Univ Western Ont, 67-69; NIH fel, Dept Plant Path, Univ Wis-Madison, 69-70. *Mem:* Am Inst Biol Scientists; Am Soc Cell Biol; Am Asn Univ Prof; Sigma Xi; AAAS. *Res:* Physiology of host-parasite relations with particular reference to obligate parasitism; cytochemical and related biochemical events in plant-parasite interaction studies in wheat rust, barley mildew and root rot of cabbage; senescence in plant and human tissue. *Mailing Add:* Dept Biol Ind Univ NW 3400 Broadway Gary IN 46408

BHATTACHARYA, RABI, MARKOV PROCESSES, NORMAL APPROXIMATION & ASYMPTOTIC EXPANSIONS. *Current Pos:* PROF MATH, IND UNIV, BLOOMINGTON, 82- *Personal Data:* b Porgola, India, Jan 11, 37; US citizen; m 67, Bithika Banerjee; c Urmi B (Holz) & Deepta. *Educ:* Calcutta Univ, BSc, 56, MSc, 59; Univ Chicago, PhD(statist), 67. *Honors & Awards:* Sr Scientific Award, Alexander von Humboldt Found, 94. *Prof Exp:* Asst prof statist, Univ Calif, Berkeley, 67-72; from assoc prof to prof math, Univ Ariz, Tucson, 72-82. *Concurrent Pos:* Assoc ed, Annals Probability, Inst Math Statist, 76-81; vis prof math, Indian Statist Inst, 78-79, Univ Bielefeld, Ger, 92 & 94, Univ Gottingen, Ger, 95; Inst Math Statist Fel, 78; assoc ed, J Multivariate Anal, 85-90, Economet Theory, 85-, J Statist Planning & Inference, 85-88. *Mem:* Fel Inst Math Statist; Int Inst Statist; Am Math Soc; Bernoulli Soc. *Res:* Probability and statistics; refinements of central limit theorems and asymptotic expansions, with applications to statistics and bootstrapping; derivation of criteria for ergodicity of markore processes; co-authored 3 research/graduate level books and over 60 research articles. *Mailing Add:* Dept Math Ind Univ Bloomington IN 47405. *Fax:* 812-855-0046; *E-Mail:* bhattach@ucs.indiana.edu

BHATTACHARYA, RABI SANKAR, ION IMPLANTATION, THIN FILM. *Current Pos:* sr scientist, 81-86, prin res scientist mat res, 86-93, MGR & CHIEF SCIENTIST, UNIV ENERGY SYSTS, 93- *Personal Data:* b Silchar, India, Feb 19, 48; m 79, Kabita Biswas; c Ratnesh & Debanjana. *Educ:* Gauhati Univ, BS, 67; Indian Inst Technol, MS, 69; Saha Inst, Univ Calcutta, PhD(physics), 75. *Prof Exp:* Vis scientist physics, Fom Inst Atomic & Molecular Physics, Amsterdam, 75-77; vis prof, Univ Giessen, WGer, 77-78; vis scientist plasma physics, Max Planck Inst Plasma Physics, WGer, 78-79; sr res assoc eng physics McMaster Univ, Can, 79-80; sr res assoc mat res, Univ Fla, 80-81. *Mem:* Am Phys Soc; Am Soc Metals; Am Vacuum Soc; Soc Tribologist & Lubrication Engs. *Res:* Applications of ion beams in materials; synthesis of novel surface alloys and composites using vapor deposition and ion beams; self-lubricating surfaces by ion beam processing, ion implantation of semiconductors. *Mailing Add:* Univ Energy Systs Inc 4401 Dayton-Xenia Rd Dayton OH 45432. *Fax:* 937-426-5718

BHATTACHARYA, SABYASACHI, EXPERIMENTAL CONDENSED MATTER PHYSICS. *Current Pos:* SR RES SCIENTIST, NEC RES INST, 90- *Personal Data:* b Calcutta, India, Oct 3, 51; m 81, Kalpana Raina. *Educ:* Univ Calcutta, India, BSc, 71; Delhi Univ, India, MSc, 73; Northwestern Univ, PhD(physics), 78. *Prof Exp:* Res assoc, Univ RI, 78-79; James Franck fel, Univ Chicago, 79-82; physicist, Exxon Res & Eng, 82-85, staff physicist, 85-87, sr staff, physicist, 87-89. *Concurrent Pos:* Vis scientist, Francis Bitter Nat Magnet Lab, Mass Inst Technol, 78-79. *Mem:* Fel Am Phys Soc. *Res:* Experimental condensed matter physics; low-dimensional conductors, superconductivity, disordered systems and complex fluids. *Mailing Add:* NEC Res Inst 4 Independence Way Princeton NJ 08540

BHATTACHARYA, SYAMAL KANTI, MINERAL METABOLISM, NEUROMUSCULAR DISEASES. *Current Pos:* res assoc med, Med Ctr, 79-80, instr, 80-82, from instr to asst prof surg, 83-86, ASST PROF MED CHEM, UNIV TENN, MEMPHIS, 85-, ASSOC PROF SURG, 86-, DIR, SURG RES LABS & CHEM & NUTRIENT DATA OUTPUT LAB, 82- *Personal Data:* b Calcutta, India, Feb 13, 49; nat US; m 69; c 3. *Educ:* Univ Calcutta, BSc Hons, 68, BA, 69; Murray State Univ, MS, 76; Washington Univ, AM, 78; Memphis State Univ, PhD(anal chem), 79; Am Bd Bioanal, dipl, 80. *Prof Exp:* Asst instr chem, Netaji Sikshyatan, Calcutta, 68-69; sr instr, Bhabanath Inst, Calcutta, 69-70; res & develop chemist, Swastik Household & Indust Prod, Bombay, 70-74; teaching asst, Murray State Univ, 74-76; sr res technician pediat, Med Ctr, Washington Univ, 76-77, teaching-res fel chem, 76-78. *Concurrent Pos:* Res fel, Memphis State Univ, 78-79; NIH Nat Res Serv Awardee, Univ Tenn, Ctr Health Sci, 79-81; prin investr, res grants, USPHS, 81-83, Muscular Dystrophy Asn Am, 83-85, Univ Physician Found, 85-86 & Am Heart Asn, 86-87; consult clin chem, William Bowld Hosp & Regional Med Ctr, Memphis, 82-, Baptist Mem & Affil Hosps, 83-, Le Bonheur Children's Med Ctr, 84-, Crittenden County Mem Hosp, Ark, 84- & St Joseph Hosp, Methodist Cent & Affil Hosps & Med Express Regional Labs, 85-; vis prof surg, Sch Med, Yale Univ, 85; vis prof pediat, Med Ctr, Univ Cincinnati & Cincinnati Children's Hosp, 85. *Mem:* Fel Am Inst Chemists; fel Royal Soc Chem; Am Chem Soc; NY Acad Sci; fel Indian Chem Soc; fel Am Col Nutrit; fel Am Heart Asn; fel Inst Chemists India; Am Fedn Clin Res; Soc Neurosci; Int Soc Brain Res; AAAS; Sigma Xi. *Res:* Mineral metabolism in muscular dystrophy and acute pancreatitis: applications of surgical procedures and calcium-antagonists to ameliorate these conditions by inhibiting intracellular calcium shift; prevention of myocardial ischemia and endotoxin-shock by calcium-antagonists and fructose 1, 6 diphosphate. *Mailing Add:* 76 S Fernway Rd Memphis TN 38117

BHATTACHARYA-CHATTERJEE, MALAYA, CLINICAL IMMUNOLOGY, IMMUNOTHERAPY. *Current Pos:* Asst cancer res sci, Dept Immunol & Immunochem, 69-71, cancer res scientist III, 72-78, CANCER RES SCIENTIST IV IMMUNOL, DEPT GYNEC ONCOL & CLIN IMMUNOL, ROSWELL PARK CANCER INST, 79- *Personal Data:* b Cooch-Behar, India, Jan 16, 46; US citizen; m 72; c 2. *Educ:* Presidency Col, Calcutta, India, BS, 63; Univ Col Sci, Calcutta, India, MS, 65, PhD(biochem), 69. *Concurrent Pos:* Prin investr grants, NIH, Bethesda, Md, 76-79, NSF, 80-81 & Am Cancer Soc, 83-86; asst res prof, Dept Exp Path, State Univ NY, Buffalo, 89-; spec reviewer, Nat Cancer Inst, Bethesda, Md, 89- & NIH Study Sect, 91- *Mem:* Am Asn Cancer Res; Am Asn Immunologists. *Res:* Tumor immunology and immunochemistry; experimental immunotherapy; vaccines and biological response modifiers. *Mailing Add:* Dept Microbiol & Immunol Univ Ky 207 Combs Cancer Res Bldg 800 Rose St Lexington KY 40536-0096

BHATTACHARYYA, ASHIM KUMAR, PHYSIOLOGY, NUTRITION. *Current Pos:* from asst prof to assoc prof, 75-89, PROF PATH & PHYSIOL, LA STATE UNIV MED CTR, 89- *Personal Data:* b Kanpur, India, July 9, 36; m 66, Bani Chatterjee; c Rupa & Gopa. *Educ:* Univ Calcutta, BSc, 57, MSc, 59, PhD(physiol), 65, DSc(physiol), 89. *Prof Exp:* Fel physiol, Univ Minn, 66-68; fel med, Clin Res Ctr, Univ Iowa, 69-70, assoc res scientist, 70-74, res scientist, 74-75. *Concurrent Pos:* Assoc mem, Sch Grad Studies, La State Univ Med Ctr, 75-, dir, Lipid Chem Lab, Dept Path, 76-78; fel, Coun on Atherosclerosis, Am Heart Asn, 71- *Mem:* Sigma Xi; Am Soc Clin Nutrit; Am Inst Nutrit; Soc Exp Biol & Med; Am Physiol Soc; NY Acad Sci. *Res:* Regulation and mechanism of sterol absorption in the gastrointestinal tract; sterol and bile acid metabolism; atherosclerosis; dietary fatty acids, their transport and tissue storage. *Mailing Add:* Dept Path La State Univ Med Ctr 1901 Perdido St New Orleans LA 70112-1393. *Fax:* 504-568-6037; *E-Mail:* abhatt@lsumc.edu

BHATTACHARYYA, BIBHUTI BHUSHAN, MATHEMATICAL STATISTICS. *Current Pos:* asst prof, 63-69, ASSOC PROF STATIST, NC STATE UNIV, 69- *Personal Data:* b Bhatpara, India, Aug 1, 35; m 62. *Educ:* Univ Calcutta, BSc, 53, MSc, 55; Univ London, PhD(economet), 59. *Prof Exp:* Res scholar statist, Indian Statist Inst, 56; vis statistician, NC State Col, 59-61; res fel economet, Inst Econ Growth, 62; lectr math & statist, Univ

Toronto, 62-63. *Mem:* Inst Math Statist. *Res:* Econometrics; mathematical programming and its application to national planning as well as production planning of individual firms; sequential estimation problems. *Mailing Add:* Dept Math NC State Univ Box 8205 Raleigh NC 27695-0001

BHATTACHARYYA, GOURI KANTA, statistics, mathematical statistics, for more information see previous edition

BHATTACHARYYA, MARYKA HORSTING, BIOCHEMISTRY, TOXICOLOGY. *Current Pos:* asst biochemist, 74-79, BIOCHEMIST, ARGONNE NAT LAB, 79- *Personal Data:* b Glen Ridge, NJ, Sept 17, 43; m 71; c 1. *Educ:* Tufts Univ, BS, 65; Univ Wis, PhD(biochem), 70. *Honors & Awards:* R & D 100 Award, Blood Cadmium Assay Kit. *Prof Exp:* Fel biochem, Univ Wis, 70-71, res assoc, 71-74. *Concurrent Pos:* Adj prof, Northern Ill Univ, 79-; mem, Task Group Neptunium, NCRP, 82- *Mem:* Soc Toxicol; Sigma Xi; Radiation Res Soc. *Res:* Influence of pregnancy, lactation, and ovariectomy on cadmium-induced bone loss; gastrointestinal absorption of metals including cadmium, lead, plutonium, and other actinides. *Mailing Add:* 1429 Clyde Dr Naperville IL 60565

BHATTACHARYYA, MOHIT LAL, ELECTROPHYSIOLOGY, MEMBRANE BIOPHYSICS. *Current Pos:* ASST PROF CELL BIOL & CARDIOVASC PHYSIOL, MEHARRY MED COL, 82- *Personal Data:* b May 28, 44; m; c 1. *Educ:* Univ Wyo, PhD(physics), 71. *Mailing Add:* Dept Physiol Meharry Med Col 1005 D B Todd Blvd Nashville TN 37208

BHATTACHARYYA, PRANAB K, PHYSICAL CHEMISTRY, ANALYTICAL CHEMISTRY. *Current Pos:* sr scientist & supvr spectros technol, Analytical Res Sect, 74-79, tech fel, Res & Diag Prod Sect, 79-83, group leader, Pharmaceut Res Prod Sect, 83-87, MGR, PHARMACEUT RES PROD SECT, QUAL CONTROL DEPT, HOFFMANN-LA ROCHE, INC, 87- *Personal Data:* b India, Aug 9, 38; m 69; c 2. *Educ:* Calcutta Univ, BS, 59, MS, 62; Columbia Univ, PhD(phys chem), 71. *Prof Exp:* Res assoc nuclear magnetic resonance,Cchem dept, Columbia Univ, 71-74. *Mem:* NY Acad Sci; Am Chem Soc; Am Phys Soc; Int Soc Magnetic Resonance. *Res:* Quantitative analysis and characterization of drug and biological molecules and complex organic compounds using nuclear magnetic resonance and molecular spectroscopy; development of analytical methods and validation of methodology for testing the purity and stability of bulk drugs and dosage forms; preparation of investigational new drug and new drug application submissions to the Food and Drug Administration on test procedures for new drug products. *Mailing Add:* 18 Valley Rd Nutley NJ 07110-2225

BHATTACHARYYA, RAMENDRA KUMAR, MATHEMATICS. *Current Pos:* ASSOC PROF MATH, PAC UNIV, 69- *Personal Data:* b India, Mar 29, 31; m. *Educ:* Univ Calcutta, BSc, 51, MSc, 53; Stanford Univ, PhD(math), 64. *Prof Exp:* Lectr math, Taki Govt Col, India, 54-57 & Jadavpur Univ, 57-59; asst prof math, Univ Ariz, 64-65 & Southern Ill Univ, Carbondale, 65-69. *Mem:* Am Math Soc; Math Asn Am; alcutta Math Soc. *Res:* Theory of affine connections; system analysis. *Mailing Add:* Dept Math Pac Univ Forest Grove OR 97116

BHATTACHARYYA, SAMIT KUMAR, NUCLEAR REACTOR PHYSICS, SAFETY & TECHNOLOGY APPLICATIONS. *Current Pos:* Asst nuclear eng, Argonne Nat Lab, 74-78, nuclear eng, 78-79, group leader saref treat upgrade proj, reactor core design, 79-80, mgr reactor physics sect, treat upgrade proj, 80-83, leader, anal proj & prog develop group, 83-84, assoc dir, eng div, 84-88, eng physics div, 88-94, ASSOC DIR, TECHNOL DEVELOP DIV, ARGONNE NAT LAB, 94- *Personal Data:* b Calcutta, India, Mar 21, 47; US citizen; m 71, Maryka Horsting; c Roby Paul. *Educ:* Indian Inst Technol, BTech Hons, 68; Univ Wis, MS, 70, PhD(nuclear eng), 73; Univ Chicago, MBA, 87. *Mem:* Am Nuclear Soc. *Res:* Experimental and analytical studies on fast reactor physics; safety related physics; reactor design for terrestrial and space applications; technologies for decommissioning and decontamination of reactor and related facilities. *Mailing Add:* 1429 Clyde Dr Naperville IL 60565. *Fax:* 630-252-4007; *E-Mail:* bhatt@anl.gov

BHATTACHARYYA, SHANKAR P, CONTROL SYSTEMS. *Current Pos:* assoc prof, 80-84, PROF ELEC ENG, TEX A&M UNIV, 84- *Personal Data:* b Rangoon, Burma, June 23, 46; US citizen; m 71, 85; c Mohadev, Krishna L & Shona L. *Educ:* Indian Inst Technol, BTech, 67; Rice Univ, MS, 69, PhD(elec eng), 71. *Honors & Awards:* Fulbright lectr, 89. *Prof Exp:* From asst prof to prof elec eng, Fed Univ, Rio de Janeiro, Brazil, 71-80, chmn dept, 78-80. *Concurrent Pos:* Nat Res Coun res fel, Marshall Space Flight Ctr, NASA, 74-75; prin investr, NSF res contracts, 82-; assoc ed, Trans on Automatic Control, Inst Elec & Electronics Engrs, 85-, bd gov, Control Syst Soc, 86; dir, Telecommun & Control Systs Lab, Tex A&M Univ, 88-92 & Systs & Control Inst, 92-93; fel Tex Eng Exp Sta, 89. *Mem:* Fel Inst Elec & Electronics Engrs; Soc Indust & Appl Math; Control Systs Soc Inst Elec & Electronics Engrs. *Res:* Design of automatic control systems with emphasis on robust linear and multivariable control systems; author of more than 120 papers. *Mailing Add:* Elec Eng Dept Tex A&M Univ College Station TX 77843. *Fax:* 409-845-6259; *E-Mail:* bhatt@ee.tamu.edu

BHATTI, ASIF, EPOXY CHEMISTRY. *Current Pos:* MGR TECH SERV, BNB ENVIRON SERV INC, 94- *Personal Data:* b Sailkot, Pakistan, 1937. *Educ:* Univ Salfard, Eng, BS, 79, PhD(appl chem), 83. *Prof Exp:* Mgr anal serv & compliance, Toltest Inc; mgr environ serv, Harp Contractors, 93-94. *Mem:* Soc Plastic Engrs; Am Soc Qual Control. *Mailing Add:* 7668 Pope Run Lane Sylvania OH 43560

BHATTI, NEELOO, ECOSYSTEM VULNERABILITY ASSESSMENT, EMISSIONS INVENTORY & FATE OF POLLUTANTS IN ENVIRONMENT. *Current Pos:* assoc, 89-90, ENVIRON SCIENTIST, ARGONNE NAT LAB, 90- *Personal Data:* b New Delhi, India, Jan 30, 55; Can citizen; m 85, James J McAndrew. *Educ:* McGill Univ, Montreal, BS, 76; Yale Univ, MES, 84, MS & MPhil, 86, PhD(environ sci), 88. *Prof Exp:* Teaching asst environ sci, Yale Univ, 83. *Concurrent Pos:* Environ effects specialist, World Bank, 89- *Mem:* Am Chem Soc; Soc Am Foresters; Sigma Xi. *Res:* Collection, analysis and evaluation of fundamental environmental data to assess the vulnerability of specific ecosystems to current and future levels of pollutant loading and other environmental pertubations; identifying the environmental pathways followed by a variety of pollutants; acidic deposition, climate change, air toxics and hazardous waste issues at the national and international levels. *Mailing Add:* 15425 Purley Ct Lockport IL 60441

BHATTI, RASHID, TUMOR IMMUNOLOGY & IMMUNOBIOLOGY, PROSTATE CANCER. *Current Pos:* DIR RES PROSTATE TUMORS, COOK COUNTY HOSP UROL RES LAB, CHICAGO, 74- *Personal Data:* b Karachi, July 7, 39; US citizen; m 70, Angela; c Lubna. *Educ:* Univ Karachi, BS, 61, MS, 63; Eastern Ill Univ, Charleston, MS, 70; Harvard Med Sch, Boston, dipl tumor biol, 76 & 92. *Honors & Awards:* Distinguished Serv Award, Cambridge, Eng. *Prof Exp:* Assoc pharmacologist drug eval, Bio-Test Labs, Northbrook, Ill, 70-71; res assoc prostate cancer, Rush Presby St Luke Med Ctr, Chicago, Ill, 72-74. *Concurrent Pos:* Lectr, Int Found Microbiol, 70-72; sr sci officer, Hektol Inst Med Res, 74-79; consult, UN, 85-; res asst prof surg, Col Med, Univ Ill, Chicago, 86-, asst prof urol; hon prof, Pakistan Acad Med Sci, 96. *Mem:* Am Asn Cancer Res; Europ Asn Cancer Res; NY Acad Sci; Asn Pakistani Scientists & Engrs NAm (secy, 87-88, vpres, 91-93, pres, 93-95); sr fel Pakistan Acad Med Sci (vpres, 90-92). *Res:* Early detection, monitoring and management of prostate cancer, tumor markers effect of variety of therapeutic modalities; dissemination, metastasis of prostatic cancer (hematogenous factors); immune modulation. *Mailing Add:* Dir Urol Res Labs Cook County Hosp 1835 W Harrison Chicago IL 60612. *Fax:* 312-633-5164

BHATTI, WAQAR HAMID, PHYTOCHEMISTRY, NUCLEAR PHARMACY. *Current Pos:* from asst prof to assoc prof, 69-83, dir chem & radiation safety, 87-90, PROF PHARMACOG, BUTLER UNIV, 83-, DIR NUCLEAR PHARM, 90- *Personal Data:* b Sohawa, WPakistan, Nov 22, 31; m 64. *Educ:* Univ Panjab, BSc, 55, MSc, 57; Philadelphia Col Pharm, PhD(pharmacog), 63; Butler Univ, BS, 79. *Prof Exp:* Lectr pharmacog, Univ Panjab, Pakistan, 57; lectr bot, Univ Peshawar, 58-59; asst biol, Philadelphia Col Pharm, 59-63; asst prof pharmacog, Sch Pharm, NDak State Univ, 63-67; res fel internal med, Univ Iowa Hosp, 67-68; res assoc, Sch Pharm, Univ Pittsburgh, 68-69. *Concurrent Pos:* Res assoc, Einstein Med Ctr, 62-63 & Vet Admin, 63-; teaching fel pharmacog, NSF Inst Prog High Sch Students & Teachers, 64, prin investr, NSF grant, 64- *Mem:* Asn Off Anal Chemists; Am Asn Cols Pharm; Am Soc Hosp Pharmacists; Am Chem Soc; Sigma Xi. *Res:* The chemical investigation of both higher and lower plants; development of analytical methods for pharmaceutical dosage form; stability studies of selected pharmaceutical dosage form. *Mailing Add:* Col Pharm Butler Univ Indianapolis IN 46208-3485

BHAUMIK, MANI LAL, PHYSICS, QUANTUM ELECTRONICS. *Current Pos:* CONSULT, 86- *Personal Data:* b Calcutta, India, Jan 5, 32; US citizen. *Educ:* Univ Calcutta, BS, 51, MS, 53; Indian Inst Technol, PhD(physics), 58. *Hon Degrees:* DSc, Indian Inst Technol, 96. *Prof Exp:* Fel chem physics, Univ Calif, Los Angeles, 59-61; group leader lasers, Xerox Corp, 61-67; sr physics specialist, Aerojet Gen Corp, 67-68; res mgr lasers, Northrop Corp, 78-86. *Concurrent Pos:* Lectr, Calif State Univ, Long Beach, 67-68. *Mem:* Fel Am Phys Soc; Inst Elec & Electronics Engrs; Optical Soc Am; Sigma Xi. *Res:* Discovery and development of new lasers; investigation of laser applications to various fields. *Mailing Add:* PO Box 24050 Los Angeles CA 90024

BHAVANANDAN, VEER P, CANCER, CYSTIC FIBROSIS. *Current Pos:* res assoc, 73-74, from asst prof to assoc prof, 75-85, PROF BIOCHEM, M S HERSHEY MED CTR, PA STATE UNIV, 86- *Personal Data:* b Jaffna, Sri Lanka, Nov 1, 36; US citizen; m 65, Esha Chara; c Sivakami & Sathy. *Educ:* Univ Edinburgh, PhD(chem), 62; DSc, 83. *Prof Exp:* Res assoc, Columbia Univ, NY, 65-67; agr chemist, Tea Res Inst, Sri Lanka, 67-71; staff scientist, Med Res Found, Okla City, 71-73. *Concurrent Pos:* Fel, Univ Edinburg, 60-62; NIH grant, 76-; Am Cancer Soc Eleanor Roosevelt Int Cancer fel, 82-83; NIH Sr Fogarty Int fel, 82 & Physiol Chem Study Sect, 96-; mem, NIH Biochem Study sect, 87-; vis prof, Univ Tokyo, 93-94; fel, Japan Soc Prom Sci, 93-94. *Mem:* Fel Royal Soc Chem; Soc Complex Carbohydrates; Am Chem Soc; Am Soc Biochemists; AAAS; NY Acad Sci. *Res:* Investigation of cancer-associated mucin glycoproteins from human cancer cells, cancer diagnostic tests, host-bacterial interaction in pulmonary infection of cystic fibrosis patients, structure-function of mucins. *Mailing Add:* Milton Hershey Med Ctr Pa State Univ Hershey PA 17033. *Fax:* 717-531-7072

BHAVNANI, BHAGU R, BIOCHEMISTRY, PHARMACEUTICAL CHEMISTRY. *Current Pos:* DIR RES, DEPT OBSTET & GYNEC, ST MICHAEL'S HOSP, 88- *Personal Data:* b Hyderabad, India, Feb 16, 36; Can citizen; m 73; c 3. *Educ:* Univ Bombay, BS, 58 & 60, MS, 62; Mass Col Pharm, PhD(biochem), 66. *Prof Exp:* Res assoc steroid biochem, Worcester Found Exp Biol, 62-66; lectr, McGill Univ, 68-69, asst prof investigative med, 69-75; assoc scientist, Royal Victoria Hosp, Montreal, 68-75; asst prof obstet & gynec & clin biochem, Univ Toronto, 75-76, assoc prof obstet & gynec, 76-77; staff scientist, St Michael's Hosp, Toronto, 75-76; from assoc prof to prof obstet & gynec, McMaster Univ, Hamilton, 77-88, dir reprod biol res prog, 86-88; prof obstet & gynec, Univ Toronto, 88- *Concurrent Pos:* Fel biochem,

McGill Univ, 66-68; res oper grants, Med Res Coun Can, 68-, res grant, 70-75; res grants, Ontario Cancer Treatment & Res Found, 78-82; fel, Nat Cancer Inst, 81-86 & Ministry Health, 85-88. *Mem:* AAAS; Endocrine Soc; NY Acad Sci; Can Soc Endocrinol & Metab; Soc Obstet & Gynec Can; Soc Gynec Invest. *Res:* Genetic aspects of cortisol metabolism in the guinea pig; steroid formation and metabolism during pregnancy in humans; formation of ring B unsaturated estrogens in the pregnant mare; epidemiologic relation between use of exogenous estrogens and carcinoma of the endometrium; estrogen metabolism in postmenopausal women; diabetic pregnancy and fetal lung maturation; developmental aspects of fetal glycogen metabolism; infertility and luteal function; role of opiates in the regulation of the menstrual cycle; exercise induced secondary ammenhorea. *Mailing Add:* St Michaels Obstet & Gynecol Dept 7th Fl A South Rm 736 30 Bond St Toronto ON L8N 3Z5 Can

BHAVSAR, VIRENDRAKUMAR CHHABULAL, PARALLEL & DISTRIBUTED PROCESSING, LEARNING MACHINES. *Current Pos:* from asst prof to assoc prof, 83-91, PROF COMPUT SCI, UNIV NEW BRUNSWICK, 91-, DIR GRAD STUDIES, 94- *Personal Data:* b Malegaon, India; m 78, Vidya; c Shashwat & Sankalp. *Educ:* Univ Poona, BEng, 71; Indian Inst Technol, Bombay, MTech, 73, PhD(elec eng), 82. *Prof Exp:* Lectr comput sci, Indian Inst Technol, 76-82, asst prof, 82-83. *Concurrent Pos:* Vis prof comput sci, Ctr Develop Advan Comput, 90; pres, Super & Intelligent Comput Systs, Inc, 94- *Mem:* Soc Indust & Appl Math; Inst Elec & Electronics Engrs; Asn Comput Mach; Can Info Processing Soc. *Res:* Design and analysis of parallel algorithms; artificial neural networks; computer graphics; fractals; multimedia courseware; digital very large scale integrated system architectures. *Mailing Add:* Fac Comput Sci Univ NB Fredericton NB E3B 5A3 Can

BHORJEE, JASWANT S, CHROMATIN STRUCTURE FUNCTION. *Current Pos:* scientist, Rev Admin, Div Res Br, 91-93, PROG DIR, CANCER CTR BR, NAT INST CAN, NIH, 93- *Personal Data:* b Ajmer, India, July 23, 35. *Educ:* Univ Sask, Saskatoon, PhD(microbiol), 66. *Prof Exp:* Asst prof, Univ Ill, Chicago, 78-84; asst prof microbiol, Meharry Med Col, Nashville, 84-91. *Mem:* AAAS; Sigma Xi; Am Soc Cell Biol. *Mailing Add:* 10204 Amherst Ave Silver Spring MD 20902

BHOWN, AJIT SINGH, protein chemistry, for more information see previous edition

BHUSHAN, BHARAT, TRIBOLOGY, MECHANICAL ENGINEERING. *Current Pos:* OHIO EMINENT SCHOLAR & HOWARD D WINBIGLER PROF, DEPT MECH ENG, OHIO STATE UNIV, 91- *Personal Data:* b Jhinjhana, India, Sept 30, 49; m 75; c Ankur & Noopur. *Educ:* Birla Inst Technol, India, BE Hons, 70; Mass Inst Technol, MS, 71; Univ Colo, MS, 73, PhD(mech eng), 76; Rensselaer Polytech Inst, MBA, 80; Univ Trondheim, Norway, DSc, 90; Warsaw Univ Technol, Poland, Habilitate D, 96. *Honors & Awards:* Alfred Noble Prize, Am Soc Chem Engrs, Am Inst Mech Engrs, Am Soc Mech Engrs, Inst Elec & Electronics Engrs & Western Soc Engrs, 81; Norlin Award, Univ Colo, 83; Burt L Newkirk Award, Am Soc Mech Engrs, 83, Gustus L Larson Mem Award, 86; Tech Excellence Award, Am Soc Engrs; Cert Appreciation for Space Shuttle Challenger Accident, NASA, 87. *Prof Exp:* Res staff mem, Mass Inst Technol, 71-72; expert investr, Automotive Specialists, Denver, 73-76; phys tribology & prog mgr, Mech Technol Inc, NY, 76-80; res scientist, SKF Industs Inc, Pa, 80-81; develop engr & mgr, IBM Corp, Tucson, 81-86; res staff mem & mgr head-disk interface, IBM Res Div, Almaden Res Ctr, San Jose, 86-91. *Concurrent Pos:* Expert investr, Automotive Specialists, Denver, 73-76; proprietor & mgr, Time Sharing Comput Serv, India, 77-, pvt consult, 76-, merit scholar, U P State Educ Bd, India, 61-65, Govt India, 65-70; res fel, Ford Found, 70-71; grad fel, Univ Colo, 73-74; res grants, USN, USAF, NASA, Dept Energy, E I Du Pont de Nemours & Co Inc, Chrysler & United Technol Corp, 76-81; assoc ed, J Tribology, 86-90. *Mem:* Fel Am Soc Mech Engrs; Soc Tribologists & Lubrication Engrs; Am Acad Mech; Soc Automotive Engs; Sigma Xi; fel NY Acad Sci; sr mem Inst Elec & Electronics Engrs; Nat Soc Prof Engrs. *Res:* Fundamental experimental and analytical studies in microtribology/tribology including surface and mechanical characterization; friction wear, lubrication, ceramics, coatings, contamination and their industrial applications including computer storage devices; over 300 technical papers and 60 technical reports and 6 US patents. *Mailing Add:* Mech Eng Ohio State Univ 206 W 18th Ave Columbus OH 43210-1107. *Fax:* 614-292-0325; *E-Mail:* bhushan.2@osu.edu

BHUVA, ROHIT L, PROGRAMMABLE INTEGRATED CIRCUIT DESIGNER, ANALOG INTEGRATED CIRCUIT DESIGNER. *Current Pos:* Design mgr, 78-89, tech liaison officer, 90, MGR, LINEAR DESIGN CTR, TEXAS INSTRUMENTS, 91- *Personal Data:* b Balwa, India, May 24, 54; m 80; c 2. *Educ:* MS Univ, Baroda, India, BEng, 76; Ill Inst Technol, Chicago, MS, 77. *Res:* Design and development of field programmable integrated circuits. *Mailing Add:* Texas Instruments MS 90 PO Box 655012 Dallas TX 75265

BHUVANESWARAN, CHIDAMBARAM, BIOCHEMISTRY. *Current Pos:* asst prof, 77-80, ASSOC PROF BIOCHEM, UNIV ARK, MED SCI CAMPUS, 80- *Personal Data:* b India, Nov 10, 34. *Educ:* Univ Bombay, BSc, 55 & 57, PhD(biochem), 63. *Prof Exp:* Jr sci officer, Cent Food Tech Res Inst, Mysore, India, 60-64; sci officer, Atomic Energy Estab, Bombay, 64-65; res assoc biochem, Ore State Univ, 65-68; res assoc biochem, Fac Med, Univ Man, 68-72. *Mem:* AAAS; Am Chem Soc; Asn Clin Scientists; Sigma Xi. *Res:* Electron transport and oxidative phosphorylation; lipid metabolism. *Mailing Add:* Dept Biochem Univ Ark Med Sci Campus 4301 W Markham Little Rock AR 72205. *Fax:* 501-686-8169

BHUYAN, BIJOY KUMAR, CELL BIOLOGY, EXPERIMENTAL CANCER CHEMOTHERAPY. *Current Pos:* RETIRED. *Personal Data:* b Calcutta, India, Aug 30, 30; m 55; c 2. *Educ:* Utkal Univ, India, BSc, 48; Univ Calcutta, MSc, 51; Univ Wis, MS, 54, PhD(biochem), 56. *Prof Exp:* Res assoc & fel biochem, Univ Wis, 56-57; fel, Nat Res Coun Can, 57-58; sr sci officer, Hindustan Antibiotics, India, 58-59; res assoc microbiol, Upjohn Co, 60-63, res assoc biochem, 63-73, sr res scientist, Cancer Res, 73-94. *Concurrent Pos:* Assoc ed, Cancer Res, Cell & Tissue Kinetics. *Mem:* Tissue Cult Asn; Am Asn Cancer Res; Cell Kinetic Soc. *Res:* Penicillin production; anti-tumor antibiotics; tissue culture; cell cycle; cell kinetics; human tumor cloning; developing conditions under which antitumor drugs will be more effective in killing cancer cells based on studies involving cell cycle, drug combinations, drug resistance, etc. *Mailing Add:* 6907 S 12th Portage MI 49002

BIAGETTI, RICHARD VICTOR, batteries, electrochemistry & inorganic chemistry; deceased, see previous edition for last biography

BIAGGIONI, ITALO, CLINICAL PHARMACOLOGY. *Current Pos:* res fel pharmocol, 84-86, instr, 86-87, ASST PROF MED, VANDERBILT SCH MED, 87- *Personal Data:* b Lima, Peru, Sept 4, 54; m 83. *Educ:* Universidad Peruana Cayetano Heredia, MD, 80. *Prof Exp:* Intern, Cayetano Heredia Univ Hosp, 78-79, from resident to chief resident, 80-83; assoc investr med, Nat Inst Salud, Peru, 82-83. *Concurrent Pos:* Physician, Peruvian Health Serv, 79-80; clin assoc physician, Elliot V Neuman Clin Res Ctr, Vanderbilt Univ, 86- *Mem:* Am Fedn Clin Res. *Res:* The autonomic nervous system and cardiovascular control; the role of adenoisine in the cardiovascular system. *Mailing Add:* 2873 Sugar Tree Rd Nashville TN 37215

BIAGINI, RAYMOND E, IMMUNOTOXICOLOGY, BIO-MONITORING. *Current Pos:* criteria mgr, Criteria Develop Br, Nat Inst Occup Safety & Health, 77-78, res toxicologist, Chronic Toxicol Sect, Exp Toxicol Br, 78-82 & 84-89, grad student trainee, Off of Dir, 82-84, RES TOXICOLOGIST, IMMUNOCHEM RES SECT, APPL BIOL BR, NAT INST OCCUP SAFETY & HEALTH, CINCINNATI, OHIO, 89- *Personal Data:* b San Francisco, Calif, Oct 10, 49; m 76; c 2. *Educ:* Univ San Francisco, BS, 71; Univ Nev, Reno, MS, 76; Univ Cincinnati, PhD(toxicol), 84; Am Bd Toxicol, dipl, 86. *Prof Exp:* Qual control anal chemist & microbiol consult, Best Foods Div, CPC Int, San Francisco, Calif, 73-74; res biochemist, Dept Biochem, Sch Biomed Sci, Univ Nev, Reno, 76-77. *Concurrent Pos:* Sr scientist officer, USPHS; Nat Res Coun mentor, Robert A Taft Lab, Nat Inst Occup Safety & Health; expert adv, WHO. *Mem:* Am Asn Immunologists; Soc Toxicol. *Res:* Effects of xenobiotics on the immune system of animals and humans; pulmonary pharmacology; sub-cellular bioenergetics of cardiac muscle. *Mailing Add:* CDC NIOSH 4676 Columbia Pkwy MS-C26 Cincinnati OH 45226-1922

BIAGLOW, JOHN E, BIOCHEMISTRY, ONCOLOGY. *Current Pos:* DIR, BIOCHEM DIV, DEPT RADIATION ONCOL, UNIV PA & DIR TUMOR METAB, DIV CANCER CTR. *Personal Data:* b Cleveland, Ohio, Apr 1, 37; m 60; c 9. *Educ:* John Carroll Univ, BS, 59; Loyola Univ, Chicago, MS, 61, PhD(biochem), 63. *Hon Degrees:* MA, Univ Pa, 87. *Prof Exp:* NIH fel biochem, 63-65,from asst prof to assoc prof, 65-84, prof radiation biochem, Case Western Reserve Univ 84-, dir radiation biol, 84- *Concurrent Pos:* Pres, Custom Biochem Co; asst prof radiol, Case Western Reserve Univ 67-76, assoc prof Biochem, 76-85, prof biochem & environ health, 85-, dir biochem oncol, 85-; mem, Federated Soc for Exp Biol, 76-; consult, Adamantech, Sun Oil, 85- *Mem:* Am Chem Soc; NY Acad Sci; Int Soc Oxygen Transp to Tissue; AAAS; Oxygen Soc. *Res:* Enzymology; kinetics; control and organization of enzyme systems; carcinogenesis; cell culture; oncology; physiological controls; oxygen utilization; artificial oxygen carriers. *Mailing Add:* Div Biochem 195 John Morgan Bldg Univ Pa 37th & Hamilton Walk Philadelphia PA 19104-6072

BIALAS, WAYNE FRANCIS, OPERATIONS RESEARCH, STATISTICS. *Current Pos:* ASSOC PROF INDUST ENG, STATE UNIV NY, BUFFALO, 76- *Personal Data:* b Middletown, NY, Aug 5, 49. *Educ:* Clarkson Col Technol, BS, 71; Cornell Univ, MS, 74, PhD(oper res), 75. *Prof Exp:* Res assoc & instr, Col Eng, Cornell Univ, 75. *Concurrent Pos:* Vis asst prof civil & environ eng, Cornell Univ, 81-82; vis assoc prof civil eng, Mass Inst Technol, 83-84. *Mem:* Am Statist Asn; Asn Comput Mach; Inst Indust Eng; Am Soc Civil Engrs; Inst Mgt Sci; Opers Res Soc Am. *Res:* Multilevel optimization; asymptotic properties of probability measures; economic models for flood prone regions. *Mailing Add:* Dept Indust Eng Bell Hall State Univ NY Buffalo Buffalo NY 14260-0001

BIALECKE, EDWARD P, ELECTRICAL ENGINEERING, PLASMA PHYSICS. *Current Pos:* sr engr, 69-80, TECH SPECIALIST, MCDONNELL DOUGLAS CORP, 80- *Personal Data:* b Chicago, Ill, Dec 3, 34. *Educ:* Univ Ill, BSEE, 56, MS, 58, PhD(elec eng), 63. *Prof Exp:* Asst prof elec eng, Univ Ill, 65-69. *Mem:* Inst Elec & Electronics Engrs; Geophys Union; Sigma Xi. *Res:* Gaseous electronics; plasma physics; lasers; holography; ionospheric physics; reentry physics. *Mailing Add:* McDonnell Douglas Corp PO Box 516 St Louis MO 63166

BIANCANI, PIERO, GASTROENTEROLOGY. *Current Pos:* Assoc prof, 83-85, PROF MED, RI HOSP & BROWN UNIV, 85- *Personal Data:* b Rosignano, Italy, Sept 3, 1944. *Educ:* Yale Univ, PhD(biomech), 71. *Res:* Neuro regulation gastrointestinal smooth muscle function. *Mailing Add:* Dept Med Brown Univ RI Hosp 593 Eddy St Providence RI 02902-0001

BIANCHI, CARMINE PAUL, CELL PHYSIOLOGY. *Current Pos:* prof pharmacol & chmn dept, 76-87, PROF PHARMACOL, THOMAS JEFFERSON UNIV, PHILADELPHIA, 87- *Personal Data:* b Newark, NJ, Apr 9, 27; m 57; c 3. *Educ:* Columbia Univ, AB, 50; Rutgers Univ, MS, 53, PhD(biochem, physiol), 56. *Prof Exp:* Vis scientist & res assoc, NIH, 58-60; asst mem, Inst Muscle Dis, New York, 60-61; from assoc to prof physiol, 61-68, prof pharmacol, Sch Med, Univ Pa, 68-76. *Concurrent Pos:* Res fel pub health, NIH, 56-58. *Mem:* Biophys Soc; Am Soc Zoologists; Soc Gen Physiol; Am Physiol Soc; Am Soc Pharmacol & Therapeut. *Res:* Role of mono- and divalent cations in controlling cell membrane function and metabolism. *Mailing Add:* Dept Pharmacol Thomas Jefferson Univ 1020 Locust St Philadelphia PA 19107-6731

BIANCHI, DONALD ERNEST, physiology, mycology; deceased, see previous edition for last biography

BIANCHI, JOHN J, PHYSIOLOGY, PHARMACOLOGY. *Current Pos:* SCIENTIST PHARMACOL, BERLEX LABS INC, 90- *Personal Data:* b Mt Carmel, Pa, Sept 18, 52. *Educ:* Bucknell Univ, BS, 74; Pa State Univ, PhD(physiol), 85. *Prof Exp:* Scientist pharmacol, Deborah Res Inst, 86-90. *Mem:* Am Physiol Soc; NY Acad Sci; Am Heart Asn; Am Inst Chemists. *Mailing Add:* Berlex Labs Inc 110 E Hanover Ave Cedar Knolls NJ 07927-2095

BIANCHI, ROBERT GEORGE, PHARMACOLOGY. *Current Pos:* Jr investr biol res, 50-60, SR INVESTR PHARMACOL, SEARLE LABS, 60- *Personal Data:* b Chicago, Ill, Mar 20, 25; m 48; c 4. *Educ:* Franklin & Marshall Col, BS, 45. *Mem:* Sigma Xi; AAAS. *Res:* Gastrointestinal pharmacology; discovering compounds useful in the treatment of gastrointestinal diseases. *Mailing Add:* 8336 N Caldwell Ave Niles IL 60714-2602

BIANCHINE, JOSEPH RAYMOND, PHARMACOLOGY. *Current Pos:* VPRES CLIN RES & MED DIR, NEOPROBE CORP, 97- *Personal Data:* b Albany, NY, Sept 7, 29; m 56. *Educ:* Siena Col, BS, 51; Albany Med Col, PhD(pharmacol), 59; State Univ NY, Syracuse, MD, 60. *Prof Exp:* Physician, Johns Hopkins Univ Sch Med, 66-72; prof & chmn, Dept Pharmacol, Tex Tech Univ, 72-74; prof med, Dept Med & prof & chmn, Dept Pharmacol, Ohio State Univ Sch Med, 74-83; vpres med res, Hoffman-LaRoche, 83-85 & DuPont de Nemours, 85-87; vpres & dir, Med Res Ctr, Adria Labs Erbamont, 87-97. *Concurrent Pos:* Chmn, Gen Clin Res Comt, Div Res Resources, NIH, 80-81. *Mem:* Am Soc Clin Pharmacol & Therapeut (pres, 87-88); fel Am Col Physicians; fel Am Col Clin Pharmacol; Am Soc Pharmacol & Exp Therapeut; Asn Med Sch Pharm; Soc Neurosci. *Res:* Clinical pharmacology; neurochemistry; internal medicine. *Mailing Add:* Neoprobe Corp 425 Metro Pl N Suite 400 Dublin OH 43017

BIARD, JAMES R, SEMICONDUCTOR DEVICE PHYSICS, INTEGRATED CIRCUIT DESIGN. *Current Pos:* chief scientist, Optoelectronics Div, 78-88, CHIEF SCIENTIST, MICROSWITCH DIV, HONEYWELL, 88- *Personal Data:* b Paris, Tex, May 20, 31; m 52, Amelia Ruth; c James Clark, Jan Elaine (Thomas) & Becky Dell (Brown). *Educ:* Tex A&M Univ, BS, 54, MS, 56, PhD(elec eng), 57. *Honors & Awards:* Patrick E Haggerty Innovation Award, Tex Instruments, 85. *Prof Exp:* Sr engr, Semiconductor Res & Develop Lab, Tex Instruments, 57-69; vpres res & develop, Spectronics, Inc, 69-78. *Concurrent Pos:* Adj prof, Dept Elec Eng, Tex A&M Univ, 80- *Mem:* Nat Acad Eng; fel Inst Elec & Electronics Engrs; Am Phys Soc; Sigma Xi. *Res:* Design and development of semiconductor devices and integrated circuits; holder of 31 US and 16 foreign patents. *Mailing Add:* Honeywell Microswitch Div 830 E Arapaho Rd Richardson TX 75081-2241. *Fax:* 972-270-4278; *E-Mail:* bbiard@micro.honeywell.com

BIAS, WILMA B, HUMAN GENETICS, IMMUNOLOGY. *Current Pos:* Fel med genetics, Sch Med, Johns Hopkins Univ, 63-64, from instr to prof med, 64-84, prof epidemiol, Sch Hyg, 67-94, SURG, SCH MED, JOHNS HOPKINS UNIV, 69-, PROF MED, 84- *Personal Data:* b Muskogee, Okla, Dec 23, 28; m 47; c 3. *Educ:* Univ Okla, BS, 49; Johns Hopkins Univ, PhD(genetics), 63. *Concurrent Pos:* Prof immunol & infectious dis, Sch Hyg, Johns Hopkins Univ, 73- *Mem:* AAAS; Am Soc Human Genetics; Int Transplantation Soc; Am Asn Immunol; Am Soc Histocompatibility & Immunogenetics; Clin Immunol Soc. *Res:* Immunogenetics. *Mailing Add:* Dept Med Sch Med Johns Hopkins Univ 204 E Monument St Baltimore MD 21205-2222

BIASELL, LAVERNE R(OBERT), AERONAUTICAL & ASTRONAUTICAL ENGINEERING. *Current Pos:* RETIRED. *Personal Data:* b Detroit, Mich, Oct 26, 15; m 40, Irene Hafeli; c Anne, Thomas, James & Lynn. *Educ:* Univ Detroit, AB, 37. *Honors & Awards:* Continental Aircraft Design Award, 37; Am Legion Award, 37; Space Pioneer Medal, NASA, 64. *Prof Exp:* Lab asst, Ethyl Gasoline Corp, 34-35; asst lab instr physics, Univ Detroit, 35-37; proj engr, Stinson Div, Consol Vultee Corp, 37-40; aircraft engr, Res Labs, Gen Motors Corp, 41-45; chief prod engr, Exp Eng Div, Bendix Aviation Corp, 45-46; assoc dir, Willow Run Res Ctr, Univ Mich, 46-54; chief engr, Missile Div, Chrysler Corp, 54-63, dir res & develop, Defense & Diversified Prod Divs, 65-81. *Res:* Defense and space missles, vehicles and equipment; personal aircraft. *Mailing Add:* 86 Windsor Dr Englewood FL 34223

BIBB, HAROLD DAVID, DEVELOPMENTAL BIOLOGY, NEURAL-DEVELOPMENT. *Current Pos:* ASSOC PROF ZOOL, UNIV RI, 72- *Personal Data:* b Centralia, Ill, Feb 12, 40; m 71; c 3. *Educ:* Univ Iowa, PhD(zool), 69. *Mailing Add:* 62 Enterprise Terr Kingston RI 02881

BIBB, WILLIAM ROBERT, RADIATION STUDIES. *Current Pos:* CONSULT, 93- *Personal Data:* b Salisbury, NC, May 28, 32; m 55, Pat McDuffie; c Bob & Susan. *Educ:* Univ NC, BS, 57, MS, 59, PhD(bact), 62. *Prof Exp:* Res assoc virol, Virus Lab, Sch Med, Univ NC, Chapel Hill, 62-63, USPHS trainee, 63-64, asst prof bact, 64-65; mem, Med Res Br, Div Biol & Med, US AEC, Washington, DC, 65-71, tech asst to comnr, 71-73, chief res & develop, 73-78, dir, Res Div, 78-90, asst mgr, US Dept Energy, Oak Ridge, 90-93. *Mem:* Am Soc Microbiol; Electron Micros Soc Am; Reticuloendothelial Soc; Am Nuclear Soc. *Res:* Metabolism; amino acid transport; enzyme synthesis; bacterial cell structure; amino acid decarboxylases; organ and tissue transplantation; effects of low-dose radiation; radiation protection. *Mailing Add:* PO Box 5166 Oak Ridge TN 37831-5166. *Fax:* 615-482-2423

BIBBO, MARLUCE, CYTOPATHOLOGY. *Current Pos:* res assoc, Univ Chicago, 69-70, from asst prof to assoc prof, 70-77, dir Cytol Lab & Schs Cytotechnol & Cyto Cybernet, 90-92, PROF OBSTET & GYNEC & PATH, UNIV CHICAGO, 78-; PROF PATH & CELL BIOL, JEFFERSON MED COL, PHILADELPHIA, 92- *Personal Data:* b Sao Carlos, Brazil, July 14, 39. *Educ:* Dr Alvaro Guiao Inst Educ, Brazil, BS, 57; Univ Sao Paulo, MD, 63, DSc, 68. *Honors & Awards:* Papanicolaon Award, Am Soc Cytol, 92. *Prof Exp:* Resident obstet & gynec, Univ Sao Paulo, 63-65, trainee exfoliative cytol, 65, trainee nucleic acids, 65-66, instr morphol, Fac Med, 65-68, asst prof morphol & obstet & gynec & chief cytol serv, 68-70. *Concurrent Pos:* Mem coun cylopath, Am Soc Clin Path. *Mem:* Fel Int Acad Cytol (pres elect, 90); Am Soc Cytol (pres, 83); fel Asn Clin Sci; World Asn Gynec Cancer Prev; Int Acad Path; Am Soc Clin Path. *Res:* Diagnostic and experimental cytology; computerized cell evaluations; pattern recognition; endocrinologic cell assessments; cancer detection techniques. *Mailing Add:* Thomas Jefferson Univ Hosp Dept Path 132 S Tenth St Rm 260-A Main Philadelphia PA 19107

BIBBY, MALCOLM, PHYSICAL METALLURGY. *Current Pos:* asst prof eng, 68-77, ASSOC PROF ENG, CARLETON UNIV, ONT, 77- *Personal Data:* b Mountain Park, Alta, Aug 28, 39; m 66. *Educ:* Univ Alta, BSc, 61, MSc, 63, PhD(phys metall), 65. *Prof Exp:* Mem tech staff, Solid State Device Labs, Bell Tel Labs, 66-68. *Mem:* Am Soc Metals. *Res:* Magnetic properties of materials. *Mailing Add:* Dept Eng Mech 4362 Mackenzie Carleton Univ 1125 Colonel By Dr Ottawa ON K1S 5B6 Can

BIBEAU, THOMAS CLIFFORD, FOOD COLORIMETRY. *Current Pos:* GROUP DIR, RES & DEVELOP, GRAND MET, 90- *Personal Data:* b Palmer, Mass, Mar 15, 49; m 71; c 2. *Educ:* Univ Mass, BS, 71, MS, 74 & 88, PhD(food sci), 77. *Prof Exp:* Res chemist, Heublein Inc, RJR Industs, 76-78, mgr, prod develop, 78-81, assoc mgr to mgr, 81-84, dir, beverage prod, 86-88, brand develop, 88-90. *Concurrent Pos:* Inst Food Technologists scholar, 70 & 71. *Mem:* Inst Food Technologists; Flavor & Extract Mfrs Asn. *Res:* The study of organic acid changes on processing of vegetable products; methods of measuring specific product's color; the evaluation of stability of subsidiary coal tar dyes; organic acid profiles of vegetables. *Mailing Add:* 19 Oxford Lane Windsor CT 06095-1483

BIBEL, DEBRA JAN, MEDICAL MICROBIOLOGY, MICROBIAL ECOLOGY. *Current Pos:* res assoc, 87-95, RES ASSOC FAC, KAISER FOUND, UNIV CALIF, SAN FRANCISCO, 94-; DIR, ELIE METCHNIKOFF MEM LIBR, 78- *Personal Data:* b San Francisco, Calif, Apr 6, 45; c Sara. *Educ:* Univ Calif, Berkeley, AB, 67, CPhil, 71, PhD(immunol), 72. *Prof Exp:* Bacteriologist, Letterman Army Inst Res, 72-76, microbiologist, 76-78; res assoc, Kaiser Found, 81-83; prod mgr, Tago, Inc, 83-86. *Concurrent Pos:* Lectr, Sch Pub Health, Univ Calif, Berkeley, 75, Ctr Health Studies, Antioch Col W, 75 & Univ Calif Exten, Berkeley, 77; USPHS traineeship, 67-72; tech writer, Hoefer Sci Instruments, 79; consult, 80, 86. *Mem:* Am Soc Microbiol; AAAS; Fedn Am Scientists. *Res:* Microbiology and ecology of human skin and nose; topical antimicrobial agents; host-parasite relationships; history and philosophy of medical microbiology and immunology. *Mailing Add:* 230 Orange St No 6 Oakland CA 94610-4139. *Fax:* 415-476- 8677

BIBEL, GEORGE, PRESSURE VESSEL COMPONENTS, HELICOPTER TRANSMISSION GEARING. *Current Pos:* ASSOC PROF MECH ENG, UNIV NDAK, 93- *Personal Data:* b Bedford, Ohio, June 17, 53; m 95, Mary P Holler. *Educ:* Case Western Res Univ, BS, 75, PhD(mech eng), 87; Univ Mich, MS, 80. *Prof Exp:* Sr tech specialist, BP Am, 75-87; asst prof, Univ Akron, 87-92. *Concurrent Pos:* Consult, BP Am, 87-88, US Dept Justice, 92; comt mem, Pressure Vessel Res Coun, subgroup Bolted Flange Joints, 88-; fac fel, NASA, 89, 90 & 93; prin investr, Pressure Vessel Res Coun, 89-94, NASA, 91-94 & Bolting Technol Coun, 93-94; comt mem, Boiler & Pressure Vessel Code. *Mem:* Am Soc Mech Engrs. *Res:* Design, analysis and testing of bolted flanged connections, gaskets and bolting; analysis of helicopter transmission gearing. *Mailing Add:* Univ NDak PO Box 8359 Grand Forks ND 58202

BIBEN, MAXEEN G, PRIMATOLOGY, DEVELOPMENT. *Current Pos:* ADJ INSTR, AVERETT COL, SHENANDOAH UNIV & LORD FAIRFAX COMMUNITY COL, 93- *Personal Data:* b Syracuse, NY, Oct 2, 48; m 85, Linwood R Williamson; c Seth & Lacey. *Educ:* Cornell Univ, BS, 70; Univ NC, Chapel Hill, PhD(zool), 76. *Prof Exp:* Vis lectr biol, NC Cent Univ, 76-78; Smithsonian fel, Nat Zool Park, 78-80; vis asst prof biol, Bowdoin Col, 80-81; sr staff fel, NIH, 82-89, expert, 89-93, guest researcher, 93-94. *Concurrent Pos:* Fel, Smithsonian Inst, 78-79. *Mem:* Animal Behav Soc; Am Soc Zoologists; Sigma Xi; AAAS; Am Inst Biol Sci; Am Soc Primatologists. *Res:* Auditory communication in primates with emphasis on language-like abilities and acquistion of vocal capabilities by infants; play behavior of primates and carnivores. *Mailing Add:* 2014 Martinsburg Pike Winchester VA 22603

BIBER, MARGARET CLARE BOADLE, NEUROPHARMACOLOGY. *Current Pos:* assoc prof, 75-87, interim chmn, 91-93, PROF PHYSIOL, MED COL VA, VA COMMONWEALTH UNIV, 87-, CHMN DEPT, 93- *Personal Data:* b Melbourne, Australia, Jan 18, 43; m 69, Thomas U L; c Eric G. *Educ:* Univ London, BSc, 64; Oxford Univ, DPhil(biochem, pharmacol), 67. *Prof Exp:* Res assoc pharmacol, Sch Med, Yale Univ, 68-69, from instr to asst prof, 69-75. *Concurrent Pos:* A B Coxe Mem fel pharmacol, Sch Med, Yale Univ, 67-68; estab investr, Am Heart Asn, 75-80; mem, Basic Psychopharmacol & Neuropsychopharmacol Res Rev Comt, Alcohol, Drug Abuse & Ment Health Admin, HEW, 81-85; prin investr, grant support, Nat Inst Neurol & Commun Dis & Stroke, NIH, 79-97. *Mem:* Am Soc Pharmacol & Exp Therapeut; Soc Neurosci; Am Soc Neurochem; AAAS. *Res:* Studies on the regulation of neurotransmitter formation, particularly of serotonin, by ongoing nervous activity, drugs, hormones and stressors. *Mailing Add:* Dept Physiol Med Col Va Va Commonwealth Univ Richmond VA 23298-0551. *Fax:* 804-828-7382; *E-Mail:* mbiber@gems.vcu.edu

BIBER, THOMAS U L, MEMBRANE PHYSIOLOGY. *Current Pos:* PROF PHYSIOL & BIOPHYS, MED COL VA, 75- *Educ:* Univ Bern, MD, 56. *Mailing Add:* Dept Physiol Med Col Va MCV Sta Box 551 Richmond VA 23298-0551

BIBERMAN, LUCIEN MORTON, PHYSICS. *Current Pos:* MEM SR RES STAFF, INST DEFENSE ANALYSIS, 63- *Personal Data:* b Philadelphia, Pa, May 31, 19; m; c 3. *Educ:* Rensselaer Polytech Inst, BS, 40. *Honors & Awards:* Night Vision Lab Award, US Army, 94. *Prof Exp:* Phys chemist, Congoleum-Nairn, Inc, NJ, 41-42; physicist, US Navy, SC, 42-44 & US Naval Ord Test Sta, 44-57; dir, Syst Div, Midway Labs, Univ Chicago, 57-59, assoc dir, Labs Appl Sci, 59-63. *Concurrent Pos:* Adj prof, Univ RI, 69-, vis prof, 71-72. *Mem:* AAAS; fel Optical Soc Am; fel Soc Photo-Optical Instrument Engrs; fel Inst Elec & Electronics Engrs; fel Soc Info Display. *Res:* Military applications of optics and electronics with emphasis on infrared and ultraviolet techniques. *Mailing Add:* 5904 Lenox Rd Bethesda MD 20817. *E-Mail:* lucienb@erols.com

BIBERSTEIN, ERNST LUDWIG, VETERINARY BACTERIOLOGY. *Current Pos:* asst prof vet med, Univ Calif, Davis, 56-60, assoc prof, 60- 66, chmn dept, 69-74, chief, Microbiol Serv, Vet Med Teaching Hosp, 66-75, prof, 66-90, EMER PROF MICROBIOL, UNIV CALIF, DAVIS, 90- *Personal Data:* b Breslau, Ger, Nov 11, 22; nat US; m 49; c 4. *Educ:* Univ Ill, BS, 47; Cornell Univ, DVM, 51, MS, 54, PhD(vet bact), 55; Am Col Vet Microbiologists, dipl. *Prof Exp:* Actg asst prof path, NY State Vet Col, Cornell Univ, 55-56. *Concurrent Pos:* NIH spec fel, 63-64 & 68-69. *Mem:* Am Vet Med Asn; Am Soc Microbiol; fel Am Acad Microbiol; Path Soc Gt Brit & Ireland; Am Col Vet Microbiol. *Res:* Infectious diseases of animals; pasteurellosis; haemophilus infections; clinical microbiology. *Mailing Add:* 508 12th St Davis CA 95616

BIBLARZ, OSCAR, COMBUSTION MEASUREMENTS, DISCHARGE PHYSICS. *Current Pos:* from asst prof to assoc prof, PROF AERONAUT & ASTRONAUT, NAVAL POSTGRAD SCH, MONTEREY, CALIF, 68- *Personal Data:* b Bogota, Columbia, July 4, 38; US citizen. *Educ:* Univ Calif, Los Angeles, BS, 59, MS, 63; Stanford Univ, PhD(mech eng), 68. *Prof Exp:* Develop engr, Airesearch Mfg Co, 59-61; mem tech staff, Hughes Aircraft Co, 61-63; res asst, Stanford Univ, 64-67. *Concurrent Pos:* Lady Davis fel, Technion, Israel, 76-77; vis engr, Lockhead Aircraft, 86-87; sr eng specialist, GTE Elec Prod, 87-89. *Mem:* Sigma Xi; Am Phys Soc; Am Inst Aeronaut & Astronaut; Inst Elec & Electronics Engrs Nuclear & Plasma Sci. *Res:* Lasers; unsteady flows; clusters; electric propulsion-power for space applications. *Mailing Add:* Dept Aeronaut & Astronaut Naval Postgrad Sch Monterey CA 93943-5106

BIBLER, NED EUGENE, RADIATION CHEMISTRY. *Current Pos:* Res chemist, Savannah River Lab, E I du Pont de Nemours & Co Inc, 65-73, staff chemist, 73-79, radiation chem, 79-91, RADIATION CHEM, SAVANNAH RIVER LAB, WESTINGHOUSE SAVANNAH RIVER CO, 91- *Personal Data:* b Bucyrus, Ohio, July 25, 37; m 63; c 3. *Educ:* Denison Univ, BSc, 59; Ohio State Univ, MSc, 62, PhD(chem), 65. *Mem:* Am Chem Soc; Mat Res Soc; Am Soc Testing & Mat. *Res:* Radiation chemistry associated with radioactive isotope production, nuclear fuel reprocessing, and radioactive waste storage; nuclear waste vitrification and disposal. *Mailing Add:* 813 Rollingwood Rd Aiken SC 29801-3374

BIBLIS, EVANGELOS J, WOOD SCIENCE & TECHNOLOGY. *Current Pos:* PROF WOOD TECHNOL, AUBURN UNIV, 65- *Personal Data:* b Thessaloniki, Greece, Apr 8, 29; US citizen; m 61; c 2. *Educ:* Univ Thessaloniki, BS, 53; Yale Univ, MF, 61, PhD(forestry), 65. *Prof Exp:* Qual control engr, Kaman Aircraft Corp, 61-63. *Concurrent Pos:* Consult, Indust & Atty. *Mem:* Soc Wood Sci & Technol; Forest Prod Res Soc. *Res:* Mechanical behavior of wood and wood structures. *Mailing Add:* Dept Forestry Auburn Univ Auburn AL 36849-3501

BIBRING, THOMAS, GAMETES, MICRO TUBULES. *Current Pos:* ASSOC PROF MOLECULAR BIOL, VANDERBILT UNIV, 70- *Educ:* Univ Calif, Berkeley, PhD(biophys), 62. *Mailing Add:* 6547 Brownlee Dr Nashville TN 37205

BIBYK, STEVEN B, ELECTRICAL ENGINEERING. *Current Pos:* asst prof, 84-88, ASSOC PROF ELEC ENG, OHIO STATE UNIV, 88- *Educ:* Case Western Res Univ, BS, 80, MS, 80, PhD(elec eng & appl physics), 83. *Prof Exp:* Res scientist, Electronics Div, NASA Lewis Res Ctr, Ohio Aerospace Inst, 91-92. *Concurrent Pos:* NASA-Am Soc Elec Engrs Summer Fac fel, 89, 92. *Res:* Electrical engineering; author of 6 publications. *Mailing Add:* Dept Elec Eng 205 Dreese Labs Ohio State Univ 2015 Neil Ave Columbus OH 43210

BIC, LUBOMIR, PARALLEL PROCESSING. *Current Pos:* asst prof, 80-85, ASSOC PROF COMPUT SCI, UNIV CALIF, IRVINE, 86- *Personal Data:* b Iglau, Czech, Nov 28, 51; Ger citizen; m 81; c 1. *Educ:* Tech Univ, Darmstadt, Ger, MS, 76; Univ Calif, Irvine, PhD(comput sci), 79. *Prof Exp:* Comput scientist, Siemens, Munich, Ger, 79-80. *Mem:* Asn Comput Mach; Inst Elec & Electronics Engrs. *Res:* Development of computational models suitable to highly parallel processing. *Mailing Add:* Dept ICS Univ Calif Irvine CA 92717-0001

BICE, DAVID EARL, PULMONARY IMMUNOLOGY & ASTHMA. *Current Pos:* SR SCIENTIST, INHALATION TOXICOL RES INST, LOVELACE BIOMED & ENVIRON RES INST, 75- *Personal Data:* b Cornville, Ariz, Apr 8, 38; m 60; c 6. *Educ:* Utah State Univ, BS, 62; Univ Ariz, MS, 64; La State Univ, PhD(trop med), 68. *Prof Exp:* La State Univ res assoc, Int Ctr Med Res & Training, San Jose, Costa Rica, 64-68, from instr to asst prof med & microbiol, La State Univ Med Ctr, New Orleans, 68-75. *Concurrent Pos:* Res fels immunol, La State Univ, 68-69 & Harvard Med Sch & Tufts Univ, 70-71; scientist, Dept Med, La State Univ Div, Charity Hosp, 68-75; fac affil, Dept Path, Colo State Univ & Fort Collins, Colo, 84-; consult, Nat Acad Sci; fac affil, Dept Med, Col Pharm, Univ NMex, Albuquerque, NMex. *Mem:* Am Asn Immunol; Am Thoracic Soc; AAAS. *Res:* Role of immune responses in the lung in the cause of asthma. *Mailing Add:* Inhalation Toxicol Res Inst PO Box 5890 Albuquerque NM 87185

BICHSEL, HANS, RADIATION PHYSICS, LARGE RADIATION DETECTOR. *Current Pos:* from assoc prof to prof radiol, 69-80, AFFIL PROF PHYSICS, UNIV WASH, 92-; CONSULT, 80- *Personal Data:* b Basel, Switz, Sept 2, 24; nat US; m 59; c 2. *Educ:* Univ Basel, MA & PhD(physics), 51. *Prof Exp:* Exchange fel physics, Princeton Univ, 51-52, res asst, 52-54; lectr optics, Univ Basel, 54-55; res assoc physics, Rice Inst, 55-57; asst prof physics, Univ Wash, 57-59; from asst prof to assoc prof, Univ Southern Calif, 59-68; assoc prof, Univ Calif, Berkeley, 68-69. *Concurrent Pos:* Mem, Subcomt Penetration Charged Particles Matter, Nat Acad Sci-Nat Res Coun, 62-; NSF grant, 62-64; consult, Pac Northwest Labs, Battelle Mem Inst, 66-69 & Int Comn Radiation Units & Measurements, 70-; consult, 80-; lectr, Aarhus Univ, 82; vis scientist, GSF Muenchen, 84-85; consult, IAEA, Vienna, 90- *Mem:* Am Phys Soc; Swiss Phys Soc. *Res:* Interaction of radiation with matter ultra relativistic heavy ion physics, use of radiation in medicine and biology; charged particle, photon and neutron radiation dosimetry. *Mailing Add:* 1211 22nd E Seattle WA 98112-3534. *Fax:* 206-685-4634; *E-Mail:* bichsel@npl.washington.edu

BICHTELER, KLAUS RICHARD, MATHEMATICS. *Current Pos:* asst prof, 69-71, ASSOC PROF MATH, UNIV TEX, AUSTIN, 71- *Personal Data:* b Leipzig, Ger, Mar 15, 38; m 69; c 1. *Educ:* Univ Hamburg, dipl, 62, PhD(gen relativity), 65. *Prof Exp:* Asst math, Univ Heidelberg, 65-68; asst prof, Southwest Ctr Advan Studies, 66-69. *Mem:* Am Math Soc; Math Asn Am. *Res:* Stochastic analysis. *Mailing Add:* Dept Math Univ Tex Austin TX 78712-1026

BICK, GEORGE HERMAN, ENTOMOLOGY, ZOOLOGY. *Current Pos:* RETIRED. *Personal Data:* b Neptune, La, Sept 23, 14; m 45, Juanda Bonck; c Susan A & Patricia A. *Educ:* Tulane Univ, BS, 36, MS, 38; Cornell Univ, PhD(entom), 47. *Prof Exp:* Inspector, Food & Drug Admin, USDA, La, 38-41; field biologist, State Dept Conserv, La, 41-42; asst prof, Univ Miss, 47-48 & Tulane Univ, 48-56; assoc prof, Univ Southwestern La, 56-59; prof, Clarion State Col, 59-60; prof biol, St Mary's Col, Inc, 60-80, emer prof, 80-81. *Mem:* Fel AAAS; Entom Soc Am. *Res:* Biology of Odonata. *Mailing Add:* 1928 SW 48th Ave Gainesville FL 32608

BICK, KATHERINE LIVINGSTONE, neurobiology, dementia, for more information see previous edition

BICK, KENNETH F, GEOLOGY. *Current Pos:* RETIRED. *Personal Data:* b Janesville, Wis, Feb 14, 32; m 58; c 3. *Educ:* Yale Univ, BS, 54, MS, 56, PhD(geol), 58. *Prof Exp:* Asst prof geol, Washington & Lee Univ, 58-61; assoc prof to prof geol, Col William & Mary, 61-92, chmn, Dept Geol, 62-68. *Mailing Add:* RR 2 No 84 Lexington VA 24450

BICK, PETER HAMILTON, IMMUNOLOGY. *Current Pos:* ASST PROF IMMUNOL, DEPT MICROBIOL, MED COL VA, 78- *Personal Data:* b Toledo, Ohio, Sept 30, 48; m 71; c 1. *Educ:* Albion Col, AB, 70; Univ Mich, PhD(microbiol), 75. *Prof Exp:* Guest scientist immunol, Div Immunobiol, Karolinska Inst, Stockholm, Sweden, 75-77; fel genetics, Wash Univ, 77-78. *Concurrent Pos:* Arthritis Found fel, 75-78. *Res:* Activation and regulation of immunocompetent cells. *Mailing Add:* Nat Prod Res & Develop Eli Lilly & Co Lilly Corp Ctr Indianapolis IN 46285. *Fax:* 317-276-5499

BICK, RODGER LEE, HEMATOLOGY & ONCOLOGY, THROMBOSIS & HEMOSTASIS. *Current Pos:* fel, 72-73, MEM FAC HEMAT-ONCOL, UNIV CALIF CTR HEALTH SCI, LOS ANGELES, 73-; PROF MED & PATH, SOUTHWEST MED CTR, UNIV TEX, DALLAS, 93- *Personal Data:* b San Francisco, Calif, May 21, 42. *Educ:* Univ Calif, Irvine, MD, 70. *Honors & Awards:* Outstanding Achievements, Am Soc Clin Pathologists, 93. *Prof Exp:* From intern to resident internal med, Kern Gen Hosp, Bakersfield, Calif, 70-72. *Concurrent Pos:* Dir med educ & hemat-oncol, Kern Gen Hosp, 73-74; med dir, Bay Area Hemat Oncol Res Labs, 73-92; attend hematologist, Santa Monica Med Ctr, Calif, 74-, dir oncol, 75-; attend hematologist, St John's Health Sci Ctr, Santa Monica & Univ Calif Ctr Health Sci, Los Angeles, 74-; med dir, Oncol Dept, Presby Hosp, Dallas, 92-95; mem thrombosis coun, Am Heart Asn; med dir, Calif Coagulation Labs, San Joaquin Hemat Oncol Med Group, Bakersfield, Calif, Oncol Unit, San Joaquin Community Hosp. *Mem:* Int Soc Thrombosis & Hemostasis; Am Soc Hemat; Am Cancer Soc; fel Am Col Physicians; fel Am Soc Clin Pathologists. *Res:* Hemostasis and blood coagulation; alterations of hemostasis associated with cardiopulmonary bypass; hypercoagulability and thrombosis, acquired antithrombin-III deficiency; alterations of hemostasis associated with malignancy, nature of disseminated intravascular coagulation. *Mailing Add:* Presby Hosp Oncol Dept 8200 Walnut Hill Lane Dallas TX 75231

BICK, THEODORE A, MATHEMATICS. *Current Pos:* assoc prof, 66-81, PROF MATH, UNION COL, NY, 81- *Personal Data:* b Brooklyn, NY, Dec 18, 30; m 56; c 4. *Educ:* Union Col, BS, 58; Univ Rochester, MS, 60, PhD(ergodic theory), 64. *Prof Exp:* Instr math, Hobart & William Smith Cols, 61-64, from asst prof to assoc prof, 64-66. *Mem:* Math Asn Am. *Res:* Ergodic theory; functional analysis; real variable theory; measure and integration. *Mailing Add:* Dept Math Union Col Schenectady NY 12308-2311

BICKART, THEODORE ALBERT, ELECTRICAL ENGINEERING, COMPUTER ENGINEERING. *Current Pos:* PROF ELEC ENG & DEAN ENG, MICH STATE UNIV, 89- *Personal Data:* b New York, NY, Aug 25, 35; m 58, 82, Frani Rudolph; c K Jeffrey, Lauren S & Jennifer A (Ruff). *Educ:* Johns Hopkins Univ, BES, 57, MSE, 58, DEng, 60. *Honors & Awards:* Fulbright Lectr, Kiev Polytech Inst, USSR, 81. *Prof Exp:* Instr elec eng, Johns Hopkins Univ, 58-59, lectr, 59-61; from asst prof to prof elec & computer eng, Syracuse Univ, 63-89, dean eng, 84-89. *Concurrent Pos:* Vis scholar, Dept Elec Eng & Computer Sci, Univ Calif, Berkeley, 77; vis lectr, Nanging Inst Technol, People's Repub China, 81; mem bd dirs eng, Deans Coun, Am Soc Eng Educ, 90-93; comn, Am Asn Eng Soc, 90-; hon prof, Taganroy State Univ Radio Eng, Russia, 92; academician, Int Acad Informatics, Russia & Int Higher Educ Acad Sci, Russia, 93. *Mem:* Fel Inst Elec & Electronics Engrs; Am Mat Soc; Soc Indust & Appl Math; Asn Comput Mach; Nat Soc Prof Engrs; Am Soc Eng Educ. *Res:* Nonlinear systems analysis; linear systems analysis; system simulation; numerical analysis and functional analysis in systems analysis; stability theory; digital hardware design. *Mailing Add:* Eng Dean's Off 300 Eng Bldg Mich State Univ East Lansing MI 48824-1226. *Fax:* 517-355-2288; *E-Mail:* tab@egr.msu.edu

BICKEL, EDWIN DAVID, ECONOMIC GEOLOGY, ENVIRONMENTAL GEOLOGY. *Current Pos:* GEOLOGIST & HYDROLOGIST, RECLAMATION DIV, PUB SERV COMN, 89- *Personal Data:* b Louisville, Ky, Nov 11, 41; m 67; c 2. *Educ:* Univ Louisville, AB, 63, MSc, 65; Ohio State Univ, PhD(geol), 70. *Prof Exp:* Asst prof geol, 70-73, dir coop educ, Minot State Col, 73-76; adminr geol, N Am Coal Corp, 77-83; geologist, Thames Bickel Assoc, 84-89. *Concurrent Pos:* Work-group researcher, Northern Great Plains Resources Prog, 74-75; contracted malacologist, Off Endangered Species, US Fish & Wildlife Serv, 74-; consult, 75-77; proj prin investr, NDak Regional Environ Assessment Prog, 76-77. *Mem:* Am Asn Petrol Geologists; Soc Mining Engrs; Sigma Xi; Paleont Res Inst; Am Inst Prof Geologists; Am Inst Mining Engrs; Nat Water Well Asn. *Res:* Malacology; systematics and ecology of living and fossil non-marine Mollusca; Cretaceous-Tertiary biostratigraphy, coal stratigraphy; socio-economic and environmental impacts of energy development; petroleum geology and groundwater hydrology. *Mailing Add:* PO Box 993 Bismarck ND 58502-0993

BICKEL, JOHN HENRY, NUCLEAR POWER PLANT SAFETY ANALYSIS. *Current Pos:* MGR RISK ANALYSIS, EG&G IDAHO, 89- *Personal Data:* b Chicago, IL, June 23, 50; m 73; c 3. *Educ:* Univ VT, BS, 72, MS, 74; Rensselaer Polytech Inst, MS, 76, PhD(eng sci), 80. *Honors & Awards:* Young Mem Eng Achievement Award, Am Nuclear Soc, 83. *Prof Exp:* Nuclear Eng, Combustion Eng, 75-79; Adv comt Reactor Safegards Fel, US Nuclear Regulatory Comn, 79-80; supvr probabilistic risk assessment, Northeast Utilities Serv Co, 80-89. *Concurrent Pos:* Consult & lectr, Int Atomic Energy Agency, Vienna, Soviet State Comt Supr Nuclear Energy, Moscow, Swedish Power Bd, Stockholm; lectr, Argonne Nat Lab, Nuclear power plant oper safety, 86- 87; mem peer rev, NRC, 87-88. *Mem:* Am Nuclear Soc. *Res:* Development and application of probabilistic safety and reliability methods to nuclear power plants; operational decision making and reliability improvements; reliability engineering and risk assessment. *Mailing Add:* 7622 Aldea Pl Carlsbad CA 92009

BICKEL, PETER J, PROBABILITY. *Current Pos:* From asst prof to assoc prof statist, Univ Calif, Berkeley, 63-70, chmn dept, 75-78, dean phys scis, 80-86, PROF STATIST, UNIV CALIF, BERKELEY, 70-, CHMN DEPT, 93- *Personal Data:* b Bucharest, Romania, Sept 21, 40; US citizen; m 64, Nancy Kramer; c Amanda & Stephen. *Educ:* Univ Calif, Berkeley, AB, 60, MA, 61, PhD(statist), 63. *Hon Degrees:* PhD(hc), Hebrew Univ, Jerusalem, 88. *Honors & Awards:* Comt Presidents Statist Socs Award, 79; Wald Lectr, Inst Math Statist, 80. *Concurrent Pos:* Lectr, Imp Col, Univ London, 65-66; J S Guggenheim Found fel, 70; NATO sr sci fel, 74-75; J D & Catherine T MacArthur Found fel, 84-88. *Mem:* Nat Acad Sci; fel Inst Math Statist (pres, 80); Royal Statist Soc; fel Am Statist Asn; mem Int Statist Inst; Am Acad Arts & Sci; fel AAAS; foreign mem Royal Netherlands Acad Sci. *Res:* Non-parametric methods; semi-parametric models; robustness; asymptotic methods and approximations; inference for stochastic processes; applications of statistics to molecular biology; genomics; traffic management. *Mailing Add:* Dept Statist Univ Calif Berkeley CA 94720. *Fax:* 510-642-7892; *E-Mail:* bickel@stat.berkeley.edu

BICKEL, ROBERT JOHN, MATHEMATICS. *Current Pos:* from instr to assoc prof, 46-60, actg head dept, 68-69, 73-74, PROF MATH, DREXEL UNIV, 60-, ASSOC HEAD DEPT, 63- *Personal Data:* b Louisville, Ky, Nov 8, 16; m 42. *Educ:* Univ Louisville, AB, 37; Northwestern Univ, MA, 41; Univ Pittsburgh, PhD(math), 60. *Prof Exp:* Teacher, pub schs, Ky, 37-41. *Mem:* Math Asn Am; Soc Indust & Appl Math (treas, 55-62). *Res:* Analysis; summability; divergent series. *Mailing Add:* 415 Ellis Woods Rd Pottstown PA 19464-9323

BICKEL, THOMAS FULCHER, ALGEBRA. *Current Pos:* from asst prof, 67-80, chmn dept, 85-87, PROF MATH, DARMOUTH COL, 80- *Personal Data:* b Detroit, Mich, Nov 20, 37; m 64. *Educ:* Univ Mich, BS, 59, MA, 60, PhD(math), 65. *Prof Exp:* Instr math, Mass Inst Technol, 65-67. *Mem:* Am Math Soc. *Res:* Finite group theory; theory of finite groups of Lie type; permutation groups. *Mailing Add:* Dept Math & Comput Sci Dartmouth Col 6188 Bradley Hall Hanover NH 03755-3551

BICKEL, WILLIAM SAMUEL, EXPERIMENTAL PHYSICS, SPECTROSCOPY. *Current Pos:* Res assoc physics, 65, from asst prof to assoc prof, 65-75, PROF PHYSICS, UNIV ARIZ, 75- *Personal Data:* b Ottsville, Pa, June 8, 37. *Educ:* Pa State Univ, BS, 59, PhD(physics), 65. *Mem:* Am Phys Soc; Biophys Soc; fel Am Soc Eng Educ. *Res:* Spectroscopic diagnostics; atomic physics; spectroscopy of fast excited ions; measurement of mean lives of excited ions; vacuum ultraviolet and visible spectroscopy; biophysics; time-resolved polarized light scattering from biological macromolecules, spheres, fibers and irregular particles; acoustics and physics of music; surface physics. *Mailing Add:* Dept Physics PAS Univ Ariz Tucson AZ 85721-0001

BICKELHAUPT, R(OY) E(DWARD), ceramics engineering, for more information see previous edition

BICKERT, WILLIAM GEORGE, AGRICULTURAL ENGINEERING. *Current Pos:* from res asst & instr to assoc prof, 61-72, PROF AGR ENG, MICH STATE UNIV, 72- *Personal Data:* b Bismarck, NDak, Apr 9, 37; m 61; c 2. *Educ:* NDak State Univ, BS, 59, MS, 60; Mich State Univ, PhD(agr eng), 64. *Prof Exp:* Res asst agr eng, NDak State Univ, 59-60. *Mem:* Am Soc Agr Engrs. *Res:* Livestock production facilities, ventilation systems; milking systems, equipment, design, labor utilization; environmental control. *Mailing Add:* 2962 Colony Dr East Lansing MI 48823

BICKERTON, ROBERT KEITH, PHARMACOLOGY. *Current Pos:* DIR, CO-OPER RES, YALE UNIV, 87- *Personal Data:* b East Liverpool, Ohio, Oct 1, 34; m 57; c 2. *Educ:* Univ Pittsburgh, BS, 56, MS, 58, PhD(pharmacol), 60. *Prof Exp:* Sr res pharmacologist, Norwich Pharmacol Co, 60-62, unit leader, 62-63, from asst chief to chief sect pharmacol, 63-65, dir pharmacometrics div, 65-68, dir res, 68-69, vpres res, 69-73, vpres sci affairs, 73-77, sr vpres sci affairs, 77-80; Mentor Group, Inc, 80- *Mem:* Am Pharmaceut Asn; Am Soc Pharmacol & Exp Therapeut. *Res:* Mechanism of action and development of antihypertensive drugs. *Mailing Add:* 9 Old Still Rd Woodbridge CT 06525-1101

BICKFORD, LAWRENCE RICHARDSON, SOLID STATE PHYSICS. *Current Pos:* RETIRED. *Personal Data:* b Elmira, NY, Nov 24, 21; m 43, 70; c 3. *Educ:* Alfred Univ, BS, 43; Mass Inst Technol, PhD(physics), 49. *Prof Exp:* Assoc prof physics, State Univ NY Col Ceramics, Alfred, 49-54; sr physicist res lab, IBM, 54-63, dir gen sci, Res Ctr, 62-63, dir res lab, Tokyo, Japan, 63-65, dir memory & mat res, Res Lab, NY, 65-70, mgr mat sci & technol, 70-73, res staff mem, IBM Res Lab, Calif, 73-77, prog dir tech commun, IBM White Plains, NY, 77-82; dep exec secy, Am Phys Soc, 82-84. *Mem:* Fel Am Phys Soc; Inst Elec & Electronics Engrs. *Res:* Ferrites; titanates; glass; organic conductors; contact effects on conductivity in anisotropic organic conductors; superconductivity. *Mailing Add:* 200 Bennett Ave New York NY 10040

BICKFORD, MARION EUGENE, PETROLOGY, ISOTOPE GEOCHEMISTRY. *Current Pos:* Jessie Page Heroy prof & chmn, 90-93, PROF GEOL, SYRACUSE UNIV, 93- *Personal Data:* b Memphis, Tenn, Aug 30, 32; m 54, Elizabeth Eckey; c Mark, Martha & John. *Educ:* Carleton Col, BA, 54; Univ Ill, MS, 58, PhD(geol), 60. *Prof Exp:* Asst prof geol, San Fernando Valley State Col, 60-63; asst res geophysicist, Inst Geophys, Univ Calif, Los Angeles, 63-64; from asst prof to prof geol, Univ Kans, 64-89. *Mem:* Fel Mineral Soc Am; fel Geol Soc Am; Am Geophys Union. *Res:* Crystal evolution and tectonics, Trans-Hudson, Oregon, Canada; geochronology of orogenic sequences in West Texas. *Mailing Add:* 204 Heroy Geol Lab Syracuse NY 13244-1070. *Fax:* 315-443-3363; *E-Mail:* mebickfo@suvm.acs.syr.edu

BICKFORD, REGINALD G, NEUROSCIENCES. *Current Pos:* head, EEG Lab, 69-80, prof, 69-87, EMER PROF NEUROSCI, SCH MED, UNIV HOSP, UNIV CALIF, SAN DIEGO, 87- *Personal Data:* b Brewood, Eng, Jan 20, 13; nat US; m 45; c 2. *Educ:* Cambridge Univ, BA, MD & BCh, 36; FRCP, 71. *Prof Exp:* Mayo res assoc, Univ Minn, 46-48, from assoc prof to prof physiol, 53-69. *Concurrent Pos:* Med Res Coun fel, Univ London, 37-40; consult EEG, Mayo Clin, 46-69; mem, Neurol Study Sect, USPHS, 60-64, mem, Comput Study Sect, 64-68, mem, Adv Comt Epilepsies, 64-70, mem, Clin Pract Comt Deleg to Soviet Union, 68 & mem, Sci Info Prog Adv Comt, Nat Inst Neurol Dis & Stroke, 70- *Mem:* Am EEG Soc (pres, 56); Am Physiol Soc; Int League Against Epilepsy; Am Neurol Asn. *Res:* Electrical activity of the brain in man and animals; experimentally produced changes and their relation to behavioral and psychological effects; computer analysis and automation of the electroencephalogram. *Mailing Add:* 9420 La Jolla Farms Rd La Jolla CA 92037

BICKHAM, JOHN W, CYTOGENETICS, SYSTEMATICS. *Current Pos:* from asst prof to assoc prof, 76-87, PROF WILDLIFE & FISHERIES SCI, TEX A&M UNIV, 87- *Personal Data:* b Chillicothe, Ohio, Mar 4, 49; m 81; c 2. *Educ:* Univ Dayton, BS, 71, MS, 73; Tex Tech Univ, PhD(zool), 76. *Prof Exp:* Teaching asst biol, Univ Dayton, 72-73; teacher zool, Texas Technol Univ, 73-76. *Mem:* Am Soc Mammalogists; Am Soc Ichthyologists & Herpetologists; Soc Syst Zool; AAAS. *Res:* Application of cytogenetics to the study of evolution, speciation and taxonomy of vertebrates, chiefly mammals and reptiles. *Mailing Add:* 2104 Chippendale St College Station TX 77845

BICKLEY, WILLIAM ELBERT, ENTOMOLOGY. *Current Pos:* from assoc prof to prof, 48-78, head dept, 57-71, EMER PROF ENTOM, UNIV MD, 78-; RES ASSOC, WALTER REED BIOSYSTEMATICS UNIT, SMITHSONIAN INST, 78- *Personal Data:* b Knoxville, Tenn, Jan 20, 14; m 41, Elizabeth MacGill; c 4. *Educ:* Univ Tenn, BS, 34, MS, 36; Univ Md, PhD(entom), 40. *Prof Exp:* Teacher, pub schs, Tenn, 35-37; teaching fel entom, Univ Md, 37-40, instr, 40-42; from asst entomologist to sr asst sanitarian, malaria control in war areas, USPHS, 42-46; asst prof biol, Univ Richmond, 46-49. *Concurrent Pos:* Entomologist, State Dept Pub Health, Va, 47-49; ed, Mosquito News, 73-81, emer ed, 81-; assoc ed, J Am Mosquito; control assoc, 82-95. *Mem:* Entom Soc Am; Mosquito Control Asn (pres, 61); Am Soc Trop Med & Hyg; Sigma Xi; fel Royal Entom Soc. *Res:* Chrysopidae; insect morphology; Japanese beetle; mosquitoes; vegetable insects; alfalfa weevil; dog to dog transmission of heartworm by mosquitoes. *Mailing Add:* 6516 40th Ave University Park MD 20782

BICKLING, CHARLES ROBERT, CHEMICAL ENGINEERING. *Current Pos:* Res engr, Textile Fibers Dept, 50-53, group supvr & tech supvr Chatta nylon, 53-58, tech supvr Seaford nylon, 58-63, process supvr, 63-66, fibers planning mgr, Ducilo SAIC, Arg, 66-70, sr supvr process, Va, 70-77, SPECIALIST, TEXTILE FIBERS DEPT, E I DU PONT DE NEMOURS & CO, INC, 77- *Personal Data:* b Wilmington, Del, May 29, 24; m 47. *Educ:* Univ Del, BChE, 45; Univ Wis, MS, 46, PhD(chem eng), 50. *Mem:* AAAS; Am Chem Soc; Am Inst Chem Engrs. *Mailing Add:* 916 Dundee Ct Martinsville VA 24112-5638

BICKMORE, JOHN TARRY, XEROGRAPHIC DEVELOPMENT, XEROGRAPHIC DEVELOPERS. *Current Pos:* res physicist, 55-75, SR SCIENTIST, XEROX CORP, 75- *Personal Data:* b Logan, Utah, Jan 15, 28; m 53; c 3. *Educ:* Idaho State Col, BS, 50; Univ Rochester, PhD(biophys), 56. *Prof Exp:* Res assoc, Univ Rochester, 52-55. *Mem:* AAAS; fel Soc Photog Sci & Eng. *Res:* Chemical effects of ionizing radiation; xerographic process research, particularly the mechanisms, materials properties and failure modes in the development process. *Mailing Add:* 1849 Blossom Rd Rochester NY 14625

BICKNELL, EDWARD J, COMPARATIVE PATHOLOGY, CLINICAL PATHOLOGY. *Current Pos:* ANIMAL PATHOLOGIST & EXTEN VETERINARIAN, AGR EXP STA, UNIV ARIZ, 72-; VET PATHOLOGIST, ANIMAL DIAG LAB. *Personal Data:* b Kansas City, Mo, Jan 23, 28; m 52. *Educ:* Univ Mo, BA, 48; Kans State Univ, MS, 51, DVM, 60; Mich State Univ, PhD(path), 65. *Prof Exp:* Instr path, Mich State Univ, 60-64; asst prof, Kans State Univ, 65-66; assoc prof, Iowa State Univ, 66-67; assoc prof vet sci, SDak State Univ, 68-72. *Res:* Pathology of range cattle disease; pathology of swine disease. *Mailing Add:* 26604 S Saddletree Dr Chandler AZ 85248

BICKNELL, WILLIAM EDMUND, ELECTRICAL ENGINEERING. *Current Pos:* STAFF MEM, LINCOLN LAB, MASS INST TECHNOL, 69-, ASST GROUP LEADER, 92- *Personal Data:* b Kearney, Nebr, Nov 22, 35; m 57; c 3. *Educ:* Univ Ill, BS, 57; Mass Inst Technol, MS, 58; Stanford Univ, PhD(elec eng), 64. *Prof Exp:* Electronics engr, Res & Develop Lab, US Army, 63-65; specialist, Appl Res Lab, Sylvania Elec Co, Gen Tel & Electronics Corp, 66-69. *Concurrent Pos:* Consult, Sylvania Elec Co, Gen Tel & Electronics Corp, Calif, 62 & 63; lectr, Monmouth Col, 63- *Mem:* Inst Elec & Electronics Engrs; AAAS. *Res:* Microwave and quantum electronics; maser and laser devices; electro-optic systems design and analysis; infrared systems. *Mailing Add:* Lincoln Lab MS S3-539 Mass Inst Technol PO Box 73 Lexington MA 02173

BICKNELL-BROWN, ELLEN, VIBRATIONAL SPECTROSCOPY, BIOMOLECULAR CONFORMATION. *Current Pos:* DR, NIMH, 89-93, DR, NAT CANCER INST, NIH, 93- *Personal Data:* b Jackson, Miss, Nov 24, 44; c 1. *Educ:* Rice Univ, AB, 66; Brown Univ, PhD(phys chem), 71. *Prof Exp:* Res assoc, Univ Ore, 71-73 & Univ Fla, 73-77; asst prof chem, Wayne State Univ, 77-87; spec expert chem, Nat Lib Med, 86-88. *Mem:* Am Chem Soc; Sigma Xi; AAAS. *Res:* Raman and infrared spectroscopy used to probe structure and interactions in biological molecules and systems such as membranes, proteins, lipids, and nucleic acids; resonance-enchanced near ultraviolet raman spectroscopy to investigate electronic excited states of proteins. *Mailing Add:* 4524 Everett St Kensington MD 20895

BIDANI, AKHIL, PULMONARY MEDICINE, CRITICAL CARE. *Current Pos:* PROF MED/BIOPHYS & DIR PULMONARY MED, UNIV TEX, GALVESTON, 92- *Personal Data:* b Kanpur, India, 1947. *Educ:* Univ Houston, PhD(chem eng), 75; Univ Tex, MD, 81. *Mem:* Am Col Chest Physicians; Am Soc Clin Invest. *Mailing Add:* Univ Tex Med Br E-61 Galveston TX 77550

BIDDINGTON, WILLIAM ROBERT, DENTISTRY. *Current Pos:* PROF ENDODONTICS & HEAD DEPT, SCH DENT, WVA UNIV MED CTR, 59-, DEAN SCH DENT, 68- *Personal Data:* b Piedmont, WVa, Mar 30, 25; m 47; c 1. *Educ:* Univ Md, DDS, 48. *Prof Exp:* From instr to assoc prof, Dent Sch, Univ Md, 48-59. *Concurrent Pos:* Vchmn, Joint Comn Nat Dent Exam; mem, Comn Dent Health, Coun Sports Med, US Olympic Comn, 80- *Mem:* Am Dent Asn; Int Asn Dent Res; Am Col Dent; Am Asn Endodontists. *Res:* Endodontics; periodontics. *Mailing Add:* RR 7 Morgantown WV 26505

BIDDLE, RICHARD ALBERT, INORGANIC CHEMISTRY. *Current Pos:* res chemist, Elkton Div, Morton Thiokol Inc, 57-60, head inorg & propellant chem group, Res Dept, 60-66, scientist res dept, 66-85, HEAD INGREDIENTS SYNTHESIS, ELKTON DIV, MORTON THIOKOL INC, 85- *Personal Data:* b Philadelphia, Pa, July 16, 30; m 55; c 4. *Educ:* Pa State Univ, BS, 52; Iowa State Univ, MS, 55. *Prof Exp:* Instr & res assoc chem, Iowa State Univ, 52-56. *Mem:* AAAS; Am Chem Soc; Am Defense Preparedness Asn. *Res:* Inorganic chemical syntheses with emphasis on boron hydrides and high vacuum techniques; thermal decomposition of perchlorates and kinetics of solid phase reactions; space simulation studies; thermoanalytical techniques; hygrometry; solid rocket propellant chemistry and formulation; hazards studies in propellants and explosives. *Mailing Add:* 1120 Nottingham Rd Elkton MD 21921-4742

BIDE, MARTIN JOHN, TEXTILES, DYESTUFFS. *Current Pos:* PROF TEXTILES DEPT, UNIV RI, 91- *Personal Data:* b Portsmouth, UK, Nov 7, 51. *Educ:* Univ Bradford, UK, BTech Hons, 74, PhD(dyestuff chem), 79. *Prof Exp:* Develop chemist dyes, Yorkshire Chem, UK, 77-80; develop chemist herbicides, A H Marks, Bradford, UK, 80-81; assoc prof textile chem, Southeastern Mass Univ, 81-91. *Concurrent Pos:* Consult, res proj, USDA. 83-85, dyeing indust Mass & RI, 81-; lectr, US Navy Clothing & Textile Res Facil, Natrick, Mass, 82-85 & AATCC, 85. *Mem:* Am Asn Textile Chemists & Colorists; Soc Dyes & Colorists; Royal Soc Chem. *Res:* Dyestuff chemistry; dyeing, especially wool; wool scouring; color. *Mailing Add:* Textile Dept Univ RI Quinn Hall Kingston RI 02881

BIDE, RICHARD W, TOXICOLOGY, PATHOLOGICAL CHEMISTRY. *Current Pos:* head, Biomed Sect, 84-87, DEFENSE SCIENTIST, DEFENSE RES ESTAB, SUFFIELD, RALSTON, ALTA, 87- *Personal Data:* b Calgary, Alta, Sept 5, 39; m 91, Linda Hall; c 6. *Educ:* Univ Alta, BSc, 59, MSc, 61; Aberdeen Univ, PhD(biochem), 64. *Prof Exp:* Nat Res Coun Can fel radiobiol, Atomic Energy Can, Ltd, 64-66; vet clin chem & biochem, Animal Res Inst, Lethbridge, Can Dept Agr, 66-81; toxicol & biochem residues, Animal Path Lab, Agr Can, Sask, 81-84. *Mem:* Am Asn Acoust Sci; Air & Water Mgt Asn. *Res:* Enzymology; radiobiology; veterinary pathological chemistry; biomedical profiling; toxicology. *Mailing Add:* Biomed Defense Sect Defense Res Estab Suffield Box 4000 Medicine Hat AB T1A 8K6 Can. *Fax:* 403-544-3388; *E-Mail:* rbide@dres.und.ca

BIDELMAN, WILLIAM PENDRY, ASTRONOMY. *Current Pos:* chmn dept astron, Case Western Reserve Univ & dir, Warner & Swasey Observ, 70-75, prof, 70-86, EMER PROF ASTRON, CASE WESTERN RESERVE UNIV, 86- *Personal Data:* b Los Angeles, Calif, Sept 25, 18; m 40, Verna Shirk; c Lana B, Linda B, Billie B & Barbara B. *Educ:* Harvard Univ, SB, 40; Univ Chicago, PhD(astron), 43. *Prof Exp:* Asst, Yerkes Observ, Univ Chicago, 41-43; physicist, Ballistic Res Lab, Aberdeen Proving Ground, US Ord Dept, 43-45; from instr astron to asst prof astrophys, Univ Chicago, 45-53; from asst astronr to assoc astronr, Lick Observ, Univ Calif, 53-62; prof astron, Univ Mich, 62-69 & Univ Tex, 69-70. *Mem:* Am Astron Soc; Int Astron Union. *Res:* Spectral classification; observational astrophysics; astronomical data. *Mailing Add:* 3171 Chelsea Dr Cleveland Heights OH 44118

BIDER, JOHN ROGER, POPULATIONS, BEHAVIOR. *Current Pos:* PROF ECOL, FAC AGR, McGILL UNIV, 65- *Personal Data:* b Lachine, Que, Nov 23, 32; m 56; c 6. *Educ:* Univ Montreal, BSc, 56, MSc, 59, PhD(ecol), 66. *Concurrent Pos:* Sci consult, Sci Coun Can, 69-70; consult, Environ Adv Coun, Gov Que, 73-77, Food & Agr Orgn, Rome & Can Int Develop Agency, Burundi, 74, Upper Volta, 74, Mali, 88, Environ Mgt Hydro-Que, 75-85, Coun Ecol Reserves, 75-77, Can Int Develop Agency, Haiti, 76-80, Environ Coun Gov Que, 86-90 & Cyprus, 88-93; dir, Ecomuseum, 85- *Mem:* Ecol Soc Am; Am Soc Mammalogists; Wildlife Soc; Can Soc Zoologists; Sigma Xi. *Res:* Terrestrial vertebrate ecology with emphasis on factors which affect animal activity; the temporal and spatial utilization of the environment; the relationship between activity and numbers; life history strategies and population dynamics of turtles; zoogeography. *Mailing Add:* 21111 Lakeshore Ste Anne de Bellevue PQ H9X 1C0 Can. *Fax:* 514-398-7983

BIDINOSTI, DINO RONALD, PHYSICAL CHEMISTRY. *Current Pos:* asst prof, 61-66, ASSOC PROF PHYS CHEM, UNIV WESTERN ONT, 66- *Personal Data:* b Winnipeg, Man, Mar 27, 33; m 57; c 4. *Educ:* Univ Man, BSc, 55, MSc, 56; McMaster Univ, PhD(chem), 59. *Prof Exp:* Defense Res Bd Can fel phys chem, Univ Ottawa, 59-60; res assoc & Air Res & Develop Command fel, Cornell Univ, 60-61. *Mem:* Chem Inst Can; Royal Soc Chem. *Res:* Application of mass spectrometry to chemical systems; thermochemistry. *Mailing Add:* Dept Chem Univ Western Ont London ON N6A 5B8 Can

BIDLACK, DONALD EUGENE, ANIMAL HUSBANDRY, ANIMAL SCIENCE & NUTRITION. *Current Pos:* res vet, 73-78, assoc pathologist, 78-85, RES PATHOLOGIST, SYNTEX RES, 85- *Personal Data:* b Oakwood, Ohio, Apr 16, 32; m 53; c 3. *Educ:* Ohio State Univ, BSc, 54, DVM, 57. *Prof Exp:* Pvt pract, Ind, 57-65; vet, Eaton Labs, Norwich Pharmacol Co, 65-73. *Mem:* Am Vet Med Asn. *Res:* Industrial pharmaceutical research and development. *Mailing Add:* 32510 Sunset Ridge Coarsegold CA 93614

BIDLACK, JEAN MARIE, PHARMACOLOGY OF BRAIN & LYMPHOCYTIC OPIOID RECEPTORS, AFFINITY LIGANDS FOR THE MULTIPLE OPIOID RECEPTORS. *Current Pos:* Fel, Ctr Brain Res, Univ Rochester, 79-81, asst prof, 81-87, assoc prof, Dept Pharmacol, 87-97, PROF, DEPT PHARMACOL & PHYSIOL, UNIV ROCHESTER, 97- *Personal Data:* b Rochester, NY, Dec 4, 53. *Educ:* Skidmore Col, BA, 75; Univ Rochester, MS, 77, PhD(biophys), 79. *Concurrent Pos:* Consult, Vet Admin, 86-88, Nat Inst Drug Abuse, 87-, NIH, 92-; mem, AIDS Study Sect, Nat Inst Drug Abuse, 94-, chair, AIDS Study Sect, 96- *Mem:* Am Soc Pharmacol & Exp Therapeut; Soc Neurosci; Psychoneuroimmunol Res Soc. *Res:* Central analgesic mechanisms; developing compounds for the treatment of heroin and cocaine drug addiction; understanding the pharmacological mechanisms involved in the development of opioid tolerance and dependence; characterizing opioid receptors on cells from the immune system and the function of lymphocytic opioid receptors. *Mailing Add:* Univ Rochester Med Sch Dept Pharmacol & Physiol 601 Elmwood Ave PO Box 711 Rochester NY 14642-8711. *Fax:* 716-244-9283; *E-Mail:* bidlackj@pharmacol.rochester.edu

BIDLACK, VERNE CLAUDE, JR, ORGANIC CHEMISTRY. *Current Pos:* RETIRED. *Personal Data:* b South Bend, Ind, Mar 5, 23; m 46; c 4. *Educ:* Univ Mich, BS, 44; Pa State Univ, MS, 48, PhD(chem), 50. *Prof Exp:* Res chemist, E I Du Pont de Nemours & Co, 50-51; chief org chemist pharmaceuts, Henry K Wampole Co, Inc, 51-55; sr com develop engr, Archer-Daniels-Midland Co, 55-62; mgr mkt & prod develop, Atlantic Refining Co, 62, chem mkt res, 62-64; dir long planning, Chem Group, W R Grace & Co, 64-66; develop engr & purchasing agent, FMC Corp, 66-76; mem staff, Res Dept, C Lever Co, Inc, 77-80, dir res, 80-87. *Res:* Fatty acids and vegetable oils; natural and synthetic resins; protective coatings; adhesives; medicinal chemicals; plastics; fertilizers; plastic films, dyes and pigments. *Mailing Add:* 7 Bennington Pl Newtown PA 18940

BIDLACK, WAYNE ROSS, TOXICOLOGY. *Current Pos:* Fel pharmacol, 72-74, asst prof, 74-80, ASSOC PROF PHARMACOL & NUTRIT, SCH MED, UNIV SOUTHERN CALIF, 80- *Personal Data:* b Waverly, NY, Aug 12, 44; m 68. *Educ:* Pa State Univ, Univ Park, BS, 66; Iowa State Univ, Ames, MS, 68; Univ Calif, Davis, PhD(biochem), 72. *Concurrent Pos:* Chmn bd & bd dirs, Nat Coun Against Health Fraud, 85-86; USC postgrad, 87-88; chmn, Southern Calif Inst Food Technol, 88-89, Toxicol & Safety Eval Div, 89-90. *Mem:* Am Inst Nutrit; Inst Food Technologists; Soc Toxicol; Am Soc Pharmacol & Exp Therapeut. *Res:* Hepatic drug and toxicant metabolism; evaluation of nutritional status; nutrition and the elderly; vitamin and mineral metabolism; effects of nutritional parameters. *Mailing Add:* Col Agr Calif State Polytech Univ 3801 N Temple Ave Pomona CA 91768-4041

BIDLEMAN, TERRY FRANK, ANALYTICAL CHEMISTRY, ENVIRONMENTAL CHEMISTRY. *Current Pos:* asst prof chem, 75-81, ASSOC PROF CHEM & MARINE SCI, UNIV SC, 81- *Personal Data:* b Chicago, Ill, Feb 17, 42. *Educ:* Ohio Univ, BS, 64; Univ Minn, PhD(analytical chem), 70. *Prof Exp:* Fel chem, Dalhousie Univ, 70-72; res assoc food & resource chem, Univ RI, 72-75. *Mem:* Am Chem Soc; Soc Environ Toxicol & Chem. *Res:* Pesticide residue analysis; transport of pesticides in the environment; chemical aspects of air, sea transfer; solvent extraction equilibria; equilibria in natural water systems. *Mailing Add:* Atmospheric Environ Serv 4905 Dufferin St Downsview ON M3H 5T4 Can

BIDLINGMAYER, WILLIAM LESTER, ENTOMOLOGY. *Current Pos:* RETIRED. *Personal Data:* b Cleveland, Ohio, July 7, 20; m 50; c 2. *Educ:* Univ Fla, BSA, 49, MS, 52. *Prof Exp:* Entomologist, Fla State Bd Health, 50-51; asst sanitarian, Tech Develop Lab, Commun Dis Ctr, USPHS, 51-55; entomologist, Div Health, Fla Med Entom Lab, Univ Fla, 55-79, prof, 79-87. *Mem:* Am Mosquito Control Asn; Entom Soc Am. *Res:* Biology and ecology of mosquitoes and sandflies; sampling and population dynamics of mosquito populations. *Mailing Add:* Rte 5 Box 5159 Monticello FL 32344

BIDLINGMEYER, BRIAN ARTHUR, ANALYTICAL CHEMISTRY. *Current Pos:* MGR ORG BIOSCI RES, WATERS ASSOCS, 75- *Personal Data:* b Dallas, Tex, Aug 8, 44; m 72; c 1. *Educ:* Kenyon Col, AB, 66; Purdue Univ, PhD(analytical chem), 71. *Prof Exp:* Res chemist, Standard Oil Co Ind, 71-74. *Mem:* Am Chem Soc; Am Soc Testing & Mat. *Res:* Application of liquid chromatography to difficult separations in organic and biological research, specifically pesticide residues, long-chain fatty acids and lipids; data handling, manipulation and interpretation in chromatography. *Mailing Add:* 43 Craig Lane Frazer PA 19355-1036

BIDWELL, LAWRENCE ROMAINE, PHYSICAL METALLURGY. *Current Pos:* task scientist, Aerospace Res Labs, 54-60, res metallurgist, 60-67, res metallurgist, Mat Lab, 67-70, sr res scientist, 70-76, GROUP LEADER, MAT LAB, USAF, 76- *Personal Data:* b Olean, NY, Jan 8, 31; m 52; c 4. *Educ:* Ohio State Univ, BMetE, 53, MSc, 54, PhD(thermodyn), 62. *Prof Exp:* Res assoc metall, Res Found, Ohio State Univ, 53-54. *Mem:* AAAS; Am Soc Metals; Am Inst Mining, Metall & Petrol Engrs; Sigma Xi. *Res:* Development of corrosion resistant, high temperature, rapidly solidified and aerospace structural alloys; phase equilibria and thermodynamic properties of metal and non-metal systems; electrical properties of refractory oxides; solid electrolytes. *Mailing Add:* 5787 Redbird Ct Dayton OH 45431-2919

BIDWELL, LEONARD NATHAN, MATHEMATICS. *Current Pos:* asst prof math, 62-67, ASSOC PROF MATH, RUTGERS UNIV, CAMDEN, 67- *Personal Data:* b Camden, NJ, Dec 20, 34; m 63; c 2. *Educ:* Univ Pa, BA, 56, MA, 57, PhD(math), 60. *Prof Exp:* Vis asst prof math, Haverford Col, 60-61; mathematician, Gen Elec Co, 61-62. *Mem:* Am Math Soc; Math Asn Am. *Res:* Topology; functional analysis. *Mailing Add:* Dept Math Rutgers Univ 311 N Fifth St Camden NJ 08102-1205

BIDWELL, ORVILLE WILLARD, SOIL MORPHOLOGY, ALTERNATIVE AGRICULTURE. *Current Pos:* RETIRED. *Personal Data:* b Whitehouse, Ohio, Jan 14, 18; m 44; c 2. *Educ:* Oberlin Col, AB, 40; Ohio State Univ, BSc, 42, PhD(agron), 49. *Honors & Awards:* Merit Award, Soil Conserv Soc Am, 63. *Prof Exp:* Asst agron, Ohio State Univ, 46-49; from asst prof to prof, 50-84, actg head Dept Agron, 70-71, emer prof soils, Kans State Univ, 84. *Concurrent Pos:* Vis prof, Ahmadu Bello Univ, Nigeria, 73. *Mem:* Fel AAAS; fel Am Soc Agron; fel Soil Sci Soc Am; fel Soil Conserv Soc Am. *Res:* Soil classification and development. *Mailing Add:* 3815 Emerald Circle Manhattan KS 66503-7514

BIDWELL, ROGER GRAFTON SHELFORD, PLANT PHYSIOLOGY. *Current Pos:* RETIRED. *Personal Data:* b Halifax, NS, June 8, 27; m 50, Shirley M R Mason; c Barbara, Alison, Roger & Gillian. *Educ:* Dalhousie Univ, BS, 47; Queen's Univ, Ont, BA, 50, MA, 51, PhD, 54. *Hon Degrees:* FRSC, 72. *Honors & Awards:* Queen Elizabeth II Silver Jubilee Medal, 79; Gold Medal, Can Soc Plant Physiol, 80. *Prof Exp:* Res officer, Defense Res Bd, 52-56; botanist, Atlantic Regional Lab, Nat Res Coun, 56-59; assoc prof bot, Univ Toronto, 59-65; prof biol, Case Western Res Univ, 65-69, chmn dept, 67-69; prof biol, Queen's Univ, Ont, 69-79; res prof biol, Dalhousie Univ, Halifax, NS, 81-85; dir, Atlantic Res Assocs, 82-90; dir, Atlantic Inst Biotechno, 85-88. *Concurrent Pos:* Secy, Biol Coun Can, 72-76; Nat Biotechnol Adv Comt, 83-89; dir, Cumberland Forestry Asn, 92-95; pres & bd chair, Pugwash Co-Op Ltd, 95- *Mem:* Fel AAAS; Am Soc Plant Physiol; Can Soc Plant Physiol (secy-treas, 63-65, vpres, 71-72, pres, 72-73); fel Royal Soc Can. *Res:* Intermediary metabolism in plants; carbohydrates and amino acids; process of photosynthesis; metabolism of marine algae. *Mailing Add:* Riverdell RR 1 Wallace NS B0K 1Y0 Can

BIEBEL, PAUL JOSEPH, PHYCOLOGY. *Current Pos:* from asst prof to assoc prof, 63-74, PROF BIOL, DICKINSON COL, 74- *Personal Data:* b Belleville, Ill, Feb 26, 28; m 51; c 6. *Educ:* Univ Notre Dame, BS, 49; St Louis Univ, MS, 55; Ind Univ, PhD(phycol), 63. *Honors & Awards:* DAAD Awardee. *Prof Exp:* Instr biol, Spring Hill Col, 59-63. *Mem:* Bot Soc Am; Phycol Soc Am; Am Bryol & Lichenological Soc; Int Phycol Soc; Sigma Xi. *Res:* Life cycles, morphology, taxonomy, genetics and morphogenesis of algae, especially saccoderm desmids. *Mailing Add:* PO Box 1773 Carlisle PA 17013-2896

BIEBER, ALLAN LEROY, BIOCHEMISTRY. *Current Pos:* from asst prof to assoc prof, 63-75, PROF CHEM, ARIZ STATE UNIV, 75- *Personal Data:* b Mott, NDak, Aug 14, 34; m 58; c 2. *Educ:* NDak State Univ, BS, 56, MS, 58; Ore State Univ, PhD(biochem), 62. *Prof Exp:* NIH training grant, Sch Med, Yale Univ, 61-63. *Mem:* Am Soc Biol Chemists; Am Chem Soc; Sigma Xi. *Res:* Metabolism of purines; purine analogs and their respective nucleotides; biochemistry of snake venoms and toxins. *Mailing Add:* Dept Chem Ariz State Univ Tempe AZ 85287-1604

BIEBER, FREDERICK ROBERT, HUMAN GENETICS, FORENSIC SCIENCE. *Current Pos:* instr, 83-85, asst prof, 85-91, ASSOC PROF PATH, HARVARD MED SCH, 92- *Personal Data:* m 73, Jane McNamara. *Educ:* State Univ NY, BA, 72; Univ Roch, MS, 76; Med Col Va, PhD(human genetics), 81. *Honors & Awards:* Young Investr Award, Teratology Soc, 82. *Concurrent Pos:* Assoc geneticist, Brigham Women's Hosp, 85-92, med geneticist, 92-; consult teratology, Mass Gen Hosp, 83-, pathol, Children's Hosp, 93- *Mem:* Am Acad Forensic Sci; Am Soc Human Genetics; Teratology Soc; Am Col Med Genetics. *Res:* Genetic basis of hearing loss in human populations; forensic genetics. *Mailing Add:* Dept Path Brigham Women's Hosp Boston MA 02115

BIEBER, HAROLD H, CHEMICAL ENGINEERING. *Current Pos:* sr chem engr, 56-64, Hoffmann-LaRoche, Inc, chem eng fel, 64-68, mgr process design, 68-78, proj dir, 78-79, dir eng design, 79-81, dir chem process plant dept, 82-89, ASST VPRES & DIR ENGR TECH CTR, HOFFMANN-LA ROCHE, INC, 89- *Personal Data:* b New York, NY, Apr 4, 27; m 50, Dorothy Flaxman; c Ellen, Barbara & David. *Educ:* City Col New York, BChE, 47; Polytech Inst Brooklyn, MChE, 50, DChE, 56. *Prof Exp:* Chem engr, Am Cyanamid Co, NJ, 47-54; sr res assoc, Polytech Inst Brooklyn, 54-56. *Mem:* Fel Am Inst Chem Engrs. *Res:* Unit operations; microporous membrane development. *Mailing Add:* 68 E Brook Terr Livingston NJ 07039

BIEBER, HERMAN, CHEMICAL ENGINEERING. *Current Pos:* CONSULT, BIEBER ENTERPRISES, 86- *Personal Data:* b Berleburg, Ger, Jan 13, 30; US citizen; wid; c Diane S, Judy A & Nancy L. *Educ:* Columbia Univ, BS, 52, MS, 53, DEngSci(chem eng), 62. *Prof Exp:* Instr chem eng, Columbia Univ, 53-54; engr, Esso Res & Eng Co, Linden, NJ, 55-57, group head, 57-58, sr engr, 58-61, res assoc, 61-62, sect head tech info, 62-68, sr res assoc, Corp Res Dept, 68-81, sr res assoc, Comput & Info Sci Div, 81-86. *Concurrent Pos:* Lectr, City Col New York, 54-55; adj prof, Stevens Inst Technol, 58-64; trustee, Midwest Res Inst, 67-90; mem, bd & exec comt, Eng Found, 81-91; mem bd, Eng Soc Libr, 84-90. *Mem:* Am Inst Chem Engrs; fel Am Inst Chemists; Sigma Xi. *Res:* Ion exchange kinetics; residual fuels and heavy crudes refining; information research; technology transfer; creative problem solving. *Mailing Add:* Bieber Enterprises 14 Dorset Dr Kenilworth NJ 07033-1417. *E-Mail:* hermbieber@aol.com

BIEBER, LORAN LAMOINE, BIOCHEMISTRY, SCIENCE ADMINISTRATION. *Current Pos:* PROF BIOCHEM, MICH STATE UNIV, 59-, ASSOC DEAN RES MED, 83- *Personal Data:* b Mott, NDak, Apr, 33; m 55; c 3. *Educ:* NDak State Univ, BS, 55, MS, 56; Ore State Univ, PhD(biochem), 63. *Prof Exp:* Asst agr chem, NDak State Univ, 56-57; lab technician, Hosp Lab, Ft Carson, Colo, 57-58 & Chem Ctr, Edgewood, Md, 58-59. *Concurrent Pos:* NIH fel biochem, Univ Calif, Los Angeles, 63-65; NIH fel, Mich State Univ, 66-74 & NSF fel, 67-71; vis prof cell physiol, Wenner-Gren Inst, Stockholm, 74; distinguished vis scholar, Univ Adelaide, 83. *Mem:* AAAS; Am Soc Biol Chemists; Am Chem Soc; Sigma Xi; Am Inst Nutrit. *Res:* Functions of carnitine; metabolic control; control of fatty acid and branched-chain amino acid oxidation. *Mailing Add:* Dept Biochem Mich State Univ 224 Biochem East Lansing MI 48824-1319

BIEBER, MARK ALLAN, BIOCHEMISTRY, NUTRITION. *Current Pos:* sr nutritionist, 78-80, prin nutritionist, 80-82, NUTRIT RES ASSOC, BEST FOODS, UNIT CPC INT, INC, 82- *Personal Data:* b Cleveland, Ohio, Sept 16, 46. *Educ:* Univ Pittsburgh, BS, 68; Mich State Univ, PhD(biochem), 73. *Prof Exp:* Fel nutrit, Col Physicians & Surgeons, Columbia Univ, 73-77. *Concurrent Pos:* Matheson Found fel brain res, Col Physicians & Surgeons, Columbia Univ, 73-74, vis fel Pediat, 74-77. *Mem:* Am Chem Soc; Am Oil Chemists Soc; Soc Nutrit Educ; Am Heart Asn; Am Inst Nutrit; Am Col Nutrit. *Res:* Lipids, fats and oils; essential fatty acids and deficiency; lipoproteins; atherosclerosis diet and cancer; brain growth and development; insect hormones; mass spectrometry. *Mailing Add:* Best Foods Tech Ctr 150 Pierce St Somerset NJ 08873. *Fax:* 732-627-8645

BIEBER, RAYMOND W, CELL BIOLOGY. *Current Pos:* ASSOC PROF CELL BIOL, MED CTR, UNIV NEBR, 72- *Educ:* Univ Colo, PhD(cell biol), 72. *Mailing Add:* RR 1 Lincoln NE 68583-9801

BIEBER, SAMUEL, DEVELOPMENTAL BIOLOGY. *Current Pos:* vpres acad affairs, 80-82, PROF, BIOL SCI DIV, OLD DOMINION UNIV, 80- *Personal Data:* b US, Feb 5, 26; m 49, Rosalyn L Hewitt; c Susan E (Blackwell) & Scott. *Educ:* NY Univ, BA, 44, MS, 48, PhD(vert zool), 52. *Prof Exp:* Teaching fel, Washington Sq Col, NY Univ, 48-51, res fel, 51-52; sr biologist, res labs, Burroughs Wellcome & Co, 52-62; prof biol, assoc dean sci & assoc dean grad sch, Long Island Univ, 62-64, assoc dean grad fac & spec adv to provost for sci, 64-66, dean, Conolly Col, 66-69; campus dean, Fairleigh Dickinson Univ, 69-71, prof biol sci & provost, Teaneck-Hackensack Campus, 71-78, actg vpres acad affairs, 78-80. *Concurrent Pos:* Sci collabr, New York Aquarium, 52-62; from adj asst prof to adj assoc prof grad sch, Long Island Univ, 57-62; vis fel, Cambridge Univ, 76. *Mem:* AAAS; Am Chem Soc; fel NY Acad Sci; Am Asn Cancer Res; Int Soc Develop Biol; Soc Develop Biol; Soc Exp Biol & Med; Sigma Xi. *Res:* Renotropic effects of steroids; antimetabolites and embryogenesis and regeneration; nucleic acid metabolism during gametogenesis and embryogenesis; experimental cancer chemotherapy; chemical suppression of the immune response. *Mailing Add:* 316 Westover Ave Norfolk VA 23507

BIEBER, THEODORE IMMANUEL, ORGANIC CHEMISTRY, BIOCHEMISTRY. *Current Pos:* PROF CHEM, FLA ATLANTIC UNIV, 63- *Personal Data:* b Zurich, Switz, July 6, 25. *Educ:* NY Univ, BA, 45, MS, 46, PhD(chem), 51. *Prof Exp:* Asst chem, NY Univ, 47-51; asst prof, Coe Col, 51-52, Adelphi Col, 53-56 & Ga Inst Technol, 56-57; from assoc prof to prof, Univ Miss, 57-63. *Mem:* AAAS; Am Chem Soc; NY Acad Sci; The Chem Soc; Sigma Xi. *Res:* Organophosphorus and organosulfur chemistry; stereochemistry; amide synthesis; iodine-containing dyes; heterocycles; dehydrogenation; respiratory chain phosphorylation; metallocene chemistry. *Mailing Add:* Dept Chem Fla Atlantic Univ 77 Glades Rd Boca Raton FL 33431-0991

BIEBERMAN, ROBERT ARTHUR, PETROLEUM GEOLOGY. *Current Pos:* RETIRED. *Personal Data:* b Rock Island, Ill, Apr 3, 23; m 44; c 2. *Educ:* Ind Univ, AB, 48, AM, 50. *Prof Exp:* Petrol geologist, NMex Bur Mines, 50-88. *Mem:* Am Asn Petrol Geologists. *Res:* Subsurface geology. *Mailing Add:* 601 Fitch Ave Socorro NM 87801

BIEBUYCK, JULIEN FRANCOIS, NEUROCHEMISTRY, NATIONAL ACADEMIC ADMINISTRATION. *Current Pos:* prof anesthesia, 77-83, CHMN DEPT, COL MED, PA STATE UNIV, 77-, ERIC A WALKER PROF ANESTHESTHESIA, 84-, ASSOC DEAN ACAD AFFAIRS, 91- *Personal Data:* b SAfrica, Feb 2, 35; US citizen; m 61, Jeanette A Sumner; c Gavin L, Richard M & Clare E. *Educ:* Univ Cape Town, MB & ChB, 59; Univ Oxford, Eng, DPhil(biochem), 71; FRCA, 96. *Prof Exp:* Nuffield res fel biochem, Univ Oxford, Eng, 69-72; asst prof anesthesia, Med Sch, Harvard Univ, 72-74, asst anesthetist, Mass Gen Hosp, 73-75, lectr, Med Sch, 75-76. *Concurrent Pos:* Fel, Med Found, Boston, 72-76; head, Anesthesia Metab Res Lab, Dept Anesthesia, Shriners Burns Inst & Mass Gen Hosp, Harvard Med Sch, 72-76; mem sci adv bd, Asn Univ Anesthetists, 79-82; ed, Anesthesiol, 85-; fel fac anesthesiologists, Royal Australiasian Col Surgeons, 87; co-ed, Current Opinion Anesthesiol. *Mem:* Biochem Soc Eng; Am Soc Neurochem; Am Physiol Soc; Asn Univ Anesthetists; Am Soc Anesthesiologists; Soc Acad Anesthesia (pres, 85-87); Soc Neurosci; fel Australian & NZ Col Anaesthetists. *Res:* Metabolic basis of altered consciousness including metabolic coma and anesthesia; non-respiratory functions of the lung; organ substrate utilization and metabolic control. *Mailing Add:* Dept Anesthesia Col Med Pa State Univ Hershey PA 17033. *E-Mail:* jbiebuyck@anes.hmc.psu.edu

BIEDEBACH, MARK CONRAD, BIOPHYSICS. *Current Pos:* ASSOC PROF BIOL, CALIF STATE UNIV, LONG BEACH, 67- *Personal Data:* b Pasadena, Calif, Apr 21, 32; m 64; c 2. *Educ:* Univ Southern Calif, BE, 56, MS, 58; Univ Calif, Los Angeles, PhD(biophys), 64. *Prof Exp:* NIH res fel biol systs, Calif Inst Technol, 64-65; Nat Inst Neurol Dis & Blindness res fel neurophysiol, Lab Cellular Neurophysiol, Paris, France, 65-66. *Mem:* Soc Neurosci; Sigma Xi. *Res:* Biophysics of invertebrate nervous system-integration and photoresponsive mechanisms. *Mailing Add:* Calif State Univ Dept Biol Sci 1250 Bellflower Blvd Long Beach CA 90840

BIEDENBENDER, MICHAEL DAVID, MICROWAVE DEVICES & CIRCUITS, MICROELECTRONIC PROCESS DEVELOPMENT. *Current Pos:* MEM TECH STAFF, TRW, 91- *Personal Data:* b Wichita, Kans, Apr 28, 61. *Educ:* Univ Cincinnati, BS, 84, MS, 87, PhD(elec eng), 91. *Prof Exp:* Res asst, Northrop, 84; grad asst, Univ Cincinnati, 84-85, res asst elec eng, 85-91. *Mem:* Inst Elec & Electronics Engrs; Electrochem Soc. *Res:* Designed, fabricated and characterized microwave power transistors on indium phosphide; ion implantation, encapsulation, and rapid thermal annealing of indium phosphide; indium phosphide surfaces using auger electron spectroscopy and x-ray photoelectron spectroscopy. *Mailing Add:* TRW MS D1-1050 One Space Park Redondo Beach CA 90278

BIEDENHARN, LAWRENCE C, JR, nuclear physics; deceased, see previous edition for last biography

BIEDERMAN, EDWIN WILLIAMS, JR, OIL PETROLOGY, GAS RESERVOIRS & MINEROLOGY. *Current Pos:* asst dir, 72-77, energy exten serv coordr & tech specialist, Pa Tech Assistance Prog, 77-80, SR TECH SPECIALIST, PA STATE UNIV, 80- *Personal Data:* b Stamford, Conn, June 30, 30; m 58, Margaret J White; c Robert, James, Mary (Wallace) & Jane (Haertlein). *Educ:* Cornell Univ, BA, 52; Pa State Univ, PhD(mineral), 58. *Prof Exp:* Res geologist & tech group leader, 58-68, res planner, Geochem & Sedimentology, Cities Serv Res & Develop, Co, 68-72. *Concurrent Pos:* Mem bd adv, Micropaleont Press, Am Mus Natural Hist, 70-73. *Mem:* Am Asn Petrol Geologists; Soc Econ Paleontologists & Mineralogists; Geochem Soc; Am Inst Prof Geologists; AAAS; Int Platform Soc. *Res:* Sedimentary petrology of oil and gas reservoir rocks; recent sediments; geochemistry; origin of oil; geological statistics; economic geology; photomicrography; general and physical geology; electron microscopy; glacial deposits; precious metals; 5 United States patents awarded. *Mailing Add:* 232 Mineral Sci Bldg Pa State Univ University Park PA 16802

BIEDERMAN, RONALD R, METALLURGY, MATERIALS SCIENCE. *Current Pos:* prof mech eng, 68-81, DIR ELECTRON MICROSCOPE FACIL, WORCESTER POLYTECH INST, 68-, GEORGE F FULLER PROF, 81- *Personal Data:* b Hartford, Conn, Oct 19, 38; m 62; c 1. *Educ:* Univ Conn, BS, 60, MS, 62, PhD(mat sci), 68. *Honors & Awards:* Stanley P Rockwell Mem Lectr, Am Soc Metal, 81. *Prof Exp:* Instr metall, Univ Conn, 62-68. *Concurrent Pos:* Fel, Am Soc Metals, 86- *Mem:* Fel Am Soc Metals; Am Inst Mining, Metall & Petrol Engrs; Sigma Xi; Electron Micros Soc Am; Int Metallog Soc. *Res:* Strengthening mechanisms; x-ray and electron metallography; powder metallurgy; bearing materials; high temperature materials; titanium and zirconium; ceramic membranes. *Mailing Add:* Dept Mech Eng Worcester Polytech Inst 100 Institute Rd Worcester MA 01609

BIEDERMAN-THORSON, MARGUERITE ANN, NEUROPHYSIOLOGY. *Current Pos:* CONSULT, 72- *Personal Data:* b Ft Leavenworth, Kans, Jan 9, 36; m 64, John Thorson. *Educ:* Univ Wash, Seattle, BS, 59; Univ Calif, Los Angeles, PhD(neurophysiol), 65. *Prof Exp:* NATO fel, Max Planck Inst Biol, Tubingen, 65-66 & Inst Exp Psychol, Oxford Univ, 66-67; asst res scientist neurosci, Univ Calif, San Diego, 67-69; Humboldt Stipend, Max Planck Inst Physiol Behav, 70-72. *Concurrent Pos:* Freelance translr, 72- *Res:* Neurophysiology and behavior of invertebrates and birds; editing and translating German papers and books on physiology, ecology, zoology and medicine. *Mailing Add:* Old Marlborough Arms Combe Witney Oxon OX88NQ England

BIEDLER, JUNE LEE, CELL GENETICS. *Current Pos:* ASSOC PROF BIOL, SLOAN-KETTERING DIV, GRAD SCH MED SCI, CORNELL UNIV, 73- *Personal Data:* b New York, NY, June 24, 25. *Educ:* Vassar Col, AB, 47; Columbia Univ, MA, 54; Cornell Univ, PhD(biol), 59. *Prof Exp:* Exchange investr, Inst Gustave-Roussy, France, 59-60; res fel, 59-60, res assoc, 60-62, assoc, 62-72, sect head, 66-72, assoc mem, 72-78, mem, Sloan-Kettering Inst Cancer Res, 78-, lab head, 75- *Concurrent Pos:* From instr to asst prof, Sloan-Kettering Div, Grad Sch Med Sci, Cornell Univ, 62-73; USPHS res career develop award, 63. *Mem:* Fel AAAS; Am Asn Cancer Res; Am Soc Cell Biol; Genetics Soc Am; NY Acad Sci. *Res:* Cytogenetics and somatic cell genetics; tumor biology; chromosome structure-function relationships; drug resistance of mammalian cells. *Mailing Add:* One Island Lane Greenwich CT 06830

BIEFELD, PAUL FRANKLIN, PHYSICAL CHEMISTRY. *Current Pos:* chemist, Characterization Lab, Owens-Corning Fiberglas Corp, Newark, 56, mgr, Analytical Lab, Granville, 56-71, sr scientist, 71-77, RES ASSOC, DEPT CHEM TECHNOL, TECH CTR, OWENS-CORNING FIBERGLAS CORP, 77- *Personal Data:* b Brownsville, Pa, Nov 5, 25; m 50; c 3. *Educ:* Denison Univ, BS, 48; Mich State Univ, MS, 51. *Prof Exp:* Asst, Mich State Univ, 48-51 & chem res infrared spectros, State Hwy Dept, Mich, 51-56. *Concurrent Pos:* Mem, Analytical & Phys Equip Comt, Owens-Corning Fiberglas Corp. *Mem:* Soc Appl Spectros; Coblentz Soc. *Res:* Application of instrumental analysis in the fields of glass and organic plastics and resins. *Mailing Add:* 345 Jefferson Rd Newark OH 43055

BIEGEL, JOHN E, INDUSTRIAL ENGINEERING, SYSTEMS DESIGN & SYSTEMS SCIENCE. *Current Pos:* PROF ENG, UNIV CENT FLA, 82- *Personal Data:* b Eau Claire, Wis, Nov 19, 25; m 55, Geraldine Lawrence; c Steven, N Dale & Kurt. *Educ:* Mont State Univ, BS, 48; Stanford Univ, MS, 50; Syracuse Univ, PhD(mat sci), 72. *Prof Exp:* Instr math, Mont State Col, 48-49; asst indust eng, Stanford Univ, 49-50; from instr to asst prof, Univ Ark, 50-52; engr, Ford Motor Co, 52-53 & Sandia Corp, 53-58; from asst prof to prof indust eng, Syracuse Univ, 58-78; prof, Kans State Univ, 78-82. *Concurrent Pos:* Consult, Pass & Seymour, Inc, NY, 58-64; fac fel, NSF, 64-65; adj prof, Col Environ Sci & Forestry, State Univ NY, 78. *Mem:* Inst Indust Engrs; Am Asn Artificial Intel. *Res:* Intelligent simulation training systems, intelligent simulations, object-oriented simulation; knowledge-based systems. *Mailing Add:* Dept Indust Eng Univ Cent Fla Box 25000 Orlando FL 32816. *Fax:* 407-823-3413; *E-Mail:* biegel@iems.engr.ucf.edu

BIEGELSEN, DAVID K, EXPERIMENTAL SOLID STATE PHYSICS. *Current Pos:* PRIN SCIENTIST PHYSICS, XEROX PALO ALTO RES CTR, 70- *Personal Data:* b St Louis, Mo, Oct 18, 43; m 66. *Educ:* Yale Univ, BA, 65; Wash Univ, MA & PhD(physics), 70. *Mem:* Am Phys Soc; Inst Elec & Electronics Engrs; Mat Res Soc. *Res:* Using acousto-optic probe of photoelastic properties of solids; amorphous semiconductors; heteroepitaxy; thin film crystal growth. *Mailing Add:* Xerox Palo Alto Res Ctr 3333 Coyote Hill Rd Palo Alto CA 94304

BIEGER, DETLEF, NEUROPHARMACOLOGY, NEUROPHYSIOLOGY. *Current Pos:* assoc prof, 78-84, PROF PHARMACOL, MEM UNIV, NFLD, 84- *Personal Data:* b Schoenberg, Ger, Oct 1, 39; m 66, H Mette Heners; c Tilman, Sophie & Thorben. *Educ:* Univ Kiel, WGer, Dr, 67. *Prof Exp:* Res assoc & instr pharmacol, Univ Kiel, 65-69; res assoc, Univ Toronto, 69-72; asst prof, Col Med, Univ Ill, 72-78. *Mem:* Ger Soc Pharmacol & Toxicol; Soc Neurosci; Pharmacol Soc Can; Can Asn Neurosci; Res Defence Soc Brit; Dysphagia Res Soc. *Res:* Neural basis of deglutition; neuropharmacology of esophageal myenteric ganglia; neural control of smooth muscle contractility; photo pharmacology. *Mailing Add:* Div Basic Sci Mem Univ Nfld Fac Med St John's NF A1B 3V6 Can. *Fax:* 709-737-7010; *E-Mail:* dbieger@morgan.ucs.mun.ca

BIEGLER, LORENZ THEODOR, PROCESS OPTIMIZATION, PROCESS DESIGN & CONTROL. *Current Pos:* From asst prof to assoc prof, 81-90, PROF CHEM ENG, CARNEGIE-MELLON UNIV, 90- *Personal Data:* b Chicago, Ill, Sept 10, 56; m 87; c 1. *Educ:* Ill Inst Technol, BS, 77; Univ Wis, MS, 79, PhD(chem eng), 81. *Concurrent Pos:* Presidential young investr, NSF, 85; vis scientist, Argonne Nat Lab, 90-91. *Mem:* Am Inst Chem Engrs; Am Chem Soc; Soc Indust & Appl Math; Opers Res Soc Am. *Res:* Process flowsheet optimization; nonlinear programming; parameter estimation; process simulation; process dynamics and control/optimization; synthesis of reactor networks; large-scale modelling. *Mailing Add:* Chem Eng Dept Carnegie-Mellon Univ Pittsburgh PA 15213. *Fax:* 412-268-7139; *E-Mail:* biegler@cmu.edu

BIEHL, EDWARD ROBERT, ORGANIC CHEMISTRY. *Current Pos:* from asst prof to assoc prof, 62-66, PROF CHEM, SOUTHERN METHODIST UNIV, 72- *Personal Data:* b Pittsburgh, Pa, July 14, 32; m 55; c 4. *Educ:* Univ Pittsburgh, BS, 58, PhD(chem), 61. *Prof Exp:* Sr res chemist, Monsanto Res Corp, 61-62. *Mem:* Am Chem Soc; Sigma Xi. *Res:* Benzyne chemistry. *Mailing Add:* Dept Chem Southern Methodist Univ Dallas TX 75275-0001

BIEHL, JOSEPH PARK, NEUROLOGY. *Current Pos:* from instr to prof, 50-80, EMER PROF NEUROL, COL MED, UNIV CINCINNATI, 80- *Personal Data:* b Berkeley, Calif, June 14, 22; m 49; c 4. *Educ:* Stanford Univ, AB, 43, MD, 46. *Prof Exp:* Intern internal med, Boston City Hosp, 45-46; sr asst res physician, Cincinnati Gen Hosp, 48-49, res neurologist, 49-50. *Concurrent Pos:* Fel med, Col Med, Univ Cincinnati, 50-52; consult, Vet Admin Hosp; attend neurologist, Cincinnati Gen Hosp, Drake Mem Hosp & Longview State Hosp. *Mem:* Asn Res Nerv & Ment Dis. *Res:* Clinical neurology; electroencephalography. *Mailing Add:* 5315 Hickory Trail Lane Cincinnati OH 45242

BIEHLER, SHAWN, GEOPHYSICS. *Current Pos:* ASSOC PROF, 70-, PROF GEOPHYS, UNIV CALIF, RIVERSIDE. *Personal Data:* b Jersey City, NJ, May 20, 37; m 60; c 2. *Educ:* Princeton Univ, BSE, 58; Calif Inst Technol, MS, 61, PhD(geophys), 64. *Prof Exp:* Res fel geophys, Calif Inst Technol, 64-66; asst prof, Mass Inst Technol, 66-70. *Mem:* AAAS; Am Geophys Union; Am Soc Explor Geophys; Seismol Soc Am; Europ Asn Explor Geophys. *Res:* Application of geophysics to geothermal areas; relationship of gravity anomalies to geologic structure. *Mailing Add:* Dept Earth Sci Univ Calif 900 University Ave Riverside CA 92521-0101

BIELAJEW, ALEXANDER FREDERICK, MONTE CARLO THEORY, IONIZING RADIATION THEORY. *Current Pos:* RES OFFICER, INST NAT MEASUREMENT STANDARDS, NAT RES COUN CAN, 82- *Personal Data:* b Montreal, Que, June 16, 53; m 73; c 2. *Educ:* McGill Univ, BSc, 78; Stanford Univ, PhD(physics), 82. *Honors & Awards:* Farrington Daniels Award, Am Asn Physicists Med, 85; Sylvia Fedoruk Prize, Can Orgn Med Phys, 89. *Res:* Theoretical research applied to the development of Monte Carlo techniques for use in radiation dosimetry and radiotherapy; theory of interaction of radiation with matter; theory of response of radiation-measuring instruments. *Mailing Add:* Inst Nat Measurement Standards Nat Res Coun-CN Montreal Rd Bldg M35 Ottawa ON K1A 0R6 Can

BIELAK, JACOBO, CIVIL ENGINEERING. *Current Pos:* ASSOC PROF CIVIL ENG, CARNEGIE-MELLON UNIV, 78- *Personal Data:* b Mexico City, Mex. *Educ:* Nat Univ Mex, BS, 63; Rice Univ, MS, 66; Calif Inst Technol, PhD(civil eng), 71. *Prof Exp:* Asst prof civil eng, Nat Univ Mex, 72-74, assoc prof, 74-78. *Concurrent Pos:* Sect head dynamics, Inst Eng, Nat Univ Mex, 74-78; vis assoc res engr, Univ Calif, San Diego, 77-78. *Mem:* Am Soc Chem Engrs; Am Soc Mech Engrs; Am Acad Mech; Seismol Soc Am; Sigma Xi. *Res:* Structural mechanics; analysis of structural systems; earthquake engineering with emphasis on dynamic soil-structure interaction. *Mailing Add:* Dept Civil Eng Carnegie-Mellon Univ 5000 Forbes Ave Pittsburgh PA 15213-3815

BIELAMOWICZ, MARY CLAIRE KINNEY, DIABETES & SPECIAL DIET NEEDS PROGRAMMING EFFORTS FOR TEXAS AGRICULTURE, DEVELOPMENT USDA MEAT MODULES-CONSUMER CHOICE MEAT. *Current Pos:* PROF & NUTRIT SPECIALIST, TEX AGR EXT SERV, TEX A&M UNIV, 90- *Personal Data:* b Amarillo, Tex, Nov 21, 42; m 90, Bill J; c Jessica L Sweeten, Patrick K Sweeten, Kara A & Dana L. *Educ:* Univ Tex, Austin, BS, 64; Ind Univ Med Sch, RD, 65; Okla State Univ, MS, 69; Tex A&M Univ, PhD(food sci & technol), 88. *Honors & Awards:* USDA Superior Serv Unit Award, 85. *Concurrent Pos:* Tex Agr Exp Sta Official Study Leave Grant, 87. *Mem:* Am Asn Diabetes Educ; Am Diabetes Asn; Am Inst Nutrit; Am Dietitic Asn; Am Home Econ Asn; Am Nat Cattle Women; Int Inst Food Sci & Technol; Soc Nutrit Educ; Am Meat Sci Asn; NAm Asn Study Obesity. *Res:* Contributed numerous articles to journals, publications and videos; development, execution and evaluation of nutrition programs related to special food needs for county extension agents across the state; cholesterol and fatty acid content of meat muscle and adipose tissues. *Mailing Add:* Dept Animal Sci Tex A&M Univ Kleberg Ctr Rm 220 College Station TX 77843-2471. *Fax:* 409-847-8741

BIELAT, KENNETH L, TUMOR ULTRASTRUCTURAL BIOLOGY & IMMUNOLOGY, IMPLANTOLOGY-BIOMATERIALS. *Current Pos:* CANCER RES SCIENTIST, LAB MGR & COMPUTER DATABASE MGR, PATH & ULTRASTRUCTURE, ROSWELL PARK MEM INST, 68- *Personal Data:* b Yonkers, NY, Jan 4, 45; m 82. *Educ:* Niagara Univ, BS, 66; Univ Vienna, Austria, Zeugnis, 65; State Univ NY, Buffalo, PhD(biol), 75. *Concurrent Pos:* Asst prof, Erie Community Col, 75-; immunohematologist, Buffalo Gen Hosp, 79-; tutor, Empire State Col, 85-; clin asst prof, Col Med, State Univ NY, Buffalo, 87-, res asst prof, Col Dent, 88- *Mem:* Am Asn Immunologists; Am Asn Cancer Res; Electron Micros Soc Am; Int Soc Prev Oncol; Soc Ultrastruct Path; AAAS; NY Acad Sci; Am Asn Dent Res; Int Asn Dent Res. *Res:* Ultrastructural evaluation and diagnosis of cancer; immunotherapy with monoclonal antibodies, mononuclear cells and biological response modifiers; immunoelectron microscopy and flow cytometry analyses and immunophenotyping; ultrastructural evaluation and microanalysis of tissue implants composed of various biomaterials; tumor markers; ion microscopy and x-ray microanalysis. *Mailing Add:* Dept Path Roswell Park Cancer Inst Elm & Carlton Sts Buffalo NY 14263-0001

BIELECKI, EDWIN J(OSEPH), INORGANIC CHEMISTRY. *Current Pos:* RETIRED. *Personal Data:* b North Attleborough, Mass, Mar 19, 24; m 48; c 3. *Educ:* Mass Inst Tehcnol, SB, 46. *Prof Exp:* Res engr, Beryllium Corp, 46-48, asst dir res, 48-51; proj mgr, Nat Res Corp, 51-56; develop engr, Kawecki Chem Co, 56-58, res mgr, 59-68, mgr res & develop chem, Kawecki Berylco Industs, Inc, 68-78; mgr, KBI Div, Cabot Corp, 78-81, mgr, res & develop chem, Cabot Eng Prod Group, 81-85. *Concurrent Pos:* Consult, field of rare metals. *Mem:* Am Chem Soc; Am Inst Chem Engrs; Electrochem Soc. *Res:* Rare metal; beryllium, titanium, zirconium, tantalum, columbium, boron, selenium, rubidium, germanium, cesium and others. *Mailing Add:* 310 E Sixth St Boyertown PA 19512-1212

BIELER, BARRIE HILL, MINERALOGY & PETROLOGY. *Current Pos:* RETIRED. *Personal Data:* b Pasadena, Calif, June 17, 29; m 55, Althea Rector; c Thomas, Joan & Kenneth. *Educ:* Calif Inst Technol, BS, 51, MS, 52; Pa State Univ, PhD(mineral), 55. *Prof Exp:* Field asst reconnaissance geol mapping, US Geol Surv, 52; res asst mineral, Pa State Univ, 52-55; geologist, US Geol Surv, 55-57; ceramist, Dow Chem Co, 57-67, res ceramist, Western Div, 67-70, sr res ceramist, 70-74, res specialist, 74-80, res leader, 81-86. *Concurrent Pos:* Instr adult educ progs, Acalanes & Mt Diable Sch Systs. *Mem:* Fel Photog Soc Am. *Res:* Geothermal exploration; ceramics and refractories; slags in basic oxygen surface steelmaking; melting, fining, sintering and grinding of glasses; develop porous ceramic membranes. *Mailing Add:* 737 Wiget Lane Walnut Creek CA 94598

BIELER, RUDIGER, PHYLOGENETIC SYSTEMATICS, COMPARATIVE ANATOMY. *Current Pos:* asst cur & div head, Dept Zool/Invert, 90-93, ASSOC CUR & DIV HEAD, FIELD MUS NATURAL HIST, 93- *Personal Data:* b Hamburg, Ger, Apr 9, 55. *Educ:* Univ Hamburg, MSc, 82, PhD(zool), 85. *Prof Exp:* Lectr zool, Univ Hamburg, 82-85; res fel, Smithsonian Inst, Wash, 85-86, Smithsonian Marine Sta, Ft Pierce, Fla, 86-87, NATO fel, Marine Sta, 87-88; asst cur & div head, Dept Malacol, Del Mus Natural Hist, 88-90, actg exec dir, Mus, 90. *Concurrent Pos:* Res assoc, Dept Mollusks, Mus Com Zool, Harvard Univ, 88-95; adj asst prof, Grad Col Marine Studies, Univ Delaware, 88-90; vis scientist, Smithsonian Marine Sta, 88-; counr, Am Malacol Union, 90-91, vpres, 93-95, pres, 95-96; secy, Coun Syst Malacologists, 91-94; res assoc, Div Mollusks, Nat Mus Natural Hist, Wash, 89-92; lectr, Comt Evolutionary Biol & Biol Sci Col Div, Univ Chicago, 92-; pres, Unitas Malacologiba-Int Soc Malacol, 95- *Mem:* Am Malacol Union; Soc Syst Biol; Sigma Xi; Unitas Malacol (pres, 95-). *Res:* Evolution, biology, and systematics of mollusks, especially marine snails and clams. *Mailing Add:* Field Mus Natural Hist Roosevelt Rd at Lake Shore Dr Chicago IL 60605. *Fax:* 312-663-5397; *E-Mail:* bieler@fmnh.org

BIELLIER, HAROLD VICTOR, PHYSIOLOGY. *Current Pos:* Asst prof mil sci & tactics, 50-53, assoc prof, 53-69, PROF POULTRY HUSB, UNIV MO-COLUMBIA, 69- *Personal Data:* b Bois D'Arc, Mo, Jan 22, 21; m 42; c 2. *Educ:* Univ Mo, BS, 43, PhD, 55. *Concurrent Pos:* Assoc ed, Poultry Sci, 67-82. *Mem:* Fel AAAS; Poultry Sci Asn; Sigma Xi; Worlds Poultry Sci Asn. *Res:* Endocrine and reproductive physiology of domestic poultry. *Mailing Add:* 113 W Burnam Rd Columbia MO 65203

BIELSKI, BENON H J, RADIATION CHEMISTRY. *Current Pos:* res assoc, Brookhaven Nat Lab, 58-60, assoc chemist, 60-63, chemist, 66-86, SR CHEMIST, BROOKHAVEN NAT LAB, 86- *Personal Data:* b Poland, June 12, 27; US citizen; m 69. *Educ:* Harvard Univ, BA, 51; Columbia Univ, MA, 56, PhD(chem), 57. *Prof Exp:* Asst prof chem, Univ Fla, 57-58. *Concurrent Pos:* Vis prof, State Univ NY Downstate Med Ctr, 71-83; consult, Procyte Corp, 87- *Mem:* Am Chem Soc; Am Soc Biol Chemists. *Res:* Radiation chemistry of inorganic and biological systems; chemistry of free radicals. *Mailing Add:* PO Box 535 Nading River NY 11792

BIEMANN, KLAUS, ORGANIC CHEMISTRY, ANALYTICAL CHEMISTRY. *Current Pos:* res assoc, 55-57, from instr to assoc prof, 57-63, PROF CHEM, MASS INST TECHNOL, 63- *Personal Data:* b Innsbruck, Austria, Nov 2, 26; m 56, Vera Themistocles; c Hans-Peter & Elisabeth. *Educ:* Univ Innsbruck, PhD(chem), 51. *Honors & Awards:* Stas Medal, Belg Chem Soc, 62; Powers Award, Am Acad Pharmaceut Sci, 73; Except Sci Achievement Medal, NASA, 77; Fritz Pregl Medal, Austrian Microchem Soc, 77; Field & Franklin Award Mass Spectrometry, Am Chem Soc, 86; Thomson Medal, 91; Beckman Award, Asn Biomolecular Res Facil, 95. *Prof Exp:* Instr chem, Univ Innsbruck, 51-55. *Mem:* Fel Nat Acad Sci; fel Am Acad Arts & Sci; Am Soc Mass Spectrometry; hon mem Chem Soc Belg; fel AAAS; Am Chem Soc. *Res:* Mass spectrometry of organic and biological compounds; protein chemistry and structure. *Mailing Add:* Dept Chem Rm 18-587 Mass Inst Technol Cambridge MA 02139-4307. *Fax:* 617-258-7677

BIEMPICA, LUIS, GASTROENTEROLOGY, PATHOLOGY. *Current Pos:* ATTEND PATHOLOGIST, BRONX MUNIC HOSP CTR, 78- *Personal Data:* b Orense, Spain, Aug 14, 25; US citizen; m 53; c 2. *Educ:* Univ Buenos Aires, MD, 52, cert nutrit, 56, PhD(med), 62. *Honors & Awards:* Riopedre Prize, Arg Asn Advan Sci, 69. *Prof Exp:* Resident med, Bronx Munic Hosp Ctr, 66-67 & resident path, 68-71, from asst attend to assoc attend pathologist, 71-78; from asst prof to assoc prof path, 64-78, assoc med, 64-70, asst prof med, Albert Einstein Col Med, Yeshiva Univ, 70-, clin prof pathol, 78- *Concurrent Pos:* Arg Res Coun fel, Albert Einstein Col Med, 61-62, USPHS res grant, 67-70. *Mem:* Am Asn Pathologists; Am Soc Cell Biol; Am Asn Study Liver Dis; fel Col Am Pathologists; AMA. *Res:* Liver diseases; cytochemistry; collagen degradation; ultrastructure; collagen; enzymology. *Mailing Add:* 41 Trenor Dr New Rochelle NY 10804

BIENENSTOCK, ARTHUR IRWIN, AMORPHOUS MATERIALS, SYNCHROTRON RADIATION. *Current Pos:* assoc prof mat sci, 67-72, vprovost fac affairs, 72-77, PROF MAT SCI & ENG, STANFORD UNIV, 72-, DIR, STANFORD SYNCHROTRON RADIATION LAB, 78- *Personal Data:* b New York, NY, Mar 20, 35; m 57; c 3. *Educ:* Polytech Inst Brooklyn, BS, 55, MS, 57; Harvard Univ, PhD(appl physics), 62. *Prof Exp:* Asst prof appl physics, Harvard Univ, 62-67. *Concurrent Pos:* NSF fel, Atomic Energy Res Estab, Eng, 62-63; mem ad hoc comt, Nat Acad Sci-Nat Res Coun, 69-70. *Mem:* Am Crystallog Asn; fel Am Phys Soc; NY Acad Sci; fel AAAS; Sigma Xi. *Res:* Structure and properties of imperfectly crystallized and amorphous materials; amorphous semiconductor devices; determination of atomic arrangements in amorphous materials and of the relationships of these arrangements to electrical, optical and thermal properties; synchrotron radiation. *Mailing Add:* MS 69 SLAC Stanford Univ PO Box 4349 Stanford CA 94309

BIENENSTOCK, JOHN, HYPERSENSITIVITY, NEUROIMMUNOLOGY. *Current Pos:* asst prof med, McMaster Univ, 68-74, coordr, Immunol Prog, 68-86, chmn, Dept Path, 78-89, PROF PATH & MED, MCMASTER UNIV, 74-, VPRES HEALTH SCI, 89-, DEAN FAC HEALTH SCI, 92- *Personal Data:* b Budapest, Hungary, Oct 6, 36; Brit & Can citizen; m 61, Dody Sanders; c Jimson A, Adam S & Robin A. *Educ:* Westminster Med Sch, London, MB, BS, 60; FRCP(C),76, FRCP, 80. *Honors & Awards:* Assoc Czech Soc Med (Purkynje) Medal, 89; Finkelstein Prize for Gastro Res, 96. *Prof Exp:* Fel, Harvard Med Sch, 64-66; Buswell fel, State Univ NY, Buffalo, 66-68, asst res prof med, 67-68. *Concurrent Pos:* Consult, WHO, 70-; Haddow fel, Chester Beatty Res Inst, UK, 79-80; Rayne vis prof, Univ Western Australia, 87; chair, Immunol Comt, Med Res Coun, 93. *Mem:* Fel Royal Soc Can; Can Soc Immunol (pres, 85-87); Soc Mucosal Immunol; Col Int Allergol (pres-elect); Am Asn Pathologists; AAAS; Am Soc Clin Invest. *Res:* Mucosal immunology especially that of lung and gut; allergy and hypersensitivity; mast cells and the nervous system; neuroimmunology. *Mailing Add:* 50 Albert St Dundas ON L9H 2X1 Can. *Fax:* 905-546-0800; *E-Mail:* bienens@fhs.csu.mcmaster.ca

BIENFANG, PAUL KENNETH, BIOLOGICAL OCEANOGRAPHY. *Current Pos:* DIR ENVIRON COMPLIANCE & TECHNOL, CEATECH-USE INC, 97- *Personal Data:* b Watertown, Wis, Apr 14, 48; m 73. *Educ:* Univ Hawaii, BS, 71, MS, 74, PhD, 77. *Prof Exp:* Res asst oceanog, Hawaii Inst Marine Biol, 69-73; res asst oceanog, Oceanic Inst, 73-97, sr scientist, 73-97, vpres res, 83-97. *Concurrent Pos:* Oceanog consult, Environ Consult Inc, 69-74, Oceanic Inst, 72, Sunn, Low, Tom & Hara Inc, 75 & Oceanic Eng Dept, Univ Hawaii, 76; affil fac, Dept Oceanog, Univ Hawaii. *Mem:* Am Soc Limnol & Oceanog; World Maricult Soc; Phycological Soc Am; AAAS. *Res:* Phytoplankton ecology, particularly nutritional control of sinking rates of phytoplankton and dynamics of substrate limited growth in phytoplankton; thermal pollution assessment, especially effects on phytoplankton biomass and productivity; ocean thermal energy conversion impacts and alternate uses. *Mailing Add:* Ceatech-USA Inc 7 Waterfront Pl Suite 507 Honolulu HI 96817

BIENIAWSKI, ZDZISLAW TADEUSZ, ROCK MECHANICS, MINING & TUNNELING. *Current Pos:* PROF MINERAL ENG, PA STATE UNIV, UNIV PARK, 78- *Personal Data:* b Cracow, Poland, Oct 1, 36; US citizen; m 64; c 3. *Educ:* Univ Witwatersrand, BS, 61, MS, 63; Univ Pretoria, PhD(rock mech), 68. *Honors & Awards:* Rock Mech Award, Am Inst Metall & Petrol Engrs, 84. *Prof Exp:* Sr res scientist rock mech, Coun Sci & Indust Res, 64-66, head dept geomech, 66-77. *Concurrent Pos:* Chmn, US Nat Comn Tunneling Technol, 84-85; vis prof, Stanford Univ, 85, Harvard Univ, 90; mem, US Nat Comn Rock Mech, 80-84. *Mem:* Int Soc Rock Mech (vpres, 74-79); Am Soc Eng Educ; Am Soc Mech Engrs; Am Inst Metall & Petrol Engrs; Am Soc Civil Engrs; Sigma Xi. *Res:* Improved design of longwall coal mining; geomechanics classification of rock masses; design theory and methodology. *Mailing Add:* Dept Mining Eng Pa State Univ 116 Mineral Sci University Park PA 16802-1009

BIENIEK, MACIEJ P, APPLIED MECHANICS, STRUCTURAL ENGINEERING. *Current Pos:* PROF CIVIL ENG, COLUMBIA UNIV, 69- *Personal Data:* b Wilno, Poland, Jan 5, 27; nat US; m 61; c 2. *Educ:* Danzig Tech Univ, BCivilEng & MS, 48, DSc(appl mech), 51. *Prof Exp:* Lectr mech, Danzig Tech Univ, 52-55, prof, 55-57; prof, Polish Acad Sci, 57-58; vis scholar, Columbia Univ, 58-59; vis lectr, Princeton Univ, 59-60; assoc prof civil eng & mech, Columbia Univ, 60-63; prof, Univ Southern Calif, 63-69. *Concurrent Pos:* Consult, Chinese Acad Sci, 56-57. *Mem:* Am Inst Aeronaut & Astronaut; Am Soc Civil Engrs; Sigma Xi. *Res:* Dynamics; mechanics of inelastic solids; dynamics of structures; theory of plates and shells. *Mailing Add:* 121 Cross St Demarest NJ 07027

BIENIEK, RONALD JAMES, ATOMIC & MOLECULAR COLLISION THEORY. *Current Pos:* asst prof, 81-84, ASSOC PROF PHYSICS, UNIV MO, ROLLA, 84- *Personal Data:* b South Gate, Calif, Aug 30, 48; div; c Michelle & Geoffrey. *Educ:* Univ Calif, Riverside, BS 70; Harvard Univ, AM, 73, PhD(physics), 75. *Honors & Awards:* Philips Distinguished Vis Lectr, Haverford Col, 84. *Prof Exp:* Physicist, Naval Undersea Res & Develop Ctr, 70; NSF fels, Mass Inst Technol & Harvard Univ, 70-73 & Univ Colo, Boulder, 75; asst prof phys sci, Univ Ill, Urbana-Champaign, 75-81, asst prof astron, 76-81, asst prof humanities, 78-79. *Concurrent Pos:* Mem, NSF Rev Panels, 81, 85, 90, 93 & 94; vis scientist, Paris-Meudon Observ, 85; Fulbright fel, 88-89; vis scientist, Univ Kaiserslautern, 87, 88 & 90, Univ Paris-Sud, 89, Harvard Col Obstet, 91, Oxford Univ, 92. *Mem:* Am Phys Soc; Hist Sci Soc; Am Asn Physics Teachers; Sigma Xi. *Res:* Quantum mechanical and semiclassical investigations of atomic and molecular processes, such as ionization and detachment, ultracold collisions, spectral line shapes, collisional redistribution of polarized radiation, laser-induced phenomena, vibrational-rotational excitations in molecular collisions. *Mailing Add:* Dept Physics 102 Physics Bldg Univ Mo Rolla MO 65401-0249. *Fax:* 573-341-4715; *E-Mail:* bieniek@physics.umr.edu

BIENIEWSKI, THOMAS M, MATERIAL SYNTHESIS USING DENSE PLASMAS, PLASMA SPRAYING & DEPOSITION. *Current Pos:* STAFF MEM, LOS ALAMOS NAT LAB, 72- *Personal Data:* b Posen, Poland, July 12, 36; US citizen; m 66; c 2. *Educ:* Univ Detroit, BS, 58; Calif Inst Technol, PhD(physics), 65. *Prof Exp:* Staff mem, Aerospace Res Lab, USAF, 63-72. *Res:* Atomic and molecular spectroscopy of actinide metals and compounds; development of plasma physics application for materials synthesis with plasma; handling and generating ultrapure tritium gas streams for thermonuclear energy applications. *Mailing Add:* 285 Donna Ave Los Alamos NM 87544

BIENSTOCK, D(ANIEL), CHEMICAL ENGINEERING. *Current Pos:* mgr, 77-82, DEP ASSOC DIR, COMB DIV, PITTSBURGH ENERGY RES CTR, DEPT ENERGY, 82- *Personal Data:* b Brooklyn, NY, Dec 1, 17; m 47; c 3. *Educ:* Brooklyn Col, BA, 37; NY Univ, MS, 40; Carnegie Inst Technol, MS, 57. *Honors & Awards:* Vermeil Medal, France, 79; McAfee Award, Am Inst Chem Engrs, 83. *Prof Exp:* Chemist, Edgewood Arsenal, US Dept War, 41-46; supvry chem engr, US Bur Mines, 46-60, asst proj coordr, 60-65, proj coordr, 65-77. *Mem:* Am Inst Chem Engrs; Am Soc Mech Engrs; Am Chem Soc; Nat Soc Prof Engrs; Air Pollution Control Asn; NY Acad Sci.

Res: Coal-slurry preparation and combustion; high-temperature combustion; air pollution; oxides of sulfur and nitrogen; coal-fired magnetohydrodynamics; alkalized alumina removal of sulfur oxide in flue gas; two-stage combustion in control of nitrogen oxides; Fischer-Tropsch synthesis; corrosion in hot carbonate systems. *Mailing Add:* 6611 Dalzell Pl Pittsburgh PA 15217-1441

BIENSTOCK, DANIEL, COMBINATORIAL OPTIMIZATION, DISCRETE STRUCTURES. *Current Pos:* ASSOC PROF INDUST ENG & OPERS RES, COLUMBIA UNIV, 89- *Personal Data:* b Feb 10, 60; US citizen. *Educ:* Brandeis Univ, BA, 82; Mass Inst Technol, PhD(opers res), 85. *Prof Exp:* Asst prof opers res, GSIA, Carnegie Mellon Univ, 85-86; mem tech staff, Bell Commun Res, 86-89. *Concurrent Pos:* Consult, Bell Commun Res, 90-; NSF presidential young investr award, 90. *Mem:* Opers Res Soc Am; Math Prog Soc. *Res:* Area of applied mathematics known as combinatorial optimization; discrete mathematics; theoretical computer science. *Mailing Add:* Dept Indust Eng Columbia Univ 2960 Broadway New York NY 10027-6902

BIENVENUE, GORDON RAYMOND, AUDIOLOGY, PSYCHOACOUSTICS. *Current Pos:* ASST PROF AUDIOL & PSYCHOACOUST, STATE UNIV NY, NEW PALTZ, 83- *Personal Data:* b Fall River, Mass, Oct 11, 46; m 68; c 2. *Educ:* Univ Mass, Amherst, BA, 68; Mich State Univ, MA, 69; Pa State Univ, PhD(audiol), 75; Am Speech & Hearing Asn, Clin Cert Audiol. *Prof Exp:* Chief audiol, Brooke Gen Hosp, 69-71; res asst audiol & psychoacoust, Pa State Univ, 71-83. *Concurrent Pos:* Instr audiol, US Army Med Field Serv Sch, San Antonio, Tex, 69-71; lectr audiol, Brooke Gen Hosp, 69-71; consult, Indust Audiol, 71- *Mem:* Am Speech & Hearing Asn; Sigma Xi; Acoust Soc Am; Am Audiol Soc; Mil Audiol & Speech Pathol Soc. *Res:* Investigation of psychoacoustic and physiological acoustic phenomena with particular emphasis on hearing conservation and hearing diagnostic procedures especially in the study of the effects of high level noise. *Mailing Add:* 2 Henry Ct New Paltz NY 12561

BIENZ, DARREL RUDOLPH, PLANT BREEDING. *Current Pos:* from asst prof to prof, 59-91, EMER PROF HORT, WASH STATE UNIV, 91- *Personal Data:* b Bern, Idaho, Apr 1, 26; m 50; c 5. *Educ:* Univ Idaho, BS, 50; Cornell Univ, PhD(plant breeding), 55. *Prof Exp:* Asst prof hort, Univ Idaho, 54-58, horticulturist, Agr Res Serv, USDA & Univ Idaho, 58-59. *Concurrent Pos:* Fulbright exchange prof, Turkey, 67-68; partic, Survey Tropical Agr & World Hunger, SAsia & Africa, 75-76; sr fac adv, Lambung, Mangkurat Univ Banjarbaru, S Kalimantan, Indonesia, 81; vis prof, Univ Hawaii, 75; vis res scientist, Mayaguez Agr Res Sta, PR, 85 & China Asn Sci & Technol, 85; sr adv, Jordan Valley, Jordan, 87. *Mem:* Am Soc Hort Sci; Int Hort Soc; Am Genetic Asn; Am Hort Soc; Am Inst Biol Sci. *Res:* Vegetable breeding and incompatability; general vegetable research; international agriculture; breeding all male asparagus cultivars resistant to field decline and early disease resistant tomato cultivars suitable for processing. *Mailing Add:* RR 2 Pullman WA 99163

BIER, DENNIS MARTIN, METABOLISM, MASS SPECTROMETRY. *Current Pos:* PROF PEDIAT & CHIEF NUTRIT SECT, DEPT PEDIAT, BAYLOR COL MED, 93- *Personal Data:* b Hoboken, NJ, July 24, 41; m 71; c 3. *Educ:* LeMoyne Col, BS, 62; NJ Col Med, MD, 66. *Honors & Awards:* Grace A Goldsmith Award, Am Col Nutrit; E V McCollun Award, Juv Diabetes Found; Mary Jane Keeger Award, Juv Diabetes Found. *Prof Exp:* Intern pediat, Univ Calif, San Francisco, 66-67, resident, 67-68; Bay Area Heart Asn fel, 68-69; lieutenant comdr, Naval Regional Med Ctr, US Naval Reserves, Oakland, 69-71; NIH fel, Sch Med, Wash Univ, 71-73; asst prof, Univ Calif, San Francisco, 73-76; from asst prof to assoc prof med & pediat, Sch Med, Washington Univ, 76-86, prof, 86-93. *Concurrent Pos:* Vis staff scientist, Los Alamos Sci Lab, 75- *Mem:* Inst Med-Nat Acad Sci; Am Diabetes Asn; Am Soc Mass Spectrometry; Fedn Am Soc Exp Biol; Am Soc Clin Invest; Am Soc Clin Nutrit; Soc Pediat Res. *Res:* Metabolic fuel transport; stable isotope tracers; diabetes; lipoprotein metabolism; inborn errors of metabolism. *Mailing Add:* Dir USDA ARS Childrens Nutrit Res Ctr 1100 Bates St Houston TX 77030-2600. *Fax:* 713-798-7046

BIER, MILAN, BIOPHYSICS. *Current Pos:* vis res prof chem, 62-77, PROF ENG & MICROBIOL, UNIV ARIZ, 77- *Personal Data:* b Vukovar, Yugoslavia, Dec 7, 20; nat US; m 52; c 3. *Educ:* Univ Geneva, License Sci Chim, 46; Fordham Univ, PhD(biochem), 50. *Prof Exp:* Asst prof chem, Fordham Univ, 50-62; res biophysicist, Vet Admin Hosp, 62-77. *Concurrent Pos:* Head chem res lab, Inst Appl Biol, 52-60; vis res prof chem, Univ Ariz, 62-77; consult, NASA, Abbott Sci Prod, Ionics Inc, Univs Space Res Asn & others, 73- *Mem:* Am Chem Soc; Am Soc Biol Chem. *Res:* Biomedical engineering, electrophoresis, membrane processes and artificial kidney technology; protein and enzyme biophysics, plasma fractionation, applied immunology. *Mailing Add:* Ctr Separation Sci Univ Ariz Bldg 20 Tucson AZ 85721

BIERBAUM, VERONICA MARIE, GAS PHASE ION CHEMISTRY. *Current Pos:* Vis asst prof & lectr, 74-76, res assoc, 76-78, sr res assoc chem, 78-95, spec mem grad fac, 81-95, RES PROF, UNIV COLO, BOULDER, 95- *Personal Data:* b Allentown, Pa, Aug 2, 48; m 82, Carleton J Howard; c Benjamin & Daniel. *Educ:* Cath Univ Am, BA, 70; Univ Pittsburgh, PhD(phys chem), 74. *Concurrent Pos:* Co-prin investr, Air Force Off Sci Res, 78-98, US Army Res Off, 78-88 & NSF, 79-98; mem, Joint Inst Lab Astrophys, 78-; mem, Nat Aeronaut Space Admin, 95-97. *Mem:* Am Chem Soc; Am Soc Mass Spectrometry (secy, 89-91, vpres, 94-96, pres, 96-98); Sigma Xi. *Res:* Kinetics, mechanisms and thermochemistry of gas phase ion-molecule reactions. *Mailing Add:* Dept Chem & Biochem Univ Colo Boulder CO 80309-0215. *Fax:* 303-492-5894; *E-Mail:* vmbierbaum@cuchem.colorado.edu

BIERENBAUM, MARVIN L, CARDIOLOGY, NUTRITION. *Current Pos:* DIR ATHEROSCLEROSIS RES PROJ, ST VINCENT'S HOSP, 57- *Personal Data:* b Philadelphia, Pa, Aug 30, 26; m 51; c 2. *Educ:* Rutgers Univ, BS, 47; Hahnemann Med Col, MD, 53. *Prof Exp:* Intern med, Beth Israel Hosp, Newark, NJ, 53-54; resident med & cardiol, Vet Admin Hosp, Brooklyn, 54-57. *Concurrent Pos:* Prog coordr heart dis control, NJ Dept Health, 57-; prin investr, NIH grant, 60-; consult, Fairleigh Dickinson Univ, 62-; mem coun arteriosclerosis, Am Heart Asn, 64; clin assoc prof med, NJ Col Med & Dent, 67- *Mem:* AMA; fel Am Col Physicians; Am Inst Nutrit; Am Soc Clin Invest; fel Am Col Cardiol. *Res:* Nutritional management in prevention and therapy of arteriosclerotic coronary heart disease. *Mailing Add:* Kenneth L Jordan Cardiac Ctr 48 Plymouth St Montclair NJ 07042-2625

BIERI, JOHN GENTHER, BIOCHEMISTRY, NUTRITION. *Current Pos:* NUTRIT CONSULT, 82- *Personal Data:* b Norfolk, Va, May 24, 20; m 43; c 3. *Educ:* Antioch Col, BA, 43; Pa State Col, MS, 44; Univ Minn, PhD(biochem), 49. *Honors & Awards:* Meade-Johnson Award, Am Inst Nutrit, 65. *Prof Exp:* Nutritionist, Naval Med Res Inst, 44-46; instr biochem, Univ Minn, 48-49; assoc prof, Med Br, Univ Tex, 49-55; biochemist, Nat Inst Arthritis, Metab & Digestive Dis, 55-82. *Mem:* AAAS; Am Soc Biol Chemists; Am Inst Nutrit. *Res:* Nutritional biochemistry; metabolism of vitamin E and vitamin A; polyunsaturated fatty acids; selenium. *Mailing Add:* 3612 Pimlico Pl Silver Spring MD 20906

BIERLEIN, JAMES A(LLISON), chemical engineering, physical chemistry; deceased, see previous edition for last biography

BIERLEIN, JOHN CARL, TRIBOLOGIST, METROLOGIST. *Current Pos:* SR PRIN ENGR, EATON ENG & RES CTR, SOUTHFIELD, MICH, 85- *Personal Data:* b Cleveland, Ohio, Nov 13, 36; m 60, Mary P McMath; c Paul A & Lori A (Hair). *Educ:* Mich State Univ, BS, 59; Univ Wis, MS, 61, PhD(mat eng, sci), 65; Univ Detroit, MBA, 77. *Honors & Awards:* Arch T Colwell Merit Award, Soc Automotive Engrs, Ralph R Teetor Indust Lectureship Prog. *Prof Exp:* Instr mat eng, Univ Wis, 59-65; res engr, Gen Motors Res Lab, Warren, 65-81, staff res engr mat, 81-85. *Concurrent Pos:* Adj prof, Lawrence Technol Univ, 90- *Mem:* Am Soc Metals; Am Inst Mining, Metall & Petrol Engrs; Soc Automotive Engrs; Am Soc Mech Engrs; Soc Tribological & Lubrication Engrs; Am Soc Qual Control. *Res:* Design and material development of tribosystems for lubrication, friction, wear and scoring and embedability; failure analysis; study of materials in sliding contact under marginal lubrication conditions such as bearings, elastomeric seals, gears, polymeric products and hydraulic components. *Mailing Add:* 5481 Vincent Trail Utica MI 48316. *Fax:* 248-354-6818

BIERLEIN, JOHN DAVID, MATERIAL SCIENCE-NON LINEAR OPTICS, LASER PHYSICS & ENGINEERING. *Current Pos:* Res physicist, Cent Res Dept, E I Du Pont & Co, 68-73, res assoc, Photo Prods Dept, 73-76, res supvr, 76-85, res physicist, Cent Res Dept, 85-86, res leader, 86-88, res supvr, 88-94, SR RES FEL, CENT RES DEPT, E I DU PONT & CO, 94- *Personal Data:* b May 22, 40; m 64; c 2. *Educ:* Univ Kans, BS, 63, MS, 66, PhD(physics), 68. *Honors & Awards:* Res & Develop 100 Award, 89. *Mem:* Am Phys Soc; Optical Soc Am. *Res:* Discovery and development of new non linear optical and electro-optical materials. *Mailing Add:* Cent Res Dept Du Pont Exp Sta E356/284 Wilmington DE 19898

BIERLEIN, THEO KARL, PHYSICAL CHEMISTRY. *Current Pos:* mgr phys metall unit, Reactor & Mat Technol Dept, Pac Northwest Labs, Battelle Mem Inst, 63-70, mgr damage anal, Mat Dept, 70-77, mgr alloy microstruct, Mat Eng Dept, 77-79, MGR MAT PROPERTIES, WESTINGHOUSE-HANFORD, 79- *Personal Data:* b Ansbach, Ger, Feb 6, 24; nat US; m 49; c 6. *Educ:* Univ Wash, BS, 45, PhD(chem), 50. *Prof Exp:* Chemist, Gen Elec Co, 50-52, engr, 52-55, sr scientist, 55-63. *Mem:* Am Chem Soc; Am Soc Metals; Electron Micros Soc Am; Am Nuclear Soc. *Res:* Relationship between microstructure and properties of metals and alloys; deformation and fracture mechanism; effect of reactor irradiation on structure of fuel and its cladding. *Mailing Add:* 1005 Warren Ct Richland WA 99352-2965

BIERLY, EUGENE WENDELL, METEOROLOGY, SCIENCE ADMINISTRATION. *Current Pos:* DIR ED & RES, AM GEOPHYS UNION, 92- *Personal Data:* b Pittston, Pa, Sept 11, 31; m 53, Charlotte Sima; c Jeannine, Pamela & Woody. *Educ:* Univ Pa, AB, 53; US Naval Postgrad Sch, cert, 54; Univ Mich, MS, 57, PhD, 68. *Honors & Awards:* Charles Franklin Brooks Award, Am Meteorol Soc, 90. *Prof Exp:* Asst, Dept Civil Eng, meteorol labs, Univ Mich, 56-60, asst res meteorologist, Dept Eng Mech, 60-63, lectr, 61-63; meteorologist, US AEC, 63-66; prog dir meteorol, NSF, 66-71, coordr, Global Atmospheric Res Prog, 71-74, head, Off Climate Dynamics, 74-75, head, Climate Dynamics Res Sect, 75-79, Dir, Div Atmospheric Sci, 79-92. *Concurrent Pos:* Cong fel, 70-71; mem, Health & Environ Res Adv Comt, Dept Energy, 92-; Chair, Adv Bd Sch Meteorol, Univ Okla, 94-; Chair, Adv Consul Bd, Geophys Inst, Univ Alaska, 95- *Mem:* Fel AAAS; fel Am Meteorol Soc (pres, 84); Chinese Meteorol Soc; Am Geophys Union. *Res:* Air pollution; diffusion; lake breezes; atmospheric tracers; science management; environmental problems and science policy; science education; scientific capacity building. *Mailing Add:* Am Geophys Union 2000 Florida Ave NW Washington DC 20009-1277. *Fax:* 202-328-0566; *E-Mail:* ebierly@kosmos.agu.org

BIERLY, JAMES N, JR, PHYSICS. *Current Pos:* from asst prof to assoc prof physics, 62-73, PROF PHYSICS, PHILADELPHIA COL PHARM & SCI, 73- *Personal Data:* b Lewisberg, Pa, May 6, 22; m 47. *Educ:* Kutztown State Teachers Col, BS, 43; Bucknell Univ, MS, 47; Temple Univ, PhD(physics), 61; Am Bd Radiol, dipl, 55. *Prof Exp:* Instr physics, Bucknell Univ, 47; physicist radiol dept, Jefferson Med Col, 51-55; physicist, Vet Admin Hosp, 55-56; res physicist, Franklin Inst, 56-62. *Concurrent Pos:* Consult, Misericordia Hosp; radiol physicist, Mercy Catholic Med Ctr. *Mem:* Am Phys Soc; Sigma Xi; Am Asn Physicists Med; Am Asn Physics Teachers. *Res:* Thermoelectricity in semiconductors; consulting work in medical radiation physics. *Mailing Add:* 110 Oak Ridge Ct Williamsburg VA 23188

BIERLY, MAHLON ZWINGLI, JR, MEDICINE. *Current Pos:* RETIRED. *Personal Data:* b Philadelphia, Pa, Apr 24, 22; m 44; c 2. *Educ:* Franklin & Marshall Col, BS, 43; Jefferson Med Col, MD, 46; Am Bd Pediat, dipl, 55. *Prof Exp:* Resident & asst chief, Philadelphia Hosp Contagious Dis, 49-50; resident pediat, Children's Hosp Philadelphia, 51-52; pvt pract, 52-53; mem staff, Med Dept, Wyeth Labs, 53-87. *Mem:* Am Pub Health Asn; Am Acad Pediat. *Res:* Biological agents; vaccines, toxoids and antisera. *Mailing Add:* 1707 Thomas Rd Wayne PA 19087

BIERMAN, ARTHUR, THEORETICAL PHYSICS. *Current Pos:* from asst prof to assoc prof, 64-69, actg assoc provost, 70-71, PROF PHYSICS, CITY COL, CITY UNIV NEW YORK, 69- *Personal Data:* b Vienna, Austria, Oct 14, 25; US citizen; m 83, Sandra L Riesberg; c Jessica (Kysar) & Cynthia. *Educ:* Univ Chicago, PhD(math, biol), 54; Columbia Univ, MA, 57. *Prof Exp:* Nat Found Infantile Paralysis fel, 54-55; from instr to asst prof physics, City Col New York, 58-61; sr res scientist, Lockheed-Calif Co, 62-63; assoc prof physics, Los Angeles State Col, 63. *Concurrent Pos:* Consult, Lockheed-Calif Co, 62 & Lockheed Ga Co, 65-66; US Atomic Energy Comn grant, 64-71. *Mem:* Am Phys Soc. *Res:* Theory of molecular excitons in large molecules. *Mailing Add:* 542 Arapahoe Ave Boulder CO 80302. *Fax:* 303-447-8871; *E-Mail:* arbier@aol.com

BIERMAN, EDWIN LAWRENCE, internal medicine, metabolism; deceased, see previous edition for last biography

BIERMAN, HOWARD RICHARD, MEDICINE. *Current Pos:* CLIN PROF MED, SCH MED, LOMA LINDA UNIV, 59- *Personal Data:* b Newark, NJ, Jan 27, 15; m; c 3. *Educ:* Wash Univ, BSc & MD, 39; Am Bd Internal Med, dipl. *Prof Exp:* From jr to sr intern, Barnes Hosp, 40, resident house officer, 41; clin physiologist & prin clin investr, Nat Cancer Inst, 46-53; chief clin sect, Lab Exp Oncol & assoc clin prof med, Sch Med, Univ Calif, 47-53; dir, Hosp Tumors & Allied Dis, City of Hope Med Ctr, 53-56, med dir, 56-59, chmn, Dept Internal Med & sci dir, 53-59; dir, Inst Cancer & Blood Res, Beverly Hills, 59- *Concurrent Pos:* Chief resident, St Louis Isolation Hosp, Contagious Dis, 40; spec consult, Nat Cancer Inst, 53-; emer attend physician, Los Angeles County Hosp, USN. *Mem:* Fel Am Col Physicians; fel NY Acad Sci; fel Am Col Angiol; fel Int Soc Hemat; fel Am Soc Clin Oncol. *Res:* Hematology and oncology; chemotherapy and clinical pharmacology; bone marrow metabolism; biophysical characteristics of tumors; aviation medicine; barometrics and acceleration; nutrition and vitamins; leukocyte kinetics. *Mailing Add:* 150 N Robertson Blvd Beverly Hills CA 90211

BIERMAN, SIDNEY ROY, EXPERIMENTAL NUCLEAR CRITICALITY RESEARCH, EXPERIMENTAL NEUTRON KINETICS. *Current Pos:* RETIRED. *Personal Data:* b Comfort, Tex, Jan 24, 28; m 49, Dorothy Liefeste; c Debra, Marcus & Jeffery. *Educ:* Tex Technol Univ, BS, 56; Univ Wash, MS, 63. *Prof Exp:* Process engr, Stand Oil Co, NJ, 56-59; process engr, Battelle Mem Inst, 59-63, from res scientist to sr res scientist, 63-78, staff scientist, 78-96. *Concurrent Pos:* Chmn, Nuclear Criticality Safety Div, Am Nuclear Soc, 79-80. *Mem:* Am Nuclear Soc. *Res:* Nuclear criticality; kinetics. *Mailing Add:* 2352 Enterprise Richland WA 99352. *Fax:* 509-372-4411

BIERMANN, ALAN WALES, COMPUTER SCIENCE. *Current Pos:* from asst prof to assoc prof, 74-86, PROF COMPUT SCI, DUKE UNIV, 86- *Personal Data:* b Newport News, Va, Feb 5, 39; m 68; c 2. *Educ:* Ohio State Univ, BEE & MSc, 61; Univ Calif, Berkeley, PhD(comput sci), 68. *Prof Exp:* Asst prof comput sci, San Fernando Valley State Col, 62-64 & 68-69; res assoc, Stanford Univ, 69-71; asst prof, Ohio State Univ, 71-73. *Concurrent Pos:* Pres, Asn Computational Ling, 88; vis scientist, SRI Int, Menlo Park, Calif, 88. *Mem:* Sigma Xi; Inst Elec & Electronics Engrs; Asn Comput Mach; Asn Computational Ling. *Res:* Learning and inference theory; automatic program synthesis; natural language processing; author of one book. *Mailing Add:* Dept Comput Sci Duke Univ PO Box 90129 Durham NC 27706

BIERMANN, CHRISTOPHER JAMES, PULP & PAPER CHEMISTRY. *Current Pos:* asst prof, 87-93, ASSOC PROF, DEPT FOREST PROD, ORE STATE UNIV, 93- *Personal Data:* b Winnipeg, Man, Mar 16, 58; US citizen; m 90, Lora L Jasman; c Audra & Heidi. *Educ:* Univ Maine, Orono, BS, 80; Miss State Univ, PhD(wood chem), 83. *Prof Exp:* Grad res asst, Miss Forest Prod Utilization Lab, 80-83; res asst, dept nutrit sci, Univ Wis-Madison, 84-85; res assoc, Lab Renewable Resources Eng, Purdue Univ, 85-87. *Mem:* Am Chem Soc; Forest Prod Res Soc; Soc Wood Sci & Technol; Can Pulp & Paper Asn; Tech Asn Pulp & Paper Indust. *Res:* Pretreatment of lignocellulosic materials; carbohydrate analysis; grafting of polymers onto cellulose derivatives; pulp and paper chemistry. *Mailing Add:* Dept Forest Prod Oregon State Univ Corvallis OR 97331-7402. *Fax:* 541-737-4211; *E-Mail:* biermanc@frl.orst.edu

BIERMANN, JANET SYBIL, TRAUMA, ONCOLOGY & ORTHOPEDIC ONCOLOGY. *Current Pos:* ASST PROF, UNIV MICH, 93- *Personal Data:* b Winnipeg, Man, Mar 14, 61; US citizen. *Educ:* Cornell Univ, BS, 83; Stanford Univ, MD, 87. *Prof Exp:* Internship, Univ Iowa Hosp, 87-88, orthop resident, Dept Orthop, 88-92. *Concurrent Pos:* Teaching asst, Stanford Univ, 83-84, res asst, 83-86; fel, Univ Chicago, 92-93; Ruth Jackson Orthrop travelling fel. *Mem:* Am Med Asn; Am Acad Orthop Surgeons. *Res:* Clinical and research aspects of musculoskeletal neuplasms, including primary tumors (sarcomas) and methstatic disease in both children and adults. *Mailing Add:* Sect Orthop Surg Univ Mich Hosp TC2912 Box 0328 1500 E Med Ctr Dr Ann Arbor MI 48109-0328

BIERNBAUM, CHARLES KNOX, INVERTEBRATE ZOOLOGY, CRUSTACEAN BIOLOGY. *Current Pos:* From asst prof to assoc prof, 74-86, PROF BIOL, COL CHARLESTON, 86- *Personal Data:* b Woodbury, NJ, Dec 7, 46. *Educ:* Wake Forest Univ, BS, 68; Univ Conn, PhD(biol), 74. *Mem:* Am Soc Zoologists; Crustacean Soc; Am Inst Biol Sci; Estuarine Res Fedn; Asn Southeastern Biologists. *Res:* Examination of the ecology and distribution of marine and freshwater crustaceans, especially amphipods. *Mailing Add:* 765 Stebbins St Charleston SC 29412

BIERON, JOSEPH F, ORGANIC CHEMISTRY. *Current Pos:* From asst prof to assoc prof, 66-77, dean Col Arts & Sci, 71-79, PROF CHEM, CANISIUS COL, 78-, CHMN DEPT, 84- *Personal Data:* b Buffalo, NY, Oct 19, 37; m 59; c 5. *Educ:* Canisius Col, BS, 59, MS, 61; State Univ NY Buffalo, PhD(chem), 65. *Mem:* Am Chem Soc. *Res:* Oxidation of polymeric materials and conformational analysis of organic molecules by nuclear magnetic resonance spectroscopy. *Mailing Add:* Canisius Col 2001 Main St Buffalo NY 14208

BIERSDORF, WILLIAM RICHARD, VISUAL PHYSIOLOGY, OPHTHALMOLOGY. *Current Pos:* PROF OPHTHAL, UNIV SFLA, 78-, HEALTH SCI OFFICER, VET ADMIN MED CTR, 78- *Personal Data:* b Salem, Ore, Sept 27, 25; m 66; c 2. *Educ:* Wash State Univ, BS, 50, MS, 51; Univ Wis, PhD(psychol), 54. *Prof Exp:* Exp psychologist vision, Walter Reed Army Inst Res, 54-67, asst chief, Dept Sensory Psychol, 62-66, actg chief, Dept Psychophysiol, 66-67; assoc prof ophthal, Ohio State Univ, 67-78, assoc prof biophys, 70-78, proj supvr vision res, Inst Res in Vision, 67-78. *Concurrent Pos:* US Army res grant vision, Ohio State Univ, 67-68, USPHS res grant, 68-80, 90-94; Am Psychol Asn deleg, Inter-Soc Color Coun, 66-75; adv, Comt Vision Nat Res Coun-Armed Force, 68-; mem Visual Sci Study Sect, Div Res Grants, NIH, 71-75; Vet Admin res grant, 80-88. *Mem:* Int Soc Clin Electrophysiol Vision; Asn Res Vision & Ophthal. *Res:* Human visual electrophysiology, electroretinograms and electro-oculograms from the eye, and visual evoked potentials from the brain; normal and abnormal vision, hereditary eye disease and visual brain dysfunction. *Mailing Add:* 13206 Tifton Dr Tampa FL 33618

BIERSMITH, EDWARD L, III, ORGANIC CHEMISTRY, BIO-ORGANIC CHEMISTRY. *Current Pos:* assoc prof chem, 70-77, DIR UNIV RES, NORTHEAST LA UNIV, 77- *Personal Data:* b Kansas City, Mo, Feb 26, 42; m 68; c 1. *Educ:* Rockhurst Col, AB, 63; Univ Kans, PhD(org chem), 68. *Prof Exp:* Asst chem, Rockhurst Col, 62-63; asst org chem, Univ Kans, 63-68; res assoc & instr, Univ Okla, 69-70. *Mem:* Am Chem Soc; Royal Soc Chem; Sigma Xi. *Res:* Photolysis of 2-cyclopropyl cyclohexanone: a three-carbon photochemical ring expansion; total synthesis of bicyclo heptan-2-one; isolation and identification of sterols from marine life, especially Renilla, Acrapora palmata; reactions of cyclic amides. *Mailing Add:* 1913 Richard Circle Monroe LA 71201-4559

BIERSNER, ROBERT JOHN, PHYSIOLOGICAL PSYCHOLOGY, HEALTH PSYCHOLOGY. *Current Pos:* ATTY, OCCUP SAFETY & HEALTH, 91- *Personal Data:* b Walla Walla, Wash, Sept 22, 41; m 63; c 2. *Educ:* Cent Wash Univ, BA, 63; McGill Univ, MA, 64, PhD(physiol psychol), 66. *Prof Exp:* Asst biol, Calif Inst Technol, 66-67; researcher psychol, Naval Health Res Ctr, Naval Biodynamics Lab, 70-73, human factors specialist, training eval, Naval Educ & Training Support Command, 73-76, res projs officer, Naval Submarine Med Res Lab, 76-78, prog mgr, Naval Med Res & Develop Command, 78-82, assoc dir prog planning, 82-84, cmndg officer, Naval Biodynamics Lab, 84-87; at Nat Inst Occup Safety & Health, 87-91. *Concurrent Pos:* Instr psychol, San Diego City Col & Mesa Col, 71-73; consult, NSF Antarctic Res Prog, 80-81 & Airline Pilots Rights Asn, 82-84; adv, Nat Res Coun Comt on Hearing, Bioacoust & Biomechs, 85- *Mem:* AAAS; Am Psychol Asn; US Naval Inst; Asn Mil Surgeons; Am Polar Soc; Sigma Xi. *Res:* Techniques to select individuals for stressful occupations; epidemiological designs and methods to assess effects of stressful occupations. *Mailing Add:* 9914 Capital View Ave Silver Spring MD 20910-1032

BIERSTONE, EDWARD, MATHEMATICS. *Current Pos:* PROF MATH, UNIV TORONTO. *Personal Data:* b Toronto, Ont, 46. *Educ:* Univ Toronto, BS, 69; Brandeis Univ, PhD(math), 73. *Mem:* Am Math Soc; Math Asn Am. *Res:* Mathematics. *Mailing Add:* Dept Math Univ Toronto 100 St George St Toronto ON M5S 3G3 Can

BIERWAGEN, GORDON PAUL, COLLOID & LIQUID SURFACE CHEMISTRY, CORROSION SCIENCE. *Current Pos:* PROF, POLYMERS DEPT, NDAK STATE UNIV, 90- *Personal Data:* b Wauwatosa, Wis, Mar 3, 43; m 64; c 3. *Educ:* Valparaiso Univ, BS, 64; Iowa State Univ, PhD(phys chem), 68. *Honors & Awards:* Roon Award, Fedn Socs Coatings Technol, 72. *Prof Exp:* Actg asst prof chem eng, Univ Minn, 68-69; res chemist, Dept Electrochem Eng, Battelle Mem Inst, 69-70; sr scientist,

Sherwin-Williams Res Ctr, 78-80, dir, Phys Anal Lab, Paint Res Dept, 80-90. *Concurrent Pos:* Consult, Foil Div, Gould, Inc, 74-75. *Mem:* Am Chem Soc; Am Inst Chem Engrs; AAAS; Soc Advan Mat & Process Eng; Fine Particle Soc; Electrochem Soc. *Res:* Effects of particle packing in coatings and composites; fine particle characterization; emulsion and suspension polymerization; physical chemistry of coatings; surface dynamics in thin liquid films; film formation in coatings; computer modeling of coatings properties; corrosion control by coatings; expert systems for coatings. *Mailing Add:* Dept Polymers & Coatings NDak State Univ Fargo ND 58105. *Fax:* 701-237-8439

BIERZYCHUDEK, PAULETTE F, PLANT POPULATION BIOLOGY. *Current Pos:* PROF, DEPT BIOL, LEWIS & CLARK COL, 93- *Personal Data:* b Chicago, Ill, Aug 25, 51. *Educ:* Univ Wash, BA & BS, 74; Cornell Univ, PhD(ecol & evolutionary biol), 81. *Prof Exp:* From asst prof to prof, Dept Biol, Pomona Col, 80-93, dept chair biol, 90-93. *Concurrent Pos:* Vis asst prof, Dept Bot, Duke Univ, 83-84; vis assoc prof, Dept Biol, Univ Chicago, 87. *Mem:* Ecol Soc Am; Soc Study Evolution; Coun Undergrad Res; Asn Women Sci; Soc Conserv Biol. *Res:* Evolution of plant breeding systems, especially apomixis and sex-changing; ecological consequences of producing genetically variable progeny; plant demography; evolution of flower color polymorphisms; conservation biology. *Mailing Add:* Dept Biol Lewis & Clark Col Portland OR 97219. *Fax:* 503-768-7658; *E-Mail:* bierzych@lclark.edu

BIES, DAVID ALAN, ACOUSTICS. *Current Pos:* RETIRED. *Personal Data:* b Los Angeles, Calif, Aug 15, 25; m 54; c 1. *Educ:* Univ Calif, Los Angeles, BA, 48, MA, 51, PhD, 53. *Prof Exp:* Sr consult, Bolt, Beranek & Newman, Inc, 53-72; sr res fel, Univ Adelaide, S Australia, 72-75, reader mech eng, 76-90. *Concurrent Pos:* Vis res fel, Univ Adelaide, S Australia, 90- *Mem:* AAAS; Acoust Soc Am; Australian Acoust Soc; Inst Noise Control Eng; Sigma Xi. *Res:* Sound propagation in ducts; uses of anechoic and reverberant rooms; uses of holography for study of vibration and sound radiation; general problems of noise control. *Mailing Add:* Dept Mech Eng Univ Adelaide Adelaide SA 5001 Australia

BIESELE, JOHN JULIUS, CYTOLOGY. *Current Pos:* prof zool, Univ Tex, Austin, 58-73, dir, Genetics Found, 69-77, prof zool & educ, 73-78, mem grad fac, 58-78, EMER PROF, UNIV TEX, AUSTIN, 78- *Personal Data:* b Waco, Tex, Mar 24, 18; m 43, 92, Esther A Eakin; c Marguerite A, Diana T & Elizabeth J. *Educ:* Univ Tex, AB, 39, PhD(zool), 42. *Prof Exp:* Int Cancer Res Found fel, 42 & 43-44; res assoc genetics, Carnegie Inst Technol, 44-46; asst, Sloan-Kettering Inst Cancer Res, 46, res fel, 47, head cell growth sect, 47-58, assoc, 47-55, mem, 55-58; asst prof anat, Med Col, Cornell Univ, 50-52, assoc prof biol, Grad Sch Med Sci, Sloan-Kettering Div, 52-55, prof biol, 55-58. *Concurrent Pos:* Instr, Univ Pa, 43-44; res assoc, Mass Inst Technol, 46-47; mem cell biol study sect, NIH, 58-63; assoc scientist, Sloan-Kettering Inst Cancer Res, 59-78; dir, AAAS, 60-63; counr, Cancirco, 62-90; assoc chmn, Conf Advan Sci & Math Teaching, Tex, 65, chmn, 66; mem discussion group on chem carcinogenesis, Nat Cancer Inst, 67, cancer res training comt, 69-72, res career awards, 62-77. *Mem:* Fel AAAS; Am Soc Cell Biol; Am Asn Cancer Res. *Res:* Electron microscopy; cytochemistry of cancerous and normal mammalian tissue; effects of differentiation, aging, hormones and drugs on cell chemistry and morphology; tumor chemotherapy; tissue culture; antimetabolites and mitotic poisons. *Mailing Add:* 2500 Great Oaks Pkwy Austin TX 78756

BIESIOT, PATRICIA MARIE, MARINE CRUSTACEANS. *Current Pos:* asst prof zool, 89-95, ASSOC PROF ZOOL, UNIV SOUTHERN MISS, 95- *Personal Data:* b St Cloud, Minn, Mar 23, 50; m 88, Shiao Y Wang; c Henry C. *Educ:* Bowling Green State Univ, BS, 72, MS, 75; Mass Inst Technol & Woods Hole Oceanog Inst, PhD(biol oceanog), 86. *Prof Exp:* Postdoctoral fel, Oak Ridge Nat Lab, 86-88. *Mem:* Am Soc Zool; Crustacean Soc; Sigma Xi; Western Soc Naturalists; World Aquacult Soc; Am Soc Limnol Oceanog. *Res:* Marine invertebrate zoology; physiological and biochemical adaptions of marine invertebrates; early life history stages of decapod crustaceans. *Mailing Add:* Dept Biol Sci Univ Southern Miss Hattiesburg MS 39406-5018

BIESTER, JOHN LOUIS, CHEMISTRY, ACADEMIC ADMINISTRATION. *Current Pos:* from asst prof to assoc prof chem, Beloit Col, 48-80, assoc dir field placement, 64-69, dir field placement & career coun, 69-83, EMER PROF CHEM & EMER DIR FIELD & CAREER SERV, BELOIT COL, 83- *Personal Data:* b Aurora, Ill, Aug 29, 18; wid; c Mary K & John M. *Educ:* Beloit Col, BA, 41; Syracuse Univ, MS, 43. PhD, 59. *Prof Exp:* Asst, Syracuse Univ, 42-43; res chemist, Standard Oil Co, Ind, 43; asst Syracuse Univ, 46-47. *Concurrent Pos:* Assoc prog dir, Acad Yr Insts, NSF, 61-62, consult, Sci Personnel & Educ Div, 62-69. *Res:* Science education; career education; experience based education; preparation of science teachers. *Mailing Add:* 1737 Arrowhead Dr Beloit WI 53511-3807

BIESZK, JOHN ALBERT, SOFTWARE-HARDWARE-FIRMWARE INTEGRATION, SYSTEM TESTING & ANALYSIS. *Current Pos:* PRIN RES SCIENTIST, SIEMENS MED SYSTS INC, 83- *Personal Data:* m 73, Rita A Mosher; c Stephen P, Catherine M & Christopher J. *Educ:* De Paul Univ, BS, 70, MS, 71; Univ Notre Dame, PhD(physics), 77. *Prof Exp:* Res assoc, Physics Dept, Univ Wis-Madison, 77-80; sr res scientist, Siemens Gammasonics Inc, 80-83. *Mem:* Am Asn Physicists Med; Am Phys Soc. *Res:* Single photon emission computed tomography; nuclear medicine physics; clinical nuclear medicine; integration and system testing of gamma camera systems. *Mailing Add:* Siemens Med Systs Inc 2501 N Barrington Rd Hoffman Estates IL 60195-2061. *E-Mail:* bieszk@mmg.sms.siemens.com

BIETZ, JEROLD ALLEN, PROTEIN CHEMISTRY, CEREAL CHEMISTRY. *Current Pos:* RES CHEMIST, NAT CTR AGR UTILIZATION RES, AGR RES SERV, USDA, PEORIA, 66- *Personal Data:* b Mayville, NDak, Feb 22, 42; m 63, Myrna E Blair; c Matthew J & Melanie B. *Educ:* Mayville State Col, BS, 63; Univ NDak, MS, 66. *Honors & Awards:* Geddes Award, Am Asn Cereal Chemists, 95. *Mem:* Am Chem Soc; Am Asn Cereal Chemists. *Res:* Concerning isolation, characterization and comparison of cereal endosperm proteins relates structure to functionality, quality and genetic background through peptide characterization, electrophoresis, HPLC and amino acid sequence analysis. *Mailing Add:* Nat Ctr Agr Utilization Res USDA-Agr Res Serv 1815 N University Peoria IL 61604. *Fax:* 309-681-6686; *E-Mail:* bietzja@ncaurl.ncaur.gov

BIEVER, KENNETH DUANE, BIOLOGICAL CONTROL. *Current Pos:* RES ENTOMOLOGIST, YAKIMA AGR RES LAB, AGR RES SERV, USDA, 66- *Personal Data:* b Hot Springs, SDak, Jan 8, 40; m 60; c 2. *Educ:* SDak State Univ, BS, 62; Univ Calif, Riverside, PhD(entom), 67. *Mem:* Entom Soc Am; Soc Invert Path; Int Orgn Biol Control. *Res:* Design and development of biocontrol pest management systems; biological control of insects; medical entomology; insect pathology. *Mailing Add:* One S 36th Ave Yakima WA 98902

BIGELEISEN, JACOB, NUCLEAR CHEMISTRY. *Current Pos:* vpres res & dean grad studies, State Univ NY, Stony Brook, 78-80, prof chem, 78-89, distinguished prof, 89, DISTINGUISHED EMER PROF, STATE UNIV NY, STONY BROOK, 89- *Personal Data:* b Paterson, NJ, May 2, 19; m 45, Grace A Simon; c David M, Ira S & Paul E. *Educ:* NY Univ, AB, 39; State Col Wash, MS, 41; Univ Calif, PhD(chem), 43. *Honors & Awards:* Am Chem Soc Award, 58; Gilbert N Lewis Lectr, 63; E O Lawrence Mem Award, 64. *Prof Exp:* Res scientist, Manhattan Proj, SAM Labs, Columbia Univ, 43-45; res assoc, Cryogenic Lab, Ohio State Univ, 45-46; fel, Inst Nuclear Studies, Univ Chicago, 46-48; from assoc chemist to sr chemist, Brookhaven Nat Lab, 48-68; prof chem, Univ Rochester, River Campus, 68-73, chmn dept, 70-75, Tracy H Harris prof, 73-78. *Concurrent Pos:* Vis prof, Cornell Univ, 53-54; NSF fel & hon vis prof, Swiss Fed Inst Technol, 62-63; John Simon Guggenheim fel, 74-75; chmn, Assembly Math & Phys Sci, Nat Res Coun-Nat Acad Sci, 76-80. *Mem:* Nat Acad Sci; Am Acad Arts & Sci; Am Chem Soc; Am Phys Soc; AAAS. *Res:* Theoretical basis of isotope chemistry; utilization of isotope effects; kinetics of chemical reactions; semi-quinones; photochemistry in rigid media; color of organic compounds; low temperature; spectroscopy; use of isotopes as tracers; dissociation of strong electrolytes; thermodynamics of electrolytes; acids and bases; isotope separation; intra-and inter-molecular forces in liquids and solids. *Mailing Add:* PO Box 217 St James NY 11780-0217. *Fax:* 516-632-7960; *E-Mail:* jbigeleisen@ccmail.sunysb.edu

BIGELIS, RAMUNAS, microbial fermentation, microbial metabolism, for more information see previous edition

BIGELOW, CHARLES C, CHEMISTRY, ENVIRONMENTAL EDUCATION. *Current Pos:* prof chem & dean sci, 79-89, provost, Univ Col, 95-97, EMER DEAN SCI, UNIV MAN, 90- *Personal Data:* b Edmonton, Alta, Apr 25, 28; m 53, 77, Elizabeth Sellick; c Ann (Siess) & David. *Educ:* Univ Toronto, BASc, 53; McMaster Univ, MSc, 55, PhD(chem), 57. *Prof Exp:* Nat Res Coun Can fel protein chem, Carlsberg Lab, Copenhagen, 57-59; assoc, Sloan-Kettering Inst, 59-62; from asst prof to assoc prof chem, Univ Alta, 62-65; from assoc prof to prof biochem, Univ Western Ont, 65-74; prof biochem & head dept, Mem Univ Nfld, 74-76; prof chem & dean sci, St Mary's Univ, 77-79. *Concurrent Pos:* Res grants, Nat Res Coun Can, 63-69 & 77-90; Med Res Coun Can, 65-77; vis prof biochem, Univ Toronto, 73-74, Fla State Univ, 65; vis scientist, Nat Inst Med Res, London, 84-85. *Mem:* Fel Chem Inst Can; Am Chem Soc; Am Soc Biol Chem; Can Biochem Soc; AAAS; Sigma Xi. *Res:* Physical chemistry of proteins. *Mailing Add:* Univ Man Winnipeg MB R3T 2N2 Can. *Fax:* 204-261-0021; *E-Mail:* bigelow@cc.umanitoba.ca

BIGELOW, JOHN E(ALY), CHEMICAL ENGINEERING, RADIOCHEMICAL PROCESSING. *Current Pos:* DEVELOP ENGR, OAK RIDGE NAT LAB, 61- *Personal Data:* b Hammond, Ind, Jan 28, 29; m 54; c 3. *Educ:* Purdue Univ, BS, 50; Mass Inst Technol, SM, 52, ScD(chem eng), 56. *Prof Exp:* Develop engr, Oak Ridge Nat Lab, 56-58; eng opers analyst, US Atomic Energy Comn, 58-61. *Mem:* Am Chem Soc; Am Nuclear Soc; Sigma Xi. *Res:* Chemical processing of nuclear fuel, including nonaqueous methods; production and purification of transuranium elements; design and fabrication of californium-252 neutron sources. *Mailing Add:* 111 Concord Rd Oak Ridge TN 37830-7127

BIGELOW, JOHN EDWARD, ENGINEERING, PHYSICS. *Current Pos:* RETIRED. *Personal Data:* b Worcester, Mass, July 25, 22; m 48; c 5. *Educ:* Worcester Polytech Inst, BS, 44 & 46. *Prof Exp:* Develop engr, Gen Eng Lab, Gen Elec Co, 46-54, sr engr, X-ray Dept, 54-59, mgr, Advan Eng Lab, 59-64, Info Eng Advan Tech Labs, 64-66, mgr display progs, 66- *Res:* Scientific instruments; process instruments; diagnostic devices; optical and electronic information processors; detectors; computer driven displays; data terminals. *Mailing Add:* 834 Riverview Rd Rexford NY 12148

BIGELOW, MARGARET ELIZABETH BARR, MYCOLOGY. *Current Pos:* from instr to prof, 57-89, Ray Ethan Torrey prof, 86-89, EMER PROF BOT, UNIV MASS, 89- *Personal Data:* b Elkhorn, Man, Apr 16, 23; wid. *Educ:* Univ BC, BA, 50, MA, 52; Univ Mich, PhD(bot), 56. *Prof Exp:* Nat Res Coun fel, Univ Montreal, 56-57. *Mem:* Mycol Soc Am (vpres, 79, pres, 81-82); Am Inst Biol Sci; Int Asn Plant Taxonomists; Brit Mycol Soc. *Res:* Systematics and ecology of pyrenomycetous ascomycetes; collection, identification and disposition into higher categories; improvement of classification. *Mailing Add:* 9475 Inverness Rd Sidney BC V8L 5G8 Can

BIGELOW, NICHOLAS PIERRE, LASER COOLING & TRAPPING, QUANTUM OPTICS & FLUIDS. *Current Pos:* res prof, 91-92, asst prof, 92-97, ASSOC PROF PHYSICS, UNIV ROCHESTER, 97- *Personal Data:* b Princeton, NJ, Dec 26, 58; m 81, Judith Anderson; c Ian & Eric. *Educ:* Lehigh Univ, BS, 80, BS, 81; Cornell Univ, MS, 84, PhD(physics), 89. *Prof Exp:* Mem tech staff, AT&T Bell Labs, 89-91; sr researcher, Lab Spectros Hertzienne, Ecole Normale Superieure, Paris, 91-92. *Concurrent Pos:* Sr staff scientist, Lab Laser Energetics, Rochester, 91-; vis prof, Lab Kastler-Brossel, Eccole Normale Suprieure, Paris, 92-95; Alfred P Sloan Found fel, 93-95; NSF grantee, 94-; David & Lucille Packard Found fel, 94-; Army Res Off grantee, 96- *Mem:* Am Phys Soc; Optical Soc Am. *Res:* Experimental and theoretical quantum optics; laser cooling and trapping of neutral atoms; Bose-Einstein condensation; ultra-cold collisions; condensed matter physics, magnetic resonance and spectroscopy. *Mailing Add:* Univ Rochester 63 Crescent Hill Rd Pittsford NY 14534. *Fax:* 716-275-8527; *E-Mail:* nbig@lle.rochester.edu

BIGELOW, SANFORD WALKER, SCIENCE POLICY, MEDICAL & HEALTH SCIENCE. *Current Pos:* ASSOC DIR, SAFETY & REGULATORY AFFAIRS, PFIZER, INC, 91- *Personal Data:* b Winchester, Mass, Sept 28, 56; m 82; c 3. *Educ:* Am Univ, BS, 78, MS, 81, PhD(chem), 84; Am Bd Toxicol, cert. *Prof Exp:* Chem researcher, Am Univ, 78-79; chemist, NIH, 79-85; toxicologist, Karch & Assocs, Inc, 86-87 & Environ Protection Agency, 87-89; proj dir, Food Safety, Nat Acad Sci, 89-91. *Concurrent Pos:* Consult, MultiSci, Inc, 87- *Mem:* Soc Toxicol; Inst Food Technologists; Am Chem Soc; Am Soc Plant Physiologists; Am Col Toxicol; Toxicol Forum. *Res:* Food safety, specifically in the area of purity of food additives and natural constituents in foods. *Mailing Add:* Ross Prod Div Abbott Labs 625 Cleveland Ave Columbus OH 43215

BIGELOW, WILBUR CHARLES, ELECTRON MICROSCOPY, X-RAY DIFFRACTION. *Current Pos:* res assoc res inst, 51-56, asst prof sci, 56-59, from assoc prof to prof chem & metall eng, 59-71, PROF MAT ENG, UNIV MICH, 71- *Personal Data:* b Wyoming Co, Pa, Mar 18, 23; m 50; c 2. *Educ:* Pa State Univ, BS, 44; Univ Mich, MS, 48, PhD(phys chem), 52. *Prof Exp:* Res chemist, US Naval Res Lab, Washington, DC, 44-46. *Mem:* Am Chem Soc; Electron Micros Soc Am; Microbeam Anal Soc. *Res:* Electron microscopy, diffraction and microprobe analysis; microstructures of metals and ceramics systems and their relationships to composition and physical properties. *Mailing Add:* 1136 Mixtwood St Ann Arbor MI 48103-3035. *Fax:* 313-763-4788

BIGGER, CYNTHIA ANITA HOPWOOD, GENETIC TOXICOLOGY, CHEMICAL CARCINOGENESIS. *Current Pos:* STUDY DIR, GENETIC TOXICOL DIV, MICROBIOL ASSOCS, INC, ROCKVILLE, MD, 91- *Personal Data:* b Sheffield, Ala, Mar 3, 42; m 81; c 1. *Educ:* La State Univ, Baton Rouge, BS, 66, MS, 69, PhD(microbiol), 71. *Prof Exp:* NIH fel, Dept Molecular Biol, Univ Edinburgh, 71-72; vis instr res, Dept Chem, 73, res assoc, Dept Microbiol, 74, res assoc, Sch Vet Med, La State Univ, Baton Rouge, 74-76, scientist, Basic Res Prog, Nat Cancer Inst, Frederick Cancer Res Ctr, 76-91. *Mem:* Environ Mutagen Soc; Am Asn Cancer Res. *Res:* Genetic toxicology; molecular methods in environmental mutagenesis; molecular aspects of chemical carcinogenesis, interactions of polycyclic aromatic hydrocarbons with nucleic acids. *Mailing Add:* 42 E Third St Frederick MD 21701

BIGGER, J THOMAS, JR, CARDIOLOGY, PHARMACOLOGY. *Current Pos:* instr, 66-67, assoc, 67-68, from asst prof to assoc prof med, 68-72, assoc prof, 72-75, PROF MED & PHARMACOL, COL PHYSICIANS & SURGEONS, COLUMBIA UNIV, 75- *Personal Data:* b Cambridge, Mass, Jan 17, 35. *Educ:* Emory Univ, AB, 55; Med Col Ga, MD, 60. *Prof Exp:* Intern & asst resident, Columbia Univ Med Div, Bellevue Hosp, 60-62; asst resident & resident cardiol, Presby Hosp, New York, 63-65. *Concurrent Pos:* Vis fel cardiol, Col Physicians & Surgeons, Columbia Univ, 65-66, fel, 66-67; NY Heart Asn fel, 65-68; Nat Heart & Lung Inst res career develop award, 72-77; asst physician, Presby Hosp, New York, 65-68, from asst attend physician to assoc attend physician, 68-75, attend physician, 75-; sr investr, NY Heart Asn, 68-72; assoc ed, Circulation, 70- *Mem:* Am Soc Clin Invest; Am Heart Asn; Am Physiol Soc; Am Soc Pharmacol & Exp Therapeut; fel NY Acad Sci. *Res:* Cardiac electrophysiology and arrhythmias; clinical and laboratory evaluation of cardioactive drugs, particularly cardiac antiarrhythmic drugs. *Mailing Add:* Dept Med Columbia Univ 630 W 168th St New York NY 10032-3702

BIGGERS, CHARLES JAMES, BIOLOGY, GENETICS. *Current Pos:* assoc prof, 69-77, PROF BIOL, MEMPHIS STATE UNIV, 77- *Personal Data:* b Gastonia, NC, Feb 7, 35; m 58, Shirley Hoover; c Lisa E (Pruett), Amy L (Trent) & Emily A. *Educ:* Wake Forest Col, BS, 57; Appalachian State Teachers Col, MA, 59; Univ SC, PhD(biol), 69. *Prof Exp:* Instr biol, Col Orlando, 59-61, chmn dept, 61-66, asst prof, 62-66; exten instr, Univ SC, 66-69. *Mem:* AAAS; Am Genetic Asn; Genetics Soc Am; Sigma Xi; Am Soc Mammalogists. *Res:* Genetic studies of protein polymorphisms in Peromyscus polionotus, Anthonomus grandis, Bufo woodhouseii, and Ictaluras punctatus, with primary interest in biochemical analysis and chromosomes. *Mailing Add:* 8824 Overlea Cove Cordova TN 38018. *Fax:* 901-678-4746; *E-Mail:* cbiggers@cc.memphis.edu

BIGGERS, JAMES VIRGIL, CERAMICS SCIENCE & TECHNOLOGY. *Current Pos:* from asst prof to assoc prof ceramic sci, 69-76, SR RES ASSOC, MAT RES LAB, PA STATE UNIV, UNIVERSITY PARK, 76- *Personal Data:* b Dallas, Tex, Nov 6, 28; m 56. *Educ:* Purdue Univ, BS, 60; Pa State Univ, PhD(metall), 66. *Prof Exp:* Res engr, Union Carbide Corp, 60-62; dir res, Erie Technol Corp, 66-69. *Mem:* Fel Am Ceramic Soc. *Res:* Processing and structure-property relationships in electronic ceramics. *Mailing Add:* 1321 Old Boalsburg Rd State College PA 16801

BIGGERS, JOHN DENNIS, PHYSIOLOGY. *Current Pos:* PROF PHYSIOL & MEM LAB HUMAN REPRODUCTION & REPRODUCTIVE BIOL, HARVARD MED SCH, 72- *Personal Data:* b Gt Brit, Aug 18, 23; div; c 3. *Educ:* Univ London, BSc(vet sci) & BSc(spec), 46; PhD(physiol), 52, DSc, 65. *Honors & Awards:* Hartman Award, Soc Study Reproduction, 87; Pioneer Award, Int Embryo Transfer Soc, 90; Marshall Medal, Soc Study Fertility, 90. *Prof Exp:* Student demonstr physiol, Royal Vet Col, Univ London, 44-45, demonstr, 45-47; asst lectr, Univ Sheffield, 47-48; lectr vet physiol, Univ Sydney, 48-53, sr lectr, 53-55; sr lectr physiol, Royal Vet Col, Univ London, 55-59; assoc mem, Wistar Inst & assoc prof, Sch Vet Med, Univ Pa, 59-61, King Ranch res prof reproductive physiol, 61-66; prof pop dynamics & assoc prof obstet & gynec, Johns Hopkins Univ, 66-72. *Concurrent Pos:* Vis scientist, Strangeways Res Lab, Eng, 54-55; Commonwealth fel, St John's Col, Cambridge Univ, 54-55; Damon Runyon Mem Fund grant, 60-62; NIH grant, 60-65 & 67-; Pop Coun grant, 60-; Lalor Found grant, 61; NSF grant, 61-64; adv, WHO, 64 & 71-; mem study sect reproductive biol, NIH, 67-71, adv, 69-; mem, ICRO Comt, 68-; Ford Found grant, 69-70; ed, Biol of Reproduction, 70-74; Ford Found adv, 74-; prog proj dir, NIH Grant, 74-; mem corp, Marine Biol Lab, Woods Hole. *Mem:* Am Statist Asn; Soc Study Reproduction (pres, 68-69); fel Royal Col Vet Surg; fel Royal Statist Soc; Am Inst Biol Sci; Tissue Cult Asn; Physiol Soc; Soc Study Fertility; fel AAAS. *Res:* Physiology of fertilization, preimplantation development and implantation; growth and differentiation; chemically defined media; statistics and theory of experimental design; history of reproductive biology; ethics of reproductive biology. *Mailing Add:* Dept Physiol Harvard Med Sch 25 Shattuck St Boston MA 02115-6092

BIGGERSTAFF, JOHN A, PHYSICS. *Current Pos:* PHYSICIST, OAK RIDGE NAT LAB, 62- *Personal Data:* b Berea, Ky, Sept 10, 31. *Educ:* Univ Ky, BS & MS, 53, PhD(physics), 61. *Prof Exp:* Physicist, Eng Lab, US Army Signal Corps, 55; sr engr nucleonics, Martin Co, 55-57; res assoc nuclear physics, Univ Ky, 61-63. *Mem:* Am Phys Soc. *Res:* Low energy nuclear spectroscopy; instrumentation for nuclear spectroscopy. *Mailing Add:* 517 Sandy Dr Mt Juliet TN 37122

BIGGERSTAFF, ROBERT HUGGINS, PHYSICAL ANTHROPOLOGY, ORTHODONTICS. *Current Pos:* PROF ORTHOD, UNIV TEX HEALTH SCI CTR, SAN ANTONIO, 82- *Personal Data:* b Richmond, Ky, June 1, 27; m 50; c 2. *Educ:* Howard Univ, BS, 51, DDS, 55; Univ Pa, MS, 66, PhD(anthrop), 69; cert orthod, 73. *Prof Exp:* NIH trainee, Univ Pa, 64-66, res investr, 67-69; from asst prof to assoc prof orthod, Univ Ky, 73-82. *Mem:* Am Asn Phys Anthrop; Am Anthrop Asn; Am Dent Asn; Am Asn Orthod. *Res:* Analysis of morphological and mensurational variations in the post-canine dentition; the metric description of occlusion; analysis of arch form; environmental variables which can cause deviations in tooth form. *Mailing Add:* 8206 Shallow Creek Dr San Antonio TX 78251

BIGGERSTAFF, WARREN RICHARD, ORGANIC CHEMISTRY. *Current Pos:* prof, 58-81, EMER PROF CHEM, CALIF STATE UNIV, FRESNO, 81- *Personal Data:* b Folsom, NMex, May 2, 18; m 42; c 3. *Educ:* Willamette Univ, BA, 40; Ore State Col, MS, 42; Univ Wis, PhD(org chem), 48. *Prof Exp:* Asst chem, Ore State Col, 40-42; asst, Univ Wis, 42-44, instr org chem, 47-48. *Concurrent Pos:* Chmn dept chem, Fresno State Col, 61-66, assoc vpres acad planning, 69-70; vis assoc, Sloan-Kettering Inst Cancer Res, 56-57; vis prof, Univ Lund, 67. *Mem:* Am Chem Soc; Sigma Xi. *Res:* Synthetic hormone substitutes; diethylstilbestrol and analogs related to progesterone and desoxycorticosterone; ring D metabolites of the estrogens; unsaturated thiolactones. *Mailing Add:* 2911 Juniper Ave Morro Bay CA 93442-1448

BIGGINS, JOHN, PHOTOSYNTHESIS. *Current Pos:* Asst prof bot & assoc prof biol, Brown Univ, 70-78, prof biol, 78-, chmn biochem, 85-96, CHMN BIOCHEM, BROWN UNIV, 85-, PROF BIOCHEM, 96- *Personal Data:* b Sheffield, Eng, Mar 30, 36; m 63. *Educ:* Univ London, BSc, 60; Univ Calif, Berkeley, PhD(plant physiol), 65. *Concurrent Pos:* Sr int fel, Fogarty Found. *Mem:* Am Soc Photobiol; Am Soc Plant Physiol. *Res:* Correlation of structure and biochemical function of energy transducing systems; mechanism of photosynthesis reaction centers and protein design. *Mailing Add:* Sect Biochem Brown Univ Providence RI 02912

BIGGS, ALAN RICHARD, DISEASES OF DECIDUOUS FRUITS. *Current Pos:* assoc prof, 89-95, PROF PLANT PATH, WVA UNIV, 95- *Personal Data:* b Lewisburg, Pa, June 22, 53; m 81; c 2. *Educ:* Pa State Univ, BSc, 76, MSc, 78, PhD(plant path), 82. *Honors & Awards:* Lee M Hutchins Award, Am Phytopath Soc. *Prof Exp:* Instr plant path, Pa State Univ, 82; res scientist, Agr Can, 83-89, head, Plant Path Sect, 87-89. *Concurrent Pos:* Adj prof, Dept Bot & Plant Path, Univ Toronto, 84-87, Dept Biol, Shepher Col, 93- *Mem:* Am Phytopath Soc; Int Asn Wood Anatomists; AAAS. *Res:* Fungal and bacterial diseases of deciduous tree fruits; wound response and periderm regeneration in tree bark; breeding trees for resistance to trunk and limb diseases. *Mailing Add:* Univ Exp Farm WVa Univ PO Box 609 Kearneysville WV 25430. *E-Mail:* abiggs2@wvu.edu

BIGGS, ALBERT WAYNE, ELECTRICAL ENGINEERING. *Current Pos:* assoc prof, 67-73, PROF ELEC ENG, UNIV KANS, 73- *Personal Data:* b Toledo, Ohio, Oct 4, 26; m 59; c 2. *Educ:* Wash Univ, BSEE, 47; Stanford Univ, MBA, 49; Univ Wash, PhD(elec eng), 65. *Prof Exp:* Sales analyst, Surface Combustion Co, Ohio, 50-51; standards engr, Wright Air Develop Ctr, 51-52; design engr, Boeing Co, 52-55, res engr, Aerospace Div, 57-63, res specialist, Missile & Space Info Div, 65-67; instr elec eng, Univ Wash, 55-57, res instr, 63-65. *Concurrent Pos:* Mem Comn II, Int Sci Radio Union, 65- *Mem:* Am Phys Soc; Inst Elec & Electronics Engrs; Sigma Xi; Optical Soc Am; Int Sci Radio Union. *Res:* Microwave systems, antennas and radio wave propagation; radar systems in guided missiles sources, high energy microwave and particle accelerators (neutrons). *Mailing Add:* Dept Elec Eng Univ Ala Huntsville ECE Dept Eng 263 Huntsville AL 35899

BIGGS, DAVID FREDERICK, PHARMACOLOGY. *Current Pos:* DEAN FAC PHARM, HEALTH SCI CTR, KUWAIT UNIV, 96- *Personal Data:* b London, Eng, Jan 3, 39; m 62; c 2. *Educ:* Univ Nottingham, BPharm, 61; King's Col, Univ London, 67. *Prof Exp:* Pharmacol dept head, Res Labs, May & Baker Ltd, Eng, 63-69; asst prof biopharm, Univ Alta, assoc prof, 71-78, prof pharmacol, 78-96, McCalla prof, 83-84. *Mem:* Brit Inst Biol; Brit Pharmacol Soc; Pharmaceut Soc Gt Brit; Pharmacol Soc Can. *Res:* Pharmacological properties of novel chemical compounds; relationship between structure and activity among neuromuscular blocking agents; pharmaceutical toxicology; respiratory physiology and pharmacology; toxicology of natural products; metabolism of heavy metals. *Mailing Add:* Fac Pharm Health Sci Ctr Kuwait Univ PO Box 24923 Safat Code No 13110 Kuwait

BIGGS, DOUGLAS (CRAIG), BIOLOGICAL OCEANOGRAPHY. *Current Pos:* from asst prof to assoc prof, 77-86, PROF OCEANOG, TEX A&M UNIV, 96- *Personal Data:* b Lancaster, Pa, Oct 17, 50; c 1. *Educ:* Franklin & Marshall Col, Pa, AB, 72; Mass Inst Technol, PhD(biol oceanog), 76. *Prof Exp:* Fel biol oceanog, Joint Prog, Mass Inst Technol-Woods Hole Oceanog Inst, 72-76; res assoc, Marine Sci Res Ctr, State Univ NY Stony Brook, 76-77. *Concurrent Pos:* Instr zooplankton ecol, Bermuda Biol Sta, 83, 86, 87, 89, 91; mgr, Tech Support Group Tex A&M Univ, 86-96; vchmn, UNOLS Res Vessel Tech Enhancement Comt, 93. *Mem:* Am Soc Limnol & Oceanog; AAAS; Am Geophys Union; Sigma Xi; Oceanog Soc; Marine Technol Soc. *Res:* Physiology and ecology of marine plankton; modeling of energy flow through intermediate trophic levels in open-ocean and estuarine systems; biogeochemistry of Gulf of Mexico; nutrient cycling; warm- and cold-core rings. *Mailing Add:* Dept Oceanog Tex A&M Univ College Station TX 77843-3146. *Fax:* 409-845-6331; *E-Mail:* dbiggs@ocean.tamu.edu

BIGGS, FRANK, MATHEMATICAL PHYSICS. *Current Pos:* res physicist, 65-95, STAFF MEM, SANDIA LAB, 56- *Personal Data:* b Langdon, Mo, Dec 16, 27; m 64; c 7. *Educ:* Univ Ark, BS, 56, MS, 57, PhD(physics), 65. *Concurrent Pos:* Physicist, Sandia Lab, 57-65, consult, 60-65; prof, Univ NMex, 75-76. *Mem:* Am Phys Soc; Am Soc Mech Engrs. *Res:* X-ray cross sections and instrumentation; analysis of experimental data; applied mathematics; energy studies; weapon effects. *Mailing Add:* 3515 Monte Vista Blvd NE Albuquerque NM 87106

BIGGS, HOMER GATES, BIOCHEMISTRY. *Current Pos:* CONSULT, 88-; DIR, WILLIAMS-LYNCH MED LAB & FRANKLIN PARK MED LAB, 89- *Personal Data:* b Greene, NY, Feb 16, 30; m 52, Lois Baskey; c Barbara & Betty. *Educ:* State Univ NY Binghamton, BA, 51; Univ Iowa, MS, 54, PhD(biochem), 56. *Prof Exp:* Instr & asst dir clin chem, Univ Tenn, 56-59, asst prof, Div Clin Chem, Dept Med Labs, 59-63; assoc prof path, Med Col & dir clin chem, Univ Hosp, Univ Ala, 63-70, dep dir educ, Dept Clin Path, 69-70; dir clin chem, Med Ctr, Ind Univ, Indianapolis, 70-74, prof clin path, 70-75; vpres & tech dir, Biozyme Labs, Inc, 75-78; dir, Prev Med Res Ctr of Cleveland & King James Med Labs, Inc, 79-86; pres & lab dir, BDI Labs, Inc, 86-88. *Mem:* Am Chem Soc; Am Asn Clin Chemists; AAAS; fel Asn Clin Scientists; fel Nat Acad Clin Biochem; Sigma Xi; fel Am Soc Lab Clin Scientists. *Res:* Serum proteins, minerals and enzymes. *Mailing Add:* RR 2 Box 252 Spencer IN 47460-0252

BIGGS, MAURICE EARL, SEISMOLOGY, GRAVITY. *Current Pos:* RETIRED. *Personal Data:* b Sebree, Ky, Oct 27, 21; m 46; c 4. *Educ:* Ind Univ, AB, 48, MA, 50, PhD(geophys), 74. *Prof Exp:* Head, Geophys Sect, Int Geolog Surv, 51-87, asst state geologist, 60-87. *Mem:* Sigma Xi; Europ Asn Explor Geophysicists. *Res:* Seismic refraction and reflection, gravity and magnetic methods to study the configuration and type of basement rocks in Indiana; correlate physical properties of rock with rock type. *Mailing Add:* 1213 S Brooks Dr Bloomington IN 47401

BIGGS, PAUL, petroleum engineering; deceased, see previous edition for last biography

BIGGS, R B, MARINE GEOLOGY. *Current Pos:* VPRES, NAT TECH RESOURCES DIV, R F WESTON INC, 88- *Personal Data:* b Baltimore, Md, Feb 27, 37; m 60; c 2. *Educ:* Lehigh Univ, BA, 59, MS, 61, PhD(geol), 63. *Prof Exp:* Asst geol, Lehigh Univ, 60-62; res assoc, Chesapeake Biol Lab, 62-70; from asst prof to assoc prof geol, Col Marine Studies, Univ Del, 70-88, assoc dean, 73-80. *Concurrent Pos:* Mem bd dirs, Am Geol Inst. *Mem:* AAAS; Sigma Xi; Geol Soc Am; Am Geol Inst; Am Geophys Union. *Res:* Marine geology, especially the geochemistry of modern sediments; coastal pollution. *Mailing Add:* Nat Tech Resources Dir R F Weston Inc 1 Weston Way Bldg 5-1 West Chester PA 19380

BIGGS, R DALE, CHEMICAL ENGINEERING. *Current Pos:* RETIRED. *Personal Data:* b Amarillo, Tex, Dec 14, 28; m 52; c 4. *Educ:* Rice Univ, BSChE, 50; Univ Mich, MSChE, 51, PhD(chem eng), 54. *Prof Exp:* Chem engr, Ethyl Corp, La, 54-56; proj engr, Plastics Prod Dept, Dow Chem Co, 56-59, from res engr to sr res engr, Process Fundamentals Lab, 59-67, prod develop eng supvr, Plastics Prod Dept, 67-68, spec assignment, Technol Serv & Develop, 68-69, sr res engr, Phys Res Lab, 69-70, res mgr, Dow Interdisciplinary Group, 70-74, lab dir eng, Cent Res Labs, 74-79, assoc scientist, La Div, 79-86. *Concurrent Pos:* Lectr, Grad Exten Prog, Univ Mich, Midland, 57-68. *Mem:* Am Inst Chem Eng; Am Chem Soc. *Res:* Reaction kinetics; mass transfer; fluid mechanics, particularly polymer melts and solutions; chemical process development; coal gasification; process research. *Mailing Add:* 15903 Malvern Hill Baton Rouge LA 70817

BIGGS, ROBERT HILTON, PLANT PHYSIOLOGY. *Current Pos:* From asst prof biochem to assoc prof biochem, 58-69, prof & chmn, 75-77, PROF BIOCHEM, UNIV FLA, 69- *Personal Data:* b US, May 5, 31; m 53, 78; c 3. *Educ:* ECarolina Univ, BS, 53; Purdue Univ, MS, 55, PhD(plant physiol), 58. *Concurrent Pos:* Sci & Educ Admin-Coop Res, USDA, Washington, DC, 78- *Mem:* Am Inst Biol Sci; AAAS; Sigma Xi; Am Soc Plant Physiol; Am Soc Hort Sci. *Res:* Abscission; ultraviolet light; chemical regulators; dormancy. *Mailing Add:* 5 NW 28th Terrance Gainesville FL 32607

BIGGS, RONALD C(LARKE), BUILDING SERVICES, HEAT TRANSFER. *Current Pos:* RETIRED. *Personal Data:* b Ottawa, Ont, Feb 5, 38; m 61, Deanna E; c Randal K & David D. *Educ:* Queens Univ, Ont, BSc, 61; Stanford Univ, MS, 62; McGill Univ, PhD(mech eng), 68. *Prof Exp:* Develop engr, Can Gen Elec, Ont, 63-65; assoc prof eng, Carleton Univ, Ont, 68-74; mgr energy res & develop, Pub Works Can, 74-78, dir, solar energy progs, 78-80; sr tech adv solar energy progs, Nat Res Coun Can, 80-81, head, Bldg Serv Sect, Div Bldg Res, 81-96, dir, Res Inst Const, 86-96. *Concurrent Pos:* Past chair, Can Eng Accreditation Bd. *Mem:* Am Soc Heating, Refrig & Air Conditioning Engrs; Am Soc Qual Control. *Res:* Combined free and forced convective heat transfer for laminar flow of diathermanous and althermanous gases in a vertical tube; heat transfer characteristics of turbulent boundary layer flows with the wall and pressure gradients; solar energy; building research; construction research. *Mailing Add:* 5783 Loggers Way PO Box 95 RR 1 Arnprior ON K7S 3G7 Can. *Fax:* 613-942-0822; *E-Mail:* biggs@irc.nrc.ca

BIGGS, WALTER CLARK, JR, vertebrate zoology, animal behavior, for more information see previous edition

BIGHAM, CLIFFORD BRUCE, ACCELERATOR PHYSICS, RF ENGINEERING. *Current Pos:* CONSULT, 92- *Personal Data:* b Kamloops, BC, June 12, 28; m 54, Jean C Blakey; c Joanne F, Ian B & David R. *Educ:* Queen's Univ, Ont, BS, 51, MS, 52; Univ Liverpool, PhD(nuclear physics), 54. *Prof Exp:* From assoc res officer to sr res officer reactor physics, Atomic Energy Can, Ltd, 54-66, sr res officer, Accelerator Physics Br, 66-92. *Mem:* Can Asn Physicists; Can Nuclear Soc; Am Phys Soc; Can Inst Synchrotron Radiation. *Res:* Experimental reactor physics; nuclear physics data pertaining to and parameters of nuclear reactor lattices; RF power for linear accelerators; superconducting cyclotron design; synchrotron design. *Mailing Add:* PO Box 523 Deep River ON K0J 1P0 Can

BIGHAM, ERIC CLEVELAND, MEDICINAL CHEMISTRY. *Current Pos:* proj comt leader, 85-91, SR RES SCIENTIST, BURROUGHS WELLCOME CO, 78-, SECT HEAD, 92-, PRIN SCIENTIST, 95- *Personal Data:* b Kannapolis, NC, Mar 26, 47; m 70, Rita Lentz; c Ashley. *Educ:* NC State Univ, BS, 69; Princeton Univ, MA, 71, PhD(chem), 75. *Prof Exp:* res scientist med chem, Cent Res Div, Pfizer Inc, 73-78. *Concurrent Pos:* Teaching asst, Princeton Univ, 69-73. *Mem:* Am Chem Soc; Sigma Xi. *Res:* Design and synthesis of novel chemical compounds as potential drugs; application of QSAR and computer methods to drug design; solid phase and combinatorial chemistry. *Mailing Add:* Glaxo Wellcome Inc PO Box 13398 Research Triangle Park NC 27709. *Fax:* 919-315-0430; *E-Mail:* eric_bigham@glaxo.com

BIGHAM, ROBERT ERIC, EARTHWORK IN CIVIL ENGINEERING. *Current Pos:* ENGR, BUCHANAN SOIL MECHS INC, 68- *Personal Data:* b Lampasas, Tex, Feb 10, 40; m 70; c 1. *Educ:* A&M Col Tex, BS, 63; Tex A&M Univ, MS, 69. *Prof Exp:* Res asst, Tex Transp Inst, 63-64; US Army officer, US Army, 64-67; self employed, 67-68. *Concurrent Pos:* Vchmn, Drainage Syst Adv Bd, Bryan, Tex, 86- *Mem:* Am Soc Civil Engrs; Int Soc Soil Mech & Found Eng. *Res:* Civil engineering earth-type materials and in computational methods; computational methods in civil engineering. *Mailing Add:* 102 Bellaire Ct Bellaire TX 77401

BIGLAND-RITCHIE, BRENDA RACHEL, HUMAN NEUROMUSCULAR PHYSIOLOGY, MOTOR CONTROL & MECHANISMS OF FATIGUE. *Current Pos:* from assoc prof to prof, 70-94, EMER PROF BIOL, QUINNIPIAC COL, 94- *Personal Data:* b Jordans, Eng, Sept 23, 27; m 51, J Murdoch; c Alasdair & Jocelyn. *Educ:* Univ London, BSc, 49, PhD(physiol), 68, DSc, 87. *Prof Exp:* Res asst physiol, Univ Col, Univ London, 49-51, asst lectr, 51-53; lectr pharmacol, Royal Free Hosp for Women, London, Eng, 55-56; res asst, Albert Einstein Col Med, 61-64; lectr biol, Lehman Col, 66-67; asst prof, Marymount Col, NY, 67-70. *Concurrent Pos:* Prin investr, NIH; NIH res grant, 71-96; assoc fel, John B Pierce Found, Conn, 79-85, fel, 85- *Mem:* Brit Physiol Soc; Am Physiol Soc Neurosci; fel Am Col Sports Med; Sigma Xi; Am Physiol Soc; Soc Neurosci. *Res:* Human motor control and mechanisms of fatigue. *Mailing Add:* Dept Pediat Yale Univ Sch Med 333 Cedar St New Haven CT 06520

BIGLER, RODNEY ERROL, NUCLEAR PHYSICS, BIOPHYSICS. *Current Pos:* asst prof biophys, Sloan-Kettering Div, 74-84, ASSOC PROF, MED COL, CORNELL UNIV, 84-, GRAD SCH MED SCI, 86- *Personal Data:* b Pocatello, Idaho, Mar 15, 41; m; c 4. *Educ:* Portland State Univ, BS, 66; Univ Tex, Austin, PhD(nuclear physics), 71. *Prof Exp:* Res assoc, Mem Sloan-Kettering Cancer Ctr, 71-73, assoc biophys, 73-82, asst mem, 82-84, asst lab mem, 84. *Concurrent Pos:* Res collabr, Brookhaven Nat Lab, 73-79, 83-; attend physicist, New York Hosp, 84- *Mem:* Health Physics Soc; Am Asn Physics Teachers; Am Phys Soc; Am Asn Physicists in Med; Soc Nuclear Med; AAAS; NY Acad Sci; Radiation Res Soc; Soc Magnetic Resonance Med; Sigma Xi. *Res:* New methods to diagnose, treat and evaluate the results of therapy directed primarily toward malignant disease; positron emission tomography, nuclear magnetic resonance and monoclonal antibodies. *Mailing Add:* 430 E 63rd St SE New York NY 10021

BIGLER, STUART GRAZIER, METEOROLOGY. *Current Pos:* RETIRED. *Personal Data:* b Johnstown, Pa, Oct 21, 27; m 50; c 5. *Educ:* Pa State Univ, BS, 52; Agr & Mech Col Tex, MS, 57. *Honors & Awards:* Spec Award, Am Meteorol Soc, 57; Dept Com Gold Medal, 70. *Prof Exp:* Assoc, Ill State Water Surv, 52-55; from res assoc to res scientist III, Tex A&M Univ, 55-59; meteorologist & head radar sferics unit, US Weather Bur, 59-64, supvr radiation systs sect, 64-70; dir, Alaska Region, Nat Weather Serv, 70-87. *Concurrent Pos:* Chmn, working group uses radar in meteorol, World Meteorol Orgn, 63-65; US Dept Com sci & tech training fel, 65-66. *Mem:* Fel Am Meteorol Soc. *Res:* Radar meteorology and cloud physics. *Mailing Add:* Nancy Lake PO Box 336 Willow AK 99688

BIGLER, WILLIAM NORMAN, BIOCHEMISTRY. *Current Pos:* PROF CHEM & DIR, CTR ADVAN MED TECHNOL, SAN FRANCISCO STATE UNIV, 81- *Personal Data:* b Oakland, Calif, Aug 29, 37; m 61; c 3. *Educ:* Univ Calif, Berkeley, AB, 60; San Jose State Col, MS, 63; Univ Colo, Boulder, PhD(biochem), 68. *Prof Exp:* Instr chem, Univ Colo, Boulder, 66-67; NIH fel, Univ Calif, Los Angeles, 68-70, actg asst prof biochem, 70; from asst prof to assoc prof chem, Rochester Inst Technol, 70-81, dir clin chem, 76-81. *Concurrent Pos:* Vis assoc prof biochem & biophys, Univ Hawaii, 77-78. *Mem:* NY Acad Sci; Am Asn Clin Chemists; AAAS; Am Chem Soc. *Res:* Biochemistry of cell division, regulatory enzymes, effects of ionizing radiation and slime molds; high pressure liquid chromatography, von Hipple-Lindau syndrome. *Mailing Add:* 1063 Yosemite Dr Pacifica CA 94044

BIGLEY, NANCY JANE, MICROBIOLOGY, IMMUNOLOGY. *Current Pos:* dept chmn & prog dir, Sch Med & Col Sci & Eng, 76-86, PROF MICROBIOL & IMMUNOL, WRIGHT STATE UNIV, 76- *Personal Data:* b Sewickley, Pa, Feb 1, 32. *Educ:* Pa State Univ, BS, 53; Ohio State Univ, MSc, 55, PhD(bact, immunol), 57. *Prof Exp:* Res assoc immunol, Ohio State Univ, 57-65, asst prof microbiol, 65-68, assoc prof, Fac Microbiol & Cellular Biol, 68-69; from assoc prof to prof microbiol, Chicago Med Sch, 69-76. *Concurrent Pos:* Am Found Microbiol lectr, 75-76. *Mem:* AAAS; Am Soc Microbiol; Am Asn Immunologists; Reticuloendothelial Soc; Sigma Xi. *Res:* Viral alterations of tissue components; autoimmunization; Rh antigen structural aspects; nucleic acid antigens; RNA-protein subfractions of Salmonella typhimurium involved in protective immunity; tumor-specific DNA-protein antigens; virus impairment of immunity; sex steroid differences in interferon production following picornavirus infection. *Mailing Add:* Dept Microbiol & Immunol Wright State Univ 3640 Colonel Glenn Hwy 002 MMB Dayton OH 45435-0001

BIGLEY, ROBERT HARRY, INTERNAL MEDICINE, GENETICS. *Current Pos:* From instr to assoc prof med, 60-75, PROF MED & MED GENETICS, SCH MED, ORE HEALTH SCI UNIV, 75- *Personal Data:* b Auburn, Wash, Aug 11, 29; m 59; c 2. *Educ:* Univ Wash, BS, 51; Univ Ore, MD, 53. *Concurrent Pos:* USPHS res fel coagulation, Med Sch, Univ Ore, 59-60. *Mem:* Am Soc Hemat; Int Soc Hemat. *Res:* Blood cell function; ascorbate metabolism. *Mailing Add:* 830 E Treasure Island Dr Allyn WA 98524

BIGLIANO, ROBERT P(AUL), ELECTRICAL ENGINEERING. *Current Pos:* Res engr, E I du Pont de Nemours Co Inc, 53-60, sr res engr, 60-63, res assoc, 64-72, res supvr, 72-74, eng mgr, 74-77, eng mgr, Du Pont Instrument Prod, 77-78, opers mgr, Far East Opers, 78-80, mgr Advan Instrument Systs, 86-89, MGR INST ENG, CLIN SYST DIV, E I DU PONT DE NEMOURS & CO, INC, 80- *Personal Data:* b New York, NY, Dec 6, 29; m 53; c 3. *Educ:* Rutgers Univ, BSEE, 51; Univ Del, MBA, 69. *Concurrent Pos:* Electronics res officer, Air Force Cambridge Res Ctr; pres, eng mgt & develop, Vicon Co. *Mem:* AAAS; Inst Elec & Electronics Engrs; Sigma Xi. *Res:* Instrument development for process control; adaptive systems for measurement and control; signal interpreting devices and systems; medical instrumentation; liquid chromatograph instrument development and marketing; computer displays for graphic arts color printing. *Mailing Add:* 2105 Gilpin Ave Wilmington DE 19806-2215

BIGLIERI, EDWARD GEORGE, INTERNAL MEDICINE, ENDOCRINOLOGY. *Current Pos:* CHIEF, ENDOCRINE METAB DIV, SAN FRANCISCO GEN HOSP, 62-, PROG DIR, CLIN STUDY CTR, 64- *Personal Data:* b San Francisco, Calif, Jan 17, 25; m 53; c 3. *Educ:* Univ San Francisco, BS, 48; Univ Calif, San Francisco, MD, 52. *Hon Degrees:* DSc, Univ S Fla, 85. *Honors & Awards:* Tigerstadt Award, Am Soc Hypertension, 87. *Prof Exp:* Intern, Med Ctr, Univ Calif, San Francisco, 52-53, resident, 53-54; resident, Vet Admin Hosp, San Francisco, 54-56; clin assoc, Nat Heart Inst, 56-58; asst res physician, Metab Unit, Univ Calif, San Francisco, 58-61, from asst prof to assoc prof, 62-71, prof med, Med Ctr, 71- *Concurrent Pos:* Vis scientist, Prince Henry's Hosp, Monash Univ, Australia, 67; consult, Clin Invest Ctr, Oak Knoll Naval Hosp, Calif, 67-76; mem coun high blood pressure res, Am Heart Asn; transatlantic lectr, British Endo Soc, 91. *Mem:* Asn Am Physicians; fel Am Col Physicians; Asn Am Physicians; Am Soc Clin Invest; Endocrine Soc; Am Soc Hypertension (pres). *Res:* Adrenal; mineralocorticoid hormones. *Mailing Add:* 129 Convent Ct San Rafael CA 94901

BIGNELL, RICHARD CARL, astronomy, for more information see previous edition

BIGRAS, FRANCINE JEANNE, STRESS PHYSIOLOGY, SEEDLING PRODUCTION. *Current Pos:* postdoctoral forestry, 88, RES SCIENTIST FORESTRY, FORESTRY CAN, 88- *Personal Data:* b Montreal, Que, Mar 13, 48; m 71; c Yannick & Christine. *Educ:* Univ Montreal, BS, 68; Laval Univ, MS, 72, PhD(plant sci), 87. *Prof Exp:* Teacher biol, Cegep de Sainte-Foy, 71-73; res asst biol, Laval Univ, 73-80, res asst plant sci, 87. *Concurrent Pos:* Vis scientist, Univ Minn, 84; adj prof, Laval Univ, 88- *Mem:* Can Soc Plant Physiol; Can Soc Hort Sci; Am Soc Hort Sci; Int Soc Hort Sci; Can-Fr Asn Advan Sci; Can Inst Forestry. *Res:* Conifer seedling production; stress physiology. *Mailing Add:* Forestry Can Que Region PO Box 3800 Sainte-Foy PQ G1V 4C7 Can. *Fax:* 418-648-5849

BIHLER, IVAN, BIOPHYSICS, ANIMAL PHYSIOLOGY. *Current Pos:* from asst prof to prof, 63-93, EMER PROF PHARMACOL & THERAPEUT, UNIV MAN, 93- *Personal Data:* b Osijek, Yugoslavia, Aug 12, 24; Can citizen; m 48, Lenka Kralj. *Educ:* Hebrew Univ, Jerusalem, MSc, 54, PhD(biochem), 57. *Honors & Awards:* Upjohn Award, Pharmacol Soc Can, 87- *Prof Exp:* Asst biochem, Hebrew Univ, Jerusalem, 53-58. *Concurrent Pos:* Fel pharmacol, Univ Rochester, 58-59; fel biochem, Washington Univ, 59-61; Imp Chem Indust res fel, Univ Edinburgh, 61-63; career investr, Med Res Coun, Can, 64-93. *Mem:* Am Soc Pharmacol & Exp Therapeut; Pharmacol Soc Can; NY Acad Sci; Can Biochem Soc; Int Soc Heart Res; Biochem Soc London. *Res:* Mechanisms of cell membrane permeability and its regulation; membrane transport of sugars in intestine and muscle; effect of drugs and hormones. *Mailing Add:* Dept Pharmacol & Therapeut Univ Man Winnipeg MB R3E 0W3 Can. *Fax:* 204-783-6915

BIHOVSKY, RON H(ANS), MEDICINAL CHEMISTRY, SYNTHETIC ORGANIC CHEMISTRY. *Current Pos:* SR SCIENTIST, CEPHALON INC, 92- *Personal Data:* b Ithaca, NY, Nov 9, 48; m 85, Anita J Weisberger; c Michael & Eric. *Educ:* State Univ NY, Stony Brook, BS, 70; Univ Calif, Berkeley, PhD(chem), 77. *Prof Exp:* Chemist, Entomol Res Div, USDA, 71-72; NIH fel, Univ Wis-Madison, 78-80; asst prof chem, State Univ NY, Stony Brook, 80-88; scientist, Berlex Labs, 87-92. *Mem:* Am Chem Soc. *Res:* Synthesis of medicinal compounds; peptides and enzyme inhibitors; heterocyclic compounds; peptide mimetics. *Mailing Add:* Cephalon Inc 45 Brandywine Pkwy West Chester PA 19380-4245. *Fax:* 610-344-0065

BIJOU, SIDNEY WILLIAM, DEVELOPMENTAL PSYCHOLOGY, CLINICAL PSYCHOLOGY. *Current Pos:* DISTINGUISHED PROF PSYCHOL, UNIV NEV, 93- *Personal Data:* b Baltimore, Md, Nov 12, 08; m 34, Tobias; c Robert K & Judith A. *Educ:* Univ Fla, BS, 33; Columbia Univ, MA, 36, Univ Iowa, PhD(psychol), 41. *Honors & Awards:* G Stanley Hall Award Child Develop Am Psychol Asn, 80, Edgar A Doll Award Mental Retardation, 84, Don Hake Award Basic Behav Res, 92; Career Res Sci Award, Am Acad Mental Retardation, 80. *Prof Exp:* Psychologist, Del State Hosp & Mental Health Clin, 37-39; res child psychologist, Wayne Co Training Sch, 41-42 & 46-47; asst prof psychol, Ind Univ, 46-48; prof & dir, Inst Child Develop, Univ Wash, 48-65; prof & dir, Child Behav Lab, Univ Ill, 65-75. *Concurrent Pos:* Fel, Harvard Univ, 61-62; consult, Nat Asn Retarded Citizens, 65-88, Portage Proj Early Childhood Educ, 73-; pres, Div Child Develop, Am Psychol Asn, 65-66; emer adj prof psychol, Spec Educ & Rehab, Univ Ariz, 75-93; bd mem, Intermountain Ctrs Human Develop, 77-, Desert Survivors, 82-92; Nat Adv Comt Mental Retardation Res, Univ Kans, 90- *Mem:* Am Psychol Asn; Asn Behav Analysts (pres, 77-78); Am Asn Univ Prof; Psychonomic Soc; Soc Res Child Develop; Am Psychol Soc; Am Asn Appl & Prev Psychol. *Res:* Theory and research relating to normal and deviant human development from a natural science perspective; study of language development and autistic behavior in young children. *Mailing Add:* 3313 Skyline Blvd Reno NV 89509-5658. *Fax:* 702-784-1126; *E-Mail:* swb@scs.unr.edu

BIKALES, NORBERT M, MATERIALS SCIENCE, POLYMER CHEMISTRY. *Current Pos:* dir, Polymers Prog, 76-95, HEAD, EUROP OFF, NSF, 95- *Personal Data:* b Berlin, Ger, Jan 7, 29; nat US; m 51, Gerda; c Marguerite & Edward. *Educ:* City Col, BS, 51; Polytech Inst Brooklyn, MS, 56, PhD(chem), 61. *Honors & Awards:* Great Medal, City of Paris, France, 85; Chevalier des Palmes Academiques, France, 93. *Prof Exp:* Res chemist, Am Cyanamid Co, 51-62; tech dir, Gaylord Assoc, Inc, 62-65; consult chem, 65-76; prof chem & dir continuing educ sci, Rutgers Univ, NB, 73-79. *Concurrent Pos:* Ed, Encycl Polymer Sci & Technol, 62-77; polymer workshop dir, Fairleigh Dickinson Univ, 66-68; adj prof, Upsala Col & consult to trustees, Columbia Univ & Strickman Found, 67-73; mem, Comt Lead Paints, Nat Acad Sci, 72-74, adv bd, J Polymer Sci, 78- & bd dirs, EPS Div, Soc Plastics Engrs, 79-82; titular mem & comn secy, Macromolecular Div, Int Union Pure & Appl Chem, 77-87, chmn, Working Party Recycling Polymers, 93-; ed bd, Encyclopedia Polymer Sci & Eng, 82-; chmn, Polymer Div, Am Chem Soc, 83, counr, 87-90; vis sr scientist, Ctr Res Macromolecules, Strasbourg, France, 84; chmn, Polymer Conf, Gordon Res Conf, 85, counr, 85-88, Bd Trustees, 90-; distinguished lectr, Soc Polmer Sci, Japan, 86; adv bd, J Appl Polymer Sci, 89-; sci counr, Polymer Group, France, 94- *Mem:* Fel AAAS; sr mem Soc Plastics Engrs; Am Chem Soc; fel NY Acad Sci; fel Am

Phys Soc; Mat Res Soc; hon mem Polish Chem Soc. *Res:* Polymer synthesis, reactions, and properties; chemical modification of natural polymers; water-soluble polymers; materials research; polymer education; international scientific cooperation. *Mailing Add:* NSF Europ Off Am Embassy 2 Ave Gabriel Paris 75008 France. *Fax:* 33 1 43 12 29 04; *E-Mail:* nbikales@nsf.gov

BIKERMAN, MICHAEL, GEOCHRONOLOGY. *Current Pos:* asst prof, 67-71, ASSOC PROF GEOL & PLANETARY SCI, UNIV PITTSBURGH, 71- *Personal Data:* b Berlin, Ger, July 30, 34; US citizen; m 56, Viola Odler; c Jennifer, David & Tania. *Educ:* Queens Col, NY, BS, 54; NMex Inst Mining & Technol, BS, 56; Univ Ariz, MS, 62, PhD(geol), 65. *Prof Exp:* Instr sci & eng, Ft Lewis Agr & Mech Col, 56-57; assayer, Holly Minerals, Cinnabar Mine, Idaho, 57; instr sci, Boise Jr Col, 58-60; asst geochem, geochronology lab, Univ Ariz, 63-65; asst prof geol, Wichita State Univ, 65-67. *Concurrent Pos:* Res assoc, Carnegie Mus Natural Hist, 79- *Mem:* Fel Geol Soc Am; Geochem Soc; AAAS. *Res:* Isotope geology and geochronology of volcanic rocks; isotope geology and geochronology of metamorphic terranes; history of Appalachian epeirogeny. *Mailing Add:* Dept Geol & Planetary Sci Univ Pittsburgh Pittsburgh PA 15260. *Fax:* 412-624-3914; *E-Mail:* bikerman@vms.cis.pitt.edu

BIKIN, HENRY, PHARMACEUTICAL CHEMISTRY. *Current Pos:* RETIRED. *Personal Data:* b Chicago, Ill, Oct 7, 18; m 43; c 2. *Educ:* Purdue Univ, BS, 40, MS, 48, PhD(pharmacy), 50. *Prof Exp:* Hosp pharmacist, Univ Hosp, Univ Mich, 40-41; pharmaceut chemist, Burroughs Wellcome & Co, 41-43; lab asst, Purdue Univ, 47-48; pharmaceut chemist, Eli Lilly & Co, 49-57; mgr pharmaceut develop & prod, Corvel, Inc, 57-67; res scientist, Eli Lilly & Co, 67-79. *Mem:* AAAS; fel Am Inst Chem; Am Chem Soc; Am Pharmaceut Asn. *Res:* Incompatibilities; stabilities of liquid products; tablet products; formulations; stabilities; manufacturing trouble shooter. *Mailing Add:* 109 Longhorn Trail Kerrville TX 78028-9495

BIKLE, DANIEL DAVID, INTERNAL MEDICINE, BIOCHEMISTRY. *Current Pos:* dir, Spec Diag & Treat Unit, Univ Calif-Vet Admin Med Ctr & asst prof med, 80-86, assoc prof med, 86-91, PROF MED, UNIV CALIF, SAN FRANCISCO, 91- *Personal Data:* b Harrisburg, Pa, Apr 25, 44; m 65, Elizabeth Wanneo; c 2. *Educ:* Harvard Univ, AB, 65; Univ Pa, MD, 69, PhD(biochem), 74. *Honors & Awards:* Henderson Mem Prize in Biochem; Baldwin Luckie Mem Prize; Horatio C Wood Prize in Pharmacol; Spencer Morris Prize. *Prof Exp:* Clin fel internal med, Peter Bent Brigham Hosp, 69-71; res internist internal med & biochem, Letterman Army Inst Res, 74-80. *Mem:* AAAS; Am Soc Clin Invest; Endocrinol Soc; Am Soc Bone & Mineral Res; Asn Am Physicians; Am Soc Clin Nutrit; Am Col Physicians. *Res:* Mechanism of action of Vitamin D; metabolic bone disease; keratinocyte differentiation treatment of breast cancer with vitamin D. *Mailing Add:* Dept Med Univ Calif-Vet Admin Med Ctr 4150 Clement San Francisco CA 94121. *Fax:* 415-750-6929; *E-Mail:* doctor@itsa.ucsf.edu

BIKOFF, ELIZABETH K, MAJOR HISTOCOMPATIBILITY ANTIGENS. *Current Pos:* SR RES FEL, DEPTS CELLULAR, DEVELOP BIOL, BIOCHEM & MOLECULAR BIOL, HARVARD UNIV, 92-, TUTOR BIOCHEM SCI, DEPT BIOCHEM & MOLECULAR BIOL, 93- *Personal Data:* b Cleveland, Ohio, Feb 28, 48. *Educ:* Univ Cincinnati, BS, 69; Columbia Univ, PhD(biol sci), 75. *Prof Exp:* Res fel, Dept Biochem & Biophys, Univ Calif Sch Med, San Francisco, 75-76; fel, Div Tumor Immunol, Sidney Farber Cancer Inst, Harvard Med Sch, 76-79; asst prof, Dept Microbiol & Immunol, Albert Einstein Col Med, 79-81; asst prof, Dept Obstet, Gynec & Reproductive Sci & Dept Microbiol, Mt Sanai Sch Med, NY, 81-92. *Concurrent Pos:* Helen Hay Whitney fel, 75-78; Cancer Res Inst fel, 78-79; assoc ed, J Immunol, 93. *Res:* T-cell recognition of immunoglobulin antigens; assembly and intracellular transport of products of the Major Histocompatibility Gene Complex; regulations of expression of Major Histocompatibility antigens during fetal development; contributed numerous articles to publications. *Mailing Add:* Dept Cell & Develop Biol-Biochem & Molecular Biol Harvard Univ Biol Labs 16 Divinity Ave Cambridge MA 02138. *Fax:* 617-496-6770

BILAN, M VICTOR, FOREST PHYSIOLOGY, ECOLOGY. *Current Pos:* from asst prof to assoc prof forestry, 57-66, prof tree physiol & ecol, 67-73, distiguished prof, 73-84, REGENTS PROF TREE PHYSIOL & ECOL, STEPHEN F AUSTIN STATE UNIV, 84- *Personal Data:* b Ukraine, June 6, 22; US citizen; m 57; c 4. *Educ:* Univ Munich, BS, 49; Duke Univ, MF, 54, DF, 57. *Prof Exp:* Res asst forest biol, Duke Univ, 53-57. *Concurrent Pos:* NSF travel grant, Austria, 61, res grant, 62-66; Nat Acad Sci/NSF exchange scientist, Bulgaria & Romania, 74. *Mem:* Soc Am Foresters; Ecol Soc Am; Sigma Xi; Am Inst Biol Sci. *Res:* Effect of environment on root growth; root-shoot growth correlation; seed production; growth and development of southern pines; moisture relations in trees, drought resistance. *Mailing Add:* 1100 Northwood Circle Nacogdoches TX 75961

BILANIUK, LARISSA TETIANA, NEURORADIOLOGY, MAGNETIC RESONANCE IMAGING. *Current Pos:* resident, Univ Pa, 66-67 & 68-71, assoc, 72-74, from asst prof to assoc prof, 74-82, PROF RADIOL, SCH MED, UNIV PA, 82- *Personal Data:* b Ukraine, July 15, 41; US citizen; m 64, Myron Oleksa; c Larissa Jr & Laada. *Educ:* Wayne State Univ, BA, 61, MD, 65; Am Bd Radiol, radiol specialty dipl, 71. *Honors & Awards:* St Goran lectr, Karolinska Inst, Stockholm, 84. *Prof Exp:* Intern, Philadelphia Gen Hosp, 65-66. *Concurrent Pos:* Res fel, Cancer Res Ctr, Heidelberg, Ger, 67-68; NIH fel, 68-69 & 70-71; clin fel, Am Cancer Inst, 69-70; trainee, Armed Forces Inst Path, Washington, DC, 70; Rothschild Ophthal Found fel, Paris, 72 & 80; vis prof, Univ Cattolica, Rome, 82, Grosshadern Clin, Univ Munich, Ger, 88 & Santiago, Chile, 93; mem, Radiol Study Group Res Grants, NIH, 83-86. *Mem:* Ukrainian Med Asn NAm; Radiol Soc NAm; fel Am Col Radiol; Sigma Xi; Am Soc Neuroradiol; Europ Soc Neuroradiol. *Res:* Computed tomography and magnetic resonance imaging in the diagnosis and treatment of brain tumors. *Mailing Add:* Dept Radiol Children's Hosp Philadelphia Philadelphia PA 19104-4345. *Fax:* 215-590-4127

BILANIUK, OLEKSA-MYRON, NUCLEAR & SUBNUCLEONIC STRUCTURE. *Current Pos:* from assoc prof to Swarthmore Centennial prof physics, 64-91, SWARTHMORE CENTENNIAL EMER PROF, SWARTHMORE COL, 91- *Personal Data:* b Ukraine, Dec 15, 26; US citizen; m 64, Larissa Zubal; c Larissa Jr & Laada. *Educ:* Univ Louvain, Cand Eng, 49; Univ Mich, BSE, 52, MS, 53, AM, 54, PhD(physics), 57. *Prof Exp:* Instr, Univ Mich, 57-58; asst prof physics, Univ Rochester, 59-64. *Concurrent Pos:* Vis scientist, Arg Atomic Energy Comn, 62-63; NSF sci fac fel, Max Planck Inst, Heidelberg, 67-68 & Univ Paris, Orsay, 72; Fulbright scholar, Lima, Peru, 71, Kinshasa, Zaire, 75, Rabat, Morocco, 78; Nat Acad Sci exchange scholar, Kiev, Ukraine, 76; vis scientist, Institut de Physique Nucleaire, Orsay, France, 80, Laboratori Nazionali di Frascati, Italy, 84 & Univ Munchen, Garching, Ger, 88, Inst Theor Physics, Kiev, Ukraine, 94 & Inst Med Radiol, Kharkiv, Ukraine, 96; assoc ed, Am J Physics, 84-87. *Mem:* Am Phys Soc; Europ Phys Soc; Sigma Xi; Ukrainian Acad Arts & Sci in US; foreign mem Nat Acad Sci Ukraine. *Res:* Nuclear spectroscopy; nuclear and hyper-nuclear reaction mechanisms; possibility of existence of superluminal quanta. *Mailing Add:* Dept Physics Swarthmore Col Swarthmore PA 19081-1397. *Fax:* 610-328-8260

BILBAO, MARCIA KEPLER, RADIOLOGY. *Current Pos:* CHIEF RADIOL, VET ADMIN MED CTR, GRAND JUNCTION, COLO, 82- *Personal Data:* b Rochester, Minn, Jan 14, 31; m 54; c 3. *Educ:* Univ Minn, Minneapolis, BS, 52; Columbia Univ, MD, 57; Am Bd Radiol, dipl, 62. *Honors & Awards:* Janeway Prize, Col Physicians & Surgeons, Columbia Univ, 57; Award of Merit, Am Women's Med Asn, 57; Cert of Merit, AMA, 68. *Prof Exp:* From instr to prof radiol, Med Sch, Univ Ore, 61-82. *Concurrent Pos:* Consult, Kaiser Permanaente Clin, 61-63. *Res:* Diagnostic radiology; gas contrast radiography; gastrointestinal radiography. *Mailing Add:* Vet Admin Med Ctr Dept Radiol 2121 North Ave Grand Junction CO 81501

BILD, RICHARD WAYNE, ANALYTICAL NUCLEAR CHEMISTRY, METEORITICS. *Current Pos:* mem tech staff anal chem, 78-87, sr mem tech staff radiation physics & hot cell applns, 87-93, SR MEM TECH STAFF NAT TRANSURANIC WASTE PROG, SANDIA NAT LABS, 93- *Personal Data:* b Washington, DC, June 17, 46; m 74, Karen L Robinson; c David. *Educ:* Calif Inst Technol, BS, 68; Univ Calif, Los Angeles, PhD(chem), 76. *Honors & Awards:* R F Bunshah Award, Am Vacuum Soc, 85. *Prof Exp:* Mem staff cosmochem, Max Planck Inst Nuclear Physics, 76-77; res assoc exp geochem, Lunar & Planetary Lab, Univ Ariz, 77-78. *Mem:* Meteoritical Soc; Am Nuclear Soc; Am Chem Soc. *Res:* Radio and nuclear analytical chemistry; analytical geochemistry; hot cell operations and applications; transuranic waste programs. *Mailing Add:* Dept 6801 MS 1335 Sandia Nat Labs PO Box 5800 Albuquerque NM 87185-1335. *Fax:* 505-848-0881; *E-Mail:* rwbild@sandia.gov

BILDERBACK, DAVID EARL, PLANT TISSUE CULTURE. *Current Pos:* from asst prof to assoc prof, 72-78, chmn dept, 83-88, PROF BOT, UNIV MONT, MISSOULA, 78-, ASSOC DEAN, COL ARTS & SCI, 88- *Personal Data:* b Salem, Mass, Nov 27, 43; m 70; c 2. *Educ:* Univ Ore, Eugene, BS, 65, PhD(biol), 68. *Prof Exp:* Vis asst prof, dept bot, Univ Mont, Missoula, 68-69; NIH fel, AEC Plant Res Lab, Mich State Univ, 69-70; vis asst prof, dept biol, Univ Ore, Eugene, 70-71 & dept bot sci, Univ Calif, Los Angeles, 71-72. *Mem:* Bot Soc Am; Am Soc Plant Physiologists; Sigma Xi. *Res:* Growth and development of vascular plants. *Mailing Add:* Col Arts & Sci Univ Mont Missoula MT 59812-0001

BILDERBACK, DONALD HEYWOOD, ENGINEERING PHYSICS. *Current Pos:* oper mgr, Cornell High Energy Synchrotron Source, 277 Wilson Lab, 78-83, staff scientist, 83-89, ASSOC DIR, CORNELL UNIV, 90-, ASSOC ADJ PROF APPL & ENG PHYSICS, 90- *Personal Data:* b Usumbura, Africa, March 6, 47; US citizen; m 69, Rebecca Belcher; c Douglas. *Educ:* Seattle Pac Univ, BS, 69; Purdue Univ, MS, 72, PhD(physics), 75. *Honors & Awards:* Lark-Horowitz Prize, 75; R&D 100 Award, 93. *Prof Exp:* Res mgr, X-ray Facil, Mat Sci Ctr, 75-78. *Concurrent Pos:* Pres, Multiwire Lab Ltd, NY, 81- *Mem:* Am Crystallog Asn; Am Phys Soc; AAAS. *Res:* Field of x-ray diffraction; synchrotron radiation research and two-dimensional area detectors; x-ray optics (wide bandpass monochromators, transmission and reflection x-ray mirrors, micro x-ray beams). *Mailing Add:* 2024 Slaterville Rd Ithaca NY 14850. *Fax:* 607-255-9001; *E-Mail:* dhb2@cornell.edu

BILDSTEIN, KEITH LOUIS, behavioral ecology, ornithology, for more information see previous edition

BILELLO, JOHN CHARLES, METALLURGY, MATERIALS SCIENCE. *Current Pos:* PROF MAT SCI ENG & APPL PHYSICS, UNIV MICH, ANN ARBOR, 89- *Personal Data:* b Brooklyn, NY, Oct 15, 38; m 59; c 3. *Educ:* NY Univ, BMetE, 60, MS, 62; Univ Ill, PhD(metall), 65. *Prof Exp:* Res engr, Gen Tel & Electronics Labs, Inc, 65-68; asst prof eng, State Univ NY, Stony Brook, 68-71, from assoc dean to dean, Col Eng & Appl Sci, 76-77, prof eng, 71-86; dean, Col Eng & Comput Sci, Calif State Univ, Fullerton, 86-89. *Concurrent Pos:* NATO sr fac fel, 73; vis prof, Enrico Fermi Ctr Nuclear Studies, Milan, 74; consult eng, NAm Philips Corp, 75-81, Brookhaven Nat

Lab, 78-86, NATO Sr Fac Exchange, Oxford Univ, Eng, 85-90. *Mem:* Am Inst Mining, Metall & Petrol Engrs; fel Am Soc Metals; Am Phys Soc; Sigma Xi; Mat Res Soc. *Res:* Synchrotron x-ray diffraction topography imaging; dislocation mechanisms of yielding, work hardening and fracture of ionic, semiconductor and metallic crystals; thin film processing; multilayer materials; high resolution diffraction. *Mailing Add:* 3646 W Huron River Dr Ann Arbor MI 48103-9489

BILELLO, MICHAEL ANTHONY, METEOROLOGY, CLIMATOLOGY. *Current Pos:* RETIRED. *Personal Data:* b NY, Oct 24, 24; m 51; c 5. *Educ:* Univ Wash, BS, 50; McGill Univ, MSc, 72. *Honors & Awards:* Ann Grad Award, Can Asn Geogr, 73; US-Latin Am Coop Sci Award, NSF, 75. *Prof Exp:* Meteorologist, Hydrol Sect, US Weather Bur, 51-54 & Northern Hemisphere Map Unit, 54-55, Nat Weather Anal Ctr, 55-56; meteorologist, Snow, Ice & Permafrost Res Estab, US Army Corps Engrs 56-68, res meteorologist, Geophys Sci Br, Cold Regions Res & Eng Lab, 68-82; consult, Sci & Technol Corp, 85-94. *Concurrent Pos:* Vis instr, Dartmouth Col, 64, instr glaciol sem, 68; original cataloging, Baker Lib, Dartmouth Col, 83-84; researcher river ice mgt, Ice Eng Facil, Cold Regions Res & Eng Lab, 85. *Mem:* Am Meteorol Soc; Can Geog Soc. *Res:* Meteorology and climatology in association with physical properties of snow cover; formation, growth, and decay of sea, lake and river ice; special projects on cold regions environmental research. *Mailing Add:* 2285 E Roosevelt Ave Salt Lake City UT 84108-2313

BILES, CHARLES MORGAN, MATHEMATICS. *Current Pos:* assoc prof, 69-77, PROF MATH, HUMBOLDT STATE UNIV, 77- *Personal Data:* b Yakima, Wash, Nov 29, 39; c 3. *Educ:* St Martin's Col, BS, 61; Univ Ariz, MS, 64; Univ NH, PhD(math), 69. *Prof Exp:* Instr math & chem, St Martin's Col, 64-66. *Concurrent Pos:* Mem, Comt Alliance for Progress, US Dept Com. *Mem:* Am Math Soc; Math Asn Am; Consortium Math & Appln Proj; Resource Modeling Asn (treas, 86-). *Res:* Mathematical modeling of microbial systems and renewable resource systems. *Mailing Add:* Dept Math Humboldt State Univ Arcata CA 95521-8299

BILES, JOHN ALEXANDER, PHARMACEUTICAL CHEMISTRY. *Current Pos:* from asst prof to prof, 52-57, PROF PHARMACEUT CHEM, UNIV SOUTHERN CALIF, 57-, DEAN, SCH PHARM, 68-, JOHN STAUFFER DEAN'S CHAIR, 88- *Personal Data:* b Del Norte, Colo, May 4, 23; m 43; c 2. *Educ:* Univ Colo, BS, 44, PhD(chem), 49. *Honors & Awards:* Lehn & Fink Gold Medal, 45. *Prof Exp:* Asst chem, Univ Colo, 44-47, instr pharm, 47-48, asst chem, 48-49; prof pharmaceut chem, Midwestern Univ, 49-50; asst prof pharm, Ohio State Univ, 50-52. *Concurrent Pos:* Mem bd dirs, Marion Merrell Dow, Kansas City, MO; mem, educ comt, Nat Assoc Retail Druggists; mem bd dirs, exec comt, Am Found Pharmaceut Educ. *Mem:* Fel Am Pharmaceut Asn; fel Acad Pharmaceut Sci; fel Am Asn Pharmaceut Sci; Am Asn Hosp Pharmacists; Am Asn Col Pharm (pres, 90-91). *Res:* Pharmaceutical economics; education, health care delivery systems. *Mailing Add:* Dept Pharmaceut Scis Univ Southern Calif 1985 Zonal Ave Seventh Fl Los Angeles CA 90089

BILES, ROBERT WAYNE, TOXICOLOGY. *Current Pos:* Toxicologist, Exxon Corp, 78-81, sr toxicologist, 81-83, staff toxicologist, 83-87, SR STAFF TOXICOLOGIST, SECT HEAD CHEM TOXICOL, 84-, MKT TECH SERVS, EXXON CO USA, HOUSTON. *Personal Data:* b West Palm Beach, Fla, Oct 9, 47; m 73; c 3. *Educ:* Univ Calif, Santa Barbara, BA, 70; San Diego State Univ, MS, 74; Univ Tex Med Br Galveston, PhD(environ toxicol), 78. *Concurrent Pos:* Lectr, Sch Pub Health, Columbia Univ, 79- & Rutgers Univ, 81- *Mem:* Soc Occup & Environ Health. *Res:* Biomedical, toxicological research and consultation. *Mailing Add:* Exxon USA 800 Bell St Houston TX 77002

BILES, W(ILLIAM) R(OY), CHEMICAL ENGINEERING, PROCESS CONTROL. *Current Pos:* PRES & CHIEF ENGR, W R BILES & ASSOCS, INC, 70- *Personal Data:* b Cincinnati, Ohio, Dec 20, 23; m 45; c 3. *Educ:* Univ Cincinnati, BS, 49; Pa State Univ, MS, 52, PhD(chem eng), 54. *Prof Exp:* Supvr chem prod, Am Cyanamid Co, 49-51; res chem engr, Houston Res Lab, Shell Oil Co, 54-56, group leader eng res, 56-58, group leader math & comput, 58-60, exchange scientist, Royal Dutch/Shell Lab, Amsterdam, 60-61, asst to mgr mfg res, NY, 61-62, sr technologist, 62-63, coordr comput process control, 64-69; vpres, Davis Comput Systs, Inc, 69-70. *Mem:* Am Inst Chem Engrs; Am Chem Soc; Instrument Soc Am; Inst Elec & Electronics Engrs; Am Oil Chem Soc. *Res:* Computer control of batch and continuous processes and factories.; economic evaluation and justification of applications; development of new techniques and application of standard techniques to new fields; distillation. *Mailing Add:* 6161 Savoy Suite 500 Houston TX 77036-3316

BILGER, HANS RUDOLF, RINGLASERS. *Current Pos:* from asst prof to assoc prof, 63-75, PROF ELEC ENG, OKLA STATE UNIV, 75- *Personal Data:* b Singen, Ger, May 17, 35; m 58, Edda Goemer; c Martin, Eva, Monika, Burkhard & Andrea. *Educ:* Univ Basel, PhD(solid state physics), 61. *Prof Exp:* Res assoc solid state physics, Univ Basel, 61-62; res assoc digital comput sci, Univ Ill, Urbana-Champaign, 62-63; vis scientist, Argonne Nat Lab, 65-67. *Concurrent Pos:* Res fel, Nuclear Res Ctr, Ger, 69-70; res assoc, Calif Inst Technol, 73-74; vis prof, Univ Sci & Technol, Montpellier, France, 76-78; consult, 81-; Erskine fel, Canterbury Univ, NZ, 86 & 90. *Mem:* Am Phys Soc; Am Asn Univ Profs; Sigma Xi. *Res:* Noise in semiconductors; resolution in germanium nuclear radiation detectors; space charge limited devices; ring lasers; ion implantation and backscattering; very low frequency noise; precision thermostats. *Mailing Add:* Okla State Univ 310 ES Stillwater OK 74078-5032. *Fax:* 405-744-7554; *E-Mail:* bilger@ceat.okslak.edu

BILGUTAY, NIHAT MUSTAFA, DIGITAL SIGNAL PROCESSING, COMMUNICATIONS. *Current Pos:* Drexel fel elec eng, Col Eng, Drexel Univ, 81-82, vis asst prof, 82-83, asst prof, 83-87, asst dept head, 89-90, assoc prof, 87-92, ASSOC DEAN ENG, COL ENG, DREXEL UNIV, 90-, PROF ELEC ENG, 92- *Personal Data:* b Ankara, Turkey, Mar 31, 52; US citizen; m 77, Kathleen Evans; c Canan, Aylin & Deniz. *Educ:* Bradley Univ, BS, 73; Purdue Univ, MS, 75, PhD(elec eng), 81. *Concurrent Pos:* Mem, Exec Comt, Educ Soc, Inst Elec & Electronics Engrs, 84-88, chmn, Philadelphia Sect. *Mem:* Sr mem Inst Elec & Electronics Engrs; Am Soc Nondestructive Testing; Am Soc Eng Educ; Sigma Xi. *Res:* Industrial and medical ultrasonic testing; digital signal processing; radar detection; imaging. *Mailing Add:* Col Eng Drexel Univ Philadelphia PA 19104-9984. *Fax:* 215-895-5811; *E-Mail:* bilgutay@ece.drexel.edu

BILHORN, JOHN MERLYN, ELECTROCHEMICAL ENGINEERING, BATTERY RESEARCH & ENGINEERING. *Current Pos:* SR ENG MGR, ENERGY RES CORP, 82- *Personal Data:* b Hillsdale, Mich, Apr 4, 26; m 48, Lois Hanselman; c J David, Daniel P, Debra (Towns), Doris (Simpson) & Delores (Kessenich). *Educ:* Cornell Univ, BS, 49, MS, 89; Northern Baptist Theol Sem, BD, 54, MDiv, 73. *Honors & Awards:* Young Scientist Award, Bausch & Lomb, 43. *Prof Exp:* Res engr, Pure Oil Co, 49-51; pastor, Mayfield Congregational Church, Sycamore, Ill, 54-62; mat engr mgr, Rayovac Corp, 61-75; proj mgr, Yardney Elec Corp, 75-82. *Concurrent Pos:* Pastor, Fulton Congregational Church, Edgerton, Wis, 62-75, Road Meetinghouse (First Congregational), Stonington, Conn, 75- *Mem:* Am Inst Chem Engrs; Am Sci Affil. *Res:* Research and development of nickel based batteries including machinery materials interface, plant design, start-up, quality control, profit and loss statements and forecasts. *Mailing Add:* 210 W Rollin St Edgerton WI 53534

BILIMORIA, KARL DHUNJISHAW, NAVIGATION GUIDANCE & CONTROL OF AEROSPACE VEHICLES, FLIGHT DYNAMICS. *Current Pos:* res specialist, Sterling Fed Systs Group, 94-96, AEROSPACE ENGR, AMES RES CTR, NASA, 96- *Personal Data:* b Bombay, India, June 27, 60; US citizen. *Educ:* Indian Inst Technol, BTech, 82; Va Polytech Inst & State Univ, MS, 84, PhD(aerospace eng), 86. *Prof Exp:* Asst prof aerospace eng, Ariz State Univ, 87-91, res scientist, 91-93, vis asst prof, 93-94. *Concurrent Pos:* Mem, Atmospheric Flight Mech Tech Comt, Am Inst Aeronaut & Astronaut, 95- *Mem:* Assoc fel Am Inst Aeronaut & Astronaut. *Res:* Flight vehicle dynamics, control and optimization; advanced guidance and control systems for supersonic transport aircraft; free flight concepts for future air traffic management systems; published numerous articles. *Mailing Add:* NASA Ames Res Ctr MS 262-3 Moffett Field CA 94035

BILIMORIA, MINOO HORMASJI, MICROBIOLOGY, BIOCHEMISTRY. *Current Pos:* biochemist, 68-72, SR RES SCIENTIST, IMP TOBACCO LTD, 72- *Personal Data:* b Barkhera, India, Aug 24, 30; m 67, Katy K Sadri; c Darius & Cyrus. *Educ:* Univ Bombay, BSc, 52, MSc, 54; Indian Inst Sci, PhD(microbiol), 63. *Prof Exp:* Microbiologist & chemist, Geoffrey Manners & Co Ltd, India, 54-58; res asst microbiol, Indian Inst Sci, Bangalore, 60-63; fel biochem, Sch Med, Duke Univ, 64-67. *Concurrent Pos:* Vis scientist, Path Inst, McGill Univ, Montreal, Can, 75- *Mem:* Can Biochem Soc; Indian Soc Biol Chem; Can Soc Microbiologists; NY Acad Sci; Environ Mutagen Soc; Am Soc Microbiol. *Res:* Thermophilic bacilli, microbial pectolytic enzymes; microsomal electron transport; L-asparaginases; biological effects of tobacco smoke inhalation; aryl hydrocarbon hydroxylase; mutagenic activity of chemicals and tobacco smoke in microbial systems, chemical and enzymatic treatment of tobacco to reduce biological activity. *Mailing Add:* 5210 Westmore Montreal PQ H4V 1Z5 Can

BILJETINA, RICHARD, NATURAL GAS UTILITY RESEARCH & DEVELOPMENT. *Current Pos:* From mem staff to mgr res & develop, 69-89, asst vpres, 89-92, VPRES PROD TECHNOL RES & DEVELOP, INST GAS TECHNOL, CHICAGO, 92-, VPRES GAS INDUST PROGS, DES PLAINES. *Personal Data:* b Austria, Apr 2, 47; US citizen; m 69, Mary P McCarthy; c Eric & Christine. *Educ:* Ill Inst Technol, BSCE, 69; Univ Chicago, MBA, 74. *Honors & Awards:* Gas Indust Res Award, Am Gas Asn, 96. *Mem:* Int Asn Energy Economists. *Res:* Longer term research and development needs of the gas industry; advanced combustion, cooling, distribution, storage and transportation. *Mailing Add:* Inst Gas Technol 1700 S Prospect Rd Des Plaines IL 60018. *Fax:* 847-768-0516; *E-Mail:* biljet@igt.org

BILLEN, DANIEL, MICROBIOLOGY. *Current Pos:* prof biol & dir, Oak Ridge Grad Sch Biomed Sci, Univ Tenn, 74-77, dir, Inst Radiation Biol, 77-80, prof, 74-88, EMER PROF BIOMED SCI, UNIV TENN, KNOXVILLE, 88- *Personal Data:* b New York, NY, Nov 27, 24; m 51, Eleanor Berlin; c Rhonda, Jerry & Robin. *Educ:* Cornell Univ, BS, 48; Univ Tenn, MS, 49, PhD(microbiol), 51. *Prof Exp:* Instr microbial metab, Univ Tenn, 50-51; res biologist radiobiol, Oak Ridge Nat Lab, 51-57; assoc prof, Post Grad Sch Med, Univ Tex, 57-60, biologist & prof biol & chief sect radiation biol, Univ Tex M D Anderson Hosp & Tumor Inst, 60-66; prof radiation biol & mem dept microbiol, biochem and radiol, Col Med, Univ Fla, 66-73. *Concurrent Pos:* Prog dir metab biol prog, NSF, 60-61, consult, Career Develop Rev Br, NIH, 66-70, consult radiation study sect, 69-73; ed, Microbios J & Cytobios J; hon ed, Photochem & Photobiol J, 71-73; mem, Cancer Res Manpower Rev Comt, Nat Cancer Inst, 77-80; ed-in-chief, Radiation Res, 79-88. *Mem:* Am Soc Microbiol; Radiation Res Soc. *Res:* Microbial physiology, biochemistry and cytology; radiobiology; microbiological genetics; DNA repair and replication. *Mailing Add:* 1087 W Outer Dr Oak Ridge TN 37830

BILLENSTIEN, DOROTHY CORINNE, ANATOMY. *Current Pos:* RETIRED. *Personal Data:* b Easton, Pa, Feb 27, 21. *Educ:* Boston Univ, BS, 42; Univ Colo, MS, 51, PhD(anat), 56. *Prof Exp:* From instr to asst prof anat, Albert Einstein Col Med, 56-61; from asst prof to assoc prof anat, Colo State Univ, 61-80. *Mem:* Am Asn Anatomists; Am Soc Zoologists. *Res:* Neurosecretion; neuroendocrinology. *Mailing Add:* 4821 Skyline Dr Ft Collins CO 80526

BILLER, JOSE, CEREBROVASCULAR DISEASES. *Current Pos:* PROF & CHMN, DEPT NEUROL, IND UNIV SCH MED, 94- *Personal Data:* b Montevideo, Uruguay, Jan 18, 48; US citizen; m 72; c 3. *Educ:* A V Acevedo Inst, Uruguay, BS, 65; Univ Repub Sch Med, MD, 74; Am Bd Psychiat & Neurol, cert neurol, 82. *Prof Exp:* Resident, Maciel Hosp, Pub Health Ministry, 74-76, Henry Ford Hosp, 77-78, Loyola-Univ & Hines Vet Admin Hosp, 78-79, chief resident, Loyola Univ, 79-80; fel cerebrovasc, Bowman Gray Sch Med, Wake Forest Univ, 80-81, instr neurol, 81; asst prof neurol, Stritch Med Sch, Loyola Univ, 82-84; from asst prof to assoc prof, Univ Iowa Col Med, 84-89, prof neurol, 90-91; staff physician, Northwestern Mem Hosp, 91-94. *Concurrent Pos:* Fel, Stroke Coun, Am Heart Asn, 81; lectr, Cash Co Sch Med, 83-; reviewer, J Archives Neurol & Stroke, 83-, Cerebrovasc Dis, J Stroke & Cerebrovasc Dis, 83-; consult, Neurol Serv, Vet Admin Hosp, Iowa City, 84-; prin investr, Heparinoid study, NIH Grant, Univ Iowa, 85-89, magnetic resonance imaging, 87-89. *Mem:* Fel Am Heart Asn; fel Am Acad Neurol; Am Neurol Assoc; Am Med Asn; Am Soc Neurol Invest; InterAm Col Physicians & Surgeons. *Res:* Cerebrovascular disease, its clinical aspects and therapeutic interventions. *Mailing Add:* Dept Neurol Emerson Hall Rm 125 Ind Univ Sch Med 545 Barnhill Dr Indianapolis IN 46202-5124

BILLERA, LOUIS JOSEPH, DISCRETE GEOMETRY, ALGEBRAIC COMBINATORICS. *Current Pos:* Asst prof opers res, 68-73, assoc prof opers res & math, 73-79, PROF OPERS RES & MATH, CORNELL UNIV, 80- *Personal Data:* b New York, NY, Apr 12, 43; m 64; c 2. *Educ:* Rensselaer Polytech Inst, BS, 64; City Univ New York, MA, 67, PhD(math), 68. *Concurrent Pos:* NSF fel math, Hebrew Univ, Israel, 69; vis res assoc, Brandeis Univ, 74-75; vis prof, Univ Cath Louvain, Belg, 80; prof math, Rutgers Univ, 85-89. *Mem:* Am Math Soc; Soc Indust & Appl Math; Math Asn Am. *Res:* Algebraic methods for combinatorial problems arising in geometry; convex polytopes; multivariate splines. *Mailing Add:* Cornell Univ White Hall Ithaca NY 14853-7901

BILLESBACH, DAVID P, BRILLOUIN & RAMAN SPECTROSCOPY, FERROELECTRICS. *Current Pos:* Res assoc, 88-90, vis asst prof, Dept Physics & Astron, 90- 91, RES ASST PROF, CTR LASER ANALYTICAL STUDIES TRACE GAS DYNAMICS, UNIV NEBR, 91- *Personal Data:* b Hastings, Nebr, May 22, 56. *Educ:* Univ Nebr, BS, 79, MS, 82, PhD(physics), 87. *Mem:* Am Phys Soc; Sigma Xi. *Res:* Experimental studies of structural phase transitions in solids especially brillouin scattering and birefringence; use of tunable diode lasers for the detection of trace gases in the atmosphere especially methane. *Mailing Add:* Dept Elec Eng 201 N WSEC Univ Nebr Lincoln NE 68588-0511

BILLETTE, JACQUES, CARDIAC PHYSIOLOGY, ELECTROPHYSIOLOGY. *Current Pos:* from asst prof to assoc prof, 74-87, PROF PHYSIOL, UNIV MONTREAL, 87- *Personal Data:* b Valleyfield, Que, Can, Aug 8, 40; m 79, Plamondon Lise; c Francois, Patrick, Isabelle, Marie-Helene & Oliver. *Educ:* Univ Montreal, MD, 66, PhD(physiol), 72; Can Med Coun, LMCC, 67. *Prof Exp:* Intern med, Montreal Gen Hosp, 66-67; Med Res Coun fel physiol, Univ Montreal, 67-71, lectr, 71-72; Med Res Coun fel physiol, Univ Amsterdam, 72-74. *Concurrent Pos:* Med Res Coun scholar, Univ Montreal, 74-79. *Mem:* Am Physiol Soc; Am Heart Asn; Int Soc Heart Res; Can Cardiovasc Soc; Can Physiol Soc; Can Biomed Eng Soc. *Res:* Electrophysiology of the atrioventricular node in the heart; definition of the nodal functional properties and the establishment of their cellular counterparts; rhythmic and arrhythmic responses generated by the node. *Mailing Add:* Dept Physiol Fac Med Univ Montreal CP6128 Montreal PQ H3C 3J7 Can

BILLHEIMER, FOSTER E, CELL BIOLOGY, ELECTRON MICROSCOPY. *Current Pos:* PROF BIOL, CALIFORNIA UNIV, PA, 69- *Personal Data:* b Drums, Pa, June 24, 36; m 59; c 3. *Educ:* Pa State Univ, BS, 59; Univ Tex, BA, 66; Rutgers Univ, PhD(cell biol), 69. *Prof Exp:* Teacher gen sci, Newburgh, NY, 62-65; teaching asst, Rutgers Univ, 66-69. *Concurrent Pos:* NSF fel, Acad Yr Inst, Univ Tex, 65-66; co-dir, Electron Micros Inst, 78; sr staff mem, NSF Pre-Col Teacher Develop Prog, 78-79. *Mem:* Am Soc Cell Biol; Am Soc Microbiol; Sigma Xi. *Res:* Heterotrophic nutrition and ultrastructure of the acidophilic bacterium Thiobacillus ferrooxidans; the relationship of mitochondrial DNA to mitochondrial function; cloning of cyanobacterial genes. *Mailing Add:* Dept Biol & Environ Sci Calif Univ Pa 250 Univ Ave California PA 15419-1394

BILLHEIMER, JEFFREY THOMAS, ENZYMOLOGY, LIPID METABOLISM. *Current Pos:* prin investr, 84-89, sr res biochemist, 89-93, PRIN RES BIOCHEMIST, E I DUPONT, INC, 94- *Personal Data:* b Huntington, WVa, Oct 31, 46; m 72; c Doron M, Ryan E & Aaron J. *Educ:* Purdue Univ, BS, 68; NC State Univ, Raleigh, PhD(biochem), 75. *Prof Exp:* Fel, Cornell Univ, 75-77 & Univ Mo-Columbia, 77-79; asst prof biochem, Drexel Univ, 79-84. *Mem:* Am Soc Biochem & Molecular Biol; Am Heart Asn. *Res:* Membrane-bound enzymes involved in cholesterol (sterol) metabolism in health and disease and the regulation of these enzymes: intracellular transport of lipids especially by cytosolic carrier proteins (sterol carrier protein); hypocholesterolemics; antiatherosclerotic agents. *Mailing Add:* 1618 E Lafayette Dr West Chester PA 19382. *Fax:* 302-695-8210

BILLICA, HARRY ROBERT, CHEMISTRY & PHYSICS OF MAN-MADE FIBERS. *Current Pos:* RETIRED. *Personal Data:* b Spokane, Wash, July 14, 19; m 46; c 3. *Educ:* Univ NC, BS, 41; Univ Wis, PhD(org chem), 48. *Prof Exp:* Shift supvr, Exp Sta, E I du Pont de Nemours & Co, 41-42, chemist, 42-47, res chemist, 47-50, group leader, Tech Sect, Nylon Plant, Tenn, 50-51, tech supvr, Dacron Polyester Fiber Plant, NC, 51-59, res mgr, Fiber Surface Res Sect, Textile Fibers Dept, 59-80. *Concurrent Pos:* Fiber Soc lectr, 70-71; chmn fiber sci, Gordon Res Conf, 73; consult fiber sci, 80-; lectr fiber sci, prof develop courses, 80- *Mem:* Fiber Soc (pres, 76); Textured Yarn Asn Am. *Res:* Chemical warfare; protective clothing; high pressure catalysis; hydrogenation; polymerization; catalyst development; synthetic fibers; physics and chemistry of fiber and film surfaces; polymer morphology; consulting in areas of synthetic fiber production and processing; emphasis on fiber processing finishes; polymer, fiber and fabric character, uniformity and interrelationships. *Mailing Add:* 2364 Scenic Hill Dr Spring Hill FL 23606-7012

BILLIG, FRANKLIN A, ORGANIC CHEMISTRY, SCIENCE EDUCATION. *Current Pos:* RETIRED. *Personal Data:* b Los Angeles, Calif, Feb 11, 23; m 57, Tetsuko Morinaga; c Patricia A K (Harvey). *Educ:* Univ Southern Calif, AB, 54; Kansai Gakuen Univ, Japan, MS, 67. *Prof Exp:* Res chemist, Am Potash & Chem Corp, 54-58, sr res chemist, 58-64; supvr chem labs, Univ Southern Calif, 64-75, mgr labs, 75-92, safety officer, Dept Chem, 73-92, mgr hazardous chem waste, 84-92. *Concurrent Pos:* Consult, Environ Health & Lab Safety; fel, L Pasteur Inst Advan Med Studies. *Mem:* Fel Am Inst Chemists; Am Chem Soc; fel AAAS; Sigma Xi. *Res:* Organometallics; science education techniques; theoretical organic chemistry; reduction and detoxification of hazardous waste; infrared spectra organic sulfur compounds; organoboron compounds synthesis. *Mailing Add:* Dept Chem Univ Southern Calif Los Angeles CA 90089-1062

BILLIG, FREDERICK S(TUCKY), MECHANICAL ENGINEERING. *Current Pos:* PRES & CHMN BD, PYRODYNE INC, 77- *Personal Data:* b Pittsburgh, Pa, Feb 28, 33; m 55, Margaret R Pelicano; c Linda Ann (Baumer), Donna Marie (Barten), Frederick Thomas & James Richard. *Educ:* Johns Hopkins Univ, BE, 55; Univ Md, MS, 58, PhD(mech eng), 64. *Honors & Awards:* Silver Medal, Combustion Inst, 70; Pioneer Award, Nat Aerospace Plane, 89; Hugh Dryden Lectr Res, Am Inst Aeronaut & Astronaut, 92; M M Bondarvk Award, USSR Acad Sci, 95. *Prof Exp:* Assoc engr, Appl Physics Lab, Johns Hopkins Univ, 55-58, sr engr, 58-63, proj supvr hypersonic propulsion, 64-73, prin prof staff, 65, supvr submarine physics, 77-84, asst supvr, Aeronaut Div, 77-78, chief scientist & assoc supvr, Aero Appl Physics Lab, 84-96. *Concurrent Pos:* Mem comt aeroballistics, Naval Bur Ord, 57-59; lectr, Univ Md, 65, mem grad fac, 67-91; US chmn & vpres, Int Airbreathing Propulsion Comt; mem sci adv bd, USAF, 88-92; lectr, Purdue Univ, 88- *Mem:* Nat Acad Eng; fel Am Inst Aeronaut & Astronaut; Combustion Inst. *Res:* Hypersonic aerodynamics; thermodynamics; boundary layers; heat transfer and applied research; design and development work on subsonic and supersonic combustion ramjet engines and propulsion test facilities. *Mailing Add:* 11280 Panorama Dr New Market MD 21774. *Fax:* 301-865-6028; *E-Mail:* pyrodyne@aol.com

BILLIGHEIMER, CLAUDE ELIAS, ORDINARY DIFFERENTIAL EQUATIONS. *Current Pos:* from asst prof to prof math, 66-96, EMER PROF MATH, MCMASTER UNIV, 96- *Personal Data:* b Breslau, Ger, Nov 25, 30; Can citizen; m 55. *Educ:* Univ Melbourne, BA, 52, BSc, 53, MA, 58; Univ Toronto, PhD(math), 66. *Prof Exp:* Lectr math, Royal Mil Col, Canberra, 55-57; res officer statist, Commonwealth Sci & Indust Res Orgn, Australia, 58; lectr math, Australian Nat Univ, 59-61 & Univ Toronto, 62-66. *Concurrent Pos:* Nat Res Coun Can grant, 69-; mem bd gov, Maimonides Col, Can, 75 & McMaster Univ, Can, 90. *Mem:* Sigma Xi; Am Math Soc; Can Math Soc; Australian Math Soc; Soc Indust & Appl Math; AAAS. *Res:* Mathematical analysis; ordinary differential equations; differential and difference operations; spectral theory; eigenfunction expansions; differential operators in Banach algebras; functional analysis; mathematical physics. *Mailing Add:* 42 Sterling St Hamilton ON L8S 4A7 Can

BILLINGHAM, EDWARD J, JR, ANALYTICAL CHEMISTRY. *Current Pos:* from asst prof to prof, 65-87, EMER PROF CHEM, UNIV NEV, LAS VEGAS, 88- *Personal Data:* b Lebanon, Pa, Dec 6, 34; m 58, Betty J Black. *Educ:* Lebanon Valley Col, BS, 56; Pa State Univ, PhD(chem), 61. *Prof Exp:* Assoc prof chem & chmn dept, Thiel Col, 60-65. *Mem:* Am Chem Soc. *Res:* Thermometric precipitation processes in both aqueous and fused salt media, including determination of thermodynamic properties as well as analytical implications; trace metal determinations. *Mailing Add:* 6169 Shawnee Las Vegas NV 89107-2551

BILLINGHAM, RUPERT EVERETT, CELL BIOLOGY, IMMUNOLOGY. *Current Pos:* prof & chmn dept, 71-86, EMER PROF CELL BIOL, UNIV TEX HEALTH SCI CTR, DALLAS, 90- *Personal Data:* b Warminster, Eng, Oct 15, 21; m 51; c 3. *Educ:* Oxford Univ, BA, 43, MA, 47, DPhil(zool), 50, DSc(zool), 57. *Hon Degrees:* DSc, Trinity Col, Conn, 65. *Honors & Awards:* Alvarenga Prize, Am Col Physicians, 63; Hon Award, Am Asn Plastic Surgeons, 64. *Prof Exp:* Lectr zool, Univ Birmingham, 47-51; hon res assoc, Univ Col, Univ London, 51-57; prof zool, Univ Pa, 57-71, prof med genetics & chmn dept, Sch Med, 65-71, dir, Henry Phipps Inst Med Genetics, 65-71. *Mem:* Fel Royal Soc; fel Am Acad Arts & Sci; Am Asn Immunologists; Soc Develop Biol; Am Fertil Soc. *Res:* Biology and immunology of transplantation; immunobiology of mammalian reproduction; wound healing and regeneration. *Mailing Add:* Rte 3 Box 86P Vineyard Haven MA 02568-9802

BILLINGS, CHARLES EDGAR, JR, AEROSPACE MEDICINE, ENVIRONMENTAL PHYSIOLOGY. *Current Pos:* from instr prev med to prof prev med, physiol & aviation, 60-73, mem fac, 80-83, EMER PROF, DEPT PREV MED, OHIO STATE UNIV, 83-, RES SCIENTIST, INDUST & SYSTS ENG, 92- *Personal Data:* b Boston, Mass, June 15, 29; m 55, Lillian Wilson; c Lee E. *Educ:* NY Univ, MD, 53; Ohio State Univ, MSc, 60. *Honors & Awards:* Boothby Res Award, Aerospace Med Asn, 73, Tamisea Mem Award, 80; Laura Taber Barbour Mem Medal Aviation Safety, 81; NASA Outstanding Leadership Medal, 81, 90; Jeffrey Aerospace Med Res Award, Am Inst Aeronaut & Astronaut, 86. *Prof Exp:* Resident physician, Univ Vt, 57-58; res med officer, Aviation Safety Res Off, NASA Ames Res Ctr, 73-76, chief, 76-80, asst chief res, Man-Vehicle Systs Res Div, 80-84, sr scientist, 84-89, chief scientist, 90-92. *Concurrent Pos:* Consult, Webb Assocs, 60-73; med consult, Beckett Aviation Corp, 62-73 & US Army, 64-77; tech consult, Fed Aviation Agency, 63-66, mem med adv comt, 66-70; mem comt hearing, acoust & biomech, Nat Acad Sci-Nat Res Coun, 65-69 & 75-; clin prof prev med & aviation, Ohio State Univ, 73-83, emer prof, 83-; Ames fel, 90; consult. *Mem:* Fel Aerospace Med Asn; fel Am Col Prev Med; fel Am Acad Occup Med; Int Acad Aviation & Space Med; fel Royal Aeronaut Soc; assoc fel Am Inst Aeronaut & Astronaut. *Res:* Effects of environmental stress on man's ability to perform in the work environment, particularly the flight environment; sources and prevention of human error in complex human-machine systems. *Mailing Add:* 1372 Hickory Ridge Lane Columbus OH 43235

BILLINGS, CHARLES EDGAR, OCCUPATIONAL HEALTH ENGINEERING, AEROSOL SCIENCE. *Current Pos:* ASSOC PROF, FLA STATE UNIV, 85- *Personal Data:* b Boston, Mass, May 26, 25; m 56; c 2. *Educ:* Northeastern Univ, BSME, 50; Harvard Univ, ScM, 53; Calif Inst Technol, PhD(environ health eng), 66. *Prof Exp:* Asst prof occup hyg, Harvard Sch Pub Health, 53-61, assoc prof, 62-64; res assoc aerosol sci, Calif Inst Technol, 64-66; assoc prof occup hyg, Univ Mich, 66-67; dept mgr, GCA Corp, Mass, 68-70; pres, Environ Eng Sci, 70-77; assoc prof environ sci, Johns Hopkins Univ, 77-85. *Concurrent Pos:* Air pollution spec fel, USPHS, US Dept Health, Educ & Welfare, 62-66. *Mem:* AAAS; Am Indust Hyg Asn; Brit Occup Hyg Soc; Health Physics Soc; Sigma Xi; Am Asn Aerosol Res; Air Pollution Control Asn. *Res:* Development of morphology of aerosol particle aggregates in accumulation processes; contaminant control technology; occupational hygiene. *Mailing Add:* Dept Poli Sci Fla State Univ 570 Bellamy Bldg Tallahassee FL 32306-2049

BILLINGS, MARLAND PRATT, engineering geology, petrography; deceased, see previous edition for last biography

BILLINGS, R GAIL, BIOPHYSICS, BIOMEDICAL ENGINEERING. *Current Pos:* res & develop engr, 90-94, VPRES, NEW BUSINESS DEVELOP, UTAH MED PROD, INC, 94-; DIR RES, MEDICA CORP, 97- *Personal Data:* b Orem, Utah, Apr 12, 34; m 57; c 5. *Educ:* Univ Utah, BS, 56, PhD(biophysics), 75; Utah State Univ, MS, 65. *Prof Exp:* Res engr telemetry, Lockheed Aircraft Corp, 56-58; electronics engr flight simulator, US Air Force, Hill AFB, 58-59; instrumentation engr, Marquardt Corp, 59-62; eng mgr, Thiokol Chem Corp, 62-69; res engr, Space Data Corp, 69-70; res investr heart res, Primary Children's Med Ctr, 74-76; res & develop mgr med comput, Tenet Info Systs, Inc, 76-90. *Concurrent Pos:* Nat Inst Gen Med Sci fel, 70-74. *Mem:* Inst Elec & Electronics Engrs. *Res:* Medical data processing; computer diagnosis; waveform processing. *Mailing Add:* In Medica Develop Corp 2069 Donelson Lane Salt Lake City UT 84117

BILLINGS, RONALD J, DENTISTRY. *Current Pos:* DIR, EASTMAN DENT CTR, ROCHESTER, NY. *Mailing Add:* Eastman Dent Ctr 625 Elmwood Ave Rochester NY 14620

BILLINGS, WILLIAM DWIGHT, BOTANY, ECOLOGY. *Current Pos:* from assoc prof to prof, 52-67, JAMES B DUKE PROF BOT, DUKE UNIV, 67- *Personal Data:* b Washington, DC, Dec 29, 10; m 58. *Educ:* Butler Univ, AB, 33; Duke Univ, AM, 35, PhD(bot), 36. *Hon Degrees:* DSc, Butler Univ, 55. *Honors & Awards:* Cert of Merit, Bot Soc Am, 60; Mercer Award, Ecol Soc Am, 62, Distinguished Serv Award, 81, Eminent Ecologist Award, 91. *Prof Exp:* Instr bot, Univ Tenn, 36-37; from instr to prof biol, Univ Nev, 38-52, head dept, 50-52. *Concurrent Pos:* Ed, Ecol, Ecol Soc Am, 51-56 & Ecol Monogr, 68, 69; Fulbright res scholar, Univ NZ, 59; ed, Ecol Studies, 74-93; res fel, Australian Nat Univ, 77. *Mem:* AAAS; Am Soc Naturalists; hon mem Brit Ecol Soc; Bot Soc Am; Ecol Soc Am (vpres, 60, pres, 78-79); fel Am Acad Arts & Sci. *Res:* Effect of geologic substratum on plant growth and distribution; desert, arctic and alpine ecology; physiological ecology; ecology of ecological races; environment especially carbon dioxide in biosphere. *Mailing Add:* 1628 Marion Ave Durham NC 27705-5809

BILLINGSLEY, MELVIN LEE, NEUROTOXICOLOGY, MOLECULAR NEUROBIOLOGY. *Current Pos:* PROF PHARMACOL & DIR CORE FACIL, PA STATE UNIV COL MED, 84- *Personal Data:* b Pittsburgh, Pa, Oct 31, 53; m 91, Elizabeth Magill; c Tyler, Chelsea & Andrew. *Educ:* Univ Pittsburgh, BS, 74; George Washington Univ, PhD(pharmacol), 81. *Prof Exp:* Pharmacologist, ICI Americas, 75-77; fel, Yale Univ Sch Med, 81-82; staff fel, NIH-Nat Heart, Lung & Blood Inst, 82-84. *Concurrent Pos:* Int Life Sci Inst fel, 86. *Mem:* AAAS; Am Soc Biochem & Molecular Biol; Am Soc Pharmacol & Exp Therapeut; Soc Neurosci; Sigma Xi. *Res:* Expression of neuronal genes; protein phosphorylation in nervous tissue; genetic factors which cause predisposition to nervous system damage; metal toxicity; synaptic proteins. *Mailing Add:* Dept Pharmacol Pa State Univ Hershey Med Ctr Hershey PA 17033-0850. *Fax:* 717-531-5013

BILLINGSLEY, PATRICK PAUL, MATHEMATICS. *Current Pos:* asst prof statist, 58-62, assoc prof math & statist, 62-67, PROF MATH & STATIST, UNIV CHICAGO, 67- *Personal Data:* b Sioux Falls, SDak, May 3, 25; m 53; c 5. *Educ:* US Naval Acad, BS, 48; Princeton Univ, MA, 52, PhD(math), 55. *Prof Exp:* NSF fel, Princeton Univ, 57-58. *Concurrent Pos:* Vis prof, Copenhagen Univ, 64-65; ed, Ann Probability, 76-79. *Mem:* Am Math Soc; fel Inst Math Statist. *Res:* Probability theory; stochastic process theory. *Mailing Add:* Dept Statist & Math Univ Chicago Chicago IL 60637

BILLINGTON, DAVID PERKINS, STRUCTURAL ENGINEERING. *Current Pos:* vis lectr, Princeton Univ, 58-60, assoc prof, 60-64, prof civil eng, 64-96, GORDON Y S WU PROF ENG, PRINCETON UNIV, 96- *Personal Data:* b Bryn Mawr, Pa, June 1, 27; m 51, Phyllis Bergquist; c David Jr, Elizabeth (Fox), Jane (Billington-Flucker), Philip, Stephen & Sarah. *Educ:* Princeton Univ, BSE, 50. *Hon Degrees:* LHD, Union Col, 90; DSc, Grinnell Col, 91. *Honors & Awards:* Dexter Prize, Soc Hist Technol, 79; Dana Award, Innovation in Educ, Charles Dana Found, 90. *Prof Exp:* Struct engr, Roberts & Schaefer Co, 52-60. *Concurrent Pos:* Mem del vis engrs, USSR, 58; NSF sci fac fel, Univ Delft, 66-67; visitor, Inst Advan Studies, 74-75 & 77-78; Andrew D White prof-at-large, Cornell Univ, 87-93; Fulbright fel, Belg, 50-52. *Mem:* Nat Acad Eng; Am Concrete Inst; Soc Hist Technol; Am Soc Civil Engrs. *Res:* Thin shell concrete structures; concrete cooling towers; relationship between structure and architecture; history and aesthetics of structures; life and works of Robert Maillart; design of bridges. *Mailing Add:* Dept Civil Eng Princeton Univ Princeton NJ 08544

BILLINGTON, DOUGLAS S(HELDON), materials science, inorganic chemistry; deceased, see previous edition for last biography

BILLINTON, ROY, ELECTRICAL ENGINEERING. *Current Pos:* from asst prof to assoc prof, 64-71, head dept, 76-84, PROF ELEC ENG, UNIV SASK, 71-, ASSOC DEAN GRAD STUDIES & RES, COL ENG, 86- *Personal Data:* b Leeds, Eng, Sept 14, 35; Can citizen; m 56; c 5. *Educ:* Univ Man, BScEE, 60, MSc, 63; Univ Sask, PhD(elec eng), 67. *Hon Degrees:* DSc, Univ Sask, 76. *Honors & Awards:* Sir George Nelson Award, Eng Inst Can, 65 & 67, Ross Medal, 72; Outstanding Power Eng Educr Award, Inst Elec & Electronics Engrs, 92, McNaughton Gold Medal Award, 94. *Prof Exp:* Staff engr, Man Hydro, 60-62, cost control engr, 62-64. *Concurrent Pos:* Spec lectr, Univ Man, 63-64; mem, Appl Probability Subcomt, Inst Elec & Electronics Engrs, 64-, Power Syst Eng Comt, 72-, Distrib Reliability Comt, Can Elec Asn, Consult Comt Outstage Statist, 75-; chmn, Power Syst Reliability Subsect, Can Elec Asn, 65-80 & 85-95, Appl Probability Methods Subcomt, Inst Elec & Electronics Engrs, 76-79, Power Syst Planning & Opers Sect, Can Elec Asn, 78-80, Eng & Oper Div, 80-82, Consult Comt Outstage Statist, 84- *Mem:* Can Elec Asn; fel Inst Elec & Electronics Engrs; fel Royal Soc Can; fel Eng Inst Can; fel Safety & Reliability Soc UK. *Res:* Power system analysis pertaining to operation and planning; reliability engineering, particularly power system reliability; author of several publications in field. *Mailing Add:* Dept Elec Eng Univ Sask Saskatoon SK S7N 5A9 Can

BILLMAN, FRED RICHARD, MECHANICAL METALLURGY, PHYSICAL METALLURGY. *Current Pos:* qual assurance metallurgist, Ti Forgings, Alcoa-Cleveland Works, 69-70, sr res eng, Fabricating Metall Div, 71-76, sr res eng, Ingot Casting Div, 77-78, TECH SPECIALIST RAPID SOLIDIFICATION & POWDER METALL FABRICATION PROCESSES, FABRICATING TECHNOL DIV, ALCOA LABS, 79- *Personal Data:* b El Paso, Tex, Apr 20, 43; m 66; c 3. *Educ:* Univ Tex, El Paso, BS, 65; Ohio State Univ, MS, 67. *Prof Exp:* Metallurgist ingot plant, Alcoa-Rockdale Works, 67-68; res scientist oxidation, Battelle-Metal Sci Group, 68-69. *Mem:* Am Soc Metals; Sigma Xi. *Res:* Rapid solidification; powder metallurgy; aluminum and titanium forging processes; ingot casting process development. *Mailing Add:* 52 Greenview Dr Jeannette PA 15644

BILLMAN, GEORGE EDWARD, CARDIOVASCULAR PHYSIOLOGY, AUTONOMIC NEUROPHYSIOLOGY. *Current Pos:* from asst prof to assoc prof, 84-96, PROF, OHIO STATE UNIV, 96- *Personal Data:* b Ft Worth, Tex, July 23, 54; m 75, Rosemary C Gieske; c George T & Elyse T. *Educ:* Xavier Univ, BS, 75; Univ Ky, PhD(physiol & biophys), 80. *Prof Exp:* Res assoc, Health Sci Ctr, Univ Okla, 80-82, asst prof res, 82-84. *Concurrent Pos:* Prin investr, Am Heart Asn grant, 82-84, new investr award, NIH, 83-86; consult, Glaxo Inc, 89-90; prin investr, NIH ROI grant, 86-90, NIDA ROI grant, 90-94 & F Hoffman LaRoche Contract, 90-, Hoechst Marion Roussel Contract, 94-, Merck Inc Contract, 96- *Mem:* Am Physiol Soc; Am Heart Asn; Sigma Xi. *Res:* Neural control of cardiovascular system especially control during exercise; regulation of coronary blood flow; mechanisms responsible for cardiac arrhythmias; cardiovascular effects of cocaine. *Mailing Add:* Dept Physiol Ohio State Univ 302 Hamilton Hall 1645 Neil Ave Columbus OH 43210-1239. *Fax:* 614-292-4888; *E-Mail:* billman.1@osu.edu

BILLMAN, JOHN HENRY, ORGANIC CHEMISTRY. *Current Pos:* from instr to prof, 39-78, EMER PROF ORG CHEM, IND UNIV, BLOOMINGTON, 78- *Personal Data:* b Brooklyn, NY, Feb 8, 12; m 37; c 2. *Educ:* Univ Va, BS, 34; Princeton Univ, AM, 35, PhD(chem), 37. *Prof Exp:* Instr org & inorg chem, Univ Ill, 37-39. *Concurrent Pos:* Vis lectr, Yale Univ, 46-47; prof, Univ Del, 58; consult, US Dept Health, Educ & Welfare, Am Viscose Corp & New Castle Prod; mem Pharmacol & Endocrinol Fel Panel; civilian investr, Off Sci Res & Develop. *Mem:* Am Chem Soc. *Res:* Pharmaceutical chemistry; organic synthesis; organic analytical reagents; compounds for use as plant stimulants; antitumor and antiviral agents; catalysis; amino acids. *Mailing Add:* RRO 1 10850 Main Rd East Marion NY 11939-9717

BILLMAN, KENNETH WILLIAM, STRATEGIC DEFENSE SYSTEMS & ELECTRO-OPTICS, LASERS & ENERGY SYSTEMS. *Current Pos:* chief scientist, 89-93, MGR, STRATEGIC DEFENSE SYSTS GROUP, LOCKHEED MISSILES & SPACE CO, INC, 93- *Personal Data:* b Covington, Ky, Jan 9, 33; m 54; c 4. *Educ:* Thomas More Col, AB, 55; Univ Cincinnati, MS, 58, PhD(physics), 59. *Prof Exp:* Instr physics, Univ Cincinnati, 57-59; from instr to asst prof, Mass Inst Technol, 59-67; staff physicist, Electronics Res Ctr, NASA, 67-70, staff physicist, Ames Res Ctr, 70-72, asst chief phys gas-dynamics & lasers br, 72-77, advan proj group leader, 77-79; fusion proj mgr, Elec Power Res Inst, 79-83; sr scientist, Titan Systs, Inc, 84-85, mgr, Bay Area Photonics Off. *Concurrent Pos:* Adj prof physics, Colo State Univ, 75-82. *Mem:* Am Phys Soc. *Res:* Inertial confinement fusion; orbiting mirrors for terrestrial energy supply; power transmission via laser; laser energy conversion; laser induced chemistry; isotope separation and development; space power; laser development and application; strategic defense; particle beam and laser defense weapon systems. *Mailing Add:* 1942 Limetree Lane Mountain View CA 94040

BILLMEYER, FRED WALLACE, JR, POLYMER CHEMISTRY, COLOR SCIENCE. *Current Pos:* prof, 64-84, EMER PROF CHEM, RENSSELAER POLYTECH INST, 84- *Personal Data:* b Chattanooga, Tenn, Aug 24, 19; m 51, Annette Trzcinski; c 3. *Educ:* Calif Inst Technol, BSc, 41; Cornell Univ, PhD(phys chem), 45. *Honors & Awards:* Bruning Award, Fed Soc Coatings Tech, 77; Macbeth Award, Inter-Soc Color Coun, 78, Nickerson Serv Award, 83, Godlove Award, 93; Award of Merit, Am Soc Testing & Mat, 90. *Prof Exp:* Res chemist, Plastics Dept, E I Du Pont de Nemours & Co, Inc, 45-57, res assoc, 57-64. *Concurrent Pos:* lectr, Univ Del, 52-64; vis prof, Mass Inst Technol, 60-61. *Mem:* Fel AAAS; Am Chem Soc; Inter-Soc Color Coun (pres, 69-70, secy, 70-82); fel Optical Soc Am; fel Am Phys Soc; fel Am Soc Testing Mat. *Res:* Molecular structure of polymers; color science and technology; optical properties of plastics. *Mailing Add:* 1294 Garner Ave Schenectady NY 12309-5746. *Fax:* 518-377-9511

BILLO, EDWARD JOSEPH, INORGANIC CHEMISTRY, ANALYTICAL CHEMISTRY. *Current Pos:* asst prof, 69-74, ASSOC PROF CHEM, BOSTON COL, 75- *Personal Data:* b Brantford, Ont, Aug 3, 38; m 61; c 3. *Educ:* McMaster Univ, BSc, 61, MSc, 63, PhD(chem), 67. *Prof Exp:* Res assoc, Purdue Univ, 67-69. *Mem:* Am Chem Soc. *Res:* Solution equilibria of transition metal chelates; kinetics of fast reactions of metal chelates. *Mailing Add:* Dept Chem Boston Col Chestnut Hill MA 02167-3809. *E-Mail:* joseph.billo@bc.edu

BILLS, CHARLES WAYNE, ORGANIC CHEMISTRY. *Current Pos:* RETIRED. *Personal Data:* b Meeker, Colo, Nov 6, 24; m 47, June A Paules; c 3. *Educ:* Colo Agr & Mech Col, BS, 47; Univ Colo, MS, 52, PhD(chem), 54. *Prof Exp:* Analyst, Los Alamos Sci Lab, Univ Calif, 47, org chem & radiochem synthesis, 48-50; asst, Univ Colo, 50-52, qual anal, 53; res chemist corrosion, Prod Res Dept, Stanolind Oil & Gas Co, 54-55 & Mallinckrodt Chem Works, Mo, 55-56; chief geochem & geophys, Res & Develop Br, US AEC, Colo, 56-58, nuclear chemist, Chem Separations Br, Hanford Opers Off, Wash, 58-59, dep dir, Health & Safety Div, Nat Reactor Testing Sta, Idaho Opers, 59-62, dir, Nuclear Technol Div, 62-74, asst mgr prod & tech support, Idaho Opers, Energy Res & Develop Admin, 74-77; asst to gen mgr, EG&G Serv, Inc, 77-81, vpres & mgr bus admin, 81-86. *Concurrent Pos:* Princeton Univ fel pub affairs, 62-63; ex-officio dir, Eastern Idaho Nuclear Indust Coun, 66-85 & Intermountain Sci Experience Ctr, Inc, 73-85. *Mem:* Am Chem Soc. *Res:* Aluminum stearates; geochemistry of uranium; processing nuclear power reactor fuels; transuranic and fission product recovery; nuclear reactor operations, safety and technology; geothermal, solar and low head hydroelectric technology; radioactive waste management; organizational development. *Mailing Add:* 1090 E 21st St Idaho Falls ID 83404

BILLS, DANIEL GRANVILLE, VACUUM PHYSICS. *Current Pos:* pres & chmn bd dirs, 54-88, CHMN & CHIEF EXEC OFFICER, GRANVILLE-PHILLIPS CO, 88- *Personal Data:* b Wenatchee, Wash, Sept 8, 24; m 45; c 3. *Educ:* Wash State Univ, BS, 49, MS, 51; Harvard Univ, PhD(physics), 57. *Prof Exp:* Instr physics, Wash State Univ, 55-57, asst prof, 57-60. *Mem:* Am Phys Soc; hon mem Am Vacuum Soc (treas, 67-70, pres, 72). *Res:* Surface physics; physical electronics; ultrahigh vacuum. *Mailing Add:* 460 Lipan Way Boulder CO 80303

BILLS, DONALD DUANE, FOOD SCIENCE. *Current Pos:* RETIRED. *Personal Data:* b Hillsboro, Ore, Dec 4, 32; m 56; c 4. *Educ:* Ore State Univ, BS, 59, MS, 64, PhD(food sci), 66. *Prof Exp:* From asst prof to prof food sci & technol, Ore State Univ, 65-75; chief, Plant Prod Lab, USDA, 75-96. *Mem:* Am Chem Soc; Phytochem Soc; Am Potato Asn; Sigma Xi; Inst Food Technologists. *Res:* Trace components in foods, food safety, plant biochemistry. *Mailing Add:* USDA ARS 214 Bldg 003 Beltsville MD 20705

BILLS, JAMES LAVAR, INORGANIC CHEMISTRY. *Current Pos:* From asst prof to assoc prof, 62-77, PROF CHEM, BRIGHAM YOUNG UNIV, 77- *Personal Data:* b Murray, Utah, Aug 4, 35; m 58; c 3. *Educ:* Univ Utah, BS, 58; Mass Inst Technol, PhD(inorg chem), 63. *Mem:* Am Chem Soc; Sigma Xi. *Res:* Theoretical interpretations of molecular properties. *Mailing Add:* 1720 W 1400 N Provo UT 84604-2266

BILLS, JOHN LAWRENCE, CHEMISTRY. *Current Pos:* mgr corp develop, 64-79, VPRES CORP STUDIES & PROG, KERR-MCGEE CORP, 79- *Personal Data:* b Moore, Idaho, July 11, 20; m 46, Dayle Alldredge; c Linda (Gee), Janet (deceased), Judy (Istook), Cheryl (Jaffa), Cynthia (Lords), Lori (Whipple) & Diane (Ricks). *Educ:* Stanford Univ, AB, 42, PhD(chem), 47. *Prof Exp:* Res chemist, Union Oil Co, Calif, 44-46, 47-49, group leader, 49-52; instr chem, Stanford Univ, 46-47; mkt develop engr, Brea Chem, Inc, 52-57; mgr mkt res, Am Potash & Chem Corp, 57-64. *Mem:* Am Chem Soc. *Res:* Hydroforming and desulfurization catalysts; organic synthesis of isoquinoline derivatives; oxidation and combustion of petroleum products as a synthetic tool; acetylene chemistry, hydrogen cyanide; phthalic acids; polymers; fertilizers and related products. *Mailing Add:* 4940 NW 30th Pl Oklahoma City OK 73122

BILLUPS, NORMAN FREDRICK, PHARMACY, PHARMACEUTICAL CHEMISTRY. *Current Pos:* DEAN & PROF, COL PHARM, UNIV TOLEDO, 77- *Personal Data:* b Portland, Ore, Oct 15, 34; m 57; c Tamra Mae (Conway) & Timothy Fredrick. *Educ:* Ore State Univ, BS, 58, MS, 61, PhD(pharmaceut), 63. *Honors & Awards:* Lyman Award, Am Asn Cols Pharm, 71; Res Achievement Award, Am Soc Hosp Pharmacists, 75; Norman F Billups Distinguished Serv Award, 92. *Prof Exp:* Instr pharm, Ore State Univ, 58-59, asst, 59-62, NIH res fel phys pharm, 62-63; from assoc prof to prof pharm, Univ Ky, 63-77. *Concurrent Pos:* Fel, Am Found Pharmaceut Educ, 62-63; consult, Blue Cross-Blue Shield; auth, Ann Am Drug Index, 77-; trustee, Toledo Acad Pharm & Ohio Pharmacist's Asn. *Mem:* Am Pharmaceut Asn; Am Soc Hosp Pharmacists; Am Asn Cols Pharm. *Res:* Various dosage forms of pharmaceutical products, especially disintegrating agents and ointment technology; drug release from selected ointment bases; kinetics of drug absorption and distribution; protein binding of drugs; complexation; percutaneous adsorption; socio-economics of pharmacy; pharmaceutical care research. *Mailing Add:* Dean Col Pharm Univ Toledo Toledo OH 43606-3390. *Fax:* 419-530-8407; *E-Mail:* nillup@utnet.utoledo.edu

BILLUPS, W EDWARD, ORGANIC CHEMISTRY. *Current Pos:* from asst prof to assoc prof, 70-81, PROF CHEM, RICE UNIV, 81- *Personal Data:* b Huntington, WVa, Apr 7, 39; m 66; c 1. *Educ:* Marshall Univ, BS, 61, MS, 65; Pa State Univ, PhD(chem), 70. *Prof Exp:* Res chemist, Union Carbide Corp, WVa, 61-68. *Concurrent Pos:* Alfred P Sloan fel, 73-75; consult, UNESCO, 80. *Mem:* Am Chem Soc; Royal Soc Chem. *Res:* Chemistry of small ring systems, reactive intermediates, synthetic methods; organo-transition metal chemistry. *Mailing Add:* Dept Chem Rice Univ PO Box 1892 Houston TX 77251-1892

BILODEAU, GERALD GUSTAVE, MATHEMATICAL ANALYSIS. *Current Pos:* from asst prof to assoc prof, 60-71, PROF MATH, BOSTON COL, 71- *Personal Data:* b Waterville, Maine, Nov 2, 29; m 56; c 6. *Educ:* Univ Maine, BA, 50; Harvard Univ, AM, 51, PhD(math), 59. *Prof Exp:* Sr mathematician, Westinghouse Atomic Power Div, Pa, 55-59; adv res engr, Sylvania Electronics Systs, 59-60. *Mem:* Am Math Soc; Math Asn Am; Sigma Xi; Soc Indust & Appl Math. *Res:* Orthogonal functions; integral transforms; partial differential equations. *Mailing Add:* Boston Col Chestnut Hill MA 02167-3806

BILOW, NORMAN, POLYMER CHEMISTRY, ORGANIC CHEMISTRY. *Current Pos:* RETIRED. *Personal Data:* b Chicago, Ill, Sept 9, 28; m 54, Selma H Rifkin; c Steven, Sandra & Richard. *Educ:* Roosevelt Univ, BS, 49; Univ Chicago, MS, 52, PhD(chem), 56. *Honors & Awards:* Indust Res Mag Award, 70 & 74; L A Hyland Award, Hughes Aircraft Co, 76; New Technol Awards (4), NASA. *Prof Exp:* Res chemist, Emulsol Corp, 49-52; asst, Univ Chicago, 55-56; res chemist, Dow Chem Co, 56-59; staff scientist, Hughes Aircraft Co, 59-65, sr staff chemist, 65-67, head, Chem Synthesis Group, 67-69, head, Polymer & Chem Technol Sect, Aerospace Group, 69-70, head, Polymer & Phys Chem Sect, 70-73, sr scientist, Advan Technol Lab, 73-80, chief scientist, Mat & Processes Lab, 80-84. *Concurrent Pos:* Dir, res & develop, Furane Prods Co, Subsid Rohm P Haas, 84-86, Furane Prod Co, Div Ciba Geigy, 86-89; mgr, qual assurance & consult, Ciba Geigy, 89-90. *Mem:* Am Chem Soc; Sigma Xi; fel Am Inst Chemists; NY Acad Sci; AAAS. *Res:* Stereospecific polyolefins; polyphenylenes; phenolics; ablative resins; free radicals; photochemistry; diazo compounds; surfactants; polyurethanes; intumescent paints; electrical insulation; polyferrocenes; poly-aromatic-heterocyclic polymers; thermosetting acetylene-substituted polymers; epoxy resins; microelectronic materials; high temperature polymers; polyimides; electrically conductive polyimines; conductive adhesives. *Mailing Add:* 16685 Calneva Dr Encino CA 91436

BILPUCH, EDWARD GEORGE, PHYSICS. *Current Pos:* Res assoc, Duke Univ, 56-62, from asst prof to assoc prof, 62-71, dep dir, 68-78, PROF PHYSICS, DUKE UNIV, 71-, DIR, TRIANGLE UNIV NUCLEAR LAB, 78- *Personal Data:* b Connellsville, Pa, Feb 10, 27; m 52. *Educ:* Univ NC, BS, 50, MS, 52, PhD, 56. *Concurrent Pos:* Sr US scientist Humboldt awardee, 83-84; hon prof, Fudan Univ, Shanghai, 86; Henry W Newson prof physics, Duke Univ, 87. *Mem:* Fel Am Phys Soc; AAAS. *Res:* High resolution neutron and charged particle cross section measurements; fine structure of isobaric analogue states. *Mailing Add:* Physics Dept Duke Univ Durham NC 27708-0308

BILS, ROBERT F, CYTOLOGY, ELECTRON MICROSCOPY. *Current Pos:* from asst prof to assoc prof, 61-70, PROF BIOL, UNIV SOUTHERN CALIF, 70-, DIR, CTR ELECTRON MICROSCOPY & MICROANALYSIS, 84- *Personal Data:* b Harvey, Ill, Jan 10, 31; m 54; c 3. *Educ:* Univ Ill, BS, 54, MS, 58, PhD(bot), 60. *Prof Exp:* Asst bot, Univ Ill, 56-57, Electron Micros Lab, 57-60; res assoc biol, Mass Inst Technol, 60-61. *Concurrent Pos:* NIH fel, Mass Inst Technol, 60-61; dir electron micros lab, Allan Hancock Found, 61-84; vis prof, Path Inst & Air Hyg Inst, Univ Dusseldorf, 68-69; vis prof, Res Unit Comp Animal Resp, Univ Bristol, 76-77.

Mem: Fel Royal Micros Soc; AAAS; NY Acad Sci; Electron Micros Soc Am; Am Soc Cell Biol. *Res:* Cell ultrastructure, electron microscopy; cytologic effects of toxic air pollutants on lung cells; connective tissues of lung; development and aging of cells; author of book on electron microscopy. *Mailing Add:* Dept Biol Sci Univ Southern Calif Los Angeles CA 90089

BILTONEN, RODNEY LINCOLN, BIOPHYSICAL CHEMISTRY, BIOCHEMISTRY. *Current Pos:* assoc dean med, 79-81, assoc provost res, 81-84, PROF PHARMACOL & BIOCHEM, SCH MED, UNIV VA, 77- *Personal Data:* b Sudbury, Ont, Aug 24, 37; US citizen; m 60; c 2. *Educ:* Harvard Univ, AB, 59; Univ Minn, PhD(phys chem), 65. *Prof Exp:* NIH fel, 65-66; asst prof phys chem, Johns Hopkins Univ, 66-72, assoc prof pharmacol & biochem, 72-77. *Concurrent Pos:* Counr, Biophys Soc, 83-87. *Mem:* Am Chem Soc; AAAS; Am Soc Biol Chemists; Biophys Soc. *Res:* Structure and thermodynamics of macromolecules of biological significance; thermodynamics of ligand binding to macromolecules; application of calorimetric techniques to the study of biological systems; thermodynamic aspects structural transitions of membranes; mechanism of activation of phospholipase A2. *Mailing Add:* Dept Pharm Univ Va Health Sci Ctr MC Box 448 Charlottesville VA 22908

BILYEU, RUSSELL GENE, MATHEMATICAL ANALYSIS. *Current Pos:* from asst prof to assoc prof, 60-70, PROF MATH, N TEX STATE UNIV, 70- *Personal Data:* b Krum, Tex, Jan 22, 30; m 53; c 4. *Educ:* NTex State Univ, BS, 52, MS, 57; Univ Kans, PhD(math), 60. *Prof Exp:* Engr systs eng, Chance Vought Aircraft, Inc, 52-57. *Mem:* Am Math Soc; Math Asn Am. *Res:* Normed linear spaces. *Mailing Add:* 1709 Westchester St Denton TX 76201-2552

BIMBER, RUSSELL MORROW, WATER SUPPLIES. *Current Pos:* CONSULT CHEMIST, 91- *Personal Data:* b Warren, Pa, Mar 26, 29; m 51, Constance Dowling; c Frederick, Barbara & William. *Educ:* Antioch Col, BS, 52; Western Reserve Univ, MS, 62. *Prof Exp:* From chemist to sr chemist, Diamond Shamrock Corp, 52-80, res assoc, 80-86; res assoc, Ricerca Inc, 86-91, consult, 91-95. *Concurrent Pos:* Consult, Penn Cent, 69, Pub Rel Comt Voorhees, 82. *Mem:* Am Chem Soc. *Res:* Chemical process research and development, including vapor phase catalytic reactions such as ammoxidation, chlorination and ketone synthesis; granted 25 US patents; groundwater pollution and cleanup. *Mailing Add:* 10471 Prouty Rd Painesville OH 44077

BINA, MINOU, BIOPHYSICS, MOLECULAR BIOLOGY. *Current Pos:* PROF, PURDUE UNIV, 79- *Personal Data:* b Teheran, Iran, Oct 15, 45; US citizen. *Educ:* Temple Univ, BA, 70; Yale Univ, MS, 72, PhD(chem), 74. *Honors & Awards:* Am Chem Soc Award, 68; Cancer Res Award, Lions Int, 96. *Prof Exp:* Fel biochem, Nat Cancer Inst, NIH, 75-77, sr fel virol, Nat Inst Allergy & Infectious Dis, 77-79. *Concurrent Pos:* Vis scholar, Ctr Cancer Res, Mass Inst Technol, 87-88. *Mem:* AAAS; Biophys Soc; Am Soc Biol Chem; Am Soc Cell Biol; Am Soc Microbiol; NY Acad Sci; Sigma Xi. *Res:* Protein-DNA interactions; chromatin structure; regulation of gene expression; analysis of the human genome. *Mailing Add:* Dept Chem Purdue Univ Brown Bldg West Lafayette IN 47907-1393

BINCER, ADAM MARIAN, THEORETICAL PHYSICS. *Current Pos:* from asst prof to prof, 60-96, EMER PROF PHYSICS, UNIV WIS, MADISON, 96- *Personal Data:* b Krakow, Poland, Apr 25, 30; US citizen; c Andrea (Hayward) & Ronnie. *Educ:* Mass Inst Technol, SB, 53, PhD(physics), 56. *Prof Exp:* Res assoc physics, Brookhaven Nat Lab, 56-58; asst res, Univ Calif, Berkeley, 58-60. *Concurrent Pos:* Fulbright scholar, Univ Sao Paulo, Brazil, 65. *Mem:* Am Phys Soc. *Res:* Theory of fundamental particles; analyticity properties of scattering amplitudes; group theory. *Mailing Add:* Dept Physics Univ Wis Madison WI 53706. *E-Mail:* bincer@wishep.physics.wisc.edu

BINDER, BERND R, haematology, fibrinolysis, for more information see previous edition

BINDER, BERNHARD, INORGANIC CHEMISTRY, ANALYTICAL CHEMISTRY. *Current Pos:* from asst prof to assoc prof, Southern Ore State Col, 68-80, prof chem, 80-92, chmn dept, 85-89, dir, Sch Sci, 89-92, dean, Sch Sci, 92-96, EMER PROF CHEM, SOUTHERN ORE UNIV, 92-, EMER DEAN, SCH SCI, 96- *Personal Data:* b WGer, Jan 25, 36; US citizen; m 59; c 2. *Educ:* Western NMex Univ, BA, 64; Stanford Univ, MS, 66, PhD(inorg chem), 68. *Prof Exp:* Chemist, Kennecott Copper Corp, 60-64. *Concurrent Pos:* Vis prof, Univ Konstanz, WGer, 74-75. *Mem:* Am Chem Soc; Sigma Xi. *Res:* Mixed-metal, binuclear coordination compounds; computer-assisted chemistry instruction. *Mailing Add:* Dept Chem Southern Ore Univ 1250 Siskiyou Blvd Ashland OR 97520-2268

BINDER, DANIEL, PHYSICS. *Current Pos:* RETIRED. *Personal Data:* b New York, NY, Feb 20, 27; m 56. *Educ:* City Col New York, BS, 47; Yale Univ, PhD(physics), 50. *Prof Exp:* Physicist, Oak Ridge Nat Lab, 50-60; sr staff, Hughes Aircraft Co, 60-84, sr scientist, 84-89. *Mem:* Am Phys Soc. *Res:* Radioactivity; radiation damage and dosimetry; transient radiation effects on electronics, single event upset, EMP. *Mailing Add:* PO Box 725 Monteagle TN 37356

BINDER, FRANKLIN LEWIS, MICROBIAL PHYSIOLOGY, PHARMACEUTICAL MICROBIOLOGY. *Current Pos:* prog dir med & cytotechnol, 77, PROF MICROBIOL, MARSHALL UNIV, 71-; VPRES, MICROBIOL CONSULTS, INC, 82- *Personal Data:* b Bristol, Pa, Nov 14, 45; m 65, Mary J Bradley; c Lorrie, Raymond & Molly. *Educ:* Ind Univ Pa, BA, 67; WVa Univ, MS, 69, PhD(microbiol), 71. *Honors & Awards:* Res Award, Sigma Xi, 75. *Prof Exp:* Res asst, WVa Univ, 67-71. *Concurrent Pos:* Instr microbiol, Ohio Univ, Portsmouth, 73-75; fac res grants, Marshall Univ, 75, 76, 77 & 79. *Mem:* Am Soc Microbiol; AAAS; Sigma Xi; Soc Indust Microbiol; Am Pub Health Asn. *Res:* Biochemical studies with the haustorial mycoparasite Tieghemiomyces Parasiticus in axenic culture; transport mechanism in fungi; microbial decomposition of metalworking fluids; pharmaceutical microbiology; sterilization/disinfection. *Mailing Add:* Dept Biol Sci Marshall Univ Huntington WV 25701. *Fax:* 304-696-6565

BINDER, HENRY J, INTERNAL MEDICINE, GASTROENTEROLOGY. *Current Pos:* from asst prof to assoc prof, 69-78, PROF MED, YALE UNIV, 78- *Personal Data:* b New York, NY, Dec 5, 36; m 61; c 2. *Educ:* Dartmouth Col, AB, 57; NY Univ, MD, 61; Yale Univ, MA, 78. *Hon Degrees:* MA, Yale Univ, 78. *Prof Exp:* Instr med, Yale Univ, 65-66; clin instr, Univ Calif, San Francisco, 67-68; asst prof, Univ Chicago, 68-69. *Mem:* Am Soc Clin Invest; Am Physiol Soc; Am Gastroenterol Asn; Asn Am Physicians. *Res:* Gastrointestinal physiology; intestinal transport. *Mailing Add:* Dept Internal Med Yale Univ 333 Cedar St New Haven CT 06510-3219

BINDER, IRWIN, RADIOCHEMISTRY, ENVIRONMENTAL SCIENCES. *Current Pos:* STAFF MEM RADIOCHEM, LOS ALAMOS NAT LAB, 77- *Personal Data:* b Salzburg, Austria, Apr 9, 49; US citizen; m 76; c 2. *Educ:* Univ Calif, Los Angeles, BS, 70; Univ Calif, Berkeley, PhD(chem), 77. *Mem:* Am Phys Soc; Am Chem Soc. *Res:* Analytical radiochemistry; neutron activation analysis; heavy-ion nuclear reactions; geochemistry; environmental analysis, materials studies; analytical chemistry. *Mailing Add:* 1960 Camino Mora Los Alamos NM 87544-2714. *Fax:* 505-665-3456

BINDER, MARC DAVID, NEUROPHYSIOLOGY. *Current Pos:* from asst prof to assoc prof, 78-86, PROF PHYSIOL & BIOPHYS, SCH MED, UNIV WASH, 86- *Personal Data:* b Brookline, Mass, June 8, 49; m 81, Karin Kalff; c Katrin R, & Gracie K. *Educ:* Columbia Univ, AB, 71; Univ Southern Calif, MS, 72, PHD(biol & bioeng), 74. *Honors & Awards:* Jacob Javits Neurosci Investr Award, 92. *Prof Exp:* Res asst biol, Univ Southern Calif, 72-74; consult environ impact, Ocean Sci & Eng, Inc, 72-73; res assoc neurophysiol, Pac Med Ctr, 74-75; instr, Univ Calif Davis, 75; res assoc physiol, Col Med, Univ Ariz, 75-78. *Concurrent Pos:* Vis asst prof physiol, Col Med, Univ Ariz, 78-81; vis assoc prof physiol, Harvard Med Sch, 82-83; adj prof oral biol, Univ Wash Sch Dent, 90- *Mem:* Soc Neurosci; AAAS; Sigma Xi; Am Physiol Soc. *Res:* Neural control of movement; neural modelling and computer simulation; neurophysiology; motoneuron physiology. *Mailing Add:* Dept Physiol & Biophys Sch Med Univ Wash Seattle WA 98195. *Fax:* 206-543-1540

BINDER, MICHAEL, CHEMISTRY, PHYSICS. *Current Pos:* RES SCIENTIST, US ARMY ELECTRONIC TECHNOL & DEVICES, FT MONMOUTH, NJ, 81- *Personal Data:* b Waterbury, Conn, Apr 18, 51. *Educ:* Brooklyn Col, BS, 68, MS, 72, PhD(chem-physics), 78. *Prof Exp:* Asst prof chem, Queens Col, 78-79; scientist, Power Conservation Induct, Mt Vernon, NY, 79-81. *Mem:* Electrochem Soc; Sigma Xi. *Res:* Spectroscopy and electrochemistry of nonaqueous solvents for battery applications; dielectrics. *Mailing Add:* US Army LABCOM Ft Monmouth NJ 07703-5000

BINDER, SUZANNE, PUBLIC HEALTH, EPIDEMIOLOGY. *Current Pos:* epidemic intel serv officer & med epidemiologist, Spec Studies Br, Ctr Dis Control, 84-86, med epidemiologist, Acute & Nat Hazards Studies Sect, Health Studies Br, 86-89, Lead Poisoning Prev Activ, 89-90, chief, Lead Poisoning Prev Br, 90-95, ASSOC DIR MED SCI, DIV PARASITIC DIS, NAT CTR INFECTIOUS DIS, CTR DIS PREV & CONTROL, 95- *Personal Data:* b Philadelphia, Pa, Sept 25, 55. *Educ:* McGill Univ, BS, 76; Tufts Univ, MD, 81; Am Bd Internal Med, cert, 84. *Honors & Awards:* Martin J Loeb Mem Prize, 81; Arthur S Flemming Award, 92. *Prof Exp:* From intern to resident internal med, Tufts-New Eng Med Ctr, 81-84. *Concurrent Pos:* Clin asst prof commun health, Emory Univ Sch Med, 89-93; asst dir prev, Div Environ Hazards & Health Effects, Nat Ctr Environ Health, Ctr Dis Control, 94-95. *Mem:* Am Pub Health Asn; Am Soc Trop Med & Hyg; Asn Exec Women; Comn Officers Asn. *Res:* Published numerous articles in professional publications. *Mailing Add:* Div Parasitic Dis Nat Ctr Infectious Dis Ctr Dis Control & Prev 4770 Buford Hwy NE F-22 Atlanta GA 30341-3724

BINDLOSS, WILLIAM, SOLID STATE PHYSICS, MATERIALS SCIENCE. *Current Pos:* Res scientist physics, E I DuPont de Nemours & Co, Inc, 67-70, res group leader, 70-73, res supvr, Cent Res Dept, 73-79, sr res assoc, Photo Prod Dept, 79-85, mem tech staff, 85-93, SR RES ASSOC, CENT RES DEPT, E I DUPONT DE NEMOURS & CO, INC, 93- *Personal Data:* b Westerly, RI, Dec 16, 37; m 63; c 3. *Educ:* Yale Univ, BE, 60; Univ Calif, Berkeley, PhD(physics), 67. *Mem:* Am Phys Soc; AAAS. *Res:* Magnetic, electrical, and optical properties of inorganic and organic materials. *Mailing Add:* Cent Res & Develop Dept DuPont Co Exp Sta 352 Wilmington DE 19810

BINDRA, JASJIT SINGH, ORGANIC CHEMISTRY. *Current Pos:* res chemist, Pfizer Inc, 71-74, sr res chemist, 74-76, sr res investr, 76-80, prin res investr, 80-83, asst dir, 83-89, SR SCI ADVISOR, PFIZER, INC, 89- *Personal Data:* b Rawalpindi, India, Oct 20, 42; m 70; c 2. *Educ:* Agra Univ,

MSc, 64, PhD(chem), 68. *Prof Exp:* Scientist med chem, Cent Drug Res Inst, India, 68-69; res assoc chem, Ind Univ, Bloomington, 69-71. *Mem:* Am Chem Soc. *Res:* Organic synthesis; medicinal agents. *Mailing Add:* Med Res Labs Pfizer Pharm Eastern Point Rd Groton CT 06340

BINFORD, JESSE STONE, JR, CALORIMETRY, LIPID MEMBRANE THERMODYNAMICS. *Current Pos:* assoc prof, 61-71, PROF CHEM, UNIV SFLA, 72- *Personal Data:* b Freeport, Tex, Nov 1, 28; m 55, Lolita R Fritz; c Lincoln B & Jason J. *Educ:* Rice Univ, BA, 50, MA, 52; Univ Utah, PhD(chem), 55. *Prof Exp:* Instr chem, Univ Tex, 55-58; from asst prof to assoc prof, Univ Pac, 58-61. *Concurrent Pos:* Fulbright prof chem & chmn dept, Nat Univ Honduras, 68-69; consult, Fla Consort, AID, Honduras, 69 & Exxon Prod Res Co, Houston, 74; vis scientist, Sweden Thermochem Lab, Univ Lund, 82-83; vis prof, Dept Chem Eng, Cox Biomed Eng Lab, Rice Univ, Houston, Tex, 93-94. *Mem:* AAAS; Am Chem Soc; Calorimetry Conf; Sigma Xi. *Res:* Solution calorimetry; biochemical calorimetry; thermodynamics of lipid bilayers and their interactions with amphiphilic molecules; encapsulation of drugs and hemoglobin and their stabilization in the blood stream. *Mailing Add:* 1905 E 111th Ave Tampa FL 33612

BINFORD, LAURENCE CHARLES, VERTEBRATE ZOOLOGY, ORNITHOLOGY. *Current Pos:* RETIRED. *Personal Data:* b Chicago, Ill, Jan 11, 35. *Educ:* Univ Mich, BS, 57; La State Univ, PhD(vert zool), 68. *Prof Exp:* Instr zool, La State Univ, 65-66; asst cur birds & mammals, Calif Acad Sci, 68-73, assoc cur & chmn dept, 73-80. *Concurrent Pos:* Vpres bd dirs, Point Reyes Bird Observ, 69-72, pres bd dirs, 72-76; charter mem, Calif Bird Rec Comt, 69-77, vsecy, 78-79 & 81-86; fel, Calif Acad Sci, 72; chmn ed bd, Western Birds, 73-86; mem coun, Cooper Ornith Soc, 76-78, secy bd, 78-81; mem bd dirs, Western Field Ornithologists, 76-86, pres bd dirs, 84-86. *Mem:* Am Ornith Union; Cooper Ornith Soc; Wilson Ornith Soc. *Res:* Ornithology, especially avian taxonomy; ornithogeography, particularly Mexico. *Mailing Add:* 330 Grove St Glencoe IL 60022

BINFORD, MICHAEL W, PALEOLIMNOLOGY, LANDSCAPE ECOLOGY & ENVIRONMENTAL GEOGRAPHY. *Current Pos:* from asst prof to assoc prof, 86-96, SR RES FEL, HARVARD UNIV, 96- *Personal Data:* b Hutchinson, Kans, May 21, 51; m 85, Mary V Lowry; c Elizabeth & Katherine. *Educ:* Kans State Univ, BS, 73; La State Univ, MS, 75; Ind Univ, PhD(zool & geol), 80. *Prof Exp:* Res assoc, Fla State Mus, Univ Fla, 80-86. *Concurrent Pos:* Assoc ed, J Paleolimnology, 88-; assoc, Harvard Forest. *Mem:* Ecol Soc Am; Am Soc Limnol & Oceanog; Int Asn Theoret & Appl Limnol; Sigma Xi; fel AAAS; Int Asn Landscape Ecol. *Res:* Lake-drainage basin interaction; paleolimnology; ecological relationships between land use and water quality in lakes, streams and wetlands; environment-economics interactions. *Mailing Add:* Dept Landscape Archit Grad Sch Design Harvard Univ 48 Quincy St Cambridge MA 02138. *Fax:* 617-495-5015; *E-Mail:* mbinford@gsd.harvard.edu

BING, ARTHUR, PLANT PHYSIOLOGY. *Personal Data:* b Springfield, Mass, Apr 18, 16; m 54, Hauptvogel; c 1. *Educ:* Univ Conn, BS, 39; Cornell Univ, PhD, 49. *Honors & Awards:* Gold Medal, NAm Gladiolos Soc. *Prof Exp:* Asst bot, Cornell Univ, 46-49; prof floricult, Long Island Hort Res Lab, Cornell Univ, 51-83, consult, 83-86. *Mem:* Weed Sci Soc Am; Am Soc Hort Sci; Int Soc Hort Sci; Sigma Xi. *Res:* Weed control and factors influencing flowering of ornamentals. *Mailing Add:* Long Island Hort Res Lab 39 Sound Ave Riverhead NY 11901

BING, DAVID H, IMMUNOLOGY, PROTEIN CHEMISTRY. *Current Pos:* assoc dir biol sci, 86-, SCI DIR, CBR LABS, 86- *Personal Data:* b East Cleveland, Ohio, Aug 3, 38; m 61; c 3. *Educ:* Wesleyan Univ, BA, 60; Case Western Reserve Univ, PhD(immunol), 66. *Prof Exp:* Asst prof microbiol & pub health, Mich State Univ, 68-72, assoc prof microbiol & pub health & human develop, 72-73; sr investr, Ctr Blood Res, Boston, 73- *Concurrent Pos:* Am Cancer Soc fel immunochem, Univ Calif, Berkeley, 66-68; foreign res worker, Nat Inst Health & Med Res, 70-71; res assoc, Div Immunol, Childrens Hosp Res Ctr, Boston, 72-73; prin res assoc, Dept Biol Chem, Harvard Med Sch, 73- *Mem:* Am Chem Soc; Am Asn Immunologists. *Mailing Add:* CBR Labs Ctr Blood Res 800 Huntington Ave Boston MA 02115

BING, GEORGE FRANKLIN, THEORETICAL PHYSICS. *Current Pos:* RETIRED. *Personal Data:* b Barberton, Ohio, Dec 16, 24; m 51; c 5. *Educ:* Oberlin Col, BA, 48; Case Inst Technol, MS, 51, PhD(theoret physics), 54. *Prof Exp:* Physicist, Battelle Mem Inst, 51-52; instr, Case Inst Technol, 52-54; mem staff, Lawrence Radiation Lab, Univ Calif, 54-61; asst dir nuclear test detection off, advan res proj agency, US Dept of Defense, DC, 61-63; mem staff, Lawrence Radiation Lab, Univ Calif, 63-67; sci adv to SACEUR, Supreme Hq Allied Powers Europe, 67-70; mem staff, Lawrence Livermore Nat Lab, Univ Calif, 70-88. *Mem:* Am Phys Soc. *Res:* Weapons physics; hydrodynamics; controlled thermonuclear process; problems of national defense. *Mailing Add:* 4128 Colgate Way Livermore CA 94550

BING, KURT, MATHEMATICAL LOGIC. *Current Pos:* from asst prof to prof math, 53-79, EMER PROF MATH SCI, RENSSELAER POLYTECH INST, 79- *Personal Data:* b Cologne, Ger, Apr 30, 14; nat US; m 52; c 2. *Educ:* Hebrew Univ, Jerusalem, MSc, 46; Harvard Univ, PhD(math), 53. *Prof Exp:* Assoc math, Univ Calif, 52-53. *Mem:* Am Math Soc; Math Asn Am; Asn Symbolic Logic. *Res:* Mathematical logic; foundations of mathematics. *Mailing Add:* 22 Kuhl Blvd Wynantskill NY 12198-8152

BING, OSCAR H L, MYOCARDIAL PHYSIOLOGY. *Current Pos:* RES PROF MED, SCH MED, BOSTON UNIV, 94- *Personal Data:* b New York, NY, July 13, 35; m 75, Barbara Nelson; c David, Michael, Benjamin & William. *Educ:* Washington & Lee Univ, BS, 56; Univ Md, MD, 61. *Prof Exp:* Prof med, Sch Med, Tufts Univ, 81-94. *Concurrent Pos:* Career develop award, NIH, 75-80; assoc chief of staff res & develop, Boston Vet Admin Med Ctr, 81- *Mem:* Am Heart Asn; Int Soc Heart Res; Am Physiol Soc. *Res:* Studies of mechanisms underlying heart failure due to pressure load. *Mailing Add:* Dept Med MRC 151 Boston Vet Admin Med Ctr 150 S Huntington Ave Boston MA 02130-4820. *Fax:* 617-232-2969

BING, RICHARD F, VETERINARY MEDICINE. *Current Pos:* GLOBAL DIR RES & DEVELOP, DINTEC AGR, 94- *Personal Data:* b Sandusky, Ohio, Dec 9, 41; m 66; c 2. *Educ:* Ohio State Univ, DVM, 66. *Prof Exp:* Animal sci rep, Lilly Res Labs, Eli Lilly & Co, 66-72, tech specialist, 72-74, mgr nat acct res, 74-79, mgr animal sci res & develop, Europe, Lilly Res Ctr, 79-82, prod regist mgr, Lilly Res Labs, 82-89; sr adv, Dowelance, 89-93. *Res:* Antibiotics and growth promotants for livestock and poultry. *Mailing Add:* 9330 Zionsville Rd Indianapolis IN 46268

BING, RICHARD JOHN, INTERNAL MEDICINE. *Current Pos:* EMER PROF MED, UNIV SOUTHERN CALIF, 80- *Personal Data:* b Nuremburg, Bavaria, Oct 12, 09; nat US; m 38; c 4. *Educ:* Univ Munich, MD, 34; Univ Bern, MD, 35. *Honors & Awards:* Res Accomplishment Award, Am Heart Asn, 74. *Prof Exp:* Instr physiol, Col Physicians & Surgeons, Columbia Univ, 39-41; instr, NY Univ, 41-43; instr med, Med Sch, Johns Hopkins Univ, 43-44, asst prof surg, 45-47, assoc prof surg & asst prof med, 47-51; prof exp med & clin physiol, Med Col Ala, 51-56; prof med, Washington Univ & dir univ med serv, Vet Admin Hosp, 56-59; prof med & chmn dept, Col Med, Wayne State Univ, 59-69; prof med, Univ Southern Calif, 69-80; dir exp cardiol & sci develop, Huntington Mem Hosp & Huntington Inst, Pasadena, 69- *Concurrent Pos:* Res assoc, Calif Inst Technol, 69-; Harvey Lectr, Royal Soc Med, 54-55. *Mem:* Am Soc Clin Invest; Am Physiol Soc; Harvey Soc; Soc Exp Biol & Med; Asn Am Physicians. *Res:* Physiology and biochemistry of heart muscle; clinical cardiology and internal medicine. *Mailing Add:* Dept Exp Cardiol Huntington Med Res Inst 99 N El Molino Ave Pasadena CA 91101

BINGEL, AUDREY SUSANNA, PHARMACOLOGY, REPRODUCTIVE ENDOCRINOLOGY. *Current Pos:* Assoc prof, 67-81, PROF PHARMACOL, COL PHARM, UNIV ILL, 81- *Personal Data:* b Bronx, NY. *Educ:* Hunter Col, AB, 63; Univ Ill, Chicago, PhD, 68. *Mem:* Am Inst Biol Sci; Am Soc Pharmacog; Endocrine Soc; Am Fertil Soc; Soc Study Reproduction; Sigma Xi. *Res:* Antifertility screening; ovulation timing. *Mailing Add:* Col Pharm Univ Ill Rm 310N 833 S Wood St M/C877 Chicago IL 60612

BINGER, WILSON VALENTINE, CIVIL ENGINEERING, CONSTRUCTION CONTRACT ADMINISTRATION. *Current Pos:* CONSULT ENGR, 85- *Personal Data:* b Greenwich, NY, Feb 28, 17; m 47, 86, Jane Schwarz; c Wilson V Jr, Mary B & Julia (Akgul). *Educ:* Harvard Univ, AB, 38, MSCE, 39. *Honors & Awards:* Steinmetz Award, 85. *Prof Exp:* Soils engr, US Army Engrs, Wilmington, Del, 39-40; soils & found engr, Gatun 3d Locks Proj, Panama Canal, 40-43; soils engr & resident engr, Parsons Brinckerhoff, Hogan & MacDonald, Caracas, Venezuela, 45-46, chief soils engr, Buenos Aires, Arg, 48-50; chief, Soils & Found Sect, Isthmian Canal Studies, Panama Canal, 46-47; chief, Soils Br, Mo River Div, US Army Engrs, Omaha, 47-48; vpres, Porterfield-Binger Construct Co, Youngstown, Ohio, 50-52; regional mgr, Tams Engrs & Architects, Bogota, Colombia, 52-56, assoc partner, NY, 57-61, partner, 62-84, chmn, 75-84. *Concurrent Pos:* Trustee, Robert Col, Istanbul, Turkey, 70-; mem, US Comt Large Dams. *Mem:* Nat Acad Eng; fel Am Soc Civil Engrs; fel Inst Civil Engrs; Am Consult Engrs Coun (vpres, 73-75); Int Fedn Consult Engrs (pres 81-83); foreign mem Royal Acad Eng Brit. *Res:* Large projects, construction contract administration. *Mailing Add:* 420 Lexington Ave Suite 300 New York NY 10170

BINGGELI, RICHARD LEE, NEUROPHYSIOLOGY. *Current Pos:* From instr to asst prof, 64-70, ASSOC PROF ANAT, SCH MED, UNIV SOUTHERN CALIF, 70- *Personal Data:* b Sioux Falls, SDak, May 16, 37; m 62; c 3. *Educ:* Univ Calif, Los Angeles, AB, 59, PhD(anat), 64. *Concurrent Pos:* Consult, Astropower, Inc, Douglas Aircraft Co, Inc, 63-66. *Mem:* Soc Neurosci; Am Asn Anatomists. *Res:* Neurophysiological and behavioral studies of the avian, amphibian, and mammalian visual systems; electrobiology of cancer cells. *Mailing Add:* Dept Anat Univ Southern Calif 1333 San Pablo St BMT 401 Los Angeles CA 90033

BINGHAM, BILLY ELIAS, NUCLEAR ENGINEERING. *Current Pos:* unit mgr, Nuclear Power Div, Babcock & Wilcox, 68-79, adv engr, adv reactor proj, 79-86, space power & propulsion, 86-88, ADV ENGR SPACE & DEFENCE SYSTS, BABCOCK & WILCOX, 88- *Personal Data:* b Fallston, NC, July 31, 31; m 57; c 2. *Educ:* NC State Univ, BEng, 55; Univ Va, PhD(nuclear eng), 70. *Prof Exp:* Head radiol safety, Army Biol Warfare Lab, Fort Detrick, Frederick, Md, 56-58. *Mem:* Am Nuclear Soc; Am Astronaut Soc. *Res:* Advanced reactor concepts for space and terrestrial applications; design of the reactor concept and their supporting, safety and propection systems. *Mailing Add:* 110 Old Wiggington Rd Lynchburg VA 24502

BINGHAM, CARLETON DILLE, analytical chemistry, radiochemistry, for more information see previous edition

BINGHAM, CARROL R, NUCLEAR PHYSICS. *Current Pos:* asst prof, 66-71, assoc prof, 71-77, PROF PHYSICS, UNIV TENN, KNOXVILLE, 77- *Personal Data:* b Fallston, NC, May 22, 38; m 61, Sandra Schrum; c 3. *Educ:* NC State Univ, BSNE, 60, MS, 62; Univ Tenn, PhD(nuclear physics), 65. *Prof Exp:* Res assoc nuclear spectros, Oak Ridge Nat Lab, 65-66. *Concurrent Pos:* Consult, Union Carbide Corp, 66-83 & Martin Marietta, 83- *Mem:* Am Phys Soc. *Res:* Investigation of high-spin nuclear state produced by heavy-ion bombardment of nuclei; nuclear spectroscopy from decay properties of short-lived nuclei; study of nuclear shapes and scattering potentials for heavy ions; measurement of nuclear ground state and isomer moments and isotope shifts utilizing laser spectroscopy. *Mailing Add:* Dept Physics Univ Tenn Knoxville TN 37996-1200

BINGHAM, CHRISTOPHER, STATISTICS, CHRONOBIOMETRY. *Current Pos:* assoc prof, 72-80, PROF APPL STATIST, UNIV MINN, ST PAUL, 80- *Personal Data:* b New York, NY, Apr 16, 37; m 67. *Educ:* Yale Univ, BA, 58, MA, 60, PhD(math), 64. *Prof Exp:* Res assoc math, Princeton Univ, 64-66; asst prof statist, Univ Chicago, 66-72. *Mem:* Biomet Soc; Soc Indust & Appl Math; fel Am Statist Asn; fel Inst Math Statist; Royal Statist Soc. *Res:* Probability distributions of directions; chronobiometry; time series analysis. *Mailing Add:* 792 Osceola Ave St Paul MN 55105-3326. *Fax:* 612-624-2719; *E-Mail:* kb@umnstat.stat.umn.edu

BINGHAM, EDWIN THEODORE, PLANT BREEDING. *Current Pos:* from asst prof to assoc prof 65-70, PROF AGRON, UNIV WIS-MADISON, 74- *Personal Data:* b Ogden, Utah, Nov 4, 36; m 62; c 2. *Educ:* Utah State Univ, BS, 59, MS, 61; Cornell Univ, PhD(genetics), 64. *Prof Exp:* NIH fel genetics, Univ Minn, 64-65. *Mem:* Am Soc Agron; Am Genetic Asn; Can Genetic Asn; Crop Sci Soc Am. *Res:* Genetics and breeding of alfalfa; genetics and cytogenetics of autotetraploids; germ plasma transfer in alfalfa; plant tissue culture. *Mailing Add:* Agron Moore Hall Univ Wis 1575 Linden Dr Madison WI 53706-1514

BINGHAM, EULA, CHEMICAL CARCINOGENESIS, PULMONARY DEFENSE. *Current Pos:* vpres & univ dean grad studies & res, 82-90, PROF ENVIRON HEALTH, COL MED, UNIV CINCINNATI, 77- *Personal Data:* b Covington, Ky, July 9, 29; m 58; c 3. *Educ:* Eastern Ky Univ, BS, 51; Univ Cincinnati, MS, 54, PhD(zool), 58. *Hon Degrees:* DSc, Eastern Ky Univ, 79; LLD, Mt St Joseph Col, 81. *Honors & Awards:* Rockefeller Found Pub Serv Award, 80; Julia Jones Award, Am Lung Asn, 80; Homer N Calver Award, Am Pub Health Asn, 80, Alice Hamilton Award, 84; William Lloyd Award for Occup Safety, US Steel Workers, 84. *Prof Exp:* Anal chemist, Hilton-Davis Chem Co, 51-52; res assoc, Univ Cincinnati, 53-54, res asst, 55-57, res assoc, 57-61, from asst prof to assoc prof environ health, 61-77, assoc dir grad studies, 72-77. *Concurrent Pos:* Consult, Subcomt on Carcinogenesis of Threshold Limits Comt, Am Conf Indust Hyg, 72, Panel on Vapor Phase Organic Air Pollutants, Nat Res Coun, 72-75; mem, Safety & Occup Health Study Sect, Nat Inst Occup Safety & Health, 72-76; asst secy labor, Occup Safety & Health Admin, US Dept Labor, 77-81; mem, Nat Toxicol Prog, 78-81, chair, 79-81; mem, Comt on Priority Mechanisms for Res on Agents Potentially Hazardous to Human Health, Assembly Life Sci, Nat Res Coun, 81-84, vchmn, Comt Toxicol, Comn Life Sci, 86-, mem, Comt on Toxicol Subcomt Guidelines for Spacecraft Maximum Allowable Concentrations for Space Station Contaminants, 89-91; mem working group, Int Agency for Res on Cancer, 83, chair, 84; vchmn, Comt on Methods for In Vivo Toxicity Testing of Complex Mixtures from the Environ, Comn Life Sci, Nat Acad Sci, 84-86, mem, Comt on Ground-Water Protection, Water Sci & Technol Bd, 85-86; mem, Comt on the Future of Pub Health; pres, Collegium Ramazzini, 92. *Mem:* Inst Med-Nat Acad Sci; Soc Occup & Environ Health (vpres, 75, pres-elect, 79); Am Asn Cancer Res; Sigma Xi; AAAS; Am Col Toxicol (pres, 81). *Res:* Toxicology; chemical carcinogenesis; pulmonary defense mechanisms; regulatory toxicology; occupational/environmental health. *Mailing Add:* Kettering Bldg ML056 Univ Cincinnati Med Ctr Cincinnati OH 45267

BINGHAM, FELTON WELLS, DISPOSAL OF RADIOACTIVE WASTE, RISK MANAGEMENT. *Current Pos:* mem tech staff, 64-83, distinguished mem tech staff & supvr, 83-92, DEPT MGR, SANDIA NAT LABS, 92- *Personal Data:* b Greenville, Miss, Aug 18, 35; m 59; c 4. *Educ:* Tulane Univ, BS, 57; Ind Univ, MS, 59, PhD(physics), 62. *Prof Exp:* Assoc physics, Ind Univ, 57-59, res asst, 59-62; res assoc, Univ Ill, 62-64. *Res:* Disposal of radioactive waste and uranium-mill tailings; collision and radiation processes important in high-power gas lasers; collisions between heavy ions and atoms; studies of repositories for radioactive waste; risk management. *Mailing Add:* 12608 Loyola Ave Albuquerque NM 87112. *E-Mail:* fwbingh@nwer.sandia.gov

BINGHAM, GENE AUSTIN, VETERINARY MEDICINE. *Current Pos:* INST VET & CHIEF VET MED & RESOURCES BR, NIMH, NIH, 89- *Educ:* Auburn Univ, DVM, 58; Am Bd Vet Pub Health, dipl, 66. *Prof Exp:* Vet med office, Path Div, US Army Biol Lab, Ft Detrick Md, 58-59, US Army Trop Res Med Lab, San Juan, PR, 59-60; asst chief, Animal Hosp Sect & head, Primated Quarantine Unit, Vet Resources Br, Res Resources Div, NIH, Bethesda, Md, 60-62; chief, Animal Prod & Conditioning Br, Animal Farm Div, US Army, Ft Detrick, Md, 62-67; dir, Lab Animal Facil, Sch Med, Univ Pittsburgh, 67-78, asst prof, Dept Surg, 67-73, adj assoc prof, 73-78; head, Lab Animal Resources Sect, Biol Div, Oak Ridge Nat Lab, Tenn, 78-89. *Concurrent Pos:* Bd dir, Am Asn Lab Animal Sci, 65, 71-74, Am Col Lab Animal Med, 70-72; mem var comt, Am Asn Lab Animal Sci, 68-75, Subcomt Rodent Standards, Inst Lab Animal Resources, Nat Acad Sci, 67-68; mem, Coun Accreditation, Am Asn Accreditation Lab Animal Care, 71-74, consult, 67- *Mem:* Vet Med Asn; Am Asn Lab Animal Sci (pres, 73); Am Col Lab Animal Med. *Res:* Veterinary medicine. *Mailing Add:* NIMH Bldg 36 Rm 1A27 Bethesda MD 20892-4032

BINGHAM, HARRY H, JR, physics; deceased, see previous edition for last biography

BINGHAM, J PETER, ELECTRONICS. *Current Pos:* staff mem, 82-91, PRES, PHILIPS LAB, 91- *Personal Data:* b Apr 25, 42; m; c 2. *Educ:* NY Polytech Inst, BS; Univ Md, MS & PhD. *Honors & Awards:* Antarctica geog feature named in honor, Bingham Peak. *Prof Exp:* Staff mem, David Sarnoff Res Ctr, RCA Consumer Electronics; exec vpres technol, Thomson Consumer Electronics; vpres eng, Philips CEC & Magnavox CATV Systs. *Mem:* Inst Elec & Electronics Engrs. *Res:* Experimental physics; electrical engineering; telecommunications. *Mailing Add:* Philips Res 345 Scarborough Rd Briarcliff Manor NY 10510

BINGHAM, RICHARD CHARLES, TECHNICAL MANAGEMENT, ORGANIC CHEMISTRY. *Current Pos:* res chemist, 73-78, res supvr, 78-81, PROD MGR, E I DU PONT DE NEMOURS & CO, INC, 81- *Personal Data:* b Middlebury, Vt, May 23, 44; m 72. *Educ:* Univ Vt, BS, 66; Princeton Univ, PhD(chem), 70. *Prof Exp:* Fel chem, Univ Tex, Austin, 71-72. *Mem:* Am Chem Soc. *Res:* Synthesis of novel dyes and pigments; electronic spectra of organic molecules; interpretation of the structures of molecules; theoretical organic chemistry; polymer chemistry. *Mailing Add:* J3 Montbartd Dr Chadds Ford PA 19317-9278

BINGHAM, RICHARD S(TEPHEN), JR, CHEMICAL ENGINEERING, TECHNICAL MANAGEMENT. *Current Pos:* RETIRED. *Personal Data:* b Brooklyn, NY, July 7, 24; m 49; c 4. *Educ:* Carnegie Inst Technol, BSChE, 48; Univ Wis-Oshkosh, MBA, 73. *Honors & Awards:* Brumbaugh Award, Am Soc Qual Control, 64. *Prof Exp:* Chem engr, explosives res, Hercules Powder Co, 48-50 & Pilot Plant Div, 50-51; supvr in charge, Qual Control Dept, Atlas Powder Co, 51-52, tech asst & statist consult, 52-56; sr engr qual control br, Res & Develop, Carborundum Co, 56-57, supv engr, Process Control Dept, 57-59, mgr qual control dept, Coated Abrasives Div, 59-62; mgr qual control, Consolidated Papers, Inc, 62-66, dir tech serv, 66-71, dir, mgt systs, 71-87. *Concurrent Pos:* Lectr, Univ Del, 51-52, Univ Chattanooga, 53-54 & Rochester Inst Technol, 55-72; adv conf qual control, Rutgers Univ, 57-59; ed, Have You Read Dept, Am Soc Qual Control, 61-; qual control inst, Univ Wis, 63; consult, 87- *Mem:* Fel Am Soc Qual Control (vpres, 66-69); Biomet Soc; Opers Res Soc Am; Am Inst Chem Engrs; Am Statist Asn. *Res:* Application of statistical methods to research, development and process control problems; operations research; data processing; industrial engineering. *Mailing Add:* 7349 Edinburgh Way Brooksville FL 34613

BINGHAM, ROBERT J, BIOCHEMISTRY, FOOD CHEMISTRY. *Current Pos:* PRES, WIN HY FOODS, INC, 76- *Personal Data:* b Blackfoot, Idaho, Feb 17, 32; m 59; c 5. *Educ:* Utah State Univ, BS, 59; Univ Wis, MS, 62, PhD(biochem, food sci), 64. *Prof Exp:* Health physicist, Phillips Petrol Co, AEC, Idaho, 59; res asst food sci, Univ Wis, 59-63; asst prof food chem, NC State Univ, 63-68; head agr-prod res, Beatrice Foods Co, 68-70; vpres, Nutrico, 70-74; vpres, Promarkco, 74-76. *Concurrent Pos:* Dir, Banfield of Tulsa, 73-80 & Prime Western, Inc, 75-80. *Mem:* Fel Am Inst Chem; Am Chem Soc; Inst Food Technol; Am Dairy Sci Asn. *Res:* Nutritional properties and means of protecting or enhancing nutritional value during processing and storage; utilization of by-products of food industry for high quality animal feeds. *Mailing Add:* 8620 Regency Dr Tulsa OK 74131-3625

BINGHAM, ROBERT LODEWIJK, nuclear physics, plasma physics, for more information see previous edition

BINGHAM, SAMUEL WAYNE, PLANT PHYSIOLOGY, WEED SCIENCE. *Current Pos:* assoc prof, 61-72, PROF PLANT PHYSIOL, VA POLYTECH INST & STATE UNIV, 72- *Personal Data:* b Fallston, NC, Apr 6, 29; m 55; c 3. *Educ:* NC State Col, BS, 54, MS, 56; La State Univ, PhD(weed sci), 60. *Prof Exp:* Res agronomist, Crops Div, USDA, 56-58; asst specialist, La State Univ, 60-61. *Mem:* Weed Sci Soc Am; Int Turfgrass Soc. *Res:* Weed control in turf, penetration, translocation and fate of herbicides in plants; effects of herbicides on physiological process in plants; fate of herbicides in surface water. *Mailing Add:* Dept PPWS Va Polytech Inst & State Univ Blacksburg VA 24061-0331

BINGLER, EDWARD CHARLES, geology, for more information see previous edition

BINHAMMER, ROBERT T, ANATOMY. *Current Pos:* assoc dean acad affairs, 79-86, PROF ANAT, COL MED, UNIV NEBR, 79- *Personal Data:* b Watertown, Wis, Apr 28, 29; m 52; c 3. *Educ:* Kalamazoo Col, BA, 51; Univ Tex, MA, 53, PhD(anat), 55. *Prof Exp:* From instr to prof anat, Col Med, Univ Cincinnati, 55-79, from asst dean to assoc dean, 67-79. *Mem:* Assoc mem Radiation Res Soc; Am Asn Anatomists. *Res:* Radiation biology; parabiosis in physiological studies; pituitary physiology; cytology. *Mailing Add:* 3608 S 101 St Omaha NE 68124

BINI, ALESSANDRA MARGHERITA, THROMBOSIS, ATHEROSCLEROSIS. *Current Pos:* ASST MEM, DEPT BLOOD COAGULATION BIOCHEM, LINDSEY KIMBAIL RES INST, NY BLOOD CTR, 92- *Personal Data:* b Milano, Italy, Nov 11, 50. *Educ:* Univ Milano, Italy, Doctor Biological Sci, 80; Mario Negri Inst, Italy, dipl pharmacol res, 82; Columbia Univ, MA, MPh, 86, PhD(path), 87. *Prof Exp:* Staff res assoc, Dept Med, Col Physicians & Surgeons, Columbia Univ, 84-86, sr staff res assoc, 87-88; head, Coagulation & Fibrinolysis Res Unit, Cent Res Biomed & Pharmacol, Mario Negri & Maria Imbaro Inst, Chieti, Italy, 88-92. *Concurrent Pos:* Vis scientist, Lindsley Kimball Res Ctr, NY Blood Ctr, 88-89; adj asst prof path, Col Physicians & Surgeons, Columbia Univ, 89-92 & 92- *Mem:* Am Asn Pathologists; Am Heart Asn; Int Soc Thrombosis &

Hemostasis; Soc Appl Immunohistochem; Int Fibrinogen Soc. *Res:* Pathophysiology of fibrin formation and degradation in vascular and extravascular sites in atherosclerosis, malignancy and renal disease. *Mailing Add:* NY Blood Ctr 310 E 67th St New York NY 10021. *Fax:* 212-570-3195; *E-Mail:* abini@server.nybc.org

BINKLEY, CLARK SHEPARD, FOREST ECONOMICS. *Current Pos:* DEAN & PROF FOREST RESOURCES MGT, UNIV BC, 90- *Personal Data:* b Salt Lake City, Utah, Dec 1, 49; m 72, Nadine Bonda; c Clayton B, Emily E & Alex F. *Educ:* Harvard Univ, AB, 71, MS, 76; Yale Univ, PhD(forestry), 79. *Prof Exp:* Res asst, Ctr Pop Studies, Harvard Univ, 69-71; dir, Environ Qual Div, Urban Systs Res & Eng, Inc, 71-75; actg instr, Sch Forestry & Environ Studies, Yale Univ, 78-79, from asst prof to prof, 79-90. *Concurrent Pos:* Dir, W Frasen Timber, Ltd; comt mem, Nat Acad Sci. *Mem:* AAAS; Soc Am Foresters; Can Inst Forestry; Commonwealth Forestry Asn. *Res:* Applications of economics to problems arising in public and private management; conservation of forest lands. *Mailing Add:* Univ BC Fac Forestry No 270-2357 Main Mall Vancouver BC V6T 1Z4 Can

BINKLEY, ROGER WENDELL, ORGANIC CHEMISTRY, PHOTOCHEMISTRY. *Current Pos:* From asst prof to assoc prof, 66-74, PROF CHEM, CLEVELAND STATE UNIV, 74- *Personal Data:* b Newark, NJ, Mar 9, 41; m 62; c 2. *Educ:* Drew Univ, BA, 62; Univ Wis, PhD(org chem), 66. *Concurrent Pos:* Res collab grant, 68-69. *Mem:* Am Chem Soc. *Res:* Photochemistry of carbohydrates. *Mailing Add:* H19 Hawthorne Dr Oberlin OH 44074-1425

BINKLEY, SUE ANN, BIOLOGICAL RHYTHMS, ENDOCRINOLOGY. *Personal Data:* b Dayton, Ohio, May 19, 44; m, H Randolph Tatem; c Shelley, Kyra & Jeffrey. *Educ:* Univ Colo, BA, 66; Univ Tex, Austin, PhD(zool), 71. *Prof Exp:* NIH fel physiol, Nat Inst Child Health & Human Develop, 71-72; from asst prof to assoc prof biol, Temple Univ, 73-97. *Concurrent Pos:* Mem, Regulatory Biol Panel, NSF, 80-82. *Mem:* Endocrine Soc; AAAS. *Res:* Biological basis of circadian rhythms in vertebrates and in the function of the pineal gland. *Mailing Add:* PO Box 12373 Aspen CO 81612

BINKOWSKI, FRANCIS STANLEY, METEOROLOGY. *Current Pos:* METEOROLOGIST, NAT OCEANIC & ATMOSPHERIC ADMIN, 75- *Personal Data:* b Elizabeth, NJ, 1937; m 61; c 4. *Educ:* Rutgers Univ, AB, 60; NY Univ, MS, 66, PhD(meteorol), 72. *Prof Exp:* Weather officer, Air Weather Serv, US Air Force, 60-64; asst prof meteorol, Rutgers Univ, 67-75. *Mem:* Am Meteorol Soc; Sigma Xi. *Res:* Numerical modeling for air pollution meteorology; atmospheric turbulence and diffusion. *Mailing Add:* 717 Tinkerbell Rd Chapel Hill NC 27514-3013

BINN, LEONARD NORMAN, MEDICAL & VETERINARY VIROLOGY, VIRAL VACCINES. *Current Pos:* microbiologist, 55-67, SUPVRY RES MICROBIOLOGIST, WALTER REED ARMY INST RES, 67- *Personal Data:* b Kedainiai, Lithuania, Nov 6, 27; US citizen; m 80, Ruth H Lasky; c Beth H, Shari H & David N. *Educ:* NY Univ, BA, 49; Univ Mich, MS, 51, PhD(bact), 55. *Mem:* Am Soc Microbiol; US Animal Health Asn; Am Soc Trop Med & Hyg; Am Soc Virol; Sigma Xi; Infectious Dis Soc Am. *Res:* Hepatitis viruses; stable smallpox vaccine; immunology of adenoviruses; immunity in arthropod-borne virus diseases; laboratory animal virus diseases and canine viruses. *Mailing Add:* 9626 Alta Vista Terr Bethesda MD 20814

BINNICKER, PAMELA CAROLINE, NEUROSCIENCES, CYTOLOGY. *Current Pos:* asst prof biol sci, 72-78, ASSOC PROF PHARMACEUT SCI, SCH PHARM, MERCER UNIV, 78- *Personal Data:* b Denmark, SC, July 17, 38. *Educ:* Coker Col, BA, 60; Columbia Univ, PhD(anat), 70. *Prof Exp:* Instr human biol, DeKalb Community Col, 71-72. *Concurrent Pos:* Instr anat & physiol, Sch Anestaesia, Ga Bapt Hosp, 75-86; lectr, Mercer Sch Nursing, 85-88. *Mem:* NY Acad Sci; Am Asn Cols Pharm. *Res:* Anatomy. *Mailing Add:* 1331 S Ponce De Leon Ave NE Atlanta GA 30306

BINNIE, WILLIAM HUGH, ORAL PATHOLOGY, ORAL MEDICINE. *Current Pos:* prof & chmn oral path, 79-82, prof & chmn path, 82-90, PROF & CHMN DIAG SCI, BAYLOR COL DENT, 90- *Personal Data:* b Glasgow, Scotland, Dec 24, 39; US citizen; m 97, Cheryl Weatherly; c 4. *Educ:* Glasgow Univ, BDS, 63; McGill Univ, DDS, 65; Ind Univ, MSD, 67; Royal Col Physicians & Surgeons, Glasgow, FDS, 72; Royal Col Pathologists, London, MRCPath, 75, FRCPath, 86. *Prof Exp:* Dent surgeon, Int Grenfell Asn, 63-64; from lectr to sr lectr oral path, Guy's Hosp Med Sch, 67-79. *Concurrent Pos:* Hon consult, Guy's Hosp, 75-79; consult, WHO, 75- & Baylor Univ Med Ctr, Vet Admin & Methodist Hosp, Dallas, 81-; chmn, Path Sect, Am Asn Dent Schs, 82-83; mem, Test Construction Comt, Nat Bd Oral Path & Dent Radiol, 84-88, Path/Micro, 89-92, Component B, 92-95. *Mem:* Am Acad Oral Path; Int Asn Oral Path (secy-treas, 86-92, pres elect, 92-94, pres, 94-96); Am Dent Asn; Am Asn Dent Schs; Int Asn Dent Res; Am Acad Oral Med. *Res:* Epidemiology, etiology, pathogenesis, diagnosis and management of oral mucosal disease; oral squamous cell carcinoma and salivary gland neoplasms. *Mailing Add:* Dept Diag Sci Baylor Col Dent 3302 Gaston Ave Dallas TX 75246. *Fax:* 214-828-8306

BINNIG, GERD, PHYSICS. *Current Pos:* Res staff mem, Zurich Res Lab, 78-86, GROUP LEADER, IBM PHYSICS GROUP, MUNICH UNIV, 84-, IBM FEL, 86- *Personal Data:* b Frankfurt, WGer, July 20, 47; m 69, Lore Wagler; c Iris & Marvin. *Educ:* J W Goethe Univ, dipl, 73, PhD(physics), 78. *Honors & Awards:* Nobel Prize in Physics, 86; Physics Prize, Ger Phys Soc, 82; Otto Klung Prize, 83; King Faisal Int Prize for Sci, 84; Hewlett Packard Europhysics Prize, 84; Elliot Cresson Medal, Franklin Inst, 87; Grosses Verdienstkreuz mit Stern und Schulterband des VVerdienstordens, 88; Minnie Rosen Award, Ross Univ, 88; Nat Inventors Hall of Fame, 94. *Concurrent Pos:* Fac mem, Stanford Univ, 85-86; hon prof physics, Univ Munich, WGer, 87- *Mem:* Nat Acad Sci; Europ Acad Arts, Sci & Humanities. *Res:* Atomic force microscopy; scanning tunneling microscopy. *Mailing Add:* IBM Res Div Zurich Res Lab Saeumerstrasse 4 Rueschlikon CH-8803 Switzerland

BINNING, LARRY KEITH, HORTICULTURE, WEED SCIENCE. *Current Pos:* From asst prof to assoc prof, 69-78, PROF HORT, UNIV WIS-MADISON, 78- *Personal Data:* b Fond du Lac, Wis, Aug 29, 42; m 64, Dorothy I Fisher; c Kimberly A & Heather L. *Educ:* Univ Wis, BS, 65; Mich State Univ, MS, 67, PhD(herbicide physiol, crop sci), 69. *Mem:* Weed Sci Soc Am; Hort Soc; Potato Asn Am. *Res:* Herbicide use and physiology; integrated pest management; weed ecology. *Mailing Add:* Dept Hort 385 Univ Wis Madison 1575 Linden Dr Madison WI 53706-1514. *Fax:* 608-262-4743; *E-Mail:* binning@calshp.cals.wisc.edu

BINNING, ROBERT CHRISTIE, PHYSICAL CHEMISTRY, CHEMICAL ENGINEERING. *Current Pos:* group leader, Monsanto Co, 58-61, proj mgr, 61-64, res mgr, Monsanto Res Corp, 64-65, asst dir res, 65-75, dir environ res & develop, 75-78, DIR CONTRACT RES & DEVELOP, MONSANTO RES CORP, 78- *Personal Data:* b Baton Rouge, La, Feb 11, 21; m 44; c 4. *Educ:* La State Univ, BS, 48, MS, 50, PhD(phys chem), 52. *Prof Exp:* Res chemist, Am Oil Co, 52-55, group leader, 55-58. *Mem:* Fel Am Inst Chem Engrs; Int Soc Technol Assessment; fel Am Inst Chemists; World Future Soc. *Res:* Direction of multidisciplinary research and development programs in environmental control and energy. *Mailing Add:* 3473 Tall Timber Trail Dayton OH 45409

BINNINGER, DAVID MICHAEL, MOLECULAR BIOLOGY, GENETICS. *Current Pos:* ASST PROF MOLECULAR GENETICS, FLA ATLANTIC UNIV, 90- *Personal Data:* b Kenosha, Wis; m 87, Kathleen Dailey; c Kelsey E. *Educ:* Univ SFla, BA, 79, MA, 81; Univ NC, PhD(genetics), 87. *Prof Exp:* Postdoctoral res molecular genetics, Univ Calif, Davis, Calif, 87-90. *Mem:* Sigma Xi; Sci Res Soc Am; Bioelectromagnetics Soc. *Res:* Investigation of the molecular mechanisms whereby 60 Hz electromagnetic fields are transduced into a biological signal that is capable of affecting gene expression; molecular basis of genetic recombination in eucaryotic cells. *Mailing Add:* 4220 NW Tenth St Delray Beach FL 33445. *Fax:* 561-367-2749; *E-Mail:* binninge@acc.fau.edu

BINNS, WALTER ROBERT, COSMIC RAY PHYSICS, RADIOLOGY. *Current Pos:* sr res assoc, 80-89, RES PROF, WASH UNIV, 89- *Personal Data:* b Williamsburg, Kans, Nov 7, 40; m 62; c 2. *Educ:* Univ Ottawa, BS, 62; Colo State Univ, MS, 66, PhD(physics), 69. *Prof Exp:* Scientist, Res Labs, McDonnell Douglas Corp, 69-80. *Mem:* Am Phys Soc; Am Asn Physicists Med. *Res:* Abundances of very heavy cosmic rays in the primary cosmic radiation; dosimetry and treatment verification in radiology. *Mailing Add:* 11128 Queens Way St Louis MO 63146

BINTINGER, DAVID L, COMPUTER DATA ANALYSIS, DRIFT CHAMBER CONSTRUCTION. *Current Pos:* AT BROOKHAVEN NAT LAB. *Personal Data:* b South Bend, Ind. *Educ:* Univ Notre Dame, BS, 64; Univ Chicago, PhD(physics), 75. *Prof Exp:* Res assoc, Fermi Nat Accelerator Lab, 75- *Mem:* Am Phys Soc. *Res:* Experimental high energy physics: design and supervision of construction of experimental equipment, and analysis of data. *Mailing Add:* MS 50A-2160 Lawrence Berkeley Lab Univ Calif One Cyclotron Rd Berkeley CA 94720

BINTZ, GARY LUTHER, COMPARATIVE PHYSIOLOGY, ENVIRONMENTAL PHYSIOLOGY. *Current Pos:* Asst prof physiol, 68-74, ASSOC PROF BIOL, EASTERN MONT STATE COL, 74- *Personal Data:* b Manchester, Iowa, Feb 25, 41. *Educ:* Cornell Col, BA, 63; Univ NMex, MS, 66, PhD(zool), 68. *Res:* Water metabolism, including the effects of negative water balance on whole body and tissue levels; studies on several rodents, especially ground squirrels capable of hibernation. *Mailing Add:* 731 Burlington Ave Billings MT 59101-0298

BINZ, CARL MICHAEL, ANALYTICAL CHEMISTRY. *Current Pos:* instr anal chem, 75-80, ASST PROF CHEM, LORAS COL0, 80- *Personal Data:* b Elgin, Ill, June 29, 47; m 75. *Educ:* Loras Col, BS, 69; Purdue Univ, MS, 71, PhD(chem), 74. *Prof Exp:* Res assoc, Purdue Univ, 74-75. *Res:* Determination of trace materials in air and water and their accumulated effects. *Mailing Add:* 3050 Valley View Rd Dubuque IA 52001

BIOLEAU, LUC J R, ENVIRONMENTAL HEALTH. *Current Pos:* CONSULT COORDR COMPUT, COMPUT DATA PROCESSING SOLUTIONS, 83-; CONSULT COORDR OCCUP HEALTH & SAFETY, OCCUP SAFETY HEALTH & ENVIRON CONSULTS, 85- *Personal Data:* b Schefferville, Que. *Educ:* Laurentian Univ, Ont, BSc, 79, MSc, 82. *Prof Exp:* Res assoc biol & chem, Laurentian Univ & McMaster Univ, 78-82; teacher biol, Laurentian Univ, 80-81; res coordr occup health & safety, Northeastern Ont Occup Health & Safety Resource Ctr, 82-85. *Concurrent Pos:* Researcher histochem, Carleton Univ, 80; technician sampling, Ont Res Found, 80; researcher x-ray fluorescences, Atmospheric Environ Servs, 82. *Res:* Monitor, literature search, analyses of major designated substances in Ontario; asbestos monitoring and analysis on site after sampling; substances on workplace; occupational health and safety and environmental subjects. *Mailing Add:* Occup Safety Health & Environ Consults 1233 The Kingsway Sudbury ON P3B 2E9 Can

BIOLSI, LOUIS, JR, THEORETICAL CHEMISTRY. *Current Pos:* From asst prof, to assoc prof, 68-84, PROF CHEM, UNIV MO-ROLLA, 84- *Personal Data:* b Port Jefferson, NY, Aug 21, 40; m 62; c 3. *Educ:* State Univ NY Albany, BS, 61, MS, 63; Rensselaer Polytech Inst, PhD(theoret chem), 67. *Prof Exp:* Proj assoc, Theoret Chem Inst, Univ Wis, 66-67; res assoc theoret chem, Brown Univ, 68. *Mem:* Am Phys Soc; Am Chem Soc. *Res:* Scattering and kinetic theory of polyatomic molecules and the specification of nonequilibrium states. *Mailing Add:* Dept Chem Univ Mo Rolla MO 65401

BIONDI, MANFRED ANTHONY, ATOMIC PHYSICS, AERONOMY. *Current Pos:* prof physics, 60-86, EMER PROF PHYSICS, UNIV PITTSBURGH, 86- *Personal Data:* b Carlstadt, NJ, Mar 5, 24; m 52, Elaine T Leitkam; c David M & George P. *Educ:* Mass Inst Technol, SB, 44, PhD(physics), 49. *Honors & Awards:* Davisson-Germer Prize, Am Phys Soc, 84. *Prof Exp:* Res assoc physics, Mass Inst Technol, 46-49; from res physicist to adv physicist, Westinghouse Res Lab, 49-57, mgr physics dept, 57-60. *Concurrent Pos:* Mem adv panel physics, NSF; vis fel, Joint Inst Lab Astrophys, 72-73; exchange prof, Univ Paris, 76-86; prin investr, Auroral & Airplow Studies of Earth's Upper Atmosphere, NSF, 76-; mem, Army Basic Res Steering Comt, Nat Res Coun, 85-88, chmn, 87-88. *Mem:* Fel AAAS; fel Am Phys Soc; Am Geophys Union. *Res:* Interactions and reactions involving electrons, ions and excited atoms; plasma physics; electromagnetic properties of metals at liquid helium temperatures; upper atmospheric dynamics; thermosphere and ionosphere. *Mailing Add:* Dept Physics & Astron Univ Pittsburgh Pittsburgh PA 15260. *Fax:* 412-624-9163; *E-Mail:* I:biondi@vm3.cis.pitt.edu, biondit@pitt.edu

BIONDO, FRANK X, MICROBIOLOGY, MYCOLOGY. *Current Pos:* assoc prof, 72-80, PROF HEALTH SCI, C W POST COL, LONG ISLAND UNIV, 80. *Personal Data:* b Brooklyn, NY, Mar 25, 27. *Educ:* Temple Univ, BA, 48; Athenaeum Ohio, MS, 51, PhD(exp med), 55. *Prof Exp:* Res dir bovine mastitis, Agr Res Inst, NJ, 53-54; instr microbiol, NY Med Col, 56-60; asst prof microbiol, Long Island Univ, 60-68, C W Post Col, 68-72. *Concurrent Pos:* Part time med technologist, Ital Hosp, New York, 44-60; La State Univ fel parasitol & trop med, PR Dominican Repub & Haiti, 58. *Mem:* AAAS; Am Soc Microbiol; Am Soc Trop Med & Hyg. *Res:* Medical mycology; tranplantable tumors; tissue extracts and their effect on Micrococcus pyogenes var aureus infections in mice and transplantable tumors; biochemistry of dematiaceous fungi and Candida species. *Mailing Add:* Dept Health Sci C W Post Campus Col Long Island Univ Greenvale NY 11548-1300

BIRBARA, PHILIP JAMES, CATALYIC & ABSORPTION PROCESSES, AIR WATER & SOLID WASTE POLLUTION CONTROL TECHNOLOGIES. *Current Pos:* SR PRIN SCIENTIST, HAMILTON STAND, 77. *Personal Data:* b Worcester, Mass, Aug 25, 34; m 68, Carolann Hefferan; c Charles & James. *Educ:* Moss Inst Technol, BS, 56, MS, 57; Univ Mich, PhD(chem eng), 61. *Honors & Awards:* Heros of Chem Award, Am Chem Soc, 96; Sr prin scientist, Hamilton Stand, 61-72. *Prof Exp:* Chem eng specialist, Chem Construct Corp, 73-76. *Concurrent Pos:* Prin investr advance waste mgr technol eval, Nat Acad Sci, 95-96. *Mem:* Am Soc Chem Engrs; Sigma Xi; AAAS. *Res:* Chemical process engineering and chemical engineering; patentee in field. *Mailing Add:* 52 Elm St 1 Hamilton Road Windsor Locks CT 06096

BIRCH, MARTIN CHRISTOPHER, ENTOMOLOGY, HEAD INJURIES & REHABILITATION. *Current Pos:* AT DEPT ZOOL, OXFORD UNIV, 80- *Personal Data:* b Crewe, Eng, July 14, 44; m 70; c 2. *Educ:* Oxford Univ, BA, 66, DPhil(entom), 69. *Prof Exp:* Res asst org chem, Dyson Perrins Lab, Oxford Univ, 69-70; res asst entom, Univ Calif, Berkeley, 70-73; assoc prof, Univ Calif, Davis, 73-80. *Concurrent Pos:* Royal Entom Soc fel, 65-; Headway oxford chmn, 87- *Mem:* Royal Entom Soc; Entom Soc Am; Sigma Xi; Int Soc Chem Ecol; Soc Exp Biol; Asn Study Animal Behav. *Res:* Insect behavior and physiology, particularly chemical communication; behavioral mechanisms in pheromone communication of Coleoptera and Lepidoptera. *Mailing Add:* Dept Zool Oxford Univ S Parks Rd Oxford OX1 3PS England

BIRCH, RAYMOND E(MBREE), CERAMICS ENGINEERING. *Current Pos:* RETIRED. *Personal Data:* b McConnelsville, Ohio, Dec 19, 05; m 27; c 1. *Educ:* Ohio State Univ, BCerE, 27, CerE, 37. *Honors & Awards:* Greaves-Walker Award, Nat Inst Ceramic Engrs; St Louis Award, John Jeppson Medal, Am Ceramic Soc, A V Bleininger Award. *Prof Exp:* Ceramic engr, Carlyle-Labold Co, 27-28; res engr, Eng Exp Sta, Ohio State Univ, 28-30; res engr, Harbison-Walker Refractories Co, 30-45, dir res, 45-70; res, Dresser Industs Co, 68-70. *Concurrent Pos:* Founding officer, Nat Inst Ceramic Engrs, 35; pres & founding group, St Clair Mem Hosp, Pittsburgh, 53-70; mem adv comt, Eng Depts, Ohio State Univ, Carnegie Mellon Univ & Ill Univs, 70- *Mem:* Fel AAAS; fel Am Ceramic Soc; fel Am Soc Testing & Mat; fel Geol Soc Am. *Res:* Refractories utilization of magnesia. *Mailing Add:* 45 Katherine Blvd Palm Harbor FL 34684

BIRCH, RUTH ELLEN, CLINICAL IMMUNOLOGY. *Current Pos:* RES SCI, VITEK SYSTEM, 86- *Personal Data:* b Chicago, Ill, Mar 7, 52. *Educ:* Univ Ill Med Ctr, MS, 77, PhD(immunol), 79. *Prof Exp:* Res asst prof pediat, Washington Univ, 82-86. *Mem:* Am Asn Immunol; Am Soc Microbiol; Am Soc Clin Path. *Res:* Immunoregulation and clinical assay development. *Mailing Add:* Birch Consultants 12605 Villa Hill Lane Creve Coeur MO 63141-6321

BIRCHAK, JAMES ROBERT, SENSORS, TRANSDUCER DESIGN. *Current Pos:* sr res physicist, Halliburton Logging Serv, 91-93, PRIN RES PHYSICIST, HALLIBURTON ENERGY SERVS, 93- *Personal Data:* b Latrobe, Pa, Mar 20, 39; m 63, Beatrice C Brennan; c William A & Frank L. *Educ:* Carnegie-Mellon Univ, BS, 61; Rice Univ, MA, 64, PhD(physics), 66; Wayne State Univ, MBA, 71. *Prof Exp:* Assoc sr res physicist, Gen Motors Res Lab, 66-71; sr res physicist, Southwest Res Inst, 71-76; res specialist, Babcock & Wilcox Lynchburg Res Ctr, 76-79; staff scientist & mgr, Nl Indust, 79-85; mem tech staff, Reliability Inc, 86-91. *Concurrent Pos:* Pres, Birchak Consult, 86- *Mem:* Am Phys Soc; Inst Elec & Electronics Engrs; Sigma Xi; Am Soc Nondestructive Testing; Soc Petrol Eng. *Res:* Irreversible magnetization of superconductors; magnet sources of internal friction; ultrasonics; electric and magnetic properties of materials; geophysics; solar energy; electronics; wireline and logging-while-drilling sensors for oil wells. *Mailing Add:* 3902 Cypressdale Spring TX 77388

BIRCHEM, REGINA, CELL & DEVELOPMENTAL BIOLOGY, ELECTRON MICROSCOPY. *Current Pos:* ASSOC PROF & FLORENCE MARIE SCOTT CHAIR DEVELOP BIOL, SETON HILL COL, GREENSBURG, PA, 90- *Personal Data:* b Sisseton, SDak; m 81, Dan I Bolef. *Educ:* Univ NDak, BSEd, 64; Univ Ga, MEd, 70, PhD(cell biol), 77. *Honors & Awards:* Presidential Award, Electron Micros Soc Am, 77. *Prof Exp:* Elem teacher, St Peter & Paul Sch, NDak, 58-61; sci teacher, St Francis Acad, 63-69; instr, Dept Bot, Sch Forest Resources, Univ Ga, 71, res assoc, 71-72, res assoc ultrastruct, 77-79; res assoc molecular, cellular & develop biol, Univ Colo, Boulder, 79-80 & Washington Univ, St Louis, 80-81; asst prof biol, Fontbonne Col, St Louis, 81-84, Univ Sewanee, Tenn, 84; asst res prof, Dept Neurol, St Louis Sch Med, 85-88; assoc prof biol, Pa State Univ, McKeesport, 88-90. *Concurrent Pos:* Consult. *Mem:* Int Asn Plant Tissue Culture. *Res:* Development and morphology of Volvox carteri; gametogenesis in Volvox; embryogenesis and organogenesis in pine and hardwood tissue cultures; plant cell ultrastructure; neuron and Schwann cell tissue culture; demyelinating neuropathy studies in tissue culture; education on environmental issues; writing and research on effect of environmental chemistry residues on development of organisms; micropropagation of perennnials in tissue culture. *Mailing Add:* Dept Biol Seton Hill Col Greensburg PA 15601. *E-Mail:* rbirchem@igc.apc.org

BIRCHFIELD, GENE EDWARD, ATMOSPHERIC PHYSICS, GEOPHYSICS. *Current Pos:* assoc prof, 63-74, PROF ENG & GEOL SCI, NORTHWESTERN UNIV, 74- *Personal Data:* b Bartlesville, Okla, Apr 14, 28; m 59; c 3. *Educ:* Univ Chicago, AB, 52, MS, 55, PhD(geophys sci), 62. *Prof Exp:* Asst meteorol, Univ Chicago, 56-62; NSF fel geophys sci, Univ Stockholm & Mass Inst Technol, 62-63. *Concurrent Pos:* Vis scientist, Inst Oceanog Sci, Wormley, Surrey, Eng, 72-73. *Mem:* Am Meteorol Soc; Am Geophys Union. *Res:* Geophysical fluid dynamics; physical limnology. *Mailing Add:* Dept Geol Northwestern Univ 309 Locy Hall Evanston IL 60208-0001

BIRCHFIELD, WRAY, PLANT PATHOLOGY. *Current Pos:* res plant pathologist, 59-72, nematologist, USDA, La State Univ, 72-84, CONSULT, 84- *Personal Data:* b Ware Shoals, SC, July 2, 20; m 45; c 3. *Educ:* Univ Fla, BS, 49, MS, 51; La Sa State Univ, PhD(plant path), 54. *Prof Exp:* Lab asst plant path, Univ Fla, 49-50; asst, La State Univ, 51-54; phytonematologist, Citrus Exp Sta, Fla State Plant Bd, 54-59. *Concurrent Pos:* Adj prof, La State Univ, nematol teaching, 68-84. *Mem:* Am Phytopath Soc; Soc Nematol. *Res:* Diseases of plants caused by nematodes; host-parasite relations of nematode diseases; soil microbiology and fumigation studies of soils; fungal and nematode complexes in relation to root diseases of plants; taxonomy of nematodes, fungi and plants. *Mailing Add:* 9302 Kingcrest Parkway Baton Rouge LA 70810

BIRCHLER, JAMES ARTHUR, GENETICS. *Current Pos:* assoc prof, 91-, PROF, UNIV MO. *Personal Data:* b Red Bud, Ill, Feb 7, 50. *Educ:* Eastern Ill Univ, BS, 72; Ind Univ, PhD(genetics), 77. *Prof Exp:* Investr genetics, Oak Ridge Nat Lab, 77-81; res affil, Roswell Park Mem Inst, 81-82; res affil, Dept Genetics, Univ Calif, Berkeley, 82-85; from asst prof to assoc prof, Harvard Univ, 85-91. *Mem:* Genetics Soc Am; AAAS. *Res:* Molecular genetics of eukaryotic gene expression. *Mailing Add:* Biol Sci Dept 117 Tucker Hall Univ Mo Columbia MO 65211. *Fax:* 573-882-0123; *E-Mail:* birchler@biosci.mbp.missouri.edu

BIRCKBICHLER, PAUL JOSEPH, BIOCHEMISTRY, CELL BIOLOGY. *Current Pos:* res assoc, 72-77, asst scientist, 77-81, ASSOC SCIENTIST, SAMUEL ROBERTS NOBLE FOUND, 81- *Personal Data:* b Greenville, Pa, Nov 13, 42; m 65; c 2. *Educ:* Duquesne Univ, BS, 64, PhD(biochem), 69. *Prof Exp:* Res fel, Brown Univ, 69-71; vis scientist, Bergen Univ, 71-72. *Concurrent Pos:* NSF traineeship, Duquesne Univ, 65-68; instr chem, Pa State Univ, 68-69; clin enzymologist, RI Hosp, 71. *Mem:* Am Asn Cancer Res; Tissue Cult Asn; Am Chem Soc; Am Soc Biol Chem; NY Acad Sci. *Res:* Transglutaminase and isopeptide product in normal and transformed human cells; regulation of transglutaminase activity in transformed cells; membrane proteins of normal and transformed cells. *Mailing Add:* Dept Urol 5SP330 Univ Okla Health Sci Ctr 920 Stanton L Young Blvd Oklahoma City OK 73104

BIRD, CAROLYN J, MARINE BIOLOGY. *Current Pos:* MARINE BIOLOGIST, INST MARINE BIOSCI, NAT RES COUN CAN. *Honors & Awards:* Luigi Provasoli Award, 94. *Mailing Add:* Nat Res Coun Can Inst Marine Biosci 1411 Oxford St Halifax NS B3H 3Z1 Can

BIRD, CHARLES DURHAM, BOTANY. *Current Pos:* RETIRED. *Personal Data:* b Norman, Okla, July 7, 32; Can citizen; m 57, Ann L George; c Arthur, Eric, John & Debora. *Educ:* Univ Man, BS, 56; Okla State Univ, MS, 58, PhD(bot), 60. *Honors & Awards:* Loran L Goulden Memn Award, 78. *Prof Exp:* Nat Res Coun Can fel, 60-62; asst prof bot, Univ Alta, Calgary, 62-65, actg cur herbarium, 62-79, admin off dept, 66-69, from assoc prof to prof bot, 67-79; rancher, 75-92. *Concurrent Pos:* Assoc ed bot, Can Field Naturalist, 74-; geneologist, Clan Rattray Soc. *Res:* Geneology; Ecology and wise land use policies. *Mailing Add:* Box 22 Erskine AB T0C 1G0 Can. *E-Mail:* cbird@wildrose.net

BIRD, CHARLES EDWARD, ENDOCRINOLOGY, METABOLISM. *Current Pos:* from asst prof to assoc prof, 65-75, assoc dean, Fac Med, 77-81, PROF MED, QUEEN'S UNIV, ONT, 75- *Personal Data:* b Kingston, Ont, Oct 19, 31; m 56; c 2. *Educ:* Queen's Univ, Ont, MD & CM, 56; McGill Univ, PhD(exp med), 67. *Prof Exp:* Clin asst med, Toronto Gen Hosp, Can, 61-63; clin asst, Royal Victoria Hosp, Can, 63-65. *Mem:* Can Med Asn; Endocrine Soc. *Res:* Biological disposition of progesterone; progesterone metabolism in the human fetus; androgen metabolism in carcinoma of the prostate; androgen and estrogen metabolism in carcinoma of the breast. *Mailing Add:* Watkins Three Rm 4-322 Kingston Gen Hosp 76 Stuart St Kingston ON K7L 2V7 Can

BIRD, CHARLES NORMAN, ORGANIC CHEMISTRY. *Current Pos:* RETIRED. *Personal Data:* b Rolla, Mo, Dec 27, 29. *Educ:* Col St Thomas, BS, 51; Univ Md, PhD(org chem), 57. *Prof Exp:* Coordr polyester develop, Minn Mining & Mfg Co, 3M Ctr, St Paul, 56-71, supvr graphic arts prod, 71-72, supvr photog bases & prod responsibility coordr, 72-88. *Mem:* Am Chem Soc. *Res:* Pyrolysis of esters; amides and lactones; organic synthesis; adhesives; rubber chemicals; polyester films; photographic films and chemicals. *Mailing Add:* 4102 River Rd S Afton MN 55001

BIRD, GEORGE RICHMOND, PHOTOVOLTAIC & PHOTOSENSITIZING MATERIALS, IMAGING SYSTEMS. *Current Pos:* dir sch, 71-74, PROF CHEM, SCH CHEM, RUTGERS UNIV, 69- *Personal Data:* b Bismark, NDak, Jan 25, 25; m 48, Doris Forgue; c George P, Elizabeth N & Margaret A. *Educ:* Harvard Univ, AB, 49, AM, 52, PhD(phys chem), 53. *Prof Exp:* Nat Res Coun fel, Radiation Lab, Columbia Univ, 52-53; asst prof chem, Rice Inst, 53-58; res chemist, Polaroid Corp, 58-61, mgr phys chem lab, 61-69. *Concurrent Pos:* Guggenheim fel, Photog Inst, Fed Tech Sch, Zurich, 74-75; vis lectr, Soc Photog Scientists & Engrs, 84-85. *Mem:* Am Chem Soc; fel Optical Soc Am; fel Soc Photog Sci & Eng. *Res:* Photovoltaic materials and laser dyes; imaging systems. *Mailing Add:* Dept Chem Rutgers Univ PO Box 939 Piscataway NJ 08855-0939. *Fax:* 732-932-5312

BIRD, GEORGE W, NEMATOLOGY, PLANT PATHOLOGY. *Current Pos:* PROF NEMATOL, MICH STATE UNIV, 73- *Personal Data:* b Newton, Mass, June 16, 39; m 67. *Educ:* Rutgers Univ, BS, 61, MS, 63; Cornell Univ, PhD(plant path), 67. *Honors & Awards:* CIBA-GEIGY Award, Soc Nematologists, 83. *Prof Exp:* Res scientist, Res Br, Can Dept Agr, 66-68; from asst prof to assoc prof, Dept Plant Path, Univ Ga, 68-73; dir, USDA/CSREES/SARE. *Concurrent Pos:* coordr, N Cent Sustainable Agr Res & Educ Profession Develop Prog. *Mem:* Fel Am Phytopath Soc; fel Soc Nematologists (pres, 77-78); AAAS. *Res:* Phytonematology; biology nematodes; sustainable agriculture. *Mailing Add:* Dept Entom Mich State Univ 243 Natural Sci East Lansing MI 48824-1115. *Fax:* 517-353-4354; *E-Mail:* bird@msue.msu.edu

BIRD, GORDON WINSLOW, GEOCHEMISTRY, CHEMISTRY. *Current Pos:* PORTFOLIO MGR, ENVIRON TECHNOL, ALTA RES COUN, 92- *Personal Data:* b NB, Can, Jan 30, 43; m 68, Jan Robb; c 4. *Educ:* Univ NB, BSc, 65; Univ Alta, MSc, 67; Univ Toronto, PhD(geol), 71. *Prof Exp:* Res fel mineral sci, Victoria Univ, Wellington, 71-74, sr res fel, 74-77; assoc res officer chem, Atomic Energy Can, 77-81; assoc res officer chem, Oil Sands Res Ctr, Alta Res Coun, 82-86; sr res officer & mgr fundamental res, Oil Sands & Hydrocarbon Recovery, 87-90; mgr indust contracts & bus develop, 90-92. *Concurrent Pos:* Adj prof geol, Univ Alta, Edmonton, 86-96; prog dir, Alta Oil Sands Technol & Res Authority, ARC & Can Ctr Mineral & Energy Technol, 92- *Mem:* Soc Petrol Engrs. *Res:* Geology; environmental chemistry; clay mineral dissolution, mass transport, low temperature silicate reaction kinetics; thermally enhanced oil recovery. *Mailing Add:* Alta Res Coun 250 Karl Clark Rd Edmonton AB T6N 1E4 Can. *Fax:* 403-472-6912; *E-Mail:* bird@oil.arc.ab.ca

BIRD, HAROLD L(ESLIE), JR, BIOCHEMISTRY, ORGANIC CHEMISTRY. *Current Pos:* prof, 74-84, EMER PROF CHEM, COL OF THE DESERT, CALIF, 84- *Personal Data:* b Pluckemin, NJ, Dec 9, 21; m 45; c 2. *Educ:* Rutgers Univ, BS, 43; Purdue Univ, MS, 49; Univ Ariz, PhD(biochem), 74. *Prof Exp:* Chemist, Metall & Chem Div, Naval Res Lab, 43-46; asst, Purdue Univ, 46-49; biochemist & anal chemist, Eli Lilly & Co, 49-64; asst prof, Longwood Col, 64-67; instr & lectr, Dept Chem, Univ Ariz, 67-74. *Concurrent Pos:* Lectr, Purdue Univ, 63-64. *Mem:* AAAS; Am Chem Soc. *Res:* Chromatography; biochemistry and natural products. *Mailing Add:* 47-967 Sun Corral Trail Palm Desert CA 92260-6103

BIRD, HARVEY HAROLD, PLASMA PHYSICS, GEOPHYSICS. *Current Pos:* from instr to asst prof, 62-70, ASSOC PROF PHYSICS, FAIRLEIGH DICKINSON UNIV, 70- *Personal Data:* b Montclair, NJ, Aug 25, 34; m 57; c 2. *Educ:* Johns Hopkins Univ, BA, 56; Calif Inst Technol, MS, 59; Stevens Inst Technol, PhD(physics), 69. *Prof Exp:* Mem tech staff, Space Technol Labs, Thompson-Ramo-Woolridge, Calif, 59-62. *Concurrent Pos:* US del, Int Asn Geomagnetism & Aeronomy, Madrid, Spain, 69. *Mem:* Am Phys Soc; Am Geophys Union. *Res:* Physics of the earth's magnetosphere; instability theory in plasmas. *Mailing Add:* PO Box 261 Emigrant MT 59027-0261

BIRD, JOHN MALCOLM, GEOLOGY. *Current Pos:* PROF GEOL, COL ENG, CORNELL UNIV, 72- *Personal Data:* b Newark, NJ, Dec 27, 31; m 83, Maura S Weathers; c 2. *Educ:* Union Col, NY, BS, 55; Rensselaer Polytech Inst, MS, 59, PhD(geol), 62. *Prof Exp:* From instr to prof geol, State Univ NY Albany, 61-72; chmn dept geol sci, 69-72. *Concurrent Pos:* Res grants, Geol Soc Am, 62-, NY State Geol Surv, 63-, NSF, 64, 68, 72, 73, 75, 76, 77, 78, 79, 80 & 81, US Geol Surv, 79, 80 & 81, Off Naval Res 78, 79 & 80, Nat Acad Sci Day fund, 69, Petrol Res Found, 75, Nat Geog Soc, 77, 78, 79, 80, 81, 82, 83, 84 & 86 & NASA, 85-91; mem, NY State Mus & Sci Serv, 63-67; Nat Acad Sci exchange vis scientist, Polish Acad Sci, 67; res assoc, Lamont-Doherty Geol Observ, Columbia Univ, 70, sr res assoc, 70-72; distinguished vis scientist, Am Geol Inst, 71-; assoc ed, J Geophys Res, 71-73; chmn, Appalachian Working Group, US Geodynamics Comt, 71-73; distinguished lectr, Am Asn Petrol Geologists, 77-78; vis prof, Inst Physique Globe, Univ Paris, 86. *Mem:* Fel Geol Soc Am; Am Geophys Union; fel Can Geol Soc; Sigma Xi. *Res:* Geotectonics; genesis of ore deposits; Appalachian geology; lithosphere plate tectonics; continent evolution; evolution of mountain belts; ophiolite tectonics; petrology of ultramafic rocks. *Mailing Add:* Dept Geol Sci Cornell Univ 4126 Snee Hall Ithaca NY 14853. *E-Mail:* bird@geology.cornell.edu

BIRD, JOHN WILLIAM CLYDE, CELL PHYSIOLOGY, MOLECULAR PHYSIOLOGY. *Current Pos:* From asst prof to prof physiol & biochem, Rutgers Univ, 61-78, dir, Bur Biol Res, 76-87, chmn, dept biol sci, 82-86, DISTINGUISHED PROF PHYSIOL, RUTGERS UNIV, 78- *Personal Data:* b Erie, Pa, Nov 10, 32; m 54, Evelyn S; c John & Jason. *Educ:* Univ Colo, BA, 58, MA, 59; Univ Iowa, PhD(physiol), 61. *Honors & Awards:* Outstanding Res Award, Muscular Dystrophy Asn, 82 & 85. *Concurrent Pos:* Fulbright prof biochem, Cairo Univ, 64-65; NIH career develop award, 66-71; Fulbright res scholar, Belg, 69-70; vis prof biochem, Jilin Univ, People's Repub China, 81; Fulbright prof physiol, Univ Panama, 94. *Mem:* AAAS; NY Acad Sci; Am Physiol Soc; Fedn Clin Res; fel Nat Acad Sci France. *Res:* Proteinases and proteinase inhibitors; muscle lysosomes; muscular dystrophy. *Mailing Add:* Dept Cell Develop Neural Biol Rutgers Univ PO Box 1059 Piscataway NJ 08854. *Fax:* 732-445-5870; *E-Mail:* bird@rutgers.biology.edu

BIRD, JOSEPH FRANCIS, theoretical physics, for more information see previous edition

BIRD, JOSEPH G, CLINICAL PHARMACOLOGY, MEDICINE. *Current Pos:* RETIRED. *Personal Data:* b Waycross, Ga, Oct 6, 15; m 39; c 3. *Educ:* Fla Southern Col, BS, 37; Univ Md, MD, 42, PhD(pharmacol), 49. *Prof Exp:* Rotating intern, Univ Hosp, Baltimore, Md, 42-43; asst resident med, 43-44 & 46-47; instr pharmacol, Sch Med, Univ Md, 47-54, asst med, 50-54; dir, Div Clin Res, Sterling-Winthrop Res Inst, 54-67, dir exp med, 67-70; asst dir, Ciba-Geigy Corp, 70-72, assoc dir, 73-77, dir clin pharmacol, 77-80. *Concurrent Pos:* Staff physician, Univ Hosp & Md Gen Hosp, Baltimore, 50-54; med dir, Radio Div, Bendix Corp, 49-54. *Mem:* AAAS; assoc emer Am Chem Soc; emer Am Soc Clin Pharmacol & Exp Therapeut; emer NY Acad Sci. *Res:* Pharmaceutical research; clinical trials of new drugs. *Mailing Add:* 29 Sea Spray Dr Biddeford ME 04005-9204

BIRD, KIMON T, plant tissue culture, plant biotechnology; deceased, see previous edition for last biography

BIRD, LESLIE V(AUGHN), electrical engineering, for more information see previous edition

BIRD, LUTHER SMITH, PLANT PATHOLOGY. *Current Pos:* From instr to prof, 50-86, EMER PROF PLANT PATH, TEX A&M UNIV, 86- *Personal Data:* b Greenville, SC, Nov 25, 21; m 47; c 2. *Educ:* Clemson Univ, BS, 48; Tex A&M Univ, MS, 50, PhD(genetics), 55. *Mem:* Crop Sci Soc Am; Am Phytopath Soc; Am Soc Agron; Am Genetic Asn; Sigma Xi. *Res:* Breeding for and genetics of multi-adversity resistance (diseases, insects and stress) in cotton; symbiosis genetics; seed quality and cold tolerance in cotton; nature of resistance and escape mechanisms. *Mailing Add:* 729 Shady Lane Bryan TX 77802-4322

BIRD, MARY LYNNE MILLER, ADMINISTRATION. *Current Pos:* EXEC DIR, AM GEOG SOC, 83- *Personal Data:* b Buffalo, NY, Feb 25, 34; m 58, Thomas Edward; c Matthew David & Lisa Bronwen. *Educ:* Syracuse Univ, AB, 56. *Prof Exp:* Mem res staff, Ctr Res Personality, Harvard Univ, 59-62, Ctr Int Studies, Princeton Univ, 62-66, Inst Int Soc Res, 65, Sch Int Affairs, Columbia Univ, 66-67, Coun Foreign Rels, 67-69, Twentieth Century Fund, 69-72; asst to pres, World Policy Inst, 72-74; dir develop, Fund for Peace, 74-78; dir fels prog, Exec Coun Foreign Dipl, 78-79; dir develop, Asn Vol Surg Contraception, 79-83. *Concurrent Pos:* Consult, Fedn Am Scientists, Washington, 74-75. *Mem:* AAAS; Asn Am Geogr; Soc Woman Geogr; Int Soc Spatial Sci; Inst Current World Affairs; Nat Coun Geog Educ; Int Geog Union; Conf Latin Am Geogr. *Mailing Add:* Am Geog Soc 120 Wall St No 100 New York NY 10005-3904. *Fax:* 212-422-5480; *E-Mail:* amgeosoc@earthlink.net

BIRD, MICHAEL WESLEY, GUIDANCE & CONTROL, NAVIGATION. *Current Pos:* Sr staff engr, 69-80, mgr flight mgt technol, Instrument Div, 80-87, DIR, MIL & COM SYSTS, LEAR SIEGLER INC, 87-; DIR, SYSTS ENG, SMITH INDUSTS, GRAND RAPIDS. *Personal Data:* b Grand Rapids, Mich, Sept 24, 42; m 65; c 1. *Educ:* Mich State Univ, BS, 64, MS, 66, PhD(elec eng), 69. *Mem:* Inst Elec & Electronics Engrs. *Res:* Applied research in performance optimization control theory; artificial intelligence with application to vehicle guidance systems. *Mailing Add:* Smiths Industs Grand Rapids 4141 Eastern Ave SE Grand Rapids MI 49518

BIRD, PETER, TECTONOPHYSICS, FINITE ELEMENT MODELS. *Current Pos:* From asst prof to assoc prof, 76-85, PROF EARTH & SPACE SCI, UNIV CALIF, LOS ANGELES, 85- *Personal Data:* b Cambridge, Mass, Sept 29, 51; m 72, Jean M Campbell; c Andrew. *Educ:* Harvard Univ, BA, 72; Mass Inst Technol, PhD(geophys), 76. *Mem:* Fel Am Geophys Union; fel Geol Soc Am. *Res:* Finite-element and analytic modeling of lithosphere deformation to test theories of orgeny and determine the rheology of lithosphere in situ. *Mailing Add:* Dept Earth & Space Sci Univ Calif Los Angeles CA 90095-1567

BIRD, R(OBERT) BYRON, CHEMICAL ENGINEERING, THEORETICAL CHEMISTRY. *Current Pos:* proj assoc chem eng, Univ Wis-Madison, 53-55, assoc prof, 55-57, chmn dept, 64-68, Charles F Burgess distinguished prof, 68-72, prof chem eng, 57-92, Vilas Res prof, 72-92, John D Macarthur prof, 82-92, EMER PROF, UNIV WIS-MADISON, 92- *Personal Data:* b Bryan, Tex, Feb 5, 24. *Educ:* Univ Ill, BS, 47; Univ Wis, PhD(chem), 50. *Hon Degrees:* DEng, Lehigh Univ, 72, Wash Univ,, 73 Colo sch mines, 86 & Technion-Israel Inst Technol,93-; DEng Sci, Technische Hogeschool Delft, Holland, 77; DSc, Clarkson Col Technol, 80, Eidgenossiche Tech Sch, Zurich, 94, Kyoto Univ, Japan, 96. *Honors & Awards:* Curtis McGraw Award, 59 & Westinghouse Award, 60, Corcoran Award, 87, Am Soc Eng Educ; William H Walker Award, 62, Prof Prog Award, 65 & W K Lewis Award, 74, Am Inst Chem Engrs; Bingham Medal, Soc Rheology, 74; Eringen Medal, Soc Eng Sci, 83; Nat Medal of Sci, 87; Founders Award, Am Inst Chem Engrs. *Prof Exp:* Fulbright fel, Amsterdam, 50-51; proj assoc chem, Univ Wis, 51-52; asst prof, Cornell Univ, 52-53. *Concurrent Pos:* Mem adv panel, Eng Sci Div, NSF, 61-64; Fulbright lectr, Kyoto & Nagoya Univ, 62-63; Petrol Res Fund grant, Am Chem Soc, 63; consult, Union Carbide Corp, 64-77; mem adv bd, Int Chem Eng, 65, 66; US ed, Appl Sci Res, 68-87 & 89-; mem adv bd, Indust & Eng Chem, 70-72 & J Non-Newtonian Fluid Mech, 76-; J M Burgers prof, Tech Univ, Delft, Holland, 94; vis prof, Cath Univ Louvain, Belg, 94. *Mem:* Nat Acad Sci; Nat Acad Eng; fel Am Inst Chem Engrs; fel Am Phys Soc; Am Acad Arts & Sci; foreign mem Royal Dutch Acad Arts & Sci. *Res:* Transport phenomena; viscoelastic fluid mechanics; polymer fluid dynamics and kinetic theory; molecular theory of gases and liquids; technical Japanese translation. *Mailing Add:* Dept Chem Eng Univ Wis Madison WI 53706-1691

BIRD, RICHARD PUTNAM, BIOPHYSICS. *Current Pos:* TECH WRITER, SCI TYPOGRAPHERS, 88- *Personal Data:* b Durango, Colo, July 19, 38; m 62; c 3. *Educ:* Univ Colo, BS, 60, MS, 62; Univ Calif, Berkeley, MBioradiol, 68, PhD(biophys), 72; Am Bd Toxicol, cert. *Prof Exp:* Res asst physics, Univ Colo, 61-62; health physicist, Idaho Opers Off, 62-64; phys sci adminr, San Francisco Opers Off, US AEC, 64-66; res assoc physics, Kans State Univ, 71-74; res assoc biophysics, Columbia Univ, 74-88. *Mem:* Radiation Res Soc. *Res:* Biological effect of radiation of different quality, particularly accelerator-produced radiations, using eucharyotic cell systems. *Mailing Add:* 110 Jennings Ave Patchogue NY 11772

BIRD, ROBERT EARL, MOLECULAR BIOLOGY. *Current Pos:* DIR, DRUG DEVELOP, MOLECULAR ONCOL, INC, 89- *Personal Data:* b San Antonio, Tex, Nov 4, 43; m 64. *Educ:* Kans State Univ, BS, 65, PhD(genetics), 69. *Prof Exp:* Investr molecular biol, Biol Div, Oak Ridge Nat Lab, 69-71; res dir, Dept Molecular Biol, Univ Geneva, Switz, 71-74; sr staff fel, Lab Molecular Biol, Nat Inst Arthritis, Metab & Digestive Dis, NIH, 74-77; asst prof, Dept Molecular Biol, Vanderbilt Univ, 77-; res dir, Genex Corp, 88-89. *Mem:* Genetics Soc Am; Am Soc Microbiol. *Res:* Genetics, microbiology and biochemistry as related to the regulation of chromosome replication and cell division; control and mechanism of DNA replication in vivo and in vitro. *Mailing Add:* Molecular Oncol Inc 19 Firstfield Rd Gaithersburg MD 20878

BIRD, SAMUEL OSCAR, II, INVERTEBRATE PALEONTOLOGY, SYSTEMATICS. *Current Pos:* RETIRED. *Personal Data:* b Charleston, WVa, Feb 26, 34; m 55. *Educ:* Marshall Col, BS, 55; Univ Wis, MS, 58; Univ NC, PhD(geol), 62. *Prof Exp:* From asst prof to prof geol & geog, Mary Washington Col, 62-68, prof, geol, 68-79, chmn dept, 70-79; geologist-ed, Va Div Mineral Resources, 79-85 & Va Div Energy, 85-89. *Concurrent Pos:* Exten grant for res partic, Col Teachers Prog, 65-67; proj dir, Co SIP, NSF, 70-75. *Mem:* Fel Geol Soc Am; Am Geol Inst. *Res:* Quantitative systematics; molluscan ecology and community structure; quantitative approaches to stratigraphic correlation; appalachian stratigraphy and structural geology. *Mailing Add:* 212 Wickham Ave Beckley WV 25801

BIRD, STEPHANIE J(EAN), RESEARCH ETHICS, HEALTH POLICY. *Current Pos:* staff scientist neurosci res prog, Mass Inst Technol, 79-82, Mellon fel, 82-83, vis scholar, 83-86, res assoc & lectr, 86-92, spec asst to assoc provost, 92-95, SPEC ASST TO PROVOST, MASS INST TECHNOL, 95- *Personal Data:* b Los Angeles, Calif, Oct 5, 48; m 76, Lawrence W Shannon. *Educ:* Univ Calif, Los Angeles, BA, 71; Yale Univ, MS, 72, PhD(physiol), 75. *Prof Exp:* Fel, Johns Hopkins Univ, 75-76; fel, Case Western Res Univ, 76-78, sr res assoc, 78-79. *Concurrent Pos:* Consult, Sen Edward M Kennedy Comt Policy, 82; Social Issues Comt, Soc Neurosci, 83-86, Pub Info Comt, 84-87; Nominations Comt, Asn Women Sci, 83-85, counr, 86-88, proj dir & prin investr, Mentoring Proj, 90-93; consult, Arista Omega Communs, 86-89, Med-X Med Communs, 89-90, DC Helath Chem Textbk, 92, Mass Corp Educ Telecommunications, 92- *Mem:* Soc Neurosci; Asn Women Sci (pres-elect, 88-89, pres, 90-91); fel AAAS; Coun Sci Soc Res. *Res:* Neuroscience, and it's ethical, legal & social policy implications, especially screening tests; health and science policy relating to neuroscience and or biotechnology issues. *Mailing Add:* 41 Sleepy Hollow Wrentham MA 02093. *Fax:* 617-253-1986

BIRD, THOMAS DWIGHT, NEUROLOGY, NEUROGENETICS. *Current Pos:* Neurol resident, Univ Wash, 69-70, 72-74, med genetics fel, 74-76, from asst prof to assoc prof, 76-88, PROF MED, UNIV WASH, 88-, PROF NEUROL, 96-; CHIEF NEUROL, VET ADMIN MED CTR, SEATTLE, 84- *Personal Data:* b Newark, NY, Aug 3, 42; M 67, Rosaline Merrill; c Jeffrey & Caroline. *Educ:* Dartmouth Col, BA, 64; Cornell Univ, MD, 68. *Honors & Awards:* Wartenberg Prize, Am Acad Neurol, 92; Met Life Res Award, Metrop Life Found, 95. *Concurrent Pos:* Investr, Alzheimer's Res Ctr, Univ Wash, 85-, adj prof psychiat, 95- *Mem:* Am Acad Neurol; Am Neurol Asn; Am Soc Human Genetics; AAAS. *Res:* Clinical neurogenetic research of hereditary diseases of the nervous system including Alzheimer's Disease and neuromuscular disorders. *Mailing Add:* Vet Admin Med Ctr Seattle WA 98108

BIRD, THOMAS JOSEPH, MEDICAL MICROBIOLOGY. *Current Pos:* RETIRED. *Personal Data:* b Scranton, Pa, Nov 15, 27; m 52; c 6. *Educ:* Univ Scranton, BS, 51; Univ Pa, MS, 54, PhD(med microbiol), 56. *Prof Exp:* Instr microbiol, Med Sch, Northwestern Univ, 56-58; instr, Stritch Sch Med, Loyola Univ, Ill, 58-59, asst prof, 59-60; res microbiologist, Hines Vet Admin Hosp, Hines, Ill, 64-72, chief microbiologist, 72-88. *Concurrent Pos:* Consult, Ill Dept Pub Health, 65-; vis prof microbiol, Chicago Med Sch, 70- *Mem:* Fel Am Soc Microbiol; Sigma Xi; NY Acad Sci; Brit Soc Gen Microbiol; fel Am Acad Microbiol. *Res:* Virus relationships to host; bacteriophages; lysogeny; tissue culture; drug effects on host virus system; pseudomonas infections; plasmid epidemiology; pyocins; Legionnaire's disease. *Mailing Add:* 1500 Victoria Ave Berkeley IL 60163-1465

BIRDSALL, CHARLES KENNEDY, ELECTRICAL ENGINEERING, FIRST PRINCIPLES COMPUTER SIMULATIONS OF ELECTRICAL DEVICES. *Current Pos:* prof, 55-91, PROF ELEC ENG GRAD SCH & LEADER, PLASMA THEORY & SIMULATION GROUP, UNIV CALIF, BERKELEY, 91- *Personal Data:* b New York, NY, Nov 19, 25; m 49, 81, Virginia Anderson; c Anne, Barbara, Thomas & John. *Educ:* Univ Mich, BSE, 46, MSE, 48; Stanford Univ, PhD(elec eng), 51. *Honors & Awards:* Plasma Sci & Applns Award, Inst Elec & Electronics Engrs Nuclear & Plasma Sci Soc, 88. *Prof Exp:* Res Physicist, Hughes Res & Develop Labs, 51-55, group leader electron physics, Gen Elec Microwave Lab, 55-59. *Concurrent Pos:* Lectr, Univ Calif, Los Angeles, 53-55, Stanford Univ, 55 & Univ Calif exten, 56; prof, Miller Inst Basic Res in Sci, Univ Calif, Berkeley, 63-64, chmn, Energy & Resources Prog, 72-74; assoc ed, Inst Elec & Electronics Engrs Transactions on Electron Devices, 64; NSF grantee, US-Japan Coop Sci Prog, 66; sr vis fel, Univ Reading, Eng, 76; consult, Lawrence Livermore Nat Lab, 60-86; foreign res assoc, Inst Plasma Physics, Nagoya Univ, Japan, 81 & 82, vis prof, 88; vis prof Chevron energy, Calif Inst Technol, 82; vis res scholar, Max Planck Inst Plasma Physics, Ger & Inst Theoret Physics, Univ Innsbruck, Austria, 85; Fulbright grant, Innsbruck, Austria, 91. *Mem:* Fel Inst Elec & Electronics Engrs; fel Am Phys Soc; fel AAAS. *Res:* Plasmas; computer simulation of plasmas; plasma assisted processing of materials; plasma devices, microwave tube modeling and simulation; about 160 journal publication and 27 patents. *Mailing Add:* Dept Elec Eng & Comput Sci Univ Calif Berkeley CA 94720-1770. *Fax:* 510-642-6330; *E-Mail:* birdsall@eecs.berkeley.edu

BIRDSALL, MARION IVENS, food science, social science, for more information see previous edition

BIRDSALL, THEODORE G, UNDERWATER ACOUSTIC PROPAGATION, SIGNAL PROCESSING. *Current Pos:* Res engr, Univ Mich, 50-66, assoc prof, 67-70, dir, 74-88, PROF COMMUN, PROCESSING & DETECTION THEORY COMMUN & SIGNAL PROCESSING LAB, UNIV MICH, 70- *Personal Data:* b Lakewood, Ohio, Oct 30, 27; m 51, Helen Camelle Wilson; c Edward A, Michael G, Margaret M (Kovas), Steven C, Patrick W & Robert J. *Educ:* Univ Mich, BSE, 50, MS, 52, PhD(commun sci), 66. *Concurrent Pos:* Prin investr, Off Naval Res, Univ Mich, 60- *Mem:* Inst Elec & Electronics Engrs; fel Acoust Soc Am. *Res:* Stochastic detection and estimation theory applied to underwater acoustic propagation and underwater acoustic tomography; design and conducting of experiments, applications of results. *Mailing Add:* 2450 Canyon Dr Ypsilanti MI 48197. *E-Mail:* birdsall@umich.edu

BIRDSALL, TIMOTHY CARROLL, NATUROPATHIC MEDICINE, BOTANICAL MEDICINE. *Current Pos:* TECH DIR, THORNE RES INC, 89- *Personal Data:* b Geneva Township, Wis, July 4, 51; m 72, Kathryn June Williams; c Jeremy, Lisa, Aaron, Rebecca, James, John, Andrew & Addie. *Educ:* Grace Col, BA, 72; Bastyr Univ, ND(naturopath med), 85. *Prof Exp:* Instr therapeut nutrit, Bastyr Univ, 87-90. *Concurrent Pos:* Vis lectr therapeut nutrit, Bastyr Univ, 90-94; dir, Am Asn Natropathic Physicians, 92-; ed-in-chief, Alternative Med Rev, 96- *Mem:* NY Acad Sci; Am Asn Naturopath Physicians (vpres, 96-); AAAS; fel Am Col Naturopath Obstetricians. *Res:* Therapeutic nutrition; botanical medicine; natural childbirth; homocysteine metabolism; fibromyalgia; immune dysfunction; bioflavonoids; insulin resistance syndrome. *Mailing Add:* PO Box 3200 Sandpoint ID 83864. *E-Mail:* tim@thorne.com

BIRDSALL, WILLIAM JOHN, INORGANIC CHEMISTRY. *Current Pos:* from asst prof to assoc prof, 71-83, PROF CHEM, ALBRIGHT COL, 83- *Personal Data:* b Waterbury, Conn, Oct 28, 44; m 69; c 2. *Educ:* Univ Maine, BA, 66; Pa State Univ, PhD(chem), 71. *Concurrent Pos:* Fel, Pa State Univ, 71; vis scientist, Oxford Univ, 78-79 & Danforth Assoc; vis prof, Lehigh Univ, 87-88. *Mem:* AAAS; Am Chem Soc; Sigma Xi; NY Acad Sci. *Res:* Isolation of natural products with emphasis on inorganic constituents; synthesis and structural determination of metal-purine complexes and alkaloid-metal adducts; study of bilayer phospholipid vesicles. *Mailing Add:* Sch Vet Med Univ Pa Kennett Sq PA 19348-1682

BIRDSELL, DALE CARL, MICROBIOLOGY, PHYSIOLOGY. *Current Pos:* ASSOC PROF BASIC DENT SCI, UNIV FLA, 74- *Personal Data:* b Spokane, Wash, Feb 9, 40; m 62; c 2. *Educ:* Wash State Univ, BS, 62, MS, 64; Univ Calif, Riverside, PhD(biol), 67. *Prof Exp:* Res assoc microbiol, Scripps Clin & Res Found, 67-68; asst prof, Sch Med, Univ Louisville, 69-70; asst prof, Sch Dent, Loyola Univ, 70-74. *Concurrent Pos:* NIH fel microbiol, Scripps Clin & Res Found, 68-69. *Mem:* AAAS; Am Soc Microbiol; Int Asn Dent Res. *Res:* Structure and function of the synthesis of macromolecular components of cell surfaces; membrane genesis in microorganisms; role of surfaces in diseases of oral cavity. *Mailing Add:* Foothill Hosp 1403 29th St NW Calgary AB T2N 2T9 Can

BIRDSONG, RAY STUART, biology, ichthyology; deceased, see previous edition for last biography

BIRDWHISTELL, RALPH KENTON, PHYSICAL INORGANIC CHEMISTRY. *Current Pos:* PROF CHEM & CHMN DEPT, UNIV W FLA, 67- *Personal Data:* b Columbus, Ohio, May 11, 24; m 43; c 3. *Educ:* Ohio State Univ, BSc, 49; Univ Kans, PhD(chem), 53. *Prof Exp:* Fel, Mich State Univ, 53-54, asst prof, 54-58; assoc prof chem, Butler Univ, 63-67. *Concurrent Pos:* Vis lectr, Univ Ill, 62-63. *Mem:* Am Chem Soc; Sigma Xi; AAAS; NY Acad Sci. *Res:* Synthesis and thermodynamic properties of inorganic complex compounds; species occurring in both aqueous and nonaqueous media. *Mailing Add:* Dept Chem Univ W Fla Pensacola FL 32514-5751

BIRECKA, HELENA M, PLANT PHYSIOLOGY, BIOCHEMISTRY. *Current Pos:* RETIRED. *Personal Data:* b Poland, May 13, 21; m 48; c 1. *Educ:* Univ Perm, MS, 44; Timiriazev Acad, Moscow, PhD(plant physiol), 48. *Prof Exp:* Asst prof agr chem, Agr Univ, Warsaw, 49-51, assoc prof plant physiol, 53-61, chmn dept, 54-68, prof, 61-68; assoc prof agr chem, Univ Poznan, 51-53; consult, Int Atomic Energy Agency, Vienna, 68-69; res assoc plant physiol, Yale Univ, 69-70; assoc prof plant physiol & biochem, Union Col, NY, 70-74, prof biosci, 74-91. *Concurrent Pos:* head, Plant Metab Lab, Polish Acad Sci, 60-68, chmn, Comt Use Isotopes & Nuclear Energy in Agr & Biol Sci, 62-68; prof, Isotope Lab, Inst Plant Cultivation, Warsaw, 61-68; Food & Agr Orgn fel, 64. *Mem:* Polish Bot Soc; Polish Biochem Soc; Am Soc Plant Physiol; Am Soc Agron. *Res:* Mineral nutrition of plants; alkaloid biosynthesis and metabolism; photosynthesis; long distance translocation in plants; polyamine biosynthesis; scientific papers published over 100. *Mailing Add:* 1159 Phoenix Ave Schenectady NY 12308

BIRECKI, HENRYK, LIQUID CRYSTAL TECHNOLOGY, COMPUTER DATA STORAGE. *Current Pos:* mem tech staff displays, 79-81, Hewlett Packard Labs, optical data storage, 81-83, proj mgr, 83-85, technol eval & optical comput, 85-87, proj mgr, Optical Data Storage, 87-93, PRIN PROJ SCIENTIST, DISPLAY TECHNOL, HEWLETT PACKARD LABS, 93- *Personal Data:* b Warsaw, Poland, Nov 19, 48; m 71; c 2. *Educ:* McGill Univ, BSc, 70 & MSc, 72; Mass Inst Technol, PhD(physics), 76. *Prof Exp:* Fel & mem tech staff physics liquid crystals, Lawrence Berkeley Labs, 76-79. *Mem:* Am Phys Soc; Sigma Xi; Soc Info Display. *Res:* Optical data storage concentrating on magneto-optic technology for high performance systems; display technologies concentrating on liquid crystal and phosphor physics. *Mailing Add:* 3001 Ross Rd Palo Alto CA 94303

BIRELY, JOHN H, CHEMICAL PHYSICS. *Current Pos:* group leader, asst dir & dep div leader, 74-81, assoc dir chem, Earth & Life Sci, 81-86, DEP DIR, DEFENSE, LOS ALAMOS NAT LAB, 86- *Personal Data:* b Glen Ridge, NJ, Oct 17, 39; m 82; c 1. *Educ:* Yale Univ, BS, 61; Univ Calif, Berkeley, MS, 63; Harvard Univ, PhD(phys chem), 67. *Prof Exp:* Asst phys chem, Univ Calif, Berkeley, 61-63 & Harvard Univ, 63-66; NIH fel, Cambridge Univ, 66-67; asst prof chem, Univ Calif, Los Angeles, 67-69; mem tech staff, Aerospace Corp, 69-74. *Mem:* Am Phys Soc; Am Chem Soc; AAAS. *Res:* Atomic and molecular collision physics; molecular spectroscopy; gas phase chemical kinetics and energy transfer; laser photochemistry. *Mailing Add:* 115 Piedra Loop Los Alamos NM 87544

BIRGE, ANN CHAMBERLAIN, science education; deceased, see previous edition for last biography

BIRGE, EDWARD ASAHEL, BACTERIAL GENETICS. *Current Pos:* asst prof, 72-77, ASSOC PROF MICROBIOL, ARIZ STATE UNIV, 77- , CHAIR, 91- *Personal Data:* b Madison, Wis, July 30, 42; m 84, Lori G Pearce; c Anna & Mara. *Educ:* Univ Wis-Madison, BA, 65, PhD(molecular biol), 71. *Prof Exp:* Fel, Radiobiol Lab, Yale Univ, 70-72. *Concurrent Pos:* Vis assoc prof bact, Univ Wis-Madison, 82. *Mem:* Am Soc Microbiol. *Res:* Bacterial genetics; regulation of isocitrate dehydrogenase; recombination in Escherichia coli. *Mailing Add:* Dept Microbiol Ariz State Univ Tempe AZ 85287-2701. *Fax:* 602-965-0098; *E-Mail:* edward.birge@asu.edu

BIRGE, ROBERT RICHARDS, LASER SPECTROSCOPY, MOLECULAR ELECTRONICS. *Current Pos:* PROF CHEM, SYRACUSE UNIV, 88-, DIR, CTR MOLECULAR ELECTRONICS, 88- *Personal Data:* b Washington, DC, Aug 10, 46; m 68; c 2. *Educ:* Yale Univ, BS, 68; Wesleyan Univ, PhD(chem), 72. *Honors & Awards:* Nat Sci Award, Am Cyanamid Co, 64. *Prof Exp:* Researcher chem air pollution res div, Environics Br, Kirtland Air Force Base, NMex, 72-73; NIH fel chem, Harvard Univ, 73-75; from asst prof to assoc prof, Univ Calif, Riverside, 75-84; prof chem & head dept, Carnegie-Mellon Univ, 85-87, dir, Ctr Molecular Electronics, 85-87. *Concurrent Pos:* Consult molecular spectros, Air Pollution Res Div, Environics Br, Kirtland Air Force Base, NMex, 73-75; mem & sci consult, Bice Comn Atmospheric Pollution, US Senate, 76-77; chmn, res comt, Univ Calif, 81-82; Weingart fel, Calif Inst Technol, 82-83; treas, Carnegie Inst Natural Hist, 85-86; mem, Molecular & Cellular Biophys Chem Study Sect, NIH, 84-88 & Adv Grant Rev Panel, Biophys Prog, NSF, 90; bd dir, West Penn Hosp Res Found, 87-88; Univ Calif Regents Fac fel, 76. *Mem:* Am Chem Soc; Sigma Xi; Am Phys Soc; Biophys Soc. *Res:* Theory and application of nonlinear (two-photon) laser spectroscopy to the study of biological molecules and protein bound chromophores; development and application of molecular orbital theory and molecular dynamics in biophysics; laser photocalorimetry and solvent effects. *Mailing Add:* Dept Chem Syracuse Univ Syracuse NY 13244-4100

BIRGE, ROBERT WALSH, HIGH ENERGY PARTICLE PHYSICS. *Current Pos:* Jr physicist, Univ Calif, Berkeley, 42-45, lectr, Physics Dept, 58-70, physicist, Lawrence Radiation Lab, 50-87, assoc dir physics, comput sci & math, 73-81, dep assoc dir, 82-87, EMER ASSOC DIR, LAWRENCE BERKELEY LAB, UNIV CALIF, 87- *Personal Data:* b Berkeley, Calif, Jan 30, 24; m 48, Ann C Birge; c Margit A, Bettine & Norman O. *Educ:* Univ Calif, AB, 45; Harvard Univ, AM, 47, PhD(physics), 51. *Concurrent Pos:* Orgn Europ Econ Coop sr vis fel, 60; Guggenheim fel, 61; consult, Arms Control & Disarmament Agency, 63; NATO sr fel sci, 71; vis scientist, Europ Orgn Nuclear Res, 71-72; mem sci policy comt, Stanford Linear Accelerator Ctr, 70-74. *Mem:* Am Phys Soc; AAAS. *Res:* Experimental high energy particle physics. *Mailing Add:* One Greenwood Common Berkeley CA 94708

BIRGE, WESLEY JOE, ZOOLOGY, AQUATIC TOXICOLOGY. *Current Pos:* PROF BIOL SCI, UNIV KY, LEXINGTON, 68-, PROF, GRAD CTR TOXICOL, 77-, ACTG DIR, SCH BIOL SCI, 80- *Personal Data:* b Pomeroy, Wash, Mar 11, 29; m 69. *Educ:* Eastern Wash State Col, BA, 51; Ore State Col, MS, 53, PhD(zool), 55. *Prof Exp:* Asst zool, Ore State Col, 52-53; instr, Univ Ill, 55-58, asst prof, 58-62; assoc prof, Univ Minn, Morris, 62-68. *Mem:* Soc Environ Toxicol & Chem; Am Soc Zoologists; Soc Develop Biol; Am Soc Cell Biol; Int Soc Develop Biologists. *Res:* Environmental toxicology; reproductive and developmental biology; neuroembryology; electron microscopy, histology. *Mailing Add:* Sch Biol Sci Morgan Biol Sci Bldg Univ Ky Lexington KY 40506-0001

BIRGENEAU, ROBERT JOSEPH, CONDENSED MATTER PHYSICS. *Current Pos:* prof physics, 75-82, head dept, 88-91, CECIL & IDA GREEN PROF PHYSICS, MASS INST TECHNOL, 82-, DEAN SCI, 91- *Personal Data:* b Toronto, Ont, Mar 25, 42; m 64; c 4. *Educ:* Univ Toronto, BSc, 63; Yale Univ, PhD(physics), 66. *Honors & Awards:* Morris Loeb Lectr, Harvard Univ, 86; Oliver E Buckley Prize for Condensed Matter Physics, Am Phys Soc, 87; Bertram Eugene Warren Award, Am Chem Asn, 88; Mat Sci Outstanding Accomplishment Award, Dept Energy, 88; 48th Richtmyer Mem Lectr, 89; Guiptill Lectr, Dalhousie Univ, 90; Welsh Lectr, Univ Toronto, 94; Segre Distinguished Lectr Physics, Tel Aviv Univ, 95. *Prof Exp:* Instr, Dept Eng & Appl Sci, Yale Univ, 66-67; fel, Oxford Univ, 67-68; mem tech staff, Bell Lab Inc, 68-74, head, Res Dept, 75. *Concurrent Pos:* Guest sr scientist, Brookhaven Nat Lab, 68-; vis scientist, Riso Nat Lab, Rosklde, Denmark, 71 & 79; mem, Solid State Sci Adv Panel, Nat Res Coun, 74-80; mem external rev comt, Solid State & Mat Sci Div, Argonne Nat Lab, 78-80, bd govs, 92-; co-chmn, Gordon Conf Quantum Solids & Fluids, 79; mem, Rev Panel Neutron Scattering, US Dept Energy, 80; chmn, Policy & Adv Bd, Cornell High Energy Synchrotron Source, 80-84; assoc ed, Condensed Matter Physics, Phys Rev Lett, 80-; assoc dir, Res Lab Electronics, Mass Inst Technol, 83-86; mem, Major Mat Facil Comt, Nat Acad Sci, 84, Prog Comt, High Flux Beam Reactor, Brookhaven, 84, Dept Energy & NSF Synchrotron Adv Comt, 85, Mat Sci Comt, NSF, 89-90 & bd trustees, Assoc Univs, Inc, 90-; consult, Los Alamos Nat Lab, 82-, Sandia Lab, 85-; bd trustees, Mus Sci, 92-; bd gov, Argonne Lab, 92- *Mem:* Fel Am Phys Soc; fel AAAS; fel Am Acad Arts & Sci. *Res:* Neutron and x-ray scattering spectroscopy of condensed matter, especially near magnetic, liquid crystal, and melting phase transitions; transport and scattering studies of high-temperature superconductors. *Mailing Add:* Sch Sci 6-123 Mass Inst Technol 77 Massachusetts Ave Cambridge MA 02139-4307. *Fax:* 617-253-8901; *E-Mail:* robertjb@mit.edu

BIRITZ, HELMUT, THEORETICAL PHYSICS. *Current Pos:* asst prof, 68-74, ASSOC PROF THEORET PHYSICS, GA INST TECHNOL, 74- *Personal Data:* b Vienna, Austria, Oct 4, 40; m 66. *Educ:* Univ Vienna, PhD(theoret physics), 62. *Prof Exp:* Res assoc theoret physics, Univ Vienna, 62-63 & Max Planck Inst Physics & Astrophys, 63-67. *Mem:* Am Phys Soc. *Res:* Theoretical high energy physics. *Mailing Add:* Sch Physics Ga Inst Technol Atlanta GA 30332

BIRIUK, GEORGE, MATHEMATICS. *Current Pos:* From asst prof to assoc prof, 62-70, PROF MATH, CALIF STATE UNIV, NORTHRIDGE, 70- *Personal Data:* b Sdolbunov, Russia, Apr 1, 28. *Educ:* Ind Univ, MA, 57; Univ Calif, Los Angeles, PhD(math), 63. *Concurrent Pos:* Assoc ed, Math Rev, 67-68. *Mem:* Am Math Soc. *Res:* Functional analysis, especially self adjoint and normal operators in Hilbert spaces; applications to differential operators. *Mailing Add:* Dept Math Calif State Univ Northridge CA 91330

BIRK, JAMES PETER, CHEMICAL EDUCATION, ARTIFICIAL INTELLIGENCE. *Current Pos:* assoc prof, 73-79, PROF CHEM, ARIZ STATE UNIV, 79- *Personal Data:* b Cold Spring, Minn, Aug 21, 41; m 74, Kay Gunter; c Kara. *Educ:* St John's Univ, Minn, BA, 63; Iowa State Univ, PhD(phys chem), 67. *Honors & Awards:* Nat Calalyst Award, 90. *Prof Exp:* Res assoc inorg chem, Univ Chicago, 67-68; asst prof, Univ Pa, 68-73. *Concurrent Pos:* Asst chmn, Chem Dept, Ariz State Univ, 84-86; vis prof, Eastern Mich Univ, 87-88; ed, Filtrates & Residues, J Chem Educ, 88-89; bd dir, Odyssey Sch Gifted & Talented, 85-87; adv bd, Ctr Acad Precocity; SERAPHIM fel, 87-88; comput series, J Chem Educ, 89-96 & 97. *Mem:* Am Chem Soc; Soc Col Sci Teachers; Nat Sci Teachers Asn; Asn Comput Sci & Math Teaching; Sigma Xi. *Res:* Kinetics and mechanisms of reactions of transition metal complexes in solution; oxidation-reduction reactions; substitution reactions; linkage isomerism; computers in chemical education; artificial intelligence in chemical education; inorganic chemistry. *Mailing Add:* Dept Chem Ariz State Univ Tempe AZ 85287. *E-Mail:* jbirk@asu.edu

BIRKBY, WALTER H, FORENSIC ANTHROPOLOGY. *Current Pos:* RETIRED. *Personal Data:* b Gordon, Nebr, Feb 28, 31; m 55, Carmen S Gates; c Julieanne & Jeffrey. *Educ:* Univ Kans, BA, 60, MA, 63; Univ Ariz, PhD(anthrop), 73. *Honors & Awards:* T Dale Stewart Award, Am Acad Forensic Sci, 90. *Prof Exp:* phys anthropologist, Ariz State Mus, 68-85, cur phys anthrop, 85-96. *Concurrent Pos:* Consult, Inst Forensic Sci, 71-76; chmn, Anthrop Sect, Am Acad Forensic Sci, 76-77; consult, Off Med Examr, Pima Co, Ariz, 81-; lectr, Univ Ariz, 81-89; dir, Forensic Anthrop Grad Prog, Univ Ariz, 83-96, adj res prof anthrop, 86-96; consult, USAF Hosp, Davis-Monthan, AFB, Tuscon, Ariz, 84-96; pres, Am Bd Forensic Anthrop, 85-87; adv forensic anthrop, Chief Dept Army, Armed Serv Graves Regist Off, Washington, DC, 86-93. *Mem:* Fel Am Acad Forensic Sci; Am Asn Phys Anthrop. *Res:* Analysis of unidentified recent human remains; establishment of positive identity for law enforcement agencies; medical examiners, criminal and civil attorneys. *Mailing Add:* Forensic Sci Ctr 2825 E District Tucson AZ 85714. *Fax:* 520-294-9402; *E-Mail:* wbirkby@aol.com

BIRKE, RONALD LEWIS, ELECTROCHEMISTRY, ANALYTICAL CHEMISTRY. *Current Pos:* assoc prof, 74-80, PROF CHEM, CITY COL NEW YORK, 80- *Personal Data:* b St Louis, Mo, Jan 4, 39; m 62, 75, Marilyn Sohn; c Susan A, Mimi B, Jason E & Nili T. *Educ:* Univ NC, BS, 61; Mass Inst Technol, PhD(anal chem), 65. *Prof Exp:* Res asst chem, Mass Inst Technol, 62-63, 65; vis fel, Free Univ Brussels, 65-66; instr, Harvard Univ, 66-69; from asst prof to assoc prof, Univ SFla, 69-74. *Concurrent Pos:* William F Milton Fund grant, Harvard Univ, 66-67; consult, US Army Electronic Components Commmand, NJ, 68 & US Army Harry Diamond Labs, DC, 69; NIH grant, 70-73 & 75-82, NSF grant, 79-82, 83-85, 87-91; tech exchange prog, Dept Energy, 92. *Mem:* AAAS; Am Chem Soc; Electrochem Soc; NY Acad Sci; Sigma Xi. *Res:* Thermodynamics and kinetics of electrochemical reactions in solution and interfaces; principles of electrochemical measurements; electroanalytical chemical analysis; biological redox processes and raman spectroscopy at electrodes; surface enhanced Raman Scattering. *Mailing Add:* Dept Chem City Col New York New York NY 10031. *Fax:* 212-650-6107; *E-Mail:* birke@scisan.sci.ccny.cuny.edu

BIRKEBAK, RICHARD C(LARENCE), MECHANICAL ENGINEERING. *Current Pos:* PROF SCI & TECHNOL, UNIV NATIONS, 85- *Personal Data:* b St Paul, Minn, Mar 14, 34; m 53; c 4. *Educ:* Univ Minn, BS, 55, MSME, 56, PhD(mech eng), 62. *Prof Exp:* Instr mech eng, Univ Minn, 56-62, US Pub Health Serv fel life sci, Mus Natural Hist, 62-64; asst prof mech eng, Ga Inst Technol, 64-66; assoc prof mech eng, Univ Ky, 66-70, prof, 70-84, res prof, 78-79. *Concurrent Pos:* Prin investr, USAF Aircraft Icing, 82-86. *Mem:* Am Soc Mech Engrs. *Res:* Heat transfer in icing conditions; thermal physical properties of biological materials; heat transfer in biological systems; thermal radiation property measurements and instrumentation; thermal physical property measurements at low temperatures and pressures. *Mailing Add:* 7937 Tenth Ave SW Seattle WA 98106

BIRKEDAL HANSEN, HENNING, COLLAGEN BREAKDOWN. *Current Pos:* PROF DENT, SCH DENT, UNIV ALA, 83- *Educ:* Royal Dent Col, Denmark, PhD(biochem), 77. *Mailing Add:* NIDR NIH 30 Convent Dr MSC 4326 Bldg 30 Rm 132 Bethesda MD 20892-4326

BIRKELAND, CHARLES JOHN, HORTICULTURE. *Current Pos:* RETIRED. *Personal Data:* b Warwick, NDak, Apr 16, 16; m 41; c 3. *Educ:* Mich State Col, BS, 39; Kans State Col, MS, 41; Univ Ill, PhD(hort), 47. *Prof Exp:* Res asst, Kans State Col, 39-41, asst horticulturist, 41-46; from asst to asst prof, 46-49, actg head dept, 49-50, prof hort & head dept, Univ Ill, Urbana-Champaign, 50-77. *Mem:* AAAS; fel Am Soc Hort Sci; fel Am Pomol Soc; Am Genetic Asn; Bot Soc Am; Sigma Xi. *Res:* Anatomy and photosynthesis of fruit-tree leaves; internal structure of apple leaves of varieties, species and hybrids, with special reference to growth and fruitfulness; fruit breeding. *Mailing Add:* 101 W Windsor Rd Urbana IL 61801

BIRKELAND, PETER WESSEL, GEOLOGY, SOIL SCIENCE. *Current Pos:* assoc prof, 67-72, PROF GEOL SCI, UNIV COLO, BOULDER, 72- *Personal Data:* b Seattle, Wash, Sept 19, 34; m 59, Suzanne Birkeland; c Karl & Robin. *Educ:* Univ Wash, BS, 58; Stanford Univ, PhD(geol), 62. *Honors & Awards:* Kirk Bryan Award, Geol Soc Am. *Prof Exp:* Asst prof soil morphol, Univ Calif, Berkeley, 62-67. *Mem:* Geol Soc Am; Soil Sci Soc Am; Am Quaternary Asn; Int Union Quaternary Res. *Res:* Geomorphology; Pleistocene geology; soil morphology and genesis; soil stratigraphy and mineralogy; soil development rates. *Mailing Add:* Geol Sci Univ Colo Box 250 Boulder CO 80309-0250

BIRKEMEIER, WILLIAM P, ELECTRICAL ENGINEERING. *Current Pos:* RETIRED. *Personal Data:* b Evanston, Ill, Nov 10, 27; m 51; c 3. *Educ:* Northwestern Univ, BS, 51; Univ Ark, MS, 55; Purdue Univ, PhD(elec eng), 59. *Prof Exp:* Elec engr, Collins Radio Co, Iowa, 51-54; assoc prof elec eng, Univ Ark, 59-60; assoc prof, Univ Wis-Madison, 60-65, prof elec eng, 65-, chmn dept, 80-88. *Concurrent Pos:* Consult, Emerson Elec Co, Mo, 60-61, Collins Radio Co, Iowa, 63-64 & Harris Corp, 77-78. *Mem:* Sr mem Inst Elec & Electronics Engrs; Int Union Radio Scientists. *Res:* Radio probing of the atmosphere; radar technology; biomedical engineering; coherent optics. *Mailing Add:* S 11463 Soeldner Rd Spring Green WI 53588

BIRKEN, STEVEN, ENDOCRINOLOGY, PROTEIN STRUCTURE-FUNCTION. *Current Pos:* Res assoc protein chem, 72-84, res scientist, 85-88, DIR, PROTEIN CORE FACIL, COLUMBIA UNIV, 86-, SR RES SCIENTIST, 88- *Personal Data:* b Brooklyn, NY, Dec 17, 45; m 72; c 4. *Educ:* NY Univ, BA, 67; Hofstra Univ, MA, 69; St Johns Univ, PhD(biol), 72. *Concurrent Pos:* NSF fel, 70-72; NIH fel, 73-74. *Mem:* Endocrine Soc; Am Chem Soc; AAAS; Am Soc Biol Chemists. *Res:* Protein structural and immunochemical studies of glycoprotein hormones, chiefly human choriogonadotropin. *Mailing Add:* Dept Med Columbia Univ 630 W 168th St New York NY 10032-3702

BIRKENBERGER, LORI, RESPIRATORY. *Current Pos:* ASSOC SCIENTIST, MARION MERRELL DOW INC, 92- *Personal Data:* b Waterbury, Conn, Oct 3, 62; m 87, Michael A Story. *Educ:* Univ Cincinnati, PhD(anat & cell biol), 90. *Prof Exp:* Res assoc, NIH, Nat Heart Lung & Blood Inst, 90-92. *Mem:* Am Soc Cell Biologist; Sigma Xi. *Mailing Add:* Hoechst Marion Roussel Inc 2110 E Galbraith Rd PO Box 156300 Cincinnati OH 45215-6300. *Fax:* 513-948-7345

BIRKENHAUER, ROBERT JOSEPH, TEXTILE CHEMISTRY. *Current Pos:* RETIRED. *Personal Data:* b Toledo, Ohio, Feb 7, 16; m 41, Christine; c Donald L & Diana H (Anderson). *Educ:* Univ Detroit, BS, 37; Univ Notre Dame, MS, 39, PhD(phys chem), 41. *Prof Exp:* Chemist, Gulf Refining Co, Tex, 37-38; asst, Univ Notre Dame, 38-41; res chemist, process develop viscose rayon, 41-44, prod develop, 44-46, res group leader equip develop, 46, res supvr, 46-47, plant res surv, Textile Fibers Dept, 47-53, process supt rayon, 53-58, dacron, 58-60, mgr tech serv, 60-62, asst to prod mgr dacron, E I du Pont de Nemours & Co, 62-78. *Res:* Process and development of viscose rayon and of dacron and polyester fibers. *Mailing Add:* 2518 Deepwood Dr Wilmington DE 19810

BIRKENHOLZ, DALE EUGENE, BIOLOGY. *Current Pos:* assoc prof biol sci, 62-70, PROF ECOL, ILL STATE UNIV, 70- *Educ:* Iowa State Univ, BS, 56; Southern Ill Univ, MA, 58; Univ Fla, PhD(biol), 62. *Prof Exp:* Instr biol, Univ Fla, 61-62. *Mem:* AAAS; Am Soc Mammalogists; Ecol Soc Am; Am Soc Zoologists; Am Ornith Union; Sigma Xi. *Res:* Ecology and behavior of small mammals; ornithology. *Mailing Add:* 805 Karin Dr Normal IL 61761

BIRKES, DAVID SPENCER, STATISTICS. *Current Pos:* trainee, 72-74, asst prof, 74-82, ASSOC PROF STATIST, ORE STATE UNIV, 82- *Personal Data:* b Portland, Ore, Dec 1, 42. *Educ:* Stanford Univ, BS, 64; Univ Chicago, MS, 66; Univ Wash, PhD(math), 69; Ore State Univ, MS, 72. *Prof Exp:* Res staff mem math, Inst Defense Anal, 70-71. *Mem:* Am Statist Asn; Inst Math Statist. *Res:* Linear models. *Mailing Add:* Dept Statist Ore State Univ 44 Kidder Hall Corvallis OR 97331-4606

BIRKETT, JAMES DAVIS, PHYSICAL CHEMISTRY. *Current Pos:* PROPRIETOR & CONSULT, W NECK STRATEGIES, 88- *Personal Data:* b Norwalk, Conn, Sept 30, 36; m 60; c Lucy B, John H & Benjamin T. *Educ:* Bowdoin Col, AB, 58; Yale Univ, MS, 60, PhD(chem), 63. *Prof Exp:* Chemist res & develop, Arthur D Little, Inc, 62-88. *Concurrent Pos:* Trustee, Lincoln Acad, New Castle, Maine. *Mem:* AAAS; Am Chem Soc; Water Supply Improv Asn; Int Desalination Asn; Am Water Works Asn; NAm Membrane Soc; NY Acad Sci. *Res:* Membrane permeation systems; desalination systems; water treatment technology; strategic management of technology; history of technology. *Mailing Add:* PO Box 193 Nobleboro ME 04555-0193

BIRKHAHN, RONALD H, SYNTHETIC ENERGY NUTRIENTS, FAT METABOLISM. *Current Pos:* PROF SURG & BIOCHEM, MED COL OHIO, 76- *Personal Data:* b 39; m 69, Gertrude Chan; c Ronald H & Robert H. *Educ:* Purdue Univ, PhD(phys chem), 67. *Mem:* Am Inst Nutrit; Am Soc Clin Nutrit; Am Col Nutrit; Nutrit Soc Gt Brit; Am Physiol Soc; AAAS; Am Soc Parenteral & Enternal Nutrit. *Res:* Improved parenteral nutritional support of the critically ill; ketosis and its influence on wound healing in surgical patients; nutritional interaction with tumor growth; liver regeneration. *Mailing Add:* Med Col Ohio PO Box 10008 Toledo OH 43699. *Fax:* 419-381-3057; *E-Mail:* birkhahn%portny@cutter.mco.edu

BIRKHOFF, GARRETT, mathematics; deceased, see previous edition for last biography

BIRKHOFF, ROBERT D, EXPERIMENTAL SOLID STATE PHYSICS. *Current Pos:* RETIRED. *Personal Data:* b Chicago, Ill, Jan 29, 25; m 45. *Educ:* Mass Inst Technol, BS, 45; Northwestern Univ, PhD(physics), 49. *Prof Exp:* Consult, Health Physics Div, Oak Ridge Nat Lab, 50-55, physicist, 55-67, sect chief, Radiation Physics Sect, 67-74, mem res staff, Health & Safety Res Div, 74-81; prof physics, Univ Tenn, 67-81. *Mem:* Fel Am Phys Soc; Health Physics Soc. *Res:* Beta ray spectroscopy; interaction of radiation with matter; health physics; electronic and optical properties of liquids; electronic structure of submicron objects. *Mailing Add:* 8466 N Lockwood Ridge Rd No 244 Sarasota FL 34243

BIRKIMER, DONALD LEO, STRUCTURES, APPLIED MECHANICS. *Current Pos:* RETIRED. *Personal Data:* b New Lexington, Ohio, Sept 6, 41; m 62; c 3. *Educ:* Ohio Univ, BSCE, 63; Univ Cincinnati, MS, 65, PhD(struct, appl mech), 68; Harvard Univ, PMD, 73. *Honors & Awards:* Wason Medal, Am Concrete Inst, 73; Coast Guard Meritorius Unit Commendation Award, 76. *Prof Exp:* Civil engr, Wright Patterson AFB, 63-64; res civil engr, US Army Corps Engrs, 64-68; res struct engr, Battelle Mem Inst, 68-69; actg chief res & develop, US Army Construct Eng Res Lab, 69-71; asst dir, Naval Surface Weapons Ctr, 71-75; tech dir res & develop, Coast Guard Res & Develop Ctr, Groton, 75-81; tech dir, Naval Civil Eng Lab, Port Hueneme, Calif, 81-85. *Concurrent Pos:* Tech consult, Battelle Mem Inst, Nat Standard Co & Technovation Mgt, Inc, 69-71. *Mem:* AAAS; Am Mgt Asn; Inst Mgt Sci; Am Soc Testing & Mat; Nat Soc Prof Engrs. *Res:* Oil identification; vessel traffic services; aid to navigation; domestic and polar ice technology; marine fire safety; search and rescue. *Mailing Add:* 1291 Seybolt Ave Camarillo CA 93010

BIRKS, JOHN WILLIAM, KINETICS OF ATMOSPHERIC REACTIONS, FIELD MEASUREMENTS OF ATMOSPHERIC SPECIES. *Current Pos:* assoc prof, 77-84, PROF CHEM, UNIV COLO, BOULDER, 84- *Personal Data:* b Vinita, Okla, Dec 10, 46; m 72, 90, Kathy L Rowlen; c Krishna D, Alicia S & Shannon L. *Educ:* Univ Ark, BS, 68; Univ Calif, Berkeley, MS, 70, PhD(chem), 74. *Honors & Awards:* Leo Szilard Award, Am Phys Soc, 85; Witherspoon Peace & Justice Award, Witherspoon Soc, 86; Ralph M Johnson Distinguished Guest lectr, Utah State Univ, 86; William J Probst lectr, Southern Ill Univ, 87. *Prof Exp:* Asst prof chem, Univ Ill, Urbana-Champaign, 74-77. *Concurrent Pos:* Fel, Coop Inst Res Environ Sci, Univ Calif, Boulder, 77-, actg dir, 85-86; Alfred P Sloan Found fel, 79; guest scientist, Max Planck Inst, Mainz, Ger, 81-82; mem, Comt Atmospheric Effects Nuclear Explosions, Nat Acad Sci, 83-84; John Simon Guggenheim fel, 86. *Mem:* Am Chem Soc; AAAS; Am Geophys Union. *Res:* Chemical sources, sinks and transformations in the atmosphere are studied in both the field and laboratory in order to obtain a better understanding of such problems as stratospheric ozone depletion, photochemical smog, acid precipitation and global warming; co-developer of the "nuclear winter" theory; developing the use of kites for vertical profiling of chemical species in the atmosphere. *Mailing Add:* Cires-Campus Box 449 Univ Colo Boulder CO 80309-0001. *Fax:* 303-492-1149

BIRKS, NEIL, METALLURGY, PHYSICAL CHEMISTRY. *Current Pos:* PROF MAT SCI & ENG, UNIV PITTSBURGH, 78- *Personal Data:* b Sheffield, Eng, Oct 16, 35; m 58, Mary Potts; c Jane C & David J. *Educ:* Sheffield Univ, BMet, 57, PhD(metall), 60. *Prof Exp:* NATO res fel phys chem, Max Planck Inst Phys Chem, Gottingen, 60-62, res fel, United Steel Co, 62-64; sr lectr metall, Sheffield Univ, 64-68. *Mem:* Fel Am Soc Metals Int; fel Inst Metallurgists (London); fel Inst Mat (London); Sheffield Metall & Eng Asn; Am Inst Metall Eng. *Res:* Iron and steel making; deoxidation, desulfurization, high temperature oxidation of metals; hot corrosion, scaling and decarburization; erosion-corrosion of metals. *Mailing Add:* Dept Mat Sci & Eng Univ Pittsburgh Pittsburgh PA 15261. *Fax:* 412-624-8069

BIRKY, CARL WILLIAM, JR, EVOLUTION. *Current Pos:* assoc prof, 70-76, PROF GENETICS, OHIO STATE UNIV, 76- *Personal Data:* b Urbana, Ill, June 5, 37; m 60, 84; c 1. *Educ:* Ind Univ, BA, 59, PhD(embryol), 63. *Prof Exp:* From instr to asst prof zool, Univ Calif, Berkeley, 63-70. *Concurrent Pos:* NIH fel, 69, 87, 88; Hargitt fel cell biol, Duke Univ, 77-78; mem, genetics study sect, NIH, 84-87; regional ed, Current Genetics, 85-; coun mem, Am Genetic Asn, 88-91. *Mem:* Am Inst Biol Sci; Am Soc Cell Biol; Soc Study Evolution; Int Soc Develop Biol; Genetics Soc Am; Am Genetic Asn (pres-elect, 91). *Res:* Genetics and evolution, especially of mitochondria and chloroplasts. *Mailing Add:* Dept Molecular Genetics Ohio State Univ 484 W 12th Ave Columbus OH 43210

BIRLE, JOHN DAVID, MATERIALS SCIENCE. *Current Pos:* RETIRED. *Personal Data:* b Columbus, Ohio, Sept 11, 39. *Educ:* Ohio State Univ, BChE, 62, MS, 63, PhD(mineral), 67. *Prof Exp:* Develop engr, Gen Elec Co, 67-69, prog engr, 69-93, mgr, GE Superabrasives, 93-96. *Res:* High pressure research; x-ray crystal structure analysis; acid mine drainage abatement; fossilized bacteria in sulfide minerals; crystal growth; coal and crude oil analysis; computerized automation. *Mailing Add:* 229 Columbian Ave Columbus OH 43223

BIRMAN, JOAN SYLVIA, MATHEMATICS. *Current Pos:* PROF MATH, COLUMBIA UNIV, 73- *Personal Data:* b New York, NY, May 30, 27; m 50; c 3. *Educ:* Barnard Col, Columbia Univ, BA, 48, Columbia Univ, MA, 50; NY Univ, PhD(math), 68. *Prof Exp:* Asst prof math, Stevens Inst Technol, 68-73. *Concurrent Pos:* Vis asst prof, Princeton Univ, 71. *Mem:* Am Math Soc. *Res:* Topology; group theory; Riemann surfaces. *Mailing Add:* Columbia Univ 2990 Broadway New York NY 10027-0029

BIRMAN, JOSEPH HAROLD, GEOLOGY. *Current Pos:* Chmn dept, 50-70, PROF GEOL, OCCIDENTAL COL, 50- *Personal Data:* b West Hartford, Conn, June 2, 24; m 45; c 2. *Educ:* Brown Univ, AB, 48; Calif Inst Technol, MSc, 50; Univ Calif, Los Angeles, PhD, 57. *Concurrent Pos:* Pres, Geothermal Surveys Inc, 61-; NSF grant glacial geol studies, Turkey, 63. *Mem:* Geol Soc Am; Am Inst Mining, Metall & Petrol Engrs; Sigma Xi. *Res:* Minerals exploration and development; glacial geology; shallow earth temperatures in ground water exploration. *Mailing Add:* 1617 Silverwood Dr Los Angeles CA 90041-3126

BIRMAN, JOSEPH LEON, THEORETICAL PHYSICS, CONDENSED MATTER. *Current Pos:* Henry Semat Prof, 74-87, DISTINGUISHED PROF PHYSICS, CITY COL NEW YORK, 87- *Personal Data:* b New York, NY, May 21, 27; m 50, Joan S Lyttle; c Kenneth P, Carl D & Deborah A (Shlider). *Educ:* City Col New York, BS, 47; Columbia Univ, MA, 50, PhD(theoret chem), 52. *Hon Degrees:* Dr es Sci, Univ Rennes, France, 74. *Honors & Awards:* Townsend Harris Medal; Mary Amanda Wood Vis lectr, Univ Pa, 60. *Prof Exp:* Asst, Columbia Univ, 48-52; from physicist to head, Luminescence Sect, Gen Tel & Electronics Res Labs, NY, 52-62; from assoc prof to prof physics, NY Univ, 62-74. *Concurrent Pos:* Vis prof, Univ Paris, 69-70. *Mem:* Fel Am Phys Soc; fel NY Acad Sci. *Res:* Solid state and many-body quantum theory; group theory; optical properties of condensed matter systems; mechanisms of super conductivity; queri crystals; non-linear optical probagation. *Mailing Add:* Dept Physics City Col New York 138 St Convent Ave New York NY 10031. *Fax:* 212-650-6940

BIRMAN, VICTOR MARK, COMPOSITE MATERIALS & STRUCTURES, SMART MATERIALS & STRUCTURES. *Current Pos:* assoc prof, 89-96, PROF MECH & AEROSPACE ENG, UNIV MO, ROLLA, 96- *Personal Data:* b Leningrad, Russia, Jan 13, 50; US citizen; m 77, Anna; c Michael & Shirley. *Educ:* Leningrad Shipbuilding Inst, BS, 73; Technion-Israel Inst Technol, PhD(aeronaut eng), 83. *Prof Exp:* Engr, Inst Design Steel Structures, Leningrad, Russia, 73-78; res engr, Israel Aircraft Industs, 84; asst prof to assoc prof naval archit, Univ New Orleans, 86-88. *Concurrent Pos:* Assoc ed, Composites Part B: Eng, 91-; vis, Univ Natal, SAfrica, 92, Wright-Patterson AFB, 92, 93 & 97, NASA, 93 & 94. *Mem:* Fel Am Soc Mech Engrs; assoc fel Am Inst Aeronaut & Astronaut; Int Community Composites Eng. *Res:* Composite and smart structures; over 120 publications, including more than 70 papers in referred journals. *Mailing Add:* Eng Educ Ctr Univ Mo-Rolla 8001 Natural Bridge Rd St Louis MO 63121-4401. *E-Mail:* vbirman@umr.edu

BIRMINGHAM, BRENDAN CHARLES, ENVIRONMENTAL TOXICOLOGY. *Current Pos:* pesticide res specialist, 82-83, stands coordr, 83-92, RES SCIENTIST, ONT MINISTRY ENVIRON, 92- *Personal Data:* b London, Eng, Nov 30, 45; m 69; c 3. *Educ:* Univ Col, Ireland, BSc, 67, HDipEd, 68; McGill Univ, MSc, 71; Univ Windsor, PhD(biol), 80. *Prof Exp:* Fel, Biol Dept, York Univ, 75-79, res assoc, 80-82. *Mem:* Can Soc Plant Physiologists. *Res:* Environmental physiology and toxicology measuring behavior and impact of pesticides in the aquatic ecosystem; plant productivity: measured photosynthesis and photorespiration of freshwater algae using sensitive assay of dissolved inorganic carbon; scientific risk analysis of hazardous contaminants. *Mailing Add:* Stand Develop Br 2 St Clair Ave W 12th Floor Toronto ON M4V 1A5 Can

BIRMINGHAM, MARION KRANTZ, BIOCHEMISTRY, ENDOCRINOLOGY. *Current Pos:* PROF PSYCHIAT, McGILL UNIV, 72- *Personal Data:* b Munich, Ger, Nov 2, 17; Can citizen; m 42; c 2. *Educ:* Bennington Col, BA, 41; McGill Univ, MSc, 46, PhD(exp med), 49. *Honors & Awards:* Ann Eduardo Brown Menendez Lectr. *Prof Exp:* Res biochemist, Geront Unit, 49-54, dir lab steroid biochem, Allan Mem Inst Psychiat, 54- *Concurrent Pos:* Demonstr, McGill Univ, 53-61, lectr, 54-61, hon lectr biochem, 59, from asst prof to assoc prof psychiat, 61-72; med res assoc, Med Res Coun Can. *Mem:* Am Soc Biol Chemists; Endocrine Soc; Can Physiol Soc; Can Biochem Soc; Soc Endocrinol. *Res:* Adrenal steroid biogenesis and its control. *Mailing Add:* Dept Psychiat McGill Univ 1033 Pine Ave W Montreal PQ H3A 1A1 Can. *Fax:* 514-630-3997

BIRMINGHAM, THOMAS JOSEPH, PLASMA PHYSICS, SPACE PHYSICS. *Current Pos:* Res assoc, Nat Acad Sci, 65-66, STAFF SCIENTIST SPACE PLASMA PHYSICS, GODDARD SPACE FLIGHT CTR, 66- *Personal Data:* b Milford, Mass, Sept 28, 38; m 65; c 3. *Educ:* Boston Col, BS, 60; Princeton Univ, MA, 62, PhD(physics), 65. *Concurrent Pos:* Ed, J Geophys Res & Space Physics, 86- *Mem:* Fel Am Phys Soc; Am Geophys Union; Sigma Xi. *Res:* Theoretical plasma physics. *Mailing Add:* Code 695 NASA Goddard Space Flight Ctr Greenbelt MD 20771

BIRNBAUM, DAVID, PHYSICS, COMPUTER SCIENCE. *Current Pos:* PRIN SCIENTIST, XEROX CORP, 81- *Personal Data:* b New York, NY, Mar 30, 40; m 65, Martha Rock; c Nina R, Adam M & Deborah B. *Educ:* Cornell Univ, BEngPhys, 61; Univ Rochester, MA, 63, PhD(physics), 67, MBA, 81. *Prof Exp:* Res assoc physics, Univ Rochester, 67; res physicist, Carnegie-Mellon Univ, 67-69, asst prof, 69-71; asst prof, Hamline Univ, 71-76; sr res engr, Gen Rwy Signal Co, 76-81. *Mem:* Am Phys Soc; Inst Elec & Electronics Engrs. *Res:* Electronic image processing; color reproduction; transportation systems research; physics education; astronomy. *Mailing Add:* 800 Phillips Rd Webster NY 14580

BIRNBAUM, EDWARD ROBERT, INORGANIC CHEMISTRY, BIOINORGANIC CHEMISTRY. *Current Pos:* Asst prof, 68-73, assoc prof, 73-78, PROF INORG CHEM, NMEX STATE UNIV, 78- *Personal Data:* b Brooklyn, NY, Oct 28, 43; m 68; c 3. *Educ:* Brooklyn Col, BS, 64; Univ Ill, Urbana, MS, 66, PhD(inorg chem), 68. *Concurrent Pos:* Vis prof, Univ Alta, 76-77. *Mem:* AAAS; Am Chem Soc; Am Soc Biol Chem; Biophys Soc. *Res:* Fluorescence and nuclear magnetic resonance studies of inorganic and biological complexes of the lanthanide ions. *Mailing Add:* Dept Chem Box 30001 Univ Hawaii Manoa 2545 Mall Honolulu HI 96822-0001

BIRNBAUM, ERNEST RODMAN, INORGANIC CHEMISTRY. *Current Pos:* from instr to asst prof, 63-71, assoc prof, 71-77, PROF CHEM, ST JOHN'S UNIV, NY, 77- *Personal Data:* b Newark, NJ, Oct 4, 33. *Educ:* Univ Calif, Berkeley, BA, 55; Univ Southern Calif, MS, 58; Univ Fla, PhD(chem), 61. *Prof Exp:* Sr res engr, Rocketdyne Div, NAm Aviation, Inc, 61-62; fel chem, Univ Tex, 62-63. *Mem:* Am Chem Soc; Royal Soc Chem. *Res:* Inorganic reactions in nonaqueous solvents; kinetics and mechanisms of inorganic reactions; Lewis acid-base reactions; hydrido complexes of transition metals. *Mailing Add:* Dept Chem St John's Univ Jamaica NY 11439-1001

BIRNBAUM, GEORGE, NONDESTRUCTIVE EVALUATION & PROCESS SENSING. *Current Pos:* SR SCIENTIST, NAT INST STAND & TECHNOL, 75- *Personal Data:* b July 16, 19. *Educ:* Brooklyn Col, 41; George Washington Univ, MS, 49, PhD(physics), 56. *Honors & Awards:* Gold Medal, Dept Com, 89. *Prof Exp:* Head microwave dielectric measurement group, Nat Bur Stand, Washington, DC, 46-54, head microwave frequency & spectros sect, Boulder Labs, 54-56; sr scientist & head, Quantum Physics Sect, Hughes Res Labs, Calif, 56-62; group leader, Spectros Sci Ctr, NAm Rockwell Corp, 62-75. *Concurrent Pos:* Mem USA comn I & chmn, Int Radio Sci Union, 73-76; mem & chmn, Nat Acad Sci adv panel to radio stand lab, Nat Bur Stand, 65-68; vis prof, Univ Paris, 79 & 83-85; distinguished vis lectr, Univ Tex, Austin, 80; res prof, Cath Univ Am, 89- *Mem:* Fel Am Phys Soc; fel Inst Elec & Electronics Engrs. *Res:* Infrared spectroscopy, collision induced absorption and light scattering; molecular motions and interactions in compressed fluids. *Mailing Add:* Rm B344 Bldg 223 Nat Inst Stand & Technol Gaithersburg MD 20899

BIRNBAUM, GEORGE I, STRUCTURAL CHEMISTRY. *Current Pos:* assoc res officer, 66-76, SR RES OFFICER, NAT RES COUN CAN, 76- *Personal Data:* b Cracow, Poland, July 14, 31; Can citizen; m 67; c 2. *Educ:* Columbia Univ, BS, 54, MA, 55, PhD(org chem), 61. *Prof Exp:* Res worker x-ray crystallog, Columbia Univ, 59-61, res assoc, 61-64; fel, Nat Res Coun Can, 64-65; NIH spec fel, Glasgow Univ, 65-66. *Mem:* Am Chem Soc; Am Crystallog Asn; Chem Inst Can. *Res:* X-ray structure analyses of proteins and biologically significant organic molecules. *Mailing Add:* 10264 Wild Apple Circle Gaithersburg MD 20879

BIRNBAUM, H(OWARD) K(ENT), MATERIALS SCIENCE ENGINEERING. *Current Pos:* assoc prof, 61-63, PROF METALL, UNIV ILL, URBANA-CHAMPAIGN, 63-, DIR, MAT RES LAB. *Personal Data:* b New York, NY, Oct 18, 32; m 54, Freda Silber; c Elisa, Scott & Shari. *Educ:* Columbia Univ, BS, 53, MS, 55; Univ Ill, PhD(metall), 59. *Honors & Awards:* Robert Mehl Gold Medal. *Prof Exp:* From instr to asst prof metall, Univ Chicago, 59-61. *Concurrent Pos:* Lectr, Inst Metals. *Mem:* Nat Acad Eng; fel Am Phys Soc; fel AAAS; Am Inst Mining, Metall & Petrol Engrs; fel Am Soc Metals. *Res:* Physical metallurgy; physics of solids; dislocation theory; mechanical properties of solids; hydrogen in solids; interstitial diffusion; hydrogen embrittlement. *Mailing Add:* Mat Res Lab Univ Ill 104 S Goodwin Urbana IL 61801. *Fax:* 217-244-2278; *E-Mail:* hbirnbau@uiuc.edu

BIRNBAUM, HERMANN, organic chemistry, lipid chemistry; deceased, see previous edition for last biography

BIRNBAUM, JOEL S, ARCHITECTURE. *Current Pos:* founding dir, Hewlett Packard Co, 80-84, vpres & dir, 84-86, vpres & gen mgr, Info Technol Group, 86-88, vpres & gen mgr, Info Archit Group, 88-91, SR VPRES RES & DEVELOP & DIR, HEWLETT PACKARD CO, 91- *Educ:* Cornell Univ, BS, 60; Yale Univ, MS, 61, PhD(nuclear physics), 65. *Prof Exp:* Dir comput serv, T J Watson Res Lab, IBM Corp, Yorktwon Heights, NY, 65-80. *Concurrent Pos:* Mem, Res Roundtable, Nat Acad Sci, Nat Acad Eng & Inst Med-Nat Acad Sci; mem, Eng Coun, Cornell Univ, Univ Southern Calif & Beckman Inst, Univ Ill; bd mem, Corp Nat Res Initiatives, Technion Univ Israel & Tech Mus Innovation. *Mem:* Nat Acad Eng; Inst Elec & Electronics Engrs; Asn Comput Mach. *Res:* Information architecture. *Mailing Add:* Hewlett-Packard Co 1501 Page Mill Rd Palo Alto CA 94304

BIRNBAUM, LINDA SILBER, TOXICOLOGY. *Current Pos:* sr staff fel, 79-80, RES MICROBIOLOGIST, SYST TOXICOL BR, NAT INST ENVIRON HEALTH SCI, 80- *Personal Data:* b Passaic, NJ, Dec 21, 46; m 67; c 3. *Educ:* Univ Rochester, AB, 67; Univ Ill, Urbana, MS, 69, PhD(microbiol), 72. *Prof Exp:* Asst prof microbiol, Univ Ill, Urbana, 72; fel biochem, Univ Mass, 73-74; asst prof biol, Kirkland, 74-75; res assoc biochem, Masonic Med Res Lab, 75-79. *Concurrent Pos:* adj prof, Sch Pub Health, Univ NC, Chapel Hill, 81- *Mem:* Am Soc Pharmacol & Exp Therapeut; AAAS; Soc Toxicol; Geront Soc; Am Aging Asn; Int Soc Study Xenobiotics. *Res:* Biochemistry of drug metabolism and carcinogenesis in liver and extra-hepatic tissues from organism of different ages; mechanisms of toxicity; chemical disposition. *Mailing Add:* Dept Environ Toxicol US Environ Protection Agency MD-66 Research Triangle Park NC 27711-0001

BIRNBAUM, MICHAEL HENRY, MATHEMATICAL PSYCHOLOGY, DECISION MAKING & JUDGMENT. *Current Pos:* PROF PSYCHOL, CALIF STATE UNIV, FULLERTON, 86- *Personal Data:* b Los Angeles, Calif, Mar 10, 46; m 68, 72, Bonnie Bruck; c Melissa & Kevin. *Educ:* Univ Calif, Los Angeles, BA, 68, MA, 69, PhD(psychol), 72. *Prof Exp:* NIMH fel, Univ Calif, San Diego, 72-73; asst prof psychol, Kans State Univ, 73-74; from asst prof to prof, Univ Ill, Urbana-Champaign, 74-88. *Concurrent Pos:* Consult, Rand Corp, 80- *Mem:* Fel Am Psychol Soc; Am Psychol Asn; Psychonomic Soc; Judgement & Decision Making Soc; Math Psychol Soc. *Res:* Mathematical psychology to investigate how people represent, compare and combine information to reach overall decisions or integrated judgements. *Mailing Add:* Dept Psychol Calif State Univ Fullerton CA 92634. *Fax:* 714-449-7134; *E-Mail:* mbirnbaum@fullerton.edu

BIRNBAUM, MILTON, LASERS & SPECTROSCOPY, OPTICS & OPTO ELECTRONICS. *Current Pos:* PROF RES, DEPT ELEC ENG, UNIV SOUTHERN CALIF, 86- *Personal Data:* b Brooklyn, NY, Nov 27, 20; m 57; c Robin S & David M. *Educ:* Brooklyn Col, AB, 42; Univ Md, MS, 48, PhD(physics), 53. *Prof Exp:* Nuclear physicist, Naval Res Lab, DC, 46-53; head dept physics, Bulova Res & Develop Co, 53-55; assoc prof, Polytech Inst Brooklyn, 55-61; sect head, Aerospace Corp, 61-70, head quantum optics dept, 70-72, sr scientist, 72-86. *Concurrent Pos:* Consult, Brookhaven Nat Lab, 57-58, Repub Aviation Corp, 60, Loral Electronics Corp, 60-61, Hughes Aircraft Co, 87-89, Northrop Corp, 87-89, Aerospace Corp, 86- *Mem:* Fel Am Phys Soc; fel Optical Soc Am; fel Inst Elec & Electronic Engrs; Int Soc Optical Eng. *Res:* Accelerator design; neutron binding energies; electron paramagnetic resonance; laser physics; optics; semiconductors; solid state lasers; conversion solid state lasers; saturable absorber q-switches; diode pumped solid state lasers. *Mailing Add:* 4904 Elkridge Dr Ranch Palos Verdes CA 90274

BIRNBAUM, SIDNEY, MATHEMATICS. *Current Pos:* prof math & chmn dept, 70-73, assoc dean, Sch Sci, 73-80, PROF MATH, CALIF STATE POLYTECH UNIV, POMONA, 80- *Personal Data:* b New York, NY, Sept 22, 28; m 54; c 3. *Educ:* NY Univ BA, 48, MS, 49; Univ Colo, PhD(math), 65. *Prof Exp:* Engr, Martin Co, 53-56, res scientist, 56-65; assoc prof math, Univ SC, 65-70, actg head dept, 67-68. *Concurrent Pos:* Consult, Sandia Corp, NMex, 66- *Mem:* AAAS; Am Math Soc; Math Asn Am; Soc Indust & Appl Math; Sigma Xi. *Res:* Functional analysis; spectral theory; probability; aeroelasticity. *Mailing Add:* Calif State Polytech Univ 3801 W Temple Ave Pomona CA 91768-2557

BIRNBAUMER, LUTZ, BIOCHEMISTRY, ENDOCRINOLOGY. *Current Pos:* PROF ANESTHESIOL & BIOL CHEM, SCH MED, UNIV CALIF, LOS ANGELES, 94- *Personal Data:* b Vienna, Austria, Feb 6, 39; Arg citizen; m 65. *Educ:* Univ Buenos Aires, BA, 62, BS, 64, PhD(glycogen metab), 66. *Prof Exp:* Nat Inst Arthritis, Metab & Digestive Dis fel, 68-69; staff fel endocrinol, Nat Inst Arthritis, Metab & Digestive Dis, 69-71; assoc prof physiol, Sch Med, Northwestern Univ, Chicago, 71-75; prof cell & reproductive biol, Baylor Col Med, 75-94. *Concurrent Pos:* Nat Inst Child Health & Human Develop res grant, Northwestern Univ, 71-, Nat Inst Arthritis, Metab & Digestive Dis & Nat Heart, Lung & Blood Inst grants, 76- *Mem:* Nat Acad Sci; Soc Study Reproduction; Endocrine Soc; Am Soc Biol Chemists. *Res:* Cellular, biochemical and molecular bases of hormone and catecholamine action; role of cyclic nucleotides in cellular regulation; plasma membrane biochemistry; reproductive physiology of the ovary. *Mailing Add:* Univ Calif Sch Med MC 177820 Los Angeles CA 90095

BIRNBOIM, HYMAN CHAIM, CANCER RESEARCH, MOLECULAR BIOLOGY. *Current Pos:* CAREER SCIENTIST, GEN DIV, OTTAWA REGIONAL CANCER CTR, 84- *Personal Data:* b Winnipeg, Man, Feb 29, 36; m 59; c 2. *Educ:* Univ Man, MD, 60, MSc, 63; FRCP(C), 85. *Prof Exp:* Intern, St Boniface Hosp, Winnipeg, 60-61, asst resident med, 61-62; fel biochem, Nat Cancer Inst Can, 62-63, Med Res Coun, Can, 63-67; assoc res officer, Dept Biol & Health Physics, Chalk River Nuclear Lab, Atomic Energy Can, Ltd, 67-78, sr res officer, Health Sci Div, 78-84; sr lectr, Dept Biochem, Univ Ottawa, assoc prof, Dept Med & Microbiol-Immunol, 84-87, prof, 87-, prof, Dept Biochem, 89- *Concurrent Pos:* Assoc ed, Can J Biochem, 73-78. *Mem:* Can Biochem Soc; AAAS; Am Asn Cancer Res. *Res:* Activation of oncogenes by DNA strands breaks and oxyradicals. *Mailing Add:* Ottawa Gen Hosp 501 Smythe Rd Cancer Res Labs Ottawa ON K1H 8L6 Can

BIRNEY, DAVID MARTIN, STUDIES OF PSEUDOPERICYCIC REACTIONS, STRUCTURE & ACTIVITY OF SUBSTANCE P. *Current Pos:* asst prof, 89-95, ASSOC PROF ORG CHEM, TEX TECH UNIV, 95- *Personal Data:* b Washington, DC, May 12, 56; m 80; c 3. *Educ:* Swarthmore Col, BA, 78; Yale Univ, PhD(chem), 87. *Prof Exp:* Ed, Sadtler Res Labs, 79-81. *Concurrent Pos:* Adj prof, Dept Opthal, Tex Tech Health Scis Ctr. *Mem:* Am Chem Soc. *Res:* Ab initio calculations of transition states for organic reactions; multiphoton infrared photochemistry and photoacoustic calorimetry; studies of pseudopericyclic reactions; synthesis, NMR conformations and activities of substance P analogs. *Mailing Add:* Dept Chem & Biochem Tex Tech Univ Lubbock TX 79409-1061. *Fax:* 806-742-1289; *E-Mail:* vddmb@ttu.edu

BIRNEY, DION SCOTT, JR, ASTRONOMY. *Current Pos:* RETIRED. *Personal Data:* b Washington, DC, Apr 23, 26; m 55; c 3. *Educ:* Yale Univ, BS, 50; Georgetown Univ, MA, 56, PhD(astron), 61. *Prof Exp:* Engr, Eng Res Corp, Md, 50-52, Am Instrument Co, 52-54 & Stone Straw Corp, DC, 54-56; asst astron, Georgetown Univ, 56-60; from instr to asst prof astron, Univ Va, 60-68; from assoc prof to prof astron, Wellesley Col, 74-91. *Mem:* Am Astron Soc; Sigma Xi. *Res:* Photometry of Cepheid variables and eclipsing binaries. *Mailing Add:* Whitin Observ Wellesley Col Wellesley MA 02181

BIRNEY, ELMER CLEA, MAMMALOGY, ECOLOGY. *Current Pos:* from asst prof to assoc prof, 70-81, PROF ECOL, UNIV MINN, MINNEAPOLIS, 81-, CUR MAMMAL, JAMES FORD BELL MUS NATURAL HIST, 70- *Personal Data:* b Satanta, Kans, Mar 26, 40; m 61; c 2. *Educ:* Ft Hays Kans State Univ, BS, 63, MS, 65; Univ Kans, PhD(zool), 70. *Prof Exp:* Instr biol, Kearney State Col, 65-66. *Concurrent Pos:* From managing ed to ed, J Mammal, 78-84, ed spec publ mammalogy, 84- *Mem:* Ecol Soc Am; Am Soc Mammal (1st vpres, 86-); Soc Study Evolution; Soc Syst Zool; Am Soc Naturalists. *Res:* Evolution, ecology and behavior of mammals. *Mailing Add:* Univ Minn 100 Ecol Bldg Univ Minn 10 Church St SE St Paul MN 55108

BIRNHOLZ, JASON CORDELL, ULTRASONIC IMAGING, FETAL PHYSIOLOGY. *Current Pos:* PVT PRACT, 89- *Personal Data:* b Newark, NJ, Dec 11, 42; m 71, Elaine Farrell; c Matthew, Justin & Evan. *Educ:* Union Col, NY, BS, 63; Johns Hopkins, MD, 67. *Prof Exp:* Intern internal med, Bellevue Hosp, 67-68; fel, NIH, 68-70; resident physician radiol, Mass Gen Hosp, 70-73; adv acad fel, biomed eng, Mass Inst Technol, 73-75; asst prof radiol, Stanford Univ, 75-76; assoc prof, Med Sch, Harvard Univ, 76-82; prof radiol, Rush Med Col, 82-88. *Concurrent Pos:* Var int vis professorships; res dir, E-Cal Corp. *Mem:* Fel Am Col Radiol; assoc fel Am Col Obstetricians & Gynecologists; fel Royal Col Radiol; Sigma Xi; AAAS; AMA. *Res:* Applied research in ultrasonic imaging including technical development and clinical applications; human fetal development; early pregnancy loss; menstruation; sexuality. *Mailing Add:* Diag Ultrasound Consults 120 Oak Brook Oak Brook IL 60521-2314. *Fax:* 630-954-2919; *E-Mail:* prime@egal.com

BIRNIE, RICHARD WILLIAMS, MINERALOGY. *Current Pos:* From asst prof to assoc prof, 75-87, PROF GEOL, DARTMOUTH COL, 87-, DEAN, GRAD STUDIES, 90- *Personal Data:* b Boston, Mass, Dec 8, 44; m 73; c 3. *Educ:* Dartmouth Col, AB, 68, AM, 71; Harvard Univ, PhD(geol), 75. *Mem:* Geol Soc Am; Mineral Soc Am; Soc Econ Geologists; Explorers Club; Sigma Xi. *Res:* Infrared radiation thermometry of volcanoes; remote sensing applied to prospecting for ore deposits; sulfide mineralogy and crystal chemistry. *Mailing Add:* Earth Sci Dartmouth Col Hanover NH 03755

BIRNIR, BJORN, APPLIED MATHEMATICS, DYNAMICAL SYSTEMS. *Current Pos:* assoc prof, 85-92, PROF MATH, UNIV CALIF, SANTA BARBARA, 92- *Personal Data:* b Reykjavik, Iceland, Aug 19, 53; m 80; c 2. *Educ:* Union Col, Schenectady, NY, BS, 76; Courant Inst, NY Univ, MS, 78, PhD(math), 81. *Prof Exp:* Asst prof math, Univ Ariz, Tucson, 81-83; res assoc, Univ Calif, Berkeley, 83-84; res fel math & comput, Univ Iceland, Reykjavik, 84-85. *Concurrent Pos:* Mittag-Lettler Fel, 94. *Mem:* Am Math Soc; Soc Indust & Appl Math; Icelandic Math Soc; Am Phys Soc. *Res:* Nonlinear partial differential equations, describing a variety of phenomena in physics and engineering; perturbation theory for integrable partial differential equations; dynamical systems theory of nonlinear partial differential equations, condensed matter physics, semi-conductor theory. *Mailing Add:* Math Dept Univ Calif 552 University Ave Santa Barbara CA 93106. *Fax:* 805-893-2385; *E-Mail:* birmir@math.ucsb.edu

BIRNSTIEL, CHARLES, MOVABLE BRIDGE MACHINERY ENGINEERING, STRUCTURAL ENGINEERING FOR BRIDGES & BUILDINGS. *Current Pos:* CONSULT ENGR, 74- *Personal Data:* b New York, NY, Dec 6, 29. *Educ:* NY Univ, BCE, 54, MCE, 57, EngScD, 62. *Honors & Awards:* State of the Art Award, Am Soc Civil Engrs, 81. *Prof Exp:* From instr to prof civil eng, NY Univ, 54-73; prof, Poly Inst New York, 73-74. *Concurrent Pos:* Adj prof, Columbia Univ, New York, 88- *Mem:* Fel Am Civil Engrs; Int Asn Bridge & Struct Engrs; Am Soc Eng Educ; Am Railway Eng Asn; Struct Stability Res Coun. *Res:* Elastic and inelastic stability of metal structures; cable-suspended structures; mechanisms; writing; bridges and movable structures. *Mailing Add:* 100-35 Queens Blvd Forest Hills NY 11375

BIRO, GEORGE P, CARDIOVASCULAR PHYSIOLOGY, BLOOD SUBSTITUTES & TRANSFUSION MEDICINE. *Current Pos:* RETIRED. *Personal Data:* b Budapest, Hungary, Jan 14, 38; Can citizen; m 64, Eva Gero; c Andrew W & Suzanne C. *Educ:* Queen's Univ, Kingston, Ont, MD, 63, PhD(physiol), 70. *Prof Exp:* Prof, Univ Ottawa, 72-93, assoc dean, fac med, 90-96. *Concurrent Pos:* Vis prof, Univ Calif, San Diego, 81-82. *Mem:* Can Physiol Soc; Am Physiol Soc; Int Soc Heart Res; Int Soc Oxygen Transport Tissue. *Res:* Blood substitutes including stroma-free hemoglobin solution and perfluorocarbon; oxygen supply to the myocardium; blood rheology; possible ultimate clinical applications. *Mailing Add:* Fac Med Univ Ottawa 451 Smyth Rd Ottawa ON K1H 8M5 Can. *Fax:* 613-562-5434; *E-Mail:* biromw@uottawa.ca

BIRON, CHRISTINE A, VIRAL IMMUNOLOGY. *Current Pos:* asst prof, 87-90, ASSOC PROF MED SCI, DIV BIOL & MED, BROWN UNIV, 90- *Personal Data:* b Woonsocket, RI, Aug 8, 51. *Educ:* Univ NC, Chapel Hill, PhD(immunol), 80. *Prof Exp:* asst prof path, Med Sch, Univ Mass, 83-87. *Concurrent Pos:* Scholar, Leukemia Soc Am. *Mem:* Am Asn Immunol; AAAS; Sigma Xi. *Res:* Immune response to viral infections; NK cells; T lymphocytes. *Mailing Add:* Div Biomed Brown Univ Box G-B618 Providence RI 02912-0001

BIRREN, JAMES E(MMETT), GERONTOLOGY, PSYCHOLOGY. *Current Pos:* dir, Borun Ctr Geront Res, 89-93, ASSOC DIR, CTR AGING, UNIV CALIF, LOS ANGELES, 91- *Personal Data:* b Chicago, Ill; m 42, Betty Solomon; c Barbara A, Jeffrey E & Bruce W. *Educ:* Chicago State Univ, BE, 41; Northwestern Univ, MA, 43, PhD(psychol), 47. *Hon Degrees:* PhD, Univ Gothenburg, Sweden, 82, DSc, Northwestern Univ, 86; LLD, St Thomas Univ, Fredericton, Can, 90. *Honors & Awards:* Brookdale Award, Brookdale Found, 80; Sandoz Prize Geront Res. *Prof Exp:* Chief, Sect Aging, NIMH, 51-64; head, Prog Aging, Nat Inst Child Health & Human Develop, 64-65; dir, Geront Ctr, Univ Southern Calif, 65-89, dean, Sch Geront, 75-89. *Mem:* Am Physiol Soc; Am Psychol Asn; Geront Soc (pres, 61); Am Soc Aging. *Res:* Psychophysiology of aging; changes in decision making. *Mailing Add:* 647 Toyopa Dr Pacific Palisades CA 90272. *Fax:* 310-794-0681; *E-Mail:* jbirren@medl.medsch.ucla.edu

BIRRENKOTT, GLENN PETER, JR, POULTRY SCIENCE. *Current Pos:* PROF POULTRY SCI, CLEMSON UNIV, 78- *Personal Data:* b Feb 6, 51; US citizen; m 85, Marian Moon; c Anna. *Educ:* Univ Wis, Madison, BS, 73, MS, 75, PhD(poultry sci), 78. *Mem:* AAAS; Poultry Sci Asn; World's Poultry Sci Asn; Sigma Xi. *Res:* Avian endocrinology; avian reproductive physiology; comparative endocrinology; animal physiology; stress; hyperthermia. *Mailing Add:* 213 Clemson View Dr Seneca SC 29678. *Fax:* 864-656-1033; *E-Mail:* glenn_birrenkott@quickmail.clemson.edu

BIRSHTEIN, BARBARA K, MOLECULAR IMMUNOLOGY, ANTIBODY GENE REGULATION & EXPRESSION. *Current Pos:* Fel, 71-73, from asst prof to assoc prof, 73-84, PROF, DEPT CELL BIOL, ALBERT EINSTEIN COL MED, 84- *Personal Data:* b Clarksburg, WVa, Dec 13, 44. *Educ:* Univ Mich, Ann Arbor, BS, 65; Johns Hopkins Univ, PhD(biol), 71. *Concurrent Pos:* Mem, NIH Allergy & Immunol Dis Study Sect, 81-85, Am Cancer Soc Adv Comt Immunol & Immunother, 87-91, Study Sect Israel Cancer Res Fund, 87-91, NIH Allergy, Immunol & Transplantation Res Comt, 93-; sect ed molecular genetics, J Immunol, 81-87; dir, Sue Golding Grad Div Med Sci, Albert Einstein Col Med, 90-93; Burroughs Wellcome vis prof, Loyola Univ, Chicago, 91. *Mem:* Am Asn Immunologists. *Res:* How antibody genes are rearranged and expressed exclusively in B cells. *Mailing Add:* Dept Cell Biol Albert Einstein Col Med 1300 Morris Park Ave Bronx NY 10461-1926

BIRSS, VIOLA INGRID, ELECTRCHEMISTRY, SURFACE SCIENCE. *Current Pos:* from asst prof to assoc prof, 81-86, PROF CHEM, UNIV CALGARY, 91- *Personal Data:* b Coleman, Alta, Oct 6, 50. *Educ:* Univ Calgary, BSc, 72; Univ Auckland, PhD(electrochem), 78. *Honors & Awards:* Lash Miller Award, Can Sect, Electrochem Soc, 85; Clara Bensur Award, Can Soc Chem, 93. *Prof Exp:* Res scientist, Continental Group Inc, 79-81, Alcan Int Ltd, 81-82. *Mem:* Sigma Xi; Electrochem Soc Inc; Can Inst Chem; AAAS; Am Soc Metals; Int Electrochem Soc. *Res:* Study of film-forming reactions at metal surfaces with a focus on mechanisms and rates of oxide film growth; determination of film properties and nanocompositional and structural characteristics; absorption of biologically important molecules on electrode surfaces; electrochemical properties of amorphous metal alloys. *Mailing Add:* Dept Chem Univ Calgary Calgary AB T2N 1N4 Can. *E-Mail:* birss@acs.ucalgary.ca

BIRSTEIN, SEYMOUR J, SURFACE CHEMISTRY, CLOUD PHYSICS. *Current Pos:* PRES, SJB ASSOCS, INC, 77- *Personal Data:* b Brooklyn, NY, May 1, 27; div, Diane; c 1. *Educ:* NY Univ, BA, 47; Mont State Col, MS, 49. *Prof Exp:* Res chemist res labs, Air Reduction Co, Inc, 49-50; res chemist, Air Force Cambridge Res Labs, 51-59, proj scientist, 59-68, chief aerosol interaction br, 68-76. *Mem:* Am Chem Soc; Am Meteorol Soc; Electron Micros Soc Am; Sigma Xi; fel Am Inst Chemists. *Res:* Application of aerosols in controlling the aerospace environment; basic research and its application to meteorological and weather modification processes. *Mailing Add:* 24 Pippen Rd Marlborough MA 01752. *Fax:* 508-624-7254

BIRT, ARTHUR ROBERT, medicine, dermatology, for more information see previous edition

BIRT, DIANE FEICKERT, BIOCHEMISTRY, HUMAN NUTRITION. *Current Pos:* PROF & CHMN, DEPT FOOD SCI & HUMAN NUTRIT, IOWA STATE UNIV, 97- *Personal Data:* b Petaluma, Calif, Oct 12, 49. *Educ:* Whittier Col, BA, 72; Purdue Univ, PhD(nutrit), 75. *Prof Exp:* Asst prof human nutrit, Iowa State Univ, 75-76; from asst prof to assoc prof, Eppley Inst Res Cancer, Univ Nebr Med Ctr, 76-88, assoc prof, Dept Pharmaceut Sci, Col Pharm, 82-88, assoc prof biochem, Col Med, 85-88, prof, Dept Pharmaceut Sci, Col Pharm & prof biochem & molecular biol, 88-97. *Concurrent Pos:* Prin investr, numerous res grants, Nat Cancer Inst, 78-96; mem, Chem Path Ad Hoc Study Sect, NIH, 84-87 & Metab Path Study Sect, 87-91, chmn, 89-91; mem, Comt Comp Toxicity Carcinogens, Nat Acad Sci, 93-95; mem, Prog Proj Study Sect, NIH, 94-97. *Mem:* Am Soc Nutrit Sci; Am Asn Cancer Res. *Res:* Biochemical mechanism of high fat/high dietary energy enhancement of cancer; mechanism of cancer inhibition by phytochemicals; author of numerous technical publications. *Mailing Add:* Univ Nebr Med Ctr 600 S 42nd St Omaha NE 68198-6805

BIRTCH, ALAN GRANT, SURGERY. *Current Pos:* PROF SURG & ASST CHMN, SCH MED, SOUTHERN ILL UNIV, 72-, CHMN GEN SURG, 72-, CHIEF, SECT TRANSPLANTATION, 72-, COORDR RES AFFAIRS, 79- *Personal Data:* b La Porte, Ind, Feb 3, 32; m 54; c 4. *Educ:* Johns Hopkins Univ, BA, 54; Johns Hopkins Med Sch, MD, 58. *Prof Exp:* Resident surg, Peter Bent Brigham Hosp, 58-63, asst, 63-66; instr, Harvard Med Sch, 66-67, assoc, 68-70, asst prof, 70-72. *Concurrent Pos:* Res fel surg, Harvard Med Sch, 63-64; Arthur-Tracey Cabot fel, Peter Bent Brigham Hosp, 64-65, chief resident, 64-65; res fel physiol, Harvard Med Sch, 65-66; consult surg, Robert Breck Brigham Hosp, 68-72; coordr res affairs, Southern Ill Univ, 79- *Mem:* Am Surg Asn; Transplantation Soc; Am Col Surgeons; Cent Surg Asn; Soc Univ Surgeons. *Res:* Clinical and basic transplantation immunology. *Mailing Add:* Southern Ill Univ Sch Med 800 N Rutledge Springfield IL 62708-4911

BIRTEL, FRANK T, MATHEMATICS, SCIENCE & RELIGION. *Current Pos:* from asst prof to assoc prof, Tulane Univ, 62-67, provost & dean, Grad Sch, 78-81, PROF MATH, TULANE UNIV, 67-, UNIV PROF, 82. *Personal Data:* b New Orleans, La, Apr 4, 32; m 90, Margaret Smith; c Rebecca (Madura) & Michael T. *Educ:* Loyola Univ, La, BS, 52; Univ Notre Dame, MS, 53, PhD(math), 60. *Prof Exp:* Sr mathematician, US Naval Nuclear

Power Sch, 55-57; instr math, Conn Col, 56-57; asst prof, Ohio State Univ, 60-62. *Concurrent Pos:* Lectr, res assoc & Off Naval Res fel, Yale Univ, 61-62; vis prof, Cath Univ Nijmegen, 68-69; Fulbright lectr, 68-69; assoc secy, Am Math Soc, 77-88. *Mem:* Math Asn Am; Am Math Soc. *Res:* Uniform algebras; several complex variables, harmonic analysis, topological rings and algebras; higher education; science, ethics and religion. *Mailing Add:* Dept Math Tulane Univ New Orleans LA 70118-5698. *E-Mail:* ftbirtel@mailhost.tcs.tulane.edu

BIRX, DEBORAH L, ALLERGY & IMMUNOLOGY. *Current Pos:* Intern, Walter Reed Army Med Ctr, 80-81, resident internal med, 81-83, fel allergy & clin immunol, 83-85, asst chief allergy & immunol serv, 85-89, ASST CHIEF, DEPT RETROVIRAL RES, WALTER REED ARMY INST RES, 89-; ASST PROF MED, UNIFORMED SERV UNIV HEALTH SCI, 85- *Personal Data:* b Baltimore, Md, Apr 4, 56; c 2. *Educ:* Houghton Col, BS, 76; Pa State Univ, MS & MD, 80; Am Bd Internal Med, dipl, 83; Am Bd Allergy & Immunol, 85. *Concurrent Pos:* Teaching fel, Uniformed Serv Univ Health Sci, 80-85; Acad Allergy & Immunol young investr award & travel grant, 85; sr investr cellular immunol, Walter Reed Army Med Ctr, 86-89, consult allergy immunol serv, 89- *Mem:* Am Asn Clin Res; Am Col Physicians; Am Asn Immunologists; Am Acad Allergy & Immunol. *Res:* Cation effect on lymphocyte activation; calcium and protein kinase regulation in polymorphonuclear activation; B cell dysfunction in AIDS patients; Epstein-Barr virus infection and immunoregulation in man; immunology of human imunodeficiency virus; analysis of T and B cell specific responses; author of numerous technical publications. *Mailing Add:* Div Retrovirol Walter Reed Army Inst Res 13 Taft Ct Suite 200 Rockville MD 20850-5318. *Fax:* 301-762-4177

BIS, RICHARD F, SOLID STATE PHYSICS. *Current Pos:* PHYSICIST, US NAVAL ORD LAB, 57- *Personal Data:* b Woonsocket, RI, Mar 9, 35; m 57; c 2. *Educ:* Worcester Polytech Inst, BS, 57; Univ Md, MS, 61, PhD(physics), 69. *Concurrent Pos:* Instr, Univ Md, 64- *Res:* Optical and electrical properties of tin tellurium and its alloys with lead; bulk and film samples. *Mailing Add:* 5513 Ridge Rd Mt Airy MD 21771

BISAILLON, ANDRE, VETERINARY ANATOMY, MAMMALOGY. *Current Pos:* from asst prof to assoc prof, 73-83, PROF GROSS VET ANAT, UNIV MONTREAL, 83- *Personal Data:* b Montreal, Que, Aug 9, 43; m 78; c 2. *Educ:* Col Bourget, BA, 65; Univ Montreal, DMV, 69, MScV, 73. *Prof Exp:* Instr gross vet anat, Univ Sask, 71-73. *Concurrent Pos:* Secy, Fac Med Vet, Univ Montreal. *Mem:* Am Asn Vet Anatomists; World Asn Vet Anatomists; Can Asn Vet Anatomists. *Res:* Morphology of aquatic mammals, mainly pinnipeds; study of aquatic locomotion of pinnipeds and gross anatomy of the blood vessels of semi-aquatic and aquatic mammals; morphology of the newborn pig. *Mailing Add:* Fac Vet Med Univ Montreal 3200 Sicott St St Hyacinthe PQ J2S 2M2 Can

BISBY, MARK A, MEDICAL EDUCATION, SCIENCE POLICY. *Current Pos:* HEAD PHYSIOL, QUEEN'S UNIV, 89- *Personal Data:* b Malvern, Eng, Aug 8, 46; Can citizen; m 68, Isobel Poulton; c Adam, Luke & Kate. *Educ:* Oxford Univ, Eng, MA, 69, DPhil, 72. *Prof Exp:* Prof physiol, Univ Calgary, 73-89, asst dean med, 79-84 & 86-89. *Mem:* Can Physiol Soc (secy, 84-87, pres, 93-94); Soc Neurosci; Int Soc Neurochem; Can Fedn Biol Socs (pres, 89-90). *Res:* Nerve regeneration; axonal transport; neuroplasticity; neuropathic pain. *Mailing Add:* Dept Physiol Queen's Univ Kingston ON K7L 3N6 Can. *E-Mail:* bisbym@post.queensu.ca

BISCAYE, PIERRE EGINTON, MARINE GEOCHEMISTRY, DEEP-SEA SEDIMENTATION. *Current Pos:* res assoc, 67-71, SR RES SCIENTIST, LAMONT-DOHERTY GEOL OBSERV, COLUMBIA UNIV, 71- *Personal Data:* b New York, NY, Nov 24, 35; m 58, Nedaleine R Bell; c 4. *Educ:* Wheaton Col, Ill, BS, 57; Yale Univ, PhD(geochem), 64. *Prof Exp:* Geochemist, Jersey Prod Res Co, Tulsa, Okla, 64-65; scientist, Isotopes, Inc, Westwood, NJ, 65-67. *Concurrent Pos:* Nat Acad Sci-Nat Res Coun resident res assoc, Inst Space Studies, NY, 67-69. *Mem:* AAAS; Am Geophys Union; Clay Minerals Soc; Am Geochem Soc; fel Geol Soc Am. *Res:* Isotope-, major- and trace-element geochemistry, and mineralogy to study atmospheric dusts, suspended particulates, deep-sea and continental shelf sediments; sources, sinks and transport mechanisms of marine sedimentation. *Mailing Add:* Lamont-Doherty Earth Observ Palisades NY 10964. *Fax:* 914-365-8115; *E-Mail:* biscaye@ldeo.columbia.edu

BISCHOF, NOBERT S, MATHEMATICS, LOGIC. *Current Pos:* PROF MATH, MERRILL COL, OAKLAND, CALIF, 60- *Personal Data:* b Syracuse, NY, 1933; m, Phyllis Burkart; c Otto & John. *Educ:* Syracuse Univ, BA, 55; Univ Wis, MA, 57. *Concurrent Pos:* Formed acad senate & chair, Calif Commun Cols, 68-69, pres 80-81. *Mem:* Math Asn Am. *Res:* Mathematics; logic. *Mailing Add:* 468 Michigan Ave Berkeley CA 94707-1738

BISCHOFF, ERIC RICHARD, DEVELOPMENTAL BIOLOGY, CELL BIOLOGY. *Current Pos:* asst prof, 69-76, ASSOC PROF ANAT, MED SCH, WASH UNIV, 76- *Personal Data:* b Joliet, Ill, June 16, 38; m 61; c 4. *Educ:* Knox Col, Ill, AB, 60; Wash Univ, PhD(zool), 66. *Prof Exp:* Fel anat, Univ Pa, 65-68, instr, med sch, 68-69. *Mem:* Am Soc Cell Biol; Am Soc Zoologists. *Res:* Differentiation of cultured skeletal muscle cells; skeletal muscle regeneration. *Mailing Add:* Dept Anat & Neurobiol Wash Univ Sch Med 660 S Euclid Ave St Louis MO 63110-1093. *Fax:* 314-362-3446

BISCHOFF, HARRY WILLIAM, ZOOLOGY, BOTANY. *Current Pos:* RETIRED. *Personal Data:* b Evansville, Ind, May 15, 22; m 47; c 5. *Educ:* Evansville Col, BA, 49; Vanderbilt Univ, MS, 52; Univ Tex, PhD(phycol), 63. *Prof Exp:* From instr to assoc prof, Tex Luthran Col, 50-65, dean men, 53-54, prof biol, 65- *Concurrent Pos:* NSF fel, 59-60. *Mem:* Bot Soc Am; Phycol Soc Am. *Res:* Phycology; culturing and systematics. *Mailing Add:* Dept Biol Tex Lutheran Univ Seguin TX 78155-5999

BISCHOFF, JAMES LOUDEN, GEOCHEMISTRY. *Current Pos:* geologist, 74-91, SR SCIENTIST, MARINE GEOL BR, US GEOL SURV, 91- *Personal Data:* b Los Angeles, Calif, Mar 20, 40; m 65; c 2. *Educ:* Occidental Col, AB, 62; Univ Calif, Berkeley, PhD(geochem), 66. *Honors & Awards:* US Dept Interior Award for Meritorious Serv; Hon Fel, Calif Acad Scis. *Prof Exp:* Fel marine geochem, Woods Hole Oceanog Inst, 66-67, asst scientist, 67-69; from asst prof to assoc prof geol sci, Univ Southern Calif, 69-74; consult prof, Dept Geol, Stanford Univ, 74-78. *Mem:* AAAS; Geochem Soc; Geol Soc Am; Int Asn Geochem & Cosmochem; fel Am Geophys Union. *Res:* Chemistry of water-rock interaction; metal deposits in the oceans; uranium-series dating. *Mailing Add:* US Geol Surv MS99M 345 Middle Field Rd Menlo Park CA 94025

BISCHOFF, JOYCE E, ANGIOGENESIS, GLYCOPROTEINS. *Current Pos:* ASST PROF SURG, HARVARD MED SCH, 90-; RES ASSOC, CHILDRENS HOSP, 91- *Personal Data:* b Detroit, Mich, May 4, 58; m 85, Ellis J Neufeld; c Thomas I. *Educ:* Duke Univ, AB, 80; Wash Univ, St Louis, PhD(biochem), 85. *Prof Exp:* Helen Hay Whitney fel, Whitehead Inst, 85-88, assoc, 88-90. *Concurrent Pos:* Prin investr, Am Heart Asn, 91-94, NIH, 92-; proj leader, NIH, 92- *Mem:* Am Soc Cell Biol; Am Soc Biochem & Molecular Biol. *Res:* Biochemical mechanisms of new capillary blood vessel growth and formation; role of cell surface glycoconjugates and lectins in this process known as angiogenesis. *Mailing Add:* Surg Res Lab Childrens Hosp 300 Longwood Ave Boston MA 02115-5737

BISCHOFF, KENNETH BRUCE, CHEMICAL & BIOLOGICAL ENGINEERING. *Current Pos:* chmn, Dept Chem Eng, 78-82, UNIDEL PROF BIOMED & CHEM ENG, UNIV DEL, 76- *Personal Data:* b Chicago, Ill, Feb 29, 36; m 59, Joyce Winterberg; c 2. *Educ:* Ill Inst Technol, BS, 57, PhD(chem eng), 61. *Honors & Awards:* Ebert Prize, Acad Pharmaceut Sci, 71; Prof Progress Award, Am Inst Chem Engrs, 76, Food, Pharmaceut & Bioeng Div Award, 82, R H Wilhelm Award, 87; Founders Award, Chem Inst Toxicol, 92. *Prof Exp:* NSF res fel, State Univ Ghent, 60-61; from asst prof to assoc prof chem eng, Univ Tex, Austin, 61-67; from assoc prof to prof, Univ Md, College Park, 67-70; dir, Sch Chem Eng, Cornell Univ, 70-75, Walter R Read prof eng, 70-76. *Concurrent Pos:* Consult, Exxon Res, 64-, Biomed Eng Br, NIH, 67-, Exxon Res & Eng Co, 77-, Gen Foods Corp & W R Grace Co, 80-; mem, Eng & Urban Health Sci Study Sect, Environ Protection Agency, 66-71, chmn, Planning Comt, 68-71; meeting chmn, 1st Int Symp Chem Reaction Eng, Am Inst Chem Engrs-Am Chem Soc-Europ Fedn Chem Eng, 70; mem, Artificial Kidney Chronic Uremia Contracts Rev Group, 70-76; mem, Bd Chem Sci & Technol, Nat Res Coun, 83-86; chmn, Coun Chem Res, 85, Food Pharmaceut Bioeng Div, Am Inst Chem Engrs, 85; numerous lectrs, US & foreign. *Mem:* Nat Acad Eng; fel AAAS; fel Am Inst Chem Engrs; Am Chem Soc; NY Acad Sci; Sigma Xi. *Res:* Chemical reaction, biological and medical engineering; author or co-author of 4 books and over 100 publications. *Mailing Add:* 1007 Benge Rd Hockessin DE 19707-9242. *Fax:* 302-234-1724

BISCHOFF, ROBERT FRANCIS, PHYSICAL CHEMISTRY. *Current Pos:* Prod regist mgr, Dow Chem Co, 67-89, PROD REGIST MGR, DOW ELANCO, 89- *Personal Data:* b Beech Grove, Ind, June 28, 43; m 67; c 4. *Educ:* Ind Univ, AB, 65; Purdue Univ, MS, 67. *Mem:* Am Chem Soc. *Res:* Chemical and physical properties of agricultural pesticides, optimization of these properties via formulation research; surface and colloid chemistry; registration of pesticide chemicals. *Mailing Add:* 1602 Continental Dr Zionsville IN 46077-9083

BISE, CHRISTOPHER JOHN, UNDERGROUND COAL MINING & MAINTENANCE ENGINEERING, INDUSTRIAL HEALTH & SAFETY. *Current Pos:* from asst prof to assoc prof, 80-91, PROF MINING ENG, PA STATE UNIV, 91-, CHMN MINING ENG, 93- *Personal Data:* b Philadelphia, Pa, Aug 16, 50. *Educ:* Va Polytech Inst & State Univ, BS, 72; Pa State Univ, MS, 76, PhD(mining eng), 80. *Prof Exp:* Resident engr, Consol Coal Co, 72-74. *Concurrent Pos:* Instr, Pa State Univ, 76-80. *Mem:* Soc Mining Engrs; Soc Prof Engrs; Nat Acad Forensic Engrs. *Res:* Improvement of productivity and safety in underground coal mining; mining methods; mine power systems; mine subsidence; mine health and safety. *Mailing Add:* 118 Hosler Bldg Penn State Univ University Park PA 16802

BISEL, HARRY FERREE, cancer; deceased, see previous edition for last biography

BISGAARD, SOREN, QUALITY IMPROVEMENT, MANAGEMENT. *Current Pos:* res asst, 80-85, RES ASSOC STATIST, UNIV WIS-MADISON, 86- *Personal Data:* b Umanak, Greenland, June 17, 51; Danish citizen. *Educ:* Copenhagen Col Eng, BS, 75; Tech Univ Denmark, MS, 79; Univ Wis-Madison, MS, 82, PhD(statist), 85. *Honors & Awards:* Shewell Prize, Am Soc Qual Control, 8, Brumbaugh Award 87. *Prof Exp:* Engr, exp toolmaking, WGer Quartz Smelting Works, 75-76; consult opers res, Int Serv Syst, 79 & statist, Burmeister & Wain, Copenhagen, 79-80. *Mem:* Am Statist Asn; AAAS. *Res:* Industrial and physical science application of statistics; quality control, quality improvement, design of experiments;

manufacturing and computerized manufacturing; statistical inference; management; design of environmental regulations; design of laws and standards. *Mailing Add:* Dept Indust Eng 390 Mech Eng Univ Wisc Madison 1513 University Ave Madison WI 53706-1572

BISGARD, GERALD EDWIN, VETERINARY PHYSIOLOGY, NEUROBIOLOGY. *Current Pos:* from asst prof to prof vet physiol, 71-80, prof & chmn dept comp biosci, 80-97, PROF VET SCI, DEPT COMP BIOSCI, UNIV WIS-MADISON, 80- *Personal Data:* b Denver, Colo, Aug 4, 37; m 61, Sharon Kay; c Jennifer, Kristine & Bradley. *Educ:* Colo State Univ, BS, 59, DVM, 62; Purdue Univ, MS, 67; Univ Wis, PhD(physiol), 71. *Prof Exp:* From instr to asst prof vet clins, Purdue Univ, 62-69. *Concurrent Pos:* Sr int fel, NIH Fogarty, Oxford Univ, 93- *Mem:* Am Physiol Soc; Am Vet Med Asn; Am Thoracic Soc. *Res:* Neurochemical control of respiration; hypoxia-induced plasticity of chemoreceptor reflexes. *Mailing Add:* One Julia Circle Madison WI 53705-1033

BISH, DAVID LEE, X-RAY POWDER DIFFRACTION, CLAY & ZEOLITE MINERALOGY. *Current Pos:* STAFF MEM, LOS ALAMOS NAT LAB, 80- *Personal Data:* b Arlington, Va, Mar 5, 52; m 81, Karen; c 1. *Educ:* Furman Univ, Greenville, BS, 74; Pa State Univ, PhD(mineral), 77. *Honors & Awards:* Jackson Clay Science Award, Clay Minerals Soc. *Prof Exp:* Res fel clay mineral, Dept Geol Sci, Harvard Univ, 77-80. *Concurrent Pos:* Counr, Clay Minerals Soc, 86-89; assoc ed, Mineral Soc Am, 88-91. *Mem:* Fel Mineral Soc Am; Clay Minerals Soc; Int Asn Study Clays; Am Geophys Union. *Res:* Quantitative phase analysis of mixtures using x-ray powder diffraction methods; Rietveld refinement of crystal structures using x-ray and neutron powder diffraction data; importance of zeolites and clays in a high-level radioactive waste repository. *Mailing Add:* Los Alamos Nat Lab Mail Stop D469 Los Alamos NM 87545. *Fax:* 505-665-3285; *E-Mail:* bish@essxrd.lanl.gov

BISHARA, MICHAEL NAGEEB, ATOMIC & MOLECULAR PHYSICS, TECHNICAL MANAGEMENT. *Current Pos:* CHMN ENG, SOUTHWEST VA COMMUNITY COL, 70- *Personal Data:* b Alexandria, Egypt, Apr 26, 33; US citizen; m 59; c 1. *Educ:* Cairo Univ, BAE, 57; Univ Va, MAE, 64, DSc, 69. *Honors & Awards:* Minta Martin Award, Am Asn Aeronaut & Astronaut, 64. *Prof Exp:* Eng trainee, Egyptian Ministry Indust, 59-60, asst dir tech training, 60-61; res scientist eng, Univ Va Res Labs, 64-69; eng specialist, AiResearch Mfg Co, 69-70; dir eng, S & S Corp, 79-82. *Concurrent Pos:* Mem, adv comt, Va Ctr Coal & Energy Res, 78-, Va Gov's Adv Comt Mined Land Reclamation, 79-; chmn, VCCS Chancellors Task Force Microcomput, 83; mem, Va Task Force Joint Training Partnership Act, 83; consult, Va Commonwealth Univ, 83- & Nat Independent Coal Operators' Asn, 83. *Mem:* Inst Elec & Electronics Engrs; Soc Automotive Engrs; Soc Mining Eng; Nat Soc Staff & Prof Develop; Nat Comput Graphics Asn; Sigma Xi. *Res:* Low density rarefied gas flow, including the interaction between inert gas atoms or molecules and solid surfaces; molecular and atomic beam experimentation; vacuum technology and space simulation; tribology in space environments. *Mailing Add:* 175 Valley View Dr Abingdon VA 24210

BISHARA, RAFIK HANNA, ANALYTICAL CHEMISTRY. *Current Pos:* anal chemist, 67-69, sr anal chemist, 71-75, MGR QUAL ASSURANCE, ELI LILLY & CO, 76- *Personal Data:* b Cairo, Egypt, Mar 21, 41; US citizen; m 68; c 3. *Educ:* Cairo Univ, BSc, 62; Butler Univ, MSc, 70; Purdue Univ, PhD(bionucleonics), 72. *Prof Exp:* Phamaceut chemist & head biochem unit, Chem Indust Develop Co, Egypt, 62-67. *Mem:* Am Chem Soc; Am Pharmaceut Asn; Acad Pharmaceut Sci. *Res:* Analytical methods, specifications, reference standards; investigational new drug and new drug applications for new drug substances; corresponding precursors and degradation products; chromatographic techniques and compilation of analytical data. *Mailing Add:* 40 Cool Creek Ct Carmel IN 46033-1984

BISHARA, SAMIR EDWARD, ORTHODONTICS. *Current Pos:* asst prof orthod, 70-73, assoc prof, 73-76, PROF ORTHOD, UNIV IOWA, 76- *Personal Data:* b Cairo, Egypt, Oct 31, 35; m 75. *Educ:* Univ Alexandria, BChD, 57, dipl, 66; Univ Iowa, MS, 70, DDS, 72. *Prof Exp:* From intern to mem med staff dent, Moassat Hosp, Alexandria, Egypt, 57-68. *Concurrent Pos:* Fel, Guggenheim Dent Clin, 59-60. *Mem:* Int Asn Dent Res; Am Asn Orthodontists; Am Cleft Palate Asn; Int Dent Fedn; AAAS; fel Am Col Dentists; fel Int Col Dentists. *Res:* Changes in facial and dental relations in normal orthodontic and cleft populations. *Mailing Add:* Univ Iowa Col Dentistry Iowa City IA 52240

BISHIR, JOHN WILLIAM, APPLIED MATHEMATICS. *Current Pos:* from asst prof to assoc prof, 63-68, PROF MATH, NC STATE UNIV, 68- *Personal Data:* b Joplin, Mo, Sept 23, 33; m 54, 77; c 4. *Educ:* Univ Mo, AB, 55; State Univ Iowa, MS, 57; NC State Univ, PhD(statist), 61. *Prof Exp:* From instr to asst prof math, NC State Univ, 57-62; asst prof statist, Fla State Univ, 62-63. *Mem:* Math Asn Am; Soc Industr Appl Math. *Res:* Mathematical modeling in wildlife biology, ecology, and forest evolution. *Mailing Add:* NC State Univ Box 8205 Raleigh NC 27695-8205

BISHOP, ALAN REGINALD, NONLINEAR & NONEQUILIBRIUM PHENOMENA, COMPLEX ORGANIC & INORGANIC ELECTRONIC MATERIALS. *Current Pos:* dep dir, Ctr Nonlinear Studies, 81-84, STAFF MEM, LOS ALAMOS NAT LAB, 80-, GROUP LEADER, CONDENSED MATTER THEORY, 85- *Personal Data:* b Bilston, UK, Oct 18, 47; m, Jennifer Simeons; c Nicholas, Alan, Joanna & Louise. *Educ:* Univ East Anglia, UK, BSc, 69; Cambridge Univ, UK, MSc, 70, PhD(theoret solid state), 73. *Hon Degrees:* PhD, Oxford Univ, UK, 74. *Honors & Awards:* E O Lawrence Award Mats Sci, US Dept Energy, 93. *Prof Exp:* Res fel, St Johns Col, Oxford Univ, UK, 73-76, Cornell Univ, 74-76; lectr, Univ London, UK, 76-79. *Concurrent Pos:* Sr Fulbright-Hays scholar, 74-76; consult, IBM Res Lab, Switz, 76-81, RCA Res Lab, Switz, 77-82 & Int Ctr, Theoret Physics, Italy, 89-; adj prof, Univ NMex, 93- *Mem:* Fel Am Phys Soc; Inst Physics. *Res:* Systematic application of techniques from modern mathematics and simulation governing strongly nonlinear and nonequilibrium situations; complex electronic and structural materials. *Mailing Add:* Theoret Div MSB262 Los Alamos Nat Lab Los Alamos NM 87545. *Fax:* 505-665-4063; *E-Mail:* arb@viking.lanl.gov

BISHOP, ALBERT B, INDUSTRIAL ENGINEERING, MANUFACTURING SYSTEMS. *Current Pos:* res assoc opers res & instr indust eng, 54-57, from asst prof to assoc prof, 57-65, chmn dept indust & systs eng, 74-82, PROF INDUST ENG, OHIO STATE UNIV, 65-, PROJ SUPVR, SYSTS RES GROUP, 66- *Personal Data:* b Philadelphia, Pa, Apr 7, 29; m 51; c 3. *Educ:* Cornell Univ, BEE, 51; Ohio State Univ, MS, 53, PhD(indust eng), 57. *Prof Exp:* Mem tech staff, Bell Tel Labs, 54. *Concurrent Pos:* Consult, NAm Aviation, Inc, 58-71, Indust Nucleonics Corp, 59-73, Chem Abstr Serv, 64-70, Stanford Res Inst, 65-67, US Army Combat Develop Command, 70-71, US Army Sci Adv Panel, 75-77, Galion Div, Dresser Indust, 76-, US Army Mats Systs Anal Activ, 78-79, Aerojet Electrosyst, 79-81, Ohio State Int, 79-81, Perfection Coby, 82-83, Container Recovery Corp, 83-84, Accu Ray, 85-86; vis scholar sci technol & soc & mech eng, Mass Inst Technol, 84. *Mem:* Opers Res Soc Am; fel Am Inst Indust Engrs; Inst Elec & Electronics Engrs; fel Am Soc Qual Control; Inst Mgt Sci; Soc Mfg Engrs. *Res:* Formulation and manipulation of analytic models of man-machine systems, including production and industrial systems; control-theory and mathematical programming models; product liability; principles for machine/human compatibility in manufacturing systems. *Mailing Add:* Dept Indust & Systs Eng Ohio State Univ 1971 Neil Ave Columbus OH 43210-1271

BISHOP, ALLEN DAVID, JR, INORGANIC CHEMISTRY, PHYSICAL CHEMISTRY. *Current Pos:* assoc prof, Millsaps Col, 67-74, prof chmn, 74-78, chmn, Dept Comput Sci & dir, Acad Comput, 78-91, PROF CHEM & DIR ACAD COMPUT, MILLSAPS COL, 91- *Personal Data:* b Meridian, Miss, Sept 5, 38; m 62, Julia M Dawson; c Julia M & Allen D III. *Educ:* Mills Col, BS, 60; La State Univ, Baton Rouge, MS, 63; Univ Houston, PhD(inorg chem), 67. *Prof Exp:* Chemist, Res & Develop Lab, Texaco, Inc, Tex, 63-65; fel chem, Univ Houston, 67. *Mem:* Am Chem Soc; Asn Comput Mach. *Res:* Polymerization of silicic acid under conditions similar to geologic conditions, effect of various ions on the polymerization process; complexes of oxomolybdenum V, complexes of molybdenum in the plus-5 oxidation state in an attempt to stabilize this oxidation state; thixotropic properties of clays, effect of various organic chelating agents on the thixotropic properties of clays; micro processor-instrument; CBE development in chemistry; modeling of geochemical systems; geochemistry. *Mailing Add:* Dept Chem Millsaps Col Jackson MS 39210

BISHOP, ASA ORIN, JR, ELECTRICAL ENGINEERING, COMPUTER SYSTEM DESIGN. *Current Pos:* from asst prof to assoc prof 70-80, assoc dir, Comput Ctr, 75-86, PROF ELEC ENG, UNIV TENN, KNOXVILLE, 80- *Personal Data:* b Richmond, Va, June 30, 38; m 64; c 3. *Educ:* Va Mil Inst, BS, 59; Clemson Univ, MS, 66, PhD(elec eng), 69. *Prof Exp:* Instr elec eng, Va Mil Inst, 62-64; teaching asst instr, Clemson Univ, 64-69, fel & res assoc, 69-70. *Concurrent Pos:* Consult, Duke Med Ctr, 69- & Vet Admin Hosp, 69-; spec asst financial mgt to asst secy, Navy, 78-79. *Mem:* Inst Elec & Electronics Engrs; Am Soc Engr Educ; Indust Elec & Control Inst Soc. *Res:* Feature extraction of information from the electroencephalogram and electrocardiogram using digital filter techniques and the on-line, real-time analysis of bioelectric phenomena; long range planning for data processing installations. *Mailing Add:* Elec Eng Univ Tenn 1345 Circle Park Knoxville TN 37996-0001

BISHOP, BEVERLY PETTERSON, NEUROPHYSIOLOGY, NEUROL CONTROL OF RESPIRATION. *Current Pos:* from instr to prof physiol, 58-91, DISTINGUISHED TEACHING PROF, STATE UNIV NY, BUFFALO, 92- *Personal Data:* b Corning, NY, Oct 19, 22; m 44, Charles W; c Geoffrey C. *Educ:* Syracuse Univ, BA, 44; Univ Rochester, MA, 46; State Univ NY Buffalo, PhD(physiol), 58. *Honors & Awards:* Golden Pen Award, Am Phys Ther Asn, 76, Res Award, 80. *Prof Exp:* Asst psychol, Univ Rochester, 44-46; teacher, Ohio Pub Sch, 46-48; instr bus admin, State Univ NY, Buffalo, 49-50; asst physiol, Glasgow Univ, 56-57. *Concurrent Pos:* NIH Study Sect, Respiration & Appl Physiol, 80-84, 91 & 93; mem coun, Am Physiol Soc, 88-91. *Mem:* Am Physiol Soc; Soc Neurosci; Am Cong Rehab Med; Am Asn Electrodiag Med; hon mem Am Phys Ther Asn. *Res:* Neurophysiology; neural regulation of respiration, mastication and other motor systems; integration of the diverse functions of the abdominal muscles. *Mailing Add:* Dept Physiol Sch Med Biomed Sci & Dent Med State Univ NY 124 Sherman Hall Buffalo NY 14214. *Fax:* 716-829-2344; *E-Mail:* bishop@ubmed.buffalo.edu

BISHOP, CHARLES (WILLIAM), BIOCHEMISTRY. *Current Pos:* asst prof, 47-64, ASSOC PROF BIOCHEM, SCH MED, STATE UNIV NY, BUFFALO, 64-, ASSOC PROF MED, 65- *Personal Data:* b Elmira, NY, June 30, 20; m 44, Beverly Peterson; c Geoffrey. *Educ:* Syracuse Univ, BS, 42, MS, 44; Univ Rochester, PhD(biochem), 46; Am Bd Clin Chem, dipl. *Prof Exp:* Asst chem, Syracuse Univ, 42-44; res chemist, Manhattan Proj, Univ Rochester, 44-46; instr chem, Kent State Univ, 46-47. *Concurrent Pos:* Supvr, Med Res Lab, Buffalo Gen Hosp, 47-51, asst lab dir, Chronic Dis Res Inst, 51-55; NIH spec res fel, Glasgow Univ, 55-56; founder, Blood Info Serv; head, Chem Lab, Buffalo Gen Hosp, 67-80. *Mem:* AAAS; Am Chem Soc; Am Soc

Biol Chemists; Am Asn Clin Chemists; Am Med Informatics Asn. *Res:* Red cell metabolism; carbohydrate and purine metabolism; blood storage systems; clinical chemistry; medical informatics; created framework for medical knowledge. *Mailing Add:* Dept Med Erie Co Med Ctr State Univ NY Buffalo NY 14215. *Fax:* 716-898-4493; *E-Mail:* ebishop@ubmede.buffalo.edu

BISHOP, CHARLES ANTHONY, organic chemistry, physical chemistry, for more information see previous edition

BISHOP, CHARLES FRANKLIN, PLANT PATHOLOGY. *Current Pos:* prof agr, Goshen Col, 56-63, chmn div natural sci, 68-73, prof biol, 63-86, EMER PROF BIOL, GOSHEN COL, 86-, PLANT PEST CONSULT, 88- *Personal Data:* b Doylestown, Pa, June 29, 18; m 43, Suzanne Harnish; c David F, John K, Lawrence A & Bruce E. *Educ:* Goshen Col, BA, 40; Univ WVa, MS, 42, PhD(plant path), 48. *Prof Exp:* Exten specialist plant path & entom, Univ WVa, 44-56. *Concurrent Pos:* Vis prof, Univ SFla, 73 & Univ Fla, 75-76; open fac fel, Lilly Endowment Fund, 75. *Mem:* Sigma Xi; Am Inst Biol Sci. *Res:* Purpletop of potatoes. *Mailing Add:* Dept Biol Goshen College Goshen IN 46526

BISHOP, CHARLES JOHNSON, GENETICS. *Current Pos:* RETIRED. *Personal Data:* b Sask, Can, Jan 6, 20; m 51, Katherine A Corey; c John. *Educ:* Acadia Univ, BSc, 41; Harvard Univ, AM & PhD(cytogenetics), 47. *Hon Degrees:* DSc, Acadia Univ, 82. *Honors & Awards:* Jubilee Medal, 77. *Prof Exp:* Assoc prof genetics & agr res officer, Acadia Univ, 47-52, res prof & supt exp sta, Kentville, NS, 52-58; dir res sta, Summerland, BC, 58-59; assoc dir prog, Res Br, Can Dept Agr, 59-64, res coordr hort, 64-85. *Mem:* Fel Am Soc Hort Sci; Am Pomol Soc (vpres, 57); Genetics Soc Can (pres, 58); Can Soc Hort Sci (pres, 57); fel Royal Soc Can; fel Agr Inst Can; hon life mem, Can Hort Coun. *Res:* X-ray and thermal neutron induced mutations in apples; polyploidy and scab resistance in apples; fruit and vegetable breeding; male sterility in tomatoes; editorial practices in plant science reporting; coordination of horticultural research. *Mailing Add:* 1968 Bel Air Dr Ottawa ON K2C 0W9 Can

BISHOP, CHARLES JOSEPH, ENERGY SYSTEMS ENGINEERING, SOLAR ENERGY ENGINEERING. *Current Pos:* dir tech servs, 81-84, exec dir corp technol, 84-85, VPRES, A O SMITH CORP, 85- *Personal Data:* b Gary, Ind, June 22, 41; m 63; c 2. *Educ:* Purdue Univ, BS, 63; Univ Wash, PhD(nuclear chem), 69. *Honors & Awards:* Cert of Recognition, NASA. *Prof Exp:* Mgr, Boeing Co, 69-77; br chief, Solar Energy Res Inst, 77-81. *Concurrent Pos:* Prog comt, Indust Res Inst, 87-89, chmn advan study group, 88-89, mem bd dirs, 89- *Mem:* Indust Res Inst. *Res:* Systems engineering; solar energy; energy systems; systems analysis; electrochemistry; photovoltaics. *Mailing Add:* 1455 Cedarton Pkwy Grafton WI 53024-0990

BISHOP, CLAUDE TITUS, IMMUNOCHEMISTRY, CARBOHYDRATE CHEMISTRY. *Current Pos:* RETIRED. *Personal Data:* b Liverpool, NS, May 13, 25; m 52; c 1. *Educ:* Acadia Univ, BSc, 45, BA, 46; McGill Univ, PhD(chem), 49. *Hon Degrees:* DSc, Univ Western Ont, 86. *Prof Exp:* Asst res officer, Carbohydrate Chem Sect, Div Biosci, Nat Res Coun Can, 49-55, assoc res officer, 55-60, sr res officer, 60-67, prin res officer, 67-70, asst dir, Biochem Lab, 70-72, assoc dir, Biol Res Div, 72-78, dir, Biol Sci Div, 78-87, secy gen, 87-89. *Concurrent Pos:* Ed-in-chief, Can J Res, 71-90. *Mem:* Can Biochem Soc; Chem Inst Can; Am Chem Soc; fel Royal Soc Can. *Res:* Carbohydrate chemistry; structures and immunochemistry of microbial polysaccharide antigens. *Mailing Add:* 63 Holborn Ave Nepean ON K2C 3H1 Can. *Fax:* 613-825-7479

BISHOP, DAVID FRANKLIN, MOLECULAR GENETICS OF HUMAN HEME BIOSYNTHESIS. *Current Pos:* Instr pediat, Mt Sinai Sch Med, 79-80, res asst prof pediat & genetics, 80-87, assoc prof med & molecular genetics, 87-94, assoc prof human genetics, 94-96, PROF, MT SINAI SCH MED, 96- *Personal Data:* b Morgantown, WVa, Mar 27, 45; m 81, Sandra Grow. *Educ:* Goshen Col, BA, 69; Mich State Univ, PhD(biochem), 76. *Concurrent Pos:* Prin investr hemat, NIH, 89- *Mem:* AAAS; Am Soc Human Genetics; NY Acad Sci; Harvey Soc; Soc Inherited Metab Dis. *Res:* Identification and characterization of the molecular defects causing X-linked sideroblastic anemia, the molecular genetics and regulation of human heme biosynthesis and the enzymology of the delta-aminolevulinate synthase isozymes. *Mailing Add:* Dept Human Genetics Mt Sinai Sch Med New York NY 10029-6574. *Fax:* 212-360-1809; *E-Mail:* bishop@msvax.mssm.edu

BISHOP, DAVID JOHN, PHYSICS. *Current Pos:* Mem tech staff, 78-88, DISTINGUISHED MEM TECH STAFF & HEAD, MICROSTRUCT PHYSICS RES DEPT, AT&T BELL LABS, 88- *Personal Data:* b Montgomery, Ala, Oct 6, 51; m 82, Vanessa J Levin; c Noah S. *Educ:* Syracuse Univ, BS, 73; Cornell Univ, MS, 77, PhD, 78. *Honors & Awards:* Bausch & Lomb Hon Sci Award. *Concurrent Pos:* Adj prof physics, State Univ NY, Buffalo. *Mem:* Fel Am Phys Soc. *Res:* Low temperature physics; superconductors and superfluids. *Mailing Add:* AT&T Bell Labs Rm 1D-231 600 Mountain Ave Murray Hill NJ 07974-0636. *Fax:* 908-582-3260; *E-Mail:* ojb@physics.att.com

BISHOP, DAVID MICHAEL, THEORETICAL CHEMISTRY. *Current Pos:* from asst prof to assoc prof, 63-67, PROF CHEM, UNIV OTTAWA, 72- *Personal Data:* b London, Eng, Sept 19, 36. *Educ:* Univ London, BSc, 57, PhD(chem), 60, DSc, 72. *Prof Exp:* Asst prof chem, Carnegie Inst Technol, 62-63. *Concurrent Pos:* Am Chem Soc fel, 60-62. *Mem:* Fel Royal Soc Can. *Res:* Molecular quantum chemistry. *Mailing Add:* Dept Chem Univ Ottawa Ottawa ON K1N 9B4 Can

BISHOP, EDWIN VANDEWATER, ASTRONOMY, PHYSICS. *Current Pos:* PROF ASTRON & PHYSICS, YOUNGSTOWN STATE UNIV, 69- *Personal Data:* b Jamaica, NY, May 17, 35; m 57; c 1. *Educ:* Swarthmore Col, BA, 58; Yale Univ, MS, 60, PhD(physics), 66. *Prof Exp:* Res staff astronr, Yale Univ, 66-69. *Mem:* Am Astron Soc; Am Phys Soc. *Res:* Solar-system physics; thermodynamic properties, particularly temperature-profile histories of the major planets' interiors, especially Jupiter's. *Mailing Add:* 4271 Lake Rd Youngstown OH 44511

BISHOP, EUGENE H(ARLAN), MECHANICAL ENGINEERING. *Current Pos:* PROF MECH ENG & HEAD DEPT, CLEMSON UNIV, 74- *Personal Data:* b Ellisville, Miss, Oct 29, 33; m 55; c 3. *Educ:* Miss State Univ, BS, 55; Univ Tex, PhD(mech eng), 64. *Prof Exp:* Asst engr, Eng Exten Serv, Miss State Univ, 60-61; asst heat transfer, Univ Tex, 61-64; assoc prof mech eng, Miss State Univ, 64-67; assoc prof, Mont State Univ, 67-69, prof aerospace & mech eng & head dept, 69-74. *Mem:* Am Soc Mech Engrs. *Res:* Natural convection heat transfer and fluid mechanics. *Mailing Add:* Dept Mech Eng Clemson Univ Clemson SC 29632-0001

BISHOP, FINLEY CHARLES, MINERALOGY, PETROLOGY. *Current Pos:* From instr to asst prof, 76-82, ASSOC PROF GEOL, NORTHWESTERN UNIV, EVANSTON, 82- *Personal Data:* b Minneapolis, Minn, May 1, 49. *Educ:* Carleton Col, AB, 72; Univ Chicago, SM, 74, PhD(geol), 76. *Mem:* AAAS; Am Geophys Union; Geol Soc Am; Geochem Soc; Mineral Soc Am. *Res:* Ion exchange in minerals at high temperatures and pressures; mineralogy of Archean layered igneous complexes; kimberlites and upper mantle rocks; properties of magnesian calcites. *Mailing Add:* Dept Geol Sci Northwestern Univ 1847 Sheridin Rd Evanston IL 60208-2150

BISHOP, GALE ARDEN, PALEONTOLOGY. *Current Pos:* PROF GEOL, GA SOUTHERN COL, 71- *Personal Data:* b Jamestown, NDak, Dec 10, 42; m 64; c 2. *Educ:* SDak Sch of Mines, BS, 65, MS, 67; Univ Tex, Austin, PhD(geol), 71. *Concurrent Pos:* Dir, Ga Southern Col Mus, 80-83. *Mem:* Sigma Xi; Crustacean Soc; Paleont Soc. *Res:* Cretaceous crabs; preservation processes; functional morphology; Tertiary fresh-water clams; ammonite biostratigraphic mapping and larval development; predation-produced trace fossils; paleoecology; decapod trace fossils; fossil and living ghost shrimp; coastal geology. *Mailing Add:* Dept Geol Ga Southern Univ Statesboro GA 30460-8149

BISHOP, GUY WILLIAM, ENTOMOLOGY. *Current Pos:* RETIRED. *Personal Data:* b Medford, Ore, May 16, 26; m 48; c 3. *Educ:* Ore State Col, BS, 51, MS, 53; State Col Wash, PhD(entom), 58. *Prof Exp:* Asst entom, Ore State Col, 48-52; asst, State Col Wash, 54-56; from asst entomologist to assoc entomologist, Univ Idaho, 57-74, assoc prof, 68-74, prof entom & entomologist, 74-88. *Mem:* Am Entom Soc. *Res:* Virus vectors of plants; potato insects. *Mailing Add:* 3403 N Valley View Rd Ashland OR 97520

BISHOP, JACK BELMONT, GENETICS, TOXICOLOGY. *Current Pos:* RES GENETICIST, NAT INST ENVIRON HEALTH SCI, DEPT HEALTH & HUMAN SERV, NIH, 85- *Personal Data:* b Seymour, Tex, Aug 26, 43; m 71; c 2. *Educ:* McMurry Col, BA, 67; La State Univ, Baton Rouge, MS, 70, PhD(genetics), 74. *Honors & Awards:* Commendable Serv Award, Food & Drug Admin, 80. *Prof Exp:* Res geneticist, Bee Breeding & Stock Ctr Res Lab, Agr Res Serv, USDA, 72-75; res geneticist, Nat Ctr Toxicol Res, HEW, Food & Drug Admin, 75-85. *Concurrent Pos:* Adj prof med sci, Grad Sch, Univ Ark, 80-88; spec appt, Sch Med, Univ NC, Chapel Hill, 89- *Mem:* Environ Mutagens Soc; Sigma Xi; Teratology Soc. *Res:* Developmental genetic toxicology involving studies of induced germ cell damage, such as aneuploidy and structural chromosome damage leading to abnormal development and/or reproductive failure; topoisomerase inhibitors and anti-retroviral (AIDS) drugs. *Mailing Add:* 2824 Mattlyn Ct Raleigh NC 27613. *Fax:* 919-541-4634; *E-Mail:* bishop@niehs.nih.gov

BISHOP, JACK GARLAND, physiology, for more information see previous edition

BISHOP, JACK LYNN, ENTOMOLOGY. *Current Pos:* entomologist, Shell Develop Co, Calif, 67-70, toxicologist-environmentalist, Shell Chem Co, 70-77, MEM STAFF, SHELL DEVELOP CO, CALIF, 77- *Personal Data:* b Abilene, Kans, Nov 15, 29; m 58; c 2. *Educ:* Kans State Univ, BS, 56, MS, 57, PhD, 59. *Prof Exp:* From asst prof to assoc prof entom, Va Polytech Inst & State Univ, 58-67. *Mem:* Entom Soc Am; Sigma Xi. *Res:* Forage entomology and insect toxicology. *Mailing Add:* PO Box 267 Bethel Island CA 94511-0267

BISHOP, JAMES MARTIN, PHYSICS. *Current Pos:* FAC FEL, DEPT PHYSICS, UNIV NOTRE DAME, 72- *Personal Data:* b Dodge City, Kans, Mar 13, 36; m 64; c 2. *Educ:* Kans State Teachers Col, AB, 58; Univ Wis, MS, 60, PhD(physics), 67. *Prof Exp:* Instr physics, Ohio Univ, 66-67, asst prof, 67-72. *Mem:* AAAS; Am Phys Soc; Asn Comput Mach; Sigma Xi. *Res:* Elementary particle physics; computer applications in physics. *Mailing Add:* Dept Physics Univ Notre Dame Notre Dame IN 46556-9999

BISHOP, JAY LYMAN, ENVIRONMENTAL & INDUSTRIAL CHEMISTRY, PALEOGRAPHY. *Current Pos:* CHEM & ENVIRON ENGR, US ARMY, 82- *Personal Data:* b Salt Lake City, Utah, July 7, 32; m 58; c Peggy J, Lynn W, Janet G, Nancy, Deanna T, Linda E, Lyman M,

Jay S & Michelle. *Educ:* Univ Utah, BS, 53, PhD(org chem), 62. *Prof Exp:* Res assoc org chem, Ariz State Univ, 62-63, instr & res assoc chem, 64-67; sr chemist, Ciba Pharmaceut Corp, 67-71; chief chemist & metallurgist, Assoc Smelters Int, 73 & United Refinery Inc, 73-75; chief chemist & metallurgist, US Nat Metals Inc, 75-76; pres, Western Consult, 76- *Concurrent Pos:* Pres, Bishop Mfg Co, 71-, consult chemist, 72-; lectr, Univ Utah, 60-62; traveling sci lectr, Ariz Acad Sci, 62-64; sr pres, 481st Quorum of 70, 70-71. *Res:* Heterocyclics; polymers; amine-formaldehyde alkylation; industrial processes; chemotherapeutic agents; precious metals refining and fabricating; energy research; fuel alcohol production; paleography and translation; munitions deactivation; EPA laws; history; music; religion. *Mailing Add:* 1663 S 75 East Bountiful UT 84010-5218

BISHOP, JOHN MICHAEL, VIROLOGY, BIOCHEMISTRY. *Current Pos:* from asst prof to assoc prof, 68-72, PROF MICROBIOL, UNIV CALIF, SAN FRANCISCO, 72-, PROF BIOCHEM & BIOPHYS, 82-, PROF, MED CTR, 94-; DIR, G W HOOPER RES FOUND, 81- *Personal Data:* b York, Pa, Feb 22, 36; m 59; c 2. *Educ:* Gettysburg Col, AB, 57; Harvard Univ, MD, 62. *Hon Degrees:* DSc, Gettysburg Col, 83. *Honors & Awards:* Nobel Prize in Physiol or Med, 89; Biomed Res Award, Am Asn Med Cols, 81; Albert Lasker Basic Med Res Award, 82; Armand Hammer Cancer Res Award, 84; Gen Motors Found Cancer Res Award, 84; Gairdner Found Int Award, Can, 84; Medal of Honor, Am Cancer Soc, 85; Passano Foudn Award; Lila Gruber Cancer Res Award, Am Acad Dermat. *Prof Exp:* Intern internal med, Mass Gen Hosp, Boston, 62-63, resident, 63-64; res assoc virol, NIH, 64-66, sr investr, 66-68. *Concurrent Pos:* Res grants, NIH, 68-, Cancer Res Coord Comt, Univ Calif, 68- & Calif Div, Am Cancer Soc, 69-; vis scientist, Heinrich-Pette Inst, Ger, 67-68; assoc ed, Virol, 70-89; mem bd trustees, Leukemia Soc Am, 73-78; co-chair, Gordon Conf Animal Cells & Viruses, 79; chair, Virol Sect, NIH, 80-82, mem adv comt to dir, 86-88; non-resident fel, Salk Inst, 90- *Mem:* Nat Acad Sci; Inst Med-Nat Acad Sci; Am Soc Biol Chemists; Am Soc Microbiol; Am Soc Cell Biol; Am Acad Arts & Sci; Fed Am Scientists; Am Asn Univ Prof; fel AAAS. *Res:* Biochemistry of animal viruses; replication of nucleic acids; viral oncogenesis; molecular genetics. *Mailing Add:* Box 0552 San Francisco CA 94143

BISHOP, JOHN RUSSELL, AGRICULTURAL CHEMISTRY. *Current Pos:* RETIRED. *Personal Data:* b Pa, Dec 6, 20; m 45; c 3. *Educ:* Ursinus Col, BS, 42. *Prof Exp:* Dir res & develop, Am Chem Prod Inc, 75-78; assoc dir explor & develop, Herb & Plant Growth Reg, Union Carbide Agr Prod Co Inc, 78-81. *Mem:* Am Chem Soc; Weed Sci Soc Am; Int Weed Sci Soc. *Res:* Organic chemical research pertaining to agricultural chemicals; preparation of chemicals for use as herbicides, plant hormones, plant growth regulators; defoliators; formulation of herbicides and plant growth regulators. *Mailing Add:* Ctr Dairy Res Univ Wis 1605 Linden Dr Madison WI 53706

BISHOP, JOHN WATSON, ECOLOGY, AQUATIC BIOLOGY. *Current Pos:* from asst prof to assoc prof, 66-83, PROF BIOL, UNIV RICHMOND, 83- *Personal Data:* b Glenridge, NJ, Mar 21, 38; m 62; c 2. *Educ:* Rutgers Univ, BA, 60; Cornell Univ, MS, 62, PhD(oceanog), 66. *Prof Exp:* Asst prof biol, Univ Del, 64-66. *Concurrent Pos:* Univ res found grant, Univ Del, 65-66; Off Water Resources grant, 68-70. *Mem:* Am Soc Limnol & Oceanog; Ecol Soc Am. *Res:* Zooplankton ecology; trophic relationships in aquatic ecosystems. *Mailing Add:* 4701 Cosby Rd Powhatan VA 23139-3906

BISHOP, JOHN WILLIAM, PETROLEUM CHEMISTRY. *Current Pos:* RETIRED. *Personal Data:* b Jefferson Co, Ind, June 12, 16; m 39; c 2. *Educ:* DePauw Univ, BA, 38; Western Reserve Univ, MA, 39, PhD(org chem), 42. *Prof Exp:* Chemist, Tidewater Oil Co, 42-44, group leader, res dept, 44-56, mgr opers anal, 56-68; mgr econ & eval, Getty Oil Co, 68-79, mgr strategic crude oil planning, 80-84. *Mem:* Am Chem Soc; Am Nuclear Soc; Sigma Xi; AAAS. *Res:* Hydrocarbon isomerization; lubricants; additives for lubricants; electronic computer applications in petroleum industry; planning and economic evaluations; nuclear power technology. *Mailing Add:* 982 Marisa Lane Olivenhain CA 92024-9784

BISHOP, JONATHAN S, GLYCOGEN METABOLISM. *Current Pos:* ASSOC PROF INTERNAL MED, MED SCH, UNIV MINN, 69-, LECTR PHARMACOL, 79- *Personal Data:* b Cleveland, Ohio, Apr 20, 25. *Educ:* Yale Univ, MD, 49. *Mailing Add:* 2280 W Lake of the Isle Pkwy Minneapolis MN 55405

BISHOP, JOSEPH MICHAEL, APPLIED OCEANOGRAPHY & MARINE POLICY, RESEARCH MANAGEMENT. *Current Pos:* sr scientist, Off Chief Scientist, 86-93, DIR, OFF RES & TECHNOL APPLNS, NAT OCEANIC & ATMOSPHERIC ADMIN, 93- *Personal Data:* b Syracuse, NY, Jan 6, 43; m 69, Christine Curtis; c Stacey, Laina & Stephanie. *Educ:* State Univ NY Maritime Col, BS, 66; NY Univ, MS, 70, PhD(oceanog), 73. *Prof Exp:* Asst dean, State Univ NY Maritime Col, 71-72, instr meteorol, 72-74; oceanogr, US Coast Guard, 74-76 & Nat Oceanic Atmospheric Admin, 76-80; policy adv meteorol, Fed Emergency Mgt Agency, 80-84; sr sci adv, Nat Adv Comt Oceans & Atmosphere, 84-86. *Concurrent Pos:* Instr, George Washington Univ, 77-82, Catholic Univ, 79- & Johns Hopkins Univ, 88- *Mem:* Marine Technol Soc. *Res:* Coastal circulation; wind waves; air-sea interaction; applied oceanography; meteorology; ocean affairs and policy; technology transfer; program management. *Mailing Add:* Tintagel Ct Dumfries VA 22026. *Fax:* 301-713-4100

BISHOP, KEITH C, III, ORGANOMETALLIC CHEMISTRY, CATALYSIS. *Current Pos:* res chemist, Chevron Res Co, 74-81, sr environ engr, 81-85, policy coordr chem, Chevron Res Co, SR CONSULT, CALIF STATE RELATIONS, CHEVRON, 91- *Personal Data:* b Portland, Ore, Jan 31, 47; c 2. *Educ:* Univ Calif, Santa Barbara, BS, 69; Yale Univ, PhD(chem), 73. *Prof Exp:* Fel chem, Stanford Univ, 73-74. *Concurrent Pos:* Bd dir, Main Municipal Water Dist, 79-83. *Mem:* Am Chem Soc; Sigma Xi; AAAS. *Res:* Environmental science. *Mailing Add:* Chevron Corp 1201 K Sta Suite 1910 Sacramento CA 95814-3924

BISHOP, MARGARET S, GEOLOGY. *Current Pos:* RETIRED. *Personal Data:* b Lewiston, Mich, June 21, 06; m 37; c 2. *Educ:* Univ Mich, AB, 29, MS, 31, PhD(geol), 33. *Prof Exp:* Geologist, Pure Oil Co, 29-30, asst to chief geologist, 33-38, consult geologist, 38-53; from asst prof to prof geol, Univ Houston, 53-71, emer prof, 71. *Mem:* Geol Soc Am; Am Asn Petrol Geologists. *Res:* Subsurface geology and earth science. *Mailing Add:* 4125 17th St N Texas City TX 77590

BISHOP, MARILYN FRANCES, THEORETICAL SOLID STATE PHYSICS, THEORETICAL BIOPHYSICS. *Current Pos:* ASSOC PROF PHYSICS, VA COMMONWEALTH UNIV, 86- *Personal Data:* b Sacramento, Calif, Jan 19, 50; m 85, Andrew Certner; c Benjamin & Geoffrey. *Educ:* Univ Calif, Irvine, BA, 71 & 72, MA, 73, PhD(physics), 76. *Prof Exp:* Res asst physics, Univ Calif, Irvine, 72-76; res assoc physics, Purdue Univ, 76-79; asst prof physics, Drexel Univ, 79-86. *Mem:* Am Phys Soc; Sigma Xi; AAAS; Biophysical Soc. *Res:* Interacting fermi systems; highly correlated electron systems; charge densiity waves; transport properties of metals; electron-phonon interactions; superconductivity; kinetics of polymerization of biological polymers light scattering from biological polymers. *Mailing Add:* Dept Physics Va Commonwealth Univ 1020 W Main St Richmond VA 23284-2000. *Fax:* 804-828-7073; *E-Mail:* bishop@gems.vcu.edu

BISHOP, MARVIN, CHEMICAL PHYSICS, COMPUTER SCIENCE. *Current Pos:* ASSOC PROF, MANHATTAN COL, 83- *Personal Data:* b New York, NY, Feb 17, 45; m 90; c 1. *Educ:* City Col New York, BS, 66; Columbia Univ, PhD(chem), 71; New York Univ, MS Comput Sci, 83. *Prof Exp:* Res assoc chem, Nat Bur Standards, 71-73 & Columbia Univ, 73-74; vis asst prof, Howard Univ, 74-75; res asst prof, State Univ NY Albany, 75-76; asst prof chem, Fordham Univ, Lincoln Ctr, 76-81; vis scientist, Vanderwaals Lab, Neth, 81-82; res scientist, Courant Inst Math, 82-83. *Concurrent Pos:* Nat Res Coun fel, Nat Bur Standards, 71-73; Am Chem Soc-Petrol Res Fund grant, Fordham Univ, 76-; comput grant & fac res grant, Nat Res Coun Can, 78-; type B grants, PRF-Am Chem Soc, 79-81, 84-86 & 87-89; PRF-ACS type B grants, 79-81, 84-86, 87-89; IBM grants, 85-86, 87-; vis scientist, UMIST, Univ Manchester Inst Sci & Technol, 88-91. *Mem:* Am Chem Soc; Am Phys Soc; Asn Comput Mach. *Res:* Statistical mechanics; computer simulation; polymers; liquid-crystals; fluids. *Mailing Add:* Dept Math Comput Sci Manhattan Col Riverdale NY 10471

BISHOP, MURIEL BOYD, BIOCHEMISTRY, ORGANIC CHEMISTRY. *Current Pos:* asst prof, 60-74, ASSOC PROF CHEM, CLEMSON UNIV, 74- *Personal Data:* b Billingsley, Ala, Oct 7, 28; m 60; c 1. *Educ:* Huntingdon Col, BA, 52; Emory Univ, MS, 55; Mich State Univ, PhD(chem), 58. *Prof Exp:* NSF grant pharmacol, Yale Univ, 58-59. *Mem:* Am Chem Soc. *Res:* Nucleic acid chemistry, especially enzymes associated with pyrimidine biosynthesis; structure of nucleic acids. *Mailing Add:* PO Box 1366 Clemson SC 29633-1366

BISHOP, NANCY HORSCHEL, MICROBIOLOGY, IMMUNOLOGY. *Current Pos:* from asst prof to assoc prof, 77-84, PROF BIOL, CALIF STATE UNIV, NORTHRIDGE, 84- *Personal Data:* b Yakima, Wash, Mar 15, 36. *Educ:* Wash State Univ, BS, 58, MS, 61; Univ Calif, Los Angeles, PhD(microbiol & immunol), 75. *Prof Exp:* Res asst bact, Wash State Univ, 60-62; microbiologist, Yakima Valley Mem Hosp, 62 & Greater Bakersfield Mem Hosp, 63-64; sr microbiologist, Santa Barbara Cottage Hosp, 64-68; microbiologist, Los Robles Hosp, 69-70; scholar microbiol & immunol, Univ Calif, Los Angeles, 75-77. *Mem:* Am Soc Microbiol; Am Venereal Dis Asn; AAAS. *Res:* Mechanisms of immunity in syphilis. *Mailing Add:* Dept Biol Calif State Univ 1811 Nordhoff St Northridge CA 91330. *Fax:* 818-885-2034

BISHOP, NORMAN IVAN, PLANT PHYSIOLOGY. *Current Pos:* from assoc prof to prof, 63-93, dept chmn, 86-89, EMER PROF PLANT PHYSIOL, ORE STATE UNIV, 93- *Personal Data:* b Silverton, Colo, June 29, 28; m 48, Patricia Sutherland; c Bryan, Julie, James & Diane. *Educ:* Univ Utah, BS, 51, MS, 52, PhD(physiol), 55. *Prof Exp:* Res asst biol, Univ Utah, 52-55; res assoc biochem, Univ Chicago, 55-57, asst prof, 57-60; assoc prof, Fla State Univ, 60-63. *Concurrent Pos:* Lalor Found fel, 56; Guggenheim fel, 71; Alexander von Humboldt Sr Scientist Award, 91. *Mem:* Fel AAAS; Am Soc Plant Physiol; Biophys Soc; Am Soc Biol Chemists; Am Soc Photobiol; Japanese Soc Plant Physiol. *Res:* Photosynthesis and metabolism of microorganisms; photochemistry; general biochemistry; function of carotenoids in photosynthesis. *Mailing Add:* Dept Bot Ore State Univ Corvallis OR 97331. *Fax:* 541-737-3573

BISHOP, PAUL EDWARD, MICROBIOLOGY, GENETICS. *Current Pos:* from asst prof to assoc prof, 77-90, PROF MICROBIOL, NC STATE UNIV, 90- *Personal Data:* b Portland, Ore, Feb 12, 40; m 68, Lola G Montesdeoca; c Paul E. *Educ:* Wash State Univ, BS, 64; Ore State Univ, MS, 70, PhD(food sci), 73. *Prof Exp:* Technician retinal metab, Sch Med, Univ Wash, 66-67; res assoc biochem nitrogen fixation, Ore State Univ, 73-75; res assoc genetics nitrogen fixation, Univ Wis-Madison, 75-77. *Concurrent Pos:* Prin investr,

Competitive Grants Prog, Sci & Educ Admin, USDA, 78-80, 81-83, 84-98; Agr Res Serv fel, Agr & Food Nitrogen, Univ Sussex, Brighton, UK, 84-85. *Mem:* Am Soc Microbiol. *Res:* Genetics and molecular biology of alternative nitrogen fixation systems in azotobacter vinelandii; molecular biology. *Mailing Add:* Dept Microbiol NC State Univ Raleigh NC 27650. *Fax:* 919-515-7867; *E-Mail:* peb@mbio.ncsu.edu

BISHOP, PAUL LESLIE, HAZARDOUS WASTE TREATMENT, WASTEWATER TREATMENT. *Current Pos:* William Thomas prof & head civil & environ eng, 88-93, PROF ENVIRON ENG, UNIV CINCINNATI, 93- *Personal Data:* b Hyannis, Mass, Nov 27, 45; m 71, Pamela J Neher; c Andrew P & Amanda M. *Educ:* Northeastern Univ, BSCE, 68; Purdue Univ MSCE, 70, PhD(environ eng), 72. *Prof Exp:* From asst prof to prof environ eng, Univ NH, 72-87, head, 76-82. *Concurrent Pos:* Environ eng consult, 72-; vis prof, Heriot-Watt Univ, Edinburgh, Scotland, 80 & Tech Univ Denmark, Lyngby, 86-87; bd trustees, Am Acad Environ Engrs, 88-93; liaison, Asn Environ Eng Profs, 88-93; prog comt vchair, Water Environ Fedn; mem, Hazardous Waste Comt, Am Soc Civil Engrs; mem bd dir, Accreditation Bd Eng & Technol, 90- *Mem:* Int Asn Water Quality; Am Soc Eng Educ; Am Soc Civil Engrs; Asn Environ Eng Prof (vpres, 91-92, pres, 92-93); Air & Waste Mgt Asn. *Res:* Hazardous waste treatment; biological waste treatment; solidification and stabilization of hazardous wastes; leaching mechanisms; use of biofilms for treatment; solid waste composting. *Mailing Add:* Dept Civil Eng Univ Cincinnati 2600 Clifton Ave Cincinnati OH 45220-2872. *Fax:* 513-556-2599; *E-Mail:* pbishop@uceng.uc.edu

BISHOP, RICHARD LAWRENCE, GEOMETRY. *Current Pos:* PROF MATH, UNIV ILL, URBANA-CHAMPAIGN, 59- *Personal Data:* b Lake Odessa, Mich, Aug 12, 31; m 54; c 5. *Educ:* Case Inst Technol, BS, 54; Mass Inst Technol, PhD(math), 59. *Mem:* Am Math Soc. *Res:* Relations between the topological and analytical properties of riemannian manifolds. *Mailing Add:* Univ Ill 1409 W Green St Urbana IL 61801-2917

BISHOP, RICHARD RAY, ELECTRICAL ENGINEERING, BIOENGINEERING. *Current Pos:* ASST PROF ELEC ENG & CHMN DEPT, UNIV NEW ORLEANS, 80- *Personal Data:* b Ft Worth, Tex, Mar 23, 38; m 62. *Educ:* Southern Methodist Univ, BSEE, 61, MSEE, 65; Univ Tex, Austin, PhD(elec eng), 68. *Prof Exp:* Technician, Bell Helicopter Corp, Tex, 57-61; engr, Tex Instruments, 61-62; instr elec eng, Southern Methodist Univ, 62-63; asst prof elec eng, Pa State Univ, University Park, 68-80. *Mem:* Inst Elec & Electronics Engrs; Asn Comput Mach. *Res:* Biomedical electronics; biomedical signal processing, particularly electroencephalogram analysis by computer; biomedical simulation. *Mailing Add:* Eng 910 Univ New Orleans New Orleans LA 70122

BISHOP, RICHARD STEARNS, EXPLORATION TECHNOLOGY. *Current Pos:* sr res specialist, Exxon Prof Res Co, 75-81, proj leader USA explor, 81-84, dist geol USA prod, 84-86, explorationist USA explor, 86-87, reg explor, Prod Res Co, 87-92, GEOL ASSOC, EXXON PROD RES CO, 81- PRES REGIONAL EXPL & ASSESSMENT, EXXON EXPLOR CO, 92- *Personal Data:* b Dowagiac, Mich, April 14, 45; m 71, Edythe; c Ryan & Timothy. *Educ:* Tex Christian Univ, BS, 67; Univ Mo, MA, 69; Stanford Univ, PhD(geol), 77. *Honors & Awards:* Sproule Award, 80. *Prof Exp:* Prod geologist, Univ Oil Co, Calif, 69-71. *Concurrent Pos:* Instr, La State Univ, 71; chmn, Nat Convention, Am Asn Petrol Geologists, 88,. *Mem:* Am Asn Petrol Geologists (secy, 91); fel Geol Soc Am; Soc Petrol Engrs. *Res:* Material balance model of the accumulation and dispersion of hydrocarbons in the subsurface; mechanics of diapir movement; origins of abnormal pressures; assessment methods. *Mailing Add:* 13622 Kingride Lane Houston TX 77079

BISHOP, ROBERT H, CONTROL THEORY, SPACECRAFT SYSTEMS. *Current Pos:* ASST PROF AEROSPACE, UNIV TEX, 90- *Personal Data:* b Vicenza, Italy; US citizen. *Educ:* Tex A&M Univ, BS, 79, MS, 80; Rice Univ, PhD(elec), 90. *Prof Exp:* Res staff, Charles Stark Draper Lab, 80-90. *Concurrent Pos:* Mem, Guidance, Navigation & Control Tech Comt, Am Inst Aeronaut & Astronaut, 91; mem, Spaceflight Mech Comt, Am Astronaut Soc, 93. *Mem:* Am Astronaut Soc; sr mem Am Inst Aeronaut & Astronaut; Inst Elec & Electronics Engrs. *Res:* Spacecraft guidance, navigation, and control; nonlinear control of spacecraft; interplanetary navigation analysis; adaptive control. *Mailing Add:* Dept Areospace Eng WRW 408 B Univ Tex Austin TX 78712. *E-Mail:* bishop@zeus.ae.utexas.edu

BISHOP, ROY LOVITT, ASTRONOMY. *Personal Data:* b Wolfville, NS, Sept 22, 39;; m 61, Gertrude Wellwood; c Grant, Katrina & Orinda. *Educ:* Acadia Univ, BSc, 61; McMaster Univ, MSc, 63; Univ Man, PhD(physics), 69. *Prof Exp:* Head dept, Acadia Univ, 76-83 & 86-92, prof physics, 63-94. *Concurrent Pos:* Ed Observer's Handbk, Royal Astron Soc Can, 81- *Mem:* Royal Astron Soc Can (pres, 84-86); Can Astron Soc; Int Astron Union; Am Asn Physics Teachers. *Res:* History of astronomy with an emphasis on Canada. *Mailing Add:* Dept Physics Acadia Univ Wolfville NS B0P 1X0 Can. *E-Mail:* roy.bishop@acadiau.ca

BISHOP, SANFORD PARSONS, COMPARATIVE PATHOLOGY, CARDIOVASCULAR DISEASES. *Current Pos:* PROF PATH, UNIV ALA AT BIRMINGHAM, 75- *Personal Data:* b Springfield, Vt, Aug 28, 36; m 57, Carol Fogg; c Linda (Pilkerton), Wendy (Walters) & Harold H. *Educ:* NY State Col Vet Med, Cornell Univ, DVM, 60; Ohio State Univ, MSc, 65, PhD(vet path), 68; Am Col Vet Pathologists, dipl; Am Col Vet Internal Med, dipl & cert cardiol. *Prof Exp:* Pvt pract vet med, NY, 60-62; instr cardiol, Sch Vet Med, Univ Pa, 62-63; from asst prof to assoc prof path, Col Med & Dept Vet Path, Ohio State Univ, 68-75. *Concurrent Pos:* Res career develop award, NIH, 72-75. *Mem:* AAAS; Am Soc Invest Pathology; Am Vet Med Asn; Am Heart Asn; Int Acad Path; Int Soc Heart Res (pres-elect, 91-94, pres, 94-97). *Res:* Comparative cardiovascular pathology; hypertrophy; congestive heart failure; atherosclerosis; myocardial infarction. *Mailing Add:* Dept Path Univ Ala at Birmingham 1670 University Blvd Birmingham AL 35294. *Fax:* 205-934-1775; *E-Mail:* bishop@vh.path.uab.edu

BISHOP, STEPHEN GRAY, SOLID STATE PHYSICS. *Current Pos:* PROF ELEC & COMPUT ENG, DIR, MICROELEC LAB, 88-, ADVAN RES PROJS AGENCY, UNIV ILL URBANA-CHICAGO, 93- *Personal Data:* b York, Pa, Jan 26, 39; m 63; c 2. *Educ:* Gettysburg Col, BA, 60; Brown Univ, PhD(physics), 65. *Honors & Awards:* Pure Sci Award, Res & Eng Soc Am, 77; Alan Berman Res Publ Award, Naval Res Lab, 75. *Prof Exp:* Res assoc physics, Brown Univ, 65-66; Nat Acad Sci-Nat Res Coun res assoc, Naval Res Lab, 66-88, res physicist semiconductor physics, 68-73, supvry res physicist, 74-89. *Concurrent Pos:* Vis scientist semiconductor physics, Max Planck Inst, Stuttgart, Ger, 73-74; exchange scientist, Royal Signals & Radar Estab, Great Malvern, Eng, 78-79; adj prof physics, State Univ NY, Buffalo, 84-, Univ Utah, 86- *Mem:* AAAS; fel Am Phys Soc; Sigma Xi; Mat Res Soc; Optic Soc Am; Lasers & Electro-Optics Soc. *Res:* Optical and electronic properties of crystalline and amorphous semiconductors; optical spectroscopy, luminescence and magnetic resonance techniques. *Mailing Add:* Microelec Lab Univ Ill 208 N Wright St Urbana IL 61801

BISHOP, STEPHEN HURST, BIOCHEMISTRY, COMPARATIVE PHYSIOLOGY. *Current Pos:* assoc prof, 77-79, PROF ZOOL, IOWA STATE UNIV, 79- *Personal Data:* b Philadelphia, Pa, June 22, 36; m 62; c 3. *Educ:* Gettysburg Col, BA, 58; Duke Univ, MA, 60; Rice Univ, PhD(biol), 64. *Prof Exp:* Res assoc biochem, Univ Kans Med Ctr, 64-67; asst prof biochem, Baylor Col Med, 67-77. *Concurrent Pos:* Fel biochem, Univ Kans, 64-67; mem, Inst Summer Prog, MBL, NSF, 75-77, Regulatory Biol Grant Rev Panel, 78-81, prog officer, Regulatory Biol, 86-88; coordr molecular cell develop prog, Iowa State Univ, 80-83. *Mem:* Fel AAAS; Soc Complex Carbohydrates; Am Chem Soc; Am Soc Biochem & Molecular Biol; Am Soc Zool; NY Acad Sci. *Res:* Phosphoglycoprotein structure-function; nitrogen metabolism; regulation of aminoacid metabolism; osmoregulation; enzymology. *Mailing Add:* Dept Zool & Genetics Iowa State Univ Ames IA 50011-0001

BISHOP, THOMAS PARKER, SOLID STATE PHYSICS. *Current Pos:* From asst prof to assoc prof, 67-79, prof physics, 79-91, PROF SCI EDUC, SCH EDUC, GA SOUTHERN UNIV, 91- *Personal Data:* b Richland, Ga, July 22, 36; m 62; c 2. *Educ:* Carson-Newman Col, BS, 59; Emory Univ, MS, 63; Clemson Univ, PhD, 68. *Mem:* Am Asn Physics Teachers; Am Phys Soc. *Res:* Color centers in solids; electron paramagnetic resonance; health physics. *Mailing Add:* 305 Palomino Path Statesboro GA 30458

BISHOP, VERNON S, CARDIOVASCULAR PHYSIOLOGY. *Current Pos:* PROF PHARMACOL, UNIV TEX, 68- *Mailing Add:* Dept Pharmacol Health Sci Ctr Univ Tex 7703 Floyd Curl Dr San Antonio TX 78284-7756

BISHOP, WALTON BURRELL, RELIABILITY, SEQUENTIAL ANALYSIS. *Current Pos:* res electronics engr, 66-80, CONSULT, US NAVAL RES LAB, 80- *Personal Data:* b LeRoy, Ill, Aug 25, 17; m 40, 59, Anne-Marie Delachapelle; c Gregory, Chantal & Veronique. *Educ:* Ill State Univ, BEd, 39; Boston Univ, MA, 50; Northeastern Univ, MSEE, 54; Univ Md, MA, 83, PhD(pub commun), 90. *Prof Exp:* Instr pub schs, Ill, 39-42; radio engr, Scott Field, Ill, 42-43; electronics engr & mathematician, Air Force Cambridge Res Labs, 46-66. *Concurrent Pos:* Lectr eve classes, Northeastern Univ, 60-66. *Mem:* Sigma Xi; Inst Elec & Electronics Engrs; Soc Prof Journalist; Int Commun Asn; Asn Educ Jour & Mass Commun. *Res:* Electronic means of identifying aircraft; reliability; science communication and science education; medical electronics; granted 23 patents. *Mailing Add:* 6 Balmoral Dr E Oxon Hill MD 20745-1011

BISHOP, WILLIAM P, SPACE & ENVIRONMENTAL SCIENCE. *Current Pos:* VPRES RES, DESERT RES INST, 90- *Personal Data:* b Lakewood, Ohio, Jan 18, 40; m 63, Sarah Gilbert. *Educ:* Col Wooster, BA, 62; Ohio State Univ, PhD(phys chem), 67. *Honors & Awards:* Silver Medal, Nuclear Regulatory Comn & Dept Com. *Prof Exp:* Vis res assoc chem, Ohio State Univ, 67-69; mem staff nuclear fuel cycle, Sandia Labs, 69-75; chief, Waste Mgt Br, US Nuclear Regulatory Comn, 75-76, asst dir, 76-78; dep dir Environ Observations Div, NASA, 78-81, dep dir, Life Sci Div, 81-83; dep asst admin satellites & actg asst admin environ satellite, Data & Info Serv, Nat Oceanic & Atmospheric Admin, 83-87; vpres, SAIC, 87-89. *Concurrent Pos:* Vpres tech, Am Inst Aeronaut & Astronaut, 86-87. *Mem:* AAAS; Am Nuclear Soc; Am Geophys Union; Sigma Xi; Am Meteorol Soc. *Res:* Radiation chemistry, radiation dosimetry; underground testing; nuclear fuel cycle research; nuclear waste management; remote sensing; atmospheric and oceanographic science. *Mailing Add:* Dept Energy Rm 4B014 1000 Independence Ave SW Washington DC 20585

BISHOP, YVONNE M M, BIOSTATISTICS, MATHEMATICAL STATISTICS. *Current Pos:* RETIRED. *Personal Data:* b Eng, Jan 12, 25; US citizen. *Educ:* Univ London, BA, 47; Harvard Univ, MSc, 61, PhD(statist), 67. *Prof Exp:* Math ed, Ministry Agr & Fisheries, Eng, 49-51; ed asst, J Iron & Steel Inst, 51-52; sr ed asst, Brit Coal Utilization Res Asn, 52-53; statistician, Pac Biol Sta, BC, 53-54, Int Pac Salmon Fisheries Comn, Can, 54-56, Inter-Am Trop Tuna Comn, 56-57 & St Paul's Rehab Ctr for Newly Blinded Adults, 58-61; instr statist, Sch Pub Health, Harvard Univ, 61-63, asst prof biostatist, 63-71, assoc prof, 71-80; dep asst adminr, Energy Data Opers,

Energy Info Admin, 79-81, dir, Off Statist Stand, 81-97. *Concurrent Pos:* Head, Div Biostatist & Data Processing, Sidney Farber Cancer Ctr, 66-75; mem bd dirs, Am Statist Asn, 81-83. *Mem:* Biomet Soc; fel Am Statist Asn; Int Statist Inst; fel Am Pub Health Asn. *Res:* Statistics applied to energy; development of statistical methodology, particularly quality assessment of survey data. *Mailing Add:* 5432 39th St NW Washington DC 20015-2956

BISIO, ATTILIO L, SCALEUP, PETROLEUM PROCESSES. *Current Pos:* PRIN, ATRO ASSOCS, 86- *Personal Data:* b New York, NY, Aug 21, 30; m 55, Rosemary Ronzoni; c Joseph & Thomas. *Educ:* Columbia Col, BA, 52, BS, 53, MS, 54. *Prof Exp:* Engr & mgr, Exxon Res & Eng Co, 57-81, eng adv, 81-86. *Concurrent Pos:* Adj lectr, Dept Chem Eng, Pa State Univ, 85-93; ed, Chem Eng Progress, 86-90. *Mem:* AAAS; Am Chem Soc; Inst Elec & Electronics Engrs; Asn Consult Chemists & Chem Engrs; Asn Res Dirs; Nat Asn Sci Writers. *Res:* Chemical and energy engineering; scaleup and risk emphasis; recycling. *Mailing Add:* 1 Park Dr Westfield Mountainside NJ 07092. *Fax:* 908-233-7852

BISKEBORN, MERLE CHESTER, ENGINEERING, MATERIALS SCIENCE. *Current Pos:* RETIRED. *Personal Data:* b Scotia, Nebr, Sept 22, 07; m 35; c 3. *Educ:* SDak Sch Mines & Technol, BS, 30. *Hon Degrees:* DEng, SDak Sch Mines & Technol, 61. *Prof Exp:* Mem tech staff cable develop, Bell Tel Labs, Inc, Am Tel & Tel Co, 30-38, supvr, 38-42, engr radar mfg, Western Elec Co, Md, 42-44, supvr cable develop, Bell Tel Labs, Inc, 44-51, asst toll cable engr, 51-52, toll cable engr, 52-54, sub-dept head, 54-62, head, Cable Dept, 62-72; dir res & develop, Phelps Dodge Commun Co, 72-83. *Concurrent Pos:* Consult, 83- *Mem:* Inst Elec & Electronics Engrs. *Res:* Carrier telephone cable; crosstalk and high frequency primary constants of cable; first automatic radar; microwave resonant cavities; microwave coaxials; first transatlantic telephone cable; anti-submarine cable; wire connectors; cable reclamation compound; waterproof telephone cable. *Mailing Add:* 34 Linden Lane Chatham NJ 07928

BISKUPIAK, JOSEPH E, medicinal chemistry, radiochemistry, for more information see previous edition

BISMANIS, JEKABS EDWARDS, BACTERIOLOGY. *Current Pos:* RETIRED. *Personal Data:* b Svitene, Latvia, Dec 28, 11; m 37; c 3. *Educ:* Latvian Univ, MD, 35; Med Coun Can, LMCC, 50;. *Prof Exp:* Asst bact, Latvian Univ, 35-39; in charge, Pasteur Inst, 39-44; in charge, Bact Lab, Dept Health, Riga, Latvia, 39-44; practicing physician, Ger, 44-48; lectr, Univ Ottawa, 48-51; med bacteriologist, Lab Pub Health, Regina, Sask, 51-52; from asst prof to prof bact, Univ BC, 52-77, emer prof med microbiol, 77-90. *Concurrent Pos:* Family physician, 77-88, 89-90. *Mem:* Emer mem Can Soc Microbiol; fel Royal Col Physicians Can. *Res:* Virology; activation of latent infections by immunosuppression. *Mailing Add:* 2726 Lynbrook Dr Vancouver BC V5S 2C4 Can

BISNO, ALAN LESTER, INTERNAL MEDICINE, INFECTIOUS DISEASES. *Current Pos:* CHIEF MED SERV, MIAMI VA MED CTR, 87-; PROF MED & VCHMN VET ADMIN AFFAIRS, DEPT MED, UNIV MIAMI, 87- *Personal Data:* b Memphis, Tenn, Sept 28, 36; m 63, Barbara Klearman; c Susan & Neal. *Educ:* Princeton Univ, AB, 58; Wash Univ, MD, 62. *Prof Exp:* Intern internal med, Vanderbilt Univ Hosp, 62-63, resident, 63-65; med epidemiologist, Ctr Dis Control, USPHS, 65-68; from asst prof to prof, Univ Tenn, Memphis, 69-86, chief, Sect Infectious Dis, 71-86, assoc dean acad & fac affairs, 81-87. *Concurrent Pos:* NIH training grant infectious dis, Med Sch, Univ Tenn, Memphis, 68-69; teaching & res scholar, Am Col Physicians, 69-72; Comt Rheumatic Fever & Endocarditis, Am Heart Asn, 75-89. *Mem:* Infectious Dis Soc Am; fel Am Col Physicians; Cent Soc Clin Res; Am Fedn Clin Res; Am Heart Asn; Southern Soc Clin Invest. *Res:* Host-parasite relations in infectious diseases and clinical epidemiology as it relates to infectious diseases; special interest and emphasis in streptococcal diseases and their sequelae. *Mailing Add:* Med Serv Miami Vet Admin Med Ctr 1201 NW 16 St Miami FL 33125

BISQUE, RAMON EDWARD, GEOCHEMISTRY. *Current Pos:* From asst prof to assoc prof geochem, Colo Sch Mines, 59-69, prof chem & head dept, 69-77, adj prof, 77-90, EMER PROF CHEM & GEOCHEM, COLO SCH MINES, 90- *Personal Data:* b Stambaugh, Mich, Sept 1, 31; m 54; c 5. *Educ:* St Norbert Col, BS, 53; Iowa State Col, MS, 56 & 57, PhD(geochem), 59. *Concurrent Pos:* Consult, Arthur D Little, Inc, Mass, 62-64 & Am Geol Inst, DC, 64-66; co-founder, Earth Sci, Inc, Colo, 62; assoc dir, Earth Sci Curric Proj, Colo Sch Mines, 65, dir, 65-; chmn, Earth Sci Inc, Golden, Colo, 70- *Mem:* Am Geochem Soc. *Res:* Geochemistry and analytical chemistry as applied to mineral exploration, benefication and exploitation; curriculum development in earth science. *Mailing Add:* 9113 Fern Way Golden CO 80403

BISSELL, CHARLES LYNN, PHYSICAL CHEMISTRY. *Current Pos:* From asst prof to assoc prof, 65-74, PROF CHEM, NORTHWESTERN STATE UNIV, LA, 74- *Personal Data:* b Cumberland, Iowa, Mar 22, 39; m 59; c 3. *Educ:* Tarkio Col, BA, 61; Iowa State Univ, MS, 63; Tex A&M Univ, PhD(phys chem), 65. *Mem:* Am Chem Soc. *Res:* Electrochemistry of fused salts with conductivity and electrochemical cells as the primary concern. *Mailing Add:* 1520 Williams Ave Natchitoches LA 71457

BISSELL, DWIGHT MONTGOMERY, HEPATOLOGY, GASTROENTEROLOGY. *Current Pos:* Assoc prof, 80-86, PROF MED, UNIV CALIF, SAN FRANCISCO, 86- *Personal Data:* b San Francisco, Calif, July 11, 40; m 67; c 2. *Educ:* Harvard Univ, AB, 62, MD, 67. *Concurrent Pos:* Coun, Am Asn Study Liver Dis, 90-; ed, Hepatology. *Mem:* Asn Am Physicians; Am Soc Clin Invest; Am Soc Cell Biol. *Res:* Cellular and molecular basis for liver fibrosis and cirrhosis; iron-related hepatic injury; liver disease of alcohol abuse; porphyrias. *Mailing Add:* Bldg 40 Rm 4102 San Francisco Gen Hosp San Francisco CA 94110. *E-Mail:* dmbiss@itsa.ucsf.edu

BISSELL, EUGENE RICHARD, ORGANIC CHEMISTRY. *Current Pos:* CONSULT, PROTOTEK INC & ENZYME SYSTS PROD, 87- *Personal Data:* b San Francisco, Calif, June 24, 28; m 63, Virginia Bybee. *Educ:* Univ Calif, BS, 49; Mass Inst Technol, PhD(org chem), 53. *Prof Exp:* Chemist, Lawrence Livermore Nat Lab, 53-83; chemist, Enzyme Systs Prod, 83-85. *Mem:* Am Chem Soc. *Res:* Organic synthesis; fluorine and polymer chemistry; synthesis of biologically active materials; dye synthesis. *Mailing Add:* 101 Via Lucia Alamo CA 94507

BISSELL, GLENN DANIEL, VETERINARY MEDICINE. *Current Pos:* RETIRED. *Personal Data:* b Rochester, NY, Sept 21, 35; m 73. *Educ:* Univ Calif, BS, 57, DVM, 59, MPH, 83. *Prof Exp:* Vet I diag lab, Calif Dept Agr, 59-62; med researcher, US Army Biol Labs, 62-63; vet II & III diag lab, Calif Dept Agr, 63-66. *Concurrent Pos:* Consult, Hayward State Univ, 71- & Cutter Labs, 74- *Mem:* Am Asn Lab Animal Sci; Am Vet Med Asn. *Res:* Veterinary medicine in the study of the care, breeding, utilization and diseases of laboratory animals. *Mailing Add:* 4468 Clancy Lane Vacaville CA 95688

BISSELL, GROSVENOR WILLSE, INTERNAL MEDICINE. *Current Pos:* RETIRED. *Personal Data:* b Buffalo, NY, Mar 17, 15; wid. *Educ:* Univ Buffalo, MD, 39. *Prof Exp:* Intern, Buffalo Gen Hosp, 39-40, asst res med & pediat, 40-41, chief res med, 41-42; assoc, Thorndike Mem Lab, 43-44; instr internal med, sch med Univ Buffalo, 44-46, assoc, 46-48, asst prof, 48-51; asst med dir, Armour Labs, 51-52; asst prof internal med, Sch Med, Univ Buffalo, 52-56, assoc prof med, 56-62; chief med serv, Vet Admin Hosp, Buffalo, 52-62; chief endocrine sect & assoc chief staff for res, Sunmount Vet Admin Hosp, Tupper Lake, NY, 62-65; from assoc prof to prof internal med, Sch Med, Wayne State Univ, 65-76; chief med serv, Vet Admin Hosp, Allen Park, 65-76 & Saginaw, 76-81; prof med, Mich State Univ, East Lansing, 76-81; clin prof internal med, Sch Med, Wayne State Univ, Detroit, 76-86. *Concurrent Pos:* Res fel, Thorndike Mem Lab, 42-43; instr clin path, Sch Med, Harvard Univ & vis physician, Boston City Hosp, 43-44; asst internal med, E J Meyer Mem Hosp, 44-51, attend, 52-62; chmn, Vet Admin Coop Study Oral Hypoglycemic Agents in Treatment of Diabetes Mellitus, 51-64; consult internal med, endocrinol & addictology, Vet Admin Med Ctr, Saginaw, 81. *Mem:* AAAS; AMA; Am Thyroid Asn; Endorine Soc. *Res:* Endocrinology; metabolism. *Mailing Add:* 5685 Noel Ct Saginaw MI 48603

BISSELL, HAROLD JOSEPH, geology; deceased, see previous edition for last biography

BISSELL, MICHAEL G, CLINICAL CHEMISTRY. *Current Pos:* ASSOC PROF & DIR LAB MED, UNIV TEX MED BR, GALVESTON, 93- *Personal Data:* b Ridgecrest, Calif, Mar 5, 47. *Educ:* Univ Ariz, BS(chem) & BS(math), 69; Stanford Univ, MD, 75, PhD(neuro & biobehav sci), 77; Univ Calif, Berkeley, MPH, 78; Am Bd Path, dipl clin path, 81. *Prof Exp:* Resident clin path, Martinez Vet Admin Med Ctr, Univ Calif, Davis, 78-81; sr staff assoc fel, Lab Neurochem, NIMH, 81-84; asst prof path, Pritzker Sch Med, Univ Chicago, 84-88; dir clin path, City Hope Nat Med Ctr, 88-91; clin asst prof path, Sch Med, Univ Calif, Los Angeles, 89-91; vpres & med dir, Nichols Inst, 91-93. *Concurrent Pos:* Asst dir clin chem, Med Ctr, Univ Chicago, 84-86, dir gen clin chem, Hosps, 86-88; consult, Bulk Power Facil Siting Comt, State NH Pub Utilities Comn, 85-86, Health Care Financing Admin, 87, Biomed & Environ Consults, 88-91, Clin Lab Mgt Asn, 89-91, Nat Cancer Inst, 89, Nat Comt Clin Lab Stand & Acad Med Arts & Sci, 90-91; ed, Clin Lab Mgt Asn Newslett, 89-91; mem, Coun Continuing Educ, Am Soc Clin Pathologists, 90-91. *Mem:* Am Asn Clin Chem; Am Pub Health Asn; Am Soc Clin Pathologists; Clin Lab Mgt Asn; Col Am Pathologists; Sigma Xi. *Res:* Clinical pathology; clincial chemistry; author of more than 30 technical publications. *Mailing Add:* 1721 Avenue K Galveston TX 77550-4918

BISSELL, MINA JAHAN, MOLECULAR BIOLOGY. *Current Pos:* Am Cancer Soc fel molecular biol, Univ Calif, Berkeley, 70-72, sr biochemist, 72-76, SR STAFF MEM, LAWRENCE BERKELEY LAB, UNIV CALIF, BERKELEY, 76-, CO-DIR, LAB CELL BIOL, 80-, DIR, DIV CELL & MOLECULAR BIOL, 88- *Personal Data:* b Tehran, Iran, May 14, 40; m 67; c 2. *Educ:* Radcliffe Col, AB, 63; Harvard Univ, MA, 65, PhD(molecular genetics), 69. *Prof Exp:* Milton fel, Harvard Univ, 69-70. *Mem:* Inst Med-Nat Acad Sci; Am Soc Cell Biol; AAAS; Asn Women in Sci; Tissue Cult Asn; Am Soc Biol Chemists. *Res:* Regulation of gene expression in normal and malignant cells. *Mailing Add:* Lab Cell Biol Lawrence Berkeley Lab Univ Calif Bldg 83/101 One Cyclotron Rd Berkeley CA 94720-0001

BISSETT, J(AMES) R(OBERT), civil engineering; deceased, see previous edition for last biography

BISSETT, MARJORIE LOUISE, MICROBIOLOGY. *Current Pos:* RES MICROBIOLOGIST, CALIF STATE DEPT PUB HEALTH, 65- *Personal Data:* b Miami, Ariz, Sept 21, 25. *Educ:* Univ Calif, Los Angeles, AB, 49; Univ Mich, PhD(epidemiol sci), 65. *Prof Exp:* Microbiologist, Calif State Dept Pub

Health, 49-55, asst microbiologist, 55-61; trainee epidemiol sci, Univ Mich, 61-65. *Concurrent Pos:* Mem, Diag Prod Adv Comt, Food & Drug Admin, 72-76. *Mem:* Soc Gen Microbiol; Am Soc Microbiol; NY Acad Sci; Conf State & Prov Pub Health Lab Dirs; fel Am Acad Microbiol. *Res:* Clinical and public health microbiology; microbiology and laboratory diagnosis of Neisseria gonorrheae, Yersinia species, Legionellaceae, Enterobacteriaceae, Borrelia burgdorferi and other medically important organisms. *Mailing Add:* 1751 Spruce St Berkeley CA 94704

BISSEY, LUTHER TRAUGER, CHEMISTRY, PETROLEUM ENGINEERING. *Current Pos:* Analyst, Mineral Indust Exp Sta, Col Mineral Indust, 36-38, instr, Petrol & Natural Gas Dept, 38-50, from asst prof to assoc prof, 50-73, EMER ASSOC PROF, PETROL & NATURAL GAS DEPT, PA STATE UNIV, 73- *Personal Data:* b New Britain, Pa, Aug 2, 12; m 40, Martha Anderson. *Educ:* Pa State Univ, BS, 34, MS, 42. *Mem:* Sigma Xi; Am Soc Testing Mat; Soc Petrol Engrs; Am Gas Asn. *Res:* Water-flooding; household refuse incineration; natural gas pipeline deposits; gas flow in porous media; gas reservoir mechanics; instrumentation and communications. *Mailing Add:* 930 N Atherton St State College PA 16803-3540

BISSHOPP, FREDERIC EDWARD, APPLIED MATHEMATICS. *Current Pos:* From asst prof to assoc prof math, 61-89, PROF APPL MATH, BROWN UNIV, 89- *Personal Data:* b Beloit, Wis, Oct 2, 34; m 58; c 1. *Educ:* Ill Inst Technol, BS, 54; Univ Chicago, MS, 56, PhD(physics), 59. *Res:* Fluid mechanics; partial differential equations; numerical analysis. *Mailing Add:* c/o Div Appl Math Brown Univ Providence RI 02912-9100

BISSING, DONALD EUGENE, ORGANIC CHEMISTRY. *Current Pos:* DIR, RES & DEVELOP, AGR CHEM GROUP, FMC CORP, 78- *Personal Data:* b McCook, Nebr, Sept 10, 34; m 54; c 2. *Educ:* Fort Hays State Col, BA, 59; Univ Kans, PhD(org chem), 62. *Prof Exp:* Mgr process develop, Monsanto Co, 62-74; dir chem eng res & develop chem, BASF Wyandotte Corp, 74-76, gen mgr agr chem div, 76-78. *Mem:* Am Chem Soc; Res & Eng Soc Am. *Res:* Chemistry of agricultural products, polyether polyols, graft polyols; environmental control chemistry and engineering; residue, metabolism of agricultural products. *Mailing Add:* FMC Corp Chem Res & Devlop PO Box 8 Princeton NJ 08543

BISSING, DONALD RAY, PARTICLE & FIBER IDENTIFICATION, PLANT ANATOMY & FUNCTION. *Current Pos:* POLARIZED LIGHT MICROS SUPVR, HEALTH SCI ASSOC, 90- *Personal Data:* b Poplar Bluff, Mo, Feb 18, 43; m 69, Linda Schalski; c Douglas & Jeffrey. *Educ:* Univ Md, BS, 71; Claremont Grad Sch, MA, 73, PhD(bot), 76. *Prof Exp:* Asst prof bot, Southern Ill Univ, Carbondale, 76-90. *Mem:* AAAS; Int Asn Wood Anatomists; Bot Soc Am. *Res:* Systematic and functional aspects of plant anatomy and morphology; particle and fiber identification. *Mailing Add:* PO Box 30204 Long Beach CA 90853-0204. *Fax:* 714-220-2081

BISSINGER, BARNARD HINKLE, MATHEMATICS, ENGINEERING. *Current Pos:* prof on leave, 68-69, PROF MATH SCI, PA STATE UNIV, CAPITOL CAMPUS, 70- *Personal Data:* b Lancaster, Pa, Jan 27, 18; m 50; c 2. *Educ:* Franklin & Marshall Col, BS, 38; Syracuse Univ, MA, 40; Cornell Univ, PhD(math), 43. *Prof Exp:* Instr math, Cornell Univ, 43; asst prof, Mich State Col, 44; opers res analyst, USAAF, 44 & Chennault Flying Tigers, China, 45; gen mgr, Athletic Shoe Factory, 46-52; Lehman prof math & chmn dept, Lebanon Valley Col, 53-68. *Concurrent Pos:* Assoc actuary, Pa State Univ, 68; NSF sci fac fel, Princeton Univ, 58-59. *Mem:* Am Math Soc; Math Asn Am; fel Royal Statist Soc. *Res:* Operations research; mathematical analysis; functional analogues of continued fractions; group physical mortality. *Mailing Add:* 281 W Main St Middletown PA 17057

BISSON, EDMOND E(MILE), TRIBOLOGICAL RESEARCH. *Current Pos:* CONSULT ENGR, 73- *Personal Data:* b East Barre, Vt, July 16, 16; m 47, Fernande M Trottier; c Roland A, Colette (Gregory) & Michelle (Bartell). *Educ:* Univ Fla, BS, 38, ME, 54. *Honors & Awards:* Hunt Mem Medal, Am Soc Lubrication Engrs, 54, Nat Award, 67; Jacques de Vaucanson Medal, Groupement pour l'Avancement de la Mecanque Industrielle, 66; Medal Except Sci Achievement, NASA, 68; P M Ku Medal, Am Soc Lubrication Engrs, 80; Hersey Award, Am Soc Mech Engrs, 81. *Prof Exp:* Res & proj engr lubrication & wear res, NACA/NASA, Va, 39-43, head piston ring res sect, Lewis Res Lab, 43-45, head lubrication & wear res sect, 45-55, asst chief, Fluid Syst Components Div, 55-68, assoc chief, 68-73. *Concurrent Pos:* Teacher short courses, Univ Calif, Los Angeles, Univ Tenn Space Inst, Va Polytech Inst, State Univ & Case Western Res Univ; ed-in-chief, Soc Tribologists & Lubrication Engrs, 76-90. *Mem:* Fel Am Soc Mech Engrs; fel Soc Tribologists & Lubrication Engrs (pres, 63-64); NY Acad Sci. *Res:* Friction, lubrication and wear, tribology; unconventional lubricants; bearings and seals under extreme operating conditions. *Mailing Add:* 805 Windrush Dr Unit A-1 Westlake OH 44145

BISSON, MARY A, ELECTROPHYSIOLOGY, ECOPHYSIOLOGY. *Current Pos:* from asst prof to assoc prof, 80-94, PROF, DEPT BIOL SCI, STATE UNIV NY, BUFFALO, 94- *Personal Data:* b Fairfield, Calif, Oct 24, 48; m 68, Terrence P. *Educ:* Univ Chicago, BA, 70; Duke Univ, PhD(bot), 76. *Prof Exp:* Trainee physiol, Univ NC, Chapel Hill, 76-77; res fel biophys, Univ Sydney, NSW, Australia, 78-80. *Concurrent Pos:* Guest lectr, Marine Biol Lab, 82; vis assoc prof, Cornell Univ, Ithaca, NY, 87; vis res prof, Flinders Univ, Adelaide, SAustralia, 88; mem, Cell Biol Panel, NSF, 92-; mem, Bd Univ Space Res Asn, 93- *Mem:* AAAS; Am Soc Plant Physiologists; Asn Women Sci (secy, 88-90); Sigma Xi; Am Soc Gravitational & Space Biol. *Res:* Control of ion transport in plants; control of cytoplasmic pH by active and passive proton movements; mechanisms of salt tolerance in charophyte algae; effects of gravity on differentiation. *Mailing Add:* Dept Biol Sci Cooke 109 State Univ NY Buffalo NY 14260. *Fax:* 716-645-2975; *E-Mail:* bisson@acsu.buffalo.edu

BISSON, PETER ANDRE, aquatic biology, for more information see previous edition

BISSONETTE, JOHN ALFRED, WILDLIFE ECOLOGY & MANAGEMENT, LANDSCAPE ECOLOGY. *Current Pos:* LEADER, UTAH COOP FISH & WILDLIFE RES UNIT, 85- *Personal Data:* b Colchester, Vt, July 9, 41; m 66; c Nicole E & Gabriel J. *Educ:* Univ Vt, BA, 64; Yale Univ, MFS, 70; Univ Mich, PhD(wildlife mgt & resource ecol), 76. *Prof Exp:* Vis asst prof vert ecol, Ariz State Univ, 75-76, asst prof, 76-77; asst leader wildlife, Okla Coop Wildlife Res Unit, 77-81; acting leader wildlife, Main Coop Wildlife Res Unit, US Fish & Wildlife Serv, 81-85. *Concurrent Pos:* Adj assoc prof wildlife ecol, Okla State Univ, 77-; coop assoc prof wildlife resource, Univ Maine, 81-; prof, Dept Fisheries & Wildlife & adj prof, Dept Geol & Earth Res, Utah State Univ, 91- *Mem:* Wildlife Soc; Soc Conserv Biol; Int Asn Landscape Ecol; Ecol Soc Am. *Res:* Mammals, especially ungulate ecology & behavior; collared peccary (Dicotyles tajacu) biology population dynamics; landscape ecology; American marten effects of habitat fragmentation. *Mailing Add:* Dept Fisheries & Wildlife Utah State Univ Logan UT 84322-5290. *Fax:* 435-797-4025

BISSONNETTE, GARY KENT, ENVIRONMENTAL MICROBIOLOGY, AQUATIC ECOLOGY. *Current Pos:* From asst prof to assoc prof bact, Div Plant Sci, 74-82, PROF AGR MICROBIOL, WVA UNIV, 82- *Personal Data:* b Claremont, NH, May 8, 47; m 72; c 2. *Educ:* Univ NH, BA, 69; Mont State Univ, MS, 71, PhD(microbiol), 74. *Mem:* Am Inst Biol Sci; Sigma Xi; Am Soc Microbiol; Soc Indust Microbiol; fel Am Acad Microbiol; Am Water Works Asn. *Res:* Recovery of organisms of public health significance from aquatic environments; effects of environmental stress on microorganisms. *Mailing Add:* Environ Microbiol 401 Brooks Hall WVa Univ PO Box 6057 Morgantown WV 26506-6057

BISSONNETTE, HOWARD LOUIS, PLANT PATHOLOGY. *Current Pos:* prof plant path & plant pathoologist, agr exten, 68-87, EMER PROF, UNIV MINN, MINNEAPOLIS, 87- *Personal Data:* b Detroit, Mich, Aug 28, 27; m 57, Karwyn St Onge; c Daniel, Lee Ann & Suzanne. *Educ:* Col St Thomas, BS, 52; Univ Minn, MS, 58, PhD, 64. *Prof Exp:* Res asst, Univ Minn, 53-56, plant pathologist, USDA, 57-62; plant pathologist, USDA, 57-62; exten plant pathologist, NDak State Univ, 62-68. *Concurrent Pos:* Consult, crop prod, potato storage. *Mem:* Am Phytopath Soc. *Res:* Soil mycroflora; root rot diseases of sugar beets and peas; general pathology; potato diseases; aerial application of fungicides. *Mailing Add:* Dept Plant Path Univ Minn St Paul MN 55108

BISSONNETTE, JOHN MAURICE, OBSTETRICS & GYNECOLOGY. *Current Pos:* from asst prof to assoc prof, 73-79, PROF OBSTET & GYNEC, ORE HEALTH SCI UNIV, 79-, PROF CELL BIOL & ANAT, 81- *Personal Data:* b Montreal, Can, Feb 11, 39. *Educ:* Loyola Col Montreal, BA, 60; McGill Univ, MD CM, 64. *Honors & Awards:* Duncan Reid Lectr, Harvard Univ, 84. *Prof Exp:* Rotating intern, Montreal Gen Hosp, 64-65, asst resident, 65-66; resident obstet & gynec, Johns Hopkins Hosp, Baltimore, 66-69; fel pulmonary physiol, Sch Pub Health, Johns Hopkins Univ, 69-70; asst prof obstet & gynec, Univ Calif, Irvine, 70-73. *Mem:* Am Physiol Soc; Soc Gynec Invest; AAAS. *Res:* Respiratory and cardiovascular physiology of the mammalian fetus and placenta, and membrane transport in the placenta especially ion transport; control of fetal breathing movements in utero. *Mailing Add:* Res Bldg L-458 Rm 426 Ore Health Sci Univ Portland OR 97201-3098. *Fax:* 503-494-5296

BISSOT, THOMAS CHARLES, INORGANIC CHEMISTRY, PHYSICAL CHEMISTRY. *Current Pos:* RETIRED. *Personal Data:* b Grand Rapids, Mich, Apr 20, 30; m 51; c 8. *Educ:* Aquinas Col, BS, 52; Univ Mich, MS, 53, PhD(chem), 56. *Prof Exp:* Mem staff, E I Du Pont de Nemours & Co, 55-82, sr res fel, 82-90; consult, 90- *Mem:* Am Chem Soc. *Res:* Boron hydrides; high vacuum techniques; catalysis; polymer and surface chemistry; membrane development for chloralkali cells; barrier polymers for packaging. *Mailing Add:* 25 Deer Run Rd Newark DE 19711

BISTRIAN, BRUCE RYAN, NUTRITION, MEDICINE. *Current Pos:* from clin asst prof to assoc prof, 76-90, PROF MED, HARVARD MED SCH, 90- *Personal Data:* b Southhampton, NY, Oct 22, 39; m 64; c 3. *Educ:* NY Univ, AB, 61; Cornell Univ, MD, 65; Johns Hopkins Sch Pub Health, MPH, 71; Mass Inst Technol, PhD(nutrit biochem), 76. *Prof Exp:* Intern, Bellevue Hosp, Cornell Div, 65-66; fel metab, Univ Vt Med Sch, 68-69, resident, 69-70. *Concurrent Pos:* Res assoc, Mass Inst Technol, 76-81, lectr nutrit, 81-84; mem, Nutrit Study Sect, NIH, 85-89. *Mem:* Sigma Xi; Am Soc Clin Nutrit; Fedn NAm Soc Exp Biol; Am Col Nutrit; fel Am Col Physicians; Am Soc Parental & Enteral Nutrit (pres, 89-90). *Res:* Optimal compostion of diets for the treatment of obesity; nutritional assessment and nutritional support of the hospitalized patient; dynamic aspects of protein metabolism in semistarvation, injury or infection; novel fats in clinical nutrition; effect of cytokines on intermediary metabolism. *Mailing Add:* Harvard Med Sch New Eng Deaconess Hosp 194 Pilgrim Rd Boston MA 02215

BISWAL, NILAMBAR, VIROLOGY. *Current Pos:* fel virol, 67-68, asst prof, 68-72, ASSOC PROF VIROL, BAYLOR COL MED, HOUSTON, 72- *Personal Data:* b Khamar, Orissa, India, Feb 20, 34; m 67; c 3. *Educ:* Punjab Col Vet Med, BVSc & AH, 58; Mich State Univ, MS, 63, PhD(microbiol), 65. *Prof Exp:* Asst res virologist, Virus Lab, Univ Calif, Berkeley, 65-67. *Mem:* Am Soc Microbiol; AAAS; Sigma Xi. *Res:* Basic mechanism of biosynthesis of herpes virus DNA; analysis of structure and replication of herpes virus DNA. *Mailing Add:* 8841 Doves Fly Way Laurel MD 20723-1298

BISWAS, ASIT KUMAR, ENVIRONMENTAL MANAGEMENT, AGRICULTURAL DEVELOPMENT. *Current Pos:* DIR, BISWAS & ASSOCS, OTTAWA, 76- *Personal Data:* b Balasore, India, Feb 25, 39; m, Margaret Peitsch. *Educ:* Indian Inst Technol, Kharagpur, BTech, 60, MTech, 61; Univ Strathclyde, PhD(water mgt), 67. *Hon Degrees:* DTech, Univ Lund, Sweden, 84. *Honors & Awards:* Walter L Huber Res Medal, Am Soc Civil Engrs, 74; Crystal Drop Award, Int Water Resources Asn, 94. *Prof Exp:* Asst civil engr, Ward, Ashcroft & Parkman, UK, 61-62; res fel hydraul eng, Loughborough Univ Technol, Eng, 62-63; lectr water resources eng, Univ Strathclyde, 63-67; prof water resource planning, Queen's Univ, Ont, 67-68; sr res officer, Dept Energy, Mines & Resources, 68-70; dir, Dept Environ, Ottawa, Can, 70-76. *Concurrent Pos:* Vis prof, Univ Ottawa, 68-70; sr consult, UN Environ Prog, 74-; Rockefeller Found Int Relations fel, 74-75; sr res scientist, Int Inst Appl Syst Anal, 78-79; ed, J Ecol Modeling, Water Resources Develop J & Mazingira J; sr sci adv to exec dir, UN Environ Prog, pres, Int Fund Agr Develop, UN Univ & UN Indust Develop Orgn; chmn, Middle East Water Comn, 94-97, Tech Comn, World Water Coun, 96- *Mem:* Am Soc Civil Engrs; Int Soc Ecol Modelling (pres, 76-91); Int Water Resource Asn (vpres, 79-82, pres, 88-91); Int Asn Hydraulic Res; hon mem Indian Water Resources Soc; hon mem, Egyption Eng Soc; Russ Acad Eng. *Res:* Resources management; irrigated agriculture; environmental sciences; climate and society; hydrology and water resources; rural and agricultural development. *Mailing Add:* 3691 Albion Rd S No 87 Gloucester ON K1T 1P2 Can

BISWAS, CHITRA, connective tissue biochemistry; deceased, see previous edition for last biography

BISWAS, DEBAJIT K, MOLECULAR & CELLULAR BIOLOGY. *Current Pos:* Vis asst prof microbiol & molecular genetics, Harvard Med Sch, 68-73, asst prof oral biol, Sch Dent Med, 73-81, assoc prof molecular biol, Sch Dent Med, 81-92, RES ASSOC, DIV CELL GROWTH & REGULATION, DANA-FARBER CANCER INST, HARVARD MED SCH, 92- *Personal Data:* b India, Junel, 32. *Educ:* Calcutta Univ, India, BS, 51, MS, 53 & 57, PhD(biochem), 71. *Concurrent Pos:* Sr fel, Nat Inst Sci, India, 58; spec fel, Leukemia Soc Am, 73. *Mailing Add:* 100 Prospect St Newton MA 02165

BISWAS, DIPAK R, HIGH TEMPERATURE MATERIAL PROCESSING, COATINGS ON OPTICAL FIBER CHEMICAL VAPOR DEPOSITION THIN FILM. *Current Pos:* DIR, RES & DEVELOP, FIBERGUIDE, 91- *Personal Data:* b India, Feb 3, 49; US citizen. *Educ:* Univ Calcutta, India, BTech, 70; Univ Calif, Berkeley, MS, 74, PhD(mat sci & eng), 76. *Prof Exp:* Postdoctoral fel mat sci & ceramics, Lawrence Berkeley Lab, 76-78; res assoc ceramics, Univ Utah, 78-79; mat scientist mat sci, Inst Gas Technol, 79-81; mgr & prin staff scientist optical fiber, ITT Electro Optical Prod Div & Alcatel Cable Systs, 81-88; dir res & develop optical fiber, Spectran Corp, 88-91. *Mem:* Am Ceramic Soc; Soc Photo-Optical Engrs; Optical Soc Am. *Res:* Development of specialty coatings on optical glass fibers, fiber optic sensors; high strength hermetically coated optical fibers for adverse environment; optical fibers embedded in smart skin or structures; optical fibers for medical applications. *Mailing Add:* 166 Thoreau Dr Plainsboro NJ 08536. *Fax:* 908-647-8464

BISWAS, NRIPENDRA NATH, PHYSICS. *Current Pos:* from asst prof to assoc prof, 65-76, PROF PHYSICS, UNIV NOTRE DAME, IND, 76- *Personal Data:* b Calcutta, India, Aug 1, 30; m 59; c 2. *Educ:* Univ Calcutta, BSc, 49, MSc, 51, DrPhil(physics), 55. *Prof Exp:* Res asst cosmic rays, Bose Res Inst, Calcutta, 52-55; res scholar physics, Max Planck Inst Physics, Gottingen, 55-57; res assoc, Physics Inst, Univ Bologna, 57-58; vis scientist high energy physics, Lawrence Radiation Lab, Univ Calif, Berkeley, 58-60; res scientist bubble chamber anal, Max Planck Inst Physics, Munich, 61-65. *Mem:* Sigma Xi. *Res:* Elementary particle physics, theoretical and experimental; study of cosmic rays. *Mailing Add:* Dept Physics Univ Notre Dame Notre Dame IN 46556

BISWAS, PRATIM, AEROSOL SCIENCE & ENGINEERING, PARTICLE FORMATION & GROWTH DYNAMICS IN HIGH TEMPERATURE ENVIRONMENTS. *Current Pos:* from asst prof to assoc prof, 85-93, PROF ENVIRON ENG, UNIV CINCINNATI, 93-, DIR, ENVIRON ENG & SCI DIV, 95- *Personal Data:* b Poona, Maharashtra, India, Feb 22, 58; m 86, Sujata Basu; c Vivek & Vikram. *Educ:* Indian Inst Technol, Bombay, BS, 80; Univ Calif, Los Angeles, MS, 81; Calif Inst Technol, PhD(mech eng), 85. *Honors & Awards:* Kenneth Whitby Award, Am Asn Aerosol Res, 91. *Mem:* Am Asn Aerosol Res; Air & Waste Mgt Asn; Am Soc Mech Engrs; Sigma Xi; Am Ceramic Soc; Indian Aerosol Sci & Technol Asn. *Res:* Aerosol science and engineering; air quality and pollution control; combustion and thermal sciences. *Mailing Add:* Dept Civil & Environ Eng ML-71 Univ Cincinnati Cincinnati OH 45221-0071. *E-Mail:* pratim.biswas@uc.edu

BISWAS, PROSANTO K, HORTICULTURE, PLANT PHYSIOLOGY. *Current Pos:* Asst prof hort & head dept, 62-69, PROF HORT & CHMN, DEPT PLANT & SOIL SCI, TUSKEGEE UNIV, 69- *Personal Data:* b Calcutta, India, Mar 1, 34; US citizen; m 62; c 1. *Educ:* Univ Calcutta, BS, 58; Univ Mo, MS, 59, PhD(hort), 62. *Mem:* Am Soc Plant Physiol; Am Soc Hort Sci; Weed Sci Soc Am. *Res:* Physiological responses of plants to different growth regulators; metanolism and mode of action of herbicides by plants. *Mailing Add:* Dept Agric Sci Tuskegee Inst Tuskegee AL 36088

BISWAS, ROBIN MICHAEL, HEPATITIS VIRUSES, MOLECULAR BIOLOGY. *Current Pos:* sr staff fel viral hepatitis, 87-89, LAB CHIEF VIRAL HEPATITIS, LAB HEPATITIS, CTR BIOLOGICS EVAL & RES, FOOD & DRUG ADMIN, 89- *Personal Data:* b Oxford, Eng, May 31, 42; US citizen; m 73; c 2. *Educ:* Univ Gottingen, Ger, MD, 71, PhD(med), 75. *Prof Exp:* Intern med & surg, Univ Hosps, Gottingen, Ger, 71-72; res assoc viral hepatitis, Dept Med Microbiol, Univ Gottingen, Ger, 72-78; resident path, Univ Tex, San Antonio, Bexar County Hosp, 80-81 & Univ Md Hosp, Baltimore, 81-84; staff fel med microbiol, Dept Clin Path, Clin Ctr, NIH, 84-87. *Concurrent Pos:* Instr med microbiol, Dept Med Microbiol, Univ Gottingen, Ger, 72-78. *Mem:* Soc Exp Biol & Med; Am Asn Blood Banks. *Res:* Development of tests for viral hepatitis; relationships between viral hepatitis markers and prevalence of clinical disease and the search for possibly existing unidentified viral agents of hepatitis. *Mailing Add:* 6009 Henning St Bethesda MD 20817

BISWAS, SHIB D, CHEMISTRY, BIOCHEMISTRY. *Current Pos:* fel biochem, 64-65, lectr, 65-67 & Sch Dent Hyg, 65, ASST PROF BIOCHEM & ORAL BIOL, UNIV MANITOBA, 68- *Personal Data:* b Agra, India, Feb 1, 40; m 69. *Educ:* Univ Allahabad, BSc, 57, MSc, 60, PhD(chem), 64. *Prof Exp:* Fel chem, Univ Cambridge, 64. *Res:* Lignin complexes in metal ions; etiology of perio-dontal and caries diseases processes in relation to biochemical standpoint; application of radiochemicals in the study of metabolic pathways in oral bacteria. *Mailing Add:* Dept Oral Biol D-332 Univ Manitoba Winnipeg MB R3T 2N2 Can

BITCOVER, EZRA HAROLD, LEATHER CHEMISTRY. *Current Pos:* RETIRED. *Personal Data:* b New York, NY, Jan 16, 20; m 44; c 4. *Educ:* Rutgers Univ, BS, 41; Univ Mass, PhD(agron), 51. *Prof Exp:* Jr chemist, Tenn Valley Authority, 41-43; res chemist, Prophylactic Brush Co, 43-46; soils chemist, Citrus Exp Sta, Univ Fla, 48; anal res supvr, Lindsay Chem Co, 50-52; res chemist food processing, Miner Labs, 53-56; res biochemist, Eastern Utilization Res Div, USDA, 56-80. *Mem:* AAAS; Am Leather Chem Asn; fel Sigma Xi; Am Chem Soc; fel Am Inst Chemists (secy, 58-63). *Res:* Nitrogen chemicals; processing of vegetables; tannery pollution; leather defects; collagen by-products; hide processing. *Mailing Add:* 12 Nora Lane Plainview NY 11803

BITENSKY, MARK WOLFE, PATHOLOGY. *Current Pos:* RES PROF, BIOMED ENG DEPT, VISUAL & CIRCULATORY BIOPHYS LAB, BOSTON UNIV, 96- *Personal Data:* b Brooklyn, NY, Apr 5, 34; m 57; c 2. *Educ:* Yale Univ, BA, 55, MD, 59. *Prof Exp:* Intern, Univ Div Bellevue Hosp, 59-60, asst res med, 60-61, asst res path, 61; clin assoc, Nat Inst Arthritis & Metab Dis, 61-63, spec res fel, 63-64; instr, Dept Med, NY Univ Sch Med, 64-65, asst prof med, 65-70; assoc prof path, Sch Med, Yale Univ, 70-76, dir student educ, Dept Path, 77-81, prof, 76-; sr fel, Los Alamos Nat Lab. *Concurrent Pos:* Consult, NIH extramural progs; consult, NIH grants & contracts & off cancer ctrs grants & contracts; assoc ed, J Cyclic Nucleotide Res; dir, Div Life Sci, Los Alamos Nat Lab, 81-86. *Mem:* AAAS; fel NY Acad Sci; Endocrine Soc; Harvey Soc; Am Asn Pathologists. *Res:* Cyclic nucleotide chemistry especially in the vertebrate rod; membrane biochemistry and enzyme regulatory mechanisms, especially as related to the study of cell surface regulatory mechanism and cyclic nucleotide effects on normal metbolism and disease states; genetic disorders of metabolism and regulation; diabetes mellitus and protein glucation. *Mailing Add:* 113 Bay State Rd Apt 5 Boston MA 02215-1709

BITGOOD, J(OHN) JAMES, CYTOGENETICS. *Current Pos:* from asst prof to assoc prof, 81-91, PROF POULTRY MGT & GENETICS, DEPT POULTRY SCI, UNIV WIS, 91- *Personal Data:* b Agawam, Mass, Feb 26, 40; m 64, Kathryn Puvogel; c Mark J, Gregory M & Jeffrey K. *Educ:* Univ Mass, BVA, 61; Univ Minn, MS, 75, PhD(animal sci), 80. *Prof Exp:* Res asst, Dept Animal Sci, Univ Minn, 72-80, fel, 80-81. *Mem:* Poultry Sci Asn; AAAS; Sigma Xi. *Res:* Avian cytogenetics; chromosome behavior; single gene inheritance in the chicken; development of linkage maps in the chicken. *Mailing Add:* 3105 Nightingale Lane Middleton WI 53562-1628. *Fax:* 608-262-6005; *E-Mail:* bitgood@calshp.cals.wisc.edu

BITHA, PANAYOTA, COMPUTERS. *Current Pos:* Chemist, 60-63, res chemist, 63-82, SR RES CHEMIST, LEDERLE LABS, DIV AM CYANAMID CO, 82- *Personal Data:* b Greece; US citizen. *Educ:* Polytech Sch Athens, dipl chem & eng, 58; Columbia Univ, MS, 60. *Mem:* Am Chem Soc; Sigma Xi. *Res:* Medicinals used for infectious diseases such as tetracyclines, B-lactams, natural antibiotics and quinolones; drugs for cancer chemotherapy; author of 29 publications; awarded 36 patents. *Mailing Add:* 287 Treetop Circle Nanuet NY 10954

BITLER, WILLIAM REYNOLDS, PHYSICAL METALLURGY. *Current Pos:* assoc prof, 62-69, chmn metall sect, 69-73, PROF METALL, PA STATE UNIV, 69- *Personal Data:* b Nyack, NY, Nov 25, 27; m 54; c 2. *Educ:* Carnegie Inst Technol, BS, 53, MS, 55, PhD(physics), 57. *Prof Exp:* Asst prof metall eng, Carnegie Inst Technol, 56-62. *Concurrent Pos:* Consult,

Allegheny-Ludlum Steel Corp, 57-, carrier, 79-80; sr Fulbright res prof, Inst Physics, Univ Oslo, Norway, 85-86. *Mem:* Am Phys Soc; Am Soc Metals; Am Inst Mining, Metall & Petrol Engrs; Am Electroplaters Soc. *Res:* Physical metallurgy; kinetics; statistical thermodynamics; magnetism; superconduction. *Mailing Add:* Dept Mat Sci Pa State Univ 101 Steidle Bldg University Park PA 16802-5005

BITMAN, JOEL, BIOCHEMISTRY. *Current Pos:* chemist & leader physiol invests, Dairy Cattle Res Br, 56-74, chief biochem lab, Animal Physiol & Genetics Inst, Agr Res Ctr-East, 74-79, CHEMIST, MILK SECRETION & MASTITIS LAB, USDA, 79- *Personal Data:* b Elizabeth, NJ, Nov 29, 26; m 50; c 3. *Educ:* Cornell Univ, AB, 46; Univ Minn, MS, 48, PhD(physiol chem), 50. *Prof Exp:* Asst physiol chem, Univ Minn, 47-50, res fel, 50; chemist, Div Nutrit & Physiol, Dairy Husb Res Br, USDA, 51-55; res assoc, Columbia Univ, 55-56. *Mem:* Am Chem Soc; AAAS; Am Dairy Sci Asn; Am Oil Chemists Soc; Am Soc Animal Sci; Fedn Am Soc Exp Biol. *Res:* Chemistry and metabolism of sex hormones; determination of estrogens in blood; vitamin A deficiency and cerebrospinal fluid mechanics; body temperature during the estrous cycle; chemical composition of the mammary gland during mastitis; mechanism of estrogen action in the uterus; DDT effect on carbonic anhydrase and egg-shell thickness; estrogenic effects of DDT; lipid composition of human and bovine milk; thyroid hormones in cattle. *Mailing Add:* Milk Secretion & Mastitis Lab Animal Sci Inst USDA Beltsville MD 20705

BITO, LASZLO Z, OCULAR PHYSIOLOGY & PHARMACOLOGY. *Current Pos:* From instr to asst prof, Columbia Univ, 65-74, sr res assoc, 74-77, assoc prof & head, Ocular Physiol Lab, 77-80, PROF OCULAR PHYSIOL, COLUMBIA UNIV, 80- *Personal Data:* b Budapest, Hungary, Sept 7, 34; US citizen; m, Olivia B Carino; c John & Lawrence. *Educ:* Bard Col, BA, 59; Columbia Univ, PhD, 63. *Honors & Awards:* Semmelweis Sci Soc Award, 74; Alcon Res Inst Award, Alcon Res Inst, 85; Andre Balazs Prize, Int Soc Eye Res, 88. *Concurrent Pos:* Hon res assoc, Univ Col, London, 65-66; vis prof ocular pharmacol, Univ PR, 72-88. *Mem:* Am Soc Pharmacol & Exp Therapeut; Am Physiol Soc; Int Soc Eye Res; Asn Res Vision & Ophthal. *Res:* Prostagland in transport; nature of blood-ocular and blood-brain barriers and homeostasis of ocular fluids; pathophysiology of inflammation; mechanism of accommodation and development of presbyopia; development of prostaglandin analogues for the medical management of glaucoma. *Mailing Add:* Dept Ophthal Res Col Physicians & Surgeons Columbia Univ 630 W 168th St New York NY 10032

BITONDO, DOMENIC, AERONAUTICAL ENGINEERING. *Current Pos:* PRES, BITONDO ASSOC, INC, 81- *Personal Data:* b Welland, Ont, June 7, 25; US citizen; m 49, Delphine M Dicola; c Michael L, David L, Annamarie (Conley), Marisa (Tinaglia). *Educ:* Univ Toronto, BASc, 47, MASc, 48, PhD(aerophys, aeronaut), 50. *Prof Exp:* Res engr, Nat Res Coun Can, 47; aeronaut engr, US Naval Ord Lab, Md, 48, Defense Res Bd Can, 49 & NAm Aviation, Inc, 50-51; prin investr, Aerophys Develop Corp, 52-56, chief aerodyn, 55-58, proj engr, 58-59; proj engr, Norair Div, Northrop Corp, 59; head test planning & anal sect, Space Tech Labs, 59-60; head, Dept Aeromech, Aerospace Corp, 60-61, dir advan ballistic re-entry systs prog, 61-63, dir, Vehicle Systs, 63; tech dir & head eng, Bendix Systs Div, Bendix Corp, 63-67, dir eng, Apollo Lunar Exp Prog, Aerospace Syst Div, 67-69, dir & gen mgr, Bendix Res Labs, Bendix Ctr, 69-79, exec dir res & develop, 79-80. *Concurrent Pos:* Consult, Inst Defense Anal & mem systs panel, defender prog, res planning & mgt, 63-65; lectr technol planning, Univ Mich, 83-87. *Mem:* Am Inst Aeronaut & Astronaut. *Res:* Development of shock tube as aerodynamic research tool; non-stationary fluid flow; re-entry vehicles for ballistic missiles; research management, planning and control. *Mailing Add:* 5 Manchester Court Ann Arbor MI 48104-6562

BITRAN, JACOB DAVID, BONE MARROW TRANSPLANTATION, BREAST CANCER THERAPY. *Current Pos:* DIR CANCER SERV, LUTHERAN GEN HEALTH CARE SYST, 91-; PROF MED, UNIV ILL CHICAGO, 96- *Personal Data:* b Thessalonikki, Greece, Sept 23, 47; US citizen; m 70, Linda Androw; c Lauren & Dina. *Educ:* Univ Ill, BS, 68, MD, 71. *Prof Exp:* From asst prof to prof med, 77-91, dir clin res, 84-89, prof clin med, Univ Chicago, 91- *Concurrent Pos:* Dir hemat & oncol, Lutheran Gen Hosp, 91- *Mem:* Am Col Physicians; Am Soc Clin Oncol; Am Soc Hemat; Am Asn Cancer Res; Am Fedn Clin Res. *Res:* Bone marrow transplantation; dose intensitive chemotherapy for advanced stage breast cancer; bone marrow physiology. *Mailing Add:* 1700 Luthre Ln Park Ridge IL 60068. *Fax:* 847-318-2905; *E-Mail:* j.bitran-md@advoctehealth.com

BITTAR, EVELYN EDWARD, PHYSIOLOGY. *Current Pos:* from vis assoc prof to assoc prof, 68-72, PROF PHYSIOL, UNIV WIS-MADISON, 72- *Personal Data:* b Jaffa, Israel, Oct 12, 28; m 61; c 4. *Educ:* Colby Col, BA, 51; Yale Univ, MD, 55. *Honors & Awards:* Osler Medal, Am Asn Hist Med. *Prof Exp:* Instr med, Med Sch, George Washington Univ, 59-61; chief med officer geriat, St Elizabeth's Hosp, Washington, DC, 61-63; Fulbright lectr nephrology, Univ Damascus, 63-64; vis scientist cell physiol, Bristol Univ, 64-65; Wellcome Trust investr, Cambridge Univ, 67-68. *Concurrent Pos:* NIH fel, DC Gen Hosp, 60-61; Wellcome Trust fel, Oxford Univ, 65-67; Fulbright lectr, Univ Algiers, 80; Burroughs-Wellcome vis prof, Oxford Univ, 82. *Mem:* Brit Biochem Soc; Brit Biophys Soc; Brit Soc Exp Biol; Am Physiol Soc; Am Biophys Soc; NY Acad Sci. *Res:* Cell physiology with special reference to membrane transport and ion transport in single cell preparations; mode of action of hormones and drugs. *Mailing Add:* Dept Physiol Univ Wis Madison WI 53706

BITTER, GARY G, MATHEMATICS EDUCATION, COMPUTER EDUCATION. *Current Pos:* from asst prof to assoc prof, 70-77, PROF MATH & COMPUT EDUC, ARIZ STATE UNIV, 77-, PROF MEDIA COMPUT-BASED INSTR. *Personal Data:* b Hoisington, Kans, Feb 2, 40; m 62; c 3. *Educ:* Kans State Univ, BS, 62; Emporia State Univ, MA, 65; Univ Denver, PhD(comput & math educ), 70. *Prof Exp:* Teacher math & sci, Derby High Sch, 62-65; teacher math, Forsythe Jr High Sch, 65-66; instr, Washburn Univ, 66-67; instr comput sci & math, Colo Col, 67-70. *Concurrent Pos:* Consult, Kaman Sci, 67-70; lectr, Univ Colo, 68-69; supvr student teachers & comput educ res assoc, Univ Denver, 69-70; ed, Sch Sci & Math J. *Mem:* Int Asn Comput Educ; Nat Coun Teachers Math; Math Asn Am; Sch Sci & Math Asn; Am Educ Res Asn. *Res:* Incorporation of computer into elementary and secondary school curriculum; futuristic mathematics curricula; mathematics laboratory; the application of the hand held calculator in the school; computer assisted mathematics. *Mailing Add:* Educ Media & Comput c/o Dept Curric & Instructions Ariz State Univ Tempe AZ 85287-0001

BITTERMAN, MORTON EDWARD, LEARNING, INTELLIGENCE. *Current Pos:* DIR, BEKESY LAB NEUROBIOL, 90- *Personal Data:* b New York, NY, Jan 19, 21; m 67; c 3. *Educ:* New York Univ, BA, 41; Columbia Univ, MA, 42; Cornell Univ, PhD(psychol), 45. *Honors & Awards:* Humbolt Prize, Alexander von Humboldt-Stiftung, WGer, 81. *Prof Exp:* Asst prof psychol, Cornell Univ, 45-50; assoc prof, Univ Tex, 50-55; mem, Inst Advan Study, 55-57; prof, Bryn Mawr Col, 57-70, Univ SFla, 70-71 & Univ Hawaii, 71- *Concurrent Pos:* Ed, Am Jour Psychol, 55-73; assoc ed, Animal Learning & Behavior, 73-76 & 84-88; prin investr, ONR, NSF, Nat Inst Mental Health, 57-; consult ed, J Comp Psychol, 88-92. *Mem:* Soc Exp Psychologists; Psychonomic Soc; Am Psychol Asn. *Res:* Comparative analysis of learning in vertebrates and invertebrates; evolution of intelligence. *Mailing Add:* Bekesy Lab Neurobiol 1993 East-West Rd Honolulu HI 96822

BITTERS, WILLARD PAUL, HORTICULTURE. *Current Pos:* from asst horticulturist to assoc horticulturist, 46-58, horticulturist & prof hort, 58-82, EMER HORTICULTURIST & PROF HORT, CITRUS EXP STA & AGR RES CTR, UNIV CALIF, RIVERSIDE, 82- *Personal Data:* b Eau Claire, Wis, June 4, 15; m 40; c 2. *Educ:* St Norbert Col, BA, 37; Univ Wis, MA, 40, PhD(plant physiol), 42. *Prof Exp:* Lab asst, Univ Wis, 39-40; res asst, Univ Ariz, 40-42, asst horticulturist, 42-46. *Res:* Effect of rootstocks on long term yields; fruit quality and size; effect of rootstocks in relation to disease resistance; clonal varieties of citrus; ornamental citrus; dwarfing rootstocks. *Mailing Add:* 1185 La Subida Ct Riverside CA 92507

BITTERWOLF, THOMAS EDWIN, SYNTHESIS & CHEMISTRY OF BIMETALLIC COMPLEXES, RING-SUBSTITUTED CYCLOVENTADIENYL METAL COMPLEXES. *Current Pos:* assoc prof, 88-92, prof chem & dir off Teaching Enhancement, 92-96, ASSOC DEAN, UNIV IDAHO, 96- *Personal Data:* b New Orleans, La, Jan 19, 47; m 68, Caroline Means; c Heidi E & Katharine N. *Educ:* Centenary Col La, BS, 68; WVa Univ, PhD(chem), 76. *Prof Exp:* Assoc prof chem, US Naval Acad, 83-88. *Concurrent Pos:* Vis prof chem, Univ Padova, 87. *Mem:* Am Chem Soc; Royal Soc Chem; Sigma Xi; AAAS. *Res:* Synthesis of homo- and hetero bimetallic complexes in which the geometry and proximity of the metals can be controlled; photochemistry of organometallic compounds in solution, frozen matriles & super critical fluids. *Mailing Add:* Dept Chem Univ Idaho Moscow ID 83844-2343. *Fax:* 208-885-6173; *E-Mail:* bitterte@losprey.csrv.uidaho.edu

BITTINGER, MARVIN LOWELL, MATHEMATICS. *Current Pos:* Asst prof math, Ind Univ-Purdue Univ, Indianapolis, 68-74, ASSOC PROF MATH, PURDUE UNIV, WEST LAFAYETTE, 74- *Personal Data:* b Akron, Ohio, Aug 9, 41; m 65; c 1. *Educ:* Manchester Col, BA, 63; Ohio State Univ, BS, 65; Purdue Univ, PhD(math educ), 68. *Concurrent Pos:* Consult, Addison-Wesley Publ Co, 70- *Mem:* Math Asn Am. *Res:* Mathematics education; trigonometry; logic and proof. *Mailing Add:* 3011 Whispering Tr Carmel IN 46033-3952

BITTKER, DAVID ARTHUR, CHEMICAL KINETICS. *Current Pos:* RES SCIENTIST, LEWIS RES CTR, NASA, 52- *Personal Data:* b Rochester, NY, Sept 22, 27; m 53; c 2. *Educ:* Cornell Univ, BA, 49; Univ Rochester, PhD(phys chem), 53. *Concurrent Pos:* Lectr math, Cleveland State Univ, 67- *Mem:* Am Inst Aeronaut & Astronaut. *Res:* Chemical mechanism of hydrocarbon fuel thermal degradation; complex kinetic computations of hydrocarbon combustion and pollutant formation for various combustor models. *Mailing Add:* 4095 Charlton Rd Cleveland OH 44121

BITTLE, JAMES LONG, VETERINARY MICROBIOLOGY, VIROLOGY. *Current Pos:* mem, 80-90, ADJ MEM, SCRIPPS RES INST, 90- *Personal Data:* b Norristown, Pa, Mar 7, 27; m 54, Ruth A Roberts; c James J & Barbara A. *Educ:* Univ Calif, BS, 51, DVM, 53. *Honors & Awards:* Medal Outstanding Res Achievement, Johnson & Johnson, 76. *Prof Exp:* Virologist, Virus Res Lab, Pitman-Moore Co, 58-60; supt tissue cult prod, head dept polio & virus vaccine testing & mgr biol testing, Lederle Labs, NY, 60-65; dir virus res, Pitman-Moore Co, Ind, 65-66, head dept infectious dis, Pitman-Moore Div, Dow Chem Co, 67-69, dir res, 69-76, exec vpres, 76-77, pres, 77-79. *Concurrent Pos:* Mem bd dirs, Syntro Inc & Torrey Pines Inst Molecular Studies. *Mem:* Am Col Vet Microbiologist; Am Vet Med Asn; Soc Exp Biol & Med. *Res:* Viral infectious diseases; vaccine development; production; testing. *Mailing Add:* 5353 Calle Vista San Diego CA 92109

BITTMAN, ROBERT, BIOPHYSICAL CHEMISTRY. *Current Pos:* from asst prof to prof, 66-88, DISTINGUISHED PROF CHEM, QUEENS COL, NY, 88- *Personal Data:* b New York, NY, Mar 19, 42; m 75; c 2. *Educ:* Queens Col, NY, BS, 62; Univ Calif, Berkeley, PhD(chem), 65. *Prof Exp:* NSF fel chem, Max Planck Inst Phys Chem, 65-66. *Concurrent Pos:* Res grant, Am Chem Soc, 67-71; asst secy, Org Reactions, 68, secy, 69-73, co-secy, 74-; res grants, NIH, 71-; vis res scientist, Nat Ctr Sci Res, France, 80-81. *Mem:* NY Acad Sci; Sigma Xi; Am Soc Biol Chemists; Biophys Soc; Am Chem Soc. *Res:* Fast reactions in solution; molecular interactions between lipids and sterols in membranes; biomembrane structure; mode of action of membrane-active agents; mechanisms of biochemical and organic reactions; chemical synthesis of lipids. *Mailing Add:* Dept Chem Queens Col City Univ NY Flushing NY 11367-1597

BITTNER, BURT JAMES, ELECTROMAGNETICS. *Current Pos:* CONSULT, HARRIS CORP, 87- *Personal Data:* b Ft Collins, Colo, Feb 8, 21; m 46; c 4. *Educ:* Colo State Univ, BSEE, 43. *Prof Exp:* Jr engr, Submarine Signal Co, 46-48; div supvr, Sandia Corp, 48-56; vpres & res dir, Gulton Indust Div, 57-58; sr staff scientist, Kaman Sci Corp, 58-74; group leader, Interstellar Ltd, 65-74, dir, 74; sr staff engr, Martin Marietta, Denver, 77-87. *Concurrent Pos:* Task engr, Pac Nuclear Tests, 62; secy & pres, Air Acad Bd Educ, 63-75; mem, Group Six, Int Radio Consult Comt, 64-; consult, Army Res Off, Duke Univ, 68-73, Nat Ctr Atmospheric Res, 74 & Shock Tube Lab, Univ NMex; sr consult, Kaman Sci Corp & Kaman Aerospace, 74-77; res physicist, Univ Colo, Colorado Springs, 74-75. *Mem:* Sr mem Inst Elec & Electronics Engrs; Prof Soc Protective Design. *Res:* Antennas; nuclear electromagnetic plasma. *Mailing Add:* 2580 Clinton Dr NE Palm Bay FL 32905

BITTNER, HARLAN FLETCHER, PHYSICAL CHEMISTRY, SOLID STATE CHEMISTRY. *Current Pos:* MEM TECH STAFF, AEROSPACE CORP, 80- *Personal Data:* b Eugene, Ore, Mar 26, 51; m 81, Rebecca Brittain; c Ryan C. *Educ:* Univ Ore, BA, 73; Univ Calif, San Diego, PhD(chem), 77. *Prof Exp:* Res staff mat chem, Oak Ridge Nat Lab, Union Carbide Corp, 78-80. *Mem:* Am Chem Soc; Electrochem Soc. *Res:* Reactive metal electrode passivation; lithium battery electrochemistry; oxidation of metals and alloys; hydrogen absorption by and permeation through metals and alloys; alloy and intermetallic compound formation. *Mailing Add:* M6/209 PO Box 92957 Los Angeles CA 90009

BITTNER, JOHN WILLIAM, GENERAL PHYSICS. *Current Pos:* Assoc physicist, 54-63, PHYSICIST, BROOKHAVEN NAT LAB, 63- *Personal Data:* b Iowa, Mar 6, 26; m 64; c 2. *Educ:* Univ Western Ont, BSc, 48, MS, 50, PhD, 54. *Mem:* Am Phys Soc; Inst Elec & Electronics Engrs; Sigma Xi. *Res:* Nuclear accelerators; scanning transmission electron microscope. *Mailing Add:* 462 Festubert St Duncan BC V9L 3T2 Can

BITTON, GABRIEL, ENVIRONMENTAL MICROBIOLOGY. *Current Pos:* PROF ENVIRON MICROBIOL, UNIV FLA, 74- *Personal Data:* b Marrakech, Morocco, Sept 8, 40; m 70; c 2. *Educ:* Univ Toulouse, BS & Agr Eng, 65; Laval Univ, MS, 67; Hebrew Univ, PhD(microbiol), 73. *Prof Exp:* Teacher biol, Acad Quebec, 66-68; res fel appl microbiol, Harvard Univ, 72-74. *Concurrent Pos:* Prof, Univ Perpignan, France. *Mem:* Am Soc Microbiol; Am Soc Limnol Oceanog; Soc Indust Microbiol. *Res:* Microbiology of surfaces; environmental virology; environmental toxicology. *Mailing Add:* 2616 NW 21st St Gainesville FL 32605

BITZER, DONALD L, ELECTRICAL ENGINEERING. *Current Pos:* From res asst prof to assoc prof radar, 60-67, PROF ELEC ENG & DIR, 67-, EMER PROF ELEC ENG & EMER DIR, COMPUTER-BASED EDUC RES LAB, UNIV ILL, URBANA-CHAMPAIGN; DISTINGUISHED UNIV RES PROF, NC STATE UNIV. *Personal Data:* b East St Louis, Ill, Jan 1, 34; m 55; c 1. *Educ:* Univ Ill, BS, 55, MS, 56, PhD(elec eng), 60. *Hon Degrees:* PhD, MacMurray Col, 85. *Honors & Awards:* IR 100 Award, 66; Vladimir K Zworkyin Award, Nat Acad Eng, 73; Chester F Carlson Award, Am Soc Eng Educ, 81; Educ Award, Am Fedn Info Processing Socs, 89. *Concurrent Pos:* Mem high resolution radar comt, US Dept Defense, 58-59; comput consult, US Agency Int Develop, 64. *Mem:* Nat Acad Eng; Am Soc Eng Educ; fel Inst Elec & Electronics Engrs; fel AAAS; Sigma Xi; Data Processing Mgt Asn. *Res:* Generation of large synthetic radar antennas; automatic instruction with high speed digital computers; measurement of small signals in a plasma; numerous patents, including Plato and Novanet systems. *Mailing Add:* Dept Comput Sci Box 8206 NC State Univ Raleigh NC 27695

BITZER, MORRIS JAY, AGRONOMY. *Current Pos:* EXTEN SPECIALIST GRAIN CROPS, UNIV KY, 71- *Personal Data:* b Huntington, Ind, Mar 3, 36; m 56; c 3. *Educ:* Purdue Univ, BS, 58, MS, 65, PhD(plant breeding, genetics), 68. *Prof Exp:* Teacher, high schs, Ind, 59-63; res asst hybrid wheat, Purdue Univ, 63-68; asst prof agron, Univ Ga, 68-71. *Mem:* Am Soc Agron; Crop Sci Soc Am. *Res:* Hybrid vigor and gene action in hybrid wheat; pollen dispersal and seed set for hybrid wheat production; effect of nitrogen on yields of dwarf wheats; vernalization of soft winter wheats. *Mailing Add:* 2049 Rebel Rd Lexington KY 40503

BITZER, RICHARD ALLEN, electrical & microwave engineering, aerospace engineering, for more information see previous edition

BIVENS, RICHARD LOWELL, PHYSICAL CHEMISTRY. *Current Pos:* From asst prof to assoc prof, 65-79, assoc dean, 84-88, PROF CHEM, ALLEGHENY COL, 79- *Personal Data:* b Denver, Ill, Aug 19, 39; m 63, Mary Hunter; c Jonathan & Jennifer. *Educ:* Monmouth Col, Ill, BA, 61; Case Western Res Univ, MS, 63, PhD(chem), 69. *Concurrent Pos:* Dana vis prof, Univ Rochester, 91. *Mem:* Am Chem Soc; Sigma Xi. *Res:* Structure of ion-solvent clusters; computational chemistry of small ion-molecule reactions. *Mailing Add:* Dept Chem Allegheny Col Meadville PA 16335. *E-Mail:* rbivens@alleg.edu

BIVER, CARL JOHN, JR, APPLIED PHYSICS, MATERIALS SCIENCE. *Current Pos:* INSTR CHEM ENG SCI, UNIV SFLA, TAMPA, 92- *Personal Data:* b Owensboro, Ky, July 1, 32; m 58; c 4. *Educ:* Univ Notre Dame, BS, 54, MS, 56. *Honors & Awards:* Gen Elec Co Inventors Award, 72. *Prof Exp:* Asst scientist metall, Argonne Nat Lab, 56-59; from physicist to sr physicist, X-ray Dept, Gen Elec Co, 59-66, sr physicist, Neutron Devices Dept, 66-90; head, Sci Dept & teacher math & physics, St Petersburg Jr Col, St Petersburg Campus, 90-92. *Mem:* Am Vacuum Soc; AAAS; Am Soc Metals. *Res:* Gaseous permeation phenomena; high pressure physics; thermoelectric devices physics; photoconductivity, heat transfer, transport phenomena, metallurgical and chemical kinetics; mathematical modeling. *Mailing Add:* 4 Westwood Lane Belleair Clearwater FL 34616

BIVINS, BRACK ALLEN, trauma, metabolism; deceased, see previous edition for last biography

BIXBY, ROBERT EUGENE, OPERATIONS RESEARCH. *Current Pos:* PROF COMPUT & APPL MATH, RICE UNIV, 84-; CHMN, CPLEX OPTIMIZATION, INCLINE VILLAGE, NEV, 84- *Personal Data:* b Oakland, Calif, Sept 14, 45; m 66; c 3. *Educ:* Univ Calif, Berkeley, BA, 68; Cornell Univ, MS, 70, PhD(opers res), 72. *Prof Exp:* Asst prof math, Univ Ky, 72-77; assoc prof, Northwestern Univ, 77-80, prof, 80-84. *Mem:* Nat Acad Eng; Math Prog Soc; Soc Ind & Appl Math. *Res:* Games matroids and graphs; combinatorial optimization, matroid theory and linear programming. *Mailing Add:* Rice Univ PO Box 1892 Houston TX 77251

BIXBY, W(ILLIAM) HERBERT, ELECTRICAL ENGINEERING. *Current Pos:* RETIRED. *Personal Data:* b Indianapolis, Ind, Dec 28, 06; m 63. *Educ:* Univ Mich, BSE, 30, MS, 31, PhD(elec eng), 33; Chrysler Inst Technol, MME, 35. *Prof Exp:* Res engr, Detroit Edison Co, 28-32; spec probs engr, Chrysler Corp, 33-36; from instr to prof elec eng, Wayne State Univ, 36-56; vpres appl res, Power Equip Co Div, North Elec Co, 56-80. *Concurrent Pos:* Develop engr, Power Equip Co, Detroit, 37-80. *Mem:* Fel AAAS; fel Inst Elec & Electronics Engrs. *Res:* Automatic control; dielectric materials; general and industrial electronics; electricity and magnetism; applied mathematics; time-lag in breakdown of liquid insulations as a function of voltage application; breakdown and time-lag of dielectric materials; breakdown of liquid carbon tetrachloride. *Mailing Add:* 2308 SE 21st St Ft Lauderdale FL 33316

BIXLER, DAVID, GENETICS, DENTISTRY. *Current Pos:* USPHS fel, Sch Dent, Ind Univ, Indianapolis, 56-58, asst prof dent sci, Sch Dent & Med, 59-66, asst prof med genetics, 66-70, assoc prof dent sci & med genetics, 70-74, PROF MED GENETICS & ORAL-FACIAL GENETICS & CHMN, DEPT ORAL-FACIAL GENETICS, SCHS DENT & MED, IND UNIV, INDIANAPOLIS, 74- *Personal Data:* b Chicago, Ill, Jan 7, 29; m 51, 64, Gloria Greenen; c 5. *Educ:* Ind Univ, AB, 50, PhD(zool), 56, DDS, 59; Am Bd Med Genetics, dipl, 82. *Concurrent Pos:* USPHS career develop award, 67-72. *Mem:* AAAS; Am Soc Human Genetics; Sigma Xi; Am Cleft Palate Asn; Soc Craniofacial Genetics. *Res:* Genetics of cleft lip and palate; hereditary anomalies of oral and facial structures. *Mailing Add:* Ind Univ Sch Dent 1121 W Michigan St Indianapolis IN 46202-5135

BIXLER, DEAN A, TEXTILE CHEMISTRY. *Current Pos:* DIR RES, CONE MILLS CORP, 69- *Personal Data:* b Gretna, Nebr, Oct 24, 19; m 41; c 2. *Educ:* Univ Nebr, Lincoln, BS, 40, MS, 46; Purdue Univ, PhD(agr biol), 53. *Mailing Add:* 835 Bentley Dr Naples FL 34110

BIXLER, JOHN WILSON, ANALYTICAL CHEMISTRY. *Current Pos:* assoc prof, 69-77, PROF CHEM, STATE UNIV NY COL BROCKPORT, 77- *Personal Data:* b Eau Claire, Wis, July 27, 37. *Educ:* Lakeland Col, BS, 59; Univ Minn, PhD(anal chem), 63. *Prof Exp:* Instr chem, Lake Forest Col, 63-65, asst prof, 65-69. *Concurrent Pos:* Vis prof, Purdue Univ, 75-76; vis scientist, Melbourne Univ, 77-78 & Deakin Univ, 84-85. *Mem:* Am Chem Soc. *Res:* Electroanalytical chemistry; chemical instrumentation. *Mailing Add:* Dept Chem State Univ Col Brockport NY 14420

BIXLER, OTTO C, ELECTRONICS ENGINEERING, MANAGEMENT SCIENCES. *Current Pos:* RETIRED. *Personal Data:* b Morenci, Ariz, May 9, 16; m 38, Annette E Struck; c Otto C Jr & Terry R. *Educ:* Univ Southern Calif, BS, 37; Kennedy Western Univ, PhD, 85. *Prof Exp:* Engr, Valuation Dept, Southern Calif Edison Co, Ltd, 37-42; field engr radio & sonar systs, Radio Div, Western Elec Co with Bur Ships, 42-43, sr engr, 43-45, systs engr, Elec Res Prod Div, 45-49; develop engr, AiRes Mfg Co, 49-51; dir eng & res, Magnecord, Inc, 51-53, vpres & works mgr, 53-54; tech dir, Helipot Corp Div, Beckman Instruments, 54-58; mgr prod design & mfg computer oper, Aeronutronic Div, Ford Motor Co, 58-62; asst gen mgr, Space & Systs Div, Packard Bell Electronics Corp, 62-63; vpres & mgr defense opers, Univac Div, Sperry-Rand Corp, 63-66; vpres & mgr opers, Wanlass Elec Co, 66-67; vpres mfg & distribution, Rexall Drug Co, 67-68; pres, Eng Res Prod Co & Ad Corp,

68-74; gen mgr, Waimea Dispensary & Clin, 74-84; Adminr, Hawaiian Eye Ctr, 85-86; prog mgr, QCM Res, 90-92. *Concurrent Pos:* Mem bd, Info Systs Design, Inc, 70-74; exec vpres, Info Serv Industs, 70-72. *Mem:* AAAS; Inst Elec & Electronics Engrs; Sigma Xi; Soc Motion Picture & TV Engrs; NY Acad Sci; Med Group Mgt Asn. *Res:* Microfilm systems; management information systems; first magnetic tape recorder and stereo tape recorder, computer mass memory system; first multicolor computer display terminals and USN Pacific Missile Fleet microfilm automated indentured parts control system; re-entry decoy systems; space shuttle instrumentation. *Mailing Add:* 849 Promontory Dr W Newport Beach CA 92660

BIZIOS, RENA, BLOOD COAGULATION, TRANSPORT PHENOMENA IN PULMONARY PATHOPHYSIOLOGY. *Current Pos:* ASST PROF BIOMED ENG, RENSSELAER POLYTECH INST, 81- *Personal Data:* b Larissa, Greece, July 7, 43. *Educ:* Univ Mass, BS, 68; Calif Inst Technol, MS, 71; Mass Inst Technol PhD(biomed eng), 79. *Prof Exp:* Jr scientist, Dept Lab Med, Med Sch, Univ Minn, 70-71, assoc scientist proj coordr, Dept Surg, 72-73; fel spec coagulation lab, Roger Williams Gen Hosp, 79-80. *Concurrent Pos:* Adj asst prof physiol, Albany Med Col, 82- *Mem:* Biomed Eng Soc; Soc Women Engrs; Am Inst Chem Engrs; AAAS; NY Acad Sci; Am Soc Eng Educ; Sigma Xi. *Res:* Blood coagulation; platelet and leukocyte function in health and disease; transport properties of endothelium; transport phenomena in pulmonary pathophysiology; modeling physiological process and systems. *Mailing Add:* Dept Biomed Eng Rensselaer Polytech Inst Troy NY 12180-3590

BIZZI, EMILIO, NEUROPHYSIOLOGY, NEUROBIOLOGY. *Current Pos:* Res assoc, Dept Psychol, Mass Inst Technol, 66-67, lectr, 67-68, from assoc prof to prof neurophysiol, 69-80, dir, Whitaker Col, 83-89, EUGENE MCDERMOTT PROF BRAIN SCI & HUMAN BEHAV, MASS INST TECHNOL, 80-, CHMN, DEPT BRAIN & COGNITIVE SCI, 86- *Personal Data:* b Rome, Italy, Feb 22, 33; US citizen. *Educ:* Univ Rome, MD, 58, Docenza, 68. *Honors & Awards:* Alden Spencer Award, 78; Bartlett lectr, 88. *Concurrent Pos:* Res assoc, Zool Neurophysiol Lab, Wash Univ, Mo, 63-64; vis assoc, Psychol Lab Clin Sci, NIMH, 64-66; fel, Found Fund Res Psychiat, 68; sr investr, Inst Cardiovasc Res, Univ Milan, 68-69; mem, Study Sect Vision B, NIH, 73-77; Whitaker health sci award, 78-79 & 82-83; NIH Javits neurosci investr award, 88; counr, Soc Neurosci, 88; corp mem, Boston Mus Sci, 89- *Mem:* Nat Acad Sci; Soc Neurosci; AAAS; Am Physiol Soc; Ital Physiol Soc; Int Brain Res Orgn; Am Acad Arts & Sci. *Res:* Author and co-author of numerous publications and books relating to neurophysiology and neurobiology. *Mailing Add:* Dept Brain & Cognitive Sci Mass Inst Technol 25-526 Cambridge MA 02139-4307

BIZZOCO, RICHARD LAWRENCE WEISS, CELL BIOLOGY, BOTANY. *Current Pos:* from asst prof to assoc prof, PROF BOT CALIF STATE UNIV, SAN DIEGO, 85- *Personal Data:* b New York, NY, Dec 28, 40; div; c 2. *Educ:* Univ Conn, BA, 64; Calif State Univ, Long Beach, MS, 70; Ind Univ, PhD(microbiol), 72. *Prof Exp:* Res fel bot, Univ Calif, Berkeley, 73-74; res fel cell biol, Harvard Univ, 74-76; res assoc med microbiol, Univ Calif, Irvine, 76-77. *Concurrent Pos:* Am Cancer Soc fel, Univ Calif, Berkeley, 73-74; NIH fel cell biol, Harvard Univ, 75-76; NIH grant, Calif State Univ, San Diego, 78-, NIH biomed res, 85-87; NSF, 87. *Mem:* Sigma Xi; Phycological Soc Am. *Res:* Mechanism of cell fusion; cell-cell interaction; cell differentiation cell structure; biological electron microscopy; immunoelectron micros. *Mailing Add:* Dept Biol San Diego State Univ San Diego CA 92182-4614. *Fax:* 619-594-5676; *E-Mail:* rbizzoco@sunstroke.sdsu.edu

BJARNGARD, BENGT E, RADIOLOGICAL PHYSICS. *Current Pos:* PROF RADIOL MED, BROWN UNIV, 89-; DIR PHYSICS, ROGER WILLIAMS MED CTR, 89- *Personal Data:* b N Akarp, Sweden, Oct 2, 34. *Educ:* Univ Lund, Fil Mag, 58, Fil Lic(radiation physics), 62. *Hon Degrees:* MA, Brown Univ, 90. *Honors & Awards:* R S Landaur Award, 75. *Prof Exp:* Asst radiation physics, Univ Lund, 59-61; res physicist, Atomic Energy Co, Sweden, 61-65; dir radiation physics, Controls for Radiation, Inc, 65-68; from asst prof to prof radiother, Harvard Med Sch, 68-89; dir physics, Harvard Joint Ctr Radiation Therapeut, 68-89. *Concurrent Pos:* Lectr, Harvard Sch Pub Health. *Mem:* Am Asn Physicists in Med; Europ Soc Therapeut Radiation Oncol; Radiation Res Soc; Am Soc Therapeut Radiation Oncol. *Res:* Dosimetry; medical radiological physics. *Mailing Add:* 51 Samoset Rd Winchester MA 01890-3441. *Fax:* 401-456-6550

BJELDANES, LEONARD FRANK, GENE REGULATION, DIET & CANCER. *Current Pos:* Teaching & res asst, Dept Chem, Univ Calif, Los Angeles, 68-70, fel res chemist, Berkeley, 70-72, from asst prof to assoc prof, 72-82, PROF FOOD TOXICOL, DEPT NUTRIT SCI, UNIV CALIF, BERKELEY, 82- *Personal Data:* b St Peter, Minn, Oct 31, 43. *Educ:* Univ Minn, Minneapolis, BCh, 67; Univ Calif, Los Angeles, PhD(org chem), 70. *Concurrent Pos:* NDEA grad fel, special study Sect, NIH, 84-85; vis prof, Inst Toxicol, Univ Mainz, WGer, 88. *Mem:* Am Chem Soc; Environ Mutagen Soc; Inst Food Technologists; AAAS; Am Inst Nutrit. *Res:* Mechanistic studies of the effects of dietary ligands for the Ah receptor on expression of genes involved in cell growth and steroid metabolism. *Mailing Add:* Dept Nutrit Sci Univ Calif 217 Morgan hall Berkeley CA 94720-3104. *Fax:* 510-642-0535

BJERKAAS, ALLAN WAYNE, DYNAMICAL OCEANOGRAPHY, REMOTE SENSING. *Current Pos:* SR PHYSICIST, APPL PHYSICS LAB, JOHNS HOPKINS UNIV, 73- *Personal Data:* b Alexandria, Minn, Nov 25, 44; m 65; c 4. *Educ:* Univ NDak, BS, 66; Univ Ill, Urbana, MS, 67, PhD(physics), 71. *Prof Exp:* Res assoc physics, Univ Pittsburgh, 71-73. *Concurrent Pos:* Lectr, Johns Hopkins Univ. *Mem:* Sigma Xi. *Res:* Signal processing; image processing; remote sensing. *Mailing Add:* 4922 Snowy Reach Columbia MD 21044

BJERREGAARD, RICHARD S, AGRICULTURAL FIELD RESEARCH, ECOPHYSIOLOGY. *Current Pos:* REGULATORY SERVS, DOW ELANCO, 90- *Personal Data:* b Gunnison, Utah, Jan 9, 43; m 62; c 5. *Educ:* Brigham Young Univ, BS, 67; Utah State Univ, PhD(ecol), 72. *Prof Exp:* Asst prof biol sci, Calif State Polytech Univ, 71-72; exten specialist, Exten Serv, Tex A&M Univ, 72-76; plant sci rep, Lilly Res Labs, 76-84, proj mgr, 84-90. *Res:* Agricultural research projects; agricultural extension. *Mailing Add:* 542 Shady La Greenwood IN 46142

BJORHOVDE, REIDAR, STRUCTURAL ENGINEERING, STEEL & COMPOSITE STRUCTURES. *Current Pos:* chmn, 87-91 & 95-96, PROF CIVIL ENG, UNIV PITTSBURGH, PA, 87-, DIR, 89- *Personal Data:* b Harstad, Norway, Nov 6, 41; US citizen; m 72, Patricia E Ordonez; c Ian D & Heather L. *Educ:* Norweg Inst Technol, Trondheim, MS, 64, DrIng(civil eng), 68; Lehigh Univ, Bethlehem, Pa, PhD(civil eng), 72. *Honors & Awards:* Duggan Medal, Eng Inst Can, 80; T R Higgins Lectr, 87; J James R Croes Medal, Am Soc Civil Engrs, 92; Serv Award, Am Iron & Steel Inst, 95. *Prof Exp:* Res fel struct eng, Norweg Inst Technol, 65-66, asst prof, 66-68; res asst struct eng, Fritz Eng Lab, Lehigh Univ, 68-72; regional engr steel construct, Am Inst Steel Construct, Boston, 72-74, res engr, NY, 74-77; prof civil eng, Univ Alta, Edmonton, Can, 77-81, Univ Ariz, Tucson, 81-87. *Concurrent Pos:* Tech secy, Struct Stability Res Coun, 69-71; chmn & mem, Nat & Internat Tech Comt, 72-, Nat & Internat Tech Conf, 82-; lectr, Northeastern Univ, Boston, Mass, 73; ed, J Constructional Steel Res, 86-; vis prof, Univ Paris VI, France, 87; NATO sr guest scientist fel, 87; mem related fac, Latin Am Studies & W Europ Studies, Univ Pittsburgh, 88-; vis prof & steel indust fel, Univ Witwatersrand, Johannesburg, SAfrica, 89; dir, Bridge & Struct Info Ctr, 89-; mem, Related Fac, WEurop Studies Prog, Univ Pittsburgh, 89-; res fel, Japan Soc Prom Sci, 92. *Mem:* Fel Am Soc Civil Engrs; Am Inst Steel Construct; Int Asn Bridge & Struct Eng; Asn Bridge Construct & Design; Struct Stability Res Coun; Sigma Xi; Am Welding Soc; Mex Soc Struct Eng; Norweg Soc Steel Struct; Steel Construct Inst Eng. *Res:* Strength and stability of all types of steel structures; load and resistance factor design; steel columns; composite structures; steel connections; fracture of welded and other joints; metallic materials. *Mailing Add:* 4609 Bayard St No 86 Pittsburgh PA 15213-2711. *E-Mail:* bjorh@civ.pitt.edu

BJORK, CARL KENNETH, SR, CHEMISTRY. *Current Pos:* res & develop engr, 54-59, patent agt & group leader, 59-70, mgr bioprod sect, Patent Dept, 70-78, mgr int sect, Patent Dept, 78-87, ADMIN MGR, PATENT OPERS, DOW CHEM CO, 87- *Personal Data:* b Burlington, Iowa, Mar 16, 26; m 47; c 7. *Educ:* Augustana Col, AB, 47; DePauw Univ, MA, 50; Univ Ky, PhD(inorg chem), 53. *Prof Exp:* Res chemist, Int Mining & Chem Co, 53-54. *Concurrent Pos:* Chmn, Chem & Law Div, Am Chem Soc, 85 & 86, mem, Comt Patents & Related Matters, 78- *Mem:* Am Chem Soc; Sigma Xi. *Res:* Patent law; management; US and international patent applications and prosecution. *Mailing Add:* 2712 Lambros Midland MI 48642-3948

BJORK, PHILIP R, VERTEBRATE PALEONTOLOGY. *Current Pos:* assoc prof, 75-80, PROF GEOL, SDAK SCH MINES & TECHNOL, 80-, DIR MUS GEOL, 75- *Personal Data:* b Wyandotte, Mich, Sept 14, 40; m 64; c 2. *Educ:* Univ Mich, BS, 62, PhD(geol), 68; SDak Sch Mines & Technol, MS, 64. *Prof Exp:* From asst prof to assoc prof geol, Univ Wis-Stevens Point, 68-75. *Mem:* Soc Vert Paleont; Am Paleont Soc. *Res:* Blancan carnivora in North America; Oligocene faunas of North America; Blancan faunas of North America; dinosaurs of western North America. *Mailing Add:* Mus Geol SDak Sch Mines & Technol 501 E St Joseph St Rapid City SD 57701-3901

BJORKEN, JAMES D, PHYSICS. *Current Pos:* STAFF MEM, THEORET PHYSICS DEPT, STANFORD LINEAR ACCELERATOR CTR, 89- *Personal Data:* b Chicago, Ill, June 22, 34. *Educ:* Mass Inst Technol, BS, 56; Stanford Univ, PhD, 59. *Honors & Awards:* E O Lawrence Award, US Dept Energy, 78. *Prof Exp:* Res assoc, Stanford Univ, 60, from asst prof to prof, 61-79; sr physicist, Fermi Nat Accelerator Lab, 79-84, assoc dir physics, 84-88. *Mem:* Nat Acad Sci; fel Am Phys Soc; fel Am Acad Arts & Sci. *Res:* Author and coauthor of several books. *Mailing Add:* Stanford Linear Accelerator Ctr PO Box 4349 Stanford CA 94309

BJORKHOLM, JOHN ERNST, EXPERIMENTAL PHYSICS, SOFT X RAY OPTICS. *Current Pos:* PRIN SCIENTIST, COMPONENTS RES LAB, INTEL CORP, 96- *Personal Data:* b Milwaukee, Wis, Mar 22, 39; m 64, Mary J Durbin; c Kristin & Laura. *Educ:* Princeton Univ, BSE, 61; Stanford Univ, MS, 62, PhD(appl physics), 66. *Prof Exp:* Distinguished mem tech staff, Bell Labs, 66-94. *Concurrent Pos:* Chmn, Gordon Res Conf Nonlinear Optics & Lasers, 77; mem, Exec Comt of Tech Coun, Optical Soc Am. 86-87; comptroller, CLEO/QELS, 88-91; bd dirs, Optical Soc Am, 88-90; trustee, Princeton Univ, 91-95. *Mem:* Fel Am Phys Soc; sr mem Inst Elec & Electronics Engrs; fel Optical Soc Am (treas, 92-96). *Res:* Quantum electronics; nonlinear optics; interaction of resonant light with atoms; atomic physics; high resolution two-photon spectroscopy; extreme ultraviolet lithography. *Mailing Add:* 408 Cabonia Court Pleasanton CA 94566. *E-Mail:* john_bjorkholm@ccm.sc.intel.com

BJORKLAND, JOHN A(LEXANDER), ENGINEERING PHYSICS. *Current Pos:* RETIRED. *Personal Data:* b Chicago, Ill, Oct 16, 23. *Educ:* Univ Chicago, BS, 46, MS, 50; NC State Col, PhD(eng physics), 56. *Prof Exp:* Sr engr, Cook Res Labs Div, Cook Elec Co, 56-60; assoc physicist, Armour Res Found, 60-61; assoc engr, Argonne Nat Lab, 61-85. *Res:* Nuclear reactor instrumentation and electronic pulse circuitry. *Mailing Add:* 1005 Harvard Terr Evanston IL 60202-3306

BJORKLUND, GARY CARL, QUANTUM ELECTRONICS, OPTICS. *Current Pos:* DIR ADVAN DEVELOP, OPTIVISION. *Personal Data:* b Passaic, NJ, Nov 17, 46; m 69. *Educ:* Mass Inst Technol, BS, 68; Stanford Univ, MS, 69, PhD(appl physics), 74. *Prof Exp:* Mem tech staff, Bell Tel Labs, 74-79; res staff mem, Almoden Res Ctr, IBM, 79-80, mgr, 80- *Mem:* Fel Am Phys Soc; fel Optical Soc Am; fel Inst Elec & Electronics Engrs. *Res:* Organic nonlinear optical materials and devices, frequency domain optical memories and FM spectroscopy. *Mailing Add:* Optivision 2450 Hillview Ave Palo Alto CA 94304

BJORKLUND, RICHARD GUY, ECOLOGY, CONSERVATION. *Current Pos:* from instr to prof biol, 57-68, chmn dept, 64-70, dean lib arts & sci, 73-78, PROF BIOL, BRADLEY UNIV, 68- *Personal Data:* b Milwaukee, Wis, Feb 10, 28; div; c 5. *Educ:* Mont State Univ, BS, 51, MS, 53; Univ Mich, PhD, 58. *Prof Exp:* Res asst, Univ Mich, 54-55. *Concurrent Pos:* Asst blister rust control, US Forest Serv, 48; aide, Inst Fish Res, 53-54; consult teach & res proj, 78-81 & 84-91; contract res, Avian Ecol, Ill Dept Conserv, 81 & 85. *Mem:* Am Inst Biol Sci; Sigma Xi; Colonial Waterbird Group; Wilson Ornith Soc; Am Ornithologists Union; Am Fisheries Soc. *Res:* Environmental biology; temperature sense; photoperiodism; endocrine functions; aquatic biology; ecology and natural history of herons; ecology and natural history of other birds. *Mailing Add:* RR 1 Box 162AB Topeka IL 61567-9714

BJORKMAN, OLLE ERIK, PHYSIOLOGICAL ECOLOGY, PHOTOBIOLOGY. *Current Pos:* res fel, 64-65, STAFF BIOLOGIST, DEPT PLANT BIOL, CARNEGIE INST WASH, CALIF, 66- *Personal Data:* b Jonkoping, Swed, July 29, 33; m 55; c 2. *Educ:* Univ Stockholm, MS, 57; Univ Uppsala, PhD, 60. *Honors & Awards:* Linneus Prize, Royal Physiog Soc, Swed; Selby Award, Australian Acad Sci; Stephen Hales Award, Am Soc Plant Physiologists. *Prof Exp:* Asst scientist, Dept Genetics & Plant Breeding, Royal Agr Col Sweden & Univ Uppsala, 57-61, res fel, Swed Natural Sci Res Coun, 61-63. *Concurrent Pos:* Assoc courtesy prof biol, Stanford Univ, 67-, courtesy prof, 75- *Mem:* Nat Acad Sci; Am Soc Plant Physiologists; fel AAAS; Am Acad Arts & Sci; Australian Acad Sci; Royal Swed Acad Sci. *Res:* Physiological and biochemical mechanisms of plant response and adaptation to ecologically diverse environments; environmental and biological control of photosynthesis. *Mailing Add:* Dept Plant Biol Carnegie Inst Wash 290 Panama St Stanford CA 94305

BJORKMAN, PAMELA J, PROTEIN CRYSTALLOGRAPHY, PROTEIN EXPRESSION. *Current Pos:* ASST INVESTR BIOL & CHEM, HOWARD HUGHES MED INST & DIV BIOL, CALIF INST TECHNOL, 89. *Personal Data:* b Portland, Ore, June 21, 56; m 88; c 1. *Educ:* Univ Ore, BA, 78; Harvard Univ, PhD(biochem & molecular biol), 84. *Honors & Awards:* William B Coley Award, Distinguished Res Fundamental Immunol, Cancer Res Inst, 91; Gairdner Found Int Award, 94. *Prof Exp:* Postdoctoral fel, Harvard Univ, 84-86; postdoctoral fel, Dept Microbiol & Immunol, Stanford Univ, 86-89; asst prof biol & chem, div biol, Calif Inst Technol, 89- *Concurrent Pos:* Young investr award, Am Soc Histocompatibility & Immunogenetics, 88; mem, Nat Res Coun Comt, Investigate Funding Young Investigators, 90- *Mem:* Am Crystallog Asn. *Res:* Structure and function of all surface recognition molecules found in the immune and nervous systems by x-ray crystallographic, biochemical and molecular biological techniques. *Mailing Add:* Div Biol 156-29 Calif Inst Technol 1201 E California Blvd Pasadena CA 91125-0002

BJORKMAN, THOMAS NILS ERIK, PLANT PHYSIOLOGY. *Current Pos:* asst prof, 90-96, ASSOC PROF HORT, DEPT HORT SCI, CORNELL UNIV, 96- *Personal Data:* b Uppsala, Sweden, May 12, 58; m 82, Ann Raffetto. *Educ:* Univ Calif, Davis, BS, 79; Cornell Univ, PhD(plant physiol), 87. *Prof Exp:* Postdoctoral assoc, Bot Dept, Univ Wash, 86-90. *Mem:* Bot Soc Am; Am Soc Plant Physiologists; Scandinavian Soc Plant Physiologists; Am Soc Hort Sci. *Res:* Environmental effects on root development, especially rhizosphere biology; scope ranges from cellular interactions to impact on vegetable production systems and agricultural sustainability. *Mailing Add:* Dept Hort Sci Cornell Univ Geneva NY 14456. *E-Mail:* tnbl@cornell.edu

BJORNDAHL, JAY MARK, SIGNAL TRANSDUCTION, T-LYMPHOCYTES. *Current Pos:* DIR IMMUNOL, FLOW CYTOMETRY LAB, HARRINGTON CANCER CTR, 88- *Personal Data:* b Lafayette, Ind, Nov 14, 55; m 82; c 2. *Educ:* Calif State Univ, BA, 79; Univ Kans, MS, 85, PhD(pharmacol), 87. *Prof Exp:* Assoc res scientist immunol, Okla Med Res Found, 85-88. *Concurrent Pos:* Clin asst prof, Dept Internal Med, Health Sci Ctr, Tex Tech Univ, Amarillo, 88- *Mem:* Sigma Xi; AAAS; Am Soc Microbiol; Am Asn Immunologists. *Res:* Signal transduction in human T lymphocytes; ligand-receptor interactions; surface antigen expression; flow cytometry; protein isolation/purification. *Mailing Add:* Tex Tech Univ Health Sci Ctr PO Box 51920 Amarillo TX 79159-1920

BJORNDAL, ARNE MAGNE, DENTISTRY, ENDODONTICS. *Current Pos:* from instr to prof operative dent & endodont, 55-88, EMER PROF OPERATIVE DENT & ENDODONT, COL DENT, UNIV IOWA, 88- *Personal Data:* b Ulstein, Norway, Aug 19, 16; m 52, Katharine; c 3. *Educ:* Volda State Col, BS, 39; Univ Oslo, DDS, 47; Univ Iowa, MS & DDS, 56; Am Bd Endodont, dipl, 64. *Prof Exp:* Instr pedodont, 48-52. *Concurrent Pos:* Mem, Coun Med TV, 65-; vpres, Clyde Davis Midwestern Endodontic Study Group. *Mem:* Fel Am Col Dentists; AAAS; Am Asn Endodont; Int Asn Dent Res; Norweg Dent Asn. *Res:* Endodontics in relation to hemophiliacs and blood dyscrasias. *Mailing Add:* 2510 Bluffwood Circle Iowa City IA 52245. *E-Mail:* bjorndal@blue.tweeg.uiowa.edu

BJORNERUD, EGIL KRISTOFFER, PHYSICS. *Current Pos:* MANAGING DIR, BRAATHEN INDUST SERV, OSLO, NORWAY, 84- *Personal Data:* b Hamar, Norway, May 3, 25; nat US; m 59; c 4. *Educ:* Univ Wash, BS, 49, MBA, 69; Calif Inst Technol, PhD(physics), 54. *Prof Exp:* Staff mem, Physics Dept, Rand Corp, Calif, 54-55; reactor dept, Inst Atomic Energy, Norway, 55-56; res assoc, Gen Atomic Div, Gen Dynamics Corp, 56-59, asst export mgr, 59-62; assoc dir, Sci Div, Nat Eng Sci Co, Calif, 62-64; chief, Nuclear Technol Aerospace Div, 64-67, dir laser develop, Res Div, 70-75, dir, Nuclear Projs, Eng & Construct Div, Boeing Co, 75-84. *Concurrent Pos:* Consult, AEC, India, 59-60; deleg, Int Atomic Energy Agency, Vienna, 80. *Mem:* Am Phys Soc; Am Nuclear Soc; Am Inst Aeronaut & Astronaut; fel Royal Astron Soc. *Res:* Cloud-chamber studies of elementary particle interactions; experimental studies of flame emission spectra; neutron diffusion and criticality experiments; reactor physics and nuclear technology. *Mailing Add:* 1500 38th E Seattle WA 98112

BJORNSTI, MARY-ANN, DNA TOPOISOMERASES, DNA TOPOLOGY. *Current Pos:* asst prof, 89-95, ASSOC PROF, DEPT BIOCHEM & MOLECULAR BIOL, THOMAS JEFFERSON UNIV, 95- *Personal Data:* b Brooklyn, NY, Sept 8, 56. *Educ:* NY State Univ, BS, 78; Univ Minn, PhD(genetics & cell biol), 83. *Prof Exp:* Fogarty fel, Univ Basel, Switz, 84-85; fel, Dept Biochem & Molecular Biol, Harvard Univ, 85-89. *Concurrent Pos:* Prin investr, NIH Gen Med Sci, 90-95, W W Smith Charitable Trust, 91-93 & Nat Cancer Inst, 93- *Mem:* Genetics Soc Am; AAAS. *Res:* Genetic and biochemical analyses of the function of DNA topoisomerase I and its interaction with a potent neoplastic agent, camptothecin. *Mailing Add:* Thomas Jefferson Univ 233 S Tenth St Philadelphia PA 19107. *Fax:* 215-923-9162; *E-Mail:* bjornsti@hendrix.jci.tju.edu

BLACHERE, JEAN R, CERAMICS. *Current Pos:* asst prof, 68-74, ASSOC PROF CERAMIC ENG, UNIV PITTSBURGH, 75- *Personal Data:* b Autun, France, Dec 25, 37; m 59; c 2. *Educ:* Nat Sch Advan Indust Ceramics, Dipl eng, 59; Alfred Univ, MS, 61, PhD(ceramics), 69. *Prof Exp:* Ceramic technologist, Cent Res Lab, Domtar Ltd, Can, 62-65. *Mem:* Am Ceramic Soc; Nat Inst Ceramic Engrs; Ceramic Educ Coun; Am Inst Mining, Metall & Petrol Engrs. *Res:* High temperature materials; surfaces, grain boundaries and hot corrosion; solid state reactions; mechanical properties; refractories; electromagnetic properties. *Mailing Add:* Dept Metall Eng Univ Pittsburgh 848 Benedum Hall Pittsburgh PA 15260-0001

BLACHFORD, CAMERON W, ELECTRICAL ENGINEERING. *Current Pos:* PROF ENG, UNIV REGINA, 67- *Personal Data:* b Colonsay, Sask, July 10, 31; m 56, 87; c 4. *Educ:* Univ Sask, BSc, 53; Univ Ill, MS, 59, PhD(elec eng), 63. *Prof Exp:* Salesman, English Elec Co, Ltd, 56-58; instr elec eng, Univ Ill, 60-63; from asst prof to assoc prof, Queen's Univ, Ont, 63-67, assoc vpres res, 77-92. *Concurrent Pos:* Actg vpres, Univ Regina, 93- *Mem:* Inst Elec & Electronics Engrs; fel Eng Inst Can; Asn Prof Engrs Sask; Can Soc Elec & Computer Eng. *Res:* Automatic controls; electro-mechanical energy conversion. *Mailing Add:* 6104 Brunskill Pl Regina SK S4T 7W7 Can

BLACHMAN, ARTHUR GILBERT, PHYSICS. *Current Pos:* res staff mem, Watson Lab, NY, 56-65, RES STAFF MEM RES CTR, IBM CORP, YORKTOWN HEIGHTS, 65- *Personal Data:* b Cleveland, Ohio, June 29, 26; m 53; c 3. *Educ:* Western Res Univ, BS, 50; Ohio State Univ, MS, 56; NY Univ, PhD(physics), 66. *Prof Exp:* Physicist res dept, Erie Resistor Corp, Pa, 50-51; physicist digital comput lab, Mass Inst Technol, 51-52; teacher high sch, Colo, 52-54. *Mem:* AAAS; Am Phys Soc; Am Vacuum Soc. *Res:* Semiconductor physics; hyperfine structure of atomic metastable states; structure and properties of sputtered thin films. *Mailing Add:* 215 Cedar Dr E Briarcliff Manor NY 10510

BLACHMAN, NELSON MERLE, PHYSICS, APPLIED MATHEMATICS & PROBABILITY THEORY. *Current Pos:* RETIRED. *Personal Data:* b Cleveland, Ohio, Oct 27, 23; m 53, Anne Lefkowitz; c Susan J & Nancy R. *Educ:* Case Sch Appl Sci, Cleveland, BS, 43; Harvard Univ, AM, 47, PhD(appl physics), 47. *Prof Exp:* Spec res assoc, Underwater Sound Lab, Harvard Univ, 43-45, res assoc, Ctr Commun Res, 45-46, Cruft Lab, 46; assoc physicist, Brookhaven Nat Lab, 47-51; physicist, Math Sci Div, Off Naval Res, 51-54, liaison scientist, London, 58-60 & 76-78, Naval Res Lab, Wash, 85-86; prin scientist, Govt Systs Corp, Gen Tel & Electronics Corp, 54-58, 60-76, 78-85, 86-93. *Concurrent Pos:* Lectr, Univ Md, 51-52; lectr, Eng Exten, Univ Calif, 61-63; sr Fulbright lectr, Madrid, 64-65; lectr Stanford Univ, 67; mem, Info Theory Group Bd Govs, Inst Elec & Electronics Engrs, 69-75. *Mem:* Fel AAAS; Math Asn Am; fel Inst Elec & Electronics Engrs; Soc Indust & Appl Math; fel Inst Elec Engrs London; Am Statist Asn; Union Radio Sci Int; Acoust Soc Am. *Res:* Statistical communication theory; information theory; random processes; nonlinear transformations of signals and noise; signal detection and estimation. *Mailing Add:* 33 Linda Ave No 2210 Oakland CA 94611-4819. *E-Mail:* n.blachman@ieee.org

BLACHUT, T(HEODORE) J(OSEPH), PHOTOGRAMMETRY. *Current Pos:* RETIRED. *Personal Data:* b Czestochowa, Poland, Feb 10, 15; nat US; m 48, Fanni Schawalder; c Jan, Daniel & Pietr. *Educ:* Inst Technol, Lwow, Poland, Dipl Eng, 38, Dr Techn Sc, Tech Univ Zurich (ETH), Switz. *Hon Degrees:* Techn Univ Milano (Italy), Medation of Honor, 60, Acad Mining & Metallurgy, Krakow, Hon Doc Degree, 74. *Prof Exp:* From asst to assoc scientist photogram, Swiss Fed Inst Technol & lectr cartog, Polish Univ, Camp, Switz, 41-44; geodesist & photogrammetrist, Sci Dept, Wild Co, Switz, 45-51; head photogram res, Nat Res Coun Can, 51-80. *Concurrent Pos:* Vis prof, Laval Univ; NSF vis scientist; Can deleg & officer, Pan Am Inst Geog & Hist, Orgn Am States. *Mem:* Fel Royal Soc Can; Am Soc Photogram; Can

Inst Surv; Int Soc Photogram; hon mem Brazilian Cartog Soc; hon mem Polish Scodetic & Photogr Soc; fel Polish Acad Sci. *Res:* Photogrammetric equipment and methods; introduction of aerial triangulation method based on the use of radar auxiliary data; long distance bridging; precise large-scale photogrammetry; non-cartographic photogrammetry; development of stereo-orthophoto mapping system; multipurpose cadastre as a basis of a general and dynamic land information system; over 100 scientific and technical publications, several in a book form translated and published in up to seven languages. *Mailing Add:* 61 Rothwell Dr Ottawa ON K1J 7G7 Can

BLACK, ARTHUR HERMAN, ANALYTICAL CHEMISTRY. *Current Pos:* From instr to assoc prof chem, Univ Toledo, 46-61, asst dean Col Arts & Sci, 61-64, dean men, 64-68, assoc dean, 68-84, prof chem, 70-84, EMER PROF CHEM, UNIV TOLEDO, 84- *Personal Data:* b Toledo, Ohio, Aug 16, 19; m 45, Virginia R Girkins; c Jeffrey A, Curtis D & James A. *Educ:* Univ Toledo, BS, 41, MS, 48; Univ Mich, MS, 55. *Mem:* AAAS; Am Chem Soc; Sigma Xi. *Res:* Volumetric and colorimetric methods involving various chelating agents. *Mailing Add:* 3209 Kylemore Rd Toledo OH 43606

BLACK, ARTHUR LEO, BIOCHEMISTRY. *Current Pos:* From instr to assoc prof, 51-62, PROF BIOCHEM, UNIV CALIF, DAVIS, 62- *Personal Data:* b Redlands, Calif, Dec 1, 22; m 45, Trudi E McCur; c Teresa (Townsend), Janet (Carter) & Patty (Tleimat). *Educ:* Univ Calif, BS, 48, PhD(comp physiol), 51. *Honors & Awards:* Borden Award, Am Inst Nutrit, 63. *Prof Exp:* 1st Lt, USAF, 43-46. *Mem:* AAAS; Am Soc Biol Chemists & Molecular Biol; Am Inst Nutrit Sci; Am Physiol Soc. *Res:* Gluconeogenesis and its control; metabolism of amino acids in animals; study of intermediary metabolism in intact animals, including ruminants. *Mailing Add:* Dept Molecular Biol Sci Sch Vet Med Univ Calif Davis CA 95616. *Fax:* 530-752-4698; *E-Mail:* ablack@ucdavis.edu

BLACK, ASA C, JR, ANATOMY. *Current Pos:* assoc prof, 85-95, PROF ANAT, MERCER MED SCH, 95- *Personal Data:* b Clarksville, Tenn, Jan 2, 43; m; m 71, Cynthia Woods. *Educ:* Vanderbilt Univ, BA, 65, PhD(anat), 74. *Prof Exp:* Instr anat, Vanderbilt Univ, 72; res assoc, Univ Iowa, 73-75, asst prof anat, 75-85. *Concurrent Pos:* Prof, Dept Obstet & Gynec, Mercer Univ Sch Med & Med Ctr Central Ga. *Mem:* AAAS; Am Asn Anatomists; Soc Neurosci; Am Soc Neurochem; Res Soc Alcoholism. *Res:* Role of nucleotides in neuronal function; mechanisms of action of ethanol on the nervous system; mechanisms responsible for the fetal alcohol syndrome. *Mailing Add:* Mercer Univ Sch Med 841 1400 Coleman Ave Macon GA 31207

BLACK, BETTY LYNNE, EMBRYOLOGY, CELL PHYSIOLOGY. *Current Pos:* assoc prof develop biol, 79-95, PROF ZOOL, NC STATE UNIV, 96- *Personal Data:* b St Louis, Mo, Mar 28, 46. *Educ:* Lindenwood Col, BA, 67; Vanderbilt Univ, MS, 69; Wash Univ, St Louis, PhD(biol), 76. *Honors & Awards:* Res Career Develop Award, Pub Health Serv. *Prof Exp:* Instr biol, Harris Teachers Col, 69-72; res fel, Sch Med, Wash Univ, 77-79. *Mem:* Soc Develop Biol; Am Soc Cell Biol. *Res:* Regulatory role of hormones and ions in differentiation of embryonic intestine; development of intestinal transport systems. *Mailing Add:* Dept Zool NC State Univ Campus Box 7617 Raleigh NC 27695-7617. *Fax:* 919-515-2698; *E-Mail:* betty_black@ncsu.edu

BLACK, BILLY C, II, BIOCHEMISTRY, ANALYTICAL CHEMISTRY. *Current Pos:* PROF CHEM, ALBANY STATE COL, 64-, CHMN DEPT, 61- *Personal Data:* b Beatrice, Ala, Feb 1, 37; m 61; c 1. *Educ:* Tuskegee Inst, BS, 60; Iowa State Univ, MS, 62, PhD(biochem), 64. *Prof Exp:* Res asst biochem, Iowa State Univ, 60-64. *Mem:* Am Chem Soc; Am Oil Chem Soc; Int Food Technologists; Am Inst Chemists. *Res:* Fatty acid metabolism; molecular dynamics; glyceride structure. *Mailing Add:* Pres/Chancellor Albany State Col 504 College Dr Albany GA 31705-2717

BLACK, CHARLES ALLEN, SOIL FERTILITY, SOIL CHEMISTRY. *Current Pos:* instr soils, Iowa State Univ, 39-42, res assoc, 43-44, from res asst prof to res assoc prof, 44-49, prof, 49-67, distinguished prof, 67-79, adj prof, 79-85, EMER PROF SOILS, IOWA STATE UNIV, 85- *Personal Data:* b Lone Tree, Iowa, Jan 22, 16; m 39, Marjorie Anderson; c Carol A, Richard A & Marilyn J. *Educ:* Colo State Univ, BS, 37; Iowa State Univ, MS, 38, PhD(soil fertil), 42. *Honors & Awards:* Soil Sci Award, Am Soc Agron, 57, Agron Serv Award, 86; Bouyoucos Soil Sci Distinguished Career Award, Soil Sci Soc Am, 81; Distinguished Serv Award, Am Agr Ed Asn, 79; Henry A Wallace Award, Iowa State Univ, 80; Nat Award Agr Excellence, Nat Agr-Mkt Asn, 83; Charles A Black Award, Coun Agr Sci & Technol, 86; Agron Serv Award, Am Soc Agron, 86; Award Excellence, Am Coun Sci & Health, 93. *Prof Exp:* Asst land classifier, Resettlement Admin, 37; jr soil surveyor, Soil Conserv Serv, USDA, 38. *Concurrent Pos:* Vis prof, Cornell Univ, 55-56; Kearney Found lectr, Univ Calif, 60; NSF fel, 64-65; consult, USDA, 64; chmn bd dirs, Coun Agr Sci & Technol, 72, pres, 73, exec vpres, 74-85, exec chmn bd dirs, 85-88. *Mem:* Fel AAAS; fel Am Soc Agron (pres, 70-71); fel Soil Sci Soc Am (pres, 62); fel Am Inst Chemists; Int Soc Soil Sci; Am Soc Agr Engrs. *Res:* Soil phosphorus and soil-plant relationships; selection by sequential elimination based on concordant judgments. *Mailing Add:* Dept Agron Iowa State Univ Ames IA 50011. *Fax:* 515-294-1544

BLACK, CLANTON CANDLER, JR, BIOCHEMISTRY. *Current Pos:* from assoc prof to prof biochem, 67-74, prof bot & head dept, 74-77, prof biochem, 77, RES PROF, BIOCHEM, UNIV GA, 82- *Personal Data:* b Tampa, Fla, Nov 27, 31; m 52, Betty Dantzler; c 3. *Educ:* Univ Fla, BSA, 53, MSA, 57, PhD(agron), 60. *Honors & Awards:* Merit Award, Bot Soc Am. *Prof Exp:* NIH fel biochem, Cornell Univ, 60-62; fel, Kettering Res Lab, 62-63, staff scientist, 63-67; asst prof biol, Antioch Col, 63-67. *Mem:* Am Soc Biol Chemists; Am Soc Plant Physiologists (pres-elect, 77-78, pres, 78-79); fel AAAS. *Res:* Photosynthesis; enzymology; electron transport; pyrophosphate & sucrose metabolism. *Mailing Add:* Dept Biochem & Molecular Biol Univ Ga Athens GA 30602. *Fax:* 706-542-1786; *E-Mail:* ccblack@uga.cc.uga.edu

BLACK, CRAIG C, VERTEBRATE PALEONTOLOGY. *Current Pos:* RETIRED. *Personal Data:* b Peking, China, May 28, 32; US citizen; m 54, 67; c 2. *Educ:* Amherst Col, AB, 54, MA, 57; Harvard Univ, PhD(biol), 62. *Prof Exp:* Assoc cur vert paleont, Carnegie Mus, 60-63, cur, 63-70; assoc prof ecol & systs, Mus Natural Hist, Univ Kans, 70-72; dir mus & prof geosci, Tex Tech Univ, 72-75; dir, Carnegie Mus Natural Hist, 75-82; dir, Co Mus Natural Hist, Los Angeles, 82-94. *Concurrent Pos:* Mem, Mus Panel, Nat Endowment Arts, 74-77; mem, Nat Sci Bd, 85-90. *Mem:* Soc Vert Paleont (pres, 70-71); fel Geol Soc Am; Soc Study Evolution; fel Linnean Soc London; fel AAAS. *Res:* Tertiary mammals; paleoecology and biogeography; rodent evolution. *Mailing Add:* 8 Applewood Lane NW Ranchos de Albuquerque NM 87107-6404

BLACK, CRAIG PATRICK, ANIMAL PHYSIOLOGY, ANIMAL ECOLOGY. *Current Pos:* Lectr, Dept Biol Sci, 74-75, NIH FEL, DEPT PHYSIOL, SCH MED, DARTMOUTH COL, 75- *Personal Data:* b Greeley, Colo, Apr 25, 46; m 69. *Educ:* Tufts Univ, BS, 68; Dartmouth Col, PhD(biol), 75. *Concurrent Pos:* Vis asst prof, Dept Biol Sci, Dartmouth Col, 75-76. *Mem:* Ecol Soc Am; Cooper Ornith Soc; Am Ornithologists Union; Sigma Xi. *Res:* Avian energetics; avian respiration physiology; high altitude physiology. *Mailing Add:* Dept Biol Univ Toledo 2801 W Bancroft Toledo OH 43606-3390

BLACK, CURTIS DOERSAM, NUTRITION, CLINICAL PHARMACY. *Current Pos:* from asst prof to assoc prof, 78-90, assoc dept head, 86-90, MERCK PROF CLIN PHARM, PURDUE UNIV, 90-, ASST DEAN ACAD AFFAIRS, 92- *Personal Data:* b Toledo, Ohio, Mar 23, 51; m 74, Marilyn Couch; c Andrew. *Educ:* Univ Toledo, BSPharm, 74; Purdue Univ, MS, 76, PhD(clin pharm & pharmaceuts), 78. *Prof Exp:* Asst prof, Purdue Univ, 78-84, assoc prof clin pharm, 84-90, assoc dept head, 86-90. *Concurrent Pos:* Consult, Prof Educ Bur, Searle Labs, 83-90, Clin Nutrit, Travenol Labs, 84-85; site eval team, Am Coun Pharm Ed, 88-, NIU, 88- *Mem:* Sigma Xi; Am Asn Col Pharm; Am Soc Parenteral & Enteral Nutrit; Am Col Clin Pharm. *Res:* Pharmaceutical considerations for intravenous drug and nutrient delivery; beneficial health outcomes from clinical pharmacy services 658 quality of life enhancements in cancer patients. *Mailing Add:* Dept Pharm Pract Univ Toledo Toledo OH 43606. *Fax:* 419-530-7770; *E-Mail:* cdblack@utnet.utoledo.edu

BLACK, DAVID CHARLES, THEORETICAL ASTROPHYSICS, METEORITICS. *Current Pos:* DIR, LUNAR & PLANETARY INST, 88- *Personal Data:* b Waterloo, Iowa, May 14, 43; m 67. *Educ:* Univ Minn, BS, 65, MS, 67, PhD(physics), 70. *Prof Exp:* Nat Acad Sci fel, 70-72; res scientist theoret astrophys, NASA Ames Res Ctr, 72-85, chief scientist Space Sta, 85-88. *Mem:* AAAS; NY Acad Sci. *Res:* Theoretical studies of the formation and evolution of stars and planetary systems; interpretation of rare gas isotopic data from meteorites and lunar samples. *Mailing Add:* 3600 Bay Area Blvd Houston TX 77058

BLACK, DEAN, HEALTH, FAMILY RELATIONS. *Current Pos:* DIR RES, PARKER COL CHIROPRACTIC, DALLAS, TEX, 96- *Personal Data:* b Salt Lake City, Utah, May 6, 42; m 65, Claudia Porter; c Laurie, David, Melissa, Adam, Kimberli, Christopher, Jennifer, Triana & Michael. *Educ:* Brigham Young Univ, BA, 66, MS, 69; Pa State Univ, PhD(human develop), 71. *Prof Exp:* Asst prof sociol, Univ Southern Calif, 71-74; assoc prof, Brigham Young Univ, 74-79; pres, Sunrider Naturalfife Corp, 79-84; sr mkt specialists, Comput Resources & Info Corp, 84-85; pres, Biores Found, Tapestry Press, 85-92. *Concurrent Pos:* Consult, Action, Washington, DC, 72 & 73, US State Dept, USAID, 77; independent author & lectr, 92- *Mem:* Sigma Xi. *Res:* Scientific, philosophical and political relationships between conventional medicine and natural healing therapies; influence of social and psychological factors on health; physiological correlates of various coping styles and their manifestation in physical, mental and emotional parameters; mathematical approaches to recognizing subtle patterns in complex data sets. *Mailing Add:* 618 Highland Meadows Dr Highland Village TX 75067. *Fax:* 972-317-2844; *E-Mail:* 104325.651@compuserve.com

BLACK, DONALD K, ORGANIC CHEMISTRY. *Current Pos:* RES CHEMIST, RES CTR, HERCULES, INC, 68- *Personal Data:* b Ely, Eng, Feb 23, 36. *Educ:* Univ London, BSc, 60, PhD(org chem), 63. *Prof Exp:* Res chemist, Middlesex Hosp Med Sch, London, 64-66; Nat Acad Sci resident res assoc org chem, Naval Stores Res Sta, USDA, 66-68. *Mem:* The Chem Soc. *Res:* Diterpene, resin acid and pesticide chemistry. *Mailing Add:* 215 N Star Rd Newark DE 19711

BLACK, DONALD LEIGHTON, ANIMAL PHYSIOLOGY. *Current Pos:* Assoc prof animal physiol, 59-68, PROF VET & ANIMAL SCI, UNIV MASS, AMHERST, 68- *Personal Data:* b Portland, Maine, Aug 3, 28; m 50; c 3. *Educ:* Univ Maine, BS, 54; Cornell Univ, MS, 57, PhD(animal physiol), 59. *Res:* Oviduct physiology; physiology of ovarian function. *Mailing Add:* Paige Lab Dept Animal Sci Univ Mass Amherst MA 01003-0088

BLACK, FRANCIS LEE, VIROLOGY, IMMUNITY. *Current Pos:* res assoc & lectr epidemiol, Yale Univ, 55-61, from asst prof to prof, 61-96, EMER PROF EPIDEMIOL, SCH MED, YALE UNIV, 96- *Personal Data:* b Taipei, Formosa, Jan 2, 26; Can citizen; m 52, Joyce Avison; c Mela J (Matthews), Douglas & Peter. *Educ:* Univ BC, BA, 47, MA, 49; Univ Calif, PhD(biochem), 52. *Prof Exp:* Fel virus chem, Rockefeller Found, 52-54; chemist viruses, Lab Hyg, Dept Nat Health & Welfare, Can, 54-55. *Concurrent Pos:* Consult, Maiden Biotec. *Mem:* Am Asn Phys Anthropologists; Am Soc Trop Med & Hyg; Am Epidemiol Soc; Sigma Xi. *Res:* Chemistry and functions of viruses; measles virus; infectious disease patterns in isolated populations; South American Indians; population genetics. *Mailing Add:* 109 Mill Plain Rd Branford CT 06405

BLACK, FRANKLIN OWEN, OTOLARYNGOLOGY. *Current Pos:* CHIEF DIV NEUROTOLOGY, GOOD SAMARITAN HOSP. *Personal Data:* b St Louis, Mo, Aug 8, 37. *Educ:* Southeast Mo State Univ, BA, 59; Univ Mo-Columbia, MD, 63. *Prof Exp:* Intern, Mobile Gen Hosp, 63-64; resident gen surg, Bataan Mem Hosp & Lovelace Found, 64-65 & otolaryngol, Med Ctr, Univ Colo, 65-68, instr, 68-69, assoc prof surg, 69-71 & Col Med, Univ Fla, 71-74; assoc prof & dir, div vestibular dis, Eye & Ear Hosp, Pittsburgh, 74-, vchmn otolaryngol, 76- *Concurrent Pos:* NIH spec res fel, Univ Colo, 68-69; attend physician otolaryngol, Denver Vet Admin Hosp & Denver Gen Hosp, 68-69; NIH res career develop award, Univ Fla, 72-74; pres, Pittsburgh Neurosci Soc, 77-78 & Asn for Res Otolaryngol, 78-79; chmn, Comt for Res, Am Acad Otolaryngol, 78-83; ad hoc reviewer, NIH & Am Inst Biol Sci. *Mem:* Asn for Res Otolaryngol; Am Inst Biol Sci; Am Col Surgeons; Am Acad Otolaryngol; Am Bd Otolaryngol; Sigma Xi. *Res:* Objective clinical vestibular examination methods; computerized posturography; control characteristics of human postural sway trajectories; clinical vestibulo-occular responses to rotational acceleration. *Mailing Add:* Good Samaritan Hosp Med Ctr 1040 NW 22nd Ave No 10 Portland OR 97210-3057

BLACK, HOMER SELTON, CANCER. *Current Pos:* res asst prof dermat, Baylor Col Med, 68-74, adj asst prof biochem, 69-74, assoc res prof, 74-80, PROF DERMAT, BAYLOR COL MED, 80- *Personal Data:* b Port Arthur, Tex, Sept 9, 35; m 68, Dianne Darre; c Heather & Derek. *Educ:* Agr & Mech Col Tex, BS, 56; Sam Houston State Teachers Col, MEd, 60; La State Univ, PhD(bot), 64; Univ Houston, MSA, 77. *Prof Exp:* Res chemist, Seed Protein Pioneering Res Lab, Southern Utilization Res & Develop Div, USDA, 64-65; res fel biochem, Univ Tex-M D Anderson Hosp & Tumor Inst, 65-66; asst prof biol, Sam Houston State Univ, 66-68; physiologist, Vet Admin Hosp, Houston, Tex, 68-76. *Concurrent Pos:* Nat Acad Sci-Nat Res Coun res assoc, 64-; dir, Photobiol Lab, Vet Admin Hosp, Houston, Tex, 76-; res career scientist, Vet Affairs, 82- *Mem:* Am Oil Chemists Soc; Am Soc Photobiol; Europ Soc Photobiol; Am Asn Cancer Res; Inst Prof Mgrs. *Res:* Photobiology; photo-carcinogenesis; lipid metabolism of skin; chemical carcinogenesis. *Mailing Add:* Vet Affairs Med Ctr 2002 Holcombe Blvd Houston TX 77030. *Fax:* 713-794-7638

BLACK, HOWARD CHARLES, ORGANIC CHEMISTRY. *Current Pos:* RETIRED. *Personal Data:* b Warsaw, Ind, Sept 20, 12; m 38, Mary E Fine. *Educ:* DePauw Univ, AB, 34; Univ Ill, AM, 36, PhD(biochem), 38. *Prof Exp:* Res chemist, Swift & Co, 37-41, in chg fat & oil res div, Res Labs, 41-50, asst dir res, 50-54, assoc dir, 54-63, dir, 63-70, gen mgr sci res, 70-73. *Mem:* Am Chem Soc; Am Oil Chem Soc (pres, 57). *Res:* Amino acid metabolism; fats and oils; autoxidation; antioxidants; emulsifying agents; industrial oils; fatty acids; drying oils; oil seed extraction; solvent extraction of oils; soaps and detergents; adhesives; proteins; plastics. *Mailing Add:* 12 Concordia Dr Bella Vista AR 72714-2401

BLACK, HUGH ELIAS, VETERINARY PATHOLOGY. *Current Pos:* PRES, HUGH E BLACK ASSOC, 94- *Personal Data:* b Mindemoya, Ont, Oct 30, 38; m 61; c 3. *Educ:* Ont Vet Col, DVM, 63; Ohio State Univ, MSc, 69, PhD(vet path), 72. *Prof Exp:* Pvt pract vet med, Wellesley Vet Clin, Wellesley, Ont, 63-67; path resident vet path, Ohio State Univ, 67-72; res pathologist, Procter & Gamble Co, 72-78; mem staff, Toxicol Lab, Warner-Lambert, 78-79; dir, Path Lab, Schering Corp, 79-89, vpres drug safety & metab, 89-94. *Concurrent Pos:* Adj asst prof path, Dept Vet Pathobiol, Ohio State Univ, 74- *Mem:* Am Col Vet Pathologists; Int Acad Path; Am Vet Med Asn; Can Vet Med Asn. *Res:* Parathyroid gland ultrastructure and secretory activity; calcium homeostatic mechanisms; pathophysiology of skeletal disease; toxicologic pathology. *Mailing Add:* 270 Sparta Ave Suite 205 Sparta NJ 07871

BLACK, IRA B, NEUROLOGY. *Current Pos:* PROF & CHMN NEUROL, ROBERT WOOD JOHNSON MED SCH. *Mailing Add:* Univ Med & Dent Robert Wood Johnson Med Sch Clin Acad Bldg 125 Patterson St Piscataway NJ 08901

BLACK, JAMES W(HYTE), PHARMACOLOGY. *Current Pos:* PROF ANAL PHARMACOL, SCH MED, RAYNE INST, KINGS COL, 84-; CHANCELLOR, UNIV DUNDEE, 92- *Personal Data:* b June 14, 24. *Educ:* Univ St Andrews, MB & Chb. *Hon Degrees:* Dr, Univ Edinburgh, 89; DSc, Univ Glasgow, 89. *Honors & Awards:* Nobel Prize Med, 88; Mullard Award, Royal Soc, 78. *Prof Exp:* Prof chmn, Dept Pharmacol, Univ Col, London, 73-77; dir therapeut res, Wellcome Res Labs, 78-84. *Concurrent Pos:* Asst lectr physiol, Univ St Andrews, 46; lectr, Univ Malaya, 47-50; sr lectr, Univ Glasgow Vet Sch, 50-58, ICI Pharmaceut Ltd, 58-64; head biol res, Dept Res Dir, Smith Kline & French, Welwyn Garden City, 64-73. *Mem:* Nat Acad Sci; fel Royal Col Physicians; Royal Col Vet Surgeons; Royal Soc. *Mailing Add:* Univ Purdee Dundee DD1 4HN Scotland

BLACK, JEFFREY HOWARD, herpetology, ecology; deceased, see previous edition for last biography

BLACK, JESSIE KATE, developmental biology, for more information see previous edition

BLACK, JOE BERNARD, INVERTEBRATE ZOOLOGY. *Current Pos:* PROF BIOL & CHMN DEPT, LA COL, 74- *Personal Data:* b Noxapater, Miss, Nov 1, 33; m 55; c 1. *Educ:* Miss Col, BS, 55; Tulane Univ, MS, 57, PhD(zool), 63. *Prof Exp:* Asst prof biol, La Col, 57-60; assoc prof, Miss Col, 62-64; from assoc prof to prof, McNeese State Univ, 64-74. *Mem:* Am Soc Zool; Int Soc Astacology; Am Sci Affil; Sigma Xi. *Res:* Development, taxonomy, ecology and genetics of crawfishes. *Mailing Add:* Dept Biol La Col Col Sta Pineville LA 71360

BLACK, JOHN ALEXANDER, BIOCHEMISTRY. *Current Pos:* RETIRED. *Personal Data:* b Kettle, Scotland, June 15, 40. *Educ:* Glasgow Univ, BSc, 61, PhD(biochem), 64. *Prof Exp:* Res assoc biochem, Univ BC, 64-67; from asst prof to prof biochem & med genetics, Ore Health Sci Univ, 66-85. *Res:* Structural, functional and genetic relationships of proteins. *Mailing Add:* 10815 SW 57th Ave Portland OR 97219

BLACK, JOHN B, ENDOCRINOLOGY, ANATOMY. *Current Pos:* VPRES ACAD AFFAIRS, E GA COL, SWAINSBORO, GA, 95- *Personal Data:* b Ann Arbor, Mich, Apr 11, 39; m 65; c 1. *Educ:* Mercer Univ, AB, 61; Med Col Ga, PhD(endocrinol), 69. *Prof Exp:* From asst prof to prof biol, Augusta Col, 68-69. *Concurrent Pos:* Consult, Augusta Lab Hormone Assays; actg chmn dept, Augusta Col, 75-77. *Mem:* Am Fertil & Steril Soc; Am Soc Andrology; Int Fedn Fertil Soc; Am Asn Tissue Banks Sperm Coun; Sigma Xi. *Res:* Reproductive endocrine physiology; effect of androgens on hypothalamic-hypophyseal-ovarian axis; separation and storage of sperm fractions. *Mailing Add:* Acad Affairs Off E Georgia Col 131 Col Circle Swainsboro GA 30401

BLACK, JOHN DAVID, vertebrate zoology, for more information see previous edition

BLACK, JOHN HARRY, ASTRONOMY. *Current Pos:* PROF RADIO ASTRO ONSALA SPACE OBSERV, CHALMERS UNIV TECHNOL, 96- *Personal Data:* b Indianapolis, Ind, May 7, 49; m 77. *Educ:* Harvard Univ, BA, 71, AM, 73, PhD(astron), 75. *Honors & Awards:* Robert Trumpler Award, Astron Soc Pac, 77. *Prof Exp:* Asst prof astron, Univ Minn, 75-78; res assoc astron & aeronomy, Harvard Col Observ, 78-83; assoc prof astron & assoc astronr, Steward Observ, Univ Ariz, 83-89, prof & astronr, 89-96. *Concurrent Pos:* Lectr astron, Harvard Univ, 80-83. *Mem:* Am Astron Soc; Astron Soc Pac; Royal Astron Soc; Sigma Xi; Int Astron Union. *Res:* Theoretical studies of diffuse matter; ultraviolet space astronomy; atomic and molecular processes in a variety of astronomical contexts; spectroscopy; interacting galaxies. *Mailing Add:* Onsala Space Observ Chalmers Univ S-43992 Onsala Sweden

BLACK, KENNETH ELDON, WILDLIFE MANAGEMENT. *Current Pos:* RETIRED. *Personal Data:* b Adrian, Mo, Feb 2, 22; m 44, Marjorie J Underwood; c Gerald L & Mark C. *Educ:* Wash State Univ, BS, 49. *Prof Exp:* Regional supvr river basin studies, US Fish & Wildlife Serv, 63-71, dep assoc dir environ, Washington, DC, 71-74, assoc dir environ, 74, regional dir, Atlanta, Ga, 74-81. *Concurrent Pos:* Cong fel, Am Polit Sci Asn, 66-67. *Mem:* Wildlife Soc; Am Fisheries Soc. *Res:* Waterfowl population dynamics. *Mailing Add:* 5940 Hwy 2297 Panama City FL 32404

BLACK, KIRBY SAMUEL, surgical research, cell biology, for more information see previous edition

BLACK, LAUREN ELIZABETH, REGULATORY DECISION MAKING, DRUG DEVELOPMENT. *Current Pos:* pharmacologist, Ctr Drugs, 91-95, PHARMACOLOGIST, CTR BIOLOGICS, FOOD & DRUG ADMIN, 95- *Personal Data:* b Washington, DC, Sept 1, 60. *Educ:* Carnegie Mellon Univ, BS, 82; Va Commonwealth Univ, PhD(pharmacol & toxicol), 89. *Prof Exp:* Pharmacol tech, Walter Reed Army Inst Res, 82-84; postdoctoral fel, Nat Inst Neurol Dis & Stroke, NIH, 89-91. *Concurrent Pos:* Vis lectr, Med Ctr Va, 96, Hood Col, 96 & Georgetown Univ, 97. *Mem:* Soc Toxicol. *Res:* Drug development guidance on critical animal and in vitro studies; drugs; biotechnologic therapeutics as well as tissue-containing devices for human use. *Mailing Add:* HFM-579 Food & Drug Admin 1401 Rockville Pike Rockville MD 20852. *E-Mail:* black@a1.cber.fda.gov

BLACK, LINDSAY MACLEOD, PLANT VIRUS TUMORS, INSECT VECTORS. *Current Pos:* prof, Dept Bot, 52-73 & Dept Genetics & Develop, 73-75, EMER PROF PLANT VIROL, UNIV ILL, URBANA, 75- *Personal Data:* b Edinburgh, Scotland, Apr 20, 07; US citizen; m 36, Helen M Wilhelm; c Lindsay Wilhelm, Douglas R & Anne E (Mangel). *Educ:* Univ BC, Can, BSA, 29; Cornell Univ, PhD(plant path), 36. *Honors & Awards:* Wright lectr, Purdue Univ, 67; Ruth Allen Award, Am Phytopath Soc, 78. *Prof Exp:* Teaching asst plant path, Univ BC, 29-30; teaching asst, Cornell Univ, 30-34, res asst, 34-36; res fel biol, Nat Res Coun, 36-37; res asst plant virol, Rockefeller Inst Med Res, 37-41, res assoc, 41-46; res cur, Brooklyn Bot Garden, 46-52. *Concurrent Pos:* Prin investr res grants, Am Cancer Soc, NIH & NSF, 47-75; mem growth comt, morphogenesis panel, Nat Res Coun, 50-52; ed, Virol, 55; mem etiology comt, Am Cancer Soc, 60-64; spec NIH fel, Markham's Virus Res Unit, Cambridge, Eng, 61-62; vis prof plant path, Univ Calif, Berkeley, 66-67. *Mem:* AAAS; Am Phytopath Soc. *Res:* Insect transmission of plant viruses; multiplication of plant viruses in insect vectors;

vector cell monolayer cultures; immunofluorescent assay of infections; loss of transmissibility by deletion mutations in viruses; virus-double stranded RNA; plant phloem Rickettsias; associated evolution of vector and virus; overwintering of virus in vector; genetic variation in vector's ability to transmit virus; infection of vector organs; discovered wound tumor virus of plants; NY and NJ potato yellow dwarf viruses; early micrographs of Rhabdo-, Bunya-, and Reo-viruses; lipid in a plant virus. *Mailing Add:* 550 Stratford Lane Ridge NY 11961-2038

BLACK, LOWELL LYNN, PLANT PATHOLOGY. *Current Pos:* PLANT PATHOLOGIST, ASIAN VEGETABLE RES & DEVELOP CTR, 93- *Personal Data:* b Norman, Ark, Oct 9, 38; m 60, Deanna Carner; c Todd A, Ryan M & Kevin A. *Educ:* Univ Ark, BS, 60, MS, 62; Univ Wis, PhD(plant path), 65. *Prof Exp:* Asst prof plant path, WVa Univ, 65-68; from asst prof to assoc prof, La State Univ, 68-76, prof plant path, 76-95. *Mem:* Am Phytopath Soc; Sigma Xi. *Res:* Host plant resistance; diseases of vegetables, fungal diseases. *Mailing Add:* AVRDC PO Box 42 Shahua Tainan 741 Taiwan

BLACK, MARK MORRIS, NEURONAL CYTOSKELETON, DEVELOPMENTAL NEUROSCIENCE. *Current Pos:* Asst prof, 80-86, ASSOC PROF NEUROANAT, TEMPLE UNIV, 86- *Personal Data:* m; c 1. *Educ:* Case Western Reserve Univ, PhD(anat), 78. *Mailing Add:* Dept Anat Temple Univ Med Sch 3420 N Broad St Philadelphia PA 19140-5104

BLACK, MARTIN, MEDICINE, PHARMACOLOGY. *Current Pos:* PROF HEPATOLOGY & PHARMACOL, MED SCH, TEMPLE UNIV, 73- *Personal Data:* b Dec, 37; m 74, Hester Holly Sonder; c Jocelyn & Maxwell. *Educ:* MB, BS, 61; FRCP, 80, FRCP (Edinburgh), 82. *Concurrent Pos:* Assoc Ed, Annals Internal Med, 78- *Mem:* Am Asn Study Liver Dis; Am Genetic Asn; Am Fed Clin Res; Am Soc Pharmacol & Exp Therapeut; Int Asn Study Liver Dis; fel Royal Col Physicians. *Res:* Mechanisms involved in aceteuchopheu hepetoxicity; cytodrome paso in health and disease; viral hepatitis; liver transplantation; cirrhosis. *Mailing Add:* Dept Med & Pharmacol Med Sch Temple Univ 3420 N Broad St Philadelphia PA 19140-5104. *Fax:* 215-707-2864

BLACK, PAUL H, MEDICINE, VIROLOGY. *Current Pos:* PROF MICROBIOL & MED, RES PROF SURG & CHMN, DEPT MICROBIOL, SCH MED, BOSTON UNIV, 79- *Personal Data:* b Boston, Mass, Mar 11, 30; m 62, Sandra Merkin; c Scott, Marc & Jeffrey. *Educ:* Dartmouth Col, AB, 52; Columbia Univ, MD, 56. *Prof Exp:* Intern med, Mass Gen Hosp, 56-57, asst resident, 57-58, clin & res fel, 58-60, resident, 60-61; sr surgeon, NIH, 61-67, consult, Nat Inst Allergy & Infectious Dis, 64-67; from asst prof to assoc prof med, Harvard Med Sch, 67-79. *Concurrent Pos:* Asst physician, Mass Gen Hosp, 67-70, assoc physician, 70-79, hon physician, 79- *Mem:* Am Soc Clin Invest; NY Acad Sci; Am Asn Microbiol; AMA; fel AAAS. *Res:* Oncogenic viruses and the mechanisms by which these viruses induce malignancy; cell surface changes in malignant cells; cell surface shedding; psychoneuroimmunology (effect of the mind on the immune system); immunology; infectious diseases. *Mailing Add:* 21 Dawes Rd Lexington MA 02173

BLACK, PERRY, NEUROSURGERY, NEUROPHYSIOLOGY. *Current Pos:* PROF & CHMN DEPT NEUROSURG, HAHNEMANN MED COL PHILADELPHIA, 80- *Personal Data:* b Montreal, Que, Oct 2, 30; m 63; c 3. *Educ:* McGill Univ, BSc, 51, MD, CM, 56; Am Bd Neurol Surg, dipl, 66. *Prof Exp:* Intern & asst resident med & gen surg, Jewish Gen Hosp, Montreal, 56-58; asst resident neurol, Montreal Neurol Inst, 58-59; resident neurosurg, Johns Hopkins Hosp, 59-63, from instr to asst prof, Sch Med, 64-69, asst prof psychiat, 67-70, assoc prof neurosurg, Sch Med, Johns Hopkins Univ, 69-80, assoc prof psychiat, 70-80, neurosurgeon, 64-80. *Concurrent Pos:* NIH fel physiol, Johns Hopkins Univ, 61-62; dir lab neurol sci, Friends Med Sci Res Ctr, Baltimore, Md, 64-; vis neurosurgeon, Baltimore City Hosps, 65-; neurosurg consult, NCharles Gen Hosp, Baltimore, 75-, & Good Samaritan Hosp, 70-; mem neurol A study sect, NIH, 73-77; assoc ed, Neurosurg, J Cong Neurol Surgeons, 76-; neurosurg rep, Johns Hopkins Med Sch Coun, 77-79, chmn tenure policy comt, 77-78, vchmn coun, 78-79, mem adv bd med fac, Sch Med, 78-79; chmn int comt, Cong Neurol Surgeons, 75-79. *Mem:* Int Asn Study Pain; coordr, Epilepsy Found Am, 73- Mem: Cong Neurol Surg; Am Asn Neurol Surg; Soc Neurosci; Am Neurol Asn. *Res:* Neurosurgery, particularly primate model of spinal cord injury; experimental study of recovery of motor function; clinical and experimental epilepsy. *Mailing Add:* Allegheny Univ Health Sci Hahnemannu Med Sch Broad & Vine St Philadelphia PA 19102

BLACK, PETER ELLIOTT, WATERSHED MANAGEMENT, ENVIRONMENTAL IMPACT ANALYSIS. *Current Pos:* PROF WATER & RELATED LAND RESOURCES, COL ENVIRON SCI & FORESTRY, STATE UNIV NY, 65- *Personal Data:* b New York, NY, Nov 19, 34; m 56, 87; c Steven K, Andrew G, Douglas M & Brian E. *Educ:* Univ Mich, BS, 56, MF, 58; Colo State Univ, PhD(watershed mgt), 61. *Honors & Awards:* President's Award Outstanding Serv, Am Water Resources Asn, 88. *Prof Exp:* Res forester, Coweeta Hydrol Lab, Southeastern Forest & Range Exp Sta, US Forest Serv, 56-59; asst, Coop Watershed Mgt Unit, Colo State Univ, 59-60; asst prof forestry & watershed mgt, Humboldt State Col, 61-65. *Concurrent Pos:* Watershed mgt consult, Nat Park Serv, Washington, DC, 63-64; prin, Impact Consults, Syracuse, 74-86; vis prof, dept geog, Univ Colo, 85-86. *Mem:* Am Geophys Union; Soil Conserv Soc Am; Nat Asn Environ Professionals; Am Water Resources Asn. *Res:* Forest influences; wildland hydrology; water law; environmental impact analysis; conservation policy. *Mailing Add:* Col Environ Sci & Forestry State Univ NY Syracuse NY 13210. *Fax:* 315-470-6956; *E-Mail:* peblack@syr.edu

BLACK, RICHARD H, APPLIED MATHEMATICS. *Current Pos:* ASSOC PROF MATH, CLEVELAND STATE UNIV, 68- *Personal Data:* b Deerfield, Wis, Apr 24, 25. *Educ:* Univ Wis, BS, 47, MS, 51, PhD(appl math), 63. *Prof Exp:* Instr math, Univ Wis-Milwaukee, 56-63, asst prof math & dir, Comput Ctr, 63-68. *Mem:* Asn Comput Mach; Am Math Soc. *Res:* Pattern recognition; computer science. *Mailing Add:* 11800 Edgewater Cleveland OH 44107

BLACK, ROBERT CORL, BOTANY, PLANT PHYSIOLOGY. *Current Pos:* ASSOC PROF BIOL, PA STATE UNIV, DELAWARE CO CAMPUS, 70- *Personal Data:* b Philadelphia, Pa, June 16, 41; m 63, Arlene M Bruno; c Keith. *Educ:* Pa State Univ, BS, 63, MS, 65, PhD(bot), 70. *Prof Exp:* Food technologist, Gen Foods Corp, 65-67. *Mem:* AAAS; Am Soc Plant Physiologists; Int Soc Plant Molecular Biol. *Res:* plant growth and development; biochemistry and physiology of auxin and cytokinin; plant tumorigenesis. *Mailing Add:* Dept Biol Pa State Univ Delaware County Campus Media PA 19063. *E-Mail:* rcb4@psuvm.edu.psu

BLACK, ROBERT EARL LEE, EMBRYOLOGY. *Current Pos:* RETIRED. *Personal Data:* b Cassville, Mo, Nov 20, 28; m 53; c 3. *Educ:* William Jewell Col, BA, 51; Univ Wash, PhD(zool), 57. *Prof Exp:* USPHS fel, Calif Inst Technol, 57-59; from assoc prof to prof biol, Col William & Mary, 59-93, prof marine sci, 65-93. *Mem:* AAAS; Am Soc Zool. *Res:* Embryology of marine invertebrates. *Mailing Add:* 120 Chapel Hill Lane Williamsburg VA 23188

BLACK, ROBERT L, PEDIATRICS. *Current Pos:* Instr pediat, Stanford Univ, 61-62, from asst clin prof to assoc clin prof, 62-75, CLIN PROF PEDIAT, STANFORD UNIV, 75-; PVT PRACT PEDIAT, 62- *Personal Data:* b Los Angeles, Calif, Aug 25, 30; m 53, Jean McGuire; c Donald J, Douglas & Margaret S. *Educ:* Stanford Univ, BA, 52, MD, 55. *Concurrent Pos:* Residency pediat, Stanford Univ, 58-62; mem, State Maternal, Child, Adolescent Health Bd, Calif & Inst Med, Nat Acad Sci, 83. *Mem:* Nat Acad Sci; Am Acad Pediat. *Res:* Health planning for children. *Mailing Add:* 920 Cass St Monterey CA 93940

BLACK, SAMUEL HAROLD, MEDICAL MICROBIOLOGY & MICROBIAL CYTOLOGY. *Current Pos:* head, Dept Med Microbiol & Immunol, Col Med, Tex A&M Univ, 75-91, asst dean curric & undergrad med educ, 85-87, intern dean med, 87-88, assoc dean acad affairs, 88-91, PROF MICROBIOL, DEPT MED MICROBIOL & IMMUNOL, COL MED, TEX A&M UNIV, 75- *Personal Data:* b Lebanon, Pa, May 1, 30; m 61, Elisabeth M Zandveld; c Vicki A & Alisa J. *Educ:* Lebanon Valley Col, BS, 52; Univ Mich, MS, 58, PhD(microbiol), 61. *Prof Exp:* NSF fel, Delft Technol Univ, 60-61; instr microbiol, Univ Mich, Ann Arbor, 61-62; from asst prof to assoc prof, Baylor Col Med, 62-71; from assoc prof to prof microbiol & pub health, Mich State Univ, 71-75. *Concurrent Pos:* Lectr, Univ Mich, Flint, 61-62 & Univ Houston, 64-66; guest prof, Swiss Fed Inst Technol, 69-70. *Mem:* Soc Gen Microbiol; Am Soc Microbiol; fel Am Acad Microbiol; Am Soc Cell Biol; Soc Invert Path; Electron Micros Soc Am; Sigma Xi. *Res:* Medical microbiology; microbial physiology; cytology of morphogenesis in prokaryotic and eukaryotic cells; biology of Bacillus species, of Hansenula species, and of Treponema pallidum. *Mailing Add:* Col Med Tex A&M Univ College Station TX 77843-1114. *Fax:* 409-845-3479; *E-Mail:* shblack@tamu.edu

BLACK, SIMON, BIOCHEMISTRY. *Current Pos:* chemist, NIH, 52-58, chief, Sect Biochem Amino Acids, 58-83, res chemsit, 83-87, VOL BIOCHEMIST, NIH, 87- *Personal Data:* b Deerfield, Wis, Aug 9, 17; m 44; c 3. *Educ:* Univ Wis, BS, 38, MS, 41, PhD(biochem), 42. *Prof Exp:* Asst pharmacol, Univ Chicago, 42-45, res assoc, 45-46, from instr to asst prof biochem, Dept Med, 46-51; fel, Mass Gen Hosp, 51-52. *Concurrent Pos:* Consult, Off Sci Res & Develop, 42-45; mem exec coun, Space Res Comt, Int Coun Sci Unions, 74-83; course dir, NSF, 79-80. *Mem:* AAAS; Am Soc Biol Chemists; Am Chem Soc. *Res:* Biochemistry of amino acids; enzymes of amino acid metabolism and activation; origin of life and the genetic code. *Mailing Add:* NIH Bldg 8 Bethesda MD 20892. *Fax:* 301-402-0240; *E-Mail:* simonb@bdg8.niddk.nih.gov

BLACK, SYDNEY D, ENGINEERING TECHNICAL TRAINING, PHYSICS & MATHEMATICS TRAINING. *Current Pos:* RETIRED. *Personal Data:* b Newcastle-on-Tyne, Eng, Aug 17, 15; US citizen; m 45, Harriet L Cohen; c Barbara E. *Educ:* Wash Univ, BS, 38; Ill Inst Technol, MS, 40; Univ Cincinnati, DSc(appl eng sci), 46. *Honors & Awards:* Distinguished Serv Award, Am Inst Aeronaut & Astronaut, 87. *Prof Exp:* Res assoc eng, Riverside Res Inst, 66-76; sr res engr, Grumman Data Systs, 77-78; assoc prof elec eng, US Merchant Marine Acad, 78-80; proj engr, Norden Systs, United Technol, 80-81; supvr, Digital Equip Corp, 81-83, prin engr, 83-87, consult comput mfg, 87-94. *Concurrent Pos:* Dir, Exp Physics Lab, USAF, assoc prof aero eng & chief propeller designer; consult aerophys, Goodyear Aircraft Co, 52-55; supvr, Small Aircraft Engines, Gen Elec, 55-60; sr specialist, Repub Aviation Corp, 60-62; dept head, Vehicle Eng, Gen Precision Inc, 62-65; pres, S Black & Assoc, 64-; adj assoc prof mech eng, Columbia Univ, Fairleigh Dickinson Univ & Stevens Inst Technol, 67-72; adj prof, City Col NY. *Mem:* Fel Sigma Xi; assoc fel Am Inst Aeronaut & Astronaut; sr mem Soc Mfg Engrs. *Res:* Systematic method of aircraft propeller design and stress analysis; theory of ferromagnetic fluids; supersonic aeroelasticity; exotic propulsion systems; laser weaponry development; structural dynamics. *Mailing Add:* 48 Bonaire Dr Toms River NJ 08757

BLACK, T EDWARD, ELECTRO-MECHANICAL DESIGN. *Current Pos:* CONSULT ELECTRO-MECH DESIGN ENGR, 83- *Personal Data:* b Dec 15, 32; div; c Karen N & Michael O. *Educ:* Ill Inst Technol, BSME, 62, BSEE, 71. *Honors & Awards:* Inventors Recognition Award, Abbott Labs, 89. *Prof Exp:* Mgr automation eng, TRW Cinch Inc, Ill, 80-81; mgr eng, Wico Corp, Ill, 81-83. *Mem:* Am Eng Asn. *Res:* Medical diagnostic equipment, ink-jet printing systems, automatic manufacturing tooling and special purpose machines. *Mailing Add:* 1127 Miller Lane Buffalo Grove IL 60089-4244

BLACK, TRUMAN D, SOLID STATE PHYSICS, OPTICS. *Current Pos:* from asst prof to assoc prof, 65-81, PROF PHYSICS, UNIV TEX, ARLINGTON, 82- *Personal Data:* b Houston, Tex, Sept 30, 37; m 57, Marjorie L Parker; c Elizabeth & Bryan. *Educ:* Univ Houston, BS, 59; Rice Univ, MA, 62, PhD(physics), 64. *Prof Exp:* Mem tech staff, Tex Instruments, 64-65. *Mem:* Am Phys Soc; Am Asn Physics Teachers; AAAS; Sigma Xi; Am Optical Soc. *Res:* Spin lattice interactions in paramagnetic solids; low temperature magnetic effects; laser optics; holography. *Mailing Add:* Univ Tex Physics Dept PO Box 19059 Arlington TX 76019-0059. *Fax:* 817-272-3637

BLACK, VIRGINIA H, CELL & MOLECULAR BIOLOGY. *Current Pos:* Instr anat, 67-68, from instr to asst prof, 68-73, ASSOC PROF CELL BIOL, SCH MED, NY UNIV, 73- *Personal Data:* b Detroit, Mich, Sept 24, 41; div; c 2. *Educ:* Kalamazoo Col, AB, 63; Sacramento State Col, MA, 66; Stanford Univ, PhD(anat), 68. *Concurrent Pos:* USPHS res grants, 69-87 & 90-, Am Cancer Soc res grants, 87-90; lectr, Univ Oporto, Port, 83. *Mem:* Endocrine Soc; Am Soc Cell Biologists; Am Asn Anat; NY Acad Sci; Soc Develop Biol; Sigma Xi. *Res:* Cytodifferentiation and functional modulation of steroid-secreting cells; regulation of cytochrome P450s in the adrenal cortex; role of peroxisomes in cholesterol metabolism; influence of hormones on adrenal and reproductive system development. *Mailing Add:* 110 Bleecker St New York NY 10012

BLACK, WALLACE GORDON, reproductive physiology; deceased, see previous edition for last biography

BLACK, WAYNE EDWARD, PUBLIC & ENVIRONMENTAL HEALTH, BIOCHEMISTRY. *Current Pos:* Chief radiol health res, 63-64, chief radiol health res & lab serv, 64-67, DIR LABS, ST LOUIS COUNTY HEALTH DEPT, 67- *Personal Data:* b East St Louis, Ill, Sept 15, 35; m 85, Carol Dupas. *Educ:* Ill Col, BS, 57; Univ St Louis, PhD, 64; Nat Registry Clin Chem, cert. *Concurrent Pos:* Lectr physiol chem, Wash Univ, 66-70, instr, Dept Physiol Chem, Sch Dent, 69-79; mem, Biohazard & Environ Safety Bd, St Louis Univ Med Ctr, 79 & Environ Hazard Response Team, St Louis Co, Mo, 79. *Mem:* Fel Am Inst Chemists; AAAS; Am Chem Soc; Health Physics Soc; Sigma Xi. *Res:* Laboratory work, including environmental health. *Mailing Add:* 12351 Matthews Lane St Louis MO 63127-1343

BLACK, WILLIAM BRUCE, ORGANIC CHEMISTRY, POLYMER CHEMISTRY. *Current Pos:* RETIRED. *Personal Data:* b Indianapolis, Ind, Feb 25, 23; m 45, Marie Christoffersen; c 2. *Educ:* Univ Va, BA, 50, MS, 53, PhD(org chem), 54. *Prof Exp:* Res chemist, Chemstrand Res Ctr, Monsanto Textiles Co, 54-61, group leader, 61-62, Chemstrand Co Div, Monsanto Co, 62-65, mgr polymer sci, 65-69, sr group leader, 69-80, sr fel, Monsanto Tech Ctr, 80-85. *Concurrent Pos:* Co-ed, High-Modulus Wholly Aromatic Fibers, 73, Stress Induced Crystallization Part II, 79. *Mem:* Am Chem Soc. *Res:* Synthesis, spinning and evaluation of novel polymers and fibers, especially very high modulus, very high strength aromatic fibers; the attainment of unusually high strength and high modulus fibers from conventional polymers; technical management. *Mailing Add:* 2300 N Whaley Ave Pensacola FL 32503-4972

BLACK, WILLIAM Z(ACHARY), MECHANICAL ENGINEERING. *Current Pos:* Asst prof, 67-70, assoc prof, 70-75, PROF MECH ENG, GA INST TECHNOL, 75- *Personal Data:* b Champaign, Ill, Oct 9, 40; m 62; c 2. *Educ:* Univ Ill, BS, 63, MS, 64; Purdue Univ, PhD(mech eng), 68. *Honors & Awards:* Recipient of Meriam, Am Soc Eng Educ, 86. *Mem:* Am Soc Mech Engrs; Am Soc Eng Educ; Inst Elec & Electronics Engrs; Sigma Xi; Am Soc Heating Refrig & Air Conditioning Engrs; Nat Soc Prof Engrs. *Res:* Heat transfer; fluid mechanics; thermodynamics. *Mailing Add:* Sch Mech Eng Ga Inst Technol Atlanta GA 30332-0001

BLACKADAR, ALFRED KIMBALL, METEOROLOGY. *Current Pos:* from asoc prof to prof, 56-85, head dept, 67-81, EMER PROF METEOROL PA STATE UNIV, 85- *Personal Data:* b Newburyport, Mass, July 6, 20; m 46, Beatrice Fenner; c Bruce E, Russell L & Thomas A. *Educ:* Princeton Univ, AB, 42; NY Univ, PhD(meteorol), 50. *Honors & Awards:* Charles F Brooks Award, Am Meteorol Soc, 69; Humboldt Found Sr Scientist Award, 73; Cleveland Abbe Award, Am Meteorol Soc, 86. *Prof Exp:* Res assoc prof meteorol, NY Univ, 46-56. *Concurrent Pos:* Ed, Meteorol Monogr, 61-65; mem, Nat Acad Sci-US Nat Comt Global Atmospheric Res Prog, 68-71; mem, NSF Adv Panel Atmospheric Sci, 68-71; mem comt basic sci adv to US Army, Nat Acad Sci-Nat Res Coun, 70-73, mem exec comt, Earth Sci Div. *Mem:* Fel AAAS; fel Am Meteorol Soc (secy, 65-69, pres, 71-72); fel Am Geophys Union; Deutsche Meteorol Gesellschaft. *Res:* Atmospheric energy transformation; atmospheric turbulence; atmospheric boundary layer modelling. *Mailing Add:* 805 W Foster Ave State College PA 16801. *Fax:* 814-865-3663

BLACKADAR, BRUCE EVAN, MATHEMATICS. *Current Pos:* ASST PROF MATH, UNIV NEV, RENO, 75- *Personal Data:* b Nyack, NY, Oct 22, 48. *Educ:* Princeton Univ, AB, 70; Univ Calif, Berkeley, MA, 74, PhD(math), 75. *Mem:* Am Math Soc. *Res:* Tensor products and crossed products of von Neumann algebras; induced representations of locally compact groups; representations of products and extensions of groups. *Mailing Add:* Dept Math Univ Nev Reno NV 89557-0001

BLACKADAR, ROBERT GORDON, GEOLOGY. *Current Pos:* RETIRED. *Personal Data:* b Ottawa, Ont, Mar 18, 28. *Educ:* Univ Toronto, BA, 50, MA, 51, PhD(geol), 54. *Prof Exp:* chief sci ed, Geol Surv Can, 70-79, geologist, 53-89, dir, Geol Info Div, 79-89. *Concurrent Pos:* Sci ed, Geol Surv Can, 65-70. *Mem:* Geol Soc Am; fel Arctic Inst NAm. *Res:* Precambrian geology of Arctic regions; geography and geology of the Arctic. *Mailing Add:* 65 Lock Isle Rd Nepean ON K2H 8G7 Can

BLACKARD, WILLIAM GRIFFITH, internal medicine, endocrinology; deceased, see previous edition for last biography

BLACKBURN, ARCHIE BARNARD, PSYCHIATRY. *Current Pos:* STAFF PSYCHIATRIST, VET ADMIN HOSP, HOUSTON, 73- *Personal Data:* b Austin, Tex, July 6, 38; m 67; c 2. *Educ:* Baylor Univ, BA, 60, MS & MD, 65; Am Bd Psychiat & Neurol, dipl psychiat, 74. *Prof Exp:* Resident psychiatrist, Vet Admin Hosp & Univ Tex Southwestern Med Sch Dallas, 69-70 & Vet Admin Hosp & Univ Okla, 70-72; asst prof, Health Sci Ctr, Univ Okla, 72-73; asst prof psychiat, Baylor Col Med, 73- *Concurrent Pos:* Staff psychiatrist & med dir, Drug Abuse Treatment Unit, Vet Admin Hosp, Oklahoma City, 72-73; med dir, Houston Vet Admin Therapeut Community Ward, 76-84; med staff, Mem SW Hosp, W Oaks Hosp & Belle Park Hosp, Houston, Tex, 83- *Mem:* AAAS; Am Psychiat Asn. *Res:* Clinical hypodynamics; biorhythms; methadone maintenance; application of research methodology in clinical disorders of sleep. *Mailing Add:* Vet Admin Hosp Day Treatment Ctr 2002 Holcombe Blvd Houston TX 77030

BLACKBURN, DALE WARREN, SYNTHETIC ORGANIC & NATURAL PRODUCTS CHEMISTRY, RADIOCHEMISTRY. *Current Pos:* CONSULT, SPECIALIZED CHEM TECHNOL 86- *Personal Data:* b La Porte, Ind, Sept 12, 26; m 78, Grace Adams; c Robert & Nancy (Rice). *Educ:* Purdue Univ, BS, 48, MS, 51, PhD(pharmaceut chem), 54. *Prof Exp:* Anal chemist, Whitehall Pharmacal Co, 50; instr pharmaceut chem, Purdue Univ, 51-52, asst prof, 54-56; group leader, Smith Kline Corp, 56-66, asst dir, Org Chem Sect, 66-78, assoc dir radiochem, 79-86. *Concurrent Pos:* Founder, Org Reactions Catalysis Soc, 65, Int Isotope Soc, 86; treas, Int Isotope Soc, 86- *Mem:* Am Chem Soc; Am Pharmaceut Asn; Health Physics Soc; Int Isotope Soc; Org Reaction Catalysis Soc. *Res:* Organic and radiochemical synthesis; catalysis and high pressure reactions; instrumental analysis; separation and purification; radiological defense. *Mailing Add:* 144 Ramblewood Rd Moorestown NJ 08057. *Fax:* 609-235-6801

BLACKBURN, DANIEL GLENN, REPRODUCTIVE BIOLOGY, FUNCTIONAL MORPHOLOGY. *Current Pos:* asst prof zool, histophysiol & evolution, 88-91, ASSOC PROF ZOOL, DEPT BIOL, TRINITY COL, HARTFORD, 91- *Personal Data:* b Pittsburgh, Pa, Aug 27, 52; m 85, Cora E Miller. *Educ:* Univ Pittsburgh, BSc, 75; Cornell Univ, MSc, 78, PhD(zool), 85. *Prof Exp:* Teaching asst biol, Cornell Univ, 75-85, lectr histophysiol, Dept Physiol, 85; teaching asst vet anat, NY State Col Vet Med, 81-84; res assoc, Cell Biol Dept, Vanderbilt Univ Sch Med, 86-88. *Mem:* Am Soc Zoologists; Herpetologists League; Soc Study Amphibians & Reptiles; Am Soc Ichthyologists & Herpetologists; Sigma Xi. *Res:* Placentation and fetal nutrition of reptiles and mammals; evolution of reproductive patterns, especially viviparity and lactation; functional morphology of skeletomuscular systems of reptiles and amphibians; sexual dimorphism of fish and amphibians. *Mailing Add:* 156 Pendleton Rd New Britain CT 06053. *Fax:* 860-297-2538

BLACKBURN, EDWARD VICTOR, ORGANIC CHEMISTRY. *Current Pos:* Fel, 69-70, lectr, 70-72, assoc prof chem, 72-78, PROF CHEM & ASSOC DEAN, FAC ST JEAN, UNIV ALTA, 83- *Personal Data:* b Skegness, Eng, Sept 18, 44; m 73; c 3. *Educ:* Univ London, BSc, 66; Univ Nottingham, PhD(org chem), 69. *Mem:* The Chem Soc; assoc Royal Inst Chem; Am Chem Soc; Chem Inst Can. *Res:* Photochemistry of olefins with particular reference to stilbene analogues; polar effects in radical reactions; computer assisted and computer based instructional techniques. *Mailing Add:* Dept Chem Fac St Jean 8406 91st St Edmonton AB T6C 4G9 Can

BLACKBURN, ELIZABETH HELEN, MOLECULAR BIOLOGY, BIOCHEMISTRY. *Current Pos:* fel biochem, 77-78, PROF MOLECULAR BIOL, UNIV CALIF, SAN FRANCISCO, 90- *Personal Data:* b Hobart, Australia, Nov 26, 48; m 75; c 1. *Educ:* Univ Melbourne, BS, 70, MS, 71; Cambridge Univ, PhD(molecular biol), 75. *Honors & Awards:* Eli Lilly Award Microbiol, 88; Molecular Biol Award, Nat Acad Sci, 90. *Prof Exp:* Fel biol, Yale Univ, 75-77; from asst prof to assoc prof molecular biol, Univ Calif, Berkeley, 78-90. *Mem:* Nat Acad Sci; Am Soc Cell Biol. *Res:* Repetitive DNA sequences and chromosomal structure in eukaryotes; studies on structure and function synthesis of telomeres chromosome ends; ribonucleoprotein enzyme that synthesizes telomgres has been discovered and characterized. *Mailing Add:* Dept Microbiol Univ Calif San Francisco CA 94143

BLACKBURN, GARY RAY, BIOCHEMISTRY, ONCOLOGY. *Current Pos:* GENETIC TOXICOLOGIST, MOBIL OIL CORP, 81- *Personal Data:* b Shickshinny, Pa, May 13, 46; m 75. *Educ:* Wilkes Col, BS, 68; Univ Wis, PhD(oncol), 74. *Prof Exp:* Res assoc radiation biol, Colo State Univ, 74-77; res assoc oncol, Inst Cancer Res, Fox Chase Cancer Ctr, 77-81. *Concurrent Pos:* Nat Cancer Inst fel, Colo State Univ, 75-77. *Mem:* Sigma Xi; Am Asn Cancer Res; Soc Exp Biol & Med. *Res:* Biochemical mechanisms by which chemical carcinogens effect transformation of susceptible cells in target organs, with an emphasis on these agents' alteration of cell architecture and division. *Mailing Add:* Petrolabs Inc 133 Industrial Dr Warminster PA 18974

BLACKBURN, GEORGE L, NUTRITIONAL BIOCHEMISTRY, SURGERY. *Current Pos:* MEM, DEPT NUTRIT, CANCER RES INST, BOSTON, 75-; ASSOC PROF SURG, MED SCH, HARVARD UNIV, 76- *Personal Data:* b McPherson, Kans, Feb 12, 36. *Educ:* Univ Kans, MD, 65; Mass Inst Technol, PhD(nutrit biochem), 73. *Mailing Add:* Dept Hyperaliment New Eng Cancer Res Inst 1194 Pilgrim Rd Boston MA 02215. *Fax:* 617-632-0235

BLACKBURN, HENRY WEBSTER, JR, EPIDEMIOLOGY, PUBLIC HEALTH. *Current Pos:* from asst prof to assoc prof, Univ Minn, Minneapolis, 56-68, dir physiol hyg, Sch Pub Health & prof med, Sch Med, 72-83, chmn, Div Epidemiol, 83-90, Mayo chair, Pub Health, 89-95, PROF PHYSIOL HYG, SCH PUB HEALTH, UNIV MINN, MINNEAPOLIS, 68- *Personal Data:* b Miami, Fla, Mar 22, 25; m 91, Stacy Richardson; c John, Katia & Heidi. *Educ:* Univ Miami, BS, 47; Tulane Univ, MD, 48; Univ Minn, MS, 57. *Hon Degrees:* Dr, Univ Kuopio, Finland, 82. *Honors & Awards:* Thomas Francis Award Epidemiol, 75; Naylor Dana Award Prev Med, 76; Louis Bishop Award Cardiol, 79; Res Achievement Award, Am Heart Asn, 93. *Prof Exp:* Intern, Chicago Wesley Mem, 48-49; intern, Am Hosp of Paris, 49-50; med officer-in-chg, USPHS, Austria & Ger, 50-53; chief resident med, Ancker Hosp, Minn, 56. *Concurrent Pos:* Med dir, Underwriting Mutual Serv Ins Co, Minn, 56-; temporary consult, WHO, 61, 64, 65, 70 & 71, consult, 81-; chmn coun epidemiol, Am Heart Asn, 71-73; med consult, Retail Credit Co, 69-72; vis prof, Univ Geneva, 70-71; dir electrocardiographic ctr & mem steering comt, Coronary Drug Proj, Nat Heart & Lung Inst, nat vchmn multiple risk factor intervention trial, 72-75, mem adv comt, Cardiol Br, 75-; chmn, Coun Epidemiol, Int Soc Cardiol, 86-90 & Med Sect AAAS, 91-92; mem, Study Sect Epidemiol & Dis Control, NIH & adv bd, Nat Heart, Lung & Blood Inst, 89-92. *Mem:* Fel Am Col Epidemiol; Am Heart Asn; fel Am Col Cardiol; fel Am Epidemiol Soc; Belg Royal Acad Med; Soc Fr Cardiol. *Res:* Epidemiology of cardiovascular disease; electrocardiography; internal medicine; chronic disease epidemiology and prevention; promotion of health in population-wide strategies with community-based programs and experimental design. *Mailing Add:* Div Epidemiol 1300 S Second St No 300 Minneapolis MN 55454. *Fax:* 612-624-0315; *E-Mail:* blackburn@epivax.epi.umn.edu

BLACKBURN, JACK BAILEY, CIVIL ENGINEERING. *Current Pos:* PROF ENG, ARIZ STATE UNIV, 72- *Personal Data:* b Sterling, Okla, Oct 19, 22; m 49; c 2. *Educ:* Univ Okla, BS, 47; Purdue Univ, MS, 49, PhD(civil eng), 55. *Prof Exp:* Res asst joint hwy res proj, Purdue Univ, 47-49, res engr, 49-55; assoc prof civil eng, Univ Md, 55-58; transp planning engr, Harland Bartholomew & Assocs, 58-60; prof transp eng & dir Ariz transp & traffic inst, Univ Ariz, 60-63; prof & head civil eng dept, Kans State Univ, 63-72. *Concurrent Pos:* Mem, Hwy Res Bd, Nat Acad Sci-Nat Res Coun, 48-70, Comts Durability of Concrete, 53-65, Qual Traffic Serv, 65-70, Theory Traffic Flow, 65-70 & Characteristics Traffic Flow, 65-70; contact rep, Kans State Univ, 63-72; mem bldg res adv bd, Nat Acad Sci-Nat Acad Eng, 68-71. *Mem:* Am Soc Civil Engrs; Am Arbit Asn; Nat Soc Prof Engrs. *Res:* Materials of construction; urban and regional planning; highway and airport planning, economics and design; traffic and transportation engineering; engineering statistics and design of experiments. *Mailing Add:* 4343 N 84th Pl Scottsdale AZ 85251

BLACKBURN, JACOB FLOYD, computer sciences, for more information see previous edition

BLACKBURN, JOHN GILL, PHYSIOLOGY. *Current Pos:* From instr to assoc prof, 64-86, PROF PHYSIOL, MED UNIV SC, 86- *Personal Data:* b Lake Charles, La, June 25, 35; m 56; c 2. *Educ:* Tulane Univ, BS, 59, PhD(physiol), 65. *Concurrent Pos:* USPHS res grants, 65-68, 74-87 & 88- *Mem:* Sigma Xi; Soc Gen Physiologists; Am Physiol Soc. *Res:* Epithelial transport. *Mailing Add:* Dept Physiol Med Univ SC 171 Ashley Ave Charleston SC 29425-0001

BLACKBURN, JOHN LEWIS, electrical engineering; deceased, see previous edition for last biography

BLACKBURN, JOHN ROBERT, FORENSIC & ENVIRONMENTAL CHEMISTRY. *Current Pos:* from asst prof to assoc prof, 72-84, chmn, Div Natural Sci, 82-88, PROF CHEM, GEORGETOWN COL, 84-, CHMN DEPT, 72- *Personal Data:* b Berea, Ky, Jan 30, 45; m 69, Patricia Graham; c Jennifer & Melissa. *Educ:* Westminster Col, BS, 67; Vanderbilt Univ, PhD(inorg chem), 72. *Prof Exp:* Res assoc, Vanderbilt Univ, 72. *Concurrent Pos:* Vis asst prof chem, Vanderbilt Univ, 74; vis res assoc, Univ Ky, 79, 82; vis prof chem, Va Commmonwealth Univ, 88-89. *Mem:* Am Chem Soc; Water Environ Fedn. *Res:* Chemical education; chemical dynamics; crystallography. *Mailing Add:* Dept Chem Georgetown Col No 205 Georgetown KY 40324-1696

BLACKBURN, MICHAEL N, PHYSICAL BIOCHEMISTRY OF PROTEINS. *Current Pos:* ASSOC PROF BIOCHEM, LA STATE UNIV, 75- *Personal Data:* b Oak Park, Ill, June 30, 44. *Educ:* Univ Calif, Riverside, PhD(biochem), 71. *Mem:* Am Soc Biol Chem; Am Chem Soc; Am Heart Asn. *Mailing Add:* Dept Micromolecular Sci Smith Kline Beecham Res & Develop Div PO Box 1539 King of Prussia PA 19406-0939. *Fax:* 610-270-7361

BLACKBURN, THOMAS HENRY, mathematics; deceased, see previous edition for last biography

BLACKBURN, THOMAS ROY, RESEARCH ADMINISTRATION. *Current Pos:* GRANTS OFFICER, PETRO RES FUND, AM CHEM SOC, 91- *Personal Data:* b St Louis, Mo, Nov 30, 36. *Educ:* Carleton Col, BA, 58; Harvard Univ, MA, 59, PhD(anal chem), 62. *Prof Exp:* From instr to asst prof chem, Carleton Col, 62-64; asst prof, Wellesley Col, 64-67; from asst prof to prof chem, Hobart & William Smith Col, 67-78; McGaw distinguished prof, St Andrews Presby Col, 78-91. *Concurrent Pos:* Vis prof, Swiss Fed Inst Water Pollution Control & Water Conserv, 72-73; res assoc geochem, Harvard Univ, 77; vis prof, Lab Planetary Studies, Cornell Univ, 78; vis prof, Dept Geol, Univ St Andrews, Scotland, 86. *Mem:* AAAS; Am Chem Soc; Geochem Soc. *Res:* Aquatic geochemistry; Aqueous solutions. *Mailing Add:* 1763 Park Rd NW Washington DC 20010

BLACKBURN, WILBERT HOWARD, WATERSHED MANAGEMENT. *Current Pos:* supvry hydrologist, USDA-Agr Res Serv, Boise, Idaho, 87-92, ASSOC AREA DIR, USDA-AGR RES SERV, NORTHERN PLAINS AREA, COLO, 92- *Personal Data:* b Loa, Utah, Mar 23, 41; m 65; c 5. *Educ:* Brigham Young Univ, BS, 65; Univ Nev, Reno, MS, 67, PhD, 73. *Honors & Awards:* Outstanding Achievement Award, Soc Range Mgt, 87. *Prof Exp:* Lab instr bot, Brigham Young Univ, 63-65; res aide range ecol, Intermountain Forest & Range Exp Sta, 64-65; res asst, Univ Nev, Reno, 65-66, range ecologist, 66-74, asst prof range & watershed mgt, 73-75; from assoc prof to prof watershed mgt, Tex A&M Univ, 75-87. *Concurrent Pos:* Mem, Comt Wild & Free-Roaming Horses & Burros, & Livestock Phase, Capital Reef Nat Park, Nat Res Coun & Nat Acad Sci; mem adv panel, assessment water-related technol sustaining agr semi-arid lands, Off Technol Assessment. *Mem:* Soc Range Mgt. *Res:* Pinyon-juniper invasion, condition and trend; vegetation and soil relationships; range hydrology; infiltration studies of selected vegetation; soil units; range and forest practices and water quality; water yield improvement from rangeland water sheds; soil erosion. *Mailing Add:* USDA-Agr Res Serv 1201 Oak Ridge Dr Suite 150 Fort Collins CO 80525

BLACKBURN, WILL R, pediatric-perinatal pathology, tropical medicine, for more information see previous edition

BLACKBURN, WILLIAM HOWARD, PETROLOGY, GEOCHEMISTRY. *Current Pos:* PROF & CHMN MINERAL & PETROL, UNIV WINDSOR, 89- *Personal Data:* b Ottawa, Ont, July 30, 41; m 83; c 2. *Educ:* St Francis Xavier Univ, BSc, 64; Mass Inst Technol, PhD(geol), 67. *Prof Exp:* From asst prof to prof geol & geochem, Univ Ky, 67-88. *Mem:* Geol Asn Can; Mineral Asn Can; Mineral Soc Am. *Res:* Clay minerology and environmental geochemistry; mobility of chemical elements during metamorphism and kinetics of metamorphic reactions; variation of major and minor element chemistry of granites; tectonics and basalt geochemistry. *Mailing Add:* Dept Earth Sci Univ Windsor Windsor ON N9B 3P4 Can. *Fax:* 519-973-7081; *E-Mail:* blackbu@uwindsor.ca

BLACKERBY, BRUCE ALFRED, GEOLOGY. *Current Pos:* From asst prof to assoc prof geol, 63-71, PROF GEOL, CALIF STATE UNIV, FRESNO, 71-, CHMN DEPT, 69- *Personal Data:* US citizen. *Educ:* Univ Calif, Riverside, AB , 59; Univ Calif, Los Angeles, PhD(geol), 65. *Concurrent Pos:* NSF instrl grant, 64-65; geologist, US Geol Surv, 65- *Mem:* Geol Soc Am. *Res:* Tertiary and Mesozoic volcanics; regional geology; geology of Sierra Nevada, especially batholith. *Mailing Add:* Dept Geol Calif State Univ Fresno 2345 E San Ramon Fresno CA 93740-0001

BLACKETT, DONALD WATSON, MATHEMATICS. *Current Pos:* from asst prof to prof, 53-90, EMER PROF MATH, BOSTON UNIV, 90- *Personal Data:* b Boston, Mass, May 2, 26; m 51. *Educ:* Harvard Univ, AB, 47; Princeton Univ, MA, 48, PhD(math), 50. *Prof Exp:* Instr math, Princeton Univ, 50-51, res assoc, 51-53. *Mem:* Am Math Soc; Math Asn Am. *Res:* Algebra; operations research. *Mailing Add:* 97 Eliot Ave West Newton MA 02165-1710

BLACKETT, SHIRLEY ALLART, MATHEMATICS. *Current Pos:* RETIRED. *Personal Data:* b Greenport, NY, Jan 24, 28; m 51. *Educ:* Univ Rochester, AB, 48; Pa State Univ, EdM, 51. *Prof Exp:* Test specialist, Math Test Develop Dept, Educ Testing Serv, 49-52; from instr to assoc prof math, Northeastern Univ, 53-89. *Mem:* Math Asn Am. *Res:* Testing and educational measurement. *Mailing Add:* 97 Eliot Ave West Newton MA 02165-1710

BLACKEY, EDWIN ARTHUR, JR, GEOLOGY. *Current Pos:* Geologist, 51-72, div geologist, 72-82, CONSULT ENG GEOLOGIST, NE DIV, CORPS ENGRS, 82- *Personal Data:* b Tamworth, NH, Oct 19, 27; m 55, Patricia A Matthews; c Mark E & Janet A. *Educ:* Univ NH, BS, 51. *Concurrent Pos:* Mem, Earth Removal Bd, Sudbury; dir, New Eng Sect, Asn Eng Geologists. *Mem:* Asn Eng Geologists; Am Geol Inst. *Res:* Geology. *Mailing Add:* 62 King Philip Rd Sudbury MA 01776

BLACKHAM, ANGUS UDELL, PHYSICAL ORGANIC CHEMISTRY. *Current Pos:* From asst prof to assoc prof, 52-60, PROF CHEM, BRIGHAM YOUNG UNIV, 60- *Personal Data:* b East Ely, Nev, Apr 16, 26; m 46; c 6. *Educ:* Brigham Young Univ, AB, 49; Univ Cincinnati, MS, 50, PhD, 52. *Mem:* Am Chem Soc; Sigma Xi. *Res:* Electroorganic chemistry; azoalkanes and aliphatic azines; transition metal complexes; catalytic reforming of hydrocarbons; coal combustion and gasification. *Mailing Add:* 1632 S 200 East Orem UT 84058-7805

BLACKKETTER, DENNIS O, MECHANICAL & DESIGN ENGINEERING. *Current Pos:* PROF MECH ENG, CALIF STATE UNIV, CHICO, 84- *Personal Data:* b Westville, Okla, Aug 30, 32; m 55; c 3. *Educ:* Fresno State Col, BS, 55; Univ Idaho, MS, 60; Univ Ariz, PhD, 66. *Prof Exp:* Instr mech eng, Univ Idaho, 58-60; asst prof, Sacramento State Col, 60-63; prof & dept head mech eng, Mont State Univ, 66-84. *Concurrent Pos:* Consult, Power Policy Bd, Am Soc Mech Engrs, 75-, vchmn, Energetics Div, 79. *Res:* Low frequency sound transmission in the human body. *Mailing Add:* 23553 Hickory Way Auburn CA 95602-8150

BLACKLER, ANTONIE W C, DEVELOPMENTAL BIOLOGY. *Current Pos:* assoc prof, 64-73, PROF ZOOL, CORNELL UNIV, 73- *Personal Data:* b Portsmouth, Eng, Oct 19, 31; m 70, Rochelle L Melkin; c 2. *Educ:* Univ London, BSc, 53, PhD(embryol), 56. *Prof Exp:* Sr biologist, Loughborough Col Technol, Eng, 56-57; asst lectr zool, Queen's Univ, Belfast, 57-59; Brit Empire Cancer Campaign res asst embryol, Oxford Univ, 59-61; extraordinary prof zool, Univ Geneva, 61-64. *Concurrent Pos:* Div dir, NSF, 81-82. *Mem:* Soc Develop Biol; Int Soc Develop Biol. *Res:* Origin and differentiation of amphibian sex cells; nucleo-cytoplasmic interactions in amphibian development. *Mailing Add:* Dept Genetics Cornell Univ Ithaca NY 14853-0001

BLACKLOW, NEIL RICHARD, VIROLOGY. *Current Pos:* prof med & microbiol, 76-90, CHMN DEPT MED, SCH MED, UNIV MASS, 90- *Personal Data:* b Cambridge, Mass, Feb 26, 38; m 63, Margery Brown; c John A & Peter D. *Educ:* Harvard Univ, BA, 59; Columbia Univ, MD, 63. *Prof Exp:* Resident med, Beth Israel Hosp, Harvard Univ, 63-65; res virologist, NIH, 65-68, sr scientist, 69-71; clin fel med, Mass Gen Hosp, Harvard Univ, 68-69, NIH sr scientist, 69-71; from asst to assoc prof med, Sch Med, Boston Univ, 71-76. *Concurrent Pos:* Assoc ed, Reviews of Infect Dis, 82-90, Infectious Dis Clin Pract, 90-; lectr med, Harvard Med Sch, 84- *Mem:* Am Soc Clin Invest; Infectious Dis Soc Am; Asn Am Physicians; Am Asn Immunol; Asn Prof Med; Am Clin & Climat Asn. *Res:* Viral enteritis; defective viruses; clinical virology; clinical infectious disease. *Mailing Add:* Med Ctr Univ Mass 55 Lake Ave N Worcester MA 01655

BLACKMAN, CARL F, MOLECULAR BIOLOGY, PHYSICAL CHEMISTRY. *Current Pos:* BIOLOGIST, ENVIRON PROTECTION AGENCY, 70- *Personal Data:* b Annapolis, Md, Mar 16, 41; m 67. *Educ:* Colgate Univ, AB, 63; Pa State Univ, MS, 67, PhD(biophys), 69. *Prof Exp:* Fel, Brookhaven Nat Lab, 68-70; biologist, Bur Radiol Health, 70. *Mem:* Am Soc Photobiol; Biophys Soc; Bioelectromagnetic Soc; Am Soc Cell Biol; Soc InVitro Biol. *Res:* Interactions of chemical agents and non-ionizing electromagnetic radiation--DC to 300 GHz--with biological systems at the molecular and cellular level. *Mailing Add:* Environ Protection Agency MD-68 Research Triangle Park NC 27711-2055. *Fax:* 919-541-0694; *E-Mail:* blackman.carl@.epamail.epa.gov

BLACKMAN, JEROME, MATHEMATICS. *Current Pos:* RETIRED. *Personal Data:* b New York, NY, Apr 22, 28; m 55. *Educ:* Mass Inst Technol, BS, 48; Cornell Univ, PhD(math), 51. *Prof Exp:* From instr to assoc prof, Syracuse Univ, 52-87, emer prof, 87. *Res:* Mathematical analysis, geometric quantization. *Mailing Add:* 7005 Lakeshore Dr Cicero NY 13039-9741

BLACKMAN, MARC ROY, PITUITARY GLYCOPROTEINS, CELL PHYSIOLOGY & BIOCHEMISTRY. *Current Pos:* GUEST SCIENTIST ENDOCRINOL & METAB, GERONT RES CTR, NAT INST AGING, NIH, BALTIMORE, MD, 80- *Personal Data:* b Boston, Mass, Mar 2, 46; m 71; c 3. *Educ:* Northeastern Univ, AB, 68; NY Univ, MD, 72. *Prof Exp:* Intern jr & sr asst resident internal med, Bronx Munic Hosp Ctr & Albert Einstein Col Med, 72-75; fel endocrinol, Clin Endocrinol Br, Nat Inst Arthritis, Diabetes & Digestive & Kidney Dis, NIH, Bethesda, Md, 75-77; assoc prof endocrinol & metab, Dept Med, Francis Scott Key Med Ctr & Johns Hopkins Univ Sch Med, 77- *Concurrent Pos:* Consult endocrinol, Johns Hopkins Hosp, 85-; prog dir, Gen Clin Res Ctr & chief, Div Endocrinol & Metab, Johns Hopkins Bayview Med Ctr. *Mem:* Endocrine Soc; Am Fedn Clin Res; Geront Soc Am; AAAS. *Res:* Clinical and laboratory studies of cellular mechanisms for age-related derangements in anterior pituitary hormone secretion. *Mailing Add:* Geront Res Ctr Rm 2B-20 Baltimore MD 21224

BLACKMAN, SAMUEL WILLIAM, PATENT ATTORNEY, MATHMATICAL STATISTICS. *Current Pos:* RETIRED. *Personal Data:* b New York, NY, Aug 25, 13; m 39, Clara Gershunoff; c Susan B, Elinor A & Joan S. *Educ:* Cornell Univ, AB, 34; NY Univ, MS, 37; Polytech Inst Brooklyn, PhD(chem), 60. *Prof Exp:* Dir control, Premo Pharmaceut Labs, Inc, 35-42; microanalyst, Hoffmann-La Roche, 42-44; sr chemist, Burroughs Wellcome & Co, Inc, 44-70; from assoc prof to prof chem, Yeshiva Univ, 68-80; consult indust, Chem Patents & Regulatory Affairs, 69-90, statist anal, 69-90. *Mem:* Am Chem Soc. *Res:* Polynuclear condensed heterocycles; quaternary ammonium compounds; statistical analysis of chemical analyses. *Mailing Add:* 1349 Lexington Ave New York NY 10128

BLACKMON, BOBBY GLENN, FOREST SOILS. *Current Pos:* PROF & HEAD, DEPT FOREST RESOURCES, UNIV ARK, MONTICELLO, 79- *Personal Data:* b Rodessa, La, May 17, 40; m 58; c 3. *Educ:* La Tech Univ, BS, 62; Duke Univ, MF, 63; La State Univ, PhD(forest soils), 69. *Prof Exp:* Res asst soil fertility, Univ Ark, Stuttgart, 63-65; soil scientist, Southern Hardwoods Labs, USDA Forest Serv, Stoneville, Miss, 67-72, proj leader forest soils, 72-79. *Mem:* Soil Sci Soc Am; Am Soc Agron; Soc Am Foresters; Nat Asn Prof Forestry Schs & Cols. *Res:* Forest soil fertility and tree nutrition including nutrient cycling, fertilization and nutrient changes in forest soils. *Mailing Add:* Dean Sch Forest Resources Univ Ark Box 3468 Monticello AR 71656

BLACKMON, CLINTON RALPH, PLANT BREEDING & GENETICS, VARIETY TESTING. *Current Pos:* from assoc prof to prof plant sci, Del Valley Col Sci & Agr, 64-88, chmn, Dept Hort, 69-75, dean, 75-88, AGR CONSULT & EMER PROF PLANT SCI, DEL VALLEY COL AGR, 88- *Personal Data:* b Timmonsville, SC, Aug 13, 19; m 45, Miriam LeMay; c Daniel, Rebecca, Whitney, Christopher & Jonathan. *Educ:* Clemson Col, BS, 41; Univ Mass, MS, 49; Rutgers Univ, PhD(farm crops), 55. *Prof Exp:* Instr bot, Univ Mass, 48; assoc prof agron, Nat Agr Col, 48-55, head dept, 49-55; from asst prof to assoc prof, Univ Maine, 56-62; prof & agr adv, Panama, 62-64. *Concurrent Pos:* Partic, Comn Undergrad Educ Biol Sci Teaching Conf, NSF, Washington, DC, 68 & Biol Inst, Williams Col, 68; UN agr consult Paraguay, 75; Eastern regional dir, NACTA, 78-80; consult, Opportunities Industrialization Centers Int & Advan Technol Ctr Southeastern Pa, 81-88; prof consult plant sci, Waldoboro, Maine, 90- *Mem:* Am Soc Hort Sci; Am Soc Agron; Sigma Xi; Nat Asn Col & Teachers Agr. *Res:* Plant breeding techniques; fungi spores in the plant and animal environment; varietal improvement; pollen viability in economic plants. *Mailing Add:* 5 Old Rte 1 Waldoboro ME 04572

BLACKMON, JAMES B, SPACE POWER, DIGITAL IMAGE PROCESSING. *Current Pos:* staff engr, 73-86, mgr, 86-90, SR MGR, ADVAN SPACE SYSTS, MCDONNELL DOUGLAS SPACE SYSTS CO, 90- *Personal Data:* b Charlotte, NC, Dec 6, 38; m; c 4. *Educ:* Calif Inst Technol, BS, 61; Univ Calif, Los Angeles, MS, 65, PhD(eng & appl sci), 72. *Prof Exp:* Engr & scientist, Douglas Aircraft Co, 61-65, McDonnell Douglas Astronaut Co, 65-73. *Concurrent Pos:* Adj prof & lectr ecol, Calif State Univ, Northridge, 73-76; adj prof, Orange Coast Col, 76-85; chmn, Subcomt E44-08 Solar Thermal, Am Soc Testing & Mat, 84- *Mem:* Am Inst Aeronaut & Astronaut; Am Soc Testing & Mat; fel Inst Advan Eng. *Res:* Advanced space systems; terrestrial and space solar power; space chemical and nuclear power; advanced thermal management systems; digital imaging system applications for optical evaluation of solar concentrators, spacecraft docking sensors, and large structural alignment; artificial intelligence based system design; micro gravity cryogenic fluid management. *Mailing Add:* 4845 Cove Creek Dr Brownsboro AL 35741

BLACKMON, MAURICE LEE, ELEMENTARY PARTICLE PHYSICS. *Current Pos:* DIR CLIMATE RES DIV, US DEPT COM, NAT OCEANIC & ATMOSPHERIC ADMIN, 88- *Personal Data:* b Beaumont, Tex, Aug 24, 40; m 70. *Educ:* Lamar State Col, BS, 62; Mass Inst Technol, PhD(physics), 67. *Prof Exp:* Appointee physics, Argonne Nat Lab, 67-69; asst prof, Syracuse Univ, 69-74; mem staff, Nat Ctr Atmospheric Res, 74-75, chmn, 76-80, scientist, Advan Study Prog, 81-87. *Mem:* Am Meteorol Soc. *Res:* General circulation of the atmosphere. *Mailing Add:* 1535 Kendall Dr Boulder CO 80303

BLACKMON, RONALD H, MOLECULAR BIOLOGY OF AGING, ANTIOXIDANT ENZYMES. *Current Pos:* from asst prof to assoc prof, 89-94, PROF & CHMN, BIOL DEPT, ELIZABETH CITY STATE UNIV, 95- *Personal Data:* b Philadelphia, Pa, Sept 26, 53. *Educ:* Del State Univ, BS, 80; Howard Univ, MS, 85, PhD(cell biol), 88. *Prof Exp:* Res assoc, Agr Res Serv, USDA, 88-89. *Mem:* Sigma Xi; Soc Col Sci Teachers; Soc In Vitro Biol. *Res:* Cellular and molecular biology of aging in Drosophila melanogaster; recombinant baculoviruses. *Mailing Add:* Elizabeth City State Univ Campus Box 970 Elizabeth City NC 27909. *Fax:* 919-335-3697; *E-Mail:* blackmrh@alpha.ecsu.edu

BLACKMORE, DENIS LOUIS, NONLINEAR DYNAMICS & CHAOS, MATHEMATICAL FLUID MECHANICS. *Current Pos:* actg chmn, NJ Inst Technol, 85, assoc chmn, 86-88, from asst prof to prof, 71-82, assoc dir, Ctr Non Linear Sci & Math Comput, 86-90, PROF MATH, NJ INST TECHNOL, 82-, DIR PHD PROG MATH SCI, 95- *Personal Data:* b Jamaica, NY, July 20, 43; c 1. *Educ:* Polytech Univ NY, BS, 65, MS, 66 & PhD(math), 71. *Prof Exp:* Res asst fluid mech, Polytech Univ NY, 64-65, instr math, 68-71. *Concurrent Pos:* Statistician, Elmhurst Hosp, 70-71; prin investr, NSF Grant, 72-73, 91-94 & 95-98, NJ Inst Technol, SBR, Res Grant, 81-83, Off Naval Res, 92-95 & Harlan Perlis Res Award, 93; consult, Raymar Graphic Design Co, 85; NJCST grant, 97- *Mem:* Am Math Soc; Soc Natural Philos; Sigma Xi; NY Acad Sci; Soc Indust & Appl Math. *Res:* Qualitative theory of differential equations; differential invariants of manifold; control systems; fluid mechanics; differential geometry; analysis of vortex breakdown phenomena; characterization of chaos in discrete dynamical systems; topological classification of isolated singularities and triangulation of manifolds; computer-aided geometric design. *Mailing Add:* Dept Math NJ Inst Technol Newark NJ 07102. *Fax:* 973-596-6467; *E-Mail:* deblac@chaos.njit.edu

BLACKMORE, PETER FREDRICK, HORMONE MECHANISMS, ENDOCRINOLOGY. *Current Pos:* ASSOC PROF PHARMACOL, EASTERN VA MED SCH, 88- *Personal Data:* b May 27, 47; m 71, Jill M Quirk; c David, Heather & Fiona. *Educ:* Univ NSW, Australia, PhD(biochem), 76. *Prof Exp:* Asst prof physiol & assoc investr, Howard Hughes Med Inst, Vanderbilt Univ, 78-88. *Concurrent Pos:* Adj assoc prof, Old Dominion Univ, 89- *Mem:* Am Soc Biochem & Molecular Biol. *Res:* Non-genomic steroid signal transduction mechanisms in human sperm; hormone signaling in cancer; mechanismms of calcium influx induced by hormones in hepatocytes and other cells. *Mailing Add:* Eastern Va Med Sch PO Box 1980 Norfolk VA 23501. *E-Mail:* blackmore@borg.evms.edu

BLACKSHAW, GEORGE LANSING, NUCLEAR ENGINEERING. *Current Pos:* EXEC VPRES & PROVOST, NY CHIROPRACTIC COL, 95- *Personal Data:* b Bay Shore, NY, May 9, 36; m 55; c 3. *Educ:* Hofstra Col, BA, 58; NC State Univ, MS, 62, PhD(nuclear eng), 66. *Prof Exp:* Physicist, Atomics Int Div, NAm Aviation, Inc, 58-60; from asst prof nuclear eng to assoc prof chem & nuclear eng, WVa Univ, 65-73, asst dean eng, 79-80, prof chem & nuclear eng, 73-, assoc dean eng, 80-; dean sci & eng, Fairleigh Dickinson Univ; provost & vpres acad affairs, Univ Bridgeport, 92-95. *Concurrent Pos:* Res grants, NSF, 67-79, WVa Dept Hwy, 68-70, AEC, 68, Radiation Mach Corp, 68-71 & US Environ Protection Agency, 71-77. *Mem:* Am Nuclear Soc; Am Soc Eng Educ; Am Inst Chem Engrs. *Res:* Neutron activation analysis; neutron scattering theory; process radiation; reverse osmosis; mine drainage purification and treatment; educational methodology. *Mailing Add:* NY Chiropractic Col Seneca Falls NY 13148

BLACKSHAW, ROBERT EARL, WEED CONTROL, CROPPING SYSTEMS. *Current Pos:* RES SCIENTIST, AGR & AGRI-FOOD CAN, 86- *Personal Data:* b Virden, Man, July 4, 55; m 80, Christine Maclean; c Michael, Alix & Stephen. *Educ:* Brandon Univ, BSc, 76; Univ Man, MSc, 79; Univ Guelph, PhD(weed sci), 87. *Prof Exp:* Agronomist, Alta Wheat Pool, 79-81; res officer, Dupont Can, 81-83. *Concurrent Pos:* Adj prof, Univ Lethbridge, 92- *Mem:* Weed Sci Soc Am; Int Weed Sci Soc. *Res:* Develop integrated weed management systems for annual crops grown on the Canadian prairies. *Mailing Add:* Agr/ Agri Food Can Res Ctr PO Box 3000 Lethbridge AB T1J 4B1 Can. *Fax:* 403-382-3156

BLACKSHEAR, MARGARET ANN, DRUGS OF ABUSE, CHRONIC DRUG ADMINISTRATION & RECEPTOR MODULATION. *Current Pos:* ASST PROF CELL BIOL & PHARMACOL, TENN STATE UNIV, 87- *Personal Data:* b Sweetwater, Tenn, Aug 31, 41; m, Julian Ward; c Jeffrey Ward & Lillian Marie. *Educ:* Knoxville Col, BS, 67; Meharry Med Col, PhD(pharmacol), 79. *Honors & Awards:* Fac Cert Outstanding Achievements Sci & Technol, White House Initiative Sci & Technol Adv Comt, 89. *Prof Exp:* Res assoc, Vanderbilt Univ Med Ctr, 79-82; asst prof pharmacol, Meharry Med Col, 83-87. *Concurrent Pos:* Vis prof, Meharry Med Col, 88-92; NIH neurobiol fel, Vanderbilt Univ Med Ctr, 81, Ford Found fel, 82. *Mem:* Soc Neurosci; Women Neurosci. *Res:* Molecular mechanisms involved in the behavior effects of methamphetamines; studies designed to determine whether drug-induced locomotor changes are correlated with changes in gene expression. *Mailing Add:* 4228 Home Haven Dr Nashville TN 37218. *Fax:* 615-963-5447; *E-Mail:* ablackshear@picard

BLACKSHEAR, PERRY L(YNNFIELD), JR, MECHANICAL ENGINEERING. *Current Pos:* assoc prof mech eng, 57-59, dir, Bioeng Training Prog, 69-76 & Ctr for Studies Phys Environ, 71-77, PROF MECH ENG, UNIV MINN, MINNEAPOLIS, 59-, DIR BIOENG, GRAD PROG, 80- *Personal Data:* b Atlanta, Ga, July 19, 21; m 48; c 6. *Educ:* Ga Inst Technol, BS, 43, MS, 47; Case Inst Technol, PhD(mech eng), 56. *Honors & Awards:* Res Award, Am Soc Artificial Internal Organs, 72; Herbert R Lissner Award Contrib Biomed Eng, Am Soc Mech Eng, 84; Clemson Award Appl Res Biomat, 86. *Prof Exp:* Aeronaut res scientist, Nat Adv Comt Aeronaut, 47-57, head combustion dynamics sect, 57. *Concurrent Pos:* Fulbright lectr, Stuttgart Tech Univ, 62; consult eng sect, Mayo Clin, 65-; mem comt fire res, Nat Acad Sci; consult, Aerospace Corp, Roanoke, Va, 68- & Artificial Kidney Prog, NIH, 70- *Mem:* Am Inst Aeronaut & Astronaut; Combustion Inst; Sigma Xi; Am Soc Artificial Internal Organs. *Res:* Fluid mechanics of chemically reacting systems as found in power and propulsion equipment; fluid mechanical aspects of artificial internal organs. *Mailing Add:* Dept Mech Eng Univ Minn 111 Church St SE Minneapolis MN 55455-0150

BLACKSTEAD, HOWARD ALLAN, MAGNETIC RESONANCE, LOW TEMPERATURE PHYSICS. *Current Pos:* asst prof, 69-75, ASSOC PROF PHYSICS, UNIV NOTRE DAME, 75- *Personal Data:* b Minot, NDak, Feb 24, 40; m 64. *Educ:* NDak State Univ, BS, 62; Dartmouth Col, MA, 64; Rice Univ, PhD(physics), 67. *Prof Exp:* Res assoc physics, Univ Ill, Urbana-Champaign, 67-69. *Mem:* Am Phys Soc; Sigma Xi. *Res:* Superfluid helium flow properties; ferromagnetic resonance in the heavy rare earth metals; nuclear quadrupole resonance; phonon spectroscopy. *Mailing Add:* Dept Physics Univ Notre Dame Notre Dame IN 46556

BLACKSTOCK, DAVID THEOBALD, MECHANICAL ENGINEERING. *Current Pos:* lectr mech eng, 71-81, sr lectr, 81-87, FAC RES SCIENTIST, APPL RES LABS, UNIV TEX AUSTIN, 70-, PROF MECH ENG, 87- *Personal Data:* b Austin, Tex, Feb 13, 30; m 55; c 4. *Educ:* Univ Tex, BS, 52, MA, 53; Harvard Univ, PhD(appl physics), 60. *Honors & Awards:* Silver Medal Phys Acoust, Acoust Soc Am, 85; Gold Medal, Acoust Soc Am, 93. *Prof Exp:* Physicist, Bioacoust Br, Wright Air Develop Ctr, Ohio, 54-56; sr res asst, Acoust Res Lab, Harvard Univ, 60; sr res staff mem nonlinear acoust, Res Dept, Gen Dynamics/Electronics NY, 60-63; assoc prof elec eng, Univ Rochester, 63-70. *Concurrent Pos:* Vis prof, Elec Eng Dept, Univ Rochester, 87-93 & 96. *Mem:* Nat Acad Eng; Am Asn Physics Teachers; fel Acoust Soc Am (vpres, 78-79, pres, 82-83); Sigma Xi. *Res:* Nonlinear acoustics; wave motion. *Mailing Add:* Dept Mech Eng Univ Tex Austin TX 78712-1063

BLACKSTOCK, REBECCA, IMMUNOLOGY, MICROBIOLOGY. *Current Pos:* asst prof, 76-82, ASSOC PROF PEDIAT, UNIV OKLA HEALTH SCI CTR, 82- *Personal Data:* b Oklahoma City, Okla, Feb 13, 43. *Educ:* Okla State Univ, BS, 65; Univ Okla, MS, 68, PhD(immunol), 72. *Prof Exp:* Res technician med microbiol, Univ Okla Health Sci Ctr, 67-68; res technician infectious dis, Univ Tex Southwestern Med Sch, 68-69; fel tumor immunol, Sch Med, Univ Fla, 72-76. *Concurrent Pos:* NIH fel, 72-75; Nat Res Serv-Nat Cancer Inst fel, 75-76; adj asst prof, 77-83, adj assoc prof microbiol & immunol, Univ Okla Health Sci Ctr, 83- *Mem:* Sigma Xi; AAAS; Am Soc Microbiol; Am Asn Immunologists; Soc Leukocyte Biol; Soc Exp Biol; fel Am Acad Microbiol. *Res:* Cellular immunology; tumor immunology; immune response to C neoformans; cryptococcal immunity, involving the study of macraphase regulation by suppressor T-lymphocytes; suppressor cell to down regulate the phagocytic activity in macrophages; regulation of suppressor cells in cryptococcosis. *Mailing Add:* Dept Microbiol & Immunol PO Box 26901 Oklahoma City OK 73190-0001. *Fax:* 405-271-1815

BLACKSTOCK, SILAS CHRISTOPHER, ELECTRON-TRANSFER CHEMISTRY. *Current Pos:* ASST PROF CHEM, VANDERBILT UNIV, 88- *Personal Data:* b Boston, Mass, Dec 21, 56; m 80, Brenda Daniel; c Daniel J & Christopher D. *Educ:* Baylor Univ, BS, 79; Univ Wis-Madison, PhD(chem), 85. *Prof Exp:* Fel, Univ Houston, University Park, 85-86; assoc, Yale Univ, 86-88. *Concurrent Pos:* Prin investr, NSF, 89-, Petrol Res Fund, Am Chem Soc, 89-91. *Mem:* Sigma Xi; Am Chem Soc. *Res:* Organic electron-transfer chemistry; development of new electron-transfer mediated reactions and the study of their mechanisms; organic high-spin polyradical ions are precursors to potential orgno-ferromagnetic materials. *Mailing Add:* Dept Chem Vanderbilt Univ 2201 W End Ave Nashville TN 37240-0001. *Fax:* 615-322-4936; *E-Mail:* blackscc@ctrvax.vanderbilt.edu

BLACKWELDER, BLAKE WINFIELD, COASTAL PLAIN GEOLOGY, PALEOENVIRONMENTAL ANALYSIS. *Current Pos:* SR GEOLOGIST, BRIT GAS, 89- *Personal Data:* b Buffalo, NY, June 25, 45; m 67. *Educ:* Duke Univ, BA, 67; George Washington Univ, MS, 71, PhD(geol), 72. *Prof Exp:* Geologist, US Geol Surv, 72-81; geologist, Tenneco Oil Co, 81-89. *Concurrent Pos:* Res fel assoc, Nat Acad Sci, 73. *Mem:* Am Asn Petrol Geologists. *Res:* Biostratigraphy; lithostratigraphy; structural evolution of the United States atlantic coastal plain. *Mailing Add:* 3022 Tilden St Houston TX 77025

BLACKWELDER, RON F, TURBULENT FLUID MECHANICS, TRANSITION. *Current Pos:* from asst prof to assoc prof, 70-80, PROF AEROSPACE ENG, UNIV SOUTHERN CALIF, 80- *Personal Data:* b Pratt, Kans, July 16, 41; m 65, Judy P Tiefel; c Laura J & Sherri L. *Educ:* Univ Colo, BS, 64; Johns Hopkins Univ, PhD(fluid dynamics), 70. *Prof Exp:* Teaching asst, Johns Hopkins Univ, 67-68, res asst, 68-70. *Concurrent Pos:* Vis scientist, Max Planck Inst Fluid Mech, Ger, 76-77; vis prof, Inst Nat Polytech, Grenoble, France, 83-84. *Mem:* Fel Am Phys Soc; assoc fel Am Inst Aeronaut & Astronaut; Sigma Xi. *Res:* Turbulent fluid dynamics; boundary layers and different methods for controlling turbulent mixing and for reducing the drag of objects in a moving fluid. *Mailing Add:* Dept Aerospace Eng Univ Southern Calif Los Angeles CA 90089-1191. *Fax:* 213-740-7774; *E-Mail:* ron@spock.usc.edu

BLACKWELL, BARRY M, PSYCHOPHARMACOLOGY. *Current Pos:* PROF, UNIV WIS MED SCH; GROUP DIR CLIN PSYCHIAT RES, MERRELL-NAT CO, 68- *Personal Data:* b Birmingham, Eng, July 5, 34; m 58; c 3. *Educ:* Cambridge Univ, BA, 57, MB, BChir, 60, MA & MD, 66; Univ London, DPM, 67. *Honors & Awards:* Adminr Award, NIMH, 91; Warren Williams Award, Am Psychiat Asn, 92; Exemplary Psychiatrist Award, Nat Alliance Ment Ill, 93. *Prof Exp:* Intern med & surg, Guys Hosps, Cambridge, 60-61; resident neurol, Whittington Hosp, London, 61-62; resident psychiat, Maudsley Hosp & Inst Psychiat, 62-68; asst prof psychiat, Univ Cincinnati, 68-70, prof psychiat & assoc prof pharmacol, 70-75; prof psychiat & pharmacol & chmn Dept Psychiat, Sch Med, Wright State Univ, 75- *Mem:* Royal Col Psychiat; Am Col Neuropsychopharmacol. *Res:* Interactions between foodstuffs and monoamine oxidase inhibitors; various aspects of clinical and psychopharmacology research; clinical research. *Mailing Add:* 2514 S 102nd St Suite 100 Milwaukee WI 53227

BLACKWELL, BENNIE FRANCIS, MECHANICAL ENGINEERING. *Current Pos:* MEM TECH STAFF, SANDIA NAT LAB, 79- *Personal Data:* b Magnolia, Ark, Nov 11, 41; m 60; c 2. *Educ:* Univ Ark, BS, 65; Univ NMex, MS, 67; Stanford Univ, PhD(mech eng), 73. *Prof Exp:* Mem tech staff, Sandia Lab, 65-77; asst prof mech eng, La Tech Univ, 77-79. *Concurrent Pos:* Consult, Nat Insulation Contractors Asn, 77-79, Pabco Div, La Pac Corp & Thermal Insulation Mfg Asn, 78-79. *Mem:* Fel Am Soc Mech Engrs; assoc fel Am Inst Aeronaut & Astronaut. *Res:* Heat transfer; numerical modeling; inverse heat conduction. *Mailing Add:* Orgn 1553 M/S 0826 Sandia Nat Lab PO Box 5800 Albuquerque NM 87185-0826. *Fax:* 505-844-4523; *E-Mail:* bfblack@cfd.sandia.gov

BLACKWELL, CHARLES C, JR, SYSTEMS CONTROL, DYNAMIC SYSTEMS SCIENCE. *Current Pos:* RES SCIENTIST, AMES RES CTR, NASA, 92- *Personal Data:* b Houston, Tex, Nov 25, 33; m 56; c 3. *Educ:* Rice Univ, BA, 55, BSME, 56; Southern Methodist Univ, MSME, 60; Univ Ariz, PhD(systems control), 66. *Prof Exp:* Propulsion engr, Gen Dynamics/Ft Worth, 56-60; asst prof mech eng, NMex State Univ, 64-66; prof mech eng, Univ Tex, Arlington, 71-92. *Concurrent Pos:* Consult, Off Saline Water Res Prog, NMex State Univ, Life Sci Inc, Ling-Temco-Vought, Inc, Gen Dynamics Corp; adj lectr, Santa Clara Univ. *Mem:* Am Soc Mech Engrs; Ecol Soc Am; Inst Elec & Electronics Engrs; Sigma Xi. *Res:* Optimal, robust and adaptive control, mathematical modeling, and estimation. *Mailing Add:* PO Box 391417 Mountain View CA 94039-1417. *Fax:* 915-961-0660; *E-Mail:* ccb@acontrol.arc.nasa.gov

BLACKWELL, CRIST SCOTT, VIBRATIONAL SPECTROSCOPY, NUCLEAR MAGNETIC RESONANCE SPECTROSCOPY. *Current Pos:* RES & DEVELOP FEL, UOP, 93- *Personal Data:* b Winston-Salem, NC, Feb 17, 45; m 90, Kathryn Parker. *Educ:* Univ NC, Chapel Hill, BS, 67; Mass Inst Technol, PhD(phys chem), 71. *Prof Exp:* Res assoc, Univ Southern Calif, 71-72 & Mich State Univ, 72-75; proj scientist, Union Carbide Corp, 75-79, group leader, 79-85, sr res scientist, 85-9 1, corp res fel, 91-93. *Mem:* Am Chem Soc; Soc Appl Spectros; Am Phys Soc; Am Soc Testing & Mat; Coblenz Soc. *Res:* Analytical spectroscopy with particular emphasis on use of infrared, Raman and nuclear magnetic resonance spectroscopy to solve structural chemical problems; solid state nuclear magnetic resonance; molecular sieves; catalysts. *Mailing Add:* 4 Ashcroft Ct Algonquin IL 60102-3261. *Fax:* 914-789-2204

BLACKWELL, DAVID (HAROLD), MATHEMATICS, STATISTICS. *Current Pos:* prof statist, Univ Calif, Berkeley, 54-73, dir, Study Ctr, UK & Ireland, 73-75, prof, 73-89, EMER PROF STATIST & MATH, UNIV CALIF, BERKELEY, 89- *Personal Data:* b Centralia, Ill, Apr 24, 19; m 44; c 7. *Educ:* Univ Ill, AB, 38, AM, 39, PhD(math), 41. *Hon Degrees:* DSc, Univ Ill, 66, Mich State Univ, 69, Southern Ill Univ, 71, Carnegie-Mellon Univ, Nat Univ Lesotho, 87, Amherst Col & Harvard Univ, 88, Howard Univ, Yale Univ & Univ Warwick, 90. *Honors & Awards:* W W Rouse Ball Lectr, Univ Cambridge, 74; Wald Lectr, Inst Math Statist, 77; John Von Neumann Theory Prize, Inst Mgt Sci & Opers Res Soc Am, 79. *Prof Exp:* Rosenwald fel, Inst Advan Study, 41-42; asst statistician, Off Price Admin, 42; instr math & physics, Southern Agr & Mech Col, 42-43; instr math, Clark Univ, 43-44; prof, Howard Univ, 44-54. *Concurrent Pos:* Res fel, Brown Univ, 43; mathematician, Rand Corp, 48-50; vis prof, Stanford Univ, 50-51 & Univ Calif, Berkeley, 54-55. *Mem:* Nat Acad Sci; AAAS; Am Math Soc (vpres, 68-71); fel Inst Math Statist (pres, 55); Am Acad Arts & Sci; Am Statist Asn (vpres, 78-). *Res:* Markoff chains; sequential analysis. *Mailing Add:* Dept Statist Univ Calif Berkeley CA 94720

BLACKWELL, FLOYD ORIS, ENVIRONMENTAL HEALTH, PUBLIC HEALTH ADMINISTRATION. *Current Pos:* RETIRED. *Personal Data:* b Mayfield, Idaho, Feb 27, 25; m 51, Eleanor Edwards; c Susan (Boutilier), Betsy (McCormick), Mary Ruth (Coleman) & Stephen. *Educ:* Wash State Univ, BS, 50; Univ Mass, MS, 54; Univ Calif, Berkeley, MPH, 65, DrPH, 69; Am Acad dipl. *Honors & Awards:* Walter S Mangold Award, Nat Environ Health Asn, 89. *Prof Exp:* Sanitarian, Benton-Franklin Dist Health Dept, 50-53; health & sanit adv, US AID, Pakistan, 54-56, sr sanit adv, 56-59; asst prof environ & pub health, Am Univ Beirut,59-64; assoc prof, Rutgers Univ, 67-71 & Col Med, Univ Vt, 71-74; prof environ & pub health, E Carolina Univ, 74-; prof & chmn dept, Environ Health Sci, Eastern Ky Univ, 81-90. *Concurrent Pos:* Mem pub health rev comt, Bur Health Manpower Educ, NIH, 71-73; mem bd dirs, Am Acad Sanitarians, 72-; led pub health deleg, Peoples Repub China, 87. *Mem:* Am Pub Health Asn; Nat Environ Health Asn (pres, 76). *Res:* Environmental control of communicable diseases, particularly food and water borne diseases, considering biological, microbiological, physical and social aspects in complex interrelationships; ecology of human well-being; health administration. *Mailing Add:* 305 Azalea Dr Washington NC 27889

BLACKWELL, HAROLD RICHARD, vision; deceased, see previous edition for last biography

BLACKWELL, JOHN, POLYMER SCIENCE, BIOPHYSICS. *Current Pos:* vis asst prof, Case Western Res Univ, 69-70, from asst prof to assoc prof, 69-77, chmn dept, 85-95, PROF MACROMOLECULAR SCI, CASE WESTERN RES UNIV, 77-, F ALEX NASON PROF, 91- *Personal Data:* b Sheffield, Eng, Jan 15, 42; m 65; c 2. *Educ:* Univ Leeds, BSc, 63, PhD(biophys), 67. *Honors & Awards:* Distinguished Achievement Award, Fiber Soc, 81. *Prof Exp:* Fel chem, State Univ NY Col Forestry, Syracuse Univ, 67-69. *Concurrent Pos:* Prin investr, NSF Grants, 70, NIH Grant, 70, NIH res career develop award, 73-77; mem exec comt, Biopolymer Subgroup, Biophys Soc, 74-77, chmn, 75-76; mem exec comt, High Polymer Physics Div, Am Phys Soc, 86-90, vchmn, 87-88, chmn, 88-89; bd mem, Edison Polymer Innovation Corp, 85-95. *Mem:* Soc Complex Carbohydrates; AAAS; Am Chem Soc; fel Am Phys Soc; Fiber Soc. *Res:* Study of the structure and interactions of macromolecules, using x-ray crystallography and other physical-chemical techniques; liquid-crystalline polymers; structure and morphology of cellulose, chitin and other polysaccharides; polysaccharide-protein interactions; structures of polyurethane elastomers. *Mailing Add:* Dept Macromolecular Sci Case Western Res Univ Cleveland OH 44106. *E-Mail:* jxb6@po.cwru.edu

BLACKWELL, JOHN HENRY, APPLIED MATHEMATICS. *Current Pos:* Demonstr physics, Univ Western Ont, 46-47, instr, 47-49, lectr, 49-52, from asst prof to prof, 52-62, appl math, 62-63, sr prof, 63-67, prof, head & chmn dept appl math, 67-76, exec asst to pres, 76-79, prof, 81-86, EMER PROF APPL MATH, UNIV WESTERN ONT, 86- *Personal Data:* b Melbourne, Australia, July 9, 21; m 46, Betty S Smith; c Stephen, Gerald, Patricia & Thomas. *Educ:* Univ Melbourne, BSc, 41; Univ Western Ont, MSc, 47, PhD(physics), 52. *Concurrent Pos:* Vis res fel, Australian Nat Univ, 55-56; vis Commonwealth fel, Oxford Univ, 64-65; mem, Can Nat Comt, Int Union Theoret & Appl Mech, 70-74. *Mem:* Fel Inst Math & Appln, UK; fel Can Soc Mech Eng; Can Soc Appl Math. *Res:* Heat flow and diffusion theory; non-linear mathematics. *Mailing Add:* 521 Riverside Dr 608 London ON N6G 5E2 Can

BLACKWELL, KIM LOIS, COMPUTATIONAL NEUROSCIENCE, NEURAL NETWORKS. *Current Pos:* ASSOC PROF COMPUT SCI & INFORMATICS, GEORGE MASON UNIV, 96- *Personal Data:* b East Orange, NJ, Aug 17, 59. *Educ:* Boston Univ, BS, 81; Univ Pa, VMD, 86, MS, 87, PhD(bioeng), 88. *Prof Exp:* Assoc vet, Radbill Animal Hosp, 86-87; res scientist, Environ Res Inst Mich, 88-96. *Mem:* Soc Neurosci. *Res:* Computational models of single neurons and groups of neurons involved in long term memory; biologically based computer algorithms for visual pattern recognition; psychophysical studies of perception. *Mailing Add:* George Mason Univ CSI MS-5C3 Fairfax VA 22030

BLACKWELL, LAWRENCE A, SAFETY ENGINEERING. *Current Pos:* RETIRED. *Personal Data:* b Houston, Tex, Nov 23, 31; m 57; c David A, Elaine & Sarah. *Educ:* Rice Inst, BA, 54; Duke Univ, PhD(physics), 58. *Prof Exp:* Engr microwave, Tex Instruments, 58-62; vpres res & develop, Microwave Physics Inc, 62-66; acad adminr, Rice Univ, 66-76; staff mem, Los Alamos Nat Lab, 76-88; consult, 89-95. *Mailing Add:* 2 Pepper Hill Dr Montgomery TX 77356

BLACKWELL, LEO HERMAN, PHYSIOLOGY. *Current Pos:* PROF PHYSIOL, SCH DENT, UNIV DETROIT, 78- *Personal Data:* b Austin, Tex, June 2, 34; m 63, June Wagner; c Leslie Alane, Scott Blasdel & Laurel Lynn. *Educ:* Univ Tex, BA, 55; ETex State Col, MA, 60; Mich State Univ, PhD(physiol), 64. *Prof Exp:* Res technician physics, Univ Tex M D Anderson Hosp & Tumor Inst, Houston, 56-59, res assoc, 59-60; asst biol, ETex State Col, 59; asst physiol, Mich State Univ, 62-63; resident student assoc, Argonne Nat Lab, 63-64; radiation safety officer, Univ Tenn, Memphis, 64-68, actg chmn div radiation biol, 67, from asst prof to assoc prof radiation biol & clin physiol, 64-75, asst to vchancellor acad affairs, 73-77, asst prof physiol & biophys & prof radiation oncol, 75-78. *Concurrent Pos:* Consult, City of Memphis Hosps, 67-78. *Mem:* Radiation Res Soc; Health Physics Soc; Am Physiol Soc. *Res:* Cell proliferation; biological effects of radiation; radiation dosimetry; tracer physiology. *Mailing Add:* Univ Detroit Mercy Sch Dent Outer Dr Campus 8200 Outer Dr Detroit MI 48235

BLACKWELL, LYLE MARVIN, ELECTRICAL ENGINEERING. *Current Pos:* RETIRED. *Personal Data:* b Charleston, WVa, Jan 29, 32; m 53; c 5. *Educ:* WVa Univ, BSEE, 54; Chrysler Inst, MAE, 56; Ohio State Univ, PhD(elec eng), 66. *Prof Exp:* Studio engr, Styling Div, Chrysler Corp, Mich, 54-58; asst prof elec eng, WVa Inst Tehcnol, 60-61, assoc prof & chmn dept, 61-63; res assoc, Commun & Control Systs Lab, Ohio State Univ, 64-66; dean, Sch Eng, WVa Inst Technol, 66-92. *Mem:* Am Soc Eng Educ; Inst Elec & Electronics Engrs. *Res:* Automatic control systems; application of automatic control to automotive design. *Mailing Add:* PO Box 185 Gauley Bridge WV 25085-0185

BLACKWELL, MEREDITH, BIOLOGY. *Current Pos:* assoc prof, 85-88, PROF BOT, LA STATE UNIV, 88- *Personal Data:* b Abbeville, La, Mar 27, 40; c 1. *Educ:* Univ Southwestern La, BS, 61; Univ Ala, MS, 63; Univ Tex, Austin, PhD(bot), 73. *Honors & Awards:* Alexopoulos Prize, Mycol Soc Am. *Prof Exp:* Asst prof biol, Hope Col, 75-81. *Mem:* Mycol Soc Am (secy, 86-88, vpres, 90-91, pres-elect, 91-92, pres, 92-93); Sigma Xi; Brit Mycol Soc; Soc Invert Pathol; Am Inst Biol Sci. *Res:* Biology of myxomycetes and entomogenous fungi; studies of fungal spore dispersal primarily by arthropod assemblies; other interest includes biology of desert fungi and myxomycetes; phylogeny of fungi infered from DNA sequences. *Mailing Add:* Dept Biol Sci La State Univ Baton Rouge LA 70803. *Fax:* 504-388-8459; *E-Mail:* btblac@unixl.sncc.lsu.edu

BLACKWELL, PAUL K, II, COMPUTER SCIENCE, MATHEMATICS. *Current Pos:* ASSOC PROF, 68-, PROF COMPUT SCI, UNIV MO, COLUMBIA. *Personal Data:* b Miami, Fla, July 10, 31; m 49; c 3. *Educ:* Univ Chicago, BA, 52; Syracuse Univ, MS, 61, PhD(math), 68. *Prof Exp:* Assoc prof math, Milwaukee Sch Eng, 55-57; analyst, Systs Develop Corp, 57-58; analyst defense systs, Gen Elec Co, NY, 58-61, consult, 61-63, analyst defense systs, 63-65; mathematician, Syracuse Univ Res Corp, 65-68. *Mem:* Am Math Soc; Asn Comput Mach; Inst Elec & Electronics Engrs; Math Asn Am; Soc Indust & Appl Math. *Res:* Data base systems; medical computing; combinatorics. *Mailing Add:* Dept Comput Sci Univ Mo 304 Math Sci Bldg Columbia MO 65211

BLACKWELL, RICHARD QUENTIN, biochemistry, for more information see previous edition

BLACKWELL, ROBERT JERRY, PHYSICS. *Current Pos:* mem, Prod Res Div, Humble Oil & Refining Co, 54-64 & Esso Prod Res Co, 64-74, RES SCIENTIST, EXXON PROD RES CO, 74- *Personal Data:* b Clovis, NMex, Dec 31, 25; m 55; c 3. *Educ:* Tex Christian Univ, BA, 47; Univ NC, PhD(physics), 53. *Prof Exp:* Instr physics, Univ NC, 47-52, asst prof, 53-54. *Mem:* Am Phys Soc; Am Asn Physics Teachers; Am Inst Chem Eng; Am Inst Mineral, Metall & Petrol Eng; Sigma Xi. *Res:* Cosmic rays; flow through porous media; petroleum production; enhanced oil recovery processes. *Mailing Add:* 8904 Memorial Houston TX 77024-5811

BLACKWELL, ROBERT LEIGHTON, ANIMAL SCIENCE, ANIMAL GENETICS. *Current Pos:* RETIRED. *Personal Data:* b Clayton, NMex, Nov 24, 24; m 50; c 1. *Educ:* NMex State Univ, BS, 49; Ore State Univ, MS, 51; Cornell Univ, PhD(animal genetics), 53. *Prof Exp:* From asst prof to assoc prof animal husb, NMex State Univ, 53-58; dir, Sheep Exp Sta, Agr Res Serv, USDA, 59-66; prof animal & range sci & head dept, Mont State Univ, 66-78, prof animal sci, 78-86. *Concurrent Pos:* Prin investr, Collab Res Support Prog, Small Ruminants, Peru, 79-86; actg assoc prog dir, Small Ruminant Collab Res Support Prog, Univ Calif-Davis, 86. *Mem:* Am Soc Animal Sci. *Res:* Genetics and breeding of domestic animals. *Mailing Add:* 109 Sourdough Ridge Rd Bozeman MT 59715

BLACKWELL, WILLIAM A(LLEN), ELECTRICAL NETWORK THEORY, ELECTRICAL ENGINEERING EDUCATION. *Current Pos:* head dept, 66-81, prof elec eng, 66-88, EMER PROF ELEC ENG, VA POLYTECH INST & STATE UNIV, 88- *Personal Data:* b Ft Worth, Tex, May 17, 20; m 49, Sherry L Tibbets; c David A & Rebecca R (Kates). *Educ:* Tex Tech Col, BS, 49; Univ Ill, MS, 52; Mich State Univ, PhD(elec eng), 58. *Honors & Awards:* Centennial Medal, Inst Elec & Electronics Engrs, 84; Distinguished Engr Award, Tex Tech Univ, 90. *Prof Exp:* From instr to asst prof elec eng, Tex Tech Col, 49-55; test engr, Gen Elec Co, 49-50; instr elec eng, Univ Ill, 55-56 & Mich State Univ, 56-59; proj engr, Gen Dynamics/Ft Worth, 59-61; prof elec eng, Southern Methodist Univ, 61 & Okla State Univ, 61-66. *Concurrent Pos:* Consult, aerosysts sect, Gen Dynamics/Ft Worth, 61; vis prof elec eng, US Military Acad, 81-82; res dir, Southeastern Ctr Elec Eng Educ, 84-85. *Mem:* Am Soc Eng Educ; fel Inst Elec & Electronics Engrs. *Res:* System theory; author of three textbooks. *Mailing Add:* Bradley Dept Elec Eng Va Polytech Inst & State Univ Blacksburg VA 24061. *Fax:* 540-231-3362; *E-Mail:* blackwel@vtvm1.cc.vt.edu

BLACKWOOD, ALLISTER CLARK, MICROBIOLOGY. *Current Pos:* prof, McGill Univ, 57-81, chmn dept, 57-68, dean fac & vprin Col, 72-77, EMER PROF MICROBIOL, MACDONALD COL, MCGILL UNIV, 81- *Personal Data:* b Calgary, Alta, Nov 22, 15; m 43, Mildred J Marsh; c Alan C, Marsha E & Susan M. *Educ:* Univ Alta, BS, 42, MS, 44; Univ Wis, PhD(microbiol), 49. *Concurrent Pos:* Mem, Div Appl Biol, Nat Res Coun, Ottawa, 44-46. *Mem:* Can Soc Microbiol (pres, 64-65); Am Soc Microbiol; Soc Gen Microbiol; Soc Appl Bact; Soc Indust Microbiol; Asn Faculties Agr Can (pres, 75-76). *Res:* US Patent for production of glycerol by fermentation. *Mailing Add:* 885 Berwick Rd 11 Qualicum Beach BC V9K 1N7 Can

BLACKWOOD, ANDREW W, MATERIALS SCIENCE ENGINEERING. *Current Pos:* sr mat engr, 82-87, dir anal serv, 88-93, VPRES TECH, STRUCT PROBE INC, 93- *Personal Data:* b Newton, NJ, Apr 1, 42; m 65; c 3. *Educ:* Rensselaer Polytech Inst, BMetE, 63 & PhD(mat eng), 70. *Prof Exp:* Res metallurgist, Am Smelting & Refining Co, 67-71, sect head, Tech Sales Serv, 71-73; supt, Metals Appln, ASARCO Inc, 74-79; tech dir, Enthone Inc, 80-82. *Mem:* Metall Soc; Am Soc Metals; Am Soc Testing & Mat; Am Electroplaters Soc; Nat Asn Corrosion Engrs; Int Soc Hybrid Microelectronics; Soc Die Casting Engrs; Soc Advan Mat & Process Eng; Sigma Xi. *Res:* Materials science, particularly the application of electron microscopy; surface analysis to materials characterization; problem solving and failure analysis for government, industrial academic and legal clients. *Mailing Add:* Structure Probe Inc PO Box 656 West Chester PA 19381-0656. *Fax:* 610-436-5755; *E-Mail:* ablackwood@zspi.com

BLAD, BLAINE L, AGRICULTURAL METEOROLOGY, REMOTE SENSING. *Current Pos:* From asst prof to assoc prof, 70-82, PROF AGR METEOROL, UNIV NEBR, 82-, HEAD, DEPT AGR METEOROL, 87-; ASSOC DIR, GREAT PLAINS CTR, GLOBAL ENVIRON CHANGE, 92- *Personal Data:* b Cedar City, Utah, Apr 2, 39; m 64, Virginia J Blackam; c Debra Jean, Sheryl Kay, Colleen, Kenneth L, Stephen L, Kirk L & Kerry Kim. *Educ:* Brigham Young Univ, BS, 64; Univ Minn, MS, 68, PhD(soil sci), 70. *Concurrent Pos:* Prin investr, NASA grant, 72-75, 81-94, NSF grant, Stand Oil grant, 84-86; co-investr, Off Water Res & Technol grant, 74-75, prin investr, 77-79; prin investr, USDA-SEA grant, 78-81; consult, NASA, 78-79, 81-84 & Stand Oil Co, Ohio, 84-88. *Mem:* Fel Am Soc Agron; Crop Sci Soc Am; AAAS; Am Meteorol Soc; Sigma Xi. *Res:* Crop temperature; plant water relations; improving crop water use efficiency; evapotranspiration; radiation balance of crops; remote sensing of crop and rangeland productivity; global climate change; water conservation in urban environment. *Mailing Add:* Dept Agr Meteorol Univ Nebr Lincoln NE 68583-0728

BLADES, ARTHUR TAYLOR, PHYSICAL CHEMISTRY. *Current Pos:* res chemist, Res Coun Alta, 55-87, RES ASSOC, UNIV ALTA, 87- *Personal Data:* b Milton, Ont, July 20, 26; m 50; c 3. *Educ:* Univ Western Ont, BSc, 48; Univ Wis, PhD(phys chem), 52. *Prof Exp:* Photochemist, Nat Res Coun Can, 52-54; fel nuclear chem, McMaster Univ, 54-55. *Concurrent Pos:* Mem sci adv comt, Environ Conserv Authority, Alta, 74-80. *Mem:* Chem Inst Can. *Res:* Chemical kinetics; kinetic isotope effects in gas phase reactions; chemistry in flames; ion-molecule chemistry; electrospray mass spectrometry. *Mailing Add:* 7204 119th St Edmonton AB T6G 1V6 Can

BLADES, JOHN DIETERLE, PHYSICS ELECTROMAGNETISM. *Current Pos:* RETIRED. *Personal Data:* b Cincinnati, Ohio, Nov 1, 24; m 49, Doris Vansant; c Catherine A, Jane B (Hoover) & Patricia B (Terrell). *Educ:* Western Md Col, BS, 49; Univ Cincinnati, MS, 51, PhD(physics), 54. *Prof Exp:* Sr staff scientist, Burroughs Corp, 54-65; mgr, Solid State Physics Lab, Franklin Inst Res Labs, 65-71; mgr, Solid State Physics, Develop Labs, Addressograph-Multigraph Corp, 71-77; staff engr, Burroughs Corp, 77-88. *Concurrent Pos:* Vis scientist, CENG, Grenoble, France, 63-64. *Mem:* Am Phys Soc; Mat Res Soc; Int Soc Hybrid Microelectronics; Soc Photo Scientists & Engrs; Am Ceramic Soc. *Res:* Engineering physics; solid state physics; mechanics; electromagnetism; materials science engineering; construction of computers. *Mailing Add:* 18243 Verano Dr San Diego CA 92128

BLADH, KATHERINE LAING, IGNEOUS PETROLOGY. *Current Pos:* asst prof, 78-85, ASSOC PROF GEOL , WITTENBERG UNIV, 85- *Personal Data:* b Pendleton, Ore, Feb 3, 47; m 71. *Educ:* Ore State Univ, BS, 69; Univ Ariz, MS, 72, PhD(geochem), 76. *Prof Exp:* Jr geologist, Amerada-Hess Oil Corp, 69; teaching asst geol, Univ Ariz, 71-74, lectr, 76-78. *Mem:* Geochem Soc; Asn Women Geoscientists; Nat Asn Geol Teachers; Sigma Xi. *Res:* Silicic volcanics: their textures and chemistry; rapakivi texture in a volcanic environment. *Mailing Add:* Dept Geol Wittenberg Univ Box 720 Springfield OH 45501

BLADH, KENNETH W, DESCRIPTIVE MINERALOGY. *Current Pos:* ASST PROF GEOL, WITTENBERG UNIV, 78- *Personal Data:* b Chicago, Ill, Nov 7, 47. *Educ:* Wittenberg Univ, BA, 69; Univ Ariz, MS, 73, PhD(geol), 78. *Mem:* Mineral Soc Am; Geol Soc Am; Mineral Asn Can; Sigma Xi. *Res:* Descriptive mineralogy; low temperature geochemistry of weathering. *Mailing Add:* Geol Dept Wittenburg Univ PO Box 720 Springfield OH 45501

BLAEDEL, WALTER JOHN, ANALYTICAL CHEMISTRY. *Current Pos:* RETIRED. *Personal Data:* b New York, NY, May 26, 16; m 42, Barbara J Bennett; c Mark E, Kenneth L & Robert W. *Educ:* Univ Calif, Los Angeles, BA, 38, MA, 39; Stanford Univ, PhD(chem), 42. *Prof Exp:* Instr chem, Northwestern Univ, 41-44; res assoc, Nat Defense Res Comt, 42-44; res assoc, Manhattan Proj, Univ Chicago, 44-46; res assoc, Radiation Lab, Univ Calif, 46-47; from asst prof to prof chem, Univ Wis-Madison, 47-81. *Concurrent Pos:* Mem comt postdoctoral fels in chem, Nat Acad Sci, 63-66; mem analytical chem adv comt, Nat Bur Stand-Nat Acad Sci, 67-69; mem comt analytical chem, Nat Res Coun, 75-78. *Mem:* Am Chem Soc. *Res:* Analysis in membrane systems; separations; electrochemistry; ion exchange; equipment and procedures for the electrochemical characterization of surface absorbed substances; experimental study of the legal process in Dane Co, Wis. *Mailing Add:* 714 Pebble Beach Dr Madison WI 53717-1138

BLAESE, R MICHAEL, IMMUNOLOGY, PEDIATRICS. *Current Pos:* clin assoc immunol fel, Metab Br, Nat Cancer Inst, NIH, 66-68, sr investr, 68-73, head, Cellular Immunol Sect, 73-93, dep chief, 85-93, clin dir, Nat Human Genome Res Inst, 94-96, CHIEF, CLIN GENE THER BR, NAT HUMAN GENOME RES INST, NIH, 94- *Personal Data:* b Minneapolis, Minn, Feb 16, 39; m 62, Julianne; c 2. *Educ:* Gustavus Adolphus Col, BS, 61; Univ Minn, MD, 64. *Hon Degrees:* MD, Univ Kuopio, Finland, 96. *Honors & Awards:* Mead Johnson Award, Am Acad Pediat, 80; Maxwell Finland Award, Infectious Dis Soc Am, 91; Naomi M Kanof Clin Investr Award, Soc Investigative Dermat, 94; Bertil Aberg Award, Royal Swed Acad Sci, 94; Erwin Neter Award, Am Soc Microbiol, 95; E Mead Johnson Award Lectr, Am Acad Pediat; Inaugural Alexandra J Kefalides Mem Lectr, Univ Pa Sch Med; Leo Creep Lect, Montefiore Hosp, Univ Pittsburgh Med Ctr; R L & Annie Meaher Hill Cancer Lectr, Univ SAla; Mittelstaedt Lectr, Am Col Allergy & Immunol; Daniel Y Perey Mem Lectr, McMaster Univ; Martin Van Buren Teem Sr Lectr, Kennestone Med Ctr; Markey Molecular Med Lectr, Univ Wash. *Prof Exp:* Intern, Parkland Hosp, Dallas, 64-65; resident pediat, Hosp, Univ Minn, 65-66. *Concurrent Pos:* Attend physician, Clin Ctr, NIH, 68-; assoc ed, J Immunol, 76-80; Burroughs-Wellcome vis prof, Royal Col Med, 80; med bd, Warren Grant Magnusson Clin Ctr, NIH; distinguished vis prof, Dept Immunol, Temple Univ; distinguished vis prof, Am Cancer Soc, Gainesville, Tampa & Miami. *Mem:* Am Soc Clin Invest; Am Asn Immunologists; Soc Pediat Res; Am Fedn Clin Res; fel AAAS; Asn Am Physicians; Am Soc Gene Ther. *Res:* Development of innovative treatments for human disease based on the technology of gene transfer; gene therapy; cellular immunology; primary immunodeficiency; AIDS; cancer; immunotherapy; viral vectors; gene regulation; immunoregulation; Wiskott-Aldrich syndrome; Adenosine Deaminase Deficiency; brain tumors; granted 6 patents. *Mailing Add:* Nat Human Genome Res Inst Bldg 10 Rm 10C103 NIH 10 Center Dr Bethesda MD 20892-1851

BLAGER, FLORENCE BERMAN, SPEECH PATHOLOGY. *Current Pos:* asst prof, 71-78, ASSOC PROF, DEPT OTOLARYNGOL & PSYCHIAT, UNIV COLO MED CTR, DENVER, 78- *Personal Data:* b Wheeling, WVa, July 2, 28; m 73, Morton. *Educ:* Ohio Univ, BA, 50; Univ Denver, MA, 66, PhD(speech path), 70. *Concurrent Pos:* Chief speech path & audiol, JFK Child Develop Ctr, Univ Colo Med Ctr, 71-90; adj asst prof, Dept Commun Dis, Colo State Univ, 71-78, Univ Northern Colo, 71-78, Univ Denver, 71-86; from adj asst prof to adj assoc prof, Dept Commun Dis, Univ Colo, 71-82; consult, Daycare Ctr, Colo Psychiat Hosp, 71-83, Phenylketonuria Clin, JFK Ctr, 72-78, Nat Ctr Prev Child Abuse & Neglect, Circle House Playsch, 74-78, Aurora Pub Schs & JFK Presch, 74-76, Children's Diag Ctr, 75-80, Appalachia Educ Lab Inc, Charleston, WVa, 76-78, Colo Hearing & Speech Ctr, Denver, 78-79; chief speech path & audiol serv, Nat Jewish Ctr Immunol & Respiratory Med, 85-; res assoc, Recording & Res Ctr, Denver Ctr Performing Arts, 85-, consult speech pathologist, 86- *Mem:* Am Speech Lang & Hearing Asn; NY Acad Sci; Soc Res Child Develop; Am Asn Ment Deficiency. *Res:* Laryngeal dysfunction, chronic cough, professional voice, speech, and language development in Downs infants; hearing impaired Downs infants; language of abused children. *Mailing Add:* 4200 E Ninth Ave Denver CO 80220. *Fax:* 303-757-2650

BLAHA, ELI WILLIAM, ORGANIC CHEMISTRY, POLYMER CHEMISTRY. *Current Pos:* RETIRED. *Personal Data:* b Collinsville, Ill, Oct 30, 27; m 48, Eleanor Adcock; c Jennifer & Linda. *Educ:* Univ Ill, BS, 51; Univ Iowa, PhD(org chem), 54. *Prof Exp:* Chemist, Standard Oil Co, Ind, 54-60, proj chemist, Am Oil Co Div, 60-64, sr proj chemist, Amoco Chem Corp, 64-70, group leader polystyrene process develop, 70-73, res supvr, 73-87. *Mem:* Am Chem Soc; Soc Plastics Engrs. *Res:* Discovery, development and production of motor oil additives, including detergents, dispersants, oxidation inhibitors and antiwear agents; research and development of improved polystyrene resins and new condensation polymers. *Mailing Add:* 803 Howard St Wheaton IL 60187

BLAHA, GORDON C, ANATOMY, HISTOLOGY. *Current Pos:* from instr to asst prof, 63-72, assoc prof, 72-78, PROF ANAT, COL MED, UNIV CINCINNATI, 78- *Personal Data:* b Chicago, Ill, July 21, 34. *Educ:* Northern Ill Univ, BS, 57; Univ Ill, MS, 61, PhD(anat), 63. *Prof Exp:* Instr anat, Univ Ill Col Med, 62-63. *Mem:* AAAS; Am Asn Anatomists; Geront Soc; Soc Study Reproduction; Sigma Xi. *Res:* Reproductive physiology; senescent decline in reproductive function; senescence in golden hamster. *Mailing Add:* 885 E Orleans St Paxton IL 60957

BLAHD, WILLIAM HENRY, NUCLEAR MEDICINE, INTERNAL MEDICINE. *Current Pos:* CHIEF NUCLEAR MED SERV, W LOS ANGELES VET ADMIN MED CTR, 56- *Personal Data:* b Cleveland, Ohio, May 11, 21; m 45, Weiss; c Andrea, Karen & William H Jr. *Educ:* Tulane Univ, MD, 45; Am Bd Internal Med, dipl, 53; Am Bd Nuclear Med, dipl, 72. *Prof Exp:* Ward officer metab res, Vet Admin, 51-52, asst chief radioisotope serv, 52-56. *Concurrent Pos:* Dir nuclear med, Mt Sinai Hosp, Los Angles, 55-76, St Joseph Hosp Med Ctr, Calif, 58-83, Valley Presby Med Ctr, Calif, 59-85; prof med, Univ Calif, Los Angeles, 66-; mem bd dirs, Am Bd Nuclear Med, 78-, chmn, 82-83; mem bd govs, Am Bd Internal Med, 81-83. *Mem:* Fel Am Col Physicians; AMA; Health Physics Soc; Soc Exp Biol & Med; Soc Nuclear Med (pres, 77-78). *Res:* Development of nuclear medicine techniques, study of body composition; treatment of thyroid disease; clinical applications of positron emission tomography; author of 3 textbooks on nuclear medicine and 257 scientific papers and published abstracts. *Mailing Add:* Nuclear Med Serv 691/W115 West Los Angeles Vet Admin Med Ctr Los Angeles CA 90073. *Fax:* 310-824-6952

BLAHUT, RICHARD E, ENGINEERING. *Current Pos:* PROF ELEC ENG, UNIV ILL, CHAMPAIGN, 94- *Personal Data:* b Orange, NJ, June 9, 37. *Educ:* Mass Inst Technol, BS, 60; Stevens Inst Technol, MS, 64; Cornell Univ, PhD(elec eng), 72. *Prof Exp:* Staff mem navig systs, Kearfott Div, Gen Precision, 60-64; staff mem, Fed Systs Div, IBM Corp, 64-80, fel, 80-94. *Concurrent Pos:* Courtesy prof elec eng, Cornell Univ, 73-; lectr, Int Ctr Mech Sci, Udine, Italy, 78 & 82, NATO Advan Study Inst, Bonas, France, 83, Il Ciocco, Italy, 86; fel, Japan Soc Propagation Sci, 82; adj prof, Univ Ill, distinguished vis prof elec & comput eng, 84-85, vis res prof, Coord Sci Lab; assoc ed, Inst Elec & Electronics Engrs Trans Info Theory, 85-89; vis lectr, Princeton Univ, 89; consult prof, SChina Univ Technol. *Mem:* Nat Acad Eng; fel Inst Elec & Electronics Engrs; AAAS. *Res:* Mathematical aspects of statistical information processing including information theory, communications theory, surveillance theory, error-control codes and digital signal processing. *Mailing Add:* 1308 W Main St Urbana IL 61801. *Fax:* 217-244-6280; *E-Mail:* blahut@shannon.csl.edu

BLAIKLOCK, ROBERT GEORGE, CARDIOVASCULAR TOXICOLOGY, PHYSIOLOGY. *Current Pos:* CLIN PHARMACIST, BRONX VET ADMIN MED CTR. *Personal Data:* b Newark, NJ, July 6, 40; c 4. *Educ:* Univ Vt, BA, 63; Rutgers Univ, MS, 65, PhD(physiol), 69. *Prof Exp:* Res assoc pharmacol, Med Sch, Univ Wis, 69-71; instr, Mt Sinai Sch Med, 71-73; res fel, NY Med Col, 73-74, res asst prof psychiat, 74-75, asst prof pharmacol, 75-80; sr res pharmacol, Lederle Labs, Am Cyanamid Co, 80-84; assoc prof pharmacol, Arnold & Marie Schwartz Col Pharm & Health Sci, Long Island Univ, 84- *Concurrent Pos:* Adj asst prof pharmacol, NY Med Col, 80- *Mem:* AAAS; NY Acad Sci; Sigma Xi. *Res:* Cardiovalcular pharmacology; myocardial necrosis; superoxides and membrane damage, structure and function; reperfusion injury, photooxidation and bacterial exotoxins; lipid peroxidation, hemolysis and Na-K Atpase. *Mailing Add:* 225 Washington St Glen Ridge NJ 07028

BLAINE, EDWARD HOMER, CARDIOVASCULAR, RENAL. *Current Pos:* DIR, DALTON CARDIOVASC RES CTR & PROF PHYSIOL & PHARMACOL, UNIV MO, 92- *Personal Data:* b Farmington, Mo, Jan 30, 40; m 63; c 2. *Educ:* Univ Mo, AB, 62, MA, 67, PhD(physiol), 70. *Hon Degrees:* DSc, Univ Mo, 89. *Honors & Awards:* Nelson Lectr, Univ Mo, 86. *Prof Exp:* Fel, Howard Florey Inst, 71-73; asst prof physiol, Univ Pittsburgh Sch Med, 73-77; sr res fel, Merck Inst Therapeut Res, 77-78, sr investr, 78-80, dir renal pharmacol, 80-86; dir, Cardiovasc Dis Res, Searle Res & Develop, 86-92, sr dir, Washington Univ Prog, 88-92. *Concurrent Pos:* Adj prof physiol, Temple Univ Sch Md, 77-86; mem study sect, NIH, 78-85; adj prof pharmacol, Sch Med, Washington Univ, 86-; United Way chair, Searle, St Louis, 90; bd dir, Alta Mo Affiliate, 93; bd dirs, Mo Fedn Med Res, 93- *Mem:* Am Physiol Soc; Am Soc Pharmacol Exp Therapeut; Am Soc Hypertension (vpres, 91-). *Res:* Salt and water homeostasis and hypertension; salt and water intake; cardiovascular and renal physiology and pharmacology; hormonal control of blood pressure; appetitive behavior and physiological ecology. *Mailing Add:* Univ Mo John M Dalton Res Ctr Res Park Columbia MO 65211

BLAIR, ALAN HUNTLEY, ENZYMOLOGY. *Current Pos:* RETIRED. *Personal Data:* b Vancouver, BC, Oct 20, 33; m 60; c 2. *Educ:* Univ BC, BSc, 56, MSc, 57; Univ Calif, Berkeley, PhD(biochem), 64. *Prof Exp:* Damon Runyon Cancer Res Fund fel, Biophys Res Lab, Harvard Med Sch, 64-65; assoc staff med, Peter Bent Brigham Hosp, Boston, Mass, 65; from asst prof to assoc prof, Dalhousie Univ, 66-80, prof biochem, 81-96. *Res:* Targeting of drugs by linkage to antitumor antibodies; enzymology; mechanism of action of alcohol and aldehyde dehydrogenases. *Mailing Add:* D ept Biochem Dalhousie Univ Halifax NS B3H 4H7 Can. *E-Mail:* blairah@is.dal.ca

BLAIR, BARBARA ANN, PROTEIN CHEMISTRY, ENZYMOLOGY. *Current Pos:* RETIRED. *Personal Data:* b Gastonia, NC, Oct 21, 26. *Educ:* Agnes Scott Col, BA, 48; Univ Tenn, MS, 53, PhD(chem), 56. *Prof Exp:* Res assoc, Med Sch, Univ Buffalo, 56-57 & Med Sch, Univ Va, 57-61; asst prof chem, Wilson Col, 61-62; from asst prof to prof chem, Sweet Brian Col, 62-94. *Concurrent Pos:* Vis lectr & actg head, chem dept, Women's Christian Col, Madras, India, 68-69; asst dean, Sweet Briar Col, 69-74, acad dean, 74-77. *Mem:* Fel AAAS; Am Chem Soc; Sigma Xi. *Res:* Amino acid metabolism; protein structure. *Mailing Add:* PO Box P Sweet Briar VA 24595

BLAIR, CAROL DEAN, VIROLOGY, MOLECULAR BIOLOGY. *Current Pos:* from asst prof to assoc prof microbiol, 75-85, asst dean, Col Vet Med Biomed Sci, 83-88, PROF MICROBIOL, COLO STATE UNIV, 85-, DEPT HEAD MICROBIOL, COLO STATE UNIV, 88- *Personal Data:* b Salt Lake City, Utah, Jan 31, 42; m 68, Patrick Brennan; c Deirdre, Niall & Justin. *Educ:* Univ Utah, BA, 64; Univ Calif, Berkeley, PhD(molecular biol), 68. *Hon Degrees:* MA, Dublin Univ, 74. *Prof Exp:* Fel biochem, Dublin Univ, 68-70, from jr lectr to lectr microbiol, 70-75. *Concurrent Pos:* Fel, Am Cancer Soc, 68-69, Irish Dept Educ, 69-70 & Int Union Against Cancer, Am Cancer Soc, 72-73; vis prof, Univ Colo Health Sci Ctr, 82; coun deleg, AAAS, 97- *Mem:* Am Soc Microbiol; Soc Gen Microbiol; AAAS; Am Soc Trop Med & Hyg; Sigma Xi; Am Soc Virol. *Res:* Mechanisms of animal virus replication; mechanisms of virus pathogenesis; arbovirus-vector interactions; virus genetics. *Mailing Add:* Dept Microbiol Colo State Univ Ft Collins CO 80523. *Fax:* 970-491-1815; *E-Mail:* cblair@vines.colostate.edu

BLAIR, CHARLES EUGENE, OPERATIONS RESEARCH. *Current Pos:* from asst prof to assoc prof, 76-85, PROF, DEPT BUS ADMIN, UNIV ILL, 88- *Personal Data:* b New York, NY, Dec 30, 49; m, Joan Friedman. *Educ:* Mass Inst Technol, BS, 71; Carnegie-Mellon Univ, MA, 72, PhD(math), 75. *Prof Exp:* Vis asst prof, Dept Math, NC State Univ, 75-76. *Concurrent Pos:* Vis asst prof, Ga Inst Technol, 80. *Mem:* Am Math Soc; Opers Res Soc. *Res:* Integer and linear programming; computational complexity; cryptography. *Mailing Add:* 1206 S Sixth St Box 8 Champaign IL 61820-6915. *E-Mail:* c-blair@uiuc.edu

BLAIR, CHARLES MELVIN, JR, SURFACE CHEMISTRY, SYNTHETIC ORGANIC CHEMISTRY. *Current Pos:* PRES, BLAIR PETRO CO, 86- *Personal Data:* b Vernon, Tex, Oct 24, 10; m 36, Catherine Stone; c Julian & Sally. *Educ:* Rice Univ, AB, 31, AM, 32; Calif Inst Technol, PhD(chem), 35. *Prof Exp:* Chemist, Petrolite Corp, 35-43, dir res, 43-53, pres, 53-64; vchancellor, Wash Univ, 64-67; vpres & tech dir, Magna Corp, 67-70, chmn bd dirs & sr scientist, 70-86. *Mem:* AAAS; Am Chem Soc; Soc Petrol Engrs. *Res:* Colloid and surface chemistry; demulsifiers; corrosion inhibitors; chemical processing of petroleum; chemical agents for enhancement of petroleum production; penicillin production process. *Mailing Add:* 835 Morningside Dr Fullerton CA 92835. *Fax:* 714-256-2469

BLAIR, DAVID W(ILLIAM), THERMODYNAMICS, COMBUSTION. *Current Pos:* PRES, PRINCETON SCI ENTERPRISES, 85- *Personal Data:* b Santa Barbara, Calif, Oct 5, 29; m 54, Rosemary Miles; c Karen E, Barbara A, M Maria, Amanda M, David B & Rachel P. *Educ:* Ore State Univ, BS, 52; Columbia Univ, MS, 54, PhD(combustion), 61. *Prof Exp:* Teaching asst mech eng, Columbia Univ, 52-54, instr, 54-58; res assoc aeronaut eng, Princeton Univ, 58-61; sr res engr, Aerochem Res Labs, 61-62; fel combustion & propulsion, Royal Norweg Inst Indust & Sci Res, 62-63; assoc prof mech eng, Polytech Inst Brooklyn, 63-69; sr res engr, Exxon Res & Eng Co, 69-74, eng assoc, 74-83; sr res engr, M L Energia, 83-85. *Concurrent Pos:* Lectr, Columbia Univ, 59, adj assoc prof mech eng, 75-; lectr, Stevens Inst Technol, 61-62. *Mem:* Combustion Inst; Am Phys Soc; Am Soc Mech Engrs; Am Inst Chem Engrs. *Res:* Solid propellant rocket propulsion; fluid mechanics; energy conversion; plasma physics; combustion emissions and pollutant control; coal combustion and gasification; high temperature test apparatus; tribology test apparatus; automated instrumentation; blood and hemoglobin test apparatus. *Mailing Add:* 1108 Kingston Rd Princeton NJ 08540. *E-Mail:* 76443.161@compuserve.com

BLAIR, DONALD GEORGE RALPH, BIOCHEMISTRY, CANCER RESEARCH. *Current Pos:* RETIRED. *Personal Data:* b Lloydminster, Sask, Nov 5, 32; m 59, Joan L Springsteen; c Eric Donald & Karen Jo. *Educ:* Univ Alta, BSc, 55, MSc, 56; Univ Wis, PhD, 61. *Prof Exp:* Lectr cancer res, Univ Sask, 61-63, lectr biochem, 63-67, from asst prof to assoc prof cancer res, 63-76, assoc prof biochem, 76-93. *Concurrent Pos:* Res assoc, Nat Cancer Inst Can, 71-75. *Mem:* AAAS; Am Soc Biochem & Molecular Biol; Sigma Xi; Am Asn Cancer Res; Can Biochem Soc; Can Oncol Soc. *Res:* Cell biology; rat intestinal sucrase; mechanisms and regulation of the biosynthesis of pyrimidine nucleotides; mechanisms of the resistance of mammalian cells to purine and pyrimidine analogues; RNA synthesis in neoplastic cells; RNA polymerase; polyamines and RNA synthesis. *Mailing Add:* 12 Leyden Crescent Saskatoon SK S7J 2S4 Can

BLAIR, EMIL, THORACIC SURGERY, CARDIOVASCULAR SURGERY. *Current Pos:* RETIRED. *Personal Data:* b Satu-mare, Rumania, Oct 20, 23; US citizen. *Educ:* Med Col Ga, MD, 46. *Honors & Awards:* Hektoen Award, AMA, 55. *Prof Exp:* Instr med & NIH fel, Med Ctr, Duke Univ, 52-54; Halsted fel surg, Univ Colo Med Ctr, Denver, 56-57; asst prof surg, Sch Med, Univ Md, Baltimore, 60-66; prof cardiothoracic surg, Col Med, Univ Vt, 66-69; from prof to emer prof surg, Univ Colo Med Ctr, Denver, 69-89. *Concurrent Pos:* Vis prof, Univ Uppsala, Guys Hosp, Univ Oslo, Univ Helsinki, 65-66 & Hodossoh Univ Hosp, Jerusalem, 77-80; consult, Cent Off, Vet Admin, 65-68; Career res award, 61 & fel Fogarty Int Ctr, NIH, 61. *Mem:* Am Asn Thoracic Surg; Am Col Surg; Sigma Xi; Soc Vascular Surg; Oriental Inst; Am Inst Archeol. *Res:* Hypothermia; hyperbaric oxygen; cardiovascular pulmonary physiology and surgery; shock; biomechanics of trauma; emergency medical services; education, health and hospital planning. *Mailing Add:* 1190 W Northern Pkwy Baltimore MD 21210

BLAIR, ETCYL HOWELL, ORGANIC CHEMISTRY. *Current Pos:* res chemist, 51-56, group leader, 56-65, div leader, 65-67, dir res, Britton Lab, 67-68, mgr res & develop, Agr Dept, 68-71, dir res & develop, Agr-Org Dept, 71-73, dir health & environ res, US Area Res & Develop, 73-78, VPRES & DIR HEALTH & ENVIRON SCI, DOW CHEM CO, 78- *Personal Data:* b Wynona, Okla, Oct 16, 22; m 49; c 3. *Educ:* Southwestern Col, Kans, AB, 47; Kans State Col, MS, 49, PhD(chem), 52. *Hon Degrees:* DSc, Southwestern Col, Kans, 74. *Prof Exp:* Instr org chem, Southwestern Col, Kans, 47-48; res asst, Kans State Col, 48-51. *Concurrent Pos:* mem bd dirs, Chem Indust Inst Toxicol, 77- *Mem:* Int Acad Environ Safety; AAAS; Am Chem Soc; NY Acad Sci; Sigma Xi. *Res:* Isolation and characterization of natural products; synthesis of biological active compounds; organic phosphorus compounds. *Mailing Add:* Four Crescent Ct Midland MI 48640-3310

BLAIR, GEORGE RICHARD, INORGANIC CHEMISTRY. *Current Pos:* RETIRED. *Personal Data:* b San Bernardino, Calif, Aug 17, 20; m 51; c 2. *Educ:* Univ Redlands, BA, 42. *Honors & Awards:* NASA Award for Contribution to Surveyor Prog. *Prof Exp:* Chief anal chemist, Metal Hydrides, Inc, Mass, 43-46; anal group leader, Mineral Eng Lab, Am Cyanamid Co, 50-52; chief res chemist, McMillan Lab, Inc, Mass, 52-59; head space mat group, Hughes Aircraft Co, Culver City, 59-68, head chem process, Electron Dynamics Div, 68-72, head anal servs, Hughes Aircraft Res Labs, 72-74, qual engr, 74-77, res chemist, 77-84. *Mem:* Am Chem Soc. *Res:* High vacuum studies; clean surfaces; optical fibers; instrumental analysis; fiber optics. *Mailing Add:* 10748 Cranks Rd Culver City CA 90230-5481

BLAIR, GRANT CLARK, imaging computer systems, image data retrieval & interchange, for more information see previous edition

BLAIR, JAMES BRYAN, BIOCHEMISTRY. *Current Pos:* PROF & HEAD, BIOCHEM & MOLECULAR BIOL, OKLA STATE UNIV, 90- *Personal Data:* b Waynesburg, Pa, May 26, 44; m 66; c 2. *Educ:* WVa Univ, BS, 66; Univ Va, PhD(biochem), 70. *Prof Exp:* Lab asst chem, WVa Univ, 64-66; fel, Inst Enzyme Res, Univ Wis, 69-72; from asst prof to prof biochem WVa Univ, 72-90, interim chmn, 84-85. *Concurrent Pos:* NIH fel, 70; NIH res career develop award, 78- *Mem:* AAAS; Am Soc Biol Chemists; Biophys Soc; Am Chem Soc; Sigma Xi. *Res:* Regulation of carbohydrate and lipid metabolism in mammals; kinetic and regulatory properties of hepatic pyruvate kinase; fish models of chemical carcinogenesis. *Mailing Add:* 1924 Elvin Dr Stillwater OK 74074-2140. *Fax:* 405-744-7799; *E-Mail:* jbb0bmb@olcoax.okstate.edu

BLAIR, JAMES EDWARD, PHYSICAL CHEMISTRY. *Current Pos:* CHEMIST 4, WIS STATE LAB HYG, MADISON, 87- *Personal Data:* b Cedar Rapids, Iowa, Dec 6, 35; m 61; c 2. *Educ:* Rockhurst Col, BS, 58; Univ Wis, PhD(chem), 63. *Prof Exp:* Res chemist, Photo Prod Dept, E I du Pont de Nemours & Co, 63-65; from asst prof to assoc prof, Milton Col, 65-80; assoc prof, Edgewood Col, 80-81; scientist II, Raltech, 81-86. *Concurrent Pos:* Res assoc, Enzyme Inst, 65-81; NSF fel. *Mem:* Sigma Xi. *Res:* Sedimentation studies of polymer solutions; proteins and DNA. *Mailing Add:* 2210 Ravenswood Rd Madison WI 53711

BLAIR, JOHN, electrical engineering, for more information see previous edition

BLAIR, JOHN MORRIS, EXPERIMENTAL NUCLEAR PHYSICS. *Current Pos:* from asst prof to assoc prof, 50-62, prof, 62-89, EMER PROF PHYSICS, UNIV MINN, MINNEAPOLIS, 89- *Personal Data:* b Russellville, Ark, May 24, 19; m 47; c 2. *Educ:* Okla Agr & Mech Col, BS, 40; Univ Wis, PhM, 42; Univ Minn, PhD(physics), 47. *Prof Exp:* Jr scientist, Los Alamos Sci Lab, NMex, 43-45; res assoc physics, Univ Minn, 47-48; assoc scientist, Argonne Nat Lab, 48-50. *Mem:* Am Phys Soc; Am Asn Physics Teachers; Sigma Xi. *Res:* Development of equipment to aid in teaching physics; development and use of Van de Graaf machines; reaction involving heavy ions. *Mailing Add:* Sch Physics Univ Minn Minneapolis MN 55455

BLAIR, MARTHA LONGWELL, BIOMEDICAL RESEARCH, ANIMAL PHYSIOLOGY. *Current Pos:* ASSOC PROF PHYSIOL, UNIV ROCHESTER, 77- *Personal Data:* b 1948; m 78; c 2. *Educ:* Wellesley Col, BA, 69; Univ Wash, PhD(physiol & psychol), 74. *Mailing Add:* Dept Physiol Univ Rochester Med Ctr Box 711 Rochester NY 14642-8711

BLAIR, PAUL V, BIOCHEMISTRY, REGULATION OF ENERGY METABOLISM. *Current Pos:* PROF BIOCHEM, SCH MED, UNIV IND, INDIANAPOLIS, 91- *Personal Data:* b Kimball, Nebr, Nov 11, 29; m 88, Connie P; c Benjamin, Christopher, Jennifer & Cameron. *Educ:* Utah State Univ, BS, 57; Purdue Univ, PhD(genetics & chem), 61. *Prof Exp:* Fel biochem, Inst Enzyme Res, Univ Wis, 61-64, asst prof, Univ, 64-66; asst prof, Sch Med, Univ Ind, Indianapolis, 66-69, assoc prof biochem, 69-81; pub rels & sales, Engineered Models Corp, 82-91. *Concurrent Pos:* Sabbatical, Cambridge Univ, 72-73, Univ Alaska, 79. *Mem:* Am Soc Biol Chemists; Am Soc Cell Biol. *Res:* Mitochondrial metabolism; correlation of metabolic functions with ultrastructure; metabolic regulation. *Mailing Add:* Dept Biochem & Molecular Biol Ind Univ Sch Med 635 Barnhill Dr Indianapolis IN 46202-5122

BLAIR, PHYLLIS BEEBE, IMMUNOLOGY. *Current Pos:* PROF IMMUNOL, UNIV CALIF, BERKELEY, 72- *Personal Data:* b Buffalo, NY, May 17, 31; m 55. *Educ:* Cornell Univ, BS, 53; Univ Calif, Berkeley, PhD(zool), 58. *Mem:* AAAS; Am Asn Cancer Res; Am Asn Immunologists; Am Soc Zoologists; Clin Immunol Soc. *Res:* Immune regulation. *Mailing Add:* 601 Van Ness Ave San Francisco CA 94102

BLAIR, ROBERT, ANIMAL & POULTRY NUTRITION. *Current Pos:* head, 84-91, PROF ANIMAL SCI, UNIV BC, 84- *Personal Data:* b May 29, 33; UK & Can citizen; m 58; c 2. *Educ:* Univ Glasgow, BSc, 56; Univ Aberdeen, PhD(animal & swine nutrit), 60; DSc, Univ Sask, 83. *Honors & Awards:* Decorated Knight Lufsensic Ursinius Order, Netherlands. *Prof Exp:* Sr res fel swine prod, Univ Aberdeen, 60-66; prin sci officer nutrit, Agr Res Coun, 66-75; res assoc, Cornell Univ, 69-70; dir nutrit, Swift Can Co Ltd, 76-78; from assoc prof to prof animal & poultry sci, Univ Sask, 78-84. *Concurrent Pos:* Exec dir, Prairie Swine Ctr, 78-84; pres, World Soc Animal Prod, 88-93. *Mem:* Can Soc Animal Sci; Am Soc Animal Sci; Nutrit Soc; Poultry Sci Asn; Am Inst Nutrit; Brit Soc Animal Prod. *Res:* Vitamin utilization in poultry and swine; swine nutrition; poultry nutrition; nutritional toxicology. *Mailing Add:* Dept Animal Sci Univ BC Suite 139 2357 Main Mall Vancouver BC V6T 2A2 Can. *Fax:* 604-822-4400

BLAIR, ROBERT G, ECONOMIC GEOLOGY. *Current Pos:* CHIEF GEOLOGIST, COEURD ALENE, 87- *Personal Data:* b Toledo, Ohio, Dec 6, 36. *Educ:* Dartmouth Univ, BA, 58; Univ Mich, MA, 60. *Mem:* Fel Geol Soc Am; Soc Econ Geologists; Geol Soc Can. *Mailing Add:* 7764 S Elm Ct Littleton CO 80122

BLAIR, ROBERT WILLIAM, petroleum geology, for more information see previous edition

BLAIR, ROBERT WILLIAM, NEUROPHYSIOLOGY. *Current Pos:* ASST PROF PHYSIOL, OKLA UNIV, 80- *Educ:* Univ Tex, PhD(pharmacol), 79. *Mailing Add:* Dept Physiol Univ Okla Health Sci Ctr Oklahoma City OK 73190-0001

BLAIR, WILLIAM DAVID, NON-COMMUTATIVE RING THEORY. *Current Pos:* From asst prof to assoc prof, 71-86, PROF MATH, NORTHERN ILL UNIV, 86-, DEPT CHAIR, 90- *Personal Data:* b Baltimore, Md, Apr 20, 43; m 65, Kathleen McMullen; c Carla & Stephanie. *Educ:* Johns Hopkins Univ, AB, 65; Univ Md, PhD(math), 71. *Concurrent Pos:* Vis fel, Univ Leeds, 78-79 & Univ Calif, San Diego, 85-86. *Mem:* Am Math Soc; Math Asn Am; London Math Soc; Sigma Xi. *Res:* Ring theory, noetherian rings; localizations and quotient rings. *Mailing Add:* Dept Math Sci Northern Ill Univ De Kalb IL 60115. *Fax:* 815-753-1112; *E-Mail:* blair@math.niu.edu

BLAIR, WILLIAM EMANUEL, ELECTRICAL ENGINEERING & GEOPHYSICS, POWER ENGINEERING & DATA COMMUNICATIONS. *Current Pos:* PROJ MGR, EPRI, 91- *Personal Data:* b Elmira, NY, Apr 10, 34; m 59, Patricia Ryder; c 2. *Educ:* Cornell Univ, BSEE, 58, MSEE, 60; Univ NMex, DSc, 64. *Prof Exp:* Res asst elec eng, Cornell Univ, 58-60; assoc, Univ NMex, 60-64; res engr, Stanford Res Inst, 64-68, sr res engr, 68-76; proj mgr, Elec Power Res Inst, 76-84; lead consult, Energy & Control Consults, 84-90. *Mem:* Sr mem Inst Elec & Electronics Engrs; Int Electrotech Comn. *Res:* Very-low-frequency propagation and antenna theory; ionospheric propagation theory; satellite data processing; underground and underwater antenna theory; microwave tube theory; electric utility communications, especially power-line carrier, distribution automation power system engineering. *Mailing Add:* EPRI 3412 Hillview Palo Alto CA 94304. *Fax:* 650-855-8997; *E-Mail:* bblair@epri.com

BLAIS, BURTON W, IMMUNODIAGNOSTICS, IMMUNOTECHNOLOGY & BIOTECHNOLOGY. *Current Pos:* RES SCIENTIST & CHIEF, TECH DEVELOP TRANSFER UNIT, FOOD LAB, LAB SERV DIV, AGR & AGRI-FOOD CAN, OTTAWA, 92- *Personal Data:* b Montreal, Que, June 2, 63; m 88, Lisa Morrison. *Educ:* Univ NB, BSc, 84; Carleton Univ, MSc, 86, PhD(biol & biochem), 90. *Prof Exp:* Vis fel molecular biol, Nat Lab Sexually Transmitted Dis, Lab Ctr Dis Control, Ottawa, 90-91, biologist & head Molecular Markers Sect, Pathogens, Dept Health & Welfare Can, 91-92. *Concurrent Pos:* Sci consult, Ricoh Kyosan, Inc, 89-; lectr, Dept Biol, Inst Biochem, Carleton Univ, Ottawa, 90-91; adj prof, Dept Food Sci, Univ Laval, Que. *Mem:* Can Biochem Soc; Can Fedn Biol Sci; Sigma Xi. *Res:* Development of novel immunoassay strategies for the diagnosis of human, animal and plant diseases; detection of microbial pathogens in foods and feeds; development of DNA probe and nucleic acid amplification methods for food pathogens. *Mailing Add:* Lab Serv Div Agr & Agri-Food Can Ottawa ON K1A 0C6 Can. *Fax:* 613-759-1267

BLAIS, J A RODRIGUE, ESTIMATION, INFORMATION. *Current Pos:* assoc prof, 79-87, PROF GEOMATICS ENG, UNIV CALGARY, 87- *Personal Data:* b Rimouski, Que, Dec 17, 41. *Educ:* Loyola Col, Montreal, BSc Hons, 63; Univ Toronto, MA, 65; Univ NB, PhD(geodesy), 79. *Prof Exp:* Mathematician, Topographical Surv, Surv & Mapping Br, Dept Energy, Mines & Resources, 68-74 & Geodetic Surv, 75-79. *Concurrent Pos:* Consult, Dept Energy, Mines & Resources, Ottawa, 79-, Alta Provincial Govt, 80-; vis prof, KN Toosy Univ Technol, Tehran, Iran, 91 & 93, Wuhan Tech Univ Surv & Mapping, China, 93. *Mem:* Can Math Soc; Can Asn Physicists; Can Inst Geomatics; Can Geophys Union; Int Soc Gen Relativity & Gravitation; Am Math Soc. *Res:* Estimation, numerical methods, gravitation, and geodetic applications; stochastic processes and applications; information theory and applications; earth's gravity field. *Mailing Add:* Dept Geomatics Eng Univ Calgary Calgary AB T2N 1N4 Can. *Fax:* 403-284-1980; *E-Mail:* blais@aco.ucalgary.ca

BLAIS, NORMAND C, chemical physics, for more information see previous edition

BLAIS, ROGER A, INDUSTRIAL INNOVATION, ECONOMIC GEOLOGY. *Current Pos:* assoc prof, Univ Montreal, 61-66, prof, 66-92, assoc dean res, 70-71, dean sci res, 70-80, dir Innovation Ctr, 80-92, EMER PROF ECOL POLYTECH, UNIV MONTREAL, 91- *Personal Data:* b Shawinigan, Que, Feb 4, 26; m 50; c 2. *Educ:* Laval Univ, BASc, 49, MSc, 50; Univ Toronto, PhD(geol), 54. *Honors & Awards:* Barlow Mem Gold Medal, Can Inst Mining & Metall, 62, Gold Medal, 67; Bancroft Award, Royal Soc Can, 76; Archambault Gold Medal & Alcan Prize, Fr Can Asn Advan Sci, 77; Officer, Order Canada, 85; Nat Order Que, 95. *Prof Exp:* Geologist, Que Dept Natural Resources, 53-56; chief develop engr, Iron Ore Co, Can, 56-61. *Concurrent Pos:* Dir, Eldorado Nuclear Ltd, 68-; chmn nat study group solid earth sci in Can, Sci Coun Can, 68-70; mem earth sci comt, Nat Res Coun Can, 67-69, chmn, 69; mem exec comt, Nat Adv Comt Res Geol Sci, 68-; gov, Int Develop Res Ctr, Ottawa, Ont, 74-, chmn exec comt, 76-; Arctic Inst NAm fel, 75; chmn study group mat res, Nat Res Coun Can, 76-77. *Mem:* AAAS; Geol Asn Can (pres, 69-70); Can Inst Mining & Metall (past pres); Mineral Asn Can; Soc Econ Geol; fel World Acad Arts & Sci. *Res:* Applied geostatistics; applications of the theory of regionalized variables to ore reserve estimation, grade control and mineral exploration; origin of iron ores; geology of base metal sulphide deposits and their relations to volcanic and carbonate rocks; industrial innovation. *Mailing Add:* 155 ave JJ Joubert app 502 Duvernay Laval PQ H7G 4T8 Can. *Fax:* 514-340-4173

BLAIS, ROGER NATHANIEL, MULTIPHASE FLOW INSTRUMENTATION. *Current Pos:* asst prof, Univ Tulsa, 77-81, chmn physics, 86-88, vice provost, 89-92, actg provost & vpres acad affairs, 90-91, ASSOC PROF ENG PHYSICS, UNIV TULSA, 81-, ASSOC DIR, ARTIFICIAL LIFT PROJS, 83- *Personal Data:* b Duluth, Minn, Oct 3, 44; m 71, Mary Leclerc; c Christopher & Laura. *Educ:* Univ Minn, BA, 66; Univ Okla, PhD(physics), 71. *Prof Exp:* Instr physics, Westark Community Col, 71-72; asst prof physics & geophys sci, Old Dom Univ, 72-77. *Concurrent Pos:* Dir, Test Measurement Div, Instrument Soc Am, 95- *Mem:* Am Phys Soc; AAAS; Am Geophys Union; Nat Soc Prof Engrs; Soc Petrol Engrs; Instrument Soc Am; Am Asn Physics Teachers. *Res:* Fluid dynamics; artificial lift technology, multiphase flow in pipes, atmospheric pollution diffusion modeling, remote sensing of atmospheric pollution, instrumentation, gaseous electronics. *Mailing Add:* 5348 E 30th Pl Tulsa OK 74114-6314. *Fax:* 918-631-2995; *E-Mail:* roger_blais@utulsa.edu

BLAISDELL, ERNEST ATWELL, JR, EXPERIMENTAL DESIGN. *Current Pos:* PROF & CHMN MATH DEPT, ELIZABETHTOWN COL, 68- *Personal Data:* b Brewer, Maine, Jan 10, 40; m 58; c 2. *Educ:* Univ Maine, BA, 62, MA, 64; Temple Univ, PhD(statist), 79. *Prof Exp:* Instr math, Clarkson Col Technol, 64-68. *Concurrent Pos:* Adj lectr math, Pa State Univ, 78-79; lectr statist, Temple Univ, 79- *Mem:* Am Statist Asn; Am Asn Univ Professors. *Res:* Partially balanced change-over designs on m-associate class PBIB designs; development of new series of these designs and a study of their efficiencies. *Mailing Add:* Dept Math Sci Elizabethtown Col Elizabethtown PA 17022

BLAISDELL, FRED W(ILLIAM), hydraulic engineering, for more information see previous edition

BLAISDELL, JAMES PERSHING, RANGE ECOLOGY. *Current Pos:* agr aid, US Forest Serv, USDA, 40-42, range conservationist, Soil Conserv Serv, 46, range conservationist, Forest Serv, 46-66, asst sta dir res, Intermountain Forest & Range Exp Sta, 66-80. *Personal Data:* b Holbrook, Idaho, June 29, 18; m 41; c 5. *Educ:* Utah State Univ, BS, 39; Univ Idaho, MS, 42; Univ Minn, PhD(bot), 56. *Prof Exp:* Field asst, Grazing Serv, US Dept Interior, 37-39. *Mem:* Soc Range Mgt; Ecol Soc Am. *Res:* Management of livestock and big game ranges; effects of fire on range vegetation; plant growth in relation to climate. *Mailing Add:* 2664 Shamrock Dr Ogden UT 84403

BLAISDELL, JOHN LEWIS, FOOD SCIENCE, CHEMICAL ENGINEERING. *Current Pos:* RETIRED. *Personal Data:* b Norwood, Mass, Feb 27, 35; m 57; c 5. *Educ:* Univ Mass, BSChE, 56, MS, 58; Mich State Univ, PhD(food sci), 63. *Prof Exp:* Asst instr agr eng, Univ Mass, 56-58; asst food sci, Mich State Univ, 58-63, NIH fel, 63-64; from asst prof to prof food sci & nutrit & agr eng. Ohio State Univ, 64-89. *Concurrent Pos:* Ed, Food Eng Div, Am Soc Agr Engrs. *Mem:* Am Soc Eng Educ; Am Soc Heat, Refrig & Air-Conditioning Engrs; Inst Food Technol; Am Inst Chem Engrs; Am Soc Agr Engrs; Sigma Xi. *Res:* Application of engineering to food preservation problems; natural convection in confined space; transient conduction and convection; dairy processing waste treatment; rheology; packaging; food process controls curriculum development. *Mailing Add:* 4842 Larwell Dr Columbus OH 43220

BLAISDELL, RICHARD KEKUNI, INTERNAL MEDICINE, HEMATOLOGY. *Current Pos:* chmn dept, 66-70, PROF MED, SCH MED, UNIV HAWAII, 66- *Personal Data:* b Honolulu, Hawaii, Mar 11, 25; m 62; c 2. *Educ:* Univ Redlands, AB, 45; Univ Chicago, MD, 47. *Prof Exp:* Intern med, Johns Hopkins Hosp, 48-49; asst resident, Charity Hosp, New Orleans, 49-50; instr path, Duke Univ, 54-55; resident med, Univ Chicago, 55-57, instr, 57-58; res assoc, Atomic Bomb Casualty Comn, 59-61; asst prof, Univ Chicago, 61-66. *Mem:* AAAS; Am Fedn Clin Res; Am Soc Hemat; Am Col Physicians; Am Asn Hist Med. *Res:* Hemoproliferative disorders; platelet-subendothelial interactions; Polynesian medicine. *Mailing Add:* 3333 Kaohinani Dr Honolulu HI 96817-1669

BLAISTEN-BAROJAS, ESTELA OLGA, PHYSICS. *Current Pos:* PROF COMPUT SCI, GEORGE MASON UNIV, 92. *Educ:* Univ Paris, MS, 70; PhD(physics), 74. *Prof Exp:* From asst prof to prof physics, Int Physics, Univ Nac Aut Mex, 75-92. *Concurrent Pos:* Vis scholar, Stanford Univ, 82-83, prof, Nat Inst Stand & Technol, 89-90, Johns Hopkins Univ, 90-91, NSF prof, 90-92; Fulbright fel, 82-83; investr, Nat Mex, 84- *Mem:* Am Phys Soc; Am Chem Soc; Mat Res Soc; NY Acad Sci; AAAS. *Res:* Computational simulations, microscopic modeling of structure and dynamics of aggregation and growth, melting, wetting, phase transitions, sintering, nanophase and structured materials. *Mailing Add:* Dept Physics, CSI George Mason Univ MS 3F3 Fairfax VA 22030. *Fax:* 301-869-5929; *E-Mail:* eblaiste@gmu.edu

BLAKE, ALEXANDER, MECHANICAL & STRUCTURAL ENGINEERING. *Current Pos:* RETIRED. *Personal Data:* b Poland, Sept 24, 20; m 52; c 1. *Educ:* Polish Univ, London, Dipl, 51, Univ London, 55. *Prof Exp:* Design engr indust & tractors, Vickers Armstrongs Ltd, Eng, 51-53; sr stress engr aircraft eng, de Havilland Eng, Co, Eng, 53-54; head eng sect distrib & generation elec, Elec Auth Eng , 54-56; design anal indust heating, Westinghouse Elec Corp, 56-58; sect head res appl & theoret mech, Assoc Spring Corp, 58-60; sr res engr, Kaiser Aluminum & Chem Corp, 60-61; mgr stress & Wright control, Aerojet Gen Corp, 61-66; tech adv, Boeing Airplain Co, 66-67; sr stress analyst, Nuclear Test Eng Div, Lawrence Radiation Lab, 66-90. *Mem:* Am Soc Mech Engr; Brit Inst Mech Eng. *Res:* Stredd and structural analysis; Machine disign; engineering mechanics. *Mailing Add:* 550 Escondido Circle Livermore CA 94550

BLAKE, CARL, ELECTRONICS ENGINEERING. *Current Pos:* CONSULT, 86- *Personal Data:* b Sarasota, Fla, Dec 17, 25; m 48; c 4. *Educ:* Mass Inst Technol, BS & MS, 49. *Prof Exp:* Asst prof elec eng, Univ Maine, 49-57; staff mem microwave components, Mass Inst Technol, 57-63, asst group leader, 63-65, assoc group leader, Phased Array Radars, Lincoln Lab, 65, group leader, 65-86. *Mem:* Inst Elec & Electronics Engrs. *Res:* Microwave theory and techniques, especially noise theory, low noise receivers, phased array radar systems, components and costing, and microwave integrated circuits. *Mailing Add:* 1 Pacific Lane Westford MA 01886

BLAKE, CARL THOMAS, AGRONOMY. *Current Pos:* AGRON EXTEN SPECIALIST TURF MGT NC AGR EXTEN SERV, 61- *Personal Data:* b Jacksonville, NC, Apr 14, 26; m 49; c 2. *Educ:* NC State Col, BS, 52, MS, 57; Pa State Univ, PhD(agron), 63. *Prof Exp:* Asst county agr agt, NC Agr Exten Serv, 52-53; spec acct, Carolina Tel & Tel Co, 53-54; agron exten specialist turf mgt, NC Agr Exten Serv, 54-60,; exten prof crop sci, NC State Univ, 61- *Mem:* Am Soc Agron. *Res:* Ecological and physiological aspects of plant communities, particularly production of cultivated species. *Mailing Add:* 4509 Leaf Ct Raleigh NC 27612

BLAKE, CHARLES ALBERT, NEUROENDOCRINOLOGY, REPRODUCTIVE BIOLOGY. *Current Pos:* PROF & CHMN CELL BIOL & NEUROSCI, UNIV SC SCH MED, 86- *Personal Data:* b Providence, RI, Nov 6, 43; m 72, Patricia K Cole; c Charles R & Jeffrey A. *Educ:* Brown Univ, BA, 66; Univ Houston, MS, 68; Univ Calif, Los Angeles, PhD(anat), 72. *Prof Exp:* Asst prof, Duke Univ, 72-76; assoc prof, Univ Nebr Med Ctr, 76-80, prof, 80-86. *Concurrent Pos:* Fel, Ministere de L Educ Nationale de Republique, 72; honor lectr, Middle Am State Univ Asn, 79; vis prof, Karolinska Inst, 80; mem, NIH Reproductive Biol Study Sect, 86-90. *Mem:* Soc Exp Biol & Med; Endocrine Soc; Soc Neurosci; Am Asn Anatomists; Am Physiol Soc. *Res:* Neuroendocrine control mechanisms for anterior pituitary gland hormone secretion; development of the anterior pituitary gland; brain mechanisms responsible for secretion of hypothalamic peptides; reproductive biology control mechanisms. *Mailing Add:* Dept Cell Biol & Neurosci Univ SC Sch Med Columbia SC 29208-0001. *Fax:* 803-733-3212

BLAKE, DANIEL BRYAN, PALEOBIOLOGY. *Current Pos:* from asst prof to assoc prof, 67-79, PROF GEOL, UNIV ILL, URBANA, 79-; ASSOC DIR, MUS NATURAL HIST, 94- *Personal Data:* b New York, NY, Apr 4, 39; wid. *Educ:* Univ Ill, Urbana, BS, 60; Mich State Univ, MS, 62; Univ Calif, Berkeley, PhD(paleont), 66. *Prof Exp:* Actg instr paleont, Univ Calif, Berkeley, 66-67. *Concurrent Pos:* Dir, Mus Natural Hist, 91-94. *Mem:* Soc Econ Paleontologists & Mineralogists; Paleont Soc; Int Paleont Union; Brit Paleont Asn; Sigma Xi; AAAS. *Res:* Fossil and modern asteroids; paleozoic Bryozoa; taxonomy, phylogeny, ecology of fossil and modern asteroids. *Mailing Add:* Rm 245 NHB Dept Geol Univ Ill 1301 W Green St Urbana IL 61801. *Fax:* 217-244-4996; *E-Mail:* dblake@uiuc.edu

BLAKE, DANIEL MELVIN, PHOTOCHEMISTRY, ENVIRONMENTAL CHEMISTRY. *Current Pos:* mgr mat br, 86-89, PRIN SCIENTIST, NAT RENEWABLE ENERGY LAB, 89- *Personal Data:* b Miami, Fla, Oct 23, 43; m 65; c 2. *Educ:* Colo State Univ, BS, 65; Wash State Univ, PhD(chem), 69. *Prof Exp:* Vis asst prof chem, Harvey Mudd Col, 69-70; from asst prof to prof chem, Univ Tex, Arlington, 70-81; sr scientist & mgr raw mat & chem alumina, Arco Metals Co, 81-85. *Mem:* Am Chem Soc; Metall Soc; AAAS; Am Soc Mech Engrs; Am Solar Energy Soc. *Res:* Coordination chemistry; platinum metals chemistry; organotransition metal chemistry; photochemistry; alumina chemicals; materials science; photochemistry; environmental chemistry; sanitary and environmental engineering. *Mailing Add:* Nat Renewable Energy Lab 1617 Cole Blvd Golden CO 80401-3393

BLAKE, DAVID ANDREW, PHARMACOLOGY, TERATOLOGY. *Current Pos:* ASSOC PROF GYNEC-OBSTET & PHARMACOL, SCH MED, JOHNS HOPKINS UNIV, 73-, SR ASSOC DEAN, 80- *Personal Data:* b Baltimore, Md, Aug 26, 41; m 63; c 3. *Educ:* Univ Md, Baltimore City,

BS, 63, PhD(pharmacol), 66. *Prof Exp:* Res assoc, Lab Chem Pharmacol, Nat Heart Inst, 66-67; from asst prof pharmacol to assoc prof pharmacol & toxicol, Sch Pharm, Univ Md, Baltimore City, 67-73, chmn dept, 69-73. *Concurrent Pos:* Mem, Human Embryol & Develop Study Sect, NIH, 84- *Mem:* Am Soc Pharmacol & Exp Therapeut. *Res:* Drug disposition; chemoteratogenicity; biochemical toxicology; biotransformation of volatile fluorocarbons; hepatotoxicity of halothane; mechanism of action of thalidomide; bioactivation and mutagenesis anesthetics carcinogenesis; toxicology. *Mailing Add:* Johns Hopkins Univ Sch Med 100 Admin Bldg 720 Rutland Ave Baltimore MD 21205-2109

BLAKE, EMMET REID, ornithology, for more information see previous edition

BLAKE, GEORGE HENRY, JR, ENTOMOLOGY. *Current Pos:* Assoc entomologist, Auburn Univ, 50-64, assoc prof, 64-65, prof entom & zool, 65-84, EMER PROF ENTOM & ZOOL, AUBURN UNIV, 84- *Personal Data:* b Faunsdale, Ala, June 21, 22; m 46; c 4. *Educ:* Auburn Univ, BS, 47, MS, 49; Univ Ill, PhD, 58. *Mem:* Entom Soc Am. *Res:* Teaching and graduate research. *Mailing Add:* 467 Southview Dr PO Box 2543 Auburn AL 36830

BLAKE, GEORGE MARSTON, FORESTRY. *Current Pos:* from asst prof silvicult to assoc prof forestry, 62-72, PROF FORESTRY, UNIV MONT, 72-, RES COORDR FORESTRY, 73- *Personal Data:* b Los Angeles, Calif, Jan 21, 32; m 52; c 4. *Educ:* Univ Idaho, BS, 57; Univ Minn, MS, 59, PhD, 64. *Prof Exp:* Asst, Univ Minn, 57-62. *Mem:* AAAS; Am Soc Foresters. *Res:* Genetic variation; western larch and ponderosa pine; tissue culture of western larch; selection and breeding of drought resistance in ponderosa pine for mine spoil reclamation. *Mailing Add:* 3109 Martinwood Rd Missoula MT 59802

BLAKE, GEORGE ROWLAND, soil physics, for more information see previous edition

BLAKE, IAN FRASER, ELECTRICAL ENGINEERING. *Current Pos:* chmn dept, 78-84, PROF ELEC ENG, UNIV WATERLOO, 69- *Personal Data:* b Saskatoon, Sask, June 7, 41; m 66; c 2. *Educ:* Queen's Univ, BSc, 62, MSc, 64; Princeton Univ, PhD(elec eng), 67. *Prof Exp:* Res assoc telecommun, Jet Propulsion Lab, 67-69. *Concurrent Pos:* IBM Res Lab, Yorktown Heights, NY, 75-76; M/A-COM Linkabit Inc, San Diego, 84-85. *Mem:* Fel Inst Elec & Electronics Engrs. *Res:* Communication theory; coding theory; combinatorial theory. *Mailing Add:* Dept Elec & Comp Eng Univ Waterloo Waterloo ON N2L 3G1 Can

BLAKE, J BERNARD, ASTROPHYSICS, SPACE PHYSICS. *Current Pos:* DEPT HEAD SPACE PARTICLES & FIELDS DEPT, SPACE SCI LAB, AEROSPACE CORP, 62- *Personal Data:* b New York, NY, Dec 14, 35; m 60; c 2. *Educ:* Univ Ill, BS, 57, MS, 58, PhD(physics), 62. *Prof Exp:* Res assoc physics, Univ Ill, 62. *Mem:* Fel Am Phys Soc; Am Geophys Union; Am Astron Soc; Sigma Xi. *Res:* Space plasma physics; cosmic-ray physics; nuclear astrophyics; nuclear physics. *Mailing Add:* Aerospace Corp M2/259 PO Box 92957 Los Angeles CA 90009

BLAKE, JAMES ELWOOD, INFORMATION SCIENCE. *Current Pos:* assoc ed org chem, 68-72, sr assoc ed, 72-76, SR ED CHEM INFO, CHEM ABSTR SERV, 76- *Personal Data:* b St George, Utah, Oct 4, 38; m 63; c 4. *Educ:* Brigham Young Univ, BA, 64. *Prof Exp:* Nat Defense Educ Act fel chem, Utah State Univ, 64-67, asst, 67-68. *Mem:* Am Chem Soc. *Res:* Applications and uses of chemical information; development of uses for new systems to handle chemical information. *Mailing Add:* 8480 NW Ohio Wesleyan Ct Lancaster OH 43130

BLAKE, JAMES J, ORGANIC CHEMISTRY, BIOCHEMISTRY. *Current Pos:* AT BRISTOL-MYERS SQUIBB, SEATTLE, 86- *Personal Data:* b New York, NY, June 10, 37. *Educ:* Mass Inst Technol, BS, 58; Univ Calif, PhD(chem), 65. *Prof Exp:* Develop engr, rheology, Aerojet Gen Corp, 58-60; asst res biochemist, Hormone Res Lab, Univ Calif, San Francisco, 65-85. *Concurrent Pos:* NIH fel, 65-67. *Mem:* AAAS; Am Chem Soc. *Res:* Synthesis of peptides. *Mailing Add:* 201 Galer Apt 243 Seattle WA 98109-3192

BLAKE, JAMES NEAL, SPEECH & HEARING SCIENCES. *Current Pos:* ASSOC PROF AUDIOL & SPEECH PATH, UNIV LOUISVILLE, 70- *Personal Data:* b Great Bend, Kans, July 18, 33; m 63. *Educ:* Kans State Univ, BS, 55, MS, 60; Univ Southern Miss, PhD(speech & hearing sci), 68. *Prof Exp:* Speech therapist, Charlotte-Mecklenburg Schs, 60-64; asst prof speech & hearing, Western Carolina Univ, 66-70. *Concurrent Pos:* Consult, Rauch Ctr Retarded Children, 70- *Mem:* Ling Soc Am; Speech Asn Am; Am Speech & Hearing Asn; Am Psychol Asn; Coun Except Children. *Res:* Relationship between normal and abnormal verbal behavior and various cognitive states; effects of variable verbal loadings on cognitive. *Mailing Add:* Dept Spec Educ Univ Louisville Louisville KY 40292-0001

BLAKE, JOHN ARCHIBALD, SCIENCE EDUCATION. *Current Pos:* DEPT HEAD MATH, OAKWOOD COL, 67-, DIR, SCI LEARNING CTR, 78- *Personal Data:* b Tobago, WI; m 61; c 2. *Educ:* Howard Univ, BS, 63, MS, 64; George Peabody Col Teachers, Vanderbilt Univ, EdS, 74; Univ Tenn, Knoxville, EdD, 78. *Mem:* Nat Coun Teachers Math; Nat Asn Math; Math Asn Am. *Res:* Problem solving in mathematics and students' thought processes. *Mailing Add:* Oakwood Col Huntsville AL 35896-0001

BLAKE, JOSEPH THOMAS, VETERINARY MEDICINE. *Current Pos:* from asst prof to assoc prof vet sci, Utah State Univ, 56-69, emer prof. *Personal Data:* b Provo, Utah, Jan 24, 19; m 41; c 6. *Educ:* Brigham Young Univ, BS, 49; Iowa State Univ, MS, 50, PhD, 55, DVM, 56. *Prof Exp:* Instr animal husb, Ariz State Univ, 50-51; instr dairy husb, Iowa State Univ, 51-53. *Mem:* Am Vet Med Asn; Am Soc Vet Physiol & Pharmacol; Am Soc Animal Sci; Am Asn Vet Med Cols. *Res:* Physiology and nutrition in relation to veterinary medicine. *Mailing Add:* 1314 N Oquirrh Dr Provo UT 84604

BLAKE, JULES, BIOTECHNOLOGY, TECHNOLOGY ACQUISITION. *Current Pos:* MEM BD DIRS, MARTEK BIOSCI CORP, 90-, PROCYTE CORP, 91-, GENE LOGIC, 91- *Personal Data:* b New York, NY, July 7, 24; m 49; c 3. *Educ:* Univ Pa, BS, 49, MS, 51, PhD(org chem), 54. *Prof Exp:* Res chemist, Marshall Lab, E I du Pont de Nemours & Co, Philadelphia, 54-59, res supvr, 60-65, develop supvr, 65-66; res dir, Indust Chem Div, Mallinckrodt Chem Works, 66-69, dir res & develop & gen mgr res & develop div, Chem Group, 69-71; vpres res & develop, Kendall Co, 71-72; vpres res & develop, Colgate-Palmolive Co, 73-87, vpres Corp Sci Affairs, 87-89; staff mem, Off Sci & Technol Policy, Exec Off of the President, 89-91. *Concurrent Pos:* Mem, Indust Res Inst, 67-, pres, 80-81; chmn adv comt anal, Nat Bur Standards, 70-73; mem Res & Develop Coun, Am Mgt Asn, 75-79; mem ad hoc adv comt, President's Sci Advisor, 80; bd overseers, Sch Dental Med, Univ Pa, 80-; dir, Cosmetic Toiletries Fragrance Asn, 85-; adv comt, Nat Sci Asn, Univ Pa, 85-, Res & Develop Adv Comt Conf Bd, 88; bd dirs, Immune Response Corp & Med Col Pa; chmn, Dirs Indust Res; mem, bd trustees, Forsyth Dent Ctr & Alleghany Univ Health Sci, 96- *Mem:* Am Chem Soc; Asn Res Dirs (pres); Sigma Xi. *Res:* Research management; consumer products; biotechnology start-ups. *Mailing Add:* 867 Sunset Ridge Bridgewater NJ 08807

BLAKE, LAMONT VINCENT, MICROWAVE PHYSICS, RADIO ENGINEERING. *Current Pos:* consult, 84- *Personal Data:* b Somerville, Mass, Nov 7, 13; m 38, 57, 80; c 2. *Educ:* Mass State Col, BS, 35; Univ Md, MS, 50. *Honors & Awards:* Sci Res Soc Am Appl Sci Award, 63. *Prof Exp:* Radio interference investr, Ark Power & Light Co, 37-40; physicist, Naval Res Lab, 40-67, consult physicist, Radar Div, 67-69, Head Radar Geophys Br, 69-72; sr scientist, Technol Serv Corp, Silver Spring, Md, 72-84. *Concurrent Pos:* Free lance tech writer, 60- *Mem:* AAAS; Am Phys Soc; Sigma Xi; Inst Elec & Electronics Engrs; Am Geophys Union. *Res:* Design of radar systems and components; radar maximum range theory; atmospheric absorption of radio waves; radio noise theory. *Mailing Add:* 800 Copley Lane Silver Spring MD 20904-1313

BLAKE, RICHARD D, PHYSICAL BIOCHEMISTRY. *Current Pos:* from asst prof to assoc prof, Univ Maine, 73-82, prof biochem, 82-97, prof chem, 94-97, EMER PROF CHEM, UNIV MAINE, 97- *Personal Data:* b Greenfield, Mass, Sept 24, 32; m 58; c 2. *Educ:* Tufts Col, BS, 58; Rutgers Univ, MS, 63; Princeton Univ, PhD(biochem), 67. *Prof Exp:* Res asst chem, Harvard Univ, 58-60; res asst chem, Princeton Univ, 61-63, res assoc biochem, 67-68, res staff, 68-73. *Concurrent Pos:* Dir, Worthington Biochem Corp, 68-77; prin investr, NIH, 75-; vis prof, Med Sch Hannover, Fed Repub Ger, 80; adj prof chem, Williams Col, 97- *Mem:* Am Soc Biol Chemists; Biophys Soc; Sigma Xi. *Res:* Structure and interactions of DNA; helix-coil transitions of DNA; evolution of DNA sequences; effect of water on the stability of DNA. *Mailing Add:* Dept Biochem Univ Maine Hitchner Hall Orono ME 04469-5735. *E-Mail:* rblake@williams.edu, blake@maine.maine.edu

BLAKE, RICHARD L, physics, general, for more information see previous edition

BLAKE, ROBERT GEORGE, mathematics; deceased, see previous edition for last biography

BLAKE, ROBERT L, BIOCHEMISTRY, PHARMACOLOGY. *Current Pos:* ASSOC PROF FAMILY MED, UNIV MO, COLUMBIA, 80- *Personal Data:* b Claremont, NH, Mar 21, 33; m 61; c 2. *Educ:* Bates Col, BS, 55; Univ Rochester, MS, 57; Univ Calif, San Francisco, PhD(biochem), 62. *Prof Exp:* Res assoc pharmacol, Univ Rochester, 55-57; asst biochem, Univ Calif, Berkeley & San Francisco, 57-59; USPHS fel, McArdle Mem Lab, Univ Wis-Madison, 62-64; res chemist, Med Ctr, Univ Calif, San Francisco, 64-65, Cardiovasc Res Inst fel, 65-66; from assoc to staff scientist, Jackson Lab, 66-80. *Concurrent Pos:* NSF travel fel, NATO Advan Study Inst, Bergen, Norway, 68. *Mem:* AAAS; NY Acad Sci; Brit Biochem Soc. *Res:* Biochemical control mechanisms of mammalian genetic expression; mitochondrial biogenesis, hormonal induction of enzymes; inborn errors of metabolism; pharmacogenetics. *Mailing Add:* Family/Commun Med Univ Mo M222 Health Sci Columbia MO 65212-0001

BLAKE, ROBERT WESLEY, ANIMAL SCIENCE, ANIMAL GENETICS. *Current Pos:* ASSOC PROF INT ANIMAL SCI, CORNELL UNIV, 86- *Personal Data:* b Long Beach, Calif, Oct 23, 45; m 71; c 2. *Educ:* Univ Minn, BS, 71; NC State Univ, MTech, 73, PhD(animal sci), 77. *Prof Exp:* Dairy extensionist, US Peace Corps, Peru, 68-71; res asst animal genetics, NC State Univ, 72-76; from asst prof to assoc prof dairy sci, Tex A&M univ, 77-86. *Concurrent Pos:* Livestock consult, Bahamas, Colombia, El Salvador, Brazil, Mex, Costa Rica, Honduras,Trinidad, Saudi Arabia, Venezuela, Nigeria, Kenya & Ethopia, 73,77 & 78-88. *Mem:* Am Dairy Sci Asn; Am Soc Animal Sci; AAAS. *Res:* Dairy cattle breeding, production economics, and management; correlated responses in nutrient utilization, physiological mechanisms, and tropical ruminant production. *Mailing Add:* 131 Morrison Hall-Animal Sci Cornell Univ Main Campus Ithaca NY 14853-0001

BLAKE, ROLLAND LAWS, GEOLOGY. *Current Pos:* petrol & mineral res geologist, 58-71, supvry geologist, 71-88, GEOLOGIST, US BUR MINES, 88- *Personal Data:* b Minneapolis, Minn, Jan 16, 24; m 53; c 3. *Educ:* Univ Minn, BS, 50, MS, 51, PhD(geol), 58. *Prof Exp:* Geologist, Cleveland-Cliffs Iron Co, Mich, 51-52, Minn, 52-54. *Mem:* Soc Mining Engrs. *Res:* Mineralogy; iron silicates; carbonates; iron oxides associated with iron ore deposits; manganese minerals; petrology; pre-Cambrian in Canadian shield area. *Mailing Add:* 6701 Southdale Rd Minneapolis MN 55435

BLAKE, THOMAS LEWIS, HORTICULTURE, AGRICULTURE. *Current Pos:* Agr res tech, 70-82, SUPT, HORT CROPS RES STA, NC STATE UNIV, 82- *Personal Data:* b Wilmington, NC, Nov 9, 46; m 68; c 2. *Educ:* Clemson Univ, BS, 70. *Res:* Blueberries, grapes, strawberries, potatoes, cabbage, cucumbers, asparagus, & woody ornamentals. *Mailing Add:* 400 S Bennett Burgaw NC 28425

BLAKE, THOMAS MATHEWS, ELECTROCARDIOGRAPHY. *Current Pos:* from asst prof to prof, 55-90, EMER PROF MED, SCH MED, UNIV MISS, 90- *Personal Data:* b Sheffield, Ala, Aug 4, 20. *Educ:* Univ Ala, BA, 41; Vanderbilt Univ, MD, 44; Am Bd Internal Med, dipl. *Prof Exp:* Intern med, Vanderbilt Univ Hosp, 44-45, intern path, 47-48, asst resident med, 48-49, fel cardiovasc res, Med Sch, 50-52, instr, 52-54, instr clin med, 54-55. *Concurrent Pos:* Asst resident, Strong Mem Hosp, Rochester, NY, 49-50; chief clin physiol sect, Res Lab, Vet Admin Hosp, 54-55; mem coun arteriosclerosis, Am Heart Asn. *Mem:* AMA; Am Fedn Clin; fel Am Col Cardiol; fel Am Col Chest Physicians; fel Am Col Physicians. *Res:* Electrocardiography. *Mailing Add:* Heart Sta Univ Miss Med Ctr Jackson MS 39216-4505. *Fax:* 601-984-2631

BLAKE, THOMAS R, FLUID MECHANICS, RHEOLOGY. *Current Pos:* head dept, 84-92, PROF MECH ENG, UNIV MASS, 80-, DIR, CTR MFG PRODUCTIVITY, 91-, ASSOC DEAN, COL ENG, 96- *Personal Data:* b New York, NY, Apr 5, 38; m 63, Julia Spencer; c 3. *Educ:* Polytech Inst Brooklyn, BME, 60; Rennselaer Polytech Inst, MS, 65; Yale Univ, PhD(eng), 71. *Prof Exp:* Engr, Pratt & Whitney Aircraft Div, United Technol Corp, 63-65, res scientist, Res Lab, 65-68; scientist & mgr, S-Cubed, Inc, 70-80. *Concurrent Pos:* Vis prof, dept physiol & adj prof, dept chem eng, Univ Ariz, 80-84; particle technol forum, Am Inst Chem Engrs. *Mem:* Am Inst Chem Engrs; Am Soc Mech Engrs. *Res:* Fluid mechanics with an emphasis upon the mathematical description of multiphase flow processes with chemical reaction. *Mailing Add:* Dept Mech Eng Univ Mass Amherst MA 01003-0014. *Fax:* 413-545-0724; *E-Mail:* blake@ecs.umass.edu

BLAKE, TOM, QTL ANALYSIS, MOLECULAR EVOLUTION. *Current Pos:* asst prof, 84-89, ASSOC PROF BARLEY BREEDING, MONT STATE UNIV, 89- *Personal Data:* US citizen. *Educ:* Univ Calif, BS, 76; SDak State Univ, MS, 79; Wash State Univ, PhD(genetics), 83. *Prof Exp:* Res assoc genetics, Univ Wis, 83-84. *Res:* Breeding of barley; construct genome maps and identify QTL's; genetics and forensics. *Mailing Add:* Plant & Soil Sci Dept Mont State Univ Bozeman MT 59717-3120

BLAKE, WESTON, JR, GLACIAL GEOLOGY. *Current Pos:* res scientist, 62-95, EMER RES SCIENTIST, GEOL SURV CAN, 95- *Personal Data:* b Boston, Mass, Feb 26, 30; m 60, Ingrid Olsson; c Erik W & Sven C. *Educ:* Dartmouth Col, AB, 51; McGill Univ, MSc, 53; Ohio State Univ, PhD(geol), 62; Univ Stockholm, Fil Lic(geog), 64, Fil Dr(phys geog), 75. *Prof Exp:* Res scientist & head paleoecol & geo-chronol sect, Terrain Sci Div, 69-86. *Concurrent Pos:* Chair, Can Nat Comt, Int Quaternary Asn, 93-97; docent, Dept Phys Geog, Univ Stockholm, 75-; assoc ed, Can J Earth Sci, 75-81. *Mem:* Fel Geol Asn Can; fel Arctic Inst NAm; Can Quaternary Asn; Geol Soc Finland; Swed Soc Anthrop & Geog; Am Quaternary Asn. *Res:* Glacial history and geomorphological processes in arctic regions; radiocarbon dating; pleistocene marine faunas. *Mailing Add:* 19 Madawaska Dr Ottawa ON K1S 3G5 Can. *E-Mail:* wblake@gsc.nrcan.gc.ca

BLAKE, WILLIAM KING, acoustics, fluid mechanics, for more information see previous edition

BLAKE, WILSON, MINING ENGINEERING. *Current Pos:* CONSULT MINING ENGR, 74- *Personal Data:* b San Francisco, Calif, Aug 29, 34; m; c 5. *Educ:* Univ Calif, Berkeley, BA, 57, MS, 62; Colo Sch Mines, PhD, 71. *Honors & Awards:* Peele Award, Am Inst Mining Engrs, 70; Interdisciplinary Award, US Nat Comt Rock Mech, 72. *Prof Exp:* Mining geologist, Malachite Corp, 57-58; sr sci data analyst, Lawrence Radiation Lab, Univ Calif, 61-65; res civil engr, Denver Mining Res Ctr, US Bur Mines, 65-71; res mining dir mining res, Gecamines, 72-74. *Concurrent Pos:* Adj asst prof, Colo Sch Mines, 71-72. *Mem:* Am Inst Mining, Metall & Petrol Engrs; Int Soc Rock Mech. *Res:* Rock mechanics; development and application of the broad-band microseismic method of determining rock stability; development of mathematical models of rock behavior; mechanics of rock bursts; development of microseismic monitoring systems. *Mailing Add:* PO Box 928 Hayden Lake ID 83835. *Fax:* 208-687-7056

BLAKELY, ELEANOR ALICE, RADIATION PHYSIOLOGY, BIOPHYSICS. *Current Pos:* biophysicist, 75-89, SR STAFF BIOPHYSICIST, LAWRENCE BERKELEY LAB, UNIV CALIF, 89- *Personal Data:* b Quantico, Va, July 29, 47; m 86, George Zizka; c Maria. *Educ:* Univ San Diego, AB, 69; Univ Ill, MS, 71, PhD(physiol), 75. *Concurrent Pos:* Co-investr, Nat Cancer Inst, 75-; assoc ed, Radiation Res, 84-88 & Space Solar Power Rev, 81-; mem, Diag Radiol Study Sect, Div Res Grants, NIH, 87-; mem, Diag Radiol Study Sect, Div Res Grants, NIH, 87-91, Nat Coun Radiation Protection & Measurements, sub-comt No 75, 90- *Mem:* Radiation Res Soc; AAAS; Am Soc Therapeut Radiologists; Ny Acad Sci. *Res:* Radiobiology of accelerated charged particle beams for radiotherapy; mechanisms of radiation damage in mammalian cells in vitro. *Mailing Add:* Lawrence Berkeley Lab Univ Calif Bldg 70A-1118 Berkeley CA 94720-1118. *Fax:* 510-486-4475; *E-Mail:* eablakely@macmail.lbl.gov

BLAKELY, J(OHN) M, MATERIALS SCIENCE. *Current Pos:* from asst prof physics & mat sci to assoc prof mat sci, 63-70, PROF MAT SCI, CORNELL UNIV, 70- *Personal Data:* b Scotland, Apr 8, 36; m 60, Nanette Irvine; c 2. *Educ:* Univ Glasgow, BS, 58, PhD(physics), 61. *Prof Exp:* Res fel appl physics, Harvard Univ, 61-63. *Concurrent Pos:* Guggenheim fel, Cavendish Lab, Cambridge Univ, UK, 70-71; vis scientist, Argonne Nat Lab, 76; NSF fel, Lawrence Berkeley Lab, Calif, 77; fel, Sci & Eng Res Coun, York Univ, Eng, 84. *Mem:* Am Inst Mining, Metall & Petrol Engrs; fel Am Phys Soc; fel Brit Inst Physics & Phys Soc. *Res:* Properties and structure of interfaces; surface reactions; crystalline defects; semiconductor surfaces; oxidation processes; atomic diffusion. *Mailing Add:* Dept Mat Sci Bard Hall Cornell Univ Ithaca NY 14853

BLAKELY, LAWRENCE MACE, PLANT PHYSIOLOGY. *Current Pos:* PROF BOT, CALIF STATE POLYTECH UNIV, POMONA, 63- *Personal Data:* b Los Angeles, Calif, Nov 12, 34; m 60; c 2. *Educ:* Mont State Univ, BA, 56, MA, 58; Cornell Univ, PhD(plant physiol), 63. *Prof Exp:* Asst bot, Mont State Univ, 56-58; asst plant physiol, Cornell Univ, 58-62, res assoc, 62-63, instr, 63. *Mem:* AAAS; Bot Soc Am; Am Soc Plant Physiologists; Plant Growth Regulator Soc Am; Sigma Xi; Am Inst Biol Sci. *Res:* Physiology of plant growth; lateral root initiation; plant tissue culture. *Mailing Add:* 415 Sierra Grande Rte 1 Bishop CA 93514-7011

BLAKELY, ROBERT FRASER, GEOPHYSICS. *Current Pos:* RETIRED. *Personal Data:* b Newark, NJ, Apr 1, 21; m 43, Rosanna Lieurance; c 2. *Educ:* Miami Univ, AB, 46, MA, 48; Ind Univ, PhD, 74. *Prof Exp:* Instr physics, Miami Univ, 47-49; spectrographer, Dept Conserv, State Geol Surv, Ind, 49-53, geophysicist, 53-74; from assoc prof to prof geophys, Ind Univ, 74-86. *Mem:* AAAS. *Res:* Spectrographic determination of major constituents in limestones; physical properties of Indiana sediments; computers in geology; solid earth geophysics and meteorology. *Mailing Add:* 116 Meadowbrook Ave Bloomington IN 47408-4328

BLAKEMAN, ALEXANDER, COLORING & COMPOUNDING OF PLASTIC RESINS. *Current Pos:* tech dir, 86-92, chemist, 86-92, TECH DIR, RIVERDALE COLOR MFG, INC, 92- *Personal Data:* b Leningrad, Russia, Nov 11, 60; US citizen; m 83, Inna Novofastovsky; c Naomi & Girshel. *Educ:* Leningrad Inst Technol, Russia, MS, 83. *Prof Exp:* Engr, Plastics Laminates, Russia, 83-86. *Mem:* Soc Plastics Engrs; Am Soc Testing & Mat. *Res:* Search for most optimal color and additive formulations designed to provide desired balance of properties and appearance to the plastic resin. *Mailing Add:* Riverdale Color Mfg Inc 147 Classon Ave Brooklyn NY 11205. *Fax:* 718-857-1003

BLAKEMORE, JOHN SYDNEY, SOLID STATE PHYSICS. *Current Pos:* RES ASSOC, WESTERN WASH UNIV, 89- *Personal Data:* b London, Eng, May 25, 27; m 53; c 2. *Educ:* Univ London, BSc, 48, PhD(physics), 51, DSc, 77. *Prof Exp:* Res physicist, Stand Telecommun Labs, London, 50-54; res fel, Univ BC, 54-56; staff scientist, Honeywell, Inc, 56-63; sr staff scientist, Lockheed Res Labs, 63-64; prof physics, Fla Atlantic Univ, 64-78; prof appl physics, Ore Grad Ctr, 78-89. *Concurrent Pos:* Fulbright-Hays sr fel, Univ New South Wales, 71; dir, Fla Solar Energy Ctr, 76-77. *Mem:* Fel Am Phys Soc; fel Brit Inst Physics. *Res:* Semiconducting materials; photoconductivity, recombination and trapping; charge carrier statistics. *Mailing Add:* Physics & Astron Bond Hall 152-MS 9064 Western Wash Univ Bellingham WA 98225-9064

BLAKEMORE, RICHARD PETER, MICROBIOLOGY. *Current Pos:* asst prof microbiol, 77-80, assoc prof, 81-85, PROF, UNIV NH, 86- *Personal Data:* b Schenectady, NY, July 16, 42; m 67; c 2. *Educ:* State Univ NY Albany, BS, 64, MS, 65; Univ Mass, Amherst, PhD(microbiol), 76. *Honors & Awards:* Lectr, ASM Found, CSM Traveling, ASM Div. *Prof Exp:* Asst prof biol, North Adams State Col, Mass, 66-70; investr, Woods Hole Oceanog Inst, 75-76; res assoc microbiol, Univ Ill, Urbana, 76-77. *Concurrent Pos:* NSF grants, 77-80 & 80-83, 83-85, 85-; Off Naval Res contracts, 79-81, 81-84, 85-; Nat Geog Soc grant, 80; lectr, Am Soc Microbiol found, CSM traveling, Am Soc Microbiol Div. *Mem:* Am Soc Microbiol; AAAS; Biophys Soc; Can Soc Microbiol. *Res:* Magnetism in bacteria; denitrification. *Mailing Add:* 4 Davis Ave Durham NH 03824

BLAKEMORE, WILLIAM STEPHEN, surgery; deceased, see previous edition for last biography

BLAKER, J WARREN, OPTICS. *Current Pos:* prof & chmn, Elec Eng Dept, 87-90, PROF & CHMN, DEPT PHYSICS, FAIRLEIGH DICKINSON UNIV, 90- *Personal Data:* b Wilkes-Barre, Pa, May 25, 34; m 57, 74, Judith Garland; c 3. *Educ:* Wilkes Col, BS, 55; Mass Inst Technol, PhD(chem), 58. *Honors & Awards:* Eugene S Farley Award. *Prof Exp:* Asst prof physics, Fairleigh Dickinson Univ, 58-61; mem staff, G C Dewey Co, 61-62 & John Wiley & Sons, Inc, 62-64; prof physics, Vassar Col, 64-76; vpres res & develop, Danker & Wohlk, Inc, 76-79; consult, Optical Sci, 79-82; chief exec officer, Univ Optical, 82-85. *Concurrent Pos:* Consult, Optical Sci &

Regulatory Affairs, 58- *Mem:* AAAS; Am Phys Soc; Am Chem Soc; Am Asn Physics Teachers; fel Optical Soc Am. *Res:* Optics and optical image processing; ophthalmic optics. *Mailing Add:* 3117 Palisades Ave Bronx NY 10463-4001. *E-Mail:* jwblaker@gramercy.10s.com

BLAKER, ROBERT HOCKMAN, PHYSICAL CHEMISTRY, INFORMATION SCIENCE. *Current Pos:* PRES, TECH INFO SERVS, INC, 85- *Personal Data:* b Meadow Bridge, WVa, Apr 6, 20; m 45, Anne T Pruitt; c 2. *Educ:* Berea Col, AB, 42; Calif Inst Technol, PhD(chem), 49. *Honors & Awards:* Am Dyestuff Reporter Award, 53. *Prof Exp:* Instr chem, Berea Col, 43-44 & Off Naval Res, Calif Inst Technol, 46-49; Imp Chem Industs fel, Univ Liverpool, 49-50; res chemist, Jackson lab, E I du Pont de Nemours & Co, Inc, 50-53, res supvr, Petrol Lab, 53-56, asst dir lab, 56-60, res mgr, Orchem Dept, 60-64, head patent serv, 64-70, mgr cent Patent & Report Serv, Info Systs Dept, 70-85. *Mem:* Am Chem Soc; Am Soc Info Sci. *Res:* Size and shape of high polymer molecules; theory of dyeing synthetic fibers; fuels and lubricants for internal combustion engines. *Mailing Add:* 1105 N Rodney St Wilmington DE 19806-4319

BLAKESLEE, A EUGENE, PHYSICAL CHEMISTRY, ELECTRONIC MATERIALS SCIENCE. *Current Pos:* RETIRED. *Personal Data:* b Sayre, Pa, June 20, 28; m 54; c 2. *Educ:* Pa State Univ, BS, 50; Cornell Univ, PhD(phys chem), 55. *Prof Exp:* Investr photoconductor develop, NJ Zinc Co, 55-57; mem tech staff semiconductor mat, Bell Tel Labs, 57-60; engr, Advan Semiconductor Lab, Gen Elec Co, 60-61; chemist, Components Div Lab, IBM Corp, 62-64 & World Trade Lab, 64-65, chemist, Res Div, 66-79; sr scientist, Solar Energy Res Inst, 79-89. *Concurrent Pos:* Mgt govt res contracts. *Mem:* Am Asn Crystal Growth. *Res:* X-ray crystallography; photoconductive zinc oxide powder; electrophotography; vapor and liquid phase epitaxial growth and diffusion in semiconductors; III-V compound semiconductor materials and devices; superlattices; solar cells; defects in semiconductor crystals; heteroepitaxy on silicon; metallic-organic chemical vapor deposition growth of superconductors. *Mailing Add:* 152 S Holman Way Golden CO 80401

BLAKESLEE, DENNIS L(AUREN), SCIENCE WRITER, EDITOR. *Current Pos:* SCI WRITER/ED, RES INST SCRIPPS CLIN, 89- *Personal Data:* b Wilmington, Del, July 2, 38; m 68; c 1. *Educ:* Middlebury Col, BA, 59; Columbia Univ, MS, 60; Univ Wis, MS, 67, PhD(genetics), 70. *Prof Exp:* Trainee, Dept Path, Sch Med, Univ Pa, 70-72; fel, 72-74, res scholar & asst prof, Nat Cancer Inst, Can, Dept Path, Queens Univ, 74-78; res assoc, Dept Genetics, Univ Wis, 78-80; dir sci info, Salk Inst, 80-83; sci writer, Lawrence Berkeley Lab, 83, Scripps Clin & Res Found, 84-88. *Mem:* AAAS; Genetics Soc Am; Am Asn Immunologists. *Res:* Non-technical articles on biomedical research and medical practice; editing and production of research publications and newletters. *Mailing Add:* 3133 Briand Ave San Diego CA 92122

BLAKESLEE, GEORGE M, FOREST PATHOLOGY. *Current Pos:* asst prof forest path, 76-81, assoc dir, Sch Forest Resources & Conserv, 93-95, ASSOC PROF FOREST PATH, UNIV FLA, 81- *Personal Data:* b Pa, Aug 30, 46; m 67; c 3. *Educ:* Albright Col, BS; Duke Univ, MF, 70, PhD(forest path), 75. *Prof Exp:* Asst prof forest path, Univ Vt, 75-76. *Mem:* Am Phytopath Soc; Soc Am Foresters. *Res:* Etiology, epidemiology and control of diseases of intensively managed forest trees. *Mailing Add:* Sch Forest Resources & Conserv, Box 110410 Univ Fla Gainesville FL 32611-0410

BLAKLEY, BARRY RAYMOND, IMMUNOTOXICOLOGY, VETERINARY TOXICOLOGY. *Current Pos:* Assoc prof, Vet Med, Univ Sask, 80-86, acad coordr toxicol, 85-91, actg dir, Toxicol Res Ctr, 93-94, PROF VET MED, UNIV SASK, 86-, CHMN, TOXICOL GROUP, 89-, ACTG DIR, TOXICOL RES CTR, 93- *Personal Data:* b Saskatoon, Sask, Mar 7, 49; m 82, Patricia Mathinos; c Matthew, Alicia, Bethany & Timothy. *Educ:* Univ Sask, BSc, 70, DVM, 75, MSc, 77; Univ Cincinnati, PhD(toxicol), 80. *Concurrent Pos:* Fel, Med Res Coun Can, 75-80. *Mem:* Can Vet Med Asn; fel Am Acad Vet Comp Toxicol; Soc Toxicol Can; Am Asn Vet Lab Diagnosticians. *Res:* Effects of chemicals and altered nutritional states (deficiency) on immune function; applied veterinary toxicology and nutritional toxicology. *Mailing Add:* Dept Vet Physiol Sci Univ Sask Saskatoon SK S7N 0W0 Can. *Fax:* 306-996-7376

BLAKLEY, GEORGE ROBERT, MATHEMATICS, COMPUTER SCIENCE. *Current Pos:* head dept, 70-78, PROF MATH, TEX A&M UNIV, 70- *Personal Data:* b Chicago, Ill, May 6, 32; m 57; c 3. *Educ:* Univ Md, PhD(math), 60. *Prof Exp:* Mathematician, Nat Inst Stand & Technol, 56-58; res assoc, Off Naval Res, Cornell Univ, 60-61; Nat Acad Sci-Nat Res Coun fel, Harvard Univ, 61-62; asst prof math, Univ Ill, 62-66; assoc prof, State Univ NY, Buffalo, 66-70. *Concurrent Pos:* Vis prof, Dept Comput Sci & Eng, Wright State Univ, 87-90; mem bd dirs, Int Asn Cryptologic Res, 93-95. *Mem:* AAAS; Am Math Soc; Inst Elec & Electronics Engrs; Asn Comput Mach; Int Asn Cryptologic Res. *Res:* Information theory; combinatorial theory; cryptography; secret sharing technology. *Mailing Add:* Dept Math Tex A&M Univ College Station TX 77843-3368. *Fax:* 409-845-6028; *E-Mail:* blakley@math.tamu.edu

BLAKLEY, RAYMOND L, ANTICANCER DRUGS, ACTIVE SITE STRUCTURE. *Current Pos:* CHMN PHARMACOL & MEM, ST JUDE CHILDREN'S RES HOSP, 81- *Personal Data:* b Christchurch, NZ, May 14, 26; m; m 49; c 4. *Educ:* Canterbury Univ Col, BSc, 46, MSc, 47; Univ Otago, NZ, PhD(biochem), 51;. *Hon Degrees:* DSc, Austialian Nat Univ, 65. *Prof Exp:* Actg head dept biochem, Australian Nat Univ, 65-66; prof biochem, Col Med, Univ Iowa, 68-81. *Concurrent Pos:* Vis prof, Univ Calif, 62-63; prof fel, Australian Nat Univ, 65-68; Mayre guest prof, Univ Queensland, 83. *Mem:* Am Soc Biol Chemists; Am Chem Soc; Am Asn Cancer Res. *Res:* Folic acid metabolism; dihydrofolate reductase structure function relations; mechanism of cytotoxicity of deoxyadenosine analogues; binding of antifolates to dihydrofolate reductase. *Mailing Add:* Dept Pharmacol St Jude Children's Hosp 332 N Lauderdale Memphis TN 38105

BLAKNEY, WILLIAM G G, CIVIL ENGINEERING, PHOTOGRAMMETRY. *Current Pos:* assoc prof, 58-90, SR DANFORTH ASSOC, AUBURN UNIV, 65-, EMER ASSOC PROF INDUST ENG, 90- *Personal Data:* b Moncton, NB, Apr 4, 26; m 51, Lavinia M Woodman; c Dawn M & Carol L. *Educ:* NS Tech Col, BE, 49; Ohio State Univ, MSc, 54. *Prof Exp:* Engr surv mapping, Topog Surv Div, Mines & Tech Surv, Can Govt, 50-58. *Mem:* Am Soc Photogram & Remote Sensing; Am Cong Surv & Mapping; Am Soc Eng Educ; Can Inst Surv. *Res:* Surveying; photo interpretation; geology; computer graphics; numerical control. *Mailing Add:* 603 Cary Dr Auburn AL 36830

BLALOCK, JAMES EDWIN, VIROLOGY, CELL BIOLOGY. *Current Pos:* PROF, DEPT PHYSIOL & BIOPHYS, UNIV ALA, BIRMINGHAM, 86- *Personal Data:* b Madison, Fla, Sept 29, 49. *Educ:* Univ Fla, Gainesville, BS, 71, PhD(immunol & med microbiol), 76. *Prof Exp:* Postdoctoral fel, Univ Tex Med Br, 76-77, from asst prof to prof, 77-86. *Concurrent Pos:* Prin investr, US Army Med Res & Develop Command Contract, 78-81; NIH grants, 81-; Off Naval Res grant, 84- *Mem:* Am Soc Microbiol; Am Asn Immunologists. *Res:* Interferon; vitamin A; cell biology; immunology; physiology; Bidirectional communication between the immune and neuroendocrine systems; immune system derived neuroendocrine hormones. *Mailing Add:* Dept Physiol & Biophysiol Univ Ala Sch Med 1918 Univ Blvd BHSB896 Birmingham AL 35294-0005. *Fax:* 204-934-1446

BLALOCK, THERON VAUGHN, ELECTRICAL ENGINEERING. *Current Pos:* instr elec eng, 59-63, PROF ELEC ENG, UNIV TENN, KNOXVILLE, 68- *Personal Data:* b Fayette Co, Tenn, Jan 9, 34; m 52; c 3. *Educ:* Univ Tenn, BS, 57, MS, 61, PhD(eng sci), 65. *Prof Exp:* Develop engr, Oak Ridge Nat Lab, 58-59, consult, 59-63, res engr, 63-68. *Mem:* Inst Elec & Electronics Engrs. *Res:* Measurement science; nuclear instrumentation; Johnson noise thermometry; electronics for inertial sensors. *Mailing Add:* Dept Elec Eng Univ Tenn 1345 Circle Park Knoxville TN 37996-0001

BLANC, FRANCIS LOUIS, ENTOMOLOGY. *Current Pos:* CONSULT, 75-; RES ASSOC ENTOMOL, CALIF ACAD SCI, 91- *Personal Data:* b Knoxville, Tenn, Aug 22, 16; m 38, Fern A Gambrell; c Yvonne M (Gardner) & Donna J (Frey). *Educ:* Univ Calif, BS, 38. *Prof Exp:* Inspector entom & plant quarantine, State Dept Agr, Calif, 40-43 & 45-47, syst entomologist, 47-58, supvr insect pest detection & surv, 58-71, prog supvr pest prevention, 71-75. *Mem:* Entom Soc Am. *Res:* Systematics of diptera, tephritidae; co-authored two books on fruit flies. *Mailing Add:* 5309 Spilman Ave Sacramento CA 95819-1733

BLANC, FREDERIC C, WASTEWATER TREATMENT, INDUSTRIAL WASTE TREATMENT. *Current Pos:* PROF CIVIL ENVIRON ENG, NORTHEASTERN UNIV, 69- *Personal Data:* b New York, NY, June 21, 39; m 63; c 2. *Educ:* City Col, City Univ New York, BCE, 62; NY Univ, MS, 66, PhD(civil eng), 69. *Prof Exp:* Engr, John Thatcher & Son Engrs, 62; sanitary engr, US Pub Health Serv, 62-64; lectr, City Col, City Univ New York, 64-65; fel, NY Univ, 65-69; engr, Bowe Walsh & Assocs, 69. *Concurrent Pos:* Consult, 69-; water comnr, Town in Harvard, 75-; bd mem, Town of Harvard, Bd Health, 75- *Mem:* Am Soc Civil Engrs; Water Pollution Control Fedn. *Res:* Environmental engineering: methane fermentation, rotating biological contactor applications, river modeling, combine sewer management studies and synfuel waste treatment. *Mailing Add:* Dept Civil Eng Northeastern Univ 360 Huntington Ave Boston MA 02115-5096

BLANC, JOSEPH, SOLID STATE SCIENCE, PHYSICAL CHEMISTRY. *Current Pos:* INDEPENDENT CONSULT, 87- *Personal Data:* b Cernauti, Romania, Mar 12, 30; US citizen; m 49, Anuita Margolis; c Suzanne, Alita & Dina. *Educ:* Columbia Col, AB, 54; Columbia Univ, MA, 55, PhD(phys chem), 59. *Prof Exp:* Res asst infrared spectros, Columbia Univ, 56-57 & 58-59; mem tech staff, RCA Labs, 59-87; sr scientist Princeton X-ray Laser Inc, 88-93. *Concurrent Pos:* Res assoc, Optic Electronics Lab, Nat Ctr Sci Res, Toulouse, France, 74-75; adj prof chem, Rider Col, Lawrenceville, NJ, 93-94. *Mem:* Am Phys Soc. *Res:* Chemical physics of defects in solids and in the spectroscopy of the lanthanide ions; study of defects in semiconductors; scanning capacitance microscopy; composite materials; non linear phenomena; oxidation kinetics; novel microscopies and non-destructive testing. *Mailing Add:* 12 Willow St Princeton NJ 08542

BLANC, ROBERT PETER, COMPUTER SCIENCE. *Current Pos:* proj mgr comput sci & technol, Nat Bur Standards, 72-74, sci prog analyst, 74-75, staff asst, Comput Utilization Prog, 75-78, actg chief, Prog Develop Off Comput Sci & Technol, 78-79, CHIEF, SYSTS & NETWORK ARCHIT DIV, NAT BUR STANDARDS, 79- *Personal Data:* b Pittsburgh, Pa, June 8, 46; m 69; c 2. *Educ:* Univ Pittsburgh, BS, 67, MS, 69. *Honors & Awards:* Silver Medal, Dept Com, 78. *Prof Exp:* Asst dir, Comput Ctr, Univ Pittsburgh, 69-72. *Concurrent Pos:* Mem task force, President's Comt on Right to Privacy, 73-74; course dir, AAAS, 76-77; mem, President's Reorgn Proj, 78-79. *Mem:* AAAS; Inst Elec & Electronics Engrs; Asn Comput Mach. *Res:* Computer network protocols; network access; network measurement; computer architecture; distributed processing; local area networking; automated office systems. *Mailing Add:* 20920 Lockhaven Ct Gaithersburg MD 20879

BLANC, WILLIAM ANDRE, pathology, for more information see previous edition

BLANCH, HARVEY WARREN, BIOCHEMICAL ENGINEERING, CHEMICAL ENGINEERING. *Current Pos:* assoc prof, 78-82, PROF CHEM ENG, UNIV CALIF, BERKELEY, 82-, SR FAC SCIENTIST, LAWRENCE BERKELEY LAB, 84- *Personal Data:* b Sydney, Australia, Jan 17, 47. *Educ:* Univ Sydney, BSc, 68; Univ New SWales, PhD(chem eng), 71. *Honors & Awards:* Johnson Award, Am Chem Soc; Food, Pharmaceut & Bioeng Award, Am Inst Chem Engrs, 96. *Prof Exp:* Asst I tech microbiol, Swiss Fed Inst Technol, Zurich, 71-73; res investr, E R Squibb & Co, 73-74; assoc prof chem eng, Univ Del, 75-78. *Concurrent Pos:* Ed, Bioprocess Eng & Biochem Eng J. *Mem:* Am Inst Chem Engrs; Am Chem Soc. *Res:* Fermentation systems; reaction kinetics and mass transfer in biological systems; enzyme engineering. *Mailing Add:* Dept Chem Eng Univ Calif Berkeley CA 94720-0001. *Fax:* 510-643-1228; *E-Mail:* blanch@socrates.berkeley.edu

BLANCHAER, MARCEL CORNEILLE, BIOCHEMISTRY. *Current Pos:* RETIRED. *Personal Data:* b Antwerp, Belg, Apr 4, 21; nat Can; c 2. *Educ:* Queens Univ, Ont, BA, 45, MD & CM, 46. *Prof Exp:* Assoc prof physiol, Univ Man, 48-64, head, Dept Biochem, 64-75, prof biochem, 64-93. *Concurrent Pos:* Markle scholar, 48-53; dir biochem, St Boniface Hosp, 54-64. *Mem:* Can Biochem Soc; Can Soc Clin Chem. *Res:* Medical education. *Mailing Add:* Dept Biochem & Molecular Biol Univ Man 336 Bannatyne Ave Winnepeg MB R3E 0W3 Can

BLANCHAR, ROBERT W, SOIL CHEMISTRY, BIOCHEMISTRY. *Current Pos:* PROF AGRON, UNIV MO-COLUMBIA, 68- *Personal Data:* b Sherburn, Minn, June 30, 37; m 58; c 2. *Educ:* Macalester Col, BA, 58; Univ Minn, MS, 61, PhD(soil sci), 64. *Prof Exp:* Res agronomist soil chem, Int Minerals & Chem Corp, 64-68. *Mem:* Am Soc Agron; Sigma Xi; Fel Soil Sci Am. *Res:* Polyphosphate chemistry in soils; ion products of iron, aluminum and manganese in soils; arsenic transformations in soils; chemical transformations in coal mine spoils; chemistry of the rhizosphere. *Mailing Add:* Agron Univ Mo 41 Mumford Columbia MO 65211

BLANCHARD, BRUCE, ENVIRONMENTAL SCIENCES, NATURAL RESOURCES MANAGEMENT. *Current Pos:* staff asst, Off Secy of Interior, 70-71, dir off environ proj rev, Off Secy, 71-89, DEP DIR, US FISH & WILDLIFE SERV, DEPT INTERIOR, 89- *Personal Data:* b Ft Stotsenburg, Phillippines, Dec 26, 32; US citizen; m 92, Mary J Cain. *Educ:* Mass Inst Technol, SB, 57, SM, 64. *Prof Exp:* Teaching asst surv, Mass Inst Technol, 57-59; hydraul engr, Chief Engr Off, US Bur Reclamation, Colo, 59-61, Phoenix develop off, Ariz, 61-63, civil engr, 63-64, proj planning engr, Cent Ariz Proj, 65-66; staff specialist, Water Resources Coun, 66-69. *Mem:* Am Soc Civil Engrs; Am Geophys Union; Am Water Resources Asn; AAAS. *Res:* Analysis of resource allocation and environmental problems in the management of natural resources and the protection and enhancement of environmental quality. *Mailing Add:* 80 Observatory Circle NW Washington DC 20008-3611

BLANCHARD, CONVERSE HERRICK, NUCLEAR PHYSICS. *Current Pos:* from assoc prof to prof, 61-90, ASSOC CHMN DEPT, UNIV WIS-MADISON, 75-, EMER PROF PHYSICS, 90- *Personal Data:* b Boston, Mass, Sept 25, 23; m 46; c 4. *Educ:* Harvard Univ, AB, 45; Univ Wis, PhD(physics), 50. *Prof Exp:* Nuclear physicist, Nat Bur Stands, 50-53; assoc prof physics, Pa State Univ, 53-61. *Mem:* Fel Am Phys Soc. *Res:* Theoretical nuclear and quantum physics. *Mailing Add:* Dept Physics Univ Wis Sterling Hall Madison WI 53706

BLANCHARD, DUNCAN CROMWELL, AIR-SEA INTERACTION, AEROBIOLOGY. *Current Pos:* RETIRED. *Personal Data:* b Winterhaven, Fla, Oct 8, 24; m 57, 68, 84, Julia Nugent; c Duncan, Rebecca, Andrea & Jonathan. *Educ:* Tufts Univ, BNavalSc, 45, BS, 47; Pa State Univ, MS, 51; Mass Inst Technol, PhD(meteorol), 61. *Prof Exp:* Res assoc, Res Lab, Gen Elec Co, 48-49; assoc scientist, Woods Hole Oceanog Inst, 51-68; sr res assoc, Atmospheric Sci Res Ctr, State Univ NY, Albany, 68-89. *Concurrent Pos:* Mem joint panel air & air sea interaction, Nat Acad Sci, 63-65; mem steering comt, Ocean Sci Comt Study Ocean Dumping, Nat Acad Sci-Nat Res Coun, 74-76; consult, NJ Cent Power & Light Co & McDonnell Douglas Astronaut Co; chmn, electorate nominating comt, AAAS, 80-84. *Mem:* Fel AAAS; Sigma Xi; fel Am Meteorol Soc; Am Geophys Union. *Res:* Aerosol production by the sea, bubble production in the sea, and flux of charged particles across the surface; ejection of dissolved organic matter and bacteria from water surfaces into the atmosphere. *Mailing Add:* 32 E Highland Dr Albany NY 12203

BLANCHARD, EUGENE JOSEPH, DYEING OF CELLULOSE, CROSSLINKING OF CELLULOSE. *Current Pos:* RES CHEMIST, SOUTHERN REGIONAL RES CTR, 63- *Personal Data:* b New Orleans, La, Feb 5, 36. *Educ:* Loyola Univ of the South, BS, 59; La State Univ, MS, 63. *Mem:* Am Asn Textile Chemists & Colorists; Am Chem Soc; AAAS. *Res:* Modification by chemical methods of cellulose to produce improved processes and products; dyeing of those products with acid basic, direct and disperse dyes for improved color fastness to washing. *Mailing Add:* 3125 Metairie Ct Metairie LA 70002

BLANCHARD, FLETCHER A(UGUSTUS), JR, ELECTRICAL ENGINEERING. *Current Pos:* RETIRED. *Personal Data:* b Cooperstown, NY, Nov 13, 24; m 47, Grace Hayden; c Fletcher A III & Scott H. *Educ:* Union Col, BA, 48; Lehigh Univ, MS, 50. *Prof Exp:* Instr elec eng, Lafayette Col, 48-50; from instr to prof elec eng, Univ NH, 50-88. *Res:* Instrumentation and control; ocean engineering. *Mailing Add:* 140 Haydens Haven Lane Northville NY 12134

BLANCHARD, FRANK NELSON, X-RAY DIFFRACTION. *Current Pos:* From asst prof to prof, 56-96, EMER PROF GEOL, UNIV FLA, 96- *Personal Data:* b Ann Arbor, Mich, May 24, 31; m 53, Mary G Wellington; c Frank, Douglas, Roy & Karen. *Educ:* Univ Mich, AB, 53, MS, 54, PhD(geol), 60. *Mem:* Mineral Soc Am; Nat Asn Geol Teachers; Mineral Asn Can. *Res:* Mineralogy; crystallography; petrology; petrography; x-ray analysis; x-ray powder diffraction standards for phosphate and arsenate minerals; mineralogy and geochemistry of magnesium-rich phosphorites from Florida. *Mailing Add:* 4610 NW 17 Pl Gainesville FL 32605

BLANCHARD, FRED AYRES, BIOPHYSICS. *Current Pos:* RETIRED. *Personal Data:* b Cleveland, Ohio, May 27, 23; m 48, Alice Lloyd; c Charles, Paul & Mark. *Educ:* La State Univ, BS, 44; Univ Cincinnati, MS, 48, PhD(physics), 51. *Prof Exp:* Radiochemist tracers, Dow Chem Co, 51-74, environ scientist, 74-86. *Mem:* Am Chem Soc; Sigma Xi. *Res:* Applications of radioisotopes to biological, chemical and industrial tracer problems; liquid scintillation counting; computer processing of counting data; low level counting; environmental science. *Mailing Add:* 39 Rosemary Ct Midland MI 48640

BLANCHARD, GORDON CARLTON, microbiology, for more information see previous edition

BLANCHARD, JAMES, PHARMACEUTICS, PHARMACOKINETICS. *Current Pos:* assoc prof, 71-87, PROF PHARMACEUT SCI, COL PHARM, UNIV ARIZ, 87- *Personal Data:* b Toronto, Ont, Mar 12, 40; m 62, Margaret T Falk; c John F. *Educ:* Univ Toronto, BScPharm, 63, MScPharm, 66; Univ Calif, San Francisco, PhD(biopharmaceut), 71. *Prof Exp:* Teaching asst, Univ Toronto, 63-65, Univ Calif, San Francisco, 66-68. *Concurrent Pos:* Prin investr res grants, 78-81; vis prof, Dept Clin Pharmacol, Royal Infirmary, Scotland, 80-81, Nestle Res Ctr, Lausanne, Switz, 87-88; Fogarty Sr Int Fel Award, Fogarty Int Ctr & Nat Inst Aging, 80-81; chmn-elect, Acad Pharmaceut Res & Sci Sect, Am Pharmaceut Asn, 90. *Mem:* Fel Am Pharmaceut Asn; Am Asn Col Pharm; Sigma Xi; fel Am Col Clin Pharmacol; fel Am Col Nutrit; Acad Pharmaceut Res & Sci. *Res:* Drug absorption; protein binding; drug-complexation interactions; effect of nutrition on drug metabolism; pharmacokinetics of drugs and nutrients in the elderly; formulation of controlled-release ocular drug-delivery systems; development of delivery systems for peptide/protein based drugs. *Mailing Add:* 1450 N Sarnoff Dr Tucson AZ 85715. *Fax:* 520-626-4063

BLANCHARD, JAMES PAGE, FUSION TECHNOLOGY, RADIATION DAMAGE. *Current Pos:* ASST PROF ENG, UNIV WIS, 88- *Personal Data:* b Orange, Calif, Feb 25, 60; m 91, Michelle Parker. *Educ:* Univ Calif, Los Angeles, BS, 83, MS, 84, PhD(nuclear eng), 88. *Honors & Awards:* Presidential Young Investr Award, NSF, 90. *Mem:* Am Soc Elec Eng; Am Soc Mech Eng; Asn Nuclear Scientists; AAAS; Mat Res Soc. *Res:* Study fusion technology, radiation damage, finite element hardness simulation, characterization of surfaces, fission reactor safety, reactor vessel embrizzlement and prediction of reactor vessel fluence. *Mailing Add:* Nuclear Eng 153 Eng Res Univ Wis 1500 Johnson Dr Madison WI 53706-1687. *E-Mail:* blanchar@engr.wisc.edu

BLANCHARD, JONATHAN EWART, GEOPHYSICS. *Current Pos:* RETIRED. *Personal Data:* b Truro, NS, Mar 22, 21; m 58; c 2. *Educ:* Dalhousie Univ, BSc, 40; Univ Toronto, MA, 47, PhD(geophys), 52. *Prof Exp:* Dir geophys, NS Res found Corp, 49-66, pres, 68-87. *Concurrent Pos:* From asst prof to prof geophys, Dalhousie Univ, 52-66. *Mem:* Soc Explor Geophysicists; Am Geophys Union; Can Asn Physicists; Can Inst Mining & Metall; fel Royal Soc Can. *Mailing Add:* 6470 Coburg Rd Halifax NS B3H 2A7 Can

BLANCHARD, RICHARD LEE, RADIOCHEMISTRY, ECOLOGY. *Current Pos:* CONSULT, 83- *Personal Data:* b Hutchinson, Kans, May 2, 33; m 55, 73; c 2. *Educ:* Ft Hays Kans State Col, BS, 55; Vanderbilt Univ, MS, 58; Washington Univ, PhD(chem), 63. *Prof Exp:* Chemist, Div Radiol Health, USPHS, Oak Ridge Nat Lab, 56-58, health physicist, Utah, 58-59, chemist, Robert A Taft Sanit Eng Ctr, 62-64, chg physics & bioassay group, Radiol Health Res Activities, 64-68, dep chief radiol eng lab, Bur Radiol Health, Environ Control Admin, Ohio, 68-74; dir, Radiochem & Nuclear Eng Facil, US Environ Protection Agency, 74-77; chief, Radiochem Spec Studies Br, Eastern Environ Radiation Facil, Montgomery, Ala, 77-83. *Concurrent Pos:* Adj prof nuclear eng, Univ Cincinnati, 68-77; mem N 13 subcomt, Am Nat Standards Inst, 74-76; adj prof, Auburn Univ, Montgomery, 78- *Mem:* Health Physics Soc; Sigma Xi. *Res:* Radiation dose to man from naturally occurring radionuclides and from radionuclides in the environment of nuclear power reactors; movement and concentration of radionuclides in aquatic environments. *Mailing Add:* 2215 Allendale Rd Montgomery AL 36111

BLANCHARD, ROBERT JOSEPH, ETHOPHARMACOLOGY, NEURAL & PHARMACOLOGICAL CONTROL OF FEAR ANXIETY & AGGRESSION. *Current Pos:* from asst prof to assoc prof, 64-72, PROF PSYCHOL, UNIV HAWAII, 72-, PROF NEUROSCI, 88- *Personal Data:* b Waltham, Mass, Apr 12, 37; m 62, D Caroline Hutchens; c Matthew C. *Educ:* Boston Univ, AB, 58; Univ Iowa, MA, 61, PhD(exp psychol), 62. *Concurrent Pos:* Prin investr, NIMH, Nat Inst Alcohol Abuse & Alcoholism, & NIH, 68-; exchange fel, Nat Acad Sci, USSR, 72-73; vis fel, Japan Found Sci, 81-82. *Mem:* Int Soc Res Aggression (pres, 92-94); Soc Neurosci; Behav Neurosci Soc. *Res:* Analysis and modeling of fear, anxiety and aggression; neural and pharmacologic control of these behaviors; author of numerous publications. *Mailing Add:* Bekesy Lab Neurobiol 1993 East West Rd Honolulu HI 96825. *Fax:* 808-956-5339

BLANCHARD, ROBERT OSBORN, BOTANY, PHYTOPATHOLOGY. *Current Pos:* from asst prof to assoc prof, 72-84, prof bot & plant path, 84-95, PROF & CHAIR PLANT BIOL, UNIV NH, 95- *Personal Data:* b Cumberland Center, Maine, July 5, 39; m 65; c 2. *Educ:* Southern Maine Voc Tech Inst, AAS, 59; Univ Maine, Portland-Gorham, BS, 64; Univ Ga, MEd, 69, PhD(plant path), 71. *Prof Exp:* Fel plant path, Univ Ga, 71-72. *Concurrent Pos:* Dept chmn bot & plant path, Univ NH, 73-76, chmn, Intercol Biol Sci Orgn, 76-78, assoc dean, Col Life Sci & Agr, 82- *Mem:* Sigma Xi; Mycol Soc Am; Am Phytopath Soc; Smithsonian Assocs. *Res:* Light and electron microscopic observations of fungi; host parasite interactions associated with tree diseases using electrophysiological techniques. *Mailing Add:* 86 Bucks Hill Rd Durham NH 03824-3210

BLANCHARD, SUSAN M, BIOMEDICAL ENGINEERING, CARDIAC ELECTROPHYSIOLOGY. *Current Pos:* ASSOC PROF, BIOL ENG & AGR DEPT, NC STATE UNIV, 93- *Personal Data:* b Knoxville, Tenn, 1946. *Educ:* Oberlin Col, BA, 68; Duke Univ, MS, 80, PhD(biomed eng), 82. *Prof Exp:* Asst res prof, Dept Biomed Eng, Duke Univ, 90-93. *Mem:* Sr mem Inst Elec & Electronics Engrs; sr mem Soc Women Engrs. *Mailing Add:* NC State Univ BAE Dept PO Box 7625 Raleigh NC 27695

BLANCHE, ERNEST EVRED, mathematics, statistics; deceased, see previous edition for last biography

BLANCHET, THIERRY ALAIN, TRIBOLOGY OF MATERIALS, SOLID LUBRICATION. *Current Pos:* Postdoctoral researcher, 92-93, ASST PROF MECH ENG, RENSSELAER POLYTECH INST, 93- *Personal Data:* b Huntington, NY, Dec 18, 63. *Educ:* Univ Vt, BS, 86; Dartmouth Col, MS, 88, PhD(eng sci), 92. *Honors & Awards:* Al Sonntag Award, Soc Tribologists & Lubrication Engrs, 93, Walter D Hodson Award, 97; Young Investr Award, NSF, 94. *Prof Exp:* Intern, Dow Chem Cent Res, 88. *Concurrent Pos:* Assoc ed, Soc Tribologists & Lubrication Engrs, 96-, secy, Solid Lubricant Tech Comt, 96- *Mem:* Soc Tribologists & Lubrication Engrs; Am Soc Mech Engrs; Sigma Xi. *Res:* High temperature solid lubrication of metals and ceramics; replenishment approaches for solid lubricant films; wear behavior of composite materials; wear and friction behavior of polymers and radiation processing for wear resistance; sterilization processing of polyethylene joint replacement components. *Mailing Add:* Rensselaer Polytech Inst MEAEM Troy NY 12180. *Fax:* 518-276-2623; *E-Mail:* blanct@rpi.edu

BLANCHET, WALDO W E, SCIENCE EDUCATION. *Current Pos:* prof sci & admin dean, 39-66, pres, 66-73, EMER PRES, FT VALLEY STATE COL, 73- *Personal Data:* b New Orleans, La, Aug 6, 10; m 43, Josephine Lavizzo; c Geri F & Waldo M. *Educ:* Talladega Col, AB, 31; Univ Mich, MS, 36, PhD(sci educ), 46. *Prof Exp:* Head sci dept, Ft Valley Normal & Indust Sch, 32-35, head dept & dean sch, 36-38. *Concurrent Pos:* Consult & lectr, NSF sci insts, Atlanta Univ & Albany State Col; consult spec proj, Tenn Valley Authority, 63-64; mem, Nat Adv Coun on Educ Disadvantaged Children, 70-; consult sci educ & higher educ, 73- *Mem:* AAAS; Nat Inst Sci; Nat Asn Res Sci Teaching. *Res:* Curriculum problems of general science education on college level. *Mailing Add:* 508 Camelot Dr College Park GA 30349

BLANCHET-SADRI, FRANCINE, SEMIGROUP THEORY, DISCRETE MATHEMATICS. *Current Pos:* ASSOC PROF, UNIV NC, GREENSBORO, 90- *Personal Data:* b Trois-Rivieres, Que, July 25, 53; m 79, Fereidoon Sadri; c Ahmad, Hamid & Marianne. *Educ:* Univ Que, Trois-Rivieres, BSpSc, 76; Princeton Univ, MS, 79; McGill Univ, PhD(math), 89. *Prof Exp:* Lectr, Univ Technol Isfahan, Iran, 82-84; teaching asst, McGill Univ, 84-88, lectr, 88-89, researcher, 89-90; res fel, Nat Sci & Eng Res Coun Can, 90. *Concurrent Pos:* Lectr, Univ Que, Trois-Rivieres, 76; prin investr, NSF, 91- *Mem:* Am Math Soc; Asn Comput Mach. *Res:* Decidability problem of the dot-depth hierarchy, more specifically on some congruences known to characterize the different levels of the hierarchy. *Mailing Add:* Univ NC Dept Math Greensboro NC 27412. *E-Mail:* blanchet@iris.uncg.edu

BLANCHETTE, ROBERT ANTHONY, FOREST PATHOLOGY, PLANT PATHOLOGY. *Current Pos:* from asst prof to assoc prof, 80-88, PROF, DEPT PLANT PATH, UNIV MINN, 88- *Personal Data:* b Lowell, Mass, July 30, 51; m 75, Carignan; c Ben & Chris. *Educ:* Merrimack Col, BA, 73; Univ NH, MS, 75; Wash State Univ, PhD(plant path), 78. *Prof Exp:* Lab asst forest path, USDA Forest Serv, Northeastern Sta, 74-75; res asst plant path, Wash State Univ, 75-77, res assoc, 77-80. *Concurrent Pos:* Hans Merensky fel. *Mem:* AAAS; Am Phytopath Soc; Mycol Soc Am; Soc Am Foresters; Am Soc Microbiol; Am Inst Conserv; fel Int Acad Wood Sci. *Res:* Discoloration and decay of living trees; forest products deterioration; diseases of urban and forest trees; biological delignification; canker diseases; stem rusts of hard pines; pinewood nematode; immunocytochemistry; host-pathogen interactions; biotechnology; ethromycology. *Mailing Add:* 975 County Rd E W St Paul MN 55126. *Fax:* 612-625-9728; *E-Mail:* robertb@puccini.crl.umn.edu

BLANCK, ANDREW R(ICHARD), MATERIALS SCIENCE, ELECTRICAL ENGINEERING. *Current Pos:* CONSULT, 50-; PRES, RUTHERFORD RES PROD CO, 58-; PRES, PRINCETON RES PROD CO, 64-; DIR PUB RELS, CLEARING HOUSE FOR CONSULT, NY, 66- *Personal Data:* b NY, Feb 7, 25; m 50; c 2. *Educ:* NY Univ, BA, 48; Polytech Inst Brooklyn, MA, 53; Sussex Inst Technol, ScD. *Prof Exp:* Chem engr, Interchem Corp, 48-49; chemist, Crownoil Chem Corp, 50-51; consult, Centro Res Labs, 51-53; tech serv engr, Celanese Corp Am, 53-56; chief chemist, Applications Lab & head Dielectrics Lab, Polymer Chem Div, W R Grace & Co, 56-58; mat engr, electromagnetic interference engr & coordr & consult, Ord Corps, Picatinny Arsenal, Dover, NJ, 57-66. *Concurrent Pos:* Dir pub rels, Assoc Consult Chem & Chem Engr, Inc, 66-; trustee, Hotel Salisbury, 66-68; fac mem, NY Univ, 68- *Mem:* Am Soc Testing & Mat; Inst Elec & Electronics Engrs; Am Chem Soc; Soc Plastic Engrs; Chem Industs Asn. *Res:* Plastics; electrical insulating systems and materials; surface coatings; plasticizers; instrumentation design for research and control purposes; adhesives; forensics. *Mailing Add:* Rutherford Res Corp Drawer 249 Rutherford NJ 07070

BLANCK, HARVEY F, JR, PHYSICAL CHEMISTRY. *Current Pos:* prof chem, 64-93, EMER PROF CHEM, AUSTIN PEAY STATE UNIV, 94- *Personal Data:* b North Ridgeville, Ohio, Apr 4, 32; m 60, Shirley Ritter; c Fred & Nancy. *Educ:* Miami Univ, BA, 54; Ohio State Univ, MS, 62, PhD(chem), 67. *Mem:* Am Chem Soc. *Res:* Physical chemistry. *Mailing Add:* Dept Chem Austin Peay State Univ Clarksville TN 37044. *Fax:* 615-648-5996; *E-Mail:* blanckh@apsu01.apsu.edy

BLANCK, RONALD RAY, OSTEOPATHIC MEDICINE. *Current Pos:* Med Serv Corps, US Army, 70-, resident internal med, Walter Reed Army Med Ctr, 70-73, from comdr capt to lt gen, 68-96, gen med officer, 68-70, asst chief gen med serv, 73-74, asst chief, Dept Med, 74-76, asst dean student affairs, Uniformed Serv Univ, 76-79, chief, Dept Med, Brooke Army Med Ctr, 79-82, chief med corps career activ off, Army Med Dept Personnel Support Act, 82-85, comdr, Berlin, 86-88, comdr, Frankfurt, 88-90, dir prof serv & chief med corps affairs, Off Surgeon Gen, 90-92, COMDR, WALTER REED ARMY MED CTR, 92- *Personal Data:* b Lancaster, Pa, Oct 8, 41; m 71, Donna R Ault; c Jennifer & Susan. *Educ:* Juniata Col, BS, 63; Philadelphia Col Osteop Med, DO, 67; Am Bd Internal Med, dipl. *Hon Degrees:* DSc, New Eng Col Osteop Med, 82; LLD, Philadelphia Col Osteop Med, 91. *Honors & Awards:* John Shaw Billings Award, Asn Mil Surgeons US, 76. *Concurrent Pos:* Asst prof clin med, Georgetown Univ, 72-78; clin instr med, Howard Univ, 75-77; assoc prof med, US Univ Health Serv, 76-79; clin assoc prof med, Univ Tex, 79-80, clin prof med, 80-82. *Mem:* AMA; fel Am Col Physicians; Am Acad Physician Execs; Asn Mil Surgeons US; Am Osteop Asn; Asn Mil Osteop Physicians & Surgeons; assoc Soc Med Consol Armed Forces. *Mailing Add:* Surgeon Gen 5109 Leesburg Pike Falls Church VA 22041-3258

BLANCK, THOMAS JOSEPH JOHN, MOLECULAR MECHANISMS OF ANESTHETIC ACTION. *Current Pos:* PROF ANESTHESIOL, PHYSIOL & BIOPHYS, CORNELL UNIV MED COL, 92- *Personal Data:* b Hoboken, NJ, June 9, 44; m 27, Marquerite Land; c Damian J, Tobias A & Sebastian J. *Educ:* Yale Univ, BS, 66; Univ Pa, MD, 70, PhD(biochem), 74. *Prof Exp:* Asst prof anesthiol & pharmacol, Univ Ariz, 77-81; assoc prof anesthiol & biomed eng, Johns Hopkins Univ, 81-92. *Concurrent Pos:* Dir cardiac anesthesia, Johns Hopkins Hosp, Baltimore, Md, 84-91; vchmn res, Med Col, Cornell Univ, 92; dir anesthesiol & sr scientist, Hosp Spec Surg, NY, 95- *Mem:* Am Soc Anesthiol; Int Anesthesia Res Soc; Biophys Soc; AAAS; Soc Cardiovasc Anesthesia; NY Acad Sci. *Res:* How anesthetics work; effect of volatile anesthetics on cardiac contraction; noted that volatile anesthetics alter calcium homeostasis. *Mailing Add:* Dept Anesthesiol Hosp Spec Surg 535 E 70th St New York NY 10021. *Fax:* 212-517-4481; *E-Mail:* blanckt@hss.edu

BLAND, BRIAN HERBERT, NEUROBIOLOGY, BEHAVIORAL NEUROSCIENCE. *Current Pos:* asst prof neuropsychol, 74-77, assoc prof, 77-81, PROF PSYCHOL, UNIV CALGARY, 81-, HEAD, DEPT PSYCHOL, 95- *Personal Data:* b Calgary, Alta, July 10, 43; m 64, Cheryl Pollock; c 2. *Educ:* Univ Calgary, BSc, 66, MSc, 68; Univ Western Ont, PhD(behav neurosci), 71. *Honors & Awards:* Int Sci Exchange Award, Nat Sci & Eng Res Coun Can, 90. *Prof Exp:* NATO sci fel, Inst Neurophysiol, Oslo, Norway, 71-73; asst prof, Univ Sask, 73-74. *Concurrent Pos:* mem, Psychol Grants Comt, Natural Sci & Eng Res Coun, 82-85; Killam res fel, 85 & 91. *Mem:* Can Physiol Soc; AAAS; NY Acad Sci; Soc Neurosci; Int Brain Res Orgn; World Fedn Neuroscientists. *Res:* Electrophysiological and pharmacological investigation of hippocampal formation function. *Mailing Add:* Behav Neurosci Res Group Dept Psychol Univ Calgary 2500 Univ Dr Calgary AB T2N 1N4 Can. *Fax:* 403-282-8249; *E-Mail:* bhbland@acs.ucalgary.ca

BLAND, CHARLES E, MYCOLOGY. *Current Pos:* From asst prof to assoc prof, 69-75, PROF BIOL, ECAROLINA UNIV, 76-, CHMN DEPT, 81- *Personal Data:* b Raleigh, NC, Aug 17, 43; m 63; c 2. *Educ:* Univ NC, Chapel Hill, AB, 64, PhD(mycol), 69. *Mem:* Mycol Soc Am; Soc Invert Path; World Maricult Soc. *Res:* Fungi; parasitic in marine and freshwater invertebrates. *Mailing Add:* Dept Biol ECarolina Univ 1000 E Fifth St Greenville NC 27858

BLAND, CLIFFORD J, COSMIC RAY PHYSICS, RADIATION PHYSICS. *Current Pos:* assoc prof, 68-77, prof physics, 77-97, head, Dept Physics & Astron, 85-97, EMER PROF, UNIV CALGARY, 97- *Personal Data:* b London, Eng, June 22, 36; m 63, Beatriz Urquidi; c Julie-Anne & Henry. *Educ:* Univ London, BSc, 58, PhD(physics), 61; Imp Col, Univ London, DIC, 61. *Prof Exp:* Res fel physics, Lab Cosmic Physics, La Paz, 62-63; res fel, Inst Physics, Milan, 64-68. *Concurrent Pos:* Lectr, La Paz, 62-63 & Milan, 64-68; consult, Nat Inst Nuclear Physics, Italy, 64-68; Nat Res Coun Can res grants, 68-77; vis prof, Rice Univ, 73 & Univ Extremadura, Spain, 91; vis researcher, Commonwealth Sci & Indust Res Orgn, Australia, 80-81. *Mem:* Am Geophys Union; assoc Royal Col Sci; Can Asn Phycisists. *Res:* Terrestrial radioactivity; radioactive decay data; alpha and gamma spectrometry. *Mailing Add:* Dept Physics Univ Calgary 2500 University Dr NW Calgary AB T2N 1N4 Can. *Fax:* 403-289-3331; *E-Mail:* 12582@ucdasvm1.admin.ucalgary.ca

BLAND, HESTER BETH, HEALTH SCIENCES. *Current Pos:* ADJ PROF, IND STATE UNIV, 72- *Personal Data:* b Sullivan, Ind, June 22, 06. *Educ:* Ind State Univ, BS, 42; Butler Univ, MS, 49; Ind Univ, HSD, 56. *Hon Degrees:* LLD, Ind State Univ, 73. *Honors & Awards:* William A Howe Award, Am Sch Health Asn, 75. *Prof Exp:* Supvr & teacher pub schs, Ind, 30-41, teacher, 42-47; supvr plant protection, Allison Div, Gen Motors Corp, 41-42; consult health educ, Ind State Bd Health, 47-72. *Concurrent Pos:* Lectr, Div Allied Sci, Sch Med, Ind Univ, 50-72 & Dept Health Educ, 58-; dir, Am Sch Health Asn & Pharmaceut Mfrs Asn Drug Educ Curric Proj, 69-70; consult ed, J Sch Health, 74-; consult, Med Arts Publ Found, 77-78 & McGovern Allergy Clin, Houston, 79- *Mem:* Fel Am Sch Health Asn (pres, 72-73); Am Asn Health, Phys Educ & Recreation. *Res:* Critical areas of health education, especially venereal disease, drug misuse, smoking and alcohol; school and public health. *Mailing Add:* 2511 Parkwood Dr No B Indianapolis IN 46224

BLAND, JEFFREY S, BIO-ORGANIC CHEMISTRY. *Current Pos:* Asst prof, 71-77, ASSOC PROF CHEM, UNIV PUGET SOUND, 77- *Personal Data:* b Peoria, Ill, Mar 21, 46; m; c 3. *Educ:* Univ Calif, Irvine, BS, 67; Univ Ore, PhD(chem), 71. *Honors & Awards:* Henry Schroeder Trace Mineral Res Award, 80. *Concurrent Pos:* Vis prof, Univ Hawaii, 74; sr res fel, Univ Ore, 74 & 75; clin lab dir, Nutrit Biochem, Bellevue-Redmond Med Lab, Evergreen State Col, 77- *Mem:* NY Acad Sci; Nat Acad Clin Biochem; AAAS; Am Chem Soc; Am Asn Clin Chemists. *Res:* Investigation of the effects of biological antioxidants upon the rate of photohemolysis of erythrocytes; examination of mechanisms of photodynamic processes and relation to membrane structure; trace minerals in human health and disease. *Mailing Add:* PO Box 1729 Gig Harbor WA 98335-2000

BLAND, JOHN (HARDESTY), MEDICINE. *Current Pos:* res fel cardiol, Col Med, Univ Vt, 48-49, from instr to prof med, 49-89, dir, Rheumatism Res Unit, 50-69, EMER PROF MED & RHEUMATOLOGY, COL MED, UNIV VT, 89- *Personal Data:* b Globe, Ariz, Nov 7, 17; m 44; c 4. *Educ:* Earlham Col, AB, 40; Jefferson Med Col, MD, 44; Am Bd Int Med, dipl, 52 & cert, internal med, 84. *Prof Exp:* Resident, Burlington County Hosp & Pa Hosp, Philadelphia, 44-46; chief cardiovasc sect, Sta Hosp, Ft Hood, Tex, 46-48. *Concurrent Pos:* Fel rheumatic dis, Mass Gen Hosp & New Eng Ctr Hosp, Boston, 50; hon res fel rheumatol, Univ Manchester, 58-59; vis sci worker, NIH, 72-73. *Mem:* AAAS; fel Am Col Physicians; Am Fedn Clin Res; NY Acad Sci; Am Rheumatism Asn; Sigma Xi; master Am Col Rheumatology. *Res:* Rheumatic disease; connective tissue metabolism; cervical spine anatomy; osteoarthritis; reversibility. *Mailing Add:* Rheumatology & Clin Immunol Unit Univ Vt Col Med Given Med Bldg Rm C302 Burlington VT 05401

BLAND, KIRBY ISAAC, SURGERY, ONCOLOGY. *Current Pos:* PROF & CHMN, DEPT SURG & DIR, SURG RESIDENCY PROG, BROWN UNIV SCH MED, 93-; SURGEON-IN-CHIEF, RI HOSP, 93- *Personal Data:* b Dothan, Ala, Feb 6, 42; m 66; c 3. *Educ:* Auburn Univ, BS, 64; Univ Ala, Birmingham, MD, 68. *Honors & Awards:* Lester R Dragstedt Physician Award, 86 & 93. *Prof Exp:* Intern surg, Univ Fla Col Med, 69, resident, 76; fel & res assoc surg oncol, Univ Tex, M D Anderson Hosp, 76-77; from asst prof to assoc prof surg, Univ Louisville Sch Med, 78-83; prof & assoc chmn surg, dir, Surg Residency Prog, Dept Surg, Univ Fla Col Med, 83-93. *Concurrent Pos:* Prin investr, Univ Fla, 84-; ComtSurg Educ, Soc Univ Surgeons, 84-86; dir, Am Bd Surg, 86-92; dir, Am Bd Colon & Rectal Surg, 87-93; comt surg educ, Am Col Surgeons, 88-90, chmn, Comt Young Surgeons, 85-87. *Mem:* Am Col Surgeons; Asn Acad Surg (pres, 87-88); Am Surg Asn; Soc Univ Surgeons; Soc Surg Oncol (treas, 88-90); Am Soc Clin Oncol; Int Soc Surg. *Res:* Tumor biology and metabolism; surgical oncology, especially melanoma, gastro-intestinal, breast neoplasms. *Mailing Add:* Dept Surg RI Hosp 593 Eddy St Providence RI 02903. *Fax:* 401-444-6612

BLAND, RICHARD DAVID, CARDIOPULMONARY PHYSIOLOGY, NEWBORN MEDICINE. *Current Pos:* fel pulmonary dis & newborn med, Cardiovasc Res Inst, 74, asst prof, 75-80, ASSOC PROF NEONATAL PEDIAT, UNIV CALIF, SAN FRANCISCO, 80- *Personal Data:* b New Rochelle, NY, Nov 16, 40; c 3. *Educ:* Yale Univ, BA, 62; Boston Univ, MD, 66. *Prof Exp:* Intern & resident pediat, Johns Hopkins Hosp, Baltimore, 66-69; chief newborn nurseries & staff pediatrician, Tripler Army Med Ctr, Honolulu, 69-72. *Concurrent Pos:* Staff mem, Cardiovasc Res Inst, Univ Calif, San Francisco, 75-; vis prof pediat, Univ Hawaii, Honolulu, 76; NIH grant, NIH, Bethesda, Md, 76-; mem planning comt, Ross Labs Seminars Perinatal Med, 77-; estab investr, Am Heart Asn, 79-84. *Mem:* Soc Pediat Res; Am Thoracic Soc; Am Fedn Clin Res; Am Acad Pediat. *Res:* Lung fluid balance in newborn animals and human infants; microcirculation in the developing lung; intensive care of newborn infants. *Mailing Add:* Dept Pediat Univ Utah Med Ctr 50 N Medical Dr Salt Lake City UT 84132

BLAND, RICHARD P, MATHEMATICAL STATISTICS. *Current Pos:* RETIRED. *Personal Data:* b Oklahoma City, Okla, Nov 23, 28; m 53. *Educ:* Univ Okla, BS, 52; Univ NC, PhD(math statist), 61. *Prof Exp:* Anal engr, Chance Vought Aircraft, Inc, 53-56; res asst statist, Univ NC, 60-61; asst prof, Johns Hopkins Univ, 61-63; from asst prof to assoc prof statist, Southern Methodist Univ, 63-89. *Mem:* Am Statist Asn; Am Inst Math Statist; Royal Statist Soc. *Res:* Statistical decision theory, statistical inference, Bayerian statistics. *Mailing Add:* 1436 N Cheyenne Dr Richardson TX 75080

BLAND, ROBERT GARY, OPERATIONS RESEARCH, APPLIED MATHEMATICS. *Current Pos:* asst prof, 78-81, ASSOC PROF OPERS RES, CORNELL UNIV, 81- *Personal Data:* b New York, NY, Feb 25, 48; m 74. *Educ:* Cornell Univ, BS, 69, MS, 72, PhD(oper res), 74. *Prof Exp:* Asst prof math sci, State Univ NY Binghamton, 74-78. *Concurrent Pos:* Res assoc oper res, Ctr Oper Res & Economet & lectr appl sci, Cath Univ Louvain, 75-78; vis prof, Europ Inst Advan Studies Mgt, 76-77; Alfred P Sloan Found Res fel, 78-; NSF graduate fel, 69-72. *Mem:* Am Math Soc; Opers Res Soc Am. *Res:* Mathematical programming; combinatorial optimization; matroids; graph theory; networks. *Mailing Add:* Dept Indust Eng Cornell Univ 319 Upson Hall Ithaca NY 14853-7501

BLAND, ROGER GLADWIN, NATURAL RESOURCE EDUCATION, SCANNING ELECTRON MICROSCOPY. *Current Pos:* From asst prof to assoc prof, 67-77, PROF BIOL, CENT MICH UNIV, 77- *Personal Data:* b Los Angeles, Calif, Dec 28, 39; m 64, Kathryn Poling; c Mark & Erin. *Educ:* Univ Calif, Davis, BS, 61; Ore State Univ, MS, 64; Univ Ariz, PhD(entom), 67. *Mem:* Entom Soc Am; Orthopterists Soc. *Res:* Behavior, ecology and sense organ morphology of insects. *Mailing Add:* Dept Biol Cent Mich Univ Mt Pleasant MI 48859. *E-Mail:* rgbland@cmich.edu

BLAND, WILLIAM M, JR, AEROSPACE ENGINEERING & TECHNOLOGY. *Current Pos:* INDEPENDENT MGT & TECH CONSULT, 94- *Personal Data:* b Portsmouth, Va, July 23, 22; m 49, Betty Johnson; c Ginny B (Thomason) & William H. *Educ:* NC State Col, BS, 47. *Prof Exp:* Res scientist aerodyn, Langley Res Ctr, Nat Adv Comt Aeronaut, 47-58; head, Systs Test Br, NASA, 58-60, asst chief, Eng Div, 60-62, dep mgr, Mercury Proj, 62-63, chief, Apollo Test Div, 63-64, chief, Apollo Test & Checkout, 65-66 & Apollo Reliability, Qual Assurance & Test Div, 67, dep mgr, reliability & qual assurance, Manned Spacecraft Ctr, 68-72, dep dir, safety, reliability & qual assurance, Johnson Space Ctr, 72-79; mgt & tech consult & pres, Geebs, Inc, 80-94. *Concurrent Pos:* Mem tech eval teams, Mercury Little Joe booster, Mercury & Apollo spacecraft & Little Joe II booster & mem mission & flight readiness rev bd, Mercury missions; vis prof space activ, Rice Univ, Univ Houston & La State Univ, 63-64; mem tech staff, President's Comn on Accident Three Mile Island, 79; consult, Nat Acad Sci, 80 & Nuclear Regulatory Comn, 84-85; expert witness, 80-; ed, Nuclear Safety Dept, J Hazard Prev, 81-82. *Mem:* Am Inst Aeronaut & Astronaut. *Res:* Aerodynamics, aircraft, audits, bioengineering, contracts, data analysis, health services, engineering design, expendable launch vehicles, nonmetallic materials, nuclear operations, risk management, reliability; lessons learned, manned space flight, safety, spacecraft, testing, quality assurance, management techniques; nuclear waste, technical editing and investigations and analysis of failures and accidents; author of over 70 technical publications. *Mailing Add:* 18575 Martinique Dr Houston TX 77058

BLANDER, MILTON, PHYSICAL CHEMISTRY, METEORITICS. *Current Pos:* GROUP LEADER & SR SCIENTIST, ARGONNE NAT LAB, 71- *Personal Data:* b Brooklyn, NY, Nov 1, 27; m 92, Carol Berss; c Kathryn, Daniel, Joshua, Benjamin & Alice. *Educ:* Brooklyn Col, BS, 50; Yale Univ, PhD(phys chem), 53. *Honors & Awards:* Mat Chem Award, Dept Energy; Max Bredig Award, Electrochem Soc. *Prof Exp:* Res assoc, Cornell Univ, 53-55; sr chemist, Oak Ridge Nat Lab, 55-62; mem tech staff, NAm Rockwell Sci Ctr, 62-67, group leader, 67-71. *Concurrent Pos:* Sr scientist, Quest Res, 95- *Mem:* Fel AAAS; Am Chem Soc; fel Meteoritical Soc; Electrochem Soc; Am Inst Mining, Metall & Petrol Engrs; Norweg Acad Technol Sci. *Res:* Statistical mechanics and thermodynamic measurements of molten ionic systems; vapors and alloys; pyrometallurgical research; welding chemistry and the origin of meteorites; combustion; nucleation. *Mailing Add:* Argonne Nat Lab 9700 S Cass Ave Argonne IL 60439. *Fax:* 630-252-9373

BLANDFORD, ROBERT ROY, PHYSICAL OCEANOGRAPHY, SEISMOLOGY. *Current Pos:* DIR RES, SEISMIC DATA LAB, GEOTECH, TELEDYNE, INC, 66- *Personal Data:* b Columbus, Ga, Jan 1, 37; m 66; c 1. *Educ:* Calif Inst Technol, BS, 59, PhD(geophys), 64. *Prof Exp:* Res scientist, NY Univ, 64-66. *Concurrent Pos:* Consult, Rand Corp, 57-66. *Mem:* Am Geophys Union. *Res:* Rossby waves; thermocline; internal waves; Gulf Stream dynamics; signal detection; arrays; time-series. *Mailing Add:* 1809 Paul Spring Rd Alexandria VA 22307

BLANDFORD, ROGER DAVID, ASTROPHYSICS. *Current Pos:* asst prof, 76-79, PROF THEORET ASTROPHYS, CALIF INST TECHNOL, 79-, RICHARD CHACE TOLMAN PROF THEORET ASTROPHYS, 89- *Personal Data:* b Grantham, Eng, Aug 28, 49; m 72, Elizabeth; c Jonathan & Edward. *Educ:* Cambridge Univ, BA, 70, MA & PhD(astrophys), 74. *Prof Exp:* Bye fel, Magdalene Col, Cambridge Univ, 72-73, res fel, St John's Col, 73-76. *Concurrent Pos:* Mem, Inst Advan Study, Princeton Univ, 74-75; Parisot fel, Univ Calif, Berkeley, 75. *Mem:* Am Astron Soc; fel Royal Astron Soc; fel Royal Soc Am Acad Arts & Sci. *Res:* Theoretical astrophysics. *Mailing Add:* 1772 Rose Villa St Pasadena CA 91106

BLANE, HOWARD THOMAS, PSYCHOLOGY, ALCOHOL RESEARCH. *Current Pos:* DIR, RES INST ADDICTIONS, 86- *Personal Data:* b Deland, Fla, May 10, 26; div; c 2. *Educ:* Harvard Univ, BA, 50; Clark Univ, MA, 51, PhD(psychol), 57. *Prof Exp:* Instr psychol, Harvard Med Sch, 57-66, asst clin prof, 66-70; from assoc prof to prof educ & psychol, Univ Pittsburgh, 70-86. *Concurrent Pos:* Vis res fel, Univ Hawaii, 68-69; prin investr numerous grants, NIMH, Nat Inst Alcoholic Abuse & Alcoholism, NIH, Japan & Nat Inst Drug Abuse; consult, Nat Inst Alcohol Abuse & Alcoholism, 70-; res prof psychol, State Univ NY, Buffalo, 86-; mem bd dirs, Res Found Ment Hyg. *Mem:* Am Pub Health Asn; fel Am Psychol Asn; AAAS; Res Soc Alcoholism; Soc Psychologists Addictive Behav; Health Educ Found (vpres, 75-); NY Acad Sci. *Res:* Psychological study of development of alcoholism in late adolescence and early adulthood; prevention of alcoholic disorders; substance abuse in the developmentally disabled. *Mailing Add:* 1021 Main St Buffalo NY 14203

BLANEY, DONALD JOHN, BIOCHEMISTRY. *Current Pos:* asst prof, 63-77, ASSOC PROF DERMAT, CINCINNATI GEN HOSP, 77-; ASSOC CLIN PROF DERMAT, UNIV CINCINNATI, 67- *Personal Data:* b Cincinnati, Ohio, May 18, 26; m 57; c 3. *Educ:* Xavier Univ, Ohio, BS, 49; Univ Iowa, PhD(biochem), 53; Univ Mich, MD, 57. *Prof Exp:* Res asst, Univ Mich, 53-55; intern, Philadelphia Gen Hosp, 57-58; fel dermat, Cincinnati Gen Hosp, 58-61, instr, 61-63; assoc prof, Univ Cincinnati, 65-67. *Mem:* AAAS; Am Chem Soc; Am Acad Dermat; AMA. *Res:* Immunology. *Mailing Add:* 2859 Bouidnot Ave Cincinnati OH 45238

BLANFORD, GEORGE EMMANUEL, JR, PHYSICS, PLANETARY SCIENCES. *Current Pos:* asst prof, 75-78, assoc prof, 78-86, PROF PHYSICS, UNIV HOUSTON, CLEAR LAKE CITY, 86- *Personal Data:* b Lebanon, Ky, Sept 16, 40; div; c Elizabeth & Peter. *Educ:* Cath Univ Am, BA, 64; Univ Louisville, MS, 67; Wash Univ, PhD(physics), 71. *Prof Exp:* Assoc instr physics, Univ Clermont-Ferrand, 71-73; Nat Res Coun res assoc, L B Johnson Space Ctr, 73-75. *Concurrent Pos:* Prin investr, NASA, 76-83, 93- *Mem:* Am Phys Soc; Am Asn Physics Teachers; AAAS; Am Geophys Union; Am Astron Soc. *Res:* Cosmic ray physics, planetary science, solar and planetary relationships. *Mailing Add:* Div Nat Sci 2700 Bay Area Blvd Houston TX 77058

BLANGERO, JOHN CHARLES, STATISTICAL GENETICS, GENETIC EPIDEMIOLOGY. *Current Pos:* scientist, 86-89, asst scientist, 89-92, ASSOC SCIENTIST, SW FOUND BIOMED RES, 93- *Personal Data:* b New Castle, Pa, Nov 13, 57. *Educ:* Youngstown State Univ, BA, 79; Case Western Res Univ, MA, 81, PhD(pop genetics), 87. *Honors & Awards:* Gabriel W Lasker Award, 93. *Concurrent Pos:* Prin investr, Nat Inst Diabetes & Digestive & Kidney Dis, 92- *Mem:* Am Statist Asn; Am Soc Human Genetics; Int Genetic Epidemiol Soc; Am Asn Anthrop Genetics; Am Asn Physical Anthrop; Human Biol Coun. *Res:* Statistical genetic methods; genetic epidemiology of common diseases; genotype-environment interaction; complex segregation analysis; linkage analysis; genetics of normal physiological variation; genetics of heart disease; endocrine genetics. *Mailing Add:* 10617 Alta Loma Helotes TX 78023. *Fax:* 210-670-3317

BLANK, ALBERT ABRAHAM, MATHEMATICAL PHYSICS, VISION. *Current Pos:* prof, 69-90, EMER PROF MATH, CARNEGIE-MELLON UNIV, 90- *Personal Data:* b New York, NY, Nov 29, 24; div; c Sharon, Tamara, Deborah & Irina. *Educ:* Brooklyn Col, AB, 44; Brown Univ, MS, 46; NY Univ, PhD(math), 51. *Prof Exp:* Math analyst physiol optics, Columbia Univ, 51-52; assoc info & control systs, Control Systs Lab, Univ Ill, 53-54; asst prof math, Univ Tenn, 54-59; from assoc prof to prof, Courant Inst Math Sci, NY Univ, 59-69. *Concurrent Pos:* Scientist, Magneto-Fluid Dynamics Div, Courant Inst Math Sci, NY Univ, 57-69, sr res scientist, 83-90; assoc ed, Am Math Monthly; sr res scientist & vis prof, Col Staten Island, 90- *Mem:* Fel AAAS; Am Phys Soc; Am Math Soc; Math Asn Am; Sigma Xi. *Res:* Magnetofluid dynamics; theory and computational studies of equilibrium, stability for problems in controllling thermonuclear reactions; partial differential equations and applications; binocular space perception; assistive computer technology for teaching science to blind persons. *Mailing Add:* 102 Loring Ave Pelham NY 10803-2014. *E-Mail:* blank@postbox.csi.cuny.edu

BLANK, BENJAMIN, ORGANIC CHEMISTRY, MEDICINAL CHEMISTRY. *Current Pos:* DIR BUS DEVELOP/MKT, BIOMED SCI, SRI INT, 91- *Personal Data:* b Philadelphia, Pa, May 12, 31; m 58, Libby Litt; c Eric, Robert & Jeffrey. *Educ:* Temple Univ, BA, 53, PhD(chem), 58. *Prof Exp:* Chemist, Muscular Dystrophy Asn, Vet Admin Hosp, Philadelphia, 56; sr med chemist, Smith Kline & French Labs, 58-74, sr investr, 74-79, sr proj admin, 79-80, mgr sci & admin affairs, New Compound Eval & Licensing, 81-84, sci dir, Res & Develop Acquisitions, 84-88; dir, CPD Acquisitions, Eastman Pharmaceuts, 88-89; vpres, Technol Assessment & Acquisition, Campbell Soup Co, 89-91. *Concurrent Pos:* Biochemist, Johnson Res Found, Sch Med, Univ Pa, 69-70. *Mem:* AAAS; NY Acad Sci; Am Chem Soc; Sigma Xi; Licensing Exces Soc. *Res:* Thyromimctics; peptides; nonsteroidal anti-inflammatories; inhibitors of steroidal biosynthesis and gluconeogenesis; cephalosporins; biotechnology; drug delivery. *Mailing Add:* 502 Bruce Rd Trevose PA 19053-6115. *Fax:* 609-734-2045

BLANK, CARL HERBERT, PUBLIC HEALTH, MICROBIOLOGY. *Current Pos:* DIR, STATE PUB HEALTH LAB, WYO, 92- *Personal Data:* b Toledo, Ohio, Mar 16, 27; m 50, Audrey Krohn; c Eric. *Educ:* Univ Toledo, BS, 50; Utah State Univ, MS, 57; Univ NC, MPH, 65, DrPH(lab pract & admin), 67. *Prof Exp:* Microbiologist, Div Labs, Utah State Health Dept, 51-58, actg asst dir, 58-62, asst dir, 62-64; dep dir, Bur Labs, Utah State Div Health, 67-72; chief, Exam & Documentation Br, Ctr Dis Control, 72-81, chief, Lab Training Br, 81-83, chief, Lab Consult Br, 83-85, dep dir & consult, 85-86, sr lab consult, Pub Health Pract Prog, 87-92. *Concurrent Pos:* Clin instr, Univ Utah, 68-70; consult, Ctr Dis Control, 71; bd dirs, Nat Comt Clin Lab Studies, 91-, Asn State & Territorial Pub Health Lab Dirs, 92-; chair, comt on Lab Studies & Pract, Am Pub Health Asn, 92- *Mem:* Am Pub Health Asn; Am Soc Microbiol; Conf Pub Health Laboratorians. *Res:* Incidence of Q fever; improved methods in isolation and identification of actinomyces species; toxo plasmosis; fluorescent antibody techniques; laboratory evaluation and improvement programs. *Mailing Add:* 745 Rodeo Ave Cheyenne WY 82009. *Fax:* 307-777-5402

BLANK, CHARLES ANTHONY, PHYSICAL INORGANIC CHEMISTRY, ENVIRONMENTAL SCIENCES GENERAL. *Current Pos:* CONSULT, 81-; PROF CHEM, 84- *Personal Data:* b Brooklyn, NY, Apr 15, 22; div; c 3. *Educ:* Brooklyn Col, BA, 46, MA, 49; Syracuse Univ, PhD(phys inorg chem), 54; Boston Univ, Cert biotechnol, 94. *Prof Exp:* Lab technician res, Int Flavors & Fragrances, Inc, 41-43; asst chem, Syracuse Univ, 47-48; res chemist, Film Dept, E I du Pont de Nemours & Co, 51-52, Bell Tel Labs, 54-56 & IBM Corp, 56-59; supvr tech staff, Phys Sci Dept, Melpar, Inc, Va, 59-60; phys scientist, US Dept Defense, 60-78. *Concurrent Pos:* Teacher chem, Assumption Col, Worcester, Mass, 84-85, physics, Northeastern Univ, Boston, 85-86, Curry Col, Milton Mass, 86-87; physics teacher, Worcester State Col, Worcester, Mass, 86-87; adj sci fac, Manatee Community Col, Bradenton, Fl, 89-90; chem instr, Curry Col, Milton, Mass, 93-; instr health & safety, Am Red Cross, Boston, 95-97. *Mem:* Emer mem Am Chem Soc; fel Am Inst Chemists; fel NY Acad Sci; New Eng Asn Chem Teachers; Sigma Xi. *Res:* Coordination compounds; organic and inorganic synthesis; solid state chemistry; chemistry of electronic devices and materials; physical instrumentation; geophysics; nuclear weapon effects; chemistry and physics of ionosphere; research administration; environmental sciences. *Mailing Add:* 255 Massachusetts Ave Apt 607 Boston MA 02115-3512

BLANK, GREGORY SCOTT, CELL BIOLOGY, PROTEIN CHEMISTRY. *Current Pos:* SR SCIENTIST PROCESS RECOVERY, GENENTECH, INC. *Personal Data:* b Nov 20, 54; m; c 1. *Educ:* Univ Southern Calif, PhD(biol), 81. *Prof Exp:* Res assoc, Becton Dickinson Monoclonal Ctr, 85- *Mailing Add:* Scientist Process Recovery Genentech 460 Point San Bruno Blvd MS 3 South San Francisco CA 94080

BLANK, HARVEY, dermatology, for more information see previous edition

BLANK, IRVIN H, DERMATOLOGY, PHOTO MEDICINE. *Current Pos:* ASSOC BIOCHEMIST, WELLMAN LAB, MASS GEN HOSP, 55- *Personal Data:* b Mt Carmel, Ill, Feb 20, 02; m 36, Anna D Finesinger; c Joan & Barbara. *Educ:* Univ Cincinnati, PhD(bacteriol), 28. *Honors & Awards:* Rothman Award, Soc Invest Dermat. *Mem:* Fel AAAS; NY Acad Sci; hon mem Soc Invest Dermat; Am Acad Dermat; Am Physiol Soc; Dermat Found. *Res:* Percutaneous absorption; mechanism of action of emollients. *Mailing Add:* Dept Dermat Mass Gen Hosp Boston MA 02114

BLANK, JOHN EDWARD, ARCHAEOLOGY, BIOLOGICAL ANTHROPOLOGY. *Current Pos:* Asst prof, 69-73, assoc prof anthrop, 73-, PROF DIR ARTS & SCI INSTRNL COMPUT CLEVELAND STATE UNIV. *Personal Data:* b Cleveland, Ohio, Dec 5, 42; m 66; c 2. *Educ:* Case Inst Technol, BS, 64, MA, 67; Univ Mass, PhD(anthrop), 70. *Mem:* Soc Am Archaeol; fel Am Anthrop Asn. *Res:* Cultural paleoecological adaptational systems of the Ohio Valley; conservation resource management, and public archaeology. *Mailing Add:* Dept Anthrop Cleveland State Univ Euclid Ave at E 24th Cleveland OH 44115-1123

BLANK, LELAND T, ENGINEERING ECONOMICS, RESEARCH CENTER DEVELOPMENT. *Current Pos:* head dept, 84-86, PROF INDUST ENG, TEX A&M UNIV, 78-, DIR, INST MFG SYSTS, 86-, ASST DEAN GRAD STUDIES, 88- *Personal Data:* b San Antonio, Tex, Jan 15, 44. *Educ:* St Mary's Univ, BS, 67; Okla State Univ, MS, 68, PhD(indust eng), 70. *Prof Exp:* Prof indust eng, Univ Tex, El Paso, 70-76; mgt scientist, indust eng, GTE Data Serv, 76-78. *Concurrent Pos:* Coordr, mfg systs, Tex A&M Univ, 85-86; automated mfg equip tech adv comn, Int Trade Admin, US Dept Commerce, 85-; asst dir, Tex Eng Exp Sta, 86- *Mem:* Inst Indust Engrs; Nat Soc Prof Engrs; Sigma Xi; Soc Mfg Engrs; Soc Comput Simulation; Am Soc Eng Educ. *Res:* Cost modeling and quality systems analysis for manufacturing systems; analysis of indirect costs in a computer integrated manufacturing environment. *Mailing Add:* Tex A&M Univ 201 Admin Bldg College Station TX 77843-1259

BLANK, MARTIN, PHYSIOLOGY, BIOPHYSICS. *Current Pos:* From instr to asst prof, 59-68, ASSOC PROF PHYSIOL, COL PHYSICIANS & SURGEONS, COLUMBIA UNIV, 68- *Personal Data:* b Feb 28, 33; m 55, Marion Hersch; c Donna, Jonathan & Ari. *Educ:* City Col New York, BS, 54; Columbia Univ, PhD(phys chem), 57; Univ Cambridge, PhD(colloid sci), 59. *Honors & Awards:* Yasuda Award, Bioelec Repair & Growth Soc, 90. *Concurrent Pos:* NIH fels, 60-70; res chemist, Unilever Res Lab, Eng, 64 & 67, Netherlands, 69; vis scientist, Weizmann Inst, 67, Univ Calif, 68, Hebrew Univ, 70- & Univ Victoria, Can, 95; liaison scientist, Off Naval Res, London, 74-75; vis lectr, Monash Univ, 82; biologist, Off Naval Res, Arlington, 84-85 & 86-88; ed, Bioelectrochem & Bioenergetics, J Electrochem Soc & Colloids & Surfaces & J Colloid Interface Sci; distinguished vis prof, Univ Western Australia, 82; distinguished lectr physiol, Wayne State Univ, 84; vis prof, Acad Sci USSR, Inst Electrochem, Moscow, 89, Tata Inst, Bombay, India, 92 & Univ Negev, Israel, 95. *Mem:* AAAS; Am Chem Soc; Biophys Soc; Electrochem Soc; Bioelectrochem Soc; Bioelectromagnetics Soc. *Res:* Physical chemistry of ion transport and excitation in natural membranes; permeability of surface films; natural membranes; biophysical and cellular mechanisms of electromagnetic stimulation of biosynthesis, enzymes (Nak-ATPase); theoretical aspects of membranes and biopolymers; biotechnology, biosensors, electroporation. *Mailing Add:* Col Physicians & Surgeons Columbia Univ New York NY 10032. *Fax:* 212-305-5775; *E-Mail:* mb32@columbia.edu

BLANK, STUART LAWRENCE, MATERIALS SCIENCE, CERAMIC ENGINEERING. *Current Pos:* res scientist, 69-77, supvr, Epitaxial Mat & Processes Group, 77-80, DEPT HEAD, ADVAN TECHNOL DEVELOP DEPT, BELL TEL LABS, 80- *Personal Data:* b Brooklyn, NY, Mar 4, 42; m 58; c 2. *Educ:* Alfred Univ, BS, 62; Univ Calif, Berkeley, MS, 64, PhD(mat sci), 67. *Prof Exp:* Res asst mat sci, Lawrence Radiation Labs, Univ Calif, 62-67. *Mem:* Am Ceramic Soc; Nat Inst Ceramic Engrs; Sigma Xi. *Res:* Solid state reactions; diffusion phenomena in refractory materials such as oxides; electro-optic materials research; crystal growth mechanisms; mechanical property effects of cation and anion impurities on crystals. *Mailing Add:* 125 Greenwood Ave Madison NJ 07940-1730

BLANK, ZVI, SOLID STATE & POLYMER CHEMISTRY, ENVIRONMENTAL SCIENCES. *Current Pos:* PRES, COMPLETE ANAL LAB INC, 91- *Personal Data:* b Tel-Aviv, Israel; m; c 3. *Educ:* Israel Inst Technol, BS, 60; NY Univ, MChE, 66, PhD(chem eng), 70. *Prof Exp:* Asst res scientist crystal growth, NY Univ, 65-69; staff engr solid state chem, Mat Res Ctr, Allied Chem Corp, 69-75; mgr chem & mat dept, Corp Res & Develop Lab, Singer Co, 75-80; vpres tech & eng, Radiation Tech Inc, 80-83, Enviro-Sci, Inc, 84-88; pres, ECRA Labs, 88-91. *Mem:* Am Chem Soc; Am Inst Chem Engrs; Inst Hazardous Mat Mgt; NY Acad Sci. *Res:* Liquid crystals; electrochemical materials; acousto-optic materials; solid state chemistry related to energy storage and conversion; metal hydrides; crystal growth; structure-properties relationships in inorganics and in polymers; hybrid microelectronics; adhesives; garment fabrication technology; environmental analysis; environmental remediation. *Mailing Add:* 103 Littleton Rd Morris Plains NJ 07950

BLANKE, JORDAN MATTHEW, SOFTWARE SYSTEMS. *Current Pos:* ASSOC PROF & DEPT CHAIR COMPUT SCI & COMPUT INFO SYSTS, MERCER UNIV, ATLANTA, 85- *Personal Data:* b New York, NY, Sept 16, 54; m 82, Charlene Silver; c Ilani & Zachary. *Educ:* State Univ NY Stony Brook, BS, 76, MS, 77; Emory Univ, JD, 80. *Prof Exp:* Assoc atty, Otterbourg, Steindler, Houston & Rosen, 81-83; law clerk, Justice Joseph Cohen, Bronx, NY, 83; asst prof comput sci & bus law, St John's Univ, Jamaica, NY, 83-85. *Concurrent Pos:* Adj prof, Emory Univ, Sch Law, 86-87. *Res:* Computers and the law; human factors in user interface design. *Mailing Add:* Mercer Univ 3001 Mercer University Dr Atlanta GA 30341-4155. *Fax:* 404-986-3337; *E-Mail:* blanke_j@atl1.mercer.peachet.edu

BLANKE, ROBERT VERNON, TOXICOLOGY. *Current Pos:* RETIRED. *Personal Data:* b Leavenworth, Kans, Dec 3, 24; m 50, Lois M Scholz; c Christine L, Steven R & Jonathan A. *Educ:* Northwestern Univ, BS, 49; Univ Ill, MS, 53, PhD(pharmacol), 58. *Honors & Awards:* Harger Award, Toxicol Sect, Am Acad Forensic Sci, 86. *Prof Exp:* Res asst, Univ Ill, 50-53, instr, 53-57; asst toxicologist, Med Examr Off, Md, 57-60; toxicologist, Ill, 60-63; toxicologist, Med Examr Off, Commonwealth of Va, 63-72; prof path, pharmacol & toxicol, Med Col Va, 72-87. *Concurrent Pos:* Sr chemist, Cook County Coroner's Lab, Chicago, 50-53; assoc prof, Med Col Va, 63-74, prof, 87-; consult, Vet Admin Hosp, Richmond, 64-70 & 74-87; mem toxicol study sect, Div Res Grants, NIH, 70-74; dir, Toxicol Lab, Med Col Va Hosp, 72-87. *Mem:* AAAS; Am Acad Forensic Sci; Am Chem Soc; NY Acad Sci; Soc Toxicol; Soc Forensic Toxicol; Sigma Xi; Am Asn Clin Chem; Int Asn Forensic Toxicol. *Res:* Analytical toxicology; environmental toxic substances; general toxicology. *Mailing Add:* 4222 Croatan Rd Richmond VA 23235-1116. *Fax:* 804-320-0028; *E-Mail:* rblanke@gems.vcu.edu

BLANKENBECLER, RICHARD, OPTICS. *Current Pos:* PROF, STANFORD LINEAR ACCELERATOR CTR, STANFORD UNIV, 69- *Personal Data:* b Kingsport, Tenn, Feb 4, 33; wid; c 2. *Educ:* Miami Univ, AB, 54; Stanford Univ, PhD(physics), 58. *Hon Degrees:* DSc, Miami Univ, Ohio, 90. *Prof Exp:* NSF fel physics, Princeton Univ, 58-63, assoc prof, 63-67; prof, Univ Calif, Santa Barbara, 67-69. *Concurrent Pos:* Fel, NSF & Sloan Found. *Mem:* Int Soc Optical Eng. *Res:* Particle physics, optics and theoretical high energy physics. *Mailing Add:* 974 Cottrell Way Palo Alto CA 94305. *Fax:* 650-926-3587

BLANKENHORN, PAUL RICHARD, WOOD SCIENCE & TECHNOLOGY, MATERIALS ENGINEERING. *Current Pos:* res asst nuclear eng, Breazeale Nuclear Reactor, Pa State Univ, 67-68, res asst wood sci, Sch Forest Resources, 70-72, res assoc mat sci, Pa Transp Inst, 72-75, from asst prof to assoc prof wood technol, 75-83, PROF WOOD TECHNOL, SCH FOREST RESOURCES, PA STATE UNIV, 83- *Personal Data:* b Shenandoah, Pa, Apr 16, 44; m 68, Janet A Astleford; c Kristin E & Brad D. *Educ:* Pa State Univ, BS, 66, MS, 68, PhD(wood sci, mat sci), 72. *Honors & Awards:* Wood Award, 2nd, Forest Prod Soc, 72; Eng Timber Bridge Award, Am Forest & Paper Asn, 92. *Prof Exp:* Eng aide aerospace eng, Johnsville Naval Air Sta, 66-67. *Mem:* Forest Prod Soc; Soc Wood Sci & Technol. *Res:* Physical and mechanical properties of wood and wood base composites; conversion of wood into energy; recycling and use of secondary fibers in wood polymer and wood cement composites. *Mailing Add:* Sch Forest Resources Univ Pa 310 Forest Resources Lab University Park PA 16802. *Fax:* 814-863-7193

BLANKENSHIP, JAMES EMERY, NEUROPHYSIOLOGY. *Current Pos:* assoc dean, Grad Sch Biomed Sci , 80-93, PROF PHYSIOL ANAT & NEUROSCI & MEM, DIV COMP MARINE NEUROBIOL, MARINE BIOMED INST, MED BR, UNIV TEX, GALVESTON, 70- *Personal Data:* b Sherman, Tex, Mar 19, 41; m 60; c 2. *Educ:* Austin Col, BA, 63; Yale Univ, MS, 65, PhD(neurophysiol), 67. *Prof Exp:* Fel physiol, Med Sch, NY Univ, 67-69; NIH fel neurophysiol, NIMH, 69-70. *Concurrent Pos:* NIH res grant, Nat Inst Neurol Dis & Stroke, 70, 72, 73, 86 & 89; Off Naval Res contract, 73; NSF res grant, 77, 79, 83 & 87-; dir, MD-PhD prog, Univ Tex Med Br Galveston, 82-93, dir, Neurosci Grad Prog, 87- *Mem:* AAAS; Soc Neurosci; Am Physiol Soc; Sigma Xi; Soc Gen Physiol. *Res:* Cellular electrophysiology and neuroendocrinology; comparative neurobiology, synaptic and interneuronal properties; neuropeptides and reproductive peptides; neural control of locomotion. *Mailing Add:* Marine Biomed Inst 200 University Blvd Galveston TX 77555-1069

BLANKENSHIP, JAMES LYNN, EXPERIMENTAL SOLID STATE PHYSICS, SEMICONDUCTORS. *Current Pos:* RES PROF, UNIV TENN, 91- *Personal Data:* b Knoxville, Tenn, Mar 26, 31; m 51; c 4. *Educ:* Univ Tenn, BS, 54, MS, 55, PhD(physics), 73. *Prof Exp:* Circuit develop engr, Oak Ridge Nat Lab, 55-58, res engr, 58-65, educ assignment, 65-67, physicist, 68-72, sr res staff mem, 72-91. *Mem:* Am Phys Soc. *Res:* Nuclear medicine image processing; heavy ion physics instrumentation and research; gaseous and solid state detector development. *Mailing Add:* 7508 Sea Kirk Lane Knoxville TN 37931-1747

BLANKENSHIP, JAMES W, biochemistry, for more information see previous edition

BLANKENSHIP, JAMES WILLIAM, BIOCHEMICAL PHARMACOLOGY. *Current Pos:* PROF PHARMACOL & TOXICOL, SCH PHARM, UNIV PAC, 77-, CHMN, DEPT PHYSIOL/ PHARMACOL, 90- *Personal Data:* b San Diego, Calif, June 8, 43; m 68, Loretta Mittelstaedt; c Todd & Kelly. *Educ:* Tex A&M, BS, 65, MS, 67; Univ Utah, PhD(pharmacol), 72. *Prof Exp:* Res assoc cell biol, Med Col, Ga, 72-74; asst prof pharmacol, Med Univ SC, 74-77. *Concurrent Pos:* Mem & consult, competency comt, Calif State Bd Pharm, 80-97; prin investr, NIH res grant, 80-83 & NSF, 84-87, 87-91; consult, Lawrence Hall Sci. *Mem:* Am Soc Pharmacol & Exp Therapeut; AAAS. *Res:* Biochemistry and cellular functions of polyamines; metabolism of polyamines and effects on DNA synthesis and on cell growth. *Mailing Add:* Sch Pharm Univ Pac Stockton CA 95211

BLANKENSHIP, LYTLE HOUSTON, WILDLIFE RESEARCH, CONSERVATION EDUCATION. *Current Pos:* RETIRED. *Personal Data:* b Campbellton, Tex, Mar 1, 27; m 54, Margaret Luecke; c Terry L, Kerry J, Jerry A & Sheri A. *Educ:* Tex A&M Univ, BS, 50; Univ Minn, MS, 52; Mich State Univ, PhD(physiol), 57. *Honors & Awards:* Outstanding Serv Award, Wildlife Soc, 83. *Prof Exp:* Biologist, Game Div, Mich Dept Conserv, 54-56; res biologist, Minn Div Game & Fish, 56-61; wildlife biologist, Wildlife Res Br, Bur Sport Fisheries & Wildlife, US Fish & Wildlife Serv, 61-69; res scientist, Tex A&M Univ-E African Agr & Forestry Res Orgn, 69-72; from assoc prof to prof, Agr Exp Sta, Tex A&M Univ, 72-88. *Concurrent Pos:* Consult, World Bank, Kenya, 71 & 75, Orgn Am States, Dominican Republic, 75, US Fish & Wildlife Serv, India, 81 & 82, Exxon, 82-; vis lectr, Univ Dar es Salaam, Tanzania, 78; owner & pres, Safari Adventures. *Mem:* Hon mem Wildlife Soc (pres elect, 85-86, pres, 86-88); Wildlife Soc Southern Africa; Nat Audubon Soc; Nat Wildlife Fedn; Ducks Unlimited; World Wildlife Fund; Nature Conservancy. *Res:* Ecology, behavior and diseases of doves, waterfowl, woodcock, moose and deer; physiology of deer; ecology, reproduction and meat production of large game animals in East Africa; range nutrition of plants and animals. *Mailing Add:* FM 117 Uvalde TX 78801

BLANKENSHIP, ROBERT EUGENE, PHOTOSYNTHESIS. *Current Pos:* assoc prof, 85-88, PROF CHEM, ARIZ STATE UNIV, 88- *Personal Data:* b Auburn, Nebr, Aug 25, 48; m 71; c 2. *Educ:* Nebr Wesleyan Univ, BS, 70; Univ Calif, Berkeley, PhD(chem), 75. *Prof Exp:* Postdoctoral fel, Univ Wash, 76-79; asst prof chem, Amherst Col, 79-85. *Concurrent Pos:* Dir, Ctr Study Early Events Photosynthesis, 88-91; ed-in-chief, Photosynthesis Res, 88-; chmn, Gordon Res Conf Photosynthesis, 91. *Mem:* Am Chem Soc; AAAS; Union Concerned Scientists. *Res:* Excitation and electron transfer in photosynthetic systems; evolution of biological energy conserving systems; mechanisms of electron transfer reactions in biological systems. *Mailing Add:* 1907 E Magdalena Dr Tempe AZ 85283

BLANKENSHIP, VICTOR D(ALE), FLUID MECHANICS, HEAT TRANSFER. *Current Pos:* RETIRED. *Personal Data:* b Topeka, Kans, Feb 9, 34; m 56, Virginia Gaeco; c Mark I & Scott C G. *Educ:* Univ Kans, BS, 56; Univ Notre Dame, MS, 59; Univ Mich, PhD(mech eng), 62. *Prof Exp:* Engr, Bendix Aviation Corp, 56-59; dir Off Res mark 18 & reentry systs concepts, Reentry Systs Div, Aerospace Corp, 62-68; mgr reentry systs eng, TRW Syst Group, 68-83, mgr penetration systs, 83-88, mgr spec projs, 88-97. *Concurrent Pos:* Lectr, Univ Southern Calif, 63-66 & Univ Redlands, 68, 75, 78, 84 & 85; mem, Strategic Arms Limitation Talk Support Group, 69 & 71; trustee, Valley Prep Sch, 70-71. *Mem:* Am Inst Aeronaut & Astronaut; NY Acad Sci; Sigma Xi. *Res:* Effects of oscillating boundary layers; rarefied gas dynamics; partially ionized gases; antenna breakdown; boundary layer; heat transfer; shock-shock interactions; nuclear effects; systems analysis; reentry systems; optics; microelectronics; electr static probes; penetration aids. *Mailing Add:* 1740 Canyon Rd Redlands CA 92373

BLANKESPOOR, HARVEY DALE, INVERTEBRATE ZOOLOGY, PARASITOLOGY. *Current Pos:* assoc prof biol, PROF, HOPE COL, 77- *Personal Data:* b Boyden, Iowa, Oct 15, 39; m 64; c 2. *Educ:* Westmar Col, BA, 63; Iowa State Univ, MS, 67, PhD(invert zool), 70. *Honors & Awards:* Chester A Herrick Award, Midwest Conf Parasitologists, 70. *Prof Exp:* Asst prof biol, Univ Northern Iowa, 70-71 & Trinity Christian Col, 71-72; asst prof zool, Univ Mich, Ann Arbor, 72-77. *Mem:* Am Soc Parasitol; Am Micros Soc; Am Soc Trop Med & Hyg. *Res:* Host-parasite relationships of parasitic flatworms. *Mailing Add:* Dept Biol Hope Col 35 E 12th St Holland MI 49423-3698

BLANKESPOOR, RONALD LEE, ORGANIC CHEMISTRY. *Current Pos:* assoc prof, 77-79, PROF CHEM, CALVIN COL, 79- *Personal Data:* b Hull, Iowa, Feb 22, 46; m 69; c 1. *Educ:* Dordt Col, AB, 68; Iowa State Univ, PhD(org chem), 71. *Prof Exp:* Asst prof chem, Univ Wis-Oshkosh, 71-73; asst prof chem, Wake Forest Univ, 73-77. *Mem:* Am Chem Soc; Sigma Xi. *Res:* Studies of radical ion reactions using electron spin resonance and electrochemical methods. *Mailing Add:* Dept Chem Calvin Col Grand Rapids MI 49546-4388

BLANKFIELD, ALAN, physics, mathematics, for more information see previous edition

BLANKLEY, CLIFTON JOHN, MEDICINAL CHEMISTRY, COMPUTER DRUG DESIGN. *Current Pos:* Sr res chemist, 67-80, sr res assoc, 80-89, ASSOC RES FEL, PARKE DAVIS RES DIV, WARNER-LAMBERT CO, 89- *Personal Data:* b Chicago, Ill, Apr 21, 42; m 76, Maureen F Foley. *Educ:* Stanford Univ, BS, 63; Mass Inst Technol, PhD(org chem), 67. *Mem:* Am Chem Soc; AAAS; NY Acad Sci; Sigma Xi. *Res:* Synthesis of potential anti-inflammatory agents, antibacterial agents, antitumor agents and antihypertensive agents and hypolipidemic agents; study of quantitative structure activity relationships; computer-assisted drug design and molecular modeling. *Mailing Add:* Parke Davis Pharm Res Div Warner-Lambert Co 2800 Plymouth Rd Ann Arbor MI 48106-1047. *Fax:* 313-998-2782

BLANKS, JANET MARIE, NEUROCYTOLOGY. *Current Pos:* ASST PROF OPHTHALMOL & ANAT, SCH MED, UNIV SCALIF, 78-; DIR EM LAB, ESTELLE DOHENY EYE FOUND, 78- *Personal Data:* b Berkeley, Calif, Sept 25, 44; m 67. *Educ:* Humboldt State Col, BA, 66; Univ Calif, Los Angeles, PhD(anat), 73. *Prof Exp:* Feldman fel neurocytol, Jules Stein Eye Inst, Univ Calif, Los Angeles, 73-74; vis scientist, Max Planck Inst Brain Res, 74-75; instr, Harvard Med Sch, Boston, 76-78. *Mem:* Asn Res Vision & Ophthal. *Res:* Correlation of biochemical and morphological changes which occur during synaptogenesis in the mammalian central nervous system; light and electron microscopic autoradiography and Golgi light microscopy. *Mailing Add:* Doheny Eye Found Univ Southern Calif Sch Med 1355 San Pablo St Los Angeles CA 90033

BLANKS, ROBERT F, chemical engineering, for more information see previous edition

BLANKSCHTEIN, DANIEL, COLLOID & INTERFACE SCIENCE, BIOTECHNOLOGY. *Current Pos:* Weizmann postdoctoral fel, Mass Inst Technol, 82-84, Bantrell postdoctoral fel, 84-86, Texaco-Mangelsdorf asst prof, 86-89, TEXACO-MANGELSDORF ASSOC PROF, MASS INST TECHNOL, 89- *Personal Data:* b Buenos Aires, Arg, Dec 1, 51; Israeli citizen; m 78; c 2. *Educ:* Tel-Aviv Univ BSc, 76, MSc, 79, PhD (physics), 83. *Concurrent Pos:* Vis scientist, Israel-Norway Cult Exchange, Oslo, 85; consult, Texaco & Oculon Corp, 89-; NSF presidential young investr, 89-94. *Mem:* Am Phys Soc; Am Chem Soc; Am Inst Chem Engrs; Soc Petrol Engrs; Mat Res Soc. *Res:* Statistical mechanics; thermodynamics and physical chemistry of structured fluids including micellar solutions, polymers and protein mixtures; molecular simulations and liquid state theory applications to predict the phase behavior of complex fluids; bioseparations using two-phase aqueous polymer and micellar systems. *Mailing Add:* Dept Chem Eng Mass Inst Technol 77 Massachusetts Ave Cambridge MA 02139-4307

BLANN, H MARSHALL, nuclear chemistry, for more information see previous edition

BLANPAIN, JAN E, MEDICINE. *Current Pos:* Dir, Leuven Univ Hosp, 60-70, prof, Med Sch & Sch Pub Health, 65-95, EMER PROF, LEUVEN UNIV, 95- *Personal Data:* b Diest, Belg, Feb 24, 30; m; c 2. *Educ:* Leuren Univ, MD, 56. *Concurrent Pos:* Lectr health serv mgt & health policy, Cornell Univ, Ottawa Univ, Montreal Univ, Leeds Univ, Manchester & others; consult health affairs, WHO, UN Develop Prog, Pan Am Health Orgn, World Bank, Rockefeller Found & others, 61-; vis scientist, US Nat Ctr Health Serv Res & Develop, 71; chmn & co-founder, Europ Health Policy Forum, 81- *Mem:* Inst Med-Nat Acad Sci; hon fel Am Col Healthcare Execs; hon fel Am Col Hosp Adminr; Int Epidemiol Asn; fel Am Col Hosp Adminr. *Res:* Comparative health care organization and health policy; quality assurance in health care. *Mailing Add:* Sch Pub Health Katholieke Univ Leuven Naamsestraat 22 Louvain 3000 Belgium

BLANPIED, GARY STEPHEN, INTERMEDIATE ENERGY NUCLEAR PHYSICS. *Current Pos:* from asst prof to assoc prof, 79-88, PROF PHYSICS, UNIV SC, 88- *Personal Data:* b Corpus Christi, Tex, Nov 25, 49; m 92, Deborah R Reece; c Jason, Christopher, Stephen & Isabelle. *Educ:* Auburn Univ, BS, 73; Ga Inst Technol, MS, 74; Univ Tex, PhD(physics), 77. *Prof Exp:* Res asst physics, Univ Tex, 74-77; res assoc, NMex State Univ, 77-79. *Concurrent Pos:* Fulbright res scholar, 86-87. *Mem:* Am Phys Soc. *Res:* Intermediate energy proton-nucleus scattering; pion-nucleus scattering; photo production of mesons; multistep excitations in inelastic scattering; electromagnetic measurements; polarized photon induced reactions. *Mailing Add:* Dept Physics Univ SC Columbia SC 29208. *Fax:* 803-777-3065; *E-Mail:* blanpied@cebaf

BLANPIED, GEORGE DAVID, POMOLOGY, PHYSIOLOGY. *Current Pos:* Asst prof, 55-57 & 59-64, assoc prof, 65-76, PROF POMOL, CORNELL UNIV, 76- *Personal Data:* b Ridgewood, NJ, June 29, 30; m 52; c 3. *Educ:* Dartmouth Col, BA, 52; Cornell Univ, MS, 55; Mich State Univ, PhD(pomol), 59. *Concurrent Pos:* Vis prof, Univ Dublin, 65-66, Agr Can, 74-75 & Fao Iran, 75; sabbatical leave, UK, 81-82. *Mem:* Am Soc Hort Sci. *Res:* Biological and commercial aspects of fruit maturity, storage, handling and marketing. *Mailing Add:* 2215 N Triphammer Rd Ithaca NY 14850

BLANPIED, WILLIAM ANTOINE, PARTICLE PHYSICS, SCIENCE POLICY. *Current Pos:* prog dir, Ethics & Values in Sci & Technol, NSF, 76-79, Off Spec Proj, 79-84, sr prog mgr, 84-89, SR INT ANALYST, DIV INT PROGS, NSF, 89- *Personal Data:* b Rochester, NY, May 11, 33; div; c Eric, Wendy & Jessica. *Educ:* Yale Univ, BS, 55; Princeton Univ, PhD(physics), 59. *Prof Exp:* Instr physics, Princeton Univ, 58-59; NSF fel, Synchrotron Lab, Frascati, Italy, 59-60; from instr to asst prof, Yale Univ, 60-66; assoc prof, Case Western Res Univ, 66-69 & 71-72; staff scientist, NSF, New Delhi, India, 69-71; sr res fel, Harvard Univ, 72-74; head div pub sector progs, AAAS, 74-76. *Concurrent Pos:* Yale Univ jr fac fel, Cambridge Electron Accelerator, Harvard Univ, 63-64; vis scholar, Grad Sch Int Rels & Pac Studies, Univ Calif, San Diego, 87-89; adj prof, Int Inst, George Mason Univ. *Mem:* Fel Am Phys Soc; Am Hist Sci Soc; fel AAAS. *Res:* Science and public policy; science policy in post World War II era; public understanding of science; history of science in Asia. *Mailing Add:* Div Int Progs NSF 4201 Wilson Blvd Arlington VA 22230. *Fax:* 703-306-0476; *E-Mail:* wblanpie@nsf.gov

BLANQUET, RICHARD STEVEN, INVERTEBRATE PHYSIOLOGY, BIOCHEMISTRY. *Current Pos:* instr physiol, 67-69, asst prof, dept biol, 69-73, ASSOC PROF BIOL, GEORGETOWN UNIV, 73- *Personal Data:* b Brooklyn, NY, Jan 17, 40; m 67. *Educ:* City Col New York, BS, 61; Duke Univ, PhD(zool), 66. *Prof Exp:* Res assoc zool, Lab Quant Biol, Univ Miami, 65-67. *Mem:* Am Soc Cell Biol; Am Soc Zool; Sigma Xi. *Res:* Physiology and biochemistry of lower invertebrates; problems of coelenterate nematocyst discharge and chemical nature of capsule and enclosed toxin; algal-cnidarian symbioses. *Mailing Add:* Dept Biol Georgetown Univ Washington DC 20057-0001

BLANTON, CHARLES DEWITT, JR, ORGANIC CHEMISTRY, MEDICINAL CHEMISTRY. *Current Pos:* assoc prof med chem, 68-75, dir res & grad studies, 81-85, PROF MED CHEM, SCH PHARM, UNIV GA, 75- *Personal Data:* b Kings Mountain, NC, Jan 11, 37; m 59; c 1. *Educ:* Western Carolina Col, BS, 59; Univ Miss, PhD(org chem), 63. *Prof Exp:* Fel, Dept Chem, Ind Univ, 63-64; assoc res prof pharmaceut & med chem, Sch Pharm, Auburn Univ, 64-68. *Mem:* Acad Pharmaceut Sci; Am Chem Soc; Am Pharmaceut Asn; Int Soc Heterocyclic Chem; The Chem Soc. *Res:* Synthesis of quinazolines as potential anticonvulsants; pyrrolopyridines and c-nucleosides as potential antineoplastic agents; potential prophylactic and radical curative antimalarial; indole and benzodiazepine analogues as potential psychopharmacological and antineoplastic agents. *Mailing Add:* 171 Thornhill Dr Athens GA 30607-1741

BLANTON, JACKSON ORIN, PHYSICAL OCEANOGRAPHY, LIMNOLOGY. *Current Pos:* PROF OCEAN, SKIDAWAY INST OCEANOG, 76- *Personal Data:* b Atlanta, Ga, Oct 28, 39; m 62; c 2. *Educ:* Univ Fla, BSCE, 62; Ore State Univ, MS, 64, PhD(oceanog), 68. *Prof Exp:* Consult coastal eng, Marine Adv Inc, 64-65; res assoc, Univ Fla, 65-66; asst prof phys oceanog, Marine Lab, Duke Univ, 68-70; res scientist phys limnol, Can Ctr Inland Waters, 70-74; prog mgr phys oceanog, US Energy Res & Develop Admin, 74-76. *Concurrent Pos:* Consult phys oceanog, Res Triangle Inst, NC, 68-69, NSF, 77-80 & US Fish & Wildlife Serv, 80. *Mem:* Am Geophys Union; Int Asn Great Lakes Res; Estuarine Res Fedn. *Res:* Energy dissipation in lakes, estuaries and shallow seas; processes of upwelling and water mass exchanges; maintenance and dissipation of thermoclines or frontal zones in oceans and lakes; continental shelf circulation. *Mailing Add:* Skidaway Inst Oceanog Ten Ocean Science Circle Savannah GA 31411

BLANTON, JOHN DAVID, LOW DIMENSIONAL TOPOLOGY, MORSE THEORY. *Current Pos:* dept chair, 91-94, PROF MATH, ST JOHN FISHER COL, 70- *Personal Data:* b St Louis, MO, Jan 23, 27; m 71, Claire Bickham; c Jack, Paul, Drew & Anne. *Educ:* St Louis Univ, AB, 53, MS, 55; Univ Ill, Urbana, PhD(math), 70. *Prof Exp:* Res asst, Inst Advan Study, 67-68; instr math, Rockhurst Col, 68-70. *Mem:* Am Math Soc; Math Asn Am; Sigma Xi. *Res:* Translation from the Latin of L Euler's "Introduction to Analysis of the Infinite"; principles of differential calculus. *Mailing Add:* Dept Math St John Fisher Col Rochester NY 14618. *E-Mail:* blanton@sjfc.edu

BLANTON, PATRICIA LOUISE, GROSS ANATOMY, PERIODONTICS. *Current Pos:* From asst prof to assoc prof gross anat, Baylor Dent Col, 67-75, chmn, Dept Gross Anat, 83-85, PROF GROSS ANAT & PERIODONT, BAYLOR DENT COL, 75-, ADJ PROF ANAT, 85- *Personal Data:* b Clarksville, Tex, July 9, 41. *Educ:* Hardin-Simmons Univ, BA, 62; Baylor Univ, MS, 64, PhD(anat), 67; Baylor Dent Col, DDS, 74, cert periodont, 75. *Honors & Awards:* First Place Award, Student Clinicians, Am Dent Asn, 72. *Concurrent Pos:* Mem, Nat Adv Coun Health Prof Educ, NIH, 73-74 & State Anat Bd, 82-85; consult, Am Dent Asn & Coun Dent, NIH Oral Biol-Med-Study Sect, 83-86 & Am Dent Asn, Coun Dent Educ & Comt Dent Accreditation, 81-85. *Mem:* Am Asn Anatomists; Am Acad Periodont; Int Soc Electromyographic Kinesiology; Am Dent Asn; Sigma Xi; fel Am Col Dent; Int Col Dent; Am Acad Periodont. *Res:* Electromyographic evaluation of the human head and neck musculature; masticatory under normal conditions and relative to temporomandibular joint dysfunction and occlusal discrepancies and adjustments. *Mailing Add:* Dept Gross Anat Baylor Col Dent 3302 Gaston Ave Dallas TX 75246

BLANTON, RONALD EDWARD, MOLECULAR BIOLOGY, GENERAL MEDICAL SCIENCES. *Current Pos:* ASST PROF GEOG MED, UNIV HOSPS, 86- *Personal Data:* b Houston, Tex, Mar 11, 52. *Educ:* Harvard Univ, BA, 74; Case Western Res Univ, MD, 79. *Mem:* Am Col Physicians; Am Fed Clin Res. *Res:* Molecular biology of schiztosomes with particular emphasis on gene regulation during development and vaccine production. *Mailing Add:* 2476 Derbyshire Rd Cleveland OH 44106

BLANTZ, ROLAND C, NEPHROLOGY & HYPERTENSION. *Current Pos:* HEAD DEPT & PROF NEPHROLOGY-HYPERTENSION, VET ADMIN MED CTR, 72- *Mailing Add:* Dept Med Div Nephrology-Hypertension Univ Calif San Diego & Vet Admin Med Ctr 3350 La Jolla Village Dr 111H San Diego CA 92161

BLASCHEK, HANS P, PLASMID BIOLOGY. *Current Pos:* asst prof food microbiol, 80-86, ASSOC PROF FOOD MICROBIOL, DEPT FOOD SCI, UNIV ILL, URBANA, CHAMPAIGN, 86- *Personal Data:* b Bruchsal, WGer, Mar 16, 52; US citizen; m 75; c 2. *Educ:* Rutgers Col, BA, 74; Rutgers Univ, MS, 77, PhD(food sci), 80. *Honors & Awards:* New Investr Res Award, NIH. *Prof Exp:* Res intern, Dept Food Sci, Rutgers Univ, 74-77, fel, 77-78, res asst, 78-80. *Concurrent Pos:* Consult, Food Indust. *Mem:* Am Soc Microbiol; Inst Food Technologists; AAAS; Soc Indust Microbiol. *Res:* Genetic and physiological manipulation of the clostridia. *Mailing Add:* 4012 Riverknoll Dr Champaign IL 61821

BLASCHUK, OREST WILLIAM, CELL ADHESION MOLECULES, CADHERINS. *Current Pos:* asst prof, 87-93, ASSOC PROF, MCGILL UNIV, 93-; MED RES SCIENTIST, ROYAL VICTORIA HOSP, 89- *Personal Data:* b Winnipeg, Man, Oct 20, 54. *Educ:* Univ Winnipeg, BSc, 75; Univ Man, MSc, 79; Univ Toronto, PhD(biochem), 84. *Mem:* Am Soc Cell Biol; Soc Develop Biol; Can Soc Cell Biol; Can Fertil & Andrology Soc. *Res:* Investigating the structure, function and regulation of a family of cell adhesion molecules known as the cadherins. *Mailing Add:* Royal Victoria Hosp Urol Lab Hershey Bldg 687 Pine Ave W Montreal PQ H3A 1A1 Can. *Fax:* 514-843-1457

BLASDELL, ROBERT FERRIS, SYSTEMATIC BOTANY, PLANT MORPHOLOGY. *Current Pos:* asst prof, 64-69, chmn dept, 78-81, ASSOC PROF BIOL, CANISIUS COL, 69- *Personal Data:* b Kuala Lumpur, Malaysia, May 12, 29; US citizen; m 63, Astrid Paluch; c Katie, Kirsten & Damione. *Educ:* Ohio Wesleyan Univ, BA, 51; Univ Mich, MA, 54, PhD(bot), 59. *Prof Exp:* Asst prof biol, La State Univ, 59-64. *Mem:* Am Fern Soc; Am Soc Plant Taxonomists; Sigma Xi. *Res:* Taxonomy and morphology of the vascular plants. *Mailing Add:* Dept Biol Canisius Col 2001 Main St Buffalo NY 14208

BLASE, EDWIN W(ILLIAM), CHEMICAL ENGINEERING. *Current Pos:* CONSULT 84- *Personal Data:* b St Charles, Mo, Sept 22, 23; m 45; c 3. *Educ:* Univ Kans, BSChE, 44; NY Univ, MBA, 65. *Prof Exp:* Chem engr, Chas Pfizer & Co, 46-52, develop supvr, 52-56, pharmaceut develop supvr, 56-60, asst to vpres prod, 60-61, mgr res co-ord, Pfizer Int, 61-65, mgr pharmaceut prod serv, 65-66, asst prod mgr, Brooklyn Plant, Cordis Corp 66-68, mgr pharmaceut develop, 68-69; mgr, biochem prod, 69-84. *Mem:* Am Chem Soc; Am Inst Chem Engrs. *Res:* Technical administration; biochemical reagents; pharmaceuticals and fine chemicals. *Mailing Add:* 908 N Doral Lane Venice FL 34293-3805

BLASER, DWIGHT A, NOISE & VIBRATION CONTROL, FLUID MECHANICS. *Current Pos:* assoc sr res engr noise & vibration, Gen Motors Res Labs, 71-74, sr res engr, 74-80, sect mgr, Signatur Analysis Group, 88-89, STAFF RES ENGR NOISE & VIBRATION, GEN MOTORS RES LABS, 80-, SECT MGR METAL CUTTING MECH & PWTRN NOISE & VIBRATION, 90-, DEPT HEAD BODY ENG & INTEGRATION. *Personal Data:* b Bucyrus, Ohio, Oct 5, 43; m 82; c 1. *Educ:* Ohio State Univ, BSME, 66, MS, 67, PhD(mech eng), 71. *Prof Exp:* Res asst thermodynamics, Exp Sta, Ohio State Univ, 65-66, res assoc, 67-71. *Concurrent Pos:* Lectr, Dept Mech Eng, Ohio State Univ, 67-71. *Mem:* Soc Automotive Engrs; Sigma Xi; Soc Mfg Engrs; Am Soc Mech Engrs. *Res:* Mechanics of manufacturing systems specializing in metal removal processes, quality inspection methods through signature analysis, fourier analysis techniques and duct acoustics. *Mailing Add:* Gen Motors Res & Develop MC480106256 30500 Mound Rd Warren MI 48090-9055

BLASER, MARTIN JACK, CAMPYLOBACTER & HELICOBACTER, ENTERIC BACTERIOLOGY. *Current Pos:* SCOVILLE PROF MED, DIR DIV INFECTIOUS DIS & PROF MICROBIOL & IMMUNOL, VANDERBILT UNIV SCH MED, 89- *Personal Data:* b New York, NY, Dec 18, 48; m 79, Ronna L Wineberg; c Daniel, Genia & Simone. *Educ:* Univ Pa, BA, 69; NY Univ, MD, 73. *Honors & Awards:* Young Investigator Award, Western Soc Clin Invest, 89; Squibb Award, Infectious Dis Soc Am, 92. *Prof Exp:* Intern internal med, Univ Colo Sch Med, 73-74, resident, 74-77, fel infectious dis, 77-79; EIS officer bacterial dis, Ctr Dis Control, 79-81; from asst prof to assoc prof infectious dis, Univ Colo Sch Med, 81-89. *Concurrent Pos:* Chief, Infectious Dis Sect, Vet Admin Med Ctr, Denver, 81-89, clin investr, 86-89; clin investr bacteriol & immunol, Rockefeller Univ, 87-88; nat counr, Am Fedn Clin Res, 86-89; assoc ed, Am J Epidemiol, 85-; mem, Bact & Mycol Study Sect, NIH, 90-94; mem, nat coun, Infectious Dis Soc Am, 93- *Mem:* Fel Am Col Physicians; fel Am Acad Microbiol; fel Am Col Epidemiol; Am Epidemiol Soc; Campylobacter Soc (secy, 79-83); Am Soc Clin Invest. *Res:* Normal bacterial flora of the gastrointestinal tract; exogenous enteric pathogens in the epidemiology, pathogenesis, and molecular biology of gastrointestinal and extraintestinal disease. *Mailing Add:* Div Infectious Dis Vanderbilt Univ Rm A3310 Med Ctr N Nashville TN 37232-2605. *Fax:* 615-343-6160

BLASER, ROBERT U, RESEARCH ADMINISTRATION, RESOURCE MANAGEMENT. *Current Pos:* RETIRED. *Personal Data:* b Akron, Ohio, Sept 1, 16; m 40; c 1. *Educ:* Univ Akron, BS, 37. *Honors & Awards:* Charles B Dudley Medal, 57. *Prof Exp:* Res engr, Babcock & Wilcox Co, 37-47, chief eng, Physics Sect, 47-51, chief, Nuclear Eng Sect, 49-51, asst supt, Mat Dept, Res Ctr, 51-61, staff asst, 61-64, chief plans, Res & Develop Div, 64-72, tech mgr acct, 72-81. *Concurrent Pos:* Consult, 81-; Serv Corps Ret Execs, 82- *Mem:* Am Phys Soc; Am Soc Mech Engrs; Am Nuclear Soc; Score. *Res:* Steam generating equipment; nuclear power; materials research; environmental testing; nuclear materials for fuel elements and structural parts; forecasting and planning of research, development, and allocation of resources. *Mailing Add:* 2543 S Union Ave No 5 Alliance OH 44601-5058

BLASIE, J KENT, BIOPHYSICS, PHYSICS. *Current Pos:* From asst prof to assoc prof, 72-78, PROF BIOPHYS & CHEM, UNIV PA, 78- *Personal Data:* b Flint, Mich, Apr 30, 43; m 65. *Educ:* Univ Mich, BS, 64, PhD(biophys), 68. *Concurrent Pos:* NIH fel, 64-68, career develop award, 71-76; assoc biophysicist, Brookhaven Nat Lab, 73-78, biophysicist, 78- *Mem:* Biophys Soc. *Res:* Structural and dynamical study of isolated and reconstituted biological membrane systems via static and time-resolved x-ray and neutron diffraction utilizing synchrotron and laser plasma sources, spectroscopy, optical and infrared linear dichroism. *Mailing Add:* Dept Chem Univ Pa Philadelphia PA 19104-6323

BLASING, TERENCE JACK, CLIMATOLOGY, STATISTICAL & AIR POLLUTION METEOROLOGY. *Current Pos:* res assoc, 77-84, RES STAFF MEM, ENERGY DIV, OAK RIDGE NAT LAB, 84- *Personal Data:* b Waukesha, Wis, Dec 16, 43; m 67, Carolyn Birch; c Jill M (Woods) & Keith M. *Educ:* Univ Wis-Madison, BS, 66, MS, 68, PhD(meteorol), 75. *Prof Exp:* Res assoc dendrochronology, Lab Tree-Ring Res, Univ Ariz, 71-77. *Concurrent Pos:* Adj assoc prof geog, Univ Tenn, Knoxville. *Mem:* Am Meteorol Soc; Am Geophys Union; Sigma Xi; Air & Waste Mgt Asn. *Res:* Statistical meteorology; paleoclimatology; air quality. *Mailing Add:* Bldg 4500N Oak Ridge Nat Lab MS 6200 Oak Ridge TN 37831. *Fax:* 423-574-5788; *E-Mail:* bla@ornl.gov

BLASINGAME, BENJAMIN P(AUL), ASTRONAUTICS. *Current Pos:* RETIRED. *Personal Data:* b State College, Pa, Aug 1, 18; m 42, 92, Margaret A Timmons; c Nancy J, James P, Margaret A & John R. *Educ:* Pa State Univ, BS, 40; Mass Inst Technol, ScD, 50. *Prof Exp:* Officer, USAF, 41-59, dir, Titan Intercontinental Ballistic Missile Develop, 56-58; prof astronaut & head dept, US Air Force Acad, 58-59; dir eng & res, AC Spark Plug-electronics Div, Gen Motors Corp, 59-62, mgr, Milwaukee Opers, 62-65, gen mgr, AC Electronics Div, 65-70, mgr, Delco Electronics Div, Milwaukee Opers, 70-72, mgr, Delco Electronics Div, Santa Barbara Opers, 72-79. *Concurrent Pos:* Dir, Santa Barbara Cottage Hosp, 77-88; Santa Barbara Bank & Trust, 84-94; trustee, Santa Barbara Found, 86-92, pres, 90-92; dir, Leinhurd Ctr Enhancement Eng Educ, 93- *Mem:* Nat Acad Engrs; Int Acad Astronaut. *Res:* Instrument design and development; accelerometers; gravimeters; gyroscopes. *Mailing Add:* 517 Carriage Hill Ct Santa Barbara CA 93110

BLASINGHAM, MARY CYNTHIA, PHYSIOLOGY. *Current Pos:* CONSULT, PHYSIOL, 79- *Personal Data:* b Indianapolis, Ind, Aug 27, 48. *Educ:* Duke Univ, BA, 70; Ind Univ, MS, 72, PhD(physiol), 76. *Prof Exp:* Asst, Ind Univ Med Ctr, 71-76, res assoc physiol, 76; res assoc pharmacol, Univ Tenn Ctr Health Sci, 76-79. *Mem:* Am Physiol Soc. *Res:* Metabolism of prostaglandin E by the lung during hemorrhagic shock; interrelationship among renal hormone systems, especially prostaglandin, kallikrein-kinin, and renin angiotensin in different states of electrolyte balance. *Mailing Add:* 4150 N Meridian St Indianapolis IN 46208-4015

BLASIUS, DON MALCOLM, AUTOMORPHIC FORMS, ARITHMETIC GEOMETRY. *Current Pos:* PROF MATH, UNIV CALIF, LOS ANGELES, 88- *Personal Data:* b Paterson, NJ, Sept 5, 50. *Educ:* Harvard, AB, 72; Oxford Univ, BA, 77; Princeton Univ, PhD(math), 81. *Prof Exp:* Asst prof, Columbia Univ, 81-85, Yale Univ, 85-87; assoc prof, City Univ New York, 87-89. *Concurrent Pos:* Mem, Inst Adv Study, 81 & 89-90, Max Planck Inst Math, 90, 91 & 92, Isaac Newton Inst, Cambridge Univ, 93; prin investr, NSF, 82-85 & 87; guest prof, Ecole Normale Supeneure, 89, Univ Paris, Orsay, 90. *Mem:* Am Math Soc. *Res:* Arithmetic of automorphic forms, especially shimura varieties. *Mailing Add:* Dept Math Univ Calif Los Angeles CA 90095-1555

BLASS, ELLIOTT MARTIN, PSYCHOPHYSIOLOGY, ANIMAL BEHAVIOR. *Current Pos:* PROF PSYCHOL & NUTRIT, CORNELL UNIV, 90- *Personal Data:* b New York, NY, Sept 10, 40; m 76; c 4. *Educ:* Brooklyn Col, BS, 63; Univ Conn, MS, 64; Univ Va, PhD(psychol), 67. *Prof Exp:* Fel zool, Univ Pa, 67-69; from asst prof to assoc prof psychol, Johns Hopkins Univ, 69-79, prof psychol & psychiat, 79-90. *Concurrent Pos:* Consult ed, J Comp & Physiol Psychol, 74- & Develop Psychol, 78-; John Simon Guggenheim Mem fel; Fulbright Hayes res prof, 83; Nat Acad Sci Exchange fel, 85. *Mem:* AAAS; Neurosci Soc; Psychonomic Soc; Develop Psychobiol Soc. *Res:* Development of ingestive behavior in infants, neurology and physiology of ingestion; maternal-infant relationships. *Mailing Add:* 115 Cayuga Heights Rd Ithaca NY 14850

BLASS, GERHARD ALOIS, theoretical physics; deceased, see previous edition for last biography

BLASS, JOHN P, NEUROPSYCHIATRY, BIOCHEMISTRY. *Current Pos:* BURKE PROF NEUROL & CHIEF DIV CHRONIC & DEGENERATIVE DIS, DEPT NEUROL, CORNELL UNIV MED COL, 78- *Personal Data:* b Vienna, Austria, Feb 21, 37; US citizen; m 60, Birgit Annelise Knudsen; c Charles & Lisa. *Educ:* Harvard Univ, AB, 58; Univ London, PhD(biochem), 60; Columbia Univ, MD, 65. *Prof Exp:* Intern, Mass Gen Hosp, 65-66, asst resident med, 66-67; res assoc, Molecular Dis Br, Nat Heart Inst, 67-70; from asst prof to assoc prof biochem & psychiat, Sch Med, Univ Calif, Los Angeles, 70-76. *Concurrent Pos:* Chair, Nat Panel Alzheimer's Dis, 87-91. *Mem:* Am Soc Biol Chemists; Int Brain Res Orgn; Int Soc Neurochem; Am Fedn Clin Res; Am Soc Clin Invest; Am Fedn Aging Res. *Res:* Metabolic disorders affecting the nervous system, including Alzheimer's Disease. *Mailing Add:* Dept Neurol Cornell Univ Med Col 1300 York Ave New York NY 10021-4805

BLASS, JOSEPH J(OHN), ENGINEERING MECHANICS OF SOLIDS, STRUCTURAL DESIGN METHODS & CRITERIA. *Current Pos:* MEM RES STAFF, OAK RIDGE NAT LAB, 74- *Personal Data:* b Jersey City, NJ, Dec 22, 40; m 62, Carole T Braun; c Pamela B (Bracher). *Educ:* Manhattan Col, BME, 62; Brown Univ, ScM, 64, PhD(mech of solids), 68; Univ Tenn, MBA, 81. *Prof Exp:* Mat res engr, USAF Mat Lab, 67-70, vis instr mech of solids, US Air Force Inst Technol, 68-70; asst prof mech eng sci, Wayne State Univ, 70-74. *Mem:* Am Soc Mech Engrs. *Res:* Time-dependent mechanical behavior of metals and composites; creep; fatigue; fracture; structural design methods and criteria. *Mailing Add:* 236 Gum Hollow Rd Oak Ridge TN 37830. *Fax:* 423-574-0740; *E-Mail:* blassjj@ornl.gov

BLASS, WILLIAM ERROL, MOLECULAR ASTROPHYSICS, IMAGE ENHANCEMENT. *Current Pos:* asst prof physics & astron, Univ Tenn, 67-71, assoc prof, 71-78, vdir opers, Molecular Spectros Lab, 71-78, assoc dir, Univ Comput Ctr, 90-93, DIR, MOLECULAR RES LAB, UNIV TENN, KNOXVILLE, 78-, PROF PHYSICS & ASTRON, 81- *Personal Data:* b Minneapolis, Minn, Aug 5, 37; m 59, 74, 85, Betty L. Haskin; c Stephen, Susan, Julia, Fred, James & Mark. *Educ:* St Mary's Col, Minn, BA, 59; Mich State Univ, PhD(physics), 63. *Prof Exp:* Asst prof physics, St Mary's Col, Minn, 63-67. *Concurrent Pos:* Co-prin investr, AEC Res Contract, 64-67; prin investr, Univ Tenn-NASA Grants, 68-70 & 81; mem sr sci staff, NASA Grant, 69-77; NASA/Am Soc Eng Educ summer fac fel, Goddard Space Flight Ctr, 86, 87, 90 & 91, pvt investr, NASA, 93-97; consult, Corp Res, Honeywell, Inc, 81, transp serv, Tenn Valley Authority, 88, Martin Marietta Energy Systs, Inc, 89-; nuclear res assoc, Dept Energy, Metals & Ceramic Div, Oak Ridge Nat Lab, 89; Univ Space Res Asn consult, Lab Extraterrestrial Physics, Goddard Space Flight Ctr, 92-97; fac assoc supercomput, Univ Comput Ctr, Univ Tenn, 93-96. *Mem:* Am Phys Soc; Optical Soc Am; Planetary Soc; Int Neural Network Soc; Inst Elec & Electronics Engrs Computer Soc; AAAS. *Res:* Theoretical and experimental molecular spectroscopy; planetary astrophysics; neural network computational systems; digital signal processing particularly deconvolution and image enhancement data; non-equilibrium thermal physics; information; computer networks; high performance computing; medical imaging. *Mailing Add:* Dept Physics & Astron Univ Tenn Knoxville TN 37996-1200. *Fax:* 423-974-7843; *E-Mail:* wblass@utk.edu

BLASZKOWSKI, THOMAS P, PHARMACOLOGY. *Current Pos:* PHARMACOLOGIST, NAT HEART, LUNG & BLOOD INST, NIH, 72- *Personal Data:* b Mount Pleasant, Pa, Nov 9, 34. *Educ:* Univ RI, PhD(pharmacol), 69. *Mailing Add:* 14342 Chesterfield Rd Rockville MD 20853-1923

BLATCHFORD, JOHN KERSLAKE, ORGANIC CHEMISTRY. *Current Pos:* RETIRED. *Personal Data:* b Chicago, Ill, Sept 6, 25; m 60; c Natalie. *Educ:* Univ Colo, BA, 49, MA, 56; Univ Cincinnati, PhD(org chem), 63. *Prof Exp:* Res chemist, Chicago Copper & Chem Co, 50-51; chief chemist, Edcan Labs, 57-61; res chemist, Whirlpool Corp, 63-68, staff chemist, Res & Eng Ctr, 68-71, staff scientist, 71-79; pres, Quanta Labs, Inc, 79-85; mgr chem, Phillips Eng Co, 85-92. *Concurrent Pos:* Adj fac chem, Southwestern Mich Col, 83-84. *Mem:* AAAS; Am Chem Soc; Sigma Xi; Int Soc Hybrid Microelectronics. *Res:* Organometallic compounds; polycyclic-aromatic hydrocarbons; organic synthesis; cyclopropanes; carbene chemistry; snake venoms; detergency; thick film hybrid electronics; polymer synthesis; chromatography; absorption refrigeration; corrosion. *Mailing Add:* 411 Wallace Ave St Joseph MI 49085

BLATSTEIN, IRA M, UNDERWATER ACOUSTICS. *Current Pos:* Res physicist underwater explosion effects, 67-81, HEAD, RADIATION DIV, RES & TECHNOL DEPT, WHITE OAK LAB, NAVAL SURFACE WEAPONS CTR, 81- *Personal Data:* b Hackensack, NJ, Apr 18, 44; m 68; c 2. *Educ:* Drexel Univ, BS, 67; Cath Univ Am, MS, 71, PhD(physics), 73. *Mem:* Am Phys Soc; Acoustical Soc Am. *Res:* Long range propagation of underwater explosion energy; normal mode theory; ray theory and modified ray theory; occan basin reverberation. *Mailing Add:* 600 Avon Square Ct Silver Spring MD 20904

BLATT, BEVERLY FAYE, SCIENCE COMMUNICATIONS, SCIENCE POLICY. *Current Pos:* CONSULT, BFB BIOCONSULT, 88- *Personal Data:* b Pittsburgh, Pa, Mar 17, 44; m 87, David H Filipek; c Bryan R Lavietes & Jonathan D Lavietes. *Educ:* Vassar Col, AB, 65; Case Western Res Univ, PhD(biol), 69. *Prof Exp:* Am Cancer Soc fel, NY Univ Med Ctr, 69-70, NIH fel, 70-71, asst prof path, 71-80; asst prof med, State Univ New York, Downstate Med Ctr, 80-84, Stonybrook Sch Med, 84-88; sect head res & clin immunol, Long Island Jewish Med Ctr, 86-88. *Concurrent Pos:* Am Cancer Soc fel, NY Univ, 69-70, Nat Cancer Inst fel, 70-71, res grant, 72-78; prin investr, NIH, ROI grant, 71-77 & Arthritis Found, 81-85, NY Arthritis Found, 81-84 & 86-87; adj asst prof biol, NY Univ, 77-78. *Mem:* AAAS; Am Soc Cell Biol; NY Acad Sci; Asn Women Sci; Harvey Soc. *Res:* Bench experience in developmental biology, cell biology, biochemistry, histology, rheumatology and oncology; presently explain biomedical technology to professionals who have problem in that area, eg, lawyers, financial analysts, legislators, local government officials. *Mailing Add:* BFB Bioconsulting 3265 Central Ave Alameda CA 94501-3108. *Fax:* 510-521-4108; *E-Mail:* beverly_f_blatt@bmug.org

BLATT, CARL ROGER, SOIL SCIENCE, PLANT PHYSIOLOGY. *Current Pos:* RETIRED. *Personal Data:* b Summit, NJ, July 16, 38; m 62; c 4. *Educ:* Del Valley Col Agr & Sci, BSc, 60; Rutgers Univ, MSc, 63, PhD(soils), 64. *Prof Exp:* Res scientist plant nutrit, Can Dept Agr, 64-80; res scientist plant nutrit, Kentville Agr Ctr, 80-96, agron prog leaders, 87-96. *Mem:* Am Soc Hort Sci; Can Soc Hort Sci; Coun Soil Testing & Plant Analysis. *Res:* Nutritional requirements and management studies of berry crops, such as strawberry, raspberry, high and lowbush blueberry, and vegetables, such as tomatoes, cabbage, cauliflower, broccoli, and cereal crops (wheat, etc). *Mailing Add:* 339 Lamont Rd RRI Kentville NS B4N 3V7 Can

BLATT, ELIZABETH KEMPSKE, MEDICAL PHYSIOLOGY, NEUROENDOCRINOLOGY. *Current Pos:* DEP DIR, SCI MUS, VA, 88- *Personal Data:* b Baltimore, Md, Dec 2, 36; m 58; c 3. *Educ:* Goucher Col, BA, 56; Vassar Col, MA, 58; Union Univ, PhD(life sci & syst), 71. *Prof Exp:* Instr physiol, Mt Holyoke Col, 58-59; res asst zool, Kans State Univ, 64-65; from instr to asst prof biol, Concord Col, 67-73; assoc prof physiol & chmn dept, 74-78, prof physiol & assoc dean acad affairs & basic sci, WVa Sch Osteop Med, 78-84; dean, Lake Erie Col, 84-88. *Concurrent Pos:* Fac fel, US Dept Health, Educ & Welfare, 69-70; grant-in-aid, Sigma Xi, 70; consult health planning, Appalachian Regional Comn, 73-74. *Mem:* AAAS; Sigma Xi; assoc mem Am Osteop Asn. *Res:* Influence of pineal on reproductive rhythmicity; electrophysiological correlates of melatonin activity. *Mailing Add:* Sci Mus Va 2500 W Broad St Richmond VA 23220-2057

BLATT, FRANK JOACHIM, PHYSICS. *Current Pos:* RETIRED. *Personal Data:* b Vienna, May 1, 24; nat US; m 46; c 2. *Educ:* Mass Inst Technol, BSEE, 46, MSEE, 48; Univ Wash, PhD(physics), 53. *Honors & Awards:* Fulbright lectr, LaSotho, Africa, 92. *Prof Exp:* Asst elec eng, Mass Inst Technol, 46-48; assoc, Univ Wash, 48-50, asst physics, 50-53; res assoc, Univ Ill, 53-55, res asst prof, 55-56; from asst prof to prof physics, Mich State Univ, 56-87, chmn dept, 69-73; prof physics, Univ Vt, 87-92. *Concurrent Pos:* Consult, Naval Res Lab, 55-59, Eng Res Inst, Univ Mich, 58-59 & Boeing Aircraft Co, 59; NSF fel, Oxford Univ, 59-60; consult, Argonne Nat Lab, 61-64, E I du Pont de Nemours & Co, Inc, 62-, Argonne Nat Lab, 67-75, Simon Fraser Univ, 72-78, Univ de Louvan, 81, Leed Univ, 82 & Univ N Sumatra, 85 & 86; guest prof, Swiss Fed Inst Technol, 63-64; mem prog rev comt, Solid State Sci Div, Argonne Nat Lab, 66-72; vis prof, ITM, Shah Alam, Malaysia, 86-87, West Pt Mil Acad, 91-92. *Mem:* Am Phys Soc; Biophys Soc. *Res:* Physics of solids; transport theory; thermoelectric and thermomagnetic effects. *Mailing Add:* PO Box 304 St James MI 49782

BLATT, HARVEY, PETROLOGY. *Current Pos:* FAC MEM, INST EARTH SCI, HEBREW UNIV, JERUSALEM. *Personal Data:* b New York, Sept 11, 31; m 84, Mary Marolda; c Susan, Barbara & Linda. *Educ:* Ohio State Univ, BS, 52; Univ Tex, MA, 58; Univ Calif, Los Angeles, PhD(geol), 63. *Prof Exp:* From instr to assoc prof geol, Univ Houston, 62-68; from assoc to prof, Univ Okla, 68-93. *Concurrent Pos:* Fulbright sr fel, 74-75. *Mem:* Geol Soc Am; Soc Econ Paleont & Mineral. *Res:* Sedimentary petrology; geochemistry and genesis of sandstones, limestones, dolmites and cherts; provenance studies; petrographic stratigraphy. *Mailing Add:* Inst Earth Sci Hebrew Univ Jerusalem 91904 Israel. *Fax:* 405-325-3140

BLATT, JEREMIAH LION, molecular biology, science education; deceased, see previous edition for last biography

BLATT, JOEL HERMAN, APPLIED OPTICS, INSTRUMENTATION. *Current Pos:* from asst prof to assoc prof, 70-82, PROF PHYSICS, FLA INST TECHNOL, 82- *Personal Data:* b Washington, DC, Mar 30, 38; m 68, Patricia Scherer. *Educ:* Harvard Univ, BA, 59; Univ Ala, Huntsville, MS, 67; Univ Ala, Tuscaloosa, PhD(physics), 70. *Prof Exp:* Physicist, Missile Support Command Calibration Ctr, Redstone Arsenal, US Army, 62-64, res physicist, Missile Command Propulsion Lab, 64-66; sr scientist, Hayes Int Corp, Ala, 66-67; sr res asst physics, Univ Ala, Huntsville, 68-70; chief scientist, USAF Malibar Test Site, 93-94. *Concurrent Pos:* Consult eng instrumentation, electromigration, acousto-optics; assoc ed, J Mfg Eng. *Mem:* Int Soc Optical Eng; Nat Speleol Soc; Optical Soc Am. *Res:* Mass spectrometry of organic radicals; optical spectroscopy and fluorometry; radiometry; general and computer interfaced instrumentation in optical and engineering areas; solid state physics; electromigration; acousto-optics; moire profilometry; machine/robot vision; human vision; automated inspection. *Mailing Add:* Dept Physics & Space Sci Fla Inst Technol Melbourne FL 32901. *Fax:* 407-984-8461; *E-Mail:* blatt@pss.fit.edu

BLATT, JOEL MARTIN, BIOCHEMISTRY. *Current Pos:* MGR PROCESS DEVELOP, BIOCIRCUITS CORP, 93- *Personal Data:* b Brooklyn, NY, Oct 28, 42; m 75; c 1. *Educ:* Brooklyn Col, BS, 63; Univ Wis-Madison, PhD(physiol chem), 68. *Prof Exp:* NIH fel, Purdue Univ, West Lafayette, 68-70, res assoc molecular biol, 70-72; from asst prof to assoc prof biochem, Meharry Med Col, 72-84; from staff scientist to sr staff scientist, Diag Div, Miles Inc, Elkhart, Ind, 84-92. *Concurrent Pos:* NSF res grant, Meharry Med Col, 74-75. *Mem:* AAAS; Am Chem Soc; Am Asn Clin Chem; Am Soc Microbiol; Sigma Xi; NY Acad Sci. *Res:* Interlocking control mechanisms for gene expression and enzyme activity; regulation of branched-chain amino acid biosynthesis in bacteria; dry chemistries for medical diagnostic testing; film coating and surface chemistry. *Mailing Add:* 890 Miranda Green St Palo Alto CA 94306-3716

BLATT, S LESLIE, RADIATIVE CAPTURE REACTIONS, INSTRUMENTATION. *Current Pos:* dean grad studies & res, 87-93, PROF PHYSICS, CLARK UNIV, 87- *Personal Data:* b Philadelphia, Pa, June 10, 35; m 59, Susanne Schwarz; c Daniel, Jeremy & Elliott. *Educ:* Princeton Univ, AB, 57; Stanford Univ, MS, 59, PhD(physics), 65. *Prof Exp:* Res assoc physics, Van de Graaff Accelerator Lab, Ohio State Univ, 64-66, from asst prof to prof physics, 66-87, chmn dept, 80-86. *Concurrent Pos:* Vis researcher, Nuclear Res Ctr, Strasbourg, France, 72-73; chmn, Ind Univ Cyclotron Facil,

Nat User's Group, 76-77; adj prof educ, Clark Univ, 93- *Mem:* Am Asn Univ Prof; Am Phys Soc; Am Asn Physics Teachers; Sigma Xi. *Res:* Studies of charged particle radiative capture reactions and other nuclear reactions; gamma-ray detector systems; design and applications of nuclear instrumentation and computer-based data acquisition systems; physics for non-science majors and for teachers at elementary and middle school levels. *Mailing Add:* Clark Univ Dept Physics 950 Main St Worcester MA 01610. *E-Mail:* lblatt@clarku.edu

BLATTEIS, CLARK MARTIN, NEUROSCIENCE. *Current Pos:* assoc prof, 66-74, PROF PHYSIOL & BIOPHYS, COL MED, UNIV TENN, MEMPHIS, 74- *Personal Data:* b Berlin, Ger, June 25, 32; nat US; m 58, Yolanda Fuentes; c Beatrice, Elisa & Charles. *Educ:* Rutgers Univ, BA, 54; Univ Iowa, MSc, 55, PhD(physiol), 57. *Prof Exp:* Asst physiol, Univ Iowa, 54-57; res physiologist, US Army Med Res Lab, Ft Knox, Ky, 58-61 & US Army Res Inst Environ Med, Natick, Mass, 63-66. *Concurrent Pos:* USPHS res fel, Inst Andean Biol, Lima, Peru, 61-62 & Nuffield Inst Med Res, Univ Oxford, Eng, 62-63; Orgn Am States exchange sci award, 68; vis prof physiol, Sch Med, Univ Guanajuato, 68-78; Fulbright-Hays sr scholar, 75 & 94; vis prof, Philipps-Univ, Marburg, WGer, 79, 81 & Commonwealth Sci & Indust Res Orgn, Sydney, Australia, 83. *Mem:* AAAS; Soc Neurosci; Am Physiol Soc; Soc Exp Biol & Med; corresp mem Peruvian Soc Physiol Sci; Soc Leukocyte Biol. *Res:* Central nervous system; temperature regulation; host-defense mechanisms. *Mailing Add:* Dept Physiol & Biophys Univ Tenn Col Med Memphis TN 38163

BLATTNER, FREDERICK RUSSELL, BIOPHYSICS, SOFTWARE SYSTEMS. *Current Pos:* Res assoc oncol, McArdle Lab, 68-73, asst scientist genetics, 73-74, from asst prof to assoc prof, 74-81, PROF GENETICS, UNIV WIS-MADISON, 81- *Personal Data:* b St Louis, Mo, Oct 6, 40; m 71; c 2. *Educ:* Oberlin Col, BA, 62; Johns Hopkins Univ, PhD(biophys), 68. *Concurrent Pos:* Pres, DNASTAR, Inc; cur, GenBank Adv Comt, NIH, & mem, Protein Identification Adv Comt. *Mem:* Sigma Xi. *Res:* Molecular biology, DNA sequencing, bacteriophage lambda, DNA cloning, recombination, replication, immunology, structure of immunoglobulin genes in mouse and man. *Mailing Add:* 1547 Jefferson Ave Madison WI 53711

BLATTNER, MEERA MCCUAIG, COMPUTER SCIENCES. *Current Pos:* PROF APPL SCI, UNIV CALIF, DAVIS & COMPUT SCIENTIST, LAWRENCE LIVERMORE NAT LAB, 80- *Personal Data:* b Chicago, Ill, Aug 14, 30; m 85, Minao Kamegai; c Douglas O, Robert G & William D. *Educ:* Univ Chicago, BA, 52; Univ Southern Calif, MA, 66; Univ Calif, Los Angeles, PhD(eng), 73. *Honors & Awards:* Serv Award, Asn Comput Mach. *Prof Exp:* Asst prof math, Los Angeles Harbor Col, 66-73; instr comput sci, Univ Mass; res fel, Harvard Univ, 73-74; asst prof math sci, Rice Univ, 74-81. *Concurrent Pos:* Adj prof biomath, M D Anderson Cancer Res Hosp, Univ Tex Med Ctr, 77- *Mem:* Soc Women Engrs; Asn Comput Mach; Inst Elec & Electronics Engrs. *Res:* Multimedia; user interfaces; audio interfaces. *Mailing Add:* Dept Appl Sci Univ Calif Davis PO Box 808 Livermore CA 94551. *Fax:* 510-455-5247; *E-Mail:* blattner@llnl.gov

BLATTNER, ROBERT J(AMES), LIE GROUPS, HARMONIC ANALYSIS. *Current Pos:* From instr to prof, 57-92, chmn dept, 81-84, EMER PROF MATH, UNIV CALIF, LOS ANGELES, 93- *Personal Data:* b Milwaukee, Wis, Aug 6, 31; m 56, 83, M Susan Montgomery; c Douglas, Robert & William. *Educ:* Harvard Col, AB, 53; Univ Chicago, PhD(math), 57. *Concurrent Pos:* NSF fel, Mass Inst Technol, 61-62; mem, Inst Advan Study, 64-65; prof math & head dept, Univ Mass, 73-75; vis scholar, Mass Inst Technol, 81; visitor, Univ Warwick, 81; hon fel, Univ Wis-Madison, 85; mem, Math Sci Res Inst, Berkeley, 85, 93. *Mem:* Am Math Soc; AAAS. *Res:* Representations of lie groups; theory of lie algebras and superalgebras; Hopf algebras. *Mailing Add:* Dept Math Univ Calif Box 951555 Los Angeles CA 90024-1555. *E-Mail:* blattner@math.ucla.edu

BLATTNER, WILLIAM ALBERT, EPIDEMIOLOGY, ONCOLOGY. *Current Pos:* ASSOC DIR, INST HUMAN VIROL & DIR, EPIDEMIOL & PREV, MED BIOTECH CTR, UNIV MD, BALTIMORE, 95- *Personal Data:* b St Louis, Miss, Oct 16, 43; m 74; c 5. *Educ:* Wash Univ St Louis, BA, 66, MO, 70; Am Bd Internal Med, dipl, 74. *Honors & Awards:* Fifth Annual Russel J Blattner Lectr, Tex Children's Hosp, 84. *Prof Exp:* Intern, Strong Mem Hosp, 70-71, asst resident, 71-72; assoc res, NY Cornell Med Ctr, 72-73; staff assoc, Nat Cancer Inst, 73-75; clin invest, Nat Cancer Inst, 75-76, sr clin invest, 76-81, chief, Family Studies Sect, 81-87, chief, Viral Epidemiol Sect, 87-95. *Concurrent Pos:* Mem, Epidemiol Subcomt Pub Health Serv, AIDS Exec Task Force, 85-87, co-chmn, AIDS Epidemiol & Surveillance Subcomt, 85-; mem, Div Cancer Etiol, Sr Promotions Review Comt, 86- *Mem:* Am Soc Clin Oncol; Am Fedn Clin Res; Am Assoc Adv Sci; Am Assoc Cancer Res; Int Soc Comparative Cancer Res. *Res:* Pioneering studies undertaken to define the epidemiology of human retroviruses from a national and international perspective; major focus on role of these viruses in human malignancy, neurologic disease and AIDS. *Mailing Add:* Inst Human Virol Div Epidemiol Med Biotech Ctr Univ Md 725 W Lombard St Rm 449 Baltimore MD 21201-1192

BLATZ, PAUL E, biochemistry, for more information see previous edition

BLAU, HARVEY ISAAC, ALGEBRA. *Current Pos:* from asst prof to assoc prof, 69-86, PROF MATH, NORTHERN ILL UNIV, 86- *Personal Data:* b Los Angeles, Calif, Aug 31, 42; m 68; c 2. *Educ:* Reed Col, BA, 63; Yale Univ, MA, 65, PhD(math), 69. *Prof Exp:* Asst prof math, Southern Conn State Col, 67-69. *Mem:* Am Math Soc; Sigma Xi; Math Asn Am. *Res:* Representations of finite groups. *Mailing Add:* Dept Math Northern Ill Univ De Kalb IL 60115-6772

BLAU, HELEN MARGARET, DEVELOPMENTAL BIOLOGY. *Current Pos:* from asst to assoc prof, 78-91, PROF MOLECULAR PHARM, SCH MED, STANFORD UNIV, 91- *Personal Data:* b London, Eng, May 8, 48; US citizen; m 76; c 2. *Educ:* Univ York, Eng, BA, 69; Harvard Univ, MA, 70, PhD(biol), 75. *Honors & Awards:* Women Cell Biol Recognition Award, 92. *Prof Exp:* Fel biol, Harvard Univ, 69-75; fel biochem, biophys & med genetics, Univ Calif, San Francisco, 75-78. *Concurrent Pos:* Mellon Found fac fel, 79-80; William M Hume fac scholar, 81-84; res career develop award, NIH, 84-89, Molecular Cytol Study Sect, 87-88; mem, Deleg China, Nat Acad Sci, 91; resident scholar, Bellagio Study Ctr, Rockefeller Found Italy, 92. *Mem:* Inst Med-Nat Acad Sci; fel AAAS; Soc Develop Biol (pres elect, 93-94); Am Soc Cell Biol. *Res:* Regulation of gene expression; molecular and cellular control of growth and differentiation; muscular dystrophy; cell and gene therapy; mechanisms of tumor suppression; growth control by untranslated RNA. *Mailing Add:* Dept Molecular Pharmacol Sch Med Stanford Univ Stanford CA 94305-5332

BLAU, HENRY HESS, JR, ATMOSPHERIC PHYSICS. *Current Pos:* PRES, WAYLAND RES INC, 82- *Personal Data:* b Speers, Pa, Feb 16, 30; m 58; c 3. *Educ:* Yale Univ, BS, 51; Ohio State Univ, MSc, 52, PhD(physics), 55. *Prof Exp:* Physicist, Arthur D Little, Inc, 55-66, leader physics sect, Res & Develop Div, 62-66; physicist, Space Sci Lab & group leader geophys, Missile & Space Div, Gen Elec Co, 66-67; physicist, Arthur D Little, Inc, 67-71; vpres & dir, Environ Res & Technol, Inc, 71-80; consult, 80-82. *Mem:* Fel Optical Soc Am; Am Phys Soc; AAAS; Sigma Xi. *Res:* Optical physics; molecular spectroscopy; air quality sensors. *Mailing Add:* Mt Blue Rd Weld ME 04285-9710

BLAU, LAWRENCE MARTIN, MEDICAL PHYSICS. *Current Pos:* DIR, MGT INFO SYSTS, HOSP JOINT DIS ORTHOP INST, 87- *Personal Data:* b New York, NY, Jan 6, 38; m 59; c 2. *Educ:* Princeton Univ, BA, 59; Univ Rochester, MA, 63, PhD(physics), 65. *Prof Exp:* Res assoc physics, Columbia Univ, 65-69; assoc scientist, Hosp Spec Surg & asst prof physics in radiol, Med Col, Cornell Univ, 69-87, dir comput serv, Hosp Spec Surg, 73-87. *Concurrent Pos:* Consult. *Mem:* Soc Nuclear Med; Am Phys Soc; Am Asn Physics Teachers; Orthop Res Soc; Sigma Xi. *Res:* Investigation and application of physics, mathematics and computers in nuclear medicine; application of computer technology in hospitals. *Mailing Add:* 18 Channing Pl East Chester NY 10709-1032

BLAU, MONTE, NUCLEAR MEDICINE. *Current Pos:* VIS PROF, RADIOL DEPT, HARVARD MED SCH, 83- *Personal Data:* b New York, NY, June 17, 26; m 46; c 2. *Educ:* Polytech Inst Brooklyn, BS, 48; Univ Wis, PhD(chem), 52. *Honors & Awards:* Hevesy Nuclear Pioneer Award, Soc Nuclear Med, 79 600. *Prof Exp:* Res asst, Geochronomet Lab, Yale Univ, 52-53; mem staff, Radioisotope Lab, Montefiore Hosp, 53-54; mem staff, dept biochem res, Roswell Park Mem Inst, 54-57, mem staff, dept nuclear med, 57-75; prof nuclear med & biophys, State Univ NY, Buffalo, 70-83, chmn, dept nuclear med, 75-83. *Mem:* Am Soc Nuclear Med (pres, 72-73); Am Chem Soc; Am Asn Physicists Med. *Res:* Radiopharmaceuticals; radioisotope instrumentation; nuclear magnetic resonance imaging; CT contrast agents. *Mailing Add:* Box 605 South Wellfleet MA 02663

BLAUER, AARON CLYDE, PLANT TAXONOMY, RANGE ANALYSIS. *Current Pos:* From instr to assoc prof, 66-86, PROF BOT & MICROBIOL, SNOW COL, 86- *Personal Data:* b Burley, Idaho, Apr 26, 39; m 62, Geaneen Whittle; c Alan C, Robert D, Anthony H, Lucile (Walbeck), Elizabeth, Amy G & Katie A. *Educ:* Brigham Young Univ, BS, 64, MS, 65. *Concurrent Pos:* Range res technician, Intermountain Forest & Range Exp Sta, USDA, 67-73, botanist, 74-91; pres, Snow Col Fac Asn, 70-72; mem bd dirs, Dept Higher Educ, Utah Educ Asn, 72; deleg, Int Bot Sci, SAfrica, 84. *Mem:* Bot Soc Am; Am Hort Soc; Am Inst Biol Sci. *Res:* Taxonomic and genetic research on Western range browse shrubs, primarily of the Chenopodiaceae, Rosaceae and Asteraceae. *Mailing Add:* 295 N 300 E Ephraim UT 84627

BLAUFOX, MORTON D, INTERNAL MEDICINE, NUCLEAR MEDICINE. *Current Pos:* instr med & dir sect nuclear med, 66-68, from asst prof to assoc prof radiol, 66-76, from asst prof to assoc prof med, 68-78, PROF RADIOL & NUCLEAR MED, ALBERT EINSTEIN COL MED, 76-, PROF MED, 78-, CHMN, DEPT NUCLEAR MED, 82- *Personal Data:* b New York, NY, July 19, 34; m 59; c 3. *Educ:* State Univ NY, MD, 59; Univ Minn, PhD(med), 64. *Honors & Awards:* Edgar Cigelman Award, 52; Edward Noble Found Award, 63; Albert Lasker Award, NIH, 80. *Prof Exp:* Asst, Peter Bent Brigham Hosp, 64-66. *Concurrent Pos:* Am Heart Asn advan res fel, 64-66; scholar, Harvard Col & res fel, Harvard Med Sch, 64-66; attend physician & dir, Div Nuclear Med, Hosp Albert Einstein Col Med, Montefiore Hosp & Med Ctr, Bronx Munic Hosp Ctr & NCent Bronx Hosp; mem, High Blood Pressure Res Coun & Coun Cardiovasc Radiol, Am Heart Asn; prin investr hypertension detection & follow-up prog, New York Ctr, Nat Heart & Lung Inst, 72-80; mem hypertension detection & follow-up prog, Nat Heart, Lung & Blood Inst, 79-, dietary intervention study hypertension, 80- *Mem:* Fel Am Col Physicians; Am Col Nuclear Physicians; fel Coun High Blood Pressure Res; fel NY Acad Med; Am Heart Asn; Am Fedn Clin Res; AMA; Soc Nuclear Med. *Res:* Nephrology and nuclear medicine. *Mailing Add:* Dept Nuclear Med Montefiore Med Park 1695 A Eastchester Rd Bronx NY 10461

BLAUNSTEIN, ROBERT P, ADMINISTRATION, RESEARCH & DEVELOPMENT. *Current Pos:* br chief, US Dept Energy, 73-86, prog mgr, 76-80, mgr, Div Technol Assessment, 80-83, MGR, OFF NUCLEAR SAFETY, US DEPT ENERGY, 83- *Personal Data:* b New York, NY, Nov 9, 39; m 62; c 2. *Educ:* City Col New York, BS, 61; Western Res Univ, MS,

64; Univ Tenn, PhD(physics), 68. *Prof Exp:* Res scientist radiation physics, Oak Ridge Nat Lab, 68; asst prof physics, Univ Tenn, Knoxville, 68-73. *Concurrent Pos:* vpres, AIG Consult, Washington, DC, 86- *Mem:* Am Phys Soc; Sigma Xi. *Res:* Interaction of low energy electrons with polyatomic molecules; electron attachment and scattering processes; interaction of ultra-violet light with polyatomic molecules; excimer formation inter- and intra-molecular energy transfer; environmental assessment and compliance. *Mailing Add:* 2703 Daniel Rd Chevy Chase MD 20815-3150

BLAUSCHILD, ROBERT ALAN, ELECTRICAL ENGINEERING. *Current Pos:* PRES, LINEAR DESIGN INC. *Personal Data:* b New York, NY, Dec 2, 48; m 79. *Educ:* Columbia Univ, BS, 71; Univ Calif, Berkeley, MS, 73. *Prof Exp:* MGR ANALOG RES INTEGRATED CIRCUITS, SIGNETICS CORP, 73- *Concurrent Pos:* Mem prog comt, Int Solid State Circuits Conf, 79- *Mem:* Inst Elec & Electronics Engrs. *Res:* New areas of analog integrated circuits including high speed data acquisition and conversion and linear metal-oxide-semiconductor circuits. *Mailing Add:* 22351 Hartman Dr Los Altos CA 94024

BLAUSTEIN, ANDREW RICHARD, POPULATION BIOLOGY, BEHAVIORAL ECOLOGY. *Current Pos:* asst prof, 78-, PROF ZOOL, ORE STATE UNIV. *Personal Data:* b New York, NY, July 17, 49; m 71. *Educ:* Southampton Col, BA, 71; Univ Nev, Reno, MS, 73; Univ Calif, Santa Barbara, PhD(biol sci), 78. *Prof Exp:* Teaching asst & assoc biol, Univ Calif, Santa Barbara, 73-78. *Mem:* AAAS; Ecol Soc Am; Animal Behav Soc; Am Soc Naturalists; Am Soc Mammalogists. *Res:* Population, community, behavioral and evolutionary ecology. *Mailing Add:* Dept Zool Ore State Univ Corvallis OR 97331-1801

BLAUSTEIN, BERNARD DANIEL, PHYSICAL CHEMISTRY, COAL SCIENCE. *Current Pos:* prog coordr, 77-79, div dir, 79-85, dep assoc dir, 85-87, SR SCIENTIST, PITTSBURGH ENERGY TECHNOL CTR, US DEPT ENERGY, 87- *Personal Data:* b Philadelphia, Pa, Apr 26, 29; m 54; c 3. *Educ:* Univ Pa, BSChE, 50; Johns Hopkins Univ, MA, 51, PhD(chem), 57. *Prof Exp:* Jr instr chem, John Hopkins Univ, 50-54; instr, Sch Pharm, Univ Md, 55-56; asst technologist, Res Ctr, US Steel Corp, 56-58; from instr to adj assoc prof, Univ Pittsburgh, 57-77; supvry phys chemist, 58-62, res chemist to supvry res chemist, Bur Mines, US Dept Interior, 62-75. *Mem:* Sigma Xi; AAAS; Am Chem Soc. *Res:* Chemistry of coal; coal liquefaction; bioprocessing of coal. *Mailing Add:* 339 Franklin Dr Pittsburgh PA 15241-1902

BLAUSTEIN, ERNEST HERMAN, EDUCATIONAL ADMINISTRATION, MICROBIOLOGY. *Current Pos:* From instr to assoc prof, 46-57, chmn, Dept Sci, 64-69, Col Lib Arts, 69-73, assoc dean, Col Lib Arts, 69-86, coordr, Six Yr Lib Arts Med Ed Prog 73-86, PROF BIOL, BOSTON UNIV, 57-, ASSOC VPRES DEVELOP, 86- *Personal Data:* b Boston, Mass, June 29, 21; m 42; c 2. *Educ:* Boston Col, AB, 41; Mass Inst Technol, MPH, 42; Boston Univ, PhD(microbiol), 52. *Concurrent Pos:* Spec res fel, NIH, 60-61; bk ed, J Col Sci Teaching; dir, Washington Legis Internship Prog, co-dir, Modular Med Curric; dir, Combined Degree Progs Med, Law & Mgt, Boston Univ; vis dean, Hebrew Univ, Hadassah Med Sch, 84; consult, NJ Dept Educ. *Mem:* Fel Am Acad Microbiol; fel Royal Soc Health; Am Conf Acad Deans; Asn Am Med Cols; Asn Adv Health Prof. *Res:* Virology; tissue culture; medical microbiology. *Mailing Add:* 44 Colgate Rd Newton MA 02162

BLAUSTEIN, MORDECAI P, CELL PHYSIOLOGY, NEUROPHYSIOLOGY. *Current Pos:* PROF PHYSIOL & CHMN DEPT, MED SCH, UNIV MD, 79-, PROF MED, 83-, SCI DIR, HYPERTENSION CTR, 85- *Personal Data:* b New York, NY, Oct 19, 35; m 59, Ellen R Baron; c Laura M & Marc B. *Educ:* Cornell Univ, BA, 57; Wash Univ, MD, 62. *Honors & Awards:* Robert J & Claire Pasarow Found Award Cardiovasc Res, 90; Alexander von Humboldt Sr US Scientist Award, 93. *Prof Exp:* Intern internal med, Boston City Hosp, 62-63; med res officer, US Navy, 63-66; NIH spec fel physiol, Cambridge Univ, 66-68; assoc prof physiol & biophys, Med Sch, Wash Univ, 68-75, prof, 75-80. *Concurrent Pos:* NATO sr fel, Univ Bern, Switz, 71; guest scientist, Lab Marine Biol Assoc, Plymouth, Eng, 73; vis prof, Univ Nat Autonomous Mex, 79, Univ Padua, Italy, 87, Univ La Plata, Argentina, 90; Humanitarian Cardiol Award, Heart to Heart & Int Soc on Hypertension, Blacks Inc, 93. *Mem:* Am Physiol Soc; Biophys Soc; Soc Gen Physiologists; Soc Neurosci. *Res:* Regulation of cell calcium in nerve and muscle; physiology of presynaptic nerve terminals; role of salt in the etiology of essential hypertension. *Mailing Add:* Dept Physiol Univ Md Sch Med 655 Baltimore St Baltimore MD 21201-1559. *Fax:* 410-706-8341

BLAW, MICHAEL ERVIN, PEDIATRIC NEUROLOGY. *Current Pos:* PEDIAT NEUROL, DALLAS, PEDIAT NEUROL ASSOCS, 92- *Personal Data:* b Gary, Ind, Nov 14, 27; m 50; c 4. *Educ:* Univ Chicago, PhB, 49, MD, 54; Am Bd Psychiat & Neurol, dipl. *Prof Exp:* Resident pediat, Univ Chicago, 54-56, instr pediat, 59-60; resident neurol, Univ Mich, 56-59; from asst prof to assoc prof pediat neurol, Univ Minn, Minneapolis, 60-68; prof pediat & neurol, Univ Tex Southwestern Med Sch Dallas, 68-, vchmn, Dept Neurol, 80-92. *Concurrent Pos:* Nat Inst Neurol Dis & Blindness spec trainee grant, 58 & pediat neurol training grant, 65; NIH grant, 64; consult, Scottish Rite Hosp, Dallas; mem bd trustees, United Cerebral Palsy Asn Dallas Co. *Mem:* AAAS; Int Child Neurol Asn (vpres); Child Neurol Soc; fel Am Acad Neurol. *Res:* Clinical studies related to neurological disease in childhood. *Mailing Add:* 309 Fall Creek Dr Richardson TX 75080

BLAY, GEORGE ALBERT, ANALYTICAL ELECTROCHEMISTRY. *Current Pos:* res chemist, Hoechst-Celanese, 60-63, sr res chemist, 63-68, res assoc, 68-92, SR RES ASSOC, HOECHST-CELANESE, 93- *Personal Data:* b Buenos Aires, Arg, Mar 25, 32; US citizen; m 65, Mirta Leczynski; c 2. *Educ:* Eng Technol Inst, Arg, BS, 56; Univ Buenos Aires, MS, 58, PhD(anal chem), 60. *Prof Exp:* Analyst, City Water Works Lab, Arg, 54-55; res chemist, AEC, Arg, 55-60. *Concurrent Pos:* Asst inorg & radio chem, Univ Buenos Aires, 57-60. *Mem:* Am Chem Soc; Arg Chem Asn. *Res:* Analytical chemistry; uranium processing; supervision of analytical group; electroanalysis; polarography; analytical instrumentation; computer control of bioreactors; catalytic oxidation; nylon chemistry; polyesters, terephthalic acid, wacker acetaldehyde; monstanto acetic acid, acrylic acid, ethyl acrylate chemistry; ethylene glycol/ethylene oxide; methanol carlsonylation; granted 24 patents. *Mailing Add:* Hoechst-Celanese PO Box 9077 Corpus Christi TX 78469

BLAYDEN, LEE CHANDLER, METALLURGICAL ENGINEERING, ENVIRONMENTAL ENGINEERING. *Current Pos:* Engr powder metall, Aluminum Co Am, 65-68, engr cast metals, 68-71, sr engr metal fluxing, 71-73, sr engr recycling, 73-76, staff engr metal forming, 76-78, supvr, 78-80, MGR, ENVIRON TECHNOL CTR, ALUMINUM CO AM, 80- *Personal Data:* b Opportunity, Wash, Aug 30, 41; m 67, Antoinette Perrotto; c Keith, James & Beth. *Educ:* Mich State Univ, BS, 64; Univ Wis, MS, 65. *Honors & Awards:* Arthur Vining Davis Award. *Concurrent Pos:* Consult, Off Technol Assessment, 75. *Mem:* Am Chem Soc; Sigma Xi; Am Soc Testing & Mat. *Res:* Metal forming; municipal refuse processing; scrap recycling and remelting; non-polluting molten metal purification; continuous ingot casting; environmental control systems; environmental monitoring; environmental remediation technology. *Mailing Add:* 805 Montclair Dr New Kensington PA 15068

BLAYDES, DAVID FAIRCHILD, PLANT PHYSIOLOGY, TISSUE & CELL CULTURE. *Current Pos:* from asst prof to assoc prof, 65-70, PROF BIOL, WVA UNIV, 80- *Personal Data:* b Columbus, Ohio, Aug 17, 34; m 61, Sophia Boyatzies; c Stephanie A & Jeffrey G. *Educ:* Ohio State Univ, BS, 56; Univ Wis, MS, 57; Ind Univ, PhD(bot), 62. *Prof Exp:* Res assoc, Mich State Univ, 62-65, NIH fel, 64-65. *Concurrent Pos:* Nat Inst Health Panel, 87. *Mem:* Tissue Cult Asn; Am Soc Plant Physiologists; NY Acad Sci; Sigma Xi. *Res:* Physiology and metabolism of plant effectors; tissue and cell culture; culture media; in vitro techniques and manipulations. *Mailing Add:* 652 Bellaire Dr Morgantown WV 26506-2421

BLAYLOCK, LYNN GAIL, ANIMAL NUTRITION. *Current Pos:* RETIRED. *Personal Data:* b Fromberg, Mont, Jan 23, 22; m 50; c 3. *Educ:* Colo Agr & Mech Col, BS, 48; Agr & Mech Col Tex, MS, 50, PhD(biochem & nutrit), 53. *Prof Exp:* Asst nutrit, Agr & Mech Col Tex, 48-52; asst prof poultry nutrit, Wash State Col, 52-54 & Colo Agr & Mech Col, 54-55; dir animal nutrit & res, Supersweet Feed Div, Int Milling Co, 55-67, mgr nutrit res & animal technol, 67-69, assoc dir res, 69-71, dir animal nutrit res, Supersweet Res Farm, Courtland, Minn, 71-75, vpres tech opers, Agr Prod Div, Int Multifoods Corp, 75-86. *Concurrent Pos:* Peace Corps volunteer, 83-86. *Mem:* Am Inst Nutrit; Poultry Sci Asn; Am Soc Animal Sci; Am Dairy Sci Asn. *Res:* Nutritional requirements of poultry, swine and cattle; interrelationships of environmental temperature and humidity on the physiological response of animals on various diets; food product development from animal products; pharmaceutical product development. *Mailing Add:* 276 Solomon Dr Estes Park CO 80517

BLAYLOCK, W KENNETH, DERMATOLOGY. *Current Pos:* CHIEF DERMAT, VET ADMIN. *Personal Data:* b Bristol, Va, Sept 6, 31; c 3. *Educ:* King Col, BS, 53; Med Col Va, MS, 58. *Prof Exp:* Intern, Duke Hosp, Durham, NC, 58-59, resident dermat, 59-61 & internal med, 61-62; from asst prof to assoc prof med, Med Col Va, 64-67, prof dermat, 67-, asst dean grad med educ, 72-80, chmn dept, 77-, assoc dean grad med educ, 80- *Concurrent Pos:* Dermat rep, Fed Drug Admin, 74-; chmn, Workshop Comt Eczema, NIH, 74-; mem, Resident Eval Comt, Am Asn Prof Dermat, 74- *Mem:* Am Acad Allergy; Am Acad Dermat; Am Dermat Asn; Soc Invest Dermat; Am Asn Prof Dermatologists. *Res:* Allergy and immunology. *Mailing Add:* Vet Admin 1201 Rock Blvd Richmond VA 23249

BLAZAR, BEVERLY A, IMMUNOLOGY. *Current Pos:* ASSOC PROF BIOL, WELLESLEY COL. *Personal Data:* b Providence, RI, Jan 1, 34; m 56; c Judith, Philip & Faye. *Educ:* Brown Univ, PhD. *Prof Exp:* Asst prof, Harvard Med Sch. *Mem:* Am Asn Immunologist; Am Asn Clin Immunol; Am Soc Microbiol; AAAS; Am Asn Univ Profs. *Res:* Epstein-Barr virus infection and B lymphocyte growth. *Mailing Add:* Wellesley Col Wellesley MA 02181. *E-Mail:* bblazar@lucy.wellesley.edu

BLAZER, DAN GERMAN, GERIATRIC PSYCHIATRY, PSYCHOSOCIAL EPIDEMIOLOGY. *Current Pos:* from asst prof to assoc prof, Duke Univ Med Ctr, 76-84, dir affective dis prog, 85-90, interim chair psychiat, 90-92, PROF PSYCHIAT, DUKE UNIV MED CTR, 84-, J P GIBBONS PSYCHIAT, 90-, DEAN MED EDUC, 92- *Personal Data:* b Nashville, Tenn, Feb 23, 44; m 66, Sherrill Walls; c Trey & Tasha. *Educ:* Vanderbilt Univ, BA, 65, Univ Tenn, MD, 69; Univ NC-Chapel Hill, MPH, 79, PhD(epidemiol), 80. *Honors & Awards:* Jack Weinburg Award, Am Psychiat Asn, 92; Sr Scientist Award, Am Asn Genetic Psychiat, 94. *Prof Exp:* Intern, Univ Tenn, 69-70; dir, Christian Mobile Clin, W Cameroun, Africa, 71-72; resident psychiat, Med Ctr, Duke Univ, 73-75; fel consult & liaison psychiat, Montefiore Hosp & Med Ctr, 75-76. *Concurrent Pos:* Assoc dir, Ctr Study Aging, Med Ctr, Duke Univ, 76-80, head, Div Soc & Community Psychiat, 80-85, hon teacher, 82-83, interim chmn, Dept

Psychiat, 90-; prin investr, Epidemiol Catchment Area Proj, Duke Univ, 80-84, Estab Pop Epidemiol Studies Elderly, 80-84, Clin Res Ctr Study Depression in Elderly, 84-; mem, Coun Int Affairs, Am Psychiat Asn, 82-86, MacArthur Found Proj Successful Aging, 85-; assoc ed, J Am Geriat Soc, 84-86, J Gerontol & Med Sci, 88-; mem, Epidemiol & Dis Control Study Sect, 86-88, chmn, 88- *Mem:* Inst Med-Nat Acad Sci; Am Psychiat Asn; fel Psychiat Res Soc; Am Col Psychiat; Soc Epidemiol Res; Am Pub Health Asn; Am Geriat Soc (vpres, 88). *Res:* Psychiatric disorders elderly community populations; depression in late life; cross sectional and longitudinal perspectives; social factors as they relate to the onset and outcome of psychiatric disorders. *Mailing Add:* Dept Psychiat Duke Univ Med Ctr PO Box 3005 Durham NC 27710. *Fax:* 919-681-7640; *E-Mail:* blaze001@mc.duke.edu

BLAZEVIC, DONNA JEAN, medical microbiology, for more information see previous edition

BLAZEY, RICHARD N, ELECTROOPTICS, ELECTROPHOTOGRAPHY. *Current Pos:* res assoc laser scanning, Res Labs, 69-93, Kodak Health Imagin Systs, 89-95, SYSTS CONCEPT CTR, EASTMAN KODAK CO, 95- *Personal Data:* b Rochester, NY, Aug 23, 41; m 64; c 3. *Educ:* Cornell Univ, BEE, 64; Purdue Univ, MSEE, 66. *Prof Exp:* Proj engr laser syst, Sperry Gyroscope Div, Sperry Rand, 66-69. *Mem:* Optical Soc Am; Inst Elec & Electronics Engrs. *Res:* Electrooptic systems, particularly laser systems and laser scanning systems; acoustooptic modulators and deflectors; ultrasonics, especially high frequency systems; color electrophotography; medical image printing. *Mailing Add:* Eastman Kodak Co Bldg 65 Rochester NY 14650-2123. *E-Mail:* blazey@image.com

BLAZICH, FRANK ARTHUR, PLANT PROPAGATION, TISSUE CULTURE. *Current Pos:* from asst prof to assoc prof, 78-86, PROF HORT, NC STATE UNIV, 86- *Personal Data:* b New York, NY, July 7, 45; m 76, Joan April Wooden; c Joan Michele & Frank Arthur Jr. *Educ:* Univ Vt, BS, 71, MS, 73; Pa State Univ, PhD(hort), 77. *Honors & Awards:* Distinguished Achievement Award, Am Soc Hort Sci, 92; Norman Jay Coleman Award, Am Asn Nurserymen, 96. *Prof Exp:* Res scientist, Va Truck & Ornamentals Res Sta, 77-78. *Concurrent Pos:* Assoc ed, Am Soc Hort Sci, 89-93; mem, Scientist Adv Pan, Hort Res Inst, 96- *Mem:* Int Plant Propagators' Soc; Am Soc Hort Sci; Am Hort Soc. *Res:* Propagation, culture and physiology of woody landscape plants; author or co-author of over 300 publications. *Mailing Add:* Dept Hort Sci NC State Univ Raleigh NC 27695-7609. *Fax:* 919-515-2505; *E-Mail:* frank_blazich@ncsu.edu

BLAZKOVEC, ANDREW A, immunobiology; deceased, see previous edition for last biography

BLAZQUEZ Y SERVIN, CARLOS HUMBERTO, PLANT PATHOLOGY. *Current Pos:* AGR ADV TO TECH UTIL OFF, 80-, PRES, PROJ LEADER, SENSOR SYSTS, KENNEDY SPACE CTR, 76-; RES PROF, AGR DEPT, UNIV FLA. *Personal Data:* b Mexico City, Mex, Oct 9, 26; nat US; m 65; c 2. *Educ:* Univ Calif, BS, 55; Univ Fla, MS, 57, PhD(plant path), 59. *Prof Exp:* Jr plant pathologist virus diseases, Bur Plant Path, Calif State Dept Agr, 55; plant pathologist, Firestone Rubber Plantations, Brazil, 59-61; asst plant pathologist, United Fruit Co, Honduras, 62-63; plant pathologist, Dow Chem Co, Mich, 64; plant pathologist citrus res, Univ West Indies, 64-66; asst prof plant path & asst plant pathologist, Agr Res Ctr, Univ Fla, 66-72, assoc prof plant path & assoc plant pathologist, 72- *Concurrent Pos:* Hon consult, Univ West Indies, 67; proj leader aerial appl grant, Univ Fla, 69-70; partic, Plant Protection Cong, Paris, 70; prin investr, Inst Food & Agr Sci, Univ Fla-NASA ERTS-B Prog, 73- *Mem:* Mycol Soc Am; Am Phytopath Soc; Asn Appl Biol; Am Chem Soc; Am Asn Hort Sci. *Res:* Pesticide residue analysis; remote sensing; low volume and ultra low volume aerial application methods for disease control; effect of fungicide degradation on biological activity. *Mailing Add:* 63 Westview Lane Cocoa Beach FL 32931

BLAZYK, JACK, BIOLOGICAL MEMBRANES, ANTIMICROBIAL PEPTIDES. *Current Pos:* from asst prof to assoc prof chem, 75-91, assoc dean basic sci, 90-93, PROF CHEM, OHIO UNIV, 91-, ASSOC DEAN RES, 93- *Personal Data:* b New York, NY, Sept 22, 47; m 72; c 3. *Educ:* Hamilton Col, AB, 69; Brown Univ, PhD(biochem), 75. *Prof Exp:* Vis asst prof chem, Univ SC, 74-75. *Concurrent Pos:* Fel gen med div, NIH, 75. *Mem:* Biophys Soc; Protein Soc; Am Chem Soc. *Res:* Structure and function of biological membranes; interactions with antimicrobial peptides by spectroscopic techniques. *Mailing Add:* Col Osteop Med Ohio Univ 234 Grosvenor Hall Athens OH 45701. *Fax:* 740-593-0148; *E-Mail:* jblazyk1@ohiou.edu

BLEACKLEY, ROBERT CHRISTOPHER, BIOCHEMISTRY. *Current Pos:* res assoc, Dept Biochem, Univ Alta, 75-77, prof asst, 77-81, sessional instr, 78-80, from asst prof to assoc prof, 81-89, assoc prof, Dept Immunol, 86-89, PROF, DEPT BIOCHEM, UNIV ALTA, 89-, PROF, DEPT IMMUNOL, 89- *Personal Data:* b Manchester, Eng, Feb 29, 52; m 75, Lucy M Entwistle. *Educ:* Univ Birmingham, BSc, 72, PhD(chem), 75. *Concurrent Pos:* Sci officer, Panel A, Nat Cancer Inst, 86 & 87, chmn, 88-91; grants, Nat Cancer Inst, 88-93, Med Res Coun, 90-93 & Can Diabetes Asn, 91-93. *Mem:* Can Biochem Soc; AAAS; Can Soc Immunologists; Am Asn Immunologists. *Res:* T-cell activation; human cytotoxic T-cells. *Mailing Add:* Dept Biochem Univ Alta Med Sci Bldg Edmonton AB T6G 2H7 Can

BLEAKNEY, JOHN SHERMAN, MALACOLOGY. *Current Pos:* RETIRED. *Personal Data:* b Corning, NY, Jan 14, 28; m 52; c 2. *Educ:* Acadia Univ, BSc, 49, MSc, 51; McGill Univ, PhD(zool), 56. *Prof Exp:* Cur ichthyol & herpet, Nat Mus Can, 52-58; from assoc prof to prof biol, Acadia Univ, 58-88, univ fel, 88-93. *Concurrent Pos:* Nat Res Coun Can sr res fel, Eng & Denmark, 67-68. *Mem:* Am Malacol Union; Malacol Soc London; Sigma Xi. *Res:* Herpetology and nudibranch molluscs of Eastern Canada; fauna of the Minas Basin, Nova Scotia. *Mailing Add:* PO Box 456 Wolfville NS B0P 1X0 Can

BLEAKNEY, WALKER, physics; deceased, see previous edition for last biography

BLEASDALE, JOHN EDWARD, DIABETES, INSULIN ACTION. *Current Pos:* SR SCIENTIST, UPJOHN CO, 86- *Personal Data:* b Croxdale, Eng, Feb 4, 50; m 79; c 3. *Educ:* Univ Birmingham, Eng, BSc, 71; Univ Nottingham, Eng, PhD(biochem), 74. *Prof Exp:* Fel, Forsvarets Forskningsanstalt Sundbyberg, Sweden, 74-75, Univ Mich, 75-78; instr biochem, Univ Tex Health Sci Ctr, Dallas, 78-79, asst prof obstet & gynecol, 79-85. *Concurrent Pos:* Adj assoc prof biol & chem, Univ Mich, 87- *Mem:* Biochem Soc; Am Soc Biochem & Molecular Biol. *Res:* Signal transduction particularly mechanisms of insulin action and insulin resistance; drugs that overcome insulin resistance; non-insulin dependent diabetes mellitus. *Mailing Add:* Metab Dis Res 7250-209-502 Upjohn Co 301 Henrietta St Kalamazoo MI 49001. *Fax:* 616-384-9763

BLECHER, F(RANKLIN) H(UGH), ELECTRICAL ENGINEERING, COMMUNICATIONS. *Current Pos:* RETIRED. *Personal Data:* b Brooklyn, NY, Feb 24, 29. *Educ:* Polytech Inst Brooklyn, BEE, 49, MEE, 50, DEE, 55. *Honors & Awards:* Thompson Award, Inst Elec & Electronics Engrs, 59. *Prof Exp:* Mem tech staff, Polytech Res & Develop Co, 50-52; mem tech staff, Bell Tel Labs, 52-60, dir, Carrier Transmission Lab, 60-68, Electron Device Lab, 68-74, Mobile Commun Lab, 74-82, exec dir, Integrated Circuit Design Div, 82-87, exec dir, Tech Info Systs Div, 87-89, consult Telecommun, AT&T Bell Labs, 89-90. *Concurrent Pos:* Pres, Polytech Univ Alumi Asn, 90-92; vchmn, Eng Found, 90- *Mem:* Nat Acad Eng; fel Inst Elec & Electronics Engrs (vpres, 77). *Res:* Design of solid state carrier systems for transmission over cables; design of single & multiple loop feedback amplifiers. *Mailing Add:* 6039 Collins Ave Apt 1526 Miami Beach FL 33140

BLECHER, MARVIN, NUCLEAR PHYSICS, ELEMENTARY PARTICLE PHYSICS. *Current Pos:* From asst prof to assoc prof, 68-81, PROF PHYSICS, VA POLYTECH INST & STATE UNIV, 82- *Personal Data:* b New York, NY, Sept 12, 40; m 62, Freda Fiedler; c Jennifer, Michael & Lee. *Educ:* Columbia Univ, BA, 62; Univ Ill, Urbana-Champaign, PhD(physics), 68. *Mem:* Am Phys Soc. *Mailing Add:* Dept Physics Va Polytech Inst & State Univ Blacksburg VA 24061. *Fax:* 540-231-7511; *E-Mail:* blecherm@vtinte.phys.vt.edu

BLECHER, MELVIN, BIOCHEMISTRY, BIOTECHNOLOGY PATENT LAW. *Current Pos:* assoc prof, 61-68, prof biochem, 68-88, EMER PROF BIOCHEM & MOLECULAR BIOL, SCHS MED & DENT & GRAD SCH, GEORGETOWN UNIV, 88- *Personal Data:* b Rahway, NJ, July 19, 22; m 50, 63, 73, Jocelyn M Hicks; c 2. *Educ:* Rutgers Univ, BS, 49; Univ Pa, PhD(biochem), 54; Georgetown Univ, JD, 85. *Prof Exp:* Asst instr biochem, Sch Med, Univ Pa, 49-51; res assoc, Col Physicians & Surgeons, Columbia Univ, 54-56; from instr to asst prof, Albert Einstein Col Med, 56-61; assoc atty, Lyon & Lyon, 88-91, Rothwell, Figg, Ernst & Kurz, 91-93. *Concurrent Pos:* Vis prof, Med Clin, Univ Rome; vis prof biochem, Univ Paris. *Mem:* Fel AAAS; Am Soc Biochem & Molecular Biol; Am Soc Pharmacol & Exp Therapeut; Endocrine Soc. *Res:* Mechanism of action of hormones; regulatory mechanisms; hormone receptors; membrane biochemistry; autoimmune diseases; immunology; molecular and cell biologies. *Mailing Add:* 4329 Van Ness St NW Washington DC 20016-5625

BLECHMAN, HARRY, MICROBIOLOGY. *Current Pos:* RETIRED. *Personal Data:* b Brooklyn, NY, Aug 22, 18; m 43; c 2. *Educ:* City Col New York, BS, 38; NY Univ, DDS, 51; Hunter Col, MA, 59; Am Bd Endodont, dipl, 68. *Prof Exp:* Clin bacteriologist, St John's Long Island Col Hosp & Rockaway Beach Hosp, 38-41; clin bacteriologist, Tilton Gen Hosp, 41-43; sr bacteriologist, Harlem Hosp, 46-47; chmn, Dept Microbiol, NY Univ, 51-54, from asst prof to prof, 51-68, chmn, Dept Microbiol, Prev Med & Byg, 54-68, asst dean, Col Dent, 64-68, dean, 68-75, prof endont & chmn dept, 75-80, Samuel & Hannah Holman prof & chmn, Dept Endodont, Col Dent, 80-89. *Concurrent Pos:* Exec secy, Guggenheim Inst Dent Res, 54-64; mem & chmn, Nat Bd Dent Examr; pres, Am Bd Endodont, 75; consult, Vet Admin Hosps, USPHS & NY State Narcotic Addiction Comn. *Mem:* Am Dent Asn; fel Am Col Dent; Am Soc Microbiol; Am Asn Endodontists (pres, 78); Int Asn Dent Res. *Res:* Oral microbiology; antibiosis and interactions among oral microorganisms in dental caries and periodontal disease. *Mailing Add:* 1 Washington Sq Village Apt 12-V New York NY 10012

BLECHNER, JACK NORMAN, OBSTETRICS & GYNECOLOGY, FETAL PHYSIOLOGY. *Current Pos:* PROF OBSTET & GYNEC & HEAD DEPT, SCH MED, UNIV CONN, 70-, ASSOC DEAN, CLIN AFFAIRS, 85- *Personal Data:* b New York, NY, Jan 7, 33; m 57; c 3. *Educ:* Columbia Col, BA, 54; Yale Univ, MD, 57; Am Bd Obstet & Gynec, dipl & cert, 80. *Prof Exp:* Intern, Bronx Munic Hosp Ctr, 57-58; Josiah Macy Jr Found fel physiol, Yale Univ, 58-60, 62-63; asst resident obstet & gynec, Columbia Presby Med Ctr, 60-63, chief resident, 63-65; from asst prof to assoc prof, Col Med, Univ Fla, 65-70. *Concurrent Pos:* Am Cancer Soc fel, 64; chief dept obstet & gynec, New Britain Gen Hosp, 70- & Dempsey Teaching Hosp, 75-; physician consult, dept obstet & gynec, Vet Admin Hosp, 70-, St Francis Hosp, 70-, Mt Sinai Hosp, Hartford, Conn, 70-, Hartford Hosp, 72-, Bristol Hosp, 73-, St Mary's Hosp, 78- & Meriden-Wallingford Hosp, 80-; examr, Am Bd Obstet & Gynec; vchmn, Coun Resident Educ in Obstet & Gynec, 78-79; mem coun, Soc Gynec Invest, 67. *Mem:* Am Col Obstetricians & Gynecologists; Am Gynec & Obstet Soc; Asn Univ Prof Gynec & Obstet; Soc Gynec Invest; Sigma Xi. *Res:* Fetal physiology; membrane transfer; experimental intrauterine surgery; respiratory gas exchange. *Mailing Add:* Dept Obstet & Gynec Univ Conn Sch Med Farmington CT 06032

BLECK, RAINER, METEOROLOGY, PHYSICAL OCEANOGRAPHY. *Current Pos:* assoc prof, 75-80, dept chair, 91-95, PROF METEOROL, UNIV MIAMI, 80- *Personal Data:* b Danzig, Ger, Nov 4, 39; m 66, Ilse Schmidt-Nickels; c 2. *Educ:* Free Univ Berlin, MS, 64; Pa State Univ, PhD(meteorol), 68. *Prof Exp:* Res asst meteorol, Inst Theoret Meteorol, Free Univ Berlin, 65; scientist, Nat Ctr Atmospheric Res, 67-75. *Mem:* Am Meteorol Soc; Am Geophys Union. *Res:* Weather analysis and prediction; ocean circulation modeling; climate dynamics. *Mailing Add:* Rosenstiel Sch Marine & Atmospheric Sci Univ Miami Miami FL 33149. *Fax:* 305-361-4696; *E-Mail:* bleck@rsmas.miami.edu

BLECKER, HARRY HERMAN, ORGANIC CHEMISTRY. *Current Pos:* from asst prof to prof, 57-89, chmn dept, 65-88, EMER PROF CHEM, UNIV MICH, FLINT, 89- *Personal Data:* b Philadelphia, Pa, Apr 10, 27; m 51, Charlotte Wetklo; c Harry Stephan, Barbara Ruth, Marian Louise & Karen Elisabeth. *Educ:* Bucknell Univ, BS, 51; Rutgers Univ, MS, 54, PhD(chem), 55. *Prof Exp:* Res assoc chem, Univ Mich, 54-56; asst prof, Bucknell Univ, 56-57. *Mem:* Am Chem Soc. *Res:* Bioanalytical chemistry. *Mailing Add:* 533 S Shore Dr Frankfort MI 49635

BLECKMANN, CHARLES ALLEN, ENVIRONMENTAL MICROBIOLOGY. *Current Pos:* ASST PROF, AIR FORCE INST TECHNOL, WRIGHT-PATTERSON AFB, 93- *Personal Data:* b Evansville, Ind, Nov 24, 44; m 68, Cecilia Andrews; c Mark. *Educ:* Univ Evansville, BA, 67; Incarnate Word Col, MS, 71; Univ Ariz, PhD(bot), 77. *Prof Exp:* Res assoc bot, Sch Renewable Natural Resources, Univ Ariz, 77-78; res scientist biol, Conoco Inc, 78-93, res group leader, 85-93. *Mem:* Sigma Xi; AAAS; Am Inst Biol Sci; Air & Waste Mgt Asn; Am Soc Microbiol. *Res:* Biological waste and wastewater treatment; bioremediation of soils and groundwater. *Mailing Add:* Air Force Inst Technol-ENV 2950 PST Wright-Patterson AFB OH 45433-7765. *Fax:* 937-656-4699; *E-Mail:* cbleckma@afit.af.mil

BLEDSOE, CAROLINE SHAFER, MYCORRHIZAL ECOLOGY, ROOT PHYSIOLOGY. *Current Pos:* ASSOC PROF SOIL ECOL, UNIV CALIF, DAVIS, 91- *Personal Data:* b Knoxville, Tenn, Aug 18, 41; m, Lewis J; c Mac. *Educ:* Vassar Col, AB, 63; Univ Tenn, MS, 64; Colo State Univ, PhD(plant physiol), 70. *Prof Exp:* From asst prof to prof forest ecol, Univ Wash, 75-88; sr staff assoc, NSF, 88-91. *Mem:* Ecol Soc Am; Int Asn Ecol; Soil Ecol Soc (pres, 91-93); Int Root Researcher Network. *Res:* Interactions of mycorrhizal fungi and plant roots in a variety of ecosystems from northwest conifer forests to arctic tundra to California oak savannas; studies of nitrogen and phosphorus uptake by mycorrhizal and nonmycorrhizal plant roots. *Mailing Add:* Dept Land Air & Water Res Hoagland Hall Univ Calif Davis CA 95616-8627. *Fax:* 530-752-1552; *E-Mail:* cbledsoe.lternet.edu

BLEDSOE, HORACE WILLIE LEE, PHYSICS, MATHEMATICS. *Current Pos:* asst prof, 73-78, ASSOC PROF PHYSICS, UNIV TEX, 78- *Personal Data:* b Blue Ridge, Tex, Feb 8, 44; m 71; c 2. *Educ:* Univ Tex, Austin, BS, 66, PhD(physics), 71. *Prof Exp:* Instr physics, State Univ NY, Stony Brook, 71-73. *Mem:* Am Phys Soc. *Res:* Low energy nuclear reaction theory; the origin of quantum mechanics and the connection between mass and energy. *Mailing Add:* 11301 Santa Cruz Dr Austin TX 78759

BLEDSOE, JAMES O, JR, ORGANIC CHEMISTRY. *Current Pos:* head develop lab, 78-88, SR SCIENTIST, UNION CAMP CORP, JACKSONVILLE, FL, 88- *Personal Data:* b New Bern, NC, Mar 22, 38; m 62, 86, Sarah Liddle; c Ellen & James. *Educ:* Univ NC, Chapel Hill, BS, 60; Univ Okla, PhD(org chem), 65. *Prof Exp:* Proj leader org synthesis, Int Flavors & Fragrances, Inc, 65-66; res chemist, 66-71, mgr new prod res, Org Chem Group, Glidden Durkee Div, SCM Corp, 71-78. *Mem:* Am Chem Soc. *Res:* Research and development of terpene products especially for uses in perfumery and flavors. *Mailing Add:* Bush-Boake Allen 2051 N Lane Ave Jacksonville FL 32254

BLEDSOE, LEWIS JACKSON (SAM), RESOURCE ECOLOGY, APPLIED MATHEMATICS. *Current Pos:* CONSULT SCIENTIST, COMPUT SCI CORP, 90- *Personal Data:* b Los Angeles, Calif, Dec 13, 42; m 62; c 1. *Educ:* Univ Tenn, AB, 64; Colo State Univ, MS, 68, PhD(systs ecol), 76. *Prof Exp:* Math consult, Oak Ridge Nat Lab, 61-66; instr systs ecol, Colo State Univ, 67-71; res assoc prof fisheries, Univ Wash, 72-91. *Concurrent Pos:* Prin investr, Norfish Marine Resource Proj, Univ Wash Sea Grant Off & Nat Marine Fisheries Serv, 73-82; landscape ecology, Nat Sci Found, Mt St Helens, 86-90; nitrogen fixation, NSF, High Arctic, 87-89 Salmon Run Trends Proj, US Fish & Wildlife Serv, 78-81. *Mem:* Ecol Soc Am; Am Fisheries Soc; AAAS. *Res:* Systems ecology; application of mathematics, statistics and computer technology to analysis of environmental systems or managed resources. *Mailing Add:* 18080 Country Rd Apt 70 Brooks CA 95606

BLEDSOE, WOODROW WILSON, mathematics; deceased, see previous edition for last biography

BLEECKER, EUGENE R, PULMONARY & CRITICAL CARE MEDICINE. *Current Pos:* CHIEF, PULMONARY SECT, BALTIMORE VET ADMIN MED CTR, 89-, PROF MED, DIV PULMONARY & CRITICAL CARE MED, SCH MED, UNIV MD, 89- *Personal Data:* b New York, NY, Jan 23, 43. *Educ:* NY Univ, BA, 64; State Univ NY, MD, 68; Am Bd Internal Med, dipl, 74, dipl pulmonary dis, 76. *Prof Exp:* Intern, State Univ NY, Kings County Hosp, 68-69, asst med resident, 69-70; clin assoc, Geront Res Ctr, NIH, 70-72; sr asst med resident, Johns Hopkins Hosp, 72-73; fel pulmonary dis, Dept Med, Univ Calif, San Francisco, 73-74 & Dept Med & Cardiovac Res Inst, 74-75, asst res physiologist, 75-76; from asst prof to assoc prof med, Sch Hyg & Pub Health, Johns Hopkins Univ, 76-82. *Concurrent Pos:* Prin investr, Nat Heart, Lung & Blood Inst, 75-76, 78-83 & 84-92, Nat Inst Aging, 83-88; clin dir pulmonary med, Francis Scott Key Med Ctr, 76-89; mem, Grants & Awards Comt, Am Lung Asn, 82-85, Bronchoprovocation Comt, Am Acad Allergy & Immunol, 82-, Comt Disability Determination, Am Thoracic Soc, 85-86, Steering Comt Sect Respiratory Pathophysiol, Am Col Chest Physicians, 85-87, Res Coun, Am Acad Allergy & Immunol, 89- & Expert Panel Diag & Treat Asthma, NIH, 89-; guest scientist, Geront Res Ctr, NIH, 86-; chmn, Comt Bronchoalveolar Lavage, Am Acad Allergy & Immunol, 88- & Panel Investigative Use Bronchoscopy Asthma, Nat Heart, Lung & Blood Inst, NIH, 90-; consult, Childhood Asthma Mgt Prog, Nat Heart Lung & Blood Inst, NIH, 91- *Mem:* Am Thoracic Soc; Am Fedn Clin Res; Am Col Chest Physicians; fel Am Acad Allergy & Immunol; Am Physiol Soc; Am Heart Asn; Geront Soc Am. *Res:* Pathogenesis of asthma and chronic airflow obstruction; airways hyperreactivity and bronchial inflammation; cardiopulmonary and exercise function during aging. *Mailing Add:* Div Pulmonary & Critical Care Med Rm 800 Sch Med Univ Md Ten S Pine St Baltimore MD 21201

BLEECKER, MARGIT, NEUROCHEMISTRY, NEUROENDOCRINOLOGY. *Current Pos:* FEL NEUROL, SCH MED, JOHNS HOPKINS UNIV, 76- *Personal Data:* b Vienna, Austria, Nov 20, 43; US citizen; m 64. *Educ:* NY Univ, BA, 64; State Univ NY Downstate Med, Ctr, PhD(anat), 70. *Prof Exp:* Instr anat, Sch Med, Johns Hopkins Univ, 70-72; instr anat, Sch Med, Temple Univ, 72-76. *Mem:* Am Soc Neurochem; Int Soc Psychoneuroendocrinol; Am Asn Anat; Soc Neurosci; Sigma Xi. *Res:* In vitro studies on Taurine in the rat brain. *Mailing Add:* Ctr Occup & Environ Neurol Children's Hosp 3901 Greenspring Ave Suite 101 Baltimore MD 21211

BLEEKE, JOHN RICHARD, HOMOGENEOUS CATALYSIS. *Current Pos:* asst prof, 81-87, ASSOC PROF, DEPT CHEM, WASH UNIV, ST LOUIS, 87- *Personal Data:* b Port Washington, Wis, Sept 16, 54; m 83, Marian Saeman; c Caroline, Jeremy & Laura. *Educ:* Carthage Col, BA, 76; Cornell Univ, MS, 79, PhD(chem), 81. *Prof Exp:* Assoc, Dept Chem, Univ Calif, Berkeley, 81. *Mem:* Am Chem Soc. *Res:* Synthesis of transition metal organometallic complexes; development of selective homogeneous arene hydrogenation and alkane functionalization catalysts; mechanistic studies of transition metal-catalyzed reactions; chemistry of metallacyclohexadienes and metallabenzenes. *Mailing Add:* Dept Chem Wash Univ Box 1134 1 Brookings Dr St Louis MO 63130-4862. *Fax:* 314-935-4481; *E-Mail:* bleeke@wuchem.wustl.edu

BLEFKO, ROBERT L, TOPOLOGY. *Current Pos:* ASSOC PROF MATH, WESTERN MICH UNIV, 68- *Personal Data:* b July 5, 32; US citizen. *Educ:* Pa State Univ, PhD(math), 65. *Prof Exp:* Asst prof math, Univ RI, 65-68. *Mem:* Am Math Soc; Math Asn Am. *Res:* General topology, specializing in continuous function theory. *Mailing Add:* Dept Math Western Mich Univ 1201 Oliver St Kalamazoo MI 49008-3804

BLEHAR, MARY C, PSYCHOLOGY, GENETICS. *Current Pos:* psychologist, Sci Reports Br, Div Sci & Public Info, NIMH, 78-79, exec secy, Psychol Educ Rev Comt, Off Extramural Proj Rev, 79-81, Psychopath & Clin Biol Res REv Comt, 81-85, chief clin & biol studies, Mood Disorders Prog, 85-92, CHIEF, MOOD ANXIETY & PERSONALITY DIS RES BR, GENETICS & FAMILY STUDIES PROG, NIMH, 92- *Educ:* Ind Univ, Bloominton, BA, 69; Johns Hopkins Univ, PhD(exp pschol), 73. *Prof Exp:* Res asst, Dept Psychol, Johns Hopkins Univ, 69-73, res scientist & res proj mgr, 73-75; res scientist, Dept Psychol, Univ Va, Charlottesville, 75-77. *Concurrent Pos:* Woodrow Wilson fel, 69; consult methodology & data analysis, Head Start Nat Eval Study, ARCA Corp, Washington, DC, 76-78; ed, Am J Psychiat, J Affective Dis, J Biol Rhythms & J Clin Psychiat; consult, Am Psychiat Asn, Am Psychol Asn, Am Psychol Soc & NSF. *Mem:* Am Psychopath Asn; Soc Light Treat & Biol Rhythms; Int Genetic Epidemiol Soc; Int Soc Psychiat Genetics; Nat Alliance Ment Ill Depressive & Manic Depressive Asn; Soc Women Health Res; Sigma Xi. *Mailing Add:* Div Clin & Treat Res NIMH 5600 Fisher's Lane Rm 10C-16 Rockville MD 20857. *Fax:* 301-480-8976; *E-Mail:* m.blehar@nih.gov

BLEI, IRA, BIOPHYSICAL CHEMISTRY. *Current Pos:* from asst prof to assoc prof, 67-74, PROF CHEM, COL STATEN ISLAND, 74- *Personal Data:* b Brooklyn, NY, Jan 19, 31; m 52; c 2. *Educ:* Brooklyn Col, BS, 52, MA, 54; Rutgers Univ, PhD(biophys chem), 57. *Prof Exp:* Instr chem, Rutgers Univ, 53-57; prin res chemist, Lever Bros Co Res Ctr, 57-61; supvr biophys & biodetection sect, Melpar, Inc, 61-66, mgr environ sci lab, 66-67. *Mem:* Am Chem Soc; NY Acad Sci. *Res:* Detection of extra-terrestrial life; optical rotatory dispersion; polarization of fluorescence; physical chemistry of non-aqueous phosphatide solutions; biological differentiation of sodium and potassium; mechanism of action of psychoactive drugs. *Mailing Add:* Col Staten Island 2800 Victory Blvd Bldg 65 Rm 235 Staten Island NY 10314

BLEI, RON CHARLES, ANALYSIS, FUNCTIONAL ANALYSIS. *Current Pos:* From asst prof to assoc prof, 71-81, PROF MATH, UNIV CONN, 81- *Personal Data:* b Prague, Czech, July 15, 45; US citizen; m 69; c 2. *Educ:* Univ Calif, Berkeley, BA, 67, PhD(math), 71. *Concurrent Pos:* Vis NATO prof, Inst Math, Italy, 73; vis assoc prof, Uppsala Univ, 77, Hebrew Univ, 78; vis fel, Inst Mittag Leffler, Sweden, 77; prin investr grants, NSF, 76-77, 77-79, 80-82 & 83-86; vis prof, Univ BC, Vancouver, 83-84; vis scholar, Cambridge Univ, 87. *Mem:* Am Math Soc. *Res:* Combinatorial dimension as a continuous parameter and its impact in analytic and probabilistic frame works. *Mailing Add:* Dept Math Univ Conn Storrs CT 06269-0001

BLEIBERG, MARVIN JAY, FOOD ADDITIVE TOXICITY, MECHANISM OF TOXICITY & RISK ASSESSMENT. *Current Pos:* PHARMACOLOGIST & TOXICOLOGIST, ADDITIVES EVAL BR, DIV TOXICOL, CTR FOOD SAFETY & APPL NUTRIT, US FOOD & DRUG ADMIN, WASHINGTON, DC, 75- *Personal Data:* b Brooklyn, NY, Feb 19, 28; m 60, Beulah Matt; c Lawrence R & Robert J. *Educ:* Col William & Mary, BS, 49; Med Col Va, PhD(pharmacol), 57; Am Bd Toxicol, dipl, 80, 85, 90, 95. *Prof Exp:* USPHS trainee steroid biochem, Worcester Found Exp Biol, 57-58; from instr to asst prof pharmacol, Jefferson Med Col, 58-61; pharmacologist, Food & Drug Admin, 61-62; sr scientist, Res Div, Melpar, Inc, 62-64; pharmacologist, Div Environ Toxicol, Woodard Res Corp, 64-68, dir, Div Pharmacol, 68-70, sect head, Spec Projs Dept, 70-75. *Concurrent Pos:* Chmn, DC Sect, Soc Exp Biol & Med, 84-85; vpres, Nat Capital Area Sect, Soc Toxicol. *Mem:* AAAS; Am Soc Pharmacol; Am Chem Soc; Soc Toxicol; Am Col Toxicol; NY Acad Sci; Asn Govt Toxicologist (pres). *Res:* Toxicology; biochemical and autonomic nervous system pharmacology; HPLC analysis of drugs in serum, blood; pharmacokinetics. *Mailing Add:* 3613 Old Post Rd Fairfax VA 22030. *Fax:* 202-418-3126; *E-Mail:* mjb@fdacf.dhhs.gov

BLEIBTREU, HERMANN KARL, PHYSICAL ANTHROPOLOGY. *Current Pos:* DIR, MUS NORTHERN ARIZ, 75- *Personal Data:* b Darmstadt, Ger, Aug 31, 33; US citizen; m 63; c 2. *Educ:* Harvard Univ, BA, 56, PhD, 64. *Prof Exp:* Tutor dept anthrop, Harvard Univ, 61; res asst biol, Case Western Reserve Univ, 62; asst prof anthrop, Univ Calif, Los Angeles, 64-66; from asst prof to assoc prof, Univ Ariz, 66-71, prof anthrop & dean col lib arts, 71-75. *Concurrent Pos:* NIH grant pop characteristics Pima-Papago, Univ Ariz, 67-68, NSF grants, 68 & 69-; mem bd, Prescott Col, 71- *Mem:* Fel AAAS; Am Asn Phys Anthrop; fel Am Anthrop Asn; Am Eugenics Soc. *Res:* Human microevolution; multivariate methods in anthropometrics. *Mailing Add:* 1931 N Calle Del Suerte Tucson AZ 85745

BLEICHER, MICHAEL NATHANIEL, DISCRETE GEOMETRY, ELEMENTARY NUMBER THEORY. *Current Pos:* from asst prof to assoc prof, 62-69, chmn dept, 73-75, PROF MATH, UNIV WIS-MADISON, 69- *Personal Data:* b Cleveland, Ohio, Oct 2, 35; m 57, 80, E Jeanne Smith; c 6. *Educ:* Calif Inst Technol, BS, 57; Tulane Univ, MS, 59, PhD(math), 61; Univ Warsaw, PhD(math), 61. *Prof Exp:* State Dept fel, Univ Warsaw, Poland, 60-61; NSF fel math, Univ Calif, Berkeley, 61-62. *Concurrent Pos:* Spec asst to dir energy res, US Dept Energy, 79-81; prof math, Inst Tech Mara, Shah Alam, Malaysia, 87-90; adj prof polit sci, INTI Inst Higher Learning, Malaysia, 87-88. *Mem:* Am Math Soc; Math Asn Am; Polish Math Soc; Sigma Xi; Southeast Asia Math Soc. *Res:* Geometry of numbers; convexity; number theory; foundations of mathematics; universal algebra; pedogogical reform in undergraduate mathematics. *Mailing Add:* Dept Math Univ Wis 480 Lincoln Dr Madison WI 53706-1313. *Fax:* 608-231-2141; *E-Mail:* bleicher@math.wisc.edu

BLEICHER, PAUL ALAN, DERMATOLOGY, CLINICAL TRIALS. *Current Pos:* VPRES CLIN AFFAIRS, ALPHA-BETA TECHNOL, 94- *Personal Data:* Brooklyn, NY, Dec 31, 54; m 77, Julia Greenstein; c Isaac & Shira. *Educ:* Rensselaer Polytech Inst, BS, 76; Univ Rochester, MS, MD & PhD(microbiol), 83. *Prof Exp:* Clin fel med, Harvard Med Sch, 83-85, clin fel dermat, 85-87, res fel, 87-88, instr, 88-91, asst prof, 91-92; dir, Med & Clin Serv Div, Parexel Int, 92-94. *Concurrent Pos:* Vis lectr dermat, Harvard Med Sch, 93-96; assoc, Med Ctr, Univ Mass, 94- *Mem:* Drug Info Asn; AAAS; Am Acad Immunol; fel Am Acad Dermat; Soc Investigative Dermat. *Res:* Design and implementation of clinical trials for the evaluation of immuno-modulatory drugs. *Mailing Add:* Alpha-Beta Technol 1 Innovation Dr Worcester MA 01605. *E-Mail:* bleicher@world.std.com

BLEICHER, SHELDON JOSEPH, INTERNAL MEDICINE, METABOLISM. *Current Pos:* from instr to assoc prof, 63-75, PROF MED, STATE UNIV NY DOWNSTATE MED CTR, 76-, CHMN DEPT INTERNAL MED, 77-; CHIEF DIV ENDOCRINOL & METAB & ATTEND PHYSICIAN, JEWISH HOSP & MED CTR BROOKLYN, 69-; PVT PRACT, WOODBURY, NY, 90- *Personal Data:* b New York, NY, Apr 9, 31. *Educ:* NY Univ, BA, 51; Western Ill Univ, MS, 52; State Univ NY Downstate Med Ctr, MD, 56. *Prof Exp:* Res fel med, Thorndike Mem Lab, Boston City Hosp & Harvard Med Sch, 60-63; dir, Metab Res Unit, Jewish Hosp & Med Ctr Brooklyn, 63-69. *Concurrent Pos:* USPHS fel, 61-63; NIH res career develop award; consult-expert med use radioisotopes, Int Atomic Energy Agency. *Mem:* Am Col Physicians; Am Fedn Clin. *Res:* Am Diabetes Asn; AMA; Endocrine Soc. Res: Diabetes; hypoglycemia; carbohydrate metabolism in pregnancy; fat metabolism. *Mailing Add:* 49 Eagle Chase Woodbury NY 11797

BLEICK, WILLARD EVAN, MATHEMATICAL PHYSICS. *Current Pos:* RETIRED. *Personal Data:* b Newark, NJ, Dec 8, 07; m 36; c 3. *Educ:* Stevens Inst Technol, ME, 29; Johns Hopkins Univ, PhD(appl math), 33. *Prof Exp:* Mem, Sch Math Inst Advan Study, 33-34 & 35-36; actuarial student, Prudential Ins Co, 36-38; engr, Gibbs & Cox, Inc, 38-40; instr math, Cooper Union, 39-40; from instr to asst prof, US Naval Acad, 40-46, assoc prof math & mech, 46-50, prof math & mech, Naval Postgrad Sch, 50-74. *Concurrent Pos:* Contractor, US Navy Optimum Track Ship Routing, 74-82. *Mem:* Am Math Soc; Math Asn Am. *Res:* Quantum mechanics; stress analysis; crystal lattice energies; digital computers; missile dynamics; control optimization. *Mailing Add:* Hacienda Carmel Carmel CA 93913

BLEIER, ALAN, COLLOID & SURFACE CHEMISTRY, HAZARDOUS & RADIOACTIVE WASTE DISPOSAL TECHNOLOGY. *Current Pos:* DEVELOP STAFF MEM, OAK RIDGE NAT LAB, 83- *Personal Data:* b Rochester, NY, Mar 12, 48. *Educ:* Clarkson Univ, BS, 70, MA, 73, PhD, 76. *Prof Exp:* Sr chemist, Union Carbide Corp, 74-79; Corning asst prof ceramics, Mass Inst Technol, 80-83. *Concurrent Pos:* Abstractor, Ceramics Abstracts, 85-; chmn comt, Proctor & Gamble fel, 87-88. *Mem:* NY Acad Sci; Sigma Xi; Am Chem Soc; Am Phys Soc; Int Asn Colloid Interface; Am Ceramic Soc. *Res:* Colloid and physical chemistry of waste disposal technology for hazardous and radioactive waste; colloid and physical chemistry of processing composite ceramics. *Mailing Add:* Chem Technol Div Oak Ridge Nat Lab PO Box 2008 Oak Ridge TN 37831-6202

BLEIER, FRANK P(HILIPP), AERODYNAMICS, FANS & BLOWERS. *Current Pos:* CONSULT ENGR, FAN DESIGN & DEVELOP WORK, 46- *Personal Data:* b Vienna, Austria, Jan 26, 13; nat US; m 55, Jadwiga Sudomirska; c Julie. *Educ:* Tech Univ, Vienna, Dipl Ing, 38. *Prof Exp:* Res engr, DeBothezat Fan Co, 40-42; dir res, Ilg Elec Ventilating Co, 42-46. *Mem:* Am Soc Heating, Refrig & Air Conditioning Engrs. *Res:* Increase of capacity and efficiency on various types of fans; design of axial flow fans and centrifugal fans for tank engine cooling; ventilation of invasion boats and pressure blowers; roof ventilators; fans for agricultural crop drying; multi-stage blower to pressurize flotation bags; author of one publication. *Mailing Add:* 536 W Cornelia Ave Chicago IL 60657-2742

BLEIER, WILLIAM JOSEPH, REPRODUCTIVE BIOLOGY. *Current Pos:* FROM ASST PROF TO ASSOC PROF ZOOL, NDAK STATE UNIV, 75- *Personal Data:* b Jourdanton, Tex, July 8, 47; m 73. *Educ:* Univ Tex, Austin, BA, 69; Tex Tech Univ, MS, 71, PhD(zool), 75. *Mem:* Sigma Xi; Am Soc Mammalogists. *Res:* Factors controlling embryonic development in mammals. *Mailing Add:* 3214 Maple St Fargo ND 58102

BLEIFUSS, RODNEY L, GEOLOGY, METALLURGICAL ENGINEERING. *Current Pos:* PROG DIR, METALL MINERALS DIV, NATURAL RESOURCES RES INST. *Personal Data:* b Rochester, Minn, May 13, 28; m 50; c 4. *Educ:* Univ Minn, Minneapolis, BE, 51, MS, 53, PhD(geol), 66. *Prof Exp:* Mineral engr, Appl Res Lab, US Steel Corp, 52-58; res assoc, Mineral Resources Res Ctr, Univ Minn, Minneapolis, 61-66, from asst prof to assoc prof metall eng, 66-77; assoc res consult, 77-80, div chief, Appl Res Lab, US Steel Corp, 80- *Mem:* Geol Soc Am; Am Inst Mining, Metall & Petrol Engrs; Soc Mining Engrs. *Res:* Iron ore beneficiation, agglomeration and direct reduction. *Mailing Add:* 6005 Gama Beach Rd Grand Rapids MN 55744

BLEIL, CARL EDWARD, MATERIAL SCIENCE, RESEARCH ADMINISTRATION. *Current Pos:* PRES, ENERGY MAT RES, 84- *Personal Data:* b Detroit, Mich, Oct 7, 23; m 79, Dolores Debs; c 4. *Educ:* Mich State Univ, BS, 47; Univ Okla, MS, 50, PhD(physics), 53. *Prof Exp:* Asst, Univ Okla, 51-53; dept res scientist, Res Labs, Gen Motors Corp, 53-84. *Concurrent Pos:* Mem solid state sci panel, SSS Comt, Nat Res Coun, 74-84; adj prof, Okla Univ, 87- *Mem:* AAAS; Am Phys Soc; Sigma Xi; Mat Res Soc. *Res:* Compound semiconductors; surface physics; crystal growth; coherent optics; film deposition and modification. *Mailing Add:* 132 Chalmers Dr Rochester Hills MI 48309

BLEIL, DAVID FRANKLIN, SOLID STATE PHYSICS, ELECTRIC & MAGENTICS. *Current Pos:* RETIRED. *Personal Data:* b Detroit, Mich, Dec 4, 08; m, Mildred Campbell; c Sally, David, Richard & Susanne. *Educ:* Univ Mich, BS, 34, MS, 37; Mich State Univ, PhD(physics), 48. *Prof Exp:* Dir res & assoc tech dir, Naval Ord Lab, 43-73. *Concurrent Pos:* Instr physics & math, Mich State Univ, Montgomery Jr Col, Univ Md & Bluefield State Col. *Mem:* Fel Am Phys Soc; Am Inst Physics; Sigma Xi. *Res:* Induced polarization-Geophy prospecting; magnetic properties of materials. *Mailing Add:* PO Box 429 Rupert WV 25984

BLEIL, JEFFREY D, FERTILIZATION, BIOCHEMISTRY. *Current Pos:* ASST PROF BIOCHEM, SCRIPPS CLIN RES INST, 90- *Personal Data:* b Milwaukee, Wis, Dec 17, 52. *Educ:* Lawrenceville Univ, BS, 71, MS, 75; Harvard Univ, PhD(cell biol), 81, MD, 86. *Prof Exp:* Res fel, Roche Inst Molecular Biol, 87-90. *Mem:* Am Soc Develop Biol; Am Soc Biochem; Am Soc Cell Biol; AAAS; Sigma Xi. *Mailing Add:* Dept Molecular Biol Res Inst Scripps Clin 10666 N Torrey Pines Rd La Jolla CA 92037-1027. *Fax:* 619-784-7411

BLEISTEIN, NORMAN, applied mathematics, mathematical analysis, for more information see previous edition

BLEIWEIS, ARNOLD SHELDON, MICROBIOLOGY, DENTISTRY. *Current Pos:* asst prof bact, 67-72, assoc prof microbiol, 72-76, prof microbiol & cell sci, microbiologist, inst food & agr sci, 76-85, PROF & CHMN, ORAL BIOL, UNIV FLA, 86-, GRAD RES PROF, ORAL BIOL, 88- *Personal*

Data: b Brooklyn, NY, Aug 8, 37; m 83. Educ: Brooklyn Col, BS, 58; Pa State Univ, MS, 60, PhD(microbiol), 64. Prof Exp: Lectr biol, Brooklyn Col, 58; asst microbiol, Pa State Univ, 58-63; fel epidemiol, Med Sch, Washington Univ, 64-65; asst biochem, Albert Einstein Med Ctr, 66-67. Concurrent Pos: NIH training grant epidemiol, 64-65, fel, 66-67, res grant sr investr, 69-; consult, Nat Inst Dent Res, 70-; mem, Nat Adv Dent Res Coun, NIH, 78-81; mem, US Army Basic Res Comt, Nat Res Coun, 79-81; mem, Dent Res Progs Adv Comt, NIH, 89- Mem: Am Soc Microbiol; Int Asn Dent Res; Am Asn Dent Res. Res: Structural and antigenic aspects of streptococcal cell walls and membrane; immunologic studies of cariogenic streptococci. Mailing Add: J H Miller Health Ctr Univ Fla Box J424 Gainesville FL 32610

BLEIWEISS, MAX PHILLIP, IMAGE PROCESSING, REMOTE SENSING. *Current Pos:* physicist, Dugway Proving Ground, 85-89, PHYSICIST REM SENSING, US ARMY, RES LAB, 89- *Personal Data:* b Nogales, Ariz, June 23, 44; m 63, Gail A Siebenthal; c David B & Mark D. *Educ:* Calif State Polytech Col, BS, 66; Calif State Col, Los Angeles, MS, 69. *Prof Exp:* Physicist astron, US Navy Naval Weapons Ctr, 66-70, Naval Ocean Syst Ctr, 70-77; vpres bus, Deseret Dent Supply, 77-85. *Mem:* Am Astron Soc; Am Geophys Union; Inst Elec & Electronics Engrs; Inst Elec & Electronics Engrs Comput Sci; Inst Elec & Electronics Engrs Geosci & Remote Sensing Soc. *Res:* Remote sensing of smoke obscurent clouds using multispectral imaging; atmospheric characterization using digital image processing; awarded patent for method of inserting clouds into simulations of real & synthetic scenes. *Mailing Add:* 1215 Villita Loop Las Cruces NM 88005. *E-Mail:* mbleiwei@arl.army.mil

BLEJWAS, THOMAS EDWARD, MECHANICAL ENGINEERING, STRUCTURAL ENGINEERING. *Current Pos:* ASST PROF MECH ENG, OKLA STATE UNIV, 78- *Personal Data:* b Plainfield, NJ, Sept 17, 46; m 69; c 2. *Educ:* Princeton Univ, BS, 68; Univ Southern Calif, MS, 72; Univ Colo, PhD(civil eng), 78. *Prof Exp:* Flight test engr, US Air Force Flight Test Ctr, Edwards AFB, 68-72; sr engr anal mech, Martin Marietta Aerospace, Denver Div, 72-77; res engr civil eng, Univ Calif, Berkeley, 77-78. *Concurrent Pos:* Instr, Univ Colo, 76-77. *Mem:* Sigma Xi. *Res:* Structural dynamics; earthquake engineering; vehicle and structure interaction; mechanism dynamics. *Mailing Add:* 2116 Bluecorn Maiden Ct NE Albuquerque NM 87112

BLEM, CHARLES R, VERTEBRATE ECOLOGY. *Current Pos:* Assoc prof, 69-80, PROF BIOL, VA COMMONWEALTH UNIV, 80- *Personal Data:* b Dunkirk, Ohio, Apr 18, 43; m 65; c Karen & Robert. *Educ:* Ohio Univ, BS, 65; Univ Ill, Urbana, MS, 68, PhD(zool), 69. *Mem:* Fel AAAS; Am Soc Ichthyologists & Herpetologists; Am Soc Mammal; fel Am Ornith Union; Cooper Ornith Soc; Wilson Ornith Soc. *Res:* Energetics and ecology of vertebrates, especially birds. *Mailing Add:* Dept Biol Sci 816 Park Ave Va Commonwealth Univ Richmond VA 23284-2012

BLENDEN, DONALD C, INFECTIOUS DISEASES, EPIDEMIC INVESTIGATION. *Current Pos:* prof, 57-90, EMER PROF EPIDEMIOL & PUB HEALTH, UNIV MO-COLUMBIA, 90- *Personal Data:* b Webster Groves, Mo, Aug 13, 29; m 51, Patricia Crawford; c Michael D & Elizabeth A (Kyd). *Educ:* Univ Mo, BS, 51, MS, 53, DVM, 56. *Prof Exp:* Med technician, Boone Co Hosp, 52-56; clin vet pvt pract, 56-57. *Concurrent Pos:* Emer consult, USAF, 78; consult, WHO, Pan-Am Health Orgn, Food & Agr Orgn int pub health; emer dir, WHO Collab Ctr for Training Ref in Enteric Zoonoses, 87-90. *Mem:* Fel Am Pub Health Asn; Am Vet Med Asn; Am Soc Microbiol; Sigma Xi; Am Col Vet Prev Med; fel Am Col Epidemiol. *Res:* Comparative medicine; epidemiology, pathogenesis and microbiology of zoonoses; leptospirosis; listeriosis; rabies; enteric infections; antigen detection; disaster preparedness. *Mailing Add:* 1506 N Circle Dr Columbia MO 65202

BLENDON, ROBERT JAY, HEALTH ECONOMICS, PUBLIC HEALTH PLANNING. *Current Pos:* chmn, 87-94, PROF, DEPT HEALTH POLICY & MGT, SCH PUB HEALTH & DEP DIR, DIV HEALTH POLICY RES & EDUC, HARVARD UNIV, 87- *Personal Data:* b Philadelphia, Pa, Dec 19, 42; m 77. *Educ:* Marietta Col, Ohio, BA, 64; Univ Chicago, MBA, 66; Johns Hopkins Univ, MPH, 67, ScD(health serv admin & res), 69. *Hon Degrees:* ScD, John Hopkins Univ, 69; MA, Harvard Univ, 88. *Prof Exp:* Asst assoc dean, Health Care Progs, Sch Med, Johns Hopkins Univ, 69-70; asst dir planning & develop, Off Health Care Progs, Johns Hopkins Med Insts & from instr to asst prof, Dept Med Care & Hosp, John Hopkins Sch Hyg & Pub Health, 70-71; spec asst health affairs to dep under secy policy coord & for policy develop to asst secy health & sci affairs, Dept Health, Educ & Welfare, 71-72; vpres, Robert Wood Johnson Found, 72-80, sr vpres & dir prog, 80-87. *Concurrent Pos:* Sr policy analyst, Comt Health Serv Indust, Cost Living Coun, Washington, DC, 71; consult, Fiber Comn Priv Philanthropy & Pub Needs, 77, sr consult, NBC, 78, comt corp soc responsibility, Inst Life Insurance, 75-79; comt US China rel, Coun Foreign Rel, 77-78, adv comt priv philanthropy & pub needs to secy treas, 77-79, steering comt, Int Conf Health Care Year 2000, Inst Med, 80-82, spec blue ribbon comt, corp restructuring NJ Hosp, Statewide Health Coord Coun, 82-84; partic, White House Conf Balanced Nat Growth & Econ Develop, 78; bd overseers, Sch Dent Med, Univ Pa & Leonard Davis Inst, Wharton Sch Bus, Philadelphia, 79-86; vis lectr, Woodrow Wilson Sch Pub & Int Affairs & course coordr, Princeton Univ, 80-87; adv panel long term planning to vpres health serv, Am Hosp Asn, 80-82; chmn, Inter Am Workshop Legislative Approach Prev Alcohol Rel Prob, Inst Med-Nat Acad Sci & Pan Am Health Orgn, 82-84; mem, Health Adv Coun, John Hopkins Univ Sch Hyg & Pub Health, 84-86; bd mem, Am Bd Med Spec & Am Pharmaceut Inst, 88-90; chmn, Comt Access Health Care, Inst Med, 89-; chair, Health Prog Comt, Am Asn Pub Opinion Res, 89-; sr adv, Subcomt Health, Nat Gov Asn, 89-; sr consult, Pub Opinion & Health Care, US Ways & Means Comt, 90- *Mem:* Inst Med-Nat Acad Sci; Coun Foreign Rels; Am Pub Health Asn; Am Hosp Asn; Asn Health Serv Res; Am Asn Pub Opinion Res. *Res:* Author of over 40 publications in medical and public health care. *Mailing Add:* Dept Health Policy & Mgt Sch Pub Health Harvard Univ 677 Huntington Ave Boston MA 02115

BLENKARN, KENNETH ARDLEY, MECHANICAL ENGINEERING. *Current Pos:* CONSULT, 86- *Personal Data:* b Amarillo, Tex, May 17, 29; m 52; c 2. *Educ:* Rice Univ, BA, 51, BS, 52, MS, 54, PhD(mech eng), 60. *Prof Exp:* Instr mech eng, Rice Univ, 52-54; res engr, Amoco Prod Co, 54-57, sr res engr, 60-63, staff res engr, 63-68, res assoc, 68-72, res supvr, 72-76, res dir, 76-86. *Mem:* Nat Acad Eng. *Res:* Applied mechanics treatment of oilwell drilling and production; effects of arctic ice on structures and vessels; ocean waves and vessel response; design of offshore structures; deepwater systems. *Mailing Add:* 9115 E 37th Ct Tulsa OK 74145

BLESS, ROBERT CHARLES, ASTRONOMY. *Current Pos:* res assoc, 58-61, from asst prof to assoc prof, 61-69, chmn dept, 72-76, PROF ASTRON, UNIV WIS-MADISON, 69- *Personal Data:* b Ithaca, NY, Dec 3, 27; m 70. *Educ:* Univ Fla, BS, 47; Cornell Univ, MS, 55; Univ Mich, PhD(astron), 58. *Prof Exp:* Physicist, Naval Res Lab, 47-48; lectr astron, Univ Mich, 58. *Concurrent Pos:* Nat Res Coun sr fel, Goddard Space Flight Ctr, 67-68; prin investr, High Speed Photometer, Hubble Space Telescope, 77- *Mem:* Int Astron Union; Am Astron Soc; fel AAAS. *Res:* Photoelectric spectrophotometry; space astronomy. *Mailing Add:* 101 Ely Pl Madison WI 53705

BLESSER, WILLIAM B, ELECTRICAL & MECHANICAL ENGINEERING, ENGINEERING EDUCATION. *Current Pos:* RETIRED. *Personal Data:* b Warren, Pa, Feb 19, 24; m 52, 79; c 2. *Educ:* Rensselaer Polytech Inst, BME, 50; Polytech Inst Brooklyn, MEE, 58. *Hon Degrees:* ScD, Ind Northern Univ, 74. *Prof Exp:* Plant engr, Beaunit Mills, Inc, 50-52; chief mech engr, Anton Electronic Lab, 52-53; engr, Bulova Res & Develop Lab, 53-54; instr mech eng, Polytech Inst NY, 54-57, from asst prof to assoc prof elec eng, 58-66, prof bioeng & mech eng & dir, Bioeng Prog, 66-90. *Concurrent Pos:* Lectr, navig & guid course, Bendix Aircraft, 58-59 & Rockefeller Inst, 59-60; mem fac, State Univ NY, Downstate Med Ctr, 62-; tech adv, US Army Res Off, 62-72; consult, Vet Admin & Cardiac Test Lab, Montefiore Med Ctr, Cardiac Ambulatory Testing, 80- *Mem:* Inst Elec & Electronics Engrs; NY Acad Sci; Asn Advan Med Instrumentation; Robotics Inst Am; Soc Comput Simulation. *Res:* Electromechanical and biomedical engineering; inertial guidance, navigation and control; rehabilitation engineering; bioengineering; robotics; simulation. *Mailing Add:* 14821 231st St Jamaica NY 11413

BLESSING, GERALD VINCENT, ULTRASONIC NONDESTRUCTIVE TESTING, ULTRASONIC MATERIAL PROPERTIES & ULTRASONIC IN-PROCESS SENSING. *Current Pos:* PHYSICIST, NAT INST STAND & TECHNOL, 80-, GROUP LEADER, 91- *Personal Data:* b Cincinnati, Ohio, July 7, 42; m 67, Mary L Paulson; c Denise & Dawn. *Educ:* Xavier Univ, Ohio, BS, 64; Col William & Mary, Va, MS, 66; Cath Univ Am, PhD(physics), 73. *Honors & Awards:* Research & develop 100 Award, Res & Develop J, 87. *Prof Exp:* Physicist, NASA, Langley, Va, 66; instr physics, Randolph-Macon Col, Va, 66-68; res physicist, Naval Surface Weapons Ctr, Md, 73-80. *Concurrent Pos:* UFFC assoc ed, 92-; mem, Admin Comt, Inst Elec & Electronics Engrs, 93-95. *Mem:* Am Phys Soc; Am Soc Nondestructive Testing; Inst Elec & Electronics Engrs; Sigma Xi; Am Soc Testing & Mat. *Res:* Materials research of the elastic properties of metals, ceramics and composites by ultrasonic methods; nondestructive evaluation of material defect properties by ultrasonics; surface roughness and thickness measured ultrasonically; ut sensors applied to manufacturing in-process control. *Mailing Add:* Nat Inst Stand & Technol Sound Bldg 233 A147 Gaithersburg MD 20899. *Fax:* 301-417-0514; *E-Mail:* gblessing@nist.gov

BLESSING, JOHN A, CANCER CLINICAL TRIALS, GYNECOLOGIC ONCOLOGY. *Current Pos:* GROUP STATISTICIAN CANCER RES & PRIN INVESTR, GYNEC ONCOL GROUP, 74-; ASST PROF, STATE UNIV NY, BUFFALO, 75-; CANCER RES SCIENTIST V, ROSWELL PARK MEM INST, 79- *Personal Data:* b Wilkes-Barre, Pa, June 12, 46; m 68; c 1. *Educ:* King's Col, BS, 68; State Univ NY, Buffalo, MA, 70, PhD(statist), 74. *Prof Exp:* Asst statistician cancer res, Acute Leukemia Group B, 74. *Mem:* Soc Gynec Oncologists; Am Soc Clin Oncol; Am Radium Soc; Biomet Soc; Inst Math Statist. *Res:* Clinical trials investigating the treatment of gynecologic cancer. *Mailing Add:* GOG Statist Off Roswell Park Cancer Inst Elm & Carlton Sts Buffalo NY 14263

BLESSING, ROBERT HARRY, STRUCTURAL CHEMISTRY, CRYSTALLOGRAPHY. *Current Pos:* RES SCIENTIST, MED FOUND BUFFALO, 78- *Personal Data:* b Wilkes-Barre, Pa, Apr 7, 41; m 62; c 2. *Educ:* King's Col, BS, 62; Ohio Univ, PhD(chem), 71. *Prof Exp:* Teacher math & physics, Riverside High Sch, NJ, 62-63; fel chem, Lund Univ, 69-70; fel crystallog, Univ Pittsburgh, 70-72 & State Univ NY Buffalo, 72-74; asst prof chem, Mercyhurst Col, 74-78. *Mem:* Am Chem Soc; Am Crystallog Asn. *Res:* Relationship of measurable macroscopic properties of molecules and crystals to measurable microstructure. *Mailing Add:* 291 Nassau Ave No 2 Kenmore NY 14217

BLESSINGER, MICHAEL ANTHONY, OPTOELECTRONICS, SOLID STATE ELECTRONICS. *Current Pos:* MEM TECH STAFF, CINCINNATI ELECTRONICS CORP, 89- *Personal Data:* b New Albany, Ind, Sept 14, 56. *Educ:* Purdue Univ, BS, 78; Calif Inst Technol, MS, 80. *Prof*

Exp: Mem tech staff, Jet Propulsion Lab, 80-84; sr res specialist, Rockwell Int, 85-89. *Mem:* Am Phys Soc; Inst Elec & Electronics Engrs. *Res:* Solid state infrared sensing electronics; design of integrated circuits and characterization of infrared sensors. *Mailing Add:* 5756 Thornwood Dr Goleta CA 93117

BLETNER, JAMES KARL, POULTRY HUSBANDRY. *Current Pos:* from assoc prof to prof, 58-78, EMER PROF POULTRY NUTRIT, UNIV TENN, KNOXVILLE, 78- *Personal Data:* b Mason, WVa, July 29, 12; m 35, Ruth Thornley; c Ruth A (Myers) & James T. *Educ:* WVa Univ, BS, 34, MS, 50; Ohio State Univ, PhD, 58. *Prof Exp:* Asst exten poultryman, Agr Exp Sta, WVa Univ, 35-38, asst prof poultry husb, Univ & asst poultry husbandman, Agr Exp Sta, 46-55; instr poultry husb, Ohio State Univ, 55-58. *Concurrent Pos:* Feed serviceman, Quaker Oats Co, 38-44 & 46. *Mem:* AAAS; Am Soc Nutrit Sci; Poultry Sci Asn; World Poultry Sci Asn; Sigma Xi. *Res:* Poultry nutrition and management. *Mailing Add:* 300 Essex Dr Knoxville TN 37922

BLEUER, NED KERMIT, GLACIAL GEOLOGY, ENVIRONMENTAL GEOLOGY. *Current Pos:* GLACIAL GEOLOGIST, IND GEOL SURV, BLOOMINGTON, IND, 68- *Personal Data:* b Oak Park, Ill, Nov 21, 43; div; c 2. *Educ:* Univ Wis-Madison, BS, 65, PhD(geol), 70; Univ Ill, MS, 67. *Concurrent Pos:* Adj prof, Dept Geol, Indiana Univ. *Mem:* Am Quaternary Asn. *Res:* Glacial stratigraphy and history of Indiana and the Midwest; downhole logging of glacial sequences; aquifers of glacial megasequences. *Mailing Add:* 740 W Sams Hill Rd Nashville IN 47448

BLEVINS, CHARLES EDWARD, ANATOMY. *Current Pos:* PROF & CHMN DEPT ANAT, SCH MED, IND UNIV, INDIANAPOLIS, 74- *Personal Data:* b Ritzville, Wash, Sept 5, 24; m 48; c 2. *Educ:* Stanford Univ, BA, 47, MA, 48; Univ Calif, San Francisco, PhD(anat), 61. *Prof Exp:* Instr anat, physiol & zool, Glendale Col, 49-51; instr anat physiol, Contra Costa Col, 51-58, chmn dept life sci, 61-62; res anatomist, Div Otolaryngol, Univ Calif, San Francisco, 59-60; from instr to asst prof anat, Univ Wash, 62-65; asst prof, Baylor Col Med, 65-67; assoc prof, Med Sch, Northwestern Univ, 67-74. *Mem:* AAAS; Am Asn Anat; Am Asn Clin Anatomists. *Res:* Gross and microscopic anatomy; histology; histochemistry and ultrastructure of muscles, nerves, connective tissue and joints of the middle ear and larynx; ultrastructure of the acoustic system. *Mailing Add:* Dept Anat Ind Univ Sch Med 1100 W Michigan St Indianapolis IN 46202

BLEVINS, DALE GLENN, PLANT NUTRITION, NITROGEN METABOLISM. *Current Pos:* from asst prof to assoc prof, 78-85, PROF AGRON, UNIV MO, COLUMBIA, 85- *Personal Data:* b Ozark, Mo, Aug 29, 43; m 67, Brenda; c Jeremy. *Educ:* Southwest Mo State Univ, BS, 65; Univ Mo, MS, 67; Univ Ky, PhD(plant physiol), 72. *Prof Exp:* Res assoc, Dept Bot, Ore State Univ, 72-74; asst prof bot, Univ Md, College Park, 74-77. *Mem:* Am Soc Plant Physiologists; fel Am Soc Agron; fel Crop Sci Soc Am. *Res:* Mineral element metabolism; boron and aluminum interactions. *Mailing Add:* Dept Agron Univ Mo Columbia MO 65211

BLEVINS, GILBERT SANDERS, EXPERIMENTAL PHYSICS, SYSTEMS ENGINEERING. *Current Pos:* CONSULT, 92- *Personal Data:* b Smyth Co, Va, Oct 31, 27; m 50, Eunice E; c Lucinda E (Mollish) & Minnie E. *Educ:* Va Polytech Inst & State Univ, BS, 53; Duke Univ, PhD(physics), 57. *Prof Exp:* Asst, Duke Univ, 53-57; sr res physicist, Nat Cash Register Co, 57-58; tech consult, Sperry Farragut Co, 58-60; mgr data acquisition systs, Guided Missile Range Div, Pan Am World Airways, 60-62; assoc dir appl physics, Surface Div, Westinghouse Elec Corp, 62-65; consult, US Dept Defense, 65-69; tech dir, USN Security Group, 69-83. *Concurrent Pos:* Sr tech staff, Anal Sci Corp, 83-92, consult, 92- *Mem:* AAAS. *Res:* Systems engineering; applied microwave and solid state physics; communications systems; data processing and storage systems; large phased array radars. *Mailing Add:* 11986 Hall Shop Rd Clarksville MD 21029

BLEVINS, MAURICE EVERETT, APPLIED PHYSICS, COMPUTER SCIENCES. *Current Pos:* RETIRED. *Personal Data:* b Franklinville, NJ, Mar 30, 28; m 52; c 1. *Educ:* Duke Univ, BS, 52, PhD(physics), 58. *Prof Exp:* Asst physics, Duke Univ, 52-56, res assoc, 56-59; prof, Wofford Col, 59-64; fac mem, Spartanburg Tech Educ Ctr, 64-72, head electronics dept, 66-72; sr res engr, Steel Meddle Mfg Co, Greenville, 72-89; sr res engr, Cinn Milicron, 89-90. *Concurrent Pos:* Consult, 68- *Mem:* Am Phys Soc; Am Asn Physics Teachers; Sigma Xi. *Res:* Computer controlled systems design-robots; computer programming; textile technology; electronics; low temperature physics; high energy physics; superconductivity. *Mailing Add:* 98 Canterbury Rd Spartanburg SC 29302-2167

BLEVINS, R(ALPH) W(ALLACE), MECHANICAL ENGINEERING. *Current Pos:* RETIRED. *Personal Data:* b Washington, DC, Mar 30, 23; m 46, 92, Marlene Schoen; c Marianne, Suzanne, Ralph & Carolyn. *Educ:* Northwestern Univ, BS, 45; Univ Tex, MS, 49. *Prof Exp:* Detailer, Bridge Div, Chicago, 45-46; instr civil eng, Univ Tex, 46-49 & Cornell Univ, 49-51; assoc engr, Appl Physics Lab, Johns Hopkins Univ, 51-52, sr engr, 52-53, proj supvr, 53-59, asst group supvr, 59-78, group supvr, 78-86. *Mem:* Am Soc Civil Engrs; Am Inst Aeronaut & Astronaut. *Res:* Missile and satellite structural design, development and environmental protection; transportation systems design and development; ocean energy systems design and development. *Mailing Add:* 10901 Swansfield Rd Columbia MD 21044

BLEVINS, RAYMOND DEAN, PHYSIOLOGY, HUMAN ANATOMY & BIOCHEMISTRY. *Current Pos:* prof human physiol & anat, 71-81, prof Biol Sci, 76-81, PROF HEALTH SCI, ETENN STATE UNIV, 71-, PROF BIOL SCI & BIOCHEM, 81- *Personal Data:* b Butler, Tenn, Apr 3, 38; m 62, Sandra Cowan; c Raymond, Robert, Lisa & Mary V. *Educ:* ETenn State Univ, BS, 60, MA, 61; Univ Tenn, PhD(human anat, physiol, biochem), 71. *Prof Exp:* Teacher & chmn dept sci, Va High Sch, 61-62; assoc prof biol & chair person, King Col, 62-69, chmn dept, 62-64; asst prof human physiol & anat, Univ Tenn, Knoxville, 69-71. *Concurrent Pos:* Consult, Biol Div, Oak Ridge Nat Lab, 74-; Environ Mutagen Info Ctr, 78-; adj prof, ETenn State Univ Med Sch, 74-86, Univ Va, 79. *Mem:* AAAS; Am Soc Zoologists; Am Inst Biol Sci; Am Chem Soc; Sigma Xi; Environ Mutagen Soc. *Res:* Effects of specific chemicals on the nucleic acids, protein and lipids on human cells grown in tissue culture. *Mailing Add:* 1401 Buffalo St Johnson City TN 37604-7301

BLEVINS, ROBERT L, SOIL SCIENCE. *Current Pos:* ASST PROF AGRON, UNIV KY, 67- *Personal Data:* b Finley, Ky, Oct 24, 31; m 55; c 2. *Educ:* Univ Ky, BS, 52, MS, 58; Ohio State Univ, PhD(agron), 67. *Prof Exp:* Soil scientist, Soil Conserv Serv, 58-61; mem staff, Eastern Ky Resource Develop Prog, 61-62; asst prof soil surv, Univ Ky, 62-65; res assoc agron, Ohio State Univ, 65-67. *Mem:* Am Soc Agron; Soil Sci Soc Am. *Res:* Forest soils; soil classification; genesis and land use, especially problems involving soil management. *Mailing Add:* Dept Agron Univ Ky 500 Limeston St Lexington KY 40506-0001

BLEVIS, BERTRAM CHARLES, SPACE TECHNOLOGY, COMMUNICATIONS. *Current Pos:* PRES, ASTROCOM ASSOC INC, 92- *Personal Data:* b Toronto, Ont, Feb 26, 32; m 59, Rhoda Ain; c Lisa, Barbara & Mark. *Educ:* Univ Toronto, BA, 53, MA, 54, PhD(physics), 56. *Honors & Awards:* Emmy Award, Nat Acad Television Arts & Sci, 87; Alouette Award, Can Aeronaut & Space Inst, 95. *Prof Exp:* Sci officer radio physics, Defence Res Telecommun Estab, 56-57, group leader ultra high frequency propagation, 57-62, sci officer satellite commun, 62-66; sci liaison officer, Can Defence Res Staff, Washington, DC, 66-69; leader, Satellite Commun Sect, Commun Res Ctr, 69-71, mgr, Space Systs Prog, 71-75, dir int arrangements, 75-77, dir gen space technol & appln, Commun Res Ctr, 77-87, exec dir res, Dept Commun, 85-86; dir, Govt Liaison, Can Astronaut Ltd, 87-92. *Concurrent Pos:* Mem, Can Nat Orgn, Int Radio Consult Comt, 61-74, deleg, Int Telecommun Union, 63-77; mem Can comn II, Inst Sci Radio Union, 65-75; vis prof, Indian Space Res Orgn, 83; mem, Space Adv Bd, Brit Satellite Broadcasting, 87-90; chmn, 42nd Cong Int Astronaut Fedn, 91; pres, Can Aeronaut & Space Inst, 94. *Mem:* Sr mem Inst Elec & Electronics Engrs; Can Asn Physicists; fel Can Aeronaut & Space Inst. *Res:* Gaseous discharge electronics; lunar radar; radio auroral backscattering; radio propagation, particularly application to space communications; satellite communications and broadcasting and space systems studies; science policy. *Mailing Add:* 1997 Neepawa Ave Ottawa ON K2A 3L4 Can. *Fax:* 613-722-8324; *E-Mail:* bcblevis@magi.com

BLEVISS, ZEGMUND O(SCAR), SYSTEMS ENGINEERING. *Current Pos:* RETIRED. *Personal Data:* b Calgary, Alta, Aug 19, 22; US citizen; m 51, Lea Wolff; c Deborah, Ilana, Sharon & Mara. *Educ:* Univ Calif, Berkeley, BS, 44; Calif Inst Technol, MS, 47, PhD(aeronaut math), 51. *Prof Exp:* Aeronaut res scientist, Ames Aeronaut Lab, Nat Adv Comt Aeronaut, 44-46; design specialist, Douglas Aircraft Co, Inc, 51-59; mem tech staff, Space Tech Labs, Thompson-Ramo-Wooldridge, Inc, 59-60; head dept magnetohydrodyn, Aerospace Corp, 60-64; asst prog mgr, BRMS data correlation facility, Heliodyne Corp, 64-66; chief sci, Space & Commun Group, Hughes Aircraft Co, 66-89. *Mem:* AAAS; Am Inst Aeronaut & Astronaut; Am Phys Soc. *Res:* Systems engineering and analysis; aeronautics; gas dynamics; re-entry physics; magnetohydrodynamics; plasma physics. *Mailing Add:* 9106 Monte Mar Dr Los Angeles CA 90035

BLEWETT, CHARLES WILLIAM, ORGANIC CHEMISTRY, OLEO CHEMISTRY. *Current Pos:* Chemist, 68-73, group leader, 73-84, MGR, CHEM GROUP, 84- *Personal Data:* b Norfolk, Va, Aug 15, 43; m 64, Mary Herold; c Angela, William, Mary (Beth), Michelle & Catherine. *Educ:* Thomas More Col, AB, 63; Univ Cincinnati, PhD(org chem), 69. *Concurrent Pos:* Instr, Univ Cincinnati, 75-92. *Mem:* Am Chem Soc; Am Oil Chemists Soc. *Res:* Dimer acids; isostearic acids; oleochemical applications; oleochemical processing. *Mailing Add:* Henkel Corp/Chem Group 4900 Este Ave Cincinnati OH 45232. *Fax:* 513-482-2862

BLEWETT, JOHN P, NUCLEAR PHYSICS, PARTICLE ACCELERATORS. *Current Pos:* RETIRED. *Personal Data:* b Toronto, Can, Apr 12, 10; m 36, 83, Joan Warnow. *Educ:* Univ Toronto, BAC & MAS, 32 & 33; Princeton Univ, PhD(physics), 36. *Honors & Awards:* Merit Award, Nuclear & Plasma Soc, Inst Elec & Electronics Engrs; Robert R Wilson Award, Am Phys Soc. *Prof Exp:* Physicist, Gen Elec Res Lab, 37-46; sr physicist, Brookhaven Nat Lab, 47-78. *Mem:* Fel Am Phys Soc; fel Inst Elec & Electronics Engrs; fel NY Acad Sci; fel AAAS. *Res:* Nuclear fusion; synchotron light sources; co-author book of particle accelerators; atomic physics; thermionic emission; microwave generation; particle accelerator design. *Mailing Add:* 7504 Sweetbriar Dr College Park MD 20740

BLEWETT, MYRTLE HILDRED, PHYSICS. *Current Pos:* RETIRED. *Personal Data:* b Toronto, Ont, May 28, 11; nat US; div. *Educ:* Univ Toronto, BA, 35. *Prof Exp:* Engr appl physics, Gen Elec Co, 42-47; physicist, Brookhaven Nat Lab, 47-64; sr physicist, Argonne Nat Lab, Ill, 64-69; sr physicist, Europ Orgn Nuclear Res, 69-77. *Mem:* Fel Am Phys Soc. *Res:* Particle accelerators; high energy physics. *Mailing Add:* 1666 Pendrell St Apt 1503 Vancouver BC V6G 1S9 Can

BLEYL, ROBERT LINGREN, TRANSPORTATION ENGINEERING, TRAFFIC ENGINEERING. *Current Pos:* CONSULT HWY TRAFFIC, ROBERT L BLEYL ENG, 81- *Personal Data:* b Salt Lake City, Utah, Mar 25, 36; m 61; c 4. *Educ:* Univ Utah, BS, 61, MS, 62; Pa State Univ, PhD(transp eng), 71. *Prof Exp:* Traffic engr, Utah Hwy Dept, 61-63, dep traffic engr, 64-65; res assoc hwy traffic, Yale Univ, 65-68; from instr to assoc prof traffic eng, Pa State Univ, 68-72; assoc prof transp eng, Univ NMex, 72-81. *Concurrent Pos:* Consult, 66-81. *Mem:* Inst Transp Engrs; Nat Acad Forensic Engrs (treas, 91-); Nat Soc Prof Engrs; Soc Automotive Engrs. *Res:* Author of numerous publications on traffic engineering and accident reconstruction. *Mailing Add:* PO Box 92167 Albuquerque NM 87199

BLEYMAN, LEA KANNER, GENETICS, CELL BIOLOGY. *Current Pos:* assoc prof biol, Baruch Col, City Univ NY, 73-78, dep chmn, 77-79, chmn, Dept Natural Sci, 81-84, PROF BIOL, BARUCH COL, CITY UNIV NY, 79- *Personal Data:* b Halle, Ger, Nov 9, 36; US citizen; c 1. *Educ:* Brandeis Univ, BA, 58; Columbia Univ, MA, 61; Ind Univ, Bloomington, PhD(genetics of ciliates), 66. *Prof Exp:* Res assoc zool, Univ Ill, Urbana, 64-69; res assoc, Labs Reproductive Biol, Univ NC, Chapel Hill, 69-72. *Concurrent Pos:* City Univ NY Chancellor's fel, 85-86; vis prof, Dept Anat, Albert Einstein Col Med, 84, 85-89. *Mem:* AAAS; Genetics Soc Am; NY Acad Sci; Am Soc Cell Biol; Soc Protozoologists (secy, 91-97). *Res:* Genetics of ciliates, especially inheritance and determination of mating type specificity and expression and nuclear-cytoplasmic relations in cellular development. *Mailing Add:* Box A0506 17 Lexington Ave New York NY 10010. *Fax:* 212-387-1258

BLICHER, ADOLPH, SEMICONDUCTOR DEVICES. *Current Pos:* CONSULT & SCI WRITER, 74- *Personal Data:* b Warsaw, Poland; nat US; wid, Anna E Gzynberg; c A Peter. *Educ:* Univ Toulose, France, BSEE, 28; Sch Advan Elec, Paris, France, MSEE, 33; Polytech Inst Poland, DSc(tech sci), 38. *Prof Exp:* Dir eng, Polish Broadcasting Co, 44-46; sr physicist, Radio Receptor Co, NY, 51-55; mgr spec prod develop & applns dept, RCA Corp, 55-56, mgr comput devices develop dept, Solid State Div, 56-62, mgr spec prod develop & applns dept, 63-64, mgr advan devices & applns dept, Solid State Technol Ctr, 64-72, consult, RCA Labs, Princeton, 72-74. *Mem:* Inst Elec & Electronics Engrs. *Res:* Solid state device physics and electronics; author of numerous papers, books and articles on solid state devices; awarded several US patents. *Mailing Add:* 7 Sassafras Lane Monmouth Junction NJ 08852

BLICK, EDWARD F(ORREST), AEROSPACE & MECHANICAL ENGINEERING. *Current Pos:* instr aeronaut eng, 59-63, from asst prof to assoc prof aerospace & mech eng, 63-69, asst dean Grad Col, 66-68, assoc dean, Col Eng, 68-69, prof aerospace & mech eng, 69-81, PROF PETROL & GEOL ENG, UNIV OKLA, 81- *Personal Data:* b Covington, Ky, Mar 9, 32; m 55; c 2. *Educ:* Univ Okla, BS, 58, MS, 59, PhD(eng sci), 63. *Prof Exp:* Aerodynamicist, McDonnell Aircraft Corp, 58-59. *Concurrent Pos:* Res assoc, Res Inst, Univ Okla, 59-; consult, Gulf Coastal Aircraft Co, 62-63 & F W Dodge Co, 63- & Channel Wing Corp, 69- *Mem:* Am Soc Mech Engrs; Soc Petrol Engrs. *Res:* Drilling; production; fluid flow. *Mailing Add:* 419 George L Cross Ct Norman OK 73069

BLICKENSDERFER, PETER W, ANALYTICAL CHEMISTRY. *Current Pos:* from assoc prof to prof chem, 71-87, HEAD CHEM DEPT, KEARNEY STATE COL, 87- *Personal Data:* b Cincinnati, Ohio, Nov 28, 32; m 56; c 4. *Educ:* Col Wooster, BA, 54; Univ Mo, PhD(phys chem), 63. *Prof Exp:* Instr chem, Univ Mo-Rolla, 61-62; assoc res chemist, Res Labs, Whirlpool Corp, 62-70, sr res chemist, 70-71. *Concurrent Pos:* Vis prof, Univ Nebr, Lincoln, 85-86. *Mem:* Am Chem Soc; Sigma Xi. *Res:* Adsorption of gases on solids; surface chemistry of silicate minerals; high vacuum techniques; analytical methods development for trace inorganic constituents and pesticide residues. *Mailing Add:* Dept Chem Univ Nebr Kearney NE 68849-0001

BLICKENSDERFER, ROBERT, WEAR RESISTANT MATERIALS RESEARCH, PHASE DIAGRAMS-METALS. *Current Pos:* CONSULT, R B INDUST, 90- *Personal Data:* b Cincinnati, Ohio, June 16, 29; m, Sara Spencer; c Diane, John & Carol. *Educ:* Univ Cincinnati, BS, 52; Univ Ore, MS, 60; Ore State Univ, PhD(metall engr), 71. *Honors & Awards:* Meritorius Serv Award, US Dept Interior, 88; Engr of the Yr, US Bur Mines, 89; Fed Engr of the Yr, Nat Soc Prof Engrs, 89. *Prof Exp:* Mech engr, Armco Int, 54-58; res physicist, US Bur Mines, 61-70, res metallurgist, 71-84, res group supvr, 84-89. *Concurrent Pos:* Prin investr, Bur Mines, US Dept Interior, 78-84; prof metall, Linn Benton Col, 84-87; vis prof, Univ Technol, Federico Santa Maria, 87-89. *Mem:* Fel Am Soc Metals Int; Sigma Xi; Am Inst Mining, Metall & Petrol Engrs. *Res:* Phase diagrams of materials at elevated temperatures; cladding of metals by hot rolling in vacuum; frictional ignition of methane-air mixtures; wear of materials by abrasion and repeated impacts; development of wear tests. *Mailing Add:* 1605 27th Ave SW Albany OR 97321

BLICKENSTAFF, ROBERT THERON, synthetic organic & natural products chemistry, for more information see previous edition

BLICKSTEIN, STUART I, NP-COMPLETENESS, PEDAGOGICAL PROBLEM IN MATHEMATICS. *Current Pos:* ASST PROF MGT SCI, RIDER COL, 86- *Personal Data:* b Brooklyn, NY, Mar 16, 39; m 67; c 2. *Educ:* Brooklyn Col, BS, 61; Fairleigh Dickinson Univ, MBA, 76. *Prof Exp:* Sr appl analyst, Serv Bur Subsid, Int Bus Mach, 64-66; mgr biostatist, Geigy Pharmaceut, 66-68; mgr, Data Anal, Med Studies Inc, 68-70; dir, Prod Discovery, Warner Lambert, 70-80; asst prof quant anal, Fairleigh Dickinson Univ, 80-86. *Concurrent Pos:* Chair, Pharmaceut Indust Statisticians, 72-75 & Biostatist subsect, Am Statist Asn, 75; adj prof, Fairleigh Dickinson Univ, 76-80 & 86-; adj fac mem, Grad Sch Mgt, Rutgers Univ, 84-; proj res coordr, Writing Across Curric Prog, 90- *Mem:* Inst Mgt Sci; Am Statist Asn; Pharmaceut Indust Statisticians. *Res:* Heuristic development for machine scheduling problems; application of writing techniques as an aid to teaching mathematics. *Mailing Add:* Dept Mgt Sci Rider Col 2083 Lawrenceville Rd Lawrenceville NJ 08640

BLICKWEDE, D(ONALD) J(OHNSON), METALLURGY. *Current Pos:* RETIRED. *Personal Data:* b Detroit, Mich, July 20, 20; m 43; c 2. *Educ:* Wayne State Univ, BS, 43; Mass Inst Technol, ScD (metall), 48. *Prof Exp:* Metallurgist, Curtis-Wright Corp, NJ, 43-45; asst metall, Mass Inst Technol, 45-48; head, High Temperature Alloys Sect, Naval Res Lab, 48-50; consult, 84. *Concurrent Pos:* Trustee, Am Soc Metals, 63-65. *Mem:* Am Iron & Steel Inst; Brit Iron & Steel Inst; Brit Inst Metals. *Res:* Raw materials, reduction, refining, forming, finishing and application of ferrous materials. *Mailing Add:* 891 Placita Cotonia Green Valley AZ 85614

BLIDBERG, D RICHARD, development of autonomous undersea systems, development of architectures for intelligent control, for more information see previous edition

BLIESE, JOHN C W, ZOOLOGY, ORNITHOLOGY. *Current Pos:* RETIRED. *Personal Data:* b Waterloo, Iowa, Mar 10, 13; m 39, Margaret Parrett; c John R & Carolyn E (Lind). *Educ:* Univ Northern Iowa, BA, 35; Columbia Univ, MA, 36; Iowa State Univ, PhD(zool), 53. *Honors & Awards:* Zool Lab named in honor, John C W Bliese Zool Lab, Kearney State Col, 87. *Prof Exp:* High sch instr, Iowa, 36-41; sci supvr, Campus Sch, Univ Northern Iowa, 41-42; civilian instr, US Air Force, 42-44 & Tenn Eastman Corp, 44-45; sci supvr, Campus Sch, Univ Northern Iowa, 45-47; instr biol, Cornell Col, 47-49; instr zool, Iowa State Univ, 49-53; from assoc prof to prof biol, Kearney State Col, 53-78, head dept, 62-66, prof, 79-83. *Mem:* Am Sci Affil; Nat Audubon Soc; Int Crane Found; Nature Conservancy; Whooping Crane Conserv Asn. *Res:* Photoperiodism of aquarium plants; roosting of bronzed grackles and associated birds; diurnal ecology of sandhill cranes. *Mailing Add:* 107 E 27 St Kearney NE 68847

BLIGH, JOHN, PHYSIOLOGY. *Current Pos:* DIR, INST ARCTIC BIOL, UNIV ALASKA, FAIRBANKS, 77-, PROF PHYSIOL, 80- *Personal Data:* b London, Eng, July 18, 22; m 52; c 2. *Educ:* Univ London, BSc, 50, PhD(physiol), 52, DSc(physiol), 77. *Prof Exp:* From sci officer to sr sci officer physiol, Hannah Res Inst, Ayr, Scotland, 52-56; from prin sci officer to sr prin sci officer, Inst Animal Physiol, Cambridge, Eng, 57-77. *Concurrent Pos:* Permanent deleg, Int Sci Comt Antarctic Res, Int Union Physiol Sci & chmn bd definition terms, 77-; prof animal physiol & dir, Div Life Sci, Univ Alaska, 77- *Mem:* Am Physiol Soc; Brit Physiol Soc; Peruvian Physiol Soc; Int Biometeorol Soc. *Res:* Mammalian thermoregulation; the neurophysiology of homeothermy in particular, and homeostasis generally. *Mailing Add:* Little Garth off High St Harston Cambridge CB2 5QB England

BLIM, RICHARD DON, PEDIATRICS. *Current Pos:* DIR MED AFFAIRS, ST LUKES HOSP, 89- *Mem:* Inst Med-Nat Acad Sci. *Mailing Add:* St Lukes Hosp Wornall Rd & 44th St Kent City MO 64111

BLINCOE, CLIFTON (ROBERT), PHYSICAL BIOCHEMISTRY. *Current Pos:* asst prof & asst res chemist, Univ Nev, Reno, 56-60, assoc prof, 60-69, prof biochem, 69-85, RES CHEMIST, UNIV NEV, RENO, 60-, EMER PROF BIOCHEM, 85- *Personal Data:* b Odessa, Mo, Nov 21, 26; m 49, Bertha Fisher; c 3. *Educ:* Univ Mo, BS, 47, MA, 48, PhD, 55. *Prof Exp:* From instr to asst prof dairy husb, Univ Mo, 50-56. *Concurrent Pos:* Vis prof, US-Ireland Scholar Exchange Prog, Trinity Col, Dublin, 69-70; Nat Feed Ingredients Asn travel fel, 74; vis prof phys biol, Cornell Univ, 76-77; mem, Dose Assessment Adv Group, app by US Secy Energy & Gov Nev, 85-86. *Mem:* AAAS; Am Chem Soc; Am Soc Animal Sci; Biophys Soc; Brit Soc Chem Indust. *Res:* Physical biochemistry of domestic animals, especially in relation to nutrition, as studied with radiotracers; computer simulation of biological processes. *Mailing Add:* 1041 University Terr Reno NV 89503-2722. *E-Mail:* blincoe@unr.edu

BLINDER, SEYMOUR MICHAEL, THEORETICAL CHEMISTRY, MATHEMATICAL PHYSICS. *Current Pos:* from asst prof to assoc prof, 63-70, PROF CHEM, UNIV MICH, 70- *Personal Data:* b New York, NY, Mar 11, 32; m 68, Frances E Bryant; c Michael I, Stephen E, Matthew B, Amy R & Sarah J. *Educ:* Cornell Univ, AB, 53; Harvard Univ, AM, 55, PhD(chem physics), 59. *Prof Exp:* Physicist, Appl Physics Lab, Johns Hopkins Univ, 58-61; asst prof, Carnegie Inst Technol, 61-62; res assoc, Harvard Univ, 62-63. *Concurrent Pos:* Guggenheim fel, Univ Col, Univ London, 65-66; NSF sr fel, Ctr de Mecanique Ondulatoire Appliquee, Paris, 70-71 & Math Inst, Oxford, 70-71; Rackham Res fel, 77; mem, bd ed, J Am Chem Soc, 78-80. *Mem:* Am Phys Soc; AAAS. *Res:* Applications of quantum mechanics to atomic and molecular problems; nonlinear phenomena in chemistry, physics and biology. *Mailing Add:* Dept Chem Univ Mich Ann Arbor MI 48109-1055

BLINK, JAMES ALLEN, HEAT TRANSFER, LASER PHYSICS. *Current Pos:* Mil res assoc, Lawrence Livermore Nat Lab, 76-78, consult, 78-79, engr, 79-84, physicist, 85-90, MECH ENGR, LAWRENCE LIVERMORE NAT LAB, 90- *Personal Data:* b Kenosha, Wis, Apr 21, 48; m 72, Freida (DelPapa); c Merike & David. *Educ:* Univ Nev, Reno, BS, 70; Ga Inst Technol, MS, 71; Univ Calif, Davis, PhD, 84. *Mem:* Am Nuclear Soc. *Res:* Design of inertial fusion reactors with emphasis on neutronics, activation, safety, tritium processing, and hydrodynamic response of fluids to pulsed fusion energy; design of high average power lasers; design of high level nuclear waste repositories. *Mailing Add:* L-217 Lawrence Livermore Nat Lab PO Box 808 Livermore CA 94550. *E-Mail:* james_blink@notes.ymp.gov

BLINKS, JOHN ROGERS, CALCIUM AS AN INTRACELLULAR MESSENGER, CALCIUM REGULATED PHOTOPROTEINS. *Current Pos:* PROF PHYSIOL/BIOPHYS, UNIV WASH, 90- *Personal Data:* b New York, NY, Mar 21, 31; m 53, Doris Chambers; c Susan, Sarah & Elizabeth. *Educ:* Stanford Univ, AB, 51; Harvard Univ, MD, 55. *Honors & Awards:* Otto Krayer Award, Am Soc Pharmacol & Exp Therapeut, 87; Res Achievement Award, Am Heart Asn, 89. *Prof Exp:* Med house officer, Peter Bent Brigham Hosp, Boston, 55-56; res assoc, Nat Heart Inst, Bethesda, Md, 56-58; instr pharmacol, Harvard Med Sch, 58-61, assoc, 61-64, asst prof, 64-68; head, Dept Pharmacol, Mayo Found, 68-88, distinguished investr, 85-90; from assoc prof to prof pharmacol, Mayo Grad Sch Med, Univ Minn, 73-90. *Concurrent Pos:* Markle scholar med sci, 61-66; hon res asst, Univ Col, Univ London, 62-63; estab investr, Am Heart Asn, 65-70, chmn, 79, mem, Res Comt, 75-79 & sci publ comt, 83-87; mem, prog proj comt, Nat Heart & Lung Inst, 68-71 & cardiol adv comt, 75-79; field ed, J Pharmacol & Exp Therapeut, 69-71; vis lectr, Dept Physiol, Univ Auckland, 74; Edmond A & Marion F Guggenheim Prof, Mayo Found, 81-87; mem, Pharmacol Test Comt, Nat Bd Med Examrs, 84-86. *Mem:* Biophys Soc; Cardiac Muscle Soc; Am Physiol Soc; Am Soc Pharmacol & Exp Therapeut; Soc Gen Physiologists; fel AAAS. *Res:* Physiology and pharmacology of heart muscle; the role of calcium in regulation of cell function; new calcium & pls & pls regulated photoproteins more suitable than aequorin for use as intracellular calcium & pls & pls indicators. *Mailing Add:* Univ Wash Friday Harbor Labs 620 University Rd Friday Harbor WA 98250. *E-Mail:* blinks@fhl.washington.edu

BLINN, DEAN WARD, PHYCOLOGY, AQUATIC ECOLOGY. *Current Pos:* asst prof, 71-77, assoc prof, 77-81, PROF BIOL, NORTHERN ARIZ UNIV, 81- *Personal Data:* b Carroll, Iowa, May 30, 41; m 65; c 2. *Educ:* Simpson Col, BA, 64; Univ Mont, MA, 66; Univ BC, PhD(phycol), 69. *Prof Exp:* Asst prof biol, Univ NDak, 69-71. *Concurrent Pos:* Dir, Ariz Pub Serv, 74-; dir, Nat Park Serv, 75- *Mem:* Sigma Xi. *Res:* Ecology, nutrition and life histories of freshwater species of algae; ecology of invertebrates; predator-prey interactions. *Mailing Add:* Dept Biol Sci Northern Ariz Univ Box 5640 Flagstaff AZ 86011-5640

BLINN, ELLIOTT L, INORGANIC CHEMISTRY. *Current Pos:* from asst prof to assoc prof, 68-77, PROF CHEM, BOWLING GREEN STATE UNIV, 77- *Personal Data:* b Pittsburgh, Pa, Sept 25, 40; m 69. *Educ:* Univ Pittsburgh, BS, 62; Ohio State Univ, MS, 64, PhD(inorg chem), 67. *Prof Exp:* Asst chem, Ohio State Univ, 61-62; fel, State Univ NY Buffalo, 67-68. *Mem:* Am Chem Soc; Sigma Xi. *Res:* Coordination chemistry; reaction mechanism of metal complexes. *Mailing Add:* 631 Crestview Dr Bowling Green OH 43402-2744

BLINN, JAMES FREDERICK, computer graphics, science education, for more information see previous edition

BLINN, LORENA VIRGINIA, SCIENCE EDUCATION. *Current Pos:* from instr to assoc prof, 64-85, PROF NATURAL SCI, MICH STATE UNIV, 85- *Personal Data:* b East Chicago, Ind, Sept 8, 39; m 85, Walter C; c Matthew & Elizabeth. *Educ:* Univ Ga, BS, 61, MS, 64; Mich State Univ, PhD(sci ed & geol), 71. *Prof Exp:* Teacher biol, MacIntyre Park Sr High Sch, Thomasville, Ga, 61-62. *Concurrent Pos:* Vis prof biol, Inst Technol, MARA, Malaysia, 86-87. *Mem:* Nat Sci Teachers Assn; AAAS. *Res:* History of Michigan Archaeological Society; college science teaching. *Mailing Add:* 117 N Kedzie Hall Mich State Univ East Lansing MI 48824-1031

BLINN, WALTER CRAIG, GENERAL EDUCATION IN SCIENCE. *Current Pos:* from instr to prof natural sci, 61-89, PROF, CTR INTEGRATED STUDIES GEN SCI, MICH STATE UNIV, 89- *Personal Data:* b Belleville, Ill, May 16, 30; m 85, Lorena Stoops; c Mary, David, Matthew & Elizabeth. *Educ:* Ill State Univ, BS, 51; Okla State Univ, MS, 58; Northwestern Univ, PhD(biol), 61. *Prof Exp:* Instr biol, Northwestern Univ, 60-61. *Concurrent Pos:* Consult, Welch Sci Co, 61-64; NSF res grant, 63-65; vis prof physics, Indiana Univ, Cooperative Prog, Malaysia, 86-87. *Mem:* Hist Sci Soc. *Res:* History and philosophy of science; metaphysical foundations of scientific thought. *Mailing Add:* Ctr Integrated Studies - Gen Sci Mich State Univ East Lansing MI 48824. *E-Mail:* blinnw@msu.edu

BLINT, RICHARD JOSEPH, CHEMICAL PHYSICS. *Current Pos:* assoc sr res scientist, 76-80, staff res scientist, 80-85, SR STAFF RES SCIENTIST, DEPT PHYS CHEM, GEN MOTORS RES, GEN MOTORS CORP, 85- *Personal Data:* b Fairmont, Minn, Feb 23, 45; m 66; c 3. *Educ:* St Mary's Col, Minn, BA, 67; Calif Inst Technol, PhD(chem), 72. *Honors & Awards:* John M Campbell Award. *Prof Exp:* Presidential internship, Brookhaven Nat Lab, 72-73; assoc chem, Nat Res Coun, 73-74; res assoc physics, Univ Ill, 74-76. *Mem:* Am Chem Soc; Combustion Inst. *Res:* Molecular quantum mechanics is utilized in the development of metal-zeolite automotive catalysts; molecular simulations are used to study polymer electrolytes. *Mailing Add:* 5311 Fieldcrest Shelby Township MI 48316-5209. *Fax:* 810-986-8697; *E-Mail:* blint@rpchem.gmr.com

BLISCHKE, WALLACE ROBERT, STATISTICS RELIABILITY, WARRANTY COST ANALYSIS. *Current Pos:* CONSULT STATIST ANAL, 69-, ASOC PROF, SCH BUS, UNIV SOUTHERN CALIF, 72- *Personal Data:* b Oak Park, Ill, Apr 20, 34; wid; c Scott, Michael, Elizabeth (Case), Carol Satterblom & Douglas Satterblom. *Educ:* Elmhurst Col, BS, 56; Cornell Univ, MS, 58, PhD(statist), 61. *Prof Exp:* Res fel biomath, NC State Col, 61-62; mem tech staff, Appl Math Dept, TRW Space Tech Labs, 62-64; sr statistician & proj dir, C-E-I-R, Inc, 64-69. *Mem:* Inst Math Statist; fel Am Statist Asn; Biomet Soc; Inst Mgt Sci; Am Inst Aeronaut & Astronaut. *Res:* Mathematical statistics, especially estimation, mixtures of distributions and discrete distributions; applied statistics, especially experimental design, sample surveys, regression and related data analysis techniques; economic and statistical analysis of warranties; reliability; litigation support. *Mailing Add:* Dept Info & Opers Mgt Univ Southern Calif Los Angeles CA 90089-1421. *Fax:* 213-740-8494; *E-Mail:* wblischke@kecknet.usc.edu

BLISS, ARTHUR DEAN, POLYMER ALLOYS, COMPOSITES. *Current Pos:* RETIRED. *Personal Data:* b Waterbury, Conn, Jan 7, 27; m 57; c 2. *Educ:* Yale Univ, BS, 49, PhD(org chem), 55. *Prof Exp:* Res chemist, Olin Mathieson Chem Corp, 55-57, sr res chemist, 57-63, res assoc, 63-69; sect head nylon res & develop, Am Hoechst Corp, 69-74, mgr res lab, 74-79, dir, Res Plastics Div, 79-85; tech dir, Texapol Corp, 86-87; dir res & develop, Plastics Div, Wellman Inc, 87-95. *Mem:* Am Chem Soc. *Res:* Synthesis and rearrangements of amino-alcohols; preparation of boron hydrides and organic thiophosphates; preparation and reaction of aliphatic sultams; condensation polymerization; nylon 6; nylon 12; copolyamides; addition polymerization; polystyrene; acrylonitrile butadiene styrene; nylon 66 alloys; thermoplastic polyesters; plastics recycling. *Mailing Add:* 104 E Bay St Georgetown SC 29440

BLISS, DAVID FRANCIS, SOLID STATE PHYSICS, CRYSTAL GROWTH. *Current Pos:* PHYSICIST, SOLID STATE SCI DIRECTORATE, ROME LAB, USAF, 89- *Personal Data:* b Durham, NC, Oct 18, 46; m 80, Judy Uhl; c 2. *Educ:* Case Western Res Univ, BA, 68; Mass Inst Technol, SM, 81. *Honors & Awards:* Charles E Ryan Award, 93. *Prof Exp:* Technician crystal growth, Mobil Solar Energy Corp, 73-79; res asst, Dept Mat Sci, Mass Inst Technol, 79-81; eng mgr, M/A-COM, Inc, 81-89. *Concurrent Pos:* Sr lectr, Northeastern Univ, State of the Art Eng, Inc, 82-; indust fel, Lawrence Berkeley Lab, 87-88; ed, J Electronic Mat, 91. *Mem:* Am Asn Crystal Growth; Mat Res Soc; Electrochem Soc. *Res:* Research in crystal growth and characterization of semi conductors including silicon, gallium arsenide, and indium phosphide; synthesis and growth of high melting temperature compounds at high pressure. *Mailing Add:* 14 Coolidge Rd Arlington MA 02174. *E-Mail:* bliss@eastlonex.rl.af.mil

BLISS, DOROTHY CRANDALL, ECOLOGY, BOTANY. *Current Pos:* from asst prof to assoc prof, 49-68, PROF BIOL, RANDOLPH-MACON WOMAN'S COL, 68-, EMER PROF, 83- *Personal Data:* b Westerly, RI, Feb 20, 16; wid; c Dorothy R (Raines). *Educ:* Univ RI, BS, 36, MS, 38; Univ Tenn, PhD, 57. *Prof Exp:* Teacher high sch, RI, 36-37; instr sci & math, Greenbrier Jr Col, 41-43, Southern Sem & Jr Col, 43-47; instr bot, Univ Wyo, 47-49. *Concurrent Pos:* Southern Fel Fund scholar, 55-56. *Mem:* Ecol Soc Am; Am Fern Soc; Sigma Xi. *Res:* Ferns of Rhode Island; ecological problem in the spruce-fir region of the Smoky Mountains; floristic survey of wilderness areas in Blue Ridge Mountains; taxonomy; floristics. *Mailing Add:* 322 Sumpter St Lynchburg VA 24503-4430

BLISS, ERLAN S, LASER PHYSICS & ALIGNMENT, DIAGNOSTIC & CONTROL SYSTEMS. *Current Pos:* group leader laser physics, 72-75, laser proj engr, Shiva, 76-77 & Nova, 78-84, SR SYST ENGR, LAWRENCE LIVERMORE LAB, UNIV CALIF, 85- *Personal Data:* b Chicago, Ill, Jan 18, 41. *Educ:* Lawrence Univ, Wis, 63; Carnegie-Mellon Univ, MS, 65, PhD(physics), 69. *Prof Exp:* Res physicist laser physics, Air Force Cambridge Res Lab, 68-72. *Mem:* Am Phys Soc. *Res:* Electronic properties of metals; laser-induced damage in dielectrics; propagation of intense laser beams in dielectrics, alignment and diagnostic systems for large lasers. *Mailing Add:* L-463 LLNL UCL PO Box 5508 Livermore CA 94551

BLISS, EUGENE LAWRENCE, MEDICINE, PSYCHIATRY. *Current Pos:* assoc prof, 56-61, chmn dept, 70-79, FOUND FUND PROF PSYCHIAT, COL MED, UNIV UTAH, 61- *Personal Data:* b Pittsburgh, Pa, Feb 18, 18; m 47; c 3. *Educ:* Yale Univ, BA, 39; NY Med Col, MD, 43. *Honors & Awards:* Moses Award, 55. *Prof Exp:* Lectr psychiat, Col Med, Univ Utah, 50-51, asst prof, 51-53; asst clin prof, Sch Med, Yale Univ, 53-56. *Concurrent Pos:* Consult, Vet Admin Hosp, Salt Lake City, 50-53 & 56- *Mem:* Am Psychiat Asn; AMA. *Res:* Neurochemistry; neuroendocrinology; multiple personalities. *Mailing Add:* 4224 Parkview Dr Salt Lake City UT 84124

BLISS, FREDRICK ALLEN, PLANT GENETICS, PLANT BREEDING. *Current Pos:* from asst prof to assoc prof, 66-76, PROF HORT, UNIV WIS-MADISON, 76- *Personal Data:* b Inavale, Nebr, Dec 5, 38; m 63; c 3. *Educ:* BSc, Univ Nebr, 60; Univ Wis, PhD(hort, genetics), 65. *Honors & Awards:* Assinsel Grand Prize, 86. *Prof Exp:* Fel genetics, Univ Minn, St Paul, 65-66. *Concurrent Pos:* Lectr, Univ Ife, Nigeria, 66-68; mem vis fac, Inst Agron & Plant Genetics, Univ Gottingen, 68-69. *Mem:* Am Genetics Asn; fel Am Soc Hort Sci; fel Crop Sci Soc Am. *Res:* Plant breeding and genetical research dealing with Phaseolus vulgaris; quantitative genetics studies; genetic control of protein synthesis; genetic control of nitrogen fixation; disease and insect resistance edible legumes. *Mailing Add:* 214 Inca Pl Davis CA 95616

BLISS, JAMES C(HARLES), BIOENGINEERING, ELECTRICAL ENGINEERING. *Current Pos:* TELESENSORY SYSTS INC, 71- *Personal Data:* b Ft Worth, Tex, Oct 21, 33; m 62; c 2. *Educ:* Northwestern Univ, BS, 56; Stanford Univ, MS, 58; Mass Inst Technol, PhD(elec eng), 61. *Honors & Awards:* Isabelle & Leonard H Goldenson Award, 77; John Scott Medal, 80. *Prof Exp:* Res engr character recognition, Stanford Res Inst, 56-58, res engr bioeng, 61-71. *Concurrent Pos:* Lectr, Stanford Univ, 66-; assoc prof elec eng, Stanford Univ, 68-71. *Mem:* Inst Elec & Electronics Engrs. *Res:* Studies on tactile and kinesthetic perception, visual information processing in anthropods; development of sensory aids for the blind; electrooptical techniques. *Mailing Add:* PO Box 1746 Los Altos CA 94023

BLISS, LAURA, CHEMISTRY. *Current Pos:* from instr to asst prof, Randolph-Macon Woman's Col, 45-57, assoc prof, 57-84, registr, 74-84, EMER ASSOC PROF CHEM, RANDOLPH-MACON WOMAN'S COL, 84- *Personal Data:* b Davenport, Iowa, Apr 10, 16. *Educ:* Iowa State Univ, BS, 38, PhD(enzyme chem), 43. *Prof Exp:* Patent chemist, Hercules Powder Co, Del, 43-45. *Concurrent Pos:* NSF sci fac fel, Inst Enzyme Res, 61-62; researcher, Dept Biochem, Univ Queensland, 68-69. *Mem:* Am Chem Soc. *Res:* Enzyme chemistry; phosphorylase; hydrolysis of beta-D-glucosides; phosphorylase of waxy maize; acetylesterases. *Mailing Add:* 501 VES B Rd Apt 604 Lynchburg VA 24503

BLISS, LAWRENCE CARROLL, ECOLOGY. *Current Pos:* chmn dept, 78-87, PROF BOT, UNIV WASH, 78- *Personal Data:* b Cleveland, Ohio, Nov 29, 29; m 52, Gweneth Jones; c Dwight I & Karen L. *Educ:* Kent State Univ, BS, 51, MS, 53; Duke Univ, PhD(bot), 56. *Prof Exp:* Instr biol, Bowling Green State Univ, 56-57; from instr to prof bot, Univ Ill, Urbana, 57-68; prof bot & dir controlled environ facil, Univ Alta, 68-78. *Concurrent Pos:* Fulbright res fel, NZ, 63-64; assoc ed, Oecologia, 69-75; assoc ed, Arctic & Apline Res, 69-71; dir Can tundra terrestrial ecosyst study, Int Biol Prog, 70-75; mem environ protection bd, Can Arctic Gas Pipeline Ltd, 71-75; mem consultative comt, Nat Mus Can, 75-77; dir revegetation modeling study, Alta Oil Sands, 75-78; dir ecosyst study, Mt St Helen, 81-; mem ecol panel, NSF, 81-83. *Mem:* Fel AAAS; Am Inst Biol Sci; fel Arctic Inst NAm; Ecol Soc Am (vpres, 75-77, treas, 76-81, pres elect, 81-82, pres, 82-83); Can Bot Asn. *Res:* Arctic ecosystem and manipulation studies; plant production; plant-soil relationships; microenvironmental studies; eco-physiology, including plant growth chamber research; tundra boreal forest and mountain ecology. *Mailing Add:* 1226 NW 175th St Seattle WA 98177. *Fax:* 206-685-8917

BLITHE, DIANA LYNN, GLYCOBIOLOGY, ENDOCRINOLOGY. *Current Pos:* staff fel, NIH, 82-85, sr staff fel, 86-88, spec expert, 89-94, HEAD, UNIT GLYCOBIOL, DEVELOP ENDOCRINOL BR, NAT INST, CHILD HEALTH & HUMAN DEVELOP, NIH, 94- *Personal Data:* b Camden, NJ, Apr 6, 50; m 87, Gary M Gilbert; c Michelle E (Gilbert). *Educ:* Rutgers Univ, BA, 72; Univ Pa, PhD(biochem), 79. *Prof Exp:* Nat Res Serv Award, res fel, Nat Cancer Inst, 79-81. *Mem:* Am Soc for Cell Biol; Endocrine Soc; Soc Glycobiol; AAAS; Asn Women in Sci; Women Endocrinol. *Res:* Glycobiology: glycoprotein hormones, alpha subumit-structure and function; endocrinology; reproductive endocrinology; gonadotropin function. *Mailing Add:* Natl Inst Child Health & Dev Bldg 61E Rm 8B13 Bethesda MD 20892-0001. *Fax:* 301-402-0574; *E-Mail:* 1db@cu.nih.gov

BLITSTEIN, JOHN, POLYMER CHEMISTRY. *Current Pos:* VPRES RES, TAPECOAT CO, 76- *Personal Data:* b Bucharest, Romania, May 28, 38; US citizen. *Educ:* Univ Bologna, Italy, PhD(indust chem), 66. *Prof Exp:* Res Chemist, Toni Co, 67-68; sr res chemist, Eugene Dietzgen Co, 68-70 & Lake Chem, 70-76. *Mem:* Am Chem Soc; Am Soc Testing & Mat; Nat Asn Corrosion Engrs; Soc Plastic Engrs. *Res:* Tapes; adhesives coatings; corrosion; polymers; plastic and alloys extrusion. *Mailing Add:* 5455 N Sheridan Rd Apt 2208 Chicago IL 60640

BLITZER, LEON, CELESTIAL MECHANICS. *Current Pos:* from asst prof to prof, 46-83, EMER PROF PHYSICS, UNIV ARIZ, 84- *Personal Data:* b New York, NY, Dec 13, 15; m 42; c 2. *Educ:* Univ Ariz, BS, 38, MS, 39; Calif Inst Technol, PhD(physics), 43. *Prof Exp:* Instr physics, Calif Inst Technol, 43-45, res assoc, Off Sci Res & Develop Proj, 42-46. *Concurrent Pos:* Consult, Space Technol Labs, 55-70 & Jet Propulsion Lab, Calif Inst Technol, 71-86. *Mem:* AAAS; Am Phys Soc; Am Asn Physics Teachers. *Res:* Exterior ballistics of rockets; stellar spectroscopy; spectroscopy; satellite orbit perturbations; satellite and planetary perturbation theory. *Mailing Add:* Dept Physics Univ Ariz Tucson AZ 85721

BLITZSTEIN, WILLIAM, ASTRONOMY. *Current Pos:* res assoc, Univ Pa, 47-54, asst prof astron & elec eng, 54-60, assoc prof astron, 60-64, prof astron, 64-86, prof astron & astrophysics & chmn dept, 80-85, dir, Observ, 80-86, EMER PROF ASTRON & ASTROPHYS, UNIV PA, 86- *Personal Data:* b Philadelphia, Pa, Sept 3, 20; m 44, Anna Golob; c Sybil & David. *Educ:* Univ Pa, PhD, 50. *Prof Exp:* Physicist with Dr J Razek, 41-47; res engr, Franklin Inst Labs, 47-52; electronic scientist, Frankford Arsenal, 52-54. *Concurrent Pos:* Consult, Princeton Univ Observ, 48-50, Decker Corp, Radio Corp Am & Spitz Labs, 58-64 & Frankford Arsenal, 72-77. *Mem:* Int Astron Union; Am Astron Soc; Optical Soc Am; Royal Astron Soc. *Res:* Electronic instrumentation; astronomical radiometry and polarimetry; eclipsing binaries; celestial mechanics. *Mailing Add:* 2329 Poplar Rd Havertown PA 19083-1643. *E-Mail:* blitzste@sas.upenn.edu

BLIVAISS, BEN BURTON, PHYSIOLOGY. *Current Pos:* from instr to assoc prof, 48-66, coordr, Basic Med Sci Educ, 75-77, PROF PHYSIOL, CHICAGO MED SCH, 66-, ASSOC DEAN CURRIC, 77- *Personal Data:* b Chicago, Ill, July 4, 17; m 46; c 3. *Educ:* Univ Chicago, BS, 38, MS, 40, PhD(zool), 46. *Prof Exp:* Lab asst biol, Wright Jr Col, 38-41; lab asst zool, Univ Chicago, 43-44, asst zool, Toxicity Lab, 45-46, Dept Zool, 46; instr physiol, Univ Ill, 46-47; guest investr zool, Univ Chicago, 47-48. *Mem:* AAAS; Aerospace Med Asn; Am Soc Zoologists; Endocrine Soc; Soc Exp Biol & Med. *Res:* Cryptorchidism; thyroid-gonad relations in fowl; mating behavior of fowl; thiouracil on pigment; pharmacology of respiratory poisons; testicular tumors; adrenal-gonad relations; steroid hormone metabolism; experimental arthritis; aerospace physiology; nutritional effects on implantation and gestation; experimental carcinogenesis. *Mailing Add:* 9324 Kostner Ave Skokie IL 60076

BLIVEN, FLOYD E, JR, ORTHOPEDIC SURGERY. *Current Pos:* RETIRED. *Personal Data:* b Erie, Pa, May 20, 21; m 50, Hester Spencer; c 6. *Educ:* Univ Rochester, AB & MD, 42; Am Bd Orthop Surg, dipl, 56. *Prof Exp:* From instr to asst prof, Sch Med, Univ Rochester, 52-56; chief orthop, Talmadge Mem Hosp, Augusta, 56-79; from assoc prof to prof, Med Col Ga, 56-86. *Concurrent Pos:* Consult, Battery State Hosp Tuberc, 56-65, Vet Admin Hosp, Augusta, 56-, Crippled Children Serv, Ga Dept Pub Health, 60-86, Milledgeville State Hosp, 63-78, US Army Hosp Spec Treatment Ctr, Ft Gordon, 65-80 & Eisenhower Med Ctr, US Army, Augusta, 80-97. *Mem:* Am Acad Orthop Surg; Orthop Res Soc; Am Col Surg; AMA. *Res:* Infection of bone and joint; circulation and developmental studies of the hip; disability evaluation. *Mailing Add:* 619 Scotts Way Augusta GA 30909

BLIX, HANS MARTIN, ATOMIC ENERGY. *Current Pos:* DIR GEN, INT ATOMIC ENERGY AGENCY, VIENNA, AUSTRIA, 81. *Personal Data:* b Uppsala, Sweden, June 28, 28; m 62, Eva Kettis; c Marten & Goran. *Educ:* Univ Uppsala, LLB, 51; Cambidge Univ, PhD, 59; Stockholm Univ, LLD, 60. *Prof Exp:* Assoc prof, Univ Stockholm, 60-63; legal adv, Ministry Foreign Affairs, Stockholm, 63-76, under secy state, Int Develop Corp, 76-78 & 79-81, minister foreign affairs, Sweden, 78-79. *Concurrent Pos:* Mem, Swed Del UN Gen Assembly, NY, 61-81 & Swed Del Conf Disarmament, Geneva, 62-78. *Mem:* Inst Droit Int. *Res:* Author of four publications. *Mailing Add:* Int Atomic Energy Agency Wagramerstrasse 5 P O Box 100 Vienna A-1400 Austria

BLIX, SUSANNE, CHILD PSYCHIATRY. *Current Pos:* Internship, Sch Med, Ind Univ, 75-76, resident, 77-79, fel child psychiat, 79-81, ASST PROF PSYCHIAT, SCH MED, IND UNIV, 81-, ACTG DIR SECT CHILD PSYCHIAT, 88- *Personal Data:* b Crawfordsville, Ind, Oct 29, 49. *Educ:* DePauw Univ, BA, 71; Ind Univ, MD, 75. *Concurrent Pos:* Consult, Ind Pastoral Coun Ctr, 78-79, Cummins Ment Health Ctr, 79-84, Midtown Ment Health Ctr, 84-85; dir, Univ Hosp, Riley Hosp Children, 83-85, asst dir, 83-85, dir psychiat serv, 85- *Mem:* Am Acad Child & Adolescent Psychiat; Am Psychiat Asn; Asn Acad Psychiat; Am Med Asn. *Res:* Psychiatric problems involving children including Munchausen's syndrome by proxy; multiple personality; eating disorders; affective disorders; effects on staff caring for seriously disturbed youth. *Mailing Add:* Riley Child Psychiat Clin 702 Barnhill Dr Rm 3701 Indianapolis IN 46202-5210

BLIZNAKOV, EMILE GEORGE, BIOMEDICINE, IMMUNOLOGY. *Current Pos:* BIOMED RES CONSULT, 88- *Personal Data:* b Kamen, Bulgaria, July 28, 26; US citizen; div. *Educ:* Acad Med, Fac Med, Sofia, MD, 53. *Prof Exp:* Dir, Regional Sta Hygiene & Epidemiol & chief, Dist Dept Health, Pirdop, Bulgaria, 53-55; staff scientist-microbiologist, Res Inst Epidemiol & Microbiol, Sofia, 55-59; sr staff scientist, New Eng Inst, 61-81, vpres, 74-76, pres, 76-81; pres & sci dir, Lupus Res Inst, 81-88. *Concurrent Pos:* Vis scientist, Res Inst Epidemiol & Microbiol, Moscow, USSR, 58-59; exec dir res & develop, Libra Res, 81-83. *Mem:* Fel Royal Soc Trop Med & Hyg London; AMA; Am Fedn Clin Res; Am Soc Microbiol; NY Acad Sci; Am Soc Neurochem. *Res:* Public health, preventive medicine and epidemiological control; administration of research; specific and nonspecific resistance to experimental bacterial, parasitic and viral infections and tumors; phagocytosis of particles by the reticuloendothelial system; neuropharmacology; experimental and clinical screening for drugs with anti-cancer and anti-infectious effect; bioenergetics, aging and autoimmunity; author of medical books, patent in field. *Mailing Add:* 2801 N Course Dr H-205 Pompano Beach FL 33069

BLIZZARD, ROBERT M, PEDIATRICS, PEDIATRIC ENDOCRINOLOGY. *Current Pos:* PRES & DIR, GENENTECH FOUND GROWTH & DEVELOP. *Personal Data:* b East St Louis, Ill, June 20, 24. *Educ:* Northwestern Univ, BS, 48, MD, 52; Am Bd Pediat, dipl. *Honors & Awards:* Ayerst Award, Endocrine Soc. *Prof Exp:* Rotating intern, Iowa Methodist Hosp & Raymond Blank Mem Hosp Children, Des Moines, Iowa, 52-53; from asst resident physician to resident physician, Raymond Blank Mem Hosp Children, 53-55; fel pediat endocrinol & pediatrician, Harriet Lane Home Children, Johns Hopkins Hosp, 55-57; asst prof pediat & med, Ohio State Univ, 57-59, assoc prof pediat, 59-60, assoc, Div Endocrinol & Metab, Univ Hosp, 57-60; from assoc prof to prof pediat, Johns Hopkins Hosp, 60-73, chief, Div Pediat Endocrinol, 60-73, actg chmn, Dept Pediat, 72-73; chmn, Dept Pediat, Sch Med, Univ Va, 73-93. *Concurrent Pos:* Consult, NIH, 60-; dir, Nat Pituitary Agency, 63-67; pres, Human Growth Found. *Mem:* Am Fedn Clin Res; Soc Pediat Res; Endocrine Soc; Am Pediat Soc; Am Fedn Clin Res; L Wilkins Pediat Endocrine Soc; Europ Pediat Endocrine Soc. *Mailing Add:* Genentech Found Growth Develop 1224 West Main St Suite 701 Charlottesville VA 22903

BLOBEL, GUNTER, CYTOLOGY. *Current Pos:* From asst prof to assoc prof, 69-76, PROF CELL BIOL, ROCKEFELLER UNIV, 76-; INVESTR, HOWARD HUGHES MED INST, 86- *Personal Data:* b Waltersdorf, Silesia, Ger, May 21, 36; m. *Educ:* Univ Tubingen, Ger, MD, 60; Univ Wis, PhD(oncol), 67. *Honors & Awards:* US Steel Award in Molecular Biol, Nat Acad Sci, 78, Richard Lounsbery Award, 83; Warburg Medal, Ger Biochem Soc, 83, Acad Sci, 83; V D Mattia Award, Roche Inst Molecular Biol, 86; Wilson Medal, Am Soc Cell Biol, 86; Louisa Gross Horwitz Prize, 87; Waterford Biomed Sci Award, 89. *Concurrent Pos:* Internship in var Ger Hosp, 60-62; postdoctoral fel, Lab Cell Biol, Rockefeller Univ, 67-69. *Mem:* Nat Acad Sci; Am Acad Arts & Sci; hon mem Japan Biochem Soc; Am Soc Cell Biol (pres, 90); assoc mem Europ Molecular Biol Orgn; hon mem Ger Soc Cell Biol; Am Philos Soc. *Mailing Add:* Cell Biol Lab Rockefeller Univ 66th St & York Ave New York NY 10021-6339

BLOCH, AARON NIXON, technology transfer, science policy; deceased, see previous edition for last biography

BLOCH, ALAN, PHYSICS, MATHEMATICS. *Current Pos:* SCI CONSULT & WRITER, 70- *Personal Data:* b New York, NY, Nov 28, 15; m; c 2. *Educ:* Swarthmore Col, BA, 38; Oberlin Col, MA, 39. *Prof Exp:* Teaching fel physics, Iowa State Col, 40-41; head comput develop sect, Arma Corp, 46-49; chief develop engr, Audio Instrument Co, Inc, 51-55; head syst analysis dept, GPL Div, Gen Precision Inc, 55-60, staff consult to vpres res & eng, 60-61, regional mkt mgr, Librascope Div, 61-63, staff physicist, 63-65; staff analyst, Gyrodyne Co Am, Inc, 65-70. *Mem:* AAAS; Am Phys Soc; Asn Comput Mach; Audio Eng Soc; NY Acad Sci; Sigma Xi. *Res:* Hard and social sciences, particularly system analysis and synthesis; interdisciplinary problem solving; microprocessor application design. *Mailing Add:* 333 E 30th St 14J New York NY 10016

BLOCH, ALEXANDER, BIOCHEMICAL PHARMACOLOGY, CANCER BIOLOGY. *Current Pos:* from scientist to assoc scientist, 62-74, PRIN SCIENTIST, CANCER RES, ROSWELL PARK MEM INST, 74- *Personal Data:* b Freiburg, Ger, Oct 6, 23; US citizen. *Educ:* City Col New York, BS, 54; Long Island Univ, MS, 58; Cornell Univ, PhD(microbiol, biochem), 62. *Honors & Awards:* Aaron Bendich Award, Sloan-Kettering Inst. *Prof Exp:* Asst biol, Long Island Univ, 57-58; asst microbiol, Sloan-Kettering Inst, 58-62. *Concurrent Pos:* Res prof, Niagara Univ, 68- & Canisius Col, 68-; assoc res prof, State Univ NY Buffalo, 68-75, res prof, 75- *Mem:* Soc Exp Biol & Med; fel NY Acad Sci; AAAS; Am Chem Soc; Am Asn Cancer Res; Am Soc Biol Chem; Am Soc Pharmacol & Exp Therapeut. *Res:* Experimental cancer chemotherapy; tumor cell proliferation and differentiation. *Mailing Add:* Roswell Park Cancer Inst Elm & Carlton Sts Buffalo NY 14263-0001

BLOCH, DANIEL R, CHEMISTRY. *Current Pos:* res chemist to sr res chemist, S C Johnson & Son, Inc, 70-79, mgr, Polymer Res Dept, 79-85, asst to vpres res & develop, 85-88, MGR EXTERNAL TECHNOL, S C JOHNSON & SON, INC, 88- *Personal Data:* b Brownsville, Wis, Dec 13, 40; c 2. *Educ:* Univ Wis, BS, 62; Univ Ill, MS, 67, PhD(chem), 70. *Prof Exp:* Instr inorg chem, Ctr Syst, Univ Wis, 62-65. *Concurrent Pos:* Vis prof, Univ Wis-Parkside, Univ Wis-Madison & Univ Wis-Milwaukee. *Mem:* Sigma Xi; Adhesion Soc; Fedn Soc Coatings Technol; Am Chem Soc. *Res:* Acrylic latex (emulsion) polymers; monomer sequencing; reaction kinetics; thermosetting acrylic polymers; copolymerizable surfactant-like monomers; latex particle stability parameters; electron beam polymerization kinetics; properties of aqueous amylose gels; modification of natural polysaccharides. *Mailing Add:* 5536 W Branch Trail Racine WI 53402-1946

BLOCH, EDWARD HENRY, ANATOMY. *Current Pos:* from asst prof to prof, 53-84, actg chmn dept, 80-82, EMER PROF ANAT, CASE WESTERN RESERVE UNIV, 84- *Personal Data:* b Berlin, Ger, Feb 1, 14; US citizen. *Educ:* Univ Chicago, BSc, 39, PhD(microphysiol), 49; Univ Tenn, MD, 45. *Prof Exp:* Asst, Univ Tenn, 40-44; intern, Michael Reese Hosp, Chicago, 46; assoc, Univ Chicago, 46-48. *Concurrent Pos:* Estab investr, Am Heart Asn, 50-55. *Mem:* Am Asn Trop Med & Hyg; Am Asn Immunol; Microcirculatory Soc (pres, 54 & co-founder); Am Heart Asn; Am Asn Anatomists; Europ Microcirculatory Soc. *Res:* Scanning microspectrophotometry of organs in vivo; microvascular physiology and pathology of the liver, spleen, gastrointestinal tract, muscle, kidney and lung; high speed cinephotography; systems analysis of organs; instrumentation for the microscopic study of living organs in situ; pathophysiology of schistosomiasis malaria; in vivo microscopy of alografts in transparent chambers. *Mailing Add:* Dept Anat Case Western Reserve Univ Cleveland OH 44106

BLOCH, ERIC, NUTRITION, DEVELOPMENTAL STEROID BIOCHEMISTRY. *Current Pos:* asst prof, 58-65, assoc prof, 65-76, PROF BIOCHEM, OBSTET & GYNEC, ALBERT EINSTEIN COL MED, 76- *Personal Data:* b Munich, Ger, Apr 4, 28; nat US; m 61, Pnina P Gruenberg; c Talia & Alexandra. *Educ:* City Col New York, BS, 48; Univ Tex, AM, 50, PhD(biochem), 53. *Prof Exp:* Asst, Univ Tex, 50-52; res biochemist, Worcester Found Exp Biol, 52-57; res assoc, Children's Cancer Res Found, 57-58. *Concurrent Pos:* Asst, Med Sch, Harvard Univ, 57; lectr steroid training prog, Worcester Found Exp Biol, 57, 58; res career develop award, 60-69; mem, NIH Study Sect, 78-82. *Mem:* Fel AAAS; Am Soc Biol Chemists; Endocrine Soc; Soc Gynec Invest; Sigma Xi. *Res:* Control of and drug effects on fetal adrenal and gonadal functional development; testicular control of reproductive tract differentiation; effects of nutrients in uterine pathology. *Mailing Add:* Dept Obstet Gynec & Biochem Albert Einstein Col Med Bronx NY 10461. *Fax:* 718-430-8586

BLOCH, ERICH, COMPUTER ENGINEERING. *Current Pos:* RETIRED. *Personal Data:* b Sulzburg, WGer, Jan 9, 25; US citizen; m 48, Renee Stern; c Rebecca (Rogers). *Educ:* Univ Buffalo, BSEE, 52. *Hon Degrees:* DEng, Colo Sch Mines, 84; DSc, Univ Mass, George Washington Univ & State Univ NY, Buffalo, 85, Oberlin Col, 87; Notre Dame, 88, Univ SC, 90 & Polytech Univ NY, 91. *Honors & Awards:* US Medal Technol; Founders Medal, Inst Elec & Electronics Engrs; Eugene Merchand Mfg Medal, Am Soc Mech Engrs/Soc Mech Engrs. *Prof Exp:* Mgr stretch comput syst, IBM, Armonk, NY, 58-62, mgr memory develop, 63-66, lab dir, 66-69, vpres, Components Div, 69-72, div vpres & gen mgr, 75-80, asst group exec technol, 80-81, corp vpres, 81-84; dir, NSF, 84-90. *Concurrent Pos:* Vis prof, George Mason Univ; distinguished fel coun competitiveness, Washington Univ. *Mem:* Nat Acad Eng; fel Inst Elec & Electronics Engrs; fel AAAS. *Res:* Computer system design of advanced CPU's and memory subsystem; semiconductor and packaging development; manufacturing management. *Mailing Add:* Former Dir NSF 2801 New Mexico Ave NW Washington DC 20007. *Fax:* 202-965-3180; *E-Mail:* bloche@compete.org

BLOCH, INGRAM, theoretical physics; deceased, see previous edition for last biography

BLOCH, KONRAD EMIL, BIOLOGICAL CHEMISTRY, BIOCHEMICAL EVOLUTION. *Current Pos:* Higgins prof biochem, 54-82, HIGGINS EMER PROF, HARVARD UNIV, 82- *Personal Data:* b Neisse, Ger, Jan 21, 12; nat US; m, Lowe Teutsch; c Peter & Susan. *Educ:* Tech Hochschule, Munich, Chem E, 34; Columbia Univ, PhD(biochem), 38. *Hon Degrees:* DSc Univ Nancy, 66, Columbia Univ, 67, Technische Univ Munich, 68, Brandeis Univ, 70; LLD, Hokkaido Univ. *Honors & Awards:* Nobel Prize Med Physiol, 64; Fritsche Award, Am Chem Soc, 64; Nat Medal of Sci, 88. *Prof Exp:* Instr biochem, Columbia Univ, 41-44, assoc, 44-46; from asst prof to prof, Univ Chicago, 46-54. *Concurrent Pos:* Guggenheim fel, 53, 68 & 75; prof sci, Harvard Sch Pub Health, 80-82. *Mem:* Nat Acad Sci; fel Am Acad Arts & Sci; Am Chem Soc; Am Soc Biol Chem (pres, 67); Am Philos Soc; foreign mem Royal Soc London; hon mem Bavarian Acad Sci; Japanese Biochem Soc. *Res:* Structure, biosynthesis and function of lipids; enzyme inhibitors. *Mailing Add:* Dept Chem & Chem Biol Harvard Univ Cambridge MA 02138

BLOCH, KURT JULIUS, IMMUNOLOGY. *Current Pos:* PHYSICIAN MED, MASS GEN HOSP, 74- *Personal Data:* b Ger, Oct 17, 29; US citizen; m 53; c 2. *Educ:* City Univ New York, BS, 51; New York Univ Sch Med, MD, 55. *Prof Exp:* Asst physician med, Mass Gen Hosp, 65-70, assoc physician, 70-74; from asst prof to assoc prof, 68-76, PROF MED, HARVARD MED SCH, 76- *Concurrent Pos:* Dir, Am Bd Allergy & Immunol, 76-81. *Mem:* Am Soc Clin Invest; Am Rheumatism Asn; Am Acad Allergy. *Res:* Biologic properties of antibodies. *Mailing Add:* Dept Med Harvard Univ Sch Med & Chief Clin Immunol & Allergy Units Mass Gen Hosp 32 Fruit St Boston MA 02114-2696

BLOCH, ROBERT JOSEPH, CELLULAR NEUROBIOLOGY, DEVELOPMENTAL NEUROBIOLOGY. *Current Pos:* asst prof, 80-85, ASSOC PROF, DEPT PHYSIOL, SCH MED, UNIV MD, BALTIMORE, 85- *Personal Data:* b New York, NY, Oct 18, 46; m 73; c 2. *Educ:* Columbia Univ, AB, 67; Harvard Univ, PhD(biochem), 72. *Honors & Awards:* Career Develop Award, NIH, 82. *Prof Exp:* Res fel, Bioctr, Univ Basel, Switz, 72-76; res assoc, Neurobiol Lab, Salt Inst, La Jolla, Calif, 76-80. *Concurrent Pos:* McKnight Scholar's Award, 81-84. *Mem:* AAAS; Soc Neurosci; Am Soc Cell Biol; NY Acad Sci. *Res:* Formation of synapses; formation of neuromuscular junction, to learn how the postsynaptic region of this synapse is assembled. *Mailing Add:* Dept Physiol Sch Med Univ Md 655 W Baltimore St Baltimore MD 21201-1559

BLOCH, SALMAN, SEDIMENTARY PETROLOGY, LOW TEMPERATURE GEOCHEMISTRY. *Current Pos:* RETIRED. *Personal Data:* b Afula, Israel, May 22, 45; US citizen. *Educ:* Wroclaw Univ, MS, 68; George Washington Univ, PhD(geochem), 77. *Prof Exp:* Ed, Am Geol Inst, 71-72; geologist, US Geol Surv, 74-78, Okla Geol Surv, 78-82; sr res geologist, Arco Oil & Gas Co, 82-86, prin res geologist, 86-95. *Mem:* Asn Explor Geochemists; Geochem Soc; Soc Econ Paleontologists & Mineralogists; Soc Environ Geochem & Health. *Res:* Provenance and reservoir quality of sandstones; porosity prediction in sandstones. *Mailing Add:* Arco Explor & Prod 2300 Plano Pkwy Plano TX 75075

BLOCH, SPENCER J, MATHEMATICS, NUMBER THEORY. *Current Pos:* assoc prof, 76-79, PROF MATH, UNIV CHICAGO, 79- *Personal Data:* b New York, NY, May 22, 44. *Educ:* Harvard Univ, BA, 66; Columbia Univ, PhD, 71. *Prof Exp:* Instr, Princeton Univ, 71, lectr, 72, asst prof, 73-74; assoc prof, Univ Mich, 74-76. *Concurrent Pos:* Ed, Bull Am Math Soc, Composito Math, Commun Algebra. *Mem:* Nat Acad Sci. *Res:* Research on algebraic geometry, K-theory and number theory. *Mailing Add:* Dept Math Univ Chicago 5734 S University Ave Chicago IL 60637

BLOCH, SYLVAN C, PHYSICS. *Current Pos:* from asst prof to assoc prof, 63-70, PROF PHYSICS, UNIV S FLA, 70- *Personal Data:* b Vicksburg, Miss, Nov 9, 31; m 58; c 2. *Educ:* USCG Acad, BS, 54; Univ Miami, MS, 59; Fla State Univ, PhD(physics), 62. *Prof Exp:* Physicist microwave spectros, Martin Co, Fla, 59; pres, Recon, Inc, 61, res dir, 61-63; asst prof physics, Fla State Univ, 63. *Concurrent Pos:* Consult, Recon, Inc, 63- *Mem:* Am Phys Soc; Inst Elec & Electronics Engrs; Am Asn Physics Teachers. *Res:* Theoretical and experimental plasma physics; atmospheric physics. *Mailing Add:* Box 271904 Tampa FL 33688

BLOCHER, JOHN MILTON, JR, PHYSICAL CHEMISTRY. *Current Pos:* res engr, 46-50, asst supvr, 50-58, div chief, 58-69, FEL, BATTELLE-COLUMBUS LABS, 69- *Personal Data:* b Baltimore, Md, Jan 6, 19; m 41; c 5. *Educ:* Baldwin-Wallace Col, BS, 40; Ohio State Univ, PhD(phys chem), 46. *Prof Exp:* Asst chem, Ohio State Univ, 40-43, 45, 46-47; instr physics, Capital Univ, 43-44; jr chemist, Tenn Eastman Corp, 44-45. *Mem:* Am Chem Soc; Electro-chem Soc; Am Nuclear Soc; Sigma Xi. *Res:* Thermodynamics of halide vapor equilibria; mass spectrometry; photovoltaic effect; high purity metals; refractory coatings; chemical vapor deposition. *Mailing Add:* 915 Silvoor Lane Oxford OH 45056-2439

BLOCK, A JAY, pulmonary medicine, critical care, for more information see previous edition

BLOCK, BARBARA ANN, BIOLOGICAL SCIENCES. *Current Pos:* ASST PROF BIOL SCI, STANFORD UNIV, 93-, CO-DIR, TUNA RES CONSERV CTR, 94- *Personal Data:* b Springfield, Mass, Apr 25, 58. *Educ:* Univ Vt, BA, 80; Duke Univ, PhD(zool), 86. *Honors & Awards:* Presidential Young Investr Award, NSF, 89; George Bartholowmew Award Lectr, Am Soc Zoologists, 93; Pres Medal, Soc Exp Biol, London, 94; Bowditch Award, Am Physiol Soc, 95; Scholander Lectr, Univ Alaska, 96; Hoar Lectr, Univ BC, 96; White Lectr, Univ Nev, 96; MacArthur Fel, John D & Catherine T MacArthur Found, 96; Hansen Lectr, Univ Calif, Berkeley, 97. *Prof Exp:* Muscular Dystrophy Asn postdoctoral fel biol & anat, Univ Pa, Philadelphia, 86-88; asst prof organismal biol, anat & evolutionary biol, Univ Chicago, 88-93. *Concurrent Pos:* Grant recipient, NSF, NIH, Nat Geog Soc, Packard Found, Nat Marine Fisheries Serv, 89-98; chmn sci adv bd, Pac Ocean Res Found, Kona, Hawaii, 91-; mem, Comt Marine Molecular Biol, Nat Res Coun, 92-93, pres fac fel panel, NSF, 92-93, Bluefin Tuna Rev Comt, Nat Acad Sci, 94, EEP Panel, 96-98, Archival Tag Develop Panel, Nat Marine Fisheries Serv, 96; Terman fel, Stanford Univ, 95. *Mem:* AAAS; Biophys Soc; Am Physiol Soc; Soc Comp & Integrative Biol. *Res:* Organismal biology; author of numerous publications. *Mailing Add:* Dept Biol Sci Hopkins Marine Sta Stanford Univ Pacific Grove CA 93950

BLOCK, BARTLEY C, BIOACOUSTICS, OLFACTION. *Current Pos:* SR ED, PHAROS HEALTHCARE COMMUN, 96- *Personal Data:* b Chicago, Ill, Apr 12, 33; m 63, Janet Jacobs; c Kenneth, Deborah & Steven. *Educ:* Northwestern Univ, BS, 54, MS, 55. *Prof Exp:* Asst prof biol, Lycoming Col, 59-62, Drexel Inst Technol, 63-64 & Southern Conn State Col, 65-67; from asst prof to assoc prof biol, Univ Bridgeport, 74-92; chief med writer, Pharmedica Commun, 92-96. *Concurrent Pos:* Entomologist, Agr Res Ctr, USDA, Beltsville, 58-61; consult, Williamsport, Pa, 61-62, Maimonides Med Ctr, 67-68 & Wethersfield, Conn, 76-77. *Mem:* AAAS; Am Inst Biol Sci; Am Soc Zoologists; Animal Behav Soc; Am Med Writers Asn. *Res:* Sensory physiology and behavior of insects, birds and mammals. *Mailing Add:* 25 Lajoie Lane Milford CT 06460

BLOCK, DAVID L, SOLAR ENERGY, ENGINEERING MECHANICS. *Current Pos:* DIR, FLA SOLAR ENERGY CTR, 77- *Personal Data:* b Davenport, Iowa, July 10, 39; m 61; c 2. *Educ:* Univ Iowa, BSCE, 62; Va Polytech Inst, MS, 64, PhD(eng mech), 66. *Prof Exp:* Engr, NASA Langley Res Ctr, 62-66; staff engr, Martin Marietta Corp, 66-68; assoc dean eng, Fla Technol Univ, 68-77. *Concurrent Pos:* Fla rep, Southern Solar Energy Ctr, 77-, Solar Energy Task Force, Nat Gov Conf, 77- *Mem:* Int Solar Energy Soc; Am Soc Testing & Mat; Nat Soc Prof Engrs; Am Soc Eng Educ. *Res:* Solar air conditioning systems, energy policy, solar energy standards and certification and marketing of energy systems. *Mailing Add:* 70 Barcelona Blvd Merritt Island FL 32952

BLOCK, DOUGLAS ALFRED, GEOLOGY, STRATIGRAPHY. *Current Pos:* RETIRED. *Personal Data:* b Rockford, Ill, July 12, 21; m 60; c 2. *Educ:* Wheaton Col, Ill, AB, 43; Univ Iowa, MS, 52; Univ NDak, PhD(Pleistocene geol), 65. *Prof Exp:* From instr to assoc prof geol, Wheaton Col, Ill, 45-67; prof geol, 67-71, prof geol & earth sci, Rock Valley Col, 71-92. *Mem:* Geol Soc Am; fel Am Sci Affil; Nat Asn Geol Teachers. *Res:* Glacial geology and geomorphology; sedimentary petrology; pleistocene stratigraphy. *Mailing Add:* 2301 Harlem Crest Rd Loves Park IL 61111

BLOCK, DUANE LLEWELLYN, OCCUPATIONAL MEDICINE. *Current Pos:* CONSULT, 87- *Personal Data:* b Madison, Wis, Dec 27, 26; m 49, Kathleen Smith; c Susan & Jeffrey. *Educ:* Univ Wis, BS, 49, MD, 51; Am Bd Prev Med, dipl & cert occup med, 61. *Honors & Awards:* William S Knudsen Award, Am Occup Med Asn, 75; Robert A Kehoe Award, 81; Weisfeldt Memorial Award, Med Col Wis, 76. *Prof Exp:* Plant physician, Cadillac Div, Gen Motors Corp, 52-54, med dir, Gen Motors Tech Ctr, 54-55; physician-in-chg, Rouge Med Serv, 55-70; med dir, Ford Motor Co, 70-87. *Concurrent Pos:* Mem vis staff, William Beaumont Hosp, 60-; clin asst prof occup & environ health, Med Sch, Wayne State Univ, 60-; lectr occup med, Sch Pub Health, Univ Mich, 60-; clin assoc prof dept prev, Med Univ Wis, 65-; consult prof Health Scis, Oakland Univ, 70-; chmn bd, Occup Health Inst, 72-78; mem, Mich Task Force Prev Health Serv & Mich Occup Health Stand Comn, 75-77; mem, Am Bd Prev Med, 75-84, chmn, 77-84; vchmn air pollution res adv comt, Coord Res Coun, 75-78; mem bd trustees, Det Med Ctr, 88-96; chmn bd trustees, Huron Valley Hosp, 90-96. *Mem:* Am Col of Occup & Environ Med; fel Am Acad Occup Med; Int Asn Occup Health; Fel Am Col of Prev Med; emer mem Soc Med Adminr. *Res:* Health effects of automotive emissions; effects of the work environment on worker health. *Mailing Add:* 3699 Brookside Dr Bloomfield Hills MI 48302-1503

BLOCK, EDWARD R, LUNG RESEARCH. *Current Pos:* PROF MED, COL MED, UNIV FLA, 75-, ASSOC CHIEF STAFF RES, VA MED CTR, GAINESVILLE, FLA. *Personal Data:* b Baltimore, Md, May 27, 44; c 2. *Educ:* Johns Hopkins Univ, MD, 68. *Concurrent Pos:* A Blaine Brower travelling scholar, Am Col Physicians; Edward Livingston Trudeau fel, Am Lung Asn. *Mem:* Fel Am Col Physicians; Am Physiobiol Soc; Am Thoracic Soc. *Res:* Mechanisms by which oxygen excess and oxygen deprivation damage mammaliam lungs and cause pulmonary injury, dysfunction and disease. *Mailing Add:* Dept Med Univ Fla Vet Admin Med Ctr 151 1601 SW Archer Rd Gainesville FL 32608-1197

BLOCK, ERIC, ORGANIC CHEMISTRY. *Current Pos:* PROF CHEM & DEPT CHMN, STATE UNIV NY, ALBANY, 81- *Personal Data:* b New York, NY, Jan 25, 42; m 66; c 2. *Educ:* Queens Col, NY, BS, 62; Harvard Univ, AM, 64, PhD(chem), 67. *Honors & Awards:* Am Chem Soc Award, Advancement Appln Agr & Food Chem, 87. *Prof Exp:* Fel, Harvard Univ, 67; from asst prof chem to prof, Univ Mo-St Louis, 67-81. *Concurrent Pos:* Vis assoc prof chem, Harvard Univ, 74; vis prof, Univ Frankfurt, 78 & Univ Bologna, 84; consult, Elf Aquitaine, France, 83-; John Simon Guggenheim fel, 84-85; assoc ed, Phosphorus & Sulfur, 86-; ed, Advances in Sulfur Chem, 88- *Mem:* Am Chem Soc; Royal Soc Chem. *Res:* Organic sulfur chemistry; organic photochemistry; novel methods of organic synthesis; organosilicon chemistry; garlic and onion chemistry. *Mailing Add:* Chem Dept State Univ NY Albany NY 12222-0001

BLOCK, GENE DAVID, CIRCADIAN RHYTHMS PHYSIOLOGY. *Current Pos:* from asst prof to assoc prof, 78-88, PROF BIOL, UNIV VA, 89-, PROF MED, 91- *Personal Data:* b New York, NY, Aug, 17, 48; m 70, Carol Kullback; c Megan L & Ian D. *Educ:* Stanford Univ, BS, 70; Univ Ore, MS, 73, PhD(psychol), 75. *Prof Exp:* Fel, Stanford Univ, 75-78. *Concurrent Pos:* Dir, Sci & Technol Ctr Biol Timing, NSF, 91-; vprovost res, 93- *Mem:* Soc Neurosci; AAAS. *Res:* Cellular and molecular basis of circadian rhythms including the retina of a marine gastropod containing a circadian pacemaker which is accessible for electrophysiological study. *Mailing Add:* Biol & Biodynamic Inst Univ Va Gilmer Hall Charlottesville VA 22903-2453. *E-Mail:* gdb@vinginia.edu

BLOCK, GEORGE E, surgery; deceased, see previous edition for last biography

BLOCK, HENRY WILLIAM, MATHEMATICAL RELIABILITY THEORY. *Current Pos:* from asst prof to assoc prof, 68-82, PROF MATH STATIST, UNIV PITTSBURGH, 82- *Personal Data:* b Newark, NJ, Sept 9, 41; m 68. *Educ:* Carnegie-Mellon Univ, BS, 63; Ohio State Univ, MS, 64, PhD(math), 68. *Prof Exp:* Asst math, Ohio State Univ, 63-68. *Concurrent Pos:* Vis asst prof, Rensselaer Polytech Inst, 74-75; vis assoc prof, Univ Calif, Berkeley, 75-76, Univ Sao Paulo, Brazil, 80; vis prof, Univ Rome, Italy, 81. *Mem:* Fel Inst Math Statist; Oper Res Soc Am; fel Am Statist Asn; Int Statist Inst. *Res:* Reliability theory; statistical distribution theory; concepts of statistical dependence. *Mailing Add:* Dept Math Univ Pittsburgh 922 William Pitt Lane Pittsburgh PA 15260-5998. *Fax:* 412-624-8397; *E-Mail:* hwb@ums.cis.pitt.edu

BLOCK, I(SAAC) EDWARD, MATHEMATICS. *Current Pos:* RETIRED. *Personal Data:* b Philadelphia, Pa, Aug 8, 24; m 57; c 3. *Educ:* Haverford Col, BS, 44; Harvard Univ, MS, 47, PhD(math), 52. *Prof Exp:* Res asst, Harvard Univ, 50-51; math consult, Philco Corp, 51-54; coordr comput appln, Burroughs Corp, 54-55, mgr comput ctr, 56-59; mgr, Univac Eng Comput Ctr, Remington Rand Univac, 59-61, mgr appl math dept, 61-64; tech adv, Info Sci Div, Auerbach Corp, 64-65, mgr planning, 65-66, mgr sci info civ, 66-68, vpres, Auerbach Publ, Inc, 71-76; managing dir, Soc Indust & Appl Math, 76-94. *Concurrent Pos:* Mem, Conf Bd Math Sci, 57-59 & 63-64 & Franklin Inst; ed, J Soc Indust & Appl Math. *Mem:* Am Math Soc; Math Asn Am; Soc Indust & Appl Math (secy, 52-53); Asn Comput Mach. *Res:* Singular integrals; harmonic analysis; applications of mathematics and automatic computation; technical publishing. *Mailing Add:* 7904 Cobden Rd Philadelphia PA 19038-7255

BLOCK, IRA, POLYMERIC MATERIALS. *Current Pos:* Assoc prof textiles & consumer econ, 78-92, ASSOC PROF MAT ENG, UNIV MD, 92- *Personal Data:* b Brooklyn, NY, Nov 11, 41; m, Roberta Stinehart; c Michelle & Stefanie. *Educ:* Univ Md, BS, 63, PhD(nuclear eng), 71. *Concurrent Pos:* Mem, Nat Adv Comt for Flammable Fabrics Act, 80-82; Smithsonian Inst fel, 80-81. *Mem:* Sigma Xi; Am Inst Conserv; Int Inst Conserv. *Res:* Performance of textile products; textiles conservation; conservation science; textile fabric flammability. *Mailing Add:* Dept Mat & Nuclear Eng Univ Md College Park MD 20742-0001

BLOCK, IRVING H, podiatric radiology, radiation safety; deceased, see previous edition for last biography

BLOCK, JACOB, SOL-GEL PROCESSES, WET CHEMICAL PREPARATION OF CERAMIC POWDERS. *Current Pos:* res chemist, 65-68, sr res chemist, 68-83, RES ASSOC, W R GRACE & CO, 83- *Personal Data:* b Brooklyn, NY, Mar 8, 36; m 63, Harriet Luft; c Alan & Bruce. *Educ:* Brooklyn Col, BS, 56; Case Inst Technol, PhD(anal chem), 61. *Prof Exp:* Sr res analyst, Olin Mathieson Chem Corp, 61-65. *Mem:* Am Chem Soc; Am Ceramic Soc. *Res:* Environmental chemistry; aqueous chemistry; chemical treatment of chrysotile asbestos to form non-hazardous products; chemical generation of reactive compounds via hydrolysis in aqueous solutions. *Mailing Add:* W R Grace & Co 7500 Grace Dr Columbia MD 21044. *Fax:* 410-531-4767; *E-Mail:* jacob.block@corp.wrgrace.com

BLOCK, JAMES A, FLUID DYNAMICS, HEAT TRANSFER. *Current Pos:* Engr, 70-73, head, Multiphase Div, 73-80, VPRES, CREARE INC, 76-, PRES, CREARE RES & DEVELOP INC, 80- *Personal Data:* b Evanston, Ill, Feb 23, 44; m 65; c 2. *Educ:* Northwestern Univ, BS, 66; Harvard Univ, MS, 67, PhD(mech eng), 70. *Mem:* Am Soc Mech Engrs; Am Inst Chem Engrs; Am Nuclear Soc; Combustion Inst. *Res:* Multiphase flow and heat transfer; energy systems; fluid dynamics; nuclear safety; experimental techniques and instrumentation; product development, trouble shooting and improvement; direct contact condensation; foam technology. *Mailing Add:* PO Box 71 Hanover NH 03755

BLOCK, JEROME BERNARD, ONCOLOGY, IMMUNOLOGY. *Current Pos:* CHIEF, DIV MED ONCOL, UNIV CALIF LOS ANGELES MED CTR, 82- *Personal Data:* b New York, NY, Jan 7, 31; m 56; c 3. *Educ:* Stanford Univ, BA, 52; NY Univ, MD, 56. *Honors & Awards:* Karger Int Prize Biochem of Leukemia, 64. *Prof Exp:* Intern med, Mass Mem Hosp, Boston, 56-57, NIH fel, 57-59; resident, Univ Wash, 59-60; clin assoc oncol, Nat Cancer Inst, 60-64, staff physician, 64-66, chief, Baltimore Res Ctr, Nat Cancer Inst, 66-76; mem fac, Div Med Oncol, Univ Calif, Harbor Gen Hosp, 76-82. *Concurrent Pos:* Inst med, George Washington Univ, 62-63. *Mem:* AAAS; Am Asn Cancer Res; Am Fedn Clin Res; Am Soc Hemat. *Res:* Chemotherapy; internal medicine. *Mailing Add:* Div Med Oncol Bldg C2 484 Univ Calif Los Angeles Med Ctr 1000 W Carson St Torrance CA 90502-2004

BLOCK, JOHN HARVEY, MEDICINAL CHEMISTRY. *Current Pos:* From asst prof to assoc prof, 66-78, PROF PHARMACEUT CHEM, ORE STATE UNIV, 78- *Personal Data:* b Yakima, Wash, May 11, 38; m 64, Alice McComb; c Alan, Bonnie & Charlotte. *Educ:* Wash State Univ, BS & BPharm, 61, MS, 63; Univ Wis, PhD(pharmaceut chem), 66. *Concurrent Pos:* NIH spec fel & vis scholar, Stanford Univ, 72-73; mem, Oreson Bd Pharm, 90- *Mem:* Am Pharmaceut Asn; Am Chem Soc; AAAS. *Res:* Drug design; quantitative structure activity relationship. *Mailing Add:* Col Pharm Ore State Univ Corvallis OR 97331-3507. *Fax:* 541-737-3999; *E-Mail:* blockj@ccmail.orst.edu

BLOCK, LAWRENCE HOWARD, CLINICAL PHARMACOLOGY. *Current Pos:* from asst prof to assoc prof, 70-75, PROF PHARMACEUT, SCH PHARM, DUQUESNE UNIV, 75-, CHMN DEPT PHARMACEUT CHEM & PHARMACEUT, 85- *Personal Data:* b Baltimore, Md, Nov 24, 41; m 74; c 2. *Educ:* Univ Md, BS, 62, MS, 66, PhD(pharmaceut), 69. *Prof Exp:* Asst prof pharm, Univ Pittsburgh, 68-70. *Concurrent Pos:* Consult, Thrift Drug Co, Div JC Penney, Inc, 76-; mem, Tech Adv Bd, Dept Health, Commonwealth Pa, 78- *Mem:* Am Asn Pharmaceut Sci; Am Pharmaceut Asn; Soc Cosmetic Chem; NY Acad Sci; Am Asn Col Pharm; Sigma Xi. *Res:* Mass transport; biopharmaceutics and pharmacokinetics; drug and cosmetic delivery system design; drug interactions. *Mailing Add:* Sch Pharm Duquesne Univ Mellon H Pittsburgh PA 15282

BLOCK, M S, MECHANICAL ENGINEERING. *Current Pos:* RETIRED. *Personal Data:* b Louisville, Ky, June 2, 17; m 39, Dorothy Johnson; c 2. *Educ:* Univ Louisville, BME, 39. *Prof Exp:* Develop engr, Park Aerial Serv, 39-40; engr, US Navy Bur Ord, 40-44; res engr, Aeronca Aircraft Corp, 46-47; chief engr, P Lorillard Co, 47-64, dir eng, Lorillard Div, Loew's Theatres, Inc, 64-82. *Mem:* Am Soc Mech Engrs; Nat Soc Prof Engrs; NY Acad Sci. *Res:* Engineering research on tobacco products; design and construction of special machinery; construction of manufacturing, processing and storage facilities and installation of equipment. *Mailing Add:* 818 Rollingwood Dr Greensboro NC 27410. *Fax:* 910-294-0837

BLOCK, MARTIN M, PHYSICS. *Current Pos:* chmn dept, 61-68, PROF PHSYICS, NORTHWESTERN UNIV, 61- *Personal Data:* b Newark, NJ, Nov 29, 25; m 49; c 2. *Educ:* Columbia Univ, BS, 47, MA, 48, PhD(physics), 51. *Prof Exp:* Instr math, Newark Col Eng, 47-48; asst physics, Columbia Univ, 47-51, scientist, 51; assoc, Duke Univ, 51, from asst prof to assoc prof, 52-61. *Concurrent Pos:* Guggenheim fel, 58-59. *Mem:* Fel Am Phys Soc; Italian Physics Soc. *Res:* High energy physics; liquid helium bubble chamber; neutrino physics; total cross sections at high energies. *Mailing Add:* 724 Noyes St Evanston IL 60201

BLOCK, MICHAEL JOSEPH, ORGANIC CHEMISTRY, CARBON CHEMISTRY. *Current Pos:* Res chemist, Unocal Corp, 68-76, sr res chemist, 76-80, supvr carbon & nitrogen chemicals res, 81-86, mgr, chem res, 86-90, mgr polymer res, Sci & Technol Div, 90-91, MGR AGR PRODS RES & DEVELOP, UNOCAL CORP, 91- *Personal Data:* b Chicago, Ill, June 29, 42; m 70, Karen R Plotkin; c Laura & Jeremy. *Educ:* Univ Mich, BS, 64; Harvard Univ, MA, 65, PhD(chem), 69. *Mem:* AAAS; Am Chem Soc. *Res:* Physical-organic and inorganic chemistry; petroleum coke and graphite research; agricultural chemicals research. *Mailing Add:* 757 Toussau Dr Fullerton CA 92831. *Fax:* 714-577-1800

BLOCK, RICHARD B, transfer of technology from lab to end user, for more information see previous edition

BLOCK, RICHARD EARL, MATHEMATICS, LIE ALGEBRAS. *Current Pos:* PROF MATH, UNIV CALIF, RIVERSIDE, 68- *Personal Data:* b Chicago, Ill, Mar 8, 31; m 64; c 2. *Educ:* Univ Chicago, PhD(math), 56. *Prof Exp:* Instr math, Univ Ind, 56-58; Off Naval Res res assoc, Yale Univ, 58-59; Bateman res fel, Calif Inst Technol, 59-60, asst prof, 60-64; assoc prof, Univ Ill, 64-68. *Concurrent Pos:* Consult, Jet Propulsion Lab, 62-68; prin investr, NSF Grants, 66-; res assoc, Yale Univ, 67; vis prof, Rutgers Univ, 80-81; fac res lectr, Univ Calif, Riverside, 86. *Mem:* Am Math Soc; Math Asn Am. *Res:* Algebra; Lie algebras; representations; associative and non-associative ring theory; combinatorial designs; hopf algebras; determined differentiably simple algebras; classification of restricted simple lie algebras. *Mailing Add:* Dept Math Univ Calif Riverside CA 92521-0001

BLOCK, ROBERT CHARLES, NUCLEAR PHYSICS, NUCLEAR ENGINEERING. *Current Pos:* prof, 66-96, assoc dean eng, 93-96, DIR, GAERTTNER LINEAR ACCELERATOR LAB, RENSSELEAR POLYTECH INST, 75-, EMER PROF NUCLEAR ENG, 97- *Personal Data:* b Newark, NJ, Feb 11, 29; m 52, Rita Adler; c Keith & Robin. *Educ:* Newark Col Eng, BS, 50; Columbia Univ, MA, 53; Duke Univ, PhD, 56. *Honors & Awards:* Glenn Murphy Award, Am Soc Eng Educ. *Prof Exp:* Elec engr, Nat Union Radio Corp, NJ, 50-51 & Bendix Aviation, NJ, 51-52; physicist, Oak Ridge Nat Lab, 55-66. *Concurrent Pos:* Lectr, vis scientists prog, Am Inst Physics & Am Asn Physics Teachers, 58-; exchange scientist, Atomic Energy Authority Res Estab, Harwell, Eng, 62-63; guest lectr, Rensselaer Polytech Inst, 65-66; vis prof, Kyoto Univ, Japan, 73-74; consult, Knolls Atomic Power Lab; mem, Nuclear Cross-sect Adv Comt, US AEC; vpres & treas, Becker, Block & Harris Inc, 80-92; mem vis comt, Dept Nuclear Energy, Brookhaven Nat Lab, 82-85; chmn, Dept Nuclear Eng & Eng Physics, 87-93. *Mem:* Am Phys Soc; fel Am Nuclear Soc; AAAS; Inst Elec & Electronics Engrs. *Res:* Basic and applied neutron physics research; industrial applications of radiation; radiation effects in electronics. *Mailing Add:* Sch Eng Rensselaer Polytech Inst Troy NY 12181. *Fax:* 518-276-4007; *E-Mail:* blockr@rpi.edu

BLOCK, ROBERT JAY, PHYSICAL METALLURGY, FAILURE ANALYSIS. *Current Pos:* from asst prof to assoc prof, 63-72, PROF METALL ENG, UNIV OKLA, 72- *Personal Data:* b Brooklyn, NY, Feb 18, 35; m 60; c 3. *Educ:* Mass Inst Technol, BSc, 56; Columbia Univ, MSc, 58; Univ Ill, PhD(metall), 63. *Prof Exp:* Asst metall, Mass Inst Technol, 56; asst metall eng, Columbia Univ, 56-58 & Univ Ill, 58-63. *Mem:* Am Soc Metals; Am Inst Mining, Metall & Petrol Engrs. *Res:* Plastic deformation of metals; failure analysis; physical metallurgy; crystal plasticity; dislocation arrangements in metals; products liability. *Mailing Add:* 2441 Smoking Oaks Rd Norman OK 73072

BLOCK, RONALD EDWARD, PHYSICAL CHEMISTRY, BIOPHYSICAL CHEMISTRY. *Current Pos:* ASSOC PROF BIOCHEM, DIV HEALTH PROFESSIONS, NOVA SOUTHEASTERN UNIV, 93- *Personal Data:* b Charleston, SC, Apr 29, 41; m 65, Patricia R; c 2. *Educ:* Col Charleston, BS, 63; Clemson Univ, MS, 66, PhD(phys chem), 69. *Prof Exp:* Fel chem, Univ Fla, 69-70; res scientist, Papanicolaou Cancer Res Inst, 72-73, assoc scientist biochem, Nuclear Magnetic Resonance Studies, 74-84, sr scientist, 84; nuclear magnetic resonance scientist, Mt Sinai Med Ctr, 84-90, Marine Res Inst physicist & assoc dir, Magnetic Resonance Res, 90-93. *Concurrent Pos:* Interim vis asst prof chem, Univ Fla, 70; adj asst prof neurol, Sch Med, Univ Miami, 74-76, adj assoc prof chem, 76-, adj asst prof biochem, 79-84, adj assoc prof, 84-; consult nuclear magnetic resonance proj, NIH, 75-88; sabbatical res chemist, USEPA, 80-81; mem NIH Diag Radiol Study Sect, 86-88. *Mem:* Am Chem Soc; AAAS; Soc Magnetic Res. *Res:* Magnetic resonance spectroscopy and imaging studies in vivo; application of nuclear magnetic resonance spectroscopy to studies of the structure of polymers, biological membranes, proteins, and tissue components. *Mailing Add:* 3200 S University Dr Nova Southeastern Univ 1750 NE 168th St Ft Lauderdale FL 33328

BLOCK, SEYMOUR STANTON, DISINFECTION, APPLIED MICROBIOLOGY. *Current Pos:* prof chem eng, 44-85, EMER PROF CHEM ENG, UNIV FLA, 85- *Personal Data:* b New York, NY, May 16, 18; m 42; c 2. *Educ:* Pa State Univ, BS, 39, MS, 41, PhD(agr biochem), 42. *Prof Exp:* Res chemist fermentation, Joseph E Seagram & Sons, Inc, 42-44. *Concurrent Pos:* Consult, Charles Pfizer Co, 55-60, Hooker Chem Co, 60-62, USDA, 65-66 & Martin-Marietta Co, 72; mem adv comt recommendations on basic res, US Army, 76-79; ed bk series on hazardous & toxic wastes, Marcel Dekker Publ, 78; consult, Quaker Oats Co, 78 & Recovery Tech Inc; numerous grants & contracts; res assoc, Frankford Arsenal, US Army, Philadelphia, 63, PR Nuclear Ctr, San Juan, 64 & Inst Nuclear Studies, Oak Ridge, Tenn, 68. *Mem:* Soc Indust Microbiol (treas, 64); Am Chem Soc; Sigma Xi. *Res:* Antimicrobial agents; mushroom research; coal investigations; toxic and hazardous wastes; developed culture of wild mushroom (pleurotus ostreatus) now grown commercially worldwide; editor and co-author of foremost book on disinfection and sterilization, in fourth edition, Biography of Benjamin Franklin; treatment and disposal of medical wastes. *Mailing Add:* 2906 SW Second Ave Gainesville FL 32607

BLOCK, STANLEY, PHYSICAL CHEMISTRY, CRYSTALLOGRAPHY. *Current Pos:* RETIRED. *Personal Data:* b Baltimore, Md, Feb 14, 26; m 50; c 3. *Educ:* Johns Hopkins Univ, MA, 52, PhD(chem), 55. *Honors & Awards:* S B Meyer, Jr Award, Am Ceramic Soc, 59; Gold Medal Award, US Dept Com, 74. *Prof Exp:* Chemist, Crown Cork & Seal Co, Ind, 43-50; physicist solid state, Nat Bur Standards, 54-67, chief, Crystallog Sect, 67-87, res scientist, 87-90. *Concurrent Pos:* Lectr, Am Univ, 58 & Howard Univ, 67; tech expert x-ray crystallog, UNESCO, 59-61; consult, 90- *Mem:* Am Chem Soc; Am Crystallog Asn. *Res:* Materials science, particularly the effects of high pressure on the structure and properties of inorganic and organic materials; synthesis of organic compounds, sintering and toughening of ceramics, reaction kinetics and structural transformations. *Mailing Add:* 904 N Belgrade Rd Silver Spring MD 20902-3248

BLOCK, STANLEY L, PSYCHIATRY. *Current Pos:* RETIRED. *Personal Data:* b Cincinnati, Ohio, Oct 10, 23; m 47, Helene Greenwald; c Bruce A & David M. *Educ:* Univ Cincinnati, BS, 50, MD, 47; Chicago Inst Psychoanal, cert, 64. *Prof Exp:* From instr to asst prof, Univ Cincinnati, 53-64, assoc clin prof, 64-71, assoc prof, 71-74, prof psychiat, 75-85. *Concurrent Pos:* Consult, Vet Admin Hosp, 57- & Jewish Family Serv, 62-; lectr, Hebrew Union Col, 62-; vis assoc prof, Med Ctr, Univ Ky, 64-69, vis prof, 69-; dir dept psychiat, Jewish Hosp, Cincinnati, Ohio, 67-77, vpres, 77-88. *Mem:* Fel Am Psychiat Asn; Am Psychoanal Asn; Am Asn Hist Med; Am Acad Sci; Hist Sci Soc. *Res:* Psychoanalysis; history of psychiatry; group psychotherapy. *Mailing Add:* 2451 Brookwood Lane Amberley Village OH 45237-2901

BLOCK, STANLEY M(ARLIN), INDUSTRIAL ENGINEERING. *Current Pos:* RETIRED. *Personal Data:* b Minneapolis, Minn, Feb 4, 22; m 47; c 4. *Educ:* Univ Minn, BME, 43, MBA, 50, PhD(mech eng), 56. *Prof Exp:* Indust engr, Minn Mining & Mfg Co, 47-49; from instr to asst prof indust eng, Univ Minn, 49-59; assoc prof prod mgt, Univ Chicago, 59-62; prof mgt sci, Ill Inst Technol, 62-80. *Concurrent Pos:* Consult, US Air Force, 54-55; labor arbitrator, 55-; fac adv & lectr, Span Study Group, SAfrica, 57; lectr, Japan Mgt Asn, Tokyo, 64 & Nat Develop & Mgt Found, Africa, 65. *Mem:* Am Inst Indust Engrs; Nat Acad Arbitrators; Soc Prof Dispute Resolution. *Res:* International education; labor-management relations; hand-motion, eye hand coordination and simultaneous hand motions; wage incentives; managerial financial rewards. *Mailing Add:* 6105 Palo Verde Dr Rockford IL 61114

BLOCK, STEVEN M, DEVELOPMENTAL BIOLOGY. *Current Pos:* ASSOC PROF, DEPT MOLECULAR BIOL, PRINCETON UNIV, 94- *Personal Data:* b Durham, NC, Oct 4, 52; m 85, Katheleen A Beasley. *Educ:* Oxford Univ, BA, 74, MA, 78; Univ Colo, MA, 82; Calif Inst Technol, PhD(biol), 83. *Honors & Awards:* Young Investr Award, Biophys Soc, 94. *Prof Exp:* Res asst, Calif Inst Technol, 74-75, Procter & Gamble, res fel, 83; res fel, Univ Colo, 75-76, NSF fel, 76-78, regents fel, 79-80, Stanford Univ, 84-85, Jane Corfin Childs fel, 85-87. *Concurrent Pos:* Lectr, Dept Cellular & Develop Biol, Harvard Univ, 87-91 & 93, assoc, 91-92 & 93. *Mem:* Sigma Xi; Biophys Soc; Am Soc Cell Biol; Am Soc Microbiol. *Res:* Contributed numerous articles to professional journals. *Mailing Add:* Dept Molecular Biol Princeton Univ 319 Schultz Bldg Princeton NJ 08544

BLOCK, TOBY FRAN, GENERAL CHEMISTRY, PHYSICAL & INORGANIC CHEMISTRY. *Current Pos:* LAB COORDR, GEN CHEM, SCH CHEM, GA INST TECHNOL, 80- *Personal Data:* b Brooklyn, NY, Oct 5, 49; m 77; c 3. *Educ:* Brooklyn Col, BS, 70; Univ Wis-Madison, PhD(phys chem), 76. *Prof Exp:* Asst prof chem, Univ Wis-Stevens Points, 76-80. *Mem:* Am Chem Soc; Sigma Xi. *Res:* Chemical education. *Mailing Add:* 3044 Stantondale Dr Atlanta GA 30341-4106

BLOCK, WALTER DAVID, BIOCHEMISTRY, NUTRITION. *Current Pos:* assoc prof biochem, 52-83, prof nutrit, 66-83, EMER PROF NUTRIT, UNIV MICH, ANN ARBOR, 83- *Personal Data:* b Dayton, Ohio, Oct 16, 11; m 41; c 2. *Educ:* Univ Dayton, BS, 33; Univ Mich, MS, 34, PhD(biochem), 38. *Prof Exp:* From instr to asst prof biochem, Univ Mich, Ann Arbor, 38-48; pvt consult, 48-52. *Concurrent Pos:* Res consult, Caylor-Nickel Res Found, Bluffton, Ind, 53-80, dir, 81. *Mem:* AAAS; Soc Exp Biol & Med; Am Inst Nutrit; Am Soc Biol Chemists. *Res:* Lipid metabolism; amino acid metabolism; protein research. *Mailing Add:* Sch Pub Health Univ Mich Med Ctr 3000 Glazier Way Ann Arbor MI 48105-3501

BLOCKER, HENRY DERRICK, SYSTEMATIC ENTOMOLOGY, CICADELLIDAE. *Current Pos:* From asst prof to assoc prof, 65-76, PROF ENTOM, KANS STATE UNIV, 76- *Personal Data:* b Waterboro, SC, May 18, 32; m 58; c 2. *Educ:* Clemson Univ, BS, 54, MS, 58; NC State Univ, PhD(entom), 65. *Mem:* Entom Soc Am. *Res:* Taxonomy and biology of leafhoppers. *Mailing Add:* 325 Fordham Rd Manhattan KS 66503

BLOCKSTEIN, DAVID EDWARD, DEVELOPMENT OF NATIONAL INSTITUTES FOR THE ENVIRONMENT, POLICIES TO CONSERVE BIOLOGICAL DIVERSITY. *Current Pos:* RESEARCHER BIOL, PRINCETON UNIV, 90-, SR ADV, COMT NAT INSTS ENVIRON. *Personal Data:* b Pittsburgh, Pa, Jan 1, 56. *Educ:* Univ Wis-Madison, BS, 78; Univ Minn, MS, 82, PhD(ecol), 86. *Honors & Awards:* Ernest P Edwards Award, Wilson Ornith Soc, 90. *Prof Exp:* Researcher, Univ Wis-Madison, 86-87; congressional fel, Am Inst Biol Sci, 87-88, prog assoc, 89-90; asst prof zool, Conn Col, 88-89. *Concurrent Pos:* Consult, Comt Sci, Space & Technol, US House Rep, 88-89 & Forest Serv, Bur Land Mgt, US Environ Protection Agency, 88-; exec dir, Comt Nat Insts Environ, 90-; lectr, Univ Minn, Minneapolis, 90-; chair, Pub Responsibility Comt, Am Ornith Union, 90- *Mem:* Am Ornithologists Union; Soc Conserv Biol; Animal Behav Soc; Cooper Ornith Soc; Wilson Ornith Soc; AAAS. *Res:* Assessment of national needs for environmental research and federal spending on environment research; policies to conserve biodiversity; population ecology of forest nesting birds; conservation of endangered birds. *Mailing Add:* Comt Nat Insts Environ 725 K St NW Ste 212 Washington DC 20006-1401

BLOCKSTEIN, WILLIAM LEONARD, health sciences, academic administration; deceased, see previous edition for last biography

BLODGETT, FREDERIC MAURICE, PEDIATRICS. *Current Pos:* PROF PEDIAT, MED COL WIS, 66- *Personal Data:* b Bucksport, Maine, July 3, 20; m; c 5. *Educ:* Bowdoin Col, BS, 42; Yale Univ, MD, 45; Am Bd Pediat, dipl, 55. *Honors & Awards:* Children's Bur Award, Interchange Experts Prog, Int Health Res Act, 66. *Prof Exp:* Instr pediat, Harvard Med Sch, 52-54, assoc, 54-57; from asst prof to assoc prof, Sch Med, Yale Univ, 57-66. *Concurrent Pos:* Chmn comt instr clin years, Sch Med, Yale Univ, 63-65. *Mem:* Fel Am Acad Pediat; Am Bd Pediat. *Res:* General care of children; lead poisoning. *Mailing Add:* 17455 Mierow Lane Brookfield WI 53045

BLODGETT, ROBERT BELL, CHEMISTRY. *Current Pos:* RETIRED. *Personal Data:* b Milwakee, Wis, Feb 2, 16; m 39; c 2. *Educ:* Northwestern Univ, BS, 37; Univ Wis, PhD(phys chem), 40. *Prof Exp:* Res chemist, Rayon Dept, E I du Pont de Nemours & Co, 40-46, res supvr cellophane res, 46-48; chief chemist, Robbins Mills, Inc, 48-54; res mgr, Okonite Co, NJ, 54-74; consult res, Anaconda-Enisson, Inc, 74-80, chief consult eng, Wire & Cable Div, 81-86. *Mem:* AAAS; Am Chem Soc; Inst Elec & Electronics Engrs. *Res:* High-voltage insulation; cable technology; high-tenacity rayon for fabric uses; plasticization and characterization of high polymers; fabric finishing and dyeing. *Mailing Add:* 12000 Southall Court Richmond VA 23233-1681

BLODI, FREDERICK CHRISTOPHER, MEDICINE. *Current Pos:* assoc prof, 52-66, PROF OPHTHAL, UNIV IOWA, 66- *Personal Data:* b Vienna, Austria, Jan 11, 17; nat US; m 46; c 2. *Educ:* Univ Vienna, MD, 40. *Prof Exp:* Instr ophthal, Univ Vienna, 46-47; res fel, Inst Ophthal, Columbia Univ, 47-52. *Concurrent Pos:* Head, Dept Ophthal, Univ Iowa, 67-86. *Mem:* Am Ophthal Soc; Asn Res Vision & Ophthal; Am Acad Ophthal & Otolaryngol; Sigma Xi. *Res:* Morphologic pathology of the eye; electromyography of the eye muscles. *Mailing Add:* 330 Ferson Ave Iowa City IA 52246

BLOEDEL, JAMES R, NEUROPHYSIOLOGY. *Current Pos:* CHMN, DIV NEUROBIOL, BARROW NEUROL INST, MED CTR, ST JOSEPH'S HOSP, 84-; RES PROF, DEPT PHYSIOL, UNIV ARIZ, 86- *Personal Data:* b Minneapolis, Minn, Apr 7, 40; c 3. *Educ:* St Olaf Col, BA, 62; Univ Minn, Minneapolis, PhD(physiol), 67, MD, 69. *Honors & Awards:* Javits Award, 86. *Prof Exp:* From asst prof to prof neurosurg & physiol, Univ Minn, Minneapolis, 68-84, dir, Neurosurg Res Lab, 72-84. *Concurrent Pos:* NIH awards, 70-; vis scientist, Lab Neurophysiol, Good Samaritan Hosp, Portland, Ore, 72; mem, Neurol B1 Study Sect, NIH; comnr, Ariz Dis Control Res Comn, 92- *Mem:* Am Physiol Soc; Soc Neurosci; Sigma Xi; Europ Neurosci Asn; AAAS; Neurosurg Soc Am. *Res:* Cerebellar physiology; learning and memory; motor disorders and motor control. *Mailing Add:* Neurobiol Barrow Neurol Inst Med Ctr St Joseph's Hosp 350 W Thomas Rd Phoenix AZ 85013-4496. *Fax:* 602-285-4172

BLOEMBERGEN, NICOLAAS, QUANTUM OPTICS. *Current Pos:* jr fel, Soc Fels, Harvard Univ, 49-51, from assoc prof to Gorron McKay Prof appl physics, 51-74, Rumford prof physics, 74-80, Gerhard Gode Univ prof, 80-90, EMER PROF PHYSICS, HARVARD UNIV, 90- *Personal Data:* b Dordrecht, Neth, Mar 11, 20; nat US; m 50, Huberta D Brink; c Antonia, Brink & Juliana. *Educ:* State Univ Utrecht, Phil Can, 41, Phys Drs, 43; State Univ Leiden, Dr Phil(physics), 48. *Hon Degrees:* AM, Harvard Univ, 51; DSc, Laval, Que, 87, Univ Conn, 88, Hartford Univ, 80, Univ Mass, 94, Univ Cent Fla, 96, Moscow State Univ, 97. *Honors & Awards:* Nobel Prize in physics, 81; Buckley Prize, Am Phys Soc, 58; Liebmann Prize, Inst Elec & Electronics Engrs, 59, Medal of Honor, 83; Ballantine Medal, Franklin Inst, 61; Nat Medal Sci, President US, 74; Lorentz Medal, Royal Dutch Acad Sci, 78; Frederic Ives Medal, Oht Soc Am, 79. *Prof Exp:* Asst physics, Harvard Univ, 46-47; assoc, State Univ Leiden, 47-48. *Concurrent Pos:* Guggenheim fel, 57, von Humboldt sr fel, 80; vis prof, Univ Paris, 57; Univ Calif, Berkeley, 64; Univ Leiden, 73 & Raman Inst, Bangalore, India, 80; consult, United Technols Res Ctr, 78, DARPA, 72- *Mem:* Nat Acad Sci; fel Am Phys Soc; fel Inst Elec & Electronics Eng; Am Acad Arts & Sci; fel Optical Soc Am. *Res:* Nuclear and electronic magnetic resonance; solid state masers; nonlinear optics. *Mailing Add:* Pierce Hall Harvard Univ Cambridge MA 02138

BLOEMER, MARK JOSEPH, INTEGRATED PHOTONICS, NONLINEAR OPTICS. *Current Pos:* RES PHYSICIST, US ARMY MISSILE COMMAND, 88- *Personal Data:* b Cincinnati, Ohio, Oct 22, 56; m 80, Cathy L Shaner; c Keith & Jenna. *Educ:* Univ Louisville, BS, 81, MS, 82; Univ Tenn, Knoxville, PhD(physics), 86. *Prof Exp:* Machinist, Falls City Pattern & Mold Inc, 76-80; teaching asst physics, Univ Louisville, 81-82, fel, US Dept Energy, 86-87; fel, US Dept Energy, Oak Ridge Nat Lab, 86-87. *Concurrent Pos:* Teacher physics, Louisville Col Sch, 81-82; res adv, Nat Res Coun Res Associateship Prog, 91-; assoc mem, Grad Fac, Univ Ala, Huntsville, 91- *Mem:* Optical Soc Am; Inst Elec & Electronics Engrs. *Res:* Optical and electro-optical properties of semiconductor heterojunctions grown by molecular beam epitaxy, nonlinear optics, integrated photonics, vertical-cavity surface-emitting lasers and photonic band gaps. *Mailing Add:* US Army Missile Command AMSMI-RD-WS-CM Redstone Arsenal AL 35898. *Fax:* 205-842-2507; *E-Mail:* mbloemer@ws.redstone.army.mil

BLOEMER, WILLIAM LOUIS, PHYSICAL CHEMISTRY, CHEMICAL INSTRUMENTATION. *Current Pos:* from asst prof to assoc prof, 73-84, PROF CHEM & MED TECHNOL, SANGAMON STATE UNIV, 84- *Personal Data:* b Covington, Ky, Nov 26, 47; c 1. *Educ:* Thomas More Col, BA, 67; Univ Ky, PhD(chem), 72. *Prof Exp:* Teaching asst chem, Univ Ky, 68-73. *Concurrent Pos:* Dean, Sch Lib Arts & Sci, Sangamon State Univ, 88- *Mem:* Am Chem Soc; Am Asn Clin Chem; Asn Develop Comput Based Instructional Systs. *Res:* Molecular orbital calculations; educational applications of computers. *Mailing Add:* Univ Ill Springfield BRK 472 Springfield IL 62794-9243

BLOGOSLAWSKI, WALTER, MARINE MICROBIOLOGY. *Current Pos:* RES MICROBIOLOGIST SHELLFISH DIS, NAT MARINE FISHERIES SERV, 71- *Personal Data:* b New Britain, Conn, Feb 8, 43; m 77; c 3. *Educ:* Fairfield Univ, BS, 66; Long Island Univ, MS, 68; Fordham Univ, PhD(marine microbiol), 71. *Prof Exp:* Res microbiologist water treatment, Monsanto Biodize, St Louis, Mo, 69-71. *Concurrent Pos:* Adj prof biol, Fairfield Univ, 72-; adv mem biol & climate effects stratospheric ozone reduction, Environ Protection Agency, Washington, DC, 77-78; adj assoc prof marine sci, Long Island Univ, 77- *Mem:* Int Ozone Inst (secy, 74-78, chmn, 80-84, pres, 88-89); AAAS; Int Ozone Inst; Sigma Xi; NY Acad Sci. *Res:* Marine microbial research; elimination of shellfish pathogens; disinfection of seawater; detoxification of biotoxins by ozone and other oxidants. *Mailing Add:* Milford Lab 212 Rogers Ave Milford CT 06460-6499

BLOHM, THOMAS ROBERT, BIOCHEMISTRY. *Current Pos:* CONSULT, 90- *Personal Data:* b South Bend, Ind, Oct 28, 20; m 48; c 1. *Educ:* Univ Notre Dame, BS, 42; Northwestern Univ, PhD(biochem), 48. *Prof Exp:* From instr to assoc prof biochem, Dent Br, Univ Tex, 48-52; head sect, Pharmacol Dept, Richardson-Merrell Inc, 52-56, head, Dept Biochem, 56-61, prin res chemist, Merrell-Nat Labs Div, 61-90. *Concurrent Pos:* Fel, Coun Arteriosclerosis, Am Heart Asn. *Mem:* Fel AAAS; Am Soc Biol Chem; fel Am Inst Chem; Int Soc Biochem Pharmacol; Am Chem Soc. *Res:* Biochemical pharmacology, lipid metabolism; atherisclerosis; metabolic diseases. *Mailing Add:* 6468 Oldbarn Ct Madeira OH 45243-2344

BLOM, CHRISTIAN JAMES, GEOLOGY. *Current Pos:* CONSULT, INT PETROLEUM EXPLORATION & PROD, 83- *Personal Data:* b Berkeley, Calif, Dec 3, 28; m 53, Olly Zangerl; c Monica, Christine & Karin. *Educ:* Calif Inst Technol, BS, 50; Innsbruck Univ, PhD(geol), 53. *Prof Exp:* Geologist, Stand Oil Co Calif, 55-64; geologist, Occidental Petrol Corp, 64-65, explor mgr & vpres, Occidental of Libya, Inc, 66-67, sr vpres & resident mgr, 67-69, sr vpres & coordr Libyan affairs, 69, explor mgr Eastern hemisphere, Occidental Explor & Prod Co, 69-78, vpres explor Eastern hemisphere, 78-83. *Mem:* Geol Soc Am; Am Asn Petrol Geol; Soc Petrol Engrs. *Res:* Fifteen patents. *Mailing Add:* 203 Fairway Dr Bakersfield CA 93309

BLOM, GASTON EUGENE, CHILD PSYCHIATRY, EDUCATIONAL PSYCHOLOGY. *Current Pos:* RETIRED. *Personal Data:* b Brooklyn, NY, Mar 29, 20; m 46; c 4. *Educ:* Colgate Univ, BA, 41; Harvard Univ, MD, 44; Am Bd Psychiat & Neurol, dipl & cert psychiat, 55; Boston Psychoanalysis Inst, dipl psychoanalysis, 56, dipl child analysis, 58; Am Bd Psychiat & Neurol, cert child psychiat, 59. *Prof Exp:* Resident psychiat, USPHS Hosp, Ft Worth, Tex, 46-47; vet resident, Univ Mich Hosp, Ann Arbor, 47-48; fel child psychiat, Mass Gen Hosp, Boston, 48-49 & Judge Baker Guid Ctr, 49-50; asst psychiat, Harvard Med Sch, 51-53, instr, 54-58; assoc prof, Med Sch & chief, Child Psychiat Div, Univ Colo Med Ctr, Denver, 58-63, dir, Day Care Ctr, 63-70, actg chmn, Dept Psychiat, 70-71, prof psychiat, Med Sch, 63-75, prof educ, Denver Ctr, 66-75; prof psychiat & elem & spec educ, Mich State Univ, 75-84. *Concurrent Pos:* Dir, Child Psychiat Unit, Mass Gen Hosp, 56-58; consult, Ment Health Study Sect, Div Res Grants, NIH, 60-64, mem, Conf Social Competence & Clin Pract, Nat Inst Ment Health, 65; mem, Conf on Adaptation to Change, Found Fund for Res in Psychiat, 68; consult, Nat Adv Comn on Dyslexia & Related Reading Dis, Dept Health, Educ & Welfare, 68-69 & Denver Pub Schs, 69-75; training & supvry analyst, Denver Psychoanal Inst, 69-75 & supvry child analyst, 70-75; mem, Conf on Child Psychiat in Gen Psychiat Training, 71; mem vis staff, Gentofte Hosp, Copenhagen, Denmark, 72-73; med consult, US Gen Acct Off, 74-75; consult, Ingham Intermediate Sch Dist, 76-; med coordr, Univ Ctr Int Rehab, Mich State Univ, 79-, fac coordr, Univ Resource Network on Youth Advocacy, 80-; adj prof psychol, Mich State Univ, 80-84; Mich State Spec Educ Adv Coun, 81- *Mem:* Fel Am Psychiat Asn; Am Acad Psychoanalysis; fel Am Acad Child Psychiat; Coun Except Children; Int Reading Asn. *Res:* Numerous publications on child and youth advocacy; developmental aspects of language acquisition; mental health intervention in collective disasters; stress and coping behaviors in handicapped children and adults. *Mailing Add:* 11 Wavely St No 5 Brookline MA 02416

BLOMBERG, BONNIE B, MICROBIOLOGY, IMMUNOLOGY. *Current Pos:* ASST PROF MICROBIOL & IMMUNOL, SCH MED, UNIV MIAMI. *Personal Data:* b Richmond, Calif, Oct 16, 48. *Educ:* Univ Calif, San Diego, PhD, 77. *Mailing Add:* Dept Microbiol & Immunol Univ Miami Sch Med PO Box 016960 Miami FL 33101-6960

BLOMGREN, GEORGE EARL, PHYSICAL CHEMISTRY. *Current Pos:* technol fel, 87-89, SR TECHNOL FEL, EVEREADY BATTERY CORP, 89- *Personal Data:* b Chicago, Ill, Apr 15, 31; m 56; c 3. *Educ:* Northwestern Univ, BS, 52; Univ Wash, PhD(chem), 56. *Prof Exp:* Boese fel, Columbia Univ, 56-57; res chemist, Nat Carbon Co, 57-62, group leader, Consumer Prod Div, 62-73, res group leader, Battery Prod Div, 73-75, sr technol assoc, 76-81, corp technol fel, Union Carbide Corp, 81-87. *Mem:* AAAS; Am Chem Soc; Electrochem Soc. *Res:* Infrared spectra; theory of liquids; electron spin resonance; quantum chemistry; electrolyte transport; electrode processes. *Mailing Add:* 1554 Clarence Ave Lakewood OH 44107-4844

BLOMMERS, ELIZABETH ANN, ORGANIC POLYMER CHEMISTRY. *Current Pos:* RETIRED. *Personal Data:* b Pittsburgh, Pa, Nov 21, 23. *Educ:* Bryn Mawr Col, AB, 45, MA, 46, PhD(chem), 50. *Prof Exp:* Instr chem, Wheaton Col, Mass, 50-51; instr, Wells Col, 51-52; chemist org res, Signal Corps, US Army, 52-53; chemist textile res, Quaker Chem Prods, 53-56; res chemist struct adhesives, Borden Chem Co, 56-62; sr chemist, Thiokol Chem Corp, 62-65, Koppers, Co, Inc, 65-74; sr res scientist, Arco Polymers, Inc, 74-80 & Arco Chem Co, 80-85; consult, 85- *Mem:* Am Chem Soc. *Res:* Mechanisms of organic reactions; adhesives; analysis of thermoplastic polymers; utilization of polymers with coal and/or oil. *Mailing Add:* 109 Hunt Club Lane Newton Square PA 19073

BLOMQUIST, CHARLES HOWARD, BIOCHEMISTRY. *Current Pos:* mem staff biochem, 69-77, MEM STAFF OBSTET & GYNEC, UNIV MINN, MINNEAPOLIS, 77-; RES DIR, DEPT OBSTET & GYNEC, ST PAUL-RAMSEY HOSP, 69- *Personal Data:* b Rockford, Ill, Oct 27, 33; m 62, Joyce Steindorf. *Educ:* Univ Ill, BS, 55; Univ Minn, PhD(biochem), 64. *Prof Exp:* Asst biochem, Univ Wash, 55-56; Olson Mem Found fel, Karolinska Inst, Sweden, 64-65; mem staff H-4 div, Los Alamos Sci Lab, 65-69. *Mem:* AAAS; Am Chem Soc; Am Soc Biol Chem; Soc Gynec Invest; Am Soc Cell Biol. *Res:* Steroid enzymology; kinetics and mechanisms of dehydrogenase enzymes; fluorometric methods as applied to enzyme and protein chemistry. *Mailing Add:* Dept Obstet & Gynec St Paul-Ramsey Hosp St Paul MN 55101-2595

BLOMQUIST, GARY JAMES, BIOCHEMISTRY. *Current Pos:* from asst prof to assoc prof, 77-83, PROF BIOCHEM, UNIV NEV, RENO, 83- *Personal Data:* b Iron Mountain, Mich, Apr 1, 47; m 70, Cheri A Niles; c Carianne, Adam J & Scott R. *Educ:* Univ Wis-La Crosse, BS, 69; Mont State Univ, PhD(chem), 73. *Prof Exp:* Asst prof chem, Univ Southern Miss, 73-77. *Mem:* AAAS; Am Soc Biol Chemists; Entom Soc Am; Int Soc Chem Ecol. *Res:* Lipid biochemistry; insect biochemistry; insect hydrocarbon and pheromone biosynthesis. *Mailing Add:* Dept Biochem Univ Nev Reno NV 89557-0014

BLOMQUIST, RICHARD FREDERICK, ADHESIVES, WOOD UTILIZATION. *Current Pos:* CONSULT, 76- *Personal Data:* b Mankato, Minn, Nov 25, 12; m 37, Helen M Ogburn; c John A, Frederick C & Patricia L (Robinson). *Educ:* Coe Col, AB, 34; Univ Iowa, MS, 36, PhD(org chem), 37. *Hon Degrees:* DSc, Coe Col, 82. *Honors & Awards:* Adhesives Award, Am Soc Testing & Mat, 62; Gottshalk Award, Prod Ressoc, 72; Marburg lectr, Am Soc Testing & Mat, 63. *Prof Exp:* Prof chem & chmn dept, Doane Col, 37-42; from asst chemist to assoc chemist, Div Wood Preserv, Forest Prod Lab, US Forest Serv, 42-45, proj leader glues & gluing res, 47-60, glued prod res, 60-66, proj leader housing res, Forestry Sci Lab, 66-76. *Concurrent Pos:* Sr res fel, NZ Forest Serv, 65; adj prof, Sch Forest Resources, Univ Ga, 68-76; chmn ad hoc comt on aerospace struct adhesives, Nat Adv Bd, Nat Acad Sci, 72-74; adv, Mex Forestry Serv, 73 & Induperu, Peru, 78; consult, 76- *Mem:* Am Chem Soc; Am Soc Testing & Mat; Forest Prod Res Soc (pres, 74-75); fel Am Inst Chemists; fel Int Acad Wood Sci. *Res:* Better utilization of wood products in building construction; adhesives for wood, metal and plastics; development of composite lumber products for building construction. *Mailing Add:* 156 S Stratford Dr Athens GA 30605-3024

BLOMQVIST, CARL GUNNAR, CARDIOLOGY, CARDIOVASCULAR PHYSIOLOGY. *Current Pos:* from instr to assoc prof med & physiol, 66-76, PROF MED & PHYSIOL, UNIV TEX SOUTHWESTERN MED CTR, 76- *Personal Data:* b Bararyd, Sweden, Dec 31, 31; US citizen; m 61, Joan B Bakula; c Mary J & Peter C. *Educ:* Univ Lund, BM, 54, MD, 60; Karolinska Inst, Sweden, PhD(med), 67. *Honors & Awards:* Citation Award, Am Col Sports Med, 87; Jeffries Med Res Award, Am Inst Aeron & Astronaut, 92; Lonis H Bader Founders Award, Aerospace Med Asn, 95. *Prof Exp:* Res fel cardiovasc epidemiol, Physiol Hyg Lab, Col Med Sci, Univ Minn, Minneapolis, 60-61; resident dept med, Karolinska Inst, Sweden, 62-65. *Concurrent Pos:* Sr attend physician & dir EKG lab, Parkland Mem Hosp, 68-; estab investr, Am Heart Asn, 68-72; mem ed bd, Circulation, 69-73, Med & Sci in Sports, 79-86, Clin Cardiol, 77-90, J Cardiac Rehab, 79-91, Appl Physiol, 87-92; mem study sect appl physiol & bioeng, NIH, 74-78, prin investr grants NIH, NASA; mem, Nat Acad Sci Comt on Space Biol & Med, 86-90; coun, mem Sect Med, AAAS, 91-; dir, NASA Specialized Ctr Res & Teaching Integrated Physiol, 93- *Mem:* Am Fedn Clin Res; fel Am Col Cardiol; Int Soc Cardiol; AAAS; Aerospace Med Asn; Int Acad Astronaut; fel Am Heart Asn (Council Epodemiology). *Res:* Cardiovascular regulation in man; space physiology and medicine. *Mailing Add:* Southwest Med Ctr Univ Tex Dallas TX 75235. *Fax:* 214-648-2036; *E-Mail:* blomqvist@swmed.edu

BLOMSTER, RALPH N, PHARMACOGNOSY. *Current Pos:* prof pharmacog & chmn dept, 68-80, PROF MED CHEM & PHARMACOG & CHMN DEPT, SCH PHARM, UNIV MD, BALTIMORE, 80- *Personal Data:* b Lynn, Mass, May 18, 31; m 62; c 2. *Educ:* Mass Col Pharm, BS, 53; Univ Pittsburgh, MS, 57; Univ Conn, PhD(pharmacog), 63. *Prof Exp:* Asst prof pharmacog, Univ Pittsburgh, 63-68. *Concurrent Pos:* Am Found Pharmaceut Educ fel, 59-61; Lederle Labs res fel, 62-63. *Mem:* AAAS; Am Soc Pharmacog; Am Pharmaceut Asn; Sigma Xi. *Res:* Phytochemical investigations; isolation, purification and identification of plant constituents with biological activity, mainly the genera Heimia and Catharanthus; plant tissue culture and biotransformations of natural products. *Mailing Add:* 108 Hillside Rd Baltimore MD 21228

BLOMSTROM, DALE CLIFTON, PROTEIN PURIFICATION, PROTEIN STRUCTURE. *Current Pos:* RETIRED. *Personal Data:* b Lincoln, Nebr, Dec 13, 27; m 56, Ann Gerhard; c Carol, Eric & Laurie. *Educ:* Univ Nebr, BS, 48, MS, 50; Univ Ill, PhD(chem), 53. *Prof Exp:* Res org & biochemist, Exp Sta, E I Du Pont De Nemours & Co, 53-90. *Mem:* Am Chem Soc. *Res:* Heterocyclic compounds; restricted rotation; quinone diimides; polymers; organic reaction mechanisms; protein structures; hormone controls in adipose tissue; mechanism of herbicide action; plant hormone metabolites; isolation and characterization of interferon-induced proteins from human cells. *Mailing Add:* 3333 Rockfield Dr S Wilmington DE 19810

BLONDIN, JOHN MICHAEL, THEORETICAL HIGH ENERGY ASTROPHYSICS. *Current Pos:* ASST PROF PHYSICS, NC STATE UNIV, 92- *Personal Data:* b Worcester, Mass, Oct 29, 60; m 88; c 2. *Educ:* Univ Wis-Madison, BA, 82; Univ Chicago, MS, 84, PhD(astron & astrophys), 87. *Prof Exp:* Nat Acad Sci-Nat Res Coun res assoc, Goddard Space Flight Ctr, NASA, 87-89; res assoc, Dept Astron, Univ Va, 89-92. *Mem:* Am Astron Soc. *Res:* Theoretical high-energy astrophysics and numerical hydrodynamics. *Mailing Add:* Dept Physics NC State Univ PO Box 8202 Raleigh NC 27695-8202

BLOOD, BENJAMIN DONALD, PRIMATOLOGY, SCIENCE ADMINISTRATION. *Current Pos:* CONSULT, US AGENCY INT DEVELOP, PAN AM HEALTH ORGN & OTHER PUB & PRIVATE RES INST, 81- *Personal Data:* b Wabash, Ind, June 11, 14; m 39; c 5. *Educ:* Colo State Univ, DVM, 39; Harvard Univ, MPH, 49; Am Col Vet Prev Med, dipl. *Honors & Awards:* Twelfth Int Vet Cong Prize, Am Vet Med Asn, 78; Order of Bifuracted Needle, WHO, 76. *Prof Exp:* Chief adv vet affairs, Ministry Pub Health, Govt Korea, 46-48; chief vet pub health, Pan Am Sanit Bur, Regional Off WHO, 49-53, consult, Zones V & VI, Buenos Aires, 53-57; founder & dir, Pan Am Zoonoses Ctr, Pan Am Health Orgn, Azul, Arg, 57-64; int health rep, Off Int Health, USPHS, DC, 64-66, assoc dir int orgn affairs, 66-69, int health attache, US Mission to UN & Other Int Orgn in Geneva, 69-74; exec dir, Fed Interagency Primate Steering Comt, NIH, 75-79; consult, WHO, 80-81. *Concurrent Pos:* Mem WHO-Food & Agr Orgn expert comt on zoonoses, Geneva, Switz, 50 & Stockholm, Sweden, 58; secy directing coun, Pan Am Cong Vet Med, Lima, Peru, 51, Sao Paulo, Brazil, 54 & Kansas City, Mo, 59; mem US del to directing coun, Pan Am Health Orgn, 65, 67 & 68, US rep, Exec Comt, 66-69, vchmn, 69; mem US del, Pan Am Sanit Conf, 66; mem US del to World Health Assemblies, 66-71; alt mem exec bd, WHO, 69-72; secy, Am Bd Vet Pub Health, 51-53. *Mem:* Fel Am Pub Health Asn; Am Vet Med Asn; Int Primatological Soc; NY Acad Sci; Am Soc Primatologists. *Res:* International aspects of public health; epidemiology of zoonoses and other diseases common to man and animals; comparative medicine. *Mailing Add:* 1122 Saville Lane McLean VA 22101

BLOOD, CHARLES ALLEN, JR, organic chemistry; deceased, see previous edition for last biography

BLOOD, CHRISTINE HABERERN, ADVANCED MALIGNANT CANCER BIOLOGY, ANTI-CANCER THERAPEUTICS. *Current Pos:* sr scientist tumor biol, 90-92, ASSOC PRIN SCIENTIST, SCHERING-PLOUGH RES INST, 92- *Personal Data:* b Allentown, Pa, Sept 24, 57. *Educ:* Muhlenberg Col, BS, 79; Univ Maine, Orono, MS, 81; Boston Univ Sch Med, PhD(microbiol), 86. *Prof Exp:* Fel, Childrens Hosp, Boston, Mass, 86-89; fac appoint instr surg, Children's Hosp & Harvard Med Sch, 89-90. *Mem:* Am Asn Cancer Res; Am Soc Cell Biol. *Res:* Biochemistry and cell biology of malignant cancers; employment activities; identification and validation of drug targets for oncology; drug discovery-assay development and screening; pre-clinical drug development. *Mailing Add:* Schering-Plough Res Ctr MS 4945 2015 Galloping Hill Rd Kenilworth NJ 07033-0539. *Fax:* 908-298-7115

BLOOD, ELIZABETH REID, BIOGEOCHEMISTRY, ECOSYSTEM SCIENCE. *Current Pos:* ASSOC SCIENTIST, JOSEPH W JONES ECOL RES CTR, 94- *Personal Data:* b Glasgow, Scotland, Apr 1, 51; US citizen. *Educ:* Va Commonwealth Univ, BS, 74, MS, 75; Univ Ga, PhD(ecol), 81. *Prof Exp:* Res assoc ecol, Va Commonwealth Univ, 76; lab mgr, J R Reed & Assoc, Inc, 77; proj mgr, Off Water Res & Technol, Dept Interior grants, Univ Ga, 79-80, NSF grants, 80-81; asst prog dir ecol, NSF, 81-82; Baruch res assoc & prog mgr N Inlet LTER, 82-86; asst prof, Dept Environ Health Sci, Univ SC, 86-94. *Mem:* NAm Benthological Soc; AAAS; Sigma Xi. *Res:* The biogeochemistry of major, minor and trace elements and their role in the structure and functioning of terrestrial wetland and aquatic ecosystems; development of analytical methodology, instrumentation and quality control protocol. *Mailing Add:* Joseph W Jones Ecol Res Ctr Ichaway Rte 2 PO Box 2324 Newton GA 31770

BLOODGOOD, ROBERT ALAN, CELL BIOLOGY, CELL MOTILITY. *Current Pos:* from asst prof to assoc prof, 80-91, PROF CELL BIOL, SCH MED, UNIV VA, 91- *Personal Data:* b Holyoke, Mass, Sept 24, 48; m 70, Janet Williams; c Elizabeth & Elena. *Educ:* Brown Univ, BS, 70; Univ Colo, Boulder, PhD(biol), 74. *Prof Exp:* Fel & res assoc biol, Yale Univ, 74-77; asst prof anat, Albert Einstein Col Med, 77-80. *Concurrent Pos:* Am Cancer Soc res fel, Yale Univ, 75-76, NIH fel, 76-77. *Mem:* Am Soc Cell Biol; fel AAAS. *Res:* Mechanisms of cell motility; structure and function of microtubules; flagella; dynamics of the cell surface; trans-membrane signaling. *Mailing Add:* Dept Cell Biol Univ Va Sch Med Box 439 Charlottesville VA 22908. *Fax:* 804-982-3912; *E-Mail:* rab4m@virginia.edu

BLOODSTEIN, OLIVER, STUTTERING. *Current Pos:* PROF SPEECH PATH, BROOKLYN COL, NY, 48- *Personal Data:* b New York, NY, Dec 2, 20; m 41; c 2. *Educ:* City Col NY, BA, 41; State Univ Iowa, MA, 42, PhD(speech path), 48. *Honors & Awards:* Hon, Am Speech-Lang-Hearing Asn, 89. *Concurrent Pos:* Prof, doc prog speech & hearing scis, City Univ NY, 66- *Mem:* Fel Am Speech-Lang-Hearing Asn. *Res:* Conditions under which stuttering varies in frequency; factors related to the distribution of stutterings in the speech sequence; features of early stuttering; developmental stages of stuttering. *Mailing Add:* Dept Speech Brooklyn Col Bedford Ave & Ave H Brooklyn NY 11210-2813

BLOODWORTH, JAMES MORGAN BARTOW, JR, ENDOCRINOLOGY, MEDICINE. *Current Pos:* PROF PATH, SCH MED, UNIV WIS-MADISON, 62- *Personal Data:* b Atlanta, Ga, Feb 21, 25; m 47, 72, Joan G Wiltgen; c Lowell A, Joyce L, Elizabeth C, Allison J & Ellen L. *Educ:* Emory Univ, MD, 48, Am Bd Path, cert anat path & forensic path. *Honors & Awards:* Lilly Award, Am Diabetes Asn, 63. *Prof Exp:* From intern to asst resident path, Presby Hosp, NY, 48-50; asst resident internal med, Univ Iowa Hosps, 50-51; from instr to prof path, Col Med, Ohio State Univ, 51-62, chief div path anat, 54-61, attend staff, Univ Hosp, 51-62. *Concurrent Pos:* Instr, Col Physicians & Surgeons, Columbia Univ, 49-50; attend path, Columbus State Hosp, 54-57; chief labs, Madison Vet Admin Hosp, 62-89, pathologist, 89-; ed, Endoc Path, 68 & 82. *Mem:* Am Asn Pathologists; Int Acad Path; Soc Exp Biol & Med; Am Soc Cell Biol; Endocrine Soc; Am Diabetes Asn. *Res:* Degenerative vascular disease, especially diabetic microangiopathy; related aspects of diabetes mellitus, renal disease electron microscopy, enzyme histochemistry and radioautography. *Mailing Add:* Dept Path Univ Wis WS Middleton Mem Vet Admin Hosp 2500 Overlook Terr Madison WI 53705-2254

BLOODWORTH, M(ORRIS) E(LKINS), SOIL PHYSICS, AGRICULTURAL ENGINEERING & ADMINISTRATION. *Current Pos:* RETIRED. *Personal Data:* b Axtell, Tex, Sept 18, 20; m 60; c 2. *Educ:* Agr & Mech Col Tex, BS, 41, MS, 53, PhD(soil physics), 58. *Prof Exp:* Agr engr soil & water, Soil Conserv Serv, USDA, 41-42 & 46-48; agr engr irrig & drainage, Tex Agr Exp Sta, 48-54, assoc soil physicist, 54-56; assoc prof agron, Tex A&M Univ, 56-63, prof soil physics & head, dept soil & crop sci, 63-80, prof agron, dept soil & crop sci & dir, int progs, 80-84. *Mem:* Fel AAAS; Am Soc Agr Engrs; fel Am Soc Agron; Soil Sci Soc Am; Int Soil Sci Soc. *Res:* Soil-plant-water relationships; interrelated physical and chemical factors affecting plant growth and production; engineering aspects concerning irrigation and drainage of agricultural soils; large scale international agricultural developments and operations; agricultural teaching; experiments in agriculture. *Mailing Add:* 801 N Rosemary Dr Bryan TX 77802

BLOOM, ALAN S, DRUG ABUSE, NEUROTOXICOLOGY. *Current Pos:* from asst prof to assoc prof, 76-87, PROF PHARMACOL, MED COL WIS, 88- *Personal Data:* b Buffalo, NY, May 28, 47; m 69; c 2. *Educ:* State Univ NY, Buffalo, BA, 69; Univ Louisville, MA, 71, PhD(neuropsychopharmacol), 74. *Prof Exp:* Fel pharmacol, Med Col, Va, 74-76. *Mem:* Am Soc Pharmacol & Therapeut; Soc Neurosci; AAAS. *Res:* Neurochemical measures of effects of drugs of abuse and insecticides, particularly their effects on brain membranes and their associated receptors and enzymes; aging and the brain. *Mailing Add:* Dept Pharmacol Med Col Wis 8701 Watertown Plank Rd Milwaukee WI 53226-4801

BLOOM, ALLEN, ORGANIC CHEMISTRY, PHOTOCHEMISTRY. *Current Pos:* VPRES, GEN COUN & SECY, LIPOSOME CO, 85- *Personal Data:* b New York, NY, Sept 9, 43; m 67; c 3. *Educ:* Brooklyn Col, BS, 65; Iowa State Univ, PhD(org chem), 71; NY Law Sch, JD, 80. *Prof Exp:* Res assoc x-ray crystallog, Cornell Univ, 69-72; mem tech staff org chem & photochem, RCA Labs, 72-77, mem patent coun, patent opers, David Sarnoff Res Ctr, 77-82; patent atty, Pfizer Inc, 82-85. *Mem:* Am Chem Soc. *Res:* Organic materials for optically recording and storing information; liquid crystal phenomena; electrical and photochemical properties of organic molecules. *Mailing Add:* DeChert Price & Rhoads PO Box 5218 Princeton NJ 08543-5218

BLOOM, ARNOLD LAPIN, LASERS, THIN FILMS. *Current Pos:* RETIRED. *Personal Data:* b Chicago, Ill, Mar 7, 23; m 51, Barbara Bellin; c Debra B (Fisher). *Educ:* Univ Calif, PhD(physics), 51. *Prof Exp:* Asst physics, Univ Calif, 48-51; physicist, Varian Assocs, 51-61; dir theoret res, Spectra-Physics, Inc, 61-68, chief scientist, 68-71; physicist, Coherent, Inc, 72-93. *Concurrent Pos:* Lectr, Stanford Univ, 69-70, res assoc physics, 71-74. *Mem:* Fel AAAS; fel Am Phys Soc; fel Optical Soc Am. *Res:* Optical pumping, lasers; physical optics; gas lasers; organic dye lasers; optical thin films design and computation. *Mailing Add:* 1955 Oak Ave Menlo Park CA 94025-5843

BLOOM, ARTHUR DAVID, GENETICS, ENVIRONMENTAL HEALTH. *Current Pos:* PRES, INT COMT SCIENTISTS ENVIRON & HEALTH, PARIS, 94-; PROF PEDIAT & PATHOL, UNIV VT, BURLINGTON, 95- *Personal Data:* b Boston, Mass, Oct 4, 34; m 82, Deborah Jean Schwarz; c Karen Ruth, Michelle Ester, Robert Joseph & Noah Schwarz. *Educ:* Harvard Univ, AB, 56; NY Univ, MD, 60. *Prof Exp:* Intern pediat, Bellevue Hosp, NY, 60-61; asst resident, Johns Hopkins Hosp, Baltimore, Md, 61; surgeon, USPHS, NIH, 62-64; sr asst resident, Johns Hopkins Hosp, 64-65; cytogeneticist, Atomic Bomb Casualty Comn, Nat Res Coun, Hiroshima, Japan, 65-68; from asst prof to assoc prof human genetics & res assoc pediat, Med Sch, Univ Mich, Ann Arbor, 68-70; prof pediat, Human Genetics & Develop, Col Physicians & Surgeons, Columbia Univ, 78-88; attend physician & geneticist, Berkshire Med Ctr, 86-94. *Concurrent Pos:* Consult, Bur Radiol Health, USPHS, 68-70; Atomic Bomb Casualty Comn, Nat Res Coun, 68-74; mem, Pan Am Health Orgn, 76-79, Environ Mutagen Soc Coun, 77-80, bd sci counrs, NIH, USPHS, 82-86; prog comt chmn, Am Soc Human Genetics, 80 & bd dirs, 81-83; chmn, Adv Panel Genetic Screening Workplace, Off Technol Assessment, US Cong, 81-83; med dir, Diagenetic Labs Inc, Teaneck, NJ, 83-88; pres, Environ Health Inst, Pittsfield, MA, 86-94; ed, Bull Berkshire Med Ctr, 89-93; consult res, IRI Servier, Paris, France, 96- *Mem:* AAAS; Am Soc Human Genetics; Soc Pediat Res; Radiation Res Soc; Environ Mutagen Soc; Europ Soc Human Genetics. *Res:* Biological and clinical effects of environmental chemicals and radiations. *Mailing Add:* 33 Avenue du General Sarrail 75016 Paris France. *Fax:* 33-1-40-71-63-46

BLOOM, ARTHUR LEROY, TECTONICS. *Current Pos:* from asst prof to prof, 60-96, EMER PROF GEOL SCI, CORNELL UNIV, 96- *Personal Data:* b Genesee, Wis, Sept 2, 28; m 53, Donna Schulz; c Jeffrey A, Jay C & Eric F. *Educ:* Miami Univ, AB, 50; Victoria Univ, NZ, MA, 52; Yale Univ, PhD(geol), 59. *Hon Degrees:* DSc, Univ Maine, Orono, Me, 96. *Prof Exp:* Instr geol, Yale Univ, 59-60. *Concurrent Pos:* Fulbright sr scholar, James Cook Univ NQueensland, Townsville, Australia, 73; vis scientist, Japan Soc Prom Sci, 80 & 93. *Mem:* AAAS; Geol Soc Am; Int Union Quaternary Res; Am Quaternary Asn; Sigma Xi. *Res:* Glacier controlled sea level changes in the Quaternary period and tectonic geomorphology of island arcs in western Pacific coral reef zone; Pleistocene geology; tectonic geomorphology of the Andes. *Mailing Add:* Dept Geol Sci Cornell Univ 2122 Snee Hall Ithaca NY 14853-1504. *E-Mail:* bloom@geology.cornell.edu

BLOOM, BARRY MALCOLM, ORGANIC CHEMISTRY. *Current Pos:* RETIRED. *Personal Data:* b Roxbury, Mass, Aug 12, 28; m 56, Joan Ensign; c Catherine, Brian & Joanna. *Educ:* Mass Inst Technol, SB, 48, PhD(org chem), 51. *Hon Degrees:* LHD, Conn Col, 92. *Prof Exp:* Nat Res Coun fel, Univ Wis, 51-52; res chemist, Pfizer Inc, 52-58, res supvr, 58-59, mgr, 59- 63, dir med chem res, 63-68, Med Prod Res & Develop Div, 68-72, vpres res & develop, Pfizer Pharmaceut, 69-71, pres cent res, 71- 90, mem bd dirs, 73-93, sr vpres res & develop, 90-92, exec vpres 92-93. *Concurrent Pos:* US Cong Off Tech, Assessment, 76-77; mem, Conn High Tech Coun, 83, vis comn, Univ Conn, Inst Mat Sci; mem, Cong Comn Fed Drug Approval Process, Comt Drugs Rare Dis, Pharmaceut Mgr Asn, chmn, Res & Develop Sect, 76; Polytech Inst NY fel; mem bd dirs, Oncogene Sci Inc, 86-93, Southern New Eng Telecommun Corp, 87-, Cubist Pharmaceut, Inc, 93-, Neurogen Corp, 93-, Vertex Pharmaceut, Inc, 94-, Incyte Pharmaceut, Inc, 94- & Catalytica Fine Chem, 94-; mem bd mgrs, Lawrence & Mem Hosp, 89- *Mem:* Am Chem Soc. *Res:* Publication on drug research, government regulatory policy; administration of research and development of human therapeutics, agricultural and fine specialty chemical products. *Mailing Add:* 43 Mackintosh Rd Lyme CT 06371

BLOOM, BARRY R, IMMUNOLOGY. *Current Pos:* from asst prof to prof, Dept Microbiol & Immunol, 64-73, chmn dept, 78-90, WEINSTOCK PROF MICROBIOL & IMMUNOL, ALBERT EINSTEIN COL MED, 73-, INVESTR, HOWARD HUGHES MED INST, 90- *Personal Data:* b Philadelphia, Pa, Apr 13, 37; m 63. *Educ:* Amherst Col, AB, 58; Rockefeller Univ, PhD(immunol), 63. *Hon Degrees:* DSc, Amherst Col, 90. *Honors & Awards:* Oscar Besredka Prize for Immunol, WGer, 84; Shipley lectr, Harvard Univ, 88; Wellcome Distinguished lectr, Univ Conn, 89. *Prof Exp:* NSF fel, Wright-Fleming Inst, London, 63-64. *Concurrent Pos:* Vis asst prof, Dept Microbiol, Meharry Med Col, 64-65; sect ed cellular immunol, J Immunol, 69-75; consult immunol, WHO, 71-, int health, White House, 77-78, Nat Acad Sci, 83; chmn, Steering Comt Immunol Leprosy, WHO, 77-86, Basic Sci Study Sect, Nat Mult Sclerosis Soc, 79, US-Japan Leprosy Panel, 79-83, Comt Immunol Tuberculosis, WHO, 86- & Sci & Tech Adv Comt Res & Training Trop Dis, WHO, 89-; vis scientist, Lab Molecular Biol, Imp Cancer Res Fund, 84-85; mem, Bd Int Health, Inst Med, Nat Acad Sci, 85-88, Nat Adv Coun, Nat Inst Allergy & Infectious Dis, 88 & Bd Sci & Technol Develop, Nat Res Coun, 90- *Mem:* Nat Acad Sci; Inst Med-Nat Acad Sci; Am Asn Immunologists (vpres, 84, pres, 85-86); Fr Soc Immunol; Fedn Am Socs Exp Biol (vpres, 85-86); fel AAAS; Am Acad Arts & Sci. *Res:* Cell-mediated immunity; virus-lymphocyte interactions; leprosy and tuberculosis; vaccines. *Mailing Add:* Dept Microbiol Albert Einstein Col Med Bronx NY 10461

BLOOM, EDA TERRI, IMMUNOLOGY & CELL BIOLOGY. *Current Pos:* CHIEF, CELLULAR IMMUNOL, DIV CELL & GENE THER, CTR BIOLOGICS EVAL & RES, FOOD & DRUG ADMIN, 89-, ADJ PROF MICROBIOL & IMMUNOL, SCH MED, GEORGE WASHINGTON UNIV, 90- *Personal Data:* b Los Angeles, Calif, May 11, 45; m 83; c 1. *Educ:* Univ Calif, Los Angeles, AB, 66, PhD(med microbiol & immunol), 70. *Prof Exp:* USPHS postdoctoral fel, Sloan Kettering Inst Cancer Res, 70-71; lectr med microbiol & immunol, Univ Calif, Los Angeles, 71-72, asst res immunologist, 72-78 & 80-81, assoc res immunologist, 81-88, adj prof, 88-89; asst prof res med, Univ Southern Calif, 78-80. *Concurrent Pos:* Mem, Immunother Comt Rev Panel B, Nat Cancer Inst, 77-79 & Immunobiol Study Sect, NIH, 91-; res affil, Vet Admin Wadsworth Med Ctr, Geriat Res, Educ & Clin Ctr, 80-83; prin investr, USPHS, Dept Health & Human Serv, 81-89; chief, Lab Tumor Immunol, Geriat Res, Educ & Clin Ctr & supvry res biologist, Vet Admin W Los Angeles Med Ctr, 83-89; adj scientist, Cell Biol & Metab Br, Nat Inst Child Health & Human Develop, NIH, 88; mem Immunobiol Study Sect, 91-95. *Mem:* AAAS; Sigma Xi; Transplantation Soc; Am Asn Immunologists; Am Asn Cancer Res; NY Acad Sci; Soc Exp Biol & Med; Geront Soc Am; Am Pub Health Asn; Soc Leukocyte Biol. *Mailing Add:* Div Cell & Gene Therap Ctr Biologics Eval & Res Food & Drug Admin Bldg 29A Rm 2B-20 8800 Rockville Pike Bethesda MD 20892

BLOOM, ELLIOTT D, PARTICLE PHYSICS, PARTICLE ASTROPHYSICS. *Current Pos:* Res assoc physics, 67-70, asst prof, 70-74, assoc prof, 74-80, PROF PHYSICS, LINEAR ACCELERATOR CTR, STANFORD UNIV, 80- *Personal Data:* b New York, NY, June 11, 40; m 62, Susan J Wilmer; c Wendy & Matthew (deceased). *Educ:* Pomona Col, BA, 62; Calif Inst Technol, PhD(physics), 67. *Honors & Awards:* Alexander Von Humboldt Sr Scientist Award, 82. *Concurrent Pos:* Consult, Sci Appln, Inc, 75-82, Space Appln Inc, 85-86, Theta Corp, 85-87. *Mem:* Fel Am Phys Soc; Am Astron Soc. *Res:* Study of heavy flavor production and decay, high energy electron positron colliding beams; x-ray and gamma-ray space satellite experiments. *Mailing Add:* MS-98 Stanford Linear Accelerator Ctr Stanford Univ Stanford CA 94309. *Fax:* 650-926-4335; *E-Mail:* elliott@slac.stanford.edu

BLOOM, EVERETT E, MECHANICAL ENGINEERING. *Current Pos:* Res staff mem, Mech Prop & Electron Micros Groups, 64-79, group leader, Radiation Effects & Microstruct Anal Group, 79-82, MGR MAT SCI SECT & FUSION MAT PROG, METALS & CERAMICS DIV, OAK RIDGE NAT LAB, 82- *Educ:* SD Sch Mines & Technol, BS, 63; Univ Tenn, MS, 64, PhD(metall eng) 70. *Mem:* Fel Am Soc Metals Int; Am Nuclear Soc. *Res:* Mechanical and physical metallurgy of materials with emphasis on materials for fission and fusion reactor applications; radiation effects in materials; development of improved materials for reactor applications. *Mailing Add:* 612 Dogwood Valley Kingston TN 37763

BLOOM, FLOYD ELLIOTT, NEUROSCIENCES, CYTOCHEMISTRY. *Current Pos:* dir & mem, Div Preclin Neurosci & Endocrinol, 83-89, CHMN & MEM, DEPT NEUROPHARMACOL, SCRIPPS CLIN & RES FOUND, LA JOLLA, CALIF, 89- *Personal Data:* b Minneapolis, Minn, Oct 8, 36; m; c 2. *Educ:* Southern Methodist Univ, AB, 56; Wash Univ, MD, 60. *Hon Degrees:* Dr, Southern Methodist Univ, 83, Hahnemann Univ, 85 & Univ Rochester, 85. *Honors & Awards:* A E Bennett Award, Soc Biol Psychiat, 71; A Cressy Morrison Award, NY Acad Sci, 71; Arthur S Flemming Award, 72; Mathilde Solowey Award, 73; McAplin Award, Nat Asn Ment Health, 80; Harold Cummins Mem lectr, 81; Paul Lamson lectr, Vanderbilt Univ, 82; Marjorie Guthrie lectr, NIH, 84; Albert Dorfman lectr, Univ Chicago, 87; George Klenk lectr & Medal, Univ Cologne, 87; John D DeLuca lectr, Nat Libr Med, 88; Erspamer lectr, Georgetown Univ, 89; Janssen Award, 89; Pasarow Award, 89; Hermann von Helmholtz Award, 90. *Prof Exp:* Intern & asst resident med, Barnes Hosp, St Louis, Mo, 60-62; NIMH res assoc, St Elizabeth's Hosp, Washington, DC, 62-64; USPHS spec fel anat, Sch Med, Yale Univ, 64-66, asst prof anat & pharmacol, 66-67, assoc prof pharmacol, 68; actg chief, Lab Neuropharmacol, Div Spec Ment Health Res Progs, NIMH, St Elizabeth's Hosp, 68-69 & chief, 69-75, chief, Sect Cytochem Pharmacol, 68-75, actg div dir, 73-75; dir, Arthur V Davis Ctr Behav Neurobiol, Salk Inst, San Diego, Calif, 75-83. *Concurrent Pos:* Asst med, Sch Med, Wash Univ, 60-62; assoc physiol, Sch Med, George Washington Univ, 62-64; res career develop award, Nat Inst Neurol Dis & Blindness, 66-68; consult, Merck, Sharpe & Dohme, 76-82, Nova Pharmaceut, 82-, Comt Sci, Eng & Pub Policy, Nat Acad Sci, 82- & McNeil Pharmaceut, 83-; adj prof, Depts Neurosci & Psychiat, Univ Calif, San Diego, 77, Depts Pharmacol & Psychiat, Col Med, Univ Calif, Irvine, 82-; vis prof, Col France, 79; chmn, Neurobiol Sect, Nat Acad Sci, 79-83 & 85-86, & Comt Policies Allocation Resources Biomed Rest, Inst Med, 88-90; Wellcome vis prof, Royal Soc Med, 84; co-chmn, Gordon Conf Reptiles, 88. *Mem:* Nat Acad Sci; Inst Med-Nat Acad Sci; Soc Neurosci (secy, 73-75, pres, 76-77); Am Soc Cell Biol; Am Soc Pharmacol & Exp Therapeut; Sigma Xi; Am Asn Anatomists; fel Am Col Neuropsychopharmacol; Am Physiol Soc; fel AAAS. *Res:* Chemical control of neuronal activity; neuronal basis of behavior and drug action; author of various technical publications and books. *Mailing Add:* Scripps Clin & Res Found 1055 N Torrey Pines Rd Mail Drop SBR-1 La Jolla CA 92037

BLOOM, HOWARD M, ELECTRICAL ENGINEERING. *Current Pos:* DEP DIR MFR, ENG LAB, NAT INST STAND & TECHNOL, 97- *Educ:* Univ Md, MS, 67. *Mailing Add:* Nat Inst Stand & Technol Bldg 220 Rte 270 Gaithersburg MD 20899

BLOOM, JAMES R, PLANT PATHOLOGY. *Current Pos:* from asst prof to prof, 53-87, EMER PROF, PLANT PATH, PA STATE UNIV, 87- *Personal Data:* b Clearfield, Pa, Feb 20, 24; m 47, June Farwell; c James R Jr, Heidi L, Gretchen E & Coralie A. *Educ:* Pa State Univ, BS, 50; Univ Wis, PhD, 53. *Prof Exp:* Asst plant path, Univ Wis, 50-53. *Mem:* Am Phytopath Soc; Soc Nematol. *Res:* Phytonematology and disease of vegetable crops; interactions between plant pathogens. *Mailing Add:* Dept Plant Path Buckhout Lab Pa State Univ University Park PA 16802

BLOOM, JEROME H(ERSHEL), ELECTRICAL ENGINEERING. *Current Pos:* RETIRED. *Personal Data:* b Boston, Mass, May 20, 24; m 53; c 2. *Educ:* Northeastern Univ, BS, 45. *Prof Exp:* Test engr, Sylvania Elec Prod, Inc, 45-46; electronic scientist & chief vacuum electronics sect, Air Force Cambridge Res Ctr, 46-63, phys scientist, 63-84. *Concurrent Pos:* Pvt consult vacuum deposition for semiconductor prod & res with thin films. *Mem:* AAAS; Inst Elec & Electronics Engrs; Am Vacuum Soc; Int Union Vacuum Sci Tech & Appln. *Res:* Vacuum tube materials and techniques; semi-conductor thin films; infrared sensors; electron beam lithography; ion implantation. *Mailing Add:* 37 Montclair Rd Waban MA 02168-1122

BLOOM, JOSEPH MORRIS, FRACTURE & APPLIED MECHANICS. *Current Pos:* RES SPECIALIST, RES CTR, BABCOCK & WILCOX CORP, 72- *Personal Data:* b Indianapolis, Ind, Apr 26, 37; m 63; c 2. *Educ:* Purdue Univ, BS, 59; Harvard Univ, SM, 60, PhD(appl math), 64. *Prof Exp:* Asst elasticity, Harvard Univ, 62-64; mathematician, US Army Mat Res Agency, Watertown, 64-66; prin scientist, Aeronutronic Div, Philco-Ford, 66-68; scientist, Mat Sci Lab, Lockheed-Ga Co, 68-70, sr tech specialist, McDonnell-Douglas Corp, 70-72. *Mem:* Am Soc Mech Engrs; Am Soc Testing & Mat; Sigma Xi. *Res:* Research and development in fracture mechanics of pressure vessel materials; elastic and plastic probability. *Mailing Add:* 908 22nd St NE Canton OH 44714-2039

BLOOM, KERRY STEVEN, CELL BIOLOGY, CHROMOSOME MECHANICS. *Current Pos:* from asst prof to assoc prof, 82-94, PROF BIOL, UNIV NC, CHAPEL HILL, 94- *Personal Data:* b Washington, DC, Dec 28, 53; m 83, Elaine Yeh; c 1. *Educ:* Tulane Univ, BS, 75; Purdue Univ, PhD(molecular biol), 80. *Honors & Awards:* Hettleman Award; Symp lectr ann meeting, Am Soc Cell Biologists, 83. *Prof Exp:* Teaching fel, Jane Coffin Childs Mem Fund Med Res, Univ Calif, Santa Barbara, 80-82. *Concurrent*

Pos: Instr physiol, Marine Biol Lab, Woods Hole, Mass, 85-89, co-dir physiol, 96- *Mem:* Am Soc Cell Biologists; Sigma Xi; Genetics Soc Am. *Res:* Chromosome mechanics in yeast; DNA-protein interaction at the centromere; structural organization of eukaryotic chromosomes; microtubule associated proteins; dynein structure and function. *Mailing Add:* Dept Biol Univ NC Fordham Hall CB No 3280 Chapel Hill NC 27599-3280. *Fax:* 919-962-1625; *E-Mail:* kerry_bloom@unc.edu

BLOOM, L(OUIS) R(ICHARD), TELECOMMUNICATION SCIENCES. *Current Pos:* GROUP CHIEF NEW TECHNOL, NAT TELECOMMUN & INFO ADMIN, INST TELECOMMUN SCI, BOULDER, 75- *Personal Data:* b Chicago, Ill, May 9, 14; m 42; c 4. *Educ:* Univ Ill, BS, 38, MS, 41, EE, 50. *Prof Exp:* Asst physics, Univ Ill, 36-39, asst elec eng, 40-43, asst prof, 46-53; res engr, Radio Corp Am, 43-46; head microwave tube sect, Sylvania Res Labs, 53-58, mgr phys electronics lab, 58-60, sci adv to dir res, 61-63; prog mgr mat sci & electronic devices, Gen Tel & Electronics Lab, 64-67, mgr phys electronics & electronic mat, 67-69, dir phys electronics lab & assoc dir res, 69-73; assoc div chief, Electromagnetic Div, Dept Commerce, Boulder, 73-75. *Mem:* Fel AAAS; Am Phys Soc; fel Inst Elec & Electronics Engrs; Sigma Xi; Optical Soc Am. *Res:* Microwaves; laser devices; electro-optical behavior of materials; optical communications; microwaves; electron beam devices; telecommunications; interactive information systems; fiber optical communication systems. *Mailing Add:* 2240 Linden Ave Boulder CO 80304-1617

BLOOM, MIRIAM, GENETIC TOXICOLOGY, ENVIRONMENTAL MUTAGENESIS. *Current Pos:* PRES, SCIWRITE, 89- *Personal Data:* b New York, NY, Dec 25, 34; m 60, Sherman; c Naomi & Stephanie. *Educ:* Brooklyn Col, BS, 57; Univ Utah, PhD(genetics), 72. *Prof Exp:* Instr bot & hort, Brooklyn Bot Gardens, 63-66; vis scholar chem, Univ Calif, Los Angeles, 72; asst res prof biol, Univ Utah, 73; fel, Univ Southern Fla, 74, res assoc, 75; adj prof, Hillsborough Community Col, 75-77; USPHS res training awardee, Col Med, Georgetown Univ, 77-79; geneticist, US Consumer Prod Safety Comn, 79-88. *Concurrent Pos:* Mem, Interagency Regulatory Liaison Group, 79-81; liaison, HHS Subcomt Environ Mutagenesis, Comt Coord Environ Related Probs, 80-86; appointee, Interagency Radiation Res Comt, 80-82; ed, Environ Mutagen Soc Newsletter, 85-90; counr, Environ Mutagen Soc, 87-88, & Fed Asbestos Task Force, 88-; secy, Environ Mutagen Soc, 89-91; sr ed, J Nat Cancer Inst, NIH, 92-94. *Mem:* Coun Biol Ed; Am Med Writers Asn; Environ Mutagen Soc; Int Fedn Sci Editors; Europ Asn Sci Editors. *Res:* Biochemical genetics of floral flavonoid patterning; pattern evolution; genetic toxicology of environmental chemicals; biomedical communication. *Mailing Add:* 4433 Wedgewood St Jackson MI 39211. *Fax:* 601-982-1933

BLOOM, MYER, PHYSICS, PHYSICAL PROPERTIES OF NATURAL MATERIALS. *Current Pos:* res assoc physics, 56-57, from asst prof to prof, 57-63, EMER PROF PHYSICS, UNIV BC, 94- *Personal Data:* b Montreal, Que, Dec 7, 28; m 54, Margaret Holmes; c David & Margot. *Educ:* McGill Univ, BSc, 49, MSc, 50; Univ Ill, PhD(physics), 54. *Hon Degrees:* Dr, Tech Univ Denmark, 94, Concordia Univ, Montreal Can, 95. *Honors & Awards:* Steacie Prize, 67; Jacob Biely Prize, 69; Gold Medal, Can Asn Physicists, 73; Izaak Walton Killam Mem Prize Nat Sci, 95. *Prof Exp:* Nat Res Coun Can traveling fel, Kamerlingh Onnes Lab, Univ Leiden, Holland, 54-56. *Concurrent Pos:* Alfred P Sloan fel, 61-65; Guggenheim fel, 64-65; fel, Can Inst Advan Res, 89- *Mem:* Am Phys Soc; Can Asn Physicists; Royal Soc Can; Biophys Soc. *Res:* Nuclear magnetic resonance; spin relaxation; biological membranes. *Mailing Add:* Dept Physics Univ BC 6224 Agricultural Rd Vancouver BC V6T 1Z1 Can. *Fax:* 604-822-5324; *E-Mail:* bloom@physics.ubc.ca

BLOOM, SANFORD GILBERT, CHEMICAL ENGINEERING. *Current Pos:* ENG SPECIALIST, MARTIN MARIETTA, 87- *Personal Data:* b Columbus, Ohio, Apr 11, 37; m 60, 79, Gayle Pearlman; c Craig. *Educ:* Ohio State Univ, BChE & MSc, 59, PhD(chem eng), 64. *Prof Exp:* Sr res engr, Petrol Prod, Atlantic Richfield Co, 64-66; assoc fel, Ecol & Environ Systs Div, Battelle Mem Inst, 66-77, prin scientist, Columbus Labs, 77-83, staff chem engr, Battelle Proj Mgt Div, 83-87. *Mem:* AAAS; Am Inst Chem Engrs; Soc Petrol Engrs. *Res:* Mathematical analysis of engineering problems of heat and mass transfer; atmospheric dispersion; fluid flow in porous media; hydraulic fracturing; ecosystem modeling; mathematical analysis of biological systems. *Mailing Add:* 7104 Delbourne Dr Knoxville TN 37919

BLOOM, SHERMAN, CARDIOVASCULAR PATHOLOGY, CELL BIOLOGY. *Current Pos:* PROF & CHAIR PATH, UNIV MISS COL MED, 88- *Personal Data:* b Brooklyn, NY, Jan 26, 34; m 60, Mirian Fishman; c Naomi & Stephanie. *Educ:* NY Univ, AB, 55, MD, 60. *Prof Exp:* Res trainee exp path, NY Univ, 61-65, instr path, 65-66; from asst prof to assoc prof, Univ Utah, 66-73; from assoc prof to prof path, Univ SFla, 73-77, actg chmn path, 77; prof path, George Washington Univ, 77-88. *Concurrent Pos:* Vis assoc prof physiol, Med Ctr, Univ Calif, Los Angeles, 72; consult, Nat Heart & Lung Inst, 74 & Drug Toxicol Br, Food & Drug Admin, 78-; bd dir, Scientists Ctr Animal Welfare, 81-; bd dir, Am Col Nutrit, 87- *Mem:* NY Acad Sci; Int Study Group Res Cardiac Metab; Am Soc Invest Path; Am Physiol Soc; Soc Cardiovasc Path (pres, 86-87); US & Can Acad Path. *Res:* Determinants of myocardial necrosis; role of dietary metals in cardiovascular resistance to stress; control of myocardial contractility; ultrastructure of myocardial cells and interstitium; role of cell structure in passive mechanical properties; cardiac toxicology. *Mailing Add:* Dept Path Univ Miss Med Ctr 2500 N State St Jackson MS 39216-4505. *Fax:* 601-984-1531; *E-Mail:* sbloom@pathology.umsmed.edu

BLOOM, STANLEY, ELECTRONICS, ELECTRON OPTICS. *Current Pos:* RETIRED. *Personal Data:* b Plainfield, NJ, Oct 18, 24; m 48; c 4. *Educ:* Rutgers Univ, BS, 48; Yale Univ, MS, 51, PhD(physics), 52. *Prof Exp:* Sr mem staff, RCA Labs, 52-87. *Concurrent Pos:* RCA Corp res fel, Cambridge Univ, 66-67. *Mem:* Inst Elec & Electronics Engrs; Am Phys Soc. *Res:* Microwave electronics; plasma physics; noise; quantum electronics; solid state; electron optics. *Mailing Add:* 1185 Sherlin Dr Bridgewater NJ 08807

BLOOM, STEPHEN ALLEN, QUANTITATIVE MACROBENTHIC ECOLOGY. *Current Pos:* ASST PROF MARINE ECOL & INVERT ZOOL, DEPT ZOOL, UNIV FLA, 76-, CHIEF SCIENTIST, ECOL DATA CONSULT INC, 79- *Personal Data:* b Tucson, Ariz, Mar 9, 47; m 70. *Educ:* Univ SFla, BA, 69; Univ Wash, PhD(zool), 74. *Prof Exp:* Asst, Dept Biol, Univ SFla, 74-75, vis asst prof marine ecol, 75-76. *Concurrent Pos:* Vis instr marine ecol, Duke Marine Lab, Beaufort, NC, 76; adj sr res scientist, Mote Marine Labs, Sarasota, Fla, 82- *Mem:* Ecol Soc Am; Sigma Xi; AAAS; Am Zool Soc. *Res:* Investigation of community structure, population dynamics and autecology of marine macroinfauna by descriptive and experimental approaches; development of analytical techniques for community ecology. *Mailing Add:* PO Box 760 Archer FL 32618-0760

BLOOM, STEPHEN EARL, TOXICOLOGY, CYTOGENETICS. *Current Pos:* from asst prof to assoc prof, 68-81, PROF CYTOGENETICS, CORNELL UNIV, 81-, ASSOC DIR ENVIRON TOXICOL, 86- *Personal Data:* b Brooklyn, NY, Oct 18, 41; m 90, Donna Muscarella; c 2. *Educ:* Long Island Univ, BS, 63; Pa State Univ, MS, 65, PhD(genetics), 68. *Honors & Awards:* Merck Award Sci Achievement, 89. *Prof Exp:* Asst genetics, Pa State Univ, 63-68. *Concurrent Pos:* Vis prof biol, Univ Tex M D Anderson Hosp & Tumor Inst Houston, 75; vis staff scientist, Worcester Found Exp Biol, 81. *Mem:* AAAS; Am Genetic Asn; Soc Exp Biol & Med; Poultry Sci Asn; Am Inst Biol Sci; Environ Mutagen Soc. *Res:* Cellular and molecular mechanisms of resistance and susceptibility of differentiating lymphocytes to toxic damage induced by drugs and environmental toxins; genetic and cytogenetic alterations influencing embryonic development. *Mailing Add:* Microbiol & Immunol C 4111 Vet Med Ctr Cornell Univ Ithaca NY 14853

BLOOM, STEWART DAVE, NUCLEAR PHYSICS. *Current Pos:* RETIRED. *Personal Data:* b Chicago, Ill, Aug 22, 23; m 49, Sally Shourai; c 3. *Educ:* Univ Chicago, PhD(physics), 52. *Prof Exp:* Assoc physicist, Brookhaven Nat Labs, 52-56; Guggenheim res fel, Cambridge Univ, 56-57; staff physicist, 57-69, prof appl sci, Lawrence Radiation Lab, 69-90. *Concurrent Pos:* Fulbright fel, France, 63. *Mem:* Fel Am Phys Soc. *Res:* Beta ray; nuclear reactions; nuclear astrophysics. *Mailing Add:* Lawrence Radiation Lab Livermore CA 94550

BLOOM, VICTOR, PSYCHIATRY, PSYCHOANALYSIS. *Current Pos:* CLIN ASSOC PROF PSYCHIAT, SCH MED, WAYNE STATE UNIV, 72- *Personal Data:* b New York, NY, Aug 17, 31; m 73, Shirley I Kemp-Dobie; c Dorcas, Gordon, Claire, David & Elizabeth. *Educ:* Univ Mich, BS, MD, 57; Am Bd Psychiat & Neurol, dipl & cert psychiat, 63. *Prof Exp:* Intern med, Sinai Hosp Detroit, 57-58; resident psychiat, Lafayette Clin, 58-61, staff psychiatrist, 61-67, chief adult inpatient serv, 68-72. *Concurrent Pos:* Instr, Sch Med, Wayne State Univ, 61-63, asst prof, 64-72; teacher, Lafayette Clin, 61-; lectr psychiat, Mich State Dept Ment Health, 61-69; pvt pract psychiat & psychoanal, 62-; consult group psychother, Neuropsychiat Inst, Med Sch, Univ Mich, 68-69 & Kidney Ctr, Mt Carmel Mercy Hosp, 68-82; consult group ther, Harper Hosp Sch Nursing, 72-76; lectr, individual & group psychother, Univ Psychiat Ctr, Detroit, Mich. *Mem:* Fel Am Psychiat Asn; fel Am Group Psychother Asn; hon assoc mem Inst Bioenergetic Anal Asn; assoc Am Acad Psychoanal. *Res:* Psychoanalysis; psychotherapy; group psychotherapy; suicide prevention; schizophrenia; milieu therapy; bioenergetic analysis; bioenergetics in group therapy; presentations and papers on gender of therapist; long term psychotherapy of schizophrenic patient; sociopathic physician; book and movie reviews, essays on politics, philosophy and popular culture. *Mailing Add:* 1007 Three Mile Dr Grosse Pointe Park MI 48230

BLOOMBERG, WILFRED, psychiatry, neurology; deceased, see previous edition for last biography

BLOOMER, JAMES L, ORGANIC CHEMISTRY, CHIRAL SYNTHESIS. *Current Pos:* asst prof, 65-70, ASSOC PROF ORG CHEM, TEMPLE UNIV, 70- *Personal Data:* b Knoxville, Tenn, Jan 6, 39. *Educ:* Univ Tenn, BS, 59, MS, 61; Univ London, PhD(org chem), 64. *Prof Exp:* NSF fel org chem, Harvard Univ, 64-65. *Concurrent Pos:* NSF res grant, 66-68; NIH res grant, 69-71. *Mem:* Am Chem Soc; Brit Chem Soc. *Res:* Synthetic organic chemistry. *Mailing Add:* Dept Chem 016-00 Temple Univ Philadelphia PA 19122

BLOOMER, OSCAR T(HEODORE), CHEMICAL ENGINEERING. *Current Pos:* from sr develop engr to sect supvr, coating & drying of photog films, 53-69, asst dir, 69-71, DIR MFG TECH DIV, EASTMAN KODAK CO, 71- *Personal Data:* b St Joseph, Mo, Aug 21, 23; m 48; c 3. *Educ:* Univ Kans, BS, 44; Ill Inst Technol, MS, 51, PhD(chem eng), 54. *Prof Exp:* Jr engr, chem eng design, Eastman Kodak Co, 44-48; sr res engr, gas technol, Inst Gas Technol, 48-53. *Mem:* AAAS; Am Chem Soc. *Res:* Process development; coating and drying of photographic films and papers; pressure-volume-temperature relationships; thermodynamic properties; phase equilibrium of gases at low temperatures. *Mailing Add:* 83 Coronado Dr Rochester NY 14617

BLOOMFIELD, DANIEL KERMIT, MEDICINE, BIOCHEMISTRY. *Current Pos:* RETIRED. *Personal Data:* b Cleveland, Ohio, Dec 14, 26; m 55; c 3. *Educ:* US Naval Acad, BS, 47; Western Reserve Univ, MS & MD, 54. *Prof Exp:* From intern to asst resident, Beth Israel Hosp, 54-56; resident, Mass Gen Hosp, 56-57; fel biochem, Harvard Univ, 57-59; hon asst registr, Inst Cardiol, 59-60; asst med, Western Reserve Univ, 60-64; dir cardiovasc res, Community Health Found, 64-66; assoc med, Mt Sinai Hosp, 66-69; dean, Sch Med, Univ Ill, Urbana-Champaign, 70-84, prof med, 70-84, emer prof med, 84-96. *Mem:* Fel Am Col Physicians; Am Fedn Clin Res; Sigma Xi. *Res:* Biosynthesis of unsaturated fatty acids; cardiac arrhythmias; gas chromatography of steroids; cholesterol metabolism; congenital heart disease; hypertension anticoagulant therapy; mass cardiac screening; medical education. *Mailing Add:* 103 E Michigan Urbana IL 61801

BLOOMFIELD, DAVID PETER, FUEL CELLS, ELECTROCHEMICAL ENGINEERING. *Current Pos:* PRES, ANAL POWER CORP, 84- *Personal Data:* b New York, NY, Mar 27, 38; m 58; c 2. *Educ:* Polytech Inst NY, BME, 61; Rensselaer Polytech Inst, MS, 70. *Prof Exp:* Asst proj engr, Power Systs Div, United Technologies Corp, 65-77; sr proj engr, Giner, Inc, 77-78; vpres systs div, Phys Sci Inc, 78-84. *Mem:* Am Soc Mech Engrs; Am Chem Soc; Electrochem Soc. *Res:* Power plant and chemical process systems analysis; electrochemical and heat transfer design and analysis; microcomputer software development. *Mailing Add:* 160 Commonwealth Ave No 301 Boston MA 02116-2737

BLOOMFIELD, DENNIS ALEXANDER, CARDIOLOGY, INTERNAL MEDICINE. *Current Pos:* DIR MED & CHIEF CARDIOL, CATH LAB, ST VINCENTS MED CTR, STATEN ISLAND, 75-, PROF CLIN MED, NY MED COL, 79-, ASSOC DEAN, 96- *Personal Data:* b Perth, Western Australia, May 4, 33; m 64, Elaine Raichlen; c Lisa, Leslie & Nanette. *Educ:* Univ Adelaide, MB, BS, 56. *Prof Exp:* Australian Heart Found traveling fel cardiol, Vanderbilt Univ Hosp, 62-65; fel, Inst Cardiol, London, Eng, 65-66; dir, Cardiol Cath Lab, Maimonides Med Ctr, 67-75. *Mem:* Fel Royal Col Physicians; fel Am Col Chest Physicians; fel Am Col Physicians; fel Am Col Cardiol; fel Australasian Col Physicians; fel Soc Cardiac Angiography & Interventions. *Res:* Application of indicator-dilution techniques to the measurement of regurgitant and regional blood flows; author or coauthor of over 50 publications. *Mailing Add:* 355 Bard Ave Staten Island NY 10310. *Fax:* 718-876-1135; *E-Mail:* debloom@aol.com

BLOOMFIELD, HAROLD H, family therapy & psychospiritual counseling, holistic medicine, for more information see previous edition

BLOOMFIELD, JORDAN JAY, ORGANIC CHEMISTRY. *Current Pos:* PRES, J CHEM RES, 93- *Personal Data:* b South Bend, Ind, Feb 25, 30; m 60, 84, Doris J Jameson; c Jaclyn, Linda & Janet. *Educ:* Univ Calif, Los Angeles, BS, 52; Mass Inst Technol, PhD(org chem), 58. *Honors & Awards:* St Louis Award, Am Chem Soc, 80. *Prof Exp:* Asst chem, Mass Inst Technol, 52-53, res, 55-57; instr, Univ Tex, 57-60; res assoc, Univ Ill, 60-61, Univ Ariz, 61-62; asst prof, Univ Okla, 62-66 & assoc prof on leave, 66-67; sr res specialist, 67-81, fel, Monsanto Co, 81-85; vis prof, Dept Chem, Univ Mich, 85-86; vpres res, Organic Consults Inc, 87-93. *Concurrent Pos:* Vis prof & sr res group leader, 66-67; vis assoc prof, Univ Mo, St Louis, 75, adj prof, 78-87. *Mem:* AAAS; Am Chem Soc; Royal Soc Chem. *Res:* Reaction mechanisms; transannular reactions; molecular rearrangements; small rings; bicyclic and polycyclic systems of unusual structure; organic synthesis. *Mailing Add:* 88587 Ellmaker Rd Veneta OR 97487

BLOOMFIELD, LOUIS AUB, ATOMIC & MOLECULAR PHYSICS. *Current Pos:* from asst prof to assoc prof, 85-95, PROF PHYSICS, UNIV VA, 96- *Personal Data:* b Boston, Mass, Oct 11, 56; m 83, Karen Shatkin; c Elana & Aaron. *Educ:* Amherst Col, BA, 79; Stanford Univ, PhD(physics), 83. *Honors & Awards:* Apker Award, Am Phys Soc; Pres Young Investr Award, NSF, 86; Young Investr Award, Off Naval Res, 88. *Prof Exp:* Fel physics, Stanford Univ, 83 & AT&T Bell Labs, 83-85. *Concurrent Pos:* Sloan fel, 89. *Mem:* Am Phys Soc; Sigma Xi. *Res:* Clusters of atoms and the origins of solid state behavior; atomic and molecular physics; laser physics and nonlinear optics. *Mailing Add:* Dept Physics Univ Va Charlottesville VA 22901. *Fax:* 804-924-4576; *E-Mail:* lab3e@virginia.edu

BLOOMFIELD, PHILIP EARL, SOLID STATE PHYSICS, THEORETICAL PHYSICS. *Current Pos:* res prof, Mat Eng Dept, 89-92, RES PROF, BIOMED ENG & SCI INST, DREXEL UNIV, 92- *Personal Data:* b Erie, Pa, Aug 28, 34; m 58; c 2. *Educ:* Univ Chicago, BA, 56, BS, 57, MS, 59, PhD(physics), 65. *Honors & Awards:* Army Res & Develop Award, 76. *Prof Exp:* Technician, Nat Bur Stand, Washington, DC, 56-57; physicist, Lab Appl Sci, Univ Chicago, 58-60; res asst solid state physics, Inst Study Metals, 60-64; asst prof physics, Univ Pa, 64-69; assoc prof, Drexel Univ, 69-70 & City Col New York, 70-73; physicist, Nat Bur Stand, Gaithersburg, Md, 74-76; sr res scientist, Pennwalt Corp, 76-87; vis scientist, Physics Dept, Univ Pa, 88. *Concurrent Pos:* Instr, Univ Chicago Col, 58-59; res assoc, John Crerar Libr, Ill, 57; lectr, Ill Inst Technol, 62; ed, Accelerated Instr Methods, Ill, 62-63; consult, Pittman Dunn Labs, Frankford Arsenal, Pa, 67-74; mem, Comt Ferroelectrics, Ultrasonics Ferroelectrics & Frequency Control Soc, Inst Elec & Electronics Engrs; owner, Alternative Techniques, 87-; prin scientist, Imperium Inc, 97- *Mem:* Am Phys Soc; Am Ceramic Soc; Inst Elec & Electronics Engrs; fel Sigma Xi. *Res:* Thermodynamics; statistical mechanics; electromagnetic phenomena in solids and dense media; ferroelectrics; magnetics; optical properties of metals and insulators; piezoelectric actuators and sensors; pyroelectric sensors; applications of electroactive polymers. *Mailing Add:* 210 Lone Oak Dr Bryn Mawr PA 19010

BLOOMFIELD, SAUL, CLINICAL PHARMACOLOGY. *Current Pos:* PROF MED & PHARMACOL, UNIV CINCINNATI, 77- *Personal Data:* b Montreal, Que, June 30, 25; m 49; c 3. *Educ:* Univ Geneva, MD, 53. *Concurrent Pos:* Consult drug eval, AMA, 74-; vis prof & prin investr, Oxford Univ Churchill Hosp, 80; mem orphans prod develop, initial rev group & arthritis adv comt liason, 83- *Mem:* Am Soc Clin Pharmacol & Therapeut; Am Fedn Clin Res; NY Acad Sci. *Res:* Clinical pharmacology and clinical testing of new analgesic agents for efficacy and safety; methodology of clinical trials of investigational new drugs, phases 1,2 &3. *Mailing Add:* Dept Internal Med Univ Cincinnati Med Ctr PO Box 670578 Cincinnati OH 45267-0578

BLOOMFIELD, VICTOR ALFRED, BIOPHYSICAL CHEMISTRY, MOLECULAR BIOPHYSICS. *Current Pos:* assoc prof, Univ Minn, St Paul, 70-74, prof biochem & chem, 74-79, Head, Biochem Dept, 79-91, PROF, DEPT BIOCHEM, UNIV MINN, ST PAUL, 79- *Personal Data:* b Newark, NJ, June 10, 38; m 93, Elsa G Shapiro. *Educ:* Univ Calif, Berkeley, BS, 59; Univ Wis, PhD(phys chem), 62. *Prof Exp:* NSF fel phys chem, Univ Calif, San Diego, 62-64; from asst prof to assoc prof, Univ Ill, 64-70. *Concurrent Pos:* Alfred P Sloan Found fel, 69-71; NIH career develop award, 71-76; co-chmn, Gordon Res Conf Physics & Phys Chem of Biopolymers, 74; mem, NIH Study Sect BBCB, 75-78; mem biophys panel, NSF, 80; secy, Biol Chem Div, Am Chem Soc, 81-83; Fogarty scholar, NIH, 85-86; ed, Biophys J, 92-97. *Mem:* Fel AAAS; Am Chem Soc; Am Soc Biol Chem; Biophys Soc (pres, 87); Sigma Xi. *Res:* Physical chemistry of biological macromolecules, viruses and other high polymers; biological hydrodynamics; quasi-elastic laser light scattering; DNA condensation; polyelectrolytes. *Mailing Add:* Dept Biochem Col Biol Sci Univ Minn 140 Gortner Lab St Paul MN 55108. *Fax:* 612-625-5780; *E-Mail:* victor@biosci.cbs.umn.edu

BLOOMQUIST, EUNICE, PHYSIOLOGY. *Current Pos:* From instr to assoc prof physiol, 69-76, actg chair, 80-84, PROF PHYSIOL, SCH MED, TUFTS UNIV, 84- *Personal Data:* b Worcester, Mass, Sept 9, 40; m 70; c 2. *Educ:* Simmons Col, BS, 63; Boston Univ, PhD(physiol), 68. *Mem:* Am Physiol Soc; Soc Gen Physiologists; NY Acad Sci. *Res:* Airway smooth muscle and inflammation; neuropeptides. *Mailing Add:* Dept Physiol Tufts Univ Med Sch 136 Harrison Ave Boston MA 02111-1800

BLOOMSBURG, GEORGE L, AGRICULTURAL & CIVIL ENGINEERING. *Current Pos:* DIR, IDAHO WATER RESOURCES RES INST, 84- *Personal Data:* b Salmon, Idaho, Mar 28, 31; m 55; c 3. *Educ:* Univ Idaho, BS, 57, MS, 59; Colo State Univ, PhD(civil eng), 64. *Prof Exp:* Agr engr, agr res serv, US Dept Agr, 58-59; hydraul engr, Wash State Univ, 60-61; asst res prof hydraul, Univ Idaho, 61-62, assoc prof irrig, 64-68, prof agr eng & eng sci & chmn dept eng sci, 68-76, eng res coordr, 76-79, prof agr eng & eng sci, 79- *Mem:* Am Soc Agr Engrs; Nat Soc Prof Engrs; Nat Water Well Asn. *Res:* Fluid mechanics; hydrology; irrigation and drainage. *Mailing Add:* 2680 W Wildwood Park Univ Idaho Worley ID 83876

BLOOR, COLIN MERCER, PATHOLOGY, PHYSIOLOGY. *Current Pos:* from asst prof to assoc prof, 68-74, co-chmn dept, 76-78, PROF PATH, UNIV CALIF, SAN DIEGO, 74-, DIR, MOLECULAR PATH GRAD PROG, 89- *Personal Data:* b Sandusky, Ohio, May 26, 33; m 59; c 3. *Educ:* Denison Univ, BS, 55; Yale Univ, MD, 60. *Prof Exp:* From intern to resident path, Yale Univ, 60-62. *Concurrent Pos:* USPHS trainee path, 60-62; Life Ins Med Res Fund fel physiol, Nuffield Inst Med Res, 62-63 & fel path, Yale Univ, 63-64. *Mem:* Am Physiol Soc; Am Asn Pathologists & Bacteriologists; Am Soc Exp Path; Am Col Cardiol; Int Acad Pathologists. *Res:* Cardiovascular physiology and pathology, particularly the coronary circulation and coronary artery disease; effects of exercise on the development of coronary collateral circulation; cardiovascular genetics; exercise physiology. *Mailing Add:* Dept Path Sch Med 0612 Univ Calif at San Diego 9500 Gilman Dr La Jolla CA 92093-0612

BLOOR, JOHN E, CHEMISTRY. *Current Pos:* ASSOC PROF CHEM, UNIV TENN, KNOXVILLE, 69- *Personal Data:* b Stoke on Trent, Eng, Aug 31, 29; m 61; c 2. *Educ:* Oxford Univ, BA, 52; Univ Manchester, PhD(chem), 59. *Prof Exp:* Res chemist, Clayton Aniline Co, Ciba Corp, 52-55; instr org chem, Univ Manchester, 55-57; assoc res chemist, BC Res Coun, Can, 60-63; sr res chemist, Franklin Inst Labs, 64-67; prof chem, Univ Va, 67-69. *Mem:* Am Chem Soc. *Res:* Molecular and far infrared spectroscopy; organic metallic compounds; organic reactivity; quantum chemistry; application of computers to chemical problems; quantum biochemistry and theory of drug action. *Mailing Add:* 6953 Riverwood Dr Knoxville TN 37920

BLOOR, W(ILLIAM) SPENCER, AUTOMATIC CONTROL SYSTEMS. *Current Pos:* CONSULT ENGR, 81- *Personal Data:* b Trenton, NJ, Oct 16, 18; c 2. *Educ:* Lafayette Col, Pa, BS, 40. *Hon Degrees:* DrEng, Lafayette, 81. *Prof Exp:* Elec engr, Leeds & Northrop Co, 40-55, var mgt positions, 55-75, mgr steam & nuclear power systs, 75-81. *Concurrent Pos:* Adj prof, Drexel Univ, 81-87; consult, Univ Pa, 82-, St Hudson Int, Macro Corp, Network Systs Develop Ed, ISA Transactions. *Mem:* Nat Acad Eng; Instrument Soc Am (pres, 74); Inst Elec & Electronics Engrs. *Mailing Add:* 1904 Jody Rd Meadowbrook PA 19046

BLOSS, FRED DONALD, MINERALOGY. *Current Pos:* prof, 61-72, alumni distinguished prof, 72-91, EMER PROF MINERAL, VA POLYTECH INST & STATE UNIV, 91- *Personal Data:* b Chicago, Ill, May 30, 20; m 46, Louise Land; c Terry (Kensler), Janet (Shuff) & Jill. *Educ:* Univ Chicago, BS, 47, MS, 49, PhD(geol), 51. *Prof Exp:* Asst, Univ Chicago, 47-50; instr phys sci, Univ Ill, 50-51; from asst prof to assoc prof geol & mineral, Univ Tenn, 51-57; assoc prof to prof geol, Southern Ill Univ, 57-67. *Concurrent Pos:* Consult, Tenn

Valley Authority, 55-; Geol Soc Am Penrose Fund grant-in-aid, 57-58; NSF sr fel, Cavendish Lab, Cambridge & Swiss Fed Inst Technol, 62-63; ed, The Am Mineralogist, 72-76; Caswell Silver distinguished vis prof geol, Univ NMex, 81-82. *Mem:* Fel Mineral Soc Am (vpres, 75-76, pres, 76-77); Mineral Asn Can; Mineral Soc Gt Brit & Ireland. *Res:* Crystallography. *Mailing Add:* Dept Geol Sci Va Polytech Inst & State Univ Blacksburg VA 24061

BLOSS, HOMER EARL, plant pathology, plant biochemistry; deceased, see previous edition for last biography

BLOSSER, HENRY GABRIEL, ACCELERATOR PHYSICS. *Current Pos:* from assoc prof to prof, 58-90, dir, Nat Superconducting Cyclotron Lab, 58-89, UNIV DIST PROF PHYSICS, MICH STATE UNIV, 90- *Personal Data:* b Harrisonburg, Va, Mar 16, 28; m 51, 73, Mamar Gray; c William, Emanuel, Gabe & Margo. *Educ:* Univ Va, BA, 51, MS, 52, PhD(physics), 54. *Honors & Awards:* Bonner Prize, Am Phys Soc, 92. *Prof Exp:* Physicist, Cyclotron Nuclear Res Group, Oak Ridge Nat Lab, 54-56, group leader, Cyclotron Analog Group, 56-58. *Concurrent Pos:* NSF sr fel, 66-67; John Simon Guggenheim Found fel, 73-74; adj prof, Dept Radiation Oncol, Wayne State Univ, 84- *Mem:* Fel Am Phys Soc. *Res:* Design and construction of sector focused cyclotrons of medium and high energy; design and construction of cyclotrons for cancer therapy. *Mailing Add:* NSCL Mich State Univ East Lansing MI 48824-3405. *Fax:* 517-353-5967

BLOSSER, JAMES CARLISLE, RECEPTOR PHARMACOLOGY. *Current Pos:* SR PRIN INVESTR BIOCHEM, FISONS PHARMACEUT, 88- *Personal Data:* b Goshen, Ind, July 5, 45; m 74; c 2. *Educ:* Ind Univ, BA, 67; Mich State Univ, PhD(biochem), 72. *Prof Exp:* Lt res & neurobiol, Armed Forces Radiobiol Res Inst, Bethesda, MD, 72-76; res assoc biochem, Duke Univ Med Ctr, 76-77; res assoc neurosci, Baylor Col Med, 77-79, asst prof, 79-82; prin investr pharmacol, Pennwalt Pharmaceut, 82-88. *Mem:* Am Soc Pharmacol & Exp Therapeut; Neurosci Soc. *Res:* Identification of sites for therapeutic intervention and discovery of drugs for the treatment of central nervous system diseases. *Mailing Add:* Dept Biol Div Res & Develop Astra Arcus USA PO Box 20890 Rochester NY 14602

BLOSSEY, ERICH CARL, BIOORGANIC CHEMISTRY. *Current Pos:* PROF CHEM, ROLLINS COL, 65- *Personal Data:* b Toledo, Ohio, June 10, 35; div; c Christina E, Elizabeth N & Erich G. *Educ:* Ohio State Univ, BS, 57; Iowa State Univ, MS, 59; Carnegie-Mellon Univ, PhD(chem), 63. *Prof Exp:* NIH fel chem, Stanford Univ, 62-63; res fel org chem, Syntex, S A, Mex, 63-64; teaching intern, Wabash Col, 64-65. *Concurrent Pos:* Vis prof, Univ NMex, 72-73; NIH vis fel, Univ NMex, 74-75; Arthur Vining Davis Found Fel, 78; A G Bush prof sci, 80-87; vis prof, Okla State Univ, 85-86; vis scholar, Harvard Univ, 91-92. *Mem:* Am Chem Soc; Royal Soc Chem; AAAS; NY Acad Sci. *Res:* Application of polymer-supported reagents to problems in organic and bioorganic chemistry; use of 13C NMR spectroscopy in polymeric reagent structures; capillary electrophoresis. *Mailing Add:* Dept Chem Rollins Col 1000 Holt Avenue Box 2743 Winter Park FL 32789-4499. *Fax:* 407-646-2479; *E-Mail:* erich.blossey@rollins.edu

BLOSTEIN, MAIER LIONEL, ELECTRONICS ENGINEERING. *Current Pos:* from asst prof to assoc prof, 63-77, PROF ELEC ENG, MCGILL UNIV, 77- *Personal Data:* b Montreal, Que, Oct 21, 32; m 57; c 2. *Educ:* McGill Univ, BEng, 54, MEng, 59; Univ Ill, PhD(elec eng), 63. *Prof Exp:* Electronic engr, Bell Tel Co Can, 54-55 & Can Marconi Co, 55-58; demonstr elec eng, McGill Univ, 58-59, lectr, 59-60; asst, Univ Ill, 60-61, instr, 61-63. *Mem:* Inst Elec & Electronics Engrs. *Res:* Solid state devices and circuits; circuit and system theory. *Mailing Add:* Dept Elec Eng McGill Univ 3480 Univ Rm 633 Montreal PQ H3A 2A7 Can

BLOSTEIN, RHODA, BIOCHEMISTRY. *Current Pos:* asst prof, McGill Univ, 63-73, assoc prof to PROF, DEPT MED, MONTRIAL GEN HOSP RES INST, MCGILL UNIV, 73- *Personal Data:* b Montreal, Que, Nov 4, 36; m 57; c 1. *Educ:* McGill Univ, BS, 56, MS, 57, PhD(biochem), 60. *Prof Exp:* Res assoc biochem, Univ Ill, 60-63. *Mem:* Biophys Soc; Am Biochem Soc; Can Biochem Soc. *Res:* Membrane biochemistry in relation to cellular functions. *Mailing Add:* Montreal Gen Hosp Res Inst Dept Med & Biochem McGill Univ 1650 Cedar Ave Rm L11-132 Montreal PQ H3G 1A4 Can

BLOT, WILLIAM JAMES, BIOSTATISTICS, EPIDEMIOLOGY. *Current Pos:* CHIEF EXEC OFFICER, EPIDEMIOL INST, 94- *Personal Data:* b New York, NY, Aug 30, 43; m 65; c 2. *Educ:* Univ Fla, BS, 64, MS, 66; Fla State Univ, PhD(statist), 70. *Prof Exp:* Assoc sci researcher comput prog, Oak Ridge Nat Lab, 66-67; statistician med res, Atomic Bomb Casualty Comn, 70-72; asst prof, Johns Hopkins Sch Hyg & Pub Health, 72-74; biostatistician, Environ Epidemiol Br, Nat Cancer Inst, 74-83, chief, Biostatistics Br, 84-94. *Mem:* Am Pub Health Asn; Am Statist Asn; Am Col Epidemiol; Am Epidemiol Soc. *Res:* Study of the patterns and determinants, particularly environmental, of chronic diseases in the United States and abroad. *Mailing Add:* 20004 Octavia Ct Gaithersburg MD 20879. *Fax:* 301-517-4063; *E-Mail:* blotw@compuserve.com

BLOTCKY, ALAN JAY, APPLICATION OF RESEARCH REACTOR TO MEDICAL RESEARCH, MANAGEMENT & OPERATION OF RESEARCH REACTOR. *Current Pos:* REACTOR MGR, VET ADMIN MED CTR, 57-, RADIOL SAFETY OFF, 57- *Personal Data:* b Omaha, Nebr, July 5, 30; m 53, Wanda Richmond; c 2. *Educ:* Carnegie Inst Technol, BS, 52; Creighton Univ, MS, 71. *Prof Exp:* Head, Mass Spec Maintenance & instr elec maintenance, Goodyear Atomic Corp, 53-55; pres, consult & mfg rep, Radiation Eng Org, 55-57. *Concurrent Pos:* Asst clin instr med, Creighton Univ Sch Med, 58-84; instr radiol, Univ Nebr Col Med, 62-73; lectr physics, Creighton Univ, 64-65, Univ Omaha, 66-67; co-tech prog chmn, Int Conf Nuclear Methods Environ & Energy Res, 84; consult, Int Atomic Energy Agency, 85; chmn, Isotopes & Radiation Div, Am Nuclear Soc, 88, Biol & Med Div, 93-94; co-prin investr, Vet Admin Merit Rev Proj. *Mem:* Sigma Xi; fel Am Nuclear Soc; Am Asn Physicists Med; Soc Nuclear Med; Health Physics Soc. *Res:* Development of sensitive neutron activation analysis methodology for trace elements and molecules in biological samples; the application of these methods in correlating trace element quantity with disease states. *Mailing Add:* 306 N 92nd St Omaha NE 68114-3916

BLOUET, BRIAN WALTER, EDUCATION ADMINISTRATION. *Current Pos:* STAFF MEM, DEPT GOVT, COL WILLIAM & MARY, 89- *Personal Data:* b Darlington, Eng, Jan 1, 36; US citizen; m 70; c 3. *Educ:* Univ Hull, Eng, BA, 60, PhD(geog), 64. *Prof Exp:* Lectr geog, Univ Sheffield, Eng, 64-69; from assoc prof to prof, Univ Nebr, 69-83, chmn dept, 76-80, dir, Ctr Great Plains Studies, 79-83; prof geog & head dept, Tex A&M Univ, 83-93. *Concurrent Pos:* Vis assoc prof geog, Univ Nebr, 66-67. *Mem:* Fel Royal Geog Soc; Asn Am Geographers. *Res:* Development of settlement patterns in the Americas and Europe. *Mailing Add:* Dept Govt Col William & Mary Williamsburg VA 23186

BLOUGH, HERBERT ALLEN, VIROLOGY. *Current Pos:* asst prof microbiol, 63-69, assoc prof ophthal, 70-75, head div biochem virol & membrane res, 70-92, prof ophthal, 75-91, EMER PROF, 92-, CONSULT, UNIV PA, 91- *Personal Data:* b Philadelphia, Pa, Dec 18, 29; m 54, Racelle Miller; c Linda (Shuffman), Colin L, Beth M & Lawrence. *Educ:* Pa State Col, BSc, 51; Chicago Med Sch, MD, 55. *Hon Degrees:* MA, Univ Pa, 72. *Honors & Awards:* Most Distinguished Alumnus Award, Chicago Med Sch, 75. *Prof Exp:* Intern, Cincinnati Gen Hosp, 55; univ fel, Univ Minn, 58-60, USPHS fel, 60-61; USPHS res fel virol, Univ Cambridge, 61-63. *Concurrent Pos:* Consult, US Naval Hosp, Philadelphia, Pa; symp mem & lectr, Ciba Found, 64; mem, Comn Influenza, Armed Forces Epidemiol Bd; Nat Multiple Sclerosis Soc sr fel, Oxford Univ, 71-72; vis prof, Univ Helsinki, 72, Katholieke Univ, Leuven, 85-86, Inst Pastuer, Paris, 88-89; mem virol study sect, NIH, 75-77, site vis, 81-; USPHS grant, 64-67, 74-; Damon Runyon-Walter Winchell Mem Fund Cancer Res grant, 67-70, 73-75; US Army Med Res & Develop Command grant, 67-76; chmn, Subcomt Virol, Univ Pa Cancer Ctr, 77-79; Mary Jennifer Selznick Fel, Nat Hereditary Disease Found, 78-; charter mem, Med & Sci Adv Bd, Herpes Resource Ctr, 79-82; sr res fel, French Ministry Sci, 88-89. *Mem:* AAAS; NY Acad Sci; Am Asn Immunol; Am Soc Microbiol; Am Soc Biol Chem; Am Soc Virol. *Res:* Structure and assembly of enveloped viruses; attachment of viruses to artificial membranes; lipid biochemistry; development of antivirals. *Mailing Add:* 200 Three Rivers Ct Berwyn PA 19312. *Fax:* 215-204-4660; *E-Mail:* hblough@shs1.shs.temple.edu

BLOUIN, FLORINE ALICE, NATURAL PRODUCTS CHEMISTRY. *Current Pos:* RETIRED. *Personal Data:* b New Orleans, La, July 3, 31. *Educ:* La State Univ, BS, 53, MS, 56; Univ Akron, PhD(polymer chem), 75. *Prof Exp:* Chemist, Southern Regional Res Lab, 53-86, res chemist, 80-86. *Mem:* Am Chem Soc; Sigma Xi. *Res:* Textile, cellulose, polymer, protein, pigment, and food chemical research. *Mailing Add:* 8133 Spruce St New Orleans LA 70118

BLOUIN, GLENN M(ORGAN), CHEMICAL ENGINEERING. *Current Pos:* Jr chem engr, 42-43, asst chem engr, 46-50, chem engr, 52-62, proj engr, 62-72, CHEM RES SUPVR, TENN VALLEY AUTHORITY, NAT FERTILIZER DEVELOP CTR, 72- *Personal Data:* b Houston, Tex, Nov 10, 19; m 48; c 1. *Educ:* Rice Univ, BS, 42. *Mem:* Am Chem Soc. *Res:* Development of new nitrogenous fertilizers; chemical nitrogen fertilizer processes and products. *Mailing Add:* 1202 Sorrento Rd Florence AL 35630

BLOUIN, LEONARD THOMAS, CARDIOVASCULAR PHYSIOLOGY, ANALYTICAL CHEMISTRY. *Current Pos:* RES DIR, L&F ENTERPRISES, LTD, 91- *Personal Data:* b Detroit, Mich, June 15, 30; m 67, Floyanne Burrell; c 3. *Educ:* Mich State Univ, BS, 51, MS, 56; Univ Tenn, PhD(physiol), 59. *Prof Exp:* Analytical develop chemist, Gen Elec Co, Wash, 51-55; lab asst, Mich State Univ, 55; lab asst, Univ Tenn, 56-59, instr clin physiol, 59; from assoc res physiologist to res physiologist, Parke, Davis & Co, 59-65, sect leader cardiovasc-renal physiol, 65-66, sr res physiologist & head cardiovasc-renal sect, 66-67, assoc lab dir, 67-70, dir cardiovasc-renal sect, 70-74, sr cardiovasc physiologist, Clin Res Dept, 74-81; pres, LFK Assocs, Inc, 81-86. *Concurrent Pos:* Solar energy & passive residential design, 81-; clin pharmaceut res consult, 81- *Res:* Renal physiology; hypertensive cardiovascular disease; diuretics; radioprotective compounds; electrocardiography; radio and clinical chemistry; congestive heart disease and edema; peripheral vascular disease; angina pectoris; cardiac arrhythmias; solar heating & cooling. *Mailing Add:* 4071 W Hardy Rd Tucson AZ 85742

BLOUNT, CHARLES E, PHYSICS. *Current Pos:* RETIRED. *Personal Data:* b Hobbs, NMex, Apr 8, 31; m 53; c 2. *Educ:* Tex Western Col, BS, 54; Tex A&M Univ, MS, 60, PhD(physics), 63. *Prof Exp:* Instr math, Tex Western Col, 56-58; from asst prof to assoc prof, Tex Christian Univ, 63-72, prof physics, 72- *Concurrent Pos:* Consult, El Paso Nat Gas Co, 56-58 & Gen Dynamics, Ft Worth, 64- *Mem:* Am Phys Soc; Am Asn Physics Teachers; Am Soc Metals; Am Inst Mining, Metall & Petrol Eng. *Res:* Electronic spectra of molecular solids; imperfections in molecular solids; color centers in alkali halides. *Mailing Add:* PO Box 100455 Ft Worth TX 76129-0001

BLOUNT, DON HOUSTON, PHYSIOLOGY. *Current Pos:* GRAD DEAN & VPROVOST RES, GRAD SCH, UNIV MO, COLUMBIA. *Personal Data:* b Cape Girardeau, Mo, Mar 25, 29; m 52; c 3. *Educ:* Univ Mo, BA, 50, MA, 56, PhD(physiol), 58. *Prof Exp:* Asst instr med physiol, Col Med, Univ Mo, 56-58; from instr to asst prof physiol & biophys, Col Med, Univ Vt, 58-61; asst prof, Dept Physiol, Med Ctr, WVa Univ, 61-67; head physiol br, Life Sci Labs, Melpar, Inc, 67-69; scientist adminr, Spec Progs Br, Nat Heart & Lung Inst, 69-72, chief cardiac functions br, div heart & vascular dis, 72- *Mem:* Am Physiol Asn. *Res:* Cardiovascular physiology; relationship between the biochemical and mechanical events of the heart. *Mailing Add:* 601 Westmount Ave Columbia MO 65203-3470

BLOUNT, EUGENE IRVING, THEORETICAL SOLID STATE PHYSICS. *Current Pos:* CONSULT, 89- *Personal Data:* b Boston, Mass, May 26, 27; m 55; c 3. *Educ:* Harvard Univ, AB, 47; Univ Chicago, MS, 51, PhD, 59. *Prof Exp:* Res physicist, Int Harvester Co, 50-54; res physicist, Westinghouse Elec Corp, 57-60; res physicist, AT&T Bell Labs, 60-89. *Concurrent Pos:* Guggenheim fel, 63-64. *Mem:* Fel Am Phys Soc. *Res:* Behavior of electrons in crystals; symmetry. *Mailing Add:* 13 Woodcliff Dr Madison NJ 07940

BLOUNT, HENRY N, CHEMISTRY. *Current Pos:* DIR, DEPT CHEM, NSF. *Honors & Awards:* Electrochem Award, Am Chem Soc, 95. *Mailing Add:* Dept Chem NSF 4201 Wilson Blvd Arlington VA 22230

BLOUSE, LOUIS E, JR, BACTERIOLOGY, MICROBIOLOGY. *Current Pos:* RETIRED. *Personal Data:* b San Antonio, Tex, Nov 29, 31; m 79; c 3. *Educ:* Univ Tex, BA, 53, MA, 55; La State Univ, New Orleans, PhD(microbiol), 71. *Honors & Awards:* Fisher Sci Award, 72. *Prof Exp:* Asst immunologist, Tex State Dept Health, 54-55; dir lab, El Paso City-Co Health Dept, 57-59; chief bact br, USAF Epidemiol Lab, 59-68; res microbiologist & chief exp methods function, USAF Sch Aerospace Med, 71-72, microbiologist & chief, Dis Surveillance Br, 73-75, microbiologist & chief, Microbiol Br, 76-83, chief, Lab Serv, Epidemiol Div, 83-91. *Concurrent Pos:* Mem, adv comt, United Cath Cols; mem, Biomed Minority Res Prog, NIH, 72-; mem adv comt, Ment Health Ment Retardation, Bexar Co. *Mem:* AAAS; Am Soc Microbiol; Electron Micros Soc Am; Sigma Xi; fel Am Acad Microbiol; Clin Lab Mgt Asn. *Res:* Isolation and characterization of bacteriophages; epizootiology of staphylococcal infections in canines; comparative studies on staphylococcal typing phages; epidemiology of coagulase-negative staphylococcal infections; combined viral-bacterial infection. *Mailing Add:* 206 Palo Grande St San Antonio TX 78232

BLOUT, ELKAN ROGERS, BIOCHEMISTRY. *Current Pos:* Nat Res Coun fel, Harvard Univ, 42-43, res assoc, Med Sch, 50-52 & 56-60, lectr biophys, 60-62, prof biol chem, 62-64, Edward S Harkness prof, 64-90, chmn dept, 65-69, dean acad affairs, Sch Pub Health, chmn, Dept Environ Sci & Physiol, 86-88, dir, Div Biol Sci, Pub Health, 87-91, EMER EDWARD S HARKNESS PROF BIOL CHEM, HARVARD UNIV, 90- *Personal Data:* b New York, NY, July 2, 19; m 85, Gail Ferris; c James E, Susan B (Merry), William L & Darya L. *Educ:* Princeton Univ, AB, 39; Columbia Univ, PhD(chem), 42. *Hon Degrees:* AM, Harvard Univ, 62; DSc, Loyola Univ, 76. *Honors & Awards:* Nat Medal Sci, 90. *Concurrent Pos:* Mem staff, Polaroid Corp, 43-48, assoc dir res, 48-58, vpres & gen mgr res, 58-62, consult, 62-; consult, Children's Med Ctr, 52- & NSF, 63-64; mem, Sci Adv Comt, Ctr Blood Res, Inc, 67-72 & mem Bd Dirs, 72-92; mem, Dept Chem Vis Comt, Carnegie-Mellon Univ, 68-70; mem, Sci Adv Comt, Mass Gen Hosp, Boston, 68-71; mem, Bd Visitors, Fac Health Sci, State Univ NY Buffalo, 68-70; trustee, Boston Biomed Res Inst, 72-; trustee, Bay Biochem Res, 73-83; mem, Bd Dirs, CHON Corp, 74-83, ESA, Inc, 85-91 & Nat Health Res Fund, 85-92; mem, Corp Mus Sci, Boston, 74-; mem, Adv Coun, Dept Biochem Sci, Princeton Univ, 74-83 & chmn, adv coun, dept molecular biol, 83-95; mem, Conseil de Surveillance, Compagnie Financiere du Scribe, 75-81; mem finance comt, Nat Acad Sci, 76- & mem coun, 80-92; mem bd gov, Weizmann Inst Sci, Rehovot,l Israel, 77- & sci adv coun Am Comt, 79-; mem, Assembly Math & Phys Sci, Nat Res Coun, 79-82; mem, Adv Comt USSR & Eastern Europe, Nat Acad Sci, 79-84; mem gov bd, Nat Res Coun, 80- & mem comn phys sci, math & resources; mem, Investments Adv Comt,l Fedn Am Soc Biol, 81-85; mem coun, Int Orgn Chem Sci Delvelop, 81-; vpres & treas, Int Orgn Chem Sci Develop, 85-; gen partner, Gosnold Investment Fund Ltd, 85-95; mem bd dirs & investment mgr, Auburn Investment Mgt Corp, 85-; sci adv, Affymax Res Inst, 88-; sr adv sci, Food & Drug Admin, 91- *Mem:* Nat Acad Sci (treas, 80-); Inst Med-Nat Acad Sci; fel Am Acad Arts & Sci (treas, 92-); fel NY Acad Sci; fel Optical Soc Am; fel AAAS. *Res:* Polypeptides and proteins; spectroscopy and rotatory phenomena; synthetic organic chemistry. *Mailing Add:* 1010 Memorial Dr Apt 12A Cambridge MA 02138-4856

BLOXHAM, DON DEE, CARDIOVASCULAR BIOLOGY. *Current Pos:* PROF BIOL, BRIGHAM YOUNG UNIV, 78- *Educ:* La State Col, PhD(physiol), 73. *Mailing Add:* 107 N 1540 E Springville UT 84663

BLOXHAM, JEREMY, EARTH SCIENCE. *Current Pos:* Postdoctoral res fel, Harvard Univ, 85-87, asst prof geophysics, 87-90, John L Loeb assoc prof nat sci, 90-93, PROF GEOPHYSICS, HARVARD UNIV, 93- *Personal Data:* b Eng, Apr 29, 60. *Educ:* Cambridge Univ, BA, 82, MA, 86, PhD(geophysics), 86. *Hon Degrees:* MA, Harvard Univ, 93. *Honors & Awards:* Presidential Young Investr Award, 91; Macelwane Award, Am Geophys Union, 94. *Concurrent Pos:* mem, Study Earths Interior Comt, Am Geophys Union, 88-92, chair, 92-94; Packard Found fel, 90; mem, Study Earth Deep Interior Exec Comt, Int Union Geod & Geophysics, 91-; assoc ed, J Geophys Res, 92-94; ed, Geophys J Int, 93-95, NAm managing ed, 95- *Mem:* Fel Royal Astron Soc; fel Am Geophys Union. *Res:* Planetary magnetism; dynamo theory; structure and dynamics of earth's core and lower mantle; core-mantle interactions and coupling; variations in Earth's rotation; inverse theory. *Mailing Add:* Dept Earth & Planetary Sci Harvard Univ 20 Oxford St Cambridge MA 02138. *Fax:* 617-495-8839

BLOXHAM, LAURENCE HASTINGS, SIGNAL PROCESSING, SIGNALS WARFARE. *Current Pos:* ADVAN ENG SPECIALIST, LOCKHEED AIRCRAFT SERV CO, 84- *Personal Data:* b Sandusky, Ohio, Mar 27, 45; m 68. *Educ:* Bowling Green State Univ, BS, 78, MS, 80. *Honors & Awards:* Robert E Gross Award, 88. *Prof Exp:* Analyst, Commun Electronics, Inc, 67-69; planner, Control Data Corp, 69-73, Digital Commun Corp, 74-76; teaching asst physics, Bowling Green State Univ, 78-80; programmer, Ill Inst Technol Res Inst, 80-81; task leader, Computer Sci Corp, 81-82; software engr, Watkins Johnson Co, 82-84. *Concurrent Pos:* Prin investr advan signal processing, Lockheed Aircraft Serv, 84- & focal plane signal processing for A-O receivers, 88- *Mem:* Sigma Xi; Inst Elec & Electronics Engrs; Int Soc Optical Eng. *Res:* Advanced signal processing systems for radio frequencies; spread spectrum signal intercept, automatic identification, and tracking; acousto-optic radio frequency spectrum analysis; high performance photo detection techniques; design and develop parallel digital signal processing architectures and algorithms. *Mailing Add:* 5918 Birdie Dr LaVerne CA 91750-1418

BLOZIS, GEORGE G, PATHOLOGY. *Current Pos:* prof & chmn dept, 66-88, EMER PROF ORAL PATH/DIAG, COL DENT, OHIO STATE UNIV, 88- *Personal Data:* b Chicago, Ill, Nov 3, 29; m 56; c 3. *Educ:* Ohio State Univ, DDS, 55; Univ Chicago, SM, 61; Am Bd Oral Path, dipl, 66. *Prof Exp:* Intern, Billing's Hosp, Univ Chicago, 55-56, instr oral path, Walter G Zoller Mem Dent Clin, 61-64, asst prof, 64-66. *Concurrent Pos:* Proj dir, Oral Cancer Demonstration grant, 63-66; consult oral path, Vet Admin. *Mem:* Fel AAAS; Am Dent Asn; fel Am Acad Oral Path; Sigma Xi; Int Asn Dent Res. *Res:* Parotid cytology, candida infections in the rat. *Mailing Add:* 1370 Reymond Rd Columbus OH 43220-3833

BLUDMAN, SIDNEY ARNOLD, THEORETICAL PHYSICS, ASTROPHYSICS. *Current Pos:* PROF PHYSICS, UNIV PA, 61- *Personal Data:* b New York, NY, May 13, 27; m 49, 88, Ellen Schaffer; c 3. *Educ:* Cornell Univ, AB, 45; Yale Univ, MS, 48, PhD(physics), 51. *Prof Exp:* Instr physics, Lehigh Univ, 50-52; mem staff, Lawrence Radiation Lab, lectr, Univ Calif, Berkeley, 52-61. *Concurrent Pos:* Assoc, Oceanog Inst, Woods Hole, 51; vis mem, Inst Advan Studies, 56-57, Inst Theory Phys, Univ Calif, Santa Barbara; lectr, Univ Calif, 59-60; vis res fel, Imp Col, Univ London, 67-68; vis prof, Tel-Aviv Univ, 71; Lady Davis vis prof, Hebrew Univ, 76 & 83; Guggenheim fel, 83-84; Ctr Particle Astrophys, Univ Calif, Berkeley, 90-91. *Mem:* Am Phys Soc; Sigma Xi; Am Astron Soc; Int Astron Union. *Res:* Elementary particle physics; neutrons, astrophysics and cosmology. *Mailing Add:* Dept Physics & Astron Univ Pa Philadelphia PA 19104

BLUE, E(MANUEL) M(ORSE), chemical engineering, for more information see previous edition

BLUE, JAMES LAWRENCE, MATHEMATICAL MODELING, APPLIED MATHEMATICS. *Current Pos:* MEM STAFF, COMPUT & APPL MATH LAB, NAT INST STAND & TECHNOL, 79- *Personal Data:* b Pekin, Ill, Sept 20, 40; m 66; c 2. *Educ:* Occidental Col, AB, 61; Calif Inst Technol, PhD(physics), 66. *Honors & Awards:* Gold Medal, US Dept Com, 83. *Prof Exp:* Mem tech staff, Bell Tel Labs, 66-79. *Mem:* Inst Elec & Electronics Engrs; Soc Indust Appl Math; Asn Comput Mach. *Res:* Mathematical modeling of physical systems, scientific software, magnetic microstructure, computer science algorithms, neural networks. *Mailing Add:* 1386 Kersey Lane Potomac MD 20854

BLUE, JOSEPH EDWARD, ACOUSTICS. *Current Pos:* head, Measurements Br, 71-81, SUPT, UNDERWATER SOUND REFERENCE DETACHMENT, NAVAL RES LAB, 81- *Personal Data:* b Quitman, Miss, Sept 29, 36; m 62; c 2. *Educ:* Miss State Univ, BS, 61; Fla State Univ, MS, 66; Univ Tex, Austin, PhD(acout), 71. *Prof Exp:* Res physicist acout, Mine Defense Lab, US Navy, 61-68; res physicist, Appl Res Labs, Univ Tex, 68-71. *Mem:* Fel Acoust Soc Am. *Res:* Methods and systems for characterizing transducers and other devices for the generation and reception of underwater acoustic signals and noise; sonar transduction and underwater acoustic materials. *Mailing Add:* 3313 Northglenn Dr Orlando FL 32806. *Fax:* 407-857-5101

BLUE, M(ARTS) DONALD, INFRARED & EXTREME-INFRARED TECHNOLOGY, INFRARED RADIATION DETECTION. *Current Pos:* CONSULT, 93- *Personal Data:* b Des Moines, Iowa, Feb 4, 32; m 60, Patricia Gallaway; c Marie, Molly, Stephen & Timothy. *Educ:* Iowa State Univ, BS, 52, MS, 54, PhD(physics), 56. *Prof Exp:* Asst physics, Iowa State Univ, 53, asst, Inst Atomic Res, 55-56; res scientist, Honeywell Res Ctr, 56-62, head res sect, Res Ctr, Honeywell Inc, 63-69, sci attache, Honeywell Europe, Inc, 69-72, mem opers staff, Honeywell Radiation Ctr, 72-74; prin res scientist, Ga Tech Res Inst, Ga Inst Technol, 74-93. *Concurrent Pos:* Fulbright fel, Univ Paris, 56-57; consult, US Army Missile Res, Develop & Eng Lab, Huntsville, Ala, 75, Lockheed Missiles & Space Co Inc, Rexham Aerospace & Defense Group Huntsville, Ala & Fairchild Weston Systs NY. *Mem:* Am Phys Soc; Sigma Xi. *Res:* Space-exposure effects in electro-optic systems components; literature analysis, measurements and analysis of infrared and laser systems and components; submillimeter technology, optical and atmospheric effects. *Mailing Add:* Ga Inst Technol 323 Baker Bldg Atlanta GA 30332. *Fax:* 770-565-0317; *E-Mail:* don.blue@gtri.gatech.edu

BLUE, MARIE-LUISE, CELL ADHESION MOLECULES, LYMPHOCYTE CELL SURFACE RECEPTORS. *Current Pos:* SR SCIENTIST, MILES INC, 89- *Personal Data:* b Lodoz, Poland, Dec 14, 47; US citizen; c Tanya, Julie & Elise. *Educ:* State Univ NY, Stony Brook, BS,

63, PhD(biol sci), 81. *Prof Exp:* Fel, Albert Einstein Col Med, 81-83; fel, Harvard Med Sch, 83-85, from instr to asst prof, 85-89. *Concurrent Pos:* Prin investr, NIH, 86-89. *Mem:* Am Asn Immunologists; AAAS. *Res:* Expression and function of cell surface receptors in T lymphocyte development, T cell activation and in lymphocyte adhesive interactions. *Mailing Add:* 400 Morgan Lane B31 West Haven CT 06516. *Fax:* 203-937-6923

BLUE, MICHAEL HENRY, cosmic ray physics, for more information see previous edition

BLUE, RICHARD ARTHUR, EXPERIMENTAL NUCLEAR PHYSICS, VACUUM SYSTEM ENGINEERING. *Current Pos:* SR LIAISON PHYSICIST, NAT SUPERCONDUCTING CYCLOTRON LAB, MICH STATE UNIV, EAST LANSING, 79- *Personal Data:* b Le Mars, Iowa, Nov 12, 36. *Educ:* Cornell Col, BA, 58; Univ Wis, MS, 60, PhD(physics), 63. *Prof Exp:* Fel physics, Ohio State Univ, 63-66; asst prof physics, Univ Fla, 66-73, assoc prof, 73-79. *Concurrent Pos:* Vis assoc prof, Univ Wis, 77-78. *Mem:* Am Phys Soc. *Res:* Low energy experimental nuclear physics; giant resonances observed via radiative capture reactions. *Mailing Add:* 631 Forest St East Lansing MI 48823-3221. *E-Mail:* blue@nscl.msu.edu

BLUE, WILLIAM GUARD, SOILS. *Current Pos:* from asst biochemist to assoc biochemist, 50-63, prof soil chem & fertil, 73-79, BIOCHEMIST, UNIV FLA, 63-, EMER PROF SOIL CHEM & FERTIL, 89- *Personal Data:* b Poplar Bluff, Mo, Nov 7, 23; m 47, Bernice Rankin; c Carol, Jane & Cynthia. *Educ:* Univ Mo, PhD(soils), 50. *Prof Exp:* Asst, Univ Mo, 47-50. *Concurrent Pos:* Pasture agronomist, Univ Fla-Costa Rican Contract, San Jose, 58-60; consult, Guyana, 67; lectr trop soils, Orgn Trop Studies, Costa Rica, 69; consult, Ecuador, 74 & Cameroor, 80; res ext adv, Dschang, Cameroun, 85-87. *Mem:* Fel Soil Sci Soc Am; Am Soc Agron; Am Forage & Grassland Coun; Int Grassland Asn. *Res:* Chemistry, fertility and biological studies of soils, especially chemistry and fertility of tropical soils in British Honduras, Costa Rica, Panama, Venezuela, Guyana and phosphate mine waste reclamation in Florida. *Mailing Add:* 1501 NW 31st St Gainesville FL 32605

BLUEFARB, SAMUEL M, DERMATOLOGY. *Current Pos:* RETIRED. *Personal Data:* b St Louis, Mo, Oct 15, 12; m 45; c 1. *Educ:* Univ Ill, BS, 35, MD, 37. *Prof Exp:* From instr to assoc prof, 42-57, prof dermat & chmn dept, Med Sch, Northwestern Univ, Chicago, 57-87. *Concurrent Pos:* Consult, Res Vet Hosp, 64- *Mem:* AMA; Soc Invest Dermat; Am Acad Dermat; Am Dermat Asn; Am Col Physicians. *Res:* Syphilology; reticuloendothelial system in cutaneous disorders. *Mailing Add:* 1250 Park Ave W Highland Park IL 60035

BLUEMEL, VAN (FONKEN WILFORD), QUANTUM OPTICS. *Current Pos:* Asst prof, 66-73, ASSOC PROF PHYSICS, WORCESTER POLYTECH INST, 73- *Personal Data:* b Freeport, Ill, Feb 8, 34; m 63; c 2. *Educ:* Univ Mich, BS, 56; Univ Ill, MS, 60, PhD(nuclear physics), 67. *Mem:* Am Phys Soc; Am Asn Physics Teachers; Sigma Xi. *Res:* Statistics of scattered light; applications of atomic coherent states. *Mailing Add:* Dept Physics Worcester Polytech Inst 100 Institute Rd Worcester MA 01609

BLUEMLE, LEWIS W, JR, INTERNAL MEDICINE. *Current Pos:* prof med, Jefferson Med Col & pres, 77-, HON STAFF MEM, THOMAS JEFFERSON UNIV. *Personal Data:* b Williamsport, Pa, Mar 9, 21; m 53; c 4. *Educ:* Johns Hopkins Univ, AB, 43, MD, 46. *Hon Degrees:* DSc, Philadelphia Col Pharm & Sci; LHD, Washington & Jefferson Col. *Prof Exp:* From asst instr to instr med, Univ Pa, 50-52, assoc, 52-55, from asst prof to assoc prof, 55-68, dir, Clin Res Ctr, Univ Hosp, 61-68; prof med & pres, State Univ NY Upstate Med Ctr, 68-74; prof med & pres, Univ Ore Health Sci Ctr, 74-77. *Concurrent Pos:* Markle scholar, 55-60; vis consult, Vet Hosp, Philadelphia, 55-68; consult, Nat Inst Arthritis & Metab Dis, 67-74; dir, Asn Acad Health Ctr, 80-83. *Mem:* Am Col Physicians; Am Fedn Clin Res; Am Clin & Climat Asn; Royal Col Physicians Edinburgh. *Res:* Renal disease. *Mailing Add:* Thomas Jefferson Univ 11th & Walnut St S Philadelphia PA 19107

BLUESTEIN, ALLEN CHANNING, ORGANIC CHEMISTRY. *Current Pos:* PRES, BERLINGTON ASSOCS, 79- *Personal Data:* b Lynn, Mass, Aug 25, 26; m 47, Sandra Snyder; c Marcia, Karen, David, Lorna & Roberta. *Educ:* Univ Mass, BS, 49. *Prof Exp:* Jr chemist, Advan Res & Develop Measurements Lab, Gen Elec Co, 52-55; rubber chemist, Anaconda Wire & Cable Co, 55-56, sr develop chemist, 56-61; res dir, Aerovox Corp, 61-63; tech dir, Cooke Color & Chem Co, Inc, Reichhold Chem Inc, Hackettstown, 63-71, vpres, 68-71; pres, Polymer Serv Inc, 71-79. *Concurrent Pos:* Mem, Underwriters Lab Tech Adv Comt. *Mem:* Am Chem Soc; sr mem Inst Elec & Electronics Engrs; fel Am Inst Chemists. *Res:* Rubber compounding technology; cross-linking of thermoplastics; reactions between ozone and polymers; electrical properties of polymers; plastics technology; wire and cable technology. *Mailing Add:* 232 Burlington Ave Spotswood NJ 08884

BLUESTEIN, BEN ALFRED, ORGANOMETALLIC CHEMISTRY, POLYMER CHEMISTRY. *Current Pos:* RETIRED. *Personal Data:* b Chicago, Ill, July 5, 18; m 47, Louise Wasserman; c Richard, Myra & Eileen. *Educ:* Univ Chicago, BS, 38, PhD(org chem), 41. *Prof Exp:* Res assoc chem, Univ Chicago, 41-43, asst, Metall Lab, 43-44; asst, Los Alamos Sci Lab, 44-46; chemist, Res Lab, Gen Elec Co, 46-50, res chemist, Silicone Prod Dept, 50-83. *Concurrent Pos:* Pittsburgh Plate Glass Co fel, Univ Chicago, 41-43. *Mem:* AAAS; Am Chem Soc; NY Acad Sci; fel Am Inst Chem; Sigma Xi. *Res:* Reactions of 9-formylfluorene; synthesis of organo-metallic resins; plastics; radiochemistry; organo-silicon chemistry. *Mailing Add:* 2037 Hoover Rd Schenectady NY 12309

BLUESTEIN, BERNARD RICHARD, organic chemistry; deceased, see previous edition for last biography

BLUESTEIN, CLAIRE, INDUSTRIAL ORGANIC CHEMISTRY, UV EB CURE FORMULATION. *Current Pos:* CONSULT & PRES, CAPTAN ASSOC INC, 76- *Personal Data:* b Philadelphia, Pa, May 3, 26; wid; c 4. *Educ:* Univ Pa, AB, 47; Univ Ill, MS, 48, PhD(org chem), 50. *Prof Exp:* Fel, Purdue Univ, 52-53; instr, Ext Serv, Pa State Univ, 58-59; sr res chemist, Sonneborn Chem & Refining Co Div, 59-63, group leader, Cent Res Labs, 63-75, mgr new technol, Witco Chem Corp, 75-76; vpres, Epolin Inc, 85-91. *Mem:* Am Chem Soc; Soc Plastics Engrs; Soc Advan Mat & Process Eng. *Res:* Polyurethane coatings, particularly radiation curable; high solids; aqueous emulsions; polyurethane elastomers; polyurethane chemistry; packaging coatings and adhesives technology; polymer analytical and physical characterization; plastics processing aids; petroleum sulfonates and waxes; alkaline earth salt dispersions; bicyclospirane polymerization; coatings and adhesives based on ring opening expansion polymerization. *Mailing Add:* Captan Assoc Inc PO Box 504 Brick NJ 08723. *Fax:* 732-840-1211

BLUESTEIN, HARRY GILBERT, RHEUMATOLOGY, CLINICAL IMMUNOLOGY. *Current Pos:* from asst prof to assoc prof, 71-84, PROF MED, SCH MED, UNIV CALIF, SAN DIEGO, 84- *Personal Data:* b New York, NY, Aug 8, 39; m 62; c 2. *Educ:* Mass Inst Technol, BS, 61; Albert Einstein Col Med, MD, 65. *Prof Exp:* Resident internal med, Georgetown Univ Hosp, 65-67; res assoc biochem, Lab Gen Comp Biochem, NIMH, NIH, 67-69, res fel immunol, Lab Immunol, 69-70; res fel, dept path, Sch Med, Harvard Univ, 70-71. *Concurrent Pos:* Attend physician, Univ Hosp, Univ Calif, San Diego Med Ctr, 71- & San Diego Vet Admin Hosp, 73- *Mem:* Am Soc Clin Invest; Am Asn Immunologists; Am Rheumatism Asn; Am Asn Physicians. *Res:* Elucidating the mechanisms responsible for the disordered immune function that characterizes rheumatoid arthritis and other autoimmune rheumatic diseases; diminished immunity in AIDS and other immunodeficiency diseases. *Mailing Add:* Dept Med Univ Calif-San Diego 9500 Gilman Dr La Jolla CA 92093-0656. *E-Mail:* hbluestein@ucsd.edu

BLUESTEIN, HOWARD BRUCE, SYNOPTIC & MESOSCALE METEOROLOGY, SEVERE CONVECTIVE STORMS & TORNADOES. *Current Pos:* Vis asst prof, 76-79, from asst prof to assoc prof, 79-90, PROF METEOROL, UNIV OKLA, 90- *Personal Data:* b Chelsea, Mass, Oct 8, 48; m 89, Kathleen E Welch. *Educ:* Mass Inst Technol, BS, 71, MS(elec eng) & MS(meteorol), 72, PhD(meteorol), 76. *Mem:* Fel Am Meteorol Soc. *Res:* Synoptic dynamic meteorology; severe convection; mesoscale meteorology; tropical meteorology. *Mailing Add:* Sch Meteorol Univ Okla 100 E Boyd Rm 1310 Norman OK 73019. *E-Mail:* hblue@sou.edu

BLUESTEIN, THEODORE, MISSILE AERODYNAMICS. *Current Pos:* RETIRED. *Personal Data:* b New York, NY, July 7, 34; m 57, Helen E Rothweiler; c Julie A (Rioux), Keith A, Nancy L (Uptegrove) & Mark A. *Educ:* Pa State Univ, BS, 56; Univ Southern Calif, MS, 58. *Honors & Awards:* Challenger Flag Award, Am Inst Aeronaut & Astronaut, 85. *Prof Exp:* Sr engr, Missile Syst Design, Raytheon Co, 61-65, missile mgr, Patriot Prog Off, 65-68, prin engr, 68-69, prin engr, missile eng, 71-76; rep, Piedmont Capital, 69-71; prog mgr, Govt Electronics, Motorola, 76-79; mem tech staff, Hughes Aircraft Co, 56-61, head syst engr, Roland Missile Syst, 79-80, Tow Missile sr proj engr, 81-88. *Mem:* Am Inst Aeronaut & Astronaut. *Res:* Missile aerodynamics; missile guidance and control; program management; missile and missile system design; systems engineering; design of Patriot missile. *Mailing Add:* 1531 W Sendero Cuatro Tucson AZ 85704

BLUESTONE, HENRY, ORGANIC CHEMISTRY. *Current Pos:* RETIRED. *Personal Data:* b Chicago, Ill, May 17, 14; wid; c Marlene (Suliteanu) & Judith. *Educ:* Univ Chicago, SB, 38, SM, 39. *Prof Exp:* Instr chem, Chicago City Jr Col, 39-42; res chemist, Velsicol Corp, 42-47; asst res dir, Julius Hyman & Co, 47-51; from res group leader to sr res group leader, Diamond Shamrock Corp, 51-73, staff chemist, 73-78, staff sci liaison, 78-82. *Mem:* Am Chem Soc. *Res:* Organic synthesis; diene reactions; heterocyclic compounds; polycyclic compounds; stereochemistry; bactericides; fungicides; herbicides; insecticides; plant growth regulators; nematocides. *Mailing Add:* 3050 Baker St San Francisco CA 94123

BLUESTONE, JEFFREY A, TRANSPLANTATION BIOLOGY. *Current Pos:* HEAD LAB, NAT CANCER INST, NIH, 83- *Personal Data:* b Ft Sill, Okla, Apr 8, 53. *Educ:* Cornell Univ, PhD(immunol), 80. *Mailing Add:* Dept Immunol Univ Chicago 5841 S Maryland Ave MC 1089 Chicago IL 60637-1470

BLUFORD, GUION STEWART, JR, AEROSPACE ENGINEERING. *Current Pos:* VPRES & GEN MGR, ENG SERV DIV, NYMA, INC, BROOK PARK, OHIO, 93- *Personal Data:* b Philadelphia, Pa, Nov 22, 42; m 64, Linda Tull; c Guion S & James T. *Educ:* Pa State Univ, BS, 64; USAF, Inst Technol, MS, 74, PhD(aerospace eng), 78; Univ Houston, MBA, 87. *Hon Degrees:* Several from US univs. *Honors & Awards:* Distinguished Nat Scientist Award, Nat Soc Black Engrs, 79, Ebony Black Achievement Award, 83. *Prof Exp:* F4C pilot, 12th Tactical Fighter Wing, USAF, 66-67, T-38 pilot instr, 3630th Flying Training Wing, 67-72, dep advan concepts, Air Force Flight Dynamics Lab, 75-77, chief aerodyn & airframe br, 77-78; astronaut cand, Johnson Space Ctr, NASA, 78-79, astronaut, 79-93. *Mem:* Am Inst Aeronaut & Astronaut; Nat Tech Asn. *Res:* Computational fluid dynamics; aerodynamics. *Mailing Add:* NYMA Inc 2001 Aerospace Pkwy Brook Park OH 44142

BLUHM, AARON LEO, ORGANIC CHEMISTRY. *Current Pos:* RES CHEMIST ORG CHEM, US ARMY NATICK LABS, 56- *Personal Data:* b Boston, Mass, May 26, 24; m 48; c 1. *Educ:* Northeastern Univ, BS, 51; Boston Univ, PhD(chem), 56. *Mem:* Am Chem Soc; Sigma Xi. *Res:* Synthesis; reaction mechanisms and kinetics; polymer structural research; infrared spectroscopy of organic and polymeric materials; photochromic materials; electron spin resonance studies of free radicals; photochemistry. *Mailing Add:* Five Wentworth Rd Canton MA 02021

BLUHM, HAROLD FREDERICK, ORGANIC CHEMISTRY, EXPLOSIVES. *Current Pos:* res chemist, Atlas Chem Industs, Inc, 57-66, supvr chem develop lab, 66-76, ASSOC MGR, ATLAS RES & DEVELOP LAB, ATLAS POWDER CO, 76- *Personal Data:* b Williamsport, Pa, Mar 12, 27. *Educ:* Bucknell Univ, BS, 52; Pa State Univ, MS, 54. *Prof Exp:* Asst chem, Pa State Univ, 52-54; res chemist, Hercules Powder Co, 54-57. *Mem:* AAAS; Am Mgt Asn; Am Chem Soc. *Res:* Organometallic compounds; plasticizers; synthetic resins; polymers; new explosive compounds and propellants; development of new commercial explosives. *Mailing Add:* 303 Union Ave Williamsport PA 17701-2325

BLUHM, LESLIE, FOOD FERMENTATION, ALCOHOLIC BEVERAGES. *Current Pos:* STRATEGIC MGR, FOOD & DRUG ADMIN, 92- *Personal Data:* b Winthrop, Mass, May 15, 40; m 90; c 3. *Educ:* Univ Mass, BSc, 63; Univ Ill, MS, 67, PhD(food sci), 68. *Prof Exp:* Res scientist, Miles Labs, Inc, 68-72, sect head, 72-78, sr res scientist, 76-78, dir food sci res, 78-79; mgr, distillery res & develop, 79-81, vpres res & develop, Joseph E Seagram & Sons, 81-90; consult, 90-92. *Mem:* Am Soc Microbiol; Inst Food Technologists; Am Soc Brewing Chemists; Soc Indust Microbiol. *Res:* Food fermentations; sanitary microbiology; alcohol production; enzymology, microbiology, biochemistry and analytical aspects associated with food products. *Mailing Add:* 20725 Highland Hall Dr Gaithersburg MD 20879

BLUHM, TERRY LEE, POLYMER STRUCTURE & MORPHOLOGY, X-RAY DIFFRACTION. *Current Pos:* res scientist, Xerox Res Ctr, Can, 78-92, PROJ MGR, SUPPLIES DEVELOP & MFG, THE DOCUMENT CO XEROX, 92- *Personal Data:* b Niagara Falls, NY, June 22, 47; m 71, Ellen Manwaring; c Sylvia. *Educ:* State Univ NY Col Environ Sci & Forestry, BS, 70, MS, 73, PhD(polymer chem), 76. *Prof Exp:* Fel, Inst Molecular Chem, WGer, 76-78. *Mem:* Am Chem Soc; NY Acad Sci; Mat Res Soc; Micros Soc Am. *Res:* Solid state structure and morphology of natural and synthetic polymers using x-ray scattering techniques and electron microscopy; molecular modelling of polymers and small molecules; structural studies of photoactive pigments. *Mailing Add:* 16 Pinehill Dr Pittsford NY 14534. *Fax:* 716-422-7266; *E-Mail:* terrybluhm@wb.xerox.com

BLUM, ALVIN SEYMOUR, BIOPHYSICS. *Current Pos:* REGIST PATENT AGENT. *Personal Data:* b Boston, Mass, Jan 23, 26; m 51; c 1. *Educ:* Brown Univ, ScB, 48. *Prof Exp:* Radioisotope scientist, Vet Admin Hosp, Calif, 50-52, biochemist, La, 52-53, Fla, 53-54, prin scientist, 55-61; chief scientist, Broward Gen Hosp, Ft Lauderdale, 61-86. *Concurrent Pos:* Instr, Sch Med, Univ Miami, 56-77; consult, Broward Gen Hosp, 58-61, Mt Sinai Hosp, 60-81, Vet Admin Hosp, Miami, Miami Heart Inst, 71-81 & Doctor's Gen Hosp Plantation, 71-77; regist patent agent, 81- *Mem:* Soc Nuclear Med; Am Asn Clin Chem. *Res:* Circulation; kidney function; biochemistry of thyroid; iron metabolism; pulmonary function; radio pharmaceuticals; instrumentation development. *Mailing Add:* 2350 Del Mar Pl Ft Lauderdale FL 33301. *Fax:* 954-832-0001

BLUM, BARTON MORRILL, SILVICULTURE. *Current Pos:* Res forester, Northeastern Forest Exp Sta, US Forest Serv, 57-64, from assoc silviculturist to silviculturist, 64-72, PROJ LEADER, NORTHEASTERN FOREST EXP STA, US FOREST SERV, 72- *Personal Data:* b Newark, NJ, May 17, 32; m 58; c 3. *Educ:* Rutgers Univ, BS, 54; Yale Univ, MF, 57; State Univ NY Col, PhD, (forestry). *Mem:* Soc Am Foresters. *Res:* Silviculture and ecology of northern hardwood forests; individual tree growth; physiology of maple sap flow and attendant problems; silviculture of northern conifers; northern conifer (spruce and fir) silviculture and ecology; spruce bud-worm. *Mailing Add:* Mann Hill Rd East Holden ME 04429

BLUM, BRUCE I, SOFTWARE ENGINEERING, CLINICAL INFORMATION SYSTEMS. *Current Pos:* RETIRED. *Personal Data:* b New York, NY; m 54, Harriet Roth; c 2. *Educ:* Rutgers Univ, BS, 51; Columbia Univ, MA, 55; Univ Md, MA, 64. *Prof Exp:* Mathematician, Appl Physics Lab, Johns Hopkins Univ, 62-67; vpres, Wolf Res & Develop Corp, 67-73; sr systs eng, TRW Systs, 73-74; assoc prof biomed eng, Johns Hopkins Univ, 75-93, prw staff, Appl Physics Lab, 74-94. *Concurrent Pos:* Dir, Clin Info Systs Div, Johns Hopkins Univ, 76-83. *Mem:* Asn Comput Mach; Inst Elec & Electronics Engrs; Am Asn Artificial Intel; fel Am Col Med Infermatics; fel AAAS. *Res:* Software engineering and the application of knowledge-based techniques; development, implementation and evaluation of clinical imformation systems. *Mailing Add:* 5605 Vantage Point Rd Columbia MD 21044

BLUM, EDWARD H(OWARD), CHEMICAL ENGINEERING, SYSTEMS ANALYSIS. *Current Pos:* CHIEF EXEC OFFICER, BLUM, CLARK & CO, INC, 89- *Personal Data:* b Washington, DC, Jan 1, 40; m 65, Marlene Witman; c Daniel & Matthew. *Educ:* Carnegie Inst Technol, BS, 61; Princeton Univ, MA, 63, PhD(chem eng), 65. *Honors & Awards:* Appln Mgt Sci Prize, Int Inst Mgt Sci, 74; Int Prize in Mgt Sci, NATO, 76. *Prof Exp:* Sloan fel chem eng, Princeton Univ, 64-65, asst prof, 65-67; asst to vpres res, Rand Corp, 67-68, proj leader & mem sr prof staff, New York-Rand Inst, 68-72, vpres, 72-74; sr scientist, Int Inst Appl Systs Anal, 74-76; dir advan technol, US Dept Energy, 76-80; vpres & exec dir, Merrill Lynch Capital Markets, 80-86; pres & chief exec officer, Md Nat Investment Banking Co, 86-89. *Concurrent Pos:* Consult, Union Carbide Corp & Rand Corp, 65-67 & Bur Budget, Exec Off President, 66-67; vis assoc prof, State Univ NY, Stony Brook, 69-72; trustee, Univ Detroit, 70-79; mem adv comt, NBS Fire Res Prog, Nat Acad Sci-Nat Res Coun-Nat Acad Eng, 71-74; mem adv bd, Solar Energy Res Inst, 83-89; mem Fed Private Sector Partnership Bd, 85-89; mem bd dirs, Thames Water Holdings Inc, 90-92 & Periphonics Corp, 95- *Mem:* AAAS; Am Inst Chem Engrs. *Res:* Applied mathematics; engineering and public policy; systems analysis; energy; combustion and fire protection; management science. *Mailing Add:* 2417 Luckett Ave Vienna VA 22180-6818. *Fax:* 703-860-9144; *E-Mail:* blumeh@concentric.net

BLUM, EDWARD K, MATHEMATICS, COMPUTER SCIENCE. *Current Pos:* PROF MATH, UNIV SOUTHERN CALIF, LOS ANGELES, 66- *Educ:* Columbia Univ, PhD(math), 52. *Honors & Awards:* Silver Core Award, Int Fed Info Processing, 83. *Prof Exp:* Instr, Univ Md Grad Sch, 53-55; instr, MIT Coop Prog, 55-56; instr, Univ Calif, Los Angeles, 57-62; prof math & dir comput ctr, Wesleyan Univ, 62-66. *Concurrent Pos:* Fulbright award, Univ Rome, Italy, 65; vis prof math, Univ Calif, Los Angeles, 66; managing ed, J Comput & Syst Sci; ed, J Numerical & Functional Analysis; sabbatical, Univ Paris & Hebrew Univ, 73, Oxford Univ, 79, Univ Calif, San Diego, 86. *Mailing Add:* Dept Math Univ Southern Calif Los Angeles CA 90089-0001

BLUM, FRANK D, DYNAMICS OF SURFACE ACTIVE POLYMERS & MOLECULES, NUCLEAR MAGNETIC RESONANCE SPECTROSCOPY & DIFFUSION COMPOSITE & FRICTION MATERIALS, BRAKE LININGS. *Current Pos:* from assoc prof to prof chem, 86-94, CUR PROF, UNIV MO, ROLLA, 94- *Personal Data:* Frank D Jr & Rebecca. *Educ:* Eastern Ill Univ, BS, 76, MS, 77; Univ Minn, PhD(phys chem), 81. *Prof Exp:* Teaching asst, Eastern Univ, 76-77; res & teaching asst, Univ Mo, 77-81; asst prof chem, Drexel Univ, 81-86. *Concurrent Pos:* Sr res investr, Mat Res Ctr, 89-; vis scientist, IBM Almaden Res Ctr, 92. *Mem:* Am Chem Soc; Soc Automotive Engrs. *Res:* Polymer-solvent and polymer-surface interactions; polymer characterization; dynamics in polymer solutions, bulk and absorbed polymers; colloid chemistry; structure and dynamics in microemulsions, liquid crystals, micelles and vesicles; non-asbestos friction materials; nuclear magnetic resonance spectroscopy and diffusion. *Mailing Add:* Dept Chem Univ Mo 1101 McCutcheon Rd Rolla MO 65401-2631. *E-Mail:* fblum@umr.edu

BLUM, FRED A, SOLID STATE ELECTRONICS, LASERS. *Current Pos:* PRES, SEQUEL, 86- *Personal Data:* b Austin, Tex, Nov 30, 39; m 88, Diane Harbert; c 2. *Educ:* Univ Tex, BS, 62; Calif Inst Technol, MS, 64, PhD(physics), 68. *Prof Exp:* Res scientist, Appl Sci Lab, Gen Dynamics/Ft Worth, 63-64; staff mem solid state div, Lincoln Lab, Mass Inst Technol, 68-73; prog mgr, Cent Res Labs, Tex Instruments, 73-75; dir, Solid State Electronics Dept, Sci Ctr, Rockwell Int, 75-79, vpres, Microelectronics Ctr, 79-81; chmn & Chief Exec Officer GigaBit Logic, 81-86. *Mem:* Am Phys Soc; Inst Elec & Electronics Engrs; AAAS; Optical Soc Am; Soc Photo-Optical Instrumentation Engrs. *Res:* Semiconductor electronic and electro-optical devices; integrated optics; fiber optics. *Mailing Add:* 5655 Lindero Canyon Rd Ste 404 Westlake Village CA 91362

BLUM, HAROLD A(RTHUR), CHEMICAL ENGINEERING. *Current Pos:* CHMN MECH ENG & AEROSPACE DEPT, 68-72, PROF MECH ENG, SOUTHERN METHODIST UNIV, 57-, PRES, DEVICES & SERVS CO, 77- *Personal Data:* b New York, NY, Apr 19, 21; m 43; c 4. *Educ:* Rensselaer Polytech Inst, BChE, 42; Northwestern Univ, MS, 48, PhD(chem eng), 50. *Prof Exp:* Asst engr, procurement dist, Philadelphia Sig Corps, 42-43; asst chem, Northwestern Univ, 47, res asst chem eng, 48-49; group leader petrol prod res, Atlantic Ref Co, 49-55; lectr heat transfer & chem eng, Southern Methodist Univ, 51-55; assoc prof petrol eng, Tex Tech Col, 55-57. *Concurrent Pos:* NSF grant, 61-64; Nat Aeronaut & Space Admin grant, 64-68; res grants, Alcoa Found, 72-74, Fair found, 73-76 & Dallas Power & Light Co, 73-79. *Mem:* Am Chem Soc; Am Soc Eng Educ; Am Soc Heating, Refrig & Air Conditioning Engrs; Int Solar Energy Soc; fel Am Soc Mech Engrs. *Res:* Heat transfer; thermodynamics; engineering education; information; solar energy. *Mailing Add:* 3501 Milton Ave Dallas TX 75205

BLUM, HARRY, visual shape, biological shape, for more information see previous edition

BLUM, JACOB JOSEPH, PHYSIOLOGY, BIOPHYSICS. *Current Pos:* assoc prof to prof physiol, 62-80, JAMES B DUKE PROF PHYSIOL, DUKE UNIV, 80- *Personal Data:* b New York, NY, Oct 3, 26; m 50, 60, Ruth Marsey; c Mark, Douglas, Lisa & Laura. *Educ:* NY Univ, BA, 47; Univ Chicago, MS, 50, PhD(physiol), 52. *Prof Exp:* Merck fel, Calif Inst Technol, 52-53; asst prof biochem, Univ Mich, 56-58; chief biophys sect, Geront Br, Nat Heart Inst, 58-62. *Concurrent Pos:* Merck fel, 52; Fogarty sr int fel, 92. *Mem:* Am Physiol Soc; Biophys Soc; Soc Cell Biologists; Protozool Soc; Sigma Xi; Soc Protozoologists (pres, 91). *Res:* Control and structural organization of intermediary metabolism; analysis of auditory processing in lower brain stem; biomathematics. *Mailing Add:* Dept Cell Biol Duke Univ Durham NC 27710. *Fax:* 919-684-5481

BLUM, JANICE S, AUTOIMMUNITY, HISTOCOMPATABILITY. *Current Pos:* ASSOC PROF, DEPT MICROBIOL & IMMUNOL, WALTHER ONCOL CTR, IND UNIV, 95- *Personal Data:* b Philadelphia, Pa, June 6, 57. *Educ:* Pa State Univ, BS, 79; Duke Univ, PhD(biochem), 84. *Honors & Awards:* Investr Award, Arthritis Found, 91. *Prof Exp:* Postdoctoral fel, Duke Univ, 84-87; postdoctoral fel & instr, Sch Med, Wash Univ, 87-91, affil asst prof, 91-95; asst mem, Virginia Mason Res Ctr, 91-95. *Mem:* Sigma Xi; Am Soc Cell Biol; Am Asn Immunologists. *Res:* Human immunity including disorders such as autoimmune disease and cancer. *Mailing Add:* Dept Microbiol & Immunol Sch Med Ind Univ MS 255 Indianapolis IN 46202

BLUM, JOEL DAVID, ENVIRONMENTAL GEOCHEMISTRY. *Current Pos:* asst prof, 90-94, ASSOC PROF, DARTMOUTH COL, 94- *Personal Data:* b Cleveland, Ohio, Jan 24, 60; m 83, Cynthia Smith; c Jacob & Hazel. *Educ:* Case Western Res Univ, BS, 81; Univ Alaska Fairbanks, MS, 82; Calif Inst Technol, PhD, 90. *Prof Exp:* Geologist, Mohawk Oil & Gas Inc, 82-83; geochemist, Alaska Geol Surv, 83-85. *Concurrent Pos:* Res affil, Argonne Nat Lab, 88-92; vis fac geochem, Calif Inst Technol, 90; prin investr, NSF, 91-, pres fac fel, 93-98; Sloan res fel, Alfred P Sloan Found, 92-94; prin investr, Nat Inst Environ Health Sci, 95- *Mem:* Am Geophys Union; Geol Soc Am; Geochem Soc. *Res:* Isotopic and trace element variations in soil and water are used to investigate geochemical and environmental processes that take place on the earth's surface and in its interior and to determine the chronology of geological processes. *Mailing Add:* Earth Sci Dept Dartmouth Col Hanover NH 03755. *E-Mail:* joel.blum@dartmouth.edu

BLUM, JOHN BENNETT, ELECTRONIC CERAMICS, POWDER PROCESSING. *Current Pos:* MGR MKT ENG, TOSHIBA AM ELECTRONIC COMPONENTS, 90- *Personal Data:* b Boston, Mass, Dec 22, 52; m 75, Emily Nixon; c Jennifer & Margaret. *Educ:* Brown Univ, BS, 74; Mass Inst Technol, MS, 77, PhD(ceramics), 79. *Honors & Awards:* Ralph R Teetor Award, Soc Automotive Engrs, 83. *Prof Exp:* Sr exp ceramist, AC Spark Plug Div, Gen Motors, 79-80; asst prof ceramics, Rutgers Univ, 80-86; sr res engr, Norton Co, 86-90. *Concurrent Pos:* Dir, Glenn N Howatt Lab, Electronic Ceramics Res, Rutgers Univ, 80-86. *Mem:* Fel Am Ceramic Soc; Int Elec & Electronics Engrs; Sigma Xi; Int Soc Hybrid Microelectronics. *Res:* Electronic ceramics; fundamental electronic properties of the materials used and the processing needed to produce high quality devices from these materials; electronics packaging; ceramics processing. *Mailing Add:* AMD Toshiba Am Electronics 112 Turnpike Rd Westborough MA 01581

BLUM, JOHN LEO, phycology; deceased, see previous edition for last biography

BLUM, JOSEPH, MATHEMATICS, COMPUTER SCIENCE. *Current Pos:* GROUP LEADER, INST LEARNING IN RETIREMENT, 89- *Personal Data:* b New York, NY, Mar 7, 19; m 84, Annabelle Bender; c Eleanore, Delores & David. *Educ:* City Col New York, BS, 40; George Washington Univ, AM, 48, PhD(math), 58. *Prof Exp:* Photogram engr, US Geol Surv, 41-47; res analyst cryptol, US Dept Army, 47-49; staff mem math, Los Alamos Sci Labs, 49-50; mathematician, Nat Bur Standards, 50-51 & Nat Security Agency, 51-75; from assoc prof to prof computer sci, Am Univ, 75-87. *Concurrent Pos:* Consult, Nat Security Agency, 75-80. *Mem:* Sigma Xi; Am Math Soc; Soc Indust & Appl Math. *Res:* Signal analysis in communications; computer system design and analysis; applications of queueing theory to computer systems. *Mailing Add:* 8101 Connecticut Ave Chevy Chase MD 20815

BLUM, KENNETH, PHARMACOLOGY, PSYCHIATRIC GENETICS. *Current Pos:* ADJ RES PROF, DEPT BEHAV SCI, SCH PUB HEALTH, UNIV NTEX. *Personal Data:* b Brooklyn, NY, Aug 8, 39; m 63; c 2. *Educ:* Columbia Univ, BS, 61; NJ Col Med, MS, 65; NY Med Col, PhD(pharmacol), 68. *Honors & Awards:* John B Sulivan Award. *Prof Exp:* Res assoc biol res, Southwest Found Res & Educ, 68-70, asst found scientist clin sci, 70-71; from asst prof to assoc prof, Univ Tex Health Sci Ctr, San Antonio, 71-82, prof pharmacol & chief, Div Drug & Alcohol Abuse, 82-96. *Concurrent Pos:* Pharmacol consult, Regional Ctr Drug Educ, 70-72, Lackland Air Force Drug Rehab Ctr, 71-74, Drug Educ Training & Resource Ctr, Region VII, US Off Educ, 72-73 & Southern Calif Res Inst, US Dept Hwy Traffic Safety, 85-; consult, Nat Drug Abuse Ctr, 77; chairperson, Nat Drug Abuse Conf Pharmacol Task Force, 77-79; chmn, Gordon Res Conf Alcohol & Int Neurotoxicol Conf Alcoholism, 79, 82; founder & ed-in-chief, J Substance & Alcohol Actions & Misuse, 79-85; chmn & pres, Kantroll, Inc. *Mem:* AAAS; Am Soc Col Professors; Am Soc Pharmacol & Exp Therapeut; Acad Med Educr & Substance Abuse; fel Am Found Pharmaceut Educ; Neurosci Soc. *Res:* Neuropharmacology; psychopharmacology; drug and alcohol abuse; drug identification; monomine correlates of drug-induced behavior; endorphins and alcohol; psychogenetics of drug seeking behavior; inventor of SAAVE and Tropamine nutritional adjuncts to alcohol and drug abuse treatment; discovery of D2 dopamine A1 allele association with alcoholism at other comparative behaviors; coined the term reward deficiency syndrome to describe common addiction behaviors; granted many patents in the US , Canada and Europe. *Mailing Add:* Dept Behav Sci Sch Pub Health Univ Tex Med Sch 7703 Floyd Curl Dr San Antonio TX 78284. *Fax:* 210-490-8634

BLUM, LEE M, TOXICOLOGY, FORENSIC SCIENCE. *Current Pos:* TOXICOLOGIST, NAT MED SERVS, INC, 86- *Personal Data:* b Philadelphia, Pa, Sept 17, 56; m 81; c 2. *Educ:* Pa State Univ, BS, 78; Northeastern Univ, MS, 80; Thomas Jefferson Univ, PhD(pharmacol), 85; Am Bd Forensic Toxicol, dipl. *Prof Exp:* Post doctoral fel, Cuyahoga County Coroner's Off, 85-86; res assoc, Case Western Univ Sch Med, 85-86. *Mem:* Sigma Xi; Am Acad Forensic Sci; AAAS; Am Chem Soc. *Res:* Analysis and interpretaton of exogenous substances in biological matrices. *Mailing Add:* Nat Med Servs 3701 Welsh Rd Willow Grove PA 19090

BLUM, LENORE CAROL, MATHEMATICAL LOGIC, APPLIED MATHEMATICS. *Current Pos:* lectr math, 69-71, RES ASSOC MATH, UNIV CALIF, BERKELEY, 71-; ASSOC PROF MATH, MILLS COL, 77-, LETTS-VILLARD CHAIR MATH & COMPUT SCI & LETTS-VILLARD RES PROF, 78- *Personal Data:* b New York, NY, Dec 18, 42; m 61; c 1. *Educ:* Simmons Col, BS, 63; Mass Inst Technol, PhD(math), 68. *Prof Exp:* Air Force Off Sci Res fel, 68-69. *Concurrent Pos:* Head, Dept Math & Comput Sci, Mills Col, 74-; coun mem, Conf Bd Math Sci, 76-; res scientist, Int Comput Sci Inst, Berkeley, 88- *Mem:* Asn Women Math (pres, 75-77); Asn Women Sci; Am Math Soc (vpres, 90-); fel AAAS; Sigma Xi. *Res:* Applications of mathematical logic to mathematics, in particular, applications to differential algebra; mathematical theory of inductive inference; information theory; complexity theory. *Mailing Add:* 700 Euclid Ave Berkeley CA 94708-1334

BLUM, LEON LEIB, MEDICINE, PATHOLOGY. *Current Pos:* RETIRED. *Personal Data:* b Telsiai, Lithuania, May 4, 08; nat US; m 36; c 2. *Educ:* Univ Berlin, MD, 33. *Prof Exp:* Res pathologist, Mt Sinai Hosp, Ill, 34-36; instr path bact & trop dis, Sch Nursing, Union Hosp, 37-57, dir, Sch Med Technol, 54-68, pathologist & dir labs, 37-83. *Concurrent Pos:* Pathologist & dir labs, Assoc Physicians & Surgeons' Clin, 36-83, St Anthony Hosp, 44-54, Clay County Hosp, Brazil, 50-73, Putnam County Hosp, Greencastle, 53-82, Greene County Gen Hosp, Linton, 55-82 & Vermillion County Hosp, Clinton, 56-83; sr partner, Terre Haute Med Lab, 47-83; consult, Charles Pfizer & Co, 58-65; adj prof life sci & clin dir, Ctr Med Technol, Ind State Univ, 67-83; med dir, Med Lab Asst Prog, Ind Voc Tech Col, 73-80; clin prof path, Sch Med, Ind Univ, 80-83. *Mem:* Am Soc Cytol; fel Col Am Path; Am Soc Clin Path; AMA; Pan-Am Med Asn. *Res:* Hematology. *Mailing Add:* 505 Arbor Lake Dr Naples FL 34110

BLUM, LESSER, CHEMICAL PHYSICS, STATISTICAL MECHANICS. *Current Pos:* PROF PHYSICS, UNIV PR, 69- *Personal Data:* b Berlin, Ger, Mar 6, 34; US citizen; m 64; c 3. *Educ:* Univ Buenos Aires, PhD(chem), 56. *Prof Exp:* Asst prof phys chem, Univ Buenos Aires, 58-66; res assoc, Rice Univ, 67-68. *Concurrent Pos:* Fel, Free Univ Brussels, 59-60, Nat Res Coun Can, 64 & J S Guggenheim Found, 78. *Mem:* Am Chem Soc; fel Am Phys Soc. *Res:* Statistical mechanics and thermodynamics of fluids and solutions; ionic solutions and electrodes in equilibrium. *Mailing Add:* Dept Physics Univ PR PO Box 23343 Rio Piedras PR 00931

BLUM, LINDA KAY, MICROBIAL ECOLOGY, ESTUARINE ECOLOGY. *Current Pos:* vis scientist, 84-85, res asst prof, 86-95, RES ASSOC PROF, DEPT ENVIRON SCI, UNIV VA, 95- *Personal Data:* b Kalamazoo, Mich, June 24, 50. *Educ:* Mich Technol Univ, BS, 72, MS, 74; Cornell Univ, PhD(microbial ecol), 80. *Prof Exp:* Res asst, Dept Forestry, Mich Technol Univ, 72-74, Dept Agron, Cornell Univ, 75-79; instr microbiol & gen biol, Biol Dept, State Univ NY, Buffalo, 79-80, asst prof, 80-84. *Mem:* Estuarine Res Fedn; Am Soc Microbiol; Am Soc Limnol & Oceanog; Soil Ecol Soc. *Res:* Identification of ecologically relevant functional differences in aquatic and terrestrial microbial communities and of biological, chemical and physical processes contributing to the functional differences by examining microbial abundance, biomass, productivity and community structure. *Mailing Add:* Clark Hall Univ Va Charlottesville VA 22903. *Fax:* 804-982-2137; *E-Mail:* lkb2e@virginia.edu

BLUM, MANUEL, COMPUTER SCIENCE. *Current Pos:* assoc prof, 69-72, assoc chairperson comput sci, 77-80, PROF ELEC ENG & COMPUT SCI, UNIV CALIF, BERKELEY, 72- *Personal Data:* b Caracas, Venezuela, Apr 26, 38; m 61, Lenore C Epstein; c Avrim. *Educ:* Mass Inst Technol, BS & MS, 61, PhD(math), 64. *Honors & Awards:* Alan M Turing Award, Asn Comput Mach, 95. *Prof Exp:* Res assoc elec eng, Mass Inst Technol, 64-65, asst prof math, 65-69. *Concurrent Pos:* Sloan Found fel, 71-72. *Mem:* Am Math Soc; fel Inst Elec & Electronics Engrs; fel AAAS; Asn Comput Mach. *Res:* Theory of algorithms; mathematical theory of inductive inference, automata in 2 and 3 dimensional space; cryptography and number theory; program result checking and correcting. *Mailing Add:* 700 Euclid Ave Berkeley CA 94708-1334. *E-Mail:* blum@cs.berkeley.edu

BLUM, MARVIN, applied mathematics, radar data processing, for more information see previous edition

BLUM, MELVIN S, SYNTHETIC INORGANIC & ORGANOMETALLIC CHEMISTRY NUTRITION. *Current Pos:* DIR, BURLINGTON SCI CORP, 74-; DIR, AM ROLAND CHEM CORP, 84-; CHMN ATOMERGIC CHEMETALS CORP, 91- *Personal Data:* b NY, Jan 8, 36; m 69, Paula Linda Weiss; c Lara J. *Educ:* Columbia Univ, BS, 57, MA, 59; Duke Univ, PhD(pharmacol), 64; Burlington Inst, PhD(nutrit), 70. *Hon Degrees:* PhD, Giredmet Inst, 94. *Prof Exp:* Sales mgr, Nuclear Corp Am, 62-63; gen mgr, GS Chem Mfg Corp, 63-75. *Concurrent Pos:* Hon prof, Russ State Inst Rare Metals, 94. *Mem:* NY Acad Sci; Am Chem Soc; Am Soc Metals. *Res:* Animal and insect repellents; antioxidants; pheromones; plant growth regulators; aversive agents; animal feed supplements; fungicides and biocides. *Mailing Add:* 1385 Lyon Pl Wantagh NY 11793

BLUM, MURRAY SHELDON, ENTOMOLOGY, PHYSIOLOGY. *Current Pos:* prof, 67-78, RES PROF ENTOM, UNIV GA, 78- *Personal Data:* b Philadelphia, Pa, July 19, 29; m 53, Nancy A Hilpp; c Deborah, Darcelle, Dawn & Dana. *Educ:* Univ Ill, BS, 52, MS, 53, PhD(entom), 55. *Honors & Awards:* Gold Medal, Int Soc Chem Ecol. *Prof Exp:* Entomologist, USDA, 57-58; assoc prof entom, La State Univ, Baton Rouge, 58-67. *Concurrent Pos:* consult, NSF, 74-76; Fulbright fel, Univ Paris, 84-85; ed, J Chem Ecol, 1972- *Mem:* Fel AAAS; Entom Soc Am; Acad Applied Sci; Int Soc Chem Ecol; Int

Soc Toxicol; Am Chem Soc. *Res:* Chemistry of insect pheromones and defensive secretions; biochemistry of the insect reproductive system; regulation of insect behavior by chemical releasers; chemistry and functions of arthropod natural products; biochemical strategies of insects feeding on toxic plants. *Mailing Add:* 475 Ponderosa Dr Athens GA 30605. *Fax:* 706-542-2279; *E-Mail:* mblumin@uga.cc.uga.edu

BLUM, NORMAN ALLEN, SOLID STATE SCIENCE, MICROELECTRONICS. *Current Pos:* PRIN STAFF PHYSICIST, APPL PHYSICS LAB, JOHNS HOPKINS UNIV, 70- *Personal Data:* b Boston, Mass, Dec 29, 32; m 57, Elaine R Grossman; c Scott, Wendy & Andrew. *Educ:* Harvard Univ, AB, 54; Brandeis Univ, MA, 59, PhD(physics), 64. *Prof Exp:* Sr res scientist, Res & Advan Develop Div, Avco Corp, 58-60; res staff mem, Nat Magnet Lab, Mass Inst Technol, 60-66 & NASA Electronics Res Ctr, 66-70. *Mem:* Am Phys Soc; Inst Elec & Electronics Engrs; Int Microelectronics & Packaging Soc. *Res:* Solid state physics; magnetism; Mossbauer effect; instrumentation; amorphous films; photovoltaics; optical and electronic properties of solids; microelectronics; biomedical sensors. *Mailing Add:* Appl Physics Lab Johns Hopkins Univ Laurel MD 20723. *E-Mail:* norman_blum@jhuapl.edu

BLUM, PATRICIA RAE, HYDROCARBON PROCESSING. *Current Pos:* PROJ LEADER, STANDARD OIL CO, OHIO, 77- *Personal Data:* b Dayton, Ohio, July 21, 48; m 80; c 1. *Educ:* Wright State Univ, BS, 70, MS, 72; Ohio State Univ, PhD(inorg chem), 77. *Prof Exp:* Teaching asst, Wright State Univ, 70-72; contract chemist, Wright Patterson AFB, 72-73; teaching asst, Ohio State Univ, 73-77. *Mem:* Am Chem Soc. *Res:* Catalytic processes for the selective oxidation of hydrocarbons. *Mailing Add:* BP Chem 4440 Warrensville Center Rd Cleveland OH 44128-2837

BLUM, RICHARD, MATHEMATICS. *Current Pos:* lectr, Univ Sask, 54-56, assoc prof, 56-63, prof math, 63-81, EMER PROF, UNIV SASK, 81- *Personal Data:* b Cernauti, Romania, Sept 26, 13; Can citizen; m 36; c 2. *Educ:* Univ Cernauti, Romania, Lic, 34; Univ Bucharest, PhD(math), 46. *Prof Exp:* Asst math, Univ Bucharest, 45-49; lectr, Univ Cluj, 49-50; asst prof, Acadia Univ, 53-54. *Mem:* Am Math Soc; Can Math Cong. *Res:* Differential geometry, particularly imbedding properties of Riemannian spaces in Euclidean spaces. *Mailing Add:* 2510 Munroe St Saskatoon SK S7J 1S9 Can

BLUM, RICK S, SIGNAL PROCESSING, COMMUNICATIONS & RADAR SYSTEMS. *Current Pos:* PROF ELEC ENG, LEHIGH UNIV, 94- *Personal Data:* m 89, Karen; c Karleigh Jean & Kyle James. *Educ:* Pa State Univ, BS, 84; Univ Pa, MS, 87, PhD(elec eng), 91. *Prof Exp:* Sr systs engr, Gen Elec Corp, 84-91; res initiation award, NSF, 92-96. *Concurrent Pos:* Res fel, Gen Elec Corp, 89; young investr award, Off Naval Res, 97- *Mem:* Inst Elec & Electronics Engrs; Sigma Xi. *Res:* Signal processing for radar and communication systems; distributed array processing and space-time processing; granted one US patent. *Mailing Add:* Dept Elec Eng & Comput Lehigh Univ 19 Memorial Dr W Bethlehem PA 18015

BLUM, ROBERT ALLAN, PSYCHIATRY, PSYCHOANALYSIS. *Current Pos:* ASST PROF PSYCHIAT, GEORGETOWN UNIV, 72-, CLIN ASSOC PROF PSYCHIAT, UNIFORMED SERVS, UNIV HEALTH SCIS, 87- *Personal Data:* b Philadelphia, Pa, May 16, 38; m 59; c 3. *Educ:* Mass Inst Technol, BS, 59, MS, 60; Univ Pa, MD, 64. *Prof Exp:* Engr, Gen Atronics Corp, 59-61; intern med, Mem Hosp Long Beach, Calif, 64-65; resident psychiat, Mass Ment Health Ctr, 65-66, chief resident, Clin Res Ctr, 66-67; staff assoc clin psychopharm, Div Spec Ment Health Res Progs, NIMH, 67-69, res psychiatrist, 69-71; res psychiatrist, Nat Inst Alcoholism & Alcohol Abuse, 71-74. *Concurrent Pos:* Teaching fel, Harvard Med Sch, 65-67; instr, Sch Med, George Washington Univ, 69-74; instr, Sch Med, Johns Hopkins Univ, 69-; consult, US Govt, 74-; teaching analyst, Baltimore-DC Inst Psychoanal, 78- *Mem:* AAAS; fel Am Psychiat Asn; Int Psychoanal Asn; Am Psychoanal Asn; Soc Gen Systs Res; Soc Clin Exp Hypn; Int Soc Hypn; Am Soc Indust Security. *Res:* Information theory; error correcting codes; cognitive and attentional mechanisms in schizophrenia; electrophysiologic correlates of behavior; mathematical models of behavior using automata theory; psychoanalytic models; psychobiographical analysis; behavioral aspects of terrorism. *Mailing Add:* 9819 Hill St Kensington MD 20895-3136

BLUM, SAMUEL EMIL, PHYSICAL CHEMISTRY, ATMOSPHERIC SCIENCES. *Current Pos:* CONSULT, 90- *Personal Data:* b New York, NY, Aug 28, 20; c 3. *Educ:* Rutgers Univ, BS, 42, PhD(phys chem), 50. *Prof Exp:* Prod chemist, US Rubber Co, 42-43; asst, Rutgers Univ, 46-50; prin res chemist, Battelle Mem Inst, 52-59; mem res staff, Thomas J Watson Res Lab, IBM Corp, 59-90. *Mem:* AAAS; Sigma Xi; fel Am Inst Chem. *Res:* Semiconductors; material science. *Mailing Add:* 18-1 Granada Crescent White Plains NY 10603

BLUM, SEYMOUR L, CERAMICS, ENVIRONMENTAL SCIENCE. *Current Pos:* PRES, S L B ASSOC, 86- *Personal Data:* b New York, NY, Jan 10, 25; m 48; c 1. *Educ:* Alfred Univ, BS, 48; Mass Inst Technol, ScD(ceramics), 54. *Honors & Awards:* Norton Award, Am Ceramic Soc, 73. *Prof Exp:* Plant engr, Com Decal, Inc, 48-51; res assoc, Mass Inst Technol, 51-54; mgr high temperature mat, Raytheon Co, 54-63; asst dir metals & ceramics res, IIT Res Inst, 63-65, dir ceramics res, 65-69, vpres, 69-71; dir energy & resource planning, Mitre Corp, 71-78; vpres, Northern Energy Corp, Boston, 78-83; vpres, Charles River Asn, Boston, 83-86. *Concurrent Pos:* Chmn, Nat Mat Adv Bd, Nat Acad Sci, 72-76; mem, Vis Comt, Mass Inst Technol, 73-79; mem, Mat Comt, Off Technol Assessment, US Cong, 74-; mem, Adv Comt Eng & Tech Systs, Nat Acad Sci, 83- *Mem:* AAAS; fel Am Ceramic Soc (vpres, 76-77); Am Soc Metals; Nat Soc Prof Engrs; fel Am Inst Chemists; Sigma Xi. *Res:* Materials research in ceramics, especially electronic ceramics, graphite, refractories and solid state behavior; environmental studies in pollution and waste utilization; environmental research in solar energy and recycling; United States materials policy and availability of materials. *Mailing Add:* 39 Pilgrim Path Sudbury MA 01776

BLUM, STANLEY WALTER, ORGANIC CHEMISTRY, BIOCHEMISTRY. *Current Pos:* MEM STAFF, FOOD & DRUG ADMIN, 78- *Personal Data:* b Sheboygan, Wis, July 3, 33; div; c 2. *Educ:* Univ Wis, BS, 55; Univ Ill, PhD(org chem), 60. *Prof Exp:* Res fel org chem, Univ Minn, 60-61; res assoc chem microbial prod, Rutgers Univ, 61-62; scientist, Warner-Lambert Res Inst, 62-66, sr scientist, 66-77. *Mem:* Am Chem Soc. *Res:* Biochemical pharmacology; drug metabolism; biochemistry. *Mailing Add:* 532 Meadow Hall Dr Rockville MD 20851-1556

BLUM, UDO, BOTANY, ECOLOGY. *Current Pos:* from asst prof to assoc prof, 69-81, PROF BOT, NC STATE UNIV, 81- *Personal Data:* b Ludenscheid, Ger, Nov 29, 39; US citizen; m 68. *Educ:* Franklin Col, BA, 63; Ind Univ, Bloomington, MA, 65; Univ Okla, PhD(bot), 68. *Prof Exp:* Vis asst prof bot, Univ Okla, 68-69. *Concurrent Pos:* Fac res grant, 70, NC State Univ & Agr Res Serv, USDA grants 69-91 & Carolina Power & Light Co, 73-79, Competitive Res Grant Prog, 81-85 & Lisa-USDA, 88-92; ed, Int J Biometeorol, 81-84 & 95-96. *Mem:* Int Soc Allelopahy; Ecol Soc Am; Int Soc Chem Ecol. *Res:* Plant plant interactions, such as competition and allelopathy; effects of natural and man-made stresses on the physiology of plants. *Mailing Add:* Dept Bot NC State Univ Raleigh NC 27695-7612. *Fax:* 919-515-3436; *E-Mail:* udo_blum@ncsu.edu

BLUMBERG, ALAN FRED, COASTAL CIRCULATION, NUMERICAL SIMULATION. *Current Pos:* PRIN SCIENTIST, HYDROQUAL INC, 85- *Personal Data:* b Ancon, Canal Zone, Oct 16, 48; US citizen; m 76; c 1. *Educ:* Fairleigh Dickinson Univ, BS, 70; Johns Hopkins Univ, MA, 73, PhD(phys oceanog), 75. *Prof Exp:* Asst gen oceanog, Johns Hopkins Univ, 73-75; res scientist estuarine & coastal circulation, Princeton Univ, 75-80; sr scientist & sr vpres, Dynalysis of Princeton, 80-85. *Concurrent Pos:* Consult, State Md, 78-79, State Calif, 87. *Mem:* Am Meteorol Soc; Am Geophys Union. *Res:* Fundamental research in physical oceanography and application of results to solution of practical engineering and environmental problems. *Mailing Add:* Hydroqual Inc One Lethbridge Plaza Mahwah NJ 07430

BLUMBERG, AVROM AARON, PHYSICAL CHEMISTRY, POLYMER CHEMISTRY. *Current Pos:* from asst prof to assoc prof, DePaul Univ, 63-75, head, Div Natural Sci & Math, 66-82, chmn, Chem Dept, 86-92, PROF CHEM, DEPAUL UNIV, 75- *Personal Data:* b Albany, NY, Mar 3, 28; m 55, 69, Judith Kohlager; c David, Susan & Jonathan. *Educ:* Rensselaer Polytech Inst, BS, 49; Yale Univ, PhD(phys chem), 53. *Prof Exp:* Lab instr, Rensselaer Polytech Inst, 49; Plate Glass fel, Mellon Inst, 53-59, res chemist polymer studies, 59-63. *Concurrent Pos:* Lectr, Univ Pittsburgh, 57-58. *Mem:* Am Chem Soc; Royal Inst Chem; Arms Control Asn; Sigma Xi. *Res:* Reaction kinetics; solid-liquid reactions; glassy state; differential thermal analysis; x-ray diffraction structure calculations; polymer configurations; transport phenomena in polymers and through films; kinetics of organic growth; arms control; polymer degradation; interfaces. *Mailing Add:* Dept Chem DePaul Univ 2320 N Kenmore Chicago IL 60201

BLUMBERG, BARUCH SAMUEL, EPIDEMIOLOGY, GENETICS. *Current Pos:* assoc dir clin res & sr mem, 64-86, vpres pop oncol, 86-89, SR ADV TO PRES, FOX CHASE CANCER CTR, PHILADELPHIA, 89-, DISTINGUISHED SCIENTIST, 89-; UNIV PROF MED & ANTHROP, UNIV PA, PHILADELPHIA, 77- *Personal Data:* b New York, NY, July 28, 25; m 54, Jean; c 4. *Educ:* Union Col, NY, BS, 46; Columbia Univ, MD, 51; Oxford Univ, PhD(biochem), 57; FRCP, 84. *Hon Degrees:* DSc, Univ Pittsburgh, Dickinson Col, Hahnemann Univ, 77, Franklin & Marshal Col, 78, Yeshiva Univ, 80, Ursinus Col, 82, Bard Col, 85, Elizabethtown Col, 88, Ball State Univ, 89, Univ Pa & Columbia Univ, 90; LLD, Union Col, 77, La Salle Univ, 82; LHD, Jewish Theol Sem Am, 77, Thomas Jefferson Univ & Rush Univ, 83; MA, Oxford Univ, 84, numerous others from US col & univ. *Honors & Awards:* Nobel Prize for Physiol & Med, 76; Passano Award, 74; Gairdner Found Int Award, 75; Karl Landsteiner Mem Award, Am Asn Blood Banks, 75; Richard & Hinda Rosenthal Found Award, Am Col Physicians; Pa Med Soc Distinguished Serv Award, 82; Molly & Sidney N Zubrow Award, Pa Hosp, Philadelphia, 86; Achievement Award, Sammy Davis Jr Nat Liver Inst, 87; John P McGovern Award, Am Med Writers Asn, 88; James Blundell Award, Brit Blood Transfusion Soc, 89; Gold Medal Award, Can Liver Found & Can Asn for the Study of the Liver, 90; Showa Emperor Mem Award, Japan, 94. *Prof Exp:* Intern & asst resident, First Med Div, Bellevue Hosp, 51-53; teaching fel, Dept Med, Col Physicians & Surgeons & Presby Hosp, NY, 53-55; mem, Dept Biochem, Oxford Univ, 55-57; chief, Geog Med & Genetics Sect & attend physician, Clin Ctr, NIH, Bethesda, Md, 57-64; clin prof, Dept Epidemiol, Sch Pub Health, Univ Wash, Seattle, 83-88; master, Balliol Col, Oxford Univ, Eng, 89-94. *Concurrent Pos:* Res collabr, Brookhaven Nat Lab, 60-; assoc prof clin med, Georgetown Univ Sch Med, 62-64; prof human genetics, Univ Pa, Philadelphia, 70-75, prof med, 70-, prof anthropol, 75-, mem, Grad Comt, 68-, mem, Grad Group Hist & Sociol Sci, 79-; vis fel, Trinity Col, Oxford, Eng, 72-73; sr attend physician, Philadelphia Gen Hosp, 75-76; fel, Balliol Col, Oxford Univ, 76, George Eastman vis prof, 83-84; mem, sci adv bd, Leonard Wood Mem, 77- & Am Comt for Weizmann Inst, 79-; consult, Franklin Inst, Philadelphia, 80-, Univ Wash Med Res Unit, Taipei, Taiwan, 82-, Off Surg Gen, 89-; Ashland vis prof, Univ Ky, 86-87; mem bd dirs, Zool Soc Philadelphia, 79-89, emer mem, 89-; mem sci adv bd, Stazione Zool, Naples, Italy, 87-, Fogarty Int Ctr, NIH, Bethesda, 89-; mem bd sci adv, Inst Sci Info, Philadelphia, 89- *Mem:* Nat

Acad Sci; Inst Med-Nat Acad Sci; Am Soc Human Genetics; fel Am Col Physicians; m Soc Clin Invest; Asn Am Physicians; hon fel Am Gastroenterol Asn; hon fel Am Col Gastroenterol; Am Philos Soc. *Res:* Discovery of hepatitis B virus and its vaccine; etiological role of hepatitis B virus and prevention of primary hepatocellular carcinoma. *Mailing Add:* Fox Chase Cancer Ctr 7701 Burholme Ave Philadelphia PA 19111

BLUMBERG, HAROLD, NARCOTICS, NARCOTIC ANTAGONISTS NALOXONE. *Current Pos:* res prof, 74-81, EMER RES PROF PHARMACOL, NEW YORK MED COL, 81- *Personal Data:* b Fairmont, WVa, June 19, 09; m 34, Dorothy Drasnin; c Mark A. *Educ:* Johns Hopkins Univ, ScD(biochem), 33. *Honors & Awards:* John Scott Medal Award, 82. *Prof Exp:* Asst pediat, Sch Med, Johns Hopkins Univ, 33-35, instr, 35-36; assoc biochemist, Off Child Hyg, USPHS, 36-38; res biochemist, Dept Biochem, Sch Hyg & Pub Health, Johns Hopkins Univ, 38-42; assoc toxicologist, Army Indust Hyg, US War Dept, 42-44; sr biologist, Sterling-Winthrop Res Inst, NY, 44-47; dir biol labs, Endo Labs, Inc, 47-60, assoc dir res, 60-70, assoc dir res, Endo Labs-DuPont Pharmaceut, 70-74. *Concurrent Pos:* Nat Res Coun fel, Sch Hyg & Pub Health, Johns Hopkins Univ, 34-35; consult, Nat Inst Drug Abuse. *Mem:* AAAS; Soc Toxicol; Am Soc Pharmacol & Exp Therapeut; Am Inst Nutrit; NY Acad Sci. *Res:* Vitamin E; lead poisoning; argyremia; manganese rickets; choline and liver cirrhosis; mercurial diuretics; theophylline derivatives; antispasmodics; naloxone and naltrexone narcotic antagonists; molindone tranquilizer; nalbuphine analgesic. *Mailing Add:* 1731 Beacon St Apt 213 Brookline MA 02146-4323

BLUMBERG, JEFFREY BERNARD, IMMUNOLOGY, TOXICOLOGY. *Current Pos:* asst dir, Tufts Univ, 81-87, actg assoc dir, 85-86, assoc prof nutrit, 81-88, PROF NUTRIT, USDA HUMAN NUTRIT RES CTR, TUFTS UNIV, 88-, ASSOC DIR, 88- *Personal Data:* b San Francisco, Calif, Dec 31, 45; m 71; c 2. *Educ:* Wash State Univ, BPharm & BSc(psychol), 69; Vanderbilt Univ, PhD(pharmacol), 74. *Honors & Awards:* Cert of Merit, USDA, 82. *Prof Exp:* Res psychopharmacol, Vanderbilt Univ, 74; asst prof pharmacol, Northeastern Univ, 75-78, dir toxicol prog, 78-79, assoc prof pharmacol & toxicol, 79-81, head sect pharmacol, 79-81. *Concurrent Pos:* NIH fel biochem, Univ Calgary, 74-75; co-prin investr, Am Heart Asn grant, 78-81; prin investr, USDA grant, 81-; Surgeon Gen Workshop Health Prom Aging; DHHS year 2000 Health Object Comt. *Mem:* Soc Neurosci; Sigma Xi; AAAS; Am Col Toxicol; Am Inst Nutrit; Am Col Nutrit; Am Soc Clin Nutrit; Am Aging Asn; Am Soc Parenteral Enteral Nutrit; NY Acad Sci; Union Concerned Scientists. *Res:* Gerontology; public health and epidemiology; nutrition; immunology biochemistry. *Mailing Add:* USDA Human Nutrit Res C Tufts Univ 711 Washington St Boston MA 02111-1524

BLUMBERG, LEROY NORMAN, PARTICLE ACCELERATORS. *Current Pos:* physicist, 66-80, SR PHYSICIST, BROOKHAVEN NAT LAB, 80- *Personal Data:* b Atlantic City, NJ, June 22, 29; m 57, Sydel Barkin; c Manya (Helman), Deborah (Hopkins) & Julia (Haykin). *Educ:* Mass Inst Technol, BSc, 51; Columbia Univ, MA, 55, PhD(physics), 62. *Prof Exp:* Physicist hydrodyn, Los Alamos Sci Lab, Univ Calif, 55-57, nuclear physics, 57-60; physicist, Union Carbide Nuclear Div, Oak Ridge Nat Lab, 62-65; physicist, Cambridge Electron Accelerator, Harvard Univ, 65-66. *Concurrent Pos:* Fulbright fel, 51-52; vis prof, Japan Nat High Energy Phys Lab, 75; vis scholar, Stanford Univ, 82-83; vis scientist, US Dept Energy, 86-88. *Mem:* AAAS; fel Am Phys Soc. *Res:* Shock wave hydrodynamics; fission fragment angular distributions; polarized proton scattering; pion production; K-zero decay; accelerator physics; electromagnetism; atomic and molecular physics; optics; design of electron storage rings as synchrotron radiation sources; orbit calculations and computer modeling. *Mailing Add:* Nat Synchrotron Light Source Brookhaven Nat Lab Bldg 725 Upton NY 11973. *Fax:* 516-344-3029; *E-Mail:* blumberg@bnl.gov

BLUMBERG, MARK STUART, RISK ADJUSTING USE OUTCOMES OF HEALTH CARE. *Current Pos:* dir, spec studies, RISK ADJUSTED MEASURES OUTCOMES, 70-94, KAISER FOUND HEALTH PLAN, INC, 94- *Personal Data:* b New York, NY, Nov 16, 24; m 52, 74; c 2. *Educ:* Harvard Sch Dent Med, DMD, 48; Harvard Med Sch, MD, 50. *Prof Exp:* Opers analyst, Opers Res Off, Johns Hopkins Univ, 51-54; commissioned officer, Occup Health Prog, USPHS, 54-56; from opers analyst to dir health econ, Stanford Res Inst, 56-66; dir health planning, Off Pres, Univ Calif, 66-70. *Concurrent Pos:* Consult, Pan Am Health Orgn, 66; mem, Res Adv Comt, Calif State Dept Ment Hyg, 67-70; lectr, Sch Pub Health, Univ Calif, Berkeley, 70-75; consult, Robert Wood Johnson Found, 83-87. *Mem:* Inst Med-Nat Acad Sci. *Res:* Quantitative analyses of data on health care service utilization delivery, organization, outcomes and costs; measuring risk-adjusted outcomes of health care. *Mailing Add:* 6150 Pinewood Rd Oakland CA 94611

BLUMBERG, PETER MITCHELL, CARCINOGENESIS, TUMOR PROMOTION. *Current Pos:* CHIEF, MOLECULAR MECHANISMS OF TUMOR PROM SECT, LAB CELLULAR CARCINOGENESIS & TUMOR PROM, DIV CANCER CAUSE & PREV, NAT CANCER INST, 81- *Personal Data:* b Glen Ridge, NJ, Jan 6, 49; m 49. *Educ:* Harvard Univ, AB, 70, AM, 70, PhD(biochem & molecular biol), 74. *Honors & Awards:* Rhoads Award, 87. *Prof Exp:* Asst prof pharmacol, Harvard Med Sch, 75-81, assoc prof, 81. *Concurrent Pos:* Assoc ed, Cancer Res, 81-; J Nat Cancer Inst, 85-; Phytotherapy Res, 87. *Mem:* Am Asn Cancer Res; Am Soc Cell Biol; Soc Neurosci; AAAS. *Res:* Analysis of the mode of action of tumor promoters, with particular emphasis on characterization of receptors for the phorbol esters. *Mailing Add:* Lab Cellular Carcinogenesis & Tumor Prom Nat Cancer Inst NIH 37 Convent Dr MSC 4255 Bldg 37 Rm 3A01 Bethesda MD 20892-4255

BLUMBERG, RICHARD WINSTON, PEDIATRICS. *Current Pos:* DIR, DIV PHYS HEALTH, DEKALB COUNTY HEALTH DEPT, 81- *Personal Data:* b Winston-Salem, NC, Nov 10, 14; m 69. *Educ:* Emory Univ, BS, 35, MD, 38. *Prof Exp:* Res assoc, Children's Hosp, Cincinnati, 47-48; assoc, Emory Univ, 48-51, from asst prof to assoc prof, 51-59, actg chmn dept, 51-59, prof pediat & chmn dept, Sch Med, 59-81. *Mem:* Am Acad Pediat; AMA; Am Pediat Soc. *Res:* Infectious diseases. *Mailing Add:* 2419 Woodward Way NW Atlanta GA 30305-4052

BLUME, ARTHUR JOEL, NEUROCHEMISTRY. *Current Pos:* ASST MEM NEUROCHEM, DEPT PHYSIOL CHEM, ROCHE INST MOLECULAR BIOL, 71- *Personal Data:* b New York, NY, May 19, 41; m 68; c 2. *Educ:* Univ Rochester, BA, 63; Syracuse Univ, MS, 66, PhD(molecular biol), 68. *Prof Exp:* USPHS fel neurochem, Lab Biochem Genetics, NIH, 68-71. *Mem:* Sigma Xi; Fedn Am Soc Exp Biol. *Res:* Storage and transfer of information in the nervous system; emphasis on properties of neuronal membranes. *Mailing Add:* DGI Bio-Technol 40 Talmadge Rd Edison NJ 08818

BLUME, FREDERICK DUANE, ENVIRONMENTAL PHYSIOLOGY. *Current Pos:* PROF BIOL, CALIF STATE COL, BAKERSFIELD, 72- *Personal Data:* b Mishawaka, Ind, Aug 27, 33; m 55; c 8. *Educ:* Wabash Col, AB, 55; Univ Calif, Berkeley, PhD(altitude metab), 65. *Prof Exp:* Asst res physiologist, White Mountain Res Sta, Univ Calif, 64-69, asst dir, 69-72. *Mem:* Fedn Am Soc Exp Biol. *Res:* Environmental physiology; carbohydrate metabolism at altitude; growth and development and cardiovascular changes at altitude. *Mailing Add:* 100 Haggin St Bakersfield CA 93309

BLUME, HANS-JUERGEN CHRISTIAN, ELECTRONICS ENGINEERING. *Current Pos:* RETIRED. *Personal Data:* b Braunschweig, WGer, May 10, 26; m 52; c 4. *Educ:* Tech Univ Braunschweig, WGer, dipl eng, 56, DEng, 66. *Honors & Awards:* Apollo Achievement Award, NASA, 69, Spec Achievement Award, 77, NASA Award, 67. *Prof Exp:* Patent engr, Siemens, 55-58; sr engr, NASA, 59-96. *Mem:* Inst Elec & Electronics Engrs. *Res:* Low-noise preamplification of microwaves with negative resistance amplifiers such as superconductive tunneling junction; development of microwave radiometer systems for the remote sensing of ocean surface parameters from aircrafts and satellites. *Mailing Add:* 1 Hampshire Dr Hampton VA 23669

BLUME, JOHN A(UGUST), DYNAMICS, EARTHQUAKE ENGINEERING. *Current Pos:* CONSULT, 87- *Personal Data:* b Gonzales, Calif, Apr 8, 09; m 85. *Educ:* Stanford Univ, AB, 32, Engr, 34, PhD(civil eng), 67. *Honors & Awards:* Moisseiff Award, Am Soc Civil Engrs, 53, 61 & 69, Howard Award, 62; Seismol Soc Am Medal, 87. *Prof Exp:* Mem staff, Seismol Div, US Coast & Geod Surv, 34-35; engr, Div Hwy, State Calif, 35-36; engr, Stand Oil Co Calif, 36-40, design engr, 40-45; pvt practice, 45-57; pres & chmn bd, John A Blume Assoc Engrs, 57-84, consult, URS/Blume Engrs, 84-87. *Concurrent Pos:* UNESCO expert, earthquake risk; mem, Interoceanic Canal Study Air Blast & Ground Shock Technol working groups, seismic & dynamic consult, Div Reactor Licensing, US Atomic Energy Comn; mem & past pres, Earthquake Eng Res Inst; consult, 45-57; mem, Organizing Comt, World Conf Earthquake Eng, 56; lectr, Stanford Univ, 57-84, consult prof, 80-86. *Mem:* Nat Acad Eng; hon mem Am Soc Civil Engrs; Seismol Soc Am; hon mem Am Concrete Inst; Soc Am Mil Engrs; Sigma Xi; hon mem Int Asn Earthquake Eng; hon mem Earthquake Eng Res Inst. *Res:* Structural-dynamic properties of buildings and other structures and the response of structures to earthquake, underground nuclear explosion, windstorm, blast, sonic boom and ocean swell. *Mailing Add:* 85 El Cerrito Ave Hillsborough CA 94010

BLUME, MARTIN, PHYSICS. *Current Pos:* from assoc physicist to physicist, 62-70, assoc dir, 81-84, SR PHYSICIST, BROOKHAVEN NAT LAB, 70-, ED-IN-CHIEF, AM PHYS SOC, 97- *Personal Data:* b New York, NY, Jan 13, 32; m 55, Sheila Bierman; c Frederick & Janet. *Educ:* Princeton Univ, AB, 54, Harvard Univ, AM, 56, PhD(physics), 59. *Honors & Awards:* E O Lawrence Award, 81. *Prof Exp:* Fulbright res fel physics, Univ Tokyo, 59-60; res assoc theoret physics, Atomic Energy Res Estab, Eng, 60-62. *Concurrent Pos:* Prof physics, State Univ NY, Stonybrook, 72-80, dep dir, 84-96. *Mem:* Fel Am Phys Soc; fel AAAS; fel NY Acad Sci; fel Am Acad Arts & Sci. *Res:* Theoretical solid state and atomic physics; neutron scattering; magnetism; magnetic resonance; synchrotron radiation. *Mailing Add:* Physics Dept Am Phys Soc One Res Rd Ridge NY 11961. *E-Mail:* blume@bnl.gov or blume@aps.org

BLUME, SHEILA BIERMAN, PSYCHIATRY. *Current Pos:* CLIN PROF PSYCHIAT STATE UNIV NY, STONY BROOK, 84-, MED DIR, ALCOHOLISM, CHEM DEPENDENCY & COMPULSIVE GAMBLING PROGS & DIR S OAKS INST, S OAKS HOSP, AMITYVILLE, NY, 84- *Personal Data:* b Brooklyn, NY, June 21, 34; m 55; c 2. *Educ:* Harvard Med Sch, MD, 58. *Prof Exp:* Intern pediat, Med Ctr, Children's Hosp, 58-59; Fulbright fel psychiat biochem, Sch Med, Tokyo Univ, 59-60; resident psychiat, Cent Islip Psychiat Ctr, 62-65, chief alcoholism unit, 64-79; dir, NY State Div Alcoholism & Alcohol Abuse, 79-83; med dir, Nat Coun Alcoholism, 83. *Concurrent Pos:* Clin asst prof psychiat, Sch Med, State Univ NY Stony Brook, 71-84; co-dir, Caribbean Inst Alcoholism, 75-87; bd dirs, Nat Comn Confidentiality Health Rec, 76-80, Nat Coun Alcoholism, 79- & Children of Alcoholics Found, 82-96; mem panel Alcoholism, Am Med Asn, 83-85; mem, Coun on Addiction Psychiat, 90- chair, comt on addiction treatment 95- Am Phychiat Asn, Gov Coun Pychiat & Substance Abuse Facil, Am Hosp Asn, 88-90; chair, am soc of add med, Task Force on Addiction Med 21st Century. *Mem:* Fel Am Psychiat Asn; Fel Am Soc of Addiction

Med (pres, 79-80); Am Acad Psychiat in Alcoholism & Addictions; Nat Coun Compulsive Gambling. *Res:* Addictive disorders in women, and compulsive gambling; drug dependence; clinical aspects, treatment, public policy, family aspects and confidentiality of records of alcoholism. *Mailing Add:* South Oaks Hosp 400 Sunrise Hwy Amityville NY 11701

BLUMEN, WILLIAM, FLUID DYNAMICS, METEOROLOGY. *Current Pos:* from asst prof to assoc prof, 66-74, PROF ASTROPHYS, PLANETARY & ATMOS SCI, UNIV COLO, BOULDER, 74- *Personal Data:* b Hartford, Conn, Aug 7, 31; m 60; c 2. *Educ:* Fla State Univ, BS, 57, MS, 58; Mass Inst Technol, PhD(mountain-wave drag), 63. *Prof Exp:* Res assoc, Univ Oslo, 63-64; fel meteorol, Nat Ctr Atmospheric Res, 64-66. *Concurrent Pos:* Lectr, Univ Colo, 65-66; res grants, NATO, 63-65, NSF, 68-70; NATO sr vis fel, Cambridge Univ, 70-71; Univ Colo fac fel & sci vis, Europ Centre Medium Range Weather Forecasts, Eng, 76-77; ed, J Atmospheric Sci, 78-; partic, The Alpine Exp Observ Prog, 82; sci visitor, Oxford Univ, 85; vis prof, Naval Postgrad Sch, 86-; hon prof, Dept Atmospheric Sci, Nanjing Univ, 88; ed, Meteorol Monographs Am Meteorol Soc, 84- *Mem:* Am Meteorol Soc. *Res:* Theoretical aspects of geophysical fluid dynamics, with application to the dynamics of atmospheric and oceanic circulations; wave motion, atmospheric fronts and hydrodynamic instability. *Mailing Add:* 2365 Balsam Dr Boulder CO 80304

BLUMENFELD, HENRY A, PHYSICS, PARTICLE DETECTION. *Current Pos:* MEM PHYSICS STAFF, SACLAY NUCLEAR RES CTR, FRANCE, 70- *Personal Data:* b Amsterdam, Neth, May 31, 25; US citizen; m 56, Kathleen Levy; c Yorick & Nadia. *Educ:* Harvard Univ, AB, 48; Columbia Univ, PhD(physics), 56. *Prof Exp:* Res assoc physics, Mass Inst Technol, 55-56 & Duke Univ, 56-57; mem physics staff, Princeton Univ, 58-67 & Europ Orgn Nuclear Res, Geneva, Switz, 67-70. *Mem:* Am Phys Soc. *Res:* High energy nuclear physics; experimental, elementary particles; large and rapid cycling bubble chambers; scintillation and photon dectors; data analysis. *Mailing Add:* DAPNIA SED Saclay Bat 123 Gif-sur-Yvette Cedex 91191 France. *Fax:* 33-1-69085669; *E-Mail:* hab@hep.saclay.cea.fr

BLUMENFELD, MARTIN, CELL BIOLOGY, MOLECULAR BIOLOGY. *Personal Data:* b Baltimore, Md, Sept 4, 41; m 66; c 2. *Educ:* Johns Hopkins Univ, BA, 63; Case Western Reserve Univ, PhD(biol), 68. *Prof Exp:* Fel zool, Univ Mich, 67-68; res assoc, Univ Tex, 68-72; fel genetics, Univ Wis, 72-73, res assoc, 73-74; asst prof zool, Univ Minn, Minneapolis, 74-80. *Concurrent Pos:* USPHS res grant, Inst Gen Med, 74. *Res:* Satellite DNA and molecular organization of chromosomes of drosophila. *Mailing Add:* 3901 Washburn Ave Minneapolis MN 55410

BLUMENFELD, OLGA O, BIOCHEMISTRY. *Current Pos:* from asst prof to assoc prof, 61-72, PROF BIOCHEM, ALBERT EINSTEIN COL MED, 72- *Personal Data:* b Lodz, Poland, Apr 6, 23; nat US; m 44; c 1. *Educ:* City Col New York, BS, 46; Univ Colo, MS, 48; NY Univ, PhD(biochem), 57. *Prof Exp:* Fel, Nat Res Coun & Rockefeller Inst, 57-61. *Concurrent Pos:* Sr investr, Arthritis Found, 61-67; NIH career develop award, 67. *Mem:* Am Chem Soc; Fedn Am Soc Exp Biol. *Res:* Protein structure. *Mailing Add:* Dept Biochem Albert Einstein Col Med Bronx NY 10461

BLUMENFIELD, DAVID, HORTICULTURE, PLANT PHYSIOLOGY. *Current Pos:* from asst prof to assoc prof, 59-71, PROF HORT, DEL VALLEY COL, 71- *Personal Data:* b Philadelphia, Pa, Mar 7, 28; m 59; c 2. *Educ:* Del Valley Col, BS, 50; Rutgers Univ, MS, 56, PhD(hort, plant physiol), 59. *Prof Exp:* Spec rep tech sales, Wyeth Labs, Pa, 53-55; res asst hort, Rutgers Univ, 55-59. *Mem:* AAAS; Am Soc Hort Sci; fel Nat Asn Col & Teachers Agr. *Res:* Plant nutrition; agricultural climatology. *Mailing Add:* Dept Hort Del Valley Col 700 E Butler Ave Doylestown PA 18901

BLUMENKOPF, TODD ANDREW, MEDICINAL CHEMISTRY RESEARCH-SITE-DIRECTED DELIVERY OF ANTITUMOR AGENTS, MEDICINAL CHEMISTRY RESEARCH. *Current Pos:* SR RES SCIENTIST, BURROUGHS WELLCOME CO, 86- *Personal Data:* b New York, NY, June 21, 56. *Educ:* Univ Calif, Los Angeles, BS, 78; Univ Calif, Berkeley, PhD(chem), 83. *Prof Exp:* NIH fel, Univ Calif, Irvine, 84-86. *Concurrent Pos:* Mem, Comt Chemists with Disabilities, Am Chem Soc, 80-, chmn, 88-92, alt counr, 82-84, consult, Prof Progs Planning & Coord Comt, 88-92; mem, Nat Comt Sci Educ Stand & Assessment, Nat Res Coun, 93- *Mem:* Am Chem Soc; AAAS; Found Sci & Disability; NY Acad Sci. *Res:* Design and synthesis of new medicinal agents; antiviral agents, antitumor agents, antibody conjugates for site-directed drug delivery and calcium channel blockers as cardiovascular agents. *Mailing Add:* Central Research Div Pfizer Inc Eastern Point Rd Groton CT 06340. *Fax:* 860-441-3803; *E-Mail:* todd_a_blumenkopf@groton.pfizer.com

BLUMENSON, LESLIE ELI, MATHEMATICAL BIOLOGY, BIOSTATISTICS. *Current Pos:* SR BIOSTAT, BIOSTATISTICAL CONSULT SERV, 91- *Personal Data:* b New York, NY, Mar 20, 34; c 2. *Educ:* NY Univ, AB, 55, MS, 56, PhD(math), 62. *Honors & Awards:* George W Snedcor Award, Am Statist Asn, 77. *Prof Exp:* Sr res mathematician, Electronics Res Lab, Columbia Univ, 56-63; USPHS trainee, Univ Chicago, 63-65; from sr cancer res scientist to assoc cancer res scientist, Roswell Park Mem Inst, 65-71, prin cancer res scientist, 72-91. *Concurrent Pos:* Res asst prof, Dept Biomet, State Univ NY, Buffalo, 86- *Mem:* Soc Math Biol. *Res:* Mathematical models in biological sciences; cancer research; biostatistics. *Mailing Add:* 141 Brookdale Dr Williamsville NY 14221

BLUMENSTEIN, MICHAEL, BIOCHEMISTRY. *Current Pos:* ASST PROF BIOCHEM, SCH MED, TUFTS UNIV, 75- *Personal Data:* b New York, NY, Nov 16, 47. *Educ:* City Col New York, BS, 68; Calif Inst Technol, PhD(chem), 72. *Prof Exp:* Mem tech staff biochem, Bell Labs, 73-74; res assoc, Univ Ariz, 74-75. *Concurrent Pos:* NIH fel, Univ Ariz, 75. *Mem:* AAAS; Am Chem Soc. *Res:* Nuclear magnetic resonance studies of biochemical systems; protein-hormone interactions; mechanism of action of adenine nucleotide coenzymes. *Mailing Add:* Dept Chem Hunter Coll 695 Park Ave New York NY 10021-5024

BLUMENSTOCK, BRENT J, CONDENSED MATTER PHYSICS. *Current Pos:* MEM TECH STAFF, AT&T BELL LABS, 82- *Educ:* Mich State Univ, BS, 75, MS, 77, PhD(exp condensed matter physics), 80. *Prof Exp:* Asst res engr, Univ Calif, Berkeley, 80-82. *Mem:* Am Phys Soc. *Res:* Granted 2 patents. *Mailing Add:* AT&T Bell Labs PO Box 900 Princeton NJ 08542-0900

BLUMENSTOCK, DAVID A, MEDICINE. *Current Pos:* PROF CLIN SURG, COL PHYSICIANS & SURGEONS, COLUMBIA UNIV, 74- *Personal Data:* b Newark, NJ, Feb 14, 27; m 52; c 3. *Educ:* Union Col, NY, BS, 49; Cornell Univ, MD, 53; Am Bd Surg, dipl, 59; Am Bd Thoracic Surg, dipl, 60. *Prof Exp:* Resident surgeon, Mary Imogene Bassett Hosp, 54-60, NIH res career develop award, 62-63, surgeon-in-chief, 63-86. *Mem:* Soc Univ Surgeons; Am Asn Thoracic Surg; Soc Thoracic Surgeons; Am Surg Asn; Am Fedn Clin Res; Int Transplantation Soc. *Res:* Transplantation of tissues and organs; preservation of living tissues. *Mailing Add:* 110 Braemar Dr c/o Marley Cheshire CT 06410-1614

BLUMENTHAL, GEORGE RAY, ASTROPHYSICS. *Current Pos:* from asst prof to assoc prof, 72-83, PROF ASTRON & ASTROPHYS, UNIV CALIF, SANTA CRUZ, 80- *Personal Data:* b Milwaukee, Wis, Oct 20, 45; m 77. *Educ:* Univ Wis, Milwaukee, BS, 66; Univ Calif, San Diego, PhD(physics), 71. *Prof Exp:* Sr scientist astrophys, Am Sci & Eng, 71-72. *Mem:* Am Astron Soc. *Res:* Galaxy formation; nature of active galaxies and quasistellar objects; compact x-ray sources; cosmology; cosmic rays; clusters of galaxies. *Mailing Add:* Dept Astron Univ Calif 325 Nat Sci II 1156 High St Santa Cruz CA 95064-1099

BLUMENTHAL, HAROLD JAY, MICROBIOLOGY, MICROBIAL BIOCHEMISTRY. *Current Pos:* chmn dept, 65-86, PROF MICROBIOL, STRITCH SCH MED, LOYOLA UNIV CHICAGO, 65- *Personal Data:* b New York, NY, Jan 21, 26; m 50, Doris Ceren; c Robert M, Steven M & David A. *Educ:* Ind Univ, BS, 47; Purdue Univ, MS, 49, PhD(bact), 53. *Prof Exp:* Teaching asst chem, Purdue Univ, 47-49; Am Cancer Soc fel, Inst Cancer Res, 53-54; from instr to assoc prof microbiol, Univ Mich, 54-65. *Concurrent Pos:* AEC fel, 52-53; res assoc, Rackham Arthritis Res Unit, 54-56; NIH spec res fel, 63-64; mem adv comt study, NIH Res Training Grant Progs, Nat Acad Sci, 66-75; consult, Argonne Univs Asn-Argonne Nat Lab, 71-74; Am Acad Microbiol vis prof, Cath Univ Chile, 72. *Mem:* AAAS; Am Soc Microbiol; Am Chem Soc; Am Asn Univ Profs. *Res:* Pathways of carbohydrate catabolism in microorganisms; metabolism of hexaric acids; neurodegenerative disease diagnosis. *Mailing Add:* Dept Microbiol & Immunol Loyola Univ Stritch Sch Med Maywood IL 60153. *Fax:* 708-216-9574

BLUMENTHAL, HERBERT, BIOCHEMISTRY, TOXICOLOGY. *Current Pos:* RETIRED. *Personal Data:* b New York, NY, May 1, 25; m 50; c 2. *Educ:* City Col New York, BS, 48; Univ Southern Calif, PhD(biochem), 55. *Honors & Awards:* George H Scott Mem Award, Toxicol Forum, 86. *Prof Exp:* Actg chief, Pharmaco-Dynamics Br, Div Pharmacol, Food & Drug Admin, 55-58; biochemist, Nat Inst Dent Res, NIH, 58-61; chief petitions res br, Food & Drug Admin, 61-71, dep dir, Div Toxicol, 70-74, actg dir, 74-76, dir, 76-88. *Concurrent Pos:* WHO expert, Adv Panel Food Safety; mem, Comt Food Chem Codex Inst Med, Nat Acad Sci. *Mem:* Fel AAAS; Soc Toxicol; Am Col Toxicol. *Res:* Toxicology of food additives, pesticides, colors, drugs. *Mailing Add:* 12545 Two Farm Dr Silver Spring MD 20904-2932

BLUMENTHAL, HERMAN T, PATHOLOGY. *Current Pos:* gerontol res assoc, 62-68, RES PROF GERONT, BIOPSYCHOL RES LAB, DEPT PSYCHOL, WASHINGTON UNIV, 68- *Personal Data:* b New York, NY, Apr 8, 13; m 40; c 2. *Educ:* Rutgers Univ, BS, 34; Univ Pa, MS, 36; Washington Univ, PhD(path), 38, MD, 42; Am Bd Path, dipl. *Honors & Awards:* Berg Prize, 41. *Prof Exp:* Asst path, Sch Med, Washington Univ, 39-42; resident, Jewish Hosp, St Louis, 42-43; lab dir, Jewish Hosp, Louisville, 46; dir div labs, Jewish Hosp, St Louis, 50-57, inst exp path, 57-62. *Concurrent Pos:* Attend pathologist, Vet Admin Hosp, Jefferson Barracks, Mo, 47-50, dir clin res prog aging, 60-66; co-chmn endocrinol sect, Int Cong Gerontol, London, 54, prog biol & clin med, San Francisco, 60; consult pathologist, Cochran Vet Admin Hosp, 64-; mem coun arteriosclerosis, Am Heart Asn; Adj Prof, Dept Community & Family Med, St Leeds Univ Med. *Mem:* AAAS; Soc Exp Biol & Med; Am Asn Cancer Res; Am Asn Path & Bact; Col Am Path; Sigma Xi. *Res:* Cancer; endocrinology; aging; transplantation; virus diseases; amebiasis; arteriosclerosis. *Mailing Add:* Dept Psychol Washington Univ St Louis MO 63130-4899

BLUMENTHAL, IRWIN S(IMEON), ELECTRICAL ENGINEERING. *Current Pos:* RES ENGR, RAND CORP, 76- *Personal Data:* b Derby, Conn, June 6, 25; c 2. *Educ:* Yale Univ, BE, 45, ME, 47, PhD(elec eng), 51. *Honors & Awards:* Second Prize, Inst Elec & Electronics Engrs, 52. *Prof Exp:* Test engr, Gen Elec Co, 45-46; lab asst elec eng, Yale Univ, 47-48, instr, 48-51; res engr, Northrop Aircraft, Inc, 51-53; res engr, Rand Corp, 53-73; mem staff, Off Naval Res, NATO, 73-76. *Mem:* Sigma Xi; Inst Elec & Electronics Engrs; Mil Opers Res Soc; Asn Unmanned Vehicle Safety; Am Defense Preparedness Asn. *Res:* Servomechanism; control system analysis and design; defense systems, concepts, analysis and evaluation; sonar; medical electronics; astronautics; cost-benefit health analysis, positive aspects of pollution; concepts and systems which will minimize the chance of nuclear war occurring. *Mailing Add:* 802 San Vicente Blvd Santa Monica CA 90402

BLUMENTHAL, JACK L, ENGINEERING. *Current Pos:* Chief engr, 91, ASST DIR, CTR AUTOMOTIVE TECHNOL, TRW SPACE & DEFENSE, 91- *Personal Data:* b Los Angeles, Calif, Sept 10, 36. *Educ:* Univ Calif, Los Angeles, PhD(eng), 63. *Concurrent Pos:* Chmn Bd, Marymount Col. *Mem:* Nat Acad Eng; Am Chem Soc; Am Combustion Inst. *Mailing Add:* Space & Defense Sect TRW 1 Space Park Redondo Beach CA 90278. *Fax:* 310-814-6403; *E-Mail:* jack.blumenthal@trw.com

BLUMENTHAL, KENNETH MICHAEL, BIOCHEMISTRY. *Current Pos:* from asst prof to assoc prof, 76-86, PROF BIOCHEM & MOLECULAR BIOL, COL MED, UNIV CINCINNATI, 86- *Personal Data:* b Chicago, Ill, Aug 24, 45; m 67; c 2. *Educ:* Univ Wis, BSc, 67; Univ Chicago, PhD(biochem), 71. *Prof Exp:* Fel biochem, Univ Calif, Los Angeles, 71-74; asst prof, Univ Fla, 74-76. *Concurrent Pos:* NIH fel, 71; NIH res career develop award, 77; Biochem Study Sect, NIH, 86- *Mem:* Am Chem Soc; Am Soc Biol Chemists; Sigma Xi. *Res:* Protein chemistry; polypeptide neurotoxin structure and function; structure and action of protein cytolysins. *Mailing Add:* Dept Molecular Genetics Col Med Univ Cincinnati 231 Bethesda Ave Cincinnati OH 45267-0524

BLUMENTHAL, RALPH HERBERT, PHYSICS. *Current Pos:* ADJ ASSOC PROF NATURAL SCI, HOFSTRA UNIV, 88- *Personal Data:* b New York, NY, Feb 24, 25; m 48, Renee Cohen; c David, Robert & Meryl. *Educ:* Brooklyn Col, BA, 45, MA, 49; NY Univ, PhD(sci educ), 56. *Prof Exp:* Radio engr, Hamilton Radio Corp, 45; lectr physics, Brooklyn Col, 46-48; physicist & proj leader, US Naval Supply Activ, 48-52; physicist & supvr test group, Picatinny Arsenal, 52; lectr physics, Brooklyn Col & Queens Col, NY, 52-54; tutor, City Col New York, 54-56, instr physics, 58-61; sr engr & group leader, Sperry Gyroscope Corp, NY, 58-62, assoc mem tech & mgt staff, 62-63; staff engr, Grumman Aerospace Corp, 63-70; physics teacher, Sewanhaka Cent High Sch Dist, Elmont, NY, 70-88. *Concurrent Pos:* Adj asst prof physics, Queensborough Community Col, 70-78, adj assoc prof, 78-81; adj asst prof physics, Adelphi Univ, 76-80, adj assoc prof, 80-87. *Mem:* Fel AAAS; Am Phys Soc. *Res:* History of science laser communication systems; electrooptical light modulation; microwave electronics; programmed physics instruction. *Mailing Add:* 15 Bonnie Dr Westbury NY 11590-2803

BLUMENTHAL, ROBERT ALLAN, DIFFERENTIAL GEOMETRY, FOLIATION THEORY. *Current Pos:* asst prof, 79-82, ASSOC PROF MATH, ST LOUIS UNIV, 82- *Personal Data:* b New York, NY, Sept 24, 51. *Educ:* Univ Rochester, BA, 73; Washington Univ, PhD(math), 78. *Prof Exp:* Maitre asst math, Univ de Lille, France, 78-79. *Mem:* Am Math Soc. *Res:* Differential geometry of foliations; effects of various targential and transverse structures on the global structure of a foliated manifold. *Mailing Add:* 1110 Bonsella St Walla Walla WA 99362

BLUMENTHAL, ROBERT MCCALLUM, mathematics, for more information see previous edition

BLUMENTHAL, ROBERT MARTIN, MOLECULAR GENETICS, DNA-PROTEIN INTERACTIONS. *Current Pos:* from asst prof to assoc prof, 81-93, PROF MICROBIOL, MED COL OHIO, 94- *Personal Data:* b Lafayette, Ind, Nov 3, 51; m 87, Beth M Dwoskin; c Noah, Judith & Sophia. *Educ:* Ind Univ, AB, 72; Univ Mich, MSc, 75, PhD(microbiol), 77. *Prof Exp:* Am Cancer Soc fel, Univ BC, 77-79; fel, Cold Spring Harbor Lab, 79-81. *Concurrent Pos:* Adj assoc prof microbiol & immunol, Univ Mich, 89-94; adj res scientist biophys, Univ Mich, 95- *Mem:* Am Soc Microbiol; Fedn Am Soc Exp Biol; AAAS; Am Soc Biochem & Molecular Biol. *Res:* Mechanism of protein-DNA interaction, regulation, structure, function, evolution of restriction; control of transcription. *Mailing Add:* Dept Microbiol & Immunol Med Col Ohio PO Box 10008 Toledo OH 43699-0008. *E-Mail:* blumenthal@opus.mco.edu

BLUMENTHAL, ROBERT N, PHYSICAL METALLURGY. *Current Pos:* assoc prof mech eng, 64-69, PROF MECH ENG, MARQUETTE UNIV, 69- *Personal Data:* b Oak Park, Ill, Aug 31, 34; m 57; c 2. *Educ:* Northwestern Univ, BS, 57, MS, 61, PhD(mat sci), 62. *Prof Exp:* Asst prof metall eng, Mich Technol Univ, 62-64. *Res:* Role of departures from stoichiometry of compounds on their thermodynamic and electrical properties. *Mailing Add:* Dept Mech Eng Marquette Univ PO Box 1881 Milwaukee WI 53201-1881

BLUMENTHAL, ROBERT PAUL, BIOPHYSICS, BIOCHEMISTRY. *Current Pos:* vis scientist, 72-75, sr investr biophys, 78-80, CHIEF, SECT MEMBRANE STRUCT & FUNCTION, LAB THEORET BIOL, NAT CANCER INST, 80- *Personal Data:* b Djakarta, Indonesia, July 28, 38; US citizen; m 66; c 3. *Educ:* Univ Leyden, Holland, BSc, 60, MSc, 62; Weizman Inst, Israel, PhD(phys chem), 67. *Prof Exp:* Fel neurobiol, Inst Pasteur, 68-70; res assoc, Columbia Univ Col Physicians & Surgeons, 70-71; vis assoc biophys, Nat Inst Arthritis & Metab Dis, 71-72. *Mem:* Biophys Soc; AAAS; Am Soc Microbiol; Am Soc Cell Biol. *Res:* Cell membrane structure and function; membrane transport; receptors; liposomes; mobility of cell surface receptors; reconstitutions; membrane fusion; viral entry; virology, cell biology. *Mailing Add:* NIH Bldg 10 Rm 4A01 Bethesda MD 20892-0001

BLUMENTHAL, ROSALYN D, tumor biology, experimental therapeutics, for more information see previous edition

BLUMENTHAL, SAUL, MATHEMATICAL STATISTICS. *Current Pos:* PROF STATIST, OHIO STATE UNIV, 83- *Personal Data:* b Philadelphia, Pa, Oct 5, 35; m 59; c 3. *Educ:* Cornell Univ, BME, 58, PhD(statist), 62. *Prof Exp:* Res assoc statist, Stanford Univ, 61-62; asst prof indust eng, Univ Minn, 62-64; asst prof statist, Rutgers Univ, 64-66; assoc prof indust eng, NY Univ, 66-71, prof, 71-73; prof statist, Univ Ky, 73-78; prof math, Univ Ill, 78-84. *Concurrent Pos:* Consult, Avionics Div, Minneapolis-Honeywell Regulator Co, 63-64, US Naval Appl Sci Lab, 68-70, Touche, Ross & Co, 69- & US Army Res Off, Durham; NSF res grant, 65-71; proj dir res contract, US Naval Appl Sci Lab, 68-69; reviewer, Math Rev; vis prof opers res, Cornell Univ, 72-73; USAF Off Sci Res grant, 75-78 & 84-91, NSF res grant, 79-83. *Mem:* Fel Inst Math Statist; fel Am Statist Asn; Opers Res Soc Am; Int Statist Inst. *Res:* Applied statistics; sequential methods in ranking and selection problems; reliability of complex systems; renewal processes; estimation of ordered parameters; estimation of population size with truncated data; analysis of incomplete data. *Mailing Add:* Dept Statist Ohio State Univ 1958 Neil Ave Columbus OH 43210-1247

BLUMENTHAL, SUSAN J, PSYCHIATRY, WOMEN HEALTH. *Current Pos:* DEP ASST SECY WOMEN'S HEALTH, US DEPT HEALTH & HUMAN SERVS, 94-; ASST SURGEON GEN & REAR ADM USPHS, CLIN PROF SCH MED, GEORGETWON UNIV. *Prof Exp:* Dir res progs, NIH. *Concurrent Pos:* Pres, Interagency Coun Women; US rep, Women's WHO; chair, Fed Coord Comt Breast Cancer; co-founder & sci dir, Soc Advan Women's Health Res. *Res:* Women's health and mental illness. *Mailing Add:* Office Women's Health USPHS 200 Independence Ave SW Rm 712-E Washington DC 20201

BLUMENTHAL, THOMAS, TRANSCRIPTIONAL REGULATION, GENE STRUCTURE. *Current Pos:* PROF BIOL, IND UNIV, 73- *Educ:* Johns Hopkins Univ, PhD(genetics), 70. *Mailing Add:* Dept Biol Ind Univ Bloomington IN 47405-6801

BLUMER, JEFFREY L, PHARMACOLOGY, PEDIATRIC MEDICINE. *Current Pos:* PROF PEDIAT, CASE WESTERN RESERVE UNIV, 91- *Personal Data:* b Philadelphia, Pa, 1951; m 87, Kim Continenza; c Bradley & Stephanie. *Educ:* Northwestern Univ, PhD(pharmacol), 77; Case Western Res, MD, 79. *Prof Exp:* Asst prof pharmacol, Med Sch, Case Western Res, 80-86; assoc prof pediat, Rainbow Babies & Children's Hosp, 86-90, assoc prof oncol, 86-90. *Concurrent Pos:* Prof pediat, Univ Va, 89-91. *Mem:* AAAS; Soc Pediat Res; Am Acad Pediat; Am Soc Microbiol; Soc Critical Care Med. *Res:* Pediatric clinical pharmacology; genetics of drug metabolism; pediatric critical care. *Mailing Add:* Dept Pediat Rainbow Babies & Childrens Hosp 11100 Euclid Ave Cleveland OH 44106. *Fax:* 216-844-5122

BLUMHAGEN, VERN ALLEN, ELECTRICAL & SYSTEMS ENGINEERING. *Current Pos:* RETIRED. *Personal Data:* b Ronan, Mont, July 18, 29; m 54, Marilyn Meyers; c Kevin, Geoffrey & Brenda. *Educ:* Iowa State Univ, BS, 54. *Prof Exp:* Asst elec eng, Iowa State Univ, 54-55; engr electronic instruments, x-ray div, Gen Elec Co, 55-58; sr res engr guid analysis, Rockwell Int Corp, 58-60, supvr cruise systs analysis, 60-62, chief systs eval, 62-63, guid analysis, 63-66, mgr guid & control analysis, 66-67, dir advan analysis, 67-70, mgr systs requirements & analysis, NAm Rockwell Corp, 70-72, mgr oper syst technol, 72-85, mgr, systs analysis, Autonetics Div, 85-87. *Mem:* Inst Elec & Electronics Engrs. *Res:* System analysis; operations analysis; computer applications; optimal estimation and control applied to aerospace systems; system concept development, definition, design and evaluation. *Mailing Add:* 47185 Goodpasture Rd Vida OR 97488. *E-Mail:* vblumhagen@clipper.net

BLUMHORST, MICHAEL ROSS, ENVIRONMENTAL FATE OF PESTICIDES. *Current Pos:* DIR RADIOMAT & RES SCI, EPL BIOANALYTICAL SERVS, 89- *Personal Data:* b Pickneyville, Ill, Dec 10, 61; m 86; c 2. *Educ:* Southern Ill Univ, Carbondale, BS, 84, MS, 85; NC State Univ, PhD(crop sci), 89. *Concurrent Pos:* Chair, Soil Aspects Sect, Weed Sci Soc Am, 84- *Mem:* Weed Sci Soc Am; Am Chem Soc. *Res:* Determining the environmental fate of pesticides; test systems include contained soil or aquatic samples using field-scale dissipation studies. *Mailing Add:* PO Box 109 Harristown IL 62537-0109. *Fax:* 217-963-2283; *E-Mail:* blumhors@eplbas.com

BLUMSTEIN, ALEXANDRE, POLYMER CHEMISTRY. *Current Pos:* PROF CHEM, UNIV LOWELL, 72- *Personal Data:* b Grodno, Poland, Jan 13, 30; m 59; c 2. *Educ:* Univ Paris, BS, 51; Univ Toulouse, Chem Engr, 52; Univ Strasbourg, PhD(polymer chem), 60. *Prof Exp:* Res trainee polymer chem, Nat Sci Res Ctr, France, 52-54, researcher, 54-57 & 59-60, res asst, 60; sr proj engr, Instruments Div, Budd Co, 61, eng supvr, 61-62; NSF res assoc, Univ Del, 62-64; from asst prof to assoc prof chem, Lowell Technol Inst, 64-72. *Mem:* Am Chem Soc. *Res:* Polymer structure; characterization and application of polymers; photoelasticity; matrix polymerization; polymerization in liquid-crystalline media; liquid crystalline order in polymers; functional polymers. *Mailing Add:* Two Regina Dr Chelmsford MA 01824-4519

BLUMSTEIN, ALFRED, OPERATIONS RESEARCH. *Current Pos:* prof, 69-79, J Erik Jonsson Univ prof & dean urban systs & opers res, 86-93, PROF, DEPT ENG & PUB POLICY & DIR URBAN SYSTS INST, H JOHN HEINZ III SCH PUB POLICY & MGT, CARNEGIE-MELLON UNIV, 79- *Personal Data:* b New York, NY, June 3, 30; m 58, Dolores Reguera; c Lisa, Ellen & Diane. *Educ:* Cornell Univ, BEP, 51, PhD(opers res), 60; Univ Buffalo, MA, 54. *Hon Degrees:* LLD, John Jay Col, City Univ NY, 96.

Honors & Awards: Kimball Medal, Opers Res Soc Am, 85, Pres Award, 93; Sutherland Award, Am Soc Criminol, 87. *Prof Exp:* Prin opers analyst, Cornell Aeronaut Lab, 51-61; res staff, Sci & Technol Div, Inst Defense Anal, 61-69. *Concurrent Pos:* Mem staff, Off Naval Res, 54-55 & 57; vis assoc prof, Cornell Univ, 63-64; dir, Sci & Technol Task Force, President's Comn Law Enforcement & Admin of Justice, 66-67; dir, Off Urban Res, Inst Defense Anal, 68-69; chmn, deterrence & incapacitation panel, Nat Res Coun, 76-78, CRLEAJ, 79-83, sentencing res panel, 80-82, criminal careers panel, 83-86; chmn, Pa Comn Crime & Delinq, 79-90; panel mem, Decision & Mgt Sci Prog, NSF, 82-85; overseas fel, Churchill Col, Univ Cambridge, 83; sci comn, Int Soc Criminol; mem, Comn Behav & Doc Sci & Educ, Nat Res Coun, 95-; dir, Nat Consortium Violence Res, 96- *Mem:* Fel AAAS; Opers Res Soc Am (pres, 77-78); Am Statist Asn; Inst Mgt Sci (pres, 87-88); fel Am Soc Criminol (pres, 91-92); Inst Opers Res & Mgt Sci (pres, 96). *Res:* Quantitative and policy research in law enforcement and criminal justice; urban transportation; family planning. *Mailing Add:* Heinz Sch Pub Policy & Mgt Carnegie-Mellon Univ Pittsburgh PA 15213. *Fax:* 412-268-7036; *E-Mail:* aboq@cmu.edu

BLUMSTEIN, CARL JOSEPH, ENERGY CONSERVATION & INFORMATION. *Current Pos:* RES POLICY ANALYST, UNIV CALIF ENERGY INST, BERKELEY, 81- *Personal Data:* b Minneapolis, Minn, June 7, 42; m, Janet Perlman; c 4. *Educ:* Reed Col, BA, 66; San Diego State Univ, MS, 68; Univ Calif, San Diego, PhD(chem), 74. *Prof Exp:* Staff scientist, Energy & Environ Div, Lawrence Berkeley Lab, 74-81. *Concurrent Pos:* Spec consult, Calif Energy Comn, 78-81; chmn, Am Coun Energy-Efficient Econ. *Mem:* AAAS; Am Coun Energy-Efficient Econ. *Res:* Energy use and conservation, including development of computer models of energy demand, analysis of energy conservation policies, assessment of energy conservation technologies. *Mailing Add:* 2243 Stuart St Berkeley CA 94705. *Fax:* 510-643-5180; *E-Mail:* cjblumstein@lbl.gov

BLUMSTEIN, RITA BLATTBERG, POLYMER CHEMISTRY. *Current Pos:* from asst prof to assoc prof, 75-81, PROF CHEM, UNIV LOWELL, 81- *Personal Data:* b Krakow, Poland, Jan 11, 37; French citizen; m 59; c 2. *Educ:* Univ Paris, BS, 59; Univ Strasbourg, MS, 60; Univ Del, PhD(phys chem), 65. *Prof Exp:* Asst prof chem, Merrimack Col, 65-69. *Concurrent Pos:* Mem polymer educ comt, Am Chem Soc, 76-, legis counr, 77- *Mem:* Am Chem Soc. *Res:* Polymerization within ordered systems; liquid crystalline order in polymers; morphology of blends; synthesis of oligomers. *Mailing Add:* Two Regina Dr Chelmsford MA 01824-4519

BLUNDELL, GEORGE PHELAN, HEMATOLOGY, IMMUNOLOGY. *Current Pos:* RETIRED. *Educ:* McGill Univ, MD, 48. *Prof Exp:* chief lab serv, Vet Admin Med Ctr, 80-88. *Mailing Add:* PO Box 1253 Shepherdstown WV 25443

BLUNDELL, JAMES KENNETH, MANUFACTURING SYSTEMS & ROBOTICS. *Current Pos:* mem staff, Truman Eng Labs, 81-88, assoc dir, Design Productivity Ctr, 85-88, DIR, CTR INTELLIGENT DESIGN, DEPT COMPUT SCI, UNIV MO, KANSAS CITY, 88-, ASSOC PROF COMPUT SCI, 88- *Personal Data:* b Prescot, Eng, Oct 21, 49; m 92, Janet A Rogers; c 1. *Educ:* Univ Salford, BS, 72; Loughborough Univ Technol, MS, 74; Univ Nottingham, PhD(mech eng), 77. *Prof Exp:* Res asst, Hawker Siddeley Aviation & Loughborough Univ, 73; asst lectr, Univ Nottingham, 74-76; sr proj engr, Tecquipment Ltd, Nottingham, 76-77; lectr, Univ West Indies, 77-79; from asst prof to assoc prof mech eng, Univ Mo, Columbia, 82-88. *Concurrent Pos:* Mem, Trinidad & Tobago Comn Prod Eng, 78; pres, James K. Blundell Asn, 89-93; mem comt, Unified Life Cycle Eng, Nat Acad Sci. *Mem:* Am Soc Mech Engrs; Am Soc Metals; Soc Mfg Engrs & Robotics Inst; Soc Logistics Engrs; Brit Inst Prod Engrs. *Res:* Planning and introduction of automation into manufacturing plants including basic robotics research and the simulation of industrial processes using digital computers. *Mailing Add:* Dept Comput Sci Ctr Intelligent Design Univ Mo 5100 Rockhill Rd Kansas City MO 64110-2446. *E-Mail:* blundell@cstp.unkc.edu

BLUNT, MARTIN JULIAN, RESERVOIR ENGINEERING, MULTI-PHASE FLOW IN POROUS MEDIA. *Current Pos:* ASST PROF PETROL ENG, STANFORD UNIV, 92- *Personal Data:* b London, Eng, Oct 3, 63. *Educ:* Cambridge Univ, BA, 85, PhD(theoret physics), 88. *Prof Exp:* Res physicist, Brit Petrol Res Ctr, 88-92. *Mem:* Soc Petrol Engrs; Am Phys Soc; Am Geophys Union. *Res:* Multi-phase flow in porous media with applications to recovery in oil and gas fields and subsurface cleanup of pollutants; interaction of phase behavior heterogeneity and viscous instability on porous media flows. *Mailing Add:* Dept Petrol Eng Stanford Univ Mitchell Bldg Stanford CA 94305-9991. *Fax:* 650-725-2099; *E-Mail:* blunt@pangea.stanford.edu

BLURTON, KEITH F, ELECTROCHEMICAL SYSTEMS, RESEARCH MANAGEMENT. *Current Pos:* PRES, MERRA, DETROIT, 93- *Personal Data:* b Grays, Eng, Apr 11, 40; m 66, Patricia M Kendrick; c Heather F. *Educ:* Southampton Univ, BSc, 61, PhD(chem), 66. *Honors & Awards:* Silver Medal Award, Am Electroplaters & Surface Finishers Soc, 86. *Prof Exp:* Lectr, Portsmouth Polytech, 61-66; sr chemist, Leesona Corp, 66-68; res dir, Energetics Sci Inc, Elmsford, 68-76; dir energy conversion & storage res, Inst Gas Technol, Chicago, 76-80; vpres chem res, PCK Technol Div, Kollmorgen Corp, Mellville, 80-86; gen mgr, Ctr Innovative Technol, Herndon Va, 86-93. *Mem:* Am Chem Soc; Electrochem Soc; AAAS; Royal Soc Chem. *Res:* Printed circuits; batteries; electrolytic processes; fuel cells; electroplating; electrochemical sensors; electrolysis; electroless deposition; materials selection and stability. *Mailing Add:* 30700 Ivy Glen Ct Bingham Farms MI 48025. *Fax:* 313-930-0145; *E-Mail:* keith@merra.org

BLUSH, STEVEN MICHAEL, NUCLEAR SCIENCE, SAFETY. *Current Pos:* PRES, STEVE BLUSH CONSULT, INC, 93- *Personal Data:* b Parkville, Mo, June 1, 48; m, Lynn F Rusten; c Sarah C. *Educ:* Univ Calif, BA, 70. *Honors & Awards:* Elmer B Staats Award Accountability in Govt, Am Soc Pub Admin, 91. *Prof Exp:* Investr, Korean-Am Rels, Subcomt Int Orgns, US House Reps, 77-79; task group leader & investr, Three Mile Island Subcomt Nuclear Regulation, US Senate, 79-80; chief investr, Pres Nuclear Safety Oversight Comt, 80-81; pvt consult, 81-83; sr study dir nuclear safety-related policy issues, Nat Res Coun, Nat Acad Sci, Nat Acad Eng, Inst Med, 84-90; spec consult secy energy, US Dept Energy, 89, dir nuclear safety, 90-93. *Concurrent Pos:* Mem, Ill Power Co Nuclear Rev & Audit Group, 93-; researcher, Nuclear Control Inst. *Mem:* Am Soc Qual Control. *Res:* Nuclear safety. *Mailing Add:* 15525 Edwards Ferry Rd A Poolesville MD 20837

BLUZER, NATHAN, DEVICE PHYSICS, ELECTRONICS. *Current Pos:* SR ADV PHYSICIST SEMI-CONDUCTIVITY & SUPER CONDUCTIVITY SOUD STAR SERVICES, NORTHROP & RUMMAN ADV TECH CENTER. *Personal Data:* b Tomashow Lubelsky, Poland, Jan 1, 47; US citizen. *Educ:* Univ Md, BSEE, 67, PhD(physics), 74. *Prof Exp:* Assoc engr radar, Westinghouse, Cockeysville, 67-68, engr design, Westinghouse Aerospace & Electronics Systs Div, 68-71; res asst physics, Univ Md, 71-74; sr engr, Solid State Devices, Westinghouse Advan Technol Labs, 74-77, fel physicist, 77-81 adv physicist, IR focal Plane Detectors, 81-88, sr adv physicist super conducting sensors & devisces, 90-96. *Concurrent Pos:* Vis scholar, Stanford Univ, 88-90; lectr, Dept Elec Eng & Comput Sci, John's Hopkins Univ, 94. *Mem:* Life mem Am Phys Soc; fel Inst Elec & Electronics Engrs. *Res:* Infrared detector and charge coupled devices; radiation effects in metal-nitrate-oxide silicon; superconducting sensors and devices; 30 US patents; published over 40 papers in scientific journals. *Mailing Add:* Northrop Grumman Advan Technol Ctr PO Box 1521 MS-3012 Baltimore MD 21203

BLY, CHARLES ALBERT, CELESTIAL SUBNUCLEAR FISSION CHAIN REACTION REACTORS, CELESTIAL POWER TRANSIENTS AS SELF POWERED TRANSMISSION MICROSCOPES. *Current Pos:* reactor operator, sr reactor operator & res engr, 77-83, SR REACTOR OPERATOR, UNIV VA, 95-, DIR, SILICON IRRADIATION LAB, 96- *Personal Data:* b Winchester, Va, Jan 11, 52; m 76, April Marie Bly-Monnen. *Educ:* Univ Va, BS, 78, MS, 83. *Prof Exp:* Nuclear engr, Westinghouse Nuclear Fuel, 83-92 & Beaver Valley Nuclear Power Sta, Duquesne Light Co, 92-94; prof chem physics & nuclear eng, Oak Ridge Nat Lab, 94. *Concurrent Pos:* Consult astrophys, AK Velan, Montreal, Can, 97- *Mem:* Am Phys Soc; Am Nuclear Soc; NY Acad Sci. *Res:* Celestial subnuclear fission chain reactions and the results of supercritical subnuclear fission chain reaction power transients interpreted as self-powered transmission microscopes capable of illuminating the fundamental structure of matter. *Mailing Add:* 777D Mountain Rd Charlottesville VA 22902. *Fax:* 804-982-5473; *E-Mail:* cab7t@virginia.edu

BLY, DONALD DAVID, ANALYTICAL CHEMISTRY, POLYMER CHEMISTRY. *Current Pos:* res chemist, Carothers Res Lab, E I du Pont de Nemours & Co, Inc, 63-67, sect supvr, 67-77, mgr analytical sci, Cent Res Dept, 77-90, CONSULT, E I DU PONT DE NEMOURS & CO, INC, 91- *Personal Data:* b Bryan, Ohio, Sept 24, 36; m 59; c 3. *Educ:* Kenyon Col, BA, 58; Purdue Univ, MS, 61, PhD(analytical chem), 62. *Prof Exp:* Eli Lilly fel, Purdue Univ, 62-63. *Concurrent Pos:* Chmn, Analytical Div, 85, Am Chem Soc, 87. *Mem:* Am Chem Soc; Am Soc Testing & Mat; AAAS. *Res:* Scientific expertise, educational instruction, critical examination of data and audit of procedures for clients engaged in problems in analytical chemistry, polymer chemistry or instruction. *Mailing Add:* 409 Brentwood Dr Carrcroft Wilmington DE 19803-4307. *Fax:* 302-762-7478

BLY, ROBERT STEWART, PHYSICAL ORGANIC CHEMISTRY, ORGANOMETALLIC CHEMISTRY. *Current Pos:* from asst prof to prof chem, Univ SC, 61-93, head dept, 70-73, distinguished prof chem, 93-94, DISTINGUISHED EMER PROF CHEM, UNIV SC, 94- *Personal Data:* b Lakeland, Fla, Aug 10, 29; m 56, Ruta Kramins. *Educ:* Fla Southern Col, BS, 51; Northwestern Univ, MS, 56; Univ Colo, PhD(org chem), 58. *Prof Exp:* Res chemist, Nylon Res Lab, E I du Pont de Nemours & Co, 57-59; NIH fel, Mass Inst Technol, 59-61. *Mem:* Am Chem Soc; Royal Soc Chem. *Res:* Mechanisms of reactions; carbonium ions; pi-complexes; ii-acetylenes transition-metal alkylidenes and vinylidenes, ligand rearrangements. *Mailing Add:* Dept Chem Univ SC Columbia SC 29208. *Fax:* 803-777-9521

BLY, SARA A, COMPUTER SCIENCE, COMPUTING HUMAN INTERACTIONS. *Current Pos:* CONSULT, 94- *Personal Data:* b Arkansas City, Kans, June 22, 46. *Educ:* Univ Kans, BS, 68; Stanford Univ, MS, 69; Univ Calif, Davis, PhD(computer sci), 82. *Prof Exp:* User interface designer, Xerox Palo Alto Res Ctr, 84-87, mem res staff, Syst Sci Lab, 87-94. *Mem:* Asn Comput Mach (secy, 88-90). *Res:* Computer-supported cooperative work. *Mailing Add:* 24511 NW Moreland Rd Hillsboro OR 97124

BLYE, RICHARD PERRY, REPRODUCTIVE BIOLOGY. *Current Pos:* HEALTH SCIENTIST ADMINR, CDB, CPR, NAT INST CHILD HEALTH & HUMAN DEVELOP, 71- *Personal Data:* b West Chester, Pa, Nov 11, 32; m 56; c 2. *Educ:* Trinity Coll, Conn, BS, 55; Rutgers Univ, PhD, 60. *Prof Exp:* Asst zool & gen biol, Rutgers Univ, 55-59; assoc scientist, Div Endocrinol, Ortho Pharmaceut Corp, 59-62, sr scientist, 62-63, Ortho res fel, 64-70. *Concurrent Pos:* Consult, Bur Drugs, Food & Drug Admin, 74-79. *Mem:* AAAS; NY Acad Sci; Soc Study Reprod; Am Chem Soc. *Res:* Endocrinology of reproduction; contraceptive development; contraceptive steroids pharmacology and safety. *Mailing Add:* 7352 Minkhollow Rd Highland MD 20777

BLYHOLDER, GEORGE DONALD, PHYSICAL CHEMISTRY. *Current Pos:* from asst prof to assoc prof chem, 59-67, vchmn dept, 68-72, PROF CHEM, UNIV ARK, FAYETTEVILLE, 67- *Personal Data:* b Elizabeth, NJ, Jan 10, 31; m 55, Betty Conrod; c Sylvia, Andrew & Victoria. *Educ:* Valparaiso Univ, BA, 52; Purdue Univ, BS, 53; Univ Utah, PhD(chem), 56. *Prof Exp:* Fel, Univ Minn, 56-57; assoc, Johns Hopkins Univ, 57-59. *Concurrent Pos:* Fel, Oxford Univ, Eng, 65; vis prof, Hokkaido Univ, Japan, 72, Univ Munich, Ger, 75, Cornell Univ, 80, Cambridge Univ, Eng, 88. *Mem:* Am Chem Soc; Sigma Xi; Am Asn Univ Prof. *Res:* Kinetics; catalysis; surface chemistry; molecular spectroscopy; molecular orbital theory. *Mailing Add:* Dept Chem Univ Ark Fayetteville AR 72701. *Fax:* 501-575-4049; *E-Mail:* gb24023@uafsysb.uark.edu

BLYLER, LEE LANDIS, JR, POLYMER ENGINEERING, OPTICAL FIBER TECHNOLOGY. *Current Pos:* Mem tech staff, 65-71, GROUP SUPVR, BELL LABS, 71- *Personal Data:* b New Brunswick, NJ, Oct 22, 38; m 62, Harriet Lillard; c Allison & Kristin. *Educ:* Princeton Univ, BSE, 61, MSE, 62, PhD(mech eng), 66. *Honors & Awards:* Fred O Conley Award in Eng/Technol, Soc Plastics Eng. *Mem:* Am Chem Soc; Soc Rheol; Soc Plastics Eng. *Res:* Polymer mechanics; flow and processing behavior of polymer melts; relationships between polymer properties and molecular structure; electrical charge storage in polymer dielectrics; polymeric materials for optical fiber waveguides and cables. *Mailing Add:* 55 Kensington Rd Basking Ridge NJ 07920. *Fax:* 908-582-5570; *E-Mail:* lblyler@bell-labs.com

BLYSTONE, ROBERT VERNON, CELL BIOLOGY, MICROSCOPY. *Current Pos:* From asst prof to assoc prof, Trinity Univ, 71-84, chmn, Dept Biol, 84-86, DIR VISUALIZATION LABS, TRINITY UNIV, 71-, PIPER PROF BIOL, 84- *Personal Data:* b El Paso, Tex, July 4, 43; m 64, Donna Moore; c Daniel. *Educ:* Univ Tex, El Paso, BS, 65; Univ Tex, Austin, MA, 68, PhD(zool), 71. *Concurrent Pos:* Consult var publ, 86-94; prin investr, Off Sci Res, USAF, 89-91 & NSF, 91-93, 96-99. *Mem:* Fel AAAS; Micros Soc Am; Nat Sci Teachers Asn; Am Inst Biol Sci; Am Soc Cell Biol; Sigma Xi; Asn Comput Mach. *Res:* Structures; three dimensional reconstruction of tissues and embryos. *Mailing Add:* Dept Biol Trinity Univ San Antonio TX 78212. *Fax:* 210-736-1229; *E-Mail:* rblyston@trinity.edu

BLYTAS, GEORGE CONSTANTIN, PHYSICAL CHEMISTRY, SEPARATION TECHNOLOGY. *Current Pos:* Chemist, Shell Develop Co, 61-72, sr staff res chemist, 72-81, res assoc, 81-89, res adv, 89-92, RES CONSULT, SHELL DEVELOP CO, 92- *Personal Data:* b Cairo, Egypt, Dec 20, 30; US citizen; m 63, Cora A Severson; c Constantin & Christina. *Educ:* Am Univ Cairo, BSc, 56; Univ Wis, PhD(phys chem), 61. *Concurrent Pos:* Lectr electrochem, Univ Calif, Berkeley, 66-67 & 69; chmn, Indust Eng Chem Div, Am Chem Soc, 81-82. *Mem:* Sigma Xi; Am Chem Soc; Am Inst Chem Eng. *Res:* Research and development in novel separation systems and processes; adsorbents, zeolites, ion exchange, solvent extraction, membrane separations, reactive and kinetic distillation, hydrometallurgy, chemistry in nonaqueous solvents, energy systems, environmental chemistry and engineering; supercritical systems, water soluble polymers, surface science and emulsions. *Mailing Add:* 14323 Apple Tree Houston TX 77079-6622

BLYTH, COLIN ROSS, MATHEMATICAL STATISTICS, FOUNDATIONS. *Current Pos:* RETIRED. *Personal Data:* b Guelph, Ont, Oct 24, 22; m 55, Valerie Thompson; c Mary A (Snetsinger), Georgina (Roche), Colin M, Alexander, Heather & Donald. *Educ:* Queen's Univ, Ont, BA, 44; Univ Toronto, MA, 46; Univ Calif, PhD(statist), 50. *Prof Exp:* From asst prof to prof math, Univ Ill, Urbana, 50-74; prof, Queen's Univ, Kingston, 72-87. *Concurrent Pos:* Assoc ed, J Am Statist Asn, 67-71. *Mem:* Fel Inst Math Statist; fel Am Statist Asn; Math Asn Am; Statist Soc Can. *Res:* Statistical inference. *Mailing Add:* Dept Math & Statist Queen's Univ Kingston ON K7L 3N6 Can. *E-Mail:* statistics.department@queensu.ca

BLYTHE, DAVID K(NOX), CIVIL ENGINEERING. *Current Pos:* RETIRED. *Personal Data:* b Georgetown, Ky, May 18, 17; m; c 3. *Educ:* Univ Ky, BS, 40, CE, 48; Cornell Univ, MCE, 50. *Prof Exp:* Jr civil engr, US Forest Serv, 40-41; mat engr, Ohio River Div Labs, Corps Engrs, US Army, 46-47; from instr to prof civil & hwy eng, Univ Ky, 47-87, chmn dept, 57-69, assoc dean continuing educ & exten, Col Eng, 69-87. *Concurrent Pos:* Consult, Ky Dept Hwys, 54-57 & Spindletop Res, Inc, 64-; OEEC & NSF sr vis fel, Univ Durham, 61; Fulbright lectr, Ecuador, 69. *Mem:* Am Soc Civil Engrs; Am Soc Eng Educ; Am Cong Surv & Mapping; Nat Soc Prof Engrs; Sigma Xi. *Res:* Highway planning; engineering interpretation of aerial photographs; control surveys; weighing highway vehicles in motion. *Mailing Add:* 975 Edgewater Dr Lexington KY 40502

BLYTHE, JACK GORDON, PHYSICAL GEOGRAPHY, GENERAL EARTH SCIENCES. *Current Pos:* RETIRED. *Personal Data:* b Kansas City, Mo, July 15, 22; m 48; c 4. *Educ:* Wichita State Univ, BA, 47; Northwestern Univ, MS, 50; Univ Okla, PhD(geol), 57. *Prof Exp:* Instr geol, Wichita State Univ, 49-51; assoc prof, Okla City Univ, 53-57; from assoc prof to prof geol, Wichita State Univ, 57-85, chmn dept, 65-70. *Mem:* Geol Soc Am; Am Asn Petrol Geol. *Res:* Stratigraphy; structural geology. *Mailing Add:* 557 N Broadview St Wichita KS 67208

BLYTHE, LINDA L, BEHAVIOR ETHOLOGY. *Current Pos:* asst prof, 78-90, PROF NEUROL, COL VET MED, ORE STATE UNIV, 90- *Personal Data:* b Los Angeles, Calif, Jan 11, 44; c Samantha, Jerry A Jr & Randall A. *Educ:* Univ Calif, Davis, BS, 72, DVM, 74, PhD(comp path), 79. *Concurrent Pos:* Dir racing res, Col Vet Med, Ore State Univ, 85- *Mem:* Am Vet Med Asn; Asn Am Equine Practr. *Res:* Diseases of the nervous system, especially in the horse, exercise physiology of racing animals and neurotoxicology of poymores plank. *Mailing Add:* 686 Marilyn Dr Philomath OR 97370. *Fax:* 541-737-0502

BLYTHE, PHILIP ANTHONY, APPLIED MATHEMATICS, FLUID MECHANICS. *Current Pos:* assoc prof, 68-70, PROF APPL MATH, LEHIGH UNIV, 70- *Personal Data:* b Dewsbury, Eng, Mar 30, 37; m 63; c 2. *Educ:* Univ Manchester, BSc, 58, PhD(fluid mech), 61. *Prof Exp:* Res fel aerodyn, Nat Phys Lab, Eng, 61-63, sr sci officer, 63-64; lectr, Imp Col, Univ London, 64-68. *Concurrent Pos:* Vis prof, Univ Newcastle, Eng, 74-75. *Res:* Nonlinear wave propagation; nonequilibrium flows; thermal convection; combustion; asymptotic methods. *Mailing Add:* Dept Mech Eng & Mech Lehigh Univ Packard Lab No 19 19 Memorial Dr W Bethlehem PA 18015-3006

BLYTHE, WILLIAM BREVARD, INTERNAL MEDICINE. *Current Pos:* from instr to assoc prof med, 60-70, assoc dir clin res unit, 65-66, dir clin res unit, 66-76, PROF MED, SCH MED UNIV NC, CHAPEL HILL, 70-, HEAD DIV NEPHROLOGY, 72-, MARIEN COVINGTON DISTINGUISHED PROF MED, 88- *Personal Data:* b Huntersville, NC, Sept 23, 28; m 56; c 4. *Educ:* Univ NC, AB, 48; Washington Univ, MD, 53. *Prof Exp:* Life Ins Med Res Fund fel, 58-60. *Mem:* Am Fedn Clin Res; AMA; Am Physiol Soc; Am Soc Artificial Internal Organs; fel Am Col Physicians; Am Clin & Climat Asn. *Res:* Renal physiology and disease; hemodialysis. *Mailing Add:* Dept Med Univ NC Sch Med CB 7155 Chapel Hill NC 27599-7155

BLYTHE, WILLIAM RICHARD, FAILURE ANALYSIS, AUTOMOBILE HANDLING. *Current Pos:* PRES, WILLIAM BLYTHE INC, 82- *Personal Data:* b Martinez, Calif, Aug 8, 31; m 55, Bonnie J Isakson; c William R Jr, Alison B (Carleton) & Kelly R. *Educ:* Univ Calif, Berkeley, AB, 55, MS, 57; Stanford Univ, PhD (eng mech), 62. *Prof Exp:* From assoc prof civil eng to prof civil eng, San Jose State Univ, 60-65, assoc dean grad studies, 68-69, chmn dept civil eng & appl mech, 69-81. *Concurrent Pos:* Consult, many eng firms, govt agencies. *Mem:* Am Soc Civil Engrs; Am Acad Mech; Int Soc Terrain-Vehicle Systs. *Res:* Analysis of hyperstatic structures; shells; vehicle dynamics; accident reconstruction. *Mailing Add:* Dept Civil Eng & Appl Mech San Jose State Univ San Jose CA 95114

BO, WALTER JOHN, ANATOMY, ENDOCRINOLOGY. *Current Pos:* assoc prof, 60-63, PROF ANAT, BOWMAN GRAY SCH MED, 63- *Personal Data:* b Chisholm, Minn, Aug 12, 23; m 48; c 3. *Educ:* Marquette Univ, BS, 46, MS, 47; Univ Cincinnati, PhD(anat), 53. *Prof Exp:* Instr zool, Xavier Univ, 47-49; from asst prof to assoc prof anat, Sch Med, Univ NDak, 53-60. *Mem:* Am Asn Anat; Asn Cancer Res; Histochem Soc; Soc Exp Biol & Med; Soc Study Reproduction; Sigma Xi. *Res:* Gross histochemistry and abnormal growth of the uterus, cervix and vagina; endocrinology; female reproductive system; intra uterine device effect on uterus mode of action. *Mailing Add:* Dept Anat Bowman Gray Sch Med Wake Forest Univ Medical Center Blvd Winston-Salem NC 27157-1010

BOACKLE, ROBERT J, IMMUNOLOGY. *Current Pos:* PROF IMMUNOL, MED UNIV SC, 75- *Educ:* Univ Ala, Birmingham, PhD(biochem), 74. *Mailing Add:* Dept Immunol & Microbiol Med Univ SC 171 Ashley Ave Charleston SC 29425

BOADE, RODNEY RUSSETT, GEOMECHANICS. *Current Pos:* sr res physicist, 81-88, MGR RESERVOIR APPLNS, PHILLIPS PETROL CO, 88- *Personal Data:* b Armstrong, Iowa, Aug 17, 35; m 65; c Harold & Stephanie (Silas). *Educ:* Augustana Col, SDak, BS, 57; Iowa State Univ, PhD(physics), 64. *Prof Exp:* Staff mem physics, Sandia Corp, 64-81. *Mem:* Am Phys Soc; Soc Petrol Engrs; Int Soc Rock Mech. *Res:* Energy transfer processes in gases and their influence on the propagation of sound; propagation of shock waves in porous and composite solids; explosive fracturing and in situ processing of oil shale; rock mechanics; petroleum reservoir fundamentals; subsidence. *Mailing Add:* 5410 Nowata Rd Bartlesville OK 74006

BOADLE-BIBER, MARGARET CLARE, NEUROCHEMISTRY. *Current Pos:* assoc prof, 75-87, PROF PHYSIOL, SCH BASIC HEALTH SCI, MED COL VA, VA COMMONWEALTH UNIV, 87-, CHMN, DEPT PHYSIOL, 93- *Personal Data:* b Melbourne, Australia, Jan 18, 43; US citizen; m; c 1. *Educ:* Univ London, BS, 64; Univ Oxford, PhD(biochem pharmacol), 67. *Prof Exp:* Instr pharmacol, Sch Med, Yale Univ, 69-71, asst prof, 71-75. *Concurrent Pos:* A B Coxe Mem fel, Sch Med, Yale Univ, 67-68; prin investr, Nat Inst Neurol Dis Stroke, NIH, 71-74, 79-83, 83-87, 87-90, 90-94 & 94-97, NIMH, 74-75, NSF, 74-76, Am Heart Asn, 74-77, A D Williams Found, 75-76, 86-87, Va Commonwealth Univ, Fac Grant in Aid, 78-79, 83-84, 86-86, Va Heart Asn, 79-80, Bristol Myers-Squibb, 87-92; estab investr, Am Heart Asn, 75-80. *Mem:* AAAS; Am Soc Neurochem; Am Soc Pharmacol & Exp Therapeut; Int Brain Res Orgn; Found Biomed Res; Int Soc Neurochem; NY Acad Sci; Soc Neurosci; Women Neuroscience. *Res:* The influence of physiological factors on the function of the rostrally projectin five-hydroxytryptamine neurons in the rat brain assessed by a variety of biochemical measures. *Mailing Add:* Dept Physiol Va Commonwealth Univ 1101 E Marshall St PO Box 98055 Richmond VA 23298-0551. *Fax:* 804-828-7382

BOADWAY, JOHN DOUGLAS, FLUID MECHANICS, ENVIRONMENTAL ENGINEERING. *Current Pos:* RETIRED. *Personal Data:* b Collingwood, Ont, Apr 5, 22; m 49; c 3. *Educ:* Univ Toronto, BASc, 45; Queens Univ, MSc, 65, PhD(civil eng), 66. *Prof Exp:* Res engr, Nat Res Coun, 45-46; res physicist, Shawinigan Chem Ltd, 46-52; mem res staff eng physics, Consol Paper Corp, 52-63; from asst prof to assoc prof civil eng, Queens Univ, Ont, 66-87. *Mem:* Can Pulp & Paper Asn; Chem Inst Can; Can

Soc Chem Engrs. *Res:* Vortex separating devices; computer simulations in hydraulics; paper making, especially hydraulics; sedimentation of effluents; electron microscopy. *Mailing Add:* 35 Holland Cresent Kingston ON K7M 2V7 Can

BOAG, DAVID ARCHIBALD, ANIMAL ECOLOGY. *Current Pos:* asst prof, 63-69, assoc prof, 69-76, PROF ZOOL, UNIV ALTA, 76-, DIR, R B MILLER BIOL STA, 63- *Personal Data:* b Edmonton, Alta, Jan 24, 34; m 63; c 2. *Educ:* Univ Alta, BSc, 57, MSc, 58; Wash State Univ, PhD(zool), 64. *Prof Exp:* Lectr zool, Univ Alta, 58-59, asst prof, 59-60; researcher, Zool Sta, Naples, Italy, 61. *Mem:* Am Ornith Union; Wildlife Soc; Ecol Soc Am; Can Soc Zool; Can Soc Wildlife & Fishery Biol. *Res:* Population ecology, especially waterfowl and grouse. *Mailing Add:* 6746 Amwell Dr Brentwood Bay BC V8M 1A4 Can

BOAG, THOMAS JOHNSON, PSYCHIATRY, PSYCHOANALYSIS. *Current Pos:* prof psychiat & head dept, Queen's Univ, Ont, 67-75, dean fac med, 75-82, vprin health sci, 83-88, EMER PROF PSYCHIAT, QUEEN'S UNIV. *Personal Data:* b Liverpool, Eng, Apr 11, 22; Can citizen; m 50, Lorna C Milne; c Peter Thomas, Graham Stewart, Patricia Janet & Alexander Harvey. *Educ:* Univ Liverpool, MB, ChB, 44; McGill Univ, dipl, 53; FRCP(C). *Prof Exp:* Asst psychiat, Royal Victoria Hosp, 52-53; lectr, McGill Univ, 53-55; from asst psychiatrist to assoc psychiatrist, Royal Victoria Hosp, 55-61; prof psychiat & chmn dept, Col Med, Univ Vt, 61-67; chief serv, DeGoesbriand Mem & Mary Fletcher Hosps, 61-67. *Concurrent Pos:* Asst prof, McGill Univ, 57-61; asst dir, Allan Mem Inst, 59-61; psychiatrist-in-chief, Kingston Gen Hosp, Ont, 67-75; consult, Hotel Dieu, Kingston Psychiat & St Mary's of the Lake & Kingston Gen Hosp, 67- *Mem:* Can Med Asn; Am Psychiat Asn; Can Psychiat Asn. *Res:* Human adaptation in Arctic; interaction recording and study of interview situation; psychiatric treatment milieu; history of psychiatry. *Mailing Add:* RR 2 Perth Rd Village ON K0L 2L0 Can

BOAL, DAVID HAROLD, PROPERTIES OF SURFACES & INTERFACES. *Current Pos:* from asst prof to assoc prof chem, 78-86, PROF PHYSICS, SIMON FRASER UNIV, 86- *Personal Data:* b Toronto, Ont, Jan 12, 48; m 73; c 2. *Educ:* Univ Toronto, BSc, 70, MSc, 71, PhD(physics), 75. *Prof Exp:* Vis asst prof physics, Univ Alta, 76-78. *Concurrent Pos:* Pres Res Univ Alta grant, 76-77; Nat Res Coun Can grant, 77-; vis assoc prof, Michigan State Univ, 83-84, Univ Ill, 86. *Mem:* Can Asn Physicists; Am Phys Soc. *Res:* Statistical mechanics; properties of surfaces and interfaces; computational physics. *Mailing Add:* Dept Physics Simon Fraser Univ Burnaby BC V5A 1S6 Can. *Fax:* 604-291-3592; *E-Mail:* boal@sfu.ca

BOAL, JAN LIST, APPLIED MATHEMATICS. *Current Pos:* chmn dept, 69-77, prof, 69-90, EMER PROF MATH, GA STATE UNIV, 90- *Personal Data:* b Canton, Ohio, Oct 20, 30; m 53; c 3. *Educ:* Ga Inst Technol, BME & MS, 54; Mass Inst Technol, PhD(math), 59. *Prof Exp:* Instr math, Mass Inst Technol, 59-60; from asst prof to assoc prof, Univ SC, 60-69. *Concurrent Pos:* Vis lectr cols, Math Asn Am, 64 & 68; co-owner, Veranda Hist Inn, 85- *Mem:* Math Asn Am; Am Soc Indust & Appl Math; Sigma Xi. *Res:* Numerical analysis; differential equations; function approximation. *Mailing Add:* 252 Seavy St Senoia GA 30276

BOARD, JAMES ELLERY, GROWTH DYNAMICS, ROW SPACING. *Current Pos:* PROF, DEPT AGRON, LA STATE UNIV, 80- *Personal Data:* b Sacramento, Calif, Sept 7, 48; m 87. *Educ:* Univ Calif, Davis, BS, 70, MS, 71, PhD(plant physiol), 78. *Prof Exp:* Postdoctoral fel, dept agron, Univ Calif, Davis, 79-80. *Mem:* Am Soc Agron; Crop Sci Soc Am. *Res:* Photoperiod effects in soybeans as affecting planting date in the southeastern USA; growth dynamics of soybeans in narrow, wide row culture in southeastern USA. *Mailing Add:* 9721 Siegen Lane Baton Rouge LA 70810

BOARD, JOHN ARNOLD, OBSTETRICS & GYNECOLOGY. *Current Pos:* from instr to prof, 62-96, EMER PROF OBSTET & GYNEC, MED COL VA, VA COMMONWEALTH UNIV, 96- *Personal Data:* b Altavista, Va, June 30, 31; m 59, Anne J Woodrum; c John Jr, Susan & Paul. *Educ:* Randolph-Macon Col, BS, 53; Med Col Va, MD, 55. *Prof Exp:* Intern, Louisville Gen Hosp, Ky, 55-56; from jr asst resident to resident obstet & gynec, Med Col Va Hosps, 56-59; USPHS fel reprod physiol & infertil, Sch Med, Yale Univ, 61-62. *Mem:* Am Col Obstet & Gynec; Soc Study Reproduction; Endocrine Soc; Soc Reproductive Endocrinologists; Soc Reproductive Surgeons; Am Soc Reproductive Med. *Res:* Gynecologic endocrinology and infertility. *Mailing Add:* 1627 Pope Ave Richmond VA 23227. *Fax:* 804-371-0573; *E-Mail:* jboard@gems.vcv.edu

BOARDMAN, GREGORY DALE, ENVIRONMENTAL MICROBIOLOGY, ENVIRONMENTAL TOXICOLOGY. *Current Pos:* asst prof, 76-83, coordr, Environ Eng Div, Civil Eng, 94-96, ASSOC PROF ENVIRON ENG, VA POLYTECH INST & STATE UNIV, 83-, CTR ORG & TECHNOL ADVAN FEL, 96- *Personal Data:* b Montpelier, Vt, Dec 12, 50; m 70, 87, Shelley Mitchell; c 5. *Educ:* Univ NH, BSCE, 72, MSCE, 73; Univ Maine, PhD(sanit eng), 76. *Mem:* Am Soc Civil Engrs; Water Environ Fedn; Int Asn Water Qual; Sigma Xi; Soc Environ Toxicol & Chem; Am Asn Textile Chemists & Colorists. *Res:* Hazardous waste management; treatment of industrial wastes; early assessment of toxicity. *Mailing Add:* Dept Civil Eng Va Poly Inst & State Univ 322 Norris Hall Blacksburg VA 24061. *Fax:* 540-231-7916; *E-Mail:* gboard@vt.edu

BOARDMAN, JOHN, THEORETICAL PHYSICS. *Current Pos:* instr, 62-65, asst prof, 65-80, ASSOC PROF PHYSICS, BROOKLYN COL, 80- *Personal Data:* b Turlock, Calif, Sept 8, 32; m 63; c 2. *Educ:* Univ Chicago, AB, 52; Iowa State Univ, MS, 56; Syracuse Univ, PhD(physics), 62. *Prof Exp:* Lectr physics, Queens Col, NY, 61-62. *Mem:* Am Phys Soc; Fedn Am Sci. *Res:* General theory of relativity. *Mailing Add:* Dept Physics City Univ NY Brooklyn Co 2900 Bedford Ave Brooklyn NY 11210-2813

BOARDMAN, JOHN MICHAEL, HOMOTOPY THEORY, GENERALIZED COHOMOLOGY. *Current Pos:* assoc prof, 69-72, PROF MATH, JOHNS HOPKINS UNIV, 72- *Personal Data:* b Manchester, Eng, Feb 13, 38; US citizen; div; c Susan & Andrew. *Educ:* Cambridge Univ, BA, 61, PhD(math), 65. *Prof Exp:* Fel, Dept Sci & Indust Res, Eng, 64-66; instr math, Univ Chicago, 66-67; lectr, Univ Warwick, 67-68; visitor, Haverford Col, 69. *Mem:* Am Math Soc. *Res:* Algebraic topology, particularly homotopy theory, stable and unstable homopy theory and cohomology theories. *Mailing Add:* Dept Math Johns Hopkins Univ Baltimore MD 21218. *E-Mail:* jboardman@math.jhu.edu

BOARDMAN, MARK R, MARINE GEOLOGY, CARBONATE SEDIMENTOLOGY. *Current Pos:* from asstprof assoc prof, 81-94, PROF GEOL, MIAMI UNIV, OHIO, 94- *Personal Data:* b Albany, NY, Mar 14, 50; div; c Jeremy & Jessica. *Educ:* Princeton Univ, AB, 72; Univ NC, Chapel Hill, MS, 76, PhD(marine sci), 78. *Prof Exp:* Prof geochem, Fed Univ Fluminense, Rio de Janeiro, 78-81. *Mem:* Sigma Xi; Soc Econ Paleontologists & Mineralogists; Int Asn Sedimentologists; Geol Soc Am. *Res:* Geochemical and sedimentologic characteristics of modern carbonate sediments; evaluation of facies and benthic communities; Holocene sea level. *Mailing Add:* Dept Geol Miami Univ Oxford OH 45056. *Fax:* 513-529-1542; *E-Mail:* boardman@miamiu

BOARDMAN, SHELBY JETT, MINERALOGY & PETROLOGY, PRECABRIAN GEOLOGY. *Current Pos:* from asst prof to prof, 71-88, chmn dept, 77-83, CHARLES L DENISON PROF GEOL, CARLETON COL, 88-, ACTG DEAN, 97- *Personal Data:* b Akron, Ohio, Nov 7, 44; m 66; c 2. *Educ:* Miami Univ, BA, 66; Univ Mich, MS, 69, PhD(geol), 71. *Prof Exp:* Petrol geologist, Mobil Oil Corp, 66; explor geologist, Bear Creek Mining Co, 67; res asst stratig, Mobil Res & Develop Corp, 68. *Concurrent Pos:* Res assoc, Univ Glasgow, Scotland, 78-79; dir geol prog, Assoc Cols of Midwest, 80; courtesy res assoc, Univ Kans, 81-82; pres, Coun Undergrad Res, Geol Coun, 87-89; assoc dean, Carelton Col, 94-97. *Mem:* Geol Soc Am; Sigma Xi; Nat Asn Geol Teachers; AAAS. *Res:* Geochemistry, petrology and geochronology of Precambrian rocks of Central Colorado. *Mailing Add:* Dept Geol Carleton Col Northfield MN 55057. *Fax:* 507-646-5427; *E-Mail:* sboardma@carelton.edu

BOARDMAN, WILLIAM JARVIS, PHYSICS, ASTRONOMY. *Current Pos:* Asst prof physics, 68-74, assoc prof math & physics, 74-82, PROF MATH & PHYSICS, BIRMINGHAM-SOUTHERN COL, 82-, DIR MEYER PLANETARIUM, 73- *Personal Data:* b Akron, Ohio, Aug 19, 39; m 65; c 3. *Educ:* Miami Univ, AB, 61, MS, 63; Univ Colo, PhD(astrogeophys), 68. *Mem:* Am Astron Soc; Am Phys Soc. *Res:* Radiative processes in the solar corona; temperature and density of coronal enhancement over regions of solar activity. *Mailing Add:* Dept Math & Sci Birmingham-Southern Col 900 Arkadelphia Rd Birmingham AL 35254-0001

BOARDMAN, WILLIAM WALTER, JR, physical inorganic chemistry, for more information see previous edition

BOAS, MARY LAYNE, PHYSICS. *Current Pos:* lectr, DePaul Univ, 55-56, from asst prof to assoc prof, 57-75, prof, 75-86, EMER PROF PHYSICS, DEPAUL UNIV, 86- *Personal Data:* b Prosser, Wash, Mar 10, 17; m 41, Ralph P Jr; c Ralph L, Anne L & Harold P. *Educ:* Univ Wash, BS, 38, MS, 40; Mass Inst Technol, PhD(physics), 48. *Prof Exp:* Instr, Duke Univ, 40-43 & Tufts Col, 43-48; lectr, Wellesley Col, 49-50; consult, Northwestern Nuclear Res Lab, 50-52; vis lectr physics, Northwestern Univ, 52-53. *Concurrent Pos:* Assoc ed, Am J Physics, 92-94. *Mem:* Am Phys Soc; Am Asn Physics Teachers; Math Asn Am. *Res:* Theoretical nuclear physics; photo-disintegration of H-3; mathematical physics; special relativity. *Mailing Add:* 3540 NE 147th St Seattle WA 98155-7822. *E-Mail:* mlboas@aol.com

BOAS, NORMAN FRANCIS, INTERNAL MEDICINE, RHEUMATOLOGY. *Current Pos:* RETIRED. *Personal Data:* b New York, NY, Aug 4, 22; m 45, Doris Whitehead; c Deborah (Howarth), Stephen E & Barbara J. *Educ:* Harvard Univ, MD, 45. *Prof Exp:* Intern & med resident, Michael Reese Hosp, 45-47; fel path, Mt Sinai Hosp, NY, 47-48, fel med, 48-51; sr asst surgeon, NIH, 51-54; res dir, Norwalk Hosp, 54-78, sr attend physician, 67-78; mem staff, Lawrence & Mem Hosps, New London, 76-85, consult staff, 80-84. *Concurrent Pos:* Asst clin prof med, Yale Univ, 75-78. *Mem:* Fel Am Col Rheumatology; Conn State Med Soc; Fairfield County Med Soc. *Res:* Clinical medicine. *Mailing Add:* 6 Brandon Lane Mystic CT 06355

BOAST, CHARLES WARREN, SOIL PHYSICS, AGRONOMY. *Current Pos:* From asst prof to prof, 70-87, PROF AGRON, UNIV ILL, 87- *Personal Data:* b Ames, Iowa, Nov 12, 43; m 66; c 2. *Educ:* Iowa State Univ, BS, 66, MS, 69, PhD(agron), 70. *Mem:* Soil Sci Soc Am; Am Soc Agron; Am Geophys Union. *Res:* Retention and movement of water in soil; surface and shallow sub-surface hydrology; plant-water relationships; transport of solutes and gases in soil. *Mailing Add:* Dept Agron Univ Ill 1102 S Goodwin Ave Urbana IL 61801-4709

BOATMAN, JOE FRANCIS, cloud physics, aerosol physics, for more information see previous edition

BOATMAN, RALPH HENRY, JR, PUBLIC HEALTH. *Current Pos:* chmn, Dept Pub Health Educ, Univ NC, Chapel Hill, 61-70, dir continuing educ & field serv, 68-70, dean allied health prof, 70-86, PROF PUB HEALTH EDUC, SCH PUB HEALTH, UNIV NC, CHAPEL HILL, 60-, DIR OFF CONTINUING EDUC HEALTH SCI, 74- *Personal Data:* b Carlinville, Ill, Apr 20, 21; m 43; c 2. *Educ:* Southern Ill Univ, BS, 43; Univ NC, MPH, 47, PhD(pub health), 54. *Prof Exp:* Health coordr & instr health educ & dir sch-community health proj, Southern Ill Univ, 47-54, chmn dept health educ, 48-54; dir community health serv, Chicago & Cook County Tuberc Inst, Ill, 54-60. *Concurrent Pos:* Lectr, Prof Schs, Univ Ill, 55-56, asst prof, 56-60; consult, Radiol Health Conf, WHO, 62; mem nat adv coun allied health prof, HEW, 68-; consult, NIH & Am Hosp Asn, 78-88; consult, univs & state bd of educ; gen col adv, Univ NC, Chapel Hill, 80- *Mem:* Fel Am Pub Health Asn (pres, 76-77); Am Soc Allied Health Prof (secy, 73-75, pres-elect, 75-76, pres, 77); Soc Pub Health Educr (pres, 66-67). *Res:* Public, school and allied health education; continuing education. *Mailing Add:* 750 Weaver Dairy Rd Chapel Hill NC 27514

BOATMAN, SANDRA, ORGANIC CHEMISTRY, BIOCHEMISTRY. *Current Pos:* asst prof, 67-74, assoc prof, 74-79, PROF CHEM, HOLLINS COL, 79- *Personal Data:* b Tampa, Fla, Nov 1, 39. *Educ:* Rice Univ, BA, 61; Duke Univ, PhD(chem), 65. *Prof Exp:* Fel, Univ NC, 65-66, NIH fel, 65-67. *Mem:* AAAS; Am Chem Soc; The Chem Soc; Sigma Xi. *Res:* Synthetic studies on polyanions of B-ketoaldehydes, pyridones; B-ketoenamines and related compounds; condensations of polyketo compounds; chemical modification of proteins and enzymes, especially at the active sites; stabilizing interactions in viruses, writing in science courses. *Mailing Add:* Dept Chem Hollins Col Box 9577 Roanoke VA 24020-9577

BOATNER, LYNN ALLEN, MAGNETIC RESONANCE, MATERIALS SCIENCE & CRYSTAL GROWTH. *Current Pos:* staff scientist, 77-80, sr res staff scientist & sect head, Solid State Div, 80-93, MARTIN MARIETTA ENERGY SYSTS CORP FEL, OAK RIDGE NAT LAB, 93- *Personal Data:* b Clarksville, Tex, Aug 3, 38; m 61, Martha A Goodwin; c Mark J, Ivan A & Philip G. *Educ:* Tex Tech Univ, BS, 60, MS, 61; Vanderbilt Univ, PhD(physics), 66. *Honors & Awards:* IR-100 Award, 82, 85 & 96; Mat Sci Res Competition, Dept Energy, 84; Jacquet-Lucas Award, Am Soc Metals Int, 88. *Prof Exp:* Asst physics, Tex Technol Col, 60-61; asst, Vanderbilt Univ, 61-66; res scientist, LTV Res Ctr, 66-70, prin scientist, Advan Technol Ctr, Inc, 71-74; sr res scientist, Lab Exp Physics, Fed Polytech Sch, Switz, 75-77. *Concurrent Pos:* Vis prof, Unam, Mex, 74. *Mem:* Fel AAAS; fel Am Phys Soc; assoc fel Am Inst Aeronaut & Astronaut; Mat Res Soc (exec secy, 92-93); Am Asn Crystal Growth; Am Ceramic Soc; fel Am Soc Metals Int. *Res:* Electron paramagnetic resonance investigations of transition metal ions in single crystals; studies of rare-earth and actinide ions; single crystal growth; superconductivity; investigations of the Jahn-Teller effect; ferroelectrics; nuclear waste disposal; ion-solid interactions; glass properties. *Mailing Add:* Solid State Div MS-6056 PO Box 2008 Oak Ridge TN 37831. *Fax:* 423-574-4814; *E-Mail:* lb4@ornl.gov

BOAZ, DAVID PAUL, ORGANIC CHEMISTRY, BIOCHEMISTRY. *Current Pos:* sr res chemist adhesives, 3M Co, 76-80, chemist specialist, 80-84, mgr, Specialty Chem Div, 84-87, Europ tech mgr specialty chem, 87-91, lab mgr, 91-92, mfg technol mgr, 92-94, MGR, PROCESS DEVELOPMENT CTR, SPECIALTY MAT DIV, 3M CO, 94- *Personal Data:* b Wichita, Kans, Oct 19, 44; m 65; c 3. *Educ:* Univ Dubuque, BA, 66; Univ Iowa, MS, 69, PhD(org chem), 72. *Prof Exp:* Fel, Dept Pediat, Univ Iowa, 71-72; res assoc hypertension, Dept Med, 72-73, asst res scientist, 73-76, assoc res scientist biochem, 76. *Mem:* Am Chem Soc; Sigma Xi. *Res:* Pressure sensitive adhesives; polymer chemistry; aminimids. *Mailing Add:* 8200 Emerald Lane St Paul MN 55125

BOAZ, PATRICIA ANNE, physical chemistry, analytical chemistry; deceased, see previous edition for last biography

BOBALEK, EDWARD G(EORGE), chemical engineering, polymer science; deceased, see previous edition for last biography

BOBBIN, RICHARD PETER, AUDITORY PHYSIOLOGY. *Current Pos:* asst prof pharmacol, Dept Otorhinolaryngol, Kresge Hearing Res Lab, Sch Med & Dept Pharmacol & Exp Therapeut, 71-76, ASSOC PROF PHARMACOL, LA STATE UNIV, 76- *Personal Data:* b Northampton, Mass, Dec 25, 42; m 66; c 2. *Educ:* Northeastern Univ, Boston, BS, 64; Tulane Univ, MS, 67, PhD(pharmacol), 69. *Concurrent Pos:* Guest worker, Lab Neuro-Otolaryngol, Nat Inst Neurol & Commun Disorders & Stroke, NIH, 81. *Mem:* Am Soc Pharmacol & Exp Therapeut; Acoust Soc Am; Asn Res Otolaryngol; AAAS; Sigma Xi. *Res:* Pharmacology and biochemistry of neurotransmitters, drug toxicity and cell death using the peripheral auditory and acousticolateralis organs as model systems; auditory biochemistry and pharmacology. *Mailing Add:* Dept Otolaryngol & Kresge Hearing Res Lab Univ Med Ctr 2020 Gravier St Suite AQ New Orleans LA 70112-2234

BOBBITT, DONALD ROBERT, CHIRAL-SELECTIVE ANALYSIS, ULTRASENSITIVE DETECTION. *Current Pos:* from asst prof to assoc prof, 85-93, PROF ANALYTICAL CHEM, UNIV ARK, 93- *Personal Data:* b Philadelphia, Pa, Oct 21, 56; m 80, Susan Cisson; c Justin, Christopher & Jonathan. *Educ:* Univ Ark, BS, 80; Iowa State Univ, PhD(chem), 85. *Honors & Awards:* Johnson & Johnson Award Chromatography, 93. *Prof Exp:* Chemist, E I Dupont, 79-80. *Concurrent Pos:* Dreyfus Teacher/Scholar fel, 88. *Mem:* Am Chem Soc; Sigma Xi; Soc App Spectros. *Res:* Application of lasers to problems in analytical chemistry; development of laser-based detection schemes for high performance liquid chromatography; ruthenium-based chemiluminescent detection of amino acids protocols; development of protein sequencing. *Mailing Add:* Dept Chem & Biochem Univ Ark 306 Chem Bldg Fayetteville AR 72701. *Fax:* 501-575-4049; *E-Mail:* dbobbitt@uafsysb.uark.edu

BOBBITT, JESSE LEROY, BIOCHEMISTRY. *Current Pos:* RETIRED. *Personal Data:* b Yellow Springs, Ohio, Sept 18, 33; m 56. *Educ:* Berea Col, BA, 55; Univ Louisville, PhD(biochem), 64. *Prof Exp:* Teacher pub schs, Ky, 58-60; biochemist, US Army Med Res Labs, Ft Knox, Ky, 63-66; res biochemist, Eli Lilly & Co, 66-93. *Mem:* AAAS; Sigma Xi; Am Chem Soc; Am Soc Biochem & Molecular Biol. *Res:* Protein isolation and characterization; mechanism of enzyme and hormone action. *Mailing Add:* 8101 Rosemead Lane Indianapolis IN 46240

BOBBITT, OLIVER BIERNE, CLINICAL PATHOLOGY. *Current Pos:* From instr to prof, 47-82, chmn dept & dir clin lab, Hosp, 52-71, EMER PROF CLIN PATH, MED SCH, UNIV VA, 82- *Personal Data:* b Charleston, WVa, Jan 10, 17; m 43; c 3. *Educ:* Univ Ga, BS, 39; Univ Va, MD, 43. *Mem:* AMA; Col Am Path; Am Soc Clin Path. *Res:* Blood groups. *Mailing Add:* 1113 Marion Dr Charlottesville VA 22903-4662

BOBECHKO, WALTER PETER, ORTHOPAEDIC PEDIATRIC SURGERY. *Current Pos:* DIR, ADVAN SURG INST, MED CITY, 88- *Personal Data:* b Toronto, Ont, Aug 22, 32; m 57, Mary; c Kevin, Karen, Janet, Ardys & Debra. *Educ:* Univ Toronto, MD, 57, BSc, 59; Royal Col Physicians & Surg Can, FRCS(C), 63. *Honors & Awards:* Austrailian Postage Stamp in honor of, 72. *Prof Exp:* Res scientist, Res Inst, Hosp Sick Children, 64-87; from asst prof to assoc prof orthop, Univ Toronto, 70-88, chmn orthop surg, 77-87. *Mem:* Can Orthop Soc; Paediat Orthop Soc; Scoliosis Res Soc; Int Soc Orthop Surg & Traumatology; Am Med Asn. *Res:* Designer of electro-spinal instrumentation, spinal pacemaker to correct spinal scoliosis deformities of children; designer of Double Hook spinal instrumentation for correction of severe spinal deformities without casts or braces. *Mailing Add:* Advan Surg Inst Med City Dallas 7777 Forest Lane Dallas TX 75230. *Fax:* 972-566-6009

BOBECK, ANDREW H, APPLIED PHYSICS, COMPUTER SCIENCE. *Current Pos:* RETIRED. *Personal Data:* b Tower Hill, Pa, Oct 1, 26; m 49, Mary E Orr; c Andrea, Linda & David. *Educ:* Purdue Univ, BS, 48, MS, 49. *Hon Degrees:* EngD, Purdue Univ, 72. *Honors & Awards:* Stuart Ballentine Medal, Franklin Inst, 73; M N Liebmann Award, Inst Elec & Electronics Engrs, 75; Valdemar Poulsen Gold Medal, Danish Acad Sci, 76. *Prof Exp:* Mem tech staff & supvr, Bell Labs, 49-89. *Mem:* Nat Acad Eng; Inst Elec & Electronics Engrs. *Res:* Magnetic logic and storage; development of very high density magnetic bubble devices. *Mailing Add:* 41 Ellers Dr Chatham NJ 07928

BOBECK, GENE E, FAILURE ANALYSIS, CORROSION. *Current Pos:* asst prof, 67-72, ASSOC PROF METALL, UNIV IDAHO, 72-, DEPT HEAD, 89- *Personal Data:* b Chicago, Il, May 13, 29; m 58, Janet Talbot; c Eric, Juliet, Shelley & David. *Educ:* Knox Col, BA 52; Iowa State Univ, MS, 56; Univ Denver, PhD(metall), 72. *Prof Exp:* Metallurgist, Dow Chem Co, Rocky Flats, Colo, 56-63. *Mem:* Minerals Metals & Mat Soc; Am Soc Metals Int; Northwest Mining Assn. *Res:* Structure-property relationships of materials, corrosion research, failure analysis of materials. *Mailing Add:* Dept Metall & Mat Univ Idaho 375 S Line St Moscow ID 83843-4140

BOBER, WILLIAM, FLUID MECHANICS, APPLIED MATHEMATICS. *Current Pos:* ASSOC PROF MECH ENG, FLA ATLANTIC UNIV, 82- *Personal Data:* b New York, NY, Mar 16, 30; m 54; c 3. *Educ:* City Col New York, BCE, 52; Pratt Inst, MS, 60; Purdue Univ, PhD(eng sci), 64. *Prof Exp:* Asst eng sci, Pratt Inst, 58-60; instr aerospace & eng sci, Purdue Univ, 60-64; assoc eng physicist, Cornell Aeronaut Lab, 64-68; vis asst prof eng mech, Va Polytech Inst, 68-69; assoc prof mech eng, Rochester Inst Technol, 69-81. *Concurrent Pos:* Ford Found fel, 60-63; lectr, State Univ NY, Buffalo, 65-67. *Mem:* Am Soc Mech Engrs. *Res:* Sub-sonic aerodynamics; heat transfer; numerical methods. *Mailing Add:* Dept Mech Eng Fla Atlantic Univ PO Box 3091 Boca Raton FL 33431-0991

BOBICH, JOSEPH AARON, NEUROCHEMISTRY. *Current Pos:* from asst prof to assoc prof, 73-83, PROF CHEM, TEX CHRISTIAN UNIV, 83- *Personal Data:* b Detroit, Mich, July 14, 42; m 64, Marianne Wanninger; c Tanya S & Maxwell E. *Educ:* Univ Mich, BS, 65; Univ Calif, Los Angeles, PhD(biol chem), 71. *Concurrent Pos:* Fel, US Nat Mult Sclerosis Soc, 71-73; dir chem of behav prog, Tex Christian Univ, 75-83; NIH res career develop grant, 78-83. *Mem:* Am Soc Neurochem; Soc Neurosci; Am Soc Biochem & Molecular Biol; Am Soc Cell Biol. *Res:* Structure and function of brain synapses; calcium binding proteins. *Mailing Add:* Dept Chem Tex Christian Univ Ft Worth TX 76129. *E-Mail:* babitch@gamma.is.tcu.edu

BOBISUD, LARRY EUGENE, DIFFERENTIAL EQUATIONS & APPLICATIONS. *Current Pos:* from asst prof to assoc prof, 67-74, chmn dept, 78-82, PROF MATH, UNIV IDAHO, 74- *Personal Data:* b Midvale, Idaho, Mar 16, 40; m 63, Helen M Meyer. *Educ:* Col Idaho, BS, 61; Univ NMex, MS, 63, PhD(math), 66. *Prof Exp:* Vis mem, Courant Inst Math Sci, NY Univ, 66-67. *Mem:* Am Math Soc. *Res:* Singular perturbation problems for partial differential equations; mathematical biology; nonlinear boundary value problems. *Mailing Add:* Dept Math & Statist Univ Idaho Moscow ID 83843-6417. *Fax:* 208-885-6198; *E-Mail:* mathstat@iduil

BOBKA, RUDOLPH J, PHYSICAL CHEMISTRY. *Current Pos:* RETIRED. *Personal Data:* b Akron, Ohio, July 27, 28; m 55, Marlene; c 1. *Educ:* Marietta Col, AB, 50; Miami Univ, MS, 51; Western Res Univ, PhD(phys chem), 60. *Prof Exp:* Analytical chemist, Army Chem Ctr, Md, 51-52; asst, Western Res Univ, 54-58; chemist, Res Lab, Union Carbide Corp, 58-68; from assoc prof to prof chem, State Univ NY Col Plattsburgh, 72-90. *Mem:* Am Chem Soc; Sigma Xi; Am Inst Chemist. *Res:* Low temperature calorimetry; surface chemistry; carbon technology. *Mailing Add:* 219 Dragoon Rd Altona NY 12910-9735

BOBKO, EDWARD, ORGANIC CHEMISTRY. *Current Pos:* from asst prof to assoc prof, 56-69, PROF CHEM, TRINITY COL, CONN, 69- *Personal Data:* b Cleveland, Ohio, Feb 15, 25; m; c 3. *Educ:* Western Reserve Univ, BS, 49; Northwestern Univ, PhD(org chem), 52. *Prof Exp:* Instr chem, Northwestern Univ, 52-53; res chemist, Olin Industs, Inc, 53-54; asst prof chem, Washington & Jefferson Col, 54-55, instr, 55-56. *Mem:* AAAS; Am Chem Soc. *Res:* Organometallic compounds; pyrimidines; physical organic chemistry. *Mailing Add:* 44 Ivy Lane Newington CT 06111

BOBLITT, ROBERT LEROY, MEDICINAL CHEMISTRY. *Current Pos:* Asst, 53-55, assoc prof, 56-70, asst dean, 72-76, PROF PHARMACEUT CHEM, COL PHARM, UNIV HOUSTON, 70-, ASSOC DEAN, 76- *Personal Data:* b Springfield, Ohio, Nov 1, 25; m 44; c 4. *Educ:* Ohio Northern Univ, BS, 48; Univ Minn, PhD(pharmaceut chem), 53. *Mem:* Am Chem Soc; Am Pharmaceut Asn; Sigma Xi. *Res:* Synthesis of amidines; physical and chemical properties of amidines; phytochemistry; synthesis of beta-adrenergic blocking agents. *Mailing Add:* 7622 Montglen St Houston TX 77061

BOBO, EDWIN RAY, MATHEMATICS. *Current Pos:* Asst prof, 65-70, ASSOC PROF MATH, GEORGETOWN UNIV, 70- *Personal Data:* b Oklahoma City, Okla, May 17, 38. *Educ:* Pa State Univ, BA, 60; Univ Va, MA, 62, PhD(math), 65. *Mem:* Am Math Soc; Math Asn Am. *Res:* Algebra; finite groups; automorphism groups of Jordan algebras; group representations. *Mailing Add:* Dept Math Georgetown Univ Washington DC 20057-0001

BOBONICH, HARRY MICHAEL, INORGANIC CHEMISTRY. *Current Pos:* RETIRED. *Personal Data:* b Ashland, Pa, Sept 13, 24; m 49; c 2. *Educ:* Susquehanna Univ, BA, 50; Bucknell Univ, MS, 56; Syracuse Univ, PhD(chem), 65. *Prof Exp:* Chemist, Barrett Div, Allied Chem Corp, 52-55; prof chem, Pa State Univ, 55-61 & 64-65; chmn dept, Shippensburg State Col, 69-74, actg dean grad studies, 74-75, assoc dean grad studies, 75-79, prof chem, 65-, dean grad sch, 80-91. *Res:* Synthesis of coordination compounds; use of magnetic measurements; infrared and ultraviolet spectra; conductance and x-rays to determine structure; development of new experiments for freshman chemistry programs. *Mailing Add:* 421 Scott Dr Shippensburg PA 17257-2168

BOBROW, DANIEL G, INTELLIGENT SYSTEMS. *Current Pos:* RES FEL, XEROX PALO ALTO RES CTR, 72- *Personal Data:* b New York, NY, Nov 29, 35; div; c 3. *Educ:* Rensselaer Polytech Inst, BS, 57; Harvard Univ, SM, 58; Mass Inst Technol, PhD(math), 64. *Honors & Awards:* Prog Lang Award, Asn Comput Mach, 74, Software Systs Award, 92. *Prof Exp:* Mem staff, Bolt, Beranek & Newman Inc, 62-64; asst prof elec eng, Mass Inst Technol, 64-65; vpres, Info Sci Div, Bolt, Beranek & Newman, Inc, 65-69, dir comput sci div, 69-72. *Concurrent Pos:* Fulbright fel, 72-73; lectr, Stanford Univ, 73-; ed-in-chief, Artificial Int, 77-; chair, Cognitive Sci Soc; pres, Am Asn Artificial Intel. *Mem:* AAAS; Asn Comput Mach; Asn Comput Ling; Cognitive Sci Soc; Am Asn Artificial Intel. *Res:* Development of knowledge representation languages and programming systems; development of a computer program that understands natural language; artificial intelligence; development of a designers assistant for very large scale integrated systems. *Mailing Add:* 1742 Sand Hill Rd Palo Alto CA 94304. *E-Mail:* bobrow@parc.xerox.com

BOBROW, LEONARD S(AUL), ELECTRICAL ENGINEERING. *Current Pos:* asst prof, 68-73, ASSOC PROF ELEC ENG, UNIV MASS, AMHERST, 73- *Personal Data:* b Newark, NJ, Nov 27, 40. *Educ:* Univ Miami, BSEE, 62; Northwestern Univ, MS, 64, PhD(elec eng), 68. *Prof Exp:* Res asst elec eng, Northwestern Univ, 66-67; electronic engr, Beltone Electronics Corp, 63-65. *Res:* Active network synthesis; coding theory, graph theory and the application of graph theory to coding. *Mailing Add:* Dept Elec Eng & Comput Sci Univ Mass Amherst MA 01003-0002

BOBST, ALBERT M, BIOPHYSICAL CHEMISTRY, ORGANIC BIOCHEMISTRY. *Current Pos:* asst prof, 69-74, assoc prof chem, 74-78, PROF CHEM, UNIV CINCINNATI, 78- *Personal Data:* b Zurich, Switz, Sept 10, 39; nat US; m 70; c 3. *Educ:* Univ Zurich, PhD(chem), 65. *Prof Exp:* Res fel, Inst Biophys & Biochem, Paris, 66; Swiss Nat Found fel, Univ Calif, Berkeley, 67-68; res assoc biochem, Princeton Univ, 68-69. *Concurrent Pos:* Vis scientist, Nat Inst Arthritis, Metab & Digestive Dis, 75-76 & 83-84. *Mem:* AAAS; Am Soc Biol Chem; Biophys Soc; Am Chem Soc. *Res:* Application of electron spin resonance and circular dichroism spectroscopy to biological systems; biological redox mechanisms; synthesis of nucleic acid analogs and hybridization probes. *Mailing Add:* Dept Chem 172 Univ Cincinnati Cincinnati OH 45221-0172. *E-Mail:* bobst@ucbeh

BOCARSLY, ANDREW B, PHOTOCHEMISTRY, ELECTROCHEMISTRY. *Current Pos:* from asst prof to assoc prof, 80-94, PROF CHEM, PRINCETON UNIV, 94- *Personal Data:* b Los Angeles, Calif, Apr 23, 54; m 77; c 3. *Educ:* Univ Calif, Los Angeles, BS, 76; Mass Inst Technol, PhD(inorg chem), 80. *Honors & Awards:* Solid State Chem Award, Am Chem Soc, 84. *Concurrent Pos:* A P Sloan fel, 86-88; secy-treas, Princeton Sect, Am Chem Soc, 92, chmn, 94. *Mem:* Am Chem Soc; Electrochem Soc. *Res:* Inorganic photochemistry and electrochemistry; chemically modified electrode interfaces; solar energy conversion; semiconducting electrodes; electrocatalysis and mechanism of interfacial charge transfer; sensors. *Mailing Add:* Dept Chem Princeton Univ Princeton NJ 08544. *E-Mail:* bocarsly@chemvax.princeton.edu

BOCCABELLA, ANTHONY VINCENT, ANATOMY. *Current Pos:* from instr to assoc prof, 59-67, PROF ANAT, COL MED & DENT NJ, 67-, CHMN DEPT, 71- *Personal Data:* b Brooklyn, NY; m 51; c 2. *Educ:* Seton Hall Univ, BS, 50, JD, 84; Univ Iowa, MS, 56, PhD(anat), 58. *Prof Exp:* Instr anat, Univ Iowa, 58-59. *Mem:* Endocrine Soc; Am Asn Anat; Am Soc Andrology; Am Soc Law & Med; Asn Anat Chmn; Sigma Xi; Soc Study Reproduction. *Res:* Thyroid physiology; male and female reproductive systems; muscular dystrophy; hormonal factors regulating spermatogenesis; histophysiological evaluation of the male reproductive system in various states of hormonal deprivation and repletion. *Mailing Add:* Dept Anat Col Med & Dent NJ 185 S Orange Ave Newark NJ 07103-2714

BOCHENEK, WIESLAW JANUSZ, GASTROENTEROLOGY, CLINICAL NURTRITION & INTERNAL MEDICINE. *Current Pos:* assoc dir, 88-91, dir res & develop, Metab Div, 91-93, SR DIR RES & DEVELOP, ENDOCRINOL & METAB DIV, WYETH-AYERST RES, 93- *Personal Data:* b Radymno, Poland, Nov 11, 38; US citizen; m 69, Elzbieta; c Krzysztof & Adam. *Educ:* Akad Medyczna, Wroclaw, MD, 62, PhD(physiol), 91. *Prof Exp:* Assoc prof med, Akad Medyczna, Wroclaw, 76-81; assoc prof med & gastrointestinal nutrit, Albany Med Col, 82-88. *Concurrent Pos:* Mem comt physiol, gastrointestinal tract & physiol, Polish Acad Sci, 75-81; asst prof med, Med Col Pa, 89- *Mem:* Am Heart Asn; Am Soc Clin Nutrit; Am Diabetic Asn. *Res:* Development of antidiabetic drugs; research on lipid absorption, intestinal lipoprotein secretion; proton pump inhibitors. *Mailing Add:* Wyeth-Ayerst Clin Res & Develop Dept 145 King of Prussia Rd Radnor PA 19087

BOCHNER, BARRY RONALD, FERMENTATION DEVELOPMENT, BIOTECHNOLOGY. *Current Pos:* SR SCIENTIST, GENENTECH, INC, 82- *Educ:* Univ Mich, PhD(bioeng), 76. *Mailing Add:* R&D Biol Inc 3938 Trust Way Hayward CA 94545

BOCHNER, BRUCE SCOTT, ALLERGY & IMMUNOLOGY. *Current Pos:* fel clin immunol, 85-88, instr med, 88-89, ASST PROF MED, JOHNS HOPKINS UNIV, 89- *Educ:* Johns Hopkins Univ, BA, 78; Univ Ill, MD, 82; Am Bd Internal Med, dipl; Am Bd Allergy & Immunol, dipl. *Honors & Awards:* Charles Reed lectr, Am Acad Allergy & Immunol, 93. *Prof Exp:* From intern to resident internal med, Univ Ill Hosps, Chicago, 82-85. *Concurrent Pos:* President's grant-in-ald award, Am Acad Allergy & Immunol, 87; grantee, Am Lung Asn, 88-90, NIH, 89-94 & Pfizer Inc, 91-93; developing investr award, Asthma & Allergy Found Am, 90, Burroughs Wellcome Fund, 92; assoc ed, J Allergy & Clin Immunol, 93-; mem, Immunol Coun, Johns Hopkins Univ. *Mem:* Am Asn Immunol; Am Acad Allergy & Immunol. *Res:* Progress in allergy and clinical immunology; late phase allergic reactions; pulmonary, pharmacology and toxicology; allergy, immunology and rheumatology. *Mailing Add:* Clin Immunol Unit 3 John Hopkins Univ Asthma & Allergy Ctr 5501 Hopkins Bayview Circle Baltimore MD 21224-6801

BOCK, AUGUST, MICROBIOLOGY. *Current Pos:* PROF MICROBIOLOGY, UNIV MUNICH. *Personal Data:* b Kaltenberg, Ger, Apr 23, 37. *Honors & Awards:* Osborne & Mendel Award, Am Inst Nutrit, 94. *Mem:* Bavarian Acad Sci. *Mailing Add:* Dept Biol Univ Munich Geschwister-Scholl Platz 80539 Munich Germany

BOCK, CARL E, ZOOLOGY, ECOLOGY. *Current Pos:* Asst prof biol, Univ Colo, 68-77, assoc chmn dept, 74-77, assoc prof, 74-80, PROF ENVIRON, POP & ORGANISMIC BIOL, UNIV COLO, 80- *Personal Data:* b Berkeley, Calif, Mar 29, 42; m 64. *Educ:* Univ Calif, Berkeley, AB, 64, PhD(zool), 68. *Mem:* Ecol Soc Am; Soc Study Evolution; Cooper Ornith Soc; Am Ornith Union; Brit Ecol Soc. *Res:* Animal ecology; evolution and ecology of birds; fire ecology. *Mailing Add:* EPO Biol Box 334 Univ Colo Boulder CO 80309

BOCK, CHARLES WALTER, QUANTUM & COMPUTATIONAL CHEMISTRY, MOLECULAR MODELING. *Current Pos:* asst prof chem, 72-89, ASST PROF COMPUT SCI, PHILADELPHIA COL TEXTILES & SCI, 72-, PROF CHEM & MATH, 89- *Personal Data:* b Philadelphia, Pa, Jan 19, 45; m 68, Lorraine Robinson; c Cindy & Carolyn. *Educ:* Drexel Univ, BS, 68, MS, 70, PhD(physics), 72. *Concurrent Pos:* Adj, Fox Chase Cancer Ctr, 92- *Mem:* Am Phys Soc. *Res:* Investigation of the most appropriate definitions of stabilization and destabilization energies; determination of molecular geometries for various organic and inorganic compounds using ab initio quantum mechanical calculations; determination of transition states for various chemical processes; solid state chemistry; chemical vapor deposition; organometallic chemistry. *Mailing Add:* Philadelphia Col Textiles & Sci Henry Ave Philadelphia PA 19144. *E-Mail:* chuck@hardy.texsci.edu

BOCK, ERNST, physical chemistry; deceased, see previous edition for last biography

BOCK, FRED G, biochemistry, for more information see previous edition

BOCK, JANE HASKETT, GENETICS. *Current Pos:* from asst prof to assoc prof, 69-79, PROF BIOL, UNIV COLO, 79- *Personal Data:* b Rochester, Ind, Oct 3, 36; m 64, Carl E; c Laura. *Educ:* Duke Univ, BA, 58; Ind Univ, Bloomington, MA, 60; Univ Calif, Berkeley, PhD(bot), 66. *Prof Exp:* Asst prof biol, Calif State Col, Hayward, 67-68. *Concurrent Pos:* Co-dir, Audubon Res Ranch, Elgin, Ariz, 80-91. *Mem:* Bot Soc Am; Brit Ecol Soc; Ecol Soc Am; Soc Conserv Biol; Am Inst Biol Sci. *Res:* Evolution and ecology of flowering plants; ecology of fire; conservation of native flora of the western US; herbivory in grassland and alpine; forensic botany. *Mailing Add:* 426 W Spruce Lane Louisville CO 80027. *Fax:* 303-492-8699; *E-Mail:* bock@spot.colorado.edu

BOCK, MARGARET ANN, MEDICAL RESEARCH. *Current Pos:* from asst prof to assoc prof, 83-90, ASSOC PROF FOODS & NUTRIT, DEPT HOME ECON, NMEX STATE UNIV, 90- *Educ:* Kans State Univ, BS, 68, MS, 79, PhD(foods & nutrit), 83. *Prof Exp:* Grad res asst, Nutrit Res, Am Inst Baking, Manhattan, Kans, 80-83. *Concurrent Pos:* Prog dir, Dept Home Econ, Am Dietetic Asn, 83-; consult therapeut nutrit, Thomas Hosp, El Paso, 92- *Mem:* Am Dietetic Asn; Am Soc Parenteral & Enteral Nutrit; Am Asn Cereal Chemists; Am Home Econ Asn; Inst Food Technol; Am Inst Nutrit; Sigma Xi. *Mailing Add:* NMex State Univ Box 3003 Dept 3470 Las Cruces NM 88003-8003

BOCK, MARK GARY, PEPTIDE CHEMISTRY, HETEROCYCLIC CHEMISTRY. *Current Pos:* sr res chemist, Merck & Co, Inc, 76-82, res fel med chem, 82-87, sr res fel, 87-91, SR INVESTR, MERCK & CO, INC, 91- *Personal Data:* b Munich, Ger, Oct 10, 46; US citizen; m 68; c 2. *Educ:* Rutgers Univ, BA, 69; Univ Ga, PhD(chem), 74. *Prof Exp:* Postdoctoral fel chem, Harvard Univ, 74-76. *Mem:* Am Chem Soc. *Res:* Design and synthesis of hormone antagonists for therapeutic application. *Mailing Add:* Merck Sharp & Dohme Res Labs W26A-4044 West Point PA 19486

BOCK, PAUL, hydrology & water resources, for more information see previous edition

BOCK, S ALLAN, ALLERGY, PEDIATRICS. *Current Pos:* Asst prof, 76-82, clin assoc prof, 82-90, CLIN PROF, DEPT PEDIAT, UNIV COLO SCH MED, 90-; STAFF PHYSICIAN, NAT JEWISH CTR IMMUNOL & RESPIRATORY MED, 76- *Personal Data:* b Baltimore, Md, Apr 28, 46; m 85, Judith; c Samuel, Eric, Lea & Michelle. *Educ:* Washington Univ, St Louis, AB, 68; Univ Md, MD, 72. *Concurrent Pos:* Pediat allergist, Dept Health & Hosps, Denver, 76-84. *Mem:* Am Acad Allergy; Am Acad Pediat. *Res:* Food allergy and immunologic sensitivity to food in children; immunology of the gastrointestinal tract; natural history of food allergy. *Mailing Add:* Dept Pediat 1400 Jackson St Denver CO 80206

BOCK, WALTER JOSEPH, VERTEBRATE MORPHOLOGY, EVOLUTION. *Current Pos:* from asst prof to assoc prof, 65-73, PROF EVOLUTIONARY BIOL, COLUMBIA UNIV, 73- *Personal Data:* b New York, NY, Nov 20, 33; m 57; c Katharine R, Susan R & Walter D. *Educ:* Cornell Univ, BS, 55; Harvard Univ, MA, 57, PhD(biol), 59. *Honors & Awards:* Coues Award, Am Ornithologists Union, 75. *Prof Exp:* From asst prof to assoc prof zool, Univ Ill, 61-65. *Concurrent Pos:* NSF fel, Univ Frankfurt, 59-61; res assoc ornith, Am Mus Natural Hist, 65- *Mem:* Fel AAAS; fel Am Ornithologists Union; Soc Study Evolution; Am Soc Naturalists (treas, 78-81); hon mem Ger Ornith Soc. *Res:* Functional and evolutionary morphology; morphology and classification of birds; general theories of major evolutionary changes. *Mailing Add:* Dept Biol Columbia Univ Main Div New York NY 10027. *Fax:* 212-865-8246; *E-Mail:* wb4@columbia.Edu

BOCK, WAYNE DEAN, MICROPALEONTOLOGY, ENVIRONMENTAL SCIENCE. *Current Pos:* CHIEF OPERATING OFFICER, SPECTRO ANALYTICA INC, 87- *Personal Data:* b Truman, Minn, Nov 15, 32; div; c 4. *Educ:* Univ Wis, BS, 58, MS, 61; Univ Miami, PhD(oceanog), 67. *Prof Exp:* Instr geol, Sch Marine & Atmospheric Sci, Univ Miami, 64-67, res scientist, 67-69, from asst prof to assoc prof micropaleont, 67-81; pres, Appl Eco-Tech Serv, Inc, 78-83; partner, Bock-Joensuu Ent, 84-87; vpres, Spectro Scan, 86-87, pres, 87-90. *Concurrent Pos:* Prin investr, NSF res grants, 67- *Mem:* AAAS; Paleont Soc; Paleont Res Inst. *Res:* Paleoecology of ocean sediment cores; use of Foraminifera as indicators of pollution: environmental assessment & monitoring. *Mailing Add:* 4020 Salzedo St Coral Gables FL 33146

BOCKELMAN, CHARLES KINCAID, NUCLEAR PHYSICS. *Current Pos:* from asst prof to prof, Yale Univ, 55-93, dep provost sci, 69-78, dep provost, 78-87, EMER PROF PHYSICS, YALE UNIV, 93- *Personal Data:* b San Francisco, Calif, Nov 29, 22; m 91, Christina D Giusto; c Faith. *Educ:* Univ Wis, PhD(physics), 51. *Prof Exp:* Res assoc physics, Mass Inst Technol, 51-55. *Concurrent Pos:* Fel, Univ Inst Theoret Physics, Copenhagen, 58-59; Guggenheim fel, Oxford Univ, 70. *Mem:* Fel Am Phys Soc; Sigma Xi. *Res:* Nuclear structure; electron scattering; nucleon transfer reactions. *Mailing Add:* A W Wright Nuclear Struct Lab Yale Univ New Haven CT 06520

BOCKELMANN, JOHN B(URGGRAF), CHEMICAL ENGINEERING. *Current Pos:* RETIRED. *Personal Data:* b Union City, NJ, July 24, 15; m 42; c 3. *Educ:* Columbia Univ, AB, 37, BS, 38, ChE, 39, PhD(chem eng), 41. *Prof Exp:* Sr proj chem engr, Soaps Div, Colgate-Palmolive-Peet Co, NJ, 41-45; asst tech dir & process engr, Tech Dept, F & M Schaefer Brewing Co, 45-49, tech dir, 49-70, vpres, 70-77. *Mem:* AAAS; Am Chem Soc; Am Soc Brewing Chem (pres, 63-64); Am Inst Chem Engrs; Inst Food Techologists; Sigma Xi. *Res:* Liquid extraction employing solvents near their critical temperatures; process control variables in brewing and their relation to final taste and taste testing. *Mailing Add:* 40 Sussex Rd Tenafly NJ 07670-2512

BOCKEMUEHL, R(OBERT) R(USSELL), ELECTRICAL ENGINEERING. *Current Pos:* Jr engr, physics dept, 52-54, res engr, 54-56, sr res engr, 56-62, asst head electronics & instrumentation dept, 62-73, HEAD INSTRUMENTATION DEPT, GEN MOTORS RES LABS, 73- *Personal Data:* b Omaha, Nebr, Oct 17, 27; m 52; c 1. *Educ:* Univ Mich, BSE, 52. *Mem:* Sigma Xi. *Res:* Advanced electronic instruments; solid state materials and device research. *Mailing Add:* 4800 N Harsdale Rd Bloomfield Hills MI 48302

BOCKHOFF, FRANK JAMES, PHYSICAL CHEMISTRY, POLYMER CHEMISTRY. *Current Pos:* chmn dept, 64-83, PROF CHEM, CLEVELAND STATE UNIV, 64- *Personal Data:* b Tiffin, Ohio, Mar 26, 28; m 51; c 4. *Educ:* Case Inst Technol, BS, 50; Case Western Res Univ, MS, 52, PhD(phys chem), 59. *Prof Exp:* Asst chem, Western Res Univ, 50-51; instr chem & chem eng, Fenn Col, 51-54, from asst prof to assoc prof chem, 54-64, chmn dept, 62-64. *Concurrent Pos:* Consult, Am Agile Corp, 53-61, Apex Reinforced Plastics Div, White Sewing Mach Co, 61-63 & Signal Chem Mfg Co, 60-62, Incar, Inc, Am Smelting & Refining Co, 64-67, Oatey Co, 80-84; tech consult, Re-Ox Corp, 62-67; res assoc, Cleveland Mus Natural Hist, 74- *Mem:* AAAS; Am Chem Soc; Soc Plastics Eng; Soc Plastics Indust; Am Inst Chem. *Res:* Plastics and resins development; complex-ion; thermodynamics and quantum theory; kinetics and mechanisms of anionic polymerizations; polymer development and applications. *Mailing Add:* 3015 Scarborough Rd Cleveland OH 44118

BOCKHOLT, ANTON JOHN, PLANT BREEDING, GENETICS. *Current Pos:* Res asst corn breeding, 54-55, instr, 55-66, asst prof corn breeding & leader, corn improv prog, 66-72, ASSOC PROF AGRON, TEX A&M UNIV, 72- *Personal Data:* b Westphalia, Tex, Sept 23, 30; m 52; c 2. *Educ:* Tex A&M Univ, BS, 52, MS, 58, PhD(plant breeding), 67. *Mem:* Am Soc Agron; Crop Sci Soc Am; Sigma Xi. *Res:* Plant breeding, genetics, pathology, biology-environment, entomology and nutrition and metabolism. *Mailing Add:* 1102 Timm Dr College Station TX 77840

BOCKHOP, CLARENCE WILLIAM, AGRICULTURAL ENGINEERING, THEORETICAL & APPLIED MECHANICS. *Current Pos:* RETIRED. *Personal Data:* b Paullina, Iowa, Mar 28, 21; m 49, Virginia Buhman; c Barbara L, Nancy J, Bryan W & Karl D. *Educ:* Iowa State Univ, BS, 43, MS, 55, PhD(agr eng & theoret & appl mech), 57. *Prof Exp:* Mgr serv & educ, Stewart Co, Dallas, 48-53; fac mem, Iowa State Univ, Ames, 53-57 & 60-80, prof agr eng, 60-80, head, Dept Agr Eng, 62-80; prof & head, Dept Agr Eng, Univ Tenn, 57-60; head, Int Rice Res Inst, Los Banos, Philippines, 80-86. *Concurrent Pos:* Chmn, Agr Eng Div, Am Soc Eng Educ, 66-67; chmn, Educ & Res Div, Am Soc Agr Engrs, 66-67, dir, 73-75; vis prof, Univ Ghana, 69-70. *Mem:* Fel Am Soc Agr Engrs; Am Soc Eng Educ; Sigma Xi. *Res:* Agricultural engineering. *Mailing Add:* 424 Hide-a-Way Lane E Lindale TX 75771-5215

BOCKMAN, DALE EDWARD, ANATOMY. *Current Pos:* PROF ANAT & CHMN DEPT, MED COL GA, 75- *Personal Data:* b Winona, Mo, Feb 4, 35; m 53; c 3. *Educ:* Southwest Mo State Col, BS, 56; Los Angeles State Col, MA, 58; Univ Ill, PhD(anat), 63. *Prof Exp:* Instr anat, Univ Ill, 62-63; from instr to asst prof, Univ Tenn Med Units, 63-68; from assoc prof to prof, Med Col Ohio, 68-75. *Res:* Fine structure; pancreas and gastrointestinal tract; development of lymphoid system; immunology. *Mailing Add:* Dept Anat Med Col Ga Augusta GA 30912-2000

BOCKMAN, RICHARD STEVEN, MOLECULAR BIOLOGY. *Current Pos:* assoc prof biochem, 71-75, assoc prof med, Med Ctr, 82-90, PROF MED, MED CTR, CORNELL UNIV, 90- *Personal Data:* b New York, NY, Sept 14, 41; m 73; c 2. *Educ:* Johns Hopkins Univ, BA, 62; Yale Univ, MD, 67; Rockefeller Univ, PhD(biochem), 71. *Concurrent Pos:* Assoc attending physician, Mem Hosp, 81-88, Hosp Spec Surg; attend physician, NY Hosp, 88- *Mem:* Am Col Physicians; Am Fedn Clin Res; NY Acad Sci; Sigma Xi; Endocrine Soc; Am Soc Clin Invest; Am Soc Bone & Mineral Res. *Res:* Endocrinology; mechanisms of normal and pathological bone resorption; molecular biology of bone formation. *Mailing Add:* Hosp Spec Surg 535 E 70th St New York NY 10021. *Fax:* 212-861-5031

BOCKO, MARK FREDERICK, ELECTRICAL ENGINEERING. *Current Pos:* Res assoc physics, 84-85, asst prof, 85-91, ASSOC PROF ELEC ENG, UNIV ROCHESTER, 92- *Personal Data:* b Utica, NY, May 21, 56; m 78; c 3. *Educ:* Colgate Univ, BA, 78; Univ Rochester, MA, 80, PhD(physics), 84. *Mem:* Am Phys Soc; Inst Elec & Electronics Engrs. *Res:* Superconductivity and tunneling; low noise detection; quantum non-demolition measurement techniques; measurement science; quantum measurement theory; scanning tunneling microscopy and related techniques; analog and digital superconducting electronics. *Mailing Add:* Dept Elec Eng Univ Rochester 500 Joseph C Wilson Rochester NY 14627-9000

BOCKOSH, GEORGE R, RESEARCH ADMINISTRATION. *Current Pos:* elec eng, 74-79, RES SUPVR, US BUR MINES, PITTSBURGH RES CTR, 79- *Personal Data:* b Charlerio, Pa, Jan 28, 51; div. *Educ:* Univ Pittsburgh, BS, 72, MS, 76. *Prof Exp:* Elec eng, Repub Steel Corp, 72-73, Corning Glass Works, 73-74. *Res:* Program in underground mining in the following areas: equipment design, material handling, human factors, life support (breathing apparatus development), noise control and advanced mining technology. *Mailing Add:* NIOSH Cochrans Mill Rd PO Box 18070 Pittsburgh PA 15236

BOCKRATH, BRADLEY CHARLES, ORGANIC CHEMISTRY. *Current Pos:* supvry res chemist coal chem, 74-85, CHIEF, COAL CHEM BR, FED ENERGY TECHNOL CTR, US DEPT ENERGY, 85- *Personal Data:* b Hamburg, NY, Dec 11, 42; m 65, Barbara Adams; c Diane. *Educ:* Union Col, BS, 65; State Univ NY Albany, PhD(chem), 71. *Honors & Awards:* Storch Award, 90. *Prof Exp:* Chemist, Eastman Kodak Co, 65-67; fel phys chem, Ohio State Univ, 71-74. *Mem:* Am Chem Soc. *Res:* Physical organic chemistry; mechanisms of coal liquefaction; coal chemistry; kinetics of fast organic reactions; radical anion chemistry; solvated electrons; radiation chemistry; hydrotreating catalysts. *Mailing Add:* 16 Conestoga Dr Bethel Park PA 15102-2789

BOCKRATH, RICHARD CHARLES, JR, MOLECULAR GENETICS, BIOLOGY. *Current Pos:* asst prof microbiol & med biophysics, 68-77, assoc prof microbiol, immunol & med biophysics, 77-81, PROF MICROBIOL & IMMUNOL, SCH MED, IND UNIV, INDIANAPOLIS, 81- *Personal Data:* b St Louis, Mo, May 7, 38; div; c 2. *Educ:* Yale Univ, BS, 61; Pa State Univ, MS, 63, PhD(biophys), 65. *Prof Exp:* Vis res fel microbial genetics, Univ Sussex, 65-67. *Concurrent Pos:* NIH fel, Univ Sussex, 66-67; vis researcher, Aarhus Univ Inst Molecular Biol, 72; res consult radiobiol, Stanford Univ, 74, vis scholar biol sci, 78-79; fac res partic, Biol & Med Res Div, Argonne Nat Lab, 77; vis worker, MRC Cell Mutation Unit, Univ Sussex, 85-86. *Mem:* Am Soc Photobiol. *Res:* Effects of low energy beta particles on cells; molecular biology and control; cellular accumulation of streptomycin; mutagenesis and DNA repair induced by ultraviolet radiation; radiation mutagenesis; nucleoid structure/function. *Mailing Add:* 401 W Westfield Blvd Indianapolis IN 46208

BOCKRIS, JOHN O'MARA, PHYSICAL CHEMISTRY, NUCLEAR & ENVIRONMENTAL ELECTROCHEMISTRY. *Current Pos:* RETIRED. *Personal Data:* b Johannesburg, SAfrica, Jan 5, 23; nat & US citizen; m 71, Lillian R; c Victor F & Anna M. *Educ:* Univ London, BSc, 43, PhD, 45, DSc(electrochem), 52. *Hon Degrees:* LPhd, Univ La Plora, Arg, 83. *Honors & Awards:* Medaille d'honneur, Univ Louvain, 53; Faraday Medal, Chem Soc London, 79; Lectr Award, Swed Acad, 79; Am Soc Award in Chem Contemp & Technol Prob, 88; Augustin Mushot Prize, 89; Lindf Medal, Electrochem Soc, 93. *Prof Exp:* Lectr phys chem, Imp Col, Univ London, 45-53; prof chem, Univ Pa, 53-72 & electrochem, 62-71; chmn, Dept Phys Chem, Flinders Univ, 72-78, prof phys chem, Sch Phys Sci, 72-78. *Concurrent Pos:* Founder, Inst Solar & Electrochem Energy Conversion; distinguished prof chem, Tex A&M Univ. *Mem:* Fel Royal Inst Chem; Int Soc Hydrogen Energy; Int Soc Electrochem; Swed Acad Engrs; Serbian Acad Sci; fel Am Asn Sci. *Res:* Corrosion of metals and semiconductors; photovoltaics; nonquantum methods of light to convert to energy; green inhibitors; low energy nuclear change in condensed media; waste disposal by electrochemical means; corrosion of aluminum alloys; nuclear waste disposal; nuclear electrochemistry; environmental electrochemistry. *Mailing Add:* Dept Chem Tex A&M College Station TX 77843-1248. *Fax:* 409-845-4205

BOCKSCH, ROBERT DONALD, ORGANIC CHEMISTRY. *Current Pos:* From asst prof to assoc prof chem, Whitworth Col, 58-68, chmn dept chem, 63-75, chmn dept health sci, 75-78, chmn dept chem, 78-90, PROF CHEM, WHITWORTH COL, 68- *Personal Data:* b Detroit, Mich, May 5, 31; m 58; c 5. *Educ:* Wayne State Univ, BS, 54, Univ Wis, PhD, 60. *Mem:* Am Chem Soc; Brit Chem Soc. *Res:* Synthetic organic chemistry; natural product chemistry; polynuclear hydrocarbons. *Mailing Add:* E 539 Bedivere Dr Spokane WA 99218-1801

BOCKSERMAN, ROBERT JULIAN, MATERIAL SCIENCE POLYMER FILMS & RIGID COMPONENTS DESIGN & MANUFACTURING, FOOD TOXICOLOGY & SANITATION. *Current Pos:* FOUND & PRES, CONATECH CONSULT GROUP, 85- *Personal Data:* b St Louis, Mo, Dec 20, 29; m 58, Clarice Kreisman; c Michael, Joyce & Carol. *Educ:* Univ Mo, BS, 52, MS, 55. *Prof Exp:* Chemist, Sealtest Corp, 55-56; prod mgr, Allan Drug Co, 57-58; res chemist, Agr Chem Div, Monsanto Co, 59-65, purchasing agent, Krummerich Plant, 66-67; founder & pres, Pharma-Tech Industs, Inc, 67-84; dir tech servs, Overlock-Howe Consult Group, 85. *Concurrent Pos:* Vis lectr, Univ Mo, Rolla, 79-, Univ Mo, Columbia, 83-, Univ Mo, Clayton, 91-, Kellog Grad Sch, Northwestern Univ, 91-; prin investr, Nat Inst Neurol & Commun Dis & Stroke, 88. *Mem:* Am Soc Testing & Mat; Inst Packaging Prof; Inst Food Technologists; Sigma Xi; Am Chem Soc; Int Soc Pharmaceut Engrs. *Res:* Compatability studies on product/package interface; physical chemistry of emulsifiers and stabilizers effects on food products; degradation studies of effects of ultra-violet light and sterilization methods on polymer films and rigid plastic components. *Mailing Add:* Conatech Consult Group 54 Morwood Lane Creve Coeur MO 63141-7621. *Fax:* 314-995-9766

BOCKSTAHLER, LARRY EARL, VIROLOGY, BIOCHEMISTRY. *Current Pos:* BIOCHEMIST, FOOD & DRUG ADMIN, USPHS, 69- *Personal Data:* b La Junta, Colo, May 13, 34; m 65; c 1. *Educ:* Mich State Univ, BS, 56; Univ Wis-Madison, MS, 60, PhD(biochem), 64. *Prof Exp:* NIH fel biochem, Max Planck Inst Biol, 64-67, biochemist & Humboldt fel biochem, 67-69. *Concurrent Pos:* Mem, Foreign Work/Study Prog, USPHS, Munich, Ger, 89-90. *Mem:* Am Soc Virol; Am Soc Photobiol; Biophys Soc; Radiation Res Soc Am; Sigma Xi; AAAS; Am Soc Testing & Mat; Soc Biol Chem. *Res:* Molecular biology of viruses; photobiology; radiation virology. *Mailing Add:* 626 Warfield Dr Rockville MD 20850

BOCKSTAHLER, THEODORE EDWIN, INDUSTRIAL ORGANIC CHEMISTRY. *Current Pos:* RETIRED. *Personal Data:* b Monticello, Ill, Nov 22, 20; m 43, Charlotte Brier; c Shirley & David. *Educ:* Ind Univ, AB, 42; Univ Ill, MS, 48, PhD(chem), 49. *Prof Exp:* Instr, Chem Warfare Sch, Edgewood Arsenal, 45; group leader org chem res, Rohm & Haas Bayport Inc, 49-66, mgr labs, 66-80, tech dir, Rohm & Haas Co, 80-83. *Mem:* Am Chem Soc. *Res:* Process development for plastic chemicals in laboratory and plant. *Mailing Add:* Plantation Estates No E112 Plantation Estates Rd Matthews NC 28105

BOCQUET, PHILIP E(DMUND), CHEMICAL ENGINEERING. *Current Pos:* prof & head dept, 61-69, assoc dean eng, 69-77, prof, 77-84, EMER PROF CHEM ENG, UNIV ARK, FAYETTVILLE, 84- *Personal Data:* b Beeville, Tex, Oct 6, 18; c 4. *Educ:* Agr & Mech Col Tex, BS, 40; Univ Mich, MSE, 47, PhD (chem eng), 53. *Prof Exp:* Assoc physiol, Univ Mich, 49-52; group supvr, Continental Oil Co, Okla, 53-57; assoc prof chem eng, Univ NMex, 57-61. *Concurrent Pos:* Consult, 57-; Fulbright lectr, Univ Madrid, 68-69. *Mem:* AAAS; Am Inst Chem Engrs; Am Chem Soc; Am Soc Eng Educ; Am Inst Mining, Metall & Petrol Engrs; Electrochem Soc. *Res:* Fluid mechanics; electrokinetics; static electricity in fluids; reservoir mechanics; miscible phase behavior; hydraulic fracturing; well logging in petroleum production; cryogenics; natural gas liquefaction. *Mailing Add:* 555 E North St Fayetteville AR 72701

BOCZKOWSKI, RONALD JAMES, ANALYTICAL CHEMISTRY. *Current Pos:* METHODS DEVELOP GROUP LEADER, UNION CAMP CORP, 73- *Personal Data:* b Bridgeport, Conn, Nov 14, 43; m 70; c 2. *Educ:* Canisius Col, BS, 65; Univ Notre Dame, PhD(chem), 71. *Prof Exp:* Res fel, Univ Cincinnati, 71-72; lab mgr textiles, Armtex, Inc, 72-73. *Mem:* Am Chem Soc; Anal Am Chem Soc; Am Asn Textile Chemists & Colorists. *Res:* Analytical application of electrochemical techniques; preconcentration techniques in trace analysis; analysis of minor components in paper, pulp and process liquors; analysis of chemicals from wood. *Mailing Add:* Union Camp PO Box 3301 Princeton NJ 08543-3301

BODA, JAMES MARVIN, COMPARATIVE PHYSIOLOGY. *Current Pos:* Actg instr animal husb, univ & animal husbandman, Exp Sta, Univ Calif, 52-54, from asst prof to assoc prof, 59-68, prof animal physiol, 65-80, chmn dept 68-73, EMER PROF, DEPT ANIMAL PHYSIOL, UNIV CALIF, DAVIS, 80- *Personal Data:* b Mt Victory, Ohio, July 3, 24; m 53; c 1. *Educ:* Univ Calif, BS, 48, PhD, 53. *Concurrent Pos:* Fulbright res scholar, 60-61. *Mem:* Am Physiol Soc; Am Soc Zoologists; Endocrine Soc. *Res:* Comparative endocrinology; physiological adaptations. *Mailing Add:* 96465 Ridgeway St Brookings OR 97415-9758

BODALY, RICHARD ANDREW, ICHTHYOLOGY, GENETICS. *Current Pos:* RES SCIENTIST, FRESHWATER INST, CAN DEPT FISHERIES & OCEANS, 77- *Personal Data:* b Vancouver, BC, June 24, 49; m 77, Gale D Robinson; c Megan & Scott. *Educ:* Simon Fraser Univ, BSc, 72; Univ Man, PhD(zool), 77. *Concurrent Pos:* Adj prof, Dept Zool, Univ Man, 86-; vis scientist, Environ Biol Unit, Loughborough Univ Technol, Eng, 87-88. *Mem:* Can Soc Zoologists; Am Fisheries Soc; Can Soc Environ Biologists; Sigma Xi. *Res:* Biology and taxonomy of coregonid fishes; uptake of mercury by freshwater fishes; reservoir fisheries and reservoir environmental impacts. *Mailing Add:* Freshwater Inst 501 University Crescent Winnipeg MB R3T 2N6 Can. *Fax:* 204-984-2404

BODAMER, GEORGE WILLOUGHBY, CHEMISTRY. *Current Pos:* RETIRED. *Personal Data:* b Philadelphia, Pa, Apr 12, 16; m 44, Mildred L Rementer; c Louise, George Jr, Carl & Ellen. *Educ:* Univ Pa, BS, 38; Cornell Univ, PhD(org chem), 41. *Prof Exp:* Chemist, Rohm and Haas, Philadelphia, 41-59; sr scientist, ESB, Inc, 59-61, mgr phys chem labs, 61-64, assoc dir res, 64-70; chief chemist, Int Hydronics Corp, Princeton, NJ, 70-76; chemist, C&D Batteries, 78-80; Consult, Rob Smith Assocs, 81. *Mem:* Am Chem Soc; Electrochem Soc. *Res:* Electrochemistry; ion exchange; industrial waste treatment. *Mailing Add:* 311 Franklin Ave Cheltenham PA 10912-2027

BODANSKY, DAVID, EXPERIMENTAL NUCLEAR PHYSICS, ENERGY & ENVIRONMENT. *Current Pos:* from asst prof to prof, 54-93, chmn dept, 76-84, EMER PROF PHYSICS, UNIV WASH, 93- *Personal Data:* b New York, NY, Mar 10, 24; m 52, Beverly Bronstein; c Joel & Daniel. *Educ:* Harvard Univ, BS, 43, MA, 48, PhD(physics), 50. *Prof Exp:* Instr physics, Columbia Univ, 50-52, assoc, 52-54. *Concurrent Pos:* Alfred P Sloan res fel, 59-63; Guggenheim fel, 66-67 & 74-75; vis scholar, Energy & Environ Policy Ctr, Harvard Univ, 81-82. *Mem:* Am Nuclear Soc; fel AAAS; Am Asn Physics Teachers; fel Am Phys Soc; Health Physics Soc. *Res:* Nuclear physics, nuclear astrophysics and energy policy. *Mailing Add:* Dept Physics Univ Wash FM-15 Seattle WA 98195. *Fax:* 206-685-0635; *E-Mail:* bodansky@phys.washington.edu

BODANSZKY, MIKLOS, BIO-ORGANIC CHEMISTRY. *Current Pos:* prof chem & biochem, 66-78, Charles Frederic Mabery prof res chem, 78-83, EMER PROF CHEM, CASE WESTERN RES UNIV, 83- *Personal Data:* b Budapest, Hungary, May 21, 15; US citizen; wid; c Eva. *Educ:* Budapest Tech Univ, dipl chem eng, 39, DSc(org chem), 49. *Honors & Awards:* Alan Pierce Award, Am Peptide Symposia, 77; Morley Medal, Am Chem Soc, 78; Alexander von Humboldt Award, Humboldt Found, 89. *Prof Exp:* Lectr med chem, Budapest Tech Univ, 50-56; res assoc biochem, Med Col, Cornell Univ, 57-59; sr res assoc peptide chem, Squibb Inst Med Res, 59-66. *Concurrent Pos:* USPHS grants, Case Western Reserve Univ, 66- *Mem:* Am Chem Soc; Am Soc Biol Chemists; Hungarian Acad Sci. *Res:* Peptide synthesis, structure and activity relationships of biologically active peptides; conformation of peptide hormones and peptide antibiotics. *Mailing Add:* One Markham Rd Princeton NJ 08540

BODDY, DAVID EDWIN, MECHANICAL ENGINEERING. *Current Pos:* ASSOC PROF ENG, OAKLAND UNIV, 65- *Personal Data:* b Erie, Pa, Aug 31, 36; m 65. *Educ:* Purdue Univ, BS, 58, MS, 60, PhD(elec eng), 66. *Concurrent Pos:* NSF res initiation grant, 67-68. *Mem:* Asn Comput Mach; Sigma Xi. *Res:* Computer science. *Mailing Add:* Dept Comput Sci Oakland Univ Rochester MI 48309-4401

BODDY, DENNIS WARREN, ENTOMOLOGY, ZOOLOGY. *Current Pos:* from asst prof to assoc prof, 64-87, EMER ASSOC PROF BIOL, PORTLAND STATE UNIV, 87- *Personal Data:* b Portland, Ore, Aug 26, 22. *Educ:* Univ Wash, BS, 47, PhD, 55. *Prof Exp:* Instr zool, Columbia Basin Col, 55-59, head, Sci Dept, 59-60, dean instr, 60-62. *Res:* Taxonomy of the Coleoptera Tenebrionidae; history of biology; birds of Puerto Vallarta, Mexico. *Mailing Add:* 1867 SW 14th Portland OR 97201

BODE, ARTHUR PALFREY, CLINICAL COAGULATION, BLOOD BANKING. *Current Pos:* asst prof, 86-91, ASSOC PROF PATH, ECAROLINA UNIV MED SCH, 91- *Personal Data:* b Lima, Ohio, Oct 12, 53; m 77; c 2. *Educ:* Univ NC, Chapel Hill, BA, 75, PhD(exp path), 82. *Prof Exp:* Postdoctoral fel blood bank, Univ NC, Chapel Hill, 82-84, res asst prof path, 84-86. *Concurrent Pos:* Sci dir, Clin Coagulation Lab, Pitt County Mem Hosp, Greenville, 86-, co-dir, Clin Flow Cytometry Lab, 86-89; prin investr, Am Heart Asn, 88-89 & Naval Res & Develop Command, 89-92. *Mem:* Am Asn Blood Banks; Am Heart Asn; AAAS; NY Acad Sci; Int Soc Thrombosis & Hemostasis; Am Asn Pathologists. *Res:* Storage of blood platelets for transfusion; vesiculation of platelets in vitro and in vivo; interference by platelets in heparin monitoring during open-heart surgery; post-operative bleeding in cardiac surgery; blood compatibility of foreign surfaces. *Mailing Add:* Clin Path & Diag Med ECarolina Univ Brody Greenville NC 27858-4354

BODE, DONALD EDWARD, solid state physics; deceased, see previous edition for last biography

BODE, JAMES DANIEL, PHYSICAL CHEMISTRY. *Current Pos:* RETIRED. *Personal Data:* b Pittsburgh, Pa, Sept 6, 23. *Educ:* Univ Pittsburgh, BS, 46, PhD(chem), 52. *Prof Exp:* Grad asst, Univ Pittsburgh, 46-51; proj engr, Fisher Sci Co, 51-52, head analytical chem, 52-55; sr res chemist, Jones & Laughlin Steel Corp, 55-58, res supvr, 58-60; mem tech staff, Bell Tel Labs, 60-63; sr res chemist, FMC Corp, 63-66; prin scientist, Bendix Res Labs, Bendix Corp, 66-81. *Mem:* AAAS; Am Chem Soc. *Res:* Instrumental methods; physics and chemistry of surfaces. *Mailing Add:* 70 Kings Ct Apt 4-C Santurce PR 00911

BODE, VERNON CECIL, MAMMALIAN GENETICS, MAMMALIAN DEVELOPMENT. *Current Pos:* PROF BIOL, KANS STATE UNIV, 70- *Personal Data:* b Marion County, Mo, Feb 19, 33; m 56; c 4. *Educ:* Univ Mo, BS, 55; Univ Ill, PhD(biochem), 61. *Prof Exp:* USPHS fel biochem, Sch Med, Stanford Univ, 61-64; from asst prof to assoc prof biochem, Med Sch, Univ Md, 64-70. *Concurrent Pos:* Am Cancer Soc scholar, Oxford Univ, 77-78; Eleanor Roosevelt, Int Cancer fel, Pasteur Inst, Am Cancer Soc, 84-85. *Mem:* Am Soc Biol Chem; Am Soc Microbiol; Genetics Soc Am; Soc Develop Biol. *Res:* Mouse genetics; regulation of embryological development in the mouse; selection of new mouse mutants after ethylnitrosourea mutagenesis; genetic analysis of the mouse t-complex; isolation of mouse mutants useful as models for human disease; preservation of mouse mutants by sperm freezing. *Mailing Add:* Div Biol Kans State Unvi Ackert Hall Manhattan KS 66506-4900

BODE, WILLIAM MORRIS, entomology, for more information see previous edition

BODEGOM, ERIK, PHYSICS. *Current Pos:* from asst prof to assoc prof, 85-92, PROF & CHAIR, PHYSICS DEPT, PORTLAND STATE UNIV, 92- *Educ:* Univ Technol, Neth, Ir, 77; Catholic Univ Am, PhD(physics), 82. *Prof Exp:* Teaching asst, Cath Univ Am, Washington, DC, 78-80, res asst, 79-82; res assoc, Vitreous State Lab, Washington, DC, 82-85. *Concurrent Pos:* Prin investr, NSF, Portland Agenda Funds, Sigma Xi, Dept Energy, Dept Educ. *Mem:* Sigma Xi; Am Phys Soc; Am Asn Physics Teachers. *Res:* Condensed matter physics: tensile strength of helium, tensile strength of nitrogen, heat transfer in cyrogenic liquids, polarization efficiences of polaroids, scanning tunneling microscopy; statistical mechanics: structure of directionally bonded liquid; nonlinear dynamics: oscillating waterfalls, heat transfer in liquids; author of 23 publications. *Mailing Add:* Physics Dept Portland State Univ Portland OR 97207

BODEK, ARIE, PARTICLE PHYSICS. *Current Pos:* from asst prof to assoc prof, 76-85, HIGH ENERGY PHYSICS GROUP HEAD, UNIV ROCHESTER, 85-, PROF PHYSICS, 86-, ASSOC CHAIR, 94- *Personal Data:* b Tel-Aviv, Israel, May 11, 47; US citizen; m 90, Priscilla S Auchincloss; c Haim, Esther, Avira & Avi. *Educ:* Mass Inst Technol, BS, 68, PhD(physics), 72. *Prof Exp:* Res assoc particle physics, Mass Inst Technol, 72-74; Millikan res fel particle physics, Calif Inst Technol, 74-76. *Concurrent Pos:* Sloan fel, 80-81; spokesman exp FNAL E595 & SLAC E140; Japan fel, NSF, 86, Dept Eng, 90. *Mem:* Fel Am Phys Soc. *Res:* Experimental particle physics; neutrino interactions; direct production of muons by hadrons; production of new states (charm, bottom); deep inelastic electron and muon scattering; scattering from nuclear targets; neutrino oscillations; e plus and e minus reactions; proton-antiproton collisions. *Mailing Add:* Dept Physics Univ Rochester Rochester NY 14627. *Fax:* 716-275-8527

BODELL, WILLIAM J, cancer chemotherapy, drug resistance, for more information see previous edition

BODEN, GUENTHER, METABOLISM, ENDOCRINOLOGY. *Current Pos:* from asst prof to assoc prof, 70-77, PROF MED, TEMPLE UNIV HOSP, 77- *Personal Data:* b Ludwigshafen, WGer, Jan 8, 35; m 70, Irene Dingeldein; c 4. *Educ:* Univ Heidelberg, MS, 56; Univ Munich, MD, 59. *Honors & Awards:* George Thompson Pew Diabetes Res Award, 86; Hugo Roesler lectr, TUSM, 93. *Prof Exp:* Asst biochem, Univ Tubingen, 63-65; res fel med, E P Joslin Res Lab, Harvard Sch Med, 65-67; resident, Rochester Gen Hosp, 67-70. *Concurrent Pos:* Asst med, Peter Bent Brigham Hosp, Boston, 65-67; gen med A, Study Sect, NIH, 78-82; chief, Div Metab/Endocrinol, Sch Med, Temple Univ, 87-, res award; prog dir, Gen Clin Res Ctr, Temple Univ Hosp, 89- *Mem:* Am Soc Clin Invest; Am Col Physicians; Am Endocrine Soc; Am Diabetes Asn; Am Fed Clin Res. *Res:* Metabolism; diabetes. *Mailing Add:* Temple Univ Hosp 3401 N Broad St Philadelphia PA 19140

BODEN, HERBERT S, ORGANIC CHEMISTRY. *Current Pos:* RETIRED. *Personal Data:* b Staten Island, NY, Apr 5, 32; m 57, Nancy Hawkins; c Kimberly. *Educ:* Univ Vt, BS, 54, MS, 56; Ohio State Univ, PhD(org chem), 60. *Prof Exp:* Instr gen & org chem, Ohio State Univ, 56-58; res chemist, Org Chem Dept, E I Du Pont De Nemours & Co Inc, 60-65, res chemist, Freon Prod Div, 65-70, tech assoc, 70, territory mgr, 70-72, prod & develop mgr, 72-74, nat acct mgr, 74-77, econ analysis & distrib mgr, Freon Prod Div, 77-78, mkt mgr, Fire Extinguishants, 78-79, mgr, Sales Support, 79-80, reg sales mgr, 81-88, nat sales mgr, Cleaning Agts, 88-90. *Mem:* Am Chem Soc. *Res:* Biguanide, benzo phenanthrene, fluorine and polymer chemistry; chemistry of tetra substituted amino ethylenes. *Mailing Add:* 904 Barnstable Ct Hockessin DE 19707

BODENHEIMER, PETER HERMAN, ASTROPHYSICS. *Current Pos:* asst astronr & asst prof, 67-70, assoc astronr & assoc prof astron, 70-76, ASTRONR & PROF ASTRON, UNIV CALIF, SANTA CRUZ, 76- *Personal Data:* b Seattle, Wash, June 29, 37; m 65; c Daniel & Debora. *Educ:* Harvard Univ, AB, 59; Univ Calif, Berkeley, PhD(astron), 65. *Honors & Awards:* US Sr Scientist Award, Alexander von Humboldt Found, Ger, 87. *Prof Exp:* NSF fel, Princeton Univ, 65-66, res assoc astrophys, 66-67. *Concurrent Pos:* Chmn, Bd Studies Astron & Astrophys, Univ Calif, Santa Cruz, 75-78, 82-83, 88-89; vis scientist, Max Planck Inst Physics & Astrophys, 76, 78, 80, 85, 87-88; prin investr, NSF grant, 77-; mem, Comt Planetary & Lunar Explor, Space Sci Bd, Nat Acad Sci, 85-87; prin investr, NASA grants, 86- *Mem:* Am Astron Soc; Int Astron Union; Royal Astronomical Soc. *Res:* Theoretical calculations of stellar structure and evolution, including problems involving hydrodynamics and rotation; star formation; evolution of the giant planets. *Mailing Add:* UCO Lick Observ Univ Calif Santa Cruz CA 95064. *E-Mail:* peterelick.ucsc.edu

BODENSCHATZ, EBERHARD, NONLINEAR SCIENCE. *Current Pos:* ASST PROF PHYSICS, ATOMIC & SOLID STATE LAB, CORNELL UNIV, 92- *Personal Data:* b Ger, Apr 22, 59. *Educ:* Univ Bayreuth, PhD(physics), 89. *Mailing Add:* Physic Dept Cornell Univ 618 Clark Hall Ithaca NY 14853

BODEY, GERALD PAUL, SR, ONCOLOGY, INFECTIOUS DISEASES. *Current Pos:* asst internist & asst prof, Univ Tex M D Anderson Hosp & Tumor Inst, 66-72, assoc internist & asst prof med, 72-75, chief chemother, 75-83, internist & prof med, 75-96, med dir, Cancer Clin Res Ctr, 77-81, dir, Off Protocol Res, 81-83, chmn, Dept Med Specialties, 87-96, CHIEF, SECT INFECTIOUS DIS, UNIV TEX M D ANDERSON HOSP, & TUMOR INST, 71-,. *Personal Data:* b Hazelton, Pa, May 22, 34; m 56, Nancy L Wiegner; c Robin G (Sparwasser), Gerald P, Jr & Sharon D (Brantley). *Educ:* Lafayette Col, AB, 56; Johns Hopkins Univ, MD, 60; Am Bd Internal Med, dipl, 72, cert oncol, 73 & cert infectious dis, 74. *Honors & Awards:* Am Chem Soc, Am Inst Chemists, Merck Chem & Robert B Youngman Greek Prizes, 56. *Prof Exp:* Intern, Osler Med Serv, Johns Hopkins Hosp, 60-61, resident, 61-62; clin assoc, Nat Cancer Inst, 62-65; resident, Univ Wash, 65-66. *Concurrent Pos:* From adj asst prof & clin asst prof to adj assoc prof & assoc clin prof, Baylor Col Med, 69-75, adj prof microbiol, immunol & med, 75-; Leukemia Soc scholar, 69-74; from asst prof to assoc prof, Grad Sch Biomed Sci, Univ Tex, Houston, 69-75, assoc prof, Med Sch, 73-76, prof med & pharmacol, 76-; consult, Prev Med Div, Space Flight Biotechnol Specialty Team, Manned Spacecraft Ctr, 70-71; consult, Brooke Gen Hosp, Ft Sam Houston, Tex, 71-; consult hemat-oncol, Wilford Hall USAF Med Ctr, Lackland AFB, Tex, 75-76, Comm Develop Comprehensive Cancer Care Ctr, Repub Panama, Orphan Prod Develop Initial Rev Group, FDA, 84-; fac mem, Union Int Contre le Cancer, mem, Tex Med Asn Comt Cancer, 84-, vis fac, Hoffman La Roche adv bd, sci adv bd, Liposome Co, 85-, adv comt, Immunocompromised Host Soc, 87-; mem, Am Soviet meetings cancer chemother, Collab Cancer Treat Res Prog, Pan Am Health Orgn, med/sci adv bd, SC Oncol Found, 86-, Janssen Res Coun, 86- *Mem:* Fel Am Col Physicians; AMA; Am Asn Cancer Res; fel Royal Col Med; fel Royal Soc Prom Health. *Res:* Cancer research; hematology; infectious diseases. *Mailing Add:* Univ Tex M D Anderson Hosp Tex Med Ctr 1515 Holcombe Box 047 Houston TX 77030-4095

BODFISH, RALPH E, medicine, nuclear structure, for more information see previous edition

BODI, LEWIS JOSEPH, PHYSICAL CHEMISTRY. *Current Pos:* RETIRED. *Personal Data:* b Racine, Wis, Dec 31, 24; m 50; c 4. *Educ:* DePauw Univ, BS, 50; Univ Wis, PhD(chem), 55. *Prof Exp:* Asst prof chem, Brooklyn Col, 54-60; eng specialist, Gen Tel & Electronics Labs, 60-67; dean sci & math, City Univ New York, 67-70, prof chem, 67-89, dean fac, York Col, 70-89, dean acad affairs, 74-89, vpres, dep to the pres, 85-89. *Res:* Luminescence; solid state chemistry and physics; science education. *Mailing Add:* 23 Whitney Circle Glen Cove NY 11542

BODIG, JOZSEF, WOOD SCIENCE, WOOD TECHNOLOGY. *Current Pos:* asst prof & asst forester, Agr Exp Sta, Colo State Univ, 63-66, from assoc prof to prof wood sci & technol, 66-79, prof, 79-89, EMER PROF WOOD SCI & CIVIL ENG, COLO STATE UNIV, 89-; FROM SR VPRES TO PRES, ENG DATA MGT INC, FORT COLLINS, COLO, 82- *Personal Data:* b Gonc, Hungary, Jan 20, 34; US citizen; m 62; c 3. *Educ:* Univ BC, BSF, 59; Univ Wash, MF, 61, PhD(wood technol), 63. *Honors & Awards:* L J Markwardt Wood Eng Award, Forest Prod Res Soc, 82 & Am Soc Testing & Mat, 85. *Prof Exp:* Proj leader, Fiber Res, Inc, Wash, 60-61; asst mech properties for wood, Univ Wash, 61-63. *Concurrent Pos:* Vis prof wood physics, Univ Wash, 69-70; mem tech adv comt, Am Inst Timber Construct, 70-, spec adv comt, Forest Prod Asn, 79-; vis res prof archit, Univ Forestry & Wood Technol, Sopron, Hungary, 79; vis prof, Capricornia Inst Adv Educ, 85; sr vpres, Eng Data Mgt Inc, Fort Collins, Colo, 82-88, exec vpres, 88-90, pres, 90-; tech dir, LRFD Engineered Wood Construct, 88-; dir, NATO Adv Res Workshop, RBD Engineered Wood Struct, 91. *Mem:* Forest Prod Res Soc; Soc Wood Sci & Tech; Nat Forest Prod Asn; Am Soc Testing & Mat; fel Int Acad Wood Sci; Am Nat Standards Inst. *Res:* Mechanical and rheological properties of wood and wood composites; nondestructive testing of wood; wood engineering; reliability-based design. *Mailing Add:* Eng Data Mgt Inc 2301 Research Blvd No 110 Ft Collins CO 80520

BODILY, DAVID MARTIN, PHYSICAL CHEMISTRY, FUEL TECHNOLOGY & PETROLEUM ENGINEERING. *Current Pos:* from asst prof to assoc prof fuels eng in mining, metall & fuels eng, Col Mines & Earth Sci, Univ Utah, 69-77, prof mining & fuels eng & chmn dept, 77-83, assoc dean col, 83-89, prof fuels eng, 89-92, PROF CHEM & FUELS ENG, UNIV UTAH, 92- *Personal Data:* b Logan, Utah, Dec 16, 33; m 58, BethAlene Judy; c Robert, Rebecca, Timothy & Christopher. *Educ:* Brigham Young Univ, BA, 59, MA, 60; Cornell Univ, PhD(phys chem), 64. *Prof Exp:* Res assoc, Northwestern Univ, 64-65; asst prof chem, Univ Ariz, 65-67. *Mem:* Am Chem Soc. *Res:* Coal science and cleaning; fossil fuel chemistry. *Mailing Add:* Dept Chem & Fuels Eng Univ Utah Salt Lake City UT 84112. *Fax:* 801-581-3344; *E-Mail:* david.bodily@m.cc.utah.edu

BODILY, SAMUEL EDWIN, OPERATIONS RESEARCH, PROBABILITY. *Current Pos:* JOHN TYLER PROF BUS ADMIN, DARDEN GRAD BUS SCH, UNIV VA, 77- *Personal Data:* b Logan, Utah, May 17, 47. *Educ:* Mass Inst Technol, SM, 74, PhD(opers res), 76. *Honors & Awards:* Educ Innovation Award, Decision Sci Int, 82. *Mem:* Decision Sci Int. *Res:* Decision and risk analysis; yield management; strategy decision modeling. *Mailing Add:* Darden Grad Bus Sch Univ Va Box 6550 Charlottesville VA 22906. *E-Mail:* bodilys@virginia.edu

BODIN, JEROME IRWIN, PHARMACEUTICAL CHEMISTRY. *Current Pos:* dir qual control, Carter Prod Inc, 64-69, dir analytical res & develop, 69-78, 82-83, dir develop res, 78-82, mgr tech admin, 83-85, ASSOC DIR PHARMACEUT CHEM, WALLACE LABS DIV, CARTER-WALLACE, INC, 85- *Personal Data:* b New York, NY, July 2, 30; m 58; c 2. *Educ:* Columbia Univ, BS, 52, MS, 54; Univ Wis, PhD(pharmaceut chem), 58. *Prof Exp:* Res analyst pharmaceut chem, Chas Pfizer & Co, Inc, 58-61; dir pharmaceut analysis, Drug Standards Lab, Am Pharmaceut Assoc Found, 62-63; chemist, Div of New Drugs, US Food & Drug Admin, 63-64. *Concurrent Pos:* Mem, Am Found Pharmaceut Educ. *Mem:* Am Chem Soc; Am Pharmaceut Asn; Acad Pharmaceut Res & Sci; Am Asn Pharmaceut Sci; Asn Off Anal Chemists. *Res:* Chemical kinetics and drug stability; drug availability and absorption; pharmaceutical quality control; federal drug regulation; organic chemistry; pharmaceutics. *Mailing Add:* 3 Wickman Lane Hightstown NJ 08520-1209

BODINE, PETER VAN NEST, STEROID HORMONE RECEPTORS, SIGNAL TRANSDUCTION. *Current Pos:* KENDALL-MAYO FEL, MAYO CLIN, ROCHESTER, MINN. *Personal Data:* b Syracuse, NY, Mar 14, 58; m 86, Judith M LaLonde. *Educ:* Syracuse Univ, BS, 80; Temple Univ, PhD(biochem), 88. *Honors & Awards:* Freedman Award, 84. *Prof Exp:* Res asst biol, Syracuse Univ, 80-82; fel cancer res, Fels Inst Cancer Res, 88-91; res asst prof cancer res, Jefferson Cancer Inst, 91-92. *Concurrent Pos:* Swern fel, 85; distinguished grad res award, NY Acad Sci, 88. *Mem:* AAAS; Sigma Xi; Am Soc Biochem & Molecular Biol; Endocrine Soc; Am Chem Soc; Am Asn Cancer Res; Am Soc Bone & Mineral Res. *Res:* Steroid hormone receptor biochemistry; regulation of steroid hormone action; regulation of gene expression by steroid hormones in bone cells. *Mailing Add:* C/O Wyeth-Ayerst 145 King of Prussia Rd Radnor PA 19087. *Fax:* 507-284-2053; *E-Mail:* bodine@mayo.edu

BODINE, ROBERT Y(OUNG), ENGINEERING MECHANICS, HISTORY & PHILOSOPHY SCIENCE. *Current Pos:* PRES CAD COMP INC, 87- *Personal Data:* b Peoria, Ill, Sept 7, 33. *Educ:* Bradley Univ, BS, 54; Univ Kans, MS, 58; Univ Wis, PhD(eng mech), 61. *Prof Exp:* Engr, Westinghouse Elec Corp, 54-58; instr eng mech, Univ Wis, 58-61; consult mech, A O Smith, 61-66, mgr eng systs, 66-86. *Concurrent Pos:* Dir, MacNeal-Schwendler Corp, 88-; lectr, Milwaukee Sch Eng, 86- *Mem:* Am Soc Mech Engrs; Sigma Xi. *Res:* Computer methods in engineering analysis; history of technology. *Mailing Add:* 2228 E Woodstock Pl Milwaukee WI 53202-1345

BODKIN, NORLYN L, PLANT BIOSYSTEMATICS, MID-APPALACHIAN FLORISTICS. *Current Pos:* from asst prof to assoc prof, 64-85, PROF BIOL, JAMES MADISON UNIV, 85- *Personal Data:* b Harrisonburg, Va, Jan 9, 37; m 58; c 2. *Educ:* WVa Univ, AB, 60, MS, 62; Univ Md, PhD(bot), 78. *Prof Exp:* Instr biol, Westminster Col, 62-64. *Concurrent Pos:* Teaching asst bot, Univ Md, 70-71; cur, James Madison Univ Herbarium, 73-, dir, Arboretum. *Mem:* Am Asn Plant Taxon; Int Asn Plant Taxon. *Res:* Shale barren endemics; monographic and revisionary research on the genus Melanthium; biosystematics of the varieties of Trillium pusillum; Mid-Appalachian floristic research. *Mailing Add:* 480 Myers Ave Harrisonburg VA 22801. *Fax:* 540-568-7873

BODLEY, HERBERT DANIEL, II, ANATOMY. *Current Pos:* assoc prof, 75-80, actg chmn dept, 78, PROF ANAT, CHICAGO COL OSTEOP MED, 80-, CHMN DEPT, 79- *Personal Data:* b Cleveland, Ohio, Nov 6, 39; m 61; c 2. *Educ:* Hamline Univ, BS, 61; Univ Minn, MS, 68, PhD(anat), 70. *Prof Exp:* From instr to asst prof anat, Univ Ariz, 70-75. *Mem:* Am Asn Anatomists; Electron Micros Soc Am; Am Soc Zoologists; Am Soc Cell Biol. *Res:* Ultrastructure. *Mailing Add:* Dept Anat Chicago Col Osteop Med 555 31st St Downers Grove IL 60515-8977

BODLEY, JAMES WILLIAM, BIOCHEMISTRY. *Current Pos:* from asst prof to assoc prof, 67-77, assoc head, 84-92, PROF BIOCHEM, MED SCH, UNIV MINN, MINNEAPOLIS, 77-, INTERIM HEAD, 92- *Personal Data:* b Portland, Ore, Oct 5, 37; m 60, Zickuhr; c Camille, Andrea & Cade. *Educ:* Walla Walla Col, BS, 60; Univ Hawaii, PhD(biochem), 64. *Prof Exp:* Prod control chemist, Dole Corp, 60; fel biochem, Sch Med, Univ, Wash, 64-66, actg asst prof, 66. *Concurrent Pos:* Am Cancer Soc fel, 65-66 & sr fel, 73-74. *Mem:* AAAS; Am Soc Biochem & Molecular Biol. *Res:* Mechanism and control of biological reactions involving nucleic acids. *Mailing Add:* Dept Biochem 4-225 Millard Hall Univ Minn Med Sch 425 Delaware St SE Minneapolis MN 55455. *Fax:* 612-625-2163; *E-Mail:* bodleool@maroon.tc.umn.edu

BODMAN, SAMUEL WRIGHT, III, CHEMICAL ENGINEERING. *Current Pos:* RETIRED. *Personal Data:* b Chicago, Ill, Nov 26, 38; m 61; c 3. *Educ:* Cornell Univ, BChE, 61; Mass Inst Technol, ScD(chem eng), 64. *Prof Exp:* From asst prof to assoc prof, Mass Inst Technol, 64-76, vis lectr chem eng, 76-84. *Concurrent Pos:* Tech adv, Am Res & Develop Corp, Mass, 64-70; vpres, FMR Develop Corp, Mass, 70- *Mem:* Am Inst Chem Engrs. *Res:* Heat and mass transfer; process design; applied mathematics. *Mailing Add:* 40 Battery St Boston MA 02109-1002

BODMER, ARNOLD R, PHYSICS, THEORETICAL NUCLEAR PHYSICS. *Current Pos:* PROF PHYSICS, UNIV ILL, CHICAGO, 65- *Personal Data:* b Frankfurt, Ger, May 23, 29; US citizen; m 56; c 4. *Educ:* Univ Manchester, BSc, 49, PhD(physics), 53. *Prof Exp:* Sci officer, Royal Armament Res & Design Estab, Eng, 53-56; res fel theoret physics, Univ Manchester, 56-57; res fel, Theoret Nuclear Physics, Europ Orgn Nuclear Res, Switz, 57-58; asst lectr theoret physics, Univ Manchester, 58-59, lectr, 60-65. *Concurrent Pos:* Resident res assoc, Argonne Nat Lab, 63-65, assoc physicist, 65-72, sr physicist, 72-85; vis prof, Nuclear Physics Lab, Oxford Univ, 70-71 & Justus-Liebig Univ, Giessen, 86. *Mem:* AAAS; Fedn Am Scientists; fel Am Phys Soc; Brit Inst Physics & Phys Soc. *Res:* Theoretical nuclear physics; nuclear structure and many-body problems; hypernuclei and baryon-baryon interactions; heavy-ion collisions. *Mailing Add:* Argonne Nat Lab B203 9700 S Cass Ave Argonne IL 60439

BODMER, WALTER FRED, CANCER. *Current Pos:* dir res, 79-91, GEN DIR, IMP CANCER RES FUND, 91- *Personal Data:* b Frankfurt-Am-Main, Ger, Jan 10, 36; Brit citizen; m 56; c 3. *Educ:* Cambridge Univ, BA, 56, PhD(pop genetics), 59. *Hon Degrees:* DSc, Univ Bath, 88, Univ Oxford, 88. *Honors & Awards:* William Allan Mem Award, Am Soc Human Soc, 80; Conway Evans Prize, Royal Col Physicians, Royal Soc, 82; Rabbi Shai Shacknai Mem Prize lectr immunol & cancer res, 83; Rose Payne Distinguished Scientist lectr, 85. *Prof Exp:* Res fel, Clare Col Cambridge Univ, 58-61; demonstr, Cambridge Univ, 60-61, fel, 61-62; from asst prof to prof, Stanford Univ, Calif, 62-70; prof, Univ Oxford, 70-79. *Concurrent Pos:* Coun mem, Royal Soc, 78-80 & Int Union Against Cancer, 82; hon fel, Keble Col, Oxford, 81; mem, Gen Adv Coun, Brit Broadcasting Corp, 81-; dir, Imp Cancer Res Technol Ltd, 82-; chmn exec bd, Orgn Europ Cancer Insts, 90-; pres, Human Genome Orgn, 90- *Mem:* Nat Acad Sci; hon mem Am Acad Arts & Sci; fel Royal Soc; Royal Inst (vpres, 83); Royal Col Path; Royal Statist Soc. *Res:* Genetics and biology of colon/rectal cancer human leukocyte-antigen system and immune response to cancer; human genome analysis. *Mailing Add:* Imp Cancer Res Fund PO Box 123 44 Lincoln's Inn Fields London WC2A 3PX England

BODNAR, DONALD GEORGE, ANTENNAS, ELECTROMAGNETIC THEORY. *Current Pos:* sr res engr, 73-81, chief, advan technol div, 86-89, PRIN RES ENGR, GA INST TECHNOL, 81-, DIR, ADVAN TECHNOL LAB, 89- *Personal Data:* b Ft William, Ont, Apr 30, 41; m 74; c 3. *Educ:* Ga Inst Technol, BEE, 63, PhD(elec eng), 69; Mass Inst Technol, MSEE, 64. *Honors & Awards:* Certificate of Recognition for creative technical innov, NASA, 87. *Prof Exp:* Eng staff consult, Microwave Electronics Div, Sperry Rand, 69-70; res engr consult, US Army White Sands Missile Range, 71, Res Engr, 71-73. *Concurrent Pos:* Lectr, Sch Electrical Eng, Ga Inst Technol, 71-78; paper reviewer, Inst Elec & Electronics Engrs Antenna & Propagation Soc, 75-; assoc ed, Inst Elec & Electronics Engrs Antennas & Propagation Soc Newsletter, 79-82; mem, Antenna Standards Comt, Inst Elec & Electronics Engrs, 79-, chmn, 83-, admin comt, Antennas & Propagation Soc, 84-87, 91- *Mem:* Inst Elec & Electronics Engrs Antennas & Propagation Soc (Admin Comt, 84-88); Int Test & Evaluation Asn; Antenna Measurement Techniques Asn; Asn Old Crows. *Res:* Design and evaluation of microwave antennas with primary emphasis on specially shaped reflector antennas; waveguide slotted arrays; electromechanical scanners; millimeter antennas; near-zone and far-zone radar cross section analyses and measurements. *Mailing Add:* 3568 W Hampton Dr NW Marietta GA 30064

BODNAR, LOUIS EUGENE, CHEMICAL ENGINEERING, PHYSICAL CHEMISTRY. *Current Pos:* RETIRED. *Personal Data:* b Prince Albert, Sask, Jan 29, 29. *Educ:* Univ Sask, BA, 50, MA, 51; McMaster Univ, PhD(chem), 57. *Prof Exp:* Lectr chem, Royal Mil Col, Can, 54-58; asst prof chem eng, Univ Waterloo, 60-62, assoc prof & actg chmn dept, 62-64, assoc prof, 64-76, dir first year studies, 70-73, fac admissions officer, 75-94, mem fac chem eng, 76-94. *Res:* Mechanisms of chemical reactions; thermodynamics. *Mailing Add:* Dept Chem Eng Univ Waterloo Waterloo ON N2L 3G1 Can

BODNAR, RICHARD JULIUS, ANALGESIC PROCESSES, INGESTIVE BEHAVIOR. *Current Pos:* from asst prof to assoc prof, 79-85, PROF PSYCHOL, CITY UNIV NY, 85-, HEAD NEUROPSYCHOL DOCTORAL PROG, 92- *Personal Data:* b New York, NY, Feb 21, 46; m 81, Carol Greenman; c Benjamin & Nicholas. *Educ:* Manhattan Col, BA, 67; City Col NY, MA, 73; City Univ NY, PhD(psychol), 76. *Prof Exp:* Fel, Columbia Univ, 76-78; res scientist, NY State Psychiat Inst, 78-79. *Concurrent Pos:* Adj prof pharmacol, Mt Sinai Sch Med, 89-; prin investr, Nat Inst Drug Abuse Grant, City Univ NY Res Found, 89- *Mem:* Am Pain Soc; fel Am Psychol Soc; AAAS; Soc Neurosci; Soc Study Ingestive Behav; NY Acad Sci. *Res:* Opioid receptor subtype roles in supra spinal analgesia and ingestive behaviors, aging and gender differences in stress-related and analgesic responses and nonopioid mechanisms of analgesia. *Mailing Add:* 186 Washington Ave Pleasantville NY 10570

BODNAR, ROBERT JOHN, FLUID INCLUSION ANALYSIS, GENESIS OF MINERAL DEPOSITS. *Current Pos:* from asst prof to assoc prof, 85-92, PROF GEOL, VA POLYTECH INST & STATE UNIV, 92- *Personal Data:* b McKeesport, Pa, Aug 25, 49; m 79; c 2. *Educ:* Univ Pittsburgh, BS, 75; Univ Ariz, MS, 78; Pa State Univ, PhD(geochem), 85. *Honors & Awards:* Lindgren Award, Soc Econ Geologists, 86. *Prof Exp:* Geologist, US Geol Surv, 78-80; res geochemist, Chevron Oil Field Res Co, 84-85. *Concurrent Pos:* NSF presidential young investr award, 86. *Mem:* Soc Econ Geologists; Am Mineral Soc; Am Geophys Union; Geochem Soc. *Res:* Experimental and theoretical studies of the volumetric and phase equilibrium properties of geologic fluids; fluid evolution in hydrothermal systems; magma-volatile interactions; vibrational spectroscopic analysis of materials. *Mailing Add:* Dept Geol Sci Va Polytech Inst & State Univ PO Box 0420 Blacksburg VA 24061-0420

BODNAR, STEPHEN J, CHEMICAL ENGINEERING, POLYMER CHEMISTRY. *Current Pos:* CONSULT, 86- *Personal Data:* b Carteret, NJ, July 6, 25; m 47, Louise Brechka; c Alison (Auckland), Patrice & Kristin. *Educ:* Lafayette Col, BA, 51; Univ Ill, Urbana-Champaign, PhD (chem), 54. *Prof Exp:* Chem engr, Esso Standard Oil Co, 54-60; mgr process eng sect, Res & Develop Dept, Tex-US Chem Co, 60-83; Gmelin Inst, Max Planck Soc, 84-85. *Mem:* Sigma Xi. *Res:* Process development of emulsion and solution polymerization; petro chemicals. *Mailing Add:* 408 W Nimitz St Fredericksburg TX 78624

BODNARUK, BOHDAN J, SYNTHETIC FUELS FROM COAL, ALTERNATIVE ENERGY SOURCES. *Current Pos:* PROJ MGR, US DEPT ENERGY, 80- *Educ:* Ill Inst Technol, BSc, 67, MSc, 73; Polytech Inst, Munich, DSc, 75. *Prof Exp:* Construct projs synthetic fuels, Great Plains Gasification Proj, 80-87. *Mem:* Am Inst Chem Engrs; Am Inst Mining Engrs. *Res:* Synthetic fuels from coal; environmental control in steel industry. *Mailing Add:* US Dept Energy 9800 S Cass Ave Argonne IL 60439. *Fax:* 630-252-8649; *E-Mail:* bohdan.bodnaruk@ch.doe.gov

BODNARYK, ROBERT PETER, biochemistry, physiology, for more information see previous edition

BODNER, GEORGE MICHAEL, CHEMICAL EDUCATION. *Current Pos:* from asst prof to assoc prof, 77-86, PROF CHEM EDUC, PURDUE UNIV, 87- *Personal Data:* b Rochester, NY, Mar 8, 46. *Educ:* State Univ NY Buffalo, BS, 69; Ind Univ, PhD(inorg chem), 72. *Honors & Awards:* CMA Catalyst Award in Chem Educ. *Prof Exp:* Vis asst prof gen chem, Univ Ill, 72-75; mem fac chem, Stephens Col, 75-77. *Mem:* Am Chem Soc; AAAS; Sigma Xi; The Chem Soc. *Res:* Application of educational technology in chemical education; how students learn chemistry. *Mailing Add:* Dept Chem Purdue Univ Lafayette IN 47907. *E-Mail:* gmbodner@vm.cc.purdue.edu

BODNER, SOL R(UBIN), SOLID & STRUCTURAL MECHANICS. *Current Pos:* prof mech, 64-68, prof mat eng & head dept, 68-72, HEAD, MAT MECH LAB, MECH ENG, TECHNION-ISRAEL INST TECHNOL, 65- *Personal Data:* b New York, NY, Mar 7, 29; m 52, Nechama Vardi; c Nir, Alan, Oran & Bettina. *Educ:* Polytech Inst Brooklyn, BCE, 50, PhD(appl mech), 55; NY Univ, MS, 53. *Honors & Awards:* Rothschild Prize, 81. *Prof Exp:* Res assoc appl mech, Polytech Inst Brooklyn, 51-55; sr mathematician, Repub Aviation Corp, 55-56; sr scientist, Avco Res & Advan Develop Div, 56; assoc prof eng, Brown Univ, 56-64. *Concurrent Pos:* Consult, Avco Res & Advan Develop Div, 56-64, Southwest Res Inst, 68, 73, 80-; Guggenheim fel, 62; vis prof, Cambridge Univ, 62, Weizmann Inst, 62-63, Univ Calif, 70, Univ Ill, 75, 79 & ETH Zurich, 83, 90, 94 & 97, Rice Univ, 96-97; Japan Prom Sci fel, 88. *Mem:* Soc Rheol; fel Am Soc Mech Engrs; Soc Eng Sci; fel AAAS; Sigma Xi. *Res:* Applied mechanics, dynamic plasticity, constitutive equations, penetration mechanics. *Mailing Add:* Dept Mech Eng Technion-Israel Inst Technol Haifa 32000 Israel. *Fax:* 972-4-8324533

BODNER, STEPHEN E, THEORETICAL PHYSICS. *Current Pos:* BR HEAD, NAVAL RES LAB, 74- *Personal Data:* b Rochester, NY, June 20, 39; m 67, Anne; c Jordan & Ruth. *Educ:* Univ Rochester, BS, 61; Princeton Univ, MA, 62, PhD(physics), 65. *Prof Exp:* Physicist, Lawrence Radiation Lab, Univ Calif, 64-74. *Concurrent Pos:* Instr appl sci, Univ Calif, Davis-Livermore, 66-68; OMB adv, 81-82. *Mem:* AAAS; Am Phys Soc; Optical Soc Am. *Res:* Plasma physics; turbulence; laser fusion controlled thermonuclear reaction research. *Mailing Add:* Washington DC 20375

BODONYI, RICHARD JAMES, AERONAUTICAL ENGINEERING, APPLIED MATHEMATICS. *Current Pos:* PROF AERO ENG, OHIO STATE UNIV, COLUMBUS, 86- *Personal Data:* b Cleveland, Ohio, Nov 26, 43; m 66; c 3. *Educ:* Ohio State Univ, BS, 66, PhD(aero eng), 73; Case Western Res Univ, MS, 70. *Prof Exp:* Aerospace engr fluid mech, Lewis Res Ctr, NASA, 67-68, fac fel, 77-78; fel, NSF, 69-73; asst prof aeronaut eng, Va Polytech Inst & State Univ, 74-76; from asst prof to prof appl math, Ind Univ-Purdue Univ, Indianapolis, 76-86; vis fel, sci & Eng Res Coun, Imp Col London, Eng, 83. *Mem:* Sigma Xi; Am Phys Soc; Am Inst Aeronaut & Astronaut; Am Acad Mech. *Res:* Theory of viscous flows; high Reynolds number flows; rotating flows; hydrodynamic stability; computational fluid dynamics. *Mailing Add:* Dept Aero/Astro Eng Ohio State Univ 2036 Neil Ave Mall Columbus OH 43210-1276. *Fax:* 614-292-8290; *E-Mail:* bodonyi.1@osu.edu

BODOR, NICHOLAS STEPHEN, MEDICINAL CHEMISTRY. *Current Pos:* prof & chmn, Dept Med Chem, 79-83, grad res prof med chem, 83-86, chmn dept, 89-91, GRAD RES PROF & EXEC DIR, CTR DRUG DISCOVERY, UNIV FLA, GAINESVILLE, 86- *Personal Data:* b Satu Mare, Transylvania, Romania, Feb 1, 39; nat US; m 61, 71, Sheryl L Reimann; c Miklos, Nicole & Erik. *Educ:* Bolyai Univ, Romania, BS & MS, 59; Babes-Bolyai Univ, Romania, DChem, 65. *Hon Degrees:* DSc, Tech Univ Budapest, 89, Med Univ Debreseu, 90. *Honors & Awards:* Res Achievement Award, Am Asn Pharmaceut Sci, 89. *Prof Exp:* Prin investr, Chem & Pharm Res Inst, Cluj, 61-68 & 69-70; R A Welch fel, Univ Tex, Austin, 68-69 & 70-72; sr res scientist, Alza Co, 72-73; dir med chem, Interx Res Corp, 73-79. *Concurrent Pos:* Adj prof, Univ Kans, 74-79; grantee, NIH, 76-; consult pharm cos; vpres & dir res, Pharmatec Inc, 83-; dir, Ctr Drug Design & Delivery, 86-; NAm ed, J Biopharm Sci. *Mem:* Fel Acad Pharmaceut Scientists; fel Am Asn Pharmaceut Sci; fel AAAS; hon mem Hungarian Chem Soc; Am Chem Soc; Am Pharmaceut Asn. *Res:* Pharmaceutical sciences. *Mailing Add:* Ctr Drug Discovery Univ Fla PO Box 100497 JHMHC Gainesville FL 32611

BODRE, ROBERT JOSEPH, ANALYTICAL CHEMISTRY. *Current Pos:* RETIRED. *Personal Data:* b Philadelphia, Pa, Mar 6, 21; m 45. *Educ:* St Josephs Col, Pa, BS, 43; Univ Louisville, PhD(chem), 61. *Prof Exp:* Chemist, Publicker Industs, Pa, 43-44; res chemist, Whitaker Wool Co, 44-47; res chemist, Girdler Div, Chemetron Corp, Ky, 47-55, group leader, 55-57; sr res chemist, Monsanto Co, 60-67, process specialist, 67-79, sr process specialist, 79-85. *Mem:* Am Chem Soc. *Res:* Development of analytical methods for industrial processes; monomer syntheses and polymerization reactions; catalyst development and applications; production of ethylbenzene and styrene. *Mailing Add:* 2501 Meadowlane St La Marque TX 77568

BOE, ARTHUR AMOS, HORTICULTURE. *Current Pos:* RETIRED. *Personal Data:* b Westfield Twp, Minn, Apr 27, 33; m 65; c 4. *Educ:* Utah State Univ, BS, 62, PhD(plant sci), 66. *Prof Exp:* Teaching asst hort, Utah State Univ, 62-65, agr specialist proj, Rural Indust Tech Assistance, Brazil, 66-67; from asst prof to prof plant sci & plant physiologist, Univ Idaho, 67-83; chmn, Dept Hort, NDak State Univ, 83- *Concurrent Pos:* Assoc plant physiologist, Univ Idaho, 72-77. *Mem:* Am Soc Hort Sci; Am Inst Biol Sci. *Res:* Fruit development and maturation as affected by plant hormones, light, temperature and magnetic fields; dormancy of woody plants and seeds; plant tissue culture; biotechnology. *Mailing Add:* 1125 NE First St Faribault MN 55021

BOECK, WILLIAM LOUIS, ATMOSPHERIC PHYSICS, SOFTWARE SYSTEMS. *Current Pos:* prof physics, 78-85, PROF COMPUT & INFO SCI & PHYSICS, NIAGARA UNIV, 85- *Personal Data:* b Buffalo, NY, June 23, 39; m 62; c 4. *Educ:* Canisius Col, BS, 61; Univ Notre Dame, PhD(physics), 65. *Prof Exp:* From asst prof to assoc prof physics, Niagara Univ, 65-73; sr res assoc, State Univ NY, Albany, 73-74; prof, Niagara Univ, 74-77; vis scientist, Nat Ctr Atmospheric Res, 77-78. *Concurrent Pos:* Chmn, Krypton 85 Working Group, Int Comn Atmospheric Elec, 74-, mem, Applications Atmospheric Elec, 75-; sci adv, Ecumenical Task Force, 80-88, Indust Waste Siting Bd, 88-90; vis scientist, Marshall Space Flight Ctr, NASA, 90-91, investr, Lightning Imaging Sensor. *Mem:* Am Geophys Union; Asn Comput Mach; Am Asn Physics Teachers. *Res:* Relationships between atmospheric radioactivity and cosmic rays and atmospheric electrical fields and currents; environmental radon measurements; stratospheric lightning; satellite observation of lightning. *Mailing Add:* Dept Comput Sci Niagara Univ Niagara University NY 14109-9999. *E-Mail:* boeck@niagara.edu

BOECKER, BRUCE BERNARD, RADIOBIOLOGY, HEALTH PHYSICS. *Current Pos:* Radiobiologist, Lovelace Biomed & Environ Res Inst, 61-64, asst head, Dept Radiobiol, 64-75, asst dir inhalation Toxicol Res Inst, 75-96, SR FEL LOVELACE RESPIRATORY RES INST, 96- *Personal Data:* b Aurora, Ill, July 9, 32; m 60, Eleanor Simson; c Nancy & Brian. *Educ:* Grinnell Col, BA, 54; Univ Rochester, MS, 60, PhD(radiobiol), 62; Am Bd Health Physics, dipl, 84. *Concurrent Pos:* Radiation biologist, Div Biol & Med, US AEC, 70-71; assoc ed, Radiation Res, 84-88; mem bd dirs, Health Physics Soc, 85-88; chmn, ORAU/Nat Cancer Inst, Working Group Bioassy, Detecting

Previous Radiation Exposures, 86; mem, NAS/NRC Comt, Biol Effects Ionizing Radiation (BEIR V), 86-89; mem, Nat Coun Radiation Protection & Measurements, 87-, bd dirs, 93-; mem, Environ & Health Stand Steering Group, US Dept Energy, 90-94; mem comt, Radiol Safety in Marshall Islands, Nat Acad Sci & Nat Res Coun, 92-94; clin prof, Col Pharm Univ NMex, 93- *Mem:* Fel Health Physics Soc; Radiation Res Soc; AAAS. *Res:* Deposition, retention and dosimetry of inhaled materials; inhalation toxicology; biological effects of inhaled materials on the respiratory tract and bioassay for internally deposited radionuclides. *Mailing Add:* Lovelace Respiratory Res Inst PO Box 5890 Albuquerque NM 87185-5890

BOECKMAN, ROBERT K, JR, SYNTHETIC METHODOLOGY, TOTAL SYNTHESIS. *Current Pos:* PROF CHEM, UNIV ROCHESTER, 80- *Personal Data:* b Pasadena, Calif, Aug 26, 44; m 76, Mary H Delton. *Educ:* Carnegie Inst Technol, BS, 66; Brandeis Univ, PhD(org chem), 71. *Prof Exp:* Asst prof chem, Wayne State Univ, 72-75, assoc prof, 76-78, prof, 79-80. *Concurrent Pos:* Fel, NIH, 70-72, Career Develop Award, 75-81; fel, A P Sloan Found, 76-80 & Japanese Soc Prom Sci, 90; Alexander von Humboldt Res prize, 92-93. *Mem:* Am Chem Soc; Royal Soc Chem; Soc Ger Chemists. *Res:* Methodology for applications of organic synthesis to the construction of stereochemically complex molecules, primarily natural products possessing biological activity of some type. *Mailing Add:* Dept Chem Univ Rochester Rochester NY 14627. *Fax:* 716-473-6889; *E-Mail:* rkb@rkbmac.chem.rochster.edu

BOEDEKER, RICHARD ROY, PHYSICS. *Current Pos:* from asst prof to assoc prof, 62-74, PROF PHYSICS, SOUTHERN ILL UNIV, EDWARDSVILLE, 74- *Personal Data:* b St Louis, Mo, Apr 8, 33; m 61; c 3. *Educ:* St Louis Univ, BS, 55, MS, 57, PhD(physics), 59. *Prof Exp:* Res assoc physics, St Louis Univ, 59-61; res scientist, McDonnell Aircraft Corp, 61-62. *Mem:* Am Phys Soc; Sigma Xi. *Res:* Neutron scattering in solids and liquids; temperature determination in gases by neutron scattering; lasers; nonlinear optics; scattering theory. *Mailing Add:* 639 Harvard Dr Edwardsville IL 62025-2669

BOEDTKER, OLAF A, SOLID STATE PHYSICS. *Current Pos:* assoc prof, 63-87, dir eng physics, 66-87, EMER PROF PHYSICS, ORE STATE UNIV, 87- *Personal Data:* b Colombo, Ceylon, Feb 10, 24; US citizen; m 52; c 4. *Educ:* Swiss Fed Inst Technol, BS, 49; Calif Inst Technol, MS, 58, PhD(eng physics), 61. *Prof Exp:* Res fel phys sci, Calif Inst Technol, 60-62; res scientist metals physics, Lawrence Radiation Lab, Univ Calif, 62-63. *Mem:* Am Soc Metals. *Mailing Add:* 2760 NW Johnson Ave Ore State Univ Corvallis OR 97330

BOEDTKER DOTY, HELGA, regulation of collagen gene expression, for more information see previous edition

BOEHLE, JOHN, JR, agronomy, weed science, for more information see previous edition

BOEHLER, GABRIEL D(OMINIQUE), MECHANICAL & AEROSPACE ENGINEERING. *Current Pos:* from asst prof to assoc prof aeronaut eng, 55-62, PROF MECH ENG, CATH UNIV AM, 62- *Personal Data:* b Paris, France, Aug 6, 26; nat US; m 57, Ingrid Onoager; c Pierre, Edith, Paul, Anne Marie & Elizabeth. *Educ:* Univ Paris, BS, 48; Cornell Univ, MS, 51; Cath Univ Am, PhD(aeronaut eng), 53. *Prof Exp:* Res asst, Cornell Univ, 50-51; chief aerodyn & asst to pres, Thieblot Aircraft Co, 51-56. *Concurrent Pos:* Consult, Aerophysics Co, 57-80, chmn bd, 80-; mem adv panel aeronaut, Off Secy Defense, 59-61. *Mem:* Am Inst Aeronaut & Astronaut; Am Helicopter Soc; Am Soc Heating, Refrig & Air-Conditioning Engrs; Soc Automotive Engrs; Am Defense Preparedness Asn. *Res:* Aerospace technology; aerodynamics; low speed flight; systems engineering; heating, ventilation and air conditioning; energy conservation; unmanned aerial vehicles; simulation. *Mailing Add:* 3010 Ordway St NW Washington DC 20008. *Fax:* 202-244-7501

BOEHLER, ROBERT A, CHEMICAL ENGINEERING, CHEMISTRY. *Current Pos:* RETIRED. *Personal Data:* b Chicago, Ill, Nov 18, 24; m 51, Ramona Kallal; c Kathleen, Mary, Robert S, Patricia & Carolyn. *Educ:* Loyola Univ, Los Angeles, BS, 50; Ill Inst Technol, MS, 66. *Prof Exp:* Area supt, Pharmaceut Div, Armour & Co, 50-53, supvr & process engr, Chem Div, 53-57; process eng, Nalco Chem Co, 57-67, group leader, microbiol dept, 67-69, sr prod engr, 69-81, mgr int opers, 81-87. *Mem:* Am Chem Soc; Am Inst Chem Engrs; Sigma Xi. *Res:* Pharmaceutics; fatty acid derivatives; process engineering and design; biochemistry. *Mailing Add:* RR 4 Jerseyville IL 62052-9434

BOEHLERT, GEORGE WALTER, ecology, zoology, for more information see previous edition

BOEHLJE, MICHAEL DEAN, FARM & AGRICULTURAL BUSINESS FINANCE, AGRICULTURAL POLICY. *Current Pos:* PROF AGR ECON, PURDUE UNIV, 92- *Personal Data:* b Sheffield, Iowa, Aug 6, 43. *Educ:* Iowa State Univ, BS, 65; Purdue Univ, MS, 68, PhD(agr econ), 71. *Prof Exp:* Asst prof agr econ, Okla State Univ, 70-73; from asst prof to prof econ, Iowa State Univ, 73-80, asst dean, Col Agr, 81-85; dept head, Univ Minn, 85-90, prof agr econ, 91-92. *Mem:* Am Agr Econ Asn; Southern Agr Econ Asn. *Res:* Strategic planning for firm in the banking, agribusiness and farm sectors to assist those firms in adapting to and thriving in a rapidly changing economic and political climate. *Mailing Add:* Dept Agr Econ Purdue Univ West Lafayette IN 47907-1968

BOEHM, BARRY WILLIAM, SOFTWARE ENGINEERING. *Current Pos:* DIR, CTR SOFTWARE ENG, UNIV SOUTHERN CALIF, 92- *Personal Data:* b Santa Monica, Calif, May 16, 35; m 61. *Educ:* Harvard Univ, BA, 57; Univ Calif, Los Angeles, MA, 61, PhD(math), 64. *Honors & Awards:* Cert of Merit, Air Force Systs Command, 72; Info Systs Award, Am Inst Aeronaut & Astronaut, 79; J D Warnier Prize, 84; Grace Hopper Award, 89. *Prof Exp:* Res engr, Gen Dynamics, Astronaut, 57-59; head comput systs anal group, Rand Corp, 59-71, head, Info Sci Dept, 71-73; dir software res & technol, TRW Systs & Energy, Inc, 73-86, chief scientist, Defense Systs Group, 86-89; dir, Info Sci & Technol Off, Defense Advan Res Proj Agency, 89-92. *Concurrent Pos:* Lectr, Exten, Univ Calif, Los Angeles, 65- & Grad Bus Sch, 69-; mem, NASA adv comt instrumentation & data processing, 68-70; mem, Southern Calif Sci Adv Comt to Selective Serv Syst, 69-, chmn, 70-; chmn conf comt, Am Fedn Info Processing Socs, 69-; guest lectr, USSR Acad Sci, 70; mem Nat Acad Sci panel comput sci develop in Brazil, 70-; sector ed, Comput Rev, 70-; chmn, NASA adv comt guid, control & info syst sci dept, 73-76; vis prof comput sci, Univ Southern Calif, 78-79 & Univ Calif, Los Angeles, 81- *Mem:* Nat Acad Eng; fel Asn Comput Mach; fel Am Inst Aeronaut & Astronaut; fel Inst Elec & Electronics Engrs. *Res:* Human-computer interaction; software engineering; software tools and environments; software metrics; software economics; developing nations. *Mailing Add:* Comput Sci Dept Univ Southern Calif Los Angeles CA 90089-0781

BOEHM, FELIX H, NUCLEAR PHYSICS, ATOMIC PHYSICS & ELEMENTARY PARTICLE PHYSICS. *Current Pos:* from assoc prof to prof, 59-84, William L Valentine prof, 85-95, WILLIAM L VALENTINE EMER PROF PHYSICS, CALIF INST TECHNOL, 95- *Personal Data:* b Basel, Switz, June 9, 24; nat US; m 56, Ruth Sommerhalder; c Marcus F & Claude N. *Educ:* Swiss Fed Inst Technol, dipl physics, 48, Dr nat sci(physics), 51. *Honors & Awards:* Alexander von Humboldt Award, 80 & 84; Bonner Prize, Am Phys Soc, 95. *Prof Exp:* Res asst, Swiss Fed Inst Technol, 48-51; Boese fel, Columbia Univ, 52-53; res fel physics, Calif Inst Technol, 53-57, asst prof, 58; vis prof, Univ Heidelberg, 58-59. *Concurrent Pos:* Sloan fel, 62-63; NSF sr fel, Univ Copenhagen, 65-66 & Europ Orgn Nuclear Res, Geneva, Switz, 71-72; trustee, Aspen Ctr Physics, 76-79; fel, Laue Langevin Inst, Grenoble, France, 79-80, Univ Munich, 80 & Swiss Int Nuclear Res, 81; mem, Bd Physics & Astron, Nat Res Coun; managing ed, Int J Mod Physics. *Mem:* Nat Acad Sci; fel Am Phys Soc; AAAS. *Res:* Nuclear structure; weak interaction; x-rays; neutrino physics; meson physics; parity and time reversal; atomic physics; muonic and pionic atoms; author of various publications. *Mailing Add:* 161-33 Calif Inst Technol Pasadena CA 91125. *E-Mail:* boehm@caltech.edu

BOEHM, JOHN JOSEPH, pediatrics, for more information see previous edition

BOEHM, PAUL DAVID, ORGANIC CHEMISTRY. *Current Pos:* VPRES, ARTHUR D LITTLE INC, 89- *Personal Data:* b New York, NY, Dec 26, 48; m 71; c 3. *Educ:* Univ Rochester, BS, 70; Univ RI, MS, 73, PhD(chem oceanog), 77. *Prof Exp:* Engr, Western Elec Co, 70-71; prin scientist, Energy Resources Co, Inc, 76-80, chief scientist, 81-83; res leader, Battelle Ocean Sci, 83-89. *Concurrent Pos:* Vis prof, Coastal Resources Ctr, Woods Hole Oceanog Inst, 81- *Mem:* AAAS; Am Chem Soc. *Res:* Investigations of organic chemical distributions in the ocean with emphasis on the chemical oceanography and biogeochemistry of marine organic pollutants. *Mailing Add:* Arthur D Little Inc Acorn Park Cambridge MA 02140-2303

BOEHM, ROBERT FOTY, HEAT TRANSFER, FLUID FLOW. *Current Pos:* chmn, 90-96, PROF MECH ENG, UNIV NEV, LAS VEGAS, 90- *Personal Data:* b Portland, Ore, Jan 16, 40; m 61, Marcia Pettibone; c Deborah & Robert C. *Educ:* Wash State Univ, BS, 62, MS, 64; Univ Calif, Berkeley, PhD(mech eng), 68. *Honors & Awards:* Ralph R Teetor Award, Soc Automotive Engrs, 71; Barrick Outstanding Res Award, Univ Nev, Las Vegas, 95. *Prof Exp:* Heat transfer engr, Aerospace Elec Dept, Westinghouse Elec Co, Ohio, 61; design engr, Lawrence Radiation Lab, 62; weights anal engr, Boeing Co, Wash, 63; engr, atomic power equip dept, Gen Elec Co, Calif, 64-66; res engr, Jet Propulsion Lab, Calif, 67; from asst prof to prof mech eng, Univ Utah, 68-90, chmn, Mech & Indust Eng Dept, 81-84. *Concurrent Pos:* Mem tech staff Saudia Labs, 84-85. *Mem:* Fel Am Soc Mech Engrs; Am Soc Eng Educ; Sigma Xi; Int Solar Energy Soc; Am Soc Heating, Refrig & Air Conditioning Engrs. *Res:* Applied thermodynamics, including design of thermal system; biotechnology studies; heat transfer; solar energy; geothermal energy; flow and heat transfer in porous media. *Mailing Add:* Dept Mech Eng Univ Nev Box 454027 Las Vegas NV 89154-4027. *Fax:* 702-895-3736; *E-Mail:* boehm@me.unlv.edu

BOEHM, ROBERT LOUIS, PAPER CHEMISTRY, PULP CHEMISTRY. *Current Pos:* RETIRED. *Personal Data:* b Buffalo, NY, Nov 17, 25; m 51; c 6. *Educ:* Colgate Univ, AB, 48; Lawrence Col, MS, 50, PhD(chem), 53. *Prof Exp:* Res chemist, Mead Corp, 53-57, tech asst to mgr, Mass, 57, asst tech dir, Chillicothe Div, 57-60, mgr, Leominster Div, 60-67, bus planner, Gilbert Paper Div, 67-69; staff mgr paper & paperbd opers, Am Can Co, 69-76; sr consult engr, H A Simons Int Ltd, Vancouver, 76-93. *Mem:* Am Chem Soc; Tech Asn Pulp & Paper Indust. *Res:* Introduction of chlorine atoms into cellulose; research in pulping and bleaching of wood pulps; paper machines. *Mailing Add:* 1221 Nanton Ave Vancouver BC V6H 2C7 Can

BOEHME, DIETHELM HARTMUT, pathology, neuropathology, for more information see previous edition

BOEHME, HOLLIS, ACOUSTICS. *Current Pos:* RES SCIENTIST, APPLIED RES LAB, UNIV TEX, 73- *Personal Data:* b Liberty, Okla, Nov 28, 33; m 54; c 3. *Educ:* Tex A&M Univ, BA, 60, MS, 61, PhD(physics), 67. *Prof Exp:* Engr, Boeing Airplane Co, 60; res asst, Tex A&M Univ, 60-61; engr, Tex Instruments Inc, 61-62; instr physics, 62-67; engr scientist, Tracor, Inc, 67-68, sr scientist, 68-70; pres, Synergy Inc, 70-73. *Concurrent Pos:* Consult, Tex Instruments Inc, 62-63. *Mem:* Am Phys Soc. *Res:* Nuclear magnetic resonance; acoustics. *Mailing Add:* 320 King Arthur Ct Austin TX 78746

BOEHME, WERNER RICHARD, organic chemistry; deceased, see previous edition for last biography

BOEHMS, CHARLES NELSON, PHYSIOLOGICAL ECOLOGY, FRESHWATER BIOLOGY. *Current Pos:* PROF & CHMN BIOL DEPT, GEORGETOWN COL, 87- *Personal Data:* b Nashville, Tenn, Feb 1, 31; m 52; c 2. *Educ:* George Peabody Col, BS, 56, MA, 57; Univ NC, Chapel Hill, PhD(zool), 71. *Prof Exp:* From instr to asst prof biol, Austin Peay State Univ, 57-61; instr zool, Univ NC, Chapel Hill, 62-64; from asst prof to prof biol, 65-87 Austin Peay State Univ, 65-71, dean students, 68-71, vpres student affairs, 71-82. *Concurrent Pos:* NSF fac fel, 64. *Mem:* Am Zool Soc; Am Soc Biol; Am Inst Biol Sci; NAm Benthological Soc. *Res:* Influence of temperature and photoperiod on seasonal regulation in fresh water invertebrates. *Mailing Add:* 209 Pocahontas Trail Georgetown KY 40324

BOEHNE, JOHN WILLIAM, NUTRITION. *Current Pos:* RETIRED. *Personal Data:* b Evansville, Ind, Feb 6, 21; m 46, Audrey Sattler; c Gregg W & Lynne A. *Educ:* Ind Univ, BS, 42. *Prof Exp:* Chemist, Lederle Labs Div, Am Cyanamid Co, NY, 46-48; asst, Western Reserve Univ, 48-57; biochemist div nutrit, Bur Foods, Food & Drug Admin, 57-59, asst to dir, 59-65, chief spec dietary foods br, 66-70, asst dir, 71-74, asst assoc dir nutrit & consumer sci, 74-78. *Mem:* Am Soc Nutrit Sci. *Res:* Bioanalytical nutrition; mineral metabolism; nutrient value of foods; food additives. *Mailing Add:* 10763 Kinloch Rd Silver Spring MD 20903-1227

BOEHNKE, DAVID NEAL, PHYSICAL CHEMISTRY, THEORETICAL CHEMISTRY. *Current Pos:* from asst prof to assoc prof, 69-82, FULL PROF CHEM, JACKSONVILLE UNIV, 82- *Personal Data:* b Dayton, Ky, July 25, 39; m 71, Cheryl Aldridge; c David, Mark & Sarah. *Educ:* Georgetown Col, BS, 61; Univ Ky, MS, 64; Univ Cincinnati, PhD(theoret chem), 68. *Prof Exp:* Instr chem & physics, Ky State Col, 64-65; res assoc, Univ NC, Chapel Hill, 67-69. *Mem:* Am Chem Soc. *Res:* Theory of critical viscosity; properties of critical fluids; kinetics of bimolecular reactions; synthesis and properties of detergents; environmental analysis of metals and hydrocarbons. *Mailing Add:* Dept Math & Sci Jacksonville Univ 2800 University Blvd N Jacksonville FL 32211-3321

BOEKELHEIDE, VIRGIL CARL, ORGANIC CHEMISTRY. *Current Pos:* PROF ORG CHEM, UNIV ORE, 60- *Personal Data:* b Chelsea, SDak, July 28, 19; m 45; c 3. *Educ:* Univ Minn, AB, 39, PhD(org chem), 43. *Honors & Awards:* Fulbright-Hays Distinguished Prof Award, Yugoslavia, 72; Alexander von Humboldt Award, WGer Govt; Coover Award, 81. *Prof Exp:* Instr chem, Univ Ill, 43-46; asst prof org chem, Univ Rochester, 46-51, from assoc prof to prof, 51-60. *Concurrent Pos:* Guggenheim fel, Swiss Fed Inst Technol, Zurich, 53-54; Swiss-Am Found Lectr, 60; Frontiers of Sci & Welch Symposium lectr, 68; Karl Pfister lectr, Mass Inst Technol, 69; mem adv coun, Nat Inst Environ Health Sci; chmn div chem & chem technol, Nat Res Coun-Nat Acad Sci; mem, Coun Int Exchange Scholars, 75-78. *Mem:* Nat Acad Sci; Am Chem Soc; Swiss Chem Soc; Ger Chem Soc; The Chem Soc. *Res:* Natural products, heterocycles and aromatic character in polycyclic molecules. *Mailing Add:* Dept Chem Univ Ore Eugene OR 97403

BOELL, EDGAR JOHN, BIOLOGY. *Current Pos:* from instr to prof biol, 38-46, Ross G Harrison prof exp zool, 47-75, chmn dept, 55-62, actg dean, Yale Col, 2nd term, 68-69, ROSS G HARRISON EMER PROF EXP ZOOL & SR BIOLOGIST, YALE UNIV, 75- *Personal Data:* b Rudd, Iowa, Oct 30, 06; m 32; c 2. *Educ:* Univ Dubuque, AB, 29; Univ Iowa, PhD(zool), 35. *Hon Degrees:* MA, Yale Univ, 46; DSc, Univ Dubuque, 52. *Honors & Awards:* Josiah Willard Gibbs Medal, 75. *Prof Exp:* Res assoc zool, Univ Iowa, 34-37. *Concurrent Pos:* Rockefeller Found fel, Cambridge Univ, 37-38; Fulbright award, Carlsberg Lab, Univ Copenhagen, 53-54; Guggenheim Found fel, Univ Rome, 63-64; ed, J Exp Zool, 65-85; master, Jonathan Edwards Col, 75-77. *Mem:* AAAS; Am Physiol Soc; Am Soc Zool; Soc Develop Biol; Am Soc Cell Biol; Am Acad Arts & Sci. *Res:* Chemical embryology; developmental physiology; reproductive biology; physiology of spermatozoa. *Mailing Add:* 886 Brentwood Dr Venice FL 34292

BOELLSTORFF, JOHN DAVID, stratigraphy, geochronology, for more information see previous edition

BOELTER, DON HOWARD, FORESTRY RESEARCH, SOIL PHYSICS. *Current Pos:* RETIRED. *Personal Data:* b Sanborn, Minn, Sept 1, 33; m 56; c 4. *Educ:* Iowa State Univ, BS, 55; Univ Minn, MS, 58, PhD(soil physics), 62. *Prof Exp:* Researcher soil physics, NCent Forest Exp Sta, Minn, 59-77, watershed mgt res, Forest Serv, Wash, DC, 77-80, asst sta dir, Pac Northwest Forest Exp Sta, USDA, Ore, 80-89, asst sta dir, 89-94. *Mem:* Am Soc Agron; Soil Sci Soc Am; Int Soc Soil Sci; Soil Conserv Soc Am; Soc Am Foresters. *Res:* Physical and hydrologic properties of peats and organic soil and relationship to the watershed management of bog and swamp areas in North Central United States. *Mailing Add:* 4724 Laura Lane Shoreview MN 55126

BOELTER, EDWIN D, JR, CHEMICAL ENGINEERING. *Current Pos:* RETIRED. *Personal Data:* b Greeley, Colo, Mar 3, 28; m 54; c 2. *Educ:* Univ Wash, BS, 49, PhD(chem eng), 52. *Prof Exp:* Tech investr, Electrochem Dept, E I du Pont de Nemours & Co Inc, 52-56, group leader, 57, sr supvr, 57-62, mgr pilot plants, 62-63, lab dir, 63-69, mgr works technol, 69-70, dir, Electronic Prod Div, 70-74, asst dir Cent Res Dept, 74-77, gen mgr, Elastomers Dept, 77-80, vpres, Polymer Prods Dept, 81-85. *Mem:* Am Chem Soc. *Res:* Electrokinetics; electroplating; molten salts; sodium; polymers. *Mailing Add:* Nine Point North Dr Salem SC 29676-9200

BOEN, JAMES ROBERT, BIOSTATISTICS. *Current Pos:* from asst prof to assoc prof, 64-75, PROF BIOSTATIST, SCH PUB HEALTH, UNIV MINN, MINNEAPOLIS, 75- *Personal Data:* b Fergus Falls, Minn, July 21, 32; m 57; c 1. *Educ:* Dartmouth Col, AB, 56; Univ Ill, MS, 57, PhD(math), 59. *Prof Exp:* Asst prof math, Southern Ill Univ, 59-60; res assoc, Univ Chicago, 60-61; lectr, Univ Mich, 61-62, fel biostatist, Stanford Univ, 62-64. *Mem:* Am Statist Asn; Biomet Soc; Am Pub Health Asn. *Mailing Add:* 101 Wayside Rd E Hopkins MN 55343

BOENIGK, JOHN WILLIAM, PHARMACEUTICAL CHEMISTRY. *Current Pos:* RETIRED. *Personal Data:* b Braddock, Pa, July 1, 18; m 47; c 4. *Educ:* Duquesne Univ, BS, 40; Western Reserve Univ, MS, 42; Purdue Univ, PhD(pharmaceut chem), 48. *Prof Exp:* Asst prof pharm, Univ Tex, 48-50; assoc prof, Med Col Va, 50-56; assoc prof, Univ Pittsburgh, 56-61; group leader pharm prod develop, Mead Johnson & Co, 61-67, sect leader tablet develop, 67-69, sr res assoc, 69-70, res assoc, 70-78, prin res scientist, 79-83. *Mem:* AAAS; Am Pharmaceut Asn. *Res:* Sustained release; stability; vitamins; antacids. *Mailing Add:* 2511 Bayard Park Dr Evansville IN 47714

BOER, F PETER, CHEMISTRY. *Current Pos:* PRES & CHIEF EXEC OFFICER, TIGER SCI. *Personal Data:* b 1941. *Educ:* Princeton Univ, AB, 61; Harvard Univ, PhD, 65. *Prof Exp:* Staff mem, Tex Div Lab, Dow Chem Co, 65-78; dir, vpres & mgr res & develop, Am Can Co, 78-83; from vpres to sr vpres, Pres Res Div & Corp Tech Group, W R Grace & Co, 83-89, exec vpres, Corp Tech Group, 89- *Mem:* Nat Acad Eng. *Res:* Chemistry. *Mailing Add:* Tiger Sci Inc 47 Country Rd S Boynton Beach FL 33436

BOER, KARL WOLFGANG, SOLAR ENERGY CONVERSION, PHOTOVOLTAICS. *Current Pos:* from assoc prof to prof physics, Univ Del, 62-72, prof physics & eng, 72-92, distinguished prof physics & solar energy, 92-95, UNIV RES PROF, UNIV DEL, 95- *Personal Data:* b Berlin, Ger, Mar 23, 26; US citizen; m 67, Renate Schroeder; c Ralf-Reinhard & Katarina Kalota. *Educ:* Humboldt Univ, Berlin, dipl phys, 49, Dr rer nat, 52, Dr rer nat habil, solid state physics, 55. *Honors & Awards:* C G Abbott Award, Am Solar Energy Soc, 81. *Prof Exp:* Asst physics, Humboldt Univ, Berlin, 49-52, oberasst, 52-55, docent, 55-58, prof, 58-61; res prof physics, NY Univ, 61-62. *Concurrent Pos:* Bereichs Leiter, Deutsche Acad Wiss, Berlin, 55-61; dir, IEC, Univ Del, 72-75, chief scientist, 73-, adv to pres, 75-90; chmn bd, SES Inc, 73-79, chief scientist, 79-82; dir pub, Am Solar Energy Soc, 78-84; ed-in-chief, Advances Solar Energy, 82- *Mem:* Fel Am Phys Soc; sr mem Inst Elec & Electronics Engrs; Int Solar Energy Soc; Am Solar Energy Soc (pres, 75-76, treas, 77); Electrochem Soc. *Res:* Electron transport in semiconductors; photoconductivity; photovoltaics; solar energy conversion. *Mailing Add:* Mat Sci Univ Del Newark DE 19716. *Fax:* 610-444-9472; *E-Mail:* solpax@aol.com

BOERBOOM, LAWRENCE E, CARDIOVASCULAR DISEASES, PHYSIOLOGY. *Current Pos:* ASST PROF PHYSIOL, DEPT CARDIOVASC DIS, MED COL WIS, 77- *Educ:* Univ NDak, Grand Forks, PhD(physiol), 75. *Mailing Add:* Dept Cardiothoracic Surg Med Col Wis PO Box 26099 FMLH E Milwaukee WI 53226-0099

BOERCKER, DAVID BRYAN, KINETIC THEORY, STATISTICAL PHYSICS. *Current Pos:* PHYSICIST, LAWRENCE LIVERMORE NAT LAB, 80- *Personal Data:* b St Louis, Mo, Nov 30, 49; m 71, Dale Padham; c Kevin & Janice. *Educ:* Austin Peay State Univ, BA, 70; Univ Fla, PhD(physics), 78. *Prof Exp:* Res assoc, Air Force Weapons Lab, 78-80. *Mem:* Am Phys Soc. *Res:* Evaluation of equilibrium time correlation functions and their associated transport coefficients for dense plasmas; broadening of spectral lines in plasmas; molecular dynamics modeling of tribological and other surface phenomena. *Mailing Add:* Lawrence Livermore Lab L-045 Univ Calif PO Box 808 Livermore CA 94550. *E-Mail:* boercker@llnl.gov

BOERE, RENE THEODOOR, INORGANIC HETEROCYCLIC CHEMISTRY. *Current Pos:* ASST PROF CHEM, UNIV LETHBRIDGE, 88- *Personal Data:* b Wageningen, Neth, May 31, 57; Can citizen; m 85, Brenda Ireland; c Adrian, Robyn, Alistair & Jocelyn. *Educ:* Dalhousie Univ, BSc, 79; Univ Western Ont, PhD(chem), 84. *Honors & Awards:* Silver Medal, Chem Inst Can, 78. *Prof Exp:* Res fel, Guelph-Waterloo Centre Grad Work Chem, 84-86; vis scientist & Inst fur Anorganic Anal Chemie, Free Univ Berlin, 86-87; asst prof chem, Univ Victoria, 87-88. *Concurrent Pos:* fel, Alexander von Humboldt Found, 86. *Mem:* Chem Inst Can; Can Soc Chem; Am Chem Soc. *Res:* Chemistry of the P-block elements at transition metal centres; the structures, reactivity and electronic nature of such compounds; use of these compounds in the design of new inorganic materials. *Mailing Add:* Dept Chem Univ Lethbridge Lethbridge AB T1K 3M4 Can. *Fax:* 403-329-2057; *E-Mail:* boere@hg.uleth.ca

BOERMA, H ROGER, SOYBEAN BREEDING & GENETICS, SOYBEAN GENOME MAPPING. *Current Pos:* From asst prof to prof, 73-94, RES PROF, UNIV GA, ATHENS, 94- *Personal Data:* b Lincoln, Ill, Dec 26, 46; m 68, Cynthia Wurth; c Erica & LeeAnn. *Educ:* Ill State Univ, BS, 68; Univ Ill, MS, 70, PhD(agron), 73. *Honors & Awards:* Agron Achievement Award, Am Soc Agron, 92; Soybean Prod Res Award, Am Soybean Asn, 91. *Concurrent Pos:* Coordr, Ctr Soybean Improv, Univ Ga, 92-; chmn, Plant Breeding & Genetics Div, Crop Sci Soc Am, 93. *Mem:* Fel Crop Sci Soc Am; fel Am Soc Agron; Coun Agr Sci & Technol; fel AAAS. *Res:* Genetic variation, genetic mapping and development of breeding strategies of soybean with emphasis on diseases, nematodes and insect resistance and physiological traits related to superior productivity. *Mailing Add:* Univ Ga 3111 Plant Sci Bldg Athens GA 30602-7272. *Fax:* 706-542-0914; *E-Mail:* rboerma@uga.cc.uga.edu

BOERNER, RALPH E J, FOREST ECOLOGY, NUTRIENT CYCLING. *Current Pos:* from asst prof to assoc prof, 80-93, PROF PLANT BIOL, OHIO STATE UNIV, 93- CHMN DEPT, 90- *Personal Data:* b Brooklyn, NY, Oct 2, 48; m 82, Elizabeth Wrobel; c Annalisa M. *Educ:* Col Cortland, BS, 70; Adelphi Univ, MS, 72; Rutgers Univ, MPh, 74, PhD(bot), 80. *Honors & Awards:* Oak Leaf Award, Nature Conserv, 92. *Prof Exp:* Asst prof biol, Burlington County Col, 74-80. *Mem:* Ecol Soc Am; Bot Soc Am; Sigma Xi; Soil Ecol Soc NAm; fel AAAS; Natural Areas Asn. *Res:* Structure-function relationships in forest ecosystems; successional patterns and land use; forest understory dynamics; plant environmental physiology; mycorrhizae. *Mailing Add:* Dept Plant Biol Ohio State Univ 1735 Neil Ave Columbus OH 43210. *E-Mail:* rboerner@postbox.acs.ohio_state.edu

BOERNKE, WILLIAM E, ENZYMOLOGY, PHYSIOLOGICAL ECOLOGY. *Current Pos:* PROF BIOL, NEBR WESLEYAN UNIV, 71- *Personal Data:* b Uniontown, Pa, Feb 7, 44; m 85. *Educ:* Univ Minn, BA, 66, PhD(zool), 72. *Concurrent Pos:* Vis scientist, Argonne Nat Lab, 81- *Mem:* AAAS; Am Soc Zoologists; Am Inst Biol Sci; Am Soc Biochem & Molecular Biol. *Res:* Metabolic or biochemical adaptations in vertebrate organisms; kinetic and physiochemical studies of enzymes; regulation of enzymes involved in nitrogen metabolism. *Mailing Add:* Dept Biol Nebr Wesleyan Univ 5000 St Paul Lincoln NE 68504

BOERS, JACK E, PARTICLE BEAM ACCELERATORS. *Current Pos:* PRES, THUNDERBIRD SIMULATIONS, 90- *Personal Data:* b Kalamazoo, Mich, Feb 14, 35; m 92, Carol D McInerney; c Robert S & Amanda J. *Educ:* Univ Mich, BSc, 57, MSc, 58, PhD(elec eng), 68. *Prof Exp:* Mem tech staff, Sandia Nat Lab, 67-84; Sr engr, Varian/Extrion, 84-90. *Concurrent Pos:* Consult, Los Alamos Nat Labs, EG&G. *Mem:* Am Phys Soc; Inst Elec & Electronics Engrs; Asn Comput Mach. *Res:* Computer simulation of particle beams. *Mailing Add:* 626 Bradfield Dr Garland TX 75042. *Fax:* 214-272-5858

BOERSMA, P DEE, ECOLOGY, CONSERVATION BIOLOGY. *Current Pos:* SCI ADV, PENGUIN TAXON GROUP, AM ASN ZOOL PARKS & AQUARIUMS, 93- *Personal Data:* b Mt Pleasant, Mich, Nov 1, 46. *Educ:* Cent Mich Univ, BS, 69; Ohio State Univ, PhD(zool), 74. *Prof Exp:* Lectr zool, Ohio State Univ, 74; from asst prof to prof zool & environ sci, Inst Environ Studies, Univ Wash, 74-89, assoc dir, 87-93, prof zool, 93- *Concurrent Pos:* Adv, US deleg, Status of Women Comn & World Pop Conf, UN, 74; mem, Off Endangered Species Sci Adv Comt, Dept Interior; Kellogg Nat Leadership fel, 82-85; William Evans vis fel, Univ Otago, NZ, 95; bd dirs, Bullitt Found, Peregrine Fund, Wash Nature Conservancy. *Mem:* AAAS; Ecol Soc Am; fel Am Ornith Union; Cooper Ornith Soc; Sigma Xi; Wilson Ornith Soc; fel Wildlife Conserv Soc; Soc Conserv Biol (pres). *Res:* Adaptations of organisms to predictable and unpredictable environments, reproductive strategies, sexual dimorphism, temperature regulation; seabird growth rates in relationship to food supply and population dynamics; seabirds as indicators of marine pollution; magellanic penguin population biology. *Mailing Add:* Univ Wash Box 351800 Seattle WA 98195. *Fax:* 206-543-3041; *E-Mail:* boersma@u.washington.edu

BOERTH, ROBERT CARTER, PEDIATRICS. *Current Pos:* PROF PEDIAT & PHARMACOL, UNIV SALA, COL MED, 81-, CHMN, DEPT PEDIAT, 85- *Personal Data:* b Fargo, NDak, June 3, 37; m 60, Margaret A Gludt; c Scott R & Robert J. *Educ:* Univ NDak, BS, 61; Univ Iowa, MD, 63, MS, 65, PhD(pharmacol), 66. *Honors & Awards:* Established Investigatorship Award, Am Heart Asn, 71; Award Exemplary Med Advocacy Children, Child Advocacy Ctr, Inc, 92. *Prof Exp:* Guest worker, Cardiol Br, Nat Heart Inst, 67-68; res assoc, USPHS Hosp, 68-70; asst prof pharmacol, Emory Univ, 70-72; resident pediat, Vanderbilt Univ, 72-74, asst prof pediat & pharmacol, 74-78, assoc prof, 78-81; clin assoc prof pediat, Meharry Med Col, 78-81. *Concurrent Pos:* Dir, Middle Tenn Poison Control Ctr, 78-81; dir, Div Pediat Clin Pharmacol, Vanderbilt Univ, 78-81; co-dir, Pediat Intensive Care Unit, Univ S Ala, Med Ctr, 81-84, dir, Div Pediat Cardiol, Col Med, 81-88, Div Clin Pharmacol, 81-90, interim chmn, Dept Pediat, 83-85, prog dir, Pediat Residency Prog, 83-93, dir, Pediat Intensive Care Unit, Children & Womens Hosp, 86-88, med dir, 84-; co-chmn, Pediat Intensive Care Unit, Univ SAla Med Ctr, 81-, med bd (clin chairs) comt, 86-, comt stand conduct res, 90-, chmn, pediat comt, 91-, grad med educ comt, 93-, neurol chair search comt, 93-, pres med staff, 94- *Mem:* Am Acad Pediat (pres, 93-); AAAS; Am Heart Asn; Am Pediat Soc; Am Physiol Soc; Am Soc Pharmacol & Exp Therapeut. *Res:* Pediatrics and pharmacology. *Mailing Add:* Univ SAla Dept Pediat 1504 Springhill Ave Rm 5309 Mobile AL 36604-3207

BOERTJE, STANLEY, zoology, parasitology, for more information see previous edition

BOES, ARDEL J, MATHEMATICS. *Current Pos:* asst prof, 66-69, ASSOC PROF MATH, COLO SCH MINES, 69-, HEAD DEPT, 78- *Personal Data:* b Wall Lake, Iowa, Sept 24, 37; m 63; c 2. *Educ:* St Ambrose Col, BA, 59; Purdue Univ, MS, 61, PhD(math), 66. *Prof Exp:* Instr math, Marycrest Col, 63-64. *Res:* Foundations of probability; measure theory. *Mailing Add:* Dept Math Colo Sch Mines Golden CO 80401

BOESCH, FRANCIS THEODORE, COMBINATORICS, FINITE MATHEMATICS. *Current Pos:* prof & dept head elec eng & computer sci, 79-88, PROF MATH, STEVENS INST TECHNOL, 80-, DEAN OF FAC, 88- *Personal Data:* b New York, NY; m; c 1. *Educ:* Polytech Inst New York, BS, 57, MS, 60, PhD(elec eng), 63. *Prof Exp:* Mem tech staff, Bell Labs, 58-59; instr elec eng, Polytech Inst New York, 59-62, asst prof, 62-63; mem tech staff, Bell Labs, 63-68; prof comput sci, Univ Calif, Berkeley, 68-69; mem tech staff, Bell Labs, 69-79. *Concurrent Pos:* Consult, Exec Off of Pres, 68-69; ed in chief, J Networks, 71-; ed, J Graph Theory, 79-; prin investr grants, Nat Sci Found, 81-84. *Mem:* Fel Inst Elec & Electronics Engrs; fel NY Acad Sci; Sigma Xi; Asn Comput Mach. *Res:* Theory and design of reliable large-scale networks, particularly computer networks, using graph theory and combinatorial optimization. *Mailing Add:* Stevens Inst Technol Castle Point Sta Hoboken NJ 07030

BOESCH, WILLIAM J, MATERIALS SCIENCE ENGINEERING, HIGH TEMPERATURE ALLOYS. *Current Pos:* RETIRED. *Personal Data:* b Peoria, Ill, Nov 25, 23. *Prof Exp:* Assoc dir technol, Spec Metals Corp, 85. *Mem:* Sigma Xi. *Mailing Add:* 16 Lin Rd Utica NY 13501

BOESE, GILBERT KARYLE, ANIMAL BEHAVIOR. *Current Pos:* PRES, ZOOL SOC MILWAUKEE CO, 89-; EXEC DIR, FOUND WILDLIFE CONSERV, 93- *Personal Data:* b Chicago, Ill, June 24, 37; m 86, Lillian Haeflei; c Ann C, Peter A & Sara R. *Educ:* Carthage Col, BA, 59; Northern Ill Univ, MS, 65; Johns Hopkins Univ, PhD(pathobiol), 73. *Prof Exp:* Teacher sci, pub sch, 60-62, teacher sci & head dept, 62-65; instr biol, Thornton Community Col, 65-67; asst prof biol, Elmhurst Col, 67-69; res assoc, Brookfield Zoo, 69-71, cur educ & res, 71-72, assoc dir, 72-77, dep dir, 77-80; dir, Milwaukee Co Zool Gardens, 80-89. *Concurrent Pos:* Primate adv comt mem, Baltimore Zool Soc, 71-72; adj prof, Northern Ill Univ, 72-73; vis lectr biol, Elmhurst Col, 71-80; adj prof, Univ Wis-Milwaukee, 80; consult, Howler Monkey Sanctuary, Belize, Calif, 87-, Belize Zoo & Trop Educ Ctr, 89- & Simon Boliver Zoo, 91. *Mem:* Am Asn Zool Parks & Aquariums; Animal Behav Soc; EAfrican Wildlife Soc; Int Union Dirs Zool Gardens. *Res:* Social behavior and ecology of the Guinea baboon and comparison of social behavior with other species of the genus Papio. *Mailing Add:* W 28 on 3592 Taylors Woods Rd Pewaukee WI 53072. *Fax:* 414-258-5958

BOESE, ROBERT ALAN, FORENSIC CHEMISTRY. *Current Pos:* PRES, B&W CONSULT FORENSIC CHEMISTS, INC, 86- *Personal Data:* b Chicago, Ill, Mar 30, 34; m 55, June C Franke; c Mark A & Brian A. *Educ:* Ill Inst Technol, BS, 67, MPA, 74. *Prof Exp:* investr, Crime Lab, Chicago Police Dept, 58-60, firearms examr, 60-63, sr firearms examr, 63-65, chemist, Crime Lab, 65-71, chief chemist, 71-74, tech coordr, 74-83, asst dir, Crime Lab Div, 83-86. *Concurrent Pos:* Prof, Univ Ill, Chicago; mem, Ill Adv Comt Arson Prev & Ill Arson Adv Comt; fac mem, St Xavier Col, 78-79; lectr, Northwestern Univ, Ill Inst Technol, Univ Notre Dame, & Loyola Univ Chicago. *Mem:* Fel Am Acad Forensic Sci; Am Chem Soc; Int Asn Arson Investrs; Am Firearms & Tool Marks Examrs. *Res:* Firearms identification; forensic chemistry; arson. *Mailing Add:* 5657 S Mason Ave Chicago IL 60638-3604

BOESGAARD, ANN MERCHANT, ASTRONOMY. *Current Pos:* from asst prof to assoc prof physics & astron, 67-77, PROF PHYSICS & ASTRON, INST ASTRON, UNIV HAWAII, 77- *Personal Data:* b Rochester, NY, Mar 21, 39; m 66. *Educ:* Mt Holyoke Col, AB, 61; Univ Calif, Berkeley, PhD(astron), 66. *Hon Degrees:* DSc, Mount Holyoke Col, 81. *Honors & Awards:* Muhlmann Prize, Astron Soc Pac, 90. *Prof Exp:* Res fel astrophys, Calif Inst Technol & Mt Wilson & Palomar Observ, 66-67. *Concurrent Pos:* Sabbatical leave, researcher, Nat Ctr Sci Res, France, 73-74; res assoc, Hale Observ, 74; counr, Am Astron Soc, 78-81; vis scientist, Harvard-Smithsonian Ctr Astrophysics, 80-81; Morrison visitor, Lick Observ, 85; vis assoc, Caltech, 85-87, vis prof, 87; NATO sr sci fel, 83; Guggenheim fel, 86. *Mem:* AAAS; Am Astron Soc; Int Astron Union; Astron Soc Pac (vpres, 74-76, pres, 76-78). *Res:* Stellar spectroscopy, nucleosynthesis and chemical composition of stars; stellar evolution. *Mailing Add:* 1607 Kamole St Honolulu HI 96821

BOESHAAR, PATRICIA CHIKOTAS, ASTRONOMY, ASTROPHYSICS. *Current Pos:* assoc prof physics, 88-91, PROF ASTROPHYS, DREW UNIV, 91- *Personal Data:* b Butler Twp, Pa, Sept 25, 47; m 70; c 1. *Educ:* Northwestern State Univ, La, BS, 69; Ohio State Univ, PhD(astron), 76. *Prof Exp:* Instr res assoc astron, Univ Wash, 75-77; asst prof physics & astron, Univ Ore, 77-80; res assoc, Univ Ariz, 80-81; prof physics, Rider Col, 81-88. *Concurrent Pos:* NSF grants astron, 78, 84, 85 & 86-88; consult, AT&T Bell Labs, 81-; vis scientist, Can-France-Hawaii Telescope Corp, 89, 90 & 91; prin investr, NSF, 91-93. *Mem:* Am Astron Soc; Sigma Xi; Astron Soc Pac. *Res:* Stellar spectroscopy; effects of changes in temperature, surface gravity, and chemical composition on the spectra of the coolest main sequence; subluminous and chemically peculiar evolved stars; galactic structure. *Mailing Add:* PO Box 165 Pottersville NJ 07979. *Fax:* 973-408-3572; *E-Mail:* pboeshaa@drew.drew.edu

BOETTCHER, F PETER, POLYMER CHEMISTRY, ORGANIC CHEMISTRY. *Current Pos:* RETIRED. *Personal Data:* b Berlin, Ger, Aug 23, 32; US citizen; m 64; c 4. *Educ:* T H Darmstadt, DiplIng, 58, DrIng(org chem), 61. *Prof Exp:* Res assoc org chem, Univ Mich, Ann Arbor, 61-63; res chemist polymer chem, E I DuPont Nemours & Co, Inc, 64-68, sr res chemist textile technol, 68-74, res supvr textile technol, 74-79, sr supvr polymer chem, 79-81, res mgr polymer chem, Cent Res Dept, 81-94. *Mem:* Am Chem Soc. *Res:* Polymer and intermediate synthesis; synthetic fibers; high performance polymers; liquid crystalline polymers. *Mailing Add:* 18 Woods Rd Northampton MA 01062

BOETTCHER, HAROLD P(AUL), ELECTRICAL ENGINEERING, MECHANICS. *Current Pos:* from assoc prof to prof, 61-88, EMER PROF ELEC ENG, UNIV WIS, 88- *Personal Data:* b Eagle, Wis, July 24, 23; m 48, Dorothy (Strandberg); c David Paul, Mark Alan, John Harold. *Educ:* Univ Wis, BS, 47, MS, 50, PhD(elec eng & mech), 54. *Prof Exp:* Instr mechs, Univ Wis, 46-54; supvr, Long Range Res Lab, A O Smith Corp, 54-61. *Concurrent Pos:* Mem, Nat Res Coun Conf Insulation, Nat Acad Sci. *Mem:* Inst Elec & Electronics Engrs; Am Soc Eng Educ; Sigma Xi. *Res:* Electric motor design and application; application of computers to electrical design; analysis and synthesis of networks; power semiconductor applications. *Mailing Add:* 230 S3411 Milky Way Rd Waukesha WI 53186

BOETTGER, SUSAN D, ORGANIC CHEMISTRY, PROCESS DEVELOPMENT LABORATORY ROBOTICS. *Current Pos:* res scientist, Indust Div, Bristol-Myers, 81-83, SR RES SCIENTIST, PHARMACEUT RES & DEVELOP DIV, BRISTOL-MYERS SQUIBB, 84- *Personal Data:* b Two Rivers, Wis, Oct 6, 52. *Educ:* Univ Wis-Madison, BS, 74; Cornell Univ, MS, 77, PhD(org chem), 79. *Prof Exp:* Fel, Cornell Univ, 79 & Univ Rochester, 79-81. *Mem:* Am Chem Soc. *Res:* Synthesis of B-lactam antibiotics and antiviral compounds; development of automated systems for optimization of organic reactions. *Mailing Add:* 7474 James St Fayetteville NY 13066

BOETTINGER, WILLIAM JAMES, METALLURGY. *Current Pos:* METALLURGIST ALLOY SOLIDIFICATION & PHASE TRANSFORMATIONS, NAT INST STANDARDS & TECHNOL, 74- *Personal Data:* b Baltimore, Md, July 22, 46; m 70; c 2. *Educ:* Johns Hopkins Univ, BES, 68, PhD(metall), 72. *Honors & Awards:* Mat Sci Div Award, Am Soc Mat, 89. *Prof Exp:* Nat Res Coun-Nat Acad Engrs, res assoc alloy solidification, Nat Bur Standards, 72-74. *Concurrent Pos:* Prof lectr phys metall, George Washington Univ, 77- *Mem:* Am Inst Mining, Metall & Petrol Engrs; Am Soc Mat. *Res:* Alloy solidification; x-ray diffraction. *Mailing Add:* 12398 N Debkay Ct Monrovia MD 21770

BOETTNER, EDWARD ALVIN, PHYSICS. *Current Pos:* physicist eng res inst, 46-59, res assoc, Inst Indust Health, 59-65, from asst prof to assoc prof indust health, 59-69, PROF INDUST HEALTH, UNIV MICH, 69- *Personal Data:* b Mich, Aug 28, 15; m 38; c 2. *Educ:* Lawrence Inst Technol, BSc, 37; Univ Mich, MSc, 51. *Prof Exp:* Spectroscopist, Wyandotte Chem Corp, 37-46. *Mem:* Am Indust Hyg Asn; Optical Soc Am. *Res:* Applied spectroscopy; application of physics instrumentation to the assessment of the environment. *Mailing Add:* 1271 Leisure World Mesa AZ 85206

BOETTNER, FRED EASTERDAY, PHARMACEUTICAL CHEMISTRY. *Current Pos:* RETIRED. *Personal Data:* b Murphysboro, Ill, Dec 10, 18; m 42; c 3. *Educ:* Carthage Col, AB, 40; Tulane Univ, MS, 42; Univ Ill, PhD(org chem), 47. *Prof Exp:* Asst chem, Tulane Univ, 40-42; res chemist, Monsanto Chem Co, Ala, 42-43, Higgins Indust, Inc, La, 43-44 & Armour Res Found, 44; asst org chem, Univ Ill, 44-47; sr scientist, Rohm and Haas Co, 47-76; sr scientist, Polysciences, Inc, 76-86. *Mem:* Am Chem Soc; fel Am Inst Chemists; AAAS. *Res:* Lignin utilization; plastics and resins; synthesis of new anion exchange resins; structure of amino amide formaldehyde resins; insecticides; fungicides; herbicides; surface active compounds; antineoplastic agents from plants; pharmaceuticals. *Mailing Add:* 1604 Ternberry Rd High Point NC 27262-7412. *Fax:* 910-883-0671

BOFFA, LIDIA C, MOLECULAR CARCINOGENESIS, GENES MODULATION. *Current Pos:* RES ASSOC PROF MOLECULAR CARCINOGENESIS, NAT CANCER INST, GENOA, ITALY, 82- *Personal Data:* b Monza, Italy, Aug 23, 45; c Maria-Theresa E (Vidali). *Educ:* Univ Padova, BS, 65, PhD(org chem), 69. *Prof Exp:* Postdoctoral cell biol & biochem, Inst Path, Univ Padova, 69-71; res assoc cell biol, Med Sch, Rockefeller Univ, NY, 71-75, asst prof cell biol, 76-82. *Concurrent Pos:* Adj fac, Rockefeller Univ, NY, 82-; vis prof, Med Sch, Univ CapeTown, SAfrica, 87; vis scientist, SKI Mem Cancer Ctr, NY, 93- *Mem:* Europ Asn Cancer Res; Am Asn Cancer Res; Am Asn Cell Biol; NY Acad Sci. *Res:* Determination of macromolecular targets of alkylating agents, with different degree of genotoxicity, in cells; gene sequence and the control of their expression in carcinogenesis. *Mailing Add:* Dept Chem Carcinogenesis Nat Cancer Inst IST Viale Benedetto XV n10 Genoa 16132 Italy. *Fax:* 39-10-352999

BOFINGER, DIANE P, PROTEIN CHEMISTRY, CLINICAL CHEMISTRY. *Current Pos:* res instr, 82-83, clin asst prof clin biochem, 89-90, ASST PROF CLIN BIOCHEM, STATE UNIV, NY, BUFFALO, 90- *Personal Data:* b Philadelphia, Pa, Sept 26, 51; m 88. *Educ:* East Stroudsburg State Col, BA, 73; State Univ NY, Buffalo, PhD(biochem), 82. *Prof Exp:* Res health scientist, Vet Admin Med Ctr Buffalo, 84-87; instr chem, Erie County Community Col, 88. *Mem:* Protein Soc; Am Asn Clin Chem; Am Chem Soc; AAAS; Asn Women Sci. *Res:* Intracellular signal transduction pathways involving calmodulin and protein phosphorylation; mapping drug and protein binding sites in calmodulin; identify proteins which are phosphorylated in various cells in response to a variety of external cell stimuli. *Mailing Add:* Clin Lab Sci 26 Cary Hall State Univ Buffalo NY 3435 Main St Buffalo NY 14214-3005

BOFINGER, PAUL O, CONSERVATION. *Honors & Awards:* Pres Conserv Achievement Award, Nature Conservancy, 93. *Mem:* Nature Conservancy. *Mailing Add:* 89 Mountain Rd Concord NH 03301-6933

BOGAN, DENIS JOHN, CHEMICAL KINETICS, MOLECULAR SPECTROSCOPY. *Current Pos:* ASSOC PROF CHEM, CATH UNIV AM, 85- *Personal Data:* b Winchester, Mass, Aug 10, 41; m 69; c 2. *Educ:* Northeastern Univ, AB, 65; Carnegie Mellon Univ, MS, 70, PhD(phys chem), 73. *Prof Exp:* Fel phys chem, Kans State Univ, 72-74, Nat Res Coun fel; res chemist phys chem, Naval Res Lab, 76-85. *Concurrent Pos:* Assoc, Nat Res Coun-Nat Acad Sci, 74 & 75; adj assoc prof chem, Cath Univ Am, 81-85. *Mem:* Am Chem Soc; Sigma Xi; Am Soc Photobiol; Inter-Am Photochem Soc; Combustion Inst. *Res:* Physical chemistry of reactive systems, particularly gas phase and gas surface catalytic behavior of molecules containing carbon, hydrogen, oxygen, and halogen. *Mailing Add:* 5110 Althea Dr Annandale VA 22003-4146

BOGAN, RICHARD HERBERT, CIVIL ENGINEERING. *Current Pos:* from asst prof to assoc prof civil eng, 54-65, PROF CIVIL ENG, UNIV WASH, 65- *Personal Data:* b Portland, Ore, June 11, 26; m 47, 70; c 5. *Educ:* Univ Wash, Seattle, BSCE, 49; Mass Inst Technol, SM, 52, ScD(eng), 54. *Prof Exp:* Engr, Pac Water Works Supply Co, Wash, 49-51; asst, Mass Inst Technol, 52-54. *Concurrent Pos:* Consult, eng firms, indust & govt, 55-; prog mgr, Div Advan Energy Res & Technol, NSF, 73-75; mem, Interagency Task Force Synthetic Fuel From Coal, Washington, DC, 73-75; mem, proj adv bds various alt energy proj including Batelle (Columbus), MITRE Corp, Elec Power Res Inst, US Dept Energy, 74-; mem, Solar Energy Task Force, Energy Res & Develop Admin, Washington, DC, actg br chief, Div Solar Energy, 75. *Mem:* Am Soc Civil Engrs; Am Soc Eng Educ; Sigma XI; Am Acad Environ Engrs; AAAS. *Res:* Control, measurement and removal of physical, chemical and biological entities contained in air, water and waste waters; computer simulation, analysis and design of treatment processes, water supply and waste management systems. *Mailing Add:* Dept Civil Eng FX-10 Univ Wash Seattle WA 98105

BOGAN, ROBERT L, DENTISTRY. *Current Pos:* RETIRED. *Personal Data:* b Anderson, Ind, July 28, 26; m 48; c 3. *Educ:* Butler Univ, BS, 50; Ind Univ, DDS, 54, MSD, 67. *Prof Exp:* Asst prosthetics, Sch Dent, Ind Univ, Indianapolis, 54-55, instr crown & bridge, 55-62, from asst prof to prof partial prosthodontics, 62-77, asst to dean, 64-67, asst dean, 67-73, assoc dean, 67-90. *Mem:* Am Asn Dent Schs; Int Col Dentists. *Res:* Clinical evaluation of factors contributing to stability in removable partial prosthodontics; laboratory study in soldering of high fusing gold alloys used in dental restorations. *Mailing Add:* 8148 Foxchase Circle Indianapolis IN 46256

BOGAR, LOUIS CHARLES, RADIOCHEMISTRY, HEALTH PHYSICS. *Current Pos:* vpres & mgr, environ safety & health, 85-87, vpres site remediation, 87-88, VPRES GOVT OPERS BUS UNIT, ENVIRON AFFAIRS, FEED MAT PROD CTR, WESTINGHOUSE MAT CO, OHIO, 88- *Personal Data:* b Bluefield, WVa, Aug 22, 32; m 54; c 3. *Educ:* Mass Inst Technol, SB, 54. *Prof Exp:* Resident radiochemist, Bettis Atomic Power Lab Off, Chalk River Nuclear Labs, Can, 57-60; scientist, Bettis Atomic Power Lab, Westinghouse Elec Corp, 60-63, supvr mat activation, 63-64, supvr radiation sources, 65-67, mgr radiation eng, 68-69, mgr radiation control, 69-71, mgr radiation & safety, 71-74, mgr steam generators, 78-85; spec assignment, Duquesne Light Co, Shippingport Atomic Power Sta, 74-77,. *Mem:* AAAS; Am Nuclear Soc; Am Chem Soc; Am Defense Preparedness Asn; Am Soc Testing & Mat; fel Am Inst Chem. *Res:* Fission product chemistry; fuel element release; radioactivation and transport processes in reactor coolants; low level radioactivity measurements; high temperature aqueous corrosion mechanisms; radiological controls; in vivo dosimetry; environmental radioactivities. *Mailing Add:* PO Box 187 Ross OH 45061-0187

BOGAR, THOMAS JOHN, EXPERIMENTAL FLUID DYNAMICS. *Current Pos:* RES SCIENTIST, MCDONNELL DOUGLAS RES LABS, 79- *Personal Data:* b Welland, Ont, Oct 3, 47; US citizen; m 69; c 2. *Educ:* Kalamazoo Col, BA, 69; Univ Mich, MS, 70, PhD(physics), 75. *Prof Exp:* Asst prof physics, Westminster Col, 75-79. *Mem:* Am Phys Soc; Am Inst Aeronaut & Astronaut. *Res:* Unsteady transonic internal flows with emphasis on instrumentation, data acquisition and processing, computer automation. *Mailing Add:* McDonnell Aircraft Co New Aircraft Missile Prod PO Box 516 St Louis MO 63166-0516

BOGARD, ANDREW DALE, RADIOCHEMISTRY. *Current Pos:* RETIRED. *Personal Data:* b Savannah, Mo, June 18, 15; m 46, Katherine Conley; c William Dale & Rebecca Lou. *Educ:* William Jewell Col, AB, 37; Univ Ark, MA, 39. *Prof Exp:* Asst chem, Univ Ark, 37-39; chemist coal prod & clay utilization, US Bur Mines, 39-42; chemist, Oak Ridge Nat Lab, 46-48; chemist liquid metals res, Naval Res Lab, 48-56; adv engr, Bettis Atomic Power Lab, Westinghouse Elec Corp, 56-80. *Concurrent Pos:* Consult, 80- *Mem:* Am Chem Soc. *Res:* Coal utilization; liquid metals for nuclear reactors; fallout; fission product analysis; heavy element chemistry; gamma ray spectrometry; reactor coolant radiochemistry. *Mailing Add:* 4765 Baptist Rd Pittsburgh PA 15227

BOGARD, DONALD DALE, GEOCHEMISTRY. *Current Pos:* cur, Antarctica Meteorite Collection, 78-84, discipline scientist, Planetary Mat Prog, 84-92, STAFF SCIENTIST, SOLAR SYST EXPLOR DIV, JOHNSON SPACE CTR, NASA, 68- *Personal Data:* b Fayetteville, Ark, Feb 6, 40. *Educ:* Univ Ark, Fayetteville, BS, 62, MS, 64, PhD(isotope geochem), 66. *Prof Exp:* Res fel geol sci, Calif Inst Technol, 66-68. *Concurrent Pos:* NSF fel, Calif Inst Technol, 66-67; assoc ed, J Geophys Res, Am Geophys Union, 75-77. *Mem:* AAAS; Geochem Soc; fel Meteoritical Soc (secy, 81-87). *Res:* Age and origin of planetary objects in the solar system; geochronology; isotope geochemistry nuclear reactions in nature; meteorites; over 100 published scientific papers. *Mailing Add:* 15506 Baybrook Dr Houston TX 77062. *E-Mail:* bogard@snmail.jsc.nasa.gov

BOGARD, TERRY L, ORGANIC CHEMISTRY, COMPUTER SCIENCE. *Current Pos:* res chemist, Lederle Labs Div, Am Cyanamid Co, 65-70, mgr, Process Develop & Clin Mat, Cyanamid Int Div, 71-80, mgr, Clin Mat, 81-83, mgr, Proj Analysis, Cyanamid Med Res Div, 83-87, mgr, area opers, Int Regulatory Affairs, 88-89, MGR, CL FILE & RES INFO SERV, AM CYANAMID CO, 89- *Personal Data:* b Bicknell, Ind, Aug 8, 36; m 62; c 3. *Educ:* Ohio State Univ, BSc, 58; Univ Calif, Los Angeles, PhD(org chem), 63. *Prof Exp:* Asst chem, Univ Calif, Los Angeles, 58-62; NIH fel, Swiss Fed Inst Technol, 62-64; fel, Brandeis Univ, 64-65. *Mem:* Am Chem Soc; Royal Soc Chem. *Res:* Theoretical, synthetic and natural products organic chemistry; polycyclic bridged compounds, alkaloids, terpenes and reaction mechanisms. *Mailing Add:* 102 W Prospect St Nanuet NY 10954-2633

BOGARDUS, CARL ROBERT, JR, MEDICINE, RADIOLOGY. *Current Pos:* from asst prof to assoc prof, 64-69, PROF RADIOL & VCHMN DEPT, MED CTR, UNIV OKLA, 69-, DIR DIV RADIATION THER, 66- *Personal Data:* b Hyden, Ky, June 26, 33; m 57; c 2. *Educ:* Hanover Col, BA, 55; Univ Louisville, MD, 59; Am Bd Radiol, cert therapeut radiol & nuclear med, 64; Am Bd Nuclear Med, dipl, 72. *Prof Exp:* Intern & resident therapeut radiol, Penrose Cancer Hosp, Colorado Springs, Colo, 63. *Concurrent Pos:* Res fel radiation physics, Mallinckrodt Inst Radiol, Sch Med, Wash Univ, 64. *Mem:* Am Soc Therapeut Radiol; Radiation Res Soc; Soc Nuclear Med; AMA; fel Am Col Radiol. *Res:* Cancer; radiation therapy, physics and biology; radioisotopes. *Mailing Add:* Okla Mem Hosp Radiation Ther Treatment Ctr PO Box 26307 Oklahoma City OK 73126-0307

BOGARDUS, EGBERT HAL, SOLID STATE SCIENCE. *Current Pos:* MGR ADVAN PROCESS CONTROL, SEMATECH, 92- *Personal Data:* b New York, NY, Feb 20, 31; m 53; c 3. *Educ:* Univ Tex, BS, 55; Pa State Univ, PhD(mat sci), 64. *Prof Exp:* Res assoc physics, Cornell Univ, 64-66; mem tech staff, Tex Instruments, Inc, Dallas, 66-68; staff physicist, IBM Components Div, IBM T J Watson Res Ctr, 69-73, adv physicist, 73-80, mem corp tech staff, 80-83, mgr advan mfg eng, Gen Prod Div, 83-85, mgr tech staff, Gen Technol Div, 85-86, mgr, Process Control Systs, 86-89, mfg tech staff, Gen Tech Div, 89-92. *Mem:* Am Phys Soc; Sigma Xi; Inst Elec & Electronics Engrs. *Res:* Optical characterization of III-V materials; ion implantation; magnetic properties of ferrofluids; surface properties of thin insulating films; electrical properties of ion-implanted devices. *Mailing Add:* 10802-B Pinehurst Dr Austin TX 78747. *E-Mail:* hal_bogardus@sematech.org

BOGART, BRUCE IAN, CELL BIOLOGY, GROSS ANATOMY. *Current Pos:* From instr to asst prof, 66-74, ASSOC PROF CELL BIOL, MED CTR, NY UNIV, 74-, COURSE DIR, GROSS ANAT, 79- *Personal Data:* b New York, NY, Sept 11, 39; c 2. *Educ:* Johns Hopkins Univ, BA, 61; NY Univ, PhD(basic med sci), 66. *Concurrent Pos:* Pres anat, Assoc Med Sch NY, 92-93. *Mem:* AAAS; Am Asn Anatomists; Am Soc Cell Biol; Am Asn Clin Anatomists; NY Acad Sci; Asn Res Vision & Ophthal. *Res:* Cell biology of secretion; salivary and lacrimal glands; cytophysiology, pharmacology and cytopathology of exocrine secretion; signal transduction; cell biology of tears and the interior eye. *Mailing Add:* Dept Cell Biol NY Univ Med Ctr 550 First Ave New York NY 10016. *Fax:* 212-263-8139

BOGART, KENNETH PAUL, COMBINATORICS, ORDERED SETS. *Current Pos:* from asst prof to assoc prof, 68-80, chair math & comput sci, 89-95, PROF MATH & COMPUT SCI, DARTMOUTH COL, 80- *Personal Data:* b Cincinnati, Ohio, Oct 6, 43; m 66, Ruth Tucker; c 2. *Educ:* Marietta Col, BS, 65; Calif Inst Technol, PhD(math), 68. *Prof Exp:* Asst instr, Marietta Col, 65-66; teaching asst, Calif Inst Technol, 66-68. *Concurrent Pos:* Ed, Perspectives on Discrete Appl Math, J Discrete Appl Math; trustee, Marietta Col. *Mem:* Math Asn Am; Am Math Soc; Soc Indust & Appl Math. *Res:* Abstract commutative ideal theory, noether lattices; lattice theory; ring theory; partically ordered sets; application of algebraic and combinatorial techniques to social and behavioral science problems; algebraic combinatorics; combinatorial algorithms; structural combinatories. *Mailing Add:* Dept Math & Comput Sci Dartmouth Col 6188 Bradley Hall Hanover NH 03755. *E-Mail:* k.p.bogart@dartmouth.edu

BOGART, MARCEL J(EAN) P(AUL), CHEMICAL ENGINEERING. *Current Pos:* RETIRED. *Personal Data:* b Paris, France, Apr 14, 13; nat US; m 47, 62; c 2. *Educ:* Cooper Union, BS, 33; Univ Mich, MSE, 34. *Prof Exp:* Chem engr, Lummus Co, 35-52, sr develop engr, 52-57, dir process develop, 57-62, sr process specialist, 62-67; supv develop engr, Fluor Engrs & Constructors, Inc, 67-83. *Concurrent Pos:* Guest lectr, Columbia Univ, 47-50; adj prof, Polytech Inst Brooklyn, 50-61. *Mem:* Fel Am Inst Chem Engrs; Sigma Xi; AAAS. *Res:* Reduction of pilot plant results to commercial practice; adaption of foreign processes to American industrial practice; aqua-ammonia absorption refrigeration. *Mailing Add:* 10602 Cordoba Ct Whittier CA 90601

BOGASH, R(ICHARD), CHEMICAL ENGINEERING. *Current Pos:* head, Prod Develop Lab Div, Wyeth Labs, 47-52, dir, Prod Div Div, 52-59, asst vpres res & develop, 59-68, vpres res & develop, 68-76, PRES RES & DEVELOP, WYETH LABS, 76-, CHMN & VPRES CORP DEVELOP, AM HOME PRODS, 78- *Personal Data:* b Philadelphia, Pa, Dec 26, 22; m 44; c 2. *Educ:* Univ Pa, BS, 43, MS, 47, PhD(chem eng), 49. *Prof Exp:* Asst, Manhattan Proj, Columbia Univ, 43-44; test engr, Insinger Mach Co, 44-46. *Mem:* Am Chem Soc. *Res:* Physiochemical properties of selected solvents near their critical temperatures; selective precipitation of enzymes; phenothiazines; antibiotics. *Mailing Add:* 101 Cheswold Lane Apt 4-F Haverford PA 19041-1865

BOGATY, HERMAN, RESEARCH ADMINISTRATION, TECHNOLOGY. *Current Pos:* RETIRED. *Personal Data:* b New York, NY, Apr 9, 18; m 38; c 2. *Educ:* City Col NY, BS, 40. *Prof Exp:* From sci aide to textile technologist, Bur Standards, 37-47; res assoc, Harris Res Labs, Inc, 47-58; assoc res dir, Toni Div, Gillette Co, 58-62, lab dir & vpres res & develop, 62-68; vpres res & develop, Consumer Prod Group, Warner Lambert Co, 68-75; pres, 75-81, Consult Res Mgt, Herman Bogaty Consult Corp, 81-88. *Mem:* Am Chem Soc; Fiber Soc; Soc Cosmetic Chem; AAAS; Inst Food Technol. *Res:* Research and development in toiletries, proprietaries, chewing gum and confections. *Mailing Add:* 1017 Laurel Hill Rd Chapel Hill NC 27514

BOGDAN, VICTOR MICHAEL, MATHEMATICS. *Current Pos:* assoc prof, 64-66, PROF MATH, CATH UNIV AM, 66- *Personal Data:* b Kiev, Ukraine, Jan 4, 33; nat US; m 68; c 2. *Educ:* Univ Warsaw, BS, 53, MS, 55; Polish Acad Sci, PhD(math), 60. *Prof Exp:* Asst math, Univ Warsaw, 52-53, asst, 53-55, from instr to asst prof, 55-61; res assoc, Univ Md, 61-62; from asst prof to assoc prof, Georgetown Univ, 62-64. *Concurrent Pos:* Mem res staff math inst, Polish Acad Sci, 55-61; NSF res grant, 64-65; vis scientist, Univ Montreal, 70-71; sr resident res assoc, Johnson Space Ctr, NASA, Houston, 78. *Mem:* Am Math Soc. *Res:* Functional analysis; linear methods of summability; integration theory; theory of distributions; differential equations in Banach spaces; almost periodic solutions of ordinary and partial differential equations; theory of random processes; computer mathematical software systems. *Mailing Add:* Dept Math Cath Univ Am 620 Michigan Ave NE Washington DC 20064-0001

BOGDANOFF, DAVID WELLS, SHOCK TUBES & SHOCK TUNNELS, LIGHT GAS GUNS & RAM ACCELERATORS. *Current Pos:* SR RES SCIENTIST, THERMOSCI INST, AMES RES CTR, NASA, 88- *Personal Data:* b Summit, NJ, Feb 25, 41; m 74, Sue Ellen Porter. *Educ:* McGill Univ, Montreal, BEng, 63; Princeton Univ, PhD(aerospace & mech sci), 68. *Prof Exp:* Postdoctoral fel, Princeton Plasma Physics Lab, 68-69 & Jet Propulsion Lab, 69-71; res engr, Plasma Physics Lab, Univ Calif, Los Angeles, 72, Physics Dept, Univ Southern Calif, Los Angeles, 73-75 & Aerospace & Energetics Res Prog, Univ Wash, 76-88. *Mem:* Am Inst Aeronaut & Astronaut; Aeroballistic Range Asn; Sigma Xi. *Res:* Co-invention and development of ram accelerator; improvement of performance of shock tubes; shock tunnels and light gas guns; development of gas optics-lenses, mirrors and light guides; shear layer mixing. *Mailing Add:* Ames Res Ctr NASA MS 230-2 Moffett Field CA 94035-1000

BOGDANOFF, JOHN LEE, ENGINEERING. *Current Pos:* from assoc prof to prof eng sci, 50-86, assoc head, Sch Aeronaut, Astronaut & Eng Sci, 67-72, EMER PROF AERONAUT & ASTRONAUT ENG, PURDUE UNIV, 86- *Personal Data:* b East Orange, NJ, May 25, 16; m 45; c 2. *Educ:* Syracuse Univ, BME, 38; Harvard Univ, MSE, 39; Columbia Univ, PhD(appl mech), 50. *Prof Exp:* Asst proj engr appl mech, Wright Aero Corp, 39-46; instr, Columbia Univ, 46-50. *Concurrent Pos:* Consult, Chatham Electronic Co, 47-49, Houdaille-Hersey, 53-54 & Allison Div, Gen Motors Corp, 53-63; dir & consult, Midwestern Appl Sci Corp, 57- *Mem:* Nat Acad Eng; Am Phys Soc; fel AAAS; fel Am Soc Mech Engrs. *Res:* Application of stochastic process in engineering; dynamics; vibration; elasticity; cumulative damages, fatigue and wear. *Mailing Add:* 327 Laurel Dr West Lafayette IN 47906

BOGDANSKI, DONALD FRANK, PHARMACOLOGY. *Current Pos:* PHARMACOLOGIST, LAB CHEM PHARMACOL, NAT HEART INST, 64- *Personal Data:* b Port Chester, NY, Oct 31, 28; m 59; c 4. *Educ:* Columbia Univ, BS, 50; Georgetown Univ, PhD, 54. *Prof Exp:* Lab asst pharmacol, Georgetown Univ, 52-53, lab asst biochem, 53; pharmacologist, Chem Pharmacol Lab, Nat Heart Inst, 54-58; spec res assoc from Med Sch, to Dept Neurophysiol, Walter Reed Army Inst Res, 58-64. *Mem:* AAAS; Am Soc Pharmacol & Exp Therapeut. *Res:* Binding and release of chemical transmitters in the peripheral nervous system; phylogenetic distribution of amines; transport, storage and release of chemical transmitters in the peripheral and central nervous system. *Mailing Add:* 10596 Spotted Horse Lane Columbia MD 21044-2214

BOGDEN, ARTHUR EUGENE, EXPERIMENTAL ONCOLOGY. *Current Pos:* RETIRED. *Personal Data:* b DuBois, Pa, Oct 6, 21; m 48; c 2. *Educ:* Univ Pa, BA, 52, MS, 53, PhD(med microbiol), 56. *Prof Exp:* Fel, Wistar Inst, 56-58, chief res serv, 58; chief, Div Cancer Immunol, Biochem Res Found, 58-63; dir immunobiol & exp oncol, 63, vpres, 68-; sci dir, EG&G Bodgen Lab, 84-96. *Concurrent Pos:* Sr res assoc, Med Sch, Univ Mass, 80- *Mem:* Am Asn Cancer Res; Am Asn Immunol; NY Acad Sci. *Res:* Immunobiology; immunogenetics; rat and rhesus blood groups; tumor cryopreservation; radiobiology; anti-inflammatory and hormone immunoassay viral-hormonal cocarcinogenesis; cancer chemotherapy and experimental oncology. *Mailing Add:* 7 Alden Rd West Yarmouth MA 02673

BOGDEN, JOHN DENNIS, TRACE ELEMENT NUTRITION, ENVIRONMENTAL TOXICOLOGY. *Current Pos:* Fel, NJ Med Sch, 71-72, Univ Med & Dent NJ Med Sch, from clin instr to instr, 73-75, from asst prof to assoc prof, 75-81, PROF PREV MED, UNIV MED & DENT, NJ MED SCH, 87- *Personal Data:* b Jersey City, NJ, Sept 5, 45; m 67, Doreen L Southard; c Jennifer L & Kimberly A. *Educ:* Brown Univ, ScB, 67; Seton Hall Univ, MS, 70, PhD(chem), 71. *Honors & Awards:* Labcatal Prize for Sci Res in the Field of Trace Elements, 91. *Concurrent Pos:* Prin investr, NIH, NJ Med Sch, 84-87; mem, bd dirs, Soc Environ Geochem & Health, 84-86; prin investr, Am Heart Asn, 82-83, 89-91 & 93-95, March of Dimes Birth Defects Fund, 92-93; hon vis prof, Henan Med Univ, Zhengzha, Peoples Repub China, 92. *Mem:* Am Chem Soc; Am Asn Univ Profs; Am Pub Health Asn; Am Col Nutrit; Am Inst Nutrit; Am Soc Clin Nutrit. *Res:* Trace element nutrition; trace element toxicology; lead poisoning, antioxidants; micronutrients and immune functions. *Mailing Add:* Dept Prev Med & Community Health 185 S Orange Ave Newark NJ 07103-2714. *Fax:* 973-982-7625

BOGDONOFF, MORTON DAVID, MEDICINE. *Current Pos:* exec assoc dean, 75-78, prof med, 75-, EMER PROF, CORNELL UNIV. *Personal Data:* b New York, NY, Dec 8, 25; m 51, 75, Mary P Welt; c 4. *Educ:* Cornell Univ Med Col, MD, 48. *Prof Exp:* From asst prof to prof, Duke Univ, 56-70, assoc dean, 68-70; prof & chmn, Dept Med, Univ Ill, 70-75. *Concurrent Pos:* Nat Counr, Am Fedn Clin Res, 60-65, pres, 64-65; mem, Presidential Adv Heart Panel, 71-72; ed, Clin Res, 58-64; chief ed, Archives Internal Med, 67-77, Drug Therapy, 77- & New Develop in Med 85-89. *Mem:* Asn Am Physicians; Am Soc Clin Invest; Am Fedn Clin Res; Endocrine Soc; Harvey Soc. *Res:* Metabolic processes; diabetes; autonomic nervous system; medical care; medical education. *Mailing Add:* Dept Med 1300 York Ave New York NY 10021. *Fax:* 212-746-8670

BOGDONOFF, PHILIP DAVID, JR, ANIMAL PHYSIOLOGY, ANIMAL NUTRITION. *Current Pos:* PRES, PEER GROUP, INC, 76- *Personal Data:* b Lowell, Mass, June 11, 27; wid; c Philip D III, Peter D & Paul D. *Educ:* Univ Md, BS, 51, MS, 53, PhD(physiol), 55. *Prof Exp:* Res analyst animal & human sci, Nat Acad Sci, 55-57; res nutritionist, Com Solvents Corp, 57-59, head animal nutrit res dept, 59-63; res assoc, Bio-Res Inst, Inc & Bio-Res Consult, Inc, 63-67; prof, N Shore Community Col, 70-72; vpres, Wheeler Assocs, Inc, 67-79. *Mem:* Sigma Xi. *Res:* Administration, research and educational development; consulting for personal and business asset management. *Mailing Add:* 17 Liberty Lane Exeter NH 03833

BOGDONOFF, SEYMOUR (MOSES), MECHANICAL ENGINEERING. *Current Pos:* from asst prof to prof aeronaut eng, Princeton Univ, 46-61, chmn, Dept Mech & Aerospace Eng, 73-81, Robert Porter Patterson prof aeronaut eng, 61-89, head, Gas Dynamics Lab, 53-89, EMER SR RES SCHOLAR & ROBERT PORTER PATTERSON PROF AERONAUT ENG, PRINCETON UNIV, 89- *Personal Data:* b New York, NY, Jan 10, 21; m 44; c 3. *Educ:* Rensselaer Polytech Inst, BAE, 42; Princeton Univ, MSE, 48. *Honors & Awards:* Fluid & Plasmadynamics Award, Am Inst Aeronaut & Astronaut, 83; Dryden Lectureship Res, Am Inst Aeronaut & Astronaut, 90; Except Civilian Serv Award, US Air Force. *Prof Exp:* Nat Adv Comt Aeronaut, 42-46. *Concurrent Pos:* Consult, US Air Force & various industs; mem, Fluid Mech Panel, Adv Group Aerospace Res & Develop, NATO, 67-76; mem, Aeronaut Adv Comt, NASA, 68-; mem, French Nat Academie of Air & Space, 90. *Mem:* Nat Acad Eng; fel Am Inst Aeronaut & Astronaut; Supersonic Tunnel Asn; Corresp mem Int Acad Astronaut; Am Soc Mech Engrs. *Res:* High speed gas dynamics; hypersonic and supersonic aerodynamics; energy; development of high speed research facilities, experimental research in supersonics and hypersonic low density flows; shock wave boundary layer interactions in two and three-dimensional configurations. *Mailing Add:* 39 Random Rd Princeton NJ 08540

BOGENSCHUTZ, ROBERT PARKS, PHYSIOLOGY, BIOLOGY. *Current Pos:* asst prof, 67-70, assoc prof, 70-77, PROF BIOL & PHYSIOL, CENT STATE UNIV, OKLA, 77- *Personal Data:* b Ponca City, Okla, Mar 25, 33. *Educ:* Okla State Univ, BS, 54, MS, 56; Cent State Col, Okla, BS, 61; Univ Okla, PhD(zool), 66. *Prof Exp:* Teacher, Am Sch London, 62-63; res assoc, Okla Univ Res Inst, 66; teacher, Am Int Sch, Vienna, 66-67. *Mem:* Am Inst Biol Sci; Am Soc Zool. *Res:* Effects of environmental factors on pituitary proteins and histology. *Mailing Add:* 1122 Huntington Ave Oklahoma City OK 73116

BOGER, DALE L, ORGANIC MEDICINAL CHEMISTRY. *Current Pos:* RICHARD & ALICE CRAMER CHAIR CHEM, SCRIPPS RES INST, 91- *Personal Data:* b Hutchinson, Kans, Aug 22, 53. *Educ:* Univ Kans, BS, 75; Harvard Univ, PhD(org chem), 80. *Honors & Awards:* A C Cope Scholar Award, Am Chem Soc, 88. *Prof Exp:* From asst prof to assoc prof med chem, Univ Kans, 79-85; from assoc prof to prof chem & med chem, Purdue Univ, 85-91. *Concurrent Pos:* Cottrell res grant, Res Corp, 80-81; Searle scholar, Chicago Comn Trust Co, Searle Family Found, 81-84; petrol res fund, Am Chem Soc, 81-83; career develop award, NIH, 83-88; Alfred P Sloan fel, 85-89. *Mem:* Am Chem Soc; AAAS. *Mailing Add:* Dept Chem Scripps Res Inst 10550 N Torrey Pines Rd La Jolla CA 92037. *Fax:* 619-554-6401

BOGER, EDWIN AUGUST, SR, PHYCOLOGY, MICROBIOLOGY. *Current Pos:* From instr to assoc prof, 68-80, PROF BIOL, WORCESTER STATE COL, 80- *Personal Data:* b Providence, RI, Oct 7, 23; m 46, 61, Margaret Pacey; c Christine L (Hanley) & Joanne P (Jenkins). *Educ:* Valparaiso Univ, BS, 61; Univ Conn, Storrs, MS, 68; Clark Univ, PhD(biol), 76. *Concurrent Pos:* Danforth Assoc, 77-83. *Mem:* AAAS; Sigma Xi; Am Soc Microbiol; Int Phycol Soc; Phycol Soc Am. *Res:* Chemical constituents of marine algae; nematode and other host-parasite relationships in algae; innovative science teaching and testing methods. *Mailing Add:* Dept Biol Worcester State Col 476 Chandler St Worcester MA 01602-2597

BOGER, PHILLIP DAVID, GEOLOGY. *Current Pos:* ASST PROF, DEPT GEOL, STATE UNIV NY, GENESEO, 76- *Personal Data:* b Xenia, Ohio, July 12, 43; m 75. *Educ:* Ohio State Univ, BSc, 66, PhD(geol), 76. *Prof Exp:* Grad teaching asst geol, Dept Mineral & Geol, Ohio State Univ, 70-71, grad admin assoc acad advisor, Univ Col, 71-73. *Concurrent Pos:* Res asst, Dept Mineral & Geol, Ohio State Univ, 73-74; co-prin & prin investr, NSF grants 74-76; fel, Grant-In-Aid, State Univ NY, 78-79 & Kodak, Geneseo, 78-79. *Mem:* Geol Soc Am. *Res:* Interpretation of the variation of strontium isotope ratios of various materials in terms of the geologic history of these materials. *Mailing Add:* Dept Geol Sci State Univ NY One College Circle Geneseo NY 14454

BOGER, WILLIAM PIERCE, MEDICINE. *Current Pos:* assoc prof psychiat & human behav & clin assoc prof med, 77-86, EMER PROF, JEFFERSON MED SCH, 86- *Personal Data:* b Johnstown, Pa, July 23, 13; m 43; c 2. *Educ:* Bucknell Univ, BS, 34; Harvard Univ, MD, 38; Am Bd Internal Med, dipl, 45. *Prof Exp:* Intern, Philadelphia Gen Hosp, 38-40; asst resident med, Mass Gen Hosp, 41-42; chief resident & instr, Med Col Va, 42-43; dir dept internal med & assoc, St Luke's Hosp, WVa, 43-44; assoc med dir, Sharp & Dohme, Inc, 45-51, med dir, 51-56; instr, Grad Sch & Sch Med, Univ Pa, 46-50, assoc med, 50-62; dir res & chief infectious dis, Montgomery Hosp, Norristown, 62-67; asst chief staff, Med Serv, 66-72, chief med serv, Vet Admin Hosp, Coatesville, 72-84. *Concurrent Pos:* Dir dept res therapeut, Norristown State Hosp, 52-62; dir int med affairs, McNeil Labs, 62-64; corp med dir, Miles Labs, Inc, 64-65, vpres res & med affairs, Dome Labs Div, 65-66. *Mem:* Am Col Physicians; fel Am Soc Pharmacol & Exp Therapeut; fel Endocrine Soc; fel Am Soc Clin Invest; fel Royal Soc Med. *Res:* Chemotherapy; antibiotics; internal medicine; metabolic disease. *Mailing Add:* 1675 Glenhardie Rd Wayne PA 19087-1003

BOGERT, BRUCE PLYMPTON, PHYSICS. *Current Pos:* RETIRED. *Personal Data:* b Waltham, Mass, Sept 26, 23; m 49, Marcia Mills; c Katherine & Joan. *Educ:* Mass Inst Technol, BS, 44, MS, 46, PhD(math), 48. *Honors & Awards:* Biennial Award, Acoustical Soc Am, 58. *Prof Exp:* Staff mem, Radiation Lab, Mass Inst Technol, 44-45; mem tech staff, Bell Labs, 48-81. *Mem:* Fel Acoustical Soc Am. *Res:* Digital transmission; seismic wave instrumentation and processing; underwater acoustics; digital computer analysis of time series. *Mailing Add:* 8 Penryn Way Rockport MA 01966. *E-Mail:* bpbogert@shore.net

BOGGESS, ALBERT, ACTIVE GALAXIES, SPACE INSTRUMENTATION. *Current Pos:* astrophysicist interstellar medium sect, 59-69, head observational astron br, 69-72, head astron systs br, 72-77, head advan syst develop br, 77-83, ASSOC DIR SCI, GODDARD SPACE FLIGHT CTR, NASA, 83- *Personal Data:* b Dallas, Tex, Jan 30, 29; m 52; c 3. *Educ:* Univ Tex, BA, 50; Univ Mich, MA, 52, PhD(astron), 54. *Prof Exp:* Fel, Johns Hopkins Univ, 54-55, consult, 55-56; physicist, Naval Res Lab, 55-58. *Mem:* Am Astron Soc; Int Astron Union. *Res:* Active galaxies; galactic nebulae; interstellar medium; high altitude research; stellar atmospheres; airglow. *Mailing Add:* 2420 Balsam Rd Boulder CO 80304

BOGGESS, GARY WADE, INORGANIC CHEMISTRY, CHEMICAL EDUCATION. *Current Pos:* from instr to assoc prof chem, 66-78, PROF & DEAN COL SCI, MURRAY STATE UNIV, 78- *Personal Data:* b Hardin, Ky, Aug 31, 36; m 54, Molly McKinney; c Bobby & Becky. *Educ:* Murray State Univ, BS, 62; Purdue Univ, MS, 66; Univ Tenn, PhD(chem), 73. *Prof Exp:* Teacher math & chem, Murray High Sch, 62-66. *Concurrent Pos:* Dir, NSF Integrated Sci Math Educ Proj, 77-; dir, Ctr Excellence & Reservoir Res. *Mem:* Am Chem Soc; AAAS; Sigma Xi. *Res:* High-temperature photoelectron spectroscopy; science and mathematics education for pre and in-service teachers; improvement of undergraduate inspection throughout Kentucky via PRISM an NSF-SSI initiative. *Mailing Add:* 506 Brewers Hwy Hardin KY 42048-9712

BOGGESS, NANCY WEBER, astronomy, for more information see previous edition

BOGGESS, WILLIAM RANDOLPH, FORESTRY. *Current Pos:* RETIRED. *Personal Data:* b Oakvale, WVa, Apr 9, 13; m 38; c 4. *Educ:* Concord Col, AB, 33; Duke Univ, MF, 40. *Prof Exp:* Teacher pub sch, WVa, 33-35; res assoc forester, Ala Agr Exp Sta, Ala Polytech Inst, 39-48; prof & assoc forest res, Dixon Springs Exp Sta, 48-58, prof forestry, 58-73, head dept, 69-73, emer prof forestry, Univ Ill, Urbana, 73-; environ consult, Lab Tree-Ring Res, Univ Ariz, 73-78, res assoc, 78-83. *Concurrent Pos:* Ed, Am Water Resources Asn Bull, 65-69 & 76-81. *Mem:* Soc Am Foresters; Am Soc Agron; Soil Sci Soc Am; Ecol Soc Am; Am Water Resources Asn (pres, 70, gen secy, 77-82). *Res:* Forest ecology; soils; forest influences. *Mailing Add:* 61 E Mediterranean Dr Tucson AZ 85704

BOGGIO, JOSEPH E, PHYSICAL CHEMISTRY. *Current Pos:* instr chem, 64-65, from asst prof to assoc prof, 65-75, PROF CHEM, FAIRFIELD UNIV, 75- *Personal Data:* b Holyoke, Mass, Mar 20, 36; m 58; c 2. *Educ:* Worcester Polytech Inst, BS, 58, MS, 60, PhD(phys chem), 63. *Prof Exp:* Res assoc surface chem, Brown Univ, 62-64. *Mem:* Am Phys Soc. *Res:* Theories of formation of very thin oxide films; contact potential studies of oxidizing metal surfaces; adsorption on the dropping mercury electrode; ellipsometry of metals and thin films. *Mailing Add:* Dept Chem Fairfield Univ Fairfield CT 06430

BOGGS, CAROL L, POPULATION BIOLOGY. *Current Pos:* Res assoc, 80-84, lectr biol, 84-89, CONSULT ASST PROF BIOL & PROG HUMAN BIOL, STANFORD UNIV, 89- *Personal Data:* b Ann Arbor, Mich, Apr 11, 52. *Educ:* Univ Tex, Austin, BA, 73, PhD(zool), 79. *Concurrent Pos:* Sr investr, Rocky Mountain Biol Lab, 78- *Res:* Resource allocation strategies, including male nutrient donations, using insects as a study system. *Mailing Add:* Dept Biol Sci Stanford Univ Stanford CA 94305-5020

BOGGS, GEORGE JOHNSON, PSYCHOACOUSTICS, ENGINEERING PSYCHOLOGY. *Current Pos:* MEM TECH STAFF, US WEST ADVAN TECHNOL, 90- *Personal Data:* b Beckley, WVa, Mar 2, 49. *Educ:* Marshall Univ, BS, 72, MS, 74; Purdue Univ, PhD(psychophysics), 81. *Prof Exp:* Psychologist, WVa Dept Health, Nicholas Ct Ment Health, 74-75, Cabell Ct Bd Educ, 75-77; mem tech staff, GTE Labs, 81-84, sr mem, 85-89. *Concurrent Pos:* Sr Fulbright res fel, Univ Nottingham, Eng, 84-85; Adj fac eng psychol, Northeastern Univ, 84-89. *Mem:* Acoust Soc Am; Soc Eng Psychologists; Am Psychol Asn; Asn Comput Mach; Sigma Xi; NY Acad Sci. *Res:* Mathematical and computer models of auditory signal processing; psychophysics of complex sounds and speech. *Mailing Add:* US West Advanced Technol 4001 Discovery Dr Suite 340 Boulder CO 80303

BOGGS, JAMES ERNEST, THEORETICAL CHEMISTRY, STRUCTURAL CHEMISTRY. *Current Pos:* PROF CHEM, UNIV TEX, AUSTIN, 53- *Personal Data:* b Cleveland, Ohio, June 9, 21; m 48, Ruth A Rogers; c Carol L, Ann S (McCarley) & Lynne (Cariker). *Educ:* Oberlin Col, BA, 43; Univ Mich, MS, 44, PhD(phys chem), 53. *Prof Exp:* Res chemist, Linde Air Prod Co, NY, 44-46; asst prof chem, Eastern Mich Univ, Mich, 48-52; instr, Univ Mich, 52-53. *Mem:* Am Chem Soc; Am Phys Soc. *Res:* Molecular structure and dynamics; microwave spectroscopy; theoretical chemistry. *Mailing Add:* Dept Chem Univ Tex Austin TX 78712. *Fax:* 512-471-8696; *E-Mail:* cmao757@hpcf.utexas.edu

BOGGS, JAMES H(ARLOW), MECHANICAL ENGINEERING. *Current Pos:* RETIRED. *Personal Data:* b Beaumont, Tex, Dec 10, 21; m 43; c 3. *Educ:* Okla State Univ, BS, 43, MS, 48; Purdue Univ, PhD(thermo & heat transfer), 53. *Prof Exp:* Jr engr, Airplane Div, Curtiss-Wright Corp, 43; from instr to prof mech eng, Okla State Univ, 43-57, head sch mech eng, 58-65, dean grad sch, 64-66, vpres acad affairs, 66-77, prof mech eng, 77-91, res coordr, 69-91, vpres acad affairs & res, 77-91. *Concurrent Pos:* Mem, Nat Adv Res Resources Coun, 70-74; ed, Mech Eng News. *Mem:* Fel Am Soc Mech Engrs. *Res:* Graduate education. *Mailing Add:* 924 Woodcrest Dr Stillwater OK 74074

BOGGS, JOSEPH D, PATHOLOGY. *Current Pos:* asst prof, 50-55, PROF PATH, NORTHWESTERN UNIV, CHICAGO, 55- *Personal Data:* b Bellefontaine, Ohio, Dec 31, 21. *Educ:* Ohio Univ, AB, 41; Jefferson Med Col, MD, 45. *Prof Exp:* Instr & assoc path, Harvard Univ, 46-50. *Concurrent Pos:* Dir labs, Children's Hosp, Chicago. *Mem:* Fel Am Soc Clin Pathologists; fel Col Am Pathologists. *Res:* Pediatric pathology. *Mailing Add:* Childs Mem Hosp 2300 Childrens Plaza Chicago IL 60614-3318

BOGGS, LAWRENCE ALLEN, CHEMISTRY OF CARBOHYDRATES, ISOLATION OF COMPONENTS FROM MIXTURES. *Current Pos:* RES CHEMIST, INST PAPER CHEM, APPLETON, WI, 74- *Personal Data:* b Spokane, Wash, June 14, 10; m 47; c 1. *Educ:* Univ Hawaii, BS, 38, MS, 39; Univ Minn, PhD(biochem), 51. *Prof Exp:* Asst chemist, Pac Chem & Fertilizer Co, Honolulu, 39-42; chemist, Pearl Harbor Navy Yard, Hawaii, 42-43; res chemist, 51-74. *Mem:* Am Chem Soc; AAAS. *Res:* Composition of fructosan from Hawaii Ti root; analyses of sugar components of spent sulfite liquor (paper pulp by-products); reactive solvent extraction; selective precipitation of non-sugars; isolation of sugar components of spent sulfite liquor. *Mailing Add:* 1705 Ravinia Pl Appleton WI 54915

BOGGS, PAUL THOMAS, NONLINEAR OPTIMIZATION, INTERIOR-POINT METHODS. *Current Pos:* comput scientist, 82-86, CHIEF, APPL & COMPUTATIONAL MATH DIV, NAT INST STAND & TECHNOL, 86- *Personal Data:* b Columbus, Ohio, Apr 14, 44; m 66, Judith E Watts; c Karen & Steven. *Educ:* Univ Akron, BS, 66; Cornell Univ, PhD(comput sci), 70. *Prof Exp:* Asst prof computer sci, Univ Kans, 70-72; asst prof math, Rensselear Polytech Inst, 72-75; mathematician, Math Div, US Army Res Off, 75-78, assoc dir, 78-82. *Concurrent Pos:* Adj prof, Univ NC, 76-82, NC State Univ, 76-82, Duke Univ, 78-82, Univ Colo, 82-85; assoc ed, Trans Math Software, Asn Comput Mach, 81-, Appl Math Lett, 87-, J Optimization, Soc Indust & Appl Math, 91-; chmn, activ group optimization, Soc Indust & Appl Math, 86-89. *Mem:* Soc Indust & Appl Math; Asn Comput Mach; Math Prog Soc. *Res:* Numerical methods for the solution of optimization problems, in particular, methods for constrained and unconstrained nonlinear optimization problems, and interior-point methods for large-scale linear and quadratic programming problems. *Mailing Add:* Nat Inst Stand & Technol Admin A-238 Nat Inst Stand & Technol Admin A-238 Bldg 101 Gaithersburg MD 20899. *Fax:* 301-990-4127; *E-Mail:* boggs@cam.nist.gov

BOGGS, ROBERT WAYNE, FOOD SCIENCE & TECHNOLOGY. *Current Pos:* Mem staff nutrit res, Procter & Gamble Co, 70-73, sect head, 73-76, assoc dir food & nutrit res, 76-83, ASSOC DIR CLIN & PRECLIN RES, MIAMI VALLEY LABS, PROCTER & GAMBLE CO, 78-, DIR HEALTH CARE, 83- *Personal Data:* b St Helena, Calif, Sept 17, 41; m 67, Donna Ferguson; c Jaci & Ryan. *Educ:* Fresno State Col, BS, 64; Univ Calif, Davis, PhD(nutrit & biochem), 70. *Concurrent Pos:* Vis prof, Med Sch, Univ Cincinnati, 72-73. *Mem:* Am Inst Nutrit; AAAS; Am Chem Soc; Sigma Xi. *Res:* Metabolic bone research; diabetes; exploratory biological research; animal science; clinical research; toxicology; pharmacology; physiology. *Mailing Add:* Procter & Gamble Co Health Care Res Ctr 8700 Mason-Montgomery Rd Cincinnati OH 45040. *Fax:* 513-622-0557

BOGGS, SALLIE PATTON SLAUGHTER, RADIOBIOLOGY. *Current Pos:* res asst prof med environ, 69-76, asst prof, 76-77, res assoc prof, 77-78, ASSOC PROF, MED & RADIOTHERAPY, UNIV PITTSBURGH, 78- *Personal Data:* b Roanoke, Va, Nov 25, 37; m 69; c 4. *Educ:* Emory Univ, BA, 59; Univ Calif, Berkley, MS, 63, PhD(biophys), 67. *Prof Exp:* Fel, Nat Cancer Inst, Nat Inst Health, 67-69. *Concurrent Pos:* Fel health physics, AEC, 63-67; guest worker, NIH, 64-67; fel, Leukemia Soc, 72-64, scholar, 75-80; mem adv comt blood diseases & resources, Nat Heart, Lung & Blood Inst, NIH, 76-80; mem NIH Hemat Study Sect, 86-90. *Mem:* Radiation Res Soc; Int Soc Exp Hemat; Am Soc Hemat. *Res:* Use of the murine transplant model and genetic modification to delineate mechanisms involved in leukemic transformation and regulation of normal hematopoietic stem cells in vivo. *Mailing Add:* 443 Morris St Pittsburgh PA 15218

BOGGS, SAM, JR, GEOLOGY. *Current Pos:* head, Dept Geol, 74-80, PROF GEOL SEDIMENTATION, UNIV ORE, 65- *Personal Data:* b King's Creek, Ky, July 26, 28; m 52, Sumiko Sasaki; c Barbara S (Lobasso), Steve R & Cindy L (Cady). *Educ:* Univ Ky, BS, 56; Univ Colo, PhD(geol), 64. *Prof Exp:* Explor geologist, Phillips Petrol Co, 56-61; res geologist, Jersey Prod Res Co, Exxon Res Co, NJ, 64-65. *Concurrent Pos:* Vis prof, Inst Oceanog, Nat Taiwan Univ, 72-73; res geologist, US Geol Surv, 66-81; vis prof, Res Scientists Foreign Specialists, Ocean Res Inst, Univ Tokyo, Japan, 81-82; scientist residence, Argonne Nat Lab, Univ Chicago, 82. *Mem:* Fel Geol Soc Am; Am Asn Petrol Geologists; Soc Sedimentary Geol. *Res:* Petrology of sedimentary rocks; emphasis on siliciclastic sedimentary rocks, especially provenance and diagenesis; marine geology; author of 4 books dealing with sedimentology and sedimentary petrology. *Mailing Add:* Dept Geol Sci Univ Ore Eugene OR 97403. *Fax:* 541-346-4692; *E-Mail:* sboggs@oregon.uoregon.edu

BOGGS, STEVEN ALLAN, ELECTRICAL INSULATION & DIELECTRONS, GASEOUS & SOLID DIELECTRICS. *Current Pos:* RES PROF & ASSOC DIR, ELEC INSULATION RES CTR, UNIV CONN, 93- *Personal Data:* b Mar 15, 46; US & Can citizen; m 68, Joan M Raymond. *Educ:* Reed Col, Portland, Ore, BA, 68; Univ Toronto, MS, 69, PhD(physics), 72, MBA, 88. *Prof Exp:* Sr res physicist, Ont Hydro Res, 75-87; dir res, Underground Systs, Inc, 87-93. *Concurrent Pos:* Prog comt, Conf Elec Insulation & Dielectric Phenomena, Inst Elec & Electronics Engrs, 80-, mem, Substa Comt & contrib ed, Elec Insulation Mag, 90-; adj prof elec eng, Univ Toronto, 91- *Mem:* Optical Soc Am; Inst Elec & Electronics Engrs Power Eng Soc; Inst Elec & Electronics Engrs Elec Insulation Soc; Inst Elec & Electronics Engrs Eng Mgt Soc. *Res:* High voltage systems for the transmission and control of electric power, especially those insulated with sulfur hexafluoride gas; underground transmission, including effects of soil thermal properties and the use of high temperature superconductors. *Mailing Add:* Elec Insulation Res Ctr Univ Conn Ins Math Sci Rm 102 Box U-136 Storrs CT 06269

BOGGS, WILLIAM EMMERSON, PHYSICAL CHEMISTRY, ANALYTICAL CHEMISTRY. *Current Pos:* RETIRED. *Personal Data:* b Zanesville, Ohio, May 9, 24; m 53, Hertha Faistauer; c William M & Karl E. *Educ:* Denison Univ, AB, 48; Carnegie Inst Technol, BS, 49, MS, 62. *Prof Exp:* Analytical chemist, State Health Dept, Ohio, 50; microchemist, Appl Res Lab, US Steel Corp, 51-58, sr technologist, 59-65, sr res engr, 65-66, assoc res consult, 66-82, res consult, 82-83. *Mem:* Am Chem Soc. *Res:* Oxidation of metals and alloys, tin and iron; instrumental and micro methods of chemical analysis; combustion of variable composition of gaseous fuels (coke oven gas & blast furnace gas). *Mailing Add:* 3761 Windover Rd Murrysville PA 15668

BOGITSH, BURTON JEROME, PARASITOLOGY, CYTOCHEMISTRY. *Current Pos:* assoc prof, 64-71, chmn dept, 72-75, 78-84, PROF BIOL, VANDERBILT UNIV, 71- *Personal Data:* b Brooklyn, NY, Feb 9, 29; m 51; c 4. *Educ:* NY Univ, AB, 49; Baylor Univ, MA, 54; Univ Va, PhD(biol), 57. *Honors & Awards:* Meritorious Serv Award, Southeastern Soc Parasitologists, 92. *Prof Exp:* From asst prof to prof biol, Ga Southern Col, 57-63; asst prog dir, NSF, 63-64. *Concurrent Pos:* Instr, Med Field Serv Sch, US Army, 52-54; NIH fel, Hammersmith, London, Eng, 73; Fulbright-Hayes fel, Egypt, 83; coun mem, Am Soc Parasitol, 88-90; vis researcher, Univ Leiden, Neth, 90; prog chmn, Am Soc Zoologists, 90-92. *Mem:* Am Soc Parasitol; Am Micros Soc (vpres, 78, pres, 85); Histochem Soc; Am Soc Zoologists. *Res:* Histochemistry of host-parasite relationships; ultrastructural localization of enzymes in helminths. *Mailing Add:* Dept Biol Vanderbilt Univ Box 1733 Sta B Nashville TN 37235. *Fax:* 615-343-0336

BOGLE, MARGARET L, CLINICAL NUTRITION. *Current Pos:* DIR CLIN NUTRIT, ARK CHILDREN'S HOSP, 76- *Educ:* Tex Women's Univ, PhD, 90. *Concurrent Pos:* Asst prof, Dept Pediat, Children's Hosp; chairperson, Am Dietitian Asn. *Mem:* Am Dietitians Asn. *Mailing Add:* Ark Children's Hosp 800 Marshall St Little Rock AR 72202-3591

BOGLE, ROBERT WORTHINGTON, EXPERIMENTAL PHYSICS. *Current Pos:* PRES, WORTH RES ASSOCS, 81- *Personal Data:* b Chicago, Ill, Dec 25, 18; m 42; c 3. *Educ:* Univ Mich, BS, 41, MS, 42, PhD(physics), 48. *Prof Exp:* Asst, Off Sci Res & Develop, Nat Defense Res Comt, US Navy & Manhattan Dist contracts, Univ Mich, 42-43, assoc, 43-44, physicist, 44-48; physicist, Appl Physics Lab, Johns Hopkins Univ, 48-58; sr scientist,

Santa Barbara Div, Curtiss-Wright Corp, 58-60; mgr Pac Range eng, Gen Elec Co, 60-64; mem, Appl Sci Staff, Gen Res Corp, 64-69; prog dir, Astro Res Corp, 69-71; mem, Radar Analysis Staff, US Naval Res Lab, 71-79; sect chief, US Dept Com Inst Telesci, 79-81. *Concurrent Pos:* Parsons fel, Johns Hopkins Univ, 56-57. *Mem:* Am Phys Soc; Am Inst Aeronaut & Astronaut; Am Geophys Union. *Res:* Experimental research in radar geophysics; applied research in physics; electronics; hypersonic fluid mechanics; system development and analysis. *Mailing Add:* 991 Skylark Dr La Jolla CA 92037

BOGLE, TOMMY EARL, SOLID STATE PHYSICS. *Current Pos:* from asst prof to assoc prof, 68-77, PROF PHYSICS, MCNEESE STATE UNIV, 77- *Personal Data:* b Logansport, La, Sept 4, 40; m 62; c 1. *Educ:* Va Polytech Inst, BS, 62; La State Univ, PhD(physics), 68. *Prof Exp:* Design engr, Tex Instruments, Inc, 62-63. *Mem:* Am Phys Soc; Am Inst Physics. *Res:* Investigation of Fermi surface of metals at liquid helium temperatures using the magneto-acoustic effect. *Mailing Add:* 438 Greenway St Lake Charles LA 70605

BOGNER, FRED K, STRUCTURAL MECHANICS, FINITE ELEMENT STRESS ANALYSIS. *Current Pos:* from asst prof to prof mech eng & res engr, 69-84, prof & chmn dept civil eng & eng mech, 84-96, PROF, DEPT CIVIL ENG & ENG MECH, UNIV DAYTON, 96- *Personal Data:* b Mansfield, Ohio, July 7, 39; m 59, Mary Reynolds; c Fred C & Sharon L. *Educ:* Case Inst Technol, BS, 61, MS, 64, PhD(eng mech), 67. *Prof Exp:* Mem tech staff anal mech, Bell Tel Labs, 67-69. *Mem:* Am Inst Aeronaut & Astronaut; Am Acad Mech; Am Soc Civil Engrs; Soc Eng Sci. *Res:* Finite element analysis; nonlinear structural analysis; plates and shells; structural dynamics; elastic-plastic structures; composite structures analysis. *Mailing Add:* Dept Civil Engr & Eng Mech Univ Dayton Dayton OH 45469-0243. *E-Mail:* fbogner@engr.udayton.edu

BOGNER, PHYLLIS HOLT, PHYSIOLOGY. *Current Pos:* assoc prof, 70-78, asst dean student affairs, 76-81, assoc, Educ Systs Sect, Ctr For Educ Develop, 70-73, PROF PHARMACOL, SCH BASIC MED SCI, COL MED, UNIV ILL, 78-, ASSOC DEAN CURRIC & STUDENT AFFAIRS, 81- *Personal Data:* b Middleboro, Mass, Mar 26, 30; m 56, 77; c 2. *Educ:* Tufts Univ, BS, 52; Brown Univ, MSc, 54; Univ Md, PhD, 57. *Prof Exp:* Asst, Tufts Univ, 50, Brown Univ, 52-54, Columbia Univ, 54-55 & Univ Md, 55-57; instr physiol & pharmacol, Sch Med, Univ Pittsburgh, 57-61, from asst prof to assoc prof pharmacol, 61-70. *Mem:* AAAS; Am Physiol Soc; Am Soc Zoologists; NY Acad Sci. *Res:* Development of mechanisms responsible for transport of monosaccharides across the intestinal wall; developmental physiology of the gastrointestinal tract; effectiveness of audiotutorials versus the lecture-mode of teaching at the medical school level. *Mailing Add:* 13623 Gemstone Dr Sun City West AZ 85375-5343

BOGORAD, LAWRENCE, PLANT PHYSIOLOGY, MOLECULAR BIOLOGY. *Current Pos:* chmn dept, Harvard Univ, 74-76, prof biol, 67-80, Maria Moors Cabot prof biol, 80-92, MARIA MOORS CABOT EMER PROF BIOL, HARVARD UNIV, 92- *Personal Data:* b Tashkent, Russia, Aug 29, 21; nat US; m 43, Rosalyn G Sagen; c Leonard Paul, Kiki (Gross). *Educ:* Univ Chicago, SB, 42, PhD(plant physiol), 49. *Hon Degrees:* MA, Harvard Univ, 67. *Honors & Awards:* Quantrell Award, Univ Chicago, 60; Stephen Hales Award, Am Soc Plant Physiol, 82. *Prof Exp:* Instr bot, Univ Chicago, 48-51, from asst prof to assoc prof, 53-61, prof, 61-67. *Concurrent Pos:* Nat Res Coun-Merck fel, Rockefeller Inst, 51-53; Fulbright res scholar & NSF sr fel div plant indust, Commonwealth Sci & Indust Res Orgn, Australia, 60; NSF sr fel biochem, Nobel Inst Med, Sweden, 61; NIH career award, 63-67; chmn sect molecular bot, Int Bot Cong, Seattle, 68; chmn, Gordon Conf Pyrrolic Compounds, 70 & Gordon Conf Plant Molecular Biol, 80; chmn, Bot Sect, Nat Acad Sci, 74-77; dir, Maria Moors Cabot Found, 75-87; ed-in-chief, Proceedings Nat Acad Sci, 91-95; coun mem, Nat Acad Sci, 89-92, Am Soc Cell Biol, 71-74. *Mem:* Nat Acad Sci; Am Soc Plant Physiol (pres, 68); fel Am Acad Arts & Sci; Am Soc Cell Biol; Am Soc Biol Chem; Soc Devel Biol (pres, 83-84); AAAS (bd dirs, 82-85, pres, 86-87, chmn bd dirs, 87-88); Am Philos Soc; foreign mem Royal Danish Acad Arts & Sci. *Res:* Plant molecular developmental biology; chloroplasts; eukaryotic organelle biology; molecular biology of chloroplasts and blue-green algae. *Mailing Add:* Biol Labs Harvard Univ 16 Divinity Ave Cambridge MA 02138. *Fax:* 617-495-4292, 496-5783; *E-Mail:* bogorad@biosun,harvard.edu

BOGOROCH, RITA, TOXICOLOGY. *Current Pos:* CONSULT, OCCUP HEALTH & MED RES, 87- *Personal Data:* b Montreal, Que. *Educ:* McGill Univ, BS, MS, 51; Univ Ottawa, PhD(anat & histol), 72. *Prof Exp:* Prof & res, Harvard Med Sch, 51-58, Sch Med, Univ Calif, 58-73; res mgr toxicol, Nat Health & Welfare, Ottawa, Can, 73-79; dir health effects, Nat Coun Paper Indust, 79-83; prin toxicologist, Arco Chem Co, 83-87. *Mem:* Am Soc Cell Biol. *Mailing Add:* 300 E 75th St No 18H New York NY 10021-3376

BOGOSIAN, GREGG, GENETICS. *Current Pos:* sr res biologist, 85-87, res specialist, 87-90, RES FEL, MONSANTO CORP, 90- *Educ:* Purdue Univ, PhD(biochem), 83. *Prof Exp:* Postdoctoral fel, Univ NC, 83-85. *Mem:* Fed Am Soc Exp Biol; Am Soc Microbiol. *Mailing Add:* Monsanto Corp 700 Chesterfield Pkwy N Chesterfield MO 63198

BOGUCKI, RAYMOND FRANCIS, INORGANIC CHEMISTRY. *Current Pos:* chmn dept, 68-78, PROF CHEM, UNIV HARTFORD, 68- *Personal Data:* b Wallingford, Conn, Mar 6, 28; m 54; c 5. *Educ:* Col Holy Cross, BS, 53, MS, 54; Clark Univ, PhD(chem), 59. *Prof Exp:* Instr chem, Lafayette Col, 54-56; res fel, Clark Univ, 59; from asst prof to assoc prof, Boston Col, 59-68. *Concurrent Pos:* Vis prof, Middle East Tech Inst, Ankara, 64-65, Purdue Univ, 66-68, Tex A&M Univ, 74-75 & NC State Univ, 82. *Mem:* Am Chem Soc; Sigma Xi. *Res:* Reactions of metal chelate compounds in aqueous solution; polynuclear metal chelates; metal coordination polymers. *Mailing Add:* 253 Hill Hollow Rd Petersburg NY 12138-9735

BOGUE, DONALD CHAPMAN, CHEMICAL ENGINEERING. *Current Pos:* from asst prof to prof chem eng, 60-76, ALUMNI DISTINGUISHED SERV PROF CHEM ENG, UNIV TENN, KNOXVILLE, 76- *Personal Data:* b St Petersburg, Fla, Jan 9, 32. *Educ:* Ga Inst Technol, BChE, 53; Univ Del, PhD(chem eng), 60. *Prof Exp:* Process engr, Esso Standard Oil Co, La, 53-54. *Concurrent Pos:* Vis lectr, Kyoto Univ; consult, Tenn Eastman Co, 70- *Mem:* Soc Rheol; Am Inst Chem Engrs; Am Chem Soc; Am Soc Eng Educ. *Res:* Non-Newtonian fluids and general rheological problems. *Mailing Add:* Dept Chem Eng Univ Tenn Knoxville TN 37996-2200

BOGUSLASKI, ROBERT CHARLES, IMMUNOCHEMISTRY, CLINICAL CHEMISTRY. *Current Pos:* res scientist to sr res scientist, 67-75, mgr Immunochem Lab, 75-76, dir, 76-81, VPRES RES & DEVELOP, AMES DIV, MILES LABS, INC, 81- *Personal Data:* b Grand Rapids, Mich, Feb 22, 41; m 71; c 2. *Educ:* Aquinas Col, BS, 62; Univ Notre Dame, PhD(org chem), 66. *Honors & Awards:* IC 100 Award, Indust Res Coun, 81. *Prof Exp:* Fel, Univ Calif Med Ctr San Francisco, 66-67. *Mem:* AAAS; Am Chem Soc; Sigma Xi. *Res:* Development of novel, convenient analytical methods for use in the clinical laboratory, with special emphasis on homogeneous, now-radioisotopic immunoassay methods. *Mailing Add:* Serim Res Corp PO Box 4002 Elkhart IN 46512-0002

BOGY, DAVID B, SOLID & FLUID MECHANICS. *Current Pos:* from asst prof to assoc prof mech eng, 67-75, vchmn grad studies, 77-80, PROF MECH ENG, UNIV CALIF, BERKELEY, 75-, DIR, COMPUT MECH LAB, 89-, CHMN, DEPT MECH ENG, 91-, WILLIAM S FLOYD JR ENDOWED CHAIR PROF ENG, 93- *Personal Data:* b Wabbaseka, Ark, June 4, 36; m 61, Patricia Pizzitola; c Susan & Rebecca. *Educ:* Rice Univ, BS, 59, MS, 61; Brown Univ, PhD(appl math), 66. *Prof Exp:* Res engr, Shell Develop Co, 61-62; co comdr, US Army CEngrs, 62-63; fel, Div Eng & Appl Sci, Calif Inst Technol, 66-67. *Concurrent Pos:* Eng consult, US & foreign corps, 71-; mem-at-large, US Nat Comt Theoret & Appl Mech, Nat Res Coun, 87-, chmn, Subcomt Res Directions in Mech, 92-; prin investr, Digital Equip Corp, 89-, IBM, 90- & NSF, 91-92. *Mem:* Nat Acad Eng; fel Am Soc Mech Engrs; Am Acad Mech; sr mem Inst Elec & Electronics Engrs. *Res:* Solid and fluid mechanics, especially as regards their application to mechanical aspects in computer technology; mechanics of particular configurations associated with computer magnetic recording disk drives; stability of packs of flexible disks and the study of vibrations and deflection of rotating flexible disks; mechanics of fluid jets in ink jet printers and fuser mechanics in electrophotography copiers. *Mailing Add:* Dept Mech Eng Univ Calif-6189 Etcheverry Hall Berkeley CA 94720

BOGYO, THOMAS P, GENETICS, STATISTICS. *Current Pos:* asst statistician, Wash State Univ, 62-65, assoc statistician, 65-70, from asst prof to assoc prof bot & info sci, 64-66, from assoc prof to prof genetics, 66-82, statistician, 70-82, EMER PROF GENETICS & STATISTICIAN, WASH STATE UNIV, 82- *Personal Data:* b Budapest, Hungary, July 14, 18; US citizen; m 46; c 5. *Educ:* Jozsef Nador Univ, Budapest, DSc(agr bot) 41; NC State Univ, MES, 63. *Prof Exp:* Plant breeder, Hungarian Plant Breeding Co, 41-45; asst prof genetics, Jozsef Nador Univ, Budapest, 45-46; asst dir, Hungarian Inst Genetics, 46-47; sr prof officer genetics, SAfrican Dept Agr, 56-58, chief prof officer genetics & agron, 56-60. *Mem:* Biomet Soc; Genetics Soc Am. *Res:* Genotype-environment interaction; simulation of genetic systems on electronic computers; experimental designs; selection. *Mailing Add:* 465 Sherwood Loop Florence OR 97439

BOHACEK, PETER KARL, ENGINEERING. *Current Pos:* VPRES, TANDEM COMMUNICATIONS SYSTS, 89- *Personal Data:* b Olomouc, Czech, Mar 4, 36; US citizen; m 60; c 4. *Educ:* Yale Univ, BE, 58, MEng, 59, PhD(elec eng), 63. *Prof Exp:* Instr elec eng, Mass Inst Technol, 62-63, asst prof, 63-64, Ford fel, 62-64; mem tech staff, Bell Tel Labs, Inc, 64-68, dept head, 68-80, dir, 80-83; dir, AT&T, NJ, 83-86, vpres, 86-89. *Mem:* Inst Elec & Electronics Engrs; Sigma Xi. *Res:* Synchronization of coherent detectors; distortion of signals passing through plasma; signal processing; detection theory; real time data processing and system design; switching systems engineering; network planning. *Mailing Add:* Tandem Communications Systs 1255 W 15th St Plano TX 75075

BOHACHEVSKY, IHOR O, FLUID MECHANICS, APPLIED MATHEMATICS. *Current Pos:* RETIRED. *Personal Data:* b Sokal, Ukraine, Sept 7, 28; US citizen; div; c 9. *Educ:* NY Univ, BAE, 56, PhD(math), 61. *Honors & Awards:* W O Bryans Medal, 56; Shewell Prize, 86; T Saaty Prize, 89. *Prof Exp:* Assoc res scientist, NY Univ, 60-63, adj asst prof aeronaut, 61-63; aerodyn res engr, Cornell Aeronaut Lab, 63-66; prin res scientist, Avco-Everett Res Lab, 66-68; staff mem, Bell Tel Lab, Inc, 68-75 & Los Alamos Nat Lab, 75-87; staff scientist, Rocketdyne, Div Rockwell Int, 87-93. *Mem:* Soc Indust & Appl Math; Am Inst Aeronaut & Astronaut; Sigma Xi; NY Acad Sci. *Res:* Magnetohydrodynamics; numerical methods in fluid mechanics; nonlinear wave propagation; geophysical fluid mechanics; mathematical economics; gas dynamics; problems related to laser applications and to laser initiated fusion reactor development; advanced weapons concepts; nonlinear optimization theory. *Mailing Add:* 3 Loma Vista St Los Alamos NM 87544

BOHACS, KEVIN MICHAEL, PALEOENVIRONMENTAL ANALYSIS. *Current Pos:* RES GEOLOGIST, EXXON PROD RES CO, 81- *Personal Data:* b Port Chester, NY, Oct 2, 54. *Educ:* Univ Conn, BSc, 76; Mass Inst Technol, DSc, 81. *Mem:* Soc Econ Paleontologists & Mineralogists; Sigma Xi. *Res:* Process oriented sedimentology; physical and sequence stratigraphy; operation of sediment-transport processes in depositional environments: record they leave, and how the record in the rocks may be used to interpret paleoenvironments. *Mailing Add:* 10018 Sugar Hill Dr Houston TX 77042-1540

BOHAN, THOMAS STEPHEN LYNCH, FORENSIC PHYSICS, PATENT LAW. *Current Pos:* DIR, MED & TECH CONSULTS, 82-; ATTY, THOMAS L BOHAN & ASSOC, 82- *Personal Data:* b Terre Haute, Ind, Feb 12, 38; US & Irish citizen; m 60, 87, Rhonda B Berg; c Richard M, Cecilia A & John C. *Educ:* Univ Chicago, SB, 60; Univ Ill, Urbana, MS, 64, PhD(physics), 68; Franklin Pierce Law Ctr, JD, 80. *Prof Exp:* Res physicist, Fansteel Metall Corp, 60-62; res assoc physics, Univ Ill, Urbana, 68-69; asst prof, Bowdoin Col, 69-76; lawyer, Sunenblick, Fontaine & Reben, 80-82. *Concurrent Pos:* Prin investr, Am Heart Asn, 70-76, Res Corp, 74-76; Fulbright vis prof physics, Nat Univ San Marcos, 72-73 & 73-74; forensic consult, 76-82; chair, Eng Sci Sect, Am Acad Forensic Sci, 97-98. *Mem:* Fel Am Acad Forensic Sci; Am Phys Soc; AAAS; Am Soc Testing & Mat; Soc Automotive Engrs. *Res:* Magnetic resonance spectroscopy at low temperatures; cloud seeding; motor vehicle dynamics; writing on issues related to scientific evidence. *Mailing Add:* 371 Fore St Portland ME 04101. *Fax:* 207-773-4585; *E-Mail:* tlb@mtcforensics.com, tbohan1@maine.rr.com

BOHANDY, JOSEPH, SOLID STATE PHYSICS, OPTICAL SPECTROSCOPY. *Current Pos:* RETIRED. *Personal Data:* b Barnesville, Ohio, July 9, 38; m 59; c 2. *Educ:* Ohio State Univ, BS, 60, MS, 61, PhD(physics), 65. *Prof Exp:* Sr physicist, Appl Physics Lab, Johns Hopkins Univ, 65- *Mem:* Am Phys Soc. *Res:* Electron paramagnetic resonance used for study of magnetism and magnetic properties of crystalline solids; optical spectroscopy of biologically significant molecules. *Mailing Add:* 11775 Stone Gate Lane Columbia MD 21044

BOHANNON, RICHARD WALLACE, PHYSICAL THERAPY. *Current Pos:* PROF PHYS THER, UNIV CONN, 87- *Personal Data:* b Salisbury, NC, Dec 29, 53; m 89, Lucie McKeon; c Stephanie Jean. *Educ:* Univ NC, Chapel Hill, BS, 77, MS, 82; NC State Univ, EdD(adult educ), 88. *Honors & Awards:* Res Award, Neurol Sect, Am Phys Ther Asn, 90; Hislop Award, Am Phys Ther Asn, 96. *Prof Exp:* Chief phys therapist, Univ Ill Hosp, 82; chief phys therapist, SE Regional Rehab Ctr, 83-87. *Concurrent Pos:* Asst ed, Clin Rehab, 88-; coordr clin res, Dept Rehab, Hartford Hosp, 89-; assoc edd, Percept Mot Skills, 93- *Mem:* Am Phys Ther Asn; Nat Stroke Asn; Am Soc Neurorehab; Am Congress Rehab Med. *Res:* Human movement studies; muscular function in patients with stroke; measurement of muscular performance. *Mailing Add:* Sch Allied Health U-101 Univ Conn Storrs CT 06269. *Fax:* 860-486-1588; *E-Mail:* bohannon@neca.com

BOHANNON, ROBERT ARTHUR, SOIL SCIENCE. *Current Pos:* exten specialist & agronomist crops & soils, 52-55, 56-61, asst to dean agr, 61-65, actg head dept agron, 65-66, dir int agr progs, 66-68, assoc prof, 51-61, dir exten serv, 68-76, PROF AGRON, KANS STATE UNIV, 61-, EXTEN SPECIALIST, SOIL & WATER CONSERV, 76- *Personal Data:* b Holton, Kans, Feb 5, 22; m 46; c 3. *Educ:* Mich State Univ, BS, 49; Kans State Univ, MS, 51; Univ Ill, PhD, 57. *Prof Exp:* County agent, Nemaha County, Kans, 51-52. *Concurrent Pos:* Fel, Univ Mich, 64-65; chmn exten comt, Great Plains Agr Coun, 71. *Mem:* Am Soc Agron; Soil Sci Soc Am. *Res:* Soil testing, soil fertility, and reduced tillage. *Mailing Add:* 210 York Rd Greenville NC 27858-5601

BOHANNON, ROBERT C, MOLECULAR VIROLOGY, VACCINE & IMMUNODIAGNOSTICS. *Current Pos:* MICROBIOLOGIST & VIROLOGIST, DUGWAY PROVING GROUNDS, US ARMY, 94- *Educ:* Univ Colo, BA, 86; Baylor Univ, PhD(molecular virol), 91. *Prof Exp:* Chief sci officer & res scientist, Biomed Res labs, 92-94. *Concurrent Pos:* Proj investr, MD Anderson Cancer Ctr, Tex, 92-94. *Res:* Rapid detection devices for biologic warfare agents; vaccines and immunodiagnostic devices. *Mailing Add:* US Army Dugway Proving Ground Bldg 2028 WD-L-T Dugway UT 84022

BOHANNON, ROBERT GARY, GEOLOGY. *Current Pos:* GEOLOGIST, DEPT INTERIOR, US GEOL SURV, 74- *Personal Data:* b Hollywood, Calif, Feb 17, 49; m 70. *Educ:* Glendale Col, AA, 69; Calif State Univ, Northridge, BS, 71; Univ Calif, Santa Barbara, PhD(geol), 76. *Prof Exp:* Teaching asst geol, Univ Calif, Santa Barbara, 71-74. *Mem:* Geol Soc Am. *Res:* Structural geology, geochemistry and sedimentology of the Muddy Mountains, southern Nevada; occurences of lithium in the western United States. *Mailing Add:* 577 Anchor Circle Redwood City CA 94065

BOHANON, JOSEPH TERRIL, ANALYTICAL CHEMISTRY. *Current Pos:* PROF CHEM & CHMN DEPT SCI & TECHNOL, EVANGEL COL, 63- *Personal Data:* b Los Angeles, Calif, June 10, 39; m, Margaret Coletti; c Joseph P & Jason A. *Educ:* Univ Calif, Los Angeles, BS, 60; Howard Univ, MS, 67; Univ Mo, Rolla, Phd(chem), 70. *Concurrent Pos:* Consult, Onscreen Corp, 85-88; analytical chemist, TSL Labs. *Mem:* Am Chem Soc; Sigma Xi; AAAS. *Res:* Organic chemistry. *Mailing Add:* Evangel Col 111 N Glenstone Springfield MO 65802-2191

BOHART, RICHARD MITCHELL, ENTOMOLOGY. *Current Pos:* from asst prof to assoc prof, 46-58, from vchmn to chmn dept, 57-67, prof, 58-80, EMER PROF ENTOM, COL AGR, UNIV CALIF, DAVIS, 80- *Personal Data:* b Palo Alto, Calif, Sept 28, 13; m 39. *Educ:* Univ Calif, BS, 34, MS, 35, PhD(entom), 38. *Prof Exp:* Asst, Univ Calif, 35-37; assoc entom, Univ Calif, Los Angeles, 38-39, instr & jr entomologist, Exp Sta, 39-46. *Mem:* Am Entom Soc. *Res:* Taxonomy of Strepsiptera Vespidae Chrysididae and Sphecidae; biology; taxonomy and control of mosquitoes. *Mailing Add:* Dept Entom Univ Calif Davis CA 95616

BOHEN, JOSEPH MICHAEL, ORGANIC CHEMISTRY. *Current Pos:* MGR NEW BUS DEVELOP, ELF ATOCHEM NA, 92- *Personal Data:* b Philadelphia, Pa, Feb 8, 46; m 69; c 2. *Educ:* Temple Univ, AB, 68; Univ Pa, PhD(chem), 73; St Joseph Univ, MBA, 92. *Prof Exp:* Proj leader, Pennwalt Corp, 73-80, group leader, 80-83, venture mgr, 83-92. *Concurrent Pos:* Instr, Univ Pa, 74-75. *Mem:* Am Chem Soc; Soc Plastics Engrs. *Res:* Organometallic compounds; heterocumulenes; cycloaddition reactions of heterocumulenes; photochemistry. *Mailing Add:* 540 Morwyck Dr King of Prussia PA 19406-1583

BOHI, DOUGLAS RAY, ECONOMICS. *Current Pos:* sr fel, 78-87, DIV DIR, RESOURCES FOR FUTURE, 88- *Personal Data:* b Pocatello, Idaho, Sept 9, 39; m, Marjorie A Brenner; c Heidi & James. *Educ:* Idaho State Univ, BS, 62; Wash State Univ, PhD(econ), 67. *Prof Exp:* Economist, Caterpiller Co, 69-70; prof econ, Southern Ill Univ, Carbondale, 70-78. *Concurrent Pos:* Fulbright scholar, Erasmus Univ, Neth, 77; vis prof, Monash Univ, Australia, 82; chief economist, Fed Energy Regulatory Comn, 87-88. *Mem:* Am Econ Asn. *Res:* Analyzing demand behavior; oil prices, energy security and import policy; analyzing nonrenewable resource supply. *Mailing Add:* 8121 Thoreau Dr 1616 P St NW Bethesda MD 20817

BOHINSKI, ROBERT CLEMENT, BIOCHEMISTRY. *Current Pos:* from asst prof to assoc prof chem, 71-74, PROF CHEM, JOHN CARROLL UNIV, 74- *Personal Data:* b Wilkes-Barre, Pa, Apr 11, 40; m 61; c 3. *Educ:* Scranton Univ, BS, 61; Pa State Univ, MS, 63, PhD(biochem), 65. *Honors & Awards:* Distinguished Fac Award, John Carroll Univ, 73. *Prof Exp:* Res biochemist, Charles Pfizer & Co, Inc, 65-66. *Mem:* AAAS; Sigma Xi. *Res:* Growth and survival characteristics of bacteria under conditions of phosphate, sulfate and nitrogen deficiencies with specific emphasis on sulfur metabolism and turnover of ribosomes. *Mailing Add:* Dept Chem John Carroll Univ 20700 N Park Blvd Cleveland OH 44118-4520

BOHL, ROBERT W, METALLURGICAL & NUCLEAR ENGINEERING. *Current Pos:* From instr to assoc prof metall eng, 46-59, prof, 59-81, EMER PROF METALL & NUCLEAR ENG, UNIV ILL, URBANA-CHAMPAIGN, 81- *Personal Data:* b Peoria, Ill, Sept 29, 25; m 47, Marie Reace; c Nancy (Williams), Betty (Kepley), Barbara & Robert. *Educ:* Univ Ill, BS, 46, MS, 49, PhD(metall eng), 56. *Concurrent Pos:* Partic Atomic Energy Comn-Am Soc Eng Educ Nuclear Eng Inst, Argonne Nat Lab, 57, 58, 60 & 62, Ames Lab, 58 & Hanford Lab, 62; res assoc, Argonne Nat Lab, 61, 68 & 69 & Battelle Mem Inst, 63, 64, 66 & 67. *Mem:* Fel Am Soc Metals; Am Inst Mining, Metall & Petrol Engrs; Am Soc Eng Educ; Sigma Xi. *Res:* Thermodynamics of metal alloy systems; physical metallurgy of materials for nuclear engineering; materials for nuclear engineering; failure analysis. *Mailing Add:* 2014 S George Huff Dr Urbana IL 61801. *Fax:* 217-333-2736

BOHLEN, HAROLD GLENN, CARDIOVASCULAR PHYSIOLOGY. *Current Pos:* ASST PROF PHYSIOL, IND UNIV, INDIANAPOLIS, 75- *Personal Data:* b Raleigh, NC, Oct 11, 46; m 70; c 2. *Educ:* Appalachian State Univ, BA, 68; Bowman Gray Sch Med, PhD(physiol), 73. *Prof Exp:* Am Heart Asn fel physiol, Univ Ariz, 73-75. *Mem:* Am Heart Asn; Fedn Am Soc Exp Biol. *Res:* Neural and local vascular control of the intestinal microcirculation. *Mailing Add:* Dept Physiol Ind Univ Sch Med 635 Barnhill Dr MS 342 Indianapolis IN 46202-5120

BOHLEN, STEVEN RALPH, METAMORPHIC PETROLOGY, EXPERIMENTAL PETROLOGY. *Current Pos:* CONSULT PROF, DEPT GEOL, STANFORD UNIV, 89- *Personal Data:* b Indianapolis, Ind, July 12, 52. *Educ:* Dartmouth Col, AB, 74; Univ Mich, MS, 77, PhD(geol), 79. *Prof Exp:* Res geochemist, Univ Calif, Los Angeles, 79-82; assoc prof geochem, Dept Earth & Space Sci, State Univ NY, Stony Brook, 82-89. *Concurrent Pos:* Ed, Am Mineralogist, 90-95. *Mem:* Mineral Soc Am; Am Geophys Union; Sigma Xi. *Res:* Metamorphic, experimental and field petrology; thermodynamic properties of minerals; phase equilibria; mineralogy, crystallography, geochemistry and evolution of the earth's crust. *Mailing Add:* US Geol Surv MS 910 12201 Sun Valley Dr Reston VA 22092

BOHLEN, WALTER FRANKLIN, PHYSICAL OCEANOGRAPHY. *Current Pos:* asst prof, 69-77, ASSOC PROF OCEANOG, UNIV CONN, 77- *Personal Data:* b Tarrytown, NY, June 21, 38; m 67; c 4. *Educ:* Univ Notre Dame, BSEE, 60; Mass Inst Technol, PhD(oceanog), 69. *Prof Exp:* Res asst geophys, Woods Hole Oceanog Inst, 62-63; engr electronics, Robert Taggert Inc, 63-65; res asst oceanog, Woods Hole Oceanog Inst, 65; res asst geol, Mass Inst Technol, 65-69. *Concurrent Pos:* Mem res planning adv comt, Long Island Sound Study, New Eng River Basins Comn, 72-75. *Mem:* Am Geophys Union; Marine Technol Soc; Sigma Xi. *Res:* Experimental investigations of sediment transport in coastal waters with particular emphasis on the factors governing variability, the relationship between laboratory and field data and the development of quantitative transport models. *Mailing Add:* Dept Marine Sci Univ Conn U-6 438 Whitney Storrs Mansfield CT 06269-0002

BOHLIN, JOHN DAVID, SOLAR PHYSICS, SPACE PHYSICS. *Current Pos:* prog scientist, NASA Hq, 77-78, chief, Solar Physics Disc Br, 78-90, chief scientist, Space Physics Div, 90-95, SR SCI PROG EXEC, NASA HQ, 96- *Personal Data:* b Valparaiso, Ind, Mar 19, 39; m 66; c 2. *Educ:* Wabash Col, AB, 61; Univ Colo, Boulder, PhD(solar physics), 68. *Honors & Awards:* Except Serv Award, NASA, 89. *Prof Exp:* Res fel astron, Calif Inst Technol, 67-70; astrophysicist solar physics, Naval Res Lab, 70-76. *Mem:* Am Astron Soc; Int Astron Union; Am Geophys Union. *Res:* Physics of the outer atmosphere of the sun, especially as inferred from ultraviolet wave lengths observed from space vehicles; structure and dynamics of the solar corona. *Mailing Add:* Code SR NASA Hq Washington DC 20546. *E-Mail:* david.bohlin@hq.nasa.gov

BOHLIN, RALPH CHARLES, ASTROPHYSICS. *Current Pos:* ASTRONR, GODDARD SPACE FLIGHT CTR, GREENBELT, 73- *Personal Data:* b Iowa City, Iowa, Nov 26, 43. *Educ:* Univ Iowa, BA, 66; Princeton Univ, MA, 69, PhD(astrophysics), 70. *Prof Exp:* Nat Res Coun fel, 69; res assoc astrophysics, Lab Atmospheric & Space Physics, Univ Colo, 70-73. *Concurrent Pos:* Co-investr, Astron Spacelab Payloads Proj, 74-77, Space Telescope Proj Faint Object Spectrog, 74- & Spacelab Ultraviolet Imaging Telescope, 79- *Mem:* Am Astron Soc; Int Astron Union; Sigma Xi. *Res:* Ultraviolet spectroscopy and ultraviolet imaging of astronomical objects, including early-type stars, planetary nebulae, diffuse nebulae and galaxies using data from sounding rockets and orbiting satellites; emphasis on the gas and dust in the interstellar medium. *Mailing Add:* 6621 Parkway Rd Baltimore MD 21239

BOHLMANN, EDWARD GUSTAV, GEOCHEMISTRY, CORROSION. *Current Pos:* RETIRED. *Personal Data:* b Milwaukee, Wis, July 19, 17; wid; c 3. *Educ:* Univ Wis, BS, 39, MS, 41. *Prof Exp:* Asst sanit chem, Univ Wis, 39-40, asst phys chem, 40-41; chemist, Solvay Process Co, NY, 41-42; res chemist metal lab, Manhattan Proj, Univ Chicago, 43; res chemist, Oak Ridge Nat Lab, 43-48, group leader, 45-48; res engr, Battelle Mem Inst, 48-49; sr res chemist, Oak Ridge Nat Lab, 49-52, chief corrosion sect, Reactor Exp Eng Div, 52-55, from asst dir to assoc dir, 55-61, assoc dir, Reactor Chem Div, 61-73, mem sr res staff, Chem Div, 73-80. *Mem:* AAAS; Am Chem Soc. *Res:* Physical chemistry; inorganic chemistry; aqueous corrosion; materials and corrosion in nuclear power reactors; molten salt reactors; silica and scaling in geothermal brines. *Mailing Add:* 7433 Somerset Rd Knoxville TN 37909. *E-Mail:* ingusb@icx.net

BOHM, ARNO, HIGH ENERGY PHYSICS, THEORETICAL PHYSICS. *Current Pos:* assoc prof, 68-78, PROF PHYSICS, UNIV TEX, AUSTIN, 78- *Personal Data:* b Stettin, Poland, Apr 26, 36; m 65; c 3. *Educ:* Tech Univ, Berlin, DiplPh, 62; Dr rer nat, 66. *Honors & Awards:* Humboldt Prize, 81. *Prof Exp:* Sci asst theoret physics, Univ Karlsruhe, 63-64; Int Atomic Energy Agency res fel particle physics, Int Ctr Theoret Physics, Trieste, Italy, 64-66; res assoc, Syracuse Univ, 66-68. *Concurrent Pos:* Vis prof, Chalmers Inst Technol, Sweden, Univ Brussels, Belg, Max Planck Inst, Munich, Univ Wurzburg, Ger, Los Alamos Nat Lab, NMex, Inst High Energy Physics, Serpukhov, USSR; IAEA fel, Italy, 65; Mortimer & Raymond Sackler fel, Israel, 80; Fulbright Award, 87. *Mem:* Fel Am Phys Soc. *Res:* Theoretical and elementary particle physics; mathematical physics; quantum physics. *Mailing Add:* Dept Physics Univ Tex Austin TX 78712

BOHM, BRUCE ARTHUR, BOTANY. *Current Pos:* from asst prof to assoc prof, 66-73, PROF BOT, UNIV BC, 73- *Personal Data:* b Burlington, Wis, Apr 9, 35; Can citizen; m 61; c 2. *Educ:* Alfred Univ, BS, 56; Univ RI, MS, 58, PhD(chem), 60. *Prof Exp:* Fel bot, McGill Univ, 60-61; asst prof chem, Univ Sask, 61-63; asst res prof pharmacog, Univ RI, 63-66. *Mem:* Am Bot Soc; Am Soc Plant Taxonomists; Phytochem Soc NAm (pres, 69); AAAS. *Res:* Chemical plant taxonomy utilizing secondary metabolites and comparative protein structure. *Mailing Add:* Dept Bot Univ BC 6270 University Blvd Rm 3529 Vancouver BC V6T 1Z4 Can

BOHM, GEORG G A, POLYMER PHYSICS. *Current Pos:* asst dir res, 67-95, DIR RES, BRIDGESTONE/FIRESTONE INC, 95- *Personal Data:* b Brunn, Czech, Oct 7, 35; m 61, Marga; c 2. *Educ:* Univ Vienna, PhD(physics), 62. *Prof Exp:* Staff mem, Max Planck Inst Phys Chem, Gottingen, 62-64; vis prof, Int Atomic Energy Agency, Vienna, 64-65; vis scholar, Northwestern Univ, Ill, 65-67. *Mem:* Am Phys Soc. *Res:* Polymer physics: interrelationship between polymer structure morphology and physical properties of heterogenous systems; radiation chemistry; processes occurring in polymers on exposure to radiation, polymer processing. *Mailing Add:* Bridgestone/Firestone Inc Cent Res Labs 1200 Firestone Pkwy Akron OH 44317

BOHM, HENRY VICTOR, HIGH TEMPERATURE SUPERCONDUCTIVITY. *Current Pos:* from assoc prof to prof physics, Wayne State Univ, 59-93, actg chmn dept, 62-63, vpres grad studies & res, 68-71, vpres spec projs, 71-72, provost, 72-75, dean fac, 84, interim dean, Col Lib Arts, 84-86, EMER PROF PHYSICS, WAYNE STATE UNIV, 93- *Personal Data:* b Vienna, Austria, July 16, 29; US citizen; m 50, Lucy Coons; c Victoria R & Jeffrey E T. *Educ:* Harvard Univ, AB, 50; Univ Ill, MS, 51; Brown Univ, PhD(physics), 58. *Prof Exp:* Jr physicist, Gen Elec Co, 51 & 53-54; staff mem, Arthur D Little, Inc, 58-59. *Concurrent Pos:* Consult, Aerospace Syst Command, USAF, 60-62; vis prof physics, Cornell Univ, 66-67, Purdue Univ, 77; mem bd dir, Ctr Res Libr, Chicago, Ill, 70-75, chmn, 73; consult, NCent Asn Schs & Cols, 70-80; comnr, Comn Inst High Educ, 74-78; pres, Argonne Univ Asn, 78-83. *Mem:* Am Phys Soc; AAAS. *Res:* Superconductivity. *Mailing Add:* Dept Physics Wayne State Univ Detroit MI 48202

BOHM, HOWARD A, MICROBIAL PESTICIDES, DRUG FORMULATIONS. *Current Pos:* ASST PROF CHEM, KEENE STATE COL, 92- *Personal Data:* b New York, NY, July 28, 43; m 67; c 1. *Educ:* NY Univ, BA, 66; Adelphi Univ, PhD(chem), 71. *Prof Exp:* Sr res chemist, Pennwalt Corp, 74-81; res chemist, IKapharm Div, Teva Corp, 81-85; sr res scientist, Lim Technol, 85-90; res chemist, Chevron Corp, 90-92. *Mem:* Am Chem Soc; Controlled Release Soc; Entom Soc Am. *Res:* Time release systems for food, drugs, and pesticides; microbial pesticides; microencapsulations; photochemistry; cyclodextrins; tableting; drug synthesis; analysis; polymers; sunscreening agents; liposomes. *Mailing Add:* 381 Fitzwilliam Rd Richmond NH 03470-2213

BOHMAN, VERLE RUDOLPH, ANIMAL NUTRITION. *Current Pos:* RETIRED. *Personal Data:* b Peterson, Utah, Dec 29, 24; m 45, Renee Jorgensen; c Margaret L, Verle D, Jolene R, Van R & Gregory N. *Educ:* Utah State Agr Col, BS, 49, MS, 51; Cornell Univ, PhD(animal nutrit), 52. *Honors & Awards:* Distinguished Serv Award, Am Soc Animal Sci, 84. *Prof Exp:* From asst prof & asst animal nutritionist to assoc prof animal husb & assoc animal nutritionist, Univ Nev, 52-63, chmn Div Animal Sci, 60-78, prof animal husb & nutrit, 63-86. *Concurrent Pos:* Ed-in-chief, J Animal Sci, 70-72. *Mem:* Fel AAAS; Am Inst Nutrit; fel Am Soc Animal Sci (pres-elect, 73-74, pres, 74-75); Am Dairy Sci Asn. *Res:* Range livestock nutrition; antibiotics; fat, hormones, protein and mineral metabolism; radioactive fallout. *Mailing Add:* 3924 W 3900 N Morgan UT 84050

BOHME, DIETHARD KURT, PHYSICAL CHEMISTRY, CHEMICAL PHYSICS. *Current Pos:* from asst prof to assoc prof, York Univ, 70-77, dir, Grad Prog Chem, 79-85, chmn, Dept Chem, 85-90, PROF CHEM, YORK UNIV, 77- *Personal Data:* b Boston, Mass, June 20, 41; div; c 3. *Educ:* McGill Univ, BSc, 62, PhD(phys chem), 65. *Honors & Awards:* Rutherford Mem Medal, Royal Soc Can, 81; Noranda Lect Award, Chem Inst Can, 83. *Prof Exp:* Nat Res Coun Can Overseas fel & hon res asst physics, Univ Col, Univ London, 65-67; resident res assoc aeronomy, Aeronomy Lab, Environ Sci Serv Admin, 67-69. *Concurrent Pos:* Res assoc, Nat Acad Sci, Nat Res Coun, 67-69; A P Sloan Found fel, 74-76; sr vis fel, Sci Res Coun Eng, 78-79; mem, Grant Selection Comt, Nat Sci Eng Res Coun Can, 83-86; A von Humboldt res award, 90; Killam res fel, 91-93. *Mem:* Fel Chem Inst Can; Am Chem Soc; Am Soc Mass Spectrometry. *Res:* Gas-phase ion chemistry; silicon-ion chemistry; ion chemistry in dense interstellar gas clouds, circumstellar envelopes, hydrocarbon flames and planetary ionospheres; gas-phase ion-induced polymer chemistry; ion chemistry of fullerenes. *Mailing Add:* Dept Chem York Univ North York ON M3J 1P3 Can. *Fax:* 416-736-5516; *E-Mail:* dkbohme@yorku.ca

BOHMER, HEINRICH EVERHARD, PHYSICS. *Current Pos:* MEM TECH STAFF, TRW SYSTS, REDONDO BEACH, CALIF, 76-; ASSOC RES PHYSICIST, UNIV CALIF, IRVINE, 76- *Personal Data:* b Munster, Ger, May 6, 31; m 62; c 1. *Educ:* Univ Munster, dipl, 59, PhD(diffusion in metals), 61. *Prof Exp:* Asst solid state physics, Inst Metal Res, Univ Munster, 62; res assoc surface physics, Univ Ill, Urbana, 62-63 & plasma physics, 63-65, res asst prof, 65-69, asst prof physics, Coord Sci Lab, 69-76. *Concurrent Pos:* Vis physicist, Dept Plasma Physics, Fontenay Nuclear Res Ctr, Fontenay, France, 72-73 & Dept Physics, Univ Calif, Irvine, 75- *Mem:* Am Phys Soc. *Res:* Plasma physics. *Mailing Add:* Dept Physics Attn Bohmer Univ Calif Irvine CA 92717-4575

BOHMONT, DALE W, PLANT SCIENCE, ACADEMIC ADMINISTRATION. *Current Pos:* PRES, BOHMONT CONSULT INC, 82- *Personal Data:* b Wheatland, Wyo, June 7, 22; m 69; c 2. *Educ:* Univ Wyo, BS, 48, MS, 50; Univ Nebr, PhD, 52; Harvard Univ, MPA, 59. *Prof Exp:* Asst agronomist & asst prof agron, Univ Wyo, 48-53; assoc agronomist & head dept, Univ Colo, 53-55, agronomist, prof & head dept, 55-60, head, Div Plant Sci, 59-61, assoc dir, Agr Exp Sta, Univ Colo, 61-63; prof, dean & dir, Exp Sta & Coop Exten Serv, Max C Fleischmann Col Agr, Univ Nev, 63-82. *Concurrent Pos:* Asst agronomist, USDA, Univ Nebr, 50-51; conserv fel, Harvard Univ, 58-59; sr agr consult, Develop & Resources Corp NY, 68-74; pres, Enide Corp Nev, 74-80; consult, TAMS Agr Develop Group, 75-78, Nev Agr Found, 82-, Brucheum-Wayneborough, Va, 84- *Mem:* AAAS; fel Am Soc Agron; fel Am Acad Sci; fel Plant Sci Soc; Weed Soc. *Res:* Crops, soils, weed control and public administration. *Mailing Add:* 280 Island Ave Reno NV 89501

BOHN, HINRICH LORENZ, SOIL CHEMISTRY. *Current Pos:* assoc prof agr chem, 66-76, PROF SOIL CHEM, UNIV ARIZ, 74-, PROF SOILS, WATER & ENG & RES SCIENTIST AGR CHEM, 76- *Personal Data:* b New York, NY, Aug 25, 34; m 62; c 3. *Educ:* Univ Calif, Berkeley, BS, 55, MS, 57; Cornell Univ, PhD(soil chem), 63. *Prof Exp:* Fel, Univ Calif, Riverside, 63-64; res chemist, Tenn Valley Authority, 64-66. *Mem:* Am Chem Soc; Soil Sci Soc Am. *Res:* Soil-pollutant reactions. *Mailing Add:* 3004 1/2 E Adams St Tucson AZ 85716

BOHN, PAUL WILLIAM, OPTICAL SPECTROSCOPY, THIN FILMS. *Current Pos:* asst prof, 83-89, assoc prof, 89-92, PROF CHEM, UNIV ILL, 92-, DEPT HEAD, 94- *Personal Data:* b Oct 27, 55; m 77, Raylene Lemorie; c Nathan R & Lauren E. *Educ:* Univ Notre Dame, BS, 77; Univ Wis-Madison, PhD(chem), 81. *Honors & Awards:* Coblentz Award, Coblentz Soc, 90. *Prof Exp:* Mem tech staff, Bell Labs, 81-83. *Concurrent Pos:* Vis assoc prof chem, Univ Utah, 92. *Mem:* Am Chem Soc; AAAS; Am Phys Soc. *Res:* Self-assembled and Langmuir-Blodgett layers, structure-function relationships studied by optical spectroscopy, optical semiconductors. *Mailing Add:* Dept Chem Univ Ill 600 S Mathews Ave Urbana IL 61801. *Fax:* 217-244-8068; *E-Mail:* bohn@aries.scs.uiuc.edu

BOHN, RANDY G, LOW TEMPERATURE PHYSICS, CRYOGENICS. *Current Pos:* From asst prof to assoc prof, 69-81, PROF PHYSICS, UNIV TOLEDO, 81- *Personal Data:* b Toledo, Ohio, Feb 11, 41; m 65; c 2. *Educ:* Univ Toledo, BS, 63; Ohio State Univ, PhD(physics), 69. *Mem:* Am Asn Physics Teachers; Am Phys Soc. *Res:* Thermal conductivity in solid hydrogen; vitreous solids; thermal properties of solids at low temperatures. *Mailing Add:* Dept Physics & Astron Univ Toledo Toledo OH 43606

BOHN, ROBERT K, MICROWAVE SPECTROSCOPY, AIR POLLUTANT DISPOSAL. *Current Pos:* asst prof, 65-71, assoc prof, 71-78, PROF CHEM, UNIV CONN, 78- *Personal Data:* b New York, NY, Jan 24, 39; m 64, 83; c 4. *Educ:* Univ Calif, Berkeley, BS, 59; Cornell Univ, PhD(phys chem), 64. *Prof Exp:* NATO fel electron diffraction, Univ Oslo, 64-65. *Concurrent Pos:* Vis scientist, Univ Tokyo, 71-72 & Columbia Univ, 79-81; vis prof, Univ Mich, 87-88. *Mem:* Am Chem Soc; Am Phys Soc. *Res:* Molecular structure; electron diffraction; microwave spectroscopy. *Mailing Add:* Dept Chem Univ Conn 205 Glenbrooke Rd U-60 Storrs CT 06269-4060

BOHN, SHERMAN ELWOOD, mathematics, for more information see previous edition

BOHNENBLUST, KENNETH E, PLANT BREEDING, PLANT PATHOLOGY. *Current Pos:* Asst prof, 67-78, ASSOC PROF PLANT BREEDING, UNIV WYO, 78- *Personal Data:* b Bala, Kans, Dec 9, 23; m 45; c 3. *Educ:* Kans State Univ, BS, 59; Univ Wyo, MS, 61; Univ Minn, St Paul, PhD(plant path), 66. *Prof Exp:* Instr agron, Univ Wyo, 59-61; asst prof biol, Wis State Univ, River Falls, 66-67. *Mem:* Sigma Xi. *Res:* Potato diseases; actinomycetes in plant disease; potato breeding; alfalfa breeding and pest resistance; virus diseases of plants; breeding cereals; morphology of cereal seedlings. *Mailing Add:* 1907 E Custer St Laramie WY 82070

BOHNERT, JANICE LEE, BIOCHEMISTRY, CLINICL TRIALS. *Current Pos:* SR CLIN RES ASSOC, NEORX CORP, 93- *Educ:* Bucknell Univ, BA, 70; Univ Wash, PhD(biochem), 81. *Prof Exp:* Chemist NIH, Bethesda, 70-84; res asst, Dept Biochem, Univ Wash, 74-81, fel, 81-82, res scientist II, Dept Chem Eng, 84, res assoc, 84-86, res assoc, 86-87, biochem consult, Ctr Bioeng, 89-92. *Mem:* Am Soc Biochem & Molecular Biol; Asn Women Sci. *Res:* Stabilize proteins loaded in hydrogels for controlled release applications; coordinated studies of bioadhesion with new polymer development; growth of marine bacteria for incorporation into polymer gels being developed for nonfouling surfaces; clincal trials of cancer therapy using pretargeted radioimmunotherapy; clinical trials of cytochalasin (biostent) to reduce restenosis after balloon angioplasty; granted one US patent; numerous publications. *Mailing Add:* 3538 NE 85th St Seattle WA 98115

BOHNING, DARYL EUGENE, BIOMATHEMATICS, PHYSIOLOGY. *Current Pos:* ASSOC PROF & RES SCIENTIST, BOHNING RADIOL, 93- *Personal Data:* b Belmond, Iowa, Sept 21, 41; c 3. *Educ:* Iowa State Univ, BS, 62, PhD(physics), 66. *Prof Exp:* Fel physics, Rutgers Univ, 66-69; NIH trainee biophys, Mass Gen Hosp & Harvard Univ, 69-70; asst prof physics, Miami Univ, 70-71; res scientist environ med, NY Univ, 71-75; asst prof & res assoc med, State Univ NY Stony Brook, 75-78; staff scientist biomath & med, Brookhaven Nat Lab, 78-; Philips Med Systs, Inc, 93. *Mem:* Am Phys Soc; Am Asn Physicists Med; Soc Magnetic Resonance Med. *Res:* Research and development on cardiac applications of magnetic resonance imaging and spectroscopy. *Mailing Add:* Bohning Radiol 171 Ashley Ave Charleston SC 29425-0001

BOHNING, JAMES JOEL, PHOTOCHEMISTRY, HISTORY OF CHEMISTRY. *Current Pos:* from asst prof to prof chem, Wilkes Col, 67-90, chmn dept, 70-86, prof, 87-90, chmn, Dept Earth & Environ Sci, 87090, EMER PROF CHEM, WILKES COL, 90-; ASST DIR, ORAL HIST, BECKMAN CTR HIST CHEM, 90- *Personal Data:* b Cleveland, Ohio, Apr 11, 34; m. *Educ:* Valparaiso Univ, BS, 56; NY Univ, MS, 59; Northeastern Univ, PhD(phys chem), 65. *Prof Exp:* Instr chem, Wilkes Col, 59-62; res fel, Northeastern Univ, 62-64. *Concurrent Pos:* Vis prof, Univ Ky, 80-81 & Lehigh Univ, 85, 86; chmn, Div Hist of Chem, Am Chem Soc, 86. *Mem:* Am Chem Soc. *Mailing Add:* 931 Hillside Lake Terr Gaithersburg MD 20878

BOHNSACK, KURT K, ECOLOGY, ACAROLOGY. *Current Pos:* RETIRED. *Personal Data:* b Stuttgart, Ger, Mar 23, 20; nat US; m 46, Julie Low; c Linda, Richard & Mary E. *Educ:* Ohio Univ, BS, 46; Univ Mich, MS, 47, PhD(zool), 54. *Prof Exp:* Instr zool, Univ Mich, 50-51; from instr to asst prof biol, Swarthmore Col, 51-56; from asst prof to prof zool, San Diego State Univ, 56-90, chmn dept, 64-67 & 80. *Concurrent Pos:* Investr, Oak Ridge Nat Lab, 56-57 & Arctic Res Lab, 62-64; mem bd dirs, San Diego Natural Hist Mus, 66-79. *Mem:* Acarol Soc Am; Sigma Xi; AAAS; Arctic Inst NAm; Audubon Soc; Soc Vector Ecol. *Res:* Entomology; acarology. *Mailing Add:* 4309 Mt Helix Highlands Dr La Mesa CA 91941-5609

BOHON, ROBERT LYNN, ENVIRONMENTAL SCIENCES, ANALYTICAL CHEMISTRY. *Current Pos:* RETIRED. *Personal Data:* b Decatur, Ill, July 20, 25; m 47, Lois E Dungan; c Barbara S, Elizabeth A & Bruce D. *Educ:* Univ Ill, BS, 46, PhD(phys chem), 50. *Prof Exp:* Asst phys chem, Univ Ill, 49-50; phys chemist & head infrared lab, Anderson Phys Lab, 50-56; sr chemist, Chem Res Lab, 3M Co, 56-66, supvr, 66-69, mgr, 69-75, mgr environ libr, 76-85, dir, Analysis & Properties Res Corp, 85-89. *Mem:* Am Sci Affil. *Res:* General physical chemistry; thermodynamics of solutions; thermal analysis; solid state reaction kinetics; physical properties of polymers; material science; environmental chemistry and engineering; technical management. *Mailing Add:* 5960 Hobe Lane St Paul MN 55110

BOHOR, BRUCE FORBES, SHOCKED MINERALS, CLAY MINERALOGY. *Current Pos:* geologist, 74-94, EMER SCIENTIST, BR COAL GEOL, US GEOL SURV, 95- *Personal Data:* b Chicago, Ill, May 4, 32; m 53; c 4. *Educ:* Beloit Col, BS, 53; Univ Ind, MS, 55; Univ Ill, PhD(geol), 59. *Prof Exp:* Res geologist, Prod Res Div, Res & Develop Dept, Continental Oil Co, Okla, 57-63, Explor Res Div, 63-65; geologist, Clay Resources & Clay Mineral Technol Sect, Ill State Geol Surv, 65-74. *Concurrent Pos:* Ill Clay fel; G K Gilbert fel, US Geol Surv, 85-86; NASA grant T-5175P, 88-93; Pecora fel, US Geol Surv, 95-96. *Mem:* Meteoritical Soc; Clay Minerals Soc; fel AAAS; Geochem Soc; Meteoritical Soc. *Res:* Clay minerals and geochemistry in coal exploration; industrial applications of clays and clay minerals; development of clay resources; tonsteins; shocked minerals, K/T boundary and other impact events. *Mailing Add:* US Geol Surv Br Coal Resources Fed Ctr Box 25046 Mail Stop 973 Denver CO 80225-0046. *Fax:* 303-236-3200

BOHR, AAGE, THEORETICAL PHYSICS. *Current Pos:* Res asst physics, Inst Theoret Physics, 46, PROF PHYSICS, NIELS BOHR INST, UNIV COPENHAGEN, 56- *Personal Data:* b Copenhagen, Denmark, June 19, 22. *Educ:* Univ Copenhagen, PhD(physics), 54. *Hon Degrees:* Dr, Manchester Univ, 61, Oslo Univ, 69, Heidelberg Univ, 71, Trondheim Univ, 72 & Upsala Univ, 75. *Honors & Awards:* Nobel Prize in Physics, 75; Dannie Heineman Prize, 60; Rutherford Medal, 72; John Price Wetherill Medal, 74. *Prof Exp:* Jr sci officer, Dept Sci & Indust Res, London, 43-45. *Mem:* Nat Acad Sci; Yugoslavia Acad Sci; Am Philol Soc; Finnish Acad Sci. *Mailing Add:* Niels Bohr Inst Univ Copenhagen Blegdamsgade 17 Copenhagen 2100 Denmark

BOHR, DAVID FRANCIS, CARDIOVASCULAR PHYSIOLOGY. *Current Pos:* PROF PHYSIOL, MED SCH, UNIV MICH, ANN ARBOR, 56- *Personal Data:* b Zurich, Switz, June 22, 15; US citizen; m 40; c 3. *Educ:* Univ Mich, MD, 42. *Honors & Awards:* Ciba Award, 84. *Prof Exp:* Life Inst Med Res fel, Univ Calif, San Francisco, 46-48, res fel path, 47-48; from asst prof to assoc prof physiol, Med Sch, Univ Mich, Ann Arbor, 48-55; vis prof pharmacol, Univ Calif, San Francisco, 55-56. *Concurrent Pos:* Vis prof physiol, Univ Heidelberg, 61-62; mem coun high blood pressure, Am Heart Asn, chmn, 78-80; distinguished prof, Univ Mich, 73. *Mem:* Am Physiol Soc (pres, 78-79). *Res:* Vascular smooth muscle; hypertension. *Mailing Add:* Dept Physiol Univ Mich 7708 Med Sci II Ann Arbor MI 48109-0622

BOHR, VILHELM ALFRED, DNA REPAIR. *Current Pos:* sr staff fel, 86-92, BR CHIEF, LAB MOLECULAR GENETICS, NAT INST AGING, NIH, 92- *Personal Data:* b Copenhagen, Denmark, Dec 3, 50; m 87, Diane Okumoto; c Christina & Eliot. *Educ:* Univ Copenhagen, Denmark, BS, 78, PhD(biochem) & MD, 87. *Prof Exp:* Resident med, Univ Copenhagen, 78-80; res scholar, Stanford Univ, 82-86. *Mem:* Am Asn Cancer Res; Am Asn Molecular Biol. *Res:* DNA repair. *Mailing Add:* Lab Molecular Genetics Nat Inst Aging NIH 4940 Eastern Ave Baltimore MD 21224. *Fax:* 410-558-8157; *E-Mail:* vbohr@nih.gov

BOHREN, BERNARD BENJAMIN, animal genetics; deceased, see previous edition for last biography

BOHREN, CRAIG FREDERICK, APPLIED PHYSICS. *Current Pos:* from asst prof to distinguished prof, 80-90, DISTINGUISHED PROF, DEPT METEOROL, PA STATE UNIV, 90- *Personal Data:* b San Francisco, Calif, Feb 24, 40; m 64, Nanette Malott. *Educ:* San Jose State Univ, BS, 63; Univ Ariz, MS, 65 & 71, PhD(physics), 75. *Honors & Awards:* Louis J Battan Author's Award, Am Meteorol Soc, 89. *Prof Exp:* Res asst nuclear eng, Gulf Gen Atomic, 65-67; res assoc hydrol, Sch Renewable Natural Resources, Univ Ariz, 72-75, lectr, Inst Atmospheric Physics, 74-75; res asst, Dept Appl Math & Astron, Univ Col Cardiff, 75-78; vis scholar, Inst Atmospheric Physics, Univ Ariz, 78-80. *Concurrent Pos:* Vis staff mem, Los Alamos Nat Lab, 80 & 86-87; vis scholar, Univ Ariz, 81, Dartmouth Col, 84, 85; res physicist, Cold Regions Res & Eng Lab, 84, 85; vis prof, Dartmouth Col, 86-87; ed, Appl Optics; Selby fel, Australian Acad Sci, 93; Mitchell vis distinguished prof, Trinity Univ, 94. *Mem:* Am Asn Physics Teachers; fel Optical Soc Am. *Res:* Light scattering by small particles; atmospheric physics; meteorological optics; physics of everyday phenomena. *Mailing Add:* Dept Meteorol Pa State Univ University Park PA 16802. *Fax:* 814-865-3663; *E-Mail:* bohren@ems.psu.edu

BOHRER, JAMES CALVIN, BIOCHEMISTRY. *Current Pos:* RETIRED. *Personal Data:* b Evansville, Ind, Oct 27, 23; m 49, Priscilla Beaupre; c Jeanne (Bozzay), Christine (Meckfesser), Mark, MaryEmily & William. *Educ:* Evansville Col, AB, 44; Cornell Univ, PhD, 51. *Prof Exp:* Sr proj chemist, Colgate-Palmolive Co, Piscataway, 50-83. *Concurrent Pos:* Instr, Univ Col, Rutgers Univ, 63-78. *Mem:* Am Chem Soc. *Res:* Many-membered ring compounds; detergents. *Mailing Add:* 19 Peach Orchard Dr East Brunswick NJ 08816-2720

BOHRER, RICHARD C, TECHNICAL MANAGEMENT. *Current Pos:* dir, Bur Community Health Servs, 78-80, DIR, DIV COMMUNITY & MIGRANT HEALTH, BUR PRIMARY HEALTH CARE, DEPT HEALTH & HUMAN SERVS, 81- *Prof Exp:* Prof phychol, Univ Minn, 67-69; asst, Nat Clearinghouse Smoking & Health, US Dept Health Educ & Welfare, 69-71, Community Health Servs, 72-73, Off Community Health Ctr, Bur Community Health Servs, 74-78. *Mailing Add:* Div Community & Migrant Health Dept Health & Human Servs 4350 EW Hwy 7th Flr Bethesda MD 20814

BOHRER, ROBERT EDWARD, MATHEMATICS, STATISTICS. *Current Pos:* from asst prof to assoc prof math, 68-79, PROF MATH, UNIV ILL, URBANA-CHAMPAIGN, 79- *Personal Data:* b St Paul, Minn, July 24, 39; m 60; c 1. *Educ:* SDak Sch Mines & Technol, BS, 61; Univ NC, Chapel Hill, PhD(statist), 66. *Prof Exp:* Statistician, Statist Res Div, Res Triangle Inst, 64-65; vis lectr statist, Univ Col Wales, 65-66; statistician, Statist Res Div, Res Triangle Inst, 66-68. *Concurrent Pos:* Res fel, Univ Kent, Canterbury, 72; vis assoc prof, Univ Calif, Berkeley, 74-75; vis scholar, Grad Theol Union, Berkeley, 74-75; acad vis, Imp Col, Univ London, 77; vis res assoc statistician, Univ Calif, Berkeley, 78-81, vis prof statist, 82-83. *Mem:* Math Asn Am; Inst Math Statist; Royal Statist Soc; fel Am Statist Asn. *Res:* Decision theory; confidence bounds; multiple inference; time series. *Mailing Add:* 905 Foley St Champaign IL 61820

BOHRER, THOMAS CARL, CHEMICAL ENGINEERING, PLASTICS SYNTHETIC FIBERS. *Current Pos:* PRES, TOM BOHRER CONSULT, 94- *Personal Data:* b Brooklyn, NY, Nov 8, 39; m 66, Janet Jacobs; c Scott & Jeffrey. *Educ:* Rensselaer Polytech Inst, BChE, 60. *Prof Exp:* Jr proj engr, Org Chem Div, Am Cyanamid Co, 60-62, proj engr, 62; chem engr, Celanese Res Co, 62-64, res eng, 64-67, sr res engr, 67-69, group leader fibers res, Celanese Fibers Co, 69-71, mgr, Tire Cord & Indust Yarns Develop, Celanese Fibers Mkt Co, 71-73, dir, Spec Prod Develop, 73-86, dir planning, 76, vpres tech & planning, 77-78, dir corp planning, 78-79, vpres tech, 79-81, vpres & gen mgr eng resins, Celanese Plastics & Specialties Co, 81-84, pres world wide eng resins, 84-87, pres spec prod group, Hoechst Celanese, 88, group pres, advan mat, Hoechst Celanese & Bereichsleder, Technische Konststoffe Hoechst Ag, 89-91, pres & chief operating officer, 91-94. *Concurrent Pos:* Chmn, Shell Polypropylene Co, 95-96; bd dirs, Capte Plastics Inc. *Res:* Exploratory fiber research and development; fibers application research and development in tire cord, industrial fibers, cigarette tow, floor coverings, fiberfill and civil engineering applications of fabric; plastics research and development in engineering resins, films, plastic pipe, structural composites, emulsions, water soluble polymers, and automotive coatings; specialty chemicals development for personal care, pharmaceuticals, agricultural, industrial, food and beverage. *Mailing Add:* 826 Winnebago Dr Franklin Lakes NJ 07417. *Fax:* 201-847-8858; *E-Mail:* combohrer@compuserve.com

BOHRER, VORSILA LAURENE, ETHNOBOTANY, GENERAL AGRICULTURE. *Current Pos:* DIR, SOUTHWEST ETHNOBOTANICAL ENTERPRISES, 85- *Personal Data:* b Chicago, Ill, Jan 22, 31. *Educ:* Univ Ariz, BA, 53, PhD(bot), 68; Univ Mich, MS, 54. *Honors & Awards:* Fryxell Award for Interdisciplinary Res, Soc Am Archaeol, 97. *Prof Exp:* Lectr biol, Univ Mass, Boston, 69-71, asst prof, 71-73; from res assoc prof to res prof, Paleoindian Inst, Eastern NMex Univ, 73-85. *Concurrent Pos:* Consult, Sch Am Res, Santa Fe, 72-79, Univ Ariz Field Sch, Grasshopper, 69-75, Puerco River Valley Archaeol Proj, 70-77, San Juan Valley Archaeol Proj, 72-80, Cent Ariz Ecotone Proj, 74-78, La Civdad, Phoenix, 82-87, Chambers Group Inc, 84-85 & Okla Archeol Surv, Norman, 84-89; head workshop archeobot, Univ Ariz, 84 & Southern Methodist Univ, 88; res assoc, Amerind Found, Dragoon, Ariz, 88- *Mem:* Soc Am Archaeol; Soc Econ Bot; Soc Range Mgt; Sigma Xi; Torrey Bot Soc. *Res:* Inter-relationship of plants and pre-historic man in the American Southwest; ethnobotany, palynology, plant microfossils, plant macrofossils, paleoecology. *Mailing Add:* 220 New Mexico Dr Portales NM 88130-7041

BOHRMAN, JEFFREY STEPHEN, PHARMACOLOGY, PHYSIOLOGY. *Personal Data:* b Easton, Pa, Jan 19, 44; m 70; c 2. *Educ:* Dickinson Col, Pa, BS, 67; Univ Pittsburgh, BS, 70; Univ Ill Med Ctr, MS, 72; Univ Pac, Stockton, Calif, PhD(pharmacol, physiol), 77. *Prof Exp:* investr, Oak Ridge Nat Lab, 77-80; res pharmacologist, Nat Inst Occup Safety & Health, Cincinnati, 80-89. *Mem:* AAAS; Found Sci & Handicapped; Asn Handicapped Student Servs Prog; NY Acad Sci. *Res:* Occupational chemical carcinogenesis; mechanism of tumor promotion; occupational photosensitization agents; role of prostaglandins and other inflammatory mediators both in initial and promotional phase of tumorigenesis; mechanism of inflammation and anti-inflammation; drug screening. *Mailing Add:* 5281 Courtney Pl Columbus OH 43235

BOICE, JOHN D, JR, PUBLIC HEALTH & EPIDEMIOLOGY. *Current Pos:* SCI DIR, INT EPIDEMIOL INST. *Personal Data:* b Brooklyn, NY, Dec 20, 45; m 74, Jennifer Rex; c John D III, James B, Jason A & Justin R. *Educ:* Univ Tex, El Paso, BS, 67; Rensselaer Polytech Inst, MS, 68; Harvard Univ, ScM, 74, ScD, 77. *Honors & Awards:* Meritorious Serv Medal, USPHS, 87, Distinguished Serv Medal, 91; AMSUS Gorgas Medal, 94; E O Lawrence Award, Dept Energy, 95. *Prof Exp:* Chief, Radiation Epidemiol Br, Nat Cancer Inst, 84-96. *Concurrent Pos:* Lectr epidemiol, Harvard Sch Pub Health, 79- *Mem:* Health Physics Soc; Soc Epidemiol Res; Am Pub Health Asn; Radiation Res Soc; Am Epidemiol Soc; Am Asn Cancer Res. *Res:* Epidemiologic research into the cause of disease in human populations. *Mailing Add:* Int Epidemiol Inst 1550 Research Blvd Rockville MD 20850. *E-Mail:* boicej@compuserve.com

BOIKESS, ROBERT S, ORGANIC CHEMISTRY. *Current Pos:* from asst prof to assoc prof, 68-84, PROF CHEM, RUTGERS UNIV, 84- *Personal Data:* b Brooklyn, NY, Feb 2, 37; m 69; c 2. *Educ:* Columbia Univ, BA, 57, MA, 60, PhD(org chem), 61. *Prof Exp:* Res fel org chem, Univ Calif, Los Angeles, 61-62; asst prof chem, State Univ NY Stony Brook, 63-68. *Concurrent Pos:* NSF fel, 62-63. *Mem:* Am Chem Soc. *Res:* Small rings; valency tautomerism; bicyclics; photochemistry; chemical education. *Mailing Add:* Dept Chem Rutgers Univ Busch Campus Piscataway NJ 08554

BOILEAU, OLIVER C, ELECTRICAL ENGINEERING. *Current Pos:* RETIRED. *Personal Data:* b Camden, NJ, Mar 31, 27; c 4. *Educ:* Univ Pa, BS, 51, MS, 53; Mass Inst Technol, MS, 64. *Prof Exp:* Vpres, Boeing Aerospace Co, 68-73, pres, 73-80; pres & mem bd dirs, Gen Dynamics Corp, 80-88; pres & gen mgr, B2 Div, Northrop Corp, 89-95. *Concurrent Pos:* Mem, Lawrence Inst Technol Corp & Lincoln Lab Adv Bd, Mass Inst Technol. *Mem:* Nat Acad Eng; Nat Aeronaut Asn; fel Am Inst Aeronaut & Astronaut; Am Defense Preparedness Asn. *Mailing Add:* PO Box 663 Saratoga WY 82331

BOIME, IRVING, MOLECULAR PHARMACOLOGY. *Current Pos:* assoc prof, 72-80, PROF OBSTET, GYNEC & PHARMACOL, WASH UNIV, 80- *Personal Data:* b St Louis, Mo, Feb 5, 41; m 61; c 2. *Educ:* St Louis Col Pharm, BS, 64; Purdue Univ, MS, 66; Washington Univ, PhD(pharmacol), 70. *Prof Exp:* Fel molecular biol, NIH, 70-72. *Concurrent Pos:* Am Cancer Soc fel, 70; NIH res grant, 73; Pop Coun res grant, 73. *Mem:* Fedn Am Soc Exp Biol. *Res:* Biosynthesis of peptide hormones; proinsulin and the protein hormones of human placenta. *Mailing Add:* Dept of Pharmacol Univ Wash Sch Med 660 S Euclid St Louis MO 63110-1010

BOIS, PIERRE, ANATOMY. *Current Pos:* CONSULT, UNIV MONTREAL, 91-, CLIN RES INST MONTREAL, 92- *Personal Data:* b Oka, Que, Mar 22, 24; m 53, Joyce Casey; c Monique, Marie & Louise. *Educ:* Laval Univ, BA, 48; Univ Montreal, MD, 53, PhD(exp med), 57. *Honors & Awards:* Francisco Hernandez Award, Panamerican Fedn Asn Med Schs, 86; Chevalier de l'Ordre Nat du Merite, Republique Francaise, 88; Duncan Graham Award, Royal Col Physicians & Surgeons Can, 88; Award of Merit, John P Robarts Res Inst, 91. *Prof Exp:* Res asst exp surg, Univ Montreal, 53-57, lectr endocrinol, 55-57, lectr advan endocrinol, 56-57, lectr pharmacol, 57-58; asst prof histol & embryol, Univ Ottawa, 58-60; from asst prof to assoc prof pharmacol, Univ Montreal, 60-64, head dept, 64-77, prof anat, 64-81, dean fac med, 70-81; pres, Med Res Coun Can, 81-91. *Concurrent Pos:* Grants, Med Res Coun, Muscular Dystrophy, Nat Cancer Soc & Dept Pub Health. *Mem:* AAAS; Endocrine Soc; Histochem Soc; NY Acad Sci; Am Fedn Clin Res; fel Royal Soc Can; fel Royal Col Physicians & Surgeons Can. *Res:* Lymphoid tissue; origin, distribution and function of mast cells, including the role of histamine, biosynthesis, physiology and pharmacology. *Mailing Add:* 6227 Ouest Saraguay Pierrefonds PQ H8Y 2H9 Can

BOISCLAIR, DANIEL, IMAGE ANALYSIS, HYDROACOUTICS. *Current Pos:* PROF FISH ECOL, UNIV MONTREAL, 89- *Personal Data:* b Montreal, Quebec, Can, May 9, 58; m 81, Claire Garon; c Isabelle, Guillaume & Alexandre. *Educ:* Univ Laval, BSc, 81; McGill Univ, MSc, 84, PhD(fish ecol), 89. *Prof Exp:* Fel, Dept Fisheries & Oceans, Pac Biol Sta, 89. *Res:* Fish ecology, population dynamics, bioenergetics, respiration, energy allocation, distribution, migration, hydroacoustics, image analysis, growth, energy consumption, activity costs, metabolism, trophic interactions and predator-prey relationships. *Mailing Add:* C P 6128 Succ Centreville Montreal PQ H3C 3J7 Can. *Fax:* 514-343-2293; *E-Mail:* boisclad@ere.umontreal.ca

BOISSE, NORMAN ROBERT, NEUROPHARMACOLOGY. *Current Pos:* ASST PROF PHARMACOL, NORTHEASTERN UNIV, 77- *Personal Data:* b Biddeford, Maine, Aug 18, 47. *Educ:* Univ Conn, Storrs, BS, 70; Cornell Univ, PhD(pharmacol), 76. *Prof Exp:* Res asst pharmacol, Cornell Univ Med Col, 76-77. *Mem:* AAAS; NY Acad Sci; Soc Neurosci; Sigma Xi. *Res:* Barbiturate, alcohol and benzodiazepine physical dependence and tolerance. *Mailing Add:* Pharmacol Dept Col Pharm-Allied Health Northeastern Univ Boston MA 02115-5096

BOISSY, RAYMOND E, CELL BIOLOGY, MORPHOLOGY. *Current Pos:* ASST PROF CELL BIOL, UNIV CINCINNATI, 86- *Personal Data:* b July 8, 54. *Educ:* Univ Mass, PhD(vet & animal sci), 82. *Prof Exp:* Assoc res scientist, Sch Med, Yale Univ, 82-86. *Mem:* AAAS; Am Soc Cell Biol. *Res:* Pigment cells. *Mailing Add:* Dermat Dept ML592 Univ Cincinnati Col Med 231 Bethesda Ave Cincinnati OH 45267-0592

BOISVENUE, RUDOLPH JOSEPH, MICROBIOLOGY, PARASITOLOGY. *Current Pos:* RES SCIENTIST, LILLY RES LABS, 62- *Personal Data:* b Windsor, Ont, Aug 30, 26; nat US; m 51; c 1. *Educ:* Univ Western Ont, BSc, 49; Univ Detroit, MSc, 51; Mich State Univ, PhD(microbiol), 55. *Prof Exp:* Wildlife biologist, Kellogg Bird Sanctuary & Forest, 52-55; mgr parasitol, Ralston Purina Co, 55-62. *Concurrent Pos:* Microtechnician, Sparrow Hosp, 53-55; asst, Mich State Univ, 54-55; mem fac, Dept Zool, Eve Div, Ind Cent Col, 62; mem, Livestock Insect Workshop Conf. *Mem:* Am Soc Parasitol; Am Asn Vet Parasitol; Wildlife Dis Asn; Am Heartworm Soc; Entom Soc Am; World Asn Advan Vet Parasitol. *Res:* Veterinary helminthology and entomology; biological and chemical control of major external and internal parasite species infecting domestic animals; in vitro cultivation of nematodes; antigenic nematode research. *Mailing Add:* 615 Hillcrest Lane Greenfield IN 46140

BOISVERT, RONALD FERNAND, MATHEMATICAL SOFTWARE, NUMERICAL ANALYSIS. *Current Pos:* comput scientist, Comput & Appl Math Lab, 79-92, LEADER, MATH SOFTWARE GROUP, NAT INST STAND & TECHNOL, 92- *Personal Data:* b Manchester, NH, July 26, 51; m 72, Rita Lefebvre; c Linette. *Educ:* Keene State Col, BS, 73; Col William & Mary, MS, 75; Purdue Univ, MS, 77, PhD (comput sci), 79. *Honors & Awards:* Silver Medal, US Dept Com, 92. *Concurrent Pos:* Assoc ed, Asn Comput Mach Trans Math Software, 87-93, ed-in-chief, 93-; consult, NSF, 87- *Mem:* Asn Comput Mach; Soc Indust & Appl Math; Inst Elec &

Electronics Engrs Comput Soc. *Res:* Development and maintenance of mathematical software; digital libraries; scientific computing; algorithms for high-performance computers; numerical analysis; numerical solution of elliptic boundary-value problems. *Mailing Add:* 9631 Shadow Oak Dr Gaithersburg MD 20879. *Fax:* 301-990-4127; *E-Mail:* boisvert@nist.gov

BOIVIN, LOUIS-PHILIPPE, OPTICAL RADIOMETRY. *Current Pos:* RES OFFICER, INST NAT MEASUREMENT STANDARDS, NAT RES COUN CAN, 73- *Personal Data:* b Ottawa, Ont, Mar 12, 44; m 70; c 2. *Educ:* Univ Ottawa, BSc, 65, PhD(physics, optics), 70. *Prof Exp:* Res scientist optical commun, Bell-Northern Res, 70-73. *Res:* Radiometry and photometry. *Mailing Add:* Rm 110 Inst Nat Measurement Standards Bldg M36 Montreal Rd Ottawa ON K1A 0R6 Can

BOJALIL, LUIS FELIPE, medical microbiology, for more information see previous edition

BOJANIC, RANKO, MATHEMATICAL ANALYSIS. *Current Pos:* assoc prof, 63-66, PROF MATH, OHIO STATE UNIV, 66- *Personal Data:* b Breza, Yugoslavia, Nov 12, 24; m 58; c Myra & Ivan. *Educ:* Serbian Acad Sci, PhD(math), 53. *Prof Exp:* Docent math analysis, Univ Skoplje, 54-56 & Sch Mech Eng, Univ Belgrade, 56-58; vis mem, Tata Inst Fundamental Res, India, 58-59; vis lectr math, Stanford Univ, 59-60; asst prof, Univ Notre Dame, 60-63. *Mem:* Am Math Soc; Math Asn Am. *Res:* Asymptotic analysis; Fourier series and the theory of approximation; numerical analysis. *Mailing Add:* Dept Math Ohio State Univ 231 W 18th Ave Columbus OH 43210-1174. *E-Mail:* bojanic@math.ohio_state.edu

BOJAR, ROBERT MICHAEL, SURGERY. *Current Pos:* SR CARDIOTHORACIC SURGEON, NEW ENG MED CTR, 89- *Personal Data:* b Boston, Mass, June 14, 51; m 96, Mercedes Von Deck. *Educ:* Brown Univ, BA, 73, MD, 76. *Prof Exp:* Resident gen surg, Mass Gen Hosp, 76-81; resident cardiovasc-thoracic surg, St Lukes Med Ctr, 81-89. *Concurrent Pos:* Asst prof surg, Tufts Univ Sch Med, 84-89, assoc prof, 89- *Mem:* Soc Thoracic Surgeons; Am Col Cardiol; Am Col Chest Physicians; Int Soc Heart & Lung Transplantation. *Res:* Perioperative care in cardiac surgery. *Mailing Add:* 114 Deborah Rd Newton Centre MA 02159. *Fax:* 617-636-7616; *E-Mail:* robert.bojar@es.slmc.org

BOJAR, SAMUEL, PSYCHIATRY, PSYCHOANALYSIS. *Current Pos:* RETIRED. *Personal Data:* b New York, NY, Jan 23, 15; m 47, Leah Cohen; c Judith (Kaplan) & Robert M. *Educ:* Brown Univ, AB, 36; Univ Rochester, MA, 37; Johns Hopkins Univ, MD, 41; Am Bd Psychiat & Neurol, cert, 52; Am Psychoanal Assoc, cert, 60. *Honors & Awards:* William James lectr, Harvard Divinity Sch, 71-72. *Prof Exp:* Asst psychol, Univ Rochester, 36-37; asst, Harvard Med Sch, 47, res fel, 48-51, instr. 51-61, clin assoc, 61-67, from asst prof to assoc clin prof psychiat, 67-85. *Concurrent Pos:* Internship, Jewish Hosp Brooklyn, 41-42 asst res path, 43; res, Boston Psychopath Hosp, 47-48; asst, Peter Bent Brigham Hosp, 48-49, from jr assoc to assoc, 50-58, sr assoc, 58-83, physician, 83-89; candidate, Boston Psychoanal Inst, 51-56; psychiatrist, Harvard Med Area Health Serv, 53-79; lectr, Harvard Divinity Sch, 63-81; hon physician, Brigham & Women's Hosp, 89- *Mem:* Sigma Xi; fel Am Psychiat Asn; Am Psychoanal Asn. *Res:* Psychoanalysis; psychosomatic and psychophysiological correlates of personality and behavior; motivational studies in higher education. *Mailing Add:* 10 Aston Rd Chestnut Hill MA 02167-2216

BOK, P DEAN, ANATOMY, CELL BIOLOGY. *Current Pos:* From asst prof to assoc prof, 68-76, assoc dir, Jules Stein Eye Inst, 72-78, PROF ANAT, UNIV CALIF, LOS ANGELES, 76- *Personal Data:* b Douglas Co, SDak, Nov 1, 39; m 64; c 3. *Educ:* Calvin Col, AB, 60; Calif State Univ, Long Beach, MA, 65; Univ Calif, Los Angeles, PhD(anat), 68. *Honors & Awards:* Gladys Shea Award, Univ Calif, Los Angeles, 68. *Concurrent Pos:* Nat Council Combat Blindness fel, Univ Calif, Los Angeles, 68-69, USPHS grant, 68-81; mem bd sci counselors, Nat Eye Inst, 80-, Retinal & Choroidal Dis Panel, 80-81. *Mem:* Fel AAAS; Asn Res Vision & Ophthal; Am Asn Anatomists; Am Soc Cell Biol. *Res:* Cell biology of retinal photoreceptors and pigment epithelium including interactions between these cell types that involve circadian and diurnal phenomena, vitamin A transport, membrane receptors and inherited photoreceptor degenerations. *Mailing Add:* Jules Stein Eye Inst Univ Calif Ctr Health Sci Los Angeles CA 90024

BOKE, NORMAN HILL, PLANT ANATOMY, MORPHOLOGY. *Current Pos:* PROF BOT, UNIV OKLA, 45- *Personal Data:* b Mobridge, SDak, Mar 14, 13; m 48; c 1. *Educ:* Univ SDak, AB, 34; Univ Okla, MS, 36; Univ Calif, PhD(bot), 39. *Prof Exp:* Asst bot, Univ SDak, 33-34 & Univ Okla, 34-36; asst bot, Univ Calif, 36-39, instr, 39-40, exp work in genetics & cytol, Bot Gardens, 40-41; inst biol, Univ NMex, 41-42; Johns Hopkins Univ, 42-44; opers analyst, US Army Air Force Pac Ocean Area & Seventh Air Force, 44-45. *Concurrent Pos:* Guggenheim fel, 53-54; ed-in-chief, Am J Bot, Bot Soc Am, 70-75. *Mem:* Bot Soc Am; Torrey Bot Club; Bot Soc Mex; Mex Soc Cactology; Explorers' Club. *Res:* Developmental anatomy and morphology of vascular plants; development of foliar organs; floral histogenesis; developmental morphology of Cactaceae. *Mailing Add:* 610 Broad Lane Norman OK 73069

BOKELMAN, DELWIN LEE, PATHOLOGY. *Current Pos:* pathologist, Merck Inst Therapeut Res, 64-67, dir path, 67-77, dir toxicol, 70-77, sr dir safety assessment, 77-81, exec dir safety assessment, 81-87, VPRES SAFETY ASSESSMENT, MERCK RES LABS, WEST POINT, PA, 87- *Personal Data:* b Linn, Kans, Sept 13, 34; m 58, Karen M Carlson; c Mark C, Lorrie L, John D & Amy L. *Educ:* Kans State Univ, BS & DVM, 58; Cornell Univ, PhD(path), 64. *Prof Exp:* Resident vet immunol, Plum Island Animal Dis Lab, USDA, NY, 58-59; instr path, NY State Vet Col, Cornell Univ, 60-61, NIH trainee, 61-64. *Mem:* Fel Am Vet Med Asn. *Res:* Safety assessment of pharmaceuticals. *Mailing Add:* 81 Woodview Dr Doylestown PA 18901. *Fax:* 215-652-3888

BOKLAGE, CHARLES EDWARD, HUMAN REPRODUCTIVE EPIDEMIOLOGY, BIOLOGY OF TWINNING, MALFORMATIONS AND INFANT MORTALITY. *Current Pos:* PROF GENETICS, BIOL & PEDIAT, DEPT PEDIAT, E CAROLINA UNIV, 78- *Personal Data:* b Louisville, Ky, Aug 25, 44; m 92, Brenda Taylor; c Leah, Anna, Lara, Kelly, Ginger, Georgia & Alana. *Educ:* Bellarmine Col, AB, 65; Univ Calif-San Diego, La Jolla, PhD(biol), 72. *Prof Exp:* Res assoc & vis asst prof, Biol Div, Kans State Univ, 72-75; fel med genetics, biostatist, neurobiol & develop psychol, Sch Med & Pub Health, Univ NC, 75-78. *Concurrent Pos:* Vis prof, Nat Inst Mental Health, Washington, 77, Charing Cross Hosp Med Sch, London, Eng, 78, Dept psychiat, Duke Univ, 78, Univ Alberta Med Sch, 80, dept neurol, Harvard Med Sch, 84, Katholyke Univ, Belgium, 87-; ed assoc, Behav & Brain Sci, 81- *Mem:* Fel & founding mem, Int Soc Twin Studies; Int Neuropsychol Soc; Am Soc Human Genetics; Am Statist Asn; Sigma Xi. *Res:* Work to understand the cellular events of human embryogenesis, the determinants of normal structures of brain and body and of malformations thereof, and the biology of infant mortality. *Mailing Add:* 3E132 B Brody Bldg Dept Pediat E Carolina Univ Greenville NC 27858-4354. *E-Mail:* gnboklag@ecuvm.cis.ecu.edu

BOKOCH, GARY M, SIGNAL TRANSDUCTION, GTP BINDING PROTEINS. *Current Pos:* Asst mem, 85-90, ASSOC MEM, SCRIPPS RES INST, 91- *Personal Data:* b Erie, Pa, Apr 15, 54; m 77, Janet Nicolia; c Jennifer N & Rebecca N. *Educ:* Pa State Univ, BS, 76; Vanderbilt Univ, PhD(pharmacol), 81. *Honors & Awards:* Louis N Katz Award, Am Heart Asn, 88, John J Sampson Res Award, 89; Young Investr Award, Soc Leukocyte Biol, 87. *Prof Exp:* Fel, Southwestern Med Sch, Univ Tex, 81-85. *Concurrent Pos:* Estab investr, Am Heart Asn, 86-91. *Mem:* Am Heart Asn; Am Soc Immunologists; Am Soc Biochem & Molecular Biol; Am Soc Cell Biol. *Res:* Research involves signal transduction in phagocytic cells and white blood cells by GTP-binding proteins of both the heterotrimeric (receptor-coupled) and low molecular weight (ras-like) variety. *Mailing Add:* Dept Immunol Scripps Res Inst 10550 N Torrey Pines Rd La Jolla CA 92037. *Fax:* 619-784-8218; *E-Mail:* bokoch@scripps.edu

BOKROS, J(ACK) C(HESTER), BIOMATERIALS. *Current Pos:* PRES & CHIEF EXEC OFFICER, MED CARBON RES INST, 94- *Personal Data:* b Park Falls, Wis, Feb 24, 31; m 58, Roberta Capen; c Kathleen, Carol & Linda. *Educ:* Univ Wis, BS, 54, MS, 55; Univ Calif, Berkeley, PhD(metall), 63. *Hon Degrees:* Rose-Hulman Inst Technol, DEng, 86. *Honors & Awards:* IR-100 Award, Indust Res, 71; Charles E Pettinos Award, Am Carbon Soc, 75; Clemson Univ Award, Soc Biomat, 76. *Prof Exp:* Sr res engr, Atomics Int Div, NAm Aviation Inc, 55-58; res staff mem, John Jay Hopkins Lab, Pure & Appl Sci, Div Gen Dynamics Corp, 58-69; dir, Med Prod Div, Gen Atomic Co, 69-78; pres, Carbomedics, Inc, 79-88; pres & chief exec officer, Carbon Implants, Inc, 89-94. *Concurrent Pos:* Consult, Gen Atomic Div, Gen Dynamics Corp, 60-62 & Aerojet Nuclear Div, Gen Tire & Rubber Co, 61-62. *Mem:* Am Soc Testing & Mat; Am Carbon Soc; Soc Biomat; Am Heart Asn; Am Soc Artificial Internal Organs; Am Inst Med & Biol Eng. *Res:* Physical and mechanical metallurgy; structure and properties of pyrolytic carbon; irradiation effects in pyrolytic carbon and graphite; crystallography and kinetics transformation; biomaterials; medical devices. *Mailing Add:* 2204 Manana St Austin TX 78730. *Fax:* 512-339-3636; *E-Mail:* bokros@mcritx.com

BOKSAY, ISTVAN JANOS ENDRE, MEDICINE, CLINICAL PHARMACOLOGY. *Current Pos:* PVT PRACT. *Personal Data:* b Ungvar, Hungary, June 22, 40; Ger citizen; wid; c 1. *Educ:* Univ Med Sch, Budapest, MD, 64; Inst Med Sch, Frankfurt, PhD(pharmacol), 72. *Prof Exp:* Intern, Budapest, Hungary, 63-64; resident, Hosp Neurol & Psychiat, 64-65; pharmacologist, Chem Fabrik v Heyden/Squibb, 65-68; sr pharmacologist, Hoechst AG, 68, exec res asst head, Pharmaceut Div, 70, head, Sect Clin Pharmacol & Drug Develop, 72-75; assoc dir clin res & internal med, Hoechst-Roussel Pharmaceut Inc, 75-78; dir clin res, Ayerst Labs, Div AM Home Prod Corp, 78- *Concurrent Pos:* Fel, Coun Stroke, Am Heart Asn. *Mem:* Int Soc Clin Pharmacol & Therapeut; AAAS; Int Soc Neurochem; Am Soc Clin Pharmacol & Therapeut; Int Union Biochem. *Res:* Basic research; research coordination; clinical pharmacology and clinical evaluation of new drugs in Phase I-IV analgesic, antihypertensive, antiinflammatory, beta-blocking, diuretics, hormones, psychotropic and vasoactive agents; anti-anginal drugs, immunosuppressives, and immunostimulants; biostatistics. *Mailing Add:* Seven N Crescent Maplewood NJ 07040

BOKUNIEWICZ, HENRY JOSEPH, GEOPHYSICS, MARINE GEOLOGY. *Current Pos:* from asst prof to assoc prof, 77-91, PROF GEOL OCEANOG, MARINE SCI RES CTR, STATE UNIV NY, STONY BROOK, 91- *Personal Data:* b Chicago, Ill, July 29, 49; m 71, Linda Sedey; c Roxana. *Educ:* Univ Ill, BA, 71; Yale Univ, MPhil, 73, PhD(geophysics), 76. *Prof Exp:* Res assoc geophys, Yale Univ, 76-77. *Concurrent Pos:* Res affil, US Army Engrs, 71-75, 79-, Waterways Exp Sta, 75-77, Geol Soc Am, 74-75, NY Off Gen Serv, 77-78 & 89-93, Nat Oceang & Atmospheric Admin, 80-90 & US Environ Protection Agency, 86-91; mem, Working Group on Effects of Sand & Gravel Extraction, Int Coun Explor Sea, 88-94; chair, Contaminated Sediments Comt, Nat Res Coun, 94. *Mem:* Am Geophys Union; Geol Soc Am; Estuarine Res Fed. *Res:* Sediment transport and coastal oceanography; dredging specialist; coastal groundwater hydrology; contaminated sediment-identification impacts and remediation; marine mining. *Mailing Add:* Dept Marine Sci State Univ NY 100 Nicolls Rd Stony Brook NY 11794-0001

BOL, KEES, PLASMA PHYSICS. *Current Pos:* RETIRED. *Personal Data:* b Netherlands, June 16, 25; nat US; m 47; c 4. *Educ:* Stanford Univ, PhD(physics), 50. *Prof Exp:* Proj engr electron beams res, Sperry Gyroscope Co, 49-54; asst prof physics, Adelphi Univ, 54-57; NSF fel, Harvard Univ, 57-59; mem res staff, Proj Matterhorn, 59-64, mem res staff, 64-83, mgr exp projs, Plasma Physics Lab, Princeton Univ, 83-88. *Mem:* fel Am Phys Soc. *Res:* Measurement of velocity of light; electron beam problems; problems of tokamak plasmas. *Mailing Add:* 37 Stouts Rd Skillman NJ 08558

BOLAFFI, JANICE LERNER, ENDOCRINOLOGY, NEUROENDOCRINOLOGY. *Current Pos:* RETIRED. *Personal Data:* b Boston, Mass Aug 12, 33; m 54, Andre; c David & Miriam. *Educ:* Brandeis Univ, BA, 54; Boston Univ, MA, 73, PhD(biol), 78. *Prof Exp:* Res fel endocrinol, New Eng Med Ctr Hosp, 78-81; vis asst prof physiol, Sch Med, Tufts Univ, 81-83; res biochemist, Univ Calif, San Francisco, 84-93. *Mem:* AAAS; Endocrine Soc; Am Soc Zoologists; NY Acad Sci; Sigma Xi; Am Diabetes Asn. *Res:* Regulation of secretion of and synthesis of islet hormones, especially insulin. *Mailing Add:* 2331 Bush St San Francisco CA 94115. *E-Mail:* jbolaffi@aol.com

BOLAND, JAMES P, CARDIOVASCULAR SURGERY, THORACIC SURGERY. *Current Pos:* PROF SURG, WVA UNIV, CHARLESTON, 76-; CHIEF SURG, CHARLESTON AREA MED CTR, 76- *Personal Data:* b Philadelphia, Pa, Mar 6, 31; m 63; c 6. *Educ:* St Joseph's Col, Pa, BS, 52; Jefferson Med Col, MD, 56. *Prof Exp:* From assoc prof to prof surg, Med Col Pa, 64-76. *Mem:* Soc Thoracic Surg; Am Col Surgeons. *Mailing Add:* 3110 MacCorkle Ave Charleston WV 25304-1210

BOLAND, JOHN JAMES, ATOM-RESOLVED STUDIES OF SURFACES, SEMICONDUCTOR SURFACE CHEMISTRY. *Current Pos:* ASSOC PROF, DEPT CHEM, UNIV NC, 94- *Personal Data:* b Dublin, Ireland, Feb 3, 58; m, Noeleen C Woods; c Keith P & Conor S. *Educ:* Univ Col Dublin, BS, 79; Calif Inst Technol, PhD(chem), 85. *Prof Exp:* Res staff, T J Watson Res Ctr, IBM, 84-94. *Res:* Reactions on surfaces and the growth of materials; semi-conductors and devices of nanoscale dimensions. *Mailing Add:* Dept Chem Univ NC Chapel Hill NC 27599-3290. *Fax:* 919-962-2388; *E-Mail:* boland@unc.edu

BOLAND, JOSEPH S(AMUEL), III, ELECTRICAL ENGINEERING. *Current Pos:* instr elec eng, 65-68, ASSOC DIR, CONTINUING EDUC VIDEO PROGS, GA INST TECHNOL, 92- *Personal Data:* b Montgomery, Ala, Sept 23, 39; m 62; c 2. *Educ:* Auburn Univ, BEE, 61, MSEE, 65; Ga Inst Technol, PhD(elec eng), 69. *Honors & Awards:* Western Elec Award, 77. *Prof Exp:* Instr elec eng, Auburn Univ, 61-62, res asst, Missile Attitude Control Systs, 64-65, from asst prof to prof elec eng, 68-92, assoc dean eng, 82-92. *Concurrent Pos:* Proj leader, NASA contract, 68-72; consult & proj leader, US Army Missile Command, 73-85. *Mem:* Inst Elec & Electronics Engrs; Am Soc Eng Educ. *Res:* Modern control theory and applications; attitude control of space vehicles; adaptive systems; correlation techniques. *Mailing Add:* Continuing Educ Video Progs Ga Inst Technol Atlanta GA 30332

BOLAND, W ROBERT, NUMERICAL MATHEMATICS, MATHEMATICAL SOFTWARE. *Current Pos:* MEM STAFF, LOS ALAMOS NAT LAB, 81- *Personal Data:* b Winter Haven, Fla, Sept 11, 37; m 60, Beryl A Pope; c Eric R & Kevin S. *Educ:* Davidson Col, BS, 59; Col William & Mary, MA, 63; Univ Colo, PhD(appl math), 68. *Prof Exp:* Mathematician, Langley Res Ctr, NASA, 59-63; instr math, Randolph-Macon Col, 63-64; NSF trainee, Univ Colo, 65-67; asst prof math, Drexel Univ, 67-70; from asst prof to prof, Clemson Univ, 70-81. *Mem:* Soc Indust & Appl Math. *Res:* Integral equations; operations research; computer science. *Mailing Add:* Los Alamos Nat Lab CIC-7 MS B294 PO Box 1663 Los Alamos NM 87545. *Fax:* 505-665-6333; *E-Mail:* wrb@lanl.gov

BOLANDE, ROBERT PAUL, PATHOLOGY. *Current Pos:* PROF PATH, E CAROLINA SCH MED, 82- *Personal Data:* b Chicago, Ill, Apr 16, 26; m 54; c 4. *Educ:* Northwestern Univ, BS, 48, MS & MD, 52; Am Bd Path, dipl, 58. *Honors & Awards:* Sidney Farber Mem lectr, Soc Pediat Path, 85. *Prof Exp:* Intern, Chicago Wesley Mem Hosp, 52-53; resident pediat path, Children's Mem Hosp Chicago, 53-54; from resident to chief resident path, Inst Path, Case Western Reserve Univ, 54-56, from instr to assoc prof path, Sch Med, 56-72, sr instr pediat, 58-72, chg pediat path, Inst & Hosp, 56-72; prof path, McGill Univ, 72-82, prof pediat, 75-82. *Concurrent Pos:* USPHS grants, 58 & 64; consult, Inst Path, Case Western Reserve Univ, 66-; chief pathologist & dir labs, Akron Children's Hosp, 66-72; co-ed, Perspectives in Pediat Path, 70-; dir path, Montreal Children's Hosp, 72-80. *Mem:* Am Asn Path & Bact; Int Acad Path; Soc Pediat Path. *Res:* Application of electron microscopy, histochemistry and tissue culture to the study of disease in early life, especially neoplasia and natural host resistance in neoplasia. *Mailing Add:* Dept Path E Carolina Sch Med Brody Bldg Rm 7518 Greenville NC 27834-4354

BOLANDER, RICHARD, ENGINEERING EDUCATION. *Current Pos:* from asst prof to prof math, Gen Motors Inst, 69-80, prof mech eng, 81-86, asst head, Dept Mech Eng & Mgt Inst, 82-86, PROF ENG PHYSICS & MATH, GMI ENG & MGT INST PROF & CHAIR APPL PHYSICS, 93- *Personal Data:* b Parsons, Kans, Mar 26, 40; m 59, Barbara Meriwether; c William, Deborah, Thomas & Robert. *Educ:* Mo Sch Mines, BS, 61; Tex Christian Univ, MS, 63; Univ Mo, Rolla, PhD(physics), 69. *Prof Exp:* Assoc engr, Gen Dynamics, Ft Worth, 62; instr physics, Tex Woman's Univ, 63-65; asst prof, La Polytech Inst, 65-66; from instr to asst prof ceramic eng, Univ Mo, Rolla, 67-69, res assoc cloud physics, 69. *Concurrent Pos:* Adj grad fac, Purdue Univ, 87- *Mem:* Am Soc Eng Educ; Am Phys Soc. *Mailing Add:* Dept Sci Math GMI Eng & Mgt Inst Flint MI 48504-4898. *Fax:* 810-762-9796; *E-Mail:* rbolande@nova.gmi.edu

BOLANDER, WILLIAM J, MECHANICAL ENGINEERING. *Current Pos:* ALGORITHM TECH RESOURCE LEADER & AUTOMOTIVE ENGR, GEN MOTORS POWERTRAIN, PONTIAC, MICH, 94- *Personal Data:* b Rolla, Mich, 1960; m, Beth; c 2. *Educ:* Purdue Univ, MME, 84. *Honors & Awards:* Jerome H Lemelson Prize for Excellence in Invention & Innovation, Mass Inst Technol, 95. *Res:* Granted patents for vehicle engine ignition timing system with adaptive knock retard; coast sync coast downshift control methods for clutch to clutch transmission shifting; valve position sensor diagnostic; throttle position sensor error recovery control method; fuel control system for engine during coolant failure. *Mailing Add:* Tech Ctr General Motors Corp 30200 Mound Rd Warren MI 48092-2025

BOLANOS, BENJAMIN, MEDICAL MYCOLOGY, AIR MICROBIOLOGY. *Current Pos:* ASSOC PROF MICROBIOL, UNIV PR MED SCI CAMPUS, 83- *Personal Data:* b Cali, Columbia, Apr 22, 57; m 87, Ester Ortiz. *Educ:* Univ Valle, BS, 73; Univ Antioquia, MS, 77; Duke Univ, PhD(microbiol & immunol), 83. *Prof Exp:* Res asst mycol, Int Ctr Med Res, 73-75; instr microbiol, Univ Valle, 77-78. *Concurrent Pos:* Med mycol consult, Vet Admin Med Ctr, 85-; consult, Occup & Safety Health Admin, 88 & PR Dept Health, 90-; lectr trop med, USN, 90-93. *Mem:* Int Soc Human & Vet Mycol; Am Soc Microbiol; AAAS. *Res:* Cryptococcosis in AIDS patients; interaction between the fungus Cryptococcus neoformans and the host which involves multiple virulence factors of the fungus; virulence factors of cryptococcus neoformans and purification of antigens for detection of cell mediated immunity in cryptococcosis. *Mailing Add:* Microbiol & Med Zool Univ PR PO Box 365067 San Juan PR 00936-5067. *Fax:* 787-758-4808

BOLCH, WILLIAM EMMETT, JR, ENVIRONMENTAL ENGINEERING, RADIOLOGICAL HEALTH. *Current Pos:* PROF ENVIRON ENG, UNIV FLA, 66- *Personal Data:* b Lenoir, NC, Oct 27, 35; m 59; c 2. *Educ:* Univ Tex, Austin, BS, 59, MS, 64; Univ Calif, Berkeley, PhD(sanit eng), 67. *Concurrent Pos:* Consult engr, Fla Power & Light, Miami, Fla, Environ Sci & Eng, Inc, Gainesville & Ardaman & Assoc, Orlando. *Mem:* Am Nuclear Soc; Health Physics Soc. *Res:* Radiotracer techniques; radiological health; radioactive waste disposal; radiological health and health physics; radon. *Mailing Add:* Dept Environ Eng 217 Black Hall Univ Fla Gainesville FL 32611-2013

BOLDEN, THEODORE EDWARD, DENTISTRY, PATHOLOGY. *Current Pos:* RETIRED. *Personal Data:* b Middleburg, Va, Apr 19, 20; wid, Dorothy M Forde. *Educ:* Lincoln Univ, Pa, AB, 41; Meharry Med Col, DDS, 47; Univ Ill, Chicago Circle, MS, 51, PhD(path), 58; Am Bd Oral Med, dipl, 70; Am Bd Oral Path, dipl, 72. *Hon Degrees:* LLD, Lincoln Univ, 81. *Prof Exp:* Instr periodont & oper dent, Meharry Med Col, 48-49; instr oral path, Sch Dent, Univ Ill, 55-57; asst prof oral diag & path, Seton Hall Col, 57-60, assoc prof, 60-62; prof dent & oral med, Sch Dent, Meharry Med Col, 62-69, dir res, 62-73, assoc dean, Sch Dent, 69-73, prof oral path & chmn dept, 69-77; prof path, Col Med & Dent NJ, NJ Dent Sch, 77-90, dean, 77-78. *Concurrent Pos:* Lectr, Meharry Med Col & Univ Ill, 56; attend, Med Ctr, NJ, 58-62; chmn adv health comt, Town of Montclair, NJ, 59-60, comnr urban develop, 61-62; abstractor, NY State Dent J, 60 & J Oral Therapeut & Pharmacol, 64; consult, Vet Admin Hosp, Tuskegee, Ala, 62-89, Nashville, Tenn, 68-77 & Brooklyn, Ny, 79-90; consult, Inst Advan Educ Dent Res, Colgate-Palmolive Co, 67-70; ed, Quart Nat Dent Asn, 75-82, consult, US Dept Health & Human Serv, 80 & 81; trustee, Am Fund Dent Health, 77-85, Neighborhood Coun, 85. *Mem:* Nat Dent Asn; Int Asn Dent Res; fel Am Acad Oral Path; NY Acad Sci; fel Am Acad Oral Med; Sigma Xi. *Res:* Histology; periodontal disease; salivary gland pathology; lacrimal gland pathology; pigmentation; effect of aging; experimental carcinogenesis; oral neoplasia. *Mailing Add:* 29 Montague Pl Montclair NJ 07042

BOLDRIDGE, DAVID WILLIAM, AEROSOL SCIENCE, RHEOLOGY. *Current Pos:* sr res chemist, 92-95, GROUP LEADER, CAB-O-SIL DIV, CABOT CORP, 95- *Personal Data:* b Richmond, Va, Dec 28, 54; m 79, Allison Andrews; c Cliff & Drew. *Educ:* Davidson Col, BS, 77; Univ Calif, Riverside, MS, 80, PhD(chem), 84. *Prof Exp:* Chemist res & develop, R J Reynolds Tobacco Co, 84-91. *Mem:* Am Chem Soc; Am Phys Soc; Am Asn Aerosol Res; Soc Rheol. *Res:* Aerosol properties and dynamics; fast reaction kinetics and mechanisms; laser spectroscopy; determination of morphology and chemistry of colloidal particles; relating colloidal particle properties to rheological performance. *Mailing Add:* 700 E US Hwy 36 Tuscola IL 61953

BOLDRIDGE, WILLIAM FRANKLIN, PHYSICAL CHEMISTRY. *Current Pos:* RETIRED. *Personal Data:* b Culpeper Co, Va, Sept 3, 17; m 42, Mary M Crigler; c Katherine A (Ellis) & David W. *Educ:* Randolph-Macon Col, BS, 39; WVa Univ, MS, 41, PhD(chem), 53. *Prof Exp:* Asst, WVa Univ, 39-41; chemist, Am Viscose Corp, Va, 41-43 & Clinton Labs, Oak Ridge, 44-45; asst prof physics, Randolph-Macon Col, 43-44; from asst prof to prof chem, Randolph-Macon Col, 49-83. *Mem:* Am Chem Soc. *Res:* Organic reagents as inorganic precipitants; radiochemistry; physics; radioactive tracer technique in the study of adsorption. *Mailing Add:* 11471 Ashcake Rd Ashland VA 23005

BOLDRY, ROBERT C, neuropharmacology, basal ganglia & movement disorders, for more information see previous edition

BOLDT, DAVID H, HEMATOLOGY, IMMUNOLOGY. *Current Pos:* PROF MED & CHIEF DIV HEMAT, HEALTH SCI CTR, UNIV TEX, SAN ANTONIO, 80- *Educ:* Tufts Univ, MD, 69. *Res:* Oncology. *Mailing Add:* Dept Med Health Sci Ctr Univ Tex 7703 Floyd Curl Dr San Antonio TX 78284-7842

BOLDT, ELIHU (AARON), PHYSICS. *Current Pos:* Nat Acad Sci sr res assoc cosmic ray physics, 64-66, GROUP LEADER X-RAY ASTRON, GODDARD SPACE FLIGHT CTR, 66- *Personal Data:* b New Brunswick, NJ, July 15, 31; m 71; c 3. *Educ:* Mass Inst Technol, SB, 53, PhD(physics), 58. *Prof Exp:* Guest scientist, Brookhaven Nat Lab, 55-57; res scientist physics, Mass Inst Technol, 58; asst prof, Rutgers Univ, 58-64. *Concurrent Pos:* Res assoc physics lab, Polytech Sch, Paris, 60-62. *Mem:* Fel Am Phys Soc; Am Astron Soc; Int Astron Union. *Res:* High energy astrophysics; elementary particles. *Mailing Add:* NASA Code 666 Goddard Space Flight Ctr Greenbelt MD 20771

BOLDT, ROGER EARL, BIOCHEMISTRY. *Current Pos:* RETIRED. *Personal Data:* b Milwaukee, Wis, Dec 23, 28; m 54; c 3. *Educ:* Univ Wis, BS, 51, MS, 53, PhD(biochem), 58. *Prof Exp:* Asst, Univ Wis, 51-58, proj assoc pediat, 58; USPHS cancer trainee, Univ Minn, 58-60; asst prof biochem, Univ Pittsburgh, 61; res biochemist, Directorate Med Res, Edgewood Arsenal, Md, 61-66; chief, Biochem Br, US Army Environ Hyg Agency, 66-81, non-metals anal br, 81-89, chief, Radiol & Inorg Chem Div, 89- *Concurrent Pos:* Adj prof chem, Univ Md, 64-66. *Mem:* Sigma Xi. *Res:* Analysis of pollutants in environmental and tissue samples. *Mailing Add:* 113 Duncannon Rd Bel Air MD 21014

BOLE, GILES G, INTERNAL MEDICINE, RHEUMATOLOGY. *Current Pos:* Resident physician, Univ Hosp, Univ Mich, 54-56, instr med, Med Sch, 58-61, from asst prof to assoc prof, 61-70, chief, Rheumatol Div, 76-86, sr assoc dean, 86-90, PROF INTERNAL MED, RACKHAM ARTHRITIS RES UNIT, UNIV MICH, ANN ARBOR, 70-, INTERIM DEAN, MED SCH, 90- *Personal Data:* b Battle Creek, Mich, July 28, 28; m 85; c 2. *Educ:* Univ Mich, BS, 49, MD, 53. *Concurrent Pos:* Arthritis Found fel, 61-63, sr investr, 63-68; dir, Multipurpose Arthritis Ctr, 77-86; mem, Nat Arthritis Adv Bd, 81-87; Am Bd Internal Med, 62-; Subspeciality Bd Rheumatology, 74- *Mem:* Am Rheumatism Asn (pres, 80). *Res:* Biochemistry and biomechanic studies of osteoarthritis. *Mailing Add:* 6015 W Ellsworth Rd M7324 Med Sci I Ann Arbor MI 48103

BOLEF, DAN ISADORE, SOLID STATE PHYSICS. *Current Pos:* PROF PHYSICS, WASH UNIV, 63- *Personal Data:* b Philadelphia, Pa, June 10, 21; m 44; c 3. *Educ:* Columbia Univ, AM, 48, PhD(physics), 52. *Prof Exp:* Instr physics, Stevens Inst Technol, 48-49; from instr to asst prof math & physics, State Univ NY, 49-53; res physicist, Westinghouse Res Labs, 53-63. *Concurrent Pos:* Vis prof, Empire State Col, 74-75. *Mem:* Fel Am Phys Soc. *Res:* Nuclear and electron spin-phonon interactions in solids; elastic properties of solids; acoustic magnetic resonance; acoustic absorption and dispersion in metals, ferromagnets; ultrasonic high frequency techniques. *Mailing Add:* RD 1 Box 134 Irwin PA 15642

BOLEMON, JAY S, physics, for more information see previous edition

BOLEN, DAVID WAYNE, PHYSICAL BIOCHEMISTRY. *Current Pos:* from asst prof to assoc prof, 71-81, PROF BIOCHEM, SOUTHERN ILL UNIV, CARBONDALE, 77- *Personal Data:* b Whitby, WVa, May 23, 42; m 64; c 3. *Educ:* Concord Col, BS, 64; Fla State Univ, PhD(biophys chem), 69. *Prof Exp:* NIH res fel biochem, Johns Hopkins Univ, 69-70 & Univ Minn, 70-71. *Concurrent Pos:* Sabbatical leave, Univ Chicago, 78-79 & Johns Hopkins Univ, 85-86. *Mem:* Am Chem Soc; Biophys Soc; Am Soc Biochem & Molecular Biol. *Res:* Thermodynamics; kinetics; mechanisms of interacting systems; protein folding. *Mailing Add:* Dept Human Biol Chem & Genetics Univ Tex Med Br 5-154A Med Res Bldg Galveston TX 77555-1052

BOLEN, ERIC GEORGE, WILDLIFE ECOLOGY. *Current Pos:* DEAN, GRAD SCH, UNIV NC, 88- *Personal Data:* b Plainfield, NJ, Nov 24, 37; c 2. *Educ:* Univ Maine, BS, 59; Utah State Univ, MS, 62, PhD(wildlife), 67. *Prof Exp:* Instr biol, Tex A&I Univ, 65-66; from asst prof to prof, Texas Tech Univ, 66-73, prof range & wildlife mgt & assoc dean, grad sch, 78-88, Paul Whitfield Horn prof, 81-88. *Concurrent Pos:* Asst dir, Welder Wildlife Found, 73-78; adj prof, Corpus Christi State Univ, 74-; mem, Fish & Wildlife & Park Natural Sci Adv Conf for Secy Interior, 75-78; ed, Wildlife Soc Bull, 75-78; ed bd, Conserv Biol. *Mem:* Wildlife Soc; Wilson Ornith Soc; Am Ornith Union; Am Soc Mammal; Cooper Ornith Soc; Soc Range Mgt; Forest & Conserv Hist Soc; Nat Leaders Am Conserv. *Res:* Waterfowl ecology and management; wetland ecology; non-game ecology and management; ornithology; plant ecology; environmental history; author of 3 textbooks. *Mailing Add:* Biol Dept Univ NC Wilmington NC 28403

BOLEN, LEE NAPIER, JR, ACOUSTICS. *Current Pos:* from asst prof to assoc prof, 64-70, PROF PHYSICS, UNIV MISS, 70- *Personal Data:* b Memphis, Tenn, June 11, 37; m 60; c 1. *Educ:* Univ Miss, BS, 59; Univ Va, MS, 61, PhD(physics), 64. *Prof Exp:* Res assoc physics, Univ Va, 63-64. *Mem:* Am Phys Soc; Am Asn Physics Teachers; Sigma Xi; Acoust Soc Am; AAAS; Nat Asn Acad Sci. *Res:* Instrumentation design; physical acoustics. *Mailing Add:* Dept Physics Univ Miss University MS 38677

BOLEN, MAX CARLTON, HIGH POLYMER PHYSICS-SOLUTIONS, SCIENCE EDUCATION. *Current Pos:* head dept, Univ Tex, El Paso, 65-69, prof physics, 65-87, coordr sci educ, Col Sci, 69-87, EMER PROF PHYSICS, UNIV TEX, EL PASO, 87- *Personal Data:* b Waynetown, Ind, Sept 23, 19; m 42, Lois Larkins; c Ronald L & Roger K. *Educ:* Wabash Col, AB, 41; Univ Chicago, cert meteorol, 43; Purdue Univ, MS, 50; Tex A&M Univ, PhD, 61. *Honors & Awards:* B T Slate Award Outstanding Contrib to Phys Sci, 86. *Prof Exp:* Teacher high sch, Ind, 41-42; asst physics, Purdue Univ, 46-48; from asst prof to assoc prof & chmn dept, Millikin Univ, 48-59; assoc prof & chmn dept, Trinity Univ, Tex, 59-63; assoc prof, Oklahoma City Univ, 63-65. *Concurrent Pos:* Vis asst prof, Tex A&M Univ, 57-58, Robert A Welch res fel, 58-59; consult, Prog Develop Div, Tex Educ Agency, 68-87; meteorologist, WTVP-TV Sta, Decatur, Ill, 53-55, KOCO, Oklahoma City, Okla, 64-65; sr res physicist, Southwest Res Inst, Tex, 63. *Mem:* Fel AAAS; Am Asn Physics Teachers; Am Phys Soc; Am Meteorol Soc; Nat Sci Teachers Asn. *Res:* Science education and how students learn science; high polymer physics. *Mailing Add:* 6625 Westwind Dr El Paso TX 79912-3831. *E-Mail:* wxmu21c@prodiogy.com

BOLENDER, CARROLL H, AERONAUTICAL SCIENCE. *Current Pos:* RETIRED. *Personal Data:* b Cincinnati, Ohio, Nov 2, 19; m 42; c 2. *Educ:* Wilmington Col, Ohio, BS, 41; Ohio State Univ, MBA, 49. *Honors & Awards:* Apollo Achievement Award, Apollo Mgt Team Award & Group Group Achievement Award, NASA, 69. *Prof Exp:* US Air Force, 41-, chief B-58 weapon systs proj, Detachment 1 Air Res & Develop Command, 58-61, prog dir, Skybolt, Aeronaut Systs Div, Air Force Systs command, 61-62, asst prog dir, 62, Skybolt test dir, Air Proving Ground Ctr, 62-63, dep chief staff opers, 63-64, adv study group, Off VChief Staff, Hq, Washington, DC, 64-65, Apollo mission dir, Off Manned Space Flight, hq, NASA, 65-67, lunar module prog mgr, Manned Spacecraft Ctr, Houston, 67-69, dept dir develop & acquisition, Dep Chief Staff res & develop, Hq, US Air Force Pentagon, 69-72; dep prog mgr, Hampton Opers, Syst Develop Corp, Va, 72-73, prog mgr, 73-79; consult, Eng Inc, Va, 79-81; consult, 81-84; prog mgr, Syst Develop Corp & Unisys, Va, 84-88. *Mailing Add:* 128 Randolph's Green Williamsburg VA 23185-6537

BOLENDER, CHARLES L, DENTISTRY. *Current Pos:* From instr to assoc prof, 59-68, chmn dept, 63-89, PROF PROSTHODONTICS, SCH DENT, UNIV WASH, 68- *Personal Data:* b Iowa City, Iowa, June 2, 32; m 55; c 3. *Educ:* Univ Iowa, DDS, 56, MS, 57. *Mem:* Am Prosthodontic Soc; Am Dent Asn; fel Am Col Dent; fel Acad Denture Prosthetics; Acad Osseointegration; Am Asn Dent Schs. *Res:* Tissue response to artificial dentures; dental implants. *Mailing Add:* 16730 32nd Pl NE Seattle WA 98155

BOLENDER, DAVID LESLIE, DEVELOPMENTAL & CELL BIOLOGY. *Current Pos:* ASSOC PROF, DEPT CELL BIOL & ANAT, MED COL WIS, 85- *Personal Data:* b Uniontown, Pa, June 11, 47; m 90, Joan Boorsma; c Chris, Philip, Kara, Tricia, Aaron & Angie. *Educ:* Bethany Col, WVa, BS, 69; WVa Univ, PhD(anat), 75. *Prof Exp:* Asst prof anat, Sch Med, Tex Tech Univ, 74-81; asst prof biol, Bethany Col, 81-85. *Mem:* Soc Develop Biol; Am Asn Anatomists. *Res:* Developmental and cell biology, specifically the role of extracellular matrix in mediation of cell differentiation during development of the heart and limbs in cell-cell interactions. *Mailing Add:* Med Col Wis 8701 Watertown Plank Rd Milwaukee WI 53226. *Fax:* 414-778-4293; *E-Mail:* bolender@post.its.mcw.edu

BOLENDER, ROBERT P, CELL BIOLOGY. *Current Pos:* asst prof, 75-81, ASSOC PROF BIOL STRUCT, UNIV WASH, 81- *Personal Data:* b Mt Kisco, NY, Sept 29, 38. *Educ:* State Univ NY Albany, BS, 60; Columbia Univ, MA, 65; Harvard Univ, PhD(anat), 70. *Prof Exp:* Fel anat, Univ Bern, 70-71, from asst to head asst, 71-74; lectr, Harvard Univ, 74-75. *Concurrent Pos:* Vis scholar biochem, Univ Louvain, 71-72. *Mem:* Am Soc Cell Biol; Union Swiss Socs Exp Biol; Int Soc Stereology; Am Asn Anatomists; NY Acad Sci. *Res:* Integration of stereological and biochemical information as a way of analyzing relationships of structure to function mathematically; biological membrane kinetics associated with drugs, toxins, and carcinogens; mathematical models for the liver and lung. *Mailing Add:* Dept Biol Struct Univ Wash Sch Med SM-20 Seattle WA 98195-0001

BOLES, JAMES RICHARD, SEDIMENTARY PETROLOGY. *Current Pos:* from asst prof to assoc prof, 75-81, PROF GEOL, UNIV CALIF, SANTA BARBARA, 81- *Personal Data:* b Richmond, Ind, Sept 3, 44; m 67; c 2. *Educ:* Purdue Univ, BS, 66; Univ Wyo, MS, 68; Univ Otago, NZ, PhD(geol), 72. *Prof Exp:* Fel geol, Univ Wyo, 72-73; res geologist, Geosci Group, Atlantic Richfield Co, 73-75. *Mem:* Am Asn Petrol Geologists. *Res:* Diagenesis of clastic sediments including sandstone cementation, clay diagenesis and zeolitization of volcanogenic sediments; sedimentary basin reconstructions. *Mailing Add:* Dept Geol Univ Calif 552 University Ave Santa Barbara CA 93106-0002

BOLES, ROBERT JOE, AQUATIC BIOLOGY. *Current Pos:* RETIRED. *Personal Data:* b Brandsville, Mo, Nov 7, 16; m 49; c 2. *Educ:* Southwestern Col, Kans, AB, 38; Kans State Univ, MS, 49; Okla State Univ, PhD(zool), 60. *Prof Exp:* Teacher high schs, 39-42 & 45-58; from asst prof to assoc prof, 60-70, prof biol, Emporia State Univ, 70- *Concurrent Pos:* Ed, Kans Sch Naturalist. *Res:* Farm pond dynamics and fish parasitology; productivity and management of small impoundments; parasites of freshwater fishes of Kansas. *Mailing Add:* 2007 Briarcliff Lane Emporia KS 66801

BOLEY, BRUNO ADRIAN, THEORETICAL MECHANICS, APPLIED MECHANICS. *Current Pos:* dean, Technol Inst & Walter P Murphy prof, 73-86, WALTER P MURPHY EMER PROF & DEAN ENG, NORTHWESTERN UNIV, EVANSTON, 86-; PROF CIVIL ENG & ENG MECH, COLUMBIA UNIV, 87- *Personal Data:* b Gorizia, Italy, May 13, 24; US citizen; wid, Sara R Kaufman; c Jacqueline (Acquaviva) & Daniel L. *Educ:* City Col New York, BCE, 43; Polytech Inst Brooklyn, MAeE, 45, SDc, 46. *Hon Degrees:* DSc, City Col New York, 82. *Honors & Awards:* Townsend Harris Medal, 81; Distinguished Serv Medal, Am Acad Mech & Soc Eng Sci, 87; Distinguished Serv Medal, Soc Eng Sci, 87; Theodore von Karman Medal, Am Soc Chem Engrs, 91; Lagrange Lectr, Accadenia Nazionale dei Lincei, Rome, 96. *Prof Exp:* Asst dir struct res, Aeronaut Eng Dept, Polytech Inst, 43-48; Eng specialist, Goodyear Aircraft Corp, 48-50; assoc prof aeronaut eng, Ohio State Univ, 50-52; from assoc prof to prof civil eng, Columbia Univ, 52-68; Joseph P Ripley prof eng & chmn dept theoret & appl mech, Cornell Univ, 68-72. *Concurrent Pos:* NSF sr sci fel, 64-65; mem cong comt, Int Union Theoret & Appl Mech, 70-; NATO sci fel, 72; ed, Mech Res Commun, 74-; chmn, US Nat Comt Theoret & Appl Mech, 74-76, vchmn, 76-78; gen chmn, Int Cong Struct Mech Reactor Technol, 77, adv gen, 79-; chmn, Midwest Prog Minorities Educ, Comt Instnl Coop, 77-82; chmn, Nat Acad Eng Task Force on Eng Educ, 79-81; chmn, Ill Council Res & Dev, 80-84; bd gov, Argonne Nat Lab, 83, Am Soc Med Exp, 84-86; proj bd, Am Soc Eng Educ, 87. *Mem:* Nat Acad Eng; hon mem Am Soc Mech Engrs; fel Am Inst Aeronaut & Astronaut; fel Am Acad Mech (pres, 73-74); fel Soc Eng Sci (pres, 75); fel AAAS; Int Union Theoret & Appl Mech; Am Soc Eng Educ; NY Acad Sci; Int Asn Struct Mechs. *Res:* Thermal stresses; structural theory; elasticity and inelasticity; wave propagation in solids; heat conduction and change of phase; vibrations and buckling; aerostructures and nuclear reactor structural mechanics; micromechanics of solids. *Mailing Add:* Dept Civil Eng & Eng Mech Columbia Univ 610 SW Mudd Bldg New York NY 10027-6699. *Fax:* 212-854-6267

BOLEY, CHARLES DANIEL, PLASMA PHYSICS, LASER PHYSICS. *Current Pos:* PHYSICIST, LAWRENCE LIVERMORE NAT LAB, 86- *Personal Data:* b Urbana, Ill, Dec 15, 43; m 82; c 2. *Educ:* Mass Inst Technol, SB, 66, PhD(physics), 71. *Prof Exp:* Fel Dept Physics, Univ Toronto, 71-73; res fel appl sci, Calif Inst Technol, 73-75; physicist, Argonne Nat Lab, 75-85; mem tech staff, AT&T Bell Labs, 85-86. *Mem:* Am Phys Soc; Sigma Xi. *Res:* Plasma physics; laser physics; computational physics; laser materials processing. *Mailing Add:* Lawrence Livermore Nat Lab L-490 Livermore CA 94550. *Fax:* 510-422-7748; *E-Mail:* boley@llnl.gov

BOLEY, FORREST IRVING, PLASMA PHYSICS, ASTROPHYSICS. *Current Pos:* chmn dept, 75-78, PROF PHYSICS & ASTRON, DARTMOUTH COL, 64- *Personal Data:* b Ft Madison, Iowa, Nov 27, 25; m 46, 69; c 4. *Educ:* Iowa State Univ, BS, 46, PhD(physics), 51. *Hon Degrees:* MA, Wesleyan Univ, 59; Dartmouth Col, 64. *Prof Exp:* Elec engr, Raytheon Mfg Co, 46-47; from asst prof to prof physics, Wesleyan Univ, 51-61; physicist, Lawrence Radiation Lab, Univ Calif, 61-64. *Concurrent Pos:* Ed, Am J Physics, Am Asn Physics Teachers, 66-72; distinguished vis prof, USAF Acad, 93. *Mem:* AAAS; Am Astron Soc; Am Phys Soc; Int Astron Union. *Res:* Cosmic rays; plasma phenomena; astrophysics. *Mailing Add:* Wilder Lab Dept Physics & Astron Dartmouth Col Hanover NH 03755

BOLEY, ROBERT B, BACTERIOLOGY, IMMUNOLOGY. *Current Pos:* ASSOC PROF BIOL, UNIV TEX, ARLINGTON, 65- *Personal Data:* b Big Spring, Tex, Aug 19, 28; m 60; c 1. *Educ:* Sam Houston State Univ, BS, 49; Tex A&M Univ, MS, 60; Ohio State Univ, PhD(microbiol), 63. *Prof Exp:* From instr to assoc prof biol, Tarleton State Col, 58-65. *Mem:* Am Soc Microbiol; Am Inst Biol Sci; NY Acad Sci; Brit Soc Gen Microbiol. *Res:* Intestinal flora and immune responses in small mammals. *Mailing Add:* 907 Pontiac Ct Arlington TX 76013

BOLEY, SCOTT JASON, PEDIATRIC SURGERY. *Current Pos:* DIR PEDIAT SURG, MONTEFIORE HOSP & MED CTR, 67- *Personal Data:* b Brooklyn, NY; m 50, Sandra. *Educ:* Wesleyan Univ, AB, 46; Jefferson Med Col, MD, 49. *Prof Exp:* Assoc prof, 67-71, prof surg & pediat & chief pediat surg serv, Albert Einstein Col Med, 71- *Mem:* Fel Am Acad Pediat; fel Am Col Surgeons; Am Pediat Surg Asn; Soc Surg Alimentary Tract; Am Med Writers' Asn; Am Physiol Soc; Am Gastroenterol Asn; Soc Cardiovasc & Interventional Radiol. *Res:* Vascular diseases of the intestines; Hirschprung's disease. *Mailing Add:* Albert Einstein Col Med Montefiore Med Ctr 111 E 210th St Bronx NY 10467

BOLGER, EDWARD M, MATHEMATICS. *Current Pos:* asst prof math, 67-69, asst prof math & statist, 69-75, PROF MATH & STATIST, MIAMI UNIV, 75- *Personal Data:* b Jersey City, NJ, Jan 9, 38; m 60; c 2. *Educ:* St Peter's Col, NJ, BS, 59; Pa State Univ, MA, 61, PhD(probability, statist), 64. *Prof Exp:* Asst prof math, Bucknell Univ, 64-67. *Mem:* Soc For Indust & Appl Math; Math Asn Am; Inst Math Statist. *Res:* N-person game theory. *Mailing Add:* Dept Math Miami Univ 500 E High St Oxford OH 45056-1618

BOLGER, P MICHAEL, HAZARD-RISK ASSESSMENT OF CONTAMINANTS IN FOODS. *Current Pos:* TOXICOLOGIST & PHYSIOLOGIST, FOOD & DRUG ADMIN, 80-, SUPVR, 86- *Personal Data:* b Corpus Christi, Tex, July 30, 49; c Colin, Cate & Matthew. *Educ:* Georgetown Univ, PhD(physiol & biophys), 76; Am Bd Toxicol, cert gen toxicol. *Mem:* Am Physiol Soc; Soc of Toxicol. *Res:* The development of novel approaches to assessing the hazard/risk of elemental or organic contamints, particularly those found in the food supply. *Mailing Add:* Contaminants Br HFS-308 Food & Drug Admin 200 C St SW Washington DC 20204

BOLGIANO, LOUIS PAUL, JR, ELECTRICAL ENGINEERING. *Current Pos:* from assoc prof to prof, 55-85, EMER PROF ENG, UNIV DEL, 85- *Personal Data:* b Baltimore, Md, June 20, 22; m 46, Sarah Spencer; c Amanda, Charles & Jeannette. *Educ:* Haverford Col, BS, 43; Johns Hopkins Univ, MA, 48, PhD(physics), 53. *Prof Exp:* Jr instr physics, Johns Hopkins Univ, 48-52; asst prof elec eng, US Naval Acad, 52-55. *Concurrent Pos:* Teaching internship, Ford Found, 53-54; prin investr, Res Corp, Univ Del, 56-57; res assoc, Stanford Univ, 60, 61; expert, US Army Ballistic Res Labs, 62; prin investr, Air Force Off Sci Res, 62-73, Univ Del Res Found, 73-75, NSF, 77-79. *Mem:* Inst Elec & Electronics Engrs. *Res:* Communication theory and signal processing. *Mailing Add:* 226 Cheltenham Rd Newark DE 19711

BOLGIANO, NICHOLAS CHARLES, ORGANIC POLYMER CHEMISTRY. *Current Pos:* RETIRED. *Personal Data:* b Baltimore, Md, Oct 26, 23; m 55; c 8. *Educ:* Loyola Col, Md, BS, 44; Catholic Univ, MS, 49; Univ Md, PhD(chem), 54. *Prof Exp:* Res fel, Mellon Inst, 54-56; res assoc, Armstrong World Industs, 54-89. *Mem:* Am Chem Soc. *Res:* Monomer and polymer synthesis; foamed plastics; coatings; binders; radiation curing. *Mailing Add:* 824 Dorsea Rd Lancaster PA 17601

BOLGIANO, RALPH, JR, RADIO PHYSICS, ATMOSPHERIC TURBULENCE. *Current Pos:* from assoc prof to prof, 58-90, EMER PROF ELEC ENG, CORNELL UNIV, 90- *Personal Data:* b Baltimore, Md, Apr 1, 22; m 48; c 4. *Educ:* Cornell Univ, BSEE, 44, BEE, 47, MEE, 49, PhD(radio physics), 58. *Prof Exp:* Develop engr, Electronics Lab, Gen Elec Co, 49-50, proj engr, 50-52, sect supvr, Advan Electronics Ctr, 53-54. *Concurrent Pos:* Consult, Gen Elec Co, 54-63, ADCOM, Inc, 62-63 & Rome Air Develop, Ctr, USAF, 63-64; mem, US nat body, Int Sci Radio Union, Inter-Union Comt Radiometeorol, Int Sci Radio Union-Int Union Geod & Geophys, 60-70, pres, 67-70; trustee, Univ Corp Atmos Res, 61-64, mem rep, 65-71; Guggenheim fel & Fulbright travel grant, 64-65; mem, Adv Group Aerospace Res & Develop, NATO, 68-78; gen chmn, Int Colloq Spectra of Meteorol Variables, Stockholm, 69; vis scientist, Radio & Space Res Sta, Sci Res Coun, UK & Inst Mech Statist of Turbulence, Univ Aix Marseille, 71-72; sr res assoc, Coop Inst Res Environ Sci, Univ Colo, Boulder, 79-80. *Mem:* Fel AAAS; Inst Elec & Electronics Engrs; Am Meteorol Soc; Am Geophys Union; Sigma Xi. *Res:* Scatter propagation of radio waves; radio scatter measurement of atmospheric structure; study of turbulent mixing in the atmosphere; theory of turbulence in stably stratified atmosphere. *Mailing Add:* Cornell Univ 129 Midway Rd Ithaca NY 14850

BOLHOFER, WILLIAM ALFRED, ORGANIC CHEMISTRY. *Current Pos:* RETIRED. *Personal Data:* b Jamaica, NY, May 18, 20; m 42; c 4. *Educ:* Mass Inst Technol, BS, 42, PhD(chem), 50. *Prof Exp:* Chemist, Merck & Co, 42-47; asst, Mass Inst Technol, 47-49; sr res fel, Merck Sharp & Dohme Res Lab, 49-74, sr investr, 74-82. *Mem:* AAAS; Am Chem Soc. *Res:* Medicinal chemistry; synthetic organic chemistry. *Mailing Add:* PO Box 278 Frederick PA 19435-0278

BOLHUIS, REINDER L H, TCR GAMMA DELTA LYMPHOCYTES, IMMUNOTHERAPY. *Current Pos:* RES ASSOC, ROTTERDAM RADIO THERAPEUT INST, 74-, STAFF MEM, 76- *Personal Data:* b Winschoten, Neth, July 2, 45; m; c 1. *Educ:* V Univ, Amsterdam, BS, 69; Erasmus Univ, Rotterdam, MD, 77. *Concurrent Pos:* Guest staff mem, Radiobiol Inst, TNO Health Orgn, Rijswijk, 72, dept head, 76; mem adv bd, Comprehensive Cancer Ctr, Rotterdam, 76-, Nat Working Party, Immunostimulantia, 77-; coordr, Tumor-Immunol, Erasmus Univ, Radiobiol Inst, TNO Health Orgn & Daniel den Hoed Cancer Ctr, 76-; numerous grants, Dutch Cancer Soc, 76-, Dept Econ Affairs, Leiden & Centocor, 89-91, Concerted Action Prog, 90-92; mem comt, Qual Assurance Clin Immunol, 81-; mem coun, Sci Adv, Daniel den Hoed Cancer Ctr, Nat Health & Med Res, Commonwealth Australia, 88-; extramural rev cand acad, Nat Cancer Inst, NIH, 86-; chmn, Standardization Immunodiag Leukemia & Lymphoma, 86-; founder & chmn, co-operation Immunophenotyping, Haematological Malignancies, Neth, 86-89; ad hoc rev, Europ J Cancer & Clin Oncol, Human Immunol, Hybridoma, Immunol Letters, Urologia Internationalis, J Cancer Res & Clin Oncol. *Mem:* Soc Qual Control Clin Immunol Assays; Am Asn Immunol; Am Asn Cancer Res. *Res:* Head and neck tumors; MHC-unrestricted cytotoxicity; NK cell receptor; bispecific monoclonal antibodies against renal and ovarian cancer, small cell lung carcinoma and human immune-deficiency virus syndrome. *Mailing Add:* Dept Clin & Tumorimmunol Dr Daniel den Hoed Cancer Ctr PO Box 5201 Rotterdam 3008 AE Netherlands

BOLICK, MARGARET RUTH, BOTANY, SYSTEMATICS. *Current Pos:* CURATOR & ASST PROF BOT, UNIV NEBR STATE MUS, 78- *Personal Data:* b Winston-Salem, NC, Sept 8, 50; m 78. *Educ:* Duke Univ, BS, 72, MA, 74; Univ Tex, Austin, PhD(bot), 78. *Mem:* Bot Soc Am; Am Soc Plant Taxonomists; Int Asn Plant Taxon; Sigma Xi. *Res:* Plant systematics, especially Asteraceae; pollen morphology, biology and evolution; mechanics of pollen walls. *Mailing Add:* W-530 Nebr Hall Univ Nebr State Mus Lincoln NE 68588-0514

BOLIE, VICTOR WAYNE, ELECTROPHYSICS, NEURAL NETWORKS. *Current Pos:* chmn dept elec & comput engr, 72-77, PROF ELEC & COMPUT ENGR, UNIV NMEX, 77- *Personal Data:* b Silverton, Ore, July 23, 24; m 45, Earleen Dale. *Educ:* Iowa State Univ, BS, 49, MS, 50, PhD, 52; Coe Col, BA, 57; Stanford Univ, MS, 59. *Prof Exp:* Eng res & admin, Collins Radio Co, 52-57; prof & chmn biomed eng, Iowa State Univ, 57-63; eng res & admin, NAm Rockwell Corp, 63-66; prof elec eng, Univ Ariz, 66-67; chaired prof, Okla State Univ, 67-72. *Concurrent Pos:* Prin investr aircraft collision avoidance, Collins Radio Co, 55-57, NIH & Iowa State Univ bioeng facil, 57-63, NIH & Iowa State Univ/Rockwell artificial hearts, 60-66, atmospheric phenomena, US Dept Defense, Okla State Univ, 67-69, automatic speech recognition, US Air Force, Okla State Univ, Univ NMex, 70-77, neutron beam choppers & free-electron laser controls, Los Alamos, 78-90; NSF fel, 58-59; nat chmn, Joint Comt Eng Med & Biol, 64-65; mem, Accreditation Bd Eng & Technol Eng Col Accreditation Team, 69-76; consult, NIH, NSF, US Navy, Space Labs, Aerojet, Fisher, Airesearch, Los Alamos; optical imaging & laser speckle studies, KAFB/Phillips Lab, 93- *Mem:* Fel Inst Elec & Electronics Engrs; Am Physiol Soc; Nat Soc Prof Engrs; Sigma Xi. *Res:* Electrophysics, particle beams, free electron lasers; CO2 laser imaging; optimization theory; published over 90 research papers and granted 38 patents. *Mailing Add:* Dept Elec & Comput Eng Univ NMex Albuquerque NM 87131-0001

BOLIEK, IRENE, ZOOLOGY. *Current Pos:* EMER CUR, CATAWBA SCI CTR, 74- *Personal Data:* b Hickory, NC, Apr 18, 07. *Educ:* NC Col for Women, AB, 29; Univ NC, AM, 33, PhD(zool), 36. *Prof Exp:* Teacher high sch, NC, 29-31; asst zool, Univ NC, 32-35; asst prof biol, Ala Col, 35-36; from instr to prof zool, Fla State Univ, 36-65; prof biol & chmn dept, Coker Col, 65-73. *Mem:* Sigma Xi. *Res:* Fresh water and marine invertebrates. *Mailing Add:* 1007 E Willow Park Dr Dalton GA 30720-5421

BOLIN, BERT RICHARD JOHANNE, ATMOSPHERIC PHYSICS, METEOROLOGY. *Current Pos:* Assoc prof, 56-61, prof, 61-90, EMER PROF, UNIV STOCKHOLM, 90- *Personal Data:* b Nykoping, Sweden, May 15, 25. *Educ:* Univ Uppsala, BS, 46; Univ Stockholm, MS, 49, PhD(meteorol), 56. *Honors & Awards:* Milkankovic Medal, Europ Geophys Soc, 93; Blue Planet Prize, Asahi Glass Found, 95. *Concurrent Pos:* Dir, Int Meteorol Inst, 61-91; sci dir, Europ Space Res Orgn, 65-67; sci adv, Swedish Prime Minister/Vice Prime Minister, 86-91; chmn, Intergovt Panel on Climate Change, World Meteorol Orgn/UN, 88-97. *Mem:* Foreign assoc Nat Acad Sci; Royal Swed Acad Sci; Swed Acad Eng Sci. *Mailing Add:* Kvarnasvagenle Osterskar 18451 Sweden

BOLING, JAMES A, MAGNESIUM RELATED PROBLEMS IN LACTATING BEEF COWS. *Current Pos:* PROF ANIMAL SCI, UNIV WIS, 67-, ASSOC DEAN RES, COL AGR, UNIV KY. *Educ:* Univ Wis, PhD(animal nutrit & biochem), 67. *Res:* Protein and mineral nutrition of ruminant animals. *Mailing Add:* Assoc Dean Res/Col Agr Univ Ky S-107 Agr Sci Bldg N Lexington KY 40546-0091

BOLINGER, ROBERT E, MEDICINE. *Current Pos:* From instr to assoc prof, 49-60, PROF MED & DIR CLIN RES CTR, MED CTR, UNIV KANS, 60-, LECTR HIST MED, 77- *Personal Data:* b Independence, Kans, May 31, 19. *Educ:* Univ Kans, AB, 40, MD, 43. *Res:* Insulin metabolism; computerized health care. *Mailing Add:* 2504 W 71st St Shawnee Mission KS 66208

BOLKER, ETHAN D, MATHEMATICS. *Current Pos:* PROF MATH, UNIV MASS, BOSTON, 72- *Personal Data:* b Brooklyn, NY, June 11, 38; m 60, Joan Leffert; c Jessica & Benjamin. *Educ:* Harvard Univ, AB, 59, AM, 61, PhD(math), 65. *Prof Exp:* Instr math, Princeton Univ, 64-65; from asst prof to assoc prof, Bryn Mawr Col, 65-72. *Concurrent Pos:* Res fel, Univ Calif, Berkeley, 67-68; consult, BGS Systs, 82- *Mem:* Math Asn Am; Am Math Soc; Asn Women Math; Asn Comput Mach. *Res:* Combinatorics; geometry; queueing theory. *Mailing Add:* Dept Math & Comput Sci Univ Mass Boston MA 02125-3393. *Fax:* 617-265-7173; *E-Mail:* eb@cs.umb.edu

BOLKER, HENRY IRVING, WOOD CHEMISTRY. *Current Pos:* RETIRED. *Personal Data:* b Montreal, Que, Feb 19, 26; m 53, Estelle R Samuels; c Louise (Mossey). *Educ:* Queen's Univ, Ont, BA, 48, MA, 50; Yale Univ, PhD(chem), 52. *Honors & Awards:* Montreal Medal Chem, Chem Inst Can, 84. *Prof Exp:* Fel biochem, McGill Univ, 51-54; chemist, Dominion Tar & Chem Co, 54 & DuPont of Can, Ltd, 54-60; chemist, Pulp & Paper Res Inst Can, 60-63, asst head, Wood Chem Div, 63-67, assoc div head chem, 67-69, head, Org Chem Sect, 69-72, head, Chem Processes Sect, 72-77, dir, Process Chem Div, 77-80, dir res, 80-87, dir acad affairs, 87-90; exec dir, Mech Woodpulp Network Excellence, 90-93. *Concurrent Pos:* Mem exec comt, Youth Sci Found, 61-64, pres, 65-66, mem admin coun, 69-71; res assoc chem, McGill Univ, 63-91; chmn, Sci Affairs, 67-71; mem admin coun, Int Coord Comt, UNESCO, 68-70; chmn, Educ Comt, Can Pulp & Paper Asn, 71-73; mem, Indust Liaison Comt, Ecole de Technol Superieure, 73-76; counr, Chem Inst Can, 74-77, bd dir, 77-81, chmn, 79-81. *Mem:* Chem Inst Can (vpres, 86-87, pres, 87-88); Can Pulp & Paper Asn; Am Chem Soc; The Chem Soc; fel Int Acad Wood Sci (secy-treas, 90-92). *Res:* Lignin; cellulose; chemical pulping and bleaching. *Mailing Add:* 110 Spartan Crescent Pointe Claire PQ H9R 3R5 Can

BOLL, H(ARRY) J(OSEPH), ELECTRICAL ENGINEERING, INTEGRATED CIRCUITS. *Current Pos:* RETIRED. *Personal Data:* b St Bonifacius, Minn, Mar 5, 30; m 56; c 6. *Educ:* Univ Minn, BS, 56, MS, 58, PhD(elec eng), 62. *Prof Exp:* Supvr, Bell Tel Labs, Inc, Murray Hill, NJ. *Concurrent Pos:* Elec Engineering Consult. *Mem:* Inst Elec & Electronics Engrs. *Res:* Secondary electron emission from magnesium oxide thin films; semiconductor devices. *Mailing Add:* 2780 70th St SW Naples FL 33999

BOLL, WILLIAM GEORGE, PLANT TISSUE CULTURE, BIOCHEMISTRY. *Current Pos:* RETIRED. *Personal Data:* b Manchester, Eng, Dec 5, 21; m 54; c 3. *Educ:* Univ Manchester, BSc, 48, PhD(plant physiol), 51. *Prof Exp:* Fel, Plant Res Inst, Univ Tex, 52-54, res scientist, 54-55; from asst prof to prof bot, McGill Univ, 55-90. *Mem:* Can Soc Plant Physiol. *Res:* Physiological and biochemical study of growth and morphogenesis of plants; excised root, tissue and cell suspension culture. *Mailing Add:* 34 Eighth St Roxboro PQ H8Y 1G5 Can

BOLLA, ROBERT IRVING, MOLECULAR BIOLOGY, NEMATODE BIOCHEMISTRY. *Current Pos:* PROF & CHAIR BIOL, ST LOUIS UNIV, 88-, ASSOC DEAN GRAD SCH, 96- *Personal Data:* b Dansville, NY, Aug 18, 43; m 66, Terese R Mandel; c Jennifer & Stephen. *Educ:* State Univ NY Buffalo, BS, 65; Univ Mass, Amherst, MSc, 67, PhD(zool), 70. *Prof Exp:* NIH res fel biol, Univ Notre Dame, 70-73; res fel, Roche Inst Molecular Biol, 73-76; from asst prof to prof biol, Univ Mo, St Louis, 76-88. *Concurrent Pos:* Vis asst prof microbiol, Washiington Univ Sch Med, 82-87; res assoc, Mo Bot Garden. *Mem:* AAAS; Sigma Xi; NY Acad Sci; Soc Nematologists; Am Aging Asn; Am Soc Microbiol. *Res:* Pinewood nematodes; population biology; toxin production in Bursaphelenchus xylophilus caused rapid pine wilt disease; metabolism Bursaphelenchus xylophilus; plant resistance to nematodes. *Mailing Add:* Dept Biol St Louis Univ 221 N Grand Blvd St Louis MO 63103-2097. *Fax:* 314-977-3658; *E-Mail:* bollari@sluvca.slu.edu

BOLLAG, JEAN-MARC, SOIL BIOCHEMISTRY, BIOREMEDIATION RESEARCH. *Current Pos:* from asst prof to assoc prof, 67-77, PROF SOIL BIOCHEM, PA STATE UNIV, 77-, DIR, CTR BIOREMEDIATION & DETOXIFICATION, 92- *Personal Data:* b Basel, Switz, Feb 19, 35; m 59, Brigitte Baumgartner; c Daniel, Gideon, Roni & Judy. *Educ:* Univ Basel, PhD(plant physiol), 59. *Honors & Awards:* Badge of Merit, Polish Ministry Agr; Environ Qual Res Award, Am Soc Agron. *Prof Exp:* Lectr plant physiol, Swiss Trop Inst, Basel, 58-59; Julius Baer fel, Switz, 63; fel plant genetics, Weizmann Inst Sci, Rehovot, Israel, 63-65; res assoc soil microbiol, Cornell Univ, 65-67. *Concurrent Pos:* mem, Biochem Sect, Ciba-Geigy, Basel, Switz, 75-76. *Mem:* Am Soc Microbiol; Am Soc Agron; fel Soil Sci Soc Am; Int Soc Soil Sci; Int Humic Substances Soc; fel Am Soc Agron; affil mem Am Chem Soc; fel Am Acad Microbiol. *Res:* Bioremediation, microbial control of the environment; degradation of pesticides by microbes; incorporation of xenobiotics into humic material; environmental application of immobilized enzymes. *Mailing Add:* 129 Land & Water Res Bldg Pa State Univ University Park PA 16802-3504. *Fax:* 814-865-7836; *E-Mail:* jmbollag@psu.edu

BOLLARD, R(ICHARD) JOHN H, AERONAUTICS, ASTRONAUTICS. *Current Pos:* head Dept Aeronaut & Astronaut, 61-77, PROF AERONAUT & ASTRONAUT, UNIV WASH, 61- *Personal Data:* b Hamilton, NZ, July 13, 27; m 55; c 4. *Educ:* Univ NZ, BS, 51. *Prof Exp:* Lectr aeronaut, Univ NZ, 54-56; from asst prof to prof, Purdue Univ, 56-61, assoc dir aerospace sci lab, 60-61. *Concurrent Pos:* Consult, NZ Govt, 54-56, James Aviation, Ltd, 54-, Midwest Appl Sci Corp, Ind, 56- & Math Sci Corp Calif, 60-; dir, Math Sci Northwest Inc. *Mem:* Assoc fel Am Inst Aeronaut & Astronaut; Am Soc Eng Educ. *Res:* Systems analysis; solid mechanics; structural analysis and design; vibration theory; photothermoviscoelasticity. *Mailing Add:* 6810 51st Ave NE Seattle WA 98115

BOLLE, DONALD MARTIN, ELECTROMAGNETISM. *Current Pos:* sr vpres acad affairs, 88-91; actg vpres admin, 95-96, PROF ELEC ENG, BLYTECH UNIV NY, 96- *Personal Data:* b Amsterdam, Netherlands, Mar 30, 33; US citizen; m 57; c 4. *Educ:* Univ Durham, BSc, 54; Purdue Univ, PhD(elec eng), 61; Brown Univ, MA, 66. *Honors & Awards:* Distinguished Serv Award, Oceanic Eng Soc, 80; Centennial Medal, Inst Elec & Electronics Engrs, 84. *Prof Exp:* Res engr, EMI Industs, Eng, 54-55; asst elec eng, Purdue Univ, 56, from instr to asst prof, 56-62; sr visitor appl math, Cambridge Univ, 62-63; from asst prof to assoc prof eng, Brown Univ, 63-70, prof, 70-80; chmn & Chandler-Weaver prof, Dept Elec & Comput Eng, 80-81, dean, Col Eng & Phys Sci, Lehigh Univ, 81-88. *Concurrent Pos:* Consult, Md Electronics Mfg Co, 56-58, Gen Elec Co, 58, Western Elec Co, 59, Bell Tel Labs, 60, P R Mallory & Co, 61 & Naval Underwater Systs Ctr, 69-80; NSF fel, 62-63. *Mem:* Am Soc Eng Educ; fel Inst Elec & Electronics Engrs; fel AAAS. *Res:* Electromagnetic theory, propagation, radiation, scattering; non-reciprocal devices; millimeter and submillimeter ware phenomena. *Mailing Add:* Prof elec eng, Polytech Univ 6 Metrotech Ctr Brooklyn NY 11201

BOLLER, FRANCOIS, behavioral neurology, neuropsychology, for more information see previous edition

BOLLES, THEODORE FREDERICK, INORGANIC CHEMISTRY, PHYSICAL CHEMISTRY. *Current Pos:* Res chemist, 3M Co, 66-71, supvr, Nuclear Med Res Lab, Nuclear Prod Proj, 71-76, mgr, Graphic Arts Lab, 77, tech dir, Transp & Com Graphics Div, 81-, Printing & Publishing Systs Div, TECH DIR SCI RES LAB, 3M CO. *Personal Data:* b LaCrosse, Wis, Nov 25, 40; m 62; c 5. *Educ:* Univ Wis, BS, 62; Univ Ill, PhD(inorg chem), 66. *Mem:* AAAS. Soc. *Res:* Organometallic chemistry of group IV, carbon, silicon, germanium, tin and lead; thermodynamics; calorimetry; coordination chemistry; nuclear medicine; radiopharmaceuticals; biochemistry; drug metabolism. *Mailing Add:* 7249 Courtly Rd St Paul MN 55125

BOLLET, ALFRED JAY, MEDICINE. *Current Pos:* clin prof, 80-90, VPRES ACAD AFFAIRS, DANBURY HOSP & SCH MED, YALE UNIV, 90- *Personal Data:* b New York, NY, July 15, 26; m 54. *Educ:* NY Univ, BS, 45, MD, 48; Am Bd Internal Med, dipl. *Prof Exp:* Resident physician, Chest Serv, Bellevue Hosp, New York, 50, asst resident physician, 52-53; clin res assoc, Nat Inst Arthritis & Metab Dis, 53-55; asst prof med, Col Med, Wayne State Univ, 55-59; assoc prof prev med & med, Sch Med, Univ Va, 59-65, prof internal & prev med, 65-66; prof med & chmn dept, Med Col Ga, 66-74; prof med & chmn dept, State Univ NY Downstate Med Ctr, 74-80. *Concurrent Pos:* Asst, Sch Med, Johns Hopkins Univ, 54-55; consult physician, Baltimore City Hosp, 54-55; Markle scholar med sci, 56-61; mem, Am Bd Intern Med, 71-78. *Mem:* AAAS; Am Soc Clin Invest; Am Fedn Clin Res (pres, 63-64); Am Rheumatism Asn; Harvey Soc. *Res:* Clinical and laboratory studies in the rheumatic diseases. *Mailing Add:* 22 Plum Beach Pt Rd Sands Point NY 11050

BOLLETER, WILLIAM THEODORE, ANALYTICAL CHEMISTRY, PROPELLANT CHEMISTRY. *Current Pos:* RETIRED. *Personal Data:* b Lufkin, Tex, June 29, 27; m 52; c 3. *Educ:* Tex Col Arts & Indust, BS, 48, MS, 50; Univ Tex, PhD(analytical chem), 55. *Prof Exp:* Instr chem, San Antonio Col, 50-52; res chemist, Monsanto Chem Co, 55-62; group supvr, Hercules Inc, Utah, 62-64, asst supt, 64-66, sr tech specialist, Va, 66-68, asst tech dir, 68-74, tech dir, 74-85, qual assurance & tech dir, 85-89. *Mem:* Am Chem Soc. *Res:* Spectroscopy; propellant chemistry. *Mailing Add:* 220 Price St Blacksburg VA 24060

BOLLICH, CHARLES N, AGRONOMY. *Current Pos:* RES LEADER, RICE RES UNIT, USDA, TEX. *Honors & Awards:* Agron Achievement Award, Am Soc Agron, 91. *Mailing Add:* Rice Res Unit USDA RR7 Box 999 Beaumont TX 77713-8530

BOLLING, GUSTAF FREDRIC, METALLURGICAL ENGINEERING, MANUFACTURING DEVELOPMENT. *Current Pos:* PROF MECH ENG & DIR MFG SYSTS ENG PROG, UNIV MICH, DEARBORN, 92- *Personal Data:* b Toronto, Ont, Apr 20, 31; m 54, 87, Valerie A Withington; c Steven F & Gillian B (Pines). *Educ:* Univ Toronto, BASc, 54, MASc, 55, PhD(metall eng), 57. *Prof Exp:* Nat Res Coun Can fel, Univ Birmingham, Eng, 57-58; res engr, Westinghouse Res Labs, Pa, 58-62; res scientist, Ford Motor Co, 62-72, res & planning mgr, 72-74, mat planning & strategy mgr, 74-76, exec engr, Vehicle Mat Develop & Planning, 76-81, assoc dir & dir, NAm Res Liaison Off, 81-84, dir, Mfg Develop Ctr, 84-92. *Concurrent Pos:* Demonstr appl physics, Univ Toronto, 54-55, lectr physics of metals, 55-57; fel engr, Westinghouse Res Labs, Pa, 61-62; expert consult, Orgn Am State, 68-72 & Space Shuttle Producibility Assessment, NASA, 81; consult, Lean Aircraft Initative, 93- *Mem:* Sigma Xi; Am Inst Mining, Metall & Petrol Engrs; Soc Mfg Engrs; Am Nat Stand Inst. *Res:* Solidification; structure sensitivity; economics of research; development of lightweight materials and new processes; directed advanced development from research through commercialization in the core manufacturing technologies, manufacturing systems and operations engineering, automation and machining, emphasizing applied computer technologies in manufacturing and close partnerships with customers; engineering management. *Mailing Add:* 5391 Royal Vale Lane Dearborn MI 48126. *Fax:* 313-593-5386; *E-Mail:* fred@umdsun2.umd.umich.edu

BOLLINGER, EDWARD H(ARRY), CHEMICAL ENGINEERING. *Current Pos:* RETIRED. *Personal Data:* b Milwaukee Wis, Aug 30, 26; m 56; c John, Robert, Susan & Anne. *Educ:* Rose Polytech Inst, BS, 49; Univ Ill, MS, 51; Ohio State Univ, PhD(chem eng), 58. *Prof Exp:* Res engr, Battelle Mem Inst, 51-52, consult, 53-58; asst, Ohio State Univ, 53; sr res engr, res ctr, B F Goodrich, 58-63, prog mgr, aerospace & defense div, 63-69, tech mgr corp new prod, 69-70, sect leader, aerospace res, 70-73, sr planning analyst, 73-78, mgr planning systs, Tire Div, 78-83, mgr, Com Anal, Res & Develop Ctr, 83-87. *Concurrent Pos:* Chmn, Cuyahoga River Basin Water Qual Comt; chmn, Summit County Energy Task Force, Colo Naval Res Reserve Co. *Mem:* Am Chem Soc; Am Inst Chem Engrs. *Res:* Transport phenomenon; thermochemistry; industrial chemistry; management systems; acoustics; macro economic forecasting. *Mailing Add:* 442 Mowbray Rd Akron OH 44333

BOLLINGER, FREDERICK W(ILLIAM), ORGANIC CHEMISTRY, SYNTHETIC ORGANIC & NATURAL PRODUCTS CHEMISTRY. *Current Pos:* RETIRED. *Personal Data:* b Tyndall, SDak, Aug 5, 18; m 45, Rita Handly; c Frederick Jr, Roger & Bruce. *Educ:* Univ SDak, BA, 39; Wash State Univ, MS, 41; Calif Inst Technol, MS, 43; Ill Inst Technol, PhD(chem), 51. *Honors & Awards:* Thomas Emery McKinney Prize, 39. *Prof Exp:* Asst chemist, State Chem Lab, SDak, 39; teaching fel, Wash State Univ, 39-41; asst chem, Ill Inst Technol, 48-50; fel, Col Med, Univ Ill, 50-51; sr chemist, Merck & Co, Inc, 51-87. *Concurrent Pos:* Int lectr, Chinese Am Sci Exchange, Beijing Inst, 84, Univ Kaiserslautern, Ger, 93. *Mem:* Am Chem Soc; Sigma Xi. *Res:* Stereochemistry; parkinsonism; natural products and azido compounds; co-inventor of sinemet. *Mailing Add:* 607 Lawrence Ave Westfield NJ 07090-3119

BOLLINGER, GILBERT A, GEOPHYSICS, SEISMOLOGY. *Current Pos:* RETIRED. *Personal Data:* b Edwardsville, Ill, Jan 4, 31; m 55, Jane M Berry; c Mark, Eric & James. *Educ:* St Louis Univ, PhD(geophys), 67. *Prof Exp:* Geophysicist, Calif Oil Co, 56-61; res asst seismol, St Louis Univ, 61-67; prof geophys, Va Polytech Inst & State Univ, 67-93. *Mem:* Seismol Soc Am (pres, 83-84); Am Geophys Union; AAAS. *Res:* Earthquake and engineering seismology; intraplate seismotectonics; seismic hazard. *Mailing Add:* PO Box 806 Buffalo WY 82834. *E-Mail:* gbolling@wyoming.com

BOLLINGER, JOHN G(USTAVE), MECHANICAL, ELECTRICAL & MANUFACTURING ENGINEERING. *Current Pos:* From instr to prof mech eng, 60-85, BASCON PROF ENG, COL ENG, UNIV WIS-MADISON, 73-, DEAN, 81-, PROF, DEPT ECE & IE, 85-,. *Personal Data:* b Grand Forks, NDak, May 28, 35; m 58; c 3. *Educ:* Univ Wis, BS, 57, PhD(mech eng), 61; Cornell Univ, MS, 58. *Honors & Awards:* Gustus L Larson Mem Award, Am Soc Mech Engrs, 76, Centennial Award, 80; Res Medal, Soc Mfg Engrs, 78. *Concurrent Pos:* Fulbright res fel, Aachen, Ger, 62-63; US Educ Comt intercountry lectr grant, Univs Birmingham & Manchester, 63, Cranfield Inst, 80; chmn bd, Unico, Inc, 83-89; mem, vis comt, Nat Inst Stand & Technol, 88-; mem technol adv bd, US Postal, 88-; assoc ed, J Mfg Systs, 89- *Mem:* Nat Acad Eng; fel Am Soc Mech Engrs; Am Soc Eng Educ; fel Soc Mfg Engrs; Nat Soc Prof Engrs. *Res:* Computer control of machines and processes; environmental noise control; control and design of machines; structural dynamics. *Mailing Add:* Dept Eng Univ Wis 2610 Eng Hall 1415 Eng Dr Madison WI 53706-1691. *Fax:* 608-262-6400; *E-Mail:* bollen@engr.wisc.edu

BOLLINGER, JOHN J, ATOMIC PHYSICS. *Current Pos:* PHYSICIST, NAT INST STAND & TECHNOL, 84- *Personal Data:* b June 10, 52; m 79, Lynn Christensen; c Larry & Andrew. *Educ:* Cornell Univ, BA, 74; Harvard Univ, PhD(physics), 81. *Honors & Awards:* Gold Medal, Dept Com, 85. *Prof Exp:* Fel, NSF, 74-77, Nat Res Coun, 82-84. *Mem:* Fel Am Phys Soc. *Res:* Stored-ion techniques for high resolution spectroscopy; time and frequency standards; noneutral plasmas. *Mailing Add:* Nat Inst Stand & Technol 325 Broadway Boulder CO 80303

BOLLINGER, LOWELL MOYER, EXPERIMENTAL NUCLEAR PHYSICS, SUPERCONDUCTING-LINEAR-ACCELERATOR TECHNOLOGY. *Current Pos:* dir, Physics Div, 63-72 & 73-74, dir, Super Conducting Linac Proj, 71-92-, PHYSICIST, ARGONNE NAT LAB, 51- *Personal Data:* b Greene Co, Va, Apr 28, 23; m 44; c 3. *Educ:* Oberlin Col, AB, 43; Cornell Univ, PhD, 51. *Honors & Awards:* Bonner Prize, Am Phys Soc. *Prof Exp:* Physicist, Nat Adv Comt Aeronaut, 43-46; from res asst to res assoc physics, Cornell Univ, 46-51. *Mem:* Am Phys Soc; AAAS. *Res:* Nuclear physics of neutron-induced reactions; development of the technology and design, and construction of the first superconducting heavy-ion linear accelerator; cosmic rays; combustion research. *Mailing Add:* Argonne Nat Lab Bldg 203 9700 S Cass Ave Argonne IL 60439

BOLLINGER, RALPH RANDAL, TRANSPLANTATION IMMUNOLOGY. *Current Pos:* CHIEF SURG TRANSPLANTATION, DUKE UNIV MED CTR, 83-, PROF SURG 91-, CHIEF GEN SURG, 94-, PROF IMMUNOL, 96- *Personal Data:* b Oct 3, 44; m 65, Monika Koch; c Christine L & Mark R. *Educ:* Tulane Univ, MD, MS(biochem) 70; Duke Univ, PhD(immunol), 77. *Mem:* Am Col Surgeons; Transplantation Soc; Soc Univ Surgeons; Am Soc Transplant Surgeons; Am Surg Asn; Am Asn Immunologists. *Res:* Transplantation immunology including xenotransplantation and small bowel transplantation. *Mailing Add:* Dept Surg Duke Univ Box 2910 Durham NC 27710. *Fax:* 919-684-8716

BOLLINGER, RICHARD COLEMAN, APPLIED MATHEMATICS. *Current Pos:* prof-in-charge, Behrend Col Grad Ctr, 74-79, from asst prof to prof math, Pa State Univ, 62-88, AT BEHREND COL PA STATE UNIV. *Personal Data:* b Johnstown, Pa, Feb 1, 32; m 54, 79, Linda M May; c David, Lisa, James, Jennifer & Adam. *Educ:* Univ Pittsburgh, BS, 54, MS, 57, PhD(math), 61. *Prof Exp:* Eng specialist, Westinghouse Res Labs, 54-59, res mathematician, 59-62. *Mem:* AAAS; Math Asn Am; Soc Indust & Appl Math. *Res:* Numerical analysis; mathematical analysis and applied mathematics; combinatorics and finite mathematics. *Mailing Add:* Dept Math Behrend Col Pa State Univ Station Rd Erie PA 16563

BOLLINGER, ROBERT OTTO, CONTINUING MEDICAL EDUCATION. *Current Pos:* from asst prof to assoc prof pediat, 76-94, DIR CONTINUING MED EDUC, SCH MED, WAYNE STATE UNIV, 89- *Personal Data:* b Detroit, Mich, June 15, 39; m 62, Ruth M Collins; c Christopher R & Susan L. *Educ:* Wayne State Univ, BS, 62, MS, 65, PhD(biol), 72. *Prof Exp:* Asst prof zool, Eastern Ill Univ, 69-71; res assoc, Child Res Ctr, Mich, 71-76. *Concurrent Pos:* Adj asst prof, Col Pharm & Allied Health Prof, Wayne State Univ, 73-76. *Mem:* Soc Appl Learning Technol; Am Med Info Asn. *Res:* Continuing medical education; applications of computer science in medicine and education. *Mailing Add:* Univ Health Ctr 5E Wayne State Univ 4201 St Antoine Detroit MI 48201

BOLLINGER, WILLIAM HUGH, REFORESTATION, REVEGETATION. *Current Pos:* VPRES, ENVIRON DIV, TERRATEK, 89- *Personal Data:* b Los Angeles, Calif, Aug 18, 47. *Educ:* Univ Calif, BA, 69; Univ Colo, MA, 72, PhD(ecol), 74. *Prof Exp:* Teaching asst biol, Univ Colo, 69-74; mem staff field ecol, Continuing Educ, Univ Colo, 72-74; sr mem staff ecol, VTN Corp, 74-76; vpres res, Native Plants, Inc, 76-89. *Concurrent Pos:* Mem staff bot res, Univ Calif Bot Gardens, 66-67; reforestation prog leader, US Agency Int Development, Sri Lanka, 78, reforestation proj staff, Kenya, 80; adv comt tech consult food & renewable resources prog, US Congress Off Technol Assessment, 81-82. *Mem:* Am Mus Natural Hist; Sigma Xi. *Res:* Relation between energy, environment and development: technical developments of solutions to vegetation problems, particularly the restoration of primary vegetation on severely damaged landscapes. *Mailing Add:* 374 L St Salt Lake City UT 84103

BOLLS, NATHAN J, JR, VERTEBRATE ZOOLOGY & PHYSIOLOGY. *Current Pos:* From instr to assoc prof, 63-80, PROF BIOL, WITTENBERG UNIV, 80- *Personal Data:* b De Witt, Mo, May 16, 31; m 62, Imogene Lamb; c Laurel H. *Educ:* Kans State Univ, BS, 59, MS, 61, PhD(vert physiol), 63. *Concurrent Pos:* Author & proj dir, NSF Matching Funds grant for undergrad physiol lab equip, 65-67; mem, Rocky Mountain Biol Lab, Inc. *Mem:* Am Soc Mammalogists; Am Inst Biol Sci. *Res:* Mammals; ecological physiology of tree squirrels and of freshwater turtles; mineral balance in rodents. *Mailing Add:* Dept Biol Box 720 Wittenberg Univ Springfield OH 45501

BOLLUM, FREDERICK JAMES, BIOCHEMISTRY. *Current Pos:* PRES, SUPERTECHS INC, 89- *Personal Data:* b Ellsworth, Wis, June 14, 27; div; c 4. *Educ:* Univ Minn, BA, 49, PhD(physiol chem), 56. *Honors & Awards:* K A Forster Award & Lectureship, Mainz Acad Sci, Ger, 74. *Prof Exp:* Asst physiol chem, Univ Minn, 53-55, instr, 55-56; USPHS fel, Univ Wis, 56-58; biochemist, Biol Div, Oak Ridge Nat Lab, 58-65; prof biochem, Med Sch, Univ Ky, 65-77; chmn dept, Uniformed Servs Univ Health Sci, 77-81, prof biochem, 77-89. *Concurrent Pos:* Consult radiation study sect, NIH, 67-68, biochem study sect, 69-73 & cancer treat rev panel, 75-77; vis prof, Univ Chile, 69, Johns Hopkins Univ, 83; consult, Am Cancer Soc, 71-72; USPHS spec fel, Med Ctr, Univ Calif, 72-73. *Mem:* Fel AAAS; Am Soc Biol Chem; Am Chem Soc; Sigma Xi. *Res:* Enzymes of nucleic acid synthesis; structure and function of nucleic acid; differentiation of lymphoid cells. *Mailing Add:* Supertechs Inc 9610 Med Ctr Dr No 101 Rockville MD 20850

BOLLYKY, L(ASZLO) JOSEPH, CHEMICAL ENGINEERING. *Current Pos:* PRES, BOLLYKY ASSOC, INC, 77- *Personal Data:* b Bolyok, Hungary, Dec 9, 32; US citizen; c Andrea, Paul & Thomas. *Educ:* Budapest Tech Univ, dipl, 56; Columbia Univ, MA, 61, PhD(chem), 64. *Prof Exp:* Chem engr, Nitrokemia Co, Hungary, 56; process develop chemist, Am Cyanamid Co, NJ, 57-60, sr res chemist & proj leader, Cent Res Div, 63-70; vpres & tech dir, Pollution Control Industs, Inc, 70-77, pres subsid, PCI Ozone Corp, 73-77. *Concurrent Pos:* Found & ed-in-chief, Ozone Sci & Eng, 79-84; dir, Int Ozone Asn. *Mem:* Am Chem Soc; Water Pollution Control Fedn; Am Waterworks Asn; Am Inst Chem Engrs; hon mem Int Ozone Asn (vpres). *Res:* Water, waste water treatment and air pollution control; ozone generation and application; chemiluminescent reactions; photochemistry; Ozone-UV reactions and reactor design; ozone treatment process and system design for water and waste water treatment and for industrial applications. *Mailing Add:* Bollyky Assoc Inc 31 Strawberry Hill Ave Stamford CT 06902-2608. *Fax:* 203-967-4845; *E-Mail:* ljbbai@bai-ozone.com

BOLMAN, WILLIAM MERTON, child psychiatry, for more information see previous edition

BOLMARCICH, JOSEPH JOHN, OPERATIONS RESEARCH, APPLIED MATHEMATICS. *Current Pos:* OPERS RES CONSULT & TREAS, QUANTICS INC, 77- *Personal Data:* b Philadelphia, Pa, Dec 22, 42; div; c 3. *Educ:* Drexel Univ, BS, 65; Univ Pa, PhD(appl math), 72. *Honors & Awards:* David Rist Prize, Mil Opers Res Soc, 75. *Prof Exp:* Res physicist, Frankford Arsenal, 65-72; consult opers res & math, Daniel H Wagner Assocs, 72-76. *Mem:* Inst Mgt Sci; Soc Indust & Appl Math; Mil Opers Res Soc; Math Asn Am. *Res:* Bayeslan information processing; combinatorial probability; mathematical logistics. *Mailing Add:* Quantics Inc 801 Springdale Dr Suite 120 Exton PA 19341

BOLME, DONALD W(ESTON), CHEMICAL ENGINEERING. *Current Pos:* CONSULT CHEM & PROCESS ENG, 70- *Personal Data:* b Louisville, Ky, Apr 17, 28; m 52, Alice E Kulju; c Mark W, Paul A & Edward S. *Educ:* Mich Col Mining & Technol, BS, 51; Univ Wash, MS, 55, PhD(chem eng), 57. *Prof Exp:* Chem engr, Dow Chem Co, Mich, 57-59 & Stanford Res Inst, 59-60; asst prof chem eng, Wash State Univ, 60-65; sr develop engr, Pac Northwest Labs, Battelle Mem Inst, 65-70. *Mem:* Am Chem Soc; Am Inst Chem Engrs. *Res:* Reduction and control of industrial pollution, air and water; evaluations and definition of hazards including explosions, pollutants and radiochemicals; development and analysis of process systems; kinetics; mechanisms and heat transfer; process kinetics and industrial chemistry of nitrogen oxides and nitric acid. *Mailing Add:* Bolme Eng PO Box 5820 Lynnwood WA 98046-5820

BOLMER, MICHAEL SHEPPARD, REACTION ENGINEERING. *Current Pos:* RES SCIENTIST & CHEM ENGR, ELF ATOCHEM NAM, 85- *Personal Data:* b Sharon, Conn, Aug 23, 54. *Educ:* Bucknell Univ, BS, 76; Univ Del, PhD(chem eng), 82. *Prof Exp:* Chem engr, Ethyl Corp, 76-77, Texaco Inc, 81-85. *Res:* Development of processes to produce new fluoro chemicals to replace chlorofluorocarbon, including reactors, catalysts, and purifications. *Mailing Add:* 900 First Ave King of Prussia PA 19406

BOLMER, PERCE W, ELECTROCHEMISTRY, SURFACE CHEMISTRY. *Current Pos:* RETIRED. *Personal Data:* b Springfield, Ohio, Nov 24, 28; m 56; c 1. *Educ:* Ohio Univ, BS, 50; Purdue Univ, MS, 52, PhD(anal chem), 54. *Prof Exp:* Sr res technologist, Field Res Lab, Mobil Oil Co Inc, 54-66; sr res technologist, Kaiser Aluminum & Chem Corp, 66-73, head finishing sect, 73-87, consult ctr technol, 87-90. *Mem:* Am Chem Soc; Am Electroplaters & Surface Finishers. *Res:* Electrochemistry of corrosion reactions; aluminum and other metal finishing; solid waste disposal; industrial pollution control; anodic oxides; electrodeposition; paint application technology; anodizing. *Mailing Add:* Seven Pasillo Way Hot Springs Village AR 71909-9998

BOLOGNESI, DANI PAUL, VIROLOGY, IMMUNOLOGY. *Current Pos:* from asst prof to prof surg, Duke Univ Med Ctr, 71-84, from asst prof to assoc prof microbiol & immunol, 71-80, dep dir, Duke Comprehensive Cancer Ctr, 81-87, PROF, MICROBIOL & IMMUNOL, DUKE UNIV MED CTR, 81-, JAMES B DUKE PROF, 84-, DIR, DUKE CTR AIDS RES, 87- *Personal Data:* b Forgaria, Italy, Mar 19, 41; US citizen; m 64; c 2. *Educ:* Rensselaer Polytech Inst, BS, 63, MS, 65; Duke Univ, PhD(virol), 67. *Prof Exp:* Res assoc, Dept Surg, Duke Univ Med Ctr, 67-68; NIH postdoctoral fel, Max-Planck Inst Virus Res, WGer, 68-71. *Concurrent Pos:* Mem tumor virus detection segment rev bd, Nat Cancer Inst, 73-76; consult, M D Anderson Hosp & Tumor Inst, Tex & Frederick Cancer Res Ctr, Md, 73-74; Nat Cancer Inst grant, Med Ctr, Duke Univ, 74-, USPHS grant, 74-75, Am Cancer Soc grant, 74-76 & Am Soc Fac Res award, 76-81; mem med & sci adv comt, Leukemia Soc Am; mem study sect, Am Cancer Soc, 77-80 & NIH Virol, 77-81; ed, AIDS Res & Human Retroviruses; mem, AIDS Task Force, Nat Cancer Inst, chmn subcomt, AIDS, adv, Vaccine Task Force; mem sci adv bd, Retrogenes, Inc; mem adv comt, AIDS Policy, NIH; mem sci adv comt, Am Found AIDS Res, 85-; Mem selection comt, AIDS Vaccine, Nat Inst Allergy & Infectious Dis. *Mem:* Am Soc Microbiol. *Res:* Tumor virology; tumor immunology; human cancer; representative of over two hundred full length publications. *Mailing Add:* PO Box 2926 Durham NC 27710

BOLON, ALBERT EUGENE, NUCLEAR ENGINEERING. *Current Pos:* Asst prof, 65-71, dept chair, 87-93, ASSOC PROF NUCLEAR & METALL ENG, UNIV MO, ROLLA, 71-, REACTOR DIR, 80- *Personal Data:* b Montgomery, Ala, July 19, 39; m 65, Sherrell R Roberts; c Cynthia P & Bruce T. *Educ:* Mo Sch Mines, BS, 61, MS, 62; Iowa State Univ, PhD(nuclear eng), 65. *Mem:* Am Nuclear Soc; Soc Prof Engrs; Sigma Xi; Am Soc Eng Educ. *Res:* Basic or applied research on materials related to applications of nuclear power; safety, environmental impacts and licensing of fission and fusion power plants. *Mailing Add:* 102 Fulton Hall Univ Mo Rolla MO 65409-0170. *E-Mail:* abolon@umr.umr.edu

BOLON, DONALD A, ORGANIC CHEMISTRY. *Current Pos:* RES CHEMIST, GEN ELEC CO, 62- *Personal Data:* b Cleveland, Ohio, Sept 7, 34; m 59; c 4. *Educ:* Allegheny Col, BS, 56; Univ Minn, PhD(org chem), 60. *Prof Exp:* Fel, Harvard Univ, 60-62. *Mem:* Am Chem Soc. *Res:* Carbene chemistry; free radical rearrangements and reactions; autoxidation and catalytic oxidative coupling reactions; solvolitic reactions; photochemical crosslinking; acetylene chemistry; ultraviolet light cured coatings; electrical insulation coatings; epoxy resin cure and use. *Mailing Add:* 2030 Cook Rd Ballston Lake NY 12019

BOLON, ROGER B, MATERIALS CHARACTERIZATION, SURFACE ANALYSIS TECHNIQUES. *Current Pos:* Assoc mem staff, 66-74, mem res staff & supvr, 74-80, MGR RES & DEVELOP, GEN ELEC CORP, 80- *Personal Data:* b Cleveland, Ohio, May 19, 39; m 63; c 2. *Educ:* Pa State Univ, BS, 61; Col Advan Sci, MS, 63. *Honors & Awards:* IR-100 Award, 69; Corning Award, Microbeam Anal Soc, 77. *Mem:* Microbeam Anal Soc (treas, 79-80, pres, 82-83). *Res:* New and or improved instrumentation methods and techniques for scanning electron microscopy; electron microprobe analysis; auger electron spectroscopy; photo electron spectroscopy. *Mailing Add:* GE Corp Res Ctr K & D 2C19 1 Research Circle Schenectady NY 12309

BOLOTIN, HERBERT HOWARD, NUCLEAR PHYSICS, MEDICAL PHYSICS. *Current Pos:* CHAMBER MFRS PROF PHYSICS, UNIV MELBOURNE, 71- *Personal Data:* b New York, NY, Jan 11, 30; m 51; c 2. *Educ:* City Col New York, BS, 50; Ind Univ, MS, 52, PhD(exp nuclear physics), 55. *Hon Degrees:* DSc, Univ Melbourne, 80. *Honors & Awards:* Res Medal, Royal Soc Victoria, 89. *Prof Exp:* Physicist, US Naval Radiol Defense Lab, 55-58; res fel nuclear physics, Brookhaven Nat Lab, 58-60, asst physicist, 60-61; asst prof physics, Mich State Univ, 61-62; assoc physicist, Argonne Nat Lab, 62-71. *Concurrent Pos:* Vis scientist, Univ Calif, Berkeley, 62 & Los Alamos Sci Lab, 66; chmn, Conf Slow-Neutron-Capture Gamma Rays, Argonne Nat Lab, 66; vis scientist, Brookhaven Nat Lab, 68; mem adv comt, Int Conf Neutron-Capture Gamma Rays Studies, Sweden, 69 & Int Conf Nuclear Structure Study Neutrons, Hungary, 72; vis prof nuclear physics, Osaka Univ Res Ctr, 77; consult nuclear physics, Rutgers Univ, 79; vis prof, Lawrence Berkeley Lab, 79; consult, Chinese Acad Sci, 84; chmn, Int Conf on Nuclear Structure, Univ Melbourne, 87; ed, Proc Int Conf on Nuclear Structure, Melbourne, 87. *Mem:* Fel Royal Soc Victoria (pres); fel Australian Inst Physics. *Res:* Experimental nuclear physics; beta and gamma ray, neutron and nuclear spectroscopy; lifetimes of excited nuclear states; neutron capture gamma rays; nuclear structure; interdisciplinary research in nuclear medicine investigations; static magnetic moments excited nuclear states. *Mailing Add:* Sch Physics Univ Melbourne Parkville Victoria 3052 Australia. *Fax:* 61-3-347-4783; *E-Mail:* bolotin@munkenkyu.ph.unimelb.edu.au

BOLOTIN, MOSHE, BOTANY, FORESTRY. *Current Pos:* RETIRED. *Personal Data:* b Jerusalem, Palestine, July 3, 22; US citizen; m 60; c 2. *Educ:* Univ Wash, BS, 51; Univ BC, MF, 58; Smith Col, PhD(bot), 74. *Prof Exp:* Forester growth study, State Sustained Yield Forest, Olympia, Wash, 51-52; state forester, Israel Forest Serv, 52-56, silviculture, 58-65; asst prof biol, Holyoke Community Col, 69-95. *Mem:* Sigma Xi. *Res:* Juvenility in woody plants; flowering in woody plants; tree improvement. *Mailing Add:* 87 Grantwood Dr Amherst MA 01002

BOLOTIN, VLADIMIR VASILYEVICH, MECHANICAL ENGINEERING. *Current Pos:* Asst prof, 50-53, PROF, MOSCOW POWER ENG INST, TECH UNIV, 53- *Personal Data:* b Tambov, Russia, Mar 29, 26. *Educ:* Moscow Inst Railway Engrs, PhD(eng), 50. *Hon Degrees:* DSc, Moscow Inst Railway Engrs, 52; Dr, Tech Univ Budapest, 75. *Honors & Awards:* Gold Medal, Czech Acad Sci, 77; State Prize, Sci & Tech, Russia, 84. *Concurrent Pos:* Lab Reliability, Russian Acad Sci, Moscow. *Mem:* Foreign assoc Nat Acad Eng; Russ Acad Sci; Russ Acad Eng. *Mailing Add:* Power Eng Inst Tech Univ Moscow Krasnokazarmennaya 14 111250 Moscow Russia

BOLS, NIELS CHRISTIAN, FISH CELL CULTURING, BIOTECHNOLOGY. *Current Pos:* from asst prof to assoc prof, 77-90, PROF CELL BIOL, REPRODUCTIVE PHYSIOL & BIOTECHNOL, UNIV WATERLOO, 90- *Personal Data:* b Revelstoke, BC, Feb 3, 48. *Educ:* Simon Fraser Univ, BS, 70; Univ BC, MS, 72; Univ Toronto, PhD(zool), 75. *Prof Exp:* Fel, Karolinska Inst, Sweden, 76-77. *Concurrent Pos:* Vis scientist, Univ Calif, San Diego, 83-84. *Mem:* Tissue Cult Asn; Can Soc Cell Biol; Can Fedn Biol Soc. *Res:* Development of fish cell lines and culturing technology for the study of the growth and differentiation of fish cells in vitro; contribution of animal cell cultures to biotechnology. *Mailing Add:* Dept Biol Univ Waterloo 200 University Ave W Waterloo ON N2L 3G1 Can

BOLSAITIS, PEDRO, physical metallurgy, thermodynamics, for more information see previous edition

BOLSER, DONALD C, BIOCHEMISTRY. *Current Pos:* ASSOC PRIN SCIENTIST, SCHERING-PLOUGH RES, 88- *Personal Data:* b Bethesda, Md, Jan 15, 58. *Educ:* Fla Inst Technol, BS, 80; Univ SFla, PhD(biochem), 85. *Prof Exp:* Fel, NIH, 85-88. *Mem:* Am Immunol Soc; Biochem Soc; Am Physiol Soc. *Mailing Add:* Dept Physiol Sci Univ Fla Col Vet Med PO Box 100144 Gainesville FL 32610-0144

BOLSTAD, LUTHER, plastics chemistry; deceased, see previous edition for last biography

BOLSTEIN, ARNOLD RICHARD, SURVEY SAMPLING, STATISTICAL ESTIMATION. *Current Pos:* assoc prof math, 73-84, ASSOC PROF STATIST, GEORGE MASON UNIV, 84- *Personal Data:* b New York, NY, Sept 2, 40; c Heidi Lanford. *Educ:* Wagner Col, BA, 62; Purdue Univ, MS, 64, PhD(math), 67. *Prof Exp:* Grant, Univ NC, Chapel Hill, 68, asst prof math, 67-73. *Concurrent Pos:* Consult, Acad Interscience Methodology, 77-80; prin investr statist anal surv data, Nat Marine Fisheries, 81-82, 90-96; design work sampling methodology, Va Dept Social Serv, 84-87; design survey, Alexandria, Va, 90-91, compliance measurement, US customs, 94- *Mem:* Am Statist Asn. *Res:* Measurement error in surveys; non-response error in surveys; effect of incentives on survey response; pre-election polls; estimation of rare events; categorical data analysis. *Mailing Add:* Dept Appl Statist George Mason Univ Fairfax VA 22030-4443. *E-Mail:* rbolstei@gmu.edu

BOLSTERLI, MARK, THEORETICAL NUCLEAR PHYSICS. *Current Pos:* staff mem, 68-90, lab assoc, 91-94, LAB AFFIL, LOS ALAMOS SCI LAB, 94- *Personal Data:* b New Haven, Conn, Oct 3, 30; m 74. *Educ:* Wash Univ, AB, 51, PhD(physics), 55. *Prof Exp:* Res assoc, Argonne Nat Lab, 55; Fulbright student physics, Univ Birmingham, 55-56; res assoc, Wash Univ, 56-57; from asst prof to prof physics, Univ Minn, 57-68. *Concurrent Pos:* Vis prof, Copenhagen Univ, 61-62; consult, Los Alamos Sci Lab, 63-68; Guggenheim fel, Oxford Univ, 64-65; vis staff mem, Swiss Inst Nuclear Res, 81; theoret prog dir, NSF, 92-93. *Mem:* Fel Am Phys Soc. *Res:* Theoretical nuclear physics, especially quantum field theory for systems of mesons and nucleons. *Mailing Add:* 712 Gonzales Rd Santa Fe NM 87501-8923. *Fax:* 505-667-9671; *E-Mail:* mb@t2.lanl.gov

BOLT, BRUCE A, SEISMOLOGY, APPLIED MATHEMATICS. *Current Pos:* chair, Acad Senate, 93-94, PROF SEISMOL & DIR SEISMOG STA, UNIV CALIF, BERKELEY, 63-, EMER PROF. *Personal Data:* b Largs, NSW, Australia, Feb 15, 30; m 56; c 4. *Educ:* Univ New Eng, Australia, BSc, 52; Univ Sydney, MSc, 54, PhD(math), 56. *Hon Degrees:* DSc, Univ Sydney, 72. *Honors & Awards:* H O Wood Award, Res Seismol. *Prof Exp:* Lectr appl math, Univ Sydney, 54-61, sr lectr, 62. *Concurrent Pos:* Fulbright res fel, Columbia Univ, 60; vis res scientist, Dept Geod & Geophys, Cambridge Univ, 61; consult seismologist, UK Atomic Energy Authority, 61; mem, Comt Seismol, Nat Acad Sci, 65-72 & Earthquake Eng Res Inst, 67-; ed, Bull Seismol Soc Am, 65-; consult, Vet Admin Seismic Adv Comt, 71-; mem, Gov's Earthquake Coun, Calif, 72-74 & Seismic Safety Comn, Calif, 78- *Mem:* Nat Acad Eng; fel Am Geophys Union; Seismol Soc Am (pres, 74-75); assoc Royal Astron Soc; Australian Math Soc; fel Am Geol Soc. *Res:* Classical mechanics as applied to the propagation of waves and structure of the earth; statistical and computational methods of data reduction; earthquake hazard assessment. *Mailing Add:* Seismog Sta Dept Geol & Geophys McCone Hall Univ Calif Berkeley CA 94720

BOLT, DOUGLAS JOHN, REPRODUCTIVE PHYSIOLOGY, ENDOCRINOLOGY. *Current Pos:* RES PHYSIOLOGIST, DAIRY CATTLE RES BR, AGR RES SERV, USDA, 68- *Personal Data:* b Isabel, Kans, Mar 2, 39; m 62. *Educ:* Kans State Univ, BS, 61, MS, 66, PhD(animal breeding), 68. *Prof Exp:* From res asst to res assoc animal husb, Kans State Univ, 62-67; fel obstet & gynec, Sch Med, Univ Mo, 67-68. *Mem:* Am Asn Animal Sci; Soc Study Reproduction. *Res:* Endocrinology and physiology of reproduction, especially as related to corpus luteum function. *Mailing Add:* 3627 Shenandoah Dr Beltsville MD 20705

BOLT, JAY A(RTHUR), MECHANICAL ENGINEERING. *Current Pos:* from assoc prof to prof mech eng, 54-82, prof-in-charge, Automotive Eng Lab, 70-80, EMER PROF MECH ENG, UNIV MICH, 82- *Personal Data:* b New Era, Mich, Oct 31, 11; m 38; c 2. *Educ:* Mich State Univ, BSME, 34, ME, 47; Chrysler Inst, MME, 37; Purdue Univ, MS, 40. *Prof Exp:* Asst prof mech eng, Univ Ill, 38-40 & Univ Notre Dame, 40-41; supvr aircraft carburetor res, Bendix Aviation Corp, 41-47. *Concurrent Pos:* Consult, indust, govt & legal prof. *Mem:* Fel Am Soc Mech Engrs; fel Soc Automotive Engrs; Nat Soc Prof Engrs; Inst Mech Engrs, London, Eng. *Res:* Internal combustion engine research; induction systems; fuel metering; injection and combustion for piston and turbine engines; air pollution; mechanical analysis and expert testimony in casualty cases involving internal combustion engines in vehicles and aircraft. *Mailing Add:* 111 Birdsong Way E-402 Hilton Head Island SC 29926-1366

BOLT, JOHN RYAN, VERTEBRATE ZOOLOGY, PALEOZOOLOGY. *Current Pos:* asst cur, 72-77, assoc cur, 77-89, chmn, 81-90, CUR FOSSIL REPTILES & AMPHIBIANS, FIELD MUS NATURAL HIST, 89- *Personal Data:* b Grand Rapids, Mich, May 28, 40; m 64. *Educ:* Mich State Univ, SB, 62; Univ Chicago, PhD(paleozool), 68. *Prof Exp:* Asst prof anat, Med Ctr, Univ Ill, 68-72. *Concurrent Pos:* Lectr, Comt Evolutionary Biol, Univ Chicago, 73-; assoc prof, Geol Sci, Univ Ill, Chicago, 85- *Mem:* Soc Vert Paleont; Soc Study Amphibians & Reptiles; Paleont Soc; Soc Syst Zool. *Res:* Evolution and origin of Paleozoic amphibia; evolution of Paleozoic vertebrate faunas. *Mailing Add:* 5125 S Ellis Ave Chicago IL 60615

BOLT, RICHARD HENRY, PHYSICS, ACOUSTICS. *Current Pos:* RETIRED. *Personal Data:* b Peking, China, Apr 22, 11; m 33; c 3. *Educ:* Univ Calif, AB, 33, MA, 37, PhD(physics), 39. *Honors & Awards:* Biennial Award, Acoust Soc Am, 42, Gold Medal, 76. *Prof Exp:* Nat Res Coun fel physics, Mass Inst Technol, 39-40; assoc, Univ Ill, 40; dir, Underwater Sound Lab, Mass Inst Technol, 41-43; sci liaison officer, Off Sci Res & Develop, London, 43-44; chief tech aide, Div 6, Nat Defense Res Comt, New York, 44-45; assoc prof physics, Mass Inst Technol, 46-54, dir, Acoustics Lab, 46-57, prof acoustics, 54-63, lectr polit sci, 63-70; chmn bd, Bolt Beranek & Newman, Inc, 53-76, emer chmn, 77-81. *Concurrent Pos:* Pres, Int Comn Acoust, 51-57; prin consult, NIH, 57-59; assoc dir, NSF, 60-63; fel, Ctr Advan Study Behav Sci, 63-64; mem gov bd, Am Inst Physics; adj prof archit, Mass Inst Technol, 83-85; guest lectr, Acad Sinica, Peking, China, 81. *Mem:* Nat Acad Eng; fel Acoust Soc Am (pres, 48); Am Phys Soc; fel Inst Elec & Electronics Engrs; fel Am Acad Arts & Sci. *Res:* Theoretical and experimental studies of sound distribution in enclosures; acoustics of rooms; bioacoustics; effects and control of noise; physics of sound; biophysics; science and public policy. *Mailing Add:* 39 Tabor Hill Rd Lincoln MA 01773

BOLT, ROBERT O'CONNOR, LUBRICATION, RADIATION EFFECTS ON ORGANIC MATERIALS. *Current Pos:* CONSULT, 85- *Personal Data:* b Detroit, Mich, Aug 31, 17; m 43, 89, Lois Fischer; c Sandy(Berry), Patsy (Perner) & Barbara (Almeida). *Educ:* James Millikin Univ, BS, 39; Purdue Univ, MS, 42, PhD(chem), 44. *Prof Exp:* From res chemist to sr res assoc, 46-69; mgr Mkt Serv, Chevron Res Co, 69-85. *Concurrent Pos:* Mem Air Force Aircraft Nuclear Propulsion Radiation Damage Adv Group, 53-55, Mat Adv Group, 55-58 & AEC Org Reactor Working Group, 61-63; lectr, Calpoly State Univ, San Luis Obispo, Ca, 75-; consult, lubricats, Lubrication, Elec Power Res Inst. *Mem:* Am Chem Soc; Soc Tribologists & Lubrication Engrs; Sigma Xi. *Res:* Radiolysis of materials; development of radiation resistant lubricants, fuels, nuclear reactor coolants, and other fluids; development of industrial lubricants; preparation and properties of synthetic oils; organic fluoride chemistry. *Mailing Add:* 55 Culloden Park Rd San Rafael CA 94901. *Fax:* 415-453-1179

BOLTAX, ALVIN, REACTOR FUELS TECHNOLOGY, RADIATION EFFECTS. *Current Pos:* CONSULT, 90- *Personal Data:* b Brooklyn, NY, Oct 20, 30; m 56, 85, Mary A Sinnhuber; c 3. *Educ:* Mass Inst Technol, SB, 51, ScD(phys metall), 55. *Prof Exp:* Group leader, Nuclear Metals, Inc, 55-58, proj mgr, 58-60; mgr fuel develop, Astronuclear Lab, 60-67, mgr fuels technol, Advan Energy Syst Div, Westinghouse, 67-90. *Concurrent Pos:* Lectr, Carnegie Mellon Univ, 70-81. *Mem:* Am Nuclear Soc; Am Inst Metall Eng; Am Soc Metals. *Res:* Fast reactor fuels (oxide and carbide); thermal reactor fuels (UO2 and MOX); materials development; irradiation testing; irradiation effects (creep, swelling, embrittlement); computer modeling of fuels and materials behavior; compact space reactor fuels and refractory metals; nerva graphite; coated fuel particles and carbide coatings; metals and ceramics fabrication. *Mailing Add:* 272 Baywood Ave Pittsburgh PA 15228

BOLTE, EDOUARD, REPRODUCTIVE PHYSIOLOGY, MEDICINE. *Current Pos:* from asst prof to prof physiol, 64-75, PROF MED, UNIV MONTREAL, 75- *Personal Data:* b Montreal, Que, July 23, 31; m 65; c 5. *Educ:* Univ Montreal, BA, 51, MD, 56. *Prof Exp:* Resident med, Univ Hosps, Columbia Univ, 58-60; Med Res Coun Can fel steroids, Columbia Univ, 60-62 & Univ Stockholm, 62-63. *Concurrent Pos:* Mem endocrine serv, Hotel-Dieu Hosp, 64- *Mem:* Endocrine Soc; Can Soc Clin Invest; Int Soc Res Reproduction. *Res:* Various aspects of androgen and estrogen metabolism in human beings in vivo; placental and fetal steroidogenesis. *Mailing Add:* Univ Montreal Hotel-Dieu Hosp 3840 St Urbank Montreal PQ H2W 1T8 Can

BOLTE, JOHN R, OPTICS, SCIENCE EDUCATION. *Current Pos:* asst dean, 68-87, PROF PHYSICS, UNIV CENT FLA, 68-, VPRES ADMIN & FINANCE AFFAIRS, 86- *Personal Data:* b Waterloo, Iowa, Nov 19, 29; m 48; c 3. *Educ:* Univ Northern Iowa, BA, 51, MA, 56; Okla State Univ, MS, 57; Univ Iowa, PhD(sci educ, physics), 62. *Prof Exp:* Instr pub schs, Iowa, 51-59; instr physics & sci educ, Univ Iowa, 59-62; from asst prof to assoc prof physics, San Diego State Col, 62-68. *Concurrent Pos:* Consult, Educ Testing Serv, NJ, 66-68; workshops, educ planning & budgeting. *Mem:* Am Asn Physics Teachers. *Res:* Carbon dioxide laser; use of lasers in communications applications; solar energy application; use of computers in science education. *Mailing Add:* 440 S Lake Sybelia Dr Maitland FL 32751

BOLTER, ERNST A, GEOCHEMISTRY, GEOLOGY. *Current Pos:* asst prof geol, 65-67, assoc prof geochem, 67-76, PROF GEOCHEM, UNIV MO-ROLLA, 76- *Personal Data:* b Mengen-Wuertt, Ger, Feb 16, 35. *Educ:* Univ Gottingen, PhD(mineral), 61. *Prof Exp:* Fel, Yale Univ, 61-63; fel, Rice Univ, 63-65. *Mem:* Mineral Soc Am; Geochem Soc; Am Geophys Union. *Res:* Geochemical prospecting; environmental geochemistry; water and soil pollution. *Mailing Add:* Dept Geol Univ Mo 1101 McCutcheon Rd Rolla MO 65401-2631

BOLTINGHOUSE, JOSEPH C, INSTRUMENTS, CONTROL THEORY. *Current Pos:* RETIRED. *Personal Data:* b Mt Vernon, Ohio, Nov 16, 19; m 55; c 2. *Educ:* Ohio Wesleyan Univ, BA, 40; Mass Inst Technol, SB, 42, Calif State Univ, Fullerton, MS, 82. *Honors & Awards:* Thurlow Award, Inst Navig, 74. *Prof Exp:* Proj engr, Sperry Gyroscope Co, Inc, 42-46; control engr, Gen Mach Corp, 46-47; sr res engr, Curtiss-Wright Corp, 48-50; electromech res specialist, NAm Aviation Autonetics Div, Rockwell Int, 50-67, staff scientist inertial instruments, Autonetics Marine Systs Div, 67-88. *Res:* Inertial platform design and instrument research; gas spin bearing gyros; development of electric bearing gyroscopes. *Mailing Add:* 16057 Arbela Dr Whittier CA 90603

BOLTON, BENJAMIN A, ORGANIC CHEMISTRY. *Current Pos:* RETIRED. *Personal Data:* b Wellsboro, Pa, Sept 5, 28; m 54; c 4. *Educ:* Lafayette Col, BS, 50; Northwestern Univ, MBA, 58. *Prof Exp:* Chemist, Atlas Powder Co, 50-52; chem engr, Amoco Chem Corp, 54-61, group leader org chem, 61-70, sect leader polymers & plastics, Res & Develop Dept, 70-72, res supvr, 72-76, div dir, 76-81, res supvr, 81-83, bus develop mgr, 83-86. *Mem:* Am Chem Soc. *Res:* Organic chemicals; product applications; high temperature polymers; foamed polymers; vinyl thermoplastics; process and product development on polystyrenes; condensation polymers. *Mailing Add:* Five Fern Lane Chesterton IN 46304-1008

BOLTON, CHARLES THOMAS, ASTRONOMY, STELLAR SPECTROSCOPY. *Current Pos:* From asst prof to assoc prof, 73-80, assoc dir, 78-88, PROF ASTRON, DAVID DUNLAP OBSERV, UNIV TORONTO, 80-, ASSOC DIR, 89- *Personal Data:* b Camp Forest, Tenn, Apr 15, 43; m 86, Carolyn Susan Challenger. *Educ:* Univ Ill, BS, 66; Univ Mich, MS, 68, PhD(astron), 70. *Concurrent Pos:* Instr, Scarborough Col, 71-72, asst prof, Erindale Col, 72-73. *Mem:* Am Astron Soc; Can Astron Soc; Int Astron Union; Astron Soc Pac; fel Royal Soc Can. *Res:* Spectroscopy and photometry of variable and multiple stars; spectroscopic studies of stellar atmospheres; light pollution control; mass loss from stars. *Mailing Add:* David Dunlap Observ Univ Toronto PO Box 360 Richmond Hill ON L4C 4Y6 Can. *Fax:* 905-884-2672; *E-Mail:* bolton@astro.utoronto.ed

BOLTON, DAVID C, PRION DISEASES, MOLECULAR BIOLOGY. *Current Pos:* HEAD, LAB MOLECULAR STRUCT & FUNCTION, NY STATE INST BASIC RES, 84- *Personal Data:* b Great Lakes, Ill, Sept 6, 52; m 80; c Elizabeth, Michelle & Thomas. *Educ:* Univ Calif, Davis, BS, 76, PhD(microbiol), 81. *Prof Exp:* Postdoctoral fel, Univ Calif, San Francisco, 81-84. *Concurrent Pos:* Res grant, NIH, 86-90, 91-95; consult, 91- *Mem:* AAAS; Am Soc Microbiol; Protein Soc; Am Soc Biochem & Molecular Biol. *Res:* biochemistry and molecular biology of prion diseases; awarded one US patent. *Mailing Add:* Dept Molecular Biol NY State Inst Basic Res 1050 Forest Hill Rd Staten Island NY 10314-6399

BOLTON, ELLIS TRUESDALE, BIOPHYSICS. *Current Pos:* PROF, UNIV DEL, 74-, DIR CTR MARICULT RES, COL MARINE STUDIES, 77-, EMER PROF MARINE STUDIES. *Personal Data:* b Linden, NJ, May 4, 22; m 43; c 2. *Educ:* Rutgers Univ, BSc, 43, PhD, 50. *Prof Exp:* Res Coun fel, Rutgers Univ, 46, teaching asst genetics & biol, 46-47, instr, 47-50, dir res, Serol Mus, 47-50; mem staff, Dept Terrestrial Magnetism, Carnegie Inst, 50-64, assoc dir, 64-66, dir, 66-74. *Mem:* World Maricult Soc; AAAS; Biophys Soc. *Res:* Molecular biology; mariculture; mass culturing of algae; biosynthesis in microorganisms. *Mailing Add:* RR 4 Lewes DE 19958

BOLTON, JAMES R, PHYSICAL CHEMISTRY. *Current Pos:* prof teaching & res, 70-96, dir, Photochem Unit, 79-85,EMER PROF RES, UNIV WESTERN ONT, 96- *Personal Data:* b Swift Current, Sask, June 24, 37; m 59, Wilma Hall; c Judy & Tom. *Educ:* Univ Sask, BA, 58, MA, 60; Cambridge Univ, PhD, 63. *Honors & Awards:* Noranda Lectr Award, Chem Inst Can, 76. *Prof Exp:* Boese fel & res assoc, Columbia Univ, 63-64; asst prof teaching & res, Univ Minn, 64-66, assoc prof, 66-69, prof assoc chmn, 69-70. *Concurrent Pos:* Alfred P Sloan Found fel, 66-68; grants, NSF, 64-70, Petrol Res Fund, 70-73, Nat Res Coun, 70-77; Nat Sci Eng Res Coun Can, 77-; consult, Solar Energy Res Inst, 78-86; distinguished lectr chem, Simon Fraser Univ, 80; sr res fel, Solarchem Environ Systs, 91-96; sr res chemist, Calgon Carbon Oxidation Technol, 96- *Mem:* Fel Chem Inst Can; Am Chem Soc; fel AAAS; Inter Am Photochem Soc; Solar Energy Soc Can. *Res:* Free radical intermediates in photochemistry and in model systems using optical and electron spin resonance techniques; photochemical reactions with the potential for conversion and storage of solar energy; mechanism of photodegradation of aqueous pollutants with UV light. *Mailing Add:* Dept Chem Univ Western Ont London ON N6A 5B7 Can. *Fax:* 519-661-3022; *E-Mail:* jbolton@julian.uwo.ca

BOLTON, JOSEPH ALOYSIUS, FILTRATION, VACUUM PUMPS. *Current Pos:* DIR NEW TECHNOL, AESCORP, 74- *Personal Data:* b Attleboro, Mass, Sept 18, 39; m 63; c 5. *Educ:* Northeastern Univ, BSME, 63, MS, 65. *Prof Exp:* mgr res & devel, Bird Machine Co, 65-74. *Concurrent Pos:* consult, Ahlstrom Screen Plates, 84-94; teacher hydraul, Adirondack Community Col, 85-88. *Mem:* Tech Asn Pulp & Paper Indust. *Res:* Presented over 18 technical papers on filtration, vacuum systems and screening systems for the pulp and paper industry; recipient of 23 patents. *Mailing Add:* AES Engineered Systs 436 Quaker Rd PO Box 7010 Queensbury NY 12804. *Fax:* 518-793-9392; *E-Mail:* boltonja@webtv.net

BOLTON, LAURA LEE, EXPERIMENTAL BIOLOGY, WOUND BIOLOGY. *Current Pos:* mgr wound care, 87-90, DIR WOUND CARE, CONVATEC DIV, BRISTOL-MYERS SQUIBB, 91- *Personal Data:* b Royal Oak, Mich, Oct 13, 44; m 68, Russell; c Kenneth, William & Diane. *Educ:* Univ Ill, BA, 66; Stanford Univ, MS, 69; Rutgers Univ, PhD(psychobiol), 73. *Prof Exp:* Sr scientist skin biol, Johnson & Johnson Res, 72-86. *Concurrent Pos:* Adj asst prof, Dept Surgery, Univ Med & Dent NJ, 80-87, adj assoc prof, 88- *Mem:* Sigma Xi; Asn Advan Wound Care; Soc Investigative Dermatol; AAAS; NY Acad Sci; Wound Healing Soc. *Res:* Exploration of variables affecting soft tissue repair. *Mailing Add:* 15 Franklin Pl Metuchen NJ 08840

BOLTON, RICHARD ANDREW ERNEST, NUCLEAR FUSION. *Current Pos:* DIR GEN, CAN CTR MAGNETIC FUSION, 88- *Personal Data:* b Montreal, Can, Oct 16, 39; m 74, Sandra Cassidy; c Andrew, Sarah & Philip. *Educ:* McGill Univ, BSc, 60, MSc, 63; Univ Montreal, PhD(plasma physics), 66. *Prof Exp:* Asst prof physics, Univ Montreal, 66-68; res assoc fusion, Culham Lab, UK Atomic Energy Authority, 68-73; sr scientist, Hydro-Que Res Inst, 73-82, mgr, 82-88. *Concurrent Pos:* Mem, Sci Coun Can, 87-92 & Nat Coun, Can Nuclear Soc, 84-87. *Mem:* Can Asn Physicists; Can Nuclear Soc. *Res:* Magnetic confinement of hot plasma in toroidal geometry for controlled fusion research and in view of eventual energy production. *Mailing Add:* 507 Argyle Westmount Montreal PQ H3Y 3B6 Can. *Fax:* 514-652-8625; *E-Mail:* bolton@ccfm.ireq.ca

BOLTON, W KLINE, IMMUNONEPHROLOGY, GLOMERULONEPHRITIS. *Current Pos:* PROF MED, DEPT NEPHROLOGY, SCH MED, UNIV VA, 73- *Educ:* Univ Va, MD, 69. *Res:* Cellular immunity. *Mailing Add:* Dept Internal Med Box 133 Univ Va Health Sci Ctr Charlottesville VA 22908

BOLTON, WADE E, DIAGNOSTIC ONCOLOGY, CELL ACTIVATION-PROLIFERATION. *Current Pos:* group supvr, 82-86, clin reagent mgr, 86-90, MGR RES, COULTER CORP, 90- *Personal Data:* m 76, Lois Hanson; c Jeremy, Chelsea & Dawn. *Educ:* Univ Houston, BS, 74; Columbia Pac Univ, MS, 86, PhD(cell biol), 88. *Prof Exp:* Res assoc, NASA, 69-74, Univ Tex Med Br, 74-78; res asst prof, Baylor Col Med, 78-82. *Concurrent Pos:* Assoc ed, Cancer Molecular Biol Soc, 94- *Mem:* Am Asn Cancer Res; Int Soc Analy Cytology; Cell Kinetics Soc; Am Soc Cell Biol; Int Soc Cancer Molecular Biol; NY Acad Sci. *Res:* Identification and configuration of research reagents useful in the diagnosis and clinical management of oncology patients. *Mailing Add:* 841 SW 87th Terr Plantation FL 33324. *Fax:* 305-380-2595; *E-Mail:* wadeb4@aol.com

BOLTON, WESSON DUDLEY, ANIMAL PATHOLOGY. *Current Pos:* asst animal pathologist, 47-50, chmn dept, 51-81, PROF ANIMAL PATH, UNIV VT, 51- *Personal Data:* b Hardwick, Vt, Dec 30, 22; m 46; c 5. *Educ:* Mich State Col, DVM, 44; Univ Vt, MS, 50. *Prof Exp:* Practicing vet, Vt, 44-47. *Mem:* Am Vet Med Asn; Sigma Xi. *Res:* Causes of infertility in dairy cattle. *Mailing Add:* 9 Pine Tree Terrace South Burlington VT 05403

BOLTRALIK, JOHN JOSEPH, BIOCHEMISTRY. *Current Pos:* RETIRED. *Personal Data:* b Mt Carmel, Pa, June 24, 26; m 51; c 2. *Educ:* Univ Pittsburgh, BS, 50, MS, 53. *Prof Exp:* Asst trop testing electronic equip, Univ Pittsburgh, 50-52; jr fel food technol, Mellon Inst Sci, 52-58; asst microbiol, Sch Med, Univ Pittsburgh, 58-60; jr biochemist, Ciba Pharmaceut Co, 60-67; res assoc, St Barnabas Med Ctr, 67-68; scientist, Alcon Labs Inc, 68-70, sr res scientist biochem, 70-74, head biochem, 74-83, prin scientist, 83-89, asst tech div, 89-93. *Mem:* Am Chem Soc; Acad Pharmaceut Sci. *Res:* Methods development for analysis of drugs from biological fluids; studies on absorption, distribution, metabolism and excretion of topically applied ophthalmic drugs; bioavailability of drugs and drug products; pharmacokinetics; receptor technology. *Mailing Add:* 5017 Whistler Ft Worth TX 76133

BOLTZ, ROBERT CHARLES, JR, FLOW CYTOMETRY, DIGITAL IMAGING MICROSCOPY & CONFOCAL MICROSCOPY. *Current Pos:* sr res, 78-89, res fel, 89-95, SR RES FEL IMMUNOLOGIST CELL SEPARATION & ANALYSIS, MERCK RES LABS, 95- *Personal Data:* b Aug 4, 45; US citizen; m 89, Sheryl A Martz. *Educ:* Pa State Univ, BS, 67 & 68, MS, 72, PhD(biophys), 78. *Prof Exp:* Vis scientist cell separation electrophoresis, Univs Space Res Asn, 77-78. *Mem:* Soc Anal Cytol. *Res:* Fluorescent cytometry and separation of mammalian cells. *Mailing Add:* Merck Res Labs PO Box 2000 R80-107W Rahway NJ 07065

BOLZ, HAROLD A(UGUST), mechanical engineering, for more information see previous edition

BOMAR, LUCIEN CLAY, RADAR SYSTEMS, MILLIMETER WAVES. *Current Pos:* res engr, 76-81, SR RES ENG, ENG EXP STA, GA INST TECHNOL, 81-, ASSOC DIV CHIEF, 80- *Personal Data:* b Birmingham, Ala, Aug 24, 47; m 69; c 3. *Educ:* Ga Inst Technol, BEE, 69. *Prof Exp:* Sr engr elec eng, Sperry Microwave Electronics Co, 69-76. *Concurrent Pos:* Radar consult, Martin Marietta Corp, 78 & Millimeter Wave Technol Inc, 81. *Mem:* Sr mem Inst Elec & Electronics Engrs; Sigma Xi. *Res:* Radar reflectivity characterization of cultural and man made objects; development of specialized radar equipments. *Mailing Add:* 2331 Northwoods Lake COOA Duluth GA 30136

BOMBA, STEVEN JAMES, INDUSTRIAL AUTOMATION SYSTEMS, APPLIED PHYSICS & MATHEMATICS. *Current Pos:* VPRES TECHNOL, JOHNSON CONTROLS INC, 90- *Personal Data:* b Chicago, Ill, June 28, 37; m 59; c 2. *Educ:* Univ Wis-Madison, BS, 59, MS, 61, PhD(physics), 68. *Prof Exp:* Res physicist, Field Res Lab, Mobil Res & Develop Corp, 68-72; mem tech staff, Central Res Lab, Tex Instruments, Inc, 72-75; systs engr, Collins Radio Group, Rockwell Int, 75-78; dir, Corp Technol Develop, Allen-Bradley Co, 78-85, vpres, 85-87; vpres, Adv Mfg Technol, Rockwell Int, 87-90. *Concurrent Pos:* Consult, S J Bomba & Assocs, 71- *Mem:* Am Asn Physics Teachers; Am Phys Soc; Inst Elec & Electronics Engrs; Sigma Xi; Soc Mfg Engrs; Am Soc Mech Engrs. *Res:* Industrial automation with emphasis on communications and control; materials, sensors and processes for materials conversion and assembly mostly regarding discrete parts and batch industries; miscellaneous applied classical physics; applied solid state physics in device and process development; systems science and engineering. *Mailing Add:* 875 E Birch Ave Whitefish Bay WI 53217-5360

BOMBECK, CHARLES THOMAS, III, surgery, animal physiology, for more information see previous edition

BOMBERGER, H(OWARD) B(RUBAKER), JR, METALLURGY. *Current Pos:* PROF METALL & MAT SCI, YOUNGSTOWN STATE UNIV, 82- *Personal Data:* b Lebanon, Pa, Feb 8, 22; m 43; c 3. *Educ:* Pa State Univ, BS, 42; Ohio State Univ, MS, 50, PhD(metall), 52. *Honors & Awards:* US Cong Award Metall, 80. *Prof Exp:* Metallurgist, Wright Aeronaut Corp, 43-45 & Buckeye Steel Castings Co, 46-47; self employed, 47-49; supvr fundamental res, Crucible Steel Co Am, Pa, 52-58, mgr titanium res & develop, 58-65; prod develop, RMI Co, 65-67, dir res & develop, 67-73, dir metall & res, 73-82. *Concurrent Pos:* Mem, US Mat Adv Bd, titanium, 68; grad instr metall, Youngstown State Univ, 68-71. *Mem:* Electrochem Soc; Nat Asn Corrosion Engrs; fel Am Soc Metals; Am Inst Mining, Metall & Petrol Engrs; Brit Inst Metals. *Res:* Physical metallurgy; titanium alloy development; alloy properties; kinetics; corrosion and electrochemical phenomena; author of fifty-five technical papers. *Mailing Add:* Youngstown State Univ 410 Wick Ave Youngstown OH 44555

BOMBIERI, ENRICO M, ALGEBRA, GEOMETRY. *Current Pos:* PROF, INST ADVAN STUDY, PRINCETON, NJ. *Personal Data:* b Milan, Italy, Nov 26, 40; nat US; c 1. *Educ:* Univ Milan, PhD(math), 63. *Honors & Awards:* Fields Medal, 74; Feltrinelli Prize, 76; Balzan Prize, 80. *Mem:* Nat Acad Sci; Europ Acad Sci Arts & Humanities; fel Am Acad Arts & Sci; foreign mem Royal Swedish Acad Sci; foreign mem Inst France Acad Sci. *Res:* Number theory; analysis; geometric measure theory; author of over 120 articles in specialized journals. *Mailing Add:* Inst Advan Study Princeton NJ 08540

BOMKE, HANS ALEXANDER, physics, for more information see previous edition

BOMMARAJU, TILAK V, ELECTROCHEMISTRY, ELECTROCHEMICAL ENGINEERING. *Current Pos:* res chemist, Occidental Chem Corp, 73-76, sr res chemist, 76-81, assoc scientist, 81-85, TECH MGR, OCCIDENTAL CHEM CORP, 85- *Personal Data:* b Tenali, Andhra Pradesh, India, Aug 1, 37; US Citizen; m 61, Savithri Kastala; c Mahesh, Sudha & Uma. *Educ:* Andhra Univ, BS, 55; Banaras Hindu Univ, India, MS, 57, PhD(chem), 67. *Prof Exp:* Sr sci officer, Cent Electrochem Res Inst, India, 57-67; fel, state Univ NY, Buffalo, 67-68, Univ Ottawa, 68-70; res chemist, Int Nickel Co Can, 70-73. *Mem:* Electrochem Soc. *Res:* Kinetic modelling of electrochemical reactions on planar and porous electrodes; role of adsorbed intermediates during the course of electrochemical reactions such as hydrogen and chlorine evolution and electrocatalysis; process engineering aspects. *Mailing Add:* Technol Ctr Oxychem Long Rd Grand Island NY 14072. *Fax:* 716-773-8110

BOMPART, BILLY EARL, DIOPHANTINE EQUATIONS. *Current Pos:* from assoc prof to prof math, 67-90, dept chmn, 83-88, VPRES ACAD AFFAIRS, AUGUSTA COL, 90- *Personal Data:* b Dallas, Tex, Dec 5, 33; m 57, Beverly A Boyd; c Melanie, Laura & Terri. *Educ:* Univ Tex, Austin, BS, 56, PhD(math educ), 67; Southwestern Baptist Theol Sem, MRE, 60; NTex State Univ, MEd, 64. *Prof Exp:* Teacher high schs, Tex, 58-62, 63-65; youth dir, Polytech Baptist Church, Ft Worth, 62-63. *Mem:* Nat Coun Teachers Math; Sigma Xi; Am Educ Res Asn; Am Math Assoc Two-Year Cols; Spec Interest Group Math Educ. *Res:* Theory of numbers. *Mailing Add:* VPres Acad Affairs Dept Augusta Col Augusta State Univ Augusta GA 30904-2200. *Fax:* 706-737-1777; *E-Mail:* bbompart@aug.edu

BOMSE, FREDERICK, PHYSICS. *Current Pos:* MEM PROF STAFF, CTR NAVAL ANALYSIS, 71- *Personal Data:* b New York, NY, Jan 24, 39; m 65, Barbara Benedict; c Mark, Monique & Michelle. *Educ:* Antioch Col, BS, 61; Johns Hopkins Univ, PhD(elem particle physics), 65. *Prof Exp:* Instr physics, Johns Hopkins Univ, 65-66; from instr to asst prof, Vanderbilt Univ, 66-71. *Concurrent Pos:* Mem staff, Appl Physics Lab, Johns Hopkins Univ, 76 & Inst Defense Analysis, 80-81; mem, Submarine Laser Comn, 83 & 87, Naval Res Adv Comt Environ Panel, 88 & Directed Energy Weapons, 89; dir, Anti Submarine Warfare Dept, Ctr Naval Analysis, 84-87, Advan Technol Prog, 91-92, Expeditionary Littoral Systs Prog, 92- *Mem:* Am Phys Soc; Sigma Xi. *Res:* Interactions of fundamental particles; acoustics; fluids; optics; directed energy weapons; advanced radar, missile and other weapon systems for support of naval operations in littoral areas and regional contingencies. *Mailing Add:* Ctr Naval Analyses 4401 Ford Ave PO Box 16268 Alexandria VA 22302-0268

BONA, JERRY LLOYD, FLUID MECHANICS, PARTIAL DIFFERENTIAL EQUATIONS. *Current Pos:* CAM PROF MATH & PHYSICS, TEX INST COMPUTATIONAL & APPL MATH, UNIV TEX, AUSTIN, 95- *Personal Data:* b Little Rock, Ark, Feb 5, 45; m 66, Pamela A Ross; c Rachael E & Jennifer D. *Educ:* Washington Univ, St Louis, BS, 66; Harvard Univ, PhD(math), 72. *Honors & Awards:* Britton Lectr, McMaster Univ, 86; W M Keck Award, 89; Porcelli Lectr, La State Univ, 93; Taft Lectr, Univ Cincinnati, 96. *Prof Exp:* Res fel, Fluid Mech Res Inst, Univ Essex, 70-72; L E Dickson instr, Univ Chicago, 72-73, from asst prof to prof math, 73-86; prof math, Pa State Univ, 86-95, actg chmn, 90-91, chmn dept & Raymond Shibley prof, 91-95. *Concurrent Pos:* Sr vis fel, Sci & Eng Res Coun, Univ Essex, UK, 73-75 & 77-78; vis res assoc, Brookhaven Nat Lab, 76 & 77; vis prof, Inst Budownictwa Wodnego, Polish Acad Sci, 77, Ctr Pesquisas Fisicas, Brazil, 80, Math Res Ctr, Univ Wis, Madison, 80-81, Numerical Analysis Lab, Orsay, France, 82-92, INRS-Oceanology, Univ Quebec, 82-87, Appl Math Physics Lab, Denmark, 82, Inst Math & Applications, Univ Minn, 85-91, US Navy Appl Res Lab, 86-95, Ecole Normale Superieure deCachan, 90-96, Inst Math Pura e Aplicado, Rio de Janeiro, 91-93, Academia Sinica, Beijing, 91 & Univ Paris Nord, Lab Math, 93 & 95; lectr, Int Cong Math, 78, Am Phys Soc, 79, Am Math Soc, 84 & Soc Indust Appl Math, 89; mem, Comt Educ, AAAS, 88-91, coun mem, 96-, Comt Undergrad Prog Math, Math Asn Am, 87-91, Tech Comt Systs Dynamics & Nonlinear Sci, Int Asn Math & Comput Simulation, 92-; chmn, math sect, AAAS, 94-95; Inst Appl Physics & Comp Math, Beijing, 96. *Mem:* Am Math Soc; Soc Indust & Appl Math; Soc Comput Simulations; AAAS; Math Asn Am; Asn Women Math; Africa Math Soc. *Res:* Nonlinear waves; partial differential equations; functional analysis; mathematical economics; probability theory. *Mailing Add:* Dept Math & Tex Inst Comput & Appl Math Univ Tex Austin TX 78712-1082. *Fax:* 512-471-9038; *E-Mail:* bona@math.utexas.edu

BONACCI, JOHN C, CHEMICAL ENGINEERING, CATALYSIS. *Current Pos:* PRES, FIBONACCI INC, 88- *Personal Data:* b Utica, NY, Aug 11, 35; m 57, Annette M Masella; c Carla J & JoAnne. *Educ:* Clarkson Col Technol, BChE, 57, MChE, 59; Univ Pa, PhD(chem eng), 66. *Prof Exp:* Engr, Yerkes Res Lab, E I Du Pont de Nemours & Co, Inc, 58-61, res engr, 61, supvr prod, 61-63; res eng appl res div, Mobil Res & Develop Corp, 66-68, sr res engr, 68-75; res sect head, Englehard Corp, 75-77, res mgr, Res & Develop Dept, 77-81, vpres, 82-83, vpres, Ventures Dept, 84, gen mgr, Systs Dept, 81-83, dir, mkt & technol Environ Catalyst Dept, 85-87; sr scientist, Sci Appl Int Corp, 88-89; mgr, Com Develop & dir mkt, H-R Int, 89-93. *Concurrent Pos:* Dir, NJ Energy Res Inst, 80-86, chmn, 83-84; rep, World Environ Ctr, 83-86; vis prof, Rutgers Univ, 88, adj prof, 89-91; licensed patent agent, 88- *Mem:* Fel Am Inst Chem Engrs; Am Chem Soc; Sigma Xi; NY Acad Sci; Licensing Execs Soc; Nat Soc Prof Engrs. *Res:* Gas-solid mass transfer; mass transfer in evaporating, condensing water; pilot plant, films, polymers, catalytic converters, refining processes; petrochemical ventures; commercial development; air pollution control; technology transfer; patent services. *Mailing Add:* 156 Gallinson Dr Murray Hill NJ 07975-2724. *Fax:* 908-464-3182

BONADONNA, GIANNI, ONCOLOGY. *Current Pos:* DIR, DIV MED ONCOL & HEAD, DEPT CANCER MED, NAT INST STUDY & CURE OF CANCER, 78- *Personal Data:* b July 28, 34; m 69, Noemi Candini; c Davide & Stefania. *Educ:* Milan Univ, MD, 59; FRCP, 97. *Honors & Awards:* Medal of Honor, Am Cancer Soc, 91; Int Soc Chemother Award; David A Karnorsky Mem Award, Am Soc Clin Oncol; Josef Steiner Cancer Res Prize, Univ Bern, Switz; Gen Motors Cancer Res Prize, Univ Bern, Switz; Clin Res Award, Fedn Europ Cancer Socs. *Prof Exp:* Resident, Div Path, Santa Cabrini Hosp, Montreal, 60-61; postdoctoral res fel, Div Chemother, Sloan-Kettering Cancer Ctr, 63-64; res fel, Diag Div, Nat Inst Cancer, Milan, 64-69, asst, 69-76, vpres, 74-78. *Concurrent Pos:* Grantee, Unrestricted Cancer Res Prog, Bristol-Myers Squibb, 93. *Mem:* Am Asn Cancer Res; Am Soc Clin Oncol; Europ Soc Med Oncol; Ital Soc Cancer; Ital Asn Med Oncol. *Res:* First protocol with adjuvant CMF combination chemotherapy, demonstrating its efficacy in a variety of breast cancers and as primary chemotherapy for operable breast cancer; developed the ABVD combination therapy for Hodgkins disease showing it to be non-cross resistant and superior to the traditional drug regimen. *Mailing Add:* Via Venezian 1 Milan 20133 Italy

BONAKDARPOUR, AKBAR, RADIOLOGY. *Current Pos:* From instr to assoc prof, 64-72, PROF RADIOL, HEALTH SCI CTR, TEMPLE UNIV, 72- *Personal Data:* b Esfahan, Iran. *Educ:* Univ Tehran, MD, 53; Temple Univ, MS, 58. *Mem:* Asn Univ Radiologists; fel Am Col Radiol; Radiol Soc NAm; Am Roentgen Ray Soc; Int Skeletal Soc. *Res:* Skeletal radiology. *Mailing Add:* Dept Diag Imaging Health Sci Ctr Temple Univ 3401 N Broad St Philadelphia PA 19140

BONAN, EUGENE J, AERONAUTICAL ENGINEERING, APPLIED MATHEMATICS. *Current Pos:* Design engr, Grumman Aircraft Eng Corp, 49-52, group leader heat transfer, 52-54, group leader armament control systs, 54-56, head weapon syst anal, 56-58, weapon syst proj engr, 58-59, asst dept head weapons syst, 59, dept head, 59-63, chief systs anal sect, 63-64, mgr systs eng, 64-66, dep dir systs technol, 66-70, DIR SYSTS TECHNOL, GRUMMAN AIRCRAFT ENG CORP, BETHPAGE, 70- *Personal Data:* b Pottsville, Pa, Jan 19, 23; m 48; c 2. *Educ:* Cath Univ Am, BS, 49. *Concurrent Pos:* Mem, US Navy Spec Weapons Long Range Planning Comn, 58-60. *Mem:* Am Inst Aeronaut & Astronaut; Am Ord Asn. *Res:* Selection, procurement, technical direction and monitoring of electronic hardware systems included in major weapon and space systems. *Mailing Add:* 4193 SW Oakhaven Circle Palm City FL 34990-7737

BONAR, DANIEL DONALD, MATHEMATICS. *Current Pos:* from asst prof to assoc prof, 69-77, chmn dept, 71-77 & 96-97, PROF MATH, DENISON UNIV, 77- *Personal Data:* b Murraysville, WVa, July 7, 38; m 66, Martha D Baker; c Mary M. *Educ:* WVa Univ, BSChE, 60, MS, 61; Ohio State Univ, PhD(math), 68. *Prof Exp:* From instr to asst prof math, Denison Univ, 65-67; teaching assoc, Ohio State Univ, 67-68; asst prof, Wayne State Univ, 68-69. *Concurrent Pos:* Teacher, Ohio State Univ, 85. *Mem:* Math Asn Am; Sigma Xi; Am Math Soc; Nat Coun Teachers Math. *Res:* Complex and real analysis; annular functions; topological idea of cluster sets. *Mailing Add:* Dept Math & Comp Sci Denison Univ Granville OH 43023. *E-Mail:* bonar@sunshine.mathsci.denison.edu

BONAR, ROBERT ADDISON, CHEMISTRY. *Current Pos:* RETIRED. *Personal Data:* b Kalamazoo, Mich, Aug 23, 25; m 51, Joy Walker; c Susan E (Mayer), Bruce R, David L & Nancy J (Sharpless). *Educ:* Univ Calif, AB, 49, PhD(biochem), 53. *Prof Exp:* Res fel, Med Sch, Univ Calif, Los Angeles, 53-55; res assoc, Dept Surg, Duke Univ, 55-59, asst prof, 59-63, assoc pr of biophys, Dept Surg, Sch Med; res chemist, Vet Admin Hosp, 72-87. *Concurrent Pos:* Nat Cancer Inst fel, 53-55. *Mem:* AAAS; Am Soc Biol Chemists; Sigma Xi. *Res:* Biochemical cytology; carcinogenesis; oncology. *Mailing Add:* 103 Malvern Circle Williamsburg VA 23185

BONAVENTURA, CELIA JEAN, PROTEIN CHEMISTRY, MARINE BIOMEDICINE. *Current Pos:* assoc prof, 72-90, PROF CELL BIOL, DUKE UNIV MED CTR & MARINE LAB, 90-, ASSOC DIR, MARINE BIOMED CTR, 78- *Personal Data:* b Silver City, NMex, June 19, 41; m 60; c 2. *Educ:* Calif State Univ, San Diego, BA, 64; Univ Tex, Austin, PhD(zool), 68. *Prof Exp:* Fel chem, Calif Inst Technol, 68-70; fel molecular biol, Regina Elena Inst Cancer Res, 71-72. *Concurrent Pos:* Asst dir, Marine Biomed Affairs, Duke Univ. *Mem:* Biophys Soc; Am Chem Soc; Am Soc Biol Chemists; Sigma Xi. *Res:* Allosteric control in respiratory proteins; protein engineering; pollutant interactions with hemoglobins. *Mailing Add:* Marine Biomed Ctr Duke Univ 135 Duke Marine Lab Rd Beaufort NC 28516-9721

BONAVENTURA, JOSEPH, PROTEIN CHEMISTRY. *Current Pos:* assoc prof, 72-90, PROF CELL BIOL, DUKE UNIV MED SCH & MARINE LAB, 90-, DIR, MARINE BIOMED CTR, 78- *Personal Data:* b Oakland, Calif, Feb 15, 42; m 60; c 2. *Educ:* Calif State Univ, San Diego, BA, 64; Univ Tex, Austin, PhD(zool), 68. *Prof Exp:* Fel chem, Calif Inst Technol, 68-70; fel molecular biol, Regina Elena Inst Cancer Res, 71-72. *Concurrent Pos:* Estab investr, Am Heart Asn, 75-80. *Mem:* Biophys Soc; Sigma Xi; Am Chem Soc; Am Soc Biol Chemists; Am Soc Zoologists. *Res:* Protein structure-function relationships; properties of insolubilized proteins; respiratory proteins as models for large multisubunit macromolecular complexes; biochemical basis for adaptation and acclimation. *Mailing Add:* Marine Biomed Ctr Duke Univ Marine Lab 114 Broad St Beaufort NC 28516

BONAVIDA, BENJAMIN, IMMUNOBIOLOGY OF CANCER. *Current Pos:* Assoc prof, 78-82, PROF IMMUNOL & BIOCHEM, SCH MED, UNIV CALIF, LOS ANGELES, 82- *Personal Data:* b Cairo, Egypt, Jan 29, 40. *Educ:* Univ Calif, PhD(immunochem), 68. *Mem:* Am Asn Immunologists; Am Asn Cancer Res; Soc Natural Immunity. *Res:* Biology of natural killer cells; AIDS immunology; immunobiology of cancer. *Mailing Add:* Dept Microbiol & Immunol Univ Calif Sch Med Health Sci Ctr Rm A2-084 Los Angeles CA 90024-1747. *Fax:* 213-207-2397

BONAVITA, NINO LOUIS, PHYSICS, MAXIMUM ENTROPY FORMALISM & BAYESIAN ESTIMATION METHODS. *Current Pos:* PHYSICIST, SPACE DATA DIV, GODDARD SPACE FLIGHT CTR, NASA, 59- *Personal Data:* b White Plains, NY, Sept 5, 31; m 65, Cynthia Walsh; c Nino (Lawrence) & Kevin. *Educ:* Fordham Univ, BS, 54; Cath Univ, MS, 63, PhD(physics), 71. *Prof Exp:* Physicist, Aberdeen Proving Ground, 54-55 & Naval Res Lab, 57-59. *Mem:* Am Phys Soc; Sigma Xi. *Res:* Statistical mechanics; theoretical solid state physics and magnetism; celestial mechanics; physics of condensed matter; stochastic processes and self-organization; information theory; intelligent systems; maximum entropy formalism; signal processing; Bayesian probability theory. *Mailing Add:* Goddard Space Flight Ctr Greenbelt Rd NASA Code 934 Bldg 28 Rm 5226 Greenbelt MD 20771. *Fax:* 301-286-1776; *E-Mail:* c0nlb@charney.gsfc.nasa.gov

BONAZZA, RICCARDO, GAS DYNAMICS, NON INTRUSIVE OPTICAL DIAGNOSTIC TECHNIQUES. *Current Pos:* Res fel, 92-93, ASST PROF NUCLEAR ENG, ENG PHYSICS & MECH ENG, UNIV WIS-MADISON, 93- *Personal Data:* m 94, Joan Thalken. *Educ:* Univ Ancona, Italy, Laurea, 83; Calif Inst Technol, MS, 85, PhD(aeronaut), 92. *Res:* Experimental investigation of the fuel-coolant interactions; cryogenics simulation (water-freon); prototypical simulation (tin-water); experimental investigation of shock-interface interaction inside a shock tube. *Mailing Add:* Mech Eng 240 Mech Eng Univ Wis 1513 University Ave Madison WI 53706-1572. *Fax:* 608-262-6707; *E-Mail:* ricrdo@conero.neep.wisc.edu

BOND, ALBERT F, MATHEMATICS. *Current Pos:* RETIRED. *Personal Data:* b Clarksburg, WVa, July 27, 30; m 51; c 3. *Educ:* WVa Univ, AB & MS, 56. *Prof Exp:* Develop engr, Goodyear Aircraft Corp, Ohio, 56-57; staff engr, Bendix Systs Div, 57-63; mgr, Systs Eng Dept, Brown Eng Co, 63-68; mgr Huntsville opers, Planning Res Corp, 68-70; gen mgr, Huntsville Div, Syst Sci, Inc, 70-72; dept mgr, Comput Sci Corp, Huntsville Opers, 72-77; sr proj mgr, Unisys, 77- *Concurrent Pos:* Guest lectr, Univ Mich, 59. *Mem:* Math Asn Am; Opers Res Soc Am. *Res:* Systems engineering; operations research; management sciences; applied mathematics; software engineering. *Mailing Add:* Gallalee Rd SE Huntsville AL 35801

BOND, ALBERT HASKELL, JR, NUCLEAR PHYSICS. *Current Pos:* ASSOC PROF PHYSICS, BROOKLYN COL, 74-, DIR INST NUCLEAR THEORY, 77- *Personal Data:* b Williamson, WVa, Sept 13, 40; m 68. *Educ:* Harvard Univ, AB, 61; Univ Wis, MS, 63, PhD(physics), 68. *Prof Exp:* Found for Aid to Res res assoc nuclear physics, Van Der Graaff Lab, Univ Sao Paulo, 68-74. *Res:* Fast neutron physics; fabrication techniques of lithium-germanium detectors; particle-gamma angular correlations. *Mailing Add:* Dept Physics City Univ NY Brooklyn Col 2900 Bedford Ave Brooklyn NY 11210-2813

BOND, ALECK C, AERONAUTICAL ENGINEERING. *Current Pos:* chief, Syst Eval & Develop Div, 62-63, mgr syst test & eval, 63-67, reliability & qual off & flight safety off, 67-68, asst dir chem & mech systs, 68-75, asst dir prog support, 75-77, assoc dir prog support, 77-80, DEP DIR ENG & DEVELOP DIRECTORATE, JOHNSON SPACE CTR, NASA, HOUSTON, 80- *Personal Data:* b Columbus, Ga, Jan 11, 22; m 48; c 2. *Educ:* Ga Inst Technol, BS, 43, MS, 48. *Prof Exp:* Aeronaut res scientist, Nat Adv Comt Aeronaut, Langley Field, Va, 48-58, aeronaut res scientist & proj engr, Mercury Manned Space Prog, Space Task Group, 58-59, aeronaut res scientist & head performance br, 59-60, asst chief, Flight Syst Div, 60-62. *Concurrent Pos:* Mem large launch vehicle planning group NASA & US Dept Defense, 61. *Mem:* Assoc fel Am Inst Aeronaut & Astronaut. *Res:* Ram jet performance; flight evaluation of various aircraft and missile configurations; aerodynamic heating; high temperature materials research; development and testing of manned spacecraft systems. *Mailing Add:* 234 Driftwood Dr Seabrook TX 77586

BOND, ANDREW, BIOCHEMISTRY, AGRONOMY. *Current Pos:* Instr agron, 54-58, assoc prof biochem, 65-69, assoc prof animal sci, 69-75, PROF BIOCHEM & DEAN ALLIED HEALTH PROFESSIONS, TENN STATE UNIV, 75- *Personal Data:* b Brownsville, Tenn, Aug 8, 27. *Educ:* Tenn Agr & Indust State Col, BS, 48; Tenn State Univ, MS, 52; Univ Minn, PhD(biochem), 65. *Mem:* Am Chem Soc; Nat Soc Allied Health; Am Soc Allied Health. *Res:* Carbohydrate transformations in germinating cereal seeds. *Mailing Add:* Sch Allied Health Tenn State Univ 3500 John A Merritt Blvd Nashville TN 37209-1561

BOND, ARTHUR CHALMER, PHYSICAL CHEMISTRY. *Current Pos:* RETIRED. *Personal Data:* b Salem, WVa, Feb 14, 17. *Educ:* Mich State Univ, BS, 39; Univ Mich, MS, 40, PhD(chem), 51. *Prof Exp:* Res chemist, Nat Defense Res Comt, Univ Chicago, 42-43, instr & asst, 43-46; from instr to asst prof phys chem, Univ Rochester, 51-57; from asst prof to assoc prof chem, Rutgers Univ, 57-67, prof chem, 67-82. *Concurrent Pos:* Asst ed, J Phys Chem, 51-57. *Mem:* AAAS; Am Chem Soc; Sigma Xi. *Res:* Molecular structure; inorganic reaction mechanisms. *Mailing Add:* 13 Dansfield Dr Talley Hill Wilmington DE 19803

BOND, CARL ELDON, ICHTHYOLOGY. *Current Pos:* from asst prof to assoc prof fish & game mgt, Ore State Univ, 49-64, asst dean grad sch, 69-74, prof, 64-84, EMER PROF FISHERIES, ORE STATE UNIV, 84- *Personal Data:* b Culdesac, Idaho, Sept 11, 20; m 42, Lenora Jenson; c Nancy L (Hemming) & Judith C (Gordon). *Educ:* Ore State Univ, BS, 47, MS, 48; Univ Mich, PhD(fisheries), 63. *Prof Exp:* Res asst zool, Univ Calif, 49. *Concurrent Pos:* NSF sci fac fel, 60 & 71; vis res prof, Tokyo Univ Fisheries, 72; vis lectr, Univ Chile, 79 & 85. *Mem:* Am Soc Ichthyol & Herpet; fel Am Inst Fishery Res Biol; Am Fisheries Soc; Sigma Xi. *Res:* Distribution, systematics and ecology of northwest fishes. *Mailing Add:* Dept Fisheries & Wildlife Ore State Univ Corvallis OR 97331

BOND, CHARLES EUGENE, SOLAR ENERGY, WIND POWER. *Current Pos:* from asst prof to assoc prof, 64-66, PROF AERONAUT & ASTRONAUT ENG, UNIV ILL, URBANA, 71- *Personal Data:* b Royston, Ga, Feb 1, 30; m 71; c 7. *Educ:* Ga Inst Technol, BS, 51; Univ Mich, MSE, 56, PhD(aeronaut & astronaut eng), 64. *Prof Exp:* Proj engr, Arnold Eng Develop Ctr, Aro, Inc, 51-54 & Jet Propulsion Lab, 56-57; asst aeronaut & astronaut eng, Univ Mich, 54-56 & 57-58; sr scientist, Res & Advan Develop Div, Avco Corp, 59-60, lead scientist, 60-61; assoc res engr, Univ Mich, 61-64, res engr, Aerodyn Lab, 64. *Mem:* Am Soc Heating Refrig & Air-Conditioning Engrs; Am Soc Mech Engrs; Int Solar Energy Soc. *Res:* Aerodynamics; wind tunnel research; electric arc technology; solar energy, technology and society; magnetogasdynamics. *Mailing Add:* Dept Aeronaut Eng Univ Ill 306 Talbot Lab 104 S Wright Urbana IL 61801

BOND, CLIFFORD WALTER, VIROLOGY. *Current Pos:* asst prof, 78-84, ASSOC PROF MICROBIOL, MONT STATE UNIV, 84-, ACTG HEAD, DEPT MICROBIOL, 90- *Personal Data:* b Buffalo, NY, Apr 7, 37; m; c 1. *Educ:* State Univ NY, Buffalo, BA, 66; Univ Ky, PhD(microbiol), 73. *Prof Exp:* Technician virol, Case Western Res Univ, 66-67, res fel, 67-69; res fel, Univ Ky, 69-74; Leukemia Soc Am fel virol, Univ Calif, San Diego, 74-76, USPHS trainee, 76-77, asst res pathologist, 77-78. *Mem:* Am Soc Microbiol; AAAS; Am Soc Virol. *Res:* Elucidation of molecular interactions between pathogenic viruses and their host that result in disease. *Mailing Add:* Dept Microbiol Mont State Univ Bozeman MT 59717. *Fax:* 406-994-4926; *E-Mail:* umbcb@gemini.oscs.montana.edu

BOND, ELIZABETH DUX, CLINICAL CHEMISTRY. *Current Pos:* RETIRED. *Personal Data:* b Altoona, Pa, June 17, 23; m, Arthur C. *Educ:* Pa State Univ, BS, 44, MS, 51; Rutgers Univ, PhD(chem), 73; NY Univ, MBA, 80. *Prof Exp:* Instr chem, Orlando Col, 63-67; asst chem, Rutgers Univ, 68-73, asst prof, 73-74; res chemist, Cities Serv Co, 74-76; sr scientist, Hoffman LaRoche, 76-79; sr chemist med prods, DuPont Co, 80-88. *Concurrent Pos:* Consult. *Mem:* Sigma Xi; Am Chem Soc. *Res:* Chemistry of coal and its products; electron spin resonance spectroscopy; infrared and raman spectroscopy; clinical chemistry. *Mailing Add:* 13 Dansfield Dr Talley Hill Wilmington DE 19803

BOND, ENRIQUETA CARTER, BIOLOGY, BIOCHEMICAL GENETICS. *Current Pos:* PRES, BURROUGHS WELLCOME FUND, 94- *Personal Data:* b Buenos Aires, Arg, May 22, 39; m 62, Langhorne; c Langhorne C & Prescott M. *Educ:* Wellesley Col, AB, 61; Univ Va, MA, 63; Georgetown Univ, PhD(biol & biochem genetics), 69. *Prof Exp:* Asst prof & actg chmn biol, Chatham Col, Pittsburgh, 70-73; asst prof, Dept Med Sci, Southern Ill Univ, 74-78; staff officer, Inst Med-Nat Acad Sci, 79-80, div dir, 81-88, exec officer, 89-94. *Concurrent Pos:* Bd mem health sci policy, Inst Med-Nat Acad Sci, 94-97; bd sci counrs, Nat Ctr Infectious Dis, 97- *Mem:* Inst Med-Nat Acad Sci; AAAS; Am Pub Health Asn; Am Soc Microbiol; Soc Advan Womens Health Res; Sigma Xi. *Mailing Add:* Burroughs Wellcome Fund 4709 Creekstone Dr Suite 100 Durham NC 27703-8472

BOND, FREDERICK THOMAS, ORGANIC CHEMISTRY. *Current Pos:* asst prof, 67-70, ASSOC PROF CHEM, UNIV CALIF, SAN DIEGO, 70-, PROVOST, REVELLE COL, 83- *Personal Data:* b Brooklyn, NY, Oct 26, 36; m 77; c 2. *Educ:* Mass Inst Technol, BS, 58; Univ Calif, Berkeley, PhD(chem), 62. *Prof Exp:* Asst prof chem, Ore State Univ, 62-67. *Concurrent Pos:* NIH spec fel, 72-73. *Mem:* Am Chem Soc; Sigma Xi; AAAS. *Res:* Chemistry of natural products; structure and reactivity relationships in simple and complex molecules; chemistry of divalent carbon; synthetic organic chemistry. *Mailing Add:* Univ Calif San Diego 9500 Gilman Dr Ph 0321 La Jolla CA 92093-0332

BOND, GARY CARL, MEDICAL PHYSIOLOGY. *Current Pos:* asst prof physiol, 76-78, ASSOC PROF PHYSIOL, MED COL GA, 78- *Personal Data:* b Lawrence, Kans, July 28, 42; m 65; c 1. *Educ:* Univ Kans, BS, 65, PhD(physiol), 70. *Prof Exp:* Res physiologist, St Luke's Hosp, 70-73; asst prof physiol, Med Ctr, Univ Ark, Little Rock, 73-76. *Concurrent Pos:* Lectr physiol, Med Ctr, Univ Kans, 71-73; clin asst prof, Sch Med, Univ Mo-Kansas City, 72-73. *Mem:* AAAS; Am Heart Asn; Am Physiol Soc. *Res:* Cardiovascular physiology with emphasis on cardiovascular control mechanisms involved in blood pressure and blood volume regulation. *Mailing Add:* Dept Physiol & Endocrinol Med Col Ga Augusta GA 30912

BOND, GEORGE WALTER, BIOLOGY, ICHTHYOLOGY. *Current Pos:* from asst prof to assoc prof, 73-84, PROF BIOL, FITCHBURG STATE COL, 84- *Personal Data:* b Lancaster, Pa, Mar 28, 44; m 65; c 4. *Educ:* Dartmouth Col, AB, 66; Univ RI, MS, 69, PhD(biol sci), 74. *Prof Exp:* Res asst ichthyol, Div Fishes, Smithsonian Inst, 72-73. *Mem:* Am Soc Ichthyologists & Herpetologists. *Res:* Biology of deepsea fishes, especially the family gonostomatidae. *Mailing Add:* Dept Biol Fitchburg State Col 160 Pearl St Fitchburg MA 01420-2697

BOND, GERARD C, TECTONICS, PALEOCLIMATE. *Current Pos:* SR RES SCIENTIST, LAMONT-DOHERTY GEOL OBSERV, 80- *Personal Data:* b Altus, Okla, May 20, 40; m 92, Rusty Lotti; c Derek, Justin & Alison. *Educ:* Univ Wis, PhD(geol), 70. *Prof Exp:* Asst prof geol, Williams Col, 70-72 & Univ Calif, Davis, 72-80. *Mem:* Fel Geol Soc Am; Am Geophys Union; Sigma Xi. *Res:* Tectonics of continens, especially in basins; paleoclimate; long-term history of sea level. *Mailing Add:* Lamont-Doherty Geological Observat Rte Nine West Palisades NY 10964

BOND, GUY HUGH, PHYSIOLOGY, BIOCHEMISTRY. *Current Pos:* assoc prof physiol, 75-85, PROF PHYSIOL, KIRKSVILLE COL OSTEOP MED 85- *Personal Data:* b Newark, NJ, Apr 2, 34; m 75; c 1. *Educ:* Rutgers Univ, BS, 56, MS, 61, PhD(physiol, biochem), 65. *Prof Exp:* Instr physiol & biochem, Rutgers Univ, 64-65; physiol fel, Vanderbilt Univ, 65-67; asst prof, Med Col Va, 67-75. *Mem:* Sigma Xi; Soc Gen Physiologists; Am Physiol Soc. *Res:* Membrane transport; human red cell membrane sodium plus potassium adenosine triphosphatase and calcium plus magnesium adenosine triphosphatase. *Mailing Add:* 113 Crowfield CLR Lewisburg WV 24901-1287

BOND, HOWARD EMERSON, ASTRONOMY. *Current Pos:* ASTRONR, SPACE TELESCOPE SCI INST, 84- *Personal Data:* b Danville, Ill, Oct 11, 42; m 67; c 1. *Educ:* Univ Ill, BS, 64; Univ Mich, MS, 65, PhD(astron), 69. *Honors & Awards:* Shapley lectr, Am Astron Soc, 81- *Prof Exp:* Res assoc, La State Univ, Baton Rouge, 69-70, from asst prof to prof astron, 70-84. *Concurrent Pos:* Vis prof, Univ Wash, 75-76; prin investr, NSF & NASA grants; vis prof, Univ Calif, 82-83. *Mem:* Am Astron Soc; Int Astron Union; Astron Soc Pac. *Res:* Astronomical spectroscopy and photometry; nucleosynthesis; population II stars; cataclysmic variable stars; nuclei of planetary nebulae. *Mailing Add:* Space Telescope Sci Inst 3700 San Martin Dr Baltimore MD 21218

BOND, JAMES ANTHONY, METABOLISM, PHARMACOKINETICS. *Current Pos:* dept head, biochem toxicol, 89-96, PROG MGR, CANCER CHEM INDUST INST TOXICOL, 96- *Personal Data:* b Santa Monica, Calif, Sept 11, 52; m 85. *Educ:* Pomona Col, BA, 75; Univ Wash, PhD(pharmacol), 79; Am Bd Toxicol, dipl, 83. *Honors & Awards:* Kenneth Morgareidge Award, Int Life Sci Inst, 90; Inhalation Specialty Sect Achievement Award, Soc Toxicol, 92. *Prof Exp:* Res fel, Chem Indust Inst Toxicol, 80-81; toxicologist, Lovelace Inhalation Res Inst, 81-88, group supvr, 88-89. *Concurrent Pos:* Clin asst prof, Col Pharm, Univ NMex, 85-89; mem, extrapolation models subcomt, sci adv bd, Environ Protection Agency & consult, sci adv bd, 85-; chmn, Toxicol Study Sect, NIH, 90-; mem, Comt Prudent Practices, Nat Acad Sci; adj prof, Dept Toxicol, NC State Univ & Univ NC, Chapel Hill. *Mem:* Soc Toxicol; Am Soc Pharmacol & Exp Therapeut; Am Asn Cancer Res; Int Soc Study Xenobiotics. *Res:* Biological fate of xenobiotics in various biological systems; role that metabolism plays in development of xenobiotic-induced toxicity and carcinogenicity; risk assessment. *Mailing Add:* Chem Indust Inst Toxicol PO Box 12137 Research Triangle Park NC 27709

BOND, JAMES ARTHUR, II, ecology; deceased, see previous edition for last biography

BOND, JENNY TAYLOR, NUTRITION. *Current Pos:* from instr nutrit to instr pharmacol, 70-72, fel develop nephrology, 72-74, assoc prof 74-79, assoc prof Dept Food Sci & Human Nutrit & Dept Pediat & Human Develop, 79-84, PROF, DEPT FOOD, SCI & HUMAN NUTRIT, MICH STATE UNIV, 84- *Personal Data:* b Kinston, NC, Sept 9, 39; m 76; c 2. *Educ:* Meredith Col, AB, 61; Mich State Univ, PhD(nutrit, physiol), 72. *Honors & Awards:* George Harrar Res Coun Award. *Prof Exp:* Exten agt youth, NC Agr Exten Serv, 61-64. *Concurrent Pos:* Specialist foods, NC Agr Exten Serv, 64. *Mem:* Am Soc Nephrology; Am Fedn Clin Res; Nutrit Soc Brit; Int Soc Nephrology; Am Inst Nutrit; Am Dietetic Asn; Soc Nutrit Educ. *Res:* Nutrition prenatally and postnatally; subsequent effects on development, specifically nutrition; drug interactions; xenobiotic metabolism; clinical nutrition. *Mailing Add:* Dept Food Sci & Human Nutrit Mich State Univ East Lansing MI 48824-1224

BOND, JUDITH, BIOCHEMISTRY, PHYSIOLOGY. *Current Pos:* PROF & HEAD BIOCHEM & NUTRIT, VA POLYTECH INST & STATE UNIV, 88- *Personal Data:* b New York, NY, Sept 27, 40; m 74; c 5. *Educ:* Bennington Col, BA, 61; Rutgers Univ, MS, 62, PhD(biochem & physiol), 66. *Honors & Awards:* Merit Award, NIH, 89. *Prof Exp:* NIH fel, Vanderbilt Univ, 66-68; from instr to prof biochem, Med Col Va, Va Commonwealth Univ, 68-88. *Concurrent Pos:* Vis scientist, Strangeways Res Lab, Cambridge, Eng, 78, Commonwealth Sci & Indust Res Orgn, Adelaide, Australia, 86. *Mem:* Am Soc Biochem & Molecular Biol; Am Chem Soc; Am Soc Microbiol; Biochem Soc; Am Physiol Soc. *Res:* Intracellular protein degradation; regulation of enzyme activity and concentration; diabetes; hormonal regulation of metabolism; lysosomes; mechanisms of intracellular proteinases. *Mailing Add:* Dept Biochem & Chem Pa State Univ Col Med Milton S Hershey Med Ctr Hershey PA 17033-0850

BOND, LORA, BOTANY. *Current Pos:* from assoc prof to prof biol, Drury Col, 48-82, head dept, 49-74, chmn, Div Sci & Math, 52-55, 64-67 & 79-82, EMER PROF, DRURY COL, 82- *Personal Data:* b Bryan, Tex, May 17, 17. *Educ:* Univ Tenn, BA, 38; Wellesley Col, MA, 41; Univ Wis, PhD(bot), 45. *Prof Exp:* Asst bot, Wellesley Col, 38-41 & Univ Wis, 41-43; actg instr, Univ Tenn, 43; instr biol & chem, Drury Col, 43-45 & bot, Wellesley Col, 45-48. *Concurrent Pos:* Sci fac fel, NSF, 61. *Mem:* Fel AAAS; Bot Soc Am; Sigma Xi; Am Inst Biol Sci. *Res:* Morphology of angiosperms; colchicine induction of polyploidy in petunia; edaphic factors of Hempstead Plains, Long Island; plant morphology. *Mailing Add:* 1512 N Washington Ave Springfield MO 65803-2849

BOND, MARTHA W(ILLIS), protein chemistry, molecular immunology, for more information see previous edition

BOND, MARVIN THOMAS, portable water supply, waste treatment, for more information see previous edition

BOND, NORMAN T(UTTLE), ELECTRICAL & INDUSTRIAL ENGINEERING. *Current Pos:* RETIRED. *Personal Data:* b Beverly, Mass, Aug 19, 20; m 52; c 4. *Educ:* Univ Ill, BS, 42; Ill Inst Technol, BS, 48; Clarkson Col Technol, MS, 61. *Prof Exp:* Elec engr, Delta Star Elec Co, Ill, 47-48; res engr, Alcoa Labs, Aluminum Co Am, 48-68, sr res scientist, Elec Eng Div, 68-78, staff scientist, Elec Products Div, 78-86. *Mem:* Inst Elec & Electronics Engrs; Sigma Xi. *Res:* Electric connectors and contacts; test techniques for electric connections; data analysis. *Mailing Add:* Box 181 Massena NY 13662-0181

BOND, PETER DANFORD, EXPERIMENTAL NUCLEAR PHYSICS. *Current Pos:* from asst physicist to assoc physicist, Brookhaven Nat Lab, 72-76, physicist, 76-86, assoc chmn, Physics Dept, 86-87, SR PHYSICIST, BROOKHAVEN NAT LAB, 86-, CHMN, PHYSICS DEPT, 87- *Personal Data:* b Providence, RI, Jan 30, 40; m 68, Sandra Salim; c Jennifer, Colin, Anthony S & John Shave. *Educ:* Harvard Univ, BA, 62; Western Reserve Univ, MA, 63; Case Western Reserve Univ, PhD(physics), 69. *Prof Exp:* Res assoc physics, Stanford Univ, 69-72. *Concurrent Pos:* Mem, Div Nuclear Physics Prog Comt, 77-79 & 89-90 Super Heavy-Ion Linear Accelerator Prog Adv Comt, 77-82, chmn, 81-82; vis scientist, Kernfysisch Versneller Inst, Neth, 83-84; mem Oak Ridge Nat Lab Physics Div, Adv Comt, 92-, comt vis to NSF 94, Nuclear Sci Adv Comt Dept Energy, NSF, 94-, Dean's Adv Comt Mass Inst Technol Lab Nuclear Sci, 94- *Mem:* Fel Am Phys Soc; fel AAAS. *Res:* Relativistic heavy ion collisions; the reaction mechanism in heavy ion induced transfer reactions. *Mailing Add:* Bldg 510A Brookhaven Nat Lab Upton NY 11973. *E-Mail:* bond@bnl.gov

BOND, RICHARD RANDOLPH, ACADEMIC ADMINISTRATION, ZOOLOGY. *Current Pos:* pres, 71-81, EMER PRES & PROF ZOOL, UNIV NORTHERN COLO, 81-; PRES, GREELEY AREA FOUND, 96- *Personal Data:* b Lost Creek, WVa, Dec 1, 27; m 46, Reva Stearns; c Harley D, Philip S, Josette B (Schaffer) & Michael R. *Educ:* Salem Col, WVa, BS, 48; Univ WVa, MS, 49; Univ Wis, PhD(zool), 55. *Hon Degrees:* LHD, Salem Col, 78. *Prof Exp:* Asst prof biol, Milton Col, 49-51; assoc prof, Salem Col, WVa, 55-58, dean mem, 57-58; fel col admin, Univ Mich, 58-59; dean fac, Elmira Col, 59-63; prof acad admin, Cornell Univ & arts & sci consult, Univ Liberia, 63-64, chief party, Cornell Univ Proj Liberia, 64-66; prof zool, vpres acad affairs & dean fac, Ill State Univ, 66-71; pres, Morgan Community Col, 91-96. *Concurrent Pos:* Mem, Bd Trustees, Salem Col; comnr, Educ Comn States, 74-81, 85; mem bd, Am Asn State Cols & Univs, 79-81; Colo State Legislator, 85-91; interim pres, Front Range Community Col, 91. *Mem:* AAAS; Ecol Soc Am; Sigma Xi; Am Ornith Union. *Res:* Ecology and behavior of birds; autonomic responses; problems of higher education; international education, biology and public policy. *Mailing Add:* 5601 18th St No 51 Greeley CO 80634. *E-Mail:* rrbond@bentley.univnorthco.edu

BOND, ROBERT FRANKLIN, PHYSIOLOGY. *Current Pos:* PROF PHYSIOL, SCH MED, UNIV SC, 88- *Personal Data:* b Pullman, Wash, Apr 9, 37; m 60, Carol Davis; c Susan C, Linda M & Brian R. *Educ:* Ursinus Col, BS, 59; Temple Univ, MS, 61, PhD(physiol), 64. *Honors & Awards:* James Schringhamer Mem Lectr, Mich State Univ. *Prof Exp:* Assoc physiol & cardiovasc trainee, 64-65, from instr to assoc prof physiol, Bowman Gray Sch Med, 65-73; prof physiol, chmn dept & dir, Cardiovasc Res Labs, Kirksville Col Osteop Med, 73-81; prof physiol & chmn dept, Sch Med, Oral Roberts Univ, 81-88. *Concurrent Pos:* Am Heart Asn advan res fel, 68-70; consult, Carolina Med Electronics & Electromagnetic Probe Co; fel Circulation Group, Am Physiol Soc. *Mem:* Am Heart Asn; Microcirc Soc; Shock Soc; Am Inst Biol Sci; AAAS. *Res:* Autoregulation of blood flow; control of cardiovascular reflexes in shock and hypertension; control of regional vascular beds; myocardial metabolism; hyperbaric physiology; endotoxic shock. *Mailing Add:* Dept Physiol Sch Med Univ SC Sch Med Columbia SC 29208. *Fax:* 803-733-1523; *E-Mail:* bond@med.sc.edu

BOND, ROBERT HAROLD, electrical engineering, for more information see previous edition

BOND, ROBERT LEVI, INSTRUMENTATION, PHYSICS. *Current Pos:* asst prof, 71-74, ASSOC PROF, DEPT ELECTRONICS & INSTRUMENTATION, UNIV ARK, 74- *Personal Data:* b Ozark, Ark, Feb 23, 40. *Educ:* State Col Ark, BS, 61; Univ Ark, MS, 64, PhD(instrumental sci), 68. *Prof Exp:* Sr res physicist, Southwest Res Inst, 68-71. *Mem:* AAAS; Instrument Soc Am; Optical Soc Am; Sigma Xi; Inst Elec & Electronics Engrs. *Res:* Particle optics; modern photon optics; mass spectrometry; vacuum technology; holography; interferometry; optical data processing; biophysics; bioengineering. *Mailing Add:* Univ Arkansas Dept Elec & Instrumentation 2801 Univ Ave ETAS Bldg 575 Little Rock AR 72204

BOND, ROBERT SUMNER, FOREST ECONOMICS, FOREST POLICY. *Current Pos:* RETIRED. *Personal Data:* b Cambridge, Mass, Oct 12, 25; m 50, Barbara Simmons; c Judith A & Robert C. *Educ:* Univ Mass, BS, 51; Yale Univ, MF, 52; State Univ NY Col Forestry, Syracuse Univ, PhD(forestry econ), 66. *Prof Exp:* Res forester, Fordyce Lumber Co, Ark, 52-54; dist forester, Div Forests & Parks, Mass Dept Natural Resources, 54-56; instr gen forestry, Univ Mass, Amherst, 56-63, from asst prof to prof forestry econ, 63-78; prof forest sci & dir, Sch Forest Resources, Pa State Univ, 78-89. *Mem:* Soc Am Foresters; Am Forestry Asn. *Res:* Forest oriented outdoor recreation; forest industry organization and labor; forest resource policy research. *Mailing Add:* Stratford Ponds 28 Main St Apt 65 Mashpee MA 02649-2200

BOND, STEPHON THOMAS, INORGANIC CHEMISTRY. *Current Pos:* ASSOC PROF CHEM, SALEM COL, 65-68 & 71- *Personal Data:* b Lost Creek, WVa, Jan 25, 34; m 60; c 4. *Educ:* Salem Col, BS, 60; WVa Univ, MA, 62; Kent State Univ, PhD(chem), 71. *Prof Exp:* Teacher chem, Belpre Pub Schs, 62-65. *Mem:* Am Chem Soc; Sigma Xi; Am Indust Hyg Asn. *Res:* Organometallic complexes; computer control of mass spectroscopy. *Mailing Add:* Rte 1 Box 74 Jane Lew WV 26378-9801

BOND, VICTOR POTTER, RADIATION BIOPHYSICS, EXPERIMENTAL MEDICINE. *Current Pos:* res group leader, Naval Radiol Defense Lab, Brookhaven Nat Lab, 48-55, mem staff, 55-58, head, Div Microbiol, 58-62, chmn, Med Dept, 62-67, assoc dir, 67-85, SR SCIENTIST, MED DEPT, BROOKHAVEN NAT LAB, 85- *Personal Data:* b Santa Clara, Calif, Nov 30, 19; m 46, 56; c 4. *Educ:* Univ Calif, AB, 43, MD, 45, PhD(med physics), 51. *Hon Degrees:* DSc, Long Island Univ, 65. *Honors & Awards:* Sr Alexander von Humbolt Award, 84-85; Distinguished Sci Achievement Award, Health Physics Soc, 86. *Prof Exp:* Asst, Med Sch, Univ Calif, 45. *Concurrent Pos:* Prof med, State Univ NY, Stony Brook, 68-; prof radiol, Columbia Univ, 69-; pres, Fifth Int Cong Radiation Res, 71-74; distinguished assoc award, US Dept Energy, 90. *Mem:* Am Phys Soc; Radiation Res Soc (pres, 73-74); Soc Exp Biol & Med; Soc Nuclear Med; Am Environ Mutagen Soc. *Res:* Biological effects of radiation; effects of radiation on mammalian systems; the use of particulate radiations in radiotherapy. *Mailing Add:* Brookhaven Nat Lab Upton NY 11973

BOND, WALTER D, PHYSICAL CHEMISTRY, CHEMICAL ENGINEERING. *Current Pos:* Staff mem res & develop, 57-61, GROUP LEADER, OAK RIDGE NAT LAB, 61-, SR SCIENTIST. *Personal Data:* b Lebanon, Tenn, Mar 21, 32; m 55; c 3. *Educ:* Mid Tenn State Univ, BS, 53; Vanderbilt Univ, PhD(phys chem), 57. *Honors & Awards:* IR-100 Award, Indust Res Mag, 85. *Concurrent Pos:* Guest scientist, Swiss Fed Inst Reactor Res, 71-72. *Mem:* Am Chem Soc; Am Nuclear Soc. *Res:* Chemistry of separations of transuranium elements; chemical kinetics; nuclear fuel cycle chemistry; nuclear fuel reprocessing; colloidal synthesis of ceramic materials. *Mailing Add:* 6704 Stone Mill Rd Knoxville TN 37919-7429

BOND, WILLIAM BRADFORD, PHYSICAL CHEMISTRY, ORGANIC CHEMISTRY. *Current Pos:* Res Chemist, 55-63, res supvr, 63-72, SR RES ASSOC, SPECIALITY PROD DIV, FABRICATED PRODUCTS DEPT, E I DU PONT DE NEMOURS & CO, 72- *Personal Data:* b Ithaca, NY, Oct 11, 29; m 52; c 4. *Educ:* Cornell Univ, BA, 51; Fla State Univ, PhD(chem), 55. *Mem:* AAAS; Am Chem Soc; Sigma Xi. *Res:* Free radical chemistry; polyamidation kinetics; polymer chemistry; fibers. *Mailing Add:* 101 Hillside Way Marietta OH 45750

BOND, WILLIAM H, INTERNAL MEDICINE, HEMATOLOGY. *Current Pos:* From instr to prof, 52-85, EMER PROF, INTERNAL MED, SCH MED, IND UNIV-PURDUE UNIV, INDIANAPOLIS, 85- *Personal Data:* b Toronto, Ont, Sept 20, 16; US citizen; m 49; c 4. *Educ:* Univ Chicago, SB, 40, MD, 42. *Concurrent Pos:* Consult, Vet Admin Hosp, 55-85. *Mem:* Am Fedn Clin Res; fel Am Col Physicians; Am Soc Hemat; Am Asn Cancer Res; Cent Soc Clin Res. *Res:* Cancer chemotherapy; clinical hematology. *Mailing Add:* 4525 W 59th St Indianapolis IN 46254-1207

BOND, WILLIAM PAYTON, PLANT PATHOLOGY. *Current Pos:* Asst prof bot & plant path, 67-74, assoc prof, 74-80, PROF BIOL, SOUTHEASTERN LA UNIV, 80- *Personal Data:* b Franklinton, La, Nov 18, 41; m 69; c 2. *Educ:* Southeastern La Col, BS, 63; La State Univ, MS, 66, PhD(plant path), 68. *Mem:* AAAS; Am Phytopath Soc. *Res:* Plant virology; soil transmission of plant viruses; serology. *Mailing Add:* Dept Biol Sci Southeastern La Univ 500 Western Ave Hammond LA 70402-0001

BONDADA, SUBBARAO, CELLULAR IMMUNOLOGY, IMMUNOGENETICS. *Current Pos:* from asst prof to assoc prof, 83-95, PROF, UNIV KY, 95- *Personal Data:* b Ambajheta, Andhra Pradesh, India, June 1, 48; m 80, Vimala Gadey; c Sandhya & Kavitha. *Educ:* Andhra Loyola Col, BSc, 68; Indian Inst Technol, MSc, 70; Tata Inst Fundamental Res, PhD(molecular biol), 76. *Prof Exp:* Vis fel, NIH, 76-79; res assoc, Foxchase Cancer Ctr, 79-83; vis assoc prof, Howard Hughes Med Inst, Dept Immunol, Univ Wash, Seattle. *Concurrent Pos:* Vis scientist, Stanford Univ, 78, Basel Inst Immunol, Switz, 81 & 83; mem, Markey Cancer Ctr, Univ Ky, 86-, assoc, Ctr Aging, 87- & assoc prof toxicol, 93-; vis assoc prof, Univ Wash, 93-94; mem, NIH Study Sect, 93; vis prof, Prairie View A & M Univ, 93; res career develop award, NIH; vis assoc prof, Howard Hughes Med Res Inst, Univ Wash, Seattle, 93-94; mem, Allergy, Immunol, Transplantation Res Comt, Nat Inst Allergy & Infectious Dis, NIH. *Mem:* Am Asn Immunol; AAAS; Int Cell Res Orgn. *Res:* Biology of immune response; B lymphocytes that produce antibodies; growth regulation of B lymphoma cells. *Mailing Add:* Dept Microbiol & Immunol Univ Ky 205 Sanders Brown Bldg Lexington KY 40536

BONDAR, RICHARD JAY LAURENT, ENZYMOLOGY, EXPERIMENTAL DESIGN. *Current Pos:* QUAL CONTROL LAB MGR, 3M PHARMACEUT, 96- *Personal Data:* b New York, NY, Sept 4, 40; m 61, Enid S Teicher; c Randy M & Karen R. *Educ:* McGill Univ, BSc, 62; Calif Inst Technol, MS, 65; Univ Calif, Riverside, PhD(biochem), 69. *Prof Exp:* Instr biol, La State Univ, New Orleans, 64-65; res assoc biochem, Mich State Univ, 69-71; res scientist, 71-73, sr res scientist, 73-77, head, Anal Enzymology Dept, 77-80, head develop oper, Worthington Biochem Corp, 80-83; prin develop chemist, Beckman, 83-85; mgr Process Control, Abbott Labs, 86-89; vpres res & develop, Int Medication Systs, Ltd, 89-90; mgr pharmaceut formulation develop, Banner Pharmacaps Inc, 92-96. *Concurrent Pos:* Mem subcomt on glucose ref methods, Standards Comt, Am Asn Clin Chem, 72-78; chmn subgroup reagent composition, subcomt Enzyme Assay Conditions, Stand Comt, Nat Comt Clin Lab Stand, 73-, Subcomt Methodological Principles, 78-89 principles, 78-89. *Mem:* Am Chem Soc; Am Asn Clin Chemists; Sigma Xi; fel Am Inst Chemists; Am Asn Pharmaceut Scientists. *Res:* Enzymology and protein chemistry; mechanisms of enzyme catalysis and mechanism of reactions of biological interest; analytical biochemistry; enzymology; analytical clinical chemistry; pharmaceutical formulation development for soft gelatin capsules. *Mailing Add:* 1661 S Tiara Way Anaheim CA 92802

BONDAREFF, WILLIAM, ANATOMY. *Current Pos:* AT GERONT CTR, UNIV SOUTHERN CALIF. *Personal Data:* b Washington, DC, Apr 29, 30; m 58; c 2. *Educ:* George Washington Univ, BS, 51, MS, 52; Univ Chicago, PhD(anat), 54; Georgetown Univ, MD, 62. *Prof Exp:* USPHS res fel, Nat Cancer Inst, 54-55; cytologist, Sect Aging, NIMH, 55-64; assoc prof, Med Sch, Northwestern Univ, Chicago, 64-70, prof anat & chmn dept, 70- *Mem:* Fel AAAS; Electron Micros Soc; Geront Soc; Am Asn Anatomists; Am Acad Neurologists. *Res:* Microscopic and ultrastructure of nervous system. *Mailing Add:* Dept Psych Health Sci Campus Univ Southern Calif 1237 N Mission Rd MOL 203 Los Angeles CA 90033-1026. *Fax:* 213-224-4176

BONDE, ERIK KAUFFMANN, PLANT PHYSIOLOGY. *Current Pos:* from asst prof to assoc prof, 55-67, PROF BIOL, UNIV COLO, 67- *Personal Data:* b Odense, Denmark, Oct 19, 22; nat US; m 53; c 3. *Educ:* Univ Colo, BA, 47, MA, 48; Univ Chicago, PhD(bot), 51. *Prof Exp:* Res assoc bot, Univ Calif, Los Angeles, 51-53; NSF fel, Calif Inst Technol, 53-54; asst prof bot, Univ Mo, 54-55. *Mem:* AAAS; Ecol Soc Am; Am Bot Soc; Am Soc Plant Physiol; Scandinavian Soc Plant Physiol; Sigma Xi. *Res:* Plant growth substances and inhibitors; photoperiodism; ecology. *Mailing Add:* 465 University Ave Boulder CO 80302

BONDE, MORRIS REINER, PLANT PATHOLOGY. *Current Pos:* RES PLANT PATHOLOGIST, AGR RES SERV, USDA, 74- *Personal Data:* b Presque Isle, Maine, Aug 7, 45; m 73. *Educ:* Univ Maine, BS, 67; Cornell Univ, MS, 69, PhD(plant path), 75. *Mem:* Am Phytopath Soc; Sigma Xi. *Res:* Epidemiology and control of diseases of major food crops. *Mailing Add:* 7313 Beechtree Dr Middletown MD 21769

BONDELID, ROLLON OSCAR, NUCLEAR PHYSICS. *Current Pos:* RETIRED. *Personal Data:* b Grand Forks, NDak, Jan 8, 23; m 93, Connie M Craycraft; c Claudia, Timothy & Janet. *Educ:* Univ NDak, BS, 45; Washington Univ, MS, 48, PhD(physics), 50. *Prof Exp:* Mem staff, Los Alamos Sci Lab, 50-52; physicist, Naval Res Lab, 52-63, head, Cyclotron Br, 63-80. *Mem:* Fel Am Phys Soc; Sigma Xi; Am Nuclear Soc. *Res:*

Development of sector-focusing cyclotron research facility; correlation studies of few-nucleon systems; neutron cancer therapy; absolute energy measurements of nuclear reactions. *Mailing Add:* 13218 Rollie Rd E Bishopville MD 21813

BONDER, SETH, OPERATIONS RESEARCH, RESEARCH MANAGEMENT. *Current Pos:* from asst prof to assoc prof indust eng, 65-72, dir, Systs Res Lab, 67-71, ADJ PROF INDUST & OPERS ENG, UNIV MICH, ANN ARBOR, 72-; PRES, VECTOR RES, INC, 72- *Personal Data:* b Bronx, NY, July 14, 32; div; c 2. *Educ:* Univ Md, BSME, 60; Ohio State Univ, PhD, 65. *Prof Exp:* Res asst indust eng, Ohio State Univ, 61, res assoc, 61-62, proj supvr & prin investr, 62-65. *Concurrent Pos:* Opers res consult, Joint Chiefs Staff, 73-77, Army Sci Bd, 74-78 & Dept HEW, 75-77; comptroller gen, GAO, 80; Jet Propulsion Lab, 81. *Mem:* AAAS (pres, 78-79); Opers Res Soc Am (vpres, 77-78, pres, 78-79); Nat Acad Scis; Inst Mgt Scis. *Res:* Methodology for long range planning; theories of research and development allocation strategies; studies of large-scale systems; organization of municipal governments; research on theories of search; modeling of population processes. *Mailing Add:* PO Box 1506 Ann Arbor MI 48106-1506

BONDERMAN, DEAN P, CLINICAL PATHOLOGY, TOXICOLOGY. *Current Pos:* PRES & CHIEF EXEC OFFICER, ANALYTICAL CONTROL SYSTS INC, 84- *Personal Data:* b Primghar, Iowa, July 6, 36; m 68; c 3. *Educ:* Westmar Col, BA, 62; Univ Iowa, PhD(inorg chem), 68. *Prof Exp:* Sr chemist & instr pesticide toxicol, Dept Prev Med, Univ Iowa, 66-70; from asst prof to assoc prof clin path, Med Ctr, Ind Univ, Indianapolis, 76-84. *Mem:* Am Chem Soc; Am Soc Clin Path; Am Asn Clin Chem. *Res:* High temperature thermodynamics of inorganic compounds; enzyme response to environmental stimuli; pesticide detection; enzyme kinetics and thermodynamics; development of quality control materials in clinical chemistry and hematology. *Mailing Add:* 8340 E 126th St Fishers IN 46038

BONDESON, STEPHEN RAY, MAGNETIC RESONANCE. *Current Pos:* ASST PROF CHEM, UNIV WIS, STEVENS POINT, 80- *Personal Data:* b Zion, Ill, June 9, 52; m 78. *Educ:* Univ Wis, Stevens Point, BS, 74; Duke Univ, PhD(phys chem), 78. *Prof Exp:* Res assoc, Princeton Univ, 78-80. *Mem:* Am Phys Soc; Am Chem Soc; Sigma Xi. *Res:* Experimental and theoretical aspects of low-dimensional charge-transfer solids; solid state magnetic resonance and relaxation phenomena; stochastic processes; random walk theory. *Mailing Add:* Dept Chem Univ Wis Stevens Point WI 54481

BONDI, AMEDEO, MICROBIOLOGY. *Current Pos:* chmn, microbiol dept, 47-78, dean, grad sch, 73-84, PROF MICROBIOL, HAHNEMANN MED COL, 47-73 & 84- *Personal Data:* b Springfield, Mass, Dec 13, 12; m 39; c 4. *Educ:* Univ Conn, BS, 35; Univ Mass, MS, 37; Univ Pa, PhD(microbiol), 42. *Honors & Awards:* Becton-Dickinson Award Clin Microbiol, 80. *Prof Exp:* Instr bact, Sch Med, Temple Univ, 38-40, asst prof, 42-47. *Mem:* AAAS; Am Soc Microbiol; NY Acad Sci; Am Soc Trop Med & Hyg; Sigma Xi. *Res:* Immunology of Brucellosis and whooping cough; studies on the antibiotic agents; studies on staphylococcal infections. *Mailing Add:* Rydal Park W 1515 Fairway Rydal PA 19046

BONDINELL, WILLIAM EDWARD, MEDICINAL CHEMISTRY. *Current Pos:* assoc sr investr, 73-75, sr investr, 76-87, ASST DIR MED CHEM, SMITH KLINE & FRENCH LABS, 87- *Personal Data:* b Passaic, NJ, Mar 26, 42; m 70; c 1. *Educ:* Fairleigh Dickinson Univ, NJ, BS, 63; Univ Calif, Berkeley, PhD(org chem), 68. *Prof Exp:* Fel, dept biochem, Columbia Univ, 69-71; res assoc, Am Health Found, 71-72. *Mem:* Am Chem Soc. *Res:* Design and synthesis of receptor agonists and antagonists, uptake and enzyme inhibitors as potential agents for cardiovascular, gastrointestinal and CNS diseases. *Mailing Add:* SmithKline Beecham Pharmaceut 709 Swedeland Rd PO Box 1539 King of Prussia PA 19406-0939. *Fax:* 610-270-4162

BONDURANT, BYRON L(EE), AGRICULTURAL ENGINEERING ADMINISTRATION. *Current Pos:* PROF AGR ENG, OHIO STATE UNIV, 64- *Personal Data:* b Lima, Ohio, Nov 11, 25; m 44; c 3. *Educ:* Ohio State Univ, BAE, 49; Univ Conn, MS, 53. *Prof Exp:* Eng trainee surv & inspection, Bur Reclamation, US Dept Interior, 48; lab asst agr eng, Ohio State Univ, 48-49; dist agr engr, Cornell Univ, 49-50; instr & exten engr, agr eng, Univ Conn, 50-53; assoc prof, Univ Del, 53-54; prof & head dept, Univ Maine, 54-64. *Concurrent Pos:* Adv to dean, Col Agr Eng, Punjab Agr Univ, India, 65-67, 69-71 & 72; team leader, Midwestern Consortium Int Activity, 76-77; proj mgr, UN Develop Prog, Food & Agr Orgn, 76-77; Fulbright prof, Univ Nairobi, 79-80. *Mem:* Fel AAAS; fel Am Soc Agr Engrs; Nat Soc Prof Engrs; Am Soc Civil Engrs; NY Acad Sci; Am Soc Eng Educ. *Res:* Soil and water conservation engineering; hydrology; domestic sewage disposal. *Mailing Add:* Dept Agr Eng Ohio State Univ 590 Woody Hayes Dr Columbus OH 43210-1057

BONDURANT, JAMES A(LLISON), agriculture, engineering, for more information see previous edition

BONDURANT, STUART, INTERNAL MEDICINE. *Current Pos:* PROF MED & DEAN, SCH MED, UNIV NC, 79- *Personal Data:* b Winston-Salem, NC, Sept 9, 29; m 54; c 3. *Educ:* Duke Univ, BS, 52, MD, 53. *Hon Degrees:* DSc, Indiana Univ, 80. *Honors & Awards:* Citation Distinguished Serv Res, Am Heart Asn, 69, Lyman Duff Mem Lectr, Award of Merit, 75; Alfred E Stengel Award, Am Col Physicians, 86. *Prof Exp:* Intern, Duke Hosp, Durham, NC, 53-54, resident internal med, 54-56; resident, Peter Bent Brigham Hosp, Boston, 58-59; from asst prof to prof med, Sch Med, Ind Univ, Indianapolis, 59-67, assoc dir, Med Ctr, 61-67; prof & chmn dept, Albany Med Col, 67-74, pres & dean, 74-79. *Concurrent Pos:* Chmn, Res Study Comt, Coun Circulation, Am Heart Asn, 64-67, Res Comt, 64-69, chmn, 67-68, vpres-at-large, 69-72; physician-in-chief, Albany Med Ctr Hosp, 67-74; mem, Adv Coun, Nat Heart & Lung Inst, NIH, 72-75; coun mem, Inst Med-Nat Acad Sci, 90-, Comt Sci, Eng & Pub Policy, 90- *Mem:* Inst Med-Nat Acad Sci; master Am Col Physicians (vpres, 78, pres-elect, 79-80, pres, 80-81); Am Soc Clin Invest (vpres, 74); Asn Am Physicians (treas, 74-79, pres, 85-86); Am Physiol Soc; fel Royal Col Physicians; fel AAAS; Am Clin & Climat Asn; Am Col Cardiol; AMA. *Res:* Author or co-author of over 45 books and papers. *Mailing Add:* CB 7000 125 MacNider Bldg Univ NC Sch Med Chapel Hill NC 27599-7000

BONDY, DONALD CLARENCE, GASTROENTEROLOGY. *Current Pos:* Instr med, Univ Western Ont, 62-63, lectr, 63-65, lectr physiol, 65-67, assoc prof, 67-74, from asst prof med to assoc prof med & physiol, 68-73, PROF MED & PHYSIOL, UNIV WESTERN ONT, 73- *Personal Data:* b Harrow, Ont, June 5, 32; m 56; c 2. *Educ:* Univ Western Ont, MD, 56; FRCPS(C), 61 & 71. *Concurrent Pos:* Consult gastroenterol, Westminster Hosp, 62-67, dir clin invest unit & chief of serv-gastroenterol, 67-72; consult gastroenterol, Victoria & St Joseph's Hosps, 62-67; chief of serv, Dept Gastroenterol, Univ Hosp, 73- *Mem:* Can Soc Clin Invest; Can Med Asn; Can Asn Gastroenterol. *Res:* Clinical gastroenterology. *Mailing Add:* Fac Med Univ Western Ont London ON N6A 5C1 Can

BONDY, MICHAEL F, ELECTRICAL ENGINEERING. *Current Pos:* PRES, MICHAEL BONDY ASSOCS, 90- *Personal Data:* b Vienna, Austria, Dec 6, 23; nat US; m 50, Enid Pincus; c Peter, Mark & Alan. *Educ:* George Washington Univ, BEE, 43; Univ Buffalo, MS, 61. *Prof Exp:* Res assoc, Nat Defense Res Comt, Off Sci Res & Develop, George Washington Univ, 43-45; jr engr, Raytheon Mfg Co, 46-48; intermediate scientist, Westinghouse Elec Corp, 49-50; electromech engr, Glenn L Martin Co, 50-53; res engr, Cornell Aeronaut Lab, Inc, 53-54; head autopilot & stability augmentation group, Bell Aircraft, 54-58; leader systs group, microelectronic prog, Commun Systs Div, Radio Corp Am, 58-65; pres, Dytonis, Inc, 65-90. *Concurrent Pos:* Vpres, Butler & Smith, Inc, 65-70; pres, Hap Jones Atlantic, Inc, 70-73; consult, Singer-Kearfott, 83-88 & Peterallas Assocs, Inc, 88-96. *Mem:* Sigma Xi; sr mem Inst Elec & Electronics Engrs. *Mailing Add:* Michael Bondy Assocs PO Box 123 Haworth NJ 07641-0123

BONDY, PHILIP K, FUNCTION OF POLYAMINES IN CELL DIFFERENTIATION, ENDOCRINE FUNCTION OF ADRENAL GLAND. *Current Pos:* assoc dean, Vet Admin Affairs, 83-89, prof med, 77-88, EMER PROF, SCH MED, YALE UNIV, 88- *Personal Data:* b New York, NY, Dec 15, 17; m 49, Sarah B Ernst; c Jonathan L, Jessica & Steven M. *Educ:* Columbia Univ, BA, 38; Harvard Univ, MD, 42. *Hon Degrees:* MS, Yale Univ, 60. *Honors & Awards:* Brainerd Prize, Columbia Univ, 38. *Prof Exp:* Assoc med, Sch Med, Emory Univ, 48-52; from asst prof to prof med, Sch Med, Yale Univ, 52-74, chmn dept, 65-72; prof med, Inst Cancer Res, London, UK, 72-77; assoc chief of staff res, 77-83, chief staff, Vet Admin Med Ctr, West Haven, 83-89. *Concurrent Pos:* Ed-in-chief, J Clin Invest, Am Soc Clin Invest, 56-62 & Yale J Biol Med, 79-93. *Mem:* Asn Am Physicians; Am Col Physicians; Royal Col Physicians; Am Soc Clin Invest; Endocrine Soc; Royal Soc Med; Sigma Xi. *Res:* Endocrinology, metabolism and control of differentiation; diabetes mellitus and adrenal cortical function; pattern of formation of ectopic hormones by neoplasms; polyamine metabolism, investigating the influence of these substances on growth and differentiation, especially of immune cells and cancers. *Mailing Add:* 9 Chestnut Lane Woodbridge CT 06525

BONDY, STEPHEN CLAUDE, BIOCHEMISTRY, NEUROBIOLOGY. *Current Pos:* PROF TOXICOL, DEPT COMMUNITY & ENVIRON MED, UNIV CALIF, IRVINE, 85- *Personal Data:* b Hilversum, Holland, Jan 10, 38; US citizen; m; c 3. *Educ:* Cambridge Univ, BA, 59, MA, 62; Univ Birmingham, MSc, 61, PhD(biochem), 62. *Prof Exp:* Res biochemist, Unilever Ltd, Bedford, Eng, 59; res asst, Univ Birmingham, 59-62; res scientist, NY State Psychiat Inst, 63-65; res biol chemist, Sch Med, Univ Calif, Los Angeles, 65-70; asst prof neurol, Med Ctr, Univ Colo, Denver, 70-75, assoc prof neurol & pharmacol, 75-78; head, Neurochem Sect, Lab Behav & Neurol Toxicol, Nat Inst Environ Health Sci, 78-85. *Concurrent Pos:* NIH res career develop award, 71-75; NIMH res scientist, 75-78. *Mem:* Toxicol Soc; Int Soc Neurochem; Am Soc Neurochem; Int Soc Develop Neurosci. *Res:* Neurobiology of cerebral development; neurotoxicology. *Mailing Add:* Dept Pharmacol Univ Calif Sch Med Irvine CA 92717-0001

BONDYBEY, VLADIMIR E, LASER CHEMISTRY & SPECTROSCOPY, MATRIX ISOLATION. *Current Pos:* PROF CHEM, OHIO STATE UNIV, 86- & TECH UNIV MUNICH, 88- *Personal Data:* b Prague, Czech, Jan 4, 40; US citizen; m 66, Dinny Burian; c Renee, Andrea & Frances. *Educ:* Univ Rostok, BSc, 65; Charles Univ, Prague, MSc, 68; Univ Calif, Berkeley, PhD(chem), 71. *Prof Exp:* Asst prof chem, Charles Univ, Prague, 66-69; postdoctoral fel chem, Ore State Univ, 72-73; tech staff chem, AT&T Bell Labs, 73-86, distinguished mem tech staff, 84. *Concurrent Pos:* Mem, Steering Comt Int Conf Matrix Isolation, 83-; adv ed, J Chem Physics, 84-86; consult, NSF, 86-87; chmn, Spectros Group, Optical Soc Am, 88-89 & Gordon Conf Matrix Isolation, 91. *Mem:* Am Chem Soc; fel Am Phys Soc; Optical Soc Am; AAAS; NY Acad Sci; Ger Soc Phys Chem. *Res:* Photochemistry, spectroscopy and structure of molecular ions, free radicals and other reactive intermediates; techniques for their production and low temperature studies; clusters and complexes, their formation, dynamics and chemical reactions. *Mailing Add:* Inst Phys & Theoret Chem Tech Univ Munich Lichtenbergstr 4 85748 Garching Germany

BONE, HENRY G, BONE & MINERAL DISORDERS. *Current Pos:* SR STAFF PHYSICIAN, HENRY FORD HOSP, 87- *Personal Data:* b Seattle, Wash, Apr 4, 47. *Educ:* Princeton Univ, AB, 68; Wash Univ, MD, 72. *Honors & Awards:* Dr Boy Frame Mem Award for Excellence in Bone Metab, Am Soc Bone & Mineral Res, 89. *Prof Exp:* Intern internal med, Parkland Hosp, Dallas, 72-73; resident, Univ Tex Health Sci Ctr, 73-74; scholar, Univ Calif, San Diego, 77-78, asst prof med, 78-84; dir clin res, Ciba Geigy, 84-87. *Mem:* Am Soc Bone & Mineral Res; Endocrine Soc; Am Fedn Clin Res; fel Am Col Physicians; Soc Clin Trials. *Res:* Pharmacotherapy of bone and mineral disorders. *Mailing Add:* Henry Ford Hosp Bone Mineral Div 2799 W Grand Blvd Detroit MI 48202-2608. *Fax:* 313-876-7155

BONE, JACK NORMAN, PHARMACY. *Current Pos:* RETIRED. *Personal Data:* b Montrose, Colo, Feb 10, 19; m 40; c 2. *Educ:* Univ Colo, BS, 41, MS, 48; Univ Wash, PhD(pharm), 53. *Prof Exp:* Pharm res asst, Cutter Labs, Berkeley, Calif, 41-42, supvr blood fractionation, 42-45; instr pharm, Univ Colo, 45-48; from asst prof to prof, 48-83, Univ Wyo, dean, Col Pharm, 66-83 & Col Health Sci, 68-83. *Concurrent Pos:* Fulbright lectr, Univ Baghdad, 63-64. *Res:* Synthesis and biotesting of antibacterials and antifungals. *Mailing Add:* 13952 E Marina Dr Apt 406 Aurora CO 80014

BONE, JESSE FRANKLIN, VETERINARY MEDICINE, LARGE ANIMAL MEDICINE & SURGERY. *Current Pos:* instr & res asst, 50-53, from asst prof to prof, 53-80, EMER PROF VET MED, ORE STATE UNIV, 80- *Personal Data:* b Tacoma, Wash, June 15, 16; m 50, Felizitas Endter; c Janice L, Brigitta M, Michael J & David F. *Educ:* State Col Wash, BA, 37; Wash State Univ, BS, 49, DVM, 50; Ore State Col, MS, 53. *Prof Exp:* Lab technician vet med, State Col Wash, 47-50. *Concurrent Pos:* Officer, US Army Res, 37-50; Fulbright lectr vet path, Univ Assuit, 64-65, lectr vet anat, Univ Nairobi, 80-82; consult, Univ Zimbabwe, 82; prof vet anat, Ross Univ, 84. *Mem:* Am Asn Vet Toxicologists; Am Asn Lab Animal Sci; Royal Soc Health. *Res:* Infertility in domestic animals. *Mailing Add:* 3017 Brae Burn Sierra Vista AZ 85635

BONE, LARRY IRVIN, CHEMICAL WASTE TREATMENT, PHYSICAL CHEMISTRY. *Current Pos:* mem staff, Dow Chem Co, 79-80, group leader, 80-84, environ proj mgr, Environ Serv Dept, 84-90, MGR ENVIRON REMEDIATION, DOW CHEMCO, 90- *Personal Data:* b Perry, Iowa, Aug 31, 35; m 57, Marilyn Batz; c Bruce (deceased) & Kimberly (McManus). *Educ:* Coe Col, BA, 57; Ohio State Univ, MSc, 64, PhD, 66. *Prof Exp:* Res chemist, Aerospace Res Labs, Wright-Patterson AFB, USAF, 64-67, nuclear scientist, US Dept Defense, 67-68; from asst prof to prof chem, ETex State Univ, 68-78, asst dean sci & technol, 73-78; vis prof, Appalachian State Univ, 78-79. *Concurrent Pos:* Chief, Chem Div, Nat Ctr Toxicol Res, 77-78. *Mem:* Am Chem Soc; Am Phys Soc; Am Soc Mass Spectrometry. *Res:* Mass spectrometric ion-molecule reactions; analytical mass spectrometry; chemical waste treatment and disposal; hazardous waste site remediation. *Mailing Add:* Dow Chem Co 2030 Willard H Dow Ctr Midland MI 48674

BONE, LEON WILSON, INVERTEBRATE PHYSIOLOGY. *Current Pos:* Res asst, 76-77, CO-PRIN INVESTR, DIV TOXICOL & PHYSIOL, DEPT ENTON, UNIV CALIF, RIVERSIDE, 77- *Personal Data:* b Memphis, Tenn, Aug 19, 45; m 67; c 2. *Educ:* Memphis State Univ, BS, 70, MS, 72; Univ Ark, Fayetteville, PhD(zool), 76. *Prof Exp:* Asst res biologist, Div Toxicol & Physiol, Dept Entom, Univ Calif, Riverside, 77-78; asst prof zool, Div Biol Sci, Ark State Univ, 78-80; mem fac, Physiol Dept, Southern Ill Univ, 80-82. *Mem:* Sigma Xi; Am Soc Parasitologists; Soc Protozoologists; Wildlife Dis Asn. *Res:* Pheromone communication of nematodes. *Mailing Add:* 2202 Annandale Huntsville AL 35801

BONE, ROGER C, INTERNAL MEDICINE, PULMONARY DISEASE. *Current Pos:* AT DEPT MED, RUSH PRESBYTERIAN ST LUKE'S MED CTR. *Personal Data:* b Bald Knob, Ark, Feb 8, 41; m 63; c 2. *Educ:* Hendrix Col, BA, 63; Univ Ark Med Sch, BMS, 65, MD, 67. *Prof Exp:* Asst prof, Univ Kans Med Ctr, 74-77; assoc prof med, Univ Ark Med Ctr, 77-79, prof, 79- *Concurrent Pos:* Chief pulmonary div, Univ Ark Med Ctr, 77- *Mem:* Am Thoracic Soc; Am Col Chest Physcians; Sigma Xi. *Res:* Basic mechanisms of lung injury in the adult respiratory distress syndrome. *Mailing Add:* Dept Med Med Col Ohio 300 Arlington Ave Toledo OH 43699-0008

BONEHAM, ROGER FREDERICK, GEOLOGY. *Current Pos:* From asst prof to assoc prof geol & bot, 66-78, PROF GEOL, IND UNIV, KOKOMO, 78- *Personal Data:* b Boston, Mass, July 26, 35; m 92, Sheila Webster. *Educ:* Mich Technol Univ, BS, 60; Wayne State Univ, MS, 65; Univ Mich, PhD(geol), 68. *Res:* Radon in soils; computer modeling of geologic structures. *Mailing Add:* Dept Sci Ind Univ Kokomo PO Box 9003 Kokomo IN 46904-9003. *Fax:* 765-455-9276; *E-Mail:* boneham@indiana.edu

BONEM, RENA MAE, INVERTEBRATE PALEONTOLOGY, PALEOECOLOGY. *Current Pos:* assoc prof, 81-90, PROF GEOL, BAYLOR UNIV, 90- *Personal Data:* b Tucumcari, NMex, May 6, 48. *Educ:* NMex Inst Mining & Technol, BS, 70, MS, 71; Univ Okla, PhD(geol), 75. *Prof Exp:* Lectr geol, Univ Tex, Arlington, 73; asst prof geol, Hope Col, 75-79; asst prof geol, Tex Christian Univ, 79-81. *Concurrent Pos:* Chmn, Coral Reef Ecol Specialty Protection, Nat YMCA Scuba Prog, 78-, mem adv bd, 89-; secy-treas, S Cent Sect, Geol Soc Am, 89- *Mem:* Paleont Soc; Int Paleont Asn; Geol Soc Am; Am Asn Petrol Geologists; Soc Econ Paleontologists & Mineralogists; Sigma Xi. *Res:* Development and succession of modern and ancient reefs systems; human impact on coral reefs. *Mailing Add:* Dept Geol Baylor Univ Waco TX 76798. *Fax:* 254-755-2673; *E-Mail:* bonem@earthlogic.baylor.edu

BONESS, MICHAEL JOHN, physics, for more information see previous edition

BONEWITZ, ROBERT ALLEN, ELECTROCHEMISTRY, CORROSION. *Current Pos:* Scientist corrosion, Alcoa Labs, 70-73, sr scientist, 73-75, sect head mat & corrosion sci, 75-79, mgr surface technol, 79-81, mgr, Alloy Technol Div, 81-82, mgr, Prod Eng Div, 82-83, opers dir, Mill Prod Res & Develop, 83-84, DIR, PROD DESIGN & MFG, ALCOA LABS, 84- *Personal Data:* b Ottawa, Kans, Dec 18, 43; m 80, Ruth Lasell; c Paul, Christopher & Cara. *Educ:* Lawrence Univ, BA, 65; Univ Fla, PhD(chem), 70. *Mem:* Sigma Xi; Am Soc Metals. *Mailing Add:* 5825 Marlborough Rd Pittsburgh PA 15217

BONEY, WILLIAM ARTHUR, JR, VETERINARY MEDICINE, IMMUNOLOGY. *Current Pos:* RETIRED. *Personal Data:* b Iola, Tex, May 13, 16; m 41, 61; c 1. *Educ:* Agr & Mech Col Tex, BS, 40, DVM, 42, MS, 48. *Prof Exp:* Exten poultry vet, Exten Serv, Agr & Mech Col Tex, 42-44, poultry vet, Exp Sta, 44-46, assoc prof poultry dis & poultry pathologist, 46-54; pres & dir, Boney Labs, 54-59; mgr vet technol, Int Div, Schering Corp, 59-62; res vet & virol proj leader, Nat Animal Dis Lab, USDA, 63-80. *Mem:* Am Vet Med Asn; Am Asn Avian Path; US Animal Health Asn. *Res:* Microbiology; virology; bacteriology; avian diseases. *Mailing Add:* 310 E O'Neil Dr Ames IA 50010

BONFIGLIO, MICHAEL, biology, orthopedic surgery; deceased, see previous edition for last biography

BONFIGLIO, THOMAS ALBERT, PATHOLOGY, CYTOPATHOLOGY. *Current Pos:* asst prof path, Univ Rochester Med Ctr, 72-76, assoc dir cytopath lab & sch cytotechnol, 73-76, actg dir, Surg Path Div & dir, Cytopath Lab, 75-76, from assoc prof to prof, 84-89, prof & actg chmn, Dept Path & Lab Med, 89-90, prof & chair, Dept Path & Lab Med, 90-97, CLIN PROF PATH & LAB MED, UNIV ROCHESTER MED CTR, 97- *Personal Data:* B Rochester, NY, Oct 17, 42; m 66, Mary Barat Rice; c Susan Marie, Amy Elizabeth & Megan Lynn. *Educ:* St John Fisher Col, BS, 64; Univ Rochester, MD, 69; Am Bd Path, dipl. *Honors & Awards:* Papanicolaou Award, Am Soc Cytol, 91. *Prof Exp:* Intern path, Univ Hosp Cleveland, 69-70, resident path, 69-71; chief resident path, Strong Mem Hosp, 71-72. *Concurrent Pos:* Teaching fel path, Case Western Res Univ, 69-71, asst prof path, 76-77; asst pathologist & chief, Cytopath & Surg Path Div, Mt Sinai Hosp, 76-77; consult, Rochester G Hosp, 78 & Genesee Hosp, 79-; vis prof & guest lectr, Med Col Ohio, 80, Dartmouth Hitchcock Med Ctr, 82, William Beaumont Army Med Ctr, El Paso & Med Univ NJ, 84, New Eng Deaconess Hosp, Boston, 85, Henry Ford Hosp, Detroit, 89, Loyola Univ Sch Med, Chicago, 90, St Francis Hosp, Conn, 91, Marshall Univ Sch Med WVa, 91, Univ Iowa Sch Med, 91, Univ Mass Sch Med, 94; chmn, Sci Prog Comt, Am Soc Cytol, 82-84; chmn, Coun Cytopath, 83-84; attend path & dir, Surg Path Unit, Strong Mem Hosp, 84-85, attend pathologist & dir, Anatomic Path Div, 85-, pathologist in chief, 89; mem, Cytopath Exam Comt, Am Bd Path, 84-89; vpres, Int Soc Path Coun, 88, pres, 89. *Mem:* Fel Am Soc Clin Pathologists (vpres, 90-91, pres-elect, 91-92, pres, 92-93); AMA; Am Soc Cytol (vpres, 84-85, pres-elect, 85-86, pres, 86-87); Am Soc Invest Path; Arthur Purdy Stout Soc Surg Pathologists; Asn Dirs Anat & Surg Path; Int Soc Gynec Pathologists; Col Am Pathologists; Int Acad Cytol; US/Can Acad Path. *Res:* Cytopathologic interpretation of transthoracic fine needle biopsies; gynecologic cytopathology; histologic typing of female genital tract; contributed many articles to professional journals. *Mailing Add:* Dept Path Univ Rochester Med Ctr 601 Elmwood Ave Rochester NY 14642

BONGA, JAN MAX, PLANT PHYSIOLOGY. *Current Pos:* RETIRED. *Personal Data:* b Bern, Switz, Dec 5, 29; Can citizen; m 59; c 3. *Educ:* State Univ Groningen, BSc, 54, MSc, 57; McMaster Univ, PhD(biol), 60. *Prof Exp:* Res officer forest path, Can Dept Forestry, 60-72, Forestry Can Maritimes Region, 72-95. *Mem:* Can Soc Plant Physiologists. *Res:* Physiology of tree growth. *Mailing Add:* Forestry Can Maritimes Region PO Box 4000 Fredericton NB E3B 5P7 Can

BONGARTEN, BRUCE C, FOREST GENETICS. *Current Pos:* FROM ASST PROF TO PROF, FOREST RESOURCES, UNIV GA, 78- *Personal Data:* b Pittsburgh, Pa, Mar 4, 51; m 75. *Educ:* State Univ NY Col Environ Sci & Forestry, BS, 73; Mich State Univ, PhD(forest genetics), 78. *Mem:* Soc Am Foresters. *Res:* Genetic improvement of southern hardwoods; pine hybridization; advanced generation breeding; population genetics of tree species. *Mailing Add:* 1430 Hickory Hill Dr Watkinsville GA 30677

BONGIORNI, DOMENIC FRANK, physical organic chemistry, for more information see previous edition

BONGIORNO, SALVATORE F, vertebrate ecology; deceased, see previous edition for last biography

BONHAM, CHARLES D, ECOLOGICAL RISK ANALYSIS, PLANT ECOLOGY. *Current Pos:* assoc prof, 70-75, PROF QUANT PLANT ECOL, COLO STATE UNIV, 75- *Personal Data:* b Cleburne, Tex, Feb 4, 37; m 55, Marla G Phillips; c Deborah, Gregory, Stephan, Mark & Lori. *Educ:* Abilene Christian Col, BS, 59; Utah State Univ, MS, 65; Colo State Univ, PhD(plant ecol), 66. *Honors & Awards:* Outstanding Achievement Award-Soc Range Mgt. *Prof Exp:* Grassland ecologist, Colo State Univ, 62-64; plant ecologist, Cornell Aeronaut Labs, 66-67; from asst prof to assoc prof statist ecol, Univ Ariz, 67-70. *Concurrent Pos:* Consult, Mining Ind & Inst, Range Veg; prin investr, Ecol Risk Analysis Biosolids, Data Analysis Alaska Oil Spill. *Mem:* Am Soc Range Mgt; Ecol Soc Am; Sigma Xi; Biomet Soc; Japanese Grassland Soc. *Res:* Quantitative plant ecology studies using statistical models;

vegetation description and plant community analyses using statistics and mathematical procedures; data analysis of oil spill bioremediation; ecological risk analysis. *Mailing Add:* Dept Rangeland Ecosystem Sci Colo State Univ Ft Collins CO 80523-0001. *Fax:* 970-491-2339

BONHAM, HAROLD F, JR, GEOLOGY. *Current Pos:* from asst mining geologist to assoc mining geologist, 63-74, MINING GEOLOGIST, NEV BUR MINES & GEOL, UNIV NEV, 74-, & PROF GEOL, MACKAY SCH MINES, UNIV NEV, RENO, 74-, ACTG DIR, STATE GEOLOGIST, 93- *Personal Data:* b Los Angeles, Calif, Sept 1, 28; m 52; c 3. *Educ:* Univ Calif, Los Angeles, BA, 54; Univ Nev, MS, 62. *Prof Exp:* Field geologist, Southern Pac Co, 55-57, geologist, 57-61. *Concurrent Pos:* Co-prin investr, Off Water Resources Res grant, 67-68; co-convenor, invitational res conf on zoning in volcanic & subvolcanic mineral deposits, Lake Tahoe, 81 & brecciation & ore deposits, Colorado Springs, 83; counr, Asn Explor Geochemists, 88-90; co-prin invest, Mineral Resource Inventory, Desert Nat Wildlife Range, New Nellis Air Force Range, 92- *Mem:* Fel Geol Soc Am; Soc Econ Geol; Asn Explor Geochemists. *Res:* Geology and geochemistry of metalliferous ore deposits; petrology and petrography of volcanic rocks; environmental geology; geology of epithermal precious metal deposits. *Mailing Add:* 2100 Right Hand Cyn Reno NV 89510

BONHAM, KELSHAW, RADIOBIOLOGY. *Current Pos:* RETIRED. *Personal Data:* b Seattle, Wash, Mar 19, 09; m 38; c 4. *Educ:* Univ Wash, BS, 31, MS, 35, PhD(zool), 37. *Prof Exp:* Asst prof fisheries, Agr & Mech Col Tex, 38-41; asst biologist, Fish & Wildlife Serv, US Dept Interior, Univ Wash, 41-42; biologist, State Fisheries Dept, Wash, 42-44; asst prof zool, Univ Hawaii, 44-45; res assoc prof lab radiation biol, Univ Wash, 45-68, res prof, Col Fisheries, 68-76. *Res:* Monogenea taxonomy; commercial biology of dogfish shark; low-level gamma-irradiation of salmon. *Mailing Add:* 2230 NE 46th St Seattle WA 98105-5709

BONHAM, LAWRENCE COOK, GEOLOGY. *Current Pos:* RETIRED. *Personal Data:* b Springfield, Mo, June 9, 20; m 46; c 4. *Educ:* Drury Col, BS, 42; Washington Univ, MS, 48, PhD, 50. *Prof Exp:* Photogram engr, US Coast & Geod Surv, 42-44; instr geol, Washington Univ, 46-48; supvry res geologist, Calif Res Corp, 50-64; explor geologist, Standard Oil Co, Calif, 64-66; sr res assoc, Chevron Oil Field Res Co, 66-80, mgr geol div, 80-85. *Concurrent Pos:* Instr, Eve Div, East Los Angeles Col, 65-72; adj prof, Univ Southern Calif, 78- & Univ Calif, Los Angeles, 80- *Mem:* Soc Econ Paleont & Mineral; Am Asn Petrol Geologists. *Res:* Sedimentary petrology; organic geochemistry; computer applications in geology. *Mailing Add:* 14169 Bronte Dr Whittier CA 90602

BONHAM, RUSSELL AUBREY, CHEMICAL PHYSICS. *Current Pos:* from instr to prof, 58-96, EMER PROF CHEM, IND UNIV, BLOOMINGTON, 97, RES PROF CHEM, ILL INST TECHNOL, 96- *Personal Data:* b San Jose, Calif, Dec 10, 31; m 57, Miriam Dye; c Frances, Margaret & Anne. *Educ:* Whittier Col, BA, 54; Iowa State Univ, PhD(phys chem), 58. *Honors & Awards:* Alexander von Humboldt Sr Scientist Award, WGer, 77. *Prof Exp:* Res assoc chem, Iowa State Col, 57-58. *Concurrent Pos:* Res assoc, Nat Acad Sci-Nat Res Coun & US Naval Res Lab, 60; asst prof, Univ Col, Univ Md, 60; NSF grants, Conf Magnetism & Crystallog, Japan, 61 & Winter Inst Quantum Chem & Solid State Physics, Fla, 62; Alfred P Sloan Found fel, 64-66; Guggenheim Mem Found fel, 64-65; Fulbright Found res scholar, Univ Tokyo, 64-65; Royal Norweg Sci & Indust res grant, 65; vis scientist, NSF grant under US-Japan Coop Sci Prog, Univ Tokyo & Hokkaido Univ, Japan, 69-70; mem, Nat Acad Sci Joint Brazilian-US Comt Grad Teaching & Res in Chem, 69-76; assoc ed, J Chem Physics, 74-77; mem, Comn Spin & Momentum Density, Int Union Crystallog, 76-82. *Mem:* Am Chem Soc; Am Crystallog Asn; fel AAAS; fel Am Phys Soc; Sigma Xi. *Res:* Low energy electron spectroscopy using pulsed electron beam time of flight techniques; measurement of accurate absolute total electron impact collision cross sections for atoms and molecules; measurement of secondary electron cross sections for electron impact. *Mailing Add:* 901 S Plymouth Ct No 1905 Chicago IL 60605

BONHORST, CARL W, BIOCHEMISTRY. *Current Pos:* from assoc prof to prof, 56-85, head dept, 68-73, EMER PROF CHEM, UNIV PORTLAND, 85- *Personal Data:* b Van Metre, SDak, Dec 31, 17; m 45, Harriet Witmer; c Lena (Andaya). *Educ:* SDak State Univ, BS, 43; Pa State Univ, MS, 47, PhD(biol chem), 49. *Prof Exp:* Instr chem, Univ Portland, 49-51; res assoc pharmacol, Univ Va, 51-52; assoc biochemist, SDak State Univ, 52-56. *Concurrent Pos:* Mem teacher prep-cert study, Nat Asn State Dirs Teacher Educ, 61; vis prof & NSF fac fel, Univ Wis, 62-63. *Mem:* Am Chem Soc; Sigma Xi. *Res:* Physical properties of esters, peptide synthesis, selenium metabolism, active transport and Pasteur effect; chiral metal crystals. *Mailing Add:* 4506 N Amherst St Portland OR 97203

BONI, ROBERT EUGENE, METALLURGICAL ENGINEERING. *Current Pos:* res engr, 56-61, sr res engr, 61-68, mgr appl sci, metall res dept, 68-70, dir metall res, res & technol, 70-76, asst vpres, 76, vpres, 76-78, group vpres, Steel Oper & Oil Gas Subsid, 78-82, exec vpres & chief oper officer, 82-83, pres & chief oper officer, 83-86, CHMN & CHIEF EXEC OFFICER, ARMCO STEEL CORP, 86- *Personal Data:* b Canton, Ohio, Feb 18, 28; m 52; c 2. *Educ:* Univ Cincinnati, MetE, 51; Carnegie Inst Technol, MS & PhD(metall eng), 54. *Honors & Awards:* Distinguished Eng Alumnus Award, Univ Cincinnati, 70; Benjamin F Fairless Award, Am Inst Mining, Metall & Petrol Engrs, 87. *Prof Exp:* Eng asst, Timken Roller Bearing Co, 47-51, metall engr, 54; chief ferrous metall res sect, gun tube develop, Watertown Arsenal Lab, 55-56. *Mem:* Am Soc Metals; Am Inst Mining, Metall & Petrol Engrs. *Mailing Add:* 420 Devon St Kearny NJ 07032

BONIFACINO, JUAN S, CELL BIOLOGY. *Current Pos:* vis fel, NIH, 82-85, Courtesy Int fel, 85-86, vis assoc, 86-91, VIS SCIENTIST, NAT INST CHILD HEALTH & HUMAN DEVELOP, NIH, 91- *Personal Data:* b Buenos Aires, Argentina, Feb 11, 54; c 2. *Educ:* A Mentruyt Sch, Argentina, Bachelor Gen Sci, 71; Univ Buenos Aires, Argentina, Biochemist, 77, PhD(biochem), 81. *Prof Exp:* Res fel, Nat Res Coun, Argentina, 78-82. *Concurrent Pos:* Instr, Dept Phys Chem, Univ Buenos Aires, 73-75, Dept Biol Chem, 76-82; lectr, Found Advan Educ Sci, NIH, 88- *Mem:* Am Soc Cell Biol. *Res:* Biochemistry; cell biology; author of over 50 publications. *Mailing Add:* Cell Biol & Metab Br Bldg 18T Rm 101 NICHD Nat Inst Health Bethesda MD 20892-5430

BONIFAZI, STEPHEN, CHEMISTRY. *Current Pos:* CONSULT, 86- *Personal Data:* b Hartford, Conn, Oct 31, 24; m 59, Joan Dunlop; c Karen S. *Educ:* Trinity Col, BS, 47. *Prof Exp:* Asst chem, Trinity Col, 47-49; sr chemist, Pratt Whitney Aircraft Group, West Palm Beach, Fla, 49-56, supvr chem, 56-58, proj chemist, 58-63, gen supvr chem, 63-78, fuels & lubricants specialist 78-86. *Mem:* Am Chem Soc; Am Soc Lubrication Engrs; Int Asn Hydrogen Energy; Am Soc Testing & Mat; Coord Res Coun; Am Soc Mech Eng. *Res:* High performance; rocket propellants; aerospace fuels technology; alternative fuels research; aerospace lubrication; solid lubrication; protective coatings. *Mailing Add:* 516 Kingfish Rd North Palm Beach FL 33408-4316

BONILLA, MANUEL GEORGE, ENGINEERING GEOLOGY. *Current Pos:* geologist, 47-93, EMER GEOLOGIST, US GEOL SURV, 94- *Personal Data:* b Sacramento, Calif, July 19, 20; m 49, Ruth Raleigh; c Janice, Roger & Laurie. *Educ:* Univ Calif, AB, 43; Stanford Univ, MS, 60. *Honors & Awards:* Claire P Holdredge Award, Asn Eng Geologists, 71. *Prof Exp:* Geologist, US Bur Reclamation, 46-47. *Concurrent Pos:* Mem, Am Seismol Deleg, People's Repub China, 74; mem adv group, Nuclear Regulatory Comn, Nuclear Facil Siting, US Geol Surv, 75-77; mem US comt, Int Asn Eng Geol, 85-88; mem subcomt eval site hazards, Fed Interagency Comt Seismic Safety Construct, 80-88. *Mem:* Fel Geol Soc Am; Seismol Soc Am; Asn Eng Geologists; Am Geophys Union; Int Asn Eng Geol. *Res:* Engineering geology; earthquake faults in relation to land use. *Mailing Add:* US Geol Surv MS 977 345 Middlefield Rd Menlo Park CA 94025

BONIN, JOHN H(ENRY), MECHANICAL ENGINEERING. *Current Pos:* CONSULT SCIENTIST, LOCKHEED MISSILES & SPACE CO, 77- *Personal Data:* b Buzet, France, May 18, 19; nat US; m 46; c 3. *Educ:* Ill Inst Technol, BS, 47, MS, 48. *Prof Exp:* Supvr heat power equip, Armour Res Found, 48-56; dir, Eng Div, Chicago Midway Labs, 56-59; mgr eng res div, Lockheed Propulsion Co, 59-65, dir res br, 65-77. *Mem:* Am Soc Mech Engrs; Am Inst Aeronaut & Astronaut; Sigma Xi. *Res:* Heat transfer and thermodynamics; high temperature phenomena. *Mailing Add:* 1257 Sargent Dr Sunnyvale CA 94087-2841

BONIN, KEITH DONALD, PROPERTIES OF ATOMS, NONLINEAR OPTICS. *Current Pos:* ASSOC PROF PHYSICS, WAKE FOREST UNIV, 92- *Personal Data:* b Haverhill, Mass, Dec 15, 56; m 78; c 3. *Educ:* Loyola Univ, BS, 78; Univ Md, College Park, PhD(physics), 84. *Prof Exp:* Res assoc physics, 84-85, instr, 85-86, asst prof res, dept physics, Princeton Univ, 86-92. *Concurrent Pos:* Consult physicist, Tracor-Jitco, Inc, Rockville, Md, 83-, Columbus Div, Battelle, 88-89. *Mem:* Optical Soc Am; Am Phys Soc; Inst Elec & Electronics Engrs. *Res:* Nonlinear optics, specifically generation of coherent extreme-ultraviolet radiation; developed new techniques for measuring fundamental properties of atoms and molecules, for example, excited-state oscillator strengths, absolute photoionization cross sections and atomic polarizabilities. *Mailing Add:* Dept Physics Wake Forest Univ Winston-Salem NC 27109

BONINI, WILLIAM E, GEOLOGY, GEOPHYSICS. *Current Pos:* From instr to assoc prof geol eng, Princeton Univ, 53-66, prof, 66-70, Magee prof geophys & geol eng, 70-96, EMER PROF GEOPHYS & GEOL ENG, PRINCETON UNIV, 96 *Personal Data:* b Washington, DC, Aug 23, 26; m 54, Rose Rozich; c John, Nancy, James & Jennifer. *Educ:* Princeton Univ, BSE, 48, MSE, 49; Univ Wis, PhD(geol), 57. *Concurrent Pos:* NSF sr fel, 63-64; vis scientist, Yugoslavia, Nat Acad Sci Eastern Europ Exchange Prog, 74, Spain, 81, Italy, 88; chmn, Geophys Div, Geol Soc Am, 85-86. *Mem:* Am Asn Petrol Geol; Am Geophys Union; Geol Soc Am; Soc Explor Geophys; Nat Asn Geol Teachers (pres, 84-85). *Res:* Gravity and magnetic anomalies and major tectonic features of the northwestern United States and Venezuela. *Mailing Add:* Dept Geosci Princeton Univ Princeton NJ 08544-1003. *Fax:* 609-258-1274; *E-Mail:* bonini@geo.princeton.edu

BONIS, LASZLO JOSEPH, MARKETING. *Current Pos:* MGT CONSULT, TECH FINANCE & MKT INC, 74-, PRES, 88- *Personal Data:* b Budapest, Hungary, May 31, 31; m 55, 85, Cheryl E Olsen; c Andrea C & Peter A. *Educ:* Univ Tech Sci, Budapest, DM Ing Mech Eng, 53; Mass Inst Technol, MSc, 59. *Prof Exp:* Assoc dir mat res, Electronics Inc, Budapest, 53-56; prof, Univ Tech Sci, 53-56; res asst, Mass Inst Technol, 57-60; exec vpres & tech dir, Ilikon Corp, 60-62, pres & tech dir, 62-74. *Concurrent Pos:* Pres, chmn & tech dir, Composite Container Corp, 77-88. *Mem:* Fel Am Inst Chemists; NY Acad Sci. *Res:* Technical finance and marketing. *Mailing Add:* Tech Finance & Mkt Inc 52 Haven St Dover MA 02030-2131

BONK, JAMES F, CHEMISTRY. *Current Pos:* From asst prof to assoc prof, 59-74, PROF CHEM, DUKE UNIV, 74-, SUPVR FRESHMAN INSTRUCTION, 77-, DIR UNDERGRAD STUDIES, 89- *Personal Data:* b Menominee, Mich, Feb 6, 31. *Educ:* Carroll Col, Wis, BS, 53; Ohio State Univ, PhD(chem), 58. *Mem:* Am Chem Soc. *Res:* Physical-inorganic chemistry. *Mailing Add:* Dept Chem Duke Univ Box 90353 Durham NC 27708-0353

BONKOVSKY, HERBERT LLOYD, MEDICINE, BIOCHEMISTRY. *Current Pos:* PROF MED, BIOCHEM & MOLECULAR BIOL, UNIV MASS MED CTR, 90-, DIR, DIV DIGESTIVE DIS & NUTRIT, 90-, DIR, LIVER-BILIARY-PANCREATIC CTR, 90-, DIR, CTR STUDY DISORDERS IRON & PORPHYRIN METAB, 90- *Personal Data:* b Cleveland, Ohio; m 67, Marilyn; c Laura, Sarah & Erik. *Educ:* Earlham Col, AB, 63; Western Reserve Univ, MD, 67. *Honors & Awards:* Borden Res Award; Mosby Award. *Prof Exp:* Intern, Duke Univ Med Ctr, 67-68; jr asst resident, Cleveland Metro Gen Hosp, 68-69; clin assoc, Nat Cancer Inst, 69-71; res fel & chief resident, Dartmouth-Hitchcock Med Ctr, 71-73; clin & res fel liver dis, Yale Liver Study Unit, 73-74; from asst prof to prof, Dartmouth Med Sch, 74-85, chief hepatol, Metab Lab, Dartmouth-Hitchcock Med Ctr, 77-85; chief div Digestive Dis, Vet Admin Hosp, White River Junction, Vt, 76-85; prof & dir clin res facil, Sch Med, Emory Univ, 85-90, dir, GT Lab, Emory Clin, 88-90. *Concurrent Pos:* Consult, Hitchcock Clin & Mary Hitchcock Mem Hosp, 74-; res assoc, Vet Admin, 74-76; prin investr, Vet Admin Merit Rev grant, 76-; co-prin investr, Nat Cancer Inst res grant, 76- *Mem:* Am Fedn Clin Res; Am Asn Study Liver Dis; fel Am Col Physicians; Am Soc Clin Invest; Am Gastroent Asn; Am Soc Biol Chemists. *Res:* Liver physiology, biochemistry and disease; hepatic heme metabolism; hepatic drug metabolism and drug-induced liver injury; iron storage diseases, experimental and clinical; acute and chronic hepatitis; auto-immune and metabolic liver diseases; porphria. *Mailing Add:* Med-Gastroenterol Univ Mass Med Sch 55 Lake Ave N Worcester MA 01655-0001. *Fax:* 508-856-3981; *E-Mail:* herbert.bonkovsky@ummed.edu

BONN, ETHEL MAY, ADMINISTRATIVE PSYCHIATRY, QUALITY ASSURANCE. *Current Pos:* assoc prof, 81-89, EMER PROF PSYCHIAT, SCH MED, UNIV NMEX, 89- *Personal Data:* b Cincinnati, Ohio, Oct 14, 25. *Educ:* Univ Cincinnati, BA, 47; Univ Chicago, MD, 51; Am Bd Psychiat & Neurol, cert, 58; Am Psychiat Asn, cert, 65; Am Bd Qual Assurance & Utilization Rev, cert, 82. *Honors & Awards:* President's Award, Admin Psychiat, Am Asn Psychiat Adminr, 76. *Prof Exp:* Rotating intern med, pediat, psychiat, surg & obstet-gynec, Strong Mem Hosp, Univ Rochester, NY, 51-53; psychiat residency, Menninger Sch Psychiat, Vet Admin Hosp, Topeka, Kans, 53-55, chief, Women's Neuropsychiat Sect Psychiat, 57-61, chief, North Psychiat Serv, Women's & Geriatric Psychiat, 61-62; asst hosp dir clin serv, Ft Logan Ment Health Ctr, Denver, Colo, 62-67, hosp dir, 67-76; field rep, Joint Comn Accreditation Hosps, Chicago, Ill, 76-78; chief qual assurance, Vet Admin Med Ctr, Brentwood, Calif, 78-81, chief, Psychiat Serv, Vet Admin Med Ctr, Albuquerque, NMex, 81-89. *Concurrent Pos:* Clin instr psychiat, Menninger Sch Psychiat, Topeka, Kans, 56-62; clin prof psychiat, Sch Med, Univ Colo, Denver, Colo, 62-76; consult psychiat, Fitzsimmons Army Hosp, 63-76, Vet Admin Hosps, Sheridan, Wyo, Tuscaloosa, Ala & Ft Lyon, Colo, 63-76; chmn, Psychiat Sect, Am Hosp Asn, 72-73; mem, Comt Hosp & Community Psychiat, Am Psychiat Asn, 77-81, chair, 80-81; clin prof psychiat, Sch Med, Univ Calif Los Angeles, 78-81. *Mem:* Am Hosp Asn; fel Am Psychiat Asn; fel Am Asn Psychiat Adminr (pres, 75-76); fel Am Col Ment Health Admin; fel Am Col Psychiatrists; AMA; Am Col Utilization Rev Physicians. *Res:* Published papers in psychiatric residency supervision, regressive electroshock treatment, psycho-active medications, administrative psychiatry and quality assurance. *Mailing Add:* 32 Altadena Dr Pueblo CO 81005

BONN, FERDINAND J, REMOTE SENSING, GEOGRAPHIC INFORMATION SYSTEMS. *Current Pos:* Asst lectr geog, Univ Sherbrooke, 69-71, teaching asst geog, 71-73, adj prof remote sensing & geog, 73-78, assoc prof remote sensing & geog, 78-85, dir, Cartel, 85-95, PROF REMOTE SENSING, UNIV SHERBROOKE, 82-, PROF RES, 95- *Personal Data:* b Erstein, France, Oct 7, 43; Can citizen; m 85; c 3. *Educ:* Lynee Kleber, Strasbourg, France, Lesl, 62; Univ Louis Pasteur de Strasbourg, BSc, 68; Univ Strasbourg, France, MSc, 69, PhD(geog), 75. *Honors & Awards:* Jacques-Rousseau Prize Interdisciplinary, Fr Can AAAS. *Concurrent Pos:* Vis prof, Univ Calif, Santa Barbara, 79-80; consult var industs & agencies, 82-; chmn, Car Remote Sensing Soc, 85-86; comt mem, Car Earth Sci, Natural Sci & Eng Res Coun Can, 85-88; coun mem, Car Adv Coun Remote Sensing, 87-93; vis scientist, Inst Nat Res Agr, France, 88-89. *Mem:* Am Soc Photogram & Remote Sensing; Can Remote Sensing Soc (pres, 85-86). *Res:* Remote sensing applied to natural resources management and environmental modeling; soils; geomorphology; desertification; author of various publications. *Mailing Add:* Ctr Remote Sensing Res Appln Sherbrooke Univ 2500 Blvd Univ Sherbrooke PQ J1K 2R1 Can

BONN, T(HEODORE) H(ERTZ), APPLIED COMPUTER RESEARCH. *Current Pos:* INDEPENDENT CONSULT, 85- *Personal Data:* b Philadelphia, Pa, May 27, 23; m 46, Edith Sindell; c Suzanne, Miriam & Matthew. *Educ:* Univ Pa, BS, 43, MS, 47. *Honors & Awards:* Centennial Medal, Inst Elect & Electronics Engrs, 84. *Prof Exp:* Res asst commun & noise, Moore Sch Elec Eng, Univ Pa, 43-47; develop engr, Magnetic Tape Develop, Magnetic Recording, Servo Mechanisms, Eckert-Mauchly Comput Corp, 47-49; chief sonar components, Mil Elec Equip, Naval Air Develop Ctr, 49-50; proj engr magnetic mat, Memory Devices & Amplification Devices, Eckert-Mauchly Div, Remington Rand, Inc, 50-57; chief engr Res & Peripheral Develop, Philadelphia Labs, Remington Rand Univac Div, Sperry Rand Corp, 57-64, mgr Comput Electronics Res, 64-; spec asst for res & develop to tech vpres, Electronic Data Processing Div, Honeywell, Inc, 64-68, dir Standards & Appl Res Div, 68-71; dir Comput Res Lab, Sperry Corp Res Ctr, 71-84, mgr C3I Systs Dept, Sperry Electronic Systs Div, 84-85. *Concurrent Pos:* Vpres publ, Inst Elec & Electronics Engrs, 80-82 & bd dirs, 80-84. *Mem:* Fel Inst Elec & Electronics Engrs; Sigma Xi; Inst Elec & Electronics Engrs Comput Soc (vpres, 66-70). *Res:* Applied research and engineering administration; computer technology; computer architecture; digital magnetic recording; data bases; software; command control communications and intelligence systems; thin films for magnetic recording; megacycle digital magnetic amplifiers; mass storage drums and discs. *Mailing Add:* 1601 Pelican Point Dr Apt H213 Sarasota FL 34231

BONN, WILLIAM GORDON, PLANT PATHOLOGY, BACTERIOLOGY. *Current Pos:* RES SCIENTIST PLANT PATH, CAN DEPT AGR, 73- *Personal Data:* b Toronto, Ont, Sept 28, 46; m 69; c 2. *Educ:* McGill Univ, BSc, 67; Rutgers Univ, MS, 69; Univ Wis, PhD(plant path), 73. *Prof Exp:* Res asst plant path, Rutgers Univ, 67-69 & Univ Wis, 69-73; asst plant path, Purdue Univ, 73. *Mem:* Fel Can Phytopath Soc; Am Phytopath Soc; Sigma Xi. *Res:* Bacterial diseases of plants; epidemiology of fire blight disease; control of bacterial diseases. *Mailing Add:* Can Dept Agr Harrow Res Sta Harrow ON N0R 1G0 Can. *Fax:* 519-738-2929

BONNE, ULRICH, PHYSICAL CHEMISTRY, COMBUSTION. *Current Pos:* STAFF SCIENTIST, HONEYWELL INC, 68-, PRIN RES FEL THERMOCHEM, SENSOR & SYST DEVELOP CTR. *Personal Data:* b London, Eng, Mar 10, 37; US citizen; m 68, Colleen; c 3. *Educ:* Univ Freiburg, BS, 57; Univ Goettingen, MS, 60, PhD(phys chem), 64. *Honors & Awards:* H W Sweatt Award, Honeywell Inc, 71. *Prof Exp:* Res assoc, Dept Phys Chem, Univ Gottingen, 60-65; prin res scientist combustion, Honeywell Inc, Corp Tech Ctr, 65-67; prin res scientist fire res, Factory Mutual Res Corp, 67-68. *Mem:* Optical Soc Am; Combustion Inst; Am Soc Heating, Refrig & Air-Conditioning Engrs; Am Chem Soc. *Res:* Efficiency improvement of energy conversion systems; mathematical modeling and simulation of combustion and heat pump systems; thermochemistry of coal gasification; optical, thermochemical and electrochemical gas sensing methods; development and application of microsensors. *Mailing Add:* Honeywell Inc Corp Tech Ctr 3660 Technology Dr Minneapolis MN 55418. *Fax:* 612-956-4517

BONNECAZE, ROGER T, CHEMICAL ENGINEERING. *Current Pos:* ASST PROF, DEPT CHEM ENG, UNIV TEX. *Concurrent Pos:* Fel, David & Lucile Packard Found, 94. *Mailing Add:* Dept Chem Eng Univ Tex Austin TX 78712-1062

BONNELL, DAVID WILLIAM, PHYSICAL INORGANIC CHEMISTRY, HIGH TEMPERATURE CHEMISTRY. *Current Pos:* RES CHEMIST INORG CHEM, NAT INST STANDARDS & TECHNOL, 75- *Personal Data:* b Wichita, Kans, Sept 29, 43; m 75, Pat McEwan; c Elizabeth A & Megan R. *Educ:* Rice Univ, BA, 68, PhD(phys chem), 72. *Honors & Awards:* IR 100, 80. *Prof Exp:* Res chemist, Rice Univ, 64-68, mass spectrometrist, 68-69, res assoc chem, 72-73; dir res, MCR-Houston Inc, 73-75. *Concurrent Pos:* Consult, Rice Univ, 74-75; vice chair, IUPAC, HTMC Conf, 89. *Mem:* Mat Res Soc; Minerals, Metals & Mat Soc. *Res:* Electron spectroscopic chem analysis instrumentation development; laser ablation; levitation calorimetry property measurements of high temperature materials; high temperature, high pressure molecular beam mass spectrometry; thermodynamic modeling; ultra high temperature; mass spectrometry. *Mailing Add:* Mat Sci & Eng Lab Nat Inst Stand & Technol Div 852 Ceramics MS A215 223 Gaithersburg MD 20899. *Fax:* 301-990-8729; *E-Mail:* bonnell@nist.gov

BONNELL, JAMES MONROE, ORGANIC CHEMISTRY, CHEMICAL ENGINEERING. *Current Pos:* DIR RES, TROPICANA PROD, INC, 57- *Personal Data:* b Chicago, Ill, Apr 5, 22; m 49. *Educ:* Northwestern Univ, BS, 44, BChE, 48, MS, 49; Univ Fla, PhD(chem), 55. *Prof Exp:* Asst dir res, Snow Crop, Fla, 51-55; tech dir, Orange Crystals, Inc, 55-57. *Concurrent Pos:* Vpres, Prof Eng Serv, Inc, 55- *Mem:* AAAS; Am Chem Soc; Am Inst Chem Eng; fel Am Inst Chemists; Sigma Xi. *Res:* Citrus products and by-products. *Mailing Add:* 7308 18th Ave NW Bradenton FL 34209

BONNER, BILLY EDWARD, ELEMENTARY PARTICLE PHYSICS. *Current Pos:* chmn, Physics Dept, 86-91, PROF, RICE UNIV, 85-, DIR, BONNER NUCLEAR LABS, 87- *Personal Data:* b Oak Grove, La, Dec 12, 39. *Educ:* La Polytech Inst, BS, 61; Rice Univ, MA, 63, PhD(physics), 65. *Prof Exp:* Fel physics, Rice Univ, 65-66; sr sci officer, Rutherford High Energy Lab, Sci Res Coun, Eng, 66-70; assoc res physicist, Crocker Nuclear Lab, Univ Calif, Davis, 71-72; mem staff physics, Los Alamos Sci Lab, Univ Calif, 72-85. *Concurrent Pos:* Vis prof physics, Rice Univ, 81-82; sci assoc at CERN, 83-84. *Mem:* Am Phys Soc; Sigma Xi; AAAS. *Res:* Intermediate and high energy particle physics; studies of hadron polarization, jets and spin dependent structure functions of nucleons. *Mailing Add:* Bonner Nuclear Labs Rice Univ MS 315 Houston TX 77251-1892. *Fax:* 713-285-5215; *E-Mail:* bonner@physics.rice.edu

BONNER, BRUCE ALBERT, PLANT PHYSIOLOGY. *Current Pos:* asst prof, 63-71, ASSOC PROF BOT, UNIV CALIF, DAVIS, 71- *Personal Data:* b Jamestown, NDak, Apr 14, 29; m 53; c 4. *Educ:* Univ Calif, AB, 52, PhD(bot) 57. *Prof Exp:* USPHS fel physiol genetics lab, Nat Cent Sci Res, France, 56-58; res assoc bot, Yale Univ, 58-61; instr, Harvard Univ, 61-63. *Mem:* Am Soc Plant Physiol; Bot Soc Am. *Res:* Mechanism of photomorphogenesis; growth and development. *Mailing Add:* 43248 E Oakside Pl Davis CA 95616

BONNER, DANIEL PATRICK, MICROBIOLOGY, CHEMOTHERAPY. *Current Pos:* dir microbiol, 87-89, EXEC DIR MICRO BIOL, BRISTOL-MYERS SQUIBB PHARM RES INST, 89- *Personal Data:* b Bayonne, NJ, Oct 9, 45; m 72, Marianne Neewalsh; c Timothy & Mary Kate. *Educ:* Fairleigh Dickinson Univ, BS, 67; Rutgers Univ, MS, 69, PhD(microbiol), 72. *Prof Exp:* Biol sci asst microbiol, Dept Rickettsial Dis, Walter Reed Army Inst Res, Walter Reed Army Med Ctr, 69-71; res assoc, Waksman Inst Microbiol, Rutgers Univ, 72-77, asst res prof, 77-78; res investr, Squibb Inst Med Res, 78-81, res group leader, 81-84, asst dept dir, 84-87. *Concurrent Pos:* Div A chmn, Am Soc Microbial, 89-90. *Mem:* AAAS; Am Soc Microbiol; Sigma Xi; Japan Antibiotics Res Asn; Am Acad Microbiol. *Res:* Chemotherapy of infectious diseases; beta-lactam antibiotics; polyene macrolide antibiotics. *Mailing Add:* Bristol-Myers Squibb 5 Research Pkwy PO Box 5100 Wallingford CT 06492-7660

BONNER, DAVID CALHOUN, STATISTICAL MECHANICS SOLUTIONS, POLYMER PHASE SEPARATION. *Current Pos:* vpres technol, 96-97, SR VPRES, WESTLAKE GROUP, 97- *Personal Data:* b Port Arthur, Tex, Nov 20, 46; m 73, Lillian; c 2. *Educ:* Univ Tex, Austin, BSChE, 67, MSChE, 69; Univ Calif, Berkeley, PhD(chem eng), 72. *Prof Exp:* Res engr, Union Carbide Corp, 68-69; assoc prof chem eng, Tex Tech Univ, 72-76 & Tex A&M Univ, 76-77; tech support mgr, Shell Oil Co, 77-86; dir corp res, B F Goodrich Co, 87-88, vpres res & develop, 88-92; sr vpres & chief tech officer, Premix Inc, 92-96. *Mem:* Am Inst Chem Eng; Am Chem Soc; Am Soc Compts. *Res:* Polymer phase equilibrium and solution theory. *Mailing Add:* Westlake Group 2801 Post Oak Blvd Suite 600 Houston TX 77056. *Fax:* 216-224-2766

BONNER, ERROL MARCUS, INDUCTIVELY COUPLED PLASMA EMISSION SPECTROSCOPY & ATOMIC ABSORPTION SPECTROSCOPY, CHROMATOGRAPHY. *Current Pos:* chief chemist, 80-94, SR CHEMIST, RINECO ANALYTICAL SERV, ENSCO INC, 94- *Personal Data:* m 80, Marina V Ballesteros. *Educ:* Univ Ala, BS, 65; Southeastern Baptist Theol Seminary, MDiv, 75. *Prof Exp:* Chemist, USAF Weapons Lab, 65-69; qual control chemist, A H Robins Co, 69-70, Burroughs Wellcome Co, 71-73; staff chemist, Velsicol Chem Corp, 76-80. *Concurrent Pos:* D-34 Comt Waste Mgt. *Mem:* Am Chem Soc; Int Union Pure & Appl Chem; Am Inst Chemists; Am Soc Testing & Mat. *Res:* Develop spectroscopic and chromatographic methods for determining priority pollutants in hazardous wastes; low level barium and beryllium determinations in complicated, unknown waste matrices by ion exchange separation with spectroscopic detection. *Mailing Add:* Rineco Anal Serv 629 Vulcan Rd Haskell PO Box 729 Benton AR 72015

BONNER, FRANCIS JOSEPH, PHYSICAL CHEMISTRY, CHEMICAL ENGINEERING. *Current Pos:* AT CHEM ENG DEPT, UNIV LOWELL, LOWELL, MA. *Personal Data:* b Wilmington, Del, Jan 4, 34; m 76; c 2. *Educ:* Mass Inst Technol, SB, 55, SM, 56; Univ Del, PhD(chem eng), 64; Univ Uppsala, Fil Lic & Fil Dr(phys chem), 67. *Prof Exp:* Swed Int Develop Agency lectr phys chem, Univ Uppsala, 66; sr res chem engr, Mobil Res & Develop Corp, 68-72; oberassistent, Swiss Fed Inst Technol, 72-81; prof chem eng, Vanderbilt Univ. *Concurrent Pos:* Swed Govt fel, Univ Uppsala, 64-65, Swed Natural Sci Res Coun grants, 65-68. *Mem:* Am Chem Soc; Am Inst Chem Engrs; NY Acad Sci; Sigma Xi. *Res:* Tribology, rheology, metallurgy, material science and engineering; physical-surface-interfacial chemistry, including mass transport of synthetic and natural macromolecules and emulsifiers; polymer science and engineering; applied surface chemistry. *Mailing Add:* Chem Eng Dept Univ Lowell One Univ Ave Lowell MA 01854

BONNER, FRANCIS TRUESDALE, NITROGEN CHEMISTRY, REACTION MECHANISMS. *Current Pos:* chmn dept, State Univ NY, 58-70, dean, Int Progs, 83-86, prof, 58-92, EMER PROF CHEM, STATE UNIV NY STONY BROOK, 92- *Personal Data:* b Salt Lake City, Utah, Dec 18, 21; m 94, M Jane Carlberg; c Michael, Alisa (deceased) & Rachel. *Educ:* Univ Utah, BA, 42; Yale Univ, MS, 44, PhD(phys chem), 45. *Prof Exp:* Res chemist, Manhattan Proj, Columbia Univ, 44-46, Clinton Nat Lab, Oak Ridge, 46-47 & Brookhaven Nat Lab, NY, 47-48; asst prof chem, Brooklyn Col, 48-54; Carnegie Found fel, Harvard Univ, 54-55; phys chemist, Arthur D Little, Inc, 55-58. *Concurrent Pos:* NSF sr fel, Saclay Nuclear Res Ctr, France, 64-65; consult ed, Addison-Wesley Publ Co, 56-77; res collabr, Brookhaven Nat Lab, 58-88; Rockefeller Found consult, Univ Del Valle, Colombia, 61, 64 & 68; Ford Found consult, Univ Antioquia, Colombia, 62, 63 & 68; vis scientist, EAWAG/ETH, Zurich, Switz, 73; Nat Acad Sci exchange vis scientist, Romania, 75; mem bd dirs, Res Found, State Univ NY, 76-88; vis prof, Kings Col, Univ London, 87. *Mem:* Fel AAAS; Am Chem Soc; Sigma Xi. *Res:* Eluicidation of reaction mechanisms by kinetic, isotopic and spectroscopic means; reactive intemediates; inorganic chemistry of nitrogen; redox chemistry of nitrogen oxides in aqueous solution. *Mailing Add:* Box 2063 Setauket NY 11733. *Fax:* 516-632-7960; *E-Mail:* fbonner@ccmail.sunysb.edu

BONNER, HUGH WARREN, EXERCISE PHYSIOLOGY. *Current Pos:* PROF, STATE UNIV NY, SYRACUSE, 94- *Personal Data:* b Chicago, Ill, Oct 27, 44; m 67. *Educ:* Univ Minn, BS, 67; Calif State Col, Hayward, MS, 70; Univ Calif, Berkeley, PhD(phys educ), 72. *Prof Exp:* From asst prof to assoc prof phys educ, Univ Tex, Austin, 72-86, dir, Exer Physiol Labs, 73-86; assoc dean, Sch Allied Health Sci, Tex Tech Univ, 92-94. *Mem:* AAAS; Am Asn Health Phys Educ & Recreation; Am Col Sports Med. *Res:* Determination of the influence of exercise training upon calcium transport of mitochondria and sarcoplasmin reticulum in cardiac and skeletal muscle and morphometric changes of subcellular organelles. *Mailing Add:* Health Sci Ctr State Univ NY 750 E Adams St Syracuse NY 13210

BONNER, JAMES (FREDRICK), developmental biology, biochemical genetics; deceased, see previous edition for last biography

BONNER, JAMES JOSE, MOLECULAR BIOLOGY, DEVELOPMENTAL BIOLOGY. *Current Pos:* asst prof, 79-85, ASSOC PROF BIOL, IND UNIV, BLOOMINGTON, 85-, ASSOC CHMN DEPT, 87- *Personal Data:* b Los Angeles, Calif, May 1, 50; m 74; c 1. *Educ:* Univ Calif, Berkeley, BA, 72; Mass Inst Technol, PhD(biol), 77. *Prof Exp:* Teaching asst biol, Mass Inst Technol, 72-76; scholar biochem, Univ Calif, San Francisco, 77-78. *Concurrent Pos:* Jr fac res award, Am Cancer Soc. *Mem:* Am Soc Cell Biol; AAAS; Genetics Soc Am; Soc Develop Biol; Sigma Xi. *Res:* Developmental regulation of genetic expression; genetic and biochemical analysis of molecular aspects of metabolic stress. *Mailing Add:* Dept Biol Ind Univ Bloomington IN 47405-3680

BONNER, JILL CHRISTINE, SOLID STATE PHYSICS, THERMAL PHYSICS. *Current Pos:* RETIRED. *Personal Data:* b Cottingham, UK, Aug 20, 37. *Educ:* Univ London, BSc, 59, PhD(physics), 68, DSc, 84. *Prof Exp:* Asst lectr physics, Royal Holloway Col, Univ London, 62-64, lectr, 64-67; res assoc, Carnegie-Mellon Univ, 68-70, res physicist, 72-73; eng & appl sci res fel, Yale Univ, 70-71; vis asst prof, Univ Utah, 73-74; sr res assoc math, Brookhaven Nat Lab, 74-76; assoc prof, Univ RI, 76-81, prof physics, 81- *Concurrent Pos:* Mem, Div Sci Manpower Improvement, NSF Rev Panel, 76, Adv Comt, Am Inst Physics, 75-78, 80-86 & 90-93, Prog Comt Ann Conf Magnetism & Magnetic Mat, 78, 80 & 89; NATO sci res grant, 77-80 & 84-88; consult, Mitre Corp, 78-79 & Gen Elec Corp Res & Develop Ctr, 79-82; fac fel, Bunting Inst, Radcliffe Col, 78-80; NSF sci res grant, 78-80, 80-83, 85-88; vis prof, Women Sci & Technol, Mich State Univ, 84; vis fel, Sci & Eng Res Coun UK, 85. *Mem:* Fel Am Phys Soc; Brit Inst Physics; fel AAAS; Asn Women Sci; Fedn Am Scientist; sr mem Inst Elec & Electronics Engrs. *Res:* Theoretical solid state physics; cooperative phenomena; magnetism and magneto chemistry; low-dimensional systems; interaction with experimentalists. *Mailing Add:* 118 Darrow Lane Charlestown RI 02813

BONNER, JOHN FRANKLIN, JR, BIOCHEMISTRY. *Current Pos:* PROF BIOCHEM, SCH MED, IND UNIV, INDIANAPOLIS, 61- *Personal Data:* b Smullton, Pa, Sept 11, 17. *Educ:* Rensselaer Polytech Inst, BChE, 38; Univ Rochester, MS, 40, PhD(biophys), 48. *Honors & Awards:* Fulbright lectr & guest prof, Univ Groningen, 54-55. *Prof Exp:* Res fel radiol, Univ Rochester, 39-47, from instr toxicol to asst prof radiation biol, 47-55; asst chief med res br, AEC, 55-61. *Concurrent Pos:* vis prof molecular & genetic biol, Univ Utah, 67-68; USPHS spec fel, Univ Utah, 67-68. *Mem:* AAAS; Am Chem Soc; Biophys Soc; Sigma Xi. *Res:* Modification of biomolecules by ionizing radiation; radioprotective compounds. *Mailing Add:* 2717 NW 108th St Vancouver WA 98685-4858

BONNER, JOHN TYLER, DEVELOPMENTAL BIOLOGY. *Current Pos:* From asst prof to prof biol, Princeton Univ, 47-90, chmn, Dept Biol, 65-77 & 83-84, actg chmn, Dept Biochem Sci, 83-84, George M Moffett prof, 66-90, EMER PROF BIOL, PRINCETON UNIV, 90- *Personal Data:* b New York, NY, May 12, 20; m 42, Ruth A Graham; c 4. *Educ:* Harvard Univ, BS, 41, MA, 42, PhD(biol), 47. *Hon Degrees:* DSc, Middlebury Col, 70. *Honors & Awards:* Waksman Medal, 55. *Concurrent Pos:* Instr embryol, Marine Biol Labs, Woods Hole, 51-52; Rockefeller traveling fel, France, 53; spec lectr, Univ Col, London, 57 & Brooklyn Col, 66; Guggenheim fel, Scotland, 58 & 71-72; NSF sr fel, Cambridge Univ, 63; ed of two sect, Biol Abstr, 57-82, trustee, 58-63; mem bd trustees, Princeton Univ Press, 64-68, 71 & 75-82; Bernard vis prof, Williams Col, 89; Raman prof, Indian Acad Sci, 90; vis prof, Indian Inst Sci, 93. *Mem:* Nat Acad Sci; Am Philos Soc; fel AAAS; fel Am Acad Arts & Sci; Soc Develop Biol; Am Soc Naturalists. *Res:* Development in lower organisms; cellular slime molds; evolution. *Mailing Add:* Dept Ecol & Evolutionary Biol Princeton Univ Princeton NJ 08544-1003. *Fax:* 609-258-1712; *E-Mail:* jtbonner@pucc.princeton.edu

BONNER, LYMAN GAYLORD, CHEMISTRY. *Current Pos:* RETIRED. *Personal Data:* b Kingston, Ont, Sept 16, 12; m 37, 73; c 3. *Educ:* Univ Utah, AB, 32; Calif Inst Technol, PhD(chem), 35. *Prof Exp:* Nat Res fel chem, Princeton Univ, 35-37; from instr to asst prof physics, Duke Univ, 37-44; res assoc, George Washington Univ, 44-45; tech dir, Hercules Powder Co, 45-55, mgr, Explosives Res Div, 55-58, dir develop, Explosives & chem Propulsion Dept, 58-65; dir found rels, Calif Inst Technol, 65-67, asst to pres, 67-69, dir student rels, 69-80, assoc chem, 66-87, registr, 77-89. *Res:* Infrared and Raman spectroscopy; ballistics. *Mailing Add:* 842 E Villa St No 519 Pasadena CA 91101

BONNER, NORMAN ANDREW, CHEMISTRY, PSYCHOLOGY. *Current Pos:* RETIRED. *Personal Data:* b San Francisco, Calif, Aug 3, 20; m 45, Adela G Hurni; c Eleanor (Anderson). *Educ:* Univ Calif, BS, 42; Princeton Univ, MA, 44, PhD(chem), 45; Calif State Univ, Hayward, MS, 76. *Prof Exp:* Res chemist, Manhattan Proj, Univ Calif, 41-42, Princeton Univ, 42-45, Los Alamos Sci Lab, Univ Calif, 45-46 & Gen Elec Co, NY, 46; instr chem, Wash Univ, 47-48, asst prof, 48-51; asst prof, Cornell Univ, 51-53; chemist, Lawrence Livermore Lab, Univ Calif, 53-87. *Concurrent Pos:* Mem adv coun, Bay Area Air Pollution Control Dist, 70-78. *Mem:* AAAS; Am Chem Soc. *Res:* Trace element analysis of environmental samples; radiochemistry; kinetics of reactions in solution; inorganic chemistry; chemistry of air pollution. *Mailing Add:* 1093 Nielsen Lane Livermore CA 94550

BONNER, OSCAR DAVIS, PHYSICAL CHEMISTRY. *Current Pos:* from asst prof to prof, Univ SC, 51-70, from actg head to head dept, 59-70, Robert L Sumwalt chair chem, 70-82, DISTINGUISHED EMER PROF CHEM, UNIV SC, 82- *Personal Data:* b Jackson, Miss, May 9, 17; m 96, Katherine N Riley; c Davis R, Richard E & Timothy G. *Educ:* Millsaps Col, BS, 39; Univ Miss, MS, 48; Univ Kans, PhD(chem), 51. *Honors & Awards:* Outstanding Serv Award, Am Chem Soc, 82. *Prof Exp:* With Miss Testing Lab, 40-41 & Filtrol Corp, 46-47; res partic, Oak Ridge Nat Lab, 51. *Concurrent Pos:* Fulbright advan res award, Germany, 57-58; Fulbright teaching-res award, Korea, 83. *Mem:* Sigma Xi; Am Chem Soc. *Res:* Ion exchange; thermodynamics of solutions; polyelectrolytes; structure of water; interaction of water and salts with biological systems. *Mailing Add:* Dept Chem Univ of SC Columbia SC 29208

BONNER, PHILIP HALLINDER, MYOGENESIS, NEURO-BIOLOGY. *Current Pos:* ASSOC PROF CELL BIOL, UNIV KY, 75- *Educ:* Univ Calif, San Diego, PhD(biol), 71. *Mailing Add:* Univ Ky Sch Biol Sci Lexington KY 40506-0001

BONNER, ROBERT DUBOIS, botany, for more information see previous edition

BONNER, TOM IVAN, MOLECULAR BIOLOGY. *Current Pos:* res biophysicist, 83-87, spec expert, 87-91, RES BIOLOGIST, NIMH, 91- *Personal Data:* b Boston, Mass, Mar 1, 42; m 66, Gretchen Kleinhans; c 3. *Educ:* Rice Univ, BA, 63; Univ Wis, PhD(physics), 68. *Honors & Awards:* Boehringer Ingleheim Award 1st Prize, 88. *Prof Exp:* Res assoc nuclear physics, Ctr Nuclear Studies, Univ Tex, Austin, 67-70; Carnegie fel, Carnegie Inst, 70-73, res assoc biophys, Dept Terrestrial Magnetism, 73-76; expert, Nat Cancer Inst, 76-82; scientist, Frederick Cancer Res Ctr, 82. *Concurrent Pos:* Mem, Comt Receptor Nomenclature & Drug Classification, Int Union Pharmacol, 90- *Mem:* AAAS; Am Phys Soc; Biophys Soc. *Res:* Nucleic acid reassociation techniques; nucleic acid sequence organization and regulation; evolution of nucleic acids; recombinant DNA; molecular neurobiology; molecular biology of G protein-coupled receptors. *Mailing Add:* Lab Cell Biol Bldg 36 Rm 3A-17 NIMH Bethesda MD 20892-4090. *E-Mail:* tibonner@ helix.nih.gov

BONNER, WALTER DANIEL, JR, plant biology; deceased, see previous edition for last biography

BONNER, WILLARD HALLAM, JR, ORGANIC CHEMISTRY, POLYMER SCIENCE. *Current Pos:* RETIRED. *Personal Data:* b New Haven, Conn, May 22, 28; m 48; c Margo & David. *Educ:* Wesleyan Univ, BA, 47; Univ Buffalo, MA, 48; Purdue Univ, PhD(org chem), 52. *Prof Exp:* Res chemist, Humble Oil & Refining Co, 52-54; res chemist & res fel, E I Du Pont De Nemours & Co, Inc, 54-82; consult, polymer sci & plastic foams, 82-97. *Mem:* Am Chem Soc; AAAS. *Res:* Reaction mechanisms; organic synthesis; petrochemicals; polymer chemistry; synthetic fibers; plastics foams. *Mailing Add:* Beaver Valley Georgetown ME 04548

BONNER, WILLIAM ANDREW, CHEMISTRY, ORGANIC CHEMISTRY. *Current Pos:* from instr to assoc prof, 46-59, prof org chem, 59-83, EMER PROF CHEM, STANFORD UNIV, 83- *Personal Data:* b Chicago, Ill, Dec 21, 19; m 44, 61, Norma C Loyola; c Constance, Candice, Randolph, Joseph, Jay & Teresa. *Educ:* Harvard Univ, BS, 41; Northwestern Univ, PhD(org chem), 44. *Prof Exp:* Res chemist, Corn Prod Ref Co, Ill, 42; asst org chem, Northwestern Univ, 42-44, res Univ Col, 44-46; chemist, Nat Defense Res Comt, 44-46. *Concurrent Pos:* Guggenheim fel, 53; Nat Res Coun res assoc, 70-71. *Mem:* Am Chem Soc; Int Soc Study Origin Life. *Res:* General organic chemistry, the abiotic origin and amplification of molecular chirality in nature; chemical evolution, carbohydrate chemistry, natural products, stereochemistry; organic reaction mechanisms, isotope effects; heterogenous catalysis, electrochemistry. *Mailing Add:* Dept Chem Stanford Univ Stanford CA 94305

BONNER, WILLIAM PAUL, SANITARY SCIENCE, CHEMISTRY. *Current Pos:* PROF, TENN TECHNOL UNIV, 72- *Personal Data:* b Bowdon, Ga, July 7, 31; m 56, Marjorie Rice; c Brent H, Bruce W & Brenda W. *Educ:* Univ Ga, BS, 52; Univ Fla, MSEng, 65, PhD(sanit sci), 67. *Prof Exp:* Jr engr, Union Carbide Nuclear Div, 52-54, supvr anal lab, 56-59, assoc chemist, 56-62; assoc chemist, Oak Ridge Nat Lab, 62-64, res staff mem water pollution, 67-72. *Mem:* Am Water Works Asn; Water Pollution Control Fedn; Sigma Xi. *Res:* Water pollution; radioactive waste disposal; radiological health; land-water interactions; behavior of pollutants in the environment; toxic and hazardous waste treatment management. *Mailing Add:* Dept Civil & Environ Eng Tenn Technol Univ Cookeville TN 38505

BONNET, JUAN A, JR, general environmental sciences; deceased, see previous edition for last biography

BONNETT, RICHARD BRIAN, GEOMORPHOLOGY, ENGINEERING & ENVIRONMENTAL GEOLOGY. *Current Pos:* from asst prof to assoc prof, 68-82, chmn dept, 77-92, PROF GEOL, MARSHALL UNIV, 82- *Personal Data:* b Jamestown, NY, Feb 7, 39; m 64, Kathleen A Jenkins; c 3. *Educ:* Allegheny Col, BS, 61; Univ Maine, MS, 63; Ohio State Univ, PhD(geol), 70. *Prof Exp:* Teaching asst geol, Univ Maine, 61-63 & Ohio State Univ, 63-68. *Concurrent Pos:* Consult, landslides, groundwater and blast damage. *Mem:* Geol Soc Am; Am Quaternary Asn; Sigma Xi. *Res:* Pleistocene-glacial geology; environmental geology; Pleistocene stratigraphy and geomorphology in tri-state area of Ohio, West Virginia and Kentucky; engineering geology. *Mailing Add:* 248 Township Rd 1167 Proctorville OH 45669

BONNETTE, DELLA T, OPERATING SYSTEMS. *Current Pos:* Dir, Comput Ctr, 75-83, ASST PROF COMPUT SCI, UNIV SOUTHWESTERN LA, 71-, DIR, COMPUT & INFO SERV, 83- *Personal Data:* b Bartlett, Kans, Mar 22, 36. *Educ:* Univ Southwestern La, MS, 69. *Concurrent Pos:* Mem, Spec Interest Group Bd, Asn Comput Mach, 85-, Finance Comt, 88-, alt, Computer Sci Accreditation Bd, 91- *Mem:* Asn Comput Mach. *Mailing Add:* Univ Southwestern La PO Box 44400 Lafayette LA 70504-9998

BONNEVILLE, MARY AGNES, CELL BIOLOGY. *Current Pos:* asst prof, 70-73, ASSOC PROF MOLECULAR, CELLULAR & DEVELOP BIOL, UNIV COLO, BOULDER, 73- *Personal Data:* b Pittsfield, Mass, May 30, 31. *Educ:* Smith Col, BA, 53; Amherst Col, MA, 55; Rockefeller Inst, PhD(cytol), 61. *Prof Exp:* Trainee anat, Col Physicians & Surgeons, Columbia Univ, 61-63; res assoc dermat, Sch Med, Tufts Univ, 63-64; asst prof biol, Brown Univ, 64-66; instr, Harvard Univ, 66-70. *Concurrent Pos:* Mem panel for eval of fel applns, Nat Acad Sci & NIH, 73-74. *Mem:* Am Soc Cell Biol; Electron Micros Soc Am; Am Asn Anat. *Res:* Structure and formation of the cell surface. *Mailing Add:* Dept Molecular Cell & Develop Biol Univ Colo Campus Box 347 Boulder CO 80302-0347

BONNEY, ROBERT JOHN, BIOCHEMISTRY. *Current Pos:* VPRES, BRISTOL-MYERS SQUIBB, 89- *Personal Data:* b Rumford, Maine, Feb 6, 42; m 62, Judith Perry; c Robert Jr, Mark & David. *Educ:* Univ Maine, BS, 64; State Univ NY Buffalo, MS, 67, PhD(biochem), 71. *Prof Exp:* Fel biochem, McArdle Lab Cancer Res, Univ Wis, 71-73; sr res scientist biochem, Dept Health, NY State, 73-76; res fel, Dept Immunol, Merck Inst Therapeut Res, 76-84, sr investr, 85-89. *Mem:* Am Soc Cell Biol. *Res:* The study of the role of the mononuclear phagocytes in inflammatory disease. *Mailing Add:* Dept Dermat Drug Discovery Westwood-Squibb 100 Forest Ave Buffalo NY 14213-1091. *Fax:* 716-887-7661

BONNEY, WILLIAM WALLACE, ONCOLOGY, FEMALE UROLOGY. *Current Pos:* ASSOC PROF UROL, DEPT UROL, COL MED, UNIV IOWA, 69-; STAFF PHYSICIAN, VET ADMIN MED CTR, 69- *Educ:* Univ Calif, Los Angeles, MD, 61. *Res:* Biology of the R3377 rat prostatic tumor. *Mailing Add:* 1021 Wylde Green Rd Iowa City IA 52246

BONNICHSEN, BILL, PETROLOGY, ECONOMIC GEOLOGY. *Current Pos:* SUPVRY RES GEOLOGIST, IDAHO BUR MINES & GEOL, 76- *Personal Data:* b Twin Falls, Idaho, Sept 25, 37; m 59; c 4. *Educ:* Univ Idaho, BS, 60; Univ Minn, Minneapolis, PhD(geol), 68. *Prof Exp:* Instr econ geol, Univ Minn, Minneapolis, 66-67; res assoc geol, Minn Geol Surv, 67-69; asst prof petrol, Cornell Univ, 69-76. *Mem:* Geol Soc Am; Int Asn Genesis Ore Deposits; Soc Econ Geologists. *Res:* Igneous and metamorphic petrology; economic geology of metals. *Mailing Add:* 927 E Seventh St Moscow ID 83843

BONNICHSEN, MARTHA MILLER GODCHAUX, PETROLOGY, VOLCANOLOGY. *Current Pos:* from asst prof to assoc prof, 70-95, PROF GEOL, MT HOLYOKE COL, 95- *Personal Data:* b Salem, Mass, May 2, 41; m 89, Bill; c Louise R (Godchaux). *Educ:* Wellesley Col, BA, 62; Univ Ore, PhD(geol), 69. *Prof Exp:* Fel geol, Yale Univ, 69-70 & Harvard Univ, 79-80. *Concurrent Pos:* Res assoc, Idaho Geol Surv. *Mem:* Geol Soc Am; Am Geophys Union; Sigma Xi; Int Asn Volcanol & Chem Earth's Interior. *Res:* Volcanology and eruption mechanisms; chemical nature and evolution of volcanic rocks; metamorphism of ultramafic rocks; structural geology. *Mailing Add:* Dept Geog & Geol Mt Holyoke Col South Hadley MA 01075. *E-Mail:* mgochau@mhc.mtholyoke.edu

BONO, PHILIP, aerospace; deceased, see previous edition for last biography

BONO, VINCENT HORACE, JR, INTERNAL MEDICINE, BIOCHEMISTRY. *Current Pos:* sr investr cancer chemother, Nat Cancer Inst, 64-73, head molecular biol & methods develop sect, Lab Chem & Biol, 73-76, CHIEF, INVEST DRUG BR, DIV CANCER TREATMENT, NAT CANCER INST, 76- *Personal Data:* b Brooklyn, NY, July 23, 33; m 57; c 2. *Educ:* Columbia Univ, AB, 53, MD, 57. *Prof Exp:* Intern internal med, Duke Univ Hosps, 57-58, univ res fel hemat, 58-59; resident internal med, Strong Mem Hosp, Univ Rochester, 59-60; clin assoc cancer chemother, Med Br, Nat Cancer Inst, Md, 60-63; trainee biochem, Dartmouth Med Sch, 63-64. *Res:* Mechanisms of action and clinical evaluation of new drugs for the therapy of human neoplasia. *Mailing Add:* 6192 Oxon Hill Rd Suite 506 Oxon Hill MD 20745-3114

BONORA, ANTHONY CHARLES, MECHANICAL ENGINEERING. *Current Pos:* mgr eng, 75-76, VPRES CORP TECHNOL, SILTEC CORP, 77-, GEN MGR, INSTRUMENT DIV, 80- *Personal Data:* b San Francisco, Calif, 43. *Educ:* Univ Calif, Berkeley, BS, 64, MS, 66. *Prof Exp:* Design engr, Lockheed Missiles & Space Co, 66-69; eng mgr, Semimetals, Inc, 69-73, opers mgr, 73-75. *Mem:* Electrochem Soc; Am Soc Eng Educ; Solar Energy Indust Asn. *Res:* Advanced fabrication of silicon materials; development of wafer manufacturing and processing equipment; crystal growth; wafer polishing. *Mailing Add:* 300 Felton Dr Menlo Park CA 94025

BONSACK, JAMES PAUL, INORGANIC CHEMISTRY, PHYSICAL CHEMISTRY. *Current Pos:* chemist, 62-69, scientist chem, 69-81, SR SCIENTIST, CHEM DIV, SCM CHEM, 81- *Personal Data:* b Westminster, Md, Nov 30, 32; m 57; c 5. *Educ:* Wash Col, BS, 53; Lehigh Univ, MS, 55. *Prof Exp:* Teaching asst chem, Lehigh Univ, 53-55; chemist, J T Baker Chem Co, 55-62. *Mem:* Am Chem Soc; AAAS; Am Ceramic Soc. *Res:* High temperature chemical processing; mineral chlorination; plasma-arc reaction processes; surface chemistry of silica; titanium chemistry. *Mailing Add:* 205 Hemlock Lane Aberdeen MD 21001

BONSACK, WALTER KARL, astrophysics, for more information see previous edition

BONSI, CONRAD K, AGRICULTURAL RESEARCH. *Current Pos:* from asst prof to assoc prof, Dept Agr Sci, 83-91, asst dir, Carver Agr Exp Sta, 86-87, ASSOC DIR, RES GEORGE WASHINGTON CARVER AGR EXP STA, TUSKEGEE UNIV, ALA, 86-, PROF, DEPT AGR SCI, 87- *Personal Data:* b Ghana, Dec 11, 50; m 82, Eunice Amenyenu; c Anibok, Akofa & Sesie. *Educ:* Univ Ghana, BSc 75; Tuskegee Univ, MS, 78; Cornell Univ, PhD(plant path), 82. *Prof Exp:* Res & teaching asst, Univ Ghana, Legon, 75-76; teaching asst, Tuskegee Univ, 76-78; grad res asst, Cornell Univ, 78-82; res assoc, Pa State Univ, 82-83. *Concurrent Pos:* Co-prog leader, Farmers Home Admin, USDA, 84-86; prin investr/co-investr, numerous res grants, 84-; fel, Leadership Training Prog, USDA-ESCOP, 92. *Mem:* Am Phytopath Soc; Am Soc Hort Sci; Sigma Xi; Caribbean Food Crop Soc; Soc

Nematologists; Int Soc Trop Root Crops. *Res:* Development of high yielding, disease resistant and environmental stress tolerant sweet potato cultivars with high nutritive value and production for controlled ecological life support systems; development of tomato cultivars adaptable for home gardens and limited resource; over 70 technical writings and publications. *Mailing Add:* Agr Tuskegee Univ Inst Campus Tuskegee AL 36088-1699. *Fax:* 334-724-4451; *E-Mail:* cobonsi@cad.tusk.edu

BONSIB, STEPHEN M, SURGICAL & RENAL PATHOLOGY. *Current Pos:* ASST PROF PATH, UNIV IOWA HOSP & CLIN, 83- *Educ:* Ind Univ, MD, 78. *Res:* Glomerulonephritis. *Mailing Add:* 4252 Turkey Creek Rd NE Iowa City IA 52240

BONSIGNORE, JOSEPH JOHN, ARCHAEOLOGY. *Personal Data:* b Brooklyn, NY, Dec 9, 20; m 45, Madlyn Anne Kleutsch; c Mark, Judith, Jay, Andrea, Donna & Regina. *Educ:* Trinity Col, BA, 42; Univ Chicago, MA, 45. *Honors & Awards:* Joseph Henry Medal, Smithsonian Inst, 91. *Prof Exp:* Mgr ed prod, Time Inc, Chicago, 45-69; gen mgr, Smithsonian Mag, 69-78, assoc publ, 78-81, publ, 81-91. *Mem:* Mag Publ Asn; Archaeol Inst Am. *Mailing Add:* Smithsonian Arts & Industs Bldg 900 Jefferson Dr SW Washington DC 20560-0003

BONSIGNORE, PATRICK VINCENT, POLYMER CHEMISTRY. *Current Pos:* POLYMER CHEMIST, DEGRADABLE PLASTICS, ARGONNE NAT LAB, 88- *Personal Data:* b New York, NY, May 10, 29; m 58; c 2. *Educ:* Queens Col, NY, BS, 51; Polytech Inst Brooklyn, PhD(org & polymer chem), 58. *Prof Exp:* Sr scientist plastics, Columbia Southern Div, PPG Industs, 58-59; sr scientist acrylic plastics, Rohm & Haas, 59-70; sr scientist hydrogels, Hydron Labs, 70; staff scientist reprographics, Memorex, 70-71; sci assoc fire retardancy, Aluminum Co Am, 72-82; sr scientist ion-exchange membrane technol, Electrochem Int, 84-88. *Concurrent Pos:* Fel, Univ Ill, 57-58; adj prof, Sch Med Chem, Univ Pittsburgh, 79-80; mem, Gov Task Force Degradable Plastics, State Ill. *Mem:* Soc Plastics Engrs; Am Chem Soc; Sigma Xi; Fire Retardant Chem Asn. *Res:* Characterization and improvement of fire retardancy and smoke suppression in plastics; development of controlled pore alumina as supports for biocatalysts in bioengineering applications; ion exchange membrane technology; poly(lactic acid) degradable plastics. *Mailing Add:* Argonne Nat Lab 9700 S Cass Ave ES/362 Argonne IL 60439-4815

BONTADELLI, JAMES ALBERT, INDUSTRIAL & SYSTEMS ENGINEERING. *Current Pos:* PROF INDUST ENG, UNIV TENN, 90- *Personal Data:* b St John, Wash, Sept 27, 29; m 51, Rossie Blackburn; c James A Jr & Peggy A. *Educ:* Ore State Univ, BS, 51; Stanford Univ, MS, 58; Ohio State Univ, PhD(indust eng), 72. *Prof Exp:* Asst chief, Systs Res Br, US Army Eng Maintenance Ctr, 59-60, chief, 60-62; proj leader, Systs Anal Div, Battelle Mem Inst, 62-66, assoc chief, 66-70, group leader mgt systs group, 70-74; mgr indust eng, Tenn Valley Authority, 74-89. *Concurrent Pos:* Adj prof indust eng, Univ Tenn, 75-89. *Mem:* Fel Inst Indust Engrs. *Res:* Productivity and quality improvement; engineering economic analysis; decision analysis; application of industrial engineering in construction, power production and service industry operations. *Mailing Add:* 11517 N Monticello Dr Knoxville TN 37922

BONTE, FREDERICK JAMES, RADIOLOGY, NUCLEAR MEDICINE. *Current Pos:* prof radiol & chmn dept, 56-73, dean, Southwestern Med Sch, Univ Tex Health Sci Ctr, 73-80, DIR, NUCLEAR MED RES CTR, UNIV TEX, 80- *Personal Data:* b Bethlehem, Pa, Jan 18, 22; m 52, 68, Cecile Poetzel; c 6. *Educ:* Western Reserve Univ, BS, 42, MD, 45. *Honors & Awards:* Hartman Medal, Soc Nuclear Med, 95; Pres Award, Am Col Nuclear Physicians, 97. *Prof Exp:* Fel radiobiol, Atomic Energy Med Res Proj, Western Reserve Univ, 48-49; resident physician, Univ Hosps, Cleveland, 49-52; asst prof radiol, Med Sch, Western Reserve Univ, 52-56. *Concurrent Pos:* Dir dept radiol, Parkland Mem Hosp, 56-73, consult, US Vet Admin Hosp Syst, 56-; mem bd, Nat Coun Radiation Protection & Measurements, 65-71; mem radiol training comt, Nat Inst Gen Med Sci, 65-70; mem med adv comt, Oak Ridge Assoc Univs, 68-70; trustee, Am Bd Radiol, 69-75 & Am Bd Nuclear Med, 71-73; chmn, Am Bd Nuclear Med, 77-80; Effie & Wofford Cain distinguished chair diag imaging. *Mem:* AAAS; fel Am Col Radiol; Am Roentgen Ray Soc; Radiol Soc NAm; Sigma Xi; fel Am Col Nuclear Physicians; Soc Nuclear Med. *Res:* Clinical and experimental nuclear medicine; radiobiology with special interest in physiological imaging of the heart and brain. *Mailing Add:* Southwestern Med Ctr Univ Tex Dallas TX 75235-9061

BONTEMPO, JOHN A, MICROBIOLOGY. *Current Pos:* INDEPENDENT CONSULT, 91- *Personal Data:* b Pesco, Italy, Sept 13, 30; US citizen; m 56; c 3. *Educ:* Heidelberg Col, AB & BS, 56; Fairleigh Dickinson Univ, MS, 69; Rutgers Univ, PhD(microbiol), 75. *Prof Exp:* Asst scientist, Warner-Lambert Res Inst, NJ, 56-62; from microbiologist to sr microbiologist, Hoffmann-LaRoche, Inc, 62-72, group leader, 72-75, tech fel, 75-82; dir new products, Genetech, 82-84; vpres prod develop, Interferon Sci, NJ, 84-87; dir new prod, Squib Bristol-Myers, 87-90; dir prod develop, Johnson & Johnson, 90-91. *Mem:* NY Acad Sci; Am Soc Microbiol; Sigma Xi. *Res:* Antimicrobial agents, analytical microbiology. *Mailing Add:* 9 Candle Lane East Brunswick NJ 08816

BONTING, SJOERD LIEUWE, BIOCHEMISTRY, SPACE BIOLOGY. *Current Pos:* RETIRED. *Personal Data:* b Amsterdam, Holland, Oct 6, 24; nat US; m 51, 87, Ereen Schutmann; c Marion, Paul, Elizabeth & Peter. *Educ:* Univ Amsterdam, BSc, 44, MSc, 50, PhD(biochem), 52. *Hon Degrees:* LTh, St Mark's Inst Theol, London, 75. *Honors & Awards:* Fight for Sight Award, Nat Coun Combat Blindness & Asn Res Ophthal, 61 & 62; Merit Award, Int Rescue Comt, 63; Arthur S Fleming Award, 64; Karger Mem Found Prize, 64; Pro Mundi Beneficis Award, Brazilian Acad Humanities, 75. *Prof Exp:* Instr anal chem, Univ Amsterdam, 47-49; biochemist, Neth Inst Nutrit, 50-52; res assoc physiol, Col Med, Univ Iowa, 52-55; asst prof physiol chem, Sch Med, Univ Minn, 55-56; asst prof biol chem, Col Med, Univ Ill & asst attend biochemist, Presby-St Luke's Hosp, Chicago, 56-60; head sect cell biol, Ophthal Br, Nat Inst Neurol Dis & Blindness, NIH, 60-65; prof biochem & chmn dept, Univ Nijmegen, 65-85; res scientist, NASA Ames Res Ctr, Moffett Field, Calif, 85-93. *Concurrent Pos:* Instr biochem, Univ Amsterdam, 51-52; fel, USPHS & Nat Cancer Inst, 52-54; guest scientist, Inst Animal Physiol, Cambridge, Eng, 64-65. *Mem:* AAAS; Am Soc Biol Chem; Am Soc Cell Biol. *Res:* Membrane and transport biochemistry; quantitative histochemistry; visual mechanism; space biology. *Mailing Add:* Specreyse 12 7471TH Goor Netherlands. *Fax:* 31-547-260447

BONTRAGER, ERNEST L, GAIT ANALYSIS INSTRUMENTATION, REHABILITATION ENGINEERING. *Current Pos:* ASSOC DIR ENG RES, PATHOKINESIOLOGY LAB, RANCH LOS AMIGOS MED CTR, 60- *Personal Data:* b Emmett, Idaho, 1937. *Educ:* Univ Calif, Berkeley, BS, 60; Case Inst Technol, MS, 65. *Mem:* Am Soc Mech Engrs; Biomed Eng Soc. *Mailing Add:* 8152 Strub Ave Whittier CA 90602

BONURA, THOMAS, RADIATION BIOLOGY & BIOCHEMISTRY, ARTIFICIAL INTELLIGENCE. *Current Pos:* SR SCIENTIST, APPLE COMPUT INC, 87- *Personal Data:* b New York, NY, Jan 27, 47; m 84, Lindsey Roscoe; c Caitlin & Caasi. *Educ:* Duquesne Univ, BS, 68; State Univ NY, Buffalo, MA, 71, PhD(biol), 73. *Prof Exp:* Res assoc, Dept Radiol, Radiobiol Res Div, Stanford Univ, 72-77, res asst DNA repair, 77-79, res assoc, Lab Exp Oncol, Dept Path, Sch Med, 79-81; appln eng, Intellicorp, Inc, 83-87. *Mem:* AAAS; Am Asn Artificial Intel; Asn Comput Mach. *Res:* Enzymology of DNA repair; interaction of ionizing radiation and DNA; cellular inactivation by DNA damaging agents. *Mailing Add:* 606 El Salto Dr Capitola CA 95010. *E-Mail:* bonura@acm.org

BONVENTRE, PETER FRANK, BACTERIAL TOXINS, IMMUNOBIOLOGY OF TOXIC SHOCK SYNDROME. *Current Pos:* from asst prof to prof, 58-95, EMER PROF MICROBIOL, COL MED, UNIV CINCINNATI, 95- *Personal Data:* b New York, NY, Aug 18, 28; m 63, Ruth Nacke. *Educ:* City Col New York, BS, 49; Univ Tenn, MS, 55; Univ Mich, PhD, 57. *Prof Exp:* NSF fel, Higher Inst Sanit, Italy, 57-58. *Concurrent Pos:* Vis res assoc, Dept Pharmacol, Royal Vet Col Sweden, 60; career develop award, USPHS, 63; vis scientist, Clin Res Ctr, London, UK, 75 & Scripps Res Inst, La Jolla, Calif, 87; ed, Infection & Immunity, 79-90 & J Leukocyte Biol, 82-92; Path & Immunopath Res, 83-90. *Mem:* AAAS; Am Soc Microbiol; Sigma Xi; Soc Leukocyte Biol. *Res:* Host-parasite relationships in infectious processes; mechanisms of pathogenesis. *Mailing Add:* Dept Molecular Genetics, Biochem & Microbiol Univ Cincinnati Col Med Cincinnati OH 45267-0524. *Fax:* 513-558-8474

BONVICINO, GUIDO EROS, ORGANIC CHEMISTRY, SYNTHETIC ORGANIC. *Current Pos:* assoc prof, 63-68, PROF ORG CHEM, C W POST CTR, LONG ISLAND UNIV, 68- *Personal Data:* b Castrovillari, Italy, Feb 9, 21; nat US; m 52; c 1. *Educ:* Fordham Univ, BS, 47, MS, 49, PhD(org chem), 52. *Honors & Awards:* Am Inst Chemists Medal, 47. *Prof Exp:* Instr org chem & analysis, Fordham Univ, 47-52; res chemist org, Lederle Labs, 52-63. *Mem:* Sigma Xi; fel Am Inst Chemists; sr mem Am Chem Soc; NY Acad Sci. *Res:* Thiamine; chemical reactions; antibiotics and synthetic chemotherapeutic agents; chemopsychiatric agents; reaction mechanisms. *Mailing Add:* 73 Hill Dr Oyster Bay NY 11771-3606

BONVILLIAN, JOHN DOUGHTY, CHILD PSYCHOLOGY, PSYCHOLINGUISTICS. *Current Pos:* vis assoc prof, 78-79, asst prof, 79-84, ASSOC PROF PSYCHOL, UNIV VA, 84- *Personal Data:* b Caldwell, Idaho, Sept 4, 48. *Educ:* Johns Hopkins Univ, BA, 70; Stanford Univ, PhD(psychol), 74. *Prof Exp:* Asst prof psychol, Vassar Col, 74-78. *Concurrent Pos:* Asst ed, Sign Language Studies, 78-; mem, Comt Linguistics, Univ Va, 79-, Inst Clin Psychol, 81-87; vis scholar, Gallaudet Col, 84-85; vis staff mem, Univ Canterbury, NZ, 91. *Mem:* fel Am Psychol Asn; Am Speech Lang & Hearing Asn; Linguistic Soc Am; Soc Res Child Develop. *Res:* Longuitudinal investigation of how words and manual signs are acquired by normal children and children with disabilities. *Mailing Add:* 222 Turkey Ridge Rd Charlottesville VA 22903. *Fax:* 804-982-4766; *E-Mail:* jdb5b@virginia.edu

BOODMAN, DAVID MORRIS, SYSTEMS SCIENCE. *Current Pos:* RETIRED. *Personal Data:* b Pittsburgh, Pa, July 4, 23; m 48; c 2. *Educ:* Univ Pittsburgh, BS, 44, PhD(phys chem), 50. *Prof Exp:* Sr staff mem, Opers Eval Group, Mass Inst Technol, 50-60; sr staff mem, Opers Res Sect, Arthur D Little Inc, 60-72, vpres, 72-89. *Concurrent Pos:* Opers analyst, Staff, Comdr in Chief, Pac Fleet, US Navy, 51, Oper Develop Force, 53-54 & staff, Comdr First Fleet, 58. *Mem:* Fel AAAS; Math Asn Am; Opers Res Soc Am. *Res:* Systems science-operations; military and industrial operations research. *Mailing Add:* 40 Potter Pond Lexington MA 02173

BOOHAR, RICHARD KENNETH, DEVELOPMENTAL BIOLOGY. *Current Pos:* asst prof, 67-71, ASSOC PROF LIFE SCI, UNIV NEBR, LINCOLN, 71- *Personal Data:* b Philadelphia, Pa, Mar 7, 35; m 59; c 5. *Educ:* Drew Univ, BA, 57; Univ Wis, MA, 60, PhD(zool), 66. *Prof Exp:* Asst zool, Univ Wis, 64; from instr to asst prof, Butler Univ, 64-67. *Mem:* AAAS; Am Inst Biol Sci; Sigma Xi. *Res:* Bioethics. *Mailing Add:* Sch Biol Sci Univ Nebr Lincoln NE 68588-0118

BOOJUM, BASIL JOHN, NUMERICAL ALGORITHMS, PERTURBATION THEORY. *Current Pos:* PRES & CHIEF SCI OFFICER, ARITHMURGY, INC, 87- *Personal Data:* b Allatha, Kazakhstan, Mar 15, 53; nat US. *Educ:* Ostraka Tech Univ, BS, 73 PhD(math), 76. *Prof Exp:* Res fel, Moscow State Univ, 76-78; prof math, Ostraka Tech Univ. 78-84; vis researcher, Univ Liege, 85; vis scholar, Hydrometeorol Inst, Bulgaria, 85-87. *Mem:* Soc Indust & Appl Math. *Res:* Development of novel spectral algorithms; perturbative and numerical studies of nonlinear waves, especially fluids; popular essays and commentaries on science. *Mailing Add:* 929 Greenhills Dr Ann Arbor MI 48105

BOOK, DAVID LINCOLN, COMPUTATIONAL FLUID MECHANICS, NONLINEAR MECHANICS. *Current Pos:* RES SCIENTIST, ASTRON DEPT, UNIV MD, 91- *Personal Data:* b Boston, Mass, Aug 4, 39; m 70; c 1. *Educ:* Yale Univ, BA, 59; Princeton Univ, MA, 61, PhD(physics), 64. *Prof Exp:* Staff assoc, Gen Atomic Div, Gen Dynamics Corp, 64-67; staff physicist, Lawrence Radiation Lab, 67-74; staff, Naval Res Lab, 74-91. *Concurrent Pos:* Consult, Arco Power Technologies Inc, 92-, Sci Applns Int Corp, 93- *Mem:* Am Phys Soc. *Res:* Theoretical plasma physics; controlled thermonuclear fusion; kinetic theory; solitons in optical fibers; nonneutral plasmas. *Mailing Add:* Astron Dept Univ Md College Park MD 20742. *E-Mail:* book@avl.umd.edu

BOOK, LINDA SUE, PEDIATRIC GASTROENTEROLOGY & HEPATOLOGY. *Current Pos:* resident, 72-74, Univ Utah, instr, 74-76, asst prof pediat & nursing, 76-80, ASSOC PROF PEDIAT, UNIV UTAH, 86-, DIR PEDIAT GASTROENTEROL & NUTRIT, PRIMARY CHILDREN'S MED CTR, 91-, DIR PEDIAT LIVER TRANSPLANTATION, 95- *Personal Data:* b Youngstown, Ohio, Oct 8, 46; m 70, Robert; c Lisa Suzanne, Zachary Robert & Nicholas Stephen. *Educ:* Univ Cincinnati, MD, 71. *Honors & Awards:* Res Award, Western Soc for Pediat, 74. *Prof Exp:* Intern, Univ Cincinnati, 71-72. *Concurrent Pos:* NIH fel pediat gastroenterol, Univ Utah, 74-76, fel premature infants res, 76- & Ross Lab award res in infant nutrit, 76- *Mem:* Fedn Am Soc Exp Biol; N Am Soc Pediat Gastroenterol & Nutrit; Am Gastroenterol Asn. *Res:* Infant nutrition; effect of various feeding practices on development of necrotizing enterocolitis; gastrointestinal immunology; liver disease in children. *Mailing Add:* Primary Children's 100 N Medical Dr Salt Lake City UT 84113. *Fax:* 801-588-2375; *E-Mail:* pclbook@ihc.com

BOOK, STEPHEN ALAN, STATISTICS, COST ANALYSIS. *Current Pos:* From asst prof to assoc prof, 70-79, PROF MATH, CALIF STATE UNIV, DOMINGUEZ HILLS, 79- *Personal Data:* b Newark, NJ, Dec 11, 41; m 68; c 5. *Educ:* Georgetown Univ, AB, 63; Cornell Univ, MA, 66; Univ Ore, PhD(math), 70. *Honors & Awards:* Pres Award Analytic Achievement, Aerospace Corp, 82. *Concurrent Pos:* Statist consult. *Mem:* Math Asn Am; Inst Math Statist; Am Math Soc; London Math Soc; Am Statist Asn; Soc Cost Estimating & Analysis. *Res:* Limit theorems of probability theory; large deviation probabilities; laws of large numbers; almost sure convergence; cost modeling, cost-risk analysis. *Mailing Add:* Dept Math Calif State Univ Carson CA 90747

BOOK, STEVEN ARNOLD, ENVIRONMENTAL SCIENCES, REGULATORY TOXICOLOGY. *Current Pos:* TOXICOLOGIST, DEPT HEALTH SERV, STATE OF CALIF, 96- *Personal Data:* b Albany, Calif, Dec 13, 45; m 68; c 2. *Educ:* Univ Calif, Berkeley, AB, 67; Univ Calif, Davis, MA, 69, PhD(physiol), 73. *Prof Exp:* Res radioecologist, Sch Vet Med Univ Calif, Davis, 69-73, asst res physiologist, Radiobiol Lab, 73-79, lectr radiol sci, 74-81, assoc res physiologist, 79-81, assoc adj prof, Lab Energy-Related Health Res, 81-85; environ sci, State of Calif, 85-94; mgr environ sci, Jacobs Eng Group, Sacramento, Calif, 94-96. *Mem:* Soc Environ Toxicol & Chem. *Res:* Human health risk assessment; ecological risk assessment. *Mailing Add:* PO Box 2123 Davis CA 95617

BOOKCHIN, ROBERT M, HEMATOLOGY. *Current Pos:* PROF MED, ALBERT EINSTEIN COL MED, 67- *Personal Data:* b New York, NY, Oct 14, 35. *Educ:* Wash Univ, MD, 59. *Concurrent Pos:* Macy fac scholar award; vis scholar, Physiol Lab, Univ Cambridge, 77-78. *Mem:* Asn Am Physicians; Am Soc Clin Invest; Am Soc Hemat; Am Soc Biochem & Molecular Biol; UK Physiol Soc. *Res:* Erythrocyte physiology and pathophysiology, hemoglobin-opathies red cell membrane transport. *Mailing Add:* Albert Einstein Col Med 1300 Morris Park Ave Bronx NY 10461-1975. *E-Mail:* bookchin@aecom.yu.edu

BOOKE, HENRY EDWARD, ICHTHYOLOGY. *Current Pos:* DIR, NE ANADROMOUS FISH LAB, US FISH & WILD SERV, 88- *Personal Data:* b Brooklyn, NY, Jan 14, 32; m 59; c 1. *Educ:* Cornell Univ, BS, 60; Mich State Univ, MS, 62; Univ Mich, PhD(ichthyol), 68. *Honors & Awards:* Unit Gulf Conser Award, 83. *Prof Exp:* Conserv biologist, Cortland Exp Hatchery, NY State Conserv Dept, 61-63; US Bur Com Fisheries res fel, 63-65; res asst ichthyol, Mus Zool, Fish Div, Univ Mich, 65-66, teaching asst, Dept Wildlife & Fisheries, 66-67; instr biol, Yale Univ, 68-69; asst prof, Boston Univ, 69-72; assoc prof fishery biol, Univ Wis-Stevens Point, 73-79, asst leader, Wis Coop Fishery Unit, US Dept Interior Fish & Wildlife Serv, 73-80; prof biol & unit leader, Ma Coop Fishery Res Unit, Univ Ma, Amherst, 80-88. *Concurrent Pos:* NSF res traineeship, Sport Fishing Inst Res grant & Theodore Roosevelt Mem fund grant, Am Mus Natural Hist, 66-67; Nat Oceanic & Atmospheric Admin sea grant, 75-80. *Mem:* AAAS; Am Fisheries Soc; Am Soc Ichthyologists & Herpetologists; Am Soc Zoologists. *Res:* Fish nutrition and hematology; biochemical systematics, cytotaxonomy population genetics and ecological physiology of fishes. *Mailing Add:* SO Conte Anadromous Fish Res Ctr One Migratory Way Turners Falls MA 01376. *Fax:* 413-863-9810

BOOKER, J(OHN) F, MECHANICAL ENGINEERING. *Current Pos:* asst prof mech & aerospace eng, 61-65, assoc dir, 77-80, PROF MECH & AEROSPACE ENG, CORNELL UNIV, 79- *Personal Data:* b Chicago, Ill, Dec 13, 34; m 57; c 4. *Educ:* Yale Univ, BE, 56; Chrysler Inst Eng, MAE, 58; Cornell Univ, PhD, 61. *Honors & Awards:* Henry Hess Award, Am Soc Mech Engrs, 65; Starley Premium Prize, Brit Inst Mech Engrs, 67; B P Oil Tribology Award, Brit Inst Mech Engrs, 87. *Prof Exp:* Engr, Chrysler Corp, 56-58. *Concurrent Pos:* Vis engr, Glacier Metal Co, 67; Ford Found Eng Residency, IBM Corp, 67-68; consult, Gen Motors Res Labs, 69-; sr vis fel, Univ Leeds, Eng, 74-75 & Twente Univ Technol, Netherlands, 75; mem, Am Soc Mech Engrs Res Comt Lubrication; assoc ed, J Lubrication Technol, 76-79; Fulbright fel, Eindhoven Univ Technol, Netherlands, 82; vis prof, Univ Durham, Eng, 82-83; vis prof, Colo State Univ, 88-89; assoc ed, Tribology Trans, 88-91. *Mem:* Fel Am Soc Mech Engrs; Soc Tribologists & Lubrication Engrs. *Res:* Hydrodynamic lubrication; dynamics of mechanical systems, especially those containing fluid film bearings; finite element methods. *Mailing Add:* Sch Mech Eng 105 Upson Hall Cornell Univ Ithaca NY 14853-7501

BOOKER, JOHN RATCLIFFE, GEOPHYSICS. *Current Pos:* from asst prof to assoc prof, 71-82, PROF GEOPHYS, UNIV WASH, 82- *Personal Data:* b Swanage, Eng, Apr 28, 42; US citizen; m 86; c 2. *Educ:* Stanford Univ, BS, 63; Univ Calif, San Diego, MS, 65, PhD(earth sci), 68. *Prof Exp:* Fulbright-Hays fel, Meteorol Inst, Univ Stockholm, 68-69; res assoc & lectr geophys, Stanford Univ, 69-71. *Concurrent Pos:* Mem, Earth Sci Proposal Rev Panel, NSF, 81-85; mem, Earth & Ocean Sci Adv Comts, 85-87, Continental Dynamics Proposal Rev Panel, 89- *Mem:* Fel Am Geophys Union. *Res:* Geomagnetic induction; inverse theory; thermal instabilities in viscosity stratified fluids and porous media; ocean acoustic tomography. *Mailing Add:* Geophys Prog Ak-50 Univ Wash 3900 Seventh Ave NE Seattle WA 98195-0001

BOOKHOUT, CAZLYN GREEN, MARINE ZOOLOGY. *Current Pos:* from instr to prof zool, 35-76, EMER PROF ZOOL, DUKE UNIV, 76- *Personal Data:* b Gilboa, NY, Jan 28, 07; m 36; c 2. *Educ:* St Stephens Col, AB, 28; Syracuse Univ, AM, 29; Duke Univ, PhD(zool), 34. *Prof Exp:* Instr biol, Women's Col, Univ NC, 29-31; asst zool, Duke Univ, 31-32; assoc prof biol, Elon Col, 34-35. *Concurrent Pos:* Dir, Marine Lab, Duke Univ, 50-63 & 64-68, actg dir oceanog prog, 67-70. *Mem:* AAAS; Am Soc Zool; Am Soc Limnol & Oceanog. *Res:* Germ cells of mammals; embryology of invertebrates and polychaetes; growth in relation to molting in Crustacea; larval development of Portuninae; effect of pesticides on development of crabs; effect of drilling fluids on development of crabs. *Mailing Add:* 1307 Alabama Ave Durham NC 27705

BOOKHOUT, THEODORE ARNOLD, WILDLIFE RESEARCH. *Current Pos:* assoc prof, 68-70, PROF ZOOL, OHIO STATE UNIV, 70; BIOLOGIST & LEADER, OHIO COOP FISH AND WILDLIFE RES UNIT, US FISH & WILDLIFE SERV, 64- *Personal Data:* b Salem, Ill, June 11, 31; m 52, Norma J Smith; c Paul E & Jill S. *Educ:* Southern Ill Univ, BA, 52, MS, 54; Univ Mich, PhD(wildlife mgt), 63. *Prof Exp:* Asst wildlife mgmt, Univ Mich, 56-59; game biologist, Mich Dept Conserv, 59-62; asst wildlife mgmt, Univ Mich, 62, instr, 62-63; res asst prof vert ecol, Univ Md, 63-64. *Mem:* Sigma Xi; Wildlife Soc (vpres, 78-79, pres-elect, 79-80, pres, 80-82); Am Soc Mammal. *Res:* Ecology and population dynamics of terrestrial game birds and mammals; waterfowl and wetland ecology. *Mailing Add:* Zool Ohio State Univ 1735 Neil Ave Columbus OH 43210-1220. *Fax:* 614-469-7395; *E-Mail:* tbookhou@magnus.acs.ohio.state.edu

BOOKMYER, BEVERLY BRANDON, ASTRONOMY. *Current Pos:* RETIRED. *Personal Data:* b Glen Head, NY; c 2. *Educ:* Chestnut Hill Col, AB, 46; Univ Pa, MS, 61, PhD(astron), 64. *Prof Exp:* Asst prof astron & math, Villanova Univ, 64-67; res asst prof, Univ Ariz, 67-71; from assoc prof physics & astron to prof, Clemson Univ, 71-87. *Concurrent Pos:* NSF res grant, 66 & int travel grant, 73 & 75. *Mem:* Am Astron Soc; Am Phys Soc; Int Astron Union; fel AAAS; Astron Soc Pac. *Res:* Photoelectric photometry of variable stars; analysis of observations of eclipsing binary systems; applications of computerized synthetic light curve techniques to contact binary systems; mass exchange; stellar evolution. *Mailing Add:* 631 W Stratford Ct Sequim WA 98382

BOOKSTEIN, ABRAHAM, INFORMATION SCIENCE, DATA COMPRESSION. *Current Pos:* Asst prof libr sci, Univ Chicago, 71-75, asst prof behav sci, 74-75, assoc prof, 75-82, PROF PSYCHOL, UNIV CHICAGO, 82- *Personal Data:* b New York, NY, Mar 22, 40; m 68, Marguerite Vickers. *Educ:* City Col New York, BS, 61; Univ Calif, Berkeley, MS, 66; Yeshiva Univ, PhD(physics), 69; Univ Chicago, MA, 70. *Honors & Awards:* Res Award, Am Soc Info Sci, 91. *Concurrent Pos:* Prin investr, NSF grants & organizing & prog comt prof conf; vis prof, Royal Inst Technol, Stockholm, 82, Grad Sch Libr & Info Sci, Univ Calif, Los Angeles, 85; Fulbright, 91-92. *Mem:* Am Soc Info Sci; Asn Comput Mach; Inst Elec & Electronics Engrs. *Res:* Mathematical modelling in the information sciences; information storage and retrieval; data compression (computer science); research methods. *Mailing Add:* Univ Chicago 5848 S University Ave Chicago IL 60637-1515. *E-Mail:* a-bookstein@uchicago.edu

BOOKSTEIN, FRED LEON, MORPHOMETRICS, COMPUTER GRAPHICS. *Current Pos:* Asst res scientist, Univ Mich, Ann Arbor, 77-80, assoc res scientist, 80-84, res scientist, 84-89, DISTINGUISHED RES SCIENTIST HUMAN GROWTH & DEVELOP, INST GERONT & BIOSTATIST, UNIV MICH, 89- *Personal Data:* b Detroit, Mich, July 27, 47; c 2. *Educ:* Univ Mich, BS, 66, PhD(statist & zool), 77; Harvard Univ, MA,

71. *Res:* New methods for morphometrics, the measurement of biological shape and shape change; applications involve radiology, evolutionary biology, orthodontics, plastic surgery and growth prediction. *Mailing Add:* 300 NIB 9th Level Univ Mich Ann Arbor MI 48109-0406

BOOKSTEIN, JOSEPH JACOB, RADIOLOGY. *Current Pos:* PROF RADIOL, HOSP, UNIV CALIF, SAN DIEGO, 74- *Personal Data:* b Detroit, Mich, July 25, 29; m 54; c 3. *Educ:* Wayne State Univ, BS, 50, MD, 54. *Prof Exp:* Am Cancer Soc fel, Stanford Univ, 59-60; from instr to prof radiol, Med Ctr, Univ Mich, Ann Arbor, 60-74. *Concurrent Pos:* Consult, Vet Admin Hosp, Ann Arbor, Mich, 61-74; mem coun cardiovasc radiol, Am Heart Asn. *Mem:* Asn Univ Radiol; Radiol Soc NAm; NAm Soc Cardiac Radiol. *Res:* Cardiovascular radiology; interventional radiology; renovascular hypertension; magnification angiography; translumind onycoplasty. *Mailing Add:* Dept Radiol Univ Hosp 200 W Arbor St San Diego CA 92103-8756

BOOKWALTER, GEORGE NORMAN, FOOD PROCESSING, CEREAL FOOD FORMULATIONS. *Current Pos:* RES FOOD TECHNOLOGIST & LEAD SCIENTIST, NATIONAL CTR AGR UTIL RES, AGR RES SERV, USDA, 66-, TECH ADV FOOD FOR PEACE PROG, 84- *Personal Data:* b Springfield, Ill, Nov 25, 24; m 51, Leah Huber; c Nancy J (Reynolds) & Karen A (Dahltorp). *Educ:* Univ Ill, BS, 51. *Honors & Awards:* Babcock-Hart Award, Nutrit Found, Inc & Inst Food Technologists, 86. *Prof Exp:* Food technologist, Gen Foods Corp, 51; chemist, Armour & Co, 52-55 & Pillsbury Co, 55-61; appln chemist, A E Staley Co, 61-65. *Concurrent Pos:* Mem, NC-120 Food Serv Comt, USDA, 75-; res collabr, Col Agr, Univ Ill, 81- *Mem:* Sigma Xi; fel Inst Food Technologists; Am Asn Cereal Chemists; Am Oil Chemists' Soc. *Res:* Development of processed food blends from cereals, oilseeds, and dairy products that are utilized in international food relief; cone milk product; whipped topping formulations. *Mailing Add:* 1808 W Teton Dr Peoria IL 61614

BOOLCHAND, PUNIT, EXPERIMENTAL SOLID STATE PHYSICS, EXPERIMENTAL NUCLEAR PHYSICS. *Current Pos:* from instr to asst prof, 69-75, ASSOC PROF PHYSICS, UNIV CINCINNATI, 75- *Personal Data:* b Varanasi, India. *Educ:* Punjab Univ, BS, 64, MS, 65; Case Western Res Univ, PhD(nuclear & solid state physics), 69. *Prof Exp:* Teaching asst physics, Case Western Res Univ, 65-67, grad fel, 67-69. *Concurrent Pos:* Cottrel res grant, Res Corp, 72; res assoc & vis scholar, Stanford Univ, 73-74; vis prof, Katholieke Univ, Leuven, Belg, 74-75; NSF res grant, 75; Am Philos Soc res grant, 75. *Mem:* AAAS; Am Phys Soc. *Res:* Hyperfine interactions studies by Mossbauer effect, perturbed angular correlations, nuclear magnetic resonance and nuclear orientation; structure of amorphous solids; lattice location of implanted ions in semiconductors and metals. *Mailing Add:* Dept ECE Mail Loc 30 Univ Cincinnati Cincinnati OH 45221

BOOLE, JOHN ALLEN, JR, PLANT MORPHOLOGY, PLANT PHYSIOLOGY. *Current Pos:* Assoc prof, Ga Southern Col, 55-58, head dept, 55-60, prof biol, 58-88, chmn, Div Sci & Math, 60-74, dir advisement, 74-88, EMER PROF BIOL, GA SOUTHERN COL, 88- *Personal Data:* b Exmore, Va, Dec 14, 21; m 49; c 3. *Educ:* Univ Va, BA, 49; Va Polytech Inst, MS, 51; Univ NC, PhD(bot), 55. *Mem:* AAAS; Bot Soc Am; Am Inst Biol Sci; Sigma Xi. *Res:* Systematic anatomy of the family Celastraceae; wood anatomy. *Mailing Add:* 10 Briarwood Ct Statesboro GA 30458

BOOLOOTIAN, RICHARD ANDREW, INVERTEBRATE ZOOLOGY. *Current Pos:* PRES, SCI SOFTWARE SYSTS, INC, 69-; CHMN, SCI DEPT, MIRMAN SCH GIFTED, 80- *Personal Data:* b Fresno, Calif, Oct 17, 27; div; c 3. *Educ:* Fresno State Col, BA, 51, MA, 53; Stanford Univ, PhD(biol), 57. *Honors & Awards:* Lalor Found Award, 59, 61. *Prof Exp:* Asst comp physiol, Hopkins Marine Sta, Stanford Univ, 54-57, res assoc, 58; from asst prof to assoc prof zool, Univ Calif, Los Angeles, 57-67; staff consult biol sci curric study, Univ Colo, 67-68; pres, Visual Sci Prod, Los Angeles, 68-69. *Concurrent Pos:* NIH spec fel, 65; dir, Inst Visual Med, Los Angeles, 68-79; pres, Instrnl Systs for Health Sci, 70-75. *Mem:* Fel AAAS; Challenger Soc. *Res:* Comparative physiology of marine invertebrates; comparative hematology of invertebrates. *Mailing Add:* 3576 Woodcliff Rd Sherman Oaks CA 91403. *Fax:* 818-501-7855; *E-Mail:* rabassoc@earthlink.net

BOOM, ROGER WRIGHT, LOW TEMPERATURE ENGINEERING PHYSICS. *Current Pos:* RETIRED. *Personal Data:* b Bladen, Nebr, Mar 10, 23; m 51, LaVerne Backdahl. *Educ:* Univ Nebr, AB, 44; Univ Minn, MS, 51; Univ Calif, Los Angeles, PhD(physics), 58. *Prof Exp:* Res engr space physics, NAm Aviation, La, 51-52; electronic engr product design, Hoffman Electronic Corp, La, 52-54; fel nuclear physics, Univ Bonn, Ger, 58-60; res engr appl superconductivity, Oak Ridge Nat Lab, 60-63; supvr appl superconductivity, Atomics Int Div, Rockwell Int, 63-68; prof nuclear & metall eng, Univ Wis-Madison, 68-91. *Concurrent Pos:* Superconductive magnetic energy storage dir, Appl Superconductivity Ctr, 72-91. *Mem:* Am Phys Soc; Inst Elec & Electronics Engrs; Am Soc Mining Engrs; Sigma Xi. *Res:* Applied superconductivity systems for energy storage, fusion reactor designs, magnetic ore separators, particle detection and composite conductors of aluminum-niobium titanium; including electrical, mechanical, thermal and magnetic experimental research topics in above systems. *Mailing Add:* 7450 Olivetas Ave LaJolla CA 92037. *Fax:* 619-459-9017

BOOMAN, KEITH ALBERT, TIME SERIES ANALYSIS, PHYSICAL ORGANIC CHEMISTRY. *Current Pos:* RETIRED. *Personal Data:* b Bellingham, Wash, Jan 15, 28; m 53; c 3. *Educ:* Univ Wash, BS, 50; Calif Inst Technol, PhD(chem), 56. *Prof Exp:* Res chemist, Res Labs, Rohm and Haas Co, Philadelphia, 56-59; head res lab, Redstone Arsenal Res Div, 59-63, head res lab, 63-70; tech dir, Soap & Detergent Asn, 71. *Mailing Add:* 172 Mountain Ave North Plainfield NJ 07060

BOOMS, ROBERT EDWARD, PHOTOGRAPHIC CHEMISTRY. *Current Pos:* CHEMIST, EASTMAN KODAK CO, 71- *Personal Data:* b Cleveland, Ohio, Mar 25, 45; m 68; c 1. *Educ:* Ohio State Univ, BS, 67; Univ Calif, Los Angeles, PhD(org chem), 71. *Mem:* Am Chem Soc; Soc Photog Scientists & Engrs; Sigma Xi. *Res:* Color photographic systems. *Mailing Add:* 8 Maple Grove Dr Churchville NY 14428-9339

BOON, JOHN DANIEL, JR, geology, for more information see previous edition

BOONE, BRADLEY GILBERT, ELECTROOPTICS, SIGNAL PROCESSING. *Current Pos:* sr physicist, 77-86, PHYSICIST & PRIN PROF STAFF, JOHNS HOPKINS UNIV, 86- *Personal Data:* b Sept 27, 50; m 72, Sandra Dixon; c April & Jonathan. *Educ:* Wash & Lee Univ, BS, 72; Univ Va, PhD(physics), 77. *Prof Exp:* Physicist solid state, US Army Foreign Sci & Tech Div, 77. *Concurrent Pos:* Lectr physics, Univ Va, 77; lectr elec eng, Johns Hopkins Univ, 83-, vis prof, Elec & Comput Eng Dept, 90-91; sect supvr, Image & Signal Processing Sect, 84-96, asst group supvr, 96-, group supvr, EO Systs Group, 96- *Mem:* Soc Photo-optical Instrumentation Engrs. *Res:* Experimental and analytical evaluation of optical processing architectures; radar image and signal processing; radar signal analysis and modeling; microelectronic applications of high temperature superconductivity; optical pattern recognition, electro-optical systems analysis; detectors. *Mailing Add:* Appl Physics Lab Johns Hopkins Univ Laurel MD 20723-6099

BOONE, CHARLES WALTER, PATHOLOGY, BIOCHEMISTRY. *Current Pos:* head, Cell Biol Sect, Lab Viral Carcinogenesis, 65-84, PROG DIR, CANCER CHEMOPREVENTION, NAT CANCER INST, NIH, 84- *Personal Data:* b Berkeley, Calif, Dec 21, 25; m 65; c 2. *Educ:* Univ Calif, San Francisco, MD, 51; Univ Calif, Los Angeles, PhD(biochem), 64; Am Bd Path, dipl, 60. *Prof Exp:* Gen pract med, Los Angeles, 52-56; resident path, 56-60. *Concurrent Pos:* Res fel, Albert Einstein Col Med, 64-65. *Mem:* Am Soc Exp Path; Am Soc Biol Chemists. *Res:* Isolation of pure tumor cells; production of tumor immunity; cellular mechanisms of carcinogenesis. *Mailing Add:* Nat Cancer Inst NIH 6130 Executive Blvd N Rm 201 9000 Rockville Pike Bethesda MD 20892

BOONE, DONALD JOE, CLINICAL CHEMISTRY, CLINICAL PATHOLOGY. *Current Pos:* chief, Clin Chem & Toxicol Sect, Training & Lab Improv Prog, 76-86, HEALTH SCI ADMINR, CTR DIS CONTROL, ATLANTA, 87- *Personal Data:* b Spokane, Wash, May 12, 43; m 73, Leslie LaBelle; c Mark & Laura. *Educ:* Cent State Univ, BS, 65; Iowa State Univ, MS, 67; Wash State Univ, PhD(chem), 70. *Prof Exp:* NSF fel biophys, Albert Einstein Col Med, 71-72; fel clin chem, Univ Iowa, 72-74; asst prof path, Univ Ky, 74-76. *Concurrent Pos:* Consult, Lexington Clin, 74-76; clin chemist, Vet Admin Hosp, Lexington, 74-76; chmn, Bd Comt Clin Chem, Am Chem Soc. *Mem:* Am Chem Soc; Am Asn Clin Chemists. *Res:* Trace element pathology; toxicology and clinical chemistry methodology; kidney and liver disease; health services research. *Mailing Add:* Pub Health Prac Prog Off Ctr Dis Control Atlanta GA 30333. *E-Mail:* djb2@phpdls1.em.cdc.gov

BOONE, DONALD MILFORD, plant pathology, for more information see previous edition

BOONE, GARY M, petrology, mineralogy, for more information see previous edition

BOONE, JAMES EDWARD, pediatrics, pediatric rheumatology, for more information see previous edition

BOONE, JAMES LIGHTHOLDER, INORGANIC CHEMISTRY. *Current Pos:* RETIRED. *Personal Data:* b San Antonio, Tex, Sept 11, 32; c 4. *Educ:* St Louis Univ, BS, 54; Univ Southern Calif, PhD(chem), 60. *Prof Exp:* Res asst, Univ Southern Calif, 54-59; chemist, US Borax & Chem Co, 59-75, mgr chem econ, US Borax Res Corp, 75-77, mgr eng econ, 77-91. *Mem:* Am Chem Soc; Sigma Xi. *Res:* Boron hydrides and their derivatives; organo-boron and organometallic compounds; high temperature boron compounds and refractories; engineering economics. *Mailing Add:* 254 Independence Rd Rochester WA 98579

BOONE, JAMES ROBERT, MATHEMATICS. *Current Pos:* asst prof, 68-74, ASSOC PROF MATH, TEX A&M UNIV, 74- *Personal Data:* b Buffalo, NY, Aug 9, 39; m 61; c 2. *Educ:* Tex A&M Univ, BA, 61, MS, 62; Tex Christian Univ, PhD(math), 68. *Prof Exp:* Opers res analyst, Gen Dynamics/Ft Worth, 63-64, aerodyn engr, 64-65. *Mem:* Am Math Soc; Math Asn Am. *Res:* General topology. *Mailing Add:* Dept Math Tex A&M Univ College Station TX 77843-0100

BOONE, JAMES RONALD, ORGANIC CHEMISTRY. *Current Pos:* ASST PROF CHEM, DAVID LIPSCOMB COL, 75- *Personal Data:* b Brownsville, Tenn, Nov 10, 46; m 70. *Educ:* David Lipscomb Col, BA, 68; Ga Inst Technol, PhD(chem), 74. *Prof Exp:* Instr chem, Ga Inst Technol, 69-70, fel biochem, 74-75. *Mem:* Am Chem Soc. *Res:* Stereoselective reductions of ketones by metal hydrides. *Mailing Add:* Dept Chem David Lipscomb Col Nashville TN 37204-3951

BOONE, LAWRENCE RUDOLPH, III, VIROLOGY & GENE THERAPY, RETROVIRUSES & HIV. *Current Pos:* RES INVESTR, GLAXO WELLCOME, INC, 89- *Personal Data:* b Memphis, Tenn, Apr 21, 48; m 75; c 2. *Educ:* Memphis State Univ, BS, 70; Univ Tenn, PhD(microbiol), 77. *Prof Exp:* fel virus res, Roche Inst Molecular Biol, 77-79; res assoc, Oak Ridge Nat Lab, 79-81; sr staff fel, Nat Inst Environ Health Sci, 81-87, microbiologist, 87-89. *Concurrent Pos:* Vis investr, Oak Ridge Nat Lab, 81-83. *Mem:* Am Soc Microbiol; AAAS; Int Soc Antiviral Res. *Res:* Retrovirus replication; antiviral drug discovery; design and develop viral vectors for gene therapy. *Mailing Add:* 4801 Abercroft Pl Fuquay Varina NC 27526-8657. *Fax:* 919-315-5243; *E-Mail:* boone-lr@glaxo.com

BOONSTRA, BRAM B, ELECTROCHEMISTRY. *Current Pos:* CONSULT, 77- *Personal Data:* b Arnhem, Neth, June 4, 12; m 45; c 2. *Educ:* Univ Amsterdam, PhD(electrochem), 38. *Prof Exp:* Asst prof analytical chem, Univ Amsterdam, 36-39; teacher high sch, Neth, 39-40; res chemist, Rubber Found, Neth, 40-43, mgr, Tech Rubber & Plastics Lab, 46-51; develop chemist, Royal Holland Cable Works, 43-46; sect head, Godfrey Cabot, Inc, 51-62, assoc dir res, Rubber & Plastics Lab, 62-77. *Concurrent Pos:* Chmn, Gordon Res Conf Elastomers, 67. *Mem:* Am Chem Soc. *Res:* High polymer physical chemistry and technology; carbon black. *Mailing Add:* 1562 Serenity Lane Sanibel FL 33957-4217

BOOP, WARREN CLARK, JR, NEUROSURGERY. *Current Pos:* ASSOC PROF NEUROSURG, MED CTR, UNIV ARK, LITTLE ROCK, 70- *Personal Data:* b Baltimore, Md, July 27, 33; c 3. *Educ:* Univ Tenn, BS & MD, 56; Univ Minn, MS, 64. *Prof Exp:* Intern, Baroness Erlanger Hosp, Chattanooga, Tenn, 56-57; resident, St Mary's Hosp, Knoxville, 57-58; resident neurosurg, Univ Minn, Minneapolis, 60-64; staff neurosurgeon, US Naval Hosp, Oakland, Calif, 64-66; head neurosurg serv, US Naval Hosp, Great Lakes, Ill, 66-69. *Concurrent Pos:* US Navy rep, Nat Res Coun Spinal Cord Injuries, 67; vis prof, Wesley Mem Hosp, Chicago, 68; staff neurosurgeon, Vet Admin Hosp, Little Rock, 70-; consult neurosurg, Ark Children's Hosp & Ark Crippled Children's Div, Dept Pub Welfare Hot Springs Rehab Ctr, 70- *Mem:* Cong Neurosurg; Am Asn Neurol Surg; AMA; Neurosurg Soc Am; Am Col Surg; Sigma Xi. *Res:* Circulatory effects of increased intracranial pressure. *Mailing Add:* 12240 Rivercrest Little Rock AR 72212

BOORD, ROBERT LENNIS, VERTEBRATE MORPHOLOGY, NEUROANATOMY. *Current Pos:* asst prof biol sci, Univ Del, 62-69, assoc prof, 69-77, prof, 77-92, EMER PROF HEALTH SCI, UNIV DEL, 92- *Personal Data:* b Masontown, Pa, July 29, 26; m 53, Mary Baird; c Amanda Bru. *Educ:* Washington & Jefferson Col, AB, 50; Univ Md, MS, 58, PhD(zool, comp anat), 60. *Honors & Awards:* Jacob K Javits Neurosci Investigator Award, 85. *Prof Exp:* USPHS fel, 60-61; instr zool, Duke Univ, 61-62. *Mem:* AAAS; Am Asn Anat; Am Soc Zoologists; Sigma Xi. *Res:* Comparative anatomy of vertebrate octavolateralis system; comparative neuroanatomy. *Mailing Add:* Dept Biol Univ Del Newark DE 19716

BOORE, DAVID M, GEOPHYSICS. *Current Pos:* GEOPHYSICIST, US GEOL SURV, 79- *Educ:* Stanford Univ, BS, 64, MS, 65; Mass Inst Technol, PhD(geophys), 70. *Prof Exp:* Postdoctoral res assoc, Nat Resource Coun, US Geol Surv, 70-72; asst prof geophys, Stanford Univ, 72-79. *Concurrent Pos:* Assoc ed, Bull Seismol Soc Am, 75-84, ed, 85-92; chmn, Comn Strong Motion Seismol, 77-83, mem, 84-91; mem, Panel Wind & Seismic Effects, US & Japan Coop Prog Natural Resources, 96- *Mem:* Fel Am Geophys Union. *Res:* Prediction of strong ground shaking from earthquakes, making use of theoretical and empirical analysis of the source, wave propagation and local site effects. *Mailing Add:* US Geol Surv 345 Middlefield Rd MS977 Menlo Park CA 94025

BOORMAN, GARY ALEXIS, RODENT PATHOLOGY, TOXICOLOGY. *Current Pos:* PATHOLOGIST TOXICOL, NAT INST ENVIRON HEALTH SCI, 78-, CHIEF, PATHOL BR, 85- *Personal Data:* b Leonard, Minn, June 30, 42; m 65, Natalie; c Beth & Sonja. *Educ:* Univ Minn, BS, 65, DVM, 67; Univ Mich, MS, 70; Univ Calif, Davis, PhD(path), 78; Am Col Vet Path, dipl, 77; Am Bd Toxicol, dipl, 81. *Prof Exp:* Resident, Lab Animal Med, Univ Mich, 68-70; pathologist rodent path, Inst Exp Geront, Neth, 70-74; resident path, Univ Calif, 74-75. *Concurrent Pos:* Adj asst prof, Sch Med, Univ NC, 79-; path consult, Interagency Regulatory Liaison Group, Chem Indust Inst Toxicol, 80; mem, Comt Infectious Dis Rats & Mice, Nat Res Coun, Nat Acad Sci, 82-90. *Mem:* Am Bd Toxicol; Am Soc Toxicol Pathologists; Am Asn Lab Animal Sci; Am Col Vet Path; Am Col Lab Animal Med; Am Asn Cancer Res. *Res:* Spontaneous and induced neoplasia in rats and mice; potential hazard of environmental chemicals testing to rodents; classification of cancer in rats and mice; effect of electromagnetic fields; ozone effect on lung; toxicity of water disinfection biproducts. *Mailing Add:* Nat Toxicol Prog Nat Inst Environ Health Sci PO Box 12233 Research Triangle Park NC 27709

BOORMAN, PHILIP MICHAEL, INORGANIC CHEMISTRY. *Current Pos:* from asst prof to assoc prof, 67-80, asst dean fac Arts & Sci, 70-73, head dept, 82-87, PROF CHEM, UNIV CALGARY, 80- *Personal Data:* b Hitchin, Eng, May 11, 39; m 66; c 4. *Educ:* Univ Nottingham, BSc, 61, PhD(inorg chem), 64. *Prof Exp:* Brit Titan res fel inorg chem, Univ Newcastle, 64-67. *Concurrent Pos:* Hon vis fel, Dept Chem, Univ Manchester, Eng, 73-74. *Mem:* Fel Chem Inst Can; Royal Soc Chem; Am Chem Soc. *Res:* Interaction of molybdenum and tungsten compounds with sulfur donor ligands; development and chemistry of hydrotreating; upgrading of heavy oil; mechanism of hydrodesulfurization process. *Mailing Add:* Univ Calgary Dept Chem Calgary AB T2N 1N4 Can

BOORN, ANDREW WILLIAM, ATOMIC SPECTROMETRY, QUADROPOLE MASS SPECTROMETRY. *Current Pos:* dir, Anal Instruments, 83-92, VPRES PROD & BUS DEVELOP, SCIEX, 92- *Personal Data:* b London, Eng, July 14, 54; c 2. *Educ:* Thames Polytech, BSc, 77; Ga Inst Technol, PhD(anal chem), 81; MBA, Univ Toronto, 92. *Prof Exp:* Sci officer, Lab Govt Chemist, London, Eng, 72-77; res & teaching asst chem, Ga Inst Technol, 77-81; appl engr, Spectrametrics, Subsidiary of Beckman Instruments, 81-83. *Mem:* Royal Soc Chem; Am Chem Soc. *Res:* Development of quantitative analytical methods for Fourier transform nuclear magnetic resonance (carbon 13 and phosphorus 31); analysis of foods by x-ray fluorescence; studies of sample introduction techniques for atomic spectroscopy; the last topic and development of atomic spectrometers; computer applications in analytical chemistry; ICP-MS instrument development and applications; LC-MS instrument development. *Mailing Add:* MDS SCIEX 71 Four Valley Dr Concord ON L4K 4V8 Can. *Fax:* 905-881-5329

BOORNE, RONALD ALBERT, ENGINEERING PHYSICS. *Current Pos:* RETIRED. *Personal Data:* b Ottawa, Ont, Sept 14, 26; m 89, Danise J Ferguson; c Stephen C. *Educ:* Univ Toronto, BASc, 48. *Prof Exp:* Instr, Univ Toronto, 48-49; theoret aerodynamicist, Aeroelastics Sect, Avro Aircraft Ltd, Can, 49-53; prof eng, 53-92, dir, Sch Eng, Mt Allison Univ, 56-72, dir eng & Comput Ctr, 66-72. *Concurrent Pos:* Sr consult, Seca Co Ltd, 67-72 & P A Lapp Ltd, Ottawa, 72-77. *Mem:* Asn Prof Engrs; Eng Inst Can; Can Asn Univ Teachers. *Res:* Aeroelastic vibrations of aircraft wings and other structures; impact of technology on society. *Mailing Add:* Dept Eng Mt Allison Univ Sackville NB E0A 3C0 Can

BOORSE, HENRY ABRAHAM, LOW TEMPERATURE PHYSICS. *Current Pos:* asst, Columbia Univ, 28-31, instr, 31-33, from asst prof to prof, 37-70, head dept, 37-59, actg dean fac, 57, dean fac, 59-70, actg pres, 62 & 67, spec lectr & asst to pres, 70-74, EMER PROF PHYSICS & EMER DEAN, BARNARD COL, COLUMBIA UNIV, 70- *Personal Data:* b Norristown, Pa, Sept 18, 04; wid; c Ronald H & Suzanne (Remond). *Educ:* US Naval Acad, dipl, 26; Columbia Univ, AM, 33, PhD(physics), 35. *Prof Exp:* Lydig fel, Cambridge Univ, Eng, 34-35; instr physics, City Col New York, 35-37. *Concurrent Pos:* Adams fel, Columbia Univ, 38-40, res physicist, SAM Labs, Manhattan Dist, 41-45, div dir, 45-46; consult, US AEC, 46-58 & Brookhaven Nat Lab, 51-55; chmn, Calorimetry Conf, 56-57; mem, Comn I, Int Inst Refrig & vchmn subcomt basic sci, US Nat Comt, 58-72; chmn, Tenth Int Conf on low Temperture Physics, USSR Acad Sci, 66. *Mem:* Fel Am Phys Soc. *Res:* Low temperature physics; liquefaction of gases; superconductivity; properties of liquid helium. *Mailing Add:* 5426 Queensloch Dr Houston TX 77096

BOORSTYN, ROBERT ROY, ELECTRICAL ENGINEERING. *Current Pos:* from instr to assoc prof, 61-75, PROF ELEC ENG, POLYTECH UNIV, 75- *Personal Data:* b New York, NY, May 28, 37; m 59; c 3. *Educ:* City Col New York, BEE, 58; Polytech Inst Brooklyn, MS, 61, PhD(elec eng), 66. *Prof Exp:* Engr, Sperry Gyroscope Co, 58-61. *Concurrent Pos:* Consult. *Mem:* Fel Inst Elec & Electronic Engrs. *Res:* Telecommunication networks. *Mailing Add:* Polytech Univ 333 Jay St Brooklyn NY 11201

BOOS, DENNIS DALE, MATHEMATICAL STATISTICS. *Current Pos:* PROF STATIST, NC STATE UNIV, 77- *Personal Data:* b Pensacola, Fla, Apr 27, 48; m 74; c 2. *Educ:* Fla State Univ, BS, 70, MS, 75, PhD(statist), 77. *Mem:* Inst Math Statist; Am Statist Asn. *Res:* Robust estimation; goodness of fit; asymptotic distribution theory. *Mailing Add:* Dept Statist NC State Univ PO Box 8203 Raleigh NC 27695-0001

BOOSALIS, MICHAEL GUS, PLANT PATHOLOGY. *Current Pos:* From asst prof to prof plant path, Agr Exp Sta, 51-89, chmn dept, 64-89, prof bot, 70-89, EMER PROF PLANT PATH, INST AGR & NATURAL RESOURCES, UNIV NEBR, LINCOLN, 89- *Personal Data:* b Faribault, Minn, Sept 20, 17; m 46; c 1. *Educ:* Univ Minn, BS, 41, MS, 48, PhD(plant path), 51. *Mem:* Am Phytopath Soc. *Res:* Ecology of fungi, causing root diseases of plants. *Mailing Add:* 3019 Jackson Dr Lincoln NE 68502

BOOSER, E(ARL) R(ICHARD), CHEMICAL ENGINEERING. *Current Pos:* RETIRED. *Personal Data:* b Harrisburg, Pa, Jan 7, 22; m 44, Katherine Swavely; c Joan B (Ropel) & Judith B (Gallo). *Educ:* Pa State Col, BS, 42, MS, 44, PhD(chem eng), 49. *Honors & Awards:* Nat Serv Award, Soc Tribologists and Lubrication Engrs, 83, Nat Achievement Award, 92. *Prof Exp:* Instr chem eng, Pa State Col, 43, res asst petrol ref, 44-48; engr, Thomson Lab, Gen Elec Co, 48-55, atomic power equip dept, 55-56, bearing & lubrication engr, Motor Eng Lab, 56-60, sr engr, Electromech Eng, 60-86. *Concurrent Pos:* Independent Consult Engr, 87- *Mem:* Am Chem Soc; fel Soc Tribologists & Lubrication Engrs (pres, 56-57); Am Soc Mech Engrs. *Res:* Petroleum refining; analysis of petroleum products; bearings and lubricants; hydraulics; atomic power equipment. *Mailing Add:* 65 St Stephens Lane Scotia NY 12302

BOOSKE, JOHN H, MATERIALS PHYSICS, PLASMA SCIENCE. *Current Pos:* asst prof, 90-94, ASSOC PROF, DEPT ELEC & COMPUT ENG, UNIV WIS-MADISON, 94-, FAC MEM, MAT SCI DEGREE PROG, 91- *Personal Data:* b May 17, 58; m 83, Bridget Catlin; c 2. *Educ:* Pa State Univ, BS, 80; Univ Mich, MS, 82, PhD(nuclear eng), 85. *Prof Exp:* US Dept Energy fusion tech fel, Univ Mich, Ann Arbor, 81-85; res assoc, Lab Plasma & Fusion Energy Studies, Univ Md, 85-88, mem res fac & asst res scientist, 88-89, assoc mem grad fac, 88-89. *Concurrent Pos:* engr magnetic fusion energy, Lawrence Livermore Nat Lab, 79, 80; NSF pres young investr,

90-97. *Mem:* Am Phys Soc; sr mem Inst Elec & Electronics Engrs; Univ Fusion Asn; Mat Res Soc; Am Ceramic Soc. *Res:* Materials physics, plasma science, vacuum electronics physics; charged particle beam physics; author of publications. *Mailing Add:* Dept Elec & Comput Eng Univ Wis 1415 Engineering Dr Madison WI 53706. *Fax:* 608-262-1267; *E-Mail:* booske@engr.wisc.edu

BOOSMAN, JAAP WIM, science administration, sedimentology, for more information see previous edition

BOOSS, JOHN, NEUROIMMUNOLOGY, NEUROVIROLOGY. *Current Pos:* neurovirologist, Vet Admin Med Ctr, 76-93, DIR NEUROL, VET HOSP ADMIN, 93- *Personal Data:* b New York, NY, Apr 3, 38; m 72; c 2. *Educ:* Oberlin Col, AB, 61; Albany Med Col, MD, 65. *Honors & Awards:* Sr Scientist Fel, French Ministry Res & Technol, 90. *Prof Exp:* Intern med, Cleveland Clin Hosp, 65-66; resident neurol, NY Univ-Bellevue Med Ctr, 66-69; teaching asst virol, Yale Univ, Sch Med, 69-71; neurologist, Sch Aerospace Med, US Air Force, 71-73; teaching asst virol & immunol, Jefferson Med Col, 73-75; asst prof, 76-81, assoc prof neurol & lab med, 81-, assoc dir neuroimmunilogy clin, Yale Univ Sch Med, New Haven, Conn, 90- *Concurrent Pos:* Attend physician, Neurol Serv, Yale-New Haven Hosp, 76-; consult staff, Waterbury Hosp, 92-; assoc clin prof nursing, Yale Univ Sch Nursing, 93-; prof, Dept Neurol & Lab Med, Yale Univ Sch Med, 96- *Mem:* Am Neurol Asn; fel Am Acad Microbiol; Am Soc Virol; Am Asn Immunol; Am Asn Neuropathologists; NY Acad Sci; Am Acad Neurol; Brit Neuropath Soc; Sigma Xi; Am Soc Microbiol. *Res:* Host-viral interaction in the central nervous system; modulation of the immune response by viral infection; organization of the host response in the central nervous system; immunology of brain grafting; author/co-author of two books and numerous publications. *Mailing Add:* Neurol Serv Vet Admin Med Ctr W Spring St West Haven CT 06516

BOOSTER, DEAN EMERSON, AGRICULTURAL ENGINEERING. *Current Pos:* From instr to prof, 56-87, EMER PROF AGR ENG, ORE STATE UNIV, 87- *Personal Data:* b Salem, Ore, Sept 20, 26; m, Martha Durette; c D Howard, Thomas W, Richard D, Douglas E & Kenneth B. *Educ:* Ore State Univ, BS, 54, MS, 56. *Mem:* Am Soc Agr Engrs. *Res:* Mechanical harvesting and handling of horticultural crops; electrostatic separation of field crop seeds; development of range land seeding equipment; nursery and greenhouse mechanization; conservation tillage in vegetable crop production; mechanical harvesting of oil seed crops. *Mailing Add:* 1544 NW 12th St Corvallis OR 97330-4632. *E-Mail:* boosterd@ucs.orst.edu

BOOTE, KENNETH JAY, CROP PHYSIOLOGY. *Current Pos:* From asst prof to assoc prof, 74-85, PROF CROP PHYSIOL, UNIV FLA, 85- *Personal Data:* b Hull, Iowa, Sept 12, 45; m 69; c 1. *Educ:* Iowa State Univ, BS, 67; Purdue Univ, MS, 69, PhD(crop physiol), 74. *Mem:* Am Soc Agron; Crop Sci Soc Am; Am Peanut Res & Educ Asn; Am Soc Plant Physiol; Fel, Am Soc Agron, 90; Fel, Crop Sci Soc Am, 90. *Res:* Relationships of physiological traits to productivity of peanut and soybean genotypes under varying environments; water relations and pest effects on photosynthesis and evapotranspiration of crop canopies; double cropping; soybean crop model development. *Mailing Add:* Dept Agron Univ Fla PO Box 110500 Gainesville FL 32611-0500

BOOTH, AMANDA JANE, INTERNAL MEDICINE. *Current Pos:* OWNER & VETERINARIAN, SASCENOS VET SERV LTD, 89- *Personal Data:* b Banbury, Eng, Mar 22, 62; Can citizen. *Educ:* Lakehead Univ, BSc, 79; Univ Sask, DVM, 83, MVet Sc, 86; Am Col Vet Internal Med, dipl, 90. *Prof Exp:* Intern large animal med & surg, Univ Pa, 83-84; resident internal med, Western Col Vet Med, 84-86; dir vet serv, Mercury Farm Technol Ctr, 86-89. *Mem:* Am Col Vet Internal Med; Can Vet Med Asn. *Res:* Investigation of correction of metabolic acidosis by oral fluid therapy in diarrheic neonatal calves; investigation of efficacy of desensitization therapy for horses with chronic obstructive pulmonary disease. *Mailing Add:* 5490 Sooke Rd PO Box 1085 Sooke BC V0S 1N0 Can

BOOTH, ANDREW DONALD, PHYSICS, ELECTRICAL ENGINEERING. *Current Pos:* RETIRED. *Personal Data:* b East Molesey, Eng, Feb 11, 18; m 50, D Kathleen; c Ian J M, Amanda J. *Educ:* Univ London, BSc, 40, DSc(physics), 51; Univ Birmingham, PhD(chem), 44. *Honors & Awards:* Centennial Medal, Can, 67. *Prof Exp:* Res physicist, Brit Rubber Producers' Res Asn, 44-46; lectr physics, Birkbeck Col, Univ London, 46-49; prof theoret physics, Univ Pittsburgh, 49-50; dir, Comput Proj, Univ London, 50-54, reader comput methods, Birkbeck Col, 54-57, head, Dept Comput Sci, 57-62; prof elec eng & head dept, Univ Sask, 62-63, dean eng, 63-77; pres & hon prof physics, Lakehead Univ, 72-78. *Concurrent Pos:* Nuffield fel, 46-47; Rockefeller fel & mem, Inst Advan Study, 47-48; consult physicist, Brit Rayon Res Asn, 48-55; sci adv, Int Computs & Tabulators, Ltd, 50-64; Europ sci adv, Am Mach & Foundry Co, 56-62; sci adv, Inst Aviation Med, 57- & H M Underwater Defense Estab, 59-63; ed, J Royal Micros Soc, 61-65; prof-at-large, Case Western Res Univ, 63-; mem, Can Proc, Brit Inst Electronics & Radio Engrs, 66-; bd mem, Nat Res Coun Can, 75-79; chair, Autonetics Res Assocs, Victoria, BC, 78-; hon scientist & instr ocean sci, Victoria, BC, 79-; chmn, Vancouver Island Br, Eng Inst Can, 86-, pres, Scholar Found, 87- *Mem:* Fel Inst Physics; hon fel Inst Ling; fel Brit Inst Elec Engrs; Brit Comput Soc; Royal Micros Soc; Inst Elec & Electronics Engrs; fel Inst Ling. *Res:* X-ray crystallography; computer design and application; biomedical engineering; machine linguistics; microscopy; ocean acoustics. *Mailing Add:* Timberlane 5317 Sooke Rd RR1 Sooke BC V0S 1N0 Can. *E-Mail:* abooth@ios.bc.ca

BOOTH, BEATRICE CROSBY, PHYTOPLANKTON ECOLOGY, PHYTOPLANKTON TAXONOMY. *Current Pos:* teaching asst oceanog, 74-75, instr marine Plankton, 75-78, res oceanogr, 78-80, sr oceanogr, 80-83, PRIN OCEANOGR, UNIV WASH, 83- *Personal Data:* b Minneapolis, Minn, Aug 29, 38; m 60; c 3. *Educ:* Radcliffe Col, BA, 60; Harvard Sch Educ, MAT, 62; Univ Wash, MS, 69. *Prof Exp:* Teaching asst oceanog, Univ Wash, 74-75; instr marine plankton, Univ Wash, 75-78. *Concurrent Pos:* Oceanogr, Pac Marine Environ Lab, Nat Oceanic & Atmospheric Admin, 78-79. *Mem:* Phycol Soc Am; Am Soc Limnol & Oceanog; AAAS. *Res:* Quantitative investigation, including taxonomy and ultrastructure, of nanoplankton species from the eastern subarctic pacific using electron and fluorescence microscopy on cultures and field collections; differentiation of heterotrophic from autotrophic component. *Mailing Add:* 5521 17th Ave NE Seattle WA 98105

BOOTH, BRUCE L, SOLID STATE PHYSICS, LASERS & INTEGRATED OPTICS. *Current Pos:* From res physicist to sr res physicist, E I du Pont de Nemours & Co, Inc, 67-73, res supvr, 73-74, sr supvr, 74-79, res mgr, 79-84, prin consult, 84-85, sr assoc, 85-89, RES FEL, E I DU PONT DE NEMOURS & CO, INC, 89. *Personal Data:* b Philadelphia, Pa, Mar 22, 38; m 68; c 4. *Educ:* Dartmouth Col, BA, 60; Northwestern Univ, PhD(physics), 67. *Mem:* Am Phys Soc; Optical Soc Am; Sigma Xi. *Res:* Low temperature band structure studies using de Haas-Shubnikov effect in semiconductors, mainly gray tin; supervise development of techniques and applications of laser-optical measurements for industry; manage research on medical and clinical instrumentation systems and test methods; integrated optics using polymers. *Mailing Add:* 1669 Warpath Rd West Chester PA 19382

BOOTH, CHARLES E, ANIMAL PHYSIOLOGY. *Current Pos:* asst prof, 84-89, ASSOC PROF BIOL, EASTERN CONN STATE UNIV, 89-, CHMN, BIOL DEPT, 92- *Personal Data:* b Cleveland, Ohio, Jan 9, 52; m 85, Beverly L Wimegarden. *Educ:* Col Wooster, BA, 74; Col William & Mary, MA, 77; Univ Calgary, PhD(biol), 83. *Prof Exp:* Fel, McMaster Univ, 82-84. *Concurrent Pos:* Vis investr, Huntsman Marine Lab, 83-, Fish Physiol & Toxicol Lab, Univ Wyo, 85-, Rosenstiel Sch Marine & Atmospheric Sci, Univ Miami, 87-, Col Charleston Grice Marine Biol Lab, 92 & Rosentiel Sch Marine & Atmospheric Sci, Univ Miami, 92; vis fac, Univ Miami, 87- *Mem:* AAAS; Am Soc Zoologists; Can Soc Zoologist; Am Asn Univ Profs. *Res:* Comparative respiratory, acid-base, and ionoregulatory physiology of aquatic animals; avian hematology. *Mailing Add:* 124 Brooklyn Turnpike Windham CT 06280. *Fax:* 860-465-5213; *E-Mail:* booth@ecsu.ctstateu.edu

BOOTH, DAVID, STATISTICS, ANALYTICAL CHEMISTRY. *Current Pos:* ASSOC PROF BUS ADMIN, KENT STATE UNIV, 85- *Personal Data:* b Galesburg, Ill, July 18, 49; m 71, Stephane Davies. *Educ:* Ill State Univ, BS, 71, MS, 77; Univ NC, MS, 74, PhD(chem), 84. *Prof Exp:* Asst prof math, Millikan Univ, 81-85. *Mem:* Sigma Xi; fel Am Inst Chemists; Am Chem Soc; Decision Sci Inst; Am Statist Asn. *Res:* Statistical process control, robotics, robust statistics and artificial intelligence. *Mailing Add:* Dept Admin Sci Grad Sch Mgt Col Bus Admin Kent State Univ Kent OH 44242. *Fax:* 330-672-2448; *E-Mail:* dbooth@bsaz.kent.edu

BOOTH, DAVID LAYTON, MARKETING, PRODUCTION. *Current Pos:* Res chemist, Org Div, Morton Chem Co, 65-69, supvr org res, 69-74, asst dir new prod develop, Morton Int, Inc, 74-79, res dir new prod develop, Morton-Norwich Prod, Inc, 79-83, dir res, 83-89, VPRES, DYES & ORG SPECIALTIES, MORTON INT, INC, 89- *Personal Data:* b Aurora, Ill, July 20, 39; m 62, Nancy Baker; c Edward & Andrew. *Educ:* Beloit Col, BS, 61; Univ Ore, PhD(org chem), 65. *Mem:* Am Chem Soc; Plant Growth Regulator Working Group; Coun Agr Sci & Technol; Soc Appln Mat & Process Eng; Soc Plastics Indust; Synthetic Org Chem Mfrs Asn; Chem Mfrs Asn. *Res:* Alkaloid chemistry; synthetic studies in pesticide research; liquid polysulfide polymers; sulfur chemistry; sulfur polymers; epoxy and polyester polymers. *Mailing Add:* 652 Kendallwood Ct Crystal Lake IL 60014

BOOTH, DONALD CAMPBELL, ORNAMENTAL PLANT ENTOMOLOGY, INTEGRATED PEST MANAGEMENT. *Current Pos:* ENTOMOLOGIST, BARTLETT TREE RES LAB, 83- *Personal Data:* b Syracuse, NY, May 13, 50; m 86; c 2. *Educ:* SUNY Col Environ Sci & Forestry, BS, 73, PhD(entomol), 79. *Prof Exp:* Assoc entomologist, United Brands Co, 78-81; res assoc, Univ Ga, 82-83. *Mem:* Entomol Soc Am. *Res:* Product development, pesticide efficacy trials and applications of integrated pest management techniques; pheromone traps, insecticidal soap, spray oils, pyrethoi. *Mailing Add:* Bartlett Tree Res Labs 13768 Hamilton Rd Charlotte NC 28278

BOOTH, EUGENE THEODORE, ELEMENTARY PARTICLE PHYSICS. *Current Pos:* RETIRED. *Personal Data:* b Rome, Ga, Sept 28, 12; m 40, Virginia Saffold; c Zaida & Brenda. *Educ:* Univ Ga, BS, 32, MS, 34; Oxford Univ, DPhil, 37. *Prof Exp:* Asst prof physics, Columbia Univ, 46-47, assoc prof, 47-49, prof, 49-59, dir, Hudson Labs, 51-52, Nevis Cyclotron Labs, 52-55; sci dir, Saclant Res Ctr, Italy, 59-61; dean grad studies, Stevens Inst Technol, 68-74. *Mem:* Fel Am Phys Soc. *Res:* Research and publications in fields of neutron physics, high energy particle physics and isotope separation. *Mailing Add:* 902 Pleasantville Rd Briarcliff Manor NY 10510

BOOTH, FRANK, MOLECULAR BIOLOGY, EXERCISE PHYSIOLOGY. *Current Pos:* PROF PHYSIOL, UNIV TEX, 75- *Personal Data:* b July 3, 43. *Educ:* Univ Iowa, PhD(exercise physiol), 70. *Res:* Gene transfer to study muscle promoter function during exercise; exercise mechanisms. *Mailing Add:* Dept Physiol & Cell Biol Univ Tex Med Sch PO Box 20708 Houston TX 77225-9964

BOOTH, GARY EDWIN, ORGANIC CHEMISTRY. *Current Pos:* Res chemist, 65-69, SECT HEAD PHYS ORG CHEM, MIAMI VALLEY LABS, PROCTER & GAMBLE CO, 69- *Personal Data:* b Campton, Ky, Dec 26, 40; m 62; c 2. *Educ:* Eastern Ky State Col, BS, 62; Ohio State Univ, PhD(org chem), 65. *Mem:* Am Chem Soc. *Res:* Conformational analysis; fluorescence of organic molecules; adsorption of dyestuffs onto cellulose; thin-layer chromatography. *Mailing Add:* 224 Wilmoth Ave Cincinnati OH 45215

BOOTH, GARY MELVON, ENTOMOLOGY. *Current Pos:* asst prof zool, 72-73, ASSOC PROF ZOOL, BRIGHAM YOUNG UNIV, 73- *Personal Data:* b Provo, Utah, Oct 9, 40; m 60; c 6. *Educ:* Utah State Univ, BS, 63, MS, 66; Univ Calif, Riverside, PhD(entom), 69. *Honors & Awards:* First Place Res Award, Sigma Xi, 73. *Prof Exp:* NIH fel, Univ Ill, 69-70, asst prof entom, 70-71, asst prof agr entom, 71-72. *Concurrent Pos:* Consult, Environ Protection Agency, 71; asst entomologist, Ill Nat Hist Surv, 71-72; consult, Thompson-Hayward Chem Co, 72-76; assoc ed environ entom, Entom Soc Am, 75. *Mem:* Sigma Xi; Entom Soc Am; Weed Sci Soc Am. *Res:* Metabolism toxicity and environmental behavior of insecticides, herbicides, fungicides and rodenticides in model ecosystems; fish, insects, water and soil; development of pest management research programs. *Mailing Add:* Dept Zool 697 WIDB Brigham Young Univ Provo UT 84602

BOOTH, IAN JEREMY, ACOUSTIC OCEANOGRAPHY & LOW TEMPERATURE SOLID STATE PHYSICS, FIBER OPTICS & OPTOELECTRONICS. *Current Pos:* res physicist, 85-94, DIR PHYSICS, AUTONETICS RES ASSOC, 79-; RES SCIENTIST, SDL OPTICS, 94- *Personal Data:* b Banbury, Eng, Mar 3, 60; Can citizen. *Educ:* Lakehead Univ, BSc, 77, BSc Hons, 78, MSc, 80; Univ BC, PhD(physics), 85. *Prof Exp:* Postdoctoral fel physics, Simon Fraser Univ, 85-87. *Concurrent Pos:* Consult, Autonetics Res Assoc, 89-; fel, Nat Sci & Eng Res Coun Can, 90; lectr, Univ Victoria, 90-93. *Mem:* Am Phys Soc; NY Acad Sci; Inst Elec Engrs UK. *Res:* Photoluminescence and far infrared transmission studies of various semiconductors at low temperature; investigation of anomolous thermionic emission effects; computer simulation and analysis of underwater sound propagation for research and communication; fiber optic lasers and amplifiers. *Mailing Add:* 5317 Sooke Rd RR No 1 Sooke BC V0S 1N0 Can. *Fax:* 250-544-2225; *E-Mail:* ibooth@islandnet.com

BOOTH, JAMES SAMUEL, BACTERIAL PHYSIOLOGY. *Current Pos:* asst prof biol sci, 74-76, ASSOC PROF BIOL SCI, CALIF POLYTECH STATE UNIV, SAN LUIS OBISPO, 76- *Personal Data:* b LeFlore, Okla, Nov 10, 27; m 62; c 1. *Educ:* Calif State Col, BS, 59; Univ Southern Calif, MS, 62, PhD(staphylocoagulase), 68. *Prof Exp:* Lectr microbiol, Calif State Col, Los Angeles, 63-65; asst prof bact physiol, Univ NMex, 67-74. *Mem:* Am Soc Microbiol; Sigma Xi. *Res:* Degradation of ergothioneine by alcaligenes faecalis; factors influencing in vitro levels of staphylocoagulase. *Mailing Add:* Rte 2 Box 340 Wilburton OK 74578-9661

BOOTH, JOHN AUSTIN, plant pathology, for more information see previous edition

BOOTH, LAWRENCE A(SHBY), NUCLEAR ENGINEERING, PHYSICS. *Current Pos:* RETIRED. *Personal Data:* b Louisville, Ky, Apr 10, 34; m 57; c 3. *Educ:* Purdue Univ, BS, 55; Univ Louisville, MChE, 56, PhD(chem eng), 60. *Prof Exp:* Asst, Univ Louisville, 56-58; mem staff, Los Alamos Sci Lab, 60-68, asst group leader, 68-70, staff mem, 70-74, group leader, 74-97. *Concurrent Pos:* Consult, Div Licensing & Regulations, AEC, 67-72. *Mem:* Am Chem Soc; Am Nuclear Soc; fel Am Inst Chemists; Sigma Xi. *Res:* Heat transfer; fluid dynamics; nuclear equipment and materials; gas cooled reactor technology; nuclear propulsion; laser technology; applications of laser fusion. *Mailing Add:* 115 Monte Rey Dr N Los Alamos NM 87544

BOOTH, NEWELL ORMOND, UNDERWATER ACOUSTICS, OCEAN ENGINEERING. *Current Pos:* Physicist optics, Naval Ord Test Sta, 63-65, RES PHYSICIST UNDERWATER ACOUST, NAVAL OCEAN SYSTS CTR, 71- *Personal Data:* b Pocatello, Idaho, Nov 23, 40; m 65; c 1. *Educ:* Univ Calif, Berkeley, BA, 62; Univ Calif, Los Angeles, MS, 66, PhD(physics), 71. *Mem:* Acoust Soc Am. *Res:* Adaptive matched-field array processing. *Mailing Add:* 4643 El Cerrito Dr San Diego CA 92115

BOOTH, NICHOLAS HENRY, TOXICOLOGY, PHARMACOLOGY. *Current Pos:* prof physiol & pharmacol, 74-85, EMER PROF, UNIV GA, 85- *Personal Data:* b Hannibal, Mo, Oct 22, 23; m 44, Jean Atyeo; c Richard, Debra & Diane. *Educ:* Mich State Univ, DVM, 47; Colo State Univ, MS, 51; Univ Colo, PhD, 59. *Prof Exp:* Pvt pract vet med, Hannibal, Mo, 47-48; from asst prof to prof physiol, Colo State Univ, 48-66, head dept, 56-66, dean col vet med & biomed sci, 66-71; dir div vet med res, Bur Vet Med, Food & Drug Admin, 71-74. *Concurrent Pos:* Chmn vet drug panel, Nat Res Coun-Nat Acad Sci, 66-68; consult, Div Physician Manpower, Bur Health Manpower, Dept Health, Educ & Welfare, 67-68; mem vet med rev comt, Bur Health Physicians Educ & Manpower Training, Dept Health, Educ & Welfare, NIH, 69-; mem spec comt vet med educ, Southern Regional Educ Bd, 70. *Mem:* AAAS; Am Physiol Soc; Am Vet Med Asn; Am Heart Asn; Soc Exp Biol & Med; Soc Toxicol. *Res:* Pharmacodynamic studies on d-tubo curarine chloride and succinylcholine chloride in the horse; meperidine studies in the cat; artificial respiration in large animals; electrical defibrillation of the dog heart; electro and phonocardiography studies in the lamb; cardiovascular studies in swine; veterinary pharmacology and toxicology; drug residue studies in food-producing animals; contributing author and co-editor of one book and 90 publications; hold one patent. *Mailing Add:* 3641 Newcastle Creek Dr Jacksonville FL 32277-3001

BOOTH, NORMAN E, ELEMENTARY PARTICLE PHYSICS. *Current Pos:* sr res officer, 70-76, LECTR, UNIV OXFORD, 76- *Personal Data:* b Toronto, Ont, Mar 7, 30; m 58; c 4. *Educ:* Univ Toronto, BA, 52; Queen's Univ, Ont, MA, 54; Univ Birmingham, PhD(physics), 57. *Prof Exp:* Res fel physics, Univ Birmingham, 57-58; res physicist, Lawrence Radiation Lab, Univ Calif, 59-62; from asst prof to assoc prof, Univ Chicago, 62-70. *Mem:* Fel Am Phys Soc; fel Inst Physics. *Res:* High energy physics; low temperature detectors. *Mailing Add:* Nuclear Physics Lab Univ Oxford Keble Rd Oxford 0X1 3RH England

BOOTH, PIETER NATHANIEL, NATURAL RESOURCE DAMAGE ASSESSMENT. *Current Pos:* SR SCIENTIST, PTI ENVIRON SERVS, INC, 87- *Personal Data:* b Zeist, Holland, May 3, 55; US citizen; m 82, Mary Frey; c Benjamin & Camila. *Educ:* Univ Pac, BS, 77; Univ Wash, MMS, 84. *Prof Exp:* Lab equip specialist, Cooper Labs, 78-83; scientist, Nat Oceanic & Atmospheric Admin, 83-84; environ scientist, Tetra Tech, Inc, 84-87. *Concurrent Pos:* Fac mem, Exec Enterprises, 92. *Mem:* Water Environ Fedn. *Res:* Environmental sciences. *Mailing Add:* 23628 172nd Ave SE Kent WA 98042. *Fax:* 425-643-9827

BOOTH, RACHEL Z, NURSING, ADMINISTRATION. *Current Pos:* PROF & DEAN, SCH NURSING, UNIV ALA, BIRMINGHAM, 87- *Personal Data:* b Seneca, SC, Feb 10, 36; m, Richard B; c Kevin M. *Educ:* Univ Md, BSN, 68, MS, 70, PhD(admin higher educ), 78. *Prof Exp:* Assoc dir, Dept Nursing, Univ Md Hosp, 70-76; chair, Grad Prog Dept, Univ Md, 74-79, assoc dean, Sch Nursing, 79-84; dean & asst vpres health affairs, Duke Univ, 84-87. *Concurrent Pos:* Consult, Univ Mo, 88, Shanghai Second Med Univ, China, 90 & Javeriana Univ, Columbia, 93; vis prof, Chiang Mai Univ, 89, 91 & 96, Chiba Univ, Japan, Univ PR, 97. *Mem:* Nat Acad Pract Nursing; Am Asn Col Nursing (pres-elect, 92-94, pres, 94-96); Am Nurses Asn. *Res:* Leadership, conflict management, change, administration, graduate education; strategic planning and evaluation pursued within a system context that is dynamic and futuristic. *Mailing Add:* 1701 University Blvd Birmingham AL 35294-1210. *E-Mail:* rzbooth@admin.son.uab.edu

BOOTH, RAY S, NUCLEAR ENGINEERING. *Current Pos:* head, Develop Group, Instrumentation & Controls Div, Oak Ridge Nat Lab, 68-76, head, Develop Group, Controls Sect, 76-81, prog mgr, Clinch River Breeder Reactor Proj Off, 81-83, proj mgt, Nuclear Progs, Instrumentation & Controls Div, 83-84, tech dir, Light Water Reactor Prog, Gen Technol Prog & Liquid Metal Reactor Prog, 84-91, SYSTS ENGR, ADVAN NEUTRON SOURCE PROJ, OAK RIDGE NAT LAB, 91- *Personal Data:* b Miami, Fla, Oct 5, 38; m 62; c 3. *Educ:* Univ Fla, BEE, 61, MSNE, 62, PhD(nuclear eng), 65. *Prof Exp:* Asst nuclear eng sci, Univ Fla, 61-65; asst prof physics, USAF Inst Technol, 65-68. *Mem:* Fel Am Nuclear Soc. *Res:* Neutron wave propagation in nuclear systems; neutron noise analysis in power reactors; nuclear reactors analysis; nuclear system design. *Mailing Add:* 9560 Sarasota Dr Knoxville TN 37923

BOOTH, RAYMOND GEORGE, NEUROBIOCHEMISTRY, DOPAMINE METABOLISM. *Current Pos:* ASSOC PROF MED CHEM, UNIV NC, CHAPEL HILL, 90- *Personal Data:* b Utica, NY, Aug 17, 60. *Educ:* Northeastern Univ, BS, 83; Univ Calif, San Francisco, PhD(pharm chem), 89. *Prof Exp:* NIH postdoctoral fel neuro biochem, Harvard Med Sch, 88-90; instr med chem, Northeast Univ, 90. *Concurrent Pos:* Prin investr, Univ NC, Chapel Hill, 90- *Mem:* Soc Neurosci; Am Chem Soc; Am Pharm Asn. *Res:* Research concerning central dopaminergic systems as they relate to Parkinson's disease and schizophernia; regulation of central dopamine synthesis, release, metabolism and receptor-mediated modulators; neurotoxicology of central dopaminergic systems. *Mailing Add:* Sch Pharm CB 7360 Univ NC Chapel Hill NC 27599. *Fax:* 919-966-6919; *E-Mail:* rbooth@email.unc.edu

BOOTH, RICHARD W, MEDICINE. *Current Pos:* assoc prof, 61-64, PROF MED, 64-, SCH MED, CREIGHTON UNIV, DIR MED SERV, 71. *Personal Data:* b Cincinnati, Ohio, Mar 17, 24; m 45; c 3. *Educ:* Univ Cincinnati, MD, 52; Am Bd Internal Med, dipl. *Prof Exp:* Donald L Mahanna res fel, Ohio State Univ Hosp, 56-59; asst prof med & instr aviation & prev med, Ohio State Univ, 59-61; med dir & chief of staff, S. Joseph Hosp, 71-93. *Concurrent Pos:* Consult, Vet Admin Hosp, Dayton, Ohio, 56-61 & Wright Patterson AFB, 60-61; attend physician, Ohio State Univ, 59-61 & Vet Admin Hosp, Nebr, 63-64; fel, Coun Clin Cardiol, Am Heart Asn; assoc dean, Sch Med, Creighton Univ, 72-79. *Mem:* Am Fedn Clin Res; Am Col Cardiol; Am Col Angiol; fel Am Col Physicians; Am Heart Asn. *Res:* Cardiovascular diseases. *Mailing Add:* 1616 S 187th Ave Omaha NE 68130-2809

BOOTH, ROBERT EDWIN, ORGANIC CHEMISTRY. *Current Pos:* RETIRED. *Personal Data:* b New York, NY, Mar 28, 21; m 42; c 3. *Educ:* NY State Col Forestry, Syracuse Univ, BS, 42, PhD, 50. *Prof Exp:* Asst instr org chem, Syracuse Univ, 49-50; res chemist chem & radiation labs, Chem Corps, US Army, 51-52; res chemist, Solvay Process Div, Allied Chem Corp, 55-68, sr res chemist, Indust Chem Div, 68-84. *Mem:* Am Chem Soc; The Chem Soc. *Res:* Plastics and polymers; vinyl ethers and chloride; polyesters; polyethers; phenolics; inorganic fluorine chemistry; polyurethanes; isocyanates. *Mailing Add:* 4909 South Ave Syracuse NY 13215

BOOTH, SHELDON JAMES, MICROBIOLOGY. *Current Pos:* ASST PROF, DEPT PATHOL & MICROBIOL, UNIV NEBR MED CTR, 77- *Personal Data:* b Marshalltown, Iowa, Feb 21, 45; m 76; c 4. *Educ:* Univ Iowa, BA, 68; Univ Nebr, PhD(microbiol), 75. *Prof Exp:* Biol sci asst microbiol, US Army, Dugway, Utah, 68-70; res assoc microbiol, Anaerobe Lab, Va Polytech

Inst, 75-77. *Concurrent Pos:* Fel, Va Polytech Inst Anaerobe Lab, 75. *Mem:* Am Soc Microbiol; AAAS; Sigma Xi. *Res:* Ultrastructure, genetics, and biochemistry of bacteriophage and bacteriocins of anaerobic bacteria; bacteriophage and bacteriocin typing of anaerobic bacteria; pathogenicity, ultrastructure, genetics and biochemistry of anaerobic bacteria; water pollution. *Mailing Add:* Dept Path & Microbiol Univ Nebr Med Ctr 600 S 42nd St Box 698-6495 Omaha NE 68198-6495

BOOTHBY, WILLIAM MUNGER, MATHEMATICS, SYSTEMS SCIENCE. *Current Pos:* from assoc prof to prof, 59-88, EMER PROF MATH, WASHINGTON UNIV, 88- *Personal Data:* b Detroit, Mich, Apr 1, 18; m 47, Ruth Robin; c Daniel, Thomas & Mark. *Educ:* Univ Mich, PhD, 49. *Prof Exp:* Swiss-Am Found for Sci Exchange fel, Swiss Fed Inst Technol, 50-51; from instr to asst prof math, Northwestern Univ, 48-59. *Concurrent Pos:* NSF sr fel, Inst Advan Study, Princeton, NJ, 61-62; vis mem, Inst Math, Univ Geneva, 65-66; vis prof, Univ Strasbourg, 71 & 77, Univ Cordoba, Arg, 81; vis researcher, Univ Rome II, 87. *Mem:* Math Asn Am; Am Math Soc; Soc Indust Appl Math. *Res:* Differential geometry and topology; geometric control theory. *Mailing Add:* Dept Math Wash Univ St Louis MO 63130. *E-Mail:* boothby@math.wustl.edu

BOOTHE, EDWARD MILTON, AERONAUTICAL ENGINEERING. *Current Pos:* INDEPENDENT CONSULT FLIGHT SIMULATION & TRAINING, STONE MOUNTAIN, GA, 93- *Personal Data:* b Springfield, Va, July 8, 35; m 58, Inez Gregory; c Timothy Edward, Amy Dolores & Suzanne Frances. *Educ:* George Washington Univ, BME, 58; Tex A&M Univ, MS, 65. *Honors & Awards:* Silver Medal, US Dept Transp, 89; Kitty Hawk Award, Fed Aviation Admin, 93; Silver Medal Flight Simulation, Royal Aeronaut Soc, 93; DeFlorez Training Award, Am Inst Aeronaut & Astronaut, 93. *Prof Exp:* Res engr & eng pilot, Calspan Corp, NY, 69-74; aeronaut engr & pilot, US Fed Aviation Admin, Washington, 74-78, aeronaut engr, Atlanta, 78-80, test pilot, 80-82, simulator evaluator, 82-83, mgr simulation, 83-93. *Mem:* Fel Am Inst Aeronaut & Astronaut; Royal Aeronaut Soc. *Res:* Flight simulation; contributed articles to professional journals. *Mailing Add:* 927 John Alden Rd Stone Mountain GA 30083-4755

BOOTHE, JAMES HOWARD, ORGANIC CHEMISTRY. *Current Pos:* RETIRED. *Personal Data:* b Okanogan, Wash, Nov 2, 16; m, Jane B Hill; c 2. *Educ:* State Col Wash, BS, 39; Univ Minn, PhD(pharmaceut chem), 43. *Honors & Awards:* Distinguished Serv Chem Award, Am Chem Soc. *Prof Exp:* Res chemist, Lederle Labs, 43-83. *Mem:* Am Chem Soc; NY Acad Sci. *Res:* Chemistry of pteridines; synthesis of folic acid and analogues; syntheses of thiobarbiturates; chemical modification of antibiotics to improve biological properties; chemistry and total synthesis of tetracyclines; chemistry of antibacterial substances. *Mailing Add:* 418 E Longport PO Box 966 Ocean Gate NJ 08740

BOOTHE, RONALD G, VISUAL PERCEPTION, VISUAL DEVELOPMENT. *Current Pos:* ASSOC PROF PSYCHOL & ASST PROF OPHTHAL, EMORY UNIV, 84- *Personal Data:* b Havre, Mont, May 25, 47; m; c 4. *Educ:* Concordia Col, BA, 68; Univ Wash, PhD(psychol), 74. *Prof Exp:* Sr fel, Univ Wash Sch Med, 74-77; res assoc, Univ Wash, 77-79, res asst prof, 79-82, res assoc prof psychol, 82-84. *Concurrent Pos:* Adj res prof ophthal, Univ Wash, 80-84; res affiliate, Child Develop & Mental Retardation Ctr, 77-84 & Regional Primate Res Ctr, 78-87; prin investr, NIH res grants, 78-; res assoc prof, Yerks Primate Ctr, Emory Univ, 84- *Mem:* AAAS; Asn Res Vision & Ophthal; Soc Neurosci. *Res:* Behavioral and neuroanatomical research regarding normal and abnormal development of vision in primates. *Mailing Add:* Dept Psychol Emory Univ Atlanta GA 30322-1100

BOOTHROYD, CARL WILLIAM, PLANT PATHOLOGY. *Current Pos:* From asst prof to assoc prof, 49-57, assoc head dept, 63-69, prof plant path, Col Agr & Life Sci, 57-80, EMER PROF PLANT PATH, CORNELL UNIV, 80- *Personal Data:* b Woodsville, NH, Jan 15, 15; m 41, 82; c 2. *Educ:* Dartmouth Col, AB, 38; State Col Wash, MS, 41; Cornell Univ, PhD, 50. *Concurrent Pos:* Guggenheim fel, 63. *Res:* Diseases of corn. *Mailing Add:* 308 The Parkway Ithaca NY 14850

BOOTHROYD, ERIC ROGER, cytology, for more information see previous edition

BOOTHROYD, GEOFFREY, MECHANICAL ENGINEERING. *Current Pos:* PROF INDUST & MFG ENG, UNIV RI, KINGSTON, 85-; PRES, BOOTHROYD & DEWHURST, INC, 85- *Personal Data:* b Lancashire, Eng, Nov 18, 32; m 54; c 2. *Educ:* Univ London, BSc, 57, PhD(mech eng), 62, DSc, 74. *Honors & Awards:* Nat Medal of Technol, 91. *Prof Exp:* Designer centrifugal pumps, Mather & Platt Ltd, Eng, 56-57; design engr, Eng Elec Co Ltd, 57-58; lectr mech eng, Royal Col Adv Tech, 58-60, sr lectr, 60-64; vis assoc prof, Ga Inst Tech, 64-65; sr lectr, Univ Salford, 65-66, reader, 66-67; prof mech eng, Univ Mass, Amherst, 67-85. *Mem:* Nat Acad Eng; fel Soc Mfg Engrs. *Res:* Production engineering; manufacturing research including metal machining and mechanized assembly and design for ease of assembly. *Mailing Add:* 138 Math St Wakefield RI 02879. *Fax:* 401-783-6872

BOOTON, RICHARD C(RITTENDEN), JR, ELECTRICAL ENGINEERING. *Current Pos:* staff mem, TRW Milcom, with co, 57-81, mgr electronic info systs opers, TRW Space Technol Labs, 66-78, spec asst to gen mgr, Electronic Systs Div, 78-80, chief scientist, 80-81, CHIEF SCIENTIST, ELECTRONIC SYSTS GROUP, TRW MILCOM, 81- *Personal Data:* b Dallas, Tex, July 26, 26; m 73. *Educ:* Agr & Mech Col, Tex, BS & MS, 48; Mass Inst Technol, ScD(elec eng), 52. *Honors & Awards:* Thompson Mem Prize, Inst Radio Engrs, 53. *Prof Exp:* Asst elec eng, Mass Inst Technol, 48-51, mem staff, Div Indust Coop, 52-54, lectr, 53-54, asst prof elec eng, 54-57. *Mem:* Am Inst Aeronaut & Astronaut; assoc fel Inst Elec & Electronics Engrs; Sigma Xi. *Res:* Optimization and analysis of time-varying and nonlinear systems; analogue computation; random processes. *Mailing Add:* 2983 Foothills Ranch Rd Boulder CO 80302-9368

BOOTS, MARVIN ROBERT, MEDICINAL CHEMISTRY. *Current Pos:* asst prof, 66-71, ASSOC PROF MED CHEM, MED COL VA, VA COMMONWEALTH UNIV, 71- *Personal Data:* b St Louis, Mo, Jan 29, 37. *Educ:* St Louis Col Pharm, BS, 58; Univ Wis, MS, 60; Univ Kans, PhD(pharmaceut chem), 63. *Honors & Awards:* Richardson Award, 63. *Prof Exp:* Asst prof pharmaceut chem, Univ Miss, 63-64; res org chemist, Gulf Res & Develop Co, 64-66. *Mem:* Am Chem Soc; Am Pharmaceut Asn; Asn Am Univ Professors. *Res:* Design and synthesis of potential therapeutic agents. *Mailing Add:* 8301 Spring Meadow Rd Richmond VA 23235

BOOTS, SHARON G, ORGANIC CHEMISTRY. *Current Pos:* PRES, LYNNE GRAY ASSOC; SCI ED; ENVIRON CONSULT; ALTERNATIVE HEALTH PRACTITIONER. *Personal Data:* b Grand Rapids, Mich, May 5, 39; c 1. *Educ:* Univ Wis, BA, 60; Stanford Univ, PhD(org chem), 64. *Prof Exp:* NIH fel org chem, Mass Inst Technol, 64; assoc chemist, Midwest Res Inst, 65-66; res assoc, Am Tobacco Co, 66-67 & Med Col Va, 67-76; res assoc, Dept Chem, Stanford Univ, 78-81; assoc clin toxicol, Nat Inst Environ Health Sci, Univ Wis-Madison, 81-82; ed, J Pharmaceut Sci, Am Pharmaceut Asn, 82-86. *Mem:* Soc Ecol Restoration; Nature Conserv; Audubon Soc. *Res:* Ecological restoration; study of native plant species, habitats, etc. *Mailing Add:* 414 Meadowlark Lane Naples FL 34105

BOOZER, ALLEN HAYNE, PLASMA PHYSICS. *Current Pos:* PROF PHYSICS, COL WILLIAM & MARY, 86- *Personal Data:* b Orangeburg, SC, July 28, 44; m 68; c 2. *Educ:* Univ Va, BA, 66; Cornell Univ, PhD(physics), 70. *Prof Exp:* Physicist, Princeton Plasma Physics Lab, 74-86. *Concurrent Pos:* External sci mem, Max Plank Soc Fed Repub Ger, 89- *Mem:* Fel Am Phys Soc (secy & treas, 88-90); Am Geophys Union. *Res:* Theory of plasmas primarily for application to magnetic fusion; equilibrium of and transport in three dimensional plasmas and methods of non-inductive current drive in plasmas. *Mailing Add:* Dept Physics Columbia Univ 500 W 120th St Rm 202 New York NY 10027

BOOZER, CAROL SUE NEELY, obesity, energy metabolism, for more information see previous edition

BOOZER, CHARLES (EUGENE), RUBBER CHEMISTRY. *Current Pos:* RETIRED. *Personal Data:* b Nacogdoches, Tex, Oct 4, 27; m 53, Edwina Blankinship; c Galvin, Glenda, Marshall, Mylitta, Amanda & Allen. *Educ:* Austin Col, BS, 49; Rice Inst, MA, 51, PhD(chem), 53. *Prof Exp:* Res assoc oxidation inhibitors, Iowa State Col, 53-54; assoc prof chem, La Polytech Inst, 54-59 & Emory Univ, 59-64; res supvr, Copolymer Rubber & Chem Corp, 64-67, res mgr, 67 -74, appln develop mgr, 74-87. *Concurrent Pos:* Consult, Copolymer Rubber & Chem Corp, 56-64, Houdry Div, Air Prod & Chem Corp. *Mem:* Am Chem Soc. *Res:* Secondary isotope effects; mechanism of chlorosulfite decomposition; mechanism of action of oxidation inhibitors; nitric acid and air oxidations; free radical and Ziegler polymerization; rubber technology. *Mailing Add:* 8635 Gail Dr Baton Rouge LA 70809-2908

BOOZER, REUBEN BRYAN, ZOOLOGY, BIOLOGY. *Current Pos:* RETIRED. *Personal Data:* b Jacksonville, Ala, Aug 19, 25; m 54; c 4. *Educ:* Jacksonville State Teachers Col, BS, 49; George Peabody Col Teachers, MA, 52; Auburn Univ, PhD(zool, bot), 69. *Prof Exp:* Teacher high sch, Ala, 50-54; asst prof biol, Jacksonville State Col, 54-63; instr zool, Auburn Univ, 63-68; dean, Col Arts & Sci, Jacksonville State Univ, 71-78, prof biol sci, 68-87, dean, Col Sci & Math, 71-87. *Res:* Histotechnique aging of mammals. *Mailing Add:* 6703 Nisbet Lake Rd Jacksonville AL 36265

BOPE, FRANK WILLIS, PHARMACEUTICAL CHEMISTRY. *Current Pos:* from asst prof to prof pharm, Ohio State Univ, 48-84, secy, Col Pharm, 58-84, asst dean, 70-81, assoc dean, 81-84, EMER ASSOC DEAN PHARM, OHIO STATE UNIV, 84- *Personal Data:* b Thornville, Ohio, Oct 30, 18; m 44; c 1. *Educ:* Ohio State Univ, BS, 41; Univ Minn, PhD(pharmaceut chem), 48. *Prof Exp:* Asst pharmaceut chem, Univ Minn, 41-42, jr scientist, 46-47. *Mem:* Am Pharmaceut Asn; Acad Pharmaceut Sci; Am Asn Cols Pharm; Sigma Xi. *Res:* Chemistry and pharmacology of tannins; antioxidants; preliminary phytochemical and pharmacological investigation of the tannin obtained from Pinus Caribaea Morelet; synthesis of esters of gentisic acid; synthesis of urea analogs. *Mailing Add:* 177 Desantis Dr Columbus OH 43214

BOPP, BERNARD WILLIAM, ASTRONOMY. *Current Pos:* from asst prof to prof, 74-90, DISTINGUISHED UNIV PROF ASTRON, UNIV TOLEDO, 90- *Personal Data:* b New York, NY, Jan 11, 47; m 73, Ginger; c Maria & Joanna. *Educ:* NY Univ, BA, 68; Univ Tex, Austin, PhD(astron), 74. *Prof Exp:* Res assoc astron, Univ Wyo, 73-74. *Concurrent Pos:* Vis prof, Univ Wyo, 80-81; vis scientist, Dominion Astrophys Observ, 87-88. *Mem:* Am Astron Soc; Royal Astron Soc; Int Astron Union; Sigma Xi. *Res:* Spectroscopy of variable and binary stars; study of stellar surface phenomena; stellar chromospheres. *Mailing Add:* Univ Toledo Ritter Astrophy Res Ctr Toledo OH 43606. *Fax:* 419-537-2723; *E-Mail:* bwb@utphyp.phyp.utoledo.edu

BOPP, C(HARLES) DANIEL, CHEMICAL ENGINEERING. *Current Pos:* develop Engr, 48-90, CONSULT, CHEM TECHNOL DIV, OAK RIDGE NAT LAB, 90- *Personal Data:* b Decatur, Ill, Feb 4, 23; wid. *Educ:* Purdue Univ, BS, 44. *Prof Exp:* Chemist, Tenn Eastman Co, Clinton Engr Works, 44-48. *Mem:* Am Chem Soc; Am Ceramic Soc; Am Nuclear Soc; Am Inst Chem Engrs; Sigma Xi. *Res:* Materials; corrosion; environmental effects of nuclear plants; water treatment; radiation chemistry. *Mailing Add:* 72 Outer Dr Oak Ridge TN 37830

BOPP, FREDERICK, III, GEOLOGY. *Current Pos:* geologist, 79-84, mgr geosci dept, 84-87, VPRES & TECH DIR, GEOSCI DEPT, WESTON, 87- *Personal Data:* US citizen; c 2. *Educ:* Brown Univ, BA, 66; Univ Del, MS, 73, PhD(geol), 80. *Prof Exp:* Pres & prin partner, Earth Quest Assocs, 74-76; res & univ fel, Dept Geol, Univ Del, 70-76; vis asst prof geochem, Univ SFla, 76-77; staff hydrogeologist, Waterways Exp Sta, US Army Corps Engrs, 77-79. *Mem:* Nat Water Well Asn; Geol Soc Am; Estuarine Res Fedn. *Res:* Groundwater resources evaluation; hydrogeologic evaluation of sanitary landfills and other waste disposal methods; detection and abatement of groundwater pollution; digital modelling of groundwater flow and solute transport; statistical analysis of geological and geochemical data; geochemical prospecting. *Mailing Add:* 22 Uwchlan Ave Downingtown PA 19335

BOPP, LAWRENCE HOWARD, PLASMID GENETICS, BIODEGRADATION. *Current Pos:* PROF, STATE UNIV NY MED COL, ALBANY, NY, 85- *Personal Data:* b Schenectady, NY, Mar 10, 49; m 71; c 2. *Educ:* State Univ NY, Albany, BS, 71; Rensselaer Polytech Inst, MS, 76, PhD(biol), 81. *Prof Exp:* Assoc staff microbiologist, Gen Elec Corp, 77-80, staff microbiologist, Res & Develop Ctr, 80-87. *Concurrent Pos:* Asst prof, Univ Southern Miss, 91-96. *Mem:* Am Soc Microbiol; AAAS; Sigma Xi. *Res:* Genetics and biochemistry of bacteria associated with leaching, metal resistance and transformations and the degradation of unusual compounds; genetic manipulation of such organisms. *Mailing Add:* 118 Birchwood Dr Schenectady NY 12303

BOPP, THOMAS THEODORE, PHYSICAL CHEMISTRY. *Current Pos:* From asst prof to assoc prof, 67-85, PROF CHEM, UNIV HAWAII, 85-, CHAIR CHEM DEPT, 92- *Personal Data:* b Glendale, Calif, Nov 29, 41; m 62, 73; c 4. *Educ:* Calif Inst Technol, BS, 63; Harvard Univ, PhD(chem), 68. *Mem:* Am Chem Soc. *Res:* Applications of magnetic resonance to liquid structure; molecular motion in liquids; computer simulation of spectra; multiple pulse NMR. *Mailing Add:* Dept Chem Univ Hawaii Honolulu HI 96822-1888. *Fax:* 808-956-5908; *E-Mail:* tbopp@uhunix.uhcc.hawaii.edu

BORA, SUNDER S, EDUCATIONAL ADMINISTRATION, TECHNICAL MANAGEMENT. *Current Pos:* asst lab dir, 72-74, TECH DIR CLIN LAB, NORTHERN WESTCHESTER HOSP CTR, MT KISCO, 74- *Personal Data:* b India, Oct 6, 38; US citizen; m 67; c 2. *Educ:* Agra Univ, India, BS, 57, MS, 59; Lucknow Univ, PhD(biochem), 67. *Prof Exp:* Res fel biochem, Lucknow Univ, India, 60-67; res assoc biochem, Columbia Univ, NY, 68-70; lab dir, Clin Lab, Clin Anal Serv, Hamden, Conn, 70-72. *Concurrent Pos:* Prog dir, Sch Med Technol, Northern Westchester Hosp Ctr, Mt Kisco, 75-; adj prof, Iona Col, New Rochelle, NY, 77-, Mercy Col, Dobbs Ferry, NY, 77-, King's Col, Briarcliff, NY, 78-, adj prof, Pace Univ, Pleasantville, NY, 87-; prin investr, NY Acad Sci, 88- *Mem:* Asn Clin Scientist; Am Asn Clin Chemists; assoc mem Am Soc Clin Pathologists. *Res:* Thyroid-metabolism; immunoglobulins. *Mailing Add:* Northern Westchester Hosp Ctr 400 E Main St Mt Kisco NY 10549

BORAH, KRIPANATH, PHARMACEUTICAL CHEMISTRY, ORGANIC CHEMISTRY. *Current Pos:* DIR, PHARM RES & DEVELOP, ORGANON INC, 80- *Personal Data:* b Calcutta, India, Mar 1, 31; m 64; c 2. *Educ:* Univ Calcutta, BS, 52, MS, 56; Univ Munich, PhD(pharm), 61. *Prof Exp:* Prod chemist, Ciba-Geigy Ltd, Bombay, India, 62-67, dep mgr develop dept, 68-70, mgr, 71-76; res assoc, Dept Chem, Boston Col, 76-77; sr scientist pharm res & develop, William H Rorer, Inc, 77-80. *Mem:* Am Chem Soc; Am Pharm Asn; Acad Pharm Sci. *Res:* Synthesis of local anesthetics; 19-norsteroids and total synthesis of Adriamycin; process research and formulation research and development of new drugs. *Mailing Add:* 34 Overlook Trail Morris Plains NJ 07950-1924

BORAKER, DAVID KENNETH, IMMUNOLOGY, IMMUNOGENETICS. *Current Pos:* PRES, CHROMOGEN CO, 85- *Personal Data:* b Los Angeles, Calif, Apr 21, 39; m 61; c 1. *Educ:* Univ Calif, Santa Barbara, BA, 62; Univ Calif, Los Angeles, PhD(med microbiol), 67. *Prof Exp:* Immunologist, Dept Serol, Walter Reed Army Inst Res, DC, 67-69; from asst prof to assoc prof med microbiol, Col Med, Univ Vt, 69-85. *Mem:* AAAS. *Res:* Kinetics of induction of high and low dose immunological paralysis; comparative immunology of the double thymus of the South American degu. *Mailing Add:* Chromogen Co PO 128 Milton VT 05468

BORCH, RICHARD FREDERIC, CANCER PHARMACOLOGY, CANCER DRUG DESIGN. *Current Pos:* DEAN'S PROF PHARMACOL & PROF CHEM, UNIV ROCHESTER, 82-, DIR, CANCER CTR, 93- *Personal Data:* b Cleveland, Ohio, May 22, 41; m 62. *Educ:* Stanford Univ, BS, 62; Columbia Univ, MA, 63, PhD(chem), 65; Univ Minn, MD, 75. *Prof Exp:* Fel chem, Harvard Univ, 65-66; from asst prof to assoc prof org chem, Univ Minn, Minneapolis, 66-82. *Concurrent Pos:* Resident internal med, Univ Minn Hosp, 75-76. *Mem:* Am Chem Soc; Am Asn Cancer Res; AAAS; Am Soc Pharmacol & Exp Therapeut. *Res:* Synthesis of biologically active compounds; mechanisms of action of antineoplastic compounds; reduction of antineoplastics toxicity; pharmacology. *Mailing Add:* Dept Pharmacol Univ Rochester Med Ctr Rochester NY 14642-8711. *Fax:* 716-244-9283; *E-Mail:* rickb@wotan.medicine.rochester.edu

BORCHARD, RONALD EUGENE, veterinary pharmacology; deceased, see previous edition for last biography

BORCHARDT, GLENN (ARNOLD), SOIL MINERALOGY, TECTONICS & STRATIGRAPHY PEDOCHRONOLOGY. *Current Pos:* Nat Res Coun res assoc, US Geol Surv, 69-71, geochemist, 72-77, SOIL MINERALOGIST, CALIF DIV MINES & GEOL, 77-; CONSULT, 84- *Personal Data:* b Watertown, Wis, July 28, 42; m 65, Marilyn Gerbig; c Nina & Natalie. *Educ:* Univ Wis-Madison, BS, 64, MS, 66; Ore State Univ, PhD(soil mineral), 69. *Prof Exp:* Res asst soils, Int Minerals & Chem Corp, 64. *Concurrent Pos:* Assoc ed, Geol Soc Am, 73-82. *Mem:* AAAS; Soil Sci Soc Am; Clay Minerals Soc; Geol Soc Am; Am Geophys Union; Asn Eng Geol. *Res:* Instrumental neutron activation analysis correlation of volcanic ash; multivariate similarity analysis; quantitative soil clay mineralogy; chemical stabilization of landslides; soil smectites; recency of faulting in soils; scientific worldview. *Mailing Add:* PO Box 5335 Berkeley CA 94705. *Fax:* 510-654-2935; *E-Mail:* soiltecton@aol.com

BORCHARDT, HANS J, FLUORINE CHEMISTRY. *Current Pos:* RETIRED. *Personal Data:* b Berlin, Ger, Jan 26, 30; US citizen; m 53; c 5. *Educ:* Brooklyn Col, BS, 52, MA, 53; Univ Wis, PhD(phys chem), 56. *Prof Exp:* Inorg chemist, Gen Eng Lab, Gen Elec Co, 56-59; sr res chemist, Explosives Dept, E I du Pont de Nemours & Co, 60-64, sr res chemist, Cent Res Dept, 65-69, sr res chemist org chem, 69-75, res assoc, Freon Prod Lab, 75-80. *Mem:* Am Chem Soc; Sigma Xi; Am Soc Heating, Refrig & Air Conditioning Engrs. *Res:* Differential thermal analysis; reactions in the solid state; rare earth solid state chemistry; phase equilibria; oxidation of metals; rare earth luminescence; lasers; crystal growth; fluorocarbon chemistry; chemical and physical properties of fluorocarbons. *Mailing Add:* 4062 DuPont Pkwy Townsend DE 19734

BORCHARDT, JOHN KEITH, SYNTHETIC ORGANIC CHEMISTRY, PHYSICAL ORGANIC CHEMISTRY. *Current Pos:* sr res chemist, 84-92, STAFF RES CHEMIST, SHELL DEVELOP CO, 92- *Personal Data:* b Evanston, Ill, June 2, 46. *Educ:* Ill Inst Technol, BS, 68; Univ Rochester, PhD(chem), 73. *Prof Exp:* Lab technician chem, Ill Inst Technol, 68; fel, Univ Notre Dame, 72-74; res chemist, Hercules, Inc, 74-77; sr chemist, 77-80, develop chemist, Halliburton Serv, 80-84. *Concurrent Pos:* Contrib ed, The Hexagon; counr, chmn two local sects, Am Chem Soc; mem fluid mechs & oil recovery process tech comt, Soc Petrol Engrs; prog chmn, Fiber Recycling, Tech Asn Pulp & Paper Indust. *Mem:* Soc Petrol Engrs; Tech Assoc Pulp & Paper Industs; Sigma Xi; Am Chem Soc; NY Acad Sci; Can Pulp & Paper Asn. *Res:* Mechanism of elimination reactions; mechanism of cycloaddition reactions; synthesis and modification of water soluble polymers; mechanism of cycloaddition reactions; synthesis of small and medium ring compounds; polymer chemistry; surfactant chemistry; removal of ink from used paper for paper recycling. *Mailing Add:* 8010 Vista Del Sol Dr Houston TX 77083-5039

BORCHARDT, KENNETH, MICROBIOLOGY, SEXUALLY TRANSMITTED DISEASES. *Current Pos:* asst chief, Vet Dept, Med Lab, Ger, 54-56, CHIEF CLIN MICROBIOL, USPHS HOSP, 65-, SCI DIR, 68-, STAFF MEM, AT SAN FRANCISCO STATE HOSP, 75- *Personal Data:* b Chicago, Ill, Sept 20, 28; m 54; c Greg, Jeff & Kim. *Educ:* Loyola Univ, Ill, BS, 50; Miami Univ, MS, 51; Tulane Univ, PhD(microbiol), 61. *Prof Exp:* Asst chief bact, Fitzsimmons Gen Hosp, 57-58; chief clin microbiol, Letterman Gen Hosp, 61-65. *Concurrent Pos:* Dir res, Biomed Diag, San Jose, Calif. *Mem:* Fel Am Pub Health Asn; fel Am Acad Microbiol; Sigma Xi; fel Royal Soc Trop Med & Hyg. *Res:* Clinical research in infectious disease associated with problems in urology, dermatology, ophthalmology and internal medicine; sexually transmitted diseases. *Mailing Add:* 15 Capilano Dr Novato CA 94949-5824

BORCHARDT, RONALD T, DRUG DELIVERY, DRUG DESIGN. *Current Pos:* from asst prof to prof biochem, 71-81, COURTESY PROF MED CHEM, UNIV KANS, 79-, SLOAN E SUMMERFIELD PROF BIOCHEM, 81-, SLOAN E SUMMERFIELD PROF CHEM & CHMN DEPT, 83- *Personal Data:* b Wausau, Wis, Feb 18, 44; m 66; c 3. *Educ:* Univ Wis-Madison, BS, 67; Univ Kans, Lawrence, PhD(med chem), 70. *Honors & Awards:* Sato Mem Int Award, Pharmaceut Soc Japan & Found Advan Educ Sci, 81; Dolph C Simons Sr Award Biomed Res, Univ Kans, 83. *Prof Exp:* Sr res asst, NIH, 69-71. *Concurrent Pos:* Estab investr, Am Heart Asn, 74-79; consult Merck, Sharp & Dohme Labs, 80-85, Upjohn Co, 84-, Glaxo, Inc, 87-; Victorian prof, Victorian Col Pharm, Melbourne, Australia, 83-; dir, Ctr Biomed Res, 81-88. *Mem:* Am Chem Soc; Am Soc Pharmacol & Exp Therapeut; Am Soc Biol Chemists; Soc Neurosci; Am Pharmaceut Asn; AAAS. *Res:* Biochemistry and chemistry of S-adenosylmethionine-dependent methyltransferases; central nervous system epinephrine and hypertension; mechanism of action of neurotoxins; metabolic and transport properties of isolated gastrointestinal mucosal cells and capillary endothelial cells (blood brain barrier). *Mailing Add:* Dept Pharmaceut Chem Univ Kans Sch Pharm 2095 Constant Ave Simons Res Lab Lawrence KS 66047

BORCHERS, EDWARD ALAN, PLANT BREEDING. *Current Pos:* plant breeder, Va Truck & Ornamentals Res Sta, 56-72, dir, 73-85, DIR, HAMPTON ROADS AGR EXP STA & PROF HORT, VA TECH, 85- *Personal Data:* b Spring Lake, NJ, Feb 26, 25; m 53; c 2. *Educ:* Cornell Univ, BS, 51; Univ NC, MS, 53; Univ Calif, PhD(plant path), 57. *Prof Exp:* Asst hort, State Col Agr & Eng, Univ NC, 51-53; asst veg crops, Univ Calif, 53-56. *Mem:* Am Soc Hort Sci. *Res:* Breeding of vegetable crops. *Mailing Add:* 4177 Ewell Rd Virginia Beach VA 23455

BORCHERS, HAROLD ALLISON, ENTOMOLOGY. *Current Pos:* assoc prof, 68-79, PROF BIOL, BEMIDJI STATE UNIV, 79- *Personal Data:* b Chicago Heights, Ill, June 6, 35; m 60; c 3. *Educ:* Iowa State Univ, BS, 61, MS, 64, PhD(entom, parasitol), 68. *Prof Exp:* Res assoc agr bee lab, Ohio State Univ, 63; instr zool & entom, Iowa State Univ, 65-68. *Mem:* Entom Soc Am; Sigma Xi; Soc Agr Res. *Res:* Nest-cleaning behavior of honey bees; populations of mites symbiotic on necrophilous beetles; diets of entomophagous fish. *Mailing Add:* 1636 Silver Lake Rd NW Bemidji MN 56601-2699

BORCHERS, RAYMOND (LESTER), biochemistry; deceased, see previous edition for last biography

BORCHERT, HAROLD R, ADMINISTRATION OF A RADIATION CONTROL PROGRAM, HEALTH PHYSICS IMPACTS FOR PUBLIC HEALTH & SAFETY. *Current Pos:* DIR, DIV RADIOL HEALTH, NEBR DEPT HEALTH, 85- *Personal Data:* b Fairbault, Minn, Apr 3, 40; m 84; c 4. *Educ:* NDak State Univ, BS, 64, MS, 74. *Prof Exp:* Grad asst, NDak State Univ, 70-73, asst radiation safety officer, 73-76; chief mat licensing & control sect, Kans Dept Health & Environ, 76-84; radiol assessment specialist, Kans Gas & Elec Co, 84-85. *Mem:* Conf Radiation Control Prog Dirs Inc; Health Physics Soc; Am Pharmaceut Asn; Air & Waste Mgt Asn. *Res:* Radon concentrations and dose impacts on humans including the various parameters that affect the concentrations; emergency response activities; dose impacts from radiation sources; radiation control program impacts on public health and safety. *Mailing Add:* 611 S 48th Lincoln NE 68516-3102

BORCHERT, PETER JOCHEN, ORGANIC CHEMISTRY. *Current Pos:* RETIRED. *Personal Data:* b Allenstein, Ger, Feb 6, 23; m 58; c 1. *Educ:* Univ Würzburg, BS, 48, MS, 51; Hannover Tech Univ, PhD(org chem), 53. *Prof Exp:* Chemist, Ind Farm Endoquimica, Sao Paulo, Brazil, 54, E F Drew, Sao Paulo, 55 & Fabrica de Pintura Montana, Caracas, Venezuela, 56-57; dir chem res lab, Marschall Div, Miles Labs, Inc, 58-73, dir res & develop, Sumner Div, 73-87. *Mem:* Am Chem Soc. *Res:* Animal poisons; detergents; auxiliary textile products; polymers; paints; carbohydrates; organic synthesis. *Mailing Add:* 28993 Ella Dr Elkhart IN 46514

BORCHERT, ROLF, ECOPHYSIOLOGY & PHENOLOGY OF TROPICAL TREES. *Current Pos:* assoc prof, 68-74, PROF BOT, UNIV KANS, 74- *Personal Data:* b Frankfurt-Main, Ger, May 7, 33; c 3. *Educ:* Univ Frankfurt, PhD(bot), 61. *Prof Exp:* Instr bot, Univ Frankfurt, 61-62; prof, Univ Andes, Colombia, 62-68. *Mem:* Am Soc Plant Physiol; Ecol Soc Am. *Res:* Growth and development of trees; calcium excretion by plants. *Mailing Add:* Dept Physiol & Cell Biol Univ Kans Lawrence KS 66045

BORCHERTS, ROBERT H, SYSTEMS SCIENCE, ELECTRONIC CONTROLS. *Current Pos:* VPRES, ZEXEL USA CORP, 89- *Personal Data:* b Mt Vernon, NY, Mar 22, 36; m 59; c 2. *Educ:* Gen Motors Inst, Eng dipl, 57; Univ Mich, MS, 59, PhD(electron spin resonance), 63. *Prof Exp:* Res asst radiation effects & electron spin resonance, Univ Mich, 61-63; res physicist, Inst Solid State Physics, Univ Tokyo, 63-64; res scientist, Sci Lab, Ford Motor Co, 65-83; staff res engr & activites head, Gen Motors Res Lab, 83-89. *Mem:* AAAS; Soc Automotive Engrs; Inst Elec & Electronics Engrs. *Res:* Magnetic resonance; optical spectroscopy; Josephson junctions; magnetic suspension; automotive control systems, suspension ride measurements, engine control, automotive fuel economy and emissions; vehicle systems; electronic controls; in-vehicle navigation. *Mailing Add:* Zexel USA Corp 37735 Enterprise Farmington Hills MI 48331. *E-Mail:* zexelfh@ix.netcom.com

BORDAN, JACK, education administration, for more information see previous edition

BORDELEAU, LUCIEN MARIO, MICROBIOLOGY, RESEARCH MANAGEMENT. *Current Pos:* RETIRED. *Personal Data:* b Quebec City, Can, July 6, 40; m 67; c 3. *Educ:* Laval Univ, BSc, 65, MSc, 67; Rutgers Univ, PhD(microbiol), 71. *Prof Exp:* Teacher biol, Tilly Regional Sch Bd, Que, 65-67; res officer, Can Agr, Que, 67-71, res scientist, 71-95, prog header, 76-95, group head, 86-95. *Concurrent Pos:* Assoc ed, Can J Microbiol, 75-78, Mircen J Appl Microbiol Biotech, 85-88; consult, CPVQ-Agr Que, 76-77, Nat Acad Sci, Wash, 80-, UNESCO, 81- *Mem:* Can Soc Microbiologists; Am Soc Microbiol; Can Col Microbiologists; Agr Inst Can. *Res:* Biological nitrogen fixation in the rhizobium-legumes system; bio-degradation; bio-fertilizers; inoculants technologies. *Mailing Add:* 1491 JC-Cantin Cap-Rouge PQ G1Y 2X7 Can

BORDEN, EDWARD B, INTESTINAL MOTILITY DISORDERS. *Current Pos:* DOCTOR PROCTOL, 87- *Personal Data:* b New York, NY, Dec 5, 49; m 76; c 2. *Educ:* Polytechnic Inst Brooklyn, BS, 72, MS, 72; Albert Einstein Col Med, MD, 76. *Prof Exp:* Asst prof surg, Albert Einstein Col Med, 82-87. *Concurrent Pos:* Asst attend surg, Montefiore Med Ctr, 81- *Mem:* Fel Am Col Surgeons; Inst Elec & Electronics Engrs; Am Motility Soc. *Res:* Clinical and experimental research in intestinal motility; mesenteric circulation; laboratory computer applications especially biological signal processing. *Mailing Add:* 625 Belle Terre Rd Suite 201 Port Jefferson NY 11777

BORDEN, ERNEST CARLETON, ONCOLOGY. *Current Pos:* from asst prof to prof oncol, 73-90, AM CANCER SOC PROF CLIN ONCOL, UNIV WIS, 84-; DIR, CANCER CTR & PROF MED, PEDIAT & MICROBIOL, MED COL WIS, 90- *Personal Data:* b Norwalk, Conn, July 12, 39; m 67, Louise Dise; c Kristin L & Sandra (Lanneau). *Educ:* Harvard Univ, AB, 61; Duke Univ, MD, 66. *Honors & Awards:* Gold Medal, SAfrican Soc Med Oncol, 87; Silver Medal, Singapore Malaysia Acad Med, 90. *Prof Exp:* Intern, internal med, Duke Univ, 66-67; resident internal med, Univ Pa, 67-68; med officer virol, Ctr Dis Control, 68-70; teaching fel oncol, Johns Hopkins Univ, 70-73. *Concurrent Pos:* Assoc ed, J Interferon Res, 80- & J Biol Response Modifiers, 82-90; mem decision network comt, Biol Response Modifiers Prog, Nat Cancer Inst, 82-86; consult, Triton Biosci, 83-90 & Ares-Serono, Geneva, Switz, 91- *Mem:* Fel Am Col Physicians; Am Asn Cancer Res (pres, 88-89); Am Soc Clin Oncol; Am Asn Immunologists; Int Soc Interferon Res (pres, 88-89); Soc Biol Ther (pres, 87-88); Am Soc Hemat. *Res:* Mechanism of action and clinical application of immunomodulators and interferons. *Mailing Add:* Cancer Ctr Univ Md Sch Med 22 S Greene St Baltimore MD 21201

BORDEN, GEORGE WAYNE, organic chemistry, chemical engineering, for more information see previous edition

BORDEN, JAMES B, CHEMICAL ENGINEERING. *Current Pos:* RETIRED. *Personal Data:* b Platteville, Wis, Feb 5, 27; m 51, Rita Doerrmann; c 3. *Educ:* Univ Wis, BS, 50; Mass Inst Technol, MS, 52. *Prof Exp:* Engr, textile fiber dept, Res Div, E I du Pont de Nemours & Co Inc, 52-55, Dacron Res Lab, 55-56, sr engr, Dacron Tech Div, 56-60, sr res engr, 60-61, tech supvr, Nomex Tech Div, 61-64, sr supvr, 64-69, process supt, Dacron Mfg Div, 69-72, asst to dir Dacron Mfg Div, 72-74, planning mgr, Europe, 74-76, mgr spec studies, 76-78, mgr econ & policy, Mat & Logistics Dept, 78-89, chmn Int Cross Boarder Movement Goods Study 89-90. *Concurrent Pos:* Chmn, CMA Energy Comn, 84-85; vchmn, NAM Fossil Fuels Comt, 88-90, NPRA Tech Subcomt, 89-90; consult, 90- *Mem:* Am Chem Soc. *Res:* Textile fiber and synthetic fiber process and development; economic evaluation of new processes, products and end uses; European petrochemical industry and energy economics legislation and regulation. *Mailing Add:* 19104 Stone Brook Chapel Hill NC 27514

BORDEN, JOHN HARVEY, CHEMICAL ECOLOGY, PEST MANAGEMENT. *Current Pos:* from asst prof to assoc prof, 66-75, PROF BIOL SCI, SIMON FRASER UNIV, 75-, DIR, CHEM ECOL RES GROUP, 81-, INDUST RES PROF, 91- *Personal Data:* b Berkeley, Calif, Feb 6, 38; Can citizen; m 62, Edna R; c Patrick C & Ian M. *Educ:* Wash State Univ, BSc, 63; Univ Calif, Berkeley, MSc, 65, PhD(entom), 66. *Honors & Awards:* C G Hewitt Award, Entom Soc Can, 77, Gold Medal, 88; J E Bussart Mem Award, Entom Soc Am, 84; Gold Medal Natural & Appl Sci, Sci Coun BC, 85. *Prof Exp:* Res technician entom, Univ Calif, Berkeley, 63, teaching asst, 63-64. *Concurrent Pos:* Fel, NSF, 64-66; travel fel, Nat Res Coun, Can, 76-77; assoc mem chem ecol, Plant Biotechnol Inst, Nat Res Coun, Saskatoon, Sask, 85-95; mem, Premier's Adv Coun Sci & Technol, BC, 87-91, BC Forest Res Adv Coun, 90-; Killam res fel, Can Coun, 90-91. *Mem:* Fel Entom Soc Can; Entom Soc Am; Can Inst Forestry; Nat Asn Advan Sci; Int Soc Chem Ecol; Sigma Xi. *Res:* Host selection, pheromones, basic biology, sensory perception and the use of semiochemicals in the management of economically important forest and agricultural insects. *Mailing Add:* Dept Biol Sci Ctr Pest Mgt Simon Fraser Univ Burnaby BC V5A 1S6 Can. *Fax:* 604-291-3496; *E-Mail:* borden@sfu.ca

BORDEN, KENNETH DUANE, PHYSICAL CHEMISTRY, NUCLEAR CHEMISTRY. *Current Pos:* from asst prof to assoc prof, 68-79, PROF CHEM & DEPT CHMN, IND CENT UNIV, 79- *Personal Data:* b Floyd, NMex, May 4, 40; m 65; c 3. *Educ:* Eastern NMex Univ, BS, 62; Univ Ill, MS, 64; Univ Ark, PhD(nuclear chem), 68. *Mem:* Am Chem Soc; Sigma Xi. *Res:* Mass distribution from the fast neutron induced fission of heavy elements; use of radioactive tracers in reaction rate studies and reaction mechanisms. *Mailing Add:* Univ Indianapolis 1400 Hanna Ave Indianapolis IN 46227

BORDEN, ROGER R(ICHMOND), MECHANICAL ENGINEERING. *Current Pos:* from asst prof to assoc prof mech eng, 59-88, EMER PROF MECH ENG, WORCESTER POLYTECH INST, 88-, EMER PROF, FRANKLIN INST BOSTON, 90- *Personal Data:* b Fall River, Mass, June 7, 30; m 57, Constance E Linberg; c Andrew H & Meredith A. *Educ:* Mass Inst Technol, BS, 52 & 53; Worcester Polytech Inst, ME, 61; Assumption Col, MA, 76, CAGS, 81, CAPS, 88. *Prof Exp:* Asst, Sloan Lab Aircraft & Automotive Engines, Mass Inst Technol, 52-53; in charge, mech & mach design dept, Franklin Inst Boston, 53-54, head dept, 54-57, head mech eng technol, 88-90; head mech eng technol & mech technol design options, Wentworth Inst, 57-59. *Concurrent Pos:* Consult, Children's Med Ctr, Mass, Mass State Dept Pub Health & P K Lindsay Co; fel, Trans Syst Ctr, US Dept Trans, 80-81. *Mem:* Am Mech Engrs; Am Soc Eng Educ; Sigma Xi; Soc Automotive Engrs. *Res:* Thermodynamics; engineering materials; internal combustion engines; electronics; instrumentation. *Mailing Add:* Box 445 Sterling MA 01564

BORDEN, WESTON THATCHER, ORGANIC & THEORETICAL CHEMISTRY. *Current Pos:* assoc prof, 73-77, PROF CHEM, UNIV WASH, 77- *Personal Data:* b New York, NY, Oct 13, 43; div; c Alice & Michael. *Educ:* Harvard Univ, BA, 64, MA, 66, PhD(chem), 68. *Prof Exp:* From instr to asst prof chem, Harvard Univ, 68-73. *Concurrent Pos:* Humboldt sr scientist award. *Mem:* Am Chem Soc; The Chem Soc. *Res:* Theoretical organic chemistry; synthesis of molecules of theoretical interest; stereochemistry of organic reactions; reaction mechanisms. *Mailing Add:* Dept Chem Univ Wash Seattle WA 98195. *Fax:* 206-685-8665; *E-Mail:* borden@chem.washington.edu

BORDER, WAYNE ALLEN, MEDICINE. *Current Pos:* assoc prof, 83-85, PROF MED, UNIV UTAH SCH MED, 85- *Personal Data:* b Bremen, Ind, Feb 6, 43; m. *Educ:* Purdue Univ, BS, 65; Wash Univ, MD, 68; Am Bd Internal Med, dipl, 78; dipl, nephrol, 80. *Prof Exp:* Med intern, NC Mem Hosp, 68-69, med resident, 69-70; res assoc, Scripps Clin & Res Found, La Jolla, Calif, 73-75; nephrol fel, Harbor Univ Calif Los Angeles Med Ctr, Torrance, 75-76; from asst prof to assoc prof med, Univ Calif Los Angeles Sch Med, 76-82. *Concurrent Pos:* Dir immunol lab, Div Nephrol & Hypertension, Harbor Univ Calif Los Angeles Med Ctr, 76-82, assoc chief, 82; chief, Div Nephrol & Hypertension, Univ Utah Sch Med, 83-, dir, Dialysis Prog, 83- *Mem:* Am Soc Clin Invest; Am Fedn Clin Res; Am Soc Nephrol; Am Asn Immunologists; fel Am Col Physicians. *Res:* Nephrology. *Mailing Add:* Dept Med Div Nephrol Univ Utah Med Ctr Salt Lake City UT 84132-0001

BORDERS, ALVIN MARSHALL, CHEMISTRY. *Current Pos:* CONSULT, 82- *Personal Data:* b Mays, Ind, Mar 7, 14; m 37; c 3. *Educ:* Ind Univ, AB, 35, PhD(chem), 37. *Prof Exp:* Res chemist, Goodyear Tire & Rubber Co, 37-41, group leader, 41-46; chief polymer res br, Off Rubber Reserve, Reconstruction Finance Corp, DC, 46; res coordr, Goodyear Tire & Rubber Co, 47; assoc, Inst Paper Chem, Lawrence Col, 48-50; group leader res, Minn Mining & Mfg Co, 50-52, assoc dir res, 52-58, res mgr, Reflective Prod Div, 58-62, dir, Appl Res Lab, Cent Res Labs, 62-65, dir, Chem Res Lab, 65-71 & Mat Sci & Process Res, 70-74, dir, Univ related progs, Cent Res Labs, 74-79, consult, 79-80; actg patent adminr, Univ Minn, 81-82. *Mem:* Am Chem Soc. *Res:* Chemistry of rubber and rubber-like materials; styrene-diene resins; paper; fluorochemicals and adhesives; research administration. *Mailing Add:* 536 Eastlake Dr SE Rio Rancho NV 87124-1898

BORDERS, CHARLES LAMONTE, JR, BIOCHEMISTRY. *Current Pos:* PROF CHEM, COL WOOSTER, 68- *Personal Data:* b Lebanon, Ky, June 13, 42; c 3. *Educ:* Bellarmine Col, Ky, BA, 64; Calif Inst Technol, PhD(chem), 68. *Mem:* Am Chem Soc; Am Soc Biol Chemists; AAAS. *Res:* Protein chemistry; enzymology. *Mailing Add:* Dept Chem Col Wooster Wooster OH 44691

BORDERS, DONALD B, ORGANIC CHEMISTRY. *Current Pos:* PRES, BIOSOURCE PHARM INC, 93- *Personal Data:* b Logansport, Ind, Jan 12, 32; m 58, Irene Trinkun; c Linda & Noreen. *Educ:* Ind Univ, BS, 54, MA, 58; Univ Ill, PhD(chem), 63. *Prof Exp:* Res chemist, Rohm and Haas Co, 62-64; res chemist, Lederle Labs, Am Cynamid Co, 64-66, group leader fermentation & isolation dept, 66-75, group leader microbiol & chemother res dept, 75-77, group leader, Microbiol Res Dept, 87-93. *Mem:* Am Chem Soc; The Chem Soc. *Res:* Syntheses of biologically active compounds; monomer and polymer syntheses; detection, purification, identification and structure of natural products and other antibiotics. *Mailing Add:* 13 Heatherhill Lane Suffern NY 10901

BORDERS, JAMES ALAN, SOLID STATE PHYSICS. *Current Pos:* physicist, 68-78, SUPVR SURFACE CHEM & ANALYTICAL DIV, SANDIA LABS, 78- *Personal Data:* b Akron, Ohio, Aug 8, 41; m 69. *Educ:* Reed Col, BA, 63; Univ Ill, Urbana, MS, 65, PhD(physics), 68. *Prof Exp:* Res asst physics, Univ Ill, Urbana, 63-68. *Mem:* fel Am Phys Soc; Sigma Xi; Electrochem Soc; Am Vacuum Soc. *Res:* Energetic ion backscattering analysis of solid surfaces and thin films; channeling location of ion-implanted impurities; formation of non-equilibrium alloys in metals by ion implantation. *Mailing Add:* Sandia Nat Labs Orig 1823 PO Box 5800 Albuquerque NM 87185

BORDIN, GERALD M, MEDICINE, PATHOLOGY. *Current Pos:* ANAT PATHOLOGIST, HOSP SCRIPPS CLIN, 76- *Personal Data:* b San Francisco, Calif, Sept 27, 40; m 64; c 2. *Educ:* Univ Calif, Berkeley, BA, 62; St Louis Univ, MD, 66. *Prof Exp:* Surg pathologist, Med Sch, Univ NMex, 72-73; anat pathologist, Lovelace-Bataan Med Ctr, 73-74; surg pathologist, Med Sch, Univ NMex, 75-76. *Concurrent Pos:* Advan clin fel, Am Cancer Soc, 71-72, jr fac clin fel, 72-73. *Mem:* Am Soc Clin Pathologists; Am Col Pathologists; US-Can Acad Path. *Res:* Cancer epidemiology; vascular biology, pathology, thrombosis. *Mailing Add:* Dept Path 10666 N Torrey Pines La Jolla CA 92037

BORDINE, BURTON W, MICROPALEONTOLOGY, PALEOBIOLOGY. *Current Pos:* MEM STAFF, PHILLIPS PETROL CO, 81- *Personal Data:* b Monroe, Mich, Nov 28, 34; m 61; c 5. *Educ:* Western Mich Univ, BS, 63; Brigham Young Univ, MS, 65; La State Univ, PhD(paleont), 74. *Prof Exp:* Geologist-micropaleontologist, Exxon Corp, 65-68; instr, Eastern Ariz Col, 68-70 & 74-75; asst prof, Middle Tenn State Univ, 75-81. *Mem:* Am Asn Petrol Geologists. *Res:* Neogene foraminifera of northern South America; relationship of trace fossils to benthic foraminifera; cenozoic foraminifera of California. *Mailing Add:* 1601 Wilson Hill Rd Readyville TN 37149

BORDNER, CHARLES ALBERT, JR, PHYSICS. *Current Pos:* ASST PROF PHYSICS, COLO COL, 66- *Personal Data:* b Salem, Mass, Nov 19, 37; m 60; c 2. *Educ:* Colo Col, BS, 59; Harvard Univ, AM, 60, PhD(physics), 64. *Prof Exp:* Res assoc physics, Harvard Univ, 64-66. *Concurrent Pos:* Vis staff mem, Mass Inst Technol, 65-66. *Mem:* Am Phys Soc; AAAS; Am Asn Physics Teachers; Sigma Xi. *Res:* Experimental high energy physics. *Mailing Add:* Dept Physics Colo Col 14 E Cachela Poudre Colorado Springs CO 80903

BORDNER, JON D B, ORGANIC CHEMISTRY, BIOCHEMISTRY. *Current Pos:* RES ADV, PFIZER CENT RES, 85- *Personal Data:* b Massillon, Ohio, Jan 25, 40; m 69; c 3. *Educ:* Case Inst Technol, BS, 62; Univ Calif, Berkeley, PhD(org chem), 66. *Prof Exp:* Fel x-ray crystallog, Calif Inst Technol, 66-69; from asst prof to prof chem, NC State Univ, 69-85. *Concurrent Pos:* Dreyfus teacher-scholar, 72; consult, Pfizer Inc, 74-85. *Mem:* Am Chem Soc; Am Crystallog Asn; Sigma Xi. *Res:* Structure and function of steroids; insect pheromones; molecular neurochemistry; x-ray crystallographics. *Mailing Add:* Pfizer Cent Res Eastern Pt Rd Groton CT 06340-5196

BORDOGNA, JOSEPH, MANUFACTURING, SCIENCE POLICY. *Current Pos:* ASST DIR ENG, NSF, 91- *Personal Data:* b Scranton, Pa, Mar 22, 33. *Educ:* Univ Pa, BSEE, 55, PhD(elec eng), 64; Mass Inst Technol, SM, 60. *Honors & Awards:* George Westinghouse Award, Am Soc Eng Educ, 74; Centennial Medal Inst Elec Electronics Eng, 84; Am Indust Modernization Leadership Award, Nat Coalition Advan Mfg, 93. *Prof Exp:* Engr, RCA Corp, 58-64; asst prof, Univ Pa, 64, Winterstein asst prof, 64-68, from assoc prof to prof, 68-76, master, Stouffer Col House, 72-76, from assoc dean to dean eng & appl sci, 73-90, Alfred Filter Moore prof eng, 76-90, dir, Moore Sch Elec Eng, 76-90. *Concurrent Pos:* Mem, USN, 55-58; consult; mem bd dirs, Roy F Weston Inc, West Chester, Pa, AOI Int, Lowell, Mass & Univ City Sci Ctr, Philadelphia, Pa; chair, Adv Comt Eng, NSF, 89-91; mem pres comt, Nat Medal Sci, 89-91; bd dirs, Accreditation Bd Eng & Technol, 90-91; chair working group, Fed Initiative Advan Mfg Technol, 93-94. *Mem:* Fel Inst Elec & Electronics Engrs; fel Am Soc Eng Educ; fel AAAS; Nat Soc Prof Engrs. *Res:* Electro-optics; author of books in electrical engineering and technological literacy and papers on educational innovation. *Mailing Add:* NSF 4201 Wilson Blvd Arlington VA 22230. *Fax:* 703-306-0289; *E-Mail:* jbordogna@nsf.gov

BORDOLOI, KIRON, SOLID STATE PHYSICS. *Current Pos:* assoc prof eng physics, 69-78, PROF ELEC ENG, UNIV LOUISVILLE, 78- *Personal Data:* b Jorhat, India, Oct 1, 34; m 61; c 2. *Educ:* Gauhati Univ, India, BSc, 55; Univ Calcutta, MSc, 57; La State Univ, PhD(physics), 64. *Prof Exp:* Lectr physics, J B Col, India, 57-58; asst, La State Univ, 58-63; asst prof, Univ Southern Miss, 63-69. *Mem:* Am Physiol Soc; sr mem Inst Elec & Electronics Engrs; Soc Photo-Optical Instrumentation Engrs. *Res:* Low temperature physics. *Mailing Add:* 9809 Tamarisk Pkwy Louisville KY 40223

BORDWELL, FREDERICK GEORGE, ORGANIC CHEMISTRY. *Current Pos:* Procter & Gamble fel, 41-42, from instr to prof, 42-54, EMER CLARE HAMILTON HALL PROF CHEM, NORTHWESTERN UNIV, 74-, EMER PROF CHEM & RES FEL, 86- *Personal Data:* b Marmarth, NDak, Jan 17, 16; m 39, 72; c 2. *Educ:* Univ Minn, BS, 37, PhD(org chem), 41. *Hon Degrees:* Dr, Univ Goteborg, Swed, 91. *Honors & Awards:* Humble Lectr, 53 & 57; Am Chem Soc Award Petrol Chem, 86; H C Brown Lectr, 86; C K Ingold Lectr, 87; Arthur CeCope Scholar Award, 91; Weisberger-Williams Lectr, 93. *Concurrent Pos:* NSF sr fel, 57; Guggenheim fel, 80; vis prof, Univ Ill, 57, Univ Wales, 75, Univ Western Ont, 76, Univ Calif, Irvine, 79, 84, 85, 86, 87, 88. *Mem:* Am Chem Soc. *Res:* Mechanisms of organic reactions; chemistry of organic sulfur compounds; acidities of weak acids; organic electrochemistry. *Mailing Add:* Dept Chem Northwestern Univ Evanston IL 60201

BOREIKO, CRAIG JOHN, GENETIC TOXICOLOGY, EXPERIMENTAL ONCOLOGY. *Current Pos:* Assoc scientist, 79-80, SCIENTIST, CHEM INDUST INST TOXICOL, 80- *Personal Data:* b Milford, Ct, June 5, 51; m 75; c 2. *Educ:* Clark Univ, BA, 73; Univ Wis-Madison, PhD(exp oncol), 79. *Mem:* Environ Mutagen Soc; Genetic Toxicol Asn; Am Asn Cancer Res. *Res:* Chemically induced oncogenic transformation of cultured human cells; cell culture models for initiation and promotion; regulation and characteristics of the transformed state. *Mailing Add:* 102 Oakstone Dr Chapel Hill NC 27514

BOREK, CARMIA GANZ, CELL BIOLOGY. *Current Pos:* from asst prof to assoc prof, 71-81, PROF PATH & RADIOL, COLUMBIA UNIV, 81-, PROF COMMUNITY HEALTH, 94- *Personal Data:* b Tel Aviv, Israel, May 27, 37; US citizen; m 58; c 2. *Educ:* Am Univ, BSc, 59; George Washington Univ, MSc, 61; Weizmann Inst Sci, PhD(cell biol, genetics), 67. *Prof Exp:* Res asst biochem, Sch Med, Georgetown Univ, 61-62; res asst, Sect Endocrinol, Nat Inst Arthritis & Metab Dis, 63; res assoc cell physiol, Col Physicians & Surgeons, Columbia Univ, 67-69; instr path, Sch Med, NY Univ, 69-71. *Concurrent Pos:* Nat Cancer Inst fel physiol, Col Physicians & Surgeons, Columbia Univ, 67-69. *Mem:* Am Soc Cell Biol; Am Asn Cancer Res; Sigma Xi; Int Soc Develop Biol; Am Tissue Cult Asn; fel NY Acad Sci. *Res:* cellular & molecular carcinogenesis (chemical radiation), anticarcinogenesis and nutritional chemoprevention. *Mailing Add:* Dept Community Health Div Nutrit 136 Harrison Ave Boston MA 02111

BOREK, FELIX, IMMUNOCHEMISTRY, ORGANIC CHEMISTRY. *Current Pos:* RETIRED. *Personal Data:* b Cracow, Poland, May 5, 26; US citizen; div. *Educ:* Hobart Col, BSc, 50; Harvard Univ, MA, 52; Rutgers Univ, PhD(org chem), 56. *Prof Exp:* Res asst chem, Rutgers Univ, 52-55; res fel biochem, Col Physicians & Surgeons, Columbia Univ, 55-57; assoc biochemist, Armed Forces Inst Path, 58-63; vis scientist, Weizmann Inst, 63-65, sr scientist, 65-67; asst prof microbiol & immunol, Albert Einstein Col Med, 67-72; founding ed, J Immunol Methods, 71-; sr lectr microbiol, Tel-Aviv Univ, 72-74. *Concurrent Pos:* Lectr, NIH, 60-63, spec res fel, 63-65. *Mem:* AAAS; Am Asn Immunol; NY Acad Sci; Biochem Soc Israel. *Res:* Specificity of delayed hypersensitivity; immunosuppression and immune tolerance in adult hosts; relation between immunogenicity and the molecular size and structure of antigens; localization of labeled antigens in the host; steroid-protein conjugates as antigens; the function of the spleen in immune responses. *Mailing Add:* Dept Microbiol Tel-Aviv Univ Tel-Aviv Israel

BOREL, ARMAND, MATHEMATICS. *Current Pos:* PROF, INST ADVAN STUDY, 57- *Personal Data:* b Switz, May 21, 23; m 52, Gabrielle Pittet; c Dominique & Ann. *Educ:* Swiss Fed Inst Technol, MS, 47; Univ Paris, PhD, 52. *Hon Degrees:* Univ Geneva, 72. *Honors & Awards:* Brouwer Medal, Dutch Math Soc, 78; Steele Prize, Am Math Soc, 91; Balzan Prize, 92. *Prof Exp:* Supplying prof algebra, Univ Geneva, 50-52; vis lectr, Univ Chicago, 54-55; prof, Swiss Fed Inst Technol, 55-56 & 83-86. *Concurrent Pos:* Vis prof, Mass Inst Technol, 58 & 69, Tata Inst, Bombay, 61, 83 & 90, Univ Paris, 64, Univ Calif, Berkeley, 75 & Yale Univ, 78. *Mem:* Nat Acad Sci; Math Soc France; Swiss Math Soc; foreign mem Finnish Acad Sci & Lett; assoc mem French Acad Sci; Am Philos Soc; Am Math Soc; Am Acad Arts & Sci. *Res:* Algebraic topology; lie groups; algebraic and arithmetic groups. *Mailing Add:* Inst Advan Study Princeton NJ 08540

BOREL, YVES, IMMUNOLOGY TOLERANCE, AUTO IMMUNITY. *Current Pos:* ASSOC PROF PEDIAT, RHEUMATOLOGY & IMMUNOL, SCH MED, HARVARD UNIV, 76- *Educ:* Univ Geneva, MD, 57. *Mailing Add:* Dept Immunol Nestec Ltd Vers-Chez-Les-Blanc PO Box 44 CH-1000 Lausanne 26 Switzerland

BORELLA, LUIS ENRIQUE, BIOCHEMISTRY. *Current Pos:* sr res assoc biochem & pharmacol, Ayerst Res Labs, 65-75, PRIN SCIENTIST, WYETH-AYERST RES, 75- *Personal Data:* b Sept 29, 30; Can citizen; m 66, Anne Willday; c Amanda & Amelia. *Educ:* Univ Buenos Aires, BSc, 50, MSc, 54; Univ Conn, MSc, 62, PhD(pharmacol), 64. *Prof Exp:* Pharmacist, 55-58; res asst clin chem, St Raphael's Hosp, New Haven, Conn, 58-60; Anna Bradbury Springer fel pharmacol, Univ Toronto, 64-65. *Mem:* Assoc AAAS; Can Pharmacol Soc; Sigma Xi. *Res:* Gastrointestinal physiology and pharmacology; drug effects on gastric acid secretion and experimental peptic ulcer; methodology in gastrointestinal research; gastrointestinal drug absorption; pharmacologic and biochemic effects of interaction between psychoactive drugs; inflammatory bowel disease; cytoprotection; anti-flammatory agents; osteoarthritis/osteoporosis; anorexiants. *Mailing Add:* 59 Sayre Dr Princeton NJ 08540-5825. *Fax:* 732-329-6695

BOREMAN, JOHN GEORGE, JR, BIOLOGY. *Current Pos:* DIR, COOP MARINE EDUC & RES PROG, NAT OCEANIC & ATMOSPHERIC ASN, UNIV MASS, 89- *Personal Data:* b Bronx, NY, Aug 15, 48; m 70; c 2. *Educ:* State Univ NY, BS, 70; Cornell Univ, MS, 72, PhD(fishery sci), 78. *Prof Exp:* Northeast power plant specialist, 74-75, aquatic ecologist, Nat Power Plant Team, US Fish & Wildlife Serv, 75-80; sr assessment scientist, Northeast Fisheries Ctr, Nat Marine Fisheries Serv, 80-85, chief res coord sect, 85-89. *Mem:* Am Fisheries Soc. *Res:* Fish population dynamics; impacts of entrainment and impingement by power plants on fish populations; quantitative approaches to fishery management. *Mailing Add:* 171 Aubinwood Rd Amherst MA 01002

BORENFREUND, ELLEN, BIOCHEMICAL GENETICS, CARCINOGENESIS. *Current Pos:* adj assoc prof, 81-88, MEM ADJ FAC, ROCKEFELLER UNIV, 88- *Personal Data:* b Ger, Mar 15, 22; US citizen. *Educ:* Hunter Col, BS, 46; NY Univ, MS, 48, PhD(biol), 57. *Honors & Awards:* Outstanding Woman Scientist, Asn Women Sci, 83. *Prof Exp:* Technician cancer res, Mt Sinai Hosp, 40-47; asst biochem, Col Physicians & Surgeons, Columbia Univ, 48-57; from res assoc to assoc, Sloan-Kettering Div, Grad Sch Med Sci, Cornell Univ, 57-65, from asst prof to assoc prof biochem, 61-81, chair, Biochem Unit, 72-74, assoc mem, Sloan-Kettering Inst Cancer Res, 65-88. *Concurrent Pos:* NIH res career develop award, 63-66. *Mem:* Am Asn Cancer Res; Am Soc Cell Biol; Am Soc Biol Chem; Tissue Cult Asn; Harvey Soc. *Res:* Nucleic acid biochemistry; biochemical genetics; cell transformation and chemical carcinogenesis in vivo and in vitro; in vitro toxicology; tissue culture. *Mailing Add:* Lab Animal Res Ctr Rockefeller Univ 1230 York Ave New York NY 10021

BORENSTEIN, BENJAMIN, food chemistry, organic chemistry, for more information see previous edition

BORER, JEFFREY STEPHEN, CARDIOLOGY. *Current Pos:* assoc prof, 79-82, PROF MED, CORNELL UNIV MED COL, 82-, GLADYS & ROLAND HARRIMAN PROF CARDIOVASC MED, 83- *Personal Data:* b Deland, Fla, Feb 22, 45; m 78; c 2. *Educ:* Harvard Col, BA, 65; Cornell Univ Med Col, MD, 69. *Honors & Awards:* Investrs Award Prize, Europ Soc Cardiol, 78; Spec Recognition Award, Asn Thoracic & Cardiovasc Surgeons India, 85. *Prof Exp:* Intern med, Mass Gen Hosp, 69-70, resident, 70- 71; clin assoc cardiol, Nat Heart, Lung & Blood Inst, 71-74, sr investr, 75-79. *Concurrent Pos:* Sr Fulbright-Hays scholar & Glorney Raisbeck fel med sci, Guy's Hosp, Univ London, Eng, 74-75; chmn Cardiac & Renal Drugs Adv Comt, US Food & Drug Admin, 81 & 83-87; mem, Life Sci Adv Comt, NASA, 84-88, Aerospace Adv Comt, 88-; prin investr, NIH, TIMI-Cornell Ctr, 84-90; pres, NY Cardiol Soc, 90-91. *Mem:* Am Soc Clin Res; Am Col Physicians; Am Col Cardiol; Am Col Chest Physicians; Am Heart Asn; Soc Nuclear Med. *Res:* Preclinical and clinical investigations in the areas of chronic and acute coronary artery disease and valvular heart disease. *Mailing Add:* NY Hosp Cornell Med Ctr Dept Cardiol 525 68th St Rm F467 New York NY 10021

BORER, KATARINA TOMLJENOVIC, NEUROENDOCRINOLOGY, PHYSIOLOGY. *Current Pos:* res fel physiol psychol, Univ Mich, 71-73, asst res scientist, Neurosci Lab, 73-77, lectr, Dept Psychol, 73-77, asst prof, 77-81, assoc prof, Dept Phys Educ, 81-88, PROF, DEPT MOVEMENT SCI, UNIV MICH, 88- *Personal Data:* b Tuzla, Yugoslavia, Sept 17, 40; US citizen; m 90, Paul E Wenger; c Elizabeth H (Meyer), Robert C III & Richard C. *Educ:* Univ Pa, BA, 62, PhD(zool), 66. *Prof Exp:* Lectr physiol & exp psychol, Alaska Methodist Univ, 68-69; lectr biol & comp vert anat, Anchorage Community Col, 68-69; NIH fel exp marine biol, Rosenstiel Sch Marine & Atmospheric Sci, Univ Miami, 69-70. *Concurrent Pos:* Fulbright-Hayes res fel, Sweden, 91. *Mem:* Endocrine Soc; Am Physiol Soc; Am Col Sports Med; Soc Neurosci. *Res:* Neuroendocrine mechanisms in weight regulation and growth in rodents; neuroendocrine effects of exercise; alteration by exercise of neuroendocrine controls over somatic growth and reproductive function; pharmacological and neurosurgical mainipulations of the central nervous system and measurement of pulsatile release of growth hormone. *Mailing Add:* Dept Movement Sci Univ Mich 401 Washtenaw Ann Arbor MI 48109-2214. *Fax:* 313-763-2206; *E-Mail:* usergb2b@umichum.edu

BORER, PHILIP N, NUCLEAR MAGNETIC RESONANCE SPECTROSCOPY. *Current Pos:* RES ASSOC PROF CHEM, SYRACUSE UNIV, 83- *Personal Data:* b Sept 23, 45; m 88; c 3. *Educ:* Univ Calif, Berkeley, PhD(chem), 72. *Res:* Nucleic acid chemistry. *Mailing Add:* Dept Chem Syracuse Univ 100 University Pl Syracuse NY 13244-0001

BORESI, ARTHUR PETER, THEORETICAL MECHANICS, APPLIED MECHANICS. *Current Pos:* prof, 80-95, EMER PROF CIVIL ENG, UNIV WYO, 95- & EMER PROF, UNIV ILL, 79- *Personal Data:* b Toluca, Ill, Aug 27, 24; m 46, C Jean Gordon; c Jennifer A (Hill), Annette (Pueschel) & Nancy J (Broderick). *Educ:* Univ Ill, BA, 48, MS, 49, PhD(theoret & appl mech), 53. *Honors & Awards:* Archie Higdon Distinguished Educator Award, Am Soc Eng Educ, 93. *Prof Exp:* Res engr dynamics, NAm Aviation, 50; mat engr, Nat Bur Stand, 51; from instr to prof theoret & appl mech, Univ Ill, Urbana, 52-80. *Concurrent Pos:* distinguished vis prof, Clarkson Col Technol, 68-69 & Naval Post-Grad Sch, Monterey, 78-79 & 86-87. *Mem:* Am Acad Mech (treas, 74-77); fel Am Soc Mech Engrs; fel Am Soc Civil Engrs; Am Soc Eng Educ; Sigma Xi; fel Am Acad Mech. *Res:* Stress analysis; dynamics; stability; energy methods in mechanics; theory of plates and shells; approximation methods in mechanics. *Mailing Add:* Dept Civil Engr Univ Wyo PO Box 3295 Laramie WY 82071. *E-Mail:* boresi@uwyo.edu

BORG, DONALD CECIL, MEDICAL RESEARCH. *Current Pos:* CONSULT, EASTMAN PHARMACEUTS, 88- *Personal Data:* b New York, NY, July 26, 26; m 49, 79; c 5. *Educ:* Harvard Univ, BS, 46, MD, 50. *Prof Exp:* Teaching fel med, Harvard Univ, 51-52; anal officer, Armed Forces Spec Weapons Proj, 52-54; teaching fel med, Washington Univ, 54-55; res assoc, 55-57, assoc scientist, 57-62, scientist, 62-79, chmn, Dept Med, 79-84, sr scientist, Brookhaven Nat Lab, 79-90. *Concurrent Pos:* Consult, Armed Forces Spec Weapons Proj, 54-57; vis res assoc prof physiol, Mt Sinai Sch Med, 68-; biophysicist, Div Biol & Med, US AEC, 70-72; mem adv bd, Nat Biomed ESR Ctr, 76-; consult, Resources for Future, 77-79, Merck & Co, 77-79. *Mem:* AAAS; Soc Nuclear Med; NY Acad Sci; Am Physiol Soc; Radiation Res Soc; Am Soc Biochem & Molecular Biol; Soc Free Radical Res; Soc Mag Res Med. *Res:* Free radical mechanisms in biological function mechanisms of oxidative cytotoxicity; electron paramagnetic resonance; health effects of energy production and use; radioactivation analysis; radiation effects; clinical research. *Mailing Add:* 36 Crestview Dr Princeton NJ 08540-7618

BORG, IRIS Y P, EARTH SCIENCES, MINERALOGY. *Current Pos:* RETIRED. *Personal Data:* b San Francisco, Calif, Oct 6, 28; m 50; c 1. *Educ:* Univ Calif, Berkeley, BS, 51, PhD(geol), 54. *Prof Exp:* Asst geol, Princeton Univ, 54-56, vis fel, 56-59; res assoc, Univ Calif, Berkeley, 60-61; geologist, Lawrence Livermore Lab, Univ Calif, 61-90. *Concurrent Pos:* Consult, Shell Develop Co, Tex, 55-67; Geol Soc Am proj grant, 57; Guggenheim fel, 68-69; vis lectr, Am Univ Cairo, Egypt, 71; lunar investr, NASA, 72; counr, Mineral Soc Am, 74-77; mem gov bd, Am Geol Inst, 75-77; US deleg, Int Mineral Asn USSR, 78; mem, Vis Comt Earth Sci, Mass Inst Technol, 78-84; affil, Energy Resource Group, Univ Calif, Berkeley, 78- *Mem:* Fel Geol Soc Am; Am Geophys Union; fel Mineral Soc Am; Am Asn Petrol Geologists. *Res:* Natural and artificial deformation of rocks and minerals; petrofabrics; high pressure x-ray technology; shock metamorphism; energy and natural resource issues. *Mailing Add:* PO Box 405 The Sea Ranch CA 95497

BORG, RICHARD JOHN, PHYSICAL CHEMISTRY. *Current Pos:* CONSULT, 90- *Personal Data:* b Calif, Oct 18, 25; m 50; c 1. *Educ:* Univ Calif, BS, 50, MS, 52; Princeton Univ, PhD(chem), 57. *Prof Exp:* Micro-analyst, Univ Calif, 51-52, res chemist, Radiation Lab, Livermore, 52-53; asst chem, Princeton Univ, 57-58, instr, 58-59; chemist, 59-75, div leader, Lawrence Livermore Lab, Univ Calif, 75-77; lectr, Univ Calif, Davis, 59-65, prof, 65-77; res chemist, Lawrence Livermore Lab, 77-90. *Concurrent Pos:* Ed, Mineral Processing & Extractive Metall Rev. *Mem:* Fel Am Phys Soc; Am Chem Soc. *Res:* Diffusion in ionic and metallic solids; Mossbauer measurements in metals; magnetic materials. *Mailing Add:* PO Box 405 The Sea Ranch CA 95497

BORG, ROBERT MUNSON, ECOLOGY. *Current Pos:* MGR, LILLIAN P BORG MEM FOREST, OSSIPEE, NH, 81- *Personal Data:* b Smithfield, Pa, May 19, 10; m 33; c 2. *Educ:* Univ Chicago, BS, 39, MS, 40. *Prof Exp:* Asst to staff, Harvard Univ, 29-31; asst forester, Dept Conserv, Mass, 33; tech forester, US Forest Serv, 33-35, supvry wildlife mgr, Mass, 35-36; asst dist agent, US Fish & Wildlife Serv, 40-45; fumigant engr, Dow Chem Co, Mich, 45. *Mem:* Soc Am Foresters. *Res:* Industrial and soil fumigation; agricultural chemicals; development of farm-forest ecosystems; Lillian P Borg memorial forest. *Mailing Add:* 235 Granite Rd Ossipee NH 03864

BORG, SIDNEY FRED, CIVIL ENGINEERING, EARTHQUAKE ENGINEERING. *Current Pos:* head civil eng, 52-77, prof, 52-87, EMER PROF CIVIL ENG, STEVENS INST TECHNOL, 87- *Personal Data:* b New York, NY, Oct 3, 16; m 44; c 4. *Educ:* Cooper Union, BSCE, 37; Polytech Inst New York, MCE, 40; Johns Hopkins Univ, DrEng, 56; Stevens Inst Technol, MEng, 58. *Honors & Awards:* Sigma Xi. *Prof Exp:* Engr, Turner Construct Co, 40-41; struct engr, Eastern Aircraft, 41-43; asst prof civil eng, Univ Md, 43-45; assoc prof aeronaut, Naval Postgrad Sch, 45-51; res engr, Grumman Aircraft Co, 51-52. *Concurrent Pos:* Consult to various pvt firms & govt agencies in eng mech & aeronaut, 50-; Fulbright prof, Danish Tech Univ, 65; vis prof, US State Dept, Polish Acad Sci, 68, Technische Hochschule, Stuttgart, 66 & 81, Israel Inst Technol, 72, Air Force Inst Technol, 73. *Mem:* Fel NY Acad Sci; fel Am Soc Civil Engrs; fel AAAS; Am Soc Eng Educ. *Res:* Solids and fluids; matrix and tensor analysis as applied to engineering; similarity methods in engineering; physical, medical sciences and the humanities; earthquake engineering. *Mailing Add:* 655 Pomander Walk Teaneck NJ 07666

BORG, THOMAS K, CARDIAC STRUCTURE FUNCTION. *Current Pos:* PROF PATH & DIR ELECTROMICROS, MED SCH, UNIV SC, 76- *Personal Data:* b Chicago, Ill, Sept 12, 43. *Educ:* Univ Wis, PhD(entom), 69. *Mem:* Am Soc Cell Biol; Soc Int Heart Res; Electromicros Soc. *Mailing Add:* Dept Develop Biol & Anat Sch Med Univ SC Columbia SC 29208-0001

BORGAONKAR, DIGAMBER SHANKARRAO, GENETICS, CYTOLOGY. *Current Pos:* DIR, CYTOGENETICS LAB, MED CTR DEL, NEWARK, 80- *Personal Data:* b Hyderabad, India, Sept 24, 32; m 63, Manda Purandare; c Raj & Sonya. *Educ:* Osmania Univ, India, BScAgr, 53; Okla State Univ, PhD(genetics), 63. *Honors & Awards:* JBS Haldane Award, Soc Bionaturalists, India. *Prof Exp:* Res asst, Indian Dept Agr, Hyderabad & Bombay, 55-59, lectr agr bot, Parbhani, 56-57; asst, Univ Minn, 59; res assoc bot, Okla State Univ, 59-63; asst prof biol, Univ NDak, 63-64; from instr to asst prof med & head chromosome lab, Johns Hopkins Univ, 64-71, assoc prof med, Div Med Genetics, Sch Med, 72-78; dir res, Genetics Ctr & prof biol sci, NTex State Univ, Denton, 78-80. *Concurrent Pos:* Grantee, Sigma Xi, 64, Am Philos Soc, 67, NSF, 66-68 & NIMH, 69-73; adj prof, Sch Life & Health Sci, Univ Del; res prof pediat med genetics, Thomas Jefferson Univ, Philadelphia; Dr Margaret I Handy chair human genetics, Med Ctr Del, 81-; investr, Alzheimer Res, Crystal Trust, Wilmington, Del, 93. *Mem:* AAAS; Am Soc Human Genetics; Sigma Xi; Am Col Med Genetics. *Res:* Human cytogenetics and genetics; mammalian cytogenetics; computer data bases of human chromosomal abnormalties. *Mailing Add:* Cytogen Lab Christiana Hosp 4755 Ogletown Station Rd PO Box 6001 Newark DE 19718. *Fax:* 302-733-3773; *E-Mail:* borgaonkar.d@mcd.gen.de.us

BORGATTI, ALFRED LAWRENCE, MICROBIOLOGY, ENTOMOLOGY. *Current Pos:* RETIRED. *Personal Data:* b Medford, Mass, Apr 28, 28. *Educ:* Tufts Univ, BS, 51, EdM, 52; Mich State Univ, PhD(entom), 61. *Prof Exp:* Teacher math & sci, Everett Pub Schs, Mass, 54-58; instr entom, Mich State Univ, 58-61; prof biol, Salem State Col, 61-92. *Concurrent Pos:* Consult, Briggs Eng Co, 80-84. *Mem:* Sigma Xi; Entom Soc Am; Am Soc Microbiol. *Res:* Microbial diseases of insects. *Mailing Add:* 8 Normandy Dr Peabody MA 01960

BORGEAT, PIERRE, LEUKOTRIENES, INFLAMMATION. *Current Pos:* Sr researcher, 79-85, assoc prof, 85-90, PROF PHYSIOL, FAC MED, LAVAL UNIV, 90- *Personal Data:* b Montreal, Que, May 22, 47; m 71, Anne Gourdeau; c Louis, Martin & Mathieu. *Educ:* Col des Jesuites de Que, BA, 67; Laval Univ, BSc, 71, DSc, 74. *Honors & Awards:* Leo-Pariseau Prize, Can-Fr Asn Advan Sci, 88; Distinguished Scientist Award, Can Soc Clin Invest, 89. *Concurrent Pos:* Ed, Prostaglandins Leukotrienes & Essential Fatty Acids, 82-; assoc prof, Dept Pharmacol, Fac Med, Univ Sherbrooke, 90- *Mem:* Clin Res Club Que; Can-Fr Asn Advan Sci; Can Biochem Soc; Can Soc Clin Invest; Int Soc Immunopharmacol. *Res:* Physiological and pharmacological control of leukotrienes synthesis; role of leukotrienes in allergic reactions and inflammation; assay methods for lipid mediators of inflammation. *Mailing Add:* Cent Hosp de l'Univ Laval 2705 Boul Laurier Ste-Foy PQ G1V 4G2 Can. *Fax:* 418-654-2765; *E-Mail:* sec.crri@crchul.ulaval.ca

BORGENS, RICHARD BEN, DEVELOPMENTAL BIOLOGY, NEUROBIOLOGY. *Current Pos:* AT DEPT ANAT, SCH VET MED, PURDUE UNIV. *Personal Data:* b Little Rock, Ark, May 7, 46; c 2. *Educ:* NTex State Univ, BS, 70, MS, 73; Purdue Univ, PhD(biol), 77. *Prof Exp:* Res assoc biol, Purdue Univ, 77-78; res assoc biol, Yale Univ, 78-80; assoc staff scientist, Jackson Lab, Bar Harbor, Maine, 80-81; staff scientist, Inst Med Res, 81- *Concurrent Pos:* Nat Paraplegia Found fel, 78-80. *Mem:* Am Soc Zoologists; Soc Develop Biol. *Res:* General problems of development, particularly the role of endogenous electrical fields in amphibian limb regeneration; role of endogenous and applied current on spinal cord regeneration. *Mailing Add:* RR 4 Delphi IN 46923

BORGES, CARLOS REGO, MATHEMATICS. *Current Pos:* from asst prof to assoc prof, 65-72, PROF MATH, UNIV CALIF, DAVIS, 72- *Personal Data:* b Sao Miguel, Portugal, Feb 17, 39; US citizen; m 58, Margaret Freitas; c Carlos F, Michael F & Mary Lou F. *Educ:* Humboldt State Col, BA, 60; Univ Wash, PhD(math), 64. *Prof Exp:* Asst prof math, Univ Nev, 64-65. *Concurrent Pos:* NSF grants, 65-68; Fulbright-Hays scholar, 71. *Mem:* Am Math Soc. *Res:* General topology; extension and retraction theory; generalized metrizable spaces. *Mailing Add:* Dept Math Univ Calif Davis CA 95616. *E-Mail:* cborges@math.ucdavis.edu

BORGES, WAYNE HOWARD, HEMATOLOGY. *Current Pos:* RETIRED. *Personal Data:* b Cleveland, Ohio, Dec 8, 19; m 43; c 2. *Educ:* Kenyon Col, AB, 41; Western Reserve Univ, MD, 44. *Prof Exp:* Fel hemat, Harvard Med Sch, 51-52, instr pediat, 52; sr instr, Western Reserve Univ, 52-53, asst prof, 53-58; assoc prof, Univ Pittsburgh, 58-63; from assoc prof to prof, Northwestern Univ, Chicago, 63-71, The Given prof pediat, 71-; med dir educ, Children's Mem Hosp, 72-85. *Concurrent Pos:* Chief, Div Hemat, Children's Mem Hosp, 63-72. *Mem:* Soc Pediat Res; Am Pediat Soc. *Res:* Pediatrics. *Mailing Add:* 1228 White Birch Lane Carlisle PA 17013

BORGESE, ELISABETH MANN, POLITICAL SCIENCE, OCEANOGRAPHY. *Current Pos:* Killam sr fel, 79-80, PROF, DEPT POLIT SCI, DALHOUSIE UNIV, 80- *Personal Data:* b Munich, Ger, Apr 24, 18; Can citizen; m 39, Giuseppe A; c Angelica & Dominica. *Educ:* Freies Gym, Zurich, Switz, BA, 35; Music Conserv, Zurich, 37; Mt St Vincent Univ, PhD, 86. *Hon Degrees:* PhD, Mt St Vincent Univ, 86. *Honors & Awards:* Medal of High Merit, Austria; Order of Merit, Govt Columbia; Sasakawa Int Environ Prize, UN, 87; Order of Can, 87; St Francis of Assisi Int Environ Prize, 93. *Prof Exp:* Res assoc, Univ Chicago, 45-51; ed, Perspective USA, 52-57; exec secy & bd eds, Encycl Britannica, 64-66; sr fel, Ctr Study Dem Insts, Santa Barbara, Calif, 64-79. *Concurrent Pos:* Chmn planning coun, Int Ocean Inst, 72-92, hon chmn, 92; adv Austrian deleg, Third UN Conf on Law of Sea, 76-82, Prep Comn, Jamaica, 83-86; chmn, Int Ctr Ocean Develop, 86-92. *Mem:* AAAS; Acad Polit Sci; World Acad Arts & Sci; Third World Acad Sci. *Res:* Ocean development; author of several books. *Mailing Add:* Int Ocean Inst Dalhousie Univ 1226 LeMerchant St Halifax NS B3H 3P7 Can. *Fax:* 902-868-2455

BORGESE, THOMAS A, PHYSIOLOGY, BIOCHEMISTRY. *Current Pos:* from asst prof to assoc prof, 67-78, PROF BIOL SCI, HERBERT H LEHMAN COL, 78- *Personal Data:* b New York, NY, Jan 21, 29; m 58; c 3. *Educ:* NY Univ, BA, 50; Rutgers Univ, PhD(physiol, biochem), 59. *Prof Exp:* NIH fel, Harvard Med Sch, 59-61, res assoc biochem, 61-62; res assoc inst nutrit sci, Columbia Univ, 62-64, asst prof nutrit biochem, 64-67. *Mem:* AAAS; Am Chem Soc; Biophys Soc; Am Physiol Soc; Sigma Xi. *Res:* Cell physiology and biochemistry; comparative biochemistry and physiology of hemoglobin. *Mailing Add:* Dept Biol Sci Herbert H Lehman Col City Univ NY Bedford Park Blvd W Bronx NY 10468

BORGESON, DAVID P, FISH BIOLOGY. *Current Pos:* RETIRED. *Personal Data:* b Muskegon, Mich, Dec 6, 35; m 58; c 4. *Educ:* Mich State Univ, BS, 58, MS, 59. *Prof Exp:* Fishery res biologist, Calif State Dept Fish & Game, 59-66; trout-salmon specialist, Mich Dept Conserv, 66-70, chief, Inland Fisheries Sect, 70-79, asst chief, Fisheries Div, Mich Dept Natural Resources, 79. *Mem:* Am Fisheries Soc; fel Am Inst Fishery Res Biologists. *Res:* Fisheries research, particularly trout and salmon. *Mailing Add:* 610 Green St Grand Ledge MI 48837

BORGIA, GERALD, BEHAVIOR ECOLOGY. *Current Pos:* asst prof, 80-86, ASSOC PROF ZOOL, DEPT ZOOL, UNIV MD, 86- *Personal Data:* b Montebello, Calif, Apr 9, 49; m 80. *Educ:* Univ Calif, Berkeley, AB, 70; Univ Mich, MS, 73, PhD(zool), 78. *Prof Exp:* Trainee, Allec Lab Animal Behav, Univ Chicago, 79-80; univ res fel, Dept Zool, Univ Melbourne, 80-81. *Concurrent Pos:* Vis researcher, Univ Melbourne, 82-90; res assoc, Smithsonian Inst, 85-90. *Mem:* Animal Behav Soc; Soc Study Evolution; AAAS. *Res:* Use of evolutionary theory to study social behavior, particularly mate choice in animals; field studies of mate choice in bowerbirds; models of anisogamy; studies of adaptation for testing evolutionary hypothesis. *Mailing Add:* Dept Zool Univ Md College Park MD 20742

BORGIOTTI, GIORGIO V, STRUCTURAL ACOUSTICS. *Current Pos:* PROF ELEC ENG, GEORGE WASH UNIV, 88- *Personal Data:* b Rome, Italy, Nov 23, 32; m 64; c 2. *Educ:* Univ Rome, EngD, 57; Ital Univ Syst, Liberan Docenza, 71. *Prof Exp:* Scientist, Selenia, Rome, 58-65; tech staff mem, Res Triangle Inst, 65-66; sect mgr, Missile Systs Div, Raytheon, 67-71; dept mgr, CSELT, Torino, Italy, 71-72; sr res assoc, Nat Acad Sci, 74-75; tech staff mem, Jet Propulsion Lab, 76-77; res staff mem, Inst Defense Anal, 80-83; oper chief scientist, Sci Applns Int Corp, 83-88. *Concurrent Pos:* Consult, struct acoust & electromagnetics, Raythean, 80-82, Bell Labs, 88-93 & David Taylor Navy Res Ctr, 93- *Mem:* Fel Inst Elec & Electronics Engrs; Sigma Xi; Union Radio Sci Int; Acoust Soc Am. *Res:* Applied electromagnetic theory, antennas, radar systems and adaptive systems; signal processing, linear system theory and system identification; acoustic radiation and scattering; modal analysis of vibration. *Mailing Add:* 5822 Highland Dr Chevy Chase MD 20815

BORGLUM, GERALD BALTZER, BIOCHEMISTRY. *Current Pos:* PROD SPECIALIST, AGDIA, 93- *Personal Data:* b Penn Yan, NY, June 30, 33; m 54; c 4. *Educ:* Dana Col, BS, 53; Univ Nebr, PhD(dipeptidases), 66. *Prof Exp:* Sr staff scientist, Miles, Inc, 65-92. *Mem:* Am Chem Soc. *Res:* Production of agricultural diagnostic reagents. *Mailing Add:* 60208 Robin Hood Lane Elkhart IN 46517-9401

BORGMAN, LEON EMRY, STATISTICS, GEOLOGY. *Current Pos:* PROF GEOL & STATIST, UNIV WYO, 70- *Personal Data:* b Chickasha, Okla, Feb 16, 28; m 49; c 2. *Educ:* Colo Sch Mines, 53; Univ Houston, MS, 59; Univ Calif, Berkeley, PhD, 63. *Prof Exp:* Oceanog engr, Shell Oil Co, 53-59; asst prof math, Univ Calif, Davis, 62-67, assoc prof eng geosci, Univ Calif, Berkeley, 67-70. *Mem:* Am Soc Civil Engrs; Am Inst Mining & Metall Engrs; Am Geophys Union. *Res:* Statistics and mathematics applied to problems in geology, coastal engineering, hydrology, mining and various other earth science disciplines. *Mailing Add:* Dept Geol Univ Wyo Box 3006 Laramie WY 82071-3006

BORGMAN, ROBERT F, NUTRITION, HYPERTENSION. *Current Pos:* EMER PROF FOOD SCI & NUTRIT, CLEMSON UNIV, 60- *Personal Data:* b Bridgeport, Conn, 1926; m 51; c 4. *Educ:* Mich State Univ, DVM, 47, MS, 49; Kans State Univ, PhD(nutrit), 59. *Mem:* Am Inst Nutrit; Can Soc Nutrit Sci; Royal Soc Health Fel, London; Am Vet Med Asn; Sigma Xi. *Res:* Metabolism. *Mailing Add:* Rte 1 Box 715 Candler NC 28715-9140

BORGMAN, ROBERT JOHN, MEDICINAL CHEMISTRY. *Current Pos:* group leader med chem, 75-76, DIR, MED & ORG CHEM, ARNAR-STONE LABS, INC, 76- *Personal Data:* b Ft Madison, Iowa, Feb 4, 42; m 66; c 4. *Educ:* Univ Iowa, PhD(med chem), 70. *Prof Exp:* From asst prof to assoc prof med chem, WVa Univ, 70-75. *Mem:* Am Pharmaceut Asn; Am Chem Soc. *Res:* Design and synthesis of dopamine; receptor agonists in periphery and central nervous system. *Mailing Add:* 735 Victoria Way Mundelein IL 60060

BORGMAN, ROBERT P, PLANT PATHOLOGY, BOTANY. *Current Pos:* prof biol & chmn dept, Div Natural Sci, 69-77, prof, Div Natural Sci, 69-94, ASST TO PRES, BUENA VISTA COL, 77- *Personal Data:* b Chicago, Ill, Apr 5, 30; m 57; c 3. *Educ:* Cent Col, Iowa, BA, 57; Kans State Univ, MS, 59; Iowa State Univ, PhD(plant path), 62. *Prof Exp:* From asst prof to assoc prof biol, Univ Omaha, 62-69. *Mem:* Am Phytopath Soc. *Res:* Fungal and vegetable crop diseases; virus diseases of cereal crop. *Mailing Add:* 315 College St Storm Lake IA 50588. *Fax:* 712-732-2461

BORGNAES, DAN, STRUCTURAL REACTION INJECTION MOLDING, RESIN TRANSFER MOLDING. *Current Pos:* CONSULT INDUST POLYMERS, ACCESS SCI CO, 90- *Personal Data:* b New York, NY, Nov 16, 35; m 59; c 2. *Educ:* Fla State Univ, BS, 61; Univ Notre Dame, PhD(org chem), 69. *Prof Exp:* Sr res chemist, PPG Indust, Natrium, WVa, 65-71; teacher chem & tech eng, Gym Blumenthal, City of Bremen, 71-74; sr group leader, Ashland Chem Co, Dublin, Ohio, 74-84, res assoc polymer chem, 85-90; res & develop lab mgr, Dexter-Hysol Div, 84-85. *Mem:* Am Chem Soc; Asn Consult Chemists & Chem Engrs. *Res:* Product, process and formulation development of polymer systems used in the structural-reaction injection molding industry; unsaturated polyesters, polyurethanes and other thermoset polymers including additives, reinforcements, inhibitors and catalysts; inventor of first structural reaction injection molding chemical system commercialized as Arimax. *Mailing Add:* 8027 Tipperary Ct N Dublin OH 43017

BORGSTEDT, HAROLD HEINRICH, pharmacology, toxicology; deceased, see previous edition for last biography

BORIE, BERNARD SIMON, METALLURGY, SOLID STATE PHYSICS. *Current Pos:* RETIRED. *Personal Data:* b New Orleans, La, June 21, 24; div; c Kathleen, Fabienne & Marianne. *Educ:* Southwestern La Inst, BS, 44; Tulane Univ, MS, 49; Mass Inst Technol, PhD(physics), 56. *Prof Exp:* Res physicist, Metall Div, Oak Ridge Nat Lab, 49-53; Fulbright fel, Univ Paris, 56-57; group leader x-ray diffraction, Oak Ridge Nat Lab, 57-60, head fundamental res sect, 60-69, sr scientist, Metals & Ceramics Div, 69-85. *Concurrent Pos:* Prof, Univ Tenn, 63-; vis prof, Cornell Univ, 71-72 & Univ Calif, Berkeley, 80. *Mem:* Inst Mining, Metall & Petrol Engrs; Am Soc Metals; Am Crystallog Asn; Sigma Xi; AAAS. *Res:* X-ray diffraction studies of imperfect solids; order-disorder effects in solid solutions; structure of thin films; diffraction effects of thermal motion. *Mailing Add:* 13 Brookside Dr Oak Ridge TN 37830-7616

BORIEK, ALADIN MOHAMMED, PULMONARY RESEARCH, RESPIRATORY SYSTEM MECHANICS. *Current Pos:* FAC PULMONARY RES, BAYLOR UNIV, 90- *Personal Data:* b Cairo, Egypt, July 31, 57. *Educ:* Univ Mich, MS, 84; Rice Univ, PhD(mech eng), 90. *Mem:* Soc Indust & Appl Math; Am Physiol Soc. *Mailing Add:* Baylor Col Med Suite 520B One Baylor Plaza Houston TX 77030

BORING, JOHN RUTLEDGE, III, MICROBIOLOGY, EPIDEMIOLOGY. *Current Pos:* PROF PREV MED & ASSOC PROF MED, EMORY UNIV, 66- *Personal Data:* b Gainesville, Fla, July 7, 30; m 59, 78; c 2. *Educ:* Univ Fla, BS, 53, MS, 55, PhD(microbiol), 61. *Prof Exp:* Nat Res Coun Can fel, 61-62; from asst chief to chief epidemic aid lab, Ctr Dis Control, 62-66. *Concurrent Pos:* Ctr Dis Control grants, Emory Univ, 68-75. *Mem:* Am Soc Microbiol; Am Epidemiol Soc. *Res:* Host-parasite relationship between children with cystic fibrosis and the bacterium pseudomonas aeruginosa. *Mailing Add:* Dept Epidemiol Rolling Sch Pub Health Emory Univ Sch Med 1518 Clifton Rd NE Atlanta GA 30322

BORING, JOHN WAYNE, PHYSICS. *Current Pos:* Sr scientist, Res Labs Eng Sci, 60-67, from assoc prof to prof, 67-91, asst dir, Ctr Advan Studies, 68-72, EMER PROF ENG PHYSICS, UNIV VA, 91- *Personal Data:* b Reidsville, NC, Oct 9, 29; m 57, Ethel Watts; c Rebecca, Pamela & Judith. *Educ:* Univ Ky, BS, 52, MS, 54, PhD(nuclear physics), 61. *Concurrent Pos:* Consult, Int Comn Radiation Units & Measurement; vis prof, Inst Physics, Univ Aarhus, Denmark, 74-75. *Mem:* Am Phys Soc. *Res:* Atomic collision phenomena; atom-surface interactions. *Mailing Add:* 3510 W Monacan Dr Charlottesville VA 22901. *E-Mail:* jwb@virginia.edu

BORIS, JAY PAUL, COMPUTATIONAL PHYSICS, DETAILED NUMERICAL SIMULATION. *Current Pos:* div consult comput physics, 70-76, head, Plasma Dynamics Br, 76-78, CHIEF SCIENTIST & DIR LAB COMPUT PHYSICS & FLUID DYNAMICS, US NAVAL RES LAB, 78- *Personal Data:* b Buffalo, NY, May 25, 42. *Educ:* Princeton Univ, BA, 64, MA, 66, PhD(astrophys sci), 68. *Honors & Awards:* Arthur S Fleming Award, 76; Capt Robert Dexter Conrad Award for Sci Achievement, USN, 90. *Prof Exp:* Res physicst, Princeton Plasma Physics Lab, 68-70. *Concurrent Pos:* Corresp ed, Comments Plasma Physics & Controlled Fusion, 72-80; mem, Fluid Dynamics Tech Comt, Am Inst Aeronaut & Astronaut, 90-93. *Mem:* Fel Am Phys Soc; fel Am Inst Aeronaut & Astronaut; Am Astron Soc; Int Combustion Inst; Soc Comput Simulation; Sigma Xi. *Res:* Computational physics and numerical analysis; fluid dynamics and turbulence in reactive and nonreactive flow; parallel processing algorithms and technology; nonlinear plasma dynamics and inertial confinement fusion; molecular dynamics applied to physical and biological systems; large-scale simulation for civilian and military applications. *Mailing Add:* 3516 Duff Dr Falls Church VA 22041. *E-Mail:* boris@slcp.nrl.navy.mil

BORISENOK, WALTER A, PHARMACY, NUTRITION. *Current Pos:* SR VPRES MFG & OPERS FOOD FORTIFICATION, FORTITECH INC. *Personal Data:* b Brooklyn, NY, Nov 10, 23; m 55, Jean M Carrolan; c Walter & David. *Educ:* Rensselaer Polytech Inst, BS, 50. *Concurrent Pos:* Sect head parenteral res & develop. *Mem:* Am Pharmaceut Asn; Parenteral Drug Asn. *Res:* Parenteral pharmaceutical products. *Mailing Add:* 61 Miller Rd Latham NY 12110. *Fax:* 518-372-5599

BORISH, IRVIN MAX, OPTOMETRY. *Current Pos:* RETIRED. *Personal Data:* b Philadelphia, Pa, Jan 21, 13; m 36, Beatrice Silver; c Frances (Goldman). *Educ:* Northern Ill Col Optom, OD, 34, DOS, 35. *Hon Degrees:* LLD, Ind Univ, 68; DSc, Pa Col Optom, 75, State Univ NY, 84; DOS, Southern Calif Col Optom, 83, Southern Col Optom, 84. *Honors & Awards:* Apollo Award, Am Optom Asn, 68, Distinguished Serv Award, 89; Wm Feimbloom Award, Am Acad Optom, 85. *Prof Exp:* From instr to prof optom, Northern Ill Col Optom, 36-44, registr, 40-44; pvt pract, 44-72; prof, Ind Univ, Bloomington, 73-83; Benedict prof, Univ Houston, 83-93, Irvin M Borish chair optometric pract. *Concurrent Pos:* Asst chief clins, Northern Ill Eye Clin, 36-41, dir clins, 41-44; lectr & vis prof optom, Ind Univ, 53-72; vpres, Ind Contact Lens Inc, 59-; vis lectr & prof var US univs & cols, 65-; consult, Nat Study Optom Educ, Nat Comn Educ, 72-73 & Essilor Corp; int optometrist, World Cong Optom, 96. *Mem:* AAAS; Am Optom Asn; hon mem Am Acad Optom; Int Soc Contact Lens Res; Int Soc Contact Lens Practitioners. *Res:* Contact lenses; refractive techniques, especially development of new instrumentation including use of vectographic design for binocular refractive methods of visual examination. *Mailing Add:* 23371 Blue Water Circle No 114 Boca Raton FL 33433. *Fax:* 561-392-0756; *E-Mail:* irvmborish@aol.com

BORISY, GARY GUY, MOLECULAR BIOLOGY. *Current Pos:* from asst prof to assoc prof, 68-75, PROF MOLECULAR BIOL & ZOOL, UNIV WIS-MADISON, 75-, CHMN LAB MOLECULAR BIOL, 80- *Personal Data:* b Chicago, Ill, Aug 18, 42; div; c 3. *Educ:* Univ Chicago, BS, 62, PhD(biophys), 66. *Honors & Awards:* Romnes Award, 75. *Prof Exp:* NSF fel, 66-67; USPHS fel, 67-68. *Concurrent Pos:* NATO fel, 68; NIH multidisciplinary biol training rev panel, 71-73, As Hoc rev comts, postdoctoral fellowships, 74, cell biol study sect, 75-79; NIH Res Career Develop Award, 75-80; Perlman-Bascom Professership of Life Sci, 80-; NIGMS couns, 82, 84; NY State Doctoral Eval comt, 84, Am Cancer Soc Cellular & Develop Adv comt, 84, 88- *Mem:* Am Soc Cell Biol; fel AAAS. *Res:* Principles of biomolecular organization; assembly of macromolecules into functional structures at the cellular level; assembly and function of cytoplasmic microtubules; formation of the mitotic spindle and the mechanism of shromosome movement; cytokinesis; cell motility; the cytoskeleton. *Mailing Add:* 1525 Linden Dr Madison WI 53706-1514

BORK, ALFRED MORTON, PHYSICS, HISTORY OF PHYSICS. *Current Pos:* vchmn, Physics Dept, 73-78, PROF PHYSICS, INFO & COMPUT SCI, UNIV CALIF, IRVINE, 68- *Personal Data:* b Jacksonville, Fla, Sept, 18, 26; m 48; c 3. *Educ:* Ga Inst Technol, BS, 47; Brown Univ, MS, 50, PhD(physics), 53. *Prof Exp:* From asst prof to prof physics, Univ Alaska, 52-63; from assoc prof to prof, Reed Col, 63-67. *Concurrent Pos:* NSF fac fel, Harvard Univ, 62-63; chmn, Spec Interest Group Comput Use & Educ, 71, Comt Instrnl Media, Am Asn Physics Teachers, 73- & Conduit Physics Comt, 74- *Mem:* Asn Comput Mach. *Res:* Philosophy and history of science; application of computers to teaching. *Mailing Add:* Dept Info & Comput Sci Univ Calif Irvine CA 92697-3425

BORK, KENNARD BAKER, GEOLOGY, PALEONTOLOGY & HISTORY OF GEOLOGY. *Current Pos:* From asst prof to prof, 66-90, ALUMNI PROF, DENISON UNIV, 90- *Personal Data:* b Kalamazoo, Mich, Oct 13, 40; m 63, Katherine Odell; c Robert O. *Educ:* DePauw Univ, BA, 62; Ind Univ, MA, 64, PhD(geol, paleont), 67. *Concurrent Pos:* Vis prof, Chapman Col, Orange, Calif, 82; secy, US Comn Hist Geol, 82-85 & corresp mem, Int Comn Hist Geol, 84; pres, E-Cent Sect, Nat Asn Geol Teachers, 85-86. *Mem:* AAAS; fel Geol Soc Am; Sigma Xi; Hist Earth Sci Soc (secy, 87-93, pres, 94-). *Res:* History of geology; invertebrate paleontology; biostratigraphy; sedimentary petrology. *Mailing Add:* 324 Mt Parnassus Dr Granville OH 43023. *Fax:* 740-587-6714; *E-Mail:* bork@cc.denison.edu

BORKAN, HAROLD, SOLID STATE ELECTRONICS, INTEGRATED CIRCUITS. *Current Pos:* CONSULT, HARBORTECH, PRINCETON, NJ, 90- *Personal Data:* b NJ, June 2, 27; m 48, Jean Sarvetnick; c Gary, Bradley & Ronald. *Educ:* Rutgers Univ, BS, 50, MS, 54. *Prof Exp:* Res engr, RCA Labs, 50-65, eng leader, RCA Corp, Somerville, 65-68, mgr custom monolithics, 68-78, mgr spec projs, Solid State Technol Ctr, Somerville, 78-79, mgr progs & planning, Advan Technol Lab, Camden, 79-81; dir, Microelectronics Div, Electronics Technol & Devices Lab, US Army, Electronics Res & Develop Command, 81-85, dep dir, Labcom, Ft Monmouth, 85-90. *Mem:* Inst Elec & Electronics Engrs. *Res:* Integrated circuits; silicon processing; solid state image sensors; thin film semiconductor devices; television camera tubes. *Mailing Add:* 150 Longview Dr Princeton NJ 08540

BORKE, MITCHELL LOUIS, PHARMACEUTICAL CHEMISTRY, NUCLEAR CHEMISTRY. *Current Pos:* from asst prof to assoc prof, 57-64, PROF CHEM, DUQUESNE UNIV, 64- *Personal Data:* b Warsaw, Poland, Mar 23, 19; US citizen; m 49; c 2. *Educ:* Univ Ill, BS, 51, MS, 53, PhD, 57. *Honors & Awards:* Elich Prize, 51. *Prof Exp:* Instr, Univ Ill, 55-57. *Concurrent Pos:* Fulbright vis prof, Taiwan, 69-70; partic scientist exchange prog, Nat Acad Sci Bulgaria, 74, Poland, 77, Yugoslavia, 79, Bulgaria, 81, Hungary, 82. *Mem:* Am Pharmaceut Asn; Acad Pharm Pract; Sigma Xi. *Res:* Pharmaceutical and analytical chemistry; radiochemistry; neutron activation analysis using isotopic sources; gas-liquid chromatography; thin layer chromatography. *Mailing Add:* Duquesne Univ Col Pharm Pittsburgh PA 15282-0001

BORKMAN, RAYMOND FRANCIS, PHYSICAL CHEMISTRY. *Current Pos:* from asst prof to assoc prof, 68-78, PROF CHEM, GA INST TECHNOL, 78- *Personal Data:* b Los Angeles, Calif, Dec 15, 40; m 76; c 4. *Educ:* Univ Calif, Los Angeles, BS, 62; Univ Calif, Riverside, PhD(chem), 66. *Prof Exp:* Teaching asst chem, Univ Calif, Riverside, 62-63, res asst, 63-66; fel, Johns Hopkins Univ, 66-68. *Concurrent Pos:* NSF fel, Johns Hopkins Univ, 66-67; Sigma Xi res award, Ga Inst Technol, 72. *Mem:* Sigma Xi; Am Soc Photobiol; Asn Res Vision & Ophthal. *Res:* Experimental-theoretical studies in molecular spectroscopy, photochemistry, photobiology and energy transfer; Ab initio computer calculations of molecular electronic wave functions and properties; biomedical sciences, especially spectroscopic studies of cataracts in human and animal eye lenses. *Mailing Add:* Sch Chem Ga Inst Technol 225 North Ave NW Atlanta GA 30332-0001

BORKON, ELI LEROY, INTERNAL MEDICINE, NUCLEAR MEDICINE. *Current Pos:* RETIRED. *Personal Data:* b Chicago, Ill, Aug 11, 08; m 37, Claire D Binder; c Barbara E (Hewson) & Williams D. *Educ:* Univ Chicago, BS, 31, PhD(physiol), 36, MD, 37; Am Bd Internal Med, dipl. *Prof Exp:* Asst physiol, Univ Chicago, 32-36; assoc prof anat, Chicago Med Sch, 37; assoc prof physiol & Health, Southern Ill Univ, 39-46; fel internal med, Wash Univ, 46; vis lectr physiol, Southern Ill Univ, 48, adj prof, 54; chmn, Dept Med, Carbondale Clin, 54-71; from clin prof to prof med, Sch Med, Southern Ill Univ, Carbondale, 71-76, asst to dean, 71-74, asst dean develop, 74-86, emer prof med, 76-86; dir nuclear med, Mem Hosp, 76-83. *Concurrent Pos:* Vpres, Med Rev Orgn Southern Ill, 80-; mem Ill State Med Disciplinary Bd, 82-, chmn, 84-85; gov, Am Col Physicians, Downstate Ill, 80-84; vchmn mem, Driver License Med Exam Bd, Sect States Off, State Ill, 92- *Mem:* AMA; master Am Col Physicians; Am Soc Internal Med; Soc Nuclear Med. *Res:* Motor activity of intestine; endocrines; effects of minerals on thyroidparathyroid; compensatory hypertrophy of remaining organs; hazards of anticoagulants. *Mailing Add:* 14 Pinewood Dr Carbondale IL 62901

BORKOVEC, ALEXEJ B, ORGANIC CHEMISTRY, BIOCHEMISTRY. *Current Pos:* RETIRED. *Personal Data:* b Prague, Czech, Oct 17, 25; US citizen; m 51. *Educ:* Prague Tech Univ, ChE, 49; Va Polytech Inst, MS, 54, PhD(org chem), 55. *Honors & Awards:* T L Pawlett Award, Univ Sydney, Australia, 71; Bronze Medal, 3rd Int Cong Pesticide Chem, 74; Super Serv Award, USDA, 79; Gold Medal, 11th Cong Plant Protection, 87. *Prof Exp:* Res org chem, Dow Chem Co, Tex, 55-56, sr res chemist, 56-58; asst prof org chem, Va Polytech Inst, 58-60; res chemist, Agr Res Serv, USDA, 61-64, invests leader, 64-72, chief, Insect Chemosterilants Lab, 72-79, chief, Insect Reproduction Lab, Agr Res Serv, 79-92. *Concurrent Pos:* Vis prof, Hollins Col, 60-61. *Mem:* AAAS; Am Chem Soc; Entom Soc Am; Czech Soc Arts & Sci Am; NY Acad Sci. *Res:* Insect neuroscience; reaction mechanism of epoxides and aziridines; synthesis and mode of action of insect chemosterilants; biochemistry of reproduction; pest control. *Mailing Add:* 12013 Kemp Mill Rd USDA Silver Spring MD 20902

BORKOVITZ, HENRY S, MICROCOMPUTER CONTROL, MEASURING SYSTEMS. *Current Pos:* AT ASTRONAUT CORP AM, 90- *Personal Data:* b Chicago, Ill, Dec 4, 35; m 83, Leanne G Gayler; c Debra K, Benjamin J, Leah L & Sara Benson. *Educ:* Ill Inst Technol, BS, 58, MS, 62; Univ Chicago, MBA, 70. *Prof Exp:* Engr, Lindberg Eng Co, 58-62; chief develop eng, Electroseal Corp, 62-64; dir eng, Sola Elec Div, Gen Signal, 64-81; vpres eng, Realist Inc, 81-90. *Mem:* Inst Elec & Electronics Engrs. *Res:* Development level sensing and control systems utilizing microcomputer circuitry; development of software to facilitate the design and programming process including cross assemblers. *Mailing Add:* W181 Destiny Dr N8291 Menomonee Falls WI 53051

BORKOWSKI, RAYMOND P, PHYSICAL CHEMISTRY. *Current Pos:* from asst prof to assoc prof, 67-78, PROF CHEM, KING'S COL, PA, 78- *Personal Data:* b Kingston, Pa, Feb 5, 34; m 64, Alberta Kunec; c Raymond A & John A. *Educ:* King's Col, BS, 55; Cath Univ, PhD(phys chem), 61. *Prof Exp:* Nat Acad Sci-Nat Res Coun res assoc photochem & radiation chem, Nat Bur Stand, 61-63; staff scientist, Aerospace Res Ctr, Gen Precision Inc, 63-67. *Concurrent Pos:* Res fel, NASA/Am Soc Elec Engrs, 79-80. *Mem:* Am Chem Soc; Sigma Xi. *Res:* Chemical kinetics; photochemistry; radiation chemistry; phenomena of energy conversion and transfer. *Mailing Add:* Seven Salem Dr Wilkes Barre PA 18702

BORKOWSKY, WILLIAM, IMMUNOLOGY, MICROBIOLOGY. *Current Pos:* Intern pediat, NY Univ Med Ctr & Bellevue Hosp, 72-73, resident, 73-75, fel infectious dis & immunol, 75-78, instr pediat, 77-78, from asst prof to assoc prof, 78-94, CHIEF, INFECTIOUS DIS & IMMUNOL, NY UNIV MED CTR & BELLEVUE HOSP, 85-, PROF PEDIAT, 94- *Personal Data:* b Ger, Mar 6, 47; US citizen; m 69; c 3. *Educ:* City Col New York, BS, 68; NY Univ, MD, 72. *Mem:* Infectious Dis Soc Am; Am Asn Immunologists; Pediat Res Soc; Pediat Infectious Dis Soc; Am Fedn Clin Res; Harvey Soc. *Res:* Immune regulation and the role of transfer factor as a regulatory molecule; acquired immunity deficiency syndrome; autoimmune diseases, particularly juvenile diabetes; hepatitis. *Mailing Add:* Dept Pediat NY Univ Med Ctr 550 First Ave New York NY 10016-6402

BORLAUG, NORMAN ERNEST, MICROBIOLOGY. *Current Pos:* DISTINGUISHED PROF INT AGR, DEPT SOIL & CROP SCI, TEX A&M UNIV, 84-; PRES, SASAKAWA AFRICA ASN, 86- *Personal Data:* b Cresco, Iowa, Mar 25, 14; m 40, Margaret Gibson; c Norma Jean (Laube) Gibson & William G. *Educ:* Univ Minn, BS, 37, MS, 40, PhD(plant path), 42. *Hon Degrees:* Numerous from US & foreign univs. *Honors & Awards:* Nobel Prize for Peace, 70; Firs Int Serv Award Agron, Am Soc Agron, 68; McDougal Mem Lectr, 71; Gold Plate Award, Am Acad Achievement, 71; Achievement Award for Contrib World Wheat Prod, Nat Asn Wheat Growers, USA, 71; Nat Award Agr Excellence in Sci, Nat Agr Mkg Asn, 82. *Prof Exp:* With US Forest Serv, 35-38; instr plant path, Univ Minn, 41; microbiologist, E I du Pont de Nemours, Del, 42-44; res scientist in-chg, Wheat Improv Coop Mex Agr Prog, Mex Ministry Agr & Rockefeller Found, Mex, 44-60; assoc dir, CIMMYT, 64-82; A D White prof-at-large, Cornell Univ, 82-85. *Concurrent Pos:* Consult, Food & Agr Orgn UN, NAfrica & Asia, 60; consult & collabr, Nat Inst Invest Agr, Mex Ministry Agr, 60-64; mem, Citizen's Comn Sci, Law & Food Supply & Comn Critical Choices for Am, 73-74, Pres Comn World Hunger, 78-79, President's Coun Adv Sci & Technol, 90-93; bd dirs, Am Coun Sci & Health, 78-; adj prof, Dept Biol, Emory Univ, 91-92. *Mem:* Nat Acad Sci; Am Phytopath Soc; Soc Am Foresters; Am Chem Soc; hon mem Am Soc Agron; Sigma Xi; hon fel Indian Soc Genetics & Plant Breeding; fel Crop Sci Soc Am; foreign mem Royal Swed Acad Agr & forestry; Am Acad Arts & Scis; Royal Agr Soc Eng. *Res:* Wheat breeding; agronomy; fungicides; weed killers; plant pathology; forestry. *Mailing Add:* CIMMYT Lisban 27 Apdo Postal 6-641 Mexico DF 06600 Mexico

BORLE, ANDRE BERNARD, PHYSIOLOGY, ENDOCRINOLOGY. *Current Pos:* from asst prof to assoc prof, 63-74, PROF PHYSIOL, SCH MED, UNIV PITTSBURGH, 74- *Personal Data:* b La Chaux-de-Fonds, Switz, May 27, 30; m 60; c 2. *Educ:* Univ Geneva, MD, 55. *Honors & Awards:* Andre Lichtwitz Prize, 70. *Prof Exp:* Intern med, Mt Auburn Hosp, Cambridge, Mass, 56-57; res fel biochem, Harvard Med Sch, 57-59; resident, Cantonal Hosp, Geneva, Switz, 59-61; instr radiation biol, Atomic Energy Proj, Univ Rochester, 61-63. *Concurrent Pos:* Ship surgeon, Johnson Line, Stockdm, 56; asst med, Peter Bent Brigham Hosp, Boston, 57-59; Lederle med fac award, 64-67. *Mem:* AAAS; Am Physiol Soc; Endocrine Soc; Biophys Soc. *Res:* Cellular calcium metabolism; general physiology of calcium; mode of action of parathyroid hormone, calcitonin and vitamin D; membrane transport of calcium; calcium and phosphate metabolism; calcium signaling. *Mailing Add:* Dept Physiol Sch Med Univ Pittsburgh Terr & Desoto Sts Pittsburgh PA 15261-0001

BORM, ALFRED ERVIN, algebra, topology; deceased, see previous edition for last biography

BORMAN, ALECK, BIOCHEMISTRY. *Current Pos:* RETIRED. *Personal Data:* b Toledo, Ohio, July 13, 19; m 46, Roberta Axelrod; c Elizabeth S & Judith L. *Educ:* Univ Toledo, BS, 41; Univ Ill, PhD(biochem), 45. *Prof Exp:* Sr chemist & sect head biochem div, E R Squibb & Sons, 45-52, head endocrinol res sect, Squibb Inst Med Res, 52-55, head endocrinol res dept, 55-62, dir physiol sect, 62-67, mgr sci personnel rels, 67, personnel mgr res & develop, 67-71, labor rels mgr, 71-86. *Concurrent Pos:* Consult, E R Squibb & Sons, 86-89. *Mem:* AAAS; Soc Exp Biol & Med; Am Asn Cancer Res; Endocrine Soc. *Res:* Protein and steroid hormones; endocrinology. *Mailing Add:* 42 North Dr East Brunswick NJ 08816

BORMAN, GARY LEE, COMBUSTION, HEAT TRANSFER. *Current Pos:* from asst prof to assoc prof, 64-71, prof, 71-94, dir, Engine Res Ctr, 86-94, EMER PROF MECH ENG, UNIV WIS-MADISON, 94- *Personal Data:* b Milwaukee, Wis, Mar 15, 32; m 71, Marlene H Mehls. *Educ:* Univ Wis-Madison, BS, 54, MS, 56 & MS, 57, PhD(mech eng), 64. *Honors & Awards:* Ralph Teetor Award, Soc Automotive Engrs, 64, Arch Colwell Award, 66 & Horning Mem Award, 78; Fulbright Lectr, Univ Sarajevo, Yugoslavia, 70; Fulbright Distinguished Prof, Maribar, Yugoslavia, 90. *Prof Exp:* Sr engr, Gen Elec Co, 57-60. *Mem:* Nat Acad Eng; Combustion Inst; fel Soc Automotive Engrs. *Res:* Combustion; combustion engines; emissions; unsteady heat transfer, droplet vaporization and sprays in engines; engine cycle simulation and modeling of thermal systems. *Mailing Add:* 4634 Gregg Rd Madison WI 53705

BORMANN, BARBARA-JEAN ANNE, TRANS MEMBRANE ONCOGENES, RECEPTOR OLIGOMERIZATION. *Current Pos:* MGR, RES & DEVELOP OPERS, PFIZER, 96- *Personal Data:* b Bronxville, NY, Oct 5, 58; m 89; c 1. *Educ:* Fairfield Univ, BS, 79; Univ Conn, PhD(biomed sci), 85. *Honors & Awards:* Gregory Pincas Mem Award, Fedn Am Soc Exp Biologists, 83. *Prof Exp:* Fel cytoskeleton, Sch Med, Yale Univ, 85-88, res assoc signal transduction, 88-89; sr scientist, Boehringer Ingelheim, 89-90, prin scientist immunol, 91-96. *Concurrent Pos:* Res affil, Sch Med, Yale Univ, 89- *Mem:* Am Soc Cell Biol. *Res:* Analysis of protein-protein interactions in membranes; transmembrane receptors including oncogenes, growth factor receptors and adhesion molecules. *Mailing Add:* Pfizer Eastpoint Rd Groton CT 06340

BORMANN, FREDERICK HERBERT, ECOLOGY. *Current Pos:* prof biol, 69-80, prof forestry & environ studies, 80-92, OASTLER PROF FOREST ECOL, SCH FORESTRY, YALE UNIV, 66-, DIR, ECOSYSTS RES, 82-EMER PROF FORESTRY & ENVIRON STUDIES, 92- *Personal Data:* b New York, NY, Mar 24, 22; m 52; c 4. *Educ:* Rutgers Univ, BS, 48; Duke Univ, MA, 50, PhD(plant ecol), 52. *Honors & Awards:* George Mercer Award, 54; Cert of Merit, Bot Soc Am. *Prof Exp:* From instr to asst prof bot, Emory Univ, 52-56; from asst prof to prof, Dartmouth Col, 56-66. *Concurrent Pos:* Fel, Ezra Stiles Col, Yale Univ; ecologist, Boston Univ exped, Alaska, 53; vis scientist, Brookhaven Nat Lab, 63-64, Ctr Energy & Environ Studies, Princeton Univ, 84, Air Pollution Info Exchange, Repub China, 85, E-W Environ & Policy Inst, Honolulu, 87 & Univ New Eng, NSW, 90; mem adv comt, Hubbard Brook, 75-, Native Plants Inc, Salt Lake City, 82-84, World Resources Inst, 86-89, Wilderness Soc, 87-; mem, Nat Comt Scope Fire Prog, Nat Res Coun, Nat Acad Sci, 77-79, Int Environ Progs Comt, 77-80; vis prof, Ctr Advan Studies, Univ Va, 80-81; Green prof, Tex Christian Univ, Ft Worth, 87. *Mem:* Nat Acad Sci; fel AAAS; Ecol Soc Am (pres, 70-71); Am Acad Arts & Sci; Am Inst Biol Sci. *Res:* Ecology and physiology of Pinus; structure and function of root grafts; structure, function and development of forest ecosystems; author of 162 technical publications. *Mailing Add:* Sch Forestry & Environ Studies Yale Univ 205 Prospect St New Haven CT 06511

BORN, ALLEN, MINING. *Current Pos:* chief metallurgist, supt & mgr, 67-76, PRES & CHIEF OPERATING OFFICER, AMAX INC, 85-, CHIEF EXEC OFFICER, 86- & CHMN, 88- *Personal Data:* b Durango, Colo, July 4, 33; m 53, Patricia Beaubien; c Michael, Scott (deceased) & Brett. *Educ:* Univ Tex, El Paso, BS, 58. *Hon Degrees:* DEng, Colo Sch Mines, 92. *Honors & Awards:* Daniel C Jackling Award, Soc Mining Engrs. *Prof Exp:* Explor geologist, El Paso Natural Gas, 58-60; metallurgist, Vanadium Corp Am, 60-62; gen foreman, Pima Mining, 62-64; asst supt, MolyCorp, 64-67; pres & chief exec officer, Can Tungsten Mining Corp Ltd, 76-81; pres, Amax Can Ltd, 77-81; pres, chmn & chief exec officer, Placer Develop Ltd, Vancouver, 81-85. *Concurrent Pos:* Chmn bd, Alumax Inc & Amax Gold Inc; mem bd dirs, Can Tungsten Mining Corp, Aztec Mining Co Ltd, Australia & Aztec Resources. *Mem:* Am Inst Mining Engrs; Am Mining Cong. *Res:* Mining and metallurgy. *Mailing Add:* Alumax 3424 Peachtree Rd NE Ste 2100 Atlanta GA 30326

BORN, GEORGE HENRY, SATELLITE NAVIGATION, SATELLITE OCEANOGRAPHY. *Current Pos:* DIR, COLO CTR ASTRODYN RES, 85- *Personal Data:* b Westhoff, Tex, Nov 10, 39. *Educ:* Univ Tex, BS, 62, MS, 65, PhD(aeronaut eng), 68. *Prof Exp:* Engr, Ling-Temco-Vought Corp, 62-63; res engr, Tex Ctr Res, 64-67; aerospace technologist, Johnson Space Ctr, 67-70; tech group supvr, Jet Propulsion Lab, 70-83; sr res engr, Ctr Space Res, 83-85. *Concurrent Pos:* Lectr, Dept Mech Eng, Univ Houston, 68-70; ed, J Astronaut Sci, 80-83; guest ed, J Geophys Res, 83 & Marine Geod, 84; sci consult, Jet Propulsion Lab, 83-86, Gen Elec, 84-85, Naval Surface Weapons Ctr & Naval Ocean & Atmosphere Res Lab, 85-86. *Mem:* Fel Am Astronaut Soc; fel Am Inst Aeronaut & Astronaut; Inst Navig; Am Geophys Union; Am Meteorol Soc; AAAS. *Res:* Precision orbit determination; satellite navigation; mission design; satellite oceanography; satellite geodesy. *Mailing Add:* Univ Colo Campus Box 431 Boulder CO 80309

BORN, GORDON STUART, HEALTH PHYSICS, PHARMACY. *Current Pos:* From teaching asst to teaching assoc, 62-64, from instr to assoc prof, 64-74, PROF MED CHEM & HEALTH SCI, PURDUE UNIV, 74- *Personal Data:* b Hammond, Ind, Apr 26, 33; m 57; c 1. *Educ:* Purdue Univ, BS, 55, MS, 64, PhD(health physics), 66. *Honors & Awards:* Lederle Pharm Fac Award, Lederle Labs, 72. *Mem:* Health Physics Soc. *Res:* Drug and environmental toxicants and application of tracer techniques to analytical problems. *Mailing Add:* 746 Northridge Dr West Lafayette IN 47906

BORN, HAROLD JOSEPH, PHYSICS. *Current Pos:* assoc prof, 61-66, PROF PHYSICS & HEAD DEPT, ILL STATE UNIV, 66- *Personal Data:* b Evansville, Ind, Nov 22, 22; m 50; c 2. *Educ:* Rose Polytech Inst, BS, 49; Iowa State Univ, MS, 58, PhD(physics), 60. *Prof Exp:* Equip engr, Phillips Petrol Co, Okla, 52-55; res asst, Ames Lab, AEC, 55-60; res physicist, Whirlpool Corp Res Labs, Mich, 60-61. *Mem:* Am Phys Soc; Am Asn Physics Teachers. *Res:* Low temperature thermoelectric effects; thermoelectric refrigeration; solid state physics. *Mailing Add:* 806 Highpoint Rd Normal IL 61761

BORNE, RONALD FRANCIS, MEDICINAL CHEMISTRY, ORGANIC CHEMISTRY. *Current Pos:* asst prof pharmaceut chem, Univ Miss, 68-70, assoc prof med chem, 70-72, chmn dept 79-88, PROF MED CHEM, UNIV MISS, 72-,. *Personal Data:* b New Orleans, La, Nov 17, 38; m 88, Jane Stanley; c Debra, Michael & Merribeth. *Educ:* Loyola Univ, La, BS, 60; Tulane Univ, MS, 62; Univ Kans, PhD(med chem), 67. *Honors & Awards:* Nat Res Serv Award, 88; Nat Lectr Award, Rho Chi, 94; Distinguished Pharm Educr Award, Am Asn Col Pharm, 96. *Prof Exp:* Res asst chem, Ochsner Med Found, 56-62; res chemist, C J Patterson Co, Mo, 62-63 & Mallinckrodt Chem Works, 67-68. *Concurrent Pos:* Vis prof, Univ Edinburgh Med Sch, Scotland, 88-89. *Mem:* Am Chem Soc; Am Acad Pharmaceut Sci; Int Soc Heterocyclic Chem; Am Asn Cols Pharm. *Res:* Medicinal chemistry, especially organic syntheses and conformational aspects of drug action. *Mailing Add:* Dept Med Chem Univ Miss Sch Pharm University MS 38677. *Fax:* 601-232-5118

BORNEMANN, ALFRED, METALLURGICAL ENGINEERING. *Current Pos:* From asst prof to assoc prof eng chem, 30-48, prof metall & head dept, 48-74, EMER PROF METALL, STEVENS INST TECHNOL, 75- *Personal Data:* b Montclair, NJ, Apr 6, 06; m 86; c 3. *Educ:* Stevens Inst Technol, ME, 27; Dresden Tech Univ, DEng, 30. *Honors & Awards:* Award of Merit, Am Soc Metals, 70. *Concurrent Pos:* Dir, Peirce Mem Lab, 40-48; trustee, Stevens Acad, 44-74, pres, 69-73; bd mgr, Nantucket Maria Mitchell Assoc, 60-, pres, 74-80. *Mem:* Am Inst Mining, Metall & Petrol Engrs; Am Chem Soc; fel Am Soc Metals; Am Soc Testing & Mat. *Res:* Heat treatment and carburizing of steels; properties of metals; corrosion; failure analysis. *Mailing Add:* 63 Cliff Rd Nantucket MA 02554-2168

BORNEMEIER, DWIGHT D, physics, for more information see previous edition

BORNING, ALAN H, COMPUTER SCIENCE. *Current Pos:* res asst prof, 80-81, from asst prof to assoc prof, 81-93, PROF, DEPT COMPUT SCI & ENG, UNIV WASH, 93- *Personal Data:* b Moscow, Idaho, Mar 8, 50. *Educ:* Reed Col, BA, 71; Stanford Univ, MS, 74, PhD(comput sci), 79. *Prof Exp:* Mem, Learning Res Group, Xerox Palo Alto Res Ctr, 76-79; NSF postdoctoral fel, Dept Artificial Intel, Univ Edinburgh, 79-80. *Concurrent Pos:* Assoc ed, Asn Comput Mach, Comput Surv; mem bd dirs, Comput Prof Soc Responsibility, 83-87; co-organizer, Working Group Archit Interactive Systs, 86, 87, 88; vis scientist, Rank Xerox Europarc, Eng, 89-90; Fulbright grantee, Monash Univ, Australia, 97. *Res:* Constraint-based languages and systems; object-oriented languages; logic programming languages; human-computer interaction. *Mailing Add:* Dept Comput Sci & Eng Univ Wash Box 352350 Seattle WA 98195-2350. *E-Mail:* borning@cs.washington.edu

BORNMANN, JOHN ARTHUR, PHYSICAL CHEMISTRY. *Current Pos:* RETIRED. *Personal Data:* b Pittsburgh, Pa, May 1, 30; m 54, Sandra L Reel; c Patricia L & Carol A (Lietz). *Educ:* Carnegie Inst Technol, BS, 52; Technische Hockschule (physics), Stuttgart, Ger, 56-57, Ind Univ, PhD(phys chem), 58. *Prof Exp:* Res chemist, E I du Pont de Nemours & Co, 58-60; res assoc, Princeton Univ, 60-61; asst prof chem, Northern Ill Univ, 61-65; assoc prof, Lindenwood Col, 65-68, chmn, div natural sci & math, 67-71 & 74-81, chmn dept chem, 65-90, prof chem, 68-91. *Concurrent Pos:* Owner, DAS Co, 74-; vis scientist, McDonnell Douglas Res Labs, 84-; Fulbright grantee, Ger, 56-57. *Mem:* AAAS; Am Chem Soc; fel Am Inst Chemists. *Res:* Interdisciplinary applications of physical chemistry. *Mailing Add:* 3 Briarwood Lane St Charles MO 63301. *Fax:* 314-946-3426; *E-Mail:* 71623.327@Compuserve.com

BORNMANN, PATRICIA L(EE), SOLAR PHYSICS. *Current Pos:* res assoc, Univ Colo & NOAA, Space Environ Lab, 88-90, resident res assoc, Nat Res Coun, 86-88, PHYSICIST, SPACE ENVIRON LAB, NAT OCEANIC & ATMOSPHERIC ADMIN, 90- *Personal Data:* b Long Branch, NJ, Feb 22, 58; m 83. *Educ:* Calif Inst Technol, BS, 79; Univ Colo, Boulder, PhD(astrophys), 85. *Honors & Awards:* Billings Award in Astrogeophys, 85. *Prof Exp:* Teaching asst, solar physics lab, astrophys dept, Univ Colo, 79, res asst, Joint Inst Lab Astrophys, 79-85; astrophysicist, Solar Physics Br, Air Force Geophys Lab, 85-86. *Concurrent Pos:* Res asst, Big Bear Solar Observ, 77-78, Nat Radio Astron Observ, 79 & Sacramento Peak Solar Observ, 80 & 81; res grant, Richter Scholar, Calif Inst Technol, 78 & 79; travel grant, Solar Physics div, Am Astron Soc, 80 & 84; guest invest Solar Maximum Mission, 86- *Mem:* Am Astron Soc; Int Astron Union; Am Geophys Union. *Res:* Interpretation of the evolution of soft x-ray lines observed during solar flares; understanding the evolution of the high temperature flare plasma; analysis of evolution of solar active regimes and the production of solar flares. *Mailing Add:* 4261 Milliken Ct Boulder CO 80303

BORNMANN, ROBERT CLARE, MEDICINE, PHYSIOLOGY. *Current Pos:* CONSULT, LIMETREE CONSULTS, RESTON, VA, 85- *Personal Data:* b Pittsburgh, Pa, June 29, 31; m 63; c Kristin B (Kazem), Elizabeth, Jennifer (Brasiel) & John. *Educ:* Harvard Univ, AB, 52; Univ Pa, MD, 56, MS, 63; Am Bd Preventive Med, dipl. *Prof Exp:* Officer-in-chg, Cape Hallett Int Geophys Year Base, Antarctica, 58-59, med officer, Underwater Swimmers Sch, Key West, Fla, 61-62, Washington, DC, 61-65, Deep Sea Divers Sch, Wash Navy Yard, Washington, DC, 63-65 & Exp Diving Unit, 65-68, dep asst med effects, Deep Submergence Systs Proj, 68-70, exchange officer underwater med, Royal Naval Physiol Lab, Alverstoke, Eng, 70-72, head submarine & diving med, Naval Med Res & Develop Command, Bethesda, 73-78, asst med effects Naval Dep, Nat Oceanic & Atmospheric Admin, Dept Com, Washington, 78-81; staff dir, Defense Med Standardization Bd, Frederick, Md, 81-85. *Concurrent Pos:* Staff med officer, Oceanogr Navy, Washington, DC, 73-78. *Mem:* AMA; AAAS; Aerospace Med Asn; Am Col Occup Med; Royal Soc Med; Undersea Med Soc; Europ-US Biomed Soc; Marine Tech Soc; Am Polar Soc. *Res:* Submarine, diving and occupational medicine; pathogenesis and treatment of decompression sickness and air embolism; development of decompression schedules for divers; design and development of diving equipment; worker's disability. *Mailing Add:* Limetree Med Consults 11569 Woodhollow Ct Reston VA 20191-4409

BORNS, HAROLD WILLIAM, JR, QUATERNARY GEOLOGY. *Current Pos:* From instr to assoc prof, 55-68, chmn dept, 71-74, PROF GEOL, UNIV MAINE, 68-, DIR, INST QUATERNARY STUDIES, 72- *Personal Data:* b Cambridge, Mass, Nov 28, 27; m 53, 81; c 4. *Educ:* Tufts Univ, BS, 51; Boston Univ, MA, 55, PhD(geol), 59. *Concurrent Pos:* Fel, Dept Geol, Yale Univ, 63-64; vis prof, Geol Inst, Univ Bergen, Norway, 75; prog mgr glaciol, Div Polar Prog, NSF, 88-90. *Mem:* Geol Soc Am; Am Polar Soc; Glaciol Soc. *Res:* Glacial geology; quaternary history of Northeast North America, Antarctica and Norway; quaternary climates; environments of paleoindians in America. *Mailing Add:* Dept Geol Sci Univ Maine Orono ME 04469

BORNSIDE, GEORGE HARRY, BACTERIOLOGY. *Current Pos:* RETIRED. *Personal Data:* b Wakefield, RI, Oct 8, 25; m 59; c 1. *Educ:* Trinity Col, BS, 48; Univ Conn, MS, 50; Univ Iowa, PhD(bact), 55. *Prof Exp:* Instr, Univ Iowa, 55-56; assoc marine microbiol, Univ Ga, 56; microbiologist, Brooklyn Bot Garden, 56-57; from asst prof to prof, 57-86, emer prof surg & microbiol, Sch Med, LA State Univ, New Orleans, 86. *Mem:* Am Soc Microbiol; Asn Gnotobiotics (pres, 74-75); Soc Exp Biol & Med. *Res:* Surgical bacteriology; bacterial virulence; antibacterial effects of hyperbaric oxygen; intestinal bacteria. *Mailing Add:* 812 St Ferdinand St New Orleans LA 70117

BORNSLAEGER, ELAYNE A, MOLECULAR EMBRYOLOGY. *Current Pos:* PROF PATH, NORTHWESTERN UNIV, 92- *Personal Data:* b Milwaukee, Wis, Aug 27, 60. *Educ:* Univ Pa, PhD(biol), 86. *Prof Exp:* Postdoctoral neuromuscular develop, Rockefeller Univ, 87-88; fel, Dept Molecular Embryol, Sloan Kettering Inst, 88-92. *Concurrent Pos:* Nat res serv award fel, NIH, 89. *Mem:* Am Soc Cell Biol; Soc Develop Biol; AAAS. *Mailing Add:* Dept Path Northwestern Univ Med Sch 303 E Chicago Ave Olson 8333 Chicago IL 60611-3008

BORNSTEIN, ALAN ARNOLD, PHYSICAL CHEMISTRY, TECHNICAL MANAGEMENT & PATENTS. *Current Pos:* FUJI HUNT PHOTO CHEM, 89- *Personal Data:* b Brooklyn, NY, Oct 24, 50; m 72; c 2. *Educ:* Polytech Inst Brooklyn, BS, 72; Yale Univ, MS, 73. *Prof Exp:* Res scientist, Int Paper Co, 73-74; teaching fel analytical chem, Brooklyn Col, 74-75; res chemist, Vet Admin Res Found, 75-77; sr scientist, Am Can Co, 77-81; res dir, Olin Corp, 81-89. *Mem:* Am Chem Soc; Soc Appl Spectros; Soc Photographic Scientists & Engrs; Nat Asn Photographic Mfrs. *Res:* Analytical chemistry research management; spectroscopy; chromatography; classical techniques. *Mailing Add:* 16 Beech St Westwood NJ 07675-2805

BORNSTEIN, JOSEPH, AGRICULTURAL ENGINEERING. *Current Pos:* RETIRED. *Personal Data:* b Boston, Mass, June 24, 21; div; c 2. *Educ:* Univ Mass, BS, 47; Mich State Univ, MS, 49. *Prof Exp:* Asst, Mich State Col, 48; agr engr, Soil Conserv Serv, USDA, 49-54, civil engr, 54-57, agr engr, Agr Res Serv, 57-85. *Concurrent Pos:* Asst prof, Univ Vt, 61-71, adj assoc prof, 71-75; fac assoc agr eng, Univ Maine, 75-85; consult, 85- *Mem:* Am Soc Agr Engrs; fel Soil & Water Conserv Soc; Nat Soc Prof Engrs; Sigma Xi; Am Soc Civil Engrs. *Res:* Agricultural drainage; soil and water conservation engineering and education; improve farming methods for cool climate of Northeast; developing effective land drainage methods to improve environment for survival and growth of quality feed grains and forages on poorly drained cropland soils, clays, silty clay loam and fragipans. *Mailing Add:* 465 North St Burlington VT 05401-1620

BORNSTEIN, JOSEPH, SYNTHETIC ORGANIC CHEMISTRY. *Current Pos:* PROF CHEM, BOSTON COL, 50- *Personal Data:* b Boston, Mass, Feb 19, 25; m 54; c 3. *Educ:* Boston Col, BS, 46; Mass Inst Technol, PhD(chem), 49. *Prof Exp:* Chemist, Tracerlab, Inc, 49-50. *Concurrent Pos:* Consult, US Army. *Mem:* Am Chem Soc; Soc Chem Indust. *Res:* Synthesis of insecticides and synergists; organic fluorine compounds; heterocyclic compounds; carbon-14 epoxy resins. *Mailing Add:* 24 Gary Rd Needham Heights MA 02194-2417

BORNSTEIN, LAWRENCE A, HISTORY AND PHILOSOPHY OF SCIENCE. *Current Pos:* from instr to assoc prof, NY Univ, 50-68, assoc dean, 68-69, chmn dept, 69-73, assoc chmn dept, 73-82, actg dean, 84-85, PROF PHYSICS, NY UNIV, 68- *Personal Data:* b New York, NY, Sept 15, 23; m 45; c 2. *Educ:* City Col NY, BS, 44; NY Univ, MS, 51, PhD (physics), 57. *Prof Exp:* Tutor physics, City Col New York, 46-50. *Mem:* Hist Sci Soc; AAAS; Am Phys Soc; Am Asn Physics Teachers; Sigma Xi. *Res:* History of physics. *Mailing Add:* 769 Grange Rd Teaneck NJ 07666-4210

BORNSTEIN, MICHAEL, PHYSICAL PHARMACY, ANALYTICAL CHEMISTRY. *Current Pos:* RES MGR, JOHNSON & JOHNSON, 88- *Personal Data:* b Zarki, Poland, May 2, 40; US citizen; m 67; c Lori, Scott, Debbie & Lisa. *Educ:* Fordham Univ, BS, 62; Univ Iowa, PhD(phys analytical pharm), 66. *Prof Exp:* Sr pharmacist, Pitman-Moore Div, Dow Chem Co, 66-67; sr pharm chemist, Eli Lilly & Co, 68-78, res scientist, 78-88. *Mem:* Am Pharmaceut Asn; Acad Pharmaceut Sci; Sigma Xi; Parenteral Drug Asn. *Res:* Pilot plant operations in liquid and ointment development; color measurement; drug adjuvant interactions in solid dosage forms observed with diffuse reflectance spectroscopy; development of parenteral cephalosporids; protein formulation and stability, freeze-drying. *Mailing Add:* 90 Barchester Way Westfield NJ 07090. *Fax:* 908-722-5406

BORNSTEIN, PAUL, CONNECTIVE TISSUE BIOLOGY, CELL & MOLECULAR BIOLOGY. *Current Pos:* from asst prof to assoc prof, 67-73, PROF BIOCHEM & MED, UNIV WASH, 73- *Personal Data:* b Antwerp, Belg, July 10, 34; US citizen. *Educ:* Cornell Univ, BA, 54; NY Univ, MD, 58. *Honors & Awards:* Merit Award, Nat Inst Arthritis, Musculoskeletal & Skin Dis, 89. *Prof Exp:* Res investr, NIH, 65-67. *Concurrent Pos:* Lederle med fac award, 68-71; NIH res career develop award, 69-74; Macy fac scholar award, 75; vis prof, Univ Calif, San Diego & Weizmann Inst, Israel, 75-76 & Fac Med, Inst Biol Chem, France, 85-86; assoc ed, Arteriosclerosis, 80-85; Guggenheim Found fel, 85. *Mem:* Am Soc Biochem & Molecular Biol; Am Soc Cell Biol; Am Chem Soc; Am Rheumatism Asn; Asn Am Physicians; Am Soc Clin Invest. *Res:* Biology of the extracellular matrix; role of the extracellular matrix in regulating cell function; regulation of collagen and thrombospondin gene expression. *Mailing Add:* Dept Biochem SJ-70 Univ Wash Seattle WA 98195-0001

BORNSTEIN, ROBERT D, AIR POLLUTION METEOROLOGY, BOUNDARY LAYER METEOROLOGY. *Current Pos:* from asst prof to assoc prof, 69-83, PROF METEOROL, SAN JOSE STATE UNIV, 83-, CHAIR, 93- *Personal Data:* b New York, NY, July 21, 42; m 88, Ilva R Imamura; c Mike, Jeremy & Vivian. *Educ:* City Col New York, BS, 64; NY Univ, MS, 67, PhD(meteorol), 72. *Prof Exp:* Asst res scientist, NY Univ, 64-68; instr meteorol, State Univ NY Maritime Col, 68. *Concurrent Pos:* Consult, Ames Res Ctr, NASA, Calif, 69-; Fulbright Awards, 76, 84 & 93. *Mem:* Am Meteorol Soc; Air & Waste Mgt Asn. *Res:* Observation and simulation of polluted urban boundary layers. *Mailing Add:* Dept Meteorol San Jose State Univ 1 Washington Sq San Jose CA 95192-0001. *Fax:* 408-924-5191

BORODIN, ALLAN BERTRAM, COMPUTER SCIENCE. *Current Pos:* from asst prof to assoc prof, Univ Toronto, 69-77, chmn, Dept Comput Sci, 80-85 & 92, actg chair, 92-93, PROF COMPUT SCI, UNIV TORONTO, 77- *Personal Data:* Can & US citizen. *Educ:* Rutgers Univ, BA, 63; Stevens Inst Technol, MS, 66; Cornell Univ, PhD(comput sci), 69. *Prof Exp:* Systs programmer & mem tech staff, Bell Tel Labs, NJ, 63-66; res & teaching asst, Cornell Univ, 66-69. *Concurrent Pos:* Ed, J Comput, Soc Indust & Appl Math, 74, managing ed, 77-80; vis assoc prof, Dept Comput Sci, Cornell Univ, 75; vis prof, Dept Math, Univ Nice, France, 83 & Dept Elec Eng & Comput Sci, Mass Inst Technol, 93; ed, J Comput Algebra, 84-89; Lady Davis vis prof, Inst Math & Comput Sci, Hebrew Univ, Jerusalem, 85-86 & Inst Comput Sci, 93-94; Varon vis prof, Weizmann Inst Sci, Israel, 94. *Mem:* Fel Royal Soc Can. *Res:* Computational complexity; resource tradeoffs-in particular, time versus space and parallel time versus hardware; parallel computation-interconnection networks; algebraic computation and online algorithms. *Mailing Add:* Dept Comput Sci Sandford Fleming Bldg Univ Toronto Toronto ON M5S 1A4 Can

BOROM, MARCUS P(RESTON), CERAMICS ENGINEERING, MATERIALS SCIENCE. *Current Pos:* staff ceramist, Res & Develop Ctr, Gen Elec Co, 65-74, tech coordr, 74-75, prog mgr, 75-84, SR SCIENTIST, GEN ELEC CORP RES & DEVELOP, 84- *Personal Data:* b Waynesboro, Ga, Feb 21, 34; m 58; c 4. *Educ:* Ga Inst Technol, BCerE, 56; Univ Calif, Berkeley, MS, 64, PhD(ceramics eng), 65. *Honors & Awards:* Ross Coffin Purdy Award, Am Ceramic Soc, 77. *Prof Exp:* Develop engr, Ferro Corp, Ohio, 57-60, res engr, 60-61. *Mem:* Fel Am Ceramic Soc. *Res:* Physical chemistry of glass-metal interfaces; mechanisms of adherence between dissimilar materials; diffusion kinetics in multicomponent systems; high temperature phase equilibria; properties of glass and enamels; high temperature molds and cores; hard metals and ceramic cutting tool materials; ceramic high temperature structural composites. *Mailing Add:* 1444 Fox Hollow Rd Schenectady NY 12309-2530

BORON, DAVID J, BIOMASS CONVERSION TO CHEMICALS & MATERIALS, CARBON DIOXIDE UTILIZATION. *Current Pos:* res scientist, 79-83, proj mgr, 83-90, PROG MGR, US DEPT ENERGY, 90- *Personal Data:* b Shadyside, Ohio, Mar 10, 53; m 79, Audrey M Slimak; c Stephanie & Jonathan. *Educ:* Miami Univ, BS, 75; Duquesne Univ, MS, 83. *Prof Exp:* Sr proj mgr, NY State Energy Res & Develop Auth, 83-87; res scientist & mgr coal technol res, Va Tech Univ, 87-89. *Concurrent Pos:* Mem, Biotechnol Res Subcomt, Nat Sci Technol Coun, 93-96; convener, Bioenergy Coord Comt. *Mem:* Biomass Energy Res Asn; Nat Geog Soc; Am Chem Soc; Smithsonian Inst. *Res:* Facilitate the introduction of biotechnology (bioprocessing) into the chemicals industry through high productivity bioreactors and efficient product recovery approaches; convert renewables (biomass) into feedstocks suitable for use in the chemicals industry; biological-mediated chemical synthesis. *Mailing Add:* 1000 Independence Ave SW MS EE-232 5F-043 Washington DC 20585

BORON, WALTER FRANK, TRANSPORT PHYSIOLOGY, SIGNAL TRANSDUCTION. *Current Pos:* From asst prof to assoc prof physiol, 80-87, PROF CELLULAR & MOLECULAR PHYSIOL, YALE UNIV SCH MED, 87- *Personal Data:* b Elyria, Ohio, Nov 18, 49; m 74; c 2. *Educ:* St Louis Univ, BA, 71; Wash Univ, St Louis, MD & PhD(physiol), 77. *Concurrent Pos:* Assoc ed, Physiol Reviews, 85; ed J Physiol, 85; young investr award, Am Soc Nephrol & Am Heart Asn, 87. *Mem:* Am Phys Soc; Am Soc Nephrol; Soc Gen Physiologists (treas, 88-). *Res:* Regulation of intracellular acid concentration optical and electrophysiological techniques in single cells; identifying new acid-base transport processes; their control by growth factors; examining them at a molecular level using biochemical and genetic approaches. *Mailing Add:* Dept Cellular & Molecular Physiol Sch Med Yale Univ 333 Cedar St New Haven CT 06510

BOROS, DOV LEWIS, MICROBIOLOGY, IMMUNOLOGY. *Current Pos:* assoc prof, 74-80, PROF IMMUNOL & MICROBIOL, SCH MED, WAYNE STATE UNIV, 80- *Personal Data:* b Budapest, Hungary, Mar 4, 32; US citizen; m 47; c 2. *Educ:* Hadassah Med Sch, Hebrew Univ, Jerusalem,

MSc, 58, PhD(immunochem), 67. *Prof Exp:* Asst dir, Vaccine & Serum Inst, Jerusalem, 60-68; USPHS grant, Sch Med, Case Western Reserve Univ, 68-70, asst prof immunol, 70-74. *Concurrent Pos:* Fogarty Sr Int Fel, 81-82; assoc ed, J Immunol, 83-87. *Mem:* Am Soc Trop Med & Hyg; Am Asn Immunologists. *Res:* Delayed hypersensitivity type granulomatous inflammation; parasitic immunity. *Mailing Add:* Dept Immunol & Microbiol Wayne State Univ Sch Med 540 E Canfield Ave Detroit MI 48201-1908

BOROSH, ITSHAK, MATHEMATICS, NUMBER THEORY. *Current Pos:* vis asst prof, 72-74, asst prof, 74-76, ASSOC PROF MATH, TEX A&M UNIV, 76- *Personal Data:* b Fes, Morocco, Oct 22, 38; Israeli citizen; m 62; c 2. *Educ:* Hebrew Univ, Israel, MSc, 61; Weizmann Inst Sci, Israel, PhD(math), 66. *Prof Exp:* Lectr, Bar-Ilan Univ, Israel, 66-70; vis lectr, Univ Ill, Urbana, 70-72. *Mem:* Israel Math Soc; Am Math Soc; Math Asn Am. *Res:* Diophantine approximations; relations between number theory and computing. *Mailing Add:* Dept Math Tex A&M Univ College Station TX 77843-0100

BOROVETZ, HARVEY S, BIOMEDICAL ENGINEERING, CARDIOVASCULAR BIOENGINEERING. *Current Pos:* PROF SURG, UNIV PITTSBURGH MED SCH, 76- *Personal Data:* b Pittsburgh, PA, May 21, 47. *Educ:* Brandeis Univ, BA, 69; Carnegie Mellon Univ, MS, 73, PhD(bio eng), 76. *Honors & Awards:* R&D 100 Award, 92. *Prof Exp:* Res asst, Carnegie Mellon Univ, 70-76. *Mem:* Am Soc Artificial Internal Organs; Biomed Eng Soc; fel Am Inst Med & Bioeng. *Mailing Add:* Univ Pittsburgh 1249 Benedum Hall Pittsburgh PA 15260-0001

BOROVSKY, DOV, CHEMISTRY. *Current Pos:* BIOCHEMIST, FLA MED ENTOM LAB, 75- *Personal Data:* b Tel Aviv, Israel, Dec 4, 43; m 72. *Educ:* Univ Calif, Los Angeles, BA, 67; Univ Miami, PhD(biochem), 72. *Prof Exp:* From res instr to res asst prof biochem, Univ Miami, 73-75. *Mem:* AAAS; Am Chem Soc; Sigma Xi. *Res:* Starch and glycogen metabolism and structure; production of proteolytic enzymes and its regulation in insects; hormonal control of insects metabolism and egg development. *Mailing Add:* Fla Med Entom Lab Univ Fla IFAS 200 Ninth St SE Vero Beach FL 32962-4657

BOROWIECKI, BARBARA ZAKRZEWSKA, ENVIRONMENTAL SCIENCE, GEOMORPHOLOGY. *Current Pos:* From instr to assoc prof, 60-69, chmn dept, 75-80 & 83-85, PROF GEOG, UNIV WIS-MILWAUKEE, 69- *Personal Data:* b Warsaw, Poland, Nov 20, 24; US citizen; m 71; c 1. *Educ:* Ind Univ, BS, 56, MS, 57; Univ Wis, PhD(geog), 62. *Concurrent Pos:* Vis prof geog, Ind Univ, 63-64; fel, Nat Res Coun, NSF; ETS consult. *Mem:* Asn Am Geog (secy); Sigma Xi; Am Geog Soc; Int Geog Union; Polish Inst Arts & Sci in Am. *Res:* Pleistocene geomorphology; regional geomorphology of the United States; spatial terrain problems; valley evolution; loess terrain; numerical terrain analysis. *Mailing Add:* Dept Geog Univ Wis Milwaukee WI 53201

BOROWITZ, GRACE BURCHMAN, ORGANIC CHEMISTRY, SYNTHETIC ORGANIC & NATURAL PRODUCTS CHEMISTRY. *Current Pos:* from asst prof to assoc prof, 73-80, PROF CHEM, RAMAPO COL NJ, 80- *Personal Data:* b New York, NY, Dec 7, 34; m 59; c Susan D & Lisa N (Ensfield). *Educ:* City Col New York, BS, 56; Yale Univ, MS, 58, PhD(org chem), 60. *Prof Exp:* Asst, Yale Univ, 56-57; res chemist, Am Cyanamid Co, 60-62; lectr gen chem, Yeshiva Col, 67; US Dept Health, Educ & Welfare teaching fel org chem & biochem, Upsala Col, 67-68, asst prof, 68-73. *Concurrent Pos:* Sigma Xi res grants, 68-71 & 79; NSF URP grant, 70; Ramapo Col NJ State res fac develop grant, 75-85; NSF NMR grant, 85, NJDHE grants, 85, 86 & 87, Sci Enrich HS Students, Women Minorities, NJDHE-IR grant, 86; prof chem, Columbia Univ, 87- *Mem:* Am Chem Soc; fel AAAS; Sigma Xi; NY Acad Sci; Am Asn Univ Professors. *Res:* Mechanisms in organophosphorus chemistry, including nucleophilicities of tricovalent phosphorus compounds and lithium aluminum hydride reduction of phosphoranes; synthesis and studies of new ion-selective molecules and molecular modeling. *Mailing Add:* Sch Theoret & Appl Sci 505 Ramapo Valley Rd Mahwah NJ 07430-1680

BOROWITZ, IRVING JULIUS, BIO-ORGANIC CHEMISTRY, MOLECULAR GRAPHICS & MODELING. *Current Pos:* PROF, YESHIVA UNIV, 80- *Personal Data:* b Brooklyn, NY, May 15, 30; m 59, Grace Burchman; c Susan D & Lisa N. *Educ:* City Col New York, BS, 51; Ind Univ, MA, 52; Columbia Univ, PhD(org chem), 56. *Prof Exp:* Fel biochem, Columbia Univ, 56-57 & 58-59, res assoc, 59-60; fel org chem, Yale Univ, 57-58; instr, City Col New York, 60-62; from asst prof to assoc prof, Lehigh Univ, 62-66; assoc prof, Yeshiva Univ, 66-74, prof chem, Belfer Grad Sch Sci, 74-77; res assoc, Allied Chem Corp, 77-80. *Concurrent Pos:* Fel org chem, Columbia Univ, 60-62; res grants, Sigma Xi, 61-62, Am Philos Soc, 61-64, NSF, 63-72, NIH, 64-68, 69-72 & 74-78. USAF, 65-69 & Petrol Res Fund, 66-69; grants, Res Corp, 73 & Health Res Coun, NY, 73-75; mem comt econ status, Am Chem Soc, 73-74; hon res prof, Ramapo Col, 78-; chair elect, Hudson-Bergen Chem Soc, Subsection NY Am Chem Soc Chap, 93, chair, 94. *Mem:* Am Chem Soc; NY Acad Sci; Sigma Xi; Am Asn Univ Professors. *Res:* Organic synthesis; selective ion-chelation; computer graphics. *Mailing Add:* 912 Eastlawn Dr Teaneck NJ 07666-6607

BOROWITZ, JOSEPH LEO, PHARMACOLOGY. *Current Pos:* assoc prof, 69-74, PROF PHARMACOL & TOXICOL, PURDUE UNIV, WEST LAFAYETTE, 74- *Personal Data:* b Columbus, Ohio, Dec 19, 32; div; c 3. *Educ:* Ohio State Univ, BSc, 55; Purdue Univ, MS, 57; Northwestern Univ, PhD(pharmacol), 60. *Prof Exp:* Asst pharmacol, Purdue Univ, 55-57; pharmacologist, Sch Aerospace Med, Univ Tex, 60-62; fel pharmacol, Harvard Med Sch, 63-64; asst prof, Bowman Gray Sch Med, 64-69. *Concurrent Pos:* Sabbatical, Cambridge Univ Med Sch, 76 & Sandoz A G, Basel, Switz, 84. *Mem:* Am Soc Pharmacol & Exp Therapeut; Sigma Xi. *Res:* Absorption of drugs from gastrointestinal tract; metabolism and release of catecholamines; release of granule bound substances; adenosine; calcium; kidney toxicology; cyanide neuro-toxicology. *Mailing Add:* Dept Pharmacol & Toxicol Purdue Univ Lafayette IN 47907-1968

BOROWITZ, MICHAEL J, IMMUNO-PATHOLOGY, HEMATOLOGY. *Current Pos:* ASSOC PROF PATH, DUKE UNIV, 81- *Personal Data:* b New York, NY, Dec 9, 50; m; c 2. *Educ:* Duke Univ, MD & PhD(physiol), 77. *Mailing Add:* 5 Lochwynd Ct Phoenix MD 21131

BOROWITZ, SIDNEY, THEORETICAL PHYSICS. *Current Pos:* from asst prof to prof, 50-85, EMER PROF PHYSICS, NY UNIV, 85- *Personal Data:* b Brooklyn, NY, June 12, 18. *Educ:* City Col NY, BS, 37; NY Univ, MS, 41 & PhD(physics), 48. *Honors & Awards:* JF Kennedy Res Fel, Weizmann Inst, Rehovath Israel, 65-66. *Prof Exp:* Physicist, Nat Bur Standards, 41-43; engr, Western Elec, 43-45; instr physics, NY Univ, 46-48 & Harvard Univ, 48-50. *Concurrent Pos:* Dean, Univ Col, NY Univ, 69-72, provost, Univ Hts Campus, 71-72, chancellor & exec vice pres, 72-77; exec dir, NY Acad Sci, 77-82; chief exec officer, Cistron Biotechnol, 83-85; consult, NY Univ, 85. *Mem:* Am Phys Soc; AAAS; NY Acad Sci. *Res:* Theoretical physics; atomic structure; atomic and molecular scattering; quantum electrodynamics. *Mailing Add:* 70 E Tenth St New York NY 10003

BOROWSKY, HARRY HERBERT, CHEMISTRY. *Current Pos:* CONSULT CHEMIST, 73- *Personal Data:* b New York, NY, Apr 26, 14; m 40; c 2. *Educ:* Brooklyn Col, BSc, 34. *Prof Exp:* Teacher pub schs, New York, 36-41 & 43-44; chemist, Onyx Oil & Chem Co, 44-57; tech dir, Intex Chem Co, 57-61 & Nuvite Chem Co, 61-69; vpres res & prod, Control Chem Corp, 69-73. *Mem:* Am Chem Soc; Tech Asn Pulp & Paper Indust; assoc Am Dairy Sci Asn; assoc Am Pub Health Asn; Chem Specialties Mfrs Asn. *Res:* Detergents; paper chemistry; sanitary chemicals and germicides; paint removers; metal treating compounds; applied, pesticide and surface chemistry. *Mailing Add:* 205B Covered Bridge Englishtown NJ 07726-4409

BOROWSKY, RICHARD LEWIS, EVOLUTION, GENETICS. *Current Pos:* Asst prof, 70-75, ASSOC PROF BIOL, NY UNIV, 75- *Personal Data:* b New York, NY, Oct 21, 43. *Educ:* City Univ New York, BA, 64; Yale Univ, MPhil, 67, PhD(evolutionary biol), 69. *Mem:* Genetics Soc Am; Soc Study Evolution; Am Soc Human Genetics. *Res:* Population genetics; adaptive significance of biochemical and physiological variability in populations; forensic genetics; human population genetics and the biostatistical evaluation of paternity; DNA fingerprinting. *Mailing Add:* Dept Biol NY Univ Washington Sq New York NY 10003

BORRA, ERMANNO FRANCO, COSMOLOGY, INSTRUMENTATION. *Current Pos:* from asst prof to assoc prof, 75-84, PROF PHYSICS, LAVAL UNIV, 84- *Personal Data:* b Gattinara, Italy, Mar 23, 43; Can citizen. *Educ:* Univ Torino, Italy, DSC, 67; Univ Western Ont, PhD(astron), 72. *Prof Exp:* Carnegie fel astron, Hale Observ, 72-74. *Concurrent Pos:* Vis scientist astron, Steward Observ, 81-82. *Mem:* Can Astron Soc; Can Asn Physicists; Am Astron Soc; Int Astron Union. *Res:* Observational cosmology; large scale structure of the universe; quasars; instrumentation for astronomy; very large optics. *Mailing Add:* Physics Dept Laval Univ Quebec PQ G1K 7P4 Can. *Fax:* 418-656-7405; *E-Mail:* borra@phy.ulaval.ca

BORRAS, CARIDAD, RADIOLOGICAL PHYSICS. *Current Pos:* REGIONAL ADV RADIOL HEALTH, PAN AM HEALTH ORGN, 88- *Personal Data:* b Barcelona, Spain, Feb 18, 42. *Educ:* Univ Barcelona, MS, 64; Am Bd Radiol, cert, 71; Univ Barcelona, DSc(physics), 74. *Prof Exp:* Hosp physicist, Hosp de la Santa Cruz y San Pablo, Barcelona, 64-66, asst physicist, Thomas Jefferson Univ, Philadelphia, 67-73; radiological physicist, W Coast Cancer Found, 74-88. *Concurrent Pos:* Adj asst prof, Sch Med Sci, Univ of the Pac, 75-76; consult, State Calif Dept Health, 75-; clin asst prof, Dept Radiol, Univ Calif, 82- *Mem:* Am Asn Physicists Med; Health Physics Soc; Soc Nuclear Med; Am Col Radiol; Radiol Soc NAm. *Res:* Radioembryopathological effects of high LET radionuclides; radionuclide dosimetry; imaging and radiation dosimetry of computerized tomography scanners; physics of diagnostic radiology and radiation therapy. *Mailing Add:* 525 23rd St NW Washington DC 20037

BORREGO, JOSE M, MICROWAVE ENGINEERING, SOLID STATE DEVICE PHYSICS. *Current Pos:* PROF, ELEC ENG, RENSSELAER POLYTECH INST, TROY, NY, 65- *Personal Data:* b Ojuel, Durango, Mex, Mar 21, 31; US citizen; m 58; c 3. *Educ:* Instit Tecnologico de Monterrey, BSc, 55; Mass Inst Technol, MS, 57, ScD (elec eng), 61. *Honors & Awards:* Sprague Award, Mass Inst Tech, 59. *Prof Exp:* Prof, elec eng, Mass Inst Technol, 61-62; prof, elec eng, Centro de Investigacion del IPN, Mex City, 62-65. *Mem:* Inst Elec & Electronics Engr; Sigma Xi. *Res:* Electrical characterization of semiconducture electronic devices; non-destructive measurements in semiconductor materials; microwave measurement techniques; physics of semiconductor electronic devices. *Mailing Add:* Elec Comput Systs Eng Dept JEC 7020 Rensselaer Polytech Inst 110-8th St Troy NY 12180

BORREGO, JOSEPH THOMAS, MATHEMATICS. *Current Pos:* asst prof, 66-72, ASSOC PROF MATH, UNIV MASS, AMHERST, 73- *Personal Data:* b Tampa, Fla, Sept 30, 39. *Educ:* Univ Fla, BA, 61, MS, 62, PhD(math), 66. *Prof Exp:* Instr math, Univ Fla, 65-66. *Mem:* Am Math Soc. *Res:* Topological semigroups. *Mailing Add:* Dept Math Univ Mass Tower B Amherst MA 01003-0002

BORRELLI, NICHOLAS FRANCIS, OPTICAL PROPERTIES OF GLASSES. *Current Pos:* Sr res physicist, 62-74, res assoc physics, 74-76, sr res assoc physics, Corning Glass Works, 76-91, RES FEL, CORNING, INC, 91. *Personal Data:* b Philadelphia, Pa, Nov 30, 36; m 89, Kaye C Newburg; c Barbara, Stephen & Matthew. *Educ:* Villanova Univ, BS, 58; Univ Rochester, MS, 60, PhD(chem eng), 63. *Honors & Awards:* Sullivan Award, Am Chem Soc, 91. *Concurrent Pos:* Lectr math, Elmira Col, NY, 69- *Mem:* Am Chem Soc; Soc Photo Optical Instrumentation Engrs; Sigma Xi; Optical Soc Am; NY Acad Sci. *Res:* Infrared and ultra-violet properties of glass; glass lasers; magneto-optics and electrooptic properties of glasses and glass-ceramics; optical properties of single crystals; photochromic materials; gradient refractive index materials; micro optics; nonlinear optics. *Mailing Add:* Corning Inc Res & Develop Lab Sullivan Park Corning NY 14830. *Fax:* 607-974-3675; *E-Mail:* borelli_nf@corning.com

BORRELLI, ROBERT L, APPLIED MATHEMATICS. *Current Pos:* from asst prof to assoc prof, 64-73, PROF MATH, HARVEY MUDD COL, 73-, CHMN, MATH DEPT, 81-, DIR MATH CLIN, 81- *Personal Data:* b Clarksburg, WVa, Mar 4, 32; m 56; c 4. *Educ:* Stanford Univ, BS, 53, MS, 54; Univ Calif, Berkeley, PhD(appl math), 63. *Prof Exp:* Mathematician, Gen Tel & Elec Labs, 59-62; asst prof math, US Naval Postgrad Sch, 62-63; mathematician, Philco Corp, 63-64. *Mem:* Am Math Soc; Math Asn Am. *Res:* Partial differential equations; non-elliptic boundary problems. *Mailing Add:* Dept Math Harvey Mudd Col 1250 N Darthmouth Ave Claremont CA 91711-5990

BORRIS, ROBERT P, PHARMACOGNOSY, PHYTOCHEMISTRY. *Current Pos:* sr res chemist, 83-87, res fel, 87-93, SR RES FEL, MERCK RES LABS, 93- *Personal Data:* b Chicago, Ill, Nov 12, 52; m 79; c 2. *Educ:* Loyola Univ, BS, 74; Univ Ill, BS, 77, PhD(pharmacog), 81. *Prof Exp:* Fel chem, Univ Zurich, 81-82; asst prof pharmacog, Rutgers Univ, 82-83. *Concurrent Pos:* Mem exec comt, Am Soc Pharmacog, 91-94. *Mem:* Am Chem Soc; Am Soc Pharmacog (vpres, 96-97, pres, 97-98); Int Union Pure & Appl Chem; Soc Econ Bot. *Res:* Discovery of novel, biologically active compounds from natural sources with potential applications as pharmaceutical therapeutics. *Mailing Add:* 211 Fox Hollow Rd Glen Gardner NJ 08826

BORRONE, LILLIAN C, CIVIL ENGINEERING, POLITICAL SCIENCE. *Current Pos:* spec asst to dir, Terminals, Port Authority NY & NJ, 70-78, asst dir aviation, 82-84, dir mgt & budget, 84-88, DIR, PORT COMMERCE DEPT, PORT AUTHORITY NY & NJ, 88- *Personal Data:* b Patterson, NJ, Aug 13, 45. *Educ:* Am Univ, BA, 68; Manhattan Col, MS, 77. *Prof Exp:* Sr transp technician, Metrop Wash Counn Govt, 68-69; transp rep, Urban Mass Transp Admin, US Dept Transp, 69-70, assoc adminr & dep adminr, 78-81; assoc, Parrish & Chambers, 81-82. *Mem:* Nat Acad Eng; Am Soc Pub Admin; Nat Acad Pub Admin; Am Asn Port Authorities; Int Asn Port Authorities. *Res:* Management and operations of transportation systems; environmental laws and regulations and their effect on system innovation, operations and financing; system competitiveness and intermodal/modal contribution to the national and global economics and defense. *Mailing Add:* Port Authority NY & NJ 1 World Trade Ctr 345 New York NY 10048

BORROR, ALAN L, ORGANIC CHEMISTRY. *Current Pos:* RETIRED. *Personal Data:* b Ambridge, Pa, June 4, 34; m 59; c 1. *Educ:* Drexel Inst Technol, BS, 57; Princeton Univ, PhD(org chem), 61. *Prof Exp:* Fel, Harvard Univ, 61-62; from asst prof to assoc prof chem, Drexel Inst Technol, 62-67; from scientist to sr scientist, Polaroid Corp, 67-70, res group leader, 70-74, lab mgr, 74-80, dir org chem, 80-88. *Mem:* Am Chem Soc. *Res:* Synthesis and reactions of heterocyclic compounds; mechanisms of organic reactions. *Mailing Add:* 19 Cape Woods Dr Cape Elizabeth ME 04107-1250

BORROR, ARTHUR CHARLES, PROTOZOOLOGY. *Current Pos:* From asst prof to assoc prof, 61-74, PROF ZOOL, UNIV NH, 74- *Personal Data:* b Columbus, Ohio, May 27, 35; m 57; c 2. *Educ:* Ohio State Univ, BSc, 56, MSc, 58; Fla State Univ, PhD(protozool), 61. *Concurrent Pos:* Assoc dir, Shoals Marine Lab. *Mem:* Am Micros Soc; AAAS; Soc Protozool. *Res:* Morphology, ecology, systematics and distribution of marine ciliated Protozoa. *Mailing Add:* 58 Edgewood Rd Durham NH 03824

BORROWMAN, S RALPH, CHEMISTRY. *Current Pos:* RETIRED. *Personal Data:* b Bedford, Wyo, Oct 29, 18; m 41, Connie Hanson; c Sandra Lee, Barbara Ann, Judith Evelyn, Janet Elaine, Darrell Ralph & Bruce Wayne. *Educ:* Univ Idaho, BS, 41; Univ Utah, 44, PhD(chem), 50. *Prof Exp:* Chem engr, Deseret Chem Warfare Depot, 44; res chemist, US Bur Mines, 50-58, supvr res chemist, 58-80; res anal chem, Univ Utah Res Inst, 80-82. *Mem:* Am Chem Soc. *Res:* Recovery of metals from low grade domestic ores by hydrometallurgical processes such as solvent extraction and ion exchange. *Mailing Add:* 158 W 2800 S Bountiful UT 84010

BORSA, JOSEPH, RADIATION PROCESSING, RADIATION BIOLOGY. *Current Pos:* RES OFFICER, RADIATION RES BR, WHITESHELL LABS, AECL RES, 85- *Personal Data:* b Wakaw, Sask, Aug 5, 38; m 60, Donna Chycoski; c John, Tamara & Gordon. *Educ:* Univ Sask, BE, 61, MSc, 63; Univ Toronto, PhD(biophys), 67. *Prof Exp:* Nat Cancer Inst Can fel, Wistar Inst Anat & Biol, Pa, 67-69; res officer, Med Biophys Br, Whiteshell Nuclear Res Estab, Atomic Energy Can Ltd, 69-85. *Concurrent Pos:* Adj prof radiation processing food & agr, Dept Agr Eng, Univ Man. *Mem:* Am Soc Microbiol; Can Soc Cell Biol; Radiation Res Soc; Coun Agr Sci & Technol. *Res:* Radiobiology; radiation processing; mycotoxins; food microbiology. *Mailing Add:* AECL Res Whiteshell Labs Pinawa MB R0E 1L0 Can. *Fax:* 204-753-8802; *E-Mail:* borsaj@wl.aecl.ca.

BORSARI, BRUNO, ZOOLOGY, ANIMAL SCIENCE. *Current Pos:* INSTR BIOL, LA STATE UNIV, EUNICE, 91- *Personal Data:* b Cesena, Italy, Jan 11, 61; m 89. *Educ:* Bologna Univ, Italy, Doctorate(agr sci), 86. *Prof Exp:* Instr agron & animal sci, St Joseph Voc Ctr, Lunsar-Sierra Leona, WAfrica, 87-89. *Res:* Classification and propagation on a protected area of the native plants and flowers of the prairie of southwestern Louisiana. *Mailing Add:* Dept Biol La State Univ PO Box 1129 Eunice LA 70535

BORSE, GAROLD JOSEPH, THEORETICAL PHYSICS. *Current Pos:* Asst prof, 66-71, assoc prof, 71-, PROF PHYSICS & ASSOC CHAIR, LEHIGH UNIV. *Personal Data:* b Detroit, Mich, Dec 20, 40; m 63; c 1. *Educ:* Univ Detroit, BS, 62; Univ Va, MS, 64, PhD(physics), 66. *Mem:* Am Phys Soc; Am Asn Physics Teachers. *Res:* Nuclear structure theory; meson-baryon bound states. *Mailing Add:* Dept Physics Lehigh Univ Bethlehem PA 18015

BORSO, CHARLES S, SMALL ANGLE SCATTERING, ARTIFICIAL INTELLIGENCE. *Current Pos:* CONSULT, 85- *Personal Data:* b Ann Arbor, Mich, July 3, 46; m 72; c 3. *Educ:* Princeton Univ, PhD(physics), 79. *Honors & Awards:* Indust Res-100 Award, 83 & 85. *Prof Exp:* Res consult, Bell Labs, 77-79; asst biophysicist, Argonne Nat Lab, 79-85. *Mem:* AAAS. *Res:* Artificial intelligence techniques applied to automated programming algorithms; intelligent systems. *Mailing Add:* 34 S Cottonwood Lane Naperville IL 60540

BORSOS, TIBOR, CANCER, IMMUNOLOGY. *Current Pos:* res chemist, Nat Cancer Inst, 62-66, head immunochem sect, 66-76, assoc chief biol br, 71-76, head humoral immunity sect, 76-80, assoc chief, 76-85, CHIEF LAB IMMUNOBIOL, NAT CANCER INST, 85-, EMER SCIENTIST; RES PROF PATH, US UNIFORMED HEALTH SERV, 87- *Personal Data:* b Budapest, Hungary, Mar 12, 27; US citizen; m 50; c 2. *Educ:* Cath Univ, BA, 54; Johns Hopkins Univ, ScD(hyg), 58. *Honors & Awards:* Alexander von Humboldt Award, 88. *Prof Exp:* Res fel microbiol, Johns Hopkins Univ, 58-60, asst prof, 60-62. *Mem:* Am Asn Immunol. *Res:* Tumor immunology; immunochemistry; action, mechanism and characterization of complement components. *Mailing Add:* Dept Path Uniformed Serv Univ Health Sci 4301 Jones Bridge Rd Bethesda MD 20814-4799

BORST, DARYLL C, LIMNOLOGY. *Current Pos:* assoc prof, 68-73, PROF BIOL, QUINNIPIAC COL, 73- *Personal Data:* b Pontiac, Mich, July 8, 40; m 65; c 2. *Educ:* Ferris State Univ, BS, 62; Cent Mich Univ, MA, 64; Univ Ill, Urbana, PhD(zool), 68. *Prof Exp:* Chemist, Gt Lakes-Ill River Basins Proj, Fed Water Pollution Control Admin, 64. *Concurrent Pos:* Consult limnol & lake restoration, 75- *Mem:* Am Soc Limnol & Oceanog; Am Micros Soc; NAm Benthological Soc; Ecol Soc Am; Sigma Xi; NAm Lake Mgt Soc. *Res:* Limnological studies of alpine lakes and streams; limnology of lake restoration. *Mailing Add:* 97 Pool Rd North Haven CT 06473

BORST, DAVID W(ELLINGTON), ELECTRICAL ENGINEERING. *Current Pos:* appln engr, 61-62, chief appln engr, 62-65, mgr power devices, Eng Sect, 65-68, mgr devices prod eng, 68-71, mgr customer eng, 71-76, mgr rating & eval 76-78, mgr device rating & nomenclature, 78-75, MGR ENG ADMIN, INT RECTIFIER CORP, EL SEGUNDO, 85- *Personal Data:* b Jacksonville, Fla; m 41; c 3. *Educ:* Brown Univ, ScB, 40. *Prof Exp:* Test engr, Gen Elec Co, 40-41, requisition engr, 41-43, proj engr, 43-45, appln engr, 45-58, with low voltage switch gear dept, 58-61. *Concurrent Pos:* Tech mgr, Intercol Broadcasting Syst, 40-48, opers mgr & eng consult, 48-53, vpres, 53-58, pres, 58, West Coast vpres, 61-71, vchmn-West, 75-, secy, 79- *Mem:* Fel Inst Elec & Electronics Engrs; assoc Sigma Xi. *Res:* Method for supplying power to igniters in mercury arc rectifiers; method for rapid switching of a loading resistor by means of an ignitron. *Mailing Add:* 2104 Chelsea Rd Palos Verdes Estates CA 90274

BORST, DIANE ELIZABETH, cell biology, for more information see previous edition

BORST, LYLE BENJAMIN, PHYSICS, SCIENCE IN PRE-HISTORY. *Current Pos:* master, Clifford Furnas Col, 68-73, prof physics, 61-83, PROF EMER, STATE UNIV NY, BUFFALO, 83- *Personal Data:* b Chicago, Ill, Nov 24, 12; m 39, Barbara Mayer; c John B, Stephen L & Frances E. *Educ:* Univ Ill, AB, 36, AM, 37; Univ Chicago, PhD(chem), 41. *Prof Exp:* Instr chem & gen sci, Univ Chicago, 40-41, res assoc, Metall Lab, 41-43; sr physicist, Clinton Lab, Oak Ridge, 43-46; asst prof chem, Mass Inst Technol, 46-51; prof physics, Univ Utah, 51-54; chmn dept, NY Univ, 54-61. *Concurrent Pos:* Chmn dept reactor sci & eng, Brookhaven Nat Lab, 46-51. *Mem:* Fel AAAS; fel Am Phys Soc. *Res:* Neutron and general nuclear physics; nuclear reactor design and development; infrared spectroscopy; liquid helium; mathematics and astronomy in pre-history. *Mailing Add:* Phys & Astron Dept State Univ NY Buffalo NY 14260

BORST, ROGER LEE, mineralogy, for more information see previous edition

BORST, WALTER LUDWIG, ATOMIC PHYSICS, ATMOSPHERIC PHYSICS. *Current Pos:* asst prof, 71-75, ASSOC PROF PHYSICS, SOUTHERN ILL UNIV, 75- *Personal Data:* b Prague, Czech, Sept 12, 38; m 64; c 1. *Educ:* Univ Tubingen, BS, 60, MS, 64; Univ Calif, Berkeley, PhD(physics), 68. *Prof Exp:* Res assoc, Space Res Coord Ctr, Univ Pittsburgh, 68-69, res asst prof physics, 70. *Mem:* Am Phys Soc; Am Geophys Union; Sigma Xi. *Res:* Atomic and molecular collision processes; reactions between electrons, ions and atmospheric gases; metastable spectroscopy; auroral phenomena; surface physics; solar energy research; solar heating and cooling of buildings; thermal design of buildings. *Mailing Add:* Dept Phys Tex Tech Univ Lubbock TX 79409

BORST-EILERS, ELSE, MEDICINE. *Current Pos:* PROF EVAL RES CLIN MED, UNIV AMSTERDAM, 92-; MINISTER, DUTCH GOV, 94- *Personal Data:* b Amsterdam, Mar 22, 32. *Educ:* Univ Amsterdam, MD, 58, PhD, 72. *Prof Exp:* Resident pediat, Univ Amsterdam, 58-60, immunohemat, 60-65; res & lectr immunohemat, Unit Utrecht, 56-68, head bloodbank, Univ Hosp, 69-75, med dir, 76-86; vpres, Health Coun Neth, 86-94. *Concurrent Pos:* Pres, Dutch Coun Bloodtransfusion; secretariat, Int Soc Technol Assessment. *Mem:* Inst Med-Nat Acad Sci. *Res:* Cause and prevention of Rh-immunization. *Mailing Add:* Ministry Health Welfare & Sports PO Box 54062280 HK Ryswyk Netherlands

BORSTING, JACK RAYMOND, RESOURCE MANAGEMENT, OPERATIONS RESEARCH. *Current Pos:* DEAN SCH ADMIN, UNIV SOUTHERN CALIF, 88- *Personal Data:* b Portland, Ore, Jan 31, 29; m 53; c 2. *Educ:* Ore State Univ, BA, 51; Univ Ore, MA, 52, PhD(math statist), 59. *Honors & Awards:* Kimbal Medal, Oper Res Soc Am. *Prof Exp:* Instr math, Western Wash State Col, 53-54; from asst prof to prof opers res & statist, US Naval Postgrad Sch, 59-80, chmn, Dept Opers Anal, 64-71, chmn, Dept Opers Res & Admin Sci, 71-74, provost & acad dean, 74-80; asst secy defense, Pentagon, 80-83; sch bus admin, Univ Miami, 83-88. *Concurrent Pos:* Consult, Inst Defense Anal, Ctr Naval Anal; IBM lectr, 66-69; vis prof, Univ Colo, 67, 69 & 71; vis distinguished prof, Ore State Univ, 68; mem, Naval Res Adv Bd Personnel Labs, 71-78; bd dir, Inst Educ Leadership, 81. *Mem:* Am Statist Asn; Inst Mgt Sci; Opers Res Soc Am (pres, 75-76); Mil Opers Res Soc (pres, 71-72); Sigma Xi. *Res:* Statistical classification techniques; reliability technical management. *Mailing Add:* PO Box 209 Palm Desert CA 92261

BORSUK, GERALD M, MICROELECTRONICS & PHOTODETECTORS, SOLID STATE ELECTRONICS. *Current Pos:* SUPT, NAVAL RES LAB, WASHINGTON, DC, 83- *Personal Data:* b Newark, NJ, Dec 15, 44; m 71; c 2. *Educ:* Georgetown Univ, BS, 66, MS, 69, PhD(physics), 72. *Honors & Awards:* IR 100 Award, 82. *Prof Exp:* Staff physicist, ITT Electro Physics Lab, Columbia, Md, 73-77; mgr, Westinghouse Adv Tech Lab, Baltimore, Md, 77-83. *Concurrent Pos:* Dep mem, Adv Group Elec Devices, 83-; mem, Microelectronics Bd, Univ Md, 86-89; adj prof electronic eng & computer sci, George Washington Univ, 88-89. *Mem:* Sigma Xi; Inst Elec & Electronics Engrs. *Res:* Electronic research and development; formulates Naval Res Lab, Navy, and Dept Defense policy in electronics tech base. *Mailing Add:* 3547 Appleton St NW Washington DC 20008-2910

BORTHAKUR, DULAL, MICROBIAL GENETICS, NITROGEN FIXATION. *Current Pos:* asst researcher, Biotechnol Prog, 89-94, asst prof, 94-96, ASSOC PROF, UNIV HAWAII, 96- *Personal Data:* b Barua Banum Gaon, Assam, India, Mar 1, 55; m 82, Pritty Bhattacharyya; c Rajsree D & Gitasre D. *Educ:* Assam Agr Univ, Jorhat, India, BSc, 75; Punjab Agr Univ, Ludhiana, India, MSc, 77; Univ East Anglia, Norwich, Eng, PhD(molecular biol), 87. *Prof Exp:* Lectr plant breeding & genetics, Assam Agr Univ, Jorhat, India, 78-80, asst prof, 80-83; res assoc, Dept Molecular Genetics & Cell Biol, Univ Chicago, 86-89. *Concurrent Pos:* Prin investr nitrogen fixation, USDA Nat Res Initiative, 92- *Mem:* Am Soc Microbiol; Sigma Xi; Int Soc Molecular Plant-Microbe Interactions. *Res:* Genetic aspects of tropical root-nodule-bacteria; genetics of mimosine degradation by Rhizobium; genetics of nodulation competitiveness; genetics of exopolysaccharide synthesis by Rhizobium. *Mailing Add:* Dept Plant Molecular Physiol St John Bldg Rm 503 Univ Hawaii 3190 Maile Way Honolulu HI 96822. *Fax:* 808-956-3542; *E-Mail:* dulal@u.hawaii.edu

BORTIN, MORTIMER M, BONE MARROW. *Current Pos:* PROF MED & SCI DIR, INT BONE MARROW REGISTRY, MED COL WIS, 51- *Educ:* Marquette Univ, MD, 45. *Mailing Add:* 9301 N 76th St Milwaukee WI 53223

BORTNICK, NEWMAN MAYER, SYNTHETIC ORGANIC CHEMISTRY, ORGANIC POLYMER CHEMISTRY. *Current Pos:* Res chemist, Rohm & Haas Co, Bristol, 44-59, head, High Pressure Res Lab, 59-66, res supvr, 66-73, mgr explor process res, 73-81 & plastics res, 81-84, corp res fel, 84-90, CONSULT, ROHM & HAAS CO, BRISTOL, 91- *Personal Data:* b Minneapolis, Minn, May 14, 21; m 43, Lillian Ulanove; c Karl, Lynn & Wendy. *Educ:* Univ Minn, BA, 41, PhD(chem), 44. *Concurrent Pos:* Sharpe Dohme res fel. *Mem:* Fel AAAS; Am Chem Soc; Royal Soc Chem; Am Inst Chemists; Soc Plastics Engrs; Sigma Xi. *Res:* Synthetic organic chemistry; polymerization; continuous proceses for plexiglas molding powders and sheet; primene talkyl; amberlyst ion exhange catalips; triazine sythesis. *Mailing Add:* 509 Oreland Mill Rd Oreland PA 19075-2388. *Fax:* 215-781-0624; *E-Mail:* rsrnmb@rohmhaas.com

BORTOFF, ALEXANDER, PHYSIOLOGY. *Current Pos:* from asst prof to assoc prof, 62-70, PROF PHYSIOL, STATE UNIV NY UPSTATE MED CTR, 70- *Personal Data:* b Cleveland, Ohio, Sept 13, 32; m 60; c 2. *Educ:* Western Reserve Univ, BS, 53; WVa Univ, MS, 56; Univ Ill, PhD(physiol), 59. *Prof Exp:* Fel, Univ Ill, 59-60; instr ophthalmic res, Western Reserve Univ, 60-62, instr physiol, 61-62. *Mem:* AAAS; Am Physiol Soc. *Res:* Electrophysiology of smooth muscle. *Mailing Add:* Dept Physiol State Univ NY Health Sci Ctr 750 E Adams St Syracuse NY 13210-2306

BORTON, ANTHONY, ANIMAL SCIENCE. *Current Pos:* From asst prof to prof, 64-95, EMER PROF ANIMAL SCI, UNIV MASS, AMHERST, 95- *Personal Data:* b Bryn Mawr, Pa, June 6, 33; m 57; c 2. *Educ:* Haverford Col, AB, 55; Mich State Univ, MS, 61, PhD(animal sci), 64. *Mem:* Am Soc Animal Sci. *Res:* Reproduction in domestic animals; equine nutrition and physiology. *Mailing Add:* 234 Main Poland Rd Conway MA 01341

BORTON, THOMAS ERNEST, AUDIOLOGY, HEARING SCIENCE. *Current Pos:* ASSOC PROF, UNIV ALA, BIRMINGHAM, 86- *Personal Data:* b Cleveland, Ohio, Sept, 22, 42; m 70; c Thomas E & James K. *Educ:* Univ Ill, BA, 66, MA, 68, PhD(audiol), 73. *Prof Exp:* Asst prof audiol, Murray State Univ, 73-74; asst prof, Boston Univ, 74-75; assoc prof, Auburn Univ, 75-80, Univ SC, 84-86; assoc prof audiol, Univ Ala, 80-84; assoc prof, Univ SC, 84-86. *Concurrent Pos:* Assoc ed, J Speech & Hearing Asn, Ala, 76-80; ed consult, J Speech & Hearing Dis 79-86; dir, Speech & Hearing Clin, Children's Hosp, Ala, 81-83. *Mem:* Am Speech, Language & Hearing Asn; Am Auditory Soc; Am Acad Audiol. *Res:* Prevention of hearing loss resulting from exposure to intense noise; treatment of patients suffering from tinnitus aurium; development of electrophysiological diagnostic tools for evaluating the auditory system. *Mailing Add:* Univ Ala Dept Surg Div Otolaryngol 1717 Seventh Ave S Birmingham AL 35294-0001

BORTONE, STEPHEN ANTHONY, ICHTHYOLOGY, MARINE BIOLOGY. *Current Pos:* From instr to assoc prof, 73-84, PROF BIOL, UNIV WFLA, 84- *Personal Data:* b Boston, Mass, Sept 3, 46; m 68; c 2. *Educ:* Albright Col, BS, 68; Fla State Univ, MS, 70; Univ NC, Chapel Hill, PhD(marine sci), 73. *Mem:* Am Soc Ichthyologists & Herpetologists; Am Fisheries Soc; Fisheries Soc Brit Isles; Ichthyol Soc Japan; Soc Study Evolution. *Res:* Reproductive biology, systematics and life history of hermaphroditic fishes; fish communities; zoogeography of fishes; fishes-parasitic copepod relationships. *Mailing Add:* Dept Biol Univ WFla Pensacola FL 32504

BORTZ, ALFRED BENJAMIN, SCIENCE WRITING ESPECIALLY CHILDRENS SCIENCE BOOKS. *Current Pos:* CONSULT/AUTH, 96- *Personal Data:* b Pittsburgh, Pa, Nov, 20, 44; m 67, Susan Grossberger; c Brian S & Rosalie E. *Educ:* Carnegie Inst Technol, BS, 66, MS, 67; Carnegie Mellon Univ, PhD (physics), 71. *Prof Exp:* From instr to asst prof physics, Bowling Green State Univ, 70-73; res assoc, Yeshiva Univ, 73-74; sr engr, Advan Reactors Div, Westinghouse Elec Co, 74-77; staff scientist, Essex Group, Inc, United Technol, 77-79; from res scientist to sr fel, Sci & Technol Educ, Carnegie Mellon Univ, 79-94; res fel, Sch Educ, Duquesue Univ, 94-96. *Concurrent Pos:* Consult, Childrens Press, 86-89, Harper & Row Jr Books Group, 85, Franklin Watts Inc, 84-, Nat Res Coun Panel Interfaces & Thin Films, 86, Mat Res Coun, Defense Adv Res Proj Agency, 86-87, AAAS Proj 2061, 85; Grolier, 86-89 & 96-, Millbrook Pres, 89-, St Vincent Col, 93-97 & Newton's Apple, 96-; Gen Chair Nat Forum on Children Sci Bk, 92; instr, Inst Children's Lit, 96-; reviewer, pub weekly, 96- *Mem:* Am Phys Soc; AAAS; Sigma Xi; Soc Children's Bk Writers & Illustrators. *Res:* Childrens science books and articles; pre college science education; public understanding of science and technology; science writing. *Mailing Add:* 1312 Foxboro Dr Monroeville PA 15146. *Fax:* 412-372-3980; *E-Mail:* bortz@duq3.cc.duq.edu

BORUCKI, WILLIAM JOSEPH, SEARCH FOR OTHER SOLAR SYSTEMS, PHYSICS OF LIGHTNING. *Current Pos:* Res scientist spectros, 62-72, RES SCIENTIST PLANETARY SCI & PHYSICS, NASA-AMES RES CTR, 72- *Personal Data:* b Chicago, Ill, Jan 26, 39; m 63, Josephine J; c 3. *Educ:* Univ Wis-Madison, BS, 60, MS, 62. *Concurrent Pos:* Guest investr, Pioneer Venus Spacecraft, 88. *Mem:* Am Geophys Union; Am Astron Soc. *Res:* Studies of lightning in planetary atmospheres; development of a system to search for other solar systems. *Mailing Add:* Ames Res Ctr MS 245-3 NASA Moffett Field CA 94035. *Fax:* 650-604-6779; *E-Mail:* Borucki@chandon.arc.nasa.gov

BORUM, OLIN H, SCIENCE EDUCATION, SCIENCE ADMINISTRATION. *Current Pos:* RETIRED. *Personal Data:* b Spencer, NC, Nov 3, 17; m 44, 77, Beatric S Comulada; c Pamela L (Edin), Robin O & Denis R. *Educ:* Univ NC, BS, 38, AM, 47, PhD(chem), 49. *Prof Exp:* Asst anal chem, Univ NC, 46-49; res chemist, Philadelphia Lab, E I du Pont de Nemours & Co, 49-50; interim res asst prof, Cancer Res Lab, Univ Fla, 50; res adminr chem div, Off Sci Res Hq, Air Res & Develop Command, 51-52; from instr to asst prof chem, US Mil Acad, 52-55; student, USAF Air Command & Staff Col, 55-56; res adminr res div, Chem Corps Res & Develop Command, DC, 56-60 & res & tech div, Wright-Patterson AFB, Ohio, 60-64; sci adminr, Hq, Army Materiel Command, Res, Develop & Eng Directorate, 64-76. *Concurrent Pos:* Consult, Am Chem Soc Petrol Res Fund, 78. *Mem:* Am Chem Soc; fel Am Inst Chemists; Sigma Xi. *Res:* Formation of acylamido ketones from amino acids; conversion of acylamido ketones to oxazoles and thiazoles; reactions of amino acids; diene synthesis with maleic anhydride and maleimide; synthesis of dioxaspiroheptane; chemistry of chemical warfare agents; materials science; explosives science; organic chemistry. *Mailing Add:* 9002 Volunteer Dr Alexandria VA 22309-2921

BORUM, PEGGY R, HUMAN NUTRITION, CARNITINE METABOLISM. *Current Pos:* ASSOC PROF HUMAN NUTRIT, DEPT FOOD SCI & HUMAN NUTRIT, UNIV FLA, 83- *Personal Data:* b 1946. *Educ:* Univ Tenn, Knoxville, PhD(biochem), 72. *Res:* Nutritional assessment. *Mailing Add:* 3131 NW 31st St Gainesville FL 32605-2164

BORWEIN, DAVID, MATHEMATICS. *Current Pos:* vis prof, Univ Western Ont, 63-64, prof, 64-89, head dept, 67-89, EMER PROF MATH, UNIV WESTERN ONT, 89- *Personal Data:* b Kaunas, Lithuania, Mar 24, 24; m 46, Bessie Flax; c Jonathan M, Peter B & Sarah T. *Educ:* Univ Witwatersrand, BSc, 45, BSc, 48; Univ London, PhD(math), 50, DSc(math), 60. *Prof Exp:* Lectr math, Univ St Andrews, 50-63. *Concurrent Pos:* Adv prob ed, Am Math, 82-85 & co-ed, Anal Int J Anal & Its Appln. *Mem:* Am Math Soc; Can Math Soc (vpres, 73-75, pres, 85-87); London Math Soc; fel Royal Soc Edinburgh; Math Asn Am. *Res:* Theory of summability of series and integrals. *Mailing Add:* Dept Math Univ Western Ont London ON N6A 5B7 Can. *Fax:* 519-661-3610; *E-Mail:* dborwein@uwa.ca

BORWEIN, JONATHAN MICHAEL, MATHEMATICS. *Current Pos:* PROF MATH, SIMON FRASER UNIV, BURNABY, BC, 84- *Personal Data:* b St Andrews, Scotland, May 20, 51; m 73, Judith Diedre Scott Roots; c Rachel, Naomi & Tova. *Educ:* Univ Western Ont, BA, 71; Jesus Col Oxford, MSc, 72, DPhil, 74. *Honors & Awards:* Coxeter-James Lectr, AAAS, 87; Fraser Medal, Atlantic Prov Coun on Scis, 88; Chauvenet Prize, Math Asn Am, 93; Merten M Hasse Prize, 93. *Prof Exp:* Fel, Dalouisie Univ, 74-75, lectr & res assoc, 75-76, from asst to assoc prof, 76-84. *Concurrent Pos:* From asst prof to assoc prof, Carnegie-Mellon Univ, 80-82; bd dirs, AAAS, 84-88, res comt, 85-88; prof invitee, French Nat Limoges, 85; distinguishing vis prof, Ctr Math Res, Univ Montreal, 86; Sr Killan fel, Dalhousie Univ, 87-88, adj prof, Dept Math Stats & Comput Sci, 93-96; chmn, 89-91, Comn Collaborative Res Initiatives, Nat Sci & Eng Res Coun, 92-95; mem, Simon Fraser Ctr Syst Sci, 92-, Simon Fraser Univ Res Coun, 93; dir, Simon Fraser Ctr Exp & Constructive Math, 93- *Mem:* Fel Royal Soc Can; AAAS; Can Math Soc; Am Math Soc; Math Asn Am; Soc Indust & Appl Math. *Res:* Optimization, computational analysis experimental mathematics and non-linear analysis. *Mailing Add:* Dept Math & Statist Simon Fraser Univ Burnaby BC V5A 1S6 Can

BORWEIN, PETER BENJAMIN, CLASSICAL ANALYSIS, COMPUTATIONAL PURE MATHEMATICS. *Current Pos:* PROF MATH, SIMON FRASER UNIV, 93- *Personal Data:* b St Andrews, Scotland, Oct 5, 53; Can citizen; m 80, Jennifer Elaine Moore; c Alexandra, Sophie & Theresa. *Educ:* Univ Western Ont, BSc, 74; Univ BC, MA, 76, PhD, 79. *Honors & Awards:* Merten Hasse Prize & Chauvenet Prize, Math Asn Am, 93. *Prof Exp:* NATO postdoctoral fel, Oxford Univ, 79-80; prof math, Dalhousie Univ, 80-93. *Concurrent Pos:* Assoc dir, Ctr Construct & Expl Math, 93. *Mem:* Am Math Soc; Can Math Soc; Math Asn Am. *Res:* Highly computational question in pure mathematics at the interface of classical analysis and number theory; contributed more than 100 articles to professional journals. *Mailing Add:* Math Dept Simon Fraser Univ Burnaby BC V5A 1S6 Can. *Fax:* 604-291-5014

BORYSENKO, MYRIN, IMMUNOBIOLOGY. *Current Pos:* RETIRED. *Personal Data:* b Berezhani, Ukraine, June 3, 42; US citizen; m 70; c 3. *Educ:* St Lawrence Univ, BS, 64; State Univ NY Upstate Med Ctr, PhD(anat), 68; Univ Calif, Los Angeles, cert immunol, 70. *Prof Exp:* NIH fel, Univ Calif, Los Angeles, 68-70; from asst prof to assoc prof anat & cellular biol, Sch Med, Tufts Univ, 76-89; owner, Mind/Body Health Sci Inc, 89-94. *Concurrent Pos:* Vis assoc prof behav med, Harvard Med Sch, 78-79. *Mem:* Am Asn Anatomists; Transplantation Soc; Am Asn Immunologists; Am Soc Zoologists; NY Acad Sci; AAAS. *Res:* Phylogenetic and developmental aspects of the immune response; effect of stress on the immune system and disease susceptibility. *Mailing Add:* 1002 Apple Valley Rd Lyons CO 80540

BORYSKO, EMIL, MICROSCOPY, POLYMER CHARACTERIZATION. *Current Pos:* RETIRED. *Personal Data:* b Scranton, Pa, Sept 24, 18; div; c 3. *Educ:* Brooklyn Col, BA, 40; George Washington Univ, MA, 50; Johns Hopkins Univ, PhD(biol), 55. *Honors & Awards:* Phillip B Hoffmann Res Scientist Award, 85; J&J Distinguished Anal Chemist Award, 89. *Prof Exp:* Supvr, Optical Glass Plant, Nat Bur Stand, 41-46, fiber technologist, 47-50; instr, Johns Hopkins Univ, 55-56; res assoc, NY Univ, 56-58; prin res scientist, Ethicon Inc, NJ, 58-92. *Concurrent Pos:* Fel Damon Runyon Fund for Cancer Res, 51-53. *Mem:* Electron Micros Soc Am; NY Acad Sci; Am Soc Cell Biol; fel AAAS. *Res:* Comparative optical and electron microscopic studies of the structure of cells and tissues; dynamic aspects of cellular growth and division; connective tissues and collagen; thermal microscopy of organic polymers; transmission and scanning electron microscopy of biomedical materials; chemical milling of surgical needles. *Mailing Add:* 211 Love Rd Bridgewater NJ 08807

BORZELLECA, JOSEPH FRANCIS, PHARMACOLOGY. *Current Pos:* from asst prof to assoc prof, 59-67, PROF PHARMACOL, MED COL VA, VA COMMONWEALTH UNIV, 67- *Personal Data:* b Norristown, Pa, Oct 3, 30; m 55; c 6. *Educ:* St Joseph's Univ, Pa, BS, 52; Thomas Jefferson Univ Med Col, MS, 54, PhD(pharmacol), 56. *Honors & Awards:* Distinguished Serv Award, US Army, 86; Excellence in Med & Community Serv Award, Nat Italian-Am Found, 87. *Prof Exp:* Res asst, Trudeau Found, Jefferson Med Col, 54-55; instr pharmacol, Woman's Med Col Pa, 56-57, assoc, 57-59. *Concurrent Pos:* Pres, Toxicol & Pharmacol, Inc; mem comns, safe drinking water, toxicol & food safety, Nat Acad Sci-Nat Res Coun; consult, US Army, US Environ Protection Agency, indust. *Mem:* AAAS; Am Chem Soc; Am Soc Pharmacol & Exp Therapeut; Soc Exp Biol & Med; Soc Toxicol (pres); Sigma Xi; Am Col Toxicol. *Res:* Toxicology of substances of economic importance; drug absorption, distribution and metabolism. *Mailing Add:* Dept Pharmacol & Toxicol Med Col Va Box 613 September Dr Richmond VA 23298-0613

BOSACCHI, BRUNO, FLAT PANEL DISPLAYS, FUZZY LOGIC. *Current Pos:* SR MEM TECH STAFF & RES SCIENTIST, AT&T BELL LABS, 78- *Personal Data:* b Milan, Italy, Sept 24, 38; m 74, To T Nguyen; c Messino & Alessandro. *Educ:* Univ Milan, Italy, PhD(physics), 64. *Prof Exp:* Asst prof, Univ Milan, Italy, 66-69; vis scientist, Arporne Nat Lab, Univ Chicago, 69-71; assoc prof, Univ Parme, Italy, 71-76; vis prof, Univ Ariz, Tucson, 76-78. *Concurrent Pos:* Lectr solid state physics & technol, Vuesco Int Sch, Trieste, Italy, 72-74 & 79; vis fel, Princeton Univ, 73; teaching asst, AT&T Network Systs, 89-91; co-chmn, Int Conf Artificial Neural Networks, Orlando, Fla, 92; chmn, Int Conf Appln Fuzzy Logic Technol, Boston, Mass, 93. *Mem:* Inst Elec & Electronics Engrs; AAAS; Am Phys Soc; Int Neural Network Soc; Optical Soc Am. *Res:* Potential interest for applications (mostly optoelectronics and soft artificial intelligence). *Mailing Add:* Eng Res Ctr AT&T Bell Labs PO Box 900 Princeton NJ 08502. *E-Mail:* bbb@pruxp.att.com

BOSAKOWSKI, THOMAS, habitat selection in raptors, fish culture technology innovations, for more information see previous edition

BOSANQUET, LOUIS PERCIVAL, REACTION ENGINEERING, PROCESS DEVELOPMENT. *Current Pos:* PVT CONSULT, 94- *Personal Data:* b Leesburg, Fla, Sept 25, 31; m 78, Janine Warner; c Philip, Edward & James. *Educ:* Univ Fla, BS, 54; Univ Tenn, MS, 60, PhD(chem eng), 63. *Prof Exp:* Res engr, Shell Oil Co, 54-58; res engr, Monsanto Co, 63-70, process group leader, 70-78, supt reaction eng, 78-80, eng mgr, 80-87, group consult, 87-93. *Concurrent Pos:* Lectr reactive chem, Am Inst Chem Engrs. *Mem:* Fel Am Inst Chem Engrs; Sigma Xi. *Res:* Organic processes research and development; use digital computers; plant start-ups and trouble shooting; reaction engineering; emergency venting of vessels; kinetic modeling; runaway reactions; reactor kinetics and simulations. *Mailing Add:* 1372 Thornwick Dr Manchester MO 63011

BOSART, LANCE FRANK, SYNOPTIC-DYNAMIC METEOROLOGY. *Current Pos:* asst prof, 69-76, ASSOC PROF ATMOSPHERIC SCI, STATE UNIV NY, ALBANY, 76- *Personal Data:* b New York, NY, Aug 24, 42; m 69. *Educ:* Mass Inst Technol, BS, 64, MS, 66, PhD(meteorol), 69. *Prof Exp:* Res asst meteorol, Mass Inst Technol, 65-69. *Concurrent Pos:* Res Found NY fac res grant, 70-71; NSF grant, 70-78; vis assoc prof, Mass Inst Technol, 78-79. *Mem:* Am Meteorol Soc; Royal Meteorol Soc. *Res:* Frontogenesis; mesoscale-synoptic scale interaction through diagnostic and prognostic studies; synoptic meteorology; climatology. *Mailing Add:* Dept Atmospheric Sci State Univ NY 1400 Washington Ave Albany NY 12222-1000

BOSCH, ARTHUR JAMES, BIOCHEMISTRY. *Current Pos:* From instr to assoc prof, 58-69, PROF CHEM, CENT COL, IOWA, 69- *Personal Data:* b Luverne, Minn, Nov 15, 28; m 52; c 4. *Educ:* Cent Col, Iowa, BA, 51; Univ Wis, MS, 52, PhD(biochem), 58. *Mem:* AAAS; Am Chem Soc. *Res:* Organic, biological and general chemistry. *Mailing Add:* 1111 Peace St Pella IA 50219

BOSCH, WILLIAM W, APPLIED MATHEMATICS, STATISTICS. *Current Pos:* from asst prof to prof, 70-81, chmn, Dept Math & Appl Statist, 81-83, PROF MATH & APPL STATIST, UNIV NORTHERN COLO, 83- *Educ:* NDak State Univ, BS, 62, MS, 63; Univ Nebr, PhD(math), 70. *Prof Exp:* Teaching asst, NDak State Univ, 61-63; asst prof math, Northern State Col, Aberdeen, SDak, 63-65; fel, Univ Nebr, Lincoln, 65-70. *Concurrent Pos:* NSF fel, 62-63, 65-67; consult, Warzn Eng, Inc, 85-86. *Mem:* Am Math Soc; Math Asn Am; AAAS. *Res:* Teaching mathematics; applications in nontraditional areas; uniformly distributed sequences; analysis. *Mailing Add:* Dept Math & Appl Statist Univ Northern Colo Greeley CO 80631

BOSCHAN, ROBERT HERSCHEL, ORGANIC CHEMISTRY, POLYMER CHEMISTRY. *Current Pos:* RES & DEVELOP ENGR, LOCKHEED, GA, 91- *Personal Data:* b Los Angeles, Calif, Oct 12, 25; m 60; c 2. *Educ:* Univ Calif, Los Angeles, BS, 47, PhD(chem), 50. *Prof Exp:* Eli Lilly res fel, 50-51; res chemist synthetic med res, Merck & Co, Inc, 51-52; org chemist, Chem Div, Res Dept, US Naval Weapons Ctr, 52-59; res & develop specialist, Mat Methods Res & Eng Div, McDonnell Douglas Corp, 59-69; mgr chem instrumentation sect, Appl Sci Div, Analog Technol Corp, 69-71; head chem sect & sr staff chemist, Hughes Aircraft Co, 71-81; res & develop engr, Lockheed Aeronaut Syst Co, Calif, 81-91. *Concurrent Pos:* Instr, Phys Sci Exten, Univ Calif, Los Angeles, 56- *Mem:* Am Chem Soc; The Chem Soc; Sigma Xi. *Res:* Organic reaction mechanisms; organic synthesis; kinetics; organic fluorine chemistry; chemistry based instrumentation; gas chromatography; mass spectroscopy. *Mailing Add:* 5480 E Idlewood Lane Atlanta GA 30327-4712

BOSCHMANN, ERWIN, BIOINORGANIC CHEMISTRY. *Current Pos:* From asst prof to assoc prof, 68-75, PROF INORG CHEM, IND UNIV, INDIANAPOLIS, 76-, ASSOC DEAN FACIL, 88- *Personal Data:* b Fernheim, Paraguay, Jan 1, 39; m 62; c 3. *Educ:* Bethel Col, BS, 63; Univ Colo, MS, 65, PhD(metal chelates), 68. *Honors & Awards:* H F Lieber Award, 83. *Concurrent Pos:* Vis prof, Agrarian Univ, Peru, 68-69, actg chief party, Ford Found Proj, 69-70; consult, Ford Found, 74, State of Ind, 83 & Asian Develop Bank, 85; Lilly Fac Open fel, 86. *Mem:* Am Chem Soc. *Res:* Preparation and study of the chemistry of coordination compounds, especially metal chelates; preparation of new chelating agents; sulfoxide ligands. *Mailing Add:* 402 Blackford St Indianapolis IN 46202-3274. *Fax:* 317-274-5457; *E-Mail:* eboschma@indycms.iupui.edu

BOSCHUNG, HERBERT THEODORE, ICHTHYOLOGY. *Current Pos:* RETIRED. *Personal Data:* b Birmingham, Ala, July 16, 25; m 51; c 4. *Educ:* Univ Ala, BS, 48, MS, 49, PhD(zool, bot), 57. *Prof Exp:* From instr to prof biol, Univ Ala, 50-87. *Concurrent Pos:* Dir, Ala Mus Natural Hist, 66-79. *Mem:* Asn Southeastern Biologists; Sigma Xi; Am Soc Ichthyologists & Herpetologists. *Res:* Fishes of Gulf of Mexico; freshwater fishes of southeastern United States. *Mailing Add:* Six Country Club Lane Tuscaloosa AL 35401

BOSE, AJAY KUMAR, ORGANIC CHEMISTRY, MEDICINAL CHEMISTRY. *Current Pos:* assoc prof, 59-61, PROF CHEM, STEVENS INST TECHNOL, 61-, GEORGE MEADE BOND PROF CHEM, 83- *Personal Data:* b Silchar, India, Feb 12, 25; m 50; c 6. *Educ:* Univ Allahabad, India, BSc, 44, MSc, 46, Mass Inst Technol, ScD, 50. *Hon Degrees:* MEng, Stevens Inst Technol, 63. *Honors & Awards:* Jubilee Gold Medal, Univ Allahabad, 46; Meghnad Saha Mem Prize, 57; Ottens Res Award, Stevens Inst Technol, 68, Davis Res Award, 81. *Prof Exp:* Res fel chem, Harvard Univ, 50-51; lectr & asst prof, Indian Inst Technol, 51-56; res assoc, Univ Pa, 56-57; res chemist, Upjohn Co, 57-59. *Concurrent Pos:* Consult. *Mem:* Am Chem Soc; Indian Chem Soc; fel Indian Nat Acad Sci. *Res:* Penicillin chemistry; natural products; synthetic organic chemistry; biogenesis; nuclear magnetic resonance and mass spectrometry; popular science writing. *Mailing Add:* Dept Chem Stevens Inst Technol Hoboken NJ 07030

BOSE, AMAR G(OPAL), ACOUSTICS, ELECTRONICS. *Current Pos:* Res asst, Res Lab Electronics, 53-56, assoc prof, 56-66, PROF ELEC ENG, MASS INST TECHNOL, 66-; CHMN & CHIEF EXEC OFFICER, BOSE CORP, 64- *Personal Data:* b Philadelphia, Pa, Nov 2, 29; m 60; c 2. *Educ:* Mass Inst Technol, SB & SM, 52, ScD, 56. *Hon Degrees:* DSc, Farmingham State Col, 90. *Concurrent Pos:* Fulbright fel, Nat Phys Lab, New Delhi & Indian Statist Inst, Calcutta, 56-57. *Mem:* Nat Acad Eng; Audio Eng Soc; Sigma Xi; Am Acad Arts Sci; fel Inst Elec & Electronics Engrs. *Res:* Acoustical transducer design; audio-signal processing and switching techniques for high efficiency power processing; published numerous articles in professional publications. *Mailing Add:* Bose Corp The Mountain Framingham MA 01701

BOSE, ANIL KUMAR, PURE MATHEMATICS. *Current Pos:* ASSOC PROF MATH, CLEMSON UNIV, 68- *Personal Data:* b Calcutta, India, Apr 1, 29; m 59; c 1. *Educ:* Univ Calcutta, BS, 48, MS, 56; Univ NC, PhD(math), 64. *Prof Exp:* Lectr math, Goenka Col, Calcutta, 58-60; part-time instr, Univ NC, 60-63; vis prof, St Augustine's Col, 63-64; asst prof, Univ Ala, 64-68. *Mem:* Am Math Soc. *Res:* Differential equations on the properties of mean-value of the solutions of certain class of elliptic equations; mean-values are considered by taking various non-negative weight functions. *Mailing Add:* 315 Kings Way Clemson SC 29631

BOSE, ANJAN, POWER SYSTEM ENGINEERING. *Current Pos:* DISTINGUISHED PROF POWER ENG & DIR, SCH ELEC ENG & COMPUT SCI, WASH STATE UNIV, 93- *Personal Data:* b Calcutta, India, June 2, 46; m 76, Frances M Pavlas; c Rajesh P, Shonali M & Jahar R. *Educ:* Indian Inst Technol, Kharagpur, BTech, 67; Univ Calif, Berkeley, MS, 68; Iowa State Univ, Ames, PhD(elec eng), 74. *Prof Exp:* Res asst elec eng, Univ Calif, 67-68; engr syst planning, Consol Edison Co, 68-70; res asst elec eng, Iowa State Univ, 70-73, instr technol & social chg, 73-74; fel, Sci Ctr, IBM, 74-75; asst prof elec eng, Clarkson Univ, 75-76; consult, Energy Mgt Systs Div, Control Data Corp, 76-78, mgr, 78-81; from assoc prof to prof elec eng, Ariz State Univ, 81-93. *Concurrent Pos:* Lectr, Univ Minn, 76-81; vpres, Power Math Assocs, Inc, 81-84; consult, 84- *Mem:* Fel Inst Elec & Electronics Engrs; Int Conf Large High Voltage Elec Systs. *Res:* Analysis, design and control of large electric power grids; power system control centers; economic and secure operation of power grids; training simulators for power system operators. *Mailing Add:* Sch Elec Eng & Comput Sci Wash State Univ Pullman WA 99164-2752. *Fax:* 509-335-3818; *E-Mail:* bose@eecs.wsu.edu

BOSE, BIMAL K, POWER ELECTRONICS, AC MACHINE DRIVES. *Current Pos:* PROF ELEC ENG & CONDRA CHAIR EXCELLENCE POWER ELECTRONICS, UNIV TENN, KNOXVILLE, 87- *Personal Data:* b Calcutta, India, Sept 1, 32; US citizen; m 61, Arati Ghosh; c Papia & Amit. *Educ:* Calcutta Univ, BE, 56, PhD(elec eng), 66; Univ Wis-Madison, MS, 60. *Honors & Awards:* Mouat Gold Medal, Calcutta Univ, India, 70; Outstanding Achievement Award, Indust Applns Soc, Inst Elec & Electronics Engrs, 93, Region 3 Outstanding Award, 94, Lamine Medal, 96; Mittelmann Award, Inst Elec & Electronics Engrs, Indust Electronics Soc, 94. *Prof Exp:* Asst engr, Tata Power Co, Bombay, 56-58; asst prof elec eng, Bengal Eng Col, 60-71; assoc prof, Rensselaer Polytech Inst, 71-76; res engr, Gen Elec Res & Develop Ctr, 76-87. *Concurrent Pos:* Adj assoc prof, Rensselaer Polytech Inst, 76-87; chief scientist, Power Electronics Applns Ctr, 87-; distinguished lectr, Indust Appl Soc & Indust Electronics Soc, Inst Elec & Electronics Soc, 89; chmn, Indust Power Converter Comt, Inst Elec & Electronics Engrs, 90-; consult, Res Triangle Inst, NC, 90-; mem, Nat Power Electronics Comt, 90-; sr adv, Beijing Power Electronics Ctr, 90-; hon prof, Shanghai Univ, 91- & China Univ Mining & Technol, 96- *Mem:* Fel Inst Elec & Electronics Engrs. *Res:* Power electronics circuits; microcomputer control; control of AC drives; simulation; fuzzy and expert system application in power electronics. *Mailing Add:* Dept Elec Eng 419 Ferris Hall Univ Tenn Knoxville TN 37996

BOSE, DEEPAK, PHARMACOLOGY, MEDICINE. *Current Pos:* lectr, 67-71, from asst prof to assoc prof, 71-82, PROF PHARMACOL, UNIV MAN, 82-, PROF INTERNAL MED, 84-, PROF ANESTHESIA, 88- *Personal Data:* b Calcutta, India, Aug 24, 41; Can citizen; m 66; c 2. *Educ:* Vikram Univ, MBBS, 63; Univ Indore, India, MD, 66; Univ Man, PhD(pharmacol), 71. *Prof Exp:* Demonstr, MGM Med Col, Indore, 65-67. *Concurrent Pos:* Med Res Coun Can fel, Univ Man, 69-71. *Mem:* Am Physiol Soc; Am Pharmacol Soc; Can Pharmacol Soc; Int Soc Heart Res; Can Thoracic Soc. *Res:* Physiology and pharmacology of cardiac, smooth and skeletal muscle; autonomic pharmacology; malignant hyperthermia; cerebral blood flow regulation. *Mailing Add:* Dept Pharmacol & Therapeut Univ Man 770 Bannatyne Ave Winnipeg MB R3E 0W3 Can

BOSE, HENRY ROBERT, JR, MICROBIOLOGY, VIROLOGY. *Current Pos:* NSF fel, Univ Tex, Austin, 67-69, asst prof, 69-74, assoc prof, 74-80, PROF MICROBIOL, UNIV TEX, AUSTIN, 80-, DIR, INST CELLULAR & MOLECULAR BIOL, 93-, MARY BETZNER MORROW CENTENIAL CHAIR, 94- *Personal Data:* b Chicago, Ill, Sept 20, 40. *Educ:* Elmhurst Col, BS, 62; Univ Ind, Indianapolis, MS, 65, PhD(microbiol), 67. *Res:* Replication and transformation of cells by ribonucleic acid enveloped animal viruses. *Mailing Add:* RR 8 Austin TX 78733

BOSE, NIRMAL K, ELECTRICAL ENGINEERING, APPLIED MATHEMATICS. *Current Pos:* Singer prof, 86-92, DIR SPATIAL & TEMPORAL SIGNAL PROCESSING CTR, PA STATE UNIV, 86-, HRB-SYSTS PROF, 92- *Personal Data:* b Calcutta, India, Aug 19, 40; m 69, Chandra Guha; c Meenekshi & Enakshi. *Educ:* Indian Inst Technol, Kharagpur, BTech, 61; Cornell Univ, MS, 63; Syracuse Univ, PhD(elec eng), 67. *Prof Exp:* From asst prof to prof elec eng & prof math, Univ Pittsburgh, 67-86. *Concurrent Pos:* Consult, RCA Corp, Pa, 68-69; vis lectr, Col Steubenville, 68-70; vis assoc prof, Dept Archit & Eng, Am Univ Beirut, 71-, Univ Md, 72, Univ Calif, Berkeley, 73-74 & Princeton Univ, 96; Ger Acad Exchange Serv grant, 78; res & lect grant, Nat Ctr Sci Res-Inst Info & Automatic Res, France, 75. *Mem:* Fel Inst Elec & Electronics Engrs; AAAS; Sigma Xi; NY Acad Sci; Am Math Soc; Am Soc Eng Educ. *Res:* Active and passive network theory; automatic control; multidimensional systems theory; large-scale circuit layout design; computational complexity theory; signal and image processing; neural networks; multidimensional signal processing. *Mailing Add:* Dept Elec Eng Pa State Univ University Park PA 16802. *Fax:* 814-865-7065; *E-Mail:* nkb@stspnkb.psu.edu

BOSE, SAMIR K, THEORETICAL PHYSICS. *Current Pos:* from asst prof to assoc prof, 66-90, PROF PHYSICS, UNIV NOTRE DAME, 90- *Personal Data:* b Decca, Bangladesh, May 1, 34; m 61, Sudesh Koshal; c Purnima, Bilasa & Amit. *Educ:* Univ Delhi, BS, 56, MS, 58; Univ Rochester, PhD(physics), 62. *Prof Exp:* Mem, Sch Math, Inst Advan Study, 62-63; fel physics, Tata Inst Fundamental Res, India, 63-64; reader, Univ Delhi, 64-66; consult, Int Ctr Theoret Physics, UNESCO, Italy, 66. *Res:* Theoretical research in elementary particles and their strong and weak interactions; application of group theory and algebraic techniques to the same. *Mailing Add:* Dept Physics Univ Notre Dame 384 Nieuwland Sci Notre Dame IN 46556. *Fax:* 219-631-5952; *E-Mail:* bose@nd.edu

BOSE, SHYAMALENDU M, SOLID STATE PHYSICS, METAL & SEMICONDUCTOR PHYSICS. *Current Pos:* from asst prof to assoc prof, Drexel Univ, 70-83, assoc dean grad study & res, Col Arts & Sci, 92-93, sr assoc dean, 93-96, PROF PHYSICS, DREXEL UNIV, 83-, INTERIM DEAN, 96- *Personal Data:* b Dacca, Bangladesh, July 17, 39; m 63, Romola Raychaudhuri; c Ananda M & Aniruddha M. *Educ:* Calcutta Univ, BS, 58, MS, 60; Univ Md, College Park, PhD(physics), 68. *Prof Exp:* Lectr physics, Midnapore Col, 60-61; fel, Cath Univ Am, 67-70. *Concurrent Pos:* Res assoc, Cath Univ Am, 70-71; electronic struct in solids fel, Univ Liege, Belg, 76-77; consult engr, United Engrs & Constructors, Philadelphia, 80-84; vis scientist, Schlumberger-Doll Res, Ridgefield, Conn, 82; vis prof, Univ Waterloo, 86; prin investr NASA grants, 83-92 & NATO grants, 91- *Mem:* Sigma Xi; Am Phys Soc; Franklin Inst; Am Asn Univ Professors. *Res:* Many-body problem; electronic and optical properties of metals; dilute magnetic alloys; chemisorption by metals; electronic properties of disordered solids; surface and interface properties of solids and 2 to 6 compounds; high-temperature superconductor; published 85 papers in professional journals. *Mailing Add:* Dept Phys & Atmospheric Sci Drexel Univ Philadelphia PA 19104-9984. *Fax:* 215-895-4999; *E-Mail:* bose@duvm.ocs.drexel.edu

BOSE, SUBIR KUMAR, THEORETICAL PHYSICS, STATISTICAL MECHANICS. *Current Pos:* PROF PHYSICS, UNIV CENT FLA, ORLANDO, 87- *Personal Data:* b Calcutta, India, Jan 1, 39; m 65; c 2. *Educ:* Bihar Univ, BSc, 58; Patna Univ, MSc, 60; Allahabad Univ, PhD(physics), 67. *Prof Exp:* Res fel physics, Univ Delhi, 66-67; res fel, St Louis Univ, 67-68; from asst prof to prof physics, Southern Ill Univ, Carbondale, 68-87. *Concurrent Pos:* Vis scientist, Saha Inst Nuclear Physics, Calcutta, 77; res fel, Ind Univ, Bloomington, 78-79. *Mem:* Am Phys Soc; Sigma Xi. *Mailing Add:* Dept Physics Univ Cent Fla Orlando FL 32816. *Fax:* 407-823-5112; *E-Mail:* sbose@ucfivm

BOSE, SUBIR KUMAR, biology, molecular parasitology, for more information see previous edition

BOSE, TAPAN KUMAR, DIELECTRIC PROPERTIES MATERIALS, THERMODYNAMIC PROPERTIES GASES. *Current Pos:* from asst prof to assoc prof, Univ Que, 69-74, chmn, Dept Physics, 72-75, dir res physics, Dielectrics Res Group, 82-94, PROF PHYSICS, UNIV QUE, TROIS-RIVIERES, 74-, DIR, HYDROGEN RES INST, 94- *Personal Data:* b Calcutta, India, Oct 12, 38; Can citizen; m 66, Gouri P Chaudhuri; c Prosenjit & Ruma. *Educ:* Univ Calcutta, India, BSc Hons, 58, MSc, 61; Univ Louvain, Belg, PhD(physics), 65. *Honors & Awards:* Gov Gen's Commemorative Medal, 94. *Prof Exp:* Work leader physics, Kammerlingh onnes Lab Holland, 65-67; res assoc, Brown Univ, 67-69. *Concurrent Pos:* Vis prof phys chem, Univ Nancy, France, 76-77 & physics, Univ Bordeaux, France, 84; mem res comn, Fonds pour la formation des chercheurs et l'aide la recherche, Que, Can, 86-89. *Mem:* Can Asn Physicists; Am Phys Soc; Inst Elec & Electronics Engrs; Can Hydrogen Asn (pres). *Res:* Condensed matter physics-dielectric and optical properties of liquids and gases; dielectric properties of materials over a wide band-microwave and radiofrequency; phase transition; hydrogen storage, transport and use. *Mailing Add:* Hydrogen Res Inst Univ Que Trois-Rivieres Case Postale 500 Trois-Rivieres PQ G9A 5H7 Can. *Fax:* 819-376-5164; *E-Mail:* tapan_bose@uqtr.uquebec.ca

BOSEE, ROLAND ANDREW, BIOCHEMISTRY. *Current Pos:* CONSULT MED & HEALTH SCI, 77- *Personal Data:* b Hagerstown, Md, Feb 12, 10; m 41; c 2. *Educ:* Temple Univ, AB, 32; Drexel Inst, BS, 34; Syracuse Univ, PhD(biochem), 37. *Honors & Awards:* Mosely Award, Aerospace Med Asn. *Prof Exp:* Chief chemist, Cheplin Biol Labs, NY, 34-37; res chemist, Endo Prod, Inc, 37-38, dir labs, 38-41, vpres & plant supt, 46-47; asst officer in charge physiol br, Air Test Ctr, USN, Md, 47-50, officer in charge, 50-52, test dir parachute unit, Auxiliary Air Sta, 53-56, dir air crew equip lab, Air Mat Ctr, Philadelphia, Pa, 56-64, head aviation med equip br, Bur Med & Surg & Human Factors Off, Bur Naval Weapons, 64-66, dir crew systs div, Naval Air Systs Command Hq, Washington, DC, 66-68; dir res, Philadelphia Gen Hosp, 68-77. *Concurrent Pos:* Mem vision comt & hearing & bioacoust comt, Nat Acad Sci-Nat Res Coun. *Mem:* AAAS; Am Chem Soc; fel Am Inst Chemists; fel Aerospace Med Asn. *Res:* Aviation physiology; carbon monoxide and its effects on aviation personnel; safety and survival equipment. *Mailing Add:* 3084 SE Pine Valley St Port St Lucie FL 34952

BOSHART, CHARLES RALPH, PHARMACOLOGY. *Current Pos:* asst dir toxicol, 79-86, dir, Drug Regulatory Affairs Preclin, 86-92, DIR SAFETY OPERS, DRUG REGULATORY AFFAIRS, PHARMACEUT RES DIV, STERLING WINTHROP, INC, 92- *Personal Data:* b Lowville, NY, June 9, 32; m 56, Donalee White; c Susan, C Garret, Amy L & David. *Educ:* Univ Buffalo, BS, 54, MS, 58; Purdue Univ, PhD(pharmacol), 59. *Prof Exp:* Instr pharmacol, Purdue Univ, 57-58; pharmacologist, Am Cyanamid Co, 59-63, sr res scientist & group leader, 63-65, head, Dept Endocrinol Res, 65-69, head, Dept Toxicol Eval, Lederle Labs, 69-79. *Mem:* AAAS; Am Soc Pharmacol & Exp Therapeut; Regulatory Affairs Prof Soc; NY Acad Sci; Drug Info Asn. *Res:* Anticonvulsants; central nervous system barriers; biological use of tritium and other radioisotopes; metabolic effects of drugs. *Mailing Add:* Sanofi Res PO Box 3026 Malvern PA 19355. *Fax:* 610-983-6414

BOSHART, GREGORY LEW, ORGANIC CHEMISTRY. *Current Pos:* EXEC OFFICER, ACAD AIDE & PROF LECTR, UNIV CHICAGO, 68-, ASST TO DEAN, PHYS SCI DIV, 74-, DEAN STUDENTS. *Personal Data:* b Lowville, NY, Mar 21, 33. *Educ:* St Lawrence Univ, BS, 55; Mass Inst Technol, PhD(org chem), 60. *Prof Exp:* Chemist, E I du Pont de Nemours & Co, 57, Esso Res & Eng Co, 60-61, 62-64 & Enjay Chem Co, 64-68. *Res:* Organic chemistry. *Mailing Add:* 5555 N Sheridan Rd Chicago IL 60640

BOSHELL, BURIS RAYE, ENDOCRINOLOGY, INTERNAL MEDICINE. *Current Pos:* STAFF MEM, DIABETES CLIN, MED CTR EAST HOSP, 90- *Personal Data:* b Marion Co, Ala, Oct 9, 26; m 51; c 2. *Educ:* Ala Polytech Inst, BS, 47; Harvard Med Sch, MD, 53. *Prof Exp:* Intern med, Peter Bent Brigham Hosp, 53-54, from jr asst resident to sr asst resident, 54-56, asst, Thorn Lab, 56-57, jr assoc physician & asst dir, Diabetic Teaching Unit, 57-58, chief resident, 58-59; from asst prof to prof, Sch Med, Univ Ala, Birmingham, 59-72, asst dir, Dept Med, 63-76, Ruth Lawson Hanson prof med, 72-90, chief, Div Endocrinol & Metab, Diabetes Res & Educ Hosp, 76-90. *Concurrent Pos:* Am Col Physicians res fel, Thorn Lab, Peter Bent Brigham Hosp, 56-57; asst, Harvard Med Sch, 58-59; clin investr, Vet Admin Hosp, 59-62, chief med serv, 62-; asst physician-in-chief, Univ Hosp & Hillman Clins, 63- *Mem:* Endocrine Soc; Am Diabetes Asn; Am Soc Clin Pharmacol & Therapeut; fel Am Col Physicians; AMA. *Res:* Diabetes mellitus; oral diagnostic test for diabetes; insulin in blood and etiological factors in insulin resistance. *Mailing Add:* 3017 Old Ivy Rd Birmingham AL 35210-3608

BOSHES, LOUIS D, NEUROPSYCHIATRY, ADULT & PEDIATRIC NEUROLOGY. *Current Pos:* from clin assoc prof to clin prof, 63-78, dir, Consultation Clin for Epilepsy, 63-72, EMER PROF NEUROL, COL MED, UNIV ILL, 78-; PROF NEUROL, COOK CO GRAD SCH MED, 70- *Personal Data:* b Chicago, Ill, Oct 15, 08; m 94, Natalie A; c Arlene (Hirschfelder) & Judi. *Educ:* Northwestern Univ, Evanston, BS, 31, Northwestern Univ, Chicago, MD, 36; Am Bd Psychiat & Neurol, dipl & cert psychiat, 47, cert neurol, 50 & cert pediat neurol, 69. *Hon Degrees:* DHH, Pan Am Med Asn, 76. *Honors & Awards:* Hon Distinguished Physician Award, Am Col Neuropsychiatrists, 87; Lect, Dr Louis D Boshes Michael Reese Hosp, 90; Spec Medalion Award Serv, Am Psychiat Asn, 92; Rhea & Louis D Boshes Ann lectr, Col Med, Univ Ill & Med Sch, Northwestern Univ, 93. *Prof Exp:* Fel psychiat, Ill Neuropsychiat Inst, Chicago, 40-42, 46-47; prof neurol & psychiat, Sch Med, Northwestern Univ, Chicago, 47-63. *Concurrent Pos:* Assoc & attend neurologist, Cook Co Hosp, Chicago, 47-63, consult neurol, 70-, attend neurol, 84-; neuropsychiat consult, Ill State Psychiat Inst Chicago, 48-70, Columbus Mem Hosp, 48-75, Louis A Weiss Mem Hosp, 50- & Nicholas J Pritzker Ctr for Children, 64-70; sr consult neurol, Vet Admin Hosp, Downey, Ill, 54-60; assoc examr, Am Bd Psychiat & Neurol, 57- & Am Bd Neurol Surg, 63-; assoc ed, Dis Nerv Syst, 60-76, Int J Neuropsychiat, 66-69, Behav Neuropsychiat, 69- & Int Surg Neurol Sci, 77-; neurol consult, Drexel Home for the Aged, 62-70; attend physician, Res & Educ Hosps, Abraham Lincoln Sch Med, Col Med, Univ Ill, 63-78; consult ed, Current Med Dig, 65-74 & New Physician, 67 -; sr attend neurologist & psychiatrist, Michael Reese Hosp & Med Ctr, 65-, chief neurol clins, 69-75; assoc attend neurologist, St Joseph Hosp, , 74 -; sr attend neurologist, psychiatrist & child neurologist, Columbus Mem Hosp, 75 -; mem adv bd & coun, Myasthenia Gravis Found, United Parkinson Found, Epilepsy Found Am & Nat Found-March of Dimes; ambassador, Int Bur Epilepsy & League Against Epilepsy; mem, Sci Exhib Adv Comt, Mus Sci & Indust, Chicago. *Mem:* Fel Am Acad Neurol; fel Am Psychiat Asn; fel AMA; fel Am Col Physicians; fel Pan-Am Med Asn (pres, 73-); Am Epilepsy Soc; Am Med Electroencephalographic Asn; Am Med Writers Asn; Int Col Surgeons; Child Neurol Soc; Sigma Xi; fel Am Med Soc Vienna; Int League Against Epilepsy; Am Med Electroencephalographic Asn. *Res:* Neurology; child neurology; psychiatry; multiple sclerosis; parkinsonism; epilepsy; myasthenia gravis; geriatric neurology; disorders of aging in the neurologic system; history of neurology; convulsive disorders; fungus infections and inflammations of the central nervous system; adult psychiatry; author or co-author of over 390 publications. *Mailing Add:* Univ Ill Col Med 912 S Wood St Rm 855N Chicago IL 60612-7330. *Fax:* 773-929-1557

BOSHKOV, STEFAN, MINING ENGINEERING, GEOLOGY. *Current Pos:* Asst mining, Columbia Univ, 42-43, assoc, 46-51, from asst prof to prof mining, 51-80, chmn, 67-85, Henry Krumb prof, 80-88, HENRY KRUMB EMER PROF, HENRY KRUMB SCH MINES, COLUMBIA UNIV, 89- *Personal Data:* b Sofia, Bulgaria, Sept 29, 18; nat US; m 43, Bianca Amaducci; c Lynn K & Stefan R. *Educ:* Am Col Sofia, Dipl, 38; Columbia Univ, BS, 41, EM, 42. *Honors & Awards:* B Krupinski Medal, State Mining Coun, Poland, 80; Mineral Indust Educ Medal, Am Inst Mining, Metall & Petrol Engrs, 80; Drinov Medal, Acad Sci, Bulgaria, 87. *Concurrent Pos:* Consult engr, 49-; mem int orgn comt, Int Mining Cong, 62-; chmn, Int Conf Strata Control, 64; Fulbright distinguished prof & sr scientist, Yugoslavia, 69; mem, Secy Labor adv comt health & safety stand metal & non-metal mining, US Dept Labor, 78; chmn, UN Int Meeting Technologies for Develop Coal Resources in Develop Countries, Beijing, 85. *Mem:* Am Inst Mining, Metall & Petrol Engrs; Am Arbit Asn; Sigma Xi. *Res:* Barodynamics; stress analysis applied to mine design; mine plant, ventilation, valuation and economics. *Mailing Add:* 119 White Plains Ave White Plains NY 10604

BOSIN, TALMAGE R, ORGANIC CHEMISTRY. *Current Pos:* from asst prof to assoc prof, 69-78, PROF PHARMACOL, MED SCI PROG, IND UNIV, BLOOMINGTON, 78- *Personal Data:* b Fond du Lac, Wis, Mar 6, 41. *Educ:* Wheaton Col, Ill, BS, 63; Ind Univ, PhD(org chem), 67. *Prof Exp:* NIH res fel org chem, Univ Calif, Berkeley, 67-69. *Concurrent Pos:* Sr int fel, 77-78. *Mem:* Am Chem Soc; Am Soc Exp Pharmacol Therapeut; Soc Toxicol. *Res:* Biologically active indole compounds, particularly serotonin and its role in pulmonary and central nervous system functions. *Mailing Add:* 1300 S Valley Forge Rd Bloomington IN 47401

BOSKEY, ADELE LUDIN, STRUCTURAL CHEMISTRY. *Current Pos:* res assoc, Cornell Univ, 74-79, from asst prof to assoc prof, 77-85, assoc scientist, 79-83, SR SCIENTIST, HOSP SPEC SURG, CORNELL UNIV, 85-, PROF BIOCHEM MED COL, 85-, DIR, LAB ULTRASTRUCTURAL BIOCHEM, 86-, DIR RES, HOSP SPEC SURG, 93- *Personal Data:* b New York, NY, Aug 30, 43; m 70; c 1. *Educ:* Columbia Univ, BA, 64; Boston Univ, PhD(phys chem), 70. *Honors & Awards:* Merit Award, NIH. *Prof Exp:* Instr chem col lib arts, Boston Univ, 69-70; res fel crystallog, Imp Col Sci & Technol, 70-71. *Mem:* Sigma Xi; Am Crystallog Asn; Am Chem Soc; Orthop Res Soc; Am Soc Bone Mineral Res. *Res:* Mechanism of hard tissue mineralization; structure determination by x-ray crystallography and electron microscopy; role of lipids and proteoglyeans in calcification. *Mailing Add:* Four Winding Way North Caldwell NJ 07006-4043

BOSLEY, DAVID EMERSON, PHYSICAL CHEMISTRY. *Current Pos:* CONSULT, TEXTILE, 85- *Personal Data:* b Lundale, WVa, Dec 16, 27; m 52; c 4. *Educ:* Univ WVa, BS, 50; Mass Inst Technol, PhD(phys chem), 54. *Prof Exp:* Res chemist, dacron plant tech sect, E I du Pont de Nemours & Co, 54-85. *Res:* Physico-chemical properties of synthetic fibers. *Mailing Add:* Box 531 Grifton NC 28530

BOSLEY, ELIZABETH CASWELL, speech pathology, for more information see previous edition

BOSLEY, GALEN CRAIG, HUMAN PERFORMANCE INTEGRITY, FATIGUE & ERROR PREVENTION. *Current Pos:* SR SCIENTIST & PROJ LEAD HUMAN FACTORS, JIL INFO SYST, 97- *Personal Data:* b Saginaw, Mich, July 3, 48. *Educ:* Univ Mich, BA, 76; Loma Linda Univ, MPH, 77, DrPH(prevent care), 82; Am Bd Prev Med, cert. *Prof Exp:* Dietitian, Wytheville Hosp, 82-84; sci res assoc, Health & Temperance Dept, Gen Conf Seventh-day Adventists, 84-91, dir food serv, 91-97. *Concurrent Pos:* Food serv consult, Columbia Union Col, 85-; consult, Total Health Lifestyle Ctr, 89; dir res, Total Life Creation, Inc, 94-96; sr scientist, Fed Aviation Admin, 96-97. *Mem:* Fel Am Dietitic Asn; Am Col Nutrit; Am Prev Care Asn; Nat Comn Health Educ Credentialing. *Res:* Human performance and decision making in relation to business and aviation safety; fatigue and its effects on brain function; health and lifestyle in the prevention of choice diseases. *Mailing Add:* 14220 Cantrell Rd Silver Spring MD 20905. *E-Mail:* 75117.3400@compuserve.com

BOSLOW, HAROLD MEYER, psychiatry; deceased, see previous edition for last biography

BOSMA, JAMES F, PEDIATRICS. *Current Pos:* CHIEF ORAL & PHARYNGEAL DEVELOP SECT, NAT INST DENT RES, NIH, 61-; LECTR, DEPT RADIOL, JOHNS HOPKINS UNIV, 75- *Personal Data:* b Grand Rapids, Mich, Apr 29, 16; m 42; c 8. *Educ:* Calvin Col, AB, 37; Univ Mich, MD, 41. *Prof Exp:* Intern, Cleveland City Hosp & Western Reserve Hosp, 41-43, resident, 43-44; asst prof pediat, Med Sch, Univ Minn, 48-49; prof, Col Med, Univ Utah, 49-59. *Concurrent Pos:* Nat Found Infantile Paralysis fel, Univ Minn, 44-46, Kellogg fel, 46-48; NIH fel, Karolinska Inst, Sweden & Wenner Gren Cardiovasc Res Lab, 59-61; pediatrician, Salt Lake Gen Hosp, 55-59; res prof, dept pediat, Sch Med & dept pediat, Sch Dent, Univ Md. *Mem:* AAAS; Soc Pediat Res; Am Pediat Soc; Soc Res Child Develop; Int Soc Cranio-facial Biol. *Res:* Motor coordination of mouth, pharynx and larynx. *Mailing Add:* 3902 Hadley Sq W Baltimore MD 21209

BOSMAJIAN, GEORGE, ORGANIC CHEMISTRY, POLYMERS. *Current Pos:* RETIRED. *Personal Data:* b Fresno, Calif, Apr 21, 21; m 49; c 3. *Educ:* Fresno State Col, AB, 43; Univ Ill, MA, 47; Wash State Univ, PhD(org chem), 49. *Prof Exp:* Jr chemist, Shell Develop Co, 43-46; res chemist, Assoc Oil Co, 49-50; group leader, Sinclair Res Labs, 50-55; sr scientist, Southern Res Inst, 55-62; res coordr, David Taylor Naval Ship Res & Develop Ctr, 62-68, div dir, 68-84, tech adv, 84-88. *Mem:* Am Chem Soc; Am Soc Metals; Soc Automotive Engrs. *Res:* Tribology, fuel & lubricants, polymers, composites, advanced materials. *Mailing Add:* 17 Emerson Rd Severna Park MD 21146-3003

BOSMANN, HAROLD BRUCE, BIOPHYSICS, PHARMACOLOGY. *Current Pos:* assoc dean, Univ Cincinnati, 82-85, prof internal med, pharmacol & cell biophys & dir prog on aging & geriatric educ & res, 82-87, vdean, 85-87, prof psychiat, 85-87, PROF PHARM & MED, SR ASSOC

DEAN & DIR RES CTR AGING, SCH MED, UNIV CINCINNATI, 87- *Personal Data:* b Chicago, Ill, June 17, 42; m 66; c 2. *Educ:* Knox Col, AB, 64; Univ Rochester, PhD(biophys), 66. *Hon Degrees:* Cambridge Univ, MA, 67. *Prof Exp:* Asst prof, Sch Med Dent, Univ Rochester, 68-74, assoc prof pharmacol & toxicol, 74-78, assoc prof oncol, 76-78, prof pharmacol, toxicol & oncol, 78-82. *Concurrent Pos:* NSF fel biophys, Strangeways Lab, Cambridge Univ, 66-67; USPHS fel, Salk Inst Biol Studies, La Jolla, Calif, 67-68 & career develop award, Univ Rochester, 68-74; scholar award, Leukemia Soc Am, 74-79. *Mem:* Am Chem Soc; Am Soc Pharmacol & Exp Therapeut; Biophys Soc. *Res:* Membranes; pharmacology; drug resistance; synaptosomes; geriatrics; toxicology; receptor analysis. *Mailing Add:* 828 Red Stable Way Hinsdale IL 60521

BOSNAK, ROBERT J, nuclear engineering, for more information see previous edition

BOSNIACK, DAVID S, LUBRICANT TECHNOLOGY, PETROLEUM CHEMISTRY. *Current Pos:* chemist, Exxon Govt Res Lab, Exxon Res & Eng Co, 62-66, sr chemist, Prod Res Div, 66-70, res assoc, Prod Res Div, 70-77, proj head, New Proj Develop, Baytown Petrol Res Lab, 70-77, sr res assoc & sect head indust lubricants & specialties, 77-81, sr res assoc & sect head engine lubricants, Prod Res Div, 81-90, TECH ADVISOR, EXXON CO INT, 90- *Personal Data:* b New York, NY, July 10, 32; m 57, Eve Ehrenfeld; c Robert, Diana & Lesley. *Educ:* City Col New York, BS, 54; NY Univ, PhD(org chem), 61. *Prof Exp:* Chemist, GAF Corp, 60-62. *Concurrent Pos:* Instr, Cooper Union, 61-63. *Mem:* Am Chem Soc; AAAS; Soc Automotive Engrs; Am Soc Testing Mat. *Res:* Petroleum chemistry; lubrication technology including synthetic lubricants, lubrication mechanisms and additive synthesis; free radical reactions. *Mailing Add:* 13 Green Hickory Hill Scotch Plains NJ 07076

BOSNIAK, MORTON A, RADIOLOGY. *Current Pos:* PROF RADIOL, SCH MED, NY UNIV, 69- *Personal Data:* b New York, NY, Nov 13, 29; m; c 1. *Educ:* Mass Inst Technol, BS, 51; State Univ NY, MD, 55. *Prof Exp:* Intern, Mt Sinai Hosp, NY, 55-56; resident radiol, NY Hosp, 56-57, 59-61; instr, Med Sch, Cornell Univ, 60-61; assoc prof, Sch Med, Boston Univ, 64-67; assoc prof, Albert Einstein Col Med, 67-69, sr attend radiologist, Hosp, 67-69, assoc dir dept, 68-69. *Concurrent Pos:* Radiologist, Montefiore Hosp, 61-62, assoc attend, 63-; sr staff radiologist, Boston City Hosp, Mass, 64-67; assoc radiologist, Univ Hosp, Boston, 64-67; sr attend radiologist, Bronx Munic Hosp Ctr, NY, 67-; attend radiologist, NY Univ Hosp, 69-; vis attend radiologist, Bellevue Hosp; consult radiol, Vet Admin Hosp. *Mem:* Am Col Radiol; Radiol Soc NAm; Asn Univ Radiol; Am Roentgen Ray Soc. *Mailing Add:* Dept Radiol NY Univ Med Ctr Radiol 550 First Ave New York NY 10016-6402

BOSNJAK, ZELJKO J, CARDIAC ELECTRO-PHYSIOLOGY, GENERAL ANESTHETICS. *Current Pos:* ASSOC PROF ANAESTHESIOL & PHYSIOL, COL MED, UNIV WIS-MILWAUKEE, 79- *Educ:* Univ Wis-Milwaukee, PhD(physiol), 79. *Res:* Calcium antagonists. *Mailing Add:* Dept Anesthesiol Med Col Wis MFRC A100 8701 W Watertown Plank Rd Milwaukee WI 53226-0509

BOSOMWORTH, PETER PALLISER, MEDICINE, ANESTHESIOLOGY. *Current Pos:* chmn, Dept Anesthesiol, Univ Ky, 62-70, assoc dean, Col Med, 67-70, vpres, Med Ctr, 70-82, CHANCELLOR, UNIV KY, 82- *Personal Data:* b Akron, Ohio, May 2, 30; m 56; c 4. *Educ:* Kent State Univ, BSc, 51; Univ Cincinnati, MD, 55; Ohio State Univ, MMedSc, 58. *Prof Exp:* Intern, Cincinnati Gen Hosp, Ohio, 57-58; asst resident anesthesiol, Ohio State Univ Hosp, 56-57, chief resident & asst instr, 57-58, instr, 58; chief anesthesia div, US Naval Hosp, Great Lakes, Ill, 58-60; dir anesthesia res, Ohio State Univ, 60-62. *Concurrent Pos:* Consult, Vet Admin Hosp & USPHS, Lexington, 62-, Ireland Army Hosp, Ft Knox, 64-66; mem bd dir, Blue Cross Blue Shield of Ky, 64-; chief staff, Univ Ky Hosp, 66-68; vpres, Health Develop Resources Inst, 70; mem, Asn Acad Health Ctr, 70-, chmn bd, 82. *Mem:* Am Soc Anesthesiol; Am Univ Anesthetists; Am Soc Anesthesiologists; AMA; Int Anesthesia Res Soc; Sigma Xi; fel Royal Soc Med. *Res:* Cardiovascular, uterine and renal physiology as influenced by anesthetic agents; health care systems and related policy. *Mailing Add:* 2956 Four Pines Rd Lexington KY 40502

BOSRON, WILLIAM F, ENZYMOLOGY, DRUG METABOLISM. *Current Pos:* from asst prof to assoc prof, 75-86, PROF, DEPT BIOCHEM & MOLECULAR BIOL, MED SCH, IND UNIV, 86-, PROF MED. *Personal Data:* b Dayton, Ohio, Dec 28, 44; m 79, Sheila Barton. *Educ:* Bowling Green Univ, BS, 67; Univ Cincinnati, PhD(biochem), 73. *Honors & Awards:* Merit Award, Nat Inst Alcohol Abuse & Alcoholism. *Prof Exp:* Res fel biochem, Harvard Med Sch, 72-75. *Concurrent Pos:* Assoc prof, Grad Sch, Ind Univ, 81- *Mem:* Am Chem Soc; Res Soc Alcoholism; Int Soc Biomed Res Alcoholism; Am Soc Biochem & Molecular Biol. *Res:* Regulation of alcohol metabolism; structure and kinetics of alcohol dehydrogenases; enzymology of cocaine estermetabolism and ethonol-cocaine interactions. *Mailing Add:* 405 Med Sci Ind Univ Sch Med 635 Barnhill Dr Indianapolis IN 46202-5122. *Fax:* 317-274-4686; *E-Mail:* wbosron@indyvax.iupui.rdu

BOSS, ALAN PAUL, STAR & PLANET FORMATION, NUMERICAL HYDRODYNAMICS. *Current Pos:* staff assoc, 81-83, STAFF MEM, DEPT TERRESTRIAL MAGNETISM, CARNEGIE INST WASHINGTON, 83- *Personal Data:* b Lakewood, Ohio, July 20, 51; m 79, Catherine A Starkie; c Margaret & Nicholas. *Educ:* Univ SFla, BS, 73; Univ Calif, Santa Barbara, MA, 75, PhD(physics), 79. *Prof Exp:* Nat Acad Sci/Nat Res Coun resident res assoc, Space Sci Div, Ames Res Ctr, NASA, 79-81. *Concurrent Pos:* Prin investr, Theory of Star Formation, NSF Grant, 84-92, Three Dimensional Evolution Solar Nebula, NASA grant 88-, NASA Planetary Systs Sci Working Group, 88-96, chair, 95-96, NASA Origins of Solar Systs Res Prog, 89-96, chair, 94-96, Binary Star Formation, NSF grant, 93-, Solar Nebula Traces, NASA grant, 93-; mem, Comn Planetary & Lunar Explor, Nat Acad Sci/Nat Res Coun, 90-93. *Mem:* Am Astron Soc; Am Geophys Union; AAAS; Int Astron Union. *Res:* Formation of stellar and planetary sytems; convection in planetary bodies; numerical gravitational hydrodynamics. *Mailing Add:* Carnegie Inst Washington 5241 Broad Br Rd NW Washington DC 20015-1305. *Fax:* 202-364-8726; *E-Mail:* boss@dtm.ciw.edu

BOSS, CHARLES BEN, ANALYTICAL CHEMISTRY. *Current Pos:* ASST PROF CHEM, NC STATE UNIV, 77- *Personal Data:* b Foley, Ala, Dec 27, 45; m 70. *Educ:* Wake Forest Univ, BS, 68; Ind Univ, PhD(analytical chem), 77. *Mem:* Soc Appl Spectros; Am Chem Soc; Optical Soc Am. *Res:* Atomic spectrometry in flames and plasmas; trace and ultra-trace chemical analysis; on-line computer instrumentation; automated optimization; novel transducers; flame chemistry. *Mailing Add:* Dept Chem Box 8204 NC State Univ Raleigh NC 27695-8204

BOSS, KENNETH JAY, MALACOLOGY. *Current Pos:* from asst cur to cur, 66-74, PROF BIOL, HARVARD UNIV, 70- *Personal Data:* b Grand Rapids, Mich, Dec 5, 35. *Educ:* Cent Mich Col, BA, 57; Mich State Univ, MSc, 59; Harvard Univ, PhD(biol), 63. *Prof Exp:* Res systematist mollusks, US Nat Mus, Dept Interior, 63-66. *Mem:* Soc Syst Zool; Am Malacol Union; Marine Biol Asn UK. *Res:* Systematic and evolutionary studies of mollusks; comparative morphology of lamellibranchs; zoogeography. *Mailing Add:* 23 Robinson St Cambridge MA 02138

BOSS, MANLEY LEON, BIOMETRICS-BIOSTATISTICS, ENVIRONMENTAL SCIENCES. *Current Pos:* RETIRED. *Personal Data:* b Atlanta, Ga, Dec 24, 24; m 56; c 3. *Educ:* Univ Miami, BS, 49; Inter-Am Inst Agr Sci, MAgr, 51; Iowa State Col, PhD, 55. *Prof Exp:* From instr to assoc prof bot, Univ Miami, 54-63; head macrobiol sect, Fla Atlantic Univ, 63-91, prof bot, 63-91, actg dean, 91-94. *Concurrent Pos:* Environ consult, biostatist consult. *Res:* Environmental sciences. *Mailing Add:* 3308 Perimeter Rd Palm City FL 34990

BOSSARD, DAVID CHARLES, OPERATIONS RESEARCH. *Current Pos:* RETIRED. *Personal Data:* b Sellersville, Pa, Mar 23, 40; m 64; c 7. *Educ:* Drexel Univ, BSc, 62; Dartmouth Col, AM, 64 & 66, PhD(math), 67. *Prof Exp:* Assoc opers res, Daniel H Wagner Assocs, 67-73, vpres opers res, 73-81; pres, D C Bossard Inc, 81-95. *Mem:* Soc Indust & Appl Math; Inst Elec & Electronics Engrs; Asn Comput Mach. *Mailing Add:* 117 Storrs Hill Rd Lebanon NH 03766

BOSSARD, MARY JEANETTE, ENZYMOLOGY, PROTEIN CHEMISTRY & BIOCHEMISTRY. *Current Pos:* INVESTR, SMITHKLINE BEECHAM, 85- *Personal Data:* b Keosauqua, Iowa, Nov 25, 54; m 75; c 2. *Educ:* Cent Col, BA, 77; Univ Nebr, PhD(chem), 81. *Prof Exp:* Fel, Univ Calif, Berkeley, 82-83, NIH fel, 83-85. *Mem:* Am Chem Soc; Am Soc Biochem & Molecular Biol. *Res:* Mechanistic enzymology applied to rational drug design; therapeutic areas: immunosuppression, cardiovascular and antifungal; enzyme categories: prolyl isomerases, proteases, ATPases, P-450, oxygenases. *Mailing Add:* Dept Molecular Recognition SmithKline Beecham Box 1539 UW2103 King of Prussia PA 19406. *Fax:* 610-270-4162; *E-Mail:* mary.j.bossard@sbphrd.com

BOSSEN, DOUGLAS C, ELECTRICAL ENGINEERING. *Current Pos:* Staff engr, IBM Corp, 68-70, adv engr, 70-76, sr engr, 76-88, SR TECH STAFF MEM, IBM CORP, 89- *Personal Data:* b Akron, Ohio, Sept 26, 41; m 66; c 2. *Educ:* Northwestern Univ, BS, 64, MS, 66, PhD(elec eng), 68. *Mem:* Sigma Xi; fel Inst Elec & Electronics Engrs; Am Fedn Info Processing Soc. *Res:* Applied research in hardware fault-tolerent computer design, including error correcting codes, error detection and recovery techniques. *Mailing Add:* IBM Corp 11400 Burnet Rd Austin TX 78758

BOSSHART, ROBERT PERRY, FIBER FARMING. *Current Pos:* FIBER FARMING MGR, NE FOREST RESOURCES, MEAD PUBL PAPER DIV, 96- *Personal Data:* b Orange, NJ, Feb 15, 42; m 75, Madeleine T; c Robert Perry & Edward Gillett. *Educ:* Univ Ill, Urbana, BS, 64; Va Polytech Inst & State Univ, MS, 67, PhD(agron), 69. *Prof Exp:* Res plant physiologist, Vegetation Control Labs, US Army, Fort Detrick, Md, 69-70; food & agr officer, 29th Civil Affairs Co, US Army, Vietnam, 70-71; chief & agronomist, Vietnam Rice Res Proj, Int Rice Res Inst, 72-75; gen mgr for Brazil, IRI Res Inst, 75-78; assoc agronomist, soil fertility & water mgt, 78-80, Hawaiian Sugar Planters Asn, agronomist, 80-85; dep dir Southeast Asia, Potash & Phosphate Inst & Int Potash Inst, 85-89; land reclamation specialist/soil scientist, Remediation Serv Div, Horsehead Resource Develop Co Inc, 90-93; gen mgr mkt, continental challenge, 93-94. *Concurrent Pos:* Affiliate fac, Agron & Soil Sci Dept, Univ Hawaii, Honolulu, 79-85; adj prof, Calif State Univ, Fresno, 81-85; consult, RP Bosshart Assocs, Singapore, Wilmette, IL, Coplay Farmington, ME, 89- *Mem:* Am Soc Agron; Soil Sci Soc Am; Inc Soc Planters Malaysia; Am Soc Hort Sci; Am Soc Surface Mining & Reclamation; Soc Am Foresters. *Res:* Soil fertility and plant nutrition; irrigation water management; increasing crop yields. *Mailing Add:* 21 Stewart Ave PO Box 726 Farmington ME 04938-0726. *Fax:* 207-779-0718

BOSSLER, JOHN DAVID, GEODETIC SCIENCE, GEOPHYSICS. *Current Pos:* DIR, CTR MAPPING, OHIO STATE UNIV, 86-, PROF GEODETIC SCI, 86- *Personal Data:* b Johnstown, Pa, Dec 8, 36; m 63; c 1. *Educ:* Univ Pittsburgh, BS, 59; Ohio State Univ, MS, 64, PhD(geod sci), 72. *Prof Exp:* Officer, Ship COWIE, Nat Oceanic & Atmospheric Admin, 59-60, chief astron field parties, Dept Com, Nat Ocean Surv & Nat Geod Surv, 60-63, chief sci experience math formulas, 64-69, exec officer, Ship Davidson, 69-71, proj mgr, Nat Geod Surv, 73-75, dep dir, 76-81, dir, 81-83, dir, Coast & Geod Surv, 83-86. *Concurrent Pos:* Nat Oceanic & Atmospheric Admin grant; dir, Ctr Mapping, Ohio State Univ, 87-94. *Mem:* Am Soc Photogram & Remote Sensors; Am Geophys Union; Am Cong Surv & Mapping; Urban & Regional Info Systs Asn; Am Soc Civil Engrs. *Res:* Geodetic science; geophysical research; digital mapping; geographic information systems. *Mailing Add:* 8500 Davington Dr Dublin OH 43017

BOSSO, JOSEPH FRANK, ORGANIC CHEMISTRY. *Current Pos:* Res asst II, 55-58, res asst I, 58-62, sr technician, 62-66, res chemist, 66-72, res assoc, 72-77, SR RES ASSOC, COATINGS & RESINS DIV, PPG INDUSTS INC, 77- *Personal Data:* b New Kensington, Pa, May 18, 31; m 54; c 3. *Educ:* Univ Pittsburgh, BS, 70. *Honors & Awards:* IR-100 Award, Indust Res Mag, 66 & 74; Coating Award, Am Soc Metals, 73. *Res:* Synthesis and development of polymers, especially in the field of cathodic electrodeposition of organic coatings. *Mailing Add:* 428 Wedgewood Dr New Kensington PA 15068

BOST, HOWARD WILLIAM, ORGANIC CHEMISTRY. *Current Pos:* RETIRED. *Personal Data:* b Robstown, Tex, Sept 29, 24; m 50; c 3. *Educ:* SW Tex State Teachers Col, BS, 48; Univ Tex, MA, 50, PhD(org chem), 55. *Honors & Awards:* Sigma Xi. *Prof Exp:* Res chemist, Phillips Petrol Co, 50-51, res chemist & group leader liquid propellants, 54-57, res chemist & sr group leader, 57-60, group leader photochem reactions, 60-68, group leader oxidation processes, 68-70, group leader org sulfur chem, 70-74, tech recruitment rep, 74-82, patent liaison, 83-85. *Concurrent Pos:* Mem joint Army-Navy-Air Force comt on mono-propellant test methods, 59-60,. *Mem:* Am Chem Soc; Sigma Xi. *Res:* Protective coatings; nitrogen chemicals; liquid rocket propellants; photo-chemical reactions; sulfur reactions; oxidation processes; organic sulfur chemistry; perfume ingredients; flame retardants; technical recruiting. *Mailing Add:* 1334 Quail Dr Bartlesville OK 74006-4344

BOST, ROBERT ORION, TOXICOLOGY. *Current Pos:* PRES, TOXICOL CONSULTS, INC, DALLAS, 87- *Personal Data:* b Elida, NMex, Jan 15, 43; m 66; c 2. *Educ:* Univ Tex, Austin, BS, 65, MA, 67; Univ Houston, PhD(chem), 70; Am Bd Forensic Toxicol, dipl, 80. *Prof Exp:* Lab asst, Southwestern Univ, 62-64; lab asst, Univ Tex, Austin, 65-67; teaching fel, Univ Houston, 67-69, res asst, 69-70; sci res specialist, La State Univ, New Orleans, 70-72; chemist, Vet Admin Hosp, New Orleans, 72-74; assoc toxicologist, Cuyahoga County Coroner's Off, 75-82; CHIEF TOXICOLOGIST, SOUTHWESTERN INST FORENSIC SCI, DALLAS, 82- *Concurrent Pos:* Asst prof, Dept Path, Southwestern Med Ctr Dallas, Univ Tex, Dallas, 82-90, assoc prof, 90-; guest ed, J Anal Toxicol, 88; adv bd, J Forensic Med, Istanbul, Turkey, 85-; dir bd, Soc Forensic Toxicologists, 86-88, vpres, 89, pres, 90. *Mem:* Am Chem Soc; Soc Forensic Toxicologists; fel Am Acad Forensic Sci; Int Asn Forensic Toxicologists. *Res:* Forensic and clinical toxicology; forensic urine drug testing; gas chromatography; derivatives for chromatography; generation and reaction of carbenes; small ring compounds. *Mailing Add:* Toxicol Consults Inc 1818 Arundel Dr Carrollton TX 75007-3012

BOSTATER, CHARLES ROGER, JR, MARINE OPTICS, EARTH SCIENCE. *Current Pos:* ASST PROF, PHYS OCEANOG & ENVIRON SCIS, DIV MARINE & ENVIRON SYSTS, FLA INST TECHNOL, 92- *Personal Data:* m, Sarah. *Educ:* Am Univ, BS, 75, MS, 76; Univ Del, PhD(marine sci), 90. *Prof Exp:* Dir tech analysis & data mgt, Chesapeake Bay Unit, Md Dept Natural Resources, 77-83; phys oceanog, Strategic Assessments, Nat Ocean Surv, Nat Oceanic & Atmospheric Admin, 88-89; res fel, Univ Del, 90-92. *Concurrent Pos:* Sr scientist, BHS Sci Systs, 87-95 & KB Sci & Eng, 88-97; prin scientist, S & C Servs, 96-97. *Mem:* Am Geophys Union; Am Soc Limnol & Oceanog; Nat Asn Environ Prof; Sigma Xi. *Res:* Marine and freshwater optical characteristics in tropical and subtropical systems for use in hyperspectral remote sensing of the earth as a system; mathematical modeling of transport and fate of chemicals in coastal and estuarine waters; integration of optical, physical biological and atmospheric models of environmental systems. *Mailing Add:* Fla Inst Technol 150 W University Blvd Melbourne FL 32901. *Fax:* 407-779-1708; *E-Mail:* bostater@probe.ocn.fit.edu

BOSTER, THOMAS ARTHUR, SOLID STATE PHYSICS. *Current Pos:* BOSTER ASSOC INC, 80- *Personal Data:* b Columbus, Ohio, Sept 28, 36; m 62; c 3. *Educ:* Capital Univ, BS, 58; Ohio Univ, MS, 60, PhD(physics), 66. *Prof Exp:* Res engr, Nortronics Div, Northrop Corp, 60-62; fel physics, Ohio Univ, 62-65; from asst prof to assoc prof, Oklahoma City Univ, 65-69; sr physicist, 68-73, group leader, 73-75, group leader, Div Responsibility for Safety & Qual Control, Lawrence Livermore Lab, Univ Calif, 75-80. *Concurrent Pos:* Consult, Okla Bur Invest, 67-68. *Mem:* Am Soc Testing & Mat; Soc Automotive Engrs; Am Phys Soc; Am Asn Physics Teachers; Am Soc Safety Engrs; Human Factors Soc. *Res:* Absorption of x-rays; radiation damage; cryogenics; microwaves; x-ray diagnostics; x-ray spectrometers; solid state detectors; safety research; accident reconstruction. *Mailing Add:* PO Box 2049 Livermore CA 94551

BOSTIAN, CAREY HOYT, GENETICS. *Current Pos:* asst prof zool, NC State Univ, 30-36, assoc prof zool & assoc poultry genetics, 36-45, prof zool & res prof poultry genetics, 45-53, assoc dean agr, 48-53, chancellor, 53-59, prof, 59-88, EMER PROF POULTRY GENETICS, NC STATE UNIV, 88- *Personal Data:* b China Grove, NC, Mar 1, 07; m 29; c 3. *Educ:* Catawba Col, AB, 28; Univ Pittsburgh, MS, 30, PhD(genetics), 33. *Hon Degrees:* DSc, Catawba Col, 53, Wake Forest Col, 54 & Nat Univ Eng, Peru, 57. *Prof Exp:* Asst zool, Univ Pittsburgh, 28-30. *Res:* General and human genetics. *Mailing Add:* 750 Weaver Dairy Rd Chapel Hill NC 27514

BOSTIAN, CHARLES WILLIAM, ELECTRICAL ENGINEERING. *Current Pos:* From asst prof to assoc prof, 69-77, PROF ELEC ENG, VA POLYTECH INST & STATE UNIV, 77- *Personal Data:* b Chambersburg, Pa, Dec 30, 40; m 64; c 2. *Educ:* NC State Univ, BS, 63, MS, 64, PhD(elec eng), 67. *Prof Exp:* Res engr, Electronics Res Lab, Corning Glassworks, 67. *Concurrent Pos:* Consult, US Dept Defense, 69-71 & Electro-Tec Corp, 72-73. *Mem:* Inst Elec & Electronics Engrs; Sigma Xi. *Res:* Satellite communications; radio wave propagation; applied electromagnetics. *Mailing Add:* Bradley Dept Elec Eng Va Polytech Inst Blacksburg VA 24061-0111

BOSTIAN, HARRY (EDWARD), MASS TRANSFER SEPARATIONS, CONVERSION PROCESSES. *Current Pos:* ENGR & RES PROG MGR, US ENVIRON PROTECTION AGENCY, 70- *Personal Data:* b Lewisburg, Pa, Jan 16, 33; m 55, Marion E Maurer. *Educ:* Bucknell Univ, BSChE, 54; Rensselaer Polytech Inst, MChE, 56; Iowa State Univ, PhD(chem eng), 59. *Prof Exp:* Asst chem eng, Rensselaer Polytech Inst, 54-56 & Iowa State Univ, 56-59; asst prof, Univ NH, 59-61; engr, Exxon Res & Eng Co, 61-65; assoc prof, Univ Miss, 65-70. *Concurrent Pos:* Consult & reviewer, Environ Topics, 75-; session organizer tech meetings, Am Inst Chem Engrs, 75-; mem, Task Forces & Work Groups Environ Control & Regulation, US Environ Protection Agency & Water Environ Fedn, 87- *Mem:* Am Inst Chem Engrs; AAAS; Sigma Xi. *Res:* Energy/environmental research; separations fundamentals and technology; sludge processing and conversion; sludge management costs; hazardous waste site reclamation; process simulation. *Mailing Add:* 6001 Bagdad Dr Cincinnati OH 45230-1302. *Fax:* 513-569-7787

BOSTICK, EDGAR E, PHYSICAL ORGANIC CHEMISTRY. *Current Pos:* res chemist, 60-69, mgr res & develop, Insulating Mat Dept, 69-76, WITH RES & DEVELOP, LEXO PROD DEPT, GEN ELEC CO, 76- *Personal Data:* b Newville, Ala, Dec 10, 26; m 55; c 5. *Educ:* Ala Polytech Inst, BS, 50; Univ Akron, PhD(chem), 59. *Prof Exp:* Jr chem engr, Goodyear Tire & Rubber Co, 50-51, chem engr, 53-56; fel, Univ Akron, 59-60. *Mem:* Am Chem Soc; Am Inst Chem Engrs. *Res:* Ionic polymerization of vinyl, diene and heterocyclic compounds; reaction kinetics and mechanisms; characterization of polymers by chemical and physical techniques. *Mailing Add:* 57 Park Ridge Dr Mt Vernon IN 47620-9405

BOSTICK, WARREN LITHGOW, PATHOLOGY. *Current Pos:* dean, 64-74, prof, 64-88, EMER PROF PATH, COL MED, UNIV CALIF, IRVINE, 88- *Personal Data:* b Dallas, Tex, July 28, 14; m 39, Virginia Lee; c Warren A & Bruce H. *Educ:* Univ Calif, AB, 36, MD, 40. *Prof Exp:* From assoc prof to prof path, Sch Med, Univ Calif, San Francisco, 50-64, dir labs, Univ Hosps, 54-64. *Concurrent Pos:* Trustee, Calif Physicians Serv, 62-70; pres, Calif Med Asn, 63-65; deleg, Col Am Path, 78- *Mem:* AAAS; Col Am Path; Am Soc Exp Path (pres elect); Am Soc Clin Path (pres, 74-75); AMA. *Res:* Hodgkins disease; ameblasis; fibrocystic disease of pancreas; viral carcinogenesis. *Mailing Add:* Dept Path D440 Univ Calif Med Sch Irvine CA 92717-4800

BOSTOCK, JUDITH LOUISE, THEORETICAL SOLID STATE PHYSICS. *Current Pos:* CHIEF OPERATING OFFICER, SC UNIVS RES & EDUC FOUND, 91- *Personal Data:* b Gardiner, Maine. *Educ:* Trinity Col, AB, 60; Dickinson Col, BS, 63; Georgetown Univ, MS, 69, PhD(physics), 71. *Hon Degrees:* LLD, Gannon Univ, 90. *Prof Exp:* Asst physics, Univ Saarland, 70-71; from instr to assoc prof physics, Mass Inst Technol, 72-82, opers res analyst Off Mgt & Budget, 84-89, spec asst to dir & asst dir indust technol, Off Sci & Technol Policy, 89-90. *Concurrent Pos:* Consult physicist crystal physics, Naval Res Lab, 72-75; consult sr physicist, BDM Corp, Va, 75-79; fac develop workshop consult, 75-80; consult ed, Addison Wesley Publ Co, 76-80, Off Mgt & Budget, 82-84; consult-at-large, SURA, Wash DC, 91-, Los Alamos Nat Lab, 91- *Mem:* Am Phys Soc; Sigma Xi. *Res:* Lattice instabilities and superconductivity in metals at low temperatures; low temperature properties in theoretical solid state physics; non-equilibrium conditions in superconductors. *Mailing Add:* Off Comm Outreach Dept Energy 121 Chardonnay Lane Aiken SC 29803

BOSTON, ANDREW CHESTER, ANIMAL BREEDING, BEEF CATTLE PRODUCTION & MANAGEMENT. *Current Pos:* COUNTY EXTEN DIR & AGR EDUCR, PURDUE UNIV, PAOLI, IND, 89- *Personal Data:* b Divernon, Ill, Nov 17, 41; m 65, Mary LaVerne Lebus; c Virginia Bell & Donald Joseph. *Educ:* Univ Ill, Urbana-Champaign, BS, 65; Univ Mo, Columbia, MS, 66; Okla State Univ, Stillwater, PhD(animal breeding), 73. *Prof Exp:* Asst prof animal breeding & genetics, La State Univ, Baton Rouge, 73-76; provincial beef prog specialist, Man Agr, Winnipeg, 76-79; chief, rec performance beef cattle, Agr Can, Ottawa, Ont, 79-82; head, Dept Agr & Natural Resources, Morehead State Univ, Ky, 82-85, prof agr & animal sci, 82-87; livestock consult, 87-89. *Concurrent Pos:* Researcher, 76-79. *Mem:* Am Soc Animal Sci; Coun Agr Sci & Technol; Nat Asn County Agr Agents; Am Registry Prof Animal Scientists; Sigma Xi. *Res:* Pasture management levels and grazing intensity on beef cow productivity and profitability; utilization of fescue (endophyte infected and clean) with fertilization and clovers by grazing cow-calf pairs; beef cow-calf performance testing, production and financial evaluation systems. *Mailing Add:* 645 N Sandy Hook Rd Paoli IN 47454-1032. *Fax:* 812-723-4196; *E-Mail:* andy_boston@acn.purdue.edu

BOSTON, CHARLES RAY, environmental program management, for more information see previous edition

BOSTON, JOHN ROBERT, TIME SERIES MODELS, SIGNAL PROCESSING. *Current Pos:* vis assoc prof elec eng, 91-95, ASSOC PROF ELEC ENG, UNIV PITTSBURGH, 95- *Personal Data:* b Evanston, Ill, Oct 16, 42; m 71, Carol Dillon; c Christopher & Patrick. *Educ:* Stanford Univ, BS, 64, MS, 66; Northwestern Univ, PhD(elec eng), 71; Univ Pittsburgh, MBA, 92. *Prof Exp:* Res assoc health care delivery, Hosp Res & Educ Trust, 71-72; asst prof elec eng, Univ Md, 72-75; asst prof biomed eng prog & elec eng, Carnegie-Mellon Univ, 75-80; res assoc prof anesthesiol, Sch Med, Univ Pittsburgh, 80-91. *Mem:* Inst Elec & Electronics Engrs Comput Soc; Eng Med & Biol Soc; Inst Elec & Electronics Engrs. *Res:* Digital signal processing, time series modeling, decision support systems, biomedical signals and control systems, fuzzy decision systems. *Mailing Add:* 308 High Oaks Ct Wexford PA 15090. *E-Mail:* boston@ee.pitt.edu

BOSTON, ROBERT WESLEY, PEDIATRICS. *Current Pos:* RETIRED. *Personal Data:* b Athens, Ont, July 10, 32; m 58; c 2. *Educ:* Queens Univ, Ont, MD, 57; Royal Col Physicians & Surgeons Can, dipl pediat, 63. *Prof Exp:* Mead Johnson Educ Fund fel pediat, Harvard Med Sch & Boston Lying-In Hosp, 62-64; McLaughlin Found traveling fel, Univ Col Hosp, London, Eng, 64-65; from asst prof to assoc prof pediat, Queens Univ, Ont, 65-77, assoc prof obstet & gynec, 77-86, prof pediat,77-95, prof, Dept Med, 87-89, prof med, 89-95. *Concurrent Pos:* Attend physician, Kingston Gen Hosp, 65- *Mem:* Can Pediat Soc; Can Soc Clin Invest. *Res:* Neonatology; respiratory distress syndrome; assessment of the fetus in uterus and of immediate neonatal adaption. *Mailing Add:* 30 Copperfield Dr Kingston ON K7M 1M4 Can

BOSTRACK, JACK M, BOTANY. *Current Pos:* assoc prof, 63-70, PROF BIOL, UNIV WIS-RIVER FALLS, 70- *Personal Data:* b Stoughton, Wis, Apr 30, 31; m 53; c 3. *Educ:* Wartburg Col, BA, 53; Univ Wis, MS, 59, PhD(bot hort), 62. *Prof Exp:* Asst bot, Univ Wis, 57-61; asst prof biol, Wayne State Col, 61-63. *Mem:* Bot Soc Am. *Res:* Morphogenesis of plant parts; determination of form in plants, as influenced by exogenous and endogenous factors. *Mailing Add:* 384 W Park St River Falls WI 54022

BOSTROM, CARL OTTO, SPACE PHYSICS. *Current Pos:* CONSULT RES & DEVELOP MGT, SPACE PHYSICS, 92- *Personal Data:* b Port Jefferson, NY, Aug 18, 32; m 54, Sara Hertzog; c Robyn (Dagen), Carl E & Jennifer (Simmons). *Educ:* Franklin & Marshall Col, BS, 56; Yale Univ, MS, 58, PhD(physics), 62. *Hon Degrees:* ScD, Franklin & Marshall Col, 92. *Honors & Awards:* Conrad Award Sci Achievement, 95. *Prof Exp:* Sr physicist, Johns Hopkins Univ, 60-64, supvr space physics group, 64-74, chief scientist, 74-78, assoc head, 78, head, Space Dept, 79-80, asst dir space systs, 79, dep dir, 79-80, dir, Appl Physics Lab, 80-92. *Concurrent Pos:* Instr, Evening Col, Johns Hopkins Univ, 75-77. *Mem:* AAAS; Am Phys Soc; Am Geophys Union; Sigma Xi; fel Nat Acad Pub Admin. *Res:* Space particles and fields; satellite instrumentation; magnetospheric physics; solar physics; satellite systems design; research administration. *Mailing Add:* 12508 Meadowood Dr Silver Spring MD 20904

BOSTROM, ROBERT CHRISTIAN, GEOPHYSICS. *Current Pos:* assoc prof, 64-69, PROF GEOL SCI & GEOPHYS, UNIV WASH, 69- *Personal Data:* b Edinburgh, Scotland, July 22, 20; m 52; c 3. *Educ:* Oxford Univ, BA, 48, MA, 52, DPhil(geophys), 61. *Prof Exp:* Geophysicist, Explor Consults Inc, 50-53 & Standard Oil Co Calif, 53-64. *Concurrent Pos:* Seafloor eng comt, Marine Bd, Nat Res Coun, 74-76. *Mem:* Am Geophys Union; Soc Explor Geophys; Am Asn Petrol Geol; Geol Soc London; Seismol Soc Am. *Res:* Mantle circulation and plate motion mechanism; earth tides; interaction of elementary particles and earth's interior; regional mineral exploration. *Mailing Add:* Dept Geol Scis Univ Wash Box 351310 Seattle WA 98195

BOSWELL, DONALD EUGENE, ORGANIC CHEMISTRY. *Current Pos:* RETIRED. *Personal Data:* b Durham, NC, Aug 12, 34; m 56; c 3. *Educ:* Duke Univ, BS, 56; Va Polytech Inst & State Univ, MS, 61, PhD(chem), 63. *Prof Exp:* Res chemist, Cent Res Div Lab, Mobil Res & Develop Co, NJ, 63-65, asst supvr catalysis & math res, 65-67; mgr prod planning, Cincinnati Milacron, 67-68, mgr res & develop, Prod Div, 68-76; dir res & develop, Metall Div, Quaker Chem, 76-78, tech dir, 78-91, vpres, res & develop, 85-91. *Mem:* Nat Asn Corrosion Engrs; AAAS; Am Chem Soc; Am Soc Tool & Mfg Eng; Am Soc Lubrication Eng. *Res:* Chemistry of heterocyclic compounds; organometallic chemistry; metalworking synthetic lubricants; corrosion inhibitors; water purification techniques; organic analytical chemistry. *Mailing Add:* 104 Vistamar Wilmington NC 28405

BOSWELL, FRANK WILLIAM CHARLES, MODULATED CRYSTALS. *Current Pos:* assoc prof, 60-63, assoc dean sci for grad affairs, 67-76, PROF PHYSICS, UNIV WATERLOO, 63- *Personal Data:* b Hamilton, Ont, July 11, 24; m 51; c 2. *Educ:* Univ Toronto, BA, 46, MA, 47, PhD(physics), 50. *Prof Exp:* Sci officer, Dept Mines & Technol Surv, Can, 50-57, head metal physics sect, 57-60. *Mem:* Electron Micros Soc Am; Can Asn Physicists. *Res:* Solid state physics; imperfections in crystals; electron microscopy and diffraction; charge density wave modulated crystals. *Mailing Add:* Dept Physics Univ Waterloo Waterloo ON N2L 3G1 Can

BOSWELL, FRED CARLEN, AGRONOMY, SOILS. *Current Pos:* asst soil chemist, Exp Sta, Univ Ga, 60-64, assoc soil chemist, 64-78, prof agron & soils, 71-91, dept head, 82-89, EMER PROF AGRON & SOILS, EXP STA, UNIV GA, 91- *Personal Data:* b Monterey, Tenn, Aug 20, 30; m 54, Marjorie S Brown; c Elaine J (King) & Julia A (Merry). *Educ:* Tenn Polytech Inst, BS, 54; Univ Tenn, MS, 56; Pa State Univ, PhD(agron, soils), 60. *Prof Exp:* Asst res agronomist, Agr Exp Sta, Univ Tenn, 55-56 & Exp Sta, Univ Ga, 56-57; asst, Pa State Univ, 58-60. *Concurrent Pos:* Adj prof, Univ Tenn, 93- *Mem:* Fel Am Soc Agron; Int Soil Sci Soc; Coun Agr Sci & Technol; fel Soil Sci Soc Am. *Res:* Soil chemistry, fertility, microbiology and closely related subjects; nitrogen transformations, management and micronutrients as related to plant growth and physiology; heavy metal and environmental studies of soils and plants. *Mailing Add:* 748 Russell Strausse Cookeville TN 38501-4515

BOSWELL, GEORGE A, ORGANIC CHEMISTRY. *Current Pos:* res org chemist, E I du Pont de Nemours & Co, Inc, 61-67, res supvr, 67-79, res mgr, Cent Res Dept, 79-85, res fel, 86-90, RES MGR, MED PROD DEPT, PHARMACEUT DIV, E I DU PONT DE NEMOURS & CO, INC, 85-, SR RES FEL, DU PONT MERCK PHARMACEUT, 91- *Personal Data:* b Hayward, Calif, Jan 26, 32; m 52; c 4. *Educ:* Univ Calif, Berkeley, BS, 56, PhD(org chem), 59. *Prof Exp:* With Shell Develop Co, Calif, 59-61. *Mem:* Am Chem Soc. *Res:* Steroid chemistry; general organic synthesis; organic fluorine and medicinal chemistry. *Mailing Add:* 226 Sequoia Circle Blairsden CA 96103

BOSWICK, JOHN A, SURGERY. *Current Pos:* PROF SURG & CHMN SECT HAND SURG, MED CTR, UNIV COLO, DENVER, 72- *Personal Data:* b Galatia, Ill, Aug 30, 26; m 49; c 3. *Educ:* Southern Ill Univ, Carbondale, BA, 51; Loyola Univ Chicago, MS, 52, MD, 56. *Prof Exp:* Assoc prof surg, Med Sch, Northwestern Univ, 61-70; prof surg, Univ Ill Med Ctr, 70-72. *Concurrent Pos:* Dir burn unit & hand surg, Cook County Hosp, Chicago, 61-72; consult, Brooke Army Med Ctr, 70-, Great Lakes Naval Hosp, 70- & Vet Admin Hosp, Denver, 72- *Mem:* Am Asn Surg of Trauma (secy, 74-79); Am Burn Asn (pres, 74-75); Am Soc Surg of Hand (secy-treas, 72-76); Asn Am Med Cols; Int Soc Burn Injuries (secy-gen, 75-). *Res:* Hand surgery. *Mailing Add:* 2005 Franklin St No 660 Denver CO 80205-5439

BOSWORTH, KEN W, ENVIRONMENTAL MODELLING, ROBUST PARAMETER ESTIMATION & NONPARAMETRIC SMOOTHING. *Current Pos:* asst prof, 91-94, ASSOC PROF MATH, IDAHO STATE UNIV, 94- *Personal Data:* b Concord, Mass, Sept 6, 55; m 85, Mary M Hofle; c Stephen Edward. *Educ:* Rensselaer Polytech Inst, BS, 77, MS, 80, PhD(math), 84. *Prof Exp:* Asst prof math, Utah State Univ, 84-89, Utah Water Res Lab, 89-91. *Concurrent Pos:* Asst prof appl math, Chesapeake Biol Inst, Univ Md, 89-91. *Mem:* Soc Indust & Appl Math. *Res:* Robust, locally adaptive, non-parametric smoothers in environmental data analysis and modelling. *Mailing Add:* Dept Math Idaho State Univ Box 8085 Pocatello ID 83209-8085. *Fax:* 208-236-2636; *E-Mail:* bosk@wrykyn.isu.edu

BOTELHO, LYNNE H PARKER, DIABETES, ENZYMOLOGY. *Current Pos:* GROUP LEADER, CELLULAR BIOCHEM, SANDOZ RES INST, SANDOZ, INC, 79- *Educ:* Ind Univ, PhD(chem), 75. *Mailing Add:* Dept Pharm Berlex Labs Inc 110 E Hanover Ave Cedar Knolls NJ 07927-2095

BOTELHO, STELLA YATES, PHYSIOLOGY. *Current Pos:* From instr to assoc prof, 49-69, prof, 69-81, EMER PROF PHYSIOL, SCH MED, UNIV PA, 81- *Personal Data:* b Japan, Jan 14, 19; US citizen. *Educ:* Univ Pa, BA, 40; Med Col Pa, MD, 49. *Honors & Awards:* Lacrima Award, Dry Eye Inst, 84. *Concurrent Pos:* Vis prof, Cambridge Univ, 57-58; lectr, US Naval Hosp, Philadelphia, 64-70; sect chief, Philadelphia Gen Hosp, 63-74; consult, Children's Hosp Philadelphia, 63-81; mem adv panel regulatory biol prog, NSF, 73-76; mem adv comt, Coun Exchange Int Scholars; mem adv bd, Dry Eye Inst, 84- *Mem:* Am Physiol Soc; Int Soc Dacryology. *Res:* Neuromuscular physiology; secretory mechanisms, especially of the orbital glands; diseases of neuromuscular system; ocular reflexes. *Mailing Add:* Normandy Farms Estates Box 1108-C108 Blue Bell PA 19422

BOTERO, J M, BIOCHEMISTRY. *Current Pos:* med & res dir western hemisphere, 61-67, med dir develop mkt, 64-67, med dir, Dome Labs, 67-69, vpres, Ames Co, 69-79, VPRES MED AFFAIRS, PROF PROD GROUP, MILES LABS, INC, 79- *Personal Data:* b Medellin, Colombia, Nov 12, 29; m 57, Wava J Riley; c Frederick W & Phillip A. *Educ:* Univ Antioquia, BS, 48, MD, 55; Harvard Univ, dipl, 79. *Honors & Awards:* Cano Award, 48. *Prof Exp:* Head dept biochem, Univ Antioquia, 60-61. *Concurrent Pos:* Kellogg fel, 55-57; Rockefeller Found fel, 57-59. *Mem:* NY Acad Sci; AMA; Am Chem Soc. *Res:* Synthesis of proteins and nucleic acids; chemical pathology of cancer and diabetes mellitus. *Mailing Add:* Bayer Corp 1884 Miles Ave PO Box 70 Elkhart IN 46515-0070. *Fax:* 219-262-7949

BOTEZ, DAN, SEMICONDUCTOR DIODE-LASER PHYSICS, PHASE-LOCKED ARRAYS OF DIODE LASERS. *Current Pos:* PHILIP D REED PROF ELEC ENG, UNIV WIS, MADISON, 93- *Personal Data:* b Bucharest, Romania, May 22, 48; m 76, Lynda Arnold; c Anca & Adrian. *Educ:* Univ Calif, Berkeley, BS, 71, MS, 72 & PhD(elec eng), 76. *Honors & Awards:* Outstanding Young Engr Centennial-Yr Award, Inst Elec & Electronics Engrs, 84. *Prof Exp:* Fel, IBM Thomas J Watson Res Ctr, 76-77; mem tech staff, RCA David Sarnoff Res Ctr, 77-82, res leader, 82-84; dir device develop, Lytel Inc, 84-86; chief scientist & lab dir, TRW Res Ctr, 86-87, sr staff scientist, 82-91, Tech Fel, 91-93. *Concurrent Pos:* Mem, Tech Comt Semiconductor Lasers, Inst Elec & Electronics Engrs, 82-87 & 90-, chmn, 88-89; mem bd of governors, Lasers and Electro-Optics Soc, Inst Elec

& Electronics Engrs, 93- *Mem:* Fel Inst Elec & Electronics Engrs; Optical Soc Am. *Res:* Developed high-power single-spatial-mode semiconductor diode lasers and high-power phase-locked arrays of diode lasers; published work on the properties of dielectric waveguides and is co-developer of Bloch-function theory for phase-locked arrays. *Mailing Add:* 200 N Prospect Madison WI 53705. *Fax:* 608-265-4623; *E-Mail:* botez@engr.wisc.edu

BOTHAST, RODNEY JACOB, MICROBIOLOGY. *Current Pos:* microbiologist, 71-78, RES LEADER, FERMENTATION BIOCHEM RES UNIT, NORTHERN REGIONAL RES CTR, AGR RES SERV, USDA, 78- *Personal Data:* b Union City, Ind, Sept 18, 45; m 65; c 3. *Educ:* Ohio State Univ, BS, 67; Va Polytech Inst & State Univ, MS, 70, PhD, 71. *Prof Exp:* Grad res asst food microbiol, Va Polytech Inst & State Univ, 67-71. *Concurrent Pos:* Sr res specialist microbiol, Peoria Sch Med, Univ Ill, 71- *Mem:* Inst Food Technologists; Am Soc Microbiol; Sigma Xi; Am Chem Soc. *Res:* Food microbiology; mycotoxins; biodeterioration; grain preservation; grain drying; solid substrate fermentations; the fermentative conversion of agricultural commodities into new and improved products. *Mailing Add:* 311 Indian Circle East Peoria IL 61611

BOTHNER, RICHARD CHARLES, ECOLOGY, ANATOMY. *Current Pos:* from asst prof to assoc prof, 58-69, PROF BIOL, ST BONAVENTURE UNIV, 69- *Personal Data:* b New York, NY, May 16, 29; m 58; c 3. *Educ:* Fordham Univ, BS, 51, MS, 57, PhD(biol), 59. *Prof Exp:* Asst biol, Fordham Univ, 55-57; mus asst herpet, Am Mus Natural Hist, NY, 57-58. *Mem:* Am Soc Ichthyol & Herpet; Ecol Soc Am; Sigma Xi. *Res:* Herpetology; phylogenetic significance of ophidian circulatory systems. *Mailing Add:* 788 Main St Olean NY 14760-1520

BOTHNER, WALLACE ARTHUR, STRUCTURAL GEOLOGY, GEOPHYSICS. *Current Pos:* from asst prof to assoc prof, 67-82, PROF GEOL, UNIV NH, 82- *Personal Data:* b Fitchburg, Mass, May 17, 41; m 63; c 3. *Educ:* Harpur Col, BA, 63; Univ Wyo, PhD(geol), 67. *Prof Exp:* Instr geol, Univ Wyo, 66-67. *Concurrent Pos:* Br geophys, US Geol Surv, WAE, 77- *Mem:* Geol Soc Am; Fel Geol Soc Am. *Res:* Metamorphic structural geology, regional geophysics and tectonics of the northern Appalachian mountains. *Mailing Add:* Dept Earth Sci Univ NH James Hall Durham NH 03824-4724

BOTHNER-BY, AKSEL ARNOLD, BIOPHYSICAL CHEMISTRY. *Current Pos:* chmn, Dept Chem, Carnegie-Mellon Univ, 67-70, prof, 67-76, dean, 71-75, univ prof, 76-90, actg head, 87-90, EMER UNIV, PROF CHEM, CARNEGIE-MELLON UNIV, 90- *Personal Data:* b Minneapolis, Minn, Apr 29, 21; m 49, Christine Treuner; c Peter O & Anne (Sigrun). *Educ:* Univ Minn, BChem, 43; NY Univ, MS, 47; Harvard Univ, PhD(chem), 49. *Honors & Awards:* IR-100 Award. *Prof Exp:* Assoc scientist chem, Brookhaven Nat Lab, 49-53, scientist, 53; instr, Harvard Univ, 53-55, lectr, 55-58; staff fel, Mellon Inst Sci, 58-59, from asst dir res to dir res, 59-62, mem adv comt, 62-67. *Concurrent Pos:* Am Cancer Soc fel, Univ Zurich, 52-53; consult, Retina Found, 57; Fulbright lectr, Univ Munich, 62-63; adj prof, Univ Pittsburgh, 64-; vis prof, Univ Calif, San Diego, 76-77. *Mem:* Am Chem Soc; Am Soc Biochem & Molecular Biol. *Res:* Nuclear magnetic resonance; structure of biopolymers. *Mailing Add:* Dept Chem Carnegie-Mellon Univ Pittsburgh PA 15213. *Fax:* 412-268-1061; *E-Mail:* abgd@andrew.cmu.edu

BOTHWELL, ALFRED LESTER MEADOR, LYMPHOCYTE RECOGNITION AND ACTIVATION. *Current Pos:* asst prof, 82-88, ASSOC PROF BIOL & IMMUNOBIOL, MED SCH, YALE UNIV, 88- *Personal Data:* b Springfield, Mo, Apr 29, 49; m 74, 85, G Shirleen Roeder; c Sara G & Laura E. *Educ:* Wash Univ, AB, 71; Yale Univ, MPh, 74, PhD(biol), 75. *Prof Exp:* Fel virol, Cold Spring Harbor Lab, 75-76; fel, Ctr Cancer Res, Mass Inst Technol, 76-82. *Mem:* Am Soc Microbiol; Sigma Xi; Am Asn Immunologists; AAAS. *Res:* Structure and expression of genes in the immune response; T cell recognition and activation. *Mailing Add:* Sect Immunobiol Yale Med Sch 310 Cedar St PO Box 208011 New Haven CT 06520-8011. *Fax:* 203-737-1764; *E-Mail:* alfred.bothwell@yale.edu

BOTHWELL, FRANK EDGAR, OPERATIONS RESEARCH, ACOUSTICS. *Current Pos:* CONSULT, ALLIANT TECHSYST, 83- *Personal Data:* b Saginaw, Mich, Feb 25, 18; m 45, Mary Sullivan; c Carol, Joseph, Mary, Charles, Joan, James, Paul & Margaret. *Educ:* Mass Inst Technol, SB(math), 40, SB(elec eng), 41, PhD(math), 46. *Prof Exp:* Staff mem radar develop, Radiation Lab, Mass Inst Technol, 40-47; div dir guided missiles, Ord Res Lab, Univ Chicago, 47-50; assoc prof elec eng, Northwestern Univ, 50-51; dir planning rocket develop, Naval Weapons Ctr, 51-58; dir appl sci, Appl Sci Lab, Univ Chicago, 58-62; dir & chief sci syst anal, Ctr Naval Anal, 62-70; vpres, Honeywell Inc, 70-83. *Mailing Add:* 422 E Jefferson St Falls Church VA 22046-3534

BOTHWELL, MAX LEWIS, LIMNOLOGY. *Current Pos:* RES SCI ENVIRON, CAN NAT WATER RES INST, 79- *Personal Data:* b Portsmouth, Va, Dec 5, 46; m 73; c Julie & Peter. *Educ:* Univ Calif, Santa Barbara, BA, 68, MA, 71; Univ Wis-Madison, PhD(zool), 75. *Honors & Awards:* Provasoli Award. *Prof Exp:* Res assoc limnol, Ctr Gt Lakes Studies, 71-75; res assoc stream ecol, Weyerhaeuser Co, 75-78; res assoc, Ctr Great Lakes Studies, Univ Wis-Milwaukee, 78-80. *Mem:* Am Soc Limnol & Oceanog; Int Soc Theoret & Appl Limnol; Phycol Soc Am. *Res:* Phytoplankton ecology; nutrient limitation and nutrient cycling; photosynthetic pigments and carbon fixation rates; ecological effects of ozone depletion. *Mailing Add:* Pac Biol Sta 3190 Hammond Bay Rd Nanaimo BC V9S 3E3 Can. *E-Mail:* bothwellm@pbs.dfo.ca

BOTKIN, DANIEL BENJAMIN, ECOLOGY. *Current Pos:* chmn, environ studies prog, 78-85, PROF, DEPT BIOL, UNIV CALIF, SANTA BARBARA, 78-, PROF, ENVIRON STUDIES PROG, 78- *Personal Data:* b Oklahoma City, Okla, Aug 19, 37; m 60, 79; c 2. *Educ:* Univ Rochester, AB, 59; Univ Wis-Madison, MS, 62; Rutgers Univ, PhD(biol), 68. *Prof Exp:* Asst prof ecol, Sch Forestry & Environ Studies, Yale Univ, 68-74, assoc prof, 74-75; assoc prof, Ecosysts Ctr, Marine Biol Lab, Woods Hole, Mass, 75-78. *Concurrent Pos:* NSF res grants, 69-83; res grants, World Wildlife Fund, 74-76, Nat Oceanic & Atmospheric Admin, 78-80, NASA, 78-79, 80-81, 81-87, Andrew J Mellon Found, 85-88, 88-91, Pew Found, 89-91, Environ Protection Agency, 89-92, Dept Energy, 90-91; mem, Space Sci Bd, Nat Acad Sci, 80-83, Sci Adv Bd, US Marine Mammal Comn, 80-81, Acad Adv Bd, Central Europ Univ, 90; fel, Woodrow Wilson Int Ctr Scholars, Smithsonian Inst Bldg, Washington, 78-79; nat lectr, Sigma Xi, 81-83; fel, Rockefeller Bellagio Study & Conf Ctr, 86, Woodrow Wilson Int Ctr Scholars, 78-79, East-West Ctr, Honolulu, 85-86, 86-87; consult, World Bank, 88, 90-91, Nat Geog Soc, 88-90. *Mem:* Fel AAAS; Ecol Soc Am; Am Inst Biol Sci; Sigma Xi; Am Soc Naturalists. *Res:* Mineral cycling and energy flow in ecosystems; ecosystem theory and models; interactions among plants and animals; population dynamics of long-lived and endangered species. *Mailing Add:* 736 N Ontare Rd Stroud Water Res Ctr 970 Spencer Rd Santa Barbara CA 93105

BOTKIN, MERWIN P, ANIMAL SCIENCE. *Current Pos:* PROF ANIMAL BREEDING, UNIV WYO, 52- *Personal Data:* b Fruita, Colo, Sept 19, 22; m 48; c 4. *Educ:* Univ Wyo, BS, 48, MS, 49; Okla State Univ, PhD(animal breeding), 52. *Prof Exp:* Instr animal prod, Univ Wyo, 48-49; instr animal husb, Okla State Univ, 51-52. *Mem:* Am Soc Animal Sci. *Res:* Sheep breeding and physiology. *Mailing Add:* 1521 Steele St Laramie WY 82070

BOTROS, RAOUF, CHEMISTRY. *Current Pos:* SR RES CHEMIST & GROUP LEADER DYESTUFFS & INTERMEDIATES, AM COLOR & CHEM CORP, SUBSID NAM PHILIPS, 68- *Personal Data:* b Mit-Ghamr, Egypt, Aug 28, 32; m 67; c 1. *Educ:* Alexandria Univ, Egypt, BSc, 55; Duquesne Univ, PhD(org chem), 62. *Prof Exp:* Res supvr dyestuff & intermediates, Egypt Dyes & Intermediates Corp, 62-67. *Concurrent Pos:* Mgr fluids develop & prod, Eastman Kodak. *Mem:* Am Chem Soc; Am Asn Textile Chemists & Colorists. *Res:* Synthesis of novel disperse, and acid dyes in the azo and anthraquinone classes for polyesters, acetates, nylon, plastic, paper and polypropylene fibers; special interest in making intermediates and developing existing products; development of imaging fluids for inkjet printers. *Mailing Add:* 5647 Hugh Dr Centerville OH 45459-1655

BOTSARIS, GREGORY D(IONYSIOS), CHEMICAL ENGINEERING. *Current Pos:* from asst prof to assoc prof chem eng, 65-76, PROF CHEM ENG, TUFTS UNIV, 76- *Personal Data:* b Patras, Greece, Jan 6, 30; m 65. *Educ:* Nat Univ Athens, Dipl, 52; Mass Inst Technol, MS, 59, ChE, 60, PhD(chem eng), 65. *Prof Exp:* From asst to prof anal chem, Univ Athens, 52-54; chem engr, Dennison Mfg Co, 60-61. *Mem:* Am Inst Chem Engrs; Am Chem Soc; Am Asn Crystal Growth; Am Asn Univ Professors. *Res:* Crystal growth; nucleation; industrial crystallizations; stabilization of solid dispersions in liquids; coal slurries. *Mailing Add:* Dept Chem Eng Tufts Univ Medford MA 02155-5555

BOTSFORD, JAMES L, MICROBIAL PHYSIOLOGY, BIOCHEMISTRY. *Current Pos:* from asst prof to assoc prof, 70-82, PROF BIOL, NMEX STATE UNIV, 82- *Personal Data:* b Spokane, Wash, June 6, 42; m 64; c 2. *Educ:* Univ Idaho, BS, 64; Ore State Univ, PhD(microbial physiol), 68. *Prof Exp:* NIH fel, Univ Ill, 68-70. *Concurrent Pos:* Inst for Elderhostel Prog Gen Engr; vis prof, Plant Growth Lab, Univ Calif, Davis, 84. *Mem:* AAAS; Am Soc Microbiol; Sigma Xi. *Res:* Cyclic nucleotides in procaryotes; molecular biology of osmoregulation. *Mailing Add:* Dept Biol NMex State Univ Box 3AF Las Cruces NM 88003

BOTSTEIN, DAVID, MOLECULAR GENETICS, MICROBIAL PHYSIOLOGY. *Current Pos:* PROF & CHMN, DEPT GENETICS, SCH MED, STANFORD UNIV, 90- *Personal Data:* b Zurich, Switz, Sept 8, 42; US citizen; m 65. *Educ:* Harvard Univ, AB, 63; Univ Mich, PhD(human genetics), 67. *Honors & Awards:* Award in Microbiol & Immunol, Eli Lilly & Co, 78; Genetics Soc Am Medal, 88. *Prof Exp:* Instr biol, Mass Inst Technol, 67-69, from asst prof to prof genetics, Dept Biol, 69-87, Earle A Griswold prof, 87-88; vpres sci, Genentech, Inc, 88-90. *Concurrent Pos:* Mem, Study Sect, NSF, 72-76 & Am Chem Soc, 77-81; NIH career develop award, 72-77; mem sci adv bd, Collab Res, Inc, 78-87; bd dirs, Genetics Soc Am, 84, Cold Spring Harbor, 85-, Life Sci Res Found, 88- & Genomyx, Inc, 88-; mem, Prog Adv Comt Human Genome, NIH, 88-, Vis Comt Biol Sci, Rice Univ, 88-, Human Genome Ctr Adv Comt, Lawrence Berkeley Lab, 88- & Sci Resource Bd, Genentech, Inc, 89- *Mem:* Nat Acad Sci; fel AAAS; Am Soc Microbiol; Genetics Soc Am; Am Acad Arts & Sci. *Res:* Control of gene expression in temperate phages, bacteria and deoxyribonucleic acid replication. *Mailing Add:* Dept Genetics Stanford Univ Sch Med Stanford CA 94305-5120

BOTT, KENNETH F, MICROBIOLOGY, MOLECULAR GENETICS. *Current Pos:* assoc prof, 72-80, dir interdept curric genetics, 84-90, PROF MICROBIOL, UNIV NC, CHAPEL HILL, 80- *Personal Data:* b Albany, NY, Dec 19, 36; m 90, Lacola Hall; c Allison & Kenneth A. *Educ:* St Lawrence Univ, BS, 58; Syracuse Univ, MS, 60, PhD(microbiol), 63. *Prof Exp:* From instr to asst prof microbiol, Univ Chicago, 62-71. *Concurrent Pos:* Trainee microbial genetics & virol, Univ Chicago, 63-64; Merck & Co Found grant fac develop, 69; Fulbright grant & vis prof, Univ Paris, Orsay, 71; vis prof, Inst Pasteur, Paris, 77; Fulbright grant & vis researcher, Nat Ctr Sci Res, Gif sur Yvette, France, 82. *Mem:* AAAS; Am Soc Microbiol; Sigma Xi; Am

Asn Univ Prof. *Res:* Molecular and genomic characterization of several Mycoplasma species; physical map of the chromosome of M genitalium; other mycoplasma species with potential association to acquired immunodeficiency syndrome patients will be related to studies provided by M genitalium; genetic manipulation of male genitalium. *Mailing Add:* Dept Microbiol & Immunol Div Health Affairs Univ NC Chapel Hill NC 27599-7290. *Fax:* 919-962-8103; *E-Mail:* kbott@med.unc.edu

BOTT, RAOUL H, MATHEMATICS. *Current Pos:* prof, 59-74, Higgins prof, 74-77, WILLIAM CASPAR GRAUSTEIN PROF MATH, HARVARD UNIV, 77- *Personal Data:* b Budapest, Hungary, Sept 24, 23; m 47; c 4. *Educ:* McGill Univ, MEng, 46; Carnegie Inst Technol, DrSc(math), 49. *Hon Degrees:* DSc, Notre Dame Univ, 80 & McGill Univ, 87. *Honors & Awards:* Veblen prize, Am Math Soc, 64, Steele Career Prize, 90; Nat Medal Sci, 87. *Prof Exp:* Mem, Inst Adv Study, 49-51, 55-57 & 70-71; from instr to prof math, Univ Mich, 51-59. *Concurrent Pos:* Master, Dunsterhouse, Harvard Univ, 78-84; hon fel, St Catherine's Col, 85. *Mem:* Nat Acad Sci; Am Math Soc; hon mem London Math Soc. *Res:* Topology; geometry; global analysis. *Mailing Add:* Dept Math Harvard Univ Cambridge MA 02138

BOTT, THOMAS LEE, MICROBIOLOGY, HYDROBIOLOGY. *Current Pos:* from asst cur to assoc cur to assoc cur, 69-86, CUR AQUATIC MICROBIOL, STROUD WATER RES CTR, ACAD NATURAL SCI PHILIDELPHIA, 86- *Personal Data:* b Jersey City, NJ, June 15, 40; m 64; c 3. *Educ:* Wheaton Col Ill, BS, 62; Univ Wis-Madison, MS, 65, PhD(bact & zool), 68. *Prof Exp:* NIH fel, Ind Univ, 68-69. *Concurrent Pos:* Adj asst prof, Biol Dept, Univ Pa, 72-81, adj assoc prof, 81-; consult, NSF, 77-, Environ Protection Res Inst, 81-84, Ill Inst Technol Res Inst, 82- *Mem:* AAAS; Am Soc Microbiol; Am Soc Limnol & Occanog; NAm Benthological Soc; Sigma Xi. *Res:* Microbial ecology; aquatic microbiology; Clostridium botulinum type E in the Great Lakes; extreme thermophilic bacteria; microbial food webs; primary productivity; oil pollution effects on microbes; bacterial population biology; biological control of algal growths; bacterial utilization of dissolved organics; bacterial productivity, metabolic condition, and biomass in streams and rivers; gems in the environment; cellulose degradation; bioremediation of toxics. *Mailing Add:* Acad Natural Sci Philadelphia Stroud Water Res Ctr RD 1 Box 512 Avondale PA 19311

BOTTEI, RUDOLPH SANTO, ANALYTICAL CHEMISTRY, INORGANIC CHEMISTRY. *Current Pos:* Instr to assoc prof, 55-71, ASST HEAD DEPT, UNIV NOTRE DAME, 66-, PROF CHEM, 71- *Personal Data:* b Old Forge, Pa, July 19, 29; m 60, Rita Uznanski; c 4. *Educ:* Wilkes Col, AB, 50; Cornell Univ, MS, 52; Princeton Univ, PhD, 56. *Mem:* Sigma Xi; Am Chem Soc. *Res:* Electroanalytical chemistry; complex ions; organometallic compounds; boron compounds; organic reduction. *Mailing Add:* Dept Chem Univ Notre Dame Notre Dame IN 46556

BOTTGER, GARY LEE, CHEMICAL PHYSICS, PHOTOGRAPHIC SCIENCE. *Current Pos:* Res asst infrared spectros, Univ Wash, 62-63, sr res chemist, 64-71, LAB HEAD, EASTMAN KODAK CO, 71- *Personal Data:* b Los Angeles, Calif, Oct 27, 38; m 65; c 2. *Educ:* Univ Southern Calif, BS, 60; Univ Wash, PhD, 64. *Concurrent Pos:* Tech asst to Eastman Kodak dir res, 86. *Mem:* Soc Imaging Sci & Technol; AAAS; Am Chem Soc; Am Phys Soc; Soc Photog Sci & Technol Japan. *Res:* Infrared and Raman spectroscopy; molecular structure; vibrational spectra of solids; theory of the photographic process; imaging science; silver halide research. *Mailing Add:* 9 Mile Post Lane Pittsford NY 14534-2213

BOTTICELLI, CHARLES ROBERT, PHYSIOLOGY. *Current Pos:* RETIRED. *Personal Data:* b Springdale, Conn, Feb 14, 28; m 54; c 6. *Educ:* Univ Conn, BA, 53; Williams Col, MA, 55; Harvard Univ, PhD(biol), 58. *Prof Exp:* Res fel, Harvard Univ, 58-60, instr, 60-62, lectr, 62-63; asst prof physiol, Boston Univ, 64-69, assoc prof biol, 69-70; prof biol & dir sci & math, Newton Col, 70-76; res mgr life sci, Explor Res Lab, GTE Labs, 76-89. *Concurrent Pos:* Prof, Div Sci, Middlesex Community Col, Bedford, Mass; sr lectr, Biol & Med Sci, Northeastern Univ, Boston, Mass. *Mem:* AAAS; Am Soc Zool; Endocrine Soc; Am Soc Agr Consults; Am Soc Hort Sci. *Res:* Physiology of reproduction; photobiology; steroid chemistry; mechanism and action of hormones; field applications of photobiology in agriculture. *Mailing Add:* 63 Westerly Rd Weston MA 02193

BOTTING, RICHARD JOHN, METHODS TECHNOLOGY, RAND SYSTEMS OF SOFTWARE DEVELOPMENT. *Current Pos:* PROF COMPUT SCI, CALIF STATE UNIV, SAN BERNARDINO, 82- *Personal Data:* b Hampshire, Eng, Jan 12, 45. *Educ:* Brunel Univ, BTech, 67, PhD(comput sci), 71. *Prof Exp:* Lectr comput sci, Brunel Univ, Eng, 71-78; lectr structured methods, Civil Serv Col, Eng, 78-82. *Mem:* Asn Comput Mach; Int Elec & Electronics Engrs. *Res:* Studying how people develop software in theory and in practice; looking for parts of the development process where small changes may lead to large benefits. *Mailing Add:* Calif State Univ 5500 State University San Bernardino CA 92407. *E-Mail:* rbotting@wiley.csusb.edu

BOTTINI, ALBERT THOMAS, ORGANIC CHEMISTRY. *Current Pos:* From instr to assoc prof, 58-68, PROF CHEM, UNIV CALIF, DAVIS, 68- *Personal Data:* b San Rafael, Calif, June 13, 32; m 53; c 3. *Educ:* Univ Calif, BS, 54; Calif Inst Technol, PhD(chem), 57. *Mem:* Am Chem Soc; Sigma Xi. *Res:* Phytotoxins; reaction mechanisms. *Mailing Add:* 2711 Baja Ave Davis CA 95616

BOTTINO, PAUL JAMES, PLANT GENETICS. *Current Pos:* asst prof, 73-76, ASSOC PROF BOT, UNIV MD, COLLEGE PARK, 76- *Personal Data:* b Price, Utah, Aug 3, 41; m 63; c 2. *Educ:* Utah State Univ, BS, 64, MS, 65; Wash State Univ, PhD(genetics), 69. *Prof Exp:* Res assoc, Brookhaven Nat Lab, 69-73. *Mem:* AAAS; Am Genetics Asn. *Res:* In vitro culture of plant cells; genetics of somatic plant cells; induced mutation in plant cells; application of tissue culture techniques to agricultural problems. *Mailing Add:* Dept Bot Univ Md RH 3223 HJ Patterson Bldg 073 College Park MD 20742

BOTTJER, DAVID JOHN, EVOLUTIONARY PALEOECOLOGY. *Current Pos:* from asst prof to assoc prof, 79-91, PROF PALEONT, UNIV SOUTHERN CALIF, 91- *Personal Data:* b New York, NY, Oct 3, 51; m 73, Sarah Wright. *Educ:* Haverford Col, BS, 73; State Univ NY-Binghamton, MA, 76; Ind Univ, PhD(geol), 78. *Prof Exp:* Nat Res Coun fel, US Geol Surv, 78-79. *Concurrent Pos:* Res assoc, Los Angeles Co Mus Natural Hist, 79-; vis scientist, Field Mus Natural Hist, Chicago, 86, ed, Palaios, 89-96. *Mem:* Soc Sedimentary Geol; Paleont Soc; fel Geol Soc Am, 86; AAAS; Int Paleont Asn; Paleont Res Inst; Geol Soc London. *Res:* Paleoecological and paleobiological trends in the Phanerozoic history of marine metazoan life; bioturbation in marine sedimentary environments; stratigraphy and paleoenvironments of sedimentary rocks, particulary those of Mesozoil age. *Mailing Add:* Dept Earth Sci Univ Southern Calif Los Angeles CA 90089-0740. *Fax:* 213-740-8801

BOTTJER, WILLIAM GEORGE, INORGANIC CHEMISTRY. *Current Pos:* res chemist org chem dept, Jackson Lab, 63-65, develop chemist, 65-68, sr res chemist, Photo Prod Dept, 68-72, sr res chemist, Parlin, NJ, 72-75, res assoc, Photo Prod Plant, 75-82, PROCESS ASSOC MFG, E I DU PONT DE NEMOURS & CO, BREVARD, NC, 82- *Personal Data:* b New York, NY, Feb 20, 31; m 58; c 2. *Educ:* Hofstra Univ, BA, 53; Univ Conn, MS, 55; Univ NH, PhD(inorg chem), 63. *Prof Exp:* Res chemist, Gen Chem Res Lab, Allied Chem Corp, NJ, 55-59. *Mem:* Am Chem Soc; Soc Photog Scientists & Engrs; AAAS. *Res:* Solid state research; magnetic materials; transition metal and fluorine chemistry; metal oxide chemistry; photographic chemistry. *Mailing Add:* 211 Grandview Lane Hendersonville NC 28739-9719

BOTTKA, NICHOLAS, SOLID STATE PHYSICS, OPTICAL PHYSICS. *Current Pos:* RES PHYSICIST, MICHELSON LAB, NAVAL WEAPONS CTR, US DEPT NAVY, 63- *Personal Data:* b Huszt, Hungary, Dec 6, 39; US citizen; m 66; c 2. *Educ:* Univ Calif, Los Angeles, BS, 63, MS, 66; Tech Univ, Berlin, PhD(physics), 70. *Mem:* Am Phys Soc. *Res:* Optical properties of solids. *Mailing Add:* ONR Europ Off 223 Old Maryebone Rd London NWI 5th England

BOTTO, DAVID JOHN, PHYSICS. *Current Pos:* VPRES, EPL ANALYSIS INC, 85- *Personal Data:* b Pottsville, Pa, Sept 21, 51. *Educ:* Franklin & Marshall Col, BA, 73; Univ Pittsburgh, MS, 74, PhD(physics), 80. *Prof Exp:* Res scientist, Dynamics Technol Inc, 81-85. *Mailing Add:* 14805 Carona Dr Silver Spring MD 20905

BOTTO, ROBERT IRVING, ANALYTICAL CHEMISTRY, GEOCHEMISTRY. *Current Pos:* Chemist, Exxon Res & Eng Co, 75-77, sr chemist, 77-79, staff chemist, 79-82, sr staff chemist, 82-91, RES ASSOC, EXXON RES & ENG CO, 91-, GROUP HEAD, BAYTOWN CHEM PLANT LAB, EXXON CHEM AMERICAS, 95- *Personal Data:* b Buffalo, NY, Apr 22, 49; m 75, Kathleen R Abbey; c Catherine & Elizabeth. *Educ:* State Univ NY, Buffalo, BA, 71; Cornell Univ, MS, 73, PhD(geochem), 76. *Concurrent Pos:* Chmn, SE Region, Am Chem Soc, 87, SW Tex Sect, 89. *Mem:* Am Chem Soc; Soc Appl Spectros. *Res:* Elemental analysis; instrumental and wet chemical methods; inductively coupled plasma atomic emission spectroscopy; scanning electron microscopy. *Mailing Add:* Exxon Chem Co 4500 Bayway Dr Baytown TX 77520. *Fax:* 281-834-2057

BOTTOM, VIRGIL ELDON, MATHEMATICS. *Current Pos:* prof, 58-73, EMER PROF PHYSICS, MCMURRY COL, 73- *Personal Data:* b Douglas, Kans, Jan 6, 11; m 32; c 3. *Educ:* Friends Univ, AB, 31; Univ Mich, MS, 38; Purdue Univ, PhD, 49. *Hon Degrees:* DSc, McMurry Col, 83. *Honors & Awards:* Sawyer Award; Cady Award. *Prof Exp:* Teacher high sch, Kans, 33-38; prof physics & head dept, Friends Univ, 38-42; from asst prof to assoc prof,Colo state Univ, 42-47; asst instr, Purdue Univ, 47-49; prof, Colo State Univ, 49-53, actg head dept, 52-53; res physicist, Motorola Res Lab, 53-58. *Concurrent Pos:* Chmn working group frequency control devices, US Dept Defense, 58-64; Fulbright lectr, Univ Sao Paulo, 64-65. *Res:* Semiconductors; piezoelectricity and applications to communication; ferromagnetism. *Mailing Add:* 3442 S Willis Abilene TX 79605

BOTTOMLEY, FRANK, INORGANIC CHEMISTRY. *Current Pos:* from asst prof to assoc prof, 69-78, PROF CHEM, UNIV NB, 78- *Personal Data:* b Hatfield, Eng, May 14, 41. *Educ:* Univ Hull, BS, 63, MS, 65; Univ Toronto, PhD(chem), 68. *Prof Exp:* Fel lectr chem, Univ Toronto, 67-69. *Concurrent Pos:* Alexander von Humboldt fel, 75-76 & 77. *Mem:* The Chem Soc; Can Inst Chem; Ges Deutscher Chemiker. *Res:* Reactions of coordinated ligands; transition metal chemistry. *Mailing Add:* Dept Chem Univ NB Bag Serv No 45222 Fredericton NB E3B 6E2 Can

BOTTOMLEY, LAWRENCE ANDREW, ELECTROCHEMISTRY, SPECTROELECTROCHEMISTRY. *Current Pos:* assist prof, 83-86, ASSOC PROF CHEM, GA TECH, 86- *Personal Data:* b Detroit, Mich, Sept 6, 50; m 86; c 4. *Educ:* Calif State Univ, Fullerton, BS, 76; Univ Houston, PhD(anal chem), 80. *Prof Exp:* Asst prof chem, Fla State Univ, 80-83.

Concurrent Pos: Vis prof chem, Lanzhou Univ, Lanzhou, People's Repub China, 93- *Mem:* Am Chem Soc; Electrochem Soc; Soc Electroanal Chemists. *Res:* Electroanalytical chemistry; scanning tunneling and atomic force microscopy nitrogen from transfer chemistry. *Mailing Add:* Sch Chem & Biochem Ga Tech Atlanta GA 30332-0400. *Fax:* 404-894-7452

BOTTOMLEY, PAUL ARTHUR, nuclear magnetic resonance, for more information see previous edition

BOTTOMLEY, RICHARD H, INTERNAL MEDICINE, ONCOLOGY. *Current Pos:* resident internal med, Med Ctr, Univ Okla, 59-61, clin asst, Sch Med, 61-64, instr internal med & sr investr oncol, 64-65, instr res med & asst prof res biol in biochem, 65-68, res med, 67-71, assoc prof med, 71-75, head, Oncol Div, 72-80, prof med, 75-81, ASSOC PROF RES MOLECULAR BIOL, SCH MED, UNIV OKLA, 68-, CLIN PROF MED, 81-; MED DIV, CENT OKLA CANCER CTR, 89-; CHIEF STAFF, SOUTHWEST MED CTR, OKLAHOMA CITY, 94- *Personal Data:* b Arkansas City, Kans, Nov 24, 33; m 58; c Astrid E & Ian P. *Educ:* Univ Okla, BS, 54, MD, 58; Am Bd Internal Med, dipl. *Prof Exp:* Intern, Salt Lake Co Gen Hosp, 58-59. *Concurrent Pos:* Nat Cancer Inst fels, McArdle Mem Lab, 61-62 & Okla Med Res Found, 61-63, asst head cancer sect, 65-72; chief med, South Community Hosp, 83-92. *Mem:* Am Fedn Clin Res; AMA; Am Soc Clin Oncol; fel Am Col Physicians; Sigma Xi. *Res:* Biology, biochemistry and chemotherapy of human neoplastic disease. *Mailing Add:* PO Box 96798 Oklahoma City OK 73143

BOTTOMLEY, SYLVIA STAKLE, INTERNAL MEDICINE, HEMATOLOGY. *Current Pos:* resident, Med Ctr, Univ Okla, 59-61, clin asst, Sch Med, 61-64, instr, 64-67, from asst prof to assoc prof, 67-75, PROF MED, SCH MED, UNIV OKLA, 75-; ASST CHIEF HEMAT SECT, VET ADMIN HOSP, 69- *Personal Data:* b Riga, Latvia, Mar 9, 34; US citizen; m 58, Richard H; c Astrid E (Morrison) & Ian P. *Educ:* Okla State Univ, BS, 54; Univ Okla, MD, 58; Am Bd Internal Med, dipl, 65, cert hemat, 72. *Prof Exp:* Intern med, Sch Med, Univ Utah, 59. *Concurrent Pos:* USPHS res fel hemat, 61-64; res assoc, Vet Admin Hosp, Oklahoma City, 64-65, clin investr, 65-68. *Mem:* Sigma Xi; Am Fedn Clin Res; Am Soc Hemat; fel Am Col Physicians; Ctr Soc Clin Res. *Res:* Clinical hematology and erythropoiesis, especially heme synthesis, iron metabolism, 5-aminolevulinate synthase. *Mailing Add:* Hemat-Oncol Sect Vet Admin Med Ctr 921 NE 13th St Oklahoma City OK 73104. *Fax:* 405-270-1569

BOTTOMS, ALBERT MAITLAND, OPERATIONS RESEARCH, INDUSTRIAL ECONOMICS. *Current Pos:* CONSULT, 91- *Personal Data:* b Montclair, NJ, Sept 2, 25; m 57, Marjoni Syranberg; c Karen & Maitland. *Educ:* Univ Pa, BSChE, 49; Iowa State Univ, MS, 51; Mass Inst Technol, MS, 62. *Prof Exp:* Res chemist, Am Cyanamid Co, 51-52; opers analyst, Opers Eval Group, Mass Inst Technol, 52-58, Weapons Systs Eval Group, Inst Defense Anal, US Dept Defense, 58-63, Res Anal Corp, 63-64, Weapons Systs Eval Group, Inst Defense Anal, 64-67; head surface weapons, Off Chief Naval Opers, 67-68; dir, Opers Res Task Force, Chicago Police Dept, 68-69; dir, Pub Safety Div, Urban Systs Res & Eng, Mass, 69-70; pres, Fundamental Systs, Inc & res assoc, Mass Inst Technol-Harvard Joint Ctr Urban Studies, 70-72; head, Warfare Anal Dept, USN Underwater Systs Ctr, 73-77; asst tech strategies, dir, Navy Technol, 77-78; asst for Dept Defense Labs, Off Under Secy Defense Res & Eng, 78-81; dir opers & mgt, Off Asst Comdr Res & Technol, Naval Air Systs Command, 81-86; Navy chair, Defense Systs Mgt Col, Ft Belvoir, Va, 86-88; dir, Ctr Study Indust Competitiveness & Nat Security, George Washington Univ, 88-90; pres, Bottoms & Assocs, Inc, Melbourne Beach, Fla, 90-91. *Concurrent Pos:* Cadet, US Mil Acad, 43-45; consult, Nat Comn Causes & Prev Violence, 68-69, Nat Acad Sci, 69- & Fed Exec Inst, 84; sci adv to comdr, US Seventh Fleet, 75-76; adv sci & technol, Ctr Naval Warfare Studies, US Naval War Col, 84-85, US Gen Acct Off, 91-, Sandia Nat Labs, 93-, Nat Acad Sci, Naval Studies Bd consult. *Mem:* Fel AAAS; Opers Res Soc Am. *Res:* Public services systems analysis; military operations research; criminal justice system; police; undersea warfare; strategy and technology; industrial economics. *Mailing Add:* 104 Reynard Dr Charlottesville VA 22901. *Fax:* 804-295-0857

BOTTOMS, GERALD DOYLE, PHYSIOLOGY, ENDOCRINOLOGY. *Current Pos:* asst prof, 66-70, assoc prof, 70-74, PROF PHYSIOL, PURDUE UNIV, 74- *Personal Data:* b Holdenville, Okla, Apr 10, 30; m 52, Maxine Lee; c Glenda (Secor), Steve & Christie (Alfred). *Educ:* ECent State Col, BS, 55; Okla State Univ, MS, 58, PhD(physiol), 66. *Honors & Awards:* Beecham Award for Excellence in Res, 86. *Prof Exp:* Sci teacher, Holdenville, Okla, 55-63. *Mem:* AAAS; Am Physiol Soc; Sigma Xi; Shock Soc; Res Soc Alcoholism. *Res:* Endotoxin shock in domestic animals; correlation of prostaglandin levels with hemodynamic changes and the effects of treatment with antiprostaglandins; Evaluation of endocrine function in domestic animals. *Mailing Add:* 175 Harvest Dr E Lafayette IN 47905. *Fax:* 317-484-8640

BOTTONE, EDWARD JOSEPH, MICROBIOLOGY. *Current Pos:* from asst microbiologist to assoc microbiologist, Mt Sinai Hosp, 69-73, asst prof microbiol, Sch Med, 73-77, actg dir microbiol, 74-75, DIR MICROBIOL, MT SINAI HOSP, 75-; PROF MICROBIOL, MT SINAI SCH MED, 81-, PROF PATH, 85-, PROF MED, 94-, DIR, CONSULTATIVE MICROBIOL, MT SINAI HOSP, 94- *Personal Data:* b New York, NY, Feb 18, 34; m 62; c Laura & Rina. *Educ:* City Col New York, BS, 65; Wagner Col, MS, 68; St John's Univ, PhD(biol), 73. *Honors & Awards:* Biomerieux Viteil Sonnenwirth Mem Award, Am Soc Microbiol. *Prof Exp:* Bacteriologist, Greenpoint Hosp, 62-64; sr bacteriologist, Elmhurst City Hosp, 64-68. *Concurrent Pos:* Consult, Elmhurst City Hosp of Mt Sinai Serv, 74-; assoc prof microbiol, Mt Sinai Sch Med, 77-81; pres, NYC Br, Am Soc Microbiol, 88-90. *Mem:* Am Soc Microbiol. *Res:* Clinical microbiology; antifungal agents. *Mailing Add:* Div Infectious Dis Mt Sinai Sch Med PO Box 1090 New York NY 10029-6574. *Fax:* 212-534-3240

BOTTORFF, EDMOND MILTON, ORGANIC CHEMISTRY. *Current Pos:* RETIRED. *Personal Data:* b Milroy, Ind, Sept 14, 16; m 48, Mildred; c 2. *Educ:* Hanover Col, AB, 37; Univ Ill, PhD(org chem), 41. *Prof Exp:* Res chemist, Rohm and Haas Co, Philadelphia, 41-47; res chemist, Eli Lilly & Co, 47-80. *Mem:* Am Chem Soc. *Res:* Action of the Grignard reagent on sterically hindered esters. *Mailing Add:* 1043 Carters Grove Indianapolis IN 46260-2228

BOTTS, TRUMAN ARTHUR, MATHEMATICS. *Current Pos:* RETIRED. *Personal Data:* b De Land, Fla, Nov 26, 17; m 44, 64, 74, Gisela Conti; c Stephen C & Margaret K. *Educ:* Stetson Univ, BS, 38; Univ Va, MA, 40, PhD(math), 42. *Prof Exp:* Instr math, Univ Va, 41-42; asst prof, Univ Del, 46-48; from asst prof to assoc prof, Univ Va, 48-68; exec dir, Conf Bd Math Sci, 68-82. *Concurrent Pos:* Ford Found fel, 53-54; fel comput sci, Nat Bur Standards, 59; vis prof, Univ PR, 62-63; exec dir, comt support res math sci, Nat Acad Sci-Nat Res Coun, Columbia Univ, 66-67. *Mem:* Fel AAAS; Am Math Soc; Math Asn Am. *Res:* Real function theory; calculus of variations; convex sets. *Mailing Add:* 3106 N John Marshall Dr Arlington VA 22207-1375

BOTZLER, RICHARD GEORGE, WILDLIFE DISEASES, ENVIRONMENTAL ETHICS. *Current Pos:* PROF WILDLIFE, HUMBOLDT STATE UNIV, 70-, DEPT CHAIR, 96- *Personal Data:* b Detroit, Mich, Jan 27, 42; m 63, Sally Jo Nelson; c Emilisa, Tin, Dorothy, Sarah & Thomas. *Educ:* Wayne State Univ, BS, 63; Univ Mich, MWM, 67, PhD(wildlife), 70. *Prof Exp:* Asst res tissue immunity, Univ Mich Hosp, 64-68. *Concurrent Pos:* Fulbright fel, Univ Hohenheim, Stuttgart, Ger, 81-82; asst ed, J Wildlife Dis, 90-91, ed, 91-96; mem, Wildlife Dis Asn Coun, 91-96. *Mem:* Wildlife Dis Asn; Int Soc Environ Ethics; Soc Conserv Biol; Wildlife Soc. *Res:* Enzoology of Listeria species and Yersinia species; avian cholera in wildfowl; physiology and parasitology of mammals; environmental ethics. *Mailing Add:* Dept Wildlife Humboldt State Univ Arcata CA 95521. *Fax:* 707-826-4060

BOUBEL, RICHARD W, MECHANICAL ENGINEERING, ENVIRONMENTAL ENGINEERING. *Current Pos:* From instr to assoc prof, 54-60, PROF MECH ENG, ORE STATE UNIV, 67- *Personal Data:* b Portland, Ore, Aug 1, 27; m 52, Ruth Abbey; c Jane, Thomas, Elizabeth & William. *Educ:* Ore State Univ, BS, 53, MS, 54; Univ NC, PhD(air & indust hyg), 63. *Honors & Awards:* Ripperton Award, Air Pollution Control Asn, 88. *Concurrent Pos:* Consult, US Bur Mines, Ore, 63-64; environ engr, USAF, 78-79; at Defense Environ Leadership Proj, 84-86. *Mem:* Fel Am Soc Mech Engrs; Air Pollution Control Asn (pres, 78-79); Sigma Xi; Am Acad Environ Engrs; hon mem Air Waste Mgt Assn. *Res:* Combustion of wood residue; air pollutants generated during combustion; instrumentation for field studies in air pollution control. *Mailing Add:* PO Box 3630 Sunriver OR 97707. *Fax:* 541-593-6832

BOUBLIK, MILOSLAV, BIOLOGICAL MACRO-MOLECULES, ELECTRON MICROSCOPY. *Current Pos:* RETIRED. *Personal Data:* b Apr 13, 27; m 59; c 2. *Educ:* Czech Acad Sci, MS, 52, PhD(biochem), 65. *Prof Exp:* Mem, Portsmouth Polytech, Eng, 68-71; mem staff, Roche Inst Molecular Biol, 71-93. *Mem:* Am Soc Biol Chemists; Electron Micros Soc Am; AAAS; NY Acad Sci. *Res:* Conformation and interactions of proteins and nucleic acids, structure-function relationship of ribosomes by electron spectroscopic techniques. *Mailing Add:* 175 Park Ave Caldwell NJ 07006

BOUBOULIS, CONSTANTINE JOSEPH, ORGANIC CHEMISTRY. *Current Pos:* OWNER-PRES, CHEM-COMP SYSTS INC, 87- *Personal Data:* b Piraeus, Greece, Feb 23, 28; US citizen; m 60; c 3. *Educ:* Nat Univ Athens, dipl, 53; Columbia Univ, MA, 57; Univ Colo, PhD(org chem), 61. *Prof Exp:* Chemist, John Lafis & Co, Greece, 54-55; from res chemist to sr res chemist, Exxon Res & Eng Co, Inc, 61-73, staff chemist, 73-80, sr staff chemist, Exxon Chem Co. 80-86. *Mem:* Am Chem Soc; Am Inst Chemists; Sigma Xi. *Res:* Steroids; synthesis and rearrangements of bicyclic systems; condensation polymers; oxidation; amines; metal mining by solvent extraction; technical service in the use of solvents; surface protective coatings; addition polymerization; high solids coatings; computer software for coatings; financial software. *Mailing Add:* 661 Golf Terr Union NJ 07083

BOUCHARD, MICHEL ANDRE, LATE CENOZOIC STRATIGRAPHY, METEORITE CRATERS. *Current Pos:* lectr geol, 75-80, from asst prof to assoc prof, 80-92, PROF GEOL, UNIV MONTREAL, 92-, CHMN, 93- *Personal Data:* b Montreal, Que, July 26, 48; c 1. *Educ:* Univ Montreal, BA, 67, BSc, 70, MSc, 74; McGill Univ, PhD(geol), 80. *Prof Exp:* Geologist, Ministry Energy Resources, Que, 74-75. *Concurrent Pos:* Sci dir, Great Whale Pub Rev Support Off. *Mem:* Can Quaternary Asn (pres, 90-92); Int Glaciol Soc; Geol Soc Am; Geol Soc Can. *Res:* Pleistocene history and glacial geomorphology applied to the reconstruction of the North American ice sheets; applications of glacial geology to mineral exploration and environmental studies. *Mailing Add:* Dept Geol Univ Montreal PO Box 6128 Montreal PQ H3C 3J7 Can. *Fax:* 514-343-5782; *E-Mail:* bouchami@ere.umontreal.ca

BOUCHARD, RAYMOND WILLIAM, FRESH WATER BIOLOGY. *Current Pos:* ACAD NAT SCI PHILADELPHIA, 86- *Personal Data:* b Ft Bragg, Calif, May 28, 44; m 73; c 2. *Educ:* Mass State Col, BSEd, 67; Univ Tenn, PhD(zool), 72. *Honors & Awards:* Explorers Club. *Prof Exp:* Res assoc, Ctr Wetland Resources, La State Univ, 73-74; asst prof, Univ N Ala, 76-78. *Concurrent Pos:* Instr ichthyol, Reelfoot Lake Biol Sta, Tenn, 70; postdoctoral fel, Nat Mus Natural Hist Smithsonian Inst, 71; instr zool, Univ Tenn, 73; fel, Nat Mus Natural Hist, Smithsonian Inst, 74-75. *Mem:* Crustacean Soc Explorer Club; Am soc Ichthyologists & Herpetologists; Int Asn Astacol; NAm Benthological Soc; Soc Syst Zool; AAAS. *Res:* Systematics; ecology, zoogeography and evolution of freshwater decapod crustaceans and fishes. *Mailing Add:* Patrick Ctr Environ Res Acad Nat Sci 1900 Benjamin Franklin Pkwy Philadelphia PA 19103

BOUCHARD, RICHARD EMILE, CARDIOLOGY, INTERNAL MEDICINE. *Current Pos:* from instr to assoc prof med, 55-77, PROF MED & FAMILY PRACT, COL MED, UNIV VT, 77- *Personal Data:* b Colchester, Vt, Mar 31, 26; m 56; c 6. *Educ:* Univ Vt, MD, 49, MS, 51. *Prof Exp:* Fel physiol, Nat Heart Inst, 50-51, fel cardiol, 54-55. *Concurrent Pos:* Fel coun clin cardiol, Am Heart Asn, 68. *Mem:* AMA; fel Am Col Physicians; fel Am Col Cardiol. *Res:* Clinical research in cardiology. *Mailing Add:* 69 Bilodeau Ct Burlington VT 05401

BOUCHER, JOHN H, MECHANICS OF BLOOD FLOW. *Current Pos:* DIR, RHEOTECH LABS, 82- *Personal Data:* b Kansas City, Mo, Dec 15, 30. *Educ:* Mo Univ, DVM, 56; Ohio State Univ, PhD(physiol), 77. *Mem:* Am Physiol Soc; Int Soc Biorheology; Am Vet Med Asn. *Mailing Add:* Rheotech Labs 2106 Salisbury Rd Silver Spring MD 20910-1234

BOUCHER, LAURENCE JAMES, INORGANIC CHEMISTRY. *Current Pos:* PROF CHEM & DEAN, COL NAT MATH SCI, TOWSON STATE UNIV, 90- *Personal Data:* b Yonkers, NY, Sept 16, 38; m 64, Susan Calkins; c Amy & Stephen. *Educ:* Mich State Univ, BS, 61; Univ Ill, MS, 62, PhD(inorg chem), 64. *Honors & Awards:* Fulbright Lectr, Colombia, 81. *Prof Exp:* Resident res assoc, Chem Div, Argonne Nat Lab, 64-66; from asst prof to assoc prof chem, Carnegie Mellon Univ, 66-76, fel, Mellon Inst, 67-76; prof & head, Dept Inorg Chem, Metrop Univ, Iztapalapa, Mexico City, 76-78; prof chem & head dept, Western Ky Univ, 78-85; prof chem & dean, Col Arts & Sci, Ark State Univ, 85-90. *Mem:* Am Asn Univ Admin; Am Chem Soc; Sigma Xi; Nat Sci Teach Asn. *Res:* Chemistry of coordination compounds; role of metal ions in biological systems; homogeneous and heterogeneous catalysis in the conversion of coal and related products. *Mailing Add:* Col Nat & Math Sci Towson State Univ Towson MD 21204. *Fax:* 410-830-2064; *E-Mail:* d7pcns2@toa.towson.edu

BOUCHER, LOUIS JACK, DENTISTRY, ANATOMY. *Current Pos:* RETIRED. *Personal Data:* b Ashland, Wis, May 24, 22; m 49, Mary L Elsner; c 4. *Educ:* Marquette Univ, DDS, 53, PhD(anat), 61. *Honors & Awards:* Int Res Award, Int Asn Dent Res, 70. *Prof Exp:* Resident prosthodontics, Vet Admin Hosp, Wood, Wis, 53-55; instr, Sch Dent, Marquette Univ, 55-60, assoc prof, 60-65, assoc anat, Sch Med, 60-65, dir, Grad Dept, 63-65, dir, Postgrad Dept, 64-65,; coordr grad studies & res, Col Dent, Univ Ky, 65-66; from asst dean to assoc dean, Sch Dent, Med Col Ga, 66-71; prof prosthodontics & dean, Sch Dent, Fairleigh Dickinson Univ, 71-76; assoc dean, Col Med & Dent NJ, NJ Dent Sch, 76-77; prof & dir prosthodontics, Sch Dent Med, State Univ NY, Stony Brook, 77-92, assoc dean, 78-92. *Concurrent Pos:* Spec fel grant, USPHS, 61-62, res career develop award, 62-65; consult, Vet Admin Hosp, Wood, Wis, 61-64, Nat Inst Dent Res, 64-66, Div Chronic Dis, USPHS, 65-67, Vet Admin Hosp, Augusta, Ga, 67-71, US Army, Ft Jackson, SC, 67-71, Ft Gordon, Ga, 68-71 & USAF Surgeon Gen 69-71. *Mem:* Am Acad Plastics Res Dent (pres, 67); Am Equilibration Soc (pres, 76); Am Prosthodontic Soc; Int Asn Dent Res; Am Dent Asn; Am Col Prosthodontics (pres, 71-72); Fedn Prosthodontics Orgns (pres, 67-68). *Res:* Functional anatomy of temporomandibular joint; response of the stratum corneum to various dental materials; epithelial reaction to various implants; cineradiographic study of the temporomandibular joint. *Mailing Add:* 7 Cedar Rd Port Jefferson NY 11777

BOUCHER, RAYMOND, hydraulic engineering, for more information see previous edition

BOUCHER, THOMAS OWEN, PRODUCTION SYSTEM DESIGN. *Current Pos:* from asst prof to assoc prof, 81-94, PROF INDUST ENG, COL ENG, RUTGERS UNIV, 94- *Personal Data:* b Providence, RI, June 25, 42; m 74, Unn Jermstad. *Educ:* Univ RI, BS, 64; Northwestern Univ, MBA, 70; Columbia Univ, MS, 73, PhD(indust eng), 78. *Honors & Awards:* Eugene L Grant Award, Am Soc Eng Educ, 83, 86, 93. *Prof Exp:* Sr proj engr, Continental Can Co, 67-69; internal consult, ABEX Corp, 70-72; sr financial analyst, Otis Elevator Co, 74-76; asst prof, Sch Opers Res & Indust Eng, Cornell Univ, 78-81. *Mem:* Sigma Xi; NY Acad Sci; Inst Indust Engrs; Soc Mfg Engrs; Inst Elec & Electronics Engrs. *Res:* Production, organization and control; productivity and technical change; production economics; computer aided manufacturing. *Mailing Add:* 65 Douglas Rd Glen Ridge NJ 07028-1227

BOUCHILLON, CHARLES W, MECHANICAL ENGINEERING. *Current Pos:* VPRES, RES & DEVELOP, FLUID QUIP, INC, SPRINGFIELD, OH. *Personal Data:* b Louisville, Miss, July 17, 31; m 58, Barbara Owons; c C Ruston, M Scott, Leslie L & David D. *Educ:* Miss State Univ, BS, 53; Ga Inst Technol, MS, 59, PhD(mech eng), 63. *Prof Exp:* Instr & res assoc mech eng, Ga Inst Technol, 59-62; assoc prof, Miss State Univ, 62-77, coordr interdisciplinary progs, Off Res, 70-79, dir, Inst Space & Environ Sci & Eng, 69-79, prof mech eng & asst dean, Grad Sch Res, 77-80, prof mech eng, 80-94. *Mem:* Am Soc Mech Engrs; Am Soc Eng Educ; Tech Asn Pulp & Paper Indust. *Res:* Vortex phenomena; particle trajectories in hydrocyclones; turbulent flow; flow in porous media; pressure losses; heat conduction in composite slabs; thermal stresses; combustion. *Mailing Add:* 1342 Lake Valley Dr Starkville MS 39759. *Fax:* 601-324-0842

BOUCK, G BENJAMIN, BOTANY, CELL BIOLOGY. *Current Pos:* PROF BIOL, UNIV ILL, CHICAGO, 71- *Personal Data:* b New York, NY, Oct 25, 33; m 61; c 3. *Educ:* Hofstra Univ, BA, 56; Columbia Univ, MA, 58, PhD(bot), 61. *Honors & Awards:* Darbarker Prize, 79. *Prof Exp:* Training fel, Harvard Univ, 61-62; from instr to assoc prof biol, Yale Univ, 62-71. *Concurrent Pos:* Vis assoc prof, Univ Calif, Berkeley, 68-69. *Mem:* AAAS; Bot Soc Am; Am Soc Cell Biol; Int Phycol Soc. *Res:* Membrane composition and surface assembly in unicellular flagellates. *Mailing Add:* Dept Biol Sci (MC/066) Univ Ill Chicago 825 W Taylor St Chicago IL 60680-4348

BOUCK, GERALD R, AQUATIC ECOLOGY, FISHERIES PHYSIOLOGY. *Current Pos:* sr fisheries biologist, 83-86, CHIEF, RES SECT, BONNEVILLE POWER ADMIN, 86-, SR FISHERIES SCIENTIST, 91- *Personal Data:* b Owosso, Mich, Aug 22, 34; m 56; c 3. *Educ:* Cent Mich Univ, BS, 60; Mich State Univ, MS, 63, PhD(fisheries physiol), 66. *Honors & Awards:* Silver Medal, US Environ Protection Agency, 70 & Gold Medal, 76. *Prof Exp:* Res asst fisheries physiol, Mich State Univ, 60-62, res instr, 65-66; chief biol effects br, Pac Northwest Water Lab, US Environ Protection Agency, 66-70, dir, Western Fish Toxicol Sta, 70-73, vis scientist, Ore State Univ, 74-75, res physiologist, Western Fish Dis Lab, 76-83. *Mem:* Ecol Soc Am; Am Fisheries Soc; Pac Estuarine Res Soc; World Maricult Soc; Fish Health Soc. *Res:* Stress physiology; toxicology/bioassays; hyperbaric physiology; gas bubble disease; plasma enzymes; gas supersaturation; estuarine physiology; Pacific salmon water quality requirements. *Mailing Add:* 9691 SW Alsea Dr Tualatin OR 97062

BOUCK, NOEL, CANCER GENETICS, ANGIOGENESIS. *Current Pos:* from asst prof to assoc prof, 79-94, PROF MICROBIOL, NORTHWESTERN UNIV, 94- *Personal Data:* b San Francisco, Calif, Oct 23, 36; m 61, G Benjamin; c Julia, John & Laurie. *Educ:* Pomona Col, BA, 58; Columbia Univ, MA, 60; Yale Univ, PhD(microbiol), 69. *Mem:* AAAS; Am Soc Cell Biologists; Am Asn Cancer Res. *Res:* Suppressor gene function & angrogenesis; inhibitors of neovascularization, their identification, mechanism of action and application as anticancer agents. *Mailing Add:* Dept Microbiol & Immunol Northwestern Univ 303 E Chicago Ave Chicago IL 60611

BOUCOT, ARTHUR JAMES, PALEONTOLOGY, EVOLUTION. *Current Pos:* PROF GEOL, ORE STATE UNIV, 69-, PROF ZOOL, 79- *Personal Data:* b Philadelphia, Pa, May 26, 24; m 48, Pierce; c Hannah, Katharine, Samuel & Peter. *Educ:* Harvard Univ, AB, 48, AM, 49, PhD(geol), 53. *Honors & Awards:* Raymond C Moore Medal, Soc Econ Paleontologists & Mineralogists, 85; Natural Sci Award, First Class, Academia Sinica, 90. *Prof Exp:* Geologist, US Geol Surv, 49-56; Guggenheim fel, Europe, 56-57; from asst prof to assoc prof geol & geophys, Mass Inst Technol, 57-61; assoc prof, Calif Inst Technol, 61-68; prof geol, Univ Pa, 68-69. *Concurrent Pos:* Res assoc, Smithsonian Inst, 68-; US rep, Silurian Subcomt, Comt Stratig, IGC, 73-; chmn, Proj Ecostratig, IGCP-IUGS, 74- *Mem:* Geol Soc Am; Mineral Soc Am; Paleont Soc (pres, 80-81); Brit Palaeont Asn; hon corresp mem Swed Geol Soc; Int Paleont Asn (pres, 84-89). *Res:* Silurian and Devonian stratigraphy and paleontology, especially brachiopods, zoogeography and paleoecology; rates of animal evolution and extinction and their controls; evolution of behavior and coevolution. *Mailing Add:* Depts Zool & Geol Ore State Univ 3029 Cordley Hall Corvallis OR 97331-2914. *Fax:* 541-737 0501

BOUDAKIAN, MAX MINAS, FLUOROAROMATICS CHEMISTRY, PYRIDINE CHEMISTRY. *Current Pos:* CHEM CONSULT, 91- *Personal Data:* b New York, NY, Sept 8, 25; m 60, Lita Hampar; c Sara, Carl & Martha. *Educ:* City Col New York, BS, 49; Univ Mich, MS, 50; Purdue Univ, PhD(chem), 55. *Prof Exp:* Res chemist, Mathieson Chem, 50-52, group leader, Olin Mathieson Chem, 55-69, res assoc, Olin Corp, 69-77, lectr, Olin Tech Sem Prog, 69-91, sr res assoc, 77-88, consult scientist, 89-91. *Mem:* Am Chem Soc. *Res:* Aromatic fluorine chemistry; halopyridines. *Mailing Add:* 30 Candlewood Dr Pittsford NY 14534-4609

BOUDART, MICHEL, PHYSICAL CHEMISTRY. *Current Pos:* prof chem eng & chem, 64-80, William M Keck sr prof chem eng, 80-94, EMER PROF, STANFORD UNIV, 94- *Personal Data:* b Brussels, Belg, June 18, 24; m 48; c 4. *Educ:* Cath Univ Louvain, Cand Ing Civil, 44, Ing Civil Chim, 47; Princeton Univ, PhD(chem), 50. *Hon Degrees:* Dr, Univs Liege & Ghent, Belgium, Notre Dame Univ & Institut Polytech, Lorraine. *Honors & Awards:* Curtis McGraw Res Award, Am Soc Eng Educ, 62; R H Wilhelm Award, Am Inst Chem Engrs, 74; Kendall Award, Am Chem Soc, 77, Murphree Award, 85; Chem Pioneer Award, Am Inst Chemists, 91; Julian Smith Lectr, Cornell Univ, 91. *Prof Exp:* Res asst, Princeton Univ, 50-53, res assoc, 53, asst to dir proj SQUID, 53-54, from asst prof to assoc prof chem eng, 54-61; prof, Univ Calif, Berkeley, 61-64. *Concurrent Pos:* Co-founder & dir, Catalytica Assocs, Inc, 74-; vis prof, Univ Louvain, 69, Rio de Janeiro, 73, Tokyo, 75 & Paris, 80; vis fel, Clare Hall, Cambridge, 84; mem sci adv bd, Brookhaven Nat Lab & Ctr Study Nuclear Energy, Belg. *Mem:* Nat Acad Sci; Nat Acad Eng; Am Inst Chem Eng; Am Chem Soc; fel AAAS; Belgium Royal Acad. *Res:* Homogeneous and heterogeneous chemical kinetics; catalysis. *Mailing Add:* Dept Chem Eng Stanford Univ Stanford CA 94305-5025

BOUDETTE, EUGENE L, EDUCATION, GEOCHEMISTRY. *Current Pos:* ADJ PROF EARTH SCI, UNIV NH, 85- *Personal Data:* b Claremont, NH, Aug 24, 26; m 61, Beatrice Drolet. *Educ:* Univ NH, BA, 51; Dartmouth Col, MA, 59, PhD(geol), 76. *Prof Exp:* Geologist, Army Corps, 51-53, US Geol Surv, 53-85. *Concurrent Pos:* State geologist, NH, 85- *Mem:* Fel Am Geol Soc. *Res:* Lithotectonics; genesis of granite; radon in groundwater. *Mailing Add:* RR 3 PO Box 1060 Pittsfield NH 03263. *Fax:* 603-271-6588

BOUDINOT, FRANK DOUGLAS, PHARMACOKINETICS, PHARMACODYNAMICS. *Current Pos:* asst prof, 86-90, ASSOC PROF PHARMACEUT, UNIV GA, 90-, HEAD, DEPT PHARMACEUT, 92- *Personal Data:* b New Brunswick, NJ, Mar 31, 56; m 92, Sally Garrett; c Garrett. *Educ:* Springfield Col, BS, 78; State Univ NY, Buffalo, PhD(pharmaceut), 86. *Prof Exp:* Vet technician, Afton Animal Hosp, 78-79; res technician, Millard Fillmore Hosp-Clin Pharmacokinetics Lab, 79-80; grad assist pharmaceut, State Univ NY, Buffalo, 80-85. *Concurrent Pos:* Chair mem comt, E I du Pont de Nemours & Co, Marshall Lab Sect, Am Asn Pharmaceut Scientists. *Mem:* Am Asn Pharmaceut Scientists; Am Asn Cols Pharm; AAAS; Am Soc Microbiol; Soc Exp Biol & Med. *Res:* Characterizing the pharmacokinetics, biopharmaceutics, metabolism and pharmacodynamics of drugs; characterizing the pharmacokinetics of anti-HIV agents and assessing the effects of age on drug disposition, metabolism and pharmacodynamics. *Mailing Add:* 270 High Ridge Dr Athens GA 30606. *Fax:* 706-542-5346; *E-Mail:* boudinot@merc.rx.uga.edu

BOUDJOUK, PHILIP RAYMOND, SYNTHETIC & MECHANISTIC ORGANOMETALLIC CHEMISTRY. *Current Pos:* Lectr chem, Univ Calif, Davis, 71-73. *Personal Data:* b New York, NY, Feb 28, 42; m 64, Gertrude Mary Flood; c Christine, Monica, Matthew & Peter. *Educ:* St John's Univ, BS, 64; Univ Wis-Madison, PhD(chem), 71. *Honors & Awards:* Am Cancer Soc Res Award, 79. *Concurrent Pos:* High sch chem teacher, Farmingdale, NY, 64-67. *Mem:* Am Chem Soc. *Res:* Synthesis of cyclic, bicyclic and tetracyclic organometallics; reactive intermediates containing silicon, germanium and tin; Lewis acid catalyzed reactions of organometallics; bioactive silanes; sonochemistry applied to synthesis; pi-complexes; highly conducting organic and organometallic compounds polysilanes; catalysis of organometallic reactions; low temperature synthesis of semiconducting materials. *Mailing Add:* Dept Chem NDak State Univ Fargo ND 58105. *Fax:* 701-231-7947; *E-Mail:* boudjouk@plains.nodak.edu

BOUDREAU, JAY EDMOND, NUCLEAR ENGINEERING. *Current Pos:* group leader & staff mem Liquid Metal Fast Breeder Reactor Safety, 73-79, prog mgr, 79-80, DEP ASSOC DIR NUCLEAR PROGS, LOS ALAMOS NAT LAB, 81- *Personal Data:* b Santa Monica, Calif, Feb 3, 46; div; c 2. *Educ:* Univ Calif, Los Angeles, BS, 67, MS, 69, PhD(eng), 72. *Prof Exp:* Asst nuclear engr, Argonne Nat Lab, 72-73. *Mem:* Am Nuclear Soc. *Res:* Fast reactor safety; core disruptive accident analysis. *Mailing Add:* 1000 Los Pueblos St Los Alamos NM 87544

BOUDREAU, ROBERT DONALD, AVIATION METEOROLOGY, INDUSTRIAL METEOROLOGY. *Current Pos:* head meteorol, 76-88, PROF METEOROL, METROP STATE COL, DENVER, 76- *Personal Data:* b N Adams, Mass, March 9, 31. *Educ:* Tex A&M Univ, BS, 62, MS, 64, PhD(meteorol), 68. *Honors & Awards:* Skylab Award, NASA, 74. *Prof Exp:* Res meteorologist, Atmospheric Sci Lab, Ariz, 65-68, Meteorol Div, Desert Test Ctr, Utah, 68-70 & Meteorol Satellite Lab, Washington, DC, 70-71; sr atmospheric scientist, Earth Resources Lab, NASA, Mo, 71-75; asst sci staff, Naval Oceanog Lab, Mo, 75-76. *Concurrent Pos:* NSF fel & NDEA fel, 62; consult, Solar Energy Res Inst, 80 & Colo Int Corp, Boulder, 81; pres, Int FMeteorol, Aviation & Electronics Inst, 81-87; airline transport pilot, 85- *Mem:* Am Meteorol Soc; Sigma Xi; Nat Weather Asn; Int Pilot's Asn; US Pilot's Asn; Aircraft Owners & Pilot's Asn. *Res:* Aviation meteorology; media dissemination of weather information; remote sensing from aircraft and satellites. *Mailing Add:* Earth & Atmospheric Sci Dept Metrop State Col PO Box 173362 Campus Box 22 Denver CO 80217-3362. *Fax:* 303-556-4941

BOUDREAU, WILLIAM F(RANCIS), MECHANICAL ENGINEERING. *Current Pos:* CONSULT, 80- *Personal Data:* b Columbus, Ohio, Sept 29, 14; m 34, Eleanore Jones; c Penelope (Garrett) & Nancy (Sharff). *Educ:* Case Inst Technol, BSc, 36; Mass Inst Technol, MSc, 40. *Prof Exp:* With Am Rolling Mill Co, Ohio, 37-43; res scientist, Substitute Alloy Mat Lab, Columbia Univ, 43-46; engr, Union Carbide Nuclear Co, 46-63; mgr compressor develop, York Div, Borg-Warner Corp, 63-73; supvr mech engr, Catalytic, Inc, 73-75; supv mech engr, Union Carbide Nuclear Div, Union Carbide Corp, 75-79. *Mem:* Am Soc Mech Engrs. *Res:* Development of special pumps, compressors and mechanical equipment. *Mailing Add:* 102 Norman Lane Oak Ridge TN 37830

BOUDREAUX, EDWARD A, INORGANIC CHEMISTRY, CHEMICAL PHYSICS. *Current Pos:* asst prof, 62-65, ASSOC PROF CHEM, UNIV NEW ORLEANS, 65- *Personal Data:* b New Orleans, La, Oct 30, 33; m 55; c 4. *Educ:* Loyola Univ, La, BS, 56; Tulane Univ, MS, 59, PhD(chem), 62. *Prof Exp:* Res assoc chem, Tulane Univ, 56-62. *Concurrent Pos:* Consult, Kalvar Corp, 61-63; Petrol Res Fund grant, 64-66; Cancer Soc Greater New Orleans grant, 66-67 & 77-78; consult, USDA, New Orleans, 68-70; Fulbright teaching fel, Univ Zagreb, 70-71; Biomed Res Ctr grant, 78-79. *Mem:* Am Chem Soc; The Chem Soc; Sigma Xi. *Res:* Inorganic solid compounds and complexes; ligand field theory; molecular orbital calculations; diffuse reflectance electronic spectroscopy; magnetochemical research. *Mailing Add:* Dept Chem Univ New Orleans New Orleans LA 70148

BOUGAS, JAMES ANDREW, THORACIC SURGERY, CARDIOPULMONARY PHYSIOLOGY. *Current Pos:* ASSOC PROF SURG, SCH MED, BOSTON UNIV, 65- *Personal Data:* b Bismarck, NDak, Jan 25, 24; m 53; c 2. *Educ:* Harvard Med Sch, MD, 48. *Prof Exp:* Intern, Columbia Univ Serv, Bellevue Hosp, 48-49, resident surg, Presby Med Ctr & Bellevue Hosp, 49-53; dir, Cardiopulmonary Lab, New Eng Deaconess Hosp, 55-65. *Concurrent Pos:* Fel thoracic surg, Overholt Thoracic Clin, 53-55, assoc thoracic surgeon, 56-65; consult to numerous hosps, 56-; lectr, Tufts Univ & assoc staff, New Eng Med Ctr, 56-; sr active staff, New Eng Deaconess Hosp, 56-; sr active staff, New Eng Baptist Hosp, Boston, 61-; vis staff, Boston City Hosp, 65-; chief thoracic surg, Boston Univ Hosp, 67-70; chmn biomat, Gordon Res Conf, 67-; mem cardiac adv group, Regional Med Prog, NH, Mass & RI, 69-; mem coun, Mass Med Asn; mem, Comt Legis, Mass Med Soc, 84- *Mem:* AAAS; Am Asn Thoracic Surg; Soc Thoracic Surg; Am Col Surg; Am Fedn Clin Res. *Res:* Physical biology; biomaterials; cardiovascular surgery; cardiac physiology. *Mailing Add:* 125 Parker Hill Boston MA 02120. *Fax:* 617-731-5742

BOUGH, WAYNE ARNOLD, POLLUTION CONTROL, WASTE MANAGEMENT. *Current Pos:* MGR, ENVIRON AFFAIRS, MID-AM DAIRYMEN, INC, MO, 84- *Personal Data:* b Stockton, Mo, Mar 21, 43; div; c 4. *Educ:* Univ Mo, Columbia, BS, 65; Univ Minn, PhD(biochem), 69. *Prof Exp:* Res dir, Pollution Control, Am Bact & Chem Res Corp, 69-72; asst prof, Pollution Control, Dept Food Sci, Ga Exp Sta, Marine Exten Serv, Univ Ga, 72-76, assoc marine scientist seafood technol, 76-80, assoc dir, 78-80; mgr tech serv, Wastewater Div, Spec Prod, Inc, Mo, 80-84. *Concurrent Pos:* Consult, Environ Assoc Inc, 73-75, SCS Eng, 74 & Mid-Am Dairymen, Inc, 79-80; adv comt, Water & Wastewater Tech Sch, Neosho, Mo, 88-; biomass adv comt, Univ Mo, 88- *Mem:* Water Pollution Control Fedn; Inst Food Technologists; NY Acad Sci. *Res:* Recovery and utilization of by-products from food processing wastes and treatment systems; by-products evaluated for feed value; chitosan manufactured from shrimp wastes for coagulation of suspended solids in wastewaters; pretreatment systems for food processing wastes; environmental regulations. *Mailing Add:* 1908 S Broadway Ave Springfield MO 65807

BOUGHER, STEPHEN WESLEY, PLANETARY ATMOSPHERES, PLANETARY AERONOMY. *Current Pos:* res assoc, 86-89, sr res assoc, 90-95, ASST RES SCIENTIST, LUNAR & PLANETARY LAB, UNIV ARIZ, 95- *Personal Data:* b Del, Ohio, Jan 4, 55; m 80, Patricia M Haas; c Jonathan W & Timothy R. *Educ:* Northwestern Univ, BA; Univ Colo, MS, 80; Univ Mich PhD(aeronomy), 85. *Prof Exp:* Fel, Nat Ctr Atmospheric Res, 84-86. *Concurrent Pos:* Pioneer Venus guest investr, Ames Res Ctr, NASA, 88-92; co-invester, Planet-B, NASA, 95- *Mem:* Am Geophys Union; Am Astron Soc; Int Asn Geomagnetism & Aeronomy. *Res:* Planetary atmospheres via the application of remote sensing techniques and modeling schemes to determine the chemistry energetics and dynamics of the upper atmospheres of the earth and other planets; comparative examination of terrestrial planet processes and global change implications; NASA Discovery mission planning and spacecraft design. *Mailing Add:* Lunar & Planetary Lab Univ Ariz Tucson AZ 85721. *E-Mail:* sbougher@lpl.arizona.edu

BOUGHN, STEPHEN PAUL, EXPERIMENTAL PHYSICS, ASTROPHYSICS. *Current Pos:* ASSOC PROF, DEPT ASTRON, HAVERFORD COL, 86- *Personal Data:* b Wheatland, Wyo, Dec 12, 46; m 68; c 1. *Educ:* Princeton Univ, BA, 69; Stanford Univ, MS, 70, PhD(physics), 75. *Prof Exp:* Physics res assoc, W W Hansen Labs & Dept Physics, Stanford Univ, 75-78; asst prof, dept physics, Joseph Henry Labs, Princeton Univ, 79-86. *Mem:* Am Phys Soc; Am Astron Soc. *Res:* Experimental gravitation; gravitational radiation detectors; the interaction of gravitational radiation with matter; low temperature experimental physics; extragalactic astronomy; cosmic background light; primeval galaxies; missing mass; clusters of galaxies. *Mailing Add:* Dept Astron Haverford Col Haverford PA 19041

BOUGHTON, JOHN HARLAND, INORGANIC CHEMISTRY. *Current Pos:* chemist, Spunbonded div, Textile Fibers Dept, 65-67, chemist, Pigments Dept, 67-72, sr res chemist, 72-76, res assoc, 76-87, SR RES ASSOC, ELECTRONICS DEPT, E I DU PONT DE NEMOURS & CO, 88- *Personal Data:* b Niagara Falls, NY, May 7, 32; m 64; c 4. *Educ:* Ariz State Univ, BS, 53, MS, 61; Univ Colo, PhD(inorg chem), 65. *Prof Exp:* Tech rep petrol ref, Tretolite Co, 55-58; teaching asst chem, Ariz State Univ, 58-60; teaching asst, Univ Colo, 60-61, res asst, 61-65. *Mem:* Am Chem Soc; Sigma Xi. *Res:* Pseudohalide complexes; solution chemistry; x-ray surface studies; surface characterization of fine particles; ultra-pure chemicals for electronics; contamination control. *Mailing Add:* 2228 Rosewood Dr Wilmington DE 19810-2816

BOUGHTON, ROBERT IVAN, JR, LOW TEMPERATURE PHYSICS. *Current Pos:* PROF PHYSICS & CHMN DEPT, BOWLING GREEN STATE UNIV, 80- *Personal Data:* b Columbus, Ohio, Apr 2, 42; m 66; c 3. *Educ:* Ohio State Univ, BS & MS, 64, PhD(physics), 68. *Prof Exp:* Fel, Swiss Fed Inst Technol, 68-69; vis asst prof physics, Northeastern Univ, 69-70, asst prof, 70-73, assoc prof, 73-80. *Mem:* Am Phys Soc; Am Asn Physics Teachers. *Res:* Transport properties of metals at low temperatures, both normal and superconducting, including measurements of effects of boundary scattering on transport. *Mailing Add:* Dept Physics & Astron Bowling Green State Univ Bowling Green OH 43403-0001

BOUILLANT, ALAIN MARCEL, VIROLOGY. *Current Pos:* RETIRED. *Personal Data:* b Gisors, France, Aug 13, 28; Can citizen; m 65, Marie A Pouliot; c Valerie. *Educ:* Advan Sch Agr Engrs & Technicians, Paris, Agr Ing, 50; Univ Montreal, DVM, 58; Univ Wis-Madison, MS, 63; Laval Univ,

PhD(microbiol & immunol), 67. *Prof Exp:* Res asst, Dept Vet Sci, Univ Wis-Madison, 60-63; res asst instr & tutor, Dept Microbiol & Immunol, Laval Univ, 64-67; res scientist virol, Animal Dis Res Inst, 67-68, res scientist virol & tissue cult, 68-95. *Mem:* Can Vet Med Asn; AAAS; Tissue Cult Asn; Sigma Xi. *Res:* Virus diseases of animals; cytopathology; electronmicroscopy; cell transformation; retrovirus. *Mailing Add:* 142 Redempgoristls Aylmer PQ J9H 5E8 Can. *Fax:* 613-952-2285

BOUIS, PAUL ANDRE, ANALYTICAL, LANTHANIDE & SEPARATIONS SCIENCE. *Current Pos:* dir anal res, 86-94, DIR SEPARATION SCI, J T BAKER, 94- *Personal Data:* b Nice, France, Sept 21, 45; US citizen; m 67, Nancy Peterson; c Suzette, Karine & Matthew. *Educ:* Va Mil Inst, BS, 67; Univ Tenn, PhD(org chem), 74. *Prof Exp:* Res assoc org chem, Rhone Poulenc, USA, 73-76, process mgr, 76-79, anal & process mgr, 79-86. *Concurrent Pos:* Adj prof, Lafayette Col, 90-92; chmn, Reagent Chem Comt, Am Chem Soc, 92- *Mem:* Am Chem Soc. *Res:* Simplification of analytical chemistry of trace analysis in organic and inorganic matrices; novel purification techniques for high purity chemicals; analysis and purification of lanthanides; development of products for use in separation sciences. *Mailing Add:* 3875 Gloucester Bethlehem PA 18017-7593. *Fax:* 201-859-6932; *E-Mail:* pbmb1@postoffice.ptd.net

BOULANGER, JEAN BAPTISTE, PSYCHOANALYSIS. *Current Pos:* PVT PRACT, 91- *Personal Data:* b Edmonton, Alta, Aug 24, 22. *Educ:* Univ Montreal, BA, 41, MD, 48; McGill Univ, MA, 50; Univ Paris, dipl psychopath, 51, lic psychol, 54; FRCP(C), 55. *Prof Exp:* Instr psychiat, Fac Med, Univ Montreal, 53, lectr, 54, from asst prof to assoc prof, 54-59, coordr, Behav Sci Course, 69-77, prof psychiat, 70-91. *Concurrent Pos:* Attend physician neuropsychiat serv, Notre Dame Hosp, 53-61; training analyst, Can Inst Psychoanal, 57 & med dir treatment serv, 59-71; consult & dir group psychother, Ste-Justine Hosp, 59-78, hon consult child psychiat, 78; consult, Inst Albert Prevost, 60-73, Lakeshore Gen Hosp, 65-78, Verdun Gen Hosp, 65-71 & L H Lafontaine Hosp, 71-77; vis scientist, Ctr Bioethics, Clin Res Inst Montreal, 77-78; pvt pract; assoc ed, Can Psychiat Asn J, 60-; dir, Int Centre Comp Criminol, 75-; vis scientist, Dept Educ & Res Forensic Psychiat, Inst Philippe Pinel de Montreal, 78- & Dept Psychiat Educ, L H Lafontaine Hosp, 81; foreign ed, Am J Forensic Psychiat, 80. *Mem:* Can Psychoanal Soc (pres, 58, 59 & 60); fel Am Psychiat Asn; Int Psychoanal Asn; Can Psychiat Asn (pres, 75-76); NY Acad Sci. *Res:* Medical undergraduate education; postgraduate psychiatric training; psychoanalytic education and training; group psychotherapy; forensic psychiatry; adult and child neuropsychiatry. *Mailing Add:* 4544 Ste Catherine St W Montreal PQ H3Z 1S1 Can

BOULANT, JACK A, NEUROPHYSIOLOGY, TEMPERATURE REGULATION. *Current Pos:* Assoc prof, 77-84, PROF PHYSIOL, OHIO STATE UNIV, 84- *Educ:* Univ Rochester, PhD(physiol), 71. *Res:* Hypothalamus. *Mailing Add:* Physiol 201 Hamilton Hall Ohio State Univ 1645 Neil Ave Columbus OH 43210

BOULDIN, DAVID RITCHEY, SOIL FERTILITY. *Current Pos:* assoc prof, 62-69, PROF SOIL SCI, CORNELL UNIV, 69- *Personal Data:* b Sedalia, Mo, Apr 6, 26; m 60; c 2. *Educ:* Kans State Univ, BS, 52; Iowa State Univ, MS, 53, PhD(agron), 56. *Prof Exp:* Soil chemist, Tenn Valley Authority, 56-62. *Mem:* AAAS; Am Soc Agron; Am Soc Plant Physiol. *Res:* Relationships between properties of the soil-fertilizer system and plant response. *Mailing Add:* Soil Crop Atmos Sci 236 Emerson Hall Cornell Univ Ithaca NY 14853-0001

BOULDIN, RICHARD H, MATHEMATICS. *Current Pos:* from asst prof to assoc prof, Univ Ga, 69-73, head math, 89-92, actg assoc dean, 92-93, assoc dean, 93-96, PROF MATH, UNIV GA, 82- *Personal Data:* b Florence, Ala, Feb 23, 42; m 70; c Laura & Mark. *Educ:* Univ Ala, BS, 64; Univ Chicago, MS, 66; Univ Va, PhD(math), 68. *Prof Exp:* Instr math, Univ Va, 68-69. *Mem:* Am Math Soc; Math Asn Am. *Res:* Perturbation theory and approximation theory for bounded operators on a Hilbert space. *Mailing Add:* Dept Math Univ Ga Athens GA 30602. *E-Mail:* rbouldin@bigben.franklin.uga.edu

BOULET, J LIONEL, electrical engineering; deceased, see previous edition for last biography

BOULET, MARCEL, FOOD SCIENCE, BIOCHEMISTRY. *Current Pos:* RETIRED. *Personal Data:* b Montreal, Que, Dec 7, 19; m 47; c 4. *Educ:* Univ Montreal, BSc, 43; McGill Univ, MSc, 45, PhD(agr chem), 48. *Honors & Awards:* Eva Award, Can Inst Food Sci & Technol, 80. *Prof Exp:* Res officer dairy chem, Nat Res Coun Can, 47-62; prof food sci, Laval Univ, 62-87; res officer, Food Res & Develop Ctr, 88- *Mem:* Am Dairy Sci Asn; Inst Food Technologists; Can Inst Food Sci & Technol; Fr-Can Asn Advan Sci. *Res:* Inorganic chemistry of milk; control of enzyme activity in foods of vegetable origin; storage of fresh fruits and vegetables; functional properties of proteins. *Mailing Add:* 987 St Charles Chomedey PQ H7V 3T8 Can

BOULGER, FRANCIS W(ILLIAM), METALLURGY, MECHANICAL ENGINEERING. *Current Pos:* RETIRED. *Personal Data:* b Minneapolis, Minn, June 19, 13; m 40. *Educ:* Univ Minn, MetE, 34; Ohio State Univ, MS, 37. *Honors & Awards:* Hunt Medal, Am Inst Mining, Metall & Petrol Engrs, 55; Gold Medal, Soc Mfg Engrs, 67; Nat Achievement Award, Am Machinist, 75. *Prof Exp:* Draftsman, Minn State Dept Hyg, 34; metallurgist, Repub Steel Corp, Cleveland, 37; res engr, Battelle Mem Inst, 38-44, asst supvr steel res, 44-47, supv metallurgist, 47-60, metall div chief, 60-66, sr tech adv, Columbus Div, 66-84. *Concurrent Pos:* Mem metalworking comt, Orgn Econ Coop & Develop; chmn, Comt on Phys Chem of Steelmaking, Am Inst Mining, Metall & Petrol Engrs, 55-56; chmn, Metal Framing Div, Soc Mfg Engrs, 67-70, Res Grants Comt, 71-73; chmn, Handbook Comt Fabrication of Titanium, Am Soc Metals, 68-71; mem, Steering Comt Comput Aided Mfg, Nat Res Coun, 78-82, Comt Net Shape Technol, 84-86. *Mem:* Nat Acad Eng; Am Inst Mining, Metall & Petrol Engrs; fel Am Soc Mech Engrs; fel Soc Mfg Engrs; fel Am Soc Metals; hon mem Int Inst Prod Engrs (pres, 75-76); NAm Mfg Res Inst; Int Cold Forging Res Group. *Res:* Steel metallurgy; low temperature properties of metals; improved free-machining steels; prevention of cracking during cold-drawing of steels; casting, forming, forging, fabricating and manufacturing practices for metals. *Mailing Add:* 1816 Harwitch Rd Columbus OH 43221

BOULLION, THOMAS L, MATHEMATICS, STATISTICS. *Current Pos:* dept math, 81-85, HEAD, STATIST DEPT, UNIV SOUTHWEST LA, 85- *Personal Data:* b Morse, La, Nov 4, 40; m 59; c 5. *Educ:* La State Univ, BS, 61; Univ Southwestern La, MS, 63; Univ Tex, PhD(math, statist), 66. *Prof Exp:* Asst prof math, Univ Southwestern La, 66-67; from asst prof to assoc prof, Tex Tech Univ, 67-74, chmn interdisciplinary statist, 74-77, prof math & statist, 74-81. *Concurrent Pos:* Consult mathematician & statistician, Tex Ctr Res, 66-72. *Mem:* Am Statist Asn; Inst Math Statist. *Res:* Statistical inference; matrix theory. *Mailing Add:* Univ SW La PO Box 41006 Lafayette LA 70504-9998

BOULOS, BADI MANSOUR, PHARMACOLOGY. *Current Pos:* ASSOC PROF ENVIRON & OCCUP HEALTH SCI, UNIV ILL MED CTR, 72- *Personal Data:* b Alexandria, Egypt, July 3, 30; m 64; c 4. *Educ:* Univ Alexandria, MB & BCh, 53, DPh, 58, DTM&H, 60; Univ Iowa, MS, 62; Univ Mo, PhD(med pharmacol), 65. *Prof Exp:* Intern med, Univ Alexandria Hosps, 53-54; med officer, UN Relief & Welfare Agency, Gaza Strip, 54-56; instr pharmacol, Univ Alexandria, 56-60; asst radiation biol, Univ Iowa, 60-63; res assoc pharmacol, Univ Mo, 63-65; asst prof pharmacol, Univ Alexandria, 65-66; asst prof, Univ Mo-Columbia & res assoc cancer res & chemother, Ellis Fischel State Cancer Hosp, 66-70; spec postdoctoral fel clin pharmacol & toxicol, NIH, 70-72. *Concurrent Pos:* Asst scientist, Cancer Res Ctr, 68-; Vet Med Res Coun grants, 69-70; USPHS grant, 69-70; USPHS spec fel clin pharmacol & toxicol, Univ Kans Med Ctr, Kansas City, 70-72; mem & assoc dir, Int Cancer Cong, Ill State Environ Health Resource Ctr, 72-78; Univ Ill grant, 73-74; NIHES contract, 73-76; scholarship indust toxicol, Wayne State Univ, 74; NIH fel, occup med, 77; prof commun med & asst dean, Col Med, King Faisal Univ, Saudi Arabia, 78-80; diplomat, Pac Basin Chem Conf, 84; consult, clin & indust toxicol, WHO, 85-; world wide expert toxicol, UNESCO. *Mem:* Soc Toxicol; AMA; Am Soc Vet Physiol & Pharmacol; NY Acad Sci; Egyptian Soc Pharmacol & Exp Therapeut; Am Soc Pharmacol & Exp Therapeut. *Res:* Effect of antioxidant food additives on behavior and changes in biogenic amines; epidemiological studies to determine effect of barium in drinking water on hypertension; effect of polychlorinated biphenyls in water on high risk population, for example, children, using feline species as a model; placental transfer of drugs and pharmacokinetics in vivo; trace metal contaminants in health food supplements, cadmium and hypertension, aluminum, and Alzheimer's disease; approx 250 research articles in scientific journals. *Mailing Add:* Univ Ill Chicago Sch Pub Health 2121 W Taylor St Chicago IL 60612-7260

BOULOUCON, PETER, CHEMICAL ENGINEERING, APPLIED MATHEMATICS. *Current Pos:* MGR, ACRYLONITRILE TECHNOL, CYTEC INDUST, INC, 93- *Personal Data:* b Ottawa, Ont, Sept 26, 35; m 65; c 2. *Educ:* McGill Univ, BEng, 57; Univ Del, MChE, 62, PhD(chem eng), 64. *Prof Exp:* Process engr, Dow Chem Can, Ltd, 57-59; sr chem engr, Cyanamid Can Ltd, 64-68; process engr, Am Cyanamid Co, 68-69, group supvr process & systs anal 69-93. *Concurrent Pos:* Vis prof, Chem Eng Dept, Univ Va, 77-78. *Mem:* Am Inst Chem Engrs; Am Chem Soc; Sigma Xi. *Res:* Process analysis and applied mathematics in the area of chemical industry; acrylonitrile process technology. *Mailing Add:* 1952 Ormond Blvd Destrehan LA 70047

BOULPAEP, EMILE L, PHYSIOLOGY, NEPHROLOGY. *Current Pos:* asst prof psysiol, 69-72, assoc prof, 72-79, chmn dept & prof physiol, 79-89, PROF CELLULAR & MOLECULAR PHYSIOL, SCH MED, YALE UNIV, 87- *Personal Data:* b Aalst, Belg, Sept 15, 38; m 64. *Educ:* Cath Univ Louvain, BS, 58, MD, 62, MMSc, 63. *Hon Degrees:* Dr, Lourain Univ, 87. *Honors & Awards:* Order of the Crown, Belgium, 79; Order of Leopold II, Belgium, 80; Homer W Smith Award, Am Soc Nephrol, NY Heart Asn. *Prof Exp:* Res scientist physiol, Cath Univ Louvain, 62-64; res fel, Med Col, Cornell Univ, 64-66; instr-chief asst, Cath Univ Louvain, 66-68; asst prof, Med Col, Cornell Univ, 68-69. *Concurrent Pos:* Belg Govt travel grant, 63-64; Belg Am Educ Found fel, 64-65; res fel, John Polachek Found Med Res, 65-66; mem bd dirs, Belg Am Educ Found, 71-, pres, 77-; fel, Branford Col, Yale Univ, 73-; mem study sect, NIH Gen Med Br, 76-80; overseas fel, Churchill Col, Cambridge, UK, 78-; mem, Coun Kidney Cardiovasc Dis, Am Heart Asn. *Mem:* Am Soc Nephrol; Am Physiol Soc; NY Acad Sci. *Res:* Electrolyte and water transport across epithelia, particularly renal tubules; electrophysiology of the kidney. *Mailing Add:* Dept Cellular & Molecular Physiol Yale Univ Sch Med 333 Cedar St New Haven CT 06510. *Fax:* 203-785-4951

BOULTON, ALAN ARTHUR, NEUROPSYCHOPHARMACOLOGY, BIOLOGICAL PSYCHIATRY. *Current Pos:* chief res biochemist & res assoc, 68-69, assoc prof, 69-75, PROF PSYCHIAT, UNIV SASK, 75-, DIR, NEUROPSYCHIAT RES, MED RES BLDG, 71- *Personal Data:* b New Mills, Eng, Mar 14, 36; m 59, Anne; c Adrian, Alistair, Annelie & Alana. *Educ:* Univ Manchester, BSc, 58, PhD(biochem), 62, DSc, 76. *Honors & Awards:* Clark Prize, 70; Heinz Lehman Award, Can Col Neuropsychopharmacol, 89; Can 125 Commemorative Medal, 93. *Prof Exp:*

Res asst biochem, Univ Manchester, 60-62; mem, Med Res Coun Unit Res Chem Path Ment Dis, Birmingham Univ, 62-68. *Concurrent Pos:* Res fel physiol, Birmingham Univ, 62-68; consult, Can Corrections, 87-93; counr, Am Neurochem Soc, 89-93; chief ed, J Neurochem; comnr, Health Sci Utilization & Res Comn, 91-97; hon prof, Norman Bethane Univ Med Sci, Changchun & Pla Med Sch Beijing, 95. *Mem:* Can Col Neuropsychopharmacol (pres, 84-86); Can Biochem Soc; Soc Biol Psychiat; Int Neurochem Soc (treas, 80-84, pres, 84-87); Am Neurochem Soc (pres, 95-97); Col Int Neuropsychopharmacol; Am Col Neuropharmacol; fel Royal Soc Can. *Res:* Neurobiology of trace amines; neurorescue and neurorescue agents; drug discovery and development. *Mailing Add:* Neuropsychiat Res Unit Univ Sask Med Res Bldg 103 Wiggins Rd Saskatoon SK S7N 5E4 Can. *Fax:* 306-966-8830; *E-Mail:* boulton@sask.usask.ca

BOULTON, PETER IRWIN PAUL, COMPUTER SYSTEMS. *Current Pos:* from asst prof to assoc prof, 67-84, PROF COMPUT SYSTS, UNIV TORONTO, 84- *Personal Data:* b Toronto, Ont, May 11, 34; m 67; c 2. *Educ:* Univ Toronto, BASc, 60, MASc, 61, PhD(elec eng), 66. *Prof Exp:* Res engr, Electronics Div, Ferranti-Packard Elec Ltd, 61-63. *Concurrent Pos:* Consult, Elec Eng Consociates Ltd, 68- *Mem:* Sr mem Inst Elec & Electronics Engrs; Asn Comput Mach. *Res:* Computer systems software and hardware; local area networks; application of graphics; programming languages and language translators. *Mailing Add:* Dept Elec Eng Univ Toronto 10 Kings College Rd Toronto ON M5S 1A4 Can

BOULTON, ROGER BRETT, WINE FERMENTATION, WINE STABILITY. *Current Pos:* asst prof, 76-82, PROF WINERY DESIGN, UNIV CALIF, DAVIS, 82- *Personal Data:* b Melbourne, Australia, July 14, 49; m 71; c 2. *Educ:* Univ Melbourne, BEng, 70, PhD(chem), 76. *Prof Exp:* Lectr process control, Dept Chem Eng, Univ Melbourne, 74-76, process simulation, 76. *Concurrent Pos:* Enol consult, Robert Mondavi Winery, 80- *Mem:* Am Inst Chem Engrs; Am Chem Soc; Am Soc Enologists. *Mailing Add:* Viticulture & Enol Dept Univ Calif Davis CA 95616

BOULWARE, DAVID G, THEORETICAL PHYSICS. *Current Pos:* from asst prof to assoc prof, 65-73, PROF PHYSICS, UNIV WASH, 73- *Personal Data:* b Oakland, Calif, Nov 20, 37; c 2. *Educ:* Univ Calif, Berkeley, AB, 58; Harvard Univ, AM, 60, PhD(physics), 62. *Prof Exp:* Jr fel, Harvard Univ, 62-65. *Mem:* Fel Am Phys Soc; fel AAAS. *Res:* Quantum field theory; quantum electrodynamics; elementary particles and relativity; general relativity and quantum gravity. *Mailing Add:* Dept Physics FM-15 Univ Wash Seattle WA 98195

BOULWARE, RALPH FREDERICK, GENETICS. *Current Pos:* res assoc, La State Univ, 57-58, from instr to assoc prof animal husb, 58-77, prof animal sci, 77-79, EMER PROF ANIMAL SCI, LA STATE UNIV, BATON ROUGE, 79- *Personal Data:* b Stamps, Ark, Feb 15, 17; m 41, Leila Whitman; c Robie. *Educ:* Okla State Univ, BS, 49; Univ Nebr, MS, 50, PhD(animal genetics), 53. *Prof Exp:* Asst animal husb, Univ Nebr, 49-53; asst prof, Miss State Col, 53-55; mgr, Farrar Farms, La, 55-57. *Concurrent Pos:* Vis prof, US AID-Nicaraguan Ministry Agr, 68-69. *Mem:* Fel AAAS; Am Soc Animal Sci; Am Meat Sci Asn; Am Genetics Asn; Inst Food Technol; Sigma Xi. *Res:* Animal breeding. *Mailing Add:* 201 Hope Rd Stamps AR 71860-2481

BOUMA, ARNOLD HEIKO, MARINE GEOLOGY, SEDIMENTOLOGY. *Current Pos:* dir, Basin Res Inst, 89-90, head, Sch Geosci, 90-92, MCCORD CHAIRED PROF GEOL, LA STATE UNIV, 88- *Personal Data:* b Groningen, Neth, Sept 5, 32; m 60, Mechilina Kampers; c Mark A, N Robert & Lars O. *Educ:* State Univ Groningen, BS, 56; State Univ Utrecht, MS, 59, PhD(sedimentol), 61. *Honors & Awards:* Francis P Shepard Award, 82. *Prof Exp:* Geol asst, State Univ Groningen, 54-56; sedimentol asst, State Univ Utrecht, 57-59, res fel, 60-62, lectr, 63-66; assoc prof, Tex A&M Univ, 66-70, prof geol oceanog, 70-76; marine geologist, US Geol Surv, 76-80; sr scientist, mgr & vpres, Gulf Res & Develop Co, 80-85; sr res assoc, Chevron Oil Field Res Co, 85-88. *Concurrent Pos:* Fel Scripps Inst, Univ Calif, 62-63; ed-in-chief, Marine Geol, 63-66; mem pub & printing comt, Int Union Geol Sci, 65-69; co-chmn panel sedimentary processes, Gulf Univ Res Corp, 67-70; mem Gulf of Mex panel, Joint Oceanog Insts Deep-Sea Drilling Proj; chmn, Coastal Geol Sect, Div Environ Geol, Am Asn Petrol Geol. *Mem:* AAAS; Am Asn Petrol Geol; Soc Econ Paleont & Mineral; Sigma Xi. *Res:* Sediments, ancient and recent; sedimentary facies models; internal characteristics of sedimentary structures with regard to transport and sedimentation; turbidites; techniques used to study sedimentary structures; graphic presentations; pollution; architecture of sedimentary bodies; environmental geology. *Mailing Add:* Dept Geol & Geophys La State Univ Baton Rouge LA 70803. *Fax:* 504-388-2302; *E-Mail:* abouma@unix1.sncc.lsu.edu

BOUMA, HESSEL, III, BIO-MEDICAL ETHICS. *Current Pos:* asst prof, 78-82, PROF BIOL, CALVIN COL, 82- *Personal Data:* b 1950; m 72; c 4. *Educ:* Univ Tex, PhD(human genetics), 75. *Mem:* Sigma Xi; Am Soc Cell Biol; Electron Micros Soc Am; Hastings Ctr; Am Scientific Affil. *Res:* Health care for the poor; human genetics. *Mailing Add:* 6630 Burger DR SE Grand Rapids MI 49546-7212. *Fax:* 616-957-8551

BOUMAN, THOMAS DAVID, THEORETICAL CHEMISTRY. *Current Pos:* asst prof, 69-72, assoc prof, 72-77, PROF CHEM, SOUTHERN ILL UNIV, 77- *Personal Data:* b Geneva, Ohio, Nov 23, 40; m 66; c 1. *Educ:* Wash Univ, AB, 62; Univ Minn, PhD(phys chem), 67. *Honors & Awards:* Eastman Kodak Award, Univ Minn, 65. *Prof Exp:* Resident res assoc chem, Argonne Nat Lab, 67-69. *Concurrent Pos:* Vis assoc prof, Dept Chem, Univ Va, 74-75; vis prof, Chem Lab IV, H C Oersted Inst, Copenhagen Denmark, 75-76; G C Marshall Mem Fund fel, 75; Fulbright-Hays travel fel, 75; Danish NATO Comt sr sci fel, 75; sr res scholar award, Southern Ill Univ, Edwardsville, 77-78. *Mem:* AAAS; Am Chem Soc; Am Phys Soc. *Res:* Theory of optical activity; molecular orbital calculations on medium-sized molecules; calculations of magnetic properties. *Mailing Add:* 1904 Cornell Ave Edwardsville IL 62025

BOUNDS, HAROLD C, MICROBIAL ECOLOGY. *Current Pos:* From instr to asst prof, 69-74, ASSOC PROF BACT, NORTHEAST LA UNIV, 74- *Personal Data:* b Shreveport, La, Aug 13, 40; m 62; c 2. *Educ:* Centenary Col, BS, 63; La State Univ, Baton Rouge, MS, 64, PhD(microbiol), 69. *Mem:* Am Soc Microbiol. *Res:* Herbicide influence on soil bacteria; microbial flora of ponds and sewage effluent; fungal contaminants in paper mills; antimicrobial properties of plant oils; sulfur oxidation by iron-sulfur autotrophs. *Mailing Add:* 300 Hartford Pl West Monroe LA 71291

BOUNDY, RAY HAROLD, chemistry; deceased, see previous edition for last biography

BOUQUOT, JERRY ELMER, PRE-CANCER EPIDEMIOLOGY. *Current Pos:* from asst prof to assoc prof oral path, 75-84, asst prof path, 75-76, PROF ORAL PATH, SCH DENT & PROF PATH, SCH MED, WVA UNIV, 84-, CHMN DEPT ORAL PATH, 76- *Personal Data:* b St Paul, Minn, June 23, 45; m 67; c 2. *Educ:* St Olaf Col, Northfield, Minn, BA, 67; Univ Minn, Minneapolis, DDS, 71, MSD, 74; Am Bd Oral Path, dipl, 78. *Prof Exp:* Asst prof oral path, Sch Dent, Univ Minn, 74-75. *Concurrent Pos:* Clin fel surgical path, Mayo Clin, Rochester, Minn, 74-75, vis sci epidemiol & med statist, 85; vis prof Royal Col Dent, Copenhagen, Denmark, 75; consult oral path, Vet Admin Hosps, Clarksburg, WVa, Martinsburg, WVa; Children's Hosp, Pittsburgh, Pa, 76- *Mem:* Int Asn Oral Path; Am Acad Oral Path; Am Dent Asn; Am Asn Cancer Educrs; Am Asn Dent Res; Am Asn Dent Schs. *Res:* Epidemiology of malignant and benign (especially pre-cancerous) lesions of the upper aerodigestive tract; head and neck pathology; methods of professional education and continuing education; health hazards of smokeless tobacco. *Mailing Add:* Rte 7 Box 583 Morgantown WV 26505

BOURBAKIS, NIKLAOS G, COMPUTER SCIENCE. *Current Pos:* ASSOC PROF, ELEC ENG, STATE UNIV NY, BINGHAMTON, 91- *Personal Data:* b Chania-Crete, Greece, Mar 23, 50; m 77; c 2. *Educ:* Univ Athens, Greece, BS, 74; Univ Patras, PhD(comput eng image processing), 82, cert elec eng, 84. *Hon Degrees:* PhD, Univ Patras, Greece, 83. *Prof Exp:* Researcher asst & chair comput sci, Dept Comput Eng, Patras Univ, Greece, 74-75, teaching asst comput orgn & chair comput sci, 77-81, teaching asst assembly lang, 82, lab instr, 83-84, lectr microcomput, 83-84; asst prof multi-microprocessor archit, Dept Electronics & Comput Eng, George Mason Univ, Fairfax, Va, 84-89; at IBM, Calif, 89-91. *Concurrent Pos:* Res collabr, NTUA, Athens, Greece, 81, res assoc, Comput Technol Inst, Univ Patroas, 87-88; referee, Trans Syst, Man & Cybernet, Inst Elec & Electronics Engrs, 85; Int J, Pattern Recognition & Artificial Intel, Int J, Microcomput Appln & Int J Automatica. *Mem:* Inst Elec & Electronics Engrs; Asn Comput Mach; Euromicro Soc; Pattern Recognition Soc; Greek Math Soc; Eurographics Soc. *Res:* Multimicroprocessor architectures applied on real-time robot vision systems; expert systems, text analysis systems; algorithms and languages for computer vision; computer languages and environments; learning systems and artificial intelligence; knowledge based very large scale integration design; performance evaluation of multiprocessor architectures; software engineering. *Mailing Add:* Dept Elec Eng State Univ NY PO Box 6000 Binghamton NY 13902-6000

BOURCHIER, ROBERT JAMES, RENEWABLE RESOURCES POLICY. *Current Pos:* RETIRED. *Personal Data:* b London, Ont, Dec 28, 27; m 52; c 3. *Educ:* Univ Toronto, BcF, 51; Univ Alta, MSc, 55; State Univ NY Col Forestry, Syracuse, PhD, 60. *Prof Exp:* Mem res staff, Can Forestry Serv, 51-73, dir prog opers, 73-75, dir gen, Can Forestry Serv, 75-80; dir forest res, Ministry Nat Resources, Ont, 80-82; exec dir, Can Inst Forestry, 83-88; exec secy, Forest Res Adv Coun Can, 88- *Concurrent Pos:* World Bank-FAO consult on forestry res in People's Repub of China, 84. *Mem:* Sigma Xi; Can Inst Forestry. *Mailing Add:* Davos St Cantley PQ J8V 3B2 Can

BOURDEAU, JAMES EDWARD, INTERNAL MEDICINE, RENAL PHYSIOLOGY. *Current Pos:* ASSOC PROF MED, PHYSIOL & BIOPHYS, HEALTH SCI CTR, UNIV OKLA, 90- *Personal Data:* b Seattle, Wash, Feb 19, 48; m 73, 91, Teri L Mullikin; c Nicole R, Louis V & Seth C. *Educ:* Northwestern Univ, BS, 70, PhD(exp path), 73, MD, 74. *Honors & Awards:* Established Investr, Am Heart Asn. *Prof Exp:* Intern/resident, Peter Bent Brigham Hosp & Harvard Med Sch, 74-76; res assoc, Lab Kidney & Electrolyte Metabol, Nat Heart, Lung & Blood Inst, 76-79; from asst prof to assoc prof med, Northwestern Univ Med Sch, 79-84; asst prof, Sch Med, Univ Chicago, 85-89; assoc prof, Univ Ill, 89-90. *Concurrent Pos:* Prin investr, NIH res grant. *Mem:* Am Fedn Clin Res; Am Soc Nephrol; Am Physiol Soc; Int Soc Nephrol; Central Soc Clin Res; Am Soc Clin Invest. *Res:* Mechanisms and regulation of calcium transport across individual segments of the mammalian nephron; genetic regulation of distal nephron calcium-transport proteins; development of the kidney. *Mailing Add:* Nephrol Asn Waukesha SC 1111 Delafield St Suite 313 Waukesha WI 53188-3407. *Fax:* 405-270-1529; *E-Mail:* jim-bourdeau@uokhsc.edu

BOURDILLON, ANTONY JOHN, TEXTURE PROCESSING, MACROSTRUCTURAL CHARACTERIZATION. *Current Pos:* PROF MAT SCI, STATE UNIV NY, STONY BROOK, 89- *Personal Data:* b Abercorn, Zambia, Sept 9, 44; Brit citizen; m 89. *Educ:* Univ Oxford, UK, BA,

71, DPhil(physics), 76. *Prof Exp:* Res assoc physics, Cavendish Lab, Cambridge Univ, UK, 76-78; tech officer mat sci, Dept Mat Sci & Metall, Univ Cambridge, UK, 78-86; dir electron micros, Univ New South Wales, Australia, 86-89. *Concurrent Pos:* Prin investr, Royal Soc & Sci & Eng Res Coun, UK, 81-86, Metal Mfrs & DITAC, Australia, 87-89, NY State Inst Superconductivity, 91- *Mem:* Nat Inst Ceramic Engrs; Am Phys Soc; Am Ceramic Soc; AAAS. *Res:* Spectroscopy of ionic solids using synchrotron radiation; X-ray absorption and structural studies of insulators, metals and semiconductors; analytical electron microscopy; electron energy-loss spectroscopy; processing and characterization of high temmperature superconducting materials; over 100 papers written and book in preparation. *Mailing Add:* PO Box 16962 Baton Rouge LA 70893

BOURDO, ERIC A, JR, FOREST MANAGEMENT. *Current Pos:* CONSULT FOREST MGT. *Personal Data:* b Muskegon, Mich, Jan 15, 17; m 42, Charline V Leddy; c Eric III, Laura L & Michael F. *Educ:* Mich Technol Univ, BS, 43; Univ Mich, MA, 51, PhD(forestry, bot), 55. *Prof Exp:* Compounder natural & synthetic rubber prod, Goodyear Tire & Rubber Co, Ohio, 43-46; consult forester, Pomeroy & McGowan Co, Ark, 46; from instr to assoc prof, Mich Technol Univ, 47-58, dir res, Ford Forestry Ctr, 55-68, prof forestry, 58-81, dean, Sch Forestry & Wood Prod, Ford Forestry Ctr, 68-81, consult forestry, 82. *Concurrent Pos:* mem, Mich Endangered Plant Species Comt. *Mem:* Soc Am Foresters; Ecol Soc Am; Am Soc Agron; Wilson Ornith Soc; fel Soc Am Foresters; Nat Audubon Soc. *Res:* Management and utilization of northern forest types. *Mailing Add:* 2839 Middle Lake Rd Twin Lake MI 49457

BOURELL, DAVID LEE, POWDER PROCESSING. *Current Pos:* from asst prof to assoc prof, 79-91, PROF MAT SCI, UNIV TEX, AUSTIN, 91- *Personal Data:* b Dallas, Tex, Feb 26, 53; m 73, Nancy Connell; c Peter, Christopher & Kathryn. *Educ:* Tex A&M Univ, BS, 75; Stanford Univ, MS, 76, PhD(mat sci & eng), 79. *Honors & Awards:* Bradley Stoughton Award, Am Soc Metals, 86. *Prof Exp:* Asst engr, Vought Aerospace Corp, 75. *Concurrent Pos:* Alexander Von Humboldt fel, Ger, 91. *Mem:* Am Inst Mech Engrs; Am Soc Metals; Sigma Xi; Am Powder Metall Inst; Am Ceramic Soc. *Res:* Particulate processing of high temperature materials; solid freeform fabrication. *Mailing Add:* Univ Tex ETC 5160 Austin TX 78712

BOURGAIN, JEAN, GEOMETRY OF INFINITE DIMENSIONAL SPACE. *Current Pos:* PROF INST ADVAN STUDY, SCH MATH, PRINCETON UNIV, 940, J L DOOB PROF MATH, UNIV ILL, 85- *Educ:* Free Univ Brussels, PhD, 77, Habilitation degree, 79. *Hon Degrees:* Dr, Hebrew Univ, 91, Univ Marne-la-Vallce, 94, Free Univ Brussels, 95. *Honors & Awards:* Empain Prize, Belg NSF, 83, Damry-Deleeuw-Bourlart Prize, 85; Salem Prize, 83; Langevin Prize, Fr Acad, 85, E Cartan Prize, 90; Fields Medal, Int Math Union, 94. *Prof Exp:* Res fel Belg, NSF, 75-81; prof, Free Univ Brussels, 81-85; prof, Inst Des Huate Etudes Scientifiques, Paris, 85-95. *Concurrent Pos:* Lady Davis prof math, Hebrew Univ Jerusalem, 88. *Mailing Add:* Dept Math Inst Advanced Studies Olden Lane Princeton NJ 08540

BOURGAULT, PRISCILLA C, PHARMACOLOGY. *Current Pos:* RETIRED. *Personal Data:* b Winooski, Vt, Jan 1, 28. *Educ:* Trinity Col, BS, 50; Loyola Univ, Ill, PhD(pharmacol), 66. *Prof Exp:* Asst prof pharmacol, Dent Sch, Loyola Univ, Chicago, 66-92. *Mem:* Sigma Xi. *Res:* Psychopharmacology; neuropharmacology. *Mailing Add:* 680-C Versailles Circle Elk Grove Village IL 60007-3526

BOURGAUX, PIERRE, ANIMAL VIROLOGY, MOLECULAR BIOLOGY. *Current Pos:* assoc prof, 68-72, PROF MICROBIOL, MED SCH, UNIV SHERBROOKE, 72- *Personal Data:* b Woluwe-St Pierre, Belg, Feb 25, 34; m 61; c 2. *Educ:* Free Univ Brussels, MD, 59; FRCP(C), 80. *Prof Exp:* From lectr to asst prof microbiol, Med Sch, Free Univ Brussels, 60-68. *Concurrent Pos:* Med Res Coun res fel, Exp Virus Res Unit, Glasgow Univ, 63-64; Eleanor Roosevelt fel, Salk Inst Biol Studies, 68-69. *Mem:* Am Soc Microbiol; Am Genetic Asn; Can Biochem Soc; Can Soc Microbiologists. *Res:* oncogenic viruses, particularly expression of viral genes in lytic and transformation systems. *Mailing Add:* Dept Microbiol Fac Med Univ Sherbrooke Sherbrooke PQ J1H 5N4 Can

BOURGET, EDWIN, MARINE ECOLOGY. *Current Pos:* asst prof, 76-84, PROF BIOL DEPT, UNIV LAVAL, 84-, DIR, BIOL DEPT, 97- *Personal Data:* b Senneterre, Que, July 6, 46; m 69; c 2. *Educ:* Univ Laval, Que, BSc, 69, MSc, 71; Univ Col Wales, PhD(marine biol), 74. *Honors & Awards:* Michel-Jurdant Award, Asn Can Fr Advan Sci. *Prof Exp:* Prof-researcher, Nat Inst Sci Res, 74-76. *Concurrent Pos:* Sr gen, Group Interuniv Res Oceanog, 93-96. *Mem:* Am Soc Limnol & Oceanog; Can Soc Zoologists; Crustacean Soc; Soc Chem Ecol. *Res:* Structure and dynamics of marine littoral benthic communities; structure and formation of barnacle shells; behavior and settlement of marine invertebrate larvae. *Mailing Add:* Int Group Oceanog Res Univ Laval Quebec City PQ G1K 7P4 Can. *Fax:* 418-656-2339

BOURGET, SYLVIO-J, soil physics, soil conservation, for more information see previous edition

BOURGIN, DAVID GORDON, MATHEMATICS. *Current Pos:* prof, 66-71, M D ANDERSON PROF MATH, UNIV HOUSTON, 71- *Personal Data:* b New York, NY, Nov 6, 00; c 2. *Educ:* Harvard Univ, PhD(math, physics), 26. *Prof Exp:* Instr, Lehigh Univ, 25-27; assoc math, Univ Ill, 27-37, from asst prof to prof, 37-44. *Concurrent Pos:* Mem, Inst Adv Study, 40-41, 48-49; prin lectr, NSF col math conf, Univ Ore, 54; Fulbright lectr, 54-55; Fulbright res grant, Rome, 55-56; ed, Ill Jour Math & Houston Jour Math. *Mem:* Am Math Soc. *Res:* Applied mathematics; linear topological spaces; algebraic topology. *Mailing Add:* 1400 Hermann Houston TX 77004

BOURGOIGNIE, JACQUES J, NEPHROLOGY, HYPERTENSION. *Current Pos:* PROF MED & DIR DIV NEPHROL, SCH MED, UNIV MIAMI, 76- *Educ:* Cath Univ Louvaine, Belgium, MD, 58. *Res:* Internal medicine of nephrology. *Mailing Add:* Dept Med & Dir Div Nephrol Univ Miami Sch Med PO Box 016960 R-126 Miami FL 33101

BOURGOYNE, ADAM T, JR, FUEL TECHNOLOGY, PETROLEUM ENGINEERING. *Current Pos:* asst prof teaching, 71-74, assoc prof, 74-79, CHMN TEACHING, LA STATE UNIV, 77-, PROF, 79- *Personal Data:* b Baton Rouge, La, July 1, 44; m 66; c 6. *Educ:* La State Univ, BS, 66, MS, 67; Univ Tex, Austin, PhD(petrol eng), 71. *Prof Exp:* Asst drilling engr, Texaco, Inc, La, 66; res assoc reservoir, Chevron Oil Res Lab, Calif, 67; res engr enhanced res, Continental Oil Res Lab, Okla, 68, sr systs engr comput applications, 69-71. *Concurrent Pos:* Res consult, Baroid Div N L Indust, 72-74; teacher, Blowout Control Sch, La State Univ, 71-; prin investr, Blowout Prev Res, Dept Interior, US Geol Surv, 77- *Mem:* Am Soc Mech & Petrol Engrs; Am Petrol Inst; Sigma Xi. *Res:* Development of improved blowout prevention procedures for use in deepwater drilling operations. *Mailing Add:* Dept Petrol Eng La State Univ Baton Rouge LA 70803-0001

BOURGUIGNON, LILLY Y W, CELL BIOLOGY. *Current Pos:* assoc prof, 81-83, PROF CELL BIOL, SCH MED, UNIV MIAMI, 83- *Personal Data:* b Shanghai, China, June 16, 46; m 70; c 1. *Educ:* Nat Taiwan Univ, BS, 69; State Univ NY, Stony Brook, MA, 71, PhD(develop biol), 73. *Prof Exp:* Fel cell biol, Yale Univ, 73-75; fel membrane biol, Univ Calif, San Diego, 75-77; asst prof biol, Wayne State Univ, 77-81. *Concurrent Pos:* Prin investr, NIH grants, 78-79, 78-81 & 81-90, Am Cancer Soc grants, 78-79 & 81-82 & Am Heart Asn grants, 84-89; estab investr, Am Heart Asn. *Mem:* Am Soc Cell Biol; Sigma Xi. *Res:* Biochemical and immunocytochemical studies on the biosynthesis of membrane proteins and transmembrane interactions between cytoskeletal components and surface receptor proteins in lymphocytes, fibroblasts and platelets; hormone-induced signal transduction and cell activation. *Mailing Add:* Dept Anat Box 016960 Univ Miami Sch Med 1600 NW Tenth Ave Miami FL 33136-1015. *Fax:* 305-545-7166

BOURKE, JOHN BUTTS, CHEMISTRY. *Current Pos:* res specialist, Cornell Univ, 63-65, from asst prof chem to assoc prof, 65-76, prof chem & dir, Anal Div, Food Sci Dept, 76-90, EMER PROF CHEM, CORNELL UNIV, 90- *Personal Data:* b Tampa, Fla, Aug 29, 34; m 57; c 3. *Educ:* Colgate Univ, BA, 57; Ore State Univ, MS, 60, PhD(chem), 63. *Prof Exp:* Asst biochem, Ore State Univ, 62-63. *Concurrent Pos:* USDA Coop Res Serv, Washington, DC, 86-88. *Mem:* AAAS; Am Chem Soc; Entom Soc Am; Asn Off Anal Chem. *Res:* Metabolism and metabolic fate of pesticides in plants and animals; laboratory data acquisition systems using computers; agricultural regulatory chemistry; analysis toxic substances and agricultural chemicals; environmental chemistry; food chemistry. *Mailing Add:* Anal Div Food Sci Dept Cornell Univ Geneva NY 14456

BOURKE, ROBERT HATHAWAY, POLAR OCEANOGRAPHY, UNDERWATER ACOUSTICS. *Current Pos:* Assoc dean fac & grad studies, 89-91, PROF PHYS OCEANOG, NAVAL POSTGRAD SCH, 71-, CHMN, DEPT OCEANOG, 94- *Personal Data:* b Portsmouth, Va, June 23, 38; m 64, Portia Hilton; c Robert K & Christopher H. *Educ:* US Naval Acad, BS, 60; Ore State Univ, MS, 69, PhD(phys oceanog), 72. *Concurrent Pos:* Consult, 74-; prin investr, Arctic Submarine Lab, Off Naval Res, 74-; overseas fel, Churchill Col, Cambridge Univ, Eng, 81-82; assoc ed, J Underwater Acoust, US Navy, 86-93. *Mem:* Sigma Xi; Am Geophys Union; Oceanog Soc. *Res:* Physical oceanography of the Arctic marginal sea-ice zones and environmental impact on underwater sound propagation. *Mailing Add:* Dept Oceanog Naval Postgrad Sch Monterey CA 93943. *Fax:* 408-656-2712; *E-Mail:* bourke@oc.nps.navy.mil

BOURKOFF, ETAN, LASER RESEARCH, MICROWAVE ANTENNAS. *Current Pos:* PROF & CHAIR, UNIV SC, 90- *Personal Data:* b Tel-Aviv, Israel, Oct 14, 49; US citizen; c 3. *Educ:* Mass Inst Technol, BS & MS, 72; Univ Calif, Berkeley, PhD(elec eng), 79. *Prof Exp:* Sr engr, Ford Aerospace & Commun Corp, 72-76; res asst, Univ Calif, Berkeley, 76-79; mem tech staff, Hewlett-Packard Labs, 79-81; from asst prof to assoc prof, Johns Hopkins Univ, 81-89. *Concurrent Pos:* NSF presidential young investr award, 85; vis assoc prof, Columbia Univ, 89. *Mem:* Sr mem Inst Elec & Electronic Engrs; NY Acad Sci; Am Phys Soc; Optical Soc Am; Sigma Xi. *Res:* Generation and application of ultrashort laser pulses using novel mode-locking techniques; studies of femto second pulse compression, semiconductor laser modulation, and soliton propagation. *Mailing Add:* 1008 Jones Rd Irmo SC 29063

BOURLAND, CHARLES THOMAS, FOOD MICROBIOLOGY & SPACE FOOD. *Current Pos:* mgr, Space Food Develop Group, 79-87, FOOD SCIENTIST, NASA, 87- *Personal Data:* b Osceola, Mo, July 19, 37; m 63, Cindi A Archer; c 1. *Educ:* Univ Mo, Columbia, BS, 59, MS, 67, PhD(food sci & nutrit), 70. *Honors & Awards:* NASA-Johnson Space Ctr Group Achievement Award, 85, Performance Award, 88, 89, 91 & 93-96. *Prof Exp:* Qual control dairy, Adams Dairy, 63-65; asst food sci, Univ Mo, Columbia, 65-69; res scientist food, Technol Inc, 69-79. *Mem:* Inst Food Technol; Nutrit Today Soc; Int Asn Milk, Food & Environ Sanit; Am Coun Sci & Health. *Res:* Food microbiology; food safety; aerospace food systems; menu planning, food processing and packaging for the space station; advanced design studies for Lunar/Mars missions. *Mailing Add:* 2341 Broad Lawn Dr Houston TX 77058. *Fax:* 713-483-1847; *E-Mail:* charles.t.bourland1@jsc.nasa.gov

BOURLAND, FREDDIE MARSHALL, AGRONOMY, GENETICS. *Current Pos:* PROF AGRON, UNIV ARK, 88- *Personal Data:* b Blytheville, Ark, May 4, 48; m 69. *Educ:* Univ Ark, BS, 70, MS, 74; Tex A&M Univ, PhD(genetics), 78. *Prof Exp:* Res assoc plant sci, Tex Agr Exp Sta, 73-78; from asst prof to assoc prof agron, Miss State Univ, 78-87. *Mem:* Am Soc Agron; Crop Sci Soc Am; Am Soc Genetics; Coun Agr Sci Technol. *Res:* Breeding cotton for host plant resistance. *Mailing Add:* 826 Sunset Dr Fayetteville AR 72701

BOURN, ALBERTA C, NUTRITION, FOOD SCIENCE. *Current Pos:* Dep chief, 82-84, CHIEF, DEPT NUTRIT, CLIN CTR, NIH, 84- *Personal Data:* b Ala. *Educ:* Tuskegee Univ, BS, 67; Va Polytech Inst & State Univ, MS, 81. *Mailing Add:* Nutrit Dept Clin Ctr NIH BIS234 9000 Rockville Pike Bethesda MD 20894

BOURN, WILLIAM M, NEUROPHARMACOLOGY, TOXICOLOGY. *Current Pos:* DIR, DIV PHARMACOL, TOXICOL & NUCLEAR PHARM, COL PHARM & HEALTH SCI, NORTHEAST LA UNIV, 74- *Educ:* Univ Ariz, PhD(pharmacol), 74. *Mailing Add:* Northeast La Univ Sch Pharmacol Monroe LA 71212-0001

BOURNE, CAROL ELIZABETH MULLIGAN, PHYCOLOGY, CELL BIOLOGY. *Current Pos:* ADJ ASST PROF BIOL, WASHINGTON UNIV, 94-; ADJ ASST PROF BIOL, UNIV MO, ST LOUIS, 94- *Personal Data:* b Rochester, NY, May 4, 48; m 68, Godfrey R. *Educ:* Ohio Wesleyan Univ, BA, 70; Miami Univ, MS, 78; Univ Mich, PhD(natural resources), 92. *Prof Exp:* Biol lab technician, Forest Serv, USDA, 70-73; grad res asst, Dept Bot, Miami Univ, 73-75; electron microscopist, Dept Nephrology, Col Med, Univ Cincinnati, 75-76; res asst, Dept Epidemiol, Sch Pub Health, Univ Mich, 78-80, res assoc, Dept Anat & Cell Biol, Med Sch, 81-83, grad res asst, Sch Natural Resources, 83-86, grad teaching asst biol, 87; Rackham fel, Univ Mich, 88-89; res scientist, Inst Food & Agr Sci, Univ Fla, 90-92; adj prof ecol, Fla Atlantic Univ, 92-93. *Mem:* Am Inst Biol Sci; Am Soc Plant Taxonomists; Phycological Soc Am; Soc Study Evolution; Int Soc Plant Molecular Biol; Int Soc Diatom Res. *Res:* Electron microscopy and molecular detection of plant mycoplasma like organisms; molecular systematics and evolution of diatom chloroplast DNA; ecology; ultrastructure and evolution of algae. *Mailing Add:* Dept Biol Univ Mo 8001 Natural Bridge Rd St Louis MO 63121-4499. *Fax:* 314-553-6233; *E-Mail:* cbphd@aol.com

BOURNE, CHARLES PERCY, INFORMATION SCIENCE, COMPUTER SEARCH SYSTEMS. *Current Pos:* PRES, CHARLES BOURNE & ASSOC, MENLO PARK, CALIF, 70- *Personal Data:* b San Francisco, Calif, Sept 2, 31; m 53, Elizabeth A Scheidtmann; c Glen & Holly. *Educ:* Univ Calif, Berkeley, BS, 57; Stanford Univ, MS, 63. *Honors & Awards:* Ann Award of Merit, Am Doc Inst, 65; Sarada Ranganathan lectr, India, 78. *Prof Exp:* Sr res engr, Stanford Res Inst, 57-66; vpres, Info Gen Corp, 66-70; dir, Inst Libr Res & prof-in-residence, Sch Libr & Info Studies, Univ Calif, Berkeley, 71-77; vpres, Gen Info Div, Dialog Info Serv Inc, 77-92. *Concurrent Pos:* Guest lectr, Univ Calif, Berkeley, 63-66,; UNESCO consult, Indonesia & Tanzania; Nat Acad Sci consult, Ghana, 76; mem, US-Egyptian Task Force Tech Info Probs, 76 & Network Adv Comt, Libr Cong, 87-92; bd dirs, Nat Info Stand Orgn, 87-90. *Mem:* Am Soc Info Sci (pres, 70). *Mailing Add:* 1619 Santa Cruz Ave Menlo Park CA 94025-5761

BOURNE, EARL WHITFIELD, HISTOLOGY, CYTOLOGY. *Current Pos:* ASSOC PROF BIOL, UNIV NMEX, 68- *Personal Data:* b Oklahoma City, Okla, July 6, 38. *Educ:* Westminster Col, Mo, AB, 60; Okla State Univ, MS, 62, PhD(zool), 68. *Prof Exp:* Asst prof biol, Bethany Col, WVa, 62-64. *Mem:* Am Asn Cell Biol; Am Micros Soc; Sigma Xi. *Res:* Effects of carcinogenic hydrocarbons on cells in vitro; cytological effects of synthetic steroids. *Mailing Add:* Dept Biol Castetter Hall Rm 167 Univ NMex Main Campus Albuquerque NM 87131

BOURNE, HENRY C(LARK), JR, ELECTRICAL ENGINEERING. *Current Pos:* vpres acad affairs, 81-86 & 87-88, actg pres, 86-87, MEM FAC ELEC ENG, GA INST TECHNOL, 81- *Personal Data:* b Tarboro, NC, Dec 31, 21; m 53; c 4. *Educ:* Mass Inst Technol, SB, 47, SM, 48, ScD(elec eng), 52. *Honors & Awards:* Centennial Medal, Inst Elec & Electronics Engrs. *Prof Exp:* Asst prof elec eng, Mass Inst Technol, 52-54; from asst prof to assoc prof, Univ Calif, Berkeley, 54-63; prof elec eng, Rice Univ, 63-79, chmn dept, 63-74. *Concurrent Pos:* Sci fac fel, NSF, 60-61, dir div eng, NSF, 77-81. *Mem:* AAAS; Am Soc Eng Educ; Inst Elec & Electronics Engrs; Am Phys Soc; Sigma Xi. *Res:* Ferromagnetism and nonlinear magnetics. *Mailing Add:* 2877 Bainbridge Way NW Atlanta GA 30339-4250

BOURNE, HENRY R, BIOCHEMISTRY. *Current Pos:* PROF MED & PHARM, MED SCH, UNIV CALIF, SAN FRANCISCO, 80- *Personal Data:* b Danville, Va, Mar 1, 40; m; c 3. *Educ:* Johns Hopkins Univ, MD, 65. *Mem:* Nat Acad Sci. *Mailing Add:* Dept Pharmacol S-1210 Box 0450 Univ Calif Med Sch Cardiovasc Res Inst San Francisco CA 94143-0450. *Fax:* 415-476-5292

BOURNE, JOHN ROSS, ELECTRICAL ENGINEERING. *Current Pos:* From asst to prof elec & biomed eng, 77-87, PROF ELEC ENG, VANDERBILT UNIV, 87-, PROF MAN TECHNOL, 91- *Personal Data:* b Bryan, Tex, Aug 31, 44; m 68; c 2. *Educ:* Vanderbilt Univ, BE, 66; Univ Fla, MSE, 67, PhD(elec eng), 69. *Honors & Awards:* Samuel A Talbot Award, Inst Elec & Electronics Engrs Med Biol Soc, 76. *Concurrent Pos:* Vis prof, Chalmers Univ, Gothenburg, Sweden, 82; ed, CRC Critical Reviews in Bioeng, 79-; assoc ed, Inst Elec & Electronics Engrs Trans Biomed Eng, 79-82. *Mem:* Inst Elec & Electronics Eng. *Res:* Intelligent systems; pattern recognition; artificial intelligence; informatics. *Mailing Add:* Dept Elec Eng Vanderbilt Univ Nashville TN 37235. *E-Mail:* bournejr@ctrax.vanderbilt.edu

BOURNE, LARRY STUART, URBAN SYSTEMS FORM & DEVELOPMENT, HOUSING MARKETS. *Current Pos:* Dir, Ctr Urban & Community Studies, 73-84, PROF GEOG & PLANNING & DIR, PLANNING PROG, UNIV TORONTO, 66- *Personal Data:* b Ont, Dec 24, 39; m 67, Paula O'Neill; c David & Alexandra. *Educ:* Univ Western Ont, BA, 61; Univ Alta, MA, 63; Univ Chicago, PhD, 66. *Honors & Awards:* Honors Award for Scholarly Achievement, Asn Am Geog, 85; Award for Schoolarly Distinction, Can Asn Geog, 85. *Mem:* Fel Royal Soc Can; Asn Am Geogrs; Can Asn Geogrs; Int Geog Union; Regional Sci Asn Int. *Res:* The changing for and organization of metropolitan areas, with emphasis on land use and reuse, housing, governance and social inequalities. *Mailing Add:* Dept Geog Univ Toronto 100 St George St Toronto ON M5S 3G3 Can. *Fax:* 416-978-6724; *E-Mail:* bourne@geog.utoronto.ca

BOURNE, MALCOLM CORNELIUS, FOOD TEXTURE, RHEOLOGY. *Current Pos:* from asst prof to assoc prof 62-73, PROF FOOD SCI & TECHNOL, CORNELL UNIV, 74- *Personal Data:* b Adelaide, Australia, May 18, 26; m 53, Elizabeth H Schumacher; c Gwendolyn, Jonathan, Lincoln, Virginia & Andrew. *Educ:* Univ Adelaide, BSc, 48; Univ Calif, MS, 61, PhD(agr chem), 62. *Honors & Awards:* Int Award, Inst Food Technologists, 92; Scott Blair Award, Am Asn Cereal Chemists, 93. *Prof Exp:* Chief chemist, Brookers Ltd, Australia, 48-58. *Concurrent Pos:* Ed, J Texture Studies; guest lectr, food rheology Ministry Higher & Sec Educ, USSR, 83; team leader, Nat Acad Sci, China, 84; fel, Inst Food Technologists, 85; consult to food indust; Inst Food Technologists Nat Scientific Lectr, 84-87; vis prof, Univ Chihuahua, Mex. *Mem:* AAAS; Am Chem Soc; Inst Food Technol; Soc Rheol; Am Asn Cereal Chem; fel Inst Food Sci & Technol (UK). *Res:* Physical measurement of quality of foods, food processing and food rheology; international food science; post harvest food losses, horticultural products; protein beverages; measurement, specification and control of texture and rheology of foods; quality factors and processing of fruits, legumes and vegetables. *Mailing Add:* 1000 Castle Rd Geneva NY 14456. *Fax:* 315-787-2397; *E-Mail:* malcolm_bourne@cornell.edu

BOURNE, PETER, ANTHROPOLOGY, PSYCHIATRY. *Current Pos:* PROF & CHMN PSYCHIAT, ST GEORGE'S UNIV MED SCH, GRENADA, 78-; PRES, AM ASN WORLD HEALTH, 84- *Personal Data:* b Oxford, Eng, Aug 6, 39; US citizen; m 74, Mary Elizabeth Wing. *Educ:* Emory Univ, MD, 62; Stanford Univ, MA, 69. *Honors & Awards:* William C Menninger Award, Cent Neuropsychiat Asn, 67. *Prof Exp:* Res psychiatrist, Walter Reed Army Inst Res, 64-67; resident, Dept Psychiat, Sch Med, Stanford Univ, 67-69; asst prof psychiat & community health, Sch Med, Emory Univ, 69-72; dir, Ga Off Drug Abuse, Off Gov, 70-73; asst dir, Spec Action Off Drug Prev, 72-74; pres, Found Int Resources, 75-77; spec asst health to the President, 77-79; asst secy gen, UN Develop Prog & Coordr, Water Decade, 79. *Concurrent Pos:* Consult, WHO, 73-74, Drug Abuse Coun, 74-77; lectr, Dept Psychiat, Sch Med, Harvard Univ, 74-80; comnr, Presidential Comn White House Fels, 77-81; head, US deleg, UN Develop Prog Gov Coun, 78-; mem jury, Lasker Awards, 78-; assoc attend psychiatrist, MacLean Hosp, 74-80; bd dirs, Save Children Fedn. *Mem:* Am Psychiat Asn; Royal Soc Med; Am Anthrop Asn; Am Med Soc Alcoholism; World Fedn Ment Health. *Res:* Psychological and biochemical aspects of stress; health service delivery; drug abuse; AIDS psychological factors in political leadership; author or editor of nine books; author or co-author of 100 technical papers. *Mailing Add:* 2119 Leroy Pl NW Washington DC 20008. *Fax:* 202-332-5414

BOURNE, PHILIP ERIC, COMPUTATIONAL BIOLOGY. *Current Pos:* SR STAFF SCIENTIST, SAN DIEGO SUPERCOMPUT CTR. *Personal Data:* b London, Eng, Mar 22, 53; m; c 1. *Educ:* Flinders Univ SAustralia, BSc, 74, MSc, 75, PhD(crystallog), 80. *Prof Exp:* Fel res, Sheffield Univ, 79-81; res assoc, Howard Hughes Med Inst, Columbia Univ, 81-83, dir, Basic Sci Comput Systs, 83-86, sr assoc, 87- *Concurrent Pos:* Adj assoc prof, Univ Calif, San Diego. *Mem:* Am Crystallog Asn; Royal Australian Chem Inst; Asn Comput Mach; Inst Elec & Electronics Engrs. *Res:* Use of computers in molecular biology. *Mailing Add:* San Diego SuperComput Ctr PO Box 85608 San Diego CA 92186-5608. *Fax:* 619-534-5113

BOURNE, SAMUEL G, mathematics; deceased, see previous edition for last biography

BOURNIA, ANTHONY, NUCLEAR PROJECT MANAGEMENT, HEAT TRANSFER. *Current Pos:* RETIRED. *Personal Data:* b Warren, Ohio, Jan 30, 25; m 63, Arlene M Kautz; c 2. *Educ:* Univ Pittsburgh, BS, 50, PhD(chem eng), 61; Univ Idaho, MS, 54. *Prof Exp:* Res chemist, Sherwin Williams Paint Co, 50-51; engr, Hanford Atomic Prod, Gen Elec Co, 51-55; sr engr, Atomic Power Dept, Westinghouse Elec Corp, 55-60, supvr, Astronuclear Lab, 60-71, adv engr, Environ Syst Dept, 71-72; sr proj mgr, US Nuclear Regulatory Comn, 72-90; proj mgr, Sci Appl Int Corp, 91. *Mem:* Am Nuclear Soc; Am Inst Chem Engrs. *Res:* Technical review, analysis, schedule and evaluation of the nuclear safety aspects of applications for construction and operation of central nuclear power plants. *Mailing Add:* 9101 Shad Lane Potomac MD 20854

BOURNIAS-VARDIABASIS, NICOLE, TERATOLOGY, DEVELOPMENTAL BIOLOGY. *Current Pos:* PROF BIOL, CALIF STATE UNIV, SAN BERNARDINO. *Personal Data:* b Athens, Greece, July 24, 54; m 76; c 2. *Educ:* Univ Calif, Irvine, BSc, 75; Univ Essex, Eng, PhD(develop genetics), 78. *Prof Exp:* Res fel biol, City Hope Res Inst, 78-80; asst res scientist develop biol, City Hope Med Ctr, 80- *Concurrent Pos:* Adj asst prof, Occidental Col, 80-81; asst prof, Calif State Univ, 81-83. *Mem:* Tissue Cult Asn; AAAS; Teratology Soc; Differentiation Soc. *Res:* Study of developmental mechanisms, particularly mechanisms of teratogenesis gene control of early embryogenesis and organogenesis; development of in vitro assays for detecting possible teratogens. *Mailing Add:* Dept Biol Calif State Univ 5500 University Pkwy San Bernardino CA 92407-2318

BOURNS, ARTHUR N, CHEMISTRY, ORGANIC CHEMISTRY. *Current Pos:* from asst prof to prof, McMaster Univ, 47-81, dean, Grad Studies, 57-61, chmn, Dept Chem, 65-67, from vpres to pres & vchancellor sci & eng, 67-80, EMER PROF CHEM, MCMASTER UNIV, 81-, EMER PRES, 93- *Personal Data:* b Petitcodiac, NB, Dec 8, 19; m 43, Marion H Blakney; c Barbara (Brown), Susan (Milne), Robert & Brian. *Educ:* Acadia Univ, BS, 41; McGill Univ PhD(chem), 44. *Hon Degrees:* DSc, Acadia Univ, 68, McGill Univ, 77, Univ NB, 81, McMaster Univ, 81; LLD, Brock Univ, 79. *Honors & Awards:* Montreal Medal, Chem Inst Can, 76. *Prof Exp:* Res chem, Dominion Rubber Co, 44-45; lectr, Acadia Univ, 45-46. *Concurrent Pos:* Nuffield travelling fel, Univ Col London, 55-56; vchmn, Gordon Res Conf, 59-60, chmn, 61-62; mem, Nat Res Coun Can, 69-75; mem bd dirs, Asn Univ & Col Can, 74-77; mem, Natural Sci & Eng Res Coun, 78-85, vis res officer, 83-84; hon prof, Jiangxi, Peoples Repub China, 89; asst prof, Univ Saskatchewan. *Mem:* Fel Chem Inst Can; fel Royal Soc Can. *Res:* Physical organic chemistry. *Mailing Add:* 2407 Woodward Ave Unit 10 Burlington ON L7R 1V2 Can

BOURNS, THOMAS KENNETH RICHARD, PARASITOLOGY. *Current Pos:* RETIRED. *Personal Data:* b Vancouver, BC, Feb 9, 24; m 51, 83. *Educ:* Univ BC, BA, 47, MA, 49; Rutgers Univ, PhD(zool), 55. *Honors & Awards:* Wardle lectr, Can Soc Zool, 83. *Prof Exp:* Tech officer, Med & Vet Entom Lab, Can Dept Agr, 49-52; asst zool, Rutgers Univ, 54-55 & bot, 55-56; lectr zool, Queen's Univ, Ont, 56-57; from lectr to emer prof, Univ Western Ont, 57-89. *Mem:* Am Soc Parasitol; Wildlife Dis Asn; Can Soc Zool (treas, 80-84). *Res:* Schistosome trematode-host relationships; trematode life cycles; tick biology; mutidisciplinary curriculum design. *Mailing Add:* Dept Zool Biol & Geol Sci Bldg Univ Western Ont London ON N6A 5B7 Can

BOURQUE, DON PHILIPPE, MOLECULAR BIOLOGY, PLANT MOLECULAR BIOLOGY. *Current Pos:* asst prof agr biochem, 73-77, assoc prof, 77-92, PROF BIOCHEM, MOLECULAR & CELLULAR BIOL, UNIV ARIZ, 92- *Personal Data:* b St Louis, Mo, Nov 23, 42; c 1. *Educ:* Johns Hopkins Univ, AB, 64; Duke Univ, MA, 67, PhD(bot), 69. *Prof Exp:* Res asst plant biochem, Dept Bot, Duke Univ, 64-69; fel molecular genetics, Dept Biol, Univ Calif, Los Angeles, 69-72, res assoc molecular biol, 72-73. *Mem:* AAAS; Am Soc Cell Biol; Am Soc Plant Physiologists; Am Soc Biol Chem & Molecular Biol. *Res:* Molecular biology of chloroplasts; molecular basis of rhizobium-plant symbiosis; xenobiotic detoxification by transgenic plants. *Mailing Add:* Dept Biochem Univ Ariz Rm 537 Tucson AZ 85721-0001. *Fax:* 520-621-9288; *E-Mail:* bourque@biosci.arizona.edu

BOURQUE, PAUL N(ORBERT), STRUCTURAL ENGINEERING. *Current Pos:* CONSULT, 88- *Personal Data:* b Haverhill, Mass, June 6, 27; m; c 2. *Educ:* St Joseph's Univ, NB, BA, 49, BEd, 56; Univ Montreal, BTh, 53; Mass Inst Technol, MS, 61. *Prof Exp:* Prof math & physics, St Joseph's Univ, NB, 53-58; prof civil eng, 61-63; dean fac sci, Univ Moncton, 63-69; dir sch archit, 69-72, asst to director for acad affairs, Laval Univ, 72-81. *Mem:* Int Asn Shell Struct; Eng Inst Can. *Mailing Add:* Sch Archit Laval Univ Quebec City PQ G1K 7P4 Can

BOURQUIN, AL WILLIS J, BIOREMEDIATION OF CONTAMINATED SOILS & GROUNDWATER, MICROBIAL ECOLOGY. *Current Pos:* PRIN BIOREMEDIATION, CAMP DRESSER & MCKEE INC, 92-, LEADER, BIOREMEDIATION SUPPORT GROUP, 93- *Personal Data:* b Castroville, Tex, Mar 2, 43. *Educ:* Univ Houston, BS, 65, MS, 68, PhD(biol), 71. *Prof Exp:* Res assoc microbiol, Lunar Receiving Lab, Brown & Root-Northrup Corp, 67-68; res microbiologist, 72-80, chief, Microbial Ecol & Biotechnol Br, US Environ Protection Agency, 81-; vpres res & develop, Ecova Corp, 87-89. *Concurrent Pos:* Adj prof, Univ WFla, 73-75; co-ed, Develop Indust Microbiol, 74-; adj prof, Ga State Univ, 75-87, Colo State Univ, 95-; vis prof microbiol, Univ Tex, 76; vis scientist aquatic toxicol, USSR, 77- *Mem:* Am Soc Microbiol; Soc Indust Microbiol; Sigma Xi. *Res:* Application of biotechnology to environmental reclamation of contaminated soils and groundwater; transport fate; biodegradation of hydrocarbon including chlorinated solvents in groundwater. *Mailing Add:* Camp Dresser & McKee Inc 1331 17th St Suite 1200 Denver CO 80202

BOURS, WILLIAM A(LSOP), III, CHEMICAL ENGINEERING. *Current Pos:* RETIRED. *Personal Data:* b New York, NY, July 20, 18; m 41; c 4. *Educ:* Princeton Univ, AB, 39, BSE, 40; Columbia Univ, MS, 41. *Prof Exp:* Engr, E I du Pont de Nemours & Co, Inc, 41-69, asst gen mgr indust & biochem dept, 69-75, vpres & gen mgr, Fabrics & Finishes Dept, 75-78, vpres fabrics & finishes, 78-81. *Mem:* Am Inst Chem Engrs; Am Chem Soc; Soc Chem Indust; Nat Paint & Coatings Asn; Sigma Xi. *Mailing Add:* Park Plaza No 1706 1100 Lovering Ave Wilmington DE 19806-3273

BOUSEMAN, JOHN KEITH, ENTOMOLOGY. *Current Pos:* asst entomologist, 72-84, ASSOC ENTOMOLOGIST, ECON ENTOM SECT, ILL NATURAL HIST SURV, 84- *Personal Data:* b Clinton, Iowa, Aug 11, 36. *Educ:* Univ Ill, BS, 60, MS, 62. *Prof Exp:* Exped entomologist, Am Mus Natural Hist Exped, Uruguay, 63 & Bolivia, 64 & 65; instr, Univ Ill, 65-66. *Concurrent Pos:* Grant-in-aid res, Sigma Xi, 61; asst entomologist agr entom, Ill Agr Exp Sta, 72-; vis coleopterist, Fla State Collection Arthropods, 80; consult, Zambia Ministry Agr & Water Resources, 84. *Mem:* Am Registry Prof Entomologists; Entom Soc Am; Am Entom Soc. *Res:* Systematic entomology, especially Coleoptera and Hymenoptera; biology of pollination; history of the biological exploration of South America. *Mailing Add:* 1815 Larch Pl Urbana IL 61801

BOUSFIELD, ALDRIDGE KNIGHT, ALGEBRAIC TOPOLOGY. *Current Pos:* assoc prof, 72-76, PROF MATH, UNIV ILL CHICAGO, 76- *Personal Data:* b Boston, Mass, Apr 5, 41; m 68, Marie Vastersavendts. *Educ:* Mass Inst Technol, SB, 63, PhD(math), 66. *Prof Exp:* Lectr math, Brandeis Univ, 66-67, asst prof math, 67-72. *Concurrent Pos:* Off Naval Res assoc math, 66-67; NSF res grant, 67- *Mem:* Am Math Soc; Math Asn Am. *Res:* Homotopy theory; semisimplicial theory; k-theory. *Mailing Add:* Dept Math Statist & Comput Sci Univ Ill Chicago Chicago IL 60607

BOUSFIELD, EDWARD LLOYD, INVERTEBRATE ZOOLOGY. *Current Pos:* Invertebrate zoologist, 50-64, chief zoologist, 64-74, sr scientist, 74-86, EMER CUR, NAT MUS NATURAL SCI, 86-; RES ASSOC, ROYAL BC MUS. *Personal Data:* b Penticton, BC, June 19, 26; m 53, 84, 94, Joyce Bradley; c Marjorie, Katherine, Mary & Kenneth. *Educ:* Univ Toronto, BA, 48, MA, 49; Harvard Univ, PhD(zool), 54. *Honors & Awards:* Outstanding Achievement Award, Govt Can, 85. *Concurrent Pos:* Adj prof, Carleton Univ, 71-84; affil prof, Univ Wash, 80-91 & Univ Toronto, 84; mem, Can Comt Oceanog; emer cur, res assoc, Royal Ont Nus, 84- *Mem:* Fel Royal Soc Can; Can Soc Zoologists; Soc Syst Zool; Estuarine Res Fedn. *Res:* Marine zoology; Crustacea; Amphipoda; systematics and ecology; intertidal and estuarine ecology; marine fouling; stream biology; aquatic entomology; marine malacology. *Mailing Add:* 611 548 Dallas Rd Victoria BC V8V 1B3 Can

BOUSH, GEORGE MALLORY, ENTOMOLOGY. *Current Pos:* RETIRED. *Personal Data:* b Norfolk, Va, June 5, 26; m 45; c 3. *Educ:* Va Polytech Inst, BSc, 48; Ohio State Univ, MSc, 51, PhD, 55. *Prof Exp:* Asst entomologist, Va Agr Exp Sta, 49-50 & Rockefeller Found, 52-54; assoc prof entom, Univ Ky, 55-57 & Va Polytech Inst, 57-64; assoc prof entom, Univ Wis-Madison, 64-68, chmn dept, 76-80, prof, 68-90. *Concurrent Pos:* Smith-Mundt fel, Iraq, 60-61; consult, USDA, 61. *Mem:* Entom Soc Am. *Res:* insect microbial symbiotic associations; insect pathology; insect transmission of plant diseases. *Mailing Add:* 15 Cove Dr Savannah GA 31419

BOUSQUET, WILLIAM F, pharmacology, biochemistry, for more information see previous edition

BOUSTANY, KAMEL, RUBBER CHEMISTRY, FUEL TECHNOLOGY. *Current Pos:* PRES, PERMEA INC, 85- *Personal Data:* b Aleppo, Syria, Mar 22, 41; US citizen; m 64; c 4. *Educ:* Neuchatel Univ, Switz, chem eng, 64, PhD(organometallics), 67. *Prof Exp:* Sr res chemist rubber, 67-71, proj mgr, 71-74, sr proj mgr prod develop, 74-78, managing dir, Bombay, India, 78-81, bus develop dir, bus div, Monsanto Co, 81-85. *Mem:* Am Chem Soc; Soc Plastic Engr. *Res:* The effect of short fibers on the reinforcement of elastomers and plastics to improve their physical properties, processibility and performances in tires and mechanical good products; enhanced oil recovery - technology, market size, economics, gas processing; membranes for separation and filtration; adsorbtion of gas. *Mailing Add:* 212 Clarston Exec Park Baldwin MO 63011

BOUTILIER, ROBERT FRANCIS, GEOLOGY. *Current Pos:* from asst prof to assoc prof, 65-73, PROF EARTH SCI, BRIDGEWATER STATE COL, 73- *Personal Data:* b Lawrence, Mass, Nov 28, 37; m 63; c 3. *Educ:* Boston Univ, AB, 59, MA, 60, PhD(geol), 63. *Prof Exp:* Instr geol, Boston Univ, 62-65. *Mem:* AAAS; Geol Soc Am; Soc Econ Mineralogists & Paleontologists; Nat Asn Geol Teachers. *Res:* Origin of igneous and metamorphic rocks of eastern Massachusetts. *Mailing Add:* Dept Earth Sci Bridgewater State Col 131 Summer St Bridgewater MA 02324-2699

BOUTJDIR, MOHAMED, CARDIAC ELECTROPHYSIOLOGY, ION CHANNELS. *Current Pos:* fel, Dept Med, 88-89, asst prof physiol & biophys, 93-96, RES ASST PROF, DEPT ANAT & CELL BIOL, STATE UNIV NY HEALTH SCI CTR, BROOKLYN, 91-, ASSOC PROF MED & ASSOC PROF PHYSIOL & BIOPHYSICS, DEPT MED, CARDIOL DIV, 96- *Personal Data:* b Morocco, Mar 2, 58. *Educ:* Univ Paris XI, MS, 84, PhD(cardiovasc electrophysiol), 87. *Prof Exp:* Cardiovasc physiol instr, Univ Paris XI, 84-87. *Concurrent Pos:* Sr res assoc, Vet Admin Med Ctr, Brooklyn, 88-, chmn res & develop comt, 94-; merit grant, Vet Admin Cent Off, 94- *Mem:* Am Heart Asn; Biophys Soc; AAAS; Fedn Am Soc Exp Biol; Cardiac Electrophysiol Soc. *Res:* Biophysical and molecular aspects of regulation of cardiac ion channels; arrthythmias and related pathophysiology. *Mailing Add:* Cardiol Dept Vet Admin Med Ctr Brooklyn NY 11209. *E-Mail:* boutjdir@sprynet.com

BOUTON, THOMAS CHESTER, POLYMER SCIENCE. *Current Pos:* MGR PROD DEVELOP, BRIDGESTONE-FIRESTONE, 76- *Personal Data:* b Milwaukee, Wis, Dec 5, 39; m 62; c 3. *Educ:* Univ Wis, BS, 52; Univ Akron, MS, 67. *Prof Exp:* Jr engr, Firestone Res, 62-64, supvr pilot plant, 65-67, mgr process develop, 67-76. *Mem:* Am Chem Soc; Am Inst Chem Engrs. *Res:* Structure-property relationships; process simulation; kinetics solution thermodynamics. *Mailing Add:* PO Box 1361 Lake Charles LA 70602

BOUTROS, OSIRIS WAHBA, PLANT PHYSIOLOGY. *Current Pos:* RETIRED. *Personal Data:* b Beni-Suef, UAR, Aug 16, 28; US citizen; m 65; c 4. *Educ:* Cairo Univ, BSc, 52; Fla State Uniiv, MS, 62; Univ Pittsburgh, PhD(plant physiol), 68. *Prof Exp:* Instr, El-Mahallah El Kobra Sec Sch, Egypt, 52-53; instr chem, Ministry of Educ, Addis Abeba, Ethiopia, 53-59; tech asst biol & chem, Fla State Univ, 59-61; instr, Col Steubenville, 62-63; asst plant physiol, Univ Pittsburgh, Bradford, 64-68, Am Cancer Soc fel, 68-69, assoc prof biol, 69-95. *Mem:* Am Soc Plant Physiol; Am Inst Biol Sci; AAAS; Bryol Soc Am. *Res:* Physiological properties, modes of action and chemical nature of plant growth regulators; pollution indicators. *Mailing Add:* RD 1 Box 16 Limestone NY 14753

BOUTROS, SUSAN NOBLIT, ENVIRONMENTAL HEALTH. *Current Pos:* PRES, ENVIRON ASSOC LTD, 95- *Personal Data:* b Lock Haven, Pa, May 22, 42; m 65; c 4. *Educ:* Dickinson Col, BS, 64; Univ Pittsburgh, PhD(plant cytol), 67. *Prof Exp:* Instr biol, Univ Pittsburgh, 67-68, NIH traineeship human genetics, Grad Sch Pub Health, 68-69, auth gen biol lab book for col level, Bradford, 69-71, from asst prof to prof biol, 71-95. *Mem:* Am Soc Parasitologists; Am Water Works Asn; Electron Micros Soc Am. *Res:* Giardia lamblia, cryptosporidium and other water borne diseases; improved identification techniques for waterborne pathogens; differentiation of ground water from surface water. *Mailing Add:* Environ Assoc Ltd Cornell Biotech Park 95 Brown Rd Ithaca NY 14850

BOUTTON, THOMAS WILLIAM, GRASSLAND ECOLOGY, STABLE ISOTOPE BIOGEOCHEMISTRY. *Current Pos:* assoc prof, 87-94, PROF RANGELAND ECOL & PLANT PHYSIOL, TEX A&M UNIV, 94- *Personal Data:* b Lakewood, Ohio, Sept 9, 51; m 79, Janet E Cook; c Kelly & Andrew. *Educ:* St Louis Univ, AB, 73; Univ Houston, MS, 76; Brigham Young Univ, PhD(bot), 79. *Prof Exp:* Fel biol, Augustana Col, 80-81, asst prof, 81-82; fel pediat, Baylor Col Med, 82-83, instr, 83-85, asst prof pediat, 85-87. *Concurrent Pos:* Res assoc bot, Univ Nairobi, Kenya, 80-81. *Mem:* AAAS; Am Geophys Union; Brit Ecol Soc; Ecol Soc Am; Sigma Xi; Soil Sci Soc Am. *Res:* The application of stable isotope techniques to problems in grassland ecology; biogeochemistry of grassland and savanna ecosystems; plant-soil relationships; reconstruction of paleoenvironments. *Mailing Add:* Dept Rangeland Ecol & Mgt Texas A&M Univ Mail Stop 2126 College Station TX 77843-2126. *Fax:* 408-845-6430; *E-Mail:* boutton@acs.tamu.edu

BOUTWELL, ROSWELL KNIGHT, BIOCHEMISTRY, CARCINOGENESIS. *Current Pos:* Asst, McArdle Lab Cancer Res, Univ Wis-Madison, 39-44, instr cancer res, 45-49, from asst prof to prof oncol, 49-88, EMER PROF ONCOL, UNIV WIS-MADISON, 88- *Personal Data:* b Madison, Wis, Nov 24, 17; m 43, Lou Fairchild; c Paul, Philip & David. *Educ:* Beloit Col, BS, 39; Univ Wis, MS, 41, PhD(biochem), 44. *Hon Degrees:* DSc, Beloti Col, 81. *Honors & Awards:* Clowes Award, Am Asn Cancer Res, 79. *Concurrent Pos:* Fel, Univ Wis, 44-45; chief res, Radiation Energy Res Found, Hiroshima, 84-86. *Mem:* Fel AAAS; Am Asn Cancer Res; Am Soc Biol Chem. *Res:* Interaction of carcinogens with tissue constituents and metabolic consequences; prevention of cancer; mechanisms of tumor promotion. *Mailing Add:* Dept Oncol Univ Wis Med Sch 1400 Univ Madison WI 53706-1599

BOUWER, HERMAN, GROUNDWATER HYDROLOGY. *Current Pos:* res hydraul engr, 59-72, dir, 72-90, LAB EXEC, US WATER CONSERV LAB, PHOENIX, 90- *Personal Data:* b Haarlem, Neth, July 11, 27; nat US; m 52, Agnes N Temminick; c Edward J, Herman G & Annette N. *Educ:* Nat Agr Univ, Neth, BS, 49, MS, 52; Cornell Univ, PhD, 55. *Honors & Awards:* Walter Huber Res Prize, Am Soc Civil Engrs, 66, Royce J Tipton Award, 84; Hancor Award, Am Soc Agr Engrs, 88. *Prof Exp:* Assoc agr engr, Auburn Univ, 55-59. *Concurrent Pos:* Consult, Nat Acad Sci; lectr groundwater hydrol, Univ Ariz; fel, Orgn Econ Coop & Develop, 64. *Mem:* Am Geophys Union; Am Soc Civil Engrs; Am Soc Agr Engrs; Nat Water Well Asn; Int Asn Water Qual; Water Environ Fedn. *Res:* Groundwater hydrology; numerous articles in professional journals. *Mailing Add:* 338 E La Diosa Dr Tempe AZ 85282

BOUWKAMP, JOHN C, HORTICULTURE, PLANT BREEDING. *Current Pos:* Asst prof, 69-74, ASSOC PROF HORT, UNIV MD, 74- *Personal Data:* b Grant, Mich, Apr 20, 42; m 66; c 4. *Educ:* Mich State Univ, BS, 64, MS, 66, PhD(hort), 69. *Mem:* Am Genetic Asn; Am Soc Hort Sci. *Res:* Genetics and physiology of vegetable crops. *Mailing Add:* Dept Hort Univ Md College Park MD 20742-0001

BOUWSMA, WARD D, MATHEMATICS. *Current Pos:* CONSULT, 80- *Personal Data:* b Lansing, Mich, Jan 11, 35; m 60; c 2. *Educ:* Calvin Col, AB, 56; Univ Mich, MA, 57, PhD(math), 62. *Prof Exp:* Asst prof math, Pa State Univ, 60-67; assoc prof math, Southern Ill Univ, 67-80. *Mem:* Am Math Soc; Math Asn Am; Sigma Xi. *Res:* Complex variables. *Mailing Add:* 2525 Londonderry Ann Arbor MI 48104

BOUYOUCOS, JOHN VINTON, APPLIED PHYSICS. *Current Pos:* mgr, Acoust Dept, Gen Dynamics Electronics Div, 59-72, PRES & CHIEF SCIENTIST, HYDROACOUST, INC, 72- *Personal Data:* b Lansing, Mich, Nov 9, 26; m 53; c 3. *Educ:* Harvard Univ, AB, 49, AM, 50, PhD(appl physics), 55. *Prof Exp:* Asst, Harvard Univ, 51-55, asst to dir, Acoust Res Lab, 55-59. *Mem:* Fel Acoust Soc Am; fel Inst Elec & Electronics Engrs; Soc Exploration Geophysicists. *Res:* Hydrodynamic power conversion; physical acoustics; underwater sound; fluid mechanics; electric networks; electronics; servomechanisms. *Mailing Add:* Hydroacoust Inc PO Box 23447 Rochester NY 14692

BOVARD, FREEMAN CARROLL, BIO-ORGANIC CHEMISTRY. *Current Pos:* from asst prof to prof chem, Claremont Men's Col, 55-64, prof, Claremont Men's Col, Pitzer Col & Scripps Col, 64-86, EMER PROF CHEM, CLAREMONT MCKENNA COL, PITZER COL & SCRIPPS COL, 86- *Personal Data:* b Eugene, Ore, July 18, 21; m 45; c 3. *Educ:* Pomona Col, AB, 43; Iowa State Col, PhD(biochem), 52. *Prof Exp:* Jr chemist, Shell Develop Co, 43-45; res biochemist, Stine Lab, E I du Pont de Nemours & Co, 51-55. *Mem:* AAAS; Am Chem Soc; Sigma Xi. *Res:* Amylolytic enzymes; carbohydrates; drug metabolism; peptide and protein synthesis; proteolytic enzymes. *Mailing Add:* 910 W Harrison Ave Claremont CA 91711-4129

BOVARD, KENLY PAUL, ANIMAL HUSBANDRY. *Current Pos:* ASSOC PROF ANIMAL SCI, VA POLYTECH INST, 57- *Personal Data:* b Pittsburgh, Pa, Mar 23, 28; m 50; c 3. *Educ:* Cornell Univ, BS, 50; Iowa State Univ, MS, 54, PhD, 60. *Prof Exp:* Res assoc animal husb, Iowa State Col, 54-57. *Mem:* Fel AAAS; Am Soc Animal Sci; Biomet Soc; Am Genetic Asn. *Res:* Beef cattle breeding; problems dealing with heritabilities of economic characteristics of commercial production. *Mailing Add:* 505 Ascot Lane Blacksburg VA 24060

BOVAY, HARRY ELMO, JR, ENGINEERING, MATERIALS SCIENCE. *Current Pos:* PRES, MID-SOUTH TELECOMMUN CO, 87- *Personal Data:* b Big Rapids, Mich, Sept 4, 14; m 77; c 2. *Educ:* Cornell Univ, Civil Engr, 36. *Honors & Awards:* ASHRAE/ALCO Award, Am Soc Heating, Refrig & Air-Conditioning Engrs, Inc, 71; Nat Soc Prof Engr Award, 87. *Prof Exp:* Engr, Humble Oil & Refining Co, 37-46; owner, H E Bovay, Jr, Consult Engrs, 46-52, partner, 52-62; pres, Bovay Engrs, Inc, 62-73, chmn bd & chief exec officer, 73-83; pres, Mid-South Telephone Co, 83-89. *Concurrent Pos:* Am Consult Engrs Coun fel, 73- *Mem:* Nat Acad Eng; Nat Soc Prof Engrs (pres, 75-76); Am Soc Testing & Mat; Am Civil Engrs; Am Soc Heating, Refrig & Air-Conditioning Engrs. *Res:* Expansion of energy field; power generation utilization; petrochemical plant development; advancement of engineering education and ethics through study and practice. *Mailing Add:* 3355 W Alabama No 1140 Houston TX 77098-1718. *Fax:* 713-626-4181

BOVBJERG, DANA H, PSYCHONEURO IMMUNOLOGY, BEHAVIORAL MEDICINE. *Current Pos:* asst prof med, 86-89, ASST PROF NEUROSCI, CORNELL UNIV MED COL, 89-, ASST PROF NEUROL; ASST MEM NEUROL, MEM SLOAN-KETTERING CANCER CTR, 89- *Personal Data:* b St Louis, Mo; m, Margaret Ball; c Katrina, Britt & Mieke. *Educ:* Carleton Col, BA, 73; Univ Iowa, BS, 77; Univ Rochester, MS, 83, PhD(neurosci), 83. *Honors & Awards:* Jr Fac Res Award-Am Cancer Soc, 90. *Mem:* Am Asn Immunologists; Am Psychosom Soc; Soc Behav Med; Acad Behav Med; Pni Res Soc. *Res:* Study of psychological & behavioral factors in cancer, with a sub specialty in psychoneuroimmunology, the regulation of the immune system by the brain. *Mailing Add:* Psychoneuroimmunol Lab Mem Sloan-Kettering Box 457 1275 York Ave New York NY 10021-6094

BOVBJERG, RICHARD VIGGO, ANIMAL ECOLOGY. *Current Pos:* RETIRED. *Personal Data:* b Chicago, Ill, Sept 11, 19; m 42, 60; c 4. *Educ:* Univ Chicago, PhD(zool), 49. *Prof Exp:* Asst zool, Univ Chicago, 46-49; from instr to asst prof, Washington Univ, 49-55; from asst prof to prof zool, Univ Iowa, 55-89. *Concurrent Pos:* Ford Found fel, 51-52; dir, Iowa Lakeside Lab, 63- *Mem:* Ecol Soc Am; Soc Study Evolution; Am Soc Limnol & Oceanog; Am Soc Zoologists. *Res:* Ecology of aquatic invertebrates. *Mailing Add:* 1710 Ridge Rd Iowa City IA 52245

BOVE, ALFRED ANTHONY, CORONARY ARTERY DISEASE. *Current Pos:* CHIEF CARDIOL SECT, TEMPLE UNIV MED SCH, 87- *Educ:* Temple Univ, Philadelphia, MD, 66, PhD(physiol), 70. *Prof Exp:* Prof med & physiol & consult cardiovasc dis, Mayo Clin, 81 -86. *Mailing Add:* Dept Med Temple Univ Med Sch 3400 N Broad St Philadelphia PA 19140. *Fax:* 215-221-8191

BOVE, JOHN L, AZIRIDINE CHEMISTRY, PERBORATE OXIDATION & ENVIRONMENTAL CHEMISTRY. *Current Pos:* PROF CHEM & ENVIRON ENG, COOPER UNION, 70-, CHMN, CHEM DEPT. *Personal Data:* b New York, NY, Apr 15, 28; m 57, June A Burns; c Adele & Catherine. *Educ:* Bucknell Univ, BA, 49, MS, 54; Case Western Res Univ, PhD(chem), 73. *Honors & Awards:* Schweinberg Award. *Prof Exp:* Asst prof chem, Cooper Union, 57-67; dep dir, NY Dept Air Resources, Bur Tech Serv, 67-70. *Mem:* AAAS. *Res:* Aziridine chemistry; benzyne chemistry; thermolysis reactions; use of fourier transform-infrared-computer to pattern recognition of organics; use of sodium perborate in Baeyer-Villiger reactions and epoxidation reactions; asymmetric synthesis. *Mailing Add:* Chem Dept Cooper Union 51 Astor Pl New York NY 10003

BOVE, JOSEPH RICHARD, HEMATOLOGY, LABORATORY MEDICINE. *Current Pos:* From instr to prof, 59-92, assoc prof lab med, 66-70, EMER PROF MED, YALE UNIV, 92- *Personal Data:* b Orange, NJ, Apr 23, 26; m 52; c 3. *Educ:* Univ Md, BS, 51, MD, 53. *Hon Degrees:* MA, Yale Univ, 70. *Honors & Awards:* John Elliott Award, Am Asn Blood Banks. *Mem:* Am Asn Blood Banks. *Res:* Blood transfusion serology, especially alterations of red cell antigens and antibodies. *Mailing Add:* 12 Brookhaven Rd Hamden CT 06517-3220

BOVE, KEVIN E, LIVER DISEASE, NEUROMUSCULAR DISEASE. *Current Pos:* ASSOC DIR PATH, CHILDREN'S HOSP, CINCINNATI, OHIO, 68-, ACTG DIR, 94-; PROF PATH & PEDIAT, UNIV CINCINNATI, 76- *Personal Data:* b 1935; m 63, Nancy Eckert; c Stephen, Renee & Allison. *Educ:* Colgate Univ, AB, 57; Univ Buffalo, MD, 61. *Prof Exp:* Asst chief anat path, Walter Reed Gen Hosp, 66-68. *Mem:* US Can Acad Path; Am Asn Exp Pathologists; Col Am Pathologists; Soc Pediat Path (secy-treas, 79-84, pres, 90-91). *Res:* Eclectic and transdisciplinary investigation of curiosa encountered in pediatric pathology practice; childhood neoplasia. *Mailing Add:* Univ Cincinnati Col Med Children's Hosp Med Ctr Cincinnati OH 45229

BOVEE, KENNETH C, VETERINARY MEDICINE, NEPHROLOGY. *Current Pos:* from asst prof to assoc prof, 67-78, dept chmn, 79-84, PROF MED, SCH VET MED, UNIV PA, 78-, CORINNE & HENRY BOWER CHAIR MED, 80- *Personal Data:* b Chicago, Ill, Sept 1, 36; m 58; c 3. *Educ:* Ohio State Univ, BSc, 58, DVM, 61; Univ Pa, MMedSci, 69. *Prof Exp:* Intern & resident, Animal Med Ctr, New York, 61-64. *Concurrent Pos:* NIH fel, Grad Sch Med, Univ Pa, 64-67. *Mem:* Am Col Vet Internal Med; Am Soc Nephrology; Int Soc Nephrology. *Res:* Renal structure, function and disease. *Mailing Add:* Univ Pa 3900 Delancey St Philadelphia PA 19104-6010

BOVELL, CARLTON ROWLAND, MICROBIAL PHYSIOLOGY. *Current Pos:* actg instr bact, Univ Calif, Riverside, 54-56, from instr to assoc prof, 57-69, vice chancellor, 81- 84, PROF MICROBIOL, UNIV CALIF, RIVERSIDE, 69- *Personal Data:* b New York, NY, Nov 10, 24; m 67. *Educ:* Brooklyn Col, AB, 48, MA, 52; Univ Calif, PhD(microbiol), 57. *Prof Exp:* Instr biol & bact, Brooklyn Col, 50-52. *Concurrent Pos:* Asst vpres, Acad Planning & Prog Rev, Systemwide Admin, Univ Calif, 78-81, chmn Dept Biol, 87-89, vchmn, Assembly Acad Senate, 89-90, chmn, 90-91, Bd Regents, 89-91. *Mem:* Am Soc Microbiologists; AAAS. *Res:* Comparative aspects of the autotrophic and heterotrophic physiology and metabolism of hydrogen bacteria. *Mailing Add:* Dept Biol Univ Calif-Riverside 900 University Ave Riverside CA 92521-0001

BOVENKERK, HAROLD P(AUL), engineering, for more information see previous edition

BOVEY, FRANK ALDEN, POLYMER CHEMISTRY. *Current Pos:* RETIRED. *Personal Data:* b Minneapolis, Minn, June 4, 18; m 41; c 3. *Educ:* Harvard Univ, BS, 40; Univ Minn, PhD(phys chem), 48. *Honors & Awards:* Polymer Chem Award, Am Chem Soc, 69, Phillips Award, 83, Award Polymer Sci, 83, Carothers Award, 91; High Polymer Physics Award, Am Phys Soc, 74; Nichols Medal, 78; Silver Medal, Japanese Polymer Soc, 91. *Prof Exp:* Asst chief chemist, Nat Synthetic Rubber Corp, 43-45; head, Polymer Res Dept, Minn Mining & Mfg Co, 48-55, res assoc, 55-62; mem tech staff, Bell Labs, 62-71, head, Polymer Chem Res Dept, 67-91. *Mem:* Nat Acad Sci; Am Chem Soc; Am Phys Soc; NY Acad Sci. *Res:* Physical chemistry of polymers; nuclear magnetic resonance of polymers; emulsion polymerization; fluorescence; rates of conformational isomerization; optical rotary dispersion. *Mailing Add:* 78 Suggle Meadow Rd Amhurst MA 01002

BOVEY, RODNEY WILLIAM, WEED & BRUSH MANAGEMENT, HERBICIDE FATE IN PLANTS, SOILS & WATER SOURCES. *Current Pos:* res agronomist, College Station, Tex, 64-67, Mayaquez, PR, 67-68, RES AGRONOMIST, AGR RES SERV, USDA, COLLEGE STATION, TEX, 67- *Personal Data:* b Craigmont, Idaho, July 17, 34; m 56, Shirley E Deffenbaugh; c Seth I, Todd E, Shawn E & Cary L. *Educ:* Univ Idaho, BS, 56, MS, 59; Univ Nebr, PhD(agron), 64. *Honors & Awards:* Outstanding Achievement Award, Soc Range Mgt, 90. *Prof Exp:* Instr agron, Univ Nebr, 59-64. *Concurrent Pos:* Grants, US Dept Defense, 64-67, US Army, Ft Detrick, 67-68 & numerous chem co, 67-; spec adv to Secy Agr for 2,4,5-T hearing called by Environ Protection Agency, US Dept Agr, 72-74 & 78-80; adj prof plant physiol, Tex A&M Univ, 84-, instr, 88. *Mem:* Am Soc Agron; Soc Range Mgt; Coun Agr Sci & Technol; fel Weed Sci Soc Am; Sigma Xi; Plant Growth Regulator Soc Am. *Res:* Develop herbicide and nonherbicide control methods for weed and brush control in pastures and rangeland; environmental fate and safety of herbicides mode of action and fate in plants, soils and water sources; develop methods to control weeds for forage crops establishment and revegetation on pastures and rangelands. *Mailing Add:* 3006 Norton Lane College Station TX 77845

BOVILLE, BYRON WALTER, atmospheric science, for more information see previous edition

BOVING, BENT GIEDE, ANATOMY, REPRODUCTIVE BIOLOGY. *Current Pos:* RETIRED. *Personal Data:* b Washington, DC, Feb 23, 20; m 44, 74, Renee Laya; c Eric, Betsy & Peter. *Educ:* Swarthmore Col, AB, 41; Jefferson Med Col, MD, 48. *Honors & Awards:* Schering Award, 46. *Prof Exp:* Asst, Swarthmore Col, 41; asst zool, Univ Iowa, 41-42; intern, Wilmington Gen Hosp, Del, 48-49; mem staff dept embryol, Carnegie Inst, 51-70; prof obstet, gynec & anat, Sch Med, Wayne State Univ, 70-88. *Concurrent Pos:* Nat Cancer Inst fel anat, Yale Univ, 49-51; vis res scientist, Reproductive Sci Prog, Univ Mich, 90- *Mem:* AAAS; Am Asn Anat; Soc Develop Biol; Int Soc Develop Biol; Soc Study Reproduction; Sigma Xi. *Res:* Rabbit blastocyst transport, spacing, orientation and attachment to the uterus; invasive growth chemistry and mechanics. *Mailing Add:* Reproductive Sci Prog Univ Mich 41901 W Eight Mile Rd Northville MI 48167-1931

BOVOPOULOS, ANDREAS D, COMMUNICATIONS NETWORKS, COMPUTER NETWORKS. *Current Pos:* CHIP COM CORP, 94- *Personal Data:* b Argos, Greece, Mar 8, 58; m 88. *Educ:* Nat Tech Univ Athens, dipl elec eng, 82; Columbia Univ, MS, 83, PhD(elec eng), 89. *Prof Exp:* Asst prof comput sci, Washington Univ, St Louis, 88-94. *Mem:* Inst Elec & Electronic Engrs. *Res:* High speed networks; traffic control framework for automatic teller machine networks; stochastic systems. *Mailing Add:* 118 Fay Rd Framingham MA 01702

BOWDAN, ELIZABETH SEGAL, ANIMAL PHYSIOLOGY. *Current Pos:* Fel, Univ Mass, 76-79, assoc fel, 79-81, vis asst prof, 81- 92, RES ASST PROF, UNIV MASS, 92- *Personal Data:* b Kingston upon Hull, Eng; m 62; c 1. *Educ:* Univ Durham, Eng, BSc, 60; Mt Holyoke Col, MA, 62; Univ Mass, PhD, 76. *Mem:* AAAS; Am Zool Soc; Animal Behav Soc. *Res:* Insect neurophysiology specifically neurophysiological and behavioral aspects of chemosensory reception and feeding regulation. *Mailing Add:* Morrill Sci Bldg Amherst MA 01003. *Fax:* 413-545-1696; *E-Mail:* ebowdan@bio.umass.edu

BOWDEN, CHARLES MALCOLM, QUANTUM OPTICS, STATISTICAL MECHANICS. *Current Pos:* PHYSICIST, US ARMY MISSILE COMMAND, 67- *Personal Data:* b Richmond, Va, Dec 31, 33; m 60; c 3. *Educ:* Univ Richmond, BS, 56; Univ Va, MS, 59; Clemson Univ, PhD(physics), 67. *Prof Exp:* Physicist, US Naval Res Lab, 59-61; instr physics, Univ Richmond, 61-64. *Concurrent Pos:* Mem part-time fac, dept physics, Univ Ala, Huntsville. *Mem:* Am Phys Soc; AAAS; Sigma Xi. *Res:* Quantum statistical mechanics of superradiance; cooperative processes in matter-radiation field interactions; laser physics; correlation phenomena in partially coherent radiation fields; laser induced molecular excitation for subsequent chemical reactivity. *Mailing Add:* 716 Versailles Dr SE Huntsville AL 35803-1728

BOWDEN, CHARLES RONALD, ONCOLOGY. *Current Pos:* res fel endocrinol, 87-89, SECT HEAD ONCOL & ENDOCRINOL RES, JASSEN RES FOUND, 90- *Personal Data:* b Senford, Del, Dec 19, 49; m 76. *Educ:* Syracuse Univ, BS, 71; Univ Southern Calif, MS, 74, PhD(biomed eng), 78. *Prof Exp:* Res scientist endocrinol & metab res, McNeil Pharmaceut, 79-80, sr scientist, 80-85, group leader, 85-86, sect head, 86-87. *Concurrent Pos:* Vis scholar & NIH fel, Northwestern Univ, 78-79. *Mem:* Sigma Xi; Am Physiol Soc; Am Diabetes Asn. *Res:* Pharmacology and biochemical mechanism of novel-experimental cancer therapies; numerous publications. *Mailing Add:* Dept Oncol Res Janssen Res Found Welsh & McKean Rds Spring House PA 19477-0776

BOWDEN, DAVID CLARK, MATHEMATICAL STATISTICS, BIOMETRY. *Current Pos:* From instr to asst prof, 65-84, PROF STATIST, COLO STATE UNIV, 84- *Personal Data:* b Tekamah, Nebr, Nov 23, 40; m 60; c 3. *Educ:* Colo State Univ, BS, 62, MS, 65, PhD(statist), 68. *Concurrent Pos:* Consult, Colo Div Wildlife, 65-; dir statist workshops for fish & wildlife biologists, 65- *Res:* Simultaneous confidence bands for linear regression models; discrimination and confidence bands on percentiles; sample survey procedures with emphasis on techniques for fisheries and wildlife. *Mailing Add:* Dept Statist Colo State Univ Ft Collins CO 80523-0001

BOWDEN, DAVID MERLE, AGRICULTURAL RESEARCH ADMINISTRATION, ANIMAL NUTRITION. *Current Pos:* RETIRED. *Personal Data:* b Hedley, BC, Sept 2, 29; m 52; c 2. *Educ:* Univ BC, BSA, 52, MSA, 57; Ore State Univ, PhD(animal nutrit), 61. *Prof Exp:* Res scientist, Res Br, Agr Can, 52-67; animal prod officer, Food & Agr Orgn, UN, 67-69; res scientist animal nutrit, Res Sta, Summerland, BC, Agr Can, 69-80, prog specialist, Western Region Res Bur, 80-83, dir, Res Sta, Swift Current, Sask, 83-85, dir, 85-89; dep proj dir, Bard Proj, Pakistan, 89-91. *Mem:* Can Soc Animal Sci (pres, 65); Am Soc Animal Sci; Agr Inst Can. *Res:* Nutrition of the beef cow and calf; use of forage crops for ruminants; blood constituents as indicators of nutritional status in ruminants; swine nutrition. *Mailing Add:* 161 Southview Ct Kelowna BC V1V 1T6 Can

BOWDEN, DOUGLAS MCHOSE, NEUROPSYCHIATRY. *Current Pos:* from adj assoc prof to adj prof pharmacol, Med Sch, Univ Wash, 75-88, from asst dir to assoc dir, Regional Primate Res Ctr, 77-88, from asst prof to assoc prof psychiat, 69-79, dir, 88-94, CORE STAFF SCIENTIST, REGIONAL PRIMATE RES CTR, UNIV WASH, 69-, PROF PSYCHIAT & BEHAV SCI, SCH MED, 79- *Personal Data:* b Durham, NC, Apr 7, 37; m 66, Vivian L; c Carlos, Dana, Julie & Luis. *Educ:* Harvard Col, BA, 59; Stanford Univ Sch Med, MD, 65. *Prof Exp:* Exchange fel neurophsiol, Moscow State Univ, 61-62. *Concurrent Pos:* Res scientist develop award, Nat Inst Ment Health, 70-75; consult, Nat Libr Med Soviet Publ Transl, 73-85; consult, Nat Inst Aging Animal Models Aging Res, 76; subcomt chmn, Comt Animal Models Aging Res, Primate Subcomt, Nat Acad Sci, 78-79; consult ed, Am J Primatol, 80-; mem, Inst Lab Animal Resources, Nat Res Coun, 85-91; bd mem, Nat Asn Biomed Res, 92-95; mem, Nat Adv Comt, Am Med Prog, Inc, 92- *Mem:* Soc Neurosci; Am Soc Primatologists; Gerontol Soc. *Res:* Analysis of brain mechanisms of neuropsychiatric disorders such as psychosis, depression, dementia, and addiction to psychoactive drugs by application of behavioral, neurophysiological and pharmacological techniques in nonhuman primates; aging in nonhuman primates. *Mailing Add:* Regional Primate Res Box 357330 Univ Wash Seattle WA 98195. *Fax:* 206-685-0305; *E-Mail:* dmbowden@u.washington.edu

BOWDEN, DRUMMOND HYDE, PATHOLOGY. *Current Pos:* RETIRED. *Personal Data:* b Wales, Mar 10, 24; Can citizen; m 48; c 2. *Educ:* Bristol Univ, MB, ChB, 48, MD, 60. *Prof Exp:* Demonstr path, Bristol Univ, 51-52; asst pathologist, Hosp Sick Children, Toronto, 52-54, res assoc, 52-56; from asst prof to assoc prof, Sch Med, St Louis Univ, 56-64; from assoc prof to prof path, Univ Man, 64-91, head dept, 81-91, emer prof, 92. *Mem:* Am Asn Path; Int Acad Path; fel Royal Col Pathologists. *Res:* Pulmonary pathology, human and experimental. *Mailing Add:* Dept Path Rm 236 Univ Man Fac Med 770 Bannatyne Ave Winnipeg MB R3E 0W3 Can. *Fax:* 204-774-9018

BOWDEN, GEORGE TIMOTHY, ONCOLOGY, BIOCHEMISTRY. *Current Pos:* asst prof, 78-90, PROF RADIATION ONCOL, UNIV ARIZ, 90- *Personal Data:* b Cincinnati, Ohio, Dec 15, 45; m 66. *Educ:* Ohio Wesleyan Univ, BA, 67; Univ Wis, PhD(exp oncol), 74. *Prof Exp:* Staff fel chem carcinogenesis, Lab Exp Path, Nat Cancer Inst, 76-78. *Concurrent Pos:* Am Cancer Soc fel, Inst Biochem, Ger Cancer Res Ctr, Heidelberg, 74-76; dir grant proj heat & radiation cancer ther, USPHS, 78-81. *Mem:* Am Asn Cancer Res; Am Tissue Cult Soc; Environ Mutagen Soc. *Res:* The role of DNA damage and repair in mutagen, carcinogen, chemotherapeutic agent induced cytotoxicity, mutagenesis and malignant transformation of normal cells. *Mailing Add:* Dept Radiation Oncol Univ Ariz Health Sci Ctr 1501 N Campbell Ave Tucson AZ 85724

BOWDEN, JOE ALLEN, ANALYTICAL CHEMISTRY. *Current Pos:* PRES & DIR, CDS LABS, 80- *Personal Data:* b Dolores, Colo, July 13, 40; m 61; c 2. *Educ:* Adams State Col, BA, 63; Univ NDak, MS, 65, PhD(biochem), 68. *Prof Exp:* Res assoc lipoproteins, Univ Fla, 68-69, NIH fel, 69-71; asst prof biochem, La State Univ, Baton Rouge, 71-78. *Concurrent Pos:* Consult, Environ Protection Agency, 73-75; consult energy problems, 73- & hazardous materials, 78-81; mem, Solar Energy Steering Comt, La State Univ, 74-78. *Mem:* AAAS; Sigma Xi; Am Soc Biol Chemists; Am Sci Affil; Am Chem Soc. *Res:* Enzymology of metabolic diseases; environmental analysis problems; lipoprotein structure and function; biochemical aspects of mental retardation; solar energy and alternate energy sources; hazardous materials and acid rain. *Mailing Add:* CDS Labs PO Box 2605 Durango CO 81302-2605

BOWDEN, MURRAE JOHN STANLEY, POLYMER CHEMISTRY. *Current Pos:* div mgr, chem & mat sci res, 87-89, ASST VPRES, NETWORK SCI & TECHNOL RES, BELLCORE, 90- *Personal Data:* b Brisbane, Australia, Dec 15, 43; m 67; c 2. *Educ:* Univ Queensland, Australia, BSc, 64, 1st class hon, 65, PhD(polymer chem), 69. *Honors & Awards:* IR-100 Award, 77. *Prof Exp:* Mem tech staff polymer chem, 71-78, supvr, radiation sensitive mat appln, Bell Labs, 79-83, div mgr, appl chem res, Bellcore, 84-86. *Mem:* Am Chem Soc. *Res:* Effects of radiation on polymers and its application to resists for electron lithography; polymer coatings for optical fibers. *Mailing Add:* 42 Overhill Rd Summit NJ 07901

BOWDEN, ROBERT LEE, JR, MATHEMATICAL PHYSICS. *Current Pos:* ASSOC PROF PHYSICS, VA POLYTECH INST & STATE UNIV, 69- *Personal Data:* b Paris, Tenn, Apr 10, 33; m 68; c 2. *Educ:* Murray State Univ, AB, 55; Va Polytech Inst & State Univ, MS, 58, PhD(physics), 63. *Prof Exp:* Instr physics & math, Murray State Univ, 55-56; asst prof physics, Va Polytech Inst & State Univ, 63-68; vis assoc prof, Mid East Tech Univ, Turkey, 68-69. *Mem:* Am Nuclear Soc; Am Phys Soc. *Res:* Linear and nonlinear operator theory analysis arising in neutral particle transport. *Mailing Add:* Physics Va Polytech Inst & State Univ PO Box 0435 Blacksburg VA 24063-0001

BOWDEN, WARREN W(ILLIAM), CHEMICAL ENGINEERING. *Current Pos:* RETIRED. *Personal Data:* b South Penobscot, Maine, Nov 28, 25; m 53; c 3. *Educ:* Univ Maine, BS, 49; Rose Polytech Inst, MS, 59; Purdue Univ, PhD, 65. *Prof Exp:* Res engr, Res Dept, Com Solvents Corp, 49-54; specialist, US Army, 54-56; from instr to prof chem eng, Rose-Hulman Inst Technol, 56-90. *Mem:* Am Chem Soc; Am Inst Chem Engrs. *Res:* Heat transfer; mass transfer; thermodynamics of solutions. *Mailing Add:* 519 S Fifth St Terre Haute IN 47807-4307

BOWDISH, FRANK W(ILLIAM), MECHANICAL & CHEMICAL REFINING OF GLASS SAND. *Current Pos:* assoc prof & assoc mineral technologist, 62-69, prof chem eng & mineral technologist, 69-81, EMER PROF, MACKAY SCH MINES, UNIV NEV, RENO, 81- *Personal Data:* b Kalispell, Mont, June 5, 17; m 44, Virginia Jones; c Caroline C (Stewart), Harriet T (Vilman), Dana (Wheeler) & Keith F. *Educ:* Mont Sch Mines, BS, 39, MDrE, 55; Mass Inst Technol, SM, 43; Univ Kans, PhD(chem eng), 56. *Prof Exp:* Trainee, Caterpillar Tractor Co, 39-41; res engr, Mass Inst Technol, 43-46; asst metallurgist, Oliver Iron Mining Co, Minn, 46-47; asst prof mining & metall eng, Univ Kans, 48-54; engr, Iron Res Inst, IRSID, France, 56-58; sr chem engr, Colo Sch Mines Res Found, 59; prof metall eng, NMex Inst Mining & Technol, 59-62. *Concurrent Pos:* Consult, Owens-Corning Fiberglas Corp & Stewart Sand & Mats Co, 52-55, Arkhola Sand, Gravel Co, 60-71, Texasgulf, Inc, 75-77, Princeton Mining & Refining, 80-83, Dixie Exp Co & BRPM, Morocco, 81-82; process consult, L-BAR Prods Inc, 86-89. *Mem:* Am Inst Mining, Metall & Petrol Engrs. *Res:* Kinetics of grinding in a ball mill; refining of feldspathic sands for use in glass making; ion exchange in clays; flotation of chrysocolla; beneficiation of iron ores; 05386214Xn of metals and minerals. *Mailing Add:* 1531 N 16th Ave Pasco WA 99301-3535

BOWDLER, ANTHONY JOHN, HEMATOLOGY, ONCOLOGY. *Current Pos:* prof med, 80-97, EMER PROF MED, SCH MED, MARSHALL UNIV, 97- *Personal Data:* b London, Eng, Oct 16, 28; US citizen; m 55, Eleanor M Sladen; c Noelle C & Jonathan F. *Educ:* Univ London, BSc, 49, MB & BS, 52, MD, 63, PhD(hemat), 67; FRCP, 75, FACP, 79, FRCPath, 84. *Prof Exp:* House physician, Univ Col Hosp, London, 52-53, Hammersmith Hosp, London, 53 & Brompton Hosp, 56; casualty med off, Univ Col Hosp, London, 56; sr house officer, Dorking Gen Hosp, Surrey, Eng, 57-58; med registr, Univ Col Hosp, 58-61; Bilton Pollard fel, Leslie Pierce Gould scholar, Univ Col Hosp Med Sch, 61-62; Buswell sr fel, Sch Med, Univ Rochester, 62-64; sr lectr & mem, Med Res Coun Group Study of Haemolytic Dis, Univ Col Hosp Med Sch, 64-67; assoc prof, Col Human Med, Mich State Univ, 67-71, prof, 71-80. *Concurrent Pos:* Surgeon-Lt, Royal Naval Vol Res, 53-55; Fulbright scholar, 62-64; hon consult, Univ Col Hosp, 67; vis prof, Dept Med, Sch Med & Dent, Univ Rochester, 74; co-prin, Gen Hemat Serv, Dept Med, Mich State Univ, 75-79; physician, Vet Admin Med Ctr, Huntington, WVa, 80- *Mem:* Med Res Soc; Am Fedn Clin Res; Am Soc Hemat; Cent Soc Clin Res; Am Soc Clin Oncol; Brit Med Asn. *Res:* Red cell physiology; myeloproliferative disorders; pathophysiology of the spleen; the physical properties of red cells and their variation with age; relationship of blood flow properties to stroke. *Mailing Add:* 2 Compton Ct Milton WV 25541-1135. *Fax:* 304-696-7297

BOWDON, EDWARD K(NIGHT), SR, COMPUTER SCIENCE & ELECTRICAL ENGINEERING, TECHNICAL MANAGEMENT. *Current Pos:* sr software systs engr, 94-96, SR SYSTS ENGR, DSC COMMUN CORP, 96- *Personal Data:* b Kansas City, Mo, July 24, 35; m 81, Mahlona Tolleson; c Mary E, Mary C & Edward K Jr. *Educ:* Kans State Univ, BS, 56; Univ NDak, MS, 60; Univ Iowa, PhD(elec eng), 69; Christian Int MABS, 93. *Prof Exp:* Field engr, Western Elec Co, 56-59; asst, Univ NDak, 59-60; develop engr, Minneapolis Honeywell Co, 60-62; design engr, Collins Radio Co, 62-67, mem tech staff comput systs, 67-69; asst prof comput sci, Univ Ill, Urbana-Champaign, 69-76; assoc prof elec eng, Univ Ark, Fayetteville, 86-81; mgr test technol, 3M Co, 81-83; assoc prof eng tech, Col Sta, Tex A&M, 83-85; systs engr, ABC Co, Tex, 85-87; software eng mr, Electrocom Automation, Tex, 87-89; systs eng staff, Rockwell Int, 89-91; systs staff, Alcatel Network Systs, 91-93; software systs div mgr, Electro-Space Inc, 93-94. *Concurrent Pos:* Consult, Automation Technol Inc, 70-74; Nat Res Coun travel grant, 71; prin investr, NSF, 71-81. *Mem:* Inst Elec & Electronics Engrs. *Res:* Computer systems analysis, modeling and analysis of network computers employing queueing theory, scheduling theory and other operations research techniques, with emphasis on improving computer throughput; digital network design aids. *Mailing Add:* 3204 Osceola Dr Plano TX 75074

BOWE, JOSEPH CHARLES, PHYSICS. *Current Pos:* RETIRED. *Personal Data:* b Chicago, Ill, Sept 17, 21; m 53, Alice Gordon; c Mary, Joseph, Anne, Alice, John & James. *Educ:* St Procopius Col, AB, 43; DePaul Univ, MS, 46; Univ Ill, PhD(physics), 51. *Prof Exp:* Instr physics, DePaul Univ, 43-44; jr physicist, Metall Lab, Univ Chicago, 44-46; asst physics, Univ Ill, 46-51; assoc physicist, Argonne Nat Lab, 51-67; teacher physics, Benedictine Col, 67-88. *Res:* Electron mobility in gases; low energy electron-atom interactions; electronic instrumentation. *Mailing Add:* 4911 Elm St Downers Grove IL 60515

BOWE, ROBERT LOOBY, PSYCHOPHARMACOLOGY, PSYCHOPHYSIOLOGY. *Current Pos:* asst prof, 64-71, ASSOC PROF PHARMACOL, MED COL VA, 71- *Personal Data:* b Worcester, Mass, Jan 25, 25; m 57; c 4. *Educ:* Boston Col, BS, 50, MS, 57; Univ Tenn, PhD(clin physiol), 60. *Prof Exp:* Instr, New Prep Sch, Mass, 52-56; asst physiol, Boston Col, 56-57; assoc pharmacol, Med Col SC, 60-61, asst prof pharmacol & therapeut, 61-64. *Concurrent Pos:* Vis prof, Columbia State Hosp, 61-64. *Mem:* AAAS. *Res:* Central nervous system; autonomic nervous system; cardiovascular and renal physiology, pathophysiology, and pharmacology; general pathophysiology and clinical physiology; psychophysiology and pathophysiology; drug abuse. *Mailing Add:* 11305 Wimberly Dr Richmond VA 23233

BOWEN, CHARLES E, BIOCHEMISTRY. *Current Pos:* Asst prof, 69-74, assoc prof, 74-80, PROF CHEM, CALIF STATE POLYTECH COL, KELLOGG-VOORHIS, 80- *Personal Data:* b St Louis, Mo, Apr 9, 36; c 1. *Educ:* San Jose State Col, AB, 59, BS, 63, MS, 65; Univ Calif, Davis, PhD(biochem), 69. *Mem:* Sigma Xi; Conchologists Am. *Res:* Protein chemistry; enzyme mechanisms; marine biochemistry of invertebrates. *Mailing Add:* Dept Chem Calif State Polytech Univ Pomona CA 91768

BOWEN, DANIEL EDWARD, ECOLOGY, POPULATION BIOLOGY. *Current Pos:* From asst prof to assoc prof, 76-88, PROF BIOL, BENEDICTINE COL, 88-, CHMN DEPT, 82- *Personal Data:* b Morris, Minn, July 4, 44; m 67; c 2. *Educ:* Rockhurst Col, BA, 66; Kans State Univ, MS, 71, PhD(biol), 76. *Mem:* Ecol Soc Am; Am Ornithologists Union; Wildlife Soc; Am Soc Zoologists; Am Inst Biol Sci. *Res:* Regulation of prairie bird populations that live in seasonal environments; winter behavior of snowgeese, bald eagles and non game birds. *Mailing Add:* Dept Biol Benedictine Col Atchison KS 66002-1499

BOWEN, DAVID HYWEL MICHAEL, CHEMISTRY, CHEMICAL ENGINEERING. *Current Pos:* from asst ed to managing ed, Am Chem Soc, 67-72, head journals dept, 73-75, dir, Mem Div, 88-93, DEP EXEC DIR & SECY, AM CHEM SOC, 94- *Personal Data:* b Gorseinon, Wales, July 1, 39; m 67, Joy Spartin; c Jennifer & Philip. *Educ:* Univ Birmingham, BSc, 60, PhD(chem eng), 63. *Prof Exp:* Res engr, Eng Res Div, E I du Pont de Nemours & Co, Inc, 63-67. *Mem:* Am Chem Soc; Am Inst Chem Eng; AAAS. *Res:* Technical communication; information science; program administration. *Mailing Add:* Am Chem Soc 1155 16th St NW Washington DC 20036. *Fax:* 202-872-6338; *E-Mail:* m_bowen@acs.org

BOWEN, DONALD EDGAR, SOLID STATE PHYSICS. *Current Pos:* VPRES ACAD AFFAIRS, SOUTHWEST MO UNIV, 85- *Personal Data:* b Brooklyn, NY, Apr 10, 39; m 79; c 3. *Educ:* Tex Christian Univ, BA, 61, MA, 63; Univ Tex, PhD(physics), 66. *Prof Exp:* Res assoc high pressure physics, Gen Dynamics/Ft Worth, 62-63; asst, Univ Tex, El Paso, 63-66, from asst prof to assoc prof physics, 66-81, chmn dept, 71-81, asst vpres acad affairs, 81-85. *Concurrent Pos:* Res Corp Cottrell grant, 67; R A Welch Found grant, 68-71; NSF grant, 77-81. *Mem:* Inst Elec & Electronics Engrs; Sigma Xi; AAAS; Am Asn Physics Teachers; Am Phys Soc. *Res:* Properties of metal-ammonia solutions and the investigations of the acoustical properties of these solutions. *Mailing Add:* Dept Physics & Astron Stephen F Austin State Univ Box 13044 1936 North St Nacogdoches TX 75962

BOWEN, DONNELL, TRANSPORT, PHARMACOKINETICS. *Current Pos:* ASST PROF, DEPT PHARMACOL, HOWARD UNIV, 79- *Educ:* Univ NC, PhD(pharmacol), 75. *Mailing Add:* Dept Pharmacol Howard Univ 520 W St NW Washington DC 20001-2337. *Fax:* 202-806-7934

BOWEN, GEORGE HAMILTON, JR, VARIABLE STARS, STELLAR EVOLUTION. *Current Pos:* from asst prof to prof, 54-92, EMER PROF ASTROPHYS, IOWA STATE UNIV, 93- *Personal Data:* b Tulsa, Okla, June 20, 25; m 48, Marjorie Brown; c Paul, Margaret, Carol, Dorothy & Kevin. *Educ:* Calif Inst Technol, BS, 49, PhD(biophys), 53. *Prof Exp:* Assoc biologist, Oak Ridge Nat Lab, 52-54. *Mem:* AAAS; Am Astron Soc; Astron Soc Pac; Sigma Xi; Int Astron Union. *Res:* Long-period variable stars; atmospheric structure and dynamics; mass loss mechanisms; evolution; stellar pulsation; solar system formation and evolution. *Mailing Add:* Dept Physics & Astron Iowa State Univ Ames IA 50011-3160

BOWEN, H KENT, TECHNOLOGY TRANSFER. *Current Pos:* FAC, HARVARD BUS SCH, 93- *Personal Data:* b Nov 21, 41; m; c 5. *Educ:* Univ Utah, BS, 67; Mass Inst Technol, PhD, 71. *Honors & Awards:* R M Fulrath Award; F H Norton Award; Schwartzwalder-PACE Award; Ross Coffin Purdy Award; Robert Browning Sosman Award; Gordon Y Billard Award, Mass Inst Technol, Henry B Kane '24 Award. *Prof Exp:* Staff, Dept Mat Sci & Eng, Mass Inst Technol, 70-76, prof, 76-81, dir, Mat Processing Ctr, Ford prof eng, 81-93, dir leaders for mfr, 88-93. *Mem:* Nat Acad Eng; AAAS. *Res:* Materials developments; technology transfer; published numerous articles in various journals. *Mailing Add:* 178 Cross St Belmont MA 02178. *Fax:* 617-496-4072

BOWEN, HENRY DITTIMUS, AGRICULTURAL ENGINEERING. *Current Pos:* RETIRED. *Personal Data:* b Bear Lake, Mich, Oct 16, 21; m 48; c 2. *Educ:* Mich State Univ, BS, 49, MS, 51, PhD(agr eng), 53. *Prof Exp:* Asst instr agr eng, Mich State Univ, 52-53; res assoc prof, NC State Univ, Raleigh, 53-60, prof agr eng, 60- *Mem:* Am Soc Agr Engrs; Sigma Xi. *Res:* Cotton planting; application of electrostatics and servomechanisms to farm mechanization problems. *Mailing Add:* 2200 W Charlotte Ct Raleigh NC 27607

BOWEN, J HARTLEY, JR, CHEMICAL ENGINEERING. *Current Pos:* ENG CONSULT, 72- *Personal Data:* b Camden, NJ, Dec 26, 14; m 43, Evelyn Cross; c J Hartley III. *Educ:* Drexel Inst Technol, BS, 38. *Prof Exp:* Chief chemist, Nat Tube & Spool Co, Philadelphia, 38-39; jr mat engr, Naval Aircraft Factory, Philadelphia, 39-41, asst mat engr, 41-43, assoc chemist in charge chem testing & develop, 43, chemist, 43-45; sr chemist, Naval Air Exp Sta, 45-47, head chem eng div, 47-50, head high polymer div, 50-59, tech dir, Aero Mat Lab, Naval Air Eng Ctr, 59-67 & Naval Air Develop Ctr, 67-72. *Mem:* Am Chem Soc; Am Soc Testing & Mat; Am Inst Chemists; Sigma Xi. *Res:* Development of special finishes; gloss measurement of camouflage lacquer; methods of packaging of aircraft and parts with emphasis on silica gel for dehumidification; engineering applications of high polymer materials; nuclear radiation effects; research on materials for aerospace and hydrospace. *Mailing Add:* 226 Avondale Ave Haddonfield NJ 08033-2625

BOWEN, J(EWELL) RAY, CHEMICAL ENGINEERING. *Current Pos:* DEAN COL ENG & PROF CHEM ENG, UNIV WASH, SEATTLE, 81- *Personal Data:* b Duck Hill, Miss, Jan 9, 34; m 56; c 3. *Educ:* Mass Inst Technol, BS, 56, MS, 57; Univ Calif, Berkeley, PhD(chem eng), 63. *Prof Exp:* From asst prof to prof chem eng, Univ Wis-Madison, 63-81, assoc vchancellor, 70-75, chmn dept, 71-73 & 78-81. *Concurrent Pos:* NATO-NSF fel, Cambridge Univ, 62-63, NATO sr fel, Univ London, 68; Richard Merton prof, DF6, Univ Karlsruhe, 76-77. *Mem:* Combustion I; Am Phys Soc; Am Inst Chem Engrs; Am Soc Eng Educ. *Res:* Boundary layer techniques applied to heat and mass transfer; flows involving shock and detonation waves and chemical lasers. *Mailing Add:* Off of the Dean Univ Wash Col Eng FH10 PO 3922415 369 Loew Hall Seattle WA 98195

BOWEN, JAMES MILTON, virology, immunology, for more information see previous edition

BOWEN, JOHN METCALF, TOXICOLOGY, CELL CULTURE. *Current Pos:* assoc prof, 63-69, PROF PHARMACOL, COL VET MED, UNIV GA, 69-, DIR VET MED EXP STA & ASSOC DEAN RES & GRAD AFFAIRS, 76- *Personal Data:* b Quincy, Mass, Mar 23, 33; m 56; c 2. *Educ:* Univ Ga, DVM, 57; Cornell Univ, PhD(physiol), 60. *Prof Exp:* From asst prof to assoc prof physiol, Kans State Univ, 60-63; fel pharmacol, Emory Univ, 63. *Mem:* Soc Neurosci; Am Soc Pharmacol & Exp Therapeut; Am Vet Med Asn; Am Soc Vet Physiol & Pharmacol. *Res:* Development of in vitro excitable cell culture systems for evaluation of mechanisms of pharmacologic effects; toxicologic effects particulary of chemicals accumulating in the environment. *Mailing Add:* Col Vet Med Univ Ga Ag Dr Athens GA 30602-7371

BOWEN, KENNETH ALAN, mathematical logic, for more information see previous edition

BOWEN, KIRA L, ECOLOGICAL EPIDEMIOLOGY, CROP LOSSES. *Current Pos:* ASSOC PROF PLANT PATH, AUBURN UNIV, 88- *Personal Data:* b Scranton, Pa, Oct 10, 58. *Educ:* Pa State Univ, BS, 80; Univ Minn, MS, 83, Univ Ill, PhD(plant path), 87. *Prof Exp:* Res affil, NC State Univ, 87-88. *Concurrent Pos:* Chair, Plant Dis Losses Comt, Am Phytopath Soc, 89-90; assoc ed, Phytopath, 90-93; co-chair, Auburn Women's Caucus, 94-95, chair, 96-97. *Mem:* Am Phytopath Soc; Am Peanut Res & Educ Soc; Nat Asn Cols & Teachers Agr; Nat Peanut Coun. *Res:* Minimizing the risk of aflatoxin contamination in peanut through appropriate crop management; management of diseases of plants in the urban landscape. *Mailing Add:* 209 Rouse Life Sci Bldg Auburn AL 36849. *Fax:* 334-844-1947; *E-Mail:* kbowen@acesag.auburn.edu

BOWEN, KIT HANSEL, PHYSICAL CHEMISTRY. *Current Pos:* PROF CHEM, JOHNS HOPKINS UNIV. *Personal Data:* b Grenada, Miss, July 23, 48; m 76; c 1. *Educ:* Univ Miss, BS, 70; Harvard Univ, PhD, 77. *Prof Exp:* Fel, Harvard Univ, 78-80. *Concurrent Pos:* NSF fel, 78. *Mem:* Am Chem Soc; Am Phys Soc. *Res:* Negative ion photoelectron spectroscopy to study gas phase negatively-charged cluster ions. *Mailing Add:* Johns Hopkins Univ Remsen Hall 34th & N Charles St Baltimore MD 21218

BOWEN, LAWRENCE HOFFMAN, PHYSICAL CHEMISTRY. *Current Pos:* from asst prof to assoc prof, 61-70, PROF CHEM, NC STATE UNIV, 70- *Personal Data:* b Lynchburg, Va, Dec 20, 34. *Educ:* Va Mil Inst, BS, 56; Mass Inst Technol, PhD(phys chem), 61. *Honors & Awards:* Res Award, Sigma Xi, 70. *Prof Exp:* Asst chem, Mass Inst Technol, 56-58 & nuclear chem, 60-61. *Concurrent Pos:* Fac res grant tracer chem, 62-63; US AEC nuclear teaching grant, 67; NSF res grant Mossbauer spectros, 68-75, 82-88; vis res prof, Univ Gent, Belg, 87, 89, 92 & 94. *Mem:* Am Chem Soc; Clay Minerals Soc; Sigma Xi. *Res:* Mossbauer spectroscopy structure and bonding in iron oxides and related compounds; nuclear and radiochemistry applied to physicochemical problems; thermodynamics in solutions and solids. *Mailing Add:* Dept Chem NC State Univ Raleigh NC 27695-8204. *Fax:* 919-515-5079

BOWEN, PAUL TYNER, PHYSICOCHEMICAL WASTE WATER TREATMENT PROCESSES. *Current Pos:* ASST PROF CIVIL ENG, UNIV OKLA, 82- *Personal Data:* b Macon, Ga; m 80; c 2. *Educ:* Mercer Univ, BS,75; Clemson Univ, MS, 76; PhD(environ syst eng), 82. *Mem:* Am Soc Civil Engrs; Int Asn on Water Pollution Res & Control; Water Pollution Fedn; Am Water Works Asn; Am Chem Soc; Asn Environ Eng Prof. *Res:* Application of physicochemical water and wastewater treatment processes to sludge treatment and handling; removal of algal by-products from water; remediation of industrial wastes. *Mailing Add:* Metcalf & Eddy 1201 Peachtree St NE 400 Colony Sq Suite 1101 Atlanta GA 30361

BOWEN, RAFAEL LEE, DENTISTRY, POLYMER CHEMISTRY. *Current Pos:* RETIRED. *Personal Data:* b Takoma Park, Md, Dec 27, 25; m 58; c 2. *Educ:* Univ Southern Calif, DDS, 53. *Hon Degrees:* DSc, Georgetown Univ, 87. *Honors & Awards:* Hollenback Mem Prize, Acad Oper Dent, 81; Mitch Nakayama Mem Award, Japanese Sect, Pierce Fauchard Acad, 84; Wilmer Souder Award, Dent Mat Group, Int Asn Dent Res. *Prof Exp:* Pvt pract dent, San Diego, 53-55; res assoc, Am Dent Asn Res Unt, 56-70, assoc dir, 70-82; dir, Paffenbarber Res Ctr, Nat Bur Stand, 83-93. *Mem:* Am Dent Asn; Int Asn Dent Res; Sigma Xi. *Res:* Dental therapeutic materials and prevention of oral diseases; insoluble direct filling material approximating the properties and appearance of the anterior teeth; physical measurements; adhesion of dentin and enamel to dental composite restorations; glass ceramic inserts for dental composite restorations; protective tooth coatings; tooth desensitization. *Mailing Add:* Am Dent Asn Nat Inst Stand & Technol Gaithersburg MD 20899

BOWEN, RAY M, MECHANICS, APPLIED MATHEMATICS. *Current Pos:* PRES, TEX A&M UNIV, 94- *Personal Data:* b Ft Worth, Tex, Mar 30, 36; m 58; c 2. *Educ:* Tex A&M Univ, BS, 58, PhD(eng), 61; Calif Inst Technol, MS, 59. *Prof Exp:* Asst prof aeronaut eng, USAF Inst Technol, 61-64; res fel mech, Johns Hopkins Univ, 64-65; assoc prof eng mech, La State Univ, 65-67; from asst prof to prof mech, Rice Univ, 67-83, chmn dept, 72-77; dean eng, Univ Ky, 83-89, prof mech, 83-91; int pres, Okla State Univ, 93-94. *Concurrent Pos:* Dep Asst Dir Eng, NSF, 90- *Mem:* Soc Natural Philos; fel Am Soc Mech Engrs; Am Soc Eng Educ. *Res:* Nonlinear continuum mechanics. *Mailing Add:* Tex A&M Univ College Station TX 77843-1246

BOWEN, RICHARD ELI, PARASITOLOGY. *Current Pos:* RETIRED. *Personal Data:* b Oskaloosa, Kans, Sept 27, 32; m 55; c 2. *Educ:* Univ Kans, BA, 54; Kans State Univ, MS, 60, DVM, 61; Univ Mass, PhD(microbiol), 65. *Prof Exp:* Instr vet sci, Univ Mass, 61-65; sr bacteriologist, Vet Res Div, Eli Lilly & Co, 65-75, dept head, parasitol res, 75-93. *Mem:* Am Vet Med Asn; Am Soc Microbiol; Am Asn Avian Path; Wildlife Dis Asn; Indust Vet Asn; Sigma Xi. *Res:* Avian leukosis; avian respiratory diseases; bacterial diseases of swine and wildlife; disinfectants; general diagnostic bacteriology. *Mailing Add:* 5214 S State Rd 9 Greenfield IN 46140

BOWEN, RICHARD LEE, PHYSICAL GEOLOGY. *Current Pos:* assoc prof, 64-68, chmn dept, 68-74, PROF GEOL, UNIV SOUTHERN MISS, 68- *Personal Data:* b Bunn, NC, July 2, 29; m 57; c 3. *Educ:* Univ NC, AB, 49; Ind Univ, MA, 51; Univ Melbourne, PhD(geol), 60. *Prof Exp:* Teaching fel, Ind Univ, 50; geologist, US Geol Surv, 51; geologist-geophysicist, Standard

Oil Co Calif, 52-54; consult, Am Overseas Petrol Corp, 57 & petrol explor, Gulf Oil Corp, Africa, 59-61; US Agency Int Develop vis prof, Univ Rio Grande do Sul, Brazil, 62-64. *Concurrent Pos:* NATO sci conf grants, 68 & 70; instnl rep Gulf Univs Res Corp & mem sci panel. *Mem:* AAAS; Am Asn Petrol Geol; Am Geol Soc; Geophys Union; Am Inst Urban & Regional Affairs; Sigma Xi. *Res:* Petroleum and glacial geology; paleoclimatology; stratigraphy; sedimentology; Gondwana studies; oceanic geochemistry; continental margin tectonics; material balances in geology. *Mailing Add:* Univ Southern Miss Box 8152 Hattiesburg MS 39406-8152

BOWEN, RUTH JUSTICE, INORGANIC CHEMISTRY, CHEMICAL EDUCATION. *Current Pos:* From asst prof inorg chem to assoc prof chem 68-78, PROF CHEM, CALIF STATE POLYTECH UNIV, POMONA, 78- *Personal Data:* b Parkersburg, WVa, Jan 11, 42; m 72; c 1. *Educ:* Glenville State Col, BA, 63; WVa Univ, PhD(chem), 68. *Mem:* Am Chem Soc; Nat Asn Sci Teachers. *Res:* Chemical education. *Mailing Add:* Dept Chem Calif State Polytech Univ 3801 W Temple Ave Pomona CA 91768-2557

BOWEN, SAMUEL PHILIP, THEORETICAL PHYSICS, CONDENSED MATTER PHYSICS. *Current Pos:* PROG LEADER, DIV EDUC PROGS, ARGONNE NAT LAB, 89- *Personal Data:* b Council Bluffs, Iowa, Oct 12, 39; m 62; c 1. *Educ:* Iowa State Univ, BS, 62; Cornell Univ, PhD(physics), 67. *Prof Exp:* Res physicist, Univ Calif, Berkeley, 67-69; asst prof, Univ Wis, Madison, 69-74; assoc prof physics & asst dir, Va Ctr Coal & Energy, Va Polytech Inst & State Univ, 75-88, prof physics, 89. *Concurrent Pos:* Res adminr, Energy Exten, Va Coop Exten Serv; asst prof physics, Univ Wis-Madison, Admin off campus grad prog. *Mem:* AAAS; Am Phys Soc. *Res:* Dilute magnetic alloys; field theory; biophysics; solid state physics; energy conversion processes; energy conservation technologies; passive solar heating; economic analysis of energy problems; statistical properties of epilepsy. *Mailing Add:* Div Educ Progs Argonne Nat Lab 9700 S Cass Ave Argonne IL 60439. *Fax:* 630-252-3193; *E-Mail:* bowen@dep.anl.gov

BOWEN, SARANE THOMPSON, GENETICS. *Current Pos:* from instr to asst prof, 56-62, assoc prof, 63-68, PROF BIOL, SAN FRANCISCO STATE UNIV, 69- *Personal Data:* b Des Moines, Iowa, Dec 11, 27; m 54. *Educ:* Iowa State Univ, BS, 48, MS, 51, PhD(genetics, physiol), 52. *Prof Exp:* Instr biol, San Francisco Col Women, 53-54. *Mem:* Genetics Soc Am; Am Soc Human Genetics; fel AAAS. *Res:* physiological ecology; genetics of Artemia. *Mailing Add:* Dept Biol San Francisco State Col San Francisco CA 94132

BOWEN, SCOTT MICHAEL, WASTE REMEDIATION. *Current Pos:* res asst, 78, STAFF MEM CHEM, LOS ALAMOS NAT LAB, 85- *Personal Data:* b Santa Fe, NMex, Dec 7, 56. *Educ:* Univ NMex, BS, 78, MS, 81, PhD(chem), 83. *Prof Exp:* Teaching asst chem, Univ NMex, 78-79, res asst, 79-83; postdoctoral scientist chem, Idaho Nat Eng Lab, 83, scientist, 84-85. *Mem:* Am Chem Soc; AAAS. *Res:* Isolation and analysis of radioactive elements from soil and waste samples. *Mailing Add:* 1424 40th St Los Alamos NM 87544. *Fax:* 505-665-4955

BOWEN, STEPHEN HARTMAN, AQUATIC ECOLOGY, ICHTHYOLOGY. *Current Pos:* ASST PROF ZOOL, MICH TECHNOL UNIV, 78- *Personal Data:* b Ann Arbor, Mich, Jan 13, 49; m 73; c 1. *Educ:* DePauw Univ, BA, 71; Ind Univ, MA, 73; Rhodes Univ, PhD(zool), 76. *Prof Exp:* Partic, Lake Valencia Proj, Univ Colo, 76-78. *Concurrent Pos:* Consult fish ecol & cult, La Salle Found Natural Sci, Caracas, Venezuela, 77; consult subcontract environ assessment, Mich Technol Univ. *Mem:* Ecol Soc Am; AAAS; Am Fisheries Soc; Am Soc Naturalists. *Res:* Ecology of fishes with emphasis on trophic strategies, especially detritivory. *Mailing Add:* Dept Biol Sci Mich Technol Univ 1400 Townsend Dr Houghton MI 49931-1295

BOWEN, THEODORE, PHYSICS, MEDICAL PHYSICS. *Current Pos:* from assoc prof to prof physics, 62-75, PROF PHYSICS & RADIOLOGY, UNIV ARIZ, 76- *Personal Data:* b Evanston, Ill, Mar 19, 28; m 61; c 1. *Educ:* Univ Chicago, PhB, 47, SM, 50, PhD, 54. *Prof Exp:* From asst to assoc cosmic ray res, Univ Chicago, 53-55; res fel, Brazilian Centre Physics Res, 54-55; from res asst to res assoc physics, Princeton Univ, 56-62, res physicist, 62. *Concurrent Pos:* Nat Acad Sci sr res assoc, Goddard Space Flight Ctr, NASA, 68 & 78-79. *Mem:* Fel Am phys Soc; fel AAAS; NY Acad Sci; Sigma Xi. *Res:* Detector development; cosmic ray search for rare or hypothetical new particles; properties of hypernuclei; diagnostic ultrasound. *Mailing Add:* Dept Physics Univ Ariz Tucson AZ 85721

BOWEN, THOMAS EARLE, JR, PHYSIOLOGY, BIOPHYSICS. *Current Pos:* asst vchancellor, 72-79, ASSOC PROF PHYSIOL & COORDR EDUC RESOURCES, UNIV TENN CTR HEALTH SCI, 72-, VCHANCELLOR MGT SERV, 79- *Personal Data:* b Decatur, Ala, Oct 16, 38; c 2. *Educ:* Birmingham Southern Col, BS, 61; Univ Ala, cert med technol, 61, PhD(physiol), 68. *Prof Exp:* Chief technologist adult cardiac path lab, Med Col, Univ Ala, Birmingham, 61-63, chief physiol monitoring technologist, 63-65, from instr to assoc prof physiol, 67-72. *Concurrent Pos:* Porter Found vis lectr, Am Physiol Asn, 70-71. *Res:* Cardiovascular physiology; ventricular mechanics; cardiac muscle physiology; muscle mechanics. *Mailing Add:* Allied Health Prof Bldg Univ Ky 121 Washington Ave Lexington KY 40536-0003

BOWEN, VAUGHAN TABOR, geochemistry, oceanography, for more information see previous edition

BOWEN, WILLIAM DONALD, PINNIPED ECOLOGY. *Current Pos:* CHIEF, CAN DEPT FISHERIES & OCEANS, MARINE FISH DIV, BEDFORD INST OCEANOG, 84- *Personal Data:* b Oshawa, Ont, Sept 2, 48; Can citizen; m 70; c 2. *Educ:* Univ Guelph, Ont, BSc, 71, MSc, 73; Univ BC, PhD(ecol), 78. *Prof Exp:* Res scientist ecol, Can Dept Fisheries & Oceans, 78-84. *Mem:* Sigma Xi; Soc Marine Mammal. *Res:* Population dynamics of pinnipeds; ecological energetics of reproduction in seals; resource management of marine mammals and marine fishes including studies of competitive interactions between these groups. *Mailing Add:* Dept Marine Animals Bedford Inst Oceonog Dartmouth NS B2Y 4A2 Can

BOWEN, WILLIAM H, ORAL MICROBIOLOGY, IMMUNOLOGY. *Current Pos:* ACTG CHIEF CARIES PREV & RES BR, NAT CARIES PROG, NAT INST DENT RES, 73-; PROF DENT RES, SCH MED & DENT, UNIV ROCHESTER SCH MED. *Personal Data:* b Enniscorthy, Ireland, Dec 11, 33; m 58; c 5. *Educ:* Nat Univ Ireland, BDentSurg, 55; Univ Rochester, MSc, 59; Univ London, PhD(dent), 65; Univ Ireland, DSc(dent), 74; FFDRCSI, 65; FDSRCS, 74. *Hon Degrees:* DDSc, Univ Goteberg. *Honors & Awards:* Colgate-Palmolive Prize, Brit Div, Int Asn Dent Res, 63; Int Dent Fedn Prize, 64; John Tomes Prize, Royal Col Surgeons Eng, 66. *Prof Exp:* Pvt pract, 55-56; res fel dent, Eastman Dent Ctr, Rochester, NY, 56-59; Quinten Hogg fel, Royal Col Surgeons of Eng, 59-62, Nuffield Found fel, 62-65, sr res fel, 65-69, Sir Wilfred Fish fel, 69-73. *Concurrent Pos:* Lectr, Univ London, 70; mem sci coun, Europ Orgn Caries Res, 70-73; C L Roberts Mem lectr, Univ Sheffield, 71; guest lectr, Fac Dent, Univ Oslo, 71. *Mem:* Inst Med-Nat Acad Sci; Int Asn Dent Res; Am Asn Lab Animal Sci; Am Soc Zool; Int Dent Fedn; Europ Orgn Caries Res. *Res:* Microbiology and immunology of dental caries; prevention of dental disease; oral biology of primates. *Mailing Add:* Dent Med & Surg Univ Rochester Med Sch 601 Elmwood Ave Rochester NY 14642-0001

BOWEN, WILLIAM R, BOTANY, CELL BIOLOGY. *Current Pos:* PROF & HEAD BIOL DEPT, JACKSONVILLE STATE UNIV, AL, 90- *Personal Data:* b Iowa City, Iowa, Oct 15, 36; m 60, Janet A; c Jeffrey & Scott. *Educ:* Grinnell Col, BA, 60; Univ Iowa, MS & PhD(bot), 64. *Prof Exp:* Asst prof biol, Wis State Univ, Stevens Point, 64-65, Univ Ill, Chicago Circle, 65-66 & Western Ill Univ, 66-70; assoc prof, Ripon Col, 70-75; prof biol, Univ Ark, Little Rock, 75-90. *Concurrent Pos:* Res investr, Little Rock Vet Admin Med Ctr, 81-85; adj assoc prof path, Univ Ark Med Sci, 85- *Mem:* AAAS; Am Inst Biol Sci; Nat Asn Biol Teachers; Bot Soc Am; Phycol Soc Am; Electron Microscope Soc Am; Sigma Xi. *Res:* Developmental plant anatomy and ultrastructure of green algae; botanical teaching. *Mailing Add:* 1680 Church Ave SE Jacksonville AL 36265-3200

BOWEN, ZEDDIE PAUL, GEOLOGY, PALEONTOLOGY. *Current Pos:* DEAN, FAC ARTS & SCI, COL WILLIAM & MARY, 81- *Personal Data:* b Rockmart, Ga, Mar 29, 37; m 78; c 3. *Educ:* Johns Hopkins Univ, AB, 58; Harvard Univ, MA, 60, PhD(geol), 63. *Prof Exp:* From asst prof to prof geol, Univ Rochester, 62-76, chmn, dept geol sci, 74-76; provost, Beloit Col, 76-81. *Concurrent Pos:* NSF sci fac fel, 67-68. *Mem:* Geol Soc Am; Paleont Soc. *Res:* Invertebrate paleontology; evolution, paleoecology, paleobiogeography and taxonomy of the Brachiopoda; Silurian and Devonian biostratigraphy of eastern North America. *Mailing Add:* Provost/Dir Univ Richmond Richmond VA 23173

BOWER, AMY SUE, PHYSICAL OCEANOGRAPHY, LAGRANGIAN OBSERVATIONS. *Current Pos:* postdoctoral scholar, 88-89, postdoctoral investr, 89-90, ASST SCIENTIST, WOODS HOLE OCEANOG INST, 90- *Personal Data:* b Flemington, NJ, Nov 12, 59. *Educ:* Tufts Univ, BS, 81; Univ RI, PhD(oceanog), 88. *Prof Exp:* Res assoc, Univ RI, 88. *Mem:* Am Meteorol Soc; Am Geophys Union; Oceanog Soc. *Res:* Large-and meso-scale ocean circulation with emphasis on the structure and dynamics of western boundary currents and mixing processes at oceanic gyre boundaries. *Mailing Add:* Woods Hole Oceanog Inst Clark 315A Woods Hole MA 02543

BOWER, ANNETTE, NEUROENDOCRINOLOGY, HUMAN PHYSIOLOGY. *Current Pos:* Instr physiol, 67-69, from asst prof to assoc prof, 72-75, PROF BIOL SCI, MT ST MARY'S COL, CALIF, 78-, CHAIRPERSON DEPT, 72- *Personal Data:* b Rochester, NY, May 18, 33. *Educ:* Mt St Mary's Col, BS, 60; Creighton Univ, MS, 67; Univ Ariz, PhD(biol), 72. *Honors & Awards:* NSF grants. *Concurrent Pos:* Res assoc, Univ Ariz, 72-76; dir human serv prog, Mt St Mary's Col, 76-, dir NSF women in sci grant, 77-, dir NSF undergrad res grant, 78-; mem rep, Calif Allied Health Articulation Comt, 77-; Strengthing Developing Inst Prog grant, HEW; dir, NIH-MBRS at MSMC, 87. *Mem:* AAAS; Am Zool Soc; Intra-Sci Res Found; Nat Coun Aging; Am Geront Soc; Sigma Xi. *Res:* Investigation of the behavioral and neuropharmacological function of specific brain hormones in relation to osmoregulation and hypertension; the control of melanocyte stimulating hormone release and B-endorphin control. *Mailing Add:* Mt St Mary's Col 12001 Chalon Rd Los Angeles CA 90049

BOWER, CHARLES ARTHUR, SOIL CHEMISTRY. *Current Pos:* RETIRED. *Personal Data:* b Shawnee, Okla, Feb 17, 16; m 41, Mary De Bilt; c Chris A (Clements), Jennifer (Swift), Susan C (Ash) & Charles A III. *Educ:* Okla State Univ, BS, 36; Univ Wis, PhD(soils), 41. *Honors & Awards:* Soil Sci Achievement Award, Am Soc Agron, 59. *Prof Exp:* Soil scientist, US Soil Conserv Serv, 36-38; asst, Univ Wis, 38-41; chemist, NC State Dept Agr, 41-42; asst prof soils, Iowa State Col, 42-45; prin soil scientist, US Salinity Lab, 45-60, dir, 60-72; soil scientist, Univ Hawaii, 72-81. *Concurrent Pos:* Prof soil sci, Univ Calif, Riverside, 65-72; consult, 81- *Mem:* Soil Sci Soc Am; fel Am Soc Agron. *Res:* Chemistry of salt-affected and tropical soils; mineral nutrition of plants; cation exchange; water quality; agricultural development of arid and tropical lands. *Mailing Add:* 1036 B Willow Tree Dr Las Vegas NV 89128

BOWER, DAVID ROY EUGENE, FOREST BIOMETRY. *Current Pos:* FOREST BIOMETRICIAN, WEYERHAEUSER CO, 69- *Personal Data:* b Port Angeles, Wash, Sept 10, 34; m 55; c 4. *Educ:* Univ Idaho, BS, 58; Duke Univ, MF, 59. *Prof Exp:* Silviculturist, Southern Forest Exp Sta, US Forest Serv, 59-64, math statistician, 66-69. *Mem:* Soc Am Foresters. *Res:* Biologic models to describe growth of trees and stands; experimental designs for testing effects of silvicultural treatments, effects of measurement error and biological variability on growth estimation. *Mailing Add:* 1090 Rock Creek Rd Hot Springs AR 71913

BOWER, FRANK H(UGO), CHARGE-COUPLED DEVICE DEVELOPMENT PROGRAMS. *Current Pos:* RETIRED. *Personal Data:* b Rutherford, NJ, Oct 12, 21; m 47; c 2. *Educ:* Lehigh Univ, BSEE, 43. *Prof Exp:* Prod engr, Western Elec Co, Pa, 46-51, head dept prod eng semiconductor devices, 51-55, head dept automation develop, 55-56; chief prod engr, Motorola Semiconductor Prod Div, Ariz, 56-57, head dept res & develop, 57-59, prod line mgr, 59-60; mgr res & develop contracts & eng admin, Sylvania Semiconductor Div, Mass, 60-63, mgr integrated circuit prod, 62-63; mgr microelectronics mfg, Semiconductor Div, Raytheon Co, Calif, 63-64; microelectronics consult, 64-72; sr staff consult, Integrated Circuit Eng Corp, 67-72; pres, Integrated Technol Assocs, 70-72; mkt mgr, CCD Operation, 72-80, technol planning & admin mgr, Fairchild Semiconductor Div, 80-84, progs mkt mgr, Fairchild-Weston CCD Imaging Div, Advan Res & Develop Lab, 84-86. *Mem:* Sr mem Inst Elec & Electronics Engrs. *Res:* Development, characterization and mass production of semiconductor devices, integrated circuits and microelectronic systems; solid-state electronics. *Mailing Add:* 4256 Manuela Ave Palo Alto CA 94306

BOWER, GEORGE MYRON, ORGANIC POLYMER CHEMISTRY. *Current Pos:* RETIRED. *Personal Data:* b Arbuckle, Calif, May 26, 25; m 51; c 3. *Educ:* Ore State Univ, BS, 50; Univ Ore, MS, 54, PhD(chem), 57. *Prof Exp:* Sr res chemist, Westinghouse Res & Develop Ctr, 56-96. *Mem:* AAAS; Am Chem Soc. *Res:* Polyimides and other thermally stable polymers; composite technology; phenol-formaldehyde polymers and melamine formaldehyde polymers. *Mailing Add:* 2031 Sonny St Pittsburgh PA 15221

BOWER, J(OHN) R(OY), JR, CHEMICAL ENGINEERING, ORGANIC CHEMISTRY. *Current Pos:* RETIRED. *Personal Data:* b Helena, Mont, July 12, 15; m 42; c 3. *Educ:* Mont State Col, BS, 37; Univ Idaho, MS, 39; McGill Univ, PhD(chem), 43. *Prof Exp:* Sr res chemist, Am Cyanamid Co, 42-51, accountability dir, 51-53; accountability mgr, Phillips Petrol Co, 53-55, tech plant asst leader, 55-60, sr tech staff specialist, 60-66; sr tech staff specialist, Idaho Nuclear Corp, 66-71; sr tech staff specialist, Allied Chem corp, 71-81. *Mem:* AAAS; Am Chem Soc; Am Nuclear Soc; Am Inst Chem Engrs. *Res:* Radiochemical processing of spent reactor fuel; wood chemistry; high pressure; high temperature catalytic reactions; melamine; guanidines; cyanamide; cyanides; disposition and management of nuclear fuel processing wastes; nuclear fuel safeguards. *Mailing Add:* 2305 Calkins Idaho Falls ID 83402-4536

BOWER, NATHAN WAYNE, CHEMOMETRICS, ENVIRONMENTAL. *Current Pos:* PROF ANALYTICAL CHEM, COLO COL, 77-, CHAIR CHEM, 95- *Personal Data:* b USA, 51. *Educ:* Col Wooster, BA, 73; Ore State Univ, PhD(anal chem), 77. *Concurrent Pos:* Consult, Los Alamos Nat Lab, 83-93; vis scientist, Getty Conserv Inst, 91. *Mem:* Am Chem Soc; Soc Appl Spectroscopy; Sigma Xi. *Res:* Atomic spectroscopy and sampling statistics for analysis; precision of analysis and sampling precision in the archaeological, geochemical and environmental fields. *Mailing Add:* Dept Chem Colo Col Colorado Springs CO 80903. *Fax:* 719-389-6182

BOWER, RAYMOND KENNETH, MICROBIOLOGY, ANIMAL VIROLOGY. *Current Pos:* from asst prof to assoc prof, Dept Biol Sci, 68-92, EMER MEM FAC, UNIV ARK, FAYETTEVILLE, 92- *Personal Data:* b Kansas City, Mo, Oct 31, 27; m 59; c 2. *Educ:* Univ Mo-Kansas City, BA, 49; Kans State Univ, MS, 51, PhD(microbiol), 54. *Prof Exp:* Res fel pediat, Sch Med, Univ Kans, 54-55; USPHS fel microbiol, Sch Med, Univ Okla, 57-59; from instr to asst prof, Sch Med, Univ Ark, 59-63; asst prof, Grad Res Inst, Baylor Univ, 63-65, Col Dent & Grad Div, 65-68. *Concurrent Pos:* Consult microbiol, Div Pub Health Labs, Ark State Dept Pub Health, 75 & Vet Admin Hosp, 75-85. *Res:* Rous sarcoma virus-host cell relationships; genetic and immunologic interactions that underlie regression and immunity to Rous sarcoma virus-induced neoplasia in the chicken. *Mailing Add:* 1764 Applebury Pl Fayetteville AR 72701

BOWER, SUSAN MAE, PROTOZOOLOGY, SHELLFISH DISEASES. *Current Pos:* res fel, Natural Sci & Eng Res Coun, 81-83, res scientist biol Rhizocephalan parasites, 83-84, RES SCIENTIST SHELLFISH DIS, DEPT FISHERIES & OCEANS, CAN GOVT, 84- *Personal Data:* b Sioux Lookout, Ont, Nov 5, 51; m 96, Frank Chidley; c Stephen S. *Educ:* Univ Guelph, BSc, 74, MSc, 76, PhD(parasitol), 80. *Prof Exp:* Res assoc cellular immunol, Mich State Univ, 80-81. *Concurrent Pos:* Res scientist cultured abalone dis, Pac Trident Mariculture Ltd, 83-84. *Mem:* Can Soc Zoologists; Nat Shellfisheries Asn; Aquacult Asn Can; Soc Invert Path. *Res:* Biology of parasites; etiology of diseases that are of concern to the fishery and mariculture of marine fish and shellfish on the west coast of Canada. *Mailing Add:* Pac Biol Sta Dept Fisheries & Oceans Nanaimo BC V9R 5K6 Can. *Fax:* 250-756-7053; *E-Mail:* bowers@pbs.dfo.ca

BOWER, WILLIAM WALTER, FLUID MECHANICS, AERODYNAMICS. *Current Pos:* Sr engr aircraft propulsion, McDonnell Aircraft Co, 71-74, SCIENTIST AERODYN, MCDONNELL DOUGLAS RES LABS, 74- *Personal Data:* b Hammond, Ind, Jan 9, 45. *Educ:* Purdue Univ, BS, 67, MS, 69, PhD(mech eng), 71. *Mem:* Am Inst Aeronaut & Astronaut; Am Soc Mech Engrs; Sigma Xi. *Res:* Computational fluid mechanics; the aerodynamics of vertical takeoff and landing aircraft. *Mailing Add:* McDonnell Douglas Aerospace East PO Box 516 St Louis MO 63166-0516

BOWERFIND, EDGAR SIHLER, JR, INTERNAL MEDICINE. *Current Pos:* RETIRED. *Personal Data:* b Cleveland, Ohio, May 7, 24; m 56; c 4. *Educ:* Western Reserve Univ, MD, 49; Am Bd Internal Med, dipl, 58. *Prof Exp:* From intern to resident, Univ Hosps Cleveland, 50-56; demonstr, Case Western Res Univ, 56-58, from instr to sr instr, 58-65, asst prof med, Sch Med, 65-92. *Concurrent Pos:* Consult, Vet Admin Hosp, Cleveland, 56-; asst secy, Citizens Comn Grad Med Educ, 63-64, secy, 64-66. *Mem:* Am Med Soc Alcoholism & Other Drug Dependencies. *Res:* Clinical medical education; chemical dependency. *Mailing Add:* 2373 Demington Dr Cleveland OH 44106

BOWERING, JEAN, NUTRITION. *Current Pos:* PROF HUMAN NUTRIT, SYRACUSE UNIV, 77- *Personal Data:* b Yonkers, NY, Mar 16, 39; m 77, Emery Nordberg. *Educ:* Cornell Univ, BS, 60, MNS, 64; Univ Calif, Berkeley, PhD(nutrit), 69. *Prof Exp:* Res chemist, R T French Co, NY, 60-62; trainee, Inst Nutrit Cent Am & Panama, 64; res assoc nutrit, Cornell Univ, 64-66; instr dept pediat, Children's Hosp, DC & med sch, George Washington Univ, 69-70; asst prof human nutrit & foods, Cornell Univ, 70-77. *Mem:* Sigma Xi; Am Inst Nutrit; Soc Nutrit Educ; Am Dietetic Asn. *Res:* Dietary & nutritional status of humans. *Mailing Add:* Dept Nutrit & Food Mgt Syracuse Univ Slocum Hall Syracuse NY 13244-1250. *Fax:* 315-443-2562

BOWERMAN, EARL HARRY, HORTICULTURE, PLANT SCIENCE. *Current Pos:* ASST DEAN AGR & HOME ECON & PROF PLANT SCI, CALIF STATE UNIV, FRESNO, CALIF, 79- *Personal Data:* b El Dorado, Ark, Jan 18, 42; c 2. *Educ:* Univ Ark, BSA, 65, MS, 72; Rutgers Univ, PhD(hort), 75. *Prof Exp:* Assoc county exten agent, Ark Agr Exten Serv, 65-69; res asst, Univ Ark, 69-72 & Rutgers Univ, 72-75; asst prof hort, Tex A&M Univ, 75-79. *Mem:* Am Soc Hort Sci; Int Plant Propagators Soc; AAAS. *Res:* Plant reproductive histology. *Mailing Add:* Dept Plant Sci Calif State Univ 2415 E San Ramon Ave MS 72 Fresno CA 93740-8033. *Fax:* 209-278-7413; *E-Mail:* earlb@csufresno.edu

BOWERS, C(HARLES) EDWARD, CIVIL ENGINEERING, HYDRAULIC ENGINEERING. *Current Pos:* res assoc, St Anthony Falls Hydraul Lab, Univ Minn, Minneapolis, 51-59, from assoc prof to prof hydraul, Univ Minn, 59-76, prof civil eng, 76-90, EMER PROF CIVIL ENG, UNIV MINN, 90- *Personal Data:* b Hanna, Wyo, Sept 3, 19; m 46, Audrey Hanson; c 2. *Educ:* Univ Wyo, BS, 42; Univ Minn, MS, 49. *Honors & Awards:* Collingwood Award, Am Soc Civil Engrs, 50. *Prof Exp:* Hydraul engr, David Taylor Model Basin, US Dept Navy, 42-44; res fel, St Anthony Falls Hydraul Lab, Univ Minn, 48-49; hydraul engr, Bur Reclamation, Colo, 49-51. *Mem:* Fel Am Soc Civil Engrs; Am Soc Eng Educ; Int Asn Hydraul Res; Sigma Xi. *Res:* Hydrology; hydraulic engineering; storm runoff studies; spillways and related hydraulic structures. *Mailing Add:* 3385 N Oxford St Shoreview MN 55126-8137

BOWERS, CHAUNCEY WARNER, NEUROSCIENCE. *Current Pos:* ASST RES SCIENTIST & HEAD CELLULAR NEUROPHYSIOL SECT, DIV NEUROSCI, BECKMAN RES INST-CITY OF HOPE, DUARTE, CA, 89- *Personal Data:* b West Palm Beach, Fla, June 9, 53. *Educ:* Ga Inst Technol, BS, 75; Harvard Univ, PhD(pharmacol), 80. *Prof Exp:* Res fel, Dept Pharmacol, Harvard Med Sch, 80-82, Dept Physiol, Univ Calif, San Francisco, 82-85, Univ Conn, Storrs, 88-89; asst res physiologist, Univ Calif, San Francisco, 85-88. *Concurrent Pos:* Invited lectr, Stanford Univ, 84, 18th Annual Winter Conf Brain Res, 85, Univ Conn, 88, Univ Calif, 92, Univ Va, 93, XVIII Congress Mex Soc Cardio, 93. *Mem:* Am Bio-Cell Soc; Soc Neuroscience. *Res:* Neuroscience; author of 22 publications. *Mailing Add:* Div Neurosci Beckman Res Inst City Hope 1450 E Duarte Rd Duarte CA 91010-0269

BOWERS, DARL EUGENE, ZOOLOGY, ECOLOGY. *Current Pos:* PROF BIOL, MILLS COL, 54- *Personal Data:* b Fresno, Calif, Sept 23, 21; m 44; c 3. *Educ:* Univ Calif, Berkeley, AB, 48, MA, 52, PhD(zool), 54. *Concurrent Pos:* NSF grant, 61-66. *Mem:* AAAS; Ecol Soc Am; Am Inst Biol Soc; Sigma Xi. *Res:* Correlation of the distribution and characteristics of animal forms with environmental gradients and physical factor constellations; ornithological ecology; correlation of the distribution of amphipods with physical factors of beaches; salt marsh ecology. *Mailing Add:* 43 Vista Del Mar Ct Oakland CA 94611-2122

BOWERS, FRANK DANA, BRYOLOGY, PLANT TAXONOMY. *Current Pos:* asst prof, 75-80, assoc prof, 80-86, PROF BOT, UNIV WIS-STEVENS POINT, 86- *Personal Data:* b Fayetteville, Ark, Mar 21, 36; m 67, Donna Olsen. *Educ:* Southwest Mo State Univ, BS, 66; Univ Tenn, Knoxville, MS, 68, PhD(bot), 72. *Prof Exp:* Asst cur herbarium, Dept Bot, Univ Tenn, 68-72, fel, 72-74, res assoc, 74-75. *Mem:* Bryological & Lichenological Soc Am; Am Inst Biol Sci; Soc Econ Bot; Natural Areas Asn. *Res:* Moss flora of Mexico; mosses of Central America and Wisconsin; wildlife food plants; plant propagation; edible and poisonous plants. *Mailing Add:* Dept Biol Univ Wis Stevens Point WI 54481. *E-Mail:* fbowers@uwsp.edu

BOWERS, GEORGE HENRY, III, ORGANIC CHEMISTRY. *Current Pos:* RETIRED. *Personal Data:* b Philadelphia, Pa, Oct 16, 23; m 49; c 4. *Educ:* Washington & Lee Univ, BS, 44; Univ Pa, MS, 48, PhD(org chem), 51. *Prof Exp:* Asst instr chem, Univ Pa, 48-51; res chemist, E I du Pont de Nemours & Co, Inc, Chestnut Run, 51-74, res assoc, 74-85. *Mem:* Am Chem Soc; Sigma Xi; Inst Elec & Electronics Engrs. *Res:* Synthetic elastomers; high temperature organic reactions; synthetic thermo plastic; electrical insulation and systems. *Mailing Add:* 612 Foulkstone Rd Wilmington DE 19803

BOWERS, JAMES CLARK, COMPUTER AIDED DESIGN, ELECTRONIC ANALYSIS. *Current Pos:* PROF ELEC ENG, UNIV S FLA, 65- *Personal Data:* b South Bend, Ind, Feb 13, 34; m 56; c 3. *Educ:* Vanderbilt Univ, BE, 57; Univ Tenn, MS, 58; Wash Univ, ScD(automatic controls), 64. *Prof Exp:* Assoc res engr, Boeing Airplane Co, 58-59; dir eng tech staff, McDonnell Aircraft Corp, 59-65. *Concurrent Pos:* Staff consult, Honeywell, Inc, 65-73; sr consult, US Army, 72-, Am Vulcan Corp, 73-76, USAF, 76-, USN, 77- *Mem:* Inst Elec & Electronics Engrs. *Res:* Computer aided design and analysis--the applications and program development; solid-state modeling; electronics and control systems analysis. *Mailing Add:* PO Box 82215 Tampa FL 33682

BOWERS, JANE ANN (RAYMOND), FOOD SCIENCE. *Current Pos:* from asst prof to assoc prof, 67-74, actg head dept foods & nutrit, 75-76, PROF FOODS, KANS STATE UNIV, 74-, HEAD, DEPT FOODS & NUTRIT, 76- *Personal Data:* b Fredonia, Kans, Aug 19, 40; m 63; c Miriam R & Janel L. *Educ:* Kans State Univ, BS, 62, MS, 63, PhD(food, nutrit), 67. *Prof Exp:* Res assoc foods, Iowa State Univ, 63-64. *Mem:* Inst Food Technologists; Am Meat Sci Asn; Poultry Sci Asn; Coun Agr Sci & Technol; Am Home Econ Asn. *Res:* Chemical characteristics, nutrient and flavor stability in meat and poultry products and sensory analysis of food; over 70 research publications. *Mailing Add:* Foods Nutrit Justin Hall Kans State Univ Manhattan KS 66502. *Fax:* 785-532-3132

BOWERS, JOHN DALTON, AGRICULTURE. *Current Pos:* RETIRED. *Personal Data:* b West Unity, Ohio, July 15, 15; m 41; c 2. *Educ:* Ohio State Univ, BSc, 40. *Prof Exp:* Asst, Ohio State Univ, 40-42; lab dir, Borden, Morres & Ross, 42-43, supt milk dept, 46-47, lab dir, 47-51, lab dir qual control & res & develop, Mid-West Div, Borden Co, 51-70, dir prod develop, 70-72, dir qual control & res & develop, Northern Div, Borden, Inc, 72-80. *Concurrent Pos:* Mem bd dirs, Am Cultured Prod Inst, 67-70. *Mem:* Am Dairy Sci Asn. *Mailing Add:* 11327 Bob White Lane St Mary's OH 45885

BOWERS, JOHN E, APPLIED PHYSICS. *Current Pos:* PROF ELEC ENG, UNIV CALIF, SANTA BARBARA, 87- *Personal Data:* b St Paul, Minn, June 7, 54; m 77, Cynthia; c Eric & Steven. *Educ:* Univ Minn, BS, 76; Stanford Univ, MS, 78, PhD(appl physics), 81. *Honors & Awards:* Presidential Young Investr Award, NSF, 87; William Streifer Award, Lasers & Electro-Optics Soc, Inst Elec & Electronics Engrs, 96. *Prof Exp:* Scientist res, Honeywell Corp, Mat Sci Ctr, 77-78; res asst, Ginzton Lab, Stanford Univ, 76-81, res assoc, 81-82; mem tech staff, AT&T Bell Labs, 82-87. *Concurrent Pos:* NSF fel, 76; mem adv bd, Int Bd Optoelectronics, 87-92; guest ed, J Quantum Electronics, 89; bd dirs, Bach Camerata, 90-92; chmn, Subcomt on Semiconductor Lasers, Lasers & Electro-Optics Soc, 90-92, vpres conf, 97-; assoc dir, Optoelectronics Technol Ctr, 90-; distinguished lectr, Inst Elec & Electronics Engrs, 94. *Mem:* Fel Am Phys Soc; fel Inst Elec & Electronics Engrs; Optical Soc Am; Int Soc Optical Eng. *Res:* Ultra-fast optoelectronics, including high speed lasers, photodetectors and systems; fundamental limits to modulation and the femtosecond transport issues that limit the speed of response; granted 16 patents; author of 200 journal publications and five book chapters. *Mailing Add:* Dept Elec & Comput Eng Univ Calif Santa Barbara CA 93106. *Fax:* 805-893-7990; *E-Mail:* bowers@ece.dcsb.edu

BOWERS, KLAUS D, ELECTRONICS TECHNOLOGY. *Current Pos:* RETIRED. *Personal Data:* b Stettin, Ger, Dec 27, 29; nat US; m 64, Roswitha Rau; c Pamela & Colin. *Educ:* Oxford Univ, BA, 50, MA, 53, PhD(physics), 53. *Honors & Awards:* Frederik Philips Award, Inst Elec & Electronics Engrs, 89. *Prof Exp:* Res lectr, Christ Church, Oxford, 52-56; mem tech staff, Bell Labs, 56-59; various tech mgt positions, 59-71; managing dir component develop, Sandia Labs, 71-73, vpres components, 73-75; exec dir, AT&T Bell Labs, 75-79, vpres electronics technol, 79-90. *Mem:* Nat Acad Eng; fel Inst Elec & Electronics Engrs. *Res:* Quantum electronics; semiconductor devices and integrated circuits. *Mailing Add:* 2890 Golf Circle Emmaus PA 18049

BOWERS, LARRY DONALD, CLINICAL CHEMISTRY, TOXICOLOGY. *Current Pos:* PROF PATH & LAB MED, IND UNIV, 92-, PROF CHEM, IND UNIV, PURDUE UNIV INDIANAPOLIS, 92-, DIR, ATHLETIC DRUG TESTING & TOXICOL LAB, 92- *Personal Data:* b York, Pa, Nov 29, 50; m 73, Janet Pietruch; c Geoffrey & Kimberly. *Educ:* Franklin & Marshall Col, BA, 72; Univ Ga, PhD(anal chem), 75; Am Bd Clin Chem, dipl(clin chem & toxicol chem). *Honors & Awards:* L S Palmer Award in Chromatography. *Prof Exp:* Assoc fel, Univ Ore Health Sci Ctr, 75-77; from asst prof to prof clin chem, Univ Minn, 78-92. *Concurrent Pos:* Vis prof, Cornell Univ; dep dir, Doping Control Lab, Atlanta Olympic Games, 96. *Mem:* Am Chem Soc; Am Asn Clin Chem; Sigma Xi; Acad Clin Lab Physicians & Scientists; Am Soc Mass Spectrometry. *Res:* Application of high performance liquid chromatography to bioanalytical chemistry; toxicology; athletic drug testing; steroid metabolism, especially Phase II metabolism; peptide characterization by MS. *Mailing Add:* 3786 Power Dr Carmel IN 46033-4720. *Fax:* 317-274-3223; *E-Mail:* ibowers@iupui.edu

BOWERS, MARION DEANE, CHEMICAL ECOLOGY, INSECT ECOLOGY. *Current Pos:* ASSOC PROF BIOL & CUR ENTOM MUS, UNIV COLO, BOULDER, 89- *Personal Data:* b White Plains, NY, Mar 19, 52. *Educ:* Smith Col, BA, 74; Univ Mass, Amherst, PhD(zool), 79. *Prof Exp:* Asst, Stanford Univ, 79-81; asst prof biol, Harvard Univ, 81-86, assoc prof, 86-89. *Concurrent Pos:* Vis prof chem, Colo State Univ, 86-87. *Mem:* Ecol Soc Am; Entom Soc Am; Lepidopterists Soc; Soc Study Evolution; Chem Ecol Soc; Phytochem Soc. *Res:* Interactions of insects and their host plants, particularly the role of plant chemistry; predation on insect populations; larval foraging ecology; evolution of unpalatability. *Mailing Add:* 3140 24th St Boulder CO 80304. *Fax:* 303-492-8699; *E-Mail:* bowers@spot.colorado.edu

BOWERS, MARY BLAIR, STRUCTURE & FUNCTION. *Current Pos:* RETIRED. *Personal Data:* b Jackson, NC, Apr 2, 30. *Educ:* Duke Univ, AB, 52, MA, 55; Harvard Univ, PhD(biol), 61. *Prof Exp:* Instr biol, Harvard Univ, 63-65; res biologist, Nat Heart, Lung & Blood Inst, 69-95. *Concurrent Pos:* NIH fel, Harvard Univ, 61-63; staff fel, Nat Heart Inst, 66-69. *Mem:* Micros Soc Am (treas, 83-87; coun, 89-91); Histochem Soc (treas, 93-97); Am Soc Cell Biol; Soc Protozoologists. *Res:* Cell ultrastructure as related to membrane function, phagocytosis and cellular transport of macromolecules. *Mailing Add:* Rm B1-22 Bldg 3 NIH Bethesda MD 20892. *Fax:* 301-402-1519

BOWERS, MAYNARD C, BOTANY, BIOSYSTEMATICS. *Current Pos:* from asst prof to assoc prof, 66-75, actg head dept biol sci, 69-70, PROF BIOL, NORTHERN MICH UNIV, 75- *Personal Data:* b Battle Creek, Mich, Nov 5, 30; m 52, 70; c 4. *Educ:* Albion Col, AB, 56; Univ Va, MEd, 60; Univ Colo, PhD(bot), 66. *Prof Exp:* Teacher pub sch, Mich, 56-57 & Fla, 57-59; asst prof biol, Towson State Col, 60-62. *Concurrent Pos:* NSF Acad Year Inst, Univ Va, 59-60; researcher, Univ Turku, Finland, 75; Sigma Xi grant res; Peter White Scholar, N Mich Univ, 86-87; mem bd dir & regional dir, N Cent Region, Sigma Xi, 88-94. *Mem:* Am Bryol Soc; Am Inst Biol Sci; Bot Soc Am; Int Asn Plant Taxon. *Res:* Plant biosystematics; cytotaxonomy of bryophytes, especially the family Mniaceae; cytological effects of herbicides on non-target species; physiological effects of herbicides and their reversal using growth stimulators on non-target species. *Mailing Add:* Dept Biol Sci Northern Mich Univ Marquette MI 49855

BOWERS, MICHAEL THOMAS, CHEMICAL KINETICS, CHEMICAL PHYSICS. *Current Pos:* From asst prof to assoc prof, 68-76, PROF PHYS CHEM, UNIV CALIF, SANTA BARBARA, 76- *Personal Data:* b Moscow, Idaho, June 6, 39; m 64; c Molly, Sheila & Melissa. *Educ:* Gonzaga Univ, BS, 62; Univ Ill, Urbana, PhD(phys chem), 66. *Honors & Awards:* Nobel Laureate Signature Award, Am Chem Soc, 89. *Concurrent Pos:* Ed, Int J Mass Spectros & Ion Processes; ed, Int J Mass Spectrometry & Ion Processes, 86-; assoc ed, J Am Chem Soc, 89-; fac res lectr, Univ Calif, Santa Barbara, 94. *Mem:* Am Chem Soc; fel Am Phys Soc; Am Soc Mass Spectros; AAAS. *Res:* Gas phase ion chemistry; carbon and metal luster structure and chemistry; transition metal chemistry. *Mailing Add:* Dept Chem Univ Calif Santa Barbara CA 93106

BOWERS, PETER GEORGE, PHYSICAL CHEMISTRY. *Current Pos:* from asst prof to assoc prof, 68-79, chmn dept, 79-85, PROF CHEM, SIMMONS COL, 79- *Personal Data:* b Sussex, Eng, May 14, 37. *Educ:* Cambridge Univ, BA, 61; Univ BC, PhD(chem), 64. *Prof Exp:* NATO res fel, Univ Sheffield, 64-66; vis asst prof chem, Boston Univ, 67-68. *Concurrent Pos:* Vis assoc prof, Univ BC, 74-75, vis prof, Univ Ore, 82, 89, 93, 94 & 95. *Mem:* Am Chem Soc; Sigma Xi. *Res:* Reaction kinetics; self-organizing processes; bubble nucleation. *Mailing Add:* Dept Chem Simmons Col 300 Fenway Boston MA 02115

BOWERS, PHILLIP FREDERICK, radio astronomy, for more information see previous edition

BOWERS, ROBERT CHARLES, horticulture, plant science, for more information see previous edition

BOWERS, ROBERT CLARENCE, PHYSICS. *Current Pos:* RES PHYSICIST, NAVAL RES LAB, 50- *Personal Data:* b Cumberland, Md, Dec 22, 22; m 46; c 3. *Educ:* Univ Md, BS, 50. *Concurrent Pos:* Ed, ASLE Trans, Am Soc Lubrication Engrs, 77- *Mem:* Am Soc Lubrication Engrs; Sigma Xi; NY Acad Sci. *Res:* Friction; wear; lubrication; explosives; dielectrics. *Mailing Add:* 3705 Deming Dr Suitland MD 20746-2202

BOWERS, ROGER RAYMOND, DEVELOPMENTAL ANATOMY, VERTEBRATE ZOOLOGY. *Current Pos:* from asst prof to assoc prof, 72-80, PROF BIOL, CALIF STATE UNIV, LOS ANGELES, 80- *Personal Data:* b Augusta, Ga, Sept 15, 44; m 67; c 4. *Educ:* Creighton Univ, BS, 66; Univ Nebr-Lincoln, MS, 68, PhD(zool), 71. *Prof Exp:* Res asst zool, Univ Nebr-Lincoln, 70-71; asst prof, Southern Ill Univ, Carbondale, 71-72. *Concurrent Pos:* Prin investr NIH minority biomed support grants, 76-81, 84-, area grant, 86-88; vis prof microanat, Ruhr Univ Med Sch, Bochum, WGer, 85; vis prof biol, Calif Polytech, San Luis Obispo, 91. *Mem:* Int Pigment Cell Soc; Pan Am Soc Pigment Cell Res; Sigma Xi; Europ Soc Pigment Cell Res; Poultry Sci Asn. *Res:* Ultrastructure and enzymology of pigmentation in fish, amphibia and fowl, fowl models for vitiligo; previous ultrastructure and enzymology of carrageenan-induced granulomas in lung and subcutaneous tissues in the rat. *Mailing Add:* Dept Biol & Microbiol Calif State Univ 5151 State University Dr Los Angeles CA 90032

BOWERS, WAYNE ALEXANDER, PHYSICS. *Current Pos:* from assoc prof to prof, 47-84, EMER PROF PHYSICS, UNIV NC, CHAPEL HILL, 84- *Personal Data:* b Bilbao, Spain, Mar 1, 19; m 44, Mary Ellen Severinghaus; c John, Margaret, Ruth & Wayne. *Educ:* Oberlin Col, AB, 38; Cornell Univ, PhD(theoret physics), 43. *Honors & Awards:* Pegram Award, Am Phys Soc, 90. *Prof Exp:* Asst physics, Cornell Univ, 38-42, instr, 42-44; physicist, Manhattan Proj, Los Alamos, NMex, 44-46; res assoc, Mass Inst Technol, 46-47. *Concurrent Pos:* Vis prof, Mass Inst Technol, 68-69; NSF sci fac fel, 63-64; vis scholar, Cavendish Lab, Univ Cambridge, 77-78 & 84-85. *Mem:* Am Phys Soc; Am Asn Physics Teachers. *Res:* Theoretical solid state physics. *Mailing Add:* Dept Physics & Astron Univ NC Chapel Hill NC 27514

BOWERS, WILLIAM E, CELL BIOLOGY. *Current Pos:* PROF & CHMN DEPT MICROBIOL & IMMUNOL, UNIV SC, SCH MED, COLUMBIA, 88- *Personal Data:* b Sunbury, Pa, Oct 29, 38; m 62; c 2. *Educ:* Rockefeller Univ, PhD(life sci), 66. *Prof Exp:* From asst prof to assoc prof, Dept Biochem Cytol, Rockefeller Univ, 70-80; res immunologist, May Imogene Bassett Hosp, 80-90, actg sci dir, Med Res Inst, 85-88. *Mem:* Am Asn Immunol; Am Soc Biol Chemists; Cell Kinetics Soc; Sigma Xi. *Res:* Differentiation and antigen presentation of immune system dendritic cells. *Mailing Add:* Dept Microbiol & Immunol Univ SC Sch Med VA Campus Columbia SC 29208-0001. *Fax:* 803-733-3192

BOWERS, WILLIAM SIGMOND, INVERTEBRATE PHYSIOLOGY, BIOCHEMISTRY. *Current Pos:* prof & head, Dept Entom, 84-88, PROF ENTOM & CHEM ECOL, UNIV ARIZ, 88- *Personal Data:* b Chicago, Ill, Dec 24, 35; m 58, Patricia A Mikovich; c Mare W, Dana L, Erin J, Rion J & Lisa M. *Educ:* Ind Univ, AB, 57; Purdue Univ, MS, 59, PhD(entom), 62. *Honors & Awards:* J Everett Bussart Mem Award, Entom Soc Am, 80, Founders Mem Award, 91; Alexander von Humboldt Prize, Alexander von Humboldt Found, 89; Kenneth A Spencer Award, Am Chem Soc, 94. *Prof Exp:* Sr insect physiologist, Agr Res Ctr, US Dept Agr, 62-72; prof insect physiol, NY State Agr Exp Sta, Cornell Univ, 72-; vis dir res, Int Ctr Insect Physiol & Ecol, 77-83. *Concurrent Pos:* distinguished vis prof, NMex State Univ, 86-84; Fulbright scholar, Chem Ecol, 87, 93. *Mem:* Nat Acad Sci; fel Entom Soc Am; Am Chem Soc; Int Soc Chem Ecol; AAAS; Am Soc Pharmacog; Phytochem Soc Am; Western Soc Naturalists. *Res:* Discovery and development of biological/biorational strategies for plant and public health protection; chemical ecology, experimental biology and natural products chemistry; isolation identification and synthesis of insect hormones, anti-hormones and pheromones; natural product chemistry; insect-plant interactions. *Mailing Add:* Univ Ariz Forbes Bldg Rm 410 Tucson AZ 85721. *Fax:* 520-621-9166

BOWERSOX, TODD WILSON, FORESTRY, SOLAR ENERGY. *Current Pos:* Res asst forestry, 68-75, asst prof, 75-81, ASSOC PROF SILVICULT FORESTRY, PA STATE UNIV, 81- *Personal Data:* b Lewistown, Pa, Oct 4, 41; m 61; c 3. *Educ:* Pa State Univ, BS, 66, MS, 68, PhD(forest resources), 75. *Mem:* Forest Prod Res Soc; Soc Am Foresters; Sigma Xi. *Res:* Ecological and managerial aspects of culturing natural stands and plantations of hardwood species in eastern United States. *Mailing Add:* Sch Forest Resources Pa State Univ 204 Ferguson University Park PA 16802-4301

BOWES, GEORGE ERNEST, PLANT PHYSIOLOGY, PLANT BIOCHEMISTRY. *Current Pos:* from asst prof to assoc prof, 72-84, PROF BOT, UNIV FLA, 84- *Personal Data:* b London, Eng, May 22, 42; m 70, Helen Clifford; c George E & Joel A. *Educ:* Univ London, BSc Hons, 63, PhD(plant physiol), 67. *Hon Degrees:* MIBiol, Inst Biol, London, 68, CBiol, Inst Biol, London, 88, FIBiol, Inst Biol, London, 88. *Prof Exp:* Lectr biol, Regents St Polytech, London, 66-68; high sch teacher, Inner London Educ Authority, Eng, 68; vis res assoc agron, Univ Ill, Urbana, 68-71; res fel plant biol, Carnegie Inst, Stanford, Calif, 71-72. *Concurrent Pos:* Prin investr grants, Fla Dept Natural Resources, 76-93, Ctr Environ Prog, Inst Food & Agr Sci, Fla, 77-78, Sci & Educ Admin, USDA, 78-93, Gas Res Inst, 81-86 & NSF, 84-88; courtesy app prof agron, Univ Fla, 84-; panel mgr, USDA/Nat Res Initiatives Competitive Grants Photosynthesis Prog, 91-92; guest prof, Univ Aarhus, Denmark, 93. *Mem:* Am Soc Plant Physiologists; Brit Soc Exp Biol; fel Inst Biol; Sigma Xi; Aquatic Plant Mgt Soc. *Res:* Regulation of photosynthetic and photorespiratory carbon metabolism, especially in aquatic plants; aquatic weed control; improving crop productivity; photosynthesis in isolated cells and chloroplasts; ribulose bisphosphate carboxylase-oxygenase kinetics; effects of elevated atmospheric CO2 on photosynthesis and productivity; CO2 concentrating mechanisms. *Mailing Add:* 823 NW 36th Terr Gainesville FL 32605. *Fax:* 904-392-3993; *E-Mail:* bowes@nervm.nerdc.ufl.edu

BOWES, WILLIAM C, AEROSPACE ENGINEERING. *Current Pos:* PROG EXEC OFFICER, CRUISE MISSILE PROJECT, DEPT NAVY, WASHINGTON. *Honors & Awards:* Laurel Award, Space/Missiles Aviation Week & Space Technol, 91. *Mailing Add:* 245 Deer Dr Lusby MD 20657

BOWHILL, SIDNEY ALLAN, AERONOMY. *Current Pos:* RETIRED. *Personal Data:* b Dover, Eng, Aug 6, 27; US citizen; m; c 2. *Educ:* Cambridge Univ, BA, 48, MA, 50, PhD(physics), 54. *Honors & Awards:* Scostep Serv Award Int, 90. *Prof Exp:* Res engr, Marconi's Wireless Tel Co, Eng, 53-55; assoc prof elec eng, Pa State Univ, 55-62; prof, Univ Ill, Urbana-Champaign, 62-86; prof & head, Univ Lowell, 86-90, assoc dean, Dept Elec Eng, 90. *Concurrent Pos:* Fulbright grant, 55-56; ed, Antennas & Propagation Group Trans, 59-62 & Radio Sci, 67-73; mem, Radio Stand Panel, Nat Acad Sci, 61-64, Comt Potential Contamination & Interference Space Exp, 63-, Polar Res Comt, 67-70, chmn, Panel Upper Atmospheric Physics, 67-70, mem, Rocket Res Comt, 67-72, Comt Data Interchange & Data Ctrs, 67-82, Adv Panel World Data Ctr A, 69-75, Geophys Data Panel, 75-76, Earth Sci Panel for NSF Postdoctoral Fels, 68-69, Comt Solar-Terrestrial Res, 69-79; assoc ed, Radio Propagation, 64-67; chmn, US Comn 3, Int Sci Radio Union, 64-67, mem, US Nat Comt, 64-75 & 79-83, vchmn, 85-87, chmn, 88-90, Unions Comt Space Res Working Group 4 Upper Atmosphere, 66-79, co-chmn, Panel Interactions Between Neutral & Ionized Parts Atmosphere, 66-79, chmn, Sci Comn C, 79-84, Spec Comt Solar-Terrestrial Physics, 67-, Working Group 11 Neutral & Ion Chem, 68-73, Atmospheric Physics Progs Steering Comt, 74-80, Mid Atmospheric Prog Steering Comt, 77-; mem, Int Union Radio Sci Solar-Terrestrial Physics Comt, 68-72, chmn, Working Group Int Ref Ionosphere, 67-68, Comt Space Res, 69-75, vchmn, Int Comn 3, 69-72, chmn, 72-75; pres, Aeronomy Corp, 69- *Mem:* Nat Acad Eng; fel Inst Elec & Electronics Engrs; Am Soc Eng Educ; fel Am Geophys Union; fel AAAS. *Res:* Physics of ionosphere; radio propagation; rocket and satellite studies of upper atmosphere. *Mailing Add:* 555 Annursac Hill Rd Concord MA 01742. *E-Mail:* syndneya@aol.com

BOWICK, MARK JOHN, STRING THEORY, TOPOLOGICAL AND GEOMETRICAL ASPECTS OF THEORETICAL PHYSICS. *Current Pos:* asst prof, 87-93, PROF, SYRACUSE UNIV, 93- *Personal Data:* b Rotorua, NZ, Nov 29, 57; NZ citizen; m 84, Maria Cristina Marchetti; c Micol & Elena. *Educ:* Univ Canterbury, NZ, BSc, 77; Calif Inst Technol, MS, 79, PhD(physics), 83. *Prof Exp:* Res assoc, Yale Univ, 83-86; staff, Mass Inst Technol, 86-88. *Concurrent Pos:* Outstanding jr investr, VS Dept Energy, 87-93; vis scholar, Hardard Univ, 89, Inst Theoret Physics, Univ Calif, Santa Barbara, 91, 93 & 94. *Mem:* Am Phys Soc. *Res:* Theoretical particle physics' mathematical physics and the statistical mechanics of surfaces. *Mailing Add:* Physics Dept Syracuse Univ Syracuse NY 13244-1130. *Fax:* 315-443-9103; *E-Mail:* bowick@npac.syr.edu

BOWIE, ANDREW J(ACKSON), AGRICULTURAL ENGINEERING. *Current Pos:* RES HYDRAULIC ENGR, SEDIMENTATION LAB, AGR RES SERV, USDA, 58- *Personal Data:* b McCool, Miss, July 6, 23; m 48; c 3. *Educ:* Miss State Univ, BS, 49. *Prof Exp:* Consult engr, Commercial Soils Serv, Miss, 49-58. *Mem:* Am Soc Agr Engrs; Nat Soc Prof Engrs. *Res:* Compilation, tabulation and analysis of watershed runoff and sediment yield records; hydrologic and sediment data assembly; preparation of technical research reports and manuscripts for publication. *Mailing Add:* 535 W Woodland Heights Holly Springs MS 38635

BOWIE, EDWARD JOHN WALTER, HEMATOLOGY. *Current Pos:* RETIRED. *Personal Data:* b Church Stretton, Eng, Mar 10, 25; m 48, Gertrud S Ulrich; c Katherine A, Christopher J, John W & James U. *Educ:* Oxford Univ, MA, 50, BM & BCh, 52, DM, 81; Univ Minn, MS, 61. *Honors & Awards:* Trotter Medal, Univ Col Hosp, London, 51; Distinguished Career Award, Int Soc Thrombosis & Haemostasis, 91. *Prof Exp:* From instr to assoc prof, Mayo Med Sch, 66-74, prof med & lab med, 74-97. *Concurrent Pos:* Consult internal med, Mayo Clin, 61-, head, Sect Hemat, 71-89; Judson Daland travel award, 63; distinguished investr, Mayo Found, 87. *Mem:* AAAS; Am Soc Hemat; Am Soc Path; Int Soc Thrombosis & Haemostasis; Am Med Asn; Am Heart Asn; Central Soc Clin Res. *Res:* Haemostasis, bleeding and thrombosing diseases; von Willebrand disease. *Mailing Add:* Mayo Clin Rochester MN 55905. *Fax:* 507-284-5115

BOWIE, JAMES DWIGHT, RADIOLOGY, ULTRASOUND. *Current Pos:* assoc prof, 79-88, PROF RADIOL, DUKE UNIV, 88- *Personal Data:* b Sentinel, Okla, Oct 25, 41; m 68; c 2. *Educ:* Univ Okla, BA, 63, MD, 67. *Prof Exp:* Resident radiol, Univ Chicago, 71-73, resident & trainee, 73-74, instr & trainee, 74-75, from asst prof to assoc prof radiol, 75-79. *Mem:* Radiol Soc NAm; Am Inst Ultrasound Med; Soc Radiologists Ultrasound. *Res:* Clinical application of ultrasound in particular ultrasound of the pancreas, placenta, and pelvic tumors; computer texture analysis; diagnostic cost-benefit analysis. *Mailing Add:* 313 Watts St Durham NC 27701

BOWIE, LEMUEL JAMES, CLINICAL CHEMISTRY. *Current Pos:* assoc prof clin path, 83-92, PROF PATH, MED SCH, NORTHWESTERN UNIV, 93-; DIR CLIN BIOCHEM, EVANSTON HOSP, ILL, 79-, DIR, CLIN LAB, 95- *Personal Data:* b Vicksburg, Miss, Apr 23, 44; m 71; c 2. *Educ:* Xavier Univ La, BS, 66; Johns Hopkins Univ, PhD(biochem), 72. *Honors & Awards:* Samuel Natelson Award, Am Asn Clin Chem, 85; Bernard F Gerulat Award, NJ sect, Am Asn Clin Chem, 93. *Prof Exp:* Fel, Vet Admin Hosp, 72-73, staff biochemist clin chem, 73-74, asst chief clin chem lab serv, 74-79; asst prof chem & path, Univ Calif, San Diego, 74-79. *Concurrent Pos:* Mem subcomt enzyme assay conditions, Nat Comt Clin Lab Stand, 76-78; mem med admis comt, Med Sch, Univ Calif, San Diego, 77-79; co-ed, Chicago Clin Chemist, 79-82; consult, Nat Heart, Lung & Blood Inst, NIH, 79-85; mem clin chem sect, Clin Chem & Hematol Devices Panel, Bur Med Devices, Food & Drug Admin, 82-85; mem bd dirs, Am Asn Clin Chem, 87-89, Am Bd Clin Chem, 84-; vpres, Am Bd Clin Chem, 89- *Mem:* Am Asn Clin Chem (pres, 93); Nat Acad Clin Biochem; Am Acad Clin Lab Physicians & Scientists; Int Soc Clin Enzymol; Am Chem Soc; Am Soc Biol Chem. *Res:* Hemoglobinopathies; applied spectroscopy; fetal lung maturity. *Mailing Add:* Evanston Hosp 2650 Ridge Ave Evanston IL 60201

BOWIE, OSCAR L, applied mathematics, for more information see previous edition

BOWIE, WALTER C, VETERINARY PHYSIOLOGY. *Current Pos:* RETIRED. *Personal Data:* b Kansas City, Kans, June 29, 25; m 54; c 3. *Educ:* Kans State Col, DVM, 47; Cornell Univ, MS, 55, PhD(physiol), 60. *Prof Exp:* From instr to prof, Tuskegee Inst, 47-90, head, Dept Physiol & Pharmacol,

50-90, dean, Sch Vet Med, 80-90. *Concurrent Pos:* Prin investr, Mark L Morris Found Res Grant, 61-62; co-prin investr, NIH Res Grant, 61-; co-prin investr, US Army Res Grants, 61-62, prin investr, 64-71. *Mem:* Am Vet Med Asn; Am Soc Vet Physiologists & Pharmacologists. *Res:* Physiology, diagnosis and evaluation of cerebrospinal fluid of dogs; mechanisms of infection and immunity in listeriosis; factors in virulence and immunogenicity in Listeria monocytogenes; cardiovascular and ruminant physiology; movements of the mitral valve. *Mailing Add:* 707 Patterson St Tuskegee Inst AL 36088

BOWIN, CARL OTTO, GEOLOGY & GEOPHYSICS, EARTH STRUCTURE & TECTONICS. *Current Pos:* res assoc, Woods Hole Oceanog Inst, 61-63, asst scientist, 63-65, assoc scientist geophys, 65-78, SR SCIENTIST, WOODS HOLE OCEANOG INST, 78- *Personal Data:* b Los Angeles, Calif, Jan 30, 34; m 56, Jean V Entwistle; c Claire, Adria, Bret & Dara. *Educ:* Calif Inst Technol, BS, 55; Northwestern Univ, MS, 57; Princeton Univ, PhD(geol), 60. *Prof Exp:* Instr geol, Princeton Univ, 60-61. *Concurrent Pos:* Consult, NSF, 77-78; chmn, Numerical Data adv bd, Nat Res Coun, Nat Acad Sci, 80-82; pres, Zarak Corp, 77- *Mem:* Fel AAAS; fel Geol Soc Am; Am Geophys Union. *Res:* Development and use of geophysical data acquisition and processing systems utilizing digital computers; tectonics and gravity of earth and other planetary bodies. *Mailing Add:* 15 Upland Ave Falmouth MA 02540-2322. *Fax:* 508-457-2187; *E-Mail:* cbowin@whoi.edu

BOWKER, ALBERT HOSMER, MATHEMATICAL STATISTICS. *Current Pos:* RETIRED. *Personal Data:* b Winchendon, Mass, Sept 8, 19; m 42; c 3. *Educ:* Mass Inst Technol, BS, 41; Columbia Univ, PhD(statist), 49. *Hon Degrees:* LHD, City Univ, New York, 71; LLD, Brandais, 72, Amtech, 80; ScD, Morehouse, 88. *Honors & Awards:* Frederick Douglass Award, NY Urban League, 69; Shewhart Award, Am Soc Qual Control, 78; Order De Leopold II, 80. *Prof Exp:* Asst statistician, Mass Inst Technol, 41-43; asst dir statist res group, Columbia Univ, 43-45; from asst prof to prof statist, Stanford Univ, 47-53, head dept, 53-59, dean grad div, 58-63, asst to provost, 56-58; chancellor, City Univ New York, 63-71, Univ Calif, Berkeley, 71-80; dean, Sch Pub Affairs, Univ MD, 80-83, exec vpres, 83-86; vpres res found, City Univ NY, 86-92. *Concurrent Pos:* Mem-at-large, Div Math, Nat Res Coun-Nat Acad Sci, 62-65; mem adv comt, Off Statist Stand Statist Policy, 63; mem, Nat Adv Coun Exten & Continuing Educ; mem, Nat Drug Abuse Coun, 72 & Sloan Comn on Govt and Higher Educ; mem bd trustees, Univ Haifa, 71- & Bennington Col, 77-; asst secy postsecondary educ, US Dept Educ, 80-81. *Mem:* Fel AAAS; Inst Math Statist (pres, 61-62; fel Am Soc Qual Control; Opers Res Soc Am; fel Am Statist Asn (vpres, 62-64, pres elec, 63, pres, 64). *Res:* Industrial statistics; multivariate analysis. *Mailing Add:* Univ Calif 367 Evans Hall No 386C Berkeley CA 94720-3860. *E-Mail:* bowker@stat.berkeley.edu

BOWKER, DAVID EDWIN, REMOTE SENSING, ATMOSPHERIC PROPAGATION. *Current Pos:* RETIRED. *Personal Data:* b Richmond, Va, Apr 19, 28; m 55; c 4. *Educ:* Antioch Col, BS, 53; Mass Inst Technol, PhD(geophys), 60. *Prof Exp:* Sci staff physics, Mitre Corp, 60-64; sr res scientist space sci, NASA-Langley Res Ctr, 64-93. *Concurrent Pos:* Assoc prof lectr, George Washington Univ, 68- *Mem:* Soc Photo-Optical Instrumentation Engrs; AAAS; Am Soc Photogram & Remote Sensing. *Res:* Remote sensing of earth environment; lunar photography; space applications. *Mailing Add:* 292 Jolly Pond Rd Williamsburg VA 23188

BOWKER, RICHARD GEORGE, PHYSIOLOGICAL ECOLOGY, VERTEBRATE ZOOLOGY. *Current Pos:* PROF ZOOL, ALMA COL, 77- *Personal Data:* b Buffalo, NY, Dec 8, 46; m 68; c 2. *Educ:* Cornell Univ, BS, 68; Northern Ariz Univ, MS, 75, PhD(zool), 78. *Honors & Awards:* Barlow Award; Charles A Dana Prof Biol. *Prof Exp:* Res assoc zool, Nat Mus Kenya, 73-74. *Concurrent Pos:* Vis prof, Univ Coimbra, Portugal, 83-; vis scientist, Los Alamos Nat Lab; Fulbright fel. *Mem:* Am Soc Ichthyologists & Herpetologists; Ecol Soc Am; Europ Soc Herpetologists; Sigma Xi. *Res:* Thermoregulation and thermal ecology of lizards; population regulation in tropical anurans; metabolism of vertebrates. *Mailing Add:* 1075 Riverview Dr Alma MI 48801

BOWKLEY, HERBERT LOUIS, inorganic chemistry; deceased, see previous edition for last biography

BOWLAND, JOHN PATTERSON, ANIMAL NUTRITION. *Current Pos:* RETIRED. *Personal Data:* b Man, Can, Feb 10, 24; m 46; c 2. *Educ:* Univ Man, BSA, 45; Wash State Col, MS, 47; Univ Wis, PhD(biochem, animal husb), 49. *Honors & Awards:* Borden Award, Nutrit Soc Can, 66. *Prof Exp:* Agr supvr, Exp Farm, Brandon, Man, 45-46; from asst prof to prof animal sci, Univ Alta, 49-75, dean agr & forestry & Dept Animal Sci, 75-87. *Concurrent Pos:* Vis mem, Nat Inst Res Dairying, Eng, 59-60; guest prof, Animal Nutrit Inst, Swiss Fed Inst Technol, 68-69; mem comt animal nutrit, Nat Acad Sci-Nat Res Coun. *Mem:* Fel AAAS; Am Soc Animal Sci; Can Soc Animal Sci (secy-treas, 51-54); fel Agr Inst Can; Nutrit Soc Can; Sigma Xi. *Res:* Swine and rat nutrition, particularly energy, protein and amino acids. *Mailing Add:* 11243 79th Ave Univ AB Edmonton AB T6G 0P2 Can

BOWLDEN, HENRY JAMES, USER FRIENDLY SYSTEMS, KNOWLEDGE BASE APPLICATIONS. *Current Pos:* CONSULT, INTELLIGENT INTEGRATED SYSTS, 90- *Personal Data:* b Hamilton, Ont, Apr 5, 25; nat US; m 48, Agnes Stringer; c Sara Anne & Peter H. *Educ:* McMaster Univ, BA, 46; Univ Ill, MS, 47, PhD(physics), 51. *Prof Exp:* Asst physics, Univ Ill, 46-50; from asst prof to assoc prof physics & astron, Wayne State Univ, 50-57; res physicist, Parma Res Ctr, Union Carbide Corp, 57-61, group leader, 61-63; adv scientist, Info Systs & Human Sci Dept, Westinghouse Res & Develop Ctr, 63-90. *Concurrent Pos:* Res assoc, Detroit Inst Cancer Res, 52-57; consult, US Naval Res Labs, 56-60; mem working group WG 2-1, Int Fedn Info Processing, 70-, secy, 70-73; tech activ area leader, Intelligent Integrated Systs, W Res & Develop, 82-90. *Mem:* Asn Comput Mach; Am Asn Artificial Intel; Am Defense Preparedness Asn. *Res:* Artifical intelligence; computer languages and programming systems; numerical methods; semiconductor theory. *Mailing Add:* 1156 Bucknell Dr Monroeville PA 15146-4320. *E-Mail:* bowlden@acm.org

BOWLER, DAVID LIVINGSTONE, ELECTRONICS ENGINEERING. *Current Pos:* RETIRED. *Personal Data:* b New York, NY, June 7, 26; m 55; c 2. *Educ:* Bucknell Univ, BS, 48; Mass Inst Technol, MS, 51; Princeton Univ, MA, 58, PhD, 64. *Prof Exp:* Instr elec eng, Bucknell Univ, 48-49 & 53-54, asst prof, 54-55; engr, Hazeltine Corp, 51-53; from asst prof to prof elec eng, Swarthmore Col, 57-87, Howard N & Ada J Eavenson Prof Eng, 87-89. *Concurrent Pos:* Consult, JPM Co, Pa, 53-55 & Bartol Res Found, 58-64; vis fel, Queen's Univ, Belfast, 66-67; vis res assoc, Univ Fla, 71 & Univ Pa, 89-90; Fulbright lectr, Univ Col, Galway, Ireland, 84. *Mem:* Inst Elec & Electronics Engrs; Sigma Xi. *Res:* Electronic circuits; digital circuits. *Mailing Add:* 505 Yale Ave Swarthmore PA 19081

BOWLES, BOBBY LINWOOD, naturally occuring antimicrobial agents, antibotulinal agents, for more information see previous edition

BOWLES, JEAN ALYCE, MICROBIOLOGY, BIOCHEMISTRY. *Current Pos:* from asst prof to prof, 65-90, EMER PROF BIOL, METROP STATE COL, 90- *Personal Data:* b Boston, Mass, June 15, 29. *Educ:* Univ Ill, Urbana, BS, 56, MS, 58; Univ Colo Med Ctr, PhD(microbiol), 65. *Prof Exp:* Res assoc, Dept Biophys, Univ Colo Med Ctr, 57-60, res asst, Dept Microbiol, 60-61. *Mem:* Am Soc Microbiol; Am Inst Biol Sci; Sigma Xi; Fedn Am Scientists; fel Am Acad Microbiol. *Res:* Kinetics of utilization and the regulation of the metabolism of organic compounds in mycobacterium tuberculosis; development of methods of obtaining axenic cultures of cyanobacteria more quickly and efficiently; bacterial contamination of mattresses. *Mailing Add:* 1045 Olive St Denver CO 80220. *E-Mail:* bowlesje@mscd.edu

BOWLES, JOHN BEDELL, ZOOLOGY. *Current Pos:* RETIRED. *Personal Data:* b Karuizawa, Japan, July 29, 33; US citizen; m 58; c 4. *Educ:* Earlham Col, AB, 56; Univ Wash, MS, 63; Univ Kans, PhD(biol), 71. *Prof Exp:* Teacher high sch, Hawaii, 59-61; asst dir, Waikiki Aquarium, Honolulu, 61-62; asst prof biol, William Penn Col, 63-67; from asst prof to prof biol, Cent Col, Iowa, 69-93. *Mem:* AAAS; Am Soc Mammalogists; Sigma Xi. *Res:* Activity and reproductive patterns of bats, especially North and Central American; small mammal distribution in the midwest. *Mailing Add:* 1810 Ramona Circle San Marcos TX 78666

BOWLES, JOSEPH EDWARD, SOIL MECHANICS, STRUCTURAL ENGINEERING. *Current Pos:* OWNER, ENG COMPUT SOFTWARE, 80- *Personal Data:* b Rocky Mount, Va, July 12, 29; m 50. *Educ:* Univ Ala, Tuscaloosa, BSCE, 58; Ga Inst Technol, MSCE, 61. *Prof Exp:* Instr civil technol, Southern Tech Inst, Ga, 58-61; instr civil eng, Univ Wis, Madison, 61-63; from asst prof to prof civil eng, Bradley Univ, 63-80. *Mem:* Am Soc Civil Eng; Am Soc Eng Educ; Am Soc Testing & Mat; Am Concrete Inst. *Res:* Foundation engineering. *Mailing Add:* 6810 N Hi Wood Ct Peoria IL 61614

BOWLES, KENNETH LUDLAM, PHYSICS. *Current Pos:* CONSULT. *Personal Data:* b Bronxville, NY, Feb 20, 29; m 54; c 3. *Educ:* Cornell Univ, BEP, 51, MEE, 53, PhD(radio wave propagation), 55. *Honors & Awards:* Gold Medal, US Dept Com, 62. *Prof Exp:* Physicist, Nat Bur Stand, Colo, 55-65; dir comput ctr, Univ Calif, San Diego, 67-72, prof appl physics & computer sci, 65-84; chmn, Telesoft, 81-89. *Concurrent Pos:* Mem US nat comt, Int Sci Radio Union, 62-65; mem Ada Bd, US Dept Defense, 84-91. *Mem:* Inst Elec & Electronics Engrs; Asn Comput Machinery; Inst Elec & Electronics Engrs Computer Soc. *Res:* Plasma physics; physics and radar studies of the upper atmosphere, including measurements of ionization density, temperature, ionized constituents and nature of irregularities; radio and radar astronomy. *Mailing Add:* 13040 Caminito Mar Villa Del Mar CA 92014

BOWLES, LAWRENCE THOMPSON, MEDICAL ADMINISTRATION, THORACIC SURGERY. *Current Pos:* PRES, NAT BD MED EXAMRS, 93- *Personal Data:* b Mineola, NY, Sep 23, 31; m 65; c 3. *Educ:* Duke Univ, AB, 53, MD, 57; NY Univ, MS, 64, PhD(higher educ), 71. *Prof Exp:* Intern surg, NY Univ, 57-58, res surg, 58-62; res surg, Triboro Hosp, NY, 62-64; attend surg, George Washington Hosp, Children's Hosp, Nat Cancer Inst, 65-68; vis prof surg, Univ Ceylon, 68-69; from assoc prof to prof surg, George Washington Univ, 73-93. *Concurrent Pos:* vchmn Continuing Educ Comt, Am Col Surgeon, 79-80; mem, 82-86, chmn, Nat Libr, Med Bd Regents, 84-86, mem, 83-, Nat Bd Med Examiners, chmn, 87-, mem Vet Admin Spec Med Adv Group, 84-88, Coun Deans, Admin Assoc Am Med Cols, 85- *Mem:* Soc Thoracic Surgeons; Am Asn Thoracic Surg; Am Col Surgeons; Am Gerontol Soc; Am Acad Chest Physicians. *Res:* Surgery in the elderly; health promotion. *Mailing Add:* Nat Bd Med Examrs 3750 Market St Philadelphia PA 19104

BOWLES, ROLAND L, AERONAUTICAL ENGINEERING. *Current Pos:* MGR, WIND SHEAR PROG, NASA LANGLEY RES CTR. *Mailing Add:* Wind Shear Prog Off NASA Langley Res Ctr Hampton VA 23663

BOWLES, THOMAS JOSEPH, NUCLEAR PHYSICS. *Current Pos:* STAFF MEM, LOS ALAMOS NAT LAB, 79- *Personal Data:* b June 27, 50; c 1. *Educ:* Univ Colo, BS, 73; Princeton Univ, PhD(physics), 78. *Prof Exp:* Western Interstate Comn Higher Educ fel, Environ Protection Agency, Denver Fed Ctr, 73; res asst, Physics Dept, Princeton Univ, 73-76; res assoc, Argonne Nat Lab, 76-79. *Concurrent Pos:* Lab instr, Physics Dept, Princeton Univ, 74-75; co-prin investr, Los Alamos Nat Lab, 80-; US prin investr, Soviet-Am Gallium Exp, 87- *Mem:* Fel Am Phys Soc. *Res:* Solar neutrino physics; weak interactions; neutrino physics; nuclear astrophysics; photonuclear physics; nuclear structure physics; medium energy physics. *Mailing Add:* Physics Div Group P-3 Los Alamos Nat Lab PO Box 1663 Los Alamos NM 87545

BOWLES, WILLIAM ALLEN, polymer rheology, physical-organic chemistry, for more information see previous edition

BOWLES, WILLIAM HOWARD, BIOCHEMISTRY. *Current Pos:* ASSOC PROF, BAYLOR DENT CAMPUS, TEX A&M UNIV SYST, 96- *Personal Data:* b McCoy, Colo, Aug 1, 36; m 61; c 3. *Educ:* La Sierra Col, BA, 58; Univ Ariz, MS, 60, PhD(biochem), 64; Baylor Col Dent, DDS, 77. *Prof Exp:* Asst prof chem, Southwestern Union Col, 63-65; from asst prof to assoc prof, Baylor Univ, Tex, 65-73, spec instr, 73-77, assoc prof biochem, Col Dent, Grad Fac, 77-96. *Concurrent Pos:* Pvt pract dent, 77- *Mem:* Am Asn Dent Sch; Am Dent Asn; Int Asn Dent Res; fel Acad Gen Dent; Am Asn Dent Res; Sigma Xi. *Res:* Fat-soluble vitamins, lipids, hormones, dental amalgam, local anesthetics and dental plaque. *Mailing Add:* 426 Beverly Dr Richardson TX 75080

BOWLEY, DONOVAN ROBIN, BOTANY, ENVIRONMENTAL SCIENCE. *Current Pos:* asst surv analyst, Mass Dept Environ Qual Eng, 78, dir surface impoundments assessments, 78-80, sr planner, 80, coordr underground water resource protection prog, 80-82, prog mgr, Water Supply Contamination Correction, 82-91, GIS prog coordr, 89-93, ENVIRON ANALYST VI & ACTG DEP DIR, DIV WATER SUPPLY, MASS DEPT ENVIRON PROTECTION. *Personal Data:* b Waltham, Mass, May 20, 45. *Educ:* Eastern Nazarene Col, BA, 67; Boston Univ Grad Sch, MA, 70, PhD(bot), 78. *Prof Exp:* Instr sci, Col Basic Studies, Boston Univ, 75-77. *Concurrent Pos:* Consult ecol, bot & hort, Helden Assocs, 74-77 & Town Eng Assocs, 76-78. *Mem:* NY Acad Sci; Nat Water Well Asn. *Res:* Water supply protection; hydrology; mapping of groundwater contamination sources; lichenology, particularly New England, Arctic/Alpine and coastal regions; salt marsh develop in New England; development of environmental protection GIS databases; interrelation of human populations and environment. *Mailing Add:* 201 Ash St Waltham MA 02154-5116

BOWLING, ANN L, VETERINARY MEDICINE. *Current Pos:* asst res geneticist, 73-81, adj assoc prof, 81-88, ADJ PROF, UNIV CALIF, DAVIS, 88- *Personal Data:* b Portland, Ore, June 1, 43; m 80; c 1. *Educ:* Carleton Col, AB, 65; Univ Calif, Davis, PhD(genetics), 69. *Prof Exp:* Asst prof biol, Occidental Col, 69-73. *Mem:* AAAS; Sigma Xi; Am Genetics Soc; Int Soc Animal Genetics. *Res:* Immunogenetics; genetics in clinical veterinary medicine; cytogenetics. *Mailing Add:* Vet Genetics Lab Univ Calif Davis CA 95616

BOWLING, ARTHUR LEE, JR, THEORETICAL HIGH ENERGY PHYSICS. *Current Pos:* asst prof, 77-80, ASSOC PROF PHYSICS, AGNES SCOTT COL, 81- *Personal Data:* b Roanoke, Va, May 14, 47; m 70; c 2. *Educ:* Col of William & Mary, BS, 69; Univ Ill, MS, 70, PhD(physics), 74. *Prof Exp:* Asst vis prof physics, Swarthmore Col, 74-75; asst prof physics, Ohio State Univ, Mansfield, 75-77. *Concurrent Pos:* Vis res assoc, Ga Tech Res Inst, 84-85. *Res:* Weak and electromagnetic interactions. *Mailing Add:* 147 Winnona Dr Decatur GA 30030

BOWLING, CLARENCE C, ENTOMOLOGY, AGRICULTURE. *Current Pos:* RETIRED. *Personal Data:* b Salem, Ark, Nov 12, 26; m; c 3. *Educ:* Univ Ark, Fayetteville, BS, 54, MS, 55. *Prof Exp:* Asst entomologist, Tex A&M, 55-56, assoc entomologist, 66-67, asst prof, 67-70, assoc prof entom, 70-83. *Concurrent Pos:* Secy & prog chmn, Rice Tech Working Group, 68-70, chmn, 70-72. *Mem:* Entom Soc Am. *Res:* Biology, ecology, economic importance and methods of control of insect pests of the rice plant. *Mailing Add:* 1750 Wooten Rd Beaumont TX 77707

BOWLING, DAVID IVAN, PHYSICS. *Current Pos:* asst prof, 68-74, ASSOC PROF PHYSICS, CENT MO STATE UNIV, 74- *Personal Data:* b Los Angeles, Calif, May 26, 40; m 64; c 2. *Educ:* Univ Calif, Los Angeles, AB, 62; San Diego State Col, MS, 64; Okla State Univ, PhD(physics), 68. *Prof Exp:* Physicist, Naval Electronics Labs, 64. *Mem:* Am Asn Physics Teachers. *Res:* Acoustics; macromolecules; impedance of aperture in plates; effect of shipboard noise on job performance; electrooptic effects in solutions of rigid macromolecules. *Mailing Add:* 22527 Treehouse Lane Spring TX 77373-8803

BOWLING, FLOYD E, MATHEMATICS. *Current Pos:* RETIRED. *Personal Data:* b Elizabethton, Tenn, Aug 28, 11; wid; c 2. *Educ:* Lincoln Mem Univ, AB, 34; Univ Iowa, MS, 38; Univ Tenn, EdD(math), 53. *Hon Degrees:* DSc, Tenn Wesleyan Col, 76. *Honors & Awards:* Algernon Sydny Sullivan Award, 90. *Prof Exp:* Teacher & coach high sch, Tenn, 34-36; teacher math & physics, Lincoln Mem Univ, 37-42, prof math & head dept, 45-59; prof, head dept & dean students, Tenn Wesleyan Col, 59-78, dir continuing & adult educ, 78-79, emer prof math, 78-90, acad dean, 74 & 84-85. *Concurrent Pos:* Lectr, NSF Insts. *Mem:* Emer mem, AAAS; emer mem, Math Asn Am; emer mem, Nat Coun Teachers Math; emer mem, Am Asn Univ Prof. *Res:* Development of specific kinds of graph paper as a teaching aid in math; development of a technique for teaching college math, with more meaning and understanding on the part of the student. *Mailing Add:* Tenn Wesleyan Col Athens TN 37371-0040

BOWLING, FRANKLIN LEE, MEDICINE. *Current Pos:* RETIRED. *Personal Data:* b Guyman, Okla, Nov 2, 09; m 52; c 3. *Educ:* Univ Colo, PhC & BS, 33, MD, 46; Univ Denver, MS, 47; US Air Force Sch Aerospace Med, cert, 47; Harvard Univ, MPH, 52; Mass Inst Technol, cert, 55; US Missile Test Ctr, Cape Kennedy, cert, 60; Univ Mich, cert, 67; Am Bd Prev Med, dipl & cert aerospace med. *Honors & Awards:* Wisdom Award of Honor, 70. *Prof Exp:* Intern, Med Ctr, Univ Colo, 46-47; intern Med Corps, US Air Force, 48-67, dir base med serv, Hq, 15th Air Force, Strategic Air Command, Colorado Springs, 47-49, chief med output serv, March AFB, Calif, 49-50, hosp comdr, Saudi Arabia, 50-51, chief flight surgeon, Bolling AFB, DC, 51, chief prev med, Off Inspector Gen, Hq, 52-55, head dept prev med, US Air Force Sch Aviation Med, 55-58, chief prev med, Pac Air Forces Hq, 58-61, chief mil pub health & occup med, Off Surgeon Gen, 62-66, chief epidemiol br, Armed Forces Inst Path, 66-67; med dir, Colo State Dept Social Serv, 67-71, med serv policy dir, 71-74. *Concurrent Pos:* Rep, Armed Forces Epidemiol Bd, 61-66; consult, Am Bd Prev Med, 62-66; pres, Coun Fed Med Dir Occup Health, 65-66; consult to Surgeon Gen, Dept Air Force, 66-67; mem, Permanent Comn & Int Asn Occup Health, 66-; mem, US Pharm Conv, 75-; chmn comt toxicol, Nat Res Coun. *Mem:* Fel Am Pub Health Asn; fel Am Col Prev Med; fel Indust Med Asn; fel Royal Soc Health; Int Health Soc US (pres, 67-68, secy-treas, 74-83). *Res:* Anatomy, physiology and pharmacology of cystic innervation, Mus norvegicus; epidemiological factors in motor vehicle accidents for Army, Navy and US Air Force. *Mailing Add:* 1001 E Oxford Lane Englewood CO 80110

BOWLING, LLOYD SPENCER, SR, AUDIOLOGY, SPEECH PATHOLOGY. *Current Pos:* PROF SPEECH & CHMN DEPT SPEECH & DRAMA, GEORGE WASHINGTON UNIV, 67- *Personal Data:* b Newport, Md, Mar 29, 30; m 55; c 2. *Educ:* Univ Md, BS, 43, MA, 57, EdD(human develop), 64. *Prof Exp:* Clin audiologist, West Side Vet Admin Hosp, Chicago, 57-60; clin audiologist, Vet Admin Hosp, Washington, DC, 60-63, supvr audiol clin, 63-66, assoc chief audiol & speech path clin, 66-67; lectr, Sch Med, Georgetown Univ, 67. *Concurrent Pos:* Consult, Parmly Hearing Inst, Ill, 60-61, Fairfax County Health Dept, Va & Vet Admin Hosp, Washington, DC, 67-; chmn, DC and Brasilia, Brazil Partners Rehab & Educ, 73- *Mem:* Am Speech & Hearing Asn. *Res:* Methods of aural rehabilitation; clinical auditory tests; intelligibility. *Mailing Add:* Dept Speech & Hearing Sci Rm 204 Funger Hall George Washington Univ 2201 G St NW Washington DC 20006-4211

BOWLING, ROBERT EDWARD, MICROBIOLOGY. *Current Pos:* from instr to assoc prof microbiol, 57-77, PROF MICROBIOL & IMMUNOL, MED CTR, UNIV ARK, 77-, ASST DEAN, COL MED, 73- *Personal Data:* b Pauls Valley, Okla, Aug 9, 26; m 55; c 5. *Educ:* Univ Okla, BS, 48, MS, 50, PhD, 57. *Prof Exp:* Asst bacteriologist, Okla State Health Dept, 50-51; asst, Med Ctr, Univ Okla, 51-52, 55-57. *Mem:* Am Soc Microbiol; Brit Soc Gen Microbiol; Soc Cryobiol; Sigma Xi. *Res:* Antibiotic resistance; hypothermia; microbial antagonism; ecology; antibody production; pathogenesis and infection. *Mailing Add:* 4400 I St Little Rock AR 72205-2056

BOWLING, SUE ANN, METEOROLOGY. *Current Pos:* ASST PROF, GEOPHYS INST, UNIV ALASKA, 70- *Personal Data:* b Bridgeport, Conn, Feb 26, 41. *Educ:* Harvard Univ, AB, 63; Univ Alaska, MS, 67, PhD(geophys), 70. *Prof Exp:* Partic, Advan Study Prog, Nat Ctr Atmospheric Res, 71-72. *Mem:* Am Meteorol Soc. *Res:* Local meteorological variations, climatic change, Alaskan climate, paleoclimatology. *Mailing Add:* Dept Physics Univ Alaska PO Box 755920 Fairbanks AK 99775-5920

BOWMAN, BARBARA HYDE, GENETICS. *Current Pos:* PROF HUMAN GENETICS & CHMN DEPT, MED BR, UNIV TEX, 67- *Personal Data:* b Mineral Wells, Tex, Aug 5, 30. *Educ:* Baylor Univ, BS, 51; Univ Tex, MA, 55, PhD(genetics), 59. *Prof Exp:* Bacteriologist, Tex State Dept Health, 54-55; technician human genetics lab, Dept Zool, Univ Tex, 55-59, res scientist, Genetics Found, 59-64; mem staff, Rockefeller Univ, 64-65, asst prof, 65-67. *Concurrent Pos:* Prof & Chmn Dept Cellular & Struct Biol, Health Sci Ctr, Univ Tex. *Mem:* Harvey Soc; Am Soc Human Genetics; Am Soc Biol Chemists. *Res:* Biochemical genetics of humans; genetic control of protein structure and basic defects occurring in inherited diseases. *Mailing Add:* Dept C & S Biol Univ Tex Health Sci Ctr 7703 Floyd Curl Dr San Antonio TX 78284-7762. *Fax:* 210-567-3803

BOWMAN, BARRY J, MEMBRANE BIOLOGY, ION TRANSPORT. *Current Pos:* from asst prof to assoc prof, 79-89, PROF BIOL, UNIV CALIF, SANTA CRUZ, 89- *Personal Data:* b Pontiac, Mich, May 15, 46; m 71. *Educ:* Univ Wis-Milwaukee, BA, 68; Univ Mich, PhD(biol), 75. *Prof Exp:* Fel biochem, Yale Univ Sch Med, 75-79. *Concurrent Pos:* Chmn, Dept Biol, 96- *Mem:* Am Soc Biol Chem. *Res:* Proton-pumping adenosine triphosphatase of plasma membranes and vacuoles in order to understand the role of these enzymes in active transport. *Mailing Add:* Dept Biol Univ Calif Sinsheimer Labs Santa Cruz CA 95064. *E-Mail:* bowman@biology.ucsc.edu

BOWMAN, BERNARD ULYSSES, JR, MEDICAL MICROBIOLOGY. *Current Pos:* asst prof path, 64-66, from asst prof to assoc prof med microbiol, 66-72, PROF MED MICROBIOL, COL MED, OHIO STATE UNIV, 72- *Personal Data:* b Atlanta, Ga, Oct 1, 26; m 53; c 4. *Educ:* Piedmont Col, BS, 50; Emory Univ, MS, 57; Univ Okla, PhD, 63. *Prof Exp:* Instr bact & biol, Ga State Col, 58-60; guest lectr virol, Okla State Univ, 62; instr microbiol, Med Ctr, Univ Okla, 63-64. *Concurrent Pos:* NIH trainee, Univ Okla, 63-64; Am Thoracic Soc grant, Ohio State Univ, 67-68, Nat Tuberc Asn grant, 67-68, NIH career develop award, 68-72 & grant, 69-72; Merck grant, 79 & Bremer grant, 83-84. *Mem:* Am Soc Microbiol; Am Thoracic Soc. *Res:* Etiology of sarcoidosis; lipids of mycobacteria and mycobacteriophages; mechanisms of K cell action; mechanism of action of isonicotinic acid hydradize (INH). *Mailing Add:* 2002 N Edgemont Rd Columbus OH 43212

BOWMAN, BRUCE T, SOIL & PHYSICAL CHEMISTRY, SOIL PHYSICS. *Current Pos:* RES SCIENTIST SOIL CHEM, RES INST, CAN DEPT AGR, 69- *Personal Data:* b Oshawa, Ont, Jan 21, 42; m; c 2. *Educ:* Ont Agr Col, Univ Toronto, BSA, 64; Univ Guelph, MSc, 66; Univ Minn, St Paul, PhD(soil sci), 69. *Concurrent Pos:* Sci authority, Environ Green Plan Res Prog. *Mem:* Am Chem Soc; Am Soc Agron. *Res:* Use of gas-liquid chromatography, high performance liquid chromatography in studies of environmental behavior of insecticides and herbicides; absorption-desorption isotherms,; pesticide leaching-mobility studies; soil tillage-erosion studies; environmental quality studies; preferential water & land solute transport in soils. *Mailing Add:* London Res Ctr Agr Can 1391 Sanford St London ON N5V 4T3 Can

BOWMAN, C(LEMENT) W(ILLIS), CHEMICAL ENGINEERING. *Current Pos:* CHMN & DIR, BEAUTECH MGMT CORP. *Personal Data:* b Toronto, Ont, Jan 7, 30; m 54, Marjorie Greer; c Elizabeth A & John C. *Educ:* Univ Toronto, BASc, 52, MASc, 58, PhD(chem eng), 61. *Honors & Awards:* K A Clark Distinguished Serv Award, 89; Can Res Mgt Asn Medalist, 91; Alberta Sci Technol Leadership Award, 91; R S Jane Mem Award, 93. *Prof Exp:* Lab demonstr chem eng, Univ Toronto, 52-53; tech asst nylon processing, Can Industs, Ltd & Du Pont of Can, 53-57; res engr, Du Pont of Can, 57-58; res chemist, Imp Oil Enterprises, Ltd, 60-62; res mgr tar sand res, Cities Serv Athabasca & Syncrude Can, Ltd, 63-69; chem res mgr petrochem res, Imp Oil Enterprises, Ltd, 69-71, petrol res mgr, 71-75; chmn, Alta Oil Sands Technol & Res Authority, 75-84; vpres, Esso Petrol Can, Res Dept, 84-86; pres, Alta Res Coun, 87-92. *Concurrent Pos:* Panelist, World Petrol Cong, 67; prog chmn, Can Chem Eng Conf, 69; bd mem coun, Res Coun Alta, 78-; sci secy, UN Inst Training & Res Conf, 79; mem, Fed Govt Adv Group Hydrogen Opportunities, 85; dir, Inst Chem & Technol, 85-86; bd mem, Can Asn World Petrol Cong, 87-88; coun mem, Nat Res Coun Can, 87-89; chmn, Can Res Mgt Asn, 89. *Mem:* Asn Prof Engrs; Can Soc Chem Eng (vpres, 73-74, pres, 74-75); fel Chem Inst Can (pres-elect, 81-82, pres, 82-83); fel Can Acad Eng. *Res:* Petrochemical research, particularly olefins to plastics; oil-water-solid separation studies; theoretical analysis of mass tansfer from drops and bubbles; oil sand and heavy oil recovery and upgrading. *Mailing Add:* 2112 Huron Shores Dr RR5 Sarnia ON N7T 7H6 Can. *Fax:* 519-869-6840; *E-Mail:* progrid@ebtech.net

BOWMAN, CARLOS MORALES, information science, computer science, for more information see previous edition

BOWMAN, CHARLES D, NUCLEAR PHYSICS. *Current Pos:* assoc div leader basic physics, 82-85, STAFF MEM, LOS ALAMOS NAT LAB, 85- *Personal Data:* b Roanoke, Va, May 23, 35; m 56; c 2. *Educ:* Va Polytech Inst, BS, 56; Duke Univ, MA, 58, PhD(nuclear physics), 61. *Prof Exp:* Sr physicist, Lawrence Radiation Lab, Univ Calif, 61-68, res prog mgr, Livermore Electron Linac, 68-72; chief, Nuclear Sci Div, Nat Bur Standards, 72-77, leader, Neutron Measurement & Res Group, 77-82. *Concurrent Pos:* Mem nuclear cross sect adv comt, US AEC, 69-82. *Mem:* Fel Am Phys Soc; Am Nuclear Soc. *Res:* Neutron physics; development and application of techniques for partial neutron cross section studies on very heavy nuclei; resonance neutron spectrometry on medium weight nuclei; photodisintegration of heavy nuclei; inelastic scattering of neutrons; parity and time reversal invariance violation. *Mailing Add:* 1045 Las Pueblos Los Alamos NM 87544

BOWMAN, CRAIG T, MECHANICAL ENGINEERING. *Current Pos:* assoc prof, 76-81, PROF MECH ENG, STANFORD UNIV, 81- *Personal Data:* b Sept 19, 39. *Educ:* Carnegie Inst Technol, BS, 61; Princeton Univ, MA, 64, PhD(aerospace eng), 66. *Prof Exp:* Sr res scientist, United Technologies Res Ctr, 66-76. *Mem:* Combustion Inst (secy, 88-); Am Soc Mech Engrs; Am Inst Aeronaut & Astronaut. *Res:* Combustion; air pollution; propulsion systems. *Mailing Add:* Mech Eng Dept Stanford Univ Bldg 520 Stanford CA 94305-3032

BOWMAN, DAVID F(RANCIS), ELECTRONICS ENGINEERING. *Current Pos:* ANTENNA CONSULT, RCA CORP, 83- *Personal Data:* b Erie, Pa, Mar 26, 20; m 45; c 2. *Educ:* Ohio State Univ, BEE, 42. *Prof Exp:* Engr, Hazeltine Electronics Corp, 42-46; engr, Airborne Instruments Lab, 46-48, asst supv engr, 48-52; chief engr, Develop Eng Corp, 52-56; engr-in-charge r-f lab, ITE Circuit Breaker Co, 56-62; unit mgr design & develop eng, Missile & Surface Radar Div, 62-83. *Concurrent Pos:* Consult, Air Force Commun & Navig Lab, Wright-Patterson AFB, 50-52; consult, RCA Corp, 83-, NASA, 87- *Mem:* Inst Elec & Electronics Engrs. *Res:* Advanced development of antennas and related devices. *Mailing Add:* 51 Wilshire Dr Williamstown MA 01267

BOWMAN, DONALD EDWIN, BIOCHEMISTRY. *Current Pos:* from asst prof to prof biochem, Sch Med, Ind Univ, Indianapolis, 41-79, actg chmn, Dept Biochem & Pharmacol, 56-58, chmn, Dept Biochem, 58-66, EMER PROF BIOCHEM, SCH MED, IND UNIV, INDIANAPOLIS, 79- *Personal Data:* b Orrville, Ohio, Nov 12, 08; m 34, Martha J Reichenbach; c Raymond D & Ann E (Strong). *Educ:* Western Res Univ, AB, 33, AM, 35, PhD(biochem), 37. *Prof Exp:* Asst biol, Adelbert Col, Western Res Univ, 33-35, asst biochem, 35-37, instr biochem, Sch Med, 37-41. *Mem:* Fel AAAS; Am Chem Soc; Am Soc Biol Chem; Soc Exp Biol & Med; NY Acad Sci. *Res:* Enzymes; enzyme inhibitors; discoverer of Bowman-Birk inhibitor. *Mailing Add:* Dept Biochem & Molecular Biol Ind Univ Sch Med 635 Barnhill Dr Indianapolis IN 46202-5122

BOWMAN, DONALD HOUTS, AGRONOMY, CORN & RICE PRODUCTION. *Current Pos:* RETIRED. *Personal Data:* b Osage City, Kans, May 18, 11; m 35, Kathryn R Pelton; c Robert P & Patricia. *Educ:* Kans State Univ, BS, 33, MS, 35; Univ Wis, PhD(plant path, agron), 39. *Prof Exp:* Asst pathologist, Div Cereal Crops & Dis & asst plant path, Ohio Exp Sta, USDA, 39-46, plant pathologist, Tex Agr Exp Sta, 46-48, agronomist, Delta Br Exp Sta, 48-76. *Mem:* AAAS; Am Soc Agron. *Res:* Weed control, fertilization and general culture of rice; corn production. *Mailing Add:* 316 Sycamore Leland MS 38756

BOWMAN, DOUGLAS CLYDE, PHYSIOLOGY, PHARMACOLOGY. *Current Pos:* RETIRED. *Personal Data:* b St Louis, Mo, Oct 20, 25; m 55; c 3. *Educ:* Col Puget Sound, BS, 48, BEd, 49; Univ Wash, MS, 57, PhD(zool), 58. *Prof Exp:* Instr physiol, Univ Wash, 58-59; from instr to asst prof, Dent Sch, Northwestern Univ, 59-64; from asst prof to prof, Sch Dent, Loyola Univ, Chicago, 64-87. *Mem:* NY Acad Sci; Int Asn Dent Res. *Res:* Inflammation; action of salicylates; functional innervation of peridontal ligament; tongue thrust; hyoid positioning; toxic effects of methyl methacrylate. *Mailing Add:* 120 El Naranjo Green Valley AZ 85614

BOWMAN, EDWARD RANDOLPH, PHARMACOLOGY, PHYSIOLOGY. *Current Pos:* res asst, 56-58, RES ASSOC PHARMACOL, MED COL VA, 61- *Personal Data:* b Mercer Co, WVa, Feb 26, 27; m 54, Wilma Hall; c Linda G. *Educ:* Concord Col, BS, 52; WVa Univ, MS, 53; Med Col Va, PhD, 63. *Prof Exp:* Bacteriologist, Va State Dept Health, 54-55. *Concurrent Pos:* Vis investr, Royal Vet Col, Stockholm, Sweden, 61 & Inst Physiol, Santiago, Chile, 63. *Mem:* AAAS; Am Chem Soc; Am Soc Pharmacol & Exp Therapeut; Am Soc Exp Biol & Med; Sigma Xi; Nat Heart Inst. *Res:* Drug metabolism; nicotine metabolism; isolation and identification of urinary metabolites of nicotine; synthesis of pyridino compounds; whole body autoradiography; CNS pharmacology evaluation of unknown drugs for abuse potential; alcohol-nicotine interaction in CNS. *Mailing Add:* 1900 Windsordale Dr Richmond VA 23229-4029. *Fax:* 804-371-7519; *E-Mail:* erbowman@gems.vcu.edu

BOWMAN, EUGENE W, MATHEMATICS. *Current Pos:* prof, 47-75, EMER PROF MATH & EDUC, SOUTHERN ORE COL, 75- *Personal Data:* b North Powder, Ore, Mar 28, 10; wid; c E William. *Educ:* Univ Idaho, BS, 35, MS, 36, EdD(admin), 52. *Prof Exp:* Instr math & chem, Coeur d'Alene Jr Col, 36-38; supt pub schs, Wash, 38-43. *Concurrent Pos:* Educ adv, US Agency Int Develop, Ecuador, 60-62. *Res:* Personnel administration; comparative education. *Mailing Add:* 641 Torrington Dr Sunnyvale CA 94087

BOWMAN, FRANK LEE, MARINE ENGINEERING. *Current Pos:* USN, 66-, USS Simon Bolivar, exec officer, USS Pogy, USS Daniel Boone, USS Bremerton, comdr, USS City Corpus Christi, 83, USS Holland, 88-90, dep dir opers joint staff, 91-92, dir polit & mil affairs, 92-94, dep chief naval opers & chief naval personnel, 94-96, DIR, NAVAL NUCLEAR PROPULSION, USN, 96- *Personal Data:* b Chattanooga, Tenn; m, Linda Anne Rich; c Greg & Christy. *Educ:* Mass Inst Technol, MS, 73. *Mailing Add:* Naval Reactors Off US Dept Energy 2521 Jefferson Davis Hwy Rm 3N06 Arlington VA 22242-5160

BOWMAN, H(ARRY) FREDERICK, BIOMEDICAL ENGINEERING, HEAT TRANSFER. *Current Pos:* DIR CANCER HYPOTHERMIA PROG, HARVARD UNIV-MASS INST TECHNOL, 88- *Personal Data:* b Terre Hill, Pa, Sept 16, 41; m 63; c 1. *Educ:* Pa State Univ, BSME, 63; Mass Inst Technol, MS & NuclE, 66, PhD(nuclear eng), 68. *Prof Exp:* Mech engr, Humble Oil & Refining Co, 63; res asst, Mass Inst Technol, 67-68; From asst to assoc prof mech eng, Northeastern Univ, 68-79, assoc prof biomed eng, 79-93. *Concurrent Pos:* Admin officer, Harvard Univ-Mass Inst Technol prog health sci & technol, 69-74, exec officer biomat sci, 72-77, sr acad adminr, 77-; lectr, Dept Mech Eng, Mass Inst Technol, 76-; chmn & dir, Thermal Tech Inc, 86- *Mem:* Am Soc Mech Engrs; Am Nuclear Soc; Radiol Res Soc; NAm Hyperthermia Res Soc. *Res:* Biocat and mass transfer, thermal modeling; development and evaluation of techniques to quantify perfusion, thermal property measurements, tissue oxygen concentration, radiation and temperature; thermal dosimetry and thermal physics for cancer hyperthermia therapy and combined modality therapies; critical care monitoring. *Mailing Add:* Mass Inst Technol 77 Massachusetts Ave Cambridge MA 02139-4307

BOWMAN, JAMES DAVID, NUCLEAR PHYSICS, PARTICLE PHYSICS. *Current Pos:* staff mem nuclear physics, Meson Physics Facil, 73-93, STAFF MEM, PHYSICS DIV, LOS ALAMOS SCI LAB, 93- *Personal Data:* b White Plains, NY, Aug 24, 39; wid; c Njeri, Warigia & Wangeci. *Educ:* Calif Inst Technol, BS, 61, PhD(physics & math), 67. *Prof Exp:* Res fel nuclear & solid state physics, Calif Inst Technol, 67-68; prof nuclear physics, Univ Bonn,

68-70; res fel nuclear chem, Lawrence Berkeley Lab, Univ Calif, 70-73. *Mem:* Fel Am Physics Soc. *Res:* Medium energy physics; study of nuclear structure; pion nucleus interaction; muon decay and symmetry principles. *Mailing Add:* Physics Div Los Alamos Nat Lab MS H803 Los Alamos NM 87545

BOWMAN, JAMES E, PATHOLOGY, HUMAN GENETICS. *Current Pos:* asst prof med & path, 62-67, assoc prof path, med & biol, 64-71, med dir, Blood Bank, 62-80, dir Labs, 71-81, dir Comprehensive Sickle Cell Ctr, 73-83, PROF PATH, MED & GENETICS, UNIV CHICAGO, 71- *Personal Data:* b Washington, DC, Feb 19, 23; m 50; c 1. *Educ:* Howard Univ, BS, 43, MD, 46. *Prof Exp:* Chmn dept path, Provident Hosp, Chicago, 50-53 & Nemazee Hosp, Shiraz Med Ctr, Iran, 55-61; vis assoc prof path, Fac Med, Pahlavi Univ, 57-59, vis prof & chmn dept, 59-61; hon res asst, Univ Col, Univ London, 61-62. *Concurrent Pos:* NIH spec res fel, Univ Col, Univ London, 61-62; USPHS res grant, 64-66 & 73-; chief path br, Med Nutrit Lab, Fitzsimmons Army Hosp, Colo; fel, Ctr Adv Study Behav Sci, Kaiser Found Soc, Stanford, 81-82; sr scholar, Ctr Clin Med Ethics, Univ Chicago, 89- *Mem:* Fel Col Am Path; fel Am Soc Clin Path; Am Genetics Asn; Am Soc Human Genetics; NY Acad Sci; Sigma Xi. *Res:* Human and population genetics, particularly blood anthropology, serum and erythrocytic polymorphisms. *Mailing Add:* Dept Path Univ Chicago 5841 Maryland Ave Box MC0006 Chicago IL 60637

BOWMAN, JAMES FLOYD, II, sedimentology, oceanography, for more information see previous edition

BOWMAN, JAMES SHEPPARD, ENTOMOLOGY. *Current Pos:* RETIRED. *Personal Data:* b Orrville, Ohio, Oct 29, 28; m 56; c 3. *Educ:* Ohio State Univ, BS, 51, MS, 54; Univ Wis, PhD(entom), 58. *Prof Exp:* Res asst, Ohio State Univ, 51, 53-54 & Univ Wis, 55-58; entomologist, Hazleton Labs, 58-61; res entomologist, Am Cyanamid Co, 61-70; tech rep, CIBA-Giegy Corp, 70-71; from asst prof to prof entom, Univ NH, 71-97. *Mem:* Entom Soc Am; Sigma Xi; Am Asn Univ Prof. *Res:* Industrial development of agricultural pesticides; screening, metabolism and residue studies on insecticides, fungicides and herbicides. *Mailing Add:* Dept Entom Univ NH Nesmith Hall Durham NH 03824

BOWMAN, JAMES TALTON, GENETICS. *Current Pos:* From assoc prof to prof, 65-92, EMER PROF ZOOL, UTAH STATE UNIV, 92- *Personal Data:* b High Point, NC, Aug 2, 37; div; c 2. *Educ:* Duke Univ, BS, 61; Univ Calif, Davis, PhD(genetics), 65. *Mem:* AAAS; Genetics Soc Am; Sigma Xi. *Res:* Genetic finestructure and function in higher organisms. *Mailing Add:* Arbol No 329 Chapalia Guadalajara Jalisco 44540 Mexico

BOWMAN, JOEL MARK, THEORETICAL CHEMISTRY. *Current Pos:* asst prof, 74-77, Alfred P Sloan fel, 77-79, ASSOC PROF CHEM, ILL INST TECHNOL, 77- *Personal Data:* b Boston, Mass, Jan 16, 48; m 72. *Educ:* Univ Calif, Berkeley, AB, 69; Calif Inst Technol, PhD(chem), 74. *Prof Exp:* Teaching asst chem, Calif Inst Technol, 69-74. *Mem:* Sigma Xi; Am Phys Soc. *Res:* Theoretical aspects of reaction dynamics of molecular systems involving exact and approximate quantum, semiclassical and quasiclassical techniques; theoretical studies of gas-surface interactions. *Mailing Add:* Dept Chem Emory Univ Atlanta GA 30322-0001

BOWMAN, JOHN MAXWELL, PEDIATRICS. *Current Pos:* PROF PEDIAT & CHILD HEALTH, FAC MED, UNIV MAN, 71-, PROF OBSTET, GYNEC & REPRODUCTIVE SCI; MED DIR, RH LAB, 61- *Personal Data:* b Winnipeg, Man, May 24, 25; m 49, Constance; c Murray, Catherine, Anne, Mary M & Thomas. *Educ:* Univ Man, MD, 49. *Honors & Awards:* Bruce Chown Award, Can Red Cross Soc, 91. *Prof Exp:* Trainee, Children's Hosp, Winnipeg, 53, Winnipeg Gen Hosp, 54, Babies Hosp, Columbia Presby Med Ctr, 54-56, clin pediat & lectr, Dept Pediat, Fac Med, Queen's Univ, 56-57; pediat practr, Man Clin, 57-66. *Concurrent Pos:* Consult, Can Red Cross Soc, Blood Transfusion Serv, 83- *Mem:* Sr mem, Can Med Asn; Can Pediat Soc; Am Pediat Soc; Int Soc Blood Transfusion; Can Soc Transfusion Med; fel Royal Soc Can. *Mailing Add:* RH Lab Womens Hosp 735 Notre Dame Ave 5th Floor Winnipeg MB R3E 0L8 Can

BOWMAN, KENNETH AARON, ELECTROCHEMISTRY, ALUMINUM PROCESS METALLURGY. *Current Pos:* res scientist, 76-78, sr scientist, 78-80, STAFF SCIENTIST, ALCOA LABS, ALUMINUM CO AM, 80-, TECH SPECIALIST, 91- *Personal Data:* b Alexandria, Va, Mar 20, 48; m 91, Jo Ellen White; c 2. *Educ:* Tusculum Col, BS, 70; Univ Tenn, PhD(chem), 77. *Prof Exp:* Anal chemist qual control, Org Chem Div, Chemetron Corp, 70-71; teaching asst chem, Univ Tenn, 71-72, res asst, Alcoa Found, 72-76. *Mem:* Electrochem Soc; Int Soc Electrochem; Sigma Xi; Am Inst Mining Metall & Petrol Engrs. *Res:* Molten salt chemistry; the production and purification of aluminum, magnesium and calcium; aluminum melting and recycling; beverage and food can manufacturing and coatings. *Mailing Add:* 1410 Rte 56 E Apollo PA 15613-9726. *Fax:* 412-337-4849

BOWMAN, KIMIKO OSADA, MATHEMATICAL STATISTICS. *Current Pos:* sr res staff, 84-94, RES CONSULT, OAK RIDGE NAT LAB, 95- *Personal Data:* b Tokyo, Japan, Aug 15, 27; US citizen;; c 2. *Educ:* Radford Col, BS, 59; Va Polytech Inst, MS, 61, PhD(statist), 63; Univ Tokyo, Dr Eng, 87. *Honors & Awards:* Distinguished & Sustained Contrib Sci Award, Am Women in Sci, 88; Tech Achievement Award, Martin Marietta Energy Syst, Inc, 88. *Prof Exp:* From statistician to math statistician, Comput Technol Ctr, Nuclear Div, Union Carbide Corp, Tenn, 64-70; mem staff, Oak Ridge Nat Lab, 70-73; sr res staff, Comput Sci Div, Nuclear Div, Union Carbide Corp, 73-84. *Concurrent Pos:* Vis prof, Univ Ga, 68; instr, Univ Tenn, 66-67, asst prof, 71-73, res prof math, 90- *Mem:* Fel AAAS; fel Am Statist Asn; fel Inst Math Statist; Sigma Xi; Int Statist Inst; Int Asn Statist Comput. *Res:* Statistical research using high speed computing and estimating parameters. *Mailing Add:* Oak Ridge Nat Lab PO Box 2008 Oak Ridge TN 37831-6367. *Fax:* 423-574-0680; *E-Mail:* bowmanko@ornl.gov

BOWMAN, LAWRENCE SIEMAN, electrical engineering, for more information see previous edition

BOWMAN, LEO HENRY, ANALYTICAL CHEMISTRY. *Current Pos:* DEAN COL PHYS & LIFE SCI, ARK TECH UNIV, 76- *Personal Data:* b Valeda, Kans, May 12, 34; m 52; c 4. *Educ:* Univ Ottawa, Kans, BSc, 56; Mich State Univ, PhD(anal chem), 61. *Prof Exp:* Res chemist anal develop, Chem Div, Pittsburgh Plate Glass Co, 60-62; asst prof chem, Parsons Col, 62-65; chmn dept, Midwestern Col, 65-68; prof chem, Southwest Minn State Col, 68-76. *Mem:* Am Chem Soc. *Res:* Environmental science. *Mailing Add:* Dept Phys Sci Ark Technol Univ 215 W O St Russellville AR 72801-2230

BOWMAN, LEWIS WILMER, organic chemistry, for more information see previous edition

BOWMAN, MALCOLM JAMES, PHYSICAL OCEANOGRAPHY. *Current Pos:* from asst prof to assoc prof, 71-88, actg dean & dir, Marine Res Ctr, 87-88, PROF OCEANOG, MARINE SCI RES CTR, STATE UNIV NY, STONY BROOK, 88- *Personal Data:* b Auckland, NZ, July 30, 42; m 67, Waveney Olsson; c Gail, Sally, Hamish & Erinna. *Educ:* Univ Auckland, BSc, 65, MSc, 67; Univ Sask, PhD(elec eng), 70. *Prof Exp:* Res oceanogr Defense Sci Estab, Auckland, NZ, 67; mem staff, Univ Sask, 70-71. *Concurrent Pos:* Vis res fel, Univ Auckland, NZ, 78-79; managing ed, Springer Verlag, 78-92; vis prof, Univ BC, 85-86, USSR Acad Sci, 89 & Univ Osago, NZ, 94. *Mem:* Am Geophys Union; Am Meterol Soc; Can Meteorol & Oceanog Soc; Oceanog Soc; Estuarine Res Fedn; Asn Prof Eng Sask. *Res:* Oceanography of estuarine and coastal waters; shallow sea fronts; coastal upwelling. *Mailing Add:* Dept Marine Sci State Univ NY 100 Nicolls Rd Stony Brook NY 11794-0001. *Fax:* 516-632-8820

BOWMAN, MARJORIE ANN, FAMILY HEALTH. *Current Pos:* PROF & CHAIR, DEPT FAMILY & COMMUNITY MED, WAKE FOREST UNIV, 86- *Personal Data:* b Grove City, Pa, Aug 18, 53; m, Robert Choplin; c Bridget W Foley. *Educ:* Pa State Univ, BS, 74; Jefferson Med Col, MD, 76; Univ Southern Calif, Los Angeles, MPA, 83. *Prof Exp:* From intern to resident family pract, Duke Univ, 76-79; med officer, USPHS, 79-82; clin instr, Uniformed Servs Univ Health Sci, 80-83; dir family pract residency, Sch Med, Georgetown Univ, 83-86. *Mem:* Fel Am Acad Family Physicians; AMA; Am Pub Health Asn; Soc Teachers Family Med. *Res:* Family practice. *Mailing Add:* NC Baptist Hosp Bowman Gray Sch Med Medical Center Blvd Winston Salem NC 27157-1084

BOWMAN, MARK PAUL, ORGANOSILICON CHEMISTRY, CONTINUOUS REACTOR SYSTEMS. *Current Pos:* PROJ SCIENTIST PROCESS RES & DEVELOP, WITCO, 91- *Personal Data:* b Washington, DC, Apr 25, 58; m 87, Sandra L; c Joy-Rachel & Benjamin. *Educ:* Univ Calif, Los Angeles, BS, 80; Pa State Univ, PhD(chem), 86. *Prof Exp:* Chem lectr, Univ Zambia, 87-89. *Mem:* Am Chem Soc. *Res:* Developing synthetic methods for the manufacture of organofunctional silanes and their scaleup to batch or continuous reaction systems. *Mailing Add:* 1500 S State Rte 2 Friendly WV 26146. *Fax:* 304-652-8725; *E-Mail:* ampbncl@osispec.com

BOWMAN, NEWELL STEDMAN, organic chemistry; deceased, see previous edition for last biography

BOWMAN, PATRICIA IMIG, cosmetics & toiletries, for more information see previous edition

BOWMAN, PHIL BRYAN, ANALYTICAL CHEMISTRY. *Current Pos:* SR RES SCIENTIST, UPJOHN CO, 65- *Personal Data:* b Tulsa, Okla, July 2, 39; m 62; c 3. *Educ:* Kans State Univ, BS, 61; Purdue Univ, PhD(anal chem), 65. *Mem:* Am Chem Soc. *Res:* Gas liquid and high pressure liquid chromatography; electrochemistry; pharmaceutical analysis. *Mailing Add:* Upjohn Co 4822-259-277 7000 Portage Rd Kalamazoo MI 49001-3298

BOWMAN, RAY DOUGLAS, BIOCHEMISTRY, ANALYTICAL CHEMISTRY. *Current Pos:* asst prof, 73-80, ASSOC PROF NATURAL SCI, UNIV NFLA, 80- *Personal Data:* b Indianapolis, Ind, Mar 3, 42; m 85; c 1. *Educ:* Ind Univ, BA, 64; Calif Inst Technol, PhD(phys chem), 71. *Prof Exp:* Res fel, Calif Inst Technol, 71-73. *Res:* Measuring aquatic productivity by the oxygen balance technique; science education. *Mailing Add:* Dept Natural Sci Univ NFla Jacksonville FL 32224

BOWMAN, ROBERT CLARK, JR, CHEMICAL PHYSICS, SOLID STATE CHEMISTRY. *Current Pos:* MEM STAFF, JET PROPULSION LAB, CALIF INST TECHNOL, PASADENA, CALIF, 97- *Personal Data:* b Dayton, Ohio, Oct 10, 45; m 65; c 2. *Educ:* Miami Univ, BS, 67; Mass Inst Technol, MS, 69; Calif Inst Technol, PhD(chem), 83. *Prof Exp:* From res chemist to sr res chemist, Monsanto Res Corp, 69-75, res specialist, 75-83, sci fel, Mound Facil, 83-84; mem technol staff, Chem & Phys Lab, Aerospace

Corp, 84-89; sr specialist tech staff, Aerojet Electronic Systs Div, 90-97. *Mem:* Am Phys Soc; Mat Res Soc. *Res:* Nuclear magnetic resonance; electron paramagnetic resonance; radiation damage and defects in solids; physical properties of metal hydrides; raman light scattering of semiconductors; ion implantation effects; solid state diffusion. *Mailing Add:* Jet Propulsion Lab Calif Inst Technol/MS 157-316 4800 Oak Grove Dr Pasadena CA 91109

BOWMAN, ROBERT MATHEWS, SYNTHETIC ORGANIC CHEMISTRY, ANALYTICAL CHEMISTRY. *Current Pos:* MGR ANALYTICAL SERV, PHARMACEUT DIV, CIBA-GEIGY CORP, 70- *Personal Data:* b Belfast, Northern Ireland, July 18, 40; m 67; c 2. *Educ:* Queen's Univ, Belfast, BS, 62, Hons, 63, PhD, 66. *Prof Exp:* Fel nat prod chem, Univ Minn, 66-68; fel photochem, McMaster Univ, 68-70. *Mem:* Am Chem Soc. *Res:* Design and application of broad areas of synthetic organic chemistry leading to novel biologically significant agents, particularly those with analgesic, anti-convulsant and anti-tumor activity. *Mailing Add:* 6 Meadowbrook Ct Summit NJ 07901-2317

BOWMAN, ROBERT SAMUEL, PHYSICAL CHEMISTRY, ORGANIC CHEMISTRY. *Current Pos:* sr bone prod fel, 51-63, St Joseph Mineral Corp Labs sr fel, 63-78, dir, Mat Technol Div, 78-79, dir res, 79-81, VPRES, MELLON INST, CARNEGIE-MELLON UNIV, 81- *Personal Data:* b Valley View, Pa, June 26, 17. *Educ:* Pa State Col, BS, 40; Univ Pittsburgh, MS, 45, PhD(chem), 50. *Prof Exp:* Asst, Inst Animal Nutrit, Pa State Col, 40-41; res chemist, Jones & Laughlin Steel Corp, 41-45 & Gulf Res & Develop Co, 45-51. *Mem:* AAAS; Am Chem Soc; Am Inst Chemists; Am Inst Chemists; Sigma Xi. *Res:* Surface chemistry; solid phase reactions; coal tar Chemicals and technology; pyridine bases; petroleum hydrocarbons; polymerization; phenol and calcium phosphate chemistry; solid absorbents; catalysis, glass blowing; metal oxides; technical management; research administration. *Mailing Add:* Five Bayard Rd Apt 615 Pittsburgh PA 15213-1906

BOWMAN, THOMAS ELLIOT, zoology; deceased, see previous edition for last biography

BOWMAN, THOMAS EUGENE, THERMAL SCIENCE & FLUID MECHANICS. *Current Pos:* assoc prof space technol, Fla Inst Technol, 69-71, assoc prof mech eng, 71-75, dept head, 78-86, grad dean, 82-86 & 89-93, dean sci & eng, 86-88, dean eng, 88-89, actg dean, Sci & Lib Arts, 88-89, PROF MECH ENG, FLA INST TECHNOL, 75-, ASSOC VPRES ACAD AFFAIRS, 89- *Personal Data:* b Darby, Pa, Aug 3, 38; m 61, Ritva; c Paul, Katriina, Mark & Tony. *Educ:* Calif Inst Technol, BS, 60, MS, 61; Northwestern Univ, PhD(mech eng), 64. *Prof Exp:* Res scientist, Denver Div, Martin-Marietta Corp, 63-67; lectr appl math, Univ Reading, Eng, 67-68; res scientist, Denver Div, Martin-Marietta Corp, 68-69. *Concurrent Pos:* Vis lectr, Univ Colo, 67; staff engr, Orlando Div, Martin-Marietta Corp, 72; energy consult, Care, Egypt, 79; chmn, Policy Adv Bd, Fla Solar Energy Ctr, 81-83; chmn, Nat Mech Eng Dept Heads Comt, 83-84; chmn, ME Div, Am Soc Eng Educ, 90-91; mem, Eng Accreditation Comn, Accreditation Bd Eng & Technol, 93- *Mem:* Fel Am Soc Mech Engrs; Am Soc Eng Educ. *Res:* Fluid mechanics and thermal science, especially with regard to aerospace propulsion systems, low-gravity fluid behavior, and solar energy; developments in appropriate solar technology, especially solar cookers. *Mailing Add:* AVPAA Fla Inst Technol 150 W Univ Blvd Melbourne FL 32901. *Fax:* 407-768-8000, Ext 8948; *E-Mail:* bowman@fit.edu

BOWMAN, WALKER, III, CHEMICAL ENGINEERING. *Current Pos:* CONSULT, CHEM TECHNOL, 84- *Personal Data:* b Louisville, Ky, June 10, 24; m 55, Elizabeth Chester; c Walker IV, Warren & Willis. *Educ:* Princeton Univ, BS, 49; Mass Inst Technol, SM, 51, ScD, 56. *Prof Exp:* Jr proj engr, Stand Oil Co Inc, 55-58, proj engr, 58-60, sr proj engr, 60-63; res assoc, Amoco Chem Corp, 63-69, div dir, 69-73, sr consult engr, 73-84. *Mem:* Am Chem Soc; Am Inst Chem Engrs; Sigma Xi. *Res:* Process design; economics of petro chemicals; technological forecasting. *Mailing Add:* 4N011 Thorn Tree St Charles IL 60174. *Fax:* 630-584-1132; *E-Mail:* 76216.3666@compuserve.com

BOWMAN, WILFRED WILLIAM, CHEMISTRY. *Current Pos:* RES CHEMIST, SAVANNAH RIVER LAB, E I DU PONT DE NEMOURS & CO, INC, 73- *Personal Data:* b Piqua, Ohio, Dec 17, 41; m 59; c 2. *Educ:* Wilmington Col, BA, 63; Univ Rochester, PhD(chem), 68. *Prof Exp:* Res assoc chem, Cyclotron Inst, Tex A&M Univ, 68-73. *Mem:* Am Chem Soc; Am Phys Soc. *Res:* Gamma-ray spectroscopy; neutron activation analysis. *Mailing Add:* 1008 Holliday Dr North Augusta SC 29841-5204

BOWMER, RICHARD GLENN, PLANT PHYSIOLOGY. *Current Pos:* from asst prof to assoc prof, 65-77, PROF BOT, IDAHO STATE UNIV, 77- *Personal Data:* b Spokane, Wash, Dec 4, 31; m 57, Leona M Willey; c Mary, Linda, Richard, Edward, Theresa & James. *Educ:* Univ Idaho, BS, 53, MS, 57; Univ NC, PhD(bot), 60. *Prof Exp:* Asst prof biol, Lewis-Clark State Col, 60-61. *Res:* Translocation of solutes in higher plants. *Mailing Add:* Dept Biol Idaho State Univ Pocatello ID 83209

BOWN, THOMAS MICHAEL, vertebrate paleontology, fluvial sedimentology, for more information see previous edition

BOWNDS, JOHN MARVIN, MATHEMATICS. *Current Pos:* asst prof math, 68-74, ASSOC PROF MATH, UNIV ARIZ, 74- *Personal Data:* b Delta, Colo, Apr 21, 41; m 62; c 2. *Educ:* Chico State Col, BA, 64; Univ Calif, Riverside, MA, 67, PhD(math), 68. *Prof Exp:* Mathematician, US Naval Weapons Ctr, Calif, 64-65. *Concurrent Pos:* NSF grant, 79-81. *Mem:* Am Math Soc; Soc Indust & Appl Math. *Res:* Differential equations; numerical solution of integral equations. *Mailing Add:* 1000 Misty Springs Rd Knoxville TN 37932-3121

BOWNDS, M DERIC, NEUROBIOLOGY. *Current Pos:* from asst prof to assoc prof, 69-75, PROF MOLECULAR BIOL & ZOOL, UNIV WIS-MADISON, 75- *Personal Data:* b San Antonio, Tex, May 16, 42; div; c Jonathan & Sarah. *Educ:* Harvard Univ, BA, 63, PhD(biol), 67. *Prof Exp:* Instr neurobiol, Harvard Med Sch, 67-69. *Concurrent Pos:* NIH fel, 67-69 & res grant, 69- *Mem:* Soc Neurosci; Asn Res Vision & Ophthal; Biophys Soc; Soc Gen Physiologists. *Res:* Chemistry and physiology of photoreceptor and other nerve membranes; biology of mind. *Mailing Add:* Bock Labs Univ Wis Madison WI 53706. *E-Mail:* bownds@macc.wisc.edu

BOWNE, SAMUEL WINTER, JR, CHEMISTRY, GENETICS. *Current Pos:* RETIRED. *Personal Data:* b New York, NY, Nov 19, 25; m 54; c 2. *Educ:* Mass Inst Technol, BS, 48; Columbia Univ, MA, 52; Cornell Univ, MS, 53, PhD(genetics), 57. *Prof Exp:* Jr chemist, Merck & Co, Inc, 48-49; res assoc, Wash State Univ, 53-54; asst prof chem, Eastern Wash Col Educ, 57-59; assoc prof biol, Univ Wichita, 59-61; res assoc, Ohio State Univ, 61-62; from asst prof to assoc prof, Edinboro State Col, 62-68, head dept sci, 64-69, prof chem, 68-89. *Mem:* AAAS; Am Chem Soc. *Res:* Biochemical genetics; intermediate metabolism. *Mailing Add:* 5241 Tarbell Rd Edinboro PA 16412

BOWNESS, COLIN, PHYSICS. *Current Pos:* RETIRED. *Personal Data:* b London, Eng, Oct 26, 29; m 53; c 2. *Educ:* Univ London, BSc, 50 & 51, PhD(physics), 56. *Prof Exp:* Microwave engr, Elec & Musical Industs, Eng, 51-56, lab mgr, 56-57; tech dir microwaves & lasers, Raytheon Co, 57-62, mgr spec microwave devices oper, 62-92. *Mem:* Sr mem Inst Elec & Electronics Engrs; Optical Soc Am; Brit Inst Physics & Phys Soc. *Res:* Lasers; microwave component design, especially ferrite devices. *Mailing Add:* 76 Shady Hill Rd Weston MA 02193

BOWNS, BEVERLY HENRY, community health, adolescent health, for more information see previous edition

BOWSER, CARL, GEOCHEMISTRY. *Current Pos:* from asst prof to assoc prof, 64-74, PROF GEOL, UNIV WIS, MADISON, 74; GEOLOGIST, US GEOL SURV, 80- *Personal Data:* b Compton, Calif, Apr 21, 37; m 60; c 2. *Educ:* Univ Calif, Riverside, BA, 59; Univ Calif, Los Angeles, PhD(geol), 65. *Prof Exp:* Asst geol, Inst Geophys, Univ Calif, Los Angeles, 60-64. *Mem:* Geol Soc Am; Geochem Soc; Mineral Soc Am; Am Geophys Union; AAAS. *Res:* Geochemistry of non-marine salt deposits; mineralogy and chemistry of marine and fresh water ferromanganese nodules; chemical sedimentology of lakes; geochemistry of hydrothermal deposits in Red Sea; chemical evaluation of groundwater-lakewater systems. *Mailing Add:* 1802 Camelot Dr Madison WI 53705-1008

BOWSER, JAMES RALPH, ORGANOSILICON CHEMISTRY. *Current Pos:* asst prof, 80-84, ASSOC PROF CHEM, COL FREDONIA, STATE UNIV NY, 84-, CHMN DEPT, 83- *Personal Data:* b Windber, Pa, March 30, 49; m 81. *Educ:* Carion State Col, BS, 71; Duke Univ, PhD(chem), 76. *Prof Exp:* Instr chem, Univ Va, 76-78; asst prof, Colgate Univ, 78-80. *Mem:* Am Chem Soc; AAAS; Sigma Xi; NY Acad Sci. *Res:* Synthetic and spectroscopic aspects of organometallic chemistry with emphasis on organosilicon compounds and chromatographic methods for the analysis of such compounds. *Mailing Add:* Chem Dept State Univ NY Fredonia NY 14063

BOWSER, SAMUEL SCHUYLER, CELL BIOLOGY, PROTOZOOLOGY. *Current Pos:* Fel, 84-88, asst prof cell biol, 88-96, ASSOC PROF BIOMED SCI, UNIV ALBANY, 96-; RES SCIENTIST CELL BIOL, WADSWORTH CTR LABS, 88- *Personal Data:* b Middleton, NY, Jan 16, 57. *Educ:* Univ Albany, BS, 79, PhD(cell biol), 84. *Honors & Awards:* Antarctica Serv Medal, 85. *Concurrent Pos:* Adj assoc prof, Rensselaer Polytech Inst, Troy, NY. *Mem:* Am Soc Cell Biol; Sigma Xi; Soc Protozoologists; Am Chem Soc; Geol Soc Am. *Res:* Behavior and properties of primary cilia; physiological ecology. *Mailing Add:* Wadsworth Ctr Labs Res Box 509 Empire State Plaza Albany NY 12201. *E-Mail:* bowser@wadsworth.org

BOWSHER, ARTHUR LEROY, ECHINODERMATA, PALEONTOLOGY. *Current Pos:* CONSULT, 86- *Personal Data:* b Wapakoneta, Ohio, Apr 29, 17; m 67, Ruth E; c Sally J (Drake), Arthur L Jr, Anne (Alkinson) & Dale C. *Educ:* Univ Tulsa, BS, 41. *Prof Exp:* Mem staff, Tidewater Assoc Oil Co, 37-38; lab asst, Univ Tulsa, 38-41; lab asst, Univ Kans, 41-42, instr, 46-48; paleontologist, Smithsonian Inst, 48-52; chief lab, Navy Oil Unit, US Geol Surv, 52-57; staff geologist, Sinclair Oil & Gas Co, Okla, 57-69; sr geologist, Atlantic Richfield Oil Co, Tex, 69-70; sr geologist, Arabian Am Oil Co, Saudi Arabia, 70-78; chief explor strategy, Off Nat Petrol Reserve-Alaska, US Geol Surv, 78-86; explorationist, Yates Petrol Corp, Artesia, NMex, 81-86. *Concurrent Pos:* Asst geologist, Kans State Geol Surv, 41-42, geologist, 42; Capt, US CEngr, 42-46; instr, Am Univ, 49; independent oil finder, 86-94. *Mem:* Am Asn Petrol Geol; Paleont Soc; Geol Soc Am; Sigma Xi; hon mem Roswell Geol Soc. *Res:* Petroleum geology; non-metallic resources; stratigraphy and paleontology; author of more than 50 publications. *Mailing Add:* 5409 NW 66th St Oklahoma City OK 73132-7750

BOWSHER, HARRY FRED, NUCLEAR PHYSICS. *Current Pos:* assoc prof & chmn dept, 66-67, chmn dept, 71-74, PROF PHYSICS, AUGUSTA COL, 67- *Personal Data:* b Lima, Ohio, Feb 26, 31; m 55; c 3. *Educ:* Ohio State Univ, BS, 55, MS, 56, PhD(nuclear physics), 60. *Prof Exp:* Asst prof nuclear physics, Univ Tenn, 60-66. *Concurrent Pos:* Fulbright lectr, Dept Physics, Cheng Kung Univ, Taiwan, 69-70; consult, Oak Ridge Nat Lab, 60- *Mem:* Am Phys Soc. *Res:* Heavy-ion nuclear physics; reaction mechanisms. *Mailing Add:* Dept Physics/Chem Augusta Col 2500 Walton Way Augusta GA 30904-0299

BOWYER, C STUART, ASTRONOMY, SPACE SCIENCE. *Current Pos:* assoc prof, 67-74, PROF ASTRON, UNIV CALIF, BERKELEY, 74-, DIR, CTR EXTREME ULTRAVIOLET ASTROPHYS, 89-; PRES, BERKELEY PHOTONICS, 86- *Personal Data:* b Toledo, Ohio, Aug 2, 34; m 57, Jane Baker; c 3. *Educ:* Miami Univ, BS, 56; Cath Univ, PhD(physics), 65. *Hon Degrees:* DSc, Miami Univ, 85. *Honors & Awards:* Sr Scientist Award, Humboldt Found, 82; Spain Ministry Educ & Sci Award, 95. *Prof Exp:* Physicist, Nat Bur Stands, 56-58 & Naval Res Lab, 58-67; asst prof space sci, Cath Univ, 66-67. *Concurrent Pos:* Consult, NASA, 68-, & Israeli Space Agency, 89-; sr vis fel, Sci Res Coun, Eng, 74; Fulbright prof, 83; Red Star prof, France, 89; Guggenheim fel, 92. *Mem:* Am Geophys Union; Am Astron Soc; Int Astrophys Union; Astron Soc Pac; Int Acad Astronaut; Optical Soc Am. *Res:* Extreme ultraviolet astronomy; search for extraterrestrial intelligence; high energy astrophysics. *Mailing Add:* Space Sci Lab Univ Calif Berkeley CA 94720-7450

BOWYER, J(AMES) M(ARSTON), JR, FLUID MECHANICS & HEAT TRANSFER, APPLIED MATHEMATICS. *Current Pos:* CONSULT ENG, REG PROF ENG MECH CALIF, 89- *Personal Data:* b Courtland, Kans, Dec 11, 20; US citizen; m 48, Marie B Gillon; c John, Mary B & Peggy. *Educ:* Kans State Col, BS, 42, MS, 49; Univ Calif, PhD(mech eng), 56. *Prof Exp:* Trainee, Convair Div, Gen Dynamics Corp, 46-47, aerodynamics engr, 49-51; asst, Kans State Col, 47-49; jr res engr low pressures proj, Univ Calif, 51-55; sr thermodynamics engr, Convair Div, Gen Dynamics Corp, 55-57, asst res group engr, 57-59, design specialist, 59-60, staff scientist, 60-62, sr staff scientist, Astronaut & Convair Div, 62-63; from assoc prof to prof mech eng, Kans State Univ, 63-69; staff engr, TRW Systs Group, 69-70; staff mem, Gulf Radiation Technol, 70-71, sr staff engr, 71-76; mem tech staff, Jet Propulsion Lab, 76-84; prof & chmn, Dept Mech Eng, Wichita State Univ, 84-88, adj prof, 88-89. *Mem:* Assoc fel Am Inst Aeronaut & Astronaut; Sigma Xi. *Res:* Supersonic and hypersonic nonviscous and viscous flows; reacting gas flows; rarefied gas flows; nucleation kinetics; heat transfer; applied mathematics; solar energy. *Mailing Add:* 3683 Quailview Court Spring Valley CA 91977. *E-Mail:* 72355.1367@compuserve.com

BOWYER, KERN M(ALLORY), ELECTRICAL ENGINEERING, COMPUTER ENGINEERING. *Current Pos:* RETIRED. *Personal Data:* b Jersey City, NJ, Nov 12, 28; m 80; c 2. *Educ:* NY Univ, BEE, 57. *Prof Exp:* Serv engr commun equip, Winters Radio Lab, 48-49; test engr radar, Gen Elec Co, 51; sr res assoc, E I du Pont de Nemours & Co, Inc, 57-90. *Concurrent Pos:* Mem, Del State Indust Adv Comt. *Mem:* Audio Eng Soc; Inst Elec & Electronics Engrs; NY Acad Sci. *Res:* Image processing; communication electronics; anti-submarine warfare; industrial instrumentation; magnetic recording systems; computer systems applications. *Mailing Add:* 16 Lehigh Ave Wilmington DE 19805

BOX, EDITH DARROW, PARASITOLOGY. *Current Pos:* res assoc, Med Br, 48-49, from asst prof to assoc prof, 49-85, EMER PROF MICROBIOL, UNIV TEX, 85- *Personal Data:* b Glendale, Md, Jan 3, 22; m 51; c 2. *Educ:* Iowa State Col, BS, 43; Johns Hopkins Univ, DSc(parasitol), 48. *Prof Exp:* Student asst parasitol, Sch Hyg, Johns Hopkins Univ, 43-48. *Mem:* AAAS; Am Soc Trop Med & Hyg; Am Soc Parasitol; Soc Protozool; Wildlife Dis Asn. *Res:* Chemotherapy and biology of avian and rodent malaria; arthropod transmission of blood and tissue protozoa; life cycles of intracellular protozoa; taxonomy and biology of avian coccidia. *Mailing Add:* Rte 2B555 Dickinson TX 77539

BOX, GEORGE EDWARD PELHAM, INDUSTRIAL & MANUFACTURING ENGINEERING. *Current Pos:* prof, Univ Wis-Madison, 59-71, Ronald Aylmer Fisher prof, 71-80, vilas prof statist, 80-91, DIR RES, CTR QUALITY IMPROV, UNIV WIS-MADISON, 85- *Personal Data:* b Gravesend, Eng, Oct 18, 19; m 59, 85; c 2. *Educ:* Univ London, BS, 48, PhD(statist), 52, DSc, 61. *Hon Degrees:* DSc, Univ Rochester, 75; Carnegie Mellon Univ, 89. *Honors & Awards:* Brit Empire Medal, 46; Am Inst Chem Engrs Prof Progress Award, 63; Guy Medal, Royal Statist Soc, 64, Gold Medal, 93; Wilks Medal, Am Statist Asn; Shewhart Medal, Am Soc Qual Control, Deming Medal. *Prof Exp:* From statistician to head statist, Res Sect, Dyestuffs Div, Imp Chem Indust Ltd, 48-56; dir, Res Group, Dept Math, Princeton Univ, 56-59. *Concurrent Pos:* Vis prof, NC State Col, 53-54 & Univ Essex, 70-71; Ford Found vis prof, Grad Sch Bus Admin, Harvard Univ, 65-66; Guggenheim fel, 90. *Mem:* Fel AAAS; fel Am Statist Asn (pres, 78); Int Statist Inst; fel Inst Math Statist (pres, 79); fel Am Acad Arts & Sci; fel Royal Soc. *Res:* Design and analysis of experiments; time series and forecasting; statistical inference; quality improvement. *Mailing Add:* 2238 Branson Rd Oregon WI 53575. *Fax:* 608-263-1425

BOX, HAROLD C, BIOPHYSICS. *Current Pos:* sr cancer res scientist, 54-61, assoc cancer res scientist, 61-70, prin cancer res scientist, 70-76, DIR DEPT BIOPHYS, ROSWELL PARK MEM INST, 76- *Personal Data:* b Clarence, NY, Aug 19, 25; m 51; c 5. *Educ:* Canisius Col, BS, 48; Univ Buffalo, MA, 51, PhD(physics), 54. *Prof Exp:* Asst physicist, Cornell Aeronaut Lab, 51-54. *Concurrent Pos:* Asst res prof, Roswell Park, Grad Div, State Univ NY Buffalo, 62-74, adj prof physics, 74-76, res prof & chmn, 76- *Mem:* Am Phys Soc; Am Chem Soc; Biophys Soc; Radiation Res Soc; Am Crystallog Asn. *Res:* Magnetic resonance studies of carcinogens and radiation effects in biological compounds. *Mailing Add:* 170 Reist St Williamsville NY 14221-5350

BOX, JAMES ELLIS, JR, SOIL PHYSICS. *Current Pos:* RETIRED. *Personal Data:* b Georgetown, Tex, Sept 12, 31; m 56; c 4. *Educ:* Tex A&M Univ, BS, 52, MS, 56; Utah State Univ, PhD(soil & irrig), 61. *Prof Exp:* Soil scientist, Soil Conserv Serv, US Dept Agr, 56-57; asst soil physics, Utah State Univ, 57-60; res soil scientist, Soil & Water Conserv Res Ctr, US Dept Agr, 60-61, supt, US Big Spring Field Sta, 62-65, dir, 65-84, location leader, lab dir & soil scientist, 65-84, res leader, 72-81, res adv, Southesstern Region, Nat Asn Conserv Districts, 73-84, res soil scientist, Southern Piedmont Conserv Res Ctr, Agr Res Serv, 84-96. *Concurrent Pos:* US Dept Agr sponsoring scientist, Soil Physics Res, Israel Inst Technol, 66-; vis scientist, Am Soc Agron, 71-72; adv mem, Ga State Soil & Water Comt, Southeast Area Res Comt, Nat Asn Conserv Dist; mem grad fac, Univ Ga, 75-80. *Mem:* Fel Am Soc Agron; Crop Sci Soc Am; Int Soil Sci Soc; Soil Conserv Soc Am; Soil Sci Soc Am; fel Soil & Water Conserv Soc Am. *Res:* Basic aspects of plant-soil-water relationships; moisture conservation under dryland and rain fed conditions; wheat root research. *Mailing Add:* 3810 Old Lexington Rd Athens GA 30605

BOX, LARRY, CHEMICAL MODIFICATION OF CELLULOSIC FIBER, CHEMISTRY TROUBLE SHOOTING IN PROCESS & PRODUCT AREAS. *Current Pos:* PROF TUTOR, CHEYNEY UNIV, 94- *Personal Data:* b Chester, Pa, Sept 24, 39; m 60; c 3. *Educ:* Cheyney Univ, BA, 65; St Josephs Univ, MS, 77. *Prof Exp:* Lab technician res, Scott Paper Co, 65-70, promotion series res chem, 70-90, sr proj leader, Scott Worldwide, 90-94. *Concurrent Pos:* Lectr & tutor chem, Widener Univ, 71-75; founder & vchmn, AGAPE Day Care & Presch Inc, 81-91. *Mem:* Int Soc African Scientists; Tech Asn Pulp & Paper Indust. *Res:* Organic synthesis research on natural polymers; two patents. *Mailing Add:* 90 Andrien Rd Glen Mills PA 19342

BOX, MICHAEL ALLISTER, RADIATIVE TRANSFER, REMOTE SENSING. *Current Pos:* SR LECTR, UNIV NSW, 81- *Personal Data:* b Melbourne, Australia, Dec 23, 47; m 72, Gail P Hallinan; c Christopher & Pamela. *Educ:* Monash Univ, BSc, 70; Sydney Univ, PhD(physics), 75. *Prof Exp:* Res scientist, Inst Atmospheric Optics & Remote Sensing, Hampton, Va, 77-79; res assoc atmospheric radiation, Inst Atmospheric Physics, Univ Ariz, 79-81. *Mem:* Am Meteorol Soc; Am Geophys Union; Australian Inst Physics; Australian Meteorol & Oceanog Soc. *Res:* Inversion techniques in atmosphere remote sensing, especially aerosol size distribution; radiative transfer calculations; application of rigorous perturbation techniques in radiative transfer. *Mailing Add:* Sch Physics Univ NSW Sydney NSW 2052 Australia. *Fax:* 61-2-6633420; *E-Mail:* mab@newt.phys.unsw.edu.au

BOX, THADIS WAYNE, range management, for more information see previous edition

BOX, VERNON G S, PHARMACEUTICAL CHEMISTRY. *Current Pos:* assoc prof, 84-91, PROF ORG CHEM, CITY COL, CITY UNIV NY, 92- *Personal Data:* b Montego Bay, Jamaica, June 20, 46; m 76, Lynda L Tayloo; c Samantha & Ananda. *Educ:* Univ Wis, Kingston, Jamaica, BSc, 67, PhD(org chem), 71. *Prof Exp:* From asst lectr to sr lectr chem, Univ WI, Kingston, Jamaica, 69-82; sr scientist pharmaceut & prin scientist chem res, Schering-Plough Corp, Bloomfield, NJ, 82-84. *Concurrent Pos:* Prof Chem, Grad Sch, City Univ NY. *Mem:* Am Chem Soc; Inter-Am Photochem Soc; NY Acad Sci; Am Inst Chem. *Res:* Synthesis of natural products from monosaccharides; reaction mechanisms and stereo-electronic effects in monosaccharide chemistry; new protecting groups for monosaccharides. *Mailing Add:* Dept Chem City Col Convent Ave 138th St New York NY 10031. *Fax:* 212-650-6107; *E-Mail:* box@scisun_sci.ccny.cuny.edu, 75506.2113@compuserve.com

BOXENBAUM, HAROLD GEORGE, AGING RESEARCH, INTERSPECIES SCALING. *Current Pos:* DIR CLIN PHARMACOKINETICS, WYETH-AYERST RES, 93- *Personal Data:* b Philadelphia, Pa, Dec 26, 42; m 82; c 1. *Educ:* Temple Univ, BS, 65, MS, 69; Univ Calif, San Francisco, PhD(pharmaceut chem), 72. *Prof Exp:* Asst prof pharm, Col Pharm, Ohio State Univ, 72-74; sr scientist, Hoffmann-La Roche Inc, 74-77; owner & mgr, Pennyroyal Apothecary, 77-80; assoc prof pharm, Sch Pharm, Univ Conn, 80-85; res assoc, Marion Merrell Dow Inc, 85-93. *Concurrent Pos:* Adj assoc prof, Col Pharm, Univ Cincinnati, 88- *Mem:* Fel AAAS; fel Am Asn Pharmaceut Sci; Am Soc Pharmacol & Exp Therapeut; Int Soc Study Xenobiotics; Sigma Xi. *Res:* Pharmacokinetics, biopharmaceutics, clinical pharmacology, toxicology, aging and drug metabolism. *Mailing Add:* Otsuka Am Pharmaceut Inc 2440 Research Blvd Rockville MD 20850. *Fax:* 215-975-0338

BOXER, LAURENCE A, CELL BIOLOGY OF GRANULOCYTES. *Current Pos:* PROF & DIR PEDIAT HEMAT & ONCOL, UNIV MICH, 82- *Personal Data:* b May 17, 40; m 69, Grace Jordison; c David. *Educ:* Univ Colo, BA, 61; Stanford Univ, MD, 66. *Honors & Awards:* Mead Johnson Award, 83. *Prof Exp:* Intern & resident pediat, Yale Univ Med Ctr, New Haven, 66-68; resident pediat, Stanford Univ Med Sch, 68-69; maj, USAR Tripler Hosp, Honolulu, 69-72; fel hemat, Harvard Univ, 72-75; from asst prof to prof, Ind Univ, 75-82. *Concurrent Pos:* Estab investr, Am Heart Asn, 78-83; mem, Hemat Study Sect, 81-86 & 88-92; assoc ed, J Immunol & Blood, J Leukocyte Biol, J Pediat, J Clin Immunol, J Lab Clin Med & J Clin Invest. *Mem:* Soc Pediat Res (pres, 85-86); Am Soc Hemat (coun, 88-92); Am Soc

Clin Invest; Am Soc Cell Biol; Am Asn Immunol; Am Asn Pathologists; Am Asn Physicians. *Res:* Characterizing the metabolic pathways underlying granulocyte activation during adhesion and phagocytosis by these cells. *Mailing Add:* Dept Pediat Sch Med Univ Mich PO Box 0238 Ann Arbor MI 48109. *Fax:* 313-936-8520; *E-Mail:* laboxer@umich.edu

BOXER, ROBERT JACOB, ORGANIC CHEMISTRY. *Current Pos:* assoc prof, 64-72, PROF ORG CHEM, GA SOUTHERN UNIV, 72- *Personal Data:* b Brooklyn, NY, Apr 9, 35; m 63; c 2. *Educ:* Brooklyn Col, BS, 56; Rutgers Univ, PhD(org chem), 61. *Prof Exp:* From asst prof to assoc prof chem, Oglethorpe Col, 61-64. *Mem:* Am Chem Soc. *Res:* Organic halogenating agents; history of drugs of abuse. *Mailing Add:* Landrum Box 8064 Ga Southern Univ Statesboro GA 30460-1000

BOXER, STEVEN GEORGE, PHYSICAL CHEMISTRY. *Current Pos:* PROF CHEM, STANFORD UNIV, 76- *Personal Data:* b New York City, NY, Oct 18, 47; m 77; c 2. *Educ:* Tufts Univ, BS, 69; Univ Chicago, PhD(chem), 76. *Honors & Awards:* Presidential Young Investigator Award. *Concurrent Pos:* A P Sloan Fel. *Mem:* Am Chem Soc; Biophys Soc; Am Soc Photobiol. *Res:* Mechanisms of electron energy transfer in biological systems; new magnetic resonance methods; primary photochemistry of photosynthesis; effects of magnetic and electric fields on chemical reactions. *Mailing Add:* Dept Chem Stanford Univ Stanford CA 94305-5080. *Fax:* 650-725-4817

BOXILL, GALE CLARK, PHARMACOLOGY. *Current Pos:* RETIRED. *Personal Data:* b Indianapolis, Ind, Jan 28, 19; m 46, Irene V Byk; c William M & Judith A (Woulfe). *Educ:* Washington & Lee Univ, AB, 47; Univ Tenn, MS, 51, PhD(pharmacol), 54. *Prof Exp:* Jr pharmacologist, Wm S Merrell Co, 47-49; asst prof, Sch Pharm, Univ Ga, 52-53; pharmacologist, Res Lab, Mead Johnson & Co, 53-59; sr res assoc, Warner-Lambert Res Inst, 59-62, dir dept toxicol, 62-70; mgr toxicol, Wyeth Labs, 70-78, assoc dir biol res, 78-85. *Mem:* Am Soc Pharmacol & Exp Therapeut; Sigma Xi; Soc Toxicol (secy, 75-79). *Res:* Cardiovascular effect of epinephrine on pressoreceptors; effects of various drugs on blood pressure to vascular and central nervous system; toxicological evaluation of new drugs. *Mailing Add:* 34351 Whispering Oaks Blvd Ridge Manor FL 33525

BOXMAN, RAYMOND LEON, ELECTRICAL DISCHARGES & PLASMAS, METALLURGICAL COATINGS & THIN FILMS. *Current Pos:* ASSOC PROF ELEC ENG, TEL-AVIV UNIV, 75- *Personal Data:* b Philadelphia, Pa, June 9, 46; m 72, Edith E Selina; c Benjamin, Jonathan, Lillian & Yael. *Educ:* Mass Inst Technol, SB & SM, 69, PhD(elec eng), 73. *Honors & Awards:* Boris & Renee Joffe Award, Int Union Electro-Deposition & Surface Finishing, 84. *Prof Exp:* Sr res engr, Gen Elec Co, 73-75. *Concurrent Pos:* Vis assoc prof, Univ SC, 81-82; vis scientist, Brown Boveri Corp, 82, Multi-Arc Inc, Rockaway, NJ, 95; assoc ed, Inst Elec & Electronics Engrs Trans Plasma Sci, 87-94; vis prof, Drexel Univ, 89-90. *Mem:* Fel Inst Elec & Electronics Engrs; Sigma Xi; Israel Vacuum Soc; Israel Phys Soc. *Res:* Electrical discharges; high current vacuum arcs, laboratory measurements and formulation of physical models; applications of arcs to high current switching and to the deposition of metallurgical coatings and thin films. *Mailing Add:* Fac Eng Tel Aviv Univ Ramat Aviv Tel Aviv 69978 Israel. *Fax:* 972-3-641-0189; *E-Mail:* boxman@eng.tau.ac.il

BOYARCHUK, ALEXANDER A, ASTRONOMY. *Current Pos:* DIR, INST ASTRON, MOSCOW, 87- *Personal Data:* b Grozny, Russia, June 21, 31; m 55, Margarita Kropotova; c Cirill. *Educ:* Pulkovo Observ, USSR, PhD, 58, DSc, 67. *Prof Exp:* Minor scientist, Crimean Astrophys Observ, 58-62, sr scientist, 62-70, dep dir, 70-87. *Concurrent Pos:* Ed, J Sowjet Astron, 87. *Mem:* Am Astron Soc; Am Phys Soc; Russ Acad Sci; Int Astron Union (pres, 91-94); Royal Astron Soc; Int Astron Acad. *Res:* Published over 200 articles to professional journals. *Mailing Add:* Leninskij 69-3-385 Moscow 117296 Russia

BOYARSKY, ABRAHAM JOSEPH, DETERMINISTIC DYNAMICAL SYSTEMS. *Current Pos:* From asst prof to assoc prof, 73-82, PROF MATH, CONCORDIA UNIV, MONTREAL, 82- *Personal Data:* b Baranovitch, Poland, Nov 16, 46; Can citizen; m 74; c 9. *Educ:* McGill Univ, BEng, 67, MEng, 68, PhD(control theory), 71. *Mem:* Am Math Soc. *Res:* The limiting behavior of deterministic dynamical systems, including the subject known as "chaos". *Mailing Add:* Dept Math Concordia Univ 7141 Sherbrooke St W Montreal PQ H4B 1R6 Can

BOYARSKY, LILA HARRIET, BIOLOGY. *Current Pos:* RETIRED. *Personal Data:* b Brooklyn, NY, Apr 23, 21; m 41; c 2. *Educ:* Hunter Col, BA, 42; Univ Wis, MS, 43, PhD(genetics), 47. *Prof Exp:* Asst physiol reprod, Univ Wis, 42-43, animal husb, Purdue Univ, 43-45 & physiol, Univ Chicago, 45-47; instr biol, George Williams Col, 49-50; from asst prof to assoc prof, Transylvania Col, 55-61, prof biol, 61-91. *Mem:* AAAS; Am Zool Soc. *Res:* Genetics; endocrinology; physiology of reproduction; genetics of hamsters. *Mailing Add:* 1729 Traveller Rd Lexington KY 40504

BOYARSKY, LOUIS LESTER, NEUROPHYSIOLOGY. *Current Pos:* from asst prof to assoc prof, 50-59, PROF PHYSIOL & BIOPHYS, COL MED, UNIV KY, 59- *Personal Data:* b Jersey City, NJ, Sept 5, 19; m 41; c 2. *Educ:* City Col New York, BS, 41; Purdue Univ, MS, 45; Univ Chicago, PhD(physiol), 48. *Prof Exp:* Psychophysiologist, Inst Juv Res, 49-50. *Concurrent Pos:* Fulbright scholar, Univ Milan, 57-58; vis prof, Univ Hawaii, 68-69. *Mem:* Am Physiol Soc; Soc Neurosci; Biophys Soc; Soc Exp Biol & Med. *Res:* Peripheral and central nervous system; biophysics. *Mailing Add:* Dept Physiol & Biophys Univ Ky Med Sch MS507 Med Ctr Lexington KY 40536-0084

BOYARSKY, SAUL, UROLOGY, PHYSIOLOGY. *Current Pos:* CLIN PROF UROL, ST LOUIS UNIV, 90- *Personal Data:* b Burlington, Vt, July 22, 23; m 45, Rose Eiseman; c Myer W, Terry Linda (Alcorn) & Hannah Gail (Fowler). *Educ:* Univ Vt, BS, 43, MD, 46; Wash Univ, JD, 81. *Honors & Awards:* William P Burpeau Award; Urodynamics Soc & Int Continence Soc Award, 83. *Prof Exp:* Instr urol, Sch Med, Duke Univ, 54; instr, NY Univ, 55-56; from asst prof to assoc prof, Albert Einstein Col Med, 56-63; prof urol & asst prof physiol, Sch Med, Duke Urologist, Duke Hosp, 63-70; urologist, Barnes Hosp, 70-73; prof genitourinary surg & chmn dept, prof biomed eng & assoc prof pharmacol, Sch Med, Wash Univ, 70-73, prof urol, 70-89. *Concurrent Pos:* Fel surg, Col Med, Univ Vt, 47-48; USPHS fel physiol, Sch Med, NY Univ, 54-55; asst attend, Bellevue Hosp, NY, 54-56 & Univ Hosp, 56-63; asst chief urol, Bronx Vet Admin Hosp, 56-57, attend, 60-63; assoc attend, Bronx Munic Hosp, 56-62, vis urologist, 62-63; adj urologist, New Rochelle Hosp, 60-63; chief urol, Vet Admin Hosp, 63-70, dir rehab, 69-70; consult urol, St Louis City Hosp, 70-; consult, John Cochran Vet Admin Hosp, Jefferson Barracks, Jewish Hosp, Food & Drug Admin bur devices, HEW, Vet Admin Spinal Cord Injury Serv & Mo Crippled Childrens Serv, Univ Mo, 70-; mem panel review gastroenterol-urol devices, HEW, Food & Drug Admin; pvt law pract, 85- *Mem:* Am Physiol Soc; Am Asn Genitourinary Surgeons; Am Urol Asn; Am Col Surgeons; Soc Univ Urologists; Sigma Xi; Am Col Surgeons; fel Am Acad Forensic Sci; Urodyn Soc. *Res:* Renal, ureteral and bladder physiology and pharmacology; rehabilitation and bioengineering in urologic surgery; spinal cord injury care; benign prostate hypertrophy; forensic urology; reproductive medicine and surgery; medical law and legal medicine. *Mailing Add:* 45 Portland Pl St Louis MO 63108. *Fax:* 314-361-0741

BOYCE, BERT R, INFORMATION SCIENCES. *Current Pos:* assoc prof, 83-85, actg dean, 89-90, PROF, SCH LIBR & INFO SCI, LA STATE UNIV, 85-, ADJ PROF COMPUT SCI, 88-, DEAN, 90- *Personal Data:* b Sharon, Pa, Jan 10, 38; m 68, Judith I Warren; c Maria N & Gabriel A. *Educ:* Marietta Col, BA, 59; Case Western Res Univ, MSLS, 68, PhD(libr & info sci), 72. *Honors & Awards:* Shera Res Award, Am Libr Asn, 88. *Prof Exp:* Asst dir redevelop authority, Sharon, Pa, 66-67; info syst res analyst, Info Syst Off, Libr Cong, 68-69; lectr, Sch Libr Sci, Case Western Res Univ, 72; from asst prof to assoc prof info sci, Sch Libr & Info Sci, Univ Mo, 72-83, chmn, Dept Info Sci, 76-83, actg dean, 80-81. *Concurrent Pos:* HEA title II-B fel, 69-72; sr Fulbright-Hays scholar, Brazil, 74-75; recipient numerous grants, 82-90; mem, Educ Comt, Am Soc Info Sci, 82-84; mem, Res Comt, Asn Libr & Info Sci Educ, 86-89 & 92-93. *Mem:* Am Soc Info Sci; Am Libr Asn; Asn Libr & Info Sci Educ. *Res:* Author of numerous publications in field. *Mailing Add:* Sch Libr & Info Sci La State Univ 167 Coates Hall Baton Rouge LA 70803. *Fax:* 504-388-4581; *E-Mail:* lsboyc@lsuvm.swcc.lsu.edu

BOYCE, DONALD JOE, MATHEMATICS. *Current Pos:* from asst prof to assoc prof, 59-71, chmn math, comput sci & stastist dept, 79-83, PROF MATH, CENT STATE UNIV, 71-, PROF MATH & STATIST, 83- *Personal Data:* b Duncan, Okla, Dec 30, 31; m 52; c 6. *Educ:* Cent State Col, BS, 56; Okla State Univ, MS, 57, EdD(math educ), 68. *Prof Exp:* Instr math, Cent State Col, 57-58; systs analyst, Tinker AFB, 58-59. *Concurrent Pos:* NSF res grants for col teachers, 67-69. *Mem:* Math Asn Am; Nat Coun Teachers Math. *Res:* Modern differential geometry, particularly the curvature of differentiable manifolds; number theory. *Mailing Add:* Dept Math Univ Cent Okla Edmond OK 73034-5209

BOYCE, HENRY WORTH, JR, INTERNAL MEDICINE, GASTROENTEROLOGY. *Current Pos:* PROF MED & GASTROENTEROL, COL MED, UNIV SFLA, 75- *Personal Data:* b Clinton, NC, Sept 21, 30; m 52, Jean Murphy; c 5. *Educ:* Wake Forest Col, BS, 52, MD, 55; Baylor Univ, MS, 61; Am Bd Internal Med, dipl, 62, cert gastroenterol, 65. *Honors & Awards:* Rudolf Schindler Award, ASGE, 82; Rudolf J. and Anita S. Noer Distinguished Prof Award, Univ SFla, 85. *Prof Exp:* Intern, Tripler Gen Hosp, Honolulu, Hawaii, US Army, 55-56, resident internal med, Brooke Gen Hosp, San Antonio, Tex, 57-59, resident gastroenterol, 60-61; chief gastroenterol serv, Madigan Gen Hosp, Tacoma, Wash, 61-65, Brooke Gen Hosp, San Antonio, Tex, 65-66, Walter Reed Gen Hosp, 66-75. *Concurrent Pos:* Consult, Surgeon Gen, US Army, 67-75; dir, Ctr for Swallowing Disorders, Univ SFla; fel, Am Col of Gastroenterol. *Mem:* Fel Am Col Physicians; Am Soc Gastrointestinal Endoscopy; Asn Mil Surg US; Am Asn Study Liver Dis; Am Col Gastroenterol; Am Gastroenterol Asn. *Res:* Clinical internal medicine and gastroenterology; diagnosis and therapy of esophageal cancer, esophageal stents for cancer, esophageal dilation techniques, chromoendoscopy, endoscopic ultrasound staging of cancer. *Mailing Add:* 12901 Bruce B Downs Blvd Tampa FL 33612. *Fax:* 813-974-5333

BOYCE, JAMES B, CONDENSED MATTER PHYSICS. *Current Pos:* res staff, Xerox, Palo Alto Res Ctr, 73-84, sr mem res staff, 84-85, area mgr, Complex Interactive Syst Area, 85-86, area mgr, Thin-Film Semiconductor Area, 86-94, AREA MGR, ELECTRONIC MAT & INTEGRATED TECHNOL, XEROX, PALO ALTO RES CTR, 95- *Educ:* Univ Ill, BS, 66, MS, 67, PhD(physics), 72. *Prof Exp:* Res asst, US Naval Ord Lab, 66 & 67; IBM fel, Physics Dept, Univ Ill, 72-73. *Concurrent Pos:* Comt appln physics, Am Phys Soc, 87-89. *Mem:* Fel Am Phys Soc; Mat Res Soc; AAAS; Sigma Xi. *Res:* Studies of defects and imperfections in crystals, atomic motion in solids and liquids, magnetism, super-conductivity and amorphous materials; the structure and dynamics of amorphous silicon, pseudo-binary alloys and high-technetium superconductors using nuclear magnetic resonance and x-ray absorption techniques; deposition and characterization of high-temperature super- conducting and other oxide thin films and the fast-laser-pulse processing of silicon for the preparation and characterization of thin film semiconductor devices; polysilicon devices and circuits. *Mailing Add:* Xerox Palo Alto Res Ctr 3333 Coyote Hill Rd Palo Alto CA 94304. *Fax:* 650-812-4140; *E-Mail:* boyce@parc.xerox.com

BOYCE, MARK S, LIFE HISTORY EVOLUTION, ECOSYSTEM MANAGEMENT. *Current Pos:* VALLIER CHAIR ECOL & WIS DISTINGUISHED PROF, UNIV WIS, 93- *Personal Data:* b Yankton, SDak, May 24, 50; m 71, Evelyn H Merrill; c Aaron, Jonathon & Cody. *Educ:* Iowa State Univ, BS, 72; Univ Alaska, MS, 74; Yale Univ, MPhil, 75, PhD(pop biol), 77. *Prof Exp:* From instr to prof zool, Univ Wyo, 76-93. *Concurrent Pos:* NATO res fel, Univ Oxford, 82-83; vis prof, Dept Math, Univ Wyo, 84-85; dir, Nat Park Serv Res Ctr, 89-93; Fulbright fel, 91. *Mem:* Ecol Soc Am; Am Soc Naturalists; Soc Conserv Biol; Am Soc Mammalogists; Brit Ecol Soc; Wildlife Soc. *Res:* Population ecology and evolution of a variety of vertebrate species; sage grouse-parasite coevolution; conservation biology of spotted owls; ecology of Yellowstone. *Mailing Add:* Col Nat Resources Univ Wis Stevens Point WI 54481. *Fax:* 715-346-3624; *E-Mail:* mboyce@uwsp.edu

BOYCE, PETER BRADFORD, SEARCH FOR EXTRA TERRESTRIAL INTELLIGENCE, STAR FORMATION. *Current Pos:* EXEC OFFICER, AM ASTRON SOC, 79- *Personal Data:* b New York, NY, Nov 30, 36; m 58; c 2. *Educ:* Harvard Univ, AB, 58; Univ Mich, MA, 62, PhD(astron), 63. *Prof Exp:* Res astron, Lowell Observ, 63-75; adj prof, Ohio State Univ, 70-75; prog dir astron div, NSF, 73-79. *Concurrent Pos:* Vis prof, Univ Copenhagen, 72, Univ Md, 84; gov bd, Am Inst Phys, 79-; Cong Sci fel, 77-78; mem, Seti sci working group, NASA, 82-90; chair, Panel Status Profession, Nat Acad Sci Astron & Astrophys Surv Comt, 89-91. *Mem:* Fel AAAS; Am Astron Soc; Int Astron Union; Am Phys Soc; Optical Soc Am; Sigma Xi. *Res:* Photoelectric measurement of stellar, nebular and planetary spectra; astronomical instrumentation; microwave search strategies for seti; analysis of federal funding for astronomy. *Mailing Add:* 5700 Sherrier Pl NW Washington DC 20016-5320

BOYCE, RICHARD JOSEPH, RUBBER CHEMISTRY. *Current Pos:* Res chemist, 65-80, sr res chemist, 80-85, SR RES SCIENTIST, E I DU PONT DE NEMOURS & CO, INC, 86- *Personal Data:* b Schenectady, NY, Sept 15, 39; m 57; c 4. *Educ:* Rensselaer Polytech Inst, BChE, 61, PhD(phys chem), 66. *Mem:* Am Chem Soc; Soc Advan Mat & Process Eng. *Res:* Polymer physical chemistry; rheology of elastomers. *Mailing Add:* 11 Harvest Lane Glen Farms Elkton MD 21921-2027

BOYCE, RICHARD P, BIOPHYSICS. *Current Pos:* PROF BIOCHEM, SCH MED, UNIV FLA, 71- *Personal Data:* b Pocatello, Idaho, Jan 27, 28; m 50; c 2. *Educ:* Univ Utah, BA, 55; Yale Univ, PhD(biophys), 61. *Prof Exp:* From res asst to res assoc radiobiol, Sch Med, Yale Univ, 61-64, from asst prof to assoc prof, 64-71. *Concurrent Pos:* Guggenheim fel, 68-69. *Mem:* Biophys Soc; Am Soc Biol Chemists. *Res:* Enzymatic repair of irradiation damage in bacteria and bacterial viruses; molecular mechanisms of genetic recombination in bacteria. *Mailing Add:* 8800 NW Fourth Pl Gainesville FL 32607-1411

BOYCE, STEPHEN GADDY, PLANT ECOLOGY. *Current Pos:* RETIRED. *Personal Data:* b Anson Co, NC, Feb 5, 24; m 51, Helen Ashley; c Stephen A & Thomas M. *Educ:* NC State Col, BS, 49, MS, 51, PhD(bot), 53. *Prof Exp:* Instr bot, NC State Col, 52-53; asst prof, Ohio Univ, 53-58; silviculturist, Cent States Exp Sta, US Forest Serv, 58-64, asst dir, 64-66, chief genetics res, 66-67, asst to dep chief res, 67-70, dir, 70-73, chief forest ecologist, 74-84. *Concurrent Pos:* Vis lectr, Sch Forestry, Yale Univ, 79-81; vis prof natural resources, Sch Forestry, Duke Univ, 81- *Mem:* Ecol Soc Am; fel Soc Am Foresters; AAAS; Sigma Xi. *Res:* Forest and coastal dunes ecology; tree improvement; wood growth relations; ecology of forests; system dynamics. *Mailing Add:* 27 Moytoy Lane Brevard NC 28712-9437

BOYCE, STEPHEN SCOTT, MATHEMATICS, QUANTUM MECHANICS. *Current Pos:* Asst prof, 69-77, ASSOC PROF MATH & CHMN DEPT, BEREA COL, 77- *Personal Data:* b Indianapolis, Ind, Feb 23, 42; m 65; c 1. *Educ:* Earlham Col, BA, 64; Univ Wis, MA, 65, PhD(math), 69. *Mem:* Math Asn Am; Inst Mgt Sci. *Res:* Comparison and development of mathematical models for quantum mechanics; sequency and scheduling theory; combinatorial optimization. *Mailing Add:* CPO 2334 Berea Col Berea KY 40404

BOYCE, WILLIAM EDWARD, RANDOM DIFFERENTIAL EQUATIONS, EIGENVALUE PROBLEMS. *Current Pos:* from asst prof to prof math, 57-93, Edward P Hamilton prof, 93-96, EMER EDWARD P HAMILTON PROF SCI EDUC, RENSSELAER POLYTECH INST, 97- *Personal Data:* b Tampa, Fla, Dec 19, 30; m 55, Elsa E Keitzer; c James E, Carolyn E (Fox) & Ann C (Swengel). *Educ:* Rhodes Col, BA, 51; Carnegie Mellon Univ, MS, 53, PhD(math), 55. *Prof Exp:* Universal Match Found fel appl math, Brown Univ, 55-56, res assoc, 56-57. *Concurrent Pos:* Managing ed, SIAM Rev, 70-77; mem coun, Soc Indust & Appl Math, 75-77; vpres publ, 78-81. *Mem:* Am Math Soc; Soc Indust & Appl Math; Math Asn Am; Am Asn Univ Prof. *Res:* Approximate analytical and numerical methods for random initial value, boundary value, and eigenvalue problems, and application of such problems. *Mailing Add:* Dept Math Rensselaer Polytech Inst Troy NY 12180-3590. *E-Mail:* boycew@rpi.edu

BOYCE, WILLIAM HENRY, UROLOGY. *Current Pos:* from instr to assoc prof, 52-55, PROF UROL, BOWMAN GRAY SCH MED, 60- *Personal Data:* b Ansonville, NC, Sept 22, 18; m 48; c 4. *Educ:* Davidson Col, BS, 40; Vanderbilt Univ, MD, 44. *Hon Degrees:* DSc, Davidson Col, 82. *Honors & Awards:* Am Urol Asn Prize, 51, 52 & 54; H H Young Award Infections, 74; Barringer Medal Res, 81; Scott Award Educ, 86; Pioneer in Ultrasonography, 87; Keyes Medal Res, 92; Dornier Res Award, 92. *Prof Exp:* Asst res urologist, NY Hosp & Cornell Univ Med Ctr, 48-50; resident urologist, Univ Va, 50-52. *Mem:* Soc Exp Biol & Med; Am Urol Asn; Am Col Surgeons; Soc Univ Surgeons; Int Soc Urol; Am Asn Genito-Urinary Surgeons. *Res:* Plastic operations for congenital malformations of bladder and external genitalia; physiology of the urinary bladder; proteins, simple and conjugated, of urine in health and in various diseases; urinary calculous disease. *Mailing Add:* Rte 2 Box 150 Stuart VA 24171

BOYD, ALFRED COLTON, JR, INORGANIC CHEMISTRY. *Current Pos:* Asst prof chem, 57-68, asst dean col arts & sci, 69-74, ASSOC PROF CHEM, UNIV MD, COLLEGE PARK, 69- *Personal Data:* b Buffalo, NY, Dec 12, 29; m 59, Patricia A Germek; c Teresa, Lucy & Lawrence. *Educ:* Canisius Col, BS, 51; Purdue Univ, MS, 53, PhD(inorg chem), 57. *Mem:* Am Chem Soc. *Res:* Boron and organometallic chemistry. *Mailing Add:* Dept Chem Univ Md College Park MD 20742-0001

BOYD, CARL M, BIOLOGICAL OCEANOGRAPHY. *Current Pos:* From asst prof to assoc prof, 62-70, dir, Aquatron Lab, 70-75, PROF OCEANOG, DEPT OCEANOG, DALHOUSIE UNIV, 70- *Personal Data:* b Leavenworth, Kans, Mar 23, 33; m 55; c 4. *Educ:* Univ Ind, AB, 55, MA, 56; Scripps Inst, Univ Calif, PhD(marine biol), 62. *Concurrent Pos:* Sr res fel, Nat Res Coun Can, Sci Exchange, France, 68 & 69; sabbatical yr, Univ Paris, 75-76, off sci res & tech, New Caledonia & Allende Inst Mex, 82-83; assoc ed, Progress Oceanog, 81-83; res assoc, Whitney Lab, Univ Fla, 87. *Mem:* Am Soc Limnol & Oceanog. *Res:* Membrane transport of marine algae; ecology of marine plankton; designs of instruments. *Mailing Add:* Dept Oceanog Dalhousie Univ Halifax NS B3H 4J1 Can. *Fax:* 902-494-3877; *E-Mail:* in%carl.boyd@dal.ca

BOYD, CHARLES CURTIS, FORESTRY, AGRONOMY. *Current Pos:* OWNER, CEDAR VALLEY NURSERY, 86- *Personal Data:* b Ottawa, Ill, Feb 18, 43; m 70; c 1. *Educ:* Southern Ill Univ, BS, 66; Univ Hawaii, MS, 68; Wash State Univ, PhD(soils), 73. *Prof Exp:* Proj leader nursery agronomist, Weyerhaeuser Co, 74-77, sect mgr, Forest Biol Res, 77-85. *Concurrent Pos:* Res tech wheat res, US Agency Int Develop, 72. *Mem:* Agron Soc; Soil Sci Soc Am. *Res:* Development of technology for growing and handling conifer seedlings, rooted cuttings, tissue culture propagules, reforestation, vegetation control and insect control. *Mailing Add:* 3833 Mc Elfresh Rd SW Centralia WA 98531

BOYD, CLAUDE ELSON, WATER QUALITY, AQUATIC SOILS. *Current Pos:* PROF FISHERIES & ALLIED AQUACULT, AUBURN UNIV, 71- *Personal Data:* b Hatley, Miss, Nov 14, 39; m 90, Pornpimon Parasan; c Claude Jr, Stacy & Christopher. *Educ:* Miss State Univ, BS, 62, MS, 63; Auburn Univ, PhD(limnol), 66. *Honors & Awards:* Award of Excellence, Bioeng Div, Am Fisheries Soc. *Prof Exp:* Aquatic biologist, Fed Water Pollution Control Admin, 66; asst prof res, Auburn Univ, 67-68; mem res staff, Savannah River Ecol Lab, 69-71. *Concurrent Pos:* Consult to various corp, govt agencies & individuals. *Mem:* World Aquacult Soc; Am Fisheries Soc. *Res:* Water quality management in fish ponds; fish pond soils. *Mailing Add:* Dept Fisheries & Aquacult Auburn Univ Auburn AL 36830. *Fax:* 334-844-9208; *E-Mail:* ceboyd@ag.auburn.edu

BOYD, DAVID CHARLES, GLASS TECHNOLOGY. *Current Pos:* SR ASSOC, CONSUMER PROD DEVELOP, CORNING GLASS WORKS, 69- *Personal Data:* b Pittsburgh, Pa, Dec 31, 42; m 66; c 2. *Educ:* Lehigh Univ, BS, 64; Purdue Univ, MS, 66, PhD(metall eng), 69. *Mem:* Am Ceramic Soc; Sigma Xi. *Res:* Studies relating the properties of glasses and glass-ceramics to their compositions, particularly in the areas of consumer products, tableware and cookware; porcelain enamels. *Mailing Add:* 551 Hibbard Rd Horseheads NY 14845-7943

BOYD, DAVID WILLIAM, GEOMETRIC PROPERTIES OF ALGEBRAIC NUMBERS, ALGORITHMS IN NUMBER THEORY. *Current Pos:* assoc prof, 71-74, PROF MATH, UNIV BC, 74- *Personal Data:* b Toronto, Ont, Sept 17, 41; m 64; c 3. *Educ:* Carleton Univ, BSc, 63; Univ Toronto, MA, 64, PhD(math), 66. *Honors & Awards:* E W R Steacie Prize, Nat Res Coun, Can, 78; Coxeter-James Lectr, Can Math Soc, 79. *Prof Exp:* Asst prof math, Univ Alta, 66-67; from asst prof to assoc prof, Calif Inst Technol, 67-71. *Concurrent Pos:* Vis prof, Univ Paris VI, 81, 84 & 96. *Mem:* Math Asn Am; Am Math Soc; Can Math Soc (vpres, 79-81); Royal Soc Can. *Res:* Number theory, particularly the theory of the Pisot and Salem numbers; applications of computers to pure mathematics-number theory, algebra and geometry. *Mailing Add:* Dept Math Univ BC Vancouver BC V6T 1Z2 Can. *Fax:* 604-822-6074; *E-Mail:* boyd@math.ubc.ca

BOYD, DEAN WELDON, DECISION ANALYSIS, POLICY ANALYSIS. *Current Pos:* PRIN & PRES, DECISION FOCUS, INC, 77- *Personal Data:* b Shreveport, La, July 15, 41. *Educ:* Mass Inst Technol, BS, 63, MS, 65; Stanford Univ, PhD(eng & econ systs), 70. *Prof Exp:* Res engr, Jet Propulsion Lab, 65-67; decision analyst, SRI Int, 67-70; asst prof info sci, Univ Calif, Santa Cruz, 70-75; mgr consult, 75-77. *Concurrent Pos:* Consult, var pvt & pub orgn, 70-75; adj fac, Col Bus Admin, Univ Ore, 80- *Mem:* Inst Mgr Sci. *Res:* Application of decision analysis to problems in public and private sectors; development of methodologies for logical selection of portfolios of interrelated activities such as research and develop projects, capital investments and so forth; normative theories for the value, use and selection of models. *Mailing Add:* 36245 S 73 Cottage Grove OR 97424

BOYD, DEREK ASHLEY, FAR INFRARED SPECTROSCOPY, DIFFRACTIVE OPTICS. *Current Pos:* Res assoc, 73-74, from asst prof to assoc prof, 74-83, PROF PHYSICS, UNIV MD, COLLEGE PARK, 83-, CHMN DEPT, 90- *Personal Data:* b Port Elizabeth, SAfrica, Sept 27, 41; US citizen; m 67. *Educ:* Univ Cape Town, SAfrica, BS, 64, Hons, 65, MS, 67; Stevens Inst Technol, PhD(physics), 73. *Concurrent Pos:* Res assoc, UK Atomic Energy Authority, 67, 69 & 70; vis scientist, Jet Joint Undertaking, UK, 81 & 88. *Mem:* Fel Am Phys Soc. *Res:* Developing experimental and theoretical methods for using electron-cyclotron emission to measure plasma parameters in controlled thermonuclear fusion devices. *Mailing Add:* Dept Physics & Astron Univ Md College Park MD 20742

BOYD, DONALD BRADFORD, COMPUTATIONAL CHEMISTRY. *Current Pos:* RES PROF CHEM, IND UNIV-PURDUE UNIV, INDIANAPOLIS, 94- *Personal Data:* b Syracuse, NY, Oct 23, 41; m 65; c 3. *Educ:* Pa State Univ, BS, 63; Harvard Univ, AM, 65, PhD(chem), 68. *Prof Exp:* Res assoc chem, Cornell Univ, 67-68; sr phys chemist, Lilly Res Labs, Eli Lilly & Co, 68-74, res scientist, 75-89, sr res scientist, 90-93. *Concurrent Pos:* Fac mem, Quantum Chem Prog Exchange Workshops, Ind Univ, 80-81, 83-84; adj prof chem, Ind Univ-Purdue Univ, Indianapolis, 82-93; co-chmn, Symp Molecular Mech, 83; founder & co-chmn, Gordon Res Conf Comput Chem, 86 & 88; co-ed, Reviews Comput Chem, 90-, Chem Ed Serv, 94- *Mem:* Am Chem Soc; Sigma Xi. *Res:* Computational chemistry studies of pharmacological, organic, biochemical and inorganic molecules; relation between molecular structure and biological activity of drug molecules; computer-assisted molecular design & molecular modeling. *Mailing Add:* Dept Chem Indiana Univ-Purdue Univ 402 N Blackford St Indianapolis IN 46202-3274. *Fax:* 317-274-4701; *E-Mail:* boyd@chem.iupui.edu

BOYD, DONALD WILKIN, HISTORICAL GEOLOGY, INVERTEBRATE PALEONTOLOGY. *Current Pos:* from asst prof to prof, 56-93, EMER PROF GEOL, UNIV WYO, 93- *Personal Data:* b Newark, Ohio, Nov 1, 27; m 57, Margaret Sitzman. *Educ:* Ohio State Univ, BS, 49; Columbia Univ, PhD(geol), 57. *Prof Exp:* Instr geol, Union Col, NY, 53-56. *Concurrent Pos:* Res assoc, Am Mus Natural Hist, 68- *Mem:* Geol Soc Am; Paleont Soc; Soc Econ Paleont & Mineral; Am Asn Petrol Geol. *Res:* Permian and triassic pelecypods; inorganic and organic sedimentary structures; Permian biostratigraphy and depositional environments. *Mailing Add:* Dept Geol & Geophys Univ Wyo Laramie WY 82071-3006

BOYD, EARL NEAL, DAIRY SCIENCE. *Current Pos:* head dept food sci & technol, 68-70, asst dean & dir div basic sci, 70-78, ASSOC DEAN, COL AGR & LIFE SCI & ASSOC DIR, VA AGR EXP STA, VA POLYTECH INST & STATE UNIV, 78- *Personal Data:* b Trinity, Ky, Dec 20, 22; m 48; c 1. *Educ:* Eastern Ky State Col, BS, 48; Univ Ky, MS, 49; Ohio State Univ, PhD(dairy sci), 52. *Prof Exp:* Asst prof, Univ Ky, 52-55; res chemist, Swift & Co, 55-57; prin dairy technologist, US Dept Agr, 57-68. *Concurrent Pos:* Vis res scientist, Dept Dairy Sci, Pa State Univ, 63-64; dir, Va Tech Sea Grant Prog, 78- *Mem:* Am Dairy Sci Asn; Inst Food Technol. *Res:* Chemical and bacteriological research in relation to milk and milk products; effects of processing on milk constituents. *Mailing Add:* 813 McBryde Dr Blacksburg VA 24060-3218

BOYD, ELEANOR H, NEUROPHARMACOLOGY, NEUROPHYSIOLOGY. *Personal Data:* b Philadelphia, Pa, Oct 7, 35; m 64. *Educ:* Wellesley Col, BA, 56; Univ Rochester, PhD(pharmacol), 68. *Prof Exp:* Assoc physiol, Univ Rochester, 71-72, asst prof pharmacol & toxicol, Sch Med, 72-82, asst prof nursing, Sch Nursing, 73-82. *Concurrent Pos:* Prin investr, NIH grant, 78-81. *Mem:* Am Soc Pharmacol & Exp Therapeut; Soc Neurosci; AAAS. *Res:* The relationship of drug therapy to nursing practice. *Mailing Add:* 1273 Adobe Creek Rd Fredericksburg TX 78624-6463

BOYD, FRANCIS R, ULTRAMAFIC ROCKS. *Current Pos:* staff asst, 53-56, STAFF MEM, GEOPHYS LAB, CARNEGIE INST WASH, 56- *Personal Data:* b Boston, Mass, Jan 30, 26; c 2. *Educ:* Harvard Col, AB, 49; Stanford Univ, MS, 50; Harvard Univ, MS, 51, PhD, 58. *Prof Exp:* Fel, Harvard Univ, 52-53. *Mem:* Nat Acad Sci; fel Mineral Soc Am; fel Geol Soc Am; Geochem Soc (pres, secy); fel Am Geophys Union. *Res:* Phase equilibrium research at high pressures and temperatures; mantle xenoliths. *Mailing Add:* Geophys Lab Carnegie Inst Wash 5251 Broad Branch Rd NW Washington DC 20015-1305

BOYD, FRANK MCCALLA, BACTERIOLOGY. *Current Pos:* ASSOC PROF BIOL, NORTHEAST LA UNIV, 67- *Personal Data:* b Canton, Ga, Mar 16, 29. *Educ:* NGa Col, BS, 48; Univ Tenn, MS, 50; Univ Wis, PhD(bact), 59. *Prof Exp:* Bacteriologist, Ga Poultry Lab, 50-51; communicable dis ctr, USPHS, 51-54; res asst, Univ Wis, 54-58; asst poultry microbiologist, Univ Ga, 58-67. *Mem:* AAAS; Am Soc Microbiol; Poultry Sci Asn; Soc Gen Microbiol; Sigma Xi. *Res:* Agricultural and medical bacteriology. *Mailing Add:* 713 Hinke Dr Monroe LA 71203

BOYD, FREDERICK MERVIN, CHEMISTRY. *Current Pos:* chemist, 72-73, gen mgr mfg, 73-79, venture analyst, 79-80, dir res & develop, 80-86, GEN MGR, RES & ENGR, HUNTINGTON LABS, INC, 86- *Personal Data:* b Brazil, Ind, July 13, 39. *Educ:* Purdue Univ, BS, 61, MS, 63; Univ Calif, Davis, PhD(plant physiol), 67. *Prof Exp:* Chemist, E I DuPont de Nemours & Co, Inc, 67-70, mem staff, Agr Sales, 70-71; dir biol, Res & Develop, Stull Chem Co, 71-72. *Mem:* AAAS; Chem Specialists Mfrs Asn; Asn Off Anal Chemists; Am Oil Chemists Soc. *Res:* Developed production facilities for quaternary ammonuim chloride disinfectants; formulation research of products directed to the health care field and other speciality chemicals for sanitary maintenance of institutions; engineering; built hazardous materials containment building. *Mailing Add:* 1015 College Ave Huntington IN 46750

BOYD, FREDERICK TILGHMAN, agronomy; deceased, see previous edition for last biography

BOYD, GARY DELANE, ELECTRICAL ENGINEERING, APPLIED PHYSICS. *Current Pos:* Tech staff, AT&T Bell Labs, 59-94, CONSULT, BELL LABS LUCENT TECHNOL, 94- *Personal Data:* b Los Angeles, Calif, Sept 14, 32; m 64, Diana Logan; c Eric Logan & Cynthia Melinda. *Educ:* Calif Inst Technol, BS, 54, MS, 55, PhD(elec eng & physics), 59. *Concurrent Pos:* Head, Systs Elem Res Dept, AT&T Bell Labs, 73-80, & Electronic Device Res Dept, 80-84. *Mem:* Optical Soc Am; fel Inst Elec & Electronics Engrs. *Res:* Quantum electronics; specifically resonator theory, solid state and semiconductor lasers, non-linear optical phenomena; liquid crystal display; surface acoustic waves; optical neural networks; optical bistable devices, photonic switching and micro electromechanical systems. *Mailing Add:* Bell Labs Lucent Technol Rm 4B421 Holmdel NJ 07733

BOYD, GEORGE EDWARD, SURFACE CHEMISTRY, POLYMER CHEMISTRY. *Current Pos:* RETIRED. *Personal Data:* b Evansville, Ind, Sept 1, 11; m 42; c 1. *Educ:* Univ Chicago, BS, 33, PhD(phys chem), 37. *Honors & Awards:* Southern Chem Award, Am Chem Soc, 51, Nuclear Appln Award, 69; Reilly lectr, Univ Notre Dame, 54; Welch Found lectr, 75; Charles H Stone Award, 76. *Prof Exp:* Rockefeller Found fel, Univ Chicago, 37-38, from instr to assoc prof, 38-48; assoc dir, Chem Div, Oak Ridge Nat Lab, 49-54, asst lab dir, 54-70, sr sci adv, 70-73; prof chem, Univ Ga, 73-82. *Concurrent Pos:* Sect chief metall lab, Univ Chicago & Clinton Lab, Manhattan Proj, 43-46; assoc ed, J Phys Chem, 50-54 & Anal Chem, 53-55; Fulbright scholar & Guggenheim fel, Univ Leiden, 52-53; mem adv comt nuclear data, Nat Res Coun, 55-60; mem, Atoms for Peace Mission, AEC, 57; chmn, Fulbright Comt Chem, Nat Acad Sci, 57-63; vis prof, Purdue Univ, 62; Am Nuclear Soc rep, Nat Res Coun, 66-69; co-dir, NATO Advan Study Inst, 73; Am Nuclear Soc rep, Nat Res Coun, 66-69. *Mem:* Fel AAAS; Am Chem Soc; Am Phys Soc; fel Am Nuclear Soc; Coblentz Soc. *Res:* Physics and chemistry of surfaces; pure and applied nuclear chemistry; laser Raman and infrared spectra of molten salts and aqueous solutions; physical chemistry of polyelectrolyte solutions and gels; physical chemistry of concentrated electrolyte mixtures; technical management. *Mailing Add:* 4436 Meandering Way Apt 101 AZ Tallahassee FL 32039

BOYD, JAMES EMORY, NUCLEAR PHYSICS, GENERAL PHYSICS. *Current Pos:* pres, 61-71, EMER PRES, W GA COL, 74-; EMER PROF PHYSICS, GA INST TECHNOL, 74- *Personal Data:* b Tignall, Ga, July 18, 06; m 34; c 2. *Educ:* Univ Ga, AB, 27; Duke Univ, MA, 28; Yale Univ, PhD(physics), 33. *Prof Exp:* Instr physics, Univ Ga, 28-30; head math-sci dept, WGa Col, 33-35; from asst prof to assoc prof physics, Ga Inst Technol, 35-42, prof, 46-61, actg pres, 71-72, res assoc, Eng Exp Sta, 46-50, head physics div, 50-54, from asst dir to dir, 54-61. *Concurrent Pos:* Vchancellor acad develop, Bd Regents, Univ Syst Ga, 72-74. *Mem:* Sigma Xi; Am Phys Soc; AAAS. *Res:* X-rays and microwave propagation. *Mailing Add:* 150 Cottage Lane No 212 Carrollton GA 30117

BOYD, JEFFREY ALLEN, MOLECULAR GENETICS. *Current Pos:* staff fel, 88-90, HEAD, GENE EXPRESSION SECT, LAB MOLECULAR CARCINOGENESIS, NAT INST ENVIRON HEALTH SCI, NIH, 90-; PROF, MEM SLOAN KETTERING, NY. *Personal Data:* b Chapel Hill, NC, Mar 27, 58; m 87; c 2. *Educ:* Duke Univ, BS, 80; NC State Univ, MS, 82, PhD(toxicol), 86. *Prof Exp:* Postdoctoral fel, Lineberger Cancer Res Ctr, Dept Path, Univ NC, Chapel Hill, 86-88. *Mem:* Am Asn Cancer Res; Am Soc Cell Biol; Am Soc Microbiol; AAAS. *Res:* Molecular genetics and cell biology of human endometrial pathology, particularly carcinoma and endometriosis. *Mailing Add:* Mem Sloan Kettering 1275 York Ave New York NY 10021. *Fax:* 919-541-7784

BOYD, JOHN EDWARD, AGRICULTURAL BIOCHEMISTRY, DRUG METABOLISM. *Current Pos:* res chemist, 57-62, group leader, Metab Lab, 62-69, mgr, Metab & Anal Chem Sect, 69-81, DIR AGR RES, INFO SERV, AM CYANAMID CO, 81- *Personal Data:* b Albany, Ga, Jan 26, 32; m 54; c 2. *Educ:* State Teachers Col Pa, BS, 52; Lehigh Univ, MS, 54; Pa State Univ, PhD(agr chem), 57. *Prof Exp:* Asst monomer chem, Lehigh Univ, 52-54; asst pesticide chem, Pa State Univ, 54-57, instr, 55-56. *Mem:* Am Chem Soc; NY Acad Sci; AAAS. *Res:* Metabolism and mode of action of pesticides; sub-cellular biology; protein structure and synthesis; structure and function of cell wall and plasma membrane; data and information handling by computer. *Mailing Add:* Am Cyanamid Co PO Box 400 Princeton NJ 08540

BOYD, JOHN PHILIP, APPLIED MATHEMATICS, ATMOSPHERIC DYNAMICS. *Current Pos:* from asst prof to assoc prof meteorol & numerical anal, 77-88, PROF ATMOSPHERIC & OCEANIC SCI, UNIV MICH, 88- *Personal Data:* b Winchester, Mass, Feb 21, 51; m 87, Marilyn McDermott; c Ian & Emma. *Educ:* Harvard Univ, AB, 73, SM, 75, PhD(appl physics), 76. *Prof Exp:* Asst, Nat Ctr Atmospheric Res, 76. *Concurrent Pos:* Vis res assoc, Ctr Earth & Planetary Physics, Harvard Univ, 80; assoc dir, Lab Sci Comput, 86-; vis prof, Rutgers Univ, 91-92. *Mem:* Am Meteorol Soc; Soc Indust & Appl Math; Am Geophys Union. *Res:* Nonlinear and unstable planetary and equatorial waves in the atmosphere and ocean; Chebyshev and Fourier numerical methods; weakly nonlocal solitary waves. *Mailing Add:* Dept Atmospheric & Oceanic Sci Univ Mich 2455 Hayward Ave Ann Arbor MI 48109. *Fax:* 313-764-5137; *E-Mail:* jpboyd@engin.umich.edu

BOYD, JOHN T, ENGINEERING. *Current Pos:* CHMN, JOHN T BOYD CO, PITTSBURGH. *Honors & Awards:* Erskine Ramsay Gold Medal, Soc Mining, Metall & Explor, 93. *Mailing Add:* 4 Gateway Ctr Suite 1900 444 Liberty Ave Pittsburgh PA 15222-1212

BOYD, JOHN WILLIAM, PHYSICS. *Current Pos:* asst prof, 66-73, ASSOC PROF PHYSICS, KNOX COL, ILL, 73- *Personal Data:* b Ft Worth, Tex, Aug 28, 31; m 57; c 3. *Educ:* Mich State Univ, BS, 57, PhD(physics), 63. *Prof Exp:* Sr scientist, Systs Res Labs, Ohio, 63-66. *Mem:* AAAS; Am Phys Soc; Am Asn Physics Teachers; Sigma Xi. *Res:* Atomic and molecular structure and spectroscopy; optical masers; optics. *Mailing Add:* Dept Physics Knox Col Galesburg IL 61401

BOYD, JOSEPHINE WATSON, WATER POLLUTION. *Current Pos:* RETIRED. *Personal Data:* b St Paul, Minn, Feb 19, 27; m 56, William L; c Victoria, Samantha & Laurence. *Educ:* Univ Minn, BChemE & BBusAdmin, 48, MS, 53, PhD(bact), 55. *Prof Exp:* Chemist & bacteriologist, Theo Hamm Brewing Co, 48-55; asst, Univ Minn, 51-55; res assoc bact, Arctic Inst NAm, 56-57, Ohio State Univ, 58-61 & Arctic Inst NAm, Alaska, 62-63 & Can, 64; fel microbiol, Colo State Univ, 68-74; asst dir water pollution assessment facil, City of Ft Collins, 74-78; tech writer, Hach Co, 78-80, mkt publ mgr, 80-84, sr tech ed, 84-90. *Concurrent Pos:* Vis scientist, Norway, 65 & 70; fel, Colo State Univ, 68-73. *Mem:* AAAS; Sigma Xi. *Res:* Microbiology in the arctic environment; waste water and sewage sludge considered as raw materials rather than refuse. *Mailing Add:* 1313 Stover St Ft Collins CO 80524

BOYD, JUANELL N, TOXICOLOGY. *Current Pos:* SR RES TOXICOLOGIST, CORNING INC, 86- *Personal Data:* b Hollywood, Calif, Apr 10, 42. *Educ:* Westminster Col, BS, 64; Purdue Univ, MS, 66; Cornell Univ, PhD(toxicol, food chem & nutrit), 81; Am Bd Toxicol, dipl, 87. *Prof Exp:* Postdoctoral res, Cornell Univ, 81-86. *Concurrent Pos:* New investr award, NIH, 83; mem, Regulatory & Legis Affairs Comt, Soc Toxicol. *Mem:* Soc Toxicol; Am Chem Soc; NY Acad Sci; Am Indust Hyg Asn. *Mailing Add:* Corning Inc HP-ME-03-56 Corning NY 14831

BOYD, L(ANDIS) L(EE), AGRICULTURAL ENGINEERING. *Current Pos:* RETIRED. *Personal Data:* b Iowa, Dec 1, 23; m 46, Lila M Hummel; c 5. *Educ:* Iowa State Univ, BSAE, 47, MS, 48, PhD(agr eng, mech), 59. *Honors & Awards:* Metal Builders Mfrs Asn-Am Soc Agr Engrs Award, 68. *Prof Exp:* From asst prof to prof agr eng, Cornell Univ, 48-64; prof & head dept, Univ Minn, St Paul, 64-72; asst dir, Agr Exp Sta, 72-78; dir res & assoc dean, Col Agr & Home Econ, Wash State Univ, 78-85; dir-at-large, Western Asn Agr Exp Sta Dirs, 85-92. *Concurrent Pos:* Eng design analyst, Allis-Chalmers Mfg Co, 62-63; consult, Food & Agr Orgn, 64 & 69; fel, Univ Mich, 68. *Mem:* Fel Am Soc Agr Engrs; Am Soc Eng Educ. *Res:* Farm structures and related equipment; engineering mechanics; theory of models. *Mailing Add:* 1725 Concord Dr Ft Collins CO 80526-1601. *Fax:* 970-491-7396; *E-Mail:* boydll@lamar.colostate.edu

BOYD, LEROY HOUSTON, ANIMAL SCIENCE. *Current Pos:* asst prof, 63-66, assoc prof animal husb, 66-80, PROF ANIMAL SCI, MISS STATE UNIV, 80- *Personal Data:* b Arnett, Okla, May 29, 35; m 58; c 2. *Educ:* Okla State Univ, BS, 57; Univ Ky, MS, 60, PhD(animal husb), 63. *Prof Exp:* Asst animal husbandman, Univ Ky, 57-60. *Mem:* Am Soc Animal Sci. *Res:* Physiology, production and management of sheep and horses; ruminant nutrition. *Mailing Add:* Dept Animal Sci Miss State Univ PO Box 5228 Mississippi State MS 39762-5228

BOYD, LOUIS JEFFERSON, REPRODUCTIVE PHYSIOLOGY. *Current Pos:* RETIRED. *Personal Data:* b Lynn Grove, Ky, Mar 14, 28; m 48, Rebecca C Conner; c Beverly (Gallagher), Beda (Cain), Garth W & Bettina (Mize). *Educ:* Univ Ky, BS, 50, MS, 51; Univ Ill, PhD(dairy physiol), 56. *Prof Exp:* Field agent, Dairy Exten, Univ Ky, 51-53; assoc prof dairy, Univ Tenn, 56-62; from assoc prof to prof dairy physiol, Mich State Univ, 63-72; prof animal sci & chmn div, Univ Ga, 72-79, head dept, Animal & Dairy Sci, 74-79, coordr spons prog, Col Agr, 79-92, coordr int agr, 87-92. *Concurrent Pos:* Mem staff, Brit Milk Mkt Bd, 70-71; pres, Coun Agr Sci & Technol, 84-85. *Mem:* Fel AAAS; Am Dairy Sci Asn; Am Soc Animal Sci; Brit Soc Study Fertil; Sigma Xi. *Res:* Factors affecting reproductive efficiency in dairy cattle, such as production, extension, preservation and use of bull sperm and conception and gestation in the dairy cow. *Mailing Add:* 1030 Ramser Dr Bogart GA 30622

BOYD, MALCOLM R(OBERT), ELECTRICAL ENGINEERING. *Current Pos:* RETIRED. *Personal Data:* b Boulder, Colo, Jan 23, 24; m 47; c 2. *Educ:* State Univ, Colo, BS, 47; Stanford Univ, MS, 51, PhD(elec eng), 53. *Prof Exp:* Res assoc, Radio Corp Am Labs, 47-49; res asst, Microwave Lab, Stanford Univ, 49-53; res assoc, Gen Elec Res Lab, 53-64; vpres, Mictron, Inc, 64-72, dir res, 64-68, tech dir, 68-72; pres, VTM Microwaves Inc, 72-76, tech dir, 76-90, pres, 90; vpres res & develop, Genesis Electron Devices, 90-93; consult, 93- *Mem:* Inst Elec & Electronics Engrs. *Res:* Microwave electronics; microwave circuitry; gaseous electronics; ceramic sealing; vacuum technology. *Mailing Add:* Genesis Electron Devices 7240 Driel Dr Longmont CO 80501

BOYD, MARY K, PHOTOCHEMISTRY. *Current Pos:* ASST PROF ORG CHEM, LOYOLA UNIV, CHICAGO, 90- *Personal Data:* b Montreal, Que, Oct 16, 60; m 84. *Educ:* Univ Toronto, BSc, 84, PhD(chem), 88. *Prof Exp:* Postdoctoral fel org chem, State Univ NY, Stony Brook, 89-90. *Mem:* Am Chem Soc; Inter Am Photochem Soc; AAAS; Am Asn Univ Women; Am Women Sci. *Res:* Organic and bioorganic photochemistry; excited state processes particularly involving the generation and reactions of carbocations; fluorescence and phosphorescence techniques. *Mailing Add:* Chem Dept Loyola Univ 6525 N Sheridan Rd Chicago IL 60626-5311. *Fax:* 773-508-3086; *E-Mail:* yl60mkb@luccpua.it.luc.edu

BOYD, MICHAEL R, THERAPEUTICS RESEARCH. *Current Pos:* CHIEF, LAB DRUG DISCOVERY RES & DEVELOP, NAT CANCER INST, NIH, 90- *Mailing Add:* Nat Cancer Inst Frederick Cancer Res & Develop Ctr Bldg 1052 Rm 121 Frederick MD 21702-1201. *Fax:* 301-846-5372

BOYD, MILTON JOHN, MARINE ECOLOGY, INVERTEBRATE ZOOLOGY. *Current Pos:* PROF ZOOL, HUMBOLDT STATE UNIV, 72- *Personal Data:* b Jamestown, NY, June 16, 41; m 64; c 3. *Educ:* Univ Calif, Berkeley, BA, 64; Univ Calif, Davis, PhD(zool), 72. *Prof Exp:* Res assoc ecol, Lerner Marine Lab, 71-72. *Concurrent Pos:* Prin investr, Redwood Nat Park, US Nat Park Serv, 74-76 & San Francisco Dist, US Army Corps Engrs, 75-86. *Mem:* AAAS; Ecol Soc Am; Am Soc Zoologists. *Res:* Community structure of marine intertidal and benthic assemblages; patterns of primary productivity in spermatophytes of Pacific coast salt marshes. *Mailing Add:* 1400 Hilfiker Dr Arcata CA 95521-8299

BOYD, RICHARD HAYS, POLYMER SCIENCE. *Current Pos:* chmn dept mat sci & eng, 76-82, PROF CHEM ENG, MAT SCI & ENG & ADJ PROF CHEM, UNIV UTAH, 67- *Personal Data:* b Columbus, Ohio, Aug 12, 29; m 51; c 2. *Educ:* Ohio State Univ, BSc, 51; Mass Inst Technol, PhD, 55. *Honors & Awards:* High Polymer Physics Prize, Am Phys Soc, 88. *Prof Exp:* Res chemist, E I du Pont de Nemours & Co, 55-62; assoc prof chem, Utah State Univ, 62-65, prof, 65-67. *Concurrent Pos:* Vis fel, Swed Natural Res Coun; chmn, Div High Power Phys, Am Phys Soc, 85-86. *Mem:* Am Chem Soc; Sigma Xi; fel Am Phys Soc; Am Inst Chem Engrs. *Res:* Physical chemistry and physics of polymers; rheology, dielectric properties and kinetics; thermodynamics of solutions; thermochemistry. *Mailing Add:* Dept Mat Eng Univ Utah 304 Emro Bldg Salt Lake City UT 84112

BOYD, RICHARD NELSON, NUCLEAR PHYSICS, PARTICLE PHYSICS. *Current Pos:* from assoc prof to prof physics, 78-81, prof physics & astron, Ohio State Univ, 85-, ASSOC DEAN, COL MATH & PHYS SCI, 94- *Personal Data:* b Omaha, Nebr, Apr 25, 40; m 62, Sarah Anderson; c Martha A, Carol D & Rebecca J. *Educ:* Univ Mich, BSE(physics) & BSE(math), 62; Univ Minn, PhD(physics), 67. *Prof Exp:* Res assoc physics, Univ Minn, 67-68, Rutgers Univ, 68-71 & Stanford Univ, 71-72; asst prof, Univ Rochester, 72-78. *Concurrent Pos:* Consult, Lawrence Livermore Nat Lab, 86-; eminent sceintist, Inst Phys & Chem Res, Japan, 97-98. *Mem:* Fel Am Phys Soc; AAAS; Am Astron Soc. *Res:* Nuclear structure and reactions involving nuclei far from stability; nuclear astrophysics; searches for fundamental particles; stellar evolution; primordial nucleosynthesis; gamma-ray astronomy. *Mailing Add:* Dept Physics Ohio State Univ Columbus OH 43210. *E-Mail:* boyd@mps.ohioupdstate.edu

BOYD, ROBERT B, GROSS & MICROSCOPIC ANATOMY. *Current Pos:* ASSOC PROF ANAT, PA COL PODIATRIC MED, 81- *Educ:* Univ Okla, PhD(anat sci), 73. *Mailing Add:* Dept Biol Med Sci Pa Col Podiatric Med Eighth at Race St Philadelphia PA 19107. *Fax:* 215-629-1622

BOYD, ROBERT EDWARD, SR, MEDICINAL CHEMISTRY. *Current Pos:* AT DEPT CHEM, BENNETT COL. *Personal Data:* b Clarksville, Tenn, Nov 5, 27; m 60; c 3. *Educ:* Tenn State Univ, BA, 54; Fisk Univ, MA, 57; Univ RI, PhD(med chem), 74. *Prof Exp:* Res chemist, Nat Cancer Inst, NIH, 61-65, chemist, USPHS, 65-67; assoc prof chem, Livingstone Col, 67- *Mem:* AAAS; Am Chem Soc. *Res:* Synthesis of potential antidepressant agents based on derivatives of biogenic amines; isolation and characterization of naturally occurring phospholipids. *Mailing Add:* Chem Dept NC A&T State Univ Greensboro NC 27411

BOYD, ROBERT HENRY, PHYSICAL CHEMISTRY. *Current Pos:* Res chemist, 58-72, RES SUPVR, E I DU PONT DE NEMOURS & CO, 72- *Personal Data:* b Norristown, Pa, Aug 27, 32; m 56; c 4. *Educ:* Lebanon Valley Col, BS, 54; Pa State Univ, PhD(chem), 59. *Mem:* Am Chem Soc; Soc Photog Sci & Eng. *Res:* Chemistry of photographic systems. *Mailing Add:* 28 Longspur Dr Limestone Hills Wilmington DE 19808-1971

BOYD, ROBERT WILLIAM, NONLINEAR OPTICS. *Current Pos:* From asst prof to assoc prof, 77-87, PROF OPTICS, INST OPTICS, UNIV ROCHESTER, 87- *Personal Data:* b Buffalo, NY, Mar 8, 48; m 71; c 3. *Educ:* Mass Inst Technol, BS, 69; Univ Calif, Berkeley, PhD(physics), 77. *Concurrent Pos:* Prin investr, NSF, Off Naval Res, Army Res Off, NY SCAOT grants, 77-88; consult of several maj US Corp, 77-88; vis scientist, Jet Propulsion Lab, Calif Inst Technol, 82-83 & Univ Sussex, Brighton, Eng; tech coun, Optical Soc Am, 83-85; topical ed, J Optical Soc Am, 86-89; vis lectr, Univ Toronto, 87-88. *Mem:* Fel Optical Soc Am. *Res:* Nonlinear optical interactions in atomic vapors and nonlinear optical properties of materials; optical phase conjugation; deterministic chaos in nonlinear optics; development of new laser systems. *Mailing Add:* Inst Optics Univ Rochester Rochester NY 14627. *E-Mail:* boyd@optics.rochester.edu

BOYD, ROGER LEE, AVIAN ECOLOGY, ZOOLOGY. *Current Pos:* From asst prof to assoc prof, 76-87, DIR, BAKER UNIV NATURAL AREAS, 82-, PROF BIOL, BAKER UNIV, 87- *Personal Data:* b Lawrence, Kans, Nov 2, 47; m 70, Jan L Hoch; c Jonathan J. *Educ:* Baker Univ, BS, 69; Emporia State Univ, MS, 72; Colo State Univ, PhD(zool), 76. *Honors & Awards:* Paul A Stewart Mem Award, Wilson Ornith Soc, 81; E Alexander Bergstrom Mem Award, NE Bird Banding Asn, 81. *Concurrent Pos:* Frank M Chapman mem fund res award, Am Mus Natural Hist, 75; Louis Agassiz Fuertes grant-in-aid, Wilson Ornith Soc, 75; chmn, Sci Div, Baker Univ, 87- *Mem:* Sigma Xi; Am Ornithologists Union; Western Bird Banding Asn (second vpres, 75-77);

Wilson Ornith Soc; Cooper Ornith Soc; Tallgrass Prairie Asn (pres, 85-). *Res:* Habitat ordination of avian populations in Kansas deciduous forests; breeding ecology and migration patterns of Kansas shorebirds; behavioral aspects of niche separation in grassland birds; population ecology of Interior Least Tern and Snowy Plover. *Mailing Add:* PO Box 379 Baldwin City KS 66006-0379. *Fax:* 785-594-6721

BOYD, RUSSELL JAYE, THEORETICAL CHEMISTRY, QUANTUM CHEMISTRY. *Current Pos:* from asst prof to assoc prof, 75-85, PROF CHEM, DALHOUSIE UNIV, 85- *Personal Data:* b Kelowna, BC, Sept 11, 45; m 68, Susan L McKay-Keenan; c Gregory S & Heather K. *Educ:* Univ BC, BSc, 67; McGill Univ, PhD(chem), 71. *Honors & Awards:* Fraser Medal, APICS, 83; Can Nat Comt-Int Union of Pure & Appl Chem Award, 86. *Prof Exp:* Nat Res Coun fel chem, Math Inst, Univ Oxford, 71-73; Killam fel, Univ BC, 73-75. *Concurrent Pos:* Prin investr, Natural Sci & Eng Res Coun Can grant-in-aid, 76-; chmn, 8th Can Symp Theoret Chem, 83; vis prof, Lehrstuhl fur Theoretische Chemie, Univ Bonn, 84; ed, Can J Chem, 88-; vis prof, Eurkal Herriko Unibertsitatea, Spain, 87; Sr Killam fel, 89-90; chmn, Div Phys & Theoret Chem, Can Soc Chem, 90-93; mem & chair, Strategic Grant Selection Panel New Directions, Nat Sci & Eng Res Coun, 93-96; dir accreditation, Can Soc Chem, 96-99. *Mem:* Fel Chem Inst Can; Can Asn Physicists; Am Chem Soc; Can Asn Theoret Chemists; Int Soc Theoret Chem Physics; fel World Asn Theoret Org Chemists. *Res:* Electronic structure of atoms and molecules; electron correlation; topological aspects of molecular charge distributions; chemical concepts and the electron density; molecular structures and reaction mechanisms. *Mailing Add:* Dept Chem Dalhousie Univ Halifax NS B3H 3J5 Can. *Fax:* 902-494-8883; *E-Mail:* boyd@is.dal.ca

BOYD, VIRGINIA ANN LEWIS, VIROLOGY, GENETICS. *Current Pos:* assoc prof biol & dir, Biomed Sci Masters Degree Prog, Hood Col, 82-88, prof & chair biol, 88-92, actg dean, Grad Sch, 93-95, DEAN, GRAD SCH, HOOD COL, 95- *Personal Data:* b Shreveport, La, Nov 15, 44; div; c Kathryn A & David G. *Educ:* Northwestern State Univ La, BS, 65, MS, 68; La State Univ, PhD(microbiol), 71. *Prof Exp:* Med technician path, Martin Army Hosp, Ft Benning, Ga, 65-66; instr biol, Jacksonville State Univ, 68-69; fel virol, Baylor Col Med, 71-73; scientist virol, Cancer Res Facil, Nat Cancer Inst, Frederick, 73-88. *Concurrent Pos:* Virol consult, biol abstr; deleg cell biol, People to People Int, Japan & People's Repub China; chair, Am Asn Univs Am Fel, 92-94; consult, Glaxo Inc, Nat Career Inst. *Mem:* Am Soc Microbiol; Am Tissue Cult Asn; AAAS; Sigma Xi; NY Acad Sci; Am Soc Virol. *Res:* Microinjection of human epithelial cells with subgenomic DNA clones to map Epstein Barr Virus antigen and transforming regions; comparative studies of oncogene expression in mouse and human cultured cells; pleotrophic effects of oncogene proteins in cultured mouse and human cells; microinjection of proviral clones to determine infectivity and derive clonal retroviral stocks including HIV, BIV, BLV and EIAV; oncogenesis in human cells using various oncogenes and microinjection; therapeutic use of Antisense peptide-nucleic acid to neutralize oncogenic activity in enkaryotic cells. *Mailing Add:* Hodson Sci Ctr Rm 133 Hood Col Frederick MD 21701. *Fax:* 301-696-3597; *E-Mail:* hoodgrad@nimue.hood.edu

BOYD, WILLIAM LEE, BACTERIOLOGY. *Current Pos:* RETIRED. *Personal Data:* b Kingsport, Tenn, Apr 20, 26; m 56; c 3. *Educ:* Univ Tenn, BA, 50; Univ Minn, MS, 52, PhD(bact), 54. *Honors & Awards:* Antarctic Serv Medal. *Prof Exp:* Asst bact, Univ Tenn, 49-50 & Univ Minn, 50-54; asst prof, Univ Ga, 54-55; prin investr, Arctic Res Lab, Point Barrow, Alaska, 55-57; res assoc, Col Dent, Ohio State Univ, 58-59, from asst prof to assoc prof, 59-64; assoc prof, Colo State Univ, 64-67, actg head dept, 66-67, prof bact, 67-90, dir, Water Qual Lab, 82-90. *Concurrent Pos:* Prin investr, NSF grant, US Antarctic Res Prog, 61-63 & 67-68; vis scientist, Tromso Mus, Norway, 65, 70, Arctic Res Lab, Barrow, Alaska, 66, 71, Mus Natural Hist, Reykjavik, Iceland, 71, Inst Antartico Argentino, Antarctica, 67-68 & Gansu Agr Univ, China, 80-87. *Mem:* AAAS; Am Soc Microbiol; Arctic Inst NAm; Ecol Soc Am; NY Acad Sci. *Res:* Ecology and physiology of Arctic, Antarctic and Alpine microorganisms; microbes as indicators of water quality. *Mailing Add:* 1313 Stover St Ft Collins CO 80524

BOYE, CHARLES ANDREW, JR, polymer physics, for more information see previous edition

BOYE, FREDERICK C, ORGANIC CHEMISTRY. *Current Pos:* ENVIRON CONSULT, PRINTING INDUST, 96- *Personal Data:* b Buffalo, NY, May 30, 23; m; m 51, Virginia A Kroll; c Christopher K, Frederick C Jr & Suzanne R (Herman). *Educ:* Univ Buffalo, BA, 49, MA, 51, PhD(org chem), 52. *Prof Exp:* Res chemist, Cornell Aeronaut Lab, 52-53 & Indust Chem Div, Allied Chem Corp, 53-67; sr res chemist, Cowles Chem Div, Stauffer Chem Co, 67-68, Eastern Res Ctr, 68-71; sr res scientist, Paper Prod Res Div, Am Can Co, 71-72 & Consumer Prod Div, 72-78; dir regulatory affairs, Coating Div, M&T Chem, Inc, 78-81; info scientist, Paper Chem Database & Tech Bibliogr, Inst Paper Chem, 81-89; environ scientist, Govt Regulations, Printing Plant Opers, Banta Corp, 86-96. *Mem:* NY Acad Sci; Fel Am Inst Chemists; Sigma Xi. *Res:* Polyurethanes; exploratory intermediates for colors; pharmaceuticals; polymers; curing agents; specialty chemicals; process variable studies; process development; plant demonstration; chelating chemicals; amino acids; detergent builders; organic acid anhydrides; hot-melt adhesives. *Mailing Add:* 130 Cherry Ct Appleton WI 54915

BOYE, ROBERT JAMES, NUCLEAR PHYSICS, THEORETICAL PHYSICS. *Current Pos:* ASSOC PROF PHYSICS, MORGAN STATE COL, 61- *Personal Data:* b Shattock, Okla, Jan 11, 34. *Educ:* Univ Okla, BS, 55; Johns Hopkins Univ, PhD(physics), 68. *Mem:* Am Phys Soc; Am Asn Physics Teachers. *Res:* Molecular structure; nuclear three-body problem. *Mailing Add:* PO Box 18166 Baltimore MD 21220

BOYER, BARBARA CONTA, DEVELOPMENTAL BIOLOGY. *Current Pos:* from vis assoc prof to assoc prof biol, 73-96, PROF BIOL, UNION COL, NY, 96- *Personal Data:* b Ithaca, NY, Jan 23, 42; m 68, John F; c Cynthia J & Paul L. *Educ:* Univ Rochester, AB, 63; Univ Mich, MS, 64, PhD(zool), 69. *Prof Exp:* NIH trainee develop biol, Whitman Lab, Univ Chicago, 69-71. *Concurrent Pos:* Prin investr, Marine Biol Labs, Woods Hole, 83-; mem, Corp of Marine Biol Lab. *Mem:* Sigma Xi; Am Soc Zool; Western Soc Naturalists; AAAS; Soc Develop Biol. *Res:* Experimental embryology and gametogenesis of marine invertebrates, particularly turbellarian flatworms. *Mailing Add:* 1310 Garner Ave Schenectady NY 12309. *Fax:* 518-370-6429; *E-Mail:* boyerb@union.edu

BOYER, CINDA MARIE, MEDICINE. *Current Pos:* postdoctoral res fel, Div Immunol, 82-85, ASST MED RES PROF, DEPT MED, MED CTR, DUKE UNIV, DURHAM, NC, 85- *Personal Data:* b Lancaster, Pa, Aug 13, 54. *Educ:* Dickinson Col, BS, 75; Pa State Univ, DPhil(microbiol), 80; Am Bd Med Lab Immunol, dipl, 86. *Prof Exp:* Grad res asst, Dept Microbiol, M S Hershey Med Ctr, Pa, 75-80; postdoctoral res fel clin immunol, Dept Hosp Labs, NC Mem Hosp, Chapel Hill, 80-82. *Concurrent Pos:* Young investr award, Acad Clin Lab Physicians & Scientists, 82. *Mem:* Am Soc Microbiol; Am Asn Immunologists; Am Soc Histocompatibility & Immunogenetics. *Res:* Author of numerous publications. *Mailing Add:* Dept Path Duke Univ Med Ctr Box 3712 Durham NC 27710-0001. *Fax:* 919-684-5653

BOYER, DELMAR LEE, MATHEMATICS. *Current Pos:* PROF MATH, UNIV TEX, EL PASO, 65- *Personal Data:* b Salina, Kans, Oct 31, 26; div; c 6. *Educ:* Kans Wesleyan Univ, AB, 49; Univ Kans, MA, 52, PhD(math), 55. *Prof Exp:* from asst prof to assoc prof, Univ Idaho, 61-65. *Mem:* Am Math Soc; Math Asn Am. *Res:* Abelian groups. *Mailing Add:* Dept Math Univ Tex El Paso TX 79968-0514

BOYER, DON LAMAR, OCEANOGRAPHY. *Current Pos:* PROF & CHAIR, DEPT MECH & AEROSPACE ENG, ARIZ STATE UNIV, 88- *Personal Data:* b Valley View, Pa, Apr 5, 38; m 60; c 2. *Educ:* Rensselaer Polytech Inst, BS, 60; Johns Hopkins Univ, PhD(mech), 65. *Prof Exp:* Asst prof civil, mech & aerospace eng, Univ Del, 65-69; assoc prog dir fluid mech, NSF, 69-70; assoc prof civil, mech & aerospace eng, Univ Del, 70-71; sci coordr atmospheric sci, NSF, 71-75; prof mech eng & head dept, Univ Wyo, 75-88. *Mem:* Am Soc Mech Engrs; Am Meteorol Soc; Am Geophys Union; AAAS; Europ Geophys Soc. *Res:* Geophysical fluid mechanics. *Mailing Add:* 101 E Loma Vista Dr Tempe AZ 85282

BOYER, DON RAYMOND, VERTEBRATE ZOOLOGY. *Current Pos:* assoc prof, 58-66, PROF BIOL, WASHBURN UNIV, 66- *Personal Data:* b Lexington, Okla, Mar 31, 29; div; c 3. *Educ:* Univ Okla, BS, 50, MS, 53; Tulane Univ, PhD(zool), 58. *Prof Exp:* Instr zool, Tulane Univ, 58. *Mem:* AAAS; Am Soc Ichthyol & Herpet; Am Soc Zool; Am Inst Biol Sci. *Res:* Vertebrate zoology; physiology of temperature regulation and of respiratory and cardiovascular systemic responses in reptiles. *Mailing Add:* Dept Biol Washburn Univ 1700 SW College Blvd Topeka KS 66621

BOYER, DONALD WAYNE, PHYSICS, AEROPHYSICS. *Current Pos:* RETIRED. *Personal Data:* b Detroit, Mich, Jan 16, 29; m 56, 75, Charlotte MacInnes; c Richard, Barbara & Scott. *Educ:* Univ Melbourne, BSc, 53; Univ Toronto, MASc, 54, PhD(aerophys), 60. *Prof Exp:* Asst, Inst Aerospace Studies, Univ Toronto, 53-59; res aerodynamicist, Calspan Corp, 59-63, prin aerodynamicist, 63-95, head, phys gosdynamics, 91-95. *Mem:* Assoc fel, Am Inst Aeronaut & Astronaut. *Res:* Nonisentropic flows; viscous flows; hypersonic aerodynamics; chemical and ionization non-equilibrium phenomena; magneto gas dynamics; plasma-microwave interactions; infrared radiation physics; chemical kinetics; propellants and combustion. *Mailing Add:* 92 Sherbrooke Ave Amherst NY 14221

BOYER, ERNEST WENDELL, MICROBIAL PHYSIOLOGY, MICROBIAL GENETICS. *Current Pos:* SR STAFF SCIENTIST, SOLVAY ENZYMES, INC, 90- *Personal Data:* b Oconto, Nebr, Mar 18, 37; m 58, Erna K Sprung; c Brent J & Beth R. *Educ:* NCent Col, Ill, BA, 58; Iowa State Univ, PhD(bact), 69. *Prof Exp:* Res technician, Mayo Clin, Minn, 62-64; res microbiologist, Miles Labs, Inc, 68-77; sr res scientist, Miles Inc, 78-83, sr staff scientist, 84-89. *Mem:* AAAS; Am Soc Microbiol; Soc Indust Microbiol; Sigma Xi; Am Chem Soc. *Res:* Regulation of the synthesis of extracellular enzymes by bacteria and fungi; genetic engineering of industrial microorganisms; extracellular enzymes and taxonomy of alkalophilic bacillus species. *Mailing Add:* 1830 Grant Elkhart IN 46514-3949. *Fax:* 219-266-2444

BOYER, HAROLD EDWIN, ORAL SURGERY. *Current Pos:* From asst dean to dean, Sch Dent, 62-72, PROF ORAL SURG, UNIV LOUISVILLE, 59-, VPRES HEALTH AFFAIRS, 72- *Personal Data:* b St Lawrence, Pa, Aug 9, 25; div; c 2. *Educ:* Lebanon Valley Col, 46-48; Univ Pa, DDS, 52, MS, 58; Am Bd Oral Surg, dipl, 59. *Concurrent Pos:* Chief sect oral surg, Louisville Gen & Children's Hosps, 56-71; consult, Jewish & Vet Admin Hosps, 63-, Ireland Army Hosp, Ft Knox, Ky, 63- & Off Econ Opportunity, Proj Head Start, 65-66; pres, Am Bd Oral Surg. *Mem:* Am Soc Oral Surg; fel Am Col Dent; fel Int Col Dent. *Res:* Early recognition of oral cancer; oral exfoliative cytology; evaluation of emergency drugs and development of a practical office emergency kit. *Mailing Add:* Sch Dent Univ Louisville Louisville KY 40292

BOYER, HERBERT WAYNE, MICROBIOLOGY, MOLECULAR GENETICS. *Current Pos:* From asst prof to prof microbiol, 66-91, EMER PROF DIV GENETICS, DEPT BIOCHEM & BIOPHYS, UNIV CALIF, SAN FRANCISCO, 91- *Personal Data:* b Pittsburgh, Pa, July 10, 36; m 59; c 2. *Educ:* St Vincent Col, AB, 58; Univ Pittsburgh, MS, 60, PhD(bact), 63. *Hon Degrees:* DSc, St Vincent Col, 81. *Honors & Awards:* Nat Medal Technol, 89; Nat Medal Sci, 90; V D Mattia Award, Roche Inst Molecular Biol, 77; Doisy Lectr, Univ Ill, 79; Albert Lasker Basic Med Res Award, 80; Golden Plate Award, Am Acad Achievement, 81; Achievement Award, Indust Res Inst, 82; Moet Hennessy-Louis Vuitton Prize, Biotechnol Prize, 88; First Nat Biotechnol Award, 89. *Concurrent Pos:* USPHS fel, Yale Univ, 63-66; dir, Grad Prog Genetics, Univ Calif, San Francisco, 76-81; investr, Howard Hughes Med Inst, 76-83; co-founder & mem bd dirs, Genentech, Inc, 77-; mem, President's Circle, Nat Acad Sci, 89. *Mem:* Nat Acad Sci; fel Am Acad Arts & Sci; Am Soc Biol Chemists; fel AAAS. *Res:* Molecular genetics. *Mailing Add:* Dept Biochem & Biophys Univ Calif San Francisco CA 94143-0554

BOYER, JAMES LORENZEN, HEPATOLOGY. *Current Pos:* prof med, 78-96, chief, Div Digestive Dis, 82-96, DIR, LIVER STUDY UNIT, SCH MED, YALE UNIV, 78-, DIR LIVER CTR, 84-, ENSIGN PROF MED, 96- *Personal Data:* b New York, NY, Aug 28, 36; m 63; c 2. *Educ:* Haverford Col, BA, 58; Johns Hopkins Univ, MD, 62. *Honors & Awards:* Adolf Windaus Prize, 89; Distinguished Achievement Award, Am Gastroenterol Asn, 89. *Prof Exp:* Asst prof med, Sch Med, Yale Univ, 69-72; assoc prof internal med, Univ Chicago & Pritzerk Sch Med, 72-76, dir, Liver Study Unit, 72-78, prof med, 76-78. *Concurrent Pos:* Head, Liver Res Lab, Int Ctr Med Res & Training, Johns Hopkins Univ, 64-66; attend physician, Yale-New Haven Hosp & West Haven Vet Admin Ctr, 69-72 & 78-; dept chmn, Nat Digestive Dis Adv Bd, 81-84. *Mem:* Am Asn Study Liver Dis (pres, 80); Am Soc Clin Invest; Asn Am Physicians; Am Gastroenterol Asn; Int Asn Study Liver (pres, 88-90). *Res:* Mechanisms of bile formation and transport; study of liver structure and function; prognosis and treatment of chronic liver disease. *Mailing Add:* Dept Med Yale Sch Med 333 Cedar St New Haven CT 06510. *Fax:* 203-785-7273

BOYER, JERE MICHAEL, MICROBIAL PHYSIOLOGY, MYCOLOGY. *Current Pos:* DIR RES, AULTMAN HOSP, 87-; ADJ PROF MICROBIOL, NORTHEASTERN OHIO UNIVS COL MED, 89- *Personal Data:* b Lebanon, Pa, Feb 24, 46; m 71, Charlotte Bailey; c Kristin, Aimee & Susanna. *Educ:* Univ Scranton, BS, 68; Millersville State Col, MA, 71; St John's Univ, PhD(microbiol), 75. *Prof Exp:* From instr to prof microbiol, Philadelphia Col Osteop Med, 74-87, vchmn, 84-87. *Concurrent Pos:* Fel, St John's Univ, 71-74; NSF fel, 74; consult microbiol, Nat Bd Examrs Osteop Physicians & Surgeons, 75-87; res grant, Merck, Sharp & Dohme, 78-87; consult microbiol biochem, NIH & NSF, 79-; res grant, Smith, Kline & French, 80-, Am Osteop Asn, 82-87 & Adv Technol Ctr, 84-88, Roche, 88-, Janssen, 89-; adj prof microbiol & clerkship dir community med. *Mem:* fel Am Soc Microbiol; Soc Indust Microbiol; Med Mycol Soc Am; Sigma Xi; AAAS; Am Asn Bioanalysts; fel Am Acad Microbiol; Am Bd Bioanal. *Res:* Physiological studies of antifungal agents and their effects on fungi; effects of metabolites on fungi; direct fungal diagnostic laboratory; community health. *Mailing Add:* Dir Res Aultman Hosp 2600 6th St SW Canton OH 44710. *Fax:* 330-580-5513

BOYER, JOHN FREDERICK, POPULATION BIOLOGY. *Current Pos:* asst prof, 73-80, ASSOC PROF BIOL, UNION COL, 80- *Personal Data:* b Evanston, Ill, Oct 14, 41; m 68; c 2. *Educ:* Amherst Col, BA, 64; Univ Chicago, PhD(biol), 71. *Prof Exp:* Fel genetics, Dept Zool, Univ Iowa, 71-73. *Mem:* Soc Study Evolution; Ecol Soc Am; Sigma Xi; Am Soc Nat. *Res:* Evolution of life histories; genetic variation in social behavior. *Mailing Add:* Dept Biol Sci Union Col Schenectady NY 12308. *Fax:* 518-388-6789

BOYER, JOHN STRICKLAND, BIOCHEMISTRY, BIOPHYSICS. *Current Pos:* DU PONT PROF MARINE BIOCHEM & BIOPHYS, UNIV DEL, 87- *Personal Data:* b Cranford, NJ, May 1, 37; m 64, Jean R Matsunami; c 2. *Educ:* Univ Wis, MS, 61; Duke Univ, PhD(bot), 64. *Honors & Awards:* Shull Award, Am Soc Plant Physiol, 77; von Humboldt Sr Scientist Award, Ger, 83. *Prof Exp:* Vis asst prof bot, Duke Univ, 64-65; asst physiologist, Conn Agr Exp Sta, 65-66; from asst prof to prof bot & agron, Univ Ill, Urbana, 66-78; plant physiologist, USDA, 78-84; prof, Tex A&M Univ, 84-87. *Concurrent Pos:* Mem vis comt, Carnegie Inst Wash, Stanford Univ & Harvard Univ; Climate Lab fel, NZ, 72. *Mem:* Nat Acad Sci; fel Am Soc Agron; Am Soc Plant Physiol (pres, 81-82); Sigma Xi; fel Crop Sci Soc Am; fel Australian Nat Univ; fel Japan Soc Prom Sci. *Res:* Plant water relations, photosynthesis, plant growth and reproduction. *Mailing Add:* Col Marine Studies Rm 213 Univ Del 700 Pilottown Rd Lewes DE 19958

BOYER, JOSEPH HENRY, organic chemistry; deceased, see previous edition for last biography

BOYER, LEROY T, CIVIL ENGINEERING. *Current Pos:* Asst prof, 66-71, assoc prof, 71-76, PROF CIVIL ENG, UNIV ILL, URBANA, 76- *Personal Data:* b Ada, Minn, Mar 10, 37; m 61, Barbara Klug; c Therese & Kristin. *Educ:* Univ Minn, BS, 60, PhD(civil eng, math), 66. *Mem:* Am Soc Civil Engrs. *Res:* Construction engineering; computer assisted instruction and design; estimating, cost control and construction risk. *Mailing Add:* Dept Civil Eng Univ Ill Urbana IL 61801. *Fax:* 217-333-9404; *E-Mail:* l-boyer@uiuc.edu

BOYER, LESTER LEROY, DAYLIGHTING IN BUILDINGS, EARTH SHELTERED BUILDINGS. *Current Pos:* chair, Div Design Technol, Col Archit, 88-90, dir, Daylight Lab, 85-96, PROF ARCHIT, TEX A&M UNIV, 84- *Personal Data:* b Hanover, Pa, Apr 6, 37; m 58, Patricia B Hayes; c Douglas L, Blane E & Darla M. *Educ:* Pa State Univ, BArchE, 60, MS, 64; Univ Calif, Berkeley, PhD(archit), 76. *Prof Exp:* Instr archit eng, Pa State Univ, 60-64; res engr, Res & Develop Ctr, Armstrong World Industs, 64-68; sr consult, Bolt Beranek & Newman Inc, 68-70; prof archit, Okla State Univ, 70-84. *Concurrent Pos:* Course dir, Nat Soc Prof Engrs, 64-74; prin investr, earth shelter, US Dept Energy & Control Data Corp, 79-81, daylighting, NSF, 85-88; ed proc, Nat & Int Conf Earth Shelter, 80, 81, 83, 86 & 92; nat coordr, Passive Earth Cooling Prog, Am Solar Energy Soc, 81; vis prof archit, Univ NSW & Univ Queensland, Australia, 82; Fulbright scholar to Australia, Coun Int Exchange Scholars, 82; gen chmn, Int Conf Earth Sheltered Bldg, Australia, 83; vis researcher, Solar Energy Res Inst, Colo, 85; chair, Energy Res Rev Panel Fenestration, US Dept Energy, 88; mem bd dirs, Am Underground Space Asn, 89-93; guest prof archit eng, Delft Univ Technol, Holland, 92; Fulbright scholar to Holland, Coun Int Exchange Scholars, 92. *Mem:* Am Solar Energy Soc; Am Underground Space Asn; Am Soc Heating Refrig & Air-Conditioning; Illum Eng Soc. *Res:* Development and validation of preliminary prediction algorithms to evaluate daylighting, solar effects, and energy performance for selected prototypical daylighting configurations; minimum envelope systems for buildings, such as occur with underground and earth integrated buildings; author of publications on earth shelter technology. *Mailing Add:* PO Box 9901 College Station TX 77842-7905. *Fax:* 409-862-1571

BOYER, MARKLEY HOLMES, INTERNAL MEDICINE, TROPICAL MEDICINE. *Current Pos:* PROF, TUFTS UNIV, 87- *Personal Data:* b Philadelphia, Pa, Dec 29, 32; m 57; c 4. *Educ:* Princeton Univ, AB, 55; Univ Pa, MD, 63; Univ Oxford, DPhil(biol), 72; Harvard Univ, MPH, 72. *Prof Exp:* Asst resident, Univ Hosp, Cleveland, 65-67; physician, Hosp Albert Schweitzer, Haiti, 67; med officer, Radcliffe Infirmary, Eng, 68-70; USPHS fel trop pub health, Harvard Sch Pub Health, 72, asst prof trop pub health, 73-87. *Concurrent Pos:* Govt trustee, Jackson Lab, Maine, 72-; mem adv comt, Dept Biol, Princeton Univ, 76- *Mem:* AAAS; Royal Soc Med. *Res:* Immunology of parasitic diseases. *Mailing Add:* Dept Family Med & Community Health Sch Med 136 Harrison Ave Boston MA 02111

BOYER, MICHAEL GEORGE, PLANT PATHOLOGY. *Current Pos:* asst prof, 65-68, assoc prof, 68-92, EMER PROF BIOL, YORK UNIV, 92- *Personal Data:* b Toronto, Ont, May 15, 25; m 52; c 3. *Educ:* Ont Agr Col, BSA, 52, MS, 53; Iowa State Col, PhD(plant path), 58. *Prof Exp:* Lectr, Kemptville Agr Sch, Ont, 53-54; pathologist, Can Dept Forestry, 54-55, 58-65. *Concurrent Pos:* Mem, Can Comt Forest Tree Breeding. *Res:* Resistant poplar hybrids. *Mailing Add:* Dept Biol York Univ 4700 Keele St North York ON M3J 1P3 Can

BOYER, PAUL DELOS, BIOCHEMISTRY. *Current Pos:* dir, Molecular Biol Inst, 65-83, Biotechnol Prog, 85-88, prof, 63-90, EMER PROF BIOCHEM, UNIV CALIF, LOS ANGELES, 90- *Personal Data:* b Provo, Utah, July 31, 18; m 39; c 3. *Educ:* Brigham Young Univ, BS, 39; Univ Wis, MS, 41, PhD(biochem), 43. *Hon Degrees:* Doctorate, Univ Stockholm, 74. *Honors & Awards:* Nobel Prize in Chem, 97; Award, Am Chem Soc; McCoy Award Chem Res, 76; Tolman Medal, 84; Rose Award, Am Soc Biochem & Molecular Biol, 89. *Prof Exp:* Asst biochem res, Univ Wis, 39-43; instr chem, Stanford Univ, 43-45, res assoc, 43-45; from asst prof to prof biochem, Univ Minn, 45-56, Hill prof, 56-63. *Concurrent Pos:* Guggenheim fel, 55-56; mem, Biochem Study Sect, USPHS, 58-62, chmn, 64-66; ed, Ann Rev Biochem, 65-71, assoc ed, 72-88; ed, Biochem Biophys Res Commun, 69-79; ed, The Enzymes, 70- *Mem:* Nat Acad Sci; AAAS; Am Soc Biol Chem (pres, 69-70); Am Chem Soc; Am Acad Arts & Sci (vpres, 85-88). *Res:* Chemistry and mechanism of action of enzymes; oxidative phosphorylation; photophosphorylation; active transport. *Mailing Add:* Molecular Biol Inst Rm 200-A Univ Calif Los Angeles CA 90024

BOYER, ROBERT ALLEN, PHYSICS. *Current Pos:* prof & chmn dept, 41-81, EMER PROF PHYSICS, MUHLENBERG COL, 81- *Personal Data:* b Hummels Wharf, Pa, Aug 27, 16; m 39, Eleanor Moyer; c 2. *Educ:* Susquehanna Univ, AB, 38; Syracuse Univ, MA, 40; Lehigh Univ, PhD(physics), 52. *Hon Degrees:* DSc, Muhlenberg Col, 81. *Honors & Awards:* Lindback Award, 61. *Prof Exp:* Instr physics, Clarkson Col, 40-41. *Mem:* Am Asn Physics Teachers. *Res:* Ultrasonics. *Mailing Add:* 2000 Cambridge Ave No 129 Wyomissing PA 19610

BOYER, ROBERT ELSTON, GEOTECHNICAL, PAVEMENT. *Current Pos:* DIST ENG, ASPHALT INST, UNIV TEX. *Personal Data:* b Turners Sta, Ky, Apr 20, 39; m 59; c 2. *Educ:* Univ Ky, BS, 61; Purdue Univ, MS, 63, PhD(civil eng), 72. *Prof Exp:* Chief, Design Div, Eng & Construct, Tachikawa AFB, Japan, 63-66, Oper & Maintenance Div, Pleiku AFB, South Vietnam, 66-67; staff civil engr, Dir Oper, Hq Tactical Air Command, Langley AFB, Va, 67-69; primary researcher, Purdue Univ, W Lafayette, Ind, 69-72; course dir, Civil Eng Sch, Air Force Inst Technol, Wright-Patterson AFB, Ohio, 72-75, chief, Dept Eng Technol, 75-77; dir civil eng, 12th Missile Warning Group, Thule AFB, Greenland, 77-78; chief, Eng Res Div, Air Force Eng & Serv Ctr, Tyndall AFB, Fla, 79-81; comdr, 341st Civil Squadron, Malmstrom AFB, Mont, 81-83; dir, Eng & Environ Sci Lab, Air Force Eng & Serv Ctr, Tyndall AFB, Fla, 83- *Mem:* Fel Am Soc Civil Engrs; Soc Am Mil Engrs; Asn Asphalt Paving Technologists; Nat Soc Prof Engrs. *Res:* Soil mechanics: foundations, drainage, ground water and seepage; structural dynamics; pavements: design, evaluation and maintenance management systems. *Mailing Add:* Dept Geol Sci Geol Bldg Rm 118 Univ Tex Austin TX 78712

BOYER, ROBERT ERNST, GEOLOGY. *Current Pos:* From instr geol to assoc prof geol, 57-67, chmn dept, 71-80, PROF GEOL SCI & EDUC, 67-, DEAN, COL NATURAL SCI, UNIV TEX, AUSTIN, 80- *Personal Data:* b Palmerton, Pa, Aug 3, 29; m 51; c 3. *Educ:* Colgate Univ, BA, 51; Ind Univ, MA, 54; Univ Mich, PhD, 59. *Honors & Awards:* Neil A Miner Award, 80; Award Outstanding Contrib Pub Understanding Geol, Am Geol Inst, 88, William B Heroy, Jr Award Distinguished Serv, 90. *Concurrent Pos:* Ed, Tex J Sci, 62-64 & J Geol Educ, 65-68. *Mem:* Fel Geol Soc Am; Am Asn Petrol Geol; Am Asn Geol Teachers; fel AAAS; Sigma Xi. *Res:* Structural and field geology; mapping in Precambrian crystalline rocks of Wet Mountains, Colorado and Llano Region, Texas; heavy mineral studies of crystalline rocks; fracture pattern analysis; earth science teaching in secondary schools; space photography and remote sensing. *Mailing Add:* 7644 Parkview Circle Austin TX 78731-1160

BOYER, RODNEY FREDERICK, BIOCHEMISTRY, ORGANIC CHEMISTRY. *Current Pos:* from asst prof to assoc prof chem, 74-85, chair, 86-89, PROF CHEM, HOPE COL, 85- *Personal Data:* b Omaha, Nebr, Aug 25, 42. *Educ:* Westmar Col, BA, 64; Colo State Univ, MS, 67, PhD(chem), 70. *Prof Exp:* Res biochemist, Univ Mich Med Sch, 70-72; asst prof chem, Grand Valley State Cols, 72-74. *Concurrent Pos:* NIH fel biol chem, Univ Mich, 70-72; sabbatical leave, Univ Colo, Boulder, 91. *Mem:* Am Chem Soc; Am Asn Plant Physiol; Am Soc Biochem & Molecular Biol. *Res:* Singlet oxygen in biochemistry; alpha-oxidation of fatty acids; metal complexes of biochemical ligands; cellulose storage and mobilization of iron in plants and animals. *Mailing Add:* Dept Chem Hope Col PO Box 9000 Holland MI 49422-9000. *Fax:* 616-394-7923

BOYER, RODNEY RAYMOND, TITANIUM, PROCESS METALLURGY. *Current Pos:* SR PRIN ENGR, BOEING COM AIRPLANE GROUP, 65- *Personal Data:* b Aberdeen, Wash, July 4, 39; m 65, Janice M Arnold; c Bret A & Tawni L (Ruhl). *Hon Degrees:* Univ Wash, BS, 63, MS, 73. *Honors & Awards:* Russ Ogden Award, Am Soc Testing & Mat, 93; William Hunt Eisenman Award, Am Soc Mat, 97. *Prof Exp:* Engr, Aerojet Gen Corp, 63-65. *Concurrent Pos:* Mem, Handbk Comt, Am Soc Mat Int, 82-85, Aeromat Mgt Comt, 89- & Aerospace Tech Div Coun, 91-; asst chmn, Pac Northwest Mat Conf, 88-89; secy, 7th Int Conf Titanium, Am Inst Mining, Metall & Petrol Engrs, 88-92, chmn, US Deleg, 8th Int Titanium Conf, 92-; consult, Conoco, Inc, 90-91; chmn, Titanium Comt, Minerals, Metals & Mat Soc, 92-94, mem, Struct Mat Div Coun, 92-94; UD deleg, Am Soc Mat Int; mem, Panel Experts, Mat & Processing Technol Info Ctr. *Mem:* Fel Am Soc Mat Int; Am Inst Mining Metall & Petrol Engrs; Soc Advan Mat & Process Eng. *Res:* Relationship between the metallurgy of titanium and its engineering properties; increasing the utilization of titanium by making it more cost effective through advances in processing technologies; author and co-author of over 100 technical publications. *Mailing Add:* Boeing Com Airplane Group PO Box 3707 MS 6H-CJ Seattle WA 98124. *Fax:* 425-965-1440; *E-Mail:* rodney.r.boyer@boeing.com

BOYER, SAMUEL H, IV, MEDICAL GENETICS, EXPERIMENTAL HEMATOLOGY. *Current Pos:* From asst prof to assoc prof, 59-71, PROF MED & BIOL, SCH MED, JOHNS HOPKINS UNIV, 71- *Personal Data:* b Duluth, Minn, Aug 16, 24; m 52; c 3. *Educ:* Stanford Univ, AB, 50, MD, 54. *Concurrent Pos:* USPHS fels, Johns Hopkins Univ, 56-58, Univ Mich, 58 & Univ Col, Univ London, 58-59; ed, Johns Hopkins Med J, 75-82; investr, Howard Hughes Med Inst, 76-86. *Mem:* Am Soc Human Genetics (secy, 62-64); Asn Am Physicians; Am Soc Clin Invest. *Res:* Human biochemical genetics; genetic polymorphisms; comparative biochemistry of protein; regulation of protein synthesis; cells; organization and evaluation of reiterated DNA; regulation of erythropoiesis. *Mailing Add:* 6900 Charles Ridge Rd Baltimore MD 21204

BOYER, TIMOTHY HOWARD, THEORETICAL PHYSICS. *Current Pos:* from asst prof to assoc prof, 70-79, PROF PHYSICS, CITY COL NEW YORK, 80- *Personal Data:* b New York, NY, Mar 20, 41; m 77, Marilyn E Abel; c Laurette C & Michael C. *Educ:* Yale Univ, BA, 62; Harvard Univ, MA, 63, PhD(physics), 68. *Prof Exp:* Fel physics, Univ Md, 68-70. *Mem:* AAAS; Am Phys Soc. *Res:* Stochastic electrodynamics; classical electron theory; zero-point energy; relations between classical and quantum theories; classical electromagnetic. *Mailing Add:* Dept Physics City Col New York New York NY 10031

BOYER, VINCENT S, NUCLEAR ENGINEERING. *Current Pos:* CONSULT, 87- *Personal Data:* b Philadelphia, Pa, 18; m 42, Ethel Wolf; c Ruth, Suzanne & Sandra. *Educ:* Swarthmore Col, BSc; Univ Pa, MSc. *Hon Degrees:* DSc, Spring Garden Col, 79. *Honors & Awards:* James N Landis Medal, Am Soc Mech Engrs, 81. *Prof Exp:* Eng plant tests, elec opers, Philadelphia Elec Co, 39-44, supvr, Power Sta,46-53, asst supt, Cromby Sta, 53-56, supt, 56-60, supt, Peach Bottom Atomic Power Sta, 60-63, mgr, nuclear power, Elec Oprs Dept, 63-65, gen supt sta operating, 65-67, mgr, elec opers, 67-68, vpres, engr res, 68-80, sr vpres, Nuclear Power, 80-87. *Concurrent Pos:* Chmn, Philadelphia sect, Am Soc Mech Engrs, 66, pres, Philadelphia Post, 75. *Mem:* Nat Acad Eng; fel Am Nuclear Soc (pres, 76-77,96); fel Am Soc Mech Engrs; Nat Soc Prof Engrs. *Res:* Development of design of modular high temperature gas cooled reactor. *Mailing Add:* 3300 Darby Rd Apt 3305 Haverford PA 19041-1070

BOYER, WILLIAM DAVIS, FOREST ECOLOGY. *Current Pos:* res proj leader, 76-87, RES FORESTER, USDA, 55- *Personal Data:* b Dayton, Ohio, Sept 27, 24; m 52, 81, Doris A Bartels; c Catherine L, Susan M, Anne E & Mary R. *Educ:* US Merchant Marine Acad, BS, 50; State Univ NY, BS, 51, MS, 54; Duke Univ, PhD, 70. *Honors & Awards:* Tech Award, Southeastern Sect, Soc Am Foresters, 81. *Prof Exp:* Res asst water resources & power, Comn Orgn of Exec Br of Govt, 54-55. *Concurrent Pos:* Adj assoc prof, Auburn Univ. *Mem:* Ecol Soc Am; Soc Am Foresters; Sigma Xi. *Res:* Silvicultural problems of southern pine; ecology and management of longleaf pine, fire ecology. *Mailing Add:* 852 Terrace Acres Auburn AL 36830. *Fax:* 334-821-0037; *E-Mail:* boyer@forestry.auburn.edu

BOYERS, ALBERT SAGE, ENERGY CONSERVATION, SOLAR ENERGY. *Current Pos:* EXTEN SPECIALIST MECH ENG, NC STATE UNIV, RALEIGH, 68- *Personal Data:* b Plainfield, NJ, July 16, 40. *Educ:* Purdue Univ, BS, 62; Univ Ill, MS, 64. *Prof Exp:* Engr, Cornell Aeronaut Lab, 66-68. *Concurrent Pos:* Instr mech eng, State Univ NY, Buffalo, 66-67. *Mem:* Am Soc Heating Refrig & Air-Conditioning Engrs. *Res:* Passive and active solar energy systems for residential buildings; solar industrial process heat; industrial energy conservation; industrial ventilation systems. *Mailing Add:* Mech Eng NC State Univ Box 7910 Raleigh NC 27695-0001

BOYESON, MICHAEL GEORGE, NEUROPHARMACOLOGY, PSYCHOLOGY. *Current Pos:* RETIRED. *Personal Data:* b Patuxent River, Md, Jan 6, 48; m 85, Barbara Pollock; c Scott, Mathew & Nicole. *Educ:* Univ Wash, BS, 74; Univ NMex, MA, 80, PhD(physiol psychol), 83. *Prof Exp:* Prof rehab med, Univ Wis Med Sch, 84-94; prof, Southwestern Med Ctr, 94-96. *Concurrent Pos:* Ed, Am J Phys Med & Rehab, 89-93; mem, Med Issues Comt, Nat Head Injury Found; reviewer, Rehab Servs Admin. *Mem:* Soc Neurosci; Neurotrauma Soc; Am Psychol Asn. *Res:* Mechanisms of functional recovery after brain injury studied by neuropharmacological, physiological, onatomical and behavioral techniques. *Mailing Add:* 2404 Amherst Middleton WI 53562

BOYETTE, JOSEPH GREENE, VERTEBRATE ECOLOGY, ACADEMIC ADMINISTRATION. *Current Pos:* instr sci, 57-60, from asst prof to assoc prof, 60-69, asst dean, Grad Sch, 70-73, PROF BIOL, E CAROLINA UNIV, 69-, DEAN GRAD SCH, 73- *Personal Data:* b Colerain, NC, May 10, 29; m 53; c 3. *Educ:* E Carolina Col, BS, 56, MA, 57; NC State Univ, PhD, 66. *Prof Exp:* Chemist, NC State Dept Agr, 55-56; teacher, high sch, NC, 56-57. *Mem:* Fel AAAS; Am Soc Mammalogists. *Res:* Behavior of the pine mouse. *Mailing Add:* 1703 Beaumont Dr Greenville NC 27858

BOYKIN, DAVID WITHERS, JR, ORGANIC CHEMISTRY. *Current Pos:* from asst prof to assoc prof, 65-72, chmn dept, 74-92, PROF ORG CHEM, GA STATE UNIV, 72-, ASSOC DEAN MATH & NATURAL SCI, 93- *Personal Data:* b Montgomery, Ala, Jan 6, 39; m 59; c 1. *Educ:* Univ Ala, 61; Univ Va, 61, MS, 63, PhD(org chem), 65. *Prof Exp:* Fel org chem, Univ Va, 66-67. *Mem:* Am Chem Soc; Int Soc Heterocyclic Chem; Am Soc Microbiol. *Res:* Reaction mechanisms of heterocycles, small rings and alpha, beta-unsaturated ketones; oxygen-17 nmr; synthetic medicinals. *Mailing Add:* Dept Chem Ga State Univ Univerity Plaza Atlanta GA 30303-3044. *Fax:* 404-651-1416

BOYKIN, LORRAINE STITH, NUTRITION. *Current Pos:* from asst prof to assoc prof, 70-81, PROF NUTRIT, HUNTER COL, 81- *Personal Data:* b Crewe, Va, Feb 1, 31; m 53. *Educ:* Va State Col, BS, 51, MS, 54; NY Univ, MA, 59; Long Island Univ, MS, 64; Columbia Univ, prof dipl nutrit, 67, EdD(nutrit), 70. *Prof Exp:* Dietitian, New York City Dept Hosps, 51-52, A&T Col NC, 52-53 & NY Univ Hosp, 54-55; nutritionist, New York City Dept Health, 55-64; teacher home econ, New York Bd Educ, 64-65; from instr to asst prof nutrit, Pratt Inst, 65-70. *Concurrent Pos:* Adj assoc prof, NY Univ, 74-80; expert appointee nutrit, NIH, Bethesda, 78-79. *Mem:* Fel AAAS; fel NY Acad Sci; fel Am Geriat Soc; fel Am Pub Health Asn; fel Royal Soc Health. *Res:* Geriatrics and nutrition; alcoholism and nutrition; stress and nutrition; cultural nutrition. *Mailing Add:* 627 Powells Lane Westbury NY 11590-1320

BOYKIN, WILLIAM H(ENRY), JR, CONTROL SYSTEMS, ENGINEERING MECHANICS. *Current Pos:* VPRES, AMDYNE CORP, 92- *Personal Data:* b Birmingham, Ala, July 22, 38; m 61; c 2. *Educ:* Auburn Univ, BSEP, 61, MSME, 63; Stanford Univ, PhD(systs theory), 67. *Prof Exp:* Res scientist, Hayes Int Corp, 61 & 64; instr mech eng, Auburn Univ, 61-64; res asst, Stanford Univ, 66-67; asst prof eng sci & elec eng, Univ Fla, 67-75, prof eng sci & elec eng, 75-80, assoc dir, Ctr Intel Mach & Robotics, 78-80; pres, Syst Dynamics Inc, 80-92. *Concurrent Pos:* Consult, US Army Missile Command, 69-78, Sci Appln, Inc, 77-78 & Naval Training Device Ctr, 77-, Westinghouse Nuclear Serv Div, 78, Martin Marietta, 78-, Comput Sci Corp, 79-80 & Hughes Helicopters, 80. *Mem:* Soc Automotive Eng; sr mem Inst Elec & Electronics Engrs; Sigma Xi; Am Inst Aeronaut & Astronaut; Am Soc Mech Engrs. *Res:* Optimal control of complex systems including spacecraft and robots; design of missle guidance and control systems; development of analytical methods for analysis of digital control systems with multiple sampling rates; development of design and testing methods for precision laser pointing systems; optimal design of robot structures including joints and actuators. *Mailing Add:* 35 Revere Way Huntsville AL 35801

BOYKINS, ERNEST ALOYSIUS, JR, VERTEBRATE ZOOLOGY. *Current Pos:* ASSOC PROF SCI, UNIV SOUTHERN MISS, 81- *Personal Data:* b Vicksburg, Miss, Oct 5, 31; m 55; c 4. *Educ:* Xavier Univ La, BS, 53; Tex Southern Univ, MS, 58, Mich State Univ, PhD(zool), 64. *Prof Exp:* Asst prof biol, Alcorn Agr & Mech Col, 54-61, prof, 64-71, dir div arts & sci, 70-71; pres, Miss Valley State Univ, 71-81. *Mem:* AAAS; Am Ornith Union. *Res:* Effects of dichlorodiphenyltrichloroethane on non-target animals. *Mailing Add:* Nine Delond Pl Hattiesburg MS 39402

BOYLAN, D(AVID) R(AY), CHEMICAL ENGINEERING, PROCESS DESIGN. *Current Pos:* RETIRED. *Personal Data:* b Belleville, Kans, July 22, 22; m 44; c 4. *Educ:* Univ Kans, BS, 43; Iowa State Col, PhD(chem eng), 52. *Honors & Awards:* Merit Award, Am Chem Soc. *Prof Exp:* Proj engr, Gen Chem Co, 43-47; sr engr, Am Cyanamid Co, 47; from asst prof to prof, Iowa State Univ, 48-59, assoc div eng, Exp Sta, 59-66, dir, Eng Res Inst, 66-88, dean, Col Eng, 70-88, prof chem eng, 88- *Mem:* Am Chem Soc; fel Am Inst Chem Engrs; Am Soc Eng Educ; Nat Soc Prof Engrs; Sigma Xi; fel AAAS. *Res:* Fertilizers; fertilizer technology; filtration. *Mailing Add:* 1516 Stafford Ames IA 50010

BOYLAN, EDWARD S, MATHEMATICS, COMPUTER SCIENCE. *Current Pos:* chmn dept, 76-82, ASSOC PROF MATH, RUTGERS UNIV, 68- *Personal Data:* b New York, NY, Feb 8, 38. *Educ:* Columbia Univ, AB, 59; Princeton Univ, MA, 61, PhD(math), 62; Stevens Inst Technol, MS, 86. *Prof Exp:* Res assoc math, grad sch sci, Yeshiva Univ, 62-63; asst prof math, Rutgers Univ, 63-66; assoc prof math, Hunter Col, 66-68. *Concurrent Pos:* Consult, Hudson Inst, NY, 70-82. *Mem:* Am Math Soc; Asn Comput Mach; Inst Mgt Sci. *Res:* Probability and inventory theory; possible connections between ergodic theory and martingale theory; strategic issues. *Mailing Add:* Dept Math & Comput Sci Rutgers Univ Newark NJ 07102

BOYLAN, ELIZABETH S, HORMONES & DEVELOPMENT, TRANSPLACENTAL CARCINOGENESIS. *Current Pos:* PROVOST, BARNARD COL, 95- *Personal Data:* b Shanghai, China, 46; US citizen; m, Robert J; c Elizabeth B & Emily A. *Educ:* Wellesley Col, AB, 68; Cornell Univ, PhD(zool), 72. *Prof Exp:* Teaching asst embryol, Cornell Univ, 68-72; trainee fertil & reproductive physiol, Marine Biol Lab, Woods Hole, 70-71; res assoc biochem & oncol, Med Ctr, Univ Rochester, 72-73; from asst prof to assoc prof, Queens Col, City Univ New York, 73-82, prof biol, 83-, actg asst provost, 88-89, asst provost, 89-90, assoc provost, 90-92, actg provost, 92-93, assoc provost acad progs & planning, 94-95. *Concurrent Pos:* Nat Cancer Inst res grant, 75-83; mem, Breast Cancer Task Force, Nat Cancer Inst, 80-83; mem adv comt, Am Cancer Soc, 81-85; consult, Diethylstilbestrol Task Force, NIH, 85; chmn, Acad Sen, Queens Col, City Univ New York, 85-88; vis investr, Sloan Kettering Inst, Cancer Res, NY, 79-80; Grad Fac Biol, City Univ New York, 77-; res grants, Am Inst Cancer Res, 87-90 & Am Fedn Aging Res, 88-89. *Mem:* Soc Develop Biol; Endocrine Soc, Am Asn Cancer Res; Am Soc Zoologists; AAAS; Int Asn Breast Cancer Res; Sigma Xi; fel Am Coun Educ. *Res:* Effect of hormones on fetal tissue and its relation to mammary carcinogenesis; dietary fat and metastasis; granted one US patent. *Mailing Add:* Off Provost Barnard Col 3009 Broadway New York NY 10027-6598. *Fax:* 718-997-5879; *E-Mail:* liz@mkh1.qc.edu

BOYLAN, WILLIAM J, ANIMAL BREEDING, QUANTITATIVE GENETICS. *Current Pos:* assoc prof, 66-71, PROF ANIMAL SCI, UNIV MINN, ST PAUL, 71- *Personal Data:* b Bozeman, Mont, Dec 25, 29; m 58; c 4. *Educ:* Mont State Univ, BS, 52; Univ Minn, MS, 59, PhD(genetics), 62. *Prof Exp:* From asst prof to assoc prof quant genetics, Univ Man, 62-66. *Concurrent Pos:* NSF fel, Quantitative Genetics, Brown Univ, 66; Sabbatical leave, Animal Breeding Res Orgn, Edinburgh, Scotland, 72-73; Fulbright scholar, Egypt, 82, Turkey, 88. *Mem:* Am Soc Animal Sci; Am Genetic Asn. *Res:* Quantitative inheritance in animals; design and evaluation of systems of selection and crossbreeding with emphasis on genetic improvement of livestock. *Mailing Add:* 10711 50th St N Lake Elmo MN 55042

BOYLE, A(RCHIBALD) R(AYMOND), ELECTRICAL ENGINEERING. *Current Pos:* prof, 66-87, EMER PROF ELEC ENG, UNIV SASK, 88- *Personal Data:* b Sutton Coldfield, Eng, Apr 24, 20; m 45; c 2. *Educ:* Univ Birmingham, BSc, 40, PhD(phys chem), 43. *Prof Exp:* Exp officer, SRE Dept, Brit Admiralty, 45-46; tech dir, Dobbie McInnes Electronics Ltd, Scotland, 46-65. *Mem:* Can Inst Survrs; Am Cong Surv & Mapping. *Res:* Instrumentation; data handling; automatic cartography. *Mailing Add:* Dept Elec Eng Univ Sask Saskatoon SK S7N 0W0 Can

BOYLE, CAROLYN REDDING, STATISTICAL DESIGN EXPERIMENTS, APPLIED STATISTICAL METHODS. *Current Pos:* res assoc, Miss State Univ, 80-81, statistician, 81-85, sr res asst, 85-92, asst prof & biostatistician, 92-96, ASSOC PROF & BIOSTATISTICIAN, MISS STATE UNIV, 96- *Personal Data:* b New Orleans, La, Aug 16, 50; m 73, John A Jr; c Alan P. *Educ:* Univ New Orleans, BS, 72; Univ NC, MS, 78; Miss State Univ, PhD(eng), 92. *Prof Exp:* Res analyst, Hartford Ins Group, 78-79. *Mem:* Am Statist Asn; Int Biomet Soc; Sigma Xi. *Res:* Statistical methods and design of experiments; theoretical and applied research on the optimization of multiple response computer simulation experiments; statistical consulting. *Mailing Add:* Box 9825 Mississippi State MS 39762-9825. *Fax:* 601-325-1031; *E-Mail:* crb1@ra.msstate.edu

BOYLE, EDWARD A, OCEANOGRAPHY. *Current Pos:* from asst prof to assoc prof, 77-90, PROF EARTH, ATMOSPHERIC & PLANETARY SCI, MASS INST TECHNOL, 90- *Personal Data:* b May 1, 49. *Educ:* Univ Calif, San Diego, BA, 71; Mass Inst Technol, PhD(oceanog), 76. *Honors & Awards:* Huntsman Award, 94. *Prof Exp:* Postdoctoral fel, Univ Edinburgh, 76-77. *Concurrent Pos:* Guggenheim fel, 91-92; assoc ed, Paleoceanog & Marine Chem. *Mem:* Fel Am Geophys Union; Geochem Soc; Oceanog Soc; AAAS; Am Chem Soc. *Res:* Trace element marine geochemistry; quaternary paleoceanography. *Mailing Add:* Mass Inst Technol Rm E34-258 77 Massachusetts Ave Cambridge MA 02139. *Fax:* 617-253-8630; *E-Mail:* eaboyle@mit.edu

BOYLE, JAMES MARTIN, PROGRAM TRANSFORMATION, PARALLEL PROCESSING. *Current Pos:* Res assoc, Argonne Nat Lab, 67-69, asst comput scientist, 69-74, comput scientist, Math & Comput Sci Div, 74-96, COMPUT SCIENTIST, TECHNOL DEVELOP DIV, ARGONNE NAT LAB, 96- *Personal Data:* b Edwardsville, Ill, June 21, 42; m 70; c 2. *Educ:* Northwestern Univ, BS, 64, MS, 65, PhD(appl math), 70. *Mem:* Asn Comput Mach; Soc Indust & Appl Math; Sigma Xi; AAAS. *Res:* Source-to-source transformations of computer programs; program correctness; mathematical software; abstract programming; parallel programming; automated reasoning. *Mailing Add:* Technol Develop Div Bldg 207 9700 S Cass Ave Argonne IL 60439-4803. *E-Mail:* jboyle@anl.gor

BOYLE, JOHN ALOYSIUS, JR, VIROLOGY. *Current Pos:* asst prof, Miss State Univ, 78-84, assoc prof bicohem, 84-89, PROF & HEAD BIOCHEM & MOLECULAR BIOL, MISS STATE UNIV, 89-, ADJ PROF BASIC & APPL SCI, COL VET MED, 89-; EXEC DIR, MISS ACAD SCI, 90- *Personal Data:* b New Orleans, La, Nov 5, 50; m 73, Carolyn Redding; c Alan P. *Educ:* Univ New Orleans, BS, 72; Duke Univ, PhD(biochem), 78. *Honors & Awards:* Young Res Award, Sigma Xi. *Prof Exp:* Fel molecular biophysics & biochem, Yale Univ, 78. *Mem:* AAAS; Sigma Xi; Am Soc Microbiol; Am Soc Biochem & Molecular Biol. *Res:* Pathogen detection using nucleic acids; analytical techniques applied to nucleic acids; development of nucleic acid probes; use of polymerase chain reaction in analysis. *Mailing Add:* Dept Biochem PO Box 9650 Miss State Univ Mississippi State MS 39762. *Fax:* 601-325-8664; *E-Mail:* jab@ra.msstate.edu

BOYLE, JOHN JOSEPH, virology, for more information see previous edition

BOYLE, JOSEPH, III, RESPIRATORY PHYSIOLOGY, CARDIOVASCULAR PHYSIOLOGY. *Current Pos:* from asst prof to assoc prof, 66-96, ADJ ASN PROF PHYSIOL & PHARM, NJ MED SCH, UNIV MED & DENT NJ, 96- *Personal Data:* b Glen Ridge, NJ, Mar 10, 34; m 57, Patricia Allan Vreeland; c Debra Louise (Leighton), Joseph Edwin & Bruce Allan. *Educ:* Tufts Univ, BS, 56; Seton Hall Col Med, MD, 60. *Prof Exp:* Instr physiol, Seton Hall Col Med, 61-63; flight surgeon aerospace physiol, Brooks AFB, San Antonio, 63-66. *Mem:* Am Physiol Soc; Am Thoracic Soc; Sigma Xi. *Res:* Lung mechanics; effects of surfactant on lung function; computer based instruction; physiological modeling. *Mailing Add:* Dept Physiol Univ Med & Dent NJ NJ Med Sch 185 S Orange Ave Med Sci Bldg Level H Newark NJ 07103. *Fax:* 973-982-7950; *E-Mail:* boyle@umdnj.edu

BOYLE, KATHRYN MOYNE WARD DITTEMORE, ORGANIC CHEMISTRY. *Current Pos:* from asst prof to assoc prof, 75-82, PROF CHEM, FRIENDS UNIV, 82- *Personal Data:* b Wheaton, Kans; m 76; c 6. *Educ:* Univ Kans, BA, 49; Univ Iowa, PhD(chem), 74. *Prof Exp:* Instr chem, Univ Wash, 74-75. *Mem:* Am Chem Soc. *Mailing Add:* Chem Dept Friends Univ 2100 University Ave Wichita KS 67213-3379

BOYLE, MICHAEL DERMOT, IMMUNOCHEMISTRY, COMPLEMENT. *Current Pos:* PROF DEPT MICROBIOL, MED COL OHIO, TOLEDO, 88- *Personal Data:* b Belfast, Northern Ireland, Jan 4, 49; m 73, Carla Colville; c Kieron & Sarah. *Educ:* Univ Glasgow, Scotland, BSc, 71; Univ London, PhD(biochem), 74. *Prof Exp:* Vis fel, Nat Cancer Inst, Bethesda, Md, 74-76, expert, 76-80, vis scientist, 80; assoc prof immunol, Dept Immunol & Med Microbiol & Pediat, Col Med, Univ Fla, 81-85, prof, 85-88. *Concurrent Pos:* Assoc ed, Molecular & Cellular Biochem, 83-87; assoc ed, Biotechniques, 86- *Mem:* Am Asn Immunologists; Am Asn Cancer Res; Found Advan Educ Sci; Am Asn Vet Immunologists; Am Asn Microbiologists; Sigma Xi. *Res:* Immunochemistry of bacteria; complement and immuno-diagnostic technology; molecular pathogenesis. *Mailing Add:* Med Col Ohio PO Box 10008 3000 Arlington Ave Toledo OH 43614-5802. *Fax:* 419-381-3002

BOYLE, RICHARD JAMES, SOLVENT EXTRACTION. *Current Pos:* RETIRED. *Personal Data:* b Westport, NY, Apr 19, 27; m 55; c Rebecca, Susan, Stephen, Mary, Carolyn & Kevin. *Educ:* Univ Del, BS, 50; Univ Notre Dame, PhD(chem), 53. *Prof Exp:* Res chemist, Calco Chem Div, Am Cyanamid Co, 53-59, group leader, Plant Tech Dept, 59-61, tech rep, Res Dept, 61-62, mgr sales develop, Textile Chem Dept, Org Chem Div, 62-67, prod mgr, Mkt Develop Dept, 67-69, prod mgr, Decision Making Systs Dept, 69, field sales supvr, 69-70, tech dir, Indust Prod Dept, Europe-African Region, Cyanamid Int, 70-73, prod mgr, Indust & Mining Chems, 73-74, prod mgr organic chem, Cyanamid Europe-Mideast-Africa Div, 74-81, mkt develop mgr phosphine chem, Organic Chem Div, 81-84, new prod develop mgr, Cyanamid Int Chem Div, 84-91. *Mem:* Am Chem Soc. *Res:* Analogs of podophyllotoxin; vat dyes; ultraviolet absorbers; textile chemicals; luminescent chemicals; elastomers; phosphine chemicals and solvent extraction. *Mailing Add:* 266 Altamont Pl Somerville NJ 08876

BOYLE, WALTER GORDON, JR, COMPUTER APPLICATIONS FOR ANALYTICAL CHEMISTRY. *Current Pos:* RETIRED. *Personal Data:* b Seattle, Wash, June 27, 28; m 58; c 2. *Educ:* Univ Wash, BS, 50, PhD(anal chem), 56. *Prof Exp:* Group leader, Lawrence Livermore Nat Lab, 63-67, res chemist, 77-80, systs mgr chem comput, 80-84, mgr data base methodology, 84-90, comput applns anal chem, 85-90. *Concurrent Pos:* Guest, Lawrence Livermore Nat Lab, 90- *Mem:* Am Chem Soc; Sigma Xi. *Res:* Determination of trace elements in metals and alloys; atomic absorption and flame emission spectroscopy; computer applications in analytical chemistry; nuclear magnetic resonance imaging; data base methods for analytical chemistry. *Mailing Add:* 20 Holly Hill Ct Walnut Creek CA 94596-6206

BOYLE, WILLARD STERLING, PHYSICS. *Current Pos:* CONSULT, 80- *Personal Data:* b NS, Aug 19, 24; m 46; c 4. *Educ:* McGill Univ, PhD(physics), 50. *Hon Degrees:* LLD, Dalhousie Univ, 84. *Honors & Awards:* Stuart Ballantine Medal Award, Franklin Inst, 73; Morris N Liebmann Award, Inst Elec & Electronics Engrs, 74; Progress Award, Photog Am, 86. *Prof Exp:* Lectr physics, McGill Univ, 50-51; asst prof, Royal Mil Col, 51-53; mem tech staff, Bell Tel Labs, 53-62, dir explor studies, Bellcomm, Inc, 62-64, dir, Semiconductor Device Lab, Bell Tel Labs, 64-68, exec dir, 68-80. *Mem:* Nat Acad Eng; fel Inst Elec & Electronics Engrs; fel Am Phys Soc. *Res:* Study of electronic devices and systems relation to communications; solid state physics; semiconductors. *Mailing Add:* PO Box 180 Wallace NS B0Y 1Y0 Can

BOYLE, WILLIAM C(HARLES), CIVIL & ENVIRONMENTAL ENGINEERING. *Current Pos:* From asst prof to prof, 63-96, chmn dept, 84-86, EMER PROF CIVIL ENG, UNIV WIS-MADISON, 96- *Personal Data:* b Minneapolis, Minn, Apr 9, 36; m 59, Nancy Hahn; c Elizabeth L, Michele J, Jane L & Robert W. *Educ:* Univ Cincinnati, CE, 59, MS, 60; Calif Inst Technol, PhD, 63. *Honors & Awards:* Rudolf Hering Medal, Am Soc Civil Engrs, 75; Radebaugh Award, Water Pollution Control Fedn, 78; Founders Award, US Nat Comm Intl Water Pollution Res, 88; USEPA Commendation for Outstanding Leadership, Aeration Technol, 89; Harrison Prescot Eddy, Water Pollution Control Fedn, 90; Gordon Fair Medal for Environ Eng Educ, Water Environ Fedn, 92. *Concurrent Pos:* Chmn, Oxygen Trans Standards Comt, 78-, aeration comt, Am Soc Civil Eng, 81-90; chmn, Tech Pract Comm on Aeration, Water pollution Control Fedn, 83-90, Tech Prog Comt, Water Environ, Fedn, 92- & engr, Educ Comt, Am Acad, Environ Engrs, 93-95; prin engr, J M Montgomery Watson, 88-89; trustee, Am Acad Environ Engrs, 93-97; dir, Accred Bd Eng & Tech, 95-; bd dir, Water Environ Fedn, 96- *Mem:* Am Soc Civil Engrs; Am Water Works Asn; Water Environ Fedn; Int Asn Water Qual; Am Asn Environ Engr Profs; Am Acad Environ Engrs. *Res:* Water pollution control through biological waste treatment; mechanistic reactions in biosystems in waste and water treatment; oxygen transfer; on site waste treatment and disposal; waste water disinfection; leach testing solid wastes; fate of contaminants in soil. *Mailing Add:* 105 Carillon Dr Madison WI 53705. *E-Mail:* boyle@engr.wisc.edu

BOYLE, WILLIAM JOHNSTON, JR, ORGANIC CHEMISTRY, POLYMER CHEMISTRY. *Current Pos:* res chemist, 73-76, sr res chemist, 76-85, RES ASSOC, ALLIED CORP, 85- *Personal Data:* b Albany, Ga, Jan 10, 44; m 66, 86; c 1. *Educ:* Duke Univ, BS, 66; Northwestern Univ, PhD(org chem), 71. *Prof Exp:* Assoc org chem, Univ Calif, Santa Cruz, 70-73. *Concurrent Pos:* NSF fel, Univ Calif, Santa Cruz, 70-71. *Mem:* Am Chem Soc; AAAS; Sigma Xi. *Res:* Organic reaction mechanisms; synthetic organic chemistry; polymer synthesis. *Mailing Add:* Allied Signal Corp Bldg CRL 245 F 101 Columbia Rd Morristown NJ 07962

BOYLE, WILLIAM ROBERT, chemical & nuclear engineering, for more information see previous edition

BOYLEN, CHARLES WILLIAM, LIMNOLOGY, AQUATIC ECOLOGY. *Current Pos:* from asst prof to assoc prof, 72-88, DIR FRESH WATER INST, RENSSELAER POLYTECH INST, 85-, PROF BIOL, 89- *Personal Data:* b Baltimore, Md, Mar 29, 42; m 70, Kathryn L Anastasio; c Brent & Mark. *Educ:* Ind Univ, AB, 64; Univ Wis-Madison, MS, 67, PhD(microbiol), 69. *Prof Exp:* Postdoctoral microbial ecol, Life Detection Unit, Ames Res Ctr, NASA, 69-71 & Univ Wis-Madison, 71-72. *Concurrent Pos:* Site coordr, NSF Int Biol Prog, 74-76; appointee, Nat Comt Microbiol, Am Soc Microbiol, 75-78, pres, NY Br, 79-81; vis prof, Woods Hole Oceanog Inst, Mass, 82-83; co-dir environ eng & environ sci, Rensselaer Polytech Inst, 87-91; hon prof, Hrachan Atcharian Univ, Repub Armenia. *Mem:* Am Soc Microbiol; Am Soc Limnol & Oceanog; AAAS; Ecol Soc Am; NAm Lake Mgt Soc. *Res:* Limnology of acid and nutrient impacted lakes; microbial ecology of stressed ecosystems; ecology of invasive aquatic plant species; bioremediation; environmental science; freshwater ecology. *Mailing Add:* Darrin Fresh Water Inst Rensselaer Polytech Inst Troy NY 12181. *Fax:* 518-276-2080; *E-Mail:* boylec@rpi.edu

BOYLEN, JOYCE BEATRICE, BIOCHEMISTRY. *Current Pos:* RETIRED. *Personal Data:* b Weston, Ont, Aug 15, 26. *Educ:* Univ Toronto, BA, 47, MA, 49; McGill Univ, PhD(biochem), 61. *Prof Exp:* Jr res officer biol, Atomic Energy Can, Ltd, 49-53; Nuffield res asst genetics, Univ Leicester, 53-56; res asst biochem, McGill Univ, 57-60; sect head tissue culture, Frank W Horner, Ltd, Can, 60-63, sect head virol, 63-64; res biochemist, ICI Americas Inc, 64-68, clin info coordr, Stuart Pharmaceut Div, 68-90. *Concurrent Pos:* Mem, Coun Biol Ed. *Mem:* Drug Info Asn; Am Chem Soc; Am Med Writers Asn; AAAS. *Res:* Clinical studies of new drugs. *Mailing Add:* 801 Maple Ave Wilmington DE 19809

BOYLES, JAMES GLENN, PHYSICAL CHEMISTRY. *Current Pos:* from asst prof to assoc prof, 66-80, chmn dept, 77-88, PROF CHEM, BATES COL, 80- *Personal Data:* b Harrisburg, Pa, Mar 21, 37; m 60, Donna Fulton; c Kristen & Amanda. *Educ:* Pa State Univ, BS, 59; Rutgers Univ, PhD(chem), 66. *Prof Exp:* Instr chem, Rutgers Univ, 65-66. *Mem:* Am Chem Soc. *Res:* Chemical reaction kinetics and mechanisms. *Mailing Add:* 584 Poland Range Rd Pownal ME 04069. *Fax:* 207-786-6123; *E-Mail:* jboyles@bates.edu

BOYLES, JAMES MCGREGOR, MEDICAL PARASITOLOGY. *Current Pos:* MED HISTORIAN & MED PARASITOLOGIST, 97- *Personal Data:* b Birmingham, Ala, Oct 1, 26; m 89, Mary A Smith; c Robert & Catherine. *Educ:* Univ Ala, BS, 51, MS, 52, PhD(biol), 66. *Prof Exp:* Instr biol, Mobile Ctr, Univ Ala, 56-64; from instr to asst prof, Univ SAla, 64-71, assoc prof, 71-91, emer prof biol, 91-97. *Mem:* Am Soc Parasitol; Am Soc Trop Med & Hyg. *Res:* Amebic meningoencephalitis. *Mailing Add:* 6409 Gilbert Dr W Satsuma AL 36572

BOYLES, JANET, lipid transport, cytoskeletal structure, for more information see previous edition

BOYNE, PHILIP JOHN, ORAL & MAXILLOFACIAL SURGERY, ANATOMY. *Current Pos:* DIR ORAL SURG SECT, DEPT SURG, LOMA LINDA UNIV MED CTR, 78- *Personal Data:* b Houlton, Maine, May 1, 24; m 46, Mary A Young; c Kathryn & John. *Educ:* Colby Col, BA, 46; Tufts Univ, DMD, 47; Georgetown Univ, MS, 61. *Hon Degrees:* DSc, NJ Col Med & Dent, 75. *Honors & Awards:* Career Achievement Award Res-Am Soc Maxillo-Facial Surg, 75. *Prof Exp:* Instr anat, Tufts Univ, 47-49; resident oral surg, US Naval Dent Sch, Nat Naval Med Ctr, 54-55, staff guest scientist, US Naval Med Res Inst, 55-57, dir dent res dept, 65-68; prof dent, Sch Dent, Univ Calif, Los Angeles, 68-69, prof oral surg & chmn div, 69-74, asst dean, Sch Dent, 71-74; dir bone res lab, Univ Tex Health Sci Ctr, San Antonio, dean dent sch & prof oral surg, Dent & Med Schs, 74-78. *Concurrent Pos:* Guest lectr, Sch Dent, Georgetown Univ, 60-62 & US Naval Dent Sch, Nat Naval Med Ctr, 65-68; mem adv comt, Am Bd Oral & Maxillofacial Surg, 66-72, dir, 76-, vpres, 82, pres, 83. *Mem:* Am Dent Asn; Am Soc Oral Surg; fel Am Col Dent; fel Int Col Dentists; Int Asn Dent Res; Am Inst Oral Biol (pres, 70-). *Res:* Oral surgical research; bone healing; response of osseous tissues to trauma bone growth and development; tissue transplantation in maxillo-facial surgery; craniofacial surgery of congenital anomalies. *Mailing Add:* 11540 Hillcrest St Loma Linda CA 92354

BOYNE, WILLIAM JOSEPH, CHEMICAL ENGINEERING. *Current Pos:* MGR MFG PETROCHEM, ASHLAND CHEM CO, 80- *Personal Data:* b Troy, NY, Sept 28, 26; m 52; c 4. *Educ:* Purdue Univ, BS, 48, PhD(chem eng), 52. *Prof Exp:* Asst chem eng, Purdue Univ, 48-50; engr, Am Cyanamid Co, 52-54, sr engr, 54-61; tech mgr, Monochem Inc, 61-66, eng mgr, 66-68, vpres opers, 68-69; sr engr, Borden Chem Div, Borden Inc, 59-61, dir eng, 69-72, dir chem planning, eng & res & develop, 72-79. *Mem:* Am Inst Chem Engrs; Am Chem Soc. *Res:* Acetlyene; air separation; vinyl chloride; ammonia-urea; methanol; coated fabrics; phenol- and urea-formaldehyde resins; UV coatings; hot melt adhesives; aerosols; phosphoric acid and fertilizers; uranium recovery; sulfuric acid; fluosilicic acid. *Mailing Add:* 6008 Kirkwall Ct Dublin OH 43017-9001

BOYNTON, JOHN E, GENETICS. *Current Pos:* from asst prof to assoc prof, 68-77, PROF BOT, DUKE UNIV, 77- *Personal Data:* b Duluth, Minn, June 3, 38. *Educ:* Univ Ariz, BS, 60; Univ Calif, Davis, PhD(genetics), 66. *Honors & Awards:* Campbell Award, Am Inst Biol Sci, 67. *Prof Exp:* NIH Postdoctoral fel genetics, Univ Calif, Davis, 66 & Inst Genetics, Copenhagen Univ, 66-68. *Concurrent Pos:* Res career develop award, NIH, 72-77. *Mem:* Genetics Soc Am; Int Soc Plant Molecular Biol. *Res:* Genetic control of organelle structure and function. *Mailing Add:* 1808 Woodburn Rd Durham NC 27705

BOYNTON, JOHN E, ESTUARINE ECOLOGY, ECOLOGY OF PROTOZOA. *Current Pos:* ASST PROF BIOL, ST JOSEPH'S COL, 85- *Personal Data:* b New York, NY, Dec 16, 50; m 74; c 2. *Educ:* Univ Conn, BS, 73; Cent Conn State Col, MS, 76; Univ Md, PhD(marine & estuarine ecol), 85. *Prof Exp:* Teacher biol, Northeast Sch, Bristol, Conn, 74-80. *Mem:* AAAS; Am Soc Limnol & Oceanog; Soc Protozoologists; Nat Sci Teachers Asn; Nat Marine Educrs Asn; Atlantic Estuarine Res Soc. *Res:* Determination of sediment-water column exchange of nutrients, particularly ammonium, in the Patchogue River Estuary; development of nitrogen budget for Patchogue Lake. *Mailing Add:* 36 Clark St Port Jefferson Station Port Jefferson NY 11776

BOYNTON, NANCY JEAN, MATHEMATICS STATISTICS & OPERATIONS RESEARCH EDUCATION, QUEUEING THEORY. *Current Pos:* ASST PROF MATH, STATE UNIV NY, FREDONIA, 82- *Personal Data:* b Battle Creek, Mich, Aug 16, 51. *Educ:* Albion Col, BA, 73; Western Mich Univ, PhD(math), 79. *Prof Exp:* Asst prof math, Mich Technol Univ, 78-82. *Mem:* Math Asn Am; Am Statist Asn; Am Math Soc; Inst Opers Res & Mgt Sci; Asn Women Math; Sigma Xi; Caucus Women Statist. *Res:* Teaching of mathematics and related subjects; queueing theory and probability. *Mailing Add:* Dept Math Comput Sci State Univ NY Fredonia NY 14063. *E-Mail:* boynton@cs.fredonia.edu

BOYNTON, ROBERT M, PSYCHOLOGY, OPTICS. *Current Pos:* RETIRED. *Personal Data:* b Evanston, Ill, Oct 28, 24; m 47; c 4. *Educ:* Amherst Col, AB, 48; Brown Univ, ScM, 50, PhD(psychol), 52. *Honors & Awards:* Tillyer Medal, Optical Soc Am, 72; Godlove Award, Inter-Soc Color Coun, 81. *Prof Exp:* From asst prof psychol to prof psychol & optics, Univ Rochester, 52-74, chmn, Dept Psychol, 71-74; prof psychol, Univ Calif, San Diego, 74-91, assoc dean grad studies & res, 87-91. *Concurrent Pos:* Mem, Nat Res Coun-Armed Forces Comt Vision, 57-65, Exec Coun, 62-65; mem, US Nat Comt, Int Comn Illumination, 59-; NIH study fel, Eng, 60-61; dir, Ctr Visual Sci, Univ Rochester, 63-71; mem, Visual Sci Study Sect, NIH, 64-67; dir-at-large, Optical Soc Am, 66-69; vis prof, San Francisco Med Ctr, 69-70; chmn, Visual Sci B Study Sect, NIH, 73-77; dir, Asn Vision & Ophthal, 83-88, vpres, 88. *Mem:* Nat Acad Sci; fel Optical Soc Am; fel Am Psychol Asn; Soc Exp Psychologists; fel AAAS. *Res:* Psychology, physics and physiology of human vision. *Mailing Add:* Dept Psychol C-009 Univ Calif-San Diego La Jolla CA 92093

BOYNTON, W(ILLIAM) W(ENTWORTH), mining engineering; deceased, see previous edition for last biography

BOYNTON, WALTER RAYMOND, MARINE ECOLOGY. *Current Pos:* Res asst, 69-70, RES ASSOC MARINE ECOL, CHESAPEAKE BIOL LAB, UNIV MD, 75- *Personal Data:* b Lawrence, Mass, May 5, 47; m 73. *Educ:* Springfield Col, BS, 69; Univ NC, Chapel Hill, MS, 74; Univ Fla, PhD(environ eng), 75. *Mem:* Estuarine Res Fedn; Sigma Xi. *Res:* Population studies of estuarine fish populations; coastal zone management with special emphasis on power plant siting. *Mailing Add:* Henry Htchns Rd Prince Frederick MD 20678

BOYNTON, WILLIAM VANDEGRIFT, GEOCHEMISTRY, COSMOCHEMISTRY. *Current Pos:* from asst prof to assoc prof, 77-85, PROF, DEPT PLANETARY SCI, UNIV ARIZ, 86- *Personal Data:* b Bridgeport, Conn, Oct 29, 44; m 74; c 1. *Educ:* Wesleyan Univ, BA, 66; Carnegie-Mellon Univ, PhD(phys chem), 71. *Honors & Awards:* NASA Group Achievement Award. *Prof Exp:* Asst res geochemist, Univ Calif, 74-77. *Concurrent Pos:* Team leader & prin investr, Mars Observer Mission. *Mem:* AAAS; Meteoritical Soc; Am Chem Soc; Am Geophys Union. *Res:* Theromdynamics of trace element condensation from the solar nebula; trace element solid solution formation; neutron activation analysis; meteorites; comets; planetary surface composition; gamma-ray spectrometry. *Mailing Add:* Lunar & Planetary Lab Univ Ariz Tucson AZ 85721-0001

BOYSE, EDWARD A, IMMUNOGENETICS. *Current Pos:* DISTINGUISHED PROF MICROBIOL & IMMUNOL, UNIV ARIZ, 89- *Personal Data:* b Worthing, Eng, Aug 11, 23; UK & US citizen. *Educ:* Univ London, MB & BS, 52, MD, 57. *Honors & Awards:* Harvey lectr, 75; Cancer Res Inst Award, Tumor Immunol, 75; Isaac Adler Award, Rockefeller & Harvard Univ, 76. *Prof Exp:* Staff, Dept Path, Guy's Hosp, London, 55-56, res fel path, 57-60; pub health lab serv, Bact & Virol Sect, London, 56-57; res fel path, Sch Med, NY Univ, 60-61, asst prof, 61-64; assoc prof, Grad Sch Med Sci, Cornell Univ, 66-69, prof biol, 69-89. *Concurrent Pos:* Casualty Off & Ear, Nose & Throat Off, Essex Co Hosp, Colchester, 52, house surgeon, 53; house phys, Metrop Hosp, London, 55, med registr, 54-55; staff, Dept Path, Guy's Hosp, London, 55-56, Pub Health Lab Serv, 56-57; assoc scientist, Sloan-Kettering Inst Cancer Res, 62-64, assoc mem, 64-67, mem, 67-89; adj assoc prof path, Sch Med, NY Univ, 64-71, adj prof, 71-; immunobiol study sect, NIH, 65-69; mem, Clin Rev Bd & Exec Comt, Monell Chem Senses Ctr, Philadelphia; sci adv bd, Showa Univ Res Inst Biomed, St Petersburg, Fla; Am Cancer Soc Res prof, Cell Surface Immunogenetics, 77; sci adv coun, Roswell Park Mem Inst, Buffalo, NY; Am Cancer Soc res prof cell surface immunogenetics, 77; outstanding investr award, Nat Cancer Inst, 85. *Mem:* Nat Acad Sci; fel Royal Soc; Am Acad Arts & Sci. *Mailing Add:* Univ Ariz Dept Microbiol & Immunol Health Sci Ctr Tucson AZ 85715

BOZAK, RICHARD EDWARD, ORGANIC CHEMISTRY. *Current Pos:* from asst prof to assoc prof org chem, 64-76, coordr res, 66-69, PROF CHEM, CALIF STATE UNIV, HAYWARD, 76- *Personal Data:* b Aberdeen, Wash, Oct 13, 34; m 59; c 3. *Educ:* Univ Wash, BS, 56; Univ Calif, Berkeley, PhD(org chem), 59. *Prof Exp:* Fel org synthesis, Moscow State Univ, 59-60; fel ferrocene chem, Univ Ill, 60-61; res chemist, Shell Oil Co, Calif, 61-64 & Shell Develop Co, 64. *Concurrent Pos:* Consult, Lawrence Livermore Nat Lab, 70-; Fulbright res fel, Inorg Inst, Munich Tech Univ, 72-73. *Mem:* Am Chem Soc; Sigma Xi; Int Am Photochem Soc. *Res:* Natural products; organic chemistry of ferrocene; photochemistry. *Mailing Add:* Dept Chem Calif State Col Hayward CA 94542

BOZARTH, GENE ALLEN, BOTANY, PLANT PHYSIOLOGY. *Current Pos:* RES ASSOC, E I DU PONT DE NEMOURS CO, 89- *Personal Data:* b Rumsey, Ky, Nov 10, 41; m 68; c 2. *Educ:* Univ Ky, BS, 63; Auburn Univ, MS, 66, PhD(biochem), 69. *Prof Exp:* Fel fungus physiol, Univ Mo-Columbia, 69-71; sr res analyst, Space Sci Lab, Northrop Serv, Inc, 71-74, prin scientist, bot area, Johnson Spaceflight Ctr, 74-75; plant physiologist, 76-80, mgr, Plant Physiol Dept, 81-83, sr res biologist, Shell Develop Co, 84-89. *Mem:* Weed Sci Soc Am; Sigma Xi; Aquatic Plant Mgt Soc; Int Weed Sci Soc. *Res:* Herbicide evaluation; weed control; weed biology and plant growth regulators; rice agronomy; rice weed control; rice diseases. *Mailing Add:* 15 Nathalie Dr Newark DE 19713

BOZARTH, ROBERT F, PLANT VIROLOGY. *Current Pos:* PROF LIFE SCI, IND STATE UNIV, 76- *Personal Data:* b Herrin, Ill, Feb 23, 30; m 51; c 3. *Educ:* Univ Fla, BSc, 52, MSc, 57; Cornell Univ, PhD(plant path), 62. *Prof Exp:* Res assoc, Virol Pioneering Lab, USDA, 61-62; virologist, Boyce Thompson Inst Plant Res, 62-76. *Mem:* Sigma Xi; Am Soc Virol; Am Phytopath Soc; Am Soc Microbiol. *Res:* Physico-chemical properties of fungal and plant viruses. *Mailing Add:* Dept Life Sci Ind State Univ Terre Haute IN 47809-0001

BOZDECH, MAREK JIRI, HEMATOLOGY, ONCOLOGY. *Current Pos:* PVT PRACTICE, 90- *Personal Data:* b Wildflecken, WGer, Oct 12, 46; US citizen; m 67; c 3. *Educ:* Univ Mich, Ann Arbor, AB, 67; Wayne State Univ, Detroit, MD, 72. *Prof Exp:* Res asst otolaryngol, Kresge Hearing Res Inst, Univ Mich, Ann Arbor, 67-69; intern, Univ Wis-Madison, 72-73, resident internal med, 73-75, from asst prof to assoc prof, 78-85, dir, Clin Hemat Lab, 78-82, dir, Bone Marrow Transplantation Prog, 84-85; fel hemat & oncol, Univ Calif, San Francisco, 75-78, clin instr internal med, 77-78, assoc prof med & dir, Adult Bone Marrow Transplantation Serv, 85-90. *Concurrent Pos:* Res assoc, Cancer Res Inst, Univ Calif, San Francisco, 77-78; Nat Cancer Inst fel, NIH, 77-78; vis fel, Fred Hutchinson Cancer Res Ctr, Seattle, Wash, 80. *Mem:* AAAS; Am Soc Hemat; Am Fedn Clin Res; Am Col Physicians. *Res:* Bone marrow transplantation; abrogation of graft-versus-host disease; manipulation of the graft-versus-leukemia effect; in vitro treatment of allogeneic and autologous marrow; study of the immune and hematopoietic systems after transplantation; use of marrow transplants for treatment of genetic defects. *Mailing Add:* 50 La Placita Ct Novato CA 94945

BOZEMAN, F MARILYN, MICROBIOLOGY. *Current Pos:* RETIRED. *Personal Data:* b Washington, DC, Dec 3, 27; m 64. *Educ:* Univ Md, BS, 48, MS, 50. *Prof Exp:* Bacteriologist, Am Type Cult Collection, 48-49; microbiologist, Dept Rickettsial Dis, Walter Reed Army Inst Res, 50-73; microbiologist, Div Virol, Bur Biologics, Food & Drug Admin, 73-84, br chief, 77-84. *Mem:* Am Soc Microbiol; Tissue Cult Asn; Am Asn Immunologists. *Res:* Rickettsiology and virology; cell and tissue culture. *Mailing Add:* 4008 Queen Mary Dr Olney MD 20832

BOZEMAN, JOHN RUSSELL, PLANT ECOLOGY. *Current Pos:* asst chief, Marsh & Beach Sect, Coastal Resources Div, Brunswick, 75-89, PROG MGR, GA NATURAL HERITAGE PROG, GA DEPT NATURAL RESOURCES, 89- *Personal Data:* b Bleckley Co, Ga, Apr 2, 35; m 58, Elizabeth Aspinwall; c J Darek, Russell J & Cheron E. *Educ:* Ga Southern Col, BS, 61; Univ NC, Chapel Hill, MA, 65, PhD(bot, ecol), 71. *Prof Exp:* Teaching asst bot, Univ NC, Chapel Hill, 61-64; instr biol, Ga Southern Col, 64-66; cur herbarium, Univ NC, Chapel Hill, 66-68, instr bot, 68; from asst prof to assoc prof biol, Ga Southern Col, 68-75. *Concurrent Pos:* Consult veg analyst, Inst Natural Resources, Univ Ga, 72-75; consult resource assessment & mgt, Dept Natural Resources, Off Planning & Res, State Ga, Atlanta, 74-75. *Res:* Functional role of vegetation in aquatic and terrestrial ecosystems; stabilizing and disruptive processes, mineral cycling and storage in ecosystems; vegetational surveys of the Coastal Plain, vegetational mapping and remote sensing; resource assessment, dune stabilization, coastal processes; habitat assessment of rare and endangered species. *Mailing Add:* Ga Dept Natural Resources 2117 US Hwy 278 SE Social Circle GA 30279. *Fax:* 706-557-3033; *E-Mail:* natural_heritage@mail.dnr.state.ga.us

BOZEMAN, SAMUEL RICHMOND, BIOCHEMISTRY. *Current Pos:* assoc dean, Col Basic Med Sci, 70-72, PROF MICROBIOL, COL BASIC MED SCI, UNIV TENN CTR HEALTH SCI, MEMPHIS, 70-, EXEC ASST TO THE CHANCELLOR, 72- *Personal Data:* b Knoxville, Tenn, Nov 15, 15; m 44. *Educ:* Univ Tenn, BA, 39, MS, 40; Va Polytech Inst, PhD(bact), 45. *Prof Exp:* From bacteriologist to asst dir biol prod div, Mich State Dept Health, 44-48; chief lab, Br Pub Health & Welfare, Gen Hq Supreme Comdr Allied Powers, 48-51, UN Command, 50-51; asst dir in chg qual control, Biol Labs, Pitman-Moore Co, 52, dir, 52-57, vpres, 57-63; asst mgr biol prod, Lederle Labs, 63-67, mgr clin lab aids dept, 67-69, gen mgr acquisitions, 69-70. *Concurrent Pos:* Teaching fel bact, State Col Wash, 40-42. *Mem:* Am Pub Health Asn; NY Acad Sci. *Res:* Iso and hetero-haemagglutinogens; autoantibodies; physiology of genus bacillus, antibiotics; methodology of vaccine, toxoid, antitoxin, antiserum production and control. *Mailing Add:* 2398 Kirby Woods Cove Memphis TN 38119

BOZIAN, RICHARD C, BIOCHEMISTRY, INTERNAL MEDICINE. *Current Pos:* assoc prof, Univ Cincinnati, 63-70, asst prof biochem & dir, Div Nutrit, 63-85, prof med, 70-85, EMER PROF MED, UNIV CINCINNATI, COL MED, 85-, DIR RES, MONARCH FOUND, CINCINNATTI, 91. *Personal Data:* b Springfield, Mass, Aug 12, 19; m 51, Wilkinson; c Robin Ann, Joanna Lee, Russell Charles, Richard Aram & James Wilkinson. *Educ:* Rutgers Univ, BS, 39; Albany Med Col, MD, 50; Am Bd Internal Med, dipl, 58; Am Bd Nutrit, dipl, 68. *Prof Exp:* Instr med, Sch Med, Bellevue Med Ctr, NY Univ, 53-55, USPHS trainee metab, 54-55, asst prof med & assoc vis physician & dir clins, 55-58; clin investr, Vet Admin Hosp, Nashville, Tenn, 61-63. *Concurrent Pos:* USPHS res grant, 58 & 64; mem, Coun Arteriosclerosis, Am Heart Asn, 55-; assoc attend physician, Knickerbocker Hosp & consult, St Barnabas Hosp, NY, 56-58; Am Cancer Soc res grant, 63 & 64; lectr, Coun Food & Nutrit, 65-80. *Mem:* AAAS; Am Soc Bone Mineral Res; Harvey Soc; Am Fedn Clin Res; Sigma Xi; Am Inst Nutrit. *Res:* Nutritional biochemistry; Clinical Nutrition; lipid and trace metal metabolism. *Mailing Add:* 471 W Galbraith Cincinnati OH 45215. *Fax:* 513-521-2391

BOZLER, CARL O, ELECTRICAL ENGINEERING. *Current Pos:* SCIENTIST MICROELECTRONICS, LINCOLN LAB, MASS INST TECHNOL, 74- *Personal Data:* b Columbus, Ohio, Aug 24, 41; m 66; c 2. *Educ:* Ohio State Univ, BEE & MSc, 65, PhD(elec eng), 69. *Honors & Awards:* Baker Prize Award, Inst Elec & Electronics Engrs. *Prof Exp:* Res assoc elec eng, Ohio State Univ, 64-69; res engr electronic devices, F W Bell, Inc, 68-70; res engr microwave devices, Sperry Rand Corp, 70-74. *Mem:* Inst Elec & Electronics Engrs. *Res:* Material properties; characterization; crystal growth; impurity; implantation of gallium arsenide and other semiconductors; new fabrication techniques; new electronic devices made from semiconductors, metals and insulators; inventor and developer of the permeable base transistor. *Mailing Add:* 6001 Stearns Hill Rd Waltham MA 02154

BOZLER, EMIL, physiology; deceased, see previous edition for last biography

BOZNIAK, EUGENE GEORGE, AQUATIC ECOLOGY, PHYCOLOGY. *Current Pos:* From asst prof to assoc prof, 69-80, PROF & CHMN BOT, WEBER STATE COL, 80- *Personal Data:* b Radway, Alta, Oct 15, 42; m 65. *Educ:* Univ Alta, BSc, 63, MSc, 66; Wash Univ, PhD(aquatic ecol), 69. *Mem:* AAAS; Water Pollution Control Fedn; Am Soc Limnol & Oceanog; Ecol Soc Am; Phycol Soc Am. *Res:* Natural and synthetic phytoplankton community cultivation and ecology; effects of synthetic organic compounds upon defined phytoplankton communities; algal ecology of the Ogden River drainage system; waste stabilization ponds in the tropics. *Mailing Add:* 5148 Pierce Ave Ogden UT 84403

BOZOKI, GEORGE EDWARD, HIGH ENERGY PHYSICS, COSMIC RAY PHYSICS. *Current Pos:* RES SCIENTIST, BROOKHAVEN NAT LAB, 78- *Personal Data:* b Kunhegyes, Hungary, June 21, 30; US citizen; m 56; c 1. *Educ:* Eotvos Lorand Univ & Hungarian Acad Sci, PhD(nuclear physics), 63. *Honors & Awards:* Schmid Prize, Roland Eotvos Phys Soc, 65. *Prof Exp:* Sr res group leader high energy physics & cosmic rays & vhead dept cosmic rays, Cent Res Inst Physics, Budapest, 53-70; sr res assoc high energy physics, Inst Nuclear Physics, Paris, 70-71; sr res assoc, Dept Physics, Univ Pa, 71-74; physicist, Breeder Reactor Div, Burns & Roe, Inc, Oradell, NY, 74-78. *Concurrent Pos:* From asst prof to assoc prof nuclear physics, Fac Atomic Physics, Eotvos Lorand Univ, 59-64. *Mem:* Am Phys Soc; NY Acad Sci. *Res:* Neutrino related research; nuclear radiation safety at reactors and accelerators; risk and accident analysis of nuclear plants. *Mailing Add:* 200 Winston Dr Apt 1803 Cliffside Park NJ 07010-3224

BOZOKI-GOMBOSI, EVA S, HIGH ENERGY PHYSICS. *Current Pos:* MEM STAFF ACCELERATOR PHYSICS, BROOKHAVEN NAT LAB, 78- *Personal Data:* b Budapest, Hungary, US citizen; c 1. *Educ:* Eotvos Lorand Univ, Budapest, MS, 58; Hungarian Acad Sci, PhD(high energy physics), 62. *Prof Exp:* Sr res assoc high energy physics, Cent Res Inst Physics, Budapest, 58-71; vis res assoc, Joint Inst Nuclear Res, Dubna, USSR, 64-65, Lab Accelerateur Lineaire, Orsay, France, 70-71 & Univ Pa, Philadelphia, 71-72; sr systs analyst comput applns, Indust, 72-77. *Mem:* Am Phys Soc; Asn Comput Mach. *Res:* Hadronic interactions of high energy elementary particles; application of programmed control and simulation in accelerator physics and in various engineering fields. *Mailing Add:* Six Lantern Ct Stonybrook NY 11790

BOZOVIC, IVAN, COMPLEX OXIDES, NANOENGINEERING. *Current Pos:* SR RES SCIENTIST, VARIAN RES CTR, 89- *Personal Data:* b Belgrade, Yugoslavia, May 18, 47; US citizen; m 70, Natasha Radonjic; c Dolores & Marijeta. *Educ:* Univ Belgrade, BSc, 70, MSc, 72, PhD(physics), 75. *Honors & Awards:* Inst Physics Prize, 75; Int Award Microphotog, Polaroid Corp, 89; Fulbright Award, Fulbright Found, 82. *Prof Exp:* Docent, Fac Sci, Univ Belgrade, Yugoslavia, 78-84; sr researcher, Inst Physics, Belgrade, Yugoslavia, 84-87. *Concurrent Pos:* Head, Physics Dept, Fac Sci, Univ Belgrade, Yugoslavia, 79-81; vis prof, Univ Notre Dame, Belg, 80, 82 & 85, Stanford Univ, 87-88; vis scholar, Univ Calif, Berkeley, 82-83, Univ Pa, 85-86. *Mem:* Fel Int Soc Optical Eng; Am Phys Soc; Mat Res Soc. *Res:* Atomic layer-by-layer engineering of thin films, heterostructures and super lattices of cuprate conductors, titanate ferroelectrics and manganite ferromagnets; structure, transport properties and spectra; design, fabrication and characterization of all-oxide electronic devices. *Mailing Add:* K-114 Varian Res Ctr 3075 Hansen Way Palo Alto CA 94304-1025. *Fax:* 650-424-6988; *E-Mail:* ivan.bozovic@grc.varian.com

BOZOZUK, MICHAEL, GEOTECHNICAL ENGINEERING. *Current Pos:* RETIRED. *Personal Data:* b Poland, Nov 10, 29; m 57, Marcelle F Daoust; c Lyne, Sylvie & Camille. *Educ:* Univ Man, BSc, 52, MSc, 54; Purdue Univ, PhD(geotech), 72. *Honors & Awards:* Can Eng Centennial Silver Medal, 87; John B Stirling Medal, Eng Inst Can, 90; R F Legget Award, Can Geotech Soc, 94. *Prof Exp:* Res officer, Geotech Sect, Div Bldg Res, Nat Res Coun Can, 53-89, consult, 89-93. *Concurrent Pos:* Mem, Comt Soil & Rock Instrumentation, Transp Res Bd & Comt Found Bridges & Other Structs, 72-81; vis prof, Univ Ottawa, 76; mem, Res Comt Silo Found, Ont Silo Asn, 78-82; Cross Can tour lectr, 79; chmn, Div Comt Safety & Health, Div Bldg Res, 80-85; mem, Tech Comt Found, Can Stand Asn, 83-90; mem, Can Geosci Coun, 85-91; SE China tour lectr, 86; hon prof, Chengdu Univ, China, 86; consult pvt pract, 89-93; exec dir, Eng Inst Can, 94- *Mem:* Fel Eng Inst Can; Nat Res Coun Can; Can Geotech Soc; Int Soc Soil Mech; Can Soc Civil Eng. *Res:* Geoscience; geotechnics; civil engineering; bearing capacity of sensitive clays; negative skin friction on piles; settlement of structures on clay soils due to dessication from trees. *Mailing Add:* 691 Sandra Ave Ottawa ON K1G 2Z7 Can

BOZZELLI, JOSEPH WILLIAM, PHYSICAL CHEMISTRY, ANALYTICAL CHEMISTRY. *Current Pos:* DISTINGUISHED PROF CHEM, NJ INST TECHNOL, 75- *Personal Data:* b East Orange, NJ, Sept 16, 42; m 68; c 3. *Educ:* Marietta Col, BS, 64; Princeton Univ, MS, 70, PhD(chem), 72. *Prof Exp:* Fel chem physics, Univ Pittsburgh, 73-75. *Concurrent Pos:* Consult, NJ Environ Protection Agency, 77-, res grant, 77-81 & 86-90; consult, US Environ Protection Agency, 78-91, res grant, 78-85; res grant, NSF, NJ Inst Technol & Univ Ind Ctr, 84-91. *Mem:* Am Chem Soc; Sigma Xi. *Res:* Chemical kinetics of small molecule and atom reactions in the vapor phase; detection of trace levels of air pollutants; thermal and catalytic reactions of toxic halocarbons with water vapor and hydrogen; kinetics in combustional chloro hydrocarbons, kiv. *Mailing Add:* Dept Chem Eng & Chem NJ Inst Technol 323 ML King Dr Newark NJ 07102-1824

BOZZOLA, JOHN JOSEPH, BOTANY. *Current Pos:* assoc prof, 85-93, DIR ELECTRON MICROS CTR, SOUTHERN ILL UNIV, CARBONDALE, 83-, PROF, BOT DEPT, 93- *Personal Data:* b Herrin, Ill, Oct 22, 46. *Educ:* Southern Ill Univ, PhD, 77. *Prof Exp:* Instr, Med Col Pa, 76-79, asst prof microbiol, 79-83. *Concurrent Pos:* Young investr award, Nat Inst Dent Res, 78. *Mem:* Electron Micros Soc Am; Am Soc Microbiol; Sigma Xi. *Res:* Electron microscopy. *Mailing Add:* 113 W Seventh St Johnston City IL 62951

BOZZUTO, CARL RICHARD, PROCESS DESIGN, PILOT PLANT DEVELOPMENT & SCALE UP. *Current Pos:* Mgr fuel technol, ABB Combustion Eng, 73-74, mgr energy systs, 74-80, dir advan systs, 80-82, chief technologist, 82-84 dir utility mkt, 84-86, gen mgr fluid bed, 86-88, dir KDL, 88-93, VPRES TECHNOL, ABB COBUSTION ENG, 94- *Personal Data:* b Waterbury, Conn, June 17, 47; m 71; c 3. *Educ:* Mass Inst Technol, BS, 70, MS, 70; Hartford Grad Ctr, MS, 84. *Concurrent Pos:* Tech opportunities planning, Am Soc Mech Engrs, 76-86, solar energy stand, 77-82; coal comb appln working group, Dept Energy, 81-83; pres, Oxce Fuel Co, 89-93. *Mem:* Am Soc Mech Engrs; Am Inst Chem Engrs; Combustion Inst. *Res:* Design development, and testing of energy processes and equipment including pulverized coal, fluidized bed, and coal gasification power plants; author of various publications; granted 15 patents. *Mailing Add:* One Parky Dr Enfield CT 06082-6107

BRAASCH, NORMAN L, ENTOMOLOGY. *Current Pos:* from asst prof to assoc prof zool, 63-77, PROF BIOL, SOUTHEAST MO STATE COL, 77- *Personal Data:* b Pierce, Nebr, July 29, 28; m 53; c 1. *Educ:* Univ Nebr, BS, 50, MA, 55, PhD(entom), 65. *Prof Exp:* Instr, Nebr Pub Schs, 55-57; res asst entom, Univ Nebr, 58-63. *Mem:* AAAS; Am Soc Zoologists; Entom Soc Am. *Res:* Invertebrate zoology. *Mailing Add:* 2524 Marvin St Cape Girardeau MO 63701

BRAATEN, DAVID A, BOUNDARY LAYER TURBULENCE, AEROSOL PHYSICS. *Current Pos:* ASST PROF ATMOSPHERIC SCI, DEPT PHYSICS & ASTRON, UNIV KANS, 89- *Personal Data:* b New York, NY, Nov 22, 55. *Educ:* State Univ NY, Oswego, BS, 77; San Jose State Univ, MS, 81; Univ Calif, Davis, PhD(atmospheric sci), 88. *Prof Exp:* Meteorologist, Henningson, Durham & Richardson, Inc, 77-80; res asst, Univ Calif, Davis, 81-88, postgrad researcher, 88-89. *Mem:* Am Meteorol Soc; Am Asn Aerosol Research. *Res:* Laboratory and atmosphere experimental investigations of turbulent structures which are important in physical processes such as aerosol resuspension, aerosol deposition, momentum flux, mass flux and heat flux. *Mailing Add:* 940 Maine St Lawrence KS 66044

BRAATEN, MELVIN OLE, STATISTICS, ENGINEERING. *Current Pos:* ENGR, ROCKWELL INT, 76-; ASSOC PROF BUS, UNIV IOWA, 76- *Personal Data:* b Greenbush, Minn, Sept 6, 34; m 56; c 2. *Educ:* NDak State Univ, BS, 56, MS, 61; NC State Univ, PhD(statist), 65. *Prof Exp:* Asst prof forest biomet, Duke Univ, 65-69; assoc prof indust eng & radiol sci, Univ Mo-Columbia, 69-76. *Mem:* Am Statist Asn; Biomet Soc. *Res:* Computer applications in human engineering; operations research systems modeling in medical service; engineering statistical modeling. *Mailing Add:* 640 Stuart Ct Coralville IA 52241

BRAATZ, JAMES ANTHONY, BIOCHEMISTRY, POLYMER CHEMISTRY. *Current Pos:* sr res biochemist, Res Div, 84-86, res assoc, Res Div, 86-94, SR RES ASSOC, W R GRACE & CO, 94- *Personal Data:* b Baltimore, Md, July 17, 43; m 64, Geraldine L Waldecker; c James III, Ronald & Mary. *Educ:* Johns Hopkins Univ, BS, 68, PhD(biochem), 73. *Honors & Awards:* Incentive Award, Dept Com, 84. *Prof Exp:* Staff fel, NIH, 73-84, head biochem sect, Biol Response Modifiers Prog, Nat Cancer Inst, 81-84. *Concurrent Pos:* Consult, Abbott Labs, North Chicago, Ill, 81-84 & Hoffman-LaRoche, Nutley, NJ, 83-84. *Mem:* Am Chem Soc; Am Soc Biochem & Molecular Biol; AAAS; Protein Soc. *Res:* Blood-material interactions; new methodology for immobilization of proteins, chemistry of biocompatible polymers; immunoassays for protein-polymer interactions. *Mailing Add:* W R Grace & Co 7500 Grace Dr Columbia MD 21044. *Fax:* 410-531-4243; *E-Mail:* braatz@wrc.wrgrace.com

BRABANDER, HERBERT JOSEPH, ORGANIC CHEMISTRY. *Current Pos:* RES CHEMIST, LEDERLE LABS, AM CYANAMID CO, 53- *Personal Data:* b Brooklyn, NY, Apr 17, 32; m 63; c 3. *Educ:* LI Univ, BS, 53; Stevens Inst Technol, MS, 58. *Mem:* Am Chem Soc. *Res:* Pharmaceutical chemical research for the development of new drugs, particularly agents which act upon the central nervous system. *Mailing Add:* 10 Robert Pl Nanuet NY 10954

BRABB, EARL EDWARD, GEOLOGY. *Current Pos:* Geologist, 59-94, proj chief, San Francisco Bay Region Geol, 90-94, EMER GEOLOGIST, US GEOL SURV, 94- *Personal Data:* b Detroit, Mich, May 27, 29; m 57, Gisela Reichel; c Robin & Kristin. *Educ:* Dartmouth Col, AB, 51; Univ Mich, MS, 52; Stanford Univ, PhD(geol), 60. *Honors & Awards:* Group Award, Achievement & Spec Serv, US Geol Surv, 82; Meritorious Award, US Dept Interior, 83; Distinguished Practice Award, Geol Soc Am, 88; Ital Nat Res Coun Citation & Medal Distinguished Serv, 95. *Concurrent Pos:* Geotech adv, City San Jose, 71-74; expert witness, Nuclear Regulatory Comn, 77-81 & comt mudslides, Nat Acad Sci-Nat Res Coun, 81-82; deleg, Am Comn Stratig Nomenclature, US Geol Surv, 78-82; chmn, US-Japan Landslide Conf, 79 & Landslide Proj Third World Countries, UNESCO, 81; chief, US Landslide Hazard Mapping, 81-90, Regional Landslide Res Group, 82-85; coordr, USGS-Ital CNR hazard courses, Perugia, 88-92. *Mem:* Int Asn Eng Geologists; Am Geophys Union. *Res:* Regional landslide hazard mapping; digital cartography for geologic mapping; seismic zonation for land-use planning; air photo interpretation; environmental geology; San Andreas fault. *Mailing Add:* US Geol Surv 345 Middlefield Rd MS975 Menlo Park CA 94025. *Fax:* 650-329-4936; *E-Mail:* ebrabb@isdmnl.wr.usgs.gov

BRABHAM, DALE EDWIN, DISCHARGE LAMP DESIGN, DISCHARGE LAMP CHEMISTRY. *Current Pos:* SR CONTRIBUTOR, WELCH ALLYN, 97- *Personal Data:* b Gainesville, Fla, Dec 26, 47; m 67, Linda Grant; c Michael, John, David, Christina, Emily & Ellen. *Educ:* Univ Fla, BS, 68; Fla State Univ, PhD(molecular biophysics), 73. *Prof Exp:* Res asst, Univ Fla, 73-74; NIH fel, Univ Ga, 74-76; vis prof biophysics, Fed Univ Paraiba, Brazil, 76-78; asst prof phys chem, Elmira Col, 81-84; sr engr, Philips

Lighting Co, 84-93; sr engr, Imaging & Sensing Technol, 93-97. *Concurrent Pos:* Vis asst prof, Univ Fla, 78-81; vis asst prof, Univ Rochester, 82-83; lectr phys chem, Elmira Col, 93-97; light source comt, Illuminating Eng Soc, 96-98. *Mem:* Illuminating Eng Soc; Am Chem Soc; Soc Appl Spectros. *Res:* Design and chemistry of discharge lamps; development of spectral diagnostics; product performance and life are central themes of lamp development. *Mailing Add:* 221 Feldspar Dr Syracuse NY 13219. *Fax:* 315-685-4178; *E-Mail:* brabhamd@mail.welchallyn.com

BRABSON, BENNET BRISTOL, ELEMENTARY PARTICLE PHYSICS. *Current Pos:* from asst prof to assoc prof, 68-76, sci assoc, 72-78, PROF PHYSICS, IND UNIV, BLOOMINGTON, 76- *Personal Data:* b Washington, DC, July 29, 38; m 63; c 2. *Educ:* Carleton Col, BA, 60; Mass Inst Technol, PhD(physics), 66. *Prof Exp:* Res assoc physics, 66-67, NSF fel, Mass Inst Technol, 67-68. *Mem:* Sigma Xi; fel Am Phys Soc. *Res:* Study of strong and electromagnetic interactions, including meson spectroscopy, utilizing spark, streamer, bubble, proportional and drift chambers and counter systems; Electron-positron collisions at high energies; exotics, hybrids and gluebulk. *Mailing Add:* Dept Physics Swain Hall W Ind Univ Bloomington IN 47405

BRABSON, GEORGE DANA, JR, SPECTROSCOPY, INSTRUMENTAL ANALYSIS. *Current Pos:* ASSOC PROF CHEM, UNIV NMEX, 94- *Personal Data:* b Washington, DC, Feb 18, 35; m 59, Shirley Stebbins; c 3. *Educ:* Case Inst Technol, BS, 56; Univ Calif, Berkeley, MS, 62, PhD(chem), 65. *Honors & Awards:* Tech Achievement Award, Air Force Syst Command, 72. *Prof Exp:* Chem engr, Dow Chem Co, Mich, 56; engr, Armed Forces Spec Weapons Proj, Sandia Base, NMex, 56-61; from instr to assoc prof chem, USAF Acad, 62-70, dir chem, F J Seiler Res Lab, 71-74; high energy laser prog, Air Force Weapons Labs, 74-78; dep dir, Mat Lab, Wright-Patterson AFB, Ohio, 78-81; dean res & info, Defense Systs Mgt Col. Ft Belvoir, Va, 81-83; asst prof chem, Ind Univ, 83-84; assoc prof chem, Univ Va, 88-94. *Concurrent Pos:* Vis prof chem, Univ NMex, 84-88. *Mem:* Sigma Xi; Am Phys Soc; Am Chem Soc. *Res:* Spectroscopy of high temperature molecules isolated in frozen inert gas matrices. *Mailing Add:* 9008 Natalie Ave NE Albuquerque NM 87111

BRABY, LESLIE ALAN, RADIOLOGICAL PHYSICS, RADIATION BIOPHYSICS. *Current Pos:* RES SCIENTIST RADIOL PHYSICS & BIOPHYS, PAC NORTHWEST LAB, BATTELLE MEM INST, 63-, MGR, RADIATION PHYSICST CHEM, 93- *Personal Data:* b Kelso, Wash, Jan 12, 41; m 66, Barbara Shearer; c 3. *Educ:* Linfield Col, BA, 63; Ore State Univ, PhD(radiol physics), 72. *Mem:* Sigma Xi; Radiation Res Soc; Am Phys Soc; Health Physics Soc; AAAS. *Res:* Investigation of the physical and biological processes which determine the response of cells and organisms to ionizing radiation. *Mailing Add:* 3708 Winridge Bryan TX 77802. *Fax:* 509-376-9944

BRACCO, DONATO JOHN, PHYSICAL CHEMISTRY, ANALYTICAL CHEMISTRY. *Current Pos:* LECTR CHEM DEPT, SUFFOLK UNIV, BOSTON, 83- *Personal Data:* b Neresine, Lussino, Italy, Feb 16, 21; nat US; m 50, Elsie Toivonen; c Mark, Celia, Linda, Robert, Pamela & Lisa. *Educ:* City Col New York, BChE, 41. *Prof Exp:* Res chemist, Peter J Schweitzer, Inc, 41-42; chem engr, Titanium Div, Nat Lead Co, 42-45 & AEC, 47; sect head phosphor & cathode ray tube chem, Physics Labs, Sylvania Elec Prod, Inc, 47-55, mgr, Chem Lab, 55-57 & Planning Res Labs, 58-61, mgr mat anal, Gen Tel & Electronics Labs, 61-69, dir mat res lab, GTE Labs, 69-72, dir, Cent Serv Lab, 72-74, dir mat eng lab, 75-78, dir, Elec Equip Technol, 78-83. *Mem:* Fel, AAAS; Electrochem Soc; Inst Elec & Electronics Engrs; Am Soc Qual Control; Solar Energy Soc; Am Chem Soc; fel Am Inst Chemists. *Res:* Instrumental analysis; process monitoring; materials engineering; solar energy thermal conversion; cathode ray tube screen processing; black and white and color, luminescent materials. *Mailing Add:* 348 Hayward Mill Rd Concord MA 01742-4606

BRACE, C LORING, PHYSICAL ANTHROPOLOGY. *Current Pos:* assoc prof, 67-71, PROF ANTHROP, UNIV MICH, ANN ARBOR, 71-, CUR PHYS ANTHROP, MUS ANTHROP, 67- *Personal Data:* b Hanover, NH, Dec 19, 30; m 57; c 3. *Educ:* Williams Col, BA, 52; Harvard Univ, MA, 58, PhD(anthrop), 62. *Prof Exp:* Instr anthrop, Univ Wis, Milwaukee, 60-61; from asst prof to assoc prof, Univ Calif, Santa Barbara, 61-67. *Concurrent Pos:* Vis prof anthrop, Univ Auckland, 73. *Mem:* AAAS; Am Asn Phys Anthrop; fel Am Anthrop Asn; Soc Study Human Biol; Int Asn Human Biologists; mem Dent Anthropol Asn (pres, 88-90). *Res:* History of biological anthropology; evolutionary theory and study of human evolution as it is expressed in the human fossil record; analysis of the origin of contemporary human physical diversity; dental anthropology. *Mailing Add:* 1020 Ferdon Rd Univ Mich Ann Arbor MI 48104

BRACE, JOHN WELLS, PURE MATHEMATICS. *Current Pos:* From instr to prof, 53-64, PROF EMER MATH, UNIV MD, COLLEGE PARK, 85- *Personal Data:* b Evanston, Ill, Jan 19, 26; m 50, Patricia A Demarest; c James, George, Ann, Nancy & Catherine. *Educ:* Swarthmore Col, BA, 49; Cornell Univ, AM, 51, PhD(math), 53. *Concurrent Pos:* Vis, dept pure math & math statist, Cambridge Univ, Eng, 66-67, 73-74 & 80-81. *Mem:* Am Math Soc; Math Asn Am. *Res:* Applications of functional analysis, ranging through theoretical functional analysis to applied engineering. *Mailing Add:* PO Box 227 Cherryfield ME 04622

BRACE, LARRY HAROLD, IONOSPHERIC PHYSICS. *Current Pos:* RETIRED. *Personal Data:* b Saginaw, Mich, Feb 19, 29; m 53; c 3. *Educ:* Univ Mich, BS, 58. *Honors & Awards:* NASA Medal for Exceptional Sci Achievement, 80. *Prof Exp:* Res assoc, Space Physics Res Lab, Univ Mich, 58-60, dir, 60-62; res physicist, Goddard Space Flight Ctr, NASA, 62-90; vis res scientist, Space Physics Res Lab, Univ Mich, 90-91. *Concurrent Pos:* Mem Ionosphere Subcomt, NASA, 65-67 & MARS Sci Working Group, 89-90. *Mem:* Am Phys Soc; Am Geophys Union. *Res:* Rocket and satellite borne instruments in studies of the processes controlling the electron energy balance of the ionosphere; exploration of the ionosphere of Venus by in-situ measurements. *Mailing Add:* 4203 Russell Ave Mt Rainier MD 20712

BRACE, NEAL ORIN, ORGANIC CHEMISTRY, FLUORINE CHEMISTRY. *Current Pos:* From assoc prof to prof chem, 66-68, EMER PROF CHEM, WHEATON COL, ILL, 88- *Personal Data:* b Osceola, Wis, Apr 12, 22; m 45; c 7. *Educ:* Univ Minn, BA, 46; Univ Ill, PhD(org chem), 48. *Honors & Awards:* Humboldt Prize, Ger, 72. *Prof Exp:* Res chemist, Tenn Eastman Corp, 48-49; res chemist, Org Chem Dept, E I du Pont de Nemours & Co, 49-63; assoc prof chem, North Park Col, 63-66, head dept, 64-66. *Concurrent Pos:* Sr US Scientist, Alexander von Humboldt-Stiftung, Ger, 72; Richard Merton prof & hon Fulbright prof, GH Wuppertal, Ger, 78. *Mem:* Am Chem Soc; Am Sci Affil. *Res:* Perfluoroalkyl-substituted alkenyl radical cyclization, perfluoroalkyl-alkanoic acids and alkanols; mechanisms of substitution and elimination reactions of perfluoroalkyl-substituted iodoalkanes; phase transfer-catalyzed substitution and elimination reactions; synthesis of vinyl sulfones; alkylation of amides by alkyl halides. *Mailing Add:* 2881 65th St N St Petersburg IL 33710

BRACE, ROBERT ALLEN, CARDIOVASCULAR PHYSIOLOGY. *Current Pos:* PROF REPRODUCTIVE MED, UNIV CALIF, SAN DIEGO, 84- *Personal Data:* b Marlette, Mich, May 4, 48; m 69. *Educ:* Mich State Univ, BS, 70, MS, 71, PhD(chem eng), 73. *Prof Exp:* Instr, Univ Miss, 73-75, asst prof physiol & biophys, Med Ctr, 75-77; assoc prof physics, Marshall Univ, 77-78; assoc prof physiol, Loma Linda Univ, 78-83, prof, 83-84. *Mem:* Microcirculatory Soc; Am Physiol Soc; Soc Gynec Invest; Perinatal Res Soc; Int Lymphol Soc. *Res:* Dynamics and control of fluid volumes in fetus and adult, including blood volume control, lymph flow, transcapillary forces, drinking, urinary output and amniotic fluid volume. *Mailing Add:* Dept Reproductive Med Univ Calif San Diego La Jolla CA 92093-0802. *Fax:* 619-543-2919

BRACE, WILLIAM FRANCIS, STRUCTURAL GEOLOGY. *Current Pos:* RETIRED. *Personal Data:* b Littleton, NH, Aug 26, 26; m 55; c 3. *Educ:* Mass Inst Technol, BS, 49, PhD(geol), 53. *Honors & Awards:* Walter Bacher Medal, Am Geol Soc, 89. *Prof Exp:* Fulbright fel, Mass Inst Technol, Austria, 53-54, from asst prof to prof geol, 55-80, Cecil & Ida Green prof & head dept, 80-88. *Mem:* Nat Acad Sci; Geol Soc Am; Am Soc Civil Engrs. *Res:* Application of mechanics to problems of structural geology. *Mailing Add:* Dept Earth & Planet Sci Bldg 54-722 Mass Inst Technol Cambridge MA 02139

BRACEWELL, RONALD NEWBOLD, ASTRONOMY, COMPUTER SCIENCE. *Current Pos:* prof, 55-91, Lewis M Terman prof, 74-79, EMER LEWIS M TERMAN PROF ELEC ENG, STANFORD UNIV, 91- *Personal Data:* b Sydney, Australia, July 22, 21; m 53, Helen M L Elliott; c Catherine Wendy & Mark Cecil. *Educ:* Univ Sydney, BSc, 41, BE, 43, ME, 48; Cambridge Univ, PhD(physics), 50. *Honors & Awards:* Heinrich Hertz Gold Medal, Inst Elec & Electronics Engrs. *Prof Exp:* Sr res officer, Radiophys Div, Commonwealth Sci & Indust Res Orgn, Australia, 42-46, 49-55. *Concurrent Pos:* Fulbright vis prof, Univ Calif, 54-55; Christensen fel, St Catherine's Col, Oxford, 87; vis astronr, Astrophys Dept, Oxford Univ, 87; fel commoner, Churchill Col, Cambridge, 88; sr vis fel, Inst Astron, Cambridge, 88. *Mem:* Int Astron Union; fel Inst Elec & Electronics Engrs; fel AAAS; Royal Astron Soc; Am Astron Soc; Astron Soc Australia; Int Sci Radio Union. *Res:* Solar physics; tomography; earth's atmosphere; fast alogorithms; radio wave propagation; antennas; radio telescopes; electromagnetic theory; solar activity; image construction; astronomy; fourier analysis; Hartley transform. *Mailing Add:* 836 Santa Fe Ave Stanford CA 94305. *Fax:* 650-725-7126; *E-Mail:* bracewell@star.stanford.edu

BRACH, EUGENE JENŐ, AGRICULTURAL ENGINEERING. *Current Pos:* proj engr, Eng Res Serv, 62-65, RES SCIENTIST, ENG & STATIST RES INST, RES BR, CAN AGR, 65-, TECH/SCI ADV, MEAT & POULTRY PROD DIV, FP&I, 88- *Personal Data:* Tokaj, Hungary, Aug 28, 28; Can citizen; m 53; c 4. *Educ:* Tech Univ Budapest, cert Eng, 53; Acad Mil Eng, cert mil eng, 53. *Prof Exp:* Develop engr, Defence Res, 53-56; proj engr, Sangamo Elec Co, 57-62. *Concurrent Pos:* Adj prof, Dept Plant Sci, Fac Agr, Univ Man, 78-84. *Mem:* Inst Elec & Electronics Engrs. *Res:* Grading and inspection of agricultural commodities by machine vision; electro-optics; agricultural research in breeding and disease control using field spectroscopy; instrument development in aid of agriculture. *Mailing Add:* Meat & Poultry Prods Halledon FP&I Br Agr Can 2255 Carline Ave Ottawa ON K1A 0Y9 Can

BRACH, RAYMOND M, MECHANICAL ENGINEERING, ACOUSTICS. *Current Pos:* asst prof eng sci, 65-70, ASSOC PROF AEROSPACE & MECH ENG, UNIV NOTRE DAME, 70- *Personal Data:* b Chicago, Ill, Oct 18, 34; m 56; c 7. *Educ:* Ill Inst Technol, BS, 58, MS, 62; Univ Wis, PhD(eng mech), 65. *Prof Exp:* Assoc res engr, IIT Res Inst, 58-62; sr res engr, Continental Can Co, 62-63. *Concurrent Pos:* Eng res consult; lic prof eng, State of Ind. *Mem:* Am Soc Mech Engrs; Acoust Soc Am; Am Soc Eng Educ; Soc Automotive Engrs; Inst Noise Control Engrs. *Res:* Vibrations, mechanical engineering design; acoustics; vehicle dynamics; mechanics of particle and rigid body impact with applications ranging from collision analysis of automotive vehicles to the analysis of erosion and wear data and the rebound and collection of solid aerosol particles. *Mailing Add:* Dept Aerospace & Mech Eng Univ Notre Dame Notre Dame IN 46556

BRACHER, KATHERINE, ASTRONOMY. *Current Pos:* from asst prof to assoc prof, 67-81, PROF ASTRON, WHITMAN COL, 81- *Personal Data:* b San Francisco, Calif, Oct 26, 38. *Educ:* Mt Holyoke Col, AB, 60; Ind Univ, AM, 62, PhD(astron), 66. *Prof Exp:* From instr to asst prof astron, Univ Southern Calif, 65-67. *Concurrent Pos:* Chair, Hist Astron Div, Am Astron Soc, 89-91. *Mem:* Sigma Xi; Am Astron Soc; Astron Soc Pac. *Res:* Archaeoastronomy; history of astronomy. *Mailing Add:* Dept Astron Whitman Col Walla Walla WA 99362-2082

BRACHFELD, NORMAN, BIOCHEMISTRY, CARDIOVASCULAR PHYSIOLOGY. *Current Pos:* from instr to asst prof, 60-68, ASSOC PROF MED, MED COL, CORNELL UNIV, 68- *Personal Data:* b New York, NY, Oct 16, 27. *Educ:* Columbia Univ, AB, 49; Wash Univ, MD, 53. *Prof Exp:* Intern med, Maimonides Hosp, Brooklyn, 53-54; intern surg, Peter Bent Brigham Hosp, Boston, 54-55, asst resident, 55-56, asst med, 57-59; asst resident med, NY Hosp, 59-60. *Concurrent Pos:* Teaching & res fel, Peter Bent Brigham Hosp, Boston, 56-57; teaching fel, Harvard Univ Med Sch, 56-57, res fel med, 57-59, Samuel A Levine fel, 58-59; res fel physiol, Sloan Kettering Inst, 57; sr res fel, NY Heart Asn, 61-62; career scientist award, City of NY Health Res Coun, 62-68; career develop award, NIH, 68-73; physician, Outpatient Dept, NY Hosp, 60-62, asst attend, 62-68, assoc attend, 68-; asst dir, Comprehensive Care & Teaching Prog, Med Col, Cornell Univ, 60-65, assoc dir, 65-68; res assoc, Inst Muscle Dis Inc, 60-66, head, Div Myocardial Metab & assoc mem, 66-73; med res collabr, Brookhaven Nat Lab, 61-63; asst vis physician, Sec Med Div, Bellevue Hosp, 63-68. *Mem:* Am Fedn Clin Res; Am Heart Asn; Harvey Soc; fel Am Col Physicians; fel Am Col Cardiol. *Res:* Metabolic and hemodynamic changes in the ischemic heart; cardiovascular research; clinical cardiology. *Mailing Add:* 920 Park Ave New York NY 10028

BRACHMAN, MALCOLM K, THEORETICAL PHYSICS. *Current Pos:* PRES, NORTHWEST OIL CO, 56- *Personal Data:* b Ft Worth, Tex, Dec 9, 26; m 51, Minda Delugach; c Lynn (Gryll), Mac & Lisa. *Educ:* Yale Univ, BA, 45; Harvard Univ, MA, 47, PhD(physics), 49. *Prof Exp:* Asst prof physics, Southern Methodist Univ, 49-50; assoc physicist, Argonne Nat Lab, 50-53; res physicist, Tex Instruments, Inc, 53-54. *Concurrent Pos:* Chmn and chief exec officer, Pioneer Am Ins Co, 54-79. *Mem:* Am Phys Soc; Inst Elec & Electronics Engrs; Am Math Soc; Am Inst Mining; Soc Explor Geophys. *Mailing Add:* Northwest Oil Co Inc 3232 McKinney Ave Suite 770 Dallas TX 75204-2423. *Fax:* 214-871-2764

BRACHMAN, PHILIP SIGMUND, medicine, for more information see previous edition

BRACIALE, THOMAS JOSEPH, JR, INFLUENZA VIROLOGY, T-LYMPHOCYTE CLONES. *Current Pos:* assoc pathologist, Barnes Hosp, 82-92, PROF PATHOL & MICROBIOL, 92-, DIR, BEIRNE B CARTER CTR IMMUNOL RES, 92- *Personal Data:* b Philadelphia, Pa, Oct 22, 46; m 72; c 3. *Educ:* St Joseph's Col, BS, 68; Univ Pa, PhD(microbiol), 74, MD, 75. *Prof Exp:* Intern/resident path, Sch Med, Wash Univ, 75-76; vis fel microbiol, Australian Nat Univ, 76-78; asst pathologist, Barnes Hosp, 78-82; from asst prof to assoc prof, 78-88, PROF PATH, SCH MED, WASH UNIV, 88- *Concurrent Pos:* Fel, Jan Coffin Child's Mem Found, 76-78; assoc ed, J Immunol, 82-86; mem, Exp Virol Study Sect, NIH, 83-87; sect ed, J Immunol, 87- *Mem:* Am Asn Immunologists; Am Asn Pathologists; Am Soc Microbiol; AAAS. *Res:* Analysis of the function and properties of cloned populations of thymus-derived lymphocytes from man and experimental animals. *Mailing Add:* Beirne B Cater Ctr Immunol Res Univ Va Charlottesville VA 22908-0001

BRACIALE, VIVIAN LAM, VIRAL IMMUNOLOGY, LYMPHOKINES & RECEPTORS. *Current Pos:* ASSOC PROF MICROBIOL, HEALTH SCI CTR, UNIV VA, 91- *Personal Data:* b New York, NY, June 5, 48; div; c 3. *Educ:* Cornell Univ, AB, 69; Univ Pa, PhD(microbiol, 73. *Prof Exp:* Fel immunol, Univ Pa Sch Med, 74-75 & Wash Univ Sch Med, 75-76; vis fel, Australian Nat Univ, 76-78; res instr path, Sch Med, Wash Univ, 78-83, res asst prof, 83-89, asst prof, 89-91. *Concurrent Pos:* Mem & consult, Clin Sci Study Sect, NIH, 85-89; assoc ed, J Immunol, 89-91; sect ed, J Immunol, 95- & J Lenkocyte Biol, 97- *Mem:* Am Asn Immunologists; AAAS. *Res:* Role of T lymphocytes in the immune response and events in their induction and differentiation using cloned cell populations. *Mailing Add:* Health Sci Ctr Univ Va Beirne Carter Immunol Ctr MR4 Bldg Box 4012 Charlottesville VA 22908-0001. *Fax:* 804-924-1221; *E-Mail:* vlb9u@virginia.edu

BRACK, KARL, ORGANIC POLYMER CHEMISTRY, PHOTOCHEMISTRY. *Current Pos:* TECH DIR, MACE ADHESIVES & COATINGS, 92- *Personal Data:* b Kuttingen, AG, Switz, Nov 22, 23; US citizen; m 88, Karen L Imondi; c Karl E & Hans P. *Educ:* Swiss Fed Inst Technol, MS, 49, PhD(org chem), 51. *Prof Exp:* Res chemist pesticides, Hercules Inc, 52-57, res chemist polymers, 57-71; sr chemist inks & coatings, Dennison Mfg Co, 71-75, res assoc inks & coatings, 75-78; group leader adhesives & coatings, Polymer Industs, 78-83; mgr adhesives & coatings, Upaco Adhesives, 83-87; instr, Univ Lowell, Mass, 87-90. *Mem:* Am Chem Soc; Soc Mfg Engrs; Asn Finishing Processes; Sigma Xi. *Res:* Synthesis of radiation-curable oligomers, prepolymers and polymers; research and development of radiation-curable inks, coatings and adhesives; urethane type adhesives and coatings; polyester adhesives and coatings; biodegradable polymers. *Mailing Add:* 19 Proctor St Worcester MA 01606. *E-Mail:* kbracksr@aol.com

BRACKBILL, JEREMIAH U, COMPUTER MODELLING. *Current Pos:* LAB FEL, LOS ALAMOS NAT LAB, 83- *Personal Data:* b Harrisburg, Pa, Jan 19, 41; m 65, Isabel Mueller; c 2. *Educ:* Lehigh Univ, BS, 63; Univ Wis, Madison, MS, 70, PhD(physics), 71. *Prof Exp:* Staff mem, Los Alamos Nat Lab, 71-78 & 80-85; res prof comput physics, Courant Inst, NY Univ, 78-80; prof appl math & numerical modelling, Brown Univ, 85-86. *Concurrent Pos:* Assoc ed, J Comput Physics, 87-; spec topics ed, Comput Physics Commun, 87-; vis prof, Dept Math, Univ NMex, 88-89, prof math, Univ NMex/Los Alamos Lab, 92- *Mem:* Fel Am Phys Soc; AAAS; Am Geophys Union. *Res:* Develop implicit and adaptive grid methods for magnetohydrodynamic and plasma kinetic problems with multiple time and space scales; model unstable flow and transport in laboratory and space plasmas. *Mailing Add:* 820 Los Pueblos Los Alamos NM 87544. *E-Mail:* jub@lanl.gov

BRACKELSBERG, PAUL O, ANIMAL BREEDING. *Current Pos:* Assoc prof, 66-77, PROF ANIMAL SCI, IOWA STATE UNIV, 77- *Personal Data:* b Mohall, NDak, Aug 27, 39; m 61; c 3. *Educ:* NDak State Univ, BS, 61; Univ Conn, 63; Okla State Univ, PhD(animal breeding), 66. *Mem:* Am Soc Animal Sci. *Res:* Application of genetic principles to applied animal breeding, with emphasis on growth and carcass traits; livestock production. *Mailing Add:* Dept Animal Sci Iowa State Univ Ames IA 50011-2010

BRACKEN, RONALD CLAY, ELECTRONIC PACKAGING OF SEMICONDUCTOR DEVICES. *Current Pos:* DIR PACKAGING SCI, SEMICONDUCTOR RES CORP, 95- *Personal Data:* m 59, Mary; c Clay, Sysan, John & Thomas. *Educ:* Rice Univ, BA, 56; Purdue Univ, PhD(chem), 61. *Prof Exp:* Res chemist, Physics Res Labs, Tex Instruments Inc, Dallas, 61, res chemist gas solid reactions, Mat Res & Develop Labs, 61-69, sect head, Process Develop Lab, Components Group, Stafford, 69-71, mgr process eng, Circuits Design Pilot Line, 71-74, mgr process eng, Photomask Serv Dept, 74-78; mgr, Photomask & Comput Aided Design Serv, Mostek Corp, 78-80, mgr functional probe, Photomask & Comput Aided Design Serv, 81-82; dir comput aided design & photomask, RCA/Gen Elec, 82-89; dir advan packaging develop, Harris Semiconductor, 89-95. *Mem:* Am Chem Soc; Electrochem Soc. *Res:* Catalytic activity of semiconductors. *Mailing Add:* 109 Mel Oaks Chapel Hill NC 27516

BRACKENBURY, ROBERT WILLIAM, DEVELOPMENTAL BIOLOGY. *Current Pos:* ASSOC PROF, UNIV CINCINNATI MED CTR, 87- *Personal Data:* b Long Beach, Calif, May 19, 48; m 69; c 1. *Educ:* Calif Inst Technol, BS, 70; Brandeis Univ, PhD(biol), 76. *Prof Exp:* Jane Coffin Childs fel, 75-77, asst prof, Rockefeller Univ, 78-87. *Mem:* Harvey Soc. *Res:* Structure and function of cell-surface molecules and cell-cell interactions during development; role of alterations in adhesion and motility in tumor cell invasiveness and metastasis; developmental neurobiology. *Mailing Add:* Univ Cincinnati Med Ctr 231 Bethesda Ave Cincinnati OH 45267. *Fax:* 513-558-4454

BRACKENRIDGE, DAVID ROSS, ORGANIC CHEMISTRY. *Current Pos:* chemist, Ethyl Corp, 66-76, sr res chemist res & develop, 76-85, sr res specialist, 85-90, RES ADV, RES & DEVELOP, ETHYL CORP, 90- *Personal Data:* b Buffalo, NY, Jan 31, 38; m 64; c 2. *Educ:* Canisius Col, BS, 60; Ohio State Univ, MS, 65, PhD(org chem), 66. *Mem:* Am Chem Soc. *Res:* Synthetic, organic chemistry; reaction mechanisms; bromo-organic compounds; flame retardants; lube oil additives. *Mailing Add:* 5232 Halls Ferry Baton Rouge LA 70817-2421

BRACKENRIDGE, JOHN BRUCE, CLASSICAL MECHANICS. *Current Pos:* from asst prof to assoc prof, 59-66, PROF PHYSICS, LAWRENCE UNIV, 66- *Personal Data:* b Youngstown, Ohio, Apr 20, 27; m 54; c 4. *Educ:* Muskingum Col, BS, 51; Brown Univ, MS, 54, PhD(physics), 59; London Univ, MSc, 74. *Honors & Awards:* Chapman Chair of Physics, Lawrence Univ, 63. *Prof Exp:* Asst prof physics, Muskingum Col, 55-59. *Concurrent Pos:* Res grants, Res Corp, 55-60 and NSF, 60-65, 68; vis scholar, Imp Col, Univ London, 74-75; fel, Nat Endowment Humanities, 80-81, 87-88, 90-93. *Mem:* Am Acoust Soc; Am Asn Physics Teachers; Hist Sci Soc. *Res:* Subaqueous acoustics; fluid dynamics; application of schlieren interferometry systems to measurements of fluid flow; history philosophy of science; 17th and 18th century physics and astronomy with attention to Newton's Principia. *Mailing Add:* 218 N Union St Appleton WI 54911

BRACKER, CHARLES E, FUNGAL CYTOLOGY. *Current Pos:* from asst prof to assoc prof, 64-73, PROF BOT & PLANT PATH DEPT, PURDUE UNIV, WEST LAFAYETTE, 73- *Personal Data:* b Portchester, NY, Feb 3, 38; m 63; c 2. *Educ:* Univ Calif, Davis, BS, 60, PhD(plant path), 64. *Honors & Awards:* Ruth Allen Award, Am Phytopathol Soc, 83. *Prof Exp:* Res asst plant path, Univ Calif, Davis, 60-64. *Concurrent Pos:* Ann lectr, Mycological Soc Am, 91. *Mem:* Fel AAAS; Mycol Soc Am; Brit Mycological Soc; Electron Micros Soc; Am Soc Cell Biol. *Res:* Fungal ultrastructure and development; developmental cytology; cell wall formation; endomembrane system and organelles; cell growth and reproduction; morphogenesis cell ultrastructure. *Mailing Add:* Dept Path & Bot Purdue Univ West Lafayette IN 47907-1057. *Fax:* 765-494-5896

BRACKETT, BENJAMIN GAYLORD, ANIMAL PHYSIOLOGY, NEW MAMMALIAN REPRODUCTIVE TECHNOLOGY. *Current Pos:* head, 83-95, PROF, DEPT PHYSIOL & PHARMACOL, COL VET MED, UNIV GA, ATHENS, 83- *Personal Data:* b Athens, Ga, Nov 18, 38; m 59, Ann T Crawford; c Laura E, Jeffrey C & David G. *Educ:* Univ Ga, BSA, 64, DVM, 62, MS, 64, PhD(biochem), 66; Am Col Theriogenologists, dipl. *Hon Degrees:* MA, Univ Pa, 71. *Prof Exp:* Mark L Morris Animal Found fel & Am Vet Med Asn fel, Univ Ga, 62-64,; Nat Inst Child Health & Human Develop fel, Univ Ga, 64-66; assoc reproductive biol, Univ Pa, 66-68, from asst prof to prof, Dept Obstet & Gynec & managing dir, Primate Colony, 68-74, prof animal reproduction, Dept Clin Studies, 74-83. *Concurrent Pos:* Consult, Nat Inst Child Health & Human Develop, 68-; mem sci adv bd, Mark L Morris Animal Found, 71-74, mem, Primate Res Ctrs Adv Comt, 74-78; consult, Univ Wis Regional Primate Ctr, US Congress Off Technol Assessment, 86-88, Contraceptive Res & Develop Prog, 86-; pres & chmn bd, Reproductive Biol, Assoc, Atlanta, GA, 83-88. *Mem:* Am Vet Med Asn; Soc Theriogenology; Int Embryo Transfer Soc (pres, 84-85); Am Fertil Soc; Soc Study Reproduction (secy, 82-86); Am Physiol Soc. *Res:* Basic research involving preimplantation stages of mammalian reproduction, especially fertilization of mammalian ova in vitro and development of new reproductive and genetic technologies in animals. *Mailing Add:* Dept Physiol & Pharmacol Col Vet Med Univ Ga Athens GA 30602. *Fax:* 706-542-3015; *E-Mail:* brackett.b@calc.vet.uga.edu

BRACKETT, ROBERT E, FOOD MICROBIOLOGY, FOOD SAFETY. *Current Pos:* ASSOC PROF, FOOD SCI DIV, UNIV GA. *Personal Data:* b Milwaukee, Wis, Nov 28, 53; m 75; c 2. *Educ:* Univ Wis, BS, 76, MS, 79, PhD(food sci), 81. *Prof Exp:* Res asst, Univ Wis, 76-81; food safety specialist, NC State Univ, 81- *Mem:* Int Asn Milk Food & Environ Sanitarians; Inst Food Technologists; Am Soc Microbiol. *Res:* Microbiology of fruits and vegetables; survival and behavior of Listeria monocytogenes in foods; psychotropic pathogens in foods. *Mailing Add:* 1820 Pinecrest Dr Griffin GA 30223

BRACKETT, ROBERT GILES, IMMUNOLOGY. *Current Pos:* CONSULT, 81- *Personal Data:* b Nyack, NY, Oct 8, 30; m 51; c 5. *Educ:* Rutgers Univ, BS, 53, MS, 57, PhD(bact), 60. *Prof Exp:* Asst bact, Rutgers Univ, 56-59, instr, 59-60; asst res microbiologist cell cult, Parke, Davis & Co, 60-62, res microbiologist cell cult & virol, 62-66, dir, Virol Sect, 66-70, dir clin immunol, 70-81. *Concurrent Pos:* Jr microbiologist, Merck & Co, Inc, NJ, 56; bacteriologist, E R Squibb & Sons, 57-58. *Mem:* Am Soc Microbiol; Tissue Cult Asn; Soc Cryobiol. *Res:* Laboratory and/or clinical research and development of bacterial, plasmodial, and viral vaccines, skin test antigens, and blood products with emphasis on the immunology of these biological products. *Mailing Add:* 220 N Marcella Rd Mt Prospect IL 60056-2613

BRACKIN, EDDY JOE, ALGEBRA. *Current Pos:* From instr to asst prof, 69-74, ASSOC PROF MATH, UNIV N ALA, 74- *Personal Data:* b Town Creek, Ala, Feb 27, 45; m 66. *Educ:* Florence State Univ, BS, 67; Univ Ala, MA, 68, PhD(algebra), 70. *Mem:* Am Math Asn. *Res:* Theory of semirings. *Mailing Add:* Dept Math & Comput Sci Univ N Ala 1 University Florence AL 35632-0001

BRACKMANN, RICHARD THEODORE, MASS SPECTROMETRY, ATOMIC PHYSICS. *Current Pos:* MGR ENG, EXTRANUCLEAR LABS, INC, 73- *Personal Data:* b Kansas City, Mo, Nov 23, 30; m 86, Patti C Helsley; c 3. *Educ:* Univ Kans, BS, 53. *Prof Exp:* Asst, Gen Atomic Div, Gen Dynamics Corp, 56-58, mem res staff, 58-63; assoc res prof physics & elec eng, Univ Pittsburgh, 63-72, pres, 66-72. *Mem:* Am Phys Soc; Am Soc Mass Spectrometry. *Res:* Atomic research using modulated crossed beam, mass spectrometric, cryogenic, counting and high vacuum techniques; development of state of the art quadrupole mass spectrometric equipment and techniques used in ambient, environmental, process control and GC-LC/MS/DS. *Mailing Add:* Rte 1 Box 114 Collins MO 64738

BRADBEER, CLIVE, BIOCHEMISTRY. *Current Pos:* from asst prof to assoc prof, 64-79, PROF BIOCHEM, MED SCH, UNIV VA, 79- *Personal Data:* b Tynemouth, Eng, Feb 20, 33; m 60, Wilma Jean Youngert; c Suzanne Mary & Thomas Clive. *Educ:* Univ Durham, BSc, 54, PhD(plant biochem), 57. *Prof Exp:* Jr res biochemist, Univ Calif, Berkeley, 57-59; jr res biochemist, Univ Calif, Davis, 59; proj assoc biochem, Univ Wis, 59-60; lectr microbiol, Queen Mary Col, Univ London, 60-62; vis scientist, Nat Heart Inst, 62-64. *Concurrent Pos:* Vis lectr biochem, Univ Otago, Dunedin, New Zealand, 82-83, 93. *Mem:* Am Soc Biochem & Molecular Biol. *Res:* Structure-function relationships in bacterial cell envelopes, with special attention to the transport of vitamin B12; effects of vitamin B12 deficiency upon the developing nervous system in ventebrate embryos. *Mailing Add:* Dept Biochem Univ Va Med Sch Charlottesville VA 22908-0001. *Fax:* 804-924-5069; *E-Mail:* cb7f@virginia.edu

BRADBURD, ERVIN M, ENGINEERING. *Current Pos:* RETIRED. *Personal Data:* b Philadelphia, Pa, May 29, 20; m 41; c Daniel & Ralph. *Educ:* Columbia Univ, BS, 41, MS, 43. *Prof Exp:* Asst elec eng, Columbia Univ, 41-43; head, Dept Transmitter Eng Develop, Fed Telecommun Labs, Inc, 43-58; mgr advan commun technol, Radio Corp Am, 58-66, Advan Commun Lab, 66-68; vpres & dir eng, Defense Commun Div, Int Tel & Tel Corp, Nutley, NAm, 68-75, tech dir, Telecommun & Electronics Group, 75-85. *Mem:* Fel Inst Elec & Electronics Engrs. *Res:* Communications engineering; high power transmitter development; communication systems, techniques and technology. *Mailing Add:* White Birch Dr Pomona NY 10970

BRADBURN, GREGORY RUSSELL, CHEMICAL KINETICS. *Current Pos:* RES ASST, WASH UNIV, 91- *Personal Data:* b Wichita, Kans, Feb 23, 55; m 77, Teri C Scholfield; c Anne L. *Educ:* USAF Acad, BSc, 77; Univ Mo, St Louis, MSc, 88; Washington Univ, 90- *Prof Exp:* Laser physicist, Air Force Weapons Lab, 77-80; IR res physicist, Air Force Geophysics Lab, 80-82; res scientist, McDonnell Douglas Res Lab, 82-90. *Concurrent Pos:* Adj prof, Lindenwood Col, 90. *Mem:* Am Chem Soc. *Res:* Measurement of photophysics of semiconductor nanoclusters and other nanocrystalline materials. *Mailing Add:* 9001 Olden St Overland MO 63114. *Fax:* 314-935-4481; *E-Mail:* bradburn@wuchem_wustl.edu

BRADBURY, DONALD, mechanical engineering, for more information see previous edition

BRADBURY, E MORTON, CHEMISTRY. *Current Pos:* DIR, LIFE SCI DIV, LOS ALAMOS NAT LAB, NMEX, 88- *Personal Data:* b May 25, 33. *Educ:* Univ London, BSc Hons, 55, PhD(biophys), 58. *Prof Exp:* Res scientist, Courtauld Res Lab, 58-62; head, Dept Molecular Biol & reader biophys, Portsmouth Polytech, 62-79; PROF & CHAIRPERSON, DEPT BIOL CHEM, SCH MED, UNIV CALIF, DAVIS, 79- *Concurrent Pos:* Mem, Biol Sci Comt, Sci Res Coun UK, 71-75, Neutron Beam Res Comt, 71-76, Brit Nat Comt Biophys, 71-79, Int Coun Magnetic Resonance in Biol, 72-80, sci coun, Inst Laue Langevin, France, 75-80 & prog comt, Argonne & Los Alamos Nat Labs, 83-; chmn, Brit Biophys Soc, 73, Int Coun Magnetic Resonance in Biol, 76-80 & Neutron-Biol Comt, Inst Laue Langevin, 76-80. *Res:* Author of numerous publications. *Mailing Add:* Dept Biol Chem Rm 4110 Univ Calif Sch Med Med Sci Bldg 1A Davis CA 95616

BRADBURY, ELMER J(OSEPH), CHEMICAL ENGINEERING. *Current Pos:* RETIRED. *Personal Data:* b Kokomo, Ind, June 26, 17; m 46, 73; c 2. *Educ:* Purdue Univ, BS, 42; Ohio State Univ, MS, 49. *Prof Exp:* Pilot plant supvr, Merck & Co, NJ, 42-45; res engr, Battelle Mem Inst, 45-50, prin chem engr, 50-58, proj leader, 58-62, sr res chemist, 62-69, proj leader res chem, 69- 80, prin res scientist, 80-85. *Mem:* AAAS; Am Chem Soc; Am Inst Chem Engrs; Am Soc Testing Mat; Sigma Xi. *Res:* High pressure polymerizations and reactions; processing and fabrication of conventional and high temepraturе resins; structural composites, materials and fabrication techniques. *Mailing Add:* 8400 Steitz Rd Powell OH 43065-9728

BRADBURY, JACK W, ANIMAL BEHAVIOR, SOCIOBIOLOGY. *Current Pos:* from asst prof to assoc prof, 76-83, PROF BIOL, UNIV CALIF, SAN DIEGO, 83- *Personal Data:* b Los Angeles, Calif, Sept 28, 41; m 73, Sandra Vehrencamp; c Kristin & Katrina. *Educ:* Reed Col, BS, 63; Rockefeller Univ, PhD(animal behav), 68. *Prof Exp:* NIH training grant to Rockefeller Univ taken at William Beebe Trop Res Sta, Simla, Trinidad, WI, 68-69; asst prof neurobiol & behav, Cornell Univ, 69-72; asst prof, Rockefeller Univ, 72-75. *Concurrent Pos:* Richard King Mellon fel, Rockefeller Univ, 73-75; mem, Psychobiol Panel, NSF, 78-80; mem, Comt Direction Lab d'Ecol Trop, Ctr Nat Res Sci, France, 78-80; ed, Behav Ecol & Sociobiol, 89- *Mem:* Ecol Soc Am; Sigma Xi; AAAS; Asn Study Animal Behav; Soc Study Evolution. *Res:* Field studies on resource utilization and social evolution in tropical bats and antelopes; evolution of lek behavior in bats and birds; communication in parrots. *Mailing Add:* Dept Biol 0116 Univ Calif San Diego La Jolla CA 92093-0116. *Fax:* 619-534-7108; *E-Mail:* jbradbury@ucsd.edu

BRADBURY, JAMES CLIFFORD, GEOLOGY. *Current Pos:* From asst geologist to geologist, 49-82, head, Indust Minerals Sect, 68-81, actg head, Geol Group, 81-82, prin geol & head, Geol Group, 82-84, EMER PRIN GEOLOGIST, ILL STATE GEOL SURV, 84- *Personal Data:* b US, July 7, 18; c 3. *Educ:* Univ Ill, AB, 41; Harvard Univ, AM, 49, PhD, 58. *Honors & Awards:* Hardinge Award, Am Inst Mining, Metal & Petrol Engrs, 85. *Mem:* Fel AAAS; Am Inst Mining, Metall & Petrol Engrs; fel Geol Soc Am; fel Soc Econ Geologists; Int Asn Genesis Ore Deposits; distinguished mem, Soc Mining Engrs, 85. *Res:* Geology of mineral deposits of Illinois. *Mailing Add:* 101 W Windsor Rd Urbana IL 61802-6697

BRADBURY, JAMES NORRIS, EXPERIMENTAL PHYSICS. *Current Pos:* group leader, 73-85, DEP DIV LEADER, MEDIUM ENERGY PHYSICS DIV, LOS ALAMOS NAT LAB, 86- *Personal Data:* b Palo Alto, Calif, May 25, 35; m 61; c 2. *Educ:* Pomona Col, BA, 56; Stanford Univ, PhD(physics), 65. *Prof Exp:* Res scientist, Lockheed Palo Alto Res Lab, 66-73. *Mem:* Am Geophys Union; Am Phys Soc; Am Asn Physicists in Med. *Res:* Applications of LAMPF to biomedical and environmental research. *Mailing Add:* 1069 Camino Manaua Santa Fe NM 87501

BRADBURY, JAMES THOMAS, ENDOCRINOLOGY. *Current Pos:* ADJ PROF, MONT STATE UNIV, 74- *Personal Data:* b Cody, Wyo, Apr 7, 06; m 29; c 2. *Educ:* Mont State Col, BS, 28; Univ Mich, MS, 30, ScD(zool), 32. *Prof Exp:* Asst, Dept Obstet & Gynec, Univ Hosp, Univ Mich, 32-37, instr, 37-40; endocrinologist, Bur Dairy Indust, USDA, 40-44; from asst prof to prof, 44-74, EMER PROF OBSTET & GYNEC, UNIV HOSP, UNIV IOWA, 74- *Concurrent Pos:* Assoc prof, Univ Louisville, 49-52. *Mem:* Am Physiol Soc; Am Asn Anat; Endocrine Soc; Soc Exp Biol & Med. *Res:* Physiology, biochemistry and histology in study of the actions of hormones in processes of sex and reproduction. *Mailing Add:* 1020 E Olive St Bozeman MT 59715-3855

BRADBURY, MARGARET G, ICHTHYOLOGY, EVOLUTION. *Current Pos:* RETIRED. *Personal Data:* b Chicago, Ill, July 15, 27. *Educ:* Roosevelt Univ, BS, 55; Stanford Univ, PhD(biol), 63. *Prof Exp:* From asst prof to prof biol, San Francisco State Univ, 63-94. *Concurrent Pos:* Res assoc, Calif Acad Sci, 68- *Mem:* Am Soc Ichthyologists & Herpetologists; Sigma Xi. *Res:* Systematic ichthyology; monographic treatment of the lophiiform family ogcocephalidae, their distribution and natural history. *Mailing Add:* Moss Landing Marine Labs PO Box 450 Moss Landing CA 95039-0450. *E-Mail:* bradbury@mlml.calstate.edu

BRADBURY, MICHAEL WAYNE, mammalian developmental genetics, molecular biology embryos, for more information see previous edition

BRADBURY, NORRIS EDWIN, PHYSICS. *Current Pos:* RETIRED. *Personal Data:* b Santa Barbara, Calif, May 30, 09; m 33; c 3. *Educ:* Pomona Col, AB, 29; Univ Calif, PhD(physics, math), 32. *Hon Degrees:* ScD, Pomona Col, 51; LLD, Univ NMex, 53; DSc, Case Inst Technol, 56. *Honors & Awards:* Enrico Fermi Award, AEC, 70. *Prof Exp:* Nat Res fel physics, Mass Inst Technol, 32-34; from asst prof to prof, Stanford Univ, 34-51; prof physics, Univ Calif, 51-70, dir, Los Alamos Sci Lab, 45-70. *Mem:* Nat Acad Sci; fel Am Phys Soc. *Res:* Conduction of electricity in gases; properties of ions; atmospheric electricity; nuclear physics. *Mailing Add:* 1451 47th St Los Alamos NM 87544

BRADBURY, PHYLLIS CLARKE, PROTOZOOLOGY. *Current Pos:* from asst prof to assoc prof, 67-77, PROF ZOOL, NC STATE UNIV, 77- *Personal Data:* b Oakland, Calif. *Educ:* Univ Calif, Berkeley, AB, 58, MA, 61, PhD(zool), 65. *Prof Exp:* USPHS training fel, Rockefeller Univ, 65-67. *Concurrent Pos:* Prin investr, USPHS grant, 68-71; NATO fel, Sta Biologique de Roscoff, 73-74; mem, Trop Med & Parasitol Study Sect, Pub Health Serv, NIH, 77-81; co-ed, J Protozool, 80-, managing ed, 83-88. *Mem:* Soc Protozoologists (pres, 77-78); Am Soc Zoologists; Am Micros Soc. *Res:* Fine structure of morphogenesis in protozoa; taxonomy of ciliated protozoa; differentiation of sexual stages of malarial parasites; genesis of organelles in protozoa; protozoan parasites of crustacea. *Mailing Add:* Dept Zool NC State Univ Box 7617 Raleigh NC 27695-7617

BRADDOCK, JOSEPH V, PHYSICS. *Current Pos:* FOUNDER, BDM CORP, 60-, SR VPRES, BDM INT INC, 85- *Personal Data:* b Hoboken, NJ, Dec 10, 29; m 65, Bertha Soto; c Joseph A & Robert T. *Educ:* St Peter's Col, BS, 51; Fordham Univ, MS, 52, PhD(physics), 59. *Prof Exp:* Instr physics, Fordham Univ, 53-58; asst prof, Iona Col, 58-60. *Concurrent Pos:* Mem, Weapons Syst Vulnerability Working Groups, Defense Nuclear Agency & Serv Develop Agencies, 65-75; mem, Sci Adv Bd, Nat Security Agency, 76-83, DNA Sci Adv Group on Effects, 77-85, Army Sci Bd, Dept Army, 77-84 & Defense Sci Bd, 84-93. *Mem:* Am Phys Soc; Inst Elec & Electronics Engrs. *Res:* Weapon system design and analysis; neutron and solid state physics; atomic and molecular spectra. *Mailing Add:* 1501 BDM Way McLean VA 22102

BRADDOCK, WILLIAM A, FIELD GEOLOGY. *Current Pos:* from instr to assoc prof, 56-70, PROF GEOL, UNIV COLO, 70- *Personal Data:* b Rifle, Colo, Feb 3, 29. *Educ:* Univ Colo, BA, 51; Princeton Univ, PhD(geol), 59. *Prof Exp:* Geologist, US Geol Surv, 52-56. *Concurrent Pos:* Geologist, US Geol Surv, 56- *Mem:* Geol Soc Am; Am Geophys Union. *Res:* Structural geology; igneous and metamorphic petrology; Precambrian geology. *Mailing Add:* 2137 Grove Circle W Boulder CO 80302

BRADEN, CHARLES HOSEA, NUCLEAR PHYSICS, SYSTEM DYNAMICS. *Current Pos:* RETIRED. *Personal Data:* b Chicago, Ill, Mar 21, 26; m 52, Sara McKinley; c Patsy & Jack. *Educ:* Columbia Univ, BS, 46; Wash Univ, PhD(physics), 51. *Prof Exp:* From asst prof to regents prof physics, Ga Inst Technol, 51-91; consult, Fernbank Mus Natural Hist, 90-96. *Concurrent Pos:* Assoc dir physics prog, NSF, 59-60. *Mem:* Am Phys Soc; Syst Dynamics Soc. *Res:* Nuclear spectroscopy and structure; socio-economic modeling. *Mailing Add:* 1645 Berkeley Lane NE Atlanta GA 30329

BRADEN, CHARLES MCMURRAY, MATHEMATICS. *Current Pos:* RETIRED. *Personal Data:* b Santiago, Chile, June 9, 18; US citizen; m 43; c 4. *Educ:* Northwestern Univ, BS, 39; Univ Minn, MS, 50, PhD(math), 57. *Honors & Awards:* Thomas Jefferson Award, 70. *Prof Exp:* Instr math, Inst Technol, Univ Minn, 46-56; from asst prof to assoc prof, 56-60, dean fac, 69-72, prof math, Macalester Col, 60- *Concurrent Pos:* NSF fac fel, 59-60. *Mem:* Am Math Soc; Math Asn Am. *Res:* Partial difference equations; logic; heat engines. *Mailing Add:* 1666 Coffman St No 218 St Paul MN 55108

BRADER, WALTER HOWE, JR, ORGANIC CHEMISTRY. *Current Pos:* sr res chemist, 59-62, sr proj chemist, 62-64, supvr explor res, 64-67, coordr, 67-70, mgr com develop, 70-71, DIR RES & DEVELOP, JEFFERSON CHEM CO, 71- *Personal Data:* b Beaumont, Tex, Oct 30, 27; m 44; c 3. *Educ:* Rice Univ, BA, 50; Ga Inst Technol, PhD(org chem), 54. *Prof Exp:* Res chemist, Standard Oil Co, Ind, 54-59. *Mem:* Am Chem Soc. *Res:* Petrochemicals synthesis; application of catalysis to organic synthesis; new process development; economic evaluations; development of new product sales. *Mailing Add:* 8803 Crest Ridge Circle Austin TX 78750-3043

BRADFIELD, ROBERT B, CLINICAL NUTRITION, BIOCHEMISTRY. *Current Pos:* PRES, NUTRITION SCIENCE, POLICY & LAW, ORINDA, CALIF, 80- *Personal Data:* b Columbia, Mo, Nov 15, 28; m 55; c 3. *Educ:* Cornell Univ, BA, 51, MNS, 53, PhD(biochem, nutrit), 55; Univ Calif, Berkeley, JD, 76; Am Bd Nutrit, dipl, 78. *Honors & Awards:* Joseph Goldberger Award, AMA, 78, Gold Award. *Prof Exp:* Serv officer, Interam Pub Health Serv, US State Dept, Peru, 55-62; USPHS sr fel, Cornell Univ, 62-63, & London Sch Trop Med, 63-64; clin prof human nutrit, Univ Calif, Berkeley, 64-80. *Concurrent Pos:* Appt field dir, Latin Am, Harvard Sch Pub Health, Harvard Univ; grants, William Waterman Fund, 57, 58, 60, 62, 64, 68, NIH, 62-67, 69-72, 73-75, Rockefeller Found, 58, 60, 62, 63-64, 67, 68, 69, 71, US Dept Agr, 69-71 & Brit Nutrit Found, 69, 71, 79; fels, Rockefeller Found, 64, 72, 77 WHO, 65, 67, 74, 79 & Guggenheim, 69; consult var worldwide orgns, 64; consult & lectr, Peace Corps, 64-80; ed, Am J Clin Nutrit, 66-78; mem food & nutrit bd subcomt, Nat Res Coun, 77-79; mem, Latin Am Sci Bd, NSF, 78-80, arbitrator, NASP & AAA, 82- & White House Task Force Nutrit, 85; chief party, Child Survival Proj, Cairo, Egypt, 89-90. *Mem:* Fel Am Inst Chem; fel Royal Soc Trop Med & Hyg; fel Royal Soc Health; fel Int Col Pediat; fel AAAS; fel Brazilian Soc Health; fel Royal Soc Photog Soc. *Mailing Add:* Nutrit, Sci, Policy & Law 120 Village Sq Suite 122 Orinda CA 94563

BRADFORD, DAVID S, ORTHOPEDIC SURGERY. *Current Pos:* PROF & CHMN DEPT ORTHOP SURG, UNIV CALIF, SAN FRANCISCO, 90- *Personal Data:* b Charlotte, NC, Oct 15, 36; c 3. *Educ:* Davidson Col, BS, 58; Univ Pa, MD, 62. *Prof Exp:* From resident gen surg to resident orthop surg, Columbia-Presby Med Ctr, 62-66, Annie C Kane jr fel, 68-69; from asst prof to prof orthop surg, Univ Minn, Minneapolis, 70-90. *Mem:* Fel Am Col Surgeons; Orthop Res Soc; Am Acad Orthop Surgeons; Scoliosis Res Soc (pres, 86). *Res:* Connective tissue diseases; diseases of growth and development; idiopathic scoliosis; congenital malformation. *Mailing Add:* Dept Orthop Surg Univ Calif Parnassus Ave Rm MU-320 W San Francisco CA 94143-0728

BRADFORD, EDMOND JAMES, IDENTIFICATION & RECOGNITION OF WORLD CLASS RESEARCH IN CHEMISTRY. *Current Pos:* mgr, Col Prog, Am Chem Soc, 84-88, Nat Chem Week mgr, 88-92, spec asst to exec dir, 92-95, AWARDS ADMINR, AM CHEM SOC, 95- *Personal Data:* b Okarche, Okla, Oct 14, 52; m 89, Monica Marie Creamer; c Megan, Emily, Allison & Colleen. *Educ:* Wichita State Univ, BA, 75; Western Ill Univ, MS, 77; Univ Mo, Columbia, PhD(adult educ/chem), 84. *Prof Exp:* Spec contract chemist, Ill Environ Protection Agency, 76; instr gen, org & phys chem, Lincoln Trail Col, 76-81. *Concurrent Pos:* Vis prof eng & org chem, Univ Mo, 81-94. *Mem:* Am Chem Soc; AAAS. *Res:* Identification and recognition of world-class research in chemistry. *Mailing Add:* Am Chem Soc 1155 16th St NW Washington DC 20036. *E-Mail:* j_bradford@acs.org

BRADFORD, G ERIC, GENETICS OF REPRODUCTION, INTERNATIONAL AGRICULTURE. *Current Pos:* from asst prof to prof, 57-93, chair, Animal Sci Dept, 73-78 & 90-93, EMER PROF ANIMAL SCI, UNIV CALIF, DAVIS, 93- *Personal Data:* b Kingsey, Que, Nov 2, 29; m 54; c 4. *Educ:* McGill Univ, BSc, 51; Univ Wis, MS, 52, PhD(genetics, animal husb), 56. *Honors & Awards:* J R Prentice Mem Award, Am Soc Animal Sci, 85. *Prof Exp:* Res asst animal sci, Univ Wis, 51-55; asst prof animal sci & genetics, Macdonald Col, McGill Univ, 55-57. *Concurrent Pos:* Prin investr, Small Ruminants Collab Res Support Prog, USAID-Univ Calif, 78-96; ed, Breed & Genetics Sect, J Animal Sci, 79-80; mem, Coun Agr Sci & Technol. *Mem:* Am Soc Animal Sci; fel AAAS; Brit Soc Animal Prod. *Res:* Genetics of growth and reproduction in livestock and laboratory animals, with emphasis on genetics of prenatal survival and litter size; sheep breeding; major genes. *Mailing Add:* Dept Animal Sci Univ Calif Davis Davis CA 95616-5224. *Fax:* 530-752-0175; *E-Mail:* gebradford@ucdavis.edu

BRADFORD, HAROLD R(AWSEL), metallurgy; deceased, see previous edition for last biography

BRADFORD, HENRY BERNARD, JR, bacteriology, microbiology, for more information see previous edition

BRADFORD, JAMES C, MATHEMATICS. *Current Pos:* CONSULT, 86- *Personal Data:* b Wichita Falls, Tex, Aug 28, 30; m 51; c 3. *Educ:* NTex State Col, BS, 51, MS, 52; Univ Okla, PhD(math), 57. *Prof Exp:* Assoc prof math, Abilene Christian Col, 57-61; res mathematician, Teledyne Systs Co, 61-65; prof math & chmn dept, Abilene Christian Col, 65-79; gov, Math Asn Am, 83-85. *Concurrent Pos:* Consult, Chance-Vought Aircraft, 57-61; vis scientist, Tex Acad Sci, 60-61. *Mem:* Am Math Soc; Math Asn Am; Sigma Xi. *Res:* Functions of a real variable; abstract analysis; analysis stationary time series applied to geophysics. *Mailing Add:* Abilene Christian Univ Box 8012 Sta ACU Abilene TX 79699-8012

BRADFORD, JAMES CARROW, teratology, for more information see previous edition

BRADFORD, JOHN NORMAN, ATOMIC PHYSICS, NUCLEAR PHYSICS. *Current Pos:* RETIRED. *Personal Data:* b Carthage, Mo, May 28, 31; m 63, Phyllis Cameron; c Janet & Margaret. *Educ:* Kans State Univ, BS, 54; Iowa State Univ, PhD(physics), 65. *Prof Exp:* Sr physicist, Gen Dynamics & Astronaut, 62-63; asst prof physics, Univ Mont, 65-67 & Kans State Univ, 67-69; res physicist, Air Force Cambridge Res Lab, Bedford, 69-76, dep electronics technol, 76-96. *Mem:* Am Phys Soc; Sigma Xi. *Res:* Nuclear physics, particularly photonuclear reactions; chnanneling and energy loss; x-ray induced electron emission; x-ray imaging; radiation effects in electronics. *Mailing Add:* 3540 Beaver Creek Rd St James Plantation Southport NC 28461

BRADFORD, JOHN R(OSS), CHEMICAL ENGINEERING. *Current Pos:* VPRES DEVELOP, CHEM PLANT SERV GROUP INC. *Personal Data:* b Amarillo, Tex, Nov 26, 22; m; c 2. *Educ:* Tex Tech Col, BS, 42, MS, 48; Case Western Reserve Univ, PhD, 53. *Prof Exp:* Lectr physics, Tex Tech Col, 46-48; dir, Radioisotopes Lab, Case Western Reserve Univ, 50-54; res consult, US Radium Corp, 54-55; prof chem eng & dean col, Tex Tech Univ, 55-, chmn, Dept Systs, 76- *Concurrent Pos:* Mem, US Nat Comn, World Energy Conf, 78- *Mem:* Am Soc Eng Educ; Am Inst Chem Engrs; Am Chem Soc; Am Soc Testing & Mat. *Res:* Industrial applications of radioisotopes; activation analysis; engineering education. *Mailing Add:* 3112 42nd St Lubbock TX 79413

BRADFORD, LAURA SAMPLE, BREAST FEEDING OF PREMATURE INFANTS, DEVELOPMENTAL ISSUES IN NEONATAL INTENSIVE CARE UNIT. *Current Pos:* Level D staff nurse, 81-96, nurse, Neonatal apnea eval prog, 82-96, CLIN NURSE COORDR, SPEC CARE NURSERY, RUSH-PRESBY-ST LUKE'S MED CTR, 96- *Personal Data:* b St Louis, Mo, Dec 5, 45; c 2. *Educ:* Grinnell Col, BA, 67; Wash Univ, PhD(biol), 71; Rush Univ, BSN, 81. *Prof Exp:* Fel genetics, dept biol, Univ Chicago, 71-73; asst prof biol, Roosevelt Univ, 73-79. *Mem:* Asn Womens Health Obstet & Neonatal Nurses; Nat Asn Neonatal Nurses; Int Soc Nurses Genetics; Nat Perinatal Asn. *Res:* Effects of discharge teaching to parents of infants with breathing abnormalities (apnea, periodic breathing) on family functioning; effects of infant massage on developmental outcome; genetics; breast feeding outcomes in premature infants. *Mailing Add:* 5647 S Blackstone Chicago IL 60637

BRADFORD, LAWRENCE GLENN, MOLECULAR BIOLOGY, MICROBIOLOGY. *Current Pos:* ASST PROF BIOL, BENEDICTINE COL, ATCHISON, KANS, 89- *Personal Data:* b Atlanta, Kans, May 24, 39. *Educ:* Univ Kans, BA, 61, PhD(microbiol), 89; Northwestern Univ, MAT, 70. *Prof Exp:* High Sch teacher sci & math, Trego Community High Sch, Wakeeney, Kans, 70-73, Raymore-Peculiar High Sch, Peculiar, Mo, 73-76 & Maur Hill Prep Sch, Atchison, Kans, 76-82. *Mem:* Am Soc Microbiol; Sigma Xi. *Res:* Characterization of human epidermal cell lines which had been immortalized by transfection with SV40 T-antigen and with Harvey murine sarcoma virus ras oncogene. *Mailing Add:* Biol Dept Benedictine Col 1020 N Second St Atchison KS 66002-1499

BRADFORD, MARION MCKINLEY, BIOCHEMISTRY. *Current Pos:* res biochemist, 81-83, sr res chemist, 83-92, RES SCIENTIST, AE STALEY MFG CO, DECATUR, ILL, 92- *Personal Data:* b Rome, Ga, Oct 28, 46; m 71; c 2. *Educ:* Shorter Col, Ga, BA, 67; Univ Ga, MS, 74, PhD(biochem), 75. *Prof Exp:* Res assoc, Univ Ga, 75-77, asst res scientist biochem, 77-81. *Mem:* Am Chem Soc. *Res:* Hydrolyzed vegetable protein flavors; microbial and human nutrition; food starch chemistry; biomass utilization; biocatalysis. *Mailing Add:* A E Staley Mfg Co 2200 E Eldorado St Decatur IL 62521

BRADFORD, PHILLIPS VERNER, ELECTRICAL ENGINEERING, MICROWAVE PHYSICS. *Current Pos:* EXEC DIR, COLO ADVAN TECHNOL INST, 89- *Personal Data:* b Washington, DC, June 15, 40; m 63, 72, Camille Quarrier; c Phillip & Anthony. *Educ:* Johns Hopkins Univ, BES, 62; Univ Va, MEE, 64; Columbia Univ, EngScD(elec eng), 68. *Prof Exp:* Res asst, Res Labs Eng Sci, Univ Va, 63-64; res asst, Plasma Lab, Dept Elec Eng, Columbia Univ, 65-67; mem tech staff, Bell Tel Labs, Holmdel, 67-69; dir, Precision Optics, Inc, 70-72; staff, Drexel Firestone, 72-73; indust specialist, Merrill Lynch Pierce Fenner & Smith, 73-76; staff scientist, Ametek, Inc, 76-77; mgr, Phelps Dodge Industs, 77-82; dir corp res, Rutgers Univ, 82-84; dir, Kans Advan Technol Comn, 84-87; assoc dir, NY State Ctr Advan Technol, Comput & Info Systs, 88-89. *Concurrent Pos:* Staff, Dominick & Dominick, 69-72. *Mem:* Inst Elec & Electronics Engrs; NY Acad Sci; assoc mem Am Soc Heating, Refrig & Air-Conditioning Engrs; Electrochem Soc. *Res:* Interaction of microwaves with matter; use of microwaves to diagnose some properties of plasma; propagation of microwaves in communication paths to earth satellites; solar energy; economics; technology transfer. *Mailing Add:* 11515 Quivas Way Denver CO 80234. *Fax:* 303-620-4789; *E-Mail:* pvb@csn.org

BRADFORD, REAGAN HOWARD, biochemistry, for more information see previous edition

BRADFORD, SAMUEL ARTHUR, METALLURGY, CORROSION. *Current Pos:* prof, 67-94, EMER PROF METALL, UNIV ALTA, 94- *Personal Data:* b Rolla, Mo, July 19, 28; m 57, Evelin Carlston; c Ellen, George, Charles & Benjamin. *Educ:* Univ Mo, Rolla, BS, 51, MS, 56; Iowa State Univ, PhD(phys metall), 61. *Prof Exp:* Asst chief chemist, Pillsbury Mills, Inc, NY, 53-55; asst phys metall, Ames Lab, AEC, 57-61; engr, Homer Res Labs, Bethlehem Steel Co, 61-67. *Concurrent Pos:* Vis fel, Ohio State Univ, 77-78. *Mem:* Nat Asn Corrosion Engrs; Am Soc Metals. *Res:* Oxidation and corrosion of metals; stability of metal oxides; thermodynamics of solid state diffusion and reaction; effects of impurities on physical and mechanical properties of metals; crystal structures. *Mailing Add:* Dept Mining Metall & Petrol Engrs Univ Alta Edmonton AB T6G 2G6 Can

BRADFORD, WILLIAM DALTON, PATHOLOGY, PEDIATRICS. *Current Pos:* asst prof path & assoc pediat, Duke Univ, 66-70, assoc dean grad med educ, 70-71, 74-78 & 84-87, asst to chancellor, health affairs, 87-89, PROF PATH, DUKE UNIV, 70- *Personal Data:* b Rochester, NY, Nov 2, 31; m 61, Anne Harden; c Scott H & Lisa (Graham). *Educ:* Amherst Col, AB, 54; Western Res Univ, MD, 58; Am Bd Pediat, dipl, 63; Am Bd Path, dipl anat path, 67. *Prof Exp:* Intern path, Children's Hosp Med Ctr, Boston, 58-59, asst resident pediat, 59-61; resident path, Boston Hosp for Women, 63-64; New Eng Deaconess Hosp, Boston, 64-65. *Concurrent Pos:* Teaching fel, Harvard Univ, 63-64; Mead Johnson res fel pediat, 63-64; fel path, Duke Univ, 65-66, Liaison Comt Med Educ, Survey Team Sec, 77- *Mem:* Am Asn Path; Soc Pediat Res; Int Acad Path; Sigma Xi; Soc Pediat Path (pres, 87). *Res:* Iron metabolism; infectious diseases; medical education. *Mailing Add:* Dept Path Duke Univ Med Ctr Box 3712 Durham NC 27710-5129

BRADFORD, WILLIS WARREN, AGRONOMY. *Current Pos:* CONSULT, 89- *Personal Data:* b Lincolnton, Ga, Mar 13, 22; m 41; c 2. *Educ:* Univ Ga, BSA, 47, MS, 48; Agr & Mech Col Tex, PhD(plant breeding), 54. *Prof Exp:* Assoc agronomist, Univ Ga, 48-50; geneticist, Inst de Fomento Algodonera, Colombia, SAm, 50; agronomist, Coastal Plain Exp Sta, Ga, 52-57; agronomist, Miss, Delta & Pine Land Co, 57-59, mem staff admin cotton breeding, Western Div, 59-89. *Res:* Cotton breeding. *Mailing Add:* 454 West K St Brawley CA 92227

BRADFUTE, OSCAR E, PLANT VIROLOGY, DETECTION OF PLANT VIRUSES. *Current Pos:* PROF PLANT PATH, OARDC, OHIO STATE UNIV, 81- *Educ:* Univ Calif, Berkeley, PhD(plant path), 63. *Mailing Add:* 102 Adobe St Santa Cruz CA 95060. *Fax:* 216-263-3841

BRADHAM, GILBERT BOWMAN, SURGERY. *Current Pos:* Assoc, Med Univ SC, 64-65, from asst prof to assoc prof, 65-72, prof, 72-80, CLIN PROF SURG, MED UNIV SC, 80-, DEAN, STUDENT LIFE, 88- *Personal Data:* b Sumter, SC, Aug 5, 31; c 2. *Educ:* Med Univ SC, MD, 56. *Mem:* AMA; Soc Univ Surg. *Mailing Add:* Harper Student Ctr Med Univ SC 171 Ashley Ave Charleston SC 29425

BRADHAM, LAURENCE STOBO, BIOCHEMISTRY. *Current Pos:* asst prof, 71-74, ASSOC PROF BIOCHEM, UNIV TENN, MEMPHIS, 74- *Personal Data:* b Charleston, SC, Dec 3, 29; m 58; c 4. *Educ:* Univ of the South, BS, 51; Univ Tenn, MS, 53, PhD(biochem), 58. *Prof Exp:* Instr pharmacol, Vanderbilt Univ, 58-59; res assoc, Rockefeller Inst, 59-63; res biochemist, Vet Admin Hosp, Little Rock, 63-71. *Mem:* Am Chem Soc; Fedn Am Soc Exp Biol; Am Soc Biol Chemists. *Res:* Metabolism of sulfur compounds; biochemistry of hormone action; enzymology. *Mailing Add:* Dept Biochem Univ Tenn Memphis TN 38163-0001

BRADISH, JOHN PATRICK, mechanical & nuclear engineering, for more information see previous edition

BRADLAW, JUNE A, CELL BIOLOGY, MICROBIOLOGY. *Current Pos:* res microbiologist genetic toxicol, Div Toxicol, 65-86, LEADER, IN VITRO TOXICOL TEAM, FOOD & DRUG ADMIN, 85- *Personal Data:* b Norwich, Conn, July 22, 36; div. *Educ:* Conn Col, AB, 58; Univ Md, College Park, MS, 64; George Washington Univ, PhD(microbiol), 74. *Honors & Awards:* Award Merit, Food & Drug Admin, 71, Commendable Serv Award, 87. *Prof Exp:* Biologist microbial metab, Agr Res Serv, USDA, 58-65. *Concurrent Pos:* Adj assoc prof microbiol, George Washington Univ, 81-89, lectr, Biochem Dept; lectr, Anat Dept, Univ Sask, Can; chmn, Toxicity, Carcinogenesis & Mutagenesis Eval Comt, Tissue Cult Asn, 82-, ed, J Tissue Cult Methods, 85-; secy, Tissue Cult Asn, 88-92; corporator, Norwich Free Acad, 93- *Mem:* Am Soc Microbiol; Tissue Cult Asn; Am Soc Cell Biol; Environ Mutagen Soc; Sigma Xi; Grad Women Sci; Am Acad Microbiol. *Res:* Mammalian cell culture applications in toxicology and in vitro toxicity testing; chemical mutagenesis; somatic cell genetics; DNA repair mechanisms; enzyme induction; structure-activity relationships. *Mailing Add:* 5706 Ridgway Ave Rockville MD 20851

BRADLEY, A FREEMAN, respiration, for more information see previous edition

BRADLEY, ARTHUR, SURFACE CHEMISTRY, MELT-BLOWN POLYMER FIBERS. *Current Pos:* APPL RES COORDR, PALL CORP, 76- *Personal Data:* b New York, NY, Apr 6, 26; m 74, Patricia White; c Peter, Lesly & Corine. *Educ:* Columbia Univ, AB, 48, MA, 50, PhD(chem), 52. *Prof Exp:* Res assoc phys org chem, George Washington Univ, 52-53; org chemist, US Naval Ord Lab, 53-55; radiochemist, Associated Nucleonics, Inc, 55-58; dir res, Radiation Res Corp, 58-69; vpres, Surface Activation Corp, 69-76. *Concurrent Pos:* Vpres dir, Solar Conversion Prod, Inc, 78-80. *Mem:* Am Chem Soc. *Res:* Organic reaction mechanisms and analytical techniques; polymer films and fibers; surface grafting; reactions in gas discharges. *Mailing Add:* 146 Beech St Floral Park NY 11001-3302

BRADLEY, CHARLES, CLINICAL CHEMISTRY. *Current Pos:* DIR CHEM, CLIN PATH LAB, TEX TECH UNIV, 87-, ASSOC PROF CHEM, MED SCH, 87- *Res:* Clinical chemistry. *Mailing Add:* Tex Tech Univ 3601 Fourth St Lubbock TX 79430

BRADLEY, DANIEL JOSEPH, PHYSICAL CHEMISTRY, PETROLEUM ENGINEERING. *Current Pos:* dir int progs, 87-89, MEM STAFF, MONT COL MINERAL SCI & TECHNOL, 79-, HEAD PETROL ENG DIV, 89- *Personal Data:* b Portage la Prairie, Man, Aug 3, 49; US citizen; m 81; c 3. *Educ:* Mich State Univ, BSc, 73, PhD(chem), 77; Mont Tech, BSC, 82; Univ Tulsa, MS, 83. *Prof Exp:* Fel, Metals & Ceramics Div, Oak Ridge Nat Lab, 75-77; fel chem, Univ Calif, Berkeley & Lawrence Berkeley Lab, 78-79. *Concurrent Pos:* Consult, Daqing Petrol Admin Bur, 86 & 87, Mont Dept State Lands, 90, various attys, petrol eng, 83- *Mem:* Am Chem Soc; Soc Petrol Engrs. *Res:* Thermodynamics of mixtures; high temperature electrolyte solutions; flow through porous material; petroleum reservior modeling; pressure transient analysis. *Mailing Add:* Dept Petrol Eng Mont Tech Butte MT 59701-8997

BRADLEY, DORIS P, SPEECH PATHOLOGY, AUDIOLOGY. *Current Pos:* chair person, Dept Speech-Hearing Sci, 81-88, PROF SPEECH & HEARING, UNIV SOUTHERN MISS, HATTIESBURG, 88- *Personal Data:* b Laurel, Miss, Oct 21, 32; m 57. *Educ:* Univ Southern Miss, BS, 53; Univ Fla, MA, 57; Univ Pittsburgh, PhD(speech path), 63. *Prof Exp:* Dir speech clin, Miss Soc Crippled Children, 53-54; speech therapist, Gulfport Schs, 54-56; speech clinician, Los Angeles Soc Crippled Children, 57-58; instr speech path, Med Sch, Univ Ore, 58-61; dir speech clin, Children's Hosp, Pittsburgh, Pa, 63-65; asst prof speech path & coordr grad prog speech & audiol, Med Sch, Univ Ore, 65-68; res assoc, Univ NC, Chapel Hill, 68-70, assoc prof oral biol & dir oral facial & commun dis prog, Dent Sch, 70-74; prof, Dept Logopedics, Wichita State Univ & head clin serv, Inst Logopedics, 74-80. *Concurrent Pos:* NIH grant, 65-; consult, United Cerebral Palsy, 54-56 & Ore State Dept Educ, 58-61; res assoc, Cleft Palate Res Ctr, Pa, 63-65; prof commun disorders, Univ Cent Florida, 80-81. *Mem:* Am Cleft Palate Asn; Am Speech & Hearing Asn; Soc Res Child Develop. *Res:* Speech problems associated with cleft palate; development of normal human communication skills in children; modification of aerodynamics of speech production through speech therapy; phonological rules in southern dialect; multiple phonemic articulation therapy; development of models of program evaluation; effectiveness of language intervention systems. *Mailing Add:* Dept Speech-Hearing Sci Univ Southern Miss Box 5092 Southern Sta Hattiesburg MS 39406-5092

BRADLEY, EDWIN LUTHER, JR, STATISTICS. *Current Pos:* from asst prof to assoc prof, 70-88, PROF BIOSTATIST, UNIV ALA, BIRMINGHAM, 88- *Personal Data:* b Jacksonville, Fla, July 16, 43; m 63, Dorothy Hill; c Edwin, Dana & Douglas. *Educ:* Univ Fla, BS, 64, MStat, 67, PhD(statist), 69. *Prof Exp:* Assoc sci programmer, Lockheed-Ga Co, 65. *Concurrent Pos:* Consult statistician. *Mem:* Am Statist Asn; Biomet Soc. *Res:* Application of statistical techniques. *Mailing Add:* Dept Biostatist Univ Ala Birmingham Birmingham AL 35294. *E-Mail:* ebradley@uab.edu

BRADLEY, ELIHU F(RANCIS), PHYSICAL METALLURGY, MATERIALS ENGINEERING. *Current Pos:* metallurgist, 41-45, design metallurgist, 45-57, eng metallurgist, 57-61, CHIEF MAT ENG, PRATT & WHITNEY AIRCRAFT DIV, UNITED AIRCRAFT CORP, 61- *Personal Data:* b Allentown, Pa, Oct 26, 17; m 42; c 4. *Educ:* Yale Univ, BE, 39. *Prof Exp:* Chemist, Seymour Mfg Co, 39-41. *Concurrent Pos:* Mem adv comt aircraft engine mat, NASA, 66-; mem comt titanium, Mat Adv Bd, 68-69. *Mem:* Fel Am Soc Metals; Am Soc Testing & Mat. *Res:* Aircraft engine materials, particularly gamma prime strengthened nickel, high temperature superalloys, cobalt alloys, titanium alloys, protective coatings and refractory metals; columbium alloys and coatings. *Mailing Add:* 71 Crestwood Rd West Hartford CT 06107

BRADLEY, EUGENE BRADFORD, MOLECULAR PHYSICS, ELECTRICAL ENGINEERING. *Current Pos:* from asst prof to assoc prof, 64-75, Univ res prof, 82-83, actg chmn, 84-85, PROF ELEC ENG, UNIV KY, 75- *Personal Data:* b Georgetown, Ky, Nov 4, 32; m 58; c 2. *Educ:* Georgetown Col, BS, 55; Univ Ky, MS, 57; Vanderbilt Univ, PhD(infrared spectros), 64. *Prof Exp:* Elec engr, Elec Parts Corp, 56; lectr physics, Vanderbilt Univ, 62-63, instr, 63-64. *Concurrent Pos:* From instr to asst prof elec eng, Univ Ky, 56-60. *Mem:* Am Phys Soc. *Res:* Far-infrared spectroscopy, laser Raman spectroscopy. *Mailing Add:* Dept Elec Eng Univ Ky 453 Anderson Hall Lexington KY 40506-0046

BRADLEY, FRANCIS J, HEALTH PHYSICS. *Current Pos:* CONSULT, 91- *Personal Data:* b New York, NY, Jan 15, 26; m 51; c 5. *Educ:* Manhattan Col, BEE, 49; Univ Pittsburgh, MS, 53; Ohio State Univ, PhD(physics, chem), 61. *Prof Exp:* Engr, Westinghouse Elec Corp, 50-53; supt radiation safety, Ohio State Univ, 53-61; tech adv, Int Atomic Energy Agency, 61-62; asst prof health physics, Univ Pittsburgh, 62-65; head health physics sect, Isotopes, Inc, 65-66; prin radiophysicist, Radiol Health Sect, NY State Dept Labor, 66-91. *Mem:* AAAS; Am Phys Soc; Health Physics Soc. *Res:* Environmental factors effecting solid state dosimeters; applications of TLD monitors; human radioisotope body burden assessment by bioassay and whole body counting; radiation protection administration and legislation; laser and microwave exposure studies. *Mailing Add:* 605 E 82nd St New York NY 10028

BRADLEY, GEORGE ALEXANDER, HORTICULTURE. *Current Pos:* From asst prof to prof, Univ Ark, Fayetteville, 55-91, dir sec sci training prog plant sci, 65, head dept hort, 68-91, EMER PROF HORT & FORESTRY, UNIV ARK, FAYETTEVILLE, 91- *Personal Data:* b Staunton, Va, Dec 4, 26; m 57, Freda Matthews; c Steven G & Susan (Pospisil). *Educ:* Univ Del, BS, 51; Cornell Univ, MS, 53, PhD(veg crops), 55. *Mem:* Fel AAAS; fel Am Soc Hort Sci. *Res:* Mineral nutrition; soils; physiology of vegetable crops. *Mailing Add:* 1700 Viewpoint Fayetteville AR 72701-2546

BRADLEY, GUY MARTIN, EMULSIONS, FOOD PRODUCT DEVELOPMENT. *Current Pos:* SCIENTIST, GFA BRANDS, INC, 94- *Personal Data:* b Bridgeport, WVa, Mar 28, 44; m 67, Diane R Hayduk; c Kevin, Keith & Christopher. *Educ:* Carnegie-Mellon Univ BS, 66; Univ Calif, Berkeley, PhD(phys chem), 71. *Prof Exp:* Scientist, Calgon Corp, 71-76 & Petrolite Corp, 76-93. *Mem:* Inst Food Technologists; Am Chem Soc. *Res:* Develop consumer products utilizing special emulsion technology, especially food products; commercialize products, including pilot plant studies, equipment design and construction, quality assurance, quality control method development and plant trials. *Mailing Add:* 14288 Forest Crest Chesterfield MO 63017-2817

BRADLEY, H(OWARD) B(ISHOP), PETROLEUM ENGINEERING. *Current Pos:* CONSULT, SOC PETROL ENGRS, 82- *Personal Data:* b Chicago, Ill, Mar 24, 20; m 40, Ophelia Brown; c Christopher H & Earlene G (Smith). *Educ:* Univ Tex, BS, 44, MS, 50. *Honors & Awards:* Distinguished Serv Award, Soc Petrol Engrs, 86. *Prof Exp:* Asst geologist, Bur Econ Geol, Tex, 46-48, res engr, Tex Petrol Res Comt, 48-49; asst prof petrol & natural gas eng, Univ Ala, 49-51; sr res technologist, field res labs, Magnolia Petrol Co, 53-60, supvr tech training, Socony Mobil Oil Co, Tex, 60-68; adv tech educ & training, Mobil Oil Corp, 68-75, corp mgr, tech training, 75-82. *Concurrent Pos:* Asst prof, Univ Tex, 48, 51. *Mem:* Am Inst Mining, Metall & Petrol Engrs; Sigma Xi; Soc Petrol Engrs. *Res:* Technical training of professional personnel of Mobil; petroleum reservoir and chemical engineering. *Mailing Add:* 215 Fresh Meadow Dr Roanoke TX 76262

BRADLEY, HARRIS WALTON, CHEMISTRY. *Current Pos:* pres, 64-82, ASST TO PRES, NC FOAM INDUST, 82- *Personal Data:* b Charlotte, NC, Jan 13, 15; m 44; c 4. *Educ:* Davidson Col, BS, 37; Univ Va, PhD(org chem), 42. *Prof Exp:* Res chemist, Jackson Lab, E I du Pont de Nemours & Co, 42-43, supvr plant opers, Chambers Works, 43-45, res chemist, Jackson Lab, 45-57; tech dir, E R Carpenter Co, 57-60; consult, 60-61; mgr res & develop, Carolina Indust Plastics Div, Essex Wire Corp, 61-64. *Mem:* AAAS; Am Chem Soc. *Res:* Textile chemicals; water-repellents for textiles; sulfoxidation of hydrocarbons; azo dyes; detergents; neoprene latex; rubber chemicals; blowing agents; polyurethanes. *Mailing Add:* NC Foam Industs, Inc Box 1528 Mt Airy NC 27030-1528

BRADLEY, HUGH EDWARD, INDUSTRIAL ENGINEERING. *Current Pos:* dir, Info Systs, 84-90, dir, MIS, 90, VPRES & CHIEF INFO OFFICER, SHAKLEE CORP, DIV YAMANOUCHI PHARMACEUT CO, 90- *Personal Data:* b Olean, NY; m 73, Carolyn Hoag. *Educ:* Mass Inst Technol, SB & SM, 57; Johns Hopkins Univ, PhD(indust eng), 63. *Honors & Awards:* Kimball Medal, Opers Res Soc Am, 90. *Prof Exp:* Asst prof indust eng, Univ Mich, 63-67; group mgr, Upjohn Co, 67-79; dir, Corp Info Systs, Syntex Corp, 79-81; assoc dir, Kaiser Aluminum Corp, 81-84. *Concurrent Pos:* Adj assoc prof, Western Mich Univ, 67-73; ed, Int Abstracts Opers Res, 69-79 & Opers Res, 89-91; adj prof, Grad Mgt Sch, Grand Valley Col, Mich, 75-78. *Mem:* Opers Res Soc Am (treas, 80-83 & 89-90, pres 85-86); Inst Mgt Sci (vpres, 77-80); Pharmaceut Mgt Sci Asn. *Mailing Add:* 408 Wawona Lane Clayton CA 94517

BRADLEY, JAMES HENRY STOBART, NUMERICAL ANALYSIS, SYSTEMS ANALYSIS. *Current Pos:* PRES, ATLANTIC CONSULTS, 82- *Personal Data:* b London, Eng, Mar 26, 33; m 66, Estella Bennett. *Educ:* Oxford Univ, BA, 54; Univ Toronto, MA, 60; Univ Mich, PhD(meteorol), 67. *Prof Exp:* Scientist isotope geol, Geol Serv Can, 57-59; scientist instrumentation, Can Meteorol Serv, 59-63; res asst meteorol, Univ Mich, 63-67; prof, Pa State Univ, 67-68; res assoc, McGill Univ, 68-70; prof physics, Drexel Univ, 70-76; sr mem tech staff, Electronic Assocs, Inc, West Long Branch, 76-82. *Concurrent Pos:* Consult, Govt Can, 68-70, US Govt, 68- *Mem:* Soc Comput Simulation. *Res:* Computational partial differential equations; real-time numerical methods; training simulators; tests of software; simulation. *Mailing Add:* 46 Rabbit Run Wallingford PA 19086-6218

BRADLEY, JAMES T, INSECT OOGENESIS. *Current Pos:* PROF ZOOL, AUBURN UNIV, 91- *Personal Data:* c 2. *Educ:* Univ Wis-Madison, BS, 70; Univ Wash, Seattle, PhD(develop biol), 76. *Mem:* Am Soc Cell Biol; Am Soc Develop Biol; Am Soc Zool; AAAS. *Res:* Multiple aspects of insect and fish vitellogenesis including vitellogenin biochemistry and endocrine regulation of protein synthesis; polyacrylamide gel electrophoresis; monoclonal antibodies; ultracryomicrotomy. *Mailing Add:* Dept Zool Auburn Univ 101 Cary Hall Auburn AL 36849-5414. *Fax:* 334-844-9234

BRADLEY, JOANN D, PHARMACOLOGY, PHYSIOLOGY. *Current Pos:* ASSOC DIR EXP BIOL, ALLIANCE PHARMACEUT CORP, 91- *Personal Data:* b Fairfax, Va, Sept 27, 61. *Educ:* Univ Va, BS, 83; Vanderbilt Univ, MS, 85, PhD(biol eng), 88. *Prof Exp:* Res fel chem eng & pharmacol, St Louis Univ, 88-91. *Mem:* Am Physiol Soc; Biomed Eng Soc. *Mailing Add:* Alliance Pharmaceut Corp 3040 Science Park Rd San Diego CA 92121

BRADLEY, JOHN SAMUEL, GEOLOGY. *Current Pos:* RETIRED. *Personal Data:* b US, Feb 23, 23; m 51, Janet Rich; c Anne, Elizabeth & James. *Educ:* Colo Sch Mines, GeolE, 48; Univ Wash, PhD(geol), 52. *Prof Exp:* Geologist, Geol Res Sect, Humble Oil & Refining Co, 50-54; marine geologist, Inst Marine Sci, Tex, 54-56; geologist, Res & Develop Dept, Atlantic Refining Co, 56-64 & Geol Res Dept, Amoco Prod Co, 64-92. *Mem:* Geol Soc Am; Am Asn Petrol Geologists; Soc Econ Paleont & Mineral; Am Geophys Union. *Res:* Rock mechanics; hydrogeology; photogeology. *Mailing Add:* 3355 S Braden Ave Tulsa OK 74135-5235

BRADLEY, JOHN SPURGEON, mathematics, for more information see previous edition

BRADLEY, JULIUS ROSCOE, JR, ENTOMOLOGY. *Current Pos:* Asst prof, 67-72, assoc prof, 72-78, PROF ENTOM, NC STATE UNIV, 78- *Personal Data:* b Minden, La, Mar 25, 40; m 63; c 1. *Educ:* La Polytech Inst, BS, 62; La State Univ, MS, 64, PhD(entom), 67. *Mem:* Entom Soc Am. *Res:* Ecology and control of the boll weevil; pest management of Heliothis species; pesticide interactions. *Mailing Add:* 117 Barcliff Cary NC 27511

BRADLEY, LAURENCE A, CHRONIC PAIN, BEHAVIORAL MEDICINE. *Current Pos:* assoc prof, 89-92, prof psychol & med, 92-94, PROF MED, UNIV ALA, BIRMINGHAM, 94-, DIR EDUC, EPIDEMIOL & HEALTH SERV RES, MULTIPURPOSE ARTHRITIS & MUSCULOSKELETAL DIS CTR, 91- *Personal Data:* b Cleveland, Ohio, Sept 13, 49. *Educ:* Vanderbilt Univ, BA, 71 & PhD(psychol), 75. *Honors & Awards:* Distinguished Investr Award, Arthritis Health Professions Asn. *Prof Exp:* Intern psychol, Duke Univ Med Ctr, 75-76; asst prof psychol, Univ Tenn, Chattanooga, 76-77 & Fordham Univ, 77-80; from asst prof to assoc prof med psychol, Bowman Gray Sch Med, 80-89. *Concurrent Pos:* Vis behav scientist, Dept Occup Med, Örebro Med Ctr, Sweden, 86-88; assoc prof, Grad Sch, Wake Forest Univ, 84-89, adj assoc prof, Univ NC, Greensboro, 85-89. *Mem:* Sigma Xi; fel Soc Personality Assessment; Int Asn Study Pain; Am Pain Soc; Arthritis Health Prof Asn; fel Am Psychol Asn. *Res:* Study on the measurement and management of chronic pain due to arthritis and gastro-intestinal disorders; medical psychology; studies on pain perception and health care seeking; behavior in persons with fibromyalgia. *Mailing Add:* 475 Boshell Diabetes Bldg Div Clin Immunol & Rheumatol Univ Ala Birmingham Univ Sta Birmingham AL 35294. *Fax:* 205-934-1477; *E-Mail:* larry.bradley@ccc.uab.edu

BRADLEY, LEE CARRINGTON, III, OPTICAL PHYSICS. *Current Pos:* RETIRED. *Personal Data:* b Birmingham, Ala, May 31, 26. *Educ:* Princeton Univ, AB, 46; Oxford Univ, DPhil(physics), 50. *Prof Exp:* Instr physics, Princeton Univ, 50-54; asst prof, Mass Inst Technol, 54-64, from staff physicist to sr staff physicist, 64-92. *Mem:* Am Phys Soc; Optical Soc Am. *Res:* Laser beam propagation. *Mailing Add:* 201 Somerset St Belmont MA 02178

BRADLEY, MARSHALL RICE, UNDERWATER ACOUSTICS, WAVE PROPAGATION. *Current Pos:* SR SCIENTIST, PLANNING SYST INC, 77- *Personal Data:* b Hattiesburg, Miss, Jan 11, 51; m 74; c 2. *Educ:* Univ Miss, BA, 73, MS, 74; Univ Va, PhD(appl math), 77. *Prof Exp:* Instr appl math, Univ Va, 76-77. *Mem:* Acoust Soc Am; Soc Indust & Appl Math. *Res:* Mathematical modeling of acoustical phenomena; elastic wave propagation; statistical analysis of acoustic data; probability theory. *Mailing Add:* Planning Systs Inc PSI Sci Ctr 115 Christian Lane Slidell LA 70458

BRADLEY, MICHAEL DOUGLAS, RESOURCE MANAGEMENT, PHYSICAL GEOGRAPHY. *Current Pos:* asst prof, 72-77, ASSOC PROF WATER RESOURCES, DEPT HYDROL & WATER RESOURCES, UNIV ARIZ, 77- *Personal Data:* b Wichita, Kans, May 20, 38; m 61. *Educ:* Univ NMex, BA, 67; Univ Mich, MPubAd, 68, PhD(resource planning & conserv), 71. *Prof Exp:* Asst res marine sci affairs, Ctr Marine Affairs, Scripps Inst Oceanog, Univ Calif, San Diego, 71-72. *Concurrent Pos:* Vis prof natural environ & resources, Grad Sch Archit & Urban Planning, Univ Calif, Los Angeles, 80-81; consult water rights, State NMex, 83- *Mem:* AAAS; Am Water Resources Asn; Asn Am Geographers; Am Geophys Union. *Res:* Water resource management in both large scale (large marine ecosystems, multi-state water systems) and small-scale(localized groundwater aquifers); rational use of scientific and technical information in court and adjudicative proceedings. *Mailing Add:* Dept Hydrol Col Eng & Mines Rm 122 Univ Ariz Tucson AZ 85721-0001

BRADLEY, MICHAEL JOHN, COMPLEX GEOMETRY, MATHEMATICS EDUCATION. *Current Pos:* ASSOC PROF MATH, MERRIMACK COL, 83- *Personal Data:* b Lawrence, Mass, Dec 12, 56; m 81, Arleen B Potvin; c Kelly A & Brian M. *Educ:* Merrimack Col, BA, 78; Univ Notre Dame, MA, 81, PhD(math), 83. *Mem:* Math Asn Am. *Res:* Complex geometry, general mathematics and computer science education. *Mailing Add:* 11 McCarthy Rd Lawrence MA 01843. *E-Mail:* mbradley@merrimack.edu

BRADLEY, PETER MICHAEL, TISSUE CULTURE, EXTRACELLULAR MATRIX. *Current Pos:* ASST PROF BIOTECHNOL, WORCESTER STATE COL, 93- *Personal Data:* b Corbridge, Eng, Apr 7, 48; US citizen; m 72, Rosslyn M Fleming; c Christopher H & Sarah E. *Educ:* Univ Aberdeen, Scotland, BS, 71; Worcester Polytech Inst, PhD(biomed sci), 84. *Prof Exp:* Technician, Imp Col, Eng, 72-74; res asst, State Univ NY, Buffalo, 74-75, Univ Mass Med Sch, 75-77, Worcester Polytech Inst, 77-84; res assoc, Northeastern Univ, 84-92; NIH trainee, Boston Univ Sch Med, 92-93. *Concurrent Pos:* Tech adv, Am Radio Relay League, 79-89; adj instr, Worcester Polytech Inst, 83; Northeast Algal Soc (secy). *Mem:* AAAS; Int Asn Plant Tissue Cult; Sigma Xi; Am Soc Cell Biol; Tissue Cult Asn. *Res:* Development of somatic plant embryos, symbiosis, marine plant polysaccharides, algae, and proteins of the extracellular matrix; use techniques of molecular biology and tissue culture. *Mailing Add:* Biol Dept Worcester State Col 486 Chandler St Worcester MA 01602-2597. *E-Mail:* pbradley@worc.mass.edu

BRADLEY, RALPH ALLAN, STATISTICS. *Current Pos:* RETIRED. *Personal Data:* b Can, Nov 28, 23; nat US; m 46; c 2. *Educ:* Queen's Univ, Ont, BA, 44, MA, 46; Univ NC, PhD(math statist), 49. *Honors & Awards:* Horsely Award, Va Acad, 57; Brumbaugh Award, Am Soc Qual Control, 56; Founders Award, Am Statist Asn. *Prof Exp:* Asst prof math, McGill Univ, 49-50; from assoc prof to prof statist, Va Polytech Inst, 50-59; prof, Fla State Univ, 59-70, head dept, 59-78, distinguished prof statist, 70-83, emer prof statist, 83-; res prof, Univ Ga, 82-93. *Concurrent Pos:* Ed, Biometrics, 57-62; chmn, Gordon Res Conf, 65; Ford Found Prog specialist, Cairo Univ, 66-67, Ford Found consult, 68-76; mem, Comt Statist, Nat Acad Sci, 82-88. *Mem:* Fel AAAS; fel Inst Math Statist; fel Am Statist Asn (vpres, 76-79, pres 81); Biomet Soc (pres, 65); Int Statist Inst. *Res:* Mathematical statistics; statistical methods for sensory difference testing. *Mailing Add:* 1221 Hickory Hill Dr Watkinsville GA 30677. *E-Mail:* ralph@rolf.stat.uga.edu

BRADLEY, RAYMOND STUART, CLIMATOLOGY, PALEOCLIMATOLOGY. *Current Pos:* From instr to assoc prof, 73-84, PROF GEOG, UNIV MASS, AMHERST, 84- *Personal Data:* b Cheshire, UK, June 13, 48; m 72; c 2. *Educ:* Univ Southampton, UK, BSc, 69; Univ Colo, Boulder, MA, 71, PhD(geog), 74. *Concurrent Pos:* Prin investr grants climate dynamics & polar progs, NSF, 75-88 & US Dept Energy, 81-88; Nat Acad Comt Trends Acid Deposition, 83-85; lectr, Acad Sinica, Beijing, 84; Advan Res Workshop, NATO, 85; vis fel, Clare Hall, Cambridge, 87; US-USSR Bilateral Meeting of Experts on Climatic Change, Leningrad, 86. *Mem:* Am Meteorol Soc; Am Quaternary Asn; Int Glaciol Soc. *Res:* Climate and climatic change; paleoclimatology; environmental change in mountain and arctic regions. *Mailing Add:* Dept Geol & Geog Univ Mass Amherst MA 01003-0002

BRADLEY, RICHARD CRANE, PHYSICS. *Current Pos:* assoc prof physics, Colo Col, 62-66, chmn dept, 70-73, dean, 73-79, prof, 66-87, EMER PROF PHYSICS, COLO COL, 87- *Personal Data:* b Chicago, Ill, May 14, 22; m 47, Dorothy Holden; c 4. *Educ:* Dartmouth Col, AB, 43; Univ Calif, PhD(physics), 53. *Prof Exp:* Tech aid, Calif Inst Technol, 43; asst physics, Univ Calif, 47-53; res assoc, Cornell Univ, 53-56, from instr to assoc prof, 56-62. *Concurrent Pos:* Consult, Kaman Nuclear, Inc, 63 & Penrose Cancer Res Inst, 64- *Mem:* AAAS; fel Am Phys Soc; Am Asn Physics Teachers. *Res:* Sputtering; secondary ion emissions; surfaces of solids; mass spectrometry; field emission microscopy. *Mailing Add:* 1035 Broadview Pl Colorado Springs CO 80904

BRADLEY, RICHARD CRANE, JR, LIMIT THEOREMS, DEPENDENT RANDOM VARIABLES. *Current Pos:* from asst prof to assoc prof, 80-91, PROF MATH, IND UNIV, 91- *Personal Data:* b Berkeley, Calif, Mar 27, 50. *Educ:* Mass Inst Technol, BS, 72; Univ Calif, San Diego, PhD(math), 78. *Prof Exp:* Asst prof statist, Columbia Univ, 78-80. *Mem:* Sigma Xi; Inst Math Statist; Am Math Soc. *Res:* Properties of strong mixing conditions for sequences of dependent random variables; limit theorems for random sequences under strong mixing conditions. *Mailing Add:* Dept Math Ind Univ Bloomington IN 47405. *E-Mail:* bradleyr@indiana.edu

BRADLEY, RICHARD E, PARASITOLOGY, VETERINARY MEDICINE. *Current Pos:* ADJ PROF BIOL, ROANE STATE COMMUNITY CO, 91- *Personal Data:* b Decatur, Ill, Oct 18, 27; m 80, Alla Parnell; c David, Donald, Richard, Jr (deceased), Douglas & Meghann. *Educ:* Fla State Univ, BS, 49; Univ Ga, MS, 53, DVM, 54; Univ Ga, PhD, 65. *Honors & Awards:* Merck Found Award, 80; Beecham Res Award, 83. *Prof Exp:* Asst zool, Univ Ga, 49-50, lab asst bact & instr zool, 50-54, instr parasitol, 54-55; instr, Univ Ill, 55-56; pvt practr vet med, Ill, 56-62; instr zool, Danville Jr Col, 62 & vet med, Univ Ga, 63; asst parasitologist, Univ Fla, 65-69, assoc parasitologist, 69-74, prof vet med, 75-90, actg chmn dept, 84-90. *Concurrent Pos:* Int consult control of parasitism in food animals; assoc vet, Animal Health Adv. *Mem:* Am Vet Med Asn; Am Soc Parasitol; Am Soc Trop Med & Hyg; Am Asn Vet Parasitol. *Res:* Canine filariasis; ruminant nematode parasites; anthelmintics; parasitic protozoa; gnotobiology; pathology and pathogenesis of parasites; immunology of parasitism; equine parasitic diseases. *Mailing Add:* RR 3 Box 441 Open Range Rd Crossville TN 38555

BRADLEY, RICHARD E, DENTISTRY, PERIODONTICS. *Current Pos:* CLIN PROF, DEPT SURG SPECIALTIES, COL DETN, UNIV NEBR MED CTR, 90- *Personal Data:* b Omaha, Nebr, Mar 9, 26; m 46, Doris McGowan; c 3. *Educ:* Univ Nebr, BSD, 50, DDS, 52; Univ Iowa, MS, 58. *Prof Exp:* Instr periodont, Univ Iowa, 57-58; asst prof, Creighton Univ, 58-59; asst prof periodont, Col Dent, Univ Nebr, Lincoln, 59-61, assoc prof, 61-65, prof, 65-80, chmn dept, 61-80, dean, Col Dent, 68-80; pres & dean, Baylor Col Dent, Dallas, 80-90. *Concurrent Pos:* Consult, Vet Admin Hosp, Omaha, 60-80, Dallas, 80-90, attend, Vet Admin Hosp, Lincoln, 60-80; cent off consult, Vet Admin, 65-72; mem, Nat Adv Coun Health Professions, Pub Health Serv, 82-86. *Mem:* Am Soc Periodont (secy, 64); Am Acad Periodont; Am Dent Asn; Int Asn Dent Res; AAAS; Sigma Xi. *Res:* Histochemistry of oral enzymology; clinical periodontics. *Mailing Add:* 6424 Crooked Creek Dr Lincoln NE 68516

BRADLEY, ROBERT FOSTER, CHEMICAL ENGINEERING. *Current Pos:* Res engr, Sabine River Works, 65-66, Savannah River Lab, 66-70, res supvr, Savannah River Lab, 70-78, chief supvr, Savannah River Plant, 78-81, res supvr, 81-85, supt, Savannah River Lab, E I du Pont, 86-89, MGR, FACIL SAFETY EVALUATION, WESTINGHOUSE SAVANNAH RIVER CO, 89- *Personal Data:* b Columbia, SC, Mar 26, 40; m 69, Doris McAlpin; c Robert Foster V, Susanne Habershaun & Melrose. *Educ:* Univ SC, BS, 62, MS, 64; Vanderbilt Univ, PhD(chem eng), 66; AMA Exten Inst, cert bus mgt, 80. *Mem:* Am Inst Chem Engrs. *Res:* Reaction kinetics, radiation chemistry, liquid metal distillation, transplutonium process development, safety analyses, near-term and long-term nuclear waste management, large-scale development of nuclear waste vitrification processes; cost-benefit analyses; nuclear safety oversight. *Mailing Add:* 631 Sandhurst Pl Aiken SC 29801

BRADLEY, ROBERT LESTER, JR, DAIRY TECHNOLOGY, FOOD SCIENCE. *Current Pos:* PROF FOOD SCI, UNIV WIS-MADISON, 64- *Personal Data:* b Beverly, Mass, Jan 14, 33; m 91, Karen; c 2. *Educ:* Univ Mass, BS, 58; Mich State Univ, MS, 60, PhD(food sci), 64. *Mem:* Am Dairy Sci Asn; Int Asn Milk, Food & Environ Sanitarians; fel Asn Off Anal Chemists. *Res:* Fate of and antagonism of environmental contaminants in foods on humans and animals; functions of dairy ingredients in food systems. *Mailing Add:* Dept Food Sci Univ Wis 103 Babcock Hall 1605 Linden Dr Madison WI 53706-1519

BRADLEY, ROBERT MARTIN, SENSORY PHYSIOLOGY, DEVELOPMENTAL PHYSIOLOGY. *Current Pos:* from asst prof to assoc prof dent, 72-79, assoc prof physiol, 80-92, PROF DENT, SCH DENT, UNIV MICH, 79-, PROF, DEPT PHYSIOL, 92- *Personal Data:* b Bury, Eng, Oct 15, 39; m 68; c 2. *Educ:* Univ London, BDS, 63; Univ Wash, MSD, 66; Fla State Univ, PhD(biol sci), 70. *Honors & Awards:* Claude Pepper Award, Nat Inst Deafness & Other Commun Dis. *Prof Exp:* House surgeon dent, Royal Dent Hosp, London, 63; house officer, St Marys Hosp, London, 64; res assoc fetal physiol, Nuffield Inst Med Res, Eng, 70-72. *Mem:* Am Physiol Soc; Soc Neurosci; Europ Chemoreceptor Res Orgn; Asn Chemoreception Sci. *Res:* Functional and anatomical development of taste receptors and central taste pathways in fetal and neonatal mammals; central control of salivary secretion; central control of swallowing. *Mailing Add:* Dept Biol & Mat Sci Sch Dent Univ Mich Ann Arbor MI 48109-1078. *Fax:* 313-764-7406

BRADLEY, RONALD JAMES, NEUROPHARMACOLOGY, ELECTROPHYSIOLOGY. *Current Pos:* PROF PSYCHIAT & PHARMACOL, LA STATE UNIV MED CTR, SHREVEPORT, 92- *Personal Data:* b Enniskillen, NIreland, Feb 17, 43; m 66, Doris M Brown; c Nicola M, Jason S & Steven J. *Educ:* Queens Univ, Belfast, BSc, 64; Univ Edinburgh, PhD(psychopharmacol), 67. *Honors & Awards:* AE Bennett Award, Soc Biol Psychiat, 67. *Prof Exp:* Fel, Dept Psychiat, Yale Univ, 67-70, Dept Psychol, Univ NMex, Albuquerque, 70-72; from asst prof to prof psychiat, Univ Ala Sch Med, Birmingham, 72-92. *Concurrent Pos:* Ed, Int Rev Neurobiol, 75- *Mem:* AAAS; Biophys Soc; Neurosci Soc. *Res:* Effects of neurotransmitters on receptor gated ion channels in cultured neuronal cells; mode of action of alcohols and anesthetics on the kinetics of channel opening and closing. *Mailing Add:* Dept Psychiat La State Univ Med Ctr PO Box 33932 Shreveport LA 71130. *Fax:* 318-674-6148

BRADLEY, RONALD W, ADHESIVE FORMULATION, INK FORMULATION. *Current Pos:* Asst chemist, Owens Brockway Glass, 60-62, assoc engr, 62- 64, engr, 64-88, SR ENGR, OWENS BROCKWAY GLASS, 88- *Personal Data:* b Mansfield, Ohio, Nov 11, 36; m 58, Charlene M Bayer; c Paul R & Brad W. *Educ:* Ashland Col, BS, 58. *Concurrent Pos:* Chmn, Test Procedures, Soc Glass Decorators, 70-72, group chmn, 72-76, dir, 80-82. *Mem:* Am Chem Soc; Soc Glass Decorators (treas, 76-80). *Res:* Labeling and decorating of glass bottles; pressure sensitive labeling; electrostatic spraying; pad printing; screen printing; offset printing. *Mailing Add:* 4526 Rambo Lane Toledo OH 43623

BRADLEY, STANLEY EDWARD, MEDICINE. *Current Pos:* from asst prof to prof, Columbia Univ, 47-59, chmn dept, 59-70, Bard prof, 60-78, EMER BARD PROF MED, COL PHYSICIANS & SURGEONS, COLUMBIA UNIV, 78- *Personal Data:* b Columbia, SC, Mar 24, 13; m 36; c Jane E Alavi. *Educ:* Johns Hopkins Univ, AB, 34; Univ Md, MD, 38. *Hon Degrees:* Dr, Univ Strasbourg, 78. *Honors & Awards:* Gibbs Prize, NY Acad Med, 47; Distinguished Achievement Award, Am Asn Study Liver Dis, 93. *Prof Exp:* Intern, Univ Hosp, Baltimore, 38-40; instr med, Sch Med, Boston Univ, 42-45, asst prof, 45-47. *Concurrent Pos:* Commonwealth Fund fel, Col Med, NY Univ, 40-42; asst clin vis physician, Bellevue Hosp, New York, 40-42; asst vis physician, Evans Mem Hosp, Mass, 42-47 & Presby Hosp, New York, 47-51, assoc vis physician, 51-59, dir med serv, 59-70, attend physician, 59-78, consult, 78-; ed-in-chief, J Clin Invest, 52-57; mem bd sci consult, Sloan Kettering Inst, 62-72; trustee, Mt Desert Island Lab, 71-81; vis prof clin pharmacol, Univ Bern, 78-90. *Mem:* Asn Am Physicians; Am Soc Clin Invest (pres, 57); Am Physiol Soc; fel Am Acad Arts & Sci; Soc Exp Biol & Med; Am Heart Asn; fel AAAS. *Res:* Normal pathologic physiology of the kidney and liver; hemodynamic adjustments; water movement through soils and lakes. *Mailing Add:* 200 N Wynnewood Ave A516 Wynnewood PA 19096-1426

BRADLEY, STERLING GAYLEN, MICROBIOLOGY & IMMUNOTOXICOLOGY, BIOTECHNOLOGY. *Current Pos:* VPRES ACAD AFFAIRS, UNIV MD, BIOTECH INST, 96- *Personal Data:* b Springfield, Mo, Apr 2, 32; m 51, 74, Judith Schneider; c Don, John, Phillip, Evelyn & Kevin. *Educ:* Southwest Mo State Univ, BA & BS, 50; Northwestern Univ, MS, 52, PhD(biol), 54. *Honors & Awards:* Charles Porter Award, Soc Indust Microbiol, 82. *Prof Exp:* Instr biol, Northwestern Univ, 54; from instr to assoc prof microbiol, Univ Minn, 56-63, prof microbiol & genetics, 63-68; chmn microbiol, Va Commonwealth Univ, 68-82, dean basic health sci, 82-93, prof microbiol, 68-96, prof pharmacol, 79-96. *Concurrent Pos:* Eli Lilly fel, Univ Wis-Madison, 54-55, NSF fel, 55-56; consult, Upjohn Co, 60-68, Minneapolis Vet Admin Hosp, 61-68 & E R Squibb & Sons, 69-76; mem coun, Soc Exp Biol & Med, 64-66 & Am Soc Microbiol, 68-74; mem exec bd, Int Comt Syst Bacteria, 66-74; mem & chmn bd sci counr, Nat Inst Allergy & Infectious Dis, 68-72; ed, Am Soc Microbiol, 70-77; coordr proj 3, US/USSR Joint Working Group Microbiol, 79-82; pres, US Fed Cult Collections, 84-86; pres, Found Immunotoxicol, 90-; bd trustees, SE Univ Res Asn, 90-93. *Mem:* Soc Indust Microbiol (pres, 64-65); Am Asn Immunol; fel AAAS; Am Acad Microbiol; Soc Exp Biol & Med; Soc Toxicol; Am Soc Microbiol (treas, 85-91); Am Soc Pharmacol & Exp Therapeut. *Res:* Proteases and protease inhibitors; biology of actinomycetes and actinophages; regulation of cellular phenotype; immunotoxicology; pathophysiology of ameboflagellates. *Mailing Add:* 178 Crescent Dr Hershey PA 17033. *Fax:* 301-403-4440; *E-Mail:* bradley@umbi.umd.edu

BRADLEY, STEVEN ARTHUR, MATERIALS SCIENCE ENGINEERING. *Current Pos:* RES SCIENTIST, UOP, INC, 84- *Personal Data:* b Chicago, Ill, Sept 21, 49; m; c 1. *Educ:* Northwestern Univ, BS, 70, PhD(mat sci), 75; Roosevelt Univ, MBA, 79. *Prof Exp:* Res mat scientist, Universal Oil Prod, Inc, 74-76, group leader, 76-81, res mgr, 81-84. *Concurrent Pos:* Instr, Sch Bus, Roosevelt Univ, 79-; co-organizer, Frontiers Electron Micros in Mat Sci meetings & co-ed proceedings. *Mem:* Am Soc Metals; Am Chem Soc; Nat Asn Corrosion Engrs; Am Soc Testing Mat; Sigma Xi; Electron Micros Soc Am; Am Ceramics Soc. *Res:* New product development in materials development areas; materials testing and analysis including materials failure analyses; catalyst development; ceramics and composites; application of electron microscopy for characterizing ceramics, catalysts, and metals; polymer characterization. *Mailing Add:* UOP 50 E Algonquin Rd Des Plaines IL 60017

BRADLEY, TED RAY, PLANT TAXONOMY, ECOLOGY. *Current Pos:* Asst prof, 67-74, ASSOC PROF BIOL, GEORGE MASON UNIV, 74- *Personal Data:* b Kansas City, Mo, Feb 1, 40. *Educ:* Rollins Col, BS, 62; Univ NC, MA, 66, PhD(plant taxon), 67. *Mem:* Am Soc Plant Taxon. *Res:* Evolution of the genus Triodanis, especially hybridization between species. *Mailing Add:* Dept Biol George Mason Univ 4400 University Dr Fairfax VA 22030-4443

BRADLEY, THOMAS BERNARD, JR, internal medicine, hematology, for more information see previous edition

BRADLEY, TIMOTHY JUD, INSECT PHYSIOLOGY, COMPARATIVE PHYSIOLOGY. *Current Pos:* from asst prof to assoc prof, 79-90, PROF, DEPT ECOL & EVOLUTIONARY BIOL, UNIV CALIF, IRVINE, 90- *Personal Data:* b Colorado City, Tex, Mar 12, 48; m 92; c 5. *Educ:* Vanderbilt Univ, BA, 71; Univ Okla, MS, 73; Univ BC, Can, PhD(zool), 76. *Mem:* Fel AAAS; Am Soc Zoologists; Am Physiol Soc; Am Mosquito Control Asn; Soc Vector Ecologists. *Res:* Comparative physiology, particularly aspects of epithelial function, ion transport and energy metabolism; evolution of physiological systems and the role of an organisms physiology in its ecology. *Mailing Add:* Dept Ecol & Evolutionary Biol Univ Calif Irvine CA 92717

BRADLEY, W(ILLIAM) E(ARLE), ENGINEERING PHYSICS. *Current Pos:* CONSULT, 73- *Personal Data:* b Pa, Jan 7, 13; wid; c 2. *Educ:* Univ Pa, BS, 35. *Prof Exp:* Res engr, Philco Corp, 37-59, tech dir res div, 46-59; assoc dir res, Inst Defense Anal, 59-63, asst vpres, 63-69; pres, Puredesal, Inc, 70-73. *Concurrent Pos:* Mem subcomts, Nat TV Syst Comt; consult to White House, 57-62 & Dept of Defense, 57-; consult, NASA, 80-81; mem, subcomt technol innovation, bd sci & technol int develop, Nat Acad Sci, 81-83. *Mem:* Fel Inst Elec & Electronics Engrs; AAAS; Franklin Inst. *Res:* Color television; microwave systems; physical optics; electron optics; transistors and related semiconducting devices; communications; physical chemistry; water desalination. *Mailing Add:* Willow Hill Farm 5151 Ridge Rd RFD 2 New Hope PA 18938

BRADLEY, WALTER L, FRACTURE & FAILURE ANALYSIS, MECHANICAL PROPERTIES. *Current Pos:* PROF MECH ENG, TEX A&M UNIV, 76- *Personal Data:* b Dec 27, 43; m 65, Carol A James; c Sharon (Perry) & Steven W. *Educ:* Univ Tex, Austin, BS, 65, PhD(mat sci), 68. *Prof Exp:* From asst prof to assoc prof metall eng, Colo Sch Mines, 68-76. *Mem:* Fel Am Soc Mat; Am Soc Mech Engrs; Am Soc Testing & Mat; Am Soc Plastics Engrs. *Res:* Micromechanisms of fracture in metals, plastics and composites; characterization of fracture toughness in materials, relationship of chemical bonding and microstructure to mechanical properties, failure analysis. *Mailing Add:* Mech Eng Tex A&M Univ College Station TX 77843-3123. *Fax:* 409-845-3081; *E-Mail:* wlb3621@zeus.tamu.edu

BRADLEY, WILLIAM CRANE, GEOLOGY. *Current Pos:* RETIRED. *Personal Data:* b Madison, Wis, Feb 22, 25; m 58, Alice L Babcock; c Cameron, Melanie & Mark. *Educ:* Univ Wis, BS, 51; Stanford Univ, MS, 53, PhD(geol), 56. *Honors & Awards:* Distinguished Career Award, Geol Soc Am, 94. *Prof Exp:* From instr to prof geol, Univ Colo, Boulder, 55-89, chmn dept, 68-72. *Concurrent Pos:* Res scientist, Univ Tex, 65-66; vis lectr, Univ Adelaide, S Australia, 73-74, Univ Wales, Aberystwyth, 82-83. *Mem:* Geol Soc Am; Colo Sci Soc. *Res:* Geomorphology of coasts, rivers, and weathering. *Mailing Add:* 2885 16th St Boulder CO 80304-3527

BRADLEY, WILLIAM ROBINSON, industrial hygiene, toxicology, for more information see previous edition

BRADLEY, WILLIAM W(HITNEY), METALLURGY. *Current Pos:* RETIRED. *Personal Data:* b Brooklyn, Iowa, Nov 9, 22; m 49, Betty L Hickle; c Marilyn J, William A (deceased), Carol A, Katherine A & Margaret I. *Educ:* Univ Chicago, BS, 44; Univ Colo, BS, 48, MS, 49; Mass Inst Technol, ScD, 65. *Prof Exp:* Asst res engr, Univ Colo, 48-49; mem tech staff, Bell Tel Labs, 49-61; Ford fel, Mass Inst Technol, 61-64; assoc prof civil eng, Clark Univ, 64-86. *Mem:* Am Soc Eng Educ; Electrochem Soc; Sigma Xi. *Res:* Environmental deterioration of materials; corrosion of metals; materials science. *Mailing Add:* 115 Market St Potsdam NY 13676

BRADLOW, HERBERT LEON, ORGANIC, BIOLOGICAL CHEMISTRY, ENDOCRINOLOGY CANCER & CHEMO PREVENTION. *Current Pos:* PROF DEPT SURG, CORNELL UNIV MED SCH, 91- *Personal Data:* b Philadelphia, Pa, Mar 21, 24; m 47, Hattie Gottlieb; c Ellen, Jarel & Alec.

Educ: Univ Pa, BS, 45; Univ Kans, MS, 47, PhD(chem), 49. *Prof Exp:* Fel, Univ Calif, 49-50; assoc, Sloan Kettering Cancer Inst, 63-77; prof biochem, Albert Einstein Col Med, 71-77; prof, Rockefeller Univ Hosp, 77-89. *Concurrent Pos:* Assoc prof biochem, Albert Einstein Col Med, 68-71; adj assoc prof, Rockefeller Univ, 71-74, adj prof, 74- *Mem:* Am Chem Soc; Am Soc Biol Chemists; Endocrine Soc; Brit Soc Endocrinol; Royal Soc Chem; Am Asn Cancer Res; Am Asn Canccer Prev. *Res:* Fluoraromatic compounds; cholesterol metabolism; steroid hormone metabolism; endocrinology; cancer research; chemo prevention. *Mailing Add:* 86-25 Palo Alto St Holliswood NY 11423. *Fax:* 212-746-5413; *E-Mail:* leon@rockrux.rockefeller.edu

BRADNER, HUGH, EXPERIMENTAL PHYSICS, GEOPHYSICS. *Current Pos:* prof, 64-80, RES PHYSICIST, INST GEOPHYS & PLANETARY PHYSICS, UNIV CALIF, SAN DIEGO, 61-, EMER PROF ENG PHYSICS & GEOPHYS, 80- *Personal Data:* b Tonopah, Nev, Nov 5, 15; m 43, Marjorie Hall; c Barbara C (Cornet). *Educ:* Miami Univ, AB, 36; Calif Inst Technol, PhD(physics), 41. *Hon Degrees:* DSc, Miami Univ, 61. *Prof Exp:* Mem res dept, Champion Paper & Fiber Co, 36-37; asst, Calif Inst Technol, 39-41; mem res staff design & test magnetic mines, US Naval Ord Lab, Wash, 41-43; mem res staff, Manhattan Dist, Los Alamos, NMex, 43-46 & Radiation Lab, Univ Calif, Berkeley, 46-61. *Concurrent Pos:* Var consult civilian & mil. *Mem:* Fel Am Phys Soc; Seismol Soc Am; Am Geophys Union. *Res:* High energy physics; applied engineering physics; malacology. *Mailing Add:* 0225 Inst Geophys & Planetary Physics Univ Calif San Diego La Jolla CA 92093. *Fax:* 619-534-5332, 459-0657; *E-Mail:* hbradner@ucsd.edu

BRADNER, MEAD, ENGINEERING, ENGINEERING MECHANICS. *Current Pos:* CONSULT, 84- *Personal Data:* b Tonopah, Nev, Sept 23, 14; m 43; c 6. *Educ:* Mass Inst Technol, SB, 38. *Prof Exp:* Res physicist, Champion Paper & Fibre Co, Ohio, 35-36; student, Foxboro Co, 37 & R R Donnelley & Sons, Ill, 38-40; contract employee, Naval Ord Lab, 40-43; consult engr, Westinghouse Elec Co, Pa, 43-45; res engr, Foxboro Corp, 45-50, res dir, 50-62, int eng coordr, 62-68, tech dir res, develop & eng, 66-71, mkt planner, 71-73, tech consult, 73-77, tech dir ideas, 77-84. *Mem:* AAAS; fel Am Soc Mech Engrs; fel Instrument Soc Am; Am Nat Stand Inst. *Res:* Industrial instruments; underwater ordnance. *Mailing Add:* 30 Water St Foxboro MA 02035

BRADNER, WILLIAM TURNBULL, BACTERIOLOGY, ONCOLOGY. *Current Pos:* sr res scientist cancer chemother screening, Bristol Labs, Bristol-Myers, 58-65, asst dir pharmacol res, 65-73, asst dir microbiol res, 73-77, dir antitumor biol dept, 77-85, dir admin preclin anticancer res, 85-86, PRES RES ADV, BRISTOL-MYERS, 87- *Personal Data:* b NJ, Aug 16, 24; m 51; c 3. *Educ:* Lehigh Univ, BA, 48, MS, 49, PhD(bact), 52. *Prof Exp:* Assoc bact, Brown Univ, 53-55; asst mem exp chemother, Sloan Kettering Inst, 55-58. *Concurrent Pos:* Assoc, Med Col, Cornell Univ, 56-58, asst prof bact, 58; consult, cancer res. *Mem:* AAAS; Am Asn Cancer Res; NY Acad Sci; Am Soc Clin Oncol. *Res:* Amoebicidal agents; bacterial associates of Endamoeba histolytica; bacteriology of radiation infection; in vivo screening of antitumor agents, host defense against cancer; experimental cancer chemotherapy toxicity of anticancer drugs; clinical development of cancer drugs. *Mailing Add:* 4903 Briarwood Circle Manlius NY 13104

BRADSHAW, AUBREY SWIFT, fresh water ecology; deceased, see previous edition for last biography

BRADSHAW, GAY, MATHEMATICAL ECOLOGY, SPATIAL STATISTICS. *Current Pos:* ASST PROF, DEPT FOREST SCI, ORE STATE UNIV, 91-; RES MATHEMATICIAN, USDA FOREST SERV, 91- *Educ:* Univ Calif, Santa Barbara, BA, 78; Stanford Univ, MSc, 86; Ore State Univ, PhD(forest ecol), 91. *Res:* Mathematical ecology; spatial statistics. *Mailing Add:* Forest Sci Lab 3200 SW Jefferson Way Corvallis OR 97333

BRADSHAW, GORDON VAN RENSSELAER, MAMMALOGY. *Current Pos:* prof, 61-80, chairperson dept, 76-80, EMER PROF BIOL, PHOENIX COL, 80- *Personal Data:* b Kansas City, Mo, Aug 8, 31; m 53; c 2. *Educ:* Cent Mo State Col, BS, 53; Kans State Univ, MS, 56; Univ Ariz, PhD(zool), 61. *Prof Exp:* Asst prof biol, The Citadel, 60-61. *Mem:* AAAS; Am Soc Mammal; Sigma Xi. *Res:* Natural history of southwestern bats. *Mailing Add:* HC 63 Box 5655 Mayer AZ 86333-9802

BRADSHAW, JERALD SHERWIN, ORGANIC CHEMISTRY. *Current Pos:* assoc prof chem, Brigham Young Univ, 66-73, asst chmn, 80-86, prof, 73-93, REED M IZATT PROF CHEM, BRIGHAM YOUNG UNIV, 93- *Personal Data:* b Cedar City, Utah, Nov 28, 32; m 54, Karen Lee; c Donna & Melinda. *Educ:* Univ Utah, BS, 55; Univ Calif, Los Angeles, PhD(chem), 63. *Honors & Awards:* Maeser Res Award, Brigham Young Univ, 77; Utah Award, Am Chem Soc, 89; Medal for Sci & Technol, Utah Gov, 91; Nat Award Separations Sci & Technol, Am Chem Soc, 96. *Prof Exp:* NFS fel, Calif Inst Tech, 62-63; chemist, Chevron Res Co, 63-66. *Concurrent Pos:* Nat Acad Sci exchange prof, Univ Ljubljana, Yugoslavia, 72-73; chem res, Univ Sheffield, Eng, 78; Sigma Xi ann lectr, Brigham Young Univ, 88; Nat Sci Exchange Prof, James Cook Univ, Townsville, Australia, 88. *Mem:* Am Chem Soc; Int Soc Heterocyclic Chem. *Res:* Synthesis and complexation properties of macrocyclic compounds; synthesis of polysiloxane stationaty phases for capillary gas and supercritical fluid chromatography. *Mailing Add:* 1244 E 2300 N Provo UT 84604. *Fax:* 801-378-5474

BRADSHAW, JOHN ALDEN, ELECTROPHYSICS. *Current Pos:* CONSULT, 78- *Personal Data:* b Ann Arbor, Mich, Dec 9, 19. *Educ:* Harvard Univ, BA, 41, MS, 48, PhD(electrophysics), 54. *Prof Exp:* Res assoc, Res Lab, Gen Elec Co, 54-62; assoc prof elec eng, Rensselaer Polytech Inst, 62-78. *Mem:* AAAS; Am Asn Physics Teachers; sr mem Inst Elec & Electronics Engrs; Am Solar Energy Soc. *Res:* Electron beam dynamics; wave propagation in overmoded guides and plasma; microwave scattering from waveguide obstacles. *Mailing Add:* 223 Green St Schenectady NY 12305-1401

BRADSHAW, JOHN STRATLII, BIOLOGICAL OCEANOGRAPHY. *Current Pos:* ASSOC PROF BIOL, UNIV SAN DIEGO, 67- *Personal Data:* b High Wycombe, Eng, Oct 15, 27; nat US; m 48; c 4. *Educ:* San Diego State Col, BS, 50; Univ Calif, MS & PhD(oceanog), 58. *Prof Exp:* Jr res biologist, Scripps Inst Oceanog, Univ Calif, San Diego, 58-67. *Mem:* Am Soc Limnol & Oceanog; Ecol Soc Am; Sigma Xi. *Res:* Ecology of recent foraminifera and coastal lagoons; physiological ecology. *Mailing Add:* 308 Camino Califia San Marcos CA 92069

BRADSHAW, MARTIN DANIEL, ELECTRICAL ENGINEERING. *Current Pos:* from asst prof to assoc prof elec eng, 63-76, asst dean, Col Eng, 74-76, PROF ELEC & COMPUT ENG, UNIV NMEX, 76- *Personal Data:* b Pittsburg, Kans, June 24, 36; m 83; c 3. *Educ:* Univ Wichita, BS, 58, MS, 61; Carnegie Inst Technol, PhD(elec eng), 64. *Honors & Awards:* Western Elec Fund Award, Gulf-Southwest Sect, Am Soc Eng Educ, 69; George Westinghouse Award, Am Soc Eng Educ, 73. *Prof Exp:* Jr engr, Boeing Airplane Co, Kans, 58-59, res engr, 61; instr elec eng, Univ Wichita, 59-61; asst, Carnegie Inst Technol, 61-63. *Concurrent Pos:* Engr, State Elec Comn, Victoria, Australia, 78. *Mem:* Sr mem Inst Elec & Electronics Engrs. *Res:* Electromagnetic fields; antennas; electric power; large scale systems; effective teaching techniques; large scale systems with particular emphasis on electromagnetic fields and electric power systems; application of diakoptics techniques to solution of electromagnetics problems. *Mailing Add:* EE Prob Solvers PO Box 786 Placitas NM 87043

BRADSHAW, PETER, AERODYNAMICS, ENGINEERING. *Current Pos:* THOMAS V JONES PROF ENG, STANFORD UNIV, 88- *Personal Data:* b Torquay, Eng, Dec 26, 35; m 59, 68, Sheila Dorothy Brown. *Educ:* Cambridge Univ, Eng, BA, 57. *Hon Degrees:* DSc, Exeter Univ, Eng, 90. *Honors & Awards:* Bronze Medal, Royal Aeronaut Soc, 71; Busk Prize, 72; Fluid Dynamics Award, Am Inst Aeronaut & Astronaut, 94. *Prof Exp:* Sci officer, Nat Physics Lab, Teddington, Eng, 57-69; prof, Imp Col Sci & Technol, London, 69-88. *Res:* Author of several books and nearly 200 journal articles on aerodynamics. *Mailing Add:* Dept Mech Eng Stanford Univ Stanford CA 94305

BRADSHAW, RALPH ALDEN, BIOCHEMISTRY. *Current Pos:* PROF & CHMN, DEPT BIOL CHEM, UNIV CALIF, IRVINE, 82- *Personal Data:* b Boston, Mass, Feb 14, 41; m 61; c 2. *Educ:* Colby Col, BA, 62; Duke Univ, PhD(biochem), 66. *Honors & Awards:* Gold Medal, Ital Nat Res Coun, 87. *Prof Exp:* Res assoc biochem, Ind Univ, 66-67; sr fel, dept biochem, Univ Wash, Seattle, 67-68, actg res asst prof, 68-69; from asst prof to prof, dept biol chem, Wash Univ, St Louis, 69-82. *Concurrent Pos:* USPHS fel chem, Ind Univ, 66-67; USPHS fel, Univ Wash, 67-68; USPHS career res develop award, 70-74; Physiol Chem Study Sect, NIH, 75-79, chmn, 78-79, Biomed Sci Study Sect, 80-85; sci adv bd, Hereditary Dis Found, 83-87; Coun Thrombosis, Am Heart Asn, 84-86; external adv bd, Cleveland Clin Prog Hypertension, 85-88; Nat Comt Biochem, Nat Acad Sci-Nat Res Coun, 87-; vis scientist, Univ Zurich, 69; vis lectr, Duke Univ Marine Sta, Beaufort, NC, 72, Univ Sydney, New S Wales, Australia, 77, Univ Ky, 87 & Univ Camerino, Italy, 87; Josiah Macy fac scholar, Howard Florey Inst, Univ Melbourne, 77-78; consult, Durrum Chem Co, Dionex Corp, Sunnyvale, Calif, 70-78, Cortex Pharmaceut, Irvine, Calif, 87-; sci adv, Int Genetic Eng, Santa Monica, Calif, 82-89; sci adv bd, Nucleic Acid Res Inst-ICN, Costa Mesa, Calif, 86-87, bd dirs, 86-91. *Mem:* fel AAAS; Am Chem Soc; NY Acad Sci; Am Soc Biol Chem; Am Soc Neurochem; Sigma Xi; Endocrine Soc; Am Soc Cell Biol; Soc Neurosci; Int Soc Neurochem; Protein Soc (pres, 86-87). *Res:* Structure-function relationships in proteins and enzymes; chemistry of growth factors and related hormones. *Mailing Add:* Dept Biochem Rm D240 Col Med Univ Calif Irvine CA 92717-1700. *Fax:* 714-856-8036

BRADSHAW, SAMUEL LOCKWOOD, JR, PSYCHIATRY. *Current Pos:* staff psychiatrist, 72-75, asst chief, 75-77, CHIEF PSYCHIAT, VET ADMIN HOSP, TOPEKA, KANS, 77- *Personal Data:* b Columbus, Ohio, Jan 30, 37; m 61; c 2. *Educ:* Univ Southern Calif, BM, 58, MD, 65; Univ Ill, MM, 54. *Prof Exp:* Intern med, Univ Calif, Los Angeles, 65-66; resident psychiat, Menninger Sch Psychiat, 69-72. *Concurrent Pos:* Dir interdisciplinary students, Menninger Sch Psychiat, 72-74, dir spec student prog, dir med student prog & fac mem, 72- *Mem:* Am Psychiat Asn; AAAS. *Res:* Effects of the use of names on attitudes of hospital employees; the effect of a hospital milieu. *Mailing Add:* Vet Admin Hosp 2200 Gage Blvd Topeka KS 66622

BRADSHAW, WILLARD HENRY, MICROBIOLOGY. *Current Pos:* asst prof, 61-65, assoc prof bact, 65-80, ASSOC PROF MICROBIOL, BRIGHAM YOUNG UNIV, 80- *Personal Data:* b Orem, Utah, Feb 11, 25. *Educ:* Brigham Young Univ, BS, 52, MS, 53; Univ Calif, Berkeley, PhD(comp biochem), 57. *Prof Exp:* Asst biochem, Univ Calif, 56-57; res assoc, Univ Ill, 57-59; res asst, Brigham Young Univ, 59-60; sr biochemist, Wallace Labs, 60-61. *Concurrent Pos:* Hon lectr, Stanford Univ, 67-68. *Mem:* Am Soc Microbiol; Am Chem Soc; Brit Soc Gen Microbiol. *Res:* Microbial metabolism and physiology; microbial genetics; enzyme chemistry. *Mailing Add:* 1318 Lakeview Dr Provo UT 84604

BRADSHAW, WILLIAM EMMONS, POPULATION BIOLOGY, EVOLUTION. *Current Pos:* from asst prof to assoc prof, 71-84, res assoc, Tall Timbers Res Sta, 77-78, PROF BIOL, UNIV ORE, 84- *Personal Data:* b Orange, NJ, May 16, 42; m 71, Christina M Holzapfel; c Pilar A. *Educ:* Princeton Univ, AB, 64; Univ Mich, MS, 65, PhD(zool), 69. *Honors & Awards:* Guggenheim & Fulbright Awards. *Prof Exp:* NIH res fel, Harvard Univ, 69-71. *Concurrent Pos:* Guggenheim fel, 86; Fulbright Grantee, 86; acad vis, Imp Col, Silwood Park, 86. *Mem:* Am Soc Naturalists; Ecol Soc Am; Entom Soc Am; Am Mosquito Control Asn; Soc Study Evolution; Genetics Soc Am. *Res:* Population, behavioral and community ecology; photoperiodism and seasonal development; biogeography insect diapause; mosquito ecology and physiology; life history evolution. *Mailing Add:* 1210 Dept Biol Univ Ore Eugene OR 97403-1210. *Fax:* 541-346-2364

BRADSHAW, WILLIAM NEWMAN, ENVIRONMENTAL ENGINEERING, SCIENCE ADMINISTRATION. *Current Pos:* RETIRED. *Personal Data:* b Louisville, Ky, Nov 2, 28; m 56; c 2. *Educ:* Austin Col, BA, 51; Univ Tex, MA, 56, PhD, 62. *Prof Exp:* Asst prof biol, McMurry Col, 57-61; lectr zool, Univ Tex, 61; from asst prof to prof, WVa Univ, 62-76, dir environ biol prog, 67-71; environ scientist & proj mgr, Stearns-Roger Eng Corp, 76-84, prin environ scientist, Stearns Catalytic Corp, 84-86, prin environ scientist, Stearns-Roger Div, United Engrs & Constructors Inc, 86-89; environ proj supvr, Western Opers, United Engrs & Constructors Inc, 89. *Concurrent Pos:* Vis assoc prof, M D Anderson Hosp & Tumor Inst, Univ Tex, 70-71; NIH spec res fel, 70-71; dir, Acad Assocs Inc, 73-76. *Mem:* Nat Asn Environ Prof; Am Soc Mammal; Sigma Xi; Ecol Soc Am. *Res:* Population biology and ecology; cytogenetics, speciation and behavior; terrestial, wildlife ecology, impact analysis and pollution abatement. *Mailing Add:* 4705 S Huron Englewood CO 80110-6438

BRADSHAW, WILLIAM S, BIOCHEMISTRY, DEVELOPMENTAL BIOLOGY. *Current Pos:* assoc prof, 70-85, PROF ZOOL, BRIGHAM YOUNG UNIV, 85- *Personal Data:* b Salt Lake City, Utah, Oct 29, 37; m 61; c 5. *Educ:* Harvard Univ, AB, 63; Univ Ill, PhD(biochem), 68. *Prof Exp:* Res fel, Biol Div, US AEC, Oak Ridge Nat Lab, 68-70. *Mem:* Soc Develop Biol. *Res:* Biochemistry of development; biochemical effects of environmental teratogens; synthesis of pancreatic enzymes during development; early immediate genes in RSV infected cells. *Mailing Add:* Dept Zool Brigham Young Univ Provo UT 84602

BRADSHER, CHARLES KILGO, ORGANIC CHEMISTRY. *Current Pos:* from instr to prof, Duke Univ, 39-65, chmn dept, 65-70, James B Duke prof, 65-79, EMER JAMES B DUKE PROF CHEM, DUKE UNIV, 79- *Personal Data:* b Petersburg, Va, July 13, 12; m 38, Dorothy Tideman; c Thorston, Catherine (Dunnagan) & Marien. *Educ:* Duke Univ, AB, 33; Harvard Univ, AM, 35, PhD(org chem), 37. *Honors & Awards:* Herty Medal Award, Am Chem Soc, (Ga Sect), 87. *Prof Exp:* Rohm & Haas fel, Univ Ill, 37-38, du Pont fel, 38. *Concurrent Pos:* Nat Res fel, 41-42; Fulbright lectr, State Univ Leiden, 51-52; NSF sr fel, Swiss Fed Inst Technol, 59-60. *Mem:* Am Chem Soc; Chem Soc London. *Res:* Aromatic cyclodehydration; quinolizinium derivatives; cationic polar cycloaddition. *Mailing Add:* Gross Chem Lab Duke Univ Durham NC 27706

BRADT, HALE VAN DORN, X-RAY ASTRONOMY. *Current Pos:* From instr to assoc prof, 61-72, PROF PHYSICS, MASS INST TECHNOL, 72- *Personal Data:* b Colfax, Wash, Dec 7, 30; m 58; c 2. *Educ:* Princeton Univ, AB, 52; Mass Inst Technol, PhD(physics), 61. *Concurrent Pos:* Assoc ed, Astrophys J Lett, 73-76. *Mem:* Am Phys Soc; Am Astron Soc. *Res:* X-ray astronomy. *Mailing Add:* 30 Clover St Belmont MA 02178

BRADT, PATRICIA THORNTON, AQUATIC ECOLOGY. *Current Pos:* DONNA & DAVID LONG PROF ENVIRON SCI, MUHLENBERG COL, 96- *Personal Data:* b Philadelphia, Pa, Oct 4, 30; m 52; c 3. *Educ:* Cornell Univ, BA, 52; Lehigh Univ, MS, 70, PhD(biol), 74. *Prof Exp:* Technician, Dept Gynec & Obstet, Med Sch, Yale Univ, 53-55; teaching asst bot, biol & ecol, Lehigh Univ, 73-74, asst prof, 74-77, adj asst prof, 77-81; prin investr, Liv Lakes, Inc, 87-90; res scientist, Dept Nat Resources, Cornell Univ, 84-88, res assoc, 90-91; prin res scientist, Lehigh Univ, 90-96. *Concurrent Pos:* Lectr intro biol & ecol, Lafayette Col, 75-79; prin investr, Off Water Res & Technol, US Dept Interior, 76-77; comt mem, Air & Water Tech Adv Comt, Pa Dept Environ Resources, 79-; consult, Environ Resources Mgt, Inc, 80-82; adj fac assoc, Ctr Social Res, Lehigh Univ, 80-, adj assoc prof, 81-84; environ sci fel, AAAS, 85; res consult, US Man & Biosphere, Human Dominated Systs Directorate, 90-; vis prof, Muhlenberg Col, 92- *Mem:* Fel AAAS; Sigma Xi; Asn Women Sci; NAm Benthological Soc; Am Inst Biol Sci. *Res:* Study of freshwater ecosystems; benthic macroinvertebrate fauna; water chemistry and relation to all components of ecosystem; impact of pesticides on freshwater ecosystems; effect of acid precipitation on freshwater organisms and water chemistry; biological responses to nutrient loadings. *Mailing Add:* Dept Biol Muhlenberg Col 2400 Chew St Allentown PA 18104. *E-Mail:* bradt@hal.muhlberg.edu

BRADT, RICHARD CARL, PHYSICAL CERAMICS, MATERIALS SCIENCE. *Current Pos:* DEAN, MACKAY SCH MINES, UNIV NEV, 89- *Personal Data:* b St Louis, Mo, Nov 17, 38; m 60; c 2. *Educ:* Mass Inst Technol, BSc, 60; Rensselaer Polytech Inst, MS, 65, PhD(mat eng), 67. *Honors & Awards:* R M Fulrath Award, 80; T J Planje Award, 88. *Prof Exp:* Res metallurgist, Fansteel Metall Corp, 60-62, ceramist, V-R/Wesson Div, 62-63; res fel mat eng, Rensselaer Polytech Inst, 63-67; from asst prof to prof ceramic sci, Pa State Univ, 67-78, head, Mat Sci & Eng, 78-83; head, Dept Mat Sci & Eng, Univ Wash, 83-86, Kyocera prof ceramics, 86-89. *Mem:* Fel Am Ceramic Soc; Am Soc Metals; Am Inst Mining, Metall & Petrol Engrs; Brit Ceramic Soc; Sigma Xi; Am Asn Univ Professors; Am Soc Eng Educ; Am Soc Testing & Mat; Mat Res Soc; Mineral Soc Am; Nat Inst Ceramic Engrs; Int Acad Ceramics. *Res:* Diffusion, sintering, electrical and mechanical properties and the transmission electron microscopy of ceramics, composite materials and cutting tool materials. *Mailing Add:* Dept Metallurgical & Mat Sci Univ Ala Box 870202 Tuscaloosa AL 35487

BRADWAY, KEITH E, PULP & PAPER TECHNOLOGY, ORGANIC CHEMISTRY. *Current Pos:* RETIRED. *Personal Data:* b Indianapolis, Ind, Dec 31, 26; m 50, Rita D Godschalx; c Daniel, Thomas, Patricia & Barbara. *Educ:* Purdue Univ, BSChE, 48; Inst Paper Chem, MS, 50, PhD(org chem), 53. *Honors & Awards:* Hugh D Camp Award, 68. *Prof Exp:* Res chemist, Camp Mfg Co, NJ, 53-54, asst tech dir, 54-56, supt process eng, Union Bag Camp Paper Corp, 56-60, tech control, 60-62, res scientist, 62-77, sr scientist, Union Camp Corp, NJ, 77-91. *Mem:* Am Tech Asn Pulp & Paper Indust. *Res:* Technology of manufacture of white papers, unbleached paper and paperboard, with emphasis on printability and opacity of white papers and converting characteristics of unbleached products. *Mailing Add:* 8044 N State Rd 135 Morgantown IN 46160

BRADY, ALLAN JORDAN, BIOPHYSICS. *Current Pos:* advan res fel, Los Angeles County Heart Asn Cardiovasc Res Lab, Med Ctr, 58-60, estab investr, 60-65, assoc prof in residence, Sch Med, 62-66, PROF PHYSIOL, SCH MED, UNIV CALIF, LOS ANGELES, 66-, CAREER DEVELOP AWARDS, LOS ANGELES COUNTY HEART ASN CARDIOVASC RES LAB, MED CTR, 65- *Personal Data:* b Fairview, Utah, May 23, 27; m 52; c 2. *Educ:* Univ Utah, BA, 51, MS, 52; Univ Wash, PhD(biophys), 56. *Prof Exp:* Asst physiol & biophys, Sch Med, Univ Wash, 55-56, Am Heart Asn fel, 56-57; Am Heart Asn fel, Physiol Lab, Univ Cambridge, 57-58. *Concurrent Pos:* Mem basic sci exec comt, Am Heart Asn, 62- *Mem:* Biophys Soc; Am Physiol Soc. *Res:* Electrical and ionic basis of single fiber activity; excitation-contraction coupling; muscle mechanics. *Mailing Add:* Dept Chem & Biochem Univ Tex Austin TX 78712-1167

BRADY, ALLEN H, MATHEMATICS, COMPUTER SCIENCES. *Current Pos:* assoc res prof comput sci, Desert Res Inst, Univ Nev Reno, 68-69, asst dir acad uses, Comput Ctr, Univ Syst, 69-79, prof math, 79-85, prof, 85-94, chair comput sci, 91-94, PROF EMER COMPUT SCI, UNIV NEV, RENO, 94- *Personal Data:* b Sewal, Iowa, Mar 17, 34; m 59, Yvonne C Gates; c 3. *Educ:* Univ Colo, BS, 56; Univ Wyo, MS, 59; Ore State Univ, PhD(math), 65. *Prof Exp:* Jr engr, Mat Res Lab, Collins Radio Co, Calif, 55; physicist, Cent Radio Propagation Lab, Nat Bur Standards, Colo, 56-64; asst prof comput sci, Univ Notre Dame, 65-66; dir, Comput Data Processing Ctr, Ball State Univ, 66-68. *Concurrent Pos:* Vis prof comput sci, Am Univ, Cairo, 85-87. *Mem:* Math Asn Am; Asn Comput Mach; Inst Elec & Electronics Engrs; Sigma Xi. *Res:* Artificial intelligence; turing computability; computer organization. *Mailing Add:* Dept Comput Sci Univ Nev Reno NV 89557. *E-Mail:* al@cs.unr.edu

BRADY, ALLEN ROY, SYSTEMATIC ZOOLOGY. *Current Pos:* from asst prof to assoc prof, 66-72, PROF ZOOL, HOPE COL, 72-, CHMN DEPT, 80- *Personal Data:* b Houston, Tex, Feb 7, 33; m 58, Sara Choplin; c 4. *Educ:* Univ Houston, BS, 55, MS, 59; Harvard Univ, PhD(biol), 64. *Prof Exp:* Res fel arachnology, Mus Comp Zool, Harvard Univ, 63-64; Kettering intern biol, Hope Col, 64-65; asst prof, Albion Col, 65-66. *Concurrent Pos:* Vis prof zool, Univ Fla, Gainesville, 72-73. *Mem:* Am Arachnol Soc; Am Soc Zoologists; Soc Syst Zool. *Res:* Systematics and zoogeography of spiders. *Mailing Add:* Dept Biol Hope Col 137 E 12th St Holland MI 49423-3698

BRADY, BARRY HUGH GARNET, mining engineering, for more information see previous edition

BRADY, BRIAN T, materials science, applied mathematics, for more information see previous edition

BRADY, DENNIS PATRICK, STATISTICAL METHODS TO SOLVE BUSINESS PROBLEMS. *Current Pos:* Sr statistician, 76-80, prof scientist, 80-91, DEVELOP SCIENTIST, UNION CARBIDE CORP, 91- *Personal Data:* b Mitchell, SDak, Feb 18, 49; m 72; c 2. *Educ:* St John's Univ, Minn, BA, 71; SDak Sch Mines & Technol, MS, 73; Mont State Univ, PhD(statist), 76. *Concurrent Pos:* Adj prof, Col Grad Studies, WVa Univ, 77-80. *Mem:* Am Soc Qual Control; Am Statist Asn. *Res:* Application of statistical methods to solve problems in industrial research, marketing, sales, strategic planning, production, and litigation. *Mailing Add:* 507 Woodcliff Rd Charleston WV 25314

BRADY, DONALD R, CONTINUING EDUCATION. *Current Pos:* DEAN ADMIS & SPEC PROGS, AM TECH INST, 85- *Personal Data:* b Alamosa, Colo, June 28, 39. *Educ:* Cornell Univ, PhD(biochem), 70. *Prof Exp:* Dept Chem, Memphis State Univ, 73-80, Ctr Nuclear Studies, 80-85. *Concurrent Pos:* Res grant, Memphis State Univ, NIH, 80-84. *Mem:* Am Soc Biochemists; NY Acad Sci; AAAS. *Mailing Add:* 5184 Verosa Memphis TN 38117-2128

BRADY, DONNIE GAYLE, ORGANIC CHEMISTRY, POLYMER CHEMISTRY. *Current Pos:* Res chemist, Phillips Petrol Co, 66-71, sr res chemist, 71-77, resin develop engr, Phillips Chem Co, 77-78, sect supvr, Plastics Compounding, 78-80, mgr polymer applications, 80-83, mgr Thermoplastic Composites, 83-86, mgr, Polymers & Mat Div, 86-92, WW MGR POLYETHYLENE, PHILLIPS PETROL CO, 92- *Personal Data:* b

Campbell, Mo, Sept 9, 40; m 62; c 1. *Educ:* Southern Ill Univ, BS, 62; Purdue Univ, PhD(org chem), 66. *Mem:* Am Chem Soc; Soc Plastics Engrs; Soc Mfg Eng. *Res:* Organo sulfur chemistry; organo halogen chemistry; organo metallic chemistry; flame retardant additives for polymers; engineering thermoplastics; polyolefins; advanced composites. *Mailing Add:* Phillips 66 Co PO Box 58966 Houston TX 77258-8966

BRADY, DOUGLAS MACPHERSON, digital transmission, signal processing, for more information see previous edition

BRADY, EDWARD CLARENCE, COMMAND & CONTROL SYSTEMS, ADVANCED DISTRIBUTED SIMULATION. *Current Pos:* MANAGING PARTNER, STRATEGIC PERSPECTIVES INC, 91- *Personal Data:* b New London, Conn, July 1, 41; m 90, Faye M Maloney; c Alexandrea, Tara & Christine. *Educ:* US Naval Acad, BS, 63; Am Univ, MS, 84. *Honors & Awards:* Vance R Wanner Award, Mil Opers Res Soc. *Prof Exp:* Second lt-maj, US Army, 63-71; intel specialist, US Govt, 71-74; tech staff, Mitre Corp, 74-83, vpres, 83-86, sr vpres & gen mgr, 86-90, group vpres, 90-91. *Concurrent Pos:* Mem, US Army Sci Bd, 87-94 & 97-; trustee, Ga Tech Res Corp, 90-93; consult, Defense Sci Bd, 97- *Mem:* AAAS; fel Am Inst Aeronaut & Astronaut; Inst Elec & Electronics Engrs; fel Mil Opers Res Soc. *Res:* Design and development of complex computer and telecommunications systems; design and development of globally distributed simulation systems. *Mailing Add:* Strategic Perspectives Inc 7704 Lakeloft Ct Fairfax Station VA 22039-2956. *Fax:* 703-764-2699; *E-Mail:* fbrady1@aol.com

BRADY, FRANK OWEN, BIOCHEMISTRY, MOLECULAR BIOLOGY. *Current Pos:* from asst prof to assoc prof, 73-82, PROF BIOCHEM, SCH MED, UNIV SDAK, 82-, DEAN HEALTH SCI, 92- *Personal Data:* b Chicago, Ill, Feb 8, 44; m 66, Patriciann Furnari; c Sean A, David O & Danielle R. *Educ:* Carnegie-Mellon Univ, BS, 65; Duke Univ, PhD(biochem), 70. *Prof Exp:* Fel, Inst Cancer Res, Columbia Univ, 69-73. *Concurrent Pos:* NIH fel, Nat Cancer Inst, 70-72 & trainee, 72-73; NIH career develop award, Nat Inst Environ Health Sci, 76-81; vis scientist, Med Res Coun, Toxicol Unit, Carshalton, UK, 79-80; Kelloggs Found Nat Leadership fel, 88-91, Bush fel, 93. *Mem:* Oxygen Soc; Am Soc Biochem & Molecular Biol; Am Heart Asn. *Res:* Hormonal control metallothionein of metal metabolism and molecular biology. *Mailing Add:* Div Health Sci Sch Med Univ SDak 414 E Clark St Vermillion SD 57069. *Fax:* 605-677-6569; *E-Mail:* fbrady@sunflowr.usd.edu

BRADY, FRANKLIN PAUL, NUCLEAR PHYSICS. *Current Pos:* from asst prof to assoc prof, 62-74, PROF PHYSICS, UNIV CALIF, DAVIS, 74-, ASSOC DIR, CROCKER NUCLEAR LAB, 75- *Personal Data:* b Winnipeg, Man, Aug 14, 31; m 64. *Educ:* Univ Man, BS, 53; Princeton Univ, AM, 54, PhD(physics), 60. *Prof Exp:* Res assoc nuclear physics, Princeton Univ, 60-61; physicist, Schlumberger Ltd, 61-62. *Concurrent Pos:* Ford Found vis prof prin investr, NSF grant, 72-, Nat Cancer Inst grant, 75-79, Dept Energy grant, 81-; sr Fulbright, Karlsruhe, Fed Repub Ger,82-83. *Mem:* Fel Am Phys Soc. *Res:* Geophysics; experimental nuclear physics; nuclear reactions; cyclotron design. *Mailing Add:* Dept Physics Univ of Calif Davis CA 95616

BRADY, GEORGE W, PHYSICAL CHEMISTRY. *Current Pos:* RETIRED. *Personal Data:* b Quebec, Que, Jan 22, 21; m 49; c 2. *Educ:* Laval Univ, BSc, 42; McGill Univ, PhD, 49. *Prof Exp:* Asst, Univ Chicago, 49-51; res fel, Harvard Univ, 51-52; mem tech staff, Bell Labs, 52-78; mem staff, Div Labs-Res, NY State Dept Health, 78-90. *Concurrent Pos:* Adj prof, State Univ NY, Albany, 76-; adj prof physics, Rensselaer Polytech Inst. *Mem:* Fel Am Phys Soc; fel NY Acad Sci; Biophys Soc; Am Crystallog Asn. *Res:* Chemical kinetics; surface chemistry; structure of liquids; x-ray diffraction; critical state phenomena; structure of membranes and DNA. *Mailing Add:* 233 1/2 Center St Corinth NY 12822

BRADY, JAMES EDWARD, INORGANIC CHEMISTRY. *Current Pos:* instr, 65-70, ASSOC PROF CHEM, ST JOHN'S UNIV, NY, 70- *Personal Data:* b New York, NY, Jan 26, 38; m 60; c 1. *Educ:* Hofstra Col, BA, 59; Pa State Univ, PhD(inorg chem), 64. *Prof Exp:* Staff scientist chem, Res Ctr, Aerospace Group, Gen Precision, Inc, 64-65. *Mem:* Am Chem Soc; NY Acad Sci. *Res:* Reaction mechanisms of coordination compounds by means of high pressure techniques; synthesis of inorganic luminescent materials at high temperatures. *Mailing Add:* Dept Chem St John's Univ Grand Cent & Utopia Pkwy Jamaica NY 11439

BRADY, JOHN F, MECHANICAL ENGINEERING. *Current Pos:* RETIRED. *Personal Data:* b Taunton, Mass, July 12, 28; m 52; c 4. *Educ:* Mass Inst Technol, BS, 48, MS, 50. *Honors & Awards:* Excellence Sci & Technol Award, Naval Underwater Ord Sta, 63. *Prof Exp:* Asst thermodyn, Mass Inst Technol, 48-50; mech engr, US Naval Torpedo Sta, 50-51; proj officer, Wright Air Develop Ctr, 51-52; br head proj mgt, Underwater Ord Sta, US Naval Underwater Systs Ctr, 52-56, asst, Div Syst Eng, 56-60, div head propulsion, 60-61, head, Dept Appl Sci, 61-64, head, Dept Res, 64-68, assoc dir, Underwater Weapons Sta, 68-72, assoc dir, Newport Lab, 70-71,assoc dir weapons res, 71-72, head, Weapons Dept, 72-76; consult tech staff, Submarine Signal Div, Raytheon Corp, 76-93. *Mem:* Am Inst Aeronaut & Astronaut; Am Soc Mech Engrs. *Res:* Underwater propulsion; partial admission turbines; underwater vehicle systems. *Mailing Add:* 206 Immokolee Dr Portsmouth RI 02871

BRADY, JOHN PAUL, PSYCHIATRY. *Current Pos:* from assoc prof to prof, 63-74, chmn dept, 74-82, KENNETH E APPEL PROF PSYCHIAT, SCH MED, UNIV PA, 74- *Personal Data:* b Boston, Mass, June 23, 28; m 63, Christeen Nelson; c James P, June P, Pamela (Eros) & David D. *Educ:* Boston Univ, AB, 51, MD, 55. *Hon Degrees:* MA, Univ Penn, 70. *Honors & Awards:* Strecker Award, 72. *Prof Exp:* Resident psychiat, Inst Living, Hartford, Conn, 56-59; res psychiatrist, Sch Med, Ind Univ, 59-63. *Concurrent Pos:* Co-founder & assoc ed, Behav Ther, 69-; consult panel anal of impact of basic res on ment health, Comt Brain Sci, Nat Res Coun, 72-74. *Mem:* Asn Advan Behav Ther (pres, 70-71); Soc Biol Psychiat (pres, 79-80); Psychiat Res Soc; Pavlovian Soc NAm; Am Psychiat Asn. *Res:* Applications of principles of learning to disorders of behavior; biobehavioral approaches to medical disorders. *Mailing Add:* 524 Prescott Rd Merion PA 19066

BRADY, JOSEPH VINCENT, BEHAVIORAL BIOLOGY, NEUROSCIENCE. *Current Pos:* PROF BEHAV BIOL & CTR DIR, SCH MED, JOHNS HOPKINS UNIV, 67-, PROF NEUROSCI, 83- *Personal Data:* b New York, NY, Mar 28, 22. *Educ:* Fordham Univ, BS, 43; Univ Chicago, PhD, 51. *Honors & Awards:* Eddy Award Distinguished Sci Contrib, Col Probs Drug Abuse. *Prof Exp:* Chief clin psychologist, Neuropsychiat Ctr, Europ Command, Ger, 46-48; student officer psychol, Univ Chicago, 48-51; chief, Dept Exp Psychol, Walter Reed Army Inst Res, 51-64, dep dir, Div Neuropsychiat, 64-70. *Concurrent Pos:* Prof, Univ Md, 55-69; pres & chmn-of-bd trustees & dir res, Inst Behav Resources. *Mem:* Fel AAAS; fel Am Col Neuropsychopharmacology; fel Soc Behav Med; fel Col Probs Drug Dependence. *Res:* Experimental analysis of behavior; behavioral physiology; behavioral pharmacology; comparative psychosomatics. *Mailing Add:* Behav Biol Res Ctr Johns Hopkins Univ Sch Med 5510 Nathan Shock Dr Baltimore MD 21224

BRADY, KEITH BRYAN CRAIG, ACID MINE DRAINAGE, HYDROGEOLOGY. *Current Pos:* HYDROGEOLOGIST, DEPT ENVIRON RESOURCES, BUR MINING & RECLAMATION, 80- *Personal Data:* b Dulphin Co, Pa, Apr 23, 54. *Educ:* Alaska Methodist Univ, BA, 76; Univ Maine, MS, 82. *Mem:* Geol Soc Am; Asn Groundwater Scientists & Engrs; AAAS; Am Quaternary Asn; Am Sci Affil. *Res:* Prediction of surface coal mine drainage quality; means of preventing acid mine drainage occurrence by considering variables imposed by geologic, geochemical, hydrologic and man induced controls. *Mailing Add:* 323 Williams St Harrisburg PA 17113

BRADY, LAWRENCE LEE, GEOLOGY, ECONOMIC GEOLOGY. *Current Pos:* chief mineral resources sect, Kans Geol Surv, 75-83, res assoc geol, 71-77, chief geol invests, 87-92, assoc dir, 92-94, DEP DIR, KANS GEOL SURV, 94- *Personal Data:* b Topeka, Kans, Nov 6, 36; m 60, Mary E Antenen; c Beth A & Geoffrey S. *Educ:* Kans State Univ, BS, 58; Univ Kans, MS, 67, PhD(geol), 71. *Prof Exp:* Eng geologist, US Army Corps Engr, Kansas City Dist, 58-63; asst prof geol, Okla State Univ, 71. *Mem:* Asn Eng Geologists; Am Asn Petrol Geologists; Soc Econ Paleontologists & Mineralogists; Geol Soc Am. *Res:* Coal geology and resources; quality and distribution of Kansas mineral resources; engineering geology related to mineral development; clastic sedimentology. *Mailing Add:* 1930 Constant Ave Campus West Univ Kans Lawrence KS 66047. *Fax:* 785-864-5317

BRADY, LEONARD EVERETT, ORGANIC CHEMISTRY. *Current Pos:* assoc prof, 66-70, chmn dept, 75-81, PROF CHEM, UNIV TOLEDO, 71- *Personal Data:* b Brooklyn, NY, Feb 24, 28; m 51; c 1. *Educ:* Wagner Col, BS, 51; NC State Col, MS, 54; Mich State Univ, PhD(org chem), 58. *Prof Exp:* Asst, Mich State Univ, 53-57; res chemist, Abbott Labs, 57-61; res assoc chem, Univ Ill, 61-63, instr, 63-64; assoc prof chem, Ill State Univ, 64-66. *Concurrent Pos:* Vis scholar, Cambridge Univ, 73-74; vis prof, Mich State Univ, 85. *Mem:* Am Chem Soc; Am Soc Pharmacog. *Res:* Mechanisms; structure proof; stereochemistry; natural products. *Mailing Add:* Dept Chem Univ Toledo 2801 W Bancroft St Toledo OH 43606

BRADY, LUTHER WELDON, JR, NUCLEAR MEDICINE, RADIOLOGY & RADIATION ONCOLOGY. *Current Pos:* Asst prof med & radiol, 59-66, prof radiol, 66-70, PROF RADIATION ONCOL & NUCLEAR MED & CHMN DEPT, HAHNEMANN UNIV HOSP, 70-, DIR RADIATION ONCOL, 59-, AM CANCER SOC CLIN ONCOL PROF, 75- *Personal Data:* b NC, 1925. *Educ:* George Washington, Univ AB, 46, MD, 48. *Hon Degrees:* DFA, Colgate Univ, 88; DSc, Lehigh Univ, 90; MD, Toyama Univ, 96. *Honors & Awards:* Mark Blum lectr, Monmouth Med Ctr, 77; Elsa Pardee lectr, Midland Med Ctr, 79; Medal, Nat Med Soc Ecuador, 80; Gold Medal, Am Radium Soc, 81; Gold Medal, Am Col Radiol, 83; Maurice Lenz Mem lectr, Columbia Presby Med Ctr, 83; Gilbert H Fletcher Gold Medal, 84; John McAfee lect, State Univ NY, Syracuse, 84; Swedish Acad Med Medal, 86; Gold Medal, Am Soc Therapeut Radiol & Oncol, 87; Gold Medal, Radiol Soc NAm, 89; Probstein Oncol lectr, MallincKrodt Inst, 91; Joeseph Keelty lectr, John Hopkins Univ, 92; Cancer Control Award, Am Cancer Soc, 92. *Prof Exp:* At Jefferson Med Col, 53-55, Sch Med, Univ Pa, 55-59, Sch Med, Columbia Univ, 59 & Harvard Med Sch, 62-63. *Concurrent Pos:* Consult, Vet Admin Hosp, 60-, Crozer-Chester Med Ctr, Pa Hosp, Philadelphia, Lankenau Hosp, Philadelphia, West Jersey Hosp, Camden, NJ, Garden State Hosp, Cherry Hill, NJ & St Luke's Hosp, Bethlehem, Pa; asst prof, Harvard Med Sch, 62-63; lectr, Herman Holthusen Inst, Ger, 92. *Mem:* Fel Am Col Radiol; Radiol Soc NAm; Am Radium Soc (past pres); Am Soc Therapeut Radiol (past pres); Am Soc Clin Oncol; Am Asn Cancer Res; hon fel Med Radiol Soc Italy; hon fel Royal Col Radiologists; hon fel Ger Roentgenol Soc; hon fel Royal Acad Med Belg. *Res:* Effects of radiation on pulmonary function on bone marrow using ferrochromokinetics in patients with established diagnosis of malignancy and on kidney function, monoclonal antibodies in cancer treatment; radiation oncology. *Mailing Add:* Radiation Oncol & Nuclear Med Allegheny Univ Hahnemann Div Broad & Vine Sts Philadelphia PA 19102. *Fax:* 215-762-8523

BRADY, NYLE C, AGRONOMY, SOIL & SOIL SCIENCE. *Current Pos:* SR CONSULT, UN DEVELOP PROG, 89- *Personal Data:* b Manassa, Colo, Oct 25, 20; m 36; c 4. *Educ:* Brigham Young Univ, BS, 41; NC State Col, PhD(soil sci), 47. *Hon Degrees:* PhD, Brigham Young Univ, 79 & Ohio State Univ, 91. *Honors & Awards:* Int Agron Award, Am Soc Agron, 87; Int Soil Sci Award, Soil Sci Am, 90. *Prof Exp:* Jr agronomist, NC State Col, 42-44, res instr, 46, asst prof agron, 47; from asst prof to prof soil sci, NY State Col Agr, Cornell Univ, 48-73, head Dept Agron, 55-63, dir Agr Exp Sta, 65-73, assoc dean, 70-73; dir gen, Int Rice Res Inst, Philippines, 73-81, sen asst, Admin Sci & Tech, 81-89. *Concurrent Pos:* Dir sci & educ, USDA, 63-65; chmn agr bd, Nat Res Coun, 67-70; ed, Proc Soil Sci Soc Am; ed, Agron J, 65-90. *Mem:* AAAS; Soil Sci Soc Am; Am Soc Agron; Soil Conserv Soc Am; Am Inst Biol Sci. *Res:* Physiology of the peanut plant; fundamental effects of lime on soil; influence of fertilizer on the yield of corn, rice and coffee; influence of soil temperature on nutrient uptake. *Mailing Add:* 521 S Catalina St Gilbert AZ 85233

BRADY, ROBERT FREDERICK, JR, POLYMER CHEMISTRY, ORGANIC CHEMISTRY. *Current Pos:* HEAD, COATINGS SECT, NAVAL RES LAB, 82- *Personal Data:* b Washington, DC, July 20, 42; m 65, Sharon A Callison; c Sheila M (Speth), Robert M & Patrick C. *Educ:* Univ Va, BSChem, 64, PhD(org chem), 67. *Honors & Awards:* Roon Found Award, Fedn Socs Coatings Technol, 92. *Prof Exp:* Chemist, Nat Bur Stand, 67-72 & US Customs Serv, 72-75; chief, Paints Br, Fed Supply Serv, 75-82. *Concurrent Pos:* NASA fel, 64-67; contrib ed, J Protective Coatings & Linings, 86-90; vis scientist, Defense Mat Res Lab, Melbourne, Australia, 90-91; tech ed, J Coatings Technol, 92-97. *Mem:* Sigma Xi; Am Chem Soc; Fed Socs Coatings Technol; Royal Soc Chem. *Res:* Synthetic, structural, and physical chemistry of polymers and natural products; coatings technology, testing and specifications. *Mailing Add:* 706 Hope Lane Gaithersburg MD 20878-1883

BRADY, ROBERT JAMES, MICROBIOLOGY. *Current Pos:* RETIRED. *Personal Data:* b Detroit, Mich, Apr 13, 27; m 55; c 4. *Educ:* Univ Detroit, BS, 51, MS, 54; Univ Md, PhD(microbiol), 57. *Prof Exp:* Asst biol, Univ Detroit, 53-55; asst microbiol, Univ Md, 54-57; from asst prof to assoc prof, Miami Univ, 57-69, chmn dept, 73-78, prof microbiol, 69. *Mem:* Am Soc Microbiol; Brit Soc Gen Microbiol. *Res:* Microbial physiology and genetics. *Mailing Add:* Miami Univ Rm 40 Biol Sci Bldg Oxford OH 45056

BRADY, ROSCOE OWEN, BIOCHEMISTRY, GENETIC DISORDERS. *Current Pos:* chief lipid chem sect, 54-70, asst chief lab neurochem, 70-72, CHIEF DEVELOP & METAB NEUROL BR, NAT INST NEUROL & COMMUN DIS, 72- *Personal Data:* b Philadelphia, Pa, Oct 11, 23; m 72, Bennett C Manning; c Roscoe O Jr & Randoph O. *Educ:* Harvard Univ, MD, 47. *Honors & Awards:* Gairdner Int Award, 73; Cotsias Award, Am Acad Neurol, 80; Passano Found Award, 82; Lasker Found Award, 82; SACMS Award, Child Neurol Soc, 90; Kovalenko Medal, Nat Acad Sci, 91. *Prof Exp:* Intern, Univ Hosp, Univ Pa, 47-48; officer-in-chg, Chem Labs, Naval Med Ctr, 52-54. *Concurrent Pos:* Nat Res Coun fel med sci, Univ Hosp, Univ Pa, 48-50, fel, 50-51, USPHS fel, 51-52, fel, Endocrine Sect, Med Clin, 52-54; prof lectr, Sch Med, George Washington Univ, 63-73; adj prof biochem, Georgetown Univ, 67-; staff mem, Children's Nat Med Ctr, Washington, DC. *Mem:* Nat Acad Sci; Inst Med-Nat Acad Sci; Am Soc Biol Chem & Molecular Biol; Am Soc Human Genetics; Am Soc Human Gene Ther; Am Acad Neurol. *Res:* Complex lipid metabolism; genetic diseases; viral carcinogenesis; neurochemistry; biosynthesis of fatty acids and complex lipids of the nervous system; gene therapy; enzyme replacement therapy. *Mailing Add:* 6026 Valerian Lane Rockville MD 20852-3410. *Fax:* 301-496-9480; *E-Mail:* robrady@codon.mch.gov

BRADY, SCOTT T, CELLULAR NEUROBIOLOGY, CELL MOTILITY. *Current Pos:* ASSOC PROF CELL BIOL & NEUROSCI, UNIV TEX SOUTHWESTERN MED CTR, DALLAS, 85- *Personal Data:* b San Antonio, Tex, Nov 11, 50. *Educ:* Mass Inst Technol, ScB (biol) & ScB (physics), 73, Univ Southern Calif, PhD(cellular & molecular biol), 78. *Honors & Awards:* Jordi Folch-Pi Mem Award, Am Soc Neurochem, 88. *Prof Exp:* Sr res assoc cell biol, Case Western Reserve Univ, 80-85. *Concurrent Pos:* Investr, Marine Biol Lab. *Mem:* Soc Neurosci; Am Soc Cell Biol; Am Soc Neurochem; AAAS; Am Phys Soc; Int Soc Neurochem. *Res:* Indentification and characterization of the molecular mechanisms of axonal transport, resulting in discovery of kinesin-based form of intracellular transport; role of neuronal cytoskeleton in growth and regeneration. *Mailing Add:* Dept Cell Biol & Neurosci Univ Tex Southwestern Med Ctr 5323 Harry Hines Blvd Dallas TX 75235-9111. *Fax:* 214-648-1801; *E-Mail:* bradyO3@ utsw

BRADY, STEPHEN FRANCIS, MEDICINAL CHEMISTRY. *Current Pos:* sr res chemist, 70-79, from res fel to sr res fel, 79-93, SR INVESTR, MERCK RES LABS, DIV MERCK & CO, INC, 93- *Personal Data:* b New York, NY, Oct 17, 41; m 66, Jadwiga Starzec; c Sara. *Educ:* Columbia Univ, BA, 63; Stanford Univ, PhD(chem), 67. *Prof Exp:* Res assoc, Dept Chem, Northwestern Univ, 67-70. *Mem:* Am Chem Soc; Sigma Xi; Am Peptide Soc. *Res:* Structue-based design/synthesis of potential therapeutic agents; development of methods for peptide and peptidomimetic synthesis; studies of enzyme action/inhibition and receptor properties as applied to drug discovery; chemistry and biology of amino acids and peptides. *Mailing Add:* 8803 Crefeld St Philadelphia PA 19118. *Fax:* 215-652-6345

BRADY, STEPHEN W, MATHEMATICS. *Current Pos:* ASSOC PROF MATH, WICHITA STATE UNIV, 67- *Personal Data:* b Indianapolis, Ind, Jan 12, 41; m 65. *Educ:* Ind Univ, BA, 63, MA, 65, PhD(math), 68. *Concurrent Pos:* Consult, Math & Biol Corp, 67-68. *Mem:* Soc Indust & Appl Math; Am Math Soc; Math Asn Am; NY Acad Sci. *Res:* Functional and numerical analysis; differential equations; mathematics applied to physiology. *Mailing Add:* 9823 W Second St N Wichita KS 67212-3902

BRADY, THOMAS E, SYNTHETIC ORGANIC CHEMISTRY, AGRICULTURAL CHEMISTRY. *Current Pos:* Res chemist, Org Chem Div, 67-74, sr res chemist, Chem Res Div, 74-83, SR RES CHEMIST, AGR RES DIV, AM CYANAMID CO, NJ, 83- *Personal Data:* b Elizabeth, NJ, Apr 2, 41; m 70; c Jeanne, Maureen & Mary Catherine. *Educ:* St Vincent Col, BS, 63; Fordham Univ, PhD(org chem), 68. *Mem:* Am Chem Soc; NY Acad Sci. *Res:* Synthesis of dyes and detergent additives; flame retardants; antioxidants, light stabilizers, photo initiators, herbicides, PGRs, insecticides. *Mailing Add:* 8 Dorset Lane White House Station NJ 08889-9417

BRADY, WILLIAM GORDON, APPLIED MATHEMATICS. *Current Pos:* RETIRED. *Personal Data:* b Zanesville, Ohio, May 31, 23; m 48; c 2. *Educ:* Univ Cincinnati, Aero Eng, 50; Brown Univ, MS, 53. *Prof Exp:* Asst res engr appl mech, Cornell Aeronaut Lab Inc, NY, 52-55, assoc res engr, 55-58, res engr, 58-60, prin engr, 60-70; from asst prof to prof math, Erie Community Col, 70-88. *Mem:* Sigma Xi. *Res:* Aeroelasticity; low speed aerodynamics. *Mailing Add:* 44 Pryor Ave Tonawanda NY 14150

BRADY, WILLIAM THOMAS, PHYSICAL ORGANIC CHEMISTRY. *Current Pos:* from asst prof to assoc prof, 62-68, PROF CHEM, NTEX STATE UNIV, 68- *Personal Data:* b Ventura, Calif, Sept 25, 33; m 54; c 2. *Educ:* NTex State Univ, BA, 55, MS, 56; Univ Tex, PhD(chem), 60. *Prof Exp:* Res chemist, Tex Eastman Co, Eastman Kodak Co, 56-57 & 60-62; res scientist, Clayton Found Biochem Inst, 57-60. *Mem:* Am Chem Soc. *Res:* Ketene chemistry. *Mailing Add:* Dept Chem NTex State Univ Box 5068 Denton TX 76203-0068

BRADY, WRAY GRAYSON, MATHEMATICS. *Current Pos:* dean, Grad Sch, 69-72, prof, 72-87, EMER PROF MATH, SLIPPERY ROCK STATE COL, 87- *Personal Data:* b Benton Harbor, Mich, July 20, 18; m 43, Emilie Peterson; c Wray Gordon & Susan Maes. *Educ:* Washington & Jefferson Col, BS, 40, MA, 42; Univ Pittsburgh, PhD(math), 53. *Prof Exp:* Instr math, Washington & Jefferson Col, 40-42, prof math,51-66; asst, Stanford Univ, 46-47; instr, Univ Wyo, 47-50; Bernard prof math & chmn dept, Univ Bridgeport, 66-69. *Concurrent Pos:* Consult, Atomic Energy Bd, Westinghouse Elec Bettis Plant. *Mem:* fel AAAS; Am Math Soc; Math Asn Am; Fibonacci Asn. *Res:* Infinite series; number theory; mathematical statistics. *Mailing Add:* APDO 330 45900 Chapala Jalisco Mexico

BRADY, YOLANDA J, FISH DISEASE DIAGNOSIS, ELECTRON MICROSCOPY. *Current Pos:* Res assoc diag, 84-85, ASST PROF FISH HEALTH, AUBURN UNIV, 86- *Personal Data:* b Greenwood, Miss, Aug 7, 56. *Educ:* Univ Miss, BS, 78; Univ Southern Miss, MS, 82; Auburn Univ, PhD(fish health), 85. *Mem:* Am Fisheries Soc; World Aquacult Soc. *Res:* Bacterial and viral disease mechanisms in warm-water fish, crustaceans, and mollusks. *Mailing Add:* 1424 Azalea Dr Auburn AL 36830

BRAEKEVELT, CHARLIE ROGER, ELECTRON MICROSCOPY, MORPHOLOGY. *Current Pos:* from lectr to assoc prof, 60-87, PROF ANAT, UNIV MAN, 87- *Personal Data:* b Sarnia, Ont, Aug 27, 42; m 69; c 2. *Educ:* Univ Western Ont, BA, 64, MSc, 66, PhD(anat), 69. *Prof Exp:* Demonstr zool, Univ Western Ont, 64-66, demonstr anat, 66-69. *Concurrent Pos:* Ont Grad fel, 65-68; Nellie L Farthing mem fel, 68-69; Med Res Coun Can fel, 70-71; vis prof ophthal, Cath Univ Louvain, 76; vis res fel, Univ Western Australia, 84-85; vis scientist, Med Res Coun Can, 84-85; WHO fel, 84-85. *Mem:* Can Soc Zoologists; Am Soc Zoologists; Can Asn Anatomists; Am Asn Anatomists; Asn Res Vision & Ophthal; Int Soc Eye Res. *Res:* Fine structure of normal and abnormal eye; effects of toxic substances on the vertebrate retina; cell renewal within the vertebrate retina. *Mailing Add:* Dept Anat Univ Man 730 William Ave Winnipeg MB R3E 0W3 Can

BRAEMER, ALLEN C, LICENSING, BUSINESS DEVELOPMENT. *Current Pos:* CONSULT, 92- *Personal Data:* b Woodhaven, NY, May 8, 30; m 81; c 3. *Educ:* State Univ NY Vet Col, Cornell Univ, DVM, 55. *Prof Exp:* Vet, Pine Tree Vet Hosp, Augusta, Maine, 55-56, Crawford Animal Hosp, Garden City, NY, 56-58 & Mindell Animal Hosp, Albany, 58-61; assoc res biologist, Sterling-Winthrop Res Inst, Rensselaer, NY, 61-62, group leader, 62-64, res biologist, 64-66, res vet & group leader, Exp Farm, 66-67; dir animal clin sect, Norwich Pharmacal Co, 67-69, chief vet bact sect, 69-73; asst dir, Inst Agrisci, Syntex Res, 76-85, head, Dept Vet Microbiol, 77-80, dir vet biol res, 80-85, head, Dept Animal Sci, 73-85, dir technol acquisition, 85-92. *Mem:* AAAS; Am Vet Med Asn; Am Indust Vet Asn. *Res:* Chemotherapy and immunology of microbial diseases; veterinary vaccines; licensing of technology; business development. *Mailing Add:* PO Box 3295 Sun River OR 97707-0295

BRAENDLE, DONALD HAROLD, MICROBIOLOGY. *Current Pos:* SR SCIENTIST, ABBOTT LABS, 58- *Personal Data:* b Flushing, NY, Nov 8, 27; m 57. *Educ:* Rice Inst, BA, 52; Rutgers Univ, PhD(microbiol), 57. *Prof Exp:* Waksman-Merck fel, Rutgers Univ, 57-58. *Mem:* AAAS; Am Soc Microbiol; Brit Soc Gen Microbiol; Sigma Xi. *Res:* Microbial genetics, especially that of filamentous microorganisms, their physiology, and their production of antibiotics and other microbial products. *Mailing Add:* 239 E Washington Lake Bluff IL 60044-2156

BRAGAGNOLO, JULIO ALFREDO, photovoltaic solar cells, electronic devices, for more information see previous edition

BRAGDON, ROBERT WRIGHT, CHEMISTRY. *Current Pos:* WRITER, 89- *Personal Data:* b Marblehead, Mass, Jan 19, 22; m 43; c 3. *Educ:* Bowdoin Col, BS, 43. *Prof Exp:* Analytical chemist, Manhattan Proj, Mallinckrodt Chem Works, 43-46; res chemist, United Shoe Mach Corp, 46-47; sr res chemist, Metal Hydrides, Inc, 47-52, assoc dir res, 52-60, dir res, 60-65; sr scientist, Simplex Wire & Cable Co, 65-69; mgr new prod develop, Hampshire Chem, 70-79, dir res, 79-81, vpres new prod develop, 81-84, vpres res & develop, Org Chem Div, W R Grace & Co, 84-89. *Concurrent Pos:* Consult, Ventron Corp, 69-70. *Mem:* Am Chem Soc; Com Develop Asn. *Res:* Borohydrides; aluminohydrides; alkali and alkaline earth hydrides; sodium metal cable; chelates; amino acids; hydrogen cyanide chemistry; nitroparaffins; hydrogen cynanide based products. *Mailing Add:* Rte 2 Box 69B Harpswell ME 04079-9605

BRAGG, DAVID GORDON, MEDICINE, RADIOLOGY. *Current Pos:* PROF RADIOL & CHMN DEPT, COL MED, UNIV UTAH, 70- *Personal Data:* b Portland, Ore, May 1, 33; m 55; c 4. *Educ:* Stanford Univ, AB, 55; Univ Ore, MD, 59; Am Bd Radiol, dipl, 66. *Prof Exp:* Intern, Philadelphia Gen Hosp, 59-60; resident radiol, Col Physicians & Surgeons, Columbia Univ, 62-64, chief resident, 64-65, from instr to asst prof, Med Col, Cornell Univ, 65-70. *Concurrent Pos:* Chmn dept diag radiol, Sloan-Kettering Cancer Ctr, NY, 67-70, consult, 70-; res grant, Microwave Methods Lung Water Measurement. *Mem:* AMA; Radiol Soc NAm; Am Roentgen Ray Soc; Soc Surg Oncol; Am Gastroenterol Asn. *Res:* Oncological and gastrointestinal radiology; diagnostic oncology, microwave radiology; quantitation of distribution of Lung Water by nuclear magnetic resonance. *Mailing Add:* 4403 Covecrest Dr Salt Lake City UT 84124

BRAGG, DENVER DAYTON, POULTRY SCIENCE. *Current Pos:* assoc prof poultry sci & exten specialist, 49-73, EMER ASSOC PROF POULTRY SCI, VA POLYTECH INST & STATE UNIV, 73- *Personal Data:* b Duffy, WVa, Apr 13, 15; m 41; c 2. *Educ:* WVa Univ, BS, 40; Va Polytech Inst & State Univ, MS, 53. *Prof Exp:* Poultry serviceman, Ralston Purina Co, 40; asst rural rehab supvr, Farm & Home Admin, 40-42; county 4-H Club agent, Agr Exten Serv, WVa, 46, from asst county agent to assoc county agent, 46-49. *Mem:* Poultry Sci Asn. *Res:* Egg production and processing. *Mailing Add:* 1512 Hollyhill Pl Blacksburg VA 24060-6200

BRAGG, GORDON MCALPINE, FLUID MECHANICS. *Current Pos:* Asst prof, 65-70, ASSOC PROF MECH ENG, UNIV WATERLOO, 70- *Personal Data:* b Flin Flon, Man, May 13, 39; m 63; c 3. *Educ:* Univ Toronto, BASc, 62; Cambridge Univ, PhD(aeronaut eng), 65. *Concurrent Pos:* Res asst, Univ Toronto, 61-62; mem cent comt, Can Cong Appl Mech. *Mem:* Am Soc Mech Engrs; Can Soc Mech Engrs. *Res:* Subsonic flow; turbulence; air and gas handling equipment; turbomachinery; air pollution control; wind power. *Mailing Add:* Dept Mech Eng Univ Waterloo Waterloo ON N2L 3G1 Can

BRAGG, LINCOLN ELLSWORTH, CONTINUUM PHYSICS, TRANSVERSE MERCATOR MAP PROJECTION COMPUTATION. *Current Pos:* SOFTWARE ENG SPECIALIST & ENG SPECIALIST, RAYTHEON E-SYSTS, GARLAND OPER, CAC OPER, 87- *Personal Data:* b Buffalo, NY, Jan 25, 36; m 61, 72; c Willa G (Whitright), Henry E & Angela R. *Educ:* Carnegie Inst Technol, BS, 59, MS, 60, PhD(continuum mech), 64. *Prof Exp:* Asst, US Steel Res Lab, Pa, 60, Mellon Inst, 62 & 64; res asst prof continuum mech, Inst Fluid Dynamics & Appl Math, Univ Md, College Park, 63-66; Dunham Jackson instr math, Univ Minn, Minneapolis, 66-67; asst prof, Univ Ky, 67-71 & Fla Inst Technol, 71-75; mathematician & comput specialist, Sea Automated Data Systs Off, 76-80; mem tech staff, Comput Sci Corp, 80-83, Calspan Corp, 83-85, Qual Systs, Inc, 85-87. *Mem:* Am Asn Physics Teachers; Am Cartog Asn; Am Cong Surv & Mapping. *Res:* Electromagnetic behavior of deformable materials; theory of constitutive relations; concepts of electrodynamics and their historical development; gravitational theory; transverse mercator map projection computation. *Mailing Add:* 704 Four Mile Rd Alexandria VA 22305

BRAGG, LOUIS HAIRSTON, BOTANY & SEED STRUCTURE, ELECTRON MICROSCOPY. *Current Pos:* from instr to assoc prof, 60-84, PROF BIOL, UNIV TEX, ARLINGTON, 84- *Personal Data:* b Chicora, Miss, Sept 12, 28; m 54, Shirley J Windsor; c Deborah, Susan & David. *Educ:* NTex State Col, BS, 53, MS, 57; Univ Tex, PhD(bot), 64. *Prof Exp:* Tutor biol, NTex State Col, 53-54; teacher, Pub Schs, Tex, 54-60. *Concurrent Pos:* Res scientist, Univ Tex, 64. *Mem:* Bot Soc Am; Sigma Xi; Electron Micros Soc Am. *Res:* Experimental plant ecology; seed structure; biochemical systematics; plant cytology; electron microscopy. *Mailing Add:* Dept Biol Box 19498 Univ Tex Arlington TX 76019-0001

BRAGG, LOUIS RICHARD, MATHEMATICS. *Current Pos:* PROF MATH, OAKLAND UNIV, 67- *Personal Data:* b Weston, WVa, Aug 5, 31; m; c 2. *Educ:* WVa Univ, AB, 52, MS, 53; Univ Wis, PhD(math), 55. *Prof Exp:* From instr to asst prof math, Duke Univ, 55-59; assoc prof, WVa Univ, 59-61; from asst prof to assoc prof, Case Inst Technol, 61-67. *Concurrent Pos:* Chmn, Oakland Univ, 75-78. *Mem:* Am Math Soc; Math Asn Am; Soc Indust & Appl Math. *Res:* Partial differential equations, transmutations, and special functions; numerical integration. *Mailing Add:* Dept Math Scis Oakland Univ Rochester MI 48309-4401

BRAGG, PHILIP DELL, BIOCHEMISTRY. *Current Pos:* RETIRED. *Personal Data:* b Gillingham, Eng, July 2, 32; m 88, Diana Alpen; c 3. *Educ:* Bristol Univ, BSc, 54, PhD(org chem), 58. *Hon Degrees:* DSc, 86. *Prof Exp:* Fel org chem, Queen's Univ, Ont, 57-59; res assoc biochem, Sch Med, La State Univ, 59-61; res assoc biochem, Univ BC, 61-64, from asst prof to prof, 64-74, dept head, 86-94. *Concurrent Pos:* Med Res Coun Can scholar, Univ BC, 64-69. *Mem:* Royal Soc Chem; Am Soc Microbiol; Can Biochem Soc; Am Soc Biochem & Molecular Biol. *Res:* Bioenergetics, especially of micro organisms; electron transport; oxidative phosphorylation; cellular membranes; control mechanisms; membrane transport. *Mailing Add:* Dept Biochem & Molecular Biol Univ BC Vancouver BC V6T 1Z3 Can. *Fax:* 604-822-5227; *E-Mail:* pbragg@unixg.ubc.ca

BRAGG, ROBERT H(ENRY), CARBON SCIENCE, MATERIALS CHARACTERIZATION. *Current Pos:* prof, 69-87, chmn dept, 78-81, EMER PROF MAT SCI, UNIV CALIF, BERKELEY, 87- *Personal Data:* b Jacksonville, Fla, Aug 11, 19; m 47, Violette McDonald; c Robert H III & Pamela. *Educ:* Ill Inst Technol, BS, 49, MS, 51, PhD(physics), 60. *Prof Exp:* Asst physicist, Res Lab, Portland Cement Asn, 51-54, assoc physicist, 54-56; assoc physicist, Ill Inst Technol Res Inst, 56-57, res physicist, 57-59, sr physicist, 59-61; res scientist, Palo Alto Res Lab, Lockheed Missiles & Space Co, 61-63, sr staff scientist, 63-69. *Concurrent Pos:* Consult, Univ Ill & Atomic Energy Comn, Arg, 66, Jamaica Bauxite Inst, 77; prin investr, Mat & Molecular Div, Lawrence Berkeley Lab, 69-, mem, comt Sci & Technol Appl Mat Processing Space, Nat Acad Sci, 77-78, Mat Res Adv Comt, Div Mat Res, NSF, 82-88, Eval Panel, Res Assoc Prog, Nat Res Coun, 84-; vis prof, Howard Univ, 77, Musashi Inst Technol, Japan, 89; prog dir, Div Mat Sci, Dept Energy, 81-82; chair, Eval Panel, Ctr Mat Sci, Nat Bur Standards, 81-84; vis scientist, Centre Nat de Recherche Scientifique, Univ Bordeaux, France, 83 & 86; J W Fulbright res scholar, Obafemi Awolowo Univ, Nigeria, 92-93. *Mem:* Am Ceramic Soc; Am Phys Soc; Am Crystallog Asn; Am Inst Mining & Metall Eng; Am Carbon Soc; Am Asn Univ Prof; fel Nat Soc Black Physicists. *Res:* Structure of carbon and composite materials; x-ray diffraction, small angle scattering; electron microscopy and diffraction; characterization of structure of materials; correlation of structure with electrical, magnetic, mechanical and thermophysical properties. *Mailing Add:* Dept Mat Sci & Mineral Eng Univ Calif Berkeley CA 94720. *Fax:* 510-643-5792; *E-Mail:* petebragg@aol.com

BRAGG, SUSAN LYNN, OPTICAL PHYSICS & CHEMISTRY, LASER SPECTROSCOPY. *Current Pos:* PRES, BLUEWILLOW SCI, 94- *Personal Data:* b Wheeling, WVa, Nov 16, 53; m 87. *Educ:* Wash Univ, Mo, BA, 75, MA, 77, PhD(earth & planetary sci), 81. *Prof Exp:* Sr scientist, McDonnell Douglas Res Labs, McDonnell Douglas Corp, 82-90; sr proj scientist, Metaphase Corp, 90-94. *Concurrent Pos:* Vis fel, Somerville Col, Oxford Univ, UK, 83-84. *Mem:* Optical Soc Am. *Res:* Experimental high resolution spectroscopy of atoms and small molecules; investigation of atmospheric propagation in visible and near infrared spectral regions; development of laser spectroscopic methods. *Mailing Add:* 6920 Pershing St Louis MO 63130

BRAGG, THOMAS BRAXTON, PLANT ECOLOGY, ECOLOGY. *Current Pos:* Asst prof, 74-78, ASSOC PROF BIOL, UNIV NEBR, OMAHA, 78- *Personal Data:* b San Francisco, Calif, June 4, 38; m 63; c 2. *Educ:* Calif State Polytech Univ, BS, 63; Kans State Univ, MS, 71, PhD(biol), 74. *Mem:* Ecol Soc Am; Soc Range Mgt; Am Inst Biol Sci; AAAS. *Res:* Fire ecology of native prairie and forest ecosystems with emphasis on prairie vegetation; ecosystem management; grassland restoration. *Mailing Add:* Dept Biol Univ Nebr Omaha NE 68182-0001

BRAGIN, JOSEPH, PHYSICAL CHEMISTRY. *Current Pos:* asst prof, 70-74, assoc prof, 74-, PROF CHEM, CALIF STATE UNIV, LOS ANGELES, ASSOC DEAN, SCH LETT & SCI. *Personal Data:* b Brooklyn, NY, Jan 23, 39; m 68. *Educ:* Brooklyn Col, BS, 59; Univ Wis, PhD(chem), 67. *Prof Exp:* Fel chem, Univ SC, 67-70. *Res:* Vibrational spectroscopy as a probe of chemical and biological activity. *Mailing Add:* Chem Calif State Univ 5151 State Univ Dr Los Angeles CA 90032-8000

BRAGINSKI, ALEKSANDER IGNACE, MAGNETISM, SOLID STATE ELECTRONICS. *Current Pos:* DIR INST THIN FILMS & ION TECHNOL, KFA & PROF PHYSICS, UNIV WYPERTAL, GER. *Personal Data:* b Warsaw, Poland, Apr 23, 29; US citizen; m; c 1. *Educ:* Wroclaw Tech Univ, MSc, 51; Polish Acad Sci, PhD, 60; Warsaw Tech Univ, DSc, 65. *Honors & Awards:* Heavy Mach Indust Award, Poland, 59; Polish Nat Prize, 64. *Prof Exp:* Jr engr, Nat Inst Telecommun, Wroclaw, 51-52; sr engr, Radio Works, Warsaw, 52-53, sect mgr powder cores, 53-54, lab mgr ferrites, 54-55; dept mgr, HF Ceramics Factory, 55-56; tech dir, Polfer Magnetic Mat Factory, 56; head, Polfer Res Lab, 56-66; res engr, Lignes Telegraphiques & Telephoniques, France, 66-67; sr scientist, Westinghouse Elec Co, 67-69, fel scientist, 69-71, adv scientist, 71-72, mgr solid state magnetics, 72-75, mgr superconducting mat, 75-87, consult scientist, Res & Develop Ctr, 87-89. *Concurrent Pos:* Consult, Inst Comput, Polish Acad Sci, 56-60; lectr, Warsaw Tech Univ, 58 & 64-66; from res asst to res leader, Lab Magnetism & Solid Physics, Nat Ctr Sci Res, 60-61; vis scientist, Res Ctr Juelich, (ISI-KFA), 89- *Mem:* Sr mem Inst Elec & Electronic Engrs; Am Phys Soc. *Res:* Microwave magnetics; induced anisotropy and aftereffects; ferrites; cylindrical domain memory technology; superconducting materials; Josephson junction technology, HTS; high-temperature superconductor electronic. *Mailing Add:* Steinstr Allee 58 52428 Juelich Germany

BRAGINSKY, STANISLAV IOSIFOVICH, PLASMA PHYSICS. *Current Pos:* GEOPHYSICIST & RESEARCHER, INST GEOPHYS/ PLANETARY PHYSICS, UNIV CALIF, LOS ANGELES, 89- *Personal Data:* b Moscow, Apr 15, 26; m 55, Maya A Boyarskaya; c Galina & Leonid. *Educ:* Moscow Inst Mech, Degree eng & physics, 48; Inst Atomic Energy, Moscow, cand sci, 53, DSc, 66. *Honors & Awards:* Lenin Prize for Res in Plasma Physics, Acad Sci, USSR, 58; John Adam Fleming Medal, Am Geophys Union, 93. *Prof Exp:* Sr scientist, I V Kurchatov Inst Atomic Energy, Moscow, 48-78, O Yu Schmidt Inst Physics of Earth, 78-88. *Res:* Development of two-temperature equations of plasma dynamics; theory of the pinch-effect in high power electrical discharges in gases; advancement of theory of hydromagnetic dynamo of the Earth and theory of geomagnetic secular variations; contributed numerous articles to professional journals. *Mailing Add:* Inst Geophys & Planetary Physics Rm 3879 Slichter Hall Univ Calif-Los Angeles 405 Hilgard Ave Los Angeles CA 90095

BRAGOLE, ROBERT ANTHONY, ADHESIVES & COATING TECHNOLOGY, POLYMER SYNTHESIS. *Current Pos:* dir res & develop, 85-87, VPRES RES & DEVELOP, WORTHEN INDUST, 87- *Personal Data:* b Somerville, Mass, Oct 17, 36; m 62, Jean D Beaulieu; c Linda, Lisa, Robert II, Michele & John. *Educ:* Boston Univ, AB, 58; Northeastern Univ, MS, 60; Yale Univ, PhD(org chem), 65. *Prof Exp:* Teaching fel, Boston Univ, 57-58; teaching fel & res asst, Northeastern Univ, 58-60; teaching fel, Yale Univ, 60-62, res asst, 62-64; res chemist, Carwin Res Labs, 65-66; sr res chemist, USM Chem Co, 66-69, mgr appl res, 70-73, lab mgr, Bostik Div, USM Corp, 73-78; tech dir, Bostik Div, Emhart Corp, 78-80, lab mgr, Bostik Div, 80-85. *Concurrent Pos:* Instr, Southern Conn State Col, 65-66. *Mem:* Sr mem Am Chem Soc; Soc Mfg Engrs; Soc Plastics Engrs. *Res:* Synthesis of polyurethanes; development of multiple adhesive and coating systems; lamination, diecutting, polyolefin treatments and adhesive systems; photochemistry; adhesives; coatings and laminates for interior trim applications in the automotive industry. *Mailing Add:* 5 Innis Dr Danvers MA 01923. *Fax:* 603-888-7945

BRAGONIER, JOHN ROBERT, OBSTETRICS & GYNECOLOGY. *Current Pos:* CHMN, DEPT OBSTET & GYNEC, CIGNA HEALTH PLANS CALIF, LOS ANGELES, 85- *Personal Data:* b Cedar Falls, Iowa, July 4, 37; m 59; c 3. *Educ:* Iowa State Univ, BS, 60; Univ Nebr, MS, 63, MD, 64, PhD(med sci, biochem), 67. *Prof Exp:* Intern, Univ Nebr Hosp, 64-65, resident obstet & gynec, 65; resident obstet & gynec & instr, Jefferson Med Col Hosp, 66-68; res assoc, Inst Child Health & Human Develop, NIH, 68-70; head physician, Dept Obstet & Gynec, Harbor Gen Med Ctr, Torrance, 70-85; asst prof obstet & gynec, Univ Calif, Los Angeles, 70-76, adj assoc prof, 76-82, adj prof, 82-85. *Concurrent Pos:* Adj prof, Univ Calif, Riverside, 82- *Mem:* Fel Am Col Obstetricians & Gynecologyists; Am Fertil Soc; Am Pub Health Asn; AAAS. *Res:* Medical biochemistry; biochemical teratology; social issues in obstetrics and gynecology (family planning, sex education, problem pregnancy); training of paramedical personnel; prevention of preterm birth; health care delivery systems. *Mailing Add:* 1640 Harper Ave Redondo Beach CA 90278-2725

BRAGONIER, WENDELL HUGHELL, BOTANY. *Current Pos:* prof bot & plant path & dean grad sch, 63-75, asst dir, Exp Sta, 79-82, EMER PROF BOT & PLANT PATH & EMER DEAN GRAD SCH, COLO STATE UNIV, 75- *Personal Data:* b Geneseo Twp, Iowa, Aug 5, 10; m 34, 87, Edna Teague; c J Robert, James W, Mary Ellen (Vogt), Lorraine (Holcomb), Donna (Miller), Barbara (Taniguchi) & Beverly (Suarez). *Educ:* Iowa State Teachers Col, BA, 33; Iowa State Univ, MS, 41, PhD(plant path), 47. *Prof Exp:* High sch teacher, Iowa, 33-34, Tenn, 34-35 & Iowa, 35-39; instr bot, Iowa State Univ, 40-42, res assoc & asst to dir, Indust Sci Res Inst, 42-47, assoc prof bot, 47-49, prof & head dept bot & plant path, 50-63, assoc dir, Camp Dodge Br, 46-47. *Concurrent Pos:* Chmn sci adv coun, Am Seed Res Found, 59-85; consult, Colo State Dept Agr, 79-82. *Mem:* Fel AAAS; Bot Soc Am; Sigma Xi. *Res:* Plant pathology and morphology; teaching of botany; umbrella disease of Rhus glabra L caused by Botryosphaeria ribis G & D; ethanol production from grain and agricultural wastes. *Mailing Add:* 900 Arbor Ave Unit 13 Ft Collins CO 80526

BRAHAM, HOWARD WALLACE, VERTEBRATE ZOOLOGY, MARINE ECOLOGY. *Current Pos:* supvr wildlife biol, 75-84, DIR NAT MARINE MAMMAL LAB, NAT MARINE FISHERIES SERV, NAT OCEANIC & ATMOSPHERIC ADMIN, 84- *Personal Data:* b Los Angeles, Calif, Dec 4, 42; c 4. *Educ:* Calif State Univ, Los Angeles, BS, 66; Calif Polytech State Univ, San Luis Obispo, MS, 72; Ohio State Univ, Columbus, PhD(ecol), 75. *Honors & Awards:* Admin Award, Nat Oceanic & Atomospheric Admin, 83. *Prof Exp:* Cryptographer, US Dept Justice, Fed Bur Invest, Los Angeles, 63-64; police officer, West Covina, Calif, 64-68; teacher math & phys educ, El Rancho Sch Dist, Calif, 68-69; teaching & res assoc, Calif Tech State Univ, San Luis Obispo, 69-72; teaching & res assoc, Ohio State Univ, 72-75. *Concurrent Pos:* Steering Comt, US-USSR Comn for Environ Protection Marine Mammals, 76-; manuscript ed, Fisheries Bulletin, 77-80; mem, Comt Sci Adv, Int Whaling Comn, 79- *Mem:* Soc Marine Mammal. *Res:* Population biology of marine mammals, especially endangered whales, specializing in the ecology of the Bowhead Whale, Gray Whale and Northern Sea Lion and arctic species. *Mailing Add:* Nat Marine Mammal Lab NOAA 7600 Sand Point Way NE Bldg 4 Seattle WA 98115-0070

BRAHAM, ROSCOE RILEY, JR, CLOUD PHYSICS, THUNDERSTORMS. *Current Pos:* SCHOLAR IN RESIDENCE, NC STATE UNIV, 91- *Personal Data:* b Yates City, Ill, Jan 3, 21; m 43, Mary A Moll; c Ruth A, Nancy K, Richard R & Jean L. *Educ:* Ohio Univ, BS, 42; Univ Chicago, SM, 48, PhD(meteorol), 51. *Honors & Awards:* Losey Award, Inst Aeronaut Sci, 50; Silver Medal, US Dept Com, 50; Rossby Gold Medal, Am Meteorol Soc, 81, C F Brooks Award, 87; Schaefer Award, Weather Modification Asn, 87. *Prof Exp:* Sr analyst & officer in chg thunderstorm proj, US Weather Bur, 46-49; res asst meteorol, Univ Chicago, 49-50; res meteorologist cloud physics & weather modification, NMex Inst Mining & Technol, 50-51; sr meteorologist, Univ Chicago, 51-56, from assoc prof to prof meteorol, 56-91. *Concurrent Pos:* Assoc ed, J Am Meteorol Soc, 53-69; dir, Inst Atmospheric Physics & assoc prof, Univ Ariz, 54-56; mem bd trustees, Univ Corp Atmospheric Res, 65-67, 73-77 & 79-86; prin investr, Proj Metromex, NSF, 70-78; mem adv comt, Proj Stormfury, Nat Oceanic & Atmospheric Admin, Nat Acad Sci, 72-80; mem weather modification adv comt, US Dept Com, 77-78. *Mem:* Fel AAAS; fel Am Meteorol Soc (pres, 88); Am Geophys Union (pres, Meteorol Sect, 76-77); Sigma Xi; fel Royal Meteorol Soc. *Res:* Cloud physics and weather modification; urban meteorology; thunderstorms and severe weather; understanding the physics of clouds and precipitation and determining the extent to which they can be, and are being, influenced by activities of man. *Mailing Add:* Marine Earth & Atmospheric Sci Dept NC State Univ Raleigh NC 27695

BRAHANA, THOMAS ROY, MATHEMATICS. *Current Pos:* from asst prof to prof, 54-91, EMER PROF MATH, UNIV GA, 91- *Personal Data:* b Champaign, Ill, June 26, 26; m 51, Mary A Weiss; c Elizabeth, Joan, Patrick & Daniel. *Educ:* Univ Ill, AB, 47; Univ Mich, MA, 50, PhD(math), 55. *Prof Exp:* Instr math, Dartmouth Col, 53-54. *Concurrent Pos:* Mem, Inst Advan Study, 57-58; Fulbright lectr, Univ Zagreb, Yugoslavia, 71-72. *Mem:* Am Math Soc. *Res:* Algebraic topology and geometry. *Mailing Add:* Dept Math Univ Ga Athens GA 30602

BRAHEN, LEONARD SAMUEL, psychiatry, for more information see previous edition

BRAHMA, CHANDRA SEKHAR, GEOTECHNICAL ENGINEERING, STRUCTURAL ENGINEERING. *Current Pos:* PROF CIVIL ENG, CALIF STATE UNIV, FRESNO, 80- *Personal Data:* b Calcutta, India, Oct 5, 41; US citizen; m 72, Purnima Sinha; c Charanjit & Barunashish. *Educ:* Calcutta Univ, India, BE, 62; Mich State Univ, MSc, 65; Ohio State Univ, PhD(civil eng), 69. *Honors & Awards:* AT&T Found Award, Am Soc Eng Educ, 91; Edmund Friedman Prof Recognition Award, Am Soc Civil Engrs, 93. *Prof Exp:* Asst engr, Govt West Bengal, India, 62-63; proj engr, Frank H Lehr Assoc, East Orange, NJ, 69-70; sr engr, John G Reutter Assoc, Camden, NJ, 70-72; asst prof civil eng, Worcester Polytech Inst, Mass, 72-73; chief geotech engr, Daniel, Mann, Johnson & Mendenhall, Baltimore, Md, 73-79; sr engr, Sverdrup & Parcel, St Louis, Mo, 79-80. *Concurrent Pos:* Res asst, Mich State Univ, 63-65; teaching & res assoc, Ohio State Univ, 65-69; assoc, SAFE Internation Inc, Philadelphia, Pa, 72-74; consult, Expert Resources, Inc, Peoria Heights, Ill, 81- & Twinning Labs, Inc, 82-; spec consult, Sverdrup & Parcel, St Louis, Mo, 80-; secy, Am Soc Civil Engrs, 81-83, vpres, 83-84, pres, 84-85, dir, 85-86; vis prof, eng dept, Univ Republica, Montevidio, Uruguay, 84; Fulbright Cert, Bd Foreign Scholars, 84; Fulbright grant, Coun Int Exchange Scholars, 84; consult, Marderosian & Swanson Law Firm, Fresno, Calif, 85-, & Hurlbutt, Clevenger, Long & Vortman, Visalia, Calif, 88-; Hugh B William fel, Asn Drilled Shaft Contractors, 86. *Mem:* Fel Am Soc Civil Engrs; Am Soc Testing & Mat; Sigma Xi; Int Soc Soil Mech & Found Eng; Int Soc Rock Mech; Am Soc Eng Educ; Nat Soc Prof Engrs. *Res:* Soft-ground and hard rock tunneling; deep excavations; soil-structure interaction; deep foundations; stochastic behavior of soils; physical and creep behavior of soils; specialized engineering constructions; landslides; computer-aided design in foundation engineering; underground engineering; forensic engineering; professional issues in engineering. *Mailing Add:* Dept Civil Eng Calif State Univ Fresno CA 93740-0094. *Fax:* 209-278-6759; *E-Mail:* Chandra_brahma@csufresno.edu

BRAHMBHATT, SUDHIR R, CHEMICAL ENGINEERING, GENERAL ENVIRONMENTAL SCIENCES. *Current Pos:* applications engr, Messer Griesheim Industs, 84-86, sr proj engr, 86-88, mgr oxygen & chem group, 88-92, res & develop dept head, 92-95, MGR PULP & PAPER, CHEM, HOECHST GROUP, MESSER GRIESHEIM INDUSTS, 95- *Personal Data:* b Dabhoi, Gujarat State, India, Apr 4, 51; m 77, Ashaben Amarsingh; c Tejal S & Nisha S. *Educ:* Nadiad Inst Technol, India, BEngg, 73; Stevens Inst Technol, MEng, 75; Fairleigh Dickinson Univ, MBA, 82; Kennedy Western Univ, PhD(chem eng), 91. *Prof Exp:* Res asst, Stevens Inst Technol, 75-77; chem engr, Exxon Co, USA, 77-79; sr process engr, Air Prod & Chem Inc, 79-84. *Mem:* Am Inst Chem Engrs; Am Chem Soc; Am Ceramic Soc; Am Soc Metals; Tech Asn Pulp & Paper Inst; Am Powder Metall Inst. *Res:* System for regulated atmosphere; air oxygen, fuel, oxygen burner system; chlorofluorocarbon recovery system; compact system for chlorofluorocarbons recovery; granted 5 patents. *Mailing Add:* 1700 Countrytop Ct Glencoe MO 63038-1446

BRAHMI, ZACHARIE, TUMOR IMMUNOLOGY, IMMUNO GENETICS. *Current Pos:* PROF MED, DEPT IMMUNOL, SCH MED, IND UNIV, 78- *Educ:* Ind Univ, PhD(immunol), 70. *Mailing Add:* Dept Med Riley 0615 Ind Univ Sch Med 702 Barnhill Dr Indianapolis IN 46202-5200. *Fax:* 317-274-1108

BRAID, THOMAS HAMILTON, EXPERIMENTAL PHYSICS, INSTRUMENTS. *Current Pos:* PHYSICIST, ARGONNE NAT LAB, 56- *Personal Data:* b Heriot, Scotland, Dec 21, 25; m 51; c 2. *Educ:* Univ Edinburgh, BSc, 47, PhD(physics), 51. *Prof Exp:* Nat Res Coun Can res fel physics, Atomic Energy Can, Ltd, 50-52; res asst, Princeton Univ, 52-55, instr, 55-56, res assoc, 56. *Concurrent Pos:* Vis physicist, Atomic Energy Res Establishment, Eng, 66-67; assoc ed, Appl Physics Lett, 74-79; ed, Rev Sci Instruments, 79- *Mem:* Fel Am Phys Soc. *Res:* Nuclear reactions and structure; radiation detection and instrumentation; reactor safety; scientific instruments. *Mailing Add:* 7619 S Sussex Creek Dr Apt 301 Darien IL 60559. *Fax:* 630-252-6371; *E-Mail:* rsi@anl.gov

BRAIDA, LOUIS BENJAMIN DANIEL, ELECTRICAL ENGINEERING. *Current Pos:* HENRY ELLIS WARREN PROF ELEC ENG, MASS INST TECHNOL. *Mailing Add:* Dept Elec Eng & Comput Sci Mass Inst Technol Cambridge MA 02139

BRAIDEK, JOHN GEORGE, AGRICULTURE. *Current Pos:* AGRICULTURIST, WESTERN PRODUCER, SASKATOON, CAN. *Honors & Awards:* Fel Award, Agr Inst Can, 92. *Mailing Add:* Western Producer PO Box 2500 Saskatoon SK S7K 2C4 Can

BRAIDS, OLIN CAPRON, SOIL CHEMISTRY, WATER CHEMISTRY. *Current Pos:* ASSOC, GERAGHTY & MILLER, INC, 96- *Personal Data:* b Providence, RI, Apr 29, 38; m 62, Elaine Heal; c Sally. *Educ:* Univ NH, BA, 60, MS, 63; Ohio State Univ, PhD(agron, soil chem), 66. *Prof Exp:* Res assoc, Univ Ill, Urbana-Champaign, 66-67, asst prof soil org chem, 67-72; hydrologist, US Geol Surv, 72-75; sr scientist, Geraghty & Miller, Inc, 75-80, assoc, 80-89; prin scientist, Blasland, Bouck & Lee, 89-90, vpres, 91-93; vpres, Eder Assoc, 93-96. *Concurrent Pos:* Abstractor, Chem Abstr Serv, 67-77; NSF guest lectr, Univ Calif, Riverside, 70; guest lectr, Aramco Oil, Dhahran, Saudi Arabia, 86; consult surface clean-up & mobilization processes, US Environ Protection Agency, 90. *Mem:* Am Chem Soc; Am Soc Agron; Soil Sci Soc Am; Asn Ground-Water Sci & Eng; Nat Water Well Asn; Water Environ Fedn. *Res:* Effect of land disposal of municipal sludges on soils and plants; influence of waste disposal practice on ground-water quality; chemistry of contaminants from waste in aquifers; chemistry of petroleum-related contaminants in aquifers. *Mailing Add:* 14497 N Dale Mabry Hwy Suite 115 Tampa FL 33618. *Fax:* 813-264-1850; *E-Mail:* obraids@gmgw.com

BRAIDWOOD, CLINTON ALEXANDER, ORGANIC CHEMISTRY. *Current Pos:* BRAIDWOOD CHEM CONSULT, 81- *Personal Data:* b Snover, Mich, Nov 14, 14; m 42; c 3. *Educ:* Mich State Univ, BS, 40. *Prof Exp:* Mem staff motor prod develop, US Rubber Co, 40-42; asst dir res, Reichold Chem, Inc, 42-49; vpres mfg & res develop, Schenectady Chems, Inc, 49-71, exec vpres, 71-73, pres, 73-80. *Mem:* AAAS; Am Inst Chemists; Am Chem Soc. *Res:* Alkylation of phenol and synthesis of phenolic resins from alkyl phenols; polymerization chemistry; terpene resins. *Mailing Add:* 6541 East Shore Rd Traverse City MI 49684-1820

BRAILOVSKY, CARLOS ALBERTO, PSYCHOMETRICS. *Current Pos:* PROF, OFF EVAL HEALTH SCI, UNIV LAVAL, 88-, DIR, CTR MEASUREMENT & EVAL HEALTH SCI, 92-, PROF, DEPT FAMILY MED, 95- *Personal Data:* b Buenos Aires, Arg, Oct 16, 39; Can citizen; m 91, Nancy Ouei; c Rodrigo, Javier & Martin. *Educ:* Buenos Aires Univ, MD, 61; Univ Laval, MA, 87. *Honors & Awards:* Squibb Award, Arg Med Asn, 57. *Prof Exp:* Buenos Aires Univ fel, Inst Res Sci Cancer, Villejuif, France, 63-65, res assoc virol, 65-68; invited scientist path, Univ Montreal, 69; assoc prof, Univ Sherbrooke, 70-80, prof cell biol, fac med, 80-87. *Concurrent Pos:* Consult eval, Col Physicians Quebec, 89-, Law Soc Upper Can, Toronto, Can, 93-; consult testing & assessment, Col Family Physicians Can, 94- *Mem:* Am Med Facil Can. *Res:* Psychometric caracteristics of tools for assessment of clinical competence. *Mailing Add:* Cessul Med Sch Univ Laval Quebec PQ G1K 7P4 Can. *E-Mail:* cbrailovsky@cessul.ulaval.ca

BRAILSFORD, ALAN DAVID, PHYSICS. *Personal Data:* b Mansfield, Eng, Apr 3, 30; m 52, Yvonne J Perkins; c Amanda, Melanie & Gavin. *Educ:* Birmingham Univ, Eng, BSc, 53, PhD(math physics), 56. *Hon Degrees:* DSc, Birmingham Univ. *Prof Exp:* Res physicist, Bell Tel Labs, 56-57, Sci Labs, Ford Motor Co, 57-71; prof fel, Theoret Physics Div Harwell, 71-73; sr staff scientist, Sci Labs, Ford Motor Co, 73-89, mgr physics, Ford Res Lab, 89-91. *Concurrent Pos:* Lectr, Physics Dept, Wayne State Univ, 64-66; consult, Metals & Ceramics Div, Oak Ridge Nat Lab, 75- *Mem:* Fel Am Phys Soc; fel Inst Physics; Mat Res Soc; fel Am Soc Metals Int; AAAS. *Res:* Sensor physics, irradiation effects in metals; electronic and ionic transport properties of materials; point defect and dislocation properties in materials. *Mailing Add:* 1212 Beechmont Dearborn MI 48124

BRAIN, CARLOS W, STATISTICAL METHODOLOGY, DESIGN OF EXPERIMENTS. *Current Pos:* ASSOC PROF & CHMN STATIST, FLA INT UNIV, 73- *Personal Data:* b Lima, Peru; US citizen. *Educ:* Univ Agraria, Peru, BS, 60, Ing Agr, 64; WVa Univ, MS, 69, PhD(appl statist), 75. *Concurrent Pos:* Bk rev ed, J Qual Technol, 85-87. *Mem:* Am Statist Asn; Biometric Soc. *Res:* Statistical methodology; development of procedures for testing distributional assumptions. *Mailing Add:* 13020 SW 116th St Miami FL 33186. *Fax:* 305-348-4172; *E-Mail:* Bitnet: brainc@servax

BRAIN, DEVIN KING, ORGANIC CHEMISTRY. *Current Pos:* RETIRED. *Personal Data:* b Mt Vernon, Ohio, Jan 7, 26; m 50, 83, Jeanne Hoffman; c 3. *Educ:* Univ Ariz, BS, 48, MS, 49; Ohio State Univ, PhD(org chem), 54. *Prof Exp:* Res chemist, Procter & Gamble Co, 54-88, tech mgt, 57-88. *Mem:* Am Chem Soc; Am Soc Mass Spectrometry; AAAS. *Res:* Soap and detergent products; application of, separation and instrumental techniques, especially gas chromatography, gas chromatography and mass spectrometry, mass spectrometry, nuclear magnetic resonance, irridescent radiation and x-ray techniques, to product development; industrial organic chemistry, analysis of waste water; analytical chemistry. *Mailing Add:* Three Walsh Lane Cincinnati OH 45208. *E-Mail:* decide@tso.cin.ix.net

BRAIN, JOSEPH DAVID, PHYSIOLOGY, ENVIRONMENTAL HEALTH. *Current Pos:* Res assoc physiol, Harvard Sch Pub Health, 66-68, from asst prof to assoc prof, 68-78, actg assoc dean acad affairs, 76-77, dir, respiratory biol prog, 81-93, DIR HARVARD PULMONARY SPECIALIZED CTR RES, HARVARD SCH PUB HEALTH, 77-, PROF PHYSIOL, 78-, CHMN, DEPT ENVIRON HEALTH & DIR PHYSIOL PROG. *Personal Data:* b Paterson, NJ, Jan 20, 40; m 61, Judith Boll; c Don S, Derek J & Jason M. *Educ:* Harvard Univ, SM, 62, SMHyg, 63, SDHyg, 66. *Honors & Awards:* Chadwick Medal. *Concurrent Pos:* NIH res career develop award, 69-74; mem comt, Cardiovascular & Pulmonary Study Sect, NIH, 75-79; mem prog proj res rev comt, Nat Heart, Lung & Blood Inst, 80-83. *Mem:* Am Physiol Soc; Am Thoracic Soc; Reticuloendothelial Soc; Sigma Xi; fel AAAS. *Res:* Function and structure of macrophages; pulmonary responses to inhaled gases and particles; health effects of air pollution; deposition and clearance of inhaled particles; occupational lung disease; drug delivery to and through the lungs. *Mailing Add:* Dept Environ Health Harvard Sch Pub Health 665 Hungtinton Ave Rm 1409 Boston MA 02115-6021

BRAINARD, ALAN J, CHEMICAL ENGINEERING. *Current Pos:* asst prof, 67-71, ASSOC PROF CHEM ENG, UNIV PITTSBURGH, 71- *Personal Data:* b Cleveland, Ohio, June 30, 36; m 64; c 2. *Educ:* Fenn Col, BS, 59; Univ Mich, MS, 61, PhD(chem eng), 64. *Prof Exp:* Engr, Esso Res Labs, 64-67. *Concurrent Pos:* NSF res grant, 68. *Mem:* Assoc Am Inst Chem Engrs; Am Chem Soc; Am Soc Eng Educ. *Res:* Phase equilibria of multicomponent systems; behavior of entropy at low temperatures; entropy maximum principle and the conditions of equilibrium; non-equilibrium thermodynamics; anisotropic heat conduction; carbon oxidation catalysis. *Mailing Add:* Dept Chem Eng Univ Pittsburgh 1249 Benedum Hall Pittsburgh PA 15260-0001

BRAINARD, JAMES R, ISOTOPE. *Current Pos:* MEM TECH STAFF CHEM & ENVIRON RES DEVELOP, LOS ALAMOS NAT LAB. *Educ:* Hope Col, Holland, BA, 71; Ind Univ, PhD(chem), 79. *Res:* Bioremediation of contaminated sites and process streams; magnetic resonance imaging contrast agents; applications of nuclear magnetic resonance and stable isotopes to the study of metabolism and structure; author of numerous publications; granted one patent. *Mailing Add:* Los Alamos Nat Lab CST-18 MSC 345 Los Alamos NM 87544

BRAINERD, BARRON, MATHEMATICS, QUANTITATIVE STYLISTICS. *Current Pos:* from asst prof to assoc prof, 59-67, prof, 67-89, EMER PROF MATH & LING, UNIV TORONTO, 89- *Personal Data:* b New York, NY, Apr 13, 28; Can citizen. *Educ:* Mass Inst Technol, SB, 49; Univ Mich, MS, 51, PhD(math), 54. *Prof Exp:* Instr math, Univ BC, 54-57; asst prof math, Univ Western Ont, 57-59. *Concurrent Pos:* Vis fel, Australian Nat Univ, 62-63. *Mem:* Modern Lang Asn; Asn Comput & Humanities; Can Ling Asn. *Res:* Theory of partially ordered rings; rings of continuous functions; operators on function spaces; mathematical linguistics; statistics of literary style; stochastic models in linguistics. *Mailing Add:* 7070 Alcorn Ave Toronto ON M4V 1E4 Can

BRAINERD, JEROME J(AMES), FLUID MECHANICS. *Current Pos:* head, Fluid & Thermal Sci Sect & chmn, Fluid & Thermal Eng Facil, Univ Ala, 68-70, chmn, Dept Mech Eng, 73-78, assoc prof, 65-91, EMER PROF AEROSPACE ENG, UNIV ALA, HUNTSVILLE, 91- *Personal Data:* b San Angelo, Tex, Sept 15, 32; m 56; c 6. *Educ:* Univ Notre Dame, BS, 54, MS, 56; Cornell Univ, PhD(aerospace eng), 63. *Prof Exp:* Sr aerodyn engr, Gen Dynamics/Convair, 60-62 & space sci lab, Gen Dynamics/Astronaut, 62-63, staff scientist, 63-65. *Mem:* Am Inst Aeronaut & Astronaut; Sigma Xi; Am Geophys Union; Am Phys Soc. *Res:* Various phases of fluid dynamics including magnetogasdynamics; aerodynamics; hypersonic and high enthalpy flows; perturbation theory; chemically reacting flows; hypervelocity impact; turbomachinery. *Mailing Add:* Space Sci Lab ES-84 NASA/Marshall Space Flight Ctr Huntsville AL 35812

BRAINERD, WALTER SCOTT, MATHEMATICS, COMPUTER SCIENCE. *Current Pos:* PRES, UNICOMP, INC, 91- *Personal Data:* b Des Moines, Iowa, May 27, 36; m 58; c 3. *Educ:* Univ Colo, BA, 58; Univ Md, MA, 61; Purdue Univ, PhD(comput sci), 67. *Prof Exp:* Instr math, Naval Postgrad Sch, 63-65, asst prof comput sci, 67-69; asst prof math statist, Columbia Univ, 69-72; prof math, Harvey Mudd Col, 72-73; sr systs specialist, Burroughs Corp, 73-78; mem staff, Los Alamos Nat Lab, 78-81; prof comput sci, Univ NMex, 81-90; sr software engr, Sun Micro Systs, 90-91. *Concurrent Pos:* Vis asst prof, Univ Calif, San Diego, 68. *Mem:* Asn Comput Mach; Am Nat Stand Inst. *Res:* Programming languages, theory of computation. *Mailing Add:* 1874 San Bernardino Dr NE Albuquerque NM 87122

BRAITHWAITE, CHARLES HENRY, JR, ORGANIC CHEMISTRY, CHEMICAL & FORENSIC ENGINEERING. *Current Pos:* CONSULT, BRAITHWAITE CONSULT, 87- *Personal Data:* b Chicago, Ill, Dec 16, 20; m 49, Bernice Hyde; c Charles H III & Betty S. *Educ:* Univ Calif, Los Angeles, AB, 41; Univ Mich, BSE, 43; Carnegie Inst Technol, MS, 48, DSc, 49. *Prof Exp:* Insulation engr, Westinghouse Elec Corp, 43-46; sr chemist, Shell Oil Co, 49-51; dir lab, WestVaco ChlorAlkal Div, FMC Corp, 51-57; dir research & develop, Productol Co, 57-58; pres, Cal Colonial Chemsolve, 58-87. *Concurrent Pos:* Consult, Res Dept, US Borax Corp, 58-65, W R Grace Res Corp, 59-70, Piezo Ceramic Div, Gulton Indust, 64-75 & Stratos Div, Fairchild Indust, 76-; dir, Jacksons Prods Corp, 70-88. *Mem:* Am Chem Soc; Am Inst Chem Engrs; Soc Plastics Engrs; Sigma Xi. *Res:* Coatings; plastics; materials engineering. *Mailing Add:* Braithwaite Consults 11232 Tigrina Whittier CA 90603. *Fax:* 562-947-8380

BRAITHWAITE, JOHN GEDEN NORTH, optics, for more information see previous edition

BRAJTER-TOTH, ANNA F, BIOANALYTICAL CHEMISTRY, ELECTROANALYTICAL CHEMISTRY. *Current Pos:* asst prof, 83-88, ASSOC PROF ANAL CHEM, UNIV FLA, 88- *Personal Data:* b Warsaw, Poland; US citizen; m 79, John P; c Peter H & Gregory L. *Educ:* Univ Warsaw, Poland, MS, 74; Southern Ill Univ, PhD(chem), 79. *Prof Exp:* Res asst, Univ Warsaw, 74-75; res assoc, Univ Okla, 79-80; asst prof anal chem, Univ Maine, 80-83. *Concurrent Pos:* Assoc ed, J Electrochem Soc, 89-90. *Mem:* Am Chem Soc; Soc Electroanal Chem; Electrochem Soc. *Res:* Development of electroanalytical methods for bioanalysis; on-line electrochemistry, mass spectrometry; sensors. *Mailing Add:* Dept Chem Univ Fla Gainesville FL 32611. *Fax:* 904-392-4651

BRAKEFIELD, JAMES CHARLES, COMPUTER THEORY, INTELLIGENT SYSTEMS. *Current Pos:* RES ENGR, KRUG INT, 75- *Personal Data:* b Janesville, Wis, Nov 28, 44; m 78. *Educ:* Univ Wis-Madison, BS, 71, MS(elec eng) & MS(comput sci), 72. *Prof Exp:* Systs analyst, Tex Instruments, 73-74. *Mem:* Inst Elec & Electronics Engrs; Asn Comput Mach; Int Neurol Network Soc. *Res:* Select, integrate, program and support computer equipment for scientific research; image processing and implementation of a facility for image filtering; modeling and implementation of bio-physical models; color video display generator (real time). *Mailing Add:* Conceptual Mindworks Inc 4318 Woodcock Dr San Antonio TX 78228

BRAKENSIEK, DONALD LLOYD, AGRICULTURAL, WATERSHED HYDROLOGY. *Current Pos:* RES ASSOC, UNIV MD. *Personal Data:* b Alexis, Ill, Nov 5, 28; m 56; c 3. *Educ:* Univ Ill, BS(agr) & BS(agr eng), 51, MS, 52; Iowa State Univ, PhD(agr eng), 55. *Prof Exp:* Agr engr, Agr Res Serv, USDA, Colo, 56, hydraul engr, Ohio, 57-59 & Md, 60-61, res hydraul engr, Hydrograph Lab & chief engr, Plant Indust Sta, 68-72, staff scientist, Watershed Hydrol, Nat Prog Staff, 72-74, location & res leader, Northwest Watershed Res Ctr, 74-85. *Mem:* Am Soc Agr Engrs; Am Geophys Union. *Res:* Analytical hydrology; soil water process modeling and watershed hydrology models; author of 120 publications. *Mailing Add:* 881 E Pennsylvania Dr Boise ID 83706

BRAKER, WILLIAM PAUL, ICHTHYOLOGY. *Current Pos:* RETIRED. *Personal Data:* b Chicago, Ill, Nov 3, 26; m 50, Patricia Reese. *Educ:* Northwestern Univ, BS, 50; George Washington Univ, MS, 53. *Prof Exp:* Mem staff, John G Shedd Aquarium, Chicago, 53-94, dir, 64-94. *Concurrent Pos:* Asst secy, Shedd Aquarium Soc, 60-65, secy, 65- *Mem:* Am Fisheries Soc; Am Soc Ichthyologists & Herpetologists; Am Asn Zool Parks & Aquariums; Soc Marine Mammal. *Res:* Aquatic biology. *Mailing Add:* 4121 Sunset Rd Matteson IL 60443

BRAKKE, MYRON KENDALL, PLANT VIROLOGY. *Current Pos:* RETIRED. *Personal Data:* b Preston, Minn, Oct 23, 21; m 47, Betty-Jean Einbecker; c Kenneth A, Thomas W, Joan P & Karen E. *Educ:* Univ Minn, BS, 43, PhD(biochem), 47. *Hon Degrees:* DSc, Univ Nebr-Lincoln, 96. *Honors & Awards:* Superior Serv Award, USDA, 68 & 86; Ruth Allen Award, Am Phytopath Soc, 68; Outstanding Res & Creative Activity Award, Univ Nebr, 82; Sci Hall of Fame, 87; Award of Distinction, Am Phytopath Soc, 88. *Prof Exp:* Asst biochem, Univ Minn, 43-44, instr, 44-47; res assoc, Brooklyn Bot Garden, 47-52 & Dept Bot, Univ Ill, 52-55; chemist, Agr Res Serv, USDA & prof plant path, Univ Nebr, Lincoln, 55-86. *Mem:* Nat Acad Sci; fel AAAS; Am Chem Soc; fel Am Phytopath Soc; Sigma Xi; Am Soc Virol. *Res:* Purification and characterization of plant viruses and their nucleic acids; vectors of plant viruses and control of plant virus diseases. *Mailing Add:* 406 Plant Sci Hall Univ Nebr Lincoln NE 68583-0722

BRALLEY, JAMES ALEXANDER, ORGANIC CHEMISTRY. *Current Pos:* mgr qual control, 76-79, MGR QUAL ASSURANCE, C H DEXTER DIV, DEXTER CORP, 79- *Personal Data:* b Bath Co, Va, Aug 18, 16; m 46; c 3. *Educ:* Univ Va, BS, 36, PhD(org chem), 41. *Prof Exp:* Res chemist, BF Goodrich Co, 41-46; develop chemist, Rohm and Haas Co, 46-56; dir res, AE Staley Mfg Co, 56-61, vpres res & develop, 61-70; vpres res & develop, Puritan Chem Co, 71-76. *Mem:* Sigma Xi; AAAS; Am Chem Soc. *Res:* Morphine alkaloids; vinyl and acrylic resins; plasticizers; inhibitors; starch chemistry, processing and industrial uses; vegetable oils and proteins; epoxy resins; fermentation chemistry; amylose and amylopectin; amino acids; organic syntheses; detergents; disinfectants; insecticides; herbicides; waxes; synthetic polymer formulations. *Mailing Add:* 3040 Sawtooth Circle Alpharetta GA 30202-5400

BRALOW, S PHILIP, gastroenterology, internal medicine, for more information see previous edition

BRAM, RALPH A, MEDICAL VETERINARY ENTOMOLOGY. *Current Pos:* res entomologist, Animal Parasite Dis Lab, Entom Res Div, Agr Res Serv, USDA, 68-71, res entomologist, Insects Affecting Man & Animals Res Lab, 71-72, vet entomologist, Animal & Plant Health Inspection Serv, 72-81, NAT PROG LEADER, AGR RES SERV, USDA, 81- *Personal Data:* b Washington, DC, Dec 10, 32; m 56, Antoinette M Houck; c Regina R (Howard), Timothy R, Simone A (Moran) & Jennifer M. *Educ:* Univ Md, BS, 56, MS, 61, PhD(entom), 64. *Honors & Awards:* USDA Departmental Award, Super Serv, 92; Screwworm Medal, Food & Agr Orgn, 92. *Prof Exp:* Instr entom, Univ Md, 63-64; asst prof, Purdue Univ, 64-65; entomologist, Smithsonian Inst, 65-68. *Concurrent Pos:* Consult, Food & Agr Orgn, Rome, Italy, 74-76, 82-92, Int Atomic Energy Agency, Vienna, Australia, 82-89; chmn, Sect D, Entom Soc Am, 84-85. *Mem:* AAAS; Entom Soc Am; Acarology Soc Am. *Res:* Veterinary and medical entomology; mosquito systematics and zoogeography; general entomology and pathogen-vector relationships; tick and tick-borne disease transmission and control. *Mailing Add:* 104 Tamarisk Ct Greenbelt MD 20770

BRAMAN, ROBERT STEVEN, ANALYTICAL CHEMISTRY, INSTRUMENTATION. *Current Pos:* from asst prof to assoc prof, 67-73, PROF CHEM, UNIV S FLA, 73- *Personal Data:* b Lansing, Mich, Aug 31, 30; m 54; c 2. *Educ:* Mich State Univ, BS, 52; Northwestern Univ, PhD(chem), 56. *Prof Exp:* Group leader anal chem res & develop, Callery Chem Co, 56-59; res chemist, Res Inst, Ill Inst Technol, 59-64, sr chemist, 64-67. *Mem:* Am Chem Soc; Sigma Xi. *Res:* Development of analytical instrumentation; environmental chemistry. *Mailing Add:* Dept Chem Univ of S Fla Tampa FL 33620

BRAMANTE, PIETRO OTTAVIO, PATHOLOGY, PHYSIOLOGY. *Current Pos:* RETIRED. *Personal Data:* b Rome, Italy, May 21, 20; US citizen; m 57, Aurora De Valle. *Educ:* Univ Rome, MD, 44, MS, 50; Drexel Univ, MS, 64. *Prof Exp:* Instr internal med, Sch Med, Univ Rome, 45-46, asst prof, 46-51; res fel, Sch Med, Univ Stockholm & King Gustaf's Res Inst, 51-52; from res assoc to assoc prof physiol, Sch Med, St Louis Univ, 52-65; assoc prof physiol, Univ Ill Col Med, 65-70, prof, 70-75; pathologist, Wm Beaumont Army Med Ctr, El Paso, 78-79; pathologist, Sun Bay Community Hosp, Fla, 81-82. *Concurrent Pos:* Tech med consult, Court of Justice, Rome, 48-51; Fulbright fel, 52; Heart Inst fel, Drexel Univ, 62-64. *Mem:* Am Physiol Soc; Am Soc Clin Path; Col Am Pathologists; Soc Exp Biol & Med. *Res:* Pituitary in uremia; liver function; body electrolyte; hypotension; thyroid function; innervation of nasal mucosa; methodology of energy metabolism; allometry; experimental tumorigenesis; calorigenic drugs; exercise and metabolism; experimental myocardial necrosis; experimental dyslipoproteinemia. *Mailing Add:* 2022 Camelot Dr Apt 33 Clearwater FL 34623-4249

BRAMBL, ROBERT MORGAN, PLANT BIOLOGY. *Current Pos:* from asst prof to assoc prof, 71-80, PROF, DEPT PLANT PATH & PLANT BIOL, UNIV MINN, 80- *Personal Data:* b Ft Smith, Ark, April 26, 42; m 65; c 1. *Educ:* Hendrix Col, BA, 65; Univ Nebr, PhD(bot-biochem), 69. *Prof Exp:* NIH fel & res assoc, Dept Biol Sci & Path, Stanford Univ, 69-71. *Concurrent Pos:* Proj leader, Univ Minn Agr Exp Sta, 71- & 81-83; prin investr, Nat Inst Gen Med Sci res grant, 74-; vis scientist, Inst Physiol Chem & Phys Biochem, Univ Munich, 77-80; co-prin investr, McKnight Found res grant, 83-87, USDA res grant, 85- *Mem:* Am Soc Biochem & Molecular Biol; Am Chem Soc; Am Soc Microbiol; AAAS. *Res:* Purification and characterization of mitochondrial respiratory enzymes of fungi; coordination of nuclear and mitochondrial genes in mitochondrial biogenesis; regulation of mitochondrial gene expression; structural characterization and expression of nuclear and mitochondrial genes for mitochondrial proteins in fungi and plants; mechanisms of assembly of multiple-subunit respiratory enzymes; membrane translocation of enzyme sub-units; post-transcriptional regulation of gene expression; regulation of heat shock gene expression; cellular localization and functions of stress proteins; molecular responses of plant pollen and seed embryos to environmental and biotic stresses; role of plant seed lectins in plant seed defense against fungi; biochemistry of fungi spore dormancy and germination; numerous publications. *Mailing Add:* Dept Plant Biol Univ Minn 220 Biol Sci Ctr St Paul MN 55108-1095. *Fax:* 612-625-1738

BRAMBLE, JAMES H, APPLIED MATHEMATICS, NUMERICAL ANALYSIS. *Current Pos:* PROF MATH, A&M UNIV, TEX. *Personal Data:* b Annapolis, Md, Dec 1, 30; m 55, 77; c 4. *Educ:* Brown Univ, AB, 53; Univ Md, MA, 55, PhD(math), 58. *Hon Degrees:* DSc, Chalmers Univ Technol, Gothenburg, Sweden, 85. *Prof Exp:* Mathematician, Gen Elec Co, 57-59 & US Naval Ord Lab, 59-60; res asst prof math, Univ Md, 60-63, from res assoc prof to res prof, 63-68; dir, Ctr Appl Math, Cornell Univ, 74-80, assoc chmn math, 79-84, prof math, 68- *Concurrent Pos:* Consult, Nat Bur Stand, 60-66; vis lectr, Soc Indust & Appl Math, 62-65; NSF sr fel, 66-67; vis prof, Univ Rome, 66-67, Chalmers Univ Technol, Gothenburg, Sweden, 70, 72-73, 76; vis staf mem, Los Alamos Sci Lab, Univ Calif, 74-76; consult, Brookhaven Nat Lab, 76-, Ecole Poly, Paris, 78, Lausanne, Switzerland, 79, Univ Paris, 81, Australian Nat Univ, 90. *Mem:* Am Math Soc; Soc Indust & Appl Math. *Res:* Partial differential equations; numerical analysis. *Mailing Add:* Dept Math Tex A&M Univ College Station TX 77843

BRAMBLE, WILLIAM CLARK, FORESTRY. *Current Pos:* prof forestry & head, Dept Forestry & Conserv, 58-72, EMER PROF FORESTRY, PURDUE UNIV, 72- *Personal Data:* b Baltimore, Md, Nov 7, 07; m 39; c 2. *Educ:* Pa State Univ, BS, 29; Yale Univ, MF, 30, PhD(bot), 32. *Prof Exp:* Instr bot, Carleton Col, 32-37; Nat Res fel, Univ Zurich, 35-36; from asst prof to prof forestry, Pa State Univ, 37-58, head, Dept Forest Mgt, 54-58, actg dir sch forestry, 55-58. *Concurrent Pos:* Collabr, USDA, 34-72; mem div biol & agr, Nat Res Coun, 70-73; ed, Hoosier Conserv, 75-78. *Mem:* Soc Am Foresters; Ecol Soc Am; Swiss Bot Soc; Sigma Xi. *Res:* Forest ecology and management; silviculture. *Mailing Add:* 200 Lindberg Rd West Lafayette IN 47906-2110

BRAMBLETT, CLAUD ALLEN, PHYSICAL ANTHROPOLOGY, PRIMATOLOGY. *Current Pos:* from asst prof to assoc prof, 73-81, PROF ANTHROP, UNIV TEX, AUSTIN, 81- *Personal Data:* b Crystal City, Tex, Oct 8, 39; m 61; c 2. *Educ:* Univ Tex, Austin, BA, 62, MA, 65; Univ Calif, Berkeley, PhD(anthrop), 67. *Honors & Awards:* Alban-Heiser Award, Zool Soc Houston. *Prof Exp:* Mgr, Darajani Primate Res Ctr, Southwest Found Res, 63-64. *Mem:* Am Asn Phys Anthrop; Int Primatol Soc. *Res:* Behavior as a risk factor in coronary heart disease; acquisition of social signals in developing vervet monkeys; behavioral regulators. *Mailing Add:* Dept Anthrop Univ Tex Austin TX 78712. *Fax:* 512-471-6535; *E-Mail:* cbramblett@mail.utexas.edu

BRAMBLETT, RICHARD LEE, APPLIED PHYSICS, NUCLEAR PHYSICS. *Current Pos:* PRES, APPL PHYSICS ASSOCS, 93- *Personal Data:* b Dallas, Tex, Aug 15, 35; m 57; c 3. *Educ:* Rice Univ, BA, 56, MA, 57, PhD(physics), 60. *Prof Exp:* Physicist, Lawrence Radiation Lab, Univ Calif, 60-67; br mgr, Gulf Energy & Environ Systs, Calif, 68-73; sect mgr, photon logging, Schumberger Well Serv, 80-93. *Mem:* Am Phys Soc; Am Nuclear Soc; Inst Nuclear Mat Mgt. *Res:* Experimental photonuclear and neutron physics using electron accelerator technology; spectroscopy and cross-section measurements for photons and neutrons; application of accelerators, reactors and radioisotopes to non-destructive isotopic assays. *Mailing Add:* 302 Glades Circle Largo FL 33771

BRAME, EDWARD GRANT, JR, ANALYTICAL CHEMISTRY, POLYMER SPECTROSCOPY. *Current Pos:* CONSULT, CECON GROUP, INC, 85- *Personal Data:* b Shiloh, NJ, Mar 20, 27; m 57, Grace Adolphsen. *Educ:* Dickinson Col, BS, 48; Columbia Univ, MS, 50; Univ Wis, PhD(anal chem), 57. *Prof Exp:* Asst chem, Columbia Univ, 48-50; res anal chemist, Corn Prod Refining Co, 50-53; asst, Univ Wis, 53-56; res chemist, Plastics Dept, E I Du Pont De Nemours & Co, Inc, 57-64, res chemist, Elastomer Chem Dept, 64-79, res assoc, Polymer Prod Dept, 80-85. *Concurrent Pos:* Ed, Appl Spectros Rev; researcher, Acad Affairs Comt, Winterthur Mus, Del; mem res associateships eval panel, Nat Res Coun, 74-76; chmn, Fedn Anal Chem & Spectros Socs, 76; ed-in-chief, Practical Spectros & ed, Appln Polymer Spectros, 78; Nat Acad Sci exchangee to USSR, 81, 83, 85 & 90; exhib dir, Fedn Anal Chem & Spectros Soc, 86-92. *Mem:* Sigma Xi; Am Chem Soc; Soc Appl Spectros (pres, 78); NY Acad Sci. *Res:* Infrared spectroscopy; nuclear magnetic resonance spectroscopy; electron paramagnetic resonance spectroscopy; instrumental methods of analysis; nuclear quadrupole resonance spectroscopy; surface spectroscopy. *Mailing Add:* 13 N Cliffe Dr Wilmington DE 19809-1623. *Fax:* 302-994-8837

BRAMFITT, BRUCE LIVINGSTON, FERROUS PHYSICAL METALLURGY. *Current Pos:* res engr, Bethlehem Steel Corp, 66-79, supvr metall eng, 79-84, sr scientist, 84-87, res fel, 87-, res consult, 92-95, SR RES CONSULT, BETHLEHEM STEEL CORP, 95- *Personal Data:* b Troy, NY, Feb 4, 38; m 63, Joan F Sunukjian; c Christopher L & David L. *Educ:* Univ Mo, Rolla, BS, 60, MS, 62, PhD(metall eng), 66. *Honors & Awards:* Joseph Vilella Award, Am Soc Testing & Mat, 74; C D Moore Award, Am Inst Mining, Petrol & Metall Eng, 77 & 79, Michael Tenenbaum Award, Iron & Steel Soc, 87; Bradley Stoughton Award, Am Soc Metals Int, 91. *Prof Exp:* Instr, Univ Mo, Rolla, 60-66. *Mem:* Fel Am Soc Metals Int; Am Inst Mining, Petrol & Metall Eng; Int Metall Soc; distinguished mem Iron & Steel Soc. *Res:* Physical metallurgy with emphasis on microstructure and its relationship to the properties of steel; design of new alloys based on various strengthening mechanisms. *Mailing Add:* 2057 Pleasant Dr Bethlehem PA 18015

BRAMHALL, JOHN SHEPHERD, molecular biology, for more information see previous edition

BRAMLAGE, WILLIAM JOSEPH, POSTHARVEST PHYSIOLOGY. *Current Pos:* asst prof hort, 64-69, assoc prof plant physiol, 69-76, PROF PLANT SCI, UNIV MASS, AMHERST, 76- *Personal Data:* b Dayton, Ohio, Mar 27, 37; m 67, Georgene Moizuk; c William, Ann & Catherine. *Educ:* Ohio State Univ, BS, 59; Univ Md, MS, 61, PhD(hort), 63. *Prof Exp:* Horticulturist, agr mkt serv, USDA, 63-64. *Concurrent Pos:* Vis prof, Univ Nebr, Lincoln, 76-77; vis scientist, E Malling Res Sta, Kent, Eng, 84, DSIR, Fruit & Trees, Auckland, NZ, 91. *Mem:* AAAS; Am Soc Plant Physiol; fel Am Soc Hort Sci. *Res:* Physiological disorders of fruit; stress physiology. *Mailing Add:* Dept Plant & Soil Sci Bowditch Hall Univ Mass Amherst MA 01003

BRAMLET, ROLAND C, RADIOLOGICAL PHYSICS. *Current Pos:* RETIRED. *Personal Data:* b Wallowa, Ore, June 11, 21; m 61; c 2. *Educ:* Ore State Univ, BS, 48; NY Univ, MS, 61; St John's Univ, NY, PhD(biol), 66. *Prof Exp:* Fel, Sloan-Kettering Inst Cancer Res, 58-59; jr physicist, Queens Gen Hosp, Jamaica, NY, 59-61, radioisotope physicist, 61-69; physicist, Highland Hosp, Rochester, NY, 69-91. *Concurrent Pos:* Clin asst prof radiation oncol, Sch Med & Dent, Univ Rochester, NY, 85-91. *Mem:* Am Asn Physicists Med. *Res:* Clinical radioisotopic instrumentation; radiation biology; radiation oncology. *Mailing Add:* 226 Castleman Rd Rochester NY 14620

BRAMMER, ANTHONY JOHN, ACOUSTICS PHYSICS. *Current Pos:* res fel, 67-68, asst res officer, 69-76, ASSOC RES OFFICER ACOUSTICS, NAT RES COUN, CAN, 76- *Personal Data:* b Watford, Eng, May 30, 42; Brit & Can citizen; m 67. *Educ:* Univ Exeter, Eng, BSc, 63, PhD(physics), 68. *Prof Exp:* Engr vacuum tube develop, Standard Tel & Cables, Ltd, 67. *Concurrent Pos:* Lectr physics & math, Exeter Tech Col, 66-67; sessional lectr, Carleton Univ, 69-71; adj assoc prof, Univ Windsor, 72- *Mem:* Acoust Soc Am; Can Acoust Asn. *Res:* Hand-arm vibration; vibration isolation systems; vibration standards; non-linear acoustics applicable to internal combustion engines; industrial noise control. *Mailing Add:* 4792 Massey Lane Ottawa ON K1A 0R5 Can

BRAMMER, FOREST E(VERT), ELECTRICAL ENGINEERING. *Current Pos:* head dept, 60-70, prof, 60-68, EMER PROF ELEC ENG, WAYNE STATE UNIV, 68- *Personal Data:* b Mabscott, WVa, July 21, 13; m 42; c 4. *Educ:* NC State Col, BS, 33; Concord Col, AB, 33; Case Inst Technol, PhD(elec eng), 51. *Prof Exp:* Teacher high sch, NC, 33-36; dist engr geophys, Schlumberger Well Surv Corp, 37-42; supvr underwater res group, Appl Physics Lab, Johns Hopkins Univ, 46-48; prof lectr elec eng, Case Inst Technol, 48-51, assoc prof, 51-60. *Concurrent Pos:* Mem, Nat Electronics Conf; consult, Goodyear Aircraft Corp, 54-58 & Repub Steel Corp, 59- *Mem:* Inst Elec & Electronics Engrs. *Res:* Antennas; solid state devices; analog computers. *Mailing Add:* Wayne State Univ Detroit MI 48202

BRAMMER, LEE, CRYSTALLOGRAPHY. *Current Pos:* ASST PROF INORG CHEM, UNIV MO, 90- *Personal Data:* b Barnsley, Eng, Apr 23, 63. *Educ:* Univ Bristol, UK, BSc hons, 83, PhD(inorg chem), 87. *Prof Exp:* N Atlantic Treaty Orgn fel chem, Univ New Orleans, 87-88; fel chem, Brookhaven Nat Lab, 88-90. *Mem:* Am Crystallog Asn; Am Chem Soc. *Res:* Single crystal x-ray and neutron diffraction; structure, bonding and electronic properties of organometallic compounds, particularly transition metal cluster compounds and compounds with transition metal-hydrogen interactions. *Mailing Add:* Dept Chem Univ Mo St Louis St Louis MO 63121-4499

BRAMWELL, FITZGERALD BURTON, PHYSICAL CHEMISTRY. *Current Pos:* assoc prof, 71-80, PROF CHEM, BROOKLYN COL, 80- *Personal Data:* b Brooklyn, NY, May 16, 45; m 73; c 3. *Educ:* Columbia Univ, BA, 66; Univ Mich, MS, 67, PhD(chem), 70. *Prof Exp:* Res chemist, Esso Res & Eng Co, 70-71. *Concurrent Pos:* Mem tech staff, Bell Tel Labs, 74-75, consult, 77-78; Nat Res Coun, Grad Fel Eval Panel, 81-84; BD ADVS, CHEMTECH, 85-; sci consult, Bd Educ, New York, 85; dir-at-large, NY sect, Am Chem Soc, 86. *Mem:* Am Chem Soc; NY Acad Sci. *Res:* Electron spin resonance of triplets; free radicals in solution; organic metals; charge transfer complexes; Jan-Teller distortions; aryl tin radicals. *Mailing Add:* Dept Chem City Univ NY Brooklyn Col 2901 Bedford Ave Brooklyn NY 11210-2813

BRANAHL, ERWIN FRED, AERONAUTICAL ENGINEERING. *Current Pos:* RETIRED. *Personal Data:* b St Louis, Mo, Mar 8, 22; m 44; c 2. *Educ:* Wash Univ, BS, 43, MS, 51. *Prof Exp:* Stress analyst, Curtiss-Wright Corp, 43-44; res engr, McDonnell Co, 46-47, design engr, 47-51, dynamics engr, 51-52; chief dynamics engr, McDonnell Douglas Astronaut Co, St Louis, 52-54, chief aeromech engr, 54-59, mgr aeromech, 59-60, asst chief engr, Missile Eng Div, 60-61, mgr space & missile eng progs, 61-68, vpres eng, 68-74, vpres & gen mgr, 74-86, exec vpres, 86-87. *Concurrent Pos:* Vpres & dir, McDonnell Douglas Tech Serv Co, 74-; dir, Vitek Syst, Inc, 77-; corp vpres, McDonnell Douglas Corp, 78-, vpres, McDonnell Douglas Ltd, 80- *Mem:* Assoc fel Am Inst Aeronaut & Astronaut. *Res:* Missile aerodynamics; automatic control systems; dynamics; propulsion; structures; thermodynamics. *Mailing Add:* 14 Lake Pembroke Dr St Louis MO 63135

BRANCA, ANDREW A, CELL BIOLOGY. *Current Pos:* SR SCIENTIST, DEPT CELL BIOL, PROCYTE CORP, 89- *Personal Data:* b New Rochelle, NY, Aug 20, 50. *Educ:* N Adams State Col, BA, 75; Univ NH, MS, 78, PhD(biochem), 80. *Prof Exp:* Asst prof biochem, Albany Med Col, 82-89. *Concurrent Pos:* Fel, Nat Cancer Inst, NIH, 81-82, new investr res award, Nat Inst Allergy & Infectious Dis Inst, 85-88. *Mem:* AAAS; Int Soc Interferon Res; Am Soc Biochem & Molecular Biol; Sigma Xi; Tissue Cult Asn. *Mailing Add:* Procyte Corp 12040 115th Ave NE Kirkland WA 98034-6900

BRANCATO, EMANUEL L, ELECTRICAL ENGINEERING. *Current Pos:* RETIRED. *Personal Data:* b Brooklyn, NY, Nov 3, 14; m 58; c 2. *Educ:* Columbia Univ, BA, 36, BS, 37, MS, 38. *Honors & Awards:* Centennial Award Medal, Inst Elec & Electronics Engrs, 84, T W Dakin Distinguished Tech Achievement. *Prof Exp:* Jr elec engr develop & design, Boston Naval Shipyard, 38-39; elec engr, Sci Sect, Develop & Res, NY Naval Shipyard, 39-46; sect head, Shipboard Power Systs, US Naval Res Lab, 46-54, head, Insulation Sect, Solid State Div, 54-67, head, Solid State Appl Br, 67-70, consult to dir res, 70-76, head consult staff, 76-78. *Concurrent Pos:* Consult, Elec Power Res Inst & Naval Res Lab, 79. *Mem:* Fel Inst Elec & Electronics Engrs; Sigma Xi. *Res:* Investigation of the effects of ionizing radiation on dielectric and semiconductor materials and devices. *Mailing Add:* 7370 Hallmark Rd Clarksville MD 21029. *Fax:* 301-490-4343

BRANCATO, LEO J(OHN), MECHANICAL ENGINEERING. *Current Pos:* RETIRED. *Personal Data:* b New York, NY, Oct 27, 22; m 48, Lucy Pennino; c Leo, Lorraine & Lenore. *Educ:* Cooper Union Sch Eng, BME, 50; Columbia Univ, MS, 52. *Prof Exp:* Develop engr, Edward Ermold Co, 49-52; mgr eng, Heli-Coil Corp, 52-53, chief engr design & develop, 53-56, vpres, 56-58, exec vpres & mem bd, 58-70; vpres & mem bd, Mite Corp, 70-74, pres, 75-88. *Mem:* Fel Am Soc Mech Engrs; Am Soc Metals; NY Acad Sci. *Res:* Automatic machinery; metal fabrication; screw thread fastener technology; granted 11 US patents. *Mailing Add:* 137 Chambers Rd Danbury CT 06811

BRANCH, CLARENCE JOSEPH, animal biology, radiation biology, for more information see previous edition

BRANCH, DAVID REED, ASTROPHYSICS. *Current Pos:* from asst prof to assoc prof, 73-81, chmn dept, 85-90, PROF PHYSICS & ASTRON, UNIV OKLA, 81- *Personal Data:* b Coaldale, Pa, Mar 12, 42; m 69, Sheila Myers; c Alissa & Alexander. *Educ:* Rensselaer Polytech Inst, BS, 64; Univ Md, PhD(astron), 69. *Honors & Awards:* Sr US Scientist Award, Alexander Humboldt Found, 88. *Prof Exp:* Res assoc solar physics, Goddard Space Flight Ctr, NASA, 69; res fel astrophys, Calif Inst Technol, 69-70; sr res fel, Royal Greenwich Observ, 70-73. *Concurrent Pos:* George Lynn Cross res prof, 87- *Mem:* Int Astron Union; Am Astron Soc. *Res:* Cosmology; supernovae. *Mailing Add:* Dept Physics & Astron Univ Okla Norman OK 73019-0225. *Fax:* 405-325-7557; *E-Mail:* branch@phyast.nhn.uoknor.edu

BRANCH, GARLAND MARION, JR, MEDICAL TECHNOLOGY. *Current Pos:* RETIRED. *Personal Data:* b Plant City, Fla, Apr 16, 22; m 45, Carolyn V Howes; c Virginia, Garland M III, Charles & Helen. *Educ:* Stetson Univ, BS, 43; Cornell Univ, PhD(physics), 51. *Prof Exp:* Res asst nuclear reactor physics, Manhattan Proj, 43-46; asst physics, Cornell Univ, 46-48, res asst cosmic ray physics, 48-51; res assoc electron physics, Res Lab, Gen Elec

Med Systs Div, Milwaukee, 51-58, liaison scientist, 58-60, consult microwave physicist, Superpower Microwave Tube Lab, 60-63, mgr electron beam & circuit res, Tube Dept, 63-75, sr develop engr, 75-79; prof elec engr & comput sci, Union Col, 79-85. *Concurrent Pos:* Adj prof, Union Col, NY, 67-72. *Mem:* Inst Elec & Electronics Engrs; Am Phys Soc; Am Asn Physics Teachers; NY Acad Acad Sci; Soc Photo-optical Engrs; Sigma Xi. *Res:* Microwave electronics; electron optics; cosmic rays; satellite communication systems; high-energy particle accelerators. *Mailing Add:* 1401 Via Del Mar Schenectady NY 12309-4319

BRANCH, JOHN CURTIS, PARASITOLOGY. *Current Pos:* From asst prof to assoc prof, 64-72, chmn dept, 66-80, PROF BIOL, OKLAHOMA CITY UNIV, 72- *Personal Data:* b Buffalo, Okla, Oct 1, 34; m 60, Jacqueline Davis; c Kim Renee, Karla Jean & Kay Lynn. *Educ:* Northwestern State Col, Okla, BS, 59; Univ Okla, MS, 62, PhD(prev med, pub health), 65; Oklahoma City Univ, JD, 80. *Concurrent Pos:* Atty; pres, John C Branch Prof Corp. *Mem:* AAAS; Am Soc Parasitol; Am Inst Biol Sci; Sigma Xi. *Res:* Parasite metabolism; transfer of learning via brain extracts. *Mailing Add:* 2705 Abbey Rd Oklahoma City OK 73120

BRANCH, LYN CLARKE, CONSERVATION BIOLOGY. *Current Pos:* Asst prof, 90-95, ASSOC PROF CONSERV BIOL, UNIV FLA, 95- *Personal Data:* b Greenwood, Miss, Sept 25, 53. *Educ:* Miss State Univ, BS, 75; Miami Univ, MS, 77; Univ Calif, Berkeley, PhD(wildland resource sci), 89. *Mem:* Ecol Soc Am; Am Soc Mammalogists; Soc Conserv Biol; Asn Trop Biol; Wildlife Soc. *Res:* Conservation biology; evolution of vertebrate social systems; role of animals in structuring plant communities; tropical ecology. *Mailing Add:* 7121 NE 19th Ave Gainesville FL 32601

BRANCH, ROBERT ANTHONY, CLINICAL PHARMACOLOGY. *Current Pos:* CHIEF, DIV CLIN PHARMACOL, DEPT MED, UNIV PITTSBURGH, 91-, DIR, CTR CLIN PHARMACOL, MED CTR, 91-, DIR, GEN CLIN RES CTR, 91- *Personal Data:* b Nairobi, Kenya, Oct 8, 42; c 3. *Educ:* Bristol Univ, MB & ChB, 65; RCOG, 67; MRCP, 68; Bristol Univ, MD, 76. *Prof Exp:* House surgeon, United Bristol Hosp, 65-66, physician, 66, sr house surgeon, 66-67; registrar nephrology, Welsh Nat Sch Med, 68-69; registrar gastroenterol, Univ Bristol, 69-71; res fel, Vanderbilt Univ, 71-73, from asst prof to prof med & pharmacol, 73-91. *Concurrent Pos:* Lectr clin pharmacol, Univ Bristol, 73-75. *Mem:* Brit Soc Pharmacol; Am Soc Clin Invest; fel Royal Col Physicians. *Res:* Drug disposition in normal and disease states; hepatic and renal disease; regulation of renin release. *Mailing Add:* Univ Pittsburgh Med Ctr 623 Scaife Hall Pittsburgh PA 15261-0001. *Fax:* 412-648-7107

BRANCH, WILLIAM DEAN, PEANUT BREEDING & GENETICS. *Current Pos:* asst geneticist, 78-84, assoc prof, 85-90, PROF, UNIV GA, 90- *Personal Data:* b Duncan, Okla, Sept 14, 50; m 72, Milla Pruitt; c Joshua & Mia. *Educ:* Okla State Univ, BS, 72, MS, 74, PhD(crop sci), 76. *Prof Exp:* Res asst, Okla State Univ, 72-77; res assoc, Auburn Univ, 77-78. *Mem:* Am Soc Agron; Crop Sci Soc Agron; Am Peanut Res & Educ Soc; Am Genetic Asn; Coun Agr Sci & Technol; Nat Peanut Coun. *Res:* Georgia peanut breeding and genetic research program. *Mailing Add:* Univ Ga Dept Agron Coastal Plain Exp Sta Tifton GA 31793-0748. *Fax:* 912-386-7293

BRANCHINI, BRUCE ROBERT, ORGANIC CHEMISTRY, BIO-ORGANIC CHEMISTRY. *Current Pos:* asst prof, 76-80, ASSOC PROF CHEM, UNIV WIS-PARKSIDE, 81- *Personal Data:* b New Haven, Conn, Oct 22, 50. *Educ:* Lehigh Univ, BS, 72; Johns Hopkins Univ, MA, 73, PhD(chem), 75. *Prof Exp:* Fel Biochem, Harvard Univ, 75-76. *Concurrent Pos:* Vis prof chem, Johns Hopkins Univ, 81-82. *Mem:* Am Chem Soc; AAAS. *Res:* Bioluminescence; chemiluminescence; cystic fibrosis; enzyme inhibitors; new substrates. *Mailing Add:* Chem Dept Conn Col Box 5401 270 Mohegan Ave New London CT 06320-4196

BRAND, EUGENE DEW, PSYCHIATRY, PSYCHOPHARMACOLOGY. *Current Pos:* LOCUM TENENS, 90- *Personal Data:* b CZ, Mar 10, 24; m 53, 72, Nancy Clark; c Francesca (Sarver), Bryan, Alice (Wilkinson), Romney, Cynthia (Hopkins) & Nancy J. *Educ:* Univ Va, BA, 44; Harvard Univ, MD, 50; Am Bd Psychiat & Neurol, cert, 79. *Prof Exp:* Instr physiol, Sch Med, Univ Va, 48, intern med, Univ Hosp, 50-51; resident, Univ Utah, 51-52, asst pharm, 52-53; asst prof, Univ Va Hosp, 53-61, assoc prof pharmacol, Sch Med, 61-74, resident psychiat, Univ Hosp, 70-74; med dir & staff psychiatrist, Mid Peninsula North Neck Ment Health Serv, 74-77; chmn psychiat, Rappahanock Gen Hosp, 77-86. *Mem:* Am Psychiat Asn; AMA. *Res:* Physiology; traumatic shock; psychiatry; ethology. *Mailing Add:* PO Box 26 Wicomico Church VA 22579

BRAND, JERRY JAY, PHOTOBIOLOGY, PHYCOLOGY & CRYOBIOLOGY. *Current Pos:* from asst prof to assoc prof, 74-88, PROF BOT, UNIV TEX, AUSTIN, 88- *Personal Data:* b Waterloo, Ind, Sept 20, 41; m 67, Mary L Cormany; c Eileen & Karin. *Educ:* Manchester Col, BS, 63; Purdue Univ, PhD(biol sci), 71. *Prof Exp:* Sec sch teacher chem & physics, Nigeria, 63-65; res assoc bot, Ind Univ, 71-74. *Concurrent Pos:* Vis scientist, Carnegie Inst, Stanford, Calif, 82, Inst Basic Biol, Japan, 87. *Mem:* Sigma Xi; Am Soc Plant Physiologists; Am Chem Soc; Phycol Soc Am; Soc Cryobiol. *Res:* Cryopreservation of algae; photobiology of algae. *Mailing Add:* Dept Bot B10311 Univ Tex Austin TX 78712. *E-Mail:* jbrand@utxsvs.cl.utexas.edu

BRAND, JOEL A, INTER-DISCIPLINARY INSTRUMENTATION. *Current Pos:* SR SCIENTIST, MONITOR LABS INC, 94- *Personal Data:* b Van Nuys, Calif, July 7, 65; m 89, Ann M Carter. *Educ:* Univ Mo, Rolla, BS, 86, MS & PhD(physics), 94; Colo State Univ, MS, 88. *Prof Exp:* Optical physicist, Ophir Corp, 94. *Concurrent Pos:* Founder, Advan Vacuum Instrumentation, 94- *Mem:* Air & Waste Mgt Asn. *Res:* Advancing techniques in atomic, molecular and optical physics to solve difficult analysis and instrumentation problems; integration of optoelectronics, spectroscopy and applied mathematics. *Mailing Add:* 76 Inverness Dr E Englewood CO 80112. *E-Mail:* jbrand@monitorlabs.com

BRAND, JOHN C D, CHEMICAL PHYSICS, SPECTROSCOPY. *Current Pos:* prof chem, 69-86, EMER PROF CHEM, UNIV WESTERN ONT, 86- *Personal Data:* b Durban, S Africa, 21; m 43, Evelyn G Meek; c David. *Educ:* Univ London, PhD(chem), 47, DSc, 56. *Honors & Awards:* Herzberg Award, Spectros Soc Can, 82; Medal, Can Inst Chem, 86. *Prof Exp:* Prof chem, Vanderbilt Univ, 64-69. *Mem:* Can Asn Physicists; fel Can Inst Chemists; fel Royal Soc Can. *Res:* Chemical physics; spectroscopy. *Mailing Add:* PO Box 2068 Bayfield ON N0M 1G0 Can

BRAND, JOHN S, BIOPHYSICS. *Current Pos:* UNIT DIR, EASTMAN KODAK. *Personal Data:* b Buffalo, NY, May 2, 38; m 60; c 4. *Educ:* LeMoyne Col, BS, 59; Univ Rochester, MS, 64, PhD, 66. *Prof Exp:* Fel, Univ Rochester, 66-68, asst prof, 68-75, assoc prof radiation biol & biophys, 75-, assoc prof orthop & radiol, 79-, dir musculoskeletal res, 79- *Concurrent Pos:* NIH career develop award, 75-80; vis scientist Nat Inst Med Res, Mill Hill, London, Eng, 77-78; mem B Study Sect, NIH Gen Med, 79- *Mem:* AAAS; Sigma Xi; Orthop Res Soc. *Res:* Hormonal regulation of bone cell metabolism. *Mailing Add:* 88 Ellery Rd Rochester NY 14612

BRAND, KARL GERHARD, MICROBIOLOGY. *Current Pos:* RETIRED. *Personal Data:* b Lübeck, Ger, June 10, 22, US citizen; m 49; c 2. *Educ:* Univ Hamburg, MD, 49; Trop Inst Hamburg, dipl, 54; Free Univ Berlin, DPH, 56. *Prof Exp:* Resident instr internal med, Med Acad Lübeck, 49-52; asst prof trop med, Trop Inst Hamburg, 52-54; assoc prof pub health & microbiol, Free Univ Berlin, 55-57; from asst prof to prof microbiol, Sch Med, Univ Minn, Minneapolis, 57-85; physician, WGer, 85-88. *Concurrent Pos:* Vis prof, Univ de Los Andes Mérida Venezuela, 60 & Kawasaki Med Sch, 81. *Mem:* Am Asn Immunol; Soc Exp Biol & Med; Am Soc Microbiol. *Res:* Serological problems in influenza, mumps, psittacosis, viral pneumonia; foreign body carcinogenesis; antigenic structure of cells, tissues, tumors; cancer-aging relationships; asbestos cancer; schistosomiasis cancer. *Mailing Add:* 561 Bay Rd Durham NH 03824

BRAND, LEONARD, MEDICINE, ANESTHESIOLOGY. *Current Pos:* from instr to assoc prof, 55-72, PROF CLIN ANESTHESIOL, COLUMBIA UNIV, 72- *Personal Data:* b New York, NY, Dec 21, 23; m 51; c 3. *Educ:* Yale Univ, BS, 46; Columbia Univ, MD, 49; Am Bd Anesthesiol, dipl, 59. *Prof Exp:* Intern med, Long Island Col Hosp, 49-50; resident gen med, Leo N Levi Mem Hosp, Ark, 50-51; resident anesthesiol, Presby Hosp, 53-55. *Concurrent Pos:* Asst anesthesiologist, Presby Hosp, New York, 55-57, asst attend anesthesiologist, 57-66, attend anesthesiologist, 66-, dir, Pain Treat Serv. *Mem:* Am Soc Anesthesiol. *Res:* Pharmacology and physiology of intravenous agents; fate and distribution of barbiturates in man; passage of substances into central nervous system; respiratory physiology; anesthesia for trauma and orthopedic cases; treatment of acute and chronic pain. *Mailing Add:* Dept Anesthesiol Columbia Univ Col Physicians & Surgeons 622 W 168th St New York NY 10032-3702

BRAND, LEONARD ROY, VERTEBRATE ZOOLOGY, PALEONTOLOGY. *Current Pos:* From asst prof to assoc prof, 69-78, chmn dept, 71-86, PROF BIOL & PALEONTOLOGY, LOMA LINDA UNIV, 78-, CHMN DEPT, 88- *Personal Data:* b Harvey, NDak, May 17, 41; m 74; c 2. *Educ:* La Sierra Col, BA, 64; Loma Linda Univ, MA, 66; Cornell Univ, PhD(vertebrate zool), 70. *Honors & Awards:* A Brazier Howell Award, Am Soc Mammalogists, 67. *Mem:* Sigma Xi; Am Soc Mammalogists; Animal Behav Soc; Geol Soc Am; Soc Vert Paleont. *Res:* Vertebrate typhonomy and fossil trackways; behavior and ecology of mammals. *Mailing Add:* Dept Biol & Paleontol Loma Linda Univ Loma Linda CA 92350-0001

BRAND, LUDWIG, BIOCHEMISTRY. *Current Pos:* from asst prof to assoc prof, 62-74, PROF BIOL, JOHNS HOPKINS UNIV, 74- *Personal Data:* b Vienna, Austria, Jan 3, 32; nat US; m 58, Sheila Gallay. *Educ:* Harvard Univ, BA, 55; Ind Univ, PhD, 60. *Prof Exp:* Asst biochem, Ind Univ, 55-59; Nat Found fel, 59-62. *Concurrent Pos:* Fel, Brandeis Univ, 59-61 & Weizmann Inst, 61-62. *Mem:* Am Soc Biol Chem; Biophys Soc; Am Soc Photobiol; Am Chem Soc; Protein Soc. *Res:* Mechanism of enzyme action; fluorescence studies with proteins; fluorescence lifetimes; fluorescence probe studies of biological membranes. *Mailing Add:* Dept Biol Mudd Hall Johns Hopkins Univ 3400 N Charles St Baltimore MD 21218. *Fax:* 410-516-5213; *E-Mail:* lenny@brand.bio,jhu.edu

BRAND, PAUL HYMAN, PHYSIOLOGY. *Current Pos:* asst prof, 75-80, ASSOC PROF PHYSIOL, MED COL OHIO, 80- *Personal Data:* b Yonkers, NY, June 19, 40; m 71; c 2. *Educ:* City Col New York, BS, 62; Univ Rochester, MSc & PhD(physiol), 72. *Prof Exp:* Fel dept physiol, Univ Rochester, 72-73; fel, Col Med, Univ Ariz, 73-75. *Mem:* Am Physiol Soc; Sigma Xi. *Res:* Mechanism of transport of metabolites in the kidney; epithelial transport. *Mailing Add:* CS 10008 Dept Physiol Med Col Ohio 3000 Arlington Ave Toledo OH 43699-0008. *Fax:* 419-382-7395

BRAND, RAYMOND HOWARD, ANIMAL ECOLOGY, SPRINGTAIL SPECIES DIVERSITY. *Current Pos:* from assoc prof to prof, 59-93, chmn dept, 73-80, EMER PROF BIOL, WHEATON COL, ILL, 93-; RES ASSOC, MORTON ARBORETUM, LISLE, ILL, 880. *Personal Data:* b Highland Park, Mich, Sept 22, 28; m 51, Shirley I Winch; c Barbara, Timothy & Stephen. *Educ:* Wheaton Col, Ill, BA, 50; Univ Mich, MS, 51, PhD(zool), 55. *Prof Exp:* Asst prof biol, Westmont Col, 55-57, actg chmn div sci, 57-59. *Concurrent Pos:* NSF basic res found grant, 62-64; grant, Inst Radiolbiol, Argonne Nat Lab, 65; consult ecol & environ mgt; vpres, Partners Lincoln Marsh, 93-; Dupage Count Environ Commission, 95. *Mem:* Ecol Soc Am; fel Am Sci Affil (vpres, 94, pres, 95); Sigma Xi; Am Inst Biol Sci; AAAS. *Res:* Population dynamics; animal behavior; temperature adaptations; diversity of species of insects in the order Collembola (springtails) in mid-western native and restored prairies; effects of fire on surface arthropods for different fire management programs. *Mailing Add:* Morton Arboretum 4100 Illinois Rte 53 Lisce IL 60532. *Fax:* 630-719-2433; *E-Mail:* rbrand@mortonarb.org

BRAND, RONALD S(COTT), MECHANICAL ENGINEERING. *Current Pos:* RETIRED. *Personal Data:* b Springfield, Mass, Jan 31, 19; m 41; c 3. *Educ:* Worcester Polytech Inst, BS, 40; Univ Mich, MS, 49; Brown Univ, PhD(appl math), 60. *Prof Exp:* Instr mech, Rensselaer Polytech Inst, 41-44; from instr to assoc prof mech eng, Univ Conn, 46-57, prof, 57-79, dept head, 68-74. *Concurrent Pos:* NSF res fel, Norweg Inst Technol, 62-64; vis prof, Inst Sound & Vibration Res, Univ Southampton, Eng, 71-72. *Mem:* AAAS; Am Soc Mech Engrs; Sigma Xi. *Res:* Fluid mechanics. *Mailing Add:* 20 Church Rd Box 236 Eastford CT 06242-0236

BRAND, SAMSON, METEOROLOGY, ATMOSPHERIC SCIENCE. *Current Pos:* HEAD, DECISION AID SECT, NAVAL RES LAB, 92- *Personal Data:* b New York, NY, Apr 30, 43; m 69, Helen S Meyer; c Adam & Joel. *Educ:* City Col New York, BS, 64; Fla State Univ, MS, 66. *Prof Exp:* Navy weather res facil, Naval Environ Prediction Res Facil, 66-71, res meteorologist, 71-89; head, Naval Warfare Support Dept, Naval Oceanog & Atmospheric Res Lab, 89-92. *Mem:* Am Meteorol Soc; Nat Weather Asn. *Res:* Applied meteorological research with primary emphasis in severe marine weather problems and decision making; environmental effects on weapon systems and tactical decision aid development; published over 100 articles, mostly technical in nature. *Mailing Add:* Marine Meteorol Div Naval Res Lab Monterey CA 93943-5006. *Fax:* 408-656-4769; *E-Mail:* brand@nrlmry.navy.mil

BRAND, VANCE DEVOE, ASTRONAUTICS. *Current Pos:* astronaut, 66-92, ASST CHIEF FLIGHT OPERS DIRECTORATE, DRYDEN FLIGHT RES CTR, NASA, 94- *Personal Data:* b Longmont, Colo, May 9, 31; m 53, 79, Beverly Ann Whitnel; c Susan Nancy, Stephanie, Patrick Richard, Kevin Stephen, Erik Ryan & Dane Vance. *Educ:* Univ Colo, BS, 53, BS, 60; Univ Calif, Los Angeles, MBA, 64. *Prof Exp:* Flight test engr, Lockheed-Calif Co, 60-62, traveling engr rep, 62-63, eng test pilot, 63-66; chief plans, Nat Aero-Space Plane Joint Prog Off, Wright-Patterson AFB, 92-94. *Concurrent Pos:* Command module pilot, Apollo-Soyuz mission, Johnson Space Ctr, NASA, 75, comdr, STS-5 Mission, 82, comdr, STS 41-B Mission, 84, comdr, STS-35 Mission, 90. *Mem:* Fel Am Astron Soc; Soc Exp Test Pilots; Am Inst Aeronaut & Astronaut. *Mailing Add:* PO Box 1149 Tehachapi CA 93581

BRAND, WILLIAM WAYNE, ORGANIC CHEMISTRY, CHEMOMETRICS. *Current Pos:* res assoc, corp res, 83-87, SUPVR, TESTING SERV, ICI POLYURETHANES, ICI AM INC, 87- *Personal Data:* b Garrett, Ind, Mar 9, 44; m 81, Peggy S Woodard; c Peggy S, Michael, Joe, Shandra & Louis. *Educ:* Manchester Col, BA, 66; Purdue Univ, PhD(org chem), 70. *Prof Exp:* Res chemist synthesis-agr, Am Cyanamid Co, 70-76; sr res chemist, Diamon Shamrock Corp, 76-78, res assoc agr, 78-83. *Concurrent Pos:* Chmn, Polyurethanes Raw Mat Analysis Comt, Soc Plastics Indust. *Mem:* Am Chem Soc; Ctr Process Anal Chem. *Res:* Synthetic organic chemistry, particularly in sulfur chemistry and small ring heterocycles; pesticide chemistry. *Mailing Add:* ICI Polyurethanes 286 Mantua Grove Rd West Deptford NJ 08066-1732. *Fax:* 609-423-8503

BRANDA, NEIL R, SUPRAMOLECULAR CHEMISTRY, MOLECULAR RECOGNITON. *Current Pos:* ASST PROF, DEPT CHEM, UNIV ALTA, 96- *Personal Data:* b Montevideo, Uruguay, Feb 25, 67; Can citizen; m 91, Erica M Rubin; c Ian Samuel. *Educ:* Univ Toronto, BSc, 89; Mass Inst Technol, PhD(org chem), 94. *Prof Exp:* Nat Sci & Eng Res Coun Can Postdoctoral fel, Univ Louis Pasteur, 94-96, Col France res assoc, 95. *Mem:* Am Chem Soc; AAAS. *Res:* Design of non-convalent self-assemblies for use as supramolecular catalysts, transporters and molecular reaction chambers. *Mailing Add:* Dept Chem Univ Alta Edmonton AB T6G 2G2 Can. *Fax:* 403-492-8231; *E-Mail:* neil.branda@ualberta.ca

BRANDAU, BETTY LEE, INORGANIC CHEMISTRY, NUCLEAR CHEMISTRY. *Current Pos:* CONSULT, 81- *Personal Data:* b Easton, Pa; m 62; c 1. *Educ:* Ursinus Col, BS, 53; Carnegie Inst Technol, MS, 55, PhD(inorg chem), 60. *Prof Exp:* Chemist, Sun Oil Co, Pa, 54, Dow Chem Co, Mich, 56, Y-12 Plant, Union Carbide Nuclear Corp, Tenn, 60-64 & Oak Ridge Assoc Univs, 64-65 & 69; res assoc, Rosenstiel Inst Marine & Atmospheric Sci, Univ Miami, 65-68; asst dir, Appl Isotope Studies, Univ Ga, 69-71, assoc dir, 78-81. *Concurrent Pos:* Intergovernmental Personnel Act, Nat Oceanic & Atmospheric Admin, Rockville, Md, 81-82. *Mem:* AAAS; Am Chem Soc; fel Am Inst Chemists; Sigma Xi. *Res:* Marine sediment and radiocarbon dating; geochemistry; natural radioactivity environmental problems; chemical archaeology; marine pollution. *Mailing Add:* 220 Pine Crest Athens GA 30605

BRANDAUER, CARL M(ARTIN), COMMUNICATIONS SYSTEMS. *Current Pos:* RES ASSOC, UNIV COLO, 77- *Personal Data:* b Peking, China, Oct 23, 24; nat US; m 48, 69; c 4. *Educ:* Columbia Univ, BA, 51, MA, 52, PhD(psychol), 58. *Prof Exp:* Instr psychol, Columbia Univ, 54-55; mem tech staff, Bell Tel Labs, Inc, 55-58; res psychologist, Haskins Labs, 58-60; mem tech staff, Bell Tel Labs, Inc, NJ, 60-66; scientist, Nat Ctr Atmospheric Res, 66-70; mem tech staff, Bell Tel Labs, 70-82; pres, Daemon Assoc, Inc, 82-96. *Concurrent Pos:* Res assoc psychol, Univ Colo, 76-80, EPO biol, 92- *Mem:* Acoust Soc Am. *Res:* Speech communications; systems analysis; auditory localization. *Mailing Add:* 1760 Sunset Blvd Boulder CO 80302

BRANDEAU, MARGARET LOUISE, MANUFACTURING SYSTEMS RESEARCH, MANAGEMENT SCIENCE APPLICATIONS. *Current Pos:* asst prof, 85-92, ASSOC PROF INDUST ENG, STANFORD UNIV, 92- *Personal Data:* b New York, NY, Aug 28, 55; m 88, Joseph Eschbach; c John & Paul. *Educ:* Mass Inst Technol, BS, 77, MS, 78; Stanford Univ, PhD(eng-econ systs), 85. *Concurrent Pos:* NSF presidential young investr award, 88-93; elected coun mem, Oper Res Soc Am, 93- *Mem:* Sigma Xi; Opers Res Soc Am; Inst Mgt Sci. *Res:* Manufacturing systems design models; policy analysis of Acquired Immune Deficiency syndrome screening and intervention; facility location models. *Mailing Add:* Indust Eng Dept Stanford Univ Terman Eng Ctr Stanford CA 94305-9991. *E-Mail:* ng.mlb@forsythe.stanford.edu

BRANDEBERRY, JAMES E, ELECTRICAL ENGINEERING, SYSTEMS THEORY. *Current Pos:* PRES, SIMULATION TECHNOL, 80-; DEAN ENG & COMPUT SCI, WRIGHT STATE UNIV, 84- *Personal Data:* b Toledo, Ohio, Oct 10, 39; m 62; c 2. *Educ:* Univ Toledo, BSEE, 61, MSEE, 63; Marquette Univ, PhD(elec eng), 69. *Prof Exp:* Sr proj engr, AC Electronics Div, Gen Motors Corp, 63-66; asst prof eng, Wright State Univ, 69-76, assoc prof comput sci & eng & chmn, Dept Comput Sci, 76-80. *Concurrent Pos:* Consult, Nat Cash Register Co, 69-70. *Mem:* Inst Elec & Electronics Engrs; Soc Indust & Appl Math; Am Soc Eng Educ. *Res:* Stability and optimal control of stochastic systems; modeling of man-machine systems. *Mailing Add:* Wright State Univ 3640 Colonel Glenn Dayton OH 45435-0001

BRANDELL, BRUCE REEVES, anatomy, zoology, for more information see previous edition

BRANDENBERGER, ARTHUR J, PHOTOGRAMMETRY, GEODESY & CARTOGRAPHY. *Current Pos:* RETIRED. *Personal Data:* b St Gallen, Switz, July 2, 16; m 49, Paulette E Hertig; c Elizabeth & Marie-Therese. *Educ:* Swiss Fed Inst Technol, MS, 40, PhD(photogram), 47. *Honors & Awards:* Antarctic Serv Medal, US Dept State, 70; Medal Honor, Lt Gov Que, 95. *Prof Exp:* Photogram engr, Switz, 40-44; res assoc & lectr photogram, Swiss Fed Inst Technol, 45-49; expert, Ministry Pub Works, Greece, 49-50; prof photogram, Eng Sch Istanbul, Turkey, 50-54; chief engr, City of Istanbul, 53; vis prof & res assoc photogram, Ohio State Univ, 55-56, assoc prof & chief res assoc, 57-59, prof & res supvr, 59-65; dir, Dept Photogram, Laval Univ, 65-75, res prof, 75-76, pres assemblee of prof, Geodesy Sect, Fac Forestry & Geomatics, 83-88. *Concurrent Pos:* Mem archaeol exped to Mt Ararat, Turkey, 60; mem, Adv Comt Hwy Design Aids, Hwy Res Coun Ohio, 61-63; leader, Byrd Sta Traverse, Antarctica Exped, 62-63; consult, UN, USAF & other orgn, 63-64, world cartog, UN, 75-; hon vis prof, Nat Sci Coun, Repub China, 69-70; vpres, Comt Thematic Cartog, Panam Inst Geog & Hist, OSA, 77-81; expert consult world air photo index, Food & Agr Orgn, 80-; invited scientist, Chinese Soc Geod, Photogram & Cartog, 81; hon prof, Wuhan Tech Univ Surv & Mapping, China, 82. *Mem:* Am Soc Photogram & Remote Sensing; hon mem Am Inst Navig; Am Geog Soc; Am Polar Soc; hon mem Indian Soc Photogram; French Soc Photogram & Remote Sensing; hon mem Brazilian Soc Cartog; Can Inst Surv; Am Cong Surv & Mapping. *Res:* Geodesy; cartography; navigation; photogrammetry space science; polar research; archaeology; glaciology; world cartography; space triangulation from satellite imagery. *Mailing Add:* 2590 Plaza No 611 Sillery Quebec PQ G1T 1X2 Can. *Fax:* 418-656-7411

BRANDENBERGER, JOHN RUSSELL, ATOMIC PHYSICS, LASER SPECTROSCOPY. *Current Pos:* from asst prof to prof, 68-93, chmn dept, 73-75 & 81-84, PROF PHYSICS & CHMN DEPT, LAWRENCE UNIV, 91-, MEM COUN UNDERGRAD RES, 93- *Personal Data:* b Danville, Ill, May 13, 39; m 64, Caroline Melhorn; c 2. *Educ:* Carleton Col, AB, 61; Brown Univ, ScM, 64, PhD(physics), 68. *Prof Exp:* Instr physics, Col Wooster, 64-66. *Concurrent Pos:* Res fel, Harvard Univ, 75-76; consult, Los Alamos Sci Lab, Univ Calif, 75-78; vis prof, Univ Reading, 81; Sci Fac Develop Fel, NSF, 81-82; vis sr scientist, Oxford Univ, 82; counr, Coun Undergrad Res; Fulbright fel sch, 90-91; vis scientist, Mass Inst Technol, 95-96. *Mem:* Am Phys Soc; Sigma Xi. *Res:* Measurement of Sommerfeld fine structure constant by level-crossing in atomic hydrogen; fast atomic beam spectroscopy; time-resolved fluorescence spectroscopy; high resolution laser spectroscopy. *Mailing Add:* Dept Physics Lawrence Univ Appleton WI 54912

BRANDENBERGER, ROBERT H, COSMOLOGY, PARTICLE PHYSICS. *Current Pos:* asst prof, 86-91, ASSOC PROF PHYSICS, BROWN UNIV, 91- *Personal Data:* b Bern, Switz, 1954; US citizen. *Educ:* Swiss Fed Inst Technol, Zurich, dipl physics, 78; Harvard Univ, MA, 79, PhD(physics), 83. *Prof Exp:* Postdoctoral fel physics, Inst Theoret Physics, Univ Calif, Santa Barbara, 83-85 & Dept Appl Math & Theoret Physics, Univ Cambridge, 85-87. *Concurrent Pos:* US Dept Energy outstanding jr investr, 88; A P Sloan fel, 88-92. *Res:* Using particle physics and field theory to develop models for the origin of galaxies and other structures in the universe; cosmic string models and inflationary universe scenarios. *Mailing Add:* Physics Dept Brown Univ Providence RI 02912

BRANDENBERGER, STANLEY GEORGE, ORGANIC CHEMSTRY. *Current Pos:* Res chemist, Houston Res Lab, Shell Oil Co, 56-63, sr res chemist, 63-64, group leader, 64-68, sect head, Royal Dutch/Shell Lab, Holland, 68-69, staff res chemist, Houston Res Lab, Deerpark, 69-72, STAFF RES CHEMIST, SHELL DEVELOP CO, 72- *Personal Data:* b Houston, Tex, Jan 18, 30; m 67; c 2. *Educ:* Rice Univ, BA, 52; Univ Tex, PhD(org chem), 56. *Mem:* Am Chem Soc; Southwest Catalysis Soc. *Res:* Physical organic chemistry; heterogeneous catalysis. *Mailing Add:* 5726 Kuldell Houston TX 77096

BRANDENBURG, GEORGE WARNER, HEAVY QUARK SPECTROSCOPY, PARTICLE DETECTOR RESEARCH & DEVELOPMENT. *Current Pos:* SR RES FEL & DIR, HIGH ENERGY PHYSICS LAB, HARVARD UNIV, 80- *Personal Data:* b Hempstead, NY, July 26, 44; m 65, Ellen Louise Boyd; c Peter & Anna. *Educ:* Harvard Univ, AB, 65, PhD(physics), 69. *Prof Exp:* Postdoctoral fel, Max Planck Inst, 69-71; res fel, Stanford Linear Accelerator Ctr, 71-74; assoc prof, Mass Inst Technol, 74-80. *Mem:* Fel Am Phys Soc. *Res:* Heavy quark and leyton production; experimental elementary particle physics. *Mailing Add:* High Energy Phys Lab Harvard Univ 42 Oxford St Cambridge MA 02138. *E-Mail:* brandenburg@physics.harvard.edu

BRANDENBURG, JAMES H, OTOLARYNGOLOGY. *Current Pos:* from asst prof to assoc prof, 64-72, PROF & CHMN OTOLARYNGOL, MED SCH, UNIV WIS-MADISON, 72- *Personal Data:* b Green Bay, Wis, July 17, 30; m 54; c 4. *Educ:* Univ Wis, BA, 52, MS, 56; Am Bd Otolaryngol, dipl, 63. *Honors & Awards:* Cert of Achievement, Armed Forces Inst Path, Walter Reed Hosp, 64. *Prof Exp:* Intern, William Beaumont Gen Hosp, El Paso, Tex, 57, ear, nose & throat preceptorship, 58; ear, nose & throat resident, Brooke Gen Hosp, San Antonio, 61. *Concurrent Pos:* Attend consult otolaryngol, Vet Admin Hosp, Madison, 64-; mem fac, Home Study Course, Am Acad Otolaryngol & Ophthal, 67-; prin investr prototype comprehensive network demonstration proj head & neck cancer, NIH Contract, 74- *Mem:* Fel Am Acad Ophthal & Otolaryngol; fel Am Laryngol, Rhinol & Otol Soc; Am Coun Otolaryngol; Am Soc Head & Neck Surg; AMA. *Res:* Combination therapy for epidermoid carcinoma of the head and neck; carcinoma of the larynx; study of the guinea pig cochlea by electron microscopy; study of the changes seen in the cochlea of the guinea pig following noise exposure; traumatic injuries to the larynx. *Mailing Add:* 600 Highland Ave Madison WI 53792-0001

BRANDENBURG, ROBERT O, MEDICINE. *Current Pos:* CLIN PROF MED, UNIV ARIZ, 85- *Personal Data:* b Minneapolis, Minn, Aug 5, 18; m 44; c 5. *Educ:* Univ NDak, BS, 40; Univ Pa, MD, 43. *Prof Exp:* Intern, Presby Hosp, Pa, 44; intern, Nutrit Clin, Hillman Hosp, Ala, 47-48; fel, Mayo Clin, 48-51, consult med, 51-84, from asst prof to assoc prof med, 58-69, coordr continuing med educ, Outreach Prog, 76-84, PROF MED, MAYO MED SCH, 69- *Concurrent Pos:* Chmn div cardiovasc dis, Mayo Clin, 69-74. *Mem:* AMA; Am Heart Asn; fel Am Col Physicians; fel Am Col Cardiol (vpres, 78); Am Asn Univ Prof. *Res:* Congenital and rheumatic cardiovascular disease. *Mailing Add:* 701 Mission Twin Butts Rd Green Valley AZ 85614-1322

BRANDENSTEIN, DANIEL CHARLES, ASTRONAUTICS. *Current Pos:* EXEC VPRES, KISTLER AEROSPACE CORP, 96- *Personal Data:* b Watertown, Wis, Jan 17, 43; m 66, Jane A Wade; c Adelle. *Educ:* Univ Wis, BS, 65. *Honors & Awards:* Yuri Gagarin Gold Medal, Fedn Aeronaut Int, 90; Ivan C Kinchloe Award, Soc Exp Test Pilots, 92; Laurel Award, Space/ Missiles, Aviation Week & Space Technol, 93; Haley Space Flight Award, Am Inst Aeronaut & Astronaut, 93. *Prof Exp:* USN, 65-93; astronaut, NASA Johnson Space Ctr, 78-93, chief astronaut off, 87-93; dir prog develop, Loral Space Info Syst, 93-96. *Mem:* Am Inst Aeronaut & Astronaut; Soc Exp Test Pilots; Asn Space Explorers. *Mailing Add:* 20532 127th Ave SE Snohomish WA 98296-3936

BRANDEWIE, RICHARD A(NTHONY), LASERS & OPTICAL SYSTEMS. *Current Pos:* INDEPENDENT CONSULT, 92- *Personal Data:* b Sidney, Ohio, Feb 4, 36; m 59, Arlene Warner; c Leo & Frances. *Educ:* Univ Detroit, BEE, 59; Carnegie Inst Technol, MS, 60, PhD(elec eng), 63. *Honors & Awards:* Nat Sci & Technol Award, IRIS Active Systems, 92. *Prof Exp:* Res asst elec eng, Carnegie Inst Technol, 59-60; res specialist, Autonetics Div, NAm Aviation Inc, Rockwell Int, 63-69, supvr, Laser Dept, NAm Rockwell Corp, 69-80, dir adv tech, Rocketdyne Div, 80-85, prog mgr, Rocketdyne Div, 85-92. *Mem:* Am Phys Soc; Inst Elec & Electronics Engrs. *Res:* Laser radar; coherent laser receivers; spectroscopy; plasma physics; adaptive optics, gas & solid state lasers. *Mailing Add:* 25760 Vista Verde Dr Monte Nido CA 91302-2164

BRANDFONBRENER, MARTIN, INTERNAL MEDICINE, CARDIOLOGY. *Current Pos:* PROF MED, MED SCH, NORTHWESTERN UNIV, CHICAGO, 67- *Personal Data:* b New York, NY, July 25, 27; m 56; c 4. *Educ:* Albany Med Col, MD, 49. *Prof Exp:* Rotating intern, Med Ctr, Univ Ind, 49-50; resident internal med, Boston City Hosp, 50-51; resident, Dept Physiol, Western Reserve Univ, 51-52; res assoc cardiol, Sect Geront, Nat Heart Inst, 53-54; asst resident med, Univ Hosp, Univ Cleveland, 54-55; asst resident cardiol, Presby Hosp, NY, 55-56; fel cardiorespiratory med, Col Physicians & Surgeons, Columbia Univ, 56-58; chief cardiol sect, Vet Admin Res Hosp, Chicago, 58-63; assoc prof med, Univ NMex, 63-67. *Concurrent Pos:* USPHS fel, Sch Med, Western Reserve Univ, 51-52. *Mem:* Am Fedn Clin Res (secy, 62); fel Am Col Physicians; Am Physiol Soc. *Res:* Myocardial metabolism and coronary flow. *Mailing Add:* 707 N Fairbanks Ct Chicago IL 60611-3042

BRANDHORST, BRUCE PETER, DEVELOPMENTAL BIOLOGY, MOLECULAR & CELL BIOLOGY. *Current Pos:* PROF & DIR, INST MOLECULAR BIOL & BIOCHEM, SIMON FRASER UNIV, 89- *Personal Data:* b Galveston, Tex, Nov 14, 44; m, Elaine Golds; c Gregory Golds & Gary Golds. *Educ:* Harvard Univ, AB, 66; Univ Calif, San Diego, PhD, 71. *Prof Exp:* Res assoc, Univ Colo, Boulder, 71-73; from asst prof to prof, McGill Univ, 73-89. *Concurrent Pos:* Grantee, Nat Sci & Eng Res Coun Can, 73-, NIH, 84-90; instr embryol, Marine Biol Lab, Woods Hole, Mass, 80-82, co-dir embryol course, 83-88. *Mem:* Am Soc Molecular Marine Biol & Biotechnol; Can Soc Biochem Cell & Molecular Biol; Soc Develop Biol; AAAS. *Res:* Regulation of gene expression in developing embryos; cellular interactions in embryos. *Mailing Add:* Inst Molecular Biol Simon Fraser Univ Burnaby BC V5A 1S6 Can. *Fax:* 604-291-5583; *E-Mail:* brandhor@sfu.ca

BRANDHORST, HENRY WILLIAM, JR, PERFORMANCE MEASUREMENTS. *Current Pos:* researcher, NASA, 61-67, head, Solar Cell Res Sect, 67-79, chief, Space Photovoltaic Br, 79-84, CHIEF, POWER TECHNOL DIV, LEWIS RES CTR, NASA, 84- *Personal Data:* b Omaha, Nebr, Sept 18, 36; m 56, V Louise Stephenson; c Deborah K, Henry W III & Robert W. *Educ:* Univ Okla, BS, 57; Purdue Univ, PhD(chem), 61. *Honors & Awards:* William R Cherry Award, Inst Elec & Electronics Engrs, 84. *Mem:* Sigma Xi. *Res:* Space power technology: photovoltaics, electrochemical storage, power management and distribution, spacecraft environmental interactions; solar nuclear dynamic systems: concentrators, thermal storage, free piston stirling engines, brayton and rankine cycles, advanced radiators. *Mailing Add:* 272 Westbridge Dr Berea OH 44017-1544

BRANDINGER, JAY J, ELECTRICAL ENGINEERING, MATHEMATICAL STATISTICS. *Current Pos:* EXEC DIR, NJ COMN SCI & TECHNOL, 91- *Personal Data:* b Bronx, NY, Jan 2, 27; m 51, Alice Levite; c Paul, Donna & Norman. *Educ:* Cooper Union, BEE, 51; Rutgers Univ, MSEE, 62, PhD(elec eng), 68. *Honors & Awards:* David Sarnoff Achievement Award, RCA-David Sarnoff Res Ctr, 52, 70 & 73. *Prof Exp:* Mem tech staff commun res, Res Lab, RCA Corp, 51-60, group leader TV systs, Consumer Electronics Res Lab, 60-74, vpres TV eng, Consumer Electronics Div, 74-79, div vpres, Selectavision Videodisc Oper, 79-86, staff vpres & systs eng, RCA Electronic Prods & Labs, 84-85, gen mgr, 84-86; vpres mfg & mat res, Sarnoff Res Ctr, 86-90, vpres strategic ventures, 90-91. *Concurrent Pos:* Gov's appointee, Sci & Technol Coun States, Nat Gov's Asn. *Mem:* Fel Inst Elec & Electronics Engrs; NY Acad Sci; fel Soc Info Display; Inst Math Statist; Sigma Xi; AAAS. *Res:* Consumer TV systems; statistical communications theory and application in coding, modulation, networks and detection; optical communications; electro-optic techniques; optical information processing; display techniques and systems; video discs. *Mailing Add:* Two Queens Lane Pennington NJ 08534. *Fax:* 609-292-5920; *E-Mail:* jjb@njcst.gov

BRANDLER, PHILIP, FOOD STABILIZATION, FOOD SERVICE EQUIPMENT ENGINEERING. *Current Pos:* syst analyst, US Army Natick Res & Develop Ctr, 71-73, opers res analyst, 73-75, prin investr, 75-77, supvry opers res analyst, 77-81, dir, Systs Anal, 82-85, asst tech dir prog integration, 85-88, dir food eng, 88-93, dir, sustainability, 93-95, DIR, US ARMY NATICK RES & DEVELOP CTR, 96- *Personal Data:* b New York, NY, Feb 2, 43; m 85, Rosemary E Caffarelli. *Educ:* Columbia Col, BA, 64; Brown Univ, MS, 69; Northeastern Univ, MS, 71, MBA, 73. *Honors & Awards:* Rohland Isker Award, Res & Develop Assocs for Food & Packaging Indust, 82. *Prof Exp:* Physicist, NASA Electronics Res Ctr, 67-70. *Mem:* Inst Food Technologists; Mil Opers Res Soc; Opers Res Soc Am. *Res:* Research, development and engineering in military rations, ranging from basic food chemistry to product development and testing; military field service/support equipment and systems (e.g. kitchens, showers, lutrines, launderies, heaters) ranging from basic combustion technology to development and testing of complete mobile kitchens and bakeries; field shelters (tents and rigid wall) ranging from structural dynamics and EMI shielding to product development; personnel and cargo airdrop systems ranging from modeling to development and testing of precision guided parafoils; personnel protection systems for the full spectrum of battlefield and environmental threats ranging from ballistic materials to integrated chemical protection suits. *Mailing Add:* US Army Natick Res & Develop Ctr Code SATNC-W Natick MA 01760. *Fax:* 508-233-5061

BRANDLI, HENRY WILLIAM, METEOROLOGY. *Current Pos:* RETIRED. *Personal Data:* b Boston, Mass, Nov 5, 37; m 59; c 4. *Educ:* Tufts Univ, BSME, 59; Mass Inst Technol, MS(meteorol) & MS(aeronaut & astronaut), 65. *Prof Exp:* Satellite meteorologist, Environ Res Technol, 76-78; chief scientist, Fla Weather Serv, 78-85. *Concurrent Pos:* Consult, Lockheed Harris. *Mem:* Fel Am Meteorol Soc; Nat Weather Asn; Cousteau Soc. *Res:* Satellite meteorology; remote sensing. *Mailing Add:* 3165 Sharon Dr Melbourne FL 32904

BRANDMAIER, HAROLD EDMUND, MECHANICAL ENGINEERING. *Current Pos:* MGR ENG SYSTS, BURNS & ROE, INC, 73- *Personal Data:* b New York, NY, Nov 9, 26; m 51; c 4. *Educ:* Columbia Univ, BS, 47, MS, 48, ME, 62. *Prof Exp:* Asst mech eng, Columbia Univ, 47-48; proj engr, Worthington Corp, 48-54; chief proj engr, Curtiss-Wright Corp, 56-71; proj engr, RCA Astroelectronics, 71-73. *Mem:* Am Inst Aeronaut & Astronaut; Am Soc Mech Engrs. *Res:* Fluid mechanics; thermodynamics; energy conversion; composite materials. *Mailing Add:* 63 Florence Rd Harrington Park NJ 07640

BRANDMAN, HAROLD A, ORGANIC CHEMISTRY. *Current Pos:* Chemist, 68-74, group leader, 75-78, prod chem, 78-80, dir fragrance mfg, 80-82, dir flavor, fragrance mfg, 82-84, DIR CHEM FLAVOR FRAGRANCE MFG, GIVAUDAN CORP, 85- *Personal Data:* b Newark, NJ, Jan 29, 41; m 64; c 2. *Educ:* Univ Pa, BA, 62; Seton Hall Univ, MS, 66, PhD(chem), 68. *Mem:* Am Chem Soc; Sigma Xi. *Res:* Synthesis and development of antimicrobial agents used as industrial biocides. *Mailing Add:* 7 Adams Pl Glen Ridge NJ 07028

BRANDNER, JOHN DAVID, INDUSTRIAL CHEMISTRY. *Current Pos:* RETIRED. *Personal Data:* b Bethlehem, Pa, Mar 23, 10; wid; c Susan, Julia & John D Jr. *Educ:* Lehigh Univ, BS, 32, MS, 34; Columbia Univ, PhD(chem), 43. *Prof Exp:* Chemist, Exp Lab, Atlas Powder Co, 34-37; asst, Columbia Univ, 38-40; asst dir control lab, Ravenna Ord Works, 41-42; chemist, Atlas Chem Industs, 42-44, dir res lab, 44-47, asst dir cent res lab, 48-51, mgr, 51-55, mgr phys chem & anal sect, Res Dept, 55-61, assoc dir, Chem Res Dept, 61-70, dir, Chem Res Dept, 70-75. *Concurrent Pos:* Mem comt specifications, Food Chem Codex Proj, Nat Res Coun & Food & Agr Orgn-WHO Expert Comt Food Additives. *Mem:* AAAS; Am Chem Soc; fel Am Inst Chem. *Res:* Calorimetry; kinetics; alkylene oxide reactions; food additives. *Mailing Add:* 2313 E Mall Wilmington DE 19810

BRANDOLINI, ANITA JEAN, NUCLEAR MAGNETIC RESONANCE, FOURIER TRANSFORM INFRARED. *Current Pos:* Res chemist, 83-90, SR RES CHEMIST, MOBIL CHEM CO, 90- *Personal Data:* b Chester, Pa, Mar 4, 56. *Educ:* Drexel Univ, BS, 79; Univ Del, MA, 81, PhD(phys chem), 83. *Mem:* Am Chem Soc; Soc Plastics Engrs; Soc Appl Spectros. *Res:* Utilize nuclear magnetic resonance and infrared spectroscopies for the study of polymeric materials and polymerization catalysts, including structural characterization, bulk properties, additive degradation and on-line analysis. *Mailing Add:* Mobil Chem Co PO Box 3029 Edison NJ 08818-3029. *Fax:* 732-321-6230; *E-Mail:* abrandol@interserv.com

BRANDOM, WILLIAM FRANKLIN, DEVELOPMENTAL BIOLOGY, CYTOGENETICS. *Current Pos:* RETIRED. *Personal Data:* b Oklahoma City, Okla, Jan 2, 26; m 52; c 4. *Educ:* Stanford Univ, AB, 51, MA, 54, PhD(biol), 59. *Prof Exp:* Asst biol, Stanford Univ, 53-58; Nat Cancer Inst fel, Princeton Univ, 58-59; from instr to asst prof zool, Newcomb Col, Tulane Univ, 59-65, asst prof path, Sch Med, 65-67; asst prof, Delta Primate Res Ctr, 67-68; assoc prof biol sci, Univ Denver, 68-74, prof, 74-92. *Concurrent Pos:* Nat Inst Child Health & Human Develop fel, Univ St Andrews, 66. *Mem:* AAAS; Am Soc Zool; Soc Develop Biol; Tissue Cult Asn; Sigma Xi. *Res:* Developmental biology of amphibians; developmental genetics; polyploidy; hybridization; pigment pattern formation in heteroploid hybrids; karyotyptes and idiograms of amphibian chromosomes; lampbrush chromosomes; somatic cell genetics; human radiation cytogenetics; chromosome biology. *Mailing Add:* 61125 Country Rd 129 Steamboat Springs CO 80477

BRANDON, CLEMENT EDWIN, PULP AND PAPER SCIENCE & ENGINEERING. *Current Pos:* CONSULT, 83- *Personal Data:* b Yorkshire, Ohio, Oct 3, 15; m 39, Marian Steingass; c Ralph E & William L. *Educ:* Defiance Col, AB, 36; State Univ NY, Syracuse, MS, 42. *Honors & Awards:* Testing Div Award of Merit, Tech Asn Pulp & Paper Indust, 68; Merit Award, Am Soc Testing & Mat, 90. *Prof Exp:* Teacher math, Bradford High Sch, Ohio, 36-37; chemist pulp & paper technol, Aetna Paper Co, 37-40; chief chemist, Howard Paper Co, 41-51, asst tech dir, 51-57, tech dir, 57-58; chmn, Dept Pulp & Paper Sci & Eng, Miami Univ, 58-81, dir, Coop Prog, Paper Sci & Eng Dept, 81-83. *Concurrent Pos:* Mem steering comt testing div, Tech Asn Pulp & Paper Indust, 54-64, chmn testing div, 58-61; exec dir, Miami Univ Pulp & Paper Found, 60-88; mem exec comt D-6 on paper, Am Soc for Testing & Mat, 60-, chmn, 70-72; chmn US adv comt, Int Orgn Stand Tech Comt 6 on pulp & paper, 63-69, US rep, 65-; mem testing adv bd, Tech Asn Pulp & Paper Indust, 65-80; mem comt P-3 on paper, Am Nat Stand Inst, 69-84. *Mem:* Fel Tech Asn Pulp & Paper Indust; Am Soc Testing & Mat; Paper Indust Mgt Asn; Sigma Xi. *Res:* Development of paper testing methods; hygroexpansivity of paper. *Mailing Add:* 121 Oakhill Dr Oxford OH 45056

BRANDON, DAVID LAWRENCE, IMMUNOLOGY, BIOCHEMISTRY. *Current Pos:* RES BIOCHEMIST, WESTERN REGIONAL RES CTR, USDA, 78- *Personal Data:* b New York, NY, Sept 4, 46. *Educ:* Harvard Univ, AB, 67, PhD(biochem), 74. *Prof Exp:* Res fel immunol, Nat Inst Med Res, London, UK, 74-76 & Univ Calif, Berkeley, 76-77. *Concurrent Pos:* Nat Multiple Sclerosis Soc fel, 74-76; lectr, Univ Calif, Berkeley, 79. *Mem:* Am Chem Soc; Asn Off Anal Chem Int. *Res:* Immunochemical analysis of foods; regulation of the immune response; cell membrane biochemistry; immunotoxicology; immunological studies of phytohormones and their receptors; biosensors. *Mailing Add:* USDA West Region Res Ctr 800 Buchanan St Albany CA 94710-1100

BRANDON, JAMES KENNETH, CRYSTALLOGRAPHY, PHYSICS. *Current Pos:* asst prof, 70-76, assoc chmn dept, 78-83, ASSOC PROF PHYSICS, UNIV WATERLOO, 77- *Personal Data:* b Sarnia, Ont, May 21, 40; m 62; c 3. *Educ:* McMaster Univ, BSc, 62, PhD(physics), 67. *Hon Degrees:* MA, Cambridge Univ, 68. *Prof Exp:* Res asst physics, Cavendish Lab, Cambridge Univ, 68-70. *Concurrent Pos:* Res fel, Clare Hall Cambridge Univ & NATO fel, Cavendish Lab, 68-70. *Mem:* Can Asn Physicists; Am Crystallog Asn. *Res:* Inorganic crystal structure analyses using x-ray diffraction; metal and alloy crystal structures. *Mailing Add:* Dept Physics Univ Waterloo Waterloo ON N2L 3G1 Can

BRANDON, ROBERT L, MATHEMATICS. *Current Pos:* ASSOC PROF & PROF MATH, EASTERN ORE STATE COL, 81- *Personal Data:* b Seattle, Wash, Apr 4, 40. *Educ:* Univ Wash, BS, 62; Calif State Univ, MS, 69; Colo State Univ, PhD(math), 72. *Prof Exp:* Instr, Calif State Univ, 68-69; from instr to assoc prof math, Univ Maine, Presque Isle, 72-81. *Concurrent Pos:* Vis lectr, Math, Maine Sec Schs, 72-74; adj fac, Univ Southern Calif, 74 & 76; res consult, Colo State Univ, 84 & 89. *Mem:* Am Math Soc; Math Asn Am; Am Statist Asn. *Res:* Algebraic theory of semigroups, especially the semigroup of binary relations; statistics and modeling especially as they relate to the current undergraduate mathematics curriculum. *Mailing Add:* Eastern Ore State Col 1410 L Ave La Grande OR 97850-2899

BRANDON, RONALD ARTHUR, VERTEBRATE ZOOLOGY. *Current Pos:* from asst prof to assoc prof, 63-74, chmn, 80-87, PROF ZOOL, SOUTHERN ILL UNIV, CARBONDALE, 74- *Personal Data:* b Mt Pleasant, Mich, Dec 3, 33; m 54, Doris M Huston; c Connie J, Elizabeth M (Ritter) & Jennifer R (Radtke). *Educ:* Ohio Univ, BS, 56, MS, 58; Univ Ill, PhD(zool), 62. *Prof Exp:* Asst prof biol, Univ Ala, 62-63. *Mem:* Soc Conserv Biol; Soc Study Amphibians & Reptiles; Am Soc Ichthyologists & Herpetologists; Soc Study Evolution; Am Soc Zoologists; Soc Syst Biol. *Res:* Amphibian systematics; biology of salamanders. *Mailing Add:* Dept Zool Southern Ill Univ Carbondale IL 62901-6501. *Fax:* 618-453-4110; *E-Mail:* ga3884@siucvmb.bitnet

BRANDON, WALTER WILEY, JR, ROCKET PROPULSION SYSTEMS. *Current Pos:* AEROSPACE TECHNOLOGIST PROPULSION SYSTS, MARSHAL SPACE FLIGHT CTR, NASA, 87- *Personal Data:* b Gainesville, Ga, Dec 1, 29; m 57, Patricia Donham; c Dean, Miles & Nancy. *Educ:* Emory Univ, BA, 52, MS, 53. *Prof Exp:* Scientist, Redstone Res Labs, Rohm and Haas Co, 53-65; res specialist, space div, Boeing Co, 65-67; scientist, Redstone Res Labs, Rohm and Haas Co, 67-71; physicist, US Army Missile Command, 72-87. *Mem:* Assoc fel Am Inst Aeronuat & Astronaut. *Res:* Nuclear radiation spectroscopy; liquid and solid rocket propulsion; combustion instability of rockets; detonation of rocket propellants and explosives; instrumentation; microwaves; atmospheric optics. *Mailing Add:* 1902 Colice Rd SE Huntsville AL 35801

BRANDOW, BAIRD H, THEORETICAL PHYSICS. *Current Pos:* mem staff, 74-91, GUEST SCIENTIST, LOS ALAMOS NAT LAB, 91- *Personal Data:* b San Diego, Calif, June 9, 35; m 66, Bodil Kristensen; c Anna M & Teresa. *Educ:* Calif Inst Technol, BS, 57; Cornell Univ, PhD(theoret physics), 64. *Prof Exp:* NSF fel, Niels Bohr Inst, Copenhagen Univ, 63-65; docent theoret nuclear physics, Nordic Inst Theoret Atomic Physics, Denmark, 65-66; instr physics, Cornell Univ, 66-69; fel, Battelle-Seattle Res Ctr, 69-71, Staff, Battelle Mem Inst, Ohio, 71-74. *Mem:* Am Phys Soc. *Res:* Nuclear many-body problem; linked-cluster perturbation theory; theory of liquid and solid helium; theory of magnetic insulators and associated metal-insulator transitions; theory of effective pi-electron hamiltonians; theory of valence fluctuation and heavy-electron behavior in rare earth and actinide compounds; theory of high-temperature superconductors. *Mailing Add:* Ctr Nonlinear Studies Los Alamos Nat Lab PO Box 1663 Los Alamos NM 87545

BRANDRETH, DALE ALDEN, CHEMICAL ENGINEERING, PHYSICAL CHEMISTRY. *Current Pos:* ADJ PROF CHEM ENG, WIDENER UNIV, 83- *Personal Data:* b Phoenixville, Pa, Dec 17, 31; m 66; c 2. *Educ:* Univ Pa, BSc, 53, MSc, 58; Univ Toronto, PhD(chem eng), 65. *Prof Exp:* Tech serv engr plastics processing, Welding Engrs Inc, 55-56; res asst high energy fuels, Inst Coop Res, Univ Pa, 56-57; res engr solid propellant technol, Atlantic Res Corp, 58-61; sr res engr high temperature mat, Westinghouse Astronuclear Lab, 65-66; sr res engr surface chem thermodynamics, E I Du Pont De Nemours & Co, 66-83. *Mem:* Am Chem Soc. *Res:* Thermodynamics; energy conservation; surface chemistry; chlorofluorocarbons and alternatives; thermodynamic data analysis. *Mailing Add:* 721 Whitebriar Rd Hockessin DE 19707

BRANDRISS, MARJORIE C, GENE EXPRESSION, CELLULAR PHYSIOLOGY. *Current Pos:* asst prof, Microbiol Dept, 81-87, assoc prof, Dept Microbiol & Molecular Genetics, 87-93, PROF, NJ MED SCH, UNIV MED & DENT, NJ, 93- *Personal Data:* b New York, NY, Apr 10, 49; m 76. *Educ:* Cornell Univ, AB, 71; Mass Inst Technol, PhD(microbiol), 75. *Prof Exp:* Instr molecular biol, Biol Dept, Mass Inst Technol, 75-76, fel, 76-81. *Concurrent Pos:* NIH Study Sect Panelist, 88-92. *Mem:* Am Soc Microbiol; Genetics Soc Am; AAAS. *Res:* Regulation of gene expression in the pathways of proline metabolism in the yeast, Saccharomyces cerevisiae; transcriptional regulation. *Mailing Add:* Dept Microbiol & Molecular Genetics Univ Med & Dent NJ 185 S Orange Ave Newark NJ 07103-2757

BRANDRISS, MICHAEL W, IMMUNOLOGY, INFECTIOUS DISEASES. *Current Pos:* asst prof, 65-69, ASSOC PROF MED, SCH MED & DENT, UNIV ROCHESTER, 69- *Personal Data:* b Brooklyn, NY, Oct 3, 31; m 55; c 4. *Educ:* Kenyon Col, AB, 53; NY Univ, MD, 57. *Prof Exp:* Intern med, Johns Hopkins Hosp, 57-58, asst resident, 58-59; asst resident, Baltimore City Hosps, 59-60; clin assoc, Nat Inst Allergy & Infectious Dis, 60-62, clin investr, 62-63, sr investr, 63-65. *Concurrent Pos:* Consult med, Vet Admin Hosp, Batavia, NY, 65-; Nat Inst Allergy & Infectious Dis grants, 66-; attend physician, Rochester Gen Hosp, NY; sr assoc physician, Strong Mem Hosp, Rochester. *Mem:* Am Fedn Clin Res; Am Asn Immunol; Infectious Dis Soc Am. *Res:* Delayed hypersensitivity in animals; antimetabolites in autoimmune states; immunologic studies on penicillin and related antigens; human immune response to haptens and to protein and polysaccharide antigens; human immune response to viral infections. *Mailing Add:* Dept Med Rochester Gen Hosp 1425 Portland Ave Rochester NY 14621-3095. *Fax:* 716-544-1504

BRANDS, ALVIRA BERNICE, psychiatric nursing, for more information see previous edition

BRANDSMA, JANET LOUISIE, VIROLOGY, ONCOLOGY. *Current Pos:* asst prof, 89-93, ASSOC PROF, YALE UNIV SCH MED, 93- *Personal Data:* b Wilmington, Del, July 15, 48; m 75, John Meerts; c Sarah, Lisa & Charles M. *Educ:* Syracuse Univ, AB, 70; Wesleyan Univ, Conn, MAT, 71; Yale Univ, PhD(epidemiol), 81. *Prof Exp:* Fel, Cold Spring Harbor Lab, 81-83; sr fel, Dept Otolaryngol, Long Island Jewish Med Ctr, 83-84, head, Sect Molecular Epidemiol, 84-89. *Concurrent Pos:* Swebilius Cancer Res Award, 89-90; Argall L & Anna G Hull Cancer Res Award, 91-92. *Res:* Develop a papillomavirus vaccine to prevent tumors from forming and/or to induce their regression; author of various publications; define the genetic determinants of papillomavirus-induced disease. *Mailing Add:* 1597 Durham Rd Guilford CT 06437. *Fax:* 203-785-7499; *E-Mail:* janet_brandsma@qm.yale.edu

BRANDSTETTER, ALBIN, HYDROLOGY, NUCLEAR WASTE ISOLATION. *Current Pos:* SR STAFF CONSULT, INTERA INC, 92- *Personal Data:* b Schildorn, Austria, Mar 20, 32; US citizen; m 56, Glenda J Mann; c Peter J & Erich R. *Educ:* Col Agr Vienna, Dipl Ing, 58; Univ Calif, Davis, MS, 66, PhD(hydrol), 71. *Prof Exp:* Bridge design engr, Ore State Hwy Dept, 58-59; invests engr, Ore State Water Resources Bd, 59-62; hydrol res engr, Univ Calif, Davis, 65-70; sr res scientist & proj mgr, Pac Northwest Labs, Battelle Mem Inst, 70-80, proj mgr, 80-90; sr hydrologist, Sci Appln Int Corp, 90-92. *Mem:* Am Geophys Union; Am Inst Hydrology; Am Nuclear Soc. *Res:* Hydrologic research, including the mathematical modeling of precipitation-runoff relationships, ground and surface water flow and quality; environmental planning and assessments; mathematical modeling and safety assessments of nuclear waste repositories. *Mailing Add:* 350 Humboldt Dr N Henderson NV 89014-1300. *Fax:* 702-295-4730; *E-Mail:* brandsteta@aol.com

BRANDT, ALLAN M, MEDICAL HISTORY. *Current Pos:* PROF HIST SCI, HARVARD UNIV, 92-, AMALIE MOSES KASS PROF HIST MED, DEPT SOCIAL MED, 92- *Personal Data:* b Washington, DC, Dec 18, 53. *Educ:* Brandeis Univ, BA, 74; Columbia Univ, MA, 75, MPhil, 78, PhD(Am hist), 83. *Prof Exp:* Res assoc, Proj Value & Ethics in Health Care, Col Physicians & Surgeons, Columbia Univ, 77-82, teaching fel humanities, Fac Med, 79-82; instr, Dept His, Smith Col, 82; instr, Dept Social Med & Health Policy, Med Sch & instr, Dept Hist Sci, Harvard Univ, 82, asst prof hist med & sci, Dept Social Med & Health Policy & asst prof, Dept Hist Sci, 83-87, assoc prof, 87-90; assoc prof, Dept Social Med & Dept Hist, Univ NC, Chapel Hill, 90-92. *Concurrent Pos:* Rockefeller Found fel humanities, 85-86; mem, Hastings Ctr Study Group AIDS & Civil Liberties, 85-87, fel, 93-; mem, Comt Monitoring Social Impact of AIDS, Nat Acad Sci, 89-91; mem sect hist med, Nat Libr Med Study, NIH, 89-91; consult, AIDS/HIV Prog WHO, Pan Am Health Orgn, 90; Charles E Culpeper scholar med humanities, 92- *Mem:* Inst Med-Nat Acad Sci; Hist Sci Soc; Soc Health & Human Values; Am Asn Hist Med. *Res:* Contributed articles to professional journals. *Mailing Add:* Dept Social Med Harvard Univ 641 Huntington Ave Boston MA 02115-6019

BRANDT, BRUCE LOSURE, PHYSICS, INSTRUMENTATION. *Current Pos:* DIR, DC USER PROG, FLA STATE UNIV, 92- *Personal Data:* b Seattle, Wash, Nov 3, 41; m 63; c 2. *Educ:* Pomona Col, BA, 63; Univ Rochester, PhD, 69. *Prof Exp:* Res assoc neurobiol, Salk Inst Biol Studies, 73-76; staff scientist, Neurosci Res Prog, F Bitter Nat Magnet Lab, 76-77, assoc head, Instrumentation & Opers Group, 77-91. *Concurrent Pos:* NIH fel genetics, Sch Med, Stanford Univ; Nat Multiple Sclerosis Soc fel. *Mem:* Am Phys Soc. *Res:* Properties of thin film superconductors; molecular genetics of bacteria and cultured cells; neuromuscular junction formation; electromagnetic measurements in high magnetic fields. *Mailing Add:* Nat High Magnetic Field Lab Fla State Univ Tallahassee FL 32306-4005. *Fax:* 850-644-0534; *E-Mail:* brandt@nhmfl.gov

BRANDT, CARL DAVID, VIROLOGY. *Current Pos:* from asst prof to assoc prof, 69-94, EMER PROF PEDIAT, MED SCH, GEORGE WASH UNIV, 94- *Personal Data:* b Bridgeport, Conn, Jan 19, 28; m 64, Elsa Erickson; c Karen & Erik. *Educ:* Univ Conn, BS, 49; Univ Mass, MS, 51; Harvard Univ, PhD(bact), 58. *Prof Exp:* Instr vet sci, Univ Mass, 49-52 & 54; res virologist, Charles Pfizer & Co, 58-62; assoc, Dept Epidemiol, Pub Health Res Inst, New York, 62-66; instr, Med Sch, Georgetown Univ, 66-69; res assoc, virol res, Children's Nat Med Ctr, 66-79, sr res assoc, 79-86, sr scientist, 86-94. *Concurrent Pos:* Asst prof pediat, Med Sch, George Wash Univ, 69-74, assoc prof, 74- *Mem:* Fel Infectious Dis Soc; Am Soc Microbiol; fel Am Acad Microbiol; Soc Epidemiol Res; fel Am Col Epidemiol; AAAS; Sigma Xi. *Res:* Polymerase chain reaction procedures for the diagnosis and study of pediatric human immunodeficiency virus infection; virus epidemiology; enteric and respiratory tract pathogens; rapid virus diagnosis; electron microscopy. *Mailing Add:* 819 E Franklin Ave Silver Spring MD 20901. *E-Mail:* brandtcd@aol.com

BRANDT, CHARLES LAWRENCE, PHOTOBIOLOGY, NEUROPHYSIOLOGY. *Current Pos:* RETIRED. *Personal Data:* b Prescott, Ariz, Dec 18, 25; m 54, Eleanor Chistensen. *Educ:* Stanford Univ, AB, 49, PhD(biol sci), 55. *Prof Exp:* Asst gen physiol, Stanford Univ, 50-54; instr zool, Univ Tex, 55-57; from assoc prof to prof biol, San Diego State Univ, 57-92, chmn dept, 67-69. *Concurrent Pos:* Res assoc, Hopkins Marine Sta, 56; NIH fel, Ctr Nat de la Res Sci, Marseille France, 66-67; res assoc, Naval Ocean Systs Ctr, San Diego, CA, 80-84. *Mem:* AAAS; Soc Gen Physiol; Am Soc Photobiol; Sigma Xi. *Res:* Neurosciences; photophysiology; cellular and general physiology; mechanism by which visible light inhibits the autoactive spiking and hyperpolrizes the ventral photresponsive neuron in the aplysia abdominal ganglion. *Mailing Add:* 6361 Rockhurst Dr San Diego CA 92120-3802

BRANDT, EDWARD NEWMAN, JR, ACADEMIC ADMINISTRATION, MEDICINE. *Current Pos:* exec dean, 89-92, PROF, COL MED, UNIV OKLA, 89- *Personal Data:* b Oklahoma City, Okla, July 3, 33; m 53, Patricia Lawson; c Patrick J, Edward N III, Rex C. *Educ:* Univ Okla, BS, 54; Okla State Univ, MS, 55, MD, 60, PhD(biostatist), 63. *Hon Degrees:* LHD, Med Univ SC, 84, Rush Univ, 85; DSc, NY Inst Technol, 84. *Honors & Awards:* Cert of Merit, AMA, 68; Am Col Int Physicians Award, 82; R Arnold Griswold Lectr, Univ Louisville, 83; Harvey Wiley Award, Food & Drug Admin, 84; Convocation Medalist, Am Col Cardiol, 85; Spec Recognition Award, Asn Am Med Cols, 85; Pub Health Award, Am Acad Family Physicians, 92. *Prof Exp:* From instr to prof prev med & pub health, Med Ctr, Univ Okla, 61-70, dir, Biostatist Unit & Med Res Comput Ctr, 62-70, assoc prof, Dept Internal Med, 63-70, assoc dean sch med & assoc dir, Med Ctr, 68-70; dean grad sch, Med Br, Univ Tex, Galveston, 70-74, dean med sch, 74-76, exec dean, 76-77, prof prev med & family med, 70-81, Univ Syst vpres health affairs, 77-81; asst secy health, Dept Health & Human Serv, Washington, DC, 81-84; chancellor, Univ Md, Baltimore, 85-88, pres, 88-89. *Concurrent Pos:* Consult, Civil Aeromed Res Inst, Okla, 62-67, Med Res Div, Upjohn Co, 63-67, comn evol foreign Med Schs, Fed State Med Bds, 80-81 & Coun Med Educ & Hosps, Tex Med Asn, 74-81; mem Bd Regents, Am Soc Clin Pharmacol & Therapeut, 68-73; fac adv, Nat Coun Student Sci Forums, 70-77; mem, Adv Comt, Primate Res Ctr, Div Res Resources, NIH, 75-79; mem, Panel Comput Technol & Physician Competence, Off Technol Assessment, Cong US, 78-79; chmn, Interagency Radiation Res Comt, US Govt, 81-82; mem, Nat Arthritis Bd, Dept Health & Human Serv, Nat Digestive Dis Bd, 81-84; mem, Fed Coord Coun Sci, Eng & Technol, US Govt, 81-84; mem, Working Group Food Safety, US Cabinet Coun Human Resources, 81-84; mem bd dirs, Nat AIDS Network, 86-88; prin, Ctr Excellence Govt, 86-; mem, Gov Coun, Inst Med-Nat Acad Sci, 86-, vchmn, 87-; mem, Adv Coun Hazardous Substances Res & Training, Nat Inst Environ Health Sci, 87-; ed, AIDS & Pub Policy J, 88-; adj prof, Dept Family Med, Col Med, Health Sci Ctr, Univ Okla, 89-, Dept Health Admin, Col Pub Health, 89-, Dept Biostatist & Epidemiol, 89-; pres, Inst Sci Soc, 90-93; Regentis prof, 96. *Mem:* Inst Med-Nat Acad Sci; fel AAAS; AMA; Am Acad Family Physicians; Assoc Am Med Cols; Sigma Xi; hon fel Am Col Cardiol. *Res:* Educational administration; published numerous articles in various journals. *Mailing Add:* Col Med Univ Okla PO Box 26901 Oklahoma City OK 73190. *Fax:* 405-271-3397

BRANDT, GERALD BENNETT, OPTICAL PHYSICS. *Current Pos:* CONSULT MANTIS SOLUTIONS, 92- *Personal Data:* b Pittsburgh, Pa, Apr 20, 38; m 61; c 4. *Educ:* Harvard Univ, AB, 60; Carnegie Inst Technol, MS, 63, PhD(physics), 66. *Prof Exp:* Engr, Westinghouse Res Labs, 60-66, sr engr, 66-70, fel scientist, 70-74, mgr electroptics, 74-82, adv scientist, Appl Physics Dept, Westinghoouse Sci & Technol Ctr, 82-91. *Concurrent Pos:* Lectr, Carnegie-Mellon Univ, 69 & 70 & Community Col Allegheny Co, 93-; assoc ed, J Optical Soc Am, 72-77. *Mem:* Optical Soc Am; Am Phys Soc; Soc Photo-Optical Instrumentation Engrs. *Res:* Integrated optics; optical and digital signal processing; optical design and instrumentation; coherent optics and holography; low temperature physics; electronic properties of metals; ultrasonics; computer applications; optical instrumentation. *Mailing Add:* 1600A Trimont Tower One Trimont Lane Pittsburgh PA 15211

BRANDT, GERALD H, SOIL PHYSICS. *Current Pos:* OWNER & OPERATOR, FARVIEW ORCHARDS, 93- *Personal Data:* b Lompoc, Calif, Feb 25, 33; m 58, Evelyn M Sallberg; c Clarence Andrew, Leanne Marie, Ruth Anne & Gwynne Janine (Kadiofske). *Educ:* Ore State Univ, BS, 55; Mich State Univ, MS, 60, PhD(soil sci), 63. *Prof Exp:* Asst soil sci, Mich State Univ, 60-63; chemist, Dow Chem Co, 63-72, group leader, 73-84, recruiting mgr, 84-86, res assoc, 86-93. *Concurrent Pos:* Mem, Comt Soil Physiochem Phenomena, Transp Res Bd, Nat Acad Sci, 71-75, Soil Chem Stabilization Comt, 72-75. *Mem:* Am Soc Agron; Clay Minerals Soc; Soil Sci Soc Am; Int Soc Soil Sci; Sigma Xi; Am Ceramics Soc; Am Chem Soc. *Res:* Dissolved oxygen in soils; clay-chemical phenomena; modifying soil physical properties with chemicals; erosion and sediment control; soil stabilization; frost heave in soils; environmental effects of deicing salts; chemicals research management; general applications research; ceramics forming and injection molding. *Mailing Add:* PO Box 626 Suttons Bay MI 49321. *Fax:* 616-271-4495

BRANDT, H(ARRY), MECHANICAL ENGINEERING. *Current Pos:* assoc prof, 64-69, chmn dept, 69-74 & 86-91, PROF MECH ENG, UNIV CALIF, DAVIS, 69- *Personal Data:* b Amsterdam, Neth, Nov 14, 25; nat US; m 53, Muriel R Harman; c Joyce E, Marilyn A & Robert A. *Educ:* Univ Calif, BS, 49, MS, 50, PhD(mech eng), 54. *Prof Exp:* From asst to assoc, Univ Calif, 50-54, res engr, Inst Eng Res, 51-52; supvr res engr, Chevron Res Corp, 54-64. *Concurrent Pos:* Consult, Lawrence Livermore Nat Lab, 69- & State Calif, 70-; dir, Adaptive Technol Inc, Sacramento, 81-82 & Los Alamos Nat Lab, 82-; tech dir, Aquatech Serv Inc, 92-96. *Mem:* Am Inst Aeronaut & Astronaut; Am Soc Mech Engrs. *Res:* Fluid mechanics; heat transfer; refrigeration; solar energy; robot welding machines. *Mailing Add:* 26934 Middle Golf Dr Box 3195 El Macero CA 95618. *E-Mail:* hbrandi@ucdavis.edu

BRANDT, HOWARD EDWARD, QUANTUM FIELD THEORY, GENERAL RELATIVITY. *Current Pos:* PHYSICIST, US ARMY RES LAB, 77- *Personal Data:* b Emerado, NDak, Jan 2, 39; m 72, Marilyn Kay McKinstry; c Karen & Sonja. *Educ:* Mass Inst Technol, BS, 62; Univ Wash, MS, 63, PhD(physics), 70. *Prof Exp:* Eng aid, Boeing Co, 58-62, physicist, Boeing Sci Res Lab, 62-64; postdoctoral teaching assoc, Univ Wash, 70-71; teacher physics & math, Seattle Prep Sch, 71-72; res assoc physics, Univ Md, 72-73; physicist, Lulejan & Assocs, Inc, 73-76, Sci Appln, Inc, 76-77. *Concurrent Pos:* Physics instr, Univ Md, 87; physicist, Strategic Defense Initiative Orgn, 87-94; ed, Int Soc Optical Eng, 91. *Mem:* Am Phys Soc;

Optical Soc Am; Am Math Soc; Am Asn Physics Teachers; Math Asn Am; Int Soc Optical Eng. *Res:* Quantum electrodynamics; general relativity; theory of radiative instability; high power microwave sources; nonlinear optics; quantum cryptography; quantum computation; differential geometry and other areas of pure and applied physics. *Mailing Add:* 2713 Shanandale Dr Silver Spring MD 20904. *E-Mail:* hbrandt@lamp0.arl.army.mil

BRANDT, IRA KIVE, PEDIATRICS, MEDICAL GENETICS. *Current Pos:* Prof, 70-89, EMER PROF, DEPTS PEDIAT & MED GENETICS, IND UNIV, INDIANAPOLIS, 89- *Personal Data:* b New York, NY, Nov 9, 23; m 47, Dorothy Godfrey; c Elizabeth, Laura, William & Rena. *Educ:* NY Univ, AB, 42; Columbia Univ, MD, 45; Am Bd Pediat, cert pediat, 52; Am Bd Med Genetics, cert clin & clin-biochem genetics, 82. *Prof Exp:* Res fel pediat & biochem, Yale Univ, 55-57, from asst prof to assoc prof, pediat, 57-68; chmn dept, Children's Hosp, San Francisco, 68-70; clin prof, Univ Calif, San Francisco, 70. *Mem:* Soc Pediat Res; Am Acad Pediat; Soc Inherited Metabolic Disorders; Am Pediat Soc; Am Soc Human Genetics; Am Col Med Genetics. *Res:* Metabolic and genetic disorders of children. *Mailing Add:* 972 Loma Vista Pl Santa Paula CA 93060-1330

BRANDT, J LEONARD, INTERNAL MEDICINE, GERIATRICS. *Current Pos:* CHIEF MED, HEBREW HOME & HOSP, HARTFORD, 79- *Personal Data:* b New York, NY, Aug 3, 19; m 50, Irma Silver; c Stephanie A & James D. *Educ:* Univ Mich, AB, 40; Long Island Col Med, MD, 43; Am Bd Internal Med, dipl. *Prof Exp:* Intern, Mt Sinai Hosp, Cleveland, 44; res assoc, Sch Trop Med, Columbia Univ, San Juan, PR, 45; asst res pathologist, Montefiore Hosp, New York, 48; from instr to assoc prof med, Col Med, State Univ NY, 49-59; lectr, Sch Med, McGill Univ, 59-70, assoc prof med, 70-79; sr physician, Jewish Gen Hosp, Montreal, 59-78. *Concurrent Pos:* Physician-in-chief, Jewish Gen Hosp, Montreal, 59-79; actg chief med, Mt Sinai Hosp, Hartford, 79-80; assoc prof med, Sch Med, Univ Conn, 79-87, clin prof med, 88. *Mem:* AAAS; Am Fedn Clin Res; Soc Exp Biol & Med; Am Physiol Soc; Harvey Soc; Am Geriat Soc; Geront Soc Am. *Res:* Hepatic and renal physiology; geriatrics. *Mailing Add:* Dept Med Univ Conn 61 Bonny View Rd West Hartford CT 06107-3402. *E-Mail:* lenbrandt@aol.com

BRANDT, JOHN T, HEMOSTASIS. *Current Pos:* ASST PROF PATH, OHIO STATE UNIV, 81-87, ASSOC PROF, OHIO STATE UNIV, 87- *Personal Data:* b Milwaukee, Wis, Sept 15, 48. *Educ:* Univ Mo, Columbia, MD, 76. *Mem:* Col Am Pathologists; Am Soc Clin Pathologists; AMA; Am Soc Hemat; Am Heart Asn. *Mailing Add:* Clin Labs Dept Path 164 Hamilton Hall Ohio State Univ Col Med 1645 Neil Ave Columbus OH 43210-1239. *Fax:* 614-292-7072

BRANDT, JON ALAN, PRICE ANALYSIS, COMMODITY MODELING. *Current Pos:* PROF & HEAD, DEPT AGR & RESOURCE ECON, NC STATE UNIV, 91- *Personal Data:* b Sidney, Ohio, Sept 10, 47; m 78, Cinda Edwards; c Melissa L & Ryan E. *Educ:* Ohio State Univ, BS & MS, 70; Univ Calif, Davis, PhD(agr econ), 77. *Prof Exp:* Res asst price anal, Dept Agr Econ, Ohio State Univ, 70; res asst commodity anal, Dept Agr Econ, Univ Calif, Davis, 73-77; from asst prof to assoc prof price anal, Dept Agr Econ, Purdue Univ, 77-86; prof, Univ Mo, 86-91. *Concurrent Pos:* Vis assoc prof, Dept Agr Econ, Univ Mo, 84-85. *Mem:* Am Agr Econ Asn; Int Inst Forecasters. *Res:* Agricultural price analysis and forecasting research activities related to livestock commodities; livestock modeling and policy analysis. *Mailing Add:* Dept Agr & Resource Econ NC State Univ Raleigh NC 27695-8109. *Fax:* 919-515-6268; *E-Mail:* jon_brandt@ncsu.edu

BRANDT, KARL GARET, INSTRUCTIONAL ADMINISTRATION. *Current Pos:* from asst prof to assoc prof, Purdue Univ, 66-75, asst dean grad sch, 81-84, actg dean agr, 86-87, PROF BIOCHEM, 75-, ASSOC DEAN AGR, PURDUE UNIV, 84- *Personal Data:* b Galveston, Tex, Oct 15, 38; m 65; c 2. *Educ:* Rice Univ, BA, 60; Mass Inst Technol, PhD(org chem), 64. *Prof Exp:* NSF fel, Johnson Res Found, Univ Pa, 64-65; NIH fel, Cornell Univ, 65-66. *Mem:* Am Chem Soc; Am Soc Biol Chemists; AAAS. *Res:* Mechanism of enzyme action; structure-function relationships; kinetics of enzyme-catalyzed reactions. *Mailing Add:* Agr Admin Bldg Purdue Univ West Lafayette IN 47907-1140. *Fax:* 765-494-8477

BRANDT, LUTHER WARREN, PHYSICAL CHEMISTRY. *Current Pos:* RETIRED. *Personal Data:* b Gradan, Kans, Oct 1, 20; m 42; c 1. *Educ:* Ft Hays Kans State Col, AB, 41; Kans State Univ, PhD(phys chem), 50. *Prof Exp:* Chemist fission prod anal, Clinton Labs, E I du Pont de Nemours & Co, 44 & Hanford Eng Works, E I du Pont de Nemours & Co & Gen Elec Co, 44-47; res chemist high polymers, E I du Pont de Nemours & Co, 50-52; phys chemist, US Bur Mines, 52-59, chief res div, 59-61, chief helium res ctr, Tex, 61-62, res dir, 62-70, polymer chemist, Spokane Mining Res Ctr, Wash, 70-72, res chemist, Tuscaloosa Mining Res Lab, 72-81. *Mem:* AAAS; Am Chem Soc; fel Am Inst Chemists; Sigma Xi. *Res:* Surface chemistry relating to mineral tailings; electrophoresis of serum proteins of certain animals; phase equilibria and thermodynamics of gases. *Mailing Add:* 378 Riverdale Rd Tuscaloosa AL 35406

BRANDT, MANUEL, ANALYTICAL CHEMISTRY. *Current Pos:* RETIRED. *Personal Data:* b Columbus, Ohio, Jan 7, 15; m 47, Cecelia Schalit; c David Adam & Michael Jillel. *Educ:* Ohio State Univ, BA, 36, MA, 37. *Prof Exp:* Asst physiol chem, Ohio State Univ, 36-38; chemist, US Army Ord, 40-43 & Tenn Eastman Corp, 43-45; chemist, Ethyl Corp, 45-50, group leader, 50-58, asst supvr, 58-66, supvr, Res & Develop Dept, 66-81. *Mem:* Am Chem Soc. *Res:* Microchemical analyses; trace and ultratrace metal analyses. *Mailing Add:* 641 Beaker Pl Columbus OH 43213

BRANDT, PHILIP WILLIAMS, ANATOMY, PHYSIOLOGY. *Current Pos:* from asst to asst prof, 57-70, assoc prof, 70-87, PROF ANAT; COL PHYSICIANS & SURGEONS, COLUMBIA UNIV, 88- *Personal Data:* b Cleveland, Ohio, Sept 23, 30; m 54; c 2. *Educ:* Swarthmore Col, BA, 52; Univ Pa, MS, 57; Columbia Univ, PhD(anat), 60. *Prof Exp:* Asst instr anat, Univ Pa, 53-57. *Concurrent Pos:* Guggenheim fel, 68-69; NIH career develop award, 68-73; computer prog. *Mem:* Am Soc Cell Biol; Am Asn Anat; Soc Gen Physiol. *Res:* Biophysics; muscle. *Mailing Add:* Col Physicians & Surgeons Columbia Univ 630 W 168th St New York NY 10032-3702

BRANDT, RICHARD BERNARD, BIOCHEMISTRY. *Current Pos:* asst prof, 70-74, ASSOC PROF BIOCHEM, MED COL VA, VA COMMONWEALTH UNIV, 74- *Personal Data:* b Brooklyn, NY, July 3, 34; m 56; c 3. *Educ:* Queens Col, NY, BS, 56; Brooklyn Col, MA, 61; NY Univ, PhD(biochem), 68. *Prof Exp:* Res asst, Sloan-Kettering Inst Cancer Res, NY, 56-58; substitute instr, Brooklyn Col, 59-61, chem & biol warfare grant proj leader, 61-62; res assoc, Inst Med Res & Studies, NY, 62-69; guest res assoc, Brookhaven Nat Labs, NY, 68-70. *Concurrent Pos:* Anal chemist, F D Snell, Inc, NY, 58. *Mem:* AAAS; Am Chem Soc; Soc Exp Biol & Med; Am Inst Nutrit; NY Acad Sci; Sigma Xi. *Res:* Vitamin A in trauma; D-lactate metabolism; enzyme systems in cell growth, especially glyoxalase I and II. *Mailing Add:* Dept Biochem & Prev Med Med Col Va PO Box 980614 Richmond VA 23298-0614. *Fax:* 804-786-1473

BRANDT, RICHARD CHARLES, SOLID STATE PHYSICS. *Current Pos:* PRES, OARBICK INSTRUCTIONAL SOFTWARE SYSTS, 86- *Personal Data:* b Philadelphia, Pa, Dec 18, 40; m 63; c 2. *Educ:* Calif Inst Technol, BS, 62; Univ Ill, MS, 64, PhD(physics), 67. *Prof Exp:* Staff mem solid state physics, Lincoln Lab, Mass Inst Technol, 67-71; res asst prof physics, Univ Utah, 71-93. *Mem:* Am Phys Soc; Asn Comput Mach; Soc Appl Learning Tech. *Res:* Infrared optical properties of solids; development of computer-aided instruction. *Mailing Add:* 2059 E 900 S Salt Lake City UT 84108

BRANDT, RICHARD GUSTAVE, SURFACE PHYSICS. *Current Pos:* PHYSICIST, OFF NAVAL RES, 68- *Personal Data:* b Albany, NY, Nov 2, 36; div; c Richard, Catherine & Susan. *Educ:* Yale Univ, BS, 58, MS, 59, PhD(physics), 65. *Prof Exp:* Res staff physicist, Yale Univ, 64-65; mem tech staff, Defense Res Corp, 65-68. *Mem:* Am Phys Soc; AAAS; Am Vacuum Soc. *Res:* Surface physics; superconductivity; electrooptics; solid state physics; ionospheric physics. *Mailing Add:* Code 312 Off Naval Res 800 N Quincy St Arlington VA 22217-5000

BRANDT, STEPHEN BERNARD, BIOLOGICAL OCEANOGRAPHY, FISHERIES ECOLOGY. *Current Pos:* DIR, GREAT LAKES CTR, 94- *Personal Data:* b Milwaukee, Wis, May 12, 50; m 74; c 2. *Educ:* Univ Wis-Madison, BA, 72, MS, 75, PhD(oceanog & limnol), 78. *Prof Exp:* Res technician, Lab Limnol, Univ Wis-Madison, 70-72, res specialist, 72, res asst, 73-78; res scientist, Marine Lab, Div Fisheries Res, Commonwealth Sci & Indust Res Orgn, 78-82, sr res scientist, 82-94. *Mem:* AAAS; Am Fisheries Soc; Am Soc Limnol & Oceanog; Int Asn Great Lakes Res; Australian Marine Sci Asn; Sigma Xi. *Res:* Assessment of the effects of oceanic thermal fronts on biological processes; effects of warm-core eddies on microplankton off East Australia; ecological study of oceanic squid. *Mailing Add:* Great Lakes Ctr 1300 Elmwood Ave Bldg C215 Buffalo NY 14222

BRANDT, WALTER EDMUND, VIROLOGY. *Current Pos:* dep proj mgr, 85-88, PROJ MGR, USA MED MAT DEVELOP ACT, 88- *Personal Data:* b Columbia, Pa, Apr 11, 35; m 91, Jane Sembower; c Cynthia & Patricia. *Educ:* Univ Md, BS, 60, MS, 64, PhD(microbiol), 67. *Honors & Awards:* Am Soc Microbiol Found Lectr, 83-84. *Prof Exp:* Microbiologist, Walter Reed Army Inst Res, 60-67, supvr, 67-70, asst chief virol, 70-85. *Concurrent Pos:* Consult, NIH, 71-75; instr eve div, Univ Md, 66-74, lectr microbiol, 70-78, asst proj dir extramural contracts, 78-84; consult, Vaccine Steering Comt, WHO, 84-90, chair, 88-90. *Mem:* Am Asn Immunologists; Am Soc Microbiol; Am Soc Trop Med & Hyg; Sigma Xi; Am Soc Virol; fel Am Acad Microbiol. *Res:* Dengue fever virus infection of cultured vertebrate and invertebrate cells; isolation of particulate and soluble antigens for study of dengue in humans; attenuated live virus vaccines; antigenic determinants; antibody-mediated infection; vaccine production; IND submissions. *Mailing Add:* SAIC 19933 Spur Hill Dr Gaithersburg MD 20879-1435. *Fax:* 301-698-6188

BRANDT, WERNER WILFRIED, PHYSICAL CHEMISTRY. *Current Pos:* chmn, Dept Chem, 76-78, ASSOC PROF CHEM, UNIV WIS-MILWAUKEE, 65-, MEM, LAB SURFACE STUDIES, 77- *Personal Data:* b Friedensdorf, Ger, Feb 13, 27; US citizen; m 52; c 4. *Educ:* Univ Heidelberg, BS, 49; Polytech Inst Brooklyn, PhD(phys chem), 56. *Prof Exp:* Anal chemist, Merck & Co, Inc, NJ, 50 & 52; res chemist, E I du Pont de Nemours & Co, Del, 55-59; asst prof chem, Ill Inst Technol, 59-65. *Mem:* Am Chem Soc; Am Phys Soc; fel Am Inst Chemists. *Res:* Rate processes, especially diffusion; plasma chemistry; solid state electrochemistry. *Mailing Add:* Dept Chem Univ Wis-Milwaukee Milwaukee WI 53228-1668

BRANDT, WILLIAM HENRY, BOTANY, PHYTOPATHOLOGY. *Current Pos:* from instr to assoc prof, 56-90, EMER ASSOC PROF BOT, ORE STATE UNIV, 90- *Personal Data:* b Great Falls, Mont, May 25, 27; div; c Eric & Ellen (Chairman). *Educ:* Univ Mont, BA, 50; Ohio State Univ, MSc, 51, PhD, 54. *Prof Exp:* Asst oak wilt, Ohio Agr Exp Sta, 52-54; res biologist, B F Goodrich Res Ctr, 54-56. *Concurrent Pos:* NIH spec res fel, 69-70; guest investr, Rockefeller Univ, 69-70. *Mem:* AAAS; Am Phytopath Soc; Mycol Soc Am. *Res:* Physiology of fungi; morphogenesis in fungi; vascular wilt diseases. *Mailing Add:* 2040 NW Larch Ave Ore State Univ Corvallis OR 97330. *E-Mail:* bill.brandt@cmug.com

BRANDTS, JOHN FREDERICK, PHYSICAL CHEMISTRY, BIOCHEMISTRY. *Current Pos:* from asst prof to assoc prof, 62-71, PROF CHEM, UNIV MASS, AMHERST, 71- *Personal Data:* b Celina, Ohio, June 15, 34; m 52; c 6. *Educ:* Miami Univ, BA, 56; Univ Minn, PhD(phys chem), 61. *Prof Exp:* NIH fel, 61-62. *Concurrent Pos:* NIH res grant, 63-66. *Mem:* Am Chem Soc. *Res:* Physical biochemistry; conformation and stability of globular proteins. *Mailing Add:* c/o MicroCal Inc 22 Ind Dr E Northampton MA 01060

BRANDVOLD, DONALD KEITH, BIOCHEMISTRY, PHYSICAL CHEMISTRY. *Current Pos:* asst prof, 65-74, ASSOC PROF CHEM, NMEX INST MINING & TECHNOL, 74- *Personal Data:* b Maddock, NDak, Aug 12, 36; m 61; c 1. *Educ:* NDak State Univ, BS, 62, PhD(chem), 65. *Prof Exp:* Technician, NDak State Univ, 59-62. *Mem:* AAAS; Am Chem Soc. *Res:* Submolecular and electronic biology; general molecular biology; vitamins and hormones mode of action; virus research; pesticide residues; ore leaching by bacteria; water chemistry and pollution. *Mailing Add:* Dept Chem NMex Inst Mining & Technol Socorro NM 87801-4796

BRANDWEIN, BERNARD JAY, BIOCHEMISTRY. *Current Pos:* Assoc prof, 55-69, PROF CHEM, SDAK STATE UNIV, 69- *Personal Data:* b Chicago, Ill, Apr 19, 27; m 51; c 3. *Educ:* Purdue Univ, BS, 48, MS, 51, PhD, 55. *Mem:* AAAS; Am Chem Soc; Inst Food Technologists; Sigma Xi. *Res:* Isolation, identification and proof of structure of naturally occurring carbohydrates, glycosides and vitamins; reversion products of carbohydrates. *Mailing Add:* 414 State Ave Brookings SD 57006

BRANDWEIN, PAUL FRANZ, PHYTOPATHOLOGY OF CEREAL GRAINS, MAINTENANCE OF SPECIAL ECOLOGIES. *Current Pos:* WRITER, 88- *Personal Data:* b Austria, Apr 2, 12; nat US; m 33. *Educ:* NY Univ, AB, 34, MS, 37, PhD(bot), 40. *Hon Degrees:* DSc, Colo Col, 52, Northern Mich Univ, 74. *Honors & Awards:* Distinguished Serv Award, NAm Asn Environ Sci Educ, 85; Carleton Award, Nat Sci Teachers Asn, 86. *Prof Exp:* Asst, Littauer Pneumonia Lab, 29-31; asst pharmacol, NY Univ, 31-34, teaching fel biol, 34-36, lectr ecol, 36; instr, High Sch, New York, 36-40, chmn, Dept Sci, 41-52; sci ed, Harcourt Brace Jovanovich, 52-54, sr sci ed & dir res, 54-65, pres Ctr Study Instr, 66-70, dir, Sch Dept & sr vpres, 70-78, vchmn, 70-78, sci co publ, 79-84. *Concurrent Pos:* Lectr, Columbia Univ, 42-54; consult, NY Pub Schs, 54-; sr ed, Science, 54-; assoc ed, Sci Teacher; dir educ, Conserv Found, 54-58; dir, Pinchot Int Conserv Studies, 63-; adj prof conserv & educ, Univ Pittsburgh, 60-63; vis prof, Colo Col, 62-72, Iowa Univ, 74-76. *Mem:* Fel AAAS; Am Phytopath Soc; Nat Asn Res Sci Teaching; Nat Sci Teachers Asn; NY Acad Sci; Sigma Xi; NAm Asn Environ Educ. *Res:* Environmental chemistry; aquatic microorganisms; phytopathology; cereal fungi; ekistical bases, human and natural ecologies. *Mailing Add:* PO Box 326 Unionville NY 10988

BRANEN, ALFRED LARRY, FOOD SCIENCE. *Current Pos:* assoc dean & dir resident instr, 83-86, dean, Col Agr, 86-93, PROF FOOD SCI, UNIV IDAHO, 93- *Personal Data:* b Caldwell, Idaho, Jan 5, 45; m 72, Bruss; c Arick, Greg & Josh. *Educ:* Univ Idaho, BS, 67; Purdue Univ, PhD(food sci), 70. *Prof Exp:* Asst prof food sci, Univ Wis, 70-73; from asst prof to assoc prof & chmn food sci, Wash State Univ, 74-81; prof food sci & head dept, Univ Nebr, 81-83. *Concurrent Pos:* Regional communicator, Inst Food Technologists, 79-81; mem bd dir, Am Inst Coop, Consortium Int Develop, Idaho Res Found. *Mem:* Inst Food Technologists; Nat Asn Cols & Teachers Agr. *Res:* Toxicology of food additives; preservation of foods with naturally occurring biochemicals; autoxidation and antioxidant function. *Mailing Add:* 23960 Middle Rd Wilder ID 83676

BRANGAN, PAMELA T, BIOLOGY, ANATOMY. *Current Pos:* ASSOC PROF, DEPT DENT HYG, OLD DOMINION UNIV, 83- *Personal Data:* b Davenport, Iowa, Nov 20, 44. *Educ:* Smith Col, BA, 67; Yale Univ, MFS, 70, PhD(biol), 77. *Prof Exp:* Res assoc biol, Harvard Univ, 74-76; cur mammals, Chicago Zool Soc, 76-79; asst prof ecol & systs, Cornell Univ, 79-83. *Concurrent Pos:* Lectr, Univ Chicago, 76-78. *Mem:* Am Soc Zool; Am Soc Mammal; Australian Soc Mammal; Soc Vert Paleont. *Res:* Functional morphology, mammalogy, behavior and evolution; mammalian herbivores and plant communities in the semiarid region of Australia. *Mailing Add:* Sch Dent Hyg Old Dominion Univ Norfolk VA 23529-0499

BRANGES, LOUIS DE, MATHEMATICS. *Current Pos:* assoc prof, 62-63, PROF MATH, PURDUE UNIV, 63- *Personal Data:* b Paris, France, Aug 21, 32; US & French citizen; m 80. *Educ:* Mass Inst Technol, BS, 53; Cornell Univ, PhD(math), 57. *Honors & Awards:* Alexander von Humboldt Prize, 85; Alexander Ostrowski Prize, 89. *Prof Exp:* Asst prof math, Lafayette Col, 58-59; mathematician, Inst Advan Study, 59-60; lectr, Bryn Mawr Col, 60-61; mem, Courant Inst Math Sci, 61-62. *Concurrent Pos:* Sloan Found Fel, 63-65; Guggenheim Found Fel, 67-68. *Mem:* Am Math Soc. *Res:* Functional analysis, operator theory. *Mailing Add:* 331 Hollowood Dr West Lafayette IN 47906

BRANHAM, JOSEPH MORHART, DEVELOPMENTAL BIOLOGY, ECOLOGY. *Current Pos:* chmn, Lake County Resource Adv Comt County Comn, 74-80, LAKE COUNTY WATER AUTHORITY ADV BD, 81- *Personal Data:* b Washington, DC, Jan 31, 35; m 56; c 2. *Educ:* Fla State Univ, BS, 56, MS, 58, PhD(exp biol), 63. *Prof Exp:* Asst prof biol, Oglethorpe Univ, 62-64, assoc prof, 63-65; NIH fel, Inst Animal Genetics, Univ Edinburgh, 65-67; asst prof zool, Univ Hawaii, 69-72; fel biol, Univ Utah, 72-73; sci teacher, Leesburg High Sch, Fla, 74-90. *Concurrent Pos:* Instr invertebrate zool, Marine Resources Ctr, Univ Ga, 79-84. *Mem:* AAAS; Am Soc Zoologists; Am Inst Biol Sci; NY Acad Sci; Sigma Xi. *Res:* Fertilization, sea urchin and rabbit gamete physiology; insect physiology and ecology, coral reef biology. *Mailing Add:* 801 Wilson Ave Leesburg FL 34748-6866

BRANLEY, FRANKLYN M, ASTRONOMY. *Current Pos:* SCI WRITER, 72- *Personal Data:* b New Rochelle, NY, June 5, 15; m 38; c 2. *Educ:* NY Univ, BS, 42; Columbia Univ, MA, 46, EdD(sci educ), 57. *Honors & Awards:* Edison Award. *Prof Exp:* Teacher sci, NY Pub Schs, 36-54 & State Teachers Col NY, 54-56; assoc astronr, Am Mus-Hayden Planetarium, 56-63, asst chmn, 64-68, chmn 68-72, Astronr 63-72. *Concurrent Pos:* Mem, Comn Teacher Educ & Cert, AAAS, 61-62 & Adv Comn, Nat Sci Exhib, Worlds Fair, Wash, 62; proposals referee, NSF, 62. *Mem:* Fel AAAS; Am Astron Soc; Nat Sci Teachers Asn; fel Royal Astron Soc. *Res:* Science education, especially astronomy and full use of planetaria. *Mailing Add:* Harbor Island Dr Sag Harbor NY 11963

BRANN, BENJAMIN SANDFORD, IV, PEDIATRICS, NEONATOLOGY. *Current Pos:* Asst prof, 85-93, ASSOC PROF PEDIAT & NEONATOLOGY, SCH MED, UNIV NMEX, 93- *Personal Data:* b San Antonio, Tex, Aug 17, 54. *Educ:* Univ Kans, BA, 76; Univ Ala, MD, 80. *Concurrent Pos:* Prin investr, Whitaker Found, 90-93, NMex Am Heart Asn, 90-91. *Mem:* Soc Pediat Res; Western Soc Pediat Res; Am Acad Pediat; AMA. *Res:* Bilirubin effects in developing organisms, endothelial cells, diagnostic imaging of central nervous system, and hydrocephalus in newborns. *Mailing Add:* 5607 Hunterwood Lane Arlington TX 76017. *Fax:* 505-272-6845; *E-Mail:* bbrann@medusa.unm.edu

BRANN, DARRELL WAYNE, NEUROENDOCRINOLOGY, REPRODUCTION. *Current Pos:* Fel neuroendocrinol, 90-91, asst prof, 92-95, ASST RES SCIENTIST, MED COL GA, 91-, ASSOC PROF, 95- *Personal Data:* b Dallas, Tex, May 4, 58; m, Jennifer Walker. *Educ:* Henderson State Univ, BA, 84; Med Col Ga, PhD(endocrinol), 90. *Honors & Awards:* Nat Res Serv Award, NIH, 89; Distinguished Leadership Award, Am Biog Inst Inc, 91. *Concurrent Pos:* Grant, Med Col Ga Res Inst, 91-92. *Mem:* Endocrine Soc; Soc Neurosci; Soc Study Reproduction. *Res:* Neuroendocrine mechanisms involved in the secretion of gonadotropin hormones in the female; numerous publications. *Mailing Add:* Dept Physiol & Endocrinol Med Col Ga Augusta GA 30912-3000

BRANNEN, ERIC, NUCLEAR PHYSICS, QUANTUM ELECTRONICS. *Current Pos:* RETIRED. *Personal Data:* b Manchester, Eng, Sept 25, 21; m 46, Dorothy Jordan; c Linda, Karen & Keith. *Educ:* Univ Toronto, BA, 44, MA, 46; McGill Univ, PhD(nuclear physics), 48. *Prof Exp:* Demonstr, Univ Toronto, 45-46, McGill Univ, 46-48 & Univ Toronto, 48-49; instr physics, Univ Western Ont, 49-50, lectr, 50-51, from asst prof to prof, 51-55, sr prof, 55-90. *Mem:* Am Phys Soc; Can Asn Physicists. *Res:* Racetrack microtron electron accelerator; submillimeter radiation; photon correlation; far infrared maser. *Mailing Add:* Dept Physics Univ Western Ont London ON N6A 3K7 Can

BRANNEN, WILLIAM THOMAS, JR, ORGANIC CHEMISTRY. *Current Pos:* tech dir, Elco Corp, 67-71, vpres res & mfg, 71-77, exec vpres, 77-93, SPECIALTY PROD MGR, ELCO CORP, 94- *Personal Data:* b Chicago, Ill, Sept 30, 36; div; c Elizabeth, Catherine, Colleen, Mary & Christopher. *Educ:* DePaul Univ, BS, 58; Northwestern Univ, PhD(org chem), 62. *Honors & Awards:* Outstanding Sr Chem Award, Am Inst Chemists. *Prof Exp:* Res asst org chem, Northwestern Univ, 59-62; proj chemist, Am Oil Co Div, Standard Oil Co, Ind, 62-65, sr proj chemist, Amoco Chem Corp Div, 65-67. *Concurrent Pos:* Vpres, Detrex Chem Indust, 84-93. *Mem:* Am Chem Soc; Nat Lubricating Grease Inst. *Res:* Mechanistic studies of organic and enzyme reactions; synthetic organic and inorganic chemistry. *Mailing Add:* 2050 Radcliffe Dr Westlake OH 44145. *Fax:* 864-591-0055

BRANNIGAN, DAVID, ZOOLOGY. *Current Pos:* ASSOC PROF BIOL, STATE UNIV NY, BROCKPORT, 74- *Personal Data:* b Cambridge, Mass, Apr 12, 41; m 74; c 1. *Educ:* Suffolk Univ, BS, 68; Univ NH, MS, 72, PhD(zool), 74. *Prof Exp:* Instr biol, Adelphi Univ, 71-74. *Mem:* Animal Behav Soc; AAAS. *Res:* Effect of behavior on the atherosclerolic process. *Mailing Add:* 243 Evergreen Rd Brockport NY 14420

BRANNON, DONALD RAY, ORGANIC CHEMISTRY, TOXICOLOGY. *Current Pos:* sr scientist, Lilly Res Labs, 67-71, res scientist, 71-73, head microbiol & fermentation prod red div, 73-77, head toxicity testing, 77-84, dir toxicol studies, 84-86, dir process res & develop div, 86-89, DIR ENVIRON AFFAIRS, LILLY RES LABS, 86- LILLY RES LABS, 86- *Personal Data:* b Fort Peck, Mont, May 30, 39; m 67. *Educ:* Okla State Univ, BS, 61, PhD(org chem), 65. *Prof Exp:* Res asst, Okla State Univ, 61-65. *Mem:* Am Chem Soc. *Res:* Toxicity testing; hazard evaluation; ecological hazard assessments; process chemistry. *Mailing Add:* Lily Corp Ctr Indianapolis IN 46285

BRANNON, H RAYMOND, JR, petroleum engineering, civil engineering; deceased, see previous edition for last biography

BRANNON, PATSY M, NUTRITION. *Current Pos:* PROF NUTRIT & FOOD SCI & CHAIR, DEPT NUTRIT & FOOD SCI, UNIV MD, COLLEGE PARK, 94- *Educ:* Cornell Univ, PhD(nutrit & biochem), 79. *Prof Exp:* from asst prof to prof nutrit & food sci, Univ Ariz, 82-94. *Concurrent Pos:* Nutrit Study Sect, NIH & Div Res Grants, 90-94. *Mem:* Am Inst Nutrit; Sigma Xi; Am Dietetics Asn; AAAS; Inst Food Technologists; Am Pancreatic Asn. *Res:* Nutritional influence on pancreatic functions; regulation of lipid metabolism; adaptation of pancreatic enzymes; dietary regulation of gene expression. *Mailing Add:* Univ Md 3304 Marie Mount Hall College Park MD 20742. *Fax:* 301-314-9327

BRANNON, PAUL J, SPECTROSCOPY. *Current Pos:* mem staff upper atmospheric physics, 68-70, mem staff, Laser Fusion Physics, 70-79, MEM STAFF, LASER PHYSICS, SANDIA LABS, 79- *Personal Data:* b Flint, Mich, Apr 12, 35; m 65; c 2. *Educ:* Univ Mich, BS, 57, MS, 59, PhD(physics, infrared spectros), 65. *Prof Exp:* Mem staff upper atmospheric physics, Sandia Labs, 65-67; fel infrared spectros, Univ Tenn, 67-68. *Res:* Laser physics and spectroscopy applied to upper atmospheric research, line shape and shifts in gases; optoelectronics; waveguides; xenon infrared laser. *Mailing Add:* 207 Wells NE Albuquerque NM 87123

BRANNON, WILLIAM LESTER, EPILEPTOLOGY, STROKE. *Current Pos:* PROF NEUROPSYCHIAT & DIR DIV NEUROL, SCH MED, UNIV SC, 80- *Personal Data:* b Olar, SC, Jan 11, 36; m 59, Darrell Meeks; c Debra (DeMarco), William Bert & Victoria (Diaz). *Educ:* Univ SC, BA, 95; Med Univ SC, MD, 61. *Prof Exp:* Chmn neurol, Nat Naval Med Ctr, 69-79. *Concurrent Pos:* Consult neurol, attend physician US Capitol, 69-79, White House Physician, 69-79 & Surgeon Gen US Navy, 69-79; prof, Uniformed Serv Univ Health Servs, 74-79. *Mem:* Am Acad Neurol; Am Epilepsy Soc; Am Col Physicians; Asn Univ Profs Neurol. *Res:* Clinical treatment of stroke patients. *Mailing Add:* 3555 Harden St Exten Suite 104B Columbia SC 29203. *Fax:* 803-434-3792; *E-Mail:* wlb@npsy.ceb.sc.edu

BRANNON-PEPPAS, LISA, BIOMATERIALS, CONTROLLED DRUG DELIVERY. *Current Pos:* PRES, BIOGEL TECHNOL INC, 91- *Personal Data:* b Houston, Tex, Sept 19, 62; m, Nicholas Peppas. *Educ:* Rice Univ, BS, 84; Purdue Univ, MS, 86, PhD(chem eng), 88. *Prof Exp:* Sr formulations chemist, Eli Lilly & Co, 88-91. *Concurrent Pos:* Dir, Food, Pharmaceut & Bioeng Div, Am Inst Chem Engrs, 91-94, Mat Div, 92-95, chair, 96-97; mem bd givs, Controlled Release Soc, 92-95. *Mem:* Am Inst Chem Engrs; Am Chem Soc; Controlled Release Soc (treas, 95-); Am Asn Pharmaceut Scientists. *Res:* Research, development and preparation of polymeric materials in biotechnology, bioengineering, medical sciences and industrial pharmacy including controlled drug delivery, bioadhesives, wound healing films and other biomaterials. *Mailing Add:* Biogel Technol Inc 9521 Valparaiso Ct Indianapolis IN 46268. *Fax:* 317-872-2799; *E-Mail:* lisabp@biogel.org

BRANS, CARL HENRY, MATHEMATICAL PHYSICS. *Current Pos:* From instr to assoc prof, 60-70, PROF PHYSICS, LOYOLA UNIV, LA, 70- *Personal Data:* b Dallas, Tex, Dec 13, 35; m 57; c 4. *Educ:* Loyola Univ, La, BS, 57; Princeton Univ, PhD(physics), 61. *Concurrent Pos:* NSF grant, 62-66; vis prof physics, Princeton Univ, 73-74, Inst Advan Studies, 93; res grant, Res Corp, 75. *Mem:* Am Phys Soc. *Res:* Varying gravitational constant in general relativity; mathematical methods in general relativity; differential geometry and topology; group theory; application of computers to general relativity. *Mailing Add:* Dept Physics Loyola Univ New Orleans LA 70118. *E-Mail:* brans@music.loynu.edu

BRANSCOMB, ELBERT WARREN, MOLECULAR BIOLOGY. *Current Pos:* Physicist theoret physics, 64-69, PHYSICIST MOLECULAR BIOL, LAWRENCE LIVERMORE LAB, 69- *Personal Data:* b Yakima, Wash, Mar 31, 35; m 81; c 1. *Educ:* Reed Col, BA, 57; Syracuse Univ, PhD(physics), 64. *Res:* Genetic toxicology: assays for in-vivo somatic point mutation injury in humans and in experimental animals; accuracy in the intracellular transfer of genetic information in DNA replication and in gene expression. *Mailing Add:* Lawrence Livermore Lab L-452 PO Box 808 Livermore CA 94551

BRANSCOMB, LEWIS MCADORY, INFORMATION SCIENCE, INFORMATION TECHNOLOGY. *Current Pos:* Albert Pratt pub serv prof, 86-96, AETNA EMER PROF PUB POLICY & CORP MGT, JOHN F KENNEDY SCH GOVT, HARVARD UNIV, 96- *Personal Data:* b Asheville, NC, Aug 17, 26; m 51; c 2. *Educ:* Duke Univ, AB, 45; Harvard Univ, MS, 47, PhD(physics), 49. *Hon Degrees:* DSc, Western Mich Univ, 69, Univ Rochester, 71, Univ Colo, 73, Duke Univ, 74, Lycoming Col, 79, Polytech Inst, NY, 80, Clarkson Col Technol, 81, Pace Univ, 82, Univ Ala, 83, Pratt Inst, 83, Rutgers Univ, 84, Lehigh Univ, 84, Notre Dame Univ, 86, State Univ NY, Binghamton, 89. *Honors & Awards:* Arthur Fleming Award, 58; Samuel Wesley Stratton Award; Proctor Prize, Sci Res Soc Am; Arthur M Bueche Award, Nat Acad Eng, 87. *Prof Exp:* Instr physics, Harvard Univ, 50, jr fel, Soc Fels, 49-51; physicist, Nat Bur Stand, 51-54, chief, Atomic Physics Sect, 54-59, chief div, 59-62, chmn, Joint Inst Lab Astrophys, 62-65, chief lab, Astrophys Div, 62-69, dir, 69-72; chief scientist, IBM Corp, 72, vpres & chief scientist, 72-86. *Concurrent Pos:* Rockefeller pub serv fel, Univ Col, Univ London, 57-58; prof-adjoint physics, Univ Colo, 62-69; mem, President's Sci Adv Comt, 65-68 & President's Comn Medal Sci, 70-74; mem, Int Comt Weights & Measures, 69-72; mem bd dirs, Am Nat Stand Inst, 69-72, General Foods Corp, 75-85, Mobil Corp, 78-, Lord Corp, 87-, Mitre Corp, 87-, C S Draper Labs, 88-; ed, Rev Mod Physics, 69-72; mem bd overseers, Harvard Univ, 69-; mem, Adv Comt Sci & Foreign Affairs, US Dept State, 72-74; mem, Adv Comt Energy Res & Develop, Fed Energy Agency, 73-75; trustee, Carnegie Inst, Washington, 74-90, Polytech Inst, NY, 74-78, Vanderbilt Univ, 80-, Rand Corp, Woods Hole Oceanog Inst, 85-; mem, Physics Vis Comt, Mass Inst Technol, 74-79; chmn, Panel Appl Sci & Technol, Off Assessment, US Cong, 77-79; chmn, Comt Scholarly Commun with People's Repub China, Nat Acad Sci, 77-80; mem, US-USSR Joint Comn Sci & Technol, 77-80; mem, Nat Sci Bd, 79-, chmn, 80-; chmn, Carnegie Form Task Force on Teaching as a Prof, 86, mem, Carnegie Commn Sci Technol & Govt, 89- *Mem:* Nat Acad Sci; Inst Med-Nat Acad Sci; Nat Acad Eng; Nat Acad Pub Admin; fel Am Acad Arts & Sci; Sigma Xi (pres, 85-86); fel Am Philos Soc. *Res:* Gaseous electronics; spectra of diatomic molecules; physics of the upper atmosphere; physics of negative ions; science and technology policy; information systems technology; science and technology policy; education reform. *Mailing Add:* Harvard Univ J F Kennedy Sch Govt 79 J F Kennedy St Cambridge MA 02138

BRANSOME, EDWIN D, JR, ENDOCRINOLOGY, CLINICAL PHARMACOLOGY. *Current Pos:* clin dir 9C MS Lab, 73-88, PROF MED, PHYSIOL & ENDOCRINOL, MED COL GA, 70- *Personal Data:* b New York, NY, Oct 27, 33; m 59, Janet Williams; c Edwin D III & April G. *Educ:* Yale Univ, AB, 54; Columbia Univ, MD, 58. *Prof Exp:* House officer, Peter Brent Brigham Hosp, 58-59, asst med, 59-61, asst resident, 61-62; res assoc, Columbia Univ, 62-63; assoc endocrinol, Scripps Clin & Res Found, 64-66; from asst prof to assoc prof exp med, Mass Inst Technol, 66-70; instr med, Harvard Med Sch, 66-70. *Concurrent Pos:* NIH res fel, Harvard Med Sch, 59-61; vis fel biochem, Columbia Univ, 62-63; Am Cancer Soc fel, 62-64, fac res assoc award, 65-70; Am specialist, US Dept State, 61; asst physician, Vanderbilt Clin, 62-64; chmn, comt rev, Adv Panel Endocrinol, US Pharmacopeia, 75-90, subcomt biochem microbiol 80-90, mem bd trustees, 90- & deleg, US Pharmacopoeial Conv, Med Asn Ga; mem bd dir, Am Diabetes Asn, 85-88; chmn Gov't Relations Comt, 86-88; chmn coun, Health Care Delivery & Pub Health, 88-90; consult, Stereochemical Genetics Inc, 87-; chmn, Ga Drug Utilization Rev Bd, 92- *Mem:* Am Diabetes Asn; Endocrine Soc; Am Physiol Soc; Am Col Clin Pharmacol; Am Chem Soc. *Res:* Internal medicine; mechanism of hormone and drug action on cellular metabolism and growth; drug design. *Mailing Add:* Dept Med Physiol & Endocrin Med Col Ga Augusta GA 30912. *Fax:* 706-721-6918

BRANSON, BRANLEY ALLAN, ICHTHYOLOGY, MALACOLOGY. *Current Pos:* mem fac, 66-67, assoc prof, 67-70, FOUND PROF BIOL, EASTERN KY UNIV, 70- *Personal Data:* b San Angelo, Tex, Feb 11, 29; m 64, Mary L Lewis; c Rogers McGowan. *Educ:* Okla State Univ, BS, 56, MS, 57, PhD(zool), 60. *Prof Exp:* Spec instr zool, Okla State Univ, 56-57; asst prof, Kans State Col Pittsburg, 60-66. *Concurrent Pos:* Res grants, NSF, 60-61, Sigma Xi, 62-64 & NIH, 64-66; ed, Ky Acad Sci Trans, 81- *Mem:* AAAS; Am Soc Ichthyologists & Herpetologists; Soc Study Evolution; Soc Syst Zool; Am Micros Soc. *Res:* Comparative morphology of the sensory systems of teleost fishes; ecological adaptations of fishes as regards their sensory system; zoogeography and taxonomy of fishes and mollusks. *Mailing Add:* 100 Walnut Hill Dr Richmond KY 40475

BRANSON, BRUCE WILLIAM, SURGERY. *Current Pos:* Asst prof, 62-65, assoc prof, 65-77, PROF SURG, LOMA LINDA UNIV, 77-, CHMN DEPT, 78- *Personal Data:* b Athol, Mass, Oct 20, 27; m 51; c 2. *Educ:* Loma Linda Univ, MD, 50; Am Bd Surg, dipl, 63. *Mailing Add:* 11370 Anderson St Loma Linda CA 92354

BRANSON, DAN E(ARLE), STRUCTURAL & CIVIL ENGINEERING. *Current Pos:* PROF CIVIL & ENVIRON ENG, UNIV IOWA, 63- *Personal Data:* b Dallas, Tex, Nov 13, 28; m 55; c 1. *Educ:* Auburn Univ, BCE, 54, MCE, 56; Univ Fla, PhD(struct eng), 60. *Honors & Awards:* Martin P Korn Award, Prestressed Concrete Inst, 71. *Prof Exp:* Instr civil eng, Auburn Univ, 55-56, asst prof, 57, assoc prof, 62-63; instr eng mech, Univ Fla, 59-60; assoc prof civil eng, Univ Ala, 60-62. *Concurrent Pos:* Consult, Hayes Int Corp, Ala, 61-65 & concrete & steel struct, 64-; Alexander von Humboldt US sr scientist award, WGer, 80. *Mem:* Fel Am Soc Civil Engrs; fel Am Concrete Inst; Prestressed Concrete Inst; Int Asn Bridge & Struct Eng; Am Soc Eng Educ. *Res:* Creep and shrinkage of different weight concretes; time-dependent deformation and load-deflection response of uncracked and cracked reinforced beams and slabs; prestressed structures; author of numerous papers and books. *Mailing Add:* 1104 Tower Ct Iowa City IA 52246

BRANSON, DOROTHY SWINGLE, clinical microbiology, for more information see previous edition

BRANSON, FARREL ALLEN, plant ecology, for more information see previous edition

BRANSON, HERMAN RUSSELL, physics, deceased, see previous edition for last biography

BRANSON, TERRY FRED, entomology, for more information see previous edition

BRANSTETTER, DANIEL G, CANCER RESEARCH. *Current Pos:* VET PATHOLOGIST & TOXICOLOGIST, UPJOHN CO, 84- *Personal Data:* b Cedar Rapids, Iowa, Sept 26, 50. *Educ:* Med Col Ohio, Toledo, PhD(path), 85; Am Col Vet Pathologists, dipl. *Prof Exp:* Instr, Med Col Ohio, 79-84. *Mem:* Vet Med Asn. *Mailing Add:* 1727 S Eighth St Kalamazoo MI 49009

BRANT, ALBERT WADE, FOOD TECHNOLOGY, POULTRY HUSBANDRY. *Current Pos:* agriculturist, 59-85, EMER AGRICULTURIST FOOD TECHNOL, COOP EXTEN, DEPT FOOD SCI & TECHNOL, UNIV CALIF, DAVIS, 86- *Personal Data:* b Isabel, Kans, Mar 28, 19; m 40; c 2. *Educ:* Kans State Col, BS, 40; Mich State Col, MS, 42; Iowa State Col, PhD, 49. *Prof Exp:* Instr, State Col Wash, 42-44 & 46-47; poultry husbandman, Agr Res Serv, USDA, 49-57, chief, Poultry Res Br, Animal Husb Res Div, 57-59. *Mem:* Coun Agr Sci Technol; Poultry Sci Asn; Inst Food Technologists; World Poultry Sci Asn. *Res:* Methods of determining interior quality of eggs; physical properties of meat, eggs and poultry related to quality; microbiology of meat, shell eggs and poultry; technology of animal products; processing of poultry, egg and red-meat products. *Mailing Add:* 44096 N El Macero Dr El Macero CA 95618

BRANT, DANIEL (HOSMER), vertebrate ecology, for more information see previous edition

BRANT, LARRY JAMES, STATISTICS, COMPUTER PROGRAMMING. *Current Pos:* CHIEF STATIST SCI SECT, GERONT RES CTR, NAT INST AGING, NIH, 80- *Personal Data:* b Sept 1, 46; c 2. *Educ:* Frostburg State Col, BS. 68; Pa State Univ, MA, 72; Johns Hopkins Univ, PhD(biostatist), 78. *Prof Exp:* Chief biostatist br, Alaska Invest Div, Ctrs Dis Control, 78-80. *Concurrent Pos:* Adj clin prof, Univ Hawaii, Sch Pub Health, Manoa, 84-; adj prof Math & Statist, Penn State Univ, 87-; adj assoc prof, Johns Hopkins Sch Hygiene & Pub Health, 89- *Mem:* Am Statist Asn; Biomet Soc; Am Math Soc; Math Asn Am; NY Acad Sci; Geront Soc Am; Int Asn Human Biol. *Res:* Statistical methodology and combinatorial objects applicable to statistical designs; mathematical and statistical modeling; statistical computing; longitudinal data analysis; applications to gerontology, polar populations and biological sciences. *Mailing Add:* Geront Res Ctr Nat Inst Aging 4949 Eastern Ave Baltimore MD 21224

BRANT, RUSSELL ALAN, GEOLOGY, COAL GEOLOGY & RESOURCES. *Current Pos:* sr geologist & head coas sect, 76-81, res geologist, 81-86, EMER GEOLOGIST, KY GEOL SURV, UNIV KY, 86-, RES ASST, DEPT PREV MED; CONSULT GEOLOGIST, 86- *Personal Data:* b Brooklyn, NY, Mar 18, 19; m 45, Elizabeth Dewey; c Wanda Phyllis, Robert Alan, Duane James & Daniel Paul. *Educ:* Univ Mich, BS, 48, MS, 49. *Prof Exp:* Asst chemist rubber chem, Monarch Rubber Co, 42-44; geologist, Fuels Br, US Geol Surv, 49-52; from asst head to head coal sect, Ohio Geol Surv, Columbus, 52-57, areal geol sect, 57-60, asst state geologist, 60-68, sr res geologist, 68. *Concurrent Pos:* Mine Drainage Specialist, Water Resources Ctr, Ohio State Univ, 68; res asst, Dept Prev Med, Univ Ky. *Mem:* Geol Soc Am; Am Inst Prof Geologists. *Res:* Coal and coal resources; areal; geochemistry; water geology; acid mine water; mining; underground injection of waste water; aerial surveillance, air photo interpretation; Lake Erie geology and shore erosion; gas chromotography. *Mailing Add:* 463 Pasadena Dr Lexington KY 40503. *E-Mail:* rbrant@ukcc.uky.edu

BRANTHAVER, JAN FRANKLIN, PORPHYRIN CHEMISTRY. *Current Pos:* PROG MGR, WESTERN RES INST, LARAMIE, WYO, 83- *Personal Data:* b Davenport, Iowa, Mar 12, 36. *Educ:* Millikin Univ, Decatur, Ill, BA, 58; NDak State Univ, Fargo, PhD(chem), 76. *Prof Exp:* Res assoc, Dept Chem, NDak State Univ, 64-76, instr chem, 67; res chemist, Laramie Energy Technol Ctr, US Dept Energy, 76-83. *Concurrent Pos:* Adj prof, Dept Chem, Univ Wyo, 81- *Mem:* Am Chem Soc; Sigma Xi. *Res:* Organic geochemistry of petroleum, tar sand, and oil shale with emphasis on metal chelates in these materials; relationships between chemical composition of asphalts and their physical properties. *Mailing Add:* Western Res Inst 365 N 9th St Laramie WY 82070-3370

BRANTINGHAM, CHARLES ROSS, preventive podiatric medicine, public health; deceased, see previous edition for last biography

BRANTINGHAM, PATRICIA LOUISE, CRIME PATTERN ANALYSIS, CRIMINAL EVENT SIMULATION. *Current Pos:* from asst prof to assoc prof, 77-89, PROF CRIMINOL, SIMON FRASER UNIV, 89- *Personal Data:* b St Louis, Mo, June 28, 43; Can citizen; m 67, Paul J; c Paul J Jr. *Educ:* Columbia Univ, BA, 65; Fordham Univ, MA, 66; Fla State Univ, MSP, 74, PhD(planning), 77. *Prof Exp:* Systs analyst, Johnson & Johnson, 66-67, Technicon Corp, 67-68 & Hunt-Wesson, 68-69; res assoc, Inst Criminol, Cambridge Univ, 69-70; systs analyst, Census Processing Ctr, Fla State Univ, 72-74, instr, Dept Urban & Regional Planning, 74-77. *Mem:* Am Planning Asn; Am Soc Criminol. *Res:* Epidemiology and quantitative patterns in crime and violence; criminal event simulation; crime prevention theory and practice. *Mailing Add:* 4680 Eastridge Rd North Vancouver BC V7G 1K4 Can. *Fax:* 604-291-4140; *E-Mail:* pbrantin@sfu.ca

BRANTINGHAM, PAUL JEFFREY, CRIME PATTERN ANALYSIS, CRIME PREVENTION THEORY. *Current Pos:* From asst prof to assoc prof criminol, 71-85, assoc dean, Fac Interdisciplinary Studies, 80-82, PROF CRIMINOL, SIMON FRASER UNIV, 85- *Personal Data:* b Long Beach, Calif, June 29, 43; Can citizen; m 67, Patricia L Matthews; c Paul J Jr. *Educ:* Columbia Univ, BA, 65, JD, 68; Cambridge Univ, dipl crim, 70. *Concurrent Pos:* Assoc prof criminol, Fla State Univ, 75-77; dir spec rev, Pub Serv Comn Can, 85-87. *Mem:* AAAS; Am Soc Criminol; Acad Criminal Justice Sci; fel Western Soc Criminol. *Res:* Epidemiology and quantitative patterns in crime; criminal event simulation and modelling; crime analysis; crime prevention theory and practice. *Mailing Add:* Sch Criminol Simon Fraser Univ Burnaby BC V5A 1S6 Can. *Fax:* 604-291-4140; *E-Mail:* branting@sfu.ca

BRANTLEY, LEE REED, PHYSICAL CHEMISTRY, ADHESION. *Current Pos:* prof educ, Curric Res & Develop Group, 67-72, consult, 72-73, EMER PROF EDUC, UNIV HAWAII, 72- *Personal Data:* b Herrin, Ill, Sept 23, 06; m 84, Ruth Thomas. *Educ:* Univ Calif, AB, 27; Calif Inst Technol, MS, 29, PhD(chem), 30. *Honors & Awards:* John R Kuebler Award, Alpha Chi Sigma, 73. *Prof Exp:* Reader physics, Univ Calif, Los Angeles, 26-29; asst chem, Calif Inst Technol, 28-30; instr chem & physics, Occidental Col, 30-36, from asst prof to prof chem, 36-67, head dept, 40-62. *Concurrent Pos:* Res fel, Calif Inst Technol, 36-43, asst & Nat Defense Res Coun consult, 43-44; teacher schs, Calif, 41-42; Petrol Res Fund award, 58-59; consult, Crescent Eng Co, 44-46, Pac Rocket Soc, 44-51, Nat Bur Stands, 51-54 & Corn Indust Res Found, 57-59; dir contracts, US Off Naval Res, 49-58 & Off Qm Gen, 52-58; vis prof, Lehigh Univ, 58-59; vpres, Alpha Chi Sigma Educ Found, 58-63, trustee, 63-; vis prof, Univ Hawaii, 62-63 & 65-66, res prof, 85-; consult chem engr, 73- *Mem:* Fel AAAS; Am Chem Soc; Electrochem Soc; Hawaiian Acad Sci. *Res:* Preparation and properties of xenon trioxide; relation of air borne fungal spores and pollen to asthma in Hawaii; x-ray fluoreseence spectroscopy characterization of adhesion,; chemistry of building materials; building materials technology; structural performance and environmental impact (McGraw-Hill, 96); food technology. *Mailing Add:* 2908 Robert Pl Honolulu HI 96816-1720

BRANTLEY, SUSAN LOUISE, AQUEOUS GEOCHEMISTRY, HYDROTHERMAL GEOCHEMISTRY. *Current Pos:* ASST PROF GEOCHEM, PA STATE UNIV, 86- *Personal Data:* b winter Park, Fla, Aug 11, 58. *Educ:* Princeton Univ, AB, 80, MA, 83, PhD(geol & geophys sci), 87. *Concurrent Pos:* NSF presidential young investr, 87; consult, Sawyer Res Prod, Inc, 88- *Mem:* Geochem Soc; Am Geophys Union; AmChem Soc; AAAS; Asn Women Geosci. *Res:* Thermodynamics and Kinetics of rock-water interaction over the temperature range 25 to 600 degrees centigrade; dissolution and precipitation reactions of minerals, natural brines, mineral surface chemistry, and alteration of porosity and permeability. *Mailing Add:* Dept Geosci 209 Deike Bldg Pa State Univ University Park PA 16802-2711

BRANTLEY, WILLIAM ARTHUR, MATERIALS SCIENCE, DENTAL BIOMATERIALS. *Current Pos:* SECT RESTORATIVE & PROSTHETIC DENT, COL DENT, OHIO STATE UNIV, 89- *Personal Data:* b Roanoke Rapids, NC, Jan 19, 41; m 67. *Educ:* NC State Col, BS, 63; Carnegie Inst Technol, MS, 65, Carnegie-Mellon Univ, PhD(metall & mat sci), 68. *Prof Exp:* Res metall engr & lectr, Carnegie-Mellon Univ, 67-68; tech staff mem & group leader, Ceramic Res Lab, US Army Mat & Mech Res Ctr, 68-70; mem tech staff, Bell Labs, 70-74; asst prof, Dept Dent Mat, Marquette Univ, 74-79, assoc prof & actg chmn, 79-80, prof & chmn, 80-89. *Mem:* Am Ceramic Soc; Am Soc Metals; Am Inst Mining, Metall & Petrol Engrs; Int Asn Dent Res; Am Asn Dent Res. *Res:* Dental biomaterials; biomechanics; mechanical properties of materials; defect characterization in crystalline materials. *Mailing Add:* Sect Restorative, Prosthedontics & Endodontic Dent Col Ohio State Univ 305 W 12th Ave Columbus OH 43210-1241

BRANTLEY, WILLIAM CAIN, JR, COMPUTER ORGANIZATION, ARCHITECTURE. *Current Pos:* SR ENGR, IBM RS 6000 DIV, 90- *Personal Data:* b Raleigh, NC, Feb 16, 49; m 70; c 2. *Educ:* NC State Univ, BS, 71; Univ NMex, MS, 73; Carnegie-Mellon Univ, PhD(elec eng), 78. *Prof Exp:* Staff mem, Los Alamos Sci Lab, 71-74; res staff, IBM Res, 78-89. *Mem:* Inst Elec & Electronics Engrs; Asn Comput Mach. *Res:* High performance computer organization and architectures; vector, pipeline and multiprocessors; language oriented processors and the design automation of applicators for multiprocessors (graph-partitioning). *Mailing Add:* 2905 Creeks Edge Pkwy Austin TX 78733. *E-Mail:* brantleyw@acm.org

BRANTLEY, WILLIAM HENRY, NUCLEAR PHYSICS. *Current Pos:* ASSOC PROF PHYSICS, FURMAN UNIV, 66-, CHMN DEPT, 67- *Personal Data:* b Forsyth, Ga, Aug 23, 38; m 61; c 2. *Educ:* Mercer Univ, AB, 60; Vanderbilt Univ, MA, 63, PhD(nuclear physics), 66. *Prof Exp:* Sci cooperator low energy nuclear physics, Tech Univ Delft, 65-66. *Mem:* Am Phys Soc. *Res:* Research on the energy concept; educational research; environmental research; low energy nuclear physics, including beta and gamma ray spectroscopy. *Mailing Add:* Dept Physics Furman Univ Greenville SC 29613

BRANTON, DANIEL, CELL BIOLOGY, BOTANY. *Current Pos:* PROF BIOL, & HIGGINS CHAIR PROF BIOL, HARVARD UNIV, 72- *Personal Data:* b Antwerp, Belgium, Jan 13, 32; US citizen; m 57, Lana L Brennan; c Benjamin D & Hilary C (Pellicer). *Educ:* Cornell Univ, AB, 54; Univ Calif, Davis, MS, 57; Univ Calif, Berkeley, PhD(plant physiol), 61. *Honors & Awards:* Storer lectr, Univ Calif, Davis, 84. *Prof Exp:* NSF fel, Swiss Fed Inst Technol, 61-63; from asst prof to prof bot, Univ Calif, Berkeley, 63-72. *Concurrent Pos:* Miller Res Prof, 67-68; Guggenheim fel, 70-71; distinguished lectr, Rosewell Park Mem Inst, 88; distinguished vis scientist, Univ Calif, 91. *Mem:* Nat Acad Sci; Am Acad Arts & Sci; Am Soc Cell Biol (pres, 84-85); Biophys Soc; AAAS. *Res:* Cell and membrane structure; cell biology. *Mailing Add:* Biol Labs Harvard Univ Cambridge MA 02138

BRANTON, PHILIP EDWARD, VIROLOGY, MOLECULAR BIOLOGY. *Current Pos:* PROF & CHMN BIOCHEM, MCGILL UNIV, 90- *Personal Data:* b Toronto, Ont, June 8, 43; m 70; c 1. *Educ:* Univ Toronto, BSc, 66, MSc, 68, PhD(med biophys), 72. *Prof Exp:* Fel biol, Mass Inst Technol, 72-74; asst prof cell biol, Univ Sherbrooke, 74-75; from asst prof to prof path, McMaster Univ, 75-90. *Concurrent Pos:* Nat Cancer Inst Can Hunter res fel, 72-74; res scholar, Nat Cancer Inst Can, 74-79, mem fel panel, 76-79, res assoc, mem molecular biol panel, 80-84 & chmn, molecular biol panel, 84-85, mem adv comt res, 88- *Mem:* Am Soc Microbiol; Can Soc Cell Biol. *Res:* Studies on the structure and function of early region 1 proteins of human adenoviruses and on the isolation and characterization of phosphotyrosyl protein phosphatases. *Mailing Add:* Biochem McGill Univ Fac Med 3655 Drummond Rm 802 Montreal PQ H3G 1Y6 Can

BRAQUET, PIERRE G, CHEMISTRY. *Current Pos:* GEN MGR & DIR RES, IPSEN BEAUFOUR GROUP, 82-; PROF, LA STATE UNIV, NEW ORLEANS, 88- *Personal Data:* b Dakar, Senegal, June 13, 47; m; c 3. *Educ:* Univ Bordeaux II Med Sch, Pharmacien, 70; Univ Bordeaux I, DSc, 71; Univ Paris V Med Sch, PhD(pharm), 74. *Honors & Awards:* Award by Royal Soc Med London for Discovery of PAF Antagonists, Europ Biol Res Asn. *Prof Exp:* Post grad res assoc chem, Col de France, 72; res assoc, Uniformed Army Serv Res Ctr, 72-74; dir, Dept Opers Res, Direction Centrale, Santne01 des Armne01es, 74-78; res dir, Fournier Lab, France, 78-79; dir develop, Merck, Sharp & Dohme, France, 79-82. *Concurrent Pos:* Assoc prof, Dept Chem, Univ Bordeaux Med Sch, Bordeaux, France, 69-72; vis prof, Georgetown Univ Med Sch, Wash, 84-86, Univ Sherbrook Med Sch, Can, 84-, Univ Milan Med Sch, Italy, 86-; numerous invited lectrs, US & foreign, 87- *Mem:* Am Asn Immunologists; Int Soc Heart Res; fel NY Acad Sci; Am Heart Asn; Am Soc Exp Therapeut; Am Thoracic Soc; Int Soc Immunopharmacol; Int Soc Xenobiotics. *Res:* PAF antagonists; antihypertensive agents; antiallergy drugs; antiasthmatic drugs; antibacterials; antiinflammatory agents; antibrain edema agents; antiulcer agents; antivirals/anti AIDS; aspartyl protease antagonists; diuretics; hypdipemic agents; ion transport inhibitors; immunoregulators; leukotriene antagonists; prostaglandins agonists and antagonists; somatostatine analogues. *Mailing Add:* Chmn & CEO Dir Res Biol-I Nova DNA Tech Corp 48-52 Rue de la gare Plaisir F78380 France. *Fax:* 331-30-546-151

BRAS, RAFAEL LUIS, STOCHASTIC HYDROLOGY. *Current Pos:* from asst prof to assoc prof, 76-84, dir, Ralph M Parsons Lab, 83-91, HEAD, WATER RESOURCES & ENVIRON ENG DIV, MASS INST TECHNOL, 83-, PROG HYDOL, 84, HEAD, DEPT CIVIL & ENVIRON ENG, 91- *Personal Data:* b San Juan, PR, Oct 28, 50; m 74; c 2. *Educ:* Mass Inst Technol, BS, 72, MS, 74, ScD, 75. *Honors & Awards:* Horton Award, Am Geophys Union, 81, James B Macelwane Award, 82; Huber Award, 93. *Prof Exp:* Asst prof hydrol & hydraul, Univ PR, 75-76. *Concurrent Pos:* Consult govt & private indust, 74-; ad honorem prof, Univ PR, 76-78; prin investr basic res sponsored by govt & indust, 76-; Chmn, Gilbert Winslow career develop award, Mass Inst Technol, 79-82 & William E Leonhard, 89-; assoc ed, Water Resources Res, Am Geophys Union, 81-88; John Simon Guggenheim Found fel, 82-83; vis assoc prof, Univ Simon Bolivar, Venezuela, 82-83; vis scholar, Int Inst Appl Syst Anal, 83; mem ed bd, J Hydrol, 84-; chmn, Bd J Ed, Am Geophys Union, 84-88 & Budget & Finance, 90-; dir, Mass Inst Technol, MITES Prog, 87; adv bd, eng directorate, NSF, 89-; vis prof, Univ Iowa, 89-90; chmn bd, Atmospheric Sci & Climate, NRC, 89-; assoc dir, Ctr Global Change Sci, Mass Inst Technol, 90- *Mem:* Am Soc Civil Engrs; Am Geophys Union; AAAS; Sigma Xi; Am Metrol Soc; Int Asn Hydraulic Res. *Res:* Use of probability theory in geophysics; streamflow and rainfall forecasting; soil moisture estimation and modelling; the estimation of random fields from point data; data collection network design. *Mailing Add:* Dept Civil Eng Mass Inst Technol 77 Massachusetts Ave Cambridge MA 02139-4307. *Fax:* 617-253-4546; *E-Mail:* rlbras@mit.edu

BRASCH, FREDERICK MARTIN, JR, ELECTRICAL ENGINEERING, COMPUTER SCIENCE. *Current Pos:* SUPVR, AT&T BELL LABS, 81- *Personal Data:* b Mexico City, Mex, Sept 12, 43; US citizen; m 66; c 3. *Educ:* Rice Univ, BA, 65, BS, 66, PhD(elec eng), 70. *Prof Exp:* Asst prof elec eng, Northwestern Univ, 70-75, asst prof comput sci, 71-75, assoc prof elec eng & comput sci, 75-81. *Mem:* Inst Elec & Electronics Engrs; Asn Comput Mach. *Res:* Distributed processing; real time systems; control systems. *Mailing Add:* AT&T Info Systs 11900 N Pecos 30F82 Denver CO 80234

BRASCH, KLAUS RAINER, CELL BIOLOGY, ELECTRON MICROSCOPY. *Current Pos:* prof & chair biol, 90-94, DEAN, SCH NATURAL SCIS, CALIF STATE UNIV, SAN BERNARDINO, 94- *Personal Data:* b Berlin, WGermany, Dec 19, 40; Can citizen; m 66, Margaret Schoning; c Madeleine. *Educ:* Concordia Univ, BS, 65; Carleton Univ, MS, 68, PhD(biol), 71. *Prof Exp:* Asst prof biol, Carleton Univ, Ottawa, 72-73; from asst prof to assoc prof, Queen's Univ, Kingston, 73-83; assoc prof, Univ Tulsa, 83-87, prof biol, 87-90. *Concurrent Pos:* Mem bd dirs, Can Soc Cell Biol, 76-77; vis scientist, dept med genetics, City Hope Med Ctr, Duarte, Calif, 79-80. *Mem:* AAAS; Am Soc Cell Biol; Can Soc Cell Biol; Asn Lunar Planetary. *Res:* Functional organization of eukaryotic chromosomes and cell nuclei; role of nuclear proteins and steroid hormones in gene expression and cellular development; molecular analysis of human chromosomes and genetic disorders. *Mailing Add:* Sch Natural Sci Calif State Univ San Bernardino CA 92407. *Fax:* 909-880-7005; *E-Mail:* kbrasch@wiley.csusb.edu

BRASCHO, DONN JOSEPH, RADIOLOGY. *Current Pos:* from asst prof to assoc prof, 66-74, PROF RADIATION THER, UNIV ALA, BIRMINGHAM, 74- *Personal Data:* b Syracuse, NY, Jan 9, 33; m 56; c 6. *Educ:* Hobart Col, BS, 54; State Univ NY, MD, 58. *Prof Exp:* Asst chief radiol, Madigan Gen Hosp, Tacoma, Wash, 62-64, chief radiother, 62-64 & 65-66; radiologist, 121st Evacuation Hosp, Korea, 64-65. *Mem:* AMA; Radiol Soc NAm, fel Am Col Radiol; NY Acad Sci; Am Soc Therapeut Radiol. *Res:* Clinical radiation oncology. *Mailing Add:* 142 Holiday Estates Dr Cropwell AL 35054

BRASE, DAVID ARTHUR, PHARMACOLOGY. *Current Pos:* RES ASSOC DEPT PHARMACOL & TOXICOL, MED COL VA, 84- *Personal Data:* b Orange, Calif, May 9, 45. *Educ:* Chapman Col, BS, 67; Univ Va, PhD(pharmacol), 72. *Prof Exp:* Fel pharmacol, Univ Calif, San Francisco, 72-76; asst prof pharmacol, Eastern Va Med Sch, 76-84. *Concurrent Pos:* Res starter grantee, Pharmaceut Mfrs Asn Found, 77-78; adj asst prof, Old Dominion Univ, 77-84. *Mem:* Soc Neurosci; Am Soc Pharmacol & Exp Therapeut. *Res:* Pharmacology of narcotic drugs and endogenous opioids; interactions of central nervous system neurotransmitters. *Mailing Add:* Ctr Drug Eval & Res Fed Drug Admin Rm 9B45 HFD-170 5600 Fishers Lane Rockville MD 20857

BRASEL, JO ANNE, PEDIATRICS, ENDOCRINOLOGY. *Current Pos:* PROF PEDIAT, SCH MED, UNIV CALIF, LOS ANGELES, 79-, PROF MED, 80-, CHIEF, DIV PEDIAT ENDOCRINOL, 81- *Personal Data:* b Salem, Ill, Feb 15, 34. *Educ:* Univ Colo, Boulder, BA, 56; Univ Colo, Denver, MD, 59. *Prof Exp:* From intern to resident pediat, NY Hosp-Cornell Univ Med Ctr, 59-62; fel pediat endocrinol, Sch Med, Johns Hopkins Univ, 62-65, asst prof, 65-68; from asst prof to assoc prof, Cornell Univ, Med Col, 69-72; from assoc prof to prof pediat, dir, Div Growth & Develop & asst dir, Inst Human Nutrit, Col Physicians & Surgeons, Columbia Univ, 72-79. *Concurrent Pos:* Irma T Hirschl trust career scientist award, 73-77; Nat Inst Child Health & Human Develop res career develop award, 74-79; spec consult, Endocrine & Metab Adv Comt, Food & Drug Admin, 71-75; mem nutrit study sect, NIH, 74-78; sr fulbright sabbatical res award, 80; mem, Comt Nutrit Mother & Presch Child, Food & Nutrit Bd, Nat Acad Sci, 80-82; mem, Select Panel Prom Child Health, HEW, 79-80; mem, Task Force Women, Minorities & Handicapped Sci & Tech, US Govt, 87-89. *Mem:* Soc Pediat Res; Am Pediat Soc; Endocrine Soc; Lawson Wilkins Pediat Soc; Am Soc Clin Nutrit; Am Inst Nutrit. *Res:* Growth and development, pediatric endocrinology, exercise and growth. *Mailing Add:* Harbor Univ Calif Los Angeles Med Ctr 1000 W Carson St PO Box 446 Torrance CA 90509-2910

BRASELTON, WEBB EMMETT, JR, ENDOCRINOLOGY. *Current Pos:* assoc prof, 78-84, PROF PHARM & TOXICOL, MICH STATE UNIV, 84-, DIR, ANALYTICAL TOXICOL SECT, 78- *Personal Data:* b Americus, Ga, July 17, 41; m 64; c 2. *Educ:* Univ Wis, BS, 63, MS, 66, PhD(endocrinol), 69; Am Bd Toxicol, dipl, 81. *Prof Exp:* Assoc biol chem, Harvard Med Sch, 71-73; asst res prof med, Med Col Ga, 73-77, asst prof endocrinol, 73-77, assoc res prof med, 77-78, dir, Gas Chromatography-Mass Spectrometry Facil, 73-78. *Concurrent Pos:* Res fel biol chem, Harvard Med Sch, 69-71; fel biochem, Mass Gen Hosp, Boston, 69-73. *Mem:* Am Soc Mass Spectrometry; Endocrine Soc; Am Chem Soc; Asn Off Anal Chem; Am Asn Vet Lab Diagnosticians; Am Acad Vet Comp Toxicol. *Res:* Metabolism and pharmacokinetics of drugs and xenobiotics; extraction, purification and physiochemical characterization of the anterior pituitary gonadotropic hormones; enzymes and mechanisms involved in steroid biosynthesis and metabolism; analytical methods development for organics and trace metals. *Mailing Add:* 1373 Red Leaf Lane East Lansing MI 48823

BRASH, JOHN LAW, BIOMEDICAL ENGINEERING, BIOMATERIALS. *Current Pos:* assoc prof chem eng, 72-76, PROF CHEM ENG, MCMASTER UNIV, 76-, DEPT CHAIR, 97- *Personal Data:* b Glasgow, Scotland, Mar 8, 37; m 64, Vicki Brown; c Andrew, Christopher & Matthew. *Educ:* Glasgow Univ, BSc, 58, PhD(chem), 61. *Hon Degrees:* Dr, Univ Paris XIII, 96. *Honors & Awards:* Clemson Award Basic Res, Soc Biomat, 94. *Prof Exp:* Nat Res Coun Can fel, Div Pure Chem, Ottawa, Ont, 61-63; res chemist, Yerkes Lab, E I du Pont de Nemours & Co, 63-64; polymer chemist, Stanford Res Inst, 64-69, sr polymer chemist, 69-72. *Concurrent Pos:* Vis scientist, Ctr Res Macromolecules, Strasbourg, France, 78-79; vis prof, Univ Paris-Nord, France, 86-87, 94 & Univ Linkoping, Sweden, 94; ed, Colloids & Surfaces B, Biointerfaces, 92-; chair, Gordon Res Conf Biocompatibility & Biomats, 93. *Mem:* AAAS; Am Chem Soc; Am Soc Artificial Internal Organs; Can Biomat Soc; Soc for Biomaterials. *Res:* Biomaterials; blood-surface interactions; adsorption of macromolecules, especially proteins; kinetics of polymerization reactions, segmented polyurethanes, bioactive polymers. *Mailing Add:* Dept Chem Eng McMaster Univ Hamilton ON L8S 4L8 Can. *Fax:* 905-521-1350; *E-Mail:* brashjl@mcmail.cis.mcmaster.ca

BRASHIER, CLYDE KENNETH, PLANT TAXONOMY, PLANT MORPHOLOGY. *Current Pos:* chmn dept math & sci, Dakota State Col, 67-74, acad dean, 74-76, prof biol, 76-82 & 85-86, chmn dept, 82-85, CHMN DEPT BIOL, DAKOTA STATE COL, 86- *Personal Data:* b Marion, La, May 21, 33; m 70; c 3. *Educ:* La Polytech Inst, BSc, 55; Univ Nebr, MSc, 57, PhD(bot), 61. *Prof Exp:* Prof bot & bact, Wis State Univ, Superior, 61-67. *Concurrent Pos:* Grant, Wis State Univ, 63-64; NSF fel, 63 & 68; dir, NSF Summer Insts, 64-67; grants, Dakota State Col, 68-78, 80-82 & 87-89. *Mem:* Bot Soc Am; Int Soc Plant Morphol. *Res:* Lake pollution research; environmental and career education. *Mailing Add:* 928 E Maplewood Dr Madison SD 57042

BRASITUS, THOMAS, MEDICINE, GASTROENTEROLOGY. *Current Pos:* Mem staff, Joseph B Kirsner Ctr Study Digestive Dis, DIR GASTROENTEROL/NUTRIT SECT, UNIV CHICAGO, 85-, WALTER L PALMER DISTINGUISHED PROF MED, 87- *Educ:* Jefferson Med Col, MD, 71. *Concurrent Pos:* Chmn, gen med study sect, NIMH/Nat Inst Diabetes, Digestive & Kidney Dis. *Mem:* Am Asn Physicians; Am Soc Clin Invest; Am Gastroenterol Asn (secy, 91-). *Res:* Pathogenesis and prevention of colon cancer; biocellular actions of vitamin D3 and it's metabolites. *Mailing Add:* Dept Med MC4076 Univ Chicago 5841 S Maryland Ave Chicago IL 60637-1463. *Fax:* 773-702-2182

BRASLAU, NORMAN, PHYSICS. *Current Pos:* CONSULT, 93- *Personal Data:* b Galveston, Tex, July 21, 31; m 55; c 2. *Educ:* Agr & Mech Col, Tex, BS, 51; Ohio State Univ, MS, 52; Univ Calif, Berkeley, PhD(physics), 60. *Prof Exp:* Physicist, USAF Cambridge Res Ctr, Mass, 52-56; staff mem, Lawrence Radiation Lab, Univ Calif, 60; res staff mem, IBM Watson Res Ctr, 61-90, assoc ed, IBM J Res & Develop, 90-93. *Concurrent Pos:* Vis fel, Ecole Normale Superieure, Paris, 60-61, vis prof, 75-76; vis prof, Technion, Haifa, Israel, 90. *Mem:* Am Phys Soc; Sigma Xi. *Res:* Semiconductor device physics; non-linear optics; current instabilities in semiconductors; atmospheric physics. *Mailing Add:* 194C Heritage Hills Dr Somers NY 10589

BRASLOW, JUDITH BERENSON, SCIENCE ADMINISTRATION. *Current Pos:* prog specialist, Bur Health Personnel Develop Serv, Health Serv Admin, US Dept Health & Human Servs, 80-81, legis officer, 81-82, legis officer, Bur Health Maintenance Orgn & Resource Develop, Health Resources & Servs Admin, 82-86, dep dir, Div Facil Compliance, Off Health Facil, Bur Resources Develop, 86-87, exec dir, Intragovt Task Force AIDS Health Care Delivery, 87-88, actg dir, Off Spec Projs, Bur Maternal Child Health & Resources Develop, 89-90, actg dir, Div Trauma & Emergency Med Systs, Bur Health Resources Develop Health Resources & Servs Admin, 92-94, DIR, DIV TRANSPLANTATION, OFF SPEC PROGS, HEALTH RESOURCES & SERVS ADMIN, US DEPT HEALTH & HUMAN SERVS, 90- *Personal Data:* b Sept 25, 44; m, Lawrence; c 1. *Educ:* Boston

Univ, BA, 66; Univ Md, MA, 68. *Honors & Awards:* Surgeon Gen Exemplary Serv Award, 92. *Prof Exp:* Dir cult affairs, Univ Md, 68-69, dir student parent orientation, 69-70, dir student develop, 70-74, asst dir admin/adminr, Univ Health Ctr, 74-76; legis analyst & spec asst to pres women in med, Asn Am Med Cols, 76-80; exec dir, Intragovt Task Force AIDS Health Care Delivery, 87-88. *Concurrent Pos:* Fel, WHO, 92. *Mem:* Am Col Health Asn; Am Med Women's Asn; Am Pub Health Asn; Asn Am Med Cols. *Res:* Organ transplantation; bone marrow donorship; health professions education related to donation and transplantation; allocation of organs; performance of organ procurement organizations; pediatric transplantation; HIV and hepatitis B. *Mailing Add:* Div Transplantation Health Resources & Serv Admin 5600 Fishers Lane Parklawn Bldg Rm 7-29 Rockville MD 20857

BRASS, ERIC PAUL, CLINICAL PHARMACOLOGY, DRUG DEVEOLPMENT. *Current Pos:* PROF & CHAIR, DEPT MED, HARBOR MED CTR, UNIV CALIF, LOS ANGELES, 94- *Personal Data:* b Brooklyn, NY, Sept 3, 52; m 94, Kathy Sietsema; c Carl, Courtney & Alex. *Educ:* Case Western Res Univ, BS, 73, MS, 74, PhD (pharmacol), 79, MD, 80. *Honors & Awards:* Young Investr Award, Am Soc Cliln Pharmacol & Therapeut, 86; Clin Pharmacol Award, Burroughs Welcome Fund, 89. *Prof Exp:* Asst prof med, Univ Colo, 83-89; assoc prof, Case Western Res Univ, 89-93; asst dir, Calif Clin Trials, 93-94. *Concurrent Pos:* Mem Pharmacol Sci Comt, NIH, 92-96; mem, Non-Prescription Drugs Adv Comt, Food & Drug Admin, 95- *Mem:* Fel Am Col Physicians; Am Soc Clin Invest; Am Soc Clin Pharmacol & Therapeut; Am Soc Pharmacol & Exp Therapeut. *Res:* Mechanisms of metabolic regulation in cells; how this regulation is altered by disease and how therapies can be designed to correct metabolic dysfunction; general issues in drug development and clinical trials. *Mailing Add:* Harbor Univ Calif Los Angeles Med Ctr 1000 W Carson St Torrance CA 90509-2910

BRASSARD, ANDRE, COMPARATIVE PATHOLOGY, IMMUNOPATHOLOGY. *Current Pos:* asst prof, 65-70, ASSOC PROF COMP PATH, LAVAL UNIV, 70- *Personal Data:* b Quebec City, Que, May 31, 33; m 59; c 2. *Educ:* Laval Univ, BA, 55; Univ Montreal, DVM, 60; Univ Pa, MSc, 62, PhD(comp path), 64. *Prof Exp:* Asst comp pathologist, Univ Pa, 60-62, assoc comp pathologist, 62-64. *Mem:* NY Acad Sci; Int Union Conserv of Nature. *Res:* Experimental autoimmune glomerulonephritis. *Mailing Add:* 2891 La Promenade Ste-Foy PQ G1W 2J5 Can. *Fax:* 418-651-2893

BRASTINS, AUSEKLIS, ELECTRICAL ENGINEERING, ELECTRONICS. *Current Pos:* RETIRED. *Personal Data:* b Riga, Latvia, July 27, 25; US citizen; m 57, Emily D Fridenbergs; c Anita S & Linda L. *Educ:* Carnegie Inst Technol, BS, 54, MS, 55, PhD(elec eng), 60. *Prof Exp:* Res engr, Res Labs, Westinghouse Elec Corp, 60-61, sr engr, 61-64; res engr, Gulf Res & Develop Co, 64-68, sr res engr, 68-83. *Res:* High frequency loss mechanism in ferrites; semiconductor circuitry; seismic instrumentation; computer systems. *Mailing Add:* 108 Rutledge Dr Pittsburgh PA 15215-1920

BRASUNAS, ANTON DES, METALLURGY & PHYSICAL METALLURGICAL ENGINEERING. *Current Pos:* Prof metall eng, 64-84, assoc dean, 75-80, EMER PROF METALL ENG, UNIV MO, 84- *Personal Data:* b Elizabeth, NJ, Mar 11, 19; m 46, Ellen Wirth; c James, Kay & Anne. *Educ:* Antioch Col, BS, 43; Ohio State Univ, MS, 46; Mass Inst Technol, DSc, 50. *Honors & Awards:* Fullbright Award, Colombia, SAm, 84. *Prof Exp:* Res metallurgist, Oak Ridge Nat Lab, 50-56; dir metals & mats, Eng Inst, 56-64. *Mem:* Fel Am Soc Metals; fel US Metric Asn. *Res:* High temperature corrosion of high temperature alloys; high temperature mechanical properties. *Mailing Add:* 8030 Daytona Dr St Louis MO 63105. *Fax:* 314-516-5434; *E-Mail:* brasunas@umr.edu

BRASUNAS, JOHN CHARLES, OUTER PLANET EXPLORATION, SPECTROMETER DEVELOPMENT. *Current Pos:* ASTROPHYSICIST, NASA GODDARD SPACE FLIGHT CTR, 84- *Personal Data:* b Elizabeth, NJ, Feb 6, 52; m 86, Kathleen A McCann; c Madeline & John. *Educ:* Princeton Univ, AB, 74; Harvard Univ, AM, 76, PhD(physics), 81. *Prof Exp:* Mem tech staff, Lincoln Lab, Mass Inst Technol, 81-84. *Concurrent Pos:* Conf cochair, Superconductivity Appln Infrared & Microwave Devices, Int Soc Optical Eng, 90 & 91; prin investr, high-temperature-superconductor bolometers planetary missions, NASA, 90-97. *Mem:* Am Phys Soc; Am Astron Soc; Optical Soc Am; Am Geophys Union; AAAS. *Res:* Spectroscopic, remote sensing of the Earth's upper atmosphere and of the outer planets; infrared sensor development; development of spectrometer systems; high-temperature superconductors developed for use as sensors. *Mailing Add:* NASA Goddard Code 693 Greenbelt MD 20771. *Fax:* 301-286-1683; *E-Mail:* john.c.brasunas.1@gsfc.nasa.gov

BRASWELL, EMORY HAROLD, BIOPHYSICS, BIOPHYSICAL CHEMISTRY. *Current Pos:* asst prof chem, Univ Conn, 62-64, bact, 64-68, biol, 68-73, assoc prof biol, 73-87, PROF MOLECULAR & CELL BIOL, UNIV CONN, 87-, HEAD, NAT ANAL ULTRACENTRIFUGATION FAC, 86- *Personal Data:* b Brooklyn, NY, Jan 22, 32; m 52, 71; c 3. *Educ:* Polytech Inst Brooklyn, BS, 52, MS, 55; NY Univ, PhD(phys chem), 61. *Prof Exp:* Res chemist, cent lab, Gen Foods Corp, 54-56; lectr chem, Hunter Col, 56-57; NIH fel, Univ Birmingham, 60-62. *Mem:* Am Chem Soc; Biophys Soc; Sigma Xi. *Res:* Physical biochemistry; physical chemistry of biomacromolecules; studies on dextran, gelatin, DNA and heparin, using techniques such as light scattering, analytical ultracentrifugation, viscosity, conductivity and dye binding; lactic dehydrogenase kinetics and subunit interaction; protein association. *Mailing Add:* Dept Molecular & Cell Biol U-125 Univ Conn Storrs CT 06269-3125. *Fax:* 860-486-4331

BRASWELL, ROBERT NEIL, SYSTEMS ENGINEERING. *Current Pos:* DIR COMPUT & PROF, FLA STATE UNIV, 86- *Personal Data:* b Boaz, Ala, July 23, 32; m 54; c 2. *Educ:* Univ Ala, BS, 57, MS, 59; Okla State Univ, PhD(eng), 64. *Honors & Awards:* more than fifty awards for outstanding res and develop. *Prof Exp:* Mgr opers anal, Brown Eng Co, Inc, Ala, 59-61, sr proj engr, 61-62, mgr systs eng dept, Cape Kennedy, 62-64; prof indust & systs eng, Univ Fla, 64-73, chmn dept, 65-73, resident dir genesys, 64-66, dir systs res ctr, 68-72; scientist, 72-73, tech dir, Armament Div, Eglin AFB, Fla, 73-85; dir math & comput sci, USAF, Washington, DC, 85-86. *Concurrent Pos:* Asst prof, Redstone Grad Sch, Univ Ala, 59-62; lectr, Ariz State Univ, 61-62; pres, Sole Educ Found Inc, 69- *Mem:* Am Inst Indust Engrs; Am Soc Eng Educ; Nat Soc Prof Engrs; Opers Res Soc Am; Sigma Xi. *Res:* Supercomputing; robotics with applications in large scale design. *Mailing Add:* 804 Tarpon Dr Ft Walton Beach FL 32548

BRATCHER, THOMAS LESTER, BAYESIAN INFERENCE, SURVIVAL ANALYSIS. *Current Pos:* ASSOC PROF STATIST & MATH, BAYLOR UNIV, 79- *Personal Data:* b Fortworth, Tex, July 9, 42; c 2. *Educ:* Univ Tex, Arlington, BS, 63; Southern Methodist Univ, MS, 65, PhD(statist), 69. *Prof Exp:* Tech staff statist, Sandia Nat Labs, 65-67; assoc prof, Univ Southwestern La, 69-79. *Concurrent Pos:* Statistician, Nat Ctr Toxicol Res, 75-78. *Mem:* Am Statist Asn; Sigma Xi. *Res:* Statistical inference including estimation, multiple comparisons, selection and interval estimation; biostatistics: models to analyze animal experiment data for tumors and birth defects. *Mailing Add:* 202 Shady Place Dr Waco TX 76712

BRATENAHL, ALEXANDER, plasma physics, space science, for more information see previous edition

BRATER, D(ONALD) CRAIG, NEPHROLOGY. *Current Pos:* PROF INTERNAL MED, SCH MED, IND UNIV, 86- *Educ:* Duke Univ, MD, 71. *Prof Exp:* Assoc prof pharmacol & internal med, Southwestern Med Sch, Univ Tex, 77-86. *Mailing Add:* Wishard Mem Hosp WOP 320 1001 W Tenth St Indianapolis IN 46202-2879. *Fax:* 317-630-8185

BRATERMAN, PAUL S, INORGANIC CHEMISTRY. *Current Pos:* PROF CHEM, UNIV NTEX, 88- *Personal Data:* b London, UK, Aug 28, 38; m 88, Rebecca Waugh; c Geoffrey, Russell & Laura. *Educ:* Oxford Univ, BA, 60, MA & DPhil, 63. *Hon Degrees:* DSc, Oxford Univ, 85. *Prof Exp:* Lectr chem, Glasgow Univ, 65-77, sr lectr, 77-88, reader, 88. *Concurrent Pos:* Vis scientist, Univ Calif, San Diego/NSCORT, 93. *Mem:* Am Chem Soc; fel Royal Soc Chemistry; Int Soc Study Origin Life; Sigma Xi; AAAS. *Res:* Spectroscopy and electrochemistry of inorganic and other species in solution; morphology and development, form and pattern in inorganic precipitates; origins of life. *Mailing Add:* Univ N Tex Dept Chem Denton TX 76203-5068. *Fax:* 817-565-4824; *E-Mail:* psb@bob.unt.edu

BRATHOVDE, JAMES ROBERT, ENVIRONMENTAL MANAGEMENT, ENVIRONMENTAL SCIENCES. *Current Pos:* prof chem & chmn dept, 67-70, dean col sci & humanistic studies, 70-72, prof, 72-84, EMER PROF ENVIRON SCI & CHEM, NORTHERN ARIZ UNIV, 84- *Personal Data:* b Glasgow, Mont, June 8, 26; m 49, Bonnie D Cornwell; c James Edgar, Robert Dean, Line (McDonald) & Tonna (Williams). *Educ:* Eastern Wash Col, BA, 50; Univ Wash, MS, 55, PhD(phys chem), 56. *Prof Exp:* Teacher, pub sch syst, Wash, 50-51; supvr, freshman labs, Univ Wash, 53-54, instr phys chem lab, 54; assoc prof chem, Whitworth Col, Wash, 56-57, chmn dept, 56-60; mem staff, phys sci res dept, Sandia Labs, NMex, 60-62 & aerospace nuclear safety prog, 62-63; assoc prog dir, undergrad educ sci, NSF, 63-64; prof chem & dir comput ctr, State Univ NY Binghamton, 64-67. *Mem:* Am Crystallog Asn; AAAS; Sigma Xi. *Res:* X-ray and neutron diffraction; molecular and crystal structures; ambient air and water quality; waste water operations; small scale energy converters; geothermal exploration. *Mailing Add:* 1664 S Fort Apache Rd Camp Verde AZ 86322

BRATINA, WOYMIR JOHN, solid state physics; deceased, see previous edition for last biography

BRATSCHUN, WILLIAM R(UDOLPH), CERAMIC ENGINEERING, MATERIALS SCIENCE. *Current Pos:* MGR, MAT & FAILURE ANALYSIS LAB, MOTOROLA, 87- *Personal Data:* b Chicago, Ill, June 1, 31; m 54; c Neal W, Alan R & Thomas D. *Educ:* Univ Ill, BS, 53, MS, 57, PhD(ceramic eng), 59. *Prof Exp:* Ceramic engr, Gen Elec Co, NY, 53-54; sr res scientist, Honeywell Res Ctr, 59-64; dir res, Channel Industs, Inc, 64-67; res scientist, Ill Inst Technol, Res Inst, 67-72; mgr anal chem & mfg serv, Zenith Radio Corp, 72-87. *Mem:* Fel Am Ceramic Soc; Nat Inst Ceramic Engrs; Int Soc Hybrid Microelectronics; Am Soc Metals; Inst Elec & Electronic Engrs. *Res:* Glasses; dielectrics; thick film materials; semiconductors; piezoelectrics; electronic applications of materials; failure analysis, reliability of electrical materials. *Mailing Add:* 127 N Ashland Ave La Grange IL 60525

BRATT, ALBERTUS DIRK, ENTOMOLOGY. *Current Pos:* asst prof, 64-70, chmn dept, 73-79, PROF BIOL, CALVIN COL, 70- *Personal Data:* b Bozeman, Mont, Apr 2, 33; m 55; c 4. *Educ:* Calvin Col, BS, 55; Mich State Univ, MS, 57; Cornell Univ, PhD(entom), 64. *Prof Exp:* Instr biol, Calvin Col, 58-61; asst entom, Cornell Univ, 61-64. *Mem:* Am Inst Biol Sci. *Res:* Morphology and taxonomy of Acalyptrate Diptera; fresh-water biology; morphology of immature insects. *Mailing Add:* 2843 Mulford Dr SE Grand Rapids MI 49546-4388

BRATT, BENGT ERIK, OPERATIONS RESEARCH, STATISTICS. *Current Pos:* CONSULT ENGR, 85- *Personal Data:* b Willstad, Sweden, May 18, 22; US citizen; m 66, Gerlinde Frohner; c Steve. *Educ:* Tech Col, Gothenburg, Sweden, ME, 46; West Coast Univ, MSSE, 67; Western Colo Univ, PhD(sci), 77. *Prof Exp:* Systs engr systs res, Gen Dynamics, San Diego, 56-61; res engr space probs, Inst Nat Defense, Stockholm, Sweden, 61-62; res engr rocket propulsion, Northrop Space Labs, Los Angeles, 62-64; res scientist math & statist, Lockheed Res Ctr, Los Angeles, 64-67; systs engr forecasting & statist, Metrop Water Dist, 67-85. *Concurrent Pos:* Lectr, Calif State Univ, Los Angeles. *Mem:* Svenska Teknolog foreningen, Sweden; fel AAAS. *Res:* Systems analysis; statistical methods and computer application. *Mailing Add:* 1942 Lemoyne St Los Angeles CA 90026

BRATT, PETER RAYMOND, SOLID STATE PHYSICS. *Current Pos:* MEM TECH STAFF, SANTA BARBARA RES CTR, 63- *Personal Data:* b Syracuse, NY, Nov 11, 29; m 54; c 5. *Educ:* Syracuse Univ, BS, 54, PhD(physics), 65. *Prof Exp:* Sr res scientist, Spencer Labs, Raytheon Co, 60-63. *Mem:* Am Phys Soc; Sigma Xi. *Res:* Photoconductivity in solids; semiconductor physics; infrared detection; solid state lasers. *Mailing Add:* 6505 Camino Venturoso Goleta CA 93117-1526

BRATTAIN, MICHAEL GENE, BIOCHEMISTRY. *Current Pos:* ASSOC PROF, DEPT PHARMACOL, BAYLOR COL MED. *Personal Data:* b Ponca City, Okla, Oct 31, 47. *Educ:* Rutgers Univ, BS, 70, PhD(biochem), 74. *Prof Exp:* Res assoc path, 74-76, from instr to asst prof path, Univ Ala, Birmingham, 76-78, asst prof biochem, 78- *Concurrent Pos:* Assoc scientist, Comprehensive Cancer Ctr, Univ Ala, Birmingham, 76- *Mem:* Am Asn Cancer Res. *Res:* Biochemical pathology of human cancer. *Mailing Add:* Dept Biochem Med Col Ohio PO Box 10008 Toledo OH 43699-0008. *Fax:* 419-382-7395

BRATTON, GERALD ROY, VETERINARY ANATOMY. *Current Pos:* AT DEPT VET ANAT, TEX A&M UNIV. *Personal Data:* b San Antonio, Tex, Sept 25, 42; m 65; c 3. *Educ:* Tex A&M Univ, BS, 65, DVM, 66, MS, 70, PhD(vet anat), 77. *Prof Exp:* From instr to asst prof vet anat, Tex A&M Univ, 66-75; Assoc prof vet anat in chg anat progs, Dept Animal Sci & Vet Med, Univ Tenn, Knoxville, 75- *Mem:* Am Asn Vet Anatomists; Am Vet Med Asn. *Res:* Developing an immunological method for tracing anatomical connections of the basal ganglia, and the use of horseradish peroxidase tracer methods to localize the anatomical positions of the medullary respiratory centers. *Mailing Add:* 3000 Bolero St College Station TX 77845-6545

BRATTON, SUSAN POWER, PLANT ECOLOGY. *Current Pos:* RES BIOLOGIST. *Personal Data:* b Wilmington, Del, Oct 11, 48. *Educ:* Barnard Col, Columbia Univ, AB, 70; Cornell Univ, PhD(bot), 75, Univ Ga, Athens, cert environ ethics, 85; Fuller Seminary, MA, 87. *Prof Exp:* Res biologist & res coordr ecol, Field Res Lab, Great Smoky Mountains Nat Park, US Dept Interior, 74-81; res biologist, US Nat Park Serv Coop, Univ Ga, 81- *Concurrent Pos:* Instr, AuSable Inst. *Mem:* Ecol Soc Am; Brit Ecol Soc; Torrey Bot Club; Southern Appalachian Bot Club; Soc Conserv Biol. *Res:* Impact of over-grazing and exotic species on native plant communities; ecology of the European wild boar; structure and diversity patterns of herbaceous plant communities; rare and endangered plants; human trampling effects; deer browse; park management, ecotheology; landscape history. *Mailing Add:* Lindaman Ctr Whitworth Col Spokane WA 99251

BRATTSTEN, LENA B, BIOCHEMICAL TOXICOLOGY. *Current Pos:* PROF ENTOM, RUTGERS, 87- *Personal Data:* b Gothenburg, Sweden. *Educ:* Univ Lund, Sweden, Fil kand, 67; Univ Ill, Urbana, PhD(insecticide biochem & toxicol), 71. *Prof Exp:* Fel biochem, Cornell Univ, 71-72, res assoc, 72-77; asst prof biochem & ecol, Univ Tenn, Knoxville, 77-83; sr res biologist, DuPont, 83-87. *Mem:* Sigma Xi; AAAS; Entom Soc Am; Am Chem Soc; Int Soc Chem Ecol. *Res:* Comparative biochemical toxicology of xenobiotics; insect-plant interactions, chemical ecology; insecticide resistance mechanisms. *Mailing Add:* PO Box 231 Georges & Jones New Brunswick NJ 08903

BRATTSTROM, BAYARD HOLMES, HERPETOLOGY, SOCIAL BEHAVIOR & CONSERVATION. *Current Pos:* from asst prof to prof, 60-94, EMER PROF ZOOL, CALIF STATE UNIV, FULLERTON, 94- *Personal Data:* b Chicago, Ill, July 3, 29; m 52, 83, Martha A Marsh; c Theodore A & David A. *Educ:* San Diego State Col, BS, 51; Univ Calif, Los Angeles, MA, 53, PhD(zool), 59. *Prof Exp:* Asst cur herpet, Natural Hist Mus, San Diego, 49-51, dir educ, 50-51; asst zool, Univ Calif, Los Angeles, 52-55; fel paleoecol, Calif Inst Technol, 55-56; instr biol, Adelphi Univ, 56-60. *Concurrent Pos:* Res assoc, Los Angeles Co Mus, 61-; former pres & bd mem, Fullerton Youth Mus & Natural Sci Ctr; sr fel Monash Univ, Australia, 66-67; vis prof zool, Univ Sydney, 78 & Univ Queensland, 84; consult var govt agencies & pvt orgn; vis researcher, James Cook Univ, Australia, 93-94. *Mem:* Fel AAAS; Am Soc Ichthyologists & Herpetologists; Ecol Soc Am; Am Soc Mammalogists; Am Ornith Union; fel Herpetologists League. *Res:* Ecology, behavior, paleontology, zoogeography and physiology of reptiles and amphibians; paleoecology and paleoclimates; social behavior of vertebrates; thermoregulation; ecology of tropics; population and repopulation problems; habitat loss; conservation; deserts; noise pollution. *Mailing Add:* Dept Biol Calif State Univ Fullerton CA 92634-6850. *Fax:* 714-278-3426; *E-Mail:* bbrattstrom@fullerton.edu

BRATZ, ROBERT DAVIS, BIOLOGY, ECOLOGY. *Current Pos:* From asst prof to prof, 53-83, EMER PROF, BIOL, COL IDAHO, 83- *Personal Data:* b Sherman, Tex, Dec 14, 20; m 47, Dorothy A Davis; c Barbara L (Trevor), Kenneth G & Cyndy. *Educ:* Sam Houston State Teachers Col, BS, 41; Ore State Univ, MS, 50, PhD(zool, bot), 52. *Mem:* AAAS. *Res:* General biology and ecology; biogeography of Mexico and western United States; writing on Mexico, geography and natural history. *Mailing Add:* 1400 Willow St Caldwell ID 83605

BRAU, CHARLES ALLEN, FREE-ELECTRON LASERS, ACCELERATOR PHYSICS & LASER PHYSICS. *Current Pos:* prof physics & dir, Free-Electron Laser Ctr, 88-95, PROF PHYSICS, VANDERBILT UNIV, 95- *Personal Data:* b Brooklyn, NY, Nov 4, 38; m 66, Jean Stewart; c Peter S, Rebecca A & Jennifer L. *Educ:* Cornell Univ, BEP, 61; Harvard Univ, BA, 62, PhD(appl physics), 65. *Prof Exp:* Sr staff phys chem, Avco Everett Res Lab, 65-70; NATO fel molecular physics, Kammerlingh-Onnes Lab, Univ Leiden, Neth, 70-71; sr staff laser physics, Avco Everett Res Lab, 71-76; assoc group leader laser develop & free-electron laser prog mgr, Los Alamos Nat Lab, 76-86. *Concurrent Pos:* Vis prof, Univ Calif, Santa Barbara, 86-87, Dept Nuclear Physics, Univ Oxford, 88. *Mem:* Am Phys Soc. *Res:* Laser chemistry; excimer lasers; free electron lasers. *Mailing Add:* 415 Fairfax Ave Nashville TN 37212

BRAU, JAMES EDWARD, EXPERIMENTAL HIGH ENERGY PHYSICS. *Current Pos:* PROF PHYSICS, UNIV ORE, 88- *Personal Data:* b Tacoma, Wash, Nov 10, 46; m 69, Mary Lou Williams; c Benjamin P & Daniel J. *Educ:* US Air Force Acad, BS, 69; Mass Inst Technol, MS, 70, PhD(physics), 78. *Prof Exp:* Physicist, Cent Inertial Guid Test Facil, 70-71 & Air Force Weapons Lab, 71-74; res assoc, Stanford Linear Accelerator Ctr, 78-82; from assoc prof to prof physics & astron, Univ Tenn, 82-88. *Mem:* Am Phys Soc; AAAS. *Res:* Experimental investigations of the fundamental particles and their interactions, specifically the production and decay of neutral intermediate vector boson in electron-positron annihilation; emphasis on calorimetric techniques and microvertex detection. *Mailing Add:* Physics Dept Univ Ore Eugene OR 97403

BRAUCHI, JOHN TONY, PSYCHIATRY. *Current Pos:* MED DIR, PARKSIDE, INC, UNIV OKLA, TULSA, 89- *Personal Data:* b Sayre, Okla, Dec 23, 27; m 48; c 3. *Educ:* Univ Okla, MD, 55; Am Bd Psychiat & Neurol, dipl, 62. *Prof Exp:* Intern, Hillcrest Med Ctr, 55-56; resident, Univ Hosps, Okla, 56-58; resident, Med Ctr, Univ Kans, 58-59, from instr to prof psychiat, 58-75, dir inpatient serv, 60-61, dir residency training, 64-69, dir prof serv psychiat, 64-75, assoc chmn, Dept Psychiat, 68-75; prof psychiat, family med & chmn, Dept Psychiat, Sch Med, La State Univ, 75-89. *Concurrent Pos:* Dir, Atchison Co Guid Clin, Kans, 59-60, consult, 60-61; psychiat consult, Vet Admin Consol Ctr, Wadsworth, 59-61; actg chief psychiat serv, Vet Admin Hosp, Kansas City, Mo, 61-63; psychiat consult, Vet Admin Hosp, Shreveport, La, 75-; chief psychiat, Confed Mem Med Ctr, Shreveport, 75- *Mem:* Fel Am Asn Social Psychiat; Am Asn Chmn Depts Psychiat; fel Am Psychiat Asn; fel Am Col Psychiat; AMA. *Res:* Scintillation measurement of gross locomotor behavior; electroconvulsive shock and retroactive inhibitions; sleep deprivation; concept identification in thinking disorders; psychopharmacology; government; biofeedback. *Mailing Add:* 5806 S Atlanta Ave Tulsa OK 74105

BRAUD, HARRY J, AGRICULTURAL ENGINEERING. *Current Pos:* From asst prof to assoc prof, 61-72, PROF AGR ENG, LA STATE UNIV, 72- *Personal Data:* b Hope Villa, La, Sept 9, 35; m 69; c 2. *Educ:* La State Univ, BS, 57, MS, 59; Okla State Univ, PhD(eng), 62. *Mem:* Am Soc Agr Engrs. *Res:* Environmental control for orchards and fields; hydraulic discharge through slits in an elastic pipe wall; flow of water in porous medium with respect to subirrigation. *Mailing Add:* 13519 Bluff Rd Geismar LA 70734

BRAUDE, GEORGE LEON, CHEMISTRY, CHEMICAL ENGINEERING. *Current Pos:* RETIRED. *Personal Data:* b Samara, Russia, Mar 2, 18; US citizen; m 49, Monique Colsenet. *Educ:* Wilna Univ, Lithuania, dipl, 42; Univ Halle, PhD(org chem), 45, Dr Econ Sc, 46. *Honors & Awards:* Award of Merit, Am Chem Soc, 68. *Prof Exp:* Res asst chem, Rohm & Haas fel, Univ Halle, 42-45 & Univ Frankfurt, 46-47; res chemist, Prosynthese Co, Paris, 48-52 & Imperial Paper Corp, Collins & Aikman Co, NY, 52-55; dir com res, Alcolac Chem Corp, Baltimore, 56-57; res supvr, W R Grace & Co, Md, 57-66, sect mgr, 66-68, dir spec proj dept, 68-70, mgr org res, 70-71; chief, Chem Indust Pract Br, US Food & Drug Admin, Washington, DC, 72-80, asst dir, Contaminant Coord, 81-83. *Concurrent Pos:* Consult, 83- *Mem:* Am Chem Soc. *Res:* Environmental contaminants of foods; waste treatment; organic intermediates; foams and aerosols; pharmaceuticals; detergents; pigments; polymers; specialty chemicals. *Mailing Add:* 2410 Parkway Cheverly MD 20785

BRAUDE, MONIQUE COLSENET, PHARMACY, TOXICOLOGY. *Current Pos:* chief preclin pharmacol, Biomed Res Br, Div Res, Nat Inst Drug Abuse, 74-87, CONSULT, 87- *Personal Data:* b Lisieux, France, Nov 13, 25; US citizen; m 49, George L. *Educ:* Univ Paris, dipl, 48; Ohio State Univ, MS, 54; Univ Md, PhD(pharmacol), 63. *Honors & Awards:* Scientist Emer Award, Soc Exp Biol & Med, 90. *Prof Exp:* Res pharmacist, Blaque Labs, Paris, 49-53; from res assoc to res asst prof pharmacol psychiat, Sch Med, Univ Md, Baltimore City, 62-65; pharmacologist, US Food & Drug Admin, 66-69; chief biomed sect, Ctr Studies Narcotics & Drug Abuse, NIMH, 70-74. *Mem:* AAAS; Am Soc Pharmacol & Exp Therapeut; Soc Toxicol; Soc Exp Biol & Med. *Res:* Neuropharmacology, psychopharmacology, perinatology and toxicology of drugs of abuse, marihuana, other central nervous system agents. *Mailing Add:* 462 Severnside Dr Severna Park MD 21146-2216

BRAUER, FRED, MATHEMATICS. *Current Pos:* from asst prof to assoc prof, 60-66, PROF MATH, UNIV WIS-MADISON, 66- *Personal Data:* b Konigsberg, Ger, Feb 3, 32; nat Can; m 58, Esther Luterman; c David, Deborah & Michael. *Educ:* Univ Toronto, BA, 52; Mass Inst Technol, SM, 53, PhD(math), 56. *Prof Exp:* From asst to instr, Mass Inst Technol, 53-56; instr, Univ Chicago, 56-58; from lectr to asst prof math, Univ BC, 58-60. *Mem:* Am Math Soc; Math Asn Am; Can Math Soc; Soc Indust & Appl Math; Sigma Xi. *Res:* Ordinary differential equations; biomathematics. *Mailing Add:* Dept Math Univ Wis Madison WI 53706. *Fax:* 608-263-8891; *E-Mail:* brauer@math.wisc.edu

BRAUER, GEORGE ULRICH, MATHEMATICS. *Current Pos:* from instr to asst prof, 53-66, ASSOC PROF MATH, UNIV MINN, MINNEAPOLIS, 66- *Personal Data:* b Ger, Mar 18, 27; m 68, Barbara Buchman. *Educ:* Univ Toronto, BA, 49; Univ Mich, MA, 50, PhD(math), 54. *Prof Exp:* Res asst, Univ Mich, 50-52, teaching fel, 52-53. *Mem:* Am Math Soc; Math Asn Am. *Res:* Summation of infinite series; Dirichlet series; functional analysis; real and complex variables. *Mailing Add:* Sch Math Univ Minn 127 Vincent Hall Minneapolis MN 55455-0338

BRAUER, JOHN ROBERT, FINITE ELEMENT ANALYSIS, COMPUTER-AIDED ENGINEERING. *Current Pos:* SR CONSULT ENGR FINITE ELEMENTS, ANSOFT CORP, 96- *Personal Data:* b Kenosha, Wis, Apr 18, 43; m 82, Susan McCord. *Educ:* Marquette Univ, BEE, 65; Univ Wis-Madison, MSEE, 66, PhD(elec eng), 69. *Prof Exp:* Res asst elec eng, Univ Wis-Madison, 66-68, teaching asst elec eng, 68-69; res scientist elec mach, A O Smith Corp, 69-75, sr consult engr finite elements, A O Smith Data Systs Inc, 75-88. *Concurrent Pos:* Lectr, Short Course on Finite Elements Anal, Marquette Univ, 88-; bd dirs, Appl Computational Electromag Soc. *Mem:* Fel, Inst Elec & Electronics Engrs; Sigma Xi. *Res:* Area of expertise is finite element analysis of electromagnetic fields; authored computer codes, one book and over 120 technical papers involving calculation of electromagnetic fields of frequencies from O to microwaves. *Mailing Add:* 929 N Astor St Apt 506 Milwaukee WI 53202. *E-Mail:* brauer@ansoft.com

BRAUER, JOSEPH B(ERTRAM), METALLURGY, CHEMISTRY & SOLID STATE PHYSICS. *Current Pos:* Proj officer mat eng, USAF, 51-53, chief Prod Develop Unit, 53-55, Electronic Mat Sect, 55-58, Appl Physics Sect, 58-62, chief, Solid State Appln Sect, 62-79, chief, Microelectronics Br, 79-85, CHIEF, MICROELECTRONICS RELIABILITY DIV, ROME AIR DEVELOP CTR, USAF, 85- *Personal Data:* b Lawrenceburg, Ind, Feb 12, 30; m 54, Sally Ann Maxted; c Michael, Judy, Joseph P, David & Susan. *Educ:* Purdue Univ, BSMetE, 51; Syracuse Univ, MChemE, 60. *Mem:* Am Soc Metals; fel Am Inst Chemists. *Res:* Metallurgy, chemistry and physics of solid state materials, especially work on magnetics, insulators, thermoelectrics, conductors, photoconductors and semiconductors, design and application of electronic devices and equipment employing these materials. *Mailing Add:* Rome Air Develop Ctr 1309 Carroll St Rome NY 13440-2607

BRAUER, RALPH WERNER, PHARMACOLOGY. *Current Pos:* RETIRED. *Personal Data:* b Berlin, Ger, June 18, 21; nat US. *Educ:* Columbia Univ, AB, 40; Univ Rochester, MSc, 41, PhD(biochem), 43. *Hon Degrees:* DSc, Univ NC, 97. *Honors & Awards:* Mary Scott Newbold lectr, Philadelphia Col Physicians, 62; Behnke Award, Undersea Med Soc, 70. *Prof Exp:* Res chemist, Wyandotte Chem Co, 43 & Distillation Prod Co, NY, 43-44; instr pharmacol, Harvard Med Sch, 44-47; asst prof, Sch Med, La State Univ, 47-51; head, Pharmacol Br, US Naval Radiol Defense Lab, Calif, 51-66; prof physiol & pharmacol, Sch Med, Duke Univ, 66-71; prof marine physiol & dir, Inst Marine Bio-med Res, Univ NC, Wilmington, 71-86. *Concurrent Pos:* Dir, Wrightsville Marine Bio-Med Lab, 66-71. *Mem:* Marine Technol Soc; Am Soc Pharmacol & Exp Therapeut; Soc Exp Biol & Med; NY Acad Sci; Radiation Res Soc; Am Physiol Soc. *Res:* Liver physiology; bile secretion; enzyme and fat chemistry; neutral phosphate esters as cholinesterase inhibitors; bromsulphthalein excretion; liver and plasma proteins; autoxidation of betaeleostearic acid; delayed radiation effects; nutrition and aging; environmental physiology; comparative history of science. *Mailing Add:* Inst Res Interrelation Sci & Cult 1601 Doctors Circle Wilmington NC 28401

BRAUER, ROGER L, SAFETY ENGINEERING, FACILITIES MANAGEMENT. *Current Pos:* TECH DIR, BD CERT SAFETY PROFESSIONALS, 90- *Personal Data:* b Julesburg, Colo; m 67, Charlotte Shepherd; c Michelle & David. *Educ:* Valparaiso Univ, BS & BA, 65; Univ Ill, Urbana-Champaign, MS, 67, PhD(mech eng), 72. *Honors & Awards:* Charles V Culbertson Award, Am Soc Safety Engrs, 85. *Prof Exp:* Engr, Boeing Co, 67-68; sr res engr, Roy C Ingersall Res Ctr, Borg-Warner Corp, 68-69; prin investr, Construct Eng Res Lab, US Army C Engr, 72-86, team leader, 87-90. *Concurrent Pos:* Adj asst prof safety eng, Mech & Indust Eng Dept, Univ Ill, Urbana-Champaign, 78-94; adminr, Eng Div, Am Soc Safety Engrs, 83-84, chmn, Acad Accreditation Coun, 86-90, vpres prof develop, 90-94; dir, Bd Cert Safety Professionals, 84-90. *Mem:* Am Soc Safety Engrs; Bd Cert Safety Professionals (secy-treas, 86-87, vpres, 88, pres, 89). *Res:* Facilities planning and management; ergonomics; safety engineering. *Mailing Add:* 602 W Austin St Tolono IL 61880

BRAUGHLER, JOHN MARK, NEUROPHARMACOLOGY & BIOCHEMICAL PHARMACOLOGY, FREE RADICAL BIOLOGY. *Current Pos:* res scientist, 83-84, sr res scientist, CNS Res, 85-89, assoc dir, Acquisitions Rev, 89-90, DIR, ACQUISITIONS REV, UPJOHN CO, 91- *Personal Data:* b Pittsburgh, Pa, Dec 29, 50; m 72, Elisabeth Headrick; c Jason, Tim & Amanda. *Educ:* Point Park Col, BS, 72; Univ Pittsburgh, PhD(pharmacol), 77. *Prof Exp:* Res assoc, Sch Med, Univ Pittsburgh, 77; res fel clin pharmacol, Univ Va, 77-79; from asst prof to assoc prof pharmacol, Col Med, Northeastern Ohio Univ, 79-83; asst prof biol & chem, Kent State Univ, 79-82. *Mem:* NY Acad Sci; Am Soc Pharmacol & Exp Therapeut; Soc Neurosci. *Res:* Pharmacological treatment of central nervous system injury and ischemia; biochemistry of central nervous system trauma and ischemia; pharmacology and therapeutics of antioxidants and radical scavengers; biochemical mechanisms of lipid peroxidation; membrane damage; drug development. *Mailing Add:* Upjohn Pharm 7000 Portage Rd Kalamazoo MI 49001

BRAULT, JAMES WILLIAM, solar physics, atomic spectroscopy, for more information see previous edition

BRAULT, MARGARET A, chemistry, for more information see previous edition

BRAULT, ROBERT GEORGE, POLYMER CHEMISTRY. *Current Pos:* RETIRED. *Personal Data:* b Hoquiam, Wash, Dec 4, 18; m 48; c 2. *Educ:* Whitworth Col, Wash, BS, 42; Mich State Col, PhD(org chem), 48. *Prof Exp:* Asst, Armour & Co, 49-51; asst org chem, Sinclair Res Labs, Inc, 51-54; mkt res engr, Callery Chem Co, 54-59; res chemist, Hughes Aircraft Co, 59-85. *Mem:* Am Chem Soc; Sigma Xi. *Res:* Organic synthesis; fatty acid derivatives; organo-metallics; borane chemistry; organic photochromic compounds; photopolymerization; radiation resists. *Mailing Add:* 924 Princeton St Santa Monica CA 90403-2220

BRAUMAN, JOHN I, CHEMISTRY. *Current Pos:* from asst prof to prof, 63-80, chmn dept, 79-83 & 95-96, J G JACKSON-C J WOOD PROF CHEM, STANFORD UNIV, 80- *Personal Data:* b Pittsburgh, Pa, Sept 7, 37; m 64, Sharon Kruse; c Kate A. *Educ:* Mass Inst Technol, BS, 59; Univ Calif, Berkeley, PhD(chem), 63. *Honors & Awards:* Pure Chem Award, Am Chem Soc, 73 & Harrison Howe Award, 76 & James Flack Norris Award phys org chem, 86; Arthur C Cope Scholar Award, 86. *Prof Exp:* NSF fel chem, Univ Calif, Los Angeles, 62-63. *Concurrent Pos:* Mem, Chem Adv Panel, NSF, 74-78; Guggenheim fel, 78-79; mem, Bd Chem Sci & Technol, Nat Res Coun, 78-81 & 83-, Comt Surv Opportunities Chem Sci, 82-; Christensen fel, Oxford Univ, 83-84; dep ed phys sci, Science, 85- *Mem:* Nat Acad Sci; Am Acad Arts & Sci; Am Chem Soc; Chem Soc; fel AAAS. *Res:* Physical organic chemistry; gas phase ionic reactions; electron photodetachment spectroscopy; reaction mechanisms. *Mailing Add:* Dept Chem Stanford Univ Stanford CA 94305-5080

BRAUMAN, SHARON K(RUSE), PHYSICAL ORGANIC CHEMISTRY. *Current Pos:* AT LOCKHEED RES LAB, 83- *Personal Data:* b Elizabeth, NJ, Apr 14, 39; m 64; c 1. *Educ:* Mt Holyoke Col, BA, 61; Univ Calif, Berkeley, PhD(org chem), 65. *Prof Exp:* Sr chemist, SRI Int, 65-83. *Concurrent Pos:* Lectr chem, Stanford Univ, 75-76. *Mem:* Am Chem Soc; AAAS. *Res:* Polymer degradation, combustion and fire retardance; biocompatible polymers; membrane transport; chemistry of difluoramino compounds. *Mailing Add:* Chem Dept Stanford Univ Stanford CA 94305-5080

BRAUN, ALVIN JOSEPH, PLANT PATHOLOGY. *Current Pos:* from asst prof to prof, 45-76, EMER PROF PLANT PATH, NY STATE AGR EXP STA, GENEVA, 76- *Personal Data:* b Chicago, Ill, July 10, 15; m 39, Edith K Neidle; c Kenneth, Robert & Andrea. *Educ:* Univ Chicago, BS, 37; Univ Wis, PhM, 38; Ore State Col, PhD(plant path), 47. *Prof Exp:* Asst, Univ Wis, 37-38 & Ore State Col, 38-42; analytical chemist, Sherwin-Williams Co, Ill, 42-43; asst pathologist, Guayule Res Proj, Bur Plant Indust, Soils & Agr Eng, USDA, Calif, 43-44, pathologist, 44-45. *Concurrent Pos:* Agr off, Food & Agr Orgn, UN, Res & Training Ctr for Rice Prod, Bangkok, Thailand, 66-67; vis prof, Res Inst Pomol, Poland, 75. *Mem:* Am Phytopath Soc; Sigma Xi. *Res:* Fungus and virus diseases; nematode and physiological problems of small fruits and grapes; fungicides; fumigants; spray machinery. *Mailing Add:* 509 North St Geneva NY 14456

BRAUN, CHARLES LOUIS, PHYSICAL CHEMISTRY. *Current Pos:* res instr, 65-66, chair, dept chem, 82-85, from asst prof to assoc prof, 66-72, PROF CHEM, DARTMOUTH COL, 77- *Personal Data:* b Webster, SDak, June 4, 37; m 58; c 2. *Educ:* SDak Sch Mines & Technol, BS, 59; Univ Minn, PhD(phys chem), 63. *Prof Exp:* Chief process control training sect, Eng Reactors Group, US Army, Ft Belvoir, Va, 64-65. *Concurrent Pos:* Dartmouth Col fac fel, Phys Inst, Univ Stuttgart, 69-70; vis prof, dept chem, Cornell Univ, 79-80; consult, Eastman Kodak Co, 79- *Mem:* Am Chem Soc; Am Phys Soc. *Res:* Photoionization and photoconductivity in molecular liquids and solids; electronically excited states of organic molecules. *Mailing Add:* Dept Chem Dartmouth Col Hanover NH 03755-1477

BRAUN, CLAIT E, WILDLIFE BIOLOGY. *Current Pos:* wildlife researcher, 73-80, WILDLIFE RES LEADER, COL DIV WILDLIFE, 81- *Personal Data:* b Kansas City, Mo, Oct 4, 39; m 60, Nancy J Kitzmiller; c Jennifer A, Clait R & Laurel R. *Educ:* Kans State Univ, BS, 62; Univ Mont, MS, 65; Colo State Univ, PhD(wildlife biol), 69. *Honors & Awards:* USDA Soil Conserv Serv Merit Award, 65; Prof Award, CMPS, Wildlife Soc, 89. *Prof Exp:* Soil scientist, Soil Conserv Serv, 61-69; asst wildlife researcher, Colo Div Game, Fish & Parks, 69-73. *Concurrent Pos:* Assoc, Mont Forest Conserv Exp Sta, 63-65, Am Mus Natural Hist, 69-70 & Inst Arctic & Alpine Res, 70-79; mem grad fac, Colo State Univ, 69-; ed, J Wildlife Mgt, 81-83. *Mem:* AAAS; Wildlife Soc (vpres, 95-96, pres, 96-97); Am Soc Mammal; Cooper Ornith Soc; Wilson Ornith Soc (pres, 83-84); Am Ornith Union. *Res:* Population ecology of grouse, native columbids and alpine ecology. *Mailing Add:* Wildlife Res Ctr 317 W Prospect Rd Ft Collins CO 80526. *Fax:* 970-490-2621

BRAUN, DONALD E, ANALYTICAL CHEMISTRY. *Current Pos:* PROF CHEM, PAC COL, CALIF, 57- *Personal Data:* b Dinuba, Calif, Dec 15, 30; m 56; c 2. *Educ:* Fresno State Col, AB, 52, MA, 54; Univ of the Pac, PhD(chem), 65. *Prof Exp:* Lab technician, Biochem & Virus Lab, Univ Calif, Berkeley, 54-55; med technician, Bethel Deaconess Hosp, Newton, Kans, 56-57. *Concurrent Pos:* NSF lab asst, Univ of the Pac, 63, partic, NSF res participation chem teachers, Ore State Univ, 68-69; consult, Braun, Skaffs & Kevorkian, 66- *Mem:* Am Chem Soc. *Res:* Development and refinement of analytical procedures in water and biochemical samples. *Mailing Add:* Fresno Pac Col Fresno CA 93702-4798

BRAUN, DONALD PETER, CANCER IMMUNOLOGY, MACROPHAGE IMMUNOBIOLOGY IN CANCER. *Current Pos:* asst prof oncol, 78-82, assoc prof, 83-87, ASSOC PROF ONCOL & IMMUNOL, RUSH MED COL, 87-, DIR, RES PROG DEVELOP, RUSH CANCER INST, PROF MED & IMMUNOL MICROBIOL, 93- *Personal Data:* b New York, NY, Mar 7, 50; m 74; c 3. *Educ:* Univ Ill, Urbana, BS, 72; Univ Ill, MS, 74 & PhD(microbiol), 76. *Prof Exp:* Instr immunol, Univ Ill Med Ctr, 76-78. *Concurrent Pos:* Mem, Small Bus Innovations Rev, Nat Cancer Inst, 83-85, Exp Therapeut Study Sect, 84-, Ariz Dis Control Comn, 86-88, Exp Immunol Study Sect Am Cancer Soc, 94. *Mem:* NY Acad Sci; Am Asn Cancer Res; AAAS; Am Soc Reproductive Med; Soc Biol Res Modifers; Am Chem Soc. *Res:* Elucidating how malignant disease influence immune function in patients with solid tumors; patients with AIDS; patients with endometriosis. *Mailing Add:* Sect Med Oncol Rush Med Col Suite 821 Prof Bldg Chicago IL 60612. *Fax:* 312-942-3192

BRAUN, ELDON JOHN, PHYSIOLOGY, COMPARATIVE PHYSIOLOGY. *Current Pos:* Asst prof, 72-77, ASSOC PROF PHYSIOL, COL MED, UNIV ARIZ, 77- *Personal Data:* b Glen Ullin, NDak, Jan 14, 37. *Educ:* Concordia Col, Moorhead, Minn, BA, 60; Univ Ariz, PhD(zool, biochem), 69. *Concurrent Pos:* NIH fel, Univ Ariz Col Med, 69-72. *Mem:* Am Ornith Union; Cooper Ornith Soc; Am Soc Nephrology; Int Nephrology Soc; Am Physiol Soc. *Res:* Comparative renal physiology; regulation of individual nephron function; measurement of single nephron glomerular filtration rates; function of countercurrent multiplier system changes in intrarenal blood flow patterns. *Mailing Add:* Dept Physiol Univ Ariz Health Sci Ctr PO Box 245051 Tucson AZ 85724-5051. *Fax:* 520-626-4884

BRAUN, JANET K, ZOOLOGY, MAMMALOGY. *Current Pos:* Curatorial specialist, 85-95, STAFF CUR, OKLA MUS NATURAL HIST, 95- *Personal Data:* b Kittery, Maine, June 8, 56. *Educ:* Univ Memphis, BS, 78, MS, 84; Univ Okla, PhD(biol), 93. *Concurrent Pos:* Fulbright scholar, Nat Univ Tucuman, Arg, 95, Crigyt, Mendoza, Argentina, 96. *Mem:* Am Women Sci; Am Soc Mammologists; Soc Systematic Zool; Southwestern Asn Naturalists. *Res:* Mammal systematics, evolution and natural history. *Mailing Add:* Okla Mus Nat Hist Univ Okla 1335 Asp Ave Norman OK 73019. *Fax:* 405-325-7699; *E-Mail:* jkbraun@ou.edu

BRAUN, JOSEPH CARL, nuclear science & engineering, for more information see previous edition

BRAUN, JUERGEN HANS, INORGANIC CHEMISTRY, PHYSICAL CHEMISTRY. *Current Pos:* From res chemist to sr res chemist, 55-71, RES ASSOC, CHEM & PIGMENTS DEPT, E I DU PONT DE NEMOURS & CO, INC, 71- *Personal Data:* b Hof, Ger, Nov 6, 27; US citizen; div; c 3. *Educ:* Tech Univ, Berlin, Dipl Ing, 51; Univ Tex, PhD(inorg chem), 56. *Honors & Awards:* Roon Found Award, Fedn Socs Coatings Technol, 89. *Mem:* Am Chem Soc. *Res:* Hydrothermal crystallization; crystal growth of semiconductors; chemistry of liquid ammonia; small particle technology; technology of white and colored pigments; pigment optics. *Mailing Add:* 614 Loveville Rd Bldg E Apt 1H Hockessin DE 19707-1616

BRAUN, LEWIS TIMOTHY, ECONOMIC GEOLOGY. *Current Pos:* CONSULT, 85- *Personal Data:* b Sacramento, Calif, Oct 27, 23; m 50; c 3. *Educ:* Univ Calif, Berkeley, BS, 48. *Prof Exp:* Jr geologist, Atlantic Refining Co, Wyo, 48-49; asst mining geologist, Calif Div Mines, 49-51; geologist, Geophoto Serv, Inc, Colo, 51-55, proj mgr, Cagayan Basin, Geophoto Explor, Ltd, Philippines, 55-57; admin geologist, Geophoto Serv, Inc, 57-59, chief geologist, Geophoto Serv, Ltd, Alta, 59-64, proj mgr, Geophoto Serv, Inc, 64-71, dep mgr, Geophoto, Australia, 71-72, mgr, Geophoto Serv, Dallas, 72-77; explor geologist, Tex Pac Oil Co, Inc, Denver, 77-80; geol mgr, Hrubetz Oil Co, Denver, 80-85. *Mem:* Am Asn Petrol Geologists; Am Inst Prof Geologists; fel Geol Soc Am; Can Soc Petrol Geologists. *Res:* Regional stratigraphic and structural geology and its relation to petroleum, mineral deposits and geothermal energy. *Mailing Add:* 7950 E Bethany Pl Denver CO 80234

BRAUN, LOREN L, ORGANIC CHEMISTRY. *Current Pos:* from asst prof to assoc prof, 57-66, PROF CHEM, IDAHO STATE UNIV, 66- *Personal Data:* b Waseca, Minn, June 12, 29; m 64; c 3. *Educ:* Mankato State Col, BS, 51; Univ Nebr, MS, 53, PhD(chem), 56. *Prof Exp:* Chemist, Mead Johnson & Co, 56-57. *Mem:* Am Chem Soc; Sigma Xi. *Res:* Aliphatic diazo compounds; N-Bromosuccinimide reactions; nitrogen bridgehead compounds. *Mailing Add:* 1242 E Alameda Rd Pocatello ID 83201-3028

BRAUN, LUDWIG, TECHNOLOGY IN EDUCATION. *Current Pos:* RETIRED. *Personal Data:* b Brooklyn, NY, May 14, 26; m 47, Eva M Taylor; c Barbara A, Edith E, Anne C & John L. *Educ:* Polytech Inst Brooklyn, BS, 50, MS, 55, DEE, 59. *Honors & Awards:* Paul Pair Award, 91. *Prof Exp:* Elec engr, Allied Control Co, 50-51; elec engr, Anton Electronics Labs, 51-52, head, Electronics Dept, 52-55; from instr to prof elec eng, Polytech Inst Brooklyn, 55-72; dir, Huntington Three Comput Proj, State Univ NY, Stony Brook, 81-82, prof eng, 72-82, dir, Lab Persona Comput Educ, 79-82; prof comput sci, Acad Comput Lab, NY Inst Technol, 82-87; res prof, NY Univ, 87-89. *Concurrent Pos:* Sr lectr, Dept Med, State Univ NY Downstate Med Ctr; mem prof staff, Dept Med, Kings County Hosp; consult, Grumman Aircraft Eng Co, 59-61, Gen Elec Co, 62-65, McGraw-Hill, 70-72, Albert Einstein Med Ctr, Nat Inst Educ & Div Sci Educ Develop & Res, NSF & Int Bus Mach, 78-94. *Mem:* Int Soc Technol in Educ; Sigma Xi; Nat Sci Teachers Asn. *Res:* Feedback control theory; system analysis and design; medical engineering; technology in education; simulation; educational policy. *Mailing Add:* 11 Parsons Dr Dix Hills NY 11746. *Fax:* 516-243-0248; *E-Mail:* ludbraun@ix.netcom.com

BRAUN, MARTIN, APPLIED MATHEMATICS. *Current Pos:* asst prof, 75-80, assoc prof, 80-85, PROF MATH, QUEENS COL CITY UNIV NEW YORK, 86- *Personal Data:* b New York, NY, July 26, 41. *Educ:* Yeshiva Univ, BA, 63; NY Univ, MS, 65, PhD(math), 68. *Prof Exp:* Instr math, NY Univ, 67-68 & Courant Inst Math Sci, 68; asst res prof appl math, Brown Univ, 68-70, asst prof, 70-75. *Mem:* Soc Indust & Appl Math; Am Math Soc. *Res:* Qualitative theory of ordinary differential equations. *Mailing Add:* Dept Math Queens Col City Univ NY Flushing NY 11367

BRAUN, PETER ERIC, BIOLOGICAL MEMBRANES, NEUROBIOLOGY. *Current Pos:* assoc prof, 73-83, PROF BIOCHEM, MCGILL UNIV, MONTREAL, 84- *Personal Data:* b BC, May 24, 39; m 79; c 2. *Educ:* Univ BC, Vancouver, BScP, 61, MSc, 64; Univ Calif, Berkeley, PhD(biochem), 67. *Prof Exp:* Asst prof biochem, Univ Pa, Philadelphia, 69-73. *Mem:* Am Soc Biol Chem; Am Soc Neurochem; Soc Neurosci. *Res:* Biological assembly of neural membranes; structure and function of myelin; demyelinating and dysmyelinating disorders. *Mailing Add:* Dept Biochem McGill Univ 3655 Drummond St Montreal PQ H3G 1Y6 Can. *Fax:* 514-398-7384

BRAUN, PHYLLIS C, MYCOLOGY. *Current Pos:* from asst prof to assoc prof, 80-89, PROF MOLECULAR BIOL, DEPT BIOL, FAIRFIELD UNIV, 89- *Personal Data:* b Bridgeport, Conn, Jan 19, 53; m 75, Kevin F; c Ryan C & Jessica P. *Educ:* Fairfield Univ, BS, 75; Georgetown Univ, PhD(microbiol), 78. *Prof Exp:* Postdoctoral fel, Health Ctr, Univ Conn, 78-80. *Concurrent Pos:* Consult, Int Schoeffel Industs, 84-86 & Miles Pharmaceut, 84-90. *Mem:* Am Soc Microbiol; NY Acad Sci; Med Mycol Asn Am; AAAS; Am Asn Women Sci. *Res:* Determining the mode of action of antifungal compounds and the action of these agents on the regulation of chitin synthetase, a membrane bound enzyme found in most fungii. *Mailing Add:* Dept Biol Fairfield Univ Fairfield CT 06430. *Fax:* 203-254-4126

BRAUN, RICHARD JOSEPH, APPLICATIONS OF MATHEMATICS TO VISCOUS FLUID FLOW & PHASE CHANGE PROBLEMS. *Current Pos:* ASST PROF MATH, UNIV DEL, 95- *Personal Data:* b Redding, Calif, Oct 13, 61; m 85, Mary Duffy; c Rebecca D & Elise C. *Educ:* Santa Clara Univ, BS, 83, MS, 87; Northwestern Univ, PhD(appl math), 91. *Prof Exp:* Engr, Hewlett Packard Co, 84-87; Nat Res Coun postdoctoral fel, Nat Inst Stand & Technol, 91-93, res mathematician, 93-95. *Concurrent Pos:* Res mathematician, Nat Inst Stand & Technol, 96- *Mem:* Am Phys Soc; Soc Indust & Appl Math; Am Soc Mech Engrs; Am Asn Crystal Growth. *Res:* Computational and asymptotic methods theories of viscous free surface flows such as spreading and drainage; theories of phase change like solidification and ordering. *Mailing Add:* Dept Math Sci Univ Del Newark DE 19716-2553. *Fax:* 302-831-4511; *E-Mail:* braun@math.udel.edu

BRAUN, RICHARD P, INTELLIGENT TRANSPORTATION SYSTEMS, TRANSPORTATION MANAGEMENT. *Current Pos:* RETIRED. *Educ:* Univ Minn, BSCE, 48, MSCE, 55. *Honors & Awards:* James Laurie Prize, Am Soc Civil Engrs, 94; John I Parcel-Leif J Severdrup Civil Eng Mgt Award, 97. *Prof Exp:* Comnr transp, State of Minn, 79-86; chmn, Twin Cities Area Metrop Airports Comn, 92-94. *Concurrent Pos:* Spec consult transp. *Mailing Add:* 1275 Lincoln Terr NE Columbia Heights MN 55421. *Fax:* 612-631-8958

BRAUN, ROBERT DENTON, ANALYTICAL & CORROSION CHEMISTRY, ELECTROCHEMISTRY. *Current Pos:* from asst prof to assoc prof 77-86, PROF CHEM UNIV SOUTHWESTERN LA, 86- *Personal Data:* b Santa Ana, Calif, June 28, 43; div. *Educ:* Univ Colo, BA, 65; Univ Conn, MS, 70, PhD(analytical chem), 72. *Prof Exp:* High sch teacher, Conn, 65-66; instr & fel anal chem, Univ Mich, 72-73; vis asst prof anal chem, Univ Ill, 73-74; asst prof chem, Vassar Col, 74-77. *Mem:* Electrochem Soc; Am Chem Soc; Sigma Xi; NY Acad Sci; Nat Assoc Corrosion Engrs; Am Waterwork Asn. *Res:* Electrochemistry of biochemical compounds; electrochemistry and electroanalysis in nonaqueous solvents; corrosion. *Mailing Add:* Dept Chem Univ Southwestern La Box 4-4370 Lafayette LA 70504-4370. *Fax:* 318-482-5676; *E-Mail:* rdbraun@usl.edu

BRAUN, ROBERT LEORE, PHYSICAL CHEMISTRY, COMPUTER MODELING. *Current Pos:* CHEMIST, LAWRENCE LIVERMORE NAT LAB, 66- *Personal Data:* b New England, NDak, Dec 25, 36; m 62; c 2. *Educ:* Univ Wash, BS, 59, PhD(phys chem), 66. *Honors & Awards:* Robert Peele Mem Award, Am Inst Mining, Metall & Petrol Engrs, 75. *Prof Exp:* Chemist, Hanford Labs, Gen Elec Co & Pac Northwest Labs, Battelle Mem Inst, 59-66. *Mem:* Am Inst Chem Engrs. *Res:* Computer modeling of physical and chemical processes related to recovery of natural resources. *Mailing Add:* 2529 Glen Isle Ave Vallejo CA 94591

BRAUN, WALTER G(USTAV), CHEMICAL ENGINEERING, PETROLEUM REFINING. *Current Pos:* asst petrol refining, Pa State Univ, 43-47, from instr to assoc res prof, 47-76, asst dean, Col Eng, 70-74, prof, 74-80, EMER PROF CHEM ENG & ASSOC DEAN INSTR, PA STATE UNIV, 80- *Personal Data:* b Springfield, Mass, June 23, 17; m 48, Gloria McCurdy; c Karen B (Edenfield) & Kenneth W. *Educ:* Cooper Union, BChE, 42; Pa State Univ, MS, 48, PhD(chem eng), 55. *Prof Exp:* Jr chemist, Tidewater Assoc Oil Co, 36-42. *Mem:* Fel Am Inst Chemists; Am Chem Soc; Am Inst Chem Engrs; Am Soc Eng Educ; Sigma Xi. *Res:* Raman and absorption spectroscopy; mass transfer; petroleum refining; thermodynamics. *Mailing Add:* 500 E Marylyn Ave No 74E State College PA 16801-6269

BRAUN, WERNER HEINZ, PHARMACOKINETICS, TOXICOLOGY. *Current Pos:* sr res chemist metab, Dow Chem USA, 72-77, group leader, 77-82, health & environmental affairs mgr, 82-88, biotransformation, Div Toxicol, 77-92, ENVIRON ISSUES MGR, DOW CHEM USA, 92- *Personal Data:* b Stuttgart, Ger, Mar 29, 45; US citizen; m 66; c 4. *Educ:* St Edward's Univ, BS, 67. *Prof Exp:* Anal chem, Dow Life Sci, 67-79, res chemist spectros, 69-72. *Mem:* Soc Toxicol. *Res:* Application of pharmacokinetics and metabolism to hazard assessment. *Mailing Add:* 3413 Greenbrier Terr Midland MI 48642

BRAUN, WILLI KARL, MICROPALEONTOLOGY, STRATIGRAPHY. *Current Pos:* from asst prof to assoc prof, 64-74, prof paleont & stratig, 74-93, EMER PROF, UNIV SASK, 93- *Personal Data:* b Reutlingen, WGer, Sept 22, 31; m 58; c 3. *Educ:* Univ Tuebingen, WGer, Dr rer nat, 58. *Prof Exp:* From paleontologist to sr paleontologist, Shell Can Ltd, Alta, 58-64. *Concurrent Pos:* Consult to oil co, 64- *Mem:* Fel Geol Soc Am; Paleont Soc; Brit Palaeont Asn; fel Geol Asn Can. *Res:* Paleozoic and Jurassic-Lower Cretaceous microfaunas and biostratigraphy of Western and Arctic Canada; tertiary to recent microfaunas and biostratigraphy of Mackenzie Delta-Beaufort Sea region, Arctic Canada. *Mailing Add:* Dept Geol Univ Sask Saskatoon SK S7N 0W0 Can

BRAUNDMEIER, ARTHUR JOHN, JR, PHYSICS. *Current Pos:* Assoc prof, 70-80, PROF PHYSICS, SOUTHERN ILL UNIV, EDWARDSVILLE, 80- *Personal Data:* b Granite City, Ill, Feb 28, 43; m 64; c 1. *Educ:* Eastern Ill Univ, BSEd, 65; Univ Tenn, Knoxville, MS, 69; Oak Ridge Assoc Univ, PhD(physics), 70. *Concurrent Pos:* Consult, Oak Ridge Nat Lab, 71- *Mem:* Am Phys Soc; Am Asn Physics Teachers; Optical Soc Am; Health Physics Soc; Am Vacuum Soc. *Res:* Vacuum and thin film technology; optical constants of solids in the vacuum ultraviolet; solid state plasma oscillations; spectroscopy as a tool for measuring air pollution; detectors for ultraviolet radiation. *Mailing Add:* Dept Physics Southern Ill Univ Edwardsville IL 62026-1002

BRAUNE, MAXIMILLIAN O, VIROLOGY, IMMUNOCHEMISTRY. *Current Pos:* RETIRED. *Personal Data:* b Bethlehem, Pa, Nov 21, 32; m 61; c 1. *Educ:* Moravian Col, BS, 55; Univ Maine, MS, 58; Pa State Univ, PhD(bact, biochem), 63. *Prof Exp:* Instr rest vet sci, Pa State Univ, University Park, 58-63, asst prof vet sci, 63- *Mem:* AAAS; Am Soc Microbiol; Sigma Xi. *Res:* Isolation and serological relationships of pleuropneumonia-like organisms; differential diagnosis of viral respiratory diseases by fluorescent antibody techniques. *Mailing Add:* Paradise Valley Gardiner MT 59030

BRAUNER, KENNETH MARTIN, ANALYTICAL CHEMISTRY. *Current Pos:* RETIRED. *Personal Data:* b San Francisco, Calif, Dec 29, 27; m 54, Deesse Watson; c Clark D, Lisa K (Averett) & Alison E (Larson). *Educ:* Univ Calif, BS, 49; Univ Chicago, PhD, 59. *Prof Exp:* Chemist, A Schilling & Co, 49-50 & Tidewater Assoc Oil Co, 52-53; res chemist, E I du Pont de Nemours & Co, 57-63; chief chem div, Dugway Proving Ground, 63-90. *Mem:* Soc Appl Spectros. *Res:* Electrochemistry; trace analyses; chemical separations; physical methods of analysis. *Mailing Add:* 1675 E Granada Dr Sandy UT 84093-3743

BRAUNER, PHYLLIS AMBLER, ANALYTICAL CHEMISTRY, INORGANIC CHEMISTRY. *Current Pos:* RETIRED. *Personal Data:* b Natick, Mass, Oct 2, 16; m 43; c 2. *Educ:* Wheaton Col, BA, 38; Wellesley Col, MA, 40; Boston Univ, PhD, 59. *Honors & Awards:* Hill Award, Am Chem Soc. *Prof Exp:* Head, Sci Dept, Winnwood Sch, NY, 39; analytical chemist, Bellevue Hosp, 41; asst, Purdue Univ, 41-43; analytical chemist, Gen Elec Co, Mass, 44-45; asst, Northeastern Univ, 45-46; instr, Swarthmore Col, 46-48; asst chem, Simmons Col, 49-51, from instr to assoc prof, 51-66, prof, 67-83, emer prof chem, 83. *Concurrent Pos:* NSF fel, Switz, 60-61; res assoc, Royal Inst Technol, Sweden, 64-65; vis res assoc, Swiss Fed Inst Water Res & Water Pollution Control, 70-71; vis lectr chem, Framingham-Mass State Col; teacher, Univ Md, Overseas Prog, Japan & Gaum, 84. *Mem:* AAAS; Am Chem Soc. *Res:* Physical methods of analysis; complexometry and homogeneous precipitation; solution equilibria; ionic speciation in natural waters; preparation of complex inorganic compounds. *Mailing Add:* 15 Benton St Wellesley MA 02181-6903

BRAUNFELD, PETER GEORGE, mathematics, for more information see previous edition

BRAUNLICH, PETER FRITZ, EXPERIMENTAL SOLID STATE PHYSICS, ATOMIC PHYSICS. *Current Pos:* from assoc prof to prof, 76-90, ADJ PROF PHYSICS, WASH STATE UNIV, 90- *Personal Data:* b Ger, Feb 25, 37; m 63, Elke Rumpf; c Andreas & Kristina. *Educ:* Univ Marburg, pre-dipl, 58; Univ Giessen, dipl, 61, Dr rer nat(physics), 63. *Prof Exp:* Sci asst physics, Univ Giessen, 63-65; res assoc, mat res lab, Pa State Univ, 65-66; sr physicist, 66-70, sr proj physicist, Bendix Res Labs, 70-75, sr prin scientist, 75-76. *Concurrent Pos:* Adj prof eng sci, Wayne State Univ, 74-76; pres, Int Sensor Technol, 82- *Mem:* Am Phys Soc. *Res:* Luminescence; thermally stimulated processes; photoconductivity; electron kinetics; exolectron emission; laser spectroscopy; interaction of laser light with matter; surface physics; dosimetry. *Mailing Add:* Res & Tech Pk Int Sensor Technol Inc NE 1425 Terre View Dr Pullman WA 99163. *Fax:* 509-335-7237

BRAUN-MUNZINGER, PETER, NUCLEAR STRUCTURE. *Current Pos:* From asst prof to assoc prof, 78-82, PROF PHYSICS, STATE UNIV NY, STONY BROOK, 82- *Personal Data:* b Heidelburg, Germany, Aug 26, 46. *Educ:* Univ Heidelburg, PhD(physics), 72. *Mem:* Am Phys Soc. *Res:* Nuclear Physics; physics with relativistic heavy ions. *Mailing Add:* Dept Physics State Univ NY Stony Brook NY 11794

BRAUNSCHWEIGER, CHRISTIAN CARL, MATHEMATICS EDUCATION. *Current Pos:* chmn dept, 70-73, prof math, 67-93, EMER PROF, MARQUETTE UNIV, 93- *Personal Data:* b Wellsville, NY, Oct 18, 26; m 53, H Patricia Kearns; c Michael V, Susan K B (Hickman), Kathleen A B (Piel), Steven C & Mary Pat B (Hall). *Educ:* Alfred Univ, BA, 50; Univ Wis, MS, 51, PhD(math), 55. *Prof Exp:* Teaching asst, Univ Wis, 52-55; instr math, Purdue Univ, 55-57; from asst prof to assoc prof, Univ Del, 57-67. *Concurrent Pos:* NSF fac fel, Univ Heidelberg, 64-65 & Univ Tubingen, 80-81. *Mem:* Am Math Soc; Math Asn Am. *Res:* Functional analysis and topology; geometric models of abstract linear topological spaces. *Mailing Add:* Dept Math Statist & Comput Sci Marquette Univ PO Box 1881 Milwaukee WI 53233-1881

BRAUNSCHWEIGER, PAUL G, CELL & TUMOR BIOLOGY. *Current Pos:* ASSOC PROF & CHIEF, DIV LAB RES, DEPT RADIOLOGICAL ONCOL, UNIV MIAMI, 90- *Personal Data:* b Troy, Ohio, Oct 18, 47; m 69, 88; c 3. *Educ:* State Univ NY, Buffalo, BA, 69, PhD(radiation biol), 74. *Prof Exp:* Fel, Allegheny-Singer Res Corp, Allegheny Gen Hosp, 74-75, res assoc, 75-76, asst biologist, 76-77, assoc biologist cell kinetics, 77-81, sr staff scientist, Cancer Res Lab, 81-82, chief, Exp Therapeut AMC Cancer Ctr, 82-90. *Concurrent Pos:* Instr physiol, LaRouche Col, 78-79. *Mem:* AAAS; Radiation Res Soc; Am Asn Cancer Res; Cell Kinetics Soc; Sigma Xi; Soc Magnetic Resonance Imaging. *Mailing Add:* Dept Radiol Oncol D-31 PO Box 016960 Miami FL 33101

BRAUNSTEIN, DAVID MICHAEL, ORGANIC CHEMISTRY, POLYMER CHEMISTRY. *Current Pos:* MGR RES & ENG, TECHNOL DEVELOP & PLANNING, ARCO CHEM CO, 79- *Personal Data:* b New York, NY, Dec 9, 42; m 65, Diana; c Miriam & Neil. *Educ:* Polytech Inst Brooklyn, BS, 64; Purdue Univ, PhD(org chem), 68. *Prof Exp:* Assoc chemist, Gen Foods Corp, 64; res chemist, Celanese Corp Am, 68-74, group leader, 74-76, res assoc, 76-77; proj mgr, Shell Develop Co, 77-78; dir res & develop, Certainteed Corp, 78-79. *Concurrent Pos:* Adj prof, Middlesex County Col, 71, Richmond Col, City Univ New York, 71. *Mem:* Am Chem Soc. *Res:* Polymer product and process development; thermoplastic resins, structural foams; stabilization, fire retardants; regulatory agency approvals; technical liaison with foreign affiliates; organic derivative synthesis; urethane chemistry. *Mailing Add:* 540 Green Hill Lane Berwyn PA 19312-1958. *Fax:* 610-359-3374; *E-Mail:* cnsdmba@arcochem.com

BRAUNSTEIN, GLENN DAVID, ENDOCRINOLOGY. *Current Pos:* from asst prof to assoc prof, 73-81, PROF MED, UNIV CALIF, LOS ANGELES, 81- *Personal Data:* b Greenville, Tex, Feb 29, 44; m 65, Jacquelyn Moose; c Scott M & Jeffrey T. *Educ:* Univ Calif, San Francisco, BS, 65, MD, 68. *Prof Exp:* Med intern, Peter Bent Brigham Hosp, Boston, 68, med resident, 69; clin assoc, Reproduction Res Br, NIH, 70-72; chief resident endocrinol, Harbor Gen Hosp, 72-73. *Concurrent Pos:* Dir, Div Endocrinol, Cedars Sinai Med Ctr, 73-86, chmn, Dept Med, 86- *Mem:* Am Col Physicians; Endocrine Soc; Am Fedn Clin Res; Am Soc Clin Invest; Am Fert Soc; Am Asn Physicians. *Res:* Ectopic hormone production; placental endocrinology; fertility regulation. *Mailing Add:* Dept Med Rm B118 8700 Beverly Blvd Los Angeles CA 90048. *Fax:* 310-289-5207; *E-Mail:* braunstein@csms.edu

BRAUNSTEIN, HELEN MENTCHER, SCIENCE WRITING, INFORMATION SCIENCE. *Current Pos:* RETIRED. *Personal Data:* b NY, Feb 5, 25; m 45; c 3. *Educ:* Univ Maine, BA, 64, MS, 65, PhD(phys chem), 71. *Prof Exp:* Res assoc solution chem, Reactor Chem Div, Oak Ridge Nat Lab, 72-73; document coordr environ & health sci, Environ Resource Ctr, Oak Ridge Nat Lab, 74-83. *Mem:* Am Chem Soc; Am Soc Info Sci; AAAS; Soc Tech Info; Sigma Xi. *Res:* Environmental and health literature research. *Mailing Add:* 101 Parsons Rd Oak Ridge TN 37830

BRAUNSTEIN, HERBERT, PATHOLOGY, MICROBIOLOGY & INFECTIOUS DISEASES. *Current Pos:* RETIRED. *Personal Data:* b New York, NY, Jan 10, 26; m 54; c 4. *Educ:* City Univ New York, BS, 44; Hahnemann Univ Med Col, MD, 50. *Prof Exp:* Intern, Montefiore Hosp, New York, 50-51; asst resident path, Univ Mich, 51-52; resident, Univ Cincinnati, 52-54, from instr to assoc prof, 54-64, dir, Inter-Dept Path Res Lab, 56-64; prof path, Chicago Med Sch & dir, Dept Path, Michael Reese Hosp & Med Ctr, 64-65; from assoc prof to prof, Univ Ky, 65-70; clin prof path, Sch Med, Univ Calif, Los Angeles, 75-83, prof-in residence biomed sci, Univ Calif, Riverside, 78-83; dir labs, San Bernardino Co Gen Hosp, 70-88; clin prof path, Med Sch, Loma Linda Univ, 70-92. *Concurrent Pos:* Fel gastroenterol, Univ Cincinnati, 52-54; USPHS res career develop award, 58-64; asst & actg chief path, Vet Admin Hosp, 54-56, attend pathologist,

56-64; admin supvr, Cent Labs, Cincinnati Gen Hosp, 56-64. *Mem:* Col Am Pathologists; Am Asn Pathologists; Histochem Soc; US-Can Acad Path; Am Soc Clin Path; Sigma Xi. *Res:* Pathology of diseases of liver and cardiovascular systems; histochemistry of neoplasms and cardiovascular system; clinical microbiology and infectious diseases. *Mailing Add:* 28372 Via Anzar San Juan Capistrano CA 92675-2936

BRAUNSTEIN, JERRY, PHYSICAL CHEMISTRY. *Current Pos:* group leader, Chem Div, 66-90, CONSULT, OAK RIDGE NAT LAB, 92- *Personal Data:* b New York, NY, Dec 24, 22; m 45, 77, Catherine Vallet; c Arthur, David, Michael & Sarah. *Educ:* City Col New York, BS, 42; Wesleyan Univ, MA, 47; Northwestern Univ, PhD(chem), 51. *Prof Exp:* Chemist, Manhattan Proj, Columbia Univ, 42-45; fel chem, Univ Wash, 50-52; physicist, Gen Elec Co, 52-54; from asst prof to prof chem, Univ Maine, 54-66. *Concurrent Pos:* Res assoc, Oak Ridge Nat Lab, 60-61; lectr molten salt chem, Northampton Col Advan Technol, London, 64; lectr chem, Univ Maine, 66-; ed, Advan Molten Salt Chem, 70-87; Chmn, Gordon Res Conf Molten Salt, 79. *Mem:* AAAS; Am Chem Soc; fel Am Inst Chem; Electrochem Soc. *Res:* Molten salts; thermodynamics; electrochemistry; concentrated aqueous electrolytes; solution chemistry; theoretical chemistry. *Mailing Add:* 432 Farmers Hollow Rd Clinton TN 37716. *E-Mail:* 102510.3341@compuserve.com

BRAUNSTEIN, JOSEPH DAVID, IMMUNOLOGY, CELL BIOLOGY. *Current Pos:* CLIN CHEM, JERSEY CITY MED CTR, 93- *Personal Data:* b Long Island City, NY, Sept 19, 43; m 79; c 2. *Educ:* Cornell Univ, BA, 64; Univ Minn, PhD(chem), 72. *Prof Exp:* Asst Hebrew Univ, Jerusalem, 71-72; res assoc cell immunol, Sloan Kettering Inst, NY, 73-77; res assoc cell biol, Albert Einstein Med Sch, 77-81; asst prof path, Montefiore Hosp, 81-88; asst dir chem, Mt Sinai Hosp, 88-92. *Mem:* Am Asn Immunol; Am Asn Clin Chem; NY Acad Sci. *Res:* Investigation of the relationship between the biochemistry, cell biology and endocrinology of cancer to the immune system. *Mailing Add:* 19 Ellsworth Ave Yonkers NY 10705

BRAUNSTEIN, RUBIN, PHYSICS. *Current Pos:* PROF PHYSICS, UNIV CALIF, LOS ANGELES, 64- *Personal Data:* b New York, NY, May 6, 22; m 48. *Educ:* NY Univ, BS, 48; Syracuse Univ, MS, 51, PhD(physics), 54. *Prof Exp:* Asst physics, Syracuse Univ, 48-51, res asst molecular beams, 51-52; res assoc, Columbia Univ, 52-53; mem res staff, Solid State Physics, Radio Corp Am Labs, 53-64. *Concurrent Pos:* Consult, RCA Labs, 64-; Sci Res Coun fel, Oxford Univ, 74-75. *Mem:* AAAS; fel Am Phys Soc; NY Acad Sci. *Res:* Molecular beams; radiofrequency and microwave spectroscopy; solid state; quantum electronics. *Mailing Add:* Dept Physics Univ Calif 405 Hilgard Ave Los Angeles CA 90024

BRAUNWALD, EUGENE, INTERNAL MEDICINE, CARDIOLOGY. *Current Pos:* Hersey prof, Harvard Med Sch, 72-96, chmn dept, 80-96, Hermann Blumgart prof med, 80-89, DISTINGUISHED HERSEY PROF MED & FAC DEAN, BRIGHAM & WOMEN'S & MASS GEN HOSP, HARVARD MED SCH, 96-, SR PHYSICIAN, 96-; VPRES ACAD PROG, PARTNERS HEALTHCARE SYSTS, 96- *Personal Data:* b Vienna, Austria, Aug 15, 29; nat US; m 52; c 3. *Educ:* NY Univ, AB, 49, MD, 52; Am Bd Internal Med, 60; Am Bd Internal Med, Cardiovasc Dis, 65; FRCP, 79. *Hon Degrees:* MA, Harvard Univ, 72; MD, Univ Libson, 84, Univ Rome, 91, Med Sch, Univ Porto, 92, Nat Univ LaPlata, 95, Univ Vienna, 95; ScD, Mt Sinai Med Ctr, 91. *Honors & Awards:* Numerous named lectureships, 64-94; Einthoven Medal, Dutch Cardiac Soc, 70; Drake Achievement Award, 72; Res Achievement Award, Am Heart Asn, 72, James B Herrick Award, 81, Paul D White Award, 95; Lilly Medal, Royal Col Physicians, London, 79; Wiggers Award, Am Physiol Soc, 80; Distinguished Scientist Award, Am Col Cardiol, 86; Williams Award, Asn Prof Med, 87; Theordore E Cummings Mem Prize, 88; Bayer Outstanding Cardiovasc Mentor Award, 89; Ferrari Prize, 90; John Phillips Mem Award, Am Col Physicians, 91; Distinguished Achievement Cardiovasc Res, Bristol Myers Squibb, 93; J Allyn Taylor Int Prize Med, 93; George W Thorn Award, 95. *Prof Exp:* Intern & resident, Mt Sinai Hosp, NY, 52-54; clin assoc physiol, Nat Heart Inst, 55-57, resident med, 56-57; resident, Johns Hopkins Univ, 57-58, chief cardiol sect, Nat Heart Inst, 58-68, clin dir, 66-68; prof med & chmn dept, Sch Med, Univ Calif, San Diego, 68-72; physician in chief, Brigham & Beth Israel Hosp, 72-89. *Concurrent Pos:* Fel med, Columbia Univ, 54-55; lectr physiol, Sch Med, George Washington Univ, 59-62, med, Sch Med, Johns Hopkins Univ, 60-68; from asst clin prof to clin prof med, Sch Med, Georgetown Univ, 60-68; R T Hall vis prof, Cardiac Soc Australia & NZ, 61; Eastman vis prof, Univ Rochester, 63; vis prof med, numerous foreign & US Univs, 66-89; physician-in-chief pro team, Peter Bent Bringham Hosp, 68; mem, Expert Adv Panel Cardiovasc Dis, WHO, 68-92; mem, Pres Sci Adv Comt, Biol & Med Sci, Off Sci & Technol, White House, 69-72, Heart Dis, 72; Balfour vis prof, Mayo Clin & Found, Univ Minn, 70; mem, US/USSR Res Proj Heart Dis, Nat Heart & Lung Inst, 72; consult med, W Roxbury Vet Admin Med Ctr & Brockton Vet Admin Med Ctr, 72-90; consult cardiol, Children's Hosp Med Ctr, Boston, Mass, 72-92 & Brockton Ved Admin Med Ctr, 72-90; Sir Henry Dale vis prof, Med Sch, Johns Hopkins Univ, 73; Bromberg vis prof, Univ Tex Southwestern Med Sch, 73; chmn, Biomed Res & Training Comt, Asn Am Med Cols, 73-75; Morgan vis prof, Vanderbilt Univ, 74; James Howard Means vis prof, Mass Gen Hosp, 85; Zucker vis prof, Cornell Med Col, 92; Brautbar vis prof, Univ Southern Calif, 92; chmn, Expert Panel Clin Pract Guidlines Treatment Unstable Angina, Agency Health Care Policy & Res, 93-95; Simon Dack vis prof, Mt Sinai Med Ctr, 94; trustee, Partners Healthcare Syst, 94-, vpres acad progs, 96-; sr consult, Mass Gen Hosp, 95- *Mem:* Nat Acad Sci; Inst Med-Nat Acad Sci; master Am Col Physicians; Am Physiol Soc; Am Fedn Clin Res (pres, 69-70); fel Am Acad Arts & Sci; fel AAAS; Am Soc Clin Invest (pres, 74-75); Asn Am Physicians; Asn Prof Med (pres, 74-75); fel Am Col Chest Physicians; Am Soc Pharmacol & Exp Therapeut; Soc Exp Biol & Med; Royal Soc Med; Brit Cardiac Soc; Am Heart Asn; NY Acad Sci; Int Soc Cardiol; fel Am Col Cardiol (vpres, 67); hon mem Am Soc Internal Med. *Res:* Cardiovascular hemodynamics and diagnostic techniques; clinical cardiology. *Mailing Add:* Harvard Med Sch Boston MA 02115

BRAUSE, ALLAN R, FOOD CHEMISTRY. *Personal Data:* b New York, NY, July 27, 42; m 70; c 2. *Educ:* Polytech Inst Brooklyn, BS, 63; Univ Wis, MS, 65; Univ Cincinnati, PhD(org chem), 67. *Prof Exp:* Res chemist, Phys Res Lab, Dow Chem Co, 67-68; chemist, Coatings & Chems Lab, US Army, 68-70; chemist, Res Div, US Indust Chem Co, 70-72; sr food chemist, Kroger Co, 72-84; chief chemist, Unique Anal Serv, 84-85; chief analytical chemist, Gen Physics Corp, 85-89. *Mem:* Am Chem Soc; Asn Off Anal Chemists; Inst Food Technologists; Sigma Xi. *Res:* Verification of authenticity of natural products, especially fruit juices and vanilla, by instrumental analysis; food and flavor chemistry; nutritional analysis; vitamins and fats by gas chromatography and liquid chromatography. *Mailing Add:* 9151 Rumsey Rd No 190 Columbia MD 21045-1929

BRAUTH, STEVEN EARLE, NEUROPSYCHOLOGY. *Current Pos:* from asst prof to assoc prof psychol, 75-89, PROF, UNIV MD, COL PARK, 89- *Personal Data:* b Trenton, NJ, Apr 12, 47. *Educ:* Rensselaer Polytech Inst, BS, 67; NY Univ, PhD(psychol), 73. *Prof Exp:* Res fel biol, Calif Inst Technol, 72-74; res assoc anat, State Univ NY Stony Brook, 74-75. *Res:* Comparative neuroanatomy and neurophysiology of the vertebrate brain; study of the evolution of the brain-behavior relationships; comparative neurobiology of the basal ganglia. *Mailing Add:* Dept Psychol Univ Md Rm No 1145 B Zool-Psychol Bldg, 144 College Park MD 20742-0001

BRAUTIGAN, DAVID L, PROTEIN PHOSPHORYLATION, HORMONE ACTION. *Current Pos:* from asst prof to assoc prof, 81-91, PROF MED SCI, BROWN UNIV, 91- *Personal Data:* b Detroit, Mich, 1950. *Educ:* Kalamazoo Col, Mich, BA, 72; Northwestern Univ, BS, 73, PhD(biochem), 77. *Prof Exp:* Fel biochem, Univ Wash Med Sch, 77-80, res asst prof, 80-81. *Concurrent Pos:* Consult, Kemin Indust, Des Moines. *Mem:* AAAS; Am Chem Soc; Am Soc Biochem & Molecular Biol; Am Soc Cell Biol. *Res:* Mechanism of action of insulin and growth factors; protein phosphorylation of serine and tyrosine residue; protein phosphatases; protein structure and function. *Mailing Add:* Dir Ctr Cell Signaling Univ Va Box 577 Hospital W Charlottesville VA 22908-0001. *Fax:* 804-924-1236

BRAVENEC, EDWARD V, MATERIAL FAILURE ANALYSIS. *Current Pos:* VPRES ENGR, DIR & CONSULT, ANDERSON & ASSOC INC, 84- *Personal Data:* b Temple, Tex, Aug 25, 30; m 56, Aileen D Titsworth; c David. *Educ:* Univ Tex, El Paso, BS, 56; Univ Houston, MS, 61; Pac Western Univ, PhD(metall), 79. *Honors & Awards:* Meritorious Serv, Am Soc Mech Engrs. *Prof Exp:* Engr, Eastern State Petrol Co, 56-57; res metall, Hughes Tool Co, 57-58; mgr, metall, Armco, Inc. *Concurrent Pos:* Consult, Exxon, NASA, Prudential Life Ins, Union Carbide, et al, 84- *Mem:* Fel Am Soc Metals Int; fel Am Soc Mech Engrs; sr mem Am Soc Qual Control. *Res:* Material fracture mechanisms, material high-low temperature properties, corrosion properties, quality control and quality assurance management. *Mailing Add:* 206 Sleepy Hollow Ct Seabrook TX 77586. *Fax:* 713-481-9115

BRAVERMAN, IRWIN MERTON, MEDICINE, DERMATOLOGY. *Current Pos:* from asst prof to assoc prof, 62-73, PROF DERMAT, SCH MED, YALE UNIV, 73- *Personal Data:* b Boston, Mass, Apr 17, 29; m 55, Muriel Freedman; c Paula, David & Michael. *Educ:* Harvard Univ, BA, 51; Yale Univ, MD, 55. *Honors & Awards:* Taub Int Mem Award, 80; Litchfield lectr, Oxford Univ, 84; Master Dermat Award, Am Acad Dermat, 93. *Prof Exp:* Intern, Med Serv, Yale Hosp, 55-56, asst resident med, 58-59. *Concurrent Pos:* Helen Hay Whitney Found res fel dermat, Sch Med, Yale Univ, 59-62; vis scientist, Dept Biol Struct, Univ Wash, 69-70; mem bd dirs, Am Acad Dermat, 80-84 & Soc Investigative Dermat, 82-87. *Mem:* Soc Invest Dermat (pres, 92-94); Am Fedn Clin Res; Am Acad Dermatologists; Am Dermat Asn; Am Asn Physicians. *Res:* Autoimmune disorders; lupus erythematosus; scleroderma and dermatomyositis, both from clinical and research aspects; microcirculation in skin, both from clinical and from electron microscopic aspects. *Mailing Add:* Sect Dermat Yale Univ New Haven CT 06520. *Fax:* 203-785-7637; *E-Mail:* brauerman@biomed.med.yale.edu

BRAVO, JUSTO BALADJAY, INORGANIC CHEMISTRY. *Current Pos:* prof, West Chester State Col, 64-83, chmn dept, 67-68, EMER PROF CHEM, WEST CHESTER UNIV, 83- *Personal Data:* b Philippines, Dec 5, 17; nat US; m 42; c 3. *Educ:* Adamson Univ, Manila, BSChE, 40; Univ Kans, PhD(chem), 53. *Prof Exp:* Instr chem, Univ St Tomas, Philippines, 46-49; asst instr, Univ Kans, 49-50, res assoc, 50-53; res chemist, Wyandotte Chem Corp, Mich, 53 & Oldbury Electrochem Co, 54-56; res proj engr, Am Potash & Chem Corp, 56-57; sr res chemist, Foote Mineral Co, Pa, 57-59, group leader, 59-60; res supvr, Sun Oil Co, 60-63; sr res scientist, Glidden Co, Md, 63-64. *Concurrent Pos:* Sr consult, Wastex Industs Co, Inc, 71-77; grad coordr, West Chester State Col, 76-83. *Mem:* Sigma Xi. *Res:* Uninegative rhenium; inorganic pigments and phosphorus compounds; lithium metal and inorganic lithium compounds; electrochemicals; gas-solid reactions; fused system electrolysis; powder metallurgy; electrode processes; fuel cell development; synthesis, structure and properties of inorganic complex compounds. *Mailing Add:* 3000 22nd Ave Rio Rancho NM 87124-1658

BRAWER, JAMES ROBIN, NEUROCYTOLOGY, NEUROENDOCRINOLOGY. *Current Pos:* from asst prof to assoc prof obstet, gynec & anat, 75-81, assoc scientist, 76-78, MED SCIENTIST, MCGILL UNIV-ROYAL VICTORIA HOSP, 78-, PROF OBSTET & GYNEC, MED SCH, 81-, PROF ANAT, 83- *Personal Data:* b Patterson, NJ, Dec 15, 44; m 68; c 5. *Educ:* Tufts Univ, BS, 66; Harvard Univ, PhD(neurocytol), 71. *Prof Exp:* NIH fel, Harvard Med Sch, 71-72; from asst prof to assoc prof anat, Med Sch, Tufts Univ, 72-75. *Concurrent Pos:* Med Res Coun Can scholar, 76; assoc mem, Dept Med, Div Exp Med, McGill

Univ, 77-, dir, Ctr Study Reproduction, 87-90. *Mem:* Soc Study Reproduction; Am Asn Anatomists; Sigma Xi. *Res:* Cytophysiology of neuroendocrine transducers in the medial basal hypothalamus; regulation of brain, pituitary, ovarian axis, polycystic ovarian disease. *Mailing Add:* Dept Anat & Cell Biol McGill Univ Strathcone Anat & Dent Bldg 3640 University St Montreal PQ H3A 2B2 Can

BRAWER, STEVEN ARNOLD, PHYSICS. *Current Pos:* PHYSICIST, LAWRENCE LIVERMORE LAB, 77- *Personal Data:* b Paterson, NJ, Oct 7, 41; m 67; c 2. *Educ:* Rutgers Univ, BA, 64; Univ Colo, PhD(physics), 72. *Prof Exp:* Res assoc, Mat Res Lab, Pa State Univ, 72-77. *Mem:* Am Phys Soc; Am Ceramic Soc. *Res:* Optical properties of dielectric glasses. *Mailing Add:* Six Dickson Dr Westfield NJ 07090

BRAWERMAN, GEORGE, BIOCHEMISTRY. *Current Pos:* PROF BIOCHEM, SCH MED, TUFTS UNIV, 70- *Personal Data:* b Biala Podlaska, Poland, June 12, 27; US citizen; m 53; c 2. *Educ:* Univ Brussels, BS, 48; Columbia Univ, PhD(biochem), 53. *Prof Exp:* Res assoc biochem, Col Physicians & Surgeons, Columbia Univ, 56-60, asst prof, 60-61; from asst prof to assoc prof, Yale Univ Sch Med, 61-70. *Concurrent Pos:* USPHS career develop award, 63-70. *Mem:* AAAS; Am Soc Biol Chemists. *Res:* Biochemistry of gene expression; structure and function of messenger RNA; protein biosynthesis. *Mailing Add:* 29 Jeffrey Rd Wayland MA 01778

BRAWLEY, JOEL VINCENT, JR, ALGEBRA, COMBINATORICS & FINITE MATHEMATICS. *Current Pos:* from asst prof to prof, 65-82, actg head dept, 77-78, ALUMNI DISTINGUISHED PROF MATH SCI, CLEMSON UNIV, 82- *Personal Data:* b Mooresville, NC, Feb 2, 38; m 59, Frances Owen; c Vincent, Daniel & Francy. *Educ:* NC State Univ, BS, 60, MS, 62, PhD(math), 64. *Prof Exp:* Instr math, NC State Univ, 64-65. *Concurrent Pos:* Vis lectr statist, Southern Regional Educ Bd, 67-69; vis lectr, Math Asn Am, 68-, sect lectr, 75-76; lectr, Nat High Sch & Jr Col Math Club, 70-; vis assoc prof, NC State Univ, 71-72; vis prof, Univ Tenn, Knoxville, 79-80. *Mem:* Math Asn Am; Am Math Soc; Sigma Xi. *Res:* Linear and abstract algebra, combinatorics; finite field theory; numerous research publications and one book. *Mailing Add:* Math Sci Dept Clemson Univ Clemson SC 29634-1907. *Fax:* 864-656-5230; *E-Mail:* jvbrw@clemson.clemson.edu

BRAWLEY, SUSAN HOWARD, PHYCOLOGY, COMMUNITY ECOLOGY. *Current Pos:* assoc prof, 91-94, PROF SCH MARINE SCI & DEPT BIOL SCI, UNIV MAINE, 94- *Personal Data:* b Charlotte, NC, Oct 6, 51; m 95; c Anne Charlotte. *Educ:* Wellesley Col, BA, 73; Univ Calif, Berkeley, PhD(bot), 78. *Honors & Awards:* Career Advan Award, NSF, 88-89. *Prof Exp:* Res assoc, Smithsonian Inst, 79-83 & physiol dept, Univ Conn Health Ctr, 81-83; asst prof, 83-90, assoc prof biol, Vanderbilt Univ, 90-91. *Concurrent Pos:* NSF traineeship, Univ Calif, 73-74, regents fel, 74-75; Luce scholar, Univ Tokyo, 76-77; Smithsonian fel, 78-79; sci scholar, Bunting Inst, Radcliffe Col, 81-83; prin investr ecol, Nat Geog Soc grants, Qingdao, China, 86, Sweden, 93, 94 & 95, NSF Grants, 84-87 & 88-91, 92-97, 94-97; assoc ed, J Phycol, 89-92, ed chief, 96-; pres, NE Algal Soc, 94-96; mem, Comt Biol Diversity Marine Systs, Nat Res Coun, 94-95. *Mem:* Am Soc Cell Biol; Ecol Soc Am; Phycol Soc Am (treas, 89-91); Int Phycol Soc; Soc Develop Biol; Am Soc Plant Physiol. *Res:* Early embryogenesis; polyspermy blocks; marine ecol; effects of small herbivores upon algal community structure; fertilization ecology; physiology. *Mailing Add:* Sch Marine Sci & Dept Biol Sci Univ Maine 5722 Deering Hall Orono ME 04469-5722. *E-Mail:* brawley@maine.maine.edu

BRAWN, MARY KAREN, biochemistry, for more information see previous edition

BRAWNER, THOMAS A, MICROBIOLOGY, VIROLOGY. *Current Pos:* chair, Div Nat Sci, 90-93, CHAIRPERSON, DEPT BIOL, CARTHAGE COL, 89- *Personal Data:* b Cleveland, Ohio, Dec 8, 45; m 67; c 2. *Educ:* Albion Col, BA, 67; Univ Tex, Austin, PhD(microbiol), 72. *Prof Exp:* Fel virol, Univ Tex, San Antonio, 71-73; asst prof microbiol, Univ Mo, Columbia, 73-81, assoc prof, 81; mem staff, Abbott Labs, 81-89. *Mem:* Sigma Xi; Am Soc Microbiol; AAAS. *Res:* Process of viral RNA replication; RNA viral biochemistry and genetics; replication of Hepatitis B virus; Hepatitis B viral markers; Delta virus replication and markers. *Mailing Add:* Dept Biol Carthage Col Kenosha WI 53140. *E-Mail:* brawnel@carthage.edu

BRAY, A PHILIP, MECHANICAL ENGINEERING. *Current Pos:* PRES & CHIEF EXEC OFFICER, ENERGEO. *Personal Data:* b San Francisco, Calif, Sept 23, 33; m 56; c 6. *Educ:* Univ Calif, Berkeley, BS, 55. *Honors & Awards:* Lawrence Mem Award, US Dept Energy. *Prof Exp:* Mem staff, Gen Elec Co, 55-79, vpres & gen mgr, Nuclear Power Systs Div, 79-84; sr vpres, Mgt Anal Co, 84-85, exec vpres, 84-86, pres & chief exec officer, 86- *Concurrent Pos:* Chmn, Goose Lake Lumber Co, 87- & Teal Tech Inc, 87-; mem bd, Sequoia Nat Bank, Energeo, Inc, Thomas Res Corp, Thermal Energy Storage, Inc. *Mem:* Nat Acad Eng. *Mailing Add:* Energeo 567 Mississippi San Francisco CA 94107

BRAY, BONNIE ANDERSON, GLYCOSAMINOGLYCANS & GLYCOPROTEINS EXTRA CELLULAR MATRIX. *Current Pos:* res assoc, 69-83, assoc res scientist, 83-94, res scientist, 93-94, SPECIAL RES SCIENTIES, DEPT MED, COL PHYSICIANS & SURGEONS, COLUMBIA UNIV, 94- *Personal Data:* b Lincolnton, Ga, Oct 27, 29; wid. *Educ:* Univ Ga, BS, 50; Columbia Univ, PhD(biochem), 63. *Prof Exp:* Asst chemist, Union Carbide Corp, 50-51, jr chemist, 51-52; jr biologist, Oak Ridge Nat Lab, 52-59; res assoc biochem & med, Col Physicians & Surgeons, Columbia Univ, 63-66; NIH fel, Lab Biophys Chem, Nat Inst Arthritis & Metab Dis, 66-67; res assoc, NY Blood Ctr, 67-69. *Mem:* Soc Glycobiol; Am Chem Soc; Am Soc Biochem & Molecular Biol; Biochem Soc; Soc Exp Biol & Med. *Res:* Glycosaminoglycan biochemistry; linkage of glysosaminoglycans to protein; Glycosaminoglycan-Protein interactions in extra cellular matrix; fibrinogen and fibronectin, especially tissue fibronectin; basement membrane biochemistry and immunology; extracellular matrix of lung and placenta; angiogenesis. *Mailing Add:* St Lukes-Roosevelt Hosp Ctr AJA Rm 101 1000 Tenth Ave New York NY 10019-1105. *Fax:* 212-523-7442

BRAY, BRUCE G(LENN), CHEMICAL ENGINEERING. *Current Pos:* RETIRED. *Personal Data:* b Deckerville, Mich, Mar 17, 30; m 54; c 3. *Educ:* Univ Mich, BS, 53, MS, 54, PhD(chem eng), 57. *Prof Exp:* Res assoc, Eng Res Inst, 53-57; res engr, Continental Oil Co, Okla, 57-59, sr res engr, 59-61, res group leader, 61-65, res assoc, 65-66; dir eng, CER Geonuclear Corp, 67-73; dir spec projs, Continental Oil Co, 73-79; mgr, Mining Res Div, Conoco/Dupont, 80-85. *Concurrent Pos:* Mem, Indust Adv Comt Gen Eng, Univ Nev, Las Vegas, 71-73 & Indust Adv Comt, Sch Technol, Okla State Univ, 75-76. *Mem:* AAAS; Am Inst Chem Engrs; Sigma Xi; Am Inst Mining, Metall & Petrol Engrs. *Res:* Applied thermodynamics; effects of gamma radiation on several polysulfone reactions; hydrocarbon processing; reservoir engineering; low temperature processing; peaceful uses of nuclear explosives; in situ leaching; coal preparation, treating; hydraulic transport; mining research; coal characterization. *Mailing Add:* 2500 Donner Ponca City OK 74604

BRAY, DALE FRANK, ENTOMOLOGY. *Current Pos:* RETIRED. *Personal Data:* b Paw Paw, Mich, Mar 2, 22; m 47; c 2. *Educ:* Mich State Col, BS, 47, MS, 49; Rutgers Univ, PhD(entom), 54. *Prof Exp:* Grad asst entom, Mich State Col, 47-49; from instr to asst prof, Univ Del, 49-55; assoc entomologist, Bartlett Tree Res Labs, 55-58; prof entom & chmn dept, Univ Del, 58-80, emer prof, 80-83; pres & entomologist, Bray Entom Serv, 83-87. *Mem:* Entom Soc Am; hon mem Nat Pest Control Asn; Am Entom Soc. *Res:* Economic entomology; shade tree and ornamental plant insects; microlepidoptera-urban entomology. *Mailing Add:* PO Box 85 Dimock PA 18816

BRAY, DONALD JAMES, POULTRY NUTRITION. *Current Pos:* RETIRED. *Personal Data:* b Anamosa, Iowa, Nov 8, 23; m 48; c 5. *Educ:* Iowa State Col, BS, 50; Kans State Col, MS, 52, PhD, 54. *Prof Exp:* From asst prof to assoc prof animal sci, Univ Ill, Urbana, Champaign, 54-68, prof, 68-80; mem staff, Coop State Res Serv, USDA, 80-83. *Mem:* AAAS; Poultry Sci Asn; World Poultry Sci Asn; Am Inst Nutrit; Sigma Xi. *Res:* Nutritional and environmental factors as they influence laying hens. *Mailing Add:* 6604 191st St Seattle WA 98155

BRAY, ELIZABETH ANN, PLANT HORMONES, REGULATION OF GENE EXPRESSION. *Current Pos:* asst prof, 85-92, ASSOC PROF, DEPT BOT & PLANT SCI, UNIV CALIF, RIVERSIDE, 92- *Personal Data:* b Ithaca, NY, Aug 18, 54. *Educ:* Mt Holyoke Col, BA, 76; Univ Minn, St Paul, MS, 78, PhD(plant physiol), 82. *Prof Exp:* Res assoc, MSU-Dept Energy Plant Res Lab, 82-83, Wash Univ, 83-85. *Concurrent Pos:* Res assoc, Statewide Air Pollution Res Ctr, Univ Calif, Riverside, 91- *Mem:* Am Soc Plant Physiologists; Int Soc Plant Molecular Biol. *Res:* Regulation of gene expression by the plant hormone abscisic acid during periods of drought stress and other environmental stresses. *Mailing Add:* Dept Bot & Plant Sci Univ Calif 3121 Batchelor Hall Riverside CA 92521-0001. *Fax:* 909-787-4437

BRAY, GEORGE A, MEDICINE & NUTRITION. *Current Pos:* DIR, PENNINGTON BIOMED RES CTR, LA STATE UNIV, BATON ROUGE, 89- *Personal Data:* b Evanston, Ill, July 25, 31; c 4. *Educ:* Brown Univ, AB, 53; Harvard Univ, MD, 57. *Honors & Awards:* Osborne & Mendel Award, AIN, 88; McCollum Award, Am Soc Clin Nutrit, 89. *Prof Exp:* From asst prof to assoc prof med, Sch Med, Tufts Univ, 64-70; from assoc prof to prof med, Sch Med, Univ Calif, Los Angeles, 70-81; dir clin study ctr, Harbor Gen Hosp, Torrance, Calif, 70-78; prof med & chief, Div Diabetes & Clin Nutrit, Univ Southern Calif, Los Angeles, 81-89. *Concurrent Pos:* NSF fel, Nat Inst Med Res, 61-62; NIH fel, New Eng Med Ctr Hosps, 62-64; NIH res grants, Harbor Gen Hosp, 67 & 70; assoc chief, Div Endocrinol & Metab, Harbor Gen Hosp, 70-; chmn, Fogarty Ctr Conf Obesity, 73; consult, Food & Drug Admin, 71 & Dept Health & Welfare, Can, 74; invited witness, Select Comt Nutrit & Human Needs, US Sen, 74. *Mem:* Asn Am Physicians; Am Soc Clin Invest; Sigma Xi; NAm Asn Study Obesity; Endocrine Soc; fel AAAS; fel Am Col Physicians. *Res:* Etiology, treatment and management of experimental animal and human obesity. *Mailing Add:* Pennington Biomed Res Ctr 6400 Perkins Rd Baton Rouge LA 70808. *Fax:* 504-765-0935

BRAY, JAMES WILLIAM, THEORETICAL SOLID STATE PHYSICS, SUPERCONDUCTIVITY. *Current Pos:* mgr, Phys Sci Br, 79-82, Electronic Mat Sci Br, 82-87, MGR, HIGH TEMPERATURE SUPERCONDUCTORS PROG, GE CORP RES & DEVELOP, 87- *Personal Data:* b Atlanta, Ga, Feb 6, 48. *Educ:* Ga Inst Technol, BS, 70; Univ Ill, MS, 71, PhD(physics), 74. *Prof Exp:* Physicist, Gen Elec Res & Develop Ctr, 74-79. *Mem:* Am Phys Soc. *Res:* Theoretical study of magnetic and transport properties of quasi-one-dimensional system; superconductivity. *Mailing Add:* Gen Elec Res & Develop Ctr PO Box 8 Schenectady NY 12301. *Fax:* 518-387-7597; *E-Mail:* bray@crd.ge.com

BRAY, JOAN LYNNE, ELECTRON MICROSCOPY. *Current Pos:* ASST PROF BIOL, UNIV N FLA, 76- *Personal Data:* b Yankton, SD, Oct 10, 35. *Educ:* Rosary Col, BA, 64; Purdue Univ, MS, 69, PhD(biol), 75. *Mem:* AAAS; Nat Asn Biol Teachers. *Res:* Ultrastructure of algal development. *Mailing Add:* Univ NFla 4567 St Johns Bluff S Jacksonville FL 32224-2646

BRAY, JOHN ROGER, ECOLOGY. *Current Pos:* CONSULT ECOLOGIST, 66- *Personal Data:* b Belleville, Ill, June 20, 29; m 61, Gwendolyn J Struik; c Naomi Struik, Hanna Moata & Melissa Struik. *Educ:* Univ Ill, BA, 50; Univ Wis, PhD(bot), 55. *Prof Exp:* Asst, Univ Wis, 50-54; vis lectr, Univ Minn, 55-57; asst prof, Univ Toronto, 57-62; prin sci officer, Dept Sci & Indust Res, 63-66. *Concurrent Pos:* Vis prof, Univ Minn, 69; fel, Australian Nat Univ, 80. *Mem:* Fel AAAS; Ecol Soc Am; Brit Ecol Soc; NZ Ecol Soc. *Res:* Quantitative techniques for sampling and classifying vegetation; productivity and efficiency of terrestrial vegetation; ecologic theory; historical climatology; influence of solar and volcanic activity on climate; forest regeneration dynamics. *Mailing Add:* PO Box 494 Nelson New Zealand

BRAY, JOHN THOMAS, ANALYTICAL CHEMISTRY, BIOCHEMISTRY. *Current Pos:* asst prof dept surg & dir, Trace Elements Labs, 78-84, ASSOC PROF SHARED RES RESOURCES LABS & GROUP LEADER, ELEMENTAL ANALYSIS GROUP, SCH MED, E CAROLINA UNIV, 84- *Personal Data:* b Terre Haute, Ind, Apr 13, 44; m 67; c 2. *Educ:* Rose-Hulman Inst Technol, BS, 67; Johns Hopkins Univ, MA, 70, PhD(chem oceanog, geochem), 73. *Prof Exp:* Res asst dept earth & planetary sci, Chesapeake Bay Inst, Johns Hopkins Univ, 67-77, assoc res scientist dept geog & environ eng, 73-74; chem prog coordr, Ecol Anal, Inc, 74-78. *Mem:* Am Chem Soc; Am Soc Limnol & Oceanog; AAAS; Sigma Xi; Soc Appl Spectros; Soc Environ Geochem & Health. *Res:* Analytical chemistry of trace elements in biomedical, environmental and geological matrices; biogeochemical cycling of trace elements in the environment and the role of trace elements in nutrition and other physiological functions. *Mailing Add:* Metrics Inc PO Box 4035 Greenville NC 27836

BRAY, NORMAN FRANCIS, PHYSICAL CHEMISTRY. *Current Pos:* ASST PROF CHEM, LEHMAN COL, 69- *Personal Data:* b Louisville, Ky, May 27, 38; m 66; c 2. *Educ:* Univ Louisville, BS, 60, PhD(phys chem), 63. *Prof Exp:* Res scientist, NASA, Ohio, 63-64; from instr to asst prof chem, Hunter Col, 64-69. *Mem:* Am Chem Soc. *Res:* Structure determination by nuclear magnetic resonance; solution thermodynamics. *Mailing Add:* H H Lehman Col Bedford Park Blvd W Bronx NY 10468-1590

BRAY, PHILIP JAMES, SOLID STATE PHYSICS. *Current Pos:* from assoc prof to prof, Brown Univ, 55-85, chmn dept, 63-68, Hazard prof physics, 85-90, EMER HAZARD PROF PHYSICS, BROWN UNIV, 90- *Personal Data:* b Kansas City, Mo, Aug 25, 25; m 51; c Carolyn, James & Katherine. *Educ:* Brown Univ, ScB, 48; Harvard Univ, MA, 49, PhD(physics), 53. *Honors & Awards:* George W Morey Award, Am Ceramic Soc, 70; Sir Nevil Mott Award, 91. *Prof Exp:* Asst prof physics, Rensselaer Polytech Inst, 52-55. *Concurrent Pos:* NSF sr fel, 61-62; John Simon Guggenheim fel, 68-69; vis prof, Dept Glass Technol, Univ Sheffield, 61-62 & 68-69; vis prof, Dept Chem, Univ Exeter, 75-76. *Mem:* Fel AAAS; fel Am Phys Soc; Am Acad Arts & Sci; fel Soc Glass Technol; fel Am Ceramic Soc. *Res:* Nuclear magnetic resonance and nuclear quadrupole resonance studies of the structure of glasses and crystalline materials. *Mailing Add:* Dept Physics Brown Univ Box 1843 Providence RI 02912. *Fax:* 401-863-2024; *E-Mail:* ph400000@brownum.brown.edu

BRAY, RALPH, SOLID STATE PHYSICS. *Current Pos:* From instr to assoc prof, 45-65, prof, 65-89, EMER PROF PHYSICS, PURDUE UNIV, 89- *Personal Data:* b Russia, Sept 11, 21; nat US; m 48; c 3. *Educ:* Brooklyn Col, BA, 42; Purdue Univ, PhD(physics), 49. *Honors & Awards:* vis Scientist Award, Japan Soc Prom Sci, 78. *Concurrent Pos:* Nat Res Coun fel, Tech Univ Delft, 51-52; consult, Univ Reading, 52-53, Battelle Mem Inst & Nat Cash Register Co; vis scientist, Gen Atomic Div, Gen Dynamics Corp, 60-61; Guggenheim fel, 69-70; vis scientist, Clarendon Lab, Oxford Univ, 69-70 & Becton Ctr, Yale Univ, 70 & Max Planck Inst, 85-86; fac adv, Tex Instruments, Gen Tel Res & Electronics Lab; vis prof, Univ Osaka, 90; von Humboldt Sr Scientist Award, 85-86; Guggenheim Mem Fel Award, 69. *Mem:* Fel Am Phys Soc; Sigma Xi. *Res:* Semiconductors; nonequilibrium phenomena; acoustoelectric effects; instabilities; brillouin scattering. *Mailing Add:* Physics Dept Purdue Univ West Lafayette IN 47907

BRAY, RICHARD NEWTON, FISH ECOLOGY, MARINE ECOLOGY. *Current Pos:* lectr, 78-79, asst prof, 79-88, PROF BIOL, CALIF STATE UNIV, LONG BEACH, 88- *Personal Data:* b San Diego, Calif, Apr 14, 45; m 76; c 2. *Educ:* San Diego State Univ, BS, 67; Univ Calif, Santa Barbara, MA, 74, PhD(biol), 78. *Honors & Awards:* Stoye Award, Am Soc Ichthyologists & Herpetologists, 78. *Prof Exp:* Res asst biol, Univ Calif, Santa Barbara, 74-78. *Mem:* AAAS; Am Soc Ichthyologists & Herpetologists; Western Soc Naturalists; Ecol Soc Am; Am Soc Limnol Oceangr. *Res:* Role of fishes in the food web of subtidal reef communities. *Mailing Add:* Dept Biol Calif State Univ 3702 Csulb Long Beach CA 90840-0004

BRAY, ROBERT S, METALLURGY, ALLOYS. *Current Pos:* EMER PROF CHEM MAT ENG, CALIF STATE POLYTECH UNIV, POMONA, 80- *Personal Data:* b Feb 3, 27. *Educ:* Yale Univ, BE, 53, ME, 54. *Mem:* Fel Am Soc Metals. *Mailing Add:* 411 Pinata Pl Fullerton CA 92635

BRAY, TAMMY M, ANTIOXIDANT NUTRIENTS & FREE RADICAL METABOLISM, NUTRITIONAL TOXICOLOGY. *Current Pos:* from asst prof to assoc prof, 78-89, PROF, DEPT NUTRIT SCI, UNIV GUELPH, 89- *Personal Data:* b China, Feb 14, 47; US & Can citizen; m 68, John; c James, Jannine & Jacob. *Educ:* Fu-Jen Univ, BSc, 67; Washington State Univ, MSc, 70, PhD(nutrit), 74. *Prof Exp:* Res assoc, Dept Animal Sci, Washington State Univ, 74-78. *Concurrent Pos:* Vis prof, Dept Food Sci & Nutrit, Fu-Jen Univ, 85-86, Dept Vet Pharmacol & Toxicol, Univ Calif, 85-86; coordr, Dept Nutrit Sci, Univ Guelph, 88-92, actg chair, 91-92, actg assoc vpres acad, 92-94. *Mem:* Am Inst Nutrit; Can Soc Nutrit Sci (pres, 91-92); fel Oxygen Soc; Soc Toxicol; Soc Exp Biol Med; Sigma Xi. *Res:* Free radical metabolism in health and disease; understanding of the biochemical and metabolic basis of the foodborne toxin-induced disease; nutrition and stress. *Mailing Add:* Dept Human Nutrit Ohio State Univ 1787 Neil Ave Campbell Hall Rm 347 Columbus OH 43210-1295. *Fax:* 519-763-5902; *E-Mail:* tbray@uoguelph.ca

BRAYER, KENNETH, DATA COMMUNICATIONS ENGINEERING, SIMULATION & MODELING. *Current Pos:* Tech staff mem, Mitre Corp, 65-79, dept staff, 79-82, group leader, 82-89, proj mgr, 89-94, PRIN CONSULT, MITRE CORP, 95- *Personal Data:* b New York, NY, July 3, 41. *Educ:* City Col NY, BEE, 64; Columbia Univ, MS, 65. *Concurrent Pos:* Jr res engr, Columbia Univ Electronics Res Labs, 64-; res referee, Eng Div, NSF, 69-; ed, Inst Elec & Electronics Engrs Press, 74-75, Commun Mag, 84, J Selected Topics Commun, 87, Trans Commun, 87-90; instr, George Washington Univ, 76-77; organizer, Milcom Conf, 86- *Mem:* Fel Inst Elec & Electronics Engrs. *Res:* Digital data communications; high frequency radio; error detection and correction coding; computer communication and networking; adaptive computer systems; rapid prototyping; coding and modulation. *Mailing Add:* Mitre Corp 202 Burlington Rd Bedford MA 01730. *Fax:* 781-271-5810; *E-Mail:* k.brayer@ieee.org

BRAYMER, HUGH DOUGLAS, MOLECULAR BIOLOGY. *Current Pos:* from asst prof to assoc prof, 66-74, PROF MICROBIOL, LA STATE UNIV, BATON ROUGE, 86-, VPRES ACAD AFFAIRS. *Personal Data:* b Oklahoma City, Okla, Mar 28, 33; m 56, Marilyn Province; c 2. *Educ:* Univ Okla, BS, 55, MS, 57, PhD(biochem), 60. *Prof Exp:* Biochemist gene action res, Radiobiol Br, USAF Sch Aerospace Med, 60-63; USPHS fel biochem genetics, Stanford Univ, 63-66. *Concurrent Pos:* Mem fac, Trinity Univ, 60-63; vis prof, Univ Edinburgh, Scotland, 83. *Mem:* Am Chem Soc; Genetics Soc Am; Am Soc Microbiol; Am Soc Biol Chemists; Brit Biochem Soc. *Res:* Biochemical genetics; gene action; genetics of obesity; metabolic control mechanisms. *Mailing Add:* Pennington Biomed Res Ctr La State Univ 6400 Perkins Rd Baton Rouge LA 70808. *Fax:* 504-388-5524; *E-Mail:* hdb@lanmail.ocs.lsu.edu

BRAYTON, ROBERT K, COMPUTER AIDED DESIGN. *Current Pos:* vis McKay Prof, 85-86, PROF, DEPT ELEC ENG & COMPUT SCI, UNIV CALIF, BERKELEY, 87- *Personal Data:* b Des Moines, Iowa; m, Ruth; c Jane, Jim & Mike. *Educ:* Iowa State Univ, BS, 56; Mass Inst Technol, PhD(math), 61. *Prof Exp:* Elec engr, Remington Rand Univac, 56-57; res asst artificial intel, Mass Inst Technol, 57-61, mgr, Differential Equations & Numerical Anal, 63-81, vis assoc prof, 66-67; asst dir, Math Sci Dept, IBM Res, 71-72; vis prof elec eng, Imp Col, London, 75-76; mgr, Logic Design, 81-85, second level mgr differential equations & comput algebra, 81-84, second level mgr math algorithms, 84-87; vis prof elec eng, TU Delft, 92-93. *Concurrent Pos:* Res staff mem, IBM Thomas J Watson Res Ctr, 61-67. *Mem:* Nat Acad Eng; fel Inst Elec & Electronics Engrs; fel AAAS. *Res:* Mathematics; circuits and systems; computer aided design; numerous technical publications. *Mailing Add:* Dept Elec Eng & Comput Sci Cory Hall Univ Calif Berkeley CA 94720. *Fax:* 510 643-5052; *E-Mail:* brayton@ic.berkeley.edu

BRAZEAU, GAYLE A, PHARMACOKINETICS, PHYSICAL PHARMACY. *Current Pos:* ASST PROF PHARMACEUT, COL PHARM, UNIV HOUSTON, 89- *Personal Data:* b Toledo, Ohio, May 27, 57; m 79. *Educ:* Univ Toledo, BS, 80, MS, 83; State Univ NY, Buffalo, PhD(pharmaceut), 89. *Prof Exp:* Grad teaching asst pharmaceut, Univ Toledo, 80-83; grad res asst pharmaceut, State Univ NY, Buffalo, 83-89. *Concurrent Pos:* Sigma Xi res award, State Univ NY, Buffalo, 87. *Mem:* Am Asn Pharmaceut Scientists; Am Asn Cols Pharm; assoc mem Soc Exp Biol & Med. *Res:* Mechanisms muscle damage upon intramuscular injection; drug disposition-neuromuscular diseases; lipoproteins of drug delivery systems. *Mailing Add:* Dept Pharmaceut Univ Fla PO Box 100484 Gainesville FL 32610-0484

BRAZEE, ROSS D, AEROSOL PHYSICS, TRANSPORT PROCESSES. *Current Pos:* agr engr, dept agr eng res, Agr Res Serv, 57-62, leader, Pioneering Lab, Fine Particle Physics, 62-72, res leader, Agr Eng Res Unit, 72-85, RES LEADER, APPLN TECH RES UNIT, AGR RES SERV, USDA, 85- *Personal Data:* b Adrian, Mich, Oct 9, 30; m 53, M Jean Roth; c Kathleen M (Thompson), Karen M (Mork), Kay M (Wagner) & Kevin M. *Educ:* Mich State Univ, BS, 52, MS, 53, PhD(agr eng), 57. *Prof Exp:* Grad res asst, Mich State Univ, 52-53 & 55-57. *Concurrent Pos:* Adj prof, Ohio Agr Res & Develop Ctr, 60- & Ohio State Univ, 63- *Mem:* AAAS; NY Acad Sci; Am Geophys Union; Am Soc Agr Engrs; Sigma Xi. *Res:* Agricultural micrometeorology; crop protection; atmospheric turbulence and diffusion in plant populations; image processing; electrostatics; fluid mechanics. *Mailing Add:* Ohio Agr Res & Develop Ctr USDA Agr Res Serv Wooster OH 44691

BRAZEL, ANTHONY JAMES, CLIMATOLOGY, MICROCLIMATOLOGY. *Current Pos:* PROF GEOG, ARIZ STATE UNIV, 74- *Educ:* Rutgers Univ, BA, 63, MA, 65; Univ Mich, PhD(geog), 72. *Prof Exp:* Res scientist, US Army Corps Eng, 69-70; prof geog, Windsor Univ, Can, 71-74. *Concurrent Pos:* Prin investr, Jet Propulsion, Pasadena, 86-; prin investr, Salt River Proj, Phoenix, Ariz, 87-; state climatologist, Arizona, 79- *Mem:* Asn Am Geographers; Royal Meteorol Soc; Am Meteorol Soc; Nat Weather Asn; Int Mountain Soc. *Res:* Climatology of Arizona; study desertification and acolian processes, energy and moisture budgets of urban areas and arid environments. *Mailing Add:* Dept Geog Ariz State Univ Box 870104 Tempe AZ 85287-0104

BRAZELTON, WILLIAM T(HOMAS), CHEMICAL ENGINEERING. *Current Pos:* Instr mech & chem eng, 43-47, from asst prof to assoc prof, 47-63, PROF CHEM ENG & ASSOC DEAN TECHNOL INST, NORTHWESTERN UNIV, 63- *Personal Data:* b Danville, Ill, Jan 22, 21; m 44; c 2. *Educ:* Northwestern Univ, BS, 43, MS, 47, PhD(chem eng), 52. *Mem:* Am Chem Soc; Am Soc Eng Educ; Am Inst Chem Engrs. *Res:* Heat and mass transfer operations; fluidization. *Mailing Add:* 10 E Willow Rd Prospect Heights IL 60070-1332

BRAZIER, MARY A B, neurophysiology; deceased, see previous edition for last biography

BRAZINSKY, IRV, CHEMICAL ENGINEERING. *Current Pos:* assoc prof, 85-91, CHMN, DEPT CHEM ENG, COOPER UNION SCH ENG, 89-, PROF CHEM ENG, 91- *Personal Data:* b New York, NY, Oct 27, 36; m 59, Rosalie Seligson; c Howard & Michael. *Educ:* Cooper Union, BS, 58; Lehigh Univ, MS, 60; Mass Inst Technol, ScD(chem eng), 67. *Honors & Awards:* Schweinburg Award; Campbell & Schiff Award. *Prof Exp:* Res engr rocket vehicle res, NASA, 59-61; res engr non-Newtonian fluid dynamics, Polaroid Corp, 66-69; sr res engr, Celanese Res Co, 69-76; sr res & develop engr, Halcon Int, 76-81; process mgr, Foster Wheeler Energy Corp, 81-85. *Concurrent Pos:* Adj prof, Newark Col Eng, 71-81; fel, Petrol Res Fund, Proctor & Gamble & Arthur D Little. *Mem:* Am Inst Chem Engrs; Sigma Xi; NY Acad Sci; Am Soc Eng Educ; Am Chem Soc; Soc Plastics Engrs. *Res:* Heat transfer and mass transfer; flow of non-Newtonian fluids; fiber spinning; chemical reaction kinetics; thermodynamics; crystal growth from the melt; municipal waste treatment; rapid chilling of beverages. *Mailing Add:* 6 Rustic Lane Matawan NJ 07747. *Fax:* 212-353-4341

BRAZIS, A(DOLPH) RICHARD, MICROBIOLOGY. *Current Pos:* RETIRED. *Personal Data:* b Bridgeport, Conn, Nov 14, 26; m 52; c 2. *Educ:* Norwich Univ, BS, 49; Univ Mo, MS, 51, PhD(dairy husb, bact), 54. *Honors & Awards:* USPHS Commendation Medal, 63; Award of Merit, Food & Drug Admin, 76. *Prof Exp:* Asst instr dairy husb & bact, Univ Mo, 52-54; sr scientist, Robert A Taft Sanit Eng Ctr, 54-69, chmn appl lab methods comt, 64-78; lab cert officer, Div Microbiol, Food & Drug Admin, 69-70, chief lab develop prog, 70-78, actg chief, Lab Qual Assurance Br, Div Microbiol, 77-78; corp microbiologist, Fairmont Foods Co, 78-80; mgr, Sanit Microbiol, W A Golomski & Assoc, 81-84. *Concurrent Pos:* Chmn screening test subcomt, Nat Mastitis Coun, 67-; pres, Int Asn of milk food & environ sanitarians, Inc, 83-84. *Mem:* Sigma Xi; Int Asn Milk, Food & Environ Sanit (pres, 83-84); Inst Food Technol; Am Soc Microbiologists; Am Dairy Sci Asn. *Res:* Water supply and pollution germicidal agents investigations; sanitation of radionuclide removal processes; laboratory evaluation and services; milk and food microbiology; administration and collegiate teaching; industry processing and laboratory quality assurance. *Mailing Add:* 1006 Martin Dr Bellevue NE 68005-4702

BRAZY, PETER C, EPITHELIAL TRANSPORT, CELLULAR METABOLISM. *Current Pos:* ASSOC PROF & HEAD NEPHROLOGY SECT, UNIV WIS, 88- *Personal Data:* b 1946; c 2. *Educ:* Washington Univ, St Louis, MD, 72. *Prof Exp:* Asst prof & chief nephrol, Duke Univ Med Ctr, 74-88. *Mailing Add:* Univ Wis Clin Sci Ctr 600 Highland Ave H4/510 Madison WI 53792-0001. *Fax:* 608-263-0568

BREAKEFIELD, XANDRA OWENS, BIOCHEMICAL GENETICS, NEUROSCIENCE. *Current Pos:* ASSOC GENETICIST, DEPT NEUROGENETICS, MASS GEN HOSP, 71- *Personal Data:* b Boston, Mass, Oct 6, 42; m 74; c 2. *Educ:* Wilson Col, AB, 65; Georgetown Univ, PhD(microbial genetics), 71. *Honors & Awards:* Mathilde Solowey Award Neurosci, FAES, NIH, 86. *Prof Exp:* Fel neurobiol, Nat Heart & Lung Inst, 71-73, staff fel, 73-74; asst prof human genetics, Sch Med, Yale Univ, 74-; assoc prof neurol, Harvard Med Sch; dir, Molecular Neurogenetics, E K Shriver Ctr. *Concurrent Pos:* Prin investr res grants, Nat Inst Neurol Dis & Stroke, 75-78, March of Dimes, 76-79, Dystonia Med Res Found, 77-80 & Nat Inst Gen Med Sci, 78-81; assoc geneticist, neurol sci, Mass Gen Hosp; McKnight Neurosci Develop Award, 82-84; Jants Neurosci Investr Award, 85-92. *Mem:* Am Soc Neurochem; Int Soc Neurochem; Am Soc Human Genetics; Soc for Neurosci. *Res:* Genetic control of neurotransmitter metabolism; catecholamines; monoamine oxidase; cell culture; gene mapping; inheritance of monoamine oxidase in human population; inherited neurologic diseases. *Mailing Add:* Dept Neurogenetics Mass Gen Hosp 6th Fl Bldg 149 E 13th St Charlestown MA 02129

BREAKER, LAURENCE COATES, SATELLITE REMOTE SENSING, OCEAN CIRCULATION. *Current Pos:* SR RES PHYS SCIENTIST, NAT CTR ENVIRON PREDICTION, NAT WEATHER SERV, 87- *Personal Data:* b Cutchogue, NY, Mar 10, 39; m 85, Robin R Singer. *Educ:* Bucknell Univ, BS, 61; Univ Miami, MS, 69; Naval Postgrad Sch, PhD(oceanog), 83. *Prof Exp:* Oceanogr, US Naval Oceanographic Off, 61-74 & Nat Environ Satellite & Info Servs, Nat Oceanic Atmospheric Admin, 74-82; adj prof oceanog, Naval Postgrad Sch, 83-86; vis scientist, Moss Landing Marine Labs, 86-87. *Concurrent Pos:* Sr scientist, Sci Appln Int, 84-85; instr environ sci, Grad Sch, US Dept Agr, 96-; mem, Environ Policy Comn, City of Alexandria, Va, 97. *Mem:* Am Meteorol Soc; Am Geophys Union. *Res:* Application of remote sensing techniques to study coastal ocean circulation; development of new algorithms to infer physical properties of the ocean using recently developed satellite instruments. *Mailing Add:* 810 Chalfonte Dr Alexandria VA 22305

BREAKEY, DONALD RAY, BIOLOGY. *Current Pos:* RETIRED. *Personal Data:* b Snohomish, Wash, June 1, 27; m 48; c 2. *Educ:* Willamette Univ, BS, 50; Mich State Univ, MS, 52; Univ Calif, Berkeley, PhD(zool), 61. *Prof Exp:* From instr to prof biol, Willamete Univ, 54-92, chmn dept, 68-83. *Concurrent Pos:* Past pres, Malheur Field Sta Consortium, Pac NW Bird & Mammal Soc & Great Basin Soc. *Mem:* Sigma Xi; Am Soc Mammal; Australian Mammal Soc. *Res:* Vertebrate mammalian populations and distribution; ecological habitats and their evaluation in relation to animal forms present; athropod and life histories. *Mailing Add:* PO Box 3698 Salem OR 97302-0698

BREAKIRON, LEE ALLEN, ATOMIC TIMEKEEPING, STATISTICS. *Current Pos:* ASTRONOMER, US NAVAL OBSERV, 86- *Personal Data:* b Arlington, Va, July 26, 48; m 87, Teiko Hirasawa; c Jason. *Educ:* Univ Va, BS, 70; Univ Pittsburgh, MS, 73, PhD(astron), 77. *Prof Exp:* Postdoctoral res, Wesleyan Univ, 76-80; admin asst, NSF, 80-85; res prof, Univ Pittsburgh, 85-86. *Concurrent Pos:* Consult, Stand Coord Comt No 27, Inst Elec & Electronics Engrs, 91-94. *Mem:* Am Astron Soc; Int Astron Union; Sigma Xi. *Res:* Designed, implemented, and continue to refine the computer algorithm producing the official atomic time scale of the United States; atomic clock performance. *Mailing Add:* Time Serv Dept US Naval Observ Washington DC 20392. *Fax:* 202-762-1511; *E-Mail:* lab@tycho.usno.navy.mil

BREAKSTONE, ALAN M, PARTICLES AND FIELDS. *Current Pos:* ASST PHYSICIST, UNIV HAWAII, MANOA, 84- *Personal Data:* b Racine, Wis, Oct 13, 50; m 86. *Educ:* Calif Inst Technol, BS, 72; Univ Calif, Santa Cruz, MS, 74, PhD(physics), 80. *Prof Exp:* Postdoctoral fel, Ames Lab, Iowa State Univ, 80-84. *Mem:* Am Phys Soc. *Res:* Experimental elementary particle physics. *Mailing Add:* 887 W Knickerbocker Dr Sunnyvale CA 94087

BREAM, CHARLES ANTHONY, MEDICINE. *Current Pos:* RETIRED. *Personal Data:* b Midland, Pa, Mar 15, 15; m 41; c 4. *Educ:* Grove City Col, BS, 36; Temple Univ, MD, 40. *Prof Exp:* Intern, Mercy Hosp, Pa, 40-41; vis physician, St Vincent's Hosp, Pa, 46-48; instr radiol, Col Physicians & Surgeons, Columbia Univ, 51-52; from asst prof to prof radiol, Sch Med, Univ NC, Chapel Hill, 52-84. *Concurrent Pos:* Mellon res fel, Mercy Hosp, Pa, 41-42; instr med, Sch Med, Univ Pittsburgh, 40-41; asst vis physician, Hamot Hosp, Pa, 46-48; attend radiologist, NC Mem Hosp, Univ NC, 52-; consult, Watts Hosp, 53- & Womack Army Hosp, 58-; vis attend radiologist, Vet Admin Hosp, Durham, 55- *Mem:* Roentgen Ray Soc; Radiol Soc NAm; Asn Am Med Cols; Asn Univ Radiologists; fel Am Col Radiol. *Res:* Improvement of techniques, methods and scope of investigation of the retioperitoneal space; extend the usefulness of excretory urography in various nephropathies. *Mailing Add:* 3 Buttons Rd Chapel Hill NC 27514

BREARLEY, HARRINGTON C(OOPER), JR, ELECTRICAL ENGINEERING, COMPUTER SCIENCE. *Current Pos:* from assoc prof to prof, 65-95, EMER PROF ELEC ENG & COMPUT SCI, IOWA STATE UNIV, 95- *Personal Data:* b Greenville, SC, Jan 17, 26; m 57, Mary J Bradford; c Ann, William & Caroline. *Educ:* Ga Inst Technol, BEE, 46; Univ Ill, MS, 50, PhD(elec eng), 54. *Prof Exp:* Mem tech staff, Bell Tel Labs, 47-49; engr, Gen Elec Co, 53-59; res asst prof elec eng, Univ Ill, 59-65. *Mem:* Inst Elec & Electronics Engrs; Sigma Xi. *Res:* Computer science; switching theory. *Mailing Add:* 1537 Linden Dr Ames IA 50010-5533

BREAULT, GEORGE OMER, DRUG METABOLISM. *Current Pos:* Sr res biochemist drug metab, Merck Inst Therapeut Res, 70-72, res fel, 72-76, sr res fel, 76-80. *Personal Data:* b Providence, RI, Nov 30, 42; m 67; c 2. *Educ:* Univ Notre Dame, AB, 64; Univ RI, MS, 67; Univ Mich, PhD(pharm chem), 70. *Mem:* AAAS; Am Chem Soc. *Res:* Development of analytical methods for drugs in biological systems. *Mailing Add:* Analytical Develop Corp 4405 N Chestnut St Colorado Springs CO 80907-3812

BREAZEALE, ALMUT FRERICHS, POLYMER CHEMISTRY, ORGANIC CHEMISTRY. *Current Pos:* RETIRED. *Personal Data:* b Berlin, Germany, May 4, 38; US citizen; m 64, Robert David; c Steven David & Daniel Robert. *Educ:* Univ Ill, BS, 60; Univ Wash, PhD(org chem), 65. *Prof Exp:* Res assoc, E I Du Pont de Nemours & Co, 65-92. *Mem:* Am Chem Soc; Sigma Xi. *Res:* Structure-property relationships of thermoset and thermoplastic polymers, including elastomers and fluorinated polymers. *Mailing Add:* 1306 Necomb Rd Wilmington DE 19803-5108. *E-Mail:* almutb@aol.com

BREAZEALE, MACK ALFRED, PHYSICAL ACOUSTICS, SOLID STATE PHYSICS. *Current Pos:* DISTINGUISHED RES PROF PHYSICS, UNIV MISS, 88- *Personal Data:* b Leona Mines, Va, Aug 15, 30; m 90, Louise Scott; c Jennifer, David & William. *Educ:* Berea Col, BA, 53; Univ Mo, Rolla, MS, 54; Mich State Univ, PhD(physics), 57. *Honors & Awards:* Silver Medal Phys Acoust, Acoust Soc Am, 88. *Prof Exp:* Asst physics, Univ Mo, Rolla, 53-54; asst, Mich State Univ, 54-57, asst prof, 57-58 & 59-62; Fulbright res grant,

Phys Inst, Stuttgart Tech Inst, 58-59; from assoc prof to prof physics, Univ Tenn, Knoxville, 67-95. *Concurrent Pos:* Consult, Oak Ridge Nat Lab, 62-72, Naval Res Lab, 72-74 & Leeds & Northrup, 79-81; mem orgn comt, Int Symp Nonlinear Acoust, Moscow, 75, Blacksburg, Va, 76, Paris, 78, Leeds, 79, Kobe, 84, Novosibirsk, 87 & Austin, Tex, 90; guest prof, Tech Univ Denmark, 77; assoc ed, J Acoust Soc Am, 77-; vis prof, Tech Univ Denmark, 77, Univ Paris VI, 77; tech prog chmn, Acoust Soc Am, 85; distinguished lectr, Inst Elec & Electronics Engrs, 87-88, President's lectr, 87. *Mem:* Am Asn Univ Professors; fel Acoust Soc Am; Am Phys Soc; fel Inst Elec & Electronic Engrs; fel Inst Acoust Gt Brit. *Res:* Ultrasonics; nonlinear solid state and liquid state phenomena. *Mailing Add:* Nat Ctr Phys Acoust Univ Miss Coliseum Dr University MS 38677. *Fax:* 601-232-7494; *E-Mail:* breazeal@sunset.backbone.olemiss.edu

BREAZEALE, ROBERT DAVID, ORGANIC CHEMISTRY. *Current Pos:* res chemist, 64-71, RES SUPVR, AUTOMOTIVE PROD DEPT, RES DIV, E I DU PONT DE NEMOURS & CO, INC, 71- *Personal Data:* b Ames, Iowa, Aug 30, 35; m 64, Almut Frerichs; c Steven & Daniel. *Educ:* SDak State Col, BS, 57; Univ Wash, PhD(org chem), 64. *Prof Exp:* Res chemist, Sinclair Res Labs, Inc, 57-59. *Mem:* Am Chem Soc. *Res:* Polymer and petroleum chemistry; non-benzenoid aromatic chemistry; finishes and adhesives technology. *Mailing Add:* E I du Pont de Nemours Automotive Prod Marshall Lab 3500 Grays Ferry Ave Philadelphia PA 19146

BREAZEALE, WILLIAM HORACE, JR, PHYSICAL CHEMISTRY, CHEMICAL SAFETY. *Current Pos:* assoc prof, 70-71, assoc dean, 73-75, PROF CHEM & PHYSICS, FRANCIS MARION COL, 71-, CHMN DEPT, 70- *Personal Data:* b Greensboro, NC, Aug 30, 38; m 63, 85; c 3. *Educ:* Univ SC, BS, 61, PhD(phys chem), 66. *Prof Exp:* Asst prof chem, Winthrop Col, 66-70. *Mem:* Sigma Xi; Am Chem Soc. *Res:* Chemical education; thermodynamics of solutions; chemical safety. *Mailing Add:* 897 Ivanhoe Dr Florence SC 29505

BREAZILE, JAMES E, NEUROANATOMY, NEUROPHYSIOLOGY. *Current Pos:* MEM FAC, COL VET MED, OKLA STATE UNIV, 80- *Personal Data:* b Rockport, Mo, Dec 31, 34; m 57; c 3. *Educ:* Univ Mo, BS, 58, DVM, 58; Univ Minn, PhD(anat, physiol), 63. *Prof Exp:* Pvt pract vet med, 58-60; NIH fel, 61-63; asst prof physiol, Okla State Univ, 63-67; assoc prof vet anat, Univ Mo, Columbia, 67-68, chmn dept, 69-70 & 72-77, dir grad studies vet anat, 72-77, prof vet anat, 68-80. *Concurrent Pos:* NIH res grant, 64-; consult, 77- *Mem:* AAAS; Am Vet Med Asn; Am Asn Vet Anat; Am Soc Vet Physiol & Pharmacol; Am Asn Anatomists; Sigma Xi. *Res:* Studies of normal structure of the central nervous system of vertebrates correlated with physiological phenomena, especially pain and autonomic control mechanisms; gross anatomy. *Mailing Add:* Physiol Sci Okla State Univ Univ Col Vet Med Stillwater OK 74074-0353. *Fax:* 405-744-6743

BREBBIA, CARLOS ALBERTO, COMPUTATIONAL MECHANICS, ENGINEERING. *Current Pos:* DIR, WESSEX INST TECHNOL, SOUTHAMPTON, 81-; PRES, COMPUTATIONAL MECH INC, 84-; PROF, UNIV PORTSMOUTH, 91- *Personal Data:* b Rosario, Arg, Dec 13, 48; m 71, Carolyn S Stones; c Alexander C & Isabel E. *Educ:* Univ Litoral, Rosario, dipl, 68; Univ Southampton, Eng, PhD(civil eng), 72. *Hon Degrees:* PhD, Polytroh Univ Bucharest, Romania, 95. *Honors & Awards:* Ville France Medal, 78. *Prof Exp:* Lectr, Univ Southampton, 70-75, reader, 76-79; asst prof, Princeton Univ, 75-76; prof, Univ Calif, Irvine, 79-81. *Mem:* Int Soc Boundary Elements (pres, 89-); Am Soc Civil Engrs; fel Inst Mech Engrs. *Res:* Development of the main concept of the boundary element method, of innovative computational techniques and of an industrial computer aided design code based on boundary element methods. *Mailing Add:* Comput Mech Inc 25 Bridge St Billerica MA 01821

BREBRICK, ROBERT FRANK, JR, SOLID STATE CHEMISTRY. *Current Pos:* from assoc prof to prof, 70-96, EMER PROF, DEPT MECH ENG MAT SCI PROG, MARQUETTE UNIV, 96- *Personal Data:* b Danvers, Mont, Oct 18, 25; m 57, Marian Knodle; c 4. *Educ:* Mont State Col, BS, 47; Cath Univ Am, PhD(chem), 52. *Honors & Awards:* Meritorious Civilian Serv Award, 56. *Prof Exp:* Asst, Cath Univ Am, 47-50; phys chemist, Naval Ord Lab, 52-61, group leader, mat group, Solid State Div, 57-61; phys chemist, Solid State Div, Lincoln Lab, Mass Inst Technol, 61-70. *Res:* Physical chemistry of semiconductors; theoretical and experimental studies of the homogeneity range and thermodynamic properties of semiconducting compounds; calculation of phase diagrams. *Mailing Add:* Dept Mech Eng Marquette Univ Milwaukee WI 53233. *Fax:* 414-288-7082; *E-Mail:* 6075brebrick@vms.csd.mu.edu

BRECHER, ARTHUR SEYMOUR, BIOCHEMISTRY. *Current Pos:* assoc prof, 69-75, PROF BIOCHEM, BOWLING GREEN STATE UNIV, 75- *Personal Data:* b New York, NY, Mar 30, 28; m 66, Laura Lyman; c Benjamin & Sharon. *Educ:* City Col New York, BS, 48; Univ Calif, Los Angeles, PhD, 56. *Prof Exp:* Jr res biochemist, NY State Psychiat Inst, 48-52; asst chem, Univ Calif, Los Angeles, 53-56; asst prof biochem, Purdue Univ, 56-58; biochemist pharmacol, Food & Drug Admin, Dept Health, Educ & Welfare, 58-60; assoc res scientist, NY State Dept Ment Hyg, 60-63; asst prof biochem, Sch Med, George Washington Univ, 63-69. *Mem:* AAAS; Am Chem Soc; Soc Exp Biol & Med; Am Soc Biochem & Molecular Biol; Am Soc Neurochem; Int Soc Neurochem. *Res:* Enzyme chemistry; intermediary metabolism; drug metabolism; hypertension; alcoholism; bacterial nutrition. *Mailing Add:* Dept Chem Bowling Green State Univ Bowling Green OH 43403. *Fax:* 419-372-9809

BRECHER, AVIVA, SPACE PHYSICS, PALEOMAGNETISM. *Current Pos:* STRATEGIC PLANNING ANALYST, US DEPT TRANSP, 87- *Personal Data:* b Bucarest, Romania, July 4, 45; m 65; c 2. *Educ:* Israel Inst Technol & Mass Inst Technol, BSc & MSc, 68; Univ Calif, PhD(appl physics), 72. *Honors & Awards:* Asteroid named in honor of, Brecher 4242. *Prof Exp:* Res assoc earth & planetary sci, Mass Inst Technol, 72-77; asst prof physics, Wellesley Col, 77-79; sr staff consult, nuclear & geotech systs safety & environ safety, Arthur D Little, Inc, 79-85; dir acad-corp rels, Boston Univ, 85-87. *Concurrent Pos:* Amelia Earhard Zonta fel, 71-72; vis scientist, Mass Inst Technol, 77-79; exchange scientist, Japan Soc Prom Sci, 79-80; cong sci fel, Am Phys Soc fel & US Senate, 83-84; mem, Transp Res Bd, Nat Acad Sci. *Mem:* Am Phys Soc; AAAS; Int Astron Union. *Res:* Laser physics and solid state physics; nature of lunar magnetism; planetary magnetic fields; terrestrial paleomagnetism and continental drift; physical properties of meteorites and models of planetary evolution; risk analysis for nuclear waste disposal in geologic repositories; physico-chemical and mathematical modeling of the long-term performance of nuclear waste packages; probabilistic risk analysis for the mining industry (subsidence, flooding, earthquakes, back failure); technology assesment and strategic planning; university and industry cooperative research; advanced transportation technology and safety analysis (maglev, commercial space transporation); health effects of electromagnetic fields and radiation. *Mailing Add:* Transp Strategic Planning Anal Off US Dept Transp-Nat Transp Syst Ctr Cambridge MA 02142. *E-Mail:* aviva.brecher@tsc.dot.gov

BRECHER, CHARLES, OPTICAL MATERIALS & PHENOMENA. *Current Pos:* RES PROF, CHEM DEPT, BOSTON UNIV, 93- *Personal Data:* b Brooklyn, NY, Nov 5, 32; m 69, Roberta; c Jonathan & Andrew. *Educ:* Columbia Univ, BA, 54, MA, 55, PhD(phys chem), 59. *Prof Exp:* Res fel phys chem, Columbia Univ, 59-62; res chemist, Mat Sci Lab, Gen Tel & Electronics Labs, 62-92. *Mem:* Am Phys Soc; Sigma Xi. *Res:* Optical phenomena and materials, especially spectra of solids and liquids, as related to problems of light generation, suntillation, molecular and crystal structure, molecular interactions; energy transfer and laser phenomena. *Mailing Add:* Dept Chem Boston Univ 590 Commonwealth Ave Boston MA 02215

BRECHER, GEORGE, LABORATORY MEDICINE, HEMATOLOGY. *Current Pos:* chmn dept, 66-78, prof lab med, 66-78, EMER PROF, UNIV CALIF, BERKELEY, 78- *Personal Data:* b Olomouc, Czech, Nov 5, 13; US citizen; m 59, Eva Schneider; c 5. *Educ:* Univ Prague, MD, 38; Univ London, DTM&H, 40. *Honors & Awards:* French Legion Hon, 80. *Prof Exp:* Sr asst surgeon, USPHS, 47, surgeon, 49-51, sr surgeon, 51-53, med dir, 54-56, chief hemat serv, Dept Clin Path, 53-66. *Concurrent Pos:* Fel, Mayo Clin, 43; NIH fel, 67; assoc fac scientist, Lawrence Berkeley Labs, Donner Lab, Berkeley, 78- *Mem:* Acad Clin Lab Physicians & Scientists (pres, 71); Am Soc Hemat (pres, 73); Asn Am Physicians; Int Soc Hemat. *Res:* Morphologic hematology; kinetics of bone marrow and blood cells; laboratory automation and quality control. *Mailing Add:* 319 Yale Ave Berkeley CA 94708-1107

BRECHER, KENNETH, THEORETICAL ASTROPHYSICS, HISTORY OF SCIENCE. *Current Pos:* assoc prof, 79-81, PROF ASTRON & PHYSICS, BOSTON UNIV, 81-, DIR SCI & MATH EDUC CTR, 90- *Personal Data:* b New York, NY, Dec 7, 43; m 65, Aviva Schwartz; c Daniel & Karen. *Educ:* Mass Inst Technol, BS, 64, PhD(physics), 69. *Prof Exp:* Res physicist, Univ Calif, San Diego, 69-72; from asst prof to assoc prof physics, Mass Inst Technol, 72-79. *Concurrent Pos:* John Simon Guggenheim Mem fel, 79-80; assoc, Harvard Col Observ, 79-; sr res assoc, Nat Res Coun, NASA & Nat Acad Sci, 83-84; W K Kellog fel, 85-88. *Mem:* Fel Am Phys Soc; Am Astron Soc; Int Astron Union; Sigma Xi; Am Asn Physics Teachers; NY Acad Sci. *Res:* Theoretical high energy astrophysics; x-ray and gamma-ray astronomy; observational tests and consequences of gravitational theories; cosmology; archaeoastronomy; historical astronomy and archaeoastrophysics; informal and formal science education. *Mailing Add:* Dept Astron Boston Univ 725 Commonwealth Ave Boston MA 02215. *Fax:* 617-353-5704; *E-Mail:* brecher@bo.edu

BRECHER, PETER I, BIOCHEMISTRY. *Current Pos:* from asst prof to assoc prof biochem, 71-81, PROF BIOCHEM, SCH MED, BOSTON UNIV, 81- *Personal Data:* b New York, NY, May 19, 40; m 64; c 2. *Educ:* Ohio Univ, BS, 60; Boston Univ, PhD(biochem), 68. *Prof Exp:* Res assoc, Ben May Labs Cancer Res, Univ Chicago, 69-71. *Concurrent Pos:* Res fel biochem, Sch Med, Boston Univ, 68-69; NIH trainee physiol, 68-69. *Res:* Lipid metabolism in the arterial wall; cardiovascular diseases. *Mailing Add:* Boston Univ Sch Med 80 E Concord St Boston MA 02218-2394. *Fax:* 617-638-5258

BRECHNER, BEVERLY LORRAINE, MATHEMATICS. *Current Pos:* from asst prof to assoc prof, 68-83, PROF MATH, UNIV FLA, 83- *Personal Data:* b New York, NY, May 27, 36. *Educ:* Univ Miami, BS, 57, MS, 59; La State Univ, Baton Rouge, PhD(math), 64. *Honors & Awards:* George Polya Award, Math Asn Am, 89. *Prof Exp:* Instr math, La State Univ, New Orleans, 62-64, asst prof, 64-68. *Concurrent Pos:* Vis assoc prof math, Univ Mich, 77 & Univ Tex, 80. *Mem:* AAAS; Am Math Soc; Math Asn Am. *Res:* Topology; point set topology; spaces of homeomorphisms; locally setwise homogeneous continua; chainable continua; dimension theory; prime end theory; fixed point problems. *Mailing Add:* Univ Fla 358 Little Hall PO Box 118105 Gainesville FL 32611-8000

BRECHT, PATRICK ERNEST, PLANT PHYSIOLOGY, VEGETABLE CROPS. *Current Pos:* DIR SPEC COMMODITIES, AM PRESIDENT LINES, 81- *Personal Data:* b Beaconsfield, Eng, Jan 8, 46; US citizen; m 67; c 1. *Educ:* Whittier Col, BA, 68; Calif State Univ, Los Angeles, MS, 69; Univ Calif, Davis, PhD(plant physiol), 73. *Prof Exp:* Asst prof postharvest physiol,

Cornell Univ, 73-76; dir prod res & develop, Sea-Land Serv Inc, 76-78; dir qual control perishables, United Brands Co, 78-81. *Mem:* Am Soc Hort Sci; Am Soc Plant Physiologists; Inst Food Technologists; Sigma Xi. *Res:* Postharvest physiology and quality of vegetables and fruits. *Mailing Add:* 4733 Bodega Ave Petaluma CA 94952

BRECKE, BARRY JOHN, WEED SCIENCE, AGRONOMY. *Current Pos:* Asst prof, 75-81, ASSOC PROF WEED SCI, W FLA RES & EDUC CTR, UNIV FLA, 81- *Personal Data:* b Milwaukee, Wis, Jan 16, 47; m 69, Gayle L Naggatz; c Darren J & Suzanne M. *Educ:* Wis State Univ, River Falls, BS, 69; Cornell Univ, MS, 74, PhD(weed sci), 76. *Concurrent Pos:* Prin investr, USDA, 87-89; Co Han Inc grants, 92-96; Ctr Integrated Pest Mgt, 95-96; assoc ed, Weed Technol, 93-96. *Mem:* Weed Sci Soc Am; Plant Growth Regulator Soc Am; Am Soc Agron; Int Weed Sci Soc. *Res:* Studies of weed management systems; the effects of various cultural practices on weeds; biology of particularly troublesome weeds and weed population dynamics. *Mailing Add:* 5651 Meadowlark Ln Milton FL 32570-8770. *Fax:* 850-994-9589; *E-Mail:* bjbe@gnv.ifas.ufl.edu

BRECKENRIDGE, BRUCE (MCLAIN), PHARMACOLOGY. *Current Pos:* RETIRED. *Personal Data:* b Brooklyn, Iowa, Nov 7, 26; m 49, Mary Barber; c 3. *Educ:* Iowa State Col, BS, 47; Univ Rochester, MS, 49, PhD(physiol), 52, MD, 56. *Prof Exp:* Instr physiol, Univ Rochester, 53-56; intern med, Barnes Hosp, St Louis, 56-57; from instr to assoc prof pharmacol, Washington Univ, 57-67; chmn dept, Univ Med & Dent, NJ, Robert Wood Johnson Med Sch, 67-89, prof pharmacol, 67-95. *Concurrent Pos:* Fel pharmacol, Washington Univ, 57-59; Markle scholar med sci, 59; mem, Pharmacol A Study Sect, NIH, 68-72; adj prof med, Robert Wood Johnson Med Sch, 79-95. *Mem:* Am Soc Biochem & Molecular Biol; Am Soc Pharmacol & Exp Therapeut. *Res:* Metabolism of the nervous system; cyclic nucleotides and drug action. *Mailing Add:* 135 Leabrook Lane 675 Hoes Lane Princeton NJ 08540-3621

BRECKENRIDGE, CARL, ATHEROSCLEROSIS, CLINICAL BIOCHEMISTRY. *Current Pos:* assoc prof, 80-84, PROF BIOCHEM, DALHOUSIE UNIV, 85-, DEPT HEAD BIOCHEM, 88- *Personal Data:* b Asphodel Twp, Ont, July 29, 42; m 65; c 3. *Educ:* Queen's Univ, Ont, BSc, 65; Univ Toronto, MSc, 66, PhD(biochem), 70. *Prof Exp:* Med Res Coun Can res fel, Ctr Neurochem, Strasbourg, France, 70-72 & Montreal Neurol Inst, 72; from asst to assoc prof clin biochem, Univ Toronto, 72-80, dir, Core Lab, 72-80. *Mem:* Can Fedn Biol Socs; Am Oil Chemists Soc; Can Soc Clin Chem; Can Soc Clin Invest; Can Atherosclerosis Soc; fel Am Heart Asn. *Res:* Studies of the structure of lipid and protein constituents of human lipoproteins and their role in hyperlipoproteinemia and the development of atherosclerosis. *Mailing Add:* Dept Biochem Dalhousie Univ Halifax NS B3H 4H7 Can

BRECKENRIDGE, JOHN ROBERT, MEDICAL BIOPHYSICS. *Current Pos:* supvry physicist, 61-64, res physicist, 64-74, chief, Biophysics Br, 74-84, CONSULT, MIL ERGONOMICS DIV, US ARMY RES INST ENVIRON MED, 85- *Personal Data:* b Kingston, Pa, Oct 10, 20; m 79; c 1. *Educ:* Univ Pa, BS, 42. *Prof Exp:* Student engr, Electrometall Co, Union Carbide Corp, Ohio, 42-45; physicist, Qm Res & Eng Ctr, Mass, 46-61. *Mem:* Sigma Xi; Am Soc Heat, Refrig & Air-Conditioning Engrs. *Res:* Heat and moisture transfer from clothed man to his environment in terms of clothing parameters and environmental factors. *Mailing Add:* 63 Stonebridge Rd Wayland MA 01778

BRECKENRIDGE, MARY BARBER, MEDICAL DEMOGRAPHY, HEALTH SERVICES RESEARCH. *Current Pos:* from asst prof to assoc prof, 78-94, PROF, UNIV MED & DENT NJ, ROBERT WOOD JOHNSON MED SCH, 94- *Personal Data:* b Omaha, Nebr, Mar 4, 25; m 49, Bruce M; c Lee, Janet B (Pierrehumbert) & Ellen B (Koch). *Educ:* Iowa State Univ, BS, 47; Univ Iowa, MS, 48; Princeton Univ, PhD(demog), 76. *Prof Exp:* Fel, Princeton Univ, 76-78. *Concurrent Pos:* Vis fel, Harvard Sch Pub Health, 84-86; grad fac pub health, Rutgers Univ, 87-; prin investr, Agency for Health Care Policy & Res & Health Resources & Serv Admin, 93-95. *Mem:* Am Pub Health Asn; Am Statist Asn; Asn Health Serv Res; Pop Asn Am. *Res:* Maternal and infant outcomes of pregnancy; relation of changes in medical technology and policy to health outcomes; covariates of health care utilization. *Mailing Add:* Dept Family Med UMDNJ-Robert Wood Johnson Med Sch New Brunswick NJ 08903-0019. *Fax:* 732-246-8084; *E-Mail:* brecken@umdnj.edu

BRECKENRIDGE, ROBERT A(RTHUR), OCEAN ENGINEERING, STRUCTURAL ENGINEERING. *Current Pos:* RETIRED. *Personal Data:* b Los Angeles, Calif, Mar 29, 24; m 55, 83, Elena Maluchin; c Sharon J (Prestwich) & John A. *Educ:* Univ Southern Calif, BE, 50, MS, 53. *Prof Exp:* Mat engr, US Naval Civil Eng Lab, 50-51, civil engr, 52-54, res engr, 54-69, ocean eng prog mgr, 69-74, dir found eng div, 74-79. *Mem:* Sigma Xi; fel Am Soc Civil Engrs. *Res:* Structures and structural components; blast-resistant shelters; blast-closure devices; deep-ocean structures and structural plastics; design guidelines, equipment, tools and techniques for ocean installations. *Mailing Add:* PO Box 1207 Twin Peaks CA 92391-1207

BRECKENRIDGE, WALTER JOHN, ECOLOGY, ORNITHOLOGY & HERPETOLOGY. *Current Pos:* RETIRED. *Personal Data:* b Brooklyn, Iowa, Mar 22, 03; m 33, Dorothy Shogren; c Betsy (Norum), Thomas R & Barbara (Franklin). *Educ:* Univ Iowa, BA, 26; Univ Minn, MA, 34, PhD(ecol), 41. *Honors & Awards:* Minn Award, Nat Wildlife Soc, 67; Arthur Allen Award, Cornell Univ. *Prof Exp:* Museum preparator, Bell Mus Natural Hist, Univ Minn, 26-46, mus dir, 46-70. *Concurrent Pos:* Breckenridge chmn orinth, Univ Minn. *Mem:* Wilson Ornith Soc (pres, 51-53); fel Am Ornith Union. *Res:* Herpetology and ornithology of Minnesota. *Mailing Add:* 5800 St Croix Ave Apt 511 Minneapolis MN 55422

BRECKENRIDGE, WILLIAM H, CHEMICAL DYNAMICS, SPECTROSCOPY. *Current Pos:* from asst prof to assoc prof, 71-80, PROF CHEM, UNIV UTAH, 80- *Personal Data:* b Kansas City, Mo, Oct 14, 41; m 84, Julie; c Shanda. *Educ:* Univ Kans, BS, 63; Stanford Univ, PhD(chem), 68. *Prof Exp:* mem tech staff, Bell Labs, NJ, 70-71. *Concurrent Pos:* Dreyfus teacher Scholar, 73-78; vis scholar, Stanford Univ, 77-78, Max Planck Inst, WGer, 84-85; sr Fulbright fel, 84; vis prof, Univ Paris-South, 85; Guggenheim fel, 85. *Mem:* Am Chem Soc; Am Phys Soc. *Res:* State-to-state dynamics of chemical reactions and energy transfer processes in the gas phase, using laser techniques; spectroscopy and dynamics of van der Waals complexes of metal atoms in supersonic jets. *Mailing Add:* Dept Chem Univ Utah Salt Lake City UT 84112-1102. *Fax:* 801-581-8433; *E-Mail:* breckenridge@chemistry.utah.edu

BRECKINRIDGE, JAMES BERNARD, OPTICAL PHYSICS. *Current Pos:* co-investr, NASA Spacelab 3 & mem tech staff, 76-80, MGR, OPTICAL SCI SECT, JET PROPULSION LAB, 80-; FAC, CALIF INST TECHNOL, 81- *Personal Data:* b Cleveland, Ohio, May 27, 39; m 65, Ann M Yoder; c Douglass E & John B. *Educ:* Case Inst Technol, BSc, 61; Univ Ariz, MS, 70, PhD(optics), 76. *Prof Exp:* Asst astron, Lick Observ, Univ Calif, 61-64 & Kitt Peak Nat Observ, NSF, 64-66; engr physicist, Rauland Corp, Zenith Radio Corp, 66-67; assoc-in-res, Kitt Peak Nat Observ, NSF, 67-76. *Concurrent Pos:* Tech adv HST failure rev bd, NASA. *Mem:* Fel Optical Soc Am; Am Astron Soc; Royal Astron Soc; Int Astron Union; Inst Elec & Electronics Engrs; Sigma Xi; fel Soc Photo-Optical Instrumentation Engrs; Int Soc Photo-Optical Instrumentation Engrs (pres, 94). *Res:* Optical interferometric techniques for research in astrophysics; image evaluation; optical instruments; space telescopes. *Mailing Add:* 4565 Viro Rd La Canada CA 91011-3763

BREDAHL, EDWARD ARLAN, PHYSIOLOGY, ECOLOGY. *Current Pos:* AT DEPT MATH-SCI, SEATTLE CENT COMMUNITY COL. *Personal Data:* b Pelican Rapids, Minn, Dec 20, 37; div; c 2. *Educ:* Concordia Col, Moorhead, Minn, BA, 59; Univ NDak, MST, 64, PhD(physiol ecol), 69. *Prof Exp:* Teacher high sch, Minn, 59-62; instr cell physiol, Univ NDak, 69; asst prof biol & ecol, Stout State Univ, 69-80; mem fac, Moorhead State Col, 80- *Res:* Physiological investigation of water balance in hibernating and nonhibernating Citellus franklinii and Citellus richardsonii to develop efficiency indices for water balance relative to the environment. *Mailing Add:* 22711 Lakeview Dr Mountlake Terrace WA 98043

BREDECK, HENRY E, physiology, for more information see previous edition

BREDEHOEFT, JOHN DALLAS, HYDROLOGY, GEOLOGY. *Current Pos:* CONSULT, HYDRODYNAMICS GROUP, 94- *Personal Data:* b St Louis, Mo, Feb 28, 33; m 58; c 3. *Educ:* Princeton Univ, BSE, 55; Univ Ill, MS, 57, PhD(geol), 62. *Honors & Awards:* R E Horton Award, Am Geophys Union, 75, Horton Medal, 97; O E Meinzer Award, Geol Surv Am, 75. *Prof Exp:* Geologist, Humble Oil & Refining Co Div, Standard Oil Co, NJ, 57-59; geologist, Desert Res Inst, Nev, 62; res geologist, US Geol Surv, 62-74, dept asst chief res hydrologist, Water Resources Div, 74-79, res geologist, 85-94; regional hydrologist, Water Resource Div, Manlo Park, 80-85. *Concurrent Pos:* Vis assoc prof, Univ Ill, 67-68; res assoc, Resources for Future, 68-70. *Mem:* Nat Acad Eng; Geol Soc Am; Am Geophys Union; Am Asn Petrol Geologists; Russia Acad Nat Scis. *Res:* Ground water hydrology; physical properties of ground water systems; physics of ground water motion; transport of chemical constituents in ground-water systems. *Mailing Add:* PO Box 352 234 Scenic Dr LaHonda CA 94020. *Fax:* 650-747-0273; *E-Mail:* jdbrede@aol.com

BREDENBERG, CARL ERIC, THORACIC SURGERY, VASCULAR SURGERY. *Current Pos:* asst prof, 72-76, assoc prof, 76-80, PROF SURG, STATE UNIV NY, UPSTATE MED CTR, 80- *Personal Data:* b San Mateo, Calif, Mar 18, 40; m 66; c 2. *Educ:* Johns Hopkins Univ, MD, 64. *Prof Exp:* Intern surg, Johns Hopkins Hosp, 64-65, asst resident, 67-71, resident surgeon, 71-72. *Concurrent Pos:* Chief Thoracic Surg Sect, Syracuse Vet Admin Hosp, 73-; surgeon in charge, Vascular Surg Serv, State Univ NY, 75- *Mem:* Soc Univ Surgeons; Asn Academic Surg; Int Cardiovascular Soc; Am Asn Thoracic Surg; Am Col Surgeons. *Res:* Pulmonary and cardiovascular physiology on shock, pulmonary alveolar mechanics, pulmonary circulation and pulmonary edema. *Mailing Add:* Dept Surg Maine Med Ctr 22 Bramhall St Portland ME 04102-3175

BREDER, CHARLES VINCENT, ORGANIC POLYMER CHEMISTRY, ANALYTICAL CHEMISTRY. *Current Pos:* STAFF SCIENTIST, LAW OFF KELLER & HECKMAN, 84- *Personal Data:* b Atlantic City, NJ, Feb 15, 40; m 62; c 2. *Educ:* Carson-Newman Col, BS, 62; Vanderbilt Univ, MS, 64, PhD(org chem), 68. *Honors & Awards:* Award of Merit, FDA. *Prof Exp:* Res chemist, E I du Pont de Nemours & Co, 67-71; res chemist, Food & Drug Admin, Dept Health, Educ & Welfare, 71-84. *Mem:* Am Chem Soc; Asn Off Anal Chemists; Am Soc Testing & Mat. *Res:* Determination of the identity and quantity of chemicals that migrate from food packaging into foods. *Mailing Add:* Keller & Heckman 1001 G St NW Suite 500 W Washington DC 20001-4545

BREDEWEG, ROBERT ALLEN, ANALYTICAL CHEMISTRY. *Current Pos:* SR ASSOC SCIENTIST, DOW CHEM CO, 65- *Personal Data:* b Forest Grove, Mich, Aug 15, 41; m 63, Barbara L Young; c Todd A & Cheryl L. *Educ:* Hope Col, BA, 63; Southern Ill Univ, MA, 65. *Honors & Awards:* Vernon A Stenger Award, Dow Chem Anal Scientists, 75; IR 100 Award. *Mem:* Am Chem Soc; Instrument Soc Am. *Res:* Automation of analytical procedures; process optimization. *Mailing Add:* 233 Dewberry Dr Lake Jackson TX 77566-4903

BREDON, GLEN E, MATHEMATICS, TOPOLOGY. *Current Pos:* prof, 68-93, EMER PROF MATH, RUTGERS UNIV, NEW BRUNSWICK, 93- *Personal Data:* b Fresno, Calif, Aug 24, 32; m 63, Anne Loeb; c Joelle & Aaron. *Educ:* Stanford Univ, BS, 54; Harvard Univ, AM, 55, PhD(math), 58. *Prof Exp:* Mem, Inst Advan Study, 58-60; from asst prof to prof math, Univ Calif, Berkeley, 60-68. *Concurrent Pos:* Sloan fel, 65-67; mem, Inst Advan Study, 58-60, 66-67, 71-72, 75-76 & 80-81. *Mem:* Sigma Xi; Math Asn Am. *Res:* Topological transformation groups; algebraic and differential topology. *Mailing Add:* 58188 Trails End Rd North Fork CA 93643

BREE, ALAN V, PHYSICAL CHEMISTRY. *Current Pos:* from asst prof to assoc prof, 61-71, PROF CHEM, UNIV BC, 71- *Personal Data:* b Sydney, Australia, Nov 16, 32; m 61; c 2. *Educ:* Univ Sydney, BSc, 54, MSc, 55, PhD(phys chem), 58. *Prof Exp:* Nat Res Coun Can fel, 58-59; fel, Chem Dept, Univ Col, Univ London, 60-61. *Res:* Electronic and vibrational properties of aromatic molecules in the gas; solution and solid phases. *Mailing Add:* Dept Chem Univ BC 2329 West Mall Vancouver BC V6T 1W5 Can

BREECE, HARRY T, III, ELECTRICAL ENGINEERING, COMMUNICATIONS. *Current Pos:* VPRES ENG, SUPERIOR AUTOTRONICS, INC. *Personal Data:* b Huntington, WVa, May 3, 39; m 64; c 4. *Educ:* Univ Cincinnati, BS, 62; Rutgers Univ, MS, 64; Purdue Univ, PhD(elec eng), 69. *Prof Exp:* Engr semiconductor circuit design, Semiconductor Div, RCA, 62-64; mem tech staff digital commun systs, Bell Labs, 69-78; dist mgr strategic planning, AT&T, 78-84. *Mem:* Inst Elec & Electronics Engrs. *Res:* Digital communications; digital switching; data communications. *Mailing Add:* Superior Autotronics Inc Rm 104 533 Third Ave Huntington WV 25701

BREED, CAROL SAMETH, GEOLOGY, DESERT GEOMORPHOLOGY. *Current Pos:* GEOLOGIST, US GEOL SURV, 72- *Personal Data:* b New York, NY, Apr 21, 33; m 54, 65; c 5. *Educ:* Smith Col, BA, 54; Brown Univ, MS, 57. *Prof Exp:* Asst geol, Mus Northern Ariz, 70-72. *Concurrent Pos:* Co-investr desert studies, Nat Air & Space Mus, Smithsonian Inst, 75-; res assoc, Mus Northern Ariz, 76- *Mem:* Sigma Xi; fel Geol Soc Am. *Res:* Desert geologic processes and landforms, especially in southwestern American deserts and Eastern Sahara (NAfrica) with application to problems of geologic history, climate change and soil and water resources in arid regions. *Mailing Add:* 189 Wilson Caynon Rd Sedona AZ 86336-4103

BREED, ERNEST SPENCER, SURGERY, PHYSIOLOGY. *Current Pos:* RETIRED. *Personal Data:* b Lyndonville, NY, May 27, 13; m 44, Nadia Tichy; c Ione, Tamara, Judy & Nadia. *Educ:* Univ Mich, MD, 38; Am Bd Surg, dipl, 49. *Prof Exp:* Intern med & surg, NY Univ Div, Bellevue Hosp, 39-40, asst resident surg & path, 40-41, resident, 41-42; instr surg, Sch Med, NY Univ, 47-50, from asst prof to assoc prof surg, 50-90. *Concurrent Pos:* Res fel, Off Sci Res & Develop shock proj, Col Physicians & Surgeons, Columbia Univ, 42-44; Commonwealth Fund res fel physiol, 47-49; attend, Bellevue Hosp, 42-, Univ Hosp, 52- & Vet Admin Hosp, Manhattan, NY, 56-; consult, Misericordia Hosp, Bronx, 65- *Mem:* Soc Univ Surgeons. *Res:* Right heart catherization in patients in shock and in chronic pulmonary disease; right renal vein catheterization; renal function in relation to surgical conditions in patients, including open heart surgery and general surgical patients before, during and after surgery; direct measurement of cardiac output of the heart. *Mailing Add:* Dept Surg Sch Med New York Univ 550 First Ave New York NY 10016-6402

BREED, HELEN ILLICK, ENVIRONMENTAL HEALTH, RIGHTS FOR WOMEN. *Current Pos:* ENVIRON ADV, WOMEN'S ENVIRON & DEVELOP ORGN, 91-; INT LIAISON, NY STATE SUMMIT, 92- *Personal Data:* b New Cumberland, Pa, Mar 12, 25; m 57, Henry E; c Henry E III, Joseph I & Brenda E. *Educ:* Syracuse Univ, BS, 47, MS, 49; Cornell Univ, PhD(vert zool & biol), 53. *Prof Exp:* Asst, Dept Zool, Syracuse Univ, 47-49; teacher high sch, Lyons, NY, 49-50; instr zool & physiol, Dept Biol, Akron Univ, 54; Ford Found fel & instr physiol, Vassar Col, 54-55; asst prof biol, Russell Sage Col, 55-57; asst dir syst biol, NSF, DC, 57; res assoc prof conserv, Cornell Univ, 57-61; res assoc biol, Rensselaer Polytech Inst, 64-68; consult, Eltick Res Corp, 71-90. *Concurrent Pos:* Am-Scand fel, 59-60; mem, Rensselaer Environ Mgt Coun, 71-78; consult, Ichthyol Assoc, 71-80, UNCED, Geneva, 91. *Mem:* AAAS; Am Soc Zoologists; Soc Syst Zool; Am Soc Ichthyol & Herpet; Am Inst Biol Sci; Sigma Xi. *Res:* Ichthyology; ecology; conservation; x-ray diffraction of vertebrate hard tissue; environment and sustainable development. *Mailing Add:* RD 3 Box 245 B Troy NY 12180

BREED, HENRY ELTINGE, PHYSICS, EXPERIMENTAL PHYSICS. *Current Pos:* RETIRED. *Personal Data:* b New York, NY, Dec 5, 15; m 57, Helen Illick; c Henry E III, Joseph I & Brenda E. *Educ:* Colgate Univ, BA, 38; Rensselaer Polytech Inst, MS, 48, PhD, 55. *Honors & Awards:* Fulbright lectr optics, Nat Univ Eng, Lima, Peru, 73. *Prof Exp:* From instr to prof physics, Rensselaer Polytech Inst, 45-81. *Concurrent Pos:* Res asst, Gen Elec Res Lab, 46-48; consult, Ord Corps, US Army, 56-62; Fulbright fel, Inst Teorisk Kjemi, Trondheim, Norway, 59-60; sabbatical, Univ Oslo, 76. *Mem:* Am Phys Soc; Am Asn Physics Teachers; fel Optical Soc Am; Sigma Xi. *Res:* Electron diffraction; optics; acoustics. *Mailing Add:* Rd 3 Box 421 Troy NY 12180

BREED, LAURENCE WOODS, ORGANIC POLYMER CHEMISTRY. *Current Pos:* RETIRED. *Personal Data:* b Decatur, Ill, Dec 16, 24; m 48; c 2. *Educ:* Park Col, BA, 48; Univ Kans, MA, 50. *Prof Exp:* Asst, Univ Kans, 48-50; res chemist, Battenfeld Grease & Oil Corp, 50-53; assoc chemist, Midwest Res Inst, 53-59, sr chemist, 59-62, prin chemist, 62-67, sr adv chem, 67-77, mgr plan, 77-90. *Mem:* Am Chem Soc. *Res:* Organosilicon chemistry; organic and semiorganic polymers; organic synthesis; thermal analysis of materials. *Mailing Add:* 6400 W 66th Terr Overland Park KS 66202-4117

BREED, MICHAEL DALLAM, INSECT BEHAVIOR. *Current Pos:* From asst prof to assoc prof, 77-87, PROF BIOL, UNIV COLO, 87- *Personal Data:* b Kansas City, Mo, Sept 2, 51; m 75, Cheryl Nistig; c Elise & Ann. *Educ:* Grinnell Col, BA, 73; Univ Kans, MA, 75, PhD(entom), 77. *Concurrent Pos:* Dept chair, Univ Colo, 86-90, actg assoc dean, 91-93. *Mem:* Animal Behav Soc; Int Union Study Social Insects (secy & treas, 78-82); Asn Trop Biol; Int Bee Res Asn; Entom Soc Am. *Res:* Mechanisms of dominance in social insects; kin recognition; the behavioral ecology of aggression; territoriality and spacing behavior; comparative social behavior of bees. *Mailing Add:* Dept Environ Pop & Org Biol Univ Colo Boulder CO 80309-0334. *Fax:* 303-492-8699; *E-Mail:* breed_m@spot.colorado.edu

BREED, WILLIAM JOSEPH, writer, tour leader, for more information see previous edition

BREEDEN, JOHN ELBERT, PLANT ECOLOGY. *Current Pos:* RETIRED. *Personal Data:* b Charlotte, Tenn, Nov 11, 31; m 53; c 3. *Educ:* Austin Peay State Univ, BS, 53, MA, 54; Vanderbilt Univ, PhD(plant ecol), 68. *Prof Exp:* Prof biol, David Lipscomb Univ, 68-96. *Mem:* Sigma Xi. *Mailing Add:* 1221 Parker Pl Brentwood TN 37027

BREEDING, J ERNEST, JR, WATER WAVES, BEACH PROCESSES. *Current Pos:* oceanogr, Naval Oceanog Off, 88, RES PHYSICIST, NAVAL RES LAB-STENNIS SPACE CTR, 88- *Personal Data:* b Peoria, Ill, Mar 17, 38; m 70, 90, Rebecca Darden; c Della G, David & Michael. *Educ:* Drake Univ, BA, 60; Columbia Univ, PhD(geophys), 72. *Prof Exp:* Res asst physics, Univ Tenn, Knoxville, 60-61; res physicist, Naval Coastal Systs Ctr, 62-78; vis assoc prof oceanog, Fla State Univ, Tallahassee, 77-79; assoc prof, oceanog & ocean eng, Fla Inst Technol, 79-87. *Concurrent Pos:* Res asst phys oceanog, Lamont-Doherty Earth Observ, Columbia Univ, 65-70. *Mem:* AAAS; Am Asn Physics Teachers; Am Geophys Union; Soc Explor Geophysicists; Sigma Xi; Am Meteorol Soc; Acoust Soc Am. *Res:* Modification and prediction of water waves in coastal waters; wave refraction; wave induced beach processes; ambient noise in underwater sound. *Mailing Add:* 115 Blackbeard Dr Slidell LA 70461. *Fax:* 504-643-8540; *E-Mail:* travel@communique.net

BREEDLOVE, CHARLES B, SCIENCE EDUCATION. *Current Pos:* prof, 64-80, EMER PROF PHYSICS, EASTERN MICH UNIV, 80- *Personal Data:* b Chico, Tex, Dec 5, 16; m 42; c 2. *Educ:* McMurry Col, BS, 37; Southern Methodist Univ, MS, 38; Wayne State Univ, EdD, 63. *Prof Exp:* Teacher pub high schs, Tex, 38-42 & Mich, 43-58; head dept chem, Henry Ford High Sch, 58-64. *Concurrent Pos:* Mem, State Sci Curriculum Comt, Mich, 64-65; dir, Five Year NSF Proj, 70-75. *Mem:* Nat Asn Sci Teachers; Nat Asn Res Sci Teaching; Am Asn Physics Teachers; Am Chem Soc. *Res:* Science teacher education and science curriculum projects. *Mailing Add:* 555 Pleasant St Birmingham MI 48009-4437

BREEN, DALE H, metallurgy, for more information see previous edition

BREEN, GAIL ANNE MARIE, NEUROSCIENCES, MOLECULAR BIOLOGY. *Current Pos:* AT BIOL PROG DIV, UNIV TEX, DALLAS. *Personal Data:* b Pembroke, Ont, Can. *Educ:* Univ Toronto, BSc, 70; Univ Calif, Los Angeles, PhD(neurosci), 74. *Prof Exp:* From res asst pharm to res asst immunol, Univ Toronto, 68-70; res asst neurosci, Univ Calif, Los Angeles, 70-74; Med Res Coun Can fel & res assoc molecular biol, Roswell Park Mem Inst, 74- *Concurrent Pos:* Achievement Rewards for Col Scientists Found fel, 70-72. *Mem:* Soc Neurosci; Sigma Xi. *Res:* Genetics and biochemistry of various lysosomal enzymes, especially beta-galactosidase; regulation of gene expression during development and differentiation, especially of the nervous system. *Mailing Add:* Dept Molecular & Cell Biol Univ Tex-Dallas PO Box 830 688 M-S FO 3 1 Richardson TX 75083. *Fax:* 972-690-2409

BREEN, JAMES LANGHORNE, OBSTETRICS & GYNECOLOGY. *Current Pos:* DIR, DEPT OBSTET & GYNEC, ST BARNABAS MED CTR, 69-, CHMN, 97- *Personal Data:* b Chicago, Ill, Sept 5, 26; m 51; c 5. *Educ:* Northwestern Univ, BS, 48, MD, 52; Am Bd Obstet & Gynec, dipl. *Prof Exp:* Rotating intern, Walter Reed Army Hosp, 52-53, resident obstet & gynec, 54-57, asst chief, 57-58; from asst chief to chief, Second Gen Hosp, Landstuhl, Ger, 58-60; assoc prof, Seton Hall Col Med & Dent, 61-69. *Concurrent Pos:* Res fel obstet, gynec & breast path, Armed Forces Inst Path, 60-61; attend obstetrician & gynecologist, Margaret Hague Maternity Hosp, Jersey City, 61-63; gynecologist & obstetrician-in-chief, Newark City Hosp, 63-; attend gynecologist, Med Ctr, Jersey City, 63-; consult, St Elizabeth Hosp & Monmouth Med Ctr, 63- & St Barnabas Med Ctr, 64-; clin prof obstet & gynec, Jefferson Med Col, 76- & NJ Med Sch, 86. *Mem:* Fel Am Col Obstet & Gynec; fel Am Col Surgeons; Asn Mil Surgeons US; NY Acad Sci; Am Soc Cytol; Soc Gynec Surgeons (pres, 88-89). *Res:* Oncology surgery; research cytology; biochemical assays of female genital malignancy; ovarian tumors. *Mailing Add:* St Barnabas Med Ctr Old Short Hills Rd Livingston NJ 07039

BREEN, JOHN E(DWARD), CIVIL ENGINEERING, STRUCTURAL ENGINEERING. *Current Pos:* res engr, Univ Tex, Austin, 59-62, from asst prof to prof civil eng, 62-77, J J McKetta prof eng, 77-81, Carol Cockrell Curran Chair Eng, 81-84, NASSER I AL-RASHID CHAIR CIVIL ENG, UNIV TEX, AUSTIN, 84- *Personal Data:* b Buffalo, NY, May 1, 32; m 53, Marian Killian; c Mary, Michael, Dennis, Sheila, Sean, Kerry & Christopher. *Educ:* Marquette Univ, BCE, 53; Univ Mo, MS, 57; Univ Tex, PhD, 62. *Honors & Awards:* Wason Medal, Am Concrete Inst, 72 & 83, Raymond C Reese Res Medal, 72 & 78; T Y Lin Award, Am Soc Civil Engrs, 85, 89 & 91; Arthur A Anderson Award, Am Concrete Inst, 87; J Boase Award, Reinforced Concrete Res Coun, 87; Fedn Internationale de Precontrainte Medal, 90; Lindau Award, Am Concrete Inst, 94. *Prof Exp:* Res engr, Univ Mo, 56-57, asst prof civil eng, 57-59. *Concurrent Pos:* Consult engr, 58- *Mem:* Nat Acad Eng; hon mem Am Concrete Inst; fel Am Soc Civil Engrs; Int Asn Bridge & Struct Eng; foreign mem Swiss Acad Eng Sci. *Res:* Structural design and behavior of reinforced and prestressed concrete; codes and standards for building and bridge structures; construction safety in concrete construction. *Mailing Add:* Ferguson Struct Eng Lab 10100 Burnet Rd Bldg 177 Austin TX 78758-4497. *Fax:* 512-471-1944; *E-Mail:* jbreen@mail.utexas.edu

BREEN, JOSEPH JOHN, ENVIRONMENTAL HEALTH, POLLUTION PREVENTION. *Current Pos:* RETIRED. *Personal Data:* b Waterbury, Conn, July 22, 42. *Educ:* Fairfield Univ, BS, 64; Duke Univ, PhD(chem), 73. *Honors & Awards:* Silver Medal, Environ Protection Agency, 84; Bronze Medal, Environ Protection Agency, 85, 86, 87 & 91. *Prof Exp:* NIH fel, Biophysics & Microbiol Dept, Univ Pittsburgh, 72-74; chemist, Lab Officiel des Analyses, Rech Chimiques, Casablanca, Morocco, 74-75 & Inst Agronomique, Veternaire-Hassan II, Rabat, Morocco, 75-76; supvr chemist, Environ Protection Agency, Wash, DC, 77-85, br chief, Off Toxic Substances, 85-91, br chief pollution prev & toxics, 91-97. *Concurrent Pos:* Consult, The Br Sch, Morocco, 74-76; adj prof, Southeastern Univ, Washington, DC, 84-85; exec dir, Green Chem Inst. *Mem:* Am Chem Soc; Sigma Xi; Am Pub Health Asn; Asn Off Anal Chem. *Res:* Promote pollution prevention in industrial chemistry processes; process analytied chemistry; environmentally benign chemical synthesis and processing; lead poisoning in children; chemometrics. *Mailing Add:* Green Chem Inst 1650 Research Blvd Rockville MD 20850. *Fax:* 202-260-0481

BREEN, MARILYN, GEOMETRY. *Current Pos:* Vis instr, 70-71, from asst prof to assoc prof, 72-82, PROF MATH, UNIV OKLA, 82- *Personal Data:* b Anderson, SC, Nov 8, 44; m 75, Walter Kelley; c Joyce Kelley. *Educ:* Agnes Scott Col, BA, 66; Clemson Univ, MS, 68, PhD(math), 70. *Mem:* Math Asn Am; Am Math Soc. *Res:* Convexity and combinatorial geometry; convex polytopes; m-convex sets; starshaped sets. *Mailing Add:* Dept Math Univ Okla Norman OK 73019

BREEN, MOIRA, BIOCHEMISTRY. *Current Pos:* RETIRED. *Personal Data:* b Madras, India, Dec 18, 23; US citizen. *Educ:* Univ Madras, BS, 44; Vassar Col, MS, 51; Northwestern Univ, PhD(biochem), 60. *Prof Exp:* Asst biochem & physiol, Univ Madras, 44-49; asst physiol, Vassar Col, 49-52; instr, Sch Nursing, Johns Hopkins Univ, 52-53; asst nutrit, Harvard Univ, 53-54; instr biochem, Northwestern Univ, 60-62; res assoc med, Univ Va, 62-63; res assoc physiol, Univ Chicago, 64-65; sr res biochemist, Res-in-Aging Lab, Vet Admin Hosp, North Chicago, Ill, 65-88; assoc prof, Dept Path, Univ Health Sci, Chicago Med Sch North Chicago, Ill, 79-96. *Mem:* AAAS; Am Chem Soc; Am Soc Biol Chemists; Complex Carbohydrate Soc. *Res:* Complex carbohydrates in central nervous system and other tissues. *Mailing Add:* 139 Woodland Rd Libertyville IL 60048-1701

BREENE, WILLIAM MICHAEL, FOOD SCIENCE, BIOCHEMISTRY. *Current Pos:* from asst prof to assoc prof, 68-80, PROF FOOD SCI & NUTRIT, UNIV MINN, ST PAUL, 80- *Personal Data:* b Adams, Wis, May 10, 30; m 63. *Educ:* Univ Wis, BS, 57, MS, 61, PhD(dairy & food industs), 64. *Prof Exp:* Res asst dairy & food industs, Univ Wis, 58-64, proj asst, 64; res assoc dairy industs, Univ Minn, 64-66, asst prof food sci & industs, 66-67; asst prof, Mich State Univ, 67. *Mem:* Inst Food Technologists; Am Soc Hort Sci; Am Asn Cereal Chem. *Res:* Spray drying fruits and vegetables using skim milk as a carrier; carotenoid oxidation, fruit and vegetable texture, soybean foods, adzuki beans, bean sprouts. *Mailing Add:* 225 Food Sci N Ctr Dept Food Sci Univ Minn 1334 Eckles Ave St Paul MN 55108-1040

BREESE, GEORGE RICHARD, PHARMACOLOGY, NEUROBIOLOGY. *Current Pos:* from asst prof to assoc prof, 68-76, PROF PSYCHIAT & PHARMACOL, SCH MED, UNIV NC, CHAPEL HILL, 76- *Personal Data:* b Richmond, Ind, Dec 27, 36; m 60, Joan C Skates; c Charles R & Alicia D. *Educ:* Butler Univ, BS, 59, MS, 61; Univ Tenn, PhD(pharmacol), 65. *Prof Exp:* Instr pharmacol, Med Sch, Univ Ark, 65-66; res assoc pharmacol & toxicol, Nat Inst Gen Med Sci, 66-68. *Concurrent Pos:* NIH grant; NIMH grant, Study Sect; USPHS grant. *Mem:* AAAS; Am Soc Pharmacol & Exp Therapeut; Soc Neurosci; Am Col Neuropsychopharmacol; Res Soc Alcohol; Int Soc Neurochem. *Res:* Developmental neuropsychopharmacology; neuropharmacology; depression; alcohol; neurocytotoxic compounds; peptides; Lesch-Nyhan disease; pharmacology of antidepressant drugs; gene therapy; self injurious behavior. *Mailing Add:* 3007 Thurston-Bowles Bldg Univ NC Sch Med Chapel Hill NC 27599-7178. *E-Mail:* gbreese@css.unc.edu

BREESE, SYDNEY SALISBURY, JR, VETERINARY VIROLOGY. *Current Pos:* RETIRED. *Personal Data:* b New York, NY, Apr 11, 22; m 53, A Elaine Higgins; c John S, Constance E & Peter J. *Educ:* Antioch Col, BS, 44; Univ Md, MS, 53. *Prof Exp:* Biophysicist virol, Walter Reed Army Inst Res, 48-53; physicist, Children's Cancer Res Found, 54-55, Plum Island Animal Dis Ctr, USDA, 55-78; assoc dir, Cent Electron Micros Facil, Med Sch, Univ Va, 79-84, res asst prof, anat, 80-84; electron micros, Marine Sci Ctr, Suffolk Co Community Col, 86-92. *Concurrent Pos:* Prog chmn & ed, 4th Int Cong Electron Micros, 62; chmn, Gordon Res Conf Immuno-Electron Micros, 72. *Mem:* AAAS; Electron Micros Soc Am (pres, 64); Am Soc Cell Biol; Soc Gen Microbiol Gt Brit. *Res:* Physical properties and purification of viruses; electron microscopy and ultracentrifugation techniques for virology problems; development and identification of viruses; immunochemical techniques in electron microscopy. *Mailing Add:* 1700 Cedar Beach Rd Southold NY 11971-2042

BREG, WILLIAM ROY, PEDIATRICS, CYTOGENETICS. *Current Pos:* From clin instr to assoc clin prof, 55-77, prof, 77-93, EMER PROF GENETICS & PEDIAT, YALE UNIV, 93- *Personal Data:* b Arlington, Tex, Sept 6, 23; m 48, Margaret Meston; c 4. *Educ:* Yale Univ, MD, 47. *Concurrent Pos:* Consult, physician & dir, Res Lab, Southbury Training Sch, 54-77; consult, Nat Inst Child Health & Human Develop, 65-69. *Mem:* Am Acad Pediat; Am Asn Ment Deficiency; Soc Pediat Res; Am Soc Human Genetics; Am Pediat Soc. *Res:* Human chromosomal abnormalities. *Mailing Add:* 1737 Bucks Hill Rd Southbury CT 06488-2404

BREGAR, WILLIAM S, PROBLEM SOLVING. *Current Pos:* asst prof, 75-81, ASSOC PROF COMPUTER SCI, ORE STATE UNIV, 81- *Personal Data:* b Chicago, Ill, Jan 11, 41; m 63; c 3. *Educ:* Miami Univ, BA, 63; Univ Wis, Madison, MS, 69, PhD(comput sci), 74. *Prof Exp:* Res assoc comput aided instr, Pa State Univ, 74-75. *Mem:* Asn Comput Mach; Sigma Xi; Asn Develop Comput Based Instr Systs. *Res:* Artificial intelligence emphasizing cognitive aspects of problem solving, knowledge representation and their application to computer based instruction. *Mailing Add:* 17 Hillshire Dr Lake Oswego OR 97034-7374

BREGLIA, RUDOLPH JOHN, TOXICOLOGY. *Current Pos:* CONSULT TOXICOLOGIST, BP OIL INC, 88- *Personal Data:* b New York, NY, Nov 6, 47; m 74; c 3. *Educ:* St John's Col Pharm, BS, 70; St John's Univ, MS, 72; New York Med Col, PhD(pharmacol), 79. *Honors & Awards:* Chevron USA Award, 84. *Prof Exp:* Toxicologist, Texaco, Inc, 79-81, sr toxicologist, 81-85, corp toxicologist, 85-88. *Mem:* Assoc Soc Toxicol. *Res:* Designing, monitoring and evaluating toxicity testing for a wide variety of experimental materials and commercial products. *Mailing Add:* British Petrol 200 Pub Square-7H Cleveland OH 44114-2375

BREGMAN, ALLYN A(ARON), CELL BIOLOGY, CYTOGENETICS. *Current Pos:* From asst prof to assoc prof, 67-85, PROF BIOL, STATE UNIV NY, COL NEW PALTZ, 85-, ASSOC DEAN LIBERAL ARTS & SCI, 92- *Personal Data:* b Brooklyn, NY, Apr 29, 41; m 65, Sybil Brewster; c Susannah & Naomi. *Educ:* Brooklyn Col, BS, 62; Univ Rochester, MS, 64, PhD(biol), 68. *Concurrent Pos:* NIMH grant; vis scholar, Duke Univ, 75. *Mem:* AAAS; Am Soc Cell Biol. *Res:* Cell biology; auth of 1 book. *Mailing Add:* Dept Biol State Univ NY Col New Paltz NY 12561

BREGMAN, DAVID, CARDIOVASCULAR SURGERY. *Current Pos:* From asst prof to assoc prof, 75-83, ASSOC CLIN PROF SURG, COL PHYSICIANS & SURGEONS, COLUMBIA PRESBY MED CTR, COLUMBIA UNIV, 83-; CHMN, DEPT SURG, ST JOSEPH'S HOSP & MED CTR, NJ, 82- *Personal Data:* b New York, NY, Apr 24, 40; m 77; c 4. *Educ:* NY Univ, BA, 61; State Univ NY, MD, 65. *Concurrent Pos:* Asst attending surgeon, Presby Hosp, New York, 75-80, assoc attending surgeon, 80-; overall chmn, subcomt Formulation Nat Standards, Am Soc Artificial Internal Organs, 77-; mem, Comt Cardiovasc Surg, Am Col Chest Physicians, 77-; prof surg, Sch Grad Med Educ, Seton Hall Univ, South Orange, NJ, 89- *Mem:* Fel Am Col Cardiol; fel Am Col Chest Physicians; fel Am Col Surgeons; Am Soc Artificial Internal Organs; Soc Thoracic Surgeons; Am Asn Thoracic Surg. *Res:* Artificial organs with emphasis on mechanical circulatory support techniques; pioneered in clinical applications of intra-aortic balloon pumping and pulsatile assist device during open heart surgery. *Mailing Add:* 268 Martin Luther King Blvd St Michaels Med Ctr Newark NJ 07102

BREGMAN, JACOB ISRAEL, ENVIRONMENTAL MANAGEMENT. *Current Pos:* PRES, BREGMAN & CO INC, 84- *Personal Data:* b Hartford, Conn, Sept 17, 23; m 48, Mona Madan; c Janet, Marcia & Barbara. *Educ:* Providence Col, BS, 43; Polytech Inst Brooklyn, MS, 48, PhD(chem), 51. *Prof Exp:* Chemist, Fels & Co, 47-48; sr chemist, Nat Aluminate Corp, 50-52, head dept phys chem, 52-59; supvr phys chem, IIT Res Inst, 59-63, asst dir chem res, 63-65, dir chem sci res & mgr water res ctr, 65-67; dep asst secy, US Dept Interior, 67-69; pres & chmn bd, Wapora, Inc, 69-82; vpres, Dynamic Corp, 83-84. *Concurrent Pos:* Chmn, Northeast Ill Metrop Area Air Pollution Control Bd, 62-63, Ill Air Pollution Control Bd, 63-67, Adv Comt Saline Water Conversion to Sci & Tech Comt, NATO Parliamentarians Coun, 63 & Water Resources Res Coun, 64-66; ed, Int Series Chem & Allied Sci, Spartan Book Co, 64-67; co-ed, Series on Water Pollution, Acad Press, 69-80. *Mem:* Am Chem Soc; Sigma Xi; Am Inst Chemists. *Res:* Ion exchange; corrosion; water treatment; saline water conversion; air and water pollution; environment. *Mailing Add:* 5630 Old Chester Rd Bethesda MD 20814. *Fax:* 301-652-4819

BREHM, BERTRAM GEORGE, JR, BOTANY, SYSTEMATICS. *Current Pos:* from asst prof to prof 62-93, EMER PROF BIOL, REED COL, 93- *Personal Data:* b Cleveland, Ohio, Nov 26, 26; m 50; c 6. *Educ:* Western Res Univ, BS, 50, MS, 52; Univ Tex, PhD(bot), 62. *Prof Exp:* Instr biol, Lee Col, Tex, 55-61. *Concurrent Pos:* NSF grants, 63 & 67. *Mem:* AAAS; Bot Soc Am; Int Asn Plant Taxon; Am Asn Plant Taxon. *Res:* Systematics and evolution of higher plants as determined by comparative chemistry; plant-insect interactions. *Mailing Add:* 727 SW Chestnut Portland OR 97219

BREHM, JOHN JOSEPH, PHYSICS, NONLINEAR DYNAMICS. *Current Pos:* assoc prof, 67-71, PROF PHYSICS, UNIV MASS, AMHERST, 71- *Personal Data:* b Memphis, Tenn, Dec 6, 34; m 59, Mary Ellen Kempers; c John, Robert, Richard & Jennifer. *Educ:* Univ Md, BS, 56, PhD(physics), 63; Cornell Univ, MS, 59. *Prof Exp:* Physicist, US Naval Ord Lab, 58-62; NSF fel particle physics, Princeton Univ, 62-63; from asst prof to assoc prof high energy physics, Northwestern Univ, 63-67. *Res:* Theoretical physics, elementary particle physics; nonlinear dynamics. *Mailing Add:* Dept Physics Univ Mass Amherst MA 01003. *Fax:* 413-545-0648; *E-Mail:* jjb@phast.umass.edu

BREHM, LAWRENCE PAUL, HOLOGRAPHY & DIFFERENTIAL HOLOGRAPHY, WAVEGUIDE OPTICS. *Current Pos:* STAFF PHYSICIST, IBM CORP, 85- *Personal Data:* b Berwyn, Ill, Dec 24, 48; m 87; c 1. *Educ:* Manhattan Col, BS, 70; Rensselaer Polytech Inst, MS, 78; Univ Del, PhD(physics), 84. *Prof Exp:* Teacher physics, Barlow Sch, 72-75; teaching asst & res trainee physics, Rensselaer Polytech Inst, 75-78; teacher physics, Simon's Rock Bard Col, 78-79; instr & res fel physics, Univ Del, 79-84. *Mem:* Sigma Xi; Am Phys Soc; Biophys Soc; Am Asn Physics Teachers. *Res:* Optoelectronics; metrology and analysis of optical digital data communications systems; electronic packaging. *Mailing Add:* 7 Vincent St Binghamton NY 13905-4512

BREHM, WARREN JOHN, CHEMISTRY, PATENTS. *Current Pos:* RETIRED. *Personal Data:* b New York, NY, Nov 2, 25; m 49, 78, Marcia J Gray; c 2. *Educ:* NY Univ, AB, 44; Harvard Univ, AM, 46, PhD(org chem), 48. *Prof Exp:* Chemist, Carbide & Carbon Chem Corp, Tenn, 45-46; Jewett fel, Columbia Univ, 48-49; instr, NY Univ, 49-52; chemist, E I Du Pont de Nemours & Co Inc, 52-56, from supvr to sr supvr, 56-68, res labsupt, Plastics Dept, Fluorocarbons Div, Exp Sta, 68, sr supvr, Res & Develop Div, 68-82, patents consult, 82-90. *Mem:* Am Chem Soc; NY Acad Sci; Royal Soc Chem. *Res:* Structure of strychnine; antimalarials; reaction mechanisms; polymers and plastics. *Mailing Add:* 111 W Pembrey Dr Pembrey Wilmington DE 19803-2006

BREHM, WILLIAM FREDERICK, RADIOACTIVE MATERIAL TRANSPORT, CORROSION. *Current Pos:* sr engr & fel engr, 70-76, mgr, Corrosion Technol, 76-87, FEL ENGR, WESTINGHOUSE HANFORD CO, 89- *Personal Data:* b Franklin, Pa, May 26, 40. *Educ:* Mass Inst Technol, BS, 62; Cornell Univ, MS, 64, PhD(mats sci), 67. *Prof Exp:* Res engr, Sci Lab, Ford Motor Co, 62; teaching asst, Cornell Univ, 62-63, res asst, 63-67; sr scientist, Battelle Northwest Labs, 67-70, staff scientist & group leader, 87-88. *Mem:* Sigma Xi; Minerals, Metals & Mat Soc; Am Soc Metals Int; Am Nuclear Soc; Nat Asn Corrosion Engrs. *Res:* Materials compatibility and radioactive mass transport in fluid systems especially sodium and lithium; methods for cleaning sodium and lithium from components and requalifying them for continued service; engineering problems associated with fluid systems and cover gas; corrosion of container materials in nuclear waste repository environments; engineering: plant chemist and system cognizant engineer, fast flux test facility-Department of Energy test reactor; chemistry and engineering aspects of high-level nuclear waste storage. *Mailing Add:* 727 Snyder Rd Richland WA 99352-1704

BREHME, ROBERT W, THEORETICAL PHYSICS. *Current Pos:* From asst prof to assoc prof, 59-68, EMER PROF PHYSICS, WAKE FOREST UNIV, 68- *Personal Data:* b Washington, DC, Mar 6, 30; m 54; c 4. *Educ:* Roanoke Col, BS, 51; Univ NC, MS, 54, PhD(physics), 59. *Concurrent Pos:* Res assoc, Univ NC, 64-65. *Mem:* Am Asn Physics Teachers; AAAS; Sigma Xi; Am Phys Soc. *Res:* Field theory; astronomy; quantum electrodynamics; relativity. *Mailing Add:* Dept Physics Wake Forest Univ Winston-Salem NC 27109-3818

BREHMER, MORRIS LEROY, AQUATIC BIOLOGY. *Current Pos:* dir environ opers, 71-76, exec mgr environ serv, 76-83, CORP SCIENTIST, VA POWER, 83- *Personal Data:* b Strasburg, Ill, Apr 10, 25; m 54. *Educ:* Eastern Ill Univ, BS, 50; Mich State Univ, MS, 56, PhD, 58. *Prof Exp:* Tech asst, Ill Nat Hist Surv, 51; fisheries biologist, Ill Dept Conserv, 51-55; tech asst, Inst Paper Chem, 55; student conserv aide, Mich Inst Fisheries Res, 55-58; assoc biologist, Va Inst Marine Sci, 58-63, sr marine scientist, 63-67, asst dir, 67-71, head div appl marine sci & ocean eng, 69-71. *Mem:* Air Pollution Control Asn; Water Pollution Control Fedn. *Res:* Aquatic ecology; toxicology; electric fields. *Mailing Add:* 9099 Fenway Dr Mechanicsville VA 23116

BREHOB, W(AYNE) M, MECHANICAL ENGINEERING. *Current Pos:* DEVELOP ENGR, GEN MOTORS, 96- *Personal Data:* b Indianapolis, Ind, June 19, 36; m 56, Marie L Schrader; c 6. *Educ:* Purdue Univ, BS, 58, MS, 60, PhD(mech eng), 63. *Prof Exp:* Instr mech eng, Purdue Univ, 59-63; res engr, Ford Motor Co, 63-70, prin res engr emission, 70-75, exec engr components & emission res, 75-78, exec engr advanced eng, prod planning Res, Ford Motor Co, 78-81; chmn, Mech Eng Dept, Lawrence Inst Technol, 81-95; prof mech eng, Lawrence Tech Univ, 89-, dept chmn, 91-96. *Mem:* Soc Automotive Engrs; Combustion Inst; Am Soc Mech Engrs. *Res:* Emission control through engine design and after treatment systems; emission regulations and tests; drivetrain and vehicle modifications for fuel economy improvement; alternate engines, engine fuels and fuel sources. *Mailing Add:* 538 N Franklin Dearborn MI 48128-1518

BREIDENBACH, MARTIN, PHYSICS. *Current Pos:* res assoc, Stanford Linear Accelerator Ctr, Stanford Univ, 72-77, staff physicist, 77-89, controls sect head, Accelerator Dept, 88-89, PROF, STANFORD LINEAR ACCELERATOR CTR, STANFORD UNIV, 89- *Personal Data:* b NJ, Oct 10, 43. *Educ:* Mass Inst Technol, BS, 65, PhD(physics), 70. *Prof Exp:* Res assoc, Mass Inst Technol, 69-71; jr vis scientist, Europ Orgn Nuclear Res, 71-72. *Mem:* Fel Am Phys Soc. *Mailing Add:* Stanford Linear Accelerator Ctr Stanford Univ PO Box 4349 Bin 96 Stanford CA 94305

BREIDENBACH, ROWLAND WILLIAM, PLANT BIOCHEMISTRY, CELL CULTURE. *Current Pos:* asst prof, 70-71, asst agronomist, Exp Sta, 67-76, assoc agronomist, 76-82, LECTR AGRON & RANGE SCI, UNIV CALIF, DAVIS, 76-, AGRONOMIST, 82-, DIR, PLANT GROWTH LAB, 87- *Personal Data:* b Dayton, Ohio, Feb 1, 35; m 57; c 2. *Educ:* Univ Fla, BS, 59; Univ Calif, Davis, MS, 63, PhD(plant physiol), 66. *Honors & Awards:* NY Bot Garden Award, 68. *Prof Exp:* NIH fel biol sci, Purdue Univ, 66-67. *Concurrent Pos:* NSF fel, 68-70; Du Pont Young fac award, Univ Calif, Davis, 70-71. *Mem:* AAAS; Am Soc Plant Physiol. *Res:* Cell and molecular biology; biomembranes, compartmentation and metabolic regulation; mechanisms of environmental stress effects on plants. *Mailing Add:* 1525 Redwood Lane Davis CA 95616

BREIG, EDWARD LOUIS, QUANTUM THEORY, ATOMIC COLLISIONS. *Current Pos:* RES SCIENTIST, UNIV TEX, DALLAS, 72- *Personal Data:* b St Marys, Mo, Oct 6, 32. *Educ:* Southeast Mo State Col, BS, 54; Univ Okla, MS, 63, PhD(physics), 66. *Prof Exp:* Res engr, Autonetics-NAm Rockwell, 61-62; theoret physicist, Aerospace Corp, Los Angeles, 66-72. *Mem:* Am Phys Soc; Am Asn Physics Teachers; Am Geophys Union. *Res:* Theoretical atomic and molecular physics, with applications to physics and chemistry of planetary atmospheres; atomic processes in lasers; mathematical analysis of ionospheric measurements from satellites. *Mailing Add:* 529 W Lookout Dr Richardson TX 75080

BREIG, MARVIN L, SOLID STATE PHYSICS. *Current Pos:* Asst prof, 63-64, assoc prof, 64-76, PROF PHYSICS, EASTERN ILL UNIV, 76- *Personal Data:* b St Mary's, Mo, Oct 9, 34; m 61; c 1. *Educ:* Southeast Mo State Col, BS, 56; Univ Okla, MS, 59, PhD(physics), 63. *Res:* Dislocation study in ionic crystals; pyroelectric effect in triglycene sulfate; electron spin resonance and nuclear magnetic resonance. *Mailing Add:* 521 Hall Ct Charleston IL 61920-3011

BREIL, DAVID A, BRYOLOGY, PLANT MORPHOLOGY. *Current Pos:* PROF BIOL, LONGWOOD COL, 68- *Personal Data:* b Brockton, Mass, Mar 27, 38; m 93, Phyllis Williams; c 4. *Educ:* Univ Mass, Amherst, BS, 60, MA, 63; Fla State Univ, PhD(bot), 68. *Prof Exp:* Instr bot, Pa State Univ, 63-65; Tall Timbers Res Sta grant, Fla, 66-68. *Mem:* Am Bryol & Lichenological Soc; Bot Soc Am. *Res:* Liverwort flora of Florida; bryophytes of Virginia; ecology of bryophytes. *Mailing Add:* Dept Natural Sci Longwood Col 201 High St Farmville VA 23909-7895

BREIL, SANDRA J, CELL PHYSIOLOGY, PLANT HISTOCHEMISTRY. *Current Pos:* ASSOC PROF BIOL, LONGWOOD COL, 69- *Personal Data:* b Springfield, Mass, Apr 30, 37. *Educ:* Univ Vt, BA, 58; Univ Mass, PhD(bot), 63. *Prof Exp:* Instr biol, Wilson Col, 63-65; fel, Inst Molecular Biophys, Fla State Univ, 66-68. *Mailing Add:* Nat Sci Dept Longwood Col 201 High St Farmville VA 23909-1895

BREILAND, JOHN GUSTAVSON, meteorology; deceased, see previous edition for last biography

BREILLATT, JULIAN PAUL, JR, BIOMATERIALS, TISSUE ENGINEERING. *Current Pos:* Baxter res scientist, 86-90, res dir, 90-94, SR RES DIR, BAXTER HEALTH CARE CORP, 95- *Personal Data:* b Pensacola, Fla, Mar 2, 38; m 62, Gaye Sorensen; c Elise, Adrienne, Alain & Andre. *Educ:* Univ Calif, Berkeley, AB, 59; Univ Utah, PhD(biochem), 67. *Honors & Awards:* IR-100 Award, Indust Res, 77. *Prof Exp:* Res assoc, Oak Ridge Nat Lab, 67-69, res scientist, 69-74, actg dir, Molecular Anat Prog, 74-76, sr res scientist biol div, 76-77; res supvr, E I du Pont de Nemours & Co, 77-78, sr res chemist, 78-85. *Mem:* AAAS; Am Soc Artificial Internal Organs; Biomat Soc; Int Soc Artificial Organs. *Res:* Ex vivo blood cell separation; immunodepletion; zonal centrifugation; artificial organs; bioresponse inducing materials; tissue engineering. *Mailing Add:* Baxter Healthcare Corp Baxter Technology Park Round Lake IL 60073-0490. *Fax:* 847-270-4414

BREINER, SHELDON, GEOPHYSICS. *Current Pos:* PRES & FOUNDER, QUORUM SOFTWARE, 88-; CHMN & CHIEF EXEC OFFICER, PARA MAGNETIC LOGGING INC, 83- *Personal Data:* b Milwaukee, Wis, Oct 23, 36; m 62; c 2. *Educ:* Stanford Univ, BS, 59, MS, 62, PhD(geophys), 67. *Prof Exp:* Res geophysicist, Varian Assocs, 61-68; geophysicist & pres, Geometrics, 69-83; pres & founder, Syntelligence, 83-87. *Concurrent Pos:* Res assoc, NSF grant, 65-67; res assoc, dept geophys, Stanford Univ, 67-, consult prof, dept appl earth sci, 74-78. *Mem:* AAAS; Soc Explor Geophys; Am Geophys Union; Europ Asn Explor Geophysicists; Sigma Xi. *Res:* Remote sensing, magnetic and gamma ray surveys for mineral and petroleum exploration; airborne and marine magnetic gradient studies; earthquake prediction; micropulsations; magnetic surveys for archaeological exploration; author of one book. *Mailing Add:* 45 Buckeye Portola Valley CA 94028-8015. *Fax:* 650-323-3111; *E-Mail:* sheldon.breiner@quorum.com

BREIPOHL, ARTHUR M, ELECTRICAL ENGINEERING. *Current Pos:* PROF, SCH ELEC & COMPUT ENG, UNIV OKLA, 84- *Personal Data:* b Higginsville, Mo, Nov 14, 31; m 55; c 2. *Educ:* Univ Mo, BS, 54; Univ NMex, MS, 60, ScD(elec eng), 64. *Prof Exp:* Trainee engr, Westinghouse Elec Corp, 54-55; staff mem, Sandia Corp, 57-64; from asst prof to prof, Okla State Univ, 64-70; chmn, Dept Elec Eng, Univ Kans, 70-79, prof, 80-84. *Concurrent Pos:* Res asst eng, Univ NMex, 62-63; consult, Sandia Corp, 62-63 & 64-65, Kans Corp Comn, 78-84; vis prof eng econ systs, Stanford Univ, 79. *Mem:* Fel Inst Elec & Electronics Engrs; Power Eng Soc. *Res:* Statistical system studies; electric power pricing; reliability; estimation from data and engineering knowledge. *Mailing Add:* Sch Elec & Comput Eng Univ Okla 202 W Boyd Rm 219 Norman OK 73019

BREISCH, ERIC ALAN, MORPHOMETRY. *Current Pos:* ASST PROF ANAT, DEPT SURG, UNIV CALIF, SAN DIEGO, 79- *Personal Data:* b Woodbury, NJ, Nov 5, 50; m 73; c 2. *Educ:* Temple Univ, BS, 72, PhD(anat), 77. *Prof Exp:* Fel cardiovasc anat/physiol, Dept Med, Temple Univ, 77-79. *Mem:* Am Asn Anatomists; Am Physiol Soc; AAAS. *Res:* Influence of pressure overload stimuli on the myocradium and the resulting cardiac hypertrophy is then studied from both an ultrastructural and physiologic point of view; morphometric and myocardial blood flow techniques. *Mailing Add:* Dept Path Children's Hosp 3020 Children's Way San Diego CA 92123. *Fax:* 619-576-0642

BREITBEIL, FRED W, III, ORGANIC CHEMISTRY. *Current Pos:* asst prof, 63-75, chmn dept, 69-77, PROF ORG CHEM, DE PAUL UNIV, 75- *Personal Data:* b Cincinnati, Ohio, Sept 25, 31; m 56, Barbara A; c Stephan, Kenneth, Theresa & James. *Educ:* Xavier Univ, Ohio, BS, 53, MS, 57; Univ Cincinnati, PhD(org chem), 60. *Prof Exp:* Res chemist, Proctor & Gamble Co, 60-62; assoc, Iowa State Univ, 62-63. *Mem:* Am Chem Soc. *Res:* Halogen additions to heterocyclics; synthesis of esters via acid anhydrides; synthesis of flavor and fragrance compounds. *Mailing Add:* 531 Cocoa Lane Orlando FL 32804

BREITENBACH, E A, PETROLEUM ENGINEERING. *Current Pos:* PRES, CHIEF EXEC OFFICER & CHMN, SCI SOFTWARE CORP, 70- *Personal Data:* b Los Angeles, Calif, Dec 17, 36; m 55, Jean L VanDerwilt; c Kenneth A, Randall H & Kristin J. *Educ:* Stanford Univ, BS, 58, MS, 59, PhD(petrol eng), 64. *Prof Exp:* Petrol engr, Socony Mobil Oil Co, Inc, 59-61; instr formation eval, Stanford Univ, 62-64; adv res scientist, Denver Res Ctr, Marathon Oil Co, 64-68. *Mem:* Am Inst Mining, Metall & Petrol Engrs; Soc Petrol Engrs; Soc Prof Well Log Analysts. *Res:* Reservoir engineering, including primary, secondary and tertiary recovery and formation evaluation. *Mailing Add:* 4491 Marigold Lane Littleton CO 80123

BREITENBACH, ROBERT PETER, ZOOLOGY, ENDOCRINOLOGY. *Current Pos:* from asst prof to assoc prof, Univ Mo, Columbia, 59-67, chmn dept, 64-68, assoc dir, Div Biol Sci, 75-79, prof, 67-87, dir undergrad studies, Biol Div, 79-87, EMER PROF ZOOL, UNIV MO, COLUMBIA, 87- *Personal Data:* b Madison, Wis, Oct 10, 23; m 48; c 3. *Educ:* Univ Wis, BS, 49, MS, 50, PhD(zool, endocrinol), 58. *Prof Exp:* Instr zool, Univ Wis, Milwaukee, 56-59. *Mem:* AAAS; Am Physiol Soc; Soc Exp Biol & Med. *Res:* Avian physiology; development of immunological maturity, reproductive physiology, calcium metabolism, endocrines and development and avian behavior. *Mailing Add:* 1326 S Rustic Rd Columbia MO 65201-9011

BREITENBERGER, ERNST, HISTORY & PHILOSOPHY OF SCIENCE, SCIENCE EDUCATION. *Current Pos:* prof, 63-94, EMER PROF PHYSICS, OHIO UNIV, 94- *Personal Data:* b Graz, Austria, June 11, 24; c Roland, Caroline, Gisela & Erich. *Educ:* Univ Vienna, DPhil(math), 50; Cambridge Univ, PhD(physics), 56. *Prof Exp:* Res assoc, Radiuminstitut, Vienna, 50-51; Brit Coun res scholar, Univ Cambridge, 51-54; lectr physics, Univ Malaya, 54-58; from assoc prof to prof, Univ SC, 58-63. *Concurrent Pos:* Guest prof, Univ Bonn, 69-70, Univ New SWales, Sydney, 88. *Mem:* Am Phys Soc; Brit Math Asn; Math Asn Am; NY Acad Sci; AAAS; Hist Sci Soc; Gauss-Gesellschaft. *Res:* Theoretical physics; probability and statistics; mathematical methods; science history; teaching mathematics to physics students. *Mailing Add:* Dept Physics Ohio Univ Athens OH 45701-2979. *Fax:* 740-593-0433

BREITHAUPT, LEA JOSEPH, JR, PAPER CHEMISTRY, CELLULOSE CHEMISTRY. *Current Pos:* From res chemist to tech dir, Non-Wovens Div, 69-71, sr res assoc, 72-76, MGR ANALYTICAL SCI, ERLING RIIS RES LAB, INT PAPER CO, 77- *Personal Data:* b Natchez, Miss, Sept 16, 29; m 59, 79; c 3. *Educ:* St Louis Univ, BS, 51; La State Univ, MS, 56. *Mem:* Tech Asn Pulp & Paper Indust; Am Chem Soc. *Res:* Pulp processing reactions, especially dissolving pulps, cellulose derivatives and reactions; analytical chemistry. *Mailing Add:* 10 Paddock Dr Fairhope AL 36532-1118

BREITMAN, THEODORE RONALD, BIOCHEMISTRY. *Current Pos:* RES BIOCHEMIST, NIH, 63- *Personal Data:* b Brooklyn, NY, Feb, 25, 31; m 58; c 2. *Educ:* City Col New York, BS, 53; Ohio State Univ, MS, 56, PhD(biochem), 58. *Prof Exp:* Nat Cancer Inst fel, USPHS, Brandeis Univ, 58-60; res biochemist, Lederle Labs, 60-62. *Concurrent Pos:* Assoc ed, In Vitro Cellular & Develop Biol. *Mem:* AAAS; Tissue Cult Asn; Am Soc Biol Chemists; Am Asn Cancer Res. *Res:* Hormones and growth factors with particular emphasis on control of cell growth and differentiation. *Mailing Add:* Nat Cancer Inst NIH Bldg 37 Rm 5D02 Bethesda MD 20892-4255

BREITMAYER, THEODORE, CHEMICAL ENGINEERING. *Current Pos:* RETIRED. *Personal Data:* b Grants Pass, Ore, June 21, 22; m 47, Estelle Leming; c Diane, Laurie & Allen. *Educ:* Ore State Univ, BS, 44; Univ Wash, MS, 48. *Honors & Awards:* Prof Progress Award, NorCal, Am Inst Chem Engrs, 94. *Prof Exp:* Res engr, Crown Zellerbach Corp, 48-57; process design engr, Monsanto Chem Co, 51-55; sr process engr, C F Braun & Co, 55-64; chief process engr, Bechtel Group Inc, 64-88, consult, 88-97. *Mem:* Fel Am Inst Chem Engrs; Am Nuclear Soc. *Mailing Add:* 148 Draeger Dr Moraga CA 94556

BREITSCHWERDT, EDWARD B, INTERNAL MEDICINE, INFECTIOUS DISEASE. *Current Pos:* assoc prof, 82-91, PROF INTERNAL MED & INFECTIOUS DIS, COL VET MED, NC STATE UNIV, 91- *Personal Data:* b Baltimore, Md, Oct 25, 48; m 80, Anne Shepherd; c Brett & Kyle. *Educ:* Univ Md, BS, 70; Univ Ga, DVM, 74; Am Col Vet Internal Med, cert, 79. *Honors & Awards:* Small Animal Res Award, Ralston Purina, 85; Pfizer Animal Health Award, Res Excellence, 95; Excellence In Canine Res, Am Kennel Club, 95. *Prof Exp:* Intern, Sch Vet Med, Univ Miss, 74-75, resident, 75-77; from asst prof to assoc prof internal med, Sch Vet Med, La State Univ, 77-82. *Concurrent Pos:* Serv chief, Vet Teaching Hosp, La State Univ, 79-82; assoc ed, J Vet Internal Med, 86-91; vis Coughlin prof, Univ Tenn, 93. *Mem:* Am Vet Med Asn; Am Animal Hosp Asn; Am Col Vet Internal Med (pres, 85-88, vpres, 96-); Am Soc Rickettsial Dis; Am Asn Vet Immunologists; Am Soc Microbiol. *Res:* Aspects of recognition and characterization of various naturally occurring diseases of companion animals; immunologic response to infectious agents (Rickettsia rickettsii, Bartonella species), immunodeficiency diseases and intestinal immunity; clinical immunology. *Mailing Add:* Col Vet Med NC State Univ 4700 Hillsborough St Raleigh NC 27606. *Fax:* 919-829-4336

BREITWIESER, CHARLES J(OHN), ELECTRONICS ENGINEERING. *Current Pos:* DIR, T-SYSTS INC, SAN DIEGO, 76- *Personal Data:* b Colorado Springs, Colo, Sept 23, 10; m 43; c 2. *Educ:* Univ NDak, BSEE, 30; Calif Inst Technol, MS, 33. *Hon Degrees:* DSc, Univ NDak, 47. *Prof Exp:* Engr, United Sound Prod Corp, 33-34; owner, C J Breitwieser & Co, 35-37; chief engr & vpres, Caldo Corp, 37-39; secy-treas, Conducto-Therm Corp, 39-42; chief electronics & res labs, Electronic & Guid Sect, Consol-Vultee Aircraft Mfg Co, 42-51; dir eng & exec asst to vpres in chg eng, P R Mallory, 51-54; vpres eng & gen mgr res & develop, Lear Inc, 54-57; pres, Metrolog Corp Div, 57-61; vpres, Air Logistics Corp, 57-61; exec vpres & gen mgr, Cubic Corp, 61-76. *Concurrent Pos:* Consult engr, Dept Police & Fire, Los Angeles, 32-35; consult mfg commercial res, 34-37; consult engr & chief engr res, DeForest Labs, 37-41; bd mem, Swan Electronics Corp & US Elevator Corp, chmn bd, 72-76; mgt consult to staff, Calif Pac Univ, San Diego, 76-; consult to trustees, Mesa Col, San Diego, 77- *Mem:* Inst Elec & Electronics Engrs; Aerospace Indust Asn Am; Am Ord Asn; Am Inst Aeronaut & Astronaut. *Res:* Management and direction of applied research in automation; solid state devices; guidance systems for missiles and space vehicles; elevators; computers; business machinery field. *Mailing Add:* 2738 Caminito Prado La Jolla CA 92037-4009

BREKKE, CLARK JOSEPH, FOOD SCIENCE, FUNCTIONAL PROPERTIES. *Current Pos:* from asst prof to asst prof, 76-83, actg chmn, 81-84, PROF, DEPT FOOD SCI & HUMAN NUTRIT, WASH STATE UNIV, 83- *Personal Data:* b Salem, Ore, May 23, 44; m 67; c 3. *Educ:* Rutgers Univ, BS, 66; Cornell Univ, MS, 68; Univ Wis, PhD(food sci), 72. *Prof Exp:* Res asst food sci, Cornell Univ, 66-68; res asst meat sci, 68-72; asst prof food sci, Univ Maine, 72-76. *Concurrent Pos:* Vis scientist, Dept Food Sci, Univ BC, Vancouver, BC, 86. *Mem:* Inst Food Technologists; Am Meat Sci Asn; Sigma Xi; Poultry Sci Asn; Coun Agr Sci & Technol; Nat Asn Cols & Teachers Agr. *Res:* Meat, poultry and seafood products technology; biochemical, microbial and physical changes influencing product quality; muscle protein biochemistry; protein modification and functionality. *Mailing Add:* Dept Food Sci Univ Tenn 2509 River Rd Knoxville TN 37996

BREMEL, ROBERT DUANE, ANIMAL PHYSIOLOGY, BIOCHEMISTRY. *Current Pos:* ASST PROF DAIRY SCI, UNIV WIS-MADISON, 74 - *Personal Data:* b Eau Claire, Wis, Dec 19, 45; m 66; c 2. *Educ:* Univ Wis-Madison, BS, 67; St Louis Univ, PhD(biochem), 72. *Prof Exp:* Fel anat-biophys, Med Ctr, Duke Univ, 72-74. *Mem:* Am Dairy Sci Asn; Am Chem Soc; Sigma Xi. *Res:* Mechanistic studies of hormone action and the measurement and control of stress in food producing animals; genetic control of milk secretion; production of transgenic animals which produce alternate proteins in their milk. *Mailing Add:* Dept Dairy Sci 266 Animal Sci Univ Wis 1675 Observatory Dr Madison WI 53706-1205

BREMER, HANS, MOLECULAR BIOLOGY. *Current Pos:* from asst prof to assoc prof biol, 66-73, PROF BIOL, SOUTHWEST CTR ADVAN STUDIES, UNIV TEX, DALLAS, 73- *Personal Data:* b Hamburg, Ger, Aug 26, 27; m 57; c 4. *Educ:* Univ Heidelberg, Vordiplom, 49; Univ Gottingen, PhD(biol), 57. *Prof Exp:* Res fel zool, Univ Gottingen, 57-59; asst genetics, Univ Cologne, 59-62; res microbiologist, Univ Calif, Berkeley, 62-65; asst genetics, Univ Cologne, 65-66. *Concurrent Pos:* Ger Res Soc fel, 58-59; Fulbright travel grant, 62. *Res:* Developmental physiology; synthesis of ribonucleic acid; DNA replication. *Mailing Add:* Div Biol Univ Tex-Dallas Box 830688 Richardson TX 75083-0688

BREMERMANN, HANS J, EPIDEMIOLOGY OF THE HUMAN IMMUNE DEFICIENCY VIRUS, MATH MODELS OF HIV-IMMUNE SYSTEM INTERACTIONS. *Current Pos:* assoc prof math, 59-64, assoc prof math & biophys, 64-66, PROF MATH & BIOPHYSICS, UNIV CALIF, BERKELEY, 66- *Personal Data:* b Bremen, Ger, Sept 14, 26; nat US; m 54.

Educ: Univ Munster, MA & PhD(math), 51. *Prof Exp:* Instr math, Univ Munster, 52; res assoc, Stanford Univ, 52-53, vis asst prof, 53-54; asst prof, Univ Munster, 54-55; staff mem, inst Advan Study, 55-57 &58-59; asst prof, Univ Wash, 57-58. *Concurrent Pos:* Res fel, Harvard Univ, 53; indust consult; mem, exec comt grad group biophysics & med physics, Univ Calif, Berkeley, 64-68, grad group bioeng, Berkeley, 72-76 & San Francisco, 91- *Mem:* Am Math Soc; Austrian Math Soc; Am Asn Artificial Intel; Ger Math Asn; Biophys Soc; fel AAAS. *Res:* Several complex variables; Schwartz Distributions; physics; dispersion relations; renormalization; information theory; limitations of genetic control; evolution processes; self-organizing systems; biological algorithm; complexity theory; mathematical ethology; pattern recognition; model verification; optimization; control; medical applications of nonlinear control; mathematical models of epidemics and host-pathogen dynamics; conformation of proteins; artificial intelligence; nerve nets; evolution of sex; HIV epidemiology; mathematical models of the immune system; interactions of HIV with the immune system. *Mailing Add:* 1873 San Ramon Ave Berkeley CA 94707

BREMMER, BART J, ORGANIC CHEMISTRY, POLYMER CHEMISTRY. *Current Pos:* org res chemist, 57-64, proj leader org chem, 64-66, sect head, 66-69, develop mgr, 69-72, res mgr org chem, 72-78, lab dir, 78-84, ELECTRONIC INDUST DEV MGR, DOW CHEM CO, 84- *Personal Data:* b Waddinxveen, Netherlands, Sept 4, 30; US citizen; m 53; c 3. *Educ:* State Univ Leiden, BS, 50; Mich State Univ, MS, 62. *Prof Exp:* Anal chemist, Gouda Apollo, Netherlands, 50-51; res chemist, Grand Rapids Varnish Co, 54-55; chemist, Kelvinator Div, Am Motors Corp, 55-57. *Mem:* Am Chem Soc; Com Develop Asn. *Res:* Thermoset resins, especially epoxy and phenolic resins with emphasis on fire-retardant resins; episulfide chemistry; chemistry of halogenated aromatic compounds, especially those containing amine groups; pyridine chemistry; materials used in electronics industry. *Mailing Add:* 5609 Woodview Pass Midland MI 48642-3147

BREMNER, JOHN MCCOLL, AGRICULTURE, ENVIRONMENTAL SCIENCES. *Current Pos:* assoc prof soil biochem, Iowa State Univ, 59-61, prof agron & biochem, 61-93, Charles F Curtiss Distinguished prof agr, 75-93, DISTINGUISHED EMER PROF AGR, IOWA STATE UNIV, 93- *Personal Data:* b Dumbarton, Scotland, Jan 18, 22; nat US; m 50, Eleanor M Williams; c Stuart & Carol. *Educ:* Glasgow Univ, BSc, 44; Univ London, PhD(chem), 48. *Hon Degrees:* DSc, Univ Glasgow, 87, Univ London, 59. *Honors & Awards:* Soil Sci Achievement Award, Am Soc Agron, 67 & Agron Res Award, 85; Alexander von Humboldt Award, Humboldt Found, 82; Gov's Sci Achievement Medal, Gov Iowa, 83; Harvey Wiley Award, Asn Off Anal Chemists, 84; Spencer Award, Am Chem Soc, 87; Environ Qual Res Award, Soil Sci Soc Am, 89. *Prof Exp:* From sci officer to prin sci officer, Chem Dept, Rothamsted Exp Sta, Eng, 45-59. *Concurrent Pos:* Rockefeller Found fel, 57-58; tech expert, Int Atomic Energy Agency, Yugoslavia, 64-65; Guggenheim Found fel, 68-69. *Mem:* Nat Acad Sci; fel Soil Sci Soc Am; fel Am Soc Agron; Am Chem Soc; fel Am Acad Microbiol; fel AAAS. *Res:* Soil biochemistry and microbiology; environmental problems related to agriculture. *Mailing Add:* 18910 No 2 Caminito Cantilena San Diego CA 92128

BREMNER, RAYMOND WILSON, science education; deceased, see previous edition for last biography

BREMNER, WILLIAM JOHN, INTERNAL MEDICINE, REPRODUCTIVE ENDOCRINOLOGY. *Current Pos:* from asst prof to assoc prof med, obstet & gynec, 82-87, PROF & VCHAIR, DEPT MED, UNIV WASH, 87-; CHIEF MED SERV, VET ADMIN, 87- *Personal Data:* b Bellingham, Wash, July 5, 43; m 65; c 4. *Educ:* Harvard Univ, BA, 64; Univ of Wash, MD, 69; Monash Univ, Melbourne, Australia, PhD(physiol), 78. *Honors & Awards:* Wyeth Award, Pac Coast Fertil Soc, 74. *Prof Exp:* Sr res fel, Univ Wash, 72-74; sr res officer, Nat Health & Med Res Coun, Australia, 74-77; chief endocrinol, Vet Admin Med Ctr, Seattle, 79-87. *Concurrent Pos:* Hon physician endocrinol & diabetes, Prince Henry's Hosp, Melbourne, Australia, 74-77; steering comt, Prog Res Human Reproduction, WHO, 84- *Mem:* Endocrine Soc; Am Soc Andrology; Am Soc Clin Invest; Asn Am Physicians. *Res:* Human and animal reproductive endocrinology. *Mailing Add:* Endocrinol Sect Vet Admin Med Ctr 1660 S Columbian Way Seattle WA 98108-1597

BRENCHLEY, GAYLE ANNE, INVERTEBRATE ZOOLOGY, MARINE ECOLOGY. *Current Pos:* RETIRED. *Personal Data:* b Washington, DC, Sept 21, 51. *Educ:* Univ Md, College Park, BS, 73, MS, 75; Johns Hopkins Univ, PhD(ecol), 78. *Prof Exp:* Asst prof ecol, Univ Calif, Irvine, 78-87. *Concurrent Pos:* Scholar, Woods Hole Oceanog Inst, 78-79; Steps Toward Independence fel, Marine Biol Lab, 80-81. *Mem:* Am Soc Zool; Ecol Soc Am; Am Soc Naturalists; Sigma Xi; AAAS. *Res:* Ecology of marine soft-bottom communities; competition and predation among invertebrates; population ecology of mud snails (Ilyanassa) and mud shrimp (Callianassa, Upogebia). *Mailing Add:* 1734 NW Market Seattle WA 98107

BRENCHLEY, JEAN ELNORA, MICROBIAL ENZYMES. *Current Pos:* head, Dept Molecular & Cell Biol, 84-87, dir, Bioltechnol Inst, 84-90, PROF MICROBIOL & BIOTECHNOL, PA STATE UNIV, 90- *Personal Data:* b Towanda, Pa, Mar 6, 44; m 90, Bernard Asbell. *Educ:* Mansfield State Col, BS, 65; Univ Calif, San Diego, MS, 67, Univ Calif, Davis, PhD(microbiol), 70. *Hon Degrees:* Dr, Lycoming Col, 92. *Honors & Awards:* Becton-Dickenson lectr, 80; Waksman Award, 85. *Prof Exp:* Res assoc biol, Mass Inst Technol, 70-71; from asst prof to assoc prof microbiol, Pa State Univ, 71-77; from assoc prof to prof biol, Purdue Univ, West Lafayette, 77-81; res dir, Genex Corp, Rockville, MD, 81-84. *Concurrent Pos:* Found lectr, Am Soc Microbiol, 75-76; ed, J Appl & Environ Microbiol, 81-85; Microbiol Rev, 92-; elected nominating comts, AAAS, 87 & 89; mem, Nat Biotechnol Policy Bd, 90-93; mem, Adv Panel, NSF; mem bd trustees, Biosis; trustee, Found Microbiol. *Mem:* Am Soc Microbiol (pres, 86); Am Soc Biol Chemists; Soc Indust Microbiol; Am Chem Soc; Genetics Soc Am; fel AAAS. *Res:* Discovery of novel microbial cold-active enzymes; microbial genetics; biotechnology. *Mailing Add:* Pa State Univ Dept Biochem & Molecular Biol 209 S Frear Lab University Park PA 16802-0001. *Fax:* 814-863-7024; *E-Mail:* jeb7@psu.edu

BRENDEL, KLAUS, PHARMACOLOGY. *Current Pos:* assoc prof pharmacol & toxicol, 70-76, PROF PHARMACOL, HEALTH SCI CTR, UNIV ARIZ, 76- *Personal Data:* b Berlin, Ger, July 14, 33; m 57; c 3. *Educ:* Free Univ Berlin, cand chem, 55, dipl chem, 59, Dr rer nat(chem), 62. *Prof Exp:* From asst prof to assoc prof pharmacol, Duke Univ, 67-70. *Concurrent Pos:* Fel, Ger Chem Indust, Free Univ Berlin, 62-63; NATO fel, Univ Pac, 63-64 & Duke Univ, 65-67; Am Heart Asn estab investr, Duke Univ & Univ Ariz, 65-70, fel, Coun Arteriosclerosis. *Mem:* Ger Chem Soc; Am Chem Soc; Am Soc Pharmacol & Exp Therapeut; Sigma Xi. *Res:* Bioorganic chemistry; drug metabolism; drugs and intermediary metabolism; toxicology; analytical organic and clinical chemistry. *Mailing Add:* Dept Pharmacol Univ Ariz Health Sci Ctr Tucson AZ 85724-5050. *Fax:* 520-626-2204

BRENDER, RONALD FRANKLIN, INFORMATION SCIENCE. *Current Pos:* CONSULT ENGR & SUPVR COMPUT LANG DEVELOP, SOFTWARE ENG DEPT, DIGITAL EQUIP CORP, 70- *Personal Data:* b Wyandotte, Mich, Sept 22, 43; m 75. *Educ:* Univ Mich, BSE, 65, MS, 68, PhD(comput sci), 69. *Concurrent Pos:* Mem, Am Nat Stand Comt, X3J3, Fortran Lang, 73-78; vis scientist, Dept Comput Sci, Carnegie-Mellon Univ, 78-79; Ada Bd Fed Adv Comt, 83-88 mem, Int Stand Orgn ISO/IEC JTC1/SC22/WG9, Ada lang stand, 83-90. *Mem:* Asn Comput Mach; Inst Elec & Electronics Engrs. *Res:* Computer language/compiler design and development; implementation languages for system software; software development methodology. *Mailing Add:* Digital Equip Corp ZK02-3/N30 Nashua NH 03062-2698

BRENDLEY, WILLIAM H, JR, PHYSICAL CHEMISTRY, POLYMER CHEMISTRY. *Current Pos:* res chemist, 66-67, group leader thermoplastic polymer coatings, 67-72, lab head indust coatings, 72-74, DEPT MGR COATINGS TECH SERV, ROHM AND HAAS CO, 74- *Personal Data:* b Philadelphia, Pa, Mar 26, 38; m 67. *Educ:* St Joseph's Col, Pa, BS, 60, MS, 62; Univ Pa, PhD(phys chem), 65. *Prof Exp:* Chemist, Rohm and Haas Co, 60-62; NSF fel, Univ Pa, 65-66. *Mem:* Am Chem Soc; Fedn Paint Socs; Am Inst Chemists. *Res:* Radiotracer and vacuum line techniques; volume expansion of alkali metals in liquid ammonia; physical chemistry of polymeric coatings and industrial application; polymeric coatings. *Mailing Add:* 2450 Exton Rd Hatboro PA 19040-2507

BRENDLINGER, DARWIN, PROSTHODONTIC DENTISTRY, EDUCATION. *Current Pos:* ASSOC CLIN PROF, SCH DENT, TEMPLE UNIV. *Personal Data:* b Reading, Pa, Nov 29, 34; m 54, 90, Shirley Becker; c Amy (Boyer), Lori (Suggins), Eric, Denise (Brossman), Cheryl (Fassak), Lisa (Staub) & Brian (Brossman). *Educ:* Temple Univ Sch Dent, DDS, 58; Tufts Univ, MS, 68; FACP, 72. *Prof Exp:* Chief prosthodontist, USAF Regional Hosp, 68-72, USAF Med Ctr, Wiesbaden, Ger, 72-76, USAF Regional Hosp, Sheppard AFB, Tex, 76-79; dir dent serv, USAF Med Ctr, Wright Patterson AFB, 79-80, staff officer prof, USAF Dent Serv, 80-82, dep corps chief, 82-86; assoc dir, Dentsply Int Inc, 86-87, dir res & develop, 89-93; prosthodontics consult, 87-89. *Concurrent Pos:* Air Force rep, NIH adv; consult, Surgeon Gen, USAF, 72-86, Dentsply Int, 86-94. *Mem:* Am Dent Asn; Am Col Prosthodontists; Am Acad Fixed Prosthodontics. *Res:* Rate of wear of dissimilar dental materials; clinical research into practical application of castable ceramic material for inlays, onlay, crowns and bridges; utilization of light cured resins in denture construction and relines. *Mailing Add:* 205 Fairview Ave Langhorne PA 19047

BRENEMAN, EDWIN JAY, VISUAL PSYCHOPHYSICS, COLOR SCIENCE. *Current Pos:* RETIRED. *Personal Data:* b Orrville, Ohio, Sept 29, 27; m 49; c 3. *Educ:* Ohio Wesleyan Univ, BA, 50; Ohio State Univ, MSc, 52. *Prof Exp:* Res physicist visual perception & photog reproduction, Eastman Kodak Co Res Labs, 52-68; res assoc, Macbeth Div, Kollmorgen Corp, 68-73; res assoc visual perception & photog reproduction, Eastman Kodak Co Res Labs, 73-86. *Concurrent Pos:* Consult, 87- *Mem:* Optical Soc Am. *Res:* Visual perception and photographic color reproduction. *Mailing Add:* 5 Tuxford Rd Pittsford NY 14534-1517

BRENEMAN, WILLIAM C, SILICONE CHEMISTRY, CHEMICAL PLANT DESIGN. *Current Pos:* TECHNOL MGR SPECIALTY SILICONES, OSI SPECIALTIES, INC, 93- *Personal Data:* b Braddock, Pa, July 9, 41; m 68; c William C Jr. *Educ:* Carnegie-Mellon Univ, BS, 63; Ohio Univ, MS, 71, MBA, 75. *Honors & Awards:* Cert of Recognition, NASA, 81, 82; Chem Pioneer, Am Inst Chemists, 85. *Prof Exp:* Res & develop engr, Union Carbide Corp, 66-75, proj scientist, 75-79, develop engr, 79-82, lead process engr, 82-84, technol mgr, chief design engr, 84-85, mgr process res & develop, 85-93. *Mem:* Am Inst Chemists; Am Inst Chem Engrs; AAAS. *Res:* Development of a practical large scale process for production of ultra high purity silane used in manufacture of polycrystalline silicon; development of processes for manufacture of organo modified silicones, antifoams and emulsions; new product introduction. *Mailing Add:* 809 Main St Sistersville WV 26175-1221. *Fax:* 304-652-1175

BRENGELMANN, GEORGE LESLIE, BODY TEMPERATURE REGULATION, SKIN-BLOOD FLOW. *Current Pos:* PROF PHYSIOL, UNIV WASH, 66- *Personal Data:* b Mar 7, 35; m 59; c 3. *Educ:* Univ Wash, PhD(physiol), 67. *Mem:* Am Physiol Soc. *Mailing Add:* Dept Physiol Box 357290 Univ Wash Seattle WA 98195

BRENHOLDT, IRVING R, NUCLEAR INSTRUMENTATION, INDUSTRIAL SENSORS. *Current Pos:* PRES, BRENHOLDT INDUSTS INC, 85- *Personal Data:* b Sept 2, 15; m 58, Mary J Fee; c Ginna. *Educ:* Univ Minn, BSEE, 41. *Honors & Awards:* Vannevar Bush Award, US Off Sci Res & Develop, 43; Henry L Stimson Award, US War Dept, 45. *Prof Exp:* Sect head, Mass Spectrometer & Electronics, Kellex Corp, 41-45; dir, Refiner Automation, Standard Oil Co, Chicago, 46-52; chief engr, Farrand Optical Co, 52-64, dir res & develop, 70-73; vpres, Pentron Electronics Corp, 64-65; mgr & chief engr, Electro-Optics Div, Gen Precision Corp, 65-70; dir, Instrument & Systs Develop, St Regis Corp, Champion Int Corp, 73-85. *Concurrent Pos:* Mem, Advan Sensors Crit Rev Panel, US Dept Energy; dir technol, Lektrox Co, 92; prin investr & recipient of two consecutive grants, US Dept Energy, 92, 93 & 95. *Mem:* NY Acad Sci. *Res:* Technical problem solving and invention; development, design and engineering utilizing technologies of the applied physical sciences including mechanics, electronics, optics, physical optics, electro-optics, opto-electronics and electrokinetics; holder of 34 patents. *Mailing Add:* 248 B South Tr Stratford CT 06497. *Fax:* 203-922-1267

BRENNAN, DANIEL JOSEPH, STRATIGRAPHY, SEDIMENTOLOGY. *Current Pos:* PRES, REGULATORY COMPLIANCE SPECIALIST INC, 91-; CONSULT, 91- *Personal Data:* b South Bend, Ind, Sept 11, 29; m 55; c 7. *Educ:* Univ Notre Dame, BS, 51; SDak Sch Mines & Technol, MS, 53; Univ Ariz, PhD(geol), 57. *Prof Exp:* Geologist, Shell Oil Co, 57-60; from geologist to sr geologist, Sunray DX Oil Co, 60-64; from asst prof to assoc prof geol, Wichita State Univ, 64-68; from assoc prof to prof, State Univ NY, Col Cortland, 68-80, chmn dept, 70-80; geologist, Border Explor Co, 80-92; chief geologist, Coquina Oil Corp, 82-83; dist geologist, ANR Prod Co, 83-84; exec dir, Ariz Oil & Gas, 86-90. *Concurrent Pos:* Consult geologist, 68-; prin investr, NY State Sea Grant Prog, 71-74. *Mem:* Fel Geol Soc Am; Am Asn Petrol Geologists; Soc Econ Paleont & Mineral; AAAS. *Res:* Petroleum and mineral exploration; stratigraphy; sedimentation and sediment-binding mechanism; higher education in marine science. *Mailing Add:* 101 Westwood Lane Kerryville TX 78028

BRENNAN, DAVID MICHAEL, endocrine physiology; deceased, see previous edition for last biography

BRENNAN, JAMES GERARD, THEORETICAL PHYSICS. *Current Pos:* from instr to assoc prof, 52-61, chmn dept, 61-74, assoc dean grad prog, Arts & Sci, 74-77, PROF PHYSICS, CATH UNIV AM, 61- *Personal Data:* b Hazleton, Pa, Aug 30, 27; m 51; c 5. *Educ:* Univ Scranton, BS, 48; Univ Wis, MS, 50, PhD(physics), 52. *Prof Exp:* Asst, Univ Wis, 48-52. *Concurrent Pos:* Consult, Naval Ord Lab, 55-; sci liaison, Off Naval Res, London, Eng, 65-66. *Res:* Theoretical nuclear physics; theoretical interior ballistics; atomic physics; ion implantation studies; electronic stopping power calculations. *Mailing Add:* Dept Physics Cath Univ Am Washington DC 20064-0001

BRENNAN, JAMES ROBERT, PLANT ANATOMY, CYTOLOGY. *Current Pos:* chmn, dept biol, 83-87, actg vpres, acad affairs, 87-88, from instr to assoc prof, 61-69, PROF BOT, BRIDGEWATER STATE COL, 69- *Personal Data:* b Crawfordsville, Ind, Nov 14, 30; m 53; c 7. *Educ:* Va Polytech Inst, BS, 52, MS, 55; Univ Md, PhD(bot), 58. *Prof Exp:* From instr to asst prof biol, Norwich Univ, 58-61. *Concurrent Pos:* Dir, NSF Biol Sci Curric Study, Bridgewater State Col, 63- 67, NSF, Coop Col-Sch Proj, 66; seasonal ranger-naturalist, Nat Park Serv, 72-80, vis prof, Open Univ, Milton Keynes, Eng, 78, & Australian Nat Univ, Canberra, 86. *Mem:* Int Soc Plant Morphologists; Bot Soc Am; Sigma Xi; AAAS. *Res:* Plant anatomical studies in relation to taxonomy and phylogeny; ultrastructural effects of chemical agents on meristematic plant cells; development of cell shape in differentiating plant cells. *Mailing Add:* 37 Maple Ave Bridgewater MA 02324-2512

BRENNAN, JAMES THOMAS, radiotherapy, radiobiology, for more information see previous edition

BRENNAN, JOHN JOSEPH, PHYSICS, CLINICAL PHARMACOKINETICS & PHARMACODYNAMICS. *Current Pos:* dir drug metab & pharmacokinetics, 92-94, DIR, CLIN PHARMACOL, SOLVAY PHARMACEUT, 94- *Personal Data:* b Cold Spring, NY, Oct 2, 51; m 73, Marsha Schattner; c 2. *Educ:* Temple Univ, BA, 73; Philadelphia Col Pharm Sci, PhD, 80. *Prof Exp:* Sr med scientist, Bristol Myers Squibb, 86-88, from asst med dir to assoc med dir, 88-92. *Mem:* Am Col Clin Pharm; Am Asn Pharm Sci. *Res:* Single and multiple dose pharmacokinetics and pharmacodynamics of CNS, CV, hormonal and AI drugs in humans; bioanalytical chemistry and drug metabolism studies of new chemical entities; beta decay; nuclear magnetic resonance; molecular rotations in solids. *Mailing Add:* 415 Holly Stream Trail Roswell GA 30075. *Fax:* 770-565-3311

BRENNAN, JOHN PAUL, HIGH PERFORMANCE COMPUTER & COMMUNICATION SYSTEMS IN MEDICINE, COMPUTER GRAPHICS & IMAGING IN MEDICINE. *Current Pos:* ASSOC DIR OBSTET & GYNEC, LONG ISLAND COL HOSP, 89- *Personal Data:* b New York, NY, Sept 6, 53; m 82, Jais A Bamberger. *Educ:* Haverford Col, BA, 75; Columbia Univ, MD, 85; Am Bd Obstet & Gynec, dipl. *Prof Exp:* Resident physician obstet & gynec, Albert Einstein Col Med, Yeshiva Univ, 85-88, chief resident, 88-89. *Concurrent Pos:* Instr obstet & gynec, State Univ NY Health Sci Ctr, Brooklyn, 89-90, clin asst prof, 90- *Mem:* Am Med Informatics Asn; Image Soc; Soc Computer Assisted Radiol. *Res:* Application of high performance computing and communications technologies to biomedical problems; telemedicine, virtual and dynamic environments, modelling and simulation; obstetrics and gynecology. *Mailing Add:* 76 Pierrepont St Brooklyn NY 11201. *Fax:* 718-780-1392; *E-Mail:* jbrennan@panix.com

BRENNAN, LAWRENCE EDWARD, ELECTRONICS, RADAR. *Current Pos:* RETIRED. *Personal Data:* b Oak Park, Ill, Jan 29, 27; m 47; c 4. *Educ:* Univ Ill, BA, 48, MA, 49, PhD(elec eng), 51. *Prof Exp:* Res assoc electronic dynamics, Univ Ill, 49-51; specialist systs analysis, NAm Aviation, Inc, 51-52; engr, Chicago Midway Labs, 52-55, Lockheed Missile Systs Div, 55, Aeronaut Systs Inc, 56, Off Naval Res, 57 & Rand Corp, 58-67; sr scientist, Technol Serv Corp, 67-80; vpres, Adaptive Sensors, Inc, 80-91; consult, 92-94. *Mem:* Fel Inst Elec & Electronics Engrs. *Res:* Radar systems; electronic counter-countermeasures; adaptive signal processors. *Mailing Add:* 9196 Neumann Dr Elberta AL 36530. *Fax:* 334-987-1664; *E-Mail:* lbrennan@gulftel.com

BRENNAN, MICHAEL EDWARD, ORGANIC CHEMISTRY. *Current Pos:* ASST PROF, CHATTANOOGA STATE TECH COMMUNITY COL, 92- *Personal Data:* b Covington, Ky, July 8, 41; m 65, Joyce Royal; c Sharon & Catherine. *Educ:* Univ Dayton, BS, 62; Univ Fla, MS, 65, PhD(org chem), 67. *Prof Exp:* Sr res chemist, Monsanto Co, 67-69; res assoc chem, Univ Ga, 69-70; sr res chemist, Arco Chem Co, 70-76, proj chemist, 76-85, sr proj chemist, 85-87, prin res chemist, 87-91. *Mem:* Am Chem Soc. *Res:* Organic synthesis; homogeneous catalysis; reaction mechanisms; bridged polycyclic compounds; small-ring chemistry; photochemistry; nuclear magnetic resonance spectra; polyurethanes; flammability. *Mailing Add:* Chattanooga St Tech Community Col Math Sci Div 4501 Amnicola Hwy Chattanooga TN 37406-1097. *E-Mail:* mbrennan@cstcc.cc.tn.us

BRENNAN, MICHAEL JAMES, MEDICINE. *Current Pos:* PRES & MED DIR, MICH CANCER FOUND, 66- *Personal Data:* b Mt Clemens, Mich, June 11, 21; m 45; c 8. *Educ:* Univ Detroit, BS, 41; Stritch Sch Med, MD, 47. *Honors & Awards:* Horace H Rackam Award. *Prof Exp:* Assoc physician, Hemat Dept, Henry Ford Hosp, Detroit, 50-52; chief, Med & Lab Sect, US Army Hosp, Ft Monmouth, NJ, 53-54; physician-in-chg, Oncol Div, Henry Ford Hosp, 54-65, chief div, 65-66; prof med, Col Med, Wayne State Univ, 66-76. *Concurrent Pos:* Dir, Meyer L Prentis Comprehensive Cancer Ctr, Detroit, 78-87. *Mem:* AMA; Am Col Physicians; Am Asn Cancer Res; Am Soc Hematologists; Am Fedn Clin Res. *Res:* Clinical hematology and oncology; host tumor relationships; experimental and clinical chemotherapy. *Mailing Add:* 31 Willison Grosse Pointe Shores MI 48236-1564

BRENNAN, MURRAY F, SURGICAL ENDOCRINOLOGY, SURGICAL ONCOLOGY. *Current Pos:* CHIEF GASTRIC & MIXED TUMOR SERV, MEM SLOAN-KETTERING CANCER CTR, 81-, MEM, SLOAN-KETTERING INST CANCER RES, 82-, ALFRED P SLOAN PROF SURG, 84-, CHMN DEPT, 85- *Personal Data:* b Auckland, NZ, Apr 2, 40; US citizen; m 73, Susan Chambers; c Christopher S, Timothy R, Meghan L & Patrick K. *Educ:* Univ NZ, BSc, 61; Univ Otago, MB, ChB, 64, MD & Ch M, 83; FRCS(I), 90. *Hon Degrees:* Dr Med, Univ Goteborg, Sweden, 91. *Prof Exp:* Sr investr, vis scientist & head surg metab, Nat Cancer Inst, NIH, Washington, DC, 75-81. *Concurrent Pos:* Consult surg, Harvard Med Sch & Peter Bent Brigham Hosp, Boston, 75-79; clin instr surg, Georgetown Univ, 76-81; consult biochem res, Grad Sch Arts & Sci, George Washington Univ, 78-80; attend surgeon, NY Hosp, 81- & gastric & mixed tumor serv, & nutrit & endocrinol serv, Mem Sloan-Kettering Cancer Ctr, 81-; vis physician, Rockefeller Univ, 81-93, consult, 93-95; prof surg, Cornell Univ Med Col, 81- *Mem:* Inst Med-Nat Acad Sci; Am Soc Clin Invest; Am Surg Asn; Soc Surg Oncol; Soc Clin Surg; fel Royal Australasian Col Surgeons; fel Am Col Surgeons; fel Brazilian Col Surgeons; Soc Univ Surgeons. *Res:* Intermediary metabolism of the cancer patient and metabolic response to treatment and nutritional support; development of integrated multimodality therapy for soft tissue sarcoma; outcome analysis in management of cancer. *Mailing Add:* Mem Sloan-Kettering Cancer Ctr 1275 York Ave New York NY 10021. *Fax:* 212-794-3184

BRENNAN, PATRICIA CONLON, MICROBIOLOGY, IMMUNOLOGY. *Current Pos:* PROF MICROBIOL & RES, NAT COL CHIROPRACTIC, 85-, DEAN RES, 89- *Personal Data:* b Chicago, Ill, Nov 20, 32; m 58, Ralph C; c 3. *Educ:* Albion Col, AB, 54; Univ Wis, MS, 57; Loyola Univ, Ill, PhD(microbiol), 68. *Prof Exp:* Technician bact, G D Searle & Co, 54-55; bacteriologist, Animal Dis Diag Lab, Wis Dept Agr, 57-58; microbiologist, Univ Chicago Hosps & Clins, 60-63; sci asst microbiol, Argonne Nat Lab, 63-68, asst microbiologist, 68-72, microbiologist, Div Biol & Med Res, 72-81; sr immunologist, Packard Instruments, 81-85. *Mem:* AAAS; Am Soc Microbiol; Am Asn Immunologists; Am Pub Health Asn. *Res:* Mechanisms of pathogenicity; mechanisms of inflamation; free oxygen radicals; chemiluminescence. *Mailing Add:* 200 E Roosevelt Lombard IL 60148. *Fax:* 630-268-6800

BRENNAN, PATRICK JOSEPH, MICROBIOLOGY, BIOCHEMISTRY. *Current Pos:* ASSOC PROF MICROBIOL, COLO STATE UNIV. *Personal Data:* b Boyle, Ireland, Mar 16, 38; m 68; c 3. *Educ:* Nat Univ Ireland, BSc, 61, MSc, 63; Trinity Col, Univ Dublin, PhD(biochem), 65; fel Royal Acad Med, Ireland, 75. *Hon Degrees:* MA, Trinity Col, Univ Dublin, 67. *Prof Exp:*

Fel biochem, Univ Calif, Berkeley, 65-67; jr lectr, Trinity Col, Dublin, 67-71; lectr, Univ Col, Dublin, 71-76; sr res scientist, Nat Jewish Hosp, 76-81, mem staff, 81- *Concurrent Pos:* USPHS Int fel, Univ Calif, Berkeley, 65-67; Nat Sci Coun grants, Ireland, 68-74; traveling fel, Royal Irish Acad, 69; vis asst prof virol, Baylor Col Med, 72-73; NIH grants & contracts, 78-, USDA grant, 81-; asst prof microbiol, Univ Colo Med Ctr, Denver, 78-81, adj assoc prof, 81-; mem study sect, NIH, 81- *Mem:* Biochem Soc; Am Soc Microbiol; Int Leprosy Asn. *Res:* Immunochemistry of mycoracteria; antigen structure in mycobacteria; pathogenesis of mycoglycoconjugates bacteria; leprosy. *Mailing Add:* Dept Microbiol B-308 Colo State Univ Ft Collins CO 80523. *Fax:* 970-491-1815

BRENNAN, PAUL JOSEPH, CIVIL ENGINEERING, STRUCTURAL ENGINEERING & PLANNING. *Current Pos:* chmn dept, 58-77, prof civil eng, 58-77, assoc dean res & grad affairs, Col Eng, 88-91, DAVID S RUTTY PROF ENG, SYRACUSE UNIV, 77-, RES PROF, 91- *Personal Data:* b Auburn, NY, June 29, 20; m 51, Virginia A Burns; c Patricia A, Margaret M, Maureen E, William H, Elizabeth A, John R, Kathleen A, Nancy E, Virginia A & Mary E. *Educ:* Univ Detroit, BArchE, 43; Yale Univ, MEng, 44, DEng(civil eng), 51. *Prof Exp:* Plant eng dept, Mich Steel Casting Co, 42-43; asst civil eng, Yale Univ, 46-48, asst prof, 48-53; prof civil eng, Univ Del, 53-58, chmn dept, 53-55, chmn, Dept Civil Eng & Eng Mech, 55-88. *Mem:* Sigma Xi; Am Soc Civil Engrs. *Res:* Structures; structural dynamics; steel and reinforced concrete; wind energy. *Mailing Add:* Link Hall L C Smith Col Eng Syracuse Univ Syracuse NY 13244

BRENNAN, THOMAS MICHAEL, PHOTOBIOLOGY. *Current Pos:* asst prof, 78-84, assoc prof biol, 84-95, PROF BIOL, DICKINSON COL, 95- *Personal Data:* b Jacksonville, Ill, June 7, 41; m 63, Kathleen Curtis; c Daniel & Thomas. *Educ:* Univ Ill, BS, 65; Rutgers Univ, MS, 75, PhD(bot), 77. *Prof Exp:* Engr, Southwestern Bell Tel Co, 65-68; comput analyst, Bell Tel Labs, 68-71; res assoc, Princeton Univ, 77-78. *Concurrent Pos:* Res assoc, Dept Biol, Univ Ill-Chicago, 79; vis scientist, Dept Biol Sci, Univ, Md Baltimore Co, 85-86; dept chmn biol, Dickinson Col, 86-92. *Mem:* Am Soc Photobiol; Am Soc Plant Physiologists. *Res:* Plant photosensitizers; light-dependent oxygen radical formation in photosynthetic systems; writing on photosensitizers, photosynthesis and related topics for general readership. *Mailing Add:* Dept Biol Dickinson Col Carlisle PA 17013. *Fax:* 717-245-1899; *E-Mail:* brennant@dickinson.edu

BRENNECKE, HENRY MARTIN, CHEMICAL ENGINEERING. *Current Pos:* RETIRED. *Personal Data:* b Saratoga, Tex, 24; m 50; c 1. *Educ:* Tex A&M Univ, BS, 47; Univ Tex, PhD(chem eng), 54. *Prof Exp:* Chem engr, Delhi-Taylor, 47-49; sr res engr, Explosives Dept, E I DuPont Nemours Co, Inc, 54-76, tech assoc, Petrochem Dept, 76-84. *Mem:* AAAS; Am Chem Soc; Am Inst Chem Engrs; Am Inst Mining Engrs. *Res:* Research and development of chemical processes. *Mailing Add:* 5261 River Oaks Corpus Christi TX 78413

BRENNECKE, LLEWELLYN F(RANCIS), chemical engineering, for more information see previous edition

BRENNEMAN, JAMES ALDEN, MYCOLOGY. *Current Pos:* From asst prof to assoc prof, 70-88, PROF BIOL, UNIV EVANSVILLE, 88- *Personal Data:* b Elida, Ohio, Aug 26, 43; m 67, Sandra Schloneger; c Kerry & Kent. *Educ:* Goshen Col, BA, 65; WVa Univ, MS, 67; La State Univ, Baton Rouge, PhD(plant path), 70. *Mem:* AAAS; Am Inst Biol Sci; Nat Asn Biol Teachers; Sigma Xi; Mycol Soc Am; Nat Audubon Soc. *Mailing Add:* Dept Biol Univ Evansville Evansville IN 47722. *Fax:* 812-479-2320; *E-Mail:* jb45@evansville.edu

BRENNEMAN, TIMOTHY BRANNER, APPLIED EPIDEMIOLOGY & MANAGEMENT OF PLANT DISEASE. *Current Pos:* Asst prof, 86-91, ASSOC PROF, PEANUT & PECAN DIS, UNIV GA, 91- *Personal Data:* b Harrisonburg, Va, Oct 21, 57. *Educ:* Goshen Col, BA, 81; Va Polytech Inst & State Univ, PhD(plant path), 86. *Honors & Awards:* Bailey Award, Am Peanut Res & Educ Soc, 86. *Mem:* Am Phytopath Soc; Am Peanut Res & Educ Soc. *Res:* Emphasis on developing management programs for peanut and pecan diseases that are economically and environmentally sound. *Mailing Add:* Dept Plant Path Coastal Plain Exp Sta Tifton GA 31793

BRENNEMANN, ANDREW E(RNEST), JR, ELECTRICAL ENGINEERING. *Current Pos:* RETIRED. *Personal Data:* b Cincinnati, Ohio, Dec 6, 25. *Educ:* Univ Cincinnati, MSEE, 50; Syracuse Univ, MS, 61. *Prof Exp:* Res staff mem cathode ray tube storage, IBM Res Lab, 50-54, res staff mem ferroelectric applns, 54-57, res staff mem applns of superconductivity to comput circuitry, 57-64, res staff mem semiconductor surfaces & integrated circuits, 64-68, res staff mem comput commun, 69-72, res staff mem automation res, 72-85, advan robotic technol, 86-93. *Mem:* Inst Elec & Electronics Engrs. *Mailing Add:* 4 Morningside Ct Ossining NY 10562

BRENNEN, CHRISTOPHER E, FLUID MECHANICS. *Current Pos:* Fulbright res fel, 68-69, dean students, 88-92, FAC MEM, CALIF INST TECHNOL, PASADENA, 76-, PROF MECH ENG, 82- *Personal Data:* b Belfast, NIreland. *Educ:* Oxford Univ, BA, 63, MS, 66, DPhil, 66. *Honors & Awards:* R T Knapp Award, Am Soc Mech Engrs, 78 & 81, Centennial Medallion, 80, Fluids Eng Award, 92; New Technol Award, NASA, 80. *Concurrent Pos:* Assoc ed, J Fluids Eng. *Mem:* Am Soc Mech Engrs. *Res:* Cavity flows; cavitation inception and noise; turbomachinery and rotordynamics; mechanics of granular material flow. *Mailing Add:* Dept Eng & Appl Sci 128-95 Calif Inst Technol 1201 E California Pasadena CA 91125-0001

BRENNER, ABNER, ELECTROCHEMISTRY. *Current Pos:* PRES, N-Q ELECTROCHEM RES CORP, 71- *Personal Data:* b Kansas City, Mo, Aug 5, 08; m 36; c 4. *Educ:* Univ Mo, AB, 29; Univ Wis, MS, 30; Univ Md, PhD(chem), 39. *Honors & Awards:* Gold Medal, US Dept Com, 63; Proctor Award, Am Electroplaters Soc, 49, Sci Achievement Award, 62; Hothersall Award, Brit Inst Metal Finishing, 61; Electrochem Eng & Technol Award, Electrochem Soc, 74. *Prof Exp:* Asst to Dr Kahlenburg, Univ Wis, 29-30; jr chemist, Nat Bur Standards, 30-35, assoc chemist, 35-50, chief electrodeposition, 50-71. *Mem:* Am Electroplaters Soc; Am Chem Soc; Electrochem Soc; Brit Inst Metal Finishing. *Res:* Electrodeposition of metals and alloys; measurement of physical properties and of thickness and metal coatings; electrodeposition of metals from organic and fused salt baths; vapor deposition of tungsten; electroless plating; electrochemical calorimetry and galvanostalametry. *Mailing Add:* 7204 Pomander Lane Chevy Chase MD 20815-3135

BRENNER, ALAN, INORGANIC CHEMISTRY, PHYSICAL CHEMISTRY. *Current Pos:* Asst prof, 75-80, assoc prof, 80-83, PROF CHEM, WAYNE STATE UNIV, 83- *Personal Data:* b Washington, DC, Apr 30, 46; m 68, Elizabeth A Reier; c Brian, Sarah & Anne. *Educ:* Johns Hopkins Univ, BA, 68; Northwestern Univ, PhD(chem), 75. *Concurrent Pos:* Consult, various chem co. *Mem:* Catalysis Soc; Am Chem Soc; AAAS; Sigma Xi. *Res:* Synthesis; characterization and applications of novel heterogeneous catalysts; surface chemistry; organometallic chemistry. *Mailing Add:* 679 Westchester Rd Grosse Pointe Park MI 48230-1823

BRENNER, ALFRED EPHRAIM, PHYSICS, HIGH PERFORMANCE COMPUTING. *Current Pos:* DEP DIR, COMPUT & SOFTWARE ENG DIV, INST DEFENSE ANALYSIS, 93- *Personal Data:* b Brooklyn, NY, Sept 11, 31; div; c Tamara, Kendra & Lyle. *Educ:* Mass Inst Technol, SB, 53, PhD(physics), 58. *Prof Exp:* Ford Found fel physics, Europ Orgn Nuclear Res, 58-59; instr & res fel, Harvard Univ, 59-62, asst prof, 62-66, sr res assoc, 66-70; physicist & dir comput, Fermi Nat Accelerator Lab, 70-85; pres, Consortium Sci Comput, 85-86; dir applns res, Supercomput Res Ctr, 86-93. *Concurrent Pos:* Consult, Dept Energy, 72-86 & Summagraphics Corp, 73-84; mem subcomt supercomput, US Activ Bd, Inst Elec & Electronics Engrs, 83-90; chmn, Nat Res Coun, Panel Comput & Appl Math, Nat Inst Stand & Technol, 85-91; ed, J Supercomput, 86- & Int J High Speed Comput, 89-; chair, Comput Soc Tech Comt, Supercomput Applns, 90-93; mem, Comput Soc Subcomt & Sci Supercomput, 91- *Mem:* AAAS; fel Am Phys Soc; Asn Comput Mach; Inst Elec & Electronics Engrs; NY Acad Sci; Soc Indust & Appl Math. *Res:* Computational science; high performance computer architectures and data processing; experimental high energy physics. *Mailing Add:* Inst Defense Anal 1801 Beauregard St Alexandria VA 22311-1772. *E-Mail:* abrenner@ida.org

BRENNER, BARRY MORTON, INTERNAL MEDICINE, NEPHROLOGY. *Current Pos:* SAMUEL A LEVINE PROF MED, HARVARD MED SCH & DIR, RENAL DIV & LAB KIDNEY & ELECTROLYTE PHYSIOL, BRIGHAM & WOMENS HOSP, BOSTON, 76- *Personal Data:* b Brooklyn, NY, Oct 4, 37; m 60, Jane Deutsch; c Robert & Jennifer. *Educ:* Long Island Univ, BS, 58; Univ Pittsburgh, MD, 62. *Hon Degrees:* AM, Harvard Univ, 76; DSc, Long Island Univ, 87; DMSc, Univ Paris, 92. *Honors & Awards:* Merit Award, NIH; Homer Smith Award, Am Soc Nephrol; Richard Bright Award, Am Soc Hypertension. *Prof Exp:* From asst prof med to prof med & physiol, Univ Calif, San Francisco, 72-76. *Concurrent Pos:* Sr staff mem, Cardiovasc Res Inst, Univ Calif, San Francisco, 74-76; physician, Brigham & Womens Hosp, Boston, 76- *Mem:* Am Soc Clin Invest; Am Physiol Soc; Am Soc Nephrol; Asn Am Physicians; fel AAAS; Am Soc Cell Biol; Am Soc Hypertension. *Res:* Renal regulation of ion, water and macromolecule transport; regulation of renal glomerular filtration; pathophysiology of renal disorders. *Mailing Add:* Renal Div Brigham & Womens Hosp 75 Francis St Boston MA 02115

BRENNER, DAEG SCOTT, NUCLEAR CHEMISTRY, NUCLEAR PHYSICS. *Current Pos:* from asst prof to assoc prof, Clark Univ, 67-79, chmn dept, 78-81, assoc provost, 83-87, chair fac, 88-91, PROF CHEM, CLARK UNIV, 79- *Personal Data:* b Reading, Pa, Aug 9, 39; m 89, Debra Schwartz; c Bethia M, Scott H, Jennifer L, Jonathan S & Daniel E. *Educ:* Rensselaer Polytech, BS, 60; Mass Inst Technol, PhD(chem), 64. *Prof Exp:* Ford Fund fel nuclear chem, Niels Bohr Inst, Copenhagen, Denmark, 64, NATO fel, 65; res assoc, Brookhaven Nat Lab, 65-67. *Concurrent Pos:* Consult & Res collabr, Brookhaven Nat Lab. *Mem:* Am Chem Soc; Am Phys Soc; Sigma Xi. *Res:* Atomic mass measurements; nuclear spectroscopy; nuclear fission; nuclear structure. *Mailing Add:* Chem Dept Clark Univ Worcester MA 01610-1477. *Fax:* 508-793-7703; *E-Mail:* dbrenner@clarku.edu

BRENNER, DOUGLAS, POLYMER SCIENCE. *Current Pos:* res physicist, 69-73, sr res physicist, corp res lab, Exxon Res & Eng Co, 73-86, MEM TECH STAFF, AT&T BELL LABS, 86- *Personal Data:* b Washington, DC, Dec 31, 38; m 68; c 3. *Educ:* Johns Hopkins Univ, BA, 61; Harvard Univ, MA, 63, PhD(physics), 68. *Prof Exp:* Res fel atomic physics, Harvard Univ, 68-69, instr physics, 69. *Mem:* Am Phys Soc; Inst Elec & Electronics Engrs. *Res:* Physical aspects of elastomer and plastic multiphase systems and blends; polymers containing appended ionic groups; filled and reinforced polymers; photoelectron spectroscopy of polymer surfaces; radio frequency spectroscopy; adhesion studies; system engineering of computer and telecommunication systems. *Mailing Add:* 61 E Sherbrooke Pkwy Livingston NJ 07039

BRENNER, EGON, ELECTRICAL ENGINEERING. *Current Pos:* RETIRED. *Personal Data:* b Vienna, Austria, July 1, 25; US citizen; m 50, Rhoda Greenberg; c 2. *Educ:* City Col NY, BEE, 44; Polytech Inst Brooklyn, MEE, 49, DEE, 55. *Prof Exp:* Tutor elec eng, City Col NY, 46-50, from lectr to prof, 50-67, dean grad studies, 61-71, dean, Sch Eng, 71-76, actg chancellor acad affairs, 76-77, dep chancellor, 77-81, prof elec eng, 81-96. *Concurrent Pos:* Exec vpres, Yeshiva Univ, NY, 81-96. *Mem:* Fel Inst Elec & Electronics Engrs; Am Soc Eng Educ; fel AAAS. *Res:* Higher education; system theory. *Mailing Add:* 61 W 62nd St New York NY 10023

BRENNER, FIVEL CECIL, PERFORMANCE TESTING. *Current Pos:* RETIRED. *Personal Data:* b Norfolk, Va, Sept 20, 18; m 72, Margaret Becker; c Zoe D & Vivian I. *Educ:* Va Polytech Inst, BS, 40; Polytech Inst Brooklyn, MS, 42, PhD(chem), 50. *Honors & Awards:* Apparel Res Found Honor Award, 67; Merit Award & Appreciation Award, Am Soc Testing & Mat, 78; Superior Achievement Award, US Dept Transp, 76 & 78. *Prof Exp:* Asst, Polytech Inst Brooklyn, 40-42; teacher, Army Serv Col, Ger, 45-46; asst prof phys chem, Vanderbilt Univ, 49-51; sr res scientist, Johnson & Johnson, 51-60; sr group leader, Chemstrand Res Ctr, 60-66; chief textiles & apparel technol ctr, Inst Appl Technol, Nat Bur Stand, 66-70; chief tire systs div, Safety Res Lab, 70-78, chief consumer info, Nat Hwy Traffic Safety Admin, 78-83; sr statistician statist policy br, Environ Protection Agency, 87-90. *Mem:* Am Chem Soc; Fiber Soc; Am Soc Testing & Mat; Brit Textile Inst; Stand Eng Soc. *Res:* Cellulose chemistry; fiber physics and mechanics; textile mechanics; statistical design; tire test method development; highway-vehicle interaction, tire performance testing, air quality. *Mailing Add:* 1917 Rookwood Rd Silver Spring MD 20910

BRENNER, FREDERIC J, ECOLOGY, BEHAVIORAL BIOLOGY. *Current Pos:* from asst prof to assoc prof, 69-85, PROF BIOL, GROVE CITY COL, 85- *Personal Data:* b Warren, Ohio, Dec 25, 36; c 2. *Educ:* Thiel Col, BS, 58; Pa State Univ, MS, 60, PhD(zool), 64. *Prof Exp:* Asst biol, Thiel Col, 57-58; asst zool, Pa State Univ, 58-64; first Kettering teaching intern, Denison Univ, 64-65; asst prof biol, Thiel Col, 65-69. *Concurrent Pos:* Grants, Am Philos Soc & Sigma Xi, 65-66, 70, NSF, 66-67, Off Water Resources, 71-72 & 75-77, Nat Wildlife Fedn, 73, Nat Geog Soc, 73-75, Nat Rifle Asn, 79-81, Nat Wild Turkey Fedn & Pa Wild Resources Fund; vis prof, Pa State Univ, 83; consult for coal indust; ed, Newsletter, Pa Acad Sci, 72-76 & 86- *Mem:* AAAS; Am Soc Ichthyol & Herpet; Am Soc Mammal; Am Ornith Union; Am Soc Zool; Ecol Soc Am. *Res:* Hibernation and migration within animal populations; reclamation of surface mine and lands as related to wildlife and fishery management; productivity and fish populations of strip mine lakes; limnology of strip mine lakes and mine drainage streams; wildlife fisheries management of wetland systems. *Mailing Add:* Dept Biol Grove City Col Grove City PA 16127

BRENNER, GEORGE MARVIN, PHARMACOLOGY. *Current Pos:* PROF, COL OSTEOP MED, OKLA STATE UNIV, 76-, CHMN, PHARMACOL DEPT, 89- *Personal Data:* b Ottawa, Kans, Sept 19, 43; m 66, Mary Ann Robinson; c Sharon & John. *Educ:* Univ Kans, BS, 66, PhD(pharmacol), 71; Baylor Univ, MS, 68. *Prof Exp:* Asst prof pharmacol, SDak State Univ, 71-76. *Concurrent Pos:* Vis lectr, Oral Roberts Univ; adj prof, N Eastern Okla State Univ & Univ Tulsa. *Mem:* Am Soc Pharm Exp Ther; Sigma Xi; Soc Exp Biol Med. *Res:* Transdermal iontophoresis; alpha-2; adrenergic pharmacology; drug development. *Mailing Add:* 12520 S Elwood Jenks OK 74037. *Fax:* 918-561-8414; *E-Mail:* brenneg@okway.okstate.edu

BRENNER, GERALD STANLEY, PHYSICAL ORGANIC CHEMISTRY, PHARMACEUTICAL. *Current Pos:* From res fel to sr res fel, 76-80, dir, 80-93, SR DIR, MERCK & CO, INC, 94- *Personal Data:* b Brooklyn, NY, July 8, 34; m 59, Linda Byer; c Jeffrey, Elizabeth & Susan. *Educ:* City Col New York, BS, 56; Univ Wis, PhD, 61. *Mem:* Am Chem Soc; Am Asn Pharm Scientist. *Res:* Structure determination; development of organic processes; synthetic organic chemistry; medicinal chemistry; physical organic chemistry; preformulation research; biopharmaceutics; analytical chemistry; pharmaceutical chemistry. *Mailing Add:* 3007 Oakwood Dr Norristown PA 19401

BRENNER, GILBERT J, PALYNOLOGY. *Current Pos:* from asst prof to assoc prof geol, 64-70, res grant, 64-65, PROF GEOL, STATE UNIV NY COL, NEW PALTZ, 70- *Personal Data:* b New York, NY, Jan 18, 33; m 56; c 2. *Educ:* City Col New York, BS, 55; NY Univ, MS, 58; Pa State Univ, PhD(geol), 62. *Prof Exp:* Sci asst micropaleont, Am Mus Natural Hist, 56-58; teaching asst geol, Pa State Univ, 58-62; res paleontologist, Stand Oil Co Calif, 62-64. *Concurrent Pos:* NSF res grant, 65-68; Am Philos Soc Penrose Fund grant, 70; vis res scientist, Geol Surv Israel, 70-71; NSF res grant, 80. *Mem:* AAAS; Am Paleont Soc; Nat Asn Geol Teachers; Am Asn Stratig Palynologists; Bot Soc Am; Sigma Xi. *Res:* Paleogeography and ecology of recent Foraminifera; Cretaceous angiosperm pollen and spores; origin of angiosperms; plant evolution, paleogene palynomorphs from the Atlantic Coastal Plain; cretaceous floral provinces and paleoclimatology. *Mailing Add:* Dept Geol Sci State Univ NY Col 75 S Manheim Blvd New Paltz NY 12561-2400

BRENNER, HENRY CLIFTON, MAGNETIC RESONANCE & LUMINESC SPECTROSCOPY. *Current Pos:* asst prof, 75-80, ASSOC PROF CHEM, NY UNIV, 80- *Personal Data:* b Rochester, NY, Nov 21, 46; m 82, Kristine Cohen; c David. *Educ:* Mass Inst Technol, SB, 68; Univ Chicago, MS, 69, PhD(chem), 72. *Prof Exp:* Res assoc chem, Univ Calif, Berkeley, 72-75. *Concurrent Pos:* NSF energy related fel, Univ Calif, Berkeley, 75; Alfred P Sloan fel, 77-79; Fulbright scholar, Soviet Union, 90. *Mem:* Am Chem Soc; AAAS; Am Phys Soc; Biophys Soc; Am Soc Photobiol; Sigma Xi. *Res:* Electron spin resonance and optical spectroscopic studies of molecular crystals and biological systems; excited state energy transfer; coherence and laser spectroscopy; optically detected magnetic resonance; luminescence under high pressure. *Mailing Add:* Dept Chem NY Univ New York NY 10003. *Fax:* 212-260-7905; *E-Mail:* brenner@is2.nyu.edu

BRENNER, HOWARD, CHEMICAL ENGINEERING. *Current Pos:* WILLARD HENRY DOW PROF CHEM ENG, MASS INST TECHNOL, 81- *Personal Data:* b New York, NY, Mar 16, 29; div; c Leslie, Joyce & Suzanne. *Educ:* Pratt Inst, BChE, 50; NY Univ, MChE, 54, DEngSc, 57. *Honors & Awards:* Hon Scroll Award, Am Chem Soc, 61, Kendall Award Colloid Surface Chem, 88; Alpha Chi Sigma Award, Am Inst Chem Engrs, 75, Walker Award, 85; Bingham Medal, Soc Rheology, 80; Matthew Van Winkle Lectr, Univ Tex, Austin, 86; Lindsay Lectr, Tex A&M Univ, 87; B F Dodge Lectr, Yale Univ, 87; Reilly Lectr, Univ Notre Dame, 91; Gen Elec Sr Res Award Gold Medal, Am Soc Eng Educ, 96. *Prof Exp:* From instr to prof chem eng, NY Univ, 55-66; prof, Carnegie-Mellon Univ, 66-77; prof & chmn dept, Univ Rochester, 77-81. *Concurrent Pos:* Vis assoc prof chem eng, Univ Minn, 63-64; sr vis fel, Sci Res Coun Gr Brit, 74; Fairchild distinguished scholar, Calif Inst Technol, 75-76; Guggenheim fel, 88-89; Chevron vis prof chem eng, Calif Inst Technol, 88-89; vis prof mech eng, Technion, 89; distinguished lectr, Clarkson Univ, 90; Gulf vis prof chem eng, Carnegie Mellon Univ, 91; distinguished vis lectr, Univ Calgary, 92; vis prof, Inst Mech & Mat, Univ Calif, San Diego, 95, Univ Calif, Berkeley, 96, Dept Mat Sci, Inst Polymer Sci, Inst Polymers, Swiss Fed Inst Technol, Switz, 96; Lady Davis vis prof, Techion, Israel Inst Technol, 96. *Mem:* Nat Acad Eng; Am Chem Soc; fel Am Inst Chem Engrs; fel Am Acad Mech; fel AAAS; Am Phys Soc; Int Asn Colloid & Interface Scientists; Soc Natural Philos; Soc Rheology. *Res:* Liminar chaotic transport processes; complex fluids-suspension and emulsion rheology; magnetic fluids; interfacial transport processes and rheology; low Reynolds number hydrodynamics; physicochemical hydrodynamics; statistical mechanics of colloidal and polymeric systems; Brownian motion; Osmotic Phenomena; macrotransport processes; generalized Taylor dispersion phenomena; aerosol and hydrosol deposition processes; multiphase flow and transport processes in porous media; author of over 200 publications. *Mailing Add:* Dept Chem Eng Mass Inst Technol Cambridge MA 02139. *Fax:* 617-258-8224; *E-Mail:* hbrenner@mit.edu

BRENNER, JOHN FRANCIS, BIOMEDICAL IMAGE ANALYSIS. *Current Pos:* PRES, IMAGE LAB, 92- *Personal Data:* b Charleston, SC, Sept 13, 41; m 64; c 2. *Educ:* Mass Inst Technol, SB, 62, SM, 66; Tufts Univ, PhD(physics), 73. *Prof Exp:* Instr therapeut radiol, Sch Med, Tufts Univ, 72-75, asst prof, 75-92. *Concurrent Pos:* Physicist spec & sci staff radiation oncol, New Eng Med Ctr Hosp, 72-; consult, Abbott Labs, 74-; mem task force automated differential cell counters, Ctr Dis Control, 76-77; assoc dir image processing res, Dept Therapeut Radiol, New Eng Med Ctr Hosp, 76-77, dir, Image Anal Lab, 77-; assoc ed, Comput in Biol & Med, Cytometry. *Mem:* AAAS; Int Acad Cytol; Soc Anal Cytol; Sigma Xi. *Res:* Computer assisted biomedical image analysis. *Mailing Add:* 19A Crosby Dr Bedford MA 01867

BRENNER, LORRY JACK, IMMUNOLOGY. *Current Pos:* from asst prof to assoc prof, 65-74, PROF BIOL, CLEVELAND STATE UNIV, 74- *Personal Data:* b Atlanta, Ga, May 16, 23; m 54; c 2. *Educ:* Emory Univ, BA, 47; Univ Mich, MS, 49; Western Reserve Univ, PhD(immunol), 55. *Prof Exp:* Asst immunol, Dept Path, Western Reserve Univ, 54-57, instr microbiol, 57-65; immunologist, Highland View Hosp, 57-62. *Concurrent Pos:* Asst, St Luke's Hosp, Cleveland, 62; consult immunologist, Highland View Cuyahoga County Hosp, 62-78; adj, Div Prof Affairs, Cleveland Clin Found, 76- *Mem:* Am Soc Zoologists; Soc Invert Path; Am Asn Immunologists; Soc Protozoologists; Electron Microscopy Soc Am. *Res:* Ciliates and antibodies; syphilis serology; immunohematology; leukemia. *Mailing Add:* 3064 Coleridge Rd Cleveland Heights OH 44118

BRENNER, MARK, ANALYTICAL CHEMISTRY. *Current Pos:* From asst prof to assoc prof, 69-80, PROF HORT SCI, UNIV MINN, ST PAUL, 80-, ASSOC DEAN, GRAD SCH, 89- *Personal Data:* b Boston, Mass, June 19, 42; m 64; c 2. *Educ:* Univ Mass, BS, 64, MS, 65; Mich State Univ, PhD(hort), 70. *Concurrent Pos:* Mem, Plant Growth Regulator Working Group. *Mem:* Fel Am Soc Hort Sci; Am Soc Plant Physiol; Sigma Xi; Int Plant Growth Substances Asn; Crops Soc Am. *Res:* Physiology of growth and development of plants; hormone metabolism in plant tissue; development and use of new methods for plant hormone extraction and identification. *Mailing Add:* Dept Hort Sci Alderman Hall Univ Minn 1970 Fowell Ave St Paul MN 55108-6007

BRENNER, RICHARD JOSEPH, MEDICAL ENTOMOLOGY, VECTOR BIOLOGIST. *Current Pos:* res entomologist, Screwworm Res Lab, 82-84, RES ENTOMOLOGIST, MED & VET ENTOM RES LAB, AGR RES SERV, USDA, 84- *Personal Data:* b Kankakee, Ill, Aug 22, 53; m 79, Joann Perkins; c Anthony W Perkins. *Educ:* Univ Ill, Urbana-Champaign, BS, 75, MS, 76; Cornell Univ, Ithaca, PhD(med entom), 80. *Honors & Awards:* Tech Transfer Award, Fed Lab Consortium, 89, 90. *Prof Exp:* Grad tech asst med entom, Entom Dept, Univ Ill, Urbana, 75-76 & Cornell Univ, 76-80; postdoctoral res entomologist, Univ Calif, Riverside, 80-82. *Mem:* Entom Soc Am; Am Soc Trop Med & Hyg; Soc Vector Ecologists; Am Mosquito Control Asn; Royal Soc Trop Med & Hyg. *Res:* Behavior and ecology of insects adversely affecting humans, domestic animals, homes, and structures; allergies in humans caused by arthropods; microclimate in structures and the impact on household pests. *Mailing Add:* 6501 NW 50th Lane Gainesville FL 32653. *Fax:* 352-374-5818

BRENNER, ROBERT MURRAY, CYTOLOGY. *Current Pos:* assoc scientist & assoc prof, 64-68, SR SCIENTIST & PROF, ORE REGIONAL PRIMATE RES CTR, UNIV ORE HEALTH SCI CTR, 68-, HEAD, DIV REPROD BIOL & BEHAV, 83- *Personal Data:* b Lynn, Mass, Feb 6, 29; m 53; c 2. *Educ:* Boston Univ, AB, 50, AM, 51, PhD(biol), 55. *Honors & Awards:* Wyeth Award, 72. *Prof Exp:* From asst scientist to sr asst scientist, USPHS, 55-57; from instr to asst prof biol, Brown Univ, 57-64. *Concurrent Pos:* Res grants, USPHS, 64 -; mem, Reproductive Endocrinol Study Sect, NIH, 85-89. *Mem:* AAAS; Endocrine Soc; Am Soc Cell Biol; Soc Study Reproduction; Am Fertil Soc. *Res:* Electron microscopy; endocrinology; reproductive biology; steroid receptors; immunocytochemistry. *Mailing Add:* Ore Regional Primate Res Ctr 505 NW 185th St Beaverton OR 97006-3448. *Fax:* 503-690-5563

BRENNER, SIDNEY S(IEGFRIED), metallurgy, for more information see previous edition

BRENNER, STEPHEN LOUIS, BIOPHYSICS. *Current Pos:* group leader, 84-85, res supvr, 86-87, RES MGR, STRUCTURAL BIOL, DUPONT CO, 87- *Personal Data:* b Brooklyn, NY, Apr 10, 48; c 3. *Educ:* State Univ NY Binghamton, BA, 69; Ind Univ, PhD(chem physics), 72. *Honors & Awards:* Victor K LaMer Award, Colloid & Surface Chem Div, Am Chem Soc, 74. *Prof Exp:* Asst prof chem, Univ Ky, 72-74; staff fel biophys, NIH, 74-80, res chem, 80-84. *Concurrent Pos:* Adj Prof chem, Univ Del, 88- *Mem:* Biophys Soc; Protein Soc. *Res:* Biophysics of genetic recombination; DNA-protein interactions; biological assembly. *Mailing Add:* DuPont Merck Pharmaceut Co PO Box 80500 Exp Sta E 500112 Wilmington DE 19880-0500. *Fax:* 302-695-1128

BRENNER, SYDNEY, MOLECULAR BIOLOGY. *Current Pos:* RES SCIENTIST, DEPT MED, UNIV CAMBRIDGE SCH CLIN MED, 92- *Personal Data:* b Germiston, SAfrica, Jan 13, 27; m 52, Mary Woolf Balkind; c 4. *Educ:* Univ Witwatersrand, MSc, 47, MB & BCh, 51; Oxford Univ, DPhil, 54. *Honors & Awards:* Carter-Wallace Lectr, Princeton Univ, 66 & 77; Warren Triennial Prize, 68; Albert Lasker Med Res Award, 71; Royal Medal, Royal Soc, 74; Charles-Leopold Mayer Prize, Fr Acad, 91; Gairdner Found Ann Award, 78, Int Award, 91; Gifford Lectr, Univ Glasgow, 78 & 79; Krebs Medal, FEBS, 80; CIBA Medal, Biochem Soc, 81; Feldberg Found Prize, 83; Dunham Lectr, Harvard Univ, 84; Rosentiel Award, Brandeis Univ, 86; Waterford Biomed Sci Award, Res Inst Scripps Clin, 88; Distinguished Achievement Award, Bristol Myers Squibb, 92. *Prof Exp:* Mem sci staff, Med Res Coun, Eng, 57-92, dir, Lab Molecular Biol, Med Res Coun, Eng, 79-86, dir, Molecular Genetics Unit, 86-91. *Concurrent Pos:* Fel, King's Col, Cambridge Univ, 59-; hon fel, Exeter Col, Oxford Univ, 85; hon prof genetic med, Univ Cambridge Clin Sch, 89-; mem staff, Scripps Res Inst, Calif, 92-94. *Mem:* Nat Acad Sci; Am Acad Sci; hon mem Int Acad Sci; hon mem Royal Soc Eng; Royal Col Physicians; hon mem Royal Col Pathologists; Max Planck Soc; Ger Acad Natural Sci Leopoldina; Am Philos Soc; fel Royal Soc; AAAS. *Mailing Add:* Univ Cambridge Sch Clin Med Dept Med Hills Rd Cambridge CB2 2QQ England

BRENNESSEL, BARBARA A, CELL MEMBRANE IN HORMONE RESPONSES. *Current Pos:* asst prof, 80-86, assoc prof, 87-91, PROF BIOL, WHEATON COL, 92- *Personal Data:* b Brooklyn, NY, Aug 15, 48; m 77, Nicholas F Picariello; c Adriana, Eianina, Marisa & Nicholas J. *Educ:* Fordham Univ, BS, 70; Cornell Univ, PhD(biochem), 75. *Prof Exp:* Instr biochem, Med Sch, Cornell Univ, 73-74; instr & res fel microbiol & immunol, Med Sch, Tulane Univ, 75-77; res fel oral biol & pathophysiol, Harvard Sch Dent Med, 77-80. *Concurrent Pos:* Vis lectr, Harvard Sch Dent Med, 83-85. *Mem:* Am Soc Cell Biol; AAAS; NY Acad Sci; Coun Undergrad Res; Sigma Xi. *Res:* Regulation of prolactin production by thyrotropin-releasing hormone and epidermal growth factor; regulation of hormone production in pituitary tumor cells; effects of artificial sweeteners on cultured cells; relationship of cell morphology to gene expression. *Mailing Add:* Dept Biol Wheaton Col Norton MA 02766

BRENNIMAN, GARY RUSSELL, ENVIRONMENTAL HEALTH. *Current Pos:* from asst prof to assoc prof, 74-94, actg dir environ & occup health sci, 86-88, PROF, UNIV ILL, CHICAGO, 94- *Personal Data:* b Mt Clemens, Mich, Aug 4, 42; m 65, Kathleen Ford; c Suzanne & Dawn. *Educ:* Cent Mich Univ, BS, 64, MS, 66; Univ Mich, Ann Arbor, MPH, 69, PhD(environ health sci), 74. *Prof Exp:* Chief basic sci br, Brooke Army Med Ctr, US Army Med Field Serv Sch, 66-68. *Concurrent Pos:* Consult, Argonne Nat Lab, 75-77, US Environ Protection Agency, Region V, 77- & Ill Dept Com & Community Affairs, 78-; dir, Off Solid Waste Mgt, 92- *Mem:* Sigma Xi; Water Environ Fedn; AAAS. *Res:* Health effects of human exposure to metals and chlorinated hydrocarbons in drinking water; characterize emissions from incineration of infections wastes; in-soil diffusion coefficient determination for hydrocarbons; municipal solid waste management. *Mailing Add:* 428 Ethel Lombard IL 60148. *Fax:* 312-413-9898

BRENT, BENNY EARL, ANIMAL NUTRITION. *Current Pos:* asst prof animal husb, 66-69, assoc prof animal sci & indust, 69-70, PROF ANIMAL SCI & INDUST, KANS STATE UNIV, 76- *Personal Data:* b Alton, Kans, July 3, 37; m 62. *Educ:* Kans State Univ, BS, 59, MS, 60; Mich State Univ, PhD(animal husb, nutrit), 66. *Prof Exp:* Chemist, Mich State Univ, 64-66. *Mem:* AAAS; Am Soc Animal Sci; Sigma Xi. *Res:* Mathematical modeling of growth; B-complex vitamins in the rumen; control of feed intake in ruminants; enzymology of the rumen. *Mailing Add:* Dept Animal Sci & Indust Kans State Univ Manhattan KS 66506. *Fax:* 785-532-7059

BRENT, CHARLES RAY, PHYSICAL CHEMISTRY, ORGANIC CHEMISTRY. *Current Pos:* assoc prof phys chem, 60-70, asst dean, Col Arts & Sci, 66-70, PROF CHEM, UNIV SOUTHERN MISS, 70-, DIR, INST ENVIRON SCI, 74-, PROF INDUST TECH, 75-, RADIATION SAFETY OFFICER, 81- *Personal Data:* b Hattiesburg, Miss, June 12, 31; m 53; c 3. *Educ:* Univ Southern Miss, BA, 53; Tulane Univ, MS, 60, PhD(phys chem), 63. *Prof Exp:* Asst chemist, Eagle Chem Co, Ala, 53. *Mem:* AAAS; Am Chem Soc; Sigma Xi; Audubon Soc; Int Solar Energy Soc. *Res:* Thermochemical studies of nitrogen heterocyclic compounds; kinetic solvent effects; environmental measurements; solar energy conversion. *Mailing Add:* 3901 Jamestown Rd Hattiesburg MS 39402-2340

BRENT, J ALLEN, SCIENCE ADMINISTRATION. *Current Pos:* chief chem, Sect Res & Develop, Minute Maid Corp, 51-62, from assoc dir res to dir res, Minute Maid Co Div, Coca-Cola Co, 62-66, dir res & develop carbonated beverages, 66-68, vpres, Coca-Cola USA Div, 68-76, VPRES, COCA-COLA CO, 76- *Personal Data:* b Carmi, Ill, Nov 21, 21; m 46; c 4. *Educ:* Eastern Ill State Col, BS, 43; Univ Fla, PhD(chem), 49. *Prof Exp:* Naval stores asst, Univ Fla, 46-49; head dept chem, Jacksonville Jr Col, 49-51. *Concurrent Pos:* With Manhattan Proj, 43-46. *Mem:* Am Chem Soc. *Res:* Vapor-liquid equilibrium; vacuum distillation; terpenes; citrus products and by-products. *Mailing Add:* 8900 Huntcliff Trace Atlanta GA 30350-1730

BRENT, MORGAN MCKENZIE, MICROBIOLOGY, ZOOLOGY. *Current Pos:* from assoc prof to prof biol, Bowling Green State Univ, 57-85, chmn dept, 64-67, dir appl microbiol, Col Health & Human Serv, 75-77, EMER PROF BIOL SCI, 85- *Personal Data:* b Evanston, Ill, Jan 31, 23; m 55, Frances Martin; c Morgan T, Victoria A & Elizabeth H. *Educ:* Northwestern Univ, BS, 48, MS, 49, PhD(biol sci), 53. *Prof Exp:* Jr res zoologist, Univ Calif, 53-54; instr microbiol, Jefferson Med Col, 54-57. *Mem:* Soc Protozool. *Res:* Effects of environmental factors on morphogenesis and transformation of amoebo-flagellates; nutrition of protozoa; biology. *Mailing Add:* Dept Biol Sci Bowling Green State Univ Bowling Green OH 43403. *E-Mail:* morganb@bgnet.bgsu.edu

BRENT, ROBERT LEONARD, EMBRYOLOGY. *Current Pos:* assoc prof pediat, Jefferson Med Col, 57-60, clin prof, 60-61, dir, Stein Res Ctr, 64-89, PROF PEDIAT, JEFFERSON MED COL, 61-, PROF RADIATION BIOL, 62-, CHMN DEPT PEDIAT, 66-, PROF ANAT, 71-; DIR, ELEANOR ROOSEVELT CANCER RES INST, 62-; HEAD, LAB CLIN & ENVIRON TERATOL, DUPONT HOSP FOR CHILDREN, 92- *Personal Data:* b Rochester, NY, Oct 6, 27; m 49, Lillian H Hoffman; c David A, James R, Lawrence H & Deborah A. *Educ:* Univ Rochester, AB, 48, MD, 53, PhD, 55. *Hon Degrees:* DSc, Univ Rochester, 88. *Honors & Awards:* Ritchie Prize, 53; R B Miller Lectr, Beth Israel Hosp Harvard Univ, 79; Third Annual Dr Peter Danis Lectr, Cardinal Glennon Children's Hosp, 87; Ruth & Harry Bakwin Mem Lectr, NY Univ Med Ctr, 88; Burlington Int Award, 90; Workany Lectr, Teratol Soc, 92; Hart String Fel Sr Lectr, Univ Fla, 94; Brookings Inst Lectr, Int Life Sci Inst, 96. *Prof Exp:* Res assoc, AEC, Univ Rochester, 47-55, asst physics, 48-49; chief radiation biol, Div Nuclear Med, Walter Reed Army Inst Res, 55-57. *Concurrent Pos:* Intern, Mass Gen Hosp, 54-55; mem, Embryol Study Sect, NIH, 70-74, chmn, Subcomt Prev Embryol, Fetal & Perinatal Dis, Fogarty Ctr; fel, Fitzwilliam Col, Cambridge Univ, 71; ed-in-chief, Teratol, 76-, managing ed, 77-80; fertil & maternal health drug comn, FDA, 81-84; Lady Davis scholar, Jerusalem, 83-84; Louis & Bess Stein prof pediat, Jefferson Med Col, 85, distinguished prof, 89; dir, Develop Biol Lab, A I du Pont Inst, 89 & Div Develop Biol, AIDI, 89-92; hon prof, Norman Bethune Univ Med Sci, China, 92; pres, First Int Cong Birth Defects, Chengdu, China, 94; clin prof pediat, Univ SFla, 96- *Mem:* Inst Med-Nat Acad Sci; Teratol Soc (pres, 68-69); AAAS; Am Asn Anatomists; Am Soc Exp Path; Am Pediat Soc; Sigma Xi; Japan Teratol Soc; Soc Pediat Res; Am Acad Pediat; Radiation Res Soc; Am Soc Immunol; Congenital Anomalies Res Asn Japan; Europ Teratol Soc; Soc Pediat Dermat; Ambulatory Pediat Asn. *Res:* Experimental embryology; radiation biology; clinical pediatric; immunology. *Mailing Add:* Alfred I Dupont Inst PO Box 269 Wilmington DE 19899. *Fax:* 302-651-6888

BRENT, THOMAS PETER, MOLECULAR BIOLOGY. *Current Pos:* from asst mem to assoc mem, 72-85, MEM, MOLECULAR PHARMACOL, ST JUDE CHILDREN'S RES HOSP, 85- *Personal Data:* b Leipzig, Ger, Nov 7, 37; US citizen; m 66, 76, Alva Wright; c Timothy & Mathew. *Educ:* Cambridge Univ, Univ, BA, 62; Univ London, PhD(biochem), 66. *Prof Exp:* Res fel cell biol, Chester Beatty Res Inst, London, 66-68; asst prof cancer res & biochem, McGill Univ, 68-72. *Concurrent Pos:* Assoc prof, Dept Biochem, Univ Tenn Ctr Health Sci, 80-89, assoc prof, Dept Pharmacol, 90-; mem, Radiation Study Sect, NIH, 81-85; prof, Pharmacol Dept, Univ Tenn Ctr Health Sci, 94- *Mem:* Brit Biochem Soc; Radiation Res Soc; Am Asn Cancer Res; AAAS. *Res:* Repair of DNA in response to radiation and alkylation; regulation of gene expression; gene therapy. *Mailing Add:* St Jude Childrens Res Hosp PO Box 318 Memphis TN 38101. *Fax:* 901-521-1668; *E-Mail:* brent@stjude.org

BRENT, WILLIAM B, STRUCTURAL GEOLOGY, STRATIGRAPHY. *Current Pos:* CONSULT GEOLOGIST, 90- *Personal Data:* b Ky, June 28, 24. *Educ:* Univ Va, BA, 49, JD, 66; Cornell Univ, MA, 52, PhD(geol), 55. *Prof Exp:* Asst prof geol, Okla State Univ, 55-61; assoc prof, La Tech Univ, 66-68; vis assoc prof, Univ Va, 69-70; chief geologist, Tenn Div Geol, 70-90. *Mem:* Fel Geol Soc Am; Sigma Xi. *Res:* Field studies of mountain systems of the United States; chiefly structural and stratigraphic field studies in the complexly folded and faulted Southern Appalachians. *Mailing Add:* 5020 Cypress Point Circle No 204 Virginia Beach VA 23455-6860

BRENTJENS, JAN R, NEPHROLOGY, IMMUNOPATHOLOGY. *Current Pos:* assoc prof, 76-81, PROF PATH, STATE UNIV NY, BUFFALO, 81-, RES PROF MED, 82-, ASSOC PROF MICROBIOL, 76- *Personal Data:* b Netherlands, Sept 22, 36; m 64; c 3. *Educ:* Univ Leiden, MD, 64; Univ Amsterdam, PhD(exp diffuse intravascular coagulation), 67; State Univ NY, MD, 79. *Prof Exp:* Resident med, Univ Hosp Groningen, 67-72; asst prof med, Univ Groningen, 72-76. *Concurrent Pos:* Res asst prof microbiol, State Univ NY, Buffalo, 72-74; fel, Henry & Bertha Buswell Fund, 72-74, Am Nat Kidney Found, 73-74. *Res:* Immunopathology in laboratory animals and in man; nephrology. *Mailing Add:* 28 Beard Ave Buffalo NY 14214

BRENTON, JUNE GRIMM, physics, mathematics; deceased, see previous edition for last biography

BRESCIA, VINCENT THOMAS, CLINICAL CHEMISTRY, QUALITY ASSURANCE. *Current Pos:* RETIRED. *Personal Data:* b New York, NY, June 2, 30; m 65, Yvonne Kuchar; c Louis, Charles, Mike & Anthony. *Educ:* Cent Col, Iowa, BA, 55; Fla State Univ, MS, 65, PhD(genetics), 73. *Prof Exp:* Instr biol, Lees Jr Col, Ky, 60-63; from asst prof to assoc prof biol, The Lindenwood Col, 69-81; dir qual assurance, Lee Sci, 82-90; staff, Vet Admin Med Ctr, St Louis, 90-96, ancillary testing coordr, 94-96. *Mem:* Sigma Xi. *Mailing Add:* 912 Wilmington Dr St Charles MO 63301-4761

BRESHEARS, WILBERT DALE, PHYSICAL CHEMISTRY. *Current Pos:* staff mem, 66-74, GROUP LEADER PHYS CHEM, LOS ALAMOS NAT LAB, 74- *Personal Data:* b Eugene, Ore, Apr 25, 39; m 60; c 4. *Educ:* Portland State Col, BS, 61; Ore State Univ, PhD(phys chem), 65. *Prof Exp:* NSF fel, Sch Chem Sci, Univ EAnglia, 65-66. *Mem:* AAAS; Am Chem Soc. *Res:* Chemical kinetics; molecular energy transfer; laser isotope separation. *Mailing Add:* Los Alamos Nat Lab MS J495 Los Alamos NM 87545-0001

BRESLAU, BARRY RICHARD, MEMBRANE TECHNOLOGY, ULTRAFILTRATION. *Current Pos:* DIR, INDUST BUS DEVELOP, FILTRON TECH. *Personal Data:* b Brooklyn, NY, Feb 10, 42; m 66. *Educ:* Polytech Inst Brooklyn, BChE, 63, PhD(chem eng), 69; Univ Mich, MChE, 64. *Prof Exp:* Engr, Pioneer Res Div, E I du Pont de Nemours & Co, Inc, 64-65, res engr, 68-71, sr engr, 71-73; dir process res, Romicon Inc, formerly. *Mem:* Am Chem Soc; Am Inst Chem Engrs; Am Soc Testing & Mat; Am Dairy Sci Asn; Water Pollution Control Fedn. *Res:* Membrane technology; hollow fiber ultrafiltration membranes; mass transfer in membrane systems. *Mailing Add:* 26 Lincoln Dr Acton MA 01720

BRESLAUER, KENNETH JOHN, PHYSIOCHEMICAL CHARACTERIZATION OF BIOLOGICAL SYSTEMS & CORELATION OF THESE PROPERTIES WITH BIOLOGICAL FUNCTIONS. *Current Pos:* from asst prof to prof, 74-91, LINUS C PAULING PROF BIOPHYS CHEM, RUTGERS UNIV, 91- *Personal Data:* b Jonkoping, Sweden, May 8, 47; US citizen; m 85, Sherrie Schwab; c Daniel & Jordan. *Educ:* Univ Wis-Madison, BS & BA, 68; Yale Univ, MPhil, 70, PhD(biophys chem), 72. *Honors & Awards:* Sunner Medal, Int Calorimetry Soc, 85; Res Discovery Award, Johnson & Johnson, 87. *Prof Exp:* Researcher, Univ Calif, Berkeley, 73-74. *Mem:* AAAS; Am Chem Soc; Biophys Soc; Calorimetry Soc; NY Acad Sci. *Res:* Combination of spectroscopic and calorimetric techniques to characterize thermodynamically the inter- and intramolecular forces that dictate and control drug-DNA recognition patterns and DNA polymorphism in solution; predict DNA structural preferences, to rationally design DNA binding drugs, and to assess the impact of mutagenic lesions. *Mailing Add:* Rutgers Univ Dept Chem PO Box 939 Piscataway NJ 08855-0939. *Fax:* 732-932-3409

BRESLER, AARON D, ELECTRICAL ENGINEERING. *Current Pos:* DEP DIR, ANTENNA SYST DIV, CUTLER-HAMMER INC, 72- *Personal Data:* b New York, NY, June 20, 24; m 50; c 4. *Educ:* City Col NY, BEE, 44; Polytech Inst Brooklyn, MS, 51, PhD(elec eng), 59. *Prof Exp:* Instr elec eng, City Col NY, 48-51; res assoc circuit theory, Microwave Res Inst, Polytech Inst Brooklyn, 51-53; instr elec eng, City Col NY, 53-55; sr res assoc propagation & electromagnetic theories, Polytech Inst Brooklyn, 55-59; sr engr, Jasik Labs, 59-63, chief engr, 63-65, vpres, 65-68; independent consult, 68-72. *Mem:* Sr mem Inst Elec & Electronics Engrs; Sigma Xi. *Res:* Antennas; electromagnetic theory; propagation of electromagnetic wave in anisotropic media. *Mailing Add:* 12 Helene Ave Merrick NY 11566-3203

BRESLER, B(ORIS), STRUCTURAL ENGINEERING. *Current Pos:* AFFIL CONSULT, WISS JANNEY ELSTNER INC, 88- *Personal Data:* b Harbin, China, Oct 18, 18; nat US; m 46; c 1. *Educ:* Univ Calif, BS, 41; Calif Inst Technol, MS, 46. *Honors & Awards:* Wason Medal for Res, Am Concrete Inst, 59; State-of-the-Art Civil Eng Award, Am Soc Civil Engrs, 68; J W Kelly Award, Am Concrete Inst, 78. *Prof Exp:* Struct designer, Kaiser Shipyards, Calif, 41-43; stress analyst, Convair Co, 43-45; lectr & mem fac, Univ Calif, Berkeley, 46-58, asst dean, Col Eng, 56-59, chmn, Div Struct Eng & Mech, 63-64, dir, Struct Mat Lab, 63-65, prof, 58-78, emer prof civil eng, 78-88. *Concurrent Pos:* Consult engr, 46-; NSF fel, 61; Guggenheim fel, 62; prin, Wiss, Janney, Elstner & Assocs, Inc, 77-; Wiff, Janey, Elstner Assoc, 77-88; consult, 88- *Mem:* Nat Acad Eng; fel Am Concrete Inst; Int Asn Bridge & Struct Engrs; Reinforced Concrete Res Coun; fel Am Soc Civil Engrs. *Res:* Behavior and distress in structures exposed to complex loading conditions and various special environments; analyses of various means of fire protection of concrete and steel structures; systematic procedures for evaluating seismic hazards of existing buildings. *Mailing Add:* 1644 San Miguel Dr Walnut Creek CA 94596

BRESLOW, DAVID SAMUEL, polymer chemistry, organic chemistry; deceased, see previous edition for last biography

BRESLOW, ESTHER M G, BIOPHYSICAL CHEMISTRY. *Current Pos:* Res assoc, Med Col, Cornell Univ, 60-64, from asst prof to assoc prof, 64-78, actg chair, biochem, 92-95, PROF BIOCHEM, MED COL, CORNELL UNIV, 78- *Personal Data:* b New York, NY, Dec 23, 31; m 55, Ronald; c Stephanie & Karen. *Educ:* Cornell Univ, BS, 53; NY Univ, MS, 55, PhD(biochem), 59. *Concurrent Pos:* NIH fel, Med Col, Cornell Univ, 59-61 & NIH res grants, 61-74; mem, Biophys & Biophys Chem Study Sect A, NIH, 73-77, Molecular & Cell Biophys Study Sect, 94-97; mem, Adv Comt Physiol Cellular Molecular Biol, Biol Inst Subcomt, NSF, 81-84. *Mem:* Fel AAAS; Am Chem Soc; Am Soc Biol Chemists; Harvey Soc; Sigma Xi. *Res:* Relationship between protein structure and biological and chemical reactivity. *Mailing Add:* 275 Broad Ave Englewood NJ 07631

BRESLOW, JAN LESLIE, METABOLISM, PEDIATRICS. *Current Pos:* DIR, LAB BIOCHEM GENETICS & METABOLISM, ROCKEFELLER UNIV, 84-, FREDERICK HENRY LEONHARDT PROF, 86- *Personal Data:* b New York, NY, Feb 28, 43; m 65; c 2. *Educ:* Columbia Col, AB, 63; Columbia Univ, MA, 64; Harvard Med Sch, MD, 68. *Honors & Awards:* E Mead Johnson Award, Am Acad Pediat, 84. *Prof Exp:* Intern pediat, Boston Children's Hosp, 68-69, jr asst res, 69-70, asst med, 73-75, chief, Metab Lab, 73-84, assoc, 75-81, chief, Metab Div, 75-84, sr assoc, 81-84; staff assoc, Molecular Dis Br, Nat Heart, Lung & Blood Inst, 70-73; instr pediat, Harvard Med Sch, 73-74, from asst prof to assoc prof, 74-84. *Concurrent Pos:* Eugene Higgins fel, Columbia Univ, 63-64; consult med, Brigham & Women's Hosp, 76-84; investr, Am Heart Asn, 81-86, mem, Path Res Study Comt, 85-; clin affil, Pediat NY Hosp, 84- *Mem:* Nat Acad Sci; Inst Med-Nat Acad Sci; Am Soc Clin Invest; Int Atherosclerosis Soc; Am Heart Asn (pres, 96-97); Soc Pediat Res. *Res:* Laboratory and clinical investigation directed at understanding human genetic susceptibility to atherosclerosis; genes that regulate lipoprotein metabolism and mutations in these genes in patients with lipoprotein abnormalities and/or premature heart disease. *Mailing Add:* Lab Biochem Genetics & Metab Rockefeller Univ 1230 York Ave H-29 New York NY 10021-6399. *Fax:* 212-327-7165

BRESLOW, LESTER, PUBLIC HEALTH, PREVENTIVE MEDICINE. *Current Pos:* prof health serv admin, Sch Pub Health, 68-70, prof prev & social med & chmn dept, Sch Med, 70-72, dean, Sch Pub Health, 72-80, PROF PUB HEALTH, UNIV CALIF, LOS ANGELES, 80- *Personal Data:* b Bismarck, NDak, Mar 17, 15; m 67, Devra Miller; c Norman, Jack & Stephen. *Educ:* Univ Minn, BA, 35, MD, 38, MPH, 41,. *Hon Degrees:* DSc, Univ Minn, 88. *Honors & Awards:* Lasker Award, 60; Sedgwick Medal, Am Pub Health Asn, 77; Dana Award Health, Dana Found, 88. *Prof Exp:* Dist health officer, State Dept Health, Minn, 41-43; chief, Bur Chronic Dis, State Dept Pub Health, Calif, 46-60, chief, Div Prev Med Serv, 60-65, dir, 65-68. *Mem:* Inst of Med of Nat Acad Sci; Am Pub Health Asn (pres, 69); Pub Health Cancer Asn Am (pres, 53); Int Epidemiol Asn (pres, 67-68); Asn Schs Pub Health (pres, 73-75). *Res:* Chronic disease epidemiology; health services; health promotion. *Mailing Add:* Sch Pub Health Univ Calif Los Angeles CA 90024

BRESLOW, NORMAN EDWARD, MEDICAL STATISTICS. *Current Pos:* from asst prof to assoc prof, 68-76, chmn dept, 83-93, PROF BIOSTATIST, UNIV WASH, 76- *Personal Data:* b Minneapolis, Minn, Feb 21, 41; m 63; c 2. *Educ:* Reed Col, BA, 62; Stanford Univ, PhD(statist), 67. *Honors & Awards:* Snedecor Award, Comn Pres Statist Soc, 95, RA Fisher Award, 95. *Prof Exp:* Vis res worker med statist, London Sch Hyg & Trop Med, 67-68. *Concurrent Pos:* Statistician, Children's Cancer Study Group, 68-72; mem, Nat Wilm's Tumor Study Comt, 70-; statistician, Int Agency Res Cancer, WHO, 72-74 & 78-79; assoc mem, Fred Hutchinson Cancer Res Ctr, 74-82, mem, 82-; consult, Nat Inst Environ Health Sci, 75, Nat Ctr Health Servs Res & NSF, 75-77; assoc ed, J Am Statist Asn, 77-80 & Int Statist Rev, 81-86; sr US scientist award, Alexander von Humboldt Found, 82-83; bd sci counrs, Nat Toxicol Prog, 83-87; mem, Bd Health Prom & Dis Prev, Inst Med, 87-; mem, Comt Appl & Theoret Statist, Nat Acad Sci-Nat Res Coun, 88-91, bd Med Follow-up Agency Inst Med, 91-, chair, 92-96, Comt Rev Effects in Vietnam Vet Exposure Herbicins, Inst Med, 92-93; assoc prof, Univ Geneva, 93- *Mem:* Inst Med-Nat Acad Sci; Biomet Soc; fel Am Statist Asn; Soc Epidemiol Res; Int Statist Asn; fel AAAS; hon fel Royal Statist Soc. *Res:* Statistics of clinical trials, especially Wilm's tumor; childhood cancer epidemiology; statistical methodology for cohert studies and case-control studies. *Mailing Add:* Dept Biostatist SC-32 Univ Wash Seattle WA 98195

BRESLOW, RONALD, ORGANIC CHEMISTRY. *Current Pos:* Nat Res Coun fel, Columbia Univ, 55-56, from instr to prof chem, 56-67, chmn dept, 76-79, S L MITCHELL PROF CHEM, COLUMBIA UNIV, 67-, UNIV PROF, 93- *Personal Data:* b Elizabeth, NJ, Mar 14, 31; m 55; c 2. *Educ:* Harvard Univ, AB, 52, AM, 54, PhD(chem), 56. *Honors & Awards:* Fresenius Award, 66; Award Pure Chemm, Am Chem Soc, 66, Harrison Howe Award, 75; Mark van Doren Medal, Columbia Univ, 69; Baekeland Medal, 69; Centenary Medal, Brit Chem Soc, 72; Remsen Medal, 77; Roussel Prize in Steroid Chem, 78; J R Norris Award, 80; T W Richard Medal, 84; A C Cope Award, 87; Nichols Medal, 89; Chem Sci Award, US Nat Acad Sci, 89; Paracelsus Medal, Swiss Chem Soc, 90; Nat Medal of Sci, 91. *Concurrent Pos:* Chmn, Div Chem, Nat Acad Sci, 74-77; chmn, Bd Sci Adv, A P Sloan Found, 81-85 & Chem Sect, AAAS, 88-89; mem, Bd Trustees, Rockefeller Univ, 81-; coun, Am Philos Soc, 87- *Mem:* Nat Acad Sci; Am Acad Arts & Sci; Am Chem Soc (pres, 96); Am Philos Soc; AAAS; Brit Chem Soc. *Res:* Aromaticity and small ring compounds; biochemical model systems; reaction mechanisms. *Mailing Add:* 275 Broad Ave Englewood NJ 07631-4350

BRESNICK, EDWARD, BIOCHEMISTRY. *Current Pos:* PROF & DIR, EPPLEY INST RES CANCER & ALLIED DIS, MED CTR, UNIV NEBR. *Personal Data:* b Jersey City, NJ, Sept 7, 30; m 57. *Educ:* St Peter's Col, BS, 52; Fordham Univ, MS, 54, PhD, 57. *Prof Exp:* Res assoc, Med Br, Univ Tex,

57-58; res biochemist, Burroughs, Wellcome & Co, 58-61; from asst prof biochem to prof pharmacol, Baylor Col Med, 70-72; prof cell & molecular biol & chmn dept, Med Col Ga, 72-78; prof biochem, Col Med, Univ Vt, 78-, chmn dept, 80- *Concurrent Pos:* Consult, Nat Inst Gen Med Sci. *Mem:* AAAS; Am Chem Soc; Am Asn Cancer Res; Am Soc Cell Biol; Am Soc Biol Chemists. *Res:* Cancer research; enzymology; regulatory mechanisms; pyrimidine and nucleic acid metabolism. *Mailing Add:* Dept Pharmacol & Toxicol Univ Mass Med Ctr 55 Lake Ave N Worchester MA 01655-0118. *Fax:* 603-650-1129

BRESSLER, BARRY LEE, THEORETICAL PHYSICS, SYSTEMS ANALYSIS. *Current Pos:* PRIN SCIENTIST, EG&G WASH ANALYTICAL SERV CTR, INC, 94- *Personal Data:* b Reading, Pa, Feb 16, 36. *Educ:* Ursinus Col, BS, 57; Va Polytech Inst & State Univ, MS, 79, PhD(physics), 86. *Prof Exp:* Physicist, Naval Surface Warfare Ctr, 58-94, acad fel, 83-85, group leader maneuvering reentry & engagement anal, 83-85, adv strategic systs, 85-89, sr scientist, 89-94. *Concurrent Pos:* Adj prof physics, quantum mech, Va Polytech Inst & State Univ, 94-; consult, Windy Knoll Enterprises, Inc, Tex, 94- *Mem:* Am Phys Soc; Coleopterists Soc; Sigma Xi. *Res:* Modeling of ballistic missiles; simulation of maneuvering reentry vehicles; threat analysis; physics of weapons effects; many-particle theory; mathematical physics; psychology of physics; systems theory; ecology; ethology; myrmecology; cerambycid taxonomy. *Mailing Add:* PO Box 1345 College Station Fredericksburg VA 22402-1345

BRESSLER, BERNARD, MEDICINE. *Current Pos:* Assoc prof, 55-59, PROF PSYCHOSOM MED, MED CTR, DUKE UNIV, 59- *Personal Data:* b Milan, Mich, May 22, 17; m 48; c 2. *Educ:* Washington Univ, AB, 38, MD, 42. *Concurrent Pos:* Instr, Washington Psychoanal Inst, 58-60, training analyst, 60-; instr, Univ NC-Duke Univ Psychoanal Inst, 60-; consult, Ft Bragg, NC, 58. *Mem:* Am Psychoanal Asn; Am Psychiat Asn; AMA; Am Psychosomatic Soc; Am Col Psychiat; Sigma Xi. *Res:* Psychosomatic medicine; psychoanalysis. *Mailing Add:* 3600 Floyd Ave Richmond VA 23221-2714

BRESSLER, BERNARD HARVEY, physiology, anatomy, for more information see previous edition

BRESSLER, DAVID WILSON, MATHEMATICS. *Current Pos:* assoc prof, 68-74, PROF MATH, CALIF STATE UNIV, SACRAMENTO, 74- *Personal Data:* b San Francisco, Calif, Sept 7, 23; m 49; c 2. *Educ:* Univ Calif, Berkeley, AB, 49, MA, 51, PhD(math), 57. *Prof Exp:* Instr math, Univ BC, 57-58; instr, Tufts Univ, 58-59; from instr to asst prof, Univ BC, 59-68. *Mem:* Am Math Soc. *Res:* Set theory and measure theory. *Mailing Add:* 401 E Eleventh St Davis CA 95616-2011

BRESSLER, MARCUS N, SCIENCE ADMINISTRATION. *Current Pos:* PRES & CHIEF CONSULT, M N BRESSLER, PE, INC, 71- *Personal Data:* b July 31, 29; m 54, Sondra Kipnes; c Eric Leigh, Lisa Ann & Karen Judith. *Educ:* Cornell Univ, BME, 52; Case Inst Technol, MSME, 60. *Hon Degrees:* MEng, Cornell Univ, 89. *Honors & Awards:* Bernard F Langer Nuclear Codes & Stand Award, Am Soc Mech Engrs, 92, J Hall Taylor Medal, 96. *Prof Exp:* Mgr prod design & develop, Taylor Forge, 70-71; supvr codes, stand & mat, Tenn Valley Auth, 71-79, sr eng specialist, 79-88. *Concurrent Pos:* Mem, Boiler & Pressure Vessel Comt, Am Soc Mech Engrs. *Mem:* Am Soc Mech Engrs; Am Soc Testing & Mat. *Res:* Nuclear engineering; codes and standards. *Mailing Add:* M N Bressler PE Inc 829 Chateaugay Rd Knoxville TN 37923. *E-Mail:* mbresslerpe@juno.com

BRESSLER, RUBIN, DIABETES, ENDOCRINOLOGY. *Current Pos.* PROF INTERNAL MED, HEAD DEPT & CHIEF, CLIN PHARMACOL, UNIV ARIZ, 69- *Educ:* Duke Univ, MD, 57. *Mailing Add:* Dept Internal Med & Pharmacol Health Sci Ctr Univ Ariz Tucson AZ 85724-0001. *Fax:* 520-626-2752

BRESSLER, STEVEN L, NEUROPHYSIOLOGY, PSYCHOBIOLOGY. *Current Pos:* assoc prof, 90-97, PROF NEUROSCI & COMPLEX SYSTS, FLA ATLANTIC UNIV, 97- *Personal Data:* b St Louis, Mo, June 7, 51; m 81; c 3. *Educ:* Johns Hopkins Univ, BA, 72; Univ Calif, Berkeley, PhD(neurophysiol), 82. *Prof Exp:* Systs neurophysiologist, EEG Systs Lab, 82-90. *Mem:* Soc Neurosci; Soc Psychophysiol Res. *Res:* Recording spatial patterns of the brain's electrical activity from people and animals performing highly controlled tasks; developing mathematical models to describe the operation of the neural circuits generating the brain's electrical activity. *Mailing Add:* Ctr Complex Systs PO Box 3091 Boca Raton FL 33431

BRESSON, CLARENCE RICHARD, APPLIED CHEMISTRY. *Current Pos:* RETIRED. *Personal Data:* b Wooster, Ohio, July 30, 25; m 60; c 3. *Educ:* Col Wooster, BA, 50; Wash State Univ, MS, 55, PhD(chem), 58. *Prof Exp:* Baking technologist cereal chem, USDA, 51-54; chemist, Phillips Petrol Co, 59-60, 61-65, sr res chemist, 66-90. *Mem:* Am Chem Soc. *Res:* Upgrading refinery by-product streams; oxo-alcohols, primary and secondary plasticizers, fluid coke, pyrolosis gasoline; applications for new products, sulfolanyl ethers; technical service; hydraulic barriers; asphaltic concrete flexure fatigue; rubberized-asphalt roofing-membranes; photopolymers; drilling mud additives; mining chemicals. *Mailing Add:* 118 Harwood Dr Bartlesville OK 74003-9561

BRESSOUD, DAVID MARIUS, COMBINATORIAL NUMBER THEORY, GENERATING FUNCTIONS. *Current Pos:* PROF MATH, MACALESTER COL, 94-, CHAIR, 95-, DE WITT WALLACE PROF, 96- *Personal Data:* b Bethlehem, Pa, Mar 27, 50; m 85. *Educ:* Swarthmore Col, BA, 71; Temple Univ, MA, 75, PhD(math), 77. *Prof Exp:* From asst prof to prof math, Pa State Univ, 77-94. *Concurrent Pos:* Mem, Inst Adv Study, 79-80; vis asst prof, Univ Wis-Madison, 80-81; Sloan Found Fel, 82-84; prof assoc, Univ Strasbourg, France, 85-86; Fulbright fel, 85-86. *Mem:* Am Math Soc; Math Asn Am; Nat Coun Teachers Math. *Res:* Partition identities; combinatorial enumeration; special functions. *Mailing Add:* Dept Math Macalester Col St Paul MN 55105

BREST, ALBERT N, MEDICINE. *Current Pos:* HEAD DIV CARDIOL, JEFFERSON MED COL & HOSP, PA, 69- *Personal Data:* b Berwick, Pa, Dec 17, 28. *Educ:* Temple Univ, MD, 53; Am Bd Internal Med, dipl, 61. *Prof Exp:* Intern, Philadelphia Gen Hosp, Pa, 53-54; resident internal med, Temple Univ Hosp, 54 & Albert Einstein Med Ctr, Pa, 56-58; instr med & dir hypertension unit, Hahnemann Med Col, 59-60, assoc, 60, from asst prof to assoc prof, 61-69, head sect hypertension & renology, 59-63, vasc dis & renology, 63-69, cardiol, 68-69. *Concurrent Pos:* Am Heart Asn res fel, Hahnemann Hosp, 58-59. *Mem:* AMA; Am Heart Asn; NY Acad Sci; Am Fedn Clin Res; fel Am Col Cardiol. *Res:* Cardiovascular diseases. *Mailing Add:* Dept Med Jefferson Med Col 1025 Walnut St Philadelphia PA 19107-5001

BRESTON, JOSEPH N(ORBERT), CHEMICAL ENGINEERING, PETROLEUM ENGINEERING. *Current Pos:* vpres & dir res & develop, 53-56, PRES, BRADFORD CHEM CO, 65-; DIR, J N BRESTON ASSOCS, 75- *Personal Data:* b Passaic, NJ, June 6, 12; m 41, Helen Walters; c Joseph W. *Educ:* Pa State Col, BS, 35, MS, 42, PhD(fuel tech), 44. *Honors & Awards:* Pioneers in Chem Award, Am Chem Soc. *Prof Exp:* Asst chem, Pa State Col, 35-36, asst petrol ref res, 37-42; assoc, Pa Grade Crude Oil Asn, 45-48, lab dir, 48-53; owner-dir, Teck Labs, 56-75. *Concurrent Pos:* Consult, Water & Waste Treat, Pollution Control. *Mem:* AAAS; Am Asn Corrosion Engrs; Am Inst Mining, Metall & Petrol Engrs; Am Chem Soc. *Res:* Petroleum refining; chemical engineering; coal technology and combustion; fuel utilization; petroleum production and secondary recovery; chemicals for oil production; water analyses and treatment; pollution control engineering; environmental engineering. *Mailing Add:* 225 Homan Ave State College PA 16801

BRETHERTON, FRANCIS P, METEOROLOGY. *Current Pos:* DIR, SPACE SCI & ENG CTR, 88- *Personal Data:* b Oxford, Eng, July 6, 35; m 59; c 3. *Educ:* Univ Cambridge, BA, 58, MA & PhD(fluid dynamics), 62. *Honors & Awards:* Res Award, Area IV, World Meteorol Orgn, 71; Buchan Prize, Royal Meteorol Soc; Meisinger Award, Am Meteorol Soc, 72. *Prof Exp:* Instr math, Mass Inst Technol, 61-62; SAR dynamical meteorol, Univ Cambridge, 62-63, ADR, 63-64, univ lectr appl math, 66-69; prof meteorol & oceanog, Johns Hopkins Univ, 69-74; pres, Univ Corp Atmospheric Res, 73-; dir, Nat Ctr Atmospheric Res, 74-88. *Concurrent Pos:* Vis prof, Univ Miami, 68-69; mem, US Comt for Global Atmospheric Res Prog, 71-76; mem, Comt Atmospheric Sci, Nat Acad Sci, 71-77. *Mem:* Am Meteorol Soc; Royal Meteorol Soc. *Res:* Mesoscale and large scale dynamics of the atmosphere and ocean; applied mathematics and the general theory of wave propagation. *Mailing Add:* 6241 S Highlands Ave Madison WI 53705

BRETHOUR, JOHN RAYMOND, RUMINANT NUTRITION, ANIMAL PRODUCTION. *Current Pos:* assoc prof, 68-75, PROF ANIMAL SCI, FT HAYS EXP STA, KANS STATE UNIV, 75- *Personal Data:* b Junction City, Kans, Sept 30, 34; m 64, Carol Thomas; c John Jr. *Educ:* Kans State Univ, BS, 55; Okla State Univ, MS, 56. *Prof Exp:* Technician radioisotopes, Univ Tenn, 56-57; asst prof animal sci, Ft Hays Exp Sta, Kans State Univ, 57-66; beef cattle prod, J R Brethour, 66-68. *Mem:* Am Soc Animal Sci; Sigma Xi; Am Registry Cert Animal Scientists, Brit Soc Animal Prod; Am Inst Ultrasound Med. *Res:* Animal nutrition; ultrasound; animal ultrasound evaluation. *Mailing Add:* 1555 W 41st St Hays KS 67601. *Fax:* 785-625-3425; *E-Mail:* lcsuarch@matt.ksu.ksu.edu

BRETON, J RAYMOND, ACOUSTICS, WAVE PROPAGATION. *Current Pos:* PRES, BR ENTERPRISES, 89- *Personal Data:* b Hartford, Conn, Nov 14, 31; m 61; c 6. *Educ:* Boston Col, MA, 57; Harvard Univ, AM, 59; Univ RI, MS, 75, PhD(elec eng), 77. *Prof Exp:* Foreign serv officer, Dept State, 61-63; lectr, San Diego State Col, 63-65; prin engr, Naval Underwater Systs Ctr, 67-82; dir, Gen Instrument Corp, 82-89. *Mem:* Inst Elec & Electronics Engrs. *Res:* Sonar system design applied to bathymetry; general propagation and hydrodynamics. *Mailing Add:* 3 Appletree Lane Walpole MA 02081. *Fax:* 508-668-2941

BRETSCHER, ANTHONY P, MICROFILAMENT, BRUSH BORDER. *Current Pos:* ASSOC PROF BIOCHEM, SECT BIOCHEM, MOLECULAR & CELL BIOL, CORNELL UNIV, 81- *Personal Data:* b 1950; m 83; c 1. *Educ:* Leeds Univ, Eng, PhD(genetics), 74. *Mem:* Am Soc Cell Biol. *Res:* Biochemical and cell biology analysis of the cytoskeleton. *Mailing Add:* Biotechnol Bldg Cornell Univ Ithaca NY 14853-0001. *Fax:* 607-255-2428

BRETSCHER, MANUEL MARTIN, NUCLEAR PHYSICS, REACTOR PHYSICS. *Current Pos:* PHYSICIST, APPL PHYSICS DIV, ARGONNE NAT LAB, 67- *Personal Data:* b River Forest, Ill, May 12, 28; m 55, Miriam Horton; c Mark H, John T, Kathryn R, Carl P & Fred M. *Educ:* Wash Univ, AB, 50, PhD(physics), 54. *Prof Exp:* Asst prof physics, Ala Polytech Inst, 54-56; from assoc prof to prof & co-chmn dept, Valparaiso Univ, 56-67. *Concurrent Pos:* Consult, Oak Ridge Nat Lab, 58-64. *Mem:* Am Phys Soc;

Am Nuclear Soc; Sigma Xi. *Res:* Particle accelerators; stripping reactions; coulomb excitation; scattering; reactor physics; plutonium capture-to-fission ratios; age measurements; mass spectrometry; inhomogeneous magnetic field spectrometers; breeding ratio measurements for liquid metal fast breeder reactors; tritium measurements; analyses for nuclear research reactors. *Mailing Add:* 7313 Seminole Ct Darien IL 60561. *Fax:* 630-256-5161; *E-Mail:* mmbretscher@anl.gov

BRETSCHER, PETER ALAN, IMMUNOLOGY. *Current Pos:* PROF IMMUNOL, UNIV SASK, 87- *Personal Data:* b Cambridge, Eng, Mar 16, 43; m 81, Calliopi Havele; c Anna Genevieve & Paul Kostas. *Educ:* Cambridge Univ, Eng, BA, 64, PhD (molecular biol), 68. *Honors & Awards:* Cinader Award, Can Soc Immunol, 96. *Prof Exp:* Postdoctoral fel, Salk Inst, 68-75; res assoc, Australian Nat Univ, 74-76; asst prof immunol, Univ Alta, 76-87. *Mem:* Am Asn Immunologists; Can Soc Immunol. *Res:* Immunological self-nonself discrimination; regulation of immune class induced by antigen; modulation of immune responses; vaccination against slowly-growing intracellar pathogens; pertinence of two signal model of lymphocyte activation to peripheral tolerance. *Mailing Add:* Dept Microbiol Univ Sask Saskatoon SK S7N 5E5 Can. *Fax:* 306-966-4311; *E-Mail:* bretschr@duke.usask.ca

BRETSCHNEIDER, CHARLES LEROY, PHYSICAL OCEANOGRAPHY, OCEAN ENGINEERING. *Current Pos:* PROF & CHMN DEPT OCEAN ENG, UNIV HAWAII, 67- *Personal Data:* b Red Owl, SDak, Nov 9, 20; m 48; c 2. *Educ:* Hillsdale Col, BS, 47; Univ Calif, Berkeley, MS, 50; Tex A&M Univ, PhD(phys oceanog), 59. *Honors & Awards:* Outstanding Contrib Coastal Eng Res Prize, Am Soc Civil Eng, 59; Dept Army, Off Chief Engr, Outstanding Performance & Cash Award. *Prof Exp:* Engr, Waves & Wave Force Proj, 50-51; engr waves & wave forces on pilings, Res Found, Tex A&M Univ, 51-56; hydraul engr & chief, Oceanog Br, Beach Erosion Bd, Corps Engr, US Army, 56-61; dir eastern opers, Nat Eng Sci Co, Washington, DC, 61-64, vpres, Vt, 64-65, geomarine technol, 66-67. *Concurrent Pos:* Lectr, Mass Inst Technol, 61-63. *Mem:* Am Soc Oceanog; Am Soc Eng Educ; Soc Naval Archit & Marine Eng; Am Soc Civil Eng; Am Geophys Union. *Res:* Variability, spectra, forecasting, generation and decay of waves; wave forces on piles; hurricane surge and waves; rubble mound breakwater stability. *Mailing Add:* 4096 Black Point Rd Honolulu HI 96816

BRETSKY, PETER WILLIAM, INVERTEBRATE PALEONTOLOGY. *Current Pos:* dir environ paleont prog, 70-76, from assoc prof to prof, 70-95, EMER PROF EARTH & SPACE SCI, STATE UNIV NY, STONY BROOK, 96- *Personal Data:* b Easton, Pa, Oct 26, 38; m 65; c 1. *Educ:* Lafayette Col, AB, 61; Southern Methodist Univ, MS, 63; Yale Univ, PhD, 68. *Prof Exp:* Instr geol, Northwestern Univ, 67-69, asst prof geol & biol sci, 69-70. *Mem:* Soc Econ Paleont & Mineral; Paleont Soc; Marine Biol Asn UK; Sigma Xi. *Res:* Paleoecology; biostratigraphy. *Mailing Add:* 401 E 56th St New York NY 10021-6943

BRETT, BETTY LOU HILTON, EVOLUTIONARY GENETICS, ICHTHYOL. *Current Pos:* VIS PROF, NAZARETH COL, ROCHESTER, 89- *Personal Data:* b Hudson, NY, Mar 25, 52; m 74. *Educ:* State Univ NY, Buffalo, BA, 74; Univ Mich, MA, 77, PhD(natural resources), 81. *Prof Exp:* Res assoc evolutionary genetics, Univ Rochester, 81-87; vis asst prof, Rochester Inst Technol, 87- *Concurrent Pos:* Adj asst prof, State Univ NY, Brockport, 86, 89-90 & Nazareth Col, Rochester, 89-91. *Mem:* Soc Study Evolution; Am Soc Ichthyologists & Herpetologists; Genetics Soc Am; AAAS; Soc Syst Zool; Sigma Xi. *Res:* Population genetics of Genesee River fishes; analyzing transmission of supernummary chromosomes and sex ratios in mealy bugs (Coccidae). *Mailing Add:* 106 Norman Rd Rochester NY 14623

BRETT, CARLTON ELLIOT, TAPHONOMY, PALEOECOLOGY. *Current Pos:* From instr to assoc prof, 78-90, PROF GEOL & PALEONT, UNIV ROCHESTER, 90-, PROF BIOL, 94- *Personal Data:* b Exeter, NH, June 19, 51; m 74, Betty Lou Hilton; c Kenton W & Leanne M. *Educ:* State Univ NY, Buffalo, BA, 73, MA, 75; Univ Mich, PhD(paleont), 78. *Honors & Awards:* Chas Schuchert Award, Paleont Soc, 90. *Concurrent Pos:* Prin investr, Nat Oceanic & Atmospheric Admin Hydrolab, St Croix, VI, 82, Am Chem Soc grant, Univ Rochester, 83-85, 89-91 & 91-, NSF grant, 83-86, 88-91 & 92-; trustee, Paleont Res Inst, 89-; NATO collab res grant, 92-; coun, Soc Sedimentary Geol. *Mem:* Paleont Soc; Paleont Res Inst; fel Geol Soc Am; Int Paleont Asn; Soc Sedimentary Geol. *Res:* Paleozoic invertebrate paleontology, taphonomy and paleoecology and sequence-event stratigraphy; systematics and paleoecology of pelmatozoan echinoderms; paleoecology and evolution of hard substrate communities, including epibionts; paleoecology of oxygen limited facies; sequence-event stratigraphy of the Ordovician-Devonian of Appalachian Basin. *Mailing Add:* Dept Earth & Environ Sci Univ Rochester 227 Hutchison Rochester NY 14627. *E-Mail:* cebh@dbl.cc.rochester.edu

BRETT, CLIFF, SOFTWARE SYSTEMS. *Current Pos:* MEM SOFTWARE RES & DEVELOP TEAM, METROLIGHT STUDIOS. *Educ:* Mass Inst Technol, BS. *Prof Exp:* Tech dir, Whitney/Demos Prod; mem res & develop staff, Wavefront Techs. *Mailing Add:* MetroLight Studios 5724 W Third St Suite 400 Los Angeles CA 90036-3078

BRETT, ROBIN, EARTH SCIENCES. *Current Pos:* GEOLOGIST, US GEOL SURV, RESTON, VA, 82- *Personal Data:* b Adelaide, S Australia, Jan 30, 35; m 86, Jill Davidson; c Abigail & Victoria. *Educ:* Univ Adelaide, BSc, 56; Harvard Univ, AM, 60, PhD(geol), 63. *Honors & Awards:* Lindgren Award, Soc Econ Geologists, 64; Except Sci Achievement Medal, NASA, 73. *Prof Exp:* Geologist, US Geol Surv, Washington, DC, 64-69; chief, Geochem Br, Johnson Space Ctr, NASA, 69-74; geologist, US Geol Surv, Reston, Va, 74-78; dir, Earth Sci Div, NSF, 78-82. *Concurrent Pos:* Hon fel, Australian Nat Univ, 67-68; assoc ed, J Geophys Res, 72-74, 83-85 & Bd Earth Sci, Nat Acad Sci-Nat Res Coun, 85-87; pres, Planetary Geol Div, Geol Soc Am, 84; pres, Geol Soc Wash, 86; vpres, 28th Int Geol Cong, 86-; chmn, US Nat Comt, Int Union Geol & Geophys, 87-; secy gen, Int Union Geol Sci, 89-96; mem, Nat Res Coun-Nat Acad Sci US Geodynamics Comn, 85-88, chmn, 91-94. *Mem:* Geochem Soc; Am Geophys Union; Soc Econ Geol; fel Meteoritical Soc (pres, 73-74); fel Geol Soc Am; Int Union Geol Sci (pres, 96-). *Res:* Mineralogy, petrology, geochemistry of lunar samples, meteorites, planetary geochemistry; meteorite impact structures, mineral deposits. *Mailing Add:* US Geol Surv 917 Reston VA 22092. *Fax:* 703-648-4227; *E-Mail:* rbrett@usgs.gov

BRETT, WILLIAM JOHN, PHYSIOLOGY. *Current Pos:* assoc prof biol, 56-59, chmn dept life sci, 64-67, PROF BIOL, IND STATE UNIV, TERRE HAUTE, 59-, CHMN DEPT LIFE SCI, 77- *Personal Data:* b Chicago, Ill, Mar 23, 23; m 48; c 1. *Educ:* Northern Ill Univ, BS, 49; Miami Univ, MS, 50; Northwestern Univ, PhD(biol), 53. *Prof Exp:* Asst, Northwestern Univ, 50-53; asst prof biol, Millsaps Col, 53-56. *Mem:* Am Soc Zool; Am Inst Biol Sci; Animal Behav Soc; Nat Asn Biol Teachers. *Res:* Biological rhythms. *Mailing Add:* Dept Life Sci Ind Univ Terre Haute IN 47809-0001

BRETTELL, HERBERT R, INTERNAL MEDICINE. *Current Pos:* resident, 51-55, asst, 54-55, from instr to assoc prof, 56-66, head, Div Family Pract, 69-75, chmn, Dept Family Med, 75-77, PROF MED, UNIV COLO MED CTR, DENVER, 75- *Personal Data:* b Rock River, Wyo, Feb 1, 21; m 47; c 4. *Educ:* Univ Wyo, BS, 42; Univ Rochester, MD, 50; Am Bd Internal Med, cert, 57; Am Bd Family Pract, cert, 74, Am Bd Internal Med, cert, 81. *Prof Exp:* Intern, Vanderbilt Univ, 50-51. *Mem:* Am Col Physicians; Am Col Clin Pharmacol & Chemother; Am Heart Asn; Soc Geol Int Med. *Res:* Cardiovascular disease; thrombosis. *Mailing Add:* Dept Med Univ Colo Health Sci 4200 E Ninth Ave Denver CO 80220-3706

BRETTHAUER, ROGER K, CELL BIOLOGY. *Current Pos:* from asst prof to assoc prof, 64-77, PROF CHEM, UNIV NOTRE DAME, 77- *Personal Data:* b Morris, Ill, Jan 4, 35; m 59; c 3. *Educ:* Univ Ill, BS, 56, MS, 58; Mich State Univ, PhD(biochem), 62. *Prof Exp:* NIH training grant bact, Univ Wis, 62-64. *Mem:* AAAS; Am Chem Soc; Am Soc Biol Chemists; Soc Complex Carbohydrates. *Res:* Complex carbohydrates, biosynthesis, structure and function. *Mailing Add:* Dept Chem & Biochem Univ Notre Dame Notre Dame IN 46556-5601. *Fax:* 219-631-6652

BRETTING, PETER KONRAD, PLANT GENETIC RESOURCE MANAGEMENT, PLANT SYSTEMATICS. *Current Pos:* RES LEADER & COORDR, NCRPIS, AGR RES SERV, USDA, 91- *Personal Data:* b Bayshore, NY, June 21, 53; m 94, Kim Lewens; c Sarah & Dan. *Educ:* Tulane Univ, BS, 75; Ind Univ, PhD(plant sci), 81. *Prof Exp:* Botanist & head, Natural Hist Div, Inst Jamaica, 82-84; res assoc, Dept Crop Sci, NC State Univ, 84-88; res prog dir, Ind Crop Improv Asn, 88-91. *Concurrent Pos:* Actg nat prog leader, Genetic Resources, Conserv & Develop, 97. *Mem:* Bot Soc Am; Crop Sci Soc Am; Soc Study Evolution; Soc Econ Bot; Am Soc Plant Taxonomists; AAAS. *Res:* Plant genetic resource management, especially of heterozygons heterogeneous germ plasm; statistical genetic approaches to analyzing genetic market data; applications of genetic markers to plant genetic resource management; plant systematics and evolution; crop plant biodiversity. *Mailing Add:* Agron Bldg Iowa State Univ Ames IA 50011

BRETTON, R(ANDOLPH) H(ENRY), CHEMICAL ENGINEERING THERMODYNAMICS. *Current Pos:* RETIRED. *Personal Data:* b Wolfeboro, NH, Apr 1, 18; m 44, Jeannette M L'Heureux; c Nancy A (Hannans), Susan M & Randolph H Jr. *Educ:* Worcester Polytech Inst, BS, 41, MS, 43; Yale Univ, DEng, 49. *Hon Degrees:* DSc, Worcester Polytech Inst, 57. *Prof Exp:* Chem serv engr, Goodyear Tire & Rubber Co, 43-44; from asst prof to assoc prof chem eng, Yale Univ, 48-67; mgr, Tech Info Serv, 67-73; mgr proc develop, Nat Distillers & Chem Corp, 73-82. *Concurrent Pos:* Lt jg, USNR, 44-46; vis assoc engr, Brookhaven Nat Lab, 49-50, consult, 50-64; consult, Nat Distillers & Chem Corp, 59-67. *Mem:* Am Chem Soc; Am Inst Chem Engrs; Sigma Xi. *Res:* Kinetics in flow systems; high pressure thermodynamic equilibria. *Mailing Add:* 1/2 Hepburn Rd Hamden CT 06517

BRETTON, RANDOLPH HENRY, JR, OPHTHALMOLOGY, EXTRACELLULAR MATRIX. *Current Pos:* res fel, Bethesda Eye Inst, 89-91, PRIN RES SCIENTIST, AM CYANAMID, 91- *Personal Data:* b New Haven, Conn, Sept 17, 55. *Educ:* Northeastern Univ, BS, 78; Univ Vt, PhD(cell biol), 85. *Prof Exp:* Fel, Dept Dermat, Yale Sch Med, 85-87; res assoc, Dept Path, Wash Univ Sch Med, 87-89. *Mem:* AAAS; Asn Res Vision & Ophthal; Am Soc Cell Biol. *Mailing Add:* 12487 Marine Ave Maryland Heights MO 63043. *E-Mail:* 71020.3205@compuserve.com, rhb@storz.com

BRETZ, MICHAEL, ADSORPTION PHYSICS. *Current Pos:* asst prof, 73-78, ASSOC PROF PHYSICS, UNIV MICH, ANN ARBOR, 78- *Personal Data:* b Harvey, Ill, June 2, 38; m 64; c 2. *Educ:* Univ Calif, Los Angeles, 61; Univ Wash, PhD(physics), 71. *Prof Exp:* Asst scientist space physics, Lockheed Res Labs, 61-65; res assoc physics, Univ Wash, 71-73. *Mem:* Am Phys Soc; AAAS. *Res:* Properties of over-layer quantum films adsorbed on homogeneous substrates; new materials for adsorption and catalysis. *Mailing Add:* Dept Physics Univ Mich Ann Arbor MI 48109

BRETZ, PHILIP ERIC, PHYSICAL METALLURGICAL ENGINEERING, FAILURE ANALYSIS & FRACTURE MECHANICS. *Current Pos:* staff engr, Aluminum Co Am, 80-84, tech specialist, 84-86, proj mgr, 86-88, div mgr, 88-90, operating supt, 90-92, mgr mfg technol, 92-93, MGR SPEC PROJ, ALUMINUM CO AM, 93- *Personal Data:* b Carlisle, Pa, Jan 28, 53; m 79, Harriet Bulkin; c Amanda & Kristen. *Educ:* Lehigh Univ, BS, 75, MS, 77, PhD(metall), 80. *Prof Exp:* Welding engr, Chicago Bridge & Iron Co, 74-75; teaching asst & res asst metall, Lehigh Univ, 75-80. *Mem:* Am Soc Metals; Am Inst Mining Metall & Petrol Engrs; Sigma Xi. *Res:* Microstructure of materials and the influence of structure on mechanical behavior; fatigue and fracture resistance of materials; aerospace aluminum alloy and aluminum-lithium alloy development; failure analysis and product liability; aluminum alloy development. *Mailing Add:* 3901 Sardis Rd Murrysville PA 15668. *Fax:* 412-337-4203

BREUER, CHARLES B, RESEARCH ADMINISTRATION. *Current Pos:* RETIRED. *Personal Data:* b Brooklyn, NY, Aug 7, 31; m 62; c 1. *Educ:* NY Univ, BA, 53; Rutgers Univ, MS, 59, PhD(biochem), 64. *Prof Exp:* Res scientist, Squibb Inst Med Res, Olin Mathieson Chem Corp, 59-61; res asst biochem, Rutgers Univ, 61-63; res scientist, Lederle Labs, Am Cyanamid Co, 63-66, group leader, 66-67, sr res scientist, 67-70, head, Biotherapeut Dept, 70-71, dir diag res & develop, 71-76, dir sci & regulatory affairs, 76-77; dir sci & regulatory affairs, Fisher Sci Co, 77-79, dir tech opers, 80-91. *Mem:* AAAS; Am Chem Soc; Am Soc Biol Chem:. *Res:* Diagnostics; immunochemistry; biology of serum proteins; in new diagnostic agents and principles. *Mailing Add:* 101 Brookwood Dr Tryon NC 28782-3435

BREUER, DELMAR W, AERONAUTICAL ENGINEERING. *Current Pos:* from asst prof to assoc prof, USAF Inst Technol, 51-61, from actg head to head dept mech, 55-76,prof mech, 61-80, head dept aeronaut & astronaut, 77-80, EMER PROF AEROSPACE ENG, USAF INST TECHNOL, 80-; CONSULT, 80- *Personal Data:* b St James, Mo, June 21, 25; m 49, Ethelene Paschal; c 2. *Educ:* Iowa State Univ, BS, 47; Mo Sch Mines, MS, 50; Ohio State Univ, PhD(aeronaut & astronaut eng), 61. *Prof Exp:* Instr mech, Mo Sch Mines, 47-50; stress analyst, NAm Aviation, 50-51. *Mem:* Am Inst Aeronaut & Astronaut; Am Soc Eng Educ; Sigma Xi. *Res:* Effect of finite deflections on vibrations of plates; thermal stresses; stability of pressurized conical shells; dynamics of variable mass systems; non-nuclear weapon effects. *Mailing Add:* 5539 Oakshire Circle Dayton OH 45440

BREUER, GEORGE MICHAEL, PHYSICAL CHEMISTRY, INDUSTRIAL HYGIENE. *Current Pos:* at UNIV HYG LAB, UNIV IOWA, OAKDALE CAMPUS, 84- *Personal Data:* b Trenton, NJ, Feb 1, 44; m 79, Elaine Roberts. *Educ:* Univ Mo-Rolla, BS, 66; Univ Calif, Irvine, PhD(chem), 72. *Prof Exp:* Asst res chemist air pollution, Statewide Air Pollution Res Ctr, Univ Calif, Riverside, 74-77; res chemist indust hyg, Nat Inst Occup Safety & Health, 77-84. *Mem:* Am Chem Soc; Am Indust Hyg Asn. *Res:* Analytical chemistry in the ambient and occupational environments. *Mailing Add:* Univ Hyg Lab 102 Oakdale Campus Iowa City IA 52242. *Fax:* 319-335-4555; *E-Mail:* george-breuer@uiowa.edu

BREUER, MAX EVERETT, CHEMICAL ENGINEERING. *Current Pos:* CHEM ENGR, UPJOHN CO, 68- *Personal Data:* b Sperry, Iowa, Sept 29, 38; m 62; c 4. *Educ:* Univ Iowa, BS, 63, MS, 64, PhD(chem eng), 67. *Prof Exp:* Chem engr, Union Carbide Corp, 66-68. *Mem:* Am Chem Soc; Am Inst Chem Engrs. *Res:* Gas mixture separation via selective permeation; crystallization; chemical process development. *Mailing Add:* 6448 Cypress Kalamazoo MI 49024

BREUER, MELVIN A, ELECTRICAL ENGINEERING. *Current Pos:* From asst prof to assoc prof elec eng, 65-79, PROF ELEC ENG & COMPUT SCI, UNIV SOUTHERN CALIF, 79- *Personal Data:* b Los Angeles, Calif, Feb 1, 38; m 63, Sandy; c Teri & Jeff. *Educ:* Univ Calif, Los Angeles, BS, 59, MS, 61; Univ Calif, Berkeley, PhD(elec eng), 65. *Honors & Awards:* Taylor L Booth Educ Award, Inst Elec & Electronics Engrs, 93. *Concurrent Pos:* Fulbright-Hays fel, 72; ed-in-chief, J Design Automation & Fault Tolerant Comput, 77-82. *Mem:* Sigma Xi; fel Inst Elec & Electronics Engrs. *Res:* Digital computer design; switching theory; design automation; fault tolerant computing; development of new algorithms for computer aided design of digital circuits, such as the min-cut and forced vector algorithms; development of new approaches to testing, such as a knowledge based system for design for test and fundamental work on automatic test vector generation. *Mailing Add:* Elec Eng Sci Div Univ Southern Calif MS 2562 Univ Park Los Angeles CA 90089. *E-Mail:* mb@poisson.usc.edu

BREUHAUS, W(ALDEMAR) O(TTO), AERONAUTICAL ENGINEERING. *Current Pos:* RETIRED. *Personal Data:* b Lowell, Ohio, Apr 26, 18; m 50, Sara J Sheeler; c George W, Babetta A & Richard S. *Educ:* Carnegie Inst Technol, BS, 40; Univ Buffalo, MS, 61. *Honors & Awards:* Laura Taber Barbour Air Safety Award, Flight Safety Found, 67; De Florez Training Award for Flight Simulation, Am Inst Aeronaut & Astronaut, 86. *Prof Exp:* Aerodynamics engr, Chance-Vought Div, United Aircraft Corp, 40-42, head, Stability & Control Group, 42-46; head, Eng Sect, Flight Res Dept, Cornell Aeronaut Lab, Inc, 46-48, asst head, 48-56, head, 56-67, dir, Flight Dynamics Div, 67-69, dir, Aerosci Div, 69-72; mem prof staff, Systs Eval Div, Inst for Defense Analysis, 73-83. *Concurrent Pos:* Mem, Res & Technol Adv Subcomt Aircraft Flight Dynamics, NASA, 67-70; chmn, Sci Adv Bd C-5A, Performance Subcomt, USAF, 70. *Mem:* Assoc fel Am Inst Aeronaut & Astronaut. *Res:* Aircraft aerodynamics, stability and control, and flying qualities requirements; variable stability aircraft use and development. *Mailing Add:* 661 Mill Rd East Aurora NY 14052

BREUNING, SIEGFRIED M, TRANSPORTATION ENGINEERING, FUTURES ANALYSIS. *Current Pos:* prof, 71-93, EMER PROF CIVIL ENG & INTERDISCIPLINARY STUDY, UNIV MASS, DARTMOUTH, 94- *Personal Data:* b Hamburg, Ger, July 25, 24; US citizen; m 51; c 3. *Educ:* Stuttgart Tech, MS, 50; Mass Inst Technol, ScD, 57. *Prof Exp:* Asst transp eng, Stuttgart Tech, 51; eng asst, Montreal Transp Comn, 51-52; res engr, Mass Inst Tech, 52-57; assoc prof civil eng, Univ Alta, 57-59; assoc prof civil eng & res, Mich State Univ, 59-63; chief, Transp Systs Div, Nat Bur Stand, 63-65; vis prof civil eng & dir, Hwy Transp Prog, Mass Inst Technol, 65-69; exec vpres, Social Technol Systs Inc, Mass, 69-71. *Concurrent Pos:* Res consult, Hwy Intersect Design, 50; comt mem, Hwy Res Bd, Nat Acad Sci, 54-78; consult transp econ, Burma, 58; adv, Traffic Res Corp, 62-63; exec secy panel transp res & develop, US Dept Com, 63-67; consult innovation, transp & social technol, 71-; consult, Cabot Corp, 72-87; vpres & dir, New Eng Energy Policy Coun, 74-78; consult future transportation, 81. *Mem:* Ger Road Res Soc; Sigma Xi. *Res:* Definitions, measurements and research of basic factors in transportation; socio-technical systems design and research; interdisciplinary studies. *Mailing Add:* 129 School St Wayland MA 01778

BREW, DAVID ALAN, GEOLOGY. *Current Pos:* geologist, 52-95, EMER GEOL PROF, US GEOL SURV, 95- *Personal Data:* b Clifton Springs, NY, Nov 22, 30; m 58, Alice P Dickerman; c Elizabeth C, A Perrin, Catherine L & Emily O. *Educ:* Dartmouth Col, AB, 52; Stanford Univ, PhD(geol), 64. *Honors & Awards:* Meritorious Serv Award, US Dept Interior, 72; Career Serv Award for Spec Achievement, Civil Serv League, 73. *Concurrent Pos:* Asst, Stanford Univ, 58-59; Fulbright scholar, Univ Vienna, 59-60. *Mem:* Geol Soc Am; Am Geophys Union; Am Asn Petrol Geologists; Geol Soc Austria; Sigma Xi; Arctic Inst NAm. *Res:* Relations of sedimentation and tectonics; structure and structural geometry; tectonic and plutonic history of northeastern Pacific rim; relations of mineral deposits to plutonic rocks. *Mailing Add:* US Geol Surv MS 904 345 Middlefield Rd Menlo Park CA 94025

BREW, KEITH, BIOCHEMISTRY. *Current Pos:* asst prof, 70-74, PROF BIOCHEM, UNIV MIAMI MED SCH, 74- *Personal Data:* b Essex, Eng, Oct 19, 41. *Educ:* Univ Col London, BSc, 62, PhD(biochem), 66. *Prof Exp:* Fel, Duke Univ, 66-68. *Concurrent Pos:* Europe res award, 72; res career develop award, NIH, 75 & 80. *Mem:* Am Biochem Soc; Am Chem Soc; AAAS. *Mailing Add:* Dept Biochem R629 Univ Miami Sch Med 1600 NW Tenth Ave Miami FL 33136-1015

BREW, WILLIAM BARNARD, CHEMISTRY. *Current Pos:* Res chemist, 36-38, chief anal chemist, 38-41, mgr org res lab, 41-55, mgr org & inorg res lab, 55-60, mgr spec prod res lab, 60-64, dir cent res labs, 64-73, DIV VPRES & DIR CENT RES LABS, RALSTON PURINA CO, 73- *Personal Data:* b Sibley, Ill, Apr 23, 13; m 41; c 5. *Educ:* Wash Univ, BS, 35, MS, 36. *Mem:* Am Chem Soc; Inst Food Technologists; Am Inst Chemists. *Res:* Vitamin chemistry; amino acid chemistry; chromatography; spectrophotometry. *Mailing Add:* 3227 Hawthorne Blvd St Louis MO 63104-1618

BREWBAKER, JAMES LYNN, PLANT GENETICS. *Current Pos:* assoc prof, 61-64, PROF HORT, UNIV HAWAII, 64- *Personal Data:* b St Paul, Minn, Oct 11, 26; m 54, 70, Kathryn Bradley; c Paul H, Philip L, Perry L & Pamela B. *Educ:* Univ Colo, BA, 48; Cornell Univ, PhD(plant breeding), 52. *Honors & Awards:* Crop Sci Res Award, Am Soc Agron, 84; Int Inventors Award, Sweden, 86; Superior Serv, USDA, 90; Genetics & Plant Breeding Award, Nat Coun Com Plant Breeders, 92. *Prof Exp:* Asst genetics, Calif Inst Technol, 48, Univ Minn, 50 & Cornell Univ, 49-52; Nat Res Found fel, Univ Lund, Sweden, 52-53; asst prof plant breeding, Univ Philippines & Cornell Univ, 53-55; assoc geneticist, Brookhaven Nat Lab, 56-61. *Concurrent Pos:* Geneticist, Rockefeller Found, Thailand, 67-68 & Int Atomic Energy Agency, Philippines, 70; consult trop agr, Nigeria, Philippines, Korea, Colombia, Taiwan, Indonesia, India, Dominican Repub & Pakistan. *Mem:* Bot Soc Am; fel Am Soc Agron; Nitrogen Fixing Tree Asn (pres, 81-90); Nat Sweet Corn Breeders Asn (pres, 87); Soc Am Foresters. *Res:* Maize breeding and genetics; breeding tropical nitrogen-fixing trees. *Mailing Add:* Dept Hort Univ Hawaii 3190 Maile Way Honolulu HI 96822. *Fax:* 808-956-3894; *E-Mail:* brewbake@uhunix.uhcc.edu

BREWEN, J GRANT, CELL BIOLOGY, MOLECULAR BIOLOGY. *Current Pos:* PRES & CHIEF EXEC OFFICER, BIOTECHNOL RES & DEVELOP CORP, 88- *Personal Data:* b Easton, Pa, Oct 2, 39; m 69; c 2. *Educ:* Johns Hopkins Univ, BA, 61, PhD(biol), 63. *Honors & Awards:* Tech Achievement Award, Allied Signal, 86. *Prof Exp:* Res assoc cytogenetics, Oak Ridge Nat Lab, 63-66; res assoc, Div Plant Indust, Commonwealth Sci & Indust Res Org, 66-67; sr res staff, Oak Ridge Nat Lab, 67-79; dir genetics, Allied Corp, 79-88. *Concurrent Pos:* Adj prof, Sch Biomed Sci, Univ Tenn, 70-78; vis prof, Univ Calif, Berkeley, 77; adv sci comt, Ill Govt, 88- *Res:* Molecular genetics; mechanisms of mutagenesis; genetic toxicology. *Mailing Add:* 119 E Pawnee Ct Peoria IL 61615

BREWER, ARTHUR DAVID, AGRICULTURAL CHEMISTRY. *Current Pos:* res chemist, Uniroyal Res Lab, 68-75, res scientist chem, 75-81, sr group leader, 75-81, MGR, SYNTHETIC RES SECT, UNIROYAL RES LAB, 87- *Personal Data:* b Evesham, Eng, Nov 14, 41; Can citizen; m 68, Margaret McWhinnie; c Jennifer A & Hazel M. *Educ:* Cambridge Univ, BA, 63, MA, 67; Univ Strathclyde, Scotland, PhD(chem), 67. *Prof Exp:* Fel chem, Univ Ariz, 67-68. *Mem:* Fel Royal Soc Chem; Can Inst Chemists; Brit Ornithologists Union; Sigma Xi. *Res:* Basic synthesis research in heterocyclic chemistry with view to discovery of new agricultural and pharmaceutical chemicals. *Mailing Add:* Uniroyal Chem Ltd PO Box 1120 Guelph ON N1H 6N3 Can

BREWER, CURTIS FRED, NUCLEAR MAGNETIC RESONANCE SPECTROSCOPY. *Current Pos:* fel, 71-73, res assoc, 73-74, from asst prof to assoc prof, 74-84, PROF PHARMACOL, ALBERT EINSTEIN COL MED, 84- *Personal Data:* b Greenville, Tex, July 17, 44; m 89, Carol K Demitz. *Educ:* Univ Calif, Santa Barbara, BA, 66, PhD(chem), 71. *Honors & Awards:* Meller Res Award, Albert Einstein Col Med, 74. *Prof Exp:* Trainee fel, NSF, 66-69. *Concurrent Pos:* Res Career Develop Award, NIH, 75-80; mem, Biomed Sci Study Sect, NIH, 84-88, chmn, 88. *Mem:* NY Acad Sci; Am Chem Soc; Am Soc Biol Chemists; AAAS. *Res:* Biochemical and biophysical studies of the interactions of carbohydrate binding proteins (lectins) with cell surface carbohydrate molecules; ligand-macromolecule interactions and enzyme catalysis. *Mailing Add:* Dept Molecular Pharmacol Albert Einstein Col Med 1300 Morris Park Ave Bronx NY 10461-1975. *Fax:* 718-829-8705; *E-Mail:* brewer@aecom.yu.edu

BREWER, DANA ALICE, SPACECRAFT SYSTEMS, SPACE ENVIRONMENT EFFECTS. *Current Pos:* environ mgr, Space Sta Freedom Prog Off, NASA, 88-94, PROG MGR SPACECRAFT SYSTS, NASA HQ, 95- *Personal Data:* b Easton, Pa, Nov 6, 50. *Educ:* Pa State Univ, BS, 72; Va Polytech Inst & State Univ, PhD(chem), 77. *Prof Exp:* Teaching asst chem, Va Polytech Inst & State Univ, 72-77; chemist, NASA Langley Res Ctr, 75, res assoc, Joint Inst Advan Flight Sci, George Washington Univ, 77-80, asst prof lectr atmospheric chem, 79-81; sr scientist, Systs & Appl Sci Corp, 81-84; res prof chem, Col William & Mary, NASA Langley Res Ctr, 85; res assoc, Vigyan Res Assocs, 86-87; mem tech staff, AT&T Bell Labs, 87. *Mem:* Am Chem Soc; Am Inst Aeronaut & Astronaut. *Res:* Atmospheric chemical reaction mechanisms; atmospheric hydrocarbon chemical models; environmental control and life support studies for space station; spacecraft advanced technology. *Mailing Add:* 1938 Lakeport Way Reston VA 20191

BREWER, DOUGLAS G, INORGANIC CHEMISTRY, ANALYTICAL CHEMISTRY. *Current Pos:* From asst prof to assoc prof analytic & inorg chem, 61-72, PROF CHEM & DEAN SCI, UNIV NB, 72- *Personal Data:* b Toronto, Ont, Dec 22, 35; m 61; c 1. *Educ:* Univ Toronto, BA, 58, PhD(chem), 61. *Concurrent Pos:* Operating grants, Nat Res Coun Can, 61-71 & NB Res & Productivity Coun, 63-64. *Mem:* Chem Inst Can. *Res:* Stability constants of metal complexes as determined by differential potentiometry and related methods; infrared, optical rotary dispersion, ultraviolet-vision, nuclear magnetic resonance and x-ray studies of metal complexes. *Mailing Add:* Dept Chem Univ NB Box 4400 Fredericton NB E3B 5A3 Can

BREWER, FRANKLIN DOUGLAS, ENTOMOLOGY. *Current Pos:* AT TUXTLA GUTIERREZ, CHIAPAS, MEX. *Personal Data:* b Electric Mills, Miss, Sept 25, 38; m 66, 88; c 3. *Educ:* Miss Col, BS, 60; Univ Southern Miss, MS, 63; Miss State Univ, PhD(entom), 70. *Prof Exp:* Instr biol, Miss Woman's Univ, 64-66; from instr microbiol to asst prof assoc biochem, Miss State Univ, 66-71; res entomologist, Screwworm Res Lab, Agr Res Serv, USDA, 71- *Mem:* Sigma Xi; Entom Soc Am. *Res:* Insect nutrition, quality control and mass rearing techniques for producing a consistent yet economical number of competitive insects for biological control purposes. *Mailing Add:* Pheba MS 39755

BREWER, GEORGE E(UGENE) F(RANCIS), coatings technology, paint solvent emission, for more information see previous edition

BREWER, GEORGE R, PHYSICS, ELECTRICAL ENGINEERING. *Current Pos:* RETIRED. *Personal Data:* b New Albany, Ind, Sept 10, 22; m 46, 84, Mary L Vollmer; c Lynn & Wendy. *Educ:* Univ Louisville, BS, 43; Univ Mich, MS, 49 & 50, PhD(elec eng), 51. *Prof Exp:* Staff mem, Radiation Lab, Mass Inst Technol, 43-44; res engr, Naval Res Labs, 44-47; res engr res inst, Univ Mich, 47-51; mgr, Electron Device Physics Dept, Hughes Res Lab, 51-81. *Concurrent Pos:* Consult, electron & ion beam syst & microelectronics, 81-86. *Mem:* Fel Inst Elec & Electronics Engrs. *Res:* Electron and ion dynamics; electron gun and beam focusing; ion propulsion; microwave electron tubes; microelectronic processes and devices; ion implantation; electron beam lithography. *Mailing Add:* 217 Peter Pan Rd Carmel CA 93923-9746. *Fax:* 408-625-4146; *E-Mail:* 102505.3004@compuserve.com

BREWER, GLENN A, JR, CHEMISTRY. *Current Pos:* sr res microbiologist, E R Squibb & Sons, Inc, 56-60, suprv anal res, 60-67, asst dir, 67-84, dir anal res, 84-90, exec dir, Worldwide Anal Systs, 90-92, CONSULT, BRISTOL-MYERS SQUIBB INST PHARMACEUT RES, 93- *Personal Data:* b New Haven, Conn, Nov 3, 27; m 57; c 4. *Educ:* Hobart Col, BS, 49; Univ Wis, MS, 52, PhD(biochem), 54. *Prof Exp:* Sr res biochemist, Com Solvents Corp, 54-56. *Mem:* Am Chem Soc; Am Asn Pharmaceut Scientists; fel AAAS. *Res:* Pharmaceutical analysis. *Mailing Add:* Bristol-Myers Squibb Inst Pharmaceut Res Princeton NJ 08903

BREWER, GREGORY J, MEMBRANE BIOCHEMISTRY & BIOPHYSICS, CYTOLOGY. *Current Pos:* Assoc prof, 80-91, PROF MED MICROBIOL, SCH MED, SOUTHERN ILL UNIV, 91- *Personal Data:* b Apr 8, 1947. *Educ:* Calif Inst Technol, BS, 68; Univ Calif, San Diego, PhD(biol), 72. *Concurrent Pos:* Dir, Res Imaging Facil. *Mem:* Soc Neurosci; Am Soc Cell Biol. *Res:* Neuron cell culture; age-related neuron function; Alzheimer disease; synaptogenesis; ganglioside function; neuron development. *Mailing Add:* Sch Med Southern Ill Univ PO Box 19230 Springfield IL 62794-1220. *Fax:* 217-524-3227

BREWER, H BRYAN, JR, METABOLIC DISEASE, ATHEROSCLEROSIS. *Current Pos:* HEAD SECT PEPTIDE CHEM, NAT HEART, LUNG & BLOOD INST, 70-, CHIEF MOLECULAR DIS BR, 76- *Personal Data:* b Casper, Wyo, Aug 17, 38; m 58; c 2. *Educ:* Johns Hopkins Univ, BA, 60; Stanford Univ, MD, 65. *Concurrent Pos:* Mem coun atherosclerosis, Am Heart Asn, 79-81. *Mem:* Fedn Am Soc Biol Chemists; Am Soc Clin Res; Am Soc Clin Invest. *Res:* Molecular structure, function and metabolism of human plasma lipoproteins; the role of plasma lipoproteins in lipid transport in normal individuals and patients with disorders of lipid metabolism and atherosclerosis. *Mailing Add:* Molecular Dis Br Bldg 10 Rm 7N115 Nat Heart Lung & Blood Inst NIH 10 Center Dr MSC 1666 Bethesda MD 20892-1666. *Fax:* 301-402-0190

BREWER, HOWARD EUGENE, plant physiology; deceased, see previous edition for last biography

BREWER, JAMES W, ALGEBRA. *Current Pos:* chair dept, 86-95, PROF MATH, FLA ATLANTIC UNIV, 85- *Personal Data:* b West Palm Beach, Fla, May 29, 42; m 89, Virginia Ganther; c Deborah L, Jill D, James C, Amy W, David R & Thomas A. *Educ:* Fla State Univ, AB, 64, PhD(math), 68. *Prof Exp:* Asst prof math, Va Polytech Inst, 68-70; from asst prof to prof, Univ Kans, 70-87. *Concurrent Pos:* Vis prof, Univ Stellenbosch, SAfrica, 77-78 & Univ Va, 78. *Mem:* Am Math Soc; SAfrica Math Soc. *Res:* Commutative algebra with special emphasis on polynomial and power series rings; algebraic control theory. *Mailing Add:* Dept Math Fla Atlantic Univ Boca Raton FL 33431. *E-Mail:* brewer@acc.fau.edu

BREWER, JEROME, CHEMICAL ENGINEERING, THERMODYNAMICS. *Current Pos:* RETIRED. *Personal Data:* b Kansas City, Mo, Mar 31, 19; m 49, Pearl Schere; c Diane, David & Kenneth. *Educ:* Iowa State Univ, BS, 40; Univ Kans, MS, 57, PhD(phase equilibria), 60. *Prof Exp:* Asst ord engr, Southwest Proving Ground, 41-42, sect head, 42-43; group leader spectrog, Pratt-Whitney Aircraft Corp, Mo, 43-44; jr engr instrumentation, Metall Lab, Univ Chicago, 44-45; asst physicist indust res, Midwest Res Inst, 45-49, assoc physicist, 49-54, sr chem engr, 54-56; sr scientist thermodyn correlations, Air Prod & Chem, Inc, 59-61; sr physicist, Midwest Res Inst, 61-65, prin physicist, 65-67, prin chem engr, 67-73; process engr, C W Nofsinger Co, 73-80. *Mem:* Am Inst Chem Engrs; Sigma Xi. *Res:* Correlation of thermodynamic properties of materials; phase equilibra; process design; measurement of second virial coefficients. *Mailing Add:* 9948 Woodson Dr Overland Park KS 66207

BREWER, JESSE WAYNE, ENTOMOLOGY, PLANT PATHOLOGY. *Current Pos:* prof, 87-95, HEAD, DEPT ENTOM, AUBURN UNIV, 95- *Personal Data:* b Rives, Mo, Oct 10, 40; m 90, Sandra J Ewald; c Laura (Davis) & Matthew W. *Educ:* Cent Mich Univ, BS, 63, MA, 65; Purdue Univ, PhD(entom), 68. *Prof Exp:* Instr biol, Muskegon Community Col, 64-65; from asst prof to assoc prof entom, Colo State Univ, 68-79, prof & coordr entom progs, 79-87. *Concurrent Pos:* Vis scientist, Nat Acad Sci, Czech, 78, 79, 83 & 87; prof & head, Dept Entomol, Mont State Univ. *Mem:* Entom Soc Am; Can Entom Soc. *Res:* Forest entomology; pollination biology. *Mailing Add:* Auburn Univ 301 Funchess Hall Auburn AL 36849. *Fax:* 334-844-5005; *E-Mail:* wbrewer@acesag.auburn.edu

BREWER, JOHN GILBERT, ANALYTICAL CHEMISTRY. *Current Pos:* assoc prof, 68-74, PROF CHEM, ARMSTRONG STATE COL, 74- *Personal Data:* b Robinson, Ga, May 11, 37. *Educ:* Univ Ga, BS, 58, MS, 63, PhD(chem), 66. *Prof Exp:* Anal develop chemist, Chemstrand Co, Monsanto Chem Co, Fla, 58-59; asst chem, Univ Ga, 60-66; asst prof, The Citadel, 66-68. *Mem:* Am Chem Soc; Sigma Xi. *Res:* Analysis of multicomponent mixtures through fitting of their excess functions via computer usage. *Mailing Add:* Armstrong State Col Savannah GA 31419

BREWER, JOHN MICHAEL, BIOCHEMISTRY, PROTEIN SCIENCE. *Current Pos:* from asst prof to assoc prof, 66-83, PROF BIOCHEM, UNIV GA, 83- *Personal Data:* b Garden City, Kans, May 13, 38; m 65, Mary S Knopp; c Elizabeth A & Michael A. *Educ:* Johns Hopkins Univ, BA, 60, PhD(biochem), 63. *Prof Exp:* Res assoc chem, Univ Ill, Urbana-Champaign, 63-66. *Mem:* Am Chem Soc; Am Soc Biol Chemists; Biophys Soc; Sigma Xi. *Res:* Protein chemistry and structure and the mechanism of enzyme action. *Mailing Add:* Dept Biochem Univ Ga Athens GA 30602. *Fax:* 706-542-1738

BREWER, KENNETH ALVIN, TRANSPORTATION ENGINEERING. *Current Pos:* assoc prof, 69-75, PROF CIVIL ENG, IOWA STATE UNIV, 75- *Personal Data:* b Wichita, Kans, Jan 24, 38; m 58; c 3. *Educ:* Kans State Univ, BSCE, 60, MS, 61, Tex A&M Univ, PhD(civil eng), 67. *Prof Exp:* Proj engr, Fuller Assocs Consults, 63-65; res asst transp eng, Tex Transp Inst, 66-67; from instr to asst prof, Tex A&M Univ, 67-69. *Concurrent Pos:* Res assoc, Tex Transp Inst, 67-68, asst res engr, 68-69. *Mem:* Inst Transp Engrs; Am Soc Civil Engrs; Nat Soc Prof Engrs; Am Soc Eng Educ; Sigma Xi. *Res:* Traffic flow theory; transportation planning; traffic safety; travel behavior; highway maintenance; highway design. *Mailing Add:* Civil Eng Iowa State Univ Ames IA 50011-2010. *Fax:* 515-292-4580

BREWER, LEO, HIGH TEMPERATURE CHEMISTRY & THERMODYNAMICS, METALLIC BONDING. *Current Pos:* Res assoc, Manhattan Dist Proj, Radiation Lab, 43-46, from asst prof to prof, 46-89, EMER PROF, DEPT CHEM, UNIV CALIF, BERKELEY, 89- *Personal Data:* b St Louis, Mo, June 13, 19; wid; c Beth, Roger & Gail. *Educ:* Calif Inst Technol, BS, 40; Univ Calif, PhD(chem), 43. *Honors & Awards:* Baekeland

Award, 53, Am Chem Soc, W Coover lectr, 67; E O Lawrence Award, Atomic Energy Comn, 61; Robert S Williams lectr, Mass Inst Technol, 63; Henry Werner lectr, Univ Kans, 63; O M Smith lectr, Okla State Univ, 64; G N Lewis lectr, Univ Calif, 64; Palladium Medal, Electrochem Soc, 71, Henry B Linford Award, 88; W D Harkins lectr, Univ Chicago, 74; William Hume-Rothery Award, Metall Soc, 83, Extractive Metall Sci Award, 91; Louis Jacob Bircher lectr, Vanderbilt Univ, 86; Eyring lectr, Ariz State Univ, 89; Extractive Metall Sci Award, Minerals, Metals & Mat Soc. *Concurrent Pos:* Assoc, Lawrence Berkeley Lab, 47-60, prin investr, 60-, head, Inorg Mat Res Div, 61-75, assoc dir, 67-75; Guggenheim mem fel, 50; secy, Comn High Temperature, Int Union Pure & Appl Chem, 57-61 & 76-, assoc mem, Comn Thermodyn & Thermochem, 74-; fac lectr, Univ Calif, 66 & corn prod lectr, Pa State Univ, 70; assoc ed, J Chem Physics; mem, Rev Comt Reactor Chem Div, Oak Ridge Nat Lab; mem, Calorimetry Conf; mem, Comt Data Needs, Nat Res Coun, 76-78, mem, 75-79, chmn, Comt High Temperature Sci & Technol, 79-81; assoc ed, J Electrochem Soc, 76-84; ed, Atomic Energy Rev Spec Issue No 7, Atomic Energy Agency, Vienna, 77-80; mem, Int Coun Alloys Phase Diagrams, Am Soc Metals & Nat Bur Stand, 78-, Basic Energy Sci Lab Progs Panel, Dept Energy, 78-82, Coun Mat Sci, 83-85, Res Assistance Task Force, 88 & Steering Comt Workshop Chem Processes & Prod Severe Reactor Accidents, Nuclear Regulatory Comn, 88; lectr, Oak Ridge Nat Lab, 79, Frontiers Chem Res, Tex A&M Univ, 81, res scholar lectr, Drew Univ, 83. *Mem:* Nat Acad Sci; fel Am Phys Soc; Am Chem Soc; Royal Soc Chem; Metall Soc; Am Optical Soc; Electrochem Soc; Am Acad Arts & Sci; fel AAAS; fel Am Soc Metals Int; fel Am Ceramic Soc. *Res:* High temperature chemistry and thermodynamics; theory of bonding in metallic solutions. *Mailing Add:* Dept Chem Univ Calif Berkeley CA 94720. *Fax:* 510-642-8369

BREWER, LEROY EARL, JR, THERMAL PHYSICS, PHENOMENOLOGY. *Current Pos:* GROUP ENGR, LOCKHEED ADVAN DEL, 92- *Personal Data:* b Hagerstown, Md, June 1, 36; m 56; c 1. *Educ:* Univ Fla, BS, 60; Univ Tenn, MS, 65; Univ Brussels, PhD(appl sci), 75. *Prof Exp:* Res engr, Arnold Eng Develop Ctr, Aro, Inc, 60-66; physicist, Space Sci Lab, Gen Elec Co, Valley Forge, Pa, 66-69, sr syst engr & phenomenologist, 85-92; prin investr, Calspan Inc, 69-77, supvr, Physics Sect, 77-80, mgr, Advan Test Diag Br, Arnold Eng Develop Ctr, 81-85. *Concurrent Pos:* Adj fac mem math, Motlow Community Col, 76-80. *Mem:* Assoc fel Am Inst Aeronaut & Astronaut; Am Phys Soc. *Res:* Fundamental and applied research in fields of emissions, combustion, infrared physics, atmospheric physics, phenomenology of plumes, backgrounds and space electric propulsion. *Mailing Add:* PO Box 1394 Marlton NJ 08053

BREWER, MAX C(LIFTON), GEOLOGICAL ENGINEERING, GEOPHYSICS. *Current Pos:* CHIEF OPERS, NAT PETROL RESERVE IN ALASKA, 77- *Personal Data:* b Blackfalds, Alta, May 7, 24; US citizen; m 54; c 5. *Educ:* Wash Univ, BS, 50. *Hon Degrees:* DSc, Univ Alaska, 65. *Honors & Awards:* USN Distinguished Pub Serv Award, 62; Edward C Sweeney Medal, Explorer's Club, 70. *Prof Exp:* Geophysicist permafrost, US Geol Surv, 50-71, dir res, Naval Arctic Res Lab, 56-71; comnr, Alaska Dept Environ Conserv, 71-74; Arctic consult, 75-76. *Mem:* Fel Arctic Inst NAm; Soc Am Mil Engrs; Am Geophys Union; Brit Glaciol Soc. *Res:* Permafrost; ocean and fresh water ice and their effect on engineering structures through measurements of thermal gradients and physical properties. *Mailing Add:* 3819 Locarno Dr Anchorage AK 99508

BREWER, NATHAN RONALD, VETERINARY PHYSIOLOGY. *Current Pos:* RETIRED. *Personal Data:* b Albany, NY, June 28, 04; m 36, Jean Lees; c Mareen (Pasik), Sandra (Ginsberg) & Jacqui (Fechter). *Educ:* Mich State Univ, BS, 30, DVM, 37; Univ Chicago, PhD(physiol), 36. *Hon Degrees:* DSc, Chicago Col Osteop Med, 77. *Honors & Awards:* Charles River Award, Am Vet Med Asn, 92; Griffin Award, Asn Lab Animal Sci. *Prof Exp:* Vet practr, 37-45; assoc prof & dir, Univ Chicago, 45-69, dir animal quarters, 45-69, emer prof physiol, 69- *Concurrent Pos:* Consult, Chicago Med Sch, Chicago Col Osteop Med, Mercy Hosp & Ill Inst Technol, Chicago, 69-92; mem bd, Inst Lab Animal Resources, Nat Res Coun, 53-60; ed, Proc Asn Lab Animal Sci, 50-62, emer ed, Lab Animal Care, 63-92. *Mem:* Hon mem Am Soc Vet Cardiol; Nat Soc Med Res; Am Asn Lab Animal Sci (pres, 50-55); Am Physiol Soc; Am Vet Med Asn; Am Col Lab Animal Med (pres, 57-59); Wildlife Dis Asn; Am Soc Primatologists. *Res:* Laboratory animal medicine; comparative physiology. *Mailing Add:* 10800 Tara Rd Potomac MD 20854-1340

BREWER, PETER GEORGE, GEOCHEMISTRY OF THE GREENHOUSE GASES, CHEMISTRY OF SEA WATER. *Current Pos:* pres & chief exec officer, 91-96, SR SCIENTIST, MONTEREY BAY AQUARIUM RES INST, 96- *Personal Data:* b Ulverston, Eng, Dec 30, 40; nat US; m 96, Hilary Williams; c Jillian A, Alastair & Erica C. *Educ:* Liverpool Univ, BSc, 62, PhD(ocean sci), 67. *Prof Exp:* Asst scientist, Woods Hole Oceanog Inst, 67-71, assoc scientist, 71-78, sr scientist, 78-91. *Concurrent Pos:* Prog dir marine chem, NSF, 81-83; adj scientist, Woods Hole Oceanog Inst, 91-; pres, Ocean Sci Sect, Am Geophys Union, 94-96; prin investr, NSF, NASA, Off Naval Res, Dept Energy. *Mem:* Fel Am Geophys Union (pres, 94-96); fel AAAS. *Res:* Chemistry of sea water; evolution of greenhouse gas signatures in the present day ocean; ocean carbon cycle; gallium hydrates. *Mailing Add:* Monterey Bay Aquarium Res Inst PO Box 628 Moss Landing CA 95039. *Fax:* 408-775-1620; *E-Mail:* grpe@mbayi.org

BREWER, RICHARD (DEAN), ECOLOGY, ORNITHOLOGY. *Current Pos:* from instr to prof, 59-96, EMER PROF BIOL, WESTERN MICH UNIV, 96- *Personal Data:* b Murphysboro, Ill, June 17, 33; div, K T Takahashi; c Philip & Steven. *Educ:* Southern Ill Univ, BA, 55; Univ Ill, MS, 57, PhD(zool), 59. *Honors & Awards:* Edwards Prize, Wilson Ornith Soc. *Prof Exp:* Res asst zool, Univ Ill, 55-56. *Concurrent Pos:* Asst dir, C C Adams Ctr Ecol Studies, 60-63, dir, 63-68; ed, Jack-Pine Warbler, 76-79. *Mem:* Fel AAAS; Ecol Soc Am; Am Ornith Union; Wilson Ornith Soc; Am Inst Biol Sci. *Res:* Competition, speciation and habitat selection in birds; organization and evolution in plant, animal communities; forest succession; conservation of species, ecosystems and landscapes. *Mailing Add:* Dept Biol Western Mich Univ Kalamazoo MI 49001. *E-Mail:* richard.brewer@wmich.edu

BREWER, RICHARD GEORGE, QUANTUM OPTICS, LASER SPECTROSCOPY. *Current Pos:* res physicist, 63-73, IBM fel, Res Lab, 73-94, EMER FEL, IBM CORP, 94- *Personal Data:* b Los Angeles, Calif, Dec 8, 28; m 54; c 3. *Educ:* Calif Inst Technol, BS, 51; Univ Calif, Berkeley, PhD, 58. *Honors & Awards:* A A Michelson Gold Medal, Franklin Inst, 79. *Prof Exp:* Researcher, Aerojet-Gen Corp, 51-53; instr, Harvard Univ, 58-60; asst prof, Univ Calif, Los Angeles, 60-63. *Concurrent Pos:* Consult, Space Technol Labs, Inc, 62-63; vis prof physics, Mass Inst Technol, Cambridge, 68-69; mem, Comt Atomic & Molecular Physics, Nat Acad Sci-Nat Res Coun, 74-77; Japan Soc Prom Sci vis prof physics & appl physics, Univ Tokyo, 75; vis prof, Univ Calif Santa Cruz, 76; consult prof appl physics, Stanford Univ, 77-; adj prof, Nat Inst Optics, Florence, Italy, 77-; assoc ed, Optics Lett, 77-80; Nat Res Coun Rev Panal, Nat Bureau Stand, 81-84; mem rev comt, San Francisco Laser Ctr, NSF, 80-83; assoc ed, J Optical Soc Am, 80-83; mem, Comt Recommendations, US Army Basic Sci Res, 82-85; mem, Bd Physics & Astron, Nat Acad Sci-Nat Res Coun, 83-86. *Mem:* Nat Acad Sci; fel Am Phys Soc; fel Optical Soc Am. *Res:* Laser spectroscopy; atomic physics and quantum optics, including coherent optical transients, ion trapping and chaos. *Mailing Add:* 730 DeSoto Dr Palo Alto CA 94303

BREWER, ROBERT FRANKLIN, HORTICULTURE. *Current Pos:* RETIRED. *Personal Data:* b Woodbury, NJ, May 25, 27; m 47; c 2. *Educ:* Rutgers Univ, BSc, 50, PhD(hort), 53. *Prof Exp:* Soil chemist, Dept Soils & Plant Nutrit, Citrus Exp Sta, Univ Calif, Riverside, 53-70, horticulturist, Plant Sci Dept, 70-88. *Mem:* Am Soc Hort Sci; Int Soc Citriculture; Air Pollution Control Asn. *Res:* Inorganic plant nutrition; effects of fluorine and ozone on plant growth; cold tolerance; frost protection; environment modification. *Mailing Add:* 6879 S Reed Ave Reedley CA 93654

BREWER, ROBERT HYDE, ANIMAL ECOLOGY, INVERTEBRATE ZOOLOGY. *Current Pos:* from asst prof to assoc prof, 68-81, PROF BIOL, TRINITY COL, CONN, 82- *Personal Data:* b Richmond, Va, Dec 24, 31; m 60; c 1. *Educ:* Hanover Col, AB, 55; Univ Chicago, PhD(zool), 63. *Prof Exp:* Asst prof biol, Ill Col, 63-65; res fel & lectr entom, Waite Agr Res Inst, Univ Adelaide, 65-68. *Mem:* Fel AAAS; Ecol Soc Am; Am Soc Zool; Am Inst Biol Sci; Sigma Xi; Am Soc Naturalists. *Res:* Physiological and population ecology of aquatic invertebrates. *Mailing Add:* Dept Biol Trinity Col Hartford CT 06106

BREWER, ROBERT NELSON, POULTRY PATHOLOGY. *Current Pos:* asst prof poultry parasitol & path, 68-74, ASSOC PROF & DEPT HEAD POULTRY SCI, AUBURN UNIV, 74- *Personal Data:* b Philcampbell, Ala, Feb 24, 34; m 53; c 1. *Educ:* Auburn Univ, BS, 55, MS, 60; Univ Ga, PhD(poultry sci), 68. *Prof Exp:* Asst co agr agent, Exten Serv, Auburn Univ, 55-58; poultry specialist, Pillsbury Co, 60-65. *Mem:* Poultry Sci Asn; Am Inst Biol Sci. *Res:* Poultry disease research, including immunity studies on roundworms, coccidiosis and epidemiological and etiological studies on Marek's disease; environment-disease interrelationships. *Mailing Add:* Dept Poultry Sci Auburn Univ 236 Animal Sci Bldg Rm 236 Auburn AL 36849

BREWER, STEPHEN WILEY, JR, ANALYTICAL CHEMISTRY. *Current Pos:* Asst prof, 69-73, assoc prof, 73-79, PROF CHEM, EASTERN MICH UNIV, 79- *Personal Data:* b Spartanburg, SC, Jan 18, 41; m 82, Ruby L Meis. *Educ:* Univ Fla, BSCh, 62; Univ Wis-Madison, PhD(anal chem), 69. *Concurrent Pos:* Vis scholar, Univ Mich. *Mem:* Soc Appl Spectros; Spectros Soc Can; Sigma Xi; Am Chem Soc. *Res:* Emission spectroscopy; electron probe microanalysis; high-speed gas chromatography. *Mailing Add:* Dept Chem Eastern Mich Univ Ypsilanti MI 48197

BREWER, WILLIAM AUGUSTUS, REMOTE SENSING, HYDROGEOLOGY OF ARID SITES. *Current Pos:* CONSULT NUCLEAR WASTE MGT, 79- *Personal Data:* b Oakland, Calif, May 27, 30. *Educ:* Univ Calif, Berkeley, BA, 54, MA, 55, PhD(eng), 65. *Prof Exp:* Sr geologist, Anaconda Co, 55-60; assoc eng, Univ Calif, Berkeley, 60-63; chief engr, Cent Intel Agency, 63-68 & Fed Systs Div, Int Bus Mach, 69-70; consult overseas mining, 70-73; exec dir, Off Gov, Wash, 73-75; prof environ eng, Univ Wash, 75-79. *Concurrent Pos:* Consult, numerous US & foreign govt agencies, 73-; sr hydrogeologist, State Wash, 83-89. *Res:* Geotechnical analysis of nuclear-toxic waste disposal sites; regional-national energy policy; environmental legislation; mapping; geophysics. *Mailing Add:* 5131 Fir Tree Rd SE Olympia WA 98501

BREWINGTON, PERCY, JR, CIVIL ENGINEERING. *Current Pos:* asst mgr construct eng, AEC/ERDA, 73-76, DEPT MGR, OAK RIDGE OPERS OFF, DEPT ENERGY, 76- *Personal Data:* b Benton, Pa, Jan 31, 30; m 51; c 3. *Educ:* Drexel Univ, BS, 54. *Prof Exp:* Staff engr, Mobile Dist Off, US Army CEngr, 58-66, asst chief spec projs br, 66-67, chief proj mgt br, Huntsville Div, 67-73, chief eng div, 73. *Mem:* Am Soc Civil Engrs; Nat Soc Prof Engrs; Res Officers Asn. *Mailing Add:* 1074 W Outer Dr Oak Ridge TN 37830

BREWSTER, JAMES HENRY, ORGANIC CHEMISTRY, STEREO CHEMISTRY. *Current Pos:* from instr to assoc prof, 49-60, PROF CHEM, PURDUE UNIV, 60- *Personal Data:* b Ft Collins, Colo, Aug 21, 22; m 54, Christine B; c Christine C, Mary E & Barbara A. *Educ:* Cornell Univ, BA, 42; Univ Ill, PhD(chem), 48. *Prof Exp:* Chemist, Atlantic Refining Co, 42-43; asst, Univ Ill, 46-47; Fels Fund fel, Univ Chicago, 48-49. *Mem:* Fel AAAS; Am Chem Soc; Royal Chem Soc; Am Asn Univ Professors; Sigma Xi. *Res:* Stereo chemistry of displacement reactions and reductions; synthesis and optical activity of highly symmetrical compounds; stereochemical notation. *Mailing Add:* 344 Hollywood Dr West Lafayette IN 47906-2146

BREWSTER, MARCUS QUINN, HEAT TRANSFER, COMBUSTION. *Current Pos:* asst prof, 86-88, ASSOC PROF MECH ENG, UNIV ILL, URBANA, 88- *Personal Data:* b Salt Lake City, Utah, Aug 20, 55; m 79; c 3. *Educ:* Univ Utah, BS, 78, ME, 79; Univ Calif, Berkeley, PhD(mech eng), 81. *Prof Exp:* Assoc mech eng, Kyoto Univ, 81-82; asst prof, Univ Utah, 82-86. *Concurrent Pos:* Presidential young investr award, NSF, 84; young investr award, Off Naval Res, 88. *Mem:* Am Soc Mech Eng; Am Inst Aeronaut & Astronaut. *Res:* Radiative heat transfer; solid propellant combustion; laser material processing; author of one book. *Mailing Add:* Dept Mech & Industrial Eng Univ Ill-Urbana 1206 W Green St Urbana IL 61801-2906

BREWSTER, MARJORIE ANN, CLINICAL BIOCHEMISTRY, ENVIRONMENTAL EXPOSURE. *Current Pos:* CONSULT, BIOTECH SERV, 96- *Personal Data:* b Conway, Ark, Mar 7, 40. *Educ:* Univ Ark, Little Rock, BS, 64, MS, 66, PhD(biochem), 71; Am Bd Clin Chem, dipl, 74. *Prof Exp:* Clin biochemist, Clin Lab, Univ Ark, 66-67 & 71-77, asst prof path, Med Ctr, 69-79, asst prof biochem, 73-79; dir chem, Lab Ark Children's Hosp, 76-87, dir, Metal Lab, 76-96, prof pediat & path, 88-96. *Concurrent Pos:* Past pres, Nat Registry Clin Chemists, mem, govt adv comn hazardous waste; mem, Chem Safety Div, Am Chem Soc; dir, Ark Reproductive Health Monitoring Syst, 82-96. *Mem:* Am Asn Clin Chemists; Nat Acad Clin Biochemists (pres, 81-82); Asn Clin Sci; Am Chem Soc; Soc Toxicol. *Res:* Birth defects; environmental, genetic, and nutritional impacts upon health; reproductive monitoring; human exposure detection. *Mailing Add:* Biotech Serv 3200 W Commerical Dr North Little Rock AR 72116

BREY, R(OBERT) N(EWTON), CHEMICAL & NUCLEAR ENGINEERING. *Current Pos:* PROJ MGR, UNITED ENGRS & CONSTRUCTORS INC, 71- *Personal Data:* b Philadelphia, Pa, Feb 2, 20; m 48; c 3. *Educ:* Univ Pa, BS, 43; Pa State Univ, cert, 43. *Prof Exp:* Head, Nuclear Syst Group, Leeds & Northrup Co, 46-60; mgr opers admin, Ballistic Missile Early Warning Syst Proj, Radio Corp Am, 60-63; spec appln adv space proj dept, Gen Elec Co, 63-69, mgr proj eng, Power Syst Oper Prog & Syst Anal, Info Syst Group, 69-71. *Mem:* Am Nuclear Soc; Am Inst Chem Engrs; Instrument Soc Am; Franklin Inst. *Res:* Design engineering and construction of nuclear and fossil fueled central station electric generating plants for utilities. *Mailing Add:* 107 W Moreland Ave Philadelphia PA 19118

BREY, WALLACE SIEGFRIED, JR, PHYSICAL CHEMISTRY, MAGNETIC RESONANCE. *Current Pos:* from asst prof to assoc prof, 52-64, PROF CHEM, UNIV FLA, 64- *Personal Data:* b Schwenksville, Pa, June 6, 22; m 55; c William W & Paul O. *Educ:* Ursinus Col, BS, 42; Univ Pa, MS, 46, PhD(chem), 48. *Honors & Awards:* Fla Award, Am Chem Soc. *Prof Exp:* Asst chemist, Warner Co, 42-44; res chemist, Publicker Indust, 44; asst prof chem, De Pauw Univ, 48-49; from asst prof to assoc prof, St Joseph's Col, Pa, 49-52. *Concurrent Pos:* Ed, J Magnetic Resonance, 69-; prog dir, NSF, 76-77. *Mem:* AAAS; Am Chem Soc; Am Phys Soc; Royal Soc Chem; Soc Magnetic Resonance; Int Soc Magnetic Resonance. *Res:* Magnetic resonance; heterogeneous catalysis and adsorption; molecular interactions in liquids; spectroscopy of biological molecules. *Mailing Add:* PO Box 117200 Gainesville FL 32611-7200

BREYER, ARTHUR CHARLES, PHYSICAL CHEMISTRY, INORGANIC CHEMISTRY. *Current Pos:* chmn, Dept Chem & Physics, 64-85, dir, Coop Educ Prog, 77-78, PROF CHEM, BEAVER COL, 64- *Personal Data:* b Brooklyn, NY, June 13, 25; m 48, Louise M Timmerman; c Richard, Carol L (Reill) & Adrienne L (Mallett). *Educ:* NY Univ, BA, 48; Columbia Univ, MA, 50; Rutgers Univ, PhD(chem), 58. *Honors & Awards:* Honor Scroll Award, Am Inst Chemists, 73; E Emmett Reid Award, Am Chem Soc, 74, Jack Flack Norris Award, 93; Nat Catalyst Award, Chem Mfg Asn, 77. *Prof Exp:* Instr chem, Columbia Univ, 48-49; from instr to asst prof, Upsala Col, 49-58; assoc prof, Ohio Wesleyan Univ, 59-63; prof, Harvey Mudd Col, 63-64. *Concurrent Pos:* Chem study proj lectr, Gatlinburg Ion-Exchange Res Conf, 62-75; dir, NSF Undergrad Res Partic Prog, 60-64, & Inst High Sch Chem Teachers, 62-75; consult, NSF, 62-85, McGraw-Hill Book Co, Inc, Charles E Merrill Books Inc & Wadsworth Publ Co; dir, Title II Eisenhower Chem Retraining Prog, 86-89. *Mem:* AAAS; Am Chem Soc; Am Sci Affil; Franklin Inst. *Res:* Chromatography and electrophoresis of plant pigments, dyes and surfactants; ion exchange catalysis; salting-out chromatography of organic compounds; high performance liquid chromatography of proteins. *Mailing Add:* Beaver Col 450 S Easton Rd Glenside PA 19038-3295

BREYER, NORMAN NATHAN, METALLURGICAL ENGINEERING. *Current Pos:* assoc prof metall, Ill Inst Technol, 64-69, prof & chmn dept, 69-84, prof metall & mat eng, 84-91, EMER PROF METALL & MAT ENGR, ILL INST TECHNOL, 91- *Personal Data:* b Detroit, Mich, June 21, 21; m 52, 89, Claire L Shore; c Matthew D, Richard M & Marjorie A. *Educ:* Mich Tech, BS, 43; Univ Mich, MS, 48; Ill Inst Technol, PhD(metall), 63. *Prof Exp:* Aeronaut res scientist, Nat Adv Comt Aeronaut, 48; chief armor sect, Detroit Tank Arsenal, 48-52; dir res cast steels & irons, Nat Roll & Foundry, 52-54; metallurgist-in-charge armor, Continental Foundry & Mach Div, Blaw-Knox Co, 55-57; mgr tech projs, La Salle Steel Co, 57-64. *Mem:* Am Soc Metals; Am Inst Mining, Metall & Petrol Engrs; Am Soc Testing & Mat. *Res:* High strength, strain aging and cold and warm deformation of steels; leaded steels; failure analysis. *Mailing Add:* Dept Metall Ill Inst Technol 3300 S Federal St Chicago IL 60616-3732

BREYERE, EDWARD JOSEPH, IMMUNOGENETICS. *Current Pos:* RETIRED. *Personal Data:* b Washington, DC, Apr 25, 27; c 1. *Educ:* Univ Md, BS, 51, MS, 54, PhD(zool), 57. *Prof Exp:* Asst, Univ Md, 54-55; from assoc prof to prof biol, Am Univ, 61-89. *Concurrent Pos:* Res fel, Nat Cancer Inst, 57-61; dir, Immunogenetics Lab, Sibley Mem Hosp, 61-79. *Mem:* AAAS; Am Asn Cancer Res; Transplantation Soc. *Res:* Transplantation immunity; maternal-fetal relationships; immunology of oncogenic viruses. *Mailing Add:* 15115 Interlachen Dr Silver Spring MD 20906

BREZENOFF, HENRY EVANS, NEUROPHARMACOLOGY. *Current Pos:* From instr to assoc prof, 69-80, asst dean, 78-80, PROF PHARMACOL, COL MED & DENT NJ, 80-, ASSOC DEAN, GRAD SCH BIOMED SCI, 81- *Personal Data:* b New York, NY, July 9, 40; m 64; c 2. *Educ:* Columbia Univ, BS, 62; NJ Col Med & Dent, PhD(pharmacol), 68. *Concurrent Pos:* Fel pharmacol, Sch Med, Univ Calif, Los Angeles, 68-69. *Mem:* Am Soc Pharmacol & Exp Therapeut; Int Soc Hypertension; AAAS. *Res:* Central control of blood pressure; hypertension; brain acetylcholine. *Mailing Add:* Dept Pharmacol Univ Med & Dent NJ Med Sch 185 S Orange Ave Newark NJ 07103-2714. *Fax:* 973-456-7148

BREZINSKI, DARLENE RITA, PAINT & COATINGS, LEAD POISONING. *Current Pos:* SR CONSULT CHEM COATINGS, CONSOL RES INC, 90- *Personal Data:* b Chicago, Ill, Oct 9, 41. *Educ:* Mundelein Col, BS, 64; Iowa State Univ, MS, 67, PhD(chem), 69; Univ Chicago, cert advan mgt, 76. *Honors & Awards:* George Baugh Heckel Award, Fed Socs Coatings Technol, 83. *Prof Exp:* Chmn & asst prof, Chem Dept, Mundelein Col, 69-73; res chem anal serv, De Soto Inc, 73-75, tech mgr, 75-80, dir anal serv, 80-90. *Concurrent Pos:* Ed, J Coatings Technol, 75- & Fed Ser Coatings Technol, 83-; consult lead poisoning, 75- *Mem:* Am Soc Testing & Mat; Fed Socs Coatings Technol; Nat Paint & Coatings Asn; Inst Elec & Electronics Engrs. *Res:* Analytical laboratory efficiency and technical management. *Mailing Add:* 1834 Moroni Dr Kingsford MI 49802

BREZNAK, JOHN ALLEN, MICROBIAL SYMBIOSES, MICROBIAL ECOLOGY. *Current Pos:* from asst prof to assoc prof, 73-84, PROF MICROBIOL, MICH STATE UNIV, 84- *Personal Data:* b Passaic, NJ, Aug 28, 44; m 68; c 2. *Educ:* Rutgers Univ, BS, 66; Univ Mass, PhD(microbiol), 71. *Honors & Awards:* Sr US Scientist Award, Alexander von Humboldt Found, 85. *Prof Exp:* NIH fel microbiol, Dept Bacteriol, Univ Wis-Madison, 71-73. *Concurrent Pos:* Prin investr, NSF Funded Res Proj, 75-; co-dir microbiol course, Marine Biol Lab, Woods Hole, Mass, 90-94; co-investr, Ctr Microbial Ecol, Mich State Univ. *Mem:* Am Soc Microbiol; Soc Gen Microbiol; Entom Soc Am; AAAS; Soc Exp Biol; Sigma Xi. *Res:* Biochemical bases for symbiosis between termites and their intestinal microbiota; anaerobic degradation of plant polysaccharides by microorganisms. *Mailing Add:* Dept Microbiol Mich State Univ East Lansing MI 48824-1101. *Fax:* 517-353-8957; *E-Mail:* 22807jab@msu.edu

BREZNER, JEROME, ENTOMOLOGY, BIOCHEMISTRY. *Current Pos:* res assoc, 61-62, from asst prof to assoc prof, 62-68, PROF ENTOM, STATE UNIV NY COL ENVIRON SCI & FORESTRY, 68- *Personal Data:* b New York, NY, July 18, 31; m 54; c 2. *Educ:* Univ Rochester, AB, 52; Univ Mo, AM, 56, PhD(entom), 59. *Prof Exp:* Asst prof biol, Elmira Col, 59-61. *Concurrent Pos:* Am Physiol Soc fel biol, Dartmouth Med Sch, 60; NIH res grant, 62-65; US Forest Serv grant, 66-69. *Mem:* AAAS; NY Acad Sci; Entom Soc Am; Soc Environ Toxicol & Chem. *Res:* Insect enzyme proteins, the species specific nature of these molecules; insect toxicology. *Mailing Add:* Dept Biol State Univ NY Col Environ Sci Syracuse NY 13210

BREZONIK, PATRICK LEE, WATER CHEMISTRY, LIMNOLOGY. *Current Pos:* PROF ENVIRON ENG, UNIV MINN, 81-, DIR WATER RESOURCES RES CTR, 85- *Personal Data:* b Sheboygan, Wis, July 17, 41; m 65; c 2. *Educ:* Marquette Univ, BS, 63; Univ Wis, MS, 65, PhD(water chem), 68. *Prof Exp:* Asst prof water chem & environ eng, Univ Fla, 66-70, assoc prof water chem, 70-76, prof environ sci, 76-81. *Concurrent Pos:* Res grants, Fed Water Pollution Control Admin, 68-71, Off Water Resources Res, 69-71, 73-75 & 78-80, Environ Protection Agency, 74-75 & 77- & NSF, 79-81; NSF sci fac fel, Swiss Fed Inst Technol, Zurich, 71-72; chmn, Panel on Nitrates in the Environ, Nat Res Coun, 75-78; vis prof, Fed Inst for Water Treatment, Zurich, 80. *Mem:* AAAS; Am Chem Soc; Am Soc Limnol & Oceanog; Asn Environ Eng Prof. *Res:* Eutrophication of lakes; nitrogen dynamics in natural waters; nutrient chemistry; acid rain; trace metals in natural waters; organic matter in water. *Mailing Add:* Univ Minn Civil Dept 500 Pillsbury Dr SE Minneapolis MN 55455-0198

BRIAN, P(IERRE) L(EONCE) THIBAUT, CHEMICAL ENGINEERING. *Current Pos:* RETIRED. *Personal Data:* b New Orleans, La, July 8, 30; m 52, Geraldine L Earl; c Evelyn A, Richard E & James E. *Educ:* La State Univ, BS, 51; Mass Inst Technol, ScD, 56. *Honors & Awards:* Prof Progress Award, Am Inst Chem Engrs, 73, Robert L Jacks Mem Award, 89. *Prof Exp:* From asst prof to prof chem eng, Mass Inst Technol, 55-72; vpres eng, Air Prod & Chem, Inc, 72-94, mem bd dirs, 73-94. *Concurrent Pos:* Overseas fel, Churchill Col, Cambridge Univ, 69-70. *Mem:* Nat Acad Eng; Am Chem Soc; Am Inst Chem Engrs; Royal Acad Eng UK. *Res:* Interphase mass transfer; chemical kinetics; heat transfer; numerical mathematics. *Mailing Add:* 3981 Lilac Rd Allentown PA 18103

BRIANT, CLYDE LEONARD, MATERIALS SCIENCE. *Current Pos:* STAFF METALLURGIST, GEN ELEC CORP, 76- *Personal Data:* b Texarkana, Ark, May 31, 48; m 77, Jacqueline Duffy; c Paul, Judith & Bonnie. *Educ:* Hendrix Col, BA, 71; Columbia Univ, BS, 71, DEngSc, 74. *Honors & Awards:* Alfred Noble Prize, Five Eng Soc, 81; Robert Lansing Hardy Gold Medal, Am Inst Mining Metall & Petrol Engrs, 78; R W Raymond Award, Am Inst Mining Metall & Petrol Engrs, 80. *Prof Exp:* Fel metall, Univ Pa, 74-76. *Concurrent Pos:* Overseas fel, Churchill Col, Cambridge, Eng, 87-88. *Mem:* Am Inst Mining Metall & Petrol Engrs; Am Soc Metals; Mat Res Soc. *Res:* Grain boundary chemistry; hydrogen embrittlement of metals; nucleation theory; chemical boarding in alloys; corrosion and stress corrosion checking; thermomechanical processing of metals; refractory metals. *Mailing Add:* 9 Wedgewood Lane Barrington RI 02806

BRICE, BARBARA GOHANNA, HYPERTENSION RESEARCH, LEAD-BASED PAINT HAZARDS. *Current Pos:* instr med rec, 77-80, asst prof, 82-88, DIR, HEALTH INFO MGT PROG, CLARK ATLANTA UNIV, 88-, ASSOC PROF ALLIED HEALTH, 93- *Personal Data:* b Newark, NJ, Feb 28, 27; div; c Carla (Ross), Rutherford II, Richard Z & Renee (Glover). *Educ:* Clark Col, BS, 70; Cent Mich Univ, MA, 75; Ga State Univ, PhD(educ admin & supv), 92. *Prof Exp:* Staff nurse, St Joseph Hosp, Atlanta, 68-71, Atlanta Regional/Resident & Man Power Ctr, 72-75; dir med rec & admis, Univ Ctr Community Health Plan, 75-77; dir med rec, WEnd Med Ctr, Atlanta, 78-80; assoc prof med rec dir, Kean Col, NJ, 80-82. *Concurrent Pos:* Consult health info mgt, SW Hosp & Med Ctr, 91; consult & mem, Site Team for Accreditation Health Educ Progs, State of Ga, 94; prin investr, Health Tech Optimum, Health 1st Found, 95- *Mem:* Nat Soc Allied Health Prof; Am Soc Allied Health Profession; Am Health Info Mgt Asn. *Res:* Environmental justice; lead-based paint hazards; to develop a report which indicates the prevalence of lead-based paint hazards within the Vine City Community, Atlanta, Georgia. *Mailing Add:* 1853 Beecher Rd SW Atlanta GA 30310. *Fax:* 404-880-6165; *E-Mail:* bbrice@cau.edu

BRICE, DAVID KENNETH, PARTICLE-SOLID INTERACTIONS. *Current Pos:* CONSULT, CONDENSED MATTER PHYSICS, 91- *Personal Data:* b Sulphur Springs, Tex, Apr 15, 33; div. *Educ:* ETex State Col, BS, 54; Univ Kans, MS, 56, PhD(physics), 63. *Prof Exp:* Distinguished mem tech staff physics, Sandia Nat Lab, 63-91. *Concurrent Pos:* Assoc prof physics, NMex Inst Mining & Technol, 67-73. *Mem:* Am Phys Soc; AAAS. *Res:* Ion implantation; radiation damage; particle-solid interactions and atomic transport in solids. *Mailing Add:* 6821 Guadalupe Trail NW Albuquerque NM 87107-6205

BRICE, DONAT B(ENNES), CHEMICAL ENGINEERING. *Current Pos:* STAFF CHEM ENGR, CALIF DEPT WATER RESOURCES, 60- *Personal Data:* b Alton, Ill, Nov 22, 20; m 48; c 2. *Educ:* Univ Ark, BS, 42; Univ Mo, MS, 47; Ohio State Univ, PhD(chem eng), 50. *Prof Exp:* Instr chem, Mo Sch Mines, 46-47; instr chem eng, Kans State Col, 47-48 & Ohio State Univ, 48-49; chem engr internal ballistics, Naval Ord Test Sta, 50-52; proj leader chem process develop, Food Mach & Chem Corp, 52-56; sr chem engr, Flour Corp, Calif, 56-60. *Concurrent Pos:* Sr officer, Int Atomic Energy Agency, Vienna, 66-67. *Mem:* Am Inst Chem Engrs; Am Chem Soc. *Res:* Saline water purification; heat transfer; thermodynamics; metallurgy; waste water reclamation and reuse. *Mailing Add:* 3831 Garden Hwy Sacramento CA 95834-9604

BRICE, JAMES COBLE, GEOMORPHOLOGY. *Current Pos:* RETIRED. *Personal Data:* b Union City, Tenn, Dec 21, 20. *Educ:* Univ Ala, BS, 42; Univ Calif, PhD(geol), 50. *Prof Exp:* From asst prof to prof geol, Wash Univ, 50-76; hydrologist, US Geol Surv, 76-84. *Mem:* Geol Soc Am; Am Soc Civil Engrs. *Res:* Fluvial geomorphology *Mailing Add:* 1277 Woodland Ave Menlo Park CA 94025

BRICE, LUTHER KENNEDY, PHYSICAL CHEMISTRY. *Current Pos:* RETIRED. *Personal Data:* b Spartanburg, SC, Jan 29, 28. *Educ:* Harvard Univ, BA, 49; Dartmouth Col, MA, 51; Duke Univ, PhD(chem), 55. *Prof Exp:* From asst prof to prof chem, Va Polytech Inst & State Univ, 54-86; adj prof, Am Univ, 86-92. *Mem:* Am Chem Soc. *Res:* Chemical education. *Mailing Add:* 1401 17th St NW No 606 Washington DC 20036

BRICE, WILLIAM RILEY, HISTORY OF GEOLOGY, PHILOSOPHY OF SCIENCE. *Current Pos:* From asst prof to assoc prof, 71-88, PROF GEOL & PLANETARY SCI, UNIV PITTSBURGH, JOHNSTOWN, 88- *Educ:* Univ Fla, BS, 58; Cornell Univ, MS, 68, PhD(geochem), 71. *Concurrent Pos:* Vis assoc prof, Cornell Univ, 76-87, vis prof geol, 88-; William Matthew fel, NB Mus, Can, 92. *Mem:* Fel Geol Soc Am; Am Inst Prof Geologists. *Res:* History of geology, especially biographical works on academic geologists. *Mailing Add:* Geol & Planetary Sci Dept Univ Pittsburgh 450 Schoolhouse Rd Johnstown PA 15904

BRICKBAUER, ELWOOD ARTHUR, SEED CERTIFICATION. *Current Pos:* RETIRED. *Personal Data:* b Elkhart Lake, Wis; m 43, Lydia E Albertin; c 3. *Educ:* Univ Wis, BS, 43, MS, 61. *Prof Exp:* Teacher, Pub Schs, 43-44; mgr, Peck Seed Farms, 44-46; co agent, Univ Wis-Madison, 46-56, exten agronomist, 57-78, from asst prof to prof agron, 57-80. *Concurrent Pos:* Secy & treas, Wis Crop Improv Asn, 62-92; hon men, Asn Seed Cert Agencies. *Mem:* Am Soc Agron. *Res:* Corn, soybeans, small grains and seed certification. *Mailing Add:* 6708 Hubbard Ave Middleton WI 53562

BRICKENKAMP, CARROLL, PHYSICS. *Current Pos:* Chief, Off Weights & Measures, 93-96, SCI ASST TO DIR, OFF MEASUREMENT SERV, NAT INST STAND & TECHNOL, 96- *Personal Data:* b Berkeley, Calif, May 10, 45. *Educ:* Univ Pittsburg, PhD(crystallog), 70. *Mailing Add:* Nat Inst Stand & Technol Rte 270 Bldg 820 Gaithersburg MD 20899. *E-Mail:* carroll.brickenkamp@nist.gov

BRICKER, CLARK EUGENE, CHEMISTRY. *Current Pos:* PROF CHEM, UNIV KANS, 63- *Personal Data:* b Shrewsbury, Pa, June 17, 18; m 42; c 3. *Educ:* Gettysburg Col, BA, 39; Haverford Col, MS, 40; Princeton Univ, PhD(anal chem), 44. *Hon Degrees:* DSc, Pikeville Col, 70. *Prof Exp:* Res chemist, Heyden Chem Corp, NJ, 43-46; asst prof chem, Johns Hopkins Univ, 46-48; from asst prof to prof, Princeton Univ, 48-61; dean, Col Wooster, 61-63. *Mem:* AAAS; Am Chem Soc. *Res:* Physicochemistry methods of analysis; electrochemistry; spectrophotometry; photochemistry. *Mailing Add:* 1329 Kasold Dr J-1 Lawrence KS 60049-3426

BRICKER, JEROME GOUGH, MEDICAL PHYSIOLOGY, FEDERAL HEALTH CARE MANAGEMENT. *Current Pos:* RETIRED. *Personal Data:* b Buffalo, NY, Jan 20, 28; m 49, Dorothy M Ballinger; c Jay G & Scott A. *Educ:* Univ Akron, BSc, 49; Ohio State Univ, MSc, 53, PhD(physiol), 63. *Prof Exp:* Res & develop adminr air force weapons, Air Res & Develop Command, USAF, 54-60, staff scientist, Air Force Systs Command, 63-66, chief, Life Sci Div, Off Aerospace Res, 66-69; sr res scientist, Geomet, Inc, Rockville, 69-72; spec asst for Legis, Off Asst Secy Defense, Health Affairs, Washington, DC, 75-80, dir spec projs, 81-83, sr policy specialist, 84-85; consult health care mgt & environ hazards, Dept Defense, 85-91. *Concurrent Pos:* Health care consult, 73-74 & 92-97; mem, Sci Panel, Agent Orange Working Group, 81-89. *Mem:* Sigma Xi. *Res:* Endocrinology, especially intermediate metabolism; respiratory and bacterial physiology; toxic effects of herbicides. *Mailing Add:* 6000 Cable Ave Suitland MD 20746-3824

BRICKER, NEAL S, INTERNAL MEDICINE. *Current Pos:* EMER PROF, DEPT INTERNAL MED, UNIV CALIF, LOS ANGELES, 86-; SR VPRES RES, NATURON, 95- *Personal Data:* b Denver, Colo, Apr 18, 27; m 51; c 3. *Educ:* Univ Colo, BA, 46, MD, 49; Am Bd Internal Med, dipl, 56. *Hon Degrees:* Dr, Univ Port. *Honors & Awards:* Gold-Headed Cane Award, Univ Colo, 49, George Norlin Silver Award, 82; Medal, Am Soc Nephrology, 83 & Am Soc Clin Invest, 84; John P Peters Award, Am Soc Nephrol, 91. *Prof Exp:* Intern & resident, Post-Grad Med Sch, NY Univ-Bellevue Med Ctr, 49-52; clin asst, Sch Med, Univ Colo, 52-54; sr resident, Peter Bent Brigham Hosp, 54-55; instr, Harvard Med Sch, 55-56; from asst prof to prof med, Sch Med, Wash Univ, 56-72, dir, Renal Div, 56-72; prof & chmn dept, Albert Einstein Col Med, 72-76; prof & vchmn dept, Univ Miami Sch Med, 76-78; prof & dir prog kidney dis, Univ Calif, Los Angeles, 78-86; distinguished prof, Loma Linda Univ, 86-91. *Concurrent Pos:* Fel, Howard Hughes Med Inst, 55-56; jr assoc & assoc dir, Cardiorenal Lab, Peter Bent Brigham Hosp, 55-56; estab investr, Am Heart Asn, 59-64; assoc ed, J Lab & Clin Med, 61-67; investr, Mt Desert Island Biol Labs, 62-66; mem sci adv bd, Nat Kidney Dis Found, 62-69, chmn res & fel grants comt, 64-65, mem exec comt, 68-71; USPHS career res award, 64-72; mem, Gen Med Study Sect, NIH, 64-68, chmn, 66-68, chmn, Renal Dis & Urol Teaching Grants Comt, 69-71; mem, Drug Efficacy Comt, Nat Acad Sci, 66-68, Comt Space Biol & Med, 71-82, Ad Hoc Panel Renal & Metab Effects Space Flight, 72-74, chmn, 72-74, mem, Space Sci Bd, 77-81; mem, Nephrol Test Comt, Am Bd Internal Med, 71-76, chmn, 73-74, bd gov, 70-78; Gulben prof sci & technol, Gulbekan Found, 94; univ prof, Univ Port. *Mem:* Inst Med-Nat Acad Sci; Am Soc Clin Invest (pres, 72-73); fel Am Col Physicians; Asn Am Physicians; Int Soc Nephrol (vpres, 66-69, treas, 69-81); Am Soc Nephrology (pres, 66-67). *Res:* Nephrology and transport across isolated membranes. *Mailing Add:* 2313 N Second Ave Upland CA 91784. *Fax:* 909-931-0490; *E-Mail:* rbricker.com@worldnet.att.net

BRICKER, OWEN P, III, GEOCHEMISTRY, HYDROLOGY & WATER RESOURCES. *Current Pos:* GEOLOGIST, US GEOL SURV, 81- *Personal Data:* b Lancaster, Pa, Mar 5, 36; m 58; c 4. *Educ:* Franklin & Marshall Col, BS, 58; Lehigh Univ, MS, 60; Harvard Univ, PhD(geol), 64. *Prof Exp:* Fel environ sci & eng, Harvard Univ, 64-65; from asst prof to assoc prof geol, Johns Hopkins Univ, 65-75; geologist, Md Geol Surv, 75-79 & Chesapeake Bay Prog, Environ Protection Agency, 79-81. *Mem:* Geochem Soc; Am Chem Soc; Mineral Soc Am; Soc Econ Geol; Geol Soc Am. *Res:* Mineral equilibria in the earth-surface environment; chemistry of weathering and supergene processes; chemistry of natural waters. *Mailing Add:* 2632 White Hall Rd White Hall MD 21161-9724

BRICKEY, PARIS MANAFORD, ENTOMOLOGY, BIOLOGY. *Current Pos:* Analyst biol, US Food & Drug Admin, 60-63, res entomologist, 63-77, chief microanalysis br, 77-92, DIR, DIV MICROANAL EVAL, US FOOD & DRUG ADMIN, 92- *Personal Data:* b Denton, Tex, Dec 13, 31; m 59. *Educ:* Univ Md, 59, MS, 60. *Honors & Awards:* Contrib Award, US Food & Drug Admin, 64. *Mem:* Fel Asn Off Analytical Chemists; Entom Soc Am; Inst Food Technologists; Am Asn Cereal Chemists; Asn Food & Drug Off. *Res:* Detection and identification of insect, rodent, other animal filth, foreign material and mold in foods and food ingredients; determine regulatory significance of filth in foods; testify as expert witness in filth in foods. *Mailing Add:* 5705 Captain Jones C Fairfax VA 22039

BRICKS, BERNARD GERARD, LASERS. *Current Pos:* PROG MGR & SR SCIENTIST, W J SCHAFER ASSOCS, 86- *Personal Data:* b Pittsburgh, Pa, Nov 28, 41; m 63, Barbara Blackwood; c Bernard G & Joshua F. *Educ:* Memphis State Univ, BS, 63; Johns Hopkins Univ, MS, 69, PhD(physics), 71. *Prof Exp:* Fel, New Eng Inst, 71-72; laser physicist, Space Sci Lab, Gen Elec

Co, 72-82, dep prog mgr systs eng, 82-86. *Mem:* Am Phys Soc; Sigma Xi. *Res:* Research and development of engineering design, farication and delivery of low to medium power, visible and near visible laser systems; requirements definition, utility analysis and assessment of laser systems for tactical and strategic platforms. *Mailing Add:* 32 Elmwood Dr Kennett Square PA 19348-2309. *Fax:* 703-812-8049

BRIDENBAUGH, PETER R, METALLURGY, MECHANICAL ENGINEERING. *Current Pos:* Group Leader Eng Dept, Aluminum Co Am, Alcoa Ctr, Pa & Evansville, IND, 68-75, mgr, 75-78, opers dir, 78-80,dir, Res & Develop, 83-84, VPRES, ALCOA LABS, ALCOA CENTER, PA, 84- *Personal Data:* b Franklin, Pa, July 28, 40; m 65; c 2. *Educ:* Lehigh Univ, BS, 62, MS, 66; Mass Inst Technol, PhD(metall & mat sci), 68. *Concurrent Pos:* Qual Assurance Mgr, Alcoa, Alcoa, Tenn, 78-80; fel Am Soc Metals Int, 87. *Mem:* Am Soc Metals; Am Inst Mining, Metall Engrs; Am Soc Eng Educ; Indust Res Inst; Sigma Xi. *Res:* Productivity of basic deformation processing; manufacturing processes; lubricants for manufacturing processes. *Mailing Add:* 55 Quail Hill Rd Pittsburgh PA 15283-1833

BRIDGE, ALAN G, CHEMICAL ENGINEERING. *Current Pos:* res engr, 69-81, SR ENG ASSOC, CHEVRON RES CO, CALIF, 81- *Personal Data:* b Eng, Jan 15, 36; m 58; c 4. *Educ:* Univ Birmingham, BSc, 56; Univ Toronto, MASc, 58; Princeton Univ, MA, 61, PhD(chem eng), 65. *Prof Exp:* Process chem engr, Celanese Corp Am, 58-59; res engr, Photo Prods Dept, E I du Pont de Nemours & Co, Inc, 60. *Mem:* Am Inst Chem Engrs. *Res:* Licensing; two phase flow; catalysis; reactor design and development. *Mailing Add:* 7976 Terrace Dr El Cerrito CA 94530

BRIDGE, DAVID S, STOCHASTIC CONTROL, STOCHASTIC CALCULUS. *Current Pos:* DEPT CHAIR & ASSOC PROF MATH & STATIST, UNIV CENT OKLA, 92- *Personal Data:* b Baltimore, Md, Aug 21, 61. *Educ:* Loyola Col, BS, 83; Carnegie Mellon Univ, 84, PhD(math), 91. *Prof Exp:* Actuary, Alexander & Alexander, Inc, 83-86. *Mem:* Math Asn Am; Am Math Soc. *Mailing Add:* Dept Math & Statist Univ Cent Okla Edmond OK 73034. *Fax:* 405-330-3847; *E-Mail:* dbridge@aixl.ucok.edu

BRIDGE, HERBERT SAGE, space physics; deceased, see previous edition for last biography

BRIDGE, THOMAS E, GEOLOGY. *Current Pos:* RETIRED. *Personal Data:* b Apr 3, 25; m 47; c 4. *Educ:* Kans State Univ, BS, 50, MS, 53; Univ Tex, PhD(geochem), 66. *Prof Exp:* Teacher pub schs, 50-53, prin, 53-56; instr geol, Colo State Univ, 56-59; asst prof, Tex Technol Col, 63-66; prof, Emporia State Univ, 66-91. *Mem:* Am Geophys Union; Meteoritical Soc Am. *Res:* Contact metamorphic rocks and ground water geology. *Mailing Add:* Rte 1 Strong City KS 66869. *E-Mail:* bridgeth@esuvm1.emporia.edu

BRIDGE, THOMAS PETER, CLINICAL TRIALS, NEUROPSYCHOPHARMACOLOGY. *Current Pos:* CHIEF CLIN TRIALS BR, MED DEVELOP DIV, NAT INST DRUG ABUSE, NIH, 92- *Personal Data:* b Nashville, Tenn, June 2, 45; m 75, Beth J Soldo. *Educ:* Duke Univ, BA, 68; Med Col Va, MD, 71. *Honors & Awards:* J D Lane Invest, US Pub Health Serv, 84; Young Invest Award, Am Geriatrics Soc, 85. *Prof Exp:* Staff fel, NIMH, Bethesda, 77-80, AIDS Coordr, 86-91, Chief Geopsychiat Unit, Washington, 80-83; sci adv, Alcohol, Drug Abuse & Mental Health, 83-86. *Mem:* Fel Col Int Neuropsychopharmacol; Am Col Neuropsychopharmacol; AAAS. *Res:* Clinical trials program at NIH to develop pharmacological treatments for opiate/cocaine dependence; neuropsychologic and pharmacologic methods and medications for cognitive impairment. *Mailing Add:* Dept Health & Human Servs Natl Inst on Drug Abuse Rm 11A55 5600 Fishers Lane Rockville MD 20857. *Fax:* 301-443-2599; *E-Mail:* pb68c@nih.gov

BRIDGEFORD, DOUGLAS JOSEPH, POLYMER CHEMISTRY, MATERIALS SCIENCE ENGINEERING. *Current Pos:* CONSULT, 91- *Personal Data:* b Grand Forks, NDak, Feb 3, 26; m 55, Catherine E Tyler; c Brian, Hugh, Barry & John. *Educ:* Univ Minn, BChem, 47. *Prof Exp:* Chemist, Teepak Inc, 48-55, res chemist polymers, 55-63, sr res chemist, 58-63, asst res mgr, 63-72, res assoc cellulose, 72-82, adv scientist polymers, 82-91. *Mem:* Am Chem Soc; fel Am Inst Chemists; Tech Asn Pulp & Paper Indust; NY Acad Sci; Union Concerned Scientists. *Res:* Film technology from amylose, cellulose, polyvinyl alcohol and cellulose derivatives; viscose modifications; lamination; printing; coatings films; organic synthesis; waste treatment; polymer composites; granted 58 US & 1400 foreign patents; author of 5 publications. *Mailing Add:* 1209 W John St Champaign IL 61821-3805

BRIDGEO, WILLIAM ALPHONSUS, ORGANIC CHEMISTRY. *Current Pos:* assoc prof, St Mary's Univ, 63-70, dean sci, 67-76, prof anal chem, 70-93, EMER DEAN SCI, ST MARY'S UNIV, NS, 93- *Personal Data:* b St John, NB, Dec 15, 27; m 55, Margaret Camillus Campbell; c Anne M (Abraham), Mary C (Lochead), Paul J & Georgina M (Fogarty). *Educ:* St Francis Xavier Univ, BSc, 48; Univ Ottawa, PhD(chem), 52. *Prof Exp:* Instr gen chem, St Mary's Col, Ind, 52-53. *Concurrent Pos:* Dir, Tech Serv Div, NS Res Found, Halifax, 53-65, dir, Chem Div, 65-69; pres, Bridco Values Ltd, 71-; dir, Can Nat Comt, Int Asn Water Pollution Res & Control, 71-85, pres, 81-82. *Mem:* Can Inst Chem; Am Inst Chemists; Can Asn Water Pollution Res & Control; NS Inst Sci; Int Asn Water Qual. *Res:* Nitrogen, strontium, and sulfur compounds; ceramic glazes; research and development on processing strontium minerals to strontium products. *Mailing Add:* PO Box 3161 Halifax NS B3J 3H5 Can. *Fax:* 902-420-5261

BRIDGER, WAGNER H, RESEARCH ADMINISTRATION, PHARMACOLOGY. *Current Pos:* PROF PSYCHIAT & PHARMACOL, MED COL PA, 82-, CHMN DEPT, 82- *Personal Data:* b New York, NY, Jan 9, 28. *Educ:* NY Univ, BA, 46, MD, 50. *Prof Exp:* From assoc prof to prof psychiat, Albert Einstein Col Med, Bronx Munic Hosp Ctr, 65-82, dir res, 65-82. *Concurrent Pos:* Vis scientist, Instituto Superiore de Sanita, Rome, Italy, 69-70; prof neurosci, Albert Einstein Col Med, 74-82, actg chmn, 76-81, attend psychiatrist, Hosp Albert Einstein Col Med, 76-82; mental health career investr, USPHS, 58-63, res career develop, 63-68; consult, Hastings Ctr, Inst Soc, Ethics & Life Sci, 77- *Mem:* Soc Psychiat Res (secy, 66-69, pres, 70-71, vpres, 86); Soc Biol Psychiat (pres, 88); fel Am Col Neuropsychopharmacol; fel Am Col Psychiatrists; Am Psychopath Asn. *Res:* Neonatal psychophysiology cross-modal transfer in premature infants; galvanic skin response conditioning effect of drugs on animal behavior; role of various neurotransmitters on animal behavior and aggression in children. *Mailing Add:* 114 Lombard St Philadelphia PA 19147

BRIDGER, WILLIAM AITKEN, BIOCHEMISTRY. *Current Pos:* from asst prof to assoc prof, 67-77, chmn, Dept Biochem, 87-93, PROF BIOCHEM, UNIV ALTA, 77-, ASSOC VPRES RES, 93- *Personal Data:* b Winnipeg, Man, May 31, 41; m 83, Irene Fecycz; c Andrea, Eric, Keith & Jocelyn. *Educ:* Univ Man, BSc, 62, MSc, 63, PhD(biochem), 66. *Honors & Awards:* Ayerst Award, Can Biochem Soc, 80. *Prof Exp:* Med Res Coun Can res fel biochem, Univ Calif, Los Angeles, 66-67. *Concurrent Pos:* Vis prof, Rockefeller Univ, NY, 84-85. *Mem:* Am Chem Soc; Can Biochem Soc (secy, 74-); Am Soc Biol Chemists; fel Royal Soc Can. *Res:* Study of structure function and assembly of enzymes. *Mailing Add:* Univ Western Ont London ON N6A 3K7 Can. *Fax:* 403-492-1438; *E-Mail:* bill_bridger@darwin.biochem.ualberta.ca

BRIDGERS, WILLIAM FRANK, PUBLIC HEALTH POLICY. *Current Pos:* assoc prof pediat, biochem & med, Univ Ala, 68-70, prof psychiat & dir neurosci prog, Sch Med, 70-73, dir sponsored progs, 73-74, spec asst to vpres health affairs, 75-76, chmn & prof, Dept Pub Health, 76-81, dean & prof, Sch Pub Health, 81-89, dir, Lister Hill Ctr, Health Policy, 87-90, prof pub health, 90-92, EMER UNIV SCHOLAR, UNIV ALA AT BIRMINGHAM, 93- *Personal Data:* b Asheville, NC, July 26, 32; m 74, Judith Ware; c Jeffrey, David, Daniel & Jana. *Educ:* Univ of the South, BA, 54; Wash Univ, MD, 59. *Prof Exp:* From instr to asst prof prev med & med, Sch Med, Wash Univ, 63-66; from asst prof to assoc prof med, Sch Med, Univ Miami, 66-68. *Concurrent Pos:* United Health Found fel, Dept Prev Med, Sch Med, Wash Univ, 63-65; assoc ed, Nutrit Rev, 63-67; mem staff, Nat Acad Sci/Nat Res Coun, 74-75; mem, Dept Health & Human Servs, Nat Comm Vital & Health Statist, 90-94; ed, Policy Watch, 92- *Res:* Neurochemistry and regulatory molecular biology of folic acid metabolism in developing, mammalian brain; writer on health policy. *Mailing Add:* 2221 English Village Lane Birmingham AL 35223

BRIDGES, ALAN L, COMPUTER GRAPHICS, COMPUTER SECURITY. *Current Pos:* SPEC ENGR & SR PRIN ENGR, LOCKHEED AERONAUT SYST CO, 83-90 & 92- *Personal Data:* b Knoxville, Tenn, Oct 10, 50; m 84, Dale M Paulk; c Alexander T & Jennifer B. *Educ:* Ga Tech, BS, 72, MS, 74. *Prof Exp:* Asst res scientist, Ga Tech Res Inst, 75-78; asst prod mgr, Humphrey Instruments, Inc, 78-79; pres & consult, ETC West, Ltd, 79-88; sr eng proj mgr, SCI Systs, Inc, 90-92. *Concurrent Pos:* Contribed, Computer Technol Rev, 83-86, 94-; pres & cons. *Mem:* Sr mem Inst Elec & Electronics Engrs; Asn Comput Mach; Int Soc Optical Eng; Soc Info Display. *Res:* Development of Lockheed standard - software engineering process standard, guidebooks on security and human factors; multimedia communications, virtual reality and interactive voice response. *Mailing Add:* 8523 Colony Club Dr Alpharetta GA 30202-5407. *E-Mail:* G538179.fsvax@decnet.lockheed.com

BRIDGES, C DAVID, RECOMBINANT DNA, BIOCHEMISTRY OF RETINOIDS. *Current Pos:* PROF BIOL SCI PHYSIOL, PURDUE UNIV, 87- *Personal Data:* b Northiam, E Sussex, Eng, Jan 16, 33; US citizen. *Educ:* Univ London, Enh, BSc, 53, PhD(physiol & biochem), 56, DSc, 83. *Honors & Awards:* Marjorie W Margolin Prize, Retina Res Found, 82, Sam & Bertha Brochstein Award, 86. *Prof Exp:* Sci staff, Med Res Coun, London, 64-67; from asst prof to prof ophthal, NY Univ Med Ctr, 67-77; prof ophthal, Baylor Col Med, 77-87, prof biochem, 80-87. *Concurrent Pos:* Dir, Ctr Res Vision, Baylor Col Med, 78-87; distributing ed, Vision Res, Pergamon Press, 79-89; trustee, Asn Res Vision & Ophthal, 82-86, vpres, 86; Pfizer traveling fel, Clin Res Inst Montreal, 83; Marc vis scientist, Fedn Am Socs Exp Biol, 83-84; mem, Behav & Neurosci Study Sect, NIH, 83-85 & VISB Study Sect, 75-79; adj prof physiol & biophys, Sch Med, Ind Univ, 90- *Mem:* Physiol Soc; Asn Res Vision & Opthal; Am Soc Biol Chemist; Soc Neurosci; Marine Biol Asn UK. *Res:* Molecular basis of the visual process; biochemistry and transport of vitamin A in light and dark adaptation; biochemical basis of ocular diseases. *Mailing Add:* Dept Biol Sci Purdue Univ West Lafayette IN 47907

BRIDGES, CHARLES HUBERT, VETERINARY PATHOLOGY. *Current Pos:* assoc prof, Tex A&M Univ, 55-59, prof, Agr Exp Sta, 59-60, head dept, 60-78, prof, 60-87, EMER PROF VET PATH, TEX A&M UNIV, 87- *Personal Data:* b Shreveport, La, Feb 23, 21; m 45; c 2. *Educ:* Agr & Mech Col, Tex, DVM, 45, MS, 54, PhD(vet path), 57; Armed Forces Inst Path, cert, 55; Am Col Vet Pathologists, dipl, 56. *Prof Exp:* Res assoc, Agr Exp Sta, La State Univ, 49-51. *Concurrent Pos:* Adj prof path, Baylor Col Med, Houston, Tex, 78-87. *Mem:* Am Col Vet Pathologists; Int Acad Path; Am Vet Med Asn. *Res:* Experimental pathology as applied to natural diseases of animals; definition of toxicological factors in good (plant toxins, trace minerals) and their role in producing disease with special evaluation of nutritional, biochemical and pathological interactions. *Mailing Add:* 1502 Glade College Station TX 77840

BRIDGES, DONALD NORRIS, NUCLEAR SAFETY. *Current Pos:* chief, Nuclear Safety Br, 76-81, chief, Reactors Br, 81-85, dir, Safety Div, 85-89, dir, Tech Support Div, 89-92, DIR, MFG DIV, DEPT ENERGY, SAVANNAH RIVER OPERS OFF, 92- *Personal Data:* b Shelby, NC, Aug 13, 36; m 59; c 4. *Educ:* NC State Univ, Raleigh, BCE, 58, MS, 60; Ga Inst Technol, MS, 68, PhD(nuclear eng), 70. *Prof Exp:* Civil engr, DuPont Co, 61-62; naval officer, Civil Eng Corps, USN, 62-66; nuclear engr, AEC, Savannah, 70-74; nuclear engr, Div Operating Reactors, Nuclear Regulatory Comn, 74-76. *Mem:* Am Nuclear Soc; Soc Am Mil Engrs; Naval Res Asn; Res Off Asn. *Res:* Spatial and feedback effects resulting from nuclear reactor transients; nuclear methods for measuring soil moisture and density. *Mailing Add:* 1002 Longleaf Ct North Augusta SC 29841

BRIDGES, E(RNEST), ELECTRICAL ENGINEERING. *Current Pos:* From lectr to assoc prof, 56-70, PROF ELEC ENG, UNIV MAN, 70- *Personal Data:* b Winnipeg, Man, Aug 4, 31; m 56; c 3. *Educ:* Univ Man, BSc, 54, MSc, 58. *Mem:* Inst Elec & Electronics Engrs; Can Asn Univ Teachers. *Res:* Microwaves; microwave measurement methods; microwave filters and antennae; semiconductor permittivity measurements. *Mailing Add:* Dept Elec & Comp Eng Univ Man Winnipeg MB R3T 2N2 Can

BRIDGES, FRANK G, MICROWAVE ABSORPTION SPECTROSCOPY OF ELECTRIC DIPOLE SYSTEMS, EXTENDED X-RAY ABSORPTION FINE STRUCTURE STUDIES OF PURE & SUBSTITUTED CRYSTALS. *Current Pos:* from asst prof to assoc prof physics, 70-81, chair physics, 82-84, PROF PHYSICS, UNIV CALIF, SANTA CRUZ, 81- *Personal Data:* m 64, Loreen Webster; c Brent & Bradd. *Educ:* Univ BC, Can, BS, 62, MS, 64; Univ Calif, San Diego, PhD(physics), 86. *Prof Exp:* Asst res physicist & lectr, Univ Calif, San Diego, 68-70. *Concurrent Pos:* Prin investr, 71-; consult, Xerox Corp, 85-; Alexander von Humboldt fel, 76-77 & 79. *Mem:* Am Phys Soc; Mat Res Soc. *Res:* Tunneling behavior of off-center ions in crystals; local structure of defect atoms in high temperature superconductors and colossal magnetoresistance systems; investigated low velocity collisions of ice particles, such as occur in Saturn's rings; superconductivity; planetary physics. *Mailing Add:* Dept Physics Univ Calif Santa Cruz CA 95064

BRIDGES, JOHN ROBERT, ENTOMOLOGY, BIOCHEMISTRY. *Current Pos:* RES ENTOMOLOGIST, FOREST SERV, USDA, 75- *Personal Data:* b Plainview, Ark, Feb 14, 44; m 68; c 2. *Educ:* Univ Ark, BS, 66, MS, 68; Univ Wis, PhD(entom), 75. *Prof Exp:* Med entomologist, USN, 69-72. *Mem:* Entom Soc Am; Am Soc Microbiol; Mycol Soc Am. *Res:* Bark beetle and associated microorganisms; insect physiology and biochemistry. *Mailing Add:* 201 14th & Independence SW PO Box 96090 Washington DC 20090-6090

BRIDGES, KENT WENTWORTH, ECOLOGY. *Current Pos:* ASST PROF BOT, UNIV HAWAII, 73- *Personal Data:* b Milwaukee, Wis, Aug 25, 41; m 65. *Educ:* Univ Hawaii, BA, 64, MS, 67; Univ Calif, Irvine, PhD(biol), 70. *Prof Exp:* Asst prof wildlife resources, Utah State Univ, 70-73. *Concurrent Pos:* Chief modeler, Desert Biome, US Int Biol Prog, 70-73. *Mem:* Ecol Soc Am; Japanese Soc Pop Ecol; Asn Comput Mach. *Res:* Computer modeling of biological problems; systems ecology. *Mailing Add:* Dept Bot Univ Hawaii-Manoa Honolulu HI 96822-2270

BRIDGES, ROBERT STAFFORD, NEUROENDOCRINOLOGY, BEHAVIORAL ENDOCRINOLOGY. *Current Pos:* PROF COMP MED, SCH VET MED, TUFTS UNIV, 90- *Personal Data:* b Northampton, Mass, Aug 5, 47; m 75; c 2. *Educ:* Earlham Col, BA, 69; Univ Conn, MS, 72, PhD(endocrinol), 74. *Prof Exp:* Fel biochem/behav, Rutgers Univ, 75-77; res assoc anat, Sch Med, Univ Calif, Los Angeles, 77-78; asst prof, Harvard Med Sch, 78-84, assoc prof anat & cell biol, 84-90. *Concurrent Pos:* Vis lectr, Woods Hole Oceanog Inst, 80-83; res scientist develop award, NIMH, 84 89. *Mem:* Soc Study Reproduction; Endocrine Soc; Am Asn Anatomists; Soc Neurosci. *Res:* Relationships among the endocrine, neural and neuroendocrine systems in the regulation of reproductive processes in mammals; control of maternal behavior and maintenance of pregnancy by the endocrine and neuroendocrine systems; neurobiology of aging. *Mailing Add:* Sch Vet 200 W Borough Grafton MA 01506

BRIDGES, THOMAS JAMES, PHYSICS, ELECTRICAL ENGINEERING. *Current Pos:* RETIRED. *Personal Data:* b Gillingham, Eng, Dec 2, 23; UK citizen; m 50, 81; c 2. *Educ:* London Univ, BS, 44. *Prof Exp:* Scientist physics & elec eng, Royal Naval Sci Serv, UK, 44-56 & 59-63; mem tech staff, AT&T Bell Labs, 56-59, mem tech staff physics & elec eng, 63-92. *Concurrent Pos:* Vis prof, Elec Eng Dept, Mass Inst Technol, 67-68. *Mem:* Inst Elec & Electronics Engrs; Optical Soc Am. *Res:* Microwave and optical electronics. *Mailing Add:* 89 Middletown Rd Holmdel NJ 07733

BRIDGES, WILLIAM BRUCE, MILLIMETER WAVE & OPTICAL TECHNOLOGY. *Current Pos:* prof elec eng & appl physics, 77-83, exec officer elec eng, 78-81, CARL F BRAUN PROF ENG, CALIF INST TECHNOL, 83- *Personal Data:* b Inglewood, Calif, Nov 29, 34; m 57, 86, Linda J McManus; c Ann M (Foote), Bruce K & Michael A. *Educ:* Univ Calif, Berkeley, BS, 56, MS, 57, PhD(elec eng), 62. *Honors & Awards:* Arthur L Schawlow Award, Laser Inst Am, 86; Quantum Electronics Award, Inst Elec & Electronics Engrs, 88. *Prof Exp:* Assoc elec eng, Univ Calif, Berkeley, 57-59; mem tech staff, Res Labs, Hughes Aircraft Co, 60-65, sr mem tech staff, 65-68, mgr laser dept, 69-70, sr scientist, 68-77. *Concurrent Pos:* Res engr, Varian Assocs, 56 & 57; lectr, Univ Southern Calif, 62-64; Sherman Fairchild distinguished scholar, Calif Inst Technol, 74-75; assoc ed, J Quantum Electronics, Inst Elec & Electronics Engrs, 77-82 & J Optical Soc Am, 78-82; consult, Hughes Res Labs, 77-; dir, Optical Soc Am, 82-84; mem bd dirs, Uniphase Corp, 85-; vis prof, Chalmers Univ, Goteborg, Sweden, 89. *Mem:* Nat Acad Sci; Nat Acad Eng; fel Optical Soc Am (vpres, 86, pres, 88); fel Inst Elec & Electronics Engrs; Fel Laser Inst Am. *Res:* Electro-optic modulation; laser devices; optical communication and instrumentation; millimeter wave devices and systems. *Mailing Add:* Calif Inst Technol 136-93 Pasadena CA 91125. *Fax:* 626-395-2137; *E-Mail:* w6fa@cco.caltech.edu

BRIDGES, WILLIAM G, algebra, combinatorics & finite mathematics; deceased, see previous edition for last biography

BRIDGEWATER, ALBERT LOUIS, JR, elementary particle physics, for more information see previous edition

BRIDGFORTH, ROBERT MOORE, JR, ROCKET TECHNOLOGY. *Current Pos:* RETIRED. *Personal Data:* b Lexington, Miss, Oct 21, 18; m 43, Florence Jarnberg; c Robert & Alice. *Educ:* Iowa State Univ, BS, 40; Mass Inst Technol, SM, 48. *Prof Exp:* Instr chem, Mass Inst Technol, 40-43, staff mem, Div Indust Coop, 43-48; assoc prof physics & chem, Emory & Henry Col, 49-51; res specialist, Boeing Co, 51-58, chief propulsion syst sect, Syst Mgt Off, 58-59, chief propulsion res unit, 59-60; chmn bd, Rocket Res Corp, 60-69. *Concurrent Pos:* Chmn bd, Explosives Corp Am, 67-69. *Mem:* Am Chem Soc; Am Astronaut Soc; fel Brit Interplanetary Soc; Am Inst Aeronaut & Astronaut; Am Inst Chemists; Am Asn Physics Teachers. *Res:* Thermodynamics of rocket propellants; development of maximum performance rocket propellants using beryllium-oxygen-hydrogen and lithium-fluorine-hydrogen; sublimation; vapor-liquid-equilibrium. *Mailing Add:* 4325 87th Ave SE Mercer Island WA 98040

BRIDGMAN, CHARLES JAMES, NUCLEAR ENGINEERING, RESEARCH ADMINISTRATION. *Current Pos:* Asst nuclear eng, USAF Inst Technol, 59-60, from instr to assoc prof, 60-68, chmn, Nuclear Eng Comn, 68-89, chmn, Sch Eng Doctoral Coun, 76-89, PROF NUCLEAR ENG, USAF INST TECHNOL, 68-, ASSOC DEAN RES, SCH ENG, 89- *Personal Data:* b Toledo, Ohio, May 6, 30; m 54, Lucy S Hull; c Charles J Jr, Kathleen M (McFadden), Stephanie B (Danahy), Kenneth M, Paula J (Bach) & Thomas A. *Educ:* US Naval Acad, BS, 52; NC State Univ, MS, 58, PhD(nuclear eng), 63. *Mem:* Fel Am Nuclear Soc; Am Soc Eng Educ; Health Physics Soc; Sigma Xi. *Res:* Nuclear weapon effects modeling especially fallout and residual radiation; military applications of nuclear power including space nuclear power. *Mailing Add:* 7362 Natoma Pl Dayton OH 45424-3049. *Fax:* 937-255-2921; *E-Mail:* bridgman@afit.af.mil

BRIDGMAN, GEORGE HENRY, MATHEMATICS. *Current Pos:* CONSULT, 93- *Personal Data:* b Minneapolis, Minn, 1940. *Educ:* Hamline Univ, BA, 61; Univ Minn, Minneapolis, MA, 64, PhD(math), 69. *Prof Exp:* Asst prof math, Wartburg Col, 69-76; lectr, Univ Minn, Duluth, 76-79; asst prof, Hamline Univ, 79-80; asst prof, Univ Wis, River Falls, 80-81; programmer/analyst, Cray Res, Inc, St Paul, 84-85; appln prog, Div Epidemiol, Univ Minn, Minneapolis, 86-93. *Concurrent Pos:* Instr, Comput Prog, Macalester Col, St Paul, 83-84. *Mem:* Math Asn Am. *Res:* Mathematical analysis; topics in calculus. *Mailing Add:* 4306 Grimes Ave S Minneapolis MN 55424-1051

BRIDGMAN, HOWARD ALLEN, climatology, air pollution, for more information see previous edition

BRIDGMAN, JOHN FRANCIS, PARASITOLOGY, ANIMAL PHYSIOLOGY. *Current Pos:* assoc prof, 72-81, PROF BIOL, COL OZARKS, 81- *Personal Data:* b Kuling, China, Sept 6, 25; US citizen; m 52; c 4. *Educ:* Davidson Col, BS, 49; La State Univ, MS, 52; Tulane Univ, PhD(biol), 68. *Honors & Awards:* George Henry Penn Award Biol, 69. *Prof Exp:* Instr biol, Delta State Teachers Col, 52 & Univ Tenn, Martin Br, 52-54; lectr, Shikoku Christian Col, 56-67, from asst prof to prof, 57-72. *Mem:* AAAS; Am Soc Parasitologists; Japanese Soc Parasitologists; Am Soc Zoologists. *Res:* Invertebrate ecology; life cycles, bionomics and ecology of parasites together with their host-parasite relations. *Mailing Add:* 700 Hillcrest Ave Clarksville AR 72830

BRIDGMAN, WILBUR BENJAMIN, PHYSICAL CHEMISTRY. *Current Pos:* from asst prof to prof, 43-78, EMER PROF CHEM, WORCESTER POLYTECH INST, 78- *Personal Data:* b New Wilmington, Pa, Jan 28, 13; m 37; c 2. *Educ:* Wis State Teachers Col, BEd, 33; Univ Wis, PhD(chem), 37. *Prof Exp:* Instr chem, Univ Wis, 37-42, Rockefeller fel, 42-43. *Mem:* Am Chem Soc. *Res:* Dipole moments; ultracentrifugal determination of particle size and shape; solution thermodynamics; surface chemistry. *Mailing Add:* 306 Madison St Wrentham MA 02093

BRIDLE, ALAN HENRY, ASTRONOMY. *Current Pos:* SCIENTIST, NAT RADIO ASTRON OBSERV, 83-; RES PROF, UNIV VA, 84- *Personal Data:* b Harrow, Eng, Sept 2, 42; m 68. *Educ:* Cambridge Univ, BA, 63, MA, 67, PhD(radio astron), 67. *Prof Exp:* UK Sci Res Coun fel, 67; from asst prof to prof physics, Queen's Univ, Ont, 72-83. *Concurrent Pos:* Vis asst scientist, US Nat Radio Astron Observ, 68, vis scientist, 80-82; adj prof, Univ NMex, 80-81. *Mem:* Am Astron Soc; Can Astron Soc; Int Astron Union. *Res:* Extragalactic radio astronomy; radio galaxies quasars. *Mailing Add:* Nat Radio Astron Observ 520 Edgemont Rd Charlottesville VA 22903-2475. *E-Mail:* abridle@nrao.edu

BRIDWELL, G PORTER, AEROSPACE ENGINEERING. *Current Pos:* eng & mgr, 62-94, DIR, NASA-MARSHALL SPACE FLIGHT CTR, 94- *Personal Data:* b Linton, Ind, Oct 4, 35; c Michael G & Kendra L. *Educ:* Purdue Univ, BS, 58. *Prof Exp:* Engr, Rocketdyne, 58-62. *Mailing Add:* 8712 Edgehill Huntsville AL 35802

BRIEADDY, LAWRENCE EDWARD, PHARMACEUTICAL CHEMISTRY, ORGANIC CHEMISTRY. *Current Pos:* Res scientist, 71-80, SECT HEAD PHARMACEUT, BURROUGHS WELLCOME CO, 80- *Personal Data:* b Syracuse, NY, May 13, 44; m 66; c 2. *Educ:* LeMoyne Col, NY, BS, 66; NC State Univ, MS, 69. *Mem:* Am Chem Soc. *Res:* Prostaglandin synthetase inhibitors; central nervous system; monoamine oxidase inhibitors; anti-inflammatory analgesic fields. *Mailing Add:* 5924 Wintergreen Dr Raleigh NC 27609-6632

BRIEGER, GERT HENRY, HISTORY OF MEDICINE. *Current Pos:* WILLIAM H WELCH PROF & DIR, INST HIST MED, JOHNS HOPKINS UNIV SCH MED, 84- *Personal Data:* b Hamburg, Ger, Jan 5, 32; US citizen; m 55; c 3. *Educ:* Univ Calif, Berkeley, AB, 53; Univ Calif, Los Angeles, MD, 57; Harvard Univ, MPH, 62; Johns Hopkins Univ, PhD, 68. *Prof Exp:* Intern med, Univ Calif, Los Angeles, 57-58; med officer, US Army Hosp, Dugway Proving Ground, 58-61; asst prof hist med, Sch Med, Johns Hopkins Univ, 66-70; assoc prof community health sci & hist, Duke Univ, 70-75; prof & chmn, Dept Hist Health Sci, Univ Calif, San Francisco, 75-84. *Concurrent Pos:* Mem coun, Am Asn Hist Med, 68-81; mem, Vis Comt, Hist Sci Dept, Bd Overseers, Harvard Univ. *Mem:* Inst Med-Nat Acad Sci; Am Asn Hist Med (vpres, 78-80, pres, 80-82); Int Acad Hist Med. *Res:* History of American medicine and public health; history of medicine in the late 19th and 20th centuries; author of 25 publications in history of medicine. *Mailing Add:* Johns Hopkins Univ Rm 320 1900 E Monument St Baltimore MD 21205

BRIEGER, GOTTFRIED, ORGANIC CHEMISTRY. *Current Pos:* from asst prof to assoc prof, 63-72, PROF CHEM, OAKLAND UNIV, 72- *Personal Data:* b Berlin, Ger, Oct 27, 35; m 59, Ingetraud V. Rennenkampff; c Kirsten V & Michael H. *Educ:* Harvard Col, BA, 57; Univ Wis, PhD(chem), 61. *Prof Exp:* Asst prof chem, Univ Calif, Berkeley, 61-63. *Concurrent Pos:* Sr Fulbright fel, Univ Heidelberg, 72-73. *Mem:* AAAS; Am Chem Soc; Royal Chem Soc; NY Acad Sci. *Res:* Synthesis and structural determination of natural products, especially terpenes; chemistry and biochemistry of insect hormones; catalytic hydrogen transfer reactions; clinical chemistry; applied chemistry; microbial degradation of xenobiotics. *Mailing Add:* Dept Chem Oakland Univ Rochester MI 48309-4401. *Fax:* 313-370-2321; *E-Mail:* gbrieger@ouchem.chem.oakland.edu

BRIEGLEB, PHILIP ANTHES, forestry; deceased, see previous edition for last biography

BRIEHL, ROBIN WALT, BIOCHEMISTRY, BIOPHYSICS. *Current Pos:* asst prof physiol, 62-66, assoc med, 65-69, assoc prof, 66-71, PROF PHYSIOL, ALBERT EINSTEIN COL MED, 71-, PROF BIOCHEM, 73-, ASST PROF MED, 69- *Personal Data:* b Vienna, Austria, June 21, 28; US citizen. *Educ:* Swarthmore Col, BA, 50; Harvard Med Sch, MD, 54. *Prof Exp:* Intern, Montefiore Hosp, New York, 54-55, asst resident med, 55-56; asst resident med & cardiol, Presby Hosp, 56-57, asst physician, 57-60. *Concurrent Pos:* NIH vis fel, Cardiopulmonary Lab, Columbia Univ, 57-60; NIH res fel biol, Harvard Univ, 60-62; career scientist, Health Res Coun, NY, 62-72; asst physician, Bronx Munic Hosp Ctr, 65- *Mem:* Am Soc Biol Chemists; AAAS; Am Fedn Clin Res; Am Soc Clin Invest; Am Physiol Soc; Sigma Xi. *Res:* Allostery; relations between the structure and function of hemoglobin; molecular bases of sickle cell disease; physical chemistry; internal medicine. *Mailing Add:* Albert Einstein Col Med 11300 Morris Park Ave Bronx NY 10461

BRIELAND, JOAN KATHRYN, LABORATORY ANIMAL MEDICINE. *Current Pos:* Fel, 85-88, special emphasis res, 88-93, ASST PROF, LAB ANIMAL MED, UNIV MICH MED SCH, 93- *Personal Data:* b Woodstock, Ill, Oct 4, 59. *Educ:* Univ Ill, BS, 80, DVM, 84. *Concurrent Pos:* Prin investr, NIH, Univ Mich, 94- *Mem:* Am Asn Lab Animal Sci; Am Asn Pathologists. *Res:* Study of inflammatory cell function during inflammatory lung disease. *Mailing Add:* 010 Animal Res Facil Univ Mich Med Sch Box 0614 ULAM Ann Arbor MI 48109-0614. *Fax:* 313-736-6476

BRIEN, JAMES FREDERICK, PHARMACOLOGY, TOXICOLOGY. *Current Pos:* from asst prof to assoc prof, 78-86, PROF PHARMACOL & TOXICOL, QUEEN'S UNIV, 86- *Personal Data:* b Windsor, Ont, Mar 3, 45; m 67; c 2. *Educ:* Univ Windsor, BSc, 66, PhD(chem), 71. *Honors & Awards:* Basmajian Award Excellence Med Res, 80. *Prof Exp:* Fel pharmacol, Univ Toronto, 71-73; res scientist, Addiction Res Found Ont, 73-78. *Concurrent Pos:* Asst prof, Dept Psychiat, Queen's Univ, 79-; Can J Physiol & Pharmacol, 83-; vis prof, Res Inst, St Joseph's Hosp, Univ W Ont, 85-86; grants, Med Res Coun & Heart & Stroke Found Ont. *Mem:* Chem Inst Can; Soc Toxicol Can; Pharmacol Soc Can. *Res:* Effects of prenatal ethanol exposure: acute and chronic studies; mechanism of action of organic nitrate vasodilator drugs; experimental and clinical studies of antiarrhythmic drugs. *Mailing Add:* Dept Pharmacol & Toxicol Queen's Univ Kingston ON K7L 3N6 Can

BRIENT, CHARLES E, NUCLEAR PHYSICS. *Current Pos:* asst prof, 64-68, ASSOC PROF PHYSICS, OHIO UNIV, 68- *Personal Data:* b El Paso, Tex, Oct 10, 34; m 59; c 4. *Educ:* Univ Tex, BS, 57, MA, 60, PhD(physics), 63. *Prof Exp:* Res assoc nuclear physics, Univ Tex, 63-64. *Concurrent Pos:* NSF res grant, 65-66; Ohio Univ Fund res grant, 66-67; AEC grant, 68. *Mem:* Am Phys Soc. *Res:* Nuclear reaction mechanisms and structure. *Mailing Add:* Dept Physics & Astron Ohio Univ Clippinger Labs Athens OH 45701. *Fax:* 740-593-1436

BRIENT, SAMUEL JOHN, JR, THIN METAL FILMS. *Current Pos:* assoc prof, 62-74, PROF PHYSICS, UNIV TEX, EL PASO, 74- *Personal Data:* b Phoenix, Ariz, Mar 24, 30; m 56; c 2. *Educ:* Univ Tex, BS, 52, PhD(physics), 59. *Prof Exp:* Res scientist, Defense Res Lab, Univ Tex, Austin, 56, Spectros Lab, 59-60, instr physics, 60-62. *Concurrent Pos:* Consult, Air Force Off Sci Res, Holloman AFB, NMex, 63, Braddock, Dunn & McDonald Inc, Tex, 63-64, Los Alamos Sci Lab, 67-70, Harry Diamond Labs, Army Res Off, 69 & NASA, Cleveland, 74-80. *Mem:* Fel AAAS; Am Vacuum Soc; Am Phys Soc; Am Asn Physics Teachers; Sigma Xi. *Res:* Conductive mechanisms in thin films experiments; Green's function equation of motion technique. *Mailing Add:* Dept Physics Univ Tex El Paso TX 79968. *Fax:* 915-747-5748

BRIENZA, MICHAEL JOSEPH, ELECTRO-OPTICS, LASERS. *Current Pos:* DIR HARDWARE ENG, NORDEN SYST UNITED TECHNOL, 86- *Personal Data:* b Mt Vernon, NY, Aug 20, 39; m 62; c 3. *Educ:* Univ Notre Dame, BS, 60, PhD(physics), 64. *Prof Exp:* Res scientist, Res Labs, United Aircraft Corp, 64-67, sr res scientist, 67-68, chief appl laser technol, 68-71, chief electrooptics, Norden Div, 71-77; dir, Advan Technol, Sewing Prod Group, Singer Corp, 77-81; vpres eng, Diag Retrieval Systs, 81-83; dir hardware eng, GSSD, Harris Corp, 83-86. *Concurrent Pos:* Consult optical & electronic prod. *Mem:* Am Phys Soc; Optical Soc Am; Sigma Xi. *Res:* Photoelectric and optical properties of metal films; hot electron ranges and devices; surface physics and thin film studies; ultra short laser pulse technology; acousto-optic signal processing; laser applications; electronics; mechanisms; product development; manufacturing engineering. *Mailing Add:* 140 Norton Rd Easton CT 06612

BRIERE, NORMAND, MICROSCOPY, TISSUE CULTURE. *Current Pos:* Asst prof dept anat, fac med, 67-73, ASSOC PROF HISTOL, DEPT ANAT & CELL BIOL, UNIV SHERBROOKE, QUE, 73- *Personal Data:* b St-Eustache, Que, Oct 24, 37; m 63; c 1. *Educ:* Univ Montreal, BA, 59, BSc, 62, MSc, 64, PhD(cancer), 67. *Concurrent Pos:* Prin investr, Med Res Coun, 84-86. *Mem:* Am Asn Anatomists; Am Soc Cell Biol; Can Asn Anatomists; Micros Soc Can; Can Soc Cell Biol. *Res:* Culture of fetal kidney in a serum-free medium in order to study the role of various growth factors and hormones on nephrogenesis. *Mailing Add:* Dept Anat & Cell Biol Univ Sherbrooke Sch Med Sherbrooke PQ J1H 5N4 Can

BRIERLEY, CORALE LOUISE, INORGANIC WASTE WATER TREATMENT, MICROBIOLOGY. *Current Pos:* GEN PARTNER, VISTATECH PARTNERSHIP, LTD, 89-; PRIN, BRIERLEY CONSULTANCY LLC, 97- *Personal Data:* b Shelby, Mont, Mar 24, 45; m 65, James A. *Educ:* NMex Inst Mining & Technol, BS, 68, MS, 71; Univ Tex, Dallas, PhD, 81. *Prof Exp:* Microbiologist planetary quarantine, Martin Marietta Corp, Denver, 68-69; chem microbiologist bact leaching, NMex Bur Mines & Mineral Resources, 71-82; pres, Advan Mineral Technol, Inc, 82-87, vpres, 87-88; chief, Environ Process Develop, Newmont Explor, Ltd, 90-91. *Concurrent Pos:* Vis prof, Dept Mining, Metall & Fuels Eng, Univ Utah, 74 & 78; vis researcher, Appl Geochem Res Group, Imp Col, 76 & Salt Lake City Metall Res Ctr, US Bur Mines, 78; vis lectr, Concordia Univ, Montreal, 79; vis scientist, Univ Tex, Dallas, 79-80; adj prof metall eng, Univ Utah, 94-96. *Mem:* Mining & Metall Soc Am; Soc Indust Microbiol; Soc Mining Engrs. *Res:* Biogenic extractive metallurgy; biological treatment methods for inorganic wastes; thermophilic chemautotrophic micro-organisms; biooxidation of minerals. *Mailing Add:* 2074 East Terrace Dr Highlands Ranch CO 80126-2692. *Fax:* 303-683-1944; *E-Mail:* clbrierley@msn.com

BRIERLEY, GERALD PHILIP, BIOCHEMISTRY. *Current Pos:* asst prof, 64-69, PROF PHYSIOL CHEM, OHIO STATE UNIV, 69- *Personal Data:* b Ogallala, Nebr, Aug 14, 31; m 54; c 2. *Educ:* Univ Md, PhD(biochem), 61. *Prof Exp:* Fel, Inst Enzyme Res, Univ Wis, 60-62, asst prof biochem, 62-64. *Concurrent Pos:* Estab investr, Am Heart Asn, 64- *Mem:* Am Soc Biol Chemists; Am Chem Soc. *Res:* Active transport and oxidative phosphorylation in heart mitochondria. *Mailing Add:* Dept Med Biochem 333 Hamilton Hall Ohio State Univ Col Med 1645 Neil Ave Columbus OH 43210-1328. *Fax:* 614-292-4118

BRIERLEY, JAMES ALAN, GEOMICROBIOLOGY, BIOHYDROMETALLURGY. *Current Pos:* CHIEF PROCESS MICROBIOL, NEWMOUNT METALL SERV, 88- *Personal Data:* b Denver, Colo, Dec 22, 38; m 65, Corale Beer. *Educ:* Colo State Univ, BS, 61; Mont State Univ, MS, 63, PhD(microbiol), 66. *Prof Exp:* Fel microbiol, Mont State Univ, 61-66; asst prof biol, NMex Inst Mining & Technol, 66-68; res scientist, Martin Marietta Corp, Colo, 68-69; asst prof, NMex Inst Mining & Technol, 69-78, prof & dept chmn biol, 78-83; dir, Advan Mineral Technol, 83-88. *Concurrent Pos:* Vis scientist, Univ Warwick, Eng, 76; vis prof, Cath Univ, Chile, 83. *Mem:* Am Soc Microbiol; Brit Soc Gen Microbiol; fel AAAS. *Res:* Microbial leaching of metals; microbial processes for metals recovery. *Mailing Add:* Newmont Metallurgical Svcs 10101 E Dry Creek Rd Englewood CO 80112. *Fax:* 801-583-8923

BRIERLEY, STEVEN K, SEMICONDUCTOR MATERIALS, OPTIMIZATION. *Current Pos:* SR PROJ SCIENTIST, RAYTHEON RES DIV, 83- *Educ:* Principia Col, BS, 68; Mass Inst Technol, SM, 75; Univ Pa, PhD(physics), 82. *Prof Exp:* Mem tech staff & proj engr, Watkins-Johnson Co, 75-78; IBM fel, 81-82; asst prof physics, Bryn Mawr Col, 82-83. *Res:* Research and development in the field of electronic materials and devices; contributed to 27 technical papers. *Mailing Add:* Adv Device Ctr Raytheon Ct 362 Lowell St Andover MA 01810

BRIESKE, THOMAS JOHN, mathematics education, for more information see previous edition

BRIGGAMAN, ROBERT ALAN, MEDICINE, DERMATOLOGY. *Current Pos:* resident, 64-65, from instr to assoc prof, 67-74, PROF, DEPT DERMAT, SCH MED, UNIV NC, CHAPEL HILL, 74-, CHAIR, 87- *Personal Data:* b Hartford, Conn, Aug 14, 34; m 60, Irene; c 2. *Educ:* Trinity Col, Conn, BS, 56; NY Univ, MD, 60. *Honors & Awards:* Merit Award, NIH, 90. *Prof Exp:* Intern internal med, Univ Va Hosp, 60-61, resident, 61-62. *Concurrent Pos:* Res fel, Univ NC, 65-67; NIH spec fel, 67-70. *Mem:* AAAS; Am Acad Dermat; Soc Invest Dermat; Tissue Cult Asn; Sigma Xi. *Res:* Epidermal-dermal interactions; tissue culture; delayed hypersensitivity; electron microscopy. *Mailing Add:* Dermat Dept 3100 Thurston-Bowles Bldg CB No 7287 Chapel Hill NC 27599-7287

BRIGGLE, LELAND WILSON, PLANT BREEDING & GENETICS, AGRONOMY. *Current Pos:* RETIRED. *Personal Data:* b Bismarck, NDak, Oct 6, 20; m 44, Harriet Dickerson; c Gary & Pamela. *Educ:* Jamestown Col, BS, 42; NDak State Univ, BS, 49, MS, 51; Iowa State Univ, PhD(plant breeding), 54. *Prof Exp:* Asst agron, NDak State Univ, 49-51; res asst, Iowa State Univ, 52-53; geneticist, Agr Res Ctr, USDA, Beltsville, MD, 54-55, res agronomist, 55-74, staff scientist, Nat Prog Staff, 75-82, res scientist, Cereal Crops Germplasm Prog, 83-89. *Mem:* FEL AAAS; fel Am Soc Agron; fel Crop Sci Soc Am; Sigma Xi. *Res:* Wheat and oat breeding and genetics and agronomic traits; transfer of genes for disease-resistance and desired agronomic traits from related species to improved breeding lines of wheat and oats. *Mailing Add:* 701 Copley Lane Silver Spring MD 20904-1312

BRIGGS, ARTHUR HAROLD, PHARMACOLOGY, MEDICINE. *Current Pos:* chmn dept, 68-93, PROF PHARMACOL, MED SCH, UNIV TEX, SAN ANTONIO, 68- *Personal Data:* b East Orange, NJ, Nov 3, 30; m 53, Elizabeth Jensen; c Kimberlee & Norman. *Educ:* Johns Hopkins Univ, BA, 52, MD, 56. *Prof Exp:* Intern internal med, Univ Hosp, Vanderbilt Univ, 56-57, asst resident, 57-58, res assoc pharmacol, Sch Med, 58-59; from asst prof to prof pharmacol, Sch Med, Univ Miss, 59-68, from instr to assoc prof med, 60-68. *Concurrent Pos:* US Govt fel, 58-60; med expert, Social Security Adm. *Mem:* Am Soc Pharmacol & Exp Therapeut; Soc Exp Biol & Med; Sigma Xi. *Res:* Smooth muscle and cardiac muscle pharmacology; alcohol. *Mailing Add:* Health Sci Ctr Dept Pharmacol Univ Tex 7703 Floyd Curl Dr San Antonio TX 78284-7764. *Fax:* 210-567-4203

BRIGGS, DALE EDWARD, CHEMICAL ENGINEERING. *Current Pos:* From instr to assoc prof, 61-79, PROF CHEM ENG, UNIV MICH, ANN ARBOR, 79- *Personal Data:* b Alton, Ill, Nov 27, 30; m 53; c 2. *Educ:* Univ Louisville, BChE, 53; Univ Mich, MSE, 58, PhD(chem eng), 68. *Concurrent Pos:* Coal consult, Consumers Power Co, Jackson, Mich, 74- *Mem:* Am Inst Chem Engrs; Am Chem Soc. *Res:* Colloid chemistry non-aqueous systems; coal liquefaction; coal gasification air pollution control. *Mailing Add:* Dept Chem Eng Univ Mich Ann Arbor MI 48109

BRIGGS, DARINKA ZIGIC, STRATIGRAPHY, INFORMATION SCIENCE. *Current Pos:* CONSULT GEOL, SYSTS ANALYSIS RES INFO CO, 68- *Personal Data:* b Belgrade, Yugoslavia, Sept 2, 32; Can citizen; m 68. *Educ:* Univ Belgrade, Dipl Geol, 57. *Prof Exp:* Field geologist, Serbian Acad Sci, Belgrade, 56; res asst paleont, Royal Ont Mus, Toronto, 58; res geologist, Imp Oil Co, Ltd, Toronto, 59; asst geol, Univ Toronto, 58-60; teacher high sch, Tilbury, Can, 62; res assoc geol, Subsurface Lab, Univ Mich, Ann Arbor, 65-68. *Concurrent Pos:* Adj scientist geol, Lab Subsurface Geol, Univ Mich, Ann Arbor, 64- *Mem:* Am Asn Petrol Geologists; Geol Soc Am; Am Asn Univ Professors; Am Soc Info Sci; Int Asn Math Geol. *Res:* Theoretical and mathematical basis for stratigraphic analysis, and the application to historical reconstructions of paleogeographies, ancient environments, and their utilization in the search for fossil energy resources. *Mailing Add:* 3451 Burbank Dr Ann Arbor MI 48105

BRIGGS, DAVID GRIFFITH, MECHANICAL ENGINEERING, THERMODYNAMICS. *Current Pos:* From asst prof to assoc prof, 64-88, PROF MECH ENG, RUTGERS UNIV, 88- *Personal Data:* b Chicago, Ill, Apr 4, 32; m 56; c 3. *Educ:* Dartmouth Col, BA, 54, MS, 55; Univ Minn, PhD(mech eng), 65. *Concurrent Pos:* NASA-Am Soc Eng Educ fac fel, Jet Propulsion Lab, Calif Inst Technol, 70. *Mem:* Am Soc Mech Engrs. *Res:* Free convection heat transfer in stratified fluids; computational fluid mechanics. *Mailing Add:* 14 Renfro St Somerset NJ 08873-2241

BRIGGS, DONALD K, MEDICINE, HEMATOLOGY. *Current Pos:* ASST PROF MED, NY UNIV, 57- *Personal Data:* b Northampton, Eng, Apr 10, 24; US citizen; m 58; c 2. *Educ:* Cambridge Univ, MA, 44, MB & BCh, 46. *Mem:* Am Soc Hemat. *Res:* Genetics; hematology. *Mailing Add:* 170 E 79th St New York NY 10021

BRIGGS, EDWARD M, OCEAN ENGINEERING. *Current Pos:* Res asst, 59-63, asst res engr, 63-65, res engr, 65-67, sr res engr, Dept Struct Res, 68-72, group leader, 72-73, mgr ocean eng, 73-76, DIR DEPT OCEAN ENG & STRUCT DESIGN, SOUTHWEST RES INST, 76- *Personal Data:* US citizen. *Educ:* Univ Tex, BS, 63. *Mem:* Marine Technol Soc; Am Soc Testing & Mat; Am Soc Mech Engrs. *Res:* Offshore experimental stress analyses of offshore platforms, submersible barges and deep ocean oil production equipment. *Mailing Add:* 6220 Culebra Rd San Antonio TX 78228-0510

BRIGGS, FAYE ALAYE, ELECTRICAL ENGINEERING, COMPUTER ENGINEERING. *Current Pos:* ASST PROF, ELEC ENG DEPT, RICE UNIV. *Personal Data:* b Abonnema, Nigeria, Sept 23, 47. *Educ:* Ahmadu Bello Univ, Zaria, Nigeria, BEng, 71; Stanford Univ, MS, 74; Univ Ill, PhD(elec eng), 77. *Prof Exp:* Asst lectr, Col Sci & Technol, Port-Harcourt, Nigeria, 71-72; res asst, Coord Sci Lab, Univ Ill, 74-76; asst prof, Sch Elec Eng, Purdue Univ, 76- *Mem:* Inst Elec & Electronics Engrs; Asn Comput Mach. *Res:* Computer architecture; multiprocessing systems; memory organizations; microprocessors and applications; operating systems. *Mailing Add:* 7202 Via Vico San Jose CA 95129

BRIGGS, FRED NORMAN, PHYSIOLOGY. *Current Pos:* PROF VA COMMONWEALTH, 86- *Personal Data:* b Oakland, Calif, Sept 12, 24; m 49; c 1. *Educ:* Univ Calif, AB, 47, MA, 48, PhD(physiol), 53. *Prof Exp:* Radiologist, US Naval Radiol Defense Lab, 48-49; instr pharm, Dent Sch, Harvard Univ, 52-55, assoc pharmacol, Med Sch, 56-58; from asst prof to assoc prof, Med Sch, Tufts Univ, 58-61; prof physiol, Sch Med, Univ Pittsburgh, 61-71; prof physiol & chmn dept, Med Col Va, Va Commonwealth Univ, 71- *Concurrent Pos:* Res fel, Harvard Univ, 55-56; sect ed, Am J Physiol; NIH-physiol, 67-70; Am Physiol Soc Ed Comt, 71-74; prof & chmn, Va Commonwealth, 71-85; NIH Cardio Pulmonary, 75-78; chmn, 78-79; NIH Manpower Nat Heart Lung & Blood Inst, 87. *Mem:* Am Soc Pharmacol & Exp Therapeut; Am Physiol Soc; Biophys Soc. *Res:* Thyroid; adrenal; muscle; physiology. *Mailing Add:* Dept Physiol Health Sci Div Med Col Va 1100 E Marshall St Richmond VA 23295-0551. *Fax:* 804-371-7382

BRIGGS, GARRETT, SEDIMENTOLOGY. *Current Pos:* PRES, PEACE COL, 88- *Personal Data:* b Dallas, Tex, Dec 31, 34; m 57; c 4. *Educ:* Southern Methodist Univ, BS, 58, MS, 59; Univ Wis, PhD(geol), 63. *Prof Exp:* Wis Alumni Res Found asst, Univ Wis, 59-60; geologist, Chevron Oil Co, La, 62-65; asst prof geol, Tulane Univ, 65-68; assoc prof, Univ Tenn, 68-74, interim head dept, 72-74, prof geol & head dept, 74-81, assoc dean, Liberal Arts Col, 77-81; dean, Sch Phys & Math Sci, NC State Univ, 81-88. *Mem:* Am Geol Soc. *Res:* General geology and sedimentation studies of late Paleozoic rocks in the Ouachita Mountains of Oklahoma; carboniferous sediments of Cumberland Plateau, Tennessee. *Mailing Add:* Peace Col 15 E Peace St Raleigh NC 27604-1194

BRIGGS, GEORGE ROLAND, PHYSICS. *Current Pos:* mem tech staff, 54-69, MEM TECH STAFF, DIGITAL SYSTS RES LAB, DAVID SARNOFF RES CTR, RCA CORP, 69- *Personal Data:* b Ithaca, NY, May 21, 24; m 48; c 2. *Educ:* Cornell Univ, AB, 47; Univ Ill, MS, 50, PhD(physics), 53. *Honors & Awards:* Achievement Awards, RCA Corp, 54 & 60. *Prof Exp:* Mem staff, Lincoln Lab, Mass Inst Technol, 52-53. *Mem:* Am Phys Soc; Inst Elec & Electronics Engrs; Asn Comput Mach. *Res:* Magnetic and ferroelectric computer memory and logic devices; electro-luminescent-magnetic computer and television displays; nuclear-radiation resistant computer memory and logic circuitry. *Mailing Add:* 37 Broadripple Dr Princeton NJ 08540

BRIGGS, HILTON MARSHALL, ANIMAL HUSBANDRY. *Current Pos:* pres, 58-75, EMER PRES & DISTINGUISHED PROF AGR, SDAK STATE UNIV, 75- *Personal Data:* b Cairo, Iowa, Jan 9, 13; m 35; c 2. *Educ:* Iowa State Univ, BS, 33; NDak State Univ, MS, 35; Cornell Univ, PhD(nutrit), 38. *Hon Degrees:* DSc, NDak State Univ, 63; Dr Higher Educ & Admin, Univ SDak, 74. *Prof Exp:* Asst, NDak State Univ, 34-35 & Cornell Univ, 35-36; from asst prof to prof animal husb, Okla Agr & Mech Col, 36-50, assoc dean agr & assoc dir exp sta, 49-50; dean col agr & dir exp sta, Univ Wyo, 50-58. *Mem:* Fel AAAS; fel Am Soc Animal Sci (secy, 47-50, vpres, 51, pres, 52); Sigma Xi. *Mailing Add:* SDak State Univ Rm 241 Libr Box 2115 Univ Sta Brookings SD 57007-1497

BRIGGS, JEFFREY L, ENVIRONMENTAL IMPACT ASSESSMENT, WETLANDS DELINEATION & PERMITTING. *Current Pos:* SR ENVIRON SCIENTIST, EARTH TECH CORP, 93- *Personal Data:* US citizen; m 65, Jean McLean; c Noah W. *Educ:* Univ Denver, BS, 65; Ore State Univ, MA, 68, PhD(ecol), 70. *Prof Exp:* Asst prof biol & zool, Univ Wis-Whitewater, 70-74; cur III, Milwaukee Pub Mus, 74-75; lectr, Univ Wis-Milwaukee, 75-78 & Univ Wis-Waukesha, 78-79; assoc prof biol, Col Med, King Faisal Univ, Damman, Saudi Arabis, 79-84; proj mgr, SCS Engrs, 84-93. *Mem:* Am Soc Ichthyologists & Herpetologists; Soc Wetland Scientists; Ecol Soc Am; Am Soc Testing & Mats. *Res:* Environmental impact assessment and wetlands delineation; field ecology studies; environmental risk assessment; flora and fauna assessment and mapping; habitat restoration; hazardous waste impact assessment and remediation; human health and ecological risk assessment. *Mailing Add:* Earth Technol Corp 1420 King St Alexandria VA 22314

BRIGGS, JOHN CARMON, ICHTHYOLOGY, HISTORICAL BIOGEOGRAPHY. *Current Pos:* chmn dept zool, Univ SFla, 64-71, prof biol, 64-75, dir grad studies, 71-75, actg chmn, Dept Marine Sci, 76-79, prof marine sci, 79-85, EMER PROF, UNIV SFLA, 85-; ADJ PROF, NAT HIST

MUS, UNIV GA, 90-, ADJ PROF, DEPT MARINE SCI, 96- *Personal Data:* b Portland, Ore, Apr 9, 20; m 48, 54, 73, Eila A Hanni; c Linda, David, Daniel, Carleton, Douglas, Katherine, Samuel, Elizabeth & Margaret. *Educ:* Ore State Univ, BS, 43; Stanford Univ, MA, 47, PhD(biol), 52. *Honors & Awards:* Phipps & Bird Award, Fla Acad Sci, 59. *Prof Exp:* Aquatic biologist, US Fish & Wildlife Serv, Ore, 45-46; asst gen biol, Stanford Univ, 47-48; instr, Ore Inst Marine Biol, 48; asst gen biol, Hopkins Marine Sta, 49; biologist, Calif State Div Fish & Game, 50-51; res assoc, Stanford Natural Hist Mus, 52-54; from instr to asst prof biol, Univ Fla, 54-57, res assoc anat, 57-58; asst prof, Univ BC, 58-59, asst prof zool, 59-61; asst prof, Hopkins Marine Sta, 61; res scientist, Inst Marine Sci, Univ Tex, 61-64. *Mem:* Am Soc Ichthyol & Herpet (vpres, 59, 64, treas, 81-85); fel Am Inst Fishery Res Biologists; Am Soc Naturalists; Am Inst Biol Sci; Am Fisheries Soc; Soc Syst Biol; Soc Study Evolution. *Res:* Ichthyology; historical biogeography; evolutionary significance of zoogeographic patterns. *Mailing Add:* Rte 1 Box 321 Arnoldsville GA 30619

BRIGGS, JOHN DORIAN, INSECT PATHOLOGY. *Current Pos:* RETIRED. *Personal Data:* b Santa Monica, Calif, Dec 20, 26; m 51; c 3. *Educ:* Univ Calif, BS, 51, PhD(entom), 56. *Prof Exp:* Assoc entomologist, Ill Nat Hist Surv, 55-59; head entom dept, Bioferm Corp, 59-62; prof entom, Ohio State Univ, 62-92, actg dean, Col Biol Sci, 68-69. *Concurrent Pos:* Fulbright sr res fel, Mexico, 80-81. *Mem:* AAAS; Entom Soc Am; Soc Invert Path (vpres, pres, 70-74). *Res:* Insect diseases; entomogenous bacteria, fungi, protozoa and viruses; invertebrate immunology; biological control of invertebrates of public health and agricultural importance; biology of aging. *Mailing Add:* 6654 Eastland Ct Worthington OH 43085

BRIGGS, JOSEPHINE P, RENAL PHYSIOLOGY. *Current Pos:* from asst prof to assoc prof, 85-93, PROF NEPHROL, UNIV MICH, 93-, ASSOC CHAIR, DEPT MED & PHYSIOL, 93- *Personal Data:* b Toronto, Ont, Dec 14, 44; US citizen; m 79; c 2. *Educ:* Harvard Univ, AB, 66, MD, 70. *Prof Exp:* Int resident internal med, Mt Sinai Med Sch, 70-76; chief resident res staff physiol, Yale Univ, 76-80; vis scientist, Univ Munich, 80-85. *Concurrent Pos:* Alexander von Humboldt fel, 80-82; estab investr, Am Heart Asn, 83-88; counr, Am Soc Clin Invest, 89- *Mem:* Women Nephrology (pres-elect, 90-91, pres, 92-94); Am Soc Clin Invest; Am Soc Nephrol; Am Fedn Clin Res. *Res:* Renal physiology; aiming to elucidate cellular mechanisms operating within the juxtaglomerular apparatus to regulate renin secretion and renal blood flow. *Mailing Add:* Dept Internal Med Univ Mich 1560 MSRB II 1150 W Medical Ctr Dr Box 0676 Ann Arbor MI 48109-0676

BRIGGS, KEITH GLYN, WHEAT BREEDING & VARIETY ADAPTATION, BARLEY DISEASES. *Current Pos:* from asst prof to prof & chair, Dept Plant Sci, Fac Agr Forestry & Home Econ, 69-83, CHAIR, UNIV ALTA, 86- *Personal Data:* b Aug 3, 43; m, Ola Workun; c Christina L & Anthony R. *Educ:* Cambridge Univ, Eng, BA Hons, 64, Dipl Agr Sci, 65; Univ Man, PhD(plant breeding), 69. *Concurrent Pos:* Sr cerealist, Can Int Develop Agency, Ministry Agr, Kenya, 81-83. *Mem:* Can Seed Growers Asn; Agr Inst Can; Genetics Soc Can; Am Soc Agron; Can Soc Agron. *Res:* Genetics plant breeding and agronomy of cereal crops; breeding early maturing wheat varieties with soil acidity tolerance. *Mailing Add:* Dept Plant Sci Univ Alta Edmonton AB T6G 2M7 Can. *Fax:* 403-492-4265; *E-Mail:* sheathco@vm.ucs.ca

BRIGGS, PHILLIP D, MATHEMATICS. *Current Pos:* PROF MATH, E CENT OKLA STATE UNIV, 65- *Personal Data:* b Ada, Okla, Dec 10, 37. *Educ:* Univ Okla, BS, 59, MA, 63. *Mem:* Math Asn Am. *Mailing Add:* E Cent State Univ Ada OK 74820

BRIGGS, REGINALD PETER, GEOLOGY OF PETROLEUM, ENVIRONMENTAL GEOLOGY & HYDROLOGY. *Current Pos:* PRES & CHIEF GEOLOGIST, GEOMEGA, INC, 76- *Personal Data:* b Port Chester, NY, Mar 12, 29; m 56; c 3. *Educ:* Wesleyan Univ, BA, 51. *Honors & Awards:* Spec Achievement Award, US Dept Interior, 76. *Prof Exp:* Geologist, 53-76, chief PR Coop Geol Mapping Proj, 64-70, proj dir greater Pittsburgh regional studies, US Geol Surv, 70-76. *Concurrent Pos:* Managing ed, Geol Penn proj, 83- *Mem:* Fel Geol Soc Am; Am Geophys Union; Am Inst Prof Geologists; Asn Eng Geologists. *Res:* Geology of volcanic rocks; Appalachian plateau geomorphology; slope stability; mineral fuels; metallic and nonmetallic mineral resources; reclamation; limestone hydrology; forensic applications. *Mailing Add:* 101 Algonquin Rd Pittsburgh PA 15241

BRIGGS, RICHARD JULIAN, plasma physics, for more information see previous edition

BRIGGS, ROBERT CHESTER, BIOLOGY, BIOCHEMISTRY. *Current Pos:* Res assoc, 76-78, res instr, 78-80, RES ASST PROF BIOCHEM, SCH MED, VANDERBILT UNIV, 80-, ASST PROF PATH, 83- *Personal Data:* b Iron Mountain, Mich, June 6, 44; m 72; c 2. *Educ:* Northern Mich Univ, BS, 66, MA, 72; Univ Vt, PhD(zool), 77. *Mem:* Am Soc Cell Biol; AAAS; Am Asn Cancer Res; Sigma Xi; Am Asn Pathologists; Am Soc Biochem & Molecular Biol. *Res:* Nuclear protein function in normal eucaryotic cell differentiation and during malignant transformation. *Mailing Add:* Dept Path TVC 4918 Vanderbilt Univ Sch Med Nashville TN 37232-5310. *Fax:* 615-343-7023

BRIGGS, ROBERT EUGENE, AGRONOMY. *Current Pos:* RETIRED. *Personal Data:* b Madison, Wis, Apr 4, 27; m 48; c 4. *Educ:* Univ Wis, BS, 50, PhD(agron), 58; Mich State Univ, MS, 52. *Prof Exp:* Asst farm crops, Mich State Univ, 50-52; asst agron, Univ Wis, 53-56; asst plant breeder, Univ Ariz, 56-57, from asst prof to assoc prof agron, 57-70, prof agron & plant genetics, 70-, agronomist, Agr Exp Sta & Exten Agronomist, Coop Exten Serv, 74- *Concurrent Pos:* Adv field crops, US AID-Brazil Prog, 64-66. *Mem:* Am Soc Agron. *Res:* Crop production; seed technology; cultural practices; fiber quality; cotton; physiology; management. *Mailing Add:* 3326 E Lester St Tucson AZ 85716

BRIGGS, ROBERT WILBUR, GENETICS, AGRICULTURE. *Current Pos:* DIR RES, CROW'S HYBRID CORN CO, 92- *Personal Data:* b Delavan, Ill, Mar 27, 34; m 62, Gail A Chelmo; c David R & Sarah A. *Educ:* Univ Ill, BS, 56, MS, 58; Univ Minn, PhD(genetics), 63. *Prof Exp:* Res assoc genetics, Brookhaven Nat Lab, 63-65, from asst geneticist to assoc geneticist, 65-69; geneticist, Funk Seeds Int, 69-78, prin res scientist, Res Dept, 79-92. *Concurrent Pos:* Fel biol, Brookhaven Nat Lab, 63-65. *Mem:* Crop Sci Soc Am; Agron Soc Am. *Res:* Chemical mutagens in plants; application of biotechnology to plant breeding and genetics; administration of corn breeding. *Mailing Add:* RR 1 Box 30 Towanda IL 61776. *Fax:* 815-889-5253

BRIGGS, RODNEY ARTHUR, agronomy; deceased, see previous edition for last biography

BRIGGS, THOMAS, BIOCHEMISTRY. *Current Pos:* RETIRED. *Personal Data:* b New York, NY, May 24, 33; div; c 3. *Educ:* Yale Univ, BS, 54; Univ Pa, PhD(biochem), 60. *Prof Exp:* Res asst med, Yale Univ, 62-63, res assoc, 63-67; asst prof biochem, Cols Med & Dent, Univ Okla, 67-70, assoc prof biochem & molecular biol, 70-94, adj assoc prof pharm, 85-94. *Concurrent Pos:* USPHS fel, Guy's Hosp Med Sch, London, 60-62; vis scientist, NIH, 81. *Mem:* Sigma Xi; AAAS; Am Chem Soc; NY Acad Sci; Brit Biochem Soc; Soc Exp Biol & Med; assoc mem Am Soc Biochem & Molecular Biol. *Res:* Bile salt chemistry and metabolism; cholesterol metabolism; comparative biochemistry; biochemical evolution; metabolism of lipoproteins. *Mailing Add:* PO Box 21076 Oklahoma City OK 73126

BRIGGS, THOMAS N, analytical chemistry, for more information see previous edition

BRIGGS, W(ILLIAM) SCOTT, ORGANIC CHEMISTRY, ANALYTICAL CHEMISTRY. *Current Pos:* develop specialist, NW Opers, 88-90, SPECIALIST-RESINS TO ADHESIVES, ORE OVERLAY DIV, SIMPSON TIMBER CO, 90- *Personal Data:* b Shelton, Wash, Aug 15, 41; m 63, 91, Kathleen Harris; c Shane, Douglas & John. *Educ:* Univ Wash, BS, 63; Stanford Univ, PhD(org chem), 68. *Prof Exp:* Res chemist, Bellingham Div, Ga-Pac Corp, 67-84; chem consult, W S Briggs & Assoc, 84-88. *Concurrent Pos:* Lectr chem, Western Wash Univ, 84-88. *Mem:* Am Chem Soc; Am Tech Asn Pulp & Paper Indust. *Res:* Wood chemistry; application of chromatographic methods and instrumental techniques for polymer characterization; production of commercial chemicals from biomass by chemical and enzymic methods; applied polymer chemistry; applied environmental chemistry. *Mailing Add:* W S Briggs & Assocs 18516 NW 47th Ave Ridgefield WA 98642. *Fax:* 503-978-2646

BRIGGS, WILLIAM EGBERT, ALGEBRA, BIOMATHEMATICS. *Current Pos:* RETIRED. *Personal Data:* b Sioux City, Iowa, Mar 26, 25; m 47; c 4. *Educ:* Morningside Col, BA, 48; Univ Colo, MA, 49, PhD(math), 53. *Hon Degrees:* DSc, Morningside Col, 68. *Prof Exp:* Instr math, Univ Colo, 48-53, res asst, 53-54; teacher pub sch, Colo, 54-55; from instr to assoc prof math, Univ Colo, Boulder, 55-64, actg dean, Col Arts & Sci, 63-64, dean, Col Arts & Sci, 64-80, prof math, 64-88. *Concurrent Pos:* Teacher high sch, Iowa, 47-48; dir acad yr inst high sch teachers, NSF, 56-60, actg chmn dept math, 59-60; NSF fel & res assoc, Univ Col, Univ London, 61-62; mem bd dirs, Educ Projs, Inc, 66-; bd dir, Coun Cols Arts & Sci, 69-73 & 74-77; mem regional selection comt, Woodrow Wilson Fel Found, 70-71; mem comn arts & sci, Nat Asn Land Grant Cols & Univs, 70-73 & 76-79. *Mem:* Coun Cols Arts & Sci (pres-elect, 74-75, pres, 75-76); Sigma Xi; Am Math Soc; Math Asn Am; London Math Soc. *Res:* Analytic number theory; prime number theory; dirichlet L-functions and Riemann zeta function; coef of power series; sequences generated by sieve processes; polynomials for protein-ligand binding. *Mailing Add:* Campus Box 426 Univ Colo Boulder CO 80309-0001

BRIGGS, WINSLOW RUSSELL, PLANT PHYSIOLOGY. *Current Pos:* dir, 73-93, EMER DIR, DEPT PLANT BIOL, CARNEGIE INST WASH, 93- *Personal Data:* b St Paul, Minn, Apr 29, 28; m 55; c 3. *Educ:* Harvard Univ, AB, 51, AM, 52, PhD(biol), 56. *Honors & Awards:* Stephen Hales Prize, Am Soc Plant Physiologists, 94; Sterling Hendricks Award, USDA & Am Chem Soc, 95. *Prof Exp:* From instr to prof biol, Stanford Univ, 55-67; prof, Harvard Univ, 67-73. *Concurrent Pos:* Prof, Stanford Univ, 73-93, emer prof, 93-; Alexander von Humboldt US Sr Scientist Award, 93-94. *Mem:* Nat Acad Sci; AAAS; Bot Soc Am; Am Soc Plant Physiol (pres, 75-76); Am Acad Arts & Sci; Akademie der Naturforscher Leopoldina; Deutsche Acad de Natur Forscher Leopoldina. *Res:* Plant growth, development; physiology, biochemistry and molecular biology of photomorphogenesis. *Mailing Add:* 480 Hale St Palo Alto CA 94301-2207

BRIGHAM, ELAINE SUSAN, CATALYSIS. *Current Pos:* SR CHEMIST, UNION CARBIDE CORP, 96- *Personal Data:* b Bryan, Tex, Mar 18, 58. *Educ:* Tex A&M Univ, BS, 80; Univ Houston, MS, 90; Univ Tex, Austin, PhD(chem), 96. *Prof Exp:* Res Tech, Shell Develop Co, 81-90. *Mem:* Am Chem Soc. *Res:* Synthesis and testing of organometallic ligands for hydroformulation. *Mailing Add:* Union Carbide Corp PO Box 2831 South Charleston WV 25303. *Fax:* 304-747-5430; *E-Mail:* aesbrd4@peabody.sct.ucarb.com

BRIGHAM, KENNETH LARRY, PULMONARY PHYSIOLOGY. *Current Pos:* from asst prof to assoc prof, 73-78, assoc biomed eng, 77-78, PROF MED, VANDERBILT UNIV, 78-, PROF BIOMED ENG, 86- *Personal Data:* b Nashville, Tenn, Oct 29, 39; m 59; c 1. *Educ:* David Lipscomb Col, BA, 62; Vanderbilt Univ, MD, 66. *Honors & Awards:* Simon Rodbard mem-lectr, Am Col Chest Physicians, 87. *Prof Exp:* From intern to asst resident internal med, Johns Hopkins Hosp, Baltimore, 66-68; med epidemiologist, Nat Commun Dis Ctr, USPHS Ecol Invest Prog, 68-70; instr internal med, Sch Med, Vanderbilt Univ, 70-71; NIH res fel pulmonary med, Cardiovasc Res Inst, Univ Calif, San Francisco, 71-73. *Concurrent Pos:* Dir, Pulmonary Res, Sch Med, Vanderbilt Univ, 73-76, Specialized Ctr Res, 76-, dir pulmonary med, Med Ctr, 78-; mem pulmonary study sect, Nat Heart & Lung Inst, 75-79; estab investr, Am Heart Asn, 75-88; mem lung res comt, Vet Admin, 76; vpres, Nashville Soc Internal Med, 85; pres-elect, Am Thoracic Soc, 88-89. *Mem:* NY Acad Sci; Am Soc Clin Invest; AAAS; Am Fedn Clin Res; Am Thoracic Soc; Am Physiol Soc; Am Asn Prof; Am Soc Cell Biol; Micros Soc. *Res:* Humoral mechanisms in the pathogenesis of pulmonary edema resulting primarily from changes in the lung circulation. *Mailing Add:* T-1217 Med Ctr N Vanderbilt Univ Sch Med Nashville TN 37232-2650

BRIGHAM, NELSON ALLEN, MATHEMATICS. *Current Pos:* RETIRED. *Personal Data:* b Holyoke, Mass, Nov 6, 15. *Educ:* Rutgers Univ, BS, 37, MS, 38; Univ Pa, PhD(math), 48. *Prof Exp:* Asst, Inst Math, Univ Pa, 38-41; sr res engr, Repub Aviation Corp, NY, 47; asst prof math, Swarthmore Ctr, Pa State Col, 47-48; asst prof, Univ Md, 48-51, mathematician, Appl Physics Lab, 51-56; sr scientist, Avco Mfg Corp, 56-59; prin mathematician, Baird-Atomic, Inc, 59-60; staff mem, Lincoln Lab, Mass Inst Technol, 60-62 & Mitre Corp, 62-64; assoc prof math, Southeastern Mass Tech Inst, 65; prof math & astron & head dept, Butler Univ, 65-70; prof math & chmn dept, Bradley Univ, 70-71; pvt tutoring serv, 71-91. *Mem:* Am Math Soc; Math Asn Am. *Res:* Analytic additive theory of numbers; applied mathematics; digital and analog simulation and programming. *Mailing Add:* 7338 E Naranja Ave Mesa AZ 85208-7223

BRIGHAM, R MARK, BEHAVIORAL ECOLOGY, ZOOLOGY. *Current Pos:* ASSOC PROF BIOL, UNIV REGINA, 90- *Personal Data:* b Barrie, Ont, Feb 24, 60; m 84, Anne C Gunter; c P Anthony & L Keltie. *Educ:* Queens Univ, BSc Hons, 83; Carleton Univ, MSc, 85; York Univ, PhD(biol), 88. *Prof Exp:* Fel, Univ Calgary, 88-90. *Mem:* Am Soc Mammalogists; Animal Behav Soc; Cooper Ornith Soc; Can Soc Zoologists; Asn Field Ornithologists. *Res:* Physiological and behavioral ecology of nocturnal insectivorous birds and bats in temperate regions. *Mailing Add:* Dept Biol Univ Regina Regina SK S4S 0A2 Can. *Fax:* 306-585-4894; *E-Mail:* brigham@max.cc.uregina.ca

BRIGHAM, RAYMOND DALE, PLANT BREEDING. *Current Pos:* CONSULT AGRONOMIST, 93- *Personal Data:* b Stamford, Tex, Apr 1, 26; m 49, Virginia M Trenfield; c 4. *Educ:* Tex Tech Col, BS, 50; Iowa State Col, MS, 52, PhD(crop breeding, plant path), 57. *Prof Exp:* Res agronomist, Agr Res Serv, USDA, 57-67; assoc prof agron, Tex Agr Exp Sta, Tex A&M Univ, Lubbock, 67-93. *Concurrent Pos:* Prog chmn, Int Sunflower Conf, Memphis, 70; vis prof, India, 81; consult, Ministry Agr, Pakistan, 82, Agr Corp, Burma, 88, Costa Rica Ministry Agr, 90, Crop Exp Sta, Korea, 91, Ministry Agr, China, 91, Nicaragua, 93, Zimbabwe & Zambia, 94. *Mem:* AAAS; Am Phytopath Soc; Crop Sci Soc Am; Am Soc Agron; NY Acad Sci. *Res:* Breeding for disease resistance in oilseed crops; inheritance of quantitative and qualitative characteristics. *Mailing Add:* 2314 61st St Lubbock TX 79412. *Fax:* 806-795-4066

BRIGHAM, ROBERT B, ISOLATION OF STREPTOMYCESE ORIENTALIS, DEVELOPMENT OF ISOMERASE. *Current Pos:* DIR RES & DEVELOP, SUNNY FRESH FOODS, 83- *Personal Data:* b Indianapolis, Ind, Mar 28, 25; m 47, Betty Burns; c Thomas, John, Janis, Nancy, Gary & Cynthia. *Educ:* Univ Ill, BS, 53; Butler Univ, MS, 60. *Honors & Awards:* Am Sanitation Award, Huge Inst, 72. *Prof Exp:* Antibiotic res microbiologist, Eli Lilly & Co, 53-65; mgr enzyme res, Standard Brands, 65-68; mgr qual assurance, Ralston Purina, 68-71; dir qual assurance-res & develop, L S Heath & Co, 71-77; dir new prods, Fisher Nut Co, 77-83. *Mem:* Am Soc Microbiol; Am Chem Soc; Nat Confectioner Asn; Am Asn Confectionary Technologists; Inst Food Technologists. *Res:* Techniques developed in antibiotic research adapted to developmental research in enzyme chemistry that has application to glucamylase, alpha amylase research and ultimately the discovery of isomerase research and ultimately the discovery of isomerase, the source of high fructose corn syrup. *Mailing Add:* Sunny Fresh Foods RR 2 Robinson IL 62454

BRIGHAM, WARREN ULRICH, aquatic biology, aquatic entomology; deceased, see previous edition for last biography

BRIGHAM, WILLIAM EVERETT, CHEMICAL ENGINEERING. *Current Pos:* assoc chmn, Dept Petrol Eng, 79-90, actg chmn, 80-81, PROF, STANFORD UNIV, 71- *Personal Data:* b Murphysboro, Ill, Apr 1, 29; m 54, Carol Cobb; c William II, Nancy (Weil), Laura (Jester), Sarah (Fletcher) & David. *Educ:* Iowa State Univ, BS, 50; Univ Okla, MS, 56, PhD(chem eng), 62. *Honors & Awards:* Ferguson Award, Soc Petrol Engrs, 77; John Franklin Carll Award, Soc Petrol Engrs, 88; Homer H Lowry Award Fossil Energy, 90. *Prof Exp:* Chem engr, S C Johnson & Sons, 50-51, 53-54; instr chem eng, Univ Okla, 56-58; res engr, Res & Develop Dept, Continental Oil Co, 58-60, sr res engr, 60-62, res group leader, 62-65, res sect leader, 65-67, res assoc, Prod Res Div, 67-71. *Concurrent Pos:* Mem, Ed Rev Comt, J Petrol Technol & Soc Petrol Engrs J, 65-69; session co-chmn, World Petrol Cong, 76; mem, Geothermal Resources Coun, 77-; Fulbright-Hays grant, Heriot-Watt Univ, Scotland, 78-79; Los Alamos Lab Adv Comt, 82-; mem, Engr Manpower Comt, Soc Petrol Engrs, 85- *Mem:* Soc Petrol Engrs; hon mem Am Inst Mining, Metall & Petrol Engrs. *Res:* Geothermal engineering; enhanced recovery of heavy oil; reservoir mixing theories; new cell test techniques; other transient flow, oil and gas recovery phenomena. *Mailing Add:* Dept Petrol Eng Stanford Univ 88 Green Earth Sci Bldg Stanford CA 94305

BRIGHT, ARTHUR AARON, EXPERIMENTAL SOLID STATE PHYSICS. *Current Pos:* RES SCIENTIST PHYSICS, IBM WATSON RES CTR, 78- *Personal Data:* b Hanover, NH, Dec 31, 46; m 69; c 2. *Educ:* Dartmouth Col, AB, 69, MA, 70; Univ Pa, PhD(physics), 73. *Prof Exp:* Res investr physics, Univ Pa, 73-75; res scientist physics, Union Carbide Corp, Carbon Prod, 75-78. *Concurrent Pos:* Chmn Thin Films Div, Am Vacuum Soc, 91. *Mem:* Am Physics Soc; Am Vacuum Soc; Mat Res Soc. *Res:* Solid state physics; plasma processing of silicon technology materials. *Mailing Add:* IBM Thomas J Watson Res Ctr PO Box 218 Yorktown Heights NY 10598

BRIGHT, DONALD EDWARD, SYSTEMATIC ENTOMOLOGY. *Current Pos:* head, Coleoptera Sect, 72-77, proj leader, Insect Pests Proj, 90-91, RES SCIENTIST, AGR & AGRI-FOOD CAN, CAN DEPT AGR, 66- *Personal Data:* b Columbus, Ohio, Feb 10, 34; m 60, 93, Barbara Barr; c Jeffrey, Jill, Jordon & Jason. *Educ:* Colo State Univ, Ft Collins, BSc, 57; Brigham Young Univ, MSc, 61; Univ Calif, Berkeley, PhD(entom), 65. *Prof Exp:* Asst res entomologist, Dept Entom, Univ Calif, 65-66. *Concurrent Pos:* Mem, Syst Res Comt, Entom Soc Am, 79-87, Sci Pol Comt, Entom Soc Can, 79-84, Biol Coun Can, 79-84; gen chmn ann meeting, Entom Soc Can, 85, mem, Ethics Comt, 89-91; vis res scientist, Inst fur Forstentomologie, Wien, Austria, 91; vis scholar, Univ Calif, Berkeley, 91-92. *Mem:* Entom Soc Am; Sigma Xi; Coleopterists Soc (secy, 84-); Entom Soc Can (treas, 86-90). *Res:* Systematics and biology of Scolytidae coleoptera; general biology of forest coleoptera; forest entomology. *Mailing Add:* Res Br Agri & Agn-Food Can Ottawa ON K1A 0C6 Can. *Fax:* 613-995-1823

BRIGHT, GEORGE WALTER, MATHEMATICS EDUCATION. *Current Pos:* PROF EDUC, UNIV NC, GREENSBORO, 90- *Personal Data:* b Port Arthur, Tex, Apr 24, 45. *Educ:* Rice Univ, BA, 68, MA, 69; Univ Tex, Austin, PhD(math educ), 71. *Prof Exp:* From asst prof to assoc prof math, Northern Ill Univ, 71-83; assoc prof, Univ Calgary, 84-85; from assoc prof to prof cur & instr, Univ Houston, 85-90. *Concurrent Pos:* Asst prof math, Emory Univ, 74-76; vis assoc prof, Univ Wis-Madison, 79-80; mem, Res Coun Diag & Prescriptive Math. *Mem:* Nat Coun Teachers Math; Math Asn Am; Am Educ Res Asn. *Res:* Supplementary instructional techniques, games and technology in teaching mathematics; effective teaching inservice; statistics education. *Mailing Add:* Sch Educ Univ NC Greensboro NC 27412-5001. *Fax:* 910-334-4120; *E-Mail:* brightg@steffi.uncg.edu

BRIGHT, GORDON STANLEY, CHEMISTRY. *Current Pos:* RETIRED. *Personal Data:* b Smethport, Pa, Apr 29, 15; m 39; c 3. *Educ:* Tusculum Col, AB, 38; Univ Cincinnati, MS, 39. *Prof Exp:* Head, Dept Sci, Pfeiffer Col, 39-40; res chemist, Texaco Inc, 40-54, supvr, Grease Res Dept, 54-62, res assoc, 62-80. *Mem:* Fel AAAS; fel Nat Lubricating Grease Inst; Am Chem Soc; Am Soc Lubrication Eng *Res:* Grease and other lubricants. *Mailing Add:* One Whitehall Lane Hendersonville NC 28739-7027

BRIGHT, HAROLD FREDERICK, STATISTICS. *Current Pos:* chmn dept statist, 58-64, assoc dean faculties, 64-66, PROF STATIST, GEORGE WASHINGTON UNIV, 58-, VPRES ACAD AFFAIRS, 66-, PROVOST, 69- *Personal Data:* b Smethport, Pa, Aug 6, 13; m 38; c 2. *Educ:* Lake Forest Col, BA, 37; Univ Rochester, MS, 44; Univ Tex, PhD(educ psychol), 52. *Prof Exp:* Asst prof math, Denison Univ, 43-44 & Univ Rochester, 44-45; registr & dir guid, San Angelo Col, 45-49; assoc dir res, Am Asn Jr Cols, Univ Tex, 49-52; chief tech serv, Human Resources Res Off, George Washington Univ, 52-54, dept dir, 54-56; specialist opers res & synthesis, Gen Elec Co, 57-58. *Mem:* AAAS; Am Psychol Asn; Inst Math Statist; Am Statist Asn; Math Asn Am; Sigma Xi. *Res:* Teaching of statistics; computing problems; operations research. *Mailing Add:* 4132 Northwest Blvd 101 Davenport IA 52806-4244

BRIGHT, PETER BOWMAN, technical management, for more information see previous edition

BRIGHT, ROBERT C, GEOLOGY. *Current Pos:* RETIRED. *Personal Data:* b Salt Lake City, Utah, Dec 27, 28. *Educ:* Univ Utah, BS, 52, MS, 60; Univ Minn, PhD(geol), 63. *Prof Exp:* Instr geol, Univ Minn, 59; NSF fel, Royal Univ Uppsala, 63-64; assoc prof geol, Univ Minn, Minneapolis, 64-, cur paleont, Mus Natural Hist, 64-, dir, Wasatch-Uinta Field Geol Camp, 67-72, assoc prof ecol, 71-; assoc dir, Bell Mus, 78- *Mem:* AAAS; Am Asn Petrol Geologists; fel Geol Soc Am; Paleont Soc; Am Soc Limnol & Oceanog; Sigma Xi. *Res:* Pleistocene stratigraphy, paleontology; paleoecology and paleolimnology. *Mailing Add:* Bell Mus 10 Church St Minneapolis MN 55455

BRIGHT, THOMAS J, BIOLOGICAL OCEANOGRAPHY. *Current Pos:* from asst prof to assoc prof oceanog, 69-81, PROF OCEANOG, TEX A&M UNIV, 81- *Personal Data:* b Millen, Ga, Sept 2, 37; m 60; c 2. *Educ:* Univ Wyo, BS, 64; Tex A&M Univ, PhD(biol oceanog), 68. *Prof Exp:* Asst prof biol & invert zool, Jacksonville Univ, 68-69. *Mem:* Am Soc Limnol & Oceanog. *Res:* Ecology of coral reefs and hard-banks. *Mailing Add:* 9812 Runaway Rd College Station TX 77845

BRIGHT, WILLARD MEAD, PHYSICAL CHEMISTRY. *Current Pos:* CHMN & DIR, ZMI CORP, 82- *Personal Data:* b New York, NY, Mar 26, 14; m 44, 81; c 1. *Educ:* Univ Toledo, BS, 36; Harvard Univ, MA, 41, PhD(chem), 42. *Prof Exp:* Res chemist, Kendall Co, 41-44; res chemist, Bauer & Black, 44-46, group leader, 46-48; dir, Clark Lab, Kendall Co, 48-52; asst res dir, Lever Bros Co, 52-54, dir res & develop, 54-60, vpres, 60-64, dir, 62-64; vpres & dir, R J Reynolds Tobacco Co, 64-68; sr vpres & dir, Warner-Lambert Pharmaceut Co, 68-70; pres, chief exec officer & dir, Kendall Co, 70-73; pres & dir, Curtiss-Wright Corp, 74-75; pres & dir, Boehringer Mannheim Corp, 75-82. *Concurrent Pos:* Mem bd vis, dept chem, Harvard, 59-61; vis com, dept chem engr, Univ Rochester, 62-64; trustee, Corn Indust Res Found, 65-68; mem, Adv Comt on Patents, US Dept Com, 66-69; chmn, Res Comt, Nat Asn Mfrs, 66-68; dir, Am Found Pharmaceut Educ, 69-71; mem bd vis, Dept Chem, Boston Univ, 77- *Mem:* Nat Asn Mfrs; AAAS; NY Acad Sci; Am Chem Soc; Indust Res Inst (pres, 67-68). *Mailing Add:* 112 Prestwick Circle Vero Beach FL 32967

BRIGHTMAN, I JAY, MEDICINE, PUBLIC HEALTH. *Current Pos:* CONSULT HEALTH PLANNING, 73- *Personal Data:* b New York, NY, Oct 28, 09; m 35; c 3. *Educ:* NY Univ, BS, 30, MD, 34, MedScD(internal med), 40; Am Bd Internal Med, dipl, 41; Columbia Univ, MPH, 43; Am Bd Prev Med, dipl, 55. *Prof Exp:* Dir res proj, Div Syphilis Control, NY State Dept Health, 41-42, dir res proj, Veneral Dis Control, Buffalo, 43-45, asst dir div, 45-46, assoc physician, Div Med Serv, 46-48, asst dir div, 48-50, asst comnr, 50-51, asst comnr welfare med serv, 52-56, exec dir, Health Resources Bd, 56-60, asst comnr chronic dis control, 60-66, dep comnr med serv & res, 66-69; dir, New York Metrop Regional Med Prog, 69-72. *Concurrent Pos:* Assoc prof, Albany Med Col, 51-; mem, Comt Welfare Serv, AMA, 54-60, consult, 60; mem, Nat Adv Community Health Comt, USPHS, 62-73. *Mem:* Fel Am Col Physicians; Am Col Prev Med. *Res:* Chronic illness, especially natural history of disease, need for specialized resources and personnel, and medical economics. *Mailing Add:* 30 South Ave Spring Valley NY 10977-5419

BRIGHTMAN, MILTON WILFRED, NEUROANATOMY. *Current Pos:* NEUROANATOMIST, LAB NEUROANAT SCI, NAT INST NEUROL DIS & BLINDNESS, 54- *Personal Data:* b Toronto, Ont, July 13, 23; nat US; m 53; c 2. *Educ:* Univ Toronto, AB, 45, AM, 48; Yale Univ, PhD(anat), 54. *Mem:* Am Asn Anat. *Res:* Perivascular spaces in brain; neurosecretion; blood supply of spinal cord; neurocytology. *Mailing Add:* Neurolbiol Lab Bldg 36 Rm 2A21 NIH 9000 Rockville Pike Bethesda MD 20892-4062

BRIGHTMAN, VERNON, DENTISTRY, ORAL MEDICINE. *Current Pos:* from assoc to prof oral med, Sch Dent Med, Univ Pa, 64-90, actg chmn dept oral med, 78-, prof otorhinolaryngol, 73-90, mem staff, 73-80, dir, Clin Res Ctr, Children's Hosp, 84-, PROG DIR, GEN CLIN RES CTR, SCH DENT MED & PROF ORAL MED, UNIV PA, 84- *Personal Data:* b Brisbane, Australia, Dec 17, 30; m 62; c 3. *Educ:* Univ Queensland, BDSc, Hons, 52, MDSc, 56; Univ Chicago, PhD(microbiol), 60; Univ Pa, DMD, 68. *Honors & Awards:* Univ Medal, Univ Queensland, 52. *Prof Exp:* Lectr dent, Univ Queensland, 52-56; asst, Zoller Dent Clin, Univ Chicago, 56-60; instr microbiol, Univ Pa, 60-62; sr lectr, Univ Queensland, 62-64. *Concurrent Pos:* Chief dent res, Philadelphia Gen Hosp, 64-72; vis prof dept anat, Sch Vet Med, Cornell Univ, 75-76; asst dean fac develop, Sch Dent Med, Univ Pa, 92- *Mem:* Fel AAAS; fel Am Acad Oral Path; fel Am Acad Oral Med; Int Asn Dent Res; Am Dent Asn. *Res:* Oral medicine and pathology. *Mailing Add:* Gen Clin Res Ctr 4001 Spruce St Philadelphia PA 19104

BRIGHTON, CARL T, ORTHOPEDIC SUGERY. *Current Pos:* from asst prof to prof, 68-77, PAUL B MAGNUSON PROF BONE & JOINT SURG, UNIV PA, 77-, CHMN DEPT ORTHOP SURG, 77-, DIR ORTHOP RES, 68- *Personal Data:* b Pana, Ill, Aug 20, 31; m 54; c 4. *Educ:* Valparaiso Univ, BA, 53; Univ Pa, MD, 57; Univ Ill, Chicago Circle, PhD(anat), 69; Am Bd Orthop Surg, dipl, 65. *Honors & Awards:* Shands Lect Award, Orthop Res Soc, 85; Merit Award, Nat Inst Arthritis & Musculoskeletal & Skin Dis, 87. *Prof Exp:* Staff orthopedist, Philadelphia Naval Hosp, USN, 62-63, Great Lakes Naval Hosp, Ill, 63-66 & USS Sanctuary, South China Sea, 66-67. *Concurrent Pos:* NIH res career develop award, 71-76; mem, NAMSD Adv Coun, NIH, 88-92. *Mem:* Orthop Res Soc; fel Am Acad Orhtop Surg; fel Am Col Surgeons; Bioelec Repair & Growth Soc; Am Orthop Asn. *Res:* Epiphyseal plate growth and development; fracture healing; arthritis and articular cartilage preservation and transplantation; bioelectricity; osteoporosis. *Mailing Add:* Dept Orthop Hosp Univ Pa 3400 Spruce St Philadelphia PA 19104-4220

BRIGHTON, JOHN AUSTIN, MECHANICAL & BIOMEDICAL ENGINEERING. *Current Pos:* CHMN DEPT MECH ENG, MICH STATE UNIV, 77- *Personal Data:* b Gosport, Ind, July 9, 34; m 53; c 2. *Educ:* Purdue Univ, BS, 59, MS, 60, PhD(mech eng), 63. *Prof Exp:* Lab technician, Schwitzer Corp, 52-57; instr mech eng, Purdue Univ, 60-62; asst prof, Carnegie Inst Technol, 62-66; assoc prof, Pa State Univ, 66-77. *Concurrent Pos:* NSF grant, 64-65; consult, Nat Heart & Lung Inst, NIH, 78; tech ed, J Biomech Eng, Am Soc Mech Engrs. *Mem:* Am Soc Mech Engrs; Am Soc Eng Educ; Sigma Xi. *Res:* Fluid mechanics; study of the structure of turbulence in the flow of incompressible fluids; the structure of hypersonic turbulent wakes and boundary layers; biofluid mechanics; cardiovascular dynamics; blood flow. *Mailing Add:* Pa State Univ 201 Old Main University Park PA 16802-1503

BRIGHTWELL, DENNIS RICHARD, mental health administration, for more information see previous edition

BRIGNAC, PAUL JOSEPH, ANALYTICAL CHEMISTRY, SPECTROSCOPY. *Current Pos:* ASSOC STATE CHEMIST & ASSOC PROF CHEM LAB, MISS STATE UNIV, 79- *Personal Data:* b New Orleans, La, Feb 2, 44; m 68, Helene Roger; c Celeste, Rene, Angelle & Nicole. *Educ:* Univ New Orleans, BS, 66, PhD(analytical chem), 69. *Prof Exp:* From asst prof to assoc prof, Northwestern State Univ, 69-79. *Mem:* Asn Official Analytical Chem; Soc Qual Assurance. *Res:* Kinetic methods of analysis; ion selective electrodes; pularography; gas chromotography; high pressure liquid chromotography; quality assurance; metal complexation; coupled enzyme assay systems. *Mailing Add:* 2415 Douglas McArthur Starkville MS 39759. *Fax:* 601-325-7807; *E-Mail:* paul@cyber1.mscl.msstate.edu

BRIGNOLI GABLE, CAROL, risk analysis, for more information see previous edition

BRILES, CONNALLY ORAN, IMMUNOGENETICS. *Current Pos:* prof biol, 69-71, PROF ANIMAL SCI, TUSKEGEE INST, 72- *Personal Data:* b Idabel, Okla, Dec 10, 19; m 45; c 2. *Educ:* Agr & Mech Col Tex, BS, 49, MS, 51; Univ Wis, PhD, 55. *Prof Exp:* Asst poultry husb, Agr Exp Sta, La State Univ, 55-57; asst to head poultry breeding sect, USDA, Md, 57-58; geneticist & dir blood grouping lab chickens, Arbor Acres Farm, Inc, 58-62; assoc prof animal sci & genetics, Macdonald Col, McGill Univ, 63-69. *Concurrent Pos:* Breeding & incubation expert, Food & Agr Orgn, UN, Karachi, Pakistan, 71-72. *Mem:* Genetics Soc Am; Poultry Sci Asn; World's Poultry Sci Asn; Int Soc Animal Blood Group Res. *Res:* Blood groups in domestic animals and humans; association of blood group genotypes with economic and morphological characteristics in chickens; general poultry breeding; basic and practical interaction of genetic traits and environment in poultry; genetic selection and utilization of nutrients in poultry. *Mailing Add:* 1001 S Dean Rd Auburn AL 36830

BRILES, DAVID ELWOOD, PATHOGENESIS, INFECTIOUS DISEASE. *Current Pos:* from asst prof to assoc prof, 78-85, PROF MICROBIOL, UNIV ALA, BIRMINGHAM, 85-, ASSOC PROF PEDIAT, 84-, SR SCIENTIST, CANCER CTR, 83- *Personal Data:* b Hempstead, NY, May 25, 45; m 83; c 2. *Educ:* Univ Tex, Austin, BA, 67; Rockefeller Univ, PhD(immunogenetics), 73. *Prof Exp:* Res instr immunol, dept microbiol, Wash Sch Med, St Louis, Mo, 75-78. *Mem:* Am Asn Immunologists; Am Soc Microbiol. *Res:* Genetic control of bacterial pathogenesis. *Mailing Add:* Dept Microbiol 658 BRBB UAB Sta Univ Ala Birmingham AL 35294-2170

BRILES, GEORGE HERBERT, ORGANIC CHEMISTRY. *Current Pos:* assoc prof, 65-80, PROF CHEM, SOUTHAMPTON COL, LONG ISLAND UNIV, 80- *Personal Data:* b Neodesha, Kans, Sept 15, 37. *Educ:* Univ Kans, BS, 60; Whittier Col, MS, 61; Univ Mass, PhD(org chem), 66. *Prof Exp:* Chemist, US Borax Res Corp, 61. *Mem:* Am Chem Soc. *Res:* Properties and reactions of pentavalent organoantimony compounds. *Mailing Add:* RR 2 Box 219 Neodesha KS 66757-9407

BRILES, WORTHIE ELWOOD, IMMUNOGENETICS, POULTRY GENETICS. *Current Pos:* prof, 70-87, ADJ PROF & EMER PROF IMMUNOGENETICS, NORTHERN ILL UNIV, 87- *Personal Data:* b Italy, Tex, Jan 31, 18; m 41; c 3. *Educ:* Univ Tex, BA, 41; Univ Wis, PhD(genetics, poultry breeding), 48. *Honors & Awards:* Res Prize, Poultry Sci Asn, 51. *Prof Exp:* Res asst genetics, Univ Wis, 41-42, 45-47, instr genetics & zool, 47; res asst genetics, Tex A&M Univ, 47-48, from asst prof to assoc prof poultry husb, 48-57; immunogeneticist, De Kalb AgRes, Inc, 57-70. *Mem:* AAAS; Genetics Soc Am; Am Genetic Asn; fel Poultry Sci Asn; Am Asn Immunol. *Res:* Blood groups of chickens; physiological effects of blood group genes; alloantigens and disease resistance. *Mailing Add:* Dept Biol Sci Northern Ill Univ De Kalb IL 60115-2861. *Fax:* 815-753-0461

BRILEY, BRUCE EDWIN, ELECTRICAL ENGINEERING. *Current Pos:* MEM STAFF, BELL TEL LABS, NAPERVILLE, 66- *Personal Data:* b Chicago, Ill, June 24, 36; m 59; c 4. *Educ:* Univ Ill, BS, 58, MS, 59, PhD(elec eng), 63. *Prof Exp:* Asst digital comput lab, Univ Ill, 59-63; sr engr, Automatic Elec Res Labs, Gen Tel & Electronics Corp, Northlake, 63-64, mgr device appln res, 64-65, mgr electronic switching systs dept, 65-66. *Concurrent Pos:* Lectr grad sch, Ill Inst Technol, 64- *Mem:* Inst Elec & Electronics Engrs. *Res:* Memory and logic devices, systems and philosophies associated with digital computer design. *Mailing Add:* 5650 S Madison La Grange IL 60525

BRILL, A BERTRAND, NUCLEAR MEDICINE. *Current Pos:* PROF RADIOL, STATE UNIV NY, STONY BROOK, 79- *Personal Data:* b New York, NY, Dec 19, 28; m 50; c 3. *Educ:* Grinnell Col, AB, 49; Univ Utah, MD, 56; Univ Calif, Berkeley, PhD(biophys), 61. *Prof Exp:* Med dir, Div Radiol Health, USPHS, 57-64; assoc prof med & radiol, Sch Med, Vanderbilt Univ, 64-71, assoc prof biomed eng & biophys, 69-71, assoc prof physics, 70-71, prof med, radiol, biomed eng, biophys & physics, 71-79. *Mem:* AAAS; Soc Nuclear Med; Radiation Res Soc; Am Thyroid Asn. *Res:* Radiation leukemogenesis; effects of radiation on thyroid function; diagnostic radioisotope studies. *Mailing Add:* Dept Nuclear Med Univ Mass Med Ctr 55 Lake Ave Worcester MA 01609-0002

BRILL, ARTHUR SYLVAN, SPECTROSCOPY & SPECTROMETRY, ELECTRON TRANSFER & REDOX PROCESSES IN METALLOPROTEINS. *Current Pos:* mem, Ctr Advan Studies, Univ Va, 68-71, prof mat, 68-73, dir, Biophys Prog, 89-93, PROF PHYSICS, UNIV VA, 73- *Personal Data:* b Philadelphia, Pa, June 11, 27; m 57, Patricia Hartig; c Julie A & Claire B. *Educ:* Univ Calif, Berkeley, AB, 49; Univ Pa, PhD(biophys), 56. *Prof Exp:* Res assoc, Electron Micros Lab, Cornell Univ, 50-61; asst prof biophys, Yale Univ, 61-64, assoc prof molecular biol & biophys, 64-68. *Concurrent Pos:* Fel med physics, Univ Pa, 56-58; Donner fel, Med Sci Div, Nat Res Coun, Clarendon Lab, Oxford Univ, 58-59; chairperson, Div Biol Physics, Am Physics Soc, 75-76 & 90-91; assoc ed, Biophys J, 78-81. *Mem:* Fel Am Phys Soc; Biophys Soc; Electron Micros Soc Am; Am Chem Soc; Am Asn Physics Teachers; Int Electron Paramagnetic Resonance Soc. *Res:* Molecular biophysics; mechanisms of enzyme action; transition metal ions in biology; protein structure and dynamics; fundamental limitations of measuring instruments; physical chemistry; electron transfer processes in proteins. *Mailing Add:* Dept Physics Univ Va Charlottesville VA 22901

BRILL, DIETER RUDOLF, THEORETICAL PHYSICS. *Current Pos:* PROF PHYSICS, UNIV MD, COLLEGE PARK, 70- *Personal Data:* b Heidelberg, Ger, Aug 9, 33; m 71, Birgit Bramstedt; c 1. *Educ:* Princeton Univ, AB, 54, MA, 56, PhD(physics), 59. *Honors & Awards:* Humboldt Found Sr US Scientist Award. *Prof Exp:* Instr physics, Princeton Univ, 59-60; Flick exchange res fel, Univ Hamburg, 60-61; from instr to assoc prof, Yale Univ, 61-70. *Concurrent Pos:* Vis prof, Univ Wurzburg ,68; vis prof, Max Planck Inst Physics & Astrophys, Garching, Ger, 72, 75, 84 & 92; vis lectr, Col de France, Paris, 77. *Mem:* Sigma Xi; fel Am Phys Soc. *Res:* General relativity and gravitation physics; foundation of quantum mechanics; light, color, perception pedagogy for non-scientists. *Mailing Add:* Dept Physics Univ Md College Park MD 20742

BRILL, JAMES P, PETROLEUM ENGINEERING, MULTI PHASE FLOW IN PIPES. *Current Pos:* prof eng, 66-87, FLOYD M STEVENSON DISTINGUISHED PROF PETROL ENG, UNIV TULSA, 87- *Personal Data:* b Minneapolis, Minn, July 18, 38. *Educ:* Univ Minn, BS, 62; Univ Tex, Austin, PhD(eng), 66. *Honors & Awards:* Prod Eng Award, Soc Petrol Engrs, 94, Distinguished Achievement Award for Petrol Eng Fac, 94. *Prof Exp:* Res engr, Chevron Oil Co, 65-66. *Mem:* Nat Acad Eng. *Mailing Add:* Dept Eng Tulsa Univ 600 S College Tulsa OK 74104. *Fax:* 918-631-5112; *E-Mail:* pe-jpb@centum.utulsa.edu

BRILL, JOSEPH WARREN, SOLID STATE PHYSICS, ACOUSTICS. *Current Pos:* from asst prof to assoc prof, 80-89, PROF PHYSICS, UNIV KY, 89- *Personal Data:* b New York, NY, Oct 3, 50; m 85, Yolanda Musgrave. *Educ:* Columbia Univ, AB, 72; Stanford Univ, MS, 76, PhD(physics), 78. *Prof Exp:* Res assoc physics, Univ Southern Calif, 78-79. *Mem:* AAAS; Am Phys Soc. *Res:* Properties of low-one-dimensional crystals; transport, thermal, optical and elastic measurements of crystals. *Mailing Add:* Dept Physics & Astron Univ Ky Lexington KY 40506-0055. *E-Mail:* jwbrill@ukcc.uky.edu

BRILL, KENNETH GRAY, JR, PALEONTOLOGY. *Current Pos:* from asst prof to prof geol, 46-79, chmn, Dept Geol & Geol Eng, 67-69, EMER PROF GEOL, ST LOUIS UNIV, 79- *Personal Data:* b St Paul, Minn, Nov 16, 10; m 39, Priscilla Ritchie; c David R & Thomas B. *Educ:* Univ Minn, AB, 35; Univ Mich, MS, 38, PhD(geol), 39. *Honors & Awards:* Fulbright lectr, Univ Tasmania, 53. *Prof Exp:* Asst geol, Yale Univ, 36-37; from instr to assoc prof geol & geog, Univ Chattanooga, 39-44; geologist, US Geol Surv, 44-45. *Concurrent Pos:* Spec coal consult, Econ Coop Admin, SKorea, 49; hon res assoc, Univ Tasmania, 78. *Mem:* Fel AAAS; Paleont Soc; fel Geol Soc Am; Am Asn Petrol Geol. *Res:* Permo-carboniferous stratigraphy and paleontology; paleozoic stratigraphy of Rocky Mountain region. *Mailing Add:* 120 W Adams Ave St Louis MO 63122

BRILL, ROBERT H, ARCHAEOLOGICAL CHEMISTRY, ART CONSERVATION. *Current Pos:* dir, 72-75, RES SCIENTIST, CORNING MUS GLASS, 60- *Personal Data:* b Irvington, NJ, May 7, 29; m 57, Margaret R; c Elizabeth R. *Educ:* Upsala Col, BS, 51; Rutgers Univ, PhD(phys chem), 55. *Honors & Awards:* Eugene C Sullivan Award, Am Chem Soc, 87. *Prof Exp:* Asst prof chem, Upsala Col, 54-60. *Concurrent Pos:* Hon chmn, Am Tech Comt, Corpus Vitrearm, 86. *Mem:* Am Chem Soc; Am Ceramic Soc; Int Inst Conserv; Sigma Xi. *Res:* Archaeological chemistry; scientific examination of archaeological materials, particularly ancient glass; history of science and technology; glass chemistry; photochemistry. *Mailing Add:* Corning Mus Glass Corning NY 14831

BRILL, THOMAS BARTON, INORGANIC CHEMISTRY, PHYSICAL CHEMISTRY. *Current Pos:* From asst prof to assoc prof, 70-79, actg chmn, 85-86, PROF CHEM, UNIV DEL, 79-, PROF ART CONSERV, 87-, PROF CHEM ENG, 92- *Personal Data:* b Chattanooga, Tenn, Feb 3, 44; m 66; c 2. *Educ:* Univ Mont, BS, 66; Univ Minn, Minneapolis, PhD(chem), 70. *Concurrent Pos:* Prin investr, Air Force Off Sci Res & Army Res Off, 74; vis prof, Univ Ore, 78; consult, Morton-Thiokol Inc, Lawrence Livermore Nat Lab, CDS Instruments, Conoco Oil, 83-; nat lectr, Sigma Xi, 84-87; chmn, Gordon Res Conf Energetic Mats, 90; vis prof, Zhongshan Univ, China. *Mem:* Am Chem Soc; Sigma Xi; Combustion Inst; Mat Res Soc; Soc Appl Spectros. *Res:* Infrared and Raman spectroscopy; solid state effects; thermal decomposition studies; explosions; supercritical water; combustion. *Mailing Add:* Dept Chem Univ Del Newark DE 19716-0002

BRILL, WILFRED G, PHYSICS. *Current Pos:* Res assoc physics, 64-67, asst prof to assoc prof, 67-74, FAC PURDUE UNIV, N CENT CAMPUS, 74- *Personal Data:* b Albion, Ind, Aug 11, 30; m 54; c 2. *Educ:* Manchester Col, BA, 52; Purdue Univ, MS, 55, PhD(physics), 64. *Mem:* Am Asn Physics Teachers. *Res:* Atomic spectroscopy. *Mailing Add:* Dept Math & Physics Purdue Univ N Cent Campus Westville IN 46391-9528

BRILL, WILLIAM FRANKLIN, OXIDATION, CATALYSIS. *Current Pos:* CONSULT, 90- *Personal Data:* b Utica, NY, 1923; m 51, Yvonne Claeys; c Naomi, Matthew & Joseph. *Educ:* Univ Conn, BS, 45, MS, 48, PhD(chem), 50. *Prof Exp:* Res assoc org chem, Univ Calif, Los Angeles, 50-52; chemist, Polymers Sect, Olin Industs, 52-55; group leader oxidations, Petro-Tex, 55-60, res assoc, 60-66; dir chem res, Princeton Chem Res, 66-69; sr scientist, Halcon Res, 69-86; Dana fel, Drew Univ, 86-90. *Concurrent Pos:* Vis fel, Princeton Univ, 90- *Mem:* Am Chem Soc; NY Acad Sci; Catalyst Soc. *Res:* Reaction mechanisms; oxidations; catalysis; asymmetric oxidations. *Mailing Add:* 914 Rte 518 Skillman NJ 08558. *Fax:* 609-921-8689

BRILL, WINSTON J, MICROBIOLOGY, BIOCHEMICAL GENETICS. *Current Pos:* PRES, WINSTON J BRILL & ASSOCS, 89- *Personal Data:* b London, Eng, June 16, 39; US citizen; m 65; c 1. *Educ:* Rutgers Univ, BS, 61; Univ Ill, Urbana, PhD(microbiol), 65. *Honors & Awards:* Eli Lilly Award Microbiol & Immunol, 79; Alexander von Humboldt Award, 79. *Prof Exp:* NIH fel biol, Mass Inst Technol, 65-67; prof bact, Univ Wis-Madison, 67-81; dir res, Agracetus, 81-89. *Concurrent Pos:* Res grants, USPHS, 68-, NIH & NSF, 69-; panel mem, Metab Biol Prog, NSF, 74-77; USDA competitive grants prog, 78; mem, NIH Recombinant DNA Adv Panel, 79-83 & Policy Adv Comt, USDA; adj prof, Univ Wis-Madison. *Mem:* Nat Acad Sci; fel AAAS; Am Soc Microbiol; Am Soc Plant Physiologists. *Res:* Electron transport; ferredoxin; regulation of catabolism; microbial physiology; nitrogen fixation; catabolite repression; soil microbiology; plant molecular biology. *Mailing Add:* 4134 Cherokee Dr Madison WI 53711. *Fax:* 608-231-6794; *E-Mail:* wbrill@vms.macc.wisc.edu

BRILL, YVONNE CLAEYS, LIQUID ROCKET PROPULSION, SOLID ROCKET PROPULSION. *Current Pos:* CONSULT, 91- *Personal Data:* b Man, Can, Dec 30, 24; US citizen; m 51, William Franklin; c Naomi, Matthew & Joseph. *Educ:* Univ Man, Winnipeg, BSc, 45; Univ Southern Calif, Los Angeles, MS, 51. *Honors & Awards:* Marvin C Demlar Award, Am Inst Aeronaut & Astronaut, 83; Achievement Award, Soc Women Engrs, 86; Resnik Challenger Medal, Soc Women Engrs, 93. *Prof Exp:* Mathematician, Aircraft Design Douglas Aircraft Co, 45-46; res analyst propulsion & propellants, Rand Corp, 46-49; group leader igniters & fuels, Marquardt Corp, 49-52; staff engr combustion, United Technol, 52-55; proj engr preliminary design, Wright Aeronaut, 55-58; consult propulsion & propellants, FMC Corp, 58-66; mgr propulsion, 66-81, staff engr preliminary design, RCA Astro Electronics, 83-86; mgr solid rocket motor, NASA Hq, 81-83; staff mem, Space Eng Int Maritime Satellite Orgn, 86-91. *Concurrent Pos:* Mem joint Army, Navy, NASA & Air Force Hydrazine Working Group, 70-77; mem liquid rocket tech comt, Am Inst Aeronaut & Astronaut, 73-76; dir student affairs, Nat Exec Comn, Soc Women Engrs, 79-80 & 83-84, treas, 80-81; mem, USAF Sci Adv Bd, 82-83; educt comt, Int Astronaut Fed, 83-85; mem, Career Enhancement Comt, Am Inst Aeronaut & Astronaut, 84-86; mem, Space Syst Technol Workshop, USAF & Am Inst Aeronaut & Astronaut, 85-86; mem, Comt Advan Solid Rocket Motor Qual & Test Prog, Nat Res Coun, 91, Comt Earth to Orbit: An Assessment of Transp Options, Nat Res Coun, 92; mem, NASA Aerospace Safety Adv Panel, 94- *Mem:* Nat Acad Eng; fel Am Inst Aeronaut & Astronaut; fel Soc Women Engrs; Acad Int Astronaut; Brit Interplanatary Soc; Sigma Xi. *Res:* Ramjet, turbojet, turbofan and spacecraft rocket propulsion. *Mailing Add:* 914 Rte 518 Skillman NJ 08558

BRILLER, STANLEY A, BIOMEDICAL ENGINEERING, CARDIOLOGY. *Current Pos:* PROF MED, MED COL PA, 88- *Personal Data:* b New York, NY, Dec 4, 22. *Educ:* Yale Univ, BS, 45; NY Univ, MD, 47. *Hon Degrees:* MA, Univ Pa, 71. *Prof Exp:* prof eng & med, Carnegie Mellon Univ, 74- *Concurrent Pos:* Dir, Heart Sta, Allegheny Gen Hosp, 73- *Mem:* Biomed Eng Soc; Biophys Soc; Sigma Xi; Harvey Soc. *Mailing Add:* 524 East Dr Sewickley PA 15143-1115

BRILLHART, DONALD D, CHEMICAL ENGINEERING. *Current Pos:* LIPO-TECH, INC CLEVELAND, OH. *Personal Data:* b McClure, Ohio, Jan 25, 18; m 48; c 2. *Educ:* Cleveland State Univ, BChE, 48. *Prof Exp:* Chemist, Aluminum Co Am, 38-43 & Stevens Grease & Oil Co, 48-53; lubrication engr, Prof-Chem, Inc, 53-69, chem engr, 69-85. *Mem:* AAAS; Asn Consult Chemists & Chem Engrs; Am Soc Lubrication Engrs; Am Chem Soc. *Res:* Lubrication; corrosion; industrial processes; lipids; synthetic organic and natural products chemistry. *Mailing Add:* R4 Box 655A Marshall TX 75670

BRILLIANT, HOWARD MICHAEL, AEROSPACE PROPULSION, AERODYNAMICS. *Current Pos:* chief spec prof off, Aero Propulsion Lab, Air Force Wright Aeronaut Lab, 86-88, dep dir, Adv Propulsion Div, Aero Propulsion Lab, 88-89, mids prog mgr, 89-90, dir systs eng, Joint Tactical Info Distrib Syst, Joint Prof Off, Electronics Systs Div, 90-91, DEP DIR, AERO PROPULSION & POWER DIRECTORATE, WRIGHT LAB, 91- *Personal Data:* b Baltimore, Md, Aug 15, 45; m 78; c Rochelle & Amy. *Educ:* Univ Pittsburgh, BSME, 66; Univ Mich, MSE, 67, PhD(aerospace eng), 71. *Prof Exp:* Proj engr, USAF, Aero Propulsion Lab, Wright-Patterson AFB, 70-75; from instr to asst prof aeronaut, USAF Acad, 75-78, assoc prof, 78-80; chief, Chem Laser Technol Group & Fluid Mech Br, Air Force Weapons Lab, 80-84, from Europ prog mgr to actg dir acquisition suppnt, Dep Propulsion, Aeronaut Systs Div, 84-86. *Concurrent Pos:* Consult, NASA Dryden Flight

Res Ctr, 76-78. *Mem:* Am Inst Aeronaut & Astronaut; Sigma Xi; Am Soc Mech Engrs; Am Soc Eng Educ. *Res:* Airbreathing propulsion including scramjets; transonic, supersonic and hypersonic aerodynamics; boundary layer flows; laser aerodynamics, kinetics, systems; power systems and technology. *Mailing Add:* 3590 Timbrook Ct Dayton OH 45431-2529

BRILLIANT, LAWRENCE BRENT, EPIDEMIOLOGY, PUBLIC HEALTH. *Current Pos:* DIR, SEVA FOUND, SAN RAFAEL, CALIF, 78-; PRES & OWNER, BRILLIANT COLOR CARDS, 89- *Personal Data:* b Detroit, Mich, May 5, 44; m 69; c 1. *Educ:* Wayne State Univ, MD, 69; Univ Mich, MPH, 77; Ctr Dis Control, cert, 77. *Honors & Awards:* Health Minister's Award, Govt India, 75; Plaque, India Soc Malaria & Other Commun Dis, 75. *Prof Exp:* Med officer epidemiol, WHO, 73-76 & 80-81; asst prof pub health, Univ Mich, 77-81, asst prof epidemiol, 81-89. *Concurrent Pos:* Consult, WHO, New Delhi, 73-; mem, WHO Secretariat, Int Comns Eradicating Smallpox, 77-78; proj dir, Ford Found Proj Environ Health Policy, Mich, 77-78; surv dir, Nepal Blindness Surv, WHO, 80-81; lectr, Dept Epidemiol, Univ Calif, Berkeley, 91- *Mem:* Int Epidemiol Asn; Am Pub Health Asn; NY Acad Sci; Am Asn World Health; Fedn Am Scientists. *Res:* Epidemiology of blindness and blindness diseases; health planning and health policy; international health. *Mailing Add:* 517 Jacoby St San Rafael CA 94901

BRILLINGER, DAVID ROSS, STATISTICS. *Current Pos:* chmn dept, 79-80, PROF STATIST, UNIV CALIF, BERKELEY, 69- *Personal Data:* b Toronto, Ont, Oct 27, 37; m 60, Lorie Silber; c Jef & Matthew. *Educ:* Univ Toronto, BA, 59; Princeton Univ, MA, 60, PhD(math), 61. *Honors & Awards:* Wald Lectr, Inst Math Statist, 82; R A Fisher Award, Comm Pres Statist Soc, 91; Gold Medal, Statist Soc Can, 92. *Prof Exp:* Soc Sci Res Coun fel, London Sch Econ, 61-62; mem tech staff statist, Bell Tel Labs, NJ, 62-64; lectr, London Sch Econ, 64-66, reader, 66-69. *Concurrent Pos:* Lectr math, Princeton Univ, 62-64. *Mem:* Fel Am Statist Asn; fel Inst Math Statist (pres, 94-95); Int Statist Inst; fel Royal Soc Can; fel AAAS; fel Am Acad Arts & Sci. *Res:* Main stream statistics and its applications to science. *Mailing Add:* Dept Statist Univ Calif 367 Evans Hall Berkeley CA 94720-0001. *Fax:* 510-642-7892; *E-Mail:* brill@stat.berkeley.edu

BRILLSON, LEONARD JACK, SURFACE PHYSICS NATURAL SCIENCE. *Current Pos:* PROF & CTR MAT RES SCHOLAR, DEPT ELEC ENG & PHYSICS, OHIO STATE UNIV, 96- *Personal Data:* b New York, NY, Dec 15, 45; m 68, Janice Coe; c Lindsay & Erica. *Educ:* Princeton Univ, AB, 67; Univ Pa, MS, 69, PhD(physics), 72. *Prof Exp:* Assoc scientist, Xerox Corp Webster Res Ctr, 72-74, scientist, 74-79, sr scientist physics, 79-85, prin scientist, 85-89, mgr interfaces & processing group, 85-89, mgr, Mat Res Lab, 89-96. *Concurrent Pos:* Mem adv bd, Ctr Joining Mat, Carnegie-Mellon Univ; adj prof, Dept Mat Sci, Univ Pa, 84-85; dir, Am Vacuum Soc, 85-86, 95-96, exec chmn, Electronic Mat & Processing Div, 85; vis scientist, Tel Aviv Univ, 84; mem, Organizing/Prog Comt, Physics & Chem Semiconductor Interfaces Conf, 89-; mem exec bd, Ctr Photoinduced Charge Transfer, NSF, 89-; secy & treas, Div Condensed Matter Physics, Am Phys Soc, 89-93; chair, Interface, Characterization Microelectronic Mat, Int Soc Optical Eng Conf, 89; mem adv bd, Int Conf Formation of Semiconductor Interfaces, 90; assoc ed, J Electronic Mat & J Vacuum Sci & Technol, 92-; chair, Forum Indust & Appl Physics, Phys Soc, 96-97. *Mem:* Fel Am Phys Soc; fel Am Vacuum Soc; Mat Res Soc; Electrochem Soc; Inst Elec & Electronics Engrs. *Res:* Surface and interface electronic structure of semiconductors and insulators, their dependence on surface chemical composition and bonding, and their influence on charge transfer across interfaces with metals. *Mailing Add:* Ohio State Univ 205 Dreese Lab 2015 Neil Ave Columbus OH 43210-1272

BRIM, CHARLES A, PLANT BREEDING. *Current Pos:* RETIRED. *Personal Data:* b Spalding, Nebr, Apr 14, 24; m 48; c 2. *Educ:* Univ Nebr, BS, 48, MS, 50, PhD(agron), 53. *Prof Exp:* Res agronomist, USDA, 53-80, prof, 69-80, Emer Prof Crop Sci & Genetics, NC State Univ, 80-; vpres res, Funk Seeds Int, 80-86. *Mailing Add:* 2 Mine Bluff Ct Durham NC 27713

BRIM, ORVILLE G, JR, LIFESPAN DEVELOPMENTS. *Current Pos:* DIR, MACARTHUR FOUND RES NETWORK SUCCESSFUL MID-LIFE DEVELOP, 89- *Personal Data:* b Apr 7, 23; m 44; c 4. *Educ:* Yale Univ, BA, 47, MA, 49, PhD(sociol), 51. *Honors & Awards:* Kurt Lewin Mem Award, Soc Psychol Study Social Issues, 79; Distinguished Sci Contrib Child Develop Res Award, Soc Res Child Develop, 85. *Prof Exp:* Sociologist, Russell Sage Found, NY, 55-64, asst secy, 60-65, pres, 64-72; pres, Found Child Develop, NY, 74-85. *Concurrent Pos:* Chmn, Spec Comt Soc Sci, NSF, 68-69; mem, Adv Comt, Child Develop, Nat Acad Sci, 71-76; vchair, Bd Trustees, Am Inst Res, 71-87, chair, 88-90; chmn, Comt Work & Personality Middle Years, Soc Sci Res Coun, 72-79; bd trustees, William T Grant Found, Inc, 75-84. *Mem:* Inst Med-Nat Acad Sci; Am Acad Arts & Sci. *Res:* Mid-life development. *Mailing Add:* MacArthur Found Res Network Successful Mid-Life Develop 1625 Tenth Ave Vero Beach FL 32960

BRIMACOMBE, JAMES KEITH, ANALYSIS & DESIGN OF METALS & MATERIALS PROCESSES, PROCESS ENGINEERING. *Current Pos:* from asst prof to prof, Univ BC, 70-80, Stelco prof, 80-85, Stelco/Natural Sci & Eng Res Coun Can prof, 85-91, prof, 91-92, DIR, CTR METALL PROCESS ENG, UNIV BC, 85-, ALCAN CHAIR MAT PROCESS ENG, 93- *Personal Data:* b Dec 7, 43; m 70, Margaret E Rutter; c Kathryn M & Jane M. *Educ:* Univ BC, BASc, 66; Univ London, PhD(process metall), 70; Imperial Col, DIC, 70. *Hon Degrees:* DSc, Univ London, 86; Dr, Colo Sch Mines, 94. *Honors & Awards:* Charles H Herty Award, Am Inst Mining & Metals Engrs, 73 & 87, John Chipman Award, 79 & 85, Robert W Hunt Silver Medal, 80, 83 & 93; Marcus A Grossman Award, Am Soc Mat Int, 77, Henry Marion Howe Medal, 80 & 85; Extractive Metall Sci Award, Minerals, Metals & Mat Soc, 79, 87 & 89, Extractive Metall Technol Award, 82 & 91; Champion H Mathewson Gold Medal, Metall Soc, Minerals, Metals & Mat Soc, 80; Arnold Markey Lectr, Steel Bar Mill Assoc, 81; Williams Prize, Metals Soc, UK, 83; Alcan Award, Metal Soc, Can Inst Metals, 88; Howe Mem Lectr, Am Inst Minerals, Metals & Mat Soc Engrs, 93; D K C MacDonald Mem Lectr, Can Mat Sci, 94. *Concurrent Pos:* Can Coun lectr, Am Soc Mat Int, 86; chmn, Natural Sci & Eng Sci Res Coun Can, Chem/Met Eng Comn, 89-90; bd dirs, Ont Ctr Mat Res, 90-92; eminent overseas speaker, Inst Engrs, Australia, 91; mem, Task Force Challenges Sci, Conf Bd Can, 92; consult. *Mem:* Foreign assoc Nat Acad Eng; Fel Minerals, Metals & Mat Soc (pres elect, 93-94 & 95-96); Iron & Steel Soc Metals & Mat Soc Engrs (pres-elect, 94-); Royal Soc Can; fel Can Acad Eng; fel Can Inst Mining, Metall & Petrol Engrs. *Res:* Analysis and design of metals and materials processes across the flowsheets of production; emphasis on the linkage between products and processes through computer modeling coupled to plant and laboratory measurements; a total of over twenty processes have been studied. *Mailing Add:* 108-5410 Balsam St Vancouver BC V6M 4B4 Can

BRIMACOMBE, ROBERT KENNETH, EXCIMER LASERS, CARBON DIOXIDE LASERS. *Current Pos:* SR SCIENTIST, LUMONICS INC, 88- *Personal Data:* b Niagara Falls, Ont, Can, Mar 11, 57; c 1. *Educ:* Royal Mil Col, Can, BEng, 80; McMaster Univ, PhD(physics), 85. *Prof Exp:* Asst prof physics, Royal Mil Col Can, 85-88. *Mem:* Optical Soc Am; Inst Elec & Electronics Engrs; Quantum Electronics & Appln Soc. *Res:* Excitation and gain mechanisms in carbon dioxide lasers; use of excimer lasers to investigate ultraviolet transmission in optical fibers; development of excimer laser products. *Mailing Add:* Lumonics Inc 105 Schneider Rd Kanata ON K2K 1Y3 Can. *Fax:* 613-592-5706

BRIMHALL, GEORGE H, ORE DEPOSITS, CRYSTAL GEOCHEMISTRY. *Current Pos:* from asst prof to assoc prof geol, 78-82, chmn dept, 86-90 & 94, PROF GEOL, UNIV CALIF, BERKELEY, 82- *Personal Data:* b Santa Monica, Calif, Aug 24, 47; m 71, Mary J Patroan; c Lara C & Hilary A. *Educ:* Univ Calif, Berkeley, BA, 69, PhD(geol), 72. *Honors & Awards:* Lindgren Award, Soc Econ Geologists, 80; McKinstry lectr, Harvard Univ, 85. *Prof Exp:* Mine geologist, Anaconda Co, 72-74, proj geologist, 74-76; asst prof, Johns Hopkins Univ, 76-78. *Concurrent Pos:* Mem, Panel Mineral Resources, Continental Sci Drilling Comt, Nat Res Coun, 81-84. *Mem:* Fel Soc Econ Geologists; fel Mineral Soc Am; fel Geol Soc Am; Am Geophys Union; Geochem Soc; Am Inst Mining & Metall. *Res:* Distribution and tranport processes of transition metals in the Earth's crust; fractionation processes involving aqueous and magmatic fluids; hydrochemical transport; rock weathering and soil forming processes; soil resources. *Mailing Add:* Dept Geol & Geophys Univ Calif 301 Earth Sci Berkeley CA 94720-0001

BRIMHALL, J(OHN) L, MATERIALS SCIENCE. *Current Pos:* SR RES SCIENTIST, PAC NORTHWEST LAB, BATTELLE MEM INST, 65- *Personal Data:* b Palo Alto, Calif, Mar 17, 37; m 66. *Educ:* San Jose State Col, BS, 59; Stanford Univ, MS, 61, PhD(mat sci), 64. *Prof Exp:* Sr engr phys metall, Gen Elec Co, 64-65. *Mem:* Am Inst Mining, Metall & Petrol Engrs; Am Soc Metals; Sigma Xi; Mat Res Soc. *Res:* Studies of interaction of radiation with materials and the relationship between crystal lattice defects and structural properties of materials. *Mailing Add:* 2502 Riverside Dr West Richland WA 99352-5251

BRIMHALL, JAMES ELMORE, PHYSICS. *Current Pos:* Teacher, WVa State Col, 66-68, chmn dept, 68-74, from assoc prof to prof physics, 81-91, vpres admin affairs, 83-94, PROF PHYSICS, WVA STATE COL, 94- *Personal Data:* b Burlington, Iowa, June 5, 36; m 58; c 2. *Educ:* Hamline Univ, BS, 59; Univ Pittsburgh, MS, 65; Union Grad Sch, PhD, 79. *Mem:* Am Phys Soc; Am Asn Physics Teachers; Nat Sci Teachers Asn; Soc Photog Technologists. *Res:* Positronium annihilation in gases; circular polarization analysis of x-rays via Compton scattering; plane polarization analysis of gamma rays via Compton scattering; momentum spectroscopy of charged particles. *Mailing Add:* WVa State Col Campus Box 200 Institute WV 25112

BRIMIJOIN, WILLIAM STEPHEN, PHARMACOLOGY, NEUROBIOLOGY. *Current Pos:* instr pharmacol, Mayo Grad Sch Med, 71-72, from asst prof to assoc prof, 72-80, assoc dir, res training & degree progs, Mayo Grad Sch Med, 83-87, prof pharmacol, 80-89, WINSTON & IRIS CLEMENT PROF, MAYO MED SCH, 89-, CONSULT, MAYO FOUND, 72-, CHAIR, DEPT PHARMACOL, 93- *Personal Data:* b Passaic, NJ, July 1, 42; m 64, Margaret Russ; c 3. *Educ:* Harvard Col, BA, 64, Harvard Univ, PhD(pharmacol), 69. *Honors & Awards:* Jacob Javits Award, Nat Inst Neurol & Commun Dis & Stroke, 87; Sr US Scientist Award, Humboldt Found, 87. *Concurrent Pos:* NIH pharmacol res assoc training prog, 69-71; NIMH grant, 71-74; assoc consult, Mayo Found, 71-72; NIH grant & career develop award, 75-80, 80-89, 82-; vis scientist, Karolinska Inst, 78-79, Univ Wurzburg, 87-88; mem, Soc Issues Comt, Soc Neurosci, 87-90; mem, Behav & Neurosci Study Sect, NIH, 89-93. *Mem:* Am Soc Pharmacol & Exp Therapeut; Am Soc Neurochem; Soc Neurosci; Int Soc Neurochem. *Res:* Chemical biology of nerve cells; mechanisms and functions of axoplasmic transport; regulation and properties of cholinesterases. *Mailing Add:* Dept Pharmacol Mayo Med Sch 200 First St SW Rochester MN 55905-0001. *Fax:* 507-284-9111

BRIN, MYRON, BIOCHEMISTRY. *Current Pos:* RETIRED. *Personal Data:* b New York, NY, July 1, 23; m 44; c 3. *Educ:* NY Univ, BS, 45; Cornell Univ, BS, 47, MS, 48; Harvard Univ, PhD(med sci, biochem), 51. *Honors & Awards:* A Cressy Morrison Award, NY Acad Sci, 62. *Prof Exp:* Sr res scientist metab radiation, New Eng Deaconess Hosp, Boston, 51-53; instr biochem, Sch Med, Harvard Univ, 53-56; chief biologist, Food & Drug Res Labs, Inc, 56-58; assoc prof biochem & med, State Univ NY Upstate Med Ctr, 58-68; prof nutrit, Univ Calif, Davis, 68-69; asst dir biochem nutrit, Hoffmann-La Roche Inc, 69-70, dir clin nutrit, 70-88. *Concurrent Pos:* Instr biochem, Sch Med, Tufts Univ, 52-53; res fel & instr, Thorndike Mem Lab, Med Sch, Harvard Univ, 53-56, mem bd tutors, Harvard Univ, 54-56; NIH sr res fel, Hadassah Med Sch, Hebrew Univ Jerusalem, 67-68; adj prof, Columbia Univ, 69- *Mem:* AAAS; Am Soc Biol Chemists; Am Inst Nutrit; Am Soc Clin Nutrit; Am Chem Soc; Sigma Xi. *Res:* Biochemistry and nutrition; vitamin function in metabolism and health maintenance, particularly vitamin B1, B6 and E adequacy, by functional tests; concept of morgual vitamin deficiency. *Mailing Add:* 129 Cocceo Dr West Orange NJ 07052

BRINCH-HANSEN, PER, PARALLEL PROGRAMMING, PROGRAMMING LANGUAGES. *Current Pos:* DISTINGUISHED PROF COMPUT SCI, SYRACUSE UNIV, 87- *Personal Data:* b Copenhagen, Denmark, Nov 13, 38; m 65, Milena Hrastar; c Mette & Thomas. *Educ:* Tech Univ Denmark, MS, 63 & Dr Techn, 78. *Prof Exp:* Software designer, Regnecentralen, Denmark, 63-70; res assoc, Carnegie-Mellon Univ, 70-72; assoc prof comput sci, Calif Inst Technol, 72-76, Henry Salvatori prof, Univ Southern Calif, 76-84, prof, Univ Copenhagen, 84-87. *Concurrent Pos:* Consult, Burroughs, Control Data, Hewlett-Packard, IBM, Jet Propulsion Lab, Los Alamos Sci Lab, Mostek, Tex Instruments, TRW & other var nat & pvt cos. *Mem:* Fel Inst Elec & Electronics Engrs; Int Fed Info Processing; Asn Comput Mach. *Res:* Parallel programs; programming languages; operating systems; computer architecture. *Mailing Add:* 5070 Pine Valley Dr Fayetteville NY 13066

BRINCK-JOHNSEN, TRULS, ENDOCRINOLOGY, BIOCHEMISTRY. *Current Pos:* res assoc steroid chem & asst prof path, Dartmouth Med Sch, 64-69, assoc prof med, 70-77, assoc prof path, 69-83, PROF PATH, DARTMOUTH MED SCH, 83- *Personal Data:* b Stavanger, Norway, Oct 10, 26; US citizen; m 52, Kari Moeser; c Trude, Kim & Toril. *Educ:* Univ Utah, MS, 56, PhD(anat, endocrinol), 59. *Prof Exp:* Res asst analytic chem, Univ Oslo, 48-49; res asst, Inst Aviation Med, Norweg Air Force, 49-50; chief chemist, French & Norweg Trop & Antarctic Whaling Expeds, 50-52 & 53-54; res assoc med biochem, Univ Oslo, 52-53, investr steroid chem, Ullevaal Hosp, 59-63, chief biochemist, Endocrine Lab, Rikshosp, 63-64. *Concurrent Pos:* Mem assoc staff, Mary Hitchcock Mem Hosp, Hanover, NH, 67-; dir, Steroid-Radioimmunoassay Lab, Dartmouth-Hitchcock Med Ctr, 72-; consult, Vet Admin Hosp, 75-; adj assoc prof, Sch Health Studies, Univ NH, 79-83, adj prof, 83. *Mem:* Endocrine Soc; fel Nat Acad Clin Biochem; fel Royal Soc Med. *Res:* Biochemistry and physiology of steroid hormones. *Mailing Add:* Dept Path Dartmouth Med Sch 1 Medical Center Dr Lebanon NH 03756-0001. *Fax:* 603-650-6120

BRINCKMAN, FREDERICK EDWARD, JR, INORGANIC CHEMISTRY, MATERIALS BIOPROCESSING. *Current Pos:* RETIRED. *Personal Data:* b Oakland, Calif, June 24, 28; m 54; c 2. *Educ:* Univ Redlands, BS, 54; Harvard Univ, AM, 58, PhD(chem), 60. *Honors & Awards:* Silver Medal, Dept Com, 74; Gold Medal, Dept Com, 80. *Prof Exp:* Res chemist & head, Propellant Br, US Naval Ord Lab, Calif, 60-61; sci staff asst head, Anal Chem Div, Gen Res Div, US Naval Propellant Plant, Md, 61-64; actg chief, Inorg Chem Sect, Nat Bur Stand, 74-75, res chemist, Chem Stability & Corrosion Div, 64-93, group leader chem biode gradation processes, 78-93, res chemist & bioprocess coordr Polymer Div, 88-93. *Concurrent Pos:* Richard Merton vis prof geosci, Univ Maine, 78; adj prof inorg chem, Univ Md, 85. *Mem:* AAAS; Am Chem Soc; fel Royal Soc Chem; NY Acad Sci; fel Am Inst Chemists; Sigma Xi. *Res:* Synthetic inorganic and organometallic chemistry; metal-nitrogen, metal-fluorine chemistry; coordination chemistry of main group elements; applications of magnetic AA and epifluorescence and mass spectrometry to environmental inorganic chemistry; dynamics and quantative structure-activity relationship of bioactive organometallic systems in aqueous phases; organometallics as intermediates in biotransformations of metals; ultratrace specification of environmental organometals in vivo and in exocellular strategic or waste materials bioprocessing. *Mailing Add:* 560 N St SW Washington DC 20024

BRINDLEY, DAVID N, LIPOPROTEIN BIOCHEMISTRY, SIGNAL TRANSDUCTION. *Current Pos:* MED SCIENTIST, HERITAGE MED RES CTR, 88-; PROF BIOCHEM, UNIV ALTA, 88- *Personal Data:* b Buxton, Eng, Mar 25, 42. *Educ:* Univ Birmingham, Eng, BSc, 63, PhD(biochem), 66, DSc, 77. *Prof Exp:* Chmn metab regulation, Univ Nottingham, England, 85-87. *Mem:* Am Soc Biochem; Brit Biochem Soc; Can Biochem Soc; NAm Soc Study Obesity. *Res:* Role of lipid second messengers in cell activation and divisional, hormonal and pharmacological control of lipoprotein metabolism in dyslipidemia, diabetes and obesity. *Mailing Add:* Heritage Med Res Ctr Univ Alta Edmonton AB T6G 2S2 Can. *Fax:* 403-492-3383

BRINE, CHARLES JAMES, BIOPOLYMERS, CELLULOSE & CELLULOSICS. *Current Pos:* DIR RES & DEVELOP, SEABORNE INC, 93- *Personal Data:* b Newark, NJ, July 4, 50. *Educ:* Worcester Polytech Inst, BS, 72; Univ Del, MS, 74, PhD(marine studies), 79. *Honors & Awards:* Nat Award Grad Res in Appl Marine Sci, US Dept Com, 77; US/Japan Res Sem Award, NSF/Japan Soc Promotion Sci, 84. *Prof Exp:* Fel marine chem, Col Marine Studies, Univ Del, 75-79, res assoc, 79-80; res chemist, FMC Corp, 80-82, mgr, explor res, Food & Pharmaceut & Prod Div, 82-88, mgr, New Technol, 88-91, sr res assoc, 91-92; sr res assoc, Novon Prod Div, Warner-Lambert Co, 92-93. *Concurrent Pos:* Chmn, Pub Rel, Agr & Food Chem Div, Am Chem Soc-AGFD, 85-89, vchmn, 89-, prog chmn, chair-elect, 90-, chmn, 91-; co-organizer, Joint US-Japan, NSF, coop seminar on chitin, chitosan, & related enzymes, 84-; session chmn Second, Third & Fourth, Int Conf Chitin & Chitosan, 82, 85 & 88; mem, Sci Adv Bd, Fourth Int Conf, Chitin & Chitosan & Sci Adv Bd, Chitin Co, 88-89; co-founder & vpres, Am Chito Sci Soc; chmn, Fifth Int Conf, Chitin & Chitosan, 91- *Mem:* Am Chem Soc; AAAS; Sigma Xi; NY Acad Sci; Controlled Release Soc; Am ChitoSci Soc. *Res:* Chitin, chitosan and related polymeric, oligomeric and monomeric derivatives; basic and pharmaceutical application of cellulose and cellulosic derivative polymers in the areas of sustained/controlled drug delivery, drug dosage form development and pharmaceutical latex drug carrier systems; cellulose/hydrocolloid fat substitutes and food additive systems; biodegradable polymer systems. *Mailing Add:* 28 Tee-Ar Pl Princeton NJ 08540-3946

BRINEN, JACOB SOLOMON, MOLECULAR SPECTROSCOPY, SURFACE CHEMICAL ANALYSIS. *Current Pos:* From res chemist to sr res chemist, 61-74, prin res chemist, 74-82, assoc res fel, 82-86, RES FEL, AM CYANAMID CO, 86- *Personal Data:* b Brooklyn, NY, Nov 16, 34; m 58, Harriet Sheveloff; c Jeffrey L & Linda S. *Educ:* Brooklyn Col, BS, 56; Pa State Univ, PhD(chem & electronic spectros), 61. *Mem:* Am Chem Soc; Am Phys Soc; Am Vacuum Soc. *Res:* Electronic absorption spectroscopy, fluorescence and phosphorescence; electron spin and photoelectron spectroscopy, SIMS and SIMS imaging of organic and inorganic surfaces. *Mailing Add:* Cytec Industs 1937 W Main St Stamford CT 06902-4850

BRINER, ROBERT C, FORENSIC SCIENCE. *Current Pos:* DIR CRIME LAB, SEMO CRIM LAB, 71- *Personal Data:* b Jeffersonville, Ind, Mar 27, 38; m 59, Janet Walker; c Joseph & Leslie. *Educ:* Ind Univ, BS, 61; Fla State Univ, PhD(org chem), 66. *Prof Exp:* Instr chem, Purdue Univ, 67; sr res chemist, Monsanto, 67-71. *Concurrent Pos:* Instr, Criminal Justice, Southern Ill Univ, 76, Southeastern Mo State Univ, 77- *Mem:* Am Acad Sci; Am Soc Crime Lab Dirs (vpres, 79). *Res:* Electrochemistry for detection of gunshot residue and toxicology to develop methods of analysis of drugs in urine; Electrophoresis of blood stains for genetic markers. *Mailing Add:* 2312 Hillbrook Cape Girardeau MO 63701. *Fax:* 573-651-2533

BRINER, WILLIAM WATSON, MICROBIOLOGY. *Current Pos:* MICROBIOLOGIST, PROCTER & GAMBLE CO, 59- *Personal Data:* b Winchester, Ind, Dec 12, 28; m 54; c 4. *Educ:* Ohio State Univ, BA, 53, MS, 57, PhD(microbiol), 59. *Concurrent Pos:* Lectr, Eve Col, Univ Cincinnati, 63-70; assoc ed, J Dent Res, 73-75. *Mem:* AAAS; Am Soc Microbiol; Int Asn Dent Res; Am Asn Dent Res; Am Acad Microbiol. *Res:* Oral microbiology; dental diseases in animals; microbial ecology. *Mailing Add:* 462 Stonehearst Lane Cincinnati OH 45231

BRINEY, ROBERT EDWARD, COMPUTER SCIENCE. *Current Pos:* assoc prof, 68-70, prof math, 70-77, chmn dept math, 71-77, PROF COMPUT SCI, SALEM STATE COL, 77-, CHMN DEPT COMPUT SCI, 77- *Personal Data:* b Benton Harbor, Mich, Dec 2, 33. *Educ:* Northwestern Univ, AB, 55; Mass Inst Technol, PhD(math), 61. *Prof Exp:* Instr math, Mass Inst Technol, 61-62; asst prof, Purdue Univ, 62-68. *Mem:* Am Math Soc; Asn Comput Mach; Soc Indust & Appl Math; AAAS; Math Asn Am. *Res:* Algebraic geometry; commutative algebra. *Mailing Add:* Dept Comput Sci Salem State Col Salem MA 01970-5353

BRINGER, ROBERT PAUL, PLASTICS ENGINEERING. *Current Pos:* sr chem engr, 3M Co, 59-62, supvr, 62-66, mgr, Chem Div, 66-72, tech dir, Film Div, 72-84, exec dir, St Paul, 84-85, STAFF VPRES, ENVIRON ENG & POLLUTION CONTROL, 3M CO, 86- *Personal Data:* b Peoria, Ill, June 5, 30; c 3. *Educ:* Purdue Univ, BS, 52, PhD(chem eng), 56. *Prof Exp:* Chem engr, Dow Chem Co, Mich, 56-57, supvr, 57-59. *Concurrent Pos:* Mem, environ comt, Nat Asn Mfgrs & Bus Roundtable; mem, corp conserv coun, Nat Wildlife Fedn; chmn, solid & hazardous waste task force, Nat Asn Mfg; bd dirs, Air Pollution Control Asn. *Mem:* Air & Waste Mgt Asn; Water Pollution Control Fedn. *Res:* Plastics, rubbers and resins, particularly fluorocarbon and high temperature; films, particularly oriented. *Mailing Add:* 103 Eastbank Ct N Hudson WI 54016

BRINGHURST, ROYCE S, PLANT BREEDING. *Current Pos:* Chmn dept, 50-76, PROF POMOL, UNIV CALIF, DAVIS, 50- *Personal Data:* b Murray, Utah, Dec 27, 18; m 45; c 6. *Educ:* Utah State Univ, BS, 47; Univ Wis, MS, 48, PhD(agron, genetics), 50. *Mem:* Genetics Soc Am; fel Am Soc Hort Sci; Am Phytopath Soc; Bot Soc Am. *Res:* Breeding and genetics of strawberries; evolution, genetics, cytogenetics and breeding of Fragaria polyploids. *Mailing Add:* 738 Mulberry Lane Davis CA 95616

BRINIGAR, WILLIAM SEYMOUR, JR, PROTEIN CHEMISTRY. *Current Pos:* from asst prof to assoc prof, 66-79, PROF CHEM, TEMPLE UNIV, 79- *Personal Data:* b Wichita, Kans, May 18, 30; m 56; c 3. *Educ:* Univ Kans, BS, 52, PhD(chem), 57. *Prof Exp:* Res assoc, Univ SC, 57-59 & Yale Univ, 59-66. *Concurrent Pos:* Vis prof, Univ Calif, San Diego, 73-74. *Mem:* Am Chem Soc; Biophys Soc. *Res:* Mechanisms of enzyme catalysis; hemoprotein chemistry; site-specific mutagenesis of hemoglobins and myoglobins. *Mailing Add:* Dept Chem Temple Univ Philadelphia PA 19122. *Fax:* 215-204-1532

BRINK, DAVID LIDDELL, WOOD CHEMISTRY. *Current Pos:* assoc forest prod chemist & lectr forestry, Univ Calif, Berkeley, 58-62, forest prof chemist & lectr wood chem & prof agr chem, 62-80, grad adv, 72-80, EMER PROF, 80- *Personal Data:* b St Paul, Minn, July 7, 17; m 43; c 3. *Educ:* Univ Minn,

BS, 39, PhD(agr biochem, forestry), 54. *Prof Exp:* Asst, Univ Minn, 39-42; res chemist, Salvo Chem Corp, 43-45; asst, Univ Minn, 47-49; group leader lignin, Mead Corp, 49-53; chemist, Develop Ctr, Weyerhaeuser Timber Col, 54-55, chief chem sect, 55-57, chief org chem sect, Cent Res Dept, 57-58. *Mem:* Am Chem Soc; Forest Prod Res Soc; Tech Asn Pulp & Paper Indust. *Res:* Lignin, cellulose, pulping, bark, extractives. *Mailing Add:* 1068 Woodside Rd Berkeley CA 94708-1721

BRINK, FRANK, JR, BIOPHYSICS OF NERVE CELLS, ION TRANSPORT. *Current Pos:* prof, Rockefeller Univ, 53-74, dean grad studies, 57-72, Detlev W Bronk prof, 74-81, EMER PROF, ROCKEFELLER UNIV, 81- *Personal Data:* b Easton, Pa, Nov 4, 10; m 39, Marjory Gaylord; c Patricia (Mayer) & David Warner. *Educ:* Pa State Col, BS, 34; Calif Inst Technol, MS, 35; Univ Pa, PhD(biophys), 39. *Hon Degrees:* DSc, Rockefeller Univ, 83. *Prof Exp:* Lalor fel, 39-40; instr physiol, Med Col, Cornell Univ, 40-41; Johnson Found fel & lectr biophys, Univ Pa, 41-47, asst prof, 47-48; assoc prof, Johns Hopkins Univ, 48-53. *Concurrent Pos:* Dir, Comn Biol & Med, NSF, 53-59; ed, Biophys J, 60-64; chmn, Pres Comt Nat Medal Sci, 63-65. *Mem:* Nat Acad Sci; Am Acad Arts & Sci; Am Physiol Soc; Soc Gen Physiol; Biophys Soc; Soc Neurosci. *Res:* Physical chemistry of nerve cells, in particular, the transport of sodium and potassium ions; biophysics and biochemistry of neurons; ionic processes directly relevent to the cycle of excitation, response and recovery in nerve fibers; energy transformations involved in linking oxidative processes of metabolism to electrochemical events on peripheral axons of nerve cells. *Mailing Add:* Rockefeller Univ 1230 York Ave New York NY 10021-6399

BRINK, GILBERT OSCAR, EXPERIMENTAL ATOMIC PHYSICS. *Current Pos:* chmn, Dept Physics & Astron, 72-74, assoc prof, 68-80, PROF PHYSICS, STATE UNIV NY, BUFFALO, 80- *Personal Data:* b Los Angeles, Calif, May 26, 29; m 57. *Educ:* Col of the Pacific, BA, 53; Univ Calif, PhD(chem), 57. *Prof Exp:* From staff res physicist to physicist, Lawrence Radiation Lab, Univ Calif, 57-63; asst res prof, Univ Pittsburgh, 62-63; prin physicist, Cornell Aeronaut Lab, 63-68. *Concurrent Pos:* Vis McDonnell distinguished prof, Wash Univ, St Louis, 81. *Mem:* Am Phys Soc; Sigma Xi; NY Acad Sci. *Res:* Atomic beam magnetic resonance; hyperfine structure anomaly measurements; nuclear spins and magnetic moments; atomic scattering by crossed beams; molecular structure; laser excitation of atomic states. *Mailing Add:* 79 Button Wood Ct East Amherst NY 14051-1644

BRINK, JAMES E, MATHEMATICS, COMPUTER SCIENCE. *Current Pos:* from asst prof to assoc prof math, 70-81, prof math & comput sci, 84-91, PROF COMPUT SCI, PAC LUTHERAN UNIV, 91- *Personal Data:* b Grand Rapids, Mich, 43. *Educ:* Hope Col, BA, 65; Iowa State Univ, MS, 68, PhD(math), 70. *Mem:* Inst Elec & Electronics Engrs; Asn Comput Mach. *Res:* Mathematics; computer science. *Mailing Add:* Dept Comput Sci Pacific Lutheran Univ 12180 Park Ave S Tacoma WA 98447-0001

BRINK, JOHN JEROME, NEUROSCIENCES. *Current Pos:* PROF BIOCHEM, CLARK UNIV, 66- *Personal Data:* b Secunderabad, India, Mar 18, 34; US cit; m 60, Virginia Broch; c 2. *Educ:* Univ Orange Free State, SAfrica, BSc, 55; Univ Witwatersrand, BSc(Hons), 56; Univ Vt, PhD(biochem), 62. *Prof Exp:* Biochemist, Stanford Res Inst, 62-64; NIH asst res biochemist, Ment Health Res Inst, Univ Mich, 64-66. *Concurrent Pos:* Vis lectr, Harvard Med Sch, 72; res assoc, Harvard Sch Pub Health, 77-79. *Mem:* AAAS; Am Soc Neurochem; NY Acad Sci; Am Soc Biol Chemists; Int Soc Neurochem; Am Inst Nutrit. *Res:* Neurochemistry of brain proteins and nucleic acids; biochemical pharmacology of nucleic acid precursor antimetabolites; vitamin B12 metabolism of mammalian nervous system. *Mailing Add:* Dept Biol Clark Univ 950 Main St Worcester MA 01610-1455. *E-Mail:* jbrink@vax.clarku.edu

BRINK, KENNETH HAROLD, SHELF DYNAMICS, COASTAL UPWELLING. *Current Pos:* assoc scientist, 80-90, SR SCIENTIST, WOODS HOLE OCEANOG INST, 90- *Personal Data:* b Buffalo, NY, Oct 4, 49. *Educ:* Cornell Univ, BS, 71; Yale Univ, MS, 73, PhD(geol & geophys), 77. *Honors & Awards:* Cody Award, 96. *Prof Exp:* Ed, Sch Oceanog, Ore State Univ, 77-80. *Mem:* Am Geophys Union; Am Meteorol Soc; fel AAAS; Oceanog Soc. *Res:* Physical oceanography of coastal upwelling and subtidal frequency fluctuations over the continental shelf and slope. *Mailing Add:* Woods Hole Oceanog Inst Clark Bldg Mail Stop 21 Woods Hole MA 02543

BRINK, KENNETH MAURICE, HORTICULTURE. *Current Pos:* PROF HORT & HEAD DEPT, COLO STATE UNIV, 68- *Personal Data:* b Cleveland, Ohio, May 11, 32; m 56; c 2. *Educ:* Purdue Univ, BS, 54, MS, 58, PhD, 65. *Prof Exp:* From instr to assoc prof hort, Purdue Univ, 58-68. *Mem:* AAAS; Am Soc Hort Sci. *Res:* Marketing horticultural crops; post-harvest physiology and economic factors. *Mailing Add:* 1913 Navajo Dr Ft Collins CO 80525

BRINK, LINDA HOLK, BIOCHEMISTRY, IMMUNOLOGY. *Current Pos:* RES ASSOC, WHO, ROCKEFELLER FOUND & HARVARD MED SCH, 78- *Personal Data:* b Fairhope, Ala, Jan 13, 44; m 67. *Educ:* Univ Ala, BS, 67; Univ London, MSc, 73, PhD(parasitol & immunol), 77; Brunel Univ, London, MSc, 77. *Prof Exp:* Microbiologist cholera, WHO, 70-71; microbiologist tuberculosis, USAID, 71-72; res fel, Rockefeller Found, Univ London, 74-77. *Concurrent Pos:* Prin investr, WHO, 79-81, Clark Found, 81-82 & Rockefeller Found, 78- *Mem:* Am Soc Trop Med & Hyg; Royal Soc Trop Med & Hyg; Brit Soc Immunol; AAAS; Am Asn Hist Med. *Res:* Effector mechanisms of schistosome immunity and isolation of antigens now being tested in pre-vaccine trials. *Mailing Add:* 9518 Kentstone Dr Bethesda MD 20817

BRINK, MARION FRANCIS, NUTRITION. *Current Pos:* RETIRED. *Personal Data:* b Golden Eagle, Ill, Nov 20, 32. *Educ:* Univ Ill, BS, 55, MS, 58; Univ Mo, PhD(nutrit), 61. *Prof Exp:* Res biologist, Biomed Div, US Naval Radiol Defense Lab, 61-62; assoc dir nutrit res, Nat Dairy Coun, 62-65, dir nutrit, 65-70, pres, 76-85; exec vpres, United Dairy Ind Asn, 85-88, chief exec officer, 88-91. *Mem:* Am Soc Clin Res; Am Soc Nutrit Sci; Soc Nutrit Educ; Am Dairy Sci Asn; Sigma Xi. *Res:* Mineral requirements; toxicology; nutrition, biochemistry and physiology of humans and animals; effects of ionizing radiation upon nutrient requirements. *Mailing Add:* 444 Highcrest Dr Wilmette IL 60091

BRINK, NORMAN GEORGE, CHEMISTRY. *Current Pos:* RETIRED. *Personal Data:* b Littleton, Colo, Aug 31, 20; m 47. *Educ:* Princeton Univ, AB, 42, PhD(chem), 44. *Prof Exp:* Res chemist, 44-50, asst dir org & biochem res, 50-56, dir bio-org chem, 56-66, dir, Univ Rels, Merck & Co, Inc, 66-76; dir indust rels, dept chem, Univ Calif, San Diego, 77-80. *Mem:* AAAS; Am Soc Biol Chem. *Res:* Isolation of biologically active natural products; intermediary metabolism in disease; enzyme inhibition; medicinal chemistry; stimulation of academic-industrial cooperation. *Mailing Add:* 7220 York Ave S No 418 Edina MN 55435

BRINKHOUS, KENNETH MERLE, PATHOLOGY. *Current Pos:* prof, 46-61, distinguished alumni prof, 61-80, EMER PROF PATH, SCH MED, UNIV NC, CHAPEL HILL, 80- *Personal Data:* b Clayton Co, Iowa, May 29, 08; m 36, Frances Benton; c William K & John R. *Educ:* Univ Iowa, AB, 29, MD, 32. *Hon Degrees:* DSc, Univ Chicago, 67. *Honors & Awards:* Ward-Burdick Awards, Am Soc Clin Path, 41 & 63; O Max Gardner Award, 61; James F Mitchell Found Int Award, 69; Gold Headed Cane Award, Am Asn Path, 81; Maude Abbott Lectr, Int Acad Path, 85; Pobert P Grant Medal, Int Soc Thrombosis Haemostasis, 85; Distinguished Serv Award, AMA, 86; Karl Landsteiner Award, Am Asn Blood Banks, 94. *Prof Exp:* Asst path, Sch Med, Univ Iowa, 32-33, instr, 33-35, assoc, 35-37, from asst prof to assoc prof, 37-46. *Concurrent Pos:* Mem, Subcomt Blood Coagulation, Nat Res Coun, 51-54, chmn, 54-62, mem, Comt Blood, 54-, mem, Thrombosis Task Force, 65-70; mem, Int Comt Haemostasis & Thrombosis, 54-, chmn, 64-66, secy gen, 66-78; consult, Armed Forces Inst Path, 56-72; mem, Univs Asn Res & Educ in Path, 64-; pres, Fedn Am Socs Exp Biol, 66-67; mem, Arteriosclerosis Task Force & Coun, Nat Heart & Lung Inst, 70-71; chief ed, Arch Path and Lab Med, 74-83; ed, Thrombosis Res, 83-86, Year Book Path, 80-91. *Mem:* Nat Acad Sci; Inst Med-Nat Acad Sci; Am Asn Path & Bact (secy-treas, 68-71, pres, 73); Int Soc Thrombosis (pres, 72); AAAS; Am Acad Arts & Sci; Am Soc Exp Path (secy-treas, 60-63, pres, 65-66). *Res:* Blood clotting; hemorrhagic and thrombotic diseases; vitamin K; atherosclerosis; blood platelets; von Willebrand factor; hemophilia and gene therapy. *Mailing Add:* 524 Dogwood Dr Chapel Hill NC 27516-2884. *Fax:* 919-966-6718

BRINKHURST, RALPH O, OLIGOCHAETE BIOLOGY, BENTHOS. *Current Pos:* EMER DIR, AQUATIC RESOURCE CTR, 91- *Personal Data:* b Croydon, Surrey, Eng, Mar 13, 33; Can citizen; m 84; c 2. *Educ:* Univ London, BSc, 55, PhD(zool), 58, DSc, 72. *Honors & Awards:* Award of Excellence, NAm Benthological Soc. *Prof Exp:* Lectr zool, Univ Liverpool, 57-65; prof, Univ Toronto, 66-72; dir, St Andrews Biol Lab, 72-75; head, Ocean Ecol Lab, Inst Ocean Sci, 76-87; scientist, 87-92. *Concurrent Pos:* Assoc, Great Lakes Inst, Univ Toronto, 67-70, Systs & Ecol, Marine Biol Lab, Woods Hole, 67-70 & Royal Ont Mus, 68-; dir, Pollution Probe, 69-73, Huntsman Marine Lab, 72-75; adj prof, Univ Victoria, 76-91, Tenn Technol Univ, Memphis State Univ & Univ Ala, Huntsville; vis prof, Royal Roads Mil Col, 80-81. *Mem:* NAm Benthological Soc (pres, 80-81); Freshwater Biol Asn UK. *Res:* Ecology and systematics of freshwater and marine benthos especially Oligochaeta. *Mailing Add:* Aquatic Resource Ctr PO Box 680818 Franklin TN 37068-0818. *Fax:* 614-790-0173; *E-Mail:* aquatres@lx.netcom.com

BRINKLEY, JOHN MICHAEL, APPLICATION OF FLUORESCENCE TO ANALYSIS OF BIOLOGICAL MATERIALS, DEVELOPMENT OF UNIFORM FLUORESCENT LATEX MICROSPHERES. *Current Pos:* PROD DEVELOP DIR, MOLECULAR PROBES, INC, 88- *Personal Data:* b Franklin, NH, Jan 23, 44; m 71; c 4. *Educ:* Culver-Stockton Col, Canton, Mo, BA, 66; Case Western Reserve Univ, Cleveland, Ohio, PhD(org chem), 70. *Prof Exp:* Sr res chemist, Shell Develop Co, 70-73; sr res chemist, Syva Co, 73-80, clin studies supvr, 80-84; clin studies dir, Sclavo West Coast, Inc, 84-88. *Concurrent Pos:* Mem bd dirs, Western Biomed Inst, 91- *Res:* Dye-protein conjugation chemistry; fluorescent dyes; development and applications of dyed latex microspheres; development of fluorescence-based analytical techniques, primarily to detect gene transfections. *Mailing Add:* 2582 W 28th Ave Eugene OR 97405

BRINKLEY, LINDA LEE, developmental biology, for more information see previous edition

BRINKMAN, CHARLES R, HIGH TEMPERATURE MATERIALS, METALS & CERAMICS. *Current Pos:* GROUP LEADER, MECH PROPERTIES GROUP, OAK RIDGE NAT LAB, 73- *Personal Data:* b Salt Lake City, Utah, Oct 21, 37; c 2; c Tyler & Erik. *Educ:* Univ Utah, BS, 60, MS, 61, PhD(metall eng), 66. *Prof Exp:* Res Engr, Idaho Nat Lab, 66-73. *Concurrent Pos:* Subcomt chmn, Properties & Performance Ceramics, Am Soc Testing & Mat, 90- *Mem:* Am Soc Mech Engrs; fel Am Soc Metals; Am Soc Testing & Mat; Am Inst Mining Metall & Petrol Engrs; Am Ceramics Soc. *Res:* Creep-fatigue interactions; mechanical properties of ceramics; creep of metals and ceramics; design methods for ceramics. *Mailing Add:* 615 E Fox Den Dr Knoxville TN 37922. *Fax:* 423-574-5118

BRINKMAN, GEORGE LORIS, AGRICULTURAL POLICY. *Current Pos:* assoc prof, 73-81, chmn, 91-96, PROF AGR POLICY, DEPT AGR ECON & BUS, UNIV GUELPH, 81- *Personal Data:* b Minneapolis, Minn, Oct 3, 42; m 65, Elizabeth A Neal; c Lori, Diane & Deborah. *Educ:* Wash State Univ, BSc, 64, ExM, 65; Mich State Univ, PhD(agr econ), 69. *Prof Exp:* Asst prof agr policy, Dept Econ, Kans State Univ, 69-73. *Concurrent Pos:* Vis prof agr policy, Dept Food & Res Econ, Univ Fla, 80-81, Univ Saskatoon, 96, Tex A&M Univ, 96-97; chmn, Can Expert Comt Rural Resource Develop, 80-83, chmn, Statist Can Adv Comt Agr, 85-93; nat counr, Agr Inst Can, 84-86; mem, Nat Farm Finance & Mgt Task Force, 90; mem, Nat Statist Coun, 92-93; consult, Agr Can, Auditor Gen Can, Fisheries & Oceans Can, Statist Can, Can Ministry Urban Affairs, Ministry State for Econ & Regional Develop, Econ Co un Can, Can Dairy Comn, NAtlantic Fisheries Task Force, Can Fed Munic, Can Farm Bus Mgt Coun, Agr Coun Ont, Ont Milk Mkt Bd. *Mem:* Fel Can Agr Econs & Farm Mgr Soc (pres, 82); Agr Inst Can; Am Agr Econs Soc. *Res:* Price and income policy, international trade, farm structure, rural development, and evaluation of public programs for agriculture. *Mailing Add:* 14 Hickory St Guelph ON N1G 2X3 Can. *Fax:* 519-767-1510; *E-Mail:* gbrinkma@uoguelph.ca

BRINKMAN, WILLIAM F, ELECTRONICS ENGINEERING, MATERIALS SCIENCE ENGINEERING. *Current Pos:* exec dir res, Physics Div, AT&T Bell Labs, 87-94, VPRES PHYS SCI RES, BELL LABS LUCENT TECHNOL, 94- *Personal Data:* b Washington, Mo, July 20, 38; m 60; c 2. *Educ:* Univ Mo-Columbia, BS, 60, MS, 62, PhD(physics), 65. *Hon Degrees:* DHL, Univ Mo, Columbia, 87. *Prof Exp:* NSF res fel physics, Oxford Univ, 65-66; head, Infrared Physics & Electronics Res Dept, Bell Labs, 72-74, dir, Chem Physics Res Lab, 74-81 & Phys Res Lab, 81-84; vpres res, Sandia Nat Labs, 84-87. *Mem:* Nat Acad Sci; Am Phys Soc; fel AAAS. *Res:* Solid state theory; itinerant magnetism and spin fluctuations; electron tunneling theory; theory of metal-insulator transitions. *Mailing Add:* AT&T Bell Labs 600 Mountain Ave Murray Hill NJ 07974

BRINKMEYER, RAYMOND SAMUEL, ORGANIC CHEMISTRY. *Current Pos:* RES ADMINR, DOW ELANCO, 89- *Personal Data:* b Lima, Ohio, Mar 22, 48; m 71; c 2. *Educ:* Univ Cincinnati, BS, 70; Colo State Univ, PhD(chem), 75. *Prof Exp:* Res scientist, Lilly Res Labs, 78-89. *Concurrent Pos:* Fel, Stanford Univ, 75-77 & Nat Cancer Inst, 76-77. *Mem:* Am Chem Soc. *Res:* Natural products; synthetic methods; plant growth regulators. *Mailing Add:* 8939 Spider Bay Ct Indianapolis IN 46236-9037

BRINKS, JAMES S, ANIMAL GENETICS. *Current Pos:* PROF ANIMAL SCI, COLO STATE UNIV, 67- *Personal Data:* b Plymouth, Mich, Jan 2, 34; m 55; c 9. *Educ:* Mich State Univ, BS, 56, MS, 57; Iowa State Univ, PhD(statist & genetics), 60. *Prof Exp:* Res geneticist, Animal Husb Res Div, Agr Res Serv, USDA, 60-67. *Mem:* Am Soc Animal Sci. *Res:* Estimation of genetic, environmental and phenotypic parameters; estimation of response to selection and inbreeding; comparisons of mating systems; performance testing. *Mailing Add:* 2405 N Overland Trail La Porte CO 80535

BRINLEY, FLOYD JOHN, JR, BIOPHYSICS. *Current Pos:* dir, Neurol Dis Prog, 79-82, dir, Convulsive, Develop & Neuromuscular Dis Prog, Nat Inst Neurol Disorders & Stroke, 82-96, DIR, DIV CONVULSIVE, IMMUNIOL & INFECTIOUS DISORDERS, NIH, 96- *Personal Data:* b Battle Creek, Mich, May 19, 30; m 55; c 3. *Educ:* Oberlin Col, AB, 51; Univ Mich, MD, 55; Johns Hopkins Univ, PhD, 61. *Prof Exp:* Intern, Los Angeles Co Gen Hosp, 55-56; sr asst surgeon neurophysiol lab, NIH, 57-59; from asst prof to assoc prof physiol, Sch Med, Johns Hopkins Univ, 61-76; prof physiol, Sch Med, Univ MD, 76-79. *Mem:* Biophys Soc; Am Physiol Soc; Soc Gen Physiol; Soc Neurosci; Am Neurol Asn; Am Acad Neurol; Am Soc Biol Chemists. *Res:* Membrane phenomena; ionic transport. *Mailing Add:* PO Box 41021 Bethesda MD 20824. *Fax:* 301-402-0302

BRINN, JACK ELLIOTT, JR, ENDOCRINOLOGY, ELECTRON MICROSCOPY. *Current Pos:* ASST PROF ANAT, ECAROLINA UNIV, 72- *Personal Data:* b Norfolk, Va, June 7, 42; m 65; c 3. *Educ:* ECarolina Col, BA, 64, MA, 66; Univ Wyo, PhD(zool), 71. *Prof Exp:* Instr biol, ECarolina Univ, 66-67; res assoc, Milton S Hershey Med Ctr, 70-72. *Mem:* Am Asn Anatomists; Am Soc Zoologists; Am Diabetes Asn; Fedn Am Soc Exp Biol. *Res:* Ultrastructure of polypeptide hormone synthesis and secretion; comparative endocrine cytology and ultracytochemistry. *Mailing Add:* Dept Anat ECarolina Univ Sch Med Greenville NC 27858

BRINSON, MARK MCCLELLAN, WETLAND ECOLOGY, ESTUARINE ECOLOGY. *Current Pos:* from asst prof to assoc prof, 73-81, dir biol grad prog, 81-86, PROF BIOL, ECAROLINA UNIV, 81- *Personal Data:* b Shelby, Ohio, Oct 6, 43; m 71; c 1. *Educ:* Heidelberg Col, BS, 65; Univ Mich, Ann Arbor, MS, 67; Univ Fla, PhD(bot), 73. *Prof Exp:* Fisheries biologist, Peace Corps, Costa Rica, 67-69. *Concurrent Pos:* Vis asst prof bot, Univ NC, Chapel Hill, 76; wetland ecologist, US Fish & Wildlife Serv, 79-80. *Mem:* Sigma Xi; Ecol Soc Am; Am Soc Limnol & Oceanog; Soc Wetland Scientists (vpres, 89-90, pres, 90-91); Int Ecol Soc; AAAS. *Res:* Wetland biogeochemistry and hydrology; aquatic macrophyte ecology. *Mailing Add:* Dept Biol ECarolina Univ Greenville NC 27834

BRINSTER, RALPH L, DEVELOPMENTAL BIOLOGY. *Current Pos:* Asst instr physiol, Sch Med, Univ Pa, 60-61, teaching fel, 61-64, instr, 64-65, from asst prof to assoc prof, Sch Vet Med, 65-70, PROF PHYSIOL, SCH VET MED, UNIV PA, 70-, RICHARD KING MELLON PROF REPRODUCTIVE PHYSIOL, 75- *Educ:* Rutgers Univ, BS, 53; Univ Pa, VMD, 60, PhD(physiol), 64. *Hon Degrees:* DSc, Univ Basque Country, Spain, 94. *Honors & Awards:* Award in Biol & Med Sci, NY Acad Sci, 83; Harvey Soc Lectr, 84; Distinguished Serv Award, USDA, 89; Pioneer Award, Int Embryo Transfer Soc, 92; Charles-Leopold Mayer Prize, Fr Acad Sci, 94; Carl Hartman Award, Soc Study Reproduction, 97; Bower Award & Prize Sci, Franklin Inst, 97. *Concurrent Pos:* Lake Placid Conf, 87. *Mem:* Nat Acad Sci; Inst Med-Nat Acad Sci; Soc Study Reproduction; Brit Soc Study Fertil; Brit Biochem Soc; Am Vet Med Asn; fel Am Acad Arts & Sci; Am Soc Cell Biol; fel AAAS; fel Am Acad Microbiol. *Res:* In vitro culture and physiology of the cleavage stages of mammalian embryos; differentiation in the mammalian embryo; gene regulation; transgenic animals; development of the mammalian egg and early embryo; germ cell formation and differentiation; regulation of eukaryotic gene expression; gene transfer into animals. *Mailing Add:* Sch Vet Med Univ Pa 3800 Spruce St Philadelphia PA 19104

BRINTON, CHARLES CHESTER, JR, MICROBIOLOGY, BIOPHYSICS. *Current Pos:* res assoc, Univ Pittsburgh, 56-59, from asst res prof to assoc prof, 59-69, PROF MICROBIOL & MEM GRAD FAC, MED SCH, UNIV PITTSBURGH, 69- *Personal Data:* b Pittsburgh, Pa, Aug 15, 26. *Educ:* Carnegie Inst Technol, BS, 49; Univ Pittsburgh, MS, 52, PhD(biophys), 55. *Prof Exp:* Asst biophys, Univ Pittsburgh, 49-51; res fel, Geneva, Switz, 55-56. *Mem:* AAAS; Biophys Soc; Am Soc Microbiol. *Res:* Bacterial and viral genetics, biophysics, physiology and serology; electrophoresis; biochemistry and physical chemistry of proteins and nucleic acids. *Mailing Add:* Dept Biol & Life Sci A-234 Langley Hall Univ Pittsburgh Pittsburgh PA 15260-0001

BRINTON, EDWARD, BIOLOGICAL OCEANOGRAPHY. *Current Pos:* From jr res biologist to res biologist, 53-73, RES BIOL, MARINE LIFE RES GROUP, SCRIPPS INST OCEANOG, UNIV CALIF, 73- *Personal Data:* b Richmond, Ind, Jan 12, 24; m 48; c 4. *Educ:* Haverford Col, BA, 49; Bryn Mawr Col, MA, 50; Scripps Inst Oceanog, Univ Calif, PhD(oceanog), 58. *Concurrent Pos:* Partic, AID-Univ Calif Proj, Southeast Asia, 60-61; UNESCO instr, Thailand, 62 & Pakistan, 64; UNESCO cur, Indian Ocean Biol Ctr, Indian Ocean Exped, Ernakulam, S India, 65-67. *Mem:* Am Soc Limnol & Oceanog; Challenger Soc. *Res:* Systematics, population biology and zoogeography of Euphausiacea, including antarctic Krill; ecology of zooplankton. *Mailing Add:* 8347 La Jolla Shores Dr La Jolla CA 92037

BRINTON, MARGO A, RNA VIRUS REPLICATION, RNA-PROTEIN INTERACTIONS. *Current Pos:* assoc prof, 89-91, PROF, DEPT BIOL, GA STATE UNIV, 91-, ASSOC PROVOST, 91- *Personal Data:* b Hanover, Pa, Feb 6, 45; m 93, Eldon Park. *Educ:* Duke Univ, BA, 66; Univ Pa, PhD(microbiol/virol), 72. *Prof Exp:* Instr, Dept Microbiol, Univ Minn, Minneapolis, 73-74, asst prof, 75-77; sr microbiologist, Riker Res Labs, 74-77; from asst prof to assoc prof, Wistar Inst, 77-89; from Wistar asst prof to Wistar assoc prof path, Univ Pa, 78-89, from Wistar asst prof to Wistar assoc prof microbiol, 82-89. *Concurrent Pos:* Consult ed, J Reticuloendothelial Soc, 82-84; mem, Neurol Study Sect C, Nat Inst Neurol & Communicative Dis & Stroke, 85; mem, Microbiol & Infectous Dis Res Comt, Nat Inst Allergy & Infectious Dis, 86-90; adj assoc prof, Dept Microbiol & Immunol, Morehouse Sch Med, 89-; vice prog chair, Am Soc Virol, 91-93, prog chair, 93-95. *Mem:* Am Soc Virol; Am Soc Microbiol; Sigma Xi. *Res:* Molecular analysis of natural resistance to flaviviruses; structural analysis of RNA-protein interactions; positive-strand RNA virus replication; host-virus interactions; structural analysis of RNA. *Mailing Add:* Dept Biol Ga State Univ University Plaza Atlanta GA 30303. *Fax:* 404-651-2509; *E-Mail:* biomab@panther.gsu.edu

BRION, CHRISTOPHER EDWARD, ELECTRON IMPACT SPECTROSCOPY, PHOTOABSORPTION. *Current Pos:* Res fel chem, Univ BC, 61-63, teaching fel, 63-64, from asst prof to assoc prof, 64-76, PROF CHEM, UNIV BC, 76- *Personal Data:* b Eng, May 5, 37; m 61, Elizabeth M Rogers; c Catherine, Peter & Susan. *Educ:* Bristol Univ, BSc, 58, PhD(chem), 61. *Honors & Awards:* Noranda Award, Chem Inst Can, 77; Herzberg Award, Spectros Soc Can, 83; John Polanyc Award, Can Soc Chem, 93. *Concurrent Pos:* Sr res fel, Nat Res Coun Can, 69-70; John Simon Guggenheim mem fel, 78-79; Killam res fel, Canada Coun, 84; Japan Soc Prom Sci fel, 86; Sr Killam res fel, Univ BC, 90; distinguished foreign scholar, Japan Inst Molecular Sci, 90; vis prof, Univ Col London, Eng, 68, FOM Inst Atomic & Molecular Physics, Amsterdam, 69, Flinders Univ, S Australia, 78, Federal Univ, Rio de Janeiro, 83, Tex Christian Univ, 84, Univ Kuwait, 86, Chinese Acad Sci, Beijing, 86, Tokyo Inst Technol, 86, Inst Molecular Sci, Okazaki, Japan, 90. *Mem:* Fel Chem Inst Can; Can Asn Physicists; Am Chem Soc; fel Royal Soc Can; Spectros Soc Can; Can Inst Synchrotron Radiation. *Res:* Excited states of ions; energy loss electron spectroscopy; electron-electron and electron-ion coincidence techniques; photoionization; orbital imaging by electron momentum spectroscopy; synchrotron radiation studies; experimental quantum chemistry. *Mailing Add:* Dept Chem Univ BC Vancouver BC V6T 1Z1 Can. *Fax:* 604-822-2847; *E-Mail:* brion@chem.ubc.ca

BRIONI, JORGE DANIEL, PHARMACEUTICAL DISCOVERY, BEHAVIORAL PHARMACOLOGY. *Current Pos:* SR RESEARCHER, ABBOTT LABS, 90- *Personal Data:* b Marcos Juarez, Cordoba, Arg, Sept 29, 56; m 81, Elsa Daprati; c Marina, Carla & Florencia. *Educ:* Nat Univ Cordoba, BS, 78, PhD(pharm), 86. *Prof Exp:* Lectr pharamacol, Nat Univ Cordoba, 82-87, asst prof, 89-90; researcher, Univ Calif, Irvine, 87-89. *Mem:* Soc Neurosci. *Res:* Identify novel compounds for the treatment of Alzheimer's disease or age-associated memory impairments; test the effect of drugs on memory, anxiety and abuse potential; neurochemical changes induced by the novel agents. *Mailing Add:* 1029 Cumberland Ct Vernon Hills IL 60061

BRISBIN, DOREEN A, BIOINORGANIC CHEMISTRY. *Current Pos:* Res assoc chem, Univ Waterloo, 60-61, lectr, 61-63, asst prof, 63-66, assoc dean sci, 75-86, ASSOC PROF CHEM, UNIV WATERLOO, 66-, ADV TO VPRES ACAD, ACAD HUMAN RESOURCES, 86- *Personal Data:* b Edmonton, Alta, Dec 19, 26; m 49; c 3. *Educ:* Univ Alta, BSc, 46; Univ Toronto, PhD(chem), 60. *Res:* Coordination chemistry; stability of metal complexes; kinetics of metalloporphyrin formation; intermolecular complexes with porphyrins. *Mailing Add:* Dept Chem Univ Waterloo 200 University Ave W Waterloo ON N2L 3G1 Can

BRISBIN, I LEHR, JR, ZOOLOGY, ECOLOGY. *Current Pos:* Adj assoc prof vert ecol, 67-68, AEC SR FEL, SAVANNAH RIVER ECOL LAB, 68-, SR ECOLOGIST, 90-; ADJ ASSOC PROF POULTRY SCI, PHARMACOL, TOXICOL & ZOOL, UNIV GA, 69- *Personal Data:* b Drexel Hill, Pa, Apr 2, 40; m 88, Brenda Robinson; c 1. *Educ:* Wesleyan Univ, AB, 62; Univ Ga, MS, 65, PhD(zool), 67. *Concurrent Pos:* Pop ecologist, US Energy Res & Develop Admin, 73-75; adj prof, Univ SC. *Mem:* Am Soc Mammal; fel Am Ornithologists Union; Am Soc Ichthyologists & Herpetologists; Ecol Soc Am; Wildlife Soc; Soc Environ Toxicol & Chem; Sigma Xi; fel AAAS. *Res:* Vertebrate ecology and bioenergetics; mammalogy, ornithology and herpetology; ecology of domestication; canine behavior and olfaction; energy-related environmental impacts, radioecology; ecotoxicology; toxicology. *Mailing Add:* Savannah River Ecol Lab PO Drawer E Aiken SC 29802. *Fax:* 803-725-3309; *E-Mail:* towns@srel.com

BRISCOE, ANNE M, BIOCHEMISTRY, PHYSIOLOGY. *Current Pos:* RETIRED. *Personal Data:* b New York, NY, Dec 1, 18; m 89, Theodore H Heinly Sr. *Educ:* Vassar Col, AM, 45; Yale Univ, PhD(physiol chem), 49. *Prof Exp:* From res assoc to asst prof biochem, Med Col, Cornell Univ, 50-56; res assoc, Sch Med, Univ Pa, 56; assoc biochem, Columbia Univ, 56-72, asst prof med, Col Physicians & Surgeons, 72-87. *Concurrent Pos:* NIH fel, Univ Pa, 49-50; lectr, Sch Gen Studies, Hunter Col, 51-64, adj asst prof, Sch Health Sci, 73-; vis asst prof, Temple Univ, 56; consult, Vet Admin Hosp, Castle Point, NY, 57-67; career scientist, New York Health Res Coun, 60-66; lectr, Sch Gen Studies, Columbia Univ, 67-68, Sch Nursing, Harlem Hosp Ctr, 68-77 & Antioch Col Physicians Asst Prog at Harlem Hosp Ctr, 71-73; spec lectr, Columbia Univ, 87- *Mem:* Fel Am Inst Chemists; Am Chem Soc; Am Soc Clin Nutrit; Asn Women Sci (pres, 78-); fel NY Acad Sci; Harvey Soc; Endocrine Soc. *Res:* Metabolism of calcium and magnesium in human subjects; metabolic acidosis; chronic renal failure. *Mailing Add:* 2116 Sea Crescent Ruskin FL 33570-6128. *E-Mail:* drannieb@aol.com

BRISCOE, CHARLES VICTOR, PHYSICS. *Current Pos:* res assoc, 58-60, from asst prof to assoc prof, 58-70, PROF PHYSICS, UNIV NC, CHAPEL HILL, 70- *Personal Data:* b Abingdon, Va, May 5, 30; m 53; c 3. *Educ:* King Col, BA, 52; Rice Inst, MA, 57, PhD(physics), 58. *Prof Exp:* Instr math, King Col, 52-53, instr physics, 53-54. *Concurrent Pos:* Vis prof, Tech Univ Karlsruhe, 66 & 67. *Mem:* Am Phys Soc; Am Asn Physics Teachers; Sigma Xi. *Res:* Superconducting properties of metallic films; position annihilation in inert gas liquids. *Mailing Add:* Physics Dept Univ NC Chapel Hill NC 27514

BRISCOE, JOHN, SANITARY & ENVIRONMENTAL ENGINEERING. *Current Pos:* sr economist & div chief, 86-96, SR WATER ADV, WORLD BANK, WASHINGTON, DC, 96- *Personal Data:* b Brakpan, SAfrica, July 30, 48; m 79, Conceicao Andrade; c Anabela, Maria & Alexa. *Educ:* Univ Cape Town, BSc, 69; Harvard Univ, MS, 71, PhD(environ eng), 76. *Prof Exp:* Engr, Govt SAfrica, 69-70; Scientist, Cholera Res Lab, Bangladesh, 76-78; res assoc, Harvard Univ, 79; engr, Govt of Mozambique, 79-81; assoc prof environ eng, Univ NC, 81-85. *Res:* Relationships between engineered water systems and health; economics of water systems; water resource management. *Mailing Add:* World Bank Washington DC 20433

BRISCOE, JOHN WILLIAM, CIVIL ENGINEERING. *Current Pos:* From instr to assoc prof, Univ Ill, Urbana-Champaign, 48-57, asst head dept civil eng, 57-59, assoc head dept, 59-65, assoc provost, 65-67, assoc chancellor admin, 67-68, vchancellor admin affairs, 68-77, PROF CIVIL ENG, UNIV ILL, URBANA-CHAMPAIGN, 57- *Personal Data:* b Westfield, Ill, Feb 24, 17; m 42; c 1. *Educ:* Univ Ill, BS, 40 & 47, MS, 53. *Concurrent Pos:* Consult, Off Civil Defense, 61-65; mem, Proj Harbor Study Comt, 63, Joint Adv Comt Continuing Educ, 64 & USAF Acad, 64. *Mem:* Am Soc Civil Engrs; Am Soc Eng Educ; Soc Hist Technol. *Res:* Behavior of reinforced concrete structures; protective construction. *Mailing Add:* 107 Whitehall Ct Urbana IL 61801

BRISCOE, MELBOURNE GEORGE, INTERNAL WAVES, AIR-SEA INTERACTIONS. *Current Pos:* scientist Phys Oceanog, Woods Hole Oceanog Inst, Off Naval Res, 69-89, sci officer, 87-89, dir appl oceanog & acoust div, 89-92, dir, Off Ocean & Earth Sci, 92-96, DIR, PROCESS & PREDICTION DIV, OFF NAVAL RES, 96- *Personal Data:* b Akron, Ohio, July 17, 41; m 83, Ellen Straus. *Educ:* Northwestern Univ, BS, 63, PhD(mech engr), 67. *Prof Exp:* Fel, von Karman Inst Fluid Dynamics, Rhode-St Genese, Belg, 67-68; fel air sea interactions, Off Naval Res, Saclant Undersea Res Ctr, NATO, La Spezia, Italy, 68-69. *Concurrent Pos:* Ed, Oceanic Internal Waves, 74-75; assoc ed, J Geophys Res, 74-77, J Phys Oceanog, 77-79 & 87-; consult, Naval Res Adv Comt, 77, Naval Oceanog Res Develop Activ, 78, Sci Appl Inc, 79-85, Joseph Wetzell Assoc, 81, EG&G, 81-, Buoy Technol, 84, Endeco, 85; chief ed, J Phys Oceanog, 85-87; dir, US Global Ocean Obj Syst, 92-96. *Mem:* Am Geophys Union; Am Meteorol Soc; Oceanog Soc; Marine Technol Soc. *Res:* Field experiments in physical oceanography to understand the pathways of energy between atmosphere and ocean; the role of the ocean in determining the climate of the earth; internal gravity wave physics. *Mailing Add:* Six W Luray Ave Alexandria VA 22301. *Fax:* 703-696-2007; *E-Mail:* briscom@onr.navy.mil

BRISCOE, WILLIAM JOHN, PHYSICS. *Current Pos:* PROF PHYSICS, GEORGE WASHINGTON UNIV, 82- *Personal Data:* b Bronx, NY, Jan 8, 47. *Educ:* Cath Univ Am, BA, 70, PhD(physics), 78; Northeastern Univ, MS, 72. *Prof Exp:* Asst prof physics,. *Res:* Physics. *Mailing Add:* Dept Physics George Washington Univ Washington DC 20052

BRISCOE, WILLIAM TRAVIS, BIOCHEMISTRY. *Current Pos:* ASST PROF BIOCHEM, SCH MED, ORAL ROBERTS UNIV, 77- *Personal Data:* b Tulsa, Okla; m 70; c 2. *Educ:* Rice Univ, BA, 70; Univ Tex, Houston, PhD(biochem), 74. *Prof Exp:* Robert A Welch Found fel biochem, M D Anderson Hosp & Tumor Inst, Univ Tex, Houston, 74; fel microbiol, Scripps Clin & Res Found, Calif, 75-77. *Mem:* Am Asn Cancer Res. *Res:* Nucleic acid and protein synthesis, especially the investigation of mutagenic sites in DNA as carcinogenic markers. *Mailing Add:* 2628 E 73rd St Tulsa OK 74136

BRISKE, DAVID D, PHYSIOLOGICAL PLANT ECOLOGY, POPULATION ECOLOGY. *Current Pos:* asst prof, 78-83, ASSOC PROF RANGELAND ECOL & MGT, TEX A&M UNIV, 83- *Personal Data:* b Grafton, NDak, Aug 27, 51; m 71, 88; c 2. *Educ:* NDak State Univ, BA, 73; Colo State Univ, PhD(range sci), 78. *Prof Exp:* Res asst, Colo State Univ, 74-77. *Concurrent Pos:* Consult, USAID, Morocco. *Mem:* Soc Range Mgt; Ecol Soc Am; Am Inst Biol Sci. *Res:* Physiology ecology and population biology of perennial grasses including developmental morphology, defoliation physiology, clonal biology, resource allocation; competitive interactions and population structure. *Mailing Add:* Rangeland Ecol & Mgt Tex A&M Univ College Station TX 77843-0100

BRISKIN, DONALD PHILLIP, MEMBRANE BIOCHEMISTRY, BIOENERGETICS. *Current Pos:* from asst prof to assoc prof, 85-92, PROF PLANT PHYSIOL, UNIV ILL, 92- *Personal Data:* b Los Angeles, Calif, Feb 28, 55. *Educ:* Univ Southern Calif, BS, 77; Univ Calif, Riverside, PhD(plant physiol), 81. *Honors & Awards:* McKnight Res Award-Plant Biol, McKnight Found, 86; Young Crop Scientist Award, Crop Sci Soc Am, 88. *Prof Exp:* Fel, McGill Univ, 82-83; plant physiologist, Agr Res Serv, USDA, 83-85. *Mem:* Am Soc Plant Physiologists; Am Asn Univ Profs; Sigma Xi. *Res:* Biochemistry and bioenergetics of membrane transport in plants, signal transduction, organization and regulation of plant metabolic pathways. *Mailing Add:* 1201 W Gregory Dr Urbana IL 61801. *E-Mail:* dbriskin@uiuc.edu

BRISLEY, CHESTER L(AVOYEN), industrial engineering, for more information see previous edition

BRISSON, GERMAIN J, NUTRITION. *Current Pos:* dir, Nutrit Res Ctr, 68-78, prof, 62-87, EMER PROF NUTRIT, LAVAL UNIV, 90- *Personal Data:* b St Jacques, Que, Apr 12, 20; m 48; c 5. *Educ:* Joliette Sem, BA, 42; Laval Univ, BSc, 46; McGill Univ, MSc, 48; Ohio State Univ, PhD(nutrit), 50. *Honors & Awards:* Prix Leo-Pariseau, Asn Can-Fran Avan Sci, 82; Prix Pierreet Celine Lhermite, Acad de Med, Paris, 83; Prix Marie-Victorin, Quebec Govt, 88. *Prof Exp:* Res officer nutrit, Can Dept Agr, 50-60, dir admin, Lennoxville Exp Sta, 60-62. *Concurrent Pos:* Sci ed, Can J Animal Sci, 63-66. *Mem:* Am Soc Animal Sci; Am Dairy Sci Asn; Nutrit Soc Can; fel Agr Inst Can; Can Soc Animal Sci. *Res:* Nutritional requirements of young ruminants; protein and fat utilization by young animals. *Mailing Add:* Animal Sci Dept Laval Univ Quebec PQ G1K 7P4 Can

BRISTOL, DOUGLAS WALTER, ORGANIC CHEMISTRY. *Current Pos:* AT NAT INST ENVIRON HEALTH SCIS, NIH, 80- *Personal Data:* b Rochester, NY, Oct 31, 40; m 64; c 1. *Educ:* St John Fisher Col, BS, 62; Syracuse Univ, PhD(chem), 69. *Prof Exp:* Res assoc chem, Columbia Univ, 69; instr, Univ Utah, 69-71; asst prof pesticides chem, NDak State Univ, 71-77; mem staff, Div Chem & Physics, Food & Drug Admin, 77-80. *Mem:* AAAS; Am Chem Soc. *Res:* Free radical chemistry; reactions and properties of primary and secondary alkoxy-radicals; reactions of pyridinium salts with nucleophiles and dihydropyridine compounds with molecular oxygen; pesticides chemistry. *Mailing Add:* NIH/NIEHS(F1-05) PO Box 12233 Research Triangle Park NC 27709

BRISTOL, JOHN RICHARD, PARASITOLOGY, PHYSIOLOGY. *Current Pos:* from asst prof to assoc prof biol, Univ Tex, El Paso, 70-85, chmn dept, 77-83, asst dean, 84-85, prof biol & asst vpres acad affairs, 85-88, VPRES ACAD AFFAIRS, UNIV TEX, EL PASO, 88- *Personal Data:* b Mattoon, Ill, Apr 11, 38; m 75; c 2. *Educ:* Cornell Col, BA, 61; Kent State Univ, MA, 66, PhD(physiol), 70. *Prof Exp:* Instr biol, Kent State Univ, 69- *Concurrent Pos:* Prog dir, Minority Biomed Support grant, NIH, 74-83; consult, Div Res Resources, NIH, 76-78. *Mem:* Am Soc Parasitologists; Am Micros Soc. *Res:* Animal parasite host interactions; physiology and biochemistry of animal parasites. *Mailing Add:* Dept Biol Univ Tex 500 W University El Paso TX 79968

BRISTOL, MELVIN LEE, ETHNOBOTANY, HORTICULTURE. *Current Pos:* OWNER, BLOOMINGFIELDS FARM, 69- *Personal Data:* b Hartford, Conn, Dec 3, 36; m 59; c 3. *Educ:* Harvard Univ, AB, 60, AM, 62, PhD(bot), 65. *Prof Exp:* USPHS fel, 65-66; asst prof bot & asst botanist, Lyon Arboretum, Univ Hawaii, 66-69. *Mem:* Soc Econ Botanists. *Res:* Ethnobotany and floristics of Colombia and Samoa; taxonomy and ethnobotany of Datura; plant domestication; horticulture; Hemerocallis. *Mailing Add:* Nine Rte 55 W Sherman CT 06784-9722

BRISTOW, JOHN DAVID, MEDICINE. *Current Pos:* prof & dir cardiovasc res & training, 81-93, EMER PROF MED, ORE HEALTH SCI UNIV, 93- *Personal Data:* b Pittsburgh, Pa, Dec 7, 28; m 50; c 3. *Educ:* Willmette Univ, BA, 49; Univ Ore, MD, 53; Am Bd Cardiovasc Dis, dipl, 70. *Prof Exp:* Instr med, 60-61, dir cardiol lab, 62-68, from asst prof to assoc prof med, 62-70, chmn dept, 71-75, chief med serv, Univ Hosp, 69-75, prof med, Med Sch, Univ Ore, 70-77, clin res assoc physiol, 65-77; prof med, Univ Calif, San Francisco, 77-81; chief cardiol, Vet Admin Hosp, San Francisco, 77-81. *Concurrent Pos:* Nat Heart Inst spec fel, Cardiovasc Res Inst, Univ Calif, 61-62 & Radcliffe Infirmary, Eng, 67-68; Markle scholar, 64-69; Am Heart Asn Coun Clin Cardiol fel; consult, US Army Hosp, Ft Lewis, Wash, 66-68; mem, Heart & Lung Prog Proj Comt, NIH, 70-74, nat adv coun, Nat Heart, Lung & Blood Inst, 78-82; mem bd gov, Am Bd Internal Med, 78- *Mem:* Fel Am Col Physicians; Asn Am Physicians; fel Am Col Cardiol; Am Soc Clin Invest; Am Fedn Clin Res. *Res:* Clinical cardiology; cardiovascular physiology; medical education. *Mailing Add:* 2622 SW Fairmount Blvd Portland OR 97201

BRISTOW, LONNIE ROBERT, INTERNAL MEDICINE, OCCUPATIONAL MEDICINE. *Current Pos:* PRIVATE PRACT MED, 61- *Personal Data:* b New York, NY, Apr 6, 30; m 61; c 4. *Educ:* Col City New York, BS, 53; NY Univ, MD, 57. *Prof Exp:* Intern, San Francisco City & Co Hosp, 57-58; resident internal med, US Vet Admin Hosp, San Francisco, 58-60 & Bronx, NY, 60-61. *Concurrent Pos:* Consult, Calif Dept Health Care Prisons, 76-77; chmn, Sickle Cell Comt, 76-79; mem, Genetic Dis Comt, 77-79; mem bd trustees, AMA, 85-94; mem, Nat Coun Health Care Tech, Washington, 80. *Mem:* Inst Med-Nat Acad Sci; Am Soc Internal Med (pres, 81-82); AMA (pres elect, 94-95, pres, 95-); fel Am Col Physicians. *Res:* Medical ethics; socialized medicine as practiced in Great Britain and Canada; health care financing in America; professional liability insurance problems; sickle cell anemia; coronary care unit utilization. *Mailing Add:* Brookside Hosp 2023 Vale Rd San Pablo CA 94806

BRISTOW, PETER RICHARD, PLANT PATHOLOGY. *Current Pos:* asst plant pathologist, 76-80, ASSOC PLANT PATHOLOGIST, PUYALLUP RES & EXTEN CTR, WASH STATE UNIV, 80- *Personal Data:* b Detroit, Mich, June 18, 46; m 70; c 1. *Educ:* Mich State Univ, BS, 68, MS, 72, PhD(plant path), 74. *Prof Exp:* Fel plant path, Univ Mo-Columbia, 74-76. *Mem:* Int Soc Plant Path; Am Phytopath Soc; Sigma Xi. *Res:* Diseases of small fruit crops, especially red raspberry, strawberry, blueberry and cranberry; biology and ecology of soil micro-organisms; root disease pathogens. *Mailing Add:* 2028 Historic Way Puyallup WA 98371

BRISTOWE, WILLIAM WARREN, PHYSICAL CHEMISTRY. *Current Pos:* MGR, COATING & TECHNOL, ENGELHARD/ICC, 95- *Personal Data:* b Philadelphia, Pa, Jan 14, 40; m 62, Cecelia Dabose; c David, Kevin & Mark. *Educ:* Temple Univ, BS, 61; Univ Del, PhD(phys chem), 65. *Prof Exp:* Res chemist, Textile Fibers Pioneering Res, E I du Pont de Nemours & Co, 65-67 & Polymer Sect, Atlas Chem Indust, 67-70; res supvr polymer group, Corp Res Lab, ICI US Inc, 70-79, mgr polymer res, 79-87; mgr, Indust Adhesives, Am Cyanamid Co, 87-90; consult, Appl Polymer Systs, 91-95. *Concurrent Pos:* AEC fel, 62-65. *Mem:* Am Chem Soc; Sigma Xi; Soc Advan Mat Process Eng; Soc Automotive Engrs; Soc Mech Engrs. *Res:* New resins for fiber reinforced composites, sheet molding compounds; ultraviolet curable resins; rim systems; powder coatings; encapsulants; water soluble polymers; high temperature polymers; structural adhesives, coatings; desiccants; zeolites; mass and heat transfer; granted 9 patents. *Mailing Add:* 3328 Altamont Dr Wilmington DE 19810. *E-Mail:* 103007.1753@compuserve.com

BRITT, DANNY GILBERT, DAIRY NUTRITION. *Current Pos:* asst prof agr, 74-80, assoc prof, 80-91, PROF & CHMN, DEPT AGR, EASTERN KY UNIV, 91- *Personal Data:* b Glasgow, Ky, Sept 19, 46; m 66; c 1. *Educ:* Western Ky Univ, BS, 68; Mich State Univ, MS, 72, PhD(dairy nutrit), 73. *Prof Exp:* Asst prof animal sci, Tex A&I Univ, 73-74. *Mem:* AAAS; Am Dairy Sci Asn; Am Soc Animal Sci. *Res:* Use of high moisture corn in dairy rations; nutrient requirements of high producing cows. *Mailing Add:* Agr Dept Eastern Ky Univ A B Carter Bldg Richmond KY 40475-3110

BRITT, DOUGLAS LEE, LIMNOLOGY, BIOLOGY. *Current Pos:* PRES, INT SCI & TECHNOL INC, STERLING, 84- *Personal Data:* b West Lafayette, Ind, Mar 10, 46; m 70; c 2. *Educ:* Purdue Univ, BS, 68; Univ Toledo, MS, 73. *Prof Exp:* Asst biol & ecol, Univ Toledo, 68-70; assoc instr zool & limnol, Ind Univ, Bloomington, 70-72; sect head fisheries & aquatic ecol, Jack McCormick & Assoc, Wapora Inc, 73-75; proj leader energy & environ prog planning, MITRE Corp, 75-78; dir environ sci & prog planning, Gen Res Corp, 78-84. *Concurrent Pos:* Mem, Fed Interagency Comt Health & Environ Effects Energy Technol, 78-81; mem, Int Expert Working Group on Environ Monitoring & Specimen Banking, 78. *Mem:* AAAS; Nat Audubon Soc; Soc Environ Toxicol & Chem. *Res:* Environmental program planning and environmental assessments of fossil fuel and advanced energy systems; development of monitoring programs for the identification of hazardous materials in aquatic and terrestrial ecosystems. *Mailing Add:* 10802 Midsummer Dr Reston VA 22091

BRITT, EDWARD JOSEPH, PHYSICS, BIOENGINEERING. *Current Pos:* physicist, 71-80, TECH DIR, RASOR ASSOC INC, 80- *Personal Data:* b Flagstaff, Ariz, Aug 17, 41; m 65; c 2. *Educ:* Univ Ariz, BS, 64, PhD(nuclear eng), 71. *Prof Exp:* Physicist, Am Atomics Corp, 70-71. *Mem:* Inst Elec & Electronics Engrs; Am Nuclear Soc; Sigma Xi. *Res:* Thermionic energy conversion; bioengineering; laser energy conversion; plasma physics; heart pacemakers; photosynthesis; solar electric power generation; cogeneration; space power; laser development. *Mailing Add:* 20850 Pepper Tree Lane Cupertino CA 95014-2968

BRITT, HAROLD CURRAN, NUCLEAR PHYSICS. *Current Pos:* mem staff, Physics Dept, 86-88, E div leader, 88-92, SR SCIENTIST, LAWRENCE LIVERMORE NAT LAB, 92- *Personal Data:* b Buffalo, NY, Sept 14, 34; m 56, Donna Case. *Educ:* Hobart Col, BS, 56; Dartmouth Col, MA, 58; Yale Univ, PhD(physics), 61. *Prof Exp:* Mem staff, Physics Div, Los Alamos Sci Lab, 61-72, group leader, 74-81, fel, Physics Div, 81-86; vis prof physics, Univ Rochester, 72-73. *Concurrent Pos:* Mem staff, Nuclear Chem Div, Lawrence Radiation Lab, Univ Calif, 64-65; mem subpanel on instrumentation & tech, Nat Acad Sci-Nat Res Coun Nuclear Physics Surv, 70; mem, Lawrence Berkeley Lab, Super Heavy Ion Linear Accelerator Users Exec Comt, 72-73 & 77-79, chmn, 78-79; consult & vis, Niels Bohr Inst, Univ Copenhagen, 76-80; mem, Oak Ridge Nat Lab, Exec Comt Heavy Ion Accelerator Users Group, 78-79; Alexander von Humboldt sr US scientist award, 79; vis prof, Univ Munich, 79-80; mem prog adv comn, Nat Superconducting Cyclotron Lab, Mich State Univ, 81-83; mem, Exec Comt Div Nuclear Physics, Am Phys Soc, 86-88; prog dir, Nuclear Physics, NSF, 92-94. *Mem:* AAAS; fel Am Phys Soc; Am Chem Soc. *Res:* Heavy ion reactions at medium and relativistic energies. *Mailing Add:* 1099 22nd St NW Apt 410 Washington DC 20037. *E-Mail:* britt1@llnl.gov

BRITT, N WILSON, AQUATIC ENTOMOLOGY, LIMNOLOGY. *Current Pos:* RETIRED. *Personal Data:* b Lucas, Ky, Jan 3, 13; m 41, Mary K Farris. *Educ:* Western Ky State Col, BS, 39; Ohio State Univ, MS, 47, PhD(hydrobiol, entom), 50. *Prof Exp:* Pub sch teacher, Ky, 33-40; high sch prin, coach & teacher, 40-42; instr meteorol, USAAF Weather Sch, Ill, 42-43, USAAF Europ Theatre, 44-46; asst ecol, Stone Inst Hydrobiol, 47-50, from asst prof to assoc prof, Ohio State Univ, 50-68, prof entom, 68-83. *Res:* Ecology; limnology, aquatic entomology, general entomology. *Mailing Add:* 1914 70th St W Bradenton FL 34209

BRITT, PATRICIA MARIE, COMPUTER SCIENCE, BIOMATHEMATICS. *Current Pos:* CONSULT, 91- *Personal Data:* b Los Angeles, Calif, May 2, 31. *Educ:* Univ Chicago, BA, 49; Univ Calif, Los Angeles, BA, 51, PhD(philos), 59. *Prof Exp:* Mathematician, Bendix Comput Corp, Los Angeles, 58-63 & Control Data Corp, 63; sr systs engr, IBM Corp, 63-66; assoc dir health sci, Univ Calif, Los Angeles, 66-78, dir, hosp comput facil, 79-90. *Concurrent Pos:* Consult, Health Serv & Ment Health Admin, 71-73 & NIH, 72-; lectr, Dept Biomath, Univ Calif, Los Angeles, 72-78. *Res:* Application of computers to research in biomedicine. *Mailing Add:* 5162 Flagler Rd Nordland WA 98358

BRITTAIN, DAVID B, PHYSIOLOGY, GENERAL MEDICAL SCIENCES. *Current Pos:* ASSOC PROF BIOL, RIPON COL, 62- *Personal Data:* b Chicago, Ill, Dec 24, 25; m; c 3. *Educ:* DePaul Univ, MA, 51. *Mailing Add:* W13679 Liner Rd Brandon WI 53919

BRITTAIN, JOHN O(LIVER), METALLURGY. *Current Pos:* chmn dept, 68-73, prof, 55-90, dir Mat Res Ctr, 76-79, EMER PROF MAT SCI & ENG, NORTHWESTERN UNIV, 90- *Personal Data:* b Pittsburgh, Pa, Feb 15, 20; m 45; c 4. *Educ:* Pa State Univ, BS, 43, PhD(metall), 51. *Honors & Awards:* Ralph A Teetor Educ Award, Soc Automotive Engrs, 77. *Prof Exp:* Asst metall, Res Labs, Aluminum Co Am, 43-44; instr, Pa State Univ, 47-48; prin metallurgist, Battelle Mem Inst, 50-51; res assoc, Columbia Univ, 51-55. *Concurrent Pos:* Air Force Off Sci Res grant, 69-71; NSF grant, 75-; mem, Eng Comt Accreditation Bd Eng Technol; Off Naval Res grant, 78-; NASA grant, 83-; guest scholar, Kyoto Univ, 86. *Mem:* Am Inst Mining, Metall & Petrol Engrs; fel Am Soc Metals; Am Soc Eng Educ; Sigma Xi. *Res:* Materials science; structure sensitive properties of solids. *Mailing Add:* 7 Finley Ct Hendersonville NC 28739

BRITTAIN, WILLIAM JOSEPH, POLYMER SYNTHESIS, PHYSICAL-ORGANIC CHEMISTRY. *Current Pos:* ASST PROF POLYMER SCI, UNIV AKRON, 90- *Personal Data:* b Rapid City, SDak, July 12, 55; m 79; c 3. *Educ:* Univ Northern Colo, BS, 77; Calif Inst Technol, PhD(org chem), 82. *Prof Exp:* Postdoctoral assoc, Dept Chem, Duke Univ, 82-84; res chemist, Cent Res, E I du Pont de Nemours & Co, Inc, 84-88, sr res chemist, Polymer Prod, 88-90. *Mem:* Am Chem Soc. *Res:* Kinetics and mechanism of polymerization; group transfer polymerization; synthesis of biomaterial model surfaces; synthesis of NLO polymers. *Mailing Add:* Dept Polymer Sci Univ Akron Akron OH 44325-3909. *Fax:* 330-972-5290; *E-Mail:* brittain@charles.polymer.uakron.edu

BRITTAN, MARTIN RALPH, VERTEBRATE ZOOLOGY, ICHTHYOLOGY & BIOGEOGRAPHY. *Current Pos:* from asst prof to prof, 53-92, EMER PROF BIOL SCI, CALIF STATE UNIV, SACRAMENTO, 92- *Personal Data:* b San Jose, Calif, Jan 28, 22; m 47, Ruth; c Penelope & Pamela (deceased). *Educ:* San Jose State Col, AB, 46; Stanford Univ, PhD(biol sci), 51. *Prof Exp:* Teaching asst biol sci, Stanford Univ, 47-49; asst prof biol, SDak Sch Mines & Technol, 49-50; from instr to asst prof zool, San Diego State Col, 50-53. *Mem:* Am Fisheries Soc; Am Soc Ichthyologists & Herpetologists; Ecol Soc Am. *Res:* Ichthyology; hydrobiology; taxonomy; evolution; biogeography fisheries. *Mailing Add:* Dept Biol Sci Calif State Univ 6000 J St Sacramento CA 95819

BRITTELLI, DAVID ROSS, ORGANIC CHEMISTRY, MEDICINAL CHEMISTRY. *Current Pos:* sect head, 95-96, RES DIR, PHARMACEUT DIV, BAYER CORP, 96- *Personal Data:* b Milwaukee, Wis, Oct 10, 44; m 73, Mavis Roberts; c Ann. *Educ:* Univ Wis, BS, 66; Univ Ill, PhD(org chem), 69. *Prof Exp:* mem staff, Cent Res & Develop Dept, duPont Co, 69-86, sr res chemist, Med Prods Dept, 86-87, group leader, 89-90; res mgr, duPont Merck Pharmaceut Co, 91-92; sect head, Pharmaceut Div, Miles Inc, 92-95. *Mem:* Am Chem Soc; AAAS. *Res:* Chemistry of natural products; heterocyclic chemistry; new synthetic procedures. *Mailing Add:* Bayer Inc 400 Morgan Lane West Haven CT 06516-4175. *Fax:* 203-812-2650

BRITTEN, EDWARD JAMES, PLANT CYTOGENETICS. *Current Pos:* head, Dept Agr, Univ Queensland, 64-73, dean, 65-66, 71, 79-80, prof, 64-80, EMER PROF AGR, UNIV QUEENSLAND, 81- *Personal Data:* b Rouleau, Sask, Mar 5, 15; Australian citizen; m 40, Noel G Powell; c Dorothy G (Gentle), Evan J & Andrew M. *Educ:* Univ Sask, BSc, 40, MSc, 41; Univ Wis, PhD(genetics), 44. *Prof Exp:* Asst supt forage crops, Dominion Exp Farm, 44-47; asst prof bot, Univ Hawaii, 47-54, asst prof agron, 54-55, from assoc prof agr & assoc agronomist to prof agron, 55-64. *Concurrent Pos:* Sr res fel, Univ Melbourne, 61-62; res consult, Thailand Inst Sci Tech Res, 79. *Mem:* Fel AAAS; Am Soc Agron; fel Australian Inst Agr Sci; Genetic Soc Australia; Trop Grassland Soc Australia. *Res:* Cytogenetics; agricultural education; conservation; tropical agriculture; legumes for semi-arid tropics; essential oil crops. *Mailing Add:* 22 Seventh Ave St Lucia Qld 4067 Australia

BRITTEN, MICHEL, DAIRY SCIENCE, PROTEIN CHEMISTRY. *Current Pos:* RES SCIENTIST DAIRY PROTEINS, AGR CAN-FOOD RES & DEVELOP CTR, 88- *Personal Data:* b Trois-Rivie res, Que, Mar 14, 60; m 82, Johanne; c Jean-Simon & Marc-Olivier. *Educ:* Laval Univ, Bsc, 83, PhD(dairy chem), 88. *Concurrent Pos:* Vis scientist, Food Res Ctr, Reading, Eng, 86-87; auxiliary prof, Laval Univ, 90- *Mem:* Am Dairy Sci Asn. *Res:* Determination of protein structural and functional properties; improvement of functional properties through biochemical or biophysical processes; storage stability of protein-based food systems. *Mailing Add:* Food Res & Develop Ctr-Agr Can 3600 Casavant Blvd W St-Hyacinthe PQ J2S 8E3 Can. *Fax:* 514-773-8461

BRITTEN, ROY JOHN, MOLECULAR BIOLOGY. *Current Pos:* STAFF MEM BIOPHYS, CARNEGIE INST, WASHINGTON DEPT TERRESTRIAL MAGNETISM, 51-; DISTINGUISHED CARNEGIE SR RES ASSOC BIOL, CALIF INST TECHNOL, 81- *Personal Data:* b Washington, DC, Oct 1, 19; m, Jacqueline Aymar; c Gregory H & Kenneth H. *Educ:* Univ Va, BA, 40; Princeton Univ, PhD, 51. *Concurrent Pos:* Vis assoc biol, Calif Inst Technol, 71-73; sr res assoc, 73-; adj prof, Univ Calif, Irvine. *Mem:* Nat Acad Sci; AAAS. *Res:* Quadrupole focussing of energetic particle beams; repeated DNA sequences in genomes of higher organisms. *Mailing Add:* Kerckhoff Marine Lab 101 Dahlia St Corona del Mar CA 92625

BRITTEN-KELLY, MICHAEL RICHARD, FRAGRANCE CHEMISTRY. *Current Pos:* TECH DIR, BUSH BOAKE ALLEN INC, 96- *Personal Data:* m 77, Janet L Markham; c 2. *Educ:* Univ Port Elizabeth, BSc, 70, MSc, 73; Nat Sch Advan Petrol, dipl ing, 74; Univ London, PhD(org chem), 77. *Prof Exp:* Res chemist, Fritzsche Dodge & Olcott Inc, 77-81, dir process develop, 81-89; tech dir, Int Flavors & Fragrances Inc, 89-96. *Mem:* Am Chem Soc; Am Soc Qual Control. *Mailing Add:* 2051 N Lane Ave Jacksonville FL 32254

BRITTIN, DOROTHY HELEN CLARK, FOOD SCIENCE, NUTRITION. *Current Pos:* from instr to assoc prof, 65-89, PROF FOOD & NUTRIT, TEX TECH UNIV, 89- *Personal Data:* b Gadsden Co, Fla, June 27, 38; m 60, Anthony N; c Ruth, Clark & Carol. *Educ:* Fla State Univ, BS, 60; Tex Tech Univ, MS, 65, PhD, 74. *Prof Exp:* Elem sch teacher, Mobile, Ala Pub Schs, 60; home economist, NY State & Nassau Co Exten Serv, 61-63. *Concurrent Pos:* Consult, var textbk publ, 69-; mem, Am Dietetic Asn Scholar & Award Comt; chmn, Int Fedn Home Econ Res Comt; vis prof, Univ Tenn, 82 & Middle E Tech Univ, Turkey, 91. *Mem:* Soc Nutrit Educ; Am Soc Animal Sci; Inst Food Technologists; Am Meat Sci Asn; Am Inst Nutrit; Am Home Econ Asn; Int Fedn Home Econ; Am Soc Enol & Viticult; fel Am Dietetic Asn. *Res:* Food composition and acceptability, sensory analysis of food; meat science; iron in food; cultural aspects of food and nutrition; food and nutrition education. *Mailing Add:* Food & Nutrit Col Human Sci Tex Tech Univ Lubbock TX 79409

BRITTIN, WESLEY E, THEORETICAL PHYSICS. *Current Pos:* Asst physics, 42-44, instr, 44-45, from asst prof to assoc prof, 47-59, chmn dept, 57-60, chmn dept physics & astrophys, 60-74, PROF PHYSICS & ASTROPHYS, UNIV COLO, BOULDER, 59-, DIR, INST THEORET PHYSICS, 68- *Personal Data:* b Philadelphia, Pa, Apr 21, 17; m 41; c 4. *Educ:* Univ Colo, BS, 42, MS, 45; Princeton Univ, MA, 47; Univ Alaska, PhD, 57. *Concurrent Pos:* Asst, Princeton Univ, 49-50. *Mem:* Am Phys Soc; Am Asn Physics Teachers. *Res:* Statistical mechanics. *Mailing Add:* 2425 Vassar Dr Boulder CO 80303

BRITTON, CARLTON M, RANGE SCIENCE, FIRE ECOLOGY. *Current Pos:* ASSOC PROF RANGE MGT, TEX TECH UNIV, 80- *Personal Data:* b Socorro, NMex, Aug 13, 44; m 68; c 4. *Educ:* Tex Tech Univ, BS, 68, MS, 70; Tex A&M Univ, PhD(range sci), 75. *Prof Exp:* asst prof range res, Ore State Univ, 75-80. *Mem:* Soc Range Mgt; Ecol Soc Am; Sigma Xi. *Res:* Rangeland productivity; fire ecology; ecosystem analysis. *Mailing Add:* Dept Range Wildlife Tex Tech Univ Lubbock TX 79409-0001

BRITTON, CHARLES COOPER, ELECTRICAL ENGINEERING. *Current Pos:* RETIRED. *Personal Data:* b Whitley City, Ky, Apr 27, 22; m 48; c 2. *Educ:* Tex Technol Col, BS, 47; Iowa State Univ, MS, 50. *Prof Exp:* Test engr, Gen Elec Co, 47-48; instr elec eng, Iowa State Univ, 48-50; assoc prof elec eng & asst dean eng, Colo State Univ, 50- *Mem:* Inst Elec & Electronics Engrs; Instrument Soc Am; Am Soc Eng Educ. *Res:* Instrumentation engineering for wind-tunnel and hydraulic research. *Mailing Add:* 804 Birkey Pl Ft Collins CO 80526

BRITTON, DONALD MACPHAIL, CYTOGENETICS, PTERIDOLOGY. *Current Pos:* from asst prof to prof bot, 58-84, prof molecular biol & genetics, 84-88, ADJ PROF, UNIV GUELPH, 88-, EMER PROF, 93- *Personal Data:* b Toronto, Ont, Mar 6, 23; m 50, Mary A Cronyn; c Robert, Anne & Barbara. *Educ:* Univ Toronto, BA, 46; Univ Va, PhD(biol), 50. *Honors & Awards:* Gilchrist Prize, 44; Fleming Prize, 48; Lawson Medal, Can Bot Asn, 91. *Prof Exp:* Res scientist, Defense Res Bd Can, 51-52; Nat Res Coun Can fel biol, Univ Alta, 52-53; lectr genetics, 53; asst prof hort, Univ Md, 54-58. *Concurrent Pos:* Sigma Xi res grant, 59-61. *Mem:* Bot Soc Am; Am Fern Soc; Brit Pteridological Soc; Int Asn Pteridologists. *Res:* Genetics; cytotaxonomy; plant breeding; biosystematics of ferns; floristics; pteridophytes of Canada; taxonomy. *Mailing Add:* 81 James St W Guelph ON N1G 1E7 Can. *Fax:* 519-837-2075

BRITTON, DOYLE, STRUCTURAL CHEMISTRY. *Current Pos:* From asst prof to assoc prof, 55-64, PROF INORG CHEM, UNIV MINN, MINNEAPOLIS, 65- *Personal Data:* b Los Angeles, Calif, Mar 6, 30; m 62; c 3. *Educ:* Univ Calif, Los Angeles, BS, 51; Calif Inst Technol, PhD(chem), 55. *Concurrent Pos:* NSF sr fel, 63-64. *Mem:* Am Crystallog Asn. *Res:* Molecular structure; x-ray crystallography. *Mailing Add:* Dept Chem Rm 139 Smith Hall Univ Minn 207 Pleasant St SE Minneapolis MN 55455

BRITTON, MARVIN GALE, MINERALOGY, CERAMICS. *Current Pos:* RETIRED. *Personal Data:* b Corning, NY, Jan 8, 22; m 48; c 3. *Educ:* Alfred Univ, BS, 43; Ohio State Univ, MS, 49, PhD(mineral), 52. *Prof Exp:* Ceramics engr, Corning Glass Works, 43-46; res engr, Battelle Mem Inst, 48-49; res assoc mineral, Ohio State Univ, 48-52; res assoc ceramics, Corning, Inc, 52-56, develop mgr, 56-59, tech mgr govt serv, 59-61, staff res mgr, 61-63, mgr tech liaison, 63-77, mgr tech & eng educ, 78-87. *Concurrent Pos:* Mem comt aerospace & astronaut adv panel, Mat Adv Bd, Nat Acad Sci, 59-62, mem comt ceramic mat, 62-63, mem comt res-eng interaction, 65-66; instr, Fac Continuing Educ, Corning Community Col, 62-77. *Mem:* Fel Am Ceramic Soc; Sigma Xi. *Res:* Mineralogy of blast furnace slags and refractories; development of refractory ceramics. *Mailing Add:* 121 Hornby Dr Painted Post NY 14870

BRITTON, MAXWELL EDWIN, BOTANY. *Current Pos:* RETIRED. *Personal Data:* b Hymera, Ind, Jan 26, 12; m 37, 57. *Educ:* Ind State Univ, AB, 34; Ohio State Univ, MS, 37; Northwestern Univ, PhD(bot), 41. *Hon Degrees:* DSc, Ind State Univ, 67. *Prof Exp:* Jr high sch teacher, Ind, 34-35; asst bot, Ohio State Univ, 35-37; from asst to assoc prof, Northwestern Univ, 37-55; sci officer arctic res, Geog Br, Off Naval Res, 55-66, dir arctic res prog, 66-70, actg dir, Earth Sci Div, 67-69; dir arctic develop & environ prog, Arctic Inst NAm, 70-73; consult environ sci, 73-74; biol scientist, US Geol Surv, 74-80; consult environ sci, 80-82. *Concurrent Pos:* Mem exec comt geog & climatol, Nat Res Coun, 53-54; mem comt environ studies, Proj Chariot, AEC, 59-62; mem panel biol & med, Comt Polar Res, Nat Acad Sci, 71-74; mem, Environ Protection Bd, Winnipeg, Man, 72-74. *Mem:* AAAS; Ecol Soc Am; Am Soc Limnol & Oceanog; Sigma Xi. *Res:* Taxonomy of freshwater algae; microclimatology; ecological relations of bog vegetation; soil temperatures; arctic ecology. *Mailing Add:* 2330 N Vermont St Arlington VA 22207-4053

BRITTON, OTHA LEON, NUMERICAL ANALYSIS. *Current Pos:* assoc prof math, 77-80, ASST PROF COMPUT SCI, UNIV TENN, MARTIN, 80- *Personal Data:* b Portales, NMex, Aug 6, 45; m 68; c 2. *Educ:* Eastern NMex Univ, BS, 67; Drexel Univ, MS, 69, PhD(math), 72. *Prof Exp:* Asst prof math, Univ Miss, 72-77. *Mem:* Am Math Soc; Math Asn Am; Sigma Xi. *Res:* Efficient methods of finding approximate solutions to overdetermined systems of equations. *Mailing Add:* Dept Math Couput Sci Univ Tenn Martin TN 38238-0001

BRITTON, STEVEN LOYAL, CARDIOVASCULAR PHYSIOLOGY, HYPERTENSION. *Current Pos:* PROF PHYSIOL & BIOPHYS, MED COL OHIO, 81- *Personal Data:* b Oct 10, 48; m; c 2. *Educ:* Tex Tech Univ, PhD(physiol), 78. *Mem:* Am Physiol Soc. *Res:* Regulation of blood flow. *Mailing Add:* Dept Physiol & Molecular Med Med Col Ohio 3000 Arlington Ave Toledo OH 43699-0008. *Fax:* 419-382-7395

BRITTON, WALTER MARTIN, POULTRY NUTRITION. *Current Pos:* from asst prof to assoc prof, 69-91, PROF POULTRY SCI, UNIV GA, 91- *Personal Data:* b Lasker, NC, Aug 10, 39; m 61, Jean Weaver; c Sharon & Lisa. *Educ:* NC State Univ, BS, 61, MS, 63, PhD(nutrit), 67. *Prof Exp:* NIH trainee nutrit, Univ Calif, Berkeley, 67-69. *Concurrent Pos:* Vis res scientist poultry res, Spelderholt Inst, Beckbergen, Neth, 85. *Mem:* Poultry Sci Asn; World Poultry Sci Asn; Am Inst Nutrit. *Res:* Magnesium nutrition; sodium and chloride nutrition. *Mailing Add:* Dept Poultry Sci Livestock Poultry Bldg Univ Ga Athens GA 30602-2772

BRITTON, WILLIAM GIERING, PHYSICAL CHEMISTRY, INORGANIC CHEMISTRY. *Current Pos:* RETIRED. *Personal Data:* b Wilkes-Barre, Pa, Sept 25, 21; m 43; c 4. *Educ:* Millikin Univ, BS, 43; Univ Ill, MS, 47; Univ Colo, PhD(phys chem), 56. *Prof Exp:* Prof chem, Bemidji State Univ, 47-82. *Mem:* Am Chem Soc. *Res:* Inclusion of nuclear science in undergraduate instruction. *Mailing Add:* 1624 Bixby Ave Bemidji MN 56601-2619

BRITZ, GALEN C, QUALITY ASSURANCE STATISTICS, CHEMICAL ENGINEERING. *Current Pos:* Sr chem engr, Cent Res Pilot Plant, 3M Co, 66-71, sr chem engr, New Bus Ventures, 72-74, opers analysis specialist, Corp Opers Analysis, 75-81, qual assurance mgr, 81-82, process develop mgr, 82-84, qual control mgr, 85-87, tech mgr, 88-91, QUAL MGR, PERSONAL CARE & RELATED PROD DIV, 3M CO, 91- *Personal Data:* b St Paul, Minn, Apr 1, 39; m 66, Katherine W Lindig. *Educ:* Univ Minn, BS, 61; Iowa State Univ, MS, 63, PhD(chem eng), 66. *Mem:* Am Inst Chem Engrs; fel Am Soc Qual Control. *Res:* Radiation heat transfer; photopolymerization reactor engineering; photographic science and engineering; statistical experimental design; crystallization; statistic quality control. *Mailing Add:* 1169 Lakewood Dr S Maplewood MN 55119. *Fax:* 612-736-9780; *E-Mail:* gcbritz@mmm.com

BRITZ, STEVEN J, PLANT PHYSIOLOGY, PHOTOBIOLOGY. *Current Pos:* lead scientist, Plant Photobiol Lab, 80-90, RES LEADER, CLIMATE STRESS LAB, BELTSVILLE AGR RES CTR, USDA, 90- *Personal Data:* b Chicago, Ill, July 19, 49. *Educ:* Johns Hopkins Univ, BS, 71; Harvard Univ, MA, 72, PhD(biol), 77. *Prof Exp:* Res staff biologist, Yale Univ, 77-80. *Mem:* Am Soc Plant Physiologists; Am Soc Photobiol. *Res:* Photosynthesis and photosynthate partitioning; photoperiodism and circadian rhythms; photomorphogenesis. *Mailing Add:* 10549 Patuxent Ridge Way Laurel MD 20723

BRITZMAN, DARWIN GENE, ANIMAL NUTRITION, POULTRY NUTRITION. *Current Pos:* DIR NUTRIT, GTA FEEDS, HARVEST STATES CO, 65- *Personal Data:* b Watertown, SDak, May 13, 31; m 53; c 3. *Educ:* SDak State Univ, BS, 53, PhD(animal sci), 64; Univ Minn, MS, 62. *Prof Exp:* Asst turkey mgr, Sunshine State Hatchery, Watertown, SDak, 53-54, hatchery mgr, Brookings, 54-55; territory mgr feed sales, McCabe Co, Minneapolis, 55-58; asst nutritionist, Farmer's Union Grain Terminal Asn, St Paul, 58-62; res scientist poultry, Swift & Co, Chicago, 63-65. *Concurrent Pos:* Consult, Mex, China & Japan. *Mem:* Am Soc Animal Sci; Am Dairy Sci Asn; Poultry Sci Asn. *Res:* Applied poultry, livestock and pet nutrition and management. *Mailing Add:* 1900 Edgewood Rd Sioux Falls SD 57103

BRIXNER, LOTHAR HEINRICH, INORGANIC CHEMISTRY. *Current Pos:* RETIRED. *Personal Data:* b Karlsruhe, Ger, Dec 30, 28; US citizen; m 55, Marianne Luise Wielandt; c 1. *Educ:* Univ Karlsruhe, BS, 51, MS, 53, PhD(inorg chem), 55. *Honors & Awards:* Creative Invention Award, Am Chem Soc, 96; Lavoisier Medal, 97. *Prof Exp:* Asst prof inorg chem, Univ Karlsruhe, 55-56; from res chemist to sr res chemist, E I du Pont de Nemours & Co, 56-66, res assoc, Pigments Dept, 66-69, res fel inorg chem, Cent Res & Develop Dept, 69-90. *Concurrent Pos:* Fel, Mass Inst Technol, 55; vis prof mat sci, Brown Univ, 68. *Mem:* Am Chem Soc; Am Asn Crystal Growth. *Res:* Exploratory as well as crystal growth aspects of ferroelectric, ferroelastic and electrooptic materials; finding and developing novel phosphors, particularly for the application of improved medical x-ray intensifying screens; inventor of optical waveguide on KTP potassium titanyl phosphate. *Mailing Add:* 1701 W Fox Brushes Way Fox Hill Farm Glen Mills PA 19342

BRIZIO-MOLTENI, LOREDANA, reconstructive surgery, for more information see previous edition

BROACH, ROBERT WILLIAM, CRYSTAOGRAPHY, SYNCHROTRON RADIATION METHODS. *Current Pos:* SR RES ASSOC, UOP, 89- *Personal Data:* b Fayetteville, Ark, May 19, 49; c Christopher, Riley & Susan. *Educ:* Univ Ark, Fayetteville, BS, 71; Univ Wis-Madison, PhD(chem), 77. *Prof Exp:* Res asst, Univ Wis-Madison, 72-77; res asst, Argonne Nat Lab, 77-78, sr res chemist, 78-81, res scientist, 81-83, group leader, 83-87, mgr, 87-89. *Concurrent Pos:* Resident assoc, Argonne Nat Lab, 78-79. *Mem:* Am Chem Soc; Mat Res Soc; Am Crystallog Asn; Catalysis Soc. *Res:* Theoretical and experimental characterization of aerospace, automotive, and engineered materials including catalysts, adsorbents, polymers and ceramics. *Mailing Add:* UOP 50 E Algonquin Rd Des Plaines IL 60017. *E-Mail:* rwbroach@uop.com

BROACH, WILSON J, PHYSICAL CHEMISTRY. *Current Pos:* assoc prof, 57-59, PROF CHEM & DEAN COL SCI, UNIV ARK, LITTLE ROCK, 59- *Personal Data:* b Atkins, Ark, Aug 14, 15; m 42; c 4. *Educ:* Henderson State Teachers Col, BA, 37; Univ Ark, MS, 48, PhD(phys chem), 53. *Prof Exp:* Instr chem, Little Rock Jr Col, 46-48 & Univ Ark, 48-52; assoc prof, Southern State Col, 52-54; assoc prof, Northwestern State Col, La, 54-55, actg head div phys sci, 55-57. *Mem:* Am Chem Soc; AAAS. *Res:* Reaction rates in aqueous and nonaqueous solutions. *Mailing Add:* 5511 Stonewall Rd Little Rock AR 72207-4527

BROAD, ALFRED CARTER, INVERTEBRATE ZOOLOGY. *Current Pos:* RETIRED. *Personal Data:* b Yonkers, NY, Apr 29, 22; m 50; c 1. *Educ:* Univ NC, AB, 43, MA, 51; Duke Univ, PhD, 56. *Prof Exp:* Chief shrimp invests, Inst Fisheries Res, Univ NC, 48-51; res investr, Marine Lab, Duke Univ, 53-57; from asst prof to assoc prof zool, Ohio State Univ, 57-64; chmn, Dept Biol, Western Wash Univ, 64-71, actg dir, Sundquist Marine Lab, 82-85, prof biol, 64-86. *Mem:* Am Soc Zoologists; Crustacean Soc. *Res:* Sand dollar biology; arctic littoral ecology. *Mailing Add:* 1020 Indian St Bellingham WA 98225

BROADBELT, LINDA J, CHEMICAL ENGINEERING, KINETICS. *Current Pos:* ASST PROF CHEM ENG, NORTHWESTERN UNIV, 94- *Personal Data:* b Warren, Ohio, Nov 4, 66. *Educ:* Ohio State Univ, BS, 89; Univ Del, PhD(chem eng), 94. *Honors & Awards:* NSF Career Award, 96. *Mailing Add:* Dept Chem Eng Northwestern Univ 2145 Sheridan Rd Evanston IL 60208. *Fax:* 847-491-3728; *E-Mail:* broadbelt@nwu.edu

BROADBENT, FRANCIS EVERETT, SOIL MICROBIOLOGY. *Current Pos:* RETIRED. *Personal Data:* b Snowflake, Ariz, Mar 29, 22; m 44; c 6. *Educ:* Brigham Young Univ, BS, 42; Iowa State Col, MS, 46, PhD(soil bact), 48. *Prof Exp:* Instr soils, Iowa State Col, 47-48; jr chemist, Citrus Exp Sta, Univ Calif, 48-50; assoc prof soil microbiol, Cornell Univ, 50-55; assoc prof, Univ Calif, Davis, 55-61, prof soil microbiol, 61- *Concurrent Pos:* Fulbright sr res scholar, NZ, 62-63. *Mem:* Fel Am Soc Agron; Soil Sci Soc Am. *Res:* Soil organic matter chemistry; metal organic complexes; nitrogen transformations; use of stable tracer isotopes in biological systems. *Mailing Add:* 821 A St Davis CA 95616

BROADBENT, HYRUM SMITH, CHEMISTRY. *Current Pos:* from asst prof to assoc prof, 47-52, prof, 52-85, EMER PROF CHEM, BRIGHAM YOUNG UNIV, 86- *Personal Data:* b Snowflake, Ariz, July 21, 20; m 42, Katherine Miller; c Karen, David, Justin, Camille, Nathan, Thomas, Marla & Daniel. *Educ:* Brigham Young Univ, BS, 42; Iowa State Univ, PhD(org chem), 46. *Honors & Awards:* Karl G Maeser Awards, Brigham Young Univ, 68 & 70. *Prof Exp:* Lab asst chem, Brigham Young Univ, 40-42; partic, Nat Defense Res Comt & Off Sci Res & Develop Projs, Iowa State Univ, 43-44; Milton Fund fel physico-org chem, Harvard Univ, 46-47. *Concurrent Pos:* Group leader med chem, Schering Corp, 58-59; vis scientist, C F Kettering Labs, 62-63; Sigma Xi ann lectr, Brigham Young Univ, 68; res chemist, Eastman Kodak Res Labs, 70-71; vis prof chem, Kuwait Univ & Konstanz Univ, WGer, 80. *Mem:* Am Chem Soc; Royal Soc Chem; Int Soc Heterocyclic Chem. *Res:* Heterocycles; organometallic compounds; physical and general synthetic organic chemistry; contact catalysis; medicinal chemistry; environmental effects of open burning and open detonation of conventional energetic materials of war. *Mailing Add:* 1147 Aspen Ave Provo UT 84604. *Fax:* 801-378-5474

BROADBENT, NOEL DANIEL, RESEARCH ADMINISTRATION. *Current Pos:* DOCENT ARCHEOL, UPPSALA UNIV, SWEDEN, 83-; PROG DIR, OFF POLAR PROGS, NSF, 90- *Personal Data:* b Oakland, Calif, Feb 22, 46; m 73, Elaine V Rouse; c Rosanna C. *Educ:* San Diego State Univ, BA, 68; Uppsala Univ, Sweden, FK, 71, MA & PhD(archeol), 79. *Honors & Awards:* Svea Order, Stockholm, Sweden, 74. *Prof Exp:* Lectr archeol, Uppsala Univ, Sweden, 77-81; sr lectr, Umea Univ, Sweden, 81-83, dir, Ctr Arctic Res, 83-89. *Concurrent Pos:* Lectr, Int Grad Sch, Univ Stockholm, 75-78; exchange scholar, Royal Swed Acad & Chinese Acad Soc Sci, Beijing, 85, Univ Zimbabwe, 88; consult, Swed Ed Cambridge Encycl Archeol & Times Atlas Archeol, 86 & 88, Time-Life Books; mem, Swed UNESCO man & the Biosphere Comt, 88-90; author, Swed Nat Encycl, 88-93; adj prof, Univ Umea, Sweden. *Mem:* Am Anthrop Asn; Swed Archeol Asn; Int Union Circumpolar Health; Int Arctic Social Sci Asn; fel Am Scand Found. *Res:* Multidisciplinary analysis of cultural adaptation in northern maritime societies; coastal societies during the prehistoric period in the North Bothian region of Sweden and Finland; shoreline displacement and lichenometry; historic archaeology of Antarctica. *Mailing Add:* 4505 Delmont Lane Bethesda MD 20814. *Fax:* 703-306-0139; *E-Mail:* nbroadbe@nsf.gov

BROADBOOKS, HAROLD EUGENE, ECOLOGY. *Current Pos:* from asst prof to assoc prof, 57-70, PROF ZOOL, SOUTHERN ILL UNIV, EDWARDSVILLE, 71- *Personal Data:* b Wilbur, Wash, Aug 29, 15; m 50; c 6. *Educ:* Univ Wash, BA, 37; Univ Mich, MA, 40, PhD(zool), 50. *Prof Exp:* Asst prof biol, Stephen F Austin State Col, 49-50; asst prof zool, Univ Ariz, 50-52; res assoc surg, Sch Med, Univ Wash & Radioisotope Unit, Vet Admin Hosp, 53-54; biologist, State Dept Fisheries, Wash & Ore, 54-56; asst prof zool, Shurtleff Col, 56-57. *Mem:* Am Soc Mammal; Soc Study Evolution; Ecol Soc Am; Cooper Ornith Soc; Am Behavior Soc; Sigma Xi. *Res:* Mammalogy; vertebrate ecology; behavior; distribution; evolution. *Mailing Add:* 2051 El Monte Dr Thousand Oaks CA 91362-1823

BROADDUS, CHARLES D, ORGANIC CHEMISTRY. *Current Pos:* Res chemist, 60-68, sect head res, 68-72, assoc dir, Food, Paper & Coffee Technol Div, 72-73, dir, 73-80, mgr res, 80-84, VPRES RES, PROCTER & GAMBLE CO, 84- *Personal Data:* b Irvine, Ky, Oct 17, 30; m 57; c 3. *Educ:* Centre Col Ky, AB, 52; Auburn Univ, MS, 54; Univ Fla, PhD(org chem), 60. *Res:* Metalation chemistry, base catalyzed exchange reactions. *Mailing Add:* 867 Carini Lane Cincinnati OH 45218-1511

BROADFOOT, ALBERT LYLE, PHYSICS PLANETARY ATMOSPHERES, SPACE SCIENCES. *Current Pos:* SR RES SCIENTIST, LUNAR & PLANETARY LAB, UNIV ARIZ, 83- *Personal Data:* b Milestone, Sask, Jan 8, 30; US citizen; m 64; c 2. *Educ:* Univ Sask, BE, 56, MSc, 60, PhD(physics), 63. *Honors & Awards:* Exceptional Sci Achievement Medal, NASA, 81, 86. *Prof Exp:* Engr, Defence Res Bd Can, 56-58; from asst physicist to physicist, Kitt Peak Nat Observ, 63-79; sr res scientist & assoc dir, Earth & Space Sci Inst, Univ Southern Calif, 79-83. *Concurrent Pos:* Prin investr, Ultraviolet Spectrometric Exp, Mariner 10 & Voyager Missions. *Mem:* Am Astron Soc; Am Geophys Union; Int Union Geod & Geophys; Int Asn Geomagnetism & Aeronomy. *Res:* Molecular spectroscopy; upper atmospheric physics; planetary atmosphere; airglow, aurora and associated phenomena. *Mailing Add:* 5231 E 17th Pl Tucson AZ 85711

BROADHEAD, RONALD FRIGON, PETROLEUM GEOLOGY. *Current Pos:* petrol geologist, 81-88, PETROL GEOLOGIST & HEAD DATA SECT, NMEX BUR MINES & MINERAL RESOURCES, 88- *Personal Data:* b Racine, Wis, July 22, 55. *Educ:* NMex Inst Mining & Technol, BS, 77; Univ Cincinnati, MS, 79. *Prof Exp:* Petrol geologist, Cities Serv Oil Co, 79-81. *Concurrent Pos:* Adj asst prof geol, NMex Inst Mining & Technol, 83- *Mem:* Am Asn Petrol Geologists; Soc Econ Paleontologists & Mineralogists; Sigma Xi. *Res:* Investigate and evaluate petroleum resources of New Mexico. *Mailing Add:* Campus Sta Socorro NM 87801

BROADHURST, MARTIN GILBERT, SOLID STATE PHYSICS. *Current Pos:* RETIRED. *Personal Data:* b Washington, DC, Apr 28, 32; m 55, Helen Wilson; c David M & Steven G. *Educ:* Western Md Col, BA, 55; Pa State Univ, MS, 57, PhD(physics), 59. *Honors & Awards:* Silver Medal, US Dept Com, 73, Gold Medal, 79; Samuel Stratton Award, 83; Soc Plastics Engrs Res Award, 84. *Prof Exp:* Res assoc physics, Pa State Univ, 59-60; physicist, Nat Inst Stand & Technol, 60-67, chief, Polymer Dielectrics Sect, Polymer Div, 76-70, chief, Elect Mech & Thermal Properties Sect, 70-82, dep chief, 82-83, asst chief, Polymer Div, 83-88. *Concurrent Pos:* Chmn, Conf Elec Insulation, Nat Acad Sci, 76-77; consult, 88- *Mem:* Ints Elec & Electronics Engrs; fel Am Phys Soc. *Res:* Experimental and theoretical techniques for electrical, mechanical and thermal properties of organic and polymeric solids; relations between microscopic structure and bulk physical properties; thermodynamics, statistical mechanics, piezoelectric and pyroelectric properties, conduction, aging, electrical breakdown. *Mailing Add:* 106 Fairmont Ave Box 482 Shepherdstown WV 25443. *Fax:* 304-876-1942; *E-Mail:* martyb@intrepid.net

BROADUS, JAMES MATTHEW, economics of marine minerals, marine resource economics; deceased, see previous edition for last biography

BROADWAY, ROXANNE MEYER, INSECT-PLANT INTERACTIONS, PHYTOCHEMICAL DEFENSE MECHANISMS. *Current Pos:* asst prof, 87-93, ASSOC PROF ENTOM, NY STATE AGR EXP STA, CORNELL UNIV, 93- *Personal Data:* b Maywood, Calif, Mar 31, 51; m 84. *Educ:* Univ Caif, Los Angeles, BA, 73; Univ Calif, Davis, PhD(entom), 85. *Prof Exp:* Res fel entom, Univ Calif, Davis, 85-86; res fel biochem & molecular biol, Wash State Univ, 86-87. *Res:* The biochemistry of insect-host plant interactions; determination of the mechanism of action of plant natural products on insect physiology and the molecular genetics of host plant resistance. *Mailing Add:* Cornell Univ Entom Dept NY State Agr Exp Sta Geneva NY 14456

BROADWELL, CHARLES E, AGRONOMY. *Current Pos:* RETIRED. *Personal Data:* b Kingsville, Ont, May 29, 31; c 3. *Educ:* Univ, Guelph, BSA, 54. *Prof Exp:* Gen mgr, Ont Bean Producers Mkt Bd, 68-93. *Concurrent Pos:* Pres, Ont Inst Agrologists, 64; vchmn, Kent Co Area Sch Bd, 68, Co Terr Nursing Home, 92-; chmn, Ont Pulse Com, 68-93; bd dirs, Edgewood Camp, 93- *Mem:* Int Pulse Trade & Indust Confederation (pres, 89-); Can Bean Coun (pres, 91-93); fel Agr Inst Can (pres, 87). *Mailing Add:* Ont Bean Producers 140 Raney Crescent London ON N6L 1C3 Can

BROADWELL, JAMES E(UGENE), AERONAUTICAL ENGINEERING. *Current Pos:* RETIRED. *Personal Data:* b Atlanta, Ga, Jan 15, 21; m 43, Edith Merriman; c Kathy (Haris), Susan (Schwimmer) & Ann. *Educ:* Ga Inst Technol, BS, 42; Calif Inst Technol, MS, 44; Univ Mich, PhD(aeronaut eng), 52. *Prof Exp:* Asst prof aeronaut eng, Inst Technol, USAF, 46-48; instr & asst prof, Univ Mich, 48-55, assoc prof, 55-58; staff engr, Space Technol Labs, Thompson-Ramo-Wooldrige, Inc, 58-75, sr staff engr, 75-84; sr res fel, Calif Inst Technol, 67-72, from res assoc to sr res assoc, 72-85, sr scientist, 85- *Concurrent Pos:* Design specialist, Douglas Aircraft Co, 56-57. *Mem:* Nat Acad Eng; Am Phys Soc; fel Am Inst Aeronaut & Astronaut. *Res:* Turbulent mixing and combustion; rarefied gas dynamics; cellular automata; high energy chemical lasers. *Mailing Add:* 8 Muirfield Rd Half Moon Bay CA 94019. *E-Mail:* jeboad@leland.stanford.edu

BROADWELL, RICHARD DOW, NEUROBIOLOGY & NEUROPATHOLOGY, CYTOLOGY. *Current Pos:* SR SCIENTIST & INVESTR, OFF RES INTEGRITY, USPHS, 93- *Personal Data:* b Oak Park, Ill, Nov 4, 45; m 88, Bonnie Kalberer. *Educ:* Knox Col, BA, 67; Univ Wis, MS, 71, DPhil(neurosci), 74. *Prof Exp:* Staff fel neurocytol, NIH, 74-77, sr staff fel, 77-79, staff biologist, 79-80; asst prof neuropath, Med Sch, Univ Md, Baltimore, 80-84, dir, Neurol Surg Labs, 84-93, assoc prof neuropath & neurol surg, 85-89; prog dir molecular & cellular neurobiol, NSF, 87-89; prof neurol surg, Univ Md Med Sch, 90-93. *Concurrent Pos:* Japanese Soc Prom Sci Fel, 79; Nat Inst Neurol Dis & Stroke grantee, 81-93; Burroughs Wellcome fel, 93. *Mem:* Soc Neurosci; Am Asn Anatomists; Am Soc Cell Biol; Histochem Soc. *Res:* Neurocytology; neuropathology; cell biology; blood-brain barrier; axoplasmic transport; degeneration/regeneration; brain transplants; neuroimmunology. *Mailing Add:* Off Res Integrity USPHS 5615 Security Lane Rockville MD 20852. *E-Mail:* rbroadwell@usphs.dhhs.gov

BROADWIN, ALAN, ULTRASONIC SURGICAL DEVICES, DISPOSABLES FOR SURGICAL SYSTEMS. *Current Pos:* PRIN, AINSLIE CO, 93- *Personal Data:* b New York, NY, Apr 20, 35; m 61, Naomi Pascal; c Esther B & Valerie A. *Educ:* Columbia Col, BA, 56; Columbia Univ Sch Eng, BS, 57; Stevens Inst Technol, MS, 59. *Prof Exp:* Proj engr, Intertype Div, Harris Corp, 62-69; sr engr, Cavitron Corp, 69-72, group leader, 72-75, mgr med systs, 75-79; asst to gen mgr, Cavitron Ultrasonics, 79-81; dir tech develop, Cooper Lasersonics Inc, 81-85; vpres res & develop, Cooper Labs, 85-88; dir eng, Valley lab Inc, Pfizer, 88-90, ultrasonic technol, 90-93. *Mem:* Acoust Soc Am; Ultrasonics Ferroelectrics & Frequency Control Soc; Eng Med & Biol Soc; Am Inst Ultrasound Med; Am Soc Mech Engrs; Am Soc Mat. *Res:* Product conception and design; commercialization of surgical equipment and techniques; granted over 22 patents. *Mailing Add:* 27 Pine Ridge Rd Larchmont NY 10538-2616. *Fax:* 914-833-5037

BROBECK, JOHN RAYMOND, PHYSIOLOGY. *Current Pos:* prof & chmn dept, 52-70, Herbert C Rorer prof med sci, 70-84, EMER PROF, SCH MED, UNIV PA, 84- *Personal Data:* b Steamboat Springs, Colo, Apr 12, 14; m 40; c 4. *Educ:* Wheaton Col, Ill, BS, 32; Northwestern Univ, MS, 37, PhD(neurol), 39; Yale Univ, MD, 43. *Hon Degrees:* LLD, Wheaton Col, Ill, 60; MA, Univ Pa, 71. *Prof Exp:* From instr to assoc prof physiol, Sch Med, Yale Univ, 43-52. *Mem:* Nat Acad Sci; fel Am Acad Arts & Sci; Am Physiol Soc (pres, 71-72); Am Soc Clin Invest; Am Inst Nutrit. *Res:* Physiological controls and regulations; control of energy balance; physiology of hypothalamus. *Mailing Add:* 224 Vassar Ave Swarthmore PA 19081

BROBERG, JOEL WILBUR, INORGANIC CHEMISTRY. *Current Pos:* RETIRED. *Personal Data:* b Willmar, Minn, Aug 2, 10; m 37; c 2. *Educ:* Macalester Col, BA, 32; Univ Minn, MA, 40, PhD(chem educ), 62. *Prof Exp:* From asst prof to prof chem, NDak State Univ, 41-81, dir, Inst Teaching Educ, 69-77. *Mem:* Am Chem Soc. *Res:* Molar method of teaching chemistry; synthesis of coordination compounds. *Mailing Add:* 1245 11th St N Fargo ND 58102

BROBST, DONALD ALBERT, ECONOMIC GEOLOGY. *Current Pos:* ADJ PROG GEOL, NVA COMMUNITY COL, 91- *Personal Data:* b Allentown, Pa, May 8, 25; m 50, Marie Katz; c Alice. *Educ:* Muhlenberg Col, AB, 47; Univ Minn, PhD(geol), 53. *Honors & Awards:* Herbert C Hoover Award, Am Inst Mining Metall & Petrol Engrs, 88. *Prof Exp:* Geologist, US Geol Surv, 48-80, dep chief, Off Mineral Resources, 73-76, chief, Br Eastern Mineral Resources, 78-80; consult geologist, 81-91. *Mem:* Fel Geol Soc Am; fel Mineral Soc Am; fel Soc Econ Geologists; Am Inst Mining, Metall & Petrol Eng; Int Asn Genesis Ore Deposits; Soc Mining, Metall & Explor. *Res:* Economic geology of mineral deposits, especially industrial minerals; assessment of mineral resources; petrology. *Mailing Add:* 2268 Wheelwright Ct Reston VA 20191

BROBST, DUANE FRANKLIN, VETERINARY MEDICINE. *Current Pos:* PROF VET MED, WASH STATE UNIV, 70- *Personal Data:* b Medicine Lake, Mont, Oct 8, 23; m 58; c 4. *Educ:* Univ Southern Calif, AB, 49; Wash State Univ, DVM, 54; Univ Pittsburgh, MPH, 57; Univ Wis, PhD(vet sci), 62. *Prof Exp:* Pvt vet practice, Mont, 54-56; pub health veterinarian, Allegheny County Health Dept, Pa, 57-58; proj asst vet med, Univ Wis, 58-62; asst prof vet path, Sch Vet Sci & Med, Purdue Univ, 62-70. *Concurrent Pos:* Whitley County Cancer Asn, Ind & Delta Theta Tau res grant, 62-63; consult, Am Med Asn, 63- *Mem:* Am Vet Med Asn; Am Col Vet Path. *Res:* Pathology of animal disease. *Mailing Add:* SW 630 Dawnview Pullman WA 99163

BROCARD, DOMINIQUE NICOLAS, FLUID MECHANICS, CIVIL ENGINEERING. *Current Pos:* ASSOC, METCALF & EDDY, 86- *Personal Data:* b Versailles, France. *Educ:* Mass Inst Technol, MS, 73, PhD(civil eng), 76. *Prof Exp:* Res engr environ fluid mech, Alden Res Lab, Worcester Polytech Inst, 76-78, asst prof civil eng, 76-81, lead engr, 78-82, assoc prof civil engrs, 81-86, asst dir, 82-86. *Concurrent Pos:* Adj prof, Alden Res Lab, Worcester Polytech Inst, 86- *Mem:* Am Soc Civil Engrs; Sigma Xi; Int Asn Hydraul Res. *Res:* Environmental fluid mechanics; free surface and density flows; turbulent dispersion; waste heat disposal; heat and momentum transfer. *Mailing Add:* 23 Orchard St Wellesley MA 02181

BROCCOLI, ANTHONY JOSEPH, CLIMATE MODELING, PALEOCLIMATE. *Current Pos:* RES METEOROLOGIST, GEOPHYS FLUID DYNAMICS LAB, NAT OCEANIC & ATMOSPHERIC ADMIN, 82- *Personal Data:* b Newark, NJ, Sept 14, 56; m 84. *Educ:* Rutgers Univ, BS, 77, MS, 79. *Prof Exp:* Instr meteorol, Rutgers Univ, 79-82. *Mem:* Am Meteorol Soc; Am Geophys Union; AAAS. *Res:* Use of numerical models for study of climate; climate change; paleoclimate. *Mailing Add:* 9 Kingsberry Dr Somerset NJ 08873

BROCHMANN-HANSSEN, EINAR, PHARMACEUTICAL CHEMISTRY. *Current Pos:* from asst prof to assoc prof, 49-59, PROF PHARMACEUT CHEM, SCH PHARM, UNIV CALIF, SAN FRANCISCO, 59- *Personal Data:* b Hvitsten, Norway, June 18, 17; nat US; m 43; c 2. *Educ:* Univ Oslo, Cand Pharm, 41; Purdue Univ, PhD(pharmaceut chem), 49. *Honors & Awards:* Ebert Prize, 62; Powers Award, 63; Silver Medal, Univ Helsinki, 70; Res Achievement Award in Natural Prod, Acad Pharmaceut Sci, 78. *Prof Exp:* Pharmacist, Flekkefjord Apotek, Norway, 42-44; res assoc, Univ Oslo, 44-46. *Concurrent Pos:* Instr, Univ Oslo, 45-46; partic scientist, UN Opium Res Prog, 58-; mem rev & exec comts, Nat Formulary, US Pharmacopeia, 60-70; vis prof, Robert Robinson Labs, Liverpool, 65-66; mem, US Pharmacopeial Conv, 70-75; vis prof, Nat Taiwan Univ, 74-75. *Mem:* Am Soc Pharmacog; Am Chem Soc; Am Pharmaceut Asn; NY Acad Sci; Int Pharmaceut Fedn; fel Acad Pharmaceut Sci. *Res:* Isolation, structure and physiological activity of naturally occurring substances; analytical chemistry; chromatography; alkaloid chemistry and biosynthesis. *Mailing Add:* 9 De Anza Way San Rafael CA 94903

BROCK, CAROLYN PRATT, STRUCTURAL CHEMISTRY. *Current Pos:* From asst prof to assoc prof, 72-87, PROF, DEPT CHEM, UNIV KY, 87- *Personal Data:* b Chicago, Ill, July 25, 46; m 72, Louis M. *Educ:* Wellesley Col, BA, 68; Northwestern Univ, PhD(chem), 72. *Mem:* Am Chem Soc; Am Crystallog Asn. *Res:* Systematics of packing in molecular crystals; design synthesis and characterization of solid-state molecular compounds. *Mailing Add:* Dept Chem Univ Ky Lexington KY 40506-0055. *Fax:* 606-323-1069; *E-Mail:* cpbrock@ukcc.uky.edu

BROCK, DONALD R, GYNECOLOGICAL PATHOLOGY. *Current Pos:* RETIRED. *Educ:* Northwestern Univ, MD, 50. *Prof Exp:* Dir labs, St Mary's Hosp, 61-97. *Mailing Add:* St Marys Hosp 36475 Five Mile Rd Livonia MI 48154-1971

BROCK, ERNEST GEORGE, ELECTROPHYSICS. *Current Pos:* RETIRED. *Personal Data:* b Detroit, Mich, Apr 7, 26; m 50; c 3. *Educ:* Univ Notre Dame, BS, 46, PhD(physics), 51. *Prof Exp:* Res assoc, Gen Elec Res Lab, 51-56; group leader, Linfield Res Inst, Ore, 56-58; sr physicist, Res Dept, Gen Dynamics/Electronics, 58-59, prin scientist, 59-61, mgr quantum physics lab, 61-66; head quantum electronics dept, Lab Opers, Aerospace Corp, Calif, 66-68, sr staff scientist, 68-69, sr staff engr, 69-71; sr engr, NAm Rockwell, 72; sr engr specialist, Garrett Corp, 73-74; div off tech staff mem, Laser Div, Los Alamos Nat Lab, Univ Calif, 74-90, lab assoc, 90-93. *Mem:* AAAS; Am Phys Soc; sr mem Inst Elec & Electronics Engrs; NY Acad Sci; Sigma Xi. *Res:* Laser applications to fusion and isotope separation; applications of lasers and electronics technology to advanced strategic systems planning. *Mailing Add:* 1880 Camino Redondo Los Alamos NM 87544

BROCK, FRED VINCENT, METEOROLOGY. *Current Pos:* vis scientist, 73-75, STAFF SCIENTIST METEOROL, NAT CTR ATMOSPHERIC RES, 75- *Personal Data:* b Chillicothe, Ohio, Nov 25, 32; m 60; c 2. *Educ:* Ohio State Univ, BS, 54; Univ Mich, MSE, 60; Univ Okla, PhD(meteorol), 73. *Prof Exp:* Assoc res engr meteorol, Univ Mich, 60-69; spec instr, Univ Okla, 69-73. *Concurrent Pos:* Consult, Univ Corp Atmospheric Res & White Sands Missile Range, US Army, 70-73; Nat Ctr Atmospheric Res affil prof, Univ Okla, 75- *Mem:* Am Meteorol Soc. *Res:* Meteorological measurement systems including sensors, data loggers, system analysis and data processing. *Mailing Add:* Dept Meteorol Univ Okla Main Campus 900 Asp Ave Norman OK 73019-4050

BROCK, GEOFFREY E(DGAR), METALLURGY. *Current Pos:* RETIRED. *Personal Data:* b Eng, Feb 4, 30; nat US; m 55; c 3. *Educ:* Univ Wales, BSc, 50; Pa State Univ, MS, 52, PhD(metall), 54. *Prof Exp:* Res metallurgist, NJ Zinc Co, Pa, 54; metallurgist, US Army Frankford Arsenal, 54-56; mem res staff, IBM Corp, 56-64, mgr, Mat Tech Mfg Res Dept, Components Div, 64-68, mfg res lab mgr, 68-70, asst to Components Div pres, 70-71, mgr, Plans & Controls Develop Labs, Components Div, 71-74, mgr silicon process, Technol Data Systs Div, 74-89. *Mem:* Am Soc Metals; Am Inst Mining, Metall & Petrol Engrs; Mat Res Soc. *Res:* Physical metallurgy of semiconductor materials; deformation and x-ray studies of crystal defects; phase equilibria; materials research on electronic computer components. *Mailing Add:* 126 Forest Dr Mt Kisco NY 10549

BROCK, GEORGE WILLIAM, NUCLEAR ENGINEERING. *Current Pos:* RETIRED. *Personal Data:* b Grant Co, Ind, Aug 27, 20; m 44; c 3. *Educ:* Nebr State Teachers Col, AB, 39; Air Force Inst Technol, MS, 57; Purdue Univ, MS, 64. *Prof Exp:* Radio engr, Farnsworth TV & Radio Corp, Ind, 41-42; meteorologist, US Army Air Force, 42-46; physicist, Aeronaut Ice Res Lab, 46-48, chief res, 48-50; USAF, 50-75, physicist, Wright Air Develop Ctr, Ohio, 50-59, mem staff, USAF Acad, 59-65, prof physics & actg head dept, 65-66, dir sci, Hq Air Force Systs Command, Andrews AFB, Md, 69-73, dir, F J Seiler Res Lab, USAF Acad, 73-75; sr engr, Ensco Inc, Colorado Springs, 76-81; pres, Rocky Mountain Eng Assoc, Inc, Colorado Springs, 81-90. *Concurrent Pos:* Mem subcomt icing, Nat Adv Comt Aeronaut; US deleg, NATO DRG Panel Physics & Electronics, 70-75. *Mem:* AAAS; Am Phys Soc. *Res:* Solid state physics and electronic materials. *Mailing Add:* 6118 Applewood Ridge Circle Colorado Springs CO 80918

BROCK, JAMES HARVEY, ENGINEERING. *Current Pos:* Technician telemetry, 81-84, engr computer networks, 84-88, ENGR ROBOTICS, NASA-JOHNSON SPACE CTR, 88- *Personal Data:* b Neubrueke, Ger, July 16, 57; US citizen; m 78. *Educ:* Univ Houston, Clear Lake, BS, 84. *Mem:* Am Astron Soc. *Res:* Design and develop telerobotic components for telerobotic systems; design and develop interface simulators for space craft training. *Mailing Add:* 4222 Royal Manor Pasadena TX 77505

BROCK, JAMES RUSH, CHEMICAL ENGINEERING, PHYSICS. *Current Pos:* from asst prof to prof chem eng, 60-80, K A KOBE PROF, UNIV TEX, AUSTIN, 80- *Personal Data:* b McAllen, Tex, Dec 31, 30; m 64, Mary L Waghorn; c Alison & Ianthe. *Educ:* Rice Univ, BA, 53, BS, 54; Univ Wis, MS & PhD(chem eng), 60. *Honors & Awards:* Sci Rev Award, US Environ Protection Agency, 76; Sinclair Award, Am Asn Aerosol Res, 92. *Prof Exp:* Res engr, Humble Oil & Refining Co, 54-55. *Concurrent Pos:* NSF fel, 62-63; res grant, Nat Ctr Atmospheric Res, 64; mem, Res Grants Adv Comt & Prog Planning Subcomt, Nat Air Pollution Control Admin, 69-; vis prof, Univ Paris, 73-74, Tokyo Inst Technol, 88; dir, US Environ Protection Agency, Buffalo, NY Field Study & Houston, Tex Field Study, 80, mem, Environ Protection Agency Chem & Physics Rev Comt, 80- *Mem:* AAAS; Am Chem Soc; Am Inst Chem Engrs; Sigma Xi; Am Asn Aerosol Res; Ger Asn Aerosol Res. *Res:* Aerosol physics and chemistry; author of over 150 research publications. *Mailing Add:* PO Box 5164 Austin TX 78763-5164. *Fax:* 512-471-7060

BROCK, JOEL DONALD, X-RAY SCATTERING STUDIES OF THE STRUCTURE OF CONDENSED MATTER, APPLIED PHYSICS. *Current Pos:* asst prof, 89-95, ASSOC PROF APPL PHYSICS, CORNELL UNIV, 95- *Personal Data:* b Evanston, Ill, Feb 25, 59; m 83, Susan Hajda; c Rachel H. *Educ:* Stanford Univ, BS, 81; Mass Inst Technol, PhD(physics), 87. *Prof Exp:* Staff physicist, Tektronix Inc, 81-82; postdoctoral fel, Mass Inst Technol, 87-89. *Concurrent Pos:* Young investr, NSF, 92-97, prin investr, 95-; chair user comt, Cornell High Energy Synchrotron Source, 94-96; dir grad studies appl physics, Cornell Univ, 94-; chair user exec comt, Nat Sychrotron Light Source, 96-98. *Mem:* Am Phys Soc; Sigma Xi; Mat Res Soc; Union Concerned Scientists. *Res:* X-ray scattering studies of the structure of novel phases of condensed matter, the phase transitions between these phases and the kinetics of these transitions. *Mailing Add:* Sch Appl & Eng Physics Cornell Univ Ithaca NY 14850. *E-Mail:* jdb20@cornell.edu

BROCK, KATHERINE MIDDLETON, MICROBIOLOGY, SCIENCE COMMUNICATIONS. *Current Pos:* RETIRED. *Personal Data:* b Keokuk, Iowa, June 3, 38; m 71, Thomas D; c Emily & Brian. *Educ:* Vassar Col, AB, 60; Univ Calif, Berkeley, MA, 63; Univ Mass, Amherst, PhD(microbiol), 67. *Prof Exp:* Res asst biochem, Tech Univ Norway, 63-64; asst prof microbiol, San Francisco State Col, 67-70; res assoc, Ind Univ, Bloomington, 70-71; res assoc bact, Univ Wis-Madison, 71-81; vpres, Sci Tech Publ, Inc, 81-93. *Mem:* AAAS; Sigma Xi; Am Soc Microbiol. *Res:* Microbial physiology; study of extreme environments, especially high temperature, high and low hydrogen-ion concentration and saline environments. *Mailing Add:* 1227 Dartmouth Rd Madison WI 53705

BROCK, KENNETH JACK, MINERALOGY. *Current Pos:* Asst prof, 70-74, ASSOC PROF GEOL, IND UNIV NORTHWEST, 74-, CHMN, GEOSCI, 77- *Personal Data:* b Pampa, Tex, Aug 22, 37; m 62; c 1. *Educ:* San Jose State Col, BS, 62; Stanford Univ, PhD(geol), 70. *Mem:* Mineral Soc Am; Mineral Soc Gt Brit & Ireland. *Res:* Mineralogy and genesis of skarns; mineralogy of zoned lithium micas. *Mailing Add:* Dept Geol Ind Univ Northwest 3400 Broadway Gary IN 46408-1197

BROCK, LOUIS MILTON, ENGINEERING PHYSICS. *Current Pos:* PROF ENG MECH, UNIV KY, 71- *Personal Data:* b Davenport, Iowa, Apr 16, 43; m 72, Carolyn S Pratt. *Educ:* Northwestern Univ, BS, 66, MS, 67, PhD(theoret & appl mech), 72. *Prof Exp:* Draftsman, Black & Veatch Consult Engrs, 62; tech asst, Gen Dynamics/Convair, 63-64; tech asst, Sargent-Welch Sci Co, 64; res technician, Am Can Co, 65. *Concurrent Pos:* Consult, McDonnell-Douglas Astronaut Co, 72 & Compusport, Inc, 84-87; prin investr, NSF, 72-74, 79-82, 84-87 & 90-; vis prof, Dept Eng Sci, Univ Oxford, 80-81; chmn, comm elasticity, Am Soc Civil Engrs, 83-85, corresp exec comt, eng mech div; res fel, Naval Res Lab, 83, 85, 87, 90. *Mem:* Sigma Xi; Am Soc Mech Engrs; Am Soc Civil Engrs; Am Asn Univ Professors. *Res:* Wave propagation in solids, problems in fracture, composite materials and seismology; dislocation mechanics; thermoelastodynamics. *Mailing Add:* Univ Ky 467 Anderson Hall Lexington KY 40506-0001

BROCK, MARY ANNE, GERONTOLOGY, CHRONOBIOLOGY. *Current Pos:* biologist, Geront Res Ctr, Nat Inst Aging, 60-95, GUEST RES, NAT INST DEAFNESS & OTHER COMMUNICATIVE DISORDERS, NIH, 96- *Personal Data:* b Aurora, Ill, June 29, 32. *Educ:* Grinnell Col, BA, 54; Harvard Univ, MA, 56, PhD(biol), 59. *Prof Exp:* Res assoc med, Harvard Med Sch, 59-60. *Concurrent Pos:* Consult; bd gov, Soc Cryobiol, 73-76; vis scientist, Hopkins Marine Sta, Stanford Univ, 77. *Mem:* Am Soc Cell Biol; Int Soc Chronobiol; Soc Cryobiol (secy, 71-72); fel Geront Soc Am; Sigma Xi; Soc Res Biol Rhythms; fel AAAS. *Res:* Cell biology of aging mammalian cell types; effect of temperature on cellular aging; biological clocks and aging. *Mailing Add:* 357 S Columbia St Naperville IL 60540-5415

BROCK, PATRICK W G, PETROLOGY, STRUCTURAL GEOLOGY. *Current Pos:* asst prof, 70-75, ASSOC PROF GEOL, QUEENS COL, NY, 76- *Personal Data:* b Kelowna, BC, Dec 17, 32; m, Pamela Chase; c Kenneth. *Educ:* Univ BC, BASc, 56; Univ Leeds, PhD(geol), 63. *Prof Exp:* Party leader explor geol, Western Rift Explor Co, 57-59; adv Uganda geol surv, Can External Aid Off, Can Int Develop Agency, 63-70. *Concurrent Pos:* Hon lectr, Makerere Univ, Uganda, 68-70; Fac Res Award Prog grant, Res Inst, City Univ New York, 74-75; prof staff, Cong-Bd Higher Educ grant, 78-79, 79-80 & 85-87. *Mem:* Geol Asn Can; Sigma Xi; AAAS; Geol Soc Am; Asn Geoscientists Int Develop. *Res:* Structural, metamorphic and age relationships in the rocks of the Manhattan Prong, Southeast New York; regional geology; field geology. *Mailing Add:* 61-18 157th St Flushing NY 11367-1241

BROCK, RICHARD EUGENE, MARINE ECOLOGY, FISHERIES. *Current Pos:* HEAD BENTHIC STUDIES, HAWAII INST MARINE BIOL, 75- *Personal Data:* b Astoria, Que, July 1, 43; m 70; c 1. *Educ:* Univ Hawaii, BS, 68, MS, 72; Univ Wash, Seattle, PhD(fisheries), 79. *Prof Exp:* Dir field studies, Coop Fishery Unit, Univ Hawaii, 72-73; teaching asst, Univ Wash, 73-74. *Concurrent Pos:* Consult, Oceanic Inst, 72-, Environ Consult Inc, 75-, Environ Assessment Co, Pilipili Prod, 76- & Hawaii Planning Design & Res, 77- *Mem:* Am Soc Ichthyologists & Herpetologists; Soc Syst Zool; Am Soc Naturalists; Sigma Xi. *Res:* Ecological relationships of coral reef fishes; tropical marine benthic community structure and function; management of coral reef systems; energy flow through coral reef ecosystems. *Mailing Add:* Marine Sci Bldg Univ Hawaii 1000 Pope Rd Rm 204 Honolulu HI 96822

BROCK, RICHARD R, CIVIL ENGINEERING, HYDRAULIC ENGINEERING. *Current Pos:* assoc prof, 73-77, PROF CIVIL ENG, CALIF STATE UNIV, FULLERTON, 77- *Personal Data:* b Sewickley, Pa, Mar 7, 38; c 3. *Educ:* Univ Calif, Berkeley, BS, 61, MS, 62; Calif Inst Technol, PhD(civil eng), 68. *Honors & Awards:* J C Stevens Award, Am Soc Civil Engrs, 66. *Prof Exp:* Civil Engr, Los Angeles Co Flood Control Dist, 62-63; asst prof civil eng, Univ Calif, Irvine, 67-73. *Mem:* Am Soc Civil Engrs. *Res:* Flow in open channels and through porous media hydrology. *Mailing Add:* Dept Civil Eng Calif State Univ 800 N State Col Fullerton CA 92631-3547

BROCK, ROBERT H, JR, PHOTOGRAMMETRY, REMOTE SENSING. *Current Pos:* assoc prof, 67-77, PROF PHOTOGRAM & REMOTE SENSING, STATE UNIV NY COL ENVIRON SCI & FORESTRY, 77-, CHMN, FAC FOREST ENG, 80- *Personal Data:* b New Rochelle, NY, Feb 15, 33; m 74, Dorothy L Hochmoth; c Susan, James & Douglas. *Educ:* State Univ NY, BS, 58, MS, 59; Cornell Univ, PhD(photogram, geod eng), 71. *Prof Exp:* From instr to asst prof photogram & geod, Syracuse Univ, 59-66; sr systs analyst, CBS Labs, 66-67. *Concurrent Pos:* Photogram consult var corp & law firms. *Mem:* Am Soc Photogram & Remote Sensing; Am Cong Surv & Mapping; Am Soc Agr Engrs. *Res:* Photogrammetric engineering; film shrinkage and atmospheric refraction studies; effects of edge information properties on coordinate measurement; image deformation studies; surveying with global positioning systems; digital photogrammetry. *Mailing Add:* Col Environ Sci & Forestry State Univ NY 312 Bray Hall Syracuse NY 13210. *Fax:* 315-852-6021

BROCK, THOMAS DALE, MICROBIOLOGY. *Current Pos:* E B Fred prof, 71-90, EMER PROF NATURAL SCI, UNIV WIS-MADISON, 90- *Personal Data:* b Cleveland, Ohio, Sept 10, 26; m 52, 71, Katherine Middleton; c Emily K & Brian T. *Educ:* Ohio State Univ, BSc, 49, MSc, 50, PhD(microbiol), 52. *Honors & Awards:* Fisher Award, Am Soc Microbiol, 84, Carski Award, 88. *Prof Exp:* Res microbiologist, Upjohn Co, 52-57; asst prof biol, Western Res Univ, 57-59, fel, Sch Med, 59-60; from asst prof to prof bact, Ind Univ, Bloomington, 60-71. *Concurrent Pos:* Vis biologist, Am Inst Biol Sci, 61-62; USPHS career develop award, 62-68; lectr, Found Microbiol, 71-72 & 78-79. *Mem:* Fel AAAS; hon mem Am Soc Microbiol. *Res:* Microbial ecology; aquatic microbiology; history of microbiology; computer-assisted publication. *Mailing Add:* 1227 Dartmouth Rd Madison WI 53705-2213

BROCK, TOMMY A, CELL CULTURE, ION FLUX. *Current Pos:* DIR PHARMACOL, TEX BIOTECHNOL CORP, 92- *Educ:* Univ Iowa, PhD(physiol), 78. *Prof Exp:* Asst prof path, Brigham & Women's Hosp, Harvard Med Sci, 82-89; mem, Dept Med Hypertension Prog, Univ Ala, 89-92. *Mailing Add:* Tex BioTech Corp 7000 Fannin Dr Suite 1920 Houston TX 77030

BROCKBANK, KELVIN GORDON MASHADER, CARDIO-VASCULAR GRAFT DEVELOPMENT, ORGAN & TISSUE TRANSPLANTATION. *Current Pos:* PRES, KGB ASSOC, INC, 96- *Personal Data:* b Yeovil, Somerset, Eng, Apr 22, 52; m 74, Mara Protopapa; c Kelsey & Matthew. *Educ:* Trinity Col, Dublin, BA, 73, MA, 76; Med Univ SC, PhD(exp path), 80. *Prof Exp:* Res asst, Columbia Univ, 75-77; sr scientist, Erasmus Univ, 80-85; dir res & develop, Cryolife, Inc, 85-94; vpres res & develop, Baxter Healthcare, 94-96. *Concurrent Pos:* Vis asst prof path, Med Univ SC, 85-91, adj assoc prof microbiol & immunol, 95-; adj asst prof biol, Emory Univ, 88-90. *Mem:* Am Asn Tissue Banks; Tissue Cult Asn; Soc Cryobiol; Europ Soc Vascular Surg; Acad Surg Res. *Res:* Organ and tissue transplantation, including procurement, effects of short-term storage, long-term storage by cryopreservation, transplantation and the recipient's immune response; tissue engineering of grafts. *Mailing Add:* 21 Montagu St Charleston SC 29401. *Fax:* 803-722-3111

BROCKE, RAINER H, ENDANGERED WILDLIFE MANAGEMENT. *Current Pos:* sr res assoc, 73-83, ASSOC PROF WILDLIFE ECOL, STATE UNIV NY COL ENVIRON SCI & FORESTRY, 83- *Personal Data:* b Calcutta, India, Nov 24, 33; US citizen; m 57; c 3. *Educ:* Mich State Univ, BS, 55, MS, 57, PhD(mammalian bioenergetics), 70. *Prof Exp:* Instr, Mich State Univ, 63-69. *Concurrent Pos:* Consult, Develop Sci Prog, NY, 85-88; var res grants, 71- *Mem:* NY Acad Sci; Am Soc Mammal; Wildlife Soc; Sigma Xi. *Res:* Wildlife ecology and management; physiological ecology of mammals. *Mailing Add:* 249 Illick Hall State Univ NY One Forestry Dr Syracuse NY 13210

BROCKE, STEFAN, AUTOIMMUNE DISEASES, INFECTIOUS DISEASES. *Current Pos:* SCIENTIST, NAT INFO BUR, NAT INST NEUROL DIS & STROKE, NIH, 96- *Personal Data:* b Essen, Ger, Oct 10, 58. *Educ:* Free Univ Berlin, MD, 85, PhD, 91. *Prof Exp:* Fel, Stanford Univ, 91-95, res assoc, 95-96. *Concurrent Pos:* Asst doctor, Free Univ Berlin, 89-95. *Mem:* Fel Molecular Med Soc; Am Soc Microbiol. *Res:* Analysis of the mechanisms leading to and driving inflammatory and immune disease; infection and autoimmunity. *Mailing Add:* NDS Nat Info Bur Nat Inst Neurol Dis & Stroke NIH Bethesda MD 20892-1400. *E-Mail:* sbrocke@helia.nih.gov

BROCKEMEYER, EUGENE WILLIAM, PHARMACY. *Current Pos:* Res assoc, 57-67, asst dir prod develop, 67, mgr qual control & prod develop, 67-71, dir res develop & qual control, 71-82, VPRES, RES & QUAL ASSURANCE, DORSEY LABS, 83- *Personal Data:* b Buckner, Mo, June 22, 29; m 51; c 2. *Educ:* Univ Kans, BS, 51, MS, 52; Ohio State Univ, PhD(pharm), 54. *Mem:* Am Pharmaceut Asn; Am Soc Qual Control. *Res:* Rate of absorption of drugs from pharmaceutical vehicles and sustained release forms of medication. *Mailing Add:* 1230 Twin Ridge Rd Lincoln NE 68510

BROCKENBROUGH, EDWIN C, SURGERY. *Current Pos:* Asst, Sch Med, Univ Wash, 61-64, asst prof, 64-70, clin assoc prof surg, 70-84, CLIN PROF, SCH MED, UNIV WASH, 84-; SR RES SCIENTIST, INST APPL PHYSIOL & MED, SEATTLE, 75- *Personal Data:* b Baltimore, Md, July 24, 30; m 68, Jean McClure; c John, Martha, Andrew, Ann & Susan. *Educ:* Col William & Mary, BS, 52; Johns Hopkins Univ, MD, 56. *Prof Exp:* Asst surg, Johns Hopkins Univ, 57-58; clin assoc cardiac surg, NIH, 59-61. *Concurrent Pos:* Assoc surgeon-in-chief, Harborview Med Ctr, Seattle, 70-75; chief staff, Northwest Hosp; pvt pract, 75-; pres, King Co Med Soc, 92. *Mem:* Sigma Xi; Am Col Surgeons; Am Heart Asn. *Res:* Cardiovascular physiology; thoracic surgery; cerebrovascular diseases. *Mailing Add:* 1560 N 115th St Ste 102 Seattle WA 98133-8414

BROCKERHOFF, HANS, BIOCHEMISTRY, NEUROCHEMISTRY. *Current Pos:* CHIEF SCIENTIST NEUROCHEM, NY STATE INST FOR BASIC RES IN DEVELOP DISABILITIES, 73- *Personal Data:* b Duisburg, Ger, July 8, 28; m 58; c 3. *Educ:* Univ Cologne, Dr rer nat, 58. *Prof Exp:* Researcher, Univ Wash, 58-60 & Univ Calif, Berkeley, 60-61; assoc scientist, Fisheries Res Bd, Can, 61-63, sr scientist, 63-73. *Mem:* Am Soc Biol Chemists; Am Soc Neurochem. *Res:* Lipid chemistry; structure of phospholipids and triglycerides; protein kinase; lipolytic enzymes; myelin lipids; membrane structure. *Mailing Add:* 172 Prospect Ave Staten Island NY 10301. *Fax:* 718-698-3803

BROCKETT, PATRICK LEE, MATHEMATICAL STATISTICS, PROBABILITY. *Current Pos:* from asst prof to assoc prof finance, dir actuarial sci, 86-89, PROF FINANCE & ACTURARIAL SCI, UNIV TEX, AUSTIN, 86-, PROF, DEPT MATHS, FINANCE & MGT SCI & INFO SYSTS, 89- *Personal Data:* b Monterey Park, Calif, Mar 29, 48; m 88, Linda L Golden; c Angela & Russell. *Educ:* Calif State Univ, Long Beach, BA, 70; Univ Calif, Irvine, MA, 75, PhD(math), 75. *Honors & Awards:* Halmsted Prize, Soc Actuaries. *Prof Exp:* Asst prof math, Tulane Univ, 75-77 & Univ Tex, 77-80; vis prof, Dept Statist, Univ Calif, Riverside, 80-81. *Concurrent Pos:* Dir, Ctr Cybernet Studies, Univ Tex, Austin; fel, IC2 Inst, 84- *Mem:* Fel Inst Math Statist; fel Am Statist Asn; Royal Statist Soc; Am Risk & Ins Asn; fel AAAS; Opers Res Soc. *Res:* Stochastic methodology and theory and application to actuarial science, finance, statistical signal processing and signal detection; math models in finance, operations research and management science. *Mailing Add:* Dept Finance Univ Tex Austin TX 78712-1026. *Fax:* 512-471-5073; *E-Mail:* brockett@utxvm.utexas.cc.edu

BROCKETT, ROGER WARE, APPLIED MATHEMATICS. *Current Pos:* PROF ELEC ENG & COMPUT SCI, DIV APPL SCI, PIERSAL LAB, HARVARD UNIV, 69- *Personal Data:* b Wadsworth, Ohio, Oct 22, 38; m 60; c 3. *Educ:* Case Inst Technol, BS, 60, MS, 62, PhD(eng), 64. *Honors & Awards:* Richard Bellman Award, Am Automatic Soc, 90; Control Systs & Sci Eng Award, Inst Elec & Electronics Engrs, 91; Reid Award, Soc Indust & Appl Math, 96. *Prof Exp:* From asst prof to assoc prof, Mass Inst Technol, 63-69. *Concurrent Pos:* Ford fel, 63-65; vis pos, Imp Col, London, Nagoya Univ, Univ Rome & Australian Nat Univ. *Mem:* Nat Acad Eng; Am Math Soc; fel Inst Elec & Electronics Engrs; Soc Indust & Appl Math. *Res:* Automatic control theory including optimal control and stability theory; nonlinear phenomena; mathematical system theory. *Mailing Add:* 29 Oakland St Lexington MA 02173. *Fax:* 617-496-6404; *E-Mail:* brockett@hrl.harvard.edu

BROCKHAUS, JOHN ALBERT, AERIAL PHOTOGRAMMETRY & MAPPING, REMOTE SENSING & GEOGRAPHIC INFORMATION SYSTEMS. *Current Pos:* RES ASSOC, FORESTRY DEPT, NC STATE UNIV, 84- *Personal Data:* b San Luis Obispo, Calif, Aug 30, 53; m 79, Linda Antony; c John C Junjo. *Educ:* Calif Polytech State Univ, BS, 78, MS, 80; Univ Idaho, PhD(forestry mgt), 87. *Prof Exp:* Instr aerial photogram & forestry, Calif Polytech State Univ, 78-80; systs analyst, Calif Forest Resource Assessment Prog, 81-82; instr aerial photogram & remote sensing, Univ Idaho, 82-84. *Mem:* Sigma Xi; Am Soc Photogram & Remote Sensing. *Res:* Monitoring and modeling environmental phenomena such as forest decline due to acid precipitation, groundwater pollution, water quality and biogenic volatile organic compound emissions from aerial photography and satellite imagery. *Mailing Add:* Dept Geog & Environ Eng US Military Acad West Point NY 10996. *Fax:* 919-515-3439

BROCKHOUSE, BERTRAM NEVILLE, SOLID STATE PHYSICS. *Current Pos:* prof, 62-84, chmn dept, 67-70, EMER PROF PHYSICS, MCMASTER UNIV, 84- *Personal Data:* b Lethbridge, Alta, July 15, 18; m 48, Doris Miller; c 6. *Educ:* Univ BC, BA, 47; Univ Toronto, MA, 48, PhD, 50. *Hon Degrees:* DSc, Univ Waterloo, 69, McMaster Univ, 84, Univ Toronto, 95 & Univ BC, 96, HL, Dalhousie Univ, 96. *Honors & Awards:* Nobel Prize in Phys, 94; Duddell Medal & Prize, Brit Inst Physics & Phys Soc, 63; Oliver E Buckley Prize, Am Phys Soc, 62; Medal Achievement Physics, Can Asn Physicists, 67; Tory Medal, Royal Soc Can, 73. *Prof Exp:* Lectr physics, Univ Toronto, 49-50; res officer, Atomic Energy Can, Ltd, 50-60, head, Neurton Physics Br, 60-62. *Concurrent Pos:* Guggenheim fel, 70. *Mem:* Fel Am Phys Soc; Can Asn Physicists; fel Royal Soc Can; fel Royal Soc London; foreign mem Royal Swed Acad Sci; foreign mem Am Acad Arts & Sci. *Res:* Neutron physics as applied to physics of solid and liquids; philosophy of physics. *Mailing Add:* PO Box 7338 Ancaster ON L9G 3N6 Can

BROCKINGTON, JAMES WALLACE, ORGANIC CHEMISTRY. *Current Pos:* sr res chemist, Corp Res Dept, 78-79, sect mgr, 79-81, DIR PLANNING & MULTIDISCIPLINARY PROG, CORP SCI CTR, AIR PROD & CHEM INC, 81- *Personal Data:* b Norfolk, Va, Apr 12, 43; m 63; c 2. *Educ:* Univ Richmond, BS, 65; Univ Miami, MS, 67; Va Commonwealth Univ, PhD(chem), 70. *Prof Exp:* Res chemist, Res & Develop Dept, Texaco, Inc, 70-76 & Atlas Powder Co, 76-78. *Mem:* Am Chem Soc. *Mailing Add:* 4424 Parkland Dr Allentown PA 18104-1914

BROCKMAN, DAVID DEAN, PSYCHOANALYSIS, PSYCHIATRY. *Current Pos:* from clin asst prof to clin assoc prof, 56-85, CLIN PROF PSYCHIAT, COL MED, UNIV ILL, 85-; CLIN PROF PSYCHIAT, UNIV CHICAGO, 94- *Personal Data:* b Greer, SC, Aug 4, 22; m 50; c 3. *Educ:* Furman Univ, BS, 43; Med Col SC, MD, 46. *Prof Exp:* Staff mem psychiat, NShore Health Resort, Winnetka, Ill, 51-52; asst, Clin & Med Sch, Univ Chicago, 52-53, from instr to asst prof, 53-55, actg chief, Univ, 54-55, prof lectr, 55-56. *Mem:* Fel Am Psychiat Asn; Am Psychoanal Asn; fel Am Col Psychoanalysts; emer fel Am Col Psychiatrists; fel Am Soc Adolescent Psychiat. *Res:* Late adolescence; parent loss; young adulthood. *Mailing Add:* 1030 Kenelworth Glenview IL 60601

BROCKMAN, ELLIS R, MICROBIOLOGY. *Current Pos:* PROF BIOL, CENT MICH UNIV, 69- *Personal Data:* b St Louis, Mo, Feb 10, 34; m 59; c 3. *Educ:* DePauw Univ, AB, 55; Univ Mo, AM, 60, PhD(bact), 64. *Prof Exp:* Instr bact, Univ Mo, 63; asst prof biol, Winthrop Col, 63-69. *Concurrent Pos:* Consult, Warner Lambert Res Inst, 69-75 & Bristol Labs, 77-78. *Mem:* AAAS; Am Soc Microbiol; Am Inst Biol Scientists; Nat Asn Biol Teachers; Soc Indust Microbiol. *Res:* Bacterial taxonomy; biology of the myxobacteria; bacteriology of aquatic ecosystems; screening anti-microbial compounds. *Mailing Add:* Biol Dept Cent Mich Univ Mt Pleasant MI 48859-0001

BROCKMAN, HAROLD W, MATHEMATICS. *Current Pos:* From instr to prof math, 49-92, EMER PROF MATH, CAPITAL UNIV, 92- *Personal Data:* b Sidney, Ohio, Mar 31, 22; m 54, Lorraine Loufman; c Sally. *Educ:* Capital Univ, BSEd, 48; Ohio State Univ, MA, 50, PhD(math, math educ) 62. *Concurrent Pos:* Ed, Ohio J Sch Math. *Mem:* Am Math Soc; Math Asn Am; Nat Coun Teachers Math. *Res:* Algebra; analysis. *Mailing Add:* 975 Bernhard Rd Columbus OH 43227-1226

BROCKMAN, HERMAN E, GENETICS, ENVIRONMENTAL MUTAGENESIS & ANTIMUTAGENE SIS. *Current Pos:* from assoc prof to prof, 63-82, DISTINGUISHED PROF, ILL STATE UNIV, 82- *Personal Data:* b Danforth, Ill, Dec 5, 34; m 56; c 6. *Educ:* Blackburn Col, BS, 56; Northwestern Univ, MA, 57; Fla State Univ, PhD(genetics), 60. *Honors & Awards:* Environ Mutagenesis Recognition Award, Environ Mutagen Soc, 82. *Prof Exp:* Res assoc, Biol Div, Oak Ridge Nat Lab, 60-61, Nat Acad Sci-Nat Res Found, Coun fel, 61-62, USPHS fel, 62-63. *Concurrent Pos:* USPHS spec res fel, 69-70; counr, Environ Mutagen Soc, 84-86; distinguished vis scientist, US Environ Protection Agency, 87-90. *Mem:* AAAS; Genetics Soc Am; Sigma Xi; Environ Mutagen Soc. *Res:* Comparative and environmental mutagenicity and antimutagenicity. *Mailing Add:* Dept Biol Sci 4120 Ill State Univ Normal IL 61790-4120

BROCKMAN, HOWARD LYLE, JR, PHYSICAL BIOCHEMISTRY, ENZYMOLOGY. *Current Pos:* from asst prof to assoc prof, 73-81, PROF BIOCHEM, HORMEL INST, UNIV MINN, 81-, BIOPHYS SECT LEADER, 76- *Personal Data:* b Olney, Ill, Sept 5, 44. *Educ:* DePauw Univ, BA, 66; Mich State Univ, PhD(biochem), 71. *Prof Exp:* Fel biochem, Univ Chicago, 71-73. *Concurrent Pos:* Nat Inst Arthritis & Metab Dis fel, 71-73; estab investr, Am Heart Asn, 78-82, coun, atherosclerosis. *Mem:* AAAS; Am Soc Biol Chemists; Biophys Soc. *Res:* Interfacial reactions, particularly the influence of interfacial structure on reactions catalyzed by water soluble and membrane bound enzymes. *Mailing Add:* Hormel Inst Univ Minn 801 16th Ave NE Austin MN 55912-3679. *Fax:* 507-437-9696

BROCKMAN, JOHN A, JR, immunology; deceased, see previous edition for last biography

BROCKMAN, PHILIP, ATMOSPHERIC SCIENCES, ENVIRONMENTAL SCIENCES. *Current Pos:* Researcher, 59-88, asst br head, Laser Technol & Applin Br, 88-93, SR RESEARCHER, SENSOR TECHNOL BR, NASA LANGLEY RES CTR, 93- *Personal Data:* b Boston, Mass, Nov 37. *Educ:* Univ Mass, BS, 59; Col William & Mary, MA, 63. *Mem:* Optical Soc Am; assoc fel Am Inst Aeronaut & Astronaut. *Res:* Laser systems for remote sensing of atmosphere including winds, species, and pollutants; specializing in 2 micrometer systems with experience at 10 micrometer and near infrared. *Mailing Add:* Langley Res Ctr Sensor Technol Br NASA MS 474 Hampton VA 23681-0001

BROCKMAN, ROBERT W, BIOCHEMISTRY. *Current Pos:* RETIRED. *Personal Data:* b Chester, SC, Dec 8, 24; m 48; c Jean Alison (Booth) & Anne (Andrews Hoos). *Educ:* Vanderbilt Univ, BS, 47, MS, 49, PhD(chem), 51. *Prof Exp:* Asst chem, Vanderbilt Univ, 50-51; sr chemist, Southern Res Inst, 51-57, head, Drug Resistance Sect, 58-67, prin scientist, 64-89, head, Biol Chem Div, 67-89. *Concurrent Pos:* NIH spec fel, 64-66; mem adv comt, Am Cancer Soc, 66-69 & 75-78; ed, Antibiotics & Chemother, 73-82; mem, Exp Ther Study Sect, NIH, 79-83; assoc ed, Cancer Res, 81-87. *Mem:* Am Chem Soc; Am Soc Biochem & Molecular Biol; Am Asn Cancer Res; Sigma Xi; Soc Exp Biol & Med; NY Acad Sci. *Res:* Mechanisms of drug inhibition and resistance; cancer research. *Mailing Add:* 1631 Keith Valley Rd Charlottesville VA 22901-3017

BROCKMANN, HELEN JANE, ZOOLOGY, ANIMAL BEHAVIOR. *Current Pos:* from asst prof to assoc prof, 76-89, PROF ZOOL, UNIV FLA, 89- *Personal Data:* b Louisville, Ky, Feb 25, 47. *Educ:* Tufts Univ, BS, 67; Univ Wis-Madison, MS, 72, PhD(zool), 76. *Honors & Awards:* Teaching Award, Animal Behav Soc, 95. *Concurrent Pos:* NSF res fel zool, Oxford Univ, 77-78; Harry Frank Guggenheim Found grant, 77-79; prin investr, NSF grant, 79-82, 89-94; NSF vis prof women, Princeton Univ, 85-86. *Mem:* Sigma Xi; fel Animal Behav Soc; Soc Study Evolution; Int Union Study Social Insects; Soc Integrative & Comp Biol. *Res:* Ethology; social behavior; behavioral ecology and evolution; nesting behavior of digger wasps, sphecidae; origins of sociality in insects, sex ratios, life histories; behavior of horseshoe crabs; sexual selection. *Mailing Add:* Dept Zool Univ Fla Gainesville FL 32611. *Fax:* 904-392-3704; *E-Mail:* hjb@zoo.ufl.edu

BROCKWAY, ALAN PRIEST, COMPARATIVE PHYSIOLOGY. *Current Pos:* assoc prof, 67-79, PROF BIOL, UNIV COLO, DENVER, 79-, CHMN, 89- *Personal Data:* b Hanover, NH, Aug 21, 36; m; m 72, Dottie; c Julie, Joseph & Lesley. *Educ:* St John's Col, Md, AB, 58; Western Reserve Univ, PhD(biol), 64. *Prof Exp:* Asst prof zool & entom, Ohio State Univ, 63-67. *Concurrent Pos:* Vis assoc prof oral biol, Sch Dent, Univ Colo, 73-77. *Mem:* Nat Asn Adv Health Professions. *Res:* Insect respiration; control of water loss in insects; uses of microcomputers in biology. *Mailing Add:* Dept Biol Univ Colo PO Box 173364 Denver CO 80217-3364. *Fax:* 303-556-4352; *E-Mail:* abrockway@cudnvr.denver.colorado.edu

BROCKWELL, PETER JOHN, PROBABILITY, MATHEMATICAL STATISTICS. *Current Pos:* prof statist & chmn dept, 76-77, PROF STATIST, COLO STATE UNIV, 78- *Personal Data:* b Melbourne, Australia, Oct 12, 37; m 65; c 3. *Educ:* Univ Melbourne, BEE, 58, BA, 60, MA, 62; Australian Nat Univ, PhD(math statist), 67. *Prof Exp:* Asst mathematician appl math, Argonne Nat Lab, 67-70; assoc prof statist, Mich State Univ, 71-73; prof math statist & chmn dept, La Trobe Univ, 73-76. *Concurrent Pos:* Consult, Argonne Nat Lab, 70-73; assoc ed, Math Scientist, 77-84, Stochastic Models, 85-, Theory Probability & Applications, 88-; NSF res grant, 78-87, 90-; ed, Advances Appl Probability, 82-88; vis prof, Kuwait Univ, 82-84; prof statist & chmn dept, Univ Melbourne, 88-89; bk rev ed, J Statist Planning Info, 89- *Mem:* Australian Statist Soc; Am Statist Asn; fel Inst Math Statist; Cell Kinetics Soc; Sigma Xi; Int Statist Inst. *Res:* Stochastic processes and their applications in physics, biology and hydrology; time series analysis; inference for stochastic processes. *Mailing Add:* Statist Colo State Univ Ft Collins CO 80523-0001

BROCOUM, STEPHAN JOHN, STRUCTURAL GEOLOGY, TECTONICS. *Current Pos:* ASST MGR, SITE SUITABILITY, DEPT ENERGY, 88- *Personal Data:* b New York, NY, Feb 16, 41; m 69. *Educ:* Brooklyn Col, BS, 63; Columbia Univ, PhD(geol), 71. *Honors & Awards:* Antarctic Serv Medal, NSF, 73. *Prof Exp:* Res scientist geol, Lamont-Doherty Geol Observ, Columbia Univ, 71-73; asst prof, Tex Christian Univ, 73-75; proj geologist, E D'Appolonia Consult Engrs, Inc, 75-76; res geologist, Gulf Sci & Technol Co, Gulf Oil Corp, 76-88. *Mem:* AAAS; Geol Soc Am; Am Geophys Union; Sigma Xi. *Res:* Use of remote sensing for hydrocarbon exploration; improving geological criteria for siting nuclear power plants; relationships between mid-continent tectonics and earthquakes; tectonic and strain history of the Sudbury Basin; tectonic and metamorphic history of the Adirondack lowlands. *Mailing Add:* US Dept Energy YMCO PO 30307 North Las Vegas NV 89036-0307

BRODASKY, THOMAS FRANCIS, PHYSICAL CHEMISTRY, ORGANIC CHEMISTRY. *Current Pos:* RETIRED. *Personal Data:* b New London, Conn, Oct 6, 30; m 60; c 2. *Educ:* Northeastern Univ, BS, 53, MS, 55; Rensselaer Polytech Inst, PhD(chem), 61. *Prof Exp:* Sr res scientist, Chem & Biol Screening, Upjohn Co, 87-90. *Mem:* Am Chem Soc; Sigma Xi. *Res:* Gas, high performance liquid, paper and thin-layer chromatographic separations; infrared, ultraviolet and visible absorption spectroscopy; data retrieval; antibiotic metabolism; kinetics of biological reactions; gas liquid chromatography-mass spectroscopy; isolution natural products. *Mailing Add:* 6215 Westlins Ave Kalamazoo MI 49009

BRODD, RALPH JAMES, physical chemistry, for more information see previous edition

BRODE, WILLIAM EDWARD, MITIGATION OF IMPACTS & LOSSES TO WETLANDS. *Current Pos:* ENVIRON SPECIALIST VI, TENN DEPT TRANSP, 74- *Personal Data:* b McMinn Co, Tenn, Dec 17, 29; m 60, Nancy Caplenor; c William Edward Jr, John Sidney, Paul Kirk & David Andrew. *Educ:* Univ Southern Miss, BS, 52, MA, 54, PhD(biol), 69. *Prof Exp:* Teacher biol, Copiah-Lincoln Jr Col, 55-57, Knox County Schs, Tenn, 59-60, Davidson County Schs, 60-62 & High Sch, Miss, 62-65; prof biol, Wesleyan Col, Ga, 69-74. *Concurrent Pos:* Prin investr, WE Brode. *Mem:* Asn State Wetland Mgrs Inc. *Res:* Amphibian and reptile taxonomy and ecology; impact of proposed highways on wildlife and wetlands. *Mailing Add:* Environ Planning Off Suite 900 James K Polk Bldg Nashville TN 37243-0334. *Fax:* 615-741-2508

BRODER, IRVIN, IMMUNOLOGY. *Current Pos:* clin teacher med, 63-66, assoc, 66-68, asst prof, 68-71, asst prof pharmacol, 65-75, asst prof path, 65-80, assoc prof med, 71-76, DIR, GAGE RES INST, UNIV TORONTO, 71-, PROF MED, 77-, PROF PATH, 80-, PROF OCCUP & ENVIRON HEALTH, 82- *Personal Data:* b Toronto, Ont, June 27, 30; m 54; c 3. *Educ:* Univ Toronto, MD, 55; FRCP(C), 60. *Prof Exp:* Intern, Toronto Gen Hosp, 55-56, asst resident med, 58-59, resident physician, 59-60; sr intern, Sunnybrook Hosp, Toronto, 56-57; clin instr allergy, Med Ctr, Univ Mich, 60-62. *Concurrent Pos:* Res fel endocrinol, Dept Path, Univ Toronto, 57-58; res fel immunol, Dept Pharmacol, Univ Col, Univ London, 62-63; res scholar, Med Res Coun Can, 63-66; career investr, Med Res Coun Can, 66-; mem, Inst Med Sci, 68-, & Inst Immunol, Univ Toronto, 71-82. *Mem:* Can Med Asn; Can Soc Allergy & Clin Immunol; Can Thoracic Soc; Can Soc Clin Invest; Can Soc Immunol. *Res:* Occupational lung disease research; study of human obstructive airways disease. *Mailing Add:* The Gage Res Inst 223 College St Toronto ON M5T 1R4 Can. *Fax:* 416-978-2608

BRODER, MARTIN IVAN, MEDICINE, CARDIOLOGY. *Current Pos:* assoc prof, 82-86, PROF MED, SCH MED, TUFTS UNIV, 86-; CHMN, DEPT MED, BAYSTATE MED CTR, 82- *Personal Data:* b Brooklyn, NY, June 15, 36; m 69; c 4. *Educ:* Wayne State Univ, AB, 57; Western Res Univ, MD, 61. *Prof Exp:* Chief resident, Cleveland Metrop Gen Hosp, 64-65; fel clin cardiol, Univ London Inst Cardiol, 65-66; health scientist adminr, Nat Heart Inst, 67-69; fel, Vet Admin Hosp, Washington, DC, 69-70; dir cardiac care unit, Cleveland Metrop Gen Hosp, 71-75; from asst clin prof to assoc clin prof med, Sch Med, Case Western Res Univ, 76-81; chmn, Dept Med,

Fairview Gen Hosp, 76-81. *Concurrent Pos:* Consult, Vet Admin, 71-; adj prof clin med, Ohio Col Podiat Med, 73-81; dep chmn, Dept Med, Sch Med, Tufts Univ. *Mem:* Fel Am Col Cardiol; Am Col Physicians. *Res:* Coronary artery disease; artificial heart techniques; hypertension treatment; cardiac arrhythmia. *Mailing Add:* 759 Chestnut St Springfield MA 01199

BRODER, SAMUEL, CANCER RESEARCH. *Current Pos:* SR VPRES RES & DEVELOP & CHIEF SCI OFFICER, IVAX CORP, 95- *Personal Data:* b Feb 24, 45; c 2. *Educ:* Univ Mich, BS, 66, MD, 70; Am Bd Internal Med, cert, 73, cert oncol, 77. *Honors & Awards:* Upjohn Achievement Award; Arthur S Flemming Award; Augustus B Wadsworth Lectr; Drew Award, Ciba-Geigy; Samuel Rudin Award, Columbia Presby Hosp; Dr Frederick Stohlman Lectr Award; Lifetime Sci Award, Inst Advan Studies Immunol & Aging; Harvey W Wiley Medal, Food & Drug Admin. *Prof Exp:* Clin assoc, Metab Br, Nat Cancer Inst, NIH, 72-75, investr, Med Br, 75-76, sr investr, Metab Br, 76-81, assoc dir, Clin Oncol Prog, 81-88, dir, 89-94. *Mem:* Inst Med-Nat Acad Sci; Asn Am Physicians; Am Fedn Clin Res; Am Asn Cancer Res; Am Soc Clin Oncol; Am Asn Immunologists; Clin Immunol Soc; fel Am Col Physicians; Am Soc Clin Invest. *Res:* Relationships between cancer and immunodeficiency states; anti-retroviral chemotherapy. *Mailing Add:* Ivax Corp 4400 Biscayne Blvd Miami FL 33137

BRODERICK, GLEN ALLEN, RUMINANT NUTRITION, AMINO ACID METABOLISM. *Current Pos:* RES SCIENTIST RUMINANT NUTRIT, US DAIRY FORAGE RES CTR, AGR RES SERV, US DEPT AGR, 81- *Personal Data:* b Chicago, Ill, Oct 15, 45; m 68, Bonnie Hamilton; c Sarah, Margaret & Emily. *Educ:* Univ Wis-Madison, BS, 67, MS, 70, PhD(biochem), 72. *Prof Exp:* Asst prof animal nutrit, Tex A&M Univ, 72-78, assoc prof, 78-80. *Concurrent Pos:* Prof dairy sci, Univ Wis-Madison. *Mem:* Am Dairy Sci Asn; Am Soc Animal Sci; Am Inst Nutrit; Nutrit Soc. *Res:* Ruminant protein nutrition; protein degradation and protein synthesis of rumen microorganisms; amino acid nutrition and metabolism in the lactating dairy cow. *Mailing Add:* US Dairy Forage Res Ctr USDA-ARS Univ Wis 1925 Linden Dr W Madison WI 53706-1108. *Fax:* 608-264-5147; *E-Mail:* glenb@dfrc.wisc.edu

BRODERICK, JOHN, RADIO ASTRONOMY. *Current Pos:* from asst prof to assoc prof, 74-85, PROF PHYSICS, VA POLYTECH INST & STATE UNIV, 85- *Personal Data:* b Danville, Pa, Oct 14, 40; m 79, Sandy Bussey; c Rosemarie (Milleson), Jack, Cynthia Hassler & Matthew Hassler. *Educ:* Pa State Univ, BS, 62; Brandeis Univ, MA, 64, PhD(physics), 70. *Prof Exp:* Res assoc, Nat Radio Astron Observ, 69-71 & Nat Astron & Ionospheric Ctr, 71-74. *Mem:* Int Sci Radio Union; Int Astron Union; Am Astron Soc. *Res:* Extragalactic radio astronomy; very long baseline interferometry; radio sky surveys. *Mailing Add:* Dept Physics Va Polytech Inst & State Univ Blacksburg VA 24061-0435. *Fax:* 540-231-7511; *E-Mail:* john.broderick@vt.edu

BRODERIUS, STEVEN JAMES, FISHERIES BIOLOGY, AQUATIC TOXICOLOGY. *Current Pos:* RES AQUATIC BIOLOGIST TOXICOL, US ENVIRON PROTECTION AGENCY, 78- *Personal Data:* b Hutchinson, Minn, Oct 23, 43; m 69, Margaret Olson; c Allen, Karl & Karen. *Educ:* Univ Minn, BS, 65; Ore State Univ, MS, 69, PhD(fisheries), 73. *Honors & Awards:* Sci & Technol Achievement Award, US Environ Protection Agency, 85 & 92. *Prof Exp:* Res assoc aquatic toxicol, Univ Minn, 73-78. *Mem:* Am Fisheries Soc; Sigma Xi; Soc Environ Toxicol & Chem. *Res:* Toxicity of organic and inorganic environmental contaminates to aquatic organisms; use of applied chemistry to better understand the reaction of toxicants in the aquatic environment. *Mailing Add:* US EPA Mid-Continent Ecol Div 6201 Congdon Blvd Duluth MN 55804. *Fax:* 218-720-5539; *E-Mail:* broderius.steven@epamail.epa.gov

BRODERSEN, ARTHUR JAMES, ELECTRICAL ENGINEERING. *Current Pos:* chmn dept elec & bioeng, 74-81, assoc dean, 79-86, PROF ELEC ENG, VANDERBILT UNIV, 74-,. *Personal Data:* b Fresno, Calif, Aug 31, 39; m 65; c 2. *Educ:* Univ Calif, Berkeley, BS, 61, MS, 63, PhD(elec eng), 66. *Prof Exp:* From asst prof to prof elec eng, Univ Fla, 66-74. *Mem:* Inst Elec & Electronics Engrs; Am Soc Eng Educr. *Res:* Electronic and integrated circuits; modeling of semiconductor devices; microelectronics; computer and communication technology in engineering education. *Mailing Add:* Dept Elec Eng PO Box 1628 Sta B Nashville TN 37235. *E-Mail:* broderaj@vuse.vanderbilt.edu

BRODERSEN, ROBERT W, DESIGN ANALOG INTERFACE CIRCUITS. *Current Pos:* PROF, DEPT ELEC ENG & COMPUT SCI, UNIV CALIF, BERKELEY, CALIF, 76- *Educ:* Calif State Polytech Univ, BS(elec eng), & BS(math), 66; Mass Inst Technol, MSc & MS, 68 & PhD(eng), 72. *Honors & Awards:* Solid States Award, Inst Elec & Electronics Engrs, 96. *Prof Exp:* Staff, Ctr Res Lab, Tex Instruments, 72-76. *Concurrent Pos:* Consult, var industs. *Mem:* Nat Acad Eng; fel Inst Elec & Electronics Engrs. *Res:* Speech recognition and synthesis, telecommunications, image processing, control systems and robotics. *Mailing Add:* Dept Elec Eng & Comput Sci Berkeley CA 94720. *E-Mail:* rb@eecs.berkley.edu

BRODERSON, STEVAN HARDY, ANATOMY, HISTOCHEMISTRY. *Current Pos:* Instr, 67-70, ASST PROF ANAT, UNIV WASH, 70- *Personal Data:* b Lead, SDak, Sept 23, 38; m 64; c 2. *Educ:* Ohio State Univ, BS, 60; State Univ NY, PhD(anat), 67. *Concurrent Pos:* Investr, Am Epilepsy Found, 77-78. *Mem:* Am Asn Anatomists; Histochem Soc. *Res:* Histochemistry and neurochemistry of neurotransmitters and enzymes associated with neurotransmission; histochemistry of lipids associated with biomembrane structure and function. *Mailing Add:* Dept Biol Struct SM-20 Univ Wash Sch Med Seattle WA 98195

BRODEUR, ARMAND EDWARD, PEDIATRICS RADIOLOGY, PEDIATRICS. *Current Pos:* asst dean, Sch Med, St Louis Univ, 47-49, resident radiol, 49-52, instr radiol, 52-57, sr instr, 57-60, asst prof clin radiol, 60-62, assoc prof radiol, 62-70, assoc dean sch med, 62-65, assoc prof pediat, 66-78, chmn dept, 75-78, vchmn, 78-88, PROF RADIOL, SCH MED, ST LOUIS UNIV, 70-, PROF PEDIAT, 80- *Personal Data:* b Penacook, NH, Jan 8, 22; m 47, Gloria Thompson; c Armand, Garrett, Mark, Mariette, Michelle & Paul. *Educ:* St Anselm's Col, AB, 45; St Louis Univ, MD, 47, MRd, 52; Am Bd Radiol, dipl, 52. *Hon Degrees:* LLD, St Anselm's Col, 71. *Honors & Awards:* Brodeur Lect Pediat Radiol, St Louis Univ Med Sch, 97. *Prof Exp:* Intern, St Mary's Group, 47-49; asst radiologist, City Hosp, St Louis, Mo, 52. *Concurrent Pos:* Chief radiol sect, USPHS, 52-54, consult, Div Radiol Health, 63-; spec consult, Div Spec Health Serv, Firmin Desloge Hosp, St Louis, 54-, assoc radiologist, Hosp, 57; chief radiologist, Cardinal Glennon Mem Children's Hosp, St Louis, 56; consult x-ray, Cath Health Asn, 56-88; chmn radiol, Shriners Hosp Crippled Children, St Louis, 88-; assoc vpres develop, Cardinal Glennon Childrens Hosp, 88-; health broadcaster, KMOX (CBS) radio, 80, KMOV (CBS) TV, 92-93 & KSIV radio, 96- *Mem:* Fel Am Col Radiol; Am Med Asn; Radiol Soc NAm; Soc Nuclear Med; Soc Pediat Radiol; fel Am Acad Pediat; Nat Asn Physician Broadcasters; Sigma Xi. *Res:* Pediatric radiology; reduction of radiation exposure in pediatric diagnostic radiology; child abuse; pediatric urography; author of 60 publicatons and 3 textbooks. *Mailing Add:* 400 Bambury Way St Louis MO 63131-4801

BRODIE, ANN ELIZABETH, CELL BIOLOGY. *Current Pos:* res assoc biochem, 75-92, RES ASST PROF ANIMAL SCI, ORE STATE UNIV, 93- *Personal Data:* b Chicago, Ill, Jan 21, 43; m 66. *Educ:* Purdue Univ, West Lafayette, BS, 65; Univ Calif, Berkeley, PhD(genetics), 70. *Prof Exp:* Fel cell biol, Univ Wis-Madison, 70-72, res assoc neruophys, 72-75. *Concurrent Pos:* N L Tarter res fel, 77. *Mem:* AAAS; Asn Women Sci. *Res:* Cellular synthesis and metabolism of thiol compounds and control mechanisms regulating these processes; controls thiol compounds exert on other systems; oxidative stress; protien thiols; fat cell development. *Mailing Add:* 3145 NW Seneca Pl Corvallis OR 97330

BRODIE, BRUCE ORR, VETERINARY MEDICINE. *Current Pos:* from instr to assoc prof, 54-69, PROF VET MED, UNIV ILL, URBANA-CHAMPAIGN, 69- *Personal Data:* b Allegan, Mich, Apr 19, 24; m 47, 63; c 6. *Educ:* Mich State Univ, DVM, 51; Univ Ill, MS, 58. *Prof Exp:* Pvt pract, 51-54. *Concurrent Pos:* Fulbright scholar, Zimbabwe, 92-93. *Mem:* Am Vet Med Asn; Am Asn Vet Clinicians; Am Asn Bovine Practr; Soc Theriogenology. *Res:* Infectious diseases of cattle, trichomoniasis and reproductive herd health programs. *Mailing Add:* 1406 Mayfair Champaign IL 61821

BRODIE, DAVID ALAN, PHARMACOLOGY. *Current Pos:* PRES, DISCOVERY RES CONSULTS, 90- *Personal Data:* b Albany, NY, June 2, 29; m 53; c 2. *Educ:* Philadelphia Col Pharm & Sci, BSc, 51; Ohio State Univ, MSc, 53; Univ Utah, PhD(pharmacol), 56. *Prof Exp:* Instr pharmacol, Sch Med, Johns Hopkins Univ, 56-57; res assoc neuropharmacol, Merck Inst Therapeut Res, 57-62, sr investr gastroenterol, 62-64, sr res fel, 64-66, dir gastroenterol, 66-70; mgr pharmacol, William H Rorer, Inc, Pa, 70-71; assoc dir, Smith Klein & French Labs, 71-72; mgr dept, Abbott Labs, 72-73, dir div pharmacol & med chem, 73-84; dir pharmacol, Ayerst Labs Res, Inc, 84-87; dir, CNS & CV Pharmacol, Wyeth Ayerst Res, 87-90. *Mem:* Am Soc Pharmacol & Exp Therapeut; Am Physiol Soc; Am Gastroenterol Soc. *Res:* Drug effects on gastric secretion and experimental peptic ulcer. *Mailing Add:* 585 Edison Dr East Windsor NJ 08520. *Fax:* 609-448-5622

BRODIE, DON E, SOLID STATE PHYSICS, SEMICONDUCTING FILMS. *Current Pos:* lectr, Univ Waterloo, 58-59, from asst prof to assoc prof, 61-68, dean sci, 82-90, prof, 68-95, DISTINGUISHED EMER PROF PHYSICS, UNIV WATERLOO, 96- *Personal Data:* b Bracebridge, Ont, Sept 8, 29; m 55, Naureen E Petch; c 3. *Educ:* McMaster Univ, BSc, 55, MSc, 56, PhD(solid state physics), 61; Ont Col Educ, cert, 57. *Prof Exp:* Teacher physics, Humberside Collegiate Inst, 57-58. *Concurrent Pos:* Ed, Physics Can, 69-73; mem, NSERC Strategic Grants Panel; dir, Physics Photovoltaic Group, Univ Waterloo, 79-95, founding dir, Waterloo Ctr Mats Res, 94-96. *Mem:* Can Asn Physicists. *Res:* Physics of thin films, amorphous and crystalline; electronic and optical properties; photovoltaic solar cell development. *Mailing Add:* Dept Physics Univ Waterloo Waterloo ON N2L 3G1 Can. *Fax:* 519-746-8115; *E-Mail:* dbrodie@sciberg.uwaterloo.Ca

BRODIE, DONALD CRUM, PHARMACY. *Current Pos:* assoc prof pharm, Univ Calif, San Francisco, 47-53, lectr, Med Sch, 48-58, dir pharmaceut serv, 58-68, prof pharm & pharmaceut chem, Div Ambulatory & Community Med, Sch Med, 67-73, assoc dean prof affairs, Sch Pharm, 69-73, EMER PROF CHEM & PHARMACEUT CHEM, SCH PHARM, UNIV CALIF, SAN FRANCISCO, 73- *Personal Data:* b Carroll, Iowa, Mar 29, 08; m 34. *Educ:* Univ Southern Calif, BS, 34, MS, 38; Purdue Univ, PhD(pharmaceut chem), 44. *Hon Degrees:* PdD, 81. *Prof Exp:* Lab asst, Col Dent, Univ Southern Calif, 36-38; asst, Col Pharm, Purdue Univ, 38-41, instr pharmaceut chem, 41-44; assoc pharmacol, Sch Med & Dent, Univ Rochester, 44-45; assoc prof pharmaceut chem, Col Pharm, Univ Kans, 45-47. *Concurrent Pos:* Res consult, Comn Outpatient Dispensing by Hosps & Related Facilities, 65; spec assignment, dir drug-related studies, Nat Ctr Health Serv Res & Develop, Health Serv & Ment Health Admin, HEW, 70-73; adj prof med & pharm, Univ Southern Calif, 74- *Mem:* AAAS; Am Chem Soc; Am Pharmaceut Asn; Am Soc Hosp Phamacists; Soc Hosp Pharmacists Australia. *Res:* Toxicity of drug agents; antihemorrhagic activity of the naphthoquinones; salicylate analgesics; physiology and pharmacology of vascular smooth muscle; delivery of health care; professional and clinical judgment; education programs for the health care team; health professions education; impact of new technology on pharmaceutical education. *Mailing Add:* 501 S La Posada Circle Green Valley AZ 85614-5108

BRODIE, EDMUND DARRELL, JR, HERPETOLOGY, BEHAVIORAL ECOLOGY. *Current Pos:* PROF & HEAD, DEPT BIOL, UTAH STATE UNIV, 94- *Personal Data:* b Portland, Ore, June 29, 41; c Edmund D III & Kristen M. *Educ:* Ore Col Educ, BS, 63; Ore State Univ, MS, 67, PhD(zool), 69. *Prof Exp:* Asst prof zool, Clemson Univ, 69-74; from assoc prof to prof biol, Adelphi Univ, 74-84; prof & chmn dept biol, Univ Tex, Arlington, 84-94. *Mem:* AAAS; Am Soc Ichthyologists & Herpetologists; Herpetologists' League (pres, 92-93); Soc Study Evolution; Sigma Xi. *Res:* Evolution of antipredator mechanisms including behavior, toxins, anatomy and coloration; mimicry in amphibians and reptiles. *Mailing Add:* Dept Biol Utah State Univ Logan UT 84322. *Fax:* 435-797-0532

BRODIE, HARLOW KEITH HAMMOND, PSYCHIATRY. *Current Pos:* James B Duke prof psychiat & law & chmn, Dept Psychiat, Med Ctr & chief psychiat serv, Duke Hosp, 74-82, chancellor, 82-85, pres, 85-93, EMER PRES & JAMES B DUKE PROF PSYCHIAT & PROF LAW, PSYCHOL & EXP PSYCHOL. *Personal Data:* b Stamford, Conn, Aug 24, 39; m 67, Brenda Barrowclough; c Melissa V, Cameron K, Tyler H & Bryson B. *Educ:* Princeton Univ, AB, 61; Columbia Univ, MD, 65. *Hon Degrees:* LLD, Univ Richmond, 87; DHL, High Point Univ, 91. *Honors & Awards:* Dean Echols Award, Ochsner Found Hosp, 65; A E Bennett Clin Res Award, Soc Biol Psychiat, 70; William Mennihger Award, Am Col Physicians, 94. *Prof Exp:* Intern med, Ochsner Found Hosp, New Orleans, 65-66; asst resident psychiat, Columbia-Presby Med Ctr, 66-68; clin assoc psychiat, Lab Clin Sci, NIMH, 68-70; asst prof, Sch Med, Stanford Univ, 70-74, prog dir, Gen Clin Res Ctr, 73-74. *Concurrent Pos:* Consult, Palo Alto Vet Admin Hosp, Calif, 70-72; assoc ed, Am J Psychiat, 73-80; mem, Nat Adv Coun on Alcohol & Alcohol Abuse, 74-78; examr, Am Bd Psychiat & Neurol, 74-; consult psychiat, Educ Br, NIMH, 73-75, Durham Vet Admin Hosp, NC, 74-82; mem, President's Biomed Panel Interdisciplinary Cluster Pharmacol, Substance Abuse & Environ Toxicol, 75-76; chmn, Comt Substance Abuse & Mental Health Issues, Acquired Immune Deficiency Syndrome Res, 93- *Mem:* Inst Med-Nat Acad Sci; fel Am Psychiat Asn (pres, 82-83); Sigma Xi; fel Royal Col Psychiat; fel Royal Soc Med. *Res:* Psychobiology of mood disorders in man, specifically as these are related to changes in endocrine function and neurotransmitter turnover in brain. *Mailing Add:* 63 Beverly Dr Durham NC 27707

BRODIE, HARRY JOSEPH, ENDOCRINOLOGY, CHEMISTRY & BIOCHEMISTRY. *Current Pos:* PRES, HARRY J BRODIE & CO INC, 94- *Personal Data:* b New York, NY, Apr 25, 28; m 64, Angela M Hartley; c Mark & John. *Educ:* Fordham Univ, BS, 50, MS, 52; NY Univ, PhD(org chem), 58. *Prof Exp:* Instr chem, Hunter Col, 53-56 & City Col New York, 57-58; chemist, E I du Pont de Nemours & Co, 58-60; fel, Clark & Worcester Found Exp Biol, 60-62; scientist, Worcester Found Exp Biol, 62-67, sr scientist, 67-78; exec secy, physiol chem study sect, 78-85, exec secy, endocrinol study sect, 85-92. *Mem:* AAAS; Am Chem Soc; Endocrine Soc. *Res:* Mechanism of enzyme catalyzed reactions, especially estrogen biosynthesis and oxidation and reduction of steroids; inhibition of steroid hormone biosynthesis for contraception and cancer therapy; steroid synthesis, including labeling; scientific communication. *Mailing Add:* 8373 Reservoir Rd Fulton MD 20759-9622. *Fax:* 301-490-6470; *E-Mail:* hbrodie@erols.com

BRODIE, IVOR, PHYSICAL ELECTRONICS. *Current Pos:* DIR, PHYS ELECTRONICS LAB, SRI INT, 73- *Personal Data:* b London, Eng, Apr 29, 28; m 54; c 2. *Educ:* Univ London, BSc, 50, Hons, 51, MSc, 56, PhD(physics), 59. *Hon Degrees:* DSc, London Univ, 76, Eurotechnical Res Univ. *Prof Exp:* Scientist, Res Labs, Gen Elec Co Eng, 51-56 & Nat Coal Bd, Mining Res Estab, 56-59; fel engr, Electronic Tube Div, Westinghouse Elec Corp, 59-62; sr engr, Varian Assocs, 62-65, sr scientist, 65-67, dir res, Vacuum Div, 67-69; pres, Photophysics, Inc, 69-71, chmn bd & chief exec officer, 71-73. *Mem:* Fel Am Phys Soc; Soc Info Display; sr mem Inst Elec & Electronics Engrs. *Res:* Physical electronics; electron beam lithography; field emission; microfabrication technologies; electro-photography; electro-radiography. *Mailing Add:* SRI Int 333 Ravenswood Ave Menlo Park CA 94025. *Fax:* 650-859-3090

BRODIE, JEAN PAMELA, ASTRONOMY. *Current Pos:* FEL, DEPT ASTRON & SPACE SCI LAB, UNIV CALIF, BERKELEY, 80-, PROF, 97- *Personal Data:* b London, Eng, Dec 25, 53. *Educ:* Univ London, BSc, 75; Univ Cambridge, PhD(astron), 81. *Prof Exp:* Marketer & trader, Shell Int Petrol Co, 75-77; lectr astron, Bd Extra-Mural Studies, Univ Cambridge, 78-80. *Mem:* Fel Royal Astron Soc; fel Royal Col Sci; Am Astron Soc. *Res:* Observation astronomy with particular emphasis on extragulactic research including globulue cluster, active galaxies and jets, BL LAC objects. *Mailing Add:* Dept Astron Univ Calif 1156 High St Santa Cruz CA 95064-1099

BRODIE, JONATHAN D, BRAIN IMAGING, PSYCHIATRY. *Current Pos:* from asst prof to assoc prof, 78-87, PROF PSYCHIAT, NY UNIV MED CTR, 87- *Personal Data:* b New York, NY, June 11, 38; c 3. *Educ:* Univ Wis, PhD(biochem), 62; NY Univ, MD, 75. *Prof Exp:* From asst prof to assoc prof biochem, State Univ, Buffalo, NY, 65-73. *Mem:* Am Psychiat Asn; Am Soc Biol Chemists; Am Chem Soc; Am Col Psychiatrists; Soc Nuclear Med. *Res:* Positron emission tomography, application to mental disorders and biochemical pharmacology. *Mailing Add:* Dept Psychiat NY Univ Med Ctr 550 First Ave New York NY 10016. *Fax:* 212-725-3662

BRODIE, LAIRD CHARLES, PHYSICS. *Current Pos:* from instr to prof, 55-86, EMER PROF PHYSICS, PORTLAND STATE UNIV, 86- *Personal Data:* b Portland, Ore, Aug 30, 22; m 48; c 3. *Educ:* Reed Col, BA, 44; Univ Chicago, MS, 49; Northwestern Univ, PhD(physics), 54. *Prof Exp:* Res engr, Lab Div, Radio Corp Am, 53-54; Ford Found intern, Reed Col, 54-55. *Mem:* Am Phys Soc; Am Asn Phys Teachers. *Res:* Nucleation of the vapor phase in liquid helium. *Mailing Add:* Dept Physics Portland State Univ Portland OR 97207

BRODIE, MARK S, ELECTROPHYSIOLOGY, NEUROPHARMACOLOGY. *Current Pos:* FEL, UNIV COLO, 84- *Educ:* Univ Ill, PhD(pharmacol), 84. *Mailing Add:* Dept Physiol & Biophys Univ Ill 835 S Wollcott Ave Rm E202 Chicago IL 60612-7342. *Fax:* 312-996-1414

BRODISH, ALVIN, PHYSIOLOGY. *Current Pos:* prof & chmn, 75-90, EMER PROF, DEPT PHYSIOL & PHARMACOL, BOWMAN GRAY SCH MED, 90- *Personal Data:* b Brooklyn, NY, June 11, 25; m 57; c 2. *Educ:* Drake Univ, BA, 47; Univ Iowa, MS, 50; Yale Univ, PhD(physiol), 55. *Prof Exp:* Lab instr biol, Drake Univ, 47-48; asst physiol, Univ Iowa, 49-50; asst psychiat, Yale Univ, 51-53, asst physiol, 53-54, NSF fel, 55-57, from instr to assoc prof, 57-68; prof physiol, Col Med, Univ Cincinnati, 68-75. *Concurrent Pos:* Investr, Howard Hughes Med Inst, 57-60. *Mem:* AAAS; Endocrine Soc; Am Physiol Soc. *Res:* Neuroendocrine systems; regulation of anterior pituitary secretions; nerve-muscle regeneration. *Mailing Add:* 4135 Briar Creek Rd Clemmons NC 27102

BRODKEY, JERALD STEVEN, NEUROSURGERY, BIOMEDICAL ENGINEERING. *Current Pos:* prof, 77-83, CLIN PROF NEUROSURG, CASE WESTERN RES UNIV, 83-, MED DIR, PAIN CTR, ST LUKE'S HOSP, 83-, CHIEF NEUROSURG, 84- *Personal Data:* b Omaha, Nebr, Jan 20, 34; m 71, Arielle Kozloff; c Jason & Daniel. *Educ:* Harvard Univ, AB, 55; Univ Nebr, MS, 59, MD, 60; Am Bd Neurol Surg, dipl, 71. *Prof Exp:* Intern surg, Barnes Hosp, St Louis, Mo, 60-61, asst resident, 61-62; asst resident neurosurg, Mass Gen Hosp, Boston, 62-66, clin asst, 66-67; dir sci comput sect & asst chmn dept bioeng, Presby-St Luke's Hosp, 67-69; asst prof bioeng, Univ Ill, Chicago, 65-69, clin instr neurol & neurosurg, Col Med, 67-69; chief neurosurg, Cleveland Vet Admin Hosp, 69-83. *Concurrent Pos:* Clin & res fel neurosurg, Mass Gen Hosp, Boston, 62-63; USPHS spec fel, 65-66; asst attend bioeng, Presby-St Luke's Hosp, 65-67, asst attend neurosurg, 67-69. *Mem:* AAAS; Inst Elec & Electronics Engrs; Soc Cybernet; Asn Comput Mach; NY Acad Sci. *Res:* Embedding of neurophysiological experiments in a neurological control system background; clinical neurosurgery, particularly pituitary and pain surgery. *Mailing Add:* 24755 Chagrin Blvd Suite 205 Beachwood OH 44122. *Fax:* 216-831-6025; *E-Mail:* jsb8@po.cwru.edu

BRODKEY, R(OBERT) S(TANLEY), CHEMICAL ENGINEERING. *Current Pos:* EMER PROF DEPT CHEM ENG, OHIO STATE UNIV, COLUMBUS. *Personal Data:* b Los Angeles, Calif, Sept 14, 28; m 75; c 1. *Educ:* Univ Calif, BS & MS, 50; Univ Wis, PhD(chem eng), 52. *Honors & Awards:* US Sr Scientist Award, Alexander Von Humboldt Found, 75 & 83. *Prof Exp:* Chem engr, E I du Pont de Nemours & Co, 50; res chem engr, Esso Res & Eng Co, 52-56 & Esso Stand Oil Co, 56-57. *Concurrent Pos:* Consult, fluid dynamics; sr fel sci, NATO, 72; Expository lectr, GAMM, Gottingen, 75; vis prof, Japan Soc Prom Sci, 78; sr res award, Col Eng, Ohio State Univ, 83 & 86, Am Soc Eng Educ, 85; distinguished sr res award, Ohio State Univ, 83; numerous lectrs at various American, European & Asian cols & univs; 3M Lecturship Award, Am Soc Eng Educ; outstanding res award, NAm Mixing Forum, 94; W W Clyde chair eng, Univ Utah, 94. *Mem:* Am Chem Soc; fel Am Inst Chem Engrs; fel Am Phys Soc; Soc Rheology; Soc Eng Sci; fel AAAS; fel Am Inst Chemists; Sigma Xi. *Res:* Fundamental structure of turbulence; turbulent motion, mixing, and kinetics; rheology; two-phase flow; bio-fluid flow; author and co-author of 100 scientific publications. *Mailing Add:* Dept Chem Eng Ohio State Univ 140 W 19th Ave Columbus OH 43210-1180

BRODMAN, ROBERT DAVID, HERPETOLOGY. *Current Pos:* ASST PROF BIOL, ST JOSEPHS COL, 92- *Personal Data:* b Milwaukee, Wis, Apr 9, 63; m 89, Cheryl Wistrom. *Educ:* Rutgers Univ, BA, 85; Univ Mich, MS, 87; Eastern Mich Univ, MS, 89; Kent State Univ, PhD(ecol), 92. *Honors & Awards:* Storer Award, Am Soc Ichthyologits & Herpetologists, 91. *Concurrent Pos:* Adj instr phys sci, Owens Tech Col, 87-89; adj instr biol, Univ Mich, 88-89; adj instr ecol, Kent State Univ, 92. *Mem:* Am Soc Ichthyologists & Herpetologists; Herpetologists League; Soc Study Amphibians & Reptiles. *Res:* The biography of midwest herpetofauna; the effect of acidity on salamander competition and prendation; habitat partitioning in pond breeding salamanders; long term monitoring of breeding success in pond breeding salamanders; behavioral aspects of community ecology. *Mailing Add:* Dept Biol St Josephs Col PO Box 929 Rensselaer IN 47978-0929. *E-Mail:* bobb@saintjoe.edu

BRODMANN, JOHN MILTON, GRIGNARD REATIONS. *Current Pos:* EMER PROF CHEM, CULVER-STOCKTON COL, 89- *Personal Data:* b Savannah, Ga, Aug 20, 33. *Educ:* Lynchburg Col, BS, 55; Emory Univ, MS, 59, PhD(natural prod synthesis), 67. *Prof Exp:* From instr to prof chem, Culver-Stockton Col, 57-89, chmn, Div Natural Sci, 65-76, admin asst, 89-92. *Mem:* Sigma Xi; Am Chem Soc. *Res:* Grignard addition to alpha, Beta-unsaturated ketones. *Mailing Add:* 501 S Monticello Rd Canton MO 63435-1416

BRODOFF, BERNARD NOAH, DIABETES, OBESITY. *Current Pos:* CLIN PROF MED & ADJ PROF PHYSIOL, NY MED COL. *Personal Data:* b New York, NY, Sept 8, 23. *Educ:* NY Univ, BA, 42; MD, 46. *Concurrent Pos:* Vis scientist, Brookhaven Nat Lab, 67-69. *Mem:* Fel Am Col Physicians; fel Am Col Cardiol; Am Physiol Soc. *Res:* Hypothalmic mechanisms in obesity and diabetes; lipid metabolism. *Mailing Add:* Seven Beach Court Salem SC 29676. *Fax:* 914-993-4018

BRODOWAY, NICOLAS, ORGANIC CHEMISTRY. *Current Pos:* RETIRED. *Personal Data:* b Melfort, Sask, Dec 9, 22; US citizen; m 49, Mary Greissel; c 6. *Educ:* Univ BC, BSc, 49; Univ Minn, PhD(org chem), 53. *Prof Exp:* Res chemist, Elastomer Chem Div, Polymer Prod Dept, E I DuPont de Nemours & Co, Inc, 53-80, res assoc, 80-84. *Mem:* Am Chem Soc; Sigma Xi. *Res:* Polymer synthesis, evaluation and process development. *Mailing Add:* 215 Dakota Ave Wilmington DE 19803

BRODSKY, ALLEN, HEALTH & MEDICAL PHYSICS, ENVIRONMENTAL HEALTH. *Current Pos:* ADJ PROF RADIATION SCI, GEORGETOWN UNIV, 86-, CONSULT HEALTH & MED PHYSICS. *Personal Data:* b Baltimore, Md, Nov 5, 28; m 84, Phyllis Levin; c Richard, Karen & Jay. *Educ:* Johns Hopkins Univ, BE, 49, MA, 60; Univ Pittsburgh, ScD(biostatist, radiation health), 66; Am Bd Health Physics, dipl, 60; Am Bd Indust Hyg, dipl, 66; Am Bd Radiol, dipl, 75. *Honors & Awards:* Distinguished Serv Award, Western Pa Chap, Health Physics Soc, 74; Wright Langham lectr award, Radiation Epidemiol, Univ Ky Med Ctr, 79; Failla lectr award, NY Chap Health Physics Soc & Radiol & Med Physics Soc, 87; Founders Award, Health Physics Soc, 86; Radiation Sci & Eng Award, Am Nuclear Soc, 94. *Prof Exp:* Head, Health Physics Unit, Naval Res Lab, Washington, DC, 50-52, physicist, Opers Ivy & Castle, Eniwetok & Bikini, 52-54; pres, Health Physics Servs, Inc, Baltimore, Md, 55-57; radiol defense officer, Fed Civil Defense Admin, Olney, Md, 56-57; health physicist, Health Protection Br, Div Biol & Med, US AEC, Washington, DC, 57-59, radiation physicist, Div Licensing & Regulation, US AEC, Washington, DC, 59-61; res assoc health physics & epidemiol, Dept Occup Health, Grad Sch Pub Health, Univ Pittsburgh, 61-66, assoc prof, Dept Occup Health & Dept Radiation Health, 66-71; radiation physicist & safety officer, Dept Radiol, Mercy Hosp, Pittsburgh, Pa, 71-75; sr health physicist, Off Nuclear Regulatory Res, US Nuclear Regulatory Comn, Washington, DC, 75-86. *Concurrent Pos:* Consult, Westinghouse, 62-64, Numec, 66-69, Mercy Hosp, 67-70, Case Western Reserve Univ, 68-69, SCA, Inc, 87-89, Brookhaven Nat Lab, 87-88, Dept Energy, 90, Centocor, 90, Fitzpatrick Nuclear Plant, 90-91; tech dir, Dept Radiation Med, Presby Univ Hosp, Pittsburgh, 65-70; expert witness, J Terasi, 68-71, Dept Justice, 81-83; adj res prof, Sch Pharm, Duquesne Univ, 71-75; adj prof radiation sci, Georgetown Univ, 86- *Mem:* Am Indust Hyg Asn; Health Physics Soc; Am Asn Physicists Med; Am Pub Health Asn; Am Statist Asn; fel Am Nuclear Soc. *Res:* Radiation dose measurement and interpretation; radiation hazard evaluation and standards for radiation protection; mathematical models of carcinogenesis and risk estimation from environmental agents; epidemiologic studies of environmental exposures and effects. *Mailing Add:* 2765 Ocean Pines Berlin MD 21811

BRODSKY, CARROLL M, PSYCHIATRY, ANTHROPOLOGY. *Current Pos:* RETIRED. *Personal Data:* b Lowell, Mass, Dec 23, 22; c 3. *Educ:* Cath Univ Am, AB, 49, MA, 50, PhD(anthrop), 54; Univ Calif, MD, 56. *Prof Exp:* Lectr anthrop, Cath Univ Am, 52; res assoc, Human Resources Res Off, 53; from instr to prof psychiat, Sch Med, Univ Calif, San Francisco, 60-95. *Concurrent Pos:* NIMH grant, Langley-Porter Neuropsychiat Inst, 57-60. *Mem:* Acad Psychosom Med; Am Antrop Asn; Am Col Psychiat. *Res:* Studies of human disability with emphasis on social and psychiatric factors delaying recovery from illness; problems of work. *Mailing Add:* Dept Psychiat Univ Calif Sch Med San Francisco CA 94143

BRODSKY, FRANCES M(ARTHA), IMMUNOLOGY, ENDOCYTOSIS. *Current Pos:* PROG MGR CELL BIOL, BECTON DICKINSON IMMUNOCYTOMETRY SYSTS, 82- *Educ:* Oxford Univ, DPhil, 79. *Mailing Add:* Univ Calif Hooper Found Rm HSW-1542 513 Parnassus Ave San Francisco CA 94143-0552. *Fax:* 415-476-0688

BRODSKY, MARC HERBERT, SEMICONDUCTOR TECHNOLOGY. *Current Pos:* EXEC DIR & CHIEF EXEC OFFICER, AM INST PHYSICS, 93- *Personal Data:* b Philadelphia, Pa, Aug 9, 38; m 66; c 2. *Educ:* Univ Pa, AB, 60, MS, 61, PhD(physics), 65. *Prof Exp:* Res assoc physics, Univ Pa, 65; res physicist, US Naval Ord Lab, 65-66; physicist, Night Vision Lab, US Army, 66-68; res mem staff, T J Watson Res Ctr, Int Bus Mach Corp, 68-87; prog dir, IBM Advan Gas Technol Lab, 87-89; dir, tech planning, IBM Corp, Watson Res Ctr, 89-93. *Concurrent Pos:* Adj assoc prof, Columbia Univ, 72-74; exchange prof, Univ Paris VI, 74-75. *Mem:* AAAS; fel Am Phys Soc; fel Inst Elec & Electronics Engrs. *Res:* Semiconductors, amorphous semiconductors; lattice vibrations; infrared spectroscopy; semiconductor devices and technology. *Mailing Add:* Am Inst Physics One Physics Ellipse College Park MD 20740-3843

BRODSKY, MERWYN BERKLEY, SOLID STATE PHYSICS. *Current Pos:* assoc chemist, 58-66, group leader, 66-74, SR SCIENTIST, ARGONNE NAT LAB, 74- *Personal Data:* b Chicago, Ill, Mar 4, 30; m 50; c 2. *Educ:* Roosevelt Univ, BS, 49; Ill Inst Technol, MS, 51, PhD(phys chem), 55. *Prof Exp:* Asst, Ill Inst Technol, 50-54; assoc chemist, Brookhaven Nat Lab, 54-58. *Concurrent Pos:* Sr vis res fel, Imperial Col, Univ London, 71-73. *Mem:* Am Phys Soc; Am Inst Mining, Petrol & Metall Eng. *Res:* Electron transport and magnetism of actinides; fused salt electrorefining; physical chemistry of liquid metal solutions; high temperature thermodynamics; liquid metal reactor systems. *Mailing Add:* 355 Oakwood St Park Forest IL 60466

BRODSKY, PHILIP HYMAN, ADHESIVES, PLASTICS & CHEMICAL ENGINEERING. *Current Pos:* Sr res engr, Monsanto Co, 69-73, res specialist, 73-76, group leader, 76-79, sr group leader, 79-80, mgr, 80-84, dir res & develop, 84-87, dir corp res, 87-90, dir corp res & environ technol, 91-96, VPRES, CORP RES & ENVIRON TECHNOL, MONSANTO CO, 96- *Personal Data:* b Philadelphia, Pa, July 7, 42; m 77, Sunny B Kurn; c Noah, Andrew, Amy, Melanie & Michelle. *Educ:* Cornell Univ, BChE, 65, PhD(chem eng), 69. *Mem:* Am Chem Soc; Indust Res Inst; Sigma Xi. *Res:* Compatibility in polymer blends; manufacturing processes and chemistry of condensation and addition polymers; reprographics and adhesives chemistry; technology organization development; technology management training; plastics research and development; soil remediation. *Mailing Add:* Monsanto Co 800 Lindbergh Blvd St Louis MO 63167

BRODSKY, STANLEY JEROME, HIGH ENERGY PHYSICS, THEORETICAL PHYSICS. *Current Pos:* res assoc, 66-68, assoc prof, 75-76, MEM RES STAFF, STANFORD LINEAR ACCELERATOR CTR, STANFORD UNIV, 68-, PROF, 76- *Personal Data:* b St Paul, Minn, Jan 9, 40; m 62, 86, Judith E Preis; c Stephen A & David J. *Educ:* Univ Minn, BPhys, 61, PhD(physics), 64. *Honors & Awards:* Alexander von Humboldt sr distinguished US scientist. *Prof Exp:* Res assoc theoret physics, Columbia Univ, 64-66. *Concurrent Pos:* Vis assoc prof, Dept Physics, Cornell Univ, 69; consult, Particle Data Group, Lawrence Berkeley Lab, 72-78, mem high energy physics rev comt, 78-81; mem comt fundamental constants, Nat Res Coun-Nat Acad Sci, 74-77 & prog comt, Wilson Lab, Cornell Univ, 75-79; mem prog comt, Argonne Nat Lab, 77-79; mem exec bd, Sci Forum, Weizmann Inst, Rehovot, Israel, 77-, vis prof, 78; mem prog adv comt, Fermi Nat Accelerator Lab, 78-; vis prof, Inst Theoret Physics, Univ Calif, Santa Barbara, 81, 85, & 88; mem, Dept Energy & Nat Sci Found Nuclear Sci Adv Subcomt Electromagnetic Interactions, 81-; mem sci adv panel, Southeastern Univ Res Asn, Inc, 81-; vis prof natural sci, Inst Advan Study, Princeton, 82, Max Planck Inst Nuclear Physics, Heidelberg, 87 & 88; mem sci & educ adv comt, Lawrence Berkeley Lab, Univ Calif, 86-; external sci dir, Max Planck Inst Nuclear Physics, 89-; lectr, Colloquium Series, Univ Minn, 89, Inst Nuclear Theory, Univ Wash, 90. *Mem:* Fel Am Phys Soc; Union Concerned Scientists. *Res:* Quantum electrodynamics; muonic x-rays; weak interactions; Zeeman structure; Lamb shift; lepton magnetic moments; elementary particles; electromagnetic interactions; colliding beam physics; large transverse momentum reactions; nuclear processes; photon-photon collisions; quark-model; quantum chromodynamics. *Mailing Add:* Stanford Linear Accelerator Ctr Stanford Univ PO Box 4349 Stanford CA 94305. *Fax:* 650-926-2525; *E-Mail:* sjbth@slac.stanford.edu

BRODSKY, WILLIAM AARON, PHYSIOLOGY. *Current Pos:* PROF BIOPHYS, MT SINAI SCH MED, 68-, PROF NEPHROLOGY, 83- *Personal Data:* b Philadelphia, Pa, Jan 8, 18; m 50; c 3. *Educ:* Temple Univ, BS, 38, MD, 41. *Honors & Awards:* Basic Sci Res Award, Temple Univ, Sch Med, 86- *Prof Exp:* Intern, Philadelphia Gen Hosp, 41-43; instr pediat, Univ Pa, 43-44; instr, Univ Cincinnati, 48-49; from asst prof to prof pediat, Univ Louisville, 51-68, prof exp med, 60-68. *Concurrent Pos:* Res fels pediat, Univ Cincinnati, 46-48 & 49-51; USPHS res fel, 62-; estab investr, Am Heart Asn, 55-60; Career Res Award, NIH, 61-68; prof biophys grad div, City Univ NY, 68- *Mem:* Soc Pediat Res; Am Physiol Soc; Soc Exp Biol & Med; Am Soc Clin Invest; Biophys Soc (secy & exec coun, 67-72); Sigma Xi. *Res:* Osmotic properties of tissue; ion transport mechanisms; acid-base equilibria; renal transport mechanisms. *Mailing Add:* Dept Physiol & Biophys & Med Mt Sinai Med Ctr 1 Gustave L Levy Pl PO Box 1218 New York NY 10029-6574. *Fax:* 212-860-3369

BRODWICK, MALCOLM STEPHEN, PHYSIOLOGY. *Current Pos:* asst prof, 74-79, ASSOC PROF PHYSIOL, UNIV TEX MED BR, GALVESTON, 79- *Personal Data:* b New York, NY, July 26, 44; m 69; c 2. *Educ:* San Fernando Valley State Col, Ba, 67; Univ Calif, Los Angeles, PhD(anat), 72. *Prof Exp:* Fel physiol & pharmacol, Duke Univ, 72-74. *Mem:* Soc Gen Physiologists; Biophys Soc. *Res:* Membranes controlling the flux of materials from one side to the other; active transport; excitability; neurotransmitter induced conductance; exocytosis. *Mailing Add:* Dept Physiol & Biophysics Univ Tex Mec Sch Galveston 301 University Blvd Galveston TX 77550-2708

BRODWIN, MORRIS E(LLIS), ELECTRICAL ENGINEERING. *Current Pos:* from assoc prof to prof microwave eng, 58-69, PROF ELEC ENG, NORTHWESTERN UNIV, EVANSTON, 69- *Personal Data:* b New York, NY, July 14, 24; m 49; c 2. *Educ:* Univ Nebr, BS, 47; Johns Hopkins Univ, MS, 52, DrE, 57. *Prof Exp:* Res scientist, Microwave & Syst Anal, Johns Hopkins Univ, 48-58. *Concurrent Pos:* Consult, Martin Co, 57-58 & Admiral Corp, 59. *Mem:* AAAS; Inst Elec & Electronics Engrs. *Res:* Microwave physics; propagation in anisotropic media; measurement of physical properties at microwave frequencies. *Mailing Add:* Dept Elec Eng & Comput Sci Northwestern Univ 2736 Tech Inst Evanston IL 60208-0001

BRODY, AARON LEO, food technology, packaging, for more information see previous edition

BRODY, ALFRED WALTER, PHYSIOLOGY & MECHANICS OF RESPIRATION, PULMONARY DISEASE IN INTERNAL MEDICINE & MEDICAL SCIENCE PHARMACOLOGY. *Current Pos:* from asst prof to prof physiol & pharmacol, Sch Med, Creighton Univ, 54-77, dir, Pulmonary Lab, 54-77, prof med, 60-92, chief, Chest Div, 62-77, CONSULT INTERNAL MED & PULMONARY DIS, CREIGHTON UNIV, 77-, EMER PROF, 93- *Personal Data:* b New York, NY, Feb 20, 20; m 43, Shirley Bloom; c Betty Ann (Buchsbaum), Carolyn Gail (Schwarz), Frances Linda & Robert Seymour. *Educ:* Columbia Univ, BA, 40, MA, 41; Long Island Col Med, MD, 43; Univ Pa, DSc, 53. *Prof Exp:* Fel, Grad Sch Med, Univ Pa, 51-54, instr physiol & pharmacol, 51-54. *Concurrent Pos:* Consult, Pulmonary Dis, 77- *Mem:* AAAS; Am Physiol Soc; Am Thoracic Soc; NY Acad Sci; AMA. *Res:* Mechanics of respiration; respiratory physiology; lesser circulation; bronchogenic cancer medicine; internal medicine. *Mailing Add:* Dept Med Sch Med Creighton Univ 5122 Capitol Ave Omaha NE 68132

BRODY, ARNOLD R, EXPERIMENTAL PULMONARY PATHOLOGY. *Current Pos:* PROF PATH, TULANE UNIV, 93- *Personal Data:* b Boston, Mass, March 24, 43; m 67; c 2. *Educ:* Univ Ill, MS, 67; Colo State Univ, BS, 65, PhD(cell biol), 69. *Prof Exp:* Fel, Dept Entom, Ohio State Univ, 69-72; res assoc, Univ Vt, 72-74, asst prof, 74-78; sr staff fel, Nat Inst Environ Health Sci, 78-84, res biolist, lab pulmonary pathobiol, 84-87, head pulmonary path, 78-93, prof path, 87-93. *Concurrent Pos:* Vis scientist, Pneumoconiosis Res Ctr, Med Res Coun, Wales, 74 & Dept Path, Hosp Bichat, France, 77; adj prof, dept path, Col Med, Duke Univ, 78-; John P Wyatt Traveling Fel Environ Path, 84; vis prof, Dept Path, Nat Inst Cardiol, Mexico City, 85. *Mem:* AAAS; Electron Micros Soc Am; Sigma Xi; Nat Wildlife Fedn. *Res:* Defining the mechanisms by which inhaled inorganic particulates cause lung disease; deposition patterns of asbestos and silica and the subcellular interactions of various pulmonary cells with these inhaled particulates; biology and biochemistry of macrophage-derived growth factors. *Mailing Add:* 170 Walnut St New Orleans LA 70118

BRODY, BARUCH ALTER, MEDICINE, ETHICS. *Current Pos:* assoc prof, 75-77, PROF, RICE UNIV, HOUSTON, 77-; PROF, BAYLOR COL MED, HOUSTON, 82-, DIR, CTR ETHICS, 82- *Personal Data:* b Brooklyn, NY, Apr 21, 43; m 65, Dena Grosser; c Todd, Jeremy & Myles. *Educ:* Brooklyn Col, BA, 62; Princeton Univ, PhD, 67. *Prof Exp:* Asst prof, Mass Inst Technol, 67-75. *Concurrent Pos:* Consult, NASA, 90-91. *Res:* Abortion and the sanctity of human life. *Mailing Add:* Baylor Col Med 1 Baylor Plaza Houston TX 77030-3411

BRODY, BERNARD B, MEDICINE, CHEMISTRY. *Current Pos:* from instr to asst prof med, Univ Rochester, 56-81, assoc prof path, 77-81, prof, 81-91, EMER PROF MED & PATH, UNIV ROCHESTER, 91- *Personal Data:* b New York, NY, June 24, 22; m 54, Ruth Miller; c Sarah (Epstein) & Rachel (Bandych). *Educ:* Univ Wis-Madison, BS, 43; Univ Rochester, MD, 51. *Prof Exp:* Res assoc chem, Univ Chicago, 43-45; res assoc, Monsanto Chem Corp, Ohio, 45-47; intern med, Strong Mem Hosp, Rochester, NY, 51-52, asst resident, 52-53; chief resident, Genesee Hosp, 55-56; dir med affairs, Genesee Hosp, 74-87. *Concurrent Pos:* Pvt practr, 56-67; dir clin labs, Genesee Hosp, 67-81. *Mem:* AAAS; AMA; Am Soc Internal Med; Am Asn Clin Chem; Am Col Physicians. *Res:* Clinical lab technical systems and computerization. *Mailing Add:* 12 Huntington Brook Rochester NY 14625

BRODY, BURTON ALAN, PHYSICS. *Current Pos:* PROF PHYSICS, BARD COL, 70-; ADJ RES PHYSICS, COLUMBIA UNIV, 80- *Personal Data:* b New York, NY, June 8, 42; m 80, Susan Simon. *Educ:* Columbia Col, BA, 63; Univ Mich, PhD(exp physics), 70. *Mem:* Am Phys Soc; Am Asn Physics Teachers; Fedn Am Scientists. *Res:* Superfluid helium; acoustics; electronics; photon echoes (laser physics). *Mailing Add:* Dept Physics Bard Col Annandale-on-Hudson NY 12504

BRODY, EDWARD NORMAN, RNA SYNTHESIS, RNA SPLICING. *Current Pos:* PROF & CHMN, DEPT BIOL, STATE UNIV, NY, BUFFALO, 91- *Personal Data:* b Chicago, Ill, Mar 2, 39; m 64; c 4. *Educ:* Roosevelt Univ, Chicago, BS, 59; Univ Chicago, MD, 64, PhD(biochem), 65. *Prof Exp:* Fel, Dept Biophys, Univ Chicago, 65-68 & Dept Molecular Biol, Univ Geneva, 68-70; res, Inst Biol Physics & Chem, Paris, 70-88; dir res, Ctr Molecular Genetics, Gif-Sur-Yvette, 88-91. *Concurrent Pos:* Vis res assoc, Dept Biol, Calif Inst Technol, 84. *Mem:* Europ Molecular Biol Orgn. *Res:* Regulation of transcription in E coli infected by bacteriophage T4; mechanism of RNA splicing in eukaryotes. *Mailing Add:* Dept Biol Scis Cooke 109 State Univ New York Buffalo NY 14260

BRODY, EUGENE B, PSYCHIATRY, PSYCHOANALYSIS. *Current Pos:* chief resident, 48-49,from instr to assoc prof,49-57, chmn dept, 59-76, dir, Inst Psychiat & Human Behav, 59-76, prof human behav, 76-87, EMER PROF PSYCHIAT & HUMAN BEHAV, UNIV MD, BALTIMORE, 87-; SR ASSOC, JOHNS HOPKINS SCH PUB HEALTH, 86- *Personal Data:* b Columbia, Mo, June 17, 21; m 44; c 3. *Educ:* Univ Mo, AB, 41, MA, 41; Harvard Med Sch, MD, 44; Am Bd Psychiat & Neurol, dipl, 50; Am Psychoanal Asn, cert, 60. *Honors & Awards:* Global Humanitarian, Hasserman Found Int Accord, 90. *Prof Exp:* From intern to asst resident psychiat, Yale Univ, 44-46. *Concurrent Pos:* Consult, WHO & Pan Am Health Orgn, 65-, NIMH, 68- & UNESCO, 87-; dir, Interam Ment Health Studies Prog, Am Psychiat Asn, 66- 68; ed-in-chief, J Nerv & Ment Dis, 67-; vis prof, Univ Brazil, 68, Univ West Indies, 72-75 & Univ Otago, New Zealand, 81; fel, Ctr Adv Study Behav Sci, Stanford, 75-76, Sackler Inst Adv Study, Univ Tel Aviv, 86; psychiat epidemiol, US NIMH, 75-79, AIDS, 88-; bd, Hogg Found, Univ Tex, 87-90; mem adv bd, Peruvian NIMH, 84-; secy gen, World Fedn Ment Health, 83-; exec bd, Int Soc Sci Coun, 87-90. *Mem:* Fel Am Psychiat Asn; Asn Behav Sch Med Educ (pres, 80-81); World Fedn Mental Health (pres, 81-83, secy gen, 83-); fel Am Anthrop Asn; Am Psychoanal Asn. *Res:* Social psychiatry; culture and fertility; psychoanalytic anthropology; ethics and health. *Mailing Add:* Sheppard & Enoch Pratt Hosp PO Box 6815 Baltimore MD 21285-6815

BRODY, GARRY SIDNEY, PLASTIC SURGERY. *Current Pos:* CHIEF PLASTIC SURG, SCH MED, UNIV SOUTHERN CALIF-RANCHO LOS AMIGOS HOSP, 69-, ASST CLIN PROF SURG, 77- *Personal Data:* b Edmonton, Alta, Sept 21, 32; US citizen; m 57; c 3. *Educ:* Univ Alta, MD, 56; McGill Univ, MS, 59. *Concurrent Pos:* Abstract ed, J Plastic & Reconstruct Surg, 74-; chmn, Plastic Surg Res Coun, 76. *Mem:* Am Soc Plastic & Reconstruct Surg; Asn Surg of the Hand; Med Eng Soc. *Res:* Rheology of connective tissue and scar; relationship of breast cancer and prosthetic insects; multiple clinical plastic surgery problems. *Mailing Add:* 1450 San Pablo St Suite 2000 Los Angeles CA 90033

BRODY, HAROLD, NEUROGERONTOLOGY. *Current Pos:* from asst prof to prof, 54-96, chmn dept, 71-92, DISTINGUISHED TEACHING PROF, SCH MED, STATE UNIV NY BUFFALO, 96- *Personal Data:* b Cleveland, Ohio, May 15, 23; m 51, Anne Pertz; c David A & Evan B. *Educ:* Western Res Univ, BS, 47; Univ Minn, PhD(anat), 53; Univ Buffalo, MD, 61. *Honors & Awards:* Kleemeier Award Res Geront, 79; Wilson Abernathy Distinguished lectr anesthesiol, Univ Toronto, 87. *Prof Exp:* Teaching asst anat, Univ Minn, 47-49, instr, 49-50; asst prof, Univ NDak, 50-54. *Concurrent Pos:* Fulbright sr res scholar, 63; ed-in-chief, J Geront, 75-80; ed, Neurobiol Aging, 82- *Mem:* AAAS; Am Asn Anatomists; Am Geront Soc (pres, 74-75); Int Asn Gerontol; Am Geriatric Soc. *Res:* Neuroanatomy; neuropathology; age changes in the human nervous system. *Mailing Add:* Dept Anat Sci Sch Med State Univ NY Buffalo NY 14214. *Fax:* 716-829-2915

BRODY, HAROLD DAVID, CASTING & SOLIDIFICATION OF ALLOYS, COMPUTER MODELING OF MATERIALS PROCESSING. *Current Pos:* DEAN ENG, UNIV CONN, 91-, PROF METALL & MAT ENG, 91- *Personal Data:* b Boston, Mass, Apr 13, 39; m 66, Katharine Tatem; c Michael & Shayna. *Educ:* Mass Inst Technol, SB, 60, SM, 61, ScD, 65. *Honors & Awards:* Souveur Mem Award, Am Soc Metals, 68; Foundry Educ Found Prof, 77. *Prof Exp:* Sr res engr, Monsanto Res Corp, 65-66; from asst prof to prof mat eng, Univ Pittsburgh, 66-91, chmn metall & mat eng, 71-79, dir, Casting Industs Sci & Eng Inst, 86-91. *Concurrent Pos:* Res engr, Mass Inst Technol, 65-66, vis prof mat sci & eng, 87-; Foundry educ found prof, Univ Pittsburgh, 76-91; vis prof mat sci & eng, Mass Inst Technol, 87-; dir, Stardyne, Inc, 88-93, Conn Pre-eng Prog, 91-, Inroads/Greater Hartford, Inc, 91- & Conn Acad Educ, 92- *Mem:* Am Foundrymen's Soc; fel Am Soc Metals Int; Am Inst Mining, Metall & Petrol Engrs; Am Soc Eng Educ. *Res:* Fundamental studies of the development of structure and segregation in the solidification of alloys; computer simulation of casting and welding processes; development of novel solidification and coating processes; curriculum innovation in engineering education. *Mailing Add:* Sch Eng U-237 Univ Conn Storrs CT 06269-2237. *Fax:* 860-486-0318; *E-Mail:* brody@eng2.uconn.edu

BRODY, HOWARD, PHYSICS. *Current Pos:* from instr to assoc prof, 59-77, PROF PHYSICS, UNIV PA, 77- *Personal Data:* b Newark, NJ, July 11, 32; m 54; c 3. *Educ:* Mass Inst Technol, SB, 54; Calif Inst Technol, MS, 56, PhD(physics), 59. *Prof Exp:* NSF fel, 59. *Mem:* Am Phys Soc; Am Asn Physics Teachers. *Res:* Study of elementary particles and their interactions at high energy. *Mailing Add:* Dept Physics Univ Pa Philadelphia PA 19104

BRODY, HOWARD, MEDICINE. *Current Pos:* ASSOC PROF FAMILY PRACT MED HUMANITIES & PHILOS, MICH STATE UNIV, 85-, COORDR, MED HUMANITIES PROG, 85-, PROF, FAMILY PRACT & PHILOS, DIR, CTR ETHICS & HUMANITIES, LIFE SCIS, PHILOS, 90- *Personal Data:* b Chicago, Ill, June 23, 49; m 71, Daralyn Shappee; c Sheila Lynette & Mark Davan. *Educ:* Mich State Univ, BS, 71, MD, 76, PhD, 77; Am Bd Family Pract, cert, 80. *Honors & Awards:* Soc Health & Human Values Annual Award, 95. *Prof Exp:* Asst prof family pract, med humanities & philos, Mich State Univ, 80-85, asst coordr, 80-84, actg coordr, Med Humanities Prog, 81-82 & 85-85; resident, Dept Family Pract, Univ Va Med Ctr, 77-80, chief resident, 79-80. *Concurrent Pos:* Goldberger fel, AMA, 71; Bristol Meyers vis Am prof, Sect Gen Pract, Royal Soc Med, 84; fel, Hastings Ctr, 90-; vis lectr med ethics, Royal NZ Col Gen Practitioners, 91; vis prof, Ctr Biomed Ethics, Univ Olso, 91; sr scholar residence, Agency Health Care Policy & Res, 93-94. *Mem:* Inst Med-Nat Acad Sci; Soc Health & Human Values (pres, 88-89); Soc Teachers Family Med; Soc Bioethics Consult; Am Acad Family Physicians. *Res:* Contributor of numerous publications. *Mailing Add:* Dept Family Pract Mich State Univ B-100 Clin Ctr East Lansing MI 48824-1313

BRODY, JACOB A, epidemiology, medical science, for more information see previous edition

BRODY, JEROME IRA, INTERNAL MEDICINE, HEMATOLOGY. *Current Pos:* PROF MED, MED COL PA, 75- *Personal Data:* b New York, NY, Jan 24, 28; m 59, Anita J Blumstein; c 3. *Educ:* NY Univ, AB, 47, AM, 48; Jefferson Med Col, MD, 52; Am Bd Internal Med, dipl, hematol, dipl. *Prof Exp:* Intern, Philadelphia Gen Hosp, 52-53, resident path, 53-54, resident cardiol, 54-55; resident internal med, Grad Hosp, Univ Pa, 57-58; chief hemat sect, Vet Admin Hosp, Coral Gables, Fla, 60-62; from asst prof to assoc prof internal med, Sch Med, Univ Pa, 62-75, dir hemat, Grad Hosp, 62-75. *Concurrent Pos:* USPHS res fel hemat, Sch Med, Yale Univ, 58-60; asst instr path, Sch Med, Univ Pa, 53-54, asst instr internal med, 54-55, asst physician, Grad Hosp, 62-; asst attend physician, Grace-New Haven Community Hosp, Conn, 58-60 & Jackson Mem Hosp, Miami, Fla, 60-62; asst prof, Sch Med, Univ Miami, 60-62; consult, Variety Children's Hosp, Miami, 61-62; prin investr res grant, USPHS, 62-79, prog dir training grant, 64-74; consult, Walson Army Hosp & Naval Hosp, 63-75; chief med serv, Med Col, Pa Div, Vet Admin Hosp, Philadelphia, 75-79; adj prof med, Med Col, Thomas Jefferson, Univ, 89- *Mem:* AAAS; Am Soc Clin Invest; Am Fedn Clin Res; Am Soc Hemat; Am Asn Pathologists; Am Soc Clin Path. *Res:* Relationship of hemeostasis to cardiovascular disease; influence of endothelial cell dysfunction on vascular occlusion; hemostatic aspects of cardiovascular disease. *Mailing Add:* Med Col Pa Philadelphia PA 19129

BRODY, JEROME SAUL, PULMONARY DISEASES. *Current Pos:* PROF MED, SCH MED, BOSTON UNIV, 78- *Personal Data:* b Chicago, Ill, Dec 6, 34; m 55; c 3. *Educ:* Univ Ill, BS, 55, MD, 59. *Prof Exp:* NIH fel, Univ Pa, 65-67, from asst prof to assoc prof med & physiol, 67-73; assoc prof med, 73-78, CHIEF PULMONARY SECT, UNIV HOSP & BOSTON CITY

HOSP, 73- *Mem:* Fel Am Col Physicians; Am Thoracic Soc; Am Fedn Clin Res; Am Physiol Soc; Am Soc Clin Invest. *Res:* Development, compensatory growth and repair of the mammalian lung viewed from morphologic, physiologic and biochemical points of view. *Mailing Add:* Pulm Ctr K602 Boston Univ Sch Med 80 E Concord St Boston MA 02118-2394. *Fax:* 617-536-8093

BRODY, MARCIA, photobiology, for more information see previous edition

BRODY, RICHARD SIMON, ENZYME MECHANISMS. *Current Pos:* CONSULT, 83- *Personal Data:* b Brooklyn, NY, Oct 20, 50; c 2. *Educ:* Cornell Univ, BA, 72; Harvard Univ, PhD(chem), 78. *Prof Exp:* Fel, Ohio State Univ, 79-81; asst prof chem, State Univ NY at Buffalo, 81-83. *Mem:* Am Chem Soc; Am Soc Biochem & Molecular Biol. *Res:* Mechanisms of enzymes that synthesize and degrade nucleic acids; protein-nucleic acid interactions; phosphodiesterase inhibitors; model systems. *Mailing Add:* Battelle 505 King Ave Columbus OH 43201-2693. *Fax:* 614-424-5263

BRODY, SEYMOUR STEVEN, BIOPHYSICS. *Current Pos:* assoc prof, 66-68, PROF BIOL, NY UNIV, 68- *Personal Data:* b New York, NY, Nov 29, 27; m 49; c 3. *Educ:* City Col New York, BS, 51; NY Univ, MS, 53; Univ Ill, PhD(biophys), 56. *Prof Exp:* Res asst photosynthesis, Univ Ill, 53-56, res assoc, 56-59; sect chief photobiol, US Dept Air Force, 59-60; mgr biophys, Watson Lab, Int Bus Mach Corp, 60-65. *Concurrent Pos:* Adj assoc prof, Dept Biol, Washington Square Col, NY Univ, 64-65; guest prof, Dept Biol, Jawaharlal Nehru Univ, New Delhi, India, & Dept Biophys, Univ Leiden, Holland, 82; vis scientist, Royal Inst, London, Eng, 79, Carlsberg Res Lab, Copenhagen, 80 & 85, Serv Biophys, Ctr d'Etudes Nucleaires, Saclay, France, 83; guest prof, Inst Basic Biol, Okazaki, Japan, 87; Ecole Normale Superior, Paris, France, 88. *Mem:* AAAS; Biophys Soc; Photo Biol Soc. *Res:* Photobiology; fluorescence and absorption spectroscopy of molecules; heterogeneous photocatalysis; picosecond and nonosecond phenomena in living systems and in molecules; use of monomolecular bilayers and liposomes as films, models of membranes to investigate processes in vision and photosynthesis. *Mailing Add:* Dept Biol NY Univ 100 Washington Sq E New York NY 10003-6688

BRODY, STUART, BIOCHEMICAL GENETICS. *Current Pos:* from asst prof to assoc prof, 67-82, PROF BIOL, UNIV CALIF, SAN DIEGO, 82- *Personal Data:* b Newark, NJ, June 25, 37; m 65; c 2. *Educ:* Mass Inst Technol, SB, 59; Stanford Univ, PhD(biol), 64. *Prof Exp:* Guest investr biol, Rockefeller Univ, 64-66, res assoc, 66, asst prof, 66-67. *Concurrent Pos:* Am Cancer Soc fel, 64-66; prin investr NSF grant, 66-75. *Mem:* AAAS; Am Soc Biol Chemists; Am Soc Microbiol; Genetics Soc Am. *Res:* Biochemical genetics; biochemistry and morphology of microorganisms; circadian rhythms; spore formation and germination; lipid metabolism. *Mailing Add:* Dept Biol Univ Calif San Diego La Jolla CA 92093-0116

BRODY, STUART MARTIN, FRACTIONAL DISTILLATION, CHROMATOGRAPHIC & MASS SPECTROMETRIC TECHNOLOGY. *Current Pos:* sr scientist I, Pharmaceut Div, Ciba-Geigy Corp, 69-80, sr scientist II, 81-83, sr res scientist, 84-85, asst mgr, Pharmaceut Div, 85-92, MGR, PHARMACEUT DIV, CIBA-GEIGY CORP, 92- *Personal Data:* b Brooklyn, NY, June 25, 36; m 58, Helene Levine; c Russell & Elyse. *Educ:* Queens Col NY, BSc, 58. *Prof Exp:* Jr chemist, Pharmaceuticals Co-Ciba, 58-66, lab suprv, 67-68. *Mem:* Fel Am Inst Chemists; NY Acad Sci; Asn Off Anal Chemists; Am Soc Mass Spectrometry. *Res:* Develop methodologies for analytical evaluation of chemical reaction mixtures to elucidate chemical structures; analytical systems for on-line assay of complex reaction mixtures using state-of-the-art instrumentation and computer technology; analytical chemistry research relevant to the drug discovery and development process. *Mailing Add:* 8 Timberland Dr Colonia NJ 07067. *Fax:* 908-277-7904

BRODY, THEODORE MEYER, PHARMACOLOGY, CARDIOVASCULAR PHARMACOLOGY. *Current Pos:* chmn, Dept Pharmacol & Toxicol, 66-86, prof, 66-90, EMER PROF PHARMACOL, MICH STATE UNIV, 90- *Personal Data:* b Newark, NJ, May 10, 20; m 47, Ethel Drelich; c Steven, Debra, Laura & Elizabeth. *Educ:* Rutgers Univ, BS, 43; Univ Ill, MS, 49, PhD(pharmacol), 52. *Honors & Awards:* John Jacob Abel Award, Am Soc Pharmacol & Exp Therapeuts, 55, Torald Sollmann Award, 95. *Prof Exp:* From instr to prof pharmacol, Med Sch, Univ Mich, 52-66. *Concurrent Pos:* Mem, NIH Fel Rev Panel Pharmacol & Endocrinol, 64-68 & Nat Acad Sci-Nat Res Coun Pesticide Safety Adv Comt, 64-66; consult, Random House Dict Eng Lang, 64-; mem, Pharmacol & Exp Therapeut Study Sect, NIH, 69-73; mem, Pharmacol Adv Bd, Pharmaceut Mfrs Asn Found, 73-; mem, Bd Dirs, Fedn Socs Exp Biol, 73-76; US rep, Int Union Pharmacol, 73; NSF distinguished scholar lectr, Univ Hawaii, 74; mem, Drug Abuse Rev Comt, Nat Inst Drug Abuse, 75-79; Basic Sci Coun, Am Heart Asn, 86-; ed, Human Pharmacol, Molecular to Clin, 91- *Mem:* Am Soc Pharmacol & Exp Therapeut; Soc Toxicol; Am Heart Asn; Sigma Xi. *Res:* Mode of action of drugs and poisons; cardiac glycosides; ion transport; mechanism of action of cardiac glycosides and related inotropic drugs. *Mailing Add:* Dept Pharmacol & Toxicol Life Sci Bldg Mich State Univ East Lansing MI 48824

BRODY, THOMAS P, THIN FILM PHYSICS & DEVICES, FLAT PANEL DISPLAYS. *Current Pos:* PRES, ACTIVE MATRIX ASSOCS, 91- *Personal Data:* b Budapest, Hungary, Apr 18, 20; UK citizen; m 52, Maude Myra Frost; c Louise, Francine, Christopher & Sarah. *Educ:* Univ London, BSc, 50, PhD(math physics), 53. *Honors & Awards:* Karl Ferdinand Brann Prize, Soc Info Display, 87; Edward Rhein Prize, Ger, 88. *Prof Exp:* Lectr physics, Univ London, 55-59; res scientist, Westinghouse Res, 59-62, sect mgr, 62-67, dept mgr, 67-79; pres, Panelvision Corp, 80-82, vchmn, 82-85; consult, 85-88; chief exec officer, Magnascreen Corp, 88-90. *Concurrent Pos:* Prin investr, Westinghouse, 62-78, Darpa projs, 92-; vis scientist, Carnegie Mellon Univ, 91-96. *Mem:* Am Phys Soc; Inst Elec & Electronics Engrs; fel Soc Info Display. *Res:* Invention and development of active matrix display technology; thin film physics; pattern recognition. *Mailing Add:* Active Matrix Assocs 5823 Kentucky Ave Pittsburgh PA 15232. *Fax:* 412-441-2932; *E-Mail:* pbrody@mail.lm.com

BRODY, WILLIAM R, RADIOLOGY. *Current Pos:* Martin Donner prof & dir, Dept Radiol, Biomed Eng, Elec & Comput Eng, 87-96, PRES, JOHNS HOPKINS UNIV, 96- *Personal Data:* b Stockton, Calif, Jan 4, 44; c 2. *Educ:* Mass Inst Technol, SB, 65, SM, 66; Stanford Univ, MD, 70, PhD(elec eng), 72. *Prof Exp:* USPHS, 73-75; training med fel cardiovasc surg & diag radiol, Stanford Univ, from assoc prof to prof, Dept Radiol, 77-84; founder, pres, chief exec officer, Resonex Inc, 84-87, chmn bd, 87-89. *Concurrent Pos:* Radiologist-in-chief, Johns Hopkins Hosp, 87-94, prof radiol, Univ Minn Academic Health Ctr, 94-96, provost, 94-96, spec asst to pres, 96. *Mem:* Inst Med-Nat Acad Sci; fel Am Col Radiol; fel Am Col Cardiol; fel Inst Elec & Electronics Engrs; fel Am Inst Med & Biol Eng. *Res:* Author of over 120 scientific publications in the field of medical imaging and cardiovascular disease; author of 3 textbooks and issued one US patent. *Mailing Add:* Off of Pres 242 Garland Hall 3400 N Charles St Baltimore MD 21218-2688. *Fax:* 410-516-6097

BRODZINSKI, RONALD LEE, NUCLEAR INSTRUMENTATION & APPLICATIONS. *Current Pos:* Sr res scientist, Pac Northwest Lab, Battelle Mem Inst, 68-80, staff scientist, 80-86, mgr, nuclear chem, 86-89, SR STAFF SCIENTIST, PAC NORTHWEST LAB, BATTELLE MEM INST, 89- *Personal Data:* b South Bend, Ind, Feb 14, 41; m 67, Joyce; c Belinda, Eric & Kirk. *Educ:* Purdue Univ, BS, 63, PhD(nuclear chem), 68. *Concurrent Pos:* Prin investr, NASA, 72- *Mem:* Am Chem Soc. *Res:* High-energy charged particle reactions; cosmic-radiation activation of astronauts and spacecraft; nuclear waste management; environmental research; lunar and space sciences; controlled thermonuclear reactor materials research; nuclear instrument and technique development and application; fundamental particle physics. *Mailing Add:* 2506 Albemarle Ct Richland WA 99352. *Fax:* 509-372-0672; *E-Mail:* rl_brodzinski@pnl.gov

BROECKER, WALLACE, GEOCHEMISTRY. *Current Pos:* from instr to prof, 56-77, dir, Geochem Lab, 66-80, NEWBERRY PROF EARTH & ENVIRON SCI, COLUMBIA UNIV, 77- *Personal Data:* b Chicago, Ill, Nov 29, 31; m 52; c 6. *Educ:* Columbia Col, AB, 53; Columbia Univ, MA, 56, PhD(geol), 58. *Honors & Awards:* Ewing Medal, Am Geophys Union; Day Medal, Geol Soc Am, 84; Huntsman Award, Bedford Inst Can, 85; Vetlessen Award, 87; Goldschmidt Award, 88; Nat Medal of Sci, 96. *Concurrent Pos:* Sloan fel, 64. *Mem:* Nat Acad Sci; Am Geophys Union; Geochem Soc; Am Acad Sci. *Res:* Pleistocene geochronology; carbon 14 and thorium 230 dating; chemical oceanography, including oceanic mixing based on radioisotope distribution; author of 10 technical publications and 4 books. *Mailing Add:* Dept Geol Sci Lamont-Doherty Geol Observ Columbia Univ Palisades NY 10964

BROEG, CHARLES BURTON, CHEMISTRY, AGRICULTURE & FOOD CHEMISTRY. *Current Pos:* head prod planning & develop, 58, dir tech serv, 58-61, vpres & tech dir, SuCrest Corp, 61-77, VPRES RES & TECH SERV, REVERE SUGAR CORP, 78-; PRES, APPL SUGAR LABS, INC, 71- *Personal Data:* b Princeton, Ind, Mar 15, 16; m 46. *Educ:* DePauw Univ, AB, 38; Okla Agr & Mech Col, MS, 40. *Prof Exp:* Asst, Okla Agr & Mech Col, 38-40; chemist, USDA, 41-43 & 46-58. *Concurrent Pos:* Dir, World Sugar Res Orgn, Adv, Sugar Comn Codex Alimentarius. *Mem:* Am Chem Soc; Am Soc Sugar Beet Technologists; Am Soc Sugar Cane Technologists; Am Inst Chemists; Inst Food Technologists. *Res:* Cane wax; cane juice clarification; polynitro aromatic-benzene addition compounds; color standards for sugar products; direct compression vehicles from sugar; desugaring molasses; agglomeration processes and products; new product development. *Mailing Add:* 101 Victoria Court Houma LA 70360-6276

BROEKMAN, MARINUS JOHAN, BIOCHEMISTRY. *Current Pos:* res assoc med, Cornell Univ Med Col, 76-87, instr, 77-80, asst prof, 80-86, ASSOC PROF MED, CORNELL UNIV MED COL, 86-; RES BIOCHEMIST, DEPT VET AFFAIRS MED CTR, NY, 91- *Personal Data:* b Hilversum, Neth, Oct 24, 44; US citizen; c 2. *Educ:* Univ Utrecht, Neth, BS, 67, MS, 69, PhD(biochem), 67. *Prof Exp:* Res asst nutrit, Harvard Sch Pub Health, 69-76; res biochemist, Dept Vet Affairs Med Ctr, NY, 76-87, consult, 87-91. *Concurrent Pos:* Prin investr, Pub Health Serv, 76-78; invited lectr, Gordon Conf Vascular Cell Biol, 92. *Mem:* Am Soc Biochem & Molecular Biol; Soc Study Blood; Am Heart Asn; Am Fedn Clin Res; NY Acad Sci; AAAS. *Res:* Thrombosis, atherosclerosis and inflammation with the premise that cell reactivity is affected by other cells in the local microenvironment; demonstrated 2 independent mechanisms by which human endotheliial cells reduced platelet reactivity operating independent of prostacyclin also formed by endothelial cells. *Mailing Add:* Thrombosis Res 13025 W Dept Vet Admin Med Ctr 423 E 23rd St New York NY 10010

BROEMELING, LYLE DAVID, bayesian statistics, for more information see previous edition

BROENE, HERMAN HENRY, CHEMISTRY. *Current Pos:* from assoc prof to prof, 56-84, EMER PROF CHEM, CALVIN COL, 84- *Personal Data:* b Grand Rapids, Mich, Dec 28, 19; m 44, Ruth Warner; c Mary, Jane & Thomas. *Educ:* Calvin Col, AB, 42; Purdue Univ, PhD(phys chem), 47. *Prof Exp:* Asst phys chem, Purdue Univ, 42-44; res chemist, Eastman Kodak Co, 46-56. *Mem:* Am Chem Soc. *Res:* Radio-chemistry; thermodynamics of aqueous hydrofluoric acid solutions; mechanical properties of high polymers; chemical education. *Mailing Add:* 2601 Golfridge Dr SE Calvin Col Grand Rapids MI 49546-5616

BROER, MATTHIJS MENO, OPTICAL FIBER MATERIALS, SOLID STATE LASER MATERIALS. *Current Pos:* SUPV CORNING INC, 97- *Personal Data:* b Madison, Wis, Aug 23, 56. *Educ:* Tech Univ, Delft, Netherlands, BSc, 77, Univ Wis, MSc, 79, PhD(physics), 82. *Prof Exp:* Postdoctoral mem tech staff, AT&T Bell Labs, Murray Hill, NJ, 83-85, mem tech staff res, 85-97. *Mem:* Am Phys Soc; Optical Soc Am; Mat Res Soc. *Res:* Nonlinear optics in condensed matter; optical properties of amorphous systems. *Mailing Add:* Corning Inc MS-DV01-G Corning NY 14831

BROERMAN, F S, RESEARCH ADMINISTRATION, FORESTRY. *Current Pos:* Res forester, Union Camp Corp, 65-68, sr res forester, 68-72, proj leader, 72-81, MGR WOODLANDS RES DEPT, UNION CAMP CORP, 81-, TECH RES GROUP. *Personal Data:* b Oskaloosa, Iowa, Jan 5, 38; m 61; c 2. *Educ:* Iowa State Univ, BS, 60, MS, 65. *Concurrent Pos:* Res asst, Iowa Agr Exp Sta, 63-65. *Mem:* Soc Am Foresters; Soil Sci Soc Am. *Res:* Research administration and forestry. *Mailing Add:* Woodlands Res Dept Union Camp Corp PO Box 1391 Savannah GA 31402

BROERS, ALEC N, ELECTRICAL ENGINEERING, PHYSICS. *Current Pos:* prof elec eng, 84-96, head, Dept Eng, 92-96, VCHANCELLOR, UNIV CAMBRIDGE, 96-, EMER PROF, 96- *Personal Data:* b Calcutta, India, Sept 17, 38; m 64; c 2. *Educ:* Univ Melbourne, BSc, 59; Cambridge Univ, BA, 61, PhD(elec eng), 65. *Hon Degrees:* DE, Glasgow Univ, 96, DSc, Warwick Univ, 97. *Honors & Awards:* Indust Applns Physics Prize, Am Inst Physics, 82; Cledo Brunetti Award, Inst Elec & Electronics Engrs, 85. *Prof Exp:* Mem prof staff electron optics, Thomas J Watson Res Ctr, IBM Corp, 65-67, mgr electron beam technol, 67-72, mgr photon & electron optics, IBM res, 72-80, mgr lithography syst & technol tools, E Fishkill Facil, 81-82, mgr semiconductor lithography & process develop, 82-83, mgr advan develop, 83-84, mem, Corp Tech Comt, 84. *Concurrent Pos:* IBM fel, 77. *Mem:* Foreign assoc Nat Acad Eng; hon fel Inst Elec Engrs; fel Inst Physics & Phys Soc. *Res:* Development of precision electron optical equipment and its application to the production of microcircuitry and microrecording of digital information, especially new cathodes and cathode materials, ion etching and high resolution scanning electron microscopy; general aspects of high resolution lithography for microcircuits. *Mailing Add:* VChancellor's Off Univ Cambridge Cambridge CB2-1TN England. *E-Mail:* v-c@admin.cam.ac.uk

BROERSMA, DELMAR B, ENTOMOLOGY. *Current Pos:* RETIRED. *Personal Data:* b Lynden, Wash, July 2, 34; m 60; c 3. *Educ:* Calvin Col, AB, 56; Syracuse Univ, MS, 63; Clemson Univ, PhD(entom), 65. *Prof Exp:* Teacher, Grand Rapids Christian High Sch, 56-57 & Western Mich Christian High Sch, 58-62; asst entom & zool, Clemson Univ, 63-65; res entomologist, Ill Natural Hist Surv, 65-69; from asst prof to assoc prof entom, Purdue Univ, West Lafayette, 69-94. *Mem:* AAAS; Entom Soc Am. *Res:* Insect pathology; economic entomology. *Mailing Add:* 1833 Locust Lane West Lafayette IN 47906

BROFAZI, FREDERICK R, ANALYTICAL & PHARMACEUTICAL CHEMISTRY, TECHNICAL MANAGEMENT. *Current Pos:* VPRES CORP QUAL ASSURANCE, SCHERING-PLOUGH, 91- *Personal Data:* b Jersey City, NJ, Apr 21, 33; m 56, Joan Kucinski; c Diane, Patricia & Lauren. *Educ:* Rutgers Univ, BS, 54, MS, 57, PhD(chem), 59. *Prof Exp:* Res anal chemist, Nat Cash Register Co, 59-60; res supvr, Pharmaceut Div, Ciba-Geigy Corp, 60-64, group leader, 64-66, from asst dir to dir qual control, 66-71, exec dir qual control, 71-91. *Mem:* Am Chem Soc; Am Pharmaceut Asn; Am Soc Qual Control; Sigma Xi. *Res:* Development of analytical methods; pharmaceutical analysis; quality control; quality assurance. *Mailing Add:* 72 Alpine Terr Hillsdale NJ 07642

BROGAN, GEORGE EDWARD, GEOLOGY, ENGINEERING GEOLOGY. *Current Pos:* CONSULT, BROGAN CONSULT, 92- *Personal Data:* b La Jolla, Calif, Feb 18, 44; m 68; c 2. *Educ:* San Diego State Univ, BA, 66, MS, 69. *Prof Exp:* Sr proj geologist, Woodward-Clyde Consults, 71-75, dep dir eng geol, 76-, vpres, 78-; Appl Geosci, Inc, Tustin, 92. *Concurrent Pos:* Prin investr grants, US Geol Surv & Earthquake Eng Res Inst, 77-81; adv, US Geol Surv Earthquake Hazard Reduction Prog, 77-; mem prof affairs comt, Calif State Bd Regist for Geologists & Geophysicists, 78-; mem, Calif State Mining Bd, 81-84. *Mem:* Am Geophys Union; Asn Eng Geologists; Earthquake Eng Res Inst; Int Asn Eng Geol; Seismol Soc Am; Sigma Xi. *Res:* Evaluation of youthful seismic activity of faults in diverse geographic and climatic environments, as deduced from the geologic record. *Mailing Add:* 2081 Business Ctr Dr Suite 218 Irvine CA 92715-1116

BROGAN, WILLIAM L, ELECTRICAL & MECHANICAL ENGINEERING. *Current Pos:* assoc prof systs theory, 68-72, prof systs theory, 72-90, PROF ELEC & COMPUT ENG, UNIV NEBR, LINCOLN, 90- *Personal Data:* b Vail, Iowa, Mar 11, 35; m 42; c 6. *Educ:* Univ Iowa, BSME, 58; Univ Calif, Los Angeles, MS, 61, PhD(control theory), 65. *Prof Exp:* Thermodyn engr, Gen Dynamics/Convair, Calif, 58-59; mem tech staff struct dynamics, Hughes Aircraft Co, 59-61, mem tech staff control systs, 61-65; mem tech staff guid & control systs, Aerospace Corp, 65-68, 72-73. *Concurrent Pos:* Lectr, Univ Calif, Los Angeles, 66-68; consult, Brunswick Corp, Nebr, 68-; dir systs sci prog, NSF, Washington, DC, 78-79. *Mem:* Fel Inst Elec & Electronics Engrs; Inst Navig; Am Soc Navig. *Res:* Control and systems theory; applied mathematics; dynamics; filtering and estimation theory. *Mailing Add:* Dept Elec & Comput Eng Univ Nev 4505 Maryland Pkwy Las Vegas NV 89119

BROGDON, BYRON GILLIAM, DIAGNOSTIC RADIOLOGY. *Current Pos:* prof radiol, Univ SAla, 78-89, asst dean continuing med educ, 81-89, chmn dept, 85-92, univ distinguished prof, 89-96, EMER UNIV DISTINGUISHED PROF RADIOL, COL MED, UNIV S ALA, 96- *Personal Data:* b Ft Smith, Ark, Jan 22, 29; m 51, 78, Barbara Walkow; c 3. *Educ:* Univ Ark, BS & BSM, 51, MD, 52. *Honors & Awards:* Physician Speaker Award, AMA, 79; Gold Medal, Asn Univ Radiologists, 85, Am Col Radiol, 87; Schinz Medal, Swiss Soc Med Radiol, 92; Medal, City of Brescia, Italy, 91; John B Hunt Award, Am Acad Forensic Sci, 95; Gold Medal, Am Roentgen Ray Soc, 96. *Prof Exp:* Asst prof radiol, Col Med, Univ Fla, 60-63; assoc prof radiol & radiol sci, Sch Hyg & Pub Health, Sch Med, Johns Hopkins Univ, 63-67; asst dean hosp affairs, Sch Med, Univ NMex, 70-72, prof radiol, 67-78, chmn dept, 67-77. *Concurrent Pos:* Radiologist-in-chg, Div Diag Roentgenol, Johns Hopkins Hosp, 63-67; med dir, Bernalillo County Med Ctr, 69-72; pres, Southern Radiol Conf, 67-68, secy, 84-; secy-treas, Soc Chm Acad, Radiol Dept, 69-70; mem, House Deleg, Am Med Asn, 88- *Mem:* Am Roentgen Ray Soc (vpres, 79-80); Radiol Soc NAm; Soc Pediat Radiol; Asn Univ Radiologists (pres, 73-74); Am Col Radiol (pres, 78-79); Int Skeletal Soc; fel Am Acad Forensic Sci; hon mem Swiss Soc Med Radiol. *Res:* Diagnostic roentgenology; clinical applications; determination of normal and abnormal variations; visual perception, forensic radiology. *Mailing Add:* Dept Radiol Univ SAla Med Ctr Mobile AL 36617. *Fax:* 334-471-7868

BROGE, ROBERT WALTER, INTERNATIONAL BUSINESS DEVELOPMENT. *Current Pos:* RETIRED. *Personal Data:* b Cleveland, Ohio, Oct 27, 20; m 44; c 5. *Educ:* Harvard Univ, SB, 42; Cornell Univ, PhD(phys chem), 48. *Prof Exp:* Res assoc rocket res, Nat Defense Res Comt, 42-45; res chemist, Procter & Gamble Co, 48-51, sect head basic res, 51-57 & prod res, 57-61, assoc dir, 61-67, dir prod develop, 67-71, dir res, 71-78, int tech dir, 78-83. *Mem:* AAAS; Am Chem Soc; Int Asn Dent Res. *Res:* X-ray crystallography; solutions of surface active agents; dental research; chemistry of keratin; health care product development; pharmaceutical clinical research. *Mailing Add:* 221 Compton Ridge Dr Wyoming OH 45215-4119

BROGLE, RICHARD CHARLES, HEALTH CARE PRODUCTS. *Current Pos:* PRES, RICHARD C BROGLE ASSOCS, 87- *Personal Data:* b Boston, Mass, July 12, 27; m 59; c 3. *Educ:* Mass Inst Technol, SB, 50, SM, 53, PhD(food sci), 60. *Prof Exp:* Sr chemist, Am Chicle Co, 60-62; group leader contract res, Am Chicle Co, Div Warner-Lambert Co, 63-66; dir clin res, Warner-Lambert Co, 66-69, dir proprietary toiletries res, 69-72, dir clin regulatory affairs, 72-75, vpres res serv, 75-77; vpres lab opers, Block Drug Co, 78-83, vpres-dir res & develop, 83-87. *Concurrent Pos:* Chmn subcomt, Proprietary Asn, 80-86. *Mem:* AAAS; Inst Food Technologists; Acad Pharmaceut Sci; Soc Cosmetic Chemists; Am Soc Clin Pharmacol & Therapeut; Int Asn Dent Res; Am Asn Pharmaceut Scientists. *Res:* Antacid in vitro-in vivo relationships; objective clinical testing methods; control of dental plaque; research management. *Mailing Add:* Eight Kenneth Rd Upper Montclair NJ 07043

BROIDA, THEODORE RAY, RESEARCH ADMINISTRATION. *Current Pos:* RETIRED. *Personal Data:* b Louisville, Ky, Dec 6, 28; m 52; c 2. *Educ:* Univ Calif, BS, 50, MS, 52. *Hon Degrees:* LLD, Transylvania Univ, 86. *Prof Exp:* Physicist, Nucleonics Div, US Naval Radiol Defense Lab, 50-53, Broadview Res Corp, 53-55 & Defense Atomic Support Agency, 55-57; sr opers analyst, Stanford Res Inst, 57-60; dir planning, Broadview Res Corp, 60-62; mgr, Techno-econ Res Div, Spindletop Res, Inc, 62-68, pres, 68-73; pres, QRC Res Corp, 73-94. *Concurrent Pos:* Consult, US Off Educ, 68-; mem, Comt Remote Sensing Agr, Nat Acad Sci-Nat Res Coun; consult innovation develop, Off Sci & Technol, US Dept Com, 80-81. *Mem:* Asn Comput Mach; Nat Soc Prof Engrs. *Res:* High intensity thermal radiation sources and instrumentation; measurement of air temperature; logistics; inventory management; electronic data processing; reconnaissance systems; applied industrial and regional economics; resource development; communications systems; research management. *Mailing Add:* 1933 Long Pond Walk Lexington KY 40502

BROIDE, MICHAEL LYNN, CONDENSED MATTER PHYSICS, PHYSICS OF COMPLEX FLUIDS INCLUDING COLLOIDS & PROTEINS. *Current Pos:* ASST PROF PHYSICS, LEWIS & CLARK COL, 91- *Personal Data:* b Oak Park, Ill, July 15, 58; m 87, Marjorie Rosenburg; c Sophie I. *Educ:* Univ Calif, Los Angeles, BS & MS, 81; Mass Inst Technol, PhD(physics), 89. *Prof Exp:* Res assoc, Mass Inst Technol, 88-91. *Concurrent Pos:* Vis Scientist, SPEC CE Saclay, CEA, France, 91-92. *Mem:* Am Phys Soc; Mat Res Soc. *Res:* Physics of complex fluids, including colloids and proteins; experimental study of aggregation and phase transitions in these systems; light scattering and optical instrumentation, condensed matter physics, statistical physics, biophysics. *Mailing Add:* Dept Physics Lewis & Clark Col Portland OR 97219

BROIDO, ABRAHAM, PHYSICAL CHEMISTRY. *Current Pos:* RETIRED. *Personal Data:* b Cherkassi, Russia, Sept 12, 24; nat US; wid; c 2. *Educ:* Univ Chicago, SB, 43; Univ Calif, PhD(chem), 50. *Prof Exp:* Chemist, Metall Lab, Univ Chicago & Argonne Nat Lab, 43-46; res chemist, Clinton Labs & Oak Ridge Nat Lab, 46-48; chemist, Radiation Lab, Univ Calif, 48-50 & US Naval Radiol Defense Lab, 50-56; chemist, Pac Southwest Forest & Range Exp Sta, US Forest Serv, Berkeley, 56-76. *Concurrent Pos:* Guest scientist, Hebrew Univ, Jerusalem, 64-65; res assoc, Statewide Air Pollution Res Ctr, Univ Calif, 66-, consult, Inst Eng Res, 56-; head thermal radiation br, US Naval Radiol Defense Lab, 51-53; mem, Calif Gov Radiol Defense Adv Comt, 62-66; Nat Acad Sci Adv Comt Civil Defense, 66-70. *Res:* Radiochemistry; ion exchange and solvent extraction; microchemistry; rare earth and transuranic elements; effects of thermal and nuclear radiation; forest fire and air pollution research. *Mailing Add:* 1936 Carquinez Ave Richmond CA 94805-2002

BROIDO, JEFFREY HALE, NUCLEAR PHYSICS, MECHANICAL ENGINEERING. *Current Pos:* PHYSICIST, GEN ATOMIC, INC, SAN DIEGO, 62- *Personal Data:* b New York, NY, Oct 22, 34; m 61; c 2. *Educ:* Columbia Univ, AB, 55, BS, 56; Stanford Univ, MS, 60, Engr, 62. *Prof Exp:* Res engr, Beloit Corp, 61-62. *Concurrent Pos:* Consult, Swiss Fed Inst Reactor Res, 68-69. *Mem:* Am Nuclear Soc. *Res:* Economics, dynamics and control of fast breeder nuclear reactors. *Mailing Add:* 8811 Robinhood Lane La Jolla CA 92037

BROIN, THAYNE LEO, GEOLOGY. *Current Pos:* GEOL CONSULT, 83- *Personal Data:* b Kenyon, Minn, Sept 18, 22; m 49; c 3. *Educ:* St Cloud State Col, BS, 43; Univ Colo, MA, 52, PhD(geol), 57. *Prof Exp:* Asst physics, St Cloud State Col, 42, asst biol, 43; from instr to asst prof geol, Colo State Univ, 50-57; res geologist, Cities Serv Res & Develop Co, 57-65, supvr geol div, 61-65; res coordr, Explor Div, Cities Serv Oil Co, 65-72, chief comput geologist, Explor Technol Dept, 72-78, comput technol mgr, Energy Res Group, Cities Serv Co, 78-83. *Mem:* Soc Econ Paleontologists & Mineralogists; Geol Soc Am; Am Asn Petrol Geologists; Sigma Xi. *Res:* Sedimentation; stratigraphy; subsurface facies mapping; sedimentary petrology; petroleum geology; computer mapping. *Mailing Add:* 5280 Champagne Dr Colorado Springs CO 80919

BROITMAN, SELWYN ARTHUR, MICROBIOLOGY, MEDICAL EDUCATION. *Current Pos:* Res instr path, 63-64, from asst prof to assoc prof microbiol, 65-75, PROF MICROBIOL & NUTRIT SCI, SCH MED, BOSTON UNIV, 69-, ASST DEAN ADMIS, 81-, PROF PATH, 82- *Personal Data:* b Boston, Mass, Aug 30, 31; m 53, Barbara H Shwartz; c Caryn B & Joffrey Z. *Educ:* Univ Mass, BS, 52, MS, 53; Mich State Univ, PhD(microbiol), 56. *Concurrent Pos:* Res assoc gastrointestinal res lab, Mallory Inst Path, Boston City Hosp, 56-74, res assoc nutrit path univ, 75-; assoc med, Thorndike Mem Lab, 69-; assoc med, Harvard Med Sch, 69-74; founding mem, Digestive Dis Found, 71 & Nutrit Today Soc, 74; lectr, Div Allied Health Professions, Northeastern Univ, 71-73; lectr, Sargent Col Allied Health Professions, Boston Univ, 72-76, consult, Nat Large Bowel Cancer Proj, 77-; mem comt diet, nutrit & cancer, Nat Acad Sci, 81-83; mem bd dirs, Mentor Corp, 84-87. *Mem:* Am Gastroenterol Soc; Am Soc Microbiol; Soc Exp Path; NY Acad Sci; Sigma Xi; Am Inst Nutrit; Soc Exp Biol & Med; Am Fedn Clin Res; AAAS; fel Am Col Gastroenterol. *Res:* Experimental gastroenterology; malabsorptive diseases; colon cancer; intestinal flora; bacterial and viral enteric infections. *Mailing Add:* Dept Microbiol Boston Univ Sch Med Boston MA 02118

BROKAW, BRYAN EDWARD, ANIMAL BREEDING. *Current Pos:* asst prof animal sci, 75-80, chmn & assoc prof, 80-93, BRAY COOK PROF AGR, DEPT AGR & ENVIRON, ABILENE CHRISTIAN UNIV, 93- *Personal Data:* b Pittsfield, Ill, Feb 27, 49; m 70, Janice K Hammitt; c Lori L (Partin), Lisa R & Bryan C. *Educ:* Abilene Christian Univ, BS, 71; Ore State Univ, PhD(animal breeding & genetics), 75. *Mem:* Am Soc Animal Sci; Sigma Xi; Nat Asn Cols Teachers Agr. *Res:* Relationships of physiological characteristics with performance traits in beef cattle and their value as selection criteria. *Mailing Add:* Agr & Environ Dept 210 Zona Luce Bldg Abilene Christian Univ PO Box 27986 Abilene TX 79699

BROKAW, CHARLES JACOB, CELL BIOLOGY. *Current Pos:* from asst prof to assoc prof biol, Calif Inst Technol, 61-68, exec officer, 76-80, & 85-89, assoc chmn, 80-85, PROF BIOL, CALIF INST TECHNOL, 68- *Personal Data:* b Camden, NJ, Sept 12, 34; m 55, Darlene Smith; c Bryce & Tanya. *Educ:* Calif Inst Technol, BS, 55; Univ Cambridge, PhD(zool), 58. *Prof Exp:* Res assoc biol div, Oak Ridge Nat Lab, 58-59; asst prof zool, Univ Minn, 59-61. *Concurrent Pos:* Guggenheim fel, Univ Cambridge, 70-71; chmn, NIH Cellular & Molecular Dis Rev Comt, 85-87. *Mem:* AAAS; Am Soc Cell Biol; Biophys Soc. *Res:* Motility and behavior of ciliated and flagellated cells; chemotaxis: experimental work with marine invertebrate spermatozoa and Chlamydomonas; computer simulation of theoretical models. *Mailing Add:* Kerckoff Marine Lab Calif Inst Technol 101 Dahlia Ave Corona del Mar CA 92625-0001. *Fax:* 714-675-1837

BROKAW, GEORGE YOUNG, APPLIED CHEMISTRY. *Current Pos:* RETIRED. *Personal Data:* b St Clairsville, Ohio, Sept 11, 21; m 44, Margaret Hibbs; c 4. *Educ:* Ohio Wesleyan Univ, BA, 41; Ohio State Univ, MS, 44, PhD(chem), 47. *Prof Exp:* Asst chem, Ohio State Univ, 41-43, asst, Univ Res Found, 43-44; chem engr, Naval Res Lab, Washington, DC, 44-45; res assoc, Distillation Prod Industs Div, Eastman Kodak Co, 47-63, head develop labs, 63-69; sr res assoc, Tenn Eastman Co, 69-76, coordr prod safety, 76-84. *Mem:* AAAS; emer mem Am Chem Soc. *Res:* Fats and oils; food emulsifiers; fat-soluble vitamins. *Mailing Add:* 14206 Brandermill Woods Trail Midlothian VA 23112

BROKAW, RICHARD SPOHN, PHYSICAL CHEMISTRY. *Current Pos:* RETIRED. *Personal Data:* b Orange, NJ, Mar 26, 23; wid; c James A II, Richard S Jr, Frances C & Susan E. *Educ:* Swarthmore Col, AB, 43; Princeton Univ, AM, 49, PhD(chem), 51. *Honors & Awards:* Medal for Except Sci Achievement, NASA, 72. *Prof Exp:* Asst phys chem, Calco Chem Div, Am Cyanamid Co, 43-44 & Princeton Univ, 46-52; aeronaut res scientist phys chem & combustion, Lewis Res Ctr, NASA, 52-55, from assoc head to head, Combustion Fundamentals Sect, 55-57, chief, Phys Chem Br, 57-71, chief, Physics & Chem Div, 71-72, asst chief, Phys Sci Div, 72-73; lectr chem, Baldwin-Wallace Col, 74-82. *Concurrent Pos:* Consult, Am Gas Asn Labs, 75-84. *Mem:* AAAS; Am Chem Soc; Combustion Inst; Am Inst Aeronaut & Astronaut; Sigma Xi. *Res:* Combustion, especially burning velocity and spontaneous ignition; transport properties of gases, especially heat transport in chemically reacting gases; gas phase chemical kinetics. *Mailing Add:* 7 Beacon Hill RR 1 Box 262 Strafford VT 05072-9700

BROKER, THOMAS RICHARD, MOLECULAR GENETICS, TUMOR VIROLOGY. *Current Pos:* CONSULT, 84- *Personal Data:* b Hackensack, NJ, Oct 22, 44; m 74. *Educ:* Wesleyan Univ, BA, 66; Stanford Univ, PhD(biochem), 72. *Hon Degrees:* MA, Wesleyan Univ, 81. *Prof Exp:* Res fel chem, Calif Inst Technol, 72-75; sr staff investr, Colo Spring Harbor Lab, 75-79, sr scientist, electron micros, 79-84. *Concurrent Pos:* Res fel, Helen Hay Whitney Found, 72-75. *Mem:* Sigma Xi; Am Soc Microbiol. *Res:* RNA transcription and DNA replication of human papillomaviruses; mechanisms of carcinogenesis; genetic structure, expression and regulation of human papillomavirus; diagnostic and therapeutic approaches to HPV infections of genital tract epithelium. *Mailing Add:* Dept Biochem & Molecular Genetics Univ Ala 1918 University Blvd Rm 506 Birmingham AL 35294-0005. *Fax:* 205-975-6075

BROLIN, ROBERT EDWARD, GASTROINTESTINAL SURGERY. *Current Pos:* assoc prof surg, 84-89, CHIEF GASTROINTESTINAL SURG, UNIV MED & DENT NJ, ROBERT WOOD JOHNSON MED SCH, 88-, PROF SURG, 89- *Personal Data:* b Holland, Mich, Apr 12, 48; m 70; c 2. *Educ:* DePauw Univ, BA, 70; Univ Mich, Ann Arbor, 74. *Prof Exp:* Asst prof surg, Rutgers Med Sch, Univ Med & Dent NJ, 80-84. *Mem:* Asn Acad Surg; Am Col Surgeons; Am Soc Bariatric Surg; Am Motility Soc; Soc Univ Surgeons; NAm Asn Study Obesity; Soc Surg Alimentary Tract; Am Soc Parenteral & Enternal Nutrit. *Res:* Gastrointestinal motility in relationship to ischemic bowel disease and postoperative ileus; surgery for morbid obesity. *Mailing Add:* Dept Surg CN19 UMDNJ-Robert Wood Johnson Med Sch 1 R W Johnson Pl New Brunswick NJ 08903. *Fax:* 732-418-3156

BROLLEY, JOHN EDWARD, JR, ELEMENTARY PARTICLE PHYSICS. *Current Pos:* RETIRED. *Personal Data:* b Chicago, Ill, Jan 15, 19; m 46, Joyce Hicks. *Educ:* Univ Chicago, SB, 40; Ind Univ, MS, 48, PhD(physics), 49. *Prof Exp:* Mem staff, Res Elem Particle Physics & Astrophysics, Los Alamos Nat Lab, 49-83. *Mem:* Fel AAAS; fel Am Phys Soc; Archeol Inst Am; Am Astron Soc; Am Geophysical Union; Sigma Xi. *Res:* Nuclear and particle physics; laser physics; artificial intelligence; information theory, timeseries. *Mailing Add:* 1225 Los Pueblos Los Alamos NM 87544

BROLMANN, JOHN BERNARDUS, PLANT BREEDING. *Current Pos:* RETIRED. *Personal Data:* b Holland, Nov 20, 20; m 52; c 4. *Educ:* State Agr Univ Wageningen, MS, 52; Univ Fla, PhD(agron), 68. *Prof Exp:* Plant breeder, Exp Sta Mas d'Auge, France, 52-60; asst prof agron & asst legume breeder, Agr Exp Sta, Univ Fla, 69-94. *Mem:* Am Soc Agron; Crop Sci Soc Am. *Res:* Selection and breeding of tropical and temperature climate legumes for pasture use. *Mailing Add:* 2914 Forest Terr Ft Pierce FL 34982

BROM, JOSEPH MARCH, JR, PHYSICAL CHEMISTRY, MOLECULAR SPECTROSCOPY. *Current Pos:* asst prof, 75-80, ASSOC PROF CHEM, BENEDICTINE COL, 80- *Personal Data:* b Petersburg, Va, Oct 8, 42; m 67; c 2. *Educ:* Col St Thomas, BS, 64; Iowa State Univ, PhD(phys chem), 70. *Prof Exp:* Res assoc chem, Univ Fla, 70-73; asst res physicist, Univ Calif, Santa Barbara, 73-75. *Mem:* Am Chem Soc; Am Phys Soc. *Res:* Magnetic resonance and optical spectra of trapped radicals; laser chemistry; high temperature chemistry. *Mailing Add:* Univ St Thomas Mail #4405 2115 Summit Ave St Paul MN 55105-1048

BROMBERG, ELEAZER, SCIENTIFIC COMPUTING. *Current Pos:* admin dir comput ctr & assoc prof math, NY Univ, 53-57, admin mgr, Courant Inst Math Sci, 57-59, asst dir, 59-66, vchancellor acad affairs, 70-72, dep chancellor, 72-75, prof, 57-79, EMER PROF APPL MATH & COMPUT, NY UNIV, 79; SCI ADV & MATHEMATICIAN, CTR COMPUT & APP MATH, NAT INST STAND & TECHNOL, WASHINGTON, DC, 79- *Personal Data:* b Toronto, Ont, Oct 7, 13; nat US; m 48, Edith Weiss; c Dan A, Michael A & Jeremy. *Educ:* City Col New York, BS, 33; Columbia Univ, MA, 35; NY Univ, PhD(math), 50. *Prof Exp:* Asst demonstr physics, Univ Toronto, 36-37; instr, Worcester Polytech Inst, 41-42; res mathematician, Appl Math Panel, Nat Defense Res Comt, Columbia Univ, 43-44, NY Univ, 44-45; proj engr, Reeves Instrument Corp, 45-50 & 52; head mech br, Off Naval Res, 50-53. *Concurrent Pos:* Res Scientist, Los Alamos Sci Lab, 56-57; mem bd trustees, Soc Indust & Appl Math, 74-77. *Mem:* Fel AAAS; Soc Indust & Appl Math; Asn Comput Mach (secy, 53-56); Am Math Soc; Math Asn Am. *Res:* Nonlinear vibrations; computing techniques; simulation techniques; computer operations analysis. *Mailing Add:* Comput & Appl Math Lab Nat Inst Stand & Technol N 1st North 688 Gaithersburg MD 20899-2733. *Fax:* 301-963-9137; *E-Mail:* exb@cam.nist.gov

BROMBERG, MILTON JAY, INDUSTRIAL ORGANIC CHEMISTRY. *Current Pos:* RETIRED. *Personal Data:* b Brooklyn, NY, Sept 15, 23; div; c 1. *Educ:* City Col NY, BS, 44; Columbia Univ, MS, 48. *Prof Exp:* Asst res chemist, Columbia Univ, 43-44, asst, 46-48; chief chemist, H A Brassert Co, 48-51; chief chemist, Explosive Div, Olin Mathieson Chem Corp, 51-54, chief prod engr, 54-55, tech mgr, 55-57, proj mgr, High Energy Fuels Div, 57-58, mgr qual control, 58-60, staff consult org div, 60-62, mgr qual assurance, Chem Div, Doe Run Plant, 62-72, mgr qual assurance, Chem Group, Lake Charles Complex, Olin Corp, 72-78. *Mem:* Fel Am Inst Chemists. *Res:* Chemical management; quality control programs; fluoro-aromatics; petro chemicals; toluene diisocyanate; polypropylene glycols; explosives; high energy fuels; design of laboratories. *Mailing Add:* PO Box 5274 Lake Charles LA 70606-5274

BROMBERG, R(OBERT), ENGINEERING. *Current Pos:* RETIRED. *Personal Data:* b Phoenix, Ariz, Aug 6, 21; wid; c 3. *Educ:* Univ Calif, BS, 43, MS, 45; Los Angeles, PhD, 51. *Prof Exp:* Jr engr, Univ Calif, 43-49, chmn's rep eng res & assoc engr, Los Angeles, 49-52, chmn's rep eng, res & asst prof, 52-53, asst dir, Inst Industs Co-op & assoc prof eng, 53-54; mem tech staff, Ramo-Wooldridge, Inc, 54-58, assoc dir, Astrosci Lab, TRW Space Technol Labs, 58-59, dir, Propulsion Lab, 59-60, dir, Mech Div, 61-65, vpres, Mech Div, 62, vpres & gen mgr, Appl Technol Div, 71-72, vpres res & eng, TRW Electronics & Defense, 72-82. *Concurrent Pos:* Consult, 82-90. *Mem:* Nat Acad Eng; Fel AAAS; Fel Am Inst Aeronaut & Astronaut; Am Soc Eng Educ; Sigma Xi. *Res:* Propulsion research and development; heat transfer and fluid mechanics; thermal and luminous radiation; instrumentation; hypersonic boundary layer phenomena; combustion; engineering and research management. *Mailing Add:* 1001 Westholme Ave Los Angeles CA 90024

BROMBERGER, SAMUEL H, EXPLORATION GEOLOGY. *Current Pos:* RETIRED. *Personal Data:* b New York, NY, Dec 21, 41; m 66, Margaret A Nichols; c Seth A. *Educ:* City Col New York, BS, 62; Univ Iowa, MS, 65, PhD(geol), 68. *Prof Exp:* From instr to asst prof geol, Cornell Col, 67-69; geologist, Los Angeles Div, Texaco, Inc, 69-73, regional geologist, Texaco Prod Serv Ltd, London, 73-76; div staff geol, J M Huber Corp, 76-80, mgr, Gulf Coast Explor, Oil & Gas Div, Gulf Coast Dist, 80-89; vpres explor & prod, Taurus Energy, 89-90. *Mem:* Am Asn Petrol Geologists. *Res:* Stratigraphy, hydrocarbon potential analysis of sedimentary basins; regional geology; economics. *Mailing Add:* 2744 Mid Lane St Houston TX 77027-4932. *Fax:* 713-993-9020; *E-Mail:* shbrom@taronga.com

BROMBERGER-BARNEA, BARUCH (BERTHOLD), environmental medicine, physiology; deceased, see previous edition for last biography

BROMER, WILLIAM WALLIS, BIOCHEMISTRY. *Current Pos:* RETIRED. *Personal Data:* b Racine, Wis, Oct 10, 27; m 52, Patricia A Ryan; c William R, Steven P & Maryann. *Educ:* DePauw Univ, AB, 49; Ind Univ, PhD(chem), 54. *Prof Exp:* Sr biochemist, Eli Lilly & Co, 53-60, res assoc, 60-70, res adv, 70-87. *Res:* Metabolism of essential fatty acids and cholesteryl esters; antibiotics isolation; isolation and structural analysis of proteins; glucagon; intrinsic factor and vitamin B12; insulin and proinsulin chemistry; glucagon structure and function; recombinant insulin. *Mailing Add:* 8919 Spicewood Ct Indianapolis IN 46260-1545

BROMERY, RANDOLPH WILSON, GEOLOGY, GEOPHYSICS. *Current Pos:* CHANCELLOR, BD REGENTS. *Personal Data:* b Cumberland, Md, Jan 18, 26; m 47; c 5. *Educ:* Howard Univ, BS, 56; Am Univ, MS, 62; Johns Hopkins Univ, PhD, 68. *Hon Degrees:* EdD, Western New Eng Col; DSc, Frostburg State Col; LLD, Hokkaido Univ; DPs, Westfield State Col, N Adams State Col. *Prof Exp:* Geophysicist, US Geol Surv, 48-67; assoc prof geophys, 67-69, head dept geol & geog, 69-70, vchancellor, 70-72, sr vpres & chancellor, 72-80, PROF GEOPHYS, UNIV MASS, AMHERST, 69-, EXEC VPRES, 80-, COMMONWEALTH PROF GEOPHYSICS, 80-; PRES, GEOSCI ENG CORP, 81- *Concurrent Pos:* Prof lectr, Howard Univ, 61-65; consult, AID, US Dept State, 66-72; consult, Kennecott Copper & Exxon; mem bd trustees, Johns Hopkins Univ, Mt Holyoke Col; incorporator, Woods Hole Oceanog Inst; mem bd dirs, Exxon Co, NYNEX Corp, Chem Banking Corp, John Hancock Mutual Life Ins Co. *Mem:* Am Geophys Union; Soc Explor Geophys; fel Geol Soc Am; fel AAAS. *Res:* Gravity, magnetic, radioactivity and seismic surveying methods applied to geologic mapping programs. *Mailing Add:* 75 Cherry Lane Amherst MA 01002-1520

BROMET, EVELYN J, PSYCHIATRY. *Current Pos:* PROF, DEPT PSYCHIAT, STATE UNIV NY, STONY BROOK, 86- *Personal Data:* b New Britain, Conn, Nov 10, 44; m, Dmitry Goldgaber; c Julia B(Pilkonis). *Educ:* Smith Col, BA, 66; Yale Univ, PhD(pub health & epidemiol), 71. *Honors & Awards:* Rema Lapouse Mental Health Res Award, Am Pub Health Asn. *Prof Exp:* Trainee, USPHS, Yale Univ, 66-71; res assoc, Dept Psychiat, Stanford Univ, 72-76; from asst prof to assoc prof, Dept Psychiat, Univ Pittsburgh, 76-86. *Concurrent Pos:* Prin investr, psychiat epidemiol training prog, NIMH, 77-86, three mile island accidents, 79-84, exposure to lead, psychol & behav sequalae, 81-83, psychiat epidemiol study of blue collar women, 84-86, stress & mental health mgrs & prof, 86-89; reviewer, epidemiol & serv res review comt, 83-87, epidemiol of newly diagnosed psychosis, 89-; Vet Admin Sci Adv Comt, Nat Vietnam Vet Readjust Study, 87; NIMH funded res Chernobyl, 95-98; bd mem, Sjogien's Syndrome Found, 97- *Mem:* Am Pub Health Asn; Soc Epidemiol Res; Am Psychopathol Asn. *Res:* Psychiatric epidemiology which includes studies of affective disorder, alcohol abuse and psychotic disorders. *Mailing Add:* Dept Psychiat State Univ NY Stony Brook Putnam Hall S Campus Stony Brook NY 11794-8790. *E-Mail:* ebromet@mail.psychiatry.sunysb.edu

BROMFIELD, CALVIN STANTON, GEOLOGY. *Current Pos:* GEOLOGIST, US GEOL SURV, 51- *Personal Data:* b Freeport, NY, Feb 4, 23; m 43; c 4. *Educ:* Univ Ariz, BS, 48, MS, 50; Univ Ill, PhD, 62. *Prof Exp:* Geologist, Homestake Mining Co, 49-51. *Concurrent Pos:* Asst, Univ Ill, 55-57. *Mem:* Geol Soc Am; Soc Econ Geologists; Sigma Xi. *Res:* Base metal ore deposits and regional geology, especially of Arizona, Colorado and Utah. *Mailing Add:* 3201 E Hwy 70 No 56 Stafford AZ 85546-9695

BROMFIELD, KENNETH RAYMOND, PLANT PATHOLOGY. *Current Pos:* RETIRED. *Personal Data:* b Wilkes-Barre, Pa, June 22, 22; m 46; c 5. *Educ:* Pa State Univ, BS, 49; Univ Minn, PhD(plant path), 57. *Prof Exp:* Plant pathologist epiphytology, US Army Biol Labs, 49-51 & 52-55; res asst, Dept Plant Path, Univ Minn, 51-52 & 55-56; plant pathologist forest dis, US Forest Serv, Northeastern Forest Exp Sta, NH, 57-59 & US Army Biol Defense Res Ctr, 59-71; res plant pathologist & res leader, Plant Dis Res Lab, USDA, 71-82. *Concurrent Pos:* Lectr, Frederick Community Col, 61-82. *Mem:* Am Phytopath Soc. *Res:* Etiology and epiphytology of plant rusts; evaluation of plant pathogens for damage potential; biological control of weeds by plant pathogens; ecology of plant pathogens; weather plant disease relationships; epiphytology; ecology. *Mailing Add:* 102 Mercer Ct 212A Frederick MD 21701

BROMLEY, D(AVID) ALLAN, NUCLEAR PHYSICS, SCIENCE & TECHNOLOGY POLICY. *Current Pos:* assoc prof & assoc dir, Heavy Ion Lab, Yale Univ, 60-61, prof physics, 61-72, chmn dept, 70-77, dir, A Wright Nuclear Struct Lab, 61-89, Henry Ford II prof, 72-93, STERLING PROF SCI, YALE UNIV, 93-, DEAN ENG, 94- *Personal Data:* b Westmeath, Ont, May 4, 26; US citizen; m 49, Patricia J Brassor; c David J & Karen L. *Educ:* Queen's Univ, Ont, BSc, 48, MSc, 50, DSc, 81; Univ Rochester, PhD(physics), 52; Yale Univ, MA, 61;. *Hon Degrees:* Numerous from US and foreign univs, 78-91. *Honors & Awards:* Humboldt Prize, 79, 82, 85; Presidental Medal, NY Acad Sci, 89; US Nat Medal Sci, 89. *Prof Exp:* Demonstr physics, Queen's Univ, Ont, 47; res officer, Nat Res Coun Can, 48; from instr to asst prof physics, Univ Rochester, 52-55; sr res officer, Atomic Energy Can Ltd, 55-60, sect head accelerators, 58-60; asst to pres sci & technol & dir, Off Sci & Technol Policy, White House, 89-93. *Concurrent Pos:* Mem, Panel Nuclear Struct Physics, NSF, 61; chmn, Nuclear Sci Comt, Nat Res Coun, 66-76, mem, Exec Comt, Div Phys Sci & mem-at-lg, 68-78; dir, United Nuclear Corp, 67-, Labcore Inc, 69-71, Extrion Corp, 70-75, United Illum Co, 73-89, Union Trust Co, 76-89, Northeast Bancorp Inc, 76-89, Oak Ridge Assoc Univs, 78-82, Univ Bridgeport, 81-85, Gen Ionex, 80-88 & Barnes Eng Co, 84-86; chmn, Physics Surv Comt, Nat Acad Sci, 69-73, mem, Naval Studies Bd, 74-78; consult, Oak Ridge Nat Lab, Brookhaven Nat Lab, Acad Press, Bell Tel Labs, NSF, McGraw-Hill, GT&E & IBM Corp, 69-89; mem, US Nat Comt, Int Union Pure & Appl Physics, 70-, chmn, 74-, vpres, 75-81, first vpres, 81-84 & pres, 84-87; mem, Joint US-USSR Coord Comt Fundamental Res, 72 & High Energy Physics Adv Panel, Energy Res Develop Admin, 73-78; Guggenheim fel, 77-78; chmn, US Nuclear Scientists vis Peoples Repub China, 78; mem, US Nat Comt, Int Coun Sci Unions, 81-89 & White House Sci Coun, 81-89; mem, Nuclear Sci Adv Panel, NSF & Dept Energy, 81-89; Benjamin Franklin fel, Royal Soc Arts (London); US co-chmn, India-US Presidential Initiative Sci & Technol, 82-, US chmn, Brazil-US Presidential Initiative Sci & Technol, 87-; mem, Bd Dirs, Southeastern Univ Res Asn; co-chmn, US-Japan Joint Comn, US-Europ Joint Consult Group, US-Venezuelan Comn Sci & Technol, US-Chili Comn Sci & Technol, US-China Joint Comn Sci & Technol; bd dirs, Echlin Inc. *Mem:* Nat Acad Sci; Can Asn Physicists; fel Am Acad Arts & Sci; fel AAAS (pres, 81); fel Am Phys Soc; fel Brazilian Acad Sci; fel Royal Soc SAfrica; fel Am Phys Soc. *Res:* Nuclear structure and reaction mechanisms; heavy ion physics; accelerators; science and technology policy studies. *Mailing Add:* 35 Tokeneke Dr North Haven CT 06473-4348

BROMLEY, LE ROY ALTON, CHEMICAL ENGINEERING, PHYSICAL CHEMISTRY. *Current Pos:* asst, Manhattan Dist, 43-46, from instr to prof chem eng, 46-76, EMER PROF CHEM ENG, UNIV CALIF, BERKELEY, 76- *Personal Data:* b San Jose, Calif, Sept 30, 19; m 41, Bernice Doyle; c Bruce, Karen, Karla & Kathleen. *Educ:* Univ Calif, BS, 41, PhD(chem), 48; Ill Inst Technol, MS, 43. *Honors & Awards:* Alan P Colburn, Am Inst Chem Engrs, 53. *Prof Exp:* Chemist, Nat Motor Bearing Co, Calif, 41; asst, Ill Inst Technol, 41-43. *Concurrent Pos:* Vis prof, Univ Philippines, 54-56. *Mem:* Am Inst Chem Engrs; Am Chem Soc. *Res:* Heat transfer in boiling; condensation; thermodynamic properties of halides, sulfides, carbides and nitrides; high temperature heats reaction; sea water conversion; research on air pollution control by sea water; properties of sea water. *Mailing Add:* PO Box 580 Willits CA 94590-0580

BROMLEY, STEPHEN C, DEVELOPMENTAL BIOLOGY. *Current Pos:* res assoc, Mich State Univ, 69-70, assoc prof zool & assoc prof biol sci, 70-75, prog dir, 70-92, PROF ZOOL & PROF BIOL SCI, MICH STATE UNIV, 75- *Personal Data:* b Los Angeles, Calif, Aug 31, 38; m 67; c Axel, Anna, Jacob, Asa, Jane & Calder. *Educ:* Brigham Young Univ, BS, 60; Princeton Univ, MA, 62, PhD(biol), 65. *Prof Exp:* Res asst ornith & mammal, Los Angeles County Mus, 57, 59-60; instr biol, Princeton Univ, 64-65; asst prof zool, Univ Vt, 65-69. *Mem:* AAAS; Am Soc Zoologists. *Res:* Neural and endocrine factors in regeneration of amphibian limbs; response of amphibian limbs to culture conditions. *Mailing Add:* Dept Biol Sci 203 Natural Sci Mich State Univ East Lansing MI 48824-1115

BROMUND, RICHARD HAYDEN, ANALYTICAL CHEMISTRY. *Current Pos:* From asst prof to assoc prof chem, 67-80, PROF CHEM, COL WOOSTER, 80- *Personal Data:* b Oberlin, Ohio, Apr 28, 40; div; c 2. *Educ:* Oberlin Col, AB, 62; Pa State Univ, PhD(chem), 68. *Mem:* AAAS; Am Chem Soc. *Res:* Chemical instrumentation; gas chromatography; trace organic analytical chemistry. *Mailing Add:* Dept Chem Col Wooster Wooster OH 44691-2363

BROMUND, WERNER HERMANN, ANALYTICAL CHEMISTRY, ORGANIC CHEMISTRY. *Current Pos:* From instr to prof, 37-75, EMER PROF CHEM, OBERLIN COL, 75- *Personal Data:* b Duluth, Minn, May 8, 09; wid; c 2. *Educ:* Univ Chicago, BS, 32; Oberlin Col, AM, 35; NY Univ, PhD(chem), 42. *Mem:* Am Chem Soc; Sigma Xi. *Res:* Amino sugar derivatives; adsorption characteristics of porous solids; macro and microchemical apparatus design; macro and microchemical methods of analysis; methods of analysis of pharmaceuticals; teaching methods in analytical chemistry; Kofler microfusion methods of analysis. *Mailing Add:* 26376 John Rd Apt 1010 Olmsted Falls OH 44138

BRON, WALTER ERNEST, SOLID STATE PHYSICS, LASER PHYSICS. *Current Pos:* chmn, 89-92, PROF PHYSICS, UNIV CALIF, IRVINE, 86- *Personal Data:* b Berlin, Ger, Jan 17, 30; m 52, Ann E Berend; c 2. *Educ:* NY Univ, BME, 52; Columbia Univ, MS, 53, PhD(pure sci), 58. *Honors & Awards:* Alexander von Humboldt Found award, 73. *Prof Exp:* Res assoc, Eng Res & Develop Lab, 54-56; lectr, George Washington Univ, 55-56; res physicist, Watson Lab, IBM Corp, 57-58, staff mem physics group, Res Ctr, 58-66; vis prof, Phys Inst, Univ Stuttgart, 66-67; assoc prof, Ind Univ, Bloomington, 67-69, prof physics, 69-86. *Concurrent Pos:* Res assoc & lectr, Columbia Univ, 52-58, 64; Guggenheim fel, 66-67; vis prof, Max Planck Inst for Solid State Res, 73-74 & 81-82. *Mem:* Europ Phys Soc; Am Phys Soc; Sigma Xi; Am Optical Soc; Int Soc Optical Eng; AAAS. *Res:* Defects in solid crystals; optical properties of solids; lattice dynamics; phonon transport. *Mailing Add:* Dept Physics & Astron Univ Calif Irvine CA 92697. *Fax:* 714-824-2174; *E-Mail:* wbron@uci.edu

BRONAUGH, EDWIN LEE, ELECTROMAGNETIC COMPATIBILITY & MEASUREMENT UNCERTAINTY, ANTENNA & INSTRUMENT DESIGN. *Current Pos:* prin EMC scientist, 89-92, vpres eng, 92-94, PRIN EDB EMC CONSULTS, ELECTRO-MECHANICS CO, 94- *Personal Data:* b Salina, Kans, July 22, 32; m 55, Geraldine Kelly; c Cecilia A (Snodgrass) & Dana L (Weinberg). *Educ:* East Tex State Univ, BA, 55. *Honors & Awards:* Richard R Stoddart Award, Electromagnetic Compatibility Soc, Inst Elec & Electronics Engrs; Lawrence G Cuming Award. *Prof Exp:* Res scientist, Electromagnetic Compatibility, SW Res Inst, 68-76, res dir, 76-82; dir res & develop, Electro-Mech Div, Penril Co, 82-89. *Concurrent Pos:* Chmn, SC-1, Sect Comt, C 63, Am Nat Stand Inst, 77-85, vchmn, 85-; mem, Electromagnetic Compatability Stand Comt, Inst Elec & Electronics Engrs, 80-; mem, Electromagnetic Interference Stand Tech, Soc Automotive Engrs, 75-, Electromagnetic Radiation Tech Comt, 87-; dir tech serv, Electromagnetic Compatibility Soc, 81-87, vpres, 88-89, pres, 90-92. *Mem:* Fel Inst Elec & Electronics Engrs; Soc Automotive Engrs; Nat Asn radio & Telecommun Engrs. *Res:* Electromagnetic compatibility phenomena with emphasis on instrumentation and measurement of radio noise, electromagnetic disturbance and immunity of equipment to electromagnetic interference. *Mailing Add:* 10210 Prism Dr Austin TX 78726-1364

BRONAUGH, ROBERT LEWIS, TOXICOLOGY, PHARMACOLOGY. *Current Pos:* res pharmacologist, 78-88, CHIEF, SKIN ABSORPTION & METAB SECT, US FOOD & DRUG ADMIN, 88- *Personal Data:* b Spokane, Wash, Dec, 15, 42; m 70, Virginia Lemke; c Jeffrey. *Educ:* Univ NMex, BS, 68; Univ Colo, PhD(pharmacol), 72. *Honors & Awards:* Commendable Serv Award, Food & Drug Admin, 84. *Prof Exp:* Teaching fel, Med Sch, Univ Colo, 72-74 & NY Univ, 74-76; sr pharmacologist, Interx Res Corp, 76-78. *Mem:* Soc Toxicol; Soc Cosmetic Chemists. *Res:* Determination of the absorption of chemicals through skin; mechanisms; methodology effect of vehicles; effect of physico-chemical parameters; effect of metabolism. *Mailing Add:* Food & Drug Admin Off Cosmetics & Colors 8301 Muirkirk Rd Laurel MD 20708

BRONCO, CHARLES JOHN, ATOMIC PHYSICS. *Current Pos:* INDEPENDENT RES, 91- *Personal Data:* b Gary, Ind, Jan 25, 28. *Educ:* Okla State Univ, BS, 49; Univ Tex, MA, 51; Univ Okla, PhD(physics), 59. *Prof Exp:* Sr systs design engr, Chance Vought Aircraft, Tex, 56-59, electronic systs engr, 59-60; prin physicist, Phys Sci Div, Melpar, Inc, Va, 60-61, sr scientist gaseous laser res, 61-62; asst prof math & physics, Grad Inst Technol, Univ Ark, 62-68; assoc prof physics, Ark Tech Univ, 78-82; independent res, 82-89; prof physics, Univ Ozark, 89-91. *Concurrent Pos:* Consult, Melpar, Inc, 62. *Mem:* Am Phys Soc. *Res:* Resonance excitation cross-sections; high vacuum physics; electronic systems research; molecular dissociation by electron and photon impact; laser development; focal isolation methods; laboratory techniques. *Mailing Add:* Rte 1 Dover AR 72837

BRONDYKE, KENNETH J, METALLURGY & PHYSICAL METALLURGICAL ENGINEERING. *Current Pos:* RETIRED. *Personal Data:* b Saulte Ste Marie, Mich, June 16, 22. *Educ:* Univ Mich, BS, 46. *Prof Exp:* Dir, Alcoa Lab, 83. *Mem:* Am Soc Metals; Am Inst Mining Metall & Petrol Engrs; Sci Res Soc Am. *Mailing Add:* 727 14th St Oakmont PA 15139

BRONDZ, BORIS DAVIDOVICH, EXACT ELUCIDATION OF THE MHC MOLECULE. *Current Pos:* sr sci collabr immunol, Lab Immunochem, Cancer Res Ctr, 77-87, chief sci collabr, 87-89, LEADER LAB LYMPHOCYTES, LAB REGULATORY MECH IMMUN, CARCINOGENESIS INST, CANCER RES CTR, 89- *Personal Data:* b Yaroslavle, USSR, June 21, 34; m 56, 80; c 1. *Educ:* First Moscow Med Inst, Physician, 57; Gamaleya Inst Epidemiol Microbiol, Cand Sci, 65, Dr Med Sci, 73; Cancer Res Ctr, Prof, 89. *Hon Degrees:* Vet Labour USSR, Moscow Munic Soviet of People's Deputation, 87. *Prof Exp:* Sr laboratorian immunol & oncol, Gamaleya Inst, Acad Med Sci, 61-64, jr sci collabr, 64-68, sr sci collabr, 68-77. *Concurrent Pos:* Lectr, Moscow Univ, Central Inst, 82-; comn AIDS, Acad Med Sci, 88-; comn oncol, Cancer Res Ctr, 88- *Mem:* Immunol Soc; NY Acad Sci; hon mem Am Asn Immunol. *Res:* Specific absorption-elution of different T-cell subsets and their receptors on macrophage monolayers of inbred-mutant strains of mice differing in particular histocompatibility genes; the killer T-cells differ from each other in clonal structure of their receptors; difference in clonal repertoire; fine specificity and epitopes between T-killers and antibodies and between receptors of T-killers, their memory cells and suppressor T-cells; selective markers of suppressor T-cells; mechanism of immunodeficiency. *Mailing Add:* Sci Investment Carcinogenetics Cancer Res Ctr Kashirskoye Shaussae 24 Moscow 115478 Russia. *Fax:* 7(095)230-24-50

BRONK, BURT V, BIOPHYSICS. *Current Pos:* RES PHYSICIST, ARMSTRONG LAB, USAF, 95- *Personal Data:* b Pittsburgh, Pa, 1935; m 55, Gerri Ash; c 3. *Educ:* Pa State Univ, BS, 55; Princeton Univ, PhD(physics), 65. *Prof Exp:* Res assoc physics, State Univ NY, Stony Brook, 64-66; asst prof, Queens Col, NY, 66-69; sr res assoc biol, Brookhaven Nat Lab, 69-71; assoc prof, Clemson Univ, 71-78, prof physics & microbiol, 78-87, adj prof biophys, 87-95; res physicist, Chem Res Develop & Eng Ctr, Aberdeen Proving Ground, 87-95. *Concurrent Pos:* Res collabr, Brookhaven Nat Lab, 71-72; res assoc biol, Univ Tex, Dallas, 81-92; ed, Comments on Molecular & Cellular Biophys. *Mem:* Biophys Soc; Phys Soc; Am Soc Microbiol. *Res:* Optical physics of micron- sized particles; lightscatering and fluorescence of bacterial cells; Synergy of DNA damage with thermal effects; statistical physics as applied to biological processes; synergistic effect of hyperthermia on radiation and drug damage to animal cells. *Mailing Add:* Edgewood Res & Develop & Eng Ctr Aberdeen Proving Ground MD 21010-5423

BRONK, JOHN RAMSEY, INTESTINAL TRANSPORT, CELL PHYSIOLOGY. *Current Pos:* PROF BIOCHEM, UNIV YORK, ENG, 66- *Personal Data:* b Philadelphia, Pa, Dec 20, 29; m 55, Sylvia Smith; c Richard & Christopher. *Educ:* Princeton Univ, AB, 52; Oxford Univ, PhD(biochem), 55. *Prof Exp:* From asst prof to prof zool, Columbia Univ, 58-66. *Concurrent Pos:* Guggenheim fel, 64-65. *Mem:* Am Soc Biochem & Molecular Bio; Brit Biochem Soc; Brit Physiol Soc; fel AAAS. *Res:* Peptide transport and metabolism in intestine and lung; transport and metabolism of amino acids, sugars, purines, pyrimidines and vitamins in intestine and liver; mode of action of thyroid hormones. *Mailing Add:* Dept Biol Univ York York YO1 5DD England. *Fax:* 44-904-432860; *E-Mail:* jrbs@york.ac.uk

BRONNER, FELIX, CALCIUM METABOLISM, ION REGULATION. *Current Pos:* prof oral biol, Univ Conn, Farmington, 69-86, nutrit sci, 76-89, biostruct & function, 86-89, EMER PROF, UNIV CONN, FARMINGTON, 89- *Personal Data:* b Vienna, Austria, Nov 7, 21; nat US; m 47, Leah Horowitz; c Deborah R & Ethan S. *Educ:* Univ Calif, BS, 41; Mass Inst Technol, PhD(nutrit biochem), 52. *Honors & Awards:* Andre Lichtwitz Prize, INSERM, Paris, 74. *Prof Exp:* Asst, Mass Inst Technol, 51-52, assoc, 52-54; vis investr, Rockefeller Inst, 54-56, asst, 56; assoc, Hosp Spec Surg, Med Ctr, Cornell Univ, 57-58, Bicknell assoc mineral metab, 58-61, assoc scientist & asst prof biochem, Cornell Med Col, 61-63; assoc prof physiol, Sch Med, Univ Louisville, 63-69. *Concurrent Pos:* Helen Hay Whitney fel, Rockefeller Inst, 54-55 & Arthritis & Rheumatism fel, 55-56; vis scientist, Pasteur Inst, 62 & 76, Weizmann Inst Sci, 65 & 76, Univ Capetown, 85 & 88 & MRC, 91; consult, NIH, Acad Press & USDA; organizer chmn, Gordon Res Conf Bones & Teeth 54, Sanger Symp, 24th Int Cong, 65; vis scientist, INSERM, Paris, 72, Lyon, 88; vis prof, Tel-Aviv Univ, 76, Univ Capetown, 85 & 88; co-chmn, Int Workshop Calcium & Phospate Transport Across Biomembrane, Vienna, Austria, 81, 84, 87; Varon vis prof, Weizmann Inst Sci, 88. *Mem:* Fel AAAS; fel Am Inst Nutrit; Am Soc Clin Nutrit; Am Physiol Soc; Soc Exp Biol & Med; Harvey Soc; emer mem Orthop Res Soc; Am Fedn Clin Res; Am Soc Bone & Mineral Res. *Res:* Calcium and mineral metabolism; metabolic bone disease; biologic regulation; ion movement and transport. *Mailing Add:* Dept Biostruct & Function Rm L7071 Sch Dent Med Univ Conn 263 Farmington Ave Farmington CT 06030-3705. *Fax:* 860-679-2910

BRONNES, ROBERT L(EWIS), METALLURGY. *Current Pos:* RETIRED. *Personal Data:* b Dobbs Ferry, NY, Mar 17, 24. *Educ:* Univ Ala, BS, 51. *Prof Exp:* From asst engr to engr, Nam Phillips Co, Inc, 51-57, sr engr, 57-66, staff engr metall, 66-85, sr mem res staff, 85-90. *Mem:* Am Soc Metals; Metall Soc; fel Am Inst Chem; Int Metallog Soc. *Res:* Metallurgical and metallographic phases, especially semi-conductors, metal-ceramic seals, ferrites, brazing, electroplating, thin films; surface preparation of semiconductor materials. *Mailing Add:* 21 N Eckar St Irvington NY 10533

BRONS, CORNELIUS HENDRICK, SPECTROSCOPY, GEOLOGY & BIOLOGY RELATED PROJECTS. *Current Pos:* sr res technician phys chem, electro-chem, enhanced oil recovery, RES ASSOC POLYMER & COMPLEX FLUIDS & BIO-REMEDIATION OF CONTAMINATED SOILS, EXXON RES & ENG LABS, 79- *Personal Data:* b Staten Island, NY, Jan 24, 55; m; c 3. *Educ:* Fairleigh Dickinson Univ, Madison, NJ, BA, 87. *Prof Exp:* Res technician phys chem, Merck, Sharpe & Dome Res Labs, 76-77; sr res technician mineral sci, ASAR Co, Res & Develop Labs, 77-79. *Mem:* Sigma Xi; Am Chem Soc; Geol Sci US. *Res:* Water soluble polymers; encapsulation of products; surfactant research for many applications (household, automotive and soil cleaning and washing); bio-remediation research dealing with microbial populations, nourishment, treating, cleaning and formulating nutrient packages for them; treating waste water and other contaminents; granted five patents; author of various publications. *Mailing Add:* Exxon Res & Eng Corp Rte 22 E Lab LD 343 Annandale NJ 08801

BRONS, KENNETH ALLYN, COMPUTER SCIENCE. *Current Pos:* RETIRED. *Personal Data:* b Chicago, Ill, July 21, 29; m 55; c 2. *Educ:* NCent Col, Ill, BA, 51; Univ Ill, Urbana, MS, 52, PhD(math), 56. *Prof Exp:* Appl sci rep, IBM Corp, 56-59; sr methods specialist, RCA Corp, 59-69, mgr mgt sci appln, 69-72; consult, Comput Dynamics Corp, 72-75; sr syst analyst, Cryovac Div, W R G race & Co, 75-96. *Mem:* Asn Comput Mach; Am Math Soc; Math Asn Am; Soc Indust & Appl Math; Sigma Xi. *Mailing Add:* 302 Hermitage Rd Greenville SC 29615

BRONSHTEYN, LEV, LUBRICATION & TRIBOLOGY, PHYSICAL CHEMISTRY. *Current Pos:* SR CHEMIST, WYNN OIL CO, 96- *Personal Data:* b Moscow, Russia, Sept 5, 46; m 79, Larisa Eydelman; c Serge. *Educ:* Moscow Telecommun Inst, BA, 69; Nat Petrol Res Ctr, PhD(chem eng), 75. *Prof Exp:* Res engr, Navy Res Ctr, Russia, 69-75; sr scientist, Nat Petrol Res Ctr, Russia, 75-91; postdoctoral study, Mass Inst Technol, 92-94; staff fel, Gen Motors, 94-96. *Mem:* Nat Soc Corrosion Specialists; Am Soc Testing & Mat; Soc Automotive Engrs. *Res:* Friction; wearin lubricated contacts; lubricant formulation; tribological behavior of materials; additives to lubricants. *Mailing Add:* 613 Las Riendas Fullerton CA 92835. *Fax:* 626-334-3260

BRONSON, FRANKLIN HERBERT, ECOLOGY, BEHAVIOR-ETHOLOGY. *Current Pos:* assoc prof, 68-72, PROF ZOOL, UNIV TEX, AUSTIN, 72- *Personal Data:* b Pawnee City, Nebr; m 53, 75, Rebecca Banett; c Barbara Ann & Steven Michael. *Educ:* Kans State Univ, BS, 57, MS, 58; Pa State Univ, PhD(zool), 61. *Prof Exp:* Staff scientist, Jackson Lab, 61-68. *Concurrent Pos:* Dir, Inst Reproductive Biol, Univ Tex, Austin. *Mem:* Animal Behav Soc; Soc Study Reprod; Am Soc Zoologists; Soc Study Biol Rhythms. *Res:* Environmental control of reproduction. *Mailing Add:* Dept Zool Univ Tex Austin TX 78712

BRONSON, JEFF DONALDSON, NUCLEAR PHYSICS. *Current Pos:* asst prof, 67-74, mem staff, 74-87, SR SCIENTIST, CYCLOTRON INST, TEX A&M UNIV, 87- *Personal Data:* b Dallas, Tex, Aug 12, 38. *Educ:* Rice Univ, BA, 59, MA, 61, PhD(physics), 64. *Prof Exp:* Res assoc physics, Rice Univ, 64; res fel, Univ Basel, 64-65 & Univ Wis, 65-67. *Mem:* Am Phys Soc; Sigma Xi. *Res:* Nuclear forces using 3-body nuclear reactions; determination of atomic hyperfine fields and nuclear magnetic moments using perturbed angular correlations. *Mailing Add:* Cyclotron Inst MS 3366 Tex A&M Univ College Station TX 77843

BRONSTEIN, IRENA Y, CHEMISTRY. *Current Pos:* SR STAFF SCIENTIST, ALLIED HEALTH & SCIENTIFIC PROD DIAGNOSTICS RES & DEVELOP CO, ALLIED CORP, 84- *Educ:* Bryn Mawr Col, BS, 68; Johns Hopkins Univ, PhD(photochem), 73. *Prof Exp:* Res assoc, dept biol chem, Sch Med, Univ Md, 74-75; scientist photochem & polymer chem res, Polaroid Corp, 76-78, res group leader, 78-80, sr res group leader, photochem res, 80-82, sr res group leader, Land Lab, 81-82, tech mgr, photochem res, 82-84, co-dir biotech, 83-84. *Mem:* Am Soc Photobiol; Am Chem Soc; AAAS; Am Asn Clin Chem; Sigma Xi; Soc Photographic Scientists & Engrs. *Mailing Add:* 11 Ivanhoe St Newton MA 02158-2715

BRONZAN, JOHN BRAYTON, HIGH ENERGY PHYSICS. *Current Pos:* AT SERIN PHYS LAB. *Personal Data:* b Los Angeles, Calif, Apr 5, 37; m 63; c 2. *Educ:* Stanford Univ, BS, 59; Princeton Univ, PhD(physics), 63. *Prof Exp:* From instr to assoc prof physics, Mass Inst Technol, 63-71; assoc prof physics, Rutgers Univ, prof, 75- *Mem:* Fel Am Phys Soc. *Res:* Theoretical high energy physics. *Mailing Add:* Serin Physics Lab Rutgers Univ Frelinghuysend Rd PO Box 849 Piscataway NJ 08854. *Fax:* 732-932-4343; *E-Mail:* bronzan@physics.rutgers.edu

BRONZINI, MICHAEL STEPHEN, TRANSPORTATION ENGINEERING, ECONOMICS. *Current Pos:* PROF & HEAD, DEPT CIVIL ENG, PA STATE UNIV, 86- *Personal Data:* b Johnstown, Pa, Aug 21, 44; m 67; c 3. *Educ:* Stanford Univ, BS, 67; Pa State Univ, MS, 69, PhD(civil eng), 73. *Prof Exp:* Res asst civil eng, Pa State Univ, 67-72; asst prof civil eng, Ga Inst Technol, 73-75; from assoc prof to prof civil eng, Univ Tenn, 78-86, from assoc dir to dir, Transp Ctr, 78-86; sr assoc, 75-78, SR CONSULT, CACI INC, 78- *Concurrent Pos:* Consult civil eng, govt, res & develop firms & univs, 72- *Mem:* Am Soc Civil Engrs; Inst Transp Engrs; AAAS; Sigma Xi. *Res:* Development of national freight transportation network data and models; estimation of transport cost and energy use; inland waterway system and lock capacity studies. *Mailing Add:* Oak Ridge Nat Lab Ctr Transp Analysis PO Box 2008 4500 N MS-6207 Oak Ridge TN 37831-6207

BRONZINO, JOSEPH DANIEL, BIOMEDICAL ENGINEERING, SYSTEMS ENGINEERING. *Current Pos:* asst prof, Trinity Col, 68-75, chmn, Dept Eng, 82-90, PROF ENG & VERNON ROOSE PROF APPL SCI, TRINITY COL, 77- *Personal Data:* b Brooklyn, NY, Sept 29, 37; m 61, McGrath; c Michael, Melissa & Marcella. *Educ:* Worcester Polytech Inst, BSEE, 59, PhD(elec eng), 68; US Naval Postgrad Sch, MSEE, 61. *Prof Exp:* From instr to asst prof elec eng, Univ NH, 64-67; NSF fac fel, Worcester Found Exp Biol, Shrewsbury, Mass, 67-68. *Concurrent Pos:* Mem coop staff, Worcester Found Exp Biol, 68-; res assoc, Inst Living, Conn, 68-; dir biomed eng prog, Hartford Grad Ctr, 69-; clin assoc, Dept Surg, Univ Conn Health Ctr, Farmington, 71-; ed, Newsletter, Am Soc Eng Educ, 77-79; chmn, Biomed Eng Div, Am Soc Eng Educ, 80-81; chmn, Health Care Eng Policy Comt, Inst Elec & Electronics Engrs, 86-91, Technol Policy Coun, 92-93. *Mem:* AAAS; Am Soc Eng Educ; fel Inst Elec & Electronics Engrs (pres, 85); Sigma Xi; Asn Advan Med Instrumentation; Biomed Eng Soc. *Res:* Application of engineering technology to new or different environments such as medicine, biology and the ocean; neurophysiological research; biomedical engineering. *Mailing Add:* 12 Brenthaven Avon CT 06001. *Fax:* 860-297-3531; *E-Mail:* joseph.bronzino@trincoll.edu

BROODO, ARCHIE, PHYSICAL CHEMISTRY, CHEMICAL ENGINEERING. *Current Pos:* CHIEF EXEC OFFICER, AID CONSULT ENGRS, INC, 70- *Personal Data:* b Wichita Falls, Tex, Feb 3, 25; m 51; c Marcia (Sinclair), Charlene Nathan, Jack B & Kenneth. *Educ:* Agr & Mech Col Tex, BS, 48; Univ Tex, MS, 50, PhD(chem), 54. *Concurrent Pos:* Ed, Southwest Retort, Am Chem Soc, 57-58. *Mem:* Sigma Xi; Am Chem Soc; Inst Elec & Electronics Engrs; Am Soc Metals. *Res:* Technical investigation of insurance losses; chemical and other product liability; arson determinations; explosion cause analyses; materials studies and analytical chemistry; material flammability studies; corrosion studies; tire defect analyses. *Mailing Add:* AID Consult Engrs 2639 Electric Lane Suite 110 Dallas TX 75220. *Fax:* 214-352-0338

BROOK, ADRIAN GIBBS, ORGANOSILICON CHEMISTRY. *Current Pos:* lectr, Univ Toronto, 53-56, from asst prof to prof chem, 56-89, from assoc chmn to chmn dept, 68-74, EMER PROF CHEM, UNIV TORONTO, 89- *Personal Data:* b Toronto, Ont, May 21, 24; m 54, Peg Dunn; c Michael A, Katherine & David L. *Educ:* Univ Toronto, BA, 47, PhD(chem), 50. *Honors & Awards:* F S Kipping Award, Am Chem Soc, 73; Chem Inst Can Medal, 85. *Prof Exp:* Lectr chem, Univ Sask, 50-51; Nuffield res fel, Imp Col Sci & Technol, 51-52; res assoc, Iowa State Col, 52-53. *Concurrent Pos:* Vis prof, Sch Molecular Sci, Univs Sussex, 74-75, Cambridge, 81 & Ind, 88. *Mem:* Am Chem Soc; Chem Inst Can; fel Royal Soc Can. *Res:* Organosilicon, organogermanium chemistry, silenes; organometallic compounds; stereochemistry; reaction mechanisms; acylsilanes, c-functionalized organosilicon compounds. *Mailing Add:* 7 Thornwood Rd Apt 202 Toronto ON M4W 2R8 Can. *Fax:* 416-978-8775

BROOK, ITZHAK, INFECTIOUS DISEASES, PEDIATRICS. *Current Pos:* PROF PEDIAT, SCH MED, GEORGETOWN UNIV, 91- *Personal Data:* b Afula, Israel, June 16, 41; US citizen; m 67, Joyce Reback; c 5. *Educ:* Hebrew Univ, MD, 68; Tel Aviv Univ, MS, 73. *Prof Exp:* Instr microbiol, Sch Med, Hebrew Univ, 73-74; instr pediat, Univ Calif, Irvine, 76-77; asst prof, George Wash Univ, 77-80; prof pediat & surg, Sch Med, Uniformed Serv Univ, 80-91. *Concurrent Pos:* Consult infectious dis, Hosp Sick Children, 80-; attend physician, Naval Hosp, Bethesda, 80-; sr investr, Naval Med Res Inst, 84-; consult, Antinfective Adv Comt, Food & Drug Admin, 84- *Mem:* Fel Am Soc Infectious Dis; fel Soc Pediat Res; fel Soc Pediat Infectious Dis; Am Soc Microbiol; Soc Surg Infectious Dis. *Res:* Infections and pathogenicity of anaerobic bacteria; infections in the immunocompromised host; pathogenesis and therapy; upper respiratory infections. *Mailing Add:* 4431 Albemarle St NW Washington DC 20016

BROOK, MARX, PHYSICS. *Current Pos:* res physicist, NMex Inst Mining & Technol, 54-58, from assoc prof to prof, 58-86, chmn dept, 68-78, 80-86, dir, Res & Develop Div, 78-86, EMER PROF PHYSICS, NMEX INST MINING & TECHNOL, 86-; PRES, ATMOSPHERIC PROBING TECH INC, 93- *Personal Data:* b New York, NY, July 12, 20; m 47; c 3. *Educ:* Univ NMex, BS, 44; Univ Calif, Los Angeles, MA & PhD(physics), 53. *Honors & Awards:* Outstanding NMex Scientist of Year, 78. *Prof Exp:* Asst, Univ NMex, 43-46; res physicist, Univ Calif, Los Angeles, 47-53. *Concurrent Pos:* John Wesley Powell Lectr, 65; vis scientist, Cavendish Lab, 68-69; vis lectr, Japan Soc Promotion Sci, 75. *Mem:* Fel AAAS; fel Am Phys Soc; Am Asn Physics Teachers; fel Am Meteorol Soc; Royal Meteorol Soc; Sigma Xi; fel Am Geophys Union. *Res:* Air quality; cloud physics and lightning; weather radar. *Mailing Add:* PO Box 1925 Socorro NM 87801. *E-Mail:* brook@kestrel.nmt.edu

BROOK, ROBERT H, MEDICINE. *Current Pos:* DIR, DEPT HEALTH PROG & HEALTH SCI PROG, RAND CORP, SANTA MONICA, CALIF, 74-; PROF MED, DEPT MED & PROF PUB HEALTH, SCH PUB HEALTH & MED, UNIV CALIF, LOS ANGELES, 74- *Personal Data:* b New York, NY, July 3, 43; m; c 4. *Educ:* Univ Ariz, BS, 64; Johns Hopkins Univ, MD, 68, ScD, 72; Am Bd Hyg & Pub Health, dipl, 72. *Honors & Awards:* Clarke Mem lectr, Univ Hosp, Nottingham, UK, 85; Richard & Hinda Rosenthal Found Award, Am Col Physicians, 89; Hollister Univ Award Lectr, Northwestern Univ, 89; Baxter Health Serv Res Prize, 88; Sonneburn Distinguished Lectr, Univ Pa, 88. *Concurrent Pos:* Prog dir, Robert Wood Johnson Clin Scholar Training Prog, Univ Calif, Los Angeles, 74- *Mem:* Inst Med-Nat Acad Sci; fel Am Col Physicians; Am Soc Clin Invest; Am Pub Health Asn; Int Epidemiol Asn; Am Asn Physicians. *Res:* Quality assessment and assurance; development and use of health status measurements in health policy; efficiency and effectiveness of physician behavior and performance, especially as related to academic centers and internal medicine. *Mailing Add:* 1700 Main St PO Box 2138 Santa Monica CA 90406-2138

BROOK, TED STEPHENS, ENTOMOLOGY. *Current Pos:* RETIRED. *Personal Data:* b San Antonio, Tex, Apr 19, 26; m 48, Rose Bush; c Ted Stephens II & Stephanie Crystal (Woods). *Educ:* Trinity Univ, Tex, BS, 48; Kans State Univ, MS, 50; Miss State Univ, PhD(entom), 66. *Prof Exp:* Asst entomologist, Tex Agr Exp Sta, 50-54; from asst entomologist to assoc entomologist, Agr Exp Sta, 56-70, from asst prof to assoc prof entom, Miss State Univ, 64-70; plant protection adv, Univ Mo-Columbia-US AID India Prog, Dept Agr, Bihar, 70-72; assoc prof entom, Miss Agr Exp Sta, Miss State Univ, 72-75; pest mgt specialist, Miss Coop Exten Serv, 75-84. *Res:* Household and ornamental plant pests; termite biology and control; insect biology and ecology; general entomology. *Mailing Add:* 239 Pecan St Uvalde TX 78801

BROOKBANK, JOHN WARREN, DEVELOPMENTAL BIOLOGY. *Current Pos:* from asst prof to prof zool, Univ Fla, 55-72, prof zool & microbiol, 72-76, prof microbiol & cell sci, 76-85, assoc geront, 76-85, EMER PROF MICROBIOL & CELL SCI, UNIV FLA, 85- *Personal Data:* b Seattle, Wash, Mar 3, 27; m 83, Sally Sattarberg; c Ursula, John Jr & Phoebe. *Educ:* Univ Wash, BA, 49, MS, 53; Calif Inst Technol, PhD, 55. *Prof Exp:* Asst biol, Calif Inst Technol, 52-55. *Mem:* Geront Soc; Sigma Xi. *Res:* Regulation of gene expression in development and aging. *Mailing Add:* PO Box 2688 Friday Harbor WA 98250

BROOKE, JOHN PERCIVAL, APPLIED GEOPHYSICS, GEOPHYSICS. *Current Pos:* asst prof geophys & econ geol, 61-70, assoc prof geol, geophys & eng geol, 70-78, PROF GEOL, SAN JOSE STATE UNIV, 78- *Personal Data:* b Chicago, Ill, Oct 20, 33; m 70, Sheena M Turnbull. *Educ:* Mich Technol Univ, BS, 54; Univ Utah, MS, 59, PhD(geol eng), 64. *Prof Exp:* Geophysicist, Hollanger Gold Mines, 54, Am Smelting & Refining Co, 60-61 & Hall, Relph & Assoc, 70-71; seismologist, Amoco, 59 & 65. *Mem:* Soc Explor Geophys. *Res:* Instrumental and field analysis of geochemical alteration halos surrounding ore bodies; mineral exploration; operations research and mineral economics; geophysical and geochemical prospecting; engineering and environmental geology. *Mailing Add:* Dept Geol San Jose State Univ 1 Washington Sq San Jose CA 95192-0001. *E-Mail:* jpbrooke@sjsuvm1.sjsu.edu

BROOKE, MARION MURPHY, PARASITOLOGY. *Current Pos:* AT DEPT MICROBIOL, EMORY UNIV. *Personal Data:* b Atlanta, Ga, Dec 6, 13; m 40; c 3. *Educ:* Emory Univ, AB, 35, AM, 36; Johns Hopkins Univ, ScD(protozool), 42; Am Bd Microbiol, dipl. *Prof Exp:* Instr biol, Emory Jr Col, 36-38; asst protozool, Sch Hyg & Pub Health, Johns Hopkins Univ, 38-40, instr, 40-42, assoc parasitol, 42-44; assoc prof prev med, Col Med, Univ Tenn, 44-45; chief parasitol sect, Lab Br, Ctr Dis Control, USPHS, 45-51, chief parasitol & mycol sect, 51-57, chief microbiol sect, 57-62, chief lab consult & develop sect, 62-69, dep chief licensure & develop br, 69-72, assoc dir Health Lab Manpower Develop, Lab Training & Consult Div, 72-84. *Concurrent Pos:* Dir interstate malaria surv, Bd State Health Comn Upper Mississippi River Basin, 42; assoc prof, Med Sch, Emory Univ, 46-; vis investr, Sch Trop Med, Univ PR, 46; mem joint dysentery unit, Armed Forces Epidemiol Bd Korea, 51, assoc mem comn enteric infections, 54-74; mem expert adv panel parasitic dis, WHO, 64- & Conf State & Prov Pub Health Lab Dirs; assoc prof, Sch Pub Health, Univ NC, 63-75, prof, 76-; consult, 85- *Mem:* Am Soc Parasitol; Soc Trop Med & Hyg; Am Pub Health Asn; Am Acad Microbiol. *Res:* Proficiency examinations; health laboratory manpower; malaria; amoebiasis; intestinal parasites; toxoplasmosis; programmed instruction. *Mailing Add:* Sch Elec Eng Ga Inst Technol 225 North Ave NW Atlanta GA 30332-0001

BROOKE, RALPH IAN, DENTISTRY. *Current Pos:* CHIEF DENT, UNIV HOSP, LONDON, ONT, 72-; PROF ORAL MED & CHMN DEPT, UNIV WESTERN ONT, 72-, DEAN, FAC DENT & VPROVOST HEALTH SCI, 82- *Personal Data:* b Leeds, UK; Can citizen; m 63; c 2. *Educ:* Leeds Univ, BChD, 57; Royal Col Surgeons Eng, MRCS & LRCP, 63; FDSRCS, 67. *Mem:* Fel Royal Col Dent; fel Int Col Dent; hon fel Int Acad Dent; hon mem Can Dent Asn. *Res:* Chronic facial pain. *Mailing Add:* Fac Dent Univ Western Ont London ON N6A 5C1 Can

BROOKER, DONALD BROWN, CROP DRYING, MATERIALS HANDLING. *Current Pos:* from asst prof to prof, 51-82, EMER PROF AGR ENG, UNIV MO, COLUMBIA, 82- *Personal Data:* b Troy Grove, Ill, Dec 5, 16; m 36; c 2. *Educ:* Univ Mo, Columbia, BS(agr eng), 47, BS(mech eng), 54, MS, 49. *Honors & Awards:* Massey-Ferguson Medal, Am Soc Agr Engrs, 79; Halliburton Educ Award, 80. *Prof Exp:* Instr, Purdue Univ, 49-51. *Concurrent Pos:* Dir, Am Soc Agr Engrs, 76-78; Mem, Governor's Adv Bd, Weights & Measures, 81-82. *Mem:* Am Soc Agr Engrs; Am Soc Eng Educ; Nat Soc Prof Engrs; Sigma Xi. *Res:* Author of two textbooks. *Mailing Add:* 2314 Ridgemont Columbia MO 65203

BROOKER, GARY, PHARMACOLOGY, BIOCHEMISTRY. *Current Pos:* prof & chmn, Dept Biochem, 82-86, PROF, DEPT BIOCHEM & MOLECULAR BIOL, GEORGETOWN UNIV MED CTR, 86- *Personal Data:* b San Diego, Calif, Mar 24, 42; m 64; c 2. *Educ:* Univ Southern Calif, BS, 66, PhD(cardiac pharmacol), 68. *Prof Exp:* Asst prof med, Sch Med, Univ Southern Calif, 68-72, asst prof biochem, 69-72; from assoc prof to prof pharmacol, Med Sch, Univ Va, 72-82. *Concurrent Pos:* Los Angeles County Heart Asn res grants, 68-70; Am Heart Asn res grant, 70-73; USPHS res grants, 71- *Mem:* Am Soc Biol Chemists; AAAS; Am Fedn Clin Res; Am Soc Pharmacol & Exp Therapeut. *Res:* Mechanisms of hormone and drug action as it relates to cardiac metabolism and cardiac contraction; development of methods for rapid analysis of substances of biological interest; microscopic images. *Mailing Add:* Med Ctr Dept Biochem & Molecular Biol Georgetown Univ 3900 Reservoir Rd Washington DC 20007-2188. *Fax:* 301-340-9775

BROOKER, HAMPTON RALPH, NUCLEAR MAGNETIC RESONANCE, MAGNETIC RESONANCE IMAGING. *Current Pos:* asst prof to assoc prof, 64-94, PROF PHYSICS, UNIV SFLA, 94- *Personal Data:* b Columbia, SC, Sept 11, 34; m 62, Jowel Spears; c Emily (Langston) & Mark S. *Educ:* Univ Fla, BS, 56, MS, 58, PhD(physics), 62. *Prof Exp:* Asst prof physics, Abilene Christian Col, 61-63; fel, Univ Fla, 63-64. *Concurrent Pos:* Univ res fel, Univ Nottingham, Eng, 76-77; consult, Dept Radiol, Univ Fla, 78-; vis res physicist, Ames Lab, Iowa, 78. *Mem:* Am Phys Soc; Am Asn Physics Teachers; Int Soc Magnetic Resonance Med. *Res:* Application of nuclear magnetic resonance to medicine. *Mailing Add:* Dept Physics Univ SFla Tampa FL 33620. *Fax:* 813-974-5813; *E-Mail:* dkhapaa@cfrum.cfr.usf.edu

BROOKER, ROBERT MUNRO, ORGANIC CHEMISTRY. *Current Pos:* RETIRED. *Personal Data:* b Troy Grove, Ill, Jan 3, 18; m 41; c Russell & Roberta. *Educ:* Univ Mo, BS, 47, PhD(chem), 50. *Prof Exp:* Asst, Univ Mo, 46-50; head dept chem, 50-66, Ind Cent Univ, chmn div sci & math, 66-88, Bohn prof chem, 81-88. *Concurrent Pos:* Res Chemist, Pitman-Moore Co, 50-65; consult, Dow Chem Co, 65-83; pres, Short Courses, Inc, 73- *Mem:* Am Chem Soc; Sigma Xi. *Res:* Acenaphthene; veratrum alkaloids; natural products. *Mailing Add:* 1431 Windermire Indianapolis IN 46227. *E-Mail:* rbrooker@gaudlf.unidy.edu

BROOKES, NEVILLE, PHARMACOLOGY, NEUROBIOLOGY. *Current Pos:* asst prof, 74-80, ASSOC PROF PHARMACOL, MED SCH, UNIV MD, 80- *Personal Data:* b London, Eng, Mar 12, 39; m 71; c 2. *Educ:* Pharmaceut Soc Gt Brit, MPS, 62; Univ Leeds, PhD(pharmacol), 67. *Prof Exp:* Asst lectr pharmaceut, Sch Pharm, Bristol, 62-63; res fel neuropharmacol, Univ Birmingham, 67-68; instr pharmacol, Hebrew Univ, Jerusalem, 68-70, lectr, 70-74. *Concurrent Pos:* Guest worker, Behav Biol Br, Nat Inst Child Health & Human Develop, 74-76. *Mem:* Am Soc Pharmacol & Exp Therapeut; Soc Neurosci; Pharmaceut Soc Gt Brit. *Res:* Neuropharmacology and neurotoxicology; actions of transmitters drugs and toxic agents on excitable cells. *Mailing Add:* Dept Pharmacol & Exp Therapeut Univ Md Med Sch 660 W Redwood St Baltimore MD 21201-1541

BROOKHART, MAURICE S, ORGANIC CHEMISTRY. *Current Pos:* assoc prof, 69-76, PROF ORG CHEM, UNIV NC, CHAPEL HILL, 76- *Personal Data:* b Cumberland, Md, Nov 28, 42; m 65; c 2. *Educ:* Johns Hopkins Univ, BA, 64; Univ Calif, Los Angeles, PhD(org chem), 68. *Honors & Awards:* Award in Organometallic Chem, Am Chem Soc, 92. *Prof Exp:* NATO fel, Univ Southampton, 68-69. *Concurrent Pos:* Vis prof, Oxford Univ, 82-83; A C Cope Scholar, 94. *Mem:* Am Chem Soc. *Res:* Mechanistic and synthetic organometallic chemistry; applications of transition metal complexes in organic synthesis and catalysis. *Mailing Add:* Dept Chem Univ NC Chapel Hill NC 27599-3290. *Fax:* 919-962-2476; *E-Mail:* caulder@unc.edu.internet

BROOKMAN, DAVID JOSEPH, ANALYTICAL CHEMISTRY. *Current Pos:* DIR ENVIRON CHEM, TECHNOL SCI GP INC, 92- *Personal Data:* b Ft Collins, Colo, Oct 31, 43; m 65. *Educ:* Colo State Univ, BS, 65; Univ Calif, Riverside, PhD(analytical chem), 68. *Prof Exp:* Asst prof chem, Univ Wis-Madison, 68-70; from res chemist to sr res chemist, Stauffer Chem Co, 70-73, group supvr, 74-78, mgr, Analytical Sect, 79-85, mgr, Anal/Metab Dept, 86-87; mgr, Environ Sci Dept, ICI Americas, Inc, 88-91. *Mem:* AAAS; Am Chem Soc. *Res:* Environmental chemistry; analytical separations. *Mailing Add:* 988 Leneve Pl El Cerrito CA 94530-2748

BROOKNER, ELI, ELECTRICAL ENGINEERING. *Current Pos:* sr engr, Raytheon Co, 62-64, prin engr, 64-67, mgr, Info Systs Sect, 67-69, staff engr, Wayland Lab Mgr, 69-70, CONSULT SCIENTIST, RAYTHEON CO, 70- *Personal Data:* b New York, NY, Apr 2, 31; m 55, Ethel Bobick; c Lawrence N & Richard M. *Educ:* City Col New York, BEE, 53; Columbia Univ, MS, 55, DSc, 62. *Honors & Awards:* Premium Award, Franklin Inst, 66; Centennial Medal, Inst Elec & Electronics Engrs, 84, Region One Award, 86, Meritorious Achievement Award, 90. *Prof Exp:* Res engr, Electronics Res Lab, Columbia Univ, 53-57, sr res engr, 60-62; proj engr, Fed Sci Corp, 57-60. *Concurrent Pos:* Int lectr radar technol, 78-; mem, Panel Implications Future Space Systs US Navy, Nat Acad Sci, 79-80, Air Force Ad Hoc Comt on Air Mobile MX, Army Space Initiative Panel, 85; mem, Defense Adv Res Proj Agency assessment of ultra wide band technol, 90, Advan Radar Technol Panel, Naval Studies Bd, Nat Res Coun, 90-91; distinguished lectr, Inst Elec & Electronics Engrs Antennas & Propagation Soc, 83-85, Aerospace & Electronics Systs, 87-97; mem, US Nat Comn, Int Union Radio Sci & Comn B&C. *Mem:* Fel Inst Elec & Electronics Engrs; fel Am Inst Aeroanut & Astronaut; Int Union Radio Sci. *Res:* Surveillance, defense, space-borne, pulse doppler, synthetic aperture, marine and millimeter radar design; noise studies; signal processing; detection theory; waveform analysis; decoy discrimination; ionospheric propagation; target signatures; characterization of laser and millimeter communication channels; modulation; space based radar. *Mailing Add:* Raytheon Co Equip Develop Boston Post Rd Wayland MA 01778. *E-Mail:* cli_brookner@ccmail.ed.ray.com

BROOKS, ALFRED AUSTIN, JR, PHYSICAL CHEMISTRY. *Current Pos:* mgr, Comput Appln Dept, 73-81, MGR INFO SYST, COMPUT SCI DIV, NUCLEAR DIV, UNION CARBIDE CORP, 81- *Personal Data:* b Swampscott, Mass, Aug 3, 21; m 43; c 2. *Educ:* Hobart Col, BA, 46; Ohio State Univ, PhD(chem), 50. *Prof Exp:* Chemist, Lake Ontario Ord Works, 43 & Manhattan Proj, 43-45; instr, Univ Chicago, 50-52; res chemist, Standard Oil Co, 52-54 & Upjohn Co, 54-56; phys chemist, Union Carbide Nuclear, 56-62 & Cent Data Processing Div, 62-70; head comput applns dept, Oak Ridge Nat Lab, 70-73. *Mem:* Am Chem Soc; Am Phys Soc; Asn Comput Mach; Am Soc Info Sci; Sigma Xi. *Res:* Application of high speed computers to information processing. *Mailing Add:* 100 Wiltshire Dr Oak Ridge TN 37830-4505

BROOKS, ANTONE L, GENETIC TOXICOLOGY. *Current Pos:* MGR, CELLULAR & MAMMALIAN BIOL SECT, BATELLE NW LABS, 92- *Personal Data:* b St George, Utah, July 7, 38; m 63; c 6. *Educ:* Univ Utah, BS, 61, MS, 63; Cornell Univ, PhD(phys biol), 67. *Prof Exp:* Mem sr staff, Lovelace Found, 67-92. *Concurrent Pos:* Tech rep, Dept Energy, 76-78. *Mem:* Radiation Res Soc; Environ Mutagen Soc; Nat Coun Radiation Protection & Measurements. *Res:* Distribution and uptake of radioactive fallout, effects of radiation on the chromosomes of somatic and reproductive tissue; effects of internal emitters on chromosomes; genotoxic effects of pollutants from coal utilization and diesel exhaust; carcinogenic hazards of alpha emitters. *Mailing Add:* 6802 W 13th Ave Kennewick WA 99337-1305

BROOKS, ARTHUR S, PLANKTON ECOLOGY. *Current Pos:* Postdoc fel, Ctr Great Lakes Studies, 72-73, from asst prof to assoc prof zool & limnol, Dept Zool, 78-88, PROF LIMNOL, DEPT BIOL SCI & CTR GREAT LAKES STUDIES, UNIV WIS MILWAUKEE, 88- *Personal Data:* b St Johnsbury, Vt, Apr 25, 43; m 66; c 2. *Educ:* Wash & Jefferson Col, BA, 65; Univ Vt, MS, 67; Johns Hopkins Univ, PhD(environ biol), 72. *Concurrent Pos:* Vis scientist, Freshwater Biol Asn, Windermere Lab, Eng, 83-84; fel, Fairbanks Mus Natural Sci, 88. *Mem:* Sigma Xi; AAAS; Am Soc Limnol & Oceanog; Int Asn Great Lakes Res; Int Soc Limnol; Freshwater Biol Asn. *Res:* Ecology of plankton of large lakes; physical and chemical environment in which plankton live; biological interactions and influence of human activities; long-term climactic variability on aquatic ecosystems. *Mailing Add:* 4791 N Woodburn Milwaukee WI 53211-1127

BROOKS, AUSTIN EDWARD, PHYCOLOGY. *Current Pos:* from asst prof to assoc prof, 66-80, chair, Dept Biol, 78-83, chair, Sci Div, 82-92, PROF BIOL, WABASH COL, 81- *Personal Data:* b Ft Wayne, Ind, Aug 10, 38; m 63, E Lucille Clark; c Timothy & Laura. *Educ:* Wabash Col, AB, 61; Ind Univ, PhD(microbiol), 65. *Prof Exp:* Res assoc biol, Brown Univ, 65-66. *Concurrent Pos:* Alexander von Humboldt Found fel, 74-75; consult, Thailand NSF Curric Proj, 84; Hopkins-Dana fel, dept biomed eng, Johns Hopkins Med Sch, 87-88; Lilly Open fac fel, 94- *Mem:* AAAS; Phycol Soc Am; Int Phycol Soc; Sigma Xi; Found Sci & Handicapped; Nat Sci Teachers Asn. *Res:* Morphology and physiology of green flagellated algae; physiological effects of environmental chemicals on green algae; teaching materials development for the visually impaired; calcium metabolism in vascular smooth muscle. *Mailing Add:* Dept Biol Wabash Col Crawfordsville IN 47933. *Fax:* 765-364-4295; *E-Mail:* brooka@wabash.edu

BROOKS, BARBARA ALICE, NEUROSCIENCE. *Current Pos:* asst prof, 74-78, ASSOC PROF NEUROSCI, DEPT PHYSIOL, UNIV TEX HEALTH SCI CTR, SAN ANTONIO, 78- *Personal Data:* b New York, NY, June 18, 34. *Educ:* Univ Fla, BA, 57, MA, 59; Fla State Univ, PhD(exp psychol), 64. *Prof Exp:* Vis scientist, Max Planck Inst Brain Res, Frankfurt, 65-66; NIH fel, Univ Freiburg, 66-69; vis scientist, Max Planck Inst, Bad Nauheim, 70-71 & Inst Ophthal, Univ London, 71; NIH sr fel & res asst prof, Univ Wash, 72-73. *Concurrent Pos:* Prin investr, Eye Inst, NIH res grant, 74-79. *Mem:* Am Physiol Soc; Asn Res in Vision & Ophthal; Neurosci Soc; Sigma Xi. *Res:* Neurophysiology and psychophysics of vision during normal eye movement; sensory-motor integration. *Mailing Add:* Dept Physiol Univ Tex Health Sci Ctr 7703 Floyd Curl Dr San Antonio TX 78284-0001. *Fax:* 210-691-6581

BROOKS, BRADFORD O, IMMUNOTOXICOLOGY, CLINICAL IMMUNOLOGY. *Current Pos:* sr scientist, 82-92, MGR, IBM CTR PROCESS & PROD TOXICOL, IBM CORP, 92- *Personal Data:* b May 5, 51; c 2. *Educ:* Harding Univ, BS, 73; Mont State Univ, MS, 76, PhD(immunol & microbiol), 79. *Concurrent Pos:* Pres & chief exec officer, Immunocompetence, Inc, 80- *Mem:* Am Asn Immunologists; Int Soc Immunopharmacol; Am Soc Microbiol; Royal Soc Trop Med & Hyg; Am Acad Clin Toxicol. *Res:* Influence of chemicals on the immune system; novel bioassays for detection of human chemical exposure; indoor air pollution; process and product toxicology. *Mailing Add:* IBM Corp Ctr Process/Prod Toxicol GUYA/OZIC PO Box 1900 Boulder CO 80301-9191. *Fax:* 303-924-7476

BROOKS, CHARLIE R(AY), METALLURGICAL ENGINEERING. *Current Pos:* Asst metall, 54-56, from instr to assoc prof, 55-69, PROF METALL ENG, UNIV TENN, 69- *Personal Data:* b Pressmen's Home, Tenn, Sept 20, 31; m 57; c 3. *Educ:* Univ Tenn, BS, 54, MS, 59, PhD(metall eng), 62. *Concurrent Pos:* Prof & adv engr, Univ Panama, 63-64. *Mem:* Fel Am Soc Metals; Int Metallog Soc. *Res:* Measurement of specific heats of metals from 0 to 1000 degrees centigrade; adiabatic calorimetry; order-disorder reactions; electron microscopy. *Mailing Add:* Dept Mat Sci Eng Univ Tenn Knoxville TN 37996-0001

BROOKS, CLINT DEE W, MEDICINAL CHEMISTRY, SYNTHETIC CHEMISTRY. *Current Pos:* group leader med chem, 84-87, proj leader, 87-96, DIR CHEM SCI, ABBOTT LABS, 96- *Personal Data:* b Provo, Utah, Mar 2, 52; m 72, Sheila Reed; c Aaron, Christopher & Jenae. *Educ:* Univ Lethbridge, BSc, 74; Univ Alta, PhD(chem), 78. *Prof Exp:* Fel chem, Mass Inst Technol, 78-79; asst prof, Purdue Univ, 79-84. *Mem:* Am Chem Soc; Sigma Xi. *Res:* Pharmaceutical discovery; development of new methods in medicinal chemistry research and organic synthesis; process research and development of pharmaceuticals; applications of nuclear magnetic resonance, mass spectroscopy and infrared in pharmaceutical discovery research. *Mailing Add:* Dept 41K R13-4 1401 Sheridan Rd North Chicago IL 60064. *Fax:* 847-937-9249

BROOKS, CLYDE S, PHYSICAL CHEMISTRY. *Current Pos:* CONSULT, APPL PHYS CHEM, 81-; PRES, RECYCLE METALS, 83- *Personal Data:* b Pittsburgh, Pa, May 1, 17; div, Ruth Bolton; c Suzanne (Taylor) & Philip L. *Educ:* Duke Univ, BS, 40. *Prof Exp:* Koppers Co fel tar synthetics, Mellon Inst, 41-44, jr fel coal prod phys chem, 46-49; res chemist petro physics res, Shell Develop Co, E&P Div, 49-61; sr res scientist, Res Labs, United Technologies Res Ctr, 61-81. *Concurrent Pos:* Consult, Conn Hazardous Waste Mgt, 82-86; Conn task force, 84-86. *Mem:* Int Adsorption Soc; Sigma Xi (secy, 73-75); Am Chem Soc; emer fel Am Inst Chemists; Metall Soc; NAm Catalysis Soc. *Res:* Surface chemistry; heterogeneous catalysis; colloids; application of physical chemistry to elimination of environmental pollution; applications of catalysis in fossil fuel and chemical conversion processes; fossil fuel desulfurization; recovery of waste metals; preparation of adsorbent & catalysts fuel cells and space cabins metals; characterization of metal catalysts by gas absorption/chemisorption; recovery procedures for non-ferrous. *Mailing Add:* 41 Baldwin Lane Glastonbury CT 06033

BROOKS, DANIEL RUSK, SYSTEMATIC BIOLOGY, PARASITOLOGY. *Current Pos:* assoc prof, 88-91, PROF, ZOOL DEPT, UNIV TORONTO, 91- *Personal Data:* b St Louis, Mo, Apr 12, 51; m 87, Deborah A McLennan. *Educ:* Univ Nebr, Lincoln, BS, 73, MS, 75; Univ Miss, PhD(biol), 78. *Honors & Awards:* H B Ward Medal, Am Soc Parasitologists, 85. *Prof Exp:* NIH fel, Univ Notre Dame, 78-79; mem staff, Path Dept, Zool Park, Smithsonian Inst, 79-80; from asst prof to assoc prof, Zool Dept, Univ BC, 80-88. *Concurrent Pos:* Res assoc, Royal Ont Mus. *Mem:* Soc Syst Zool; Am Soc Parasitologists; Sigma Xi. *Res:* Phylogenetics of parasitic helminths; historical ecology; evolutionary biology; tropical biodiversity. *Mailing Add:* Dept Zool Univ Toronto Toronto ON M5S 1A1 Can. *Fax:* 416-978-8532; *E-Mail:* dbrooks@zoo.toronto.edu

BROOKS, DAVID ARTHUR, PHYSICAL OCEANOGRAPHY, ATMOSPHERIC SCIENCE. *Current Pos:* asst prof phys oceanog, 78-83, ASSOC PROF OCEANOG, TEX A&M UNIV, 83- *Personal Data:* b St John, NB, May 6, 43; US citizen; m 69; c 2. *Educ:* Univ Maine, Orono, BS, 65; Univ Miami, MS, 71, PhD(phys oceanog), 75. *Prof Exp:* Syst engr elec eng, Gen Elec Co, 65-69; res asst oceanog, Univ Miami, 69-75; res assoc phys oceanog, NC State Univ, 75-78. *Concurrent Pos:* Adj asst prof, NC State Univ, 78-82. *Mem:* Am Geophys Union; AAAS; Am Meteorol Soc. *Res:* Gulf stream dynamics; generation, propagation and dissipation of meanders; continental shelf and slope dynamics; Gulf of Maine circulation. *Mailing Add:* Dept Oceanog Tex A&M Univ College Station TX 77843-0100

BROOKS, DAVID C, MATHEMATICS. *Current Pos:* PROF MATH, SEATTLE PACIFIC UNIV, 67- *Personal Data:* b Farmington, NMex, Feb 14, 36. *Educ:* Seattle Pacific Univ, BS, 58; Univ Wash, MS, 60, PhD(math), 78. *Mem:* Am Math Soc. *Mailing Add:* Dept Math Seattle Pacific Univ Seattle WA 98119

BROOKS, DAVID PATRICK, RENAL PHARMACOLOGY, RENAL PHYSIOLOGY. *Current Pos:* assoc sr investr pharmacol, 86-88, SR INVESTR PHARMACOL, SMITHKLINE & FRENCH LABS, 88-, ASST DIR PHARMACOL, SMITHKLINE BEECHAM PHARMACEUT, 88- *Personal Data:* b London, Eng, May 31, 52; US citizen; m 78; c 2. *Educ:* Univ London, BSc, 74; Southampton Univ, MSc, 76, PhD(physiol), 79. *Prof Exp:* Teaching fel physiol, Southampton Univ, 78-79; res fel, Univ Hawaii, 79-81; asst prof, Univ Tenn, Memphis, 81-86. *Concurrent Pos:* Adj asst prof, Sch Med, Univ Pa, 87- *Mem:* Am Physiol Soc; Am Soc Pharmacol & Exp Therapeut; Endocrine Soc; Soc Neurosci; Am Soc Nephrology; Am Soc Hypertension. *Res:* Mechanisms involved in hypertension and chronic renal failure; discovery of novel therapeutics for hypertension and chronic renal failure. *Mailing Add:* Smithkline Beecham Pharmaceut PO Box 1539 UW2521 King of Prussia PA 19406-0939. *Fax:* 215-270-4114

BROOKS, DERL, ENTOMOLOGY. *Current Pos:* RETIRED. *Personal Data:* b Headrick, Okla, July 25, 30; m 57; c 1. *Educ:* Tex Tech Col, BS, 57, MS, 59; Iowa State Univ, PhD(entom), 62. *Prof Exp:* Assoc prof biol, Ark State Col, 62-65; assoc prof, WTex State Univ, 65-74, prof, 74-92. *Res:* Acarology, chiefly nasal mites of birds. *Mailing Add:* 413 Foster Lane Canyon TX 79015

BROOKS, DOROTHY LYNN, EDUCATION ADMINSTRATION, ALGEBRA. *Current Pos:* RETIRED. *Personal Data:* b Trinidad, Tex, June 4, 35; m 80; c 4. *Educ:* Baylor Univ, BA, 55; Tex Christian Univ, MA, 61; NTex State Univ, PhD(higher educ admin), 81. *Prof Exp:* Teacher math, Univ High Sch, Waco, Tex, 55-58; teaching asst math, Tex Christian Univ, 59-61; instr math, Tex Wesleyan Col, 62-63; from instr to asst prof, Univ Tex, Arlington, 62-82, asst dean sci, 75-82, coordr instnl planning, 82-87, asst prof math, 87-92. *Mem:* Math Asn Am; Asn Women Math; Am Phys Soc; Sigma Xi. *Mailing Add:* 720 Briarwood Blvd Arlington TX 76013-1501

BROOKS, DOUGLAS LEE, SCIENCE POLICY. *Current Pos:* AUTHOR, 79- *Personal Data:* b New Haven, Conn, Aug 5, 16; m 41, Elizabeth Thatcher; c John C, Alan D, Kenneth T & Donald L. *Educ:* Yale Univ, BS, 38; Mass Inst Technol, SM, 43, ScD, 48. *Prof Exp:* Instr math, Hill Sch-Hotchkiss Sch, 38-42; pilot & weather officer, US Army Air Corps, 42-46; opers analyst & dir res, Naval Opers Anal, USN, 48-62; pres contract res, Travelers Res Ctr, 63-70; spec asst to dir sci policy, NSF, 70-72, exec dir, Nat Adv Coun Oceans & Atmosphere, 72-79. *Mem:* Fel NY Acad Sci; Am Meteorol Soc; AAAS; Marine Technol Soc; fel NY Acad Sci. *Res:* Atmospheric physics & environmental management; naval operations & defense policies; national, environmental & strategic policy. *Mailing Add:* 60 Loeffler Rd 303P Bloomfield CT 06002

BROOKS, EDWARD MORGAN, METEOROLOGY. *Current Pos:* PROF GEOL & GEOPHYS, BOSTON COL, 85- *Personal Data:* b New Haven, Conn, Mar 19, 16; m 41, Sarah K Bergh; c Karena B (Poonen), Daniel E, Roxana B (Kamen) (deceased), Valerie B (Samson), Marita B (Cable), Bernard R, Larimore S & Galen B. *Educ:* Harvard Univ, AB, 37; Mass Inst Technol, SM, 39, ScD(meteorol), 45. *Prof Exp:* Asst observer & asst, Blue Hill Observ, Harvard Univ, 37-39; asst & map analyst, Radiosonde Sta, Mass Inst Technol, 39; map analyst & terminal forecaster, Pan Am Airways, Hawaii, 39-40, tutor meteorol, Calif, 40-41, instr, Fla, 41-42; instr, Mass Inst Technol, 42-46; from asst prof to prof geophys, Inst Technol, St Louis, 46-61; sr meteorologist, Allied Res Assocs, Mass, 61-63; staff scientist, Geophys Corp Am, 63-65; lectr geophys, Boston Col, 65-67, prof geol & geophys, 68-81 & 85-; guest prof meteorol, King Abdul-Aziz Univ, Jeddah, Saudi Arabia, 81-84. *Concurrent Pos:* Scholar, Milton Acad, 32-33; lectr, Boston Ctr Adult Educ, Mass, 43; ed, Mt Washington Observ News Bull, 65-71; meteorologist, Wallace Howell Assoc, 67 & Edgerton, Germeshausen & Grier, 67; prof physics, State Univ NY Plattsburgh, 67-68; guest prof meteorol, McGill Univ, 67-68; consult, Ocean-Atmosphere Res Inst, 68-69, Fla Power & Light Co, 69-70, Cent Weather Bur, Taiwan, 72-73 & Int Group Training Facil, 79-80; instr & asst prof meteorol & oceanog, div grad & continuing studies, Framingham State Col, Mass, 71-73; vis prof meteorol & chmn dept, Inst Astron & Geophys, Univ Sao Paulo, Brazil, 74-77; extended forecaster, Chicago Bd Trade, 77-80, William E Simpson, Inc, 79, Farmers Export Co, 79-81 & Ralston Purina Co, 80-81. *Mem:* AAAS; Am Meteorol Soc; Am Geophys Union; Am Astron Soc; Sigma Xi. *Res:* Physical oceanography; tropical cyclones; polar front in tropics; tropical cloudiness; solar radiation; microbarography; tornadoes; Coriolis force; long range forecasting, ozone, greenhouse effect, synoptic meteorology, volcanic aerosols; isentropic analysis; satellite meteorology. *Mailing Add:* Dept Geol & Geophys Boston Col Chestnut Hill MA 02167-3809. *Fax:* 617-552-2462

BROOKS, ELWOOD RALPH, VOLCANOLOGY. *Current Pos:* chmn dept, 76-79 & 85-88, PROF GEOL, CALIF STATE UNIV, HAYWARD, 65- *Personal Data:* b Charlevoix, Mich, Aug 10, 34; m 88, Della A Hahn; c Eric, Katherine, Patricia, Michael & Maureen (Bills). *Educ:* Mich Col Mining & Technol, BS, 56; Univ Calif, Berkeley, MS, 58; Univ Wis, PhD(geol), 64. *Prof Exp:* Mine geologist, White Pine Copper Co, Mich, 59-60; lectr geol, Univ Calif, Riverside, 64-65. *Concurrent Pos:* Res grants, 64, 66-67, 70-72, 74, 77-82, 86, 88, 90, 93 & 95; mem, Penrose Conf Comt, Geol Soc Am, 81-83; chair, Short Courses Comt, Geol Soc Am, 87-89. *Mem:* Fel Geol Soc Am; Nat Asn Geol Teachers; Am Geophys Union; Int Asn Volcanology & Chem Earth's Interior. *Res:* Igneous and metamorphic petrology, particularly petrology of ancient volcanic rocks; optical mineralogy and petrography; field geology. *Mailing Add:* Dept Geol Sci Calif State Univ Hayward CA 94542-3088. *Fax:* 510-885-2035; *E-Mail:* ebrooks@csuhayward.edu

BROOKS, FREDERICK P(HILLIPS), JR, COMPUTER SCIENCE. *Current Pos:* prof, 64-75, chmn dept, 64-84, KENAN PROF COMPUT SCI, DEPT COMPUT SCI, UNIV NC, CHAPEL HILL, 75- *Personal Data:* b Durham, NC, Apr 19, 31; m 56, Nancy Lee Greenwood; c Kenneth P, Roger G & Barbara B (LaDine). *Educ:* Duke Univ, AB, 53; Harvard Univ, SM, 55, PhD(comput sci), 56. *Hon Degrees:* Dr Tech Sci, Swiss Fed Inst Technol, Zurich, 91. *Honors & Awards:* W W McDowell Award, Inst Elec & Electronics Engrs, 70, Comput Pioneer Award, 82, John von Neumann Medal, 93; Comput Sci Award, Data Processing Mgt Asn, 70; Nat Medal Technol, 85; Distinguished Serv Award, Asn Comput Mach, 87, Newell Award, 95; Harry Goode Mem Award, Am Fedn Info Processing Socs, 89; Bower Prize & Award, Franklin Inst, 96. *Prof Exp:* Assoc engr, Prod Develop Lab, IBM Corp, 56, staff engr, 56-58, adv syst planner, 58-59, mem res staff, 59-60, systs planning mgr, 60-61, corp processor mgr & syst/360 mgr, 61-64, oper syst/360 mgr, 64-65. *Concurrent Pos:* Vis instr, Vassar Col, 58; adj asst prof, Columbia Univ, 60-61; mem-at-large, Nat Coun, Asn Comput Mach, 66-70, bd dirs, Spec Interest Group Comput Archit, 73-75; vis prof, Twente Tech Univ, Enschede, Neth, 70; Guggenheim fel, 75; mem, Comput Sci & Technol Bd, Nat Res Coun, 77-80; mem, Artificial Intel Task Force, Defense Sci Bd, 83-84, Computers Simulation & Training Task Force, 86-87, chmn, Mil Software Task Force, 85-87; mem, Nat Sci Bd, 87- *Mem:* Nat Acad Eng; fel Inst Elec & Electronics Engrs; fel Asn Comput Mach; fel Am Acad Arts & Sci; Royal Neth Acad Arts & Sci; fel Royal Acad Eng UK. *Res:* Interactive computer graphics, man-machine interfaces; applications to molecular structure studies, dynamic architectural visualization (walk-through); architecture of digital computers, especially design of machine language; software engineering, especially programming-in-the-large and project management; 2 US patents. *Mailing Add:* Dept Comput Sci Univ NC Chapel Hill NC 27599-3175. *E-Mail:* brooks@cs.unc.edu

BROOKS, GARNETT RYLAND, JR, ECOLOGY. *Current Pos:* RETIRED. *Personal Data:* b Richmond, Va, Nov 25, 36; div. *Educ:* Univ Richmond, BS, 57, MS, 59; Univ Fla, PhD(zool), 63. *Prof Exp:* From instr to prof biol, Col William & Mary, 62-92. *Mem:* AAAS; Ecol Soc Am; Am Soc Ichthyologists & Herpetologists. *Res:* Physiological ecology of certain species of reptiles. *Mailing Add:* 505 Rochambeau Dr Williamsburg VA 23188

BROOKS, GEORGE AUSTIN, LACTATE METABOLISM, MITOCHONDRIAL ADAPTATIONS TO TRAINING. *Current Pos:* from actg asst prof to assoc prof, 71-81, PROF PHYS EDUC, UNIV CALIF, BERKELEY, 81- *Personal Data:* b Jamaica, NY, Nov 23, 44; c Daniel S & Timothy G. *Educ:* Univ NY, BS, 66; Univ Mich, MS, 68, PhD(exercise physiol), 70. *Honors & Awards:* Citation Award, Am Col Sports Med, 93. *Prof Exp:* Vis asst prof muscle biol, Univ Wisc, 69-71; mem, Respiratory & Appl Physiol Study Sect, NIH, 91-93. *Mem:* Fel Am Col Sports Med; Am Physiol Soc; Am Acad Kinesiology & Phys Educ. *Mailing Add:* Dept Human Biodynamics Univ Calif 103 Harmon Gym Berkeley CA 94720-4480. *Fax:* 510-642-3355; *E-Mail:* gbrooks@violel.berkeley. edu

BROOKS, GEORGE WILSON, psychiatry, for more information see previous edition

BROOKS, HAROLD KELLY, GEOLOGY. *Current Pos:* from asst prof to prof, 56-80, EMER PROF GEOL, UNIV FLA, 80- *Personal Data:* b Winfield, Kans, Nov 27, 24; m 62, Susan Robinson; c Richard, Beryl, Philip & Ellen. *Educ:* Kans State Univ, BS, 47; Harvard Univ, AM, 50, PhD, 62. *Honors & Awards:* Antarctic Serv Medal, USA. *Prof Exp:* Instr geol, Brown Univ, 50-51; instr, Oberlin Col, 51-52; asst prof, Univ Tenn, 52-54 & Univ Cincinnati, 54-56. *Concurrent Pos:* Consult, eng geol, water resources & hazardous waste. *Mem:* Am Asn Petrol Geologist; Fel Geol Soc Am. *Res:* Marine geology; sedimentology; paleontology; geology and physiology of the state of Florida with published maps of the complete state. *Mailing Add:* PO Box 729 Patillas PR 00723

BROOKS, HARVEY, SCIENCE, TECHNOLOGY & PUBLIC POLICY. *Current Pos:* prof appl physics, 50-86, dean, Div Eng & Appl Physics, Harvard Univ, 57-75, prof technol & pub policy, 75-86, BENJAMIN PIERCE EMER PROF TECHNOL & PUB POLICY, KENNEDY SCH GOVT & GORDON MCKAY EMER PROF APPL PHYSIC, HARVARD UNIV, 86- *Personal Data:* b Cleveland, Ohio, Aug 5, 15; m 45; c 4. *Educ:* Yale Univ, AB, 37; Harvard Univ, PhD, 40. *Hon Degrees:* DSc, Yale Univ, 62, Union Col, 62, Harvard Univ, 63, Kenyon Col, 63, Brown Univ, 64. *Honors & Awards:* E O Lawrence Award, Am Eng Soc, 60; Forum Award, Am Phys Soc, 93; Philip Hauge Abelson Award, AAAS, 94. *Prof Exp:* Mem staff, Underwater Sound Lab, Harvard Univ, 42-45; asst dir, Ord Res Lab, Pa State Univ, 45; res assoc, Res Lab & assoc lab head, Knolls Atomic Power Lab, Gen Elec Co, 46-50. *Concurrent Pos:* Guggenheim fel, 56-57; ed-in-chief, J Physics & Chem Solids, 56-80; chmn, Comt Undersea Warfare, Nat Res Coun, 57-63; chmn, Solid State Adv Panel, Off Naval Res; mem, Adv Comt Reactor Safeguards, Progs & Policies, AEC, 58; mem, President's Sci Adv Comt, 59-64 & Nat Sci Bd, 62-74; chmn, Comt Sci & Pub Policy, Nat Acad Sci, 66-72; chmn comn, Soc Tech Systs, Nat Res Coun, 75-78; mem, Adv Comt Sci & Technol Develop, UN, 87-91. *Mem:* Nat Acad Sci; Nat Acad Eng; sr mem Inst Med Nat Acad Sci; Am Philos Soc; fel Am Phys Soc; Am Acad Arts & Sci (pres, 70-75); fel AAAS. *Res:* Solid state physics; underwater sound; nuclear reactors; science policy; author of numerous technical publications and one book. *Mailing Add:* JFK Sch Govt Harvard Univ 79 JFK St Cambridge MA 02138

BROOKS, JACK CARLTON, PHYSIOLOGY, NEUROSCIENCE. *Current Pos:* from asst prof to assoc prof, 74-91, PROF PHYSIOL, SCH DENT, MARQUETTE UNIV, 91-, DEAN, COL HEALTH SCI, 95- *Personal Data:* b Hornell, NY, May 17, 41; m 65, Melinda; c Ryan. *Educ:* Alfred Univ, BA, 63; Univ Tex, Austin, PhD(zool, physiol), 69. *Prof Exp:* Fel enzym, Univ Wis-Madison, 69-72, fel neurosci, 72-74. *Concurrent Pos:* NIH trainee, Univ Wis-Madison, 69-72, NIH fel, 72-73; NSF grants, 83-87; NIH grant, 89-92, Nat Inst Dent Res grant, 92-94. *Mem:* Soc Neurosci; Am Soc Neurochem. *Res:* Stimulation; secretion coupling in neurons and neurosecretory cells and salivary gland cells. *Mailing Add:* Dean Col Health Sci Marquette Univ PO Box 53201-1881 Milwaukee WI 53233. *Fax:* 414-288-6843; *E-Mail:* brooksj@vms.csd.mu.edu

BROOKS, JAMES ELWOOD, GEOLOGY, APPLIED, ECONOMIC & ENGINEERING. *Current Pos:* From instr to assoc prof geol, Southern Methodist Univ, 52-62, chmn dept, 61-70, prof geol, 62-95, assoc provost & dean humanities & sci, 69-72, provost & vpres ac affairs, 72-80, pres ad interim, 80-81, pres, Inst Study Earth & Man, 81-97, EMER PROF GEOL & EMER PROVOST, SOUTHERN METHODIST UNIV, 95-, VCHMN, 97- *Personal Data:* b Salem, Ind, May 31, 25; m 49, Eleanore Nystrom; c Nancy, Kathryn & Carolyn. *Educ:* DePauw Univ, AB, 48; Northwestern Univ, MS, 50; Univ Wash, PhD(geol), 54. *Concurrent Pos:* Consult geologist, Gulf Oil Corp, 52-54, DeGolyer & MacNaughton Inc, 54-59 & Egyptian Geol Surv, 67-76. *Mem:* Fel AAAS; Am Asn Petrol Geologists; fel Geol Soc Am. *Res:* Devonian and mid-Paleozoic stratigraphy of Eastern Great Basin and Pennsylvanian sedimentary petrology of north central and west Texas; origin of Qattara Depression, Egypt; regional geology North Yemen, stratigraphy and geomorphology; history of geologic concepts; groundwater in the valley of the Nile River, Egypt in relation to the deterioration of the monuments at Giza and Abydos. *Mailing Add:* 7055 Arboreal Dr Dallas TX 75231-7315. *Fax:* 214-768-4289

BROOKS, JAMES KEITH, MATHEMATICS. *Current Pos:* from asst prof to assoc prof, 67-74, PROF MATH, UNIV FLA, 74- *Personal Data:* b Cleveland, Ohio, Sept 26, 38; m 61; c 2. *Educ:* John Carroll Univ, BS, 59, MS, 61; Ohio State Univ, PhD(math), 64. *Prof Exp:* Asst prof math, Ohio State Univ, 64-66; vis lectr, Univ Southampton, 66-67. *Mem:* Am Math Soc; Math Asn Am. *Res:* Functional analysis, measure and integration theory; probability theory. *Mailing Add:* Dept Math Univ Fla 201 Walker Hall Gainesville FL 32611-2082

BROOKS, JAMES LEE, BIOCHEMISTRY. *Current Pos:* asst prof, 67-74, asst agr biochemist, 69-74, ASSOC PROF AGR BIOCHEM & ASSOC AGR BIOCHEMIST, WVA UNIV, 74- *Personal Data:* b Toledo, Ohio, Sept 11, 37; m 62; c 3. *Educ:* San Diego State Col, BS, 59, MS, 61; Univ Calif, Davis, PhD(biochem), 65. *Prof Exp:* Res assoc biochem, Univ Calif, Davis, 65, Scripps Inst, Univ Calif, 65-66 & Okla State Univ, 66-67. *Mem:* AAAS. *Res:* Enzymes in fruit ripening; control of carbohydrate metabolism; fatty acid biosynthesis; sulfur metabolism in algae and bacteria; bacterial lipids; lignification in plants. *Mailing Add:* Plant Sci WVa Univ Box 6108 Morgantown WV 26506-0001

BROOKS, JAMES MARK, ENVIRONMENTAL CHEMISTRY, GEOCHEMISTRY. *Current Pos:* Res assoc, 73-76, RES SCIENTIST OCEANOG, TEX A&M UNIV, 76- *Personal Data:* b Kansas City, Mo, Dec 29, 47; m 75; c 4. *Educ:* Abilene Christian Univ, BS, 69; Tex A&M Univ, MS, 70, PhD(oceanog), 75. *Mem:* Am Soc Limnol & Oceanog; Am Geophys Union; AAAS; Am Chem Soc; Sigma Xi. *Res:* Dissolved gas geochemistry; geochemical prospecting; stable isotope geochemistry. *Mailing Add:* Col Geosci Tex A&M Univ 833 Graham Rd College Station TX 77845-9668

BROOKS, JAMES O, ALGEBRA. *Current Pos:* asst prof, 64-66, actg chmn dept, 68-69, chmn dept, 69-77, ASSOC PROF MATH, VILLANOVA UNIV, 66- *Personal Data:* b Evanston, Ill, July 7, 30; m 58; c 2. *Educ:* Oberlin Col, AB, 52; Univ Mich, MA, 53, PhD(math), 64. *Prof Exp:* Asst prof math, Haverford Col, 59-64. *Mem:* Am Math Soc; Math Asn Am. *Res:* Algebraic number theory. *Mailing Add:* 441 S Valley Forge Rd Wayne PA 19087

BROOKS, JAMES REED, FOOD PROTEIN FUNCTIONALITY & CHARACTERIZATION, PROTEIN ALLERGENICITY. *Current Pos:* proj leader, Abbott Labs, 87-88, sr proj leader, 88-89, res scientist, 89-90, group leader, 90-92, SR GROUP LEADER PEDIAT RES & DEVELOP, ROSS PROD DIV, ABBOTT LABS, 92- *Personal Data:* b Steubenville, Ohio, July 16, 55; m 85, Lynn Hernoon; c James R & Elizabeth K. *Educ:* Ohio State Univ, BS, 77; Clemson Univ, MS, 81, PhD(plant physiol), 84. *Prof Exp:* Asst prof food sci, Univ Ark, 84-87. *Concurrent Pos:* Secy & treas, Biotechnol Div, Inst Food Technologists, 89-90; vis fac, Ohio State Univ, 93-94. *Mem:* Inst Food Technologists; Sigma Xi. *Res:* Plant protein fractionation and characterization; food protein functionality; food allergens; starch hydrolysis and utilization; processing effects on food product stability. *Mailing Add:* 2193 Heatherfield Ave Columbus OH 43235. *Fax:* 614-624-3823

BROOKS, JERRY R, REPRODUCTIVE ENDOCRINOLOGY. *Current Pos:* RETIRED. *Personal Data:* b Barboursville, WVa, Sept 9, 30. *Educ:* WVa Univ, BS, 53, MS, 58; Univ Mo, PhD(animal husb), 61. *Prof Exp:* Asst dairy husb, Univ Mo, 61-63; Ford Found res fel reproductive physiol, Worcester Found Exp Biol, Mass, 63-65; sr endocrinologist, Merck & Co, Inc, 66-72, res fel, 72-81, sr res fel, 81-85, sr investr, 85-90. *Concurrent Pos:* Coadjutant staff, Rutgers Univ, 77. *Mem:* Sigma Xi. *Res:* Causes of and therapy for benign prostatic hyperplasia; anti-acne agents. *Mailing Add:* 111 Knollwood Dr Watchung NJ 07060-6245

BROOKS, JOHN A(LBERT), CHEMICAL ENGINEERING. *Current Pos:* RETIRED. *Personal Data:* b Denver, Colo, Nov 30, 16; m 47; c 1. *Educ:* Ill Inst Technol, BS, 46. *Prof Exp:* Chem engr, res dept, Standard Oil Co, Ind, 46-51, asst proj chem engr, 51-53, group leader, 53-60, process coordr, Am Oil Co Div, 60-65, supt tech serv, Am Oil Co, 65-68, mgr planning, scheduling & tech serv, 68-72; mgr eng & tech, Amoco Oil Co, Texas City, 72-74; dir process & synthetic fuels, Amoco Res Ctr, Amoco Oil Co, 76-78, dir contracts & admin, 78-81. *Concurrent Pos:* Stockbroker, 82-87. *Mem:* Am Chem Soc; Am Inst Chem Engrs. *Res:* Petroleum. *Mailing Add:* 227 Sea Anchor Dr Osprey FL 34229

BROOKS, JOHN BILL, BIOCHEMISTRY, MICROBIOLOGY. *Current Pos:* biochemist, 63-69, RES CHEMIST, CTR DIS CONTROL, 69- *Personal Data:* b Hyatt, Tenn, Aug 9, 29; m 51; c 2. *Educ:* Western Carolina Univ, BS, 62; Va Polytech Inst, PhD(biochem, microbiol), 69. *Honors & Awards:* Kimble Metholology Res Award, 78. *Prof Exp:* Chemist, Tenn Copper Co, 59; biol aide, Ctr Dis Control, 61-62; chemist, NIH, 62-63. *Mem:* Am Soc Microbiol; Sigma Xi. *Res:* Develop methods for rapid identification of microorganisms by analysis of their metabolites or cellular constituents both in vivo and in vitro by advanced chemical procedures such as gas chromatography and spectrophotometry; author or coauthor of sixty-six publications in this area. *Mailing Add:* Bldg 5 Rm 308 Ctrs Dis Control 1600 Clifton Rd Atlanta GA 30333

BROOKS, JOHN GRAHAM, PEDIATRICS, PEDIATRIC PULMONOLOGY. *Current Pos:* PROF & CHMN, DEPT PEDIAT, DARTMOUTH MED SCH, 94- *Personal Data:* b Cambridge, Mass, Oct 19, 42; m 72, Christina L Brown; c John G IV & Ashley H. *Educ:* Harvard Univ, BA, 64, MD, 69. *Prof Exp:* Asst prof pediat, Univ Colo, 75-79; dir, Pediat Intensive Care Unit, Univ Rochester, 79-87, from assoc prof to prof pediat, 79-94, dir pediat pulmonology, 79-94. *Concurrent Pos:* Chair, numerous comts pediat & pulmonology, 81-; vis res prof, Univ Bristol, Eng, 89-90; adj prof, Respiratory Care Prog, State Univ NY Health Sci Ctr, Syracuse, 90-94. *Mem:* Am Acad Pediat; Soc Pediat Epidemiol Res; Soc Pediat Res; Am Thoracic Soc; Am Bd Pediat. *Res:* Epidemiology of the sudden infant death syndrome, particularly diagnosis and prediction; postnatal growth of sudden infant death syndrome victims; association of sudden infant death syndrome and prone sleeping. *Mailing Add:* Dept Pediat Dartmouth-Hitchcock Med Ctr One Medical Center Dr Lebanon NH 03756

BROOKS, JOHN J, HEMATOPATHOLOGY & IMMUNOPATHOLOGY, SOFT TISSUE PATHOLOGY. *Current Pos:* from asst prof to assoc prof, 79-88, PROF PATH, UNIV PA MED SCH, 88- *Personal Data:* b Philadelphia, Pa, Feb 2, 48; m 69; c 3. *Educ:* St Josephs Univ, BS, 70; Thomas Jefferson Med Sch, MD, 74. *Prof Exp:* Resident path, Hosp Univ Pa, 74-78; asst prof, Hahnemann Med Col & Hosp, 78-79. *Concurrent Pos:* Staff pathologist, Hosp Univ Pa, 79-88; vis prof, Royal Marsden Hosp, London, 87-88. *Mem:* Am Asn Pathologists; AAAS; Int Acad Path; NY Acad Sci; Soc Hemotopath. *Res:* Using immunohistochemistry, tumor markers are studied as they apply to the diagnosis of various types of cancer and to our understanding of the growth and differentiation of cancer cells, particularly sarcomas. *Mailing Add:* Roswell Park Cancer Inst 666 Elm St Buffalo NY 14263

BROOKS, JOHN LANGDON, ECOLOGY, SYSTEMATICS. *Current Pos:* RETIRED. *Personal Data:* b New Haven, Conn, Feb 10, 20; m 53, Yvette D Gittleson; c Anne. *Educ:* Yale Univ, BS, 41, MS, 42, PhD(zool), 46. *Prof Exp:* Lab asst, Yale Univ, 42-45, asst instr, 45-46, from instr to asst prof zool, 46-56, assoc prof biol, 56-69; prog dir gen ecol, NSF, 69-75, sect head ecol & pop biol, 75, dep div dir environ biol, 75-81, dir div biotic systs & resources, 81-89; consult, Capitol Syst Group, 90. *Concurrent Pos:* Vis prof, Univ Rangoon, 48-49; ed, Syst Zool, 52-59. *Mem:* Ecol Soc Am; Am Soc Limnol & Oceanog; Soc Study Evolution. *Res:* Ecology and evolution of fresh water organisms; history of evolutionary concepts especially contributions of A R Wallace. *Mailing Add:* 3014 32nd St NW Washington DC 20008

BROOKS, JOHN ROBINSON, SURGERY. *Current Pos:* Prof surg, 70-81, CHIEF SURG, HARVARD UNIV HEALTH SERV, 62-, FRANK SAWYER PROF SURG, HARVARD MED SCH, 81- *Personal Data:* b Cambridge, Mass, Nov 15, 18; m 44; c 4. *Educ:* Harvard Univ, AB, 40, MD, 43. *Mem:* Am Col Surg; Soc Univ Surg; Am Surg Asn; Int Soc Surg; Soc Surg Alimentary Tract. *Res:* Gastrointestinal surgery; transplantation; endocrine organs. *Mailing Add:* Harvard Univ Health Serv 75 Mt Auburn St Cambridge MA 02138-4901

BROOKS, JOHN S J, SURGICAL PATHOLOGY, IMMUNOHISTOCHEMISTRY. *Current Pos:* PROF & CHMN, DEPT PATH, ROSWELL PARK CANCER INST, BUFFALO, 93-; PROF & VCHMN, DEPT PATH & LAB MED, STATE UNIV NY-BUFFALO, 93-, RES PROF EXP PATH, ROSWELL PARK GRAD DIV, 94- *Personal Data:* b Philadelphia, Pa, Feb 2, 48; m 69, Brighid Dougherty; c Brighid, Patrick & Michael. *Educ:* St Joseph's Univ, Philadelphia, BS, 70; Thomas Jefferson Med Sch, MD, 74; FRCPath, 97. *Prof Exp:* Asst prof path, Hahnemann Med Col & Hosp, 78-79; from asst prof to prof, Dept Path & Lab Med, Univ Pa, Sch Med, 79-93. *Concurrent Pos:* Nat Cancer Inst fel, 76-77, clin fel, 77-78, jr fac clin fel, 82-85; Vis prof, Royal Marsden Hosp & Inst Cancer Res, London, 87; assoc dir surg path, Hosp Univ Pa, Philadelphia, 88-; chmn sarcoma path, Eastern Coop Oncol Group, 88-93; mem, Educ Comt, US-Can Div, Int Acad Path, 89-91, co-dir, Long Course Soft Tissue Path, 95; prog dir, Arthur Purdy Stout Soc Surg Pathologists, 91-92; counr, Am Soc Clin Path, 91-, chairperson, 95-97; ed-in-chief, Int J Surg Path, 92- *Mem:* Int Acad Path; AAAS; NY Acad Sci; Soc Hematopath; Am Soc Clin Pathologists; US Can Acad Path. *Res:* Growth and differentiation of tumors of the soft tissues and hematopoietic system; monoclonal antibodies and immunohistochemistry to identify cell types in human tumors; mesenchymal cell research with in-situ hybridization. *Mailing Add:* Dept Path Roswell Park Cancer Inst Elm & Carlton Sts Buffalo NY 14263. *Fax:* 716-845-3427; *E-Mail:* brooks@sc3101.med.buffalo.edu

BROOKS, KENNETH CONRAD, GAS CHROMATOGRAPHY, LIQUID CHROMATOGRAPHY. *Current Pos:* LECTR, CHEM DEPT, UNIV ILL, URBANA-CHAMPAIGN, 86- *Personal Data:* b Chicago Heights, Ill, Apr 5, 47. *Educ:* Ill Inst Technol, BS, 69; Univ Colo, Boulder, MS, 73, PhD(analytical chem), 81. *Concurrent Pos:* Instr chem, Univ Colo, Colorado Springs, 74-79; asst prof, Univ Colo, Denver, 81-85. *Mem:* Am Chem Soc. *Res:* Analytical methods development for petrochemicals; chromatography; gel chromatography, high performance liquid chromatography, gas chromatography and mass spectrometry; high temperature super conductors; metal B-diketonates; chemical vapor deposition. *Mailing Add:* Chem Dept NM State Univ Box 30001 Dept 3C Las Cruces NM 88003

BROOKS, LISA DELEVAN, POPULATION GENETICS, GENE MAPPING. *Current Pos:* ASST PROF BIOL, BROWN UNIV, 87- *Personal Data:* b Carmel, Calif, June 21, 57. *Educ:* Stanford Univ, BS, 78; Harvard Univ, PhD(biol), 85. *Prof Exp:* Res assoc, NC State Univ, 85-87. *Mem:* AAAS; Sigma Xi; Genetics Soc Am; Am Soc Human Genetics; Soc Study Evolution; Biometrics Soc. *Res:* Methods to improve gene mapping data analysis; genetic variation for recombination in Drosephila; models of natural selection. *Mailing Add:* 127 Irving Ave Apt 5 Providence RI 02906. *Fax:* 401-863-2166; *E-Mail:* lisa_brooks@brown.edu

BROOKS, MARVIN ALAN, PHARMACEUTICAL ANALYSIS. *Current Pos:* sr res fel, 85-89, DIR PHARMACEUT ANALYSIS, MERCK, SHARP & DOHME RES LABS, 89- *Personal Data:* b Trenton, NJ, Jan 28, 45; m 68, Susan G Pristoop; c Paul & Cheryl. *Educ:* Lafayette Col, BS, 66; Univ Md, PhD(analytical chem), 71. *Prof Exp:* Res group chief drug analyst, Hoffmann-La Roche Inc, 71-85. *Mem:* Am Chem Soc; Sigma Xi; fel Am Asn Pharmaceut Sci. *Res:* Analysis of drugs in dosage forms and biological fluids using chromatographic, spectrophotometric, spectrofluorometric and electrochemical methods; use of voltammetry to solve pharmaceutical problems. *Mailing Add:* Merck & Co Inc Merck Res Labs WP 78-210 West Point PA 19486

BROOKS, MICHAEL LEE, NEURORADIOLOGY, DIAGNOSTIC RADIOLOGY. *Current Pos:* SR NEURORADIOLOGIST, GRAD HOSP, PHILADELPHIA, 88-; ASSOC DIR, HOSP GRAD IMAGING CTR, ALLEGHENY UNIV. *Personal Data:* b Philadelphia, Pa, Dec 3, 55. *Educ:* Univ Pa, BA, 73; Hahnemann Univ Med Sch, MD, 81. *Prof Exp:* Fel neuroradiol, Brigham & Women's Hosp, Harvard Med Sch, 85-87, instr radiol, 87-88. *Concurrent Pos:* Consult neuroradiol, Dana Farber Cancer Ctr, 87-88, Off Med Examr, Philadelphia, 91-, Int Inst Forensic Sci, 92-; clin asst prof dent med, Univ Pa Sch Dent Med, 89-; clin asst prof diag imaging, Sch Med, Temple Univ, 89-; clin asst prof med imaging, Thomas Jefferson Col Allied Health, 92- *Mem:* Sr mem Am Soc Neuroradiol; Radiol Soc NAm; Soc Magnetic Resonance Imaging; Int Soc Minimal Intervention Spine Surg; Soc Spine Imaging. *Res:* Clinical research in magnetic resonance imaging including imaging projectile injury to the head, imaging of battered child syndrome involving the brain, imaging (post-mortem) in sudden infant death syndrome and neuroimaging of brain tumors and AIDS. *Mailing Add:* 781 S Second St Philadelphia PA 19147. *Fax:* 215-790-0678

BROOKS, NORMAN H(ERRICK), HYDRAULICS & HYDROLOGY. *Current Pos:* From instr to prof civil eng, Calif Inst Technol, 53-76, acad officer environ eng sci, 69-74, dir, Environ Qual Lab, 74-93, James Irvine prof environ & civil eng, 76-95, exec officer environ eng sci, 85-93, EMER JAMES IRVINE PROF ENVIRON & CIVIL ENG, CALIF INST TECHNOL, 95- *Personal Data:* b Worcester, Mass, July 2, 28; m 48, Fredericka Nelson; c Diana, Alexender & Laura. *Educ:* Harvard Univ, AB,

49, MS, 50; Calif Inst Technol, PhD(civil eng, physics), 54. *Honors & Awards:* Rudolph Hering Medal, Am Soc Civil Engrs, 57, 62, Collingwood Prize, J C Stevens Award & Huber Res Prize, 59, Hilgard Hydraul Prize, 70, Hunter Rouse Hydraul Eng lectr, 86. *Concurrent Pos:* Hydraul consult govt agencies & elec utilities; vis assoc prof, Grad Sch Eng, Southeast Asia Treaty Orgn, 59-60; vis prof, Mass Inst Technol, 62-63; mem, Univs Coun Water Resources; mem assembly sci & technol adv coun, Calif State legis, 70-73; mem environ studies bd, Nat Acad Sci, 73-76; guest prof, Swiss Fed Inst Technol, 84-85; mem, Comn Eng & Tech Systs, Nat Acad Sci & Nat Acad Eng, 86-89; mem, Water Sci & Technol Bd, Nat Res Coun, Nat Acad Sci/Nat Acad Eng, 88-92, Comn Wastewater Mgt Coastal Urban Areas & chair, Panel Environ Processes, 90-93. *Mem:* Nat Acad Sci; Nat Acad Eng; fel AAAS; hon mem Am Soc Civil Engrs; Am Geophys Union; Water Pollution Control Fedn. *Res:* Hydraulic engineering; turbulence and diffusion; sediment and pollutant transport in streams; outfall engineering; dispersion of wastewater in coastal waters; density-stratified flow; environmental policy studies. *Mailing Add:* W M Keck Lab Hydraul Calif Inst Technol Pasadena CA 91125. *Fax:* 626-395-2940

BROOKS, PHILIP RUSSELL, DYNAMICS OF CHEMICAL REACTIONS. *Current Pos:* From asst prof to assoc prof, 64-75, PROF CHEM, RICE UNIV, 75- *Personal Data:* b Chicago, Ill, Dec 31, 38; m 96, JoAnne Richards; c Scott, Robin, Christopher & Steven. *Educ:* Calif Inst Technol, BS, 60; Univ Calif, Berkeley, PhD(chem), 64. *Honors & Awards:* Sr US Scientist Award, Alexander von Humboldt Found, 85. *Concurrent Pos:* Alfred P Sloan fel, 70-72; Guggenheim Found fel, 74-75; vis Erskine fel, Univ Canterbury, Christchurch, NZ, 91. *Mem:* Fel Am Phys Soc; Am Chem Soc; fel Japan Soc Prom Sci. *Res:* Molecular beam reactive scattering of oriented molecules; electron transfer processes. *Mailing Add:* Dept Chem Rice Univ 6100 Main St Houston TX 77055. *Fax:* 713-285-5155

BROOKS, RICHARD C, ELECTRICAL ENGINEERING, IMAGE PROCESSING. *Current Pos:* chief, Integrated Systs Lab, Nat Weather Serv, 89-96, DEP DIR, SYSTS ACQUISITIONS OFF, NAT OCEANOG & ATMOSPHERIC ADMIN, 96- *Personal Data:* b Philadelphia, Pa, Aug 31, 45. *Educ:* Univ Va, BEE, 67; Johns Hopkins Univ, MSE, 70; Univ Mo, Columbia, PhD(elec eng), 73; Va Polytech Inst & State Univ, MBA, 78. *Prof Exp:* Commissioned officer, USPHS, 68-70; mem tech staff, Analytic Servs Inc, 73-78; staff, Fed Govt, 78-89. *Mem:* Inst Elec & Electronics Engrs. *Mailing Add:* Nat Oceanog Atmospheric Admin 1315 East West Hwy SAO SSMCIII Silver Spring MD 20910-3282. *Fax:* 301-713-0086; *E-Mail:* richard.brooks@noaa.gov

BROOKS, ROBERT ALAN, ORGANIC CHEMISTRY. *Current Pos:* RETIRED. *Personal Data:* b Gloversville, NY, Feb 23, 24; m 51; c 1. *Educ:* Harvard Univ, BS, 44; Yale Univ, MS, 45, PhD(org chem), 49. *Prof Exp:* Instr chem, Yale Univ, 46-48; res chemist, Jackson Lab, E I Du Pont de Nemours & Co Inc, Deepwater, NJ, 48-54, res supvr, 54-57, head div dyes, 57-59, head fluorine chem, 59-61, asst lab dir, 61-62, lab mgr, 62-69, tech mgr, Dyes & Chem Div, Org Chem Dept, 69-70, dir, Dyes & Chem Res, 70-75, tech dir, Freon Prod Div, 75-80, lab dir, Petrochem Dept, Exp Sta, Wilmington, Del, 80-85. *Mem:* AAAS; Am Chem Soc; NY Acad Sci. *Res:* Synthetic and organic dyes; pigments and elastomers; chemistry of fluorine. *Mailing Add:* 32 Marlton Rd Woodstown NJ 08098

BROOKS, ROBERT FRANKLIN, ENTOMOLOGY, PHYOPATHOLOGY OF CITRUS. *Current Pos:* CONSULT, 88- *Personal Data:* b Columbus, Ohio, Mar 17, 28; m 59, Harrie Marie Huntington; c Lawrence B. *Educ:* Ohio State Univ, BS, 54, MS, 55; Univ Wis, PhD(entom), 60. *Prof Exp:* Asst entom, Ohio State Univ, 54-55; asst, Univ Wis, 56-59, instr, 59-60; asst entomologist, Citrus Exp Sta, Univ Fla, 60-67, assoc prof entom & assoc entomologist, Inst Food & Agr Sci, 67-70, prof, 70-87, emer prof entom & entomologist, Inst Food & Agr Sci, Univ Fla, 70-87. *Concurrent Pos:* Consult citrus, Stand Fruit Co Div, Castle & Cook, 66-, Sun Oil Refining Co, 87-, Cutrale Sucocitrus, Brazil, Sete Lagoas Citrus, Brazil & Alfinas Chem, Johannesburg, SAfrica. *Mem:* Entom Soc Am; Int Orgn Biol Control; Sigma Xi. *Res:* Integrated control and management of citrus pests; improving and developing more efficient application equipment for use on citrus. *Mailing Add:* 710 Hunt Dr Lake Wales FL 33853. *Fax:* 941-439-5438

BROOKS, ROBERT M, MATHEMATICS. *Current Pos:* assoc prof, 67-72, PROF MATH, UNIV UTAH, 72- *Personal Data:* b Freeport, Tex, Jan 5, 38; m 60. *Educ:* La State Univ, BS, 60, PhD(math), 63. *Prof Exp:* From instr to asst prof math, Univ Minn, 63-67. *Mem:* Am Math Soc. *Res:* Topological algebras; complex analysis. *Mailing Add:* Dept Math 1959 Longview Dr Salt Lake City UT 84112

BROOKS, ROBERT R, CARDIOVASCULAR DRUGS, ANTIINFLAMMATORY DRUGS. *Current Pos:* SR SCIENTIST, P&G PHARMACEUT, 93- *Personal Data:* b Jersey City, NJ, Nov 8, 44; m 68; c 4. *Educ:* Princeton Univ, AB, 66; Johns Hopkins Univ, PhD(biochem), 71. *Prof Exp:* Fel, NIH, 72; res assoc, Univ Fla, Gainesville, 71-73; res scientist IV, res admin, Norwich Eaton Pharmaceut Inc, 73-78, scientist V, 78-83, sci assoc, 83, group leader, 83-84, sect head res admin, 84-93. *Concurrent Pos:* Instr, State Univ NY, Morrisville, 75, Binghamton, 77-80; consult, I L Richer Co, Inc, New Berlin, NY, 81-83; mem basic sci coun, Am Heart Asn. *Mem:* Am Soc Pharmacol & Exp Therapeut; Soc Exp Biol Med; Am Chem Soc. *Res:* General and cardiovascular pharmacology, in vitro models, in vivo models in small and large animals arrhythmias, hypertension, gastric secretion, inflammation, development of drug testing systems. *Mailing Add:* P&G Pharmaceut PO Box 191 Norwich NY 13815-0191

BROOKS, ROBERT W, MATHEMATICS. *Current Pos:* vis assoc prof, 84-85, assoc prof, 85-88, PROF, DEPT MATH, UNIV SOUTHERN CALIF, 88- *Personal Data:* b Washington, DC, Sept 16, 52. *Educ:* Harvard Univ, BA & MA, 74, PhD, 77. *Prof Exp:* Instr, State Univ NY, Stony Brook, 77-79; asst prof, Univ Md, 79-84. *Concurrent Pos:* Vis mem, Courant Inst Math Sci, NY Univ, 83-84; Alfred P Sloan fel, 84; vis prof, Univ Calif, Los Angeles, 89-90, 91; assoc ed, J Geometric Anal; distinguished vis prof, Bucknell Univ, 93; Fulbright sr scholar, Israel, 93-94. *Mailing Add:* Math Dept DRB-155 Univ Southern Calif University Park Campus Los Angeles CA 90089-1113

BROOKS, RONALD JAMES, EVOLUTION, LIFE HISTORY THEORY. *Current Pos:* From asst prof to assoc prof, 69-88, PROF ZOOL, UNIV GUELPH, 88- *Personal Data:* b Toronto, Ont, Apr 16, 41; m 84, Gladys Stephenson; c Jennifer L, Hilary A & Payton W. *Educ:* Univ Toronto, BSc, 63, MSc, 66; Univ Ill, PhD(zool), 70. *Concurrent Pos:* Dir, Algonquin Wildlife Res Sta, 84- *Mem:* Am Soc Mammalogists; Animal Behav Soc; Soc Study Amphibians & Reptiles; Sigma Xi; Am Soc Naturalists; Am Soc Ichthyol & Herpetol. *Res:* Population changes in rodents; life history, evolution and population biology of turtles, Chrysemys sp, Chelydra sp, Clemmys sp, and frogs, snakes and salamanders; conservation biology and evolution. *Mailing Add:* Dept Zool Univ Guelph Guelph ON N1G 2W1 Can. *Fax:* 519-767-1656; *E-Mail:* rjbrooks@uoguelph.ca

BROOKS, SAM RAYMOND, MATHEMATICS. *Current Pos:* ASST PROF MATH, MEMPHIS STATE UNIV, 66- *Personal Data:* b Austin, Tex, Apr 1, 40. *Educ:* Univ Tex, BA, 62, MA, 64, PhD(math), 69. *Mem:* Math Asn Am; Am Math Soc. *Res:* Group theory; semigroup theory and generalizations. *Mailing Add:* Dept Math Memphis Univ 3706 Alumni St Memphis TN 38152-0001

BROOKS, SAMUEL CARROLL, BIOCHEMISTRY, ENDOCRINOLOGY. *Current Pos:* from instr to assoc prof, 59-74, PROF BIOCHEM, SCH MED, WAYNE STATE UNIV, 74- *Personal Data:* b Winchester, Va, May 12, 28; m 61; c 3. *Educ:* Carnegie Inst Technol, BS, 51; Univ Wis-Madison, MS, 55, PhD(biochem), 57. *Prof Exp:* Res scientist, John L Smith Mem Lab Cancer Res, Charles Pfizer & Co, Inc, 57-59. *Concurrent Pos:* Res assoc, Detroit Inst Cancer Res, 59-70; Fulbright res scholar, Univ Louvain, 64-65; dir, Dept Chem, Mich Cancer Found, 70-74. *Mem:* Am Chem Soc; Soc Study Reprod; Endocrine Soc; Am Asn Cancer Res; Am Soc Biol Chem. *Res:* Steroid hormone activity and metabolism. *Mailing Add:* Dept Biochem Wayne State Univ Sch Med 540 Canfield Detroit MI 48201-1908

BROOKS, SHARON LYNN, DENTISTRY. *Current Pos:* clin instr oral diag & radiol, 73-76, asst res scientist herpes virus, Dent Res Inst, 76-77, asst prof oral diag & radiol, 76-80, ASSOC PROF ORAL DIAG & RADIOL, SCH DENT, UNIV MICH, 80- *Personal Data:* b Detroit, Mich, Oct 19, 44; m 65. *Educ:* Univ Mich, ABEd, 65, DDS, 73, MS, 76, MS, 84. *Prof Exp:* Pvt pract dent, 73-76. *Mem:* Am Dent Asn; Am Acad Dent Radiol; Am Asn Dent Schools; Orgn Teachers Oral Diag (secy-treas, 85-); Int Asn Dent Res; Health Physics Soc. *Res:* Herpes simplex virus; infective endocarditis; selection criteria for dental radiographs. *Mailing Add:* Dept Oral Path & Surg Univ Mich Sch Dent 1011 N University St Ann Arbor MI 48109-1078

BROOKS, SHEILAGH THOMPSON, PHYSICAL ANTHROPOLOGY. *Current Pos:* from assoc prof to prof anthrop, 66-92, chmn dept, 73-77, EMER PROF ANTHROP, UNIV NEV, LAS VEGAS, 92- *Personal Data:* b Tampico, Mex, Dec 10, 23; US citizen; m 51; c 2. *Educ:* Univ Calif, Berkeley, BA, 44, MA, 47, PhD(phys anthrop), 51. *Honors & Awards:* T Dale Stewart Award, Am Acad Forensic Sci, 93. *Prof Exp:* Assoc trop biogeog, Chihuahua & Durango, Mex, 55-58; res assoc physiol, Univ Calif, Berkeley, 58-62; lectr anthrop, Univ Southern Calif, 59-61; lectr, Pasadena City Col, 60-62; asst prof, Univ Colo, Denver & Boulder, 63-65; res asst, Mus, Southern Ill Univ, 65; asst prof, Univ Colo, Boulder, 65-66. *Concurrent Pos:* NSF fel arch & phys anthrop, Sarawak, Malaysia, 66; consult, Clark County Sheriff's Dept, 67-; mem coord coun, Nev Archaeol Surv, 68-77; grants, Dept Health, Educ & Welfare, mus progs, Univ Nev, Las Vegas, 69-71, fac res comt, Photog Lab, 70 & Nat Endowment Humanities, Preserv Hist Sites, 72-73; mem bd, Gov Comn Nev Lost City Mus, 71-76; consult, Nev Archaeol Surv, 73-77 & Archaeol Res Ctr, 77-; mem bd trustees, Nev State Mus, 77-81; mem adv bd, Div Hist Preserv & Archaeol, Nev. *Mem:* Palaeopath Asn; Europ Anthrop Asn; Soc Vert Paleont; Am Acad Forensic Sci; Am Asn Phys Anthrop; Sigma Xi. *Res:* Archaeologically recovered skeletal populations with emphasis on demography, paleopathology and morphological differences; analysis and identification of historical burials, forensic physical anthropology; skeletal identification of age at death, sex, evidence of pathologies that occurred anti or peri-mortem. *Mailing Add:* Dept Anthrop Univ Nev 4505 Maryland Pkwy Las Vegas NV 89154

BROOKS, STUART MERRILL, PULMONARY DISEASE, OCCUPATIONAL MEDICINE. *Current Pos:* PROF & CHMN, DEPT ENVIRON & OCCUP HEALTH, UNIV SFLA, 86- *Personal Data:* b Cincinnati, Ohio, Apr 28, 36; c 3. *Educ:* Univ Cincinnati, BS, 58, MD, 62; Am Bd Internal Med & Am Bd Pulmonary Dis, dipl, 69. *Prof Exp:* Resident internal med, Boston City Hosp, 63-64, 66-67, fel pulmonary dis, 67-69; res fel med, Sch Med, Tufts Univ, 68-69; from asst prof med to asst prof environ health, Col Med, Univ Cincinnati, 69-73, prof environ health & med & chief, Div Clin Studies, 73-86. *Concurrent Pos:* Mem ad hoc comt case control studies on host factors as determinants of chronic obstructive pulmonary dis susceptibility, Nat Heart & Lung Inst, 70; attend physician, Cincinnati Gen Hosp & Vet Admin Hosp, Cincinnati, 73- *Mem:* Am Fedn Clin Res; Am Thoracic Soc; fel Am Col Physicians; fel Am Col Chest Physicians. *Res:*

Pulmonary physiology; occupational lung diseases; pathogenetic mechanisms of bronchial asthma, non-respiratory functions of lung; corticosteroid metabolism. *Mailing Add:* Col Pub Health Univ SFla 13201 Bruce B Downs Tampa FL 33612-3805

BROOKS, THOMAS, AGRICULTURE & FOOD CHEMISTRY, ORGANIC & POLYMER CHEMISTRY. *Current Pos:* ASST COMNR AGR LAB SERV, SC DEPT AGR, 90- *Personal Data:* b Wyandotte, Mich, 1933. *Educ:* The Citadel, BS, 56; Univ Fla, MS, 59, PhD(chem), 61. *Honors & Awards:* I R-100 Award, 77. *Prof Exp:* Chem Officer, US Army, 62-63; assoc res fel, Pulp Chem, 63-64; chem researcher, Merck & Co, 64-73; chem tech dir, Albany Int Corp, 73-90. *Concurrent Pos:* NATO lectr, 78. *Mem:* Am Chem Soc; fel Am Inst Chemists. *Mailing Add:* 308 Lost Creek Dr Columbia SC 29212-2487

BROOKS, THOMAS FURMAN, AEROACOUSTICS. *Current Pos:* aerospace technologist acoust, 74-81, AEROSPACE RESEARCHER, LANGLEY RES CTR, NASA, 81-, SR RES SCIENTIST. *Personal Data:* b Charlotte, NC, Oct 4, 43; m 70; c 2. *Educ:* NC State Univ, BS, 68, PhD(acoust & mech eng), 74. *Prof Exp:* Tool engr, Turbine Div, Westinghouse Elec Corp, 70. *Mem:* Acoust Soc Am; Am Inst Aeronaut & Astronaut; Am Helicopter Soc. *Res:* Basic and applied aeroacoustics; rotor, propeller and airframe noise sources; linear acoustics, aerodynamics and turbulence. *Mailing Add:* Mail Stop 461 NASA Langley Res Ctr Hampton VA 23665

BROOKS, THOMAS JOSEPH, JR, PREVENTIVE MEDICINE. *Current Pos:* asst dean in-charge student affairs, 56-73, prof & chmn dept, 52-81, EMER PROF PREV MED, SCH MED, UNIV MISS, 81- *Personal Data:* b Starkville, Miss, May 23, 16; m 41; c 4. *Educ:* Univ Fla, BS, 37; Univ Tenn, MS, 39; Univ NC, PhD(prev med), 42; Bowman Gray Sch Med, MD, 45; Am Bd Microbiol, dipl. *Prof Exp:* Instr bact & parasitol, Bowman Gray Sch Med, 42-45; intern, Bowman Gray Sch Med & NC Baptist Hosp, 45-46; assoc prof pharmacol, Sch Med, Univ Miss, 47-48; med dir, Fla State Univ Hosp, 48-52; Rockefeller Found travel grant, 52. *Concurrent Pos:* Officer-in-charge res unit, US Naval Training Ctr, Md, 53-55; consult, Vet Admin Hosp, Jackson, Miss, 56-81, UN, India, 66 & epidemiol, Miss State Dept Health, 81-; La State Univ Caribbean travel fel, 56 & 60; vis prof, Sch Med, Univ Costa Rica, 62-63, Keio Univ, Japan, 68 & Kyoto Univ, 68-69; NIH trainee, Univ Wis, 65; Alan Gregg fel, Japan & Southeast Asia, 68-69. *Mem:* Am Pub Health Asn; fel Royal Soc Health Eng; Asn Teachers Prev Med; Sigma Xi. *Res:* Treatment of filariasis; toxicology of antimony; treatment of canine filariasis with anthiomaline; tuberculosis in university students; epidemiology of streptococcal diseases; mitosis of Entamoeba histolytica; epidemiology of Echinococcus granulosus; biochemistry of schistosomes. *Mailing Add:* 750 Lenox Dr Jackson MS 39211-4105

BROOKS, VERNON BERNARD, NEUROSCIENCES. *Current Pos:* chmn dept, 71-76, prof, 71-89, EMER PROF PHYSIOL, UNIV WESTERN ONT, 89- *Personal Data:* b Berlin, Ger, May 10, 23; nat Can; m 50, Nancy Fraser; c 3. *Educ:* Univ Toronto, BA, 46, PhD(physiol), 52; Univ Chicago, ScM, 48. *Prof Exp:* Lectr physiol, McGill Univ, 50-52, asst prof, 52-56; from asst prof to assoc prof neurophysiol, Rockefeller Univ, 56-64; prof physiol, NY Med Col, 64-71, chmn dept, 64-69. *Concurrent Pos:* Vis fel, Australian Nat Univ, 54-55; fel, Neural Sci Inst, Rockefeller Univ, NY, 85. *Mem:* Am Physiol Soc; Can Physiol Soc; Soc Neurosci. *Res:* Interaction of neurones; sensorimotor integration; motor control and learning by animals and human subjects. *Mailing Add:* Dept Physiol Univ Western Ont London ON N6A 5C1 Can. *Fax:* 519-661-3827; *E-Mail:* vernon.brooks@uwc.ca

BROOKS, WALTER LYDA, physics, astronomy, for more information see previous edition

BROOKS, WAYNE MAURICE, INSECT PATHOLOGY, PROTOZOOLOGY. *Current Pos:* from asst prof to assoc prof, 66-78, PROF ENTOM, NC STATE UNIV, 78- *Personal Data:* b Lynchburg, Va, Mar 11, 39; m 85, Julia Winfree; c Brian & Greg. *Educ:* NC State Univ, BS, 61; Univ Calif, PhD(entom), 66. *Prof Exp:* Res asst entom, Univ Calif, 61-63, jr specialist, 63-66. *Concurrent Pos:* Pres, Soc Invert Path, 82-84. *Mem:* Entom Soc Am; Soc Invert Path; Sigma Xi; Soc Protozoologists; Int Orgn Biol Control. *Res:* Insect pathology with emphasis on entomophilic protozoa. *Mailing Add:* Dept Entom Box 7613 NC State Univ Raleigh NC 27695-7613

BROOKS, WENDELL V F, PHYSICAL CHEMISTRY, MOLECULAR SPECTROSCOPY. *Current Pos:* RETIRED. *Personal Data:* b Rockford Ill, Mar 7, 25; m 50, Jeanne Michelson; c Helen & Margaret. *Educ:* Swarthmore Col, BA, 48; Univ Minn, PhD, 54. *Prof Exp:* Instr chem, Univ Ariz, 52-54; NSF fel, Yale Univ, 54-55; from asst prof to prof chem, Ohio Univ, 55-67; prof chem, Univ NB, 67-89. *Concurrent Pos:* Hon res assoc chem, Harvard, 73-74; vis prof physics, Duke Univ, 80-81. *Mem:* Am Chem Soc. *Res:* Infrared and microwave spectroscopy. *Mailing Add:* 218 Colonial Heights Fredericton NB E3B 5M1 Can

BROOKS, WILLIAM HAMILTON, RESOURCE MANAGEMENT, WATERSHED PLANNING. *Current Pos:* state watershed planner, 84-90, AREA COORDR, RESOURCE CONSERV & DEVELOP, NAT RESOURCES CONSERV SERV, USDA, 90- *Personal Data:* b Wilkinsburg, Pa, Nov 9, 32; m 69; c 2. *Educ:* Pa State Univ, BS, 55; NDak State Univ, MS, 64. *Prof Exp:* Asst prof plant sci, Gonzaga Univ, 65-69; develop consult, US Dept Educ, 69-70; prog dir, Natural Resources Mgt, Pima Col, 70-74; proj leader, Ministry Agr/Water Kingdom Saudi Arabia, 74-76; dir regional develop, Off Arid Land Studies, Univ Ariz, 76-82; dir exploratory technol, Agribus Res Corp, 82-83. *Concurrent Pos:* Prin investr, Off Arid Lands Studies, Univ Ariz, 79-82; consult, Stanford Res Inst, 80-81, Elec Power Res Inst, 80-81, Riyadh Univ, 81-82, Int Union Conserv Nat Resources, Switz, 82-83, Sultanate of Oman, 83-84; regional expert, UN Econ Comn Western Asia, 81-82; consult prod, Desert Realm publ, Nat Geog Soc, 82; mem, bd dirs, Int Tree Crop Inst; fel Grad Study, NSF. *Mem:* Asn Arid Land Studies (pres, 82-83); Sigma Xi; Soc Am Foresters; fel Linnaean Soc London; fel Royal Geog Soc. *Res:* Implementation and coordination of regional and international programs in new crop assessment for arid and semiarid lands, environmental assessments and impact analysis, revegetation, afforestation, quantitative plant surveys, resources management, and salinity problems; rural economic development. *Mailing Add:* PO Box 4736 San Luis Obispo CA 93403-4736. *Fax:* 805-772-4398

BROOKSHEAR, JAMES GLENN, MATHEMATICS. *Current Pos:* ASST PROF MATH, MARQUETTE UNIV, 75- *Personal Data:* b Denton, Tex, Nov 27, 44; m 68; c 1. *Educ:* NTex State Univ, BS, 67; NMex State Univ, MS, 68, PhD(math), 75. *Mem:* Am Math Soc; Math Asn Am; Asn Comput Mach. *Res:* Rings of continuous functions and related areas. *Mailing Add:* Dept Math & Statist Marquette Univ PO Box 1881 Milwaukee WI 53201-1881

BROOKS SPRINGS, SUZANNE BETH, BIOCHEMISTRY, IMMUNOLOGY. *Current Pos:* RETIRED. *Personal Data:* b Ocala, Fla, Aug 6, 35. *Educ:* Wheaton Col, Ill, BS, 57; Univ Ill, Urbana, PhD(biochem), 62. *Prof Exp:* Res assoc biochem, Sch Med, Vanderbilt Univ, 62-63; res assoc, Sch Med, Boston Univ, 63-64, instr, 64; res assoc, Am Cancer Ctr, Denver, 70-75; res assoc, Webb-Waring Inst, Med Sch, Univ Colo, 75-80; res scientist, Fitzsimmons Army Med Ctr, 80-83. *Concurrent Pos:* Fel, Nat Cancer Inst, 62-64 & Damon Runyon Found, 64-65. *Res:* Biochemical processes involved in mechanisms of cellular immunology, especially with respect to macrophage vs tumor interactions. *Mailing Add:* 2265 Ivy St Denver CO 80207

BROOM, ARTHUR DAVIS, BIO-ORGANIC CHEMISTRY, MEDICINAL CHEMISTRY. *Current Pos:* res assoc, Utah Univ, 66-67, asst res prof, 67-69, from asst prof to assoc prof, 69-75, chmn dept, 78-96, PROF MED CHEM, COL PHARM, UNIV UTAH, 75- *Personal Data:* b Panama, CZ, July 26, 37; m 60, Mary J Duffin; c Thomas A, Laura M (Wall) & Carol S (Malvey). *Educ:* Univ Tex, Austin, BS, 59; Ariz State Univ, PhD(nucleoside methylation), 65. *Prof Exp:* Res assoc, Johns Hopkins Univ, 65-66. *Concurrent Pos:* Mem BNP study sect, NIH, 80-84; consult, Egyptian govt, 83; chair, chem sect, Am Col Pharmacol, 85-86; Fulbright sr fel, WGer, 83; mem, develop therapeut contracts rev comt, Nat Cancer Inst, 88-92, chemother hemat grants rev comt, Am Cancer Soc 86-90; Acquired Immune Deficiency Syndrome & Related Res Study Sect, NIH, 90-96; counr, Med Chem Div, Am Chem Soc, 93-95. *Mem:* Fel AAAS; Am Chem Soc; Am Asn Cancer Res; Int Soc Antiviral Res; Am Asn Col Pharm; Int Soc Nucleic Acid Chem. *Res:* Conformational analysis by nuclear magnetic resonance; antiviral polynucleotides and oligonucleotides, antifolates against opportunistic infections. *Mailing Add:* Dept Med Chem Col Pharm Univ Utah Salt Lake City UT 84112. *Fax:* 801-581-7087; *E-Mail:* abroom@deans.pharm.utah.edu

BROOMAN, ERIC WILLIAM, POLLUTION PREVENTION & ELECTROCHEMICAL TECHNOLOGY, TECHNOLOGY TRANSFER & COATING TECHNOLOGY. *Current Pos:* mgr, 93-96, PRIN TECH DIR, CONCURRENT TECHNOL CORP, 96-; MGR, NAT DEFENSE CTR ENVIRON EXCELLENCE, 93- *Personal Data:* b London, Eng, Sept 15, 40; US citizen; m 62, Irene Yelland; c Andrew C & Susan I. *Educ:* Univ Surrey, Dipl Tech, 63; Cambridge Univ, PhD(electrochem), 66. *Honors & Awards:* Silver Medal Award, Am Electroplaters & Surface Finishers Soc, 88. *Prof Exp:* Res electrochemist, Columbus Div, Battelle Mem Inst, 66-75, prin res scientist, 75-78, assoc mgr, Corrosion & Electrochem Technol Sect, 78-80, assoc mgr, Chem Process, Develop & Polymer Sci & Technol Sect, 80-85, assoc mgr, Corrosion & Electrochem Tech Dept, 85-89, res leader & bus area mgr, Advan Mat Dept, Columbus Div, 89-93. *Concurrent Pos:* Res fel & consult, Univ Salford, 72-73; mem bd dirs, Electrochem Soc, Inc, 78-80 & 88-92, corp secy & trustee, 88-92; chmn res bd, mem pub bd, Adv Planning Comt & Recognition Comt, Am Electroplaters & Surface Finishers Soc, 90- *Mem:* Electrochem Soc; Am Electroplaters & Surface Finishers Soc; Sigma Xi; Inst Hazardous Mat Mgt. *Res:* Electrochemical energy conversion and storage; primary and secondary batteries; fuel cells and water electrolyzers; corrosion science and technology; coating technologies; pollution prevention; recycling; remediation. *Mailing Add:* 8450 Gullane Ct Dublin OH 43017

BROOME, CARMEN ROSE, SYSTEMATIC BOTANY. *Current Pos:* EXAMR, PLANT VARIETY PROTECT OFF, USDA, BELTSVILLE, MD, 79- *Personal Data:* b Miami, Fla, June 19, 39; m 78. *Educ:* Univ Miami, BS, 65; Univ SFla, MA, 68; Duke Univ, PhD(bot), 74. *Prof Exp:* asst prof bot, Univ MD, College Park, 73-79. *Mem:* Sigma Xi; Am Soc Plant Taxonomists; Int Asn Plant Taxon. *Res:* Systematics of angiosperms, particularly Gentianaceae; economic plants; palynology, reproductive biology of angiosperms. *Mailing Add:* USDA-NAL-ISD 10301 Baltimore Blvd 013 Beltsville MD 20705

BROOME, CLAIRE V, INFECTIOUS DISEASES, ACUTE DISEASE EPIDEMIOLOGY. *Current Pos:* Dep chief spec pathogens, Bact Dis Div, 79-80, chief spec pathogens, 81-90, ASSOC DIR SCI, CTR DIS CONTROL, 91- *Personal Data:* b Aug 24, 49; m 88, John Head; c Gabriel & Steven. *Educ:* Harvard Univ, BA, 70; Harvard Med Sch, MD, 75; Univ Calif, San Francisco, dipl, Am Bd Internal Med, 81. *Honors & Awards:* Charles C Shepard Award, 86. *Concurrent Pos:* Clin asst, Sch Med, Emory Univ, 77-; consult, WHO; infectious dis fel, Mass Gen Hosp, 80-81; mem, Microbiol & Infectious Dis

Res Comt, Nat Inst Allergy & Infectious Dis, 87-89, Consult Group Vaccine Develop, Nat Vaccine Prog. *Mem:* Inst Med-Nat Acad Sci; Am Epidemiol Soc; Am Col Physicians; Am Soc Microbiol; Am Col Epidemiol; fel Infectious Dis Soc Am. *Res:* Develop new method for estimating vaccine efficacy of pneumococcal vaccine; responsible for epidemiology investigations of toxic-shock syndrome; haemophilus influenza, listeriosis and other causes of bacterial meningitis. *Mailing Add:* D14 Off Dir Ctr Dis Control Atlanta GA 30333

BROOME, PAUL W(ALLACE), ELECTRICAL ENGINEERING, SIGNAL PROCESSING. *Current Pos:* CHIEF EXEC OFFICER, ENSCO, 68- *Personal Data:* b Oakdale, Pa, Jan 17, 32; m 57, Joan Brown; c Ronald W, V Kathleen, Barbara G & Paul W. *Educ:* Carnegie Inst Technol, BS, 54, MS, 55, PhD(elec eng), 60. *Prof Exp:* Res engr, Gulf Res & Develop Co, 55-57; chief analog comput analyst, Gen Dynamics-Astronaut, 58-61, design specialist, 61-62; sr staff scientist, Guided Missiles Range Div, Pan Am World Airways, 62-64; sr eng specialist, Earth Sci Div, Teledyne Inc, 64-65, mgr appl res lab, 65-68. *Mem:* Sigma Xi; Inst Elec & Electronics Engrs. *Res:* Signal and noise theory; time series analysis; pattern recognition and spatial filtering; applications of signal theory. *Mailing Add:* Box 2970 Winter Park CO 80482

BROOMES, LLOYDA RENEE, CHILD & ADOLESCENT PSYCHIATRY. *Current Pos:* MED DIR, S CENT FULTON CO COMMUNITY MENT HEALTH CTR, 95- *Personal Data:* b Los Angeles, Calif, July 30, 65. *Educ:* Oakwood Col, BS, 87; Meharry Med Col, MD, 90. *Honors & Awards:* Chester Pierce Award, Nat Med Asn, 94. *Prof Exp:* Gen psychiat resident, Emory Univ, 90-93, child & adolescent psychiat resident, 93-95, chief resident, Div Child & Adolescent Psychiat, 94-95. *Concurrent Pos:* On-call physician, Wesley Woods Geriat Hosp, 92-93; consult pyschiatrist, Hillside Hosp, Atlanta, 94-95, Nyarko & Assocs Inc, 95; instr, Dept psychiat, Morehouse Sch Med, 95- *Mem:* Alternative Med Asn; Black Pschiatrists Am; Am Psychiat Asn; Am Acad Child Adolescent Psychiat; Nat Med Asn. *Mailing Add:* 1380 Martinique Ct SW Atlanta GA 30331

BROOMFIELD, CLARENCE A, BIOCHEMISTRY, MOLECULAR BIOLOGY. *Current Pos:* RES CHEMIST, ARMY MED RES INST CHEM DEFENSE, 80- *Personal Data:* b Mt Morris, Mich, Sept 18, 30; m 56, Marian L Hintz; c Richard, Cheryl & Deborah. *Educ:* Univ Mich, BS, 53; Mich State Univ, PhD(chem), 58. *Prof Exp:* Res assoc phys chem, Cornell Univ, 58-59; res biochemist, Chem Res & Develop Lab, Edgewood Arsenal, 62-68, chief protein chem, Med Res Dir, Biomed Lab, 68-80. *Concurrent Pos:* NIH fel, Cornell Univ, 60-62. *Mem:* Am Chem Soc; Sigma Xi; NY Acad Sci; Am Soc Biochem & Molecular Biol. *Res:* Secondary and tertiary protein structure; relationship of structure to biological activity; toxic proteins; cholinesterases; biochemistry of nerve transmission; enzyme engineering; organophosphate hydrolyzing enzymes. *Mailing Add:* 1917 Youngston Rd Jarrettsville MD 21084. *Fax:* 410-671-1960; *E-Mail:* broomfiel_ca@mricd1.apgea.army.mil

BROOTEN, DOROTHY, NURSING. *Current Pos:* ASSOC DEAN RES & GRAD STUDIES, CASE WESTERN RES UNIV, 96- *Personal Data:* b Hazleton, Pa, Jan 16, 42; m 63; c 2. *Educ:* Univ Pa, BSN, 66, MSN, 70, PhD(educ admin). *Honors & Awards:* Distinguished Contrib to Nursing Sci, Am Nurse's Asn, 88. *Prof Exp:* Assoc prof nursing, Thomas Jefferson Univ, 72-77; from asst prof to prof, Sch Nursing, Univ Pa, 77-90, chair, Health Care of Women & Childbearing 88-90, dir, Ctr for Low Birthweight, 90-96, over seers prof perinatal nursing, 90-96. *Concurrent Pos:* Mem, Gov Coun, Am Acad Nursing, 88-91; consult, Sch Med, Univ Utrecht, Neth, 89 & Ministry of Health, Malawi, Africa, 91. *Mem:* Inst Med-Nat Acad Sci; Am Acad Nursing. *Res:* Low birthweight prevention; postdischarge care of low birthweight infants; health care delivery. *Mailing Add:* Frances Wayne Sch Nursing Case Western Res Univ 10900 Euclid Ave Cleveland OH 44106-4904

BROPHY, GERALD PATRICK, GEOLOGY, MINERALOGY. *Current Pos:* from instr to assoc prof, 54-68, PROF GEOL, AMHERST COL, 68- *Personal Data:* b Kansas City, Mo, Sept 11, 26; m 51; c 3. *Educ:* Columbia Univ, AB, 51, MA, 53, PhD(geol), 54. *Hon Degrees:* MA, Amherst Col, 68. *Prof Exp:* Res asst geol, Columbia Univ, 51-54. *Concurrent Pos:* NIH res grants, 62-; Fulbright fel, Univ Baghdad, 65-66; cur, Pratt Mus Geol, 67-; NSF grants, 69-; consult, Bear Creek Mining Co, Cerro Corp, R T Vanderbilt & Co & Conyers Construct Co; prog mgr, Geothermal Explor USA, Div Geothermal Energy, Dept Energy, 78-80; assoc, Dunn Geoscience Inc, 81- *Mem:* Fel Geol Soc Am; Mineral Soc Am; Geochem Soc; Soc Econ Geologists; Yellowstone-Big Horn Res Asn (pres, 75-77). *Res:* Crystals chemistry of phosphates and sulphates; effects of pressure on crystallization of granitic magmas; rock alteration in geothermal systems. *Mailing Add:* Dept Geol Amherst Col Amherst MA 01002-5002

BROPHY, JOHN ALLEN, geology, for more information see previous edition

BROPHY, MARY O'REILLY, ENVIRONMENTAL PHYSIOLOGY, INDUSTRIAL HYGIENE. *Current Pos:* SR INDUST HYGIENIST, DIV SAFETY & HEALTH, NY STATE DEPT LABOR, 86- *Personal Data:* b New York, NY, Aug 3, 48; c Robert, Sara & Lena. *Educ:* Univ Mich, BS, 70, MS, 72, PhD, 79. *Prof Exp:* Technician & instr histol, Univ Idaho, 74-75; instr phys ed, Univ Ga, 77-79; fel & instr histol, State Univ NY, Upstate Med Ctr, 79-81, res asst prof, 81-84; res assoc, Syracuse Res Corp, 84-86. *Concurrent Pos:* Adj prof, State Univ NY, Albany Sch Pub Health, 91-; pres, ARLS Consult, Inc; dir, Am Bd Indust Hygiene, 95- *Mem:* Am Indust Hyg Asn; Am Conf Govt Indust Hygienists; Am Indust Hyg Asn (treas, 91-); Human Factors Soc. *Res:* Identification of the health effets of environmental pollutants, especially carcinogens and teratogens; evaluation of workplace factors associated with cumulative trauma disorders; ergonomics. *Mailing Add:* 5954 Smith Rd North Syracuse NY 13212. *E-Mail:* mbrophy@sescva.esc.edu

BROQUIST, HARRY PEARSON, BIOCHEMISTRY, NUTRITION. *Current Pos:* PROF BIOCHEM, VANDERBILT UNIV, 69-, DIR DIV NUTRIT, 72- *Personal Data:* b Chicago, Ill, Jan 23, 19; m 42; c 2. *Educ:* Beloit Col, BS, 40; Univ Wis, MS, 41, PhD(biochem), 49. *Honors & Awards:* Borden Award, Am Inst Nutrit, 68. *Prof Exp:* Group leader microbiol, Lederle Lab, Pearl River, NY, 41-46 & 49-58; from assoc prof to prof biol chem, Univ Ill, 58-69. *Concurrent Pos:* Vis lectr biochem, Mich State Univ, 63; biochem consult interdept comt nutrit nat develop, US Nutrit Surv to Nigeria, 65; NSF sr fel, Karolinska Inst, Sweden, 65-66; mem nutrit study sect, NIH, 66-70; mem food & nutrit bd, Nat Res Coun, 74-; assoc ed, Nutrit Reviews, 79- & Ann Reviews Nutrit, 81- *Mem:* Am Soc Biol Chemists; Am Inst Nutrit; Fedn Am Soc Exp Biol. *Res:* Amino acid metabolism in yeasts, molds and mammalian systems; nutritional biochemistry. *Mailing Add:* Dept Biochem Vanderbilt Univ 4629 Benton Smith Rd Nashville TN 37215-4301

BROSBE, EDWIN ALLAN, MEDICAL MICROBIOLOGY. *Current Pos:* RETIRED. *Personal Data:* b Burlington, NJ, Jan 8, 18; m 43, Lillian Mazoff; c Jeffrey R & Herbert D. *Educ:* Philadelphia Col Pharm, BS, 40; Univ Colo, MS, 47, PhD(bact), 51. *Prof Exp:* Bacteriologist, Vet Admin Hosp, Ft Logan, Colo, 47-50 & Denver, Colo, 50-53, bacteriologist & actg chief lab serv, NY, 53-55, chief tuberc res lab, Long Beach, Calif, 55-66, microbiologist, Little Rock, Ark, 66-68, clin microbiologist, Long Beach, 68-73; lectr, Calif State Univ, Long Beach, 73-86. *Mem:* Emer mem Am Soc Microbiol. *Res:* Bacteriology and chemotherapy of tuberculosis; biology and chemotherapy of coccidioidomycosis; host-parasite relationship. *Mailing Add:* 198 N Wightman St Ashland OR 97520-1390

BROSCHAT, KAY O, PROTEIN STRUCTURE & REGULATION, CELL BIOLOGY. *Current Pos:* RES SCIENTIST II, G D SEARLE/MONSANTO, 90- *Personal Data:* b Aug 10, 54. *Educ:* Ohio State Univ, Columbus, PhD(biochem), 82. *Prof Exp:* Res asst prof anat & cell biol, Univ Miami, 85-90. *Mem:* Am Soc Cell Biol; Am Soc Biochem & Molecular Biol. *Res:* Myosin mediated motility; cell motility; cell activation and signal transduction; enzyme kinetics; polymerization kinetics; protein-protein interactions; protein purification; product analysis; carbohydrate biochemistry. *Mailing Add:* Dept Health Sci T2L Monsanto Co 800 N Lindbergh Blvd St Louis MO 63167. *Fax:* 314-694-8948; *E-Mail:* kobros@monsanto.com

BROSE, DAVID STEPHEN, PALEO-ANTHROPOLOGY, HUMAN ECOLOGY. *Current Pos:* DIR, SCHIELE MUS NATURAL HIST. *Personal Data:* b Detroit, Mich, Feb 20, 39; m 65; c 2. *Educ:* Univ Mich, BA, 60, MA, 66, PhD(anthrop), 68. *Honors & Awards:* Jared Kirtland Medal, 85. *Prof Exp:* From asst prof to assoc prof anthrop, Case Western Res Univ, 68-77, chmn, 73-75; chief cur archaeol, Cleveland Mus Natural Hist, 77-92. *Concurrent Pos:* Ed, Mid Continental J Archaeol, 76-91; appointment, Interagency Archaeol Serv, US Dept Interior, 77-78; adj prof, Dept Anthrop, Case Western Res Univ, 78-80 & Cleveland State Univ, 80-91; investr, GAO Interagency Task Force, New Melones Archaeol Proj, 80-81; coordr res, Cleveland Mus Natural History, 81-; chair, Nat Hist Landmarks Comt, 85-; assoc dir, Royal Ont Mus, 92- *Mem:* Soc Prof Archaeologists (pres, 82-83); Soc Am Archaeol. *Res:* Prehistoric archaeology of eastern North America; historic sites archaeology of the great lakes and Central Gulf Coast; research focuses upon cultural adaptations to changing social and environmental conditions over time. *Mailing Add:* Schiele Mus Natural Hist 1500 E Garrison Blvd Gastonia NC 28054

BROSEGHINI, ALBERT L, ZOOLOGY. *Current Pos:* RETIRED. *Personal Data:* b Chicago, Ill, Sept 17, 32; m 58; c 2. *Educ:* Northern Ill State Teachers Col, BS, 54; Iowa State Univ, MS, 56, PhD(zool), 59. *Prof Exp:* Asst prof biol, Fresno State Col, 59-62; assoc prof physiol, Col Osteop Med & Surg, 62-64; scientist adminr, Div Res Grants, NIH, 64-65, asst endocrinol prog dir, Nat Inst Arthritis & Metab Dis, 65-66, hemat prog dir, 66-69; dir res admin, Children's Hosp, Boston, 69-87, mgr patents & lic, 76-87; vpres res admin, Mass Eye & Ear Hosp, Boston, 87-90; assoc dir, Patents & Technol Mkt, Cornell Res Found, 90-94. *Mem:* AAAS. *Res:* Comparative physiology; histochemistry of insect tissues; hematology; erythropoiesis. *Mailing Add:* 153 Winged Elm Circle Aiken SC 29803

BROSEMER, RONALD WEBSTER, BIOCHEMISTRY. *Current Pos:* from asst prof to assoc prof, 63-72, assoc dean grad sch, 75-77, PROF BIOCHEM, WASH STATE UNIV, 72-, ASSOC DEAN, DIV SCI, 84- *Personal Data:* b Oakland, Calif, Feb 17, 34; m 62; c 2. *Educ:* Univ Calif, BS, 55; Univ Ill, PhD(biochem), 60. *Prof Exp:* NSF res fel, Univ Marburg, 60-62; asst prof biochem, Univ Ill, 62-63. *Concurrent Pos:* Fulbright scholar, Univ Konstanz, 70-71. *Mem:* NY Acad Sci; Am Soc Biol Chemists. *Res:* Molecular basis of neurologic diseases. *Mailing Add:* Biochem/Biophys Prog Wash State Univ Pullman WA 99164-4660

BROSENS, PIERRE JOSEPH, MECHANICAL ENGINEERING. *Current Pos:* VPRES, GEN SCANNING, INC, 69-, VCHMN BD. *Personal Data:* b Uccle, Belgium, Oct 12, 33; US citizen; m 55; c 3. *Educ:* Mass Inst Technol, BS & MS, 56, ScD(mech eng), 59. *Prof Exp:* Asst prof mech eng, Mass Inst Technol, 59-60; proj mgr thermonics, Thermo Electron Eng Corp, 60-67; mech eng consult, 67-69. *Mem:* Am Soc Mech Engrs. *Res:* Mechanical vibrations; stress analysis; mechanical design. design; management. *Mailing Add:* 34 DunDonald Rd Belmont MA 02178

BROSHAR, WAYNE CECIL, thermal physics, for more information see previous edition

BROSILOW, COLEMAN B, CHEMICAL & SYSTEMS ENGINEERING. *Current Pos:* from asst prof to assoc prof eng, 63-73, chmn Dept Chem Eng, 80-84 PROF ENG, CASE WESTERN RES UNIV, 73- *Personal Data:* b Philadelphia, Pa, Nov 14, 34; m 62; c 2. *Educ:* Drexel Inst Technol, BS, 57; Polytech Inst Brooklyn, MChE, 59, PhD(chem eng), 62. *Honors & Awards:* Comput in Chem Eng Award, Am Inst Chem Engrs, 89. *Prof Exp:* Teaching fel chem eng, Polytech Inst Technol, Brooklyn, 57-59, asst rocket propulsion syst eng, 59-60, sr res fel, 60-62; control engr, Am Cyanamid Co, 62-63. *Mem:* Am Inst Chem Engrs. *Res:* Control of industrial processes; model predictive control; digital simulation of dynamic systems; inferential control. *Mailing Add:* Dept Chem & Eng Case Western Res Univ University Circle Cleveland OH 44106-7217

BROSIN, HENRY WALTER, MEDICINE. *Current Pos:* Prof, 51-69, EMER PROF PAYCHIAT, SCH MED, UNIV PITTSBURGH, 69-; PROF PSYCHIAT, COL MED, UNIV ARIZ, 69- *Personal Data:* b Blackwood, Va, July 6, 04; m 49; c 1. *Educ:* Univ Wis, BA, 27, MD, 33. *Prof Exp:* Intern, Cincinnati Gen Hosp, 33-34; Commonwealth fel psychiat, Sch Med, Univ Colo, 34-37; Rockefeller fel, Inst Psychoanal, Univ Chicago, 37, from instr to prof psychiat, Sch Med, 37-51. *Concurrent Pos:* Fel, Ctr Advan Study Behav Sci, Calif, 56 & 66; consult, Off Surgeon Gen; mem comt army med educ, Nat Res Coun; mem nat clearing house, NIMH. *Mem:* Fel Am Acad Arts & Sci; AAAS; fel AMA; Am Psychoanal Asn; Am Psychosom Soc. *Res:* Psychoanalysis; organic cerebral disease; psychosomatic medicine; communication theory. *Mailing Add:* Col Med Univ Ariz Tucson AZ 85724

BROSNAN, JOHN THOMAS, METABOLISM. *Current Pos:* from asst prof to assoc prof, 72-81, PROF BIOCHEM, MEM UNIV NFLD, 81-, UNIV RES PROF, 90-, HEAD DEPT, 96- *Personal Data:* b Kenmare, Ireland, Feb 13, 43; m 70, Margaret Loughney; c Edward, Eileen & Tomas. *Educ:* Nat Univ Ireland, BSc, 64, MSc, 66; Oxford Univ, DPhil(biochem), 69. *Honors & Awards:* Borden Award, Nutrit Res, 86. *Prof Exp:* Fel med res, Univ Toronto, 69-71. *Concurrent Pos:* Mem, Grants Comt Metab, Med Res Coun Can, 75-78; mem, Grants Comt, Kidney Found Can, 79-86, Can Heart Found, 82-85; chair, Grants Comt, Can Diabetes Asn, 92-94, Res Coun, 94-96. *Mem:* Biochem Soc; Can Biochem Soc; Am Soc Biol Chemists; Can Soc Nutrit Sci. *Res:* Metabolic regulation, especially the regulation of amino acid metabolism in kidney and liver. *Mailing Add:* Dept Biochem Mem Univ Nfld St John's NF A1B 3X9 Can. *Fax:* 709-737-2422; *E-Mail:* jbrosnan@morgan.ucs.mun.ca

BROSNAN, MARGARET EILEEN, ENDOCRINOLOGY, PHYSIOLOGY. *Current Pos:* Fel, 72-74, from asst to assoc prof, 74-85, PROF BIOCHEM, MEM UNIV NFLD, 85- *Personal Data:* b Tulsa, Okla, Oct 29, 42; m 70, John T; c Edward, Eileen & Tomas. *Educ:* Univ Toronto, BA, 66, MSc, 67, PhD(physiol), 72. *Concurrent Pos:* Assoc ed, Can J Physiol & Pharmacol, 78-87. *Mem:* Nutrit Soc Can; Can Fedn Biol Socs (pres, 84-85); Biochem Soc UK; Can Biochem Soc; Am Physiol Soc. *Res:* Control of enzymes of polyamine metabolism in liver and mammary glands; nutritional regulation of metabolism; metabolism of amino acids in diabetes mellitus; metabolism of orginine and of homocysteine. *Mailing Add:* Dept Biochem Mem Univ Nfld St John's NF A1B 3X9 Can. *Fax:* 709-737-2422; *E-Mail:* mbrosnan@morgan.ucs.mun.ca

BROSNIHAN, K BRIDGET, ENDOCRINOLOGY, NEUROBIOLOGY. *Current Pos:* PROF, DEPT SURG SCI, PHYSIOL & PHARMACOL, 93- *Personal Data:* b Omaha, Nebr, June 3, 41; m 75, Tony W Simmons; c 2. *Educ:* Col St Mary, BS, 65; Creighton Univ, MS, 70; Case Western Reserve Univ, PhD(physiol), 74. *Prof Exp:* Fel res, Cleveland Clin, 74-76, proj scientist, 76-77, assoc staff, 77-82, staff res, 82-93. *Concurrent Pos:* Adj assoc prof physiol, Case Western Reserve Univ Med Sch, 81-82 & Cleveland State Univ. *Mem:* Am Heart Asn; Am Physiol Soc; Endocrine Soc; Soc Neurosci; Sigma Xi; Coun High Blood Pressure Fel. *Res:* Neurohormonal interrelationships of two systems, catecholamines and renin-angiotensin; central and peripheral nervous system. *Mailing Add:* Dept Surg Sci, Physiol & Pharmacol Bowman Gray Med Sch Med Ctr Blvd Winston-Salem NC 27157-0132. *Fax:* 919-716-2456; *E-Mail:* bbrosnih@bgsm.edu

BROSS, IRWIN DUDLEY JACKSON, statistics, epidemiology; deceased, see previous edition for last biography

BROSSEAU, GEORGE EMILE, JR, GENETICS. *Current Pos:* RETIRED. *Personal Data:* b Berkeley, Calif, July 24, 30; m 78; c 3. *Educ:* Univ Calif, Berkeley, BA, 52, PhD(genetics), 56. *Prof Exp:* Am Cancer Soc fel, Biol Div, Oak Ridge Nat Lab, 56-58, res assoc genetics, 58-59; from asst prof to prof zool, Univ Iowa, 59-70; prog mgr, Nat Sci Found, 70-78; expert consult, Admin Aging, 78-79; prog analyst, NSF, 79-81, proj mgr, 81-84, prog dir, 84-93. *Mem:* Am Soc Human Genetics; AAAS; Robotics Int; Sigma Xi; World Future Soc. *Res:* Administration; applied science; interdisciplinary research; research utilization; robotics; manufacturing engineering. *Mailing Add:* 11500 Fairway Dr No 108 Reston VA 22090

BROSTOFF, STEVEN WARREN, NEUROCHEMISTRY, NEUROIMMUNOLOGY. *Current Pos:* VPRES RES & DEVELOP, IMMUNE RESPONSE CORP, 88- *Personal Data:* b Boston, Mass, Sept 10, 42; m 83; c 2. *Educ:* Mass Inst Technol, BS, 64, PhD(biochem), 68. *Prof Exp:* Fel biochem, Am Cancer Soc, Eleanor Roosevelt Inst Cancer Res, Univ Colo Med Ctr, 68-70; res assoc neurochem, Salk Inst Biol Studies, 70; sr res biochemist, Dept Exp Biol, Merck Inst Therapeut Res, 71-72; asst prof, Dept Path, Albert Einstein Col Med, 72-73; from assoc prof to prof neurochem, Depts Neurol & Immunol, Med Univ SC, 73-92, assoc dean grad studies, 77-91. *Concurrent Pos:* Prin investr, NIH, 77-, mem neurological sci study sect, 79-83; vis scientist, MRC cellular immunol unit, Univ Oxford, 83. *Mem:* AAAS; Am Chem Soc; Am Soc Neurochem; Int Soc Neurochem; Am Soc Biol Chemists; Am Asn Immunologists. *Res:* Immoregulation of autoimmune diseases; chemical and immunological properties of nervous system proteins; autoimmune demyelinating diseases. *Mailing Add:* Immune Response Corp 5935 Darwin Ct Carlsbad CA 92008

BROSTOW, WITOLD KONRAD, MATERIALS SCIENCE, ENGINEERING. *Current Pos:* PROF CHEM & PHYSICS, UNIV NTEX, DENTON, 89-, PROF MAT SCI, 95- *Personal Data:* b Warsaw, Poland, Mar 21, 34; US citizen; m 73, Anna Zujko; c Gabriel J & Diana P. *Educ:* Univ Warsaw, MS, 55, DrSc, 60; Polish Acad Sci, DSc, 65. *Prof Exp:* Asst prof, Inst Phys Chem, Polish Acad Sci, 65-68; head, Div Phys Chem, Inst Synthetics, Warsaw, 68-70; Nat Acad Sci vis scholar, Stanford Univ, 69-70; Nat Res Coun Can vis scholar, Univ Ottawa, 70-71; res prof chem, Univ Montreal, 71-76; prof, Ctr Advan Studies, Mexico City, 76-79; assoc prof mat eng, Drexel Univ, Philadelphia, 80-89. *Mem:* Mexico Nat Acad Sci; fel Royal Soc Chem; Am Phys Soc; Am Chem Soc; Mat Res Soc. *Res:* Structure and properties of polymer solutions and melts; service performance and failure of polymers; computer simulation of materials and processes; information theory; statistical mechanics and thermodynamics of liquid mixtures; biopolymers. *Mailing Add:* Dept Mat Sci Univ NTex PO Box 5308 Denton TX 76203. *Fax:* 817-565-4824; *E-Mail:* brostow@unt.edu

BROSTROM, CHARLES OTTO, PHARMACOLOGY, BIOCHEMISTRY. *Current Pos:* Asst prof biochem, Robert Wood Johnson Med Sch, Univ Med & Dent NJ, 71-72, from asst prof to assoc prof pharmacol, 72-84, actg chmn pharmacol, 89-93, PROF PHARMACOL, ROBERT WOOD JOHNSON MED SCH, UNIV MED & DENT, NJ, 84- *Personal Data:* b Downsville, Wis, Nov 2, 42; m 65, Margaret A O'Brien; c Arthur. *Educ:* Wis State Univ, River Falls, BS, 64; Univ Ill, PhD(biochem), 69. *Concurrent Pos:* USPHS fel enzym, Univ Calif, Davis, 68-70, Health Sci Advan Award, 70-71. *Mem:* Am Soc Biochem & Molecular Biol. *Res:* Cyclic nucleotide metabolism in brain; regulation of protein synthesis by calcium. *Mailing Add:* Robert Wood Johnson Med Sch Dept Pharmacol Univ Med & Dent NJ Piscataway NJ 08854

BROSTROM, MARGARET ANN, BIOCHEMISTRY, PHARMACOLOGY. *Current Pos:* Sr teaching asst, 71-72, from instr to assoc prof, 72-87, PROF PHARMACOL, ROBERT WOOD JOHNSON MED SCH, UNIV MED & DENT, NJ, 87- *Personal Data:* b Chicago, Ill, Aug 13, 41; m 65; c 1. *Educ:* Clarke Col, BA, 63; Univ Ill, PhD(biochem), 68. *Concurrent Pos:* NIH fel, Univ Calif, 69-71; prin investr various grants, 80- *Mem:* Am Soc Pharmacol & Exp Therapeut. *Res:* Calcium and cyclic nucleotides in neural and pituitary function; second messengers and translational control. *Mailing Add:* Dept Pharmacol Univ Med & Dent NJ Robert Wood Johnson Med Sch 675 Hoes Lane Piscataway NJ 08854. *Fax:* 732-235-4073

BROT, FREDERICK ELLIOT, BIOCHEMICAL GENETICS. *Current Pos:* RES INSTR & NIH TRAINEE, SCH MED, WASH UNIV, 71- *Personal Data:* b Kalamazoo, Mich, May 28, 41; m 65; c 2. *Educ:* Univ Mich, BS, 62; Stanford Univ, PhD(org chem), 66. *Prof Exp:* NIH fel, Northwestern Univ, 66-68; sr res chemist, Monsanto Co, 68-71. *Mem:* AAAS; Am Chem Soc. *Res:* Protein purification and characterization; affinity chromatography; enzyme modification; application of enzymes for correction of genetic enzyme defects; synthesis and in vivo fate of site-directed drugs. *Mailing Add:* 8145 Cornell Ct University City MO 63130-3639

BROT, NATHAN, biochemistry, for more information see previous edition

BROTAK, EDWARD ALLEN, SYNOPTIC METEOROLOGY, FOREST METEOROLOGY. *Current Pos:* CONSULT, 88- *Personal Data:* b Trenton, NJ, July 17, 48. *Educ:* Rutgers Univ, BS, 70, MS, 72; Yale Univ, PhD(biometeor), 77. *Prof Exp:* Asst prof meteorol, Kean Col NJ, 77-80; asst prof, Lyndon State Col, 80-81; assoc prof & dir atmospheric sci, Univ NC, Asheville, 81-87. *Concurrent Pos:* Vis prof, Wesleyan Univ, 76, 78-80; AV ed, Weatherwise & meteorel educ ed, Nat Weather Dig. *Mem:* Am Meteorol Soc; Nat Weather Asn; Asn Am Weather Observers; Sigma Xi. *Res:* Synoptic meteorology and climatology; weather forecasting; forest fire weather. *Mailing Add:* Dept Atmospheric Sci Univ NC Asheville One Univ Heights Asheville NC 28804-3251

BROTEN, NORMAN W, ASTRONOMY. *Current Pos:* RETIRED. *Personal Data:* b Meacham, Sask, Dec 21, 21. *Educ:* Univ Western Ont, BSc, 50 & 84. *Honors & Awards:* Rumford Medal, Am Acad Arts & Sci, 71. *Prof Exp:* Astronr solar radio, Nat Res Coun Can, 50-59, radio astronr, 59-86, head, Astron Sect, 74-86. *Concurrent Pos:* Mem, Comn 40, Int Astron Union, 70-; chmn, Comn J, Int Union Radio Sci, 75- *Mem:* Can Astron Soc; Am Astron Soc; Inst Elec & Electronics Engrs; AAAS; Royal Astron Soc Can. *Res:* Radio astronomy in very long baseline interferometry, interstellar molecules, quasars, Seyfert galaxies and extra galactic objects; ionized hydrogen regions. *Mailing Add:* 48 Pineglen Crescent Nepean ON K2E 6X9 Can

BROTHERS, ALFRED DOUGLAS, SOLID STATE PHYSICS. *Current Pos:* actg chmn, 71-72, CHMN DEPT PHYSICS, BENEDICTINE COL, 72- *Personal Data:* b Waukegan, Ill, Aug 6, 39; m 72. *Educ:* Northern Ill Univ, BS, 62; Iowa State Univ, MS, 65, PhD(physics & educ), 68. *Prof Exp:* Jr physicist, Ames Lab, US AEC, 65-66; asst prof physics, St Benedict's Col, 68-71. *Mem:* Am Asn Physics Teachers; Am Inst Physics; Sigma Xi. *Res:* Optical qualities of thin films and crystalline solids. *Mailing Add:* Dept Physics & Astron Benedictine Col Atchison KS 66002

BROTHERS, EDWARD BRUCE, ICHTHYOLOGY, ECOLOGY. *Current Pos:* ECOL CONSULT, 83- *Personal Data:* b Brooklyn, NY, Apr 25, 48; m 69, Iris Merker; c Sarah & Laura. *Educ:* Brooklyn Col, BS, 68; Univ Calif, San Diego, PhD(oceanog), 75. *Prof Exp:* Asst prof zool, Univ Calif, Berkeley, 74; res assoc, Inter-Am Trop Tuna Comn, 75; asst prof ecol & systematics, Cornell Univ, 75-83. *Concurrent Pos:* Ecol consult, 83-; vis prof, Univ Mont, 86; res affil, Smithsonian Trop Res Inst, Panama, 94-97. *Mem:* Am Soc Ichthyologists & Herpetologists; Am Fisheries Soc; Sigma Xi. *Res:* Ecology and behavior of freshwater and marine fishes; growth dynamics of individuals and populations; fisheries biology. *Mailing Add:* Three Sunset W Ithaca NY 14850. *Fax:* 607-257-7264

BROTHERS, JOHN EDWIN, GEOMETRIC MEASURE THEORY, DIFFERENTIAL GEOMETRY. *Current Pos:* Asst chmn dept, 71-73, dir undergrad studies, Math Dept, 89-91, PROF MATH, IND UNIV, BLOOMINGTON, 66- *Personal Data:* b Salt Lake City, Utah, July 6, 37. *Educ:* Univ Utah, BA, 59, MS, 60; Brown Univ, PhD(math), 64. *Concurrent Pos:* Co-recipient, NSF grant, 67-81; mem, Inst Advan Study, 73-74; ed, Ind Univ Math J, 81-91. *Mem:* Am Math Soc; Math Asn Am. *Res:* Geometric measure theory and applications to the calculus of variations with emphasis on the least area problem and the study of minimal submanifolds. *Mailing Add:* Rawles Hall Ind Univ Bloomington IN 47405-5701. *Fax:* 812-855-0046; *E-Mail:* brothers@ucs.indiana.edu

BROTHERSON, DONALD E, ENERGY & CONSTRUCTION, MAINTENANCE MANAGEMENT SYSTEMS. *Current Pos:* RETIRED. *Personal Data:* b Chicago, Ill, Sept 4, 32; m 59, Mary L Nelson; c Nancy & Elizabeth. *Educ:* Univ Ill, BS, 53, MS, 55. *Prof Exp:* Dir, Bldg Res Coun, Univ Ill, 59-93. *Concurrent Pos:* Consult, 60- *Mem:* Am Soc Testing & Mat; Am Concrete Inst; Concrete Indust Bd; Am Inst Architects. *Res:* Energy conservation; engineered maintenance management systems; building failures; roofing and waterproofing. *Mailing Add:* 3640 Yacht Club Dr Miami FL 33180

BROTHERSON, JACK DEVON, PLANT ECOLOGY. *Current Pos:* PROF ECOL, BRIGHAM YOUNG UNIV, 69- *Personal Data:* b Castle Dale, Utah, Sept 18, 38; m 64; c 4. *Educ:* Brigham Young Univ, BS, 64, MS, 67; Iowa State Univ, PhD(plant ecol), 69. *Concurrent Pos:* Consult, Indian Inst, Brigham Young Univ, 69- & Bur Reclamation, Cent Utah Proj, 72-78; mem, Am Inst Biol Comt Natural Areas State of Utah, 72-74; reviewer, Brown & Co, Publishers, 74. *Mem:* AAAS; Ecol Soc Am; Brit Ecol Soc; Soc Range Mgt; Sigma Xi. *Res:* Ecological adaptation; niche metrics; evolutionary and environmental gradient accomodation of organisms, populations, and biotic communities in the Great Basin of North America. *Mailing Add:* Dept Bot Brigham Young Univ 401 Widb Provo UT 84602-1049

BROTHERTON, ROBERT JOHN, ORGANIC CHEMISTRY, RESEARCH ADMINISTRATION. *Current Pos:* res chemist, 57-64, VPRES & DIR RES, US BORAX RES CORP, 64- *Personal Data:* b Ypsilanti, Mich, Aug 4, 28; m 50; c 4. *Educ:* Univ Ill, BS, 49; Wash State Univ, PhD, 54. *Prof Exp:* Du Pont fel & instr org chem, Univ Minn, 54-55; res chemist, Refinery Res Group, Union Oil Co, 55-57. *Mem:* Am Chem Soc. *Res:* Boron chemistry. *Mailing Add:* 424 Panorama Dr Laguna Beach CA 92651-2392

BROTZEN, FRANZ R(ICHARD), PHYSICAL METALLURGY, SCIENCE & ELECTRONIC MATERIALS. *Current Pos:* assoc prof mech eng, Rice Univ, 54-59, prof mat sci, 59-86, dean eng, 62-66, EMER PROF MAT SCI, RICE UNIV, 86- *Personal Data:* b Berlin, Ger, July 4, 15; nat US; m 50, Frances B Ridgway; c Franz & Julie. *Educ:* Case Inst Technol, BS, 50, MS, 53, PhD(phys metall), 54. *Prof Exp:* Res metallurgist, US Bur Mines, Md, 50-51; sr res assoc metall, Case Inst Technol, 51-54. *Concurrent Pos:* Consult, Naval Res Lab, 55-59; Guggenheim fel, US Sr Scientist Award, Stuttgart Tech Sch, 61-62; vis lectr & consult, Univ Brazil, 63, 65 & 70; vis prof, Swiss Fed Inst Technol, 66-67, Max-Planck Inst, Stuttgart, 73-74 & Univ Lausanne, 81. *Mem:* Fel Am Soc Metals; Am Inst Mining, Metall & Petrol Engrs; Am Inst Physics; Am Soc Eng Educ. *Res:* Lattice imperfection theory; electron emission, electronic materials phenomena; alloy theory; physical properties. *Mailing Add:* Dept Mech Eng & Mat Sci Rice Univ PO Box 1892 Houston TX 77251-1892. *Fax:* 713-285-5423; *E-Mail:* brotzen@rice.edu

BROUGHTON, M(ERVYN) B(LYTHE), automatic control, power electronics, for more information see previous edition

BROUGHTON, ROBERT STEPHEN, AGRICULTURAL & HYDRAULIC ENGINEERING. *Current Pos:* from asst prof to assoc prof, McGill Univ, 63-66, chmn, Dept Agr Eng, 65-71, coordr, Agr Sci Div, 72-75, PROF AGR ENG, MACDONALD COL, MCGILL UNIV, 74-, DIR, CTR DRAINAGE STUDIES, 87- *Personal Data:* b Corbetton, Ont, June 29, 34; m 57, Ruth M Smith; c G Anne, Sharon M, Heather L & Stephen R. *Educ:* Univ Toronto, BSA, 56, BASc, 57; Mass Inst Technol, SM, 59; McGill Univ, PhD, 72. *Hon Degrees:* LLD, Dalhousie Univ, 89. *Honors & Awards:* Maple Leaf Award, Can Soc Agr Engrs, James Beamish Award; Int Develop Award, Can Comt, Int Comn Irrigation & Drainage, 93. *Prof Exp:* Res asst fluid mech, Mass Inst Technol, 57-59; hydraul engr, Conserv Br, Ont Civil Serv, 59-61. *Concurrent Pos:* External examr agr eng, Trinidad, 70-77, Nigeria, 75-76 & Eng, 79-81; consult irrigation & drainage, Food & Agr Orgn UN Asian Develop Bank & Can Govt Aid Orgns, Trinidad, Haiti, El Salvador, Egypt, India, Pakistan, USA & Can. *Mem:* Fel Am Soc Agr Engrs; fel Can Soc Agr Engrs; Can Water Resources Asn; corresp mem Plastic Pipe Asn; Sigma Xi. *Res:* Study of the water balance of flat lands in Canada; mechanics of cavitation; vorticity problems of flood control pumping stations; water resources surveys; irrigation water requirements; drainage and irrigation engineering research. *Mailing Add:* Macdonald Campus McGill Univ Ste Anne de Bellevue PQ H9X 3V9 Can. *Fax:* 514-398-8387; *E-Mail:* broughton@agreng.lan.mcgill.ca

BROUGHTON, ROGER JAMES, NEUROPHYSIOLOGY, PSYCHOBIOLOGY. *Current Pos:* assoc prof med & pharmacol, 68-74, prof pharmacol, 74-84, PROF MED & PSYCHOL, UNIV OTTAWA, 74-, ASSOC DIR, INST MED ENG, 90-; PHYSICIAN, OTTAWA GEN HOSP, 68- *Personal Data:* b Montreal, Que, Sept 25, 36; m 59, 87, Buchesen; c 3. *Educ:* Queen's Univ, Ont, MD, CM, 60; Univ Aix-Marseille, dipl electroencephalog-neurophysiol, 64; McGill Univ, PhD(neurophysiol), 67. *Prof Exp:* Intern med, Univ Sask Hosp, 60-61; resident, Centre St Paul, Marseille, 62-64; asst prof clin neurophysiol, McGill Univ, 64-68. *Concurrent Pos:* Consult, WHO, 64-68; assoc, Med Res Coun Can, 68-; ed, Sleep Rev, 70-80; med dir, Sleep Dis Ctr & Dept Clin Neurophysiol, Ottawa Gen Hosp, 80-; dir, Human Neurosci Res Unit, Fac Med, Univ Ottawa. *Mem:* Am EEG Soc; Am Sleep Disorders Asn; Sleep Res Soc; Int League Against Epilepsy; Can Soc EEG; Sigma Xi; hon corresp mem Brazilian Acad Neurologist; hon corresp mem Latin Am Sleep Soc; hon corresp mem Czech Soc; hon corresp mem Clin Neurophysiol; hon corresp mem Cuban Neurosci Soc; hon corresp mem Western EEG Soc. *Res:* Clinical disorders of sleep and arousal; phylogeny of sleep; cerebral evoked potentials and their correlates in man; daytime sleepiness in narcolepsy; chronobiological regulation of human sleep. *Mailing Add:* Dept Med Ottawa Gen Hosp Ottawa ON K1H 8L6 Can. *Fax:* 613-737-8859

BROUGHTON, WILLIAM ALBERT, ECONOMIC GEOLOGY. *Current Pos:* prof & head dept, 48-78, EMER PROF GEOL, UNIV WIS-PLATTEVILLE, 79- *Personal Data:* b Ronan, Mont, Oct 12, 14; m 43, Marguerite Erblang; c Barbara G, Nancy J, Sally E & William J. *Educ:* Univ Wis, AB, 39. *Prof Exp:* Geologist, Wis Geol Surv, 36-41; instr petrol, State Col Wash, 41; geologist, State Div Geol, Wash, 41-45; geologist, Chicago, Milwaukee, St Paul & Pac Rwy, 45-46; consult geologist, 46. *Concurrent Pos:* US Geol Surv, 51-54; geologist-in-chg, Mineral Develop Atlas, Wis Geol Surv, 61-, prof & specialist, 79- *Mem:* Fel AAAS; Soc Econ Geologists; Am Inst Mining, Metall & Petrol Eng. *Res:* Sedimentation of Wisconsin lakes; tungsten and magnetic iron deposits of Washington; zinc-lead deposits; meteoritics. *Mailing Add:* 295 Bradford Platteville WI 53818

BROUILLARD, ROBERT ERNEST, chemistry, physics; deceased, see previous edition for last biography

BROUILLET, LUC, SYSTEMATICS, PHYTOGEOGRAPHY. *Current Pos:* PROF BOT & CUR, MARIE-VICTORIN HERBARIUM, UNIV MONTREAL, 82- *Personal Data:* b L'Assomption, Que, June 18, 54. *Educ:* Univ Montreal, BSc, 75, MSc, 77; Univ Waterloo, PhD(biol), 81. *Honors & Awards:* L Cinq-Mars Award, Can Bot Asn, 79. *Prof Exp:* Prof bot, MacDonald Campus & cur Herbarium, McGill Univ, 80-82. *Mem:* Can Bot Asn (past-pres, 87-88); Can Biol Coun; Bot Soc Am; Soc Study Evolution; Am Soc Plant Taxonomists; Am Inst Biol Sci. *Res:* Systematics, evolution and phytogeography of angiosperms, Compositae and Begoniaceae; floristics and biogeography of Quebec and Newfoundland; cytogeography and flora of North America. *Mailing Add:* Institut de Recherche en Biologie Vegetale Univ Montreal 4101 Sherbrooke St E Montreal PQ H1X 2B2 Can

BROUILLETTE, ROBERT T, NEONATOLOGY, PEDIATRIC PULMONOLOGY. *Current Pos:* PROF PEDIAT, MCGILL UNIV, 89- *Personal Data:* b Washington, DC, June 27, 47; m 74, Kathleen Muldoon; c 3. *Educ:* Providence Col, AB, 69; Wash Univ, St Louis, MD, 74. *Prof Exp:* From asst prof to prof pediat, Med Sch, Northwestern Univ, 79-89. *Concurrent Pos:* Attend physician, Children's Mem Hosp, 79-89, Montreal Children's Hosp, 89-, div head, Newborn Med, Dir Sleep Lab, Resp Med, 97- *Mem:* Soc Pediat Res; Am Physiol Soc; Am Acad Pediat; Am Thoracic Soc; Am Perinatal Asn. *Res:* Development of respiratory control and airway patency original models and human diseases; central hypoventilation syndrome and phrenic nerve pacing; clinical neonatology. *Mailing Add:* Montreal Children's Hosp 2300 Tupper St Montreal PQ H3H 1P3 Can

BROUILLETTE, WALTER, SOLID STATE PHYSICS. *Current Pos:* MEM FAC, CHEM DEPT, UNIV ALA, 80- *Personal Data:* b Port Barre, La, Aug 13, 25; m 46. *Educ:* La State Univ, BSc, 48, MSc, 50; Univ Mo, PhD(physics), 55. *Prof Exp:* Physicist, Gen Elec Co, Syracuse, 55-80. *Mem:* Am Asn Physics Teachers; Am Phys Soc. *Res:* Physical electronics; electron tube circuitry; information theory; information storage and processing; electron beam lithography. *Mailing Add:* RR 1 Jamesville NY 13078-9801

BROUN, THOROWGOOD TAYLOR, JR, INDUSTRIAL CHEMISTRY. *Current Pos:* sr res chemist, 67-75, RES COORDR, HOUSTON CHEMICAL CO DIV, PPG INDUSTS, INC, 75- *Personal Data:* b Nashville, Tenn, Apr 4, 23; m 42; c 3. *Educ:* ETex State Univ, BS, 43; Purdue Univ, PhD(chem), 51. *Prof Exp:* Res analyst, Field Res Dept, Magnolia Petrol Co, 43-44; res chemist, Chem Div, PPG Industs, Inc, 51-56, res supvr, 56-67. *Mem:* Am Chem Soc; Sigma Xi. *Res:* Applied product and process research. *Mailing Add:* 5575 Clinton Dr Beaumont TX 77706-6330

BROUNS, RICHARD JOHN, ANALYTICAL CHEMISTRY, NUCLEAR CHEMISTRY. *Current Pos:* RETIRED. *Personal Data:* b Osakis, Minn, Oct 2, 17; m 52, Katherine N Neidhold; c Margaret, Katherine, Richard, Matthew, Virginia & Thomas. *Educ:* St John's Univ, Minn, BS, 42; Iowa State

Col, MS, 44, PhD(analytical chem), 48. *Prof Exp:* Plant supvr, Cardox Corp, Okla, 44-45; res chemist, Gen Elec Co, Wash, 48-52, supvr analytical chem res, 52-61, opers res analyst, 61-64; res assoc, Pac Northwest Labs, Battelle Mem Inst, 65-86. *Mem:* Am Chem Soc; Inst Nuclear Mat Mgt. *Res:* Analytical chemistry; electrochemistry; radiochemistry; instrumentation; development of nuclear safeguards systems through materials accounting measurements and statistics. *Mailing Add:* 1424 Sanford Richland WA 99352-3139

BROUS, DON W, artificial kidney systems, for more information see previous edition

BROUS, JACK, INORGANIC CHEMISTRY, PHYSICAL CHEMISTRY. *Current Pos:* mgr chem res & develop, 70-73, SR STAFF SCIENTIST, ALPHA METALS CORP, JERSEY CITY, 73- *Personal Data:* b New York, NY, Nov 14, 26; m 51, Joan Weiss; c Robin. *Educ:* City Col NY, BS, 48; Univ Chicago, SM, 49; Polytech Inst Brooklyn, PhD(inorg chem), 53. *Prof Exp:* Develop engr, Gen Eng Labs, Gen Elec Co, 52-55 & Power Tube Dept, 55-57; develop engr, RCA, 57-58, engr leader, Chem & Phys Lab, 58-68; dir process develop, Pyrofilm Corp, NJ, 69-70. *Mem:* Am Chem Soc; Sigma Xi; Inst Interconnecting & Packaging Electronic Circuits. *Res:* Inorganic dielectrics; ferroelectrics; x-ray diffraction; thermionic electron emission studies; high vacuum technology; getter materials; thermal measurements; electronic materials; cleaning materials and processes; invented the Ionograph for measurement of residual ionic contamination; surface insulation studies; surface electrical leakage phenomena of electronic insulating surfaces and the effects which different processes and processing materials have on it. *Mailing Add:* 35 Brandon Ave Livingston NJ 07039. *Fax:* 201-434-2529

BROUSSEAU, NICOLE, OPTICS. *Current Pos:* SCI RESEARCHER OPTICS, DEPT NAT DEFENSE, 75- *Personal Data:* b Quebec, Can, Oct 5, 48. *Educ:* Laval Univ, BS, 70, MS, 72, PhD(optics), 75. *Concurrent Pos:* Res asst optics, Laval Univ, 75. *Mem:* Can Asn Physicists. *Res:* Optical processing of synthetic aperture radar data; acousto-optics optical data processing. *Mailing Add:* 6-1 Timberview Way Nepean ON K2H 9M7 Can

BROUTMAN, LAWRENCE JAY, MATERIALS & POLYMER SCIENCE. *Current Pos:* assoc prof mech & mat, 66-70, PROF MAT ENG, ILL INST TECHNOL, 70- *Personal Data:* b Chicago, Ill, Feb 9, 38; m 61; c 2. *Educ:* Mass Inst Technol, SB, 59, SM, 61, ScD(mat eng), 63. *Prof Exp:* Res engr, IIT Res Inst, 63-65, sr res engr, 65-66. *Concurrent Pos:* Consult, US Air Force Mat Lab, 66-67, Aeronca Inc, 66-69, US Army Mat & Mech Res Ctr, 69- & Atomic Energy Comn, 68- *Mem:* Soc Plastics Engrs; Soc Rheol; Soc Exp Stress Anal; Am Soc Testing & Mat; Sigma Xi. *Res:* Properties and structure of organic polymers; fracture phenomena in nonmetallic materials; structure and properties of composite materials. *Mailing Add:* Metall & Mat Ill Inst Technol 3300 S Federal St Chicago IL 60616-3732

BROUWER, HENRY, SEDIMENT REMEDIATION. *Current Pos:* ASSOC PROF CHEM, REDEEMER COL, 85- *Personal Data:* b Neth, Sept, 1943; Can citizen; m 66, Jane Nieboer; c Eric, Laura, Brenda, Darren & Duane. *Educ:* Univ Western Ont, BSc, 66, PhD(chem), 71. *Concurrent Pos:* Res assoc, Can Ctr Inland Waters, 89-95; Sci educ consult, Ont Alliance Christian Sch, 92-; fac mem, Au Sable Inst Environ Studies, 94- *Mem:* Chem Inst Can. *Res:* Curriculum development. *Mailing Add:* Redeemer Col 777 Hwy 53 E Ancaster ON L9K 1J4 Can

BROUWERS, ELISABETH M, MICROPALEONTOLOGY. *Current Pos:* ASSOC RES GEOLOGIST, GEOL DIV, US GEOL SURV, 96- *Personal Data:* b Rotterdam, Neth, Oct 27, 50. *Educ:* Univ Ill, BS, 72, MS, 77; Univ Colo, PhD(geol), 86. *Mailing Add:* Geol Div US Geol Surv MS 911 Fed Ctr Denver CO 80225. *Fax:* 303-236-5448; *E-Mail:* brouwers@usgs.gov

BROWALL, KENNETH WALTER, PHYSICAL CHEMISTRY. *Current Pos:* PHYS CHEMIST, DIV CORP RES & DEVELOP, GEN ELEC CO, 69- *Personal Data:* b Boston, Mass, May 24, 47; m 72. *Educ:* Tufts Univ, BS, 69; Rensselaer Polytech Inst, MS, 72, PhD(chem), 76. *Mem:* Am Chem Soc; Electrochem Soc; Sigma Xi. *Res:* Structure and properties of solid electrolytes; power production-conversion systems; one-dimensional conductors; batteries and fuel cells; thin film deposition. *Mailing Add:* Gen Elec Co Res & Develop Ctr PO Box 8 Schenectady NY 12301-0008

BROWDER, DAVID SHELDON, MATHEMATICS, ANALYSIS & FUNCTIONAL ANALYSIS. *Current Pos:* PROF MATH, SIMMONS COL, 71- *Personal Data:* b Chicago, Ill, Jan 18, 44; m 66, Elizabeth True; c Emily & Sarah. *Educ:* Amherst Col, BA, 66; Univ Ore, MA, 68, Phd(math), 71. *Res:* Pedagogical computer applications. *Mailing Add:* 177 Aspinwall Ave Brookline MA 02146

BROWDER, FELIX EARL, MATHEMATICAL ANALYSIS. *Current Pos:* vpres res, 86-91, UNIV PROF, RUTGERS UNIV, 86- *Personal Data:* b Moscow, Russia, July 31, 27; nat US; m 49, Eva Tuslowitz; c Thomas & William. *Educ:* Mass Inst Technol, SB, 46; Princeton Univ, MA, 47, PhD(math), 48. *Hon Degrees:* MA, Yale Univ, 62; Dr, Univ Paris, 90. *Honors & Awards:* Colloquim lectr, Am Math Soc, 76. *Prof Exp:* Moore instr math, Mass Inst Technol, 48-51; instr, Boston Univ, 51-53; asst prof, Brandeis Univ, 55-56; from asst prof to prof, Yale Univ, 56-63; prof, Univ Chicago, 63-72, chmn dept, 72-77 & 80-85, Louis Block prof, 72-82, Max Mason distinguished serv prof math, 82-86. *Concurrent Pos:* Vis mem, Inst Advan Study, 53-54 & 63-64; vis prof, Inst Advan Study, 53-54 & 63-64, Inst Pure & Appl Math, Rio de Janeiro, 60, Mass Inst Technol, 61-62 & 77-78, Princeton Univ, 68 & Univ Paris, 72, 75, 78, 81, 83 & 87; Guggenheim fels, 53-54 & 66-67; NSF sr fel, 57-58; Sloan Found fel, 59-63; ed, Bull Am Math Soc, 59-68 & 77-83, assoc ed, Ann Math, 64-69; vis assoc, Calif Inst Technol, 67, 78, Fairchild distinguished vis scholar, 75-76; sr res fel, Univ Sussex, 70-76; mem var sci comts, NSF, Nat Res Coun, Nat Acad Sci, 71- *Mem:* Nat Acad Sci; Am Math Soc; fel AAAS; fel Am Acad Arts & Sci; Sigma Xi. *Res:* Partial differential equations and nonlinear functional analysis. *Mailing Add:* 37 Quince Pl North Brunswick NJ 08902-1346. *Fax:* 732-932-5530; *E-Mail:* browder@math.rutgers.edu

BROWDER, JAMES STEVE, SOLID STATE PHYSICS, OPTICS. *Current Pos:* from asst prof to assoc prof, 71-77, PROF PHYSICS, JACKSONVILLE UNIV, 77- *Personal Data:* b Goodwater, Ala, Aug 5, 39; m 62; c 3. *Educ:* Rollins Col, BS, 61; Univ Fla, MS, 63, PhD(physics), 67. *Prof Exp:* Asst physics, Univ Fla, 64-67, res asst, 67-68, fel, 68; asst prof, Northwestern State Univ, 68-71. *Concurrent Pos:* NSF acad year exten grant, 69-71. *Mem:* Am Asn Physics Teachers; Optical Soc Am; Am Phys Soc. *Res:* Use of a three-terminal capacitance dilatometer to study the thermal expansion of solids (single crystals, polycrystals and glasses) in the temperature range from room temperature down to 16 kelvin. *Mailing Add:* Dept Math & Sci Jacksonville Univ 2300 University Blvd N Jacksonville FL 32211-3393

BROWDER, LEON WILFRED, DEVELOPMENTAL BIOLOGY. *Current Pos:* asst prof biol, 69-72, assoc prof, 72-78, PROF BIOL, UNIV CALGARY, 78- *Personal Data:* b Pueblo, Colo, Apr 19, 40; m 63; c 2. *Educ:* Univ Colo, BA, 62; La State Univ, MS, 64; Univ Minn, PhD(zool), 67. *Prof Exp:* Res assoc, Univ Colo, 67-69. *Concurrent Pos:* NIH fels, 67-69; Nat Res Coun Can grant, 70- *Mem:* Can Soc Cell Biol; Soc Develop Biol; Genetics Soc Can; Am Soc Cell Biol; AAAS; Fedn Am Soc Exp Biol. *Res:* Control of amphibian pigment cell differentiation; control of genic expression during oogenesis and early development in amphibians; nuclear differentiation during development. *Mailing Add:* Dept Biol Univ Calgary 2500 University Dr NW Calgary AB T2N 1N4 Can. *Fax:* 403-289-9311

BROWDER, LEWIS EUGENE, PLANT PATHOLOGY. *Current Pos:* RETIRED. *Personal Data:* b McQueen, Okla, Jan 29, 32; m 54; c 3. *Educ:* Okla State Univ, BS, 54, MS, 56; Kans State Univ, PhD(plant path), 65. *Prof Exp:* Plant pathologist, Okla State Univ, 56-58; plant pathologist, USDA, 58-66, res plant pathologist, 66-88; asst prof of plant path, Kans State Univ, 58-88. *Mem:* Am Phytopath Soc. *Res:* Physiologic specialization of cereal rusts. *Mailing Add:* 9890 Anderson Ave Riley KS 66531

BROWDER, WILLIAM, TOPOLOGY. *Current Pos:* chmn, 71-73, PROF, DEPT MATH, PRINCETON UNIV, 64- *Personal Data:* b New York, NY, Jan 6, 34. *Educ:* Mass Inst Technol, BS, 54; Princeton Univ, PhD(math), 58. *Prof Exp:* Instr math, Univ Rochester, 57-58; from instr to assoc prof, Cornell Univ, 58-63; mem, Inst Advan Study, 63-64 & 83. *Concurrent Pos:* NSF post doc fel, Univ Chicago, Oxford, 59-60; speaker, Int Cong Math, Moscow, 66 & Nice, 70; mem coun, Am Math Soc, 67-69, 72-74 & Colloquium lectr, 77; assoc prof, Fac Sci Orsay, Univ Paris, 67-68; John Simon Guggenheim fel, 74-75; vis fel, Harvard Univ, 74; vis lectr, Tata Inst Fundamental Res, Bombay, 75; chmn, Off Math Sci & mem, Assembly Math & Phys Sci, NSF & Nat Res Coun, 78-84; SRC sr fel, Oxford, 78-79; chmn, Panel Math, Off Sci & Technol Policy, White House, 83; vis prof, Aarhus Univ, 84, Univ Chicago & North Western Univ, 85; mem, Max Planck Inst Math, 88-89; ed, Annals Math. *Mem:* Nat Acad Sci; Am Acad Arts & Sci; Am Math Soc (vpres, 77-78, pres, 89-90). *Res:* Algebraic topology with special interests in the topology of manifolds and compact transformation groups. *Mailing Add:* Dept Math Princeton Univ Fine Hall Washington Rd Princeton NJ 08544-1000

BROWDY, CRAIG LAWRENCE, AQUACULTURE, SHRIMP MARICULTURE. *Current Pos:* RES MARINE SCIENTIST, SC WILDLIFE & MARINE RESOURCES, WADDELL MARICULT CTR, 89- *Personal Data:* b Wash, DC, June 9, 58; m 88; c 1. *Educ:* Univ Md, BA, 80, BSc, 81; Tel Aviv Univ, PhD(marine zool), 89. *Prof Exp:* Tech & res asst aquacult & invert zool, Israel Oceanog & Limnol Res, Nat Ctr Maricult, 81-89. *Concurrent Pos:* Teaching asst, Zool Dept, Tel Aviv Univ, 84-88; consult shrimp maricult, 89- *Mem:* World Aquacult Soc; Crustacean Soc; Am Soc Zoologists. *Res:* Aspects of shrimp mariculture; systems design, experimental to commercial scale for maturation and spawning; larval culture, nurseries and growout; physiology and endocrine control of reproduction in crustaceans; shrimp disease pathology. *Mailing Add:* 16 Firethorn Lane Hilton Head SC 29928

BROWE, JOHN HAROLD, PUBLIC HEALTH & EPIDEMIOLOGY. *Current Pos:* RETIRED. *Personal Data:* b Burlington, Vt, Nov 17, 15; m 39, Clare Hornbeck; c Clare M, Patricia H, James P & John G. *Educ:* Univ Vt, AB, 37, MD, 40; Columbia Univ, MPH, 50. *Prof Exp:* Res assoc med & clin dir nutrit study, Col Med, Univ Vt, 46-49; pub health physician in training, NY State Dept Health, 49-50, actg dir, Bur Nutrit, 50-51, dir, Bur Nutrit, 51-77. *Concurrent Pos:* Consult, USPHS, 47, 56-73 & Vt State Dept Health, 48-49; assoc, Albany Med Col, 52-55, instr, 58-66; mem, Am Bd Nutrit; mem panel nutrit, Life Sci Comt, Space Sci Bd, Nat Acad Sci, 62-70, mem coun epidemiol, Am Heart Asn, 66-77; mem consult group for dietitians, Albany Regional Med Prog, 69-73. *Mem:* Fel Am Pub Health Asn; Am Soc Clin Nutrit; Am Inst Nutrit; Asn State & Territorial Pub Health Nutrit Dirs (pres, 57-58); Latin Am Soc Nutrit. *Res:* Human nutrition. *Mailing Add:* 4 Locust Ave Troy NY 12180-5124

BROWELL, EDWARD VERN, LASER REMOTE SENSING, ATMOSPHERIC SCIENCES. *Current Pos:* SR RES SCIENTIST & HEAD LIDAR APPL GROUP, ATMOSPHERIC SCI DIV, LANGLEY RES CTR, NASA, 74- *Personal Data:* b Indiana, Pa, Feb 6, 47; m 69, Judith R Good; c Dean. *Educ:* Univ Fla, BSAE, 68, MS, 71, PhD(appl optics), 74. *Prof Exp:* Res asst appl optics, Aerospace Eng Dept, Univ Fla, 69-74. *Mem:* Fel Optical Soc Am; Am Meteorol Soc; Am Geophys Union; AAAS. *Res:* Remote sensing of atmospheric gases and aerosols using pulsed tunable laser systems; studies of atmospheric dynamics and chemistry in troposphere and stratosphere; atmospheric environmental sciences. *Mailing Add:* MS 401-A NASA Langley Res Ctr Hampton VA 23681-0001. *Fax:* 757-864-7790; *E-Mail:* e.v.browell@larc.nasa.gov

BROWER, ALLEN S(PENCER), ELECTRICAL ENGINEERING. *Current Pos:* mem advan eng prog, 53-56, admin staff, 56-59, mgr tech educ, NY Region, 59-61, metal rolling appln engr, 61-66, systs engr, 66-69, MGR SYSTS ADVAN DEVELOP, DRIVE SYSTS DEPT, GEN ELEC CO, 70- *Personal Data:* b Poughkeepsie, NY, Sept 28, 26; m 49; c 3. *Educ:* Columbia Univ, AB, 47, BS, 48, MSEE, 50. *Prof Exp:* Asst elec eng, Columbia Univ, 48-49, instr, 49-53. *Mem:* Inst Elec & Electronics Engrs; assoc mem Asn Iron & Steel Engrs. *Res:* Industrial process control; computer technology. *Mailing Add:* 30 Beechwood Dr Burnt Hills NY 12027

BROWER, JAMES CLINTON, INVERTEBRATE PALEONTOLOGY. *Current Pos:* From asst prof to assoc prof, 63-74, PROF GEOL, SYRACUSE UNIV, 74- *Personal Data:* b New Rochelle, NY, June 27, 34; m; c 2. *Educ:* Am Univ, BS, 59, MS, 61; Univ Wis, PhD(geol), 64. *Mem:* Soc Syst Zool; Soc Econ Paleontologists & Mineralogists; Int Asn Math Geol; Paleont Soc; Int Paleont Asn. *Res:* Paleobiology; Paleozoic crinoids; geostatistics. *Mailing Add:* Dept Geol Syracuse Univ Syracuse NY 13244-1070

BROWER, JOHN HAROLD, biological control, radiation ecology, for more information see previous edition

BROWER, KAY ROBERT, ORGANIC CHEMISTRY. *Current Pos:* assoc prof, 56-70, chmn dept, 70-77, PROF CHEM, NMEX INST MINING & TECHNOL, 70- *Personal Data:* b Altus, Okla, June 7, 28; m 48; c 2. *Educ:* Mass Inst Technol, BS, 48; Univ Maine, MS, 51; Lehigh Univ, PhD(chem), 53. *Prof Exp:* Instr chem, Lehigh Univ, 53-54; res assoc, Univ Ill, 54-56. *Mem:* Fel AAAS; Am Chem Soc. *Res:* Chlorination products of organic compounds of sulfur; coumarins and chromones; kinetics of aromatic nucleophilic substitution reactions; volumes of activation of organic reactions; odor and chemical structure; chemistry of explosive decomposition. *Mailing Add:* 1306 Vista Dr Socorro NM 87801

BROWER, KEITH LAMAR, PHYSICS. *Current Pos:* mem tech staff magnetic resonance, 66-90, COMPUT SIMULATION, SANDIA LABS, 90- *Personal Data:* b South Haven, Mich, Oct 24, 36; m 60, Elizabeth Oosterhof; c William Paul, Rebecca Jill & Hendrik Keith. *Educ:* Hope Col, AB, 58; Univ Minn, MS, 61; Univ Ill, PhD(physics), 66. *Prof Exp:* Res assoc ion & plasma physics, Electronics Group, Gen Mills, 61-62. *Mem:* Am Phys Soc. *Res:* Radiation damage in semiconductors and insulators; computer simulation of satellite systems and associated phenomenology. *Mailing Add:* Sandia Labs Org 6524 PO Box 5800 Albuquerque NM 87185-0977

BROWER, LINCOLN PIERSON, ECOLOGY, EVOLUTION & ANIMAL BEHAVIOR. *Current Pos:* PROF, 80-, DISTINGUISHED SERV PROF ZOOL, UNIV FLA, 95- *Personal Data:* b Summit, NJ, Sept 10, 31; m 90, Linda Susan Fink; c Andrew B & Tamsin (White). *Educ:* Princeton Univ, AB, 53; Yale Univ, PhD(zool), 57, Amherst Col, MA, 62. *Honors & Awards:* Linnean Gold Medal Zool, Soc London, 93; Distinguished Animal Behaviorist, Outstanding Lifetime Achievement Award, Animal Behav Soc 96. *Prof Exp:* Fulbright scholar, Oxford Univ, 57-58; from instr to prof, Amherst Col, 58-75, Stone prof biol, 75-80. *Concurrent Pos:* NIH spec fel, Oxford Univ, 63-64; res prof biol, Sweet Briar Col. *Mem:* Fel AAAS; Am Soc Naturalists (vpres, 84); Am Soc Zoologists; Am Inst Biol Sci; Soc Study Evolution (pres, 79); Int Soc Chem Ecol (pres, 84). *Res:* Experimental study of ecology; evolution; animal behavior; ecological chemistry; automimicry; migration of monarch butterfly; conservation of biodiversity. *Mailing Add:* Dept Zool Univ Fla 123 Bartram Hall Gainesville FL 32611. *E-Mail:* lpb@zoo.ufl.edu

BROWER, THOMAS DUDLEY, ORTHOPEDIC SURGERY. *Current Pos:* PROF ORTHOPED, MED CTR, UNIV KY, 64- *Personal Data:* b Birch Tree, Mo, Mar 15, 24; m 48; c 2. *Educ:* Cent Col, BS, 45; Wash Univ, MD, 47. *Prof Exp:* Intern surg, Univ Chicago Clins, 47-48; fel orthoped surg, Albany Med Col, 48-49; resident orthoped surg, Univ Chicago Clins, 49-54, instr surg, 54-55; from asst prof to assoc prof orthoped, Univ Pittsburgh, 55-64. *Mem:* Am Acad Orthoped Surg; Am Orthoped Soc. *Res:* Articular cartilage. *Mailing Add:* Div Orthoped Surg Univ Ky Med Ctr Lexington KY 40506

BROWER, WILLIAM B, JR, FLUID MECHANICS, AERONAUTICAL ENGINEERING. *Current Pos:* RETIRED. *Personal Data:* b Jersey City, NJ, Oct 29, 22; m 46; c 3. *Educ:* Rensselaer Polytech Inst, BAeroE, 50, MAeroE, 51, PhD(aeronaut eng), 61. *Prof Exp:* Res assoc aerodyn, Rensselaer Polytech Inst, 52-56, asst prof fluid mech, 56-62, assoc prof fluid mech, 62-89, assoc prof aeronaut & mech eng, 68-89. *Concurrent Pos:* Res Engr, NAm Aviation, Inc, 51-52; fel, Inst Blaise Pascal, Nat Sci Res Ctr, France, 53-54; consult, Curtiss-Wright Corp, 57, Avco Corp, 57-60, NY State Natural Gas Corp, 63-64 & Gen Elec Co, 70. *Mem:* Am Soc Mech Engrs. *Res:* Electrical analogy computation; compressible flow, especially unsteady fluid mechanics; high-speed tube transportation; flow meter inventor. *Mailing Add:* 47 Second St Troy NY 12180

BROWMAN, HOWARD IRVING, ICHTHYOPLANKTON-ZOOPLANKTON INTERACTIONS, VISION & VISUALLY-GUIDED BEHAVIOR IN FISHES. *Current Pos:* RES SCIENTIST, DEPT FISHERIES & OCEANS CAN, MAURICE-LAMONTAGNE INST, 93- *Personal Data:* b Montreal, Que, Oct 31, 58; m 92, Isabelle Bernard; c Muriel Bernard-Browman. *Educ:* McGill Univ, BSc, 82, MSc, 85; Univ Kans, PhD(syst & ecol), 89. *Prof Exp:* Asst scientist, Sea Educ Asn, Woods Hole, 84; res asst, Dept Systs & Ecol, Univ Kans, 86-89; res assoc fel, Dept Biol, Hamilton Found, Univ Mont, 89-90, Med Res Coun Can, Univ Victoria, 90-93. *Concurrent Pos:* NE regional rep, Early Life Hist Sect, Am Fisheries Soc, 90, western regional rep, 91-92; adj asst prof oceanog, Univ Que, Rimaiski, 94; adj asst prof biol, Concordia Univ, 94. *Mem:* Am Fisheries Soc; Animal Behav Soc; Am Soc Limnol & Oceanog; Int Soc Neuroethology; Soc Neurosci. *Res:* Early life history, metamorphosis and foraging behavior in fishes; sensory ecology; ontogenetic sensitive periods; neuroethology of the visual system in fishes; effects of ultraviolet radiation on organisms and ecosystems. *Mailing Add:* Marine Prod Div Maurice-Lamontagne Inst 850 Rte de la Mer Mont-Joli PQ G5H 3Z4 Can. *Fax:* 418-775-0546; *E-Mail:* heudsh_browman@qc.dfo.ca

BROWN, A HAYDEN, JR, BEEF CATTLE GENETICS & BREEDING, BEEF CATTLE ADAPTATION. *Current Pos:* From asst prof to assoc prof, 77-88, PROF ANIMAL SCI, UNIV ARK, FAYETTEVILLE, 88- *Personal Data:* b Cookeville, Tenn, Oct 13, 46; m 77, Helen Gann; c Ashley. *Educ:* Tenn Technol Univ, BS, 68; Univ Tenn, Knoxville, MS, 74, PhD(genetics), 76. *Mem:* Sigma Xi; Am Soc Animal Sci; NY Acad Sci; AAAS. *Res:* Adaptation of beef cattle to climatic and production resources, and genetic improvement through artificial selection. *Mailing Add:* E 212 Animal Sci Bldg Univ Ark Fayetteville AR 72701

BROWN, ACTON RICHARD, plant breeding; deceased, see previous edition for last biography

BROWN, ALAN CHARLTON, AERONAUTICS, STEALTH TECHNOLOGY. *Current Pos:* RETIRED. *Personal Data:* b Whitley Bay, Eng, Dec 5, 29; m 52, Gweneth E Bowler; c Yvonne, Christine, Diane & Maureen. *Educ:* Hull Tech Col, Eng, dipl, 50; Cranfield Inst Technol, Eng, MS, 52; Stanford Univ, MS, 64. *Honors & Awards:* Aircraft Design Award, Am Inst Aeronaut & Astronaut, 90. *Prof Exp:* Apprentice, Blackburn Aircraft Ltd, Eng, 45-50; aerodynamicist, Bristol Aeroplane Co, 52-56; res scientist, Univ Southern Calif, Los Angeles, 56-58, Wiancko Eng Co, 58-60, Lockheed Missiles & Space Co, 60-66; group leader, Lockheed Aeronaut Systs Co, 66-69, dept mgr, Lockheed Aerospace Systs Co, 69-78, chief engr F-117A, 78-82, dir Stealth technol, 82-89, dir eng, Lockheed Corp, 89-92. *Mem:* Nat Acad Eng; fel Am Inst Aeronaut & Astronaut; fel Royal Aero Soc. *Res:* Stealth technology; total external and materials design of Hare Blue and F-117A stealth aircraft. *Mailing Add:* 388 Aptos Ridge Circle Watsonville CA 95076-8518

BROWN, ALAN R, IMMUNO-REGULATION, PROTEIN AEROSOLS & RESPIRATORY MUCOSAL IMMUNITY. *Current Pos:* ASSOC PROF, KANS STATE UNIV, 91- *Educ:* Univ Fla, Gainesville, PhD(immunol & microbiol), 77. *Prof Exp:* asst mem immunol, St Jude's Hosp, 80-91. *Mem:* Am Asn Immunol. *Res:* Immune modulation in the respiratory tract using aerosolized proteins; aerosol vaccine development. *Mailing Add:* Dept Diag Med Pathobiol Kans State Univ Vet Med Sch Manhattan KS 66506. *Fax:* 785-532-4039

BROWN, ALBERT LOREN, VETERINARY MICROBIOLOGY. *Current Pos:* RETIRED. *Personal Data:* b Rochester, NY, Aug 27, 23; m 49; c 3. *Educ:* Cornell Univ, BS, 48, MS, 49, PhD(bact), 51. *Prof Exp:* Asst bact, Cornell Univ, 48-51; res assoc virol, Sharp & Dohme Div, Merck & Co, Inc, 51-55, tech asst to dir biol prod, 55-57; res biologist, Norden Labs, 57-61, sr res scientist, 61-84, dir molecular microbiol, Res & Develop, 84-87, distinguished scientist, 87-90. *Concurrent Pos:* NIH spec fel, Sloan-Kettering Inst Cancer Res, 64; res fel, Dept Clin Vet Med, Cambridge Univ, Eng, 79. *Mem:* Am Soc Microbiol; US Animal Health Asn; Conf Res Workers Animal Dis; Int Asn Biol Stand. *Res:* Veterinary biological products; viruses; canine distemper; rabies; leptospira; tissue culture; immunology. *Mailing Add:* 859 Moraine Dr Lincoln NE 68510

BROWN, ALEX CYRIL, ECONOMIC GEOLOGY, ORE GENESIS. *Current Pos:* from asst prof to assoc prof, 70-80, PROF ECON GEOL, ECOLE POLYTECH, UNIV MONTREAL, 80- *Personal Data:* b Petrolia, Ont, July 24, 38; m 64, 74, 83, Jane C Ledwell; c Christian. *Educ:* Univ Western Ont, BSc, 62; Univ Mich, MS, 65, PhD(geol & mineral), 68. *Honors & Awards:* Gold Medal Geol, Univ Western Ont, 62; Waldemar Lindgren Citation, Soc Econ Geologists, 71; Thoyer Lindsley Vis Lectr, Soc Econ Geologists, 93-94; Duncan R Derry Medal, Mineral Deposits Div, Geol Asn Can, 94. *Prof Exp:* Tech officer, Geol Surv Can, 62-63; dir, Mineral Explor Res Inst, Montreal, 84-85. *Concurrent Pos:* Nat Res Coun Can & NATO postdoctoral fel, Univ Liege, 68-70, Sigma Xi res grant-in-aid, 69; grants, Nat Sci & Eng Res Coun Can, Ecole Polytech, Univ Montreal, 70-, FCAC-FCAR res grants, 82-, Natural Sci & Eng Res Coun Can Strategic grant, 89-; Geol Surv Can res contracts, 74-76; sabbatical leave, Geol Surv Can, 80-81; invited prof, Inst Nat De Recherche Scientifique-Georessources, Stefoy, Que, 80-84

& 96; adj prof, Derry-Rust Res Unit, Ottawa-Carleton Ctr Geosci Studies, 84-94; sabbatical leave, Univ Col, Cardiff, Wales, 87-88, CNRS-CRPG, Nancy, France, 94, Univ Calif, Riverside, 95. *Mem:* Geol Asn Can; Mineral Asn Can; Can Inst Mining & Metall; Soc Geol Appl Mineral Deposits; Soc Econ Geologists; Geol Soc Belg. *Res:* Mineralization of sediment-hosted base metal deposits; Archean gold deposits; Mississippi Valley type lead-zinc deposits; volcanogenic massive sulfide deposits. *Mailing Add:* Ecole Polytech, Univ Montreal PO Box 6079 Sta Centre Ville Montreal PQ H3C 3A7 Can. *Fax:* 514-340-4191

BROWN, ALEXANDRA LOUISE, MOLECULAR BIOLOGY. *Current Pos:* MOLECULAR BIOLOGIST, NIH, 85- *Personal Data:* b Woking, Eng, May 26, 53; US citizen; m, Stephen P Miller; c 2. *Educ:* Univ Wash, BS, 74; Univ Wis, PhD(org chem), 80. *Prof Exp:* Fel, Johns Hopkins Univ, 80-81, McArdle Lab, Univ Wis, 82-84. *Mem:* AAAS; Am Chem Soc. *Res:* Investigation of mechanisms of heterochromatin stabilizaton and destabilization and regulation of transcription. *Mailing Add:* 11215 Ashley Dr Rockville MD 20852

BROWN, ALFRED BRUCE, JR, ELECTRON PHYSICS. *Current Pos:* RETIRED. *Personal Data:* b Oak Park, Ill, May 11, 20; m 56; c 3. *Educ:* Lehigh Univ, BS, 42; Calif Inst Technol, MS, 47, PhD(physics), 50. *Prof Exp:* Res assoc, Gen Elec Res Lab, 50-56; mem tech staff, Bell Labs, 56-62, dept head, 62-75, consult, 75-82, consult, AT&T Info Syst, 83-85. *Mem:* AAAS; Am Phys Soc; Inst Elec & Electronics Engrs. *Res:* Data transmission. *Mailing Add:* 109 Edgemont Rd Upper Montclair NJ 07043

BROWN, ALFRED EDWARD, ORGANIC CHEMISTRY. *Current Pos:* RETIRED. *Personal Data:* b Elizabeth, NJ, Nov 22, 16; m 44; c 2. *Educ:* Rutgers Univ, BSc, 38; Ohio State Univ, MSc, 40, PhD(chem), 42. *Prof Exp:* Org chemist, USDA, 42-45; res assoc, Off Sci Res & Develop, 45; res assoc & asst dir, Harris Res Labs, 45-53, from asst dir res to dir res, 53-61, from vpres to pres, 53-66; pres, Celanese Res Co, 66-75, corp dir sci affairs, Celanese Corp, 76-81. *Concurrent Pos:* Mem, adv bd mil personnel supplies & mem, Comt Fire Safety Aspects Polymeric Mat, Nat Res Coun. *Mem:* Nat Acad Eng; Asn Res Dirs (pres, 72-73); Am Asn Textile Chemists & Colorists; Am Chem Soc; fel Am Inst Chemists. *Res:* Organic polymers; resins; fibers; coatings; films; carbohydrates and proteins; consumer products; structure-property relationships. *Mailing Add:* Somerset House II 5610 Wisconsin Ave Apt 408 Chevy Chase MD 20815

BROWN, ALFRED ELLIS, CELL ULTRASTRUCTURE. *Current Pos:* ASST PROF, DEPT BOT & MICROBIOL, AUBURN UNIV, 80- *Personal Data:* b Ingelwood, Calif, Mar 4, 41; m 69; c 1. *Educ:* Calif State Col, Long Beach, BS, 66; Univ Calif, Los Angeles, PhD(microbiol), 71. *Prof Exp:* Fel, Sch Med, Ind Univ, 71-72; NIH fel & res biologist, Univ Calif, San Diego, 72-76, res chemist, 76-77; asst researcher & lectr, Univ Calif, Los Angeles, 78-80. *Concurrent Pos:* Consult, 3M Corp, 79-80. *Mem:* Am Soc Microbiol; AAAS; Sigma Xi. *Res:* Structure, function and biogenesis of membranes in both eukaryotic and prokaryotic systems; photosynthetic membrane systems. *Mailing Add:* 1220 E Samford Ave Auburn AL 36830-6335

BROWN, ALISON KAY, NAVIGATION SYSTEMS, ESTIMATION & CONTROL. *Current Pos:* PRES, NAVSYS CORP, 86- *Personal Data:* b Edinburgh, Scotland, Jan 1, 57; US citizen. *Educ:* Cambridge Univ, Eng, BA & MA, 79; Mass Inst Technol, SM, 81; Univ Calif, Los Angeles, PhD(mech & aerospace eng), 84. *Honors & Awards:* Sir George Nelson Prize for Appl Mech, Cambridge Univ, 89. *Prof Exp:* Sr engr, Litton Guidance & Control, 81-84, sr mem tech staff, Litton Aero Prod, 84-86. *Concurrent Pos:* Chmn, Comt Global Positioning Syst Integrity, 87-89, Ion Satellite Div Int Conf, 88-89; ed, Global Positioning Syst World, 90-, Global Ionospheric Studies World, 90- *Mem:* Inst Navig; Inst Elec & Electronics Engrs. *Res:* Research and development related to systems design and applications of the global positioning system. *Mailing Add:* NAVSYS 14960 Woodcarver Rd Colorado Springs CO 80921-2370

BROWN, ANTHONY WILLIAM ALDRIDGE, insect physiology, toxicology, for more information see previous edition

BROWN, ARLEN, MATHEMATICS. *Current Pos:* prof, 67-91, EMER PROF MATH, IND UNIV, BLOOMINGTON, 91- *Personal Data:* b Goshen, Ind, Sept 5, 26; m 48, 64; c 3. *Educ:* Univ Chicago, PhB, 48, BS, 49, MS, 50, PhD(math), 52. *Prof Exp:* From instr to assoc prof math, Rice Inst, 52-63; assoc prof, Univ Mich, 63-67. *Mem:* Am Math Soc. *Res:* Operators on Hilbert spaces; theory of operators. *Mailing Add:* 460 E Kenwood Pl Bloomington IN 47408

BROWN, ARLIN JAMES, PHYSICS, NUTRITION. *Current Pos:* RETIRED. *Personal Data:* b Suffern, NY, Apr 10, 33. *Educ:* Franklin & Marshall Col, BS, 55. *Prof Exp:* Instr radiol warfare, Chem Biol Radiol Warfare Sch, US Army, 59-60, physicist liquid crystals, Night Vision Lab, 61-70, physicist infrared detectors, 70-74, physicist image processing, 74-78, physicist lasers, Night Vision & Electro-Optics Lab, 78-88. *Concurrent Pos:* Dir, Arlin J Brown Info Ctr Inc, 63- *Res:* Alternative cancer treatment; preventive health; lasers. *Mailing Add:* PO Box 251 Ft Belvoir VA 22060. *Fax:* 540-752-4324

BROWN, ARNOLD, INFECTIOUS DISEASES. *Current Pos:* CHIEF STAFF, DORN VET ADMIN HOSP, TOGUS, ME, 96- *Personal Data:* b Philadelphia, Pa, July 20, 39; m 64, Marguerite Schlumpf; c Daniel, Genevieve & Dahvid. *Educ:* Univ Calif, Los Angeles, AB, 60; Univ Southern Calif, Los Angeles, MD, 64. *Prof Exp:* Intern, Peter Bent Brigham Hosp, Boston, 64-66; mem staff internal med, US Naval Dispensary, Norfolk, 66-68; sr res & fel, Stanford Univ Hosp, 68-72; fel molecular virol, Univ Geneva, Switz, 72-73; staff physician, Vet Admin Med Ctr, Pittsburgh, 73-75, chief, Infectious Dis Sect & Microbiol Lab, 75-81; assoc chief staff res, Dorn Vet Admin Hosp, Columbia, 81-96. *Concurrent Pos:* Asst prof med, Sch Med, Univ Pittsburgh, 73-81, asst prof microbiol, Grad Sch Pub Health, 75-81, assoc prof infectious dis & microbiol, 84-91; assoc prof med & microbiol/immunol, Sch Med, Univ SC, Columbia, 81-84, prof, 84-96; chief, Prev Med, US Army Med Dept Activ, Ft Jackson, 91; chief prof servs, 3270th USAR Hosp, 92-95, comdr, 95-96,; actg dep dir, DVA Cent Off, Med Res Soc, 93-94; comdr, 330th Combat Support Hosp, 96- *Mem:* Fel Infectious Dis Soc Am; Am Soc Microbiol; Am Fedn Med Res; Soc Exp Biol & Med; Asn Mil Surgeons US; AAAS. *Res:* Bacterial taxonomy; control of environmental adaptation; chemical and genetic methods to classify members of the family Legionellaceae; diagnostic probes; epidemiology and preventive medicine. *Mailing Add:* Dorn Vet Admin & Regional Off Ctr Togus ME 04330. *Fax:* 207-623-5792; *E-Mail:* brown.arnold@togus.va.gov

BROWN, ARNOLD LANEHART, JR, PATHOLOGY. *Current Pos:* DEAN & PROF PATH & LAB MED, UNIV WIS, 78- *Personal Data:* b Wooster, Ohio, Jan 26, 26; m 49; c 5. *Educ:* Med Col Va, MD, 49. *Prof Exp:* Resident path, Presby-St Lukes Hosp, 50-51; instr, Med Sch, Univ Ill, 53-59; from instr to assoc prof path, Mayo Grad Sch Med, Univ Minn, 59-71, chmn, dept path & anat, 68-78, prof path, Mayo Med Sch, 71-78. *Concurrent Pos:* Resident, Presby-St Lukes Hosp, 53-56; NIH fel, 56-59; consult, Mayo Clin, 59-; mem, Nat Cancer Adv Coun, 70-72 & Nat Cancer Adv Bd, 72-74; consult, Nat Cancer Adv Bd Carcinogenesis & Nat Organ Site Progs, 74-79, chmn comt determination carcinogenicity of cyclamates, 75-76; chmn coun of deans, Asn Am Med Cols, 84-85. *Mem:* Am Asn Path & Bact; Am Soc Exp Path; Am Soc Clin Path; Am Gastroenterol Asn; Int Acad Path; Sigma Xi. *Res:* Fine structural and biochemical aspects of pathology. *Mailing Add:* Dept Path Univ Wis Med Sch 1300 University Ave Rm 1205 Madison WI 53706-1532. *Fax:* 608-262-2327

BROWN, ARTHUR A(USTIN), ENGINEERING PHYSICS. *Current Pos:* RETIRED. *Personal Data:* b Cleveland, Ohio, Feb 12, 15; m 45; c 2. *Educ:* Oberlin Col, AB, 36; Brown Univ, MS, 37, PhD(physics), 41. *Prof Exp:* Installation lab engr, Pratt & Whitney Aircraft Div, United Aircraft Corp, 40-53; vpres & gen mgr, Bowser Tech Refrig Div, Bowser, Inc, 53; vpres eng, Frederick Res Corp, 53-54; proj engr, United Aircraft Corp, 55-68, chief qual engr, Pratt & Whitney Aircraft Div, 68-77. *Concurrent Pos:* Mem spec subcomt induction syst de-icing, Nat Adv Comt Aeronaut, 42-46, chmn, 46, mem subcomt de-icing probs, 47-53, chmn, 51-52. *Mem:* AAAS; Am Nuclear Soc; Am Soc Heating, Refrig & Air-Conditioning Engrs. *Res:* Quality control; aircraft engine performance; icing of aircraft; engine and component test equipment; environmental test equipment; nuclear test facility design. *Mailing Add:* 341 Tall Timbers Rd Glastonbury CT 06033

BROWN, ARTHUR CHARLES, PHYSIOLOGY, NEUROSCIENCES. *Current Pos:* PROF PHYSIOL & PHARMACOL, ASSOC DEAN, SCH DENT, PROF PHYSIOL, SCH MED, ORE HEALTH SCI UNIV, 77- *Personal Data:* b South Bend, Ind, Feb 7, 29; m 53; c 5. *Educ:* Univ Chicago, AB, 48, MS, 54, Univ Wash, PhD(physiol, biophys), 60. *Prof Exp:* Asst physics, Univ Chicago, 51-52; asst physics, Univ Wash, 54-55, asst physiol, 55-56; instr, State Univ NY Upstate Med Ctr, 58-60; from instr to assoc prof, Univ Wash, 60-69, prof physiol & biophys, 70-77. *Concurrent Pos:* Vis lectr physiol & actg head dept, Fac Med, Univ Malaya, 69-70; chmn, Physiol Sect, Am Asn Dent Schs, 70-71, 81-82 & 86-87; mem, Comput Biomath Sci Study Sect, NIH, 73-77; hon prof, Fac Med, Univ Hong Kong, 90-91. *Mem:* Int Asn Study Pain; Am Physiol Soc; Int Asn Dent Res; Soc Neurosci; Am Asn Dent Schs. *Res:* Temperature regulation; dental and oral physiology and biophysics; neurophysiology of pain. *Mailing Add:* Ore Health Sci Univ 611 SW Campus Dr Portland OR 97201-3097. *Fax:* 503-494-4666; *E-Mail:* brownac@ohsu.edu

BROWN, ARTHUR LLOYD, SOIL SCIENCE. *Current Pos:* RETIRED. *Personal Data:* b Edmonton, Alta, Feb 16, 15; nat US; m 44, Ruth E Oliver; c Michael, Stephen, Karen & Philip. *Educ:* Univ Alta, BSc, 39, MSc, 41; Univ Minn, PhD(soil sci), 46. *Prof Exp:* Agr asst, Can Dept Agr, 39-42; asst soil sci, Univ Minn, 43-45; analyst, Univ Alta, 46; soil surveyor, Res Coun Alta, 46-47; instr soils & jr soil technologist, Univ Calif, Davis, 47-5l, assoc specialist soils, 51-57, lectr soils, Exp Sta, 51-57, specialist, 57-8l. *Mem:* AAAS; Am Soc Agron; Soil Sci Soc Am. *Res:* Soil chemistry, particularly heavy metals, especially zinc and cadmium, in the soil in relation to amounts aquired by food products; methods of diagnosing nutrient deficiencies and excesses. *Mailing Add:* 38 Parkside Dr Davis CA 95616

BROWN, ARTHUR MORTON, PHYSIOLOGY, BIOPHYSICS. *Current Pos:* PROF & CHMN DEPT PHYSIOL & MOLECULAR BIOPHYS, BAYLOR COL MED, HOUSTON, 85- *Personal Data:* b Winnipeg, Man, Mar 3, 32; div; c 4. *Educ:* Univ Man, MD, 56; Univ London, PhD(physiol), 64. *Prof Exp:* Asst resident path, Columbia-Presby Med Ctr, 56-57; asst resident med, Col Med, Univ Utah, 57-59, trainee cardiol, 59-61; res fel, Cardiovasc Res Inst, Univ Calif, San Francisco Med Ctr, 64-66, asst prof med & physiol, 66-69, from assoc prof to prof physiol & internal med, 69-73; prof & chmn dept physiol & biophys, Univ Tex Med Br, Galveston, 73-85. *Concurrent Pos:* Chmn physiol study sect, NIH, 74-76; mem Cardiovascular B Res Comt, Am Heart Asn, 76-79. *Mem:* AAAS; Am Physiol Soc; Soc Gen Physiologists; Biophys Soc. *Res:* Membrane biophysics; phototransduction; neurocirculatory control; cardiology. *Mailing Add:* Case Western Reserve Univ 2500 Metro Health Dr Cleveland OH 44109-1998. *Fax:* 713-798-3311

BROWN, AUDREY KATHLEEN, PEDIATRICS, HEMATOLOGY. *Current Pos:* PROF PEDIAT, STATE UNIV NY DOWNSTATE MED CTR, 74-, VCHMN DEPT, 76- *Personal Data:* b New York, NY, Feb 2, 23; m 54; c 1. *Educ:* Columbia Univ, BA, 44, MA, 45, MD, 50; Am Bd Pediat, dipl, 56 & cert hematol-oncol, 74. *Prof Exp:* Intern med, Columbia Med Div, Bellevue Hosp, NY, 50-51, intern & asst resident, Children's Med Serv, 51-53; Holt fel pediat, Babies Hosp, Columbia Presby Med Ctr, 53-54; civilian pediatrician, Walter Reed Army Med Ctr, 54-55; from instr to asst prof pediat, Col Med, Wayne State Univ, 55-59; from asst prof to assoc prof, Sch Med, Univ Va, 59-67; prof, Med Col Ga, 67-73, actg chmn dept, 69-73. *Concurrent Pos:* Asst & asst pediatrician, Children's Hosp, Mich, 55-57, assoc pediatrician, 58, assoc hematologist, 58-59; sr res assoc, Child Res Ctr Mich, 55-59; assoc dir, Hemat Training Grant; pediatrician, Univ Va Hosp, 59-, dir, Pediat Hemat Clin, 60-; med coordr & dir res, Children's Rehab Ctr, Va, 59-, physician in charge ped, hematol-oncol, 74-; mem perinatal biol & infant mortality training grant rev comt, NIH. *Mem:* Fel Am Acad Pediat; Soc Pediat Res; NY Acad Sci; Am Fedn Clin Res; Am Pediat Soc (secy-treas, 83-); Sigma Xi; Harvey Soc; Soc Woman Geogr. *Res:* Hyperbilirubinemia; neonatal development of the glucuronide conjugating system; Bilirubin bending; infantile pyknocytosis; fetal hemoglobin development; sickle cell anemia; nutrition and development. *Mailing Add:* Dept Pediat State Univ NY Health Sci Col Med 450 Clarkson Ave Brooklyn NY 11203-2012

BROWN, AUSTIN ROBERT, JR, COMPUTER GRAPHICS. *Current Pos:* from assoc prof to prof math, 65-88, dir comput ctr, 65-81, EMER PROF MATH, COLO SCH MINES, 88- *Personal Data:* b Kansas City, Mo, Dec 13, 25; m 51, Ann Barnett; c Douglas, Donald & Deborah. *Educ:* Grinnell Col, BA, 49; Yale Univ, MA, 50, PhD(math) 52. *Honors & Awards:* Fulbright lectr, Cyprus, 87. *Prof Exp:* Mathematician, Ballistic Res Labs, 49-53, chief comput methods sect, 53-54; assoc prof, Drury Col, 54-56; chief ballistic comput br, Air Force Armament Ctr, 56-58 & Air Proving Ground Ctr, Eglin AFB, Fla, 58; opers analyst, Hq Air Defense Command, USAF, 58-65. *Concurrent Pos:* Lectr, Univ Del, 52-54; adj prof, Colo Col, 62-63. *Mem:* Math Asn Am; Asn Comput Mach; Sigma Xi. *Res:* Computer aided instruction in mathematics. *Mailing Add:* 407 Peery Pkwy Golden CO 80403-1539

BROWN, BARBARA ILLINGWORTH, PHYSIOLOGICAL CHEMISTRY. *Current Pos:* Asst & res asst prof physiol chem, Wash Univ, 50-64, res assoc prof biol chem, 64-74, prof, 74-89, EMER PROF BIOL CHEM, SCH MED, WASH UNIV, 89- *Personal Data:* b Hartford, Conn, May 12, 24; m 51, David H; c 3. *Educ:* Smith Col, BA, 46; Yale Univ, PhD, 50. *Concurrent Pos:* Estab investr, Am Heart Asn, 66-71. *Mem:* Am Soc Biol Chemists; Brit Biochem Soc; Am Soc Human Genetics; Soc Inherit Metab Dis. *Res:* Carbohydrate metabolism; phosphorylase; glycogen storage disease. *Mailing Add:* 6440 Cecil Ave Clayton MO 63105

BROWN, BARKER HASTINGS, BIOLOGICAL CHEMISTRY, AGRICULTURAL CHEMISTRY. *Current Pos:* CHMN & TECH ADV, VULCHEM CORP, 87- *Personal Data:* b Olathe, Colo, June 24, 10; m 37; c 4. *Educ:* Alma Col, AB, 32; Univ Mich, MS, 33, PhD(biol chem), 37. *Prof Exp:* Asst prof chem, Univ Philippines, 37-42; vis asst prof biol chem, Univ Mich, 45-46; sales mgr chem & equip, Philippine Am Drug & Soutraco, 46-48; prof chem, Univ Philippines, 48-52; sales & mkt dir, Macondray & Co, 52-76; dir & tech adv, Vulcan Indust & Mining Corp, 76-86. *Concurrent Pos:* Fel, Univ Mich, 32-33 & 36-37. *Mem:* Am Chem Soc; AAAS; Philippine AAS; Chem Soc Philippines; Nat Res Coun Philippines; NY Acad Sci. *Res:* Intermediary metabolism sulfur containing amino acids; nutrition in field of utilization of natural occurring inorganic elements, primarily calcium and iron. *Mailing Add:* Bendana Brown Pizarro Assocs Quad Alpha Centrum 6th Fl Mandaluyong Philippines

BROWN, BARRY LEE, COMPUTER SCIENCES, REPRODUCTIVE PHYSIOLOGY. *Current Pos:* RES CHEMIST ENDOCRINOL, RES UNIT, FED BUR INVEST LAB DIV, 74- *Personal Data:* b Kingman, Ariz, June 29, 44; m 77; c 2. *Educ:* Univ Ga, BSA, 66, MS, 68; Purdue Univ, PhD(physiol), 72. *Prof Exp:* Res asst, Dept Animal Sci, Univ Ga, 66-68, Purdue Univ, 68-72; res fel, Dept Pop Dynamics, Johns Hopkins Univ, 72-74. *Concurrent Pos:* Asst prof lectr, Dept Biol Sci, George Washington Univ, 75-80, assoc prof lectr, 80- *Mem:* Soc Study Reproduction; Endocrine Soc. *Res:* Biochemistry and physiology of the testis; development and application of techniques, relating principally to endocrinology and forensic science; application of computers to laboratory environment. *Mailing Add:* Res Unit FBI Lab Div 935 Pennsylvania Ave NW Washington DC 20535

BROWN, BARRY STEPHEN, IN VITRO & IN VIVO CENTRAL NERVOUS SYSTEM, CARDIAC ELECTROPHYSIOLOGY. *Current Pos:* group leader, DuPont Critical Care, 86-89, res assoc, Dupont Pharmaceut, 89-90, PRIN RES SCIENTIST, DUPONT MERCK PHARMACEUT CO, 91- *Personal Data:* b Wilkes-Barre, Pa, Oct 18, 49; m 73, Carol Sharon; c Eric & Laura. *Educ:* Pa State Univ, BS, 71; Yale Univ, MS, 73; Univ SFla, PhD(pharmacol), 79. *Prof Exp:* NIH trainee, Yale Univ, 71-73; asst, Univ SFla, 74-79; fel, Mich State Univ, 79-80; Mich Heart Asn res fel, Mich State Univ, 80-81; res investr, 81-83, sr res investr, Am Critical Care, Div of Am Hosp Supply Corp, 83-86. *Concurrent Pos:* Adj prof, Dept Biol, Univ Del, 96- *Mem:* AAAS; Am Soc Pharmacol & Exp Therapeut; Soc Neurosci. *Res:* Effects of cardiovascular and central nervous system drugs on membrane potentials and ionic currents in cardiac and brain tissue. *Mailing Add:* Dupont Merck Pharmaceut Co PO Box 80400 Exp Sta Wilmington DE 19880-0400. *Fax:* 302-695-7407; *E-Mail:* brownbs@a1.lldmpc.umc.dupont.com

BROWN, BARRY W, MATHEMATICAL BIOLOGY. *Current Pos:* assoc prof, 65-80, PROF, DEPT BIOMATH, UNIV TEX M D ANDERSON HOSP & TUMOR INST, 80- *Personal Data:* b Buffalo, NY, Dec 20, 39; m 63; c 3. *Educ:* Univ Chicago, BS, 59; Univ Calif, Berkeley, MA, 61, PhD(math), 63. *Prof Exp:* Res assoc statist & asst prof biol sci, Comput Ctr, Univ Chicago, 63-65. *Concurrent Pos:* Chief sect comput sci, M D Anderson Hosp, 72- *Mem:* Asn Comput Mach; Am Statist Asn. *Res:* Mathematical problems arising in biological sciences. *Mailing Add:* Dept Statist Rice Univ 6100 Main St Houston TX 77005-1827

BROWN, BENJAMIN LATHROP, APPLIED PHYSICS. *Current Pos:* ASST PROF, MT HOLYOKE COL, 90- *Personal Data:* b Alton, Ill, Sept 25, 47; m 83; c 1. *Educ:* Principia Col, BS, 72; New York Univ, MS, 84; Brandeis Univ, PhD(physics), 87. *Prof Exp:* Mem tech staff, Physics, AT&T Bell Labs, 84-87; res assoc, Harvard Univ, 87-88; IBM res fel, Harvard Univ, 88-89. *Concurrent Pos:* Consult, AT&T Bell Lab, 87-88. *Mem:* Am Phys Soc. *Res:* Positron negative work function measurement; search for gravitational waves with a Weber Bar; laboratory simulations of galactic positron annihilation; positron plasma studies. *Mailing Add:* Physics Dept Mt Holyoke Col South Hadley MA 01075

BROWN, BERT ELWOOD, PHYSICS, ATMOSPHERIC PHYSICS. *Current Pos:* from instr to prof, 60-83, chmn, Dept Physics, 70-80, EMER PROF PHYSICS, UNIV PUGET SOUND, 83- *Personal Data:* b The Dalles, Ore, Sept 27, 26. *Educ:* Wash State Univ, BS, 49; Calif Inst Technol, MS, 53; Ore State Univ, PhD(physics), 63. *Prof Exp:* Naval architect, Puget Sound Naval Shipyard, 53-54, physicist, 54-56. *Concurrent Pos:* Consult, 83-84 & Tacoma Metro Parks, 91- *Mem:* Am Phys Soc; Am Asn Physics Teachers; Sigma Xi. *Res:* Atomic physics; atmospheric physics; climatology. *Mailing Add:* 6842 N 11 St Tacoma WA 98406

BROWN, BEVAN W, JR, WATER RESOURCES. *Current Pos:* CONSULT, ENG PLANNING, 88- *Personal Data:* b Starr, SC, Oct 19, 28; m 86; c 3. *Educ:* Clemson Univ, BS, 49, MS, 50; Stanford Univ, MS, 68. *Prof Exp:* Sect supvr, TVA-Flood Protection Br, 50-64, asst br chief, 64-72, asst, div water mgt, 72-74, asst dir, div water mgt, 74-79, dir, Div Nat Resources, 79, deputy mgr, office Nat Resources, 79-82, dir, Div Air & Water Res, 82-88. *Concurrent Pos:* Consult, Agr Int Develop Paraguay, 83, Peoples Republic China, 84, UN, Mozambique govt, 84. *Mem:* Am Soc Civil Engrs; Int Water Resources Assoc. *Mailing Add:* 4638 Cobblestone Circle Knoxville TN 37938

BROWN, BEVERLY ANN, IMMUNOCHEMISTRY, PROTEIN CHEMISTRY. *Current Pos:* RES ASSOC, NEW ENG NUCLEAR-DUPONT, 81-88, 90- *Personal Data:* b San Antonio, Tex, July 21, 51; m 72. *Educ:* Incarnate Word Col, BS, 73; Univ Tex, MA, 74; Univ Minn, PhD(biochem), 79. *Prof Exp:* Res assoc, Harvard Med Sch, 79-81; Baxter Health, 89-90. *Mem:* Am Chem Soc; AAAS; Am Soc Med Technol; Am Soc Neurochem; Am Asn Immunologists. *Res:* Investigating the feasibility of using monoclonal antibodies against cancer antigens in the diagnosis and treatment of cancer. *Mailing Add:* Res & Develop Dept NEN Life Sci 549 Albany St Boston MA 02118-2512. *Fax:* 978-667-2555

BROWN, BILLINGS, THERMODYNAMICS. *Current Pos:* RETIRED. *Personal Data:* b Seattle, Wash, June 23, 20; m 46; c 7. *Educ:* Univ Wash, BS & MS, 51, PhD(phys chem), 53. *Prof Exp:* Assoc prof chem eng, Brigham Young Univ, 53-59; tech specialist thermodynamics, Hercules Inc, 59-63; supvr solid rockets, Boeing Co, 63-64; prof chem eng, Univ Wash, 64-65; sr tech specialist solid rockets, Hercules Inc, 65-66; mem tech staff, Inst Defense Analyses, 66-68; sr tech specialist solid rockets, Hercules, Inc, 68-83. *Concurrent Pos:* Mem joint Army Navy Air Force Thermochem Panel, 58-71 & Interagency Working Group on Safety, 72- *Mem:* Am Inst Chem Engrs. *Res:* Explosion mechanisms of solid rocket fuels. *Mailing Add:* 3501 S 3650 E Salt Lake City UT 84109

BROWN, BOYD ALEX, NUCLEAR PHYSICS. *Current Pos:* res assoc, Cyclotron Lab, Mich State Univ, 75-78, from asst prof to assoc prof, 82-90, PROF, PHYSICS & ASTRON DEPT & NAT SUPERCONDUCTING CYCLOTRON LAB, MICH STATE UNIV, 90-, HEAD, NUCLEAR THEORY GROUP, 93- *Personal Data:* b Sept 25, 48; m 84, Mary Hohenstein; c Mark & Elizabeth. *Educ:* Ohio State Univ, BA; State Univ NY, Stony Brook, MS, 71, PhD(physics), 74. *Honors & Awards:* Humboldt Res Award for Sr US Scientists, 91. *Prof Exp:* Res fel, Japan Soc Prom Sci, Univ Tokyo, 74-75; res assoc, Tech Univ Munchen, Ger, 75, State Univ NY, Stony Brook, 75; res officer, Nuclear Physics Lab, Oxford Univ, 78-82. *Concurrent Pos:* Prin investr, NSF, 87-94. *Mem:* Fel Am Phys Soc. *Res:* Nuclear physics; nuclear astrophysics; author of over 200 publications. *Mailing Add:* Cyclotron Lab Mich State Univ East Lansing MI 48824

BROWN, BRADFORD E, FISHERIES BIOLOGY, ECOLOGY. *Current Pos:* asst leader, Okla Coop Fisheries Unit, US Bur Sport Fisheries & Wildlife, leader fishery mgt biol invest, Biol Lab, 70-75, chief resource assessment div, Northeast Fisheries Ctr, 76-84, dep dir, 84-89, DIR SOUTHEAST FISHERIES CTR, NAT MARINE FISHERIES SERV, US DEPT COM, 89- *Personal Data:* b Worcester, Mass, Apr 1, 38; m 59, 74, Mable Cohen; c Jeffrey P, Gregory W, Douglas B & Bradford J. *Educ:* Cornell Univ, BS, 60; Auburn Univ, MS, 62; Okla State Univ, PhD(statist zool), 69. *Honors & Awards:* Fleming Award, 76. *Prof Exp:* Asst fish cult, Auburn Univ, 61-62; fisheries biologist, Biol Lab, US Bur Com Fisheries, 62-65. *Concurrent Pos:* Asst prof zool, Okla State Univ, 65-70; mem standing comt res & statist, Int Comn Northwest Atlantic Fisheries, 71-; adj prof biol, Bridgewater State Col, 75-; mem, Int Coun Explor of the Sea, Demersal Northern Fish Com, 75-77;

adj prof natural sci, Univ Md, Eastern Shore, 78-; mem ocean policy comt, Nat Acad Sci Fisheries Task Force; adj prof, Grad Sch Oceanog, Univ RI & fisheries, Rutgers Univ; consult multispecies fisheries, Food & Arg Orgn, 78; US sci corresp, Int Comn Conserv Atlantic Tunas, 86-, coordr, Enhanced Billfish Res Prog, 87-; adj prof, Rosenstal Sch Marine & Atmospheric Scis, Univ Miami. *Mem:* Biomet Soc; Am Fisheries Soc; AAAS; Sigma Xi; fel Am Inst Fisheries Res Biologists; Ecol Soc. *Res:* Population dynamics and ecology of fresh water environments; applications of statistical and computer technology to ecology; population dynamics of exploited marine species; ecosystem approach to marine fisheries management; statistics. *Mailing Add:* Southeast Fisheries Ctr Nat Marine Fisheries Serv NOAA Miami FL 33149. *Fax:* 305-361-4219; *E-Mail:* brad.brown@nuaa.gov

BROWN, BRUCE CLAIRE, ACCELERATOR PHYSICS, HIGH ENERGY PHYSICS. *Current Pos:* res assoc, 73-76, mem accelerator div staff, 76-82, MEM MAGNET TEST FACIL, FERMI NAT ACCELERATOR LAB, 82- *Personal Data:* b Burns, Ore, May 10, 44; div; c 2. *Educ:* Univ Rochester, BS, 66; Univ Calif, San Diego, MS, 69, PhD(physics), 73. *Prof Exp:* Res asst physics, Univ Calif, San Diego, 67-72; res assoc, Univ Mich, 72-73. *Mem:* Am Phys Soc; Inst Elec & Electronics Engrs. *Res:* Accelerator magnet testing and development; development and operation of accelerator facility; structure of protron in hadron and lepton production. *Mailing Add:* Tech Support MS 316 FermiLab PO Box 500 Batavia IL 60510. *E-Mail:* bcbrown@fnal.gov

BROWN, BRUCE ELLIOT, GEOLOGY, CRYSTALLOGRAPHY. *Current Pos:* assoc prof geol sci, 65-, EMER ASSOC PROF GEOL SCI, UNIV WIS-MILWAUKEE, 65- *Personal Data:* b Chicago, Ill, May 15, 30; m 80. *Educ:* Wheaton Col, Ill, BS, 52; Univ Wis, MS, 54, PhD(soil sci), 57, MS, 60, PhD(geol), 62. *Prof Exp:* Crystallogr, Allis-Chalmers Mfg Co, 61-65. *Mem:* Mineral Soc Am; AAAS; Am Soc Limnol & Oceanog; Nat Asn Geol Teachers. *Res:* Inorganic structure, especially clay minerals, layer silicates, feldspars and binary chalcogonides; geochemistry of carbonate lakes. *Mailing Add:* Dept Geosci Univ Wis Milwaukee WI 53201

BROWN, BRUCE STILWELL, SOLID STATE PHYSICS. *Current Pos:* Post-doctoral, 72-74, asst physicist, 74-76, physicist, Mat Sci Div, 76-79, PHYSICIST, IPNS DIV, ARGONNE NAT LAB, 79-, DIR, 86- *Personal Data:* b Chicago, Ill, Mar 15, 45; m 67, Marlene Johnson; c Rebecca. *Educ:* Miami Univ, BA, 66; Univ Ill, MS, 68, PhD(physics), 72; Univ Chicago, MBA, 84. *Mem:* Am Phys Soc; Mat Res Soc; AAAS. *Res:* Neutron scattering. *Mailing Add:* IPNS-360 Argonne Nat Lab 9700 S Cass Argonne IL 60439. *E-Mail:* bsbrown@anl.gov

BROWN, BRUCE WILLARD, ENVIRONMENTAL CHEMISTRY. *Current Pos:* from asst prof to prof, Portland State Univ, 63-93, asst dean fac, 68-70, actg dean undergrad studies, 70, asst dean acad affairs, 71, EMER PROF CHEM, PORTLAND STATE UNIV, 94- *Personal Data:* b New York, NY, Nov 25, 27; m 50; c 2. *Educ:* Polytech Inst Brooklyn, BS, 49, MS, 52; Univ Wash, PhD(chem), 61. *Prof Exp:* Instr chem, Everett Jr Col, 58-63. *Mem:* Am Chem Soc; Am Crystallog Asn; Sigma Xi. *Res:* X-ray crystallography of transition metal coordination compounds; computer programing. *Mailing Add:* Dept Chem Portland State Univ PO Box 751 Portland OR 97207-0751

BROWN, BRYAN TURNER, ornithology, avian ecology, for more information see previous edition

BROWN, BUCK F(ERGUSON), ELECTRICAL ENGINEERING. *Current Pos:* head, elec eng & computer sci & dir, Echo Res Labs, 80-89, chmn, elec & computer eng & dir res & grad studies, 90-93, DEAN RES & GRAD STUDIES, ROSE-HULMAN INST TECHNOL, 93- *Personal Data:* b Monroe, La, Oct 22, 32; m 59; c 3. *Educ:* Mass Inst Technol, SB, 55; Okla State Univ, MS, 59, PhD(elec eng), 64. *Prof Exp:* Aerophys engr, Gen Dynamics, Ft Worth, 55-56; instr elec eng, Okla State Univ, 56-64; assoc prof elec eng, La Tech Univ, 64-76, prof, 76-80; dir res & develop, Lincoln Electronics, Inc, 69-80; prog dir, NSF, 89-90. *Concurrent Pos:* Dir res & develop, Lincoln Electronics, Inc, 69-80; electronics & comput consult, US Navy, 81-; prod develop consult, ITS indust, 85-86. *Mem:* Inst Elec & Electronics Engrs; Am Soc Eng Educ; Sigma Xi; Nat Soc Prof Engrs. *Res:* Linear control system design; linear sample data systems; non-linear control system theory; high-speed electronic interconnections. *Mailing Add:* 5500 Wabash Ave Rose-Hulman Inst Technol Terre Haute IN 47803

BROWN, BURTON PRIMROSE, ELECTRICAL ENGINEERING, RADIO ENGINEERING. *Current Pos:* RETIRED. *Personal Data:* b Denver, Colo, Dec 5, 17; m 44; c 2. *Educ:* Univ Colo, BSEE, 39; Univ Vt, MS, 41. *Honors & Awards:* Charles A Coffin Award, Gen Elec Co, 51, Charles P Steinmetz Award, 75. *Prof Exp:* Mem staff, Electronic Systs Div, Gen Elec Co, 47-62, consult engr, 63-78. *Concurrent Pos:* Asst dir defense res & eng, Dept of Defense, 62-63; asst prof elec eng, Univ Vt, 66-67; mem, USAF Sci Adv Bd, Army Sci Adv Panel. *Mem:* Nat Acad Eng; fel Inst Elec & Electronics Engrs. *Mailing Add:* 50 Brown St Baldwinsville NY 13027

BROWN, BYRON WILLIAM, JR, BIOSTATISTICS. *Current Pos:* chmn, Dept Health Res & Policy, 88-96, PROF BIOSTATIST & HEAD DIV, STANFORD UNIV MED CTR, 68- *Personal Data:* b Chicago, Ill, Apr 21, 30; m 49, Janet Hyde; c 6. *Educ:* Univ Minn, BA, 52, MA, 55, PhD, 59. *Prof Exp:* Instr biostatist, Univ Minn, 53-56; asst prof, La State Univ, 56-57; from lectr to prof & head div, Sch Pub Health, Univ Minn, Minneapolis, 57-68. *Concurrent Pos:* Consult to govt agencies & indust. *Mem:* Inst Med-Nat Acad Sci; Biomet Soc; fel Am Statist Asn; fel Am Heart Asn; Inst Math Statist; Int Statist Inst; fel AAAS. *Res:* Teaching, research and consulting in applied statistics for the biomedical sciences. *Mailing Add:* Div Biostatist Stanford Univ Med Ctr Stanford CA 94305

BROWN, CARL DEE, ENTOMOLOGY. *Current Pos:* RETIRED. *Personal Data:* b New Cambria, Kans, Oct 2, 19; m 44; c 2. *Educ:* Okla Baptist Univ, BS, 47; La State Univ, MS, 47; Iowa State Col, PhD(entom), 51. *Prof Exp:* Asst entomologist, Dept Entom & Bot, Agr Exp Sta, Univ Ky, 50-52; from asst prof to prof biol, Memphis State Univ, 52-84, chmn dept, 62-84. *Mem:* Am Entom Soc. *Mailing Add:* 3622 Spottswood Ave Memphis TN 38111

BROWN, CHARLES ALLAN, ORGANIC CHEMISTRY, ORGANOMETALLIC CHEMISTRY. *Current Pos:* res scientist chem, 75-94, SR RES SCIENTIST RES & DEVELOP, IBM RES LAB, 94- *Personal Data:* b Detroit, Mich, Mar 22, 44. *Educ:* Purdue Univ, BSc, 64; Univ Calif, Berkeley, PhD(chem), 67. *Prof Exp:* Chemist mass spectrometry, Stanford Univ, 67-69; chemist pharmaceut chem, Syntex Corp, 69-70; asst prof chem, Cornell Univ, 70-75. *Concurrent Pos:* Air Force Off Sci Res fel, Stanford Univ, 67-68, NSF fel, 68-69; consult, Exxon Res & Eng Co, 74-75. *Mem:* Am Chem Soc; AAAS. *Res:* New methods of synthesis of organic and organometallic materials; structural effects on reactivity and selectivity. *Mailing Add:* IBM Dept K13D2 650 Harry Rd San Jose CA 95120-6099

BROWN, CHARLES ERIC, FOURIER TRANSFORM-ION CYCLOTRON RESONANCE MASS SPECTROMETRY, CROSS POLARIZATION. *Current Pos:* anal bus develop coordr, BP Res, 88-92, ANAL RES MGR, BP CHEM 92- *Personal Data:* b Spangler, Pa, Nov 23, 46; m 71, Kathy L Houck; c Eric N. *Educ:* State Univ NY, Buffalo, BA, 68; Northwestern Univ, PhD(biochem), 73. *Prof Exp:* Instr & fel biochem, Northwestern Univ, 73-75; res fel neurosci, Roche Inst Molecular Biol, 75-77; from asst prof to assoc prof biochem, Med Col Wis, 77-88. *Concurrent Pos:* Consult, Nicolet Instrument Corp, 84-88, Metriflow, Inc, 84-88 & Johnson Wax, 84-88. *Mem:* Am Chem Soc; Int Soc Magnetic Resonance; Am Soc Pharmacol & Exp Therapeut; Am Soc Mass Spectros; Sigma Xi; Soc Neurosci. *Res:* Identifying and providing state-of-the-art analytical technology to support of chemical product lines; spectroscopy. *Mailing Add:* Res Resources Ctr/M/C937 901 S Wolcott E102 MSB Chicago IL 60612

BROWN, CHARLES JULIAN, JR, PHYSICAL CHEMISTRY, MEMBRANE SEPARATIONS. *Current Pos:* ADJ PROF CHEM, DEL TECH & COMMUNITY COL, 92-; MEMBRANE SEPARATIONS CONSULT, 92- *Personal Data:* b Utica, Miss, Dec 31, 32; m 63, Bernadine McGrath; c Roberta, Charles, Patrick & Thomas. *Educ:* Miss Col, BS, 54; Univ Tex, PhD(chem), 59. *Prof Exp:* Fel, Univ Tex, 59-60; res chemist, Film Dept, Exp Sta, E I du Pont de Nemours & Co, Inc, 60-65, res & develop scientist, 60-92, res chemist, Org Chem Dept, 65-73, sr res chemist, Plastics Prod & Resins Dept, 73-85, res assoc, Polymer Prod Dept, 85-92. *Mem:* Am Chem Soc; AAAS; Sigma Xi. *Res:* Polymers; reverse osmosis; membrane separations. *Mailing Add:* Ten Thornberry Dr Hockessin DE 19707

BROWN, CHARLES L(EONARD), MECHANICAL ENGINEERING. *Current Pos:* prof, 59-84, EMER PROF MECH ENG, PURDUE UNIV, 84- *Personal Data:* b Ranger, Tex, June 30, 20; m 46; c 2. *Educ:* Rice Inst, BS, 40; Purdue Univ, MS, 43, PhD(mech eng), 49. *Mem:* Am Soc Mech Engrs; Am Soc Eng Educ. *Res:* Thermodynamics; engineering analysis. *Mailing Add:* Mech Eng Purdue Univ 1288 Mech Eng Bldg West Lafayette IN 47907

BROWN, CHARLES MOSELEY, ATOMIC AND MOLECULAR SPECTROSCOPY, SOLAR & LABORATORY SPECTRA OF HIGHLY IONIZED SPECIES. *Current Pos:* PHYSICIST, NAVAL RES LAB, 78- *Personal Data:* b Kansas City, Mo, July 15, 43. *Educ:* Southern Ill Univ, BA, 65; Univ Md, PhD(physics), 71. *Prof Exp:* Nat Res Coun res assoc atomic & molecular spectros, 71-73; physicist, Naval Res Lab, 73-76; mem sr sci staff, Ball Bros Res Corp, 76-77. *Mem:* Fel Optical Soc Am. *Res:* Vacuum ultraviolet spectroscopy of atomic and molecular species; spectroscopy of laser heated plasmas; solar spectroscopy; spectroscopy of highly charged ions; electron beam ion trap studies. *Mailing Add:* Code 7674B Naval Res Lab Washington DC 20375

BROWN, CHARLES MYERS, PLANT BREEDING. *Current Pos:* first asst, Univ Ill, 54-55, from asst prof to assoc prof, 55-68, prof, 68-90, assoc head dept, 71-90, EMER PROF AGRON, UNIV ILL, URBANA-CHAMPAIGN, 90- *Personal Data:* b Oswego, SC, Oct 16, 27; m 57; c 2. *Educ:* Clemson Col, BS, 50; Univ Wis, MS, 52, PhD(agron), 54. *Prof Exp:* Asst agron, Univ Wis, 50-54. *Mem:* Am Soc Agron; Sigma Xi. *Res:* Oat and wheat breeding; genetics; cytogenetics. *Mailing Add:* 804 Brighton Dr Urbana IL 61801

BROWN, CHARLES NELSON, EXPERIMENTAL PARTICLE PHYSICS. *Current Pos:* STAFF PHYSICIST, FERMI NAT ACCELERATOR LAB, 74- *Personal Data:* b Victoria, BC, Can, June 3, 41; m 67, Mary K Ehmann; c Christopher & Susan. *Educ:* Univ BC, BSc, 63; Univ Rochester, AM, 66, PhD(physics), 68. *Prof Exp:* Res fel physics, Harvard Univ, 68-71, asst prof, 71-74. *Concurrent Pos:* Dir, Elem Particle Physics Prog, NSF, 92-93. *Mem:* Am Phys Soc; fel Am Physics Soc. *Res:* Experimental study of lepton scattering and lepton and heavy quark production in high energy collisions. *Mailing Add:* Fermi Nat Accelerator Lab PO Box 500 Batavia IL 60510. *E-Mail:* chuckb@fnal.gov

BROWN, CHARLES QUENTIN, GEOLOGY. *Current Pos:* dir instnl develop, 69-79, actg dean, Sch Technol, 81-83, chmn dept geol, 67-79 & 79-88, PROF GEOL, EAST CAROLINA UNIV, 67- *Personal Data:* b Roanoke Rapids, NC, Sept 12, 28; m 50; c 2. *Educ:* Univ NC, BS, 51, MS, 53; Va Polytech Inst, PhD(geol), 59. *Prof Exp:* From instr to assoc prof geol, Clemson Univ, 54-67. *Concurrent Pos:* Mem, NC Marine Sci Coun, 71-81 & NC Coastal Resources Ctr Admin Bd, 76-79. *Mem:* Geol Soc Am; Soc Econ Paleont & Mineral; Nat Asn Geol Teachers. *Res:* Sedimentation; clay mineralogy of recent deposits. *Mailing Add:* Dept Geol East Carolina Univ Greenville NC 27858

BROWN, CHARLES S(AVILLE), CHEMICAL ENGINEERING. *Current Pos:* RETIRED. *Personal Data:* b Orange Co, Va, Oct 1, 20; m 46, Millicent Phinneu; c Keith Carter (Dubois), Charles Saville Jr & Robert Allen. *Educ:* Va Polytech Inst, BS, 41; Univ Wis, PhD(chem eng), 46. *Prof Exp:* Control engr, Nat Aniline & Chem Co, NY, 41; dept mgr, Fermentation Unit, Abbott Labs, 44-58, dir & supt prod, 58-60, vpres prod, 60-61, US & Can opers, 61-64, pharmaceut opers, 64-66, exec vpres sci & mfg opers, 66-68, sci opers, 68-70, exec vpres admin, 70-81. *Mem:* Fel AAAS; Am Chem Soc; Am Inst Chem Engrs; Sigma Xi. *Res:* Aerobic fermentations; fermentation engineering; pharmaceutical manufacturing. *Mailing Add:* 421 Tiffany Dr Waukegan IL 60085

BROWN, CHARLES THOMAS, PHYSICAL CHEMISTRY. *Personal Data:* b Paterson, NJ, Oct 27, 28; m 53; c 2. *Educ:* Ohio Wesleyan Univ, BA, 53; Rensselaer Polytech Inst, MS, 55, PhD, 57. *Prof Exp:* Prin chemist, Battelle Mem Inst, 57-60; mgr chem sect, Nuclear Div, Combustion Eng Corp, 60-61; res chemist, United Aircraft Corp Res Labs, United Aircraft Corp, 61-75, sr res chemist, United Technol Res Ctr, 75-80. *Mem:* Am Chem Soc; Electrochem Soc. *Res:* Electrochemistry of non-aqueous systems, including material compatibility. *Mailing Add:* 38 Briarcliff Rd Colchester CT 06415-5228

BROWN, CHESTER HARVEY, JR, aeronautical, structural & aeroelastic analysis, systems analysis; deceased, see previous edition for last biography

BROWN, CHRISTOPHER L, MARINE BIOLOGY. *Current Pos:* SPECIALIST, HAWAII INST MARINE BIOL, UNIV HAWAII-MANOA, KANEOHE. *Concurrent Pos:* Fulbright scholar, Univ Gothenburg, Sweden, 95. *Res:* New therapeutic agents for use in the culture of agricultural marine larvae. *Mailing Add:* Hawaii Inst Marine Biol Univ Hawaii-Manoa Kaneohe HI 96744

BROWN, CHRISTOPHER W, SPECTROSCOPY. *Current Pos:* asst prof, 68-72, assoc prof, 72-76, PROF CHEM, UNIV RI, 76- *Personal Data:* b Maysville, Ky, Apr 13, 38; m 83, Kathleen McCall; c Chris III, Frances, Shelley, Alexander & Katie S. *Educ:* Xavier Univ, BS, 60, MS, 62; Univ Minn, PhD(phys chem), 67. *Honors & Awards:* Award, Chicago Sect, Soc Appl Spectros, 66, William F Meggers Award, 94. *Prof Exp:* Res fel chem, Univ Md, 66-68. *Concurrent Pos:* Gen chair, Fedn Anal Chem & Spectros Socs Ann Meeting, 97. *Mem:* Am Chem Soc; Am Phys Soc; Soc Appl Spectros; Am Soc Testing & Mat. *Res:* Infrared, near infrared, visible, ultraviolet, and Raman spectroscopy; fourier transform infrared; spectroscopic applications, environmental and biomedical problems; analysis of air and water pollutants; analysis of petroleum and natural gas; chemical applications of lasers; computerized spectroscopy; fiberoptics; biosensors. *Mailing Add:* Dept Chem Univ RI Kingston RI 02881. *Fax:* 401-792-5072; *E-Mail:* cbrown@chm.uri.edu

BROWN, COLIN BERTRAM, CIVIL ENGINEERING. *Current Pos:* PROF CIVIL ENG, UNIV WASH, 69- *Personal Data:* b London, Eng, Jan 15, 29; m 54; c 2. *Educ:* Univ London, BSc, 53; Univ Minn, PhD(mech, mats), 62. *Prof Exp:* Eng asst, D H Lee, Eng, 53-55; bridge designer, Lindsey County Coun, 55-57; design engr, Prov of BC, 57-59; res fel eng mech, Univ Minn, 59-61; asst prof civil eng, Univ Calif, Berkeley, 62-66; assoc prof civil eng & appl mech, Columbia Univ, 66-69. *Mem:* Am Soc Civil Engrs; Sigma Xi. *Res:* Structural mechanics; theory of interface friction; incremental problems in elasticity; statistical methods in structural engineering. *Mailing Add:* Dept Civil Eng Univ Wash Box 352700 Seattle WA 98195

BROWN, CONNELL JEAN, ANIMAL BREEDING & GENETICS. *Current Pos:* from asst prof to prof animal sci, Univ Ark, Fayetteville, 54-86, sect leader, 76-79, Univ prof, 86-90, EMER PROF, UNIV ARK, FAYETTEVILLE, 90- *Personal Data:* b Everton, Ark, Mar 6, 24; m 46, Erma D Taylor; c Craig W & Marie (Allen). *Educ:* Univ Ark, BSA, 48; Okla State Univ, MS, 50, PhD(animal sci), 56. *Prof Exp:* Asst animal husb, Okla State Univ, 48-50; asst prof, Univ Ark, Fayetteville, 50-53; asst, Okla State Univ, 53-54. *Concurrent Pos:* Consult, various activities. *Mem:* Fel AAAS; NY Acad Sci; fel Am Soc Animal Sci; Genetics Soc Am; Sigma Xi (pres); Am Regist Prof Animal Scientists. *Res:* Performance records of beef cattle for economic traits; beef cattle genetics and breeding; procedures to realize improvement of various traits; history of cattle industry. *Mailing Add:* Div Animal Sci Univ Ark Fayetteville AR 72701

BROWN, CYNTHIA ANN, ANALYSIS OF ALGORITHMS. *Current Pos:* dean, Col Comput Sci, 89-93, ASSOC PROF COMPUT SCI, NORTHEASTERN UNIV, 84- *Personal Data:* b Kansas City, Mo, Oct 9, 45; m 63; c 2. *Educ:* Mich State Univ, BS, 65; Univ Mich, MA, 66, PhD(math), 77. *Prof Exp:* Lectr comput sci, Ind Univ, 76-77, from asst prof to assoc prof, 77-84. *Concurrent Pos:* Mem tech staff, GTE Labs, 82-84. *Mem:* Asn Comput Mach; Am Asn Artificial Intel; Inst Elec & Electronic Engrs Comput Soc. *Res:* Analysis and development of algorithms, specializing in algorithms for solving search problems. *Mailing Add:* 818 NE Floral Pl Portland OR 97232

BROWN, DALE GORDON, organic chemistry, agricultural chemistry, for more information see previous edition

BROWN, DALE H(ENRY), MECHANICAL ENGINEERING, THERMAL POWER SYSTEMS. *Current Pos:* RETIRED. *Personal Data:* b Oak Grove, Mo, Apr 30, 22; m 44, Janet Ryder; c Mark & Susan. *Educ:* Rensselaer Polytech Inst, BS, 42, MS, 50. *Prof Exp:* Instr mech eng & mech, Rensselaer Polytech Inst, 43-44, asst prof thermodyn & heat eng, 46-50; thermodyn engr, Gen Elec Co, 50-56, thermal systs consult engr, 56-67, systs engr, Res & Develop Ctr, 67-69, thermal & environ systs consult engr, 69-76, energy syst engr, 76-81, energy systs mgt engr, Res & Develop Ctr, 81-85. *Concurrent Pos:* Prof eng consult thermal power systs & transient thermodyn, 85- *Mem:* Am Soc Mech Engrs; Soc Automotive Engrs; NY Acad Sci; Nat Soc Prof Engrs; Sigma Xi. *Res:* Energy production and environmental effects in the biosphere; system dynamics; transient thermodynamics; simulation of power and process apparatus; advanced energy conversion from coal; advanced cogeneration systems to produce power and heat; coal fired locomotive systems; advanced diesel engines; gas and steam turbine systems. *Mailing Add:* 5 Berkley Sq Scotia NY 12302-4210. *Fax:* 518-399-3277

BROWN, DALE MARIUS, SOLID STATE PHYSICS, ELECTRICAL ENGINEERING. *Current Pos:* RES PHYSICIST, GEN ELEC RES & DEVELOP CTR, 61- *Personal Data:* b Detroit, Mich; m 58, Norma Williamson; c Katherine & Victoria. *Educ:* Univ Mich, BS, 53, MS, 55; Purdue Univ, PhD(physics), 60. *Honors & Awards:* Region I Award, Inst Elec & Electronics Engrs, 78; Nat Electronics Award, Electrochem Soc, 90. *Concurrent Pos:* Ed, J Electrochem Soc, 77-; Gen Elec Coolidge fel, 83; Inst Elec & Electonics Engrs fel, 88. *Mem:* Fel Inst Elec & Electronics Engrs. *Res:* Solid state physics; semiconductors; electronic solid state devices; integrated circuits; materials and processes; solid state imagers; charge transfer devices; silicon carbide devices; granted 53 patents; authored 88 publications. *Mailing Add:* Gen Elec Corp PO Box Eight Schenectady NY 12301

BROWN, DAN A, CIVIL ENGINEERING. *Current Pos:* ASSOC PROF, DEPT CIVIL ENG, AUBURN UNIV. *Honors & Awards:* Walter L Huber Civil Eng Res Prize, Am Soc Civil Engrs, 95. *Mailing Add:* Dept Civil Eng Auburn Univ Harbert Eng Ctr Auburn AL 36849

BROWN, DANIEL JOSEPH, PHARMACOLOGY, TOXICOLOGY. *Current Pos:* PRES, FACT INC, 91- *Personal Data:* b Elwood, Ind, June 3, 41; m 66, Bonnie J Heinrich; c Christopher, Rachel & Amelia. *Educ:* Marian Col, BS, 63; Ind Univ, PhD(toxicol), 68. *Prof Exp:* Asst prof pharmacol & toxicol, Med Ctr, Ind Univ, Indianapolis, 69-86; asst chief forensic toxicologist, Bur Forensic Sci, Ill State Police, Springfield, 86-88, chief forensic toxicologist, 88-90; assoc dir toxicol, Roche Biomed Lab, Dublin, OH, 90-91. *Concurrent Pos:* Fel pharmacol & toxicol, Univ Wash, 68-69; res assoc, Chem Defense Estab, Porton Down, Eng, 76-77, Swiss Fed Toxicol, Univ Zurich, Switz, 84-85. *Mem:* Am Acad Forensic Sci; Soc Toxicol; Int Asn Forensic Toxicol; Soc Forensic Toxicol; Int Asn Chem Testing. *Res:* Pharmacology and toxicology of alcohols and volatile organic substances. *Mailing Add:* 3953 Mill Stone Dr Springfield IL 62707. *Fax:* 217-793-5256

BROWN, DANIEL MASON, civil engineering, for more information see previous edition

BROWN, DARRELL QUENTIN, RADIATION BIOPHYSICS. *Current Pos:* radiobiologist, 70-94, RADIATION SAFETY TECH, FOX CHASE CANCER CTR, 95- *Personal Data:* b Manhattan, Kans, May 23, 32; div; c Nancy & Quentin. *Educ:* Univ Kans, AB, 54, MS, 59; Univ Chicago, PhD(biophys), 64. *Prof Exp:* Mathematician-comput programmer, Lewis Lab, NASA, Ohio, 57; lab instr radiation biophys, Univ Kans, 58; USPHS trainee biophys, Univ Chicago, 59-64, res assoc, 64; asst prof radiation biol, Univ Tenn, Knoxville, 64-70; assoc prof radiation biol, Univ Pa, 71-75 & 79-91. *Concurrent Pos:* Consult, Oak Ridge Nat Lab, 68-69. *Mem:* AAAS; Radiation Res Soc; Sigma Xi. *Res:* Chemical and radiation carcinogenesis in vitro; effects of microbeam irradiation of parts of cells; quantitative microscopy; radiation dosimetry; radiobiological basis of radiotherapy; radiation protectors and radiation sensitizers; photodynamic therapy. *Mailing Add:* Fox Chase Cancer Ctr 7701 Burholme Ave Philadelphia PA 19111

BROWN, DAVID, CHEMICAL ENGINEERING. *Current Pos:* RETIRED. *Personal Data:* b New Rochelle, NY, Apr 25, 17; m 41; c 2. *Educ:* Swarthmore Col, BA, 38; Mass Inst Technol, MS, 40. *Prof Exp:* Engr, Stand Oil Co, Calif; chemist, Thompson, Weinman & Co, 41-42; engr, M W Kellogg Co, 42-44 & Shell Develop Co, sr vpres, 63-70, exec vpres, 70-78, vchmn, Halcon Int, Inc. *Mem:* Nat Acad Eng; Am Chem Soc; Am Inst Chem Engrs. *Res:* Unit operations, especially absorption and distillation; development of commercial organic chemical processes. *Mailing Add:* 103 Andros Rd Ocean Reef Club Key Largo FL 33037

BROWN, DAVID CHESTER, physics, for more information see previous edition

BROWN, DAVID E, CARIOVASCULAR PHYSIOLOGY, CONTROL OF PERIPHERAL CIRCULATION. *Current Pos:* ASSOC PROF PHYSIOL, WVA OSTEOP SCH MED, 87- *Personal Data:* b Ottawa, Ont, Mar 1, 47; m 83, Paula Watson. *Educ:* Univ Calif, Davis, BS, 68; Univ Guelph, MS, 74; Univ Ill, Urbana, PhD(animal sci), 81. *Prof Exp:* Asst prof & asst animal sci, Univ Nev, Reno, 80-87. *Concurrent Pos:* Prin, Limestone Lamb Co. *Mem:*

Am Soc Animal Sci; Am Physiol Soc; Int Soc Biometeor; Ctr Appln Scis & Technol. *Res:* Cardiovascular physiology of repartitioning agents; environmental physiology of pregnancy. *Mailing Add:* WVa Osteop Sch Med 400 N Lee St Lewisburg WV 24901. *Fax:* 304-645-4859; *E-Mail:* brown@osteo.wvnet.edu

BROWN, DAVID EDWARD, otolaryngology; deceased, see previous edition for last biography

BROWN, DAVID FRANCIS, AGRICULTURAL CHEMISTRY, PLANT BIOCHEMISTRY. *Current Pos:* RES CHEMIST, SOUTHERN REGIONAL RES CTR, SCI & EDUC ADMIN, USDA, 74- *Personal Data:* b Seattle, Wash, July 22, 35; m 63; c 3. *Educ:* NMex Inst Mining & Technol, BS, 58; Wash State Univ, MS, 61; Utah State Univ, PhD(plant nutrit & biochem), 70. *Prof Exp:* Instr chem, Sheridan Col, 61-62 & Yakima Valley Col, 62-65; res assoc, Southern Regional Res Ctr, Sci & Educ Admin-Agr Res, USDA, 69-72; res assoc plant biochem, Food Protein Res & Develop Ctr, Tex A&M Univ, 72-74. *Mem:* Am Chem Soc; Inst Food Technologists; Sigma Xi. *Res:* Byssinosis; flavor and aroma of foods and agricultural products. *Mailing Add:* Sci Dept Heritage Col 3240 Fort Rd Toppenish WA 98948-9599

BROWN, DAVID FREDERICK, medicine, for more information see previous edition

BROWN, DAVID G, DENTAL SCIENCE, TOXICOLOGY. *Current Pos:* Chmn, dept oral biochem, 81-85, asst dean, 83-89, ASSOC DEAN, COL DENT, UNIV NEBR, 89- *Personal Data:* b London, Ont, June 4, 43; c 2. *Educ:* Univ Colo, PhD(biochem), 70. *Mem:* Am Asn Dent Res; Am Asn Dent Schs; Sigma Xi; Am Soc Pharmacol & Exp Therapeut. *Mailing Add:* Col Dent Med Ctr Univ Nebr 40th & Holdredge Sts Lincoln NE 68583-0740. *Fax:* 402-472-6681

BROWN, DAVID HAZZARD, CELL BIOLOGY. *Current Pos:* AT DEPT BIOCHEM, WASHINGTON UNIV SCH MED. *Personal Data:* b Philadelphia, Pa, Apr 22, 25; m 55; c 2. *Educ:* Rutgers Univ, BA, 51, PhD(plant path), 65; Univ Pa, MS, 54. *Prof Exp:* Res assoc, Rutgers Univ, 65; NIH fel, Biol Div, Oak Ridge Nat Lab, Union Carbide Nuclear Corp, 65-67, staff molecular anat prog, 67-70; scientist, Oak Ridge Assoc Univs, 70- *Mem:* AAAS; Am Inst Biol Sci; Am Soc Cell Biol; Sigma Xi. *Res:* Use of radiopharmaceuticals in cancer detection; comparative studies of the cellular and physiological uptake of scintiscanning agents in normal and neoplastic tissue. *Mailing Add:* 6440 Cecil Ave Clayton MO 63105-2225

BROWN, DAVID LYLE, CELL BIOLOGY. *Current Pos:* from asst prof to assoc prof, 75-82, PROF BIOL, UNIV OTTAWA, 82- *Personal Data:* b Victoria, BC, Mar 2, 43; m 62; c 1. *Educ:* Univ BC, BSc, 66; Univ Calif, Davis, MSc, 68, PhD(biol), 69. *Prof Exp:* Fel biol, Yale Univ, 69-70. *Concurrent Pos:* Grants panel, Nat Res Coun Can, 76-79; assoc ed, Can J Biochem & Cell Biol, 85- *Mem:* Can Soc Cell Biol (secy, 71-75, pres, 77-78); Am Soc Cell Biol. *Res:* Synthesis of microtubule protein and the regulation of microtubule assembly; methylmercury effects on cytoskeleton; nuclear matrix in lymphocytes. *Mailing Add:* Dept Biol Univ Ottawa Ottawa ON K1N 6N5 Can. *Fax:* 613-564-5014

BROWN, DAVID MITCHELL, DIABETES MELLITUS, KIDNEY DEVELOPMENT & DISEASE. *Current Pos:* resident pediat, Univ Minn, 61-62, fel endocrinol & metab, 62-65, from asst prof to assoc prof pediat, Lab Med & Path, 67-73, actg head, 71, assoc head, 71-84, dir clin labs, 71-84, PROF PEDIAT, LAB MED & PATH, UNIV MINN, 73-, DEAN, MED SCH, 84- *Personal Data:* b Chicago, Ill, Nov 11, 35; c 3. *Educ:* Univ Ill, BS, 56, MD, 60. *Honors & Awards:* Mary Jane Kugel Award, Juv Diabetes Found, 87. *Prof Exp:* Rotating internship, Univ Ill Res & Educ Hosps, 60-61; attend staff pediat endocrinol, Wilford Hall USAF Hosp, 65-67. *Concurrent Pos:* Career develop award, USPHS, 68-73. *Mem:* Am Physiol Soc; Am Asn Path; Endocrine Soc; Am Soc Nephrol; Am Soc Cell Biol; Am Diabetes Asn. *Res:* Biochemical and physiologic bases for kidney complications of diabetes mellitus. *Mailing Add:* Univ Minn Med Sch 420 Delaware St SE Box 293 UMHC Minneapolis MN 55455. *Fax:* 612-626-6800

BROWN, DAVID P(AUL), ELECTRICAL ENGINEERING. *Current Pos:* PROF, ELEC SCI & SYST ENG, SOUTHERN ILL UNIV, 83- *Personal Data:* b Chicago, Ill, Aug 29, 34. *Educ:* Univ Ill, BS, 56, MS, 57; Mich State Univ, PhD(elec eng), 61. *Prof Exp:* From instr to asst prof elec eng, Mich State Univ, 60-63; from vis assoc prof to assoc prof elec eng, Univ Wis-Madison, 63-68, prof, 68- *Concurrent Pos:* Vis prof, Colo State Univ, 67 & 68; consult, Surabaya Inst Tech, Indonesia, 77. *Mem:* Inst Elec & Electronics Engrs; Sigma Xi. *Res:* Circuit theory; network analysis and synthesis; system theory. *Mailing Add:* Dept Elec Eng Southern Ill Univ Carbondale IL 62901

BROWN, DAVID RANDOLPH, COMPUTER SCIENCE, ELECTRICAL ENGINEERING. *Current Pos:* RETIRED. *Personal Data:* b Los Angeles, Calif, Oct 31, 23; m 44; c Philip, Ellen, Polly Sarah & Ann. *Educ:* Univ Wash, BS, 44; Mass Inst Technol, SM, 47. *Honors & Awards:* Naval Ord Develop Award, 46. *Prof Exp:* Asst res engr, Univ Wash, 44-46; res assoc, Mass Inst Technol, 46-48, group leader, 51-58; lectr, Univ Calif, 48-51; assoc tech dir res, Mitre Corp, 58-63; asst dir, Comput Sci & Technol Div, SRI Int, 63-93. *Mem:* Fel Inst Elec & Electronics Engrs. *Res:* Computer sciences; research administration; systems design and systems science; electronics engineering. *Mailing Add:* 1470 Sand Hill Rd Apt 309 Palo Alto CA 94304. *Fax:* 650-325-5258; *E-Mail:* drbrown@pacbell.net

BROWN, DAVID ROBERT, GASTRO-INTESTINAL PHARMACOLOGY, MOLECULAR PHARMACOLOGY. *Current Pos:* asst prof vet pharmacol, Univ Minn, 84-89, asst prof neurosci, 86-89, assoc prof vet biol, neurosci & toxicol, 89-97, FULL PROF NEUROSCI, PSYCHONEUROIMMUNOL, TOXICOL, VET BIOL & VET SURG, RADIOL & ANESTHESIOL, UNIV MINN, 97- *Personal Data:* b Johnson City, NY, Oct 1, 54; m 88, Laura J Mauro. *Educ:* Univ Rochester, BA, 76; Emory Univ, PhD(pharmacol), 81. *Prof Exp:* Fel pharmacol & physiol, Univ Chicago, 81-84. *Concurrent Pos:* Consult, 3M Pharmaceut, 90-; vis assoc prof pharmacol, Univ Naples, Italy, 90-91; vis res investr, Univ Mich Med Sch, 92-93; specific field ed, GI Pharmacol, J Pharmacol Exp Ther, 92-; bd sci reviewers, Am J Vet Res, 97- *Mem:* Soc Neurosci; Am Soc Pharmacol & Exp Therapeut; AAAS. *Res:* Neural regulation and pharmacology of epithelial ion transport; molecular pharmacology of neurotransmitter receptors; pharmacology and toxicology of host defense processes in mucous membranes. *Mailing Add:* Dept Vet Path Biol Pharmacol Sect Univ Minn 1988 Fitch Ave St Paul MN 55108

BROWN, DAVID SMITH, SOIL CHEMISTRY, ENVIRONMENTAL SCIENCE. *Current Pos:* BR CHIEF, ECOSYST RES DIV, NAT EXPOSURE RES LAB, 96- *Personal Data:* b Bluffton, Ind, Apr 26, 44; m 63; c 1. *Educ:* Purdue Univ, BSA, 66; Univ Ill, MS, 68, PhD(soil phys chem), 72. *Honors & Awards:* Bronze Medal, US Environ Protection Agency, 74, 86; Sci Achievement Award, Environ Protection Agency, 90, Ord Managerial Excellence Award, 90. *Prof Exp:* Res soil scientist, US Environ Protection Agency, 71-90, actg br chief, Environ Res Lab, 90-96. *Mem:* Am Soc Agron; Soil Sci Soc Am; Am Chem Soc. *Res:* Sorption of organic pollutants on natural soils and sediments; speciation and transport of pollutant metals in groundwaters. *Mailing Add:* 565 Caldwell Circle Athens GA 30605

BROWN, DAVID T, MATHEMATICS. *Current Pos:* ASSOC PROF COMPUT SCI & MATH, ITHACA COL, 88- *Personal Data:* b Portland, Ore, May 20, 36; m 60; c 3. *Educ:* Ottawa Univ, BA, 58; Syracuse Univ, MA, 61, PhD(math), 65; WVa Univ, MS(comput sci), 87. *Prof Exp:* Asst prof math, Hiram Col, 65-68 & Univ Pittsburgh, 68-74; from asst prof to assoc prof math, 74-82, prof math & comput sci, Bethany col, WVa, 82-88. *Mem:* Math Asn Am; Asn Comput Mach. *Res:* Theory. *Mailing Add:* Dept Math & Comput Sci Ithaca Col Ithaca NY 14850

BROWN, DAWN LARUE, NEUROSCIENCES. *Current Pos:* fel psychobiol, 75-78, LAB TECHNOLOGIST II, PSYCHOBIOL, FLA STATE UNIV, 78- *Personal Data:* b Frederick, Md, Nov 13, 48; m 80. *Educ:* Boston Univ, BA, 70; Drake Univ, MA, 72; Univ NC, Greensboro, PhD(physiol psychol), 76. *Prof Exp:* Instr psychol, NC A&T State Univ, 74-75. *Concurrent Pos:* Asn Res Vision & Ophthal travel fel, 75. *Mem:* Soc Neurosci; Asn Res Vision & Ophthal; AAAS. *Res:* Neurophysiology of vision; development of mammalian visual system; correlation of behavioral and electrophysiological properties of visual system; taste preferences and psychophysics. *Mailing Add:* 14219 Otter Run Rd Tallahassee FL 32312

BROWN, DEAN RAYMOND, MATHEMATICS. *Current Pos:* From asst prof to assoc prof, 70-84, chmn, Dept Math & Comput Sci, 78-83, PROF, YOUNGSTOWN STATE UNIV, 84- *Personal Data:* b Detroit, Mich. *Educ:* Rose Polytech Inst, BS, 60; Rensselaer Polytech Inst, MS, 64; Ohio State Univ, MS, 66, PhD(math), 70. *Mem:* Nat Coun Teachers Math; Math Asn Am. *Res:* Functional analysis. *Mailing Add:* Youngtown State Univ Youngstown OH 44555

BROWN, DENISE SCOTT, URBAN PLANNING. *Current Pos:* partner, 69-89, PRIN, VENTURI SCOTT BROWN ASSOCS INC, 89- *Personal Data:* b Nkana, Zambia, Oct 3, 31; m 67, Robert Charles Venturi; c James C. *Educ:* Univ Pa, MCP, 60, MArch, 65. *Hon Degrees:* Nine from US univs, 77-94. *Prof Exp:* Asst prof, Univ Pa, 60-65; assoc prof & head, Urban Design Prog, Univ Calif, Los Angeles, 65-68. *Concurrent Pos:* Asst prof, Univ Pa, 60-65; vis prof archit, Univ Calif, Berkeley, 65, Yale Univ, 67-70. *Mem:* Am Acad Arts & Sci; Am Planning Asn; Royal Soc Encour Arts, Mfg & Comm Urban Planning. *Res:* Commendations for designs and urban planning. *Mailing Add:* Venturi Scott Brown & Assocs Inc 4236 Main St Philadelphia PA 19127-1603

BROWN, DENNIS, RENAL CELL BIOLOGY. *Current Pos:* asst prof path, 85-88, ASSOC PROF PATH, HARVARD MED SCH, 88- *Personal Data:* b Grimsby, Eng, Mar 5, 51. *Educ:* Univ East Anglica, Eng, BS, 72, PhD(biochem), 75. *Prof Exp:* Researcher histol & embryol, Inst Histol & Embryol, 75-80; sr researcher histol, Univ Med Sch Geneva, Switz, 80-85. *Mem:* Am Soc Cell Biol; Am Soc Nephrology; Swiss Soc Exp Biol. *Res:* Renal cell biology. *Mailing Add:* Dept Med Renal Unit Mass Gen Hosp E 149 13th St Charlestown MA 02129-2060

BROWN, DENNIS TAYLOR, MOLECULAR BIOLOGY. *Current Pos:* PROF MICROBIOL, UNIV TEX, AUSTIN, 78- *Personal Data:* b Farmington, Maine, June 6, 41; m 62, 78, Bernadette M; c Raymond P & Ian G. *Educ:* Univ Pa, BA, 64, PhD, 67. *Prof Exp:* Asst prof, Dartmouth Col, Hanover, 68-69; assoc prof, Univ Md, Baltimore, 69-73; dir cell res, Inst Genetics, Univ Cologne, Fed Repub Ger, 73-78. *Mem:* Cell Biol Soc; Am Soc Virol; Am Soc Microbiol; Soc Gen Microbiol. *Res:* Microbiology; numerous articles in professional journals. *Mailing Add:* Cell Res Inst Univ Tex Biol Lab 220 Austin TX 78713-0001

BROWN, DENNISON ROBERT, MATHEMATICS. *Current Pos:* assoc prof, 67-70, PROF MATH, UNIV HOUSTON, 70- *Personal Data:* b New Orleans, La, May 17, 34; m 56, 87, Betty Sexton; c Robert B, Alan, Robert R, Sally, Ann & Mary. *Educ:* Duke Univ, BS, 55; La State Univ, MS, 60, PhD(math), 63. *Prof Exp:* Assoc math, La State Univ, 58-61; from asst prof to assoc prof, Univ Tenn, 63-67. *Concurrent Pos:* Vis lectr, Math Asn Am, 65-74; prin investr, NSF grants, 65-71; mem grad coun, Univ Houston, 69-71 & dir grad studies math, 69-72; ed, Semigroup Forum, 70-96; sr investr, NASA grants, 72-77; consult, Undergrad Prog Math, 73-81, vis consult, 81-; vis prof, La State Univ, 87-88. *Mem:* Am Math Soc; Sigma Xi; Math Asn Am. *Res:* Topological and algebraic semigroups; semigroups of matrices. *Mailing Add:* Dept Math Univ Houston University Park Houston TX 77204-3476. *Fax:* 713-743-3505; *E-Mail:* dbrown@uh.edu

BROWN, DONALD D, DEVELOPMENTAL BIOLOGY. *Current Pos:* spec fel, 60-61, dir dept, 76-94, MEM STAFF BIOCHEM, DEPT EMBRYOL, CARNEGIE INST, 61- *Personal Data:* b Cincinnati, Ohio, Dec 30, 31; m 57, Linda Weil; c 3. *Educ:* Univ Chicago, MS & MD, 56. *Hon Degrees:* DSci, Univ Chicago, 76, Univ Maryland, 83, Univ Cincinnati, 92. *Honors & Awards:* US Steel Found Award Molecular Biol, Nat Acad Sci, 73; V D Mattia lectr, Roche Inst Molecular Biol, 75; Boris Pregel Award, NY Acad Sci, 77; Ross G Harrison Prize, Int Soc Develop Biologists, 81; Feodor Lynen Medal, 87; E B Wilson Award, Am Soc Cell Biol, 96. *Prof Exp:* Intern, Charity Hosp, New Orleans, La, 56-57; res assoc biochem, NIMH, 57-59; spec fel, Pasteur Inst, Paris, 59-60. *Concurrent Pos:* Prof, Johns Hopkins Univ, 69- *Mem:* Nat Acad Sci; Am Soc Biol Chem; Soc Develop Biol; Am Acad Arts & Sci; Am Soc Cell Biol (pres, 92); Am Philos Soc. *Res:* Control of genes during development; isolation of genes. *Mailing Add:* Dept Embryol Carnegie Inst Washington 115 W University Pkwy Baltimore MD 21210. *Fax:* 410-243-6311; *E-Mail:* brown@mail1.ciwemb.edu

BROWN, DONALD FREDERICK MACKENZIE, BIOLOGICAL SCIENCES. *Current Pos:* RETIRED. *Personal Data:* b Chicago, Ill, Dec 9, 19; m 45. *Educ:* Univ Mich, BA, 49, MS, 51, PhD(bot), 58. *Prof Exp:* Asst prof natural sci, Eastern Mich Univ, 56-60, from assoc prof to prof biol, 60-87. *Mem:* AAAS; Wilderness Soc; Am Inst Biol Sci; Nat Audubon Soc; Nat Parks Asn. *Res:* Taxonomy; morphology and ecology of fern genus Woodsia; zoology; botany; applied botany and zoology; pteridology. *Mailing Add:* 15 Northwick Ct Ann Arbor MI 48105

BROWN, DONALD JEROULD, NUCLEAR WASTE ISOLATION. *Current Pos:* TECH CONSULT, BABCOK & WILCOX PROTEC, INC, 95- *Personal Data:* b Salt Lake City, Utah, Nov 4, 26; m 55, Joe Ann Johnson; c Tai, Seth & Ero. *Educ:* Univ Utah, BS, 55. *Prof Exp:* Engr nuclear waste, Gen Elec Co, 55-64 & Battelle Mem Inst, 64-65; environ engr, Isochem, Inc, 65-67 & Atlantic Richfield Co, 67-77; prin scientist, Rockwell Int, 77-78, proj mgr, 78-79, dept mgr, 79-81, chief sci adv nuclear waste isolation, 81-85; adv eng, Westinghouse Hanford Co, 86-94. *Concurrent Pos:* Dept mgr sci technol, Rockwell Hanford Co, 78-85. *Mem:* Fel Geol Soc Am; Am Asn Petrol Geologists. *Res:* Environmental safety; evaluating sites for the isolation of radioactive wastes; evaluating radionuclide migration through saturated and unsaturated sediments; directing geological, geophysical and hydrological research and assessing environmental impacts. *Mailing Add:* Battelle Pac NW Nat Lab PO Box 999 Richland WA 99352

BROWN, DONALD JOHN, INORGANIC CHEMISTRY. *Current Pos:* From instr to assoc prof, 60-87, PROF CHEM, WESTERN MICH UNIV, 87- *Personal Data:* b Utica, NY, June 1, 33; m 56, Mary E Carney; c Linda, Jeffrey & James. *Educ:* Utica Col, AB, 55; Syracuse Univ, PhD(chem), 63. *Concurrent Pos:* NIH grant, 64; res fel with Prof J Lewis, Univ London, 68; res fel with Prof B Lever, York Univ, 81; dir, Sci Citizens Ctr, Western Mich Univ, 84-; Kellogg Found grants, 85, 88, 89, CS Mott Found, 86. *Mem:* AAAS; Am Chem Soc; Asn Ground Water Scientists & Engrs; NAm Lake Mgt Soc; Am Water Resources Asn. *Res:* Magnetic and spectral investigations of transition metal complexes; synthesis and investigation of new chelating agents; ground water chemisty; water resources management. *Mailing Add:* 1624 Grand Ave Western Mich Univ Kalamazoo MI 49006

BROWN, DONALD M, PETROLEUM GEOLOGY, COAL RESOURCES. *Current Pos:* PETROL GEOL CONSULT, 81-; OWNER, BROWN CO. *Personal Data:* b Canton, Ohio, Feb 11, 20; m 43, Ruth Beaumont; c Carey, Mark, Joel & Katherine. *Educ:* Mt Union Col, BS, 42; Ohio State Univ, MS, 48. *Prof Exp:* Staff, US Geol Surv, 48-51, Unoco, 51-53, Exxon, 53-62 & Clinton Int, 62-73; vpres, Rickelson Oil & Gas, 73-78; explor mgr, White Ellis Drilling, 78-81. *Mem:* Fel Geol Soc Am. *Res:* Coal resources-oil and gas studies. *Mailing Add:* 6 Winchester Lane Bella Vista AR 72714

BROWN, DOUGLAS EDWARD, OPTICAL PHYSICS. *Current Pos:* RETIRED. *Personal Data:* b Mt Morris, Mich, Mar 25, 26; m 50; c 2. *Educ:* Univ Mich, BS, 49, MS, 51, PhD(physics), 57. *Prof Exp:* Physicist, Gen Elec Co, 51-52; res assoc, Willow Run Res Ctr, 52-53; res fel, Univ Mich, 53-56; physicist, Dow Chem Co, 56-58, Bendix Systs Div, 58-60 & Inst Sci & Technol, Univ Mich, 60-71; dir eng, Syscon Int, Ind, 71-74; physicist, Dept Defense, 74-94. *Mem:* Optical Soc Am. *Res:* Infrared; semiconductors; optics; thermal; optical data processing. *Mailing Add:* 364 W Crestmont Ct Beverly Hills FL 34465

BROWN, DOUGLAS FLETCHER, GENETICS, PLANT MOLECULAR GENETICS. *Current Pos:* RETIRED. *Personal Data:* b Rouleau, Sask, Aug 13, 34. *Educ:* Univ Sask, BSA, 57, MSc, 58; Univ Wis, PhD(genetics), 63. *Prof Exp:* Res asst genetics, Univ Wis, 61-63; asst res officer biol, Atomic Energy Can, Ltd, 63-66; prof, Bishop's Univ, 66-96. *Mem:* Genetics Soc Can; Sigma Xi. *Res:* Identification of bacterial species. *Mailing Add:* 110 Chemis Clifton Sawyerville PQ J0B 3A0 Can

BROWN, DOUGLAS RICHARD, PHYSICS. *Current Pos:* staff scientist, 77-79, MGR, ADVAN NUCLEONICS DIV, SCI APPLN, INC, 79- *Personal Data:* b Sacramento, Calif, Mar 13, 42; m 66; c 2. *Educ:* Univ Calif, Berkeley, BS, 66, MA, 68; Univ Wash, PhD(physics), 74. *Prof Exp:* Res asst, Nuclear Physics Lab, Univ Wash, 66-74; res asst nuclear physics, Cyclotron Inst, Tex A&M Univ, 74-77. *Mem:* Am Phys Soc. *Res:* Study of relatively simple modes of higher lying nuclear excitation; characterization of coal using nuclear and electromagnetic techniques; developed family of on-line coal analysis instruments for process control; applied physics and computer science. *Mailing Add:* Sci Applications Inc 2950 Patrick Henry Dr Santa Clara CA 95054

BROWN, DUANE, PHYSICAL CHEMISTRY. *Current Pos:* assoc prof, 51-58, PROF CHEM, ARIZ STATE UNIV, 58- *Personal Data:* b Fredonia, Ariz, Apr 1, 18; m 42; c 2. *Educ:* Brigham Young Univ, BS, 41; Princeton Univ & Mass Inst Technol, cert, 44; Cornell Univ, PhD(phys chem), 51. *Prof Exp:* Asst chem, Univ Nebr, 41-42 & Cornell Univ, 46-51. *Concurrent Pos:* Res chemist, Nat Carbon Res Labs, Ohio, 57 & 58; consult, World Wide Refineries, Phoenix, Ariz & Prof Metal Serv, Inc, 78- *Mem:* AAAS; Am Chem Soc. *Res:* Chemical kinetics; thermodynamics; radiation chemistry; hydrometallurgy. *Mailing Add:* 104 E Huntington Dr Tempe AZ 85282

BROWN, EARL IVAN, II, CIVIL ENGINEERING. *Current Pos:* RETIRED. *Personal Data:* b Carrolton, Ga, Feb 15, 17; m 41; c 3. *Educ:* Va Mil Inst, BS, 40; NC State Col, MS, 49; Univ Tex, PhD (struct eng), 53. *Prof Exp:* Instrumentman, Tenn Valley Authority, 40; asst engr, Big Four RR, Ind, 41-42; res engr, NC, 46; instr civil eng, NC State Col, 47-49; asst prof, GA Inst Technol, 50-53; head prof civil eng, Ala Polytech Inst, 54-58, asst dean, 58-60; Jones prof civil eng & Chem Dept, Duke Univ, 60-83. *Concurrent Pos:* Vis prof, Univ Liverpool, 66-67 & Univ Whitewatersrand, SAm, 74. *Mem:* Am Soc Civil Engrs; Am Soc Eng Educ; Am Concrete Inst; Int Asn Bridge & Struct Engrs. *Res:* Concrete design. *Mailing Add:* 230 Clearbrook Dr Matthews NC 28105

BROWN, EDGAR HENRY, JR, TOPOLOGY. *Current Pos:* from asst prof to assoc prof, 58-63, PROF MATH, BRANDEIS UNIV, 63- *Personal Data:* b Oak Park, Ill, Dec 27, 26; m 54; c 2. *Educ:* Univ Wis, BS, 49; Wash State Univ, MA, 51; Mass Inst Technol, PhD, 54. *Prof Exp:* Instr math, Washington Univ, 54-55; instr, Univ Chicago, 55-57; res assoc, Brown Univ, 57-58. *Concurrent Pos:* NSF sr fel, 61-62; Guggenheim fel, 65-66; Sci Res Coun sr fel, Univ Col, London, 73-74; Sci & Eng Res Coun sr fel, Cambridge Univ, 82-83; sr res fel, Jesus Col, Oxford, 86-87. *Mem:* Am Acad Arts & Sci; Am Math Soc. *Res:* Algebraic and differential topology. *Mailing Add:* Dept Math Brandeis Univ Waltham MA 02254

BROWN, EDMOND, THEORETICAL SOLID STATE PHYSICS. *Current Pos:* RETIRED. *Personal Data:* b Brooklyn, NY, July 22, 24; m 46, Judith A Loveys; c Adrienne, Margaret & Gail. *Educ:* Univ Ill, BS, 48; Cornell Univ, PhD(physics), 54. *Prof Exp:* From asst prof to prof physics, Rensselaer Polytech Inst, 55-94. *Concurrent Pos:* Vis prof, State Univ NY Albany, 67-68; consult, Phys Sci Div, Watervliet Arsenal, 73- *Mem:* Fel Am Phys Soc; Am Asn Physics Teachers. *Res:* Electron band theory of solids; theory of two dimensional electron gases. *Mailing Add:* 4 Scott Dr Troy NY 12180

BROWN, EDMUND HOSMER, ACOUSTIC REMOTE SENSING OCEANS & ATMOSPHERE. *Current Pos:* RETIRED. *Personal Data:* b Boston, Mass, June 19, 20; m 51, 71, Rhodora L Mosele; c Edmund R III, Nathaniel W & Cecile V Jones. *Educ:* Univ Colo, BS, 55, MS, 62. *Prof Exp:* Instr math, Univ Colo, 49-55; physicist, Boulder Labs, Nat Bur Stand, 51-57, educ dir, 57-65; physicist, Wave Propagation Lab, Nat Oceanic & Atmospheric Admin, 65-81; sr res assoc, Coop Inst Res Environ Sci, Univ Colo, 81-86. *Concurrent Pos:* Prof adjoint mech eng, Univ Colo, 57-58, vis lectr, math, 58-61; researcher, Inst Henri Poincare, 67-68; assoc ed, J Acoust Soc Am, 79-; external PhD examnr, Carleton Univ, Ottawa, 80 & Univ Melbourne, Australia, 85; consult, Phys Dept, Univ Kuwait, 85-91; invited lectr, Int sch Phys Acoust, Erice, Italy, 91. *Mem:* Fel Acoust Soc Am; Int Soc Acoust Remote Sensing (secy, 83-88). *Res:* Remote sensing of depth or altitude profiles of temperature in oceans and atmosphere; applications of complex geometry in elementary particles. *Mailing Add:* 905 15 St Boulder CO 80302-7311

BROWN, EDWARD HERRIOT, JR, FISHERIES SCIENCE, ECOLOGY. *Current Pos:* RETIRED. *Personal Data:* b Dover, NJ, Jan 2, 26; m 52; c 4. *Educ:* Mich State Univ, BS, 50; Ohio State Univ, MS, 61. *Prof Exp:* Fish mgt supvr I & II, Ohio Dept Natural Resources, Div Wildlife, 52-62; asst leader & proj leader fishery res, Little Miami River Proj, Xenia, Ohio, 52-58; proj leader design fishery surv, Olentangy Wildlife Exp Sta, Delaware, Ohio, 58-62; proj leader fishery res, US Dept Interior, Bur of Com Fisheries, Ann Arbor, 62-70; proj leader fishery res, Nat Fisheries Res Ctr-Great Lakes, US Fish & Wildlife Serv, 70-93; proj leader fishery res, Great Lakes Ctr, Nat Biol Serv, 93- *Mem:* Am Inst Fishery Res Biologists; Am Fisheries Soc. *Res:* Population dynamics and ecology of Great Lakes fishes, especially the coregonines, salmonines, and clupieds. *Mailing Add:* 2552 Old Boston Ct Ann Arbor MI 48104

BROWN, EDWARD JAMES, biohydiometallurgy, environmental biotechnology, for more information see previous edition

BROWN, EDWARD MARTIN, MATHEMATICS. *Current Pos:* res instr, 64-65, from asst prof to assoc prof, 65-72, vchmn dept, 74-78, PROF MATH, DARTMOUTH COL, 72- *Personal Data:* b Philadelphia, Pa, Sept 24, 33; m 59, 74; c 3. *Educ:* Univ Pa, AB, 58, MA, 59; Mass Inst Technol, PhD(math), 63. *Hon Degrees:* AM, Dartmouth Col, 73. *Prof Exp:* Teaching asst math, Univ Pa, 57-59; teaching asst, Mass Inst Technol, 59-62, asst instr, 62-63, instr, 63-64. *Concurrent Pos:* Staff mem, Math Res Inst, Univ Warwick, 70-71. *Mem:* Am Math Soc. *Res:* General knotting structure of complexes in manifolds; topology of 3-dimensional manifolds. *Mailing Add:* Dept Math Dartmouth Col Box 6188 Hanover NH 03755

BROWN, EDWIN WILSON, JR, COMMUNITY HEALTH, TRAVEL MEDICINE. *Current Pos:* PRES, GLOBAL HEALTH SERV, LTD, 87- *Personal Data:* b Youngstown, Ohio, Mar 6, 26; m 52, Patricia Currier; c Edwin III, John C & Wende P (Camp). *Educ:* Harvard Univ, MD, 53, MPH, 57. *Prof Exp:* Intern, E J Meyer Mem Hosp, 54-55; resident pub health, Arlington Co Health Dept, Va, 55-56; asst prof prev med, Sch Med, Tufts Univ, 58-61; dep chief staff, Boston Dispensary, 61; vis prof social & prev med, Osmania Med Col, India, 61-63; asst dir, Div Int Med Educ, Asn Am Med Cols, 63-65; dir, Proj Vietnam, Washington, DC, 65-66; dir, Div Int Health, Med Ctr, Ind Univ, 66-69, assoc prof med, Sch Med, 66-68, dir int affairs, 69-77, assoc dean & dir int serv, 81-86. *Concurrent Pos:* Field dir, Harvard Epidemiol Proj, Greenland, 56-57; consult, Boston City Health Dept, 58-60 & WHO, 73-; res assoc, Sch Pub Health, Harvard Univ, 59-60; sr adv med educ, King Faisal Univ, Saudi Arabia, 77-78; chmn bd dirs, Med Assistance Progs, Inc, Ill; chmn, Coun Int Educ Health Prof, Midwestern Univs Consortium Int Activ, Inc; mem, Med Adv Comt, Iran Found; mem bd dirs, Paul Carlson Found & Care-Medico, Int Students, Inc; mem bd govs, Int Policy Forum; pres, Global Health Services, Ltd, 87- *Mem:* Nat Coun Int Health. *Res:* Problems of medical education in developing countries. *Mailing Add:* 8153 Oakland Rd Indianapolis IN 46240. *Fax:* 317-257-7455; *E-Mail:* ewbindy@aol.com

BROWN, ELEANOR D, AVIAN VOCAL COMMUNICATION, SOCIAL BEHAVIOR OF BIRDS. *Current Pos:* FOREST POLICY COORDR, PAPUA NEW GUINEA DEPT ENVIRON & CONSERVATION, 96- *Personal Data:* b Grand Rapids, Mich, Nov 20, 49. *Educ:* Mount Holyoke Col, AB, 71; Univ Md, College Park, MS, 79, PhD(zool), 83. *Prof Exp:* Staff ed, Entom Soc Am, 84; res assoc, Univ Md, 85-86, asst res scientist, 87-90; res fel, NY Zool Soc, 90-92, conserv fel, 92-93; environ consult, Govt Papua New Guinea, 93-96. *Concurrent Pos:* Res assoc, Smithsonian Inst, 84-, Smithsonian Environ Res Ctr, 92-; prin investr, NSF, 85-86 & 87-89; vis lectr, Massey Univ, NZ, 85; vis scholar, Griffith Univ, Brisbane, 87-88; vis fel, Australian Mus, Sydney, 87-88. *Mem:* Animal Behav Soc; Am Ornithologists Union. *Res:* Interactions between frugivorous and nectarivorous birds and their rainforest food plants in New Guinea; vocal communication and cooperative behavior in cooperatively breeding Australian songbirds; environmental policy issues in Papua New Guinea; rainforest conservation in Papua New Guinea. *Mailing Add:* Div Birds Nat Mus Natural Hist Smithsonian Inst Washington DC 20560. *Fax:* 675-301-1691

BROWN, ELEANOR MOORE, PHYSICAL BIOCHEMISTRY. *Current Pos:* RES CHEMIST, EASTERN REGIONAL RES CTR, USDA, 71- *Personal Data:* b East Liverpool, Ohio, Mar 19, 36; m 60; c 1. *Educ:* Ohio Wesleyan Univ, BA, 58; Drexel Univ, MS, 67, PhD(chem), 71. *Honors & Awards:* Alsop Award, Am Leather Chemist Asn, 96. *Prof Exp:* Chemist, Harshaw Chem Co, 58-61 & Calbiochem, 61-62; res asst biochem, Mich State Univ, 64; res asst phys chem, Drexel Univ, 67-71. *Concurrent Pos:* Assoc, Nat Res Coun, 71-73; fel, Dairy Res Inc, 73-75. *Mem:* Am Chem Soc; AAAS; Am Soc Biochem & Molecular Biol; Protein Soc; Sigma Xi; Am Women Sci; Am Leather Chemist Asn. *Res:* Metal-protein and protein-protein interactions; lipid-protein interactions; protein secondary structure; lipoprotein complexes; protein modification; collagen structure and tanning mechanisms. *Mailing Add:* Eastern Regional Res Ctr USDA 600 E Mermaid Lane Wyndmoor PA 19038-8598. *Fax:* 215-233-6559; *E-Mail:* ebrown@arserrc.gov

BROWN, ELISE ANN BRANDENBURGER, REGULATORY TOXICOLOGY. *Current Pos:* STAFF OFFICER TOXICOLOGIST, FOOD SAFETY & INSPECTION SERV, USDA, 79- *Personal Data:* b Jacksonville, Fla, Dec 5, 28; m 52, Arthur Brickman; c Barron B, Terrence L B & Roderick S K. *Educ:* George Washington Univ, BS, 49, MS, 50, PhD(pharmacol), 56; Am Bd Toxicol, dipl. *Prof Exp:* Asst prof pharmacol, George Washington Univ, 56-57; pharmacologist, Nat Heart, Lung & Blood Inst, 62-79. *Concurrent Pos:* Fel, McCollum-Pratt Inst, Johns Hopkins Univ & Sinai Hosp, Baltimore, Md, 57-59; lectr, Sch Med, Georgetown Univ, 64- *Mem:* Am Chem Soc; Am Soc Pharmacol & Exp Therapeut; Int Soc Study Xenobiotics; Soc Exp Biol Med; Soc Toxicol; Am Col Toxicol; Asn Govt Toxicologists. *Res:* Toxicology of food additives; pharmacology of lung tissue; effect of drugs on lipid metabolism; cancer chemotherapy; cystic fibrosis of the pancreas; para-amino-benzoic acid metabolism; Toxicology of Pesticides; environmental Toxicology. *Mailing Add:* 6811 Nesbitt Pl McLean VA 22101. *Fax:* 202-205-0080; *E-Mail:* am.brown@usda.gov

BROWN, ELLEN, ANIMAL PHYSIOLOGY. *Current Pos:* RETIRED. *Personal Data:* b San Francisco, Calif, Apr 30, 12. *Educ:* Univ Calif, BA, 34, MD, 39. *Prof Exp:* Intern, San Francisco Hosp, 38-39; from asst resident to resident med, Univ Calif Hosp, 39-43; clin instr, Univ Calif, San Francisco, 43-44, from instr to prof, 46-79, emer prof med, Med Sch, 79. *Concurrent Pos:* Asst physician, Cowell Mem Hosp, 40-42; Commonwealth Fund fel, Harvard Med Sch, 44-46; Guggenheim fel, Oxford Univ, 58. *Mem:* AAAS; Am Physiol Soc; NY Acad Sci; Am Heart Asn. *Res:* Capillary pressure and permeability; blood volume and vascular capacity; cardiac failure; cardiac complications of pregnancy; peripheral circulation in relation to pain syndromes and vascular diseases. *Mailing Add:* 1400 Geary Blvd San Francisco CA 94116

BROWN, ELLEN RUTH, COMPUTATIONAL PHYSICS, APPLIED THEORETICAL PHYSICS. *Current Pos:* PHYSICIST, NAVAL SURFACE WARFARE CTR, 95- *Personal Data:* b New York, NY, June 15, 47. *Educ:* Mary Washington Col, BS, 69; Pa State Univ, MS, 71; Univ Va, PhD(physics), 81. *Prof Exp:* Physicist, Naval Weapons Lab, 69; teacher math, Va Pub Schs, 70-71; instr physics, Lord Fairfax Community Col, 71-74; engr, Wash Anal Serv Ctr, EG&G, 79-86, head dept, 82-86, scientist, 86-90, sr scientist, 90-95. *Mem:* Am Phys Soc; Sigma Xi. *Res:* Computational physics; band bending in semiconductors; photoionization of open-shell atoms; atmospheric optical-ray tracing; meteorological effects on reentry bodies; electromagnetic pulse calculations; energy technology transfer; physics of music; missile engagement analysis. *Mailing Add:* PO Box 1397 Fredericksburg VA 22402-1397

BROWN, ELLIS VINCENT, organic chemistry; deceased, see previous edition for last biography

BROWN, ELMER BURRELL, INTERNAL MEDICINE, HEMATOLOGY. *Current Pos:* RETIRED. *Personal Data:* b New York, NY, Apr 1, 26; m 54, Phyllis Yace; c Cynthia, Joanne, Catherine & Laura. *Educ:* Oberlin Col, AB, 46; Wash Univ, MD, 50; Am Bd Internal Med, 57. *Prof Exp:* From intern to asst resident med, Presby Hosp, NY, 50-52; from instr to assoc prof, Sch Med, Wash Univ, 55-71, chief hemat clin, 59-73, dir, Div Hemat, 64-73, prof med, 71-92, assoc dean continuing med educ, 73-91 & postgrad training, 83-92. *Concurrent Pos:* USPHS trainee hemat, Sch Med, Wash Univ, 54-55, Nat Res Coun fel, 55-57; USPHS spec res fel, Enzyme Sect, Lab Cellular Physiol, Nat Heart Inst, 57-59; consult, Wash Univ Clins, 55-57 & St Louis City Hosp, 55-57; Lederle Med Fac Award, 60-63; USPHS res career develop award, 63-70; vis prof, Royal Postgrad Med Sch, London, 69-70. *Mem:* Am Soc Hemat; Am Fedn Clin Res; Soc Exp Biol & Med; Am Soc Clin Invest; Am Soc Exp Path; Am Soc Clin Nutrit; Int Soc Hemat. *Res:* Problems of iron metabolism at the clinical, physiological and biochemical levels. *Mailing Add:* 6325 Ellenwood Ave St Louis MO 63105

BROWN, ERIC, COMPLEMENT, PHAGOCYTOSIS. *Current Pos:* ASSOC PROF MED, SCH MED, WASH UNIV, 85- *Personal Data:* b Ann Arbor, Mich, 50; m 83; c 1. *Educ:* Harvard Univ, MD, 75. *Prof Exp:* Sr investr immunol, NIH, Bethesda, Md, 77-85. *Mem:* AAAS; NY Acad Sci; Am Soc Clin Immunol; Am Asn Immunol; Am Found Clin Res. *Res:* Macrophage. *Mailing Add:* Div Infectious Dis Wash Univ Sch Med PO Box 8051 660 S Euclid St Louis MO 63110-1093. *Fax:* 314-362-9230

BROWN, ERIC REEDER, CHEMISTRY, VIROLOGY. *Current Pos:* STAFF, HOSP JOINT DISEASE, 90- *Personal Data:* b Cortland, NY, Mar 16, 25; m 61; c 4. *Educ:* Syracuse Univ, BA, 48, MS, 51; Univ Kans, PhD(virol, immunol biochem), 57. *Hon Degrees:* DSc, Quincy Col, 66. *Prof Exp:* Instr, Col Med, Univ Ill, 57-59; asst prof hemat & immunol, Univ Ala, 59; asst prof, Univ Minn, 60-61; sr res assoc hemat, Hektoen Inst Med Res, 61-65; assoc prof microbiol, Med Sch, Northwestern Univ, 65-68; prof microbiol & chmn dept, Chicago Med Sch, 67-89. *Concurrent Pos:* Res fel, Am Cancer Soc, 60-63; assoc, Northwestern Univ, 63-; scholar, Leukemia Soc, Inc, 65-70; mem med adv comt, Leukemia Res Found Inc, 70-; med adv, Ill State Dir Selective Serv Syst. *Mem:* NY Acad Sci; Am Asn Cancer Res; fel Am Inst Chemists; fel Am Acad Microbiol; fel Am Pub Health Asn; Sigma Xi. *Res:* Anthrax diagnosis; bacteriophage and transduction genetics; immunochemical tumor antigens; leukemia virus and antibodies; microbiology; epidemiology; pollution. *Mailing Add:* Hosp Joint Disease 301 E 17th St Rm 1136 New York NY 10003

BROWN, ERIC RICHARD, ELECTROCHEMISTRY. *Current Pos:* RES CHEMIST, RES LABS, EASTMAN KODAK CO, 67- *Personal Data:* b Ithaca, NY, Feb 12, 42; m 66; c 2. *Educ:* Mich Technol Univ, BS, 63; Northwestern Univ, PhD(anal chem), 67. *Mem:* Am Chem Soc. *Res:* Electrochemistry, especially instrumentation and automatic data acquisition; investigation of mechanisms of organic oxidation and reduction reactions. *Mailing Add:* 178 Dickson Rd Webster NY 14580

BROWN, ERNEST BENTON, JR, PHYSIOLOGY. *Current Pos:* RETIRED. *Personal Data:* b Mortons Gap, Ky, July 13, 14; m 34; c Sylvia (Davis) & Ernest B III. *Educ:* Univ Ky, BS, 37, MS, 42; Univ Minn, PhD(physiol), 49. *Prof Exp:* Prin high sch, Ky, 38-41; asst, Univ Ky, 41-42, from instr to asst prof physiol, 42-46; asst, Univ Minn, 4648, instr physiol chem, 48-49, from asst prof to prof physiol, 49-61; prof physiol & chmn dept, 61-73, dean fac & acad affairs, 73-74, vchancellor fac & acad affairs, Med Ctr, Univ Kans, Kansas City, 74-77; prof physiol & chmn dept, Sch Med, Oral Roberts Univ, 77-80. *Concurrent Pos:* Mem, NIH Physiol Fel Panel, 62-65; ed, Am J Physiol & J Appl Physiol, 60-63; ed, Proc Soc Exp Biol & Med, 63-66, Respiration Physiol, 77-81; vis fel, Oxford Univ, 67-68. *Mem:* AAAS; Soc Exp Biol & Med; Am Physiol Soc; Am Heart Asn; Am Asn Med Cols. *Res:* Anoxia and bends at high altitude; prolonged hyperventilation in man; mechanism of continued hyperpnoea following hyperventilation; effects of very high concentrations of carbon dioxide on cardiovascular system; acid-base balance; electrolyte metabolism. *Mailing Add:* 36 Barkley Circle Ft Meyers FL 33907

BROWN, ESTHER MARIE, ANATOMY. *Current Pos:* RETIRED. *Personal Data:* b Birmingham, Mich, May 12, 23; m 63. *Educ:* Mich State Univ, BS, 46, MS, 51, PhD(path), 55. *Prof Exp:* Bacteriologist, Game Div, State Dept Conserv, Mich, 46-50; bacteriologist, Ft Detrick Proj, Mich State Univ, 50-54, asst vet path, 54-55, from asst prof to prof anat, 55-71, dir sch med technol, 66-71; prof vet anat, Sch Vet Med, Univ Mo, Columbia, 71-

Concurrent Pos: Mem vet med rev comt, NIH, 72-74. *Mem:* Am Soc Med Technol; Am Asn Anatomists; Tissue Cult Asn; Am Soc Cytol; NY Acad Sci. *Res:* Microscopic anatomy; cytology and tissue culture, particularly tissue responses of animal diseases; normal histology of the white rat. *Mailing Add:* Dept Vet Biochem Sci Univ Mo Col Vet Med Columbia OH 65211

BROWN, FARRELL BLENN, STRUCTURAL CHEMISTRY. *Current Pos:* RETIRED. *Personal Data:* b Mt Ulla, NC, Nov 29, 34; m 58; c 2. *Educ:* Lenoir-Rhyne Col, BS, 57; Univ Tenn, MS, 59, PhD(phys chem), 62. *Prof Exp:* Robert A Welch Found fel, Tex A&M Univ, 62-63; from asst prof to prof chem, Clemson Univ, 63-97, assoc dean grad studies, 77-97, actg dean, 89-91. *Mem:* Photochem Soc NAm; Am Chem Soc; Sigma Xi. *Res:* Molecular spectroscopy, structure and dynamics; far infrared spectral studies; molecular configurations; quantum mechanics of bonded systems. *Mailing Add:* Grad Sch E 106 Martin Hall Clemson Univ Clemson SC 29634-5120

BROWN, FIELDING, PHYSICS. *Current Pos:* from asst prof to assoc prof, 59-67, PROF PHYSICS, WILLIAMS COL, MASS, 67- *Personal Data:* b Berlin, NH, Jan 2, 24; m 44; c 4. *Educ:* Williams Col, Mass, BA, 47, AM, 49; Princeton Univ, PhD, 53. *Prof Exp:* Res physicist, Sprague Elec Co, Mass, 52-59. *Concurrent Pos:* Vis scientist, Lincoln Lab, Mass Inst Technol, 61-62 & Francis Bitter Nat Magnet Lab, 68-; vis prof, Univ Tokyo, 65-66; consult, Mass Inst Technol, 73-74. *Mem:* Am Phys Soc; Sigma Xi. *Res:* Cosmic rays; ferrites; ferroelectricity; nonlinear optics; far infrared; lasers. *Mailing Add:* 214 Beacon St Boston MA 02116

BROWN, FORBES TAYLOR, MECHANICAL ENGINEERING, FLUID POWER. *Current Pos:* head, Syst Dynamics Div, 84-87, PROF MECH ENG, LEHIGH UNIV, 70- *Personal Data:* b Newton, Mass, Oct 12, 34; m 63; c 3. *Educ:* Mass Inst Technol, SB & SM, 58, ME, 59, ScD, 62. *Prof Exp:* Asst mech eng, Mass Inst Technol, 56-58, from instr to assoc prof, 58-70. *Concurrent Pos:* Mem, Exec Comt, Fluids Eng Div, Am Soc Mech Engrs, 70-75; mem bd gov, Nat Conf Fluid Power, 81- *Mem:* Am Soc Mech Engrs; Fluid Power Soc. *Res:* General techniques and applications of lumped and distributed modeling and simulation of complex engineering systems, plus their design and control; fluid line dynamics and vibration; conception and development of new concepts in fluid power systems. *Mailing Add:* 1715 Sunderland Dr Bethlehem PA 18017

BROWN, FOUNTAINE CHRISTINE, BIOCHEMISTRY. *Current Pos:* PROF BIOCHEM, COL MED, UNIV TENN, MEMPHIS, 58-, RES BIOCHEMIST, TENN PSYCHIAT HOSP, 58- *Personal Data:* b Huffman, Ark, Oct 13, 23. *Educ:* Southeast Mo State Col, BA & BS, 47; Univ Mo, MA, 51; Univ Iowa, PhD(biochem), 55. *Concurrent Pos:* Fel, M D Anderson Hosp & Tumor Inst, Univ Tex, 55-58. *Mem:* AAAS; Am Soc Biol Chemists; Am Chem Soc; Am Soc Neurochem; Int Soc Neurochem; Sigma Xi. *Res:* Neurochemistry; alcohol and other drug changes in the central nervous system; mechanism of enzyme action. *Mailing Add:* 19 River Oaks Community Searcy AR 72143

BROWN, FRANK MARKHAM, ELECTRICAL ENGINEERING. *Current Pos:* ASSOC PROF, DEPT ELEC ENG, UNIV KY, 72- *Personal Data:* b San Diego, Calif, May 12, 30; m 57; c 3. *Educ:* USNaval Acad, BS, 53; USAF Inst Technol, MS, 58; Ohio State Univ, PhD(elec eng), 67. *Prof Exp:* USAF, 54-72, instr electronics, Air Training Command, USAF Inst Technol, 54-56, proj scientist, Electronic Technol Lab, Air Res & Develop Command, 58-61, from instr to assoc prof elec eng, 61-72. *Mem:* Inst Elec & Electronics Engrs. *Res:* Switching theory; boolean equations. *Mailing Add:* 1832 Southlawn Dr Fairborn OH 45324

BROWN, FRED(ERICK) R(AYMOND), HYDROLOGY & WATER RESOURCES. *Current Pos:* RETIRED. *Personal Data:* b Peoria, Ill, Feb 15, 12; m 36, Louise Ferry; c Sandra, Fred Jr & Roger. *Educ:* Univ Ill, BS, 34. *Honors & Awards:* Meritorius Civilian Serv, US Dept Army. *Prof Exp:* From hydraul engr to chief, hydrodyn br, hydraul div, US Corps Engrs Waterways Exp Sta, 34-64, chief, nuclear weapons effects div, 64, asst dir sta, 64-69, tech dir sta, 69-85. *Concurrent Pos:* Chmn City Planning Comn, Vicksburg, 60-80; consult, Alaska Pipe Line & United Arab Repub. *Mem:* Hon mem Am Soc Civil Engrs; Nat Soc Prof Engrs; Int Asn Hydraul Res. *Res:* Hydraulic design of dams and appurtenant structures; explosives effects; oceanography flood control and related subjects. *Mailing Add:* 105 Stonewall Rd Vicksburg MS 39180

BROWN, FREDERICK CALVIN, SOLID STATE PHYSICS. *Current Pos:* prof, 74-87, EMER PROF PHYSICS, UNIV ILL, URBANA, 87-; PROF PHYSICS, UNIV WASH, 87- *Personal Data:* b Seattle, Wash, July 6, 24; m 52, Joan Schauble; c Susan, Gail & Derek. *Educ:* Harvard Univ, SB, 45, MA, 47, PhD(physics), 50. *Prof Exp:* Physicist, US Naval Res Lab, 50-51; assoc physicist, Appl Physics Lab, Univ Wash, 51-52; from instr to asst prof physics, Reed Col, 51-54; from asst prof to prof, Univ Ill, Urbana-Champaign, 55-73; prin scientist, Xerox Palo Alto Res Lab, 73-74. *Concurrent Pos:* NSF sr fel, Clarendon Lab, Oxford Univ, 64-65; assoc, Ctr Advan Study, Univ Ill, 69-70; consult prof appl physics, Stanford Univ, 73-74; Alexander Humboldt sr fel award, 78. *Mem:* Fel Am Phys Soc; Sigma Xi. *Res:* Photoconducting and optical properties of ionic crystals, especially silver and alkali halides; color center phenomena and cyclotron resonance; extreme ultraviolet spectroscopy and synchrotron radiation; electronic properties of semiconductors. *Mailing Add:* 2414 E Discovery Langley WA 98260

BROWN, GARRY LESLIE, FLUID MECHANICS, AERONAUTICS. *Current Pos:* CHAIR MECH & AEROSPACE ENG DEPT, PRINCETON UNIV, 90- *Personal Data:* b Adelaide, S Australia, May 14, 42; m 67; c 3. *Educ:* Univ Adelaide, BE Hons, 64; Oxford Univ, PhD(eng sci), 67. *Prof Exp:* Sr res fel aeronaut, Calif Inst Technol, 67-71; from reader to sr lectr mech eng, Univ Adelaide, 71-78; prof aeronaut, Calif Inst Technol, 78-88; dir aeronaut res labs, Melbourne, Australia, 88-90. *Mem:* Am Inst Aeronaut & Astronaut; Inst Engrs Australia. *Res:* Turbulence; structure in turbulent shear plows; combustion in turbulent plows noise and unsteady gas dynamics. *Mailing Add:* Princeton Univ PO Box CN5263 D218 Eng Quad Princeton NJ 08544

BROWN, GARY S, ROUGH SURFACE SCATTERING, REMOTE SENSING. *Current Pos:* PROF ELEC ENG, VA POLYTECH INST & STATE UNIV, 85- *Personal Data:* b Jackson, Miss, Apr 13, 40; m 70, Mary K Connaughton; c 2. *Educ:* Univ Ill, BS, 63, MS, 64, PhD(elec eng), 67. *Honors & Awards:* R W P King Award, Inst Elec & Electronics Engrs, Soc Antennas & Propagation, 77; Group Achievement Award, NASA, 78 & 79. *Prof Exp:* Consult, Andrew Corp, 65-67; mem tech staff, TRW Systs Group, 67 & 69-70; capt, Elec Eng, US Army, 67-69; sr engr, Res Triangle Inst, 70-73; chief scientist, Appl Sci Assocs, Inc, 73-85. *Concurrent Pos:* Consult, Decision Sci Applications & Johns Hopkins Appl Physics Lab, 89-90, US Naval Res Lab & Dynamics Technol Inc, 89-91, Arete Assocs, 91-95, Waste Policy Inst, 92-, Motorola, 92-93; mem, comn B & F, Int Union Radio Sci; mem, NATO-Adv Group Aerospace Res & Develop Electromagnetic Propagation Panel, 93-; secy, US Nat Comt, Int Union Radio Sci. *Mem:* Inst Elec & Electronics Engrs Antennas & Propagation Soc (pres, 88); Inst Elec & Electronics Engrs Geosci & Remote Sensing Soc; Inst Elec & Electronics Engrs Oceanic Eng Soc; Int Union Radio Sci; Sigma Xi. *Res:* Theoretical modeling of electromagnetic scattering by randomly rough surfaces and the remote sensing applications of the results with particular emphasis on the ocean surface and sea ice. *Mailing Add:* Bradley Dept Elec Eng Va Polytech Inst & State Univ Blacksburg VA 24061-0111. *Fax:* 540-231-6390; *E-Mail:* randeb@vtvmi.cc.vt.edu

BROWN, GENE MONTE, BIOCHEMISTRY. *Current Pos:* from instr to prof biol, Mass Inst Technol, 54-67, exec officer, Dept Biol, 67-72, assoc head, 72-77, head, Dept Biol, 77-85, dean sci, 85-91, PROF BIOCHEM, MASS INST TECHNOL, 67- *Personal Data:* b Mo, Jan 21, 26; m 54, Shirley Lewis; c James L, Lindsey A & Holly A. *Educ:* Colo State Univ, BS, 49; Univ Wis, MS, 50, PhD(biochem), 53. *Prof Exp:* Assoc, Univ Tex, 52-54. *Mem:* Am Soc Biol Chem; Am Soc Microbiol; Am Chem Soc; Am Acad Arts & Sci; Fedn Am Soc Exp Biol. *Res:* Biosynthesis and function of vitamins and coenzymes; enzymology. *Mailing Add:* Dept Biol Sch Sci Mass Inst Technol Cambridge MA 02139

BROWN, GEORGE D, JR, GEOLOGY, PALEONTOLOGY. *Current Pos:* from asst prof to prof geol, Boston Col, 62-86, chmn, Dept Geol & Geophys, 70-80, CONSULT, 88- *Personal Data:* b Whiting, Ind, Sept 16, 31; m 59; c 2. *Educ:* St Joseph's Col, Ind, BS, 53; Univ Ill, Urbana, MS, 55; Ind Univ, PhD(geol), 63. *Prof Exp:* Jr geologist, Pan-Am Petrol Corp, 55-57; sedimentary engr, Youngstown Sheet & Tube Co, 57-58; instr geol, Colgate Univ, 58-59; lectr, Ind Univ, 62. *Concurrent Pos:* Sigma Xi grant, 66-67; NSF Grant, 68-70. *Mem:* Paleont Soc; Int Bryozool Asn; Sigma Xi. *Res:* Paleozoic Trepostomatous Bryozoa; litho stratigraphy and biostratigraphy of Ordovician strata in the Central States area. *Mailing Add:* Dept Geol & Geophys Boston Col 140 Commonwealth Chestnut Hill MA 02167-3800

BROWN, GEORGE EDWARD, JR, CHEMICAL ENGINEERING. *Current Pos:* SR STAFF PROCESS ENGR, CRS SIRRINE ENGRS, 87- *Personal Data:* b Lakewood, Ohio, June 14, 37; m 59, Sally Ann Stretton; c Jeffrey, Amy K (Williams), Deborah A (Carter) & Heidi. *Educ:* Va Polytech Inst, BSChemE, 59. *Honors & Awards:* W R Grace & Co Award, Am Chem Soc, 94. *Prof Exp:* Proj mgr, Pilot Opers, Firestone Synthetic Fibers, 69-74; dept proj engr, J E Sirrine, 74-78; indust specialist, Fluor Daniel, 78-84; mgr process dept, Lockwood Greene Engrs, 84-86; vpres opers, Marathon Engrs, 86-87. *Mem:* Am Chem Soc; Am Inst Chem Engrs; Nat Soc Prof Engrs. *Mailing Add:* 16 Pristine Dr Greer SC 29650-4464

BROWN, GEORGE LINCOLN, CHEMISTRY. *Current Pos:* RETIRED. *Personal Data:* b Brookings, SDak, Dec 27, 21; m 43, Carrie Phillips; c 3. *Educ:* SDak State Univ, BS, 41; Brown Univ, PhD(chem), 47. *Honors & Awards:* Potter Prize, Brown Univ, 47. *Prof Exp:* Chemist, Standard Oil Co, La, 43-45; res chemist, Rohm and Haas Co, 47-51, head lab, 51-57, res supvr, 57-63; vpres res, Polyvinyl Chem, Inc, Peabody, 63-65; tech dir, Chem Coatings Div, Mobil Chem Co, 65-68, mgr, Coatings Res & Develop, 69-80, mgr admin, 80-85. *Mem:* Am Chem Soc. *Res:* Electrochemistry; properties of electrolytic solutions; surface chemistry; polymers; polymer dispersion coatings. *Mailing Add:* 23 Essex Rd Scotch Plains NJ 07076

BROWN, GEORGE MARSHALL, NEUTRON CRYSTALLOGRAPHY, X-RAY CRYSTALLOGRAPHY. *Current Pos:* chemist, 59-60, CONSULT, OAK RIDGE NAT LAB, 90- *Personal Data:* b Rochelle, Ga, Feb 14, 21; m 62; c 1. *Educ:* Emory Univ, BA, 42, MS, 43; Princeton Univ, MA, 46, PhD(phys chem), 49. *Prof Exp:* From asst prof to assoc prof chem, Univ Md, 47-59. *Concurrent Pos:* Res fel x-ray crystallog, Calif Inst Technol, 57-58; vis scholar protein crystallog, Univ Wash, 74-75. *Mem:* Am Chem Soc; Am Crystallog Asn. *Res:* X-ray and neutron crystal structure analysis; hydrogen atom location and hydrogen bonding; sugars; triarylamines; inorganic complex compounds; heteropoly acids; protein structure refinement; low-temperature apparatus. *Mailing Add:* 124 Oklahoma Ave Oak Ridge TN 37830-8604

BROWN, GEORGE MARTIN, CHEMICAL ENGINEERING. *Current Pos:* from instr to asst prof chem eng, 43-50, ASSOC PROF CHEM ENG, NORTHWESTERN UNIV, 50- *Personal Data:* b Evanston, Ill, May 28, 19; m 91, Jan Peterson; c George D, Margaret B (Hutchinson), Barbara B (Priest), David E, & Michael G. *Educ:* Univ Mich, BSE, 40; Mass Inst Technol, SM, 41; Northwestern Univ, PhD(chem eng), 49. *Prof Exp:* Asst chem engr, Sun Oil Co, Pa, 39; chem engr, Standard Oil Co, Ind, 41-43; engr, Metall Lab, Univ Chicago, 44-45. *Concurrent Pos:* Consult Chem Engr, AEC & Manhattan Dist, 44-45; engr, Off Sci Res & Develop & USN proj, 45-58. *Mem:* Am Chem Soc; Am Inst Chem Engrs. *Res:* Thermodynamic properties of mixtures; vapor-liquid phase equilibria; distillation; process simulation; application of computers to chemical engineering. *Mailing Add:* Northwestern Univ 2333 Central St #207 Evanston IL 60201-1474. *E-Mail:* g_brown@nwu.edu

BROWN, GEORGE STEPHEN, PHYSICS. *Current Pos:* PROF PHYSICS, UNIV CALIF, SANTA CRUZ, 91-, CHAIR, DEPT PHYSICS, 96- *Personal Data:* b Santa Monica, Calif, June 28, 45; m 97, Julie Claire Dryden; c Sonya. *Educ:* Calif Inst Technol, BS, 67; Cornell Univ, PhD(physics), 73. *Prof Exp:* Mem tech staff physics, Bell Labs, 73-77; sr res assoc physics,Stanford Univ, 77-82, prof res, 82-91. *Concurrent Pos:* Consult prof, Stanford Univ. *Mem:* Fel Am Phys Soc; AAAS. *Res:* X-ray diffraction; x-ray scattering; x-ray absorption spectroscopy. *Mailing Add:* Dept Physics Univ Calif Santa Cruz CA 95064

BROWN, GEORGE WALLACE, FOREST HYDROLOGY. *Current Pos:* Head, Dept Forest Eng, 73-86, assoc dean res, 86-90, PROF FOREST HYDROL, ORE STATE UNIV, 66-, DEAN RES, 90- *Personal Data:* b Warrensburg, Mo, Jan 31, 39; m 64; c 2. *Educ:* Colo State Univ, BS, 60, MS, 62; Ore State Univ, PhD(forest hydrol), 67. *Concurrent Pos:* Consult hydrologist, Weyerhaeuser Co, 73; prin res engr, Forest Serv, USDA, 81. *Mem:* Soc Am Foresters; Forest Prod Soc. *Res:* Research administration; temperature, sediment, dissolved oxygen. *Mailing Add:* Col Forestry Ore State Univ Corvallis OR 97331-5704

BROWN, GEORGE WILLARD, JR, BIOCHEMICAL ECOLOGY, ENVIRONMENTAL CHEMISTRY. *Current Pos:* from assoc prof to prof, 67-90, EMER PROF FISHERIES, COL OCEAN & FISHERY SCI, UNIV WASH, 90- *Personal Data:* b Alameda, Calif, Oct 24, 24; m 48, 61, Susan Greison; c Lucile, Susan, Gerald, Eric, Jonathan & Rebecca. *Educ:* Univ Calif, Berkeley, BS, 50, MA, 51, PhD(comp biochem), 55. *Honors & Awards:* Belg Fourragere. *Prof Exp:* Fel, NIH, 56; res fel & res assoc physiol chem, Univ Wis, 57, from instr to asst prof, 58-61; from asst prof to assoc prof biochem, Med Br, Univ Tex, Galveston, 61-67. *Concurrent Pos:* Consult, NIH, 58, Acad Press, 62-, NASA, 66-67, Highline Col, 67, US Coast Guard, 70-73, Envirodyne, Inc, 77-78, US Fish & Wildlife Serv, 80 & Res & Eval Assocs, Inc, 84-86; vis biologist, Am Inst Biol Sci, 62-73; assoc prog mem, Nat Res Coun, Nat Acad Sci, 80-81. *Mem:* Am Chem Soc; Sigma Xi; Am Soc Biochem & Molecular Biol; Soc Protection Old Fishes (pres, 67-). *Res:* Intermediary nitrogen metabolism; biochemistry of primitive fishes; enzymology; desert biology; biochemical ecology; water pollution; urea biosynthesis. *Mailing Add:* Sch Fisheries 357980 Univ Wash Seattle WA 98195-7980

BROWN, GEORGE WILLIAM, MATHEMATICS. *Current Pos:* dean grad sch admin, 67-72, prof, 67-82, EMER PROF MGT, UNIV CALIF, IRVINE, 82- *Personal Data:* b Boston, Mass, June 3, 17; m 41; c 5. *Educ:* Harvard Univ, AB, 37, AM, 38; Princeton Univ, PhD(math), 40. *Prof Exp:* Res statistician, R H Macy & Co, 40-42; res assoc, Princeton Univ, 42-44; res engr, RCA Labs, Princeton, NJ, 44-46; from assoc prof to prof math statist, Iowa State Col, 46-48; mathematician, Rand Corp, 48-52; sr staff engr, Int Telemeter Corp, 52-57; prof bus admin & eng, Univ Calif, Los Angeles, 57-67, dir, Western Data Processing Ctr, 57-64, chmn, Dept Bus Admin, 64-65. *Concurrent Pos:* Vis prof math & eng, Univ Calif, Los Angeles, 48-57; dir & consult, Dataproducts Inc, 62-88; dir, Comput Automation Inc, 69-81; dir, Calcomp, 77-80. *Mem:* Fel AAAS. *Res:* Dynamic decision processes; mathematical and applied statistics; management science; operations research. *Mailing Add:* 2401 Bamboo St Newport Beach CA 92660

BROWN, GERALD E, PHYSICS. *Current Pos:* leading prof, 74-88, DISTINGUISHED PROF PHYSICS, STATE UNIV NY, STONY BROOK, 88- *Personal Data:* b Brookings, SDak, July 22, 26; m 53; c 3. *Educ:* Univ Wis, BA, 46; Yale Univ, MS, 48, PhD, 50; Univ Birmingham, DSc, 57. *Hon Degrees:* DSc, Univ Helsinki, 82 & Univ Birmingham, Eng, 90. *Honors & Awards:* Boris Pregel Award, NY Acad Sci, 76; Tom W Bonner Prize Nuclear Physics, 82. *Prof Exp:* Prof physics, Univ Birmingham, 59-60; prof, Nordic Inst Theoret Atomic Physics, 60-85. *Concurrent Pos:* Lectr math physics, Univ Birmingham, 55-58, reader, 58-59; dir, Nuclear Astrophys Sect, NSF Inst Theoret Physics, Univ Calif, Santa Barbara, 60; prof physics, Princeton Univ, 64-68; prof, State Univ NY, Stony Brook, 68-74; mem, Vis Comt, Theoret Div, Los Alamos Sci Lab, 76-79; chmn, Gordon Res Conf Nuclear Struct Physics, 80; Alexander von Humboldt Found sr distinguished scientist award, 87. *Mem:* Nat Acad Sci; fel Am Phys Soc; fel Am Acad Arts & Sci; hon mem Finnish Soc Sci & Lett. *Res:* Author of over 240 technical publications. *Mailing Add:* Inst Theoret Physics State Univ NY Stony Brook NY 11794

BROWN, GERALD LEONARD, APPLIED MATHEMATICS. *Current Pos:* RES STAFF MEM, SYSTS EVAL DIV, INST DEFENSE ANALYSIS, 71- *Personal Data:* b New York, NY, May 17, 36; m 67, Joy Skaller; c Amy. *Educ:* Univ Miami, BS, 58; Mass Inst Technol, MS, 60; Univ Wis, PhD(math), 65. *Prof Exp:* Tech staff mem, Math Res Dept, Sandia Corp, 65-70. *Mem:* Am Math Soc; Inst Opers Res & Mgt Sci. *Res:* Partial differential equations; systems analysis; operational testing and evaluation; command and control analysis. *Mailing Add:* SED-Inst Defense Analysis 1801 N Beauregard St Alexandria VA 22311. *Fax:* 703-845-6722

BROWN, GERALD RICHARD, POMOLOGY, VITICULTURE, FOOD SAFETY. *Current Pos:* EXTEN PROF POMOL, RES & EDUC CTR, UNIV KY, 78- *Personal Data:* b Poplar Bluff, Mo, Oct 22, 37; m 59, Mary Marta; c Craig & Kevin. *Educ:* Univ Ark, BS, 59, MS, 63, PhD(bot), 74. *Honors & Awards:* Krezdorn Award, Am Soc Hort Sci, 74. *Prof Exp:* Res asst hort, Southwest Br Exp Sta, Univ Ark, Hope, 60-61; plant quarantine inspector, Agr Res Serv, USDA, 61-69; res asst genetics, Hort Dept, Univ Ark, 69-74; res pomologist, State Fruit Exp Sta, Southwest Mo State Univ, 74-78. *Concurrent Pos:* Adv estab demonstration fruit farm, Ecuador, 84; vis prof, Scottish Crop Res Inst, Invergowrie, Dundee, Scotland, Great Britain; chmn, UK CES Food Safety & Quality Task Force; vis prof, Egypt, 96. *Mem:* Am Soc Hort Sci; Sigma Xi. *Res:* Fruit production including the basic relationship of plant growth; especially the use of growth regulators, cultivar evaluation, nutrition, pruning, and irrigation; water relations. *Mailing Add:* Res & Educ Ctr Univ Ky PO Box 469 Princeton KY 42445. *Fax:* 502-365-2667; *E-Mail:* grbrown@ca.uky.edu

BROWN, GILBERT J, TECHNOLOGY & VALUES. *Current Pos:* PROF NUCLEAR ENG, UNIV MASS, LOWELL, 73- *Personal Data:* b Bronx, NY, Apr 29, 48; m 69, Merryl; c Craig & Shana. *Educ:* Cornell Univ, BS, 69; Mass Inst Technol, MS, 72, PhD(nuclear eng), 74. *Concurrent Pos:* Vis assoc, Brookhaven Nat Lab, 77; resident assoc, Argonne Nat Lab, 78; consult, Stone & Webster Eng Corp, 81-82, Int Atomic Energy Agency, 84-85 & Yankee Atomic Elec Co, 89-90; vis assoc prof nuclear eng, Mass Inst Technol, 81-82; reactor engr, NH Yankee-Seabrook Reactor, 86; dir, Am Nuclear Soc, 86-89. *Mem:* Am Nuclear Soc; Am Soc Eng Educ; Sigma Xi; Soc Lit & Sci. *Res:* Nuclear reactor systems; reactor safety; thermal hydraulics; energy economics; cogeneration and alternative energy systems; technology and values; understanding technological risks. *Mailing Add:* Univ Mass Lowell 1 University Ave Lowell MA 01854-2881. *E-Mail:* brown@cae.uml.edu

BROWN, GILBERT MORRIS, ELECTROCHEMISTRY, PHOTOCHEMISTRY. *Current Pos:* CHEMIST, OAK RIDGE NAT LAB, 78- *Personal Data:* b Valdasta, Ga, Nov 5, 47; m 84, Mary L Ferda; c Brian, Karen & Jennifer. *Educ:* Erskine Col, BA, 70; Univ NC, Chapel Hill, PhD(chem), 74. *Prof Exp:* Res assoc, Chem Dept, Stanford Univ, 74-76 & Brookhaven Nat Lab, 76-78. *Concurrent Pos:* Res asst prof, Dept Chem, Univ Tenn, Knoxville, 89- *Mem:* Am Chem Soc; Int Am Photochem Soc; Electrochem Soc; AAAS. *Res:* Photochemistry of transition metal complexes; kinetics and mechanisms of the reactions of transition metal complexes; materials chemistry; mechanisms of electrode reactions; metallo-organic labels for biological materials including DNA. *Mailing Add:* Chem Analysis Sci Div PO Box 2008 Oak Ridge Nat Lab 4500S Oak Ridge TN 37831-6119. *Fax:* 423-574-4939

BROWN, GLEN FRANCIS, GEOLOGY. *Current Pos:* chief field party, 63-69, sr staff geologist for mideastern affairs, 69-82, CONSULT, US GEOL SURV, 82- *Personal Data:* b Graysville, Ind, Dec 14, 11; m 75, Helen Royall; c Elizabeth (Kulwin). *Educ:* NMex Sch Mines, BS, 35; Northwestern Univ, MS, 40, PhD(geol), 49. *Honors & Awards:* Distinguished Serv Gold Medal, US Dept Interior, 64. *Prof Exp:* Geologist, Philippine Bur Mines, 36-38; jr geologist, US Geol Surv, 38-41, from asst geologist to sr geologist, 41-44; sr geologist, Foreign Econ Admin, 44-46; geologist, US Geol Surv, 46-48, actg chief, Mission to Thailand, 49, chief field party, Saudi Arabia, 50-54, chief, Saudi Arabian Proj, Wash, DC, 55-57; geol adv, Kingdom Saudi Arabia, 57-58; mem, World Bank Mission to Saudi Arabia, 60 & Kuwait, 62; chief, US Geol Surv Mission to Saudi Arabia, 63, 68, 69 & 80. *Concurrent Pos:* US Geol Surv deleg, 22nd & 23rd World Geol Congs; mem, Joint Comn to Saudi Arabia, 74-76. *Mem:* Soc Econ Geologists; fel Geol Soc Am; Am Geophys Union; Am Asn Petrol Geologists; Soc Photogram; fel AAAS; Sigma Xi; fel Explorers Club. *Res:* Geology of metals and coal in the Philippine islands, Thailand and South China; geology of ground water, Mississippi, California, and Saudi Arabia; Precambrian geology in Saudi Arabia; tectonism of Arabian peninsula. *Mailing Add:* 2031 Royal Fern Ct Apt 21C Reston VA 22091

BROWN, GLENN A, geology, for more information see previous edition

BROWN, GLENN HALSTEAD, chemistry, liquid crystals; deceased, see previous edition for last biography

BROWN, GLENN LAMAR, ELECTRONIC SYSTEMS, LASER TECHNOLOGY DEVELOPMENT. *Current Pos:* PRES, RESOURCES ENG & PLANNING, 71- *Personal Data:* b Miami, Ariz, Oct 14, 23; m 58; c 4. *Educ:* Univ Calif, Los Angeles, BA, 49, MA, 51, PhD(physics), 55. *Prof Exp:* Res assoc geophysics, Univ Calif, Los Angeles, 55-57; staff mem, Ramo-Woolridge Corp, 57-59; div mgr, Space Gen Corp, 59-65; dir res, Am Nucleonics Corp, 65-71. *Mem:* Am Phys Soc; Am Geophys Union; Inst Elec & Electronics Engrs. *Res:* Electromagnetics; electronic warfare; laser effects and countermeasures; electromagnetic pulse effects and countermeasures; high power microwave effects; thin film applications to electron counter-countermeasures; multiple quantum well devices. *Mailing Add:* Resource Engineering & Planning Co 5937 Via Robles Lane El Paso TX 79912

BROWN, GLENN R(OBBINS), CHEMICAL ENGINEERING. *Current Pos:* SCI ADV TO GOV, 96- *Personal Data:* b Greensburg, Pa, June 1, 30; m 87, Jeanette G Grasselli; c Robyn L (Boebinger) & Eric R. *Educ:* Pa State Univ, BS, 52; Case Inst Technol, MS, 54, PhD, 58. *Prof Exp:* Engr, Stand Oil Co, 53-55, sr engr, 55-56, tech specialist, 56-59, group leader, 59-61, asst mgr mgt methods, 61-63, mgr mgt sci & systs, 63-64, mgr res & develop, 69-75, vpres res & eng, 75-78, vpres technol & planning, 78-79, sr vpres, coal, minerals & planning, 79-80, sr vpres minerals, res & planning, 80-83, dir, 81-86, sr vpres technol, 83-86; admin, Sohio Chem Co, 64-69; dir strategic planning, Case Western Res Univ, 86-87, dean cols, 87-90, vprovost corp res & technol transfer, 90-93. *Concurrent Pos:* Dir, Nordson Co, 86-, Soc Nat Bank, 86-92, Ferro Corp, 88- *Mem:* Am Chem Soc; Am Inst Chem Engrs; AAAS. *Res:* Petroleum and petrochemical processing; management science; economic evaluation; planning. *Mailing Add:* 150 Greentree Rd Chagrin Falls OH 44022-2424

BROWN, GORDON EDGAR, JR, MINERALOGY, GEOCHEMISTRY. *Current Pos:* from asst prof to prof mineral & crystallog, 73-92, chmn, Dept Geol, 86-92, DORREL WILLIAM KIRBY PROF EARTH SCIS, STANFORD UNIV, 92-, PROF, STANFORD SYNCHROTRON RADIATION LAB, 93- *Personal Data:* b San Diego, Calif, Sept 24, 43; m 65; c 2. *Educ:* Millsaps Col, BS, 65; Va Polytech Inst & State Univ, MS, 68, PhD(mineral), 70. *Prof Exp:* Res assoc mineral, State Univ NY Stony Brook, 70-71; asst prof, Princeton Univ, 71-73. *Concurrent Pos:* Assoc ed, Am Mineralogist, Mineral Soc Am, 75-79; co-dir, Ctr Mat Res, Stanford Univ, 86. *Mem:* Mineral Soc Am; Am Crystallog Asn; Am Chem soc; Mat Res Soc; Geochem Soc; Am Geophys Union. *Res:* Crystal chemistry of the rock-forming minerals; silicate glasses and melts; high temperature of minerals; mineral surfaces; synchrotron radiation research; mineral-water interface geochemistry. *Mailing Add:* Dept Geol & Environ Sci Stanford Univ Stanford CA 94305-2115

BROWN, GORDON ELLIOTT, NONASSOCIATIVE ALGEBRAS. *Current Pos:* asst prof, 66-69, ASSOC PROF MATH, UNIV COLO, BOULDER, 69- *Personal Data:* b Ellensburg, Wash, Sept 13, 36. *Educ:* Calif Inst Technol, BS, 58; Cornell Univ, PhD(math), 63. *Prof Exp:* From instr to asst prof math, Univ Ill, Urbana, 62-66. *Mem:* Am Math Soc. *Res:* Non-associative algebras; lie algebras. *Mailing Add:* Univ Math Campus Box 395 Univ Colo Boulder CO 80309. *E-Mail:* gbrown@euclid.colorado.edu

BROWN, GORDON MANLEY, organic chemistry, for more information see previous edition

BROWN, GORDON S, engineering; deceased, see previous edition for last biography

BROWN, GRAYDON L, SYSTEMS ENGINEERING, ELECTRONICS ENGINEERING. *Current Pos:* CONSULT ENGR, 86- *Personal Data:* b Newkirk, Okla, Aug 7, 24; m 54, Marquetta Griswold; c Gracelyn (Greenwald), G Wesley, Anitra (Rowley) & Joletta (Pugh). *Educ:* Okla State Univ, BS, 48, MS, 52. *Prof Exp:* Asst proj engr, res found, Okla State Univ, 48-51; res engr, 52-60, res group leader, res & develop dept, 60-83, dir, tech & admin serv sect, Conoco, Inc, 83-86. *Concurrent Pos:* Consult engr, 91-96. *Mem:* Inst Elec & Electronics Engrs; Soc Explor Geophys; Audio Eng Soc; Nat Soc Prof Engrs. *Res:* Exploration; geophysical instrumentation; hydraulic servomechanisms; magnetic recording instrumentation. *Mailing Add:* 1528 Autumn Rd Ponca City OK 74604

BROWN, GREGORY GAYNOR, MITOCHONDRIA, PLANT ORGANELLES. *Current Pos:* from asst prof to assoc prof biol, 81-96, PROF BIOL, MCGILL UNIV, 96- *Personal Data:* b Englewood, NJ, Aug 17, 48; m 77; c 1. *Educ:* Univ Notre Dame, BS, 70; Mt Sinai Med Sch, PhD(biochem), 77. *Prof Exp:* Res assoc biochem, State Univ NY, Stony Brook, 77-79, fel, 79-81. *Concurrent Pos:* Prin investr, Nat Sci Eng Res Coun, 81- *Mem:* Can Soc Cell Biol; Int Soc Plant Molecular Biol; Am Soc Plant Physiologists. *Res:* The structure, function, expression and evolution of genetic elements in mitochondria, particularly those in higher plants; cytoplasmic male sterility in plants; genetic engineering. *Mailing Add:* Dept Biol McGill 1205 Ave Dr Penfield Montreal PQ H3A 1B1 Can

BROWN, GREGORY NEIL, TREE PHYSIOLOGY, CRYOBIOLOGY. *Current Pos:* DEAN, COL FORESTRY & WILDLIFE RESOURCES, VA POLYTECH, 92- *Personal Data:* b Detroit, Mich, Feb 10, 38; m 61, 74; c 5. *Educ:* Iowa State Univ, BS, 59; Yale Univ, MF, 60; Duke Univ, DF, 63. *Prof Exp:* Plant physiologist, Oak Ridge Nat Lab, 63-66; from asst prof to prof forest physiol, Univ Mo, Columbia, 66-77; prof forest physiol, Iowa State Univ, 77-78; prof forest resources & head dept, Univ Minn, 78-83; dean forest resources & assoc dir, Maine Agr Exp Sta, Univ Maine, Orono, 83-87, vpres res & pub serv, 87-92. *Concurrent Pos:* Mem, Nat Tree Physiol Comt, 68-72; NSF grant, 69-71; working group leader, Int Union Forest Res Orgns, 71-83; mem adv bd, Forest Sci, 77-79, ed, 79-82; chair, Tree Physiol Working Group, Soc Am Foresters, 83-84. *Mem:* Soc Am Foresters; Japanese Soc Plant Physiol; Am Soc Plant Physiologists. *Res:* Membrane structure and function and protein characterization during the induction of cold hardiness in woody plant species. *Mailing Add:* Col Forestry & Wildlife Resources Va Polytech 324 Cheatham Hall Blacksburg VA 24061-0324

BROWN, GUENDOLINE, NUTRITION. *Current Pos:* STAFF MEM, COOP EXTEN SERV, WVA UNIV, 92- *Personal Data:* b New Albany, Miss, July 13, 36; m 58; c 3. *Educ:* Miss State Col Women, BS, 58; Univ Wyo, MS, 69; Utah State Univ, PhD(nutrit & food sci), 78. *Prof Exp:* Asst prof home econ, Univ Wyo, 69-72; asst prof food & nutrit, Weber State Col, 72-74; asst prof food sci & nutrit, Colo State Univ, 78-81; chair & assoc prof food & nutrit, NDak State Univ, 81-88; prog leader, Coop Exten Serv, Univ NH, 88-92. *Mem:* Soc Nutrit Educ; Sigma Xi; Inst Food Technol. *Res:* Nutrition education; coronary heart disease; nutrient density. *Mailing Add:* Coop Exten Serv WVa Univ PO Box 6031 Morgantown WV 26507

BROWN, H EUGENE, MEDICINE. *Current Pos:* CONSULT INTERNAL MED, SOCIAL SECURITY ADMIN, ATLANTA, 81- *Personal Data:* b Jackson, Ga, Dec 25, 15; div; c Randall, Roger, Sherry (Brown-Champeaux), Pamela (Brown-Spiegel) & Kevin. *Educ:* Emory Univ, AB, 36, AM, 37, MD, 46; Univ Calif, PhD(zool), 40. *Prof Exp:* Teaching asst zool, Univ Calif, 37-40; instr, Univ Ga, 40-43; intern internal med, Grady Mem Hosp, Atlanta, 46-47; med officer, US Army, Brooklyn, 47 & Cristobal, CZ, 48-49; asst intermediate & sr resident internal med, Lawson Vet Admin Hosp, Ga, 49-52; internist, Atomic Bomb Casualty Comn, Hiroshima, 52-53; internist & partner, Emory Univ Clin, 54-73, from instr to assoc prof med, Sch Med, Emory Univ, 53-73, phsician, Univ Student Health, 73-76, assoc prof med, Dept Oral Med, Sch Dent, 74-78. *Concurrent Pos:* Physician, Fed Reserve Bank, Atlanta, 73-81; consult int med, Social Security Admin, 81- *Mem:* Sigma Xi; AMA. *Res:* Cytology of termite flagellates; human genetics; amebiasis; antibiotics. *Mailing Add:* 622 Park Lane Decatur GA 30033-5451

BROWN, HARLEY PROCTER, INVERTEBRATE ZOOLOGY, ENTOMOLOGY. *Current Pos:* from asst prof to prof, 48-84, EMER PROF ZOOL, UNIV OKLA, 84- *Personal Data:* b Uniontown, Ala, Jan 13, 21; m 42, 89, Marie M Jenkins; c Mary (Catron). *Educ:* Miami Univ, AB & AM, 42; Ohio State Univ, PhD(zool), 45. *Prof Exp:* Asst zool, Ohio State Univ, 42-45; instr, Univ Idaho, 45-47 & Queen's Col, NY, 47-48. *Concurrent Pos:* Partic, NSF Inst Marine Biol & Trop Ecol, 64; cur invert, Stovall Mus of Sci & Hist, Okla Mus Nat Hist. *Mem:* Am Soc Zool; fel AAAS; Am Micros Soc (pres, 75); Am Inst Biol Sci; Entom Soc Am; NAm Benthol Soc. *Res:* Aquatic; ecology, life history and systematics of dryopoid beetles (Coleoptera: Elmidae, Dryopidae, Psephenidae, Eubriidae, Lutrochidae). *Mailing Add:* Dept Zool Univ Okla Norman OK 73019

BROWN, HAROLD, PHYSICS. *Current Pos:* COUNR, CTR STRATEGIC & INT STUDIES, JOHNS HOPKINS UNIV, 92- *Personal Data:* b New York, NY, Sept 19, 27; m 53; c 2. *Educ:* Columbia Univ, AB, 45, MA, 46, PhD(physics), 49. *Hon Degrees:* 11 honorary degrees. *Honors & Awards:* Numerous awards including the Presidential Medal of Freedom, 81; Enrico Fermi Award, US Dept Energy, 92. *Prof Exp:* Lectr & mem sci staff, Columbia Univ, 47-50; physicist, Lawrence Radiation Lab, Univ Calif, Berkeley, 50-52, mem staff, Livermore, 52-53, group leader, 53-55, div leader, 55-58, assoc dir, 58-59, from dep dir to dir, 59-61; dir defense res & eng, Off Secy Defense, 61-65, Secy Air Force, 65-69; pres, Calif Inst Technol, 69-76; Secy Defense, DC, 77-81; distinguished vis prof, Sch Advan Int Studies, Johns Hopkins Univ, 81-84, chmn, Foreign Policy Inst, 84-92. *Concurrent Pos:* Lectr physics, Stevens Inst Technol, 49-50; mem, Polaris Steering Comt, 56-58; adv, US Deleg Conf Experts Detection Nuclear Weapons Tests, Geneva, 58; sr sci adv, US Deleg Conf Discontinuance Nuclear Weapons Tests, 58-59; mem, Sci Adv Comt Ballistic Missiles, Secy Defense, 58-61; mem, President's Sci Adv Comt, 61; deleg, Strategic Arms Limitation Talks, Helsinki, Vienna & Geneva, 69-75; mem gen adv comt, Arms Control & Disarmament Agency, 69-76; mem exec comt, Trilateral Comn, 73-76; chmn, Technol Assessment Adv Coun, 74-75; bus consult, 81-; trustee, Rand Corp, 83-92, 94- *Mem:* Nat Acad Sci; Nat Acad Eng; Am Acad Arts & Sci; Am Phys Soc. *Res:* Nuclear and neutron physics; nuclear explosives and reactor design; weapons systems; management of research and development; technology and arms control. *Mailing Add:* Ctr Strategic & Int Studies 1800 K St NW Suite 400 Washington DC 20006

BROWN, HAROLD, MEDICINE. *Current Pos:* MED EXPERT, SOCIAL SECURITY ADMIN. *Personal Data:* b Lawrence, Mass, Sept 17, 17; m 50; c 3. *Educ:* Harvard Univ, AB, 39, MD, 43; Am Bd Internal Med, dipl, 50, recert, 73. *Prof Exp:* Asst med, Harvard Med Sch, 46-47; from instr to assoc prof, Sch Med, Univ Utah, 47-61; head metab sect & dir clin res ctr, Baylor Col Med, 62-75, prof med, 62-84, actg chmn dept, 69-70, vchmn dept med, 70-75, dep chmn, 75-84; clin prof med, Univ NMex, Col Med, 85-88. *Concurrent Pos:* From asst chief to chief med serv, Vet Admin Hosp, Salt Lake City, Utah, 48-61; vis prof, Univ Med Sci, Bangkok, 57-59, vis prof med, W China Univ Med Sci, 84-85, hon prof, 85-; officer, intern & resident, Boston City Hosp, 43-47; external exam med, Univ Hong Kong, 58; consult & dir metab res lab, Vet Admin Hosp, Houston, 62-84. *Mem:* Endocrine Soc; Am Fedn Clin Res; Am Col Physicians; Am Soc Clin Invest. *Res:* Metabolism of corticosteroids; serotonin metabolism; liver disease. *Mailing Add:* Rte 9 Box 90-14 Santa Fe NM 87505-9805

BROWN, HAROLD DAVID, applied mathematics, computer sciences, for more information see previous edition

BROWN, HAROLD HUBLEY, CLINICAL CHEMISTRY. *Current Pos:* DIR, DEPT CLIN CHEM, ALBANY MED CTR HOSP, 73- *Personal Data:* b Portsmouth, NH, Mar 14, 26; m 57; c 3. *Educ:* Marietta Col, AB, 50; Wayne State Univ, PhD(biochem), 54. *Prof Exp:* Instr biochem, Albany Med Col, 54-56; biochemist, Pawtucket Mem Hosp, RI, 56-59 & Harrisburg Polyclin Hosp, 59-64; asst prof biochem & dir Core Lab Gen Clin Res Ctr, Albany Med Col, 64-65; biochemist, Harrisburg Polyclin Hosp, Pa, 65-70; clin chemist, Berkshire Med Ctr, Pittsfield, Mass, 70-73; ASSOC PROF BIOCHEM, ALBANY MED COL, 73- *Mem:* AAAS; Am Chem Soc; Am Asn Clin Chemists. *Res:* Methodology in clinical chemistry. *Mailing Add:* 98 Sherwood Dr Lenox MA 01240-2346

BROWN, HAROLD MACK, JR, VISUAL PHYSIOLOGY, BIOPHYSICS. *Current Pos:* asst prof physiol, 70-72, assoc prof, 72-80, ASST PROF MED, SCH MED, UNIV UTAH, 71-, PROF PHYSIOL, 80- *Personal Data:* b Salt Lake City, Utah, Mar 6, 36; m 59; c 3. *Educ:* Univ Utah, BS, 58, PhD(psychol, molecular biol), 64. *Honors & Awards:* Flanagan Award, Am Inst Res, 64. *Prof Exp:* Res assoc, Scripps Inst Oceanog, 67-69; asst res prof physiol, Sch

Med, Univ Calif, Los Angeles, 69-70. *Concurrent Pos:* Vet Admin fel neurol, Col Med, Univ Utah, 64-66; NIH spec fel, Scripps Inst Oceanog, 67-69. *Mem:* AAAS; Am Physiol Soc; Soc Gen Physiol; Biophys Soc; Am Soc Photobiol; Fedn Am Soc Exp Biol. *Res:* Visual biophysics and membrane biophysics. *Mailing Add:* Dept Physiol Res Park Univ Utah Med Ctr 410 Chipeta Way Salt Lake City UT 84108

BROWN, HAROLD VICTOR, ENVIRONMENTAL HEALTH, INDUSTRIAL HYGIENE. *Current Pos:* MEM HEARING BD, SOUTHCOAST AIR QUAL MGT DIST, 85- *Personal Data:* b Los Angeles, Calif, Nov 5, 18; m 46; c 2. *Educ:* Univ Calif, Los Angeles, BA, 40, MPH, 65, DrPH, 70; Am Intersoc Acad Cert Sanit & Am Am Bd Indust Hyg, dipl. *Prof Exp:* Chemist, Eng Corps, US War Dept, 41 & 46; res chemist, Pioneer-Flintkote Co, 47; indust hygienist, State Dept Health, Calif, 47-52; indust hygienist, 52-65, Univ Calif, Los Angeles, environ health & safety officer, Campus Community Safety, 65-82, lectr, Sch Pub Health, 77-82. *Concurrent Pos:* Mem, Calif Occup Safety & Health Standards Bd, 74-76. *Mem:* AAAS; Am Indust Hyg Asn; Health Physics Soc; fel Am Pub Health Asn; Conf Govt Indust Hygienists. *Res:* Cholinesterase inhibitors; laboratory safety. *Mailing Add:* 6008 Chariton Ave Los Angeles CA 90056-1508

BROWN, HARRY ALLEN, magnetism; deceased, see previous edition for last biography

BROWN, HARRY BENJAMIN, electronics engineering, for more information see previous edition

BROWN, HARRY DARROW, BIOCHEMISTRY. *Current Pos:* RETIRED. *Personal Data:* b Newark, NJ, July 21, 25; m 45; c 3. *Educ:* Long Island Univ, BS, 50; Columbia Univ, AM, 52, PhD(bot), 57. *Prof Exp:* Asst bot, Columbia Univ, 50-53; lectr biol, Hunter Col, 54-56; asst prof plant physiol, Loyola Univ, 57-61; assoc prof, Southern Ill Univ, 61-63; biochemist, Seed Protein Lab, USDA, 63-64; asst prof biochem, Univ Tex Med Br, 64-68; assoc prof, Sch Med, Univ Mo-Columbia, 68-74; prof biochem & dean res, Cook Col, Rutgers Univ, NB, 74-97. *Concurrent Pos:* Collabr, USDA, 63-64; chmn, Biochem Sect & assoc dir, Cancer Res Ctr, 68-74; assoc dir, NJ Agr Exp Sta, 74-97. *Mem:* Am Asn Cancer Res; fel Am Inst Chemists; Biophys Soc; Biochem Soc. *Res:* Particulate enzymes; biochemical calorimetry; interfacial biochemical reactions. *Mailing Add:* 6 Llewellyn Pl New Brunswick NJ 08901

BROWN, HARRY LESTER, materials science & engineering, for more information see previous edition

BROWN, HELEN BENNETT, nutrition, cardiovascular diseases; deceased, see previous edition for last biography

BROWN, HENRY, SURGERY. *Current Pos:* Clin assoc, 63-69, asst clin prof surg, 69-77, ASSOC CLIN PROF SURG, HARVARD MED SCH, 77- *Personal Data:* b Erie, Pa, Feb 20, 20; m 45; c 5. *Educ:* Univ Mich, AB, 41; Univ Pa, MD, 44. *Concurrent Pos:* Consult surgeon & mem clin res ctr, Mass Inst Technol; dir hand surg serv, New Eng Deaconess Hosp; mem surg staff, Cambridge Hosp & Mt Auburn Hosp; hand surg consult, Ganta Hosp & Leprosarium Ganta, Liberia, WAfrica, 69, 71, 73 & 75; asst dir, Harvard Surg Unit, Boston City Hosp, 72-73. *Mem:* Soc Surg Alimentary Tract; Am Soc Surg of Hand; Am Physiol Soc; Am Chem Soc; Am Col Surg; Sigma Xi. *Res:* Surgical physiology of the liver; surgery of the hand. *Mailing Add:* New Eng Deaconess Hosp 185 Pilgrim Rd Box 26 Boston MA 02215-5399

BROWN, HENRY CLAY, ORGANIC CHEMISTRY. *Current Pos:* SR RES CHEMIST, HUNTSMAN SPECIALTY CHEM CORP, 94- *Personal Data:* b Gainesville, Fla, Oct 8, 48; m 74; c 2. *Educ:* Emory Univ, BSc, 70; Univ Ga, PhD(chem), 77. *Prof Exp:* Sr res chemist, Monsanto Co, 76-94. *Mem:* Am Chem Soc; Sigma Xi. *Res:* Homogeneous and heterogeneous catalysis; new synthetic methods; process design and development; organic electrochemical synthesis. *Mailing Add:* 910 Shadow Ridge Dr Pensacola FL 32514

BROWN, HENRY CLAY, III, ORGANIC CHEMISTRY. *Current Pos:* RETIRED. *Personal Data:* b Carbur, Fla, Mar 7, 19; m 44; c 3. *Educ:* Duke Univ, BS, 41, MA, 42; Univ Fla, PhD(chem), 50. *Prof Exp:* Res chemist, Texas Co, 42-47; prof chem & chem eng, Univ Fla, 52-81. *Mem:* Am Chem Soc; Am Inst Chem Engrs; Am Inst Chemists; Soc Plastics Engrs. *Res:* Fluorine chemistry and chemistry of fluorocarbon derivatives. *Mailing Add:* 2910 NW 13th Ct Gainesville FL 32605-5001

BROWN, HENRY SEAWELL, ECONOMIC GEOLOGY. *Current Pos:* CONSULT, 89- *Personal Data:* b Marion, NC, Mar 4, 30; m 51; c 5. *Educ:* Berea Col, BA, 52; Univ Ill, MS, 54, PhD(geol), 58. *Prof Exp:* From asst prof to assoc prof geol, Berea Col, 55-58, head dept geol & geog, 55-58; from asst prof to prof geol, NC State Univ, 58-89, head dept, 86-89. *Concurrent Pos:* Consult, Mineral Res & Develop Corp, 60-, Off Technol Assessment, US Cong, 77-78 & Interstate Mining Compact Comn, 79-81; pres, Geol Resources, Inc, 71- *Mem:* Geol Soc Am; Am Inst Mining, Metall & Petrol Engrs. *Res:* Origin and nature of mineral deposits. *Mailing Add:* 2114 Buckingham Rd Raleigh NC 27607-3115

BROWN, HERBERT, ANIMAL NUTRITION, ANIMAL HUSBANDRY. *Current Pos:* RES & DEVELOP SPECIALIST, LILLY RES LABS, ELI LILLY & CO, 63- *Personal Data:* b South Irvine, Ky, Nov 10, 30; m 55; c 1. *Educ:* Univ Ky, BS, 52, MS, 56; Iowa State Univ, PhD(animal nutrit), 59. *Prof Exp:* Assoc prof animal sci, Ill State Univ, 59-61; area swine specialist, Univ Ky, 61-63. *Mem:* Am Soc Animal Sci; Am Registry Prof Animal Scientists. *Res:* Development of products that will stimulate more efficient and economic production of livestock. *Mailing Add:* 1787 S Morristown Pike Greenfield IN 46140

BROWN, HERBERT ALLEN, VERTEBRATE ZOOLOGY. *Current Pos:* asst prof, 67-76, ASSOC PROF BIOL, WESTERN WASH STATE COL, 76- *Personal Data:* b Los Angeles, Calif, Jan 10, 40; m 65; c 2. *Educ:* Univ Calif, Los Angeles, BA, 62; Univ Calif, Riverside, PhD(vert zool), 66. *Prof Exp:* Lectr biol, Univ Calif, Riverside, 66-67. *Mem:* Soc Study Evolution; Am Soc Ichthyologists & Herpetologists; Am Soc Zoologists; Soc Study Amphibians & Reptiles. *Res:* Physiological ecology of amphibians and reptiles; amphibian speciation; reproductive adaptations of amphibians and reptiles. *Mailing Add:* Dept Biol Western Mich Univ M/S 9060 Bellingham WA 98225-5996

BROWN, HERBERT CHARLES, INORGANIC CHEMISTRY, ORGANIC CHEMISTRY. *Current Pos:* prof, 47-59, Wetherill res prof, 59-78, WETHERILL RES EMER PROF CHEM, PURDUE UNIV, WEST LAFAYETTE, 78- *Personal Data:* b London, Eng, May 22, 12; nat US; m 37; c 1. *Educ:* Univ Chicago, BS, 36, PhD(inorg chem), 38. *Hon Degrees:* DSc, Univ Chicago, 68, Wayne State Univ, Lebanon Valley Col, Long Island Univ, Hebrew Univ & Pontificia Univ, 80, Purdue Univ & Univ Wales, 81, Butler Univ & Univ SParis, 82 & Ball State Univ, 85. *Honors & Awards:* Nobel Prize, 79; Harrison Howe Lectr, 53; Nichols Medal, 59; Am Chem Soc Award, 60; Linus Pauling Medal, 68; Nat Medal of Sci, 69; Baker Lectr, 69; Roger Adams Medal, 71; Charles Frederick Chandler Medal, 73; Madison Marshall Award, 75; Ingold Mem Lectr & Medal, 78; Elliot Cresson Medal, 78; Priestly Medal, 81; Perkin Medal, 82; Gold Medal, Am Inst Chemists, 87; Japan Emperor Declaration, Order Rising Sun Gold & Silver Award, 89. *Prof Exp:* Asst, Univ Chicago, 36-38, Eli Lilly fel, 38-39, instr chem, 39-43, res investr, 41-43; from asst prof to assoc prof, Wayne State Univ, 43-47. *Concurrent Pos:* Vis prof & hon lectr, numerous US & foreign univs; mem, Group on Spec Fuels, Defense Dept, 55-60; consult, Exxon Corp & var com orgn; prin investr, NIH, US Army Res Off, Off Naval Res, Ethyl Corp & NSF; Osper Symp, Univ Cincinnati, 90, Vision in Chem Symp, Rhone Poulenc Rorer, 91. *Mem:* Nat Acad Sci; Am Acad Arts & Sci; foreign fel Indian Nat Sci Acad; hon fel Royal Soc Chem; Chem Soc Japan; Pharmacol Soc Japan; Am Chem Soc; fel AAAS. *Res:* Hydrides of boron; reactions of atoms and free radicals; nature of Friedel-Craft catalysts; reaction mechanisms; chemistry of addition compounds; steric strains; selective reductions; hydroboration; chemistry of organoboranes; asymmetric synthesis via chiral organoboranes. *Mailing Add:* H C Brown & R B Wetherill Chem Labs Purdue Univ West Lafayette IN 47907-1393

BROWN, HERBERT ENSIGN, CHRONOBIOLOGY. *Current Pos:* from asst prof to assoc prof, 56-84, EMER PROF ANAT, SCH MED, UNIV MO-COLUMBIA, 85- *Personal Data:* b Ogden, Utah; m 44; c 2. *Educ:* Univ Utah, BS, 49, MS, 51, PhD(anat), 55. *Prof Exp:* Instr, Westminster Col, 54-55; res instr, Univ Utah, 55-56. *Concurrent Pos:* Lt Colonel, US Air Force. *Mem:* Int Soc Chronobiol; Reticuloendothelial Soc; Am Asn Anatomists; Sigma Xi. *Res:* Cell biology; hematology; application of chronobiological principles to endocrinology, biochemistry and immunology for an understanding of the morphology and function of cells of the blood and blood forming organs and connective tissues. *Mailing Add:* Dept Anat M304 Univ Mo Med Ctr Columbia MO 65212

BROWN, HOMER E, ELECTRICAL ENGINEERING. *Current Pos:* TECH WITNESS, 81- *Personal Data:* b Humboldt, Minn, Apr 14, 09; m 32, Mary Swanson; c James A. *Educ:* Univ Minn, BSEE, 30. *Prof Exp:* Jr engr, Commonwealth Edison Co, 30-37, engr, 37-50, sr engr, 50-55, staff engr, 55-73; Eletrobras prof power eng, Brazil, 73-76; vis prof, NC State Univ, 76-81. *Concurrent Pos:* Consult, Manhattan Proj, Univ Chicago, 42-45, McDonnell Automation Ctr, St Louis, 62-70, Serv Bur Corp, 64, Comput Sci Corp, 68-69, IBM Corp, 69, Hidroserv, Brazil, 76 & Elec Power Res Inst, 77-78; vis prof, Iowa State Univ, 69-70, Rensselaer Polytech Inst, 70 & 71, Purdue Univ, 70-71 & Univ Ill, Chicago Circle, 71; distinguished lectr, Univ Tex, Arlington, 70. *Mem:* Fel Inst Elec & Electronics Engrs; Int Conf Large Elec Systs; fel Inst Elec & Electronics Engrs Brit; Sigma Xi. *Res:* Network analysis as applied to solution of power system problems using computers. *Mailing Add:* 705 Willow Valley Lakes Dr Willow Street PA 17584-9400

BROWN, HORACE DEAN, MEDICINAL CHEMISTRY, INFORMATION SCIENCE. *Current Pos:* RETIRED. *Personal Data:* b Gainesville, Ga, Feb 13, 19; m 40, Louise Paul; c Paul D, W Keith & Elyce A. *Educ:* Berry Col, BS, 39; Emory Univ, MS, 40; Iowa State Univ, PhD(chem), 47. *Prof Exp:* Chemist, Red Rock Cola Co, Atlanta, 40-41; instr chem, Iowa State Col, 41-43, res chemist, Manhattan Proj, 44-46, asst, 46-47; sr chem & res assoc, Merck & Co, Inc, 47-61, mgr sci info, 61-66, dir sci info, 67-78, sr dir sci info, Merck Sharp & Dohme Res Labs, 78-84. *Concurrent Pos:* Asst, Quaker Oats Co, 46-47. *Mem:* Am Chem Soc; NY Acad Sci; Am Inst Chem; Asn Comput Mach. *Res:* Structure-activity relationships; insecticides; fungicides; antiparasitic agents; scientific information. *Mailing Add:* 7130 Windover Dr Durham NC 27712-9213

BROWN, HOWARD (EARL), MECHANICAL ENGINEERING. *Current Pos:* From instr to assoc prof mech eng, 40-80, EMER PROF MECH ENG, UNIV TEX, AUSTIN, 80- *Personal Data:* b Anaheim, Calif, Nov 1, 16; m 41; c 1. *Educ:* Univ Calif, BS, 39; Univ Tex, MS, 49, PhD, 56. *Concurrent Pos:* Res engr, Defense Res Lab, 45-50; asst prog dir eng sci, NSF, 60-61. *Mem:* Am Soc Mech Engrs; Am Soc Eng Educ. *Res:* Quick freezing; automatic fuel meters; droplet dispersion in air streams; convective, boiling heat transfer. *Mailing Add:* 3504 Balcones Dr Austin TX 78731

BROWN, HOWARD HOWLAND, JR, PHYSICS. *Current Pos:* res assoc, 61-62, from asst prof to assoc prof, 63-74, PROF PHYSICS, NY UNIV, 75- *Personal Data:* b New York, NY, Sept 2, 34. *Educ:* Mass Inst Technol, BS, 56, PhD(physics), 61. *Prof Exp:* Res asst physics, Res Lab Electronics, Mass Inst Technol, 56-61. *Mem:* Am Phys Soc; Sigma Xi; AAAS. *Res:* Plasma physics; physics of electronic and atomic collisions. *Mailing Add:* Dept Physics NY Univ 4 Washington Place New York NY 10003. *E-Mail:* brownh@acfz.nyu.edu

BROWN, HOWARD S, BIOLOGY, GENETICS. *Current Pos:* RETIRED. *Personal Data:* b Lakewood, Ohio, July 30, 21; m 49, Phoebe Lo; c 4. *Educ:* Univ Calif, Los Angeles, BA, 43, MA, 49; Claremont Grad Sch, PhD, 60. *Prof Exp:* Assoc prof, Calif State Polytech Univ, 48-64, prof biol, 64-82. *Concurrent Pos:* Vis prof, Chung Chi Col, Hong Kong, 61-62. *Mem:* AAAS; Bot Soc Am; Sigma Xi. *Res:* Cytogenetics; botanica genetics. *Mailing Add:* 29853 Disney Lane Vista CA 92084

BROWN, HUGH KEITH, RADIOLOGY, NEUROCYTOLOGY. *Current Pos:* from asst prof to assoc prof anat & radiol, 75-93, CLIN ASSOC PROF RADIOL, COL MED, UNIV S FLA, 93-; PROF PHYS THER, NGA COL, 93- *Personal Data:* b Atlanta, Ga, Aug 6, 45; m 66, Jane Huntington; c Hugh R & Katherine E. *Educ:* Augusta Col, BS, 67; Med Col Ga, MS, 72; Tulane Univ, PhD(anat), 74. *Prof Exp:* Technician electron micros, Med Col Ga, 67-71. *Concurrent Pos:* Scientist, magnetic resonance imaging, Dept Radiol, Col Med, Univ SFla; pres, Fla Soc Electron Micros, 91; pres, Diag Imaging Technol, Inc. *Mem:* Am Asn Anat; Electron Microscope Soc Am; Am Asn Clin Anat; Soc Magnetic Resonance Imaging; Soc Comput Assisted Radiol; Am Phys Ther Asn. *Res:* Plasticity and regeneration of nervous tissue; quantitative synaptology; tissue characterization and mapping by nuclear magnetic resonance feature analysis. *Mailing Add:* Univ SFla Col Med 12901 N 30th St Tampa FL 33612

BROWN, HUGH NEEDHAM, NUCLEAR PHYSICS. *Current Pos:* PHYSICIST, ACCELERATOR DEPT, BROOKHAVEN NAT LAB, 56- *Personal Data:* b Champaign, Ill, Sept 12, 28; m 59; c 2. *Educ:* Univ Ill, BS, 50, MS, 52, PhD(physics), 54. *Mem:* Am Phys Soc. *Res:* Accelerator development and construction; high energy physics experimental facilities. *Mailing Add:* Accelerator Dept 35 Lawrence Dr Brookhaven Nat Lab Upton NY 11973. *Fax:* 516-282-5954

BROWN, IAN DAVID, SOLID STATE CHEMISTRY, SCIENTIFIC NUMERICAL DATABASES. *Current Pos:* Fel crystallog, 59-63, from asst prof to prof, 63-96, EMER PROF PHYSICS, MCMASTER UNIV, 96- *Personal Data:* b Edgware, Eng, Apr 11, 32; Can citizen; m 61, Mariana Paterson; c Elizabeth, Catherine & Alison. *Educ:* Univ London, BSc, 55 & 56, PhD(crystallog), 59. *Concurrent Pos:* Teaching Comn, Int Union Crystallog, 90-, chair, 93-; co-ed, Acta Crystallog, 90- *Mem:* Can Asn Physicists; Brit Inst Physics; Royal Soc Chem; fel Chem Inst Can; Am Crystallog Asn. *Res:* Structure relations and models of chemical bonding in inorganic crystals; information retrieval and transfer. *Mailing Add:* Dept Physics McMaster Univ Hamilton ON L8S 4M1 Can. *Fax:* 905-521-2773; *E-Mail:* idbrown@mcmaster.ca

BROWN, IAN MCLAREN, MAGNETIC RESONANCE. *Current Pos:* assoc scientist, 65-73, SCIENTIST, McDONNELL DOUGLAS CORP, 73- *Personal Data:* b St Andrews, Scotland, Apr 15, 35; m 62; c 2. *Educ:* St Andrews Univ, BSc, 57, PhD(physics), 62. *Prof Exp:* Res assoc chem, Wash Univ, 61-63 & physics, Argonne Nat Lab, 63-65. *Mem:* Am Phys Soc; Am Chem Soc. *Res:* Magnetic resonance of free radicals in polymers. *Mailing Add:* 718 Finch Ct Chesterfield MO 63017

BROWN, IAN ROSS, MOLECULAR NEUROBIOLOGY. *Current Pos:* from asst prof to assoc prof biol, 71-81, PROF MOLECULAR & DEVELOP BIOL, UNIV TORONTO, SCARBOROUGH CAMPUS, 81- *Personal Data:* b Douglas, Scotland, UK, Oct 23, 23; Can citizen; m 69; c 3. *Educ:* Carleton Univ, BSc, 66; Univ Tex, PhD(biol), 69. *Prof Exp:* Med Res Coun fel, Univ Calgary, 69-71. *Concurrent Pos:* Sr vis investr, Dept Molecular Biol, Res Inst Scripps Clin, 84-85 & Northwestern Univ, 91; prof res zool, Univ Toronto, 88-89, res prof, Scarborough Campus, 93-94. *Mem:* Can Soc Cell Biol; AAAS; Am Soc Cell Biol; Am Soc Neurochem; Neurosci Soc; Int Neurochem Soc. *Res:* Analysis of gene expression in the development of the mammalian brain; expression of heat shock (stress) genes in neural tissue; molecular cloning of CDNA for extracellular matrix glycoproteins. *Mailing Add:* Dept Zool Univ Toronto Scarborough Campus West Hill Toronto ON M1C 1A4 Can

BROWN, IRMEL NELSON, electrical engineering, for more information see previous edition

BROWN, J(OHN) DAVID, THERMODYNAMICS OF SELF GRAVITATING SYSTEMS, HAMILTONIAN STRUCTURE OF GENERAL RELATIVITY. *Current Pos:* POSTDOCTORAL ASSOC, INST FIELD PHYSICS, UNIV NC, 88- *Personal Data:* b Shawnee, Okla, Feb 20, 57; m 85; c 2. *Educ:* Okla State Univ, BS, 79; Univ Tex, PhD(physics), 85. *Prof Exp:* Postdoctoral asst, Inst Theoret Physics, Univ Wien, 85-87; postdoctoral assoc, Ctr Relativity & Theory Group, Univ Tex, Austin, 87-88. *Mem:* Am Phys Soc. *Res:* Gravitation theory: gravitational thermodynamics, canonical quantum gravity, quantum cosmology; mathematical physics: BRST quantization, path integral constructions, Hamiltonian structure of gravity, strings and membranes. *Mailing Add:* Physics Dept NC State Univ PO Box 8202 Raleigh NC 27695. *Fax:* 919-515-6538

BROWN, J MARTIN, RADIOBIOLOGY, ONCOLOGY. *Current Pos:* NIH fel radiation biol, Med Ctr, 68-70, res assoc, 70-71, from asst prof to assoc prof, 71-84, PROF & DIR, DIV RADIATION BIOL, 84-, DIR, CANCER BIOL RES LAB, STANFORD UNIV MED CTR, 85- *Personal Data:* b Doncaster, Eng, Oct 15, 41; m 67; c 2. *Educ:* Univ Birmingham, BSc, 63; Univ London, MSc, 65; Oxford Univ, DPhil(radiation biol), 68. *Honors & Awards:* 9th Res Award, Radiation Res Soc, 80. *Concurrent Pos:* Am Cancer Soc Dernham sr fel, 71-74; mem adv comt biol effects of ionizing radiations, Nat Acad Sci, 71- *Mem:* Brit Inst Radiol; Radiation Res Soc; AAAS; Am Asn Cancer Res; Brit Asn Cancer Res; Am Soc Therapeut Radiol & Oncol. *Res:* Mammalian cellular radiobiology; tumor radiobiology; experimental chemotherapy; bioreductive cytotoxic agents; radiation carcinogenesis. *Mailing Add:* Dept Radiation Oncol Stanford Univ Med Ctr Pasteur Dr Stanford CA 94305

BROWN, JACK HAROLD UPTON, PHYSIOLOGY, MEDICAL DEVICES & DIAGNOSTICS. *Current Pos:* assoc provost res & advan educ, 78-80, prof biol, 81-88, EMER PROF, UNIV HOUSTON, 88-; CHMN, SERV CORPS RETIRED EXECS, 96- *Personal Data:* b Nixon, Tex, Nov 16, 18; m 43, Jessie C Shulz. *Educ:* Southwest Tex State Col, BS, 39; Rutgers Univ, PhD(biochem), 48. *Honors & Awards:* Fulbright Award, 50; Spec Team Award, NASA, 78. *Prof Exp:* Instr physiol, Univ Tex, 39-41; radio engr, US Air Force, Wis, 41-43; instr physics, Southwest Tex State Col, 43-44; instr phys chem, Rutgers Univ, 44-45, res assoc biochem & nutrit, 45-48; dir, Biol Labs, Mellon Inst, 48-50; asst prof physiol, Sch Med, Univ NC, 50-52; assoc prof, Emory Univ, 52-57, actg chmn dept, 57-59, prof, 58-60; exec secy training grant, Nat Inst Gen Med Sci, NIH, 60-62, chief, Spec Res Resources Br, 62-63, chief, Gen Clin Ctr Br, 63, asst chief, Div Res Facil & Resources, 63-71, dir sci progs, Nat Inst Gen Med Sci, 70-71, from assoc dir to actg dir, 64-70; spec asst to adminr, Health Sci Ment Health Admin, 70-71, assoc dep adminr, 71-73; spec asst to admin, Health Resources Admin, 73-74; coordr, Southwest Res Consortium, 74-78; prof environ sci & physiol, Univ Tex Health Sci Ctr, San Antonio, 74-78 & prof physiol, Univ Tex Med Ctr, 74-78. *Concurrent Pos:* Lectr, Univ Pittsburgh, 48-50, Med Schs, George Washington Univ, 61- & Georgetown Univ, 64-; consult, WHO, 52; Dept Com, 67, Drexel Inst, 74, Vassar Col, 75, Vet Admin, Oak Ridge Inst Nuclear Studies, Lockheed Aircraft Co, Nat Libr Med, NASA & Teltech, Sumitomo, Japan; pres, founder & bd mem, Biomed Eng Soc & Sigma Xi; founder STex Print Soc; prof community med, Baylor Col Med; prof bus, Health Care Admin, Tex Womans Univ; prof pub admin, Univ Tex; lectr art, Continuing Educ, Univ Houston, prof biol; vchmn, Serv Corps Retired Execs, 96- *Mem:* Nat Acad Eng; sr mem Am Chem Soc; Soc Exp Biol & Med; Am Physiol Soc; Biomed Eng Soc (pres, 69); fel Inst Elec & Electronics Engrs; fel AAAS; Sigma Xi (pres, 77); sr mem Inst Responsive Educ. *Res:* Research and development in new technology for patient record systems and health care using laser card technology. *Mailing Add:* 2908 Whisper View St San Antonio TX 78230. *Fax:* 713-743-2636

BROWN, JACK STANLEY, FRESHWATER BIOLOGY. *Current Pos:* RETIRED. *Personal Data:* b New Orleans, La, Mar 12, 29; m 48, Myrtle Payne; c Patricia Ormond (Bratcher) & Jack Stanley Jr. *Educ:* Tulane Univ, BS, 48; Univ Ala, MS, 49, PhD, 56. *Prof Exp:* Asst biol, Univ Ala, 48-49 & fel, 52-54; asst prof, Jacksonville State Col, 49-52; instr zool, Auburn Univ, 54-55; med entomologist, US Air Force, 55-59; prof biol & chmn dept, Emory & Henry Col, 59-63; prof biol, Parsons Col, 63-65, dean, 65-68; dir, Inst Freshwater Biol, Univ NAla, 69-75, head dept, 74-79, prof biol, 68-91. *Mem:* Am Soc Ichthyol & Herpet; Asn Southeastern Biologists; Ala Acad Sci. *Res:* Herpetology; medical entomology; natural history; freshwater benthos; water quality indicators; macrobenthos. *Mailing Add:* 12 Brannon Ct Florence AL 35630

BROWN, JAMES DOUGLAS, PHYSICAL CHEMISTRY, MATERIALS SCIENCE. *Current Pos:* from prof to assoc prof, 67-76, chmn mat sci group, 69-75, PROF MAT SCI, UNIV WESTERN ONT, 76-, CHMN, DEPT MAT ENG, 89- *Personal Data:* b Hamilton, Ont, July 17, 34; m 57; c 4. *Educ:* McMaster Univ, BSc, 57; Univ Md, PhD(phys chem), 66. *Honors & Awards:* Corning Award, Microbeam Anal Soc, 74, 80, Presidential Award, Significant Tech Achievement, 88. *Prof Exp:* Asst solubility of plutonium compounds, Atomic Energy Can Ltd, Ont, 56; chemist, Res Dept, Imp Oil Ltd, Ont, 57-60; res chemist, Res Ctr, US Bur Mines, Md, 60-66. *Concurrent Pos:* Vis scientist, Metaalinstituut TNO Apeldoorn, Neth, 75-76; vis prof, Inst Appl Physics, Univ Vienna, Austria, 82-83. *Mem:* Am Chem Soc; Microbeam Anal Soc (secy, 71, pres, 78); Asn Prof Engrs. *Res:* Structure and properties of vacuum deposited thin films; quantitative intensity; concentration relationships in electron probe microanalysis; x-ray spectroscopy; electrostatics; secondary ion mass spectroscopy. *Mailing Add:* 95 Cumberland Crescent London ON N5X 1B7 Can

BROWN, JAMES EDWARD, BLOOD COAGULATION BIOCHEMISTRY. *Current Pos:* SR STAFF SCIENTIST, MILES INC, 84- *Personal Data:* b Columbus, Ind, Jan 9, 45; wid; c Peter & Roger. *Educ:* Iowa State Univ, BS, 67, PhD(chem), 71. *Honors & Awards:* Otto Bayer Award, Bayer, 92. *Prof Exp:* Fel, Worcester Found Exp Biol, 71-73; res biochemist, Univ Calif, San Diego, 73-82; res mgr, Hemostasis Systs, Helena Labs, 82-84. *Mem:* Int Soc Thrombosis & Haemostasis; Am Chem Soc; AAAS. *Res:* Biochemistry of FVIII; chemical modification to increase the half-life of FVIII; therapeutic proteins from milk; fibrin-glue as a surgical adhesive. *Mailing Add:* 914 Anita St Lafayette CA 94549. *Fax:* 510-705-5478

BROWN, JAMES EDWARD, IMMUNOLOGY, MOLECULAR BIOLOGY. *Current Pos:* res biochemist, Dept Toxinology, 89-92, CONTRACTING OFFICER'S REP, MIL DIS HAZARDS CONTRACT PROG, US ARMY MED RES INST INFECTIOUS DIS, 91-, DEPT CHIEF MOLECULAR BIOL & IMMUNOL, TOXINOLOGY DIV, 92- *Personal Data:* b Chester, SC, Dec 6, 48; m, Mary G; c Christopher & Benjamin. *Educ:* Furman Univ, BS, 71; NC State Univ, PhD(biochem), 77. *Prof Exp:* Res biochemist, Walter Reed Army Inst Res, 77-86; safety officer, US Army Med Comp, Air Force Res Inst Med Sch, 87-88. *Concurrent Pos:* Contract officer rep, Bact Dis Contract Prog, WRAIR, 82-86, mem bact dis contract review comt, 82-86, asst chief, Dept Biol Chem, 84-86; coordr biochem module, Mil Med Sci Fel Prog, 84; asst chief, Dept Bact, US Army Med Comp, Air Force Res Inst Med Sch, 86-89, radiation protection officer, 87-89. *Mem:* Soc Mucosal Immunol; Int Soc Toxinology; Am Soc Microbiol; assoc mem Am Soc Biol Chemists; Am Chem Soc; Sigma Xi; AAAS. *Res:* Contributed numerous articles to publications and professional journals. *Mailing Add:* 5326 Wye Creek Dr Frederick MD 21701-5011. *Fax:* 301-619-2348

BROWN, JAMES HAROLD, FOREST SOILS & GENETICS. *Current Pos:* assoc prof, Ohio Agr Res & Develop Ctr, Ohio State Univ, 70-74, prof, Dept Forestry, 74-89, assoc chair forestry, 76-89, acting dir, 91-92, assoc dir, 89-95, EMER PROF, SCH NATURAL RESOURCES, OHIO AGR RES & DEVELOP CTR, OHIO STATE UNIV, 95- *Personal Data:* b Richwood, WVa, Nov 9, 31; m 53, Yvonne Beery; c Sharon L (Beaudoin). *Educ:* WVa Univ, BSF, 53; Yale Univ, MF, 54; Mich State Univ, PhD(forestry), 67. *Prof Exp:* Res asst forestry, Northeastern Forest Exp Sta, US Forest Serv, 54-55; asst silviculturist, WVa Univ, 57-61, from asst prof to assoc prof forestry, 61-70. *Mem:* Fel Soc Am Foresters; Soil Sci Soc Am. *Res:* Problems of artifical establishment and growth of tree species, including soil, ecological and genetic considerations. *Mailing Add:* Ohio Agr Res & Develop Ctr Sch Natural Resources Ohio State Univ Wooster OH 44691. *Fax:* 216-263-3688

BROWN, JAMES HARVEY, NEUROSCIENCE, SENSORY SYSTEMS. *Current Pos:* assoc prog dir psychobiol, NSF, 68-71, prog dir neurobiol, 71-76, dep div dir behav & neural sci, 76-77 & 79-82, dep asst dir biol & behav sci, 77-79, div dir physiol cellular & molecular biol, 82-84, div dir, Molecular & Cellular Biosci, 84-95, DIV DIR, BIOL INFRASTRUCTURE, NSF, 95- *Personal Data:* b Yankton, SDak, Sept 9, 36; m 59, Betty J Pruitt; c Christopher H, Karen E & Kimberly F. *Educ:* Wesleyan Univ, BA, 57; Purdue Univ, MS, 59; Univ Va, PhD(sensory systs), 62. *Prof Exp:* Res scientist, US Army Med Res Lab, 62-65, head, Vestibular Br, 65-68. *Concurrent Pos:* Adj prof, Louisville Univ, Univ Ky & Elizabethtown Col, 62-68, George Washington Univ, 70-78. *Mem:* Soc Neurosci; Sigma Xi. *Res:* Vestibular system; use of psychophysical, behavioral and physiological techniques to assess the sensory system. *Mailing Add:* 8803 Quiet Stream Ct Potomac MD 20854. *Fax:* 703-306-0355; *E-Mail:* jhbrown@nsf.gov

BROWN, JAMES HEMPHILL, BIOGEOGRAPHY, EVOLUTION. *Current Pos:* PROF BIOL, UNIV NMEX, 87-, REGENTS PROF, 90- *Personal Data:* b Ithaca, NY, Sept 25, 42; m 65, Astrid R Kodric; c 2. *Educ:* Cornell Univ, AB, 63; Univ Mich, PhD(zool), 67. *Honors & Awards:* Merriam Award, Am Soc Mammalogists, 89; Grinnell Medal, Univ Calif, 94. *Prof Exp:* Fel zool, Univ Calif, Los Angeles, 67-68, asst prof, 68-71; from asst prof to assoc prof biol, Univ Utah, 71-75; assoc prof, 75-78, prof ecol & evolutionary biol, Univ Ariz, 78-87. *Concurrent Pos:* John Simon Guggenheim fel, 91. *Mem:* Ecol Soc Am; Am Soc Naturalists; Soc Study Evolution; Am Soc Mammalogists; Soc Conserv Biol; AAAS. *Res:* Ecology and biogeography; organization of ecological communities and distribution and diversity of species; interspecific interactions of desert ecosystems and diversification of continental biotas; macroecology; allometric scaling; complex ecological systems. *Mailing Add:* Dept Biol Univ NMex Albuquerque NM 87131

BROWN, JAMES HENRY, JR, FOREST ECOLOGY, SOILS. *Current Pos:* Res asst, 58-60, lectr, 60-62, from asst prof to assoc prof, 64-80, PROF FORESTRY, UNIV RI, 80- *Personal Data:* b Oneco, Conn, July 27, 34; m 56; c Laurie, David & Craig. *Educ:* Univ Conn, BS, 56; Univ RI, MS, 58; Duke Univ, DF(forest ecol), 65. *Concurrent Pos:* Actg chmn dept, Univ RI, 67-68; res lectr, Utah State Univ, 69-70, instr, Sch Field Studies, 84. *Mem:* Soc Am Foresters; Sigma Xi. *Res:* Site-growth relationships; impact of fire on forests of southern New England; forest regeneration and forest water budget; recreation impact on forest sites; forest biomass; impact of gypsy moth defoliation. *Mailing Add:* PO Box 993 Charlestown RI 02813. *Fax:* 401-792-4561

BROWN, JAMES K, ASTHMA. *Current Pos:* ASST CHIEF RESPIRATORY CARE, VET ADMIN MED CTR, SAN FRANCISCO, 81- *Personal Data:* b Kalamazoo, Mich, Oct 14, 45. *Educ:* Johns Hopkins Univ, MD, 72. *Mem:* Am Physiol Soc; Am Thoracic Soc. *Mailing Add:* Dept Med & Cardivasc Res Inst Univ Calif San Francisco CA 94121-1598

BROWN, JAMES KERR, FORESTRY. *Current Pos:* Res forester fire mgt, NCent Forest Exp Sta, 61-65, fire-fuel appraisal, Northern Forest Fire Lab, 65-79, PROJ LEADER FIRE EFFECTS, INTERMOUNTAIN FOREST & RANGE EXP STA, US FOREST SERV, 79- *Personal Data:* b Osborne, Kans, May 14, 38; m 60; c 2. *Educ:* Univ Minn, BS, 60; Yale Univ, MF, 61; Univ Mich, PhD(forestry), 68. *Mem:* AAAS; Soc Am Foresters. *Res:* Quantification of the physical properties of forest and range fuels; fuel and fire behavior modeling; effects of fire on fuels and vegetation; biomass estimation. *Mailing Add:* 1504 Woods Gulch Rd Missoula MT 59802

BROWN, JAMES MELTON, AGRONOMY. *Current Pos:* RETIRED. *Personal Data:* b Clayton, Ala, Dec 29, 25; m 47, Joan Thomas; c James M Jr, Ginny B (Carnell), Leigh A & Jeff T. *Educ:* Auburn Univ, BS, 49, MS, 51; NC State Univ, PhD(soils, plant nutrit), 60. *Prof Exp:* Asst prof soils, Auburn Univ, 51-53, asst agronomist, 53-55; res instr soils, NC State Univ, 55-58, exten specialist, Statewide Soils Educ Prog, 58-60; agronomist, Nat Plant Food Inst, DC, 60-61; agronomist, Nat Cotton Coun Am, 61-68, mgr agron res, 68-69 & agron & pesticide residue res, 69-71, mgr prod technol, 71-91. *Concurrent Pos:* Alt rep, Agr Res Inst, 74-, mem, Pesticide Study Panel, 75-, mem bd dirs, 76-, adv mem, Regional Res Proj S-102, 76-, mem, Technol Transfer Subcomt, 77; mem, Nat Cotton Indust-Exten Resources Comt, 77-, Agr Metrol Study Panel, 78-, vres, 79-81, pres, 81-; conf coordr & chmn prog & steering comts, Beltwide Cotton Conf, 71-, ed ann proceedings, Beltwide Cotton Prod-Mechanization Conf & Beltwide Cotton Prod Res Conf, 71-; mem, Boll Weevil Eradication Trial Tech Adv Comt, 78-; consult, State-USDA Cotton Res Task Force Rev Comt, 77- *Mem:* Am Soc Agron; Soil Sci Soc Am; Crop Sci Soc; Coun Agr Sci & Technol; Plant Growth Regulation Soc. *Res:* Soil fertility and chemistry; plant nutrition and physiology; weed control; air pollution; pesticide toxic substances; plant diseases; insect control; crop production systems; agricultural weather; legislation-regulations. *Mailing Add:* 616 Little Creek Rd Auburn AL 36832-3418

BROWN, JAMES MICHAEL, INDUSTRIAL WATER TREATMENT, ENHANCED OIL RECOVERY. *Current Pos:* proj leader, 86-94, RES ASSOC, BETZ LABS, INC, 94- *Personal Data:* b Gallatin, Tenn, Sept 26, 55. *Educ:* Western Ky Univ, BS, 77; Vanderbilt Univ, MS & PhD(phys chem), 80. *Prof Exp:* Sr chemist, Halliburton Serv, 80-85, develop chemist, 85-86. *Concurrent Pos:* Instr, N Harris Co Community Col, 85- *Mem:* Am Chem Soc. *Res:* Development of mineral scale inhibitors for industrial cooling water, reverse osmosis systems and geothermal wells; development of polymeric dispersants for industrial water treatment; development of biodegradable and environmentally friendly additives for water treatment. *Mailing Add:* 26506 Oak Ridge Dr Spring TX 77380

BROWN, JAMES RICHARD, SOIL FERTILITY, WASTE MANAGEMENT. *Current Pos:* From asst prof to assoc prof, 63-78, prof agron, 78-90, PROF SOIL SCI, UNIV MO, COLUMBIA, 90- *Personal Data:* b Charleston, Ill, Oct 6, 31; m 60, Erma Sausgaard; c Darcia (Manning), Lisa, Sandra (Murray) & Diana. *Educ:* Univ Ill, BS, 53, MS, 57; Iowa State Univ, PhD(soil fertil), 63. *Mem:* Am Soc Agron; Soil Sci Soc Am; Sigma Xi; Am Forage & Grassland Coun; Soc Range Mgt; Soil & Water Conserv Soc Am. *Res:* Soil fertility and testing; waste management; plant analysis; nutrition of forage crops. *Mailing Add:* Sch Natural Resources 144 Mumford Hall Columbia MO 65211

BROWN, JAMES ROY, NUCLEAR PHYSICS. *Current Pos:* PRIN PHYSICIST, NEUTRON PHYSICS EXP, LINEAR ACCELERATOR & PHYSICIST CHG CRITICAL EXP, GEN ATOMIC CO, 59- *Personal Data:* b Wilkinsburg, Pa, June 14, 23; m 47; c 3. *Educ:* Allegheny Col, BA, 44; Calif Inst Technol, MS, 48, PhD(physics), 51. *Prof Exp:* Asst, Calif Inst Technol & Naval Ord Test Sta, 44-45; instr physics, Allegheny Col, 42-47; sr scientist nuclear physics, Reactors, Westinghouse Bettis Atomic Power Div, 50-57, adv scientist exp reactor physics, 57-59. *Mem:* AAAS; Am Nuclear Soc; Am Phys Soc; Sigma Xi. *Res:* Solid propellant rockets; elementary physics; precision spectroscopy of gamma rays using a curved crystal focusing spectrometer; present research on neutron and reactor physics. *Mailing Add:* 12611 Sommerfield Lane Poway CA 92064

BROWN, JAMES T, JR, THEORETICAL PHYSICS, EXPERIMENTAL LIGHT SCATTERING. *Current Pos:* PROF PHYSICS, COLO SCH MINES, 67- *Personal Data:* b Jackson Heights, NY, Feb 23, 39; m 59; c 3. *Educ:* Univ Colo, BA, 61, PhD(physics), 68. *Prof Exp:* Physicist, Boulder Labs, Nat Bur Stand, Colo, 58-65. *Mem:* Am Asn Aerosol Res. *Res:* Aerosol science and particulate control; condensation and nucleation properties of respirable dust; scattering of light by small particles and surfaces. *Mailing Add:* Dept Physics Colo Sch Mines Golden CO 80401. *Fax:* 303-273-3913

BROWN, JAMES WALKER, JR, BIOCHEMISTRY. *Current Pos:* From asst prof to assoc prof, 62-69, PROF CHEM, MID TENN STATE UNIV, 69- *Personal Data:* b Hampshire, Tenn, July 10, 30; m 53; c 2. *Educ:* Mid Tenn State Col, BS, 57; NC State Col, MS, 59, PhD(dairy chem), 62. *Mem:* Sigma Xi. *Mailing Add:* 1911 Ragland Ave Murfreesboro TN 37130-4145

BROWN, JAMES WARD, APPLIED MATHEMATICS. *Current Pos:* assoc prof, 68-71, PROF MATH, UNIV MICH, DEARBORN, 71- *Personal Data:* b Philadelphia, Pa, Jan 15, 34; m 57, Jacqueline Read; c Scott & Gordon. *Educ:* Harvard Univ, AB, 57; Univ Mich, AM, 58, PhD(math), 64. *Prof Exp:* Asst prof math, Univ Mich, Dearborn, 64-66 & Oberlin Col, 66-68. *Concurrent Pos:* NSF res grantee, 69; ed consult, Math Rev, 70-84. *Mem:* Sigma Xi; Am Math Soc. *Res:* Special functions of mathematical physics; author of two books. *Mailing Add:* 1710 Morton Ave Ann Arbor MI 48104

BROWN, JARVIS HOWARD, CROP PHYSIOLOGY. *Current Pos:* from asst prof to assoc prof, 67-93,, EMER ASSOC PROF AGRON, MONT STATE UNIV, 93- *Personal Data:* b Goshen, Ind, Aug 7, 37; m 59; c 3. *Educ:* Purdue Univ, BSA, 59; Iowa State Univ, MS, 62, PhD(crop physiol), 65. *Prof Exp:* Res assoc agron, Purdue Univ Univ, 65-67. *Mem:* Am Soc Agron; Crop Sci Soc Am. *Res:* Effects of leaf orientation, leaf width and chlorophyll concentration on the water use, growth, yield and photosynthesis of barley isotypes; cold hardiness of winter wheat. *Mailing Add:* 305 S 13th Ave Bozeman MT 59715

BROWN, JASON WALTER, NEUROLOGY. *Current Pos:* clin assoc prof, 75-79, CLIN PROF, NY UNIV, 79- *Personal Data:* b New York, NY, Apr 14, 38; m 67, Jo-Ann M Gelardi; c Jonathan S & Jovana M. *Educ:* Univ Calif, Berkeley, BA, 59; Univ Southern Calif, MD, 63. *Prof Exp:* Intern, St Elizabeths Hosp, Wash, 63-64; resident neurol, Univ Calif, Los Angeles, 64-67; instr, Boston Univ Med Sch, 69-70; asst clin prof, Columbia-Presby Hosp, New York, 70-75. *Concurrent Pos:* Pvt pract neurol, 70-; vis asst prof, Albert Einstein Col Med, 72-75; vis assoc prof, Rockefeller Univ, 78-79; pres, Inst Behav Neurosci; fel, Alexander von Humboldt Found, 79-, World Rehab Fund, 82. *Res:* Aphasia, apraxia and agnosia; mind, brain and consciousness; numerous articles on neurology. *Mailing Add:* Dept Neurol NY Univ Med Ctr 550 First Ave New York NY 10016-6402

BROWN, JAY CLARK, VIRUS STRUCTURE & ASSEMBLY. *Current Pos:* from asst prof to assoc prof, 71-87, PROF MICROBIOL, SCH MED, UNIV VA, 87- *Personal Data:* b Jersey City, NJ, June 23, 42; m 65, Sallie S Dietrich; c 3. *Educ:* Johns Hopkins Univ, BS, 64; Harvard Univ, PhD(biochem), 69. *Prof Exp:* Fel molecular biol, MRC Lab Molecular Biol, Cambridge, Eng, 69-71. *Concurrent Pos:* Fel sci, NATO, 69-70; instr physiol, Marine Biol Lab, Woods Hole, Mass, 77-80; personnel comt, Am Cancer Soc, 80-86; mem, Cancer Career Develop Study Sect, Calif Tobacco-Related Dis Res Prog, 90- *Mem:* Am Soc Biochem & Molecular Biol; Am Soc Microbiol; AAAS. *Res:* Structure and assembly of the herpes simplex virus capsid; develop capsid assembly as a target for anti-viral therapeutics. *Mailing Add:* Dept Microbiol Box 441 Univ Va Health Sci Ctr Charlottesville VA 22908. *Fax:* 804-982-1071; *E-Mail:* jcb2g@avery.med.virignia.edu

BROWN, JEANETTE GRASSELLI, MOLECULAR SPECTROSCOPY, NAPHTHALENE EXTRACTION. *Personal Data:* b Cleveland, Ohio, Aug 4, 28; m 87, Glenn R Brown. *Educ:* Ohio Univ, BS, 50, Western Res Univ, 58. *Hon Degrees:* Seven from US univs, 78-95. *Honors & Awards:* Garvan Medal, Am Chem Soc, 86, Analytical Chem Award, 93; William Wright Award, Coblentz Soc, 80; Theophilus Redwood Lectr, Royal Soc Chem, 94. *Prof Exp:* Proj leader assoc, Infrared Spectroscopist, 50-78; mgr analytical sci lab, Stand Oil Co, 78-83, dir, Technol Support Dept, 83-85, dir corp res & analytical sci, 85-88; dist vis prof & dir res enhancement, Ohio Univ, 89-95. *Concurrent Pos:* chair, Analytical Div, Am Chem Soc, 90-91; chmn, US Nat Comt Int Union Pure & Appl Chem, 92-94. *Mem:* Am Chem Soc; Soc Appl Spectros (pres, 70); Coblentz Soc; Royal Soc Chem. *Res:* Author of 8 books; contributed numerous articles on molecular spectroscopy to professional journals; molecular spectroscopy; awarded one patent; naphthalene extraction. *Mailing Add:* 150 Greentree Rd Chagrin Falls OH 44022-2424

BROWN, JEANETTE SNYDER, PHOTOBIOLOGY, PHOTOSYNTHESIS. *Current Pos:* RETIRED. *Personal Data:* b Rochester, NY, Mar 6, 25; m 50, Walter; c Pamela, James & Julia. *Educ:* Cornell Univ, BS, 45, MS, 48; Stanford Univ, PhD(biol), 52. *Prof Exp:* Asst chem, NY State Agr Exp Sta, Geneva, 46-47; bacteriologist, Am Inst Radiation, Calif, 48-49; staff biologist, Carnegie Inst Wash Dept Plant Biol, 58-87. *Concurrent Pos:* NSF grant, Australia, 79-80. *Mem:* Sigma Xi; Am Inst Biol Sci. *Res:* Spectroscopic investigations of the native state of chlorophyll and other photosynthetic pigments in plant membranes and isolated protein complexes. *Mailing Add:* PO Box 334 Murphys CA 95247-0334

BROWN, JEROME ENGEL, INDUSTRIAL CHEMISTRY. *Current Pos:* RETIRED. *Personal Data:* b Buckhannon, WVa, Apr 29, 24; m 92, Lynn Jurey; c Michael L, Chris E, Beverly G & Jean E (Bryant). *Educ:* WVa Wesleyan Col, BS, 44; Univ Ill, PhD(chem), 49. *Prof Exp:* Asst res supvr, Ethyl Corp, 49-60, commercial develop rep, 60-62, mgr mkt develop, 62-70, sr assoc, 70-87. *Mem:* Am Chem Soc. *Res:* Market development and research; gasoline additives; high-vacuum techniques. *Mailing Add:* HC 73 Box 118 Dogpatch AR 72648-9714

BROWN, JERRAM L, NEUROSCIENCES. *Current Pos:* PROF BIOL SCI, STATE UNIV NY ALBANY, 78- *Personal Data:* b Glen Ridge, NJ, July 19, 30; m 53, Esther Rosenbloom; c Jeffry J, Karen B (Martin) & Sheryl D (Bolstad). *Educ:* Cornell Univ, AB, 52, MS, 54; Univ Calif, Berkeley, PhD(zool), 60. *Honors & Awards:* Brewster Medal, Am Ornith Union, 87. *Prof Exp:* NIH fel, 60-62; from asst prof to prof biol & brain res, Univ Rochester, 62-78. *Mem:* Soc Study Evolution; fel Am Ornith Union; fel Animal Behav Soc; fel AAAS; Ecol Soc Am; Soc Behav Ecol. *Res:* Neuro-ethology; evolution of behavior; ecology of aid-giving in animals; behavioral ecology. *Mailing Add:* Dept Biol Sci State Univ NY Albany NY 12222. *Fax:* 518-442-4767; *E-Mail:* Bitnet: jlb81@cnsvax.albany.edu

BROWN, JERRY, SOIL SCIENCE, PERMAFROST. *Current Pos:* RETIRED. *Personal Data:* b Boundbrook, NJ, Feb 22, 36; m 65; c 2. *Educ:* Rutgers Univ, BS, 58, PhD(soils), 62. *Prof Exp:* Soil scientist & chief, Earth Sci Br, US Army Cold Regions Res & Eng Lab, 61-85, dir tundra biome, Int Biol Prog, 70-76; head, Arctic Res Policy Staff, NSF, 85-91. *Concurrent Pos:* Mem Polar Res Bd, Nat Res Coun, Nat Acad Sci, chmn, Comt Permafrost, chmn, US Comt, Int Permafrost Asn, 85-98; adv, Arctic Res Comn. *Mem:* AAAS; Soil Sci Soc Am; Arctic Inst NAm; Ecol Soc Am; Geol Soc Am; Am Geophys Union; Am Quaternary Asn; Sigma Xi; Int Permafrost Asn (secy, 93-98). *Res:* Arctic soil science; arctic ecology; permafrost. *Mailing Add:* PO Box 7 Woods Hole MA 02543-0007. *E-Mail:* jerrybrown@igc.apc.org

BROWN, JERRY L, BIOCHEMISTRY. *Current Pos:* asst prof biochem, 67-73, ASSOC PROF BIOCHEM, MED SCH, UNIV COLO, DENVER, 73- *Personal Data:* b Malvern, Ark, Oct 3, 35; m 61; c 1. *Educ:* NTex State Univ, BS, 59, MS, 60; Univ Tex, PhD(biochem), 64. *Prof Exp:* Fel biol chem, Univ Calif, Los Angeles, 63-67. *Mem:* Am Soc Biol Chemists; Fedn Am Soc Exp Biol. *Res:* Reactions resulting in structural modifications of proteins; reactions leading to blocked amino terminal amino acids are being investigated. *Mailing Add:* Dept Biochem B126 Univ Colo Health Sci Ctr Denver CO 80262-0001. *Fax:* 303-270-8215

BROWN, JERRY WILLIAM, ANATOMY, NEUROSCIENCES. *Current Pos:* from assoc prof to prof, 64-92, EMER PROF ANAT, MED CTR, UNIV ALA, BIRMINGHAM, 92- *Personal Data:* b Wichita, Kans, July 4, 25; m 50, Mina MacNair; c Louise (Hyde), Margaret S (Hildreth) & Elizabeth L (Bardo). *Educ:* Wichita State Univ, AB, 46; Univ Kans, MA, 49, PhD(anat), 51. *Prof Exp:* From asst to instr anat, Univ Kans, 47-51; instr, Sch Med, Univ Pittsburgh, 51-56; from asst prof to assoc prof, Sch Med, Univ Mo, 56-64. *Concurrent Pos:* Guest worker, Neth Cent Inst Brain Res, Univ Amsterdam, 65-66; fel, NIH, 65-66, res award, 68-71. *Mem:* AAAS; Am Acad Neurol; Soc Neurosci; Am Asn Anat. *Res:* Embryonic development of the brainstem and telencephalon; development of sensory nuclei of V in human embryos; development of telencephalon of bat embryos; adult bat telencephalon. *Mailing Add:* Dept Cell Biol Univ Ala Birmingham Univ Sta Birmingham AL 35294-0019

BROWN, JESSE J, JR, CERAMIC ENGINEERING. *Current Pos:* from asst prof to assoc prof ceramic eng, 67-77, PROF MAT ENG & DIR, CTR ADVAN CERAMIC MAT, VA POLYTECH INST & STATE UNIV, 77- *Personal Data:* b Harrisburg, Pa, Oct 1, 39; m 61; c 2. *Educ:* Pa State Univ, BS, 61, MS, 62, PhD(ceramic technol), 64. *Prof Exp:* Res & develop engr, Sylvania Elec Prod Inc Div, Gen Tel & Electronics Corp, 64-67. *Mem:* Fel Am Ceramic Soc; Am Chem Soc. *Res:* Inorganic chemistry, especially as related to phase equilibria and crystal chemistry; properties including, luminescence, thermal expansion and related fields. *Mailing Add:* Dept Mat Sci Va Polytech Inst & State Univ Box 0237 Blacksburg VA 24063-0001

BROWN, JOAN HELLER, NEUROPHARMACOLOGY, RECEPTOR MECHANISMS. *Current Pos:* asst res pharmacologist & lectr med, 75-79, asst prof residence, 79-80, ASST PROF, DIV PHARMACOL, DEPT MED, UNIV CALIF, SAN DIEGO, 80- *Personal Data:* b Cleveland, Ohio, Feb 14, 46; m 70; c 1. *Educ:* Cornell Univ, BA, 67; Albert Einstein Col Med, PhD(pharmacol), 73. *Prof Exp:* Fel pharmacol, Univ Colo Med Ctr, 73-75. *Mem:* Am Soc Pharmacol & Exp Therapeut; Soc Neurosci; Am Women Sci; Fedn Am Soc Exp Biol. *Res:* Biochemical mechanisms of neurotransmitter action: receptor pharmacology, cyclic nucleotide and phosphatidylinositol metabolism, regulation of transmitter synthesis and release. *Mailing Add:* Dept Pharmacol 0636 Univ Calif San Diego 9500 Gilman Dr La Jolla CA 92093-0636. *Fax:* 619-534-6833

BROWN, JOE NED, JR, CRYSTALLOGRAPHY, PHYSICAL CHEMISTRY. *Current Pos:* AT CIBA-GEIGY, 89- *Personal Data:* b Bryan, Tex, Jan 24, 47. *Educ:* Tex A&M Univ, BS, 69; Univ New Orleans, PhD(phys chem), 72. *Prof Exp:* Res fel biochem, Calif Inst Technol, 72-73; asst prof chem, Ill Inst Technol, 73-79; sr res scientist, Celanese Res Co, 79- *Concurrent Pos:* Damon Runyon fel, Calif Inst Technol, 72-73, NIH fel, 73; consult, G D Searle & Co, Skokie, Ill, 74-79 & Latticeworks, Inc, 79- *Mem:* Am Crystallog Asn; Am Chem Soc; Am Inst Physics; AAAS. *Res:* Structure-activity correlations among biologically active molecules; peptide structure; hydration effects on structure. *Mailing Add:* 6 Country Lane Califon NJ 07830-3437

BROWN, JOEL EDWARD, NEUROPHYSIOLOGY, BIOPHYSICS. *Current Pos:* TACHNA PROF OPHTHAL, ALBERT EINSTEIN COL MED, 91- *Personal Data:* b Middletown, NY, May 23, 37. *Educ:* Mass Inst Technol, BS & MS, 60, PhD(physiol), 64. *Honors & Awards:* Woods Hole Marine Biol Lab Res Prize, 72 & 73; E R Cole Award, Biophys Soc, 90. *Prof Exp:* From asst prof to assoc prof physiol, Mass Inst Technol, 64-71; prof anat, Vanderbilt Univ, 71-76, prof biochem, 74-76; prof physiol, State Univ NY, Stony Brook, 76-83; Bernard Becker prof ophthal, Wash Univ, 83-91. *Concurrent Pos:* NIH fel, Sch Med, Univ Chile, 64; corp mem, Woods Hole Marine Biol Lab, trustee, 73-77; McCormick Scholar, Res Prev Blindness, Inc, 84. *Mem:* Asn Res Vision & Ophthal; Am Soc Biochem & Molecular Biol; Biophys Soc; Soc Gen Physiol; fel AAAS. *Res:* Physiology, biophysics and biochemistry of retina and photoreceptors. *Mailing Add:* Dept Ophthal & Visual Sci Albert Einstein Col Med 506 Kennedy Ctr 1410 Pelham Pkwy Bronx NY 10461. *E-Mail:* jbrown@aecom.yu.edu

BROWN, JOHN ANGUS, ORGANIC CHEMISTRY, ANALYTICAL CHEMISTRY. *Current Pos:* PRES, JOHN BROWN ASSOCS, INC, 73- *Personal Data:* b Lake Wales, Fla, Dec 13, 25; m 54; c 3. *Educ:* Emory Univ, BA, 45; Ga Inst Technol, MS, 51, PhD(org chem), 54. *Honors & Awards:* Bronze Medallion, Am Defense Preparedness Asn, 82- *Prof Exp:* Engr, Law & Co, Ga, 45-48; teaching asst chem, Ga Inst Technol, 48-54; res chemist, Esso Res & Eng Co, NJ, 54-63, sr chemist, 63-68, staff adv, 68-73. *Concurrent Pos:* Mem var ad hoc study & planning panels, Dept of Defense; pres, Passaic

Valley Chamber Com, 87-90. *Mem:* Am Chem Soc; Sigma Xi; Am Defense Preparedness Asn; Soc Advan Mat & Process Eng; Optical Soc Am; Soc Photo-Optical Instrumentation Engrs. *Res:* Research and development of lubricating oil additives, safety and sensitivity of propellants and explosives; advanced physical-chemical waste reclamation processes; analytical aspects of chemical warfare defense; analytical instrument development; electronics; optics; advanced optical filters for laser eye protection. *Mailing Add:* 15 York Pl Berkeley Heights NJ 07922-1860. *Fax:* 908-647-4202

BROWN, JOHN BOYER, PHYSICAL CHEMISTRY. *Current Pos:* From instr to prof chem, Denison Univ, 52-90, chmn dept, 61-64, 72-73 & 75-76, consult, Comput Ctr, 90-94, EMER PROF CHEM, DENISON UNIV, 90- *Personal Data:* b Lexington, Ky, Nov 12, 24; m 49, Jeane C DeGarmo; c Christopher, Margaret & Stephen. *Educ:* Univ Ky, BS, 48; Northwestern Univ, PhD, 56. *Concurrent Pos:* Vis scientist, Swedish Inst Surface Chem, 73-74; vis prof, Duke Univ, 81-82; consult, Comput Ctr, 90-94. *Mem:* Fel Am Inst Chemists; NY Acad Sci. *Res:* Cationic surfactants; physical properties of micelles; solubilization by detergents. *Mailing Add:* 121 Chapin Pl Granville OH 43023

BROWN, JOHN CLIFFORD, BIOCHEMISTRY, IMMUNOLOGY. *Current Pos:* asst prof, 76-83, ASSOC PROF MICROBIOL, UNIV KANS, 83-, COURTESY ASSOC PROF BIOCHEM, 90- *Personal Data:* b Cullman, Ala, Feb 23, 43; div; c Aaron & Rachel. *Educ:* Auburn Univ, BS, 65, MS, 67; NC State Univ, PhD(biochem), 73. *Prof Exp:* Fel immunol, Univ Calif, Berkeley, 73-76. *Concurrent Pos:* Mem genetics prog, Bioanal Res, Univ Kans, 89- *Mem:* Am Asn Immunologists; Fedn Am Soc Exp Biol; AAAS. *Res:* Rheumatic disease autoantibodies; idiotype and anti-idiotype relationships in rheumatic disease. *Mailing Add:* Dept Microbiol 8041 Haworth Hall Univ Kans Lawrence KS 66045-0001. *Fax:* 785-864-5294; *E-Mail:* jbrown@kuhub.cc.ukans.edu

BROWN, JOHN FRANCIS, JR, POLYCHLORINATED BIPHENYL CHEMISTRY & TOXICOLOGY. *Current Pos:* Res assoc, Gen Elec Co, 50-56, mgr, Reaction Studies Unit, 56-61, org chemist, 61-65, mgr, Life Sci Br, 65-82, mgr health res, 82-93, MGR ENVIRON TOXICOL PROG, RES & DEVELOP CTR, GEN ELEC CO, 93- *Personal Data:* b Providence, RI, Oct 11, 26; m 55, Eleanor A Fair; c Deborah A, Marcus F & Alice F. *Educ:* Brown Univ, BS, 47; Mass Inst Technol, PhD(chem), 50. *Concurrent Pos:* Fel clin path, Upstate Med Ctr, State Univ NY, 68-69; mem, Study Critical Environ Probs, 70. *Mem:* AAAS; Am Chem Soc; Soc Environ Toxicol Chem. *Res:* Biomedical surface chemistry; health effects of industrial chemicals; environmental fate of xenobiotics. *Mailing Add:* Gen Elec Corp-Res & Develop PO Box 8 Bldg K1 Rm 3C7 Schenectady NY 12301-0008. *Fax:* 518-387-7611

BROWN, JOHN HENRY, WOOD SCIENCE, WOOD TECHNOLOGY. *Current Pos:* RETIRED. *Personal Data:* b Kalamazoo, Mich, Nov 4, 24; m 46; c 3. *Educ:* Mich State Univ, BS, 49, MS, 50; NY State Col Forestry, Syracuse Univ, PhD(wood prod eng), 62. *Prof Exp:* Trainee, Ga Pac Plywood Co, 50-51; buyer & salesman, Olympia Wood Preserving Co, 51-54; wood technologist, Res & Develop, Potlatch Forests, Inc, 54-56; instr & res asst, Syracuse Univ, 56-62, asst prof, 62-63; technologist, Eng & Tech Serv Dept, Potlatch Corp, 63-88. *Mem:* Soc Wood Sci & Technol; Forest Prod Res Soc; Am Soc Testing & Mat. *Res:* Wood adhesion; electrical properties of wood; wood-moisture relations; energy; wood combined with other materials, plastics, metals, paper and particleboard; sawmill simulation and evaluation. *Mailing Add:* 1962 Coulter Lane Clarkston WA 99403

BROWN, JOHN LAWRENCE, JR, APPLIED MATHEMATICS, COMMUNICATION THEORY. *Current Pos:* From asst prof to prof, 52-88, EMER PROF ELEC ENG, PA STATE UNIV, UNIVERSITY PARK, 88- *Personal Data:* b Ellenville, NY, Mar 6, 25. *Educ:* Ohio Univ, BS, 48; Brown Univ, PhD(appl math), 53. *Concurrent Pos:* Gen Lew Allen, Jr Res Chair, Air Force Inst Technol, 84-85; Stocker prof elec & comput eng, Ohio Univ, 88- *Mem:* Am Math Soc; fel Inst Elec & Electronics Engrs; Math Asn Am; Soc Indust & Appl Math; Acoust Soc Am. *Res:* Statistical communication theory; applied mathematics; underwater acoustics. *Mailing Add:* 1431 Curtin St State College PA 16803-3020

BROWN, JOHN LOTT, PSYCHOPHYSIOLOGY, HUMAN FACTORS ENGINEERING. *Current Pos:* pres, 78-88, EMER PROF MED & ENG, UNIV SFLA, 88- *Personal Data:* b Philadelphia, Pa, Dec 3, 24; m 48, Catharine Hertfelder; c Patricia, Judith, Anderson & Barbara. *Educ:* Worcester Polytech Inst, BSEE, 45; Temple Univ, MA, 49; Columbia Univ, PhD(psychol), 52. *Hon Degrees:* DSc, Worcester Polytech Inst, 84. *Prof Exp:* Mem staff, Div Govt Res, Columbia Univ, 51-53, tech dir, USAF Res Proj, 53-54; head, Psychol Div, Aviation Med Acceleration Lab, Naval Air Develop Ctr, 54-59; asst prof sensory physiol, Sch Med, Univ Pa, 57-62, assoc prof, 62-65, dir grad training prog physiol, 62-65; dean grad sch, Kans State Univ, 65-66, vpres acad affairs, 66-69; prof psychol & optics, Univ Rochester, 69-78, dir, Ctr Visual Sci, 71-78. *Concurrent Pos:* USPHS sr res fel physiol, Sch Med, Univ Pa, 59-63; chmn, Comt Vision, Nat Acad Sci-Nat Res Coun, 65-70, staff adv, 68-72; mem visual sci study sect, NIH, 67-71; mem bd trustees, Worcester Polytech Inst, 71-83, Asn Res Vision & Ophthal, 74-79, Illum Eng Res Inst, 74-79; assoc ed, J Optical Soc Am, 72-77; mem, Vision Res Prog Comt, Nat Eye Inst, 74-78, chmn, 75-78. *Mem:* Fel Am Psychol Asn; fel Optical Soc Am; fel AAAS; Asn Res Vision & Ophthal (pres, 78). *Res:* Psychophysiology and electrophysiology of vision; applications of psychology and physiology to man-machine systems; sensory physiology. *Mailing Add:* 4141 Bayshore Blvd Tampa FL 33611-1802. *Fax:* 813-831-9275; *E-Mail:* jbrown@suntan.eng.usf.edu

BROWN, JOHN M, CANCER IMMUNOLOGY, MONOCLONAL ANTIBODIES. *Current Pos:* CENTO COR, INC. *Educ:* Wayne State Univ, PhD(biochem), 77. *Prof Exp:* asst prof microbiol surg, Col Med, Univ Ill, 81- *Res:* Immunotherapy. *Mailing Add:* Cento Cor Inc 200 Great Valley Pkwy Malvern PA 19355-1307. *Fax:* 215-651-6100

BROWN, JOHN WESLEY, mathematics, for more information see previous edition

BROWN, JOHN WESLEY, BIOLOGICAL CHEMISTRY. *Current Pos:* from asst prof to assoc prof biochem, 57-68, chmn dept chem, 68-71, PROF CHEM, UNIV LOUISVILLE, 68-, ASSOC DEAN GRAD SCH & DIR SPONSORED PROG, 71- *Personal Data:* b Chicago, Ill, Dec 2, 25; m 50; c 3. *Educ:* Elmhurst Col, BS, 50; Univ Ill, MS, 53, PhD, 56. *Prof Exp:* Tech rep nutrit, E I Du Pont de Nemours & Co, Inc, 56-57. *Mem:* AAAS; Sigma Xi; Am Soc Biol Chem. *Res:* Animal protein metabolism; amino acid nutrition in relation to neurotransmitter synthesis and behavior. *Mailing Add:* 1960 Meadowcreek Ave Louisville KY 40218-2438

BROWN, JOSEPH M, ELEMENTARY PARTICLE PHYSICS. *Current Pos:* RETIRED. *Personal Data:* b Fayetteville, WVa, Jan 9, 28; m 52, Jimmie Marie Dikeman; c Paul, Stephanie, Barbara & Carolyn. *Educ:* WVa Univ, BS, 46, BSME, 47; Purdue Univ, MSME, 50, PhD(eng design), 52. *Prof Exp:* Struct engr, NAm Aviation, 51-53 & Douglas Aircraft Co, 53-56; owner, Struct Specialties Inc, 56-57; sect head struct, Hughes Aircraft Co, 57-61; assoc dept head vehicle design, Aerospace Corp, 61-67; physicist, McDonnell Douglas Corp, 67-70; prof mech eng, Miss State Univ, 70-91. *Mem:* Am Phys Soc; Sigma Xi. *Res:* Engineering design methodology, all areas of structural analysis and design, research into the foundations of physics. *Mailing Add:* 310 Canterbury Rd Starkville MS 39759

BROWN, JOSEPH ROSS, MATHEMATICS. *Current Pos:* prof, 52-87, EMER PROF, BRADLEY UNIV, 89- *Personal Data:* b Parkville, Mo, Sept 24, 20; m 48, Elizabeth A Etter; c Joseph Jr, William, Kristin & Daniel. *Educ:* Park Col, AB, 41; Univ Kans, MA, 49, PhD(math), 53. *Prof Exp:* Instr math, Park Col, 46-49. *Mem:* Math Asn Am. *Res:* Non-Euclidean geometry. *Mailing Add:* 11 Cape Ct Pelcin IL 61554

BROWN, JOSHUA ROBERT CALLOWAY, cell biology; deceased, see previous edition for last biography

BROWN, JUDITH E, PRENATAL NUTRITION. *Current Pos:* COORDR PUB HEALTH NUTRIT DOCTORATE CURRIC, DIV EPIDEMIOL, SCH PUB HEALTH, UNIV MINN, 88-, PROF PUB HEALTH NUTRIT, 90- *Personal Data:* b Syracuse, NY, May 12, 48. *Educ:* Rochester Inst Technol, BS, 70; Univ Mich, MPH, 72; Fla State Univ, PhD(human nutrit), 75. *Prof Exp:* Pub health nutritionist, Migrant Health Prog, Fla Dept Health, 72-73; instr, Food & Nutrit Dept, Fla State Univ, 74-75. *Res:* Prenatal nutrition and infant outcome. *Mailing Add:* Univ Minn Sch Pub Health 1300 S Second St Suite 300 Minneapolis MN 55454

BROWN, JULIUS, electrical engineering, for more information see previous edition

BROWN, KAREN KAY (KILKER), VACCINE DEVELOPMENT, FERMENTATION. *Current Pos:* dir biol res, Animal Health Div, 85-92, DIR TECHNOL & DISCOVERY, MOBAY CORP, 92- *Personal Data:* b Manhattan, Kans, July 25, 44; m 66. *Educ:* Washburn Univ, BS, 66; Okla State Univ, PhD(molecular biol & microbiol), 72. *Honors & Awards:* Miles Sci & Technol Award, 85; Mobay Sci & Technol Awards, 86. *Prof Exp:* Res scientist, Cutter Haver Lockhart Labs, 72-75, qual assurance microbiologist, 72; sr res scientist, Bayvet Div, Miles Labs, 75-82, prin scientist, 82-83, mgr biol res, 83-85. *Concurrent Pos:* Biohazards control officer, Bayvet Div, Miles Labs & Animal Health Div, Mobay Corp, 74-; pres, Pair O'Docs Investment Enterprises, 84-; chief tech officer, Dermal Res Labs, Inc. *Mem:* AAAS; NY Acad Sci; Am Soc Microbiol; Am Asn Lab Animal Scientists; Sigma Xi. *Res:* Development of veterinary vaccines and drug products; use of biotechnology techniques for development of purified subunit vaccines and diagnostics; fermentation; tissue culture; protein purification; delivery systems. *Mailing Add:* 5501 NW Fox Hill Rd Parkville MO 64152-3427

BROWN, KARL LESLIE, PARTICLE PHYSICS, PHYSICS OF BEAMS. *Current Pos:* sr res assoc, 59-74, PROF, STANFORD LINEAR ACCELERATOR CTR, 74- *Personal Data:* b Coalville, Utah, Sept 30, 25; m 48, 77, Vera Luth; c David, Dennistoun, Adriana, Jeremy & Andrew. *Educ:* Stanford Univ, BS, 47, MS, 49, PhD(physics), 53. *Prof Exp:* Res assoc, Stanford Univ, 53-58; consult, Linear Accelerator Lab, Ecole Normale Superieure, France, 58-59; dir res, Radiation Div, Varian Assocs, 66-68. *Concurrent Pos:* Consult, Varian Assocs, 66-; vis scientist, Europ Orgn Nuclear Res, 72-74, 84-85. *Mem:* Fel Am Phys Soc. *Res:* Experimental physics; charged particle accelerators and charged particle optics. *Mailing Add:* Stanford Linear Accelerator Ctr Stanford CA 94309. *E-Mail:* klb@slac.stanford.edu

BROWN, KATHRYN MARIE, IMMUNOLOGY RESEARCH, CYTOKINE REGULATION. *Current Pos:* SCI ADV & PATENT AGENT, MORGAN & FINNEGAN, 89- *Personal Data:* b Portsmouth, Ohio. *Educ:* Ohio State Univ, BS, 76, MS, 79, PhD(microbiol/immunol), 84. *Prof Exp:* NIH fel, Albert Einstein Sch Med, 84-87; res scientist, NY Univ Med Ctr, 87-89. *Mem:* Am Asn Immunologists; Am Soc Microbiol. *Mailing Add:* Morgan & Finnegan 345 Park Ave New York NY 10154

BROWN, KEITH CHARLES, PHYSICAL ORGANIC CHEMISTRY. *Current Pos:* from res scientist to sr res scientist, Clairol Inc, 74-77, sect head, 77-78, mgr org chem, 78-83, assoc dir res, 84-91, DIR RES, CLAIROL INC, DIV BRISTOL-MYERS CO, 92- *Personal Data:* b Beverley, Eng, Dec 2, 42. *Educ:* Univ Liverpool, BSc, 64, PhD(chem), 67. *Prof Exp:* Fel, Univ Rochester, 67-69; res officer, Elec Coun Res Ctr, Capenhurst, Eng, 69-73; scientist, Environ Impact Ctr Inc, Mass, 73-74. *Mem:* Am Chem Soc; Royal Soc Chem; Soc Cosmet Chemists. *Res:* Kinetics and mechanisms of reactions of organic compounds, particularly compounds important in cosmetic chemistry; dye synthesis. *Mailing Add:* Clairol Inc 2 Blachley Rd Stamford CT 06902

BROWN, KEITH H, PLASMA PHYSICS, HIGH PRESSURE PHYSICS. *Current Pos:* RES SCIENTIST, AET CTR, HUGHES MISSILE SYSTS CO, 83- *Personal Data:* b Salt Lake City, Utah, Sept 3, 39; m 63; c 3. *Educ:* Brigham Young Univ, BA, 64, PhD(physics), 69; Univ Ill, Urbana-Champaign, MS, 65. *Prof Exp:* Asst prof, 68-72, assoc prof, 72-77, prof physics, Calif State Polytech Univ, Pomona, 77-, chmn dept, 76-83. *Concurrent Pos:* Fel, Brigham Young Univ, 74-75. *Mem:* Am Phys Soc; Am Asn Physics Teachers. *Res:* Magnetic confinement of plasmas; x-ray diffraction of liquid metals at high pressures. *Mailing Add:* AET Ctr Hughes Missile Systs Co PO Box 1973 Rancho Cucamonga CA 91729-1973

BROWN, KEITH J, METEOROLOGY. *Current Pos:* RETIRED. *Personal Data:* b Santa Monica, Calif, Apr 12, 28; m, Margaret; c Terry (Jarret) & Kathleen (Fritzley). *Educ:* Univ Calif, Los Angeles, BA, 54. *Honors & Awards:* Outstanding Contrib Advan Appl Meteorol Award, 95. *Prof Exp:* Pres, NAm Weather Coun, 94. *Mem:* Fel Am Meteorol Soc; Weather Modification Asn. *Mailing Add:* 343 Camber Lane Port Ludlow WA 98365

BROWN, KENNETH GERALD, PHYSICAL CHEMISTRY, THERMODYNAMICS & MATERIAL PROPERTIES. *Current Pos:* assoc prof, 82-88, PROF, DEPT CHEM & BIOCHEM, OLD DOMINION UNIV, 82-, CHMN DEPT, 96- *Personal Data:* b Syracuse, NY, Oct 19, 44; m 88, Mary Elizabeth Jarrett; c Elizabeth, Wyatt, Melissa & Eric. *Educ:* Syracuse Univ, BA, 66; Brown Univ, PhD(chem), 71. *Prof Exp:* NIH postdoctoral fel, Univ Ore, 71-73; departmental postdoctoral fel, Univ Fla, 73-76; from asst prof to assoc prof chem, Univ Detroit, 76-81. *Mem:* Am Chem Soc. *Res:* Development of ambient-temperature catalysts and their spectroscopic characterization; synthesis of polymers in low-gravity environment. *Mailing Add:* Old Dominion Univ Norfolk VA 23529

BROWN, KENNETH H, PEDIATRIC NUTRITION. *Current Pos:* PROF NUTRIT, DEPT NUTRIT, UNIV CALIF, DAVIS, 89- *Personal Data:* b Philadelphia, Pa, June 6, 47. *Educ:* Columbia Univ, BS, 68; Univ Pa, MD, 73. *Honors & Awards:* Kellog's Int Nutrit Res Prize. *Prof Exp:* Res fel infectious dis, Sch Hyg & Pub Health, Johns Hopkins Univ, 75-79, from asst prof to assoc prof nutrit, 79-89. *Mem:* Am Soc Clin Nutrit; Soc Int Nutrit Res (pres, 92-); Am Soc Nutrit Sci. *Res:* Pediatric nutrition. *Mailing Add:* Dept Nutrit Univ Calif Davis CA 95616

BROWN, KENNETH HENRY, PHYSICAL CHEMISTRY, ANALYTICAL CHEMISTRY. *Current Pos:* asst prof, 73-81, PROF CHEM, NORTHWESTERN OKLA STATE UNIV, 81- *Personal Data:* b Utica, NY, June 6, 39; m 61, Dale Burns; c Karin Dale, Kenneth David, Richard Kieth & Scott Daniel. *Educ:* Hope Col, BA, 60; Rutgers Univ, PhD(phys chem), 66. *Prof Exp:* Asst prof chem, Transylvania Univ, 65-72, consult, T M Regan Inc, 73. *Concurrent Pos:* Consult, Ranger Eng, 75-76 & Trex Inc, 84-93. *Mem:* Am Chem Soc; Sigma Xi; Soc Col Sci Teachers. *Res:* Chemical education; chemical separations; chemical aspects of energy resource recovery and use; environmental analytical chemistry. *Mailing Add:* Dept Chem Northwestern Okla State Univ Alva OK 73717

BROWN, KENNETH HOWARD, organic polymer chemistry, for more information see previous edition

BROWN, KENNETH LAWRENCE, BIOINORGANIC CHEMISTRY. *Current Pos:* PROF CHEM & DEPT HEAD, MISS STATE UNIV, 90- *Personal Data:* b Philadelphia, Pa, July 6, 46; m 68, Kathleen Thompson; c Elizabeth L & Dana M. *Educ:* Univ Chicago, BS, 68; Univ Pa, PhD(biochem), 71. *Prof Exp:* NSF fel, 68-71; NIH trainee, Univ Pa, 72-73; NIH fel, Univ Calif, Davis, 73-75; from asst prof to assoc prof chem, Univ Tex, Arlington, 75-86, prof, 86-89. *Concurrent Pos:* Woodrow Wilson fel, 68; prin investr, NIH, 76-79 & 92-, Robert A Welch Found, 79-85, NSF, 89-92 & 93-; vis prof, Dept Chem, Univ Paris, Orsay, 83 & 86; sr fel, Nat Res Serv Award, NIH, 87-88; vis scientist, Univ Tex Health Sci Ctr, Dallas, 87-88; dir, Univ Indust Chem Res Ctr, Miss State Univ, 90-, Miss Magnetic Resonance Fac, 93- *Mem:* AAAS; Am Chem Soc; Sigma Xi; Am Soc Biochem & Molecular Biol. *Res:* Research into the chemistry of vitamin B12 and its derivatives including reactivity, nuclear magnetic resonance, x-ray crystallography and the studies of the association with vitamin B12 binding proteins and enzymes and the structure and properties of protein-round derivatives. *Mailing Add:* Dept Chem Box 9573 Miss State Univ Mississippi State MS 39762-5613. *Fax:* 601-325-1618; *E-Mail:* k1b2@ra.msstate.edu

BROWN, KENNETH MICHAEL, EVOLUTIONARY ECOLOGY, AQUATIC ECOLOGY. *Current Pos:* ASSOC PROF ZOOL, LA STATE UNIV, 85- *Personal Data:* b Riverside, Calif, Dec 20, 48; m 74; c 1. *Educ:* Ariz State Univ, BS, 70; Wash State Univ, MS, 72; Univ Iowa, PhD(zool), 76. *Prof Exp:* Instr zool, Univ Iowa, 76-77; from asst prof to assoc prof biol sci, Purdue Univ, 77-85. *Concurrent Pos:* Prin investr, NSF grants, snail pop ecol, 79-82 & snail Community ecol, 85-88; field sta dir, Crooked Lake Biol Sta, 79-85; prin investr, Off Water Res & Technol grant, zooplankton ecol, 80-83; vis prof, Bodega Marine Lab, 85. *Mem:* Ecol Soc Am; Am Soc Naturalists; Brit Ecol Soc; Soc Study Evolution. *Res:* Population and community ecology of fresh water and marine gastropods; life history evolution; importance of competition; parasitism; predation in structuring snail assemblages. *Mailing Add:* Dept Zool & Physiol La State Univ Baton Rouge LA 70803-0001

BROWN, KENNETH STEPHEN, BIOSTATISTICS, MEDICAL STATISTICS. *Current Pos:* Lectr, Univ Waterloo, 73-74, from asst prof to assoc prof, 74-88, chair, 90-96, PROF STATIST, UNIV WATERLOO, 88- *Personal Data:* b Orillia, Ont, May 4, 49; m 71; c 2. *Educ:* Univ Waterloo, BMath, 71, PhD(statist), 74. *Concurrent Pos:* Consult, prog smoking & health, Non-Med Use Drugs Directorate, Health & Welfare Can, 74-76; mem working group health hazard appraisal, Non-Med Use Drugs Directorate & Health Prom & Prev Directorate, Health & Welfare Can, 75-78; mem, health care systs grant rev comt, Ont, 87-93; co-dir, Health Behav Res Group, Univ Waterloo; prin investr, Ontario Tabacco Res Unit, 93- & Sociobehav Cancer Res Network 95- *Mem:* Can Statist Soc; Biometrics Soc. *Res:* Mathematical models of disease processes; smoking and disease; biostatistics; smoking prevention. *Mailing Add:* Dept Statist MC 6132 Univ Waterloo Waterloo ON N2L 3G1 Can

BROWN, KENNETH STEPHEN, TERATOLOGY, HUMAN GENETICS. *Current Pos:* clin assoc, 61-63, investr, Human Genetics Br, 64-67, sect chief, Develop Genetics Sect, 67-74, INVESTR GENETICS, LAB DEVELOP BIOL & ANOMALIES, NIH, 75- *Personal Data:* b Chicago, Ill, Dec 15, 29; m 55; c 3. *Educ:* Univ Chicago, BA, 49, MD, 60. *Prof Exp:* Asst zool, Univ Chicago, 52-56; intern med, Blodgett Hosp, 60-61. *Concurrent Pos:* Instr, Found Advan Educ Sci, 66-81. *Mem:* Am Soc Human Genetics; AAAS; Teratology Soc; Soc Craniofacial Genetics (pres elect, 81); Sigma Xi. *Res:* Etiology and pathogenesis of birth defects; primary interest in craniofacial malformations, using mouse genetic defects and teratogenic agents as probes for study of genetic control of biochemical processes. *Mailing Add:* 11527 Deborah Dr Potomac MD 20854-3706

BROWN, KENNETH TAYLOR, physiology, for more information see previous edition

BROWN, KERMIT EARL, PETROLEUM ENGINEERING. *Current Pos:* RETIRED. *Personal Data:* b Haskell, Tex, Nov 2, 23; m 45; c 3. *Educ:* Tex A&M Univ, BS(mech eng) & BS(petrol eng), 48; Univ Tex, MS, 59, PhD, 62. *Prof Exp:* Petrol engr, Stanolind Oil & Gas Co, 48-51; gas lift engr, Garrett Oil Tools Inc, 51-55; from asst prof to assoc prof petrol eng, Univ Tex, Austin, 55-66, grad adv, 65-66; prof petrol eng & head dept, Univ Tulsa, 66-68, vpres res, 68-88, Halliburton prof petrol eng & chmn, Div Resources Eng, 76-88, Floyd M Stevenson prof, 81-88; consult, 88-89. *Concurrent Pos:* Consult, Otis Eng Corp, 58-; Convair award, 58-59. *Mem:* Nat Acad Sci; Am Soc Eng Educ; Soc Petrol Engrs. *Res:* Storing reactor fuel waste in salt domes; gas lift applied to oil; vertical two-phase fluid flow. *Mailing Add:* Int Training & Consult 5429 E 65th Pl Tulsa OK 74104

BROWN, KIMBERLY ELLEN, DRUG DELIVERY SYSTEMS. *Current Pos:* ASST PROF, BIOL RESOURCES ENG DEPT, UNIV MD, 95- *Personal Data:* b Washington, DC, Sept 26, 68. *Educ:* Howard Univ, BS, 90; Johns Hopkins Univ, PhD, 96. *Mem:* Am Chem Soc; AAAS. *Res:* Peptide/protein/gene delivery systems; microspheres and soluble complexes to delivery proteins and genes to mammalian cells. *Mailing Add:* Biol Resources Eng Dept Univ Md College Park MD 20742-5711. *Fax:* 301-314-9023; *E-Mail:* kb107@umail.umd.edu

BROWN, L(AURENCE) C(LAYDON), PHYSICAL METALLURGY. *Current Pos:* RETIRED. *Personal Data:* b Glasgow, Scotland, Mar 23, 37. *Educ:* Univ Strathclyde, BSc, 58; Glasgow Univ, PhD(physics), 61. *Prof Exp:* Fel metall, 61-63; from asst prof to prof metall, Univ BC, 63-92. *Mem:* Am Soc Metals. *Res:* Diffusion and phase transformations in binary and ternary metal systems. *Mailing Add:* 3948 W 24th Ave Vancouver BC V6S 1M2 Can

BROWN, L CARLTON, PHYSICS. *Current Pos:* asst, Ohio State Univ, 52-55, res assoc magnetic resonance, 55-57, from asst prof to prof physics, 57-84, CONSULT PHYSICS, OHIO STATE UNIV, 84- *Personal Data:* b Mineral Springs, Ark, Mar 26, 15; m 38, Hazel Weatherly; c Jo C. *Educ:* Henderson State Teachers Col, AB, 37; Fla State Univ, MA, 52; Ohio State Univ, PhD(physics), 55. *Prof Exp:* Instr math, Pulaski County Schs, Ark, 38-39; eng aide, Ark State Hwy Dept, 39-41 & US Army Corps Engrs, 41-43 & 46-47, US Army Air Force, 43-46; training officer, US Vet Admin, 47-48; asst engr, Ark State Hwy Dept, 48-51; asst physics, Fla State Univ, 51-52. *Concurrent Pos:* Co-supvr & chief investr, Ohio State Univ res grant, Off Naval Res & Air Force Off Sci Res, 55-84. *Mem:* Am Phys Soc; Am Asn Physics Teachers. *Res:* Nuclear magnetic resonance; electron paramagnetic resonance; x-ray and gamma ray scattering; electromagnetic theory; semiconductor physics. *Mailing Add:* Dept Physics Ohio State Univ 2170 Lane Rd Columbus OH 43220

BROWN, L JACKSON, DENTISTRY. *Current Pos:* SR DIR, HEALTH POLICY RESEARCHERS CTR, AM DENT ASN, 96- *Personal Data:* b Carrolton, Mo, June 25, 41. *Educ:* Univ Mo, Kansas City, ABA, 65, DDS, 69; Columbia Univ, PhD(social med sci), 84. *Prof Exp:* Staff, Conserv Human Res Proj, Columbia Univ, 74-75; asst prof, Sch Dent, Univ Ky, 75-76; chief,

Systs Div Sect, Div Dent, Bureau Health Prof, 77-80, dep chief, Modeling & Res Br, 81-84; eval officer, Nat Inst Dent Res, NIH, 84-86, chief, Anal Studies Br, 86-91, doctor, Div Epidemiol & Oral Dis Prev, 91-96. *Mem:* Am Dent Asn; Int Asn Dent Res; Am Asn Dent Res; Am Pub Health Asn; fel Am Col Dent; Am Asn Dent Sch; Fedn Dent Int; Asn Behav Sci & Health Servs Res. *Mailing Add:* Am Dent Asn 211 E Chicago Ave Chicago IL 60611-2678. *Fax:* 312-440-2915; *E-Mail:* brown@ada.com

BROWN, LARRY PATRICK, petroleum engineering, for more information see previous edition

BROWN, LAUREN EVANS, EVOLUTION, HERPETOLOGY. *Current Pos:* from asst prof to assoc prof, 67-77, PROF VERT ZOOL, ILL STATE UNIV, 77- *Personal Data:* b Waukesha, Wis, Sept 4, 39; m 68, Jill R Hollingshead; c Lara N, Kara A & Evan S. *Educ:* Carroll Col, Wis, BS, 61; Southern Ill Univ, Carbondale, MS, 63; Univ Tex, Austin, PhD(zool), 67. *Concurrent Pos:* Managing ed, Herpetologica, 79-81; consult endangered species; mem, Houston Toad Recovery Team, US Fish & Wildlife Serv. *Mem:* Herpetologists' League; Am Soc Ichthyologists & Herpetologists; Soc Study Amphibians & Reptiles; Int Soc Study & Conserv Amphibians. *Res:* Evolution; ecology; behavior; amphibian speciation; bioacoustics; herpetology; extinction; ecology of flood plains and sand prairies; zoogeography; natural hybridization and reproductive isolation; systematics. *Mailing Add:* Dept Biol Sci Ill State Univ Campus Box 4120 Normal IL 61790-4120

BROWN, LAURIE LIZBETH, GEOPHYSICS, PALEOMAGNETISM. *Current Pos:* From asst prof to assoc prof, 74-88, PROF GEOL, UNIV MASS, 88- *Personal Data:* b Nyack, NY, July 26, 46; m, Christopher Condit; c Ian & Cailey. *Educ:* Middlebury Col, AB, 68; Univ Wyo, MS, 72; Ore State Univ, PhD(geophys), 74. *Mem:* Am Geophys Union; Geol Soc Am; Soc Explor Geophysicists; Asn Women Geoscientists; Environ Eng Geophys Soc. *Res:* Magnetic stratigraphy; secular variation; plate tectonic reconstructions; magnetic susceptibility anisotropy. *Mailing Add:* Dept Geol & Geog Univ Mass Amherst MA 01003-0002. *Fax:* 413-545-1200; *E-Mail:* lbrown@eclogite.geo.umass.edu

BROWN, LAURIE MARK, HISTORY OF PHYSICS, THEORETICAL PHYSICS. *Current Pos:* from instr to prof, 50-93, EMER PROF PHYSICS, NORTHWESTERN UNIV, EVANSTON, 93- *Personal Data:* b Brooklyn, NY, Apr 10, 23; m 69, Brigitte Dziumbla; c Joanna, Julie, Jean & Katja. *Educ:* Cornell Univ, AB, 43, PhD(theoret physics), 51. *Prof Exp:* Res assoc, SAM labs, Columbia Univ, 43-44; asst physics, Cornell Univ, 46-48, asst, Nuclear Studies Lab, 48-50. *Concurrent Pos:* NSF fel, Inst Advan Study, 52-53; Fulbright res scholar, Italy, 58-60; consult, Argonne Nat Lab, 60-70; Int Atomic Energy Agency prof, Univ Vienna, 66; vis prof, Univ Rome, 67, Univ Sao Paulo, 72-73, Univ Wash, 78, Keio Univ, 84; mem, NSF Panel Advan Sci Sem, 68, 69; chair, Div Hist Physics, Am Phys Soc, 83. *Mem:* Fel Am Phys Soc; Hist Sci Soc. *Res:* Theoretical high energy physics; quantum electrodynamics; history of physics of 20th century. *Mailing Add:* Dept Physics & Astron Northwestern Univ Evanston IL 60208. *Fax:* 847-491-9982; *E-Mail:* brown@nuhep.phys.nwu.edu

BROWN, LAWRENCE D, MATHEMATICAL STATISTICS. *Current Pos:* MIERS BUSCH PROF STATIST, WHARTON SCH, UNIV PA, 94- *Personal Data:* b Dec 16, 40. *Educ:* Calif Inst Technol, BS, 61; Cornell Univ, PhD, 64. *Hon Degrees:* DSc, Purdue Univ, 93. *Honors & Awards:* Wald lectr, Inst Math Statist, 85. *Prof Exp:* Asst prof, Dept Statist, Univ Calif, Berkeley, 65-66; from asst prof to assoc prof, Dept Math, Cornell Univ, 66-73; prof, Dept Math, Rutgers Univ, 73-78; prof, Dept Math, Cornell Univ, 78-94. *Concurrent Pos:* Fel, Nat Acad Sci-Nat Res Coun, 64-65, Sloan Found, 69-71; assoc ed, Ann Statist, 70-80 & 83-, Ann Probability, 85-88; dir, Cornell Statist Ctr, 82-83, 86-88 & 89-93, mem, Bd Math Sci, Nat Res Coun, 89-94; Lady Davis prof, Hebrew Univ, Jerusalem; vis prof, Univ Calif, Los Angeles, 93-94; mem. Comt Appl & Theoret Statist, Nat Res Coun, 94; mem, Comt Phys Sci Math & Astron, Mat Res Coun, 96. *Mem:* Nat Acad Sci; fel Inst Math Statist; Am Statist Asn; Int Statist Inst. *Res:* Mathematics and statistics. *Mailing Add:* Statist Dept Univ Pa Philadelphia PA 19104-6302. *Fax:* 215-898-1280; *E-Mail:* lbrown@wharton.upenn.edu

BROWN, LAWRENCE E(LDON), MICROCHEMISTRY. *Current Pos:* RETIRED. *Personal Data:* b Republic Co, Kans, June 19, 14; m 39, 56, Noralie Findorff; c 1. *Educ:* SW Tex State Col, AB, 36; Univ Tex, 41; Tulane Univ, 48. *Prof Exp:* Asst chemist in charge microanal lab, US Dept Agr, 42-50, chemist, South Mkt & Nutrit Res Div, 50-73. *Mem:* Am Chem Soc; Am Oil Chem Soc; fel Am Inst Chem. *Res:* Microchemical analysis; utilization research on oilseeds, meals and oils. *Mailing Add:* 805 Andrews Ave Metairie LA 70005-2311

BROWN, LAWRENCE G, MATHEMATICS. *Current Pos:* PROF MATH, PURDUE UNIV, 74- *Personal Data:* b St Louis, Mo, Feb 6, 43. *Educ:* Harvard Univ, BA, 65, PhD(math), 68. *Mem:* Am Math Soc; Am Asn Univ Prof. *Mailing Add:* 1395 Math Sci Bldg Purdue Univ West Lafayette IN 47907-1395

BROWN, LAWRENCE S, JR, INTERNAL MEDICINE, DRUG ADDICTION. *Current Pos:* SR VPRES RES, ADDICTION RES & TREAT CORP, 86-; ASST CLIN PROF MED, HARLEM HOSP/COL PHYSICIANS & SURGEONS, COLUMBIA UNIV. *Personal Data:* b Brooklyn, NY, Dec 4, 49; m 78; c 1. *Educ:* Brooklyn Col, BA, 76; Columbia Univ, MPH, 79; NY Univ, MD, 79. *Prof Exp:* Intern med, Harlem Hosp Ctr, 79-80, resident, 80-82, chief resident, 82-83; Fel med & endocrinol, dept med, Columbia Univ, 83-86. *Concurrent Pos:* Adj prof health admin, Columbia Univ, Sch Pub Health, 88-, instr med, dept med, 86-, vis clin fel, 79-82, clin fel, 82-83; asst attend physician med & endocrinol, Harlem Hosp, 86-; mem, Panel IV Drug Use & AIDS, Nat Acad Sci, 88- *Mem:* Am Pub Health Asn; Am Soc Internal Med; Am Col Physicians; NY Acad Sci; AAAS; Nat Med Asn. *Res:* Clinical investigations of the pathogenesis of diabetes and steroid metabolism; clinical investigations of the endocrinologic and immunological associations with patterns of drug abuse and addiction. *Mailing Add:* Addiction Res & Treat Corp 22 Chapel St Brooklyn NY 11201

BROWN, LEE F(RANCIS), PHYSICAL CHEMISTRY, RISK ANALYSIS. *Current Pos:* STAFF MEM, LOS ALAMOS NAT LAB, UNIV CALIF, 81- *Personal Data:* b Elmhurst, Ill, Feb 23, 29; m 67, Monica Walsh; c Eric, Cecilia & Timothy. *Educ:* Univ Notre Dame, BS, 51; Univ Del, MChE, 55, PhD(chem eng), 63. *Prof Exp:* Chem engr, Houdry Process Corp, Pa, 51-54; res assoc, Univ Colo, 63-64, actg asst prof, 64, from asst prof to prof chem eng, 64-81, chmn dept, 80-81. *Concurrent Pos:* Univ Colo fac fel, Tech Univ Delft, Neth, 67-68; vis prof, Yale Univ, 77-78; adj prof, Univ NMex, 92- *Mem:* Am Chem Soc; Am Inst Chem Engrs; Soc Risk Analysis; Am Soc Eng Educ. *Res:* Transport in and structure of porous materials; heterogeneous kinetics and catalysis; adsorption; risk analysis. *Mailing Add:* 58 Valle Vista Los Alamos NM 87544. *Fax:* 505-665-3911; *E-Mail:* malbrown@roadrunner.com

BROWN, LELAND RALPH, ENTOMOLOGY, ECONOMICS ENTOMOLOGY. *Current Pos:* prof, 69-85, EMER PROF ENTOM, UNIV CALIF, RIVERSIDE, 85- *Personal Data:* b Springdale, Ark, Mar 7, 22; m 49, Barbara Hart; c Steven, Sally & Susan. *Educ:* Univ Calif, BS, 46; Cornell Univ, PhD(econ entom), 49. *Mem:* AAAS; Entom Soc Am. *Res:* Insecticide applicators; insects affecting ornamental shrubs, shade trees and forests; insect photography; general entomology. *Mailing Add:* 362 NE 14th Ave Canby OR 97013-2964

BROWN, LEO DALE, X-RAY CRYSTALLOGRAPHY, OPTICAL MICROSCOPY. *Current Pos:* RES ASSOC, EXXON RES & ENG CO, 77- *Personal Data:* b Waco, Tex, Apr 11, 48; m 72, Paulette Cullen; c Kenneth W, Richard L & Lisa V. *Educ:* Baylor Univ, BS, 70; Univ Calif, Berkeley, PhD(chem), 74. *Prof Exp:* Fel inorg chem, Northwestern Univ, 75-77. *Mem:* Am Chem Soc; Am Crystallog Asn; Sigma Xi. *Res:* Synthetic fuels from coal and oil shale; effects of inorganic constituents on fuel processing; x-ray structural analysis of inorganic materials; optical microscopy of oil shale, coal, coke and related materials. *Mailing Add:* Exxon Res & Develop Labs PO Box 2226 Baton Rouge LA 70821-2226

BROWN, LEONARD FRANKLIN, JR, BASIN ANALYSIS, SEISMIC-SEQUENCE STRATIGRAPHY. *Current Pos:* res scientist, Bur Econ Geol, Univ Tex, 57-60, res scientist & lectr geol, 66-71, assoc dir res, 71-84, sr res scientist, 84-89, prof geol, 71-89, EMER PROF GEOL, UNIV TEX, 90- *Personal Data:* b Seminole, Okla, June 1, 28; m 56, 82, Belle K Corn; c Ann L. *Educ:* Baylor Univ, BS, 51; Univ Wis, MS, 53, PhD(geol), 55. *Honors & Awards:* Distinguished Lectr, Am Asn Petrol Geologists, 72-73, Cheney Award, 90; Dean A McGee Int Distinguished Lectr, 94, Petrol Explor Soc, Australia, 85. *Prof Exp:* Explor geologist, Stand Oil Co Tex, 55-57; from asst prof to assoc prof geol, Baylor Univ, 60-66; dir, Tex Mining & Minerals Resources Res Inst, 81-84. *Concurrent Pos:* Ed, Baylor Geol Studies Bull, 61-66; consult, Int Petrol, 73-; continuing educ lectr, 73- *Mem:* Am Asn Petrol Geol; sr fel Geol Soc Am. *Res:* Stratigraphic studies of the Pennsylvanian system; terrigenous depositional systems; environmental geology in Texas; seismic-stratigraphy; basin analysis; sequence stratigraphy; petroleum geology; mesozoic/cenozoic stratigraphy of South Atlantic Continental Margins. *Mailing Add:* Rte 5 Box 301 Georgetown TX 78626-9805. *E-Mail:* 102564.1165@compuserve.com

BROWN, LESTER R, AGRICULTURAL SCIENCE, ECONOMICS. *Current Pos:* PRES, WORLDWATCH INST, 74- *Personal Data:* b Bridgeton, NJ, Mar 28, 34; div; c Brian & Brenda. *Educ:* Rutgers Univ, BS, 55; Univ Md, MS, 59; Harvard Univ, MA, 62. *Hon Degrees:* LHD, Dickinson Col, 75, Franklin Col, 77; LLD, Univ Md, 76, Williams Col, 77, Rutgers Univ, 78, Glassboro State Col, 79, Tufts Univ, 85, Clark Univ, 88, Col Wooster, 89, Rippon Col, 90, Otterbein Col, 90, Univ Piza, Italy, 91, McGill Univ, 91, Notre Dame, 91, Northland Col, 93, St Lawrence Univ, 94, Claremont Grad Sch, 96, Villanova Univ, 96. *Honors & Awards:* Arthur S Fleming Award, US Jaycees, 65; A H Boerma Award, UN Food & Agr Orgn, 81; Lorax Award, 85; Spec Conserv Award, Nat Wildlife Fedn, 82; UN Environ Prize, 87; Gold Medal, Worldwide Fund for Nature, 89; A Bizzozero Award, Univ Parma, 91; Windstar Found Award, 91; Pro Mundo Habitabili Award, Swed Acad Sci, 91; Delphi Int Coop Award, 91; Cert Spec Recognition, Asn Am Geographers, 93; Blue Planet Prize, 94; J Sterling Morton Arbor Day, 95; Pub Serv Award, Fed Am Scientist, 95. *Prof Exp:* Int agr economist, Econ Res Serv, USDA, 59-64, policy adv secy of agr, 64-66; adminr, Int Agr Develop Serv, 66-69, sr fel, Overseas Develop Coun, 69-74. *Concurrent Pos:* Mem, Overseas Develop Coun, Global Studies Ctr & Global Tomorrow Coalition; MacArthur Found fel, 86; bd mem, NW Environ Watch. *Mem:* Coun Foreign Rels; World Future Soc; Overseas Develop Coun; Renew Am; Global Tomorrow Coalition. *Res:* Food; population; environment; resources. *Mailing Add:* Worldwatch Inst 1776 Massachusetts Ave NW Washington DC 20036-1904. *Fax:* 202-296-7365; *E-Mail:* worldwatch@worldwatch.org

BROWN, LEWIS M, MICROPALEONTOLOGY, EARTH SCIENCE EDUCATION. *Current Pos:* PROF GEOL, LAKE SUPERIOR STATE UNIV, 79-, DEPT CHAIR GEOL, 82- *Personal Data:* b Chicago, Ill, Sept 2, 43. *Educ:* Cornell Col, BA, 65; Univ Iowa, MS, 67; Univ NMex, PhD(curric & instr), 73. *Prof Exp:* Geologist, Kerr-McGee Corp, 67-71; teacher natural sci, Albuquerque Pub Schs, 71-73; assoc prof educ, NMex State Univ, 73-79. *Concurrent Pos:* Prin investr, Mich Res Excellence Fund, 88-89, Chippewa Co, Mich Environ Health, 92-93 & 93-94, Am Chem Soc, 93-95 & Nat Geog, 96-; adj prof educ, Mich State Univ, 89-90 & 96-; res assoc, Ind Geol Surv, 95- *Mem:* Pander Soc; Am Asn Petrol Geologists; Geol Soc Am; Am Inst Prof Geologists. *Res:* Conodont (Pennsylvanian) biostratigraphic studies that emphasize biozonation and correlation, evolutionary trends, and reconstruction of depositional environments; subsurface mapping in Northern Michigan. *Mailing Add:* PO Box 2122 Sault Ste Marie MI 49783. *Fax:* 906-635-2111; *E-Mail:* lbrown@lakers.lssu.edu

BROWN, LEWIS MARVIN, PHYCOLOGY, PHYSIOLOGICAL ECOLOGY. *Current Pos:* DIR RES, CLF TECHNOL INC, 95- *Personal Data:* b Brooklyn, NY, June 9, 50; m 72; c 2. *Educ:* State Univ NY, Stony Brook, BS, 72; Univ SFla, MA, 74; Univ Toronto, PhD(bot), 78. *Prof Exp:* Vis fel marine bot, Atlantic Res Lab, Nat Res Coun Can, 78-80; asst prof, Univ Western Ont, 80-87, res assoc, Cancer Res Lab, 87-88; mgr, Algal Technol Nat Renewable Energy Lab, 89-91, proj mgr, 91-95. *Concurrent Pos:* Mem bd dirs, Can Bot Asn, 87-88; adj assoc prof environ sci, Univ Colo, 96. *Mem:* Phycol Soc Am; Int Phycol Soc; Am Soc Plant Physiologists; AAAS; Soc Indust Microbiol. *Res:* Plant molecular biology; physiological ecology of algae; biotechnological applications of microalgae; global change and carbon dioxide remediation, biomass energy, bioremediation. *Mailing Add:* CLF Technologies Inc PO Box 24036 Denver CO 80224

BROWN, LEWIS RAYMOND, BACTERIOLOGY, MICROBIOLOGY. *Current Pos:* assoc dean res, Col Arts & Sci, 71-89, PROF MICROBIOL, MISS STATE UNIV, 61- *Personal Data:* b Houston, Tex, Aug 11, 30; wid; c Donna, David & Lewis Jr. *Educ:* La State Univ, BS, 51, MS, 53, PhD(bact), 58. *Honors & Awards:* Charles Porter Award, Soc Indust Microbiol, 90, Waksman Outstanding Teaching Award, 93. *Prof Exp:* Asst br chief, US Civil Serv, Pine Bluff Arsenal, 53-55; instr bact, La State Univ, 55-58; operator, pvt consult & testing lab, 58-61. *Mem:* AAAS; Am Soc Microbiol; Am Acad Microbiologists; Int Water Resources Asn; Sigma Xi; NY Acad Sci; Soc Indust Microbiol; Water Pollution Control Fedn; Am Water Resources Asn. *Res:* Biodeterioration of metals; microbial ecology; geomicrobiological prospecting; sewage and industrial waste disposal; petroleum degradation and water pollution control; isolation, characterization and metabolism of hydrocarbon oxidizing bacteria and other recalcitrant molecules; microbial enhanced oil recovery; author of 100 publications in microbiology and granted 6 patents. *Mailing Add:* Miss State Univ PO Drawer GY Mississippi State MS 39762

BROWN, LINDA ROSE, MOLECULAR SPECTROSCOPY. *Current Pos:* SR SCIENTIST PHYSICS, JET PROPULSION LAB, 78- *Personal Data:* b Muncie, Ind, Mar 7, 45. *Educ:* Ohio State Univ, BA, 68; Fla State Univ, PhD(physics), 76. *Prof Exp:* Res assoc physics, Nat Res Coun, 76-78. *Mem:* Soc Appl Spectros; Optical Soc Am; Sigma Xi. *Res:* High resolution infrared spectroscopy of light molecules of atmospheric interest. *Mailing Add:* Jet Propulsion Lab 183-301 4800 Oak Grove Dr Pasadena CA 91109

BROWN, LINDSAY DIETRICH, AGRONOMY, PLANT PHYSIOLOGY. *Current Pos:* dir, Spec Prod Mktg, 72-81, DIR N AM MKT, INT MINERAL & CHEM CO, 81- *Personal Data:* b Lynchburg, Va, Jan 14, 29; m 52; c 2. *Educ:* Lynchburg Col, BA, 51; Va Polytech Inst, MS, 58; Mich State Univ, PhD(hort), 62. *Prof Exp:* Jr instr biol, Johns Hopkins Univ, 55-56; instr hort, Va Polytech Inst, 57-58; instr, Mich State Univ, 61-63; asst prof, Univ Ky, 63-67; supvr, Agron Serv, Southwest Potash Corp, 67-69; assoc prof hort, Va Polytech Inst & State Univ, 69-70; dir, Mkt Serv, Amax Chem Corp, 70-72. *Concurrent Pos:* Consult, USAID, SE Asia, 66. *Mem:* Am Soc Hort Sci; Am Soc Agron. *Res:* Plant breeding; mineral nutrition of higher plants; physiology of greenhouse-grown plants. *Mailing Add:* 343 Green Leaf Ave Wilmette IL 60091

BROWN, LINFIELD CUTTER, SANITARY ENGINEERING. *Current Pos:* Asst prof, 70-76, assoc prof civil eng, 76-81, PROF CIVIL ENG, TUFTS UNIV, 81- *Personal Data:* b Peterborough, NH, Sept 24, 42; m 64; c 1. *Educ:* Tufts Univ, BCE, 64, MS, 66; Univ Wis-Madison, PhD(sanit eng), 70. *Mem:* Am Water Works Asn; Water Pollution Control Fedn; Sigma Xi. *Res:* Mass transfer of oxygen into streams; statistical design of experiments; statistical modelling of systems in water pollution control. *Mailing Add:* 106 Damon Rd Medford MA 02155-2445

BROWN, LLOYD LEONARD, PHYSICAL CHEMISTRY. *Current Pos:* RETIRED. *Personal Data:* b Topeka, Kans, Jan 20, 27; m 54; c 2. *Educ:* Wichita State Univ, BS, 50, MS, 52. *Prof Exp:* Chemist, Wichita Found Indust Res, 52; chemist, Oak Ridge Sch Reactor Technol, 52-53 & Oak Ridge Nat Lab, 53-91. *Mem:* Am Chem Soc. *Res:* Chemistry of stable isotopes; chemical methods for enrichment of rare isotopes; kinetic effects; nuclear magnetic resonance spectroscopy; electron spin resonance spectroscopy. *Mailing Add:* 153 N Seneca Rd Oak Ridge TN 37830-8409

BROWN, LLOYD ROBERT, ELECTRICAL ENGINEERING, FORENSIC ENGINEERING. *Current Pos:* from assoc prof to prof, 61-87, EMER PROF ELEC ENG, WASHINGTON UNIV, 87- *Personal Data:* b Fayette, Mo, Dec 10, 24; m 49, Iris Vail; c 4. *Educ:* Mo Valley Col, AB, 47; Univ Mo-Columbia, BSEE, 49; Washington Univ, MSEE, 51, DSc(elec eng), 60. *Prof Exp:* Asst elec eng, Washington Univ, 49-51, instr elec eng, 56-58; design engr, Missile Div, McDonnell Aircraft Corp, Mo, 52-54; res engr, White-Rodgers Elec Co, 54-56; engr, Electro-Mech Res, Inc, Fla, 58-61. *Concurrent Pos:* Consult, White-Rodgers Elec Co, Mo, 56-58, Universal Match Corp, 62-66, McConnell Aircraft Corp, 64-68 & US Naval Ord Sta, Ill, 66-69; pvt fire investr, expert witness & electrical specialist, 74-; bd trustees, Mo Valley Co, 95- *Mem:* Sr mem Inst Elec & Electronics Engrs; Nat Fire Protection; Int Asn Arson Investrs; Sigma Xi. *Res:* Automatic control and electronic instrumentation; fire and accident investigation. *Mailing Add:* 4010 Stag Ct Florissant MO 63033

BROWN, LORETTA ANN PORT, INTERNAL MEDICINE, BIOCHEMICAL GENETICS. *Current Pos:* chief admitting & screening, 88-92, STAFF PHYSICIAN, VET ADMIN HOSP, HAMPTON, VA, 88-; ASST PROF MED, EASTERN VA MED SCH, 84- *Personal Data:* b Kingston, NY, July 30, 45; m 70, Robert; c Adrian. *Educ:* State Univ NY, Col New Paltz, BS, 67; Univ Mich, MS, 68; Eastern Va Med Sch, MD, 81. *Honors & Awards:* Achievement Award, Am Chem Soc; Achievement Award, Am Med Women's Asn. *Prof Exp:* NSF res partic, Albion Col, 66; USPHS trainee, Univ Mich, 67-69, lab technologist, 69-70; res instr biol-med genetics, M D Anderson Hosp & Tumor Inst, 70; res instr obstet & gynec, Baylor Col Med, 71-76; adj prof biol, Christopher Newport Col, 77-78; resident, Internal Med, Eastern Va Grad Sch Med, 81-84; staff physician, Health Am, Hampton, Va, 84-87. *Concurrent Pos:* Tidewater Pulmonary Assoc, Newport News, VA, 87-88. *Res:* Suppressor mutations of the methionine-1 locus in Neurospora crassa; arginine and polyamine metabolism and control in Neurospora crassa; protein hormones in human reproductive endocrinology; equine color genetics. *Mailing Add:* Hampton Vet Med Ctr Primary Care Clin Hampton VA 23667

BROWN, LOUIS, NUCLEAR PHYSICS. *Current Pos:* Carnegie fel, Carnegie Inst Washington, 61-64, mem physics staff, 64-94, actg dir, 91-92, EMER, DEPT TERRESTRIAL MAGNETISM, CARNEGIE INST WASHINGTON, 94- *Personal Data:* b San Angelo, Tex, Jan 7, 29; m 52, Lore Frick. *Educ:* St Mary's Univ, Tex, BS, 50; Univ Tex, PhD(physics), 58. *Honors & Awards:* Amerbach Prize, Univ Basel, 64. *Prof Exp:* Res asst physics, Inst Physics, Univ Basel, 58-61. *Mem:* Fel Am Phys Soc; Am Geophys Union; AAAS. *Res:* Experimental study of the beryllium-10 content of soils, sediments and rocks; experimental study of the isotopic composition of elements in rocks and meteorites; application of resonance ionization mass spectrometry to geochronology. *Mailing Add:* Dept Terrestrial Magnetism Carnegie Inst 5241 Broad Br Rd NW Washington DC 20015

BROWN, LOWELL SEVERT, PHYSICS. *Current Pos:* assoc prof, 68-71, PROF PHYSICS, UNIV WASH, 71- *Personal Data:* b Visalia, Calif, Feb 15, 34; m 56, Shirley I Mitchell; c Stephen C. *Educ:* Univ Calif, Berkeley, AB, 56; Harvard Univ, PhD(physics), 61. *Prof Exp:* NSF fel physics, Univ Rome, 61-62 & Imp Col, Univ London, 62-63; res assoc, Yale Univ, 63-64, from asst prof to assoc prof, 64-68. *Concurrent Pos:* NSF sr fel, Imp Col, Univ London, 71-72; John Simon Guggenheim Found fel, 79-80; mem, Inst Advan Study, Princeton, NJ, 79-80; consult, Los Alamos Sci Lab; mem, Panel Pub Affairs, Am Phys Soc, 79, exec comt, Div Particles & Fields, 82-83 & 88-91, publ comt, 83-86; chmn, Theoret Physics Panel, US Dept Energy Tech Assessment Comt Univ Progs, 82-83; mem bd trustees, Aspen Ctr Physics, 82-88 & 90-; vis prof, Columbia Univ, 90; vis scientist, Los Alamos Nat Lab, 91. *Mem:* Fel Am Phys Soc; fel AAAS. *Res:* Theoretical physics; quantum field theory; elementary particle physics. *Mailing Add:* Dept Physics Univ Wash Box 351560 Seattle WA 98195. *Fax:* 206-685-0635; *E-Mail:* brown@phys.washington.edu

BROWN, LUCY LESEUR, FUNCTIONAL NEUROANATOMY, BASAL GANGLIA. *Current Pos:* Fel, 73-76, from asst prof to assoc prof neurol, 78-95, PROF NEUROL & NEUROSCI, ALBERT EINSTEIN COL MED, 95- *Personal Data:* b Brookline, Mass, May 14, 45. *Educ:* NY Univ, BA, 68, PhD(physiol psychol), 73. *Concurrent Pos:* Prin investr, Albert Einstein Col Med, 85-; mem, Peer Rev Comt, Neurol, NIH, 94-98; mem extended fac, Gen Internal Med Women's Health Track. *Mem:* Int Basal Ganglia Soc; Soc Neurosci; Asn Res in Nerv & Ment Dis; Movement Dis Soc. *Res:* Neuroanatomy and physiology of brain regions that control movement and of brain regions whose activity can modify seizures. *Mailing Add:* 33 G Tier St City Island NY 10464. *E-Mail:* brown@aecom.yu.edu

BROWN, LUTHER PARK, MATE CHOICE, EVOLUTION. *Current Pos:* Asst prof, 78-83, ASSOC PROF BIOL, GEORGE MASON UNIV, 83- *Personal Data:* b Bloomington, Ill, Feb 18, 51; div. *Educ:* Elmhurst Col, BA, 73; Ohio State Univ, MS, 76, PhD(zool), 78. *Concurrent Pos:* Asst prof, Mountain Lake Biol Sta, Univ Va, 79. *Mem:* Animal Behav Soc; Ecol Soc Am. *Res:* Behavioral ecology, specifically in the evolution of animal social and mating systems through both natural and sexual selection. *Mailing Add:* Dept Biol George Mason Univ 4400 University Dr Fairfax VA 22030-4443

BROWN, LYNN RANNEY, ANIMAL NUTRITION. *Current Pos:* from asst prof to prof, 60-94, interim head, Dept Animal Sci, 92-94, EMER PROF DAIRY EXTEN, UNIV CONN, 94- *Personal Data:* b Waterloo, Iowa, Sept 26, 28; m 53, Marjorie Sickles; c David, Barbara, Lynda & Anne. *Educ:* Iowa State Univ, BS, 50, PhD(dairy nutrit), 59. *Prof Exp:* Teacher, Pub Schs, Iowa, 50-51 & 53-55; asst dairy nutrit, Iowa State Univ, 56-58, assoc, 58-59. *Mem:* Am Dairy Sci Asn; Am Soc Animal Sci; Sigma Xi. *Res:* Physiological factors associated with bloat; nutrition of dairy calves and cows. *Mailing Add:* Dept Animal Sci Univ Conn U-40 3636 Horsebarn Rd Ext Storrs CT 06268

BROWN, MARIE JENKINS, invertebrate zoology; deceased, see previous edition for last biography

BROWN, MARK WENDELL, FRUIT ENTOMOLOGY, BIOLOGICAL CONTROL. *Current Pos:* MEM STAFF, APPALACHIAN FRUIT RES STA, AGR RES SERV, USDA, 88- *Personal Data:* b Riverside, NJ, July 11, 53. *Educ:* Univ Maine, BSF, 75; Univ Idaho, MS, 77; Pa State Univ, MS & PhD(entom), 81. *Prof Exp:* Res asst, Univ Idaho, 75-77; teaching asst entom, Pa State Univ, 77-81; res assoc, Miss State Univ, 81-88. *Concurrent Pos:* Temp instr entom, Univ Maine, 80. *Mem:* Entom Soc Am (treas); Entom Soc Can; Int Orgn Biol Control; Sigma Xi. *Res:* Analyzing community ecology of insects in deciduous fruit orchards to develop new pest management practices; study biological control of insects in deciduous fruit orchards to use for insect control. *Mailing Add:* Appalachian Fruit Res Sta 45 Wiltshire Rd Kearneysville WV 25430

BROWN, MARK WILLIAM, CHEMISTRY. *Current Pos:* develop chemist, 85-91, TECH DIR, IPS CORP, 91- *Personal Data:* b Long Beach, Calif, Sept 20, 61; m 84, Susan Cervantes; c Mark II, Samuel, Daniel & Amanda. *Educ:* Univ Southern Calif, BS, 83. *Prof Exp:* Develop chemist, Goray Mfg, 83-85. *Mem:* Am Soc Testing & Mat. *Res:* Retardation of the yellowing of catalyst systems used for acrylic adhesives; volatile organic compounds solvent cements used for the bonding of plastic piping systems; granted 2 patents. *Mailing Add:* IPS Corp 17109 S Main St Gardena CA 90248

BROWN, MARVIN ROSS, MEDICAL PHYSIOLOGY, INTERNAL MEDICINE. *Current Pos:* PRES, ALANEX, SAN DIEGO, CALIF, 95- *Personal Data:* b Douglas, Ariz, July 25, 47; m 63; c 1. *Educ:* Univ Ariz, BS, 69, MD, 73. *Prof Exp:* Fel, Salk Inst Biol Studies, 74-75, res assoc endocrinol, 75-76, ASST RES PROF, PEPTIDE BIOL LAB, SALK INST BIOL STUDIES, 76-77; asst adj prof med, Sch Med, Univ Calif, San Diego, 77-95. *Mem:* Soc Neurosci; Am Physiol Soc; Endocrine Soc; AAAS; Am Diabetes Asn. *Res:* Study of the physiology and pharmacology of brain hormones. *Mailing Add:* Alanex 3550 Gen Atomics San Diego CA 92121. *Fax:* 619-543-5679

BROWN, MAURICE VERTNER, acoustics, geophysics, for more information see previous edition

BROWN, MAX LOUIS, MECHANICAL DESIGN & SAFETY ENGINEERING. *Current Pos:* instr math, Univ Cincinnati, 60-61, from asst prof to assoc prof, 61-75, dir grad studies & asst head, Mech & Indust Eng Dept, 80-87, actg head, 81-88, PROF MECH ENG, UNIV CINCINNATI, 75-, DIR DESIGN CLIN, 89- *Personal Data:* b Elgin, Ill, Apr 12, 36; m 63, Edna Benjamin; c Clark, Cheryl (Dunco), Debora & Dena. *Educ:* Univ Cincinnati, ME, 59; Ohio State Univ, MSc, 60, PhD(mech eng), 68. *Honors & Awards:* Ralph R Teetor Award, Soc Auto Engrs, 75; Curriculum Innovation Award, Am Soc Mech Engrs, 90. *Prof Exp:* Engr, Magna Am Corp, 53-60. *Concurrent Pos:* Dir, Mach Tool & Mfg Tech Info Ctr, 68-70 & State Tech Serv Prog Referral Network Off, Cincinnati, 68-69; design, mfg & safety consult, Cincinnati Inc, Lunkenheimer Co, Honeywell Controls Div, Jacobson Co, Aetna Casualty & Surety Co, Liberty Mutual Inc Co, Aluminum Co Am, Ford Motor Co, Mobil Oil Co, Ryder Truck Rental, Johnson & Johnson, Procter & Gamble, Brit Petrol & numerous others. *Mem:* Am Soc Mech Engrs; Am Soc Eng Educ; Soc Mfg Engrs; Soc Auto Engrs. *Res:* Optimum design of mechanical parts; strength of materials; teaching; safety, engineering economics; machine design; dynamics of machines. *Mailing Add:* Dept Mech Indust & Nuclear Eng Univ Cincinnati Cincinnati OH 45221-0072. *Fax:* 513-556-3390

BROWN, MELVIN HENRY, CHEMICAL ENGINEERING. *Current Pos:* RETIRED. *Personal Data:* b Victor, Iowa, Dec 6, 19; m 47; c 4. *Educ:* Iowa State Univ, BS, 42, MS, 44, PhD(chem eng), 49. *Prof Exp:* Engr, Alcoa Labs, Aluminum Co Am, 49-60, sci assoc, 60-72, sr sci assoc chem eng, 72-80, tech consult, 81-86. *Mem:* Am Inst Chem Engrs; Am Chem Soc; Res Soc Am; NY Acad Sci. *Res:* Corrosion; desalination; waste treatment; inhibitors; heat treatment of aluminum alloys; alloy development; applications of aluminum alloys in the chemical industry; energy systems; aluminum smelting. *Mailing Add:* 1837 Shadywide Lakewood NY 14750-9646

BROWN, MERTON F, MYCOLOGY, FOREST PATHOLOGY. *Current Pos:* asst prof, 68-72, assoc prof, 72-80, PROF FORESTRY & PLANT PATH, UNIV MO-COLUMBIA, 80- *Personal Data:* b Burlington, Vt, Sept 22, 35; m 57; c 3. *Educ:* Univ Maine, BS, 61, MS, 63; Univ Iowa, PhD(bot), 66. *Prof Exp:* Asst prof biol, Wis State Univ, Superior, 66-68. *Mem:* Mycol Soc Am; Am Phytopath Soc. *Res:* Ultrastructure and composition of fungal cell walls, plant pathogenic fungi and mycorrihizae. *Mailing Add:* Plant Path Univ Mo 108 Waters Hall Columbia MO 65211-0001

BROWN, MICHAEL, INDUSTRIAL PHARMACY, REGULATORY AFFAIRS. *Current Pos:* PRES, BROWN ASSOCS, 86- *Personal Data:* b Philadelphia, Pa, Jan 8, 39; m 63, Beryl Bogin; c David & Deborah. *Educ:* Temple Univ, BS, 60; Purdue Univ, MS, 62, PhD(phys pharm), 64. *Prof Exp:* Develop chemist pharm, Lederle Lab, Div Am Cyanamid, 64-67; group leader, Carter Prod, Div Carter-Wallace, Inc, 67-74; mgr proprietaries & toiletries res & develop, Div Schering-Plough, Plough Inc, 74-76; dir prod develop & qual assurance, Consumer Prod Div, Becton Dickinson, 76-78; vpres tech affairs, L Perrigo Co, 78-86. *Mem:* Acad Pharmaceut Sci; Am Pharmaceut Asn; Sigma Xi. *Res:* Product research and development of proprietary, toiletries products; quality control and quality assurance; physical pharmacy; technical management, business planning; FDA compliance; business consulting. *Mailing Add:* 972 N Rancho Del Jefe Loop Tucson AZ 85748-2075

BROWN, MICHAEL, METAMORPHIC PETROLOGY, GRANITES. *Current Pos:* PROF & CHAIR, DEPT GEOL, UNIV MD, 90- *Personal Data:* b Hayes, Middx, UK, Mar 19, 47; c 3. *Educ:* Univ Keele, UK, BA, 69, PhD(geol), 75. *Prof Exp:* Sr lectr, prin lectr & head, Dept Geol & Phys Sci, Oxford Brookes Univ, UK, 72-84; head & prof geol, Sch Geol Sci, Kingston Univ, UK, 84-90. *Concurrent Pos:* Subj ed, J Geol Soc London, UK, 81-86; founder & ed, J Metamorphic Geol, Blackwell, Oxford, 82-; asst dean acad affairs, Fac Sci, Kingston Univ, UK, 86-89, vis prof, 90-92; vis lectr, Dept Geol & Mineral, Kyoto Univ, Japan, 93. *Mem:* Fel Geol Soc Am; Am Geophys Union; Mineral Soc Am; fel Geol Soc London; Mineral Soc Gt Brit; Europ Union Geosci. *Res:* Petrology of high-grade metamorphic rocks, their P-T-T histories and their tectonic interpretation; petrogenesis of migmatites and granites and crustal anatexis; origin of calc-alkaline plutonic rocks; magmatism and tectonics. *Mailing Add:* Dept Geol Univ Md College Park MD 20742-4211. *Fax:* 301-314-9661; *E-Mail:* mbrown@geol.umd.edu

BROWN, MICHAEL FREDERICK, NUCLEAR MAGNETIC RESONANCE SPECTROSCOPY, MEMBRANE BIOPHYSICS. *Current Pos:* PROF CHEM & BIOCHEM, UNIV ARIZ, 87-, PROF PROG NEUROSCI, 93- *Personal Data:* b Los Angeles, Calif, Nov 24, 48. *Educ:* Univ Calif, Santa Cruz, AB, 70, PhD(biol & chem), 75. *Honors & Awards:* Res Career Develop Award, NIH, 85. *Prof Exp:* NIH fel, Univ Basel, Switz, 76-79, Univ Calif, Berkeley, 79-80; from asst prof to assoc prof chem, Univ Va, 80-87. *Concurrent Pos:* Sloan res fel, Alfred P Sloan Found, 83; vis prof phys chem, Univ Lund, Sweden, 87- *Mem:* Biophys Soc; AAAS. *Res:* Physical chemistry and biochemistry includes nuclear magnetic resonance spectroscopy of liquid crystals and lipid bilayers, investigations of structure and dynamics of biological macromolecules, studies of lipid-protein interactions in membranes, the molecular basis of vision studied by fast photochemical reaction techniques, magnetic resonance imaging of lipid deposition in human atherosclerosis. *Mailing Add:* Dept Chem Univ Ariz Tucson AZ 85721

BROWN, MICHAEL LEE, ENERGETICS, GENETICS. *Current Pos:* ASST PROF FISH CULTURE, LIMNOL & CONSERV, SDAK STATE UNIV, 93- *Personal Data:* b Ft Smith, Ark, Jan 16, 55. *Educ:* Ark Tech Univ, BS, 86; Tex A&M Univ, MS, 89, PhD(wildlife & fisheries sci), 93. *Prof Exp:* Res assoc, Tex A&M Univ, 91-93, instr, 92-93. *Res:* fish culture and nutrition; reservoir ecology; population genetics; fish energetics. *Mailing Add:* SDak State Univ Northern Biol Stress Bldg Box 2140 B Brookings SD 57007

BROWN, MICHAEL S, GENETIC ENGINEERING, MOLECULAR GENETICS. *Current Pos:* asst prof, Southwestern Med Sch, 71-74, PROF MED & GENETICS & DIR, CTR GENETIC DIS, UNIV TEX SOUTHWEST MED CTR, 77-, REGENTAL PROF, 85- *Personal Data:* b New York, NY, Apr 13, 41. *Educ:* Univ Pa, BA, 62, MD, 66. *Hon Degrees:* DSc, Rensselaer Polytech Inst, 82, Univ Chicago, 82, Univ Pa, 86, Southern Methodist Univ, 93, Univ Miami, 96; Dr, Univ Paris, 88, Univ Buenos Aires, 89. *Honors & Awards:* Nobel Prize in Physiol or Med, 85; Pfizer Award, Am Chem Soc, 74; Lounsbery Award, US Nat Acad Sci, 79; Res Achievement Award, Am Heart Asn, 84; Nat Medal of Sci, 88. *Prof Exp:* Clin assoc, NIH, 68-71. *Concurrent Pos:* Estab investr, Am Heart Asn, 74-79; mem, Molecular Cytol Study Sect, NIH, 74-79 & ed adv bd, J Lipid Res, 79-83, J Cell Biol, 81-84 & Arteriosclerosis, 81; distinguished chair biomed sci, Univ Tex Southwestern Med Ctr, Dallas, 89- *Mem:* Inst Med-Nat Acad Sci; Am Soc Clin Invest; Asn Am Physicians; fel Am Col Physicians; Am Acad Arts & Sci; Am Soc Biol Chemists; Am Philos Soc. *Res:* Published numerous articles in various journals. *Mailing Add:* Dept Molecular Genetics Rm 238 Univ Tex Southwest Med Ctr 5323 Harry Hines Blvd Dallas TX 75235-9046

BROWN, MORTON, POLYMER CHEMISTRY. *Current Pos:* res chemist, Cent Res Dept, 57-62 & Elastomer Chem Dept, 62-79, TECH CONSULT, POLYMER PROD DEPT, E I DU PONT DE NEMOURS & CO, INC, 80- *Personal Data:* b New York, NY, May 7, 31; m 57; c 3. *Educ:* Cornell Univ, AB, 52; Duke Univ, AM, 54; Mass Inst Technol, PhD(org chem), 57. *Prof Exp:* Fel, Mass Inst Technol, 57. *Mem:* Am Chem Soc; Inst Elec & Electronics Engrs. *Res:* Fluorinated organo-sulfur compounds; cyano-carbons; polyurethanes; interfacial polymerizations; thermoplastic elastomers; effect of polymer melt rheology on processing characteristics; high voltage rubber insulations. *Mailing Add:* 2409 Sweetbriar Rd Wilmington DE 19810-3413

BROWN, MORTON, MATHEMATICS. *Current Pos:* Off Naval Res fel, 58-59, from asst prof to assoc prof, 59-64, PROF MATH, UNIV MICH, ANN ARBOR, 64- *Educ:* Univ Wis-Madison, BS, 53, MS, 55, PhD(math), 58. *Honors & Awards:* Veblen Prize, Am Math Soc, 64. *Prof Exp:* Instr math, Univ Wis-Madison, 57 & Ohio State Univ, 57-58. *Concurrent Pos:* NSF fel, Inst Advan Study, Princeton Univ, 60-62; Sloan Found fel, Cambridge Univ & Univ Mich, 63-65. *Mem:* Am Math Soc; Math Asn Am; Nat Coun Teachers Math. *Res:* Topology; dynamics. *Mailing Add:* Dept Math Univ Mich Ann Arbor MI 48109-1109

BROWN, MURRAY ALLISON, DAIRY SCIENCE. *Current Pos:* PROF AGR, SAM HOUSTON STATE UNIV, 65- *Personal Data:* b Rochester, NY, Oct 29, 27; m 48; c 3. *Educ:* Mich State Univ, BS, 50; Tex A&M Univ, MS, 53, PhD(animal breeding), 56. *Prof Exp:* Instr dairy prod, Tex A&M Univ, 53 & 55-57, from asst prof to assoc prof dairy sci, 57-65. *Concurrent Pos:* Animal sci consult. *Mem:* AAAS; Am Dairy Sci Asn; Nat Asn Col & Teachers Agr (pres, 69-70, secy-treas, 72-). *Res:* Bovine reproductive physiology; artificial insemination; dairy cattle breeding. *Mailing Add:* Dept Agr Sam Houston State Univ Huntsville TX 77341-1001

BROWN, MYRTLE LAURESTINE, NUTRITION. *Current Pos:* vis prof, Va Polytech Inst & State Univ, 83-84, assoc dean grad sch, 84-86, prof, 86-88, EMER PROF BIOCHEM & NUTRIT, VA POLYTECH INST & STATE UNIV, 88- *Personal Data:* b Columbia, SC, June 1, 26. *Educ:* Bennett Col, BS, 45; Pa State Univ, MS, 48, PhD(nutrit), 57. *Prof Exp:* Nutrit specialist, Human Nutrit Res Div, Agr Res Serv, USDA, 48-63; assoc prof home econ, Univ Hawaii, 63-65, nutrit, 65-66, pub health, 66-69; assoc prof nutrit, Rutgers Univ, 69-72, prof, 72-74; staff officer, Nat Acad Sci, 74-76, exec secy, Food & Nutrit Bd, 77-83. *Mem:* AAAS; Am Inst Nutrit; Inst Food Technologists; Sigma Xi. *Res:* Nutrition and reproduction; growth and development. *Mailing Add:* 201 Fincastle Dr Blacksburg VA 24060-5060

BROWN, NANCY J, CHEMICAL PHYSICS, CHEMICAL DYNAMICS. *Current Pos:* vis scholar combustion, Lawrence Berkeley Lab, Univ Calif, Berkeley, 73, lectr chem, 73-75, res engr combustion, 75-77, staff scientist, 76-84, dep prog leader, Environ Res Group, 79-91, SR SCIENTIST, LAWRENCE BERKELEY LAB, UNIV CALIF, BERKELEY, 84-, PROG LEADER, ENVIRON RES PROG, 91- *Personal Data:* b Erie, Pa, Apr 19, 43; m 74; c 1. *Educ:* Va Polytech Inst, BS, 64; Univ Md, MS, 69, PhD(phys chem), 71. *Prof Exp:* Fel, Appl Phys Lab, Johns Hopkins Univ, 71-73. *Concurrent Pos:* Adv comt, Calif State Energy Resources Conserv & Develop Comn, 75-77; affil fac, energy & resources group, Univ Calif, Berkeley, group leader combustion res, 86, prog leader environ res, 90; Gov appointee, State Calif Acid Deposition Adv Comt; prof invitee, Univ Pierre & Marie Curie, Paris VI. *Mem:* Am Chem Soc; Am Phys Soc; Combustion Inst; Asn Women Sci. *Res:* Theoretical and experimental chemical kinetics; combustion chemistry; chemical dynamics; theoretical chemistry; energy transfer; theoretical studies of reactivity and energy transfer; functional sensitivity analysis of the interrelationship between dynamics and potential structures; modeling of combustion processes; model sensitivity and uncertainty. *Mailing Add:* Lawrence Berkeley 1 Cyclotron Rd MS 70-108 Berkeley CA 94707

BROWN, NEAL B, LOW LIGHT LEVEL SPECTROSCOPY. *Current Pos:* asst geophysicist, 68-81, ASST PROF PHYSICS, UNIV ALASKA, 81- *Personal Data:* b Moscow, Idaho, Dec 13, 38; m 64, 74, 80; c 5. *Educ:* Wash State Univ, BS, 61; Univ Alaska, MS, 66. *Prof Exp:* Researcher, Ames Res Ctr, NASA, Moffett Field, Calif, 61-62 & Am Geophys Soc, 62-63. *Concurrent Pos:* Researcher, Geophys Inst, Univ Alaska, 68-71, dir, Poker Flat Res Range, 71-88. *Mem:* Sigma Xi; AAAS; Am Geophys Union; Am Inst Aeronaut & Astronaut. *Res:* Near-infrared spectral studies of aurora & air glow; low light level color television studies of aurora; low light level imaging of transient phenomena. *Mailing Add:* 1569 La Rue Lane Fairbanks AK 99709-6631

BROWN, NEAL B, HEALTH CARE ADMINISTRATION, MENTAL HEALTH. *Current Pos:* DIR, COMMUNITY SUPPORT PROG, CTR MENT HEALTH SERV, 83- *Personal Data:* b Providence, RI, May 1, 47; m 70, Ellen-Sue Son Yin; c Andrew & Mark. *Educ:* Univ RI, BA, 69, MPA, 72; George Washington Univ, MHA, 76. *Prof Exp:* Dir, Mgt Policy Off, 74-79. *Res:* Administer national research and demonstration programs focused on community treatment and rehabilitation for individuals with severe mental illnesses. *Mailing Add:* 5600 Fishers Lane Rm 11 C-22 Rockville MD 20857. *Fax:* 301-443-0541; *E-Mail:* nbrown@samsha.gov

BROWN, NEAL CURTIS, BIOCHEMISTRY, PHARMACOLOGY. *Current Pos:* assoc prof biochem, 73-74, PROF PHARMACOL & CHMN DEPT, MED SCH, UNIV MASS, 74- *Personal Data:* b Vassalboro, Maine, Mar 15, 39; m 64; c 2. *Educ:* Cornell Univ, DVM, 62; Yale Univ, PhD(biochem pharmacol), 66. *Prof Exp:* USPHS fel, Dept Chem, Karolinska Inst, Sweden, 66-68, Swed Cancer Soc fel, 68-69; from asst prof to assoc prof cell biol & pharmacol, Sch Med, Univ Md, 69-73. *Mem:* Fedn Am Socs Exp Biol. *Res:* Metabolism of DNA and DNA precursors and its control in vitro and in vivo in prokaryotic and eukaryotic cells. *Mailing Add:* Dept Pharmacol Univ Mass Med Sch 55 N Lake Ave Worcester MA 01655-0126. *Fax:* 508-856-5080

BROWN, NEIL HARRY, pharmaceutics, packaging, for more information see previous edition

BROWN, NIGEL ANDREW, TERATOLOGY, BIOCHEMICAL TOXICOLOGY. *Current Pos:* STAFF MEM, DEPT ANAT & DEVELOP BIOL, MED RES COUN LABS, 82- *Personal Data:* b Sunderland, Eng, Jan 27, 53. *Educ:* Univ Leeds, BSc, 73; Univ Surrey, PhD(biochem), 77. *Prof Exp:* Demonstr biochem, Univ Surrey, Eng, 73-75, 76-77; res fel pharmacol, Pharmakologisches Inst Univ Mainz, Ger, 75-76; vis fel toxicol, Nat Inst Environ Health Sci, NC, 77-78; asst prof pharmacol, George Washington Univ, 78-82. *Mem:* Biochem Soc; AAAS; Fedn Am Socs Exp Biol. *Res:* Mechanisms of teratogenesis; toxicity in reproduction; xenobiotic metabolism; ligand-albumin interactions. *Mailing Add:* Dept Anat & Develop Biol St George's Hosp Med Sch Cranmer Terr London SW17 ORE England

BROWN, NORMAN, METALLURGY. *Current Pos:* from asst prof to assoc prof metall, 52-60, PROF MAT SCI, UNIV PA, 60- *Personal Data:* b Lynn, Mass, Feb 7, 21; m 95, Ampara Rendon; c 6. *Educ:* Mass Inst Technol, BS, 43; Stanford Univ, MS, 50; Univ Calif, Berkeley, PhD(metall), 52. *Prof Exp:* Jr metallurgist, Naval Torpedo Sta, RI, 43-44; metallurgist, Ballistics Res Lab, Aberdeen Proving Ground, 46-48. *Concurrent Pos:* Guggenheim fel, Cavendish Lab, 58-59; vis prof, Bristol Univ, 66-67, Physics Dept, Univ Leeds, 81-82; NIH spec fel, 66-67; consult, Australian Gas Ltd, Czech Gas Co, Philadelphia Gas, Osaka Gas. *Mem:* Am Soc Metals; fel Am Phys Soc; fel Am Soc Mat. *Res:* Mechanical behavior of polymers. *Mailing Add:* Dept Mat Sci & Eng Univ Pa LRSM Bldg K1 Philadelphia PA 19107

BROWN, NORMAN LOUIS, SMALL-SCALE SOLAR & BIOMASS-ENERGY SYSTEMS, PHYSICAL CHEMISTRY. *Current Pos:* CONSULT, 81- *Personal Data:* b Atlantic City, NJ, Dec 22, 23; m 57; c 3. *Educ:* Mass Inst Technol, SB, 47; Brown Univ, PhD(phys chem), 52. *Prof Exp:* Phys chemist, Electronics Lab, Gen Elec Co, 51-56; physicist, Nat Bur Stand, 57-63 & Nat Ctr Fish Protein Concentrate, Bur Com Fisheries, US Dept Interior, 63-67; prog leader, Fish Protein Concentrate Eng Res & Develop Prog, 67-70; prof assoc, Bd Sci & Technol for Int Develop, Off Foreign Secy, Nat Acad Sci, 70-75; country prog specialist, Off Asst Adminr Int Affairs, ERDA, 75-77, chief tech adv, Develop Country Prog Off, US Dept Energy, 77-78; spec adv energy to asst adminr & Chief, Div Sci, Tech & Environ Problems, Bur for Asia, USAID, 78-81. *Concurrent Pos:* Consult, AID, Asia Develop Bank, World Bank & UN projects in Asia, Africa, Caribbean & the Mid East. *Mem:* Fel AAAS; Int Solar Energy Soc; Soc Int Develop; Am Solar Energy Soc. *Res:* Manufacture and use of fish and other protein concentrates; applications of science and technology to problems of development; small-scale renewable-resource energy systems for developing countries. *Mailing Add:* 1746 Q St NW Washington DC 20009-2408

BROWN, OLEN RAY, OXYGEN RADICALS, EXPERT WITNESS. *Current Pos:* from instr to assoc prof, Univ Mo, Columbia, 64-77, asst dir, John M Dalton Cardiovas Res Ctr, 74-78, prof microbiol, 77-96, prof vet biomed sci, 87-96, RES INVESTR, UNIV MO, COLUMBIA, 68-, RES PROF, 96- *Personal Data:* b Hastings, Okla, Aug 18, 35; m 58, Pollyana J King; c Barbara K, Diana C & David G. *Educ:* Univ Okla, BS, 58, MS, 60, PhD(microbiol), 64; Am Bd Toxicol, dipl, 89. *Prof Exp:* Spec instr microbiol, Univ Okla, 63-64. *Concurrent Pos:* Peer & site reviewer, NIH & Nat Inst Environ Health Sci; consult, Drug Abuse Policy Off, Washington, DC, 82; guest lectr, Ross Univ, St Kitts, 84 & 88; expert witness/legal consult, Tech Adv Serv Attorneys, Teltech Consult; consult, 90- *Mem:* Fel Am Inst Chem; Soc Toxicol; Oxygen Soc; Am Chem Soc; Int Soc Study Xenobiotics; Soc Free Radical Res. *Res:* Mechanisms of toxicity of oxygen for the kynorenine pathway in the brain; effects of hyperoxia and redox-active chemicals on enzymes and coenzymes; inhibition of amino acid and nicotinamide adenine dinucleotide biosynthesis, induction of genetic stringency and prevention of these toxicity sites. *Mailing Add:* John M Dalton Cardiovasc Res Ctr Univ Mo Research Park R 222D Columbia MO 65211. *Fax:* 573-884-4232; *E-Mail:* orb@showme.missouri.edu

BROWN, OLIVER MONROE, NEUROCHEMISTRY, NEUROTRANSMITTERS. *Current Pos:* from instr to asst prof, 71-84, ASSOC PROF PHARMACOL, STATE UNIV NY, UPSTATE MED CTR, 84- *Personal Data:* b Ithaca, NY, June 11, 44; div. *Educ:* Calif State Col, Long Beach, BS, 66; Kans State Univ, PhD(biochem), 70. *Prof Exp:* Fel pharmacol, Mt Sinai Sch Med, 70-71. *Concurrent Pos:* Consult, 75-; Markey fel, 87; investr, Mt Desert Island Biol Lab, Maine, 87- *Mem:* AAAS; NY Acad Sci; Am Soc Pharmacol & Exp Therapeut; Am Heart Asn; Am Pub Health Asn. *Res:* Chemical approaches to autonomic control of the mammalian heart; drug alterations of neurotransmitters in the brain; mechanisms of neurotransmitter release; toxicology; heavy metalion toxicology. *Mailing Add:* Pharmacol Dept State Univ NY Health Sci Ctr 766 Irving Ave Syracuse NY 13210-1605. *Fax:* 315-464-8000

BROWN, PAMELA ANN MCELROY, CRYSTALLIZATION, KINETICS. *Current Pos:* VIS ASST PROF CHEM ENG, STEVENS INST TECHNOL, 93- *Personal Data:* b Bakersfield, Calif, Mar 10, 55; m 80, Harvey; c Heather, Vanessa & William. *Educ:* State Univ NY, Albany, BS, 77; Mass Inst Technol, SM, 79; Polytech Univ, PhD(chem eng), 89. *Prof Exp:* Res engr, Am Cyanamid, 78-80; staff scientist, Pall Corp, 80-81; res asst, Polytech Univ, 85-89; instr chem, Barnard Col, 92-93. *Concurrent Pos:* Adj instr chem eng, Polytech Univ, 86-90; consult environ, Dema Tech Corp, 90-; adj instr chem, Queensborough Community Col, 92-93, Nassau Community Col, 95-96. *Mem:* Am Inst Chem Engrs; Soc Advan & Mat Process Eng; Am Soc Environ Educ. *Res:* Rate of aging and purification of terephthalic acid crystals in saturated solutions due to temperature fluctuations. *Mailing Add:* 3356 Bertha Dr Baldwin NY 11510. *Fax:* 201-216-8240; *E-Mail:* pbrown@attila.stevens-tech.edu

BROWN, PATRICIA LYNN, INFORMATION SCIENCE. *Current Pos:* RETIRED. *Personal Data:* b Lafayette, La, Oct 1, 28. *Educ:* Univ Southwestern La, BS, 47; Univ Tex, MA, 49. *Prof Exp:* Instr analytical chem, Smith Col, 49-50; chemist, R&M Labs, 50; res assoc indust toxicol, Albany Med Col, 50-51; lit searcher info serv & res & eng dept, Ethyl Corp, 51-53, reference librn, 53-54, lit specialist, 54, ed asst, 54-55; sr tech writer & ed pub eng, Atomic Power Div, Westinghouse Elec Corp, 55-57, staff engr, 57; supvr info serv, Semiconductor-Components Div, Tex Instruments, Inc, 57-61, mgr info serv, Corp Res & Eng, 61-64, tech info consult, 64-66; sr researcher, Battelle Mem Inst, 66-76; assoc dir, Travenol Labs, Inc, 76-82, tech info counr, 83-86; mgr tech info serv, Stepan Co, 87-93. *Mem:* Am Chem Soc; Soc Women Engrs (pres, 61-63). *Res:* Analysis and design of information systems; techniques of document preparation, acquisition, indexing, condensation, storage, retrieval, dissemination and use; design and development of methods for useful organization and presentation of information. *Mailing Add:* 1920 Ivy Lane Glenview IL 60025-1070

BROWN, PATRICIA STOCKING, ZOOLOGY, ENDOCRINOLOGY. *Current Pos:* from asst prof to assoc prof biol, 69-80, dept head, 84-86 & 88-91, PROF BIOL, SIENA COL, NY, 80- *Personal Data:* b Cadillac, Mich, Apr 25, 42; m 65; c 2. *Educ:* Univ Mich, BS, 63, MS, 66, PhD(zool), 68. *Prof Exp:* Res assoc develop biol, State Univ NY Albany, 68-69. *Concurrent Pos:* Mellon-Wellsley fel, 78-79; NSF fel, Univ Calif, Berkeley, 80-81; vis prof, Univ Bath, Eng, 87-88. *Mem:* Am Soc Zool; Am Soc Soc Icthyologists & Herpetologists; Endocrin Soc; Asn Women Sci; AAAS; History Sci Soc. *Res:* Hormonal control of growth in amphibians and reptiles; salt and water balance in urodeles; function of prolactin in lower vertebrates; history of women scientists. *Mailing Add:* Dept Biol Siena Col Loudonville NY 12211. *Fax:* 518-783-2986; *E-Mail:* brown@siena.edu

BROWN, PATRICK MICHAEL, PHYSICAL INORGANIC CHEMISTRY. *Current Pos:* dir res, 76-88, MGR CHEM RES, CYPRUS FOOTE MINERAL CO, 74-, SR TECH CONSULT TO PRES, 89- *Personal Data:* b North Tonawanda, NY, 1938; m 59; c 4. *Educ:* Univ Miss, BS, 60; Syracuse Univ, PhD, 65. *Prof Exp:* Fel, State Univ NY, Buffalo, 65-66; chemist, W R Grace & Co, 66-73, sr res chemist, 73; pres, Biolytic's Inc, 73-74. *Mem:* Sigma Xi; Am Chem Soc; Am Ceramic Soc; Am Inst Mining Metall & Petrol Engrs. *Res:* Catalysis; materials science; lithium chemistry. *Mailing Add:* 211 Allen Dr Exton PA 19341-1770

BROWN, PAUL B, NEUROPHYSIOLOGY. *Current Pos:* from asst prof to assoc prof, 74-82, PROF PHYSIOL, MED CTR, WVA UNIV, 82- *Personal Data:* b Panama City, Panama, Nov 29, 42; US citizen; m 68. *Educ:* Mass Inst Technol, BS, 64; Univ Chicago, PhD(physiol), 68. *Honors & Awards:* Benedum Distinguished Scholar Award. *Prof Exp:* NIH fel neurophysiol, Cornell Univ, 68-72; res scientist, Boston State Hosp, 72-74. *Concurrent Pos:* Chief ed, J Electrophysiol Tech, 78-88; Fogarty sr int fel, Univ Edinburgh, 80-81. *Mem:* Soc Neurosci; Am Physiol Soc. *Res:* Mechanisms of somesthesis; spinal cord neurophysiology; human and animal psychophysics; neuroanatomy; plasticity. *Mailing Add:* Dept Physiol WVa Univ Med Ctr Morgantown WV 26506. *Fax:* 304-293-3850; *E-Mail:* pbbrown@wvnums.wvnet.edu

BROWN, PAUL EDMUND, chemical reactions in high-temperature water, for more information see previous edition

BROWN, PAUL JOSEPH, BATTERY TECHNOLOGY, ELECTRIC VEHICLE TECHNOLOGY. *Current Pos:* RETIRED. *Personal Data:* b St Louis, Mo, April 18, 24; m 51; c 2. *Educ:* Wash Univ, BSME, 49, MEA, 64. *Prof Exp:* Prod mgr, Universal Match Corp, St Louis, 56-64; mkt mgr, Am Mach & Foy, York, Pa, 64-66; dir, Off Vehicle Syst Res, Nat Bur Standards, 66-71; dir, Safety Res Lab, US Dept Transp, 71-76; dir, Elec & Hybrid Vehicle Div, US Dept Energy, 76-92. *Concurrent Pos:* Adv mech engr, Emerson Elec, St Louis, Mo, 48-56 auto safety expert, White House Sci Adv Comn, 71-72; mem adv comt, Stapp Car Crash Conf, 84- *Mem:* Soc Automotive Engrs. *Res:* Management of the federal governments research & development program of electric & hybrid vehicle technologies including batteries, fuel cells, propulsion systems & prototype vehicles. *Mailing Add:* 10611 Glenwild Rd Silver Spring MD 20901

BROWN, PAUL LAWSON, SOIL MANAGEMENT, SOIL FERTILITY. *Current Pos:* RETIRED. *Personal Data:* b Ash Grove, Kans, June 1, 18; m 46; c 2. *Educ:* Kans State Univ, BS, 41, MS, 49; Iowa State Univ, PhD(soil fertil), 56. *Prof Exp:* Soil survr, Kans Agr Exp Sta, USDA, 46-48, soil scientist, Ft Hays Exp Sta, 48-56, res soil scientist, Agr Res Serv, Mont State Univ, 56-73, res soil scientist, Agr Res Serv, Northern Plains Soil & Water Res Ctr, Ft Benton, Mont, 73-80, soil scientist, Agr Res Serv, Mont State Univ, 81-83; soil scientist, Mont State Univ, 83- *Mem:* Fel Soil Sci Soc Am; fel Am Soc Agron; Can Soc Soil Sci; Int Soc Soil Sci; Sigma Xi; Soil Conserv Soc Am. *Res:* Soil management for dryland crop production; soil, crop and land management for saline seep control. *Mailing Add:* 1624 S Third Ave Bozeman MT 59715

BROWN, PAUL LOPEZ, ZOOLOGY. *Current Pos:* RETIRED. *Personal Data:* b Anderson, SC, Feb 18, 19; m 44; c 4. *Educ:* Knoxville Col, BS, 41; Univ Ill, MS, 48, PhD(zool), 55. *Prof Exp:* From instr to assoc prof biol, Southern Univ, 48-58; prof, Fla Agr & Mech Univ, 58-59; prof biol & head dept, Norfolk State Univ, 59-74; acad dean, Clark Col, 74-78; prof biol, Atlanta Univ, 78-82, dean, Sch Arts & Sci, 82-87. *Concurrent Pos:* Mem staff, NSF, 63-64 & 74, consult, 64-; consult, Off Educ, US Dept Health, Educ & Welfare, 64- *Mem:* Am Soc Zoologists; Am Micros Soc. *Res:* Biology of crayfishes including taxonomy, life history, distribution, limnology of waters inhabited; ecology. *Mailing Add:* 855 Flamingo Dr SW Atlanta GA 30311

BROWN, PAUL WHEELER, NEUROVIROLOGY, NEUROEPIDEMIOLOGY. *Current Pos:* staff assoc virol, USPHS, 63-71, MED DIR USPHS, NAT INST NEUROL & COMMUN DIS & STROKE, NIH, 72- *Personal Data:* b Teaneck, NJ, Mar 12, 36; m 57, 82; c 4. *Educ:* Harvard Univ, AB, 57; Johns Hopkins Univ, MD, 61; Am Bd Internal Med, cert, 69. *Prof Exp:* Intern & resident, Johns Hopkins Hosp, 61-63. *Concurrent Pos:* Resident, Univ Calif, San Francisco, 65-66 & Johns Hopkins Hosp, 66-67; fel, Nat Multiple Sclerosis Soc, 71-72 & Comt Control Huntington's Dis, 73-74; vis scientist virol, NIH & Med Res, Paris, France, 71-72 & 77-78. *Mem:* Am Col Physicians; Am Epidemiol Soc; Infectious Dis Soc Am; French Neurol Soc. *Res:* Study of slow and latent central nervous system viruses; creutzfeldt-jakob disease. *Mailing Add:* NIH Bldg 36 Rm 5B20 Bethesda MD 20892

BROWN, PAUL WOODROW, HAND SURGERY, ORTHOPEDIC SURGERY. *Current Pos:* CLIN PROF ORTHOP PLASTIC & RECONSTRUCT SURG, SCH MED, YALE UNIV, 78- *Personal Data:* b New York, NY, Dec 28, 19; m, Patricia Burris; c 3. *Educ:* Univ Mich, BS, 42, MD, 50. *Prof Exp:* Resident orthop surg, Letterman Army Hosp, San Francisco, 51-55; fel hand surg, Walter Reed Army Hosp, Washington, DC, 62-63; div chmn orthop, Fitzsimons Gen Hosp, Denver, 66-69; prof surg, Med Ctr, Univ Colo, Denver, 69-72; prof, Sch Med, Univ Miami, 72-74; chmn dept surg, St Vincent's Hosp, 74-83. *Concurrent Pos:* Colonel, US Army, retired. *Mem:* Am Col Surg; Am Acad Orthop Surg; Am Soc Surg of the Hand; Int Soc Orthop Surg & Traumatol; New Eng Surg Soc. *Res:* Reconstructive surgery of the hand; peripheral nerve lesions; mechanics of wound healing; fate of exposed bone. *Mailing Add:* 3071 North St Fairfield CT 06430. *Fax:* 203-255-1047

BROWN, PETER, ORGANIC CHEMISTRY. *Current Pos:* from asst prof to assoc prof, 67-77, PROF ORG CHEM, ARIZ STATE UNIV, 77- *Personal Data:* b Lincoln, Eng, Sept 12, 38. *Educ:* Univ Southampton, BSc, 61, PhD, 64. *Prof Exp:* Res assoc mass spectrometry, Stanford Univ, 64-67. *Mem:* Am Chem Soc; Royal Soc Chem. *Res:* Cycloaddition reactions; photochemistry; mass spectrometry. *Mailing Add:* 55 Benslow Rise Hitchin Herts SG4 9OY England

BROWN, PETER H, FOOD RESEARCH, BIOCHEMISTRY. *Current Pos:* sr res scientist dairy chem, Kraft Gen Foods, 89-96, ASSOC TECHNOL PRINCIPAL, KRAFT FOODS, INC, 96- *Personal Data:* b New York, NY, 1953; m, Susan Goldstein; c Allison. *Educ:* Colgate Univ, AB, 75; Univ Dayton, MS, 77; Washington Univ, PhD(plant physiol), 82. *Prof Exp:* Fel molecular hemat, Wash Univ Sch Med, 82-85, Monsanto/Anheuser-Busch fel, 85-87, fel transitional regulation, 87-89. *Mem:* Am Soc Biochem & Molecular Biol; AAAS. *Res:* Enzyme applications in food; ingredient processing; flavor discovery. *Mailing Add:* Kraft Foods Inc 801 Waukegan Rd Glenview IL 60025. *Fax:* 847-646-7302; *E-Mail:* pbrown@kraft.com

BROWN, PHILIP EDWARD, METALLIC MINERAL DEPOSITS, METAMORPHIC PETROLOGY. *Current Pos:* from asst prof to assoc prof, 81-92, chmn, 93-96, PROF ECON GEOL, UNIV WIS-MADISON, 92- *Personal Data:* b St Louis, Mo, July 12, 52; m 74; c 3. *Educ:* Carleton Col, BA, 74; Univ Mich, MS, 76, PhD(geol), 80. *Prof Exp:* Teaching asst geol, Univ Mich, 74-79, instr econ geol, 79-80; NSF fel, US Geol Surv, Reston, 80-81. *Mem:* Am Geophys Union; Soc Econ Geologists; Mineral Soc Am; Mineral Soc Can; Sigma Xi; Geol Asn Can. *Res:* Stable isotopic and geochemical studies of metamorphic and hydrothermal fluids and the origin of contact metamorphic and metasomatic ore deposits; evolution of Archean terranes. *Mailing Add:* Dept Geol & Geophys Univ Wis Madison WI 53706. *Fax:* 608-262-0693; *E-Mail:* pbrown@geology.wisc.edu

BROWN, PHYLLIS R, CHEMISTRY, BIOCHEMISTRY. *Current Pos:* from asst prof to assoc prof, 73-80, PROF CHEM, UNIV RI, 80- *Personal Data:* b Providence, RI, Mar 16, 24; m 52, Bertram M; c Charles D, Ronald B, Judith B & Elizabeth W. *Educ:* George Washington Univ, BS, 44; Brown Univ, PhD(chem), 68. *Honors & Awards:* Tswett Medal Chromatography, 88; Dal Nogere Award Chromatography, 89; Fulbright, Israel, 87. *Prof Exp:* Res asst chem, Harris Res Lab, 44-45; fel & res assoc, Dept Pharmacol, Brown Univ, 68-71, from instr to asst prof, 71-73. *Concurrent Pos:* Vis prof, Hebrew Univ, 83. *Mem:* Am Chem Soc; Am Inst Chemists; Am Asn Clin Chemists; Am Soc Pharmacol & Exp Therapeut; Am Soc Biol Chemists; Sigma Xi; NY Acad Sci. *Res:* Development of analytical and preparative high performance liquid chromatography and cafrillary electorophoresis separations for biomedical research, biotechnology and environmental monitoring. *Mailing Add:* Dept Chem Univ RI Kingston RI 02881

BROWN, R(ONALD) A(NDERSON) S(TEVEN), CHEMICAL ENGINEERING. *Current Pos:* INDEPENDENT CONSULT, 86- *Personal Data:* b Winnipeg, Man, June 23, 34; m 62; c 3. *Educ:* Univ Alta, BSc, 56, PhD(chem eng), 63; Calif Inst Technol, MS, 57. *Prof Exp:* Asst res officer, Eng Div, Res Coun Alta, 63-70, assoc res officer, 70-81; consult, Chinook Fuel Innovations Ltd, 81-84; res mgr, Pembine Resources Ltd, 85. *Mem:* Am Inst Chem Engrs; Eng Inst Can; Chem Inst Can; Sigma Xi. *Res:* Immiscible fluids; solids pipelining; combustion of solid fuels; high temperature processing; underground coal gasification; fuel technology; coal conversion. *Mailing Add:* 8923 142nd St Edmonton AB T5R 0M6 Can

BROWN, RANDALL EMORY, WASTE DISPOSAL. *Current Pos:* RETIRED. *Personal Data:* b Eugene, Ore, May 28, 17; m 50; c 2. *Educ:* Stanford Univ, AB, 38; Yale Univ, MS, 41. *Prof Exp:* Geologist, Glacier Peak Mine, M A Hanna Co, 41, State Dept Geol & Mineral Industs, Ore, 41-42, US Geol Surv, 42-45 & Corps Engrs, US Army, 45-47; sr geologist, Hanford Atomic Prod Opers, Gen Elec Co, 47-65; sr res scientist, Water & Land Resources Dept, Pac Northwest Lab, Battelle Mem Inst, 65-71; asst prof geol, Cent Wash Univ, 71-72; instr, Columbia Basin Col, 72-73; sr res scientist, Pac Northwest Labs, Battelle Mem Inst, 73-82; instr, Joint Ctr Grad Study, Richland, 73-78; supvr, Franklin Co Conserv Dist, 73-96. *Concurrent Pos:* Adj assoc prof, Cent Wash Univ, 67-69, 79-82; geol consult, 71- *Mem:* Fel AAAS; fel Geol Soc Am; Sigma Xi; Asn Ground Water Scientists & Engrs. *Res:* Ground water geology, geology and hydrology of disposal of radioactive and other wastes; geology of eastern Washington; paleoecology. *Mailing Add:* 504 Rd 49 N Pasco WA 99301

BROWN, RAY KENT, PROTEIN CHEMISTRY. *Current Pos:* chmn dept, 63-87, prof biochem, Sch Med, 63-96 EMER PROF BIOCHEM, WAYNE STATE UNIV, 96- *Personal Data:* b Columbus, Ohio, Apr 7, 24; m 47, Gertrude L Harris; c Kim, Kitene & Kevin. *Educ:* Ohio State Univ, AB, 44, MD, 47, MS, 48; Harvard Univ, PhD(biochem), 51. *Prof Exp:* Intern, Boston City Hosp, 47-48; sr asst surgeon protein chem, NIH, 51-53; asst dir, Div Labs & Res, State Dept Health, NY, 53-59, assoc dir, 59-63. *Concurrent Pos:* From assoc prof to prof, Albany Med Sch, 56-63. *Mem:* Am Chem Soc; Am Asn Immunol; Am Soc Biol Chem; Brit Biochem Soc. *Res:* Plasma proteins; immunologic studies of ribonuclease and thyroglobulin; photolabeling of proteins; role of ds RNA. *Mailing Add:* 3820 Middle Rd Highland MI 48357-3044

BROWN, RAYMOND RUSSELL, IMMUNOLOGY & CANCER, AMINO ACID METABOLISM IN INFLAMMATORY DISEASES & EOSINOPHILIA-MYALGIA SYNDROME. *Current Pos:* res asst oncol, Univ Wis-Madison, 50-53, postdoctoral fel clin oncol, 53-55, asst prof clin oncol, 55-60, assoc prof surg, 60-65, PROF CLIN ONCOL, UNIV WIS-MADISON, 65- *Personal Data:* b Calgary, Can, Dec 23, 26; US citizen. *Educ:* Univ Alta, BS, 48, MS, 50; Univ Wis-Madison, PhD(oncol), 53. *Prof Exp:* Instr chem, Univ Alta, Edmonton, 48-50. *Concurrent Pos:* Res collabr, Brookhaven Nat Lab, 61-89; affil prof, Dept Nutrit Sci, Univ Wis, 68-91; vis prof, McEachern Cancer Lab, Edmonton, 69-70. *Mem:* Am Asn Cancer Res; Am Inst Nutrit; Am Inst Clin Nutrit; Am Soc Biol Chemists. *Res:* Tryptophan metabolism; immunological diseases and tryptophan; interferon and interleukin metabolic effects; eosinophilia/myalgia syndrome and tryptophan metabolism; nutrition and cancer relationships; autoimmune diseases and AIDS. *Mailing Add:* Dept Human Oncol Sci Ctr K4/5 Clin Univ Wis Med Sch 2817 Van Hise Ave Madison WI 53792-3619. *Fax:* 608-263-4497

BROWN, RHODERICK EDMISTON, JR, BIOLOGICAL-MODEL MEMBRANES, PHYSICO-CHEMICAL INTERACTIONS OF SPHINGOLIPIDS WITH MEMBRANE LIPIDS & PROTEINS. *Current Pos:* asst prof, 86-92, ASSOC PROF, HORMEL INST, UNIV MINN, 93- *Personal Data:* b Hendersonville, NC, Apr 7, 53; m 81, Laura Strippel; c Caroline F & Christopher H. *Educ:* Univ NC, AB(chem) & AB(zool), 75; Wake Forest Univ, PhD(biochem), 81. *Prof Exp:* Res assoc, Univ Va, 81-86. *Concurrent Pos:* fac mem, Biochem & Molecular Biol Dept, Mayo Grad Sch, Mayo Clinic, 89-; prin investr, Nat Inst Gen Med Sci; mem, Coun Basic Sci, Am Heart Asn. *Mem:* Biophys Soc; Am Soc Cell Biol; AAAS; Micros Soc Am; Am Heart Asn. *Res:* Structure and function of glycolipids and sphingolipids in biologican and model membranes; spontaneous and protein-mediated intermembrane lipid transfer with emphasis on glycolipids and gangliosides; intracellular lipid transport; monomolecular film properties of sphingolipids and their interactions with other lipids and proteins; freeze fracture electron microscopic characterization of sphingolipid morphology and model membrane surface structure; toxin and lectin localization as probes for glycolipid organization in membranes. *Mailing Add:* Hormel Inst Univ Minn 801 16th Ave NE Austin MN 55912-3698. *Fax:* 507-437-9606; *E-Mail:* reb@maroon.tc.umn.edu

BROWN, RICHARD DEE, ENVIRONMENTAL POLICY, LIMNOLOGY. *Current Pos:* PROG MGR CONSERV, HORNE ENG & ENVIRON SERVS, 94- *Personal Data:* b Chicago, Ill, June 19, 38; m 90, Peggy A Opfer; c Christopher, David, Lisa, Matthew, Amanda, Patrick, Arwen & Jorene. *Educ:* Ind Univ, BA, 64, MA, 66; Univ Del, PhD(water pollution), 70. *Honors & Awards:* Prog Achievement Award, Superfund Prog, US Environ Protection Agency, 87. *Prof Exp:* Asst prof, Ind State univ, 69-73; dir, Water Sci Div, Jack McCormick & Assoc, 73-75; lead scientist, Mitre, 75-93; prof servs consult, Brown & Assocs, 93-94. *Concurrent Pos:* Exec div, Fed Interagency Comt Health & Environ Effects of Energy Technol, 78-82. *Mem:* Am Soc Testing & Mat; Am Soc Limnol & Oceanog; Ecol Soc Am. *Res:* Dynamics of colonization and succession of rheophilic substrate diatoms and water pollution monitoring and mitigation. *Mailing Add:* 2245 Southgate Sq Reston VA 22091. *E-Mail:* nickb@erols.com

BROWN, RICHARD DON, PHARMACOLOGY, TOXICOLOGY. *Current Pos:* from asst prof to assoc 69-76, coordr grad studies, 78-81, PROF PHARMACOL, SCH MED, LA STATE UNIV, SHREVEPORT, 76- *Personal Data:* b Alexandria, La, Mar 3, 40; m 63; c 1. *Educ:* La Col, BS, 64; La State Univ, MS, 66, PhD(pharmacol), 68. *Honors & Awards:* Frank R Blood Award, Soc Toxicol, 76. *Prof Exp:* Instr pharmacol, Sch Med, La State Univ, New Orleans, 68-69. *Concurrent Pos:* USPHS gen res support grant, 68-69. *Mem:* Am Soc Pharmacol & Exp Therapeut; Acoust Soc Am; Soc Neurosci; Soc Toxicol; Am Soc Clin Pharmacol Therapeut. *Res:* Ototoxic action of the loop diuretics and aminoglycosides, pharmacokinetics and computer software development; auditory physiology and pharmacology. *Mailing Add:* Dept Pharmacol & Therapeut La State Univ Sch Med PO Box 33932 Shreveport LA 71130-3932. *Fax:* 318-674-5442

BROWN, RICHARD EMERY, ORGANIC CHEMISTRY. *Current Pos:* SR CHEM PATENT AGENT, BECTON DICKINSON & CO, 83- *Personal Data:* b Chatham, NJ, Apr 7, 29; m 51; c 4. *Educ:* Moravian Col, BS, 51; Univ Md, MS, 52, PhD(org chem), 56. *Prof Exp:* Res chemist org chem, Allied Chem Corp, 55-60; assoc dept head, Warner Lambert Res Inst, 60-77; assoc dept head med chem, Revlon Health Care Group, 77-82. *Mem:* Am Chem Soc. *Res:* Synthesis of new organic compounds for potential medicinal interest. *Mailing Add:* 1 Becton Dr Franklin Lakes NJ 07417

BROWN, RICHARD GEORGE BOLNEY, ORNITHOLOGY, MARINE BIOLOGY. *Current Pos:* RES SCIENTIST ORNITH MARINE BIOL, CAN WILDLIFE SERV, 67 - *Personal Data:* b Wolverhampton, UK, Sept 15, 35; Can citizen. *Educ:* Oxford Univ, BA, 57, DPhil(ethology), 62. *Prof Exp:* Researcher ethology, Dept Zool, Oxford Univ, 62-65; res assoc animal psychol, Dept Psychol, Dalhousie Univ, NS, 65-67. *Mem:* Am Ornithologists Union; Brit Ornithologists Union; Brit Trust Ornith; Arctic Inst NAm. *Res:* The pelagic ecology of seabirds; role of seabirds in marine ecosystems. *Mailing Add:* Can Wildlife Serv Environ Conserv Br Can Wildlife Serv PO Box 1006 Dartmouth NS B2Y 2N6 Can

BROWN, RICHARD HARLAND, mathematics, for more information see previous edition

BROWN, RICHARD JULIAN CHALLIS, PHYSICAL CHEMISTRY. *Current Pos:* assoc prof, 68-83, PROF CHEM, QUEEN'S UNIV, ONT, 83- *Personal Data:* b Sydney, Australia, Apr 10, 36; m 62; c 3. *Educ:* Univ Sydney, BSc, 57, MSc, 59; Univ Ill, PhD(phys chem), 62. *Prof Exp:* Asst prof chem, Queen's Univ, Ont, 62-66; mem staff, Australian AEC, 66-69. *Mem:* Can Soc Chem. *Res:* Nuclear quadrupole resonance; nuclear spin relaxation and molecular motion in liquids and solids; radio frequency; spectroscopy at high pressure; thermodynamics of solids. *Mailing Add:* Dept Chem Queen's Univ Kingston ON K7L 3N6 Can. *E-Mail:* brownnjc@chem.queensu.ca

BROWN, RICHARD K(EMP), ELECTRICAL ENGINEERING. *Current Pos:* RETIRED. *Personal Data:* b Miamisburg, Ohio, May 18, 17; m 49; c 1. *Educ:* Univ Mich, BS, 40, MS, 41, PhD(elec eng), 52. *Honors & Awards:* Bur Ord Res & Develop Award, 45. *Prof Exp:* Spec asst, Underwater Sound Lab, Harvard Univ, 41-43; engr electronic prod develop, Physicists Res Co, 46; from instr to prof elec eng, Res Inst, Univ Mich, Ann Arbor, 47-77, prof elec & comput eng, 77- *Mem:* Audio Eng Soc; Am Acoust Soc; Inst Elec & Electronics Engrs. *Res:* Underwater sound velocity meters; acoustics; transistors; television; microwaves; radar. *Mailing Add:* 1301 Beale Ave 2403EECS Univ Mich Ann Arbor MI 48109

BROWN, RICHARD KETTEL, MATHEMATICS. *Current Pos:* chmn dept, 65-75, PROF MATH, KENT STATE UNIV, 65-, DIR OPER INST COMPUT MATH, 86- *Personal Data:* b Long Branch, NJ, Feb 3, 28; m 55. *Educ:* Muhlenberg Col, BS, 48; Rutgers Univ, MS, 50, PhD(math), 52. *Prof Exp:* Asst prof math, Rutgers Univ, 55-58; res mathematician, US Army Electronics Labs, 58-65. *Mem:* Am Math Soc; Math Asn Am; Sigma Xi. *Res:* Function of a complex variable; univalent and multivalent functions. *Mailing Add:* Math Dept Kent State Univ Main Campus PO Box 5190 Kent OH 44242-0001

BROWN, RICHARD L, STRUCTURAL TECTONICS. *Current Pos:* PROF GEOL, CARLETON UNIV, 64- *Personal Data:* b London, Eng, 64. *Educ:* Edinburgh Univ, PhD(geol), 64. *Mem:* Geol Soc Am. *Mailing Add:* Dept Earth Sci Carleton Univ Colonel By Dr Ottawa ON K1S 5B6 Can

BROWN, RICHARD MCPIKE, PLANT TAXONOMY, PLANT ECOLOGY. *Current Pos:* RETIRED. *Personal Data:* b San Diego, Calif, Feb 17, 26; m 60; c 3. *Educ:* Pomona Col, BA, 50; Harvard Univ, MA, 52. *Prof Exp:* Park naturalist, Nat Park Serv, 57-66, res biologist, 66-81. *Mem:* Am Soc Plant Taxon; Am Bryol & Lichenological Soc; Sigma Xi. *Res:* Role of man in altering natural vegetation and fauna; restoration of natural biotic conditions and processes in national parks. *Mailing Add:* 490 Estado Way Novato CA 94945

BROWN, RICHARD MALCOLM, JR, BOTANY. *Current Pos:* AT DEPT BOT, UNIV TEX, AUSTIN, 82-, JOHNSON & JOHNSON CERTORRIAL CHAIR PLANT CELL BIOL, 82- *Personal Data:* b Pampa, Tex, Jan 2, 39; m 61; c 1. *Educ:* Univ Tex, BS, 61, PhD(bot), 64. *Honors & Awards:* Arselme Payen Award, Am Chem Soc; Darbaker Prize Phycol, Bot Soc Am. *Prof Exp:* Fel, Univ Hawaii & Univ Tex, 64-65; asst prof bot, Univ Tex, Austin, 65-68; assoc prof bot, Univ NC, Chapel Hill, 68-73, prof, 73-, dir, Electron Micros Lab, 70-82. *Concurrent Pos:* NSF fel, Univ Freiburg, 68-69 & res grant, 70-72. *Mem:* AAAS; Am Soc Cell Biol; Am Soc Plant Physiologists; Bot Soc Am. *Res:* Airborne algae; algal ecology; ultrastructure of algal viruses; algal ultrastructure; immunochemistry of algae; cytology; Golgi apparatus and cell wall formation; sexual reproduction amon algae; cellulose biogenesis. *Mailing Add:* Dept Bot Univ Tex Austin TX 78713-7640. *Fax:* 512-471-3573; *E-Mail:* rmbrown@cewf.cc.utexas.edu

BROWN, RICHARD MARTIN, CERAMIC ENGINEERING. *Current Pos:* MEM TECH STAFF, TEX INSTRUMENTS INC, 66- *Personal Data:* b Chicago, Ill, Oct 22, 37; m 60; c 3. *Educ:* Univ Ill, BS, 61, MS, 62, PhD(semiconductor glasses), 66. *Prof Exp:* Res asst ceramic eng, Univ Ill, 61-66. *Mem:* AAAS; Nat Inst Ceramic Engrs. *Res:* Ferroelectric materials; electro-optics; crystal growth. *Mailing Add:* 9612 Larchcrest Dallas TX 65238

BROWN, RICHARD MAURICE, COMPUTER SCIENCE. *Current Pos:* RETIRED. *Personal Data:* b Cambridge, Mass, May 17, 24; m 46, 62; c 4. *Educ:* Harvard Univ, AB, 44, MA, 47, PhD(physics), 50. *Prof Exp:* Asst, Oceanog Inst, Woods Hole, 44-46; asst prof physics, State Col Wash, 49-54; res prof physics & elec eng, Coord Sci Lab, Univ Ill, Urbana-Champaign, 55-67, emer prof physics & comp eng, 67. *Concurrent Pos:* Res asst prof, Control Syst Lab, Univ Ill, 52-54. *Mem:* Fel Am Phys Soc; Inst Elec & Electronics Engr; Asn Comput Mach. *Res:* Electronic computer design and use; scientific data acquisition systems design. *Mailing Add:* 101 W Windsor Urbana IL 61802

BROWN, ROBERT, SPINAL CORD INJURY, CHRONIC LUNG DISEASE. *Current Pos:* CHIEF PULMONARY MED, VET ADMIN MED CTR, WEST ROXBURY, MASS, 76- *Personal Data:* b Montreal, Que, Can, Dec 13, 41. *Educ:* McGill Univ, MDCM, 69. *Mem:* Am Thoracic Soc. *Mailing Add:* Dept Med Brockton W Roxbury Va Med Ctr 1400 VFW Pkwy West Roxbury MA 02132. *Fax:* 617-323-8786

BROWN, ROBERT A, CHEMICAL ENGINEERING. *Current Pos:* from asst prof to assoc prof, 79-84, Arthur Dehun Little prof, 86-92, dept head, 89-95, PROF CHEM ENG, MASS INST TECHNOL, 84-, WARREN K LEWIS PROF, 92-, DEAN ENG, 96- *Personal Data:* b San Antonio, Tex, July 22, 51; m 72, Beverly A Lamb; c Ryan & Keith. *Educ:* Univ Tex, BS, 73, MS, 75; Univ Minn, PhD(chem eng), 79. *Honors & Awards:* Allan P Colburn Lectr, Univ Del, 86; Allan P Colburn Award, Am Inst Chem Engrs, 86; Robert Vaughan Mem Lectr, Calif Inst Technol, 87; Stanley Corrsin Mem Lectr, Johns Hopkins Univ, 89; Ernest Thiele Lectr, Notre Dame Univ, 89; Merck Lectr, Rutgers Univ, 93; David Mason Lectr, Stanford Univ, 93; Stanley Katz Mem Lectr, City Col NY, 94; Donald L Katz Lectr, Univ Mich, 95; Richard Wilhelm Lectr, Princeton Univ, 95; Peter V Danckwerts Lectr, Inst Chem Engrs, London, 96. *Prof Exp:* Vis res assoc, Dept Comput Sci & Appl Math, Lawrence Berkeley Lab, 77; instr, Dept Chem Eng & Mat Sci, Univ Minn, 78. *Concurrent Pos:* DuPont young fac grant, 79-80; consult, Poloroid Corp, 80-82, AT&T Bell Labs, 82-84, Mobil Solar Energy Corp, 82-93, Sandia Nat Lab, 83, Hughes Res Corp, 84, Lincoln Labs, 85-87, Gen Elec, 88-90, Membrex, 90-91, Crystals Specialties Inc, 90-92, MEMC Corp, 92-, Nestec, 93-, Biosym Corp, 93-, Sematech Corp, 94-, Los Alamos Nat Lab, 95-; mem, Internal Opers Comt, Mat Processing Ctr, Mass Inst Technol, 84-88, vis comt, Dept Chem Eng, Univ Tex, 89-92, Space Sci Bd, Nat Res Coun, 89-92; exec officer, Dept Chem Eng, Mass Inst Technol, 86-88; co-dir, Mass Inst Technol Supercomput Fac, 89-94; mem, Task Force Environ Technol Defense Sci Bd, Dept Defense, 94-95; mem, Bd Chem Sci, Nat Res Coun, 95- *Mem:* Nat Acad Eng; Soc Indust & Appl Math; Am Asn Crystal Growth; Am Phys Soc; Soc Rheology; Coun Chem Res; Am Inst Chem Engrs; Am Acad Arts & Sci; Am Chem Soc. *Res:* Mathematical modelling of the fluid mechanics, heat and mass transfer and interfacial phenomena associated with melt and vapor phase crystal growth; polymer processing and coating deposition; fluid mechanics of viscoelastic fluids; numerical simulation of the flow of complex fluids; prediction and characterization of microscopic changes in interface morphology during directional solidification; efficient numerical solutions of transport problems, especially by flute element and special methods; numerical implementation of bifurcation analysis; solving free- and moving-boundary problems; laser-doppler velocimetry applied to slow flows of viscoelastic fluids and to solidification systems; experimental measurement of microscale morphologies in melt/solids interfaces during solidification; transport processes and control of growth of semiconductors from the melt and vapor, large-scale process simulations; formation of crystalline defects in crystals growth from the melt and vapor; constitutive modelling of defeat dynamics; author of about 215 publications. *Mailing Add:* Dept Chem Eng Mass Inst Technol Rm 66-342 Cambridge MA 02139. *E-Mail:* rab@mit.edu

BROWN, ROBERT ALAN, ATMOSPHERIC SCIENCE, GEOPHYSICS. *Current Pos:* res assoc boundary layer dynamics, 69-70, prin scientist boundary layer dynamics, Arctic Ice Dynamics Joint Exp, 71-77, PRIN INVESTR, RES SCIENTIST & PROF, DEPT ATMOSPHERIC SCI, UNIV WASH, 77- *Personal Data:* b Los Angeles, Calif, June 11, 34; m 57, Marcia Jobe; c Vanessa, Morgan & Tristin. *Educ:* Univ Calif, Berkeley, BS, 57, MS, 63; Univ Wash, PhD(geophys, atmospheric sci), 69. *Prof Exp:* Res engr fluid dynamics, Boeing Aircraft Co, Seattle, 64-66; advan study prog fel atmospheric fluid dynamics, Nat Ctr Atmospheric Res, 70-71. *Concurrent Pos:* Adj prof, Naval Postgrad Sch, 80; mem, Satellite Sensor Teams, NASA, numerous arctic experiment teams & Earth observing syst sci teams; vis res prof, Univ Concepcion, Chile, 96 & Polytech Inst, Univ Paris, 97. *Mem:* Fel Am Meteorol Soc; Am Geophys Union; Sigma Xi. *Res:* Planetary boundary layer modeling in connection with air-sea interaction; instabilities and secondary flows in the atmosphere and ocean; fluid mechanics of the atmosphere; climate dynamics; fluid mechanics of the atmosphere; author of texts, analytic planetary boundary layer modelling. *Mailing Add:* Dept Atmospheric Sci-AK-40 Univ Wash Seattle WA 98105. *E-Mail:* rabrown@atmos.washington.edu

BROWN, ROBERT ALAN, SCIENCE POLICY. *Current Pos:* ASTRONR, SPACE TELESCOPE SCI INST, 91-, HEAD, SPEC STUDIES OFF, 91- *Personal Data:* b Hanover, NH, Feb 8, 43; m; c 2. *Educ:* Princeton Univ, AB, 65; Harvard Univ, MA, 68, PhD(physics), 71. *Prof Exp:* Res fel, Harvard Univ, 71-75, res assoc earth & planetary physics, 75-79; res fel, Lunar & Planetary Lab, Univ Ariz, 79-82. *Concurrent Pos:* Proj scientist, Hubble Space Telescope, 83-85. *Mem:* Am Astron Soc; AAAS. *Res:* Observational studies of planetary atmospheres and environments; search for other planetary systems; planetary physics; science and exploration public policy. *Mailing Add:* Space Telescope Sci Inst Baltimore MD 21218. *E-Mail:* rbrown@stsci.edu

BROWN, ROBERT ALAN, OPERATIONS RESEARCH, INDUSTRIAL ENGINEERING. *Current Pos:* From assoc prof to prof indust eng, 67-90, chmn, Dept Indust & Systs Eng, 76-81 & 84-89, EMER PROF INDUST ENG, UNIV ALA, HUNTSVILLE, 90- *Personal Data:* b Columbus, Ohio, Sept 25, 27; m 52; c 4. *Educ:* US Naval Acad, BSc, 49; Ohio State Univ, MSc, 56, PhD(indust eng), 62. *Prof Exp:* From instr to asst prof indust eng, Ohio State Univ, 56-67. *Concurrent Pos:* Expert witness testimony. *Mem:* Inst Elec & Electronics Engrs; Sigma Xi. *Res:* Industrial and systems engineering; engineering management; engineering manpower planning; micro computer applications; applied statistics; quality and reliability engineering. *Mailing Add:* Dept Indust & Systs Eng Univ Ala Huntsville AL 35899. *E-Mail:* rbrown@iquest.com

BROWN, ROBERT BRUCE, MATHEMATICS, ACTUARIAL SCIENCE. *Current Pos:* assoc prof, 70-86, assoc dean, 87-90, PROF MATH, OHIO STATE UNIV, 86- *Personal Data:* b Portland, Ore, July 19, 38; m 62, Nancy A Gutfeld; c Tracy, Daniel & Stephanie. *Educ:* Harvard Univ, AB, 59; Univ Chicago, MS, 60, PhD(math), 64. *Prof Exp:* From instr to asst prof math, Univ Calif, Berkeley, 64-69; assoc prof, Univ Toronto, 69-70. *Concurrent Pos:* Asst actuary, Midland Mutual Life Ins, 77-78. *Mem:* Nat Coun Teachers Math; Am Math Soc; Assoc Soc Actuaries; Am Acad Actuaries. *Res:* Algebra, combinatorics and their applications; actuarial science. *Mailing Add:* Dept Math Ohio State Univ 231 W 18th Ave Columbus OH 43210-1101. *Fax:* 614-292-1479; *E-Mail:* rbbrown@math.mps.ohio_state.edu

BROWN, ROBERT CALVIN, PATHOLOGY, MEDICINE. *Current Pos:* assoc prof path, 69-74, res prof, 81-82, ADJ RES PROF DEPT PATH, SCH MED, UNIV NC, CHAPEL HILL, 88-; AT CAROLINA MED DIAG & RES LABS. *Personal Data:* b Iredell Co, NC, Jan 7, 33; m 56, Mary F Vaughn; c Anne, Cindy & Peter. *Educ:* Erskine Col, AB, 55; Univ NC, MD, 59. *Honors & Awards:* Seard-Sanford Award, Am Soc Clin Path, 59. *Prof Exp:* From intern to resident path, Sch Med, Univ NC & NC Mem Hosp, 59-64, instr, 62-64; head cellular path group, Biol Div, Oak Ridge Nat Lab, 66-69; dir, Dept Path, Rutherford Hosp, 71-81, Davis Hosp, 81-82, Lexington Mem Hosp, 82, Humana Hosp, Greensboro, 83-87. *Mem:* Am Soc Clin Path; AMA; Soc Exp Biol & Med. *Res:* Megakaryocyte structure; platelet aggregation; radiation and viral leukemogenesis; ultrastructural pathology; mammalian cytogenetics; nuclear sex chromatin; malacoplakia; viruscell interactions. *Mailing Add:* Carolina Med Diag & Res Labs P A PO Box 5686 Statesville NC 28687

BROWN, ROBERT DALE, ANIMAL NUTRITION, PHYSIOLOGY. *Current Pos:* DEPT HEAD, WILDLIFE & FISHERIES, TEX A&M UNIV, 93-; DIR, INST RENEWABLE NATURAL RESOURCES, 96- *Personal Data:* b Red Bluff, Calif, July 31, 45; m 68, 79; c 3. *Educ:* Colo State Univ, BS, 68; Pa State Univ, PhD(animal nutrit), 75. *Honors & Awards:* Outstanding Teacher Award, Tex Asn Col Teachers, 77. *Prof Exp:* Asst assoc prof animal nutrit, Tex A&I Univ, 75-81; res sci, Caesar Kleberg Wildlife Res Inst, 81-87; dept head, Miss State Univ, 87-93. *Concurrent Pos:* Dir, Forage Eval Lab, Tex A&I Univ, 75-; prin investr grants, Houston Livestock Show, 75-, Perry Found, 76-, Welder Wildlife Found, 77-, NIH, 77- & Ceaser Kleberg Wildlife Found, 78-; prog admin, Am Asn Fish & Wildlife, 87, SRAC-8 (Fish, Wildlife & Aqua) 88-; pres, Nat Asn Fish & Wildlife Prog, 95-97. *Mem:* Am Fisheries Soc; Wildlife Soc; Am Inst Nutrit; Soc Range Mgt. *Res:* Nutrition; endocrinology; environmental physiology of wild and domestic ruminant animals, bobwhite quail, deer, cattle, javalian & exotic animals; biomedical aspects of deer antler growth and human biomedical applications; osteoporosis. *Mailing Add:* Wildlife & Fisheries Dept Tex A&M 210 Nagle Hall College Station TX 77843-2258. *Fax:* 409-845-3786

BROWN, ROBERT DILLON, MATHEMATICS. *Current Pos:* from asst prof to assoc prof, 63-88, ASSOC CHAIR MATH, UNIV KANS, 79-, PROF MATH, 88- *Personal Data:* b Paris, Ark, Nov 26, 33; m 68; c 2. *Educ:* Univ Calif, Berkeley, AB, 55, PhD(math), 63. *Prof Exp:* Res mathematician, Univ Calif, Berkeley, 63. *Mem:* Am Math Soc; Math Asn Am. *Res:* Eigen value approximations; partial differential equations. *Mailing Add:* Dept Math Univ Kans Lawrence KS 66045-0001

BROWN, ROBERT DON, INDUSTRIAL HYGIENE. *Current Pos:* MEM STAFF, OFF ENVIRON ENG, LANGLEY RES CTR, NASA, 77- *Personal Data:* b Falls City, Nebr, May 30, 42; m 70; c 1. *Educ:* Northwest Mo State Univ, BS, 64; Univ Mich, MS, 69. *Prof Exp:* Health physicist, Kelsey-Seybold Clin, 69-72, from indust hygienist to sr indust hygienist, 72-77. *Mem:* Health Physics Soc; Am Indust Hyg Asn; Am Acad Indust Hyg. *Res:* Environmental factors that may pose significant health hazards, particularly noise, chemical agents and electromagnetic radiation. *Mailing Add:* 429 NASA Langley Res Ctr MS 429 Hampton VA 23681

BROWN, ROBERT EUGENE, PHYSICAL CHEMISTRY. *Current Pos:* CONSULT, 90- *Personal Data:* b Appleton City, Mo, July 7, 25. *Educ:* Univ Mo, AB, 49, PhD(phys chem), 57. *Prof Exp:* Res physicist, US Naval Ord Lab, 60-90. *Mem:* Inst Elec & Electronics Engrs. *Res:* Measurements of thermal accommodation coefficients on clean metal surfaces; rare earth magnetism; development of magnetic materials; applications of magnetic materials and superconductivity to devices. *Mailing Add:* 14 E Burnam Rd No A Columbia MO 65203

BROWN, ROBERT FREEMAN, FIXED POINT THEORY. *Current Pos:* From asst prof to assoc prof, 63-73, PROF MATH, UNIV CALIF, LOS ANGELES, 73- *Personal Data:* b Cambridge, Mass, Dec 13, 35; m 57, Brenda Webster; c Geoffrey & Matthew. *Educ:* Harvard Univ, AB, 57; Univ Wis, PhD(math), 63. *Mem:* Am Math Soc; Math Asn Am. *Mailing Add:* Dept Math Univ Calif Los Angeles CA 90024. *Fax:* 310-206-6673; *E-Mail:* rfb@math.ucla.edu

BROWN, ROBERT GEORGE, MICROBIAL BIOCHEMISTRY. *Current Pos:* from asst prof to assoc prof, 67-75, PROF BIOL, DALHOUSIE UNIV, 75- *Personal Data:* b Montreal, Que, Apr 7, 37; m 63; c 3. *Educ:* McGill Univ, BSc, 59, MSc, 61; Rutgers Univ, PhD(microbiol), 65. *Prof Exp:* Nat Res Coun Can overseas fel carbohydrate chem, Univ Stockholm, 65-67. *Concurrent Pos:* Killam sr fel, 73; vis, Univ Stockholm, 74; Unilever res, Eng, 80-81, Medicarb, Sweden, 87-88. *Mem:* Am Soc Microbiol; Can Soc Microbiol. *Res:* Structure and specificity of lectins from molluscs which bind to bacteria; catabolite repression in yeasts and fungi. *Mailing Add:* Dept Biol Sci Dalhousie Univ Halifax NS B3H 4H6 Can

BROWN, ROBERT GETMAN, INDUSTRIAL CHEMISTRY. *Current Pos:* RETIRED. *Personal Data:* b Gloversville, NY, Oct 25, 17; m 37; c 3. *Educ:* Cornell Univ, ChB, 39. *Prof Exp:* Chem microscopist, B F Goodrich Co, 39-44, chem purchasing agent, 44-46; chem salesman, EMERY Industs, 46-47; vpres, Perma Glaze Chem Corp, 47-53; asst to tech dir, Mohasco Industs, 53-57; vpres & tech dir, Perma Glaze Chem Corp, 57-69; pres, Knight Oil Corp & Wells Chem Co Inc, 69-84, treas & tech dir, 84-88. *Mem:* Am Chem Soc. *Res:* Chemical specialties development; emulsion cleaners; polishes; sanitizers; industrial degreasing compounds; chrome tanning compounds; aerosol technology. *Mailing Add:* 439 Lakeside Dr Mayfield NY 12117-9776

BROWN, ROBERT GLENN, NUTRITION, PHYSIOLOGY. *Current Pos:* head, Food Sci & Nutrit, 78-88, dir biotechnol, 88-93, PROF DEPT NUTRIT, UNIV MASS, AMHEARST, 78- *Personal Data:* b Norristown, Pa, Apr 16, 38; m 65, JoAnn Bond; c Alison S & Thomas G A. *Educ:* Drexel Inst, BSc, 60; Univ Tenn, Knoxville, PhD(nutrit & physiol), 64. *Honors & Awards:* Dr Francis S W Luken's Award, Del Valley Diabetes Asn, 69. *Prof Exp:* From asst prof to assoc prof nutrit, Drexel Inst, 64-69, actg chmn dept, 68-69; assoc prof animal sci, Univ Guelph, 69-74, prof, 74-78. *Mem:* AAAS; Am Chem Soc; Am Soc Animal Sci; Nutrit Soc Can; Am Inst Nutrit; hon mem Can Vet Med Asn. *Res:* Genetic disorders of trace mineral metabolism; collagen and connective tissue metabolism; nutrition & aging; nutrition of companion animals. *Mailing Add:* Vet & Animal Sci Rm 300 Stockbridge Hall Univ Mass Amherst MA 01003

BROWN, ROBERT GOODELL, OPERATIONS RESEARCH. *Current Pos:* consult, 71-75, PRES, MAT MGT SYSTS, INC, 75- *Personal Data:* b Evanston, Ill, Apr 14, 23; m 67, 88; c 3. *Educ:* Yale Univ, BE, 44, MA, 48. *Prof Exp:* Mem staff, Opers Eval Group, US Navy, 48-50; head dept opers res, Willow Run Res Ctr, Univ Mich, 50-53; mem staff, Arthur D Little, Inc, 53-67; vpres & exec dir opers serv, Curtiss-Wright Corp, 67-68; indust consult, Distrib Industs Mkt, Int Bus Mach Corp, 68-71. *Concurrent Pos:* Vis lectr, Amos Tuck Sch Bus Admin, 64; vis prof opers res, math & prod mgt, Yale, Northeastern, Dartmouth, Boston & Lehigh Univs. *Mem:* Int Fedn Opers Res Soc (treas, 62-65); Opers Res Soc Am; Am Soc Mech Engr; Am Math Soc; fel Am Prod Inventory Control Soc. *Res:* Statistical forecasting in discrete, nonstationary, time-series, inventory control, production planning and control systems; development, implementation, evaluation and education; author of 200 works on statistical forecasting and scientific inventory management. *Mailing Add:* PO Box 239 Thetford Center VT 05075-0239

BROWN, ROBERT GRIFFITH, CHEMICAL ENGINEERING. *Current Pos:* mgr res, 75-79, dir res, 79-87, VPRES RES & DEVELOP, DIXIE CHEM CO, 87- *Personal Data:* b Binghamton, NY, Apr 29, 41; m 80, Sharon K Myrick; c Griffith L. *Educ:* Charkson Univ, BCE, 64, PhD(chem), 72. *Prof Exp:* Res chemist, FMC Corp, Baltimore, 69-72, sr res chemist, Princeton, NJ, 72-75. *Mem:* Sigma Xi. *Res:* Development of high efficiency esterification process for esters of low boiling alcohols, of high yield and purity process for manufacture of guanamines, of process for instantaneous material balancing of gas phase process via on-line mass spectrometry and of process for production of ultra high purity nitriles; process technology for heat sensitive chemicals. *Mailing Add:* Dixie Chem Co Inc 10701 Bay Area Blvd Pasadena TX 77507

BROWN, ROBERT GROVER, AEROSPACE ENGINEERING. *Current Pos:* Instr, Iowa State Col, Ames, 48-51 & 53-55, from asst prof to prof, 55-76, distinguished prof, 76-88, EMER DISTINGUISHED PROF, IOWA STATE COL, 88- *Personal Data:* b Shenandoah, Iowa, Apr 25, 26. *Educ:* Iowa State Col, BS, 48, MS, 51, PhD, 56. *Honors & Awards:* Burka Award, Inst Navig, 78 & 84. *Concurrent Pos:* Res engr, NAm Aviation, 51-53; consult var aerospace eng cos, 56- *Mem:* Fel Inst Elec & Electronics Engrs; Inst Navig. *Res:* Lines, waves and antennas; linear systems analysis; random signals and applied Kalman filtering. *Mailing Add:* Iowa State Univ Ames IA 50011

BROWN, ROBERT HARRISON, VERTEBRATE ZOOLOGY. *Current Pos:* ASSOC PROF ZOOL, CENT WASH UNIV, 67-, CHMN DEPT, 77- *Personal Data:* b Edinburg, Tex, Feb 22, 38; m 60; c 2. *Educ:* Univ Ariz, BS, 60, MS, 62, PhD(zool), 65. *Prof Exp:* Asst prof zool, Univ Idaho, 65-67. *Mem:* Am Soc Zool. *Res:* Comparative osteology and myology of lizards and rodents. *Mailing Add:* 241 Naneum Rd Ellensburg WA 98926

BROWN, ROBERT JAMES SIDFORD, PHYSICS OF POROUS MEDIA. *Current Pos:* RETIRED. *Personal Data:* b Lawndale, Calif, Sept 7, 24; m 50, 61, 93, Margaret Steeper; c Erick, Dirk, Eleanor, Sidford & Kurt. *Educ:* Calif Inst Technol, BS, 48; Univ Minn, MS, 51, PhD(physics), 53. *Honors & Awards:* Well Logging Award, Soc Petrol Eng, 94. *Prof Exp:* Electronic technician & asst, Los Alamos Sci Lab, 44-46; asst, Univ Minn, 48-53; sr res assoc physics, Chevron Oil Field Res Co, Stand Oil Co Calif, 53-86. *Concurrent Pos:* Res consult, Univ Bologna, Italy. *Mem:* Am Phys Soc; Soc Magnetic Resonance Med; Am Geophys Union; Int Soc Magnetic Resonance; Soc Petrol Eng; Soc Prof Well Log Analysts. *Res:* Application of nuclear magnetic relaxation phenomena to study of liquids and their interactions with solid surfaces in porous media; application of electromagnetic and seismic techniques to oil exploration; study of elastic properties of porous materials. *Mailing Add:* 515 W 11th St Claremont CA 91711-3721

BROWN, ROBERT LEE, bacterial physiology, biochemistry, for more information see previous edition

BROWN, ROBERT LEE, surgery, for more information see previous edition

BROWN, ROBERT LEE, INDUSTRIAL & MANUFACTURING ENGINEERING. *Current Pos:* dir advan process res & develop, 69-92, DIR EXTERNAL TECHNOL, GILLETTE CO, 93- *Personal Data:* b Detroit, Mich, Aug 4, 36; m 59; c 4. *Educ:* Mich Col Mining & Technol, BS, 58; Mass Inst Technol, SM, 61; Mass Inst Technol, ScD, 64; Boston Univ, MBA, 73. *Prof Exp:* Mgr process res, Vasco Metals, 64-67; eng mgr, Tex Instruments, 67-69. *Mem:* Am Soc Metals; Am Inst Mining & Metall Eng; Am Soc Mfg Eng; Sigma Xi. *Res:* Manufacturing development as related to the design of advanced instrumentation, equipment and manufacturing processes for high volume production. *Mailing Add:* Gillette Co Prudential Tower Bldg Boston MA 02199. *Fax:* 617-421-8484; *E-Mail:* robert_brown@gillette.com

BROWN, ROBERT MELBOURNE, ENVIRONMENTAL ISOTOPE CHEMISTRY. *Current Pos:* ASSOC RES OFFICER, ENVIRON RES BR, ATOMIC ENERGY CAN LTD, 73- *Personal Data:* b Richmond, Que, Sept 14, 24; wid; c 3. *Educ:* Bishop's Univ, Can, BSc, 44; McGill Univ, BSc, 47, PhD(phys chem), 51. *Prof Exp:* Jr res officer, Atomic Energy Can Ltd, 51-52; sci officer, Defence Res Bd, 52-62; assoc res officer, Environ Res Br, Atomic Energy Can Ltd, 62-70; sci officer, Sect Isotope Hydrol, Int Atomic Energy Agency, Vienna, 70-73; adj prof, Dept Earth Sci, Univ Waterloo, 77-87. *Concurrent Pos:* Mem, Sub-Comt Low Level Radioactiv in Mat, Int Comn Radiol Units & MeasuremenTs, 60-62. *Mem:* Sr mem Chem Inst Can; Can Nuclear Soc. *Res:* Low level radiochemistry, including early development of low background B counters; measurement of tritium and deuterium in natural waters and their use as hydrological and meteorological tracers; carbon-14 dating by accelerator mass spectrometry. *Mailing Add:* Atomic Energy Can Ltd Chalk River ON K0J 1J0 Can. *Fax:* 613-584-1221

BROWN, ROBERT ORDWAY, chemical engineering, for more information see previous edition

BROWN, ROBERT RAYMOND, ORGANIC CHEMISTRY, POLYMER CHEMISTRY. *Current Pos:* RETIRED. *Personal Data:* b Akron, Ohio, June 30, 22; m 50. *Educ:* Univ Akron, BS, 47, MS, 50; Ohio State Univ, PhD(org chem), 55. *Prof Exp:* Chemist, Firestone Tire & Rubber Co, Ohio, 47-50; sr res chemist, Int Latex Corp, 55-57, mgr polymerization res, 57-59, mgr polymer res, 59-65, dir res, Standard Brands Chem Industs, Inc, 65-72, dir res & develop, 72-75; dir res & develop, Reichold Chem, Inc, 76-84, dir technol, Emulsion Polymers Div, 84-88. *Mem:* Am Chem Soc. *Res:* Polymer research, especially elastomers for both latex and dry polymer applications. *Mailing Add:* 1300S Farmview Dr Apt B-17 Dover DE 19901-3300

BROWN, ROBERT REGINALD, PHYSICS. *Current Pos:* lectr, Univ Calif, Berkeley, 57-58, from asst prof to assoc prof, 58-65, prof, 65- EMER PROF PHYSICS, UNIV CALIF, BERKELEY. *Personal Data:* b Alameda, Calif, Apr 4, 23; m 48; c 3. *Educ:* Univ Calif, Berkeley, AB, 44, PhD(physics), 52. *Prof Exp:* Instr physics, Princeton Univ, 52-53; asst prof, Univ NMex, 53-56; asst prog dir, NSF, 56-57. *Concurrent Pos:* Guggenheim fel & Fulbright scholar, 63-64. *Mem:* Am Geophys Union. *Res:* Cosmic ray time variations; auroral and ionospheric physics; geomagnetism. *Mailing Add:* 504 Channel View Dr Anacortes WA 98221

BROWN, ROBERT STANLEY, PHYSICAL ORGANIC CHEMISTRY. *Current Pos:* from asst prof to assoc prof, 74-84, PROF CHEM, UNIV ALTA, 84- *Personal Data:* b High River, Alta, Can, Sept 16, 46; m 68, Donna C Dubeta; c Carlyn N & Trevor S. *Educ:* Univ Alta, BSc, 68; Univ Calif, San Diego, MSc, 70, PhD(chem), 72. *Honors & Awards:* Syntex Award, Can Soc Chem, 91. *Prof Exp:* Nat Res Coun Can fel, Columbia Univ, 72-74. *Mem:* Can Soc Chem; Am Chem Soc. *Res:* Amide hydrolysis mechanistic studies; model enzyme studies; electrophilic halogenation. *Mailing Add:* Dept Chem Queens Univ Kingston ON K7L 3N6 Can. *Fax:* 403-492-8231; *E-Mail:* userrbrn@mts.ucs.ualberta.ca

BROWN, ROBERT STEPHEN, INTERNAL MEDICINE, NEPHROLOGY. *Current Pos:* asst prof internal med, 72-80, ASSOC PROF MED, HARVARD MED SCH, 80- *Personal Data:* b New York, NY, May 21, 38; m 60, Judith Kaufman; c Robert Jr & Debra. *Educ:* Harvard Univ, AB, 59; Columbia Univ, MD, 63. *Prof Exp:* Intern & asst resident internal med,

Bellevue Hosp, NY, 63-65; clin assoc med, Nat Cancer Inst, 65-67; sr asst resident internal med, Yale-New Haven Hosp, 67-68; fel renal med, Med Sch, Yale Univ, 68-69, asst prof, 69-72. *Concurrent Pos:* Med dir, Kidney Transplantation & Dialysis Serv, Yale-New Haven Hosp, 69-72 & Boston City Hosp, 72-73; clin chief renal unit, Beth Israel Hosp, Boston, 73- *Mem:* Am Fedn Clin Res; Am Soc Nephrology; fel Am Col Physicians; Int Soc Nephrology; Am Soc Transplant Physicians; Nat Kidney Found. *Res:* Potassium metabolismin renal disease; metabolic aspects of nephrolithiasis; hereditary renal cancer. *Mailing Add:* Renal Unit Beth Israel Deaconess Med Ctr Boston MA 02215. *Fax:* 617-667-5276; *E-Mail:* rbrown@bidmc.harvard.edu

BROWN, ROBERT THEODORE, PHYSICS. *Current Pos:* GROUP LEADER, LOCKHEED ADVAN DEVELOP CO, 89- *Personal Data:* b Bay City, Mich, Feb 16, 31; m 56, Arlene Schnier; c James, Daniel, Teresa & Christopher. *Educ:* Univ Calif, Riverside, BA, 58; Univ Mich, MS, 59, PhD(physics), 65. *Prof Exp:* Instr physics, Univ Mich, 65-66; asst prof space sci, Rice Univ, 66-68; sci specialist, EG & G, Inc, 68-72; staff mem, Los Alamos Sci Lab, 72-81; sr scientist, Damaskos, Inc, 81-82; sr staff scientist, Grumman Corp Res Ctr, 82-89. *Concurrent Pos:* Res Corp Cottrell grant, 67-68. *Mem:* Inst Elec & Electronics Engrs; Am Phys Soc; Am Astron Soc; Appl Comput Electromagnetics Soc. *Res:* Computational physics; atomic structure and spectra; x-ray scattering; Monte Carlo charged particle and photon transport; electromagnetic scattering and diffraction. *Mailing Add:* 25838 Vaquero Ct Valencia CA 91355

BROWN, ROBERT THORSON, PLANT ECOLOGY. *Current Pos:* RETIRED. *Personal Data:* b Rochester, Minn, Sept 29, 23; m 53, Viola Jarrenpaa; c Linda, Cynthia, Lisa & Erik. *Educ:* Univ Wis, BS, 47 & 48, MS, 49, PhD(bot), 51. *Honors & Awards:* Medal of Finnish Forestry Asn, 79; Fulbright lectr, Univ Adana, Turkey, 80-81. *Prof Exp:* Assoc prof, Mich Technol Univ, 51-62, prof biol sci, 62-88. *Concurrent Pos:* Radiation biologist, Argonne Nat Lab, 66 & USAID, India, 68; Fulbright res fel, Univ Helsinki, 71-72; lectr, Soviet Acad Sci, 72, Sigma Xi lectr, 75; Fulbright res fel, Univ West Indies, St Augustine, Trinidad, 86-87; prof, Tianjin Inst Technol, Tianjin, China, 92-93. *Mem:* Fel AAAS; Am Inst Biol Sci; Ecol Soc Am; Sigma Xi; Nat Environ Educ Asn. *Res:* Air pollution; plant growth control; seed germination; northern forest ecology; radiation biology; exogenous growth substances; mycorrhizae on conifers; allelopathy; tropical ecology. *Mailing Add:* 500 Garnet St Houghton MI 49931

BROWN, ROBERT WADE, CLAY STABILIZATION, FOUNDATION REPAIR. *Current Pos:* PRES & OWNER, ROBERT WADE BROWN & ASSOCS, 70- *Personal Data:* b Dallas, Tex, June 2, 33; m 54, Mozelle Rawson; c Robert L, Cindy R, Cathy G & Candy J. *Educ:* NTex State Univ, BA & MS, 55. *Prof Exp:* Process analyst, Temco Aircraft, 55-56; mgr, Indust Res Div, Western Co, 56-63; instr math, Odessa Jr Col, 58-59; instr, API Sch Petrol Technol, 56-63; pres & chmn bd, BPR Construct & Eng, Inc, 64-70. *Concurrent Pos:* Pres & chmn bd, Webb Properties, Inc, 68-96, Brown Found Repair & Consult, Inc, 73-, Brown Oil Prod, 78- & Soil Sta, Inc, 85-; secy & treas, ECI Serv, Inc, 83-95. *Mem:* Am Soc Civil Engrs; Soc Petrol Engrs. *Res:* Clay stabilization via base exchange chemistry; structural distress relative to differential soil movement; author of over 50 technical publications and six books. *Mailing Add:* Brown Consol Inc 2614 B Industrial Lane Garland TX 75041. *Fax:* 972-840-0153

BROWN, ROBERT WAYNE, INTERNAL MEDICINE. *Current Pos:* RETIRED. *Personal Data:* b Atwood, Kans, June 27, 23; m 45; c 2. *Educ:* Univ Colo, BA, 49; Univ Kans, MD, 55. *Prof Exp:* From asst prof to prof med, Univ Kans, 60-90; dir, Salina Health Educ Found, 77-90. *Concurrent Pos:* Coordr, Kans Regional Med Prog, 69-77; mem staff, Asbury & St Johns Hosps, Salina. *Mem:* Am Fedn Clin Res; Am Col Physicians; AMA. *Res:* Endocrinology and metabolism; diabetes. *Mailing Add:* 910 Marymount Rd Salina KS 67401

BROWN, ROBERT WILLIAM, PHYSICS. *Current Pos:* from asst prof to assoc prof, 70-81, PROF PHYSICS, CASE WESTERN RESERVE UNIV, 81-, INST PROF, 91- *Personal Data:* b St Paul, Minn, Oct 3, 41. *Educ:* Univ Minn, BS, 63; Mass Inst Technol, PhD(physics), 68. *Prof Exp:* Res assoc physics, Brookhaven Nat Lab, 68-70. *Mem:* Am Phys Soc; Soc Mag Res. *Res:* High energy physics; electromagnetism; medical physics; science education. *Mailing Add:* Dept Physics Case Western Reserve Univ Cleveland OH 44106

BROWN, ROBERT ZANES, ecology, animal behavior, for more information see previous edition

BROWN, RODGER ALAN, METEOROLOGY, CONVECTIVE STORMS. *Current Pos:* RES METEOROLOGIST, NAT SEVERE STORMS LAB, 70- *Personal Data:* b Ellicottville, NY, Mar 24, 37; m 59, Diane McLeod; c Christopher, Elizabeth & Katherine. *Educ:* Antioch Col, BS, 60; Univ Chicago, MS, 62; Univ Okla, PhD, 89. *Honors & Awards:* Antarctic Serv Medal, 65. *Prof Exp:* Res meteorologist, Univ Chicago, 60-65; assoc meteorologist, Cornell Aeronaut Lab, Inc, NY, 65-68, res meteorologist, 68-70; res meteorologist, Wave Propagation Lab, Environ Sci Serv Admin, Colo, 70. *Concurrent Pos:* Chmn, Comt Severe Local Storms, Am Meteorol Soc, 80-82; comnr comts, Nat Weather Asn, 97- *Mem:* Am Meteorol Soc; Am Geophys Union; Royal Meteorol Soc; Sigma Xi; Nat Weather Asn (secy, 94, vpres, 96). *Res:* Thunderstorm kinematics and dynamics; mesometeorology; Doppler weather radar. *Mailing Add:* Nat Severe Storms Lab 1313 Halley Circle Norman OK 73069. *E-Mail:* brown@nssl.uoknor.edu

BROWN, RODNEY DUVALL, III, SOLID STATE PHYSICS, BIOPHYSICS. *Current Pos:* PRES, FIELD CYCLING SYSTEMS INC, 93- *Personal Data:* b Carbondale, Pa, Aug 28, 31; m 50; c 7. *Educ:* Univ Scranton, BS, 54; Columbia Univ, MA, 61; NY Univ, PhD(physics), 69. *Prof Exp:* Assoc engr xerography, IBM Develop Lab, 54-57, staff mem ferroelec, IBM Watson Lab, 57, staff mem hot electrons in germanium, 57-63, staff mem quantum effects in bismuth, 63-65, staff mem automated cytol, 65-67, mem interdiv comt med electronics, 66-70, staff mem quantum effects in bismuth, 67-68, mgr mach develop, 68-70, res staff mem, T J Watson Res Ctr, 70-93. *Mem:* Am Phys Soc; NY Acad Sci. *Res:* NMRD investigation of metal and sugar binding properties of concanavalin A; nuclear magnetic relaxation in protein solutions. *Mailing Add:* PO Box 233 River Edge NJ 07661

BROWN, ROGER E, ANATOMY, SURGERY. *Current Pos:* assoc vet med & surg & dir educ resources, 69-70, prof vet med & surg & chmn dept, 70-80, prof & interim chmn Dept Vet Anat & Physiol, 80-82, EMER PROF, UNIV MO, COLUMBIA, 82- *Personal Data:* b Marcellus, Mich, Feb 20, 20; m 63; c 3. *Educ:* Mich State Univ, DVM, 50, MS, 60; Purdue Univ, PhD(anat), 64. *Prof Exp:* Instr surg, Mich State Univ, 50-53, instr anat, 60-62; pvt pract, 53-60; instr anat, Purdue Univ, 62-63; asst prof, Mich State Univ, 64-66, assoc prof anat & asst dir space utilization, 66-69. *Res:* Microcirculation of the myocardium. *Mailing Add:* 10184 Elk Lake Trail Williamsburg MI 49690

BROWN, RONALD ALAN, THEORETICAL PHYSICS, SOLID STATE PHYSICS. *Current Pos:* ASSOC PROF PHYSICS, STATE UNIV NY COL OSWEGO, 71- *Personal Data:* b Cleveland, Ohio June 19, 36; m 63; c 3. *Educ:* Drexel Inst, BS, 59; Purdue Univ, MS, 61, PhD(physics), 64. *Prof Exp:* Asst prof metall & Ford Found fel eng, Mass Inst Technol, 64-67; asst prof physics, Kent State Univ, 67-71. *Mem:* Am Phys Soc; Am Asn Physics Teachers; Sigma Xi; Nat Sci Teachers Asn; Soc Com Seed Technologists. *Res:* Recombination phenomena in semiconductors; electron-donor recombination in n-type germanium and silicon; history and philosophy of physics; physics and art; science teaching in the elementary and secondary grades; development of physics teaching materials. *Mailing Add:* Dept Physics State Univ NY Oswego NY 13126

BROWN, RONALD FRANKLIN, SOLID STATE PHYSICS. *Current Pos:* PROF PHYSICS, CALIF POLYTECH STATE UNIV, 74- *Personal Data:* b San Diego, Calif, May 22, 40; m 68, Leslie Loeb; c Justin Matthew. *Educ:* Univ Calif, Riverside, BA, 62, MA, 64, PhD(physics), 68. *Honors & Awards:* Distinguished Teaching Award. *Prof Exp:* Teaching fel physics, Harvey Mudd Col, 68-69, asst prof, 69-74. *Concurrent Pos:* Referee, Am J Physics, 75. *Mem:* Am Phys Soc; Am Asn Physics Teachers. *Res:* Low temperature solid state physics; properties of magnetic insulators; electron transport in semiconductors; superconductivity. *Mailing Add:* Dept Physics Calif Polytech State Univ San Luis Obispo CA 93407-0001. *E-Mail:* rfbrown@calpoly.edu

BROWN, RONALD HAROLD, AGRONOMY, PLANT PHYSIOLOGY. *Current Pos:* assoc prof, 68-71, PROF AGRON, UNIV GA, 72- *Personal Data:* b Dudley, Ga, July 25, 35; m 57; c 4. *Educ:* Univ Ga, BS, 57, MS, 59; Va Polytech Inst, PhD(agron), 62. *Prof Exp:* Asst prof agron, Va Polytech Inst, 61-67; assoc prof, Tex A&M Univ, 67-68. *Mem:* Am Soc Agron; Crop Sci Soc Am; Am Soc Plant Physiologists. *Res:* Physiology and microclimatology as related to growth of forage crops. *Mailing Add:* 170 Broomsedge Trl Athens GA 30605

BROWN, ROSS DUNCAN, JR, BIOCHEMISTRY. *Current Pos:* ASSOC PROF, DEPT FOOD SCI, UNIV FLA, 80- *Personal Data:* b Fairmont, WVa, July 21, 35; m 58, 82; c 4. *Educ:* WVa Univ, BS, 57; Univ Wis-Madison, MS, 65, PhD(biochem), 68. *Prof Exp:* Staff chemist, Bjorksten Res Lab, Wis, 60-62; asst prof, Va Polytech Inst & State Univ, 67-80, assoc prof biochem, 80. *Mem:* AAAS; Am Chem Soc; Inst Food Technol; Sigma Xi; Am Soc Microbiol; Soc Complex Carbohydrates. *Res:* Microbial biochemistry; cellulose degradation; mode of action of cellulases; glycoprotein structures and biosynthesis. *Mailing Add:* PO Box 12031 Univ Fla Gainesville FL 32604

BROWN, RUSSELL VEDDER, genetics, immunology, for more information see previous edition

BROWN, SAMUEL HEFFNER, physics, physical chemistry, for more information see previous edition

BROWN, SANDRA, TROPICAL FORESTS, WETLANDS. *Current Pos:* asst prof, 80-86, ASSOC PROF FORESTRY, UNIV ILL, 86- *Personal Data:* b London, Eng, Oct 3, 44; US citizen. *Educ:* Univ Nottingham, Eng, BSc, 66; Univ S Fla, MS, 73; Univ Fla, PhD(environ eng sci, ecol), 78. *Prof Exp:* Teacher sci, Christopher Wren Sch, Eng, 67-68, Pinellas Co Sch Bd, 70-74; res asst environ eng sci, Univ Fla, 74-78, res assoc, Univ Fla & Univ Ill, 78-80. *Concurrent Pos:* Mem staff, President's Coun Environ Qual, 79; co-prin investr, Trop Forests & Global Carbon Cycle, US Dept Energy, 81-90; mem comt, Role Alt Farming Methods, Bd Agr, Nat Res Coun, 85-88; mem, US Man & Biosphere Directorate Trop Ecosysts. *Mem:* Ecol Soc Am; Soc Am Foresters; Int Soc Trop Foresters; Asn Trop Biologists; Soc Wetland Scientists; Sigma Xi. *Res:* Understanding how environmental factors regulate the organic matter dynamics of tropical and wetland forests; role of tropical forests in potential climate change; tropical forest restoration. *Mailing Add:* 200 SW 35th St Corvallis OR 97333

BROWN, SEWARD RALPH, GEOCHEMISTRY, ECOLOGY. *Current Pos:* dir, Biol Sta, 59-74, from asst prof to prof, 59-84, EMER PROF BIOL, QUEEN'S UNIV, ONT, 84- *Personal Data:* b Glace Bay, NS, Mar 25, 18; m 52; c 4. *Educ:* Queen's Univ, Ont, BA, 50 & 51, MA, 52; Yale Univ, PhD(biogeochem), 62. *Prof Exp:* Lectr zool, Yale Univ, 56-58. *Mem:* Am Soc Limnol & Oceanog; Geochem Soc; Can Soc Zoologists. *Res:* Biogeochemistry; primary productivity of lakes, particularly the relationship between photosynthetic rates and absolute quantities of chlorophylls, carotenoids and their diagenetic derivatives; paleolimnology, using plant pigments from lake sediments as biochemical fossils. *Mailing Add:* PO Box 167 Sydenham ON K0H 2T0 Can

BROWN, SHELDON (JACK), PHYSICS. *Current Pos:* from asst prof to assoc prof, 56-65, PROF PHYSICS, CALIF STATE UNIV, FRESNO, 65- *Personal Data:* b Los Angeles, Calif, Oct 13, 15; wid; c 2. *Educ:* Univ Calif, Los Angeles, AB, 39, PhD(physics), 51. *Prof Exp:* Res fel, Univ Strasbourg, 52-54; asst prof physics, DePaul Univ, 54-56. *Concurrent Pos:* Guggenheim fel, 62. *Mem:* Am Phys Soc; Am Asn Physics Teachers. *Res:* Electron inertia effects; gyromagnetism; gravitation; elementary particle physics; superconductivity. *Mailing Add:* Physics Calif State Univ 808 E Fairmont Ave Fresno CA 93740-3109

BROWN, SHERMAN DANIEL, CHEMICAL ENGINEERING, MATERIALS SCIENCE. *Current Pos:* assoc prof, 68-71, prof ceramic eng, 71-87, PROF MAT SCI & ENG, UNIV ILL, URBANA-CHAMPAIGN, 87- *Personal Data:* b Salt Lake City, Utah, Sept 10, 29; m 53; c 5. *Educ:* Univ Utah, BS, 50, PhD(chem eng), 57. *Prof Exp:* Sr res engr high temperature chem, Jet Propulsion Lab, Calif Inst Technol, 57-59; head appl physics sect, Utah Div, Thiokol Chem Corp, 59-60; asst prof ceramic sci, Univ Utah, 60-64; prin scientist ceramic res, Rocketdyne Div, NAm Aviation, Inc, 64-68. *Mem:* Fel Am Ceramic Soc; Nat Inst Ceramic Engrs; Ceramic Educ Coun; Am Soc Metals; Electrochem Soc. *Res:* Glass structure; ceramic-to-metal adhesion; high-temperature reaction rates in ceramic systems; brittle fracture; wear-resistant ceramic coatings. *Mailing Add:* Dept Mat Sci & Eng Univ Ill 1304 W Green Urbana IL 61801-2920

BROWN, STANLEY ALFRED, BIOMATERIALS. *Current Pos:* ASSOC PROF BIOMED ENG, DEPT BIOMED ENG, CASE WESTERN RES UNIV. *Personal Data:* b Boston, Mass, Oct 9, 43; m 70. *Educ:* Mass Inst Technol, BS, 65; Dartmouth Col, DEng, 71. *Prof Exp:* Fel physiol, 70-72, res assoc, 72-74, asst prof surg, 74-80, assoc prof surg, Dartmouth Med Sch, 80, asst prof eng, Dartmouth Col, 78-80, assoc prof, 80; assoc prof bioeng & orthop & dir orthop res, Univ Calif, Davis, 80-, assoc prof eng, 81- *Concurrent Pos:* Assoc staff, Mary Hitchcock Mem Hosp, 72-; adj asst prof eng, Dartmouth Col, 73-; res fel, Airlift Serv Indust Fund & Inst Straumann, 78. *Mem:* Asn Advan Med Instrumentation; Am Soc Artificial Internal Organs; Inst Elec & Electronics Engrs; Biomat Soc; Orthop Res Soc. *Res:* Biocompatibility of surgical implant materials; implant site infections; fracture healing, materials for fracture fixation and methods of assessment of healing; metal allergy and implants; ultrasonics; orthopaedic materials. *Mailing Add:* 4192 Giles Rd Moreland Hills OH 44022

BROWN, STANLEY GORDON, SCIENTIFIC EDITING, MANAGEMENT. *Current Pos:* from asst ed to ed, Phys Rev D, 74-92, ED, PHYS REV LETT, AM PHYS SOC, 85-, ADMIN ED, 92- *Personal Data:* b Washington, DC, May 17, 39; m 70, Margaret Haapala; c Tracy (Lioruh) & Ethan (Spencer). *Educ:* Harvard Univ, AB, 60; Univ Pa, MS, 63, PhD(physics), 66. *Prof Exp:* Instr & res assoc physics, Cornell Univ, 66-68; res assoc, Mass Inst Technol, 68-70; adj asst prof, Univ Calif, Los Angeles, 70-72; res assoc, State Univ NY, Stony Brook, 72-74. *Concurrent Pos:* Ed, Phys Rev Abstr, 81-85; chmn, Am Inst Physics Publ Bd, 82-84. *Mem:* Am Phys Soc. *Mailing Add:* Am Phys Soc One Research Rd PO Box 9000 Ridge NY 11961. *Fax:* 516-591-4141; *E-Mail:* prl@aps.org

BROWN, STANLEY MONTY, PETROLEUM & SURFACE CHEMISTRY, CATALYSIS. *Current Pos:* group leader, Minerals & Chem Div, Engelhard Minerals & Chem Corp, 75-77, res mgr, 78-80, res dir, 80-94, VPRES RES & DEVELOP, PETROL CAT GROUP, ENGELHARD CORP, 94- *Personal Data:* b New York, NY, Apr 2, 43; m 71, Pamela Barsam; c Karma B & Tiana B. *Educ:* Queens Col, NY, BA, 64; Northwestern Univ, PhD(org chem), 69. *Prof Exp:* Res chemist, Davison Chem Div, W R Grace & Co, Md, 69-73, res supvr, 73-74, res assoc, 74-75. *Mem:* Am Chem Soc; Catalysis Soc; Sigma Xi; Soc Automotive Eng; AAAS. *Res:* Catalytic chemistry; organic reaction mechanisms; preparation, characterization and evaluation of heterogeneous catalysts and catalyst supports for industrial processes including fluid cracking, hydrotreating, hydrogenation, isomerization and polymerization; autocatalysts, nox abatement. *Mailing Add:* 1424 Sylvan Lane Scotch Plains NJ 07076

BROWN, STEPHEN CLAWSON, COMPARATIVE ENDOCRINOLOGY, INVERTEBRATE BIOMECHANICS. *Current Pos:* From asst prof to prof biol, 67-86, DISTINGUISHED TEACHING, PROF, STATE UNIV NY, ALBANY, 86- *Personal Data:* b Caracas, Venezuela, June 16, 41; m 65, Patricia Stocking; c Eric & Teresa. *Educ:* George Washington Univ, BS, 63; Univ Mich, MS, 64, PhD(zool), 66. *Mem:* AAAS; Am Physiol Soc; Am Soc Zoologists; Endocrine Soc. *Res:* Hormonal control of hydromineral balance in lower vertebrates; feeding and locomotion in marine annelids. *Mailing Add:* Dept Biol Sci State Univ NY 1400 Washington Ave Albany NY 12222. *Fax:* 518-442-4767

BROWN, STEPHEN L(AWRENCE), RISK ASSESSMENT, RISK MANAGEMENT. *Current Pos:* DIR, RISKS RADIATION & CHEM COMPOUNDS RZCZ, 93- *Personal Data:* b San Francisco, Calif, Feb 16, 37; m 61, Ann Goldsberry; c Lisa, Travis & Meredith. *Educ:* Stanford Univ, BS, 58, MS, 61; Purdue Univ, PhD(physics), 63. *Prof Exp:* Assoc exec dir, Nat Res Coun Comn Life Sci, 83-86; proj mgr, Environ Corp, 86-90, prin, 91; mgr risk assessment & toxicol, ENSR Consult & Eng, 92-93; physicist, SRI Int, 63-68, sr opers analyst systs planning, 68-74, prog mgr, 74-76, asst dept dir, 76-77, dept dir, 77-83. *Concurrent Pos:* Mem, Comt Priority Mechanisms, Nat Res Coun,Comt asbestiform fibers; mem, Sci Adv Bd, Environ Protection Agency, 91- *Mem:* AAAS; Soc Risk Analysis; Int Soc Exposure Assessment. *Res:* Chemical risk assessment; radiation risk assessment. *Mailing Add:* 4700 Grass Valley Rd Oakland CA 94605-5622. *E-Mail:* slbrown@diou.com

BROWN, STEVEN MICHAEL, ARCHITECTURAL ACOUSTICS, NOISE CONTROL ENGINEERING. *Current Pos:* sr res eng, 86-89, prin eng, 89-94, SR PRIN ENG, STEELCASE, INC, 94- *Personal Data:* b New York, NY, Dec 3, 44; m 69, Carol L Swanson; c Alycia & Daniel. *Educ:* Johns Hopkins Univ, BA, 66, MA, 69, PhD(physics, math), 72. *Honors & Awards:* Wallace Waterfall Award, Am Soc Testing & Mat. *Prof Exp:* Physicist plasma physics, US Naval Res Lab, 66-70; res assoc & instr physics, Johns Hopkins Univ, 66-72; resident & sci secy atomic physics, Ctr Theoret Studies, Univ Miami, 72-73; dir qual control eng, Allegheny Metal Stamping Co, Inc, 73; res physicist acoust, Armstrong World Industs, Inc, 73-75, res scientist, 75-79, sr res scientist, 79-86. *Concurrent Pos:* Fel, NSF & NASA; invited guest lectr, PA State Univ, Grand Valley State Univ, Mich, Millersville Univ, PA. *Mem:* Fel Acoust Soc Am; Inst Noise Control Eng; Am Soc Testing & Mat; Am Phys Soc; Am Asn Physics Teachers; Inst Elec & Electronics Engrs. *Res:* Architectural and physical acoustics; noise control engineering; application of applied mathematics; materials science of acoustical materials; software engineering; computer electronics. *Mailing Add:* 599 Rookway SE Grand Rapids MI 49546-9607. *Fax:* 616-698-4131; *E-Mail:* sbrown@steelcase-research.com

BROWN, STEWART ANGLIN, PLANT BIOCHEMISTRY. *Current Pos:* assoc prof chem, Trent Univ, 64-68, dean grad studies, 73-77, prof chem, 68-87, EMER PROF, TRENT UNIV, 87- *Personal Data:* b Peterborough, Ont, Apr 6, 25; m 86, Alicja M Burgielska. *Educ:* Univ Toronto, BSA, 47; Mich State Univ, MS, 49, PhD(biochem), 51. *Prof Exp:* From asst res officer to assoc res officer, Prairie Regional Lab, Nat Res Coun Can, 51-62, sr res officer, 62-64. *Concurrent Pos:* Vis res worker, Univ Chem Lab, Cambridge Univ, 55-56; vis prof, Col Pharm, Univ Minn, Minneapolis, 70-71. *Mem:* Phytochem Soc NAm. *Res:* Biochemistry of higher plants and plant-parasite relations; chemistry of lignification, biosynthesis of coumarins and related compounds; methodology of biosynthetic investigation in plants; analysis, localization and chemical ecology of plant coumarins. *Mailing Add:* Dept Chem Trent Univ Peterborough ON K9J 7B8 Can. *Fax:* 705-748-1625

BROWN, STEWART CLIFF, PLASTICS CHEMISTRY, POLYMER CHEMISTRY. *Current Pos:* RETIRED. *Personal Data:* b Philadelphia, Pa, Mar 15, 28; m 50; c 1. *Educ:* Philadelphia Col Pharm & Sci, BSc, 50; Univ Del, MSc, 54, PhD(org chem), 57. *Prof Exp:* Res chemist, Tex-US Chem Co, 56-59 & E I Du Pont de Nemours & Co, 59-61; res chemist & tech serv supvr polymer film develop, Avisun Corp, 61-65; mkt mgr & res supvr polymer films, Hercules Inc, 65-80, dir technol film, 81-91, mgr, Mat Sci Dept, 88-91. *Res:* Film forming plastics; effects of orientation on film properties, chemical structure and orientation versus film properties. *Mailing Add:* 1406 Pennsylvania Ave Wilmington DE 19806

BROWN, STUART HOUSTON, ORGANIC CHEMISTRY. *Current Pos:* res chemist, Lubricant Res Dept, Chevron Res Co, 69-75, sr res chemist, 75-77, sr res assoc, Greases & Indust Oils Div, 77-80, sr staff specialist, Prod Mkt Dept, 80-84, tech asst to vpres, Prod Res Dept, 84-85, sr res assoc, Lubricants Div, 85-87, unit leader fuel chem, Fuels Div, 87-90, AT CHEVRON RES CO, 90- *Personal Data:* b Bryn Mawr, Pa, Mar 25, 41; m 66; c 2. *Educ:* Williams Col, BA, 63; Stanford Univ, PhD(org chem), 68. *Prof Exp:* NIH fel, Univ Liverpool, 68-69. *Mem:* Am Chem Soc. *Res:* Alkaloid structure and biosynthesis; x-ray crystallography; synthesis of lubricating oil additives; petroleum chemistry; industrial oil product development; business planning; petroleum products marketing; marketing research; performance and quality of petroleum fuels. *Mailing Add:* 85 Main Dr San Rafael CA 94901-2517

BROWN, STUART IRWIN, OPHTHALMOLOGY. *Current Pos:* CHMN, SHILEY EYE CTR, UNIV CALIF SAN DIEGO MED SCH. *Personal Data:* b Chicago, Ill, Mar 1, 33. *Educ:* Univ Ill, BMS, 55, MD, 57. *Prof Exp:* Intern, Jackson Mem Hosp, Miami, 57-58; resident ophthal, Harvard Med Sch, 58-59; resident, Eye, Ear, Nose & Throat Hosp, Med Sch, Tulane Univ, 59-61, Heed fel, 61-62; fel ophthal, Cornea Serv, Mass Eye & Ear Infirmary, 62-66; clin asst prof ophthal & asst attend surgeon, Hosp-Cornell Univ Med Ctr, 66-70, clin assoc prof & assoc attend surgeon, 70-74, dir, Cornea Serv & Cornea Res Lab, Med Ctr, 66-74; prof ophthal & chmn dept, Eye & Ear Hosp Pittsburgh & Sch Med, Univ Pittsburgh, 74- *Mem:* Am Acad Ophthal; Soc Contemp Ophthal; Pan Am Asn Ophthal; Asn Res Vision & Ophthal. *Res:* Cornea. *Mailing Add:* Univ Calif San Diego Med Sch Shiley Eye Ctr 9415 Campus Pt Rd La Jolla CA 92093-0946

BROWN, TALMAGE THURMAN, JR, PATHOLOGY, MICROBIOLOGY. *Current Pos:* PROF PATH, NC STATE UNIV, 81- *Personal Data:* b Raleigh, NC, Apr 18, 39; m 72, Carol J; c 2. *Educ:* NC State Univ, BS, 61; Okla State Univ, DVM, 65; Cornell Univ, PhD(vet path), 73. *Honors & Awards:* J Scholar Award, Charles L David DVM Found Adv Vet Path, 75. *Prof Exp:* Res assoc path & virol, Cornell Univ, 72-73; fel comp path,

Johns Hopkins Univ, 73-74, asst prof, 74-75; asst prof path, Okla State Univ, 75-78; vet med officer virol, Nat Animal Dis Ctr, Sci & Educ Admin-Agr Res, USDA, 78-81. *Concurrent Pos:* Co-investr, Pub Health Serv grant, Nat Inst Child Health & Human Develop, 71-74; fel, Nat Inst Neurol Dis & Stroke. *Mem:* Am Col Vet Pathologists; US-Can Acad Path; Am Vet Med Asn; Conf Res Workers Animal Dis; Soc Leukocyte Biol. *Res:* Pulmonary defense mechanism modulation by infectious agents and environmental pollutants; congenital and viral-induced leukocyde disorders. *Mailing Add:* 216 Rose Common Lane Cary NC 27511. *Fax:* 919-829-4455

BROWN, THEODORE CECIL, mechanical engineering; deceased, see previous edition for last biography

BROWN, THEODORE D, COMPUTER SCIENCE, OPERATIONS RESEARCH. *Current Pos:* From asst prof to assoc prof, 70-91, PROF COMPUT SCI, QUEENS COL, NY, 91-, CHAIR, 88- *Personal Data:* b Brooklyn, NY, Apr 25, 44; m 66, Linda Charne; c Elicia & Nina. *Educ:* City Col New York, BS, 66; NY Univ, BMOR, 68, PhD(oper res), 71. *Prof Exp:* Analyst, Chem Bank Opers Res, 67-70. *Mem:* Oper Res Soc Am; Asn Comput Mach; AAAS; Int Ref Orgn Forensic Med & Sci. *Res:* Computer systems; modeling computer systems; stochastic modeling; simulation methodology. *Mailing Add:* Dept Comput Sci Queens Col NY Flushing NY 11367. *E-Mail:* brown@ra.cs.qc.edu

BROWN, THEODORE GATES, JR, PHARMACOLOGY. *Current Pos:* RETIRED. *Personal Data:* b Boston, Mass, Sept 29, 20; m 45; c 5. *Educ:* Univ Tenn, AB, 48, MS, 50; Med Col SC, PhD(pharmacol), 56. *Prof Exp:* Res asst pharmacol, Sterling-Winthrop Res Inst, 57-58, assoc mem, 58-61, group leader, 61-62, res biologist, 61-63, sr res biologist & sect head, 63-68; dir biomed res, Warren-Teed Pharmaceut, Inc, 68-74; mgr preclin res, Rohm & Haas Res Ctr, 74-77; asst dir preclin res & mgr tech licensing, 77-78, mgr product develop & licensing Adria Labs, 78-83; dir new prods, Ben Venue Lab Inc, 83-87; pres, Theodore G Brown & Assocs Inc, 83-95. *Concurrent Pos:* Lectr, Albany Med Col, 58-68; consult, Pharmaceut Res Develop Prod 83- *Mem:* AAAS; Am Soc Pharmacol; Am Chem Soc; Am Heart Asn; Regulatory Affairs Prof Soc. *Res:* Pharmacology and physiology of cardiovascular disease; general pharmacology; neoplastic diseases. *Mailing Add:* 23 Seminary St Middlebury VT 05753-1217

BROWN, THEODORE LAWRENCE, INORGANIC CHEMISTRY. *Current Pos:* From instr to assoc prof, 56-65, PROF INORG CHEM, UNIV ILL, URBANA-CHAMPAIGN, 65-; DIR, BECKMAN INST ADV SCI & TECHNOL, UNIV ILL, URBANA, 87- *Personal Data:* b Green Bay, Wis, Oct 15, 28; m 51; c 5. *Educ:* Ill Inst Technol, BS, 50; Mich State Univ, PhD(chem), 56. *Honors & Awards:* Boomer lectr, Univ Alta, Edmonton, 75. *Concurrent Pos:* Sloan fel, 62-66; NSF fel, 64-65; assoc ed, Inorg Chem, 68-78; vis scientist, Int Meteorol Inst, Stockholm, 72; Firth vis prof, Sheffield Univ, 77; Guggenheim fel, 79-80; vchancellor res & dean, Grad Col, Univ Ill, Urbana, 80-86. *Mem:* Am Chem Soc; Sigma Xi; fel AAAS. *Res:* Kinetics and mechanisms of organometallic reactions. *Mailing Add:* 309 Yankee Ridge Lane Urbana IL 61801-7115

BROWN, THOMAS ALLEN, MUCOSAL IMMUNITY, IGA SUBCLASSES. *Current Pos:* ASST PROF ORAL BIOL, UNIV FLA, 84- *Educ:* Univ Fla, PhD(microbiol), 78. *Mailing Add:* Dept Oral Biol Col Dent Univ Fla Box 100424 JHMHC Gainesville FL 32610-0424. *Fax:* 904-392-3070

BROWN, THOMAS EDWARD, PLANT PHYSIOLOGY. *Current Pos:* assoc prof biol, Atlantic Community Col, 69-70, chmn, Sci Div, 73-79, prof biol, 70- 90, adj prof, 90-93, EMER PROF, 90-, CHAIR SCI DEPT, ATLANTIC COMMUNITY COL, 93- *Personal Data:* b Dayton, Ohio, May 19, 25; m 82; c 3. *Educ:* Antioch Col, BA, 50; Ohio State Univ, MS, 51, PhD(plant physiol), 54. *Prof Exp:* Staff scientist, C F Kettering Res Lab, 55-69. *Mem:* Sigma Xi. *Res:* Photosynthesis and algal physiology; algal pollution control. *Mailing Add:* Dept Sci Atlantic Community Col 5100 Blackhorse Pike Mays Landing NJ 08330

BROWN, TONY RAY, heat transfer, engineering, for more information see previous edition

BROWN, TRUMAN ROSCOE, NUCLEAR MAGNETIC RESONANCE. *Current Pos:* CHMN, DEPT NUCLEAR MAGNETIC RESONANCE & MED SPECTROS, FOX CHASE CANCER CTR, PHILADELPHIA, PA, 83- *Personal Data:* b Oct 4, 1943; c 2. *Educ:* Mass Inst Technol, Cambridge, BS, 64, PhD(physics), 70. *Prof Exp:* Instr physics, Mass Inst Technol, Cambridge, 70-71; mem tech staff, Bell Labs, Murray Hill, NJ, 71-83. *Concurrent Pos:* NAm ed, Nuclear Magnetic Resonance in Biomed, 87-; chmn, Sci Prog Comt, Soc Magnetic Resonance Med, 88-89; adj prof, Sch Med, Univ Pa, 89- *Mem:* Fel Am Phys Soc; Biophys Soc; Am Col Radiol; Soc Magnetic Resonance Med; Soc Magnetic Resonance Imaging. *Res:* Application of nuclear magnetic resonance to the study in vivo physiology, particularly in medicine. *Mailing Add:* Fox Chase Cancer Ctr 7701 Burholme Ave Philadelphia PA 19111. *Fax:* 215-728-3655

BROWN, VERNE R, ELECTRICAL ENGINEERING, SOLID STATE PHYSICS. *Current Pos:* chmn bd, 70-76, PRES, ENMET CORP, 70-, CHIEF RES EXEC, 76- *Personal Data:* b Dover, NH, Jan 23, 35; m 61; c 3. *Educ:* Univ NH, BSc, 60; Univ Mich, MSc, 61, MSc, 64, PhD(elec eng), 66. *Prof Exp:* Res engr, Univ Mich, 64-66; asst prof elec eng, Univ Calif, 66-68; vpres, Transidyne Gen Corp, Mich, 68-70. *Mem:* Instrument Soc Am; Inst Elec & Electronics Engrs; Air Pollution Control Asn; Asn Advan Med Instrumentation; Am Indust Hyg Asn. *Res:* Electrical, optical and infrared properties of solid state materials as related to sensor development, specifically use of materials technology and thin film deposition processes for sensor development; medical research; air pollution monitoring; industrial health and safety instrumentation; industrial safety/confined space entry field. *Mailing Add:* 28 Southwick Ct Ann Arbor MI 48105

BROWN, VIRGINIA RUTH, NUCLEAR THEORY. *Current Pos:* SR RES PHYSICIST, LAWRENCE LIVERMORE LAB, 66- *Personal Data:* b Wollaston, Mass. *Educ:* Northeastern Univ, BS, 57; McGill Univ, PhD(physics), 64. *Prof Exp:* Teaching asst, Ohio State Univ, 57-59, fel, 59-61; appointee, Yale Univ, 63-64. *Concurrent Pos:* Fel, Nat Res Coun Can, 61-63; adj prof, Physics Dept, Univ Calif Davis, 86-93; vis scientist, Mass Inst Technol, Cambridge, Mass, 94- *Mem:* Fel Am Phys Soc. *Res:* Nuclear reactions; nuclear structure; nucleon-nucleon interaction in the presence of other fields. *Mailing Add:* Phys Div Rm 1015N Nat Sci Found, 4201 Wilson Blvd Arlington VA 22230

BROWN, W VIRGIL, METABOLIC DISEASES, LIPOPROTEINS. *Current Pos:* PROF MED & CHIEF, DIV METAB DIS, MT SINAI MED CTR, NY, 78- *Personal Data:* b Royston, Ga, Sept 25, 38. *Educ:* Yale Univ, MD, 64. *Concurrent Pos:* Mem, Coun Arteriosclerosis, Am Heart Asn. *Mem:* Am Soc Clin Invest; Am Fedn Clin Res; Am Heart Asn. *Res:* Lipid metabolism. *Mailing Add:* Div Arteriosclerosis & Lipid Metab Dept Med Emory Univ 2001 WMB 1639 Pierce Dr Atlanta GA 30322. *Fax:* 404-727-3917

BROWN, WALTER CREIGHTON, BIOLOGY, HERPETOLOGY. *Current Pos:* instr, Menlo Col, 53-54, chmn, Div Sci, 55-61, dean, Div Sci & Eng, 61-67, dean col, 67-74, prof, 74-78, EMER PROF BIOL, MENLO COL, 78-; FEL & RES ASSOC, CALIF ACAD SCI, 74- *Personal Data:* b Butte, Mont, Aug 18, 13; m 50, Jeanette Snyder; c Pamela, James & Julie. *Educ:* Col Puget Sound, AB, 35, MA, 38; Stanford Univ, PhD, 50. *Prof Exp:* Head dept sci high, Wash, 38-42; actg instr biol, Stanford Univ, 49-50; instr, Northwestern Univ, 51-53. *Concurrent Pos:* Fulbright lectr zool, Silliman Univ, Philippines, 54-55; res assoc biol sci, Stanford Univ, 55-74; vis prof, Stanford Univ & Harvard Univ, 62-72. *Mem:* Sigma Xi; Assoc Am Soc Ichthyol & Herpet. *Res:* Ecology, systematics and zoogeography of amphibians and reptiles in the islands of the Pacific. *Mailing Add:* Dept Herpet Golden Gate Park Calif Acad Sci San Francisco CA 94118

BROWN, WALTER JOHN, INTERNAL MEDICINE. *Current Pos:* CONSULT, 87- *Personal Data:* b North Providence, RI, Aug 25, 28; m 52; c 3. *Educ:* Brown Univ, AB, 50; Univ RI, MS, 53; Med Col Ga, MD, 60. *Prof Exp:* Trainee, Clin Cardiovasc Res Prog, Med Col Ga, 62-63, asst prof med & assoc dir, Cardiovasc Res Training Prog, 64-67, assoc prof, 67-71, prof med, 71-; assoc dir & chief med, Univ Health Serv, Univ Ga, Athens, 68-, prof therapeut med, Sch Pharm & prof med & surg, Inst Comp Med, Sch Vet Med, 69- *Concurrent Pos:* Grants, NIH coop study, 66-72, Ga Heart Asn, 66-68 & Cerebrovasc Dis, Am Heart Asn, 68; attend physician, Vet Admin Hosp, Augusta, Ga, 64-69; consult, Penitentiary Syst, State Ga, 64-69; dir, Athens High Blood Pressure Ctr; consult, Northeast Ga Health Dist; at Dept Med, Med Col Ga. *Mem:* Am Heart Asn; Sigma Xi. *Res:* Epidemiology and hemodynamics of hypertension and peripheral vascular disease; bioavailability of drugs in humans. *Mailing Add:* 801 Bolton Rd Winterville GA 30683

BROWN, WALTER LYONS, MATERIALS SCIENCE. *Current Pos:* mem tech staff, AT&T Bell Labs, 50-57, DEPT HEAD, BELL LABS LUCENT TECHNOL, 57- *Personal Data:* b Charlottesville, Va, Oct 11, 24; m 46, Lucie M Oaks; c Stephen L, Stuart N, Virginia M & Keith A. *Educ:* Duke Univ, BS, 45; Harvard Univ, AM, 48, PhD(physics), 51. *Honors & Awards:* Von Hipple Award, Mat Res Soc, 84. *Mem:* Nat Acad Sci; Nat Acad Eng; fel Am Phys Soc; Mat Res Soc. *Res:* Semiconductors; space physics; interaction of energetic particles with solids. *Mailing Add:* 138 Cambridge Dr Berkeley Heights NJ 07922. *Fax:* 908-582-4228; *E-Mail:* wlb@physics.att.com

BROWN, WALTER REDVERS JOHN, ENGINEERING PHYSICS. *Current Pos:* PRES, DAEDALON CORP, 71- *Personal Data:* b Toronto, Ont, Aug 22, 25; m 48; c 5. *Educ:* Univ Toronto, BA Sc, 47; Univ Rochester, MS, 49. *Honors & Awards:* Adolph Lomb Medal, Optical Soc Am, 56. *Prof Exp:* Sr physicist, Kodak Res Lb, 49-55; res assoc, Phys Res Lab, Boston Univ, 55-57; proj mgr, Itek Corp, 57-62; vpres res & develop, United Carr Inc, 62-69; exec vpres, Ealing Corp, 69-71. *Mem:* Fel Optical Soc Am. *Res:* Comprehensive measurements of the ability of the human eye to perceive small color differences. *Mailing Add:* Daedalon Corp PO Box 2028 Salem MA 01970

BROWN, WANDA LOIS, BIOCHEMISTRY. *Current Pos:* biochemist metab, 55-62, RES BIOCHEMIST PROTEIN METAB, US ARMY INST SURG RES, 62- *Personal Data:* b England, Ark, Oct 30, 22. *Educ:* Ouachita Baptist Col, BS, 43; Sch Med, Univ Ark, cert, 46; Trinity Univ, MS, 60. *Prof Exp:* Chemist anal, Aluminum Ore Co, 43-45; med technologist, Ark Baptist Hosp, 46-50; med technologist hemat, Brooke Army Med Ctr, 51-53, med technologist chem, 53-55. *Mem:* Am Chem Soc; AAAS; Asn Women Sci. *Res:* Protein metabolism; burn trauma. *Mailing Add:* 212 Brightwood Pl San Antonio TX 78209-3315

BROWN, WARREN SHELBURNE, JR, PSYCHOPHYSIOLOGY. *Current Pos:* asst res psychologist, 73-75, asst prof, 75-80, ASSOC PROF PSYCHOL, SCH MED, UNIV CALIF, LOS ANGELES, 80-; PROF PSYCHOL, FULLER GRAD SCH PSYCHOL, PASADENA, 81-; DIR, TRAVIS INST BIOPSYCHOSOCIAL RES, 91- *Personal Data:* b Loma Linda, Calif, Sept 8, 44; m 66; c 2. *Educ:* Point Loma Col, BA, 66; Univ Southern Calif, MA, 69, PhD(exp psychol), 71. *Prof Exp:* Trainee neurosci, Brain Res Inst, Univ Calif, Los Angeles, 71-73. *Concurrent Pos:* NIMH spec res fel, 75 & res scientist develop award, 75-80; mem, NSF US-indust countries exchange scientists, 86. *Mem:* AAAS; Am Psychol Asn; Soc Psychophysiol Res; NY Acad Sci; Int Neuropsychol Soc. *Res:* Brain mechanisms of higher mental functions in humans; electroencephalography as a means of studying cortical events; disorders of higher cognitive function in humans. *Mailing Add:* Grad Sch Psychol Fuller Theol Sem Pasadena CA 91182. *Fax:* 626-584-9630; *E-Mail:* enl6wsb@uclamvs

BROWN, WENDELL STIMPSON, COASTAL PHYSICAL OCEANOGRAPHY. *Current Pos:* from asst prof to assoc prof, 74-87, PROF OCEANOG, UNIV NH, 87- *Personal Data:* b Pompton Plains, NJ, Apr 4, 43; m 79, Leslie Ahern; c Adrian G, Dylan S & Tyler A. *Educ:* Brown Univ, BS, 65, MS, 67; Mass Inst Technol, PhD(oceanog), 71. *Prof Exp:* Asst res oceanog, Inst Geophys & Planetary Physics, Univ Calif, San Diego, 70-74. *Concurrent Pos:* Vis scholar, Scripps Inst Oceanog, 81, Harvard Univ, 88 & Dartmouth Col, 96. *Mem:* Am Geophys Union; Am Meterol Soc. *Res:* Observational/modelling studies of ocean circulation on the continental shelf, slope and marginal seas in the United States; climate change related studies in the western tropical Atlantic Ocean. *Mailing Add:* Ocean Process Anal Lab Morse Hall Univ NH Durham NH 03824. *E-Mail:* wsbrown@kelvin.sr.unh.edu

BROWN, WILBUR K, GENERAL PHYSICS, FRAGMENTATION THEORY. *Current Pos:* INSTR MATH SCI, LASSON COL, 87- *Personal Data:* b Oakland, Calif, July 6, 32; m 54, Kathryn Lumilla lind; c Walter A & Craig A. *Educ:* Univ Calif, Berkeley, AB, 54, MS, 57, PhD(eng sci), 62. *Prof Exp:* Asst, Lawrence Radiation Lab, Univ Calif, 58-62; mem staff, Res Estab, Riso, Denmark, 62-64 & Los Alamos Sci Lab, 64-70; assoc prof nuclear & mech eng, Univ Wyo, 70-72; mem staff, Los Alamos Nat Lab, 72-87. *Mem:* Am Phys Soc; Am Nuclear Soc; Sigma Xi; Am Astron Soc; Astron Soc Pac. *Res:* Cosmogony; fragmentation. *Mailing Add:* 5179 Eastshore Dr Lake Almanor CA 96137

BROWN, WILLARD ANDREW, SCIENCE EDUCATION. *Current Pos:* coordr sci educ, 66-69, prof, 66-84, EMER PROF PHYSICS & ASTRON, WESTERN WASH UNIV, 84- *Personal Data:* b Seattle, Wash, Nov 13, 21; m 48; c 2. *Educ:* Univ Wash, BS, 46; Wash State Col, MAT, 58; Univ Fla, EdD(phys sci), 63. *Prof Exp:* Data analyst, Boeing Co, 48-49; teacher high sch, 51-56; asst prof educ & supvr student teachers, Western Wash State Col, 56-60; asst prof physics, Cent Wash State Col, 60-61; asst prof phys sci & astron, San Francisco State Col, 63-66. *Concurrent Pos:* Microcomput consult. *Res:* Data processing; data analysis for implementation of educational objectives. *Mailing Add:* Dept Physics & Astron Western Wash Univ MS 9064 Bellingham WA 98225-9064

BROWN, WILLIAM ANDERSON, SURFACE CHEMISTRY, RUBBER CHEMISTRY. *Current Pos:* CONSULT, 87- *Personal Data:* b Corpus Christi, Tex, Dec 21, 29; m 52, Janet Story; c Donna (Jay). *Educ:* Univ Tex, BS, 51, MA, 53, PhD(chem), 60. *Prof Exp:* Res scientist, Defense Res Labs, Univ Tex, 53-55; res engr, Alcoa Res Labs, Aluminum Co Am, 59-64; res chemist, Houston Res Lab, Indust Chem Div, Shell Chem Co, 64-68; res chemist, Ashland Chem Co, 68-71, sr res chemist, 71-79, mgr carbon black res, 79-87. *Mem:* Am Chem Soc. *Res:* Coordination compounds; catalysis; organic coatings; corrosion; fine particles; elastomers; surface chemistry. *Mailing Add:* 1473 Chelmsford St NW North Canton OH 44720-6030

BROWN, WILLIAM ARNOLD, atomic physics, for more information see previous edition

BROWN, WILLIAM AUGUSTIN, STRUCTURAL MECHANICS. *Current Pos:* dir, Off Civil Defense Prof Adv Ctr, Manhattan Col, 69-74, chmn dept, 71-79, actg assoc dean eng, 92-93, ASSOC PROF CIVIL ENG, MANHATTAN COL, 56- *Personal Data:* b Mt Vernon, NY, Aug 1, 32; m 59, Monica F McGrath; c Mark G. *Educ:* Manhattan Col, BCE, 54; Va Polytech Inst, MS, 56; NY Univ, PhD(civil eng), 68. *Prof Exp:* Assoc engr, Sperry Gyroscope Co, NY, 55-56. *Concurrent Pos:* NSF sci fac fel, 63; consult, Off Civil Defense, Washington, DC, 65-83. *Mem:* Sigma Xi; Am Soc Civil Eng. *Res:* Structural analysis; analysis of the top slab of a skewed rigid frame bridge for extension; bars of nonprismatic open section subjected to arbitrary end loading. *Mailing Add:* 50 Smithridge Rd South Salem NY 10590-1919

BROWN, WILLIAM BERNARD, polymer chemistry, for more information see previous edition

BROWN, WILLIAM E, MICROBIOLOGY, INDUSTRIAL CHEMISTRY. *Current Pos:* vpres & tech dir, 91-96, PRES, BIOSENTRY INC, 96- *Personal Data:* b Oxford, Pa, May 26, 33; m 56; c 3. *Educ:* Univ Del, BS, 56; Univ Ga, MS, 60, PhD(food sci), 64. *Prof Exp:* Bacteriologist, Amerlab Inc, Ga, 56-58; res asst virol, Univ Ga, 58-60, res asst food sci, 60-64; microbiologist, Cornell Univ, 64-66; microbiologist, Bio-Lab Inc, 67-71, vpres & tech dir, 71-87, sr scientist, 87-89. *Mem:* Poultry Sci Asn; Inst Food Technol. *Res:* Environmental sanitation; enzymology; water treatment; water chemistry. *Mailing Add:* 2046 Meadowbrook Dr SW Conyers GA 30207. *Fax:* 770-723-7056; *E-Mail:* bill@sentry.com

BROWN, WILLIAM E(RIC), CERAMICS. *Current Pos:* RETIRED. *Personal Data:* b Philadelphia, Pa, Mar 4, 23; m 45, 78; c 2. *Educ:* Rutgers Univ, BS, 48, MS, 51, PhD(ceramics), 75. *Prof Exp:* Instr ceramics, Rutgers Univ, 50-52; res engr, Kaiser Aliminum & Chem Corp, 52-67, sr res engr, 67-82. *Mem:* Keramos Hon Soc; Sigma Xi. *Res:* Thermomechanical and thermochemical properties of inorganic materials. *Mailing Add:* 1115 Kolln St Pleasanton CA 94566-5628

BROWN, WILLIAM E, BIOCHEMISTRY, MICROBIOLOGY. *Current Pos:* PROF BIOL SCI, CARNEGIE-MELLON UNIV, 73- *Personal Data:* b Cleveland, Ohio, Mar 27, 45; c 3. *Educ:* Univ Minn, PhD(biochem), 71. *Honors & Awards:* Can Soc Tech Agr Gold Medal. *Concurrent Pos:* Consult, US Dept Health, Educ & Welfare & Environ Protection Agency; adv, Am Type Cult Collection; partic adv bd, Biotechnol & Bioeng; mem organizing comt, Intersci Conf on Antimicrobial Agents & Chemother, 78-; mem microbiol exchange comt with Soviet Union, NSF. *Mem:* AAAS; Brit Soc Gen Microbiol; NY Acad Sci; Am Chem Soc; Am Soc Microbiol. *Res:* Production of organic compounds biosynthetically; production of antibiotics, vitamins, dextran and therapeutic steroids; discovery of new anti-infectives and antibiotics; technology transfer; protein biochemistry; structure function; enzymology. *Mailing Add:* Dept Biol Sci Carnegie-Mellon Univ 4400 Fifth Ave Pittsburgh PA 15213-2683. *Fax:* 412-268-7129

BROWN, WILLIAM G, COMBINATORICS & GRAPH THEORY. *Current Pos:* assoc prof, 67-76, PROF MATH, MCGILL UNIV, 76- *Personal Data:* b Toronto, Ont, June 13, 38; m 69; c 3. *Educ:* Univ Toronto, BA, 60, PhD(math), 63; Columbia Univ, MA, 61. *Prof Exp:* Asst prof math, Univ BC, 63-67. *Mem:* Am Math Soc; Math Asn Am; Can Math Soc (treas, 77-80); London Math Soc. *Res:* Combinatorial analysis; graph theory. *Mailing Add:* Dept Math McGill Univ 805 Sherbrooke St W Montreal PQ H3A 2K6 Can. *Fax:* 514-398-3899; *E-Mail:* brown@math.mcgill.ca

BROWN, WILLIAM HEDRICK, ANIMAL NUTRITION. *Current Pos:* From asst prof to assoc prof dairy sci, 59-69, PROF ANIMAL SCI, UNIV ARIZ, 69- *Personal Data:* b Yakima, Wash, Mar 18, 33; m 57; c 2. *Educ:* State Col Wash, BS, 55; Univ Md, MS, 57, PhD(animal nutrit), 59. *Concurrent Pos:* Res grants, Dept HEW, 60-63, 64-67 & NSF, 62-64. *Mem:* Am Dairy Sci Asn; Sigma Xi. *Res:* Roughage utilization by ruminants; lipid and mineral metabolism; biochemistry of the bovine rumen; pesticide residues in milk; physiology of lactation. *Mailing Add:* Dept Animal Sci Univ Ariz 1600 E University Blvd Tucson AZ 85721-0001

BROWN, WILLIAM HENRY, ORGANIC CHEMISTRY, BIOCHEMISTRY. *Current Pos:* from asst prof to assoc prof, 64-72, PROF ORG CHEM, BELOIT COL, 73- *Personal Data:* b Ogdensburg, NY, Oct 26, 32; m 60, 90; c 4. *Educ:* St Lawrence Univ, BS, 54; Harvard Univ, MA, 55; Columbia Univ, PhD(chem), 58. *Prof Exp:* From instr to asst prof org chem, Wesleyan Univ, 58-64. *Concurrent Pos:* Res fel org chem, Calif Inst Technol, 63-64; res assoc, Univ Ariz, 67-68 & 70-71. *Mem:* Am Chem Soc. *Mailing Add:* Dept Chem Beloit Col Beloit WI 53511-5595

BROWN, WILLIAM HENRY, AGRICULTURAL & BIOLOGICAL ENGINEERING. *Current Pos:* assoc prof, La State Univ, 77-80, PROF AGR ENG & HEAD DEPT, 80- *Personal Data:* b Warrensburg, Mo, May 22, 42; m 63. *Educ:* Univ Mo, BS, 64, MS, 66, PhD(agr eng), 69. *Prof Exp:* From asst prof to assoc prof agr & biol eng, Miss State Univ, 68-77. *Mem:* Am Soc Agr Engrs; Am Inst Biol Sci; Am Soc Eng Educ; Inst Elec & Electronics Engrs; Nat Soc Prof Engrs; Sigma Xi. *Res:* Plant and animal responses to environmental factors; engineering control of environmental factors. *Mailing Add:* La Agr Exp Sta PO Box 25055 Baton Rouge LA 70894-5055

BROWN, WILLIAM J, MEMBRANE RECEPTORS. *Current Pos:* ASST PROF CELL BIOL, CORNELL UNIV, 86- *Educ:* Univ Tex, Dallas, PhD(med sci), 81. *Prof Exp:* Assoc res scientist cell biol, Sch Med, Yale Univ, 81-86. *Mailing Add:* Sect Biochem-Molecular & Cell Biol Cornell Univ 359 Biotechnol Bldg Ithaca NY 14853-0001. *Fax:* 607-255-2428

BROWN, WILLIAM JOHN, MICROBIOLOGY. *Current Pos:* From instr to asst prof microbiol, 69-74, ASSOC PROF IMMUNOL & MICROBIOL, SCH MED, WAYNE STATE UNIV, 74-; DIR MICROBIOL, HUTZEL HOSP, DETROIT, 74- *Personal Data:* b Ashland, Pa, June 7, 40; m 66; c 1. *Educ:* Univ Scranton, BS, 63; Duquesne Univ, MS, 65; WVa Univ, PhD(microbiol), 69. *Concurrent Pos:* Mich Kidney Found grant; consult microbiol, Detroit Gen Hosp. *Mem:* Am Soc Microbiol. *Res:* Basic research on lymphocytic choriomeningitis virus, particularly the virus-cell relationship; urinary tract infections from both the viral and bacteriological aspects. *Mailing Add:* 2439 Dorfield Dr Rochester MI 48307

BROWN, WILLIAM LEWIS, FOOD MICROBIOLOGY. *Current Pos:* PRES, AM BACT & CHEM RES CORP, 67- *Personal Data:* b Clover, SC, Nov 23, 28; m 51, Agnes; c 3. *Educ:* Clemson Col, BS, 49; NC State Col, MS, 51; Univ Ill, PhD(food microbiol), 56. *Prof Exp:* Asst, NC State Col, 49-51, instr meats, 51-54; asst, Univ Ill, 56; res food technologist, John Morrell & Co, 56-57, asst dir res, 57-64, vpres res, 64-67. *Mem:* Fel Am Soc Microbiol; Sigma Xi; fel Inst Food Technologists. *Res:* Bacteriology; nutrition; biochemistry. *Mailing Add:* ABC Res 3437 SW 24th Ave Gainesville FL 32607

BROWN, WILLIAM LOUIS, JR, BIOLOGY. *Current Pos:* from asst prof to assoc prof, 60-68, PROF ENTOM, CORNELL UNIV, 68- *Personal Data:* b Philadelphia, Pa, June 1, 22; m 46; c 3. *Educ:* Pa State Col, BS, 47; Harvard Univ, PhD, 50. *Honors & Awards:* Donisthorpe Prize, 63. *Prof Exp:* Asst, Pa State Col, 47; Parker fel from Harvard Univ, Australia, 50-51, Fulbright fel, 51-52; asst cur insects, Mus Comp Zool, Harvard Univ, 52-54, assoc cur, 54-60. *Concurrent Pos:* Assoc, Mus Comp Zool, Harvard Univ, 60-; Guggenheim fel, 73-74. *Mem:* Am Entom Soc; Soc Syst Zool; Soc Study Evolution (pres, 84). *Res:* Systematics, ecology and behavior of ants; general evolutionary theory; zoogeography. *Mailing Add:* Dept Entom Cornell Univ 3140 Comstock Hall Ithaca NY 14853

BROWN, WILLIAM M(ILTON), systems analysis, applied mathematics, for more information see previous edition

BROWN, WILLIAM RANDALL, GEOLOGY. *Current Pos:* from asst prof to prof, 45-84, EMER PROF GEOL, UNIV KY, 84- *Personal Data:* b Staunton, Va, Oct 31, 13; m 42, Blessing Whitmore; c Elizabeth, Denison & Elaine. *Educ:* Univ Va, BS, 38, MA, 39; Cornell Univ, PhD(mineral), 42. *Prof Exp:* From asst to assoc geologist, Va Geol Surv, 42-45. *Concurrent Pos:* Consult, Calif Co, Shell Oil Co 55-64 & US Geol Surv, 64-76; Field Inst Japan, Am Geol Inst, 67; vis prof, Univ Cent Venezuela, 69; adj prof, Transylvania Univ, 79. *Mem:* Fel Geol Soc Am; Am Asn Petrol Geol. *Res:* Igneous, metamorphic and structural geology of Piedmont Province, Virginia; mica and feldspar deposits of Virginia; Piedmont zinc and lead deposits of Virginia; park basins of Colorado; Wind River Basin, Wyoming; Wyoming overthrust belt; Pennsylvanian of eastern Kentucky. *Mailing Add:* 253 Shady Lane Lexington KY 40503

BROWN, WILLIAM ROY, NEUROPATHOLOGY, IMMUNOCYTOCHEMISTRY. *Current Pos:* res asst prof, 92-96, RES ASSOC PROF RADIOL & PATH, BOWMAN GREY SCH MED, WAKE FOREST UNIV, 96- *Personal Data:* b Kenora, Ont, June 26, 45; m 84; c 3. *Educ:* Univ Waterloo, BIS, 75; Univ Windsor, MSc, 78; Univ Guelph, PhD(cell biol), 83. *Prof Exp:* Res assoc pathol, Univ Guelph, 82-83; res assoc dermat, Univ Toronto, 83-87, asst prof, 87-92. *Mem:* NY Acad Sci; Am Asn Neuropath; Int Soc Neuropath; Soc Neurosci; Am Soc Neurochem; NAm Vascular Biol Orgn. *Res:* Pathogenesis of Alzheimer's disease; brain pathology of vascular origin: germinal matrix hemorrhage in neonates, periventricular white matte ischemia (leukoaraiosis), lipid microemboli in the brain after cardiopulmonary bypass surgery. *Mailing Add:* 5177 Huntcliff Trail Winston-Salem NC 27104-4437. *Fax:* 910-716-2029; *E-Mail:* brownb@radmin.rad.bgsm.edu

BROWN, WILLIAM SAMUEL, JR, SPEECH SCIENCE. *Current Pos:* res assoc & fel, Commun Sci Lab, Univ Fla, 68-70, asst prof, 70-75, area head phonetic sci, Inst Advan Study Commun Processes, 74-81, assoc prof speech, 75-81, PROF SPEECH & DIR, INST ADVAN STUDY COMMUN PROCESSES, UNIV FLA, 81-, CHMN, DEPT COMMUN PROCESSES & DIS, 93- *Personal Data:* b Pottstown, Pa, Apr 25, 40; m 62; c 2. *Educ:* Edinboro State Col, BS, 62; State Univ NY, Buffalo, MA, 67, PhD(speech sci), 69. *Prof Exp:* Speech & hearing therapist, Crawford County Operated Classes Handicapped, 62-65; res asst speech sci, State Univ NY, Buffalo, 65-68. *Mem:* Sigma Xi; fel Int Soc Phonetic Sci; fel Am Asn Phonetic Sci (secy-treas, 73-79); fel Am Speech-Language-Hearing Asn; fel Acoust Soc Am. *Res:* Experimental phonetics; physiological and aerodynamic study of speech articulatory behavior, laryngeal and respiratory function utilizing both normal and pathological speakers. *Mailing Add:* Inst Advan Study Commun Processes Univ Fla 63 Dauer Hall Gainesville FL 32611. *E-Mail:* wsbrown@cpo.ufl.edu

BROWN, WILLIAM STANLEY, COMPUTER ALGEBRA & LANGUAGE. *Current Pos:* CONSULT, 96- *Personal Data:* b Cleveland, Ohio, Feb 13, 35; m 56; c 2. *Educ:* Yale Univ, BS, 56; Princeton Univ, PhD(physics), 61. *Prof Exp:* Instr physics, Princeton Univ, 60-61; mem tech staff, Math Physics Dept, Bell Labs, 61-66, head, Comput Math Res Dept, 66-81, head, Info Systs Dept, 81-86, div mgr venture technologies, AT&T, 86-88, int planning dir, 88-96. *Concurrent Pos:* Mem, Working Group Numerical Software, Int Fed Info Processing, 76-82 & bd sci counr, Lister Hill Ctr, Nat Libr Med, 81-83; mem, Electronic Publ Comt, Am Inst Physics, 86-89, chmn, Subcomt Numerical Databases, 87-89; mem, Info Technol Adv Panel, Europ Inst Technol, 89-90, Sci Adv Bd, 90-91. *Res:* Computer algebra and languages; information transfer; software portability; theory of floating-point computation. *Mailing Add:* 7 Dellwood Ave Chatham NJ 07928

BROWNAWELL, WOODROW DALE, TRANSCENDENCE THEORY, EFFECTIVE ALGEBRA. *Current Pos:* From asst prof to prof, 70-90, DISTINGUISHED PROF MATH, PA STATE UNIV, 90- *Personal Data:* b Grundy Co, Mo, Apr 21, 42; m 65, Eva M Kruempelmann; c Kevin D. *Educ:* Univ Kans, BA, 64; Cornell Univ, PhD(math), 70. *Honors & Awards:* Hardy-Ramanujan Soc Award, 87. *Concurrent Pos:* Vis assoc prof, Univ Colo, 74-75; Alexander von Humboldt res scholar, Univ Cologne, 77-78; master res, Ecole Polytech, 84; mem, Inst Advan Studies, Princeton, 85-86 & Math Sci Res Inst, Berkeley, 93; vis prof, Univ Paris, Univ St Etienne, 87; fel, Univ Utrecht, 92. *Mem:* Am Math Soc; Math Asn Am; Deutsch Math Ver. *Res:* Independence properties of numbers and functions arising in classical analysis; effective algebra; especially chow forms and Hilbert Nullstellensat. *Mailing Add:* Dept Math Pa State Univ University Park PA 16802-6401. *E-Mail:* wdb@math.psu.edu

BROWNE, ALAN LAMPE, ENGINEERING MECHANICS. *Current Pos:* Assoc sr res engr lubrication tire traction, Gen Motors Res Labs, 71-76, sr res engr lubrication tire mech, 76-80, staff res eng tire mech, occupant safety, 80-87, SR STAFF RES ENGR, OCCUPANT SAFETY & STRUCT COMPOSITES, GEN MOTORS RES LABS, 87- *Personal Data:* b Hamilton, Ohio, Feb 3, 44; m 70, Susan Matthews; c Christopher, Ryan & Jordan. *Educ:* Harvard Univ, AB, 66; Northwestern Univ, PhD(mech eng), 71. *Honors & Awards:* Kumar Award, Am Soc Testing & Mat. *Concurrent Pos:* Mem adv panel, Nat Coop Highway Res Prog, 74-80; assoc ed, Tire Sci & Technol, 75- *Mem:* Am Soc Mech Engrs; Am Soc Testing & Mat; Soc Automotive Engrs; Sigma Xi. *Res:* Elastohydrodynamic lubrication; pneumatic tire hydroplaning; tire wet traction; tire power loss; structural applications of composite materials; occupant safety; impact mechanics; granted 6 patents. *Mailing Add:* BE & I Dept Gen Motors Res & Develop Ctr MC 480-106-256 Warren MI 48090-9055. *E-Mail:* abrowne@cmsa.gmr.com

BROWNE, CAROLE LYNN, CELL BIOLOGY. *Current Pos:* ASST PROF CELL & MOLECULAR BIOL & ELECTRON MICROS, WAKE FOREST UNIV, 80- *Personal Data:* b July 13, 50; m 76; c 2. *Educ:* Syracuse Univ, PhD(biol). *Mem:* Am Soc Cell Biol; Electron Micros Soc Am. *Res:* Cyclic AMP dependent protein kinase; cellular regulation of mitotic process. *Mailing Add:* Dept Biol Wake Forest Univ Reynolds Sta Box 7325 Winston-Salem NC 27109

BROWNE, CHARLES IDOL, RADIOCHEMISTRY. *Current Pos:* RETIRED. *Personal Data:* b Atlanta, Ga, Feb 8, 22; m 42; c 1. *Educ:* Drew Univ, AB, 41; Calif Inst Technol, MS, 48; Univ Calif, PhD(chem), 52. *Prof Exp:* Alt leader, Radiochem Group, 55-65, assoc div leader, Weapons Test Div, 65-70, alt div leader, 70-72, div leader, 72-74, from asst dir to assoc dir, Los Alamos Sci Lab, 74-87. *Mem:* Fel Am Phys Soc; fel Am Inst Chem; Sigma Xi. *Res:* Radiochemical diagnostics. *Mailing Add:* 428 Estante Way Los Alamos NM 87544

BROWNE, COLIN LANFEAR, CHEMISTRY. *Current Pos:* RETIRED. *Personal Data:* b Buffalo, NY, Apr 11, 28; m 49; c 2. *Educ:* Lafayette Col, BA, 49; Univ Va, MS, 51, PhD(chem), 53. *Prof Exp:* Textile res chemist, Rohm and Haas Co, 53-57; mgr indust prod develop, Hoechst Celanese Corp, 57-66, mgr, Dyeing & Finishing Lab, 66-70, mgr dyeing & finishing tech serv & develop, 70-78, res & develop mgr & tech assoc, 78-90. *Mem:* Am Chem Soc; Am Asn Textile Chemists & Colorists; Fiber Soc. *Res:* Development of specialty fibers and films, smoking products and filters. *Mailing Add:* 733 Plantation Estates Dr Apt E218 Matthews NC 28105

BROWNE, CORNELIUS PAYNE, NUCLEAR PHYSICS. *Current Pos:* from asst prof to assoc prof, 56-64, PROF PHYSICS, UNIV NOTRE DAME, 64- *Personal Data:* b Madison, Wis, Oct 30, 23; wid; c Margaret & Cornelius Jr. *Educ:* Univ Wis, AB, 46, PhD(physics), 51. *Prof Exp:* Res assoc, Mass Inst Technol, 51-56. *Concurrent Pos:* Prin investr, Notre Dame Nuclear Struct Lab, 65-94; vis prof, Univ Wis, 59-61, Univ Tex, Austin, 72-73; prog officer, Nuclear Physics, NSF, 80-81. *Mem:* Am Asn Physics Teachers; fel Am Phys Soc; Sigma Xi. *Res:* Measurement of nuclear reaction energies and nuclear energy levels; nuclear reaction mechanisms. *Mailing Add:* 1606 E Washington Ave South Bend IN 46617

BROWNE, DOUGLAS TOWNSEND, BIO-ORGANIC CHEMISTRY, BIOCHEMISTRY. *Current Pos:* asst prof, 74-76, ASSOC PROF CHEM, WORCESTER POLYTECH INST, 76- *Personal Data:* b Hamilton, Ohio, Jan 23, 42; m 74; c 2. *Educ:* Mass Inst Technol, SB, 64; Univ Ill, PhD(chem), 68. *Prof Exp:* NIH fel biochem, Harvard Univ, 68-69; asst prof chem, Univ Calif, Berkeley, 69-74. *Concurrent Pos:* Affil scientist, Worcester Found Exp Biol, 75-78; vis prof, Univ Hawaii, 84-85. *Mem:* Am Chem Soc; AAAS; NY Acad Sci. *Res:* Enzyme conformation and mechanism; nuclear magnetic resonance studies of proteins; site-specific enzyme labeling; protein chemical modification; pyrimidine and enzyme photochemistry. *Mailing Add:* 25 Silver St South Hadley MA 01075-1615

BROWNE, EDWARD TANKARD, JR, BOTANY. *Current Pos:* RETIRED. *Personal Data:* b Chapel Hill, NC, Dec 17, 26; m 50; c 3. *Educ:* Univ NC, BA, 48, MA, 50, PhD(bot), 57. *Prof Exp:* Head, Bot Slide Dept, Carolina Biol Supply Co, Elon Col, 52-55; asst prof bot, Auburn Univ, 56-59 & Univ Ga, 59-60; from asst prof to assoc prof, Univ Ky, 60-67; from assoc prof to prof, Memphis State Univ, 67-88, emer prof biol, 88- *Mem:* Am Soc Plant Taxon. *Res:* Contributions of plant embryology to systematic botany; flora of Kentucky; Liliaceae and Aletris systematics. *Mailing Add:* 486 St Nick Dr Memphis TN 38117

BROWNE, JAMES CLAYTON, MOLECULAR PHYSICS, COMPUTER SCIENCE. *Current Pos:* PROF PHYSICS & COMPUT SCI, UNIV TEX, AUSTIN, 68-, RES SCIENTIST, 73- *Personal Data:* b Conway, Ark, Jan 16, 35; m 59; c 3. *Educ:* Hendrix Col, BA, 56; Univ Tex, PhD(chem), 60. *Prof Exp:* Asst prof physics, Univ Tex, 60-64; NSF fel, 64-65; prof comput sci, Queen's Univ, Belfast, 65-68. *Concurrent Pos:* Consult, NSF. *Mem:* Am Phys Soc; Asn Comput Mach; Soc Indust & Appl Math. *Res:* Atomic and molecular processes; operating systems; symbolic mathematics. *Mailing Add:* Dept Comp Sci Univ Tex Austin TX 78712

BROWNE, JOHN CHARLES, NUCLEAR COSMOCHRONOLOGY-NUCLEAR ASTROPHYSICS, NUCLEAR FISSION. *Current Pos:* group leader nuclear physics, Los Alamos Nat Lab, 79-81, div leader physics, 81-84, assoc dir exp physics, 84-86, res, 86, defense res, 86-92, comp sci, 92-93, PROG DIR ENERGY RES, LOS ALAMOS NAT LAB, 93- *Personal Data:* b Pottstown, Pa, July 29, 42; m 85, Marti Moore; c Christopher, Adam, Courtney & Ryan. *Educ:* Drexel Univ, BS, 65; Duke Univ, PhD(physics), 69. *Prof Exp:* Instr physics, Duke Univ, 69-70; staff scientist, Lawrence Livermore Nat Lab, 70-79. *Mem:* Fel Am Phys Soc; AAAS. *Res:* Director of the Los Alamos Neutron Science Center and energy research programs; development and execution of basic and applied research programs in materials science, biological and environmental researchc, scientific computing, chemical and geological sciences and high energy and nuclear physics. *Mailing Add:* MS H845 Los Alamos Nat Lab Los Alamos NM 87545. *E-Mail:* browne@lanl.gov

BROWNE, JOHN MWALIMU, CELL BIOLOGY. *Current Pos:* assoc prof, Clark Atlanta Univ, 71-77, dir res, 83-84, chair, dept biol, 85-89, PROF BIOL, CLARK ATLANTA UNIV, 77-, PROF CELL BIOL & DIR, BIOMED RES, 89-, CHAIR, DEPT BIOL SIC, 97- *Personal Data:* b Miami, Fla, Aug 13, 39; m 91, Irene V Brown; c 3. *Educ:* Bethune-Cookman Col, BS, 62; Univ Miami, MS, 68, PhD(cell & develop biol), 70. *Prof Exp:* Instr biol, Bethune-Cookman Col, 62-65; NIH res asst develop biol, Lab Quant Biol, Univ Miami, 65-68, teaching asst, Dept Biol, 68-69, res assoc, Lab Quant Biol, 70; assoc prof biol, Bethune-Cookman Col, 70-71. *Concurrent Pos:* Res assoc, Rosensteil Sch Marine & Atmospheric Sci, 70-71; adj prof cell biol, Rockefeller Univ, 78- *Mem:* Am Soc Cell Biol; AAAS; Am Soc Biotechnol; Nato fel, 84. *Res:* Cellular regulation at the translational level in avian, piscean and mammalian systems; effects of carcinogens on the differential synthesis of cell membrane enzymes during mammary gland tumorigenesis. *Mailing Add:* Dept Biol Clark Atlanta Univ Atlanta GA 30314-4391. *Fax:* 404-880-6756; *E-Mail:* jbrowne@can.edu

BROWNE, MICHAEL EDWIN, PHYSICS. *Current Pos:* dept chmn, 67-75, PROF PHYSICS, UNIV IDAHO, 67- *Personal Data:* b Los Angeles, Calif, June 12, 30; m 51; c 7. *Educ:* Univ Calif, Berkeley, BS, 52, PhD(physics), 55. *Prof Exp:* Staff scientist, Lockheed Res Labs, 55-67; vis res physicist, Physics Inst, Zurich, 63-64. *Concurrent Pos:* Vis prof physics, Boston Univ, 77. *Mem:* Am Phys Soc; Am Asn Physics Teachers. *Res:* Solid state physics and biophysics. *Mailing Add:* 927 E Sixth St Moscow ID 83843

BROWNE, RICHARD HAROLD, STATISTICS. *Current Pos:* SR CONSULT, RHB CONSULT SERV, DALLAS, 79; ADMIN DIR RES, TEX SCOTTISH RITE HOSP, 88- *Personal Data:* b St Louis, Mo, Sept 24, 46; m 70, Dennise M Richardson. *Educ:* Univ Mo-Rolla, BS, 68; Okla State Univ, MS, 70, PhD, 73. *Prof Exp:* Asst prof, Health Sci Ctr, Univ Tex, Dallas, 73-79. *Concurrent Pos:* Asst prof, SMeth Univ, Dallas, 74-77, Health Sci Ctr, Univ Tex, 79-82; statistican, Criterion Inc, Dallas, 79-81; sr mgr analyst, Sun Co, Dallas, 81-83; sr biostatistician Teams, Inc, Dallas, 83-85; adj assoc prof, Tex Womens Univ, 84- *Mem:* Am Statist Asn; Biometric Soc. *Res:* Statist. *Mailing Add:* 12045 Inwood Rd Dallas TX 75244

BROWNE, ROBERT GLENN, MANUFACTURING TECHNOLOGY RESEARCH, APPLIED MACHINE VISION RESEARCH. *Current Pos:* PROF ELECTRONICS, DEVRY INST, 93- *Personal Data:* b Brockport, NY, Oct 6, 51; m 84; c 2. *Educ:* Univ Rochester, BS, 72, BA, 72; Princeton Univ, MA, 76, PhD(physics), 79. *Prof Exp:* Mem tech staff, RCA Labs, 78-87 & David Sarnoff Res Ctr, Inc, 87-92. *Concurrent Pos:* Adj prof physics, Middlesex County Col, 87-92. *Mem:* Am Phys Soc; Math Asn Am; sr mem Mach Vision Asn. *Res:* Manufacturing technology research including development of laser-based inspection systems; applications of machine vision systems to industrial uses; electronic technology education. *Mailing Add:* 93 Remmey St Fords NJ 08863

BROWNE, RONALD K, SCIENTIFIC COMMUNICATIONS, REGULATORY SUBMISSIONS. *Current Pos:* Mgr sci affairs, Sci Commun Inc, 76-80, dir pharmacol, 80-86, sr sci writer, 86-90, LECTR & CONSULT, SCI COMMUN INC, 91- *Personal Data:* b Chicago, Ill, Oct 21, 34. *Educ:* Loyola Univ, PhD(pharm), 72. *Concurrent Pos:* Mem, coun high blood pressure, Am Heart Asn; adj assoc prof, Univ Mo-Kansas City. *Mem:* Soc Toxicol; Am Soc Pharmacol & Exp Therapeut. *Mailing Add:* 13217 El Monte St Leawood KS 66209-4170

BROWNE, SHEILA EWING, PHYSICAL ORGANIC CHEMISTRY, POLYMER CHEMISTRY. *Current Pos:* chmn, Chem Dept, 90-93, from asst prof to assoc prof, PROF CHEM, MT HOLYOKE COL, 76- *Personal Data:* b Danville, Ky, Feb 3, 49; m 74; c Katherine & David. *Educ:* Univ Tenn, Knoxville, BS, 71; Univ Calif, Berkeley, PhD(org chem), 74. *Prof Exp:* Teaching assoc chem, Worcester Polytech Inst, 74-75; fel phys org chem, Grad Dept Biochem, Brandeis Univ, 75-76. *Mem:* Sigma Xi; Am Chem Soc; Am Indian Sci & Eng Soc. *Res:* Polymers-structural changes of polyelectrolytes; structure of carbanions using 13C nuclear magnetic resonance; biodegradable polymers. *Mailing Add:* Dept Chem Mt Holyoke Col South Hadley MA 01075. *Fax:* 413-538-2327

BROWNE, W(ILLIAM) H(OOPER), MECHANICAL ENGINEERING. *Current Pos:* RETIRED. *Personal Data:* b White Plains, NY, Aug 2, 15; m 39; c 3. *Educ:* Rensselaer Polytech Inst, ME, 36. *Prof Exp:* Apprentice engr, Caterpillar Tractor Co, 36-38, res engr diesel engines, 38-42; res engr fuels, Battelle Mem Inst, 42-45, asst supvr mech eng, 45-49, supvr, 49-51, supvr petrol eng, 51-53, mgr mech eng, 53-66, asst dir admin, Columbus Labs, 66-77. *Mem:* Am Soc Mech Engrs. *Res:* Fuels utilization; mechanical design, development and research. *Mailing Add:* 215 Middle Mountain Trail Jackson NH 03846

BROWNELL, ANNA GALE, CELLULAR DIFFERENTIATION, PROTEIN BIOCHEMISTRY. *Current Pos:* asst prof cell biol & genetics, 85-88, chair, Dept Biol, 88-90, ASSOC PROF CELL BIOL & GENETICS, CHAPMAN COL, 88- *Personal Data:* b Leipzig, Ger, June 17, 42; US citizen. *Educ:* Bowling Green State Univ, BA, 64; Northwestern Univ, PhD(biochem), 75. *Prof Exp:* Fel, Univ Southern Calif, Dent Sch, 75-77, res asst prof develop biol, 77-81; res biochemist, dept surg & orthop, Univ Calif, Los Angeles, 82-85. *Concurrent Pos:* Prin investr, NIH grant, 86-90; vis scholar, Northwestern Univ, 91-92. *Res:* Proteins of the extracellular matrix and their interactions with matrix synthesizing cells; specifically how bone matrix proteins modulate the differentiation and metabolism of bone-forming cells (osteoblasts) and bone-degrading cells (osteoclasts). *Mailing Add:* Dept Biol Chapman Univ Orange CA 92866

BROWNELL, FRANK HERBERT, III, MATHEMATICS. *Current Pos:* RETIRED. *Personal Data:* b New York, NY, Sept 20, 22; m 50; c 4. *Educ:* Yale Univ, BA, 43, MS, 47; Princeton Univ, PhD(math), 49. *Prof Exp:* Fine instr, Princeton Univ, 49-50; from asst prof to prof math, Univ Wash, 50-90. *Concurrent Pos:* Ford fel, Inst Advan Study, 53-54. *Mem:* Am Math Soc. *Res:* Nonlinear delay differential equations; operations and measures on Hilbert space and applications to quantum mechanics. *Mailing Add:* 1525 Tor Jan Hill Rd Bainbridge Island WA 98110

BROWNELL, GEORGE H, MICROBIOLOGY, BACTERIAL GENETICS. *Current Pos:* From asst prof to assoc prof microbiol, 67-80, PROF IMMUNOL & MICROBIOL, MED COL GA, 80- *Personal Data:* b Minneapolis, Minn, Oct 23, 38; m 67; c 2. *Educ:* Univ Minn, BA, 61; Univ SDak, MA, 63, PhD(microbiol), 67. *Concurrent Pos:* At Lab Molecular Virol, Nat Cancer Inst, 78-79; recipient, Bicentennial Order, Univ Los Andres, 90. *Mem:* AAAS; Am Soc Microbiol; Sigma Xi. *Res:* Nocardial genetics; microbial genetics. *Mailing Add:* Dept Biochem & Molecular Biol Med Col Ga Augusta GA 30912

BROWNELL, GEORGE L, ORGANIC CHEMISTRY. *Current Pos:* supvr indust chem res, Chem Div, Aristech Chem Corp, 60-67, assoc res consult, 75-83, SECT SUPVR RES LAB, ARISTECH CHEM CORP, 67-, SR STAFF SCIENTIST, 90- *Personal Data:* b Hoosick Falls, NY, May 20, 23; m 56; c 3. *Educ:* Rensselaer Polytech, BS, 47, MS, 48; Ohio State Univ, PhD(org chem), 53. *Prof Exp:* Res chemist, Aluminum Res Labs, 53-55; asst prof, Lehigh Univ, 55-58; res chemist, Miles Chem Co, 58-60. *Concurrent Pos:* Res consult, Aristech Chem Corp, 83- *Mem:* Am Chem Soc; Sigma Xi; Royal Soc Chem. *Res:* Electrolytic reduction, oxidation and substitution of organic compounds; pharmaceutical chemistry; chemistry of coal; lignites; esterifications; liquid phase oxidations; maleic anhydride chemistry; polymerization studies; hydroformylation studies; polyester resins; plasticizers; homogeneous catalysis; maleimido chemistry; engineering resins. *Mailing Add:* 91 Woodhaven Dr Pittsburgh PA 15228-1546

BROWNELL, GORDON LEE, MEDICAL PHYSICS. *Current Pos:* Asst physics, Mass Inst Technol, 48-50, res assoc, 50-57, from asst prof to assoc prof, 57-70, PROF NUCLEAR ENG, MASS INST TECHNOL, 70-; LECTR, HARVARD MED SCH, 50- *Personal Data:* b Duncan, Okla, Apr 8, 22; m 44, 86; c 4. *Educ:* Bucknell Univ, BS, 43; Mass Inst Technol, PhD(physics), 50. *Honors & Awards:* Aebersold Award, Soc Nuclear Med; von Heuesy Medal, Europ Soc Nuclear Med; Collidge Award, Am Asn Physicists Med. *Concurrent Pos:* From asst physicist to assoc physicist, Mass Gen Hosp, 49-61, physicist, 61-, head physics res lab; trustee, Neuro-Res Found; hon fac mem, Cuyo Univ, Arg, 54. *Mem:* AAAS; Am Asn Physicists in Med; Soc Nuclear Med; Am Phys Soc; Biophys Soc. *Res:* Imaging of positron emitting isotopes; computerized axiol tomography; reactor applications; analysis of tracer data; radiation effects and dosimetry. *Mailing Add:* Phys Res Lab Mass Gen Hosp Boston MA 02114

BROWNELL, JAMES RICHARD, SOILS, IRRIGATION. *Current Pos:* prof, 69-92, EMER PROF SOILS, CALIF STATE UNIV, FRESNO, 92-; CONSULT, SOIL FERTIL, WASTE DISPOSAL, SELF EMPLOYED, WHALEY & ASSOCS, FRESNO, CALIF. *Personal Data:* b Jeannette, Pa, Apr 20, 32; m 51, Dolly M Priester; c Vicki (Cooksey), Kathleen A (Nickel), Gerald & Christopher S. *Educ:* Pa State Univ, BS, 54; Univ Minn, MS, 57; Univ Calif, Davis, PhD(geobiol), 70. *Prof Exp:* Jr voc instr soils & irrig, Fresno State Col, 58-59, asst prof chem, 59-60; agriculturist, Di Giorgio Fruit Corp, 60-64; technician soil fertil, Univ Calif, Davis, 64-69. *Concurrent Pos:* Consult, USAID, Solar Energy Res Inst, Boyle Eng, J G Boswell, Western US & Int Egypt, Nigeria, Australia, Cent Am & Caribbean, Food & Fertilizer Tech Ctr, Taipei; Fulbright scholar, Egypt. *Mem:* Soil Sci Soc Am; Soil Conserv Soc Am; Int Humic Substances Soc. *Res:* Land use planning; waste disposal; environmental impact studies; reclamation of saline sodic soils; water measurement and quality; irrigation scheduling; soil selection for chemically stabilized brick fabrication; water application technology, crop and soil affects; agricultural energy use; swimming pool treatment; solar greenhouse design; vernal pool creation; municipal sludge use; expert witness. *Mailing Add:* 310 Stafford PO Box 1681 Cambria CA 93428

BROWNELL, JOHN HOWARD, INERTIAL CONFINEMENT FUSION, PLASMA INSTABILITY THEORY. *Current Pos:* staff mem, asst group leader, assoc group leader, PROJECT LEADER, PROG MGR & GROUP LEADER, LOS ALAMOS NAT LAB, 72- *Personal Data:* b Oneonta, NY, Oct 4, 42; c Robert & Laura. *Educ:* Mass Inst Technol, BS, 64; Stanford Univ, MS, 70, PhD(physics), 71. *Prof Exp:* Vis scientist, Inst Atomic & Molecular Physics, Neth, 71-72. *Concurrent Pos:* Consult, Quantum Physics Corp, 69-72; prin investr, High Density Plasma Physics Proj, 78- *Mem:* Am Phys Soc; Sigma Xi. *Res:* Theoretical investigation of the physics of inertial confinement and hybrid fusion schemes, including the development and use of large computer simulation codes; high pulsed power and radiation source development; technical management. *Mailing Add:* Los Alamos Nat Lab MS-B220 Los Alamos NM 87545. *E-Mail:* jhb@lanl.gov

BROWNELL, PHILIP HARRY, CELLULAR NEUROBIOLOGY, SENSORY PHYSIOLOGY. *Current Pos:* from asst prof to assoc prof, 79-95, PROF ZOOL, ORE STATE UNIV, 96- *Personal Data:* b Castro Valley, Calif, Aug 2, 47; c 2. *Educ:* Univ Calif, Berkeley, AB, 70; Univ Calif, Riverside, PhD(biol), 76. *Prof Exp:* Fel physiol & neurobiol, Univ Calif, San Francisco, 76-79. *Concurrent Pos:* Sloan Found fel, 76-77 & NIH, 77-79; prin investr, NIH & Am Heart Asn, 79-; Ger Acad Exchange Serv fel, Univ Regensburg, 90. *Mem:* Soc Neurosci; AAAS; Sigma Xi; soc Neuroethology. *Res:* Neuronal mechanisms of behavior; neural circuitry; neuroethology; neuropeptide actions in central nervous system; arthropod sensory systems and physiology, pheromone. *Mailing Add:* Dept Zool Ore State Univ Corvallis OR 97331. *Fax:* 541-737-0501; *E-Mail:* brownell@bcc.orst.edu

BROWNELL, R(ICHARD) M(ILLER), ELECTRICAL ENGINEERING, MAGNETISM. *Current Pos:* RETIRED. *Personal Data:* b Detroit, Mich, Jan 26, 30; m 53; c 5. *Educ:* Yale Univ, BS, 51, MEng, 56, DEng(magnetics), 61. *Prof Exp:* Mem tech staff, Bell Tel Labs Inc, 60-65, supvr, 65-89. *Concurrent Pos:* Lectr elec eng, Lehigh Univ, 62; mem tech prog comt, Int Nonlinear Magnetics Conf, 63-64. *Mem:* Inst Elec & Electronics Engrs. *Res:* Testing magnetic materials and devices; studies of magnetization processes by electrical techniques; sealed reed contacts; coaxial switches; ferreed and remreed switches. *Mailing Add:* 58 S Ashby Ave Livingston NJ 07039-2826

BROWNELL, ROBERT LEO, JR, MARINE MAMMALS, CETACEANS. *Current Pos:* DIR, SW FISHERIES SCI CTR, 92- *Personal Data:* b San Pedro, Calif, July 8, 43. *Educ:* San Diego State Univ, BS, 67; Univ Tokyo, DAgr, 75. *Prof Exp:* Res assoc marine mammals, Cetacean Res Lab, Little Co Mary Hosp, Calif, 63-67; chief, Marine Mammal Sect, Dept Interior, Nat Ecol Res Ctr, US Fish & Wildlife Serv, 77-92. *Concurrent Pos:* Chmn, Subcomt Small Cetaceans, 75-78 & 84-86; sci adv, Comt Sci Adv Marine Mammals, Marine Mammal Comn, Wash, DC, 75-78 & 85-90; vchmn Sci Comt Int Whaling Comn, Eng, 86-88, chmn, 89-91. *Mem:* Am Soc Mammalogists; Soc Marine Mammal (pres elec, 86-88, pres 88-90); Am Asn Zool Nomenclature; Soc Conservation Biol; Xerces Soc; Soc Vertebrate Paleont. *Res:* Natural history of marine mammals especially cetaceans. *Mailing Add:* 29641 S Western Ave San Pedro CA 90732

BROWNELL, WILLIAM EDWARD, CELL BIOLOGY OF HEARING. *Current Pos:* ENDOWDED CHAIR, BAYLOR COL MED. *Personal Data:* b Augusta, Ga, Oct 17, 42; m 68, Nancy Schulson; c 3. *Educ:* Univ Chicago, SB, 68, PhD(physiol), 73. *Honors & Awards:* Fulbright Award, Fr Fulbright Found, 84; Claude Pepper Award, Nat Inst Deafness & Other Commun Dis, 90. *Prof Exp:* From asst prof to assoc prof neurosci & surg, Univ Fla, Gainesville, 74-85; dir res & assoc prof, John's Hopkins Univ, 85-92, prof otolaryngol & neurosci, Sch Med, 91- *Concurrent Pos:* Prin investr, res grants NIH, NSF, Navy, 75-, Max Kade Found, 89-90, Hasselblad Found, 90-91; consult, Dept Army, 79, Off Naval Res, 84-89; P&P Tech Comt, Acoust Soc Am, 81-84; Res Award, Roche Res Found, 82; invited prof physiol, Univ Geneva, Switz, 82-83; mem Rev Panel Commun Dis, NIH-Nat Inst Neurol & Commun Dis & Stroke, 82-85; res prof physiol, Univ Montpellier, France, 84; mem task force, Nat Strategic Plan NIDCD, 89. *Mem:* AAAS; Soc Neurosci; Centurions Deafness Res Found; Am Acad Otolaryngol; Asn Res Otolaryngol; Acoust Soc Am. *Res:* Electromechanical transduction in outer hair cells from the mammalian inner ear; fine structure of the intracochlear electric field. *Mailing Add:* 101 Westcolt St Houston TX 77007

BROWNER, CAROL M, ENVIRONMENTAL SCIENCE. *Current Pos:* ADMINR, US ENVIRON PROTECTION AGENCY, 93- *Personal Data:* b Dec 16, 55; m 87, Michael Podhorzer; c Zachary. *Educ:* Univ Fla, BA. *Prof Exp:* Secy, Dept Environ Regulation, State Fla, 91-93. *Res:* Promoting public health by protecting air, water and land. *Mailing Add:* US Environ Protection Agency 401 M St SW MS 1101 Rm 1204 W Tower Washington DC 20460

BROWNER, ROBERT HERMAN, NEUROBIOLOGY, COMPARATIVE NEUROLOGY. *Current Pos:* Instr, 73-75, ASST PROF ANAT, NY MED COL, VALHALLA, NY, 75- *Personal Data:* b New York, NY, June 19, 43; m; c 2. *Educ:* NY Univ, BA, 65, MA, 70, PhD(biol & neurobiol), 73. *Mem:* Soc Neurosci; Am Zoologists; Sigma Xi. *Res:* Comparative neurobiology of the central auditory pathway in vertebrates; light microscopy, electron microscopy; regeneration, neurophysiology. *Mailing Add:* Dept Anat NY Med Col Basic Sci Bldg Valhalla NY 10595

BROWNIE, ALEXANDER C, BIOCHEMISTRY. *Current Pos:* asst prof path & biochem, 63-67, assoc prof biochem, 67-70, res assoc prof path, 67-76, PROF BIOCHEM, STATE UNIV NY, BUFFALO, 70-, CHMN DEPT, 76-, RES PROF PATH, 76-, RES PROF MED, 84- *Personal Data:* b Bathgate, Scotland, Mar 6, 31. *Educ:* Univ Edinburgh, BSc, 52, PhD(biochem), 55, DSc, 81. *Prof Exp:* Asst biochem, Univ Edinburgh, 53-55; Scottish Hosps Endowment Res Trust fel, Royal Infirmary, Edinburgh, 55-56; Organon res fel pharmacol, Univ St Andrews, 56-59, med res fel, 59-62, hon lectr, 60-62; USPHS fel, Univ Utah, 62-63. *Mem:* Endocrine Soc; Am Soc Biol Chemists. *Res:* Adrenal steroid biosynthesis; pituitary-adrenal function in disease; mechanism of action of ACTH; hormones and hypertension. *Mailing Add:* Dept Biochem 140 Farber Hall State Univ NY Buffalo NY 14214. *Fax:* 716-829-2086

BROWNING, CHARLES BENTON, ANIMAL NUTRITION. *Current Pos:* dean & dir, 79-97, EMER DEAN, COL AGR, AGR EXP STA, COOP EXTEN, OKLA STATE UNIV, 97- *Personal Data:* b Houston, Tex, Sept 16, 31; m 56; c 6. *Educ:* Tex Technol Col, BS, 55; Kans State Univ, MS, 56, PhD(animal nutrit), 58. *Prof Exp:* From asst prof to assoc prof dairy prod, Miss State Univ, 58-62, prof dairy sci, 62-66; chmn, Dept Dairy Sci, Univ Fla, 66-69, dean, Col Agr, 69-79. *Mem:* Am Soc Animal Sci; Am Dairy Sci Asn. *Res:* Dairy cattle nutrition and physiology. *Mailing Add:* Col Agr Okla State Univ Stillwater OK 74078-0500

BROWNING, DANIEL DWIGHT, RADON. *Current Pos:* PRES, SCI MGT SERV LTD, 86- *Personal Data:* b New Albany, Miss, Mar 24, 21; m 47; c 5. *Educ:* Miss Col, BA, 41. *Prof Exp:* Control chemist, E I du Pont de Nemours & Co, 41; fel, Mellon Inst, 42-44 & 46-50; res chemist, Armstrong Cork, Co, 50-58, mgr paint res, 58-60, mgr plastic flooring res, 60-62, gen mgr bldg prod res, 62-68, asst dir res, 68-76, vpres & dir, Bus Info Serv, 76-81, vpres & dir res, Armstrong World Ind, 81-66. *Concurrent Pos:* Mem, Bldg Res Inst. *Mem:* Am Chem Soc. *Res:* Building products. *Mailing Add:* 727 E Madison St Lancaster PA 17602

BROWNING, DAVID GUNTER, ACOUSTICS, PHYSICAL OCEANOGRAPHY. *Current Pos:* ADJ PROF, DEPT PHYSICS, UNIV RI, KINGSTON, 95- *Personal Data:* b Wakefield, RI, May 3, 37. *Educ:* Univ RI, BS, 58; Mich State Univ, MS, 61. *Prof Exp:* Res physicist acoust, Naval Underwater Systs Ctr, 65-72; exchange scientist, Defense Sci Estab, NZ, 72-73; res physicist, Naval Underwater Systs Ctr, 73-79; vis scientist oceanog, Naval Postgrad Sch, 79-80; res physicist acoust, Naval Underwater Systs Ctr, 80-82; exchange scientist, Defense Res Estab-Pac Can, 83, Naval Underwater Systs Ctr, 84-94. *Mem:* Am Phys Soc; AAAS; fel Acoust Soc Am; Australia-NZ Asn Advan Sci; Sigma Xi; US Naval Inst; Am Geophys Union. *Res:* Attenuation of sound in the sea; acoustic characteristics of the oceans of the Southern Hemisphere; physical properties of ocean fronts and eddys. *Mailing Add:* 139 Old North Rd Kingston RI 02881. *Fax:* 401-783-4362; *E-Mail:* decibeldb@aol.com

BROWNING, EDWARD T, PHARMACOLOGY, NEUROCHEMISTRY. *Current Pos:* PROF PHARMACOL, ROBERT WOOD JOHNSON MED SCH, UNIV MED & DENT NJ, 84- *Personal Data:* b Cleveland, Ohio, July 15, 39; div, Elisabeth; c Victor & Charlotte. *Educ:* Purdue Univ, BS, 61; Univ Ill Med Ctr, Chicago, MS, 64, PhD(pharmacol), 66. *Prof Exp:* Johnson Res Found fel phys biochem, Univ Pa, 66-68; from asst prof to prof pharmacol, Rutgers Med Sch, 74-84. *Mem:* Fedn Am Socs Exp Biol; Soc Neurosci; Am Soc Neurochem; Am Soc Pharmacol & Exp Therapeut. *Res:* Function of astrocytes; biochemistry and molecular biology of synaptic structures. *Mailing Add:* Dept Pharmacol Robert Wood Johnson Med Sch 675 Hoes Lane Piscataway NJ 08854. *Fax:* 732-235-4073; *E-Mail:* browning@biouax.rutgers.edu

BROWNING, HORACE LAWRENCE, JR, POLYMER CHEMISTRY, PHYSICAL CHEMISTRY. *Current Pos:* res chemist, 63-65, SR RES CHEMIST, TENN EASTMAN CO, 65- *Personal Data:* b Overton, Tex, Oct 8, 32; m 53; c 2. *Educ:* Stephen F Austin State Col, BA, 54; La State Univ, MS, 56, PhD(phys chem), 60. *Prof Exp:* Asst prof chem, Northeast La State Col, 60-63. *Concurrent Pos:* Spec lectr chem, King Col, 66-71. *Mem:* Am Chem Soc. *Res:* Gel permeation chromatography; ultracentrifugation; characterization of polymers; solution thermodynamics. *Mailing Add:* 1113 Radcliffe Ave Kingsport TN 37664-2025

BROWNING, J(OHN) ARTIE, PLANT DISEASE EPIDEMIOLOGY, IN SITU CONSERVATION OF GENETIC RESOURCES. *Current Pos:* prof & head plant sci, Tex A&M Univ, 81-85, prof & head plant path & microbiol, 85-89, prof, 90-91, EMER PROF PLANT PATH, TEX A&M UNIV, 91- *Personal Data:* b Kosse, Tex, Oct 3, 23; m 46, Arra White; c Glenn A, Donna G & John E. *Educ:* Baylor Univ, BS, 47; Cornell Univ, PhD(plant path), 53. *Prof Exp:* Asst plant path, Cornell Univ, 49-53; from asst prof to prof plant path, Iowa State Univ, 53-81. *Concurrent Pos:* Mem staff, Rockefeller Found agr prog, Colombia, 63-64; vis prof, Tel-Aviv Univ, 69, 78, 82, Plant Breeding Inst, Cambridge Univ, 78, Fulbright, 90-91; mem, US-USSR Integrated Rest Mgt Prog, 74-79; mem panel experts integrated pest control, UN-Fed Agr Orgn, 78-83; bd dirs, Am Inst Biol Sci, 83-86. *Mem:* Fel AAAS; fel Am Phytopath Soc (pres, 81-82); Am Soc Agron; Crop Sci Soc Am; Am Inst Biol Sci. *Res:* Epidemiology of cereal rusts; teaching epidemiology and plant pathology; conservation and utilization of germ plasm of indigineous crop species; how indigenous plants protect themselves from diseases and relevance of this to agroecosystems. *Mailing Add:* 3122 Hollywood Dr NE Olympia WA 98516-3000

BROWNING, RONALD ANTHONY, NEUROPHARMACOLOGY, NEUROBIOLOGY. *Current Pos:* from asst prof to assoc prof, 73-90, PROF PHYSIOL & PHARMACOL, SCH MED, SOUTHERN ILL UNIV, 90- *Personal Data:* b Washington, DC, Nov 7, 40; m 65, Cheryl A Griffith; c Dana A. *Educ:* George Washington Univ, BS, 63, MS, 68; Univ Ill, PhD(pharmacol), 71. *Prof Exp:* Fel pharmacol, Univ Chicago, 71-73. *Mem:* Am Soc Pharmacol & Exp Therapeut; Soc Neurosci; AAAS; Am Epilepsy Soc. *Res:* Understanding the neurochemistry of seizures and the mechanism of action of drugs which suppress tonic seizures; importance of subcortical pathways in seizure control and spread; monoamine neurochemistry. *Mailing Add:* Dept Med Physiol & Pharmacol Sch Med Southern Ill Univ Carbondale IL 62901

BROWNLEE, DONALD E, ASTRONOMY. *Current Pos:* PROF ASTRON, UNIV WASH, 77- *Personal Data:* b Las Vegas, Nev, Dec 21, 43; m 76; c 1. *Educ:* Univ Calif, Berkeley, BSEE, 65; Univ Wash, PhD(astron), 70. *Honors & Awards:* Medal Outstanding Sci Achievement, NASA; J L Smith Medal, Nat Acad Sci, 94. *Concurrent Pos:* Consult & prin investr, NASA, 76-; vis assoc geochem, Calif Inst Technol, 77-85. *Mem:* Nat Acad Sci; Meteoritical Soc; Am Astron Soc; Microbeam Anal Soc; AAAS; Int Astron Union. *Res:* Collection and analysis of interplanetary dust to provide information on comets and the origin of the solar system. *Mailing Add:* Dept Astron Physics Hall Univ Wash Seattle WA 98195

BROWNLEE, PAULA PIMLOTT, ORGANIC CHEMISTRY. *Current Pos:* PRES, ASN AM COLS, WASHINGTON, DC, 90- *Personal Data:* b London, Eng, June 23, 34; m 61; c 3. *Educ:* Oxford Univ, MA, 57, PhD(org chem), 59. *Hon Degrees:* LHD, Hollins Col. *Prof Exp:* Res fel org chem, Univ Rochester, 59-61; res chemist, Stamford Res Labs, Am Cyanamid Co, 61-62; from instr to assoc prof chem, Rutgers Univ, 70-76; dean fac & prof chem, Union Col, Schenectady, NY, 76-81; pres & prof chem, Hollins Col, Va, 81-90. *Concurrent Pos:* Assoc dean, Douglass Col, 72-75, actg dean, 75-76, dir & vchair, Educ Testing Serv; dir, Nat Humanities Ctr. *Mem:* Soc for Values Higher Educ; Royal Soc Chem; Am Chem Soc; Am Asn Higher Educ; Sigma Xi. *Res:* Peptide synthesis; organic sulfur compounds; charge-transfer complexes incorporating polymers. *Mailing Add:* 2107 Elliott Ave McLean VA 22101-5304

BROWNLOW, ARTHUR HUME, GEOCHEMISTRY OF NATURAL WATERS. *Current Pos:* from asst prof to assoc prof, 65-81, chmn dept, 75-79, PROF GEOL, BOSTON UNIV, 81- *Personal Data:* b Helena, Mont, July 25, 33; m 85; c 4. *Educ:* Mass Inst Technol, SB, 55, PhD(geol), 60. *Prof Exp:* Asst prof geol, Univ Mo-Rolla, 60-65. *Concurrent Pos:* NSF res grant, 70-72. *Mem:* AAAS; Geol Soc Am; Geochem Soc; Mineral Soc Am; Am Geophys Union. *Res:* Water pollution; gemstones. *Mailing Add:* Dept Earth Sci Boston Univ 675 Commonwealth Ave Boston MA 02215

BROWNLOW, ROGER W, AUTOMATIC CONTROLS, FLUID MECHANICS. *Current Pos:* SR RES SCIENTIST, EASTMAN KODAK CO, 84- *Personal Data:* b Cleveland, Ohio, Dec 26, 22; m 46; c 2. *Educ:* Bucknell Univ, BS, 48; Cornell Univ, MS, 56; Ore State Univ, PhD(mech eng), 76. *Prof Exp:* Test engr, E I du Pont de Nemours, Inc, 48-53; instr decision geom, Cornell Univ, 53-56; proj engr flight control, Rockwell Int, 56-67; lectr thermo mech, Calif State Univ, Long Beach, 67-69; asst prof mech, Gonzaga Univ, 76-79; asst prof mech controls, Mich Technol Univ, 79-81; assoc prof, Western Mich Univ, 81-84. *Concurrent Pos:* Vis scholar, Stanford Univ, 80-81; Vis scholar, Stanford Univ, 80-81. *Mem:* Sigma Xi; Am Soc Mech Eng; Am Soc Eng Educ; Am Asn Univ Professors. *Res:* Wind tunnel simulation and field measurements of atmospheric boundary layer flow; computer modeling of turbulent flow; mathematical modeling and computer simulation of a flux summing redundant, servo valve control; modal analysis. *Mailing Add:* 29 Woodshire Lane Rochester NY 14606-4629

BROWNSCHEIDLE, CAROL MARY, HISTOCHEMISTRY, MATERNAL DIABETES. *Current Pos:* ASSOC RES SCIENTIST, MED FOUND BUFFALO, 81- *Personal Data:* b Buffalo, NY, July 2, 46. *Educ:* Niagara Univ, BS, 68; State Univ NY, Buffalo, PhD(anat), 74. *Prof Exp:* Asst prof anat, Col Med, Univ Cincinnati, 74-81. *Mem:* NY Acad Sci; Sigma Xi; Am Asn Anatomists; Am Diabetes Asn; AAAS. *Res:* Placental morphology and function in maternal diabetes mellitus; teratology. *Mailing Add:* 6878 Omphalius Rd Colden NY 14033

BROWNSCOMBE, EUGENE RUSSELL, PHYSICAL CHEMISTRY. *Current Pos:* tech dir, Diag Serv Inc, 78-86, RETIRED. *Personal Data:* b National City, Calif, July 9, 06; m 32; c 1. *Educ:* Yale Univ, BS, 28, PhD(phys chem), 32. *Honors & Awards:* Anthony F Lucas Gold Medal, Soc Petrol Engrs; Pioneer of Enhance Oil Recovery, Soc Petrol Engrs & Dept Energy. *Prof Exp:* Res chemist, Biol Lab, Cold Spring Harbor, 32-34; res scientist, Atlantic Richfield Co, Pa & Tex, 34-69; dir technol, Sonics Int, Inc, 69-77. *Concurrent Pos:* Instr calculus, Bishop Col, 69-71. *Mem:* Am Soc Petrol Engrs; Am Chem Soc. *Res:* Band spectra; chemical effects of x-rays; solvent extraction; petroleum production and refining; flow of fluids through porous media; theoretical reservoir analysis; exploration methods. *Mailing Add:* 2822 Lewis Dr LaVerne CA 91750-4308

BROWNSTEIN, BARBARA L, cell biology, molecular genetics, for more information see previous edition

BROWNSTEIN, KENNETH ROBERT, QUANTUM MECHANICS. *Current Pos:* Assoc prof, 65-73, PROF PHYSICS, UNIV MAINE, ORONO, 73- *Personal Data:* b New York, NY, May 6, 36. *Educ:* Rensselaer Polytech Inst, BS, 57, PhD(physics), 66. *Mem:* Am Phys Soc; Am Asn Physics Teachers; Am Soc Eng Educ; Sigma Xi. *Res:* Bounds for scattering phase shifts; approximation methods for bound and scattering states. *Mailing Add:* Dept Physics Univ Maine Orono ME 04469-0001. *Fax:* 207-581-3410

BROWNSTEIN, MARTIN H, DERMATOPATHOLOGY. *Current Pos:* CLIN PROF DERMAT, MT SINAI MED CTR, 83- *Personal Data:* b Brooklyn, NY, Aug 20, 35. *Educ:* Harvard Col, AB, 56; Yeshiva Univ, MD, 61. *Prof Exp:* Intern, Lenox Hill Hosp, 61-62; resident internal med, Vet Admin Hosp, Brooklyn & Manhattan, 62-65; resident dermat, NY Univ Hosp, 65-66; dermatologist, McDonald Army Hosp, Fort Eustis, Va, 66-68; Osborne fel dermatopath, Armed Forces Inst Path, Washington, DC, 68-69; instr dermat, Johns Hopkins Univ Med Sch, 69-70; clin asst prof dermat, NY Med Col-Metrop Hosp Ctr, 70-73, path, 71-83, clin assoc prof dermat, 73-78, clin prof, 78-83. *Concurrent Pos:* Chmn, Comt Path, Am Acad Dermat, 80-82. *Mem:* Am Soc Dermatopath (pres, 83-84); Am Acad Dermat; fel Am Col Physicians; NY Acad Med; Brit Asn Dermatologists; Int Soc Trop Dermat; AMA. *Res:* Dermatology and dermatopathology; published over 95 publication. *Mailing Add:* Lab Dermatopath 2 N Plandome Rd Port Washington NY 11050

BROWNSTEIN, MICHAEL JAY, NEUROENDOCRINOLOGY, PHARMACOLOGY. *Current Pos:* AT LAB CELL BIOL, NIMH. *Personal Data:* b Washington, DC, Feb 27, 43; m 66; c 2. *Educ:* Columbia Univ, AB, 64; Univ Chicago, MD & PhD(pharmacol), 71. *Prof Exp:* Intern pediat, Children's Hosp Med Ctr, 71-72; res assoc pharmacol, Pharmacol Res Assoc Training Prog, Nat Inst Gen Med Sci, NIH, Bethesda, 72-74, sr staff fel, 74-76; med officer res, Lab Clin Sci, Alcohol, Drug Abuse & Ment Health Admin, NIMH, Bethesda, 76-, chief, Neuroendocrinol Unit, 78- *Mem:* Sigma Xi. *Res:* Neuroendocrine regulation; peptide biosynthesis; pineal gland; neuropharmacology; circadian rhythms. *Mailing Add:* 6515 Old Farm Lane Rockville MD 20852

BROWNSTEIN, SYDNEY KENNETH, ORGANIC CHEMISTRY, NUCLEAR MAGNETIC RESONANCE. *Current Pos:* res officer, 59-91, CONSULT, NAT RES COUN SPACE,91-, PRES, BROWNSTEIN CONSULTS, 91- *Personal Data:* b Regina, Sask, Mar 5, 31; m 54, Irene Rappaport; c Michael, Bonnie & Rani. *Educ:* Univ Sask, BA, 52; Univ Chicago, PhD(chem), 55. *Prof Exp:* Chemist, Argonne Cancer Res Hosp, 55; fel & hon asst, Univ Col, Univ London, 55-56; instr chem, Cornell Univ, 56-59. *Concurrent Pos:* Weizmann fel, 65-66; vis scholar, Cambridge, 89-90. *Mem:* Chem Inst Can; Royal Soc Chem. *Res:* Application of nuclear magnetic resonance techniques to problems in chemistry. *Mailing Add:* RR3 Lanark ON K0G 1K0 Can. *Fax:* 613-991-2384; *E-Mail:* sydney.brownstein@mc.ca

BROWNSTONE, YEHOSHUA SHIEKY, CLINICAL BIOCHEMISTRY. *Current Pos:* RETIRED. *Personal Data:* b Winnipeg, Man, May 12, 29; m 50, Ellen Gresele Weis; c Desi (Yatzhak), Deborah F & David M. *Educ:* Univ Man, BScA, 50, MSc, 56; McGill Univ, PhD(biochem), 58. *Prof Exp:* Chemist, Dominion Linseed Oil Ltd, 51-52; asst, Dept Physiol & Med Res, Univ Man, 54-56; demonstr & asst, Dept Biochem, McGill Univ, 56-58, res assoc, 58-59, lectr, 60; biochemist, Dept Biochem & Radioisotopes, Queen Mary Vet Hosp, 59-60; from asst prof to prof path chem, Univ Western Ont, 61-71, prof, Div Clin Biochem, Dept Biochem, 71-93, dir, Dept Clin Path, Victoria Hosp, 61-93. *Concurrent Pos:* Vis sci, Carlsberg Lab, Copenhagen, Denmark, 69-70. *Mem:* NY Acad Sci; Can Fedn Biol Soc; Can Biochem Soc; Can Soc Clin Chemists (pres, 73-74). *Res:* Clinical chemistry; enzymology of the normocyte; the pentose phosphate metabolic pathway; enzymes in neoplastic disease; blood preservation; effect of hormones on enzyme action; drugs; metabolism and detection; mass spectrometry. *Mailing Add:* 572 Lambton London ON N5Y 4G2 Can

BROWZIN, BORIS S(ERGEEVICH), civil engineering, hydrology & water resources, for more information see previous edition

BROXMEYER, HAL EDWARD, MEDICAL SCIENCE, BIOLOGY. *Current Pos:* assoc prof med, 83-86, PROF MED, MICROBIOL-IMMUNOL, SCH MED, IND UNIV, 86-, SCI DIR, WALTHER ONCOL CTR, 88- *Personal Data:* b Brooklyn, NY, Nov 27, 44; m 69, C Beth Biller; c Eric J & Jeffrey D. *Educ:* Brooklyn Col, BS, 66; Long Island Univ, MS, 69; NY Univ, PhD(biol), 73. *Honors & Awards:* Mellor Award, Sloan Kettering Inst, 76 & 77, Boyer Award, 83; Merit Award, Nat Cancer Inst, 87. *Prof Exp:* Res assoc med biol, Queens Univ, Ont, 73-75; assoc researcher, Sloan Kettering Inst Cancer Res, Cornell Univ, 75-76, res assoc, 76-78, asst mem, 78-82, asst prof, 78-83, assoc mem, 83. *Concurrent Pos:* Leukemia Soc Am spec fel, 76-78 & scholar award, 78-83; Am Cancer Soc grant, 78-80, Nat Cancer Inst grants, 78-81 & 81-86 & 86- *Mem:* AAAS; NY Acad Sci; Am Soc Hemat; Int Soc Exp Hemat; Am Asn Cancer Res; Am Asn Immunol. *Res:* Regulation of hematopoiesis; normal and leukemic bone marrow and blood cell proliferation; maturation in vitro and in vivo. *Mailing Add:* Microbiol Immunol/Walther Oncol Ctr Ind Univ Sch Med 975 W Walnut St Indianapolis IN 46202-5121. *Fax:* 317-274-7592; *E-Mail:* hal_broxmeyer@iucc.iupui.edu

BROXTON, DAVID EDWARD, IGNEOUS PETROLOGY, MINERALOGY & GEOCHEMISTRY. *Current Pos:* STAFF MEM GEOL & GEOCHEM, LOS ALAMOS NAT LAB, 77- *Personal Data:* b Winston-Salem, NC, Aug 19, 52; m 80, Patricia O'Rourke; c Michael & Patrick. *Educ:* Univ NC, Chapel Hill, BS, 74; Univ NMex, Albuquerque, MS, 76. *Concurrent Pos:* Prin investr, Nat Uranium Resource Eval Prog, 80-83 & Yucca Mountain Proj, 84-; mem, Environ Restoration, Los Alamos Nat Lab, 91- *Mem:* Am Geophys Union; Geol Soc Am. *Res:* Secondary minerals in tuffaceous rocks and their potential use as natural radionuclide migration barriers at potential nuclear waste repositories; chemical evolution of magmas associated large volcanic complexes; application of geology to environmental restoration investigations. *Mailing Add:* Los Alamos Nat Lab Mail Stop D462 Los Alamos NM 87545. *Fax:* 505-665-3285; *E-Mail:* dbroxton@lanl.gov

BROYLES, ARTHUR AUGUSTUS, EFFECTS OF NUCLEAR EXPLOSIONS. *Current Pos:* from assoc prof to prof, 59-86, EMER PROF PHYSICS, UNIV FLA, 86- *Personal Data:* b Atlanta, Ga, May 16, 23; m 43, Jenna A Schneider; c Rhea D, David C, Bonnie S & Frances E. *Educ:* Univ Fla, BS, 42; Yale Univ, PhD(physics), 49. *Prof Exp:* Asst prof physics, Univ

Fla, 49-50; mem staff, Los Alamos Sci Lab, 50-53; res physicist, Rand Corp, 53-59. *Concurrent Pos:* Vis prof, Univ Adelaide, Australia, 80; consult, Lawrence Livermore Nat Lab, 82-, physicist, 85-86. *Mem:* Am Asn Physics Teachers; fel Am Phys Soc. *Res:* Quantum electrodynamics; nonperturbative solution of the Schwinger-Dyson equations; global effects of nuclear war; effects of gamma rays on man. *Mailing Add:* Dept Physics 215 Williamson Hall Univ Fla Gainesville FL 32611. *E-Mail:* broyles@ufhepa.phys.ufl.edu

BROYLES, CARTER D, PHYSICS, ENGINEERING SCIENCE. *Current Pos:* RETIRED. *Personal Data:* b Eckman, WVa, Nov 1, 24; m 55; c 2. *Educ:* Univ Chattanooga, BS, 48; Vanderbilt Univ, PhD(physics), 52. *Prof Exp:* Res physicist, Sandia Lab, 52-56, supvr, Radiation Physics Div, 56-64, mgr, High Altitude Burst Physics Dept, 64-68, mgr test sci dept 9110, 68-72, dir effects exp orgn, 72-75, dir field eng, 75-89. *Concurrent Pos:* Mem staff, Vanderbilt Univ, 52. *Mem:* AAAS; fel Am Phys Soc; Am Asn Physics Teachers; Sigma Xi. *Res:* Magnetic spectrometer studies of radioactive isotopes; fluid dynamics; plasma physics; nuclear radiation measurements; radioactive waste disposal; in-situ fossil fuel technology. *Mailing Add:* 5310 Los Poblanos Lane NW Albuquerque NM 87107

BROYLES, ROBERT HERMAN, DEVELOPMENTAL BIOLOGY, TOXICOLOGY. *Current Pos:* assoc prof, 77-85, PROF BIOCHEM & MOLECULAR BIOL, COL MED, UNIV OKLA HEALTH SCI CTR, 85- *Personal Data:* b Kingsport, Tenn, Feb 16, 43; m 66, J Dianne Fields; c David C & James R. *Educ:* Wake Forest Univ, BS, 65, Bowman Gray Sch Med, PhD(biochem), 70. *Prof Exp:* NIH fel, & res assoc biochem, Fla State Univ, 70-72; asst prof zool, Univ Wis-Milwaukee, 72-77. *Concurrent Pos:* Cottrell grant, Res Corp, Inc, 73; res grant, US Sea Grant Prog, 75; NIH res grant, Nat Inst Arthritis, Metab & Digestive Dis, 76-88; sr scientist, NIH, NIDDK, 89-91; asst dir, MD/PhD Prog, Col Med, Univ Okla Health Sci Ctr, 91- *Mem:* Am Soc Cell Biol; Sigma Xi; AAAS; Am Soc Zoologists; Soc Develop Biologists; Am Soc Biol Chem; Am Soc Hemat. *Res:* Developmental biology; gene regulation and DNA-binding proteins in red blood cell differentiation; effects of drugs and environmental contaminants on vertebrate embryos and on red blood cell differentiation. *Mailing Add:* Dept Biochem & Molecular Biol Univ Okla Health Sci Ctr PO Box 26901 Oklahoma City OK 73910-0001. *Fax:* 405-271-3139

BRUALDI, RICHARD ANTHONY, MATHEMATICS. *Current Pos:* from asst prof to assoc prof, 65-73, PROF MATH, UNIV WIS-MADISON, 73- *Personal Data:* b Derby, Conn, Sept 2, 39; m 63, 78; c 2. *Educ:* Univ Conn, BA, 60; Syracuse Univ, MS, 62, PhD(math), 64. *Prof Exp:* Nat Acad Sci-Nat Res Coun fel, Nat Bur Stand, 64-65. *Concurrent Pos:* NATO fel, Univ Sheffield, 69-70. *Mem:* Am Math Soc; Math Asn Am. *Res:* Matrix theory and combinatorics. *Mailing Add:* Dept Math Univ Wis 480 Lincoln Dr Madison WI 53706-1313. *Fax:* 612-263-8891

BRUBACHER, ELAINE SCHNITKER, PRE-OCLAMPSIA PREGNANCY, RENAL NATURIESIS. *Current Pos:* ASSOC PROF BIOL, PHYSIOL & ANAT, DEPT BIOL, UNIV REDLANDS, 80- *Educ:* Univ Mich, PhD(physiol), 67. *Mailing Add:* 1200 Colton Ave Redlands CA 92373-0999

BRUBAKER, BURTON D(ALE), CERAMICS ENGINEERING. *Current Pos:* CONSULT, BRUBAKER CERAMIC SERV, 94- *Personal Data:* b Tiffin, Ohio, June 15, 35; m 59, Nancy Wittman; c Debra & Andrew. *Educ:* Ohio State Univ, BCerE & MSc, 58, PhD(ceramic eng), 62. *Prof Exp:* Res assoc ceramics eng, Exp Sta, Ohio State Univ, 58-62; res engr, Dow Chem Co, 62-68, sr res engr, 68-72, sr res specialist, 72-80, res assoc, 80-94. *Mem:* Am Ceramic Soc; Nat Inst Ceramic Engrs. *Res:* Composite structures and properties; ceramic and glass foams; thermal insulations; polymer foams; ceramic armor; whisker fibers. *Mailing Add:* 1702 Sylvan Lane Midland MI 48640-2538

BRUBAKER, CARL H, JR, inorganic chemistry, organometallic chemistry; deceased, see previous edition for last biography

BRUBAKER, CLIFFORD E, BIOMECHANICS, REHABILITATION SCIENCE. *Current Pos:* DEAN, SCH HEALTH REHAB SCI, UNIV PITTSBURGH, 91- *Personal Data:* b Muncie, Ind, 1938. *Educ:* Ball State Univ, BS, 61, MA, 64; Univ Ore, PhD, 68. *Prof Exp:* Prof bioeng, Univ Va, 73-91. *Mem:* Am Inst Med & Biol Eng. *Mailing Add:* 6819 Reynolds St Pittsburgh PA 15208

BRUBAKER, GEORGE RANDELL, INORGANIC CHEMISTRY, BIOINORGANIC CHEMISTRY. *Current Pos:* DIR LAB, US FOOD & DRUG ADMIN, 90- *Personal Data:* b New York, NY, July 17, 39; m 64; c 2. *Educ:* Columbia Univ, BA, 60; Ohio State Univ, MSc, 63, PhD(chem), 65. *Prof Exp:* Res assoc inorg chem, Univ Pittsburgh, 65-66; from asst prof to assoc prof chem, Ill Inst Technol, 66-89. *Mem:* Am Chem Soc; Royal Soc Chem. *Res:* Synthesis, characterization and reactions of transition metal complexes; biological significance of transition metal chemistry. *Mailing Add:* 11 TRI US Food & Drug Admin Chicago Lab 10 W 35th St Chicago IL 60616

BRUBAKER, INARA MENCIS, PHYSICAL CHEMISTRY. *Current Pos:* res specialist, Allied Signal Eng Mat Res Ctr, 82-84, assoc res scientist, 84-86, group leader separations, 86-88, chemicals, 88-90, mgr process technol, Allied Signal Res & Technol, 90-95, SR RES ASSOC, ALLIED SIGNAL ENG MAT RES CTR, 96- *Personal Data:* b Riga, Latvia, May 1, 38; US citizen; div; c Erika J (deceased) & Andra E (deceased). *Educ:* Ohio Northern Univ, BS, 59; Ohio State Univ, MS, 61, PhD(anal chem), 63. *Prof Exp:* Res chemist electro chem, Universal Oil Prod Co, 66-70; res assoc inorg chem, Ill Inst Technol, 76; cong fel, Am Chem Soc, 77; res chemist, UOP Res Ctr, 78-82. *Concurrent Pos:* Chmn, 80-82, task force on occup safety & health, Am Chem Soc, 80-96, chmn, 89-96. *Mem:* Am Chem Soc; AAAS. *Res:* Analytical chemistry; process technology; separations; hydrometallurgy; metals recovery and management; occupational safety and health. *Mailing Add:* 126 Ardmore Rd Des Plaines IL 60016-2117

BRUBAKER, KENTON KAYLOR, BIOLOGY, HORTICULTURE. *Current Pos:* DIR ARBORETUM, EASTERN MENNONITE UNIV, 95- *Personal Data:* b Elizabethtown, Pa, Feb 17, 32; m 94, Shirley Yoder; c 4. *Educ:* Eastern Mennonite Col, BS, 54; Ohio State Univ, MSc, 57, PhD, 59. *Prof Exp:* Assoc prof biol, Eastern Mennonite Col, 59-62; horticulturist, Congo Polytech Inst, 62-64; chg de cours bot, Free Univ of the Congo, 64-65; chmn dept, Eastern Mennonite Col, 65-74, prof biol, 65-97, coordr, int agr prog, 85-95. *Mem:* Am Sci Affil; Am Asn Bot Gardens & Arboreta. *Res:* Chemical weed control in vegetable crops; carbohydrate translocation in greenhouse tomatoes; tropical horticulture; protein content of tropical vegetables; alternative fertilizers; perennials and wild flowers for home landscaping. *Mailing Add:* Arboretum Eastern Mennonite Univ Harrisonburg VA 22801-2462

BRUBAKER, LEONARD HATHAWAY, MEDICAL ONCOLOGY, HEMATOLOGY. *Current Pos:* PROF HEMAT & ONCOL, MED COL GA, 78- *Personal Data:* b Macon, Ga, July 14, 34; m 57; c 3. *Educ:* Duke Univ, AB, 56; Emory Univ, MS & MD, 64. *Prof Exp:* Intern & resident internal med, Vet Admin Hosp & Emory Univ Hosp, 64-66; clin assoc leukemia, Nat Cancer Inst, 66-68; from asst prof to assoc prof med hemat & oncol, Sch Med, Univ Mo, 69-78. *Concurrent Pos:* Fel hematol & oncol, Ohio State Univ Hosp, 68. *Mem:* Southern Soc Clin Investigation; fel Am Col Physicians; Am Soc Hemat; Am Soc Clin Oncol; Am Fedn Clin Res. *Res:* Neutrophil kinetics in neutropenic patients; paroxysmal nocturnal hemoglobinuria; marrow neutrophil reserves; neutrophil function in malnourished cancer patients; genetic metabolic characteristics in bladder cancer. *Mailing Add:* 818 St Sebasffan Way Augusta GA 30901

BRUBAKER, MERLIN L, INTERNAL MEDICINE, PUBLIC HEALTH. *Current Pos:* UNIV PHYSICIAN & PROF HEALTH CARE ADMIN, UNIV LA VERNE, 85- *Personal Data:* b Live Oak, Calif, July 1, 22; m 43; c 6. *Educ:* Calif Col Med, MD, 46; Univ London, dipl trop med & hyg, 52; Univ La Verne, BA, 56; Univ Calif, Los Angeles, MA, 62. *Prof Exp:* Pvt pract med, Fullerton, Calif, 47-52; med supt, Garkida Leprosarium, Nigeria, 52-55; assoc prof med, Calif Col Med, 55-62, chmn curric & admis comt, 56-62, dir clin pract, 59-62; chief prog planning & eval med div, Peace Corps, 62-64; asst dir, USPHS Hosp, Staten Island, NY, 64-65 & dir, USPHS hosp, Carville, La, 65-68, dir career develop global community health, 68-70; regional adv leprosy, venereal dis & treponematosis, WHO-Pan Am Health Orgn, 70-77; USPHS rep to Commonwealth PR, 77-80; dir off refugee health affairs, Off Surgeon Gen, USPHS, 80-81, dep dir Nat Med Audiovisual Ctr, Nat Libr Med, 81-82; consult int health, 82-85. *Concurrent Pos:* Col physician & dir student health servs, La Verne Col, 56-60; asst med officer in chg, USPHS Hosp, Staten Island, NY, 64-65 & dir prof training & res, Carville, La, 65, dir, 65-68; clin assoc prof, Sch Med, La State Univ, 65-68; assoc clin prof community med & int health, Sch Med, Georgetown Univ, 68-; La State Univ fel trop med & parasitol to Mid Am. *Mem:* Am Soc Trop Med & Hyg; fel Am Pub Health Asn; fel Royal Soc Med; Int Leprosy Asn; fel Royal Soc Trop Med. *Res:* Preventive medicine; medical education. *Mailing Add:* 15101 Roddy Rd Thurmont MD 21788

BRUBAKER, PAUL EUGENE, II, TOXICOLOGY. *Current Pos:* REGULATORY AFFAIRS COORDR, TOXICOL, EXXON CORP, 79- *Personal Data:* b Indiana, Pa, Dec 31, 34; m 65; c 5. *Educ:* St Vincent Col, BA, 59; Cath Univ Am, MS, 65, PhD(biol), 68. *Prof Exp:* Jr staff fel cell biol, Nat Inst Environ Health Sci, 68-70, sr staff fel, 70-71; res biologist molecular biol, US Environ Protection Agency, 71-73, sr sci adv toxicol, 73-75; chief pathophysiol, Greenfield, Ahaway & Tyler, Consults, 75-76; sr toxicologist, Mobil Oil Corp, 76-78; mgr corp toxicol, Warner-Lambert Co, 78-79. *Concurrent Pos:* Adj prof biochem, Univ NC, 72- *Mem:* AAAS; Soc Toxicol; Air Pollution Coastal Asn; Am Petrol Inst; Sigma Xi. *Res:* Environmental health; toxicology; epidemiology; molecular biology; agriculture risk analysis and air pollution. *Mailing Add:* 3 Halstead Rd Mendham NJ 07945

BRUBAKER, ROBERT ROBINSON, MICROBIOLOGY. *Current Pos:* from asst to assoc prof, 66-79, PROF MICROBIOL, MICH STATE UNIV, 79- *Personal Data:* b Wilmington, Del, Jan 15, 33; wid; c 2. *Educ:* Univ Del, BA, 57; George Washington Univ, MA, 61; Univ Chicago, PhD(microbiol), 66. *Prof Exp:* Microbiologist, US Army Biol Labs, 64-66. *Mem:* AAAS; Am Soc Microbiol; Sigma Xi. *Res:* Biochemical mechanisms of microbial virulence; genetic determinants of virulence. *Mailing Add:* 11042 Scipio Hwy Vermontville MI 49096

BRUBAKER, THOMAS ALLEN, ELECTRICAL ENGINEERING. *Current Pos:* from asst prof to assoc prof, 69-77, PROF ELEC ENG, COLO STATE UNIV, 77- *Personal Data:* b Greeley, Colo, Jan 7, 35; m 62. *Educ:* Univ Wyo, BS, 57, MS, 58; Univ Ariz, PhD(elec eng), 63. *Prof Exp:* Instr elec eng, Univ Ariz, 61-63; engr, Burr-Brown Res Corp, 63; asst prof elec eng, Univ Wyo, 63-65 & Univ Mo-Columbia, 65-69. *Concurrent Pos:* Consult, Lawrence Radiation Lab, Calif, 64-; mem, Simulation Coun, Inc. *Res:* Hybrid computers; optimum control systems; random process theory; engineering education. *Mailing Add:* Dept Elec Eng Colo State Univ Ft Collins CO 80521

BRUCAT, PHILIP JOHN, CLUSTER ION SPECTROSCOPY, PHOTOCHEMISTRY. *Current Pos:* ASST PROF, UNIV FLA, 86- *Personal Data:* b New York, NY, Aug 22, 56. *Educ:* Mass Inst Technol, BS, 77; Stanford Univ, PhD(chem), 84. *Honors & Awards:* Res Award, Am Soc Mass Spectrometry, 87. *Prof Exp:* PRF postdoctoral, Rice Univ, 84-86. *Mem:* Am Chem Soc; Am Phys Soc; Sigma Xi. *Res:* High resolution optical spectroscopy of cold molecular ions in the gas phase. *Mailing Add:* Dept Chem Univ Fla PO Box 117200 Gainesville FL 32611

BRUCE, ALAN KENNETH, RADIOBIOLOGY. *Current Pos:* asst prof, 57-62, ASSOC PROF BIOL, STATE UNIV NY, BUFFALO, 62-, RADIATION SAFETY OFFICER, 57- *Personal Data:* b Nashua, NH, Aug 24, 27; m 48; c 4. *Educ:* Univ NH, BS, 51; Univ Rochester, MS, 54, PhD(radiation biol), 56. *Prof Exp:* Assoc Atomic Energy Proj, Univ Rochester, 53-56, jr scientist, 56; assoc biol div, Oak Ridge Nat Lab, 56-57. *Mem:* AAAS; Am Soc Microbiol; Health Physics Soc; Radiation Res Soc; Sigma Xi. *Res:* Effects of radiation on cell permeability characteristics; applications of isotopic tracer techniques to biology; modification of radiation action on cells. *Mailing Add:* Dept Biol State Univ NY Cooke Hall Buffalo NY 14260-0001

BRUCE, CHARLES ROBERT, PHYSICS. *Current Pos:* RETIRED. *Personal Data:* b Topeka, Kans, Jan 3, 25; m 49; c 5. *Educ:* Wash Univ, AB, 50, PhD(physics), 56. *Prof Exp:* Res assoc, Wash Univ, 56-57; sr res scientist, Marathon Oil Co, 57-87. *Mem:* Am Phys Soc; Sigma Xi. *Res:* Nuclear magnetic resonance; geophysics and well logging; instrumentation; data acquisition; improving prospecting techniques. *Mailing Add:* 7155 S Grant Littleton CO 80122-1135

BRUCE, CHARLES WIKOFF, PHYSICS. *Current Pos:* phys scientist systs anal, Safeguard Syst Eval Agency, 71-74, RES PHYSICIST GAS/ AEROSOL SPECTROS, ATMOSPHERIC SCI LAB, WHITE SANDS MISSILE RANGE, NMEX, 74-; PROF PHYSICS, NMEX STATE UNIV, 74- *Personal Data:* b Syracuse, NY, Jan 13, 37; m 61; c 2. *Educ:* Union Col, Schenectady, NY, BS, 59; NMex State Univ, Las Cruces, MS, 68, PhD(physics), 70. *Prof Exp:* Physicist plasmas & lasers, Air Force Weapons Lab, Albuquerque, NM, 62-65. *Res:* Pulsed laser diagnostics; laser calorimetry; interferometry of laser induced plasmas; RF excited plasmoids; photo-acoustical spectroscopic techniques and in-situ spectroscopy of atmospheric aerosols. *Mailing Add:* 715 Del Mar El Paso TX 79932

BRUCE, DAVID LIONEL, anesthesiology, medicine, for more information see previous edition

BRUCE, DAVID STEWART, ANIMAL PHYSIOLOGY, ENVIRONMENTAL PHYSIOLOGY. *Current Pos:* assoc prof, 74-78, actg chmn, Biol Dept, 89-90, PROF BIOL, WHEATON COL, 78- *Personal Data:* b Amherst, Ohio, Sept 17, 39; m 61, Janet S Foltz; c Rob & Scot. *Educ:* Taylor Univ, BA & BS, 62; Purdue Univ, MS, 65, PhD(physiol), 68. *Prof Exp:* Instr physiol, DePauw Univ, 67; instr environ biol, Purdue Univ, 67, vis asst prof, 68; asst prof, Seattle Pac Col, 68-73, assoc prof biol, 73-74. *Concurrent Pos:* Muscle researcher, Univ St Andrews, Scotland, 79 & 87; Wellcome res travel grant, Scotland, 80; chair, Teaching Sect, Am Physiol Soc, 93-96. *Mem:* AAAS; Am Physiol Soc; Am Sci Affil; Sigma Xi. *Res:* Phenomenon of hibernation, especially in the bat, Myotis lucifugus, ground squirrels, Citellus tridecemlineatus and Citellus lateralis; black bear, (Ursus americanus), and polar bear (Ursus maritimus). *Mailing Add:* Dept Biol Wheaton Col Wheaton IL 60187. *Fax:* 630-752-5996; *E-Mail:* david.s.bruce@wheaton.edu

BRUCE, EUGENE N, BIOMEDICAL SIGNAL PROCESSING. *Current Pos:* PROF BIOMED ENG, UNIV KY, LEXINGTON, 91- *Personal Data:* b Hanover, NH, 1945. *Educ:* Univ Southern Calif, BS, 67, PhD(biomed eng), 72. *Prof Exp:* Assoc prof, Case Western Res Univ, Cleveland, 86-91. *Mem:* Biomed Eng Soc; Inst Elec & Electronics Engrs. *Mailing Add:* Ctr Biomed Eng Univ Ky Col Med Werner Gren Lab Rose St Lexington KY 40506-0070

BRUCE, JAMES DONALD, ELECTRICAL ENGINEERING. *Current Pos:* Teaching asst, 58-60, from instr to assoc prof, 60-79, assoc dean, Sch Eng, 71-78, dir indust liaison, 79-82, actg dean, 77-78, dir Info Systs, 83-86, PROF ELEC ENG, 73-, VPRES INFO SYSTS, 86- *Personal Data:* b Livingston, Tex, June 28, 36; m 59; c 3. *Educ:* Lamar State Col, BS(elec eng) & BS(math), 58; Mass Inst Technol, SM, 60, ScD(optimum quantization), 64. *Concurrent Pos:* Ford Found fel eng, 64-65; consult, Farmer Elec Prod Co, 61 & Missile Systs Div, Raytheon Corp, 65-71; lectr, Bolt, Beranek & Newman's Prog Advan Study, 68-70, Cambridge Res Inst, 68-70 & Oak Ridge Nat Lab, 70; trustee, Harvard Coop Soc, 74-84, dir, Concurrent Comput Corp, NJ, 86, consult, gov't & indust, Consortium, Sci Comput, trustee, 84, vchmn, 86- *Mem:* AAAS; Inst Elec & Electronics Engrs; Am Soc Eng Educ; Soc Mgt Info Systs; Sigma Xi. *Res:* Digital signal processing; data management systems. *Mailing Add:* 12 Woodpark Circle Lexington MA 02173-7208

BRUCE, JOHN GOODALL, JR, PHYSICAL OCEANOGRAPHY, OCEAN CIRCULATION. *Current Pos:* OCEANOGR, STENNIS SPACE CTR, 83- *Personal Data:* b Richmond, Va, Oct 19, 27; m 53; c 3. *Educ:* Va Polytech Inst, BS, 51, MS, 53. *Prof Exp:* Res assoc oceanog, Woods Hole Oceanog Inst, 54-83. *Concurrent Pos:* Fulbright scholar, Univ Liverpool, 56-57; consult, US Oceanog Off, 81- *Res:* Physical oceanography of the Arabian Sea with special interest in the dynamic response of the Somali current circulation to the monsoon winds; characteristics of the large mesoscale ocean eddies ocurring during the strong southwest monsoon; circulation equatorial Atlantic Ocean. *Mailing Add:* 307 Gordon St Waveland MS 39576

BRUCE, JOHN IRVIN, parasitology, physiology, for more information see previous edition

BRUCE, KIM BARRY, SEMANTICS OF PROGRAMMING LANGUAGES, MODELS OF LAMBDA CALCULUS. *Current Pos:* PROF COMPUT SCI, WILLIAMS COL, 77- *Personal Data:* b Dearborn, Mich, Oct 16, 48; m 81, Fatma Kassamali; c Christine, Jilan, Nurjahan & Shezad. *Educ:* Pomona Col, BA, 70; Univ Wis-Madison, PhD(math), 75. *Prof Exp:* Instr math, Princeton Univ, 75-77. *Concurrent Pos:* Lectr math, Minority Eng Prog, Univ Wis, 75, 78, 79; vis scholar, Stanford Univ, 77; vis scientist, Mass Inst Technol, 80-81; consult, Prime Comput, 80-81; prin investr res grants, NSF, 82-; vis prof, Univ Pisa, Italy, 85, Stanford Univ, 91 & Ecole Normal Syerieurc, Paris, 91; mem, Asn Comput Mach & Inst Elec & Electronics Engrs Comput Soc Joint Curric Task Force, 88-91; vis scientist, Newton Inst, 95; Frederick Latimer Wells prof comput sci, Williams Col. *Mem:* Asn Comput Mach; Sigma Xi; Asn Symbolic Logic; Inst Elec & Electronics Engrs Comput Soc. *Res:* Semantics and design of programming languages, especially polymorphic and object-oriented languages; models of extensions of typed lambda calculus; mathematical logic-model theory; computer science education. *Mailing Add:* Dept Comput Sci Bronfman Sci Ctr Williams Col Williamstown MA 01267-2680. *Fax:* 413-597-4116; *E-Mail:* kim@cs.williams.edu

BRUCE, RICHARD CONRAD, ZOOLOGY. *Current Pos:* PROF BIOL, WESTERN CAROLINA UNIV, 63- *Personal Data:* b Cambridge, Mass, June 2, 36; m 58; c 3. *Educ:* Tufts Univ, BS, 58; Duke Univ, MA, 61, PhD(zool), 68. *Concurrent Pos:* Exec dir, Highland Biol Sta, Univ NC, 72-; exec secy, Highland Biol Found, Inc, 77- *Mem:* Am Soc Ichthyologists & Herpetologists; Soc Study Amphibians & Reptiles; Herpetologists League; Sigma Xi. *Res:* Ecology, evolution and reproductive biology of plethodontid salamanders; natural diversity in Southern Appalachian ecosystems. *Mailing Add:* Dept Zool & Physiol La State Univ Baton Rouge LA 70803-1725

BRUCE, ROBERT ARTHUR, MEDICINE, CARDIOLOGY. *Current Pos:* from asst prof to assoc prof med, Univ Wash, 50-59, head, Div Cardiol, 50-71, co-dir, Div Cardiol, 72-82, prof, 59-87, EMER PROF MED, SCH MED, UNIV WASH, 87- *Personal Data:* b Somerville, Mass, Nov 20, 16; m 40, 95, Jean B Laughlin; c Robert, Peter, Scott & Nancy (deceased). *Educ:* Boston Univ, BS, 38; Univ Rochester, MS, 40, MD, 43. *Honors & Awards:* Honor Award, Am Col Sports Med, 83. *Prof Exp:* Asst res physician, Strong Mem Hosp, Univ Rochester, 44-45, chief res physician, 45-46, instr med, 46-50. *Concurrent Pos:* Buswell fel, Univ Rochester, 46-50; Commonwealth Fund fel, Sch Med, Univ Wash, 65-66; fel, Coun Clin Cardiol, Am Heart Asn; vis prof, Royal Infirmary, Edinburgh, Nottingham, Birmingham, Kuala Lumpor, Life Planning Inst, Tokyo, Sir Ch Gardner Hosp, Perth, WAustralia; endowed chair cardiovasc res, Univ Wash, 88. *Mem:* Asn Am Physicians; Asn Univ Cardiol (secy-treas, 64-67, vpres, 67-68, pres, 68-69); fel Am Col Cardiol; Aerospace Med Asn. *Res:* Cardiology; exercise physiology; electrocardiography; cardiac physiology and rehabilitation; cardiovascular epidemiology. *Mailing Add:* 12533 Greenwood Ave N Seattle WA 98133-8001

BRUCE, ROBERT NOLAN, JR, CIVIL ENGINEERING. *Current Pos:* assoc prof, 62-68, PROF CIVIL ENG, TULANE UNIV, 68- *Personal Data:* b Melville, La, Oct 11, 30; m 58; c 2. *Educ:* Tulane Univ, BS, 52, MS, 53; Univ Ill, PhD(civil eng), 62. *Honors & Awards:* PCI Korn Award, BOH Chair Civil Engr, 86. *Prof Exp:* Engr, Raymond Int, Inc, 53-60. *Concurrent Pos:* Spec lectr, George Washington Univ, 64 & 65, Univ Miami & Univ Maine, 66, Univ PR, 67, Rangoon Inst Tech, 79, Univ Dundee, 85; grants, US Dept Defense, 64-65, NSF, 64-66, La Dept Hwys, 65-87; consult, Off Civil Defense, USN; chmn Comt Prestressed Concrete, Am Concrete Inst, 85-89. *Mem:* Am Soc Civil Engrs; Int Fedn Prestressing; Am Concrete Inst; Int Asn Bridge & Struct Engr. *Res:* Prestressed concrete in shear; foundations; structural response to nuclear weapons effects; fatigue in prestressed concrete; bridge durability. *Mailing Add:* Dept Civil Eng Tulane Univ 6823 St Charles Ave New Orleans LA 70118-5665

BRUCE, ROBERT RUSSELL, SOIL PHYSICS. *Current Pos:* res soil scientist, 65-95, COLLABORATOR, SOUTHERN PIEDMONT CONSERV RES CTR, FED RES, SCI & EDUC ADMIN, USDA, 95- *Personal Data:* b Jasper, Ont, Mar 27, 26; m 51, Barbara E Donald; c Robert D. *Educ:* Ont Agr Col, BSA, 47; Cornell Univ, MS, 51; Univ Ill, PhD, 56. *Prof Exp:* Soil specialist, Ont Agr Col, 47-49; asst soil physics, Cornell Univ, 49-51; lectr, Ont Agr Col, 51-53; asst, Univ Ill, 53-55; from asst prof & asst agronomist to assoc prof & assoc agronomist, Miss State Univ, 55-65. *Concurrent Pos:* Vis prof, Auburn Univ, 65-; chmn, Soil Sci Soc Am, 82. *Mem:* Fel AAAS; fel Soil Sci Soc Am; fel Am Soc Agron; Soil Conserv Soc Am; Can Soil Sci Soc. *Res:* Soil moisture in relation to plant growth; soil moisture, air and heat movement in saturated and unsaturated media; water and solute distribution in layered soils; soil erosion and crop production; modification of soil rooting environment by erosion. *Mailing Add:* 560 Forest Rd Athens GA 30605

BRUCE, RUFUS ELBRIDGE, JR, optics properties of materials, atmospheric physics and optics, for more information see previous edition

BRUCE, W ROBERT, NUTRITION & CANCER, CANCER PREVENTION. *Current Pos:* SR SCIENTIST, ONT CANCER INST, 59-; PROF MED BIOPHYS, UNIV TORONTO, 66-, PROF NUTRIT SCI, 85- *Personal Data:* b Hamheung, Korea, May 26, 29; Can citizen; m, W Margaret MacFarlane; c Graham D, Lynda J & Kevin R. *Educ:* Univ Alta, BSc, 50;

Univ Sask, MSc, 54, PhD(physics), 56; Univ Chicago, MD, 58. *Honors & Awards:* Medal for Med, Royal Col Physician & Surgeons Can, 68; Dameshek Award, Am Soc Hemat, 70; McLaughlin Gold Medal, 80. *Concurrent Pos:* Chmn, Comt Fel & Bursaries, Can Cancer Soc, Ont Div, 73-74, Royal Soc Can, 88- & Nat Inst Health Comt, Md, 92; dir, Can Soc Cell Biol, 74-75, Am Asn Cancer Res, 79-82 & Toronto Br, Ludwig Inst Cancer Res, 81-88; fel, Royal Col Phys & Surgeons Can, 78; comt mem, Oncology Coord Coun, Univ Toronto, 88- & Gen Motors Cancer Res Found, 92-93; mem, Int Union Nutrit Sci, 92- *Mem:* Am Asn Cancer Res; Can Med Asn; Soc Cell Biol; fel Royal Soc Can. *Res:* Penetration and scattering of x-rays in biological materials; sensitivity of experimental tumor cells to chemotherapeutic agents and selectivity of these agents on cells in cell cycle; differentiation and effect on genotoxic compounds on spermatogenesis; experimental and epidemiological studies of diet and colon and breast cancer. *Mailing Add:* Dept Nutrit & Sci Univ Toronto Toronto ON M5S 1A1 Can. *Fax:* 416-978-5882; *E-Mail:* bruce@ocicl.oci.utoronto.ca

BRUCH, CARL WILLIAM, DISINFECTION & STERILIZATION OF MEDICAL DEVICES, GOOD MANUFACTURING PRACTICES FOR MEDICAL DEVICES. *Current Pos:* CONSULT, 90- *Personal Data:* b Kenosha, Wis, May 25, 29; m 53, 85; c Elise Anne & Miriam Louise. *Educ:* Mich State Univ, BS, 51; Univ Wis, MS, 53, PhD(microbiol), 58. *Honors & Awards:* Microbiol Studies Prize, Soc Cosmetic Chemists, 71. *Prof Exp:* Microbiologist, US Army Biol Labs, Ft Detrick, 55; res microbiologist, Process Develop Dept, Wilmot Castle Co, NY, 58-61, lab dir, 61-62; chief microbiologist, Schwarz Labs, Inc, 62-63; microbiologist, Off Space Sci & Appln, NASA, 63-66; chief, Bact Br, Bur Sci, Food & Drug Admin, 66-70, Drug Microbiol Br, 70-72, dir, Div Res & Classification, Off Med Devices, 72-74, Div Classification & Sci Eval, 74-77, actg dir, Off Device Eval, 77-79, dep dir, 79-82; vpres qual systs & regulatory affairs, Skyland Sci Serv, 83-85; dir regulatory affairs & qual audits, St Jude Med, Inc, 85-90. *Concurrent Pos:* Fed exec fel, Brookings Inst, 68-69. *Mem:* Am Soc Microbiol; Soc Indust Microbiol; NY Acad Sci. *Res:* Sterilizationn for medical devices; bioburdens; pyrogens; biological indicators for sterilization processes; microbial challenges for sterile packaged medical devices. *Mailing Add:* 684 O'Neil Rd Hudson WI 54016. *E-Mail:* cbruch@isd.net

BRUCH, JOHN C(LARENCE), JR, NUMERICAL ANALYSIS, STRUCTURAL VIBRATION CONTROL. *Current Pos:* From asst prof to prof, 66-78, PROF ENG MECH, UNIV CALIF, SANTA BARBARA, 78- *Personal Data:* b Kenosha, Wis, Oct 11, 40; m 67, Susan Tippett. *Educ:* Univ Notre Dame, BS, 62; Stanford Univ, MS, 63, PhD(civil eng), 66. *Concurrent Pos:* Res engr, Gen Motors Defense Res Lab, Calif, 67; consult, TEMPO, Gen Elec Co, Calif, 67-68, Oceanog Serv Inc, 69-70 & Pub Works Dept City Santa Barbara, 77-78. *Mem:* Am Soc Civil Engrs; Sigma Xi; Am Sci Affil. *Res:* Ground-water flow; free boundary value problems; finite element analysis; numerical analysis; parallel computing, structural vibration control. *Mailing Add:* Dept Mech & Environ Eng Univ Calif Santa Barbara CA 93106. *Fax:* 805-893-8651

BRUCH, LUDWIG WALTER, THEORETICAL PHYSICS. *Current Pos:* From asst prof to assoc prof, 66-75, PROF PHYSICS, UNIV WIS-MADISON, 75- *Personal Data:* b Rockford, Ill, Jan 23, 40; m 66, Nancy Schlaefer; c Carl E & Andrew R. *Educ:* Univ Wis, BA, 59; Oxford Univ, BA, 61, MA, 65; Univ Calif, San Diego, PhD(physics), 64. *Concurrent Pos:* Partic NSF visiting scientist prog, Dept Physics, Tokyo Univ Educ, Japan, 72-73; vis scientist, Univ Utrecht, Neth, 77-78 & Max Planck Inst Fluid Dynamics Res; Sci & Eng Res Coun fel, Univ Sussex, 83; assoc prof, Univ Marseille II, France, 84; William C Foster Fel, US Arms Control & Disarmament Agency, 88; vis prof, Tech Univ, Denmark, 91 & 94. *Mem:* Fel Am Phys Soc. *Res:* Chemical physics; theory of superfluid helium; statistical mechanics; physical adsorption. *Mailing Add:* Dept Physics Univ Wis Madison WI 53706. *Fax:* 608-265-2334

BRUCHOVSKY, NICHOLAS, ENDOCRINOLOGY, ONCOLOGY. *Current Pos:* HEAD DEPT CANCER ENCROCRINOL, CANCER CTR AGENCY BC, 80- *Personal Data:* b Toronto, Ont, Sept 21, 36; m 68; c 1. *Educ:* Univ Toronto, MD, 61, PhD(biophys), 66; FRCP(C), 75. *Prof Exp:* Intern med, Toronto Gen Hosp, 61-62; fel med, Univ Tex Southwestern Med Sch Dallas, 66-68; from asst prof to prof med, Univ Alta, 69-80. *Concurrent Pos:* Med Res Coun Can scholar, 70-75. *Mem:* Can Soc Clin Invest; Can Soc Endocrinol & Metab; Can Oncol Soc; Endocrine Soc. *Res:* Mechanism of action of androgens in prostate; control of cell proliferation in hormone-responsive and unresponsive tumors of the breast, endometrium and prostate. *Mailing Add:* Cancer Ctr Agency BC 600 W 10th Ave Vancouver BC V5Z 4E6 Can

BRUCK, DAVID LEWIS, GENETICS BEHAVIOR-ETHOLOGY, ECOLOGY. *Current Pos:* from asst prof to assoc prof, 69-88, PROF BIOL, UNIV PR, RIO PIEDRAS, 88- *Personal Data:* b New York, NY, July 17, 33; m 69, Tanya Grudzinsky; c Natasha D. *Educ:* Columbia Univ, BS, 55, AM, 57; NC State Univ, PhD(genetics), 65. *Prof Exp:* Res assoc genetics, NC State Univ, 65; res fel, Comt Math Biol, Univ Chicago, 65-66; asst prof biol, Queens Col, NY, 66-69. *Mem:* Sigma Xi; Soc Study Evolution; Int Soc Trop Ecol; Asn Trop Biol; Am Soc Naturalists. *Res:* Ecology and evolutionary genetics of Caribbean Drosophilia, especially the dunni subgroup, including mating behavior, reproductive morphology, larval niche, and dispersal. *Mailing Add:* Dept Biol Univ PR Box 23360 Rio Piedras PR 00931-3360. *Fax:* 787-764-3875; *E-Mail:* d_bruck@upracd.upr.clu.edu

BRUCK, ERIKA, PEDIATRICS. *Current Pos:* from instr to prof, 46-78, EMER PROF PEDIAT, SCH MED, STATE UNIV NY, BUFFALO, 78- *Personal Data:* b Breslau, Ger, Apr 5, 08; nat US. *Educ:* Friedrich-Wilhelms Univ, MD, 35. *Prof Exp:* Dir, Clin Lab, 2nd Dept Internal Med, Istanbul Univ, 35-39. *Concurrent Pos:* Attend physician, Dept Pediat, Childrens Hosp, Buffalo, 46-82; consult, 82- *Mem:* Soc Pediat Res; Am Acad Pediat; Am Pediat Soc. *Res:* Renal and respiratory functions in children; electrolyte metabolism; diabetes mellitus. *Mailing Add:* Childrens Hosp 219 Bryant St Buffalo NY 14222

BRUCK, GEORGE, APPLIED PHYSICS. *Current Pos:* RETIRED. *Personal Data:* b Budapest, Hungary, Oct 20, 04; nat US; m 29. *Educ:* Tech Univ, Vienna, PhD(appl physics), 27. *Prof Exp:* Asst chief engr, Compagnie des Lamps, 29-36; resident engr, Fabbr Ital Magn Marelli, 36-41; res engr, Crosley Corp, 41-43; dir special studies, Nat Union, 43-44; chief engr, Hudson Am Corp, 44; res engr, Raytheon Mfg, 44-46; chief photo engr, Specialities Inc, 46-53; pres, Bruck Indust, Inc & consult, Radiation, Inc, 53-54; staff sci adv, Avco Corp, Ohio, 54-67, chief scientist, Electronic Div, 67-69; sci adv, 69-76. *Mem:* Fel Inst Elec & Electronics Engrs; Am Phys Soc. *Res:* Electronic devices; solid state; military electronics. *Mailing Add:* 501 Portola Rd PO Box 8082 Portola Valley CA 94028-7603. *Fax:* 650-851-5007

BRUCK, ROBERT IAN, ENVIRONMENTAL EPIDEMIOLOGY & SCIENCE, FOREST PATHOLOGY. *Current Pos:* from asst prof to assoc prof, 79-90, PROF PLANT PATH & FORESTRY, NC STATE UNIV, 90- *Personal Data:* b June 25, 52; US citizen; m 73; c Isaac, Sarah & Sonia. *Educ:* State Univ NY, Buffalo, BA, 73; State Univ NY, Syracuse, PhD(plant path), 77; Syracuse Univ, PhD(forestry), 77. *Honors & Awards:* Silver Fels Award, Israel Forestry Asn. *Prof Exp:* Res assoc plant path, Cornell Univ, 77-79. *Concurrent Pos:* Spec asst to vchancellor & coordr univ environ progs, NC State Univ; dir, Inst Environ Technol Educ. *Mem:* Am Phytopath Soc; Can Phytopath Soc; Sigma Xi; AAAS; Fedn Am Scientists. *Res:* Environmental epidemiology of plant diseases; discovery of boreal montane (spruce-fir); forest decline in eastern North America. *Mailing Add:* Dept Plant Path NC State Univ Box 7616 Raleigh NC 27616. *Fax:* 919-515-5578; *E-Mail:* bob_bruck@ncsu.edu

BRUCK, STEPHEN DESIDERIUS, BIOMATERIALS, BIOMEDICAL ENGINEERING. *Current Pos:* SCI DIR BIOMAT & MED DEVICES CONSULT GROUP, STEPHEN D BRUCK ASSOCS, INC, 78- *Personal Data:* b Budapest, Hungary, Feb 4, 27; nat US; m 91, Olga Mychalus; c Debra, Stephanie & Lewis. *Educ:* Boston Col, BS, 51; Johns Hopkins Univ, MA, 53, PhD(biochem), 55. *Hon Degrees:* DMC, Tokyo Med & Dent Univ, 83. *Prof Exp:* Jr instr, Johns Hopkins Univ, 51-55; res chemist, Dacron Res Lab, E I du Pont de Nemours & Co, NC, 55-56, res chemist, Carothers Res Lab, Textile Fibers Dept, Exp Sta, Del, 56-60; proj leader, Nat Bur Standards, Washington, DC, 61-62; actg sect head coatings mat, NASA, 62; mem sr sci staff chem, Appl Physics Lab, Johns Hopkins Univ, 62-66; actg mgr polymer chem, Watson Res Ctr, IBM Corp, 66-67; res prof chem eng, Cath Univ Am, 67-69; prog dir biomat, Nat Heart, Lung & Blood Inst, NIH, 69-78. *Concurrent Pos:* Affil prof, Washington Univ, St Louis, 78-80; adj prof, Univ Tenn, 78- & vis prof, Univ Va, 79; ed-in-chief, J Long-Term Effects Med Implants, sect ed biomat, Int J Artificial Organs, ed, CRC Crit Rev Therapeut Drug Carrier Systs, NAm ed, Med Progress through Technol; former adv bd mem, Artificial Organs, Biomat & Med Devices; Nat Acad Sci exchange scholar, Czech, 83; scholar, Japan Soc for the Promotion of Sci, 83; grants, NIH, NSF & Dept Interior. *Mem:* Fel AAAS; sr mem Am Chem Soc; Am Soc Artificial Internal Organs; Sigma Xi; NY Acad Sci. *Res:* Biostability and long-term performance of medical implants and insteriods, and therapeutic drug delivery systems; scientific editing and writing, structure and property correlation of biomedical materials; biocompatibility and toxicity; technological risk assessment of health-care products; biopolymers; macromolecular pharmacology; research and development administration. *Mailing Add:* 9 Fenton Pl Chapel Hill NC 27514. *Fax:* 919-969-7060

BRUCKENSTEIN, STANLEY, ANALYTICAL CHEMISTRY, ELECTROCHEMISTRY. *Current Pos:* prof chem, 68-73, chmn dept, 74-83, A CONGER GOODYEAR PROF, STATE UNIV NY, BUFFALO, 73- *Personal Data:* b Brooklyn, NY, Nov 1, 27; m 50; c 3. *Educ:* Polytech Inst Brooklyn, BS, 50; Univ Minn, PhD(chem), 54. *Honors & Awards:* C N Reilley Award. *Prof Exp:* From instr to assoc prof analytical chem, Univ Minn, 54-62, prof analytical chem & chief div, 62-68. *Mem:* AAAS; Am Chem Soc; Electrochem Soc. *Res:* Analytical chemistry; electroanalytical methods; phys electrochem. *Mailing Add:* Dept Chem State Univ NY Buffalo NY 14214

BRUCKER, EDWARD BYERLY, OPTICS. *Current Pos:* assoc prof, 71-74, asst dean res, 80-85, PROF PHYSICS, STEVENS INST TECHNOL, 75- *Personal Data:* b Baltimore, Md, Mar 23, 31; m 63, Margaret Miller. *Educ:* Johns Hopkins Univ, BE, 52, PhD(physics), 59. *Prof Exp:* Res assoc physics, Duke Univ, 58-61, vis asst prof, 59-60; asst prof, Fla State Univ, 61-63; vis lectr, Johns Hopkins Univ, 63-64; asst prof, Fla State Univ, 64-69; sr res assoc, Rutgers Univ, 69-70. *Mem:* Am Phys Soc; Sigma Xi; Int Soc Optical Eng. *Res:* High energy physics; interactions of fundamental particles; optical information processing. *Mailing Add:* Physics Castle Point Sta Stevens Inst Technol Hoboken NJ 07030. *Fax:* 201-216-5638; *E-Mail:* brucker@ruthep.rutgers.edu

BRUCKER, PAUL CHARLES, FAMILY MEDICINE. *Current Pos:* ALUMNI PROF FAMILY MED & CHMN DEPT, JEFFERSON MED COL, 73-, CLIN ASSOC PROF MED, 76- *Personal Data:* b Philadelphia, Pa, Nov 15, 31; m 57; c 3. *Educ:* Muhlenberg Col, BS, 53; Univ Pa, MD, 57. *Prof*

Exp: Intern, Lankenau Hosp, Philadelphia, 57-58; resident, Hunterdon Med Ctr, Flemington, NJ, 58-59 & Lankenau Hosp, Philadelphia, 59-60; pvt family pract, Ambler, Pa, 60-73. *Concurrent Pos:* Mem staff, Jefferson Med Col, Temple Univ & Univ Pa, 62-72; mem, Patient Care Systs Coun. *Mem:* Inst Med-Nat Acad Sci; AMA; Soc Teachers Family Med; Am Heart Asn; Am Acad Family Physicians. *Mailing Add:* Dept Family Med Thomas Jefferson Univ Hosp 1020 Walnut St Rm 641 Philadelphia PA 19107-5567

BRUCKNER, ADAM PETER, SPACE SYSTEMS, PROPULSION. *Current Pos:* Res assoc aerospace & energetics, 72-75, res asst prof, 75- 78, res assoc prof, 78-85, RES PROF AERONAUT & ASTRONAUT, UNIV WASH, 88- *Personal Data:* b Istanbul, Turkey, Mar 21, 43; m 72; c 1. *Educ:* McGill Univ, BEngr, 66; Princeton Univ, MA, 68, PhD(aerospace & mech sci), 72. *Honors & Awards:* Brit Asn Medal, 66; PNW Award, Am Inst Aeronaut & Astronaut, 73. *Concurrent Pos:* Consult, Math Sci Northwest, 78-84, Spectra Technol, 84-86, United Technol Res Ctr, 84-86, Olin/Rocket Res Co, 88-, Eli Lilly Co, 89- *Mem:* Am Inst Aeronaut & Astronaut; Optical Soc Am; Sigma Xi. *Res:* Energy conversion for space applications; heat transfer, laser applications; advanced space propulsion techniques; hypervelocity accelerators, hypersonics. *Mailing Add:* FL-10 Aerospace & Energetics Res Prog Univ Wash Seattle WA 98195

BRUCKNER, ANDREW M, MATHEMATICS. *Current Pos:* From asst prof to assoc prof, 59-68, actg dean grad div, 66-69, PROF MATH, UNIV CALIF, SANTA BARBARA, 68- *Personal Data:* b Berlin, Ger, Dec 17, 32; US citizen; m 57, Judith Brostoff; c Theodore & Michael. *Educ:* Univ Calif, Los Angeles, BA, 55, PhD(math), 59. *Concurrent Pos:* NSF res grant, 62-74 & 78- *Mem:* Am Math Soc; Math Asn Am. *Res:* Theory of functions of a real variable. *Mailing Add:* Dept Math Univ Calif Santa Barbara CA 93106. *E-Mail:* bruckner@math.uscb.edu

BRUCKNER, DAVID ALAN, MEDICAL PARASITOLOGY. *Current Pos:* Fel parasitol, 72-75, lectr parasitol, 75-76, ASSOC PROF, DEPT PATH & LAB MED, UNIV CALIF, LOS ANGELES, 78- *Personal Data:* b Rhinelander, Wis, June 12, 41; m 65; c 2. *Educ:* Wis State Univ, Stevens Point, BS, 66; NDak State Univ, MS, 68; Johns Hopkins Univ, ScD(parasitol), 72. *Mem:* Am Soc Trop Med & Hyg; Am Soc Parasitologists; Am Soc Microbiol. *Res:* Neurophysiological interactions of Schistosoma cercariae; in vitro cultivation of larval stages of cestodes and schistosomes; development test applications for clinical microbiology and immunology. *Mailing Add:* Pathol Univ Calif Sch Med 10833 LeConte Ave Los Angeles CA 90024-1300

BRUCKNER, JAMES VICTOR, TOXICOLOGY, PHARMACOLOGY. *Current Pos:* ASST PROF PHARM & TOXICOL, UNIV TEX MED SCH HOUSTON, 75- *Personal Data:* b Lubbock, Tex, Apr 4, 44; m 68; c 2. *Educ:* Univ Tex, Austin, BS, 68, MS, 71; Univ Mich, Ann Arbor, PhD(toxicol), 74. *Prof Exp:* Asst prof pharm & toxicol, Sch Pharm, Univ Kans, 74-75. *Concurrent Pos:* Res contract, Nat Inst Drug Abuse, 75-78, consult, 76-77; res grants, Am Heart Asn, 77-78 & Nat Heart, Lung & Blood Int, 77-79; mem toxicol subcomt, Safe Drinking Water Comt, Nat Acad Sci, 78-79; consult, US Environ Protection Agency, 78-, res grants, 80- *Mem:* NY Acad Sci; AAAS; Soc Toxicol; Am Soc Pharmacol & Exp Therapeut. *Res:* Influence of environmental pollutants on therapeutic efficacy of drugs; mechanisms of gastrointestinal drug-absorption interactions; toxic interactions of hydrocarbon solvents and drugs; in vitro screening tests for detection of toxic chemicals. *Mailing Add:* Dept Pharmacol & Toxicol Univ Ga Col Pharm Athens GA 30602. *Fax:* 706-542-3398

BRUCKNER, LAWRENCE ADAM, STATISTICAL ANALYSIS. *Current Pos:* MEM TECH STAFF, LOS ALAMOS NAT LAB, UNIV CALIF, 74- *Personal Data:* b Brooklyn, NY, Feb 16, 40; div; c 3. *Educ:* Cath Univ, BA, 62, MA, 64, PhD(probability & statist), 68. *Prof Exp:* From instr to asst prof, Cath Univ, 66-68; mem tech staff, Sandia Corp, 68-71; assoc prof math, Col Santa Fe, 71-73; asst prof, Univ Maine, Portland, 73-74. *Concurrent Pos:* Adj prof, Univ NMex. *Mem:* Am Statist Asn; Am Math Asn; Am Soc Qual Control; Am Soc Testing & Mat; Sigma Xi. *Res:* Statistical process control; statistical analysis. *Mailing Add:* Los Alamos Nat Lab MS F600 Los Alamos NM 87545-0001. *E-Mail:* larry@lanl.gov

BRUDER, JOSEPH ALBERT, RADIO FREQUENCY, WAVEGUIDE IMPLEMENTATION. *Current Pos:* SR RES ENG, ENG EXP STA, GA INST TECHNOL, 79- *Personal Data:* b Brooklyn, NY, Oct 28, 38; m 65; c 4. *Educ:* Polytech Inst NY, BSEE, 62; State Univ NY, Buffalo, MSEE, 67. *Prof Exp:* Elect engr, Sylvania Electronic Syst, 62-65; res asst, State Univ NY, Buffalo, 65-66; prin engr, Calspan Corp, 66-79. *Mem:* Sigma Xi; sr mem Inst Elec & Electronics Engrs. *Res:* Design and calibrate millimeter and monopulse instrumentation radar systems; conduct field measurements for backscatter data and monopulse signal characteristics; evaluate radar systems and recommend modification for system improvement. *Mailing Add:* 2404 Riverglenn Circle Dunwoody GA 30338-5943

BRUDNER, HARVEY JEROME, BIOPHYSICS, ELECTRONICS & MATHEMATICS. *Current Pos:* PRES, HJB ENTERPRISES, 76- *Personal Data:* b New York, NY, May 29, 31; m 63, Helen Gross; c Mae A, Terry J & Jay S. *Educ:* NY Univ, BS, 52, MS, 54, PhD(physics), 59. *Prof Exp:* Electronics engr, Pioneer Instrument Div, Bendix Corp, NJ, 52; instr atomic physics, NY Univ, 53-54; physicist, US Naval Ord Lab, 54; prin physicist, Emerson Res Labs, 54-57; res scientist, Courant Inst Math Sci, NY Univ, 57-62; prof math & physics, NY Inst Technol, 62-63, dean sci & technol, 63-64; sr res assoc, Princeton Lab, Am Can Co, 64-67; dir res & develop, Westinghouse Learning Corp, 67, from vpres to pres, 67-76. *Concurrent Pos:* Consult, Emerson Radio & Phonograph Corp, 57-59 & Emertron, Inc, 57-62; mem adv comt, Middlesex County Col; mem, Coun Latin Am; adv, William Paterson Col, NJ, 75-; expert adv comput in educ, US House Rep, adv, Comn Sci & Technol, 77; res & develop, NY Power Authority, 80-84. *Mem:* AAAS; Am Phys Soc; fel Inst Elec & Electronics Engrs; Am Educ Res Asn; Soc Motion Picture & TV Engrs. *Res:* Computers and multi-media as applied to advanced educational and training systems; Thomas-Fermi techniques for determining wave functions of excited states; electromagnetic wave propagation; biological effects of microwave radiation; medical instrumentation; operations research; babylonian doubles and pythagorean triples; symmetry of powered whole numbers; fermats last theorem and N; biophysics. *Mailing Add:* 812 Abbott St Highland Park NJ 08904-2909

BRUDVIG, GARY WAYNE, BIOPHYSICAL CHEMISTRY, BIOINORGANIC CHEMISTRY. *Current Pos:* from asst prof to assoc prof, 82-91, PROF CHEM, YALE UNIV, 91- *Personal Data:* b Grand Forks, NDak, May 10, 54. *Educ:* Univ Minn, Minneapolis, BS, 76; Calif Inst Technol, PhD(chem), 81. *Prof Exp:* Trainee, NIH, 76-80; Miller fel, Univ Calif, Berkeley, 80-82. *Concurrent Pos:* Camille & Henry Dreyfus faculty fel, 82; Searle scholar, 83-86; Alfred P Sloan fel, 86-88; prin investr, USDA, 83-84 & 90-92 & 96-, NIH, 84-, Herman Frasch Found, 87-92, NATO, 88-91. *Mem:* Am Chem Soc; Biophys Soc; fel AAAS; Am Soc Photobiol; Int Soc Photosynthesis Res. *Res:* Structural and mechanistic studies of photosynthetic water oxidation, application of electron paramagnetic resonance spectroscopy to the study of metalloproteins, biological electron-transfer reactions, structural and functional modeling of manganese enzymes. *Mailing Add:* Dept Chem Yale Univ 225 Prospect St New Haven CT 06520-8107. *E-Mail:* gary.brudvig@yale.edu

BRUECK, STEVEN ROY JULIEN, QUANTUM ELECTRONICS. *Current Pos:* PROF ELEC ENG & PHYSICS, UNIV NMEX, 85-, DIR, CTR HIGH TECHNOL MAT, 86- *Personal Data:* b New York, NY, Aug 16, 44; m 68; c 3. *Educ:* Columbia Univ, BS, 65; Mass Inst Technol, SM, 67, PhD(elec eng), 71. *Prof Exp:* Mem staff physics, Bell Tel Labs, 68; res asst elec eng, Lincoln Lab, Mass Inst Technol, 68-71, mem staff quantum electronics, 71-85. *Concurrent Pos:* Assoc ed, Optics Let, 84-86 & Inst Elec & Electronics Engrs, J Quantum Electronics, 86-89, ed, 89; pub chmn, Lasers & Electrooptics Soc, Inst Elec & Electronics Engrs, 88. *Mem:* Am Phys Soc; sr mem Inst Elec & Electronics Engrs; fel Optical Soc Am; AAAS; Mat Res Soc. *Res:* Optoelectronics, semiconductors and lasers; metrology for semiconductor manufacturing; nonlinear optics. *Mailing Add:* Univ NMex CHTM EECE Bldg Rm 125 Albuquerque NM 87131

BRUECKNER, GUENTER ERICH, DESIGN OF OPTICAL INSTRUMENTATION FOR SPACEFLIGHT, DESIGN OF SPACECRAFTS. *Current Pos:* consult, 68-72, head, Solar Spectros Sect, 72-78, HEAD & CHIEF SCIENTIST, SOLAR PHYSICS PROG, NAVAL RES LAB, 78- *Personal Data:* b Dresden, Ger, Dec 26, 34; US citizen; m 58; c 2. *Educ:* Univ Goettingen, Ger, Dr rer nat(astron & physics), 61, Habilitation, 67. *Hon Degrees:* PhD, Univ Oslo, Norway, 81. *Honors & Awards:* E O Hulburt Award, 77. *Prof Exp:* Observer astron, Univ Goettingen, Ger, 65-67; asst prof physics & astrophys, Univ Md, 67-68. *Concurrent Pos:* Prin investr, NASA, 74-; mem, Space Physics Subcomt, NASA, 88-91. *Mem:* Int Acad Astronaut; Am Astron Soc; Am Geophys Union; Optical Soc Am; fel AAAS; Int Astron Union; Europ Geophys Soc. *Res:* Physics of the solar atmosphere explored by means of optical instruments in the ultraviolet spectrum which are flown on sounding rockets and spacecraft; interaction between the sun and the upper earth atmosphere investigated by means of ultraviolet instrumentation flown on satellites. *Mailing Add:* Code 4160 Naval Res Lab Washington DC 20375-0001. *Fax:* 202-767-5636; *E-Mail:* brueckner@hrts.nrl.navy.mil

BRUECKNER, HANNES KURT, GEOCHEMISTRY, STRUCTURAL GEOLOGY. *Current Pos:* asst prof, 70-75, assoc prof, 75-78, PROF, DEPT EARTH & ENVIRON SCI, QUEENS COL NY, 78- *Personal Data:* b San Francisco, Calif, Apr 6, 40; m 87, Mary Ann Luckman; c Stephen Kurt & Laurie (Stevenson). *Educ:* Cornell Univ, BS, 62; Yale Univ, MS, 65, PhD(geol), 68. *Prof Exp:* Res assoc geosci, Univ Tex, Dallas, 67-70. *Concurrent Pos:* Sr res assoc, Lamont-Doherty Geol Observ, 70-; NSF fels, 73-75, 75-78 & 79-81. *Mem:* Am Geophys Union; Sigma Xi; Geol Soc Am. *Res:* Structural, petrological and geochemical studies of relationships between mantle and crust in orogenic zones; geochemistry of sediments, particularly chert; age dating of igneous and metamorphic rocks. *Mailing Add:* Dept Geol Queens Col Flushing NY 11367. *Fax:* 914-365-8150; *E-Mail:* hannes@ldeo.columbia.edu

BRUECKNER, KEITH ALLAN, THEORETICAL PHYSICS. *Current Pos:* RETIRED. *Personal Data:* b Minneapolis, Minn, Mar 19, 24; div; c 3. *Educ:* Univ Minn, BA, 45, MA, 47; Univ Calif, PhD(physics), 50. *Honors & Awards:* Dannie Heinemann Prize, 63. *Prof Exp:* From asst prof to prof physics, Univ Pa, 51-59, chmn dept, 59-61, dean lett & sci, 63-65, dean grad studies, 65; prof physics, Univ Calif, San Diego, 59-91, dir, Inst Radiation Physics & Aerodyn, 65-67, dir, Inst Pure & Appl Phys Sci, 67-69. *Concurrent Pos:* Consult, AEC, 53-70; physicist, Brookhaven Nat Lab, 55-56; vpres & dir res, Inst Defense Analysis, Washington, DC, 61-62; vpres & tech dir, KMS Industs, 68-70, exec vpres, KMS Fusion, Inc, 71-74. *Mem:* Nat Acad Sci. *Res:* Theoretical nuclear physics; statistical mechanics, plasma physics; interactions of lasers with matter; magnetohydrodynamics and theory of metals. *Mailing Add:* Dept Physics B-019 Univ Calif San Diego La Jolla CA 92093

BRUEGGEMEIER, ROBERT WAYNE, BIOMEDICINAL CHEMISTRY. *Current Pos:* ASST PROF MED CHEM, OHIO STATE UNIV, 79- *Personal Data:* b Toledo, Ohio, June 14, 50; m 72; c 2. *Educ:* Mich State Univ, BA, 72; Univ Mich, MS, 75, PhD(med chem), 77. *Prof Exp:* Fel assoc biochem, Harvard Med Sch, 77-79. *Concurrent Pos:* Dir, Radiochem & Anal Labs, Ohio State Univ Cancer Ctr, 79- *Mem:* Am Chem Soc; AAAS; Sigma Xi. *Res:* Steroid chemistry and biochemistry; enqymology and enzyme inhibitors; hormones and cancer. *Mailing Add:* Col Pharm Ohio State Univ Columbus OH 43210-1214

BRUEHL, GEORGE WILLIAM, PLANT PATHOLOGY. *Current Pos:* RETIRED. *Personal Data:* b Mentone, Ind, Sept 10, 19; m 49; c 2. *Educ:* Univ Ark, BSA, 41; Univ Wis, PhD(plant path), 48. *Prof Exp:* Assoc pathologist, Div Cereal Crops & Dis, USDA, SDak State Col Exp Sta, 48-52, pathologist, Div Sugar Plant Invests, 52-54; pathologist, Dept Plant Path, Wash State Univ, 54-84. *Mem:* Am Phytopath Soc; Sigma Xi. *Res:* Root rots of cereal crops; general pathology of cereals. *Mailing Add:* RR 3 Pullman WA 99163

BRUENING, GEORGE, PLANT VIROLOGY, BIOCHEMISTRY. *Current Pos:* NSF fel, Virus Lab, Univ Calif, Berkeley, 65-66, from asst prof to prof biochem, 67-84, PROF PLANT PATH, UNIV CALIF, DAVIS, 85-, DIR, CTR ENG PLANT RES AGAINST PATHOGENS, 91- *Personal Data:* b Chicago, Ill, Aug 10, 38; m 60; c 3. *Educ:* Carroll Col, Wis, 60; Univ Wis-Madison, MS, 63, PhD(biochem), 65. *Concurrent Pos:* Vis scientist plant path, Cornell Univ, 74-75; Guggenheim Mem Found fel, 74-75; vis scientist biochem, Univ Adelaide, Australia, 81; vis scientist plant indust, CSIRO, Canberra, Australia, 89. *Mem:* Nat Acad Sci; fel Am Phytopath Soc; Am Soc Biochem & Molecular Biol; Soc Microbiol UK; AAAS. *Res:* Biochemistry and chemistry of plant viruses, satellite RNA, nucleic acids and proteins. *Mailing Add:* Dept Plant Path Univ Calif Davis CA 95616

BRUENING, JAMES THEODORE, MATHEMATICS. *Current Pos:* ASST PROF MATH, BAKER UNIV, 77- *Personal Data:* b Cape Girardeau, Mo, Feb 27, 49; m 73; c 2. *Educ:* Univ Mo-Rolla, BS, 71, MS, 72, PhD(math), 77. *Prof Exp:* Instr math, Westmar Col, 76-77. *Mem:* Am Math Soc. *Res:* Inverses of transfer function matrices; linear sequential circuits. *Mailing Add:* Southeast Mo State Univ 1 University Plaza Cape Girardeau MO 63701-4710

BRUENNER, ROLF SYLVESTER, APPLIED CHEMISTRY. *Current Pos:* from res chemist to sr res chemist, 59-75, SCIENTIST, AEROJET STRATEGIC PROPULSION CO, GEN TIRE & RUBBER CO, 75- *Personal Data:* b Magdeburg, Ger, Dec 31, 21; US citizen; m 56; c 4. *Educ:* Munich Tech Univ, MS, 55, PhD(photochem), 57. *Honors & Awards:* Wyld Propulsion Award, Am Inst Aeronaut & Astronaut, 85. *Prof Exp:* Sci asst photochem, Phys Chem Inst, Munich Tech Univ, 55-57; res chemist, US Army Signals Res & Develop Labs, Ft Monmouth, NJ, 57-59. *Mem:* Am Chem Soc; Soc Ger Chem; Sigma Xi. *Res:* Mechanism of energy transfer from adsorbed dye molecules to crystal lattices; photopolymerization; photographic stabilization processing; catalysis of urethane formation; polymer chemistry; composite materials; propellants and explosives. *Mailing Add:* 7748 Excelsior Ave Orangevale CA 95662-2508

BRUES, ALICE MOSSIE, PHYSICAL ANTHROPOLOGY. *Current Pos:* chmn dept anthrop, 68-71, PROF ANTHROP, UNIV COLO, BOULDER, 65- *Personal Data:* b Boston, Mass, Oct 9, 13. *Educ:* Bryn Mawr Col, AB, 33; Radcliffe Col, PhD(phys anthrop), 40. *Honors & Awards:* Phys Anthrop Award, Am Acad of Forensic Sci, 86. *Prof Exp:* Res assoc phys anthrop, Peabody Mus, Harvard Univ, 41-42; statistician, Anthropometric Unit, Wright Field, 42-44; anthropologist, Chem Warfare Serv, 45; from asst prof to prof anat, Sch Med, Univ Okla, 46-65. *Mem:* Am Asn Phys Anthrop (vpres, 66-68, pres, 71-); Soc Study Evolution; Am Soc Naturalists; Am Acad Forensic Sci. *Res:* Regional variation in man; pigmentation; computer simulation of evolutionary change; forensic identification, cranial. *Mailing Add:* 4325 Prado Dr Boulder CO 80303-9629

BRUESCH, SIMON RULIN, anatomy; deceased, see previous edition for last biography

BRUESKE, CHARLES H, PLANT PHYSIOLOGY. *Current Pos:* From asst prof to assoc prof, 64-77, PROF BIOL, MT UNION COL, 77-, DEPT CHMN, 79- *Personal Data:* b New Ulm, Minn, Dec 18, 37; m 61, Brenda McDonnough; c 2. *Educ:* Elmhurst Col, BS, 59; Univ Southern Ill, MS, 61; Ariz State Univ PhD(bot), 65. *Concurrent Pos:* Vis prof plant path, Univ Mo, 71, Ohio Agr Res & Develop Ctr, Wooster, 79; res nematologist, Agr Res Serv, USDA, Beltsville, 80. *Mem:* AAAS; Am Soc Plant Physiol; Am Soc Micros; AAAS. *Res:* Pathogenicity of human fungal pathogens; physiology of plant diseases; ecology of rock microbes. *Mailing Add:* Dept Biol Mt Union Col 1972 Clark Ave Alliance OH 44601-3929. *Fax:* 440-821-0245

BRUETMAN, MARTIN EDGARDO, NEUROLOGY. *Current Pos:* PROF NEUROL, RUSH-PRESBY ST LUKE'S, 75-; CHIEF DIV NEUROL, CHRIST HOSP, 75- *Personal Data:* b Buenos Aires, Arg, Aug 17, 32; US citizen; m 56; c 2. *Educ:* Nat Col Buenos Aires, BS & BA, 49; Univ Buenos Aires, MD, 55. *Prof Exp:* Instr neurol, Baylor Col Med, 62-63, mem, Fac Comt Res Projs, 63-64; clin asst prof neurol & head sect, Inst Med Res, Univ Buenos Aires, 64-68; from assoc prof to prof, Chicago Med Sch, 68-74, chmn dept, 70-74; chmn, Dept Neurol & dir, Residency Training Prog, Mt Sinai Hosp Med Ctr, Chicago, 74-76; coordr, Ill Regional Med Prog, 69-73. *Concurrent Pos:* Fel neurol, Baylor Col Med, 61-62; Nat Heart Inst grant, 64-68; coordr coop study cerebrovascular insufficiency, NIH, 61-64; assoc investr, Neurol Res Ctr, Inst Torcuato di Tella, Arg, 64-68; adv to secy pub health training progs, Govt Arg, 66-68; mem, Coun Cerebrovascular Dis, Am Heart Asn, 68- *Mem:* Am Epilepsy Soc; Am Acad Neurol; NY Acad Sci; Arg Soc Neurol; Arg Col Neurol. *Res:* Medical education; natural history and incidence of cerebrovascular diseases; epidemiology; community resources in relation to cerebrovascular diseases. *Mailing Add:* 11800 Southwest Hwy Palos Heights IL 60463-1029

BRUGAM, RICHARD BLAIR, LIMNOLOGY, ECOLOGY. *Current Pos:* from asst prof to assoc prof, 78-84, PROF BIOL, SOUTHERN ILL UNIV, EDWARDSVILLE, 85-, DEPT CHAIR BIOL SCI, 96- *Personal Data:* b Philadelphia, Pa, Dec 23, 46; m 70, Sue Oren; c Amy & Matthew. *Educ:* Lehigh Univ, BA, 68; Yale Univ, MPhil, 74, PhD(biol), 75. *Honors & Awards:* J Willard Gibbs Prize, 68. *Prof Exp:* Res assoc limnol, Limnol Res Ctr, Univ Minn, 75-78. *Concurrent Pos:* Vis scholar zool, Univ Wash, Seattle, 84-85. *Mem:* Ecol Soc Am; Am Quaternary Asn; Sigma Xi. *Res:* Paleolimnology, especially the long-term history of cultural eutrophication in lakes; fossil diatoms to reconstruct limnological conditions over post-glacial time; neutralization of acidic lakes on coal mine sites. *Mailing Add:* Dept Biol Sci Southern Ill Univ Edwardsville IL 62025. *E-Mail:* rbrugam@siuc.edu

BRUGGE, JOHN F, PHYSIOLOGY. *Current Pos:* NIH fel, 63-66, asst prof, 66-71, assoc prof, 71-77, PROF NEUROPHYSIOL, SCH MED, UNIV WIS-MADISON, 77- *Personal Data:* b Brooklyn, NY, Apr 24, 37; m 60; c 3. *Educ:* Luther Col, Iowa, BA, 59; Univ Ill, Urbana-Champaign, MS, 61, PhD(physiol), 63. *Mem:* Soc Neurosci; Am Physiol Soc; Int Brain Res Orgn; fel Acoust Soc Am. *Res:* Physiology and anatomy of auditory system. *Mailing Add:* Dept Neurophys Univ Wis Med Sch 1300 University Ave Madison WI 53706-1585

BRUGGEMAN, GORDON ARTHUR, PHYSICAL METALLURGY, MATERIALS PROCESSING. *Current Pos:* RETIRED. *Personal Data:* b Detroit, Mich, Sept 24, 33; m 56; c 2. *Educ:* Mass Inst Technol, SB, 55, ScD(phys metall), 60. *Prof Exp:* Instr phys metall, Mass Inst Technol, 55-57; phys metallurgist, Manlabs, Inc, Mass, 60-61; phys metallurgist, Mat & Mech Res Ctr, US Army Mat Technol Lab, 62-81, chief, Process Technol Div, 82-86, dir, Emergency Mat Div, 87-89, assoc dir, 90-93. *Concurrent Pos:* Lectr, Northeastern Univ, 63-74. *Mem:* Am Soc Metals; Am Inst Mining, Metall & Petrol Engrs. *Res:* Phase transformations and their relation to mechanical properties; failure analysis and fracture; materials processing; grain boundary structure. *Mailing Add:* 9 Fieldstone Lane Natick MA 01760

BRUGGER, ROBERT MELVIN, NEUTRON PHYSICS. *Current Pos:* dir, Res Reactor Facil, 84-81, EMER PROF NUCLEAR ENG PROG, UNIV MO, 91- *Personal Data:* b Oklahoma City, Okla, Jan 13, 29; m 53; c 2. *Educ:* Colo Col, BA, 51; Rice Inst, MA, 53, PhD(physics), 55. *Prof Exp:* Asst, Rice Inst, 51-54; res physicist, Nuclear Physics Br, Atomic Energy Div, Phillips Petrol Co, 55-61, head, Solid State Physics Sect, 61-66; head, Solid State Physics Sect, Idaho Nuclear Corp, 66-68; mgr nuclear technol div, Aerojet Nuclear Co, 68-74. *Concurrent Pos:* Mem, UK Atomic Energy Res Estab, Harwell, 62-63; comr, Idaho Nuclear Energy Comn, 70-74; sabbatical leave, Los Alamos Nat Lab, 81-82. *Mem:* Fel Am Phys Soc; fel Am Nuclear Soc. *Res:* Neutron cross sections; neutron inelastic scattering; neutron diffraction; gamma detection; high pressure research; reactor conception; design and operation; metallurgy and materials testing. *Mailing Add:* 1012 Bourn Ave Columbia MO 65203

BRUGGER, THOMAS C, CHILD PSYCHIATRY. *Current Pos:* asst prof, 75-94, COORDR CHILDREN'S SERV, CASE WESTERN RES UNIV, 75-, ACTG DIR, DIV CHILD PSYCHIAT, 87-, EMER PROF CHILD PSYCHIAT, 94-, MED DIR BEECH BROOK, 94- *Personal Data:* b Fond du Lac, Wis, Jan 19, 27; m 54; c 5. *Educ:* Univ Wis, BNS, 48, BS, 50, MD, 53. *Prof Exp:* Staff psychiatrist, Winebago State Hosp, 53; resident, Cincinnati Dept Psychiat, Cincinnati Gen Hosp, 56-58; trainee child psychiat, Dept Child Psychiat, Child Guid Home, Ohio, 58-60; staff psychiatrist, instr & asst dir children's clins, Sch Med, Univ Cincinnati, 60-61; asst prof child psychiat & dir, Child Guid & Eval Clin, Wash Univ, 61-75. *Concurrent Pos:* Consult, Cincinnati Speech & Hearing Ctr, Ohio, 59-61, Diag Clin Ment Retarded Children, 59-61 & Miriam Sch, 63-75. *Mem:* AAAS; Am Psychiat Asn; Am Orthopsychiat Asn. *Res:* Child psychiatry. *Mailing Add:* Div Child Psychiat Beech Brook Resid Treatment Ctr 3737 Lander Rd Cleveland OH 44124

BRUGH, MAX, JR, VETERINARY MEDICINE, MEDICAL MICROBIOLOGY. *Current Pos:* RES VETERINARIAN NEWCASTLE DIS, SOUTHEAST POULTRY RES LAB, USDA, 73- *Personal Data:* b Roanoke, Va, Dec 16, 38. *Educ:* Univ Ga, DVM, 64, PhD(med microbiol), 68. *Prof Exp:* Res veterinarian foot & mouth dis, Plum Island Animal Dis Lab, USDA, 68-70; virologist, Pan Am Foot & Mouth Dis Ctr, Pan Am Health Orgn, 70-73. *Mem:* Am Vet Med Asn; Am Asn Avian Pathologists; Am Asn Vet Lab Diagnosticians; World Poultry Sci Asn; Sigma Xi. *Res:* Development of methods for control of viral diseases in food animals; development and improvement of vaccines, diagnostic methods and serologic tests for control of Newcastle disease and avian influenza. *Mailing Add:* 187 Stafford Dr Athens GA 30605

BRUHN, H(JALMAR) D(IEHL), MECHANICAL & AGRICULTURAL ENGINEERING. *Current Pos:* From instr to prof agr eng, 33-78, chmn dept agr eng, 62-66, EMER PROF AGR ENG, UNIV WIS, MADISON, 78- *Personal Data:* b Spring Green, Wis, Aug 5, 07; m 38, Janet Weber; c Janet (Jeffcott). *Educ:* Univ Wis, BS, 31 & 33; Mass Inst Technol, MS, 37. *Honors & Awards:* McCormick-Case Gold Medal, Am Soc Agr Eng, 92. *Concurrent*

Pos: Consult agr eng, 78- *Mem:* Am Soc Agr Eng; AAAS; Nat Soc Prof Engrs; NY Acad Sci; Soc Green Veg Res; Am Asn Univ Professors. *Res:* Farm power and machinery with emphasis on forage harvesting, crushing, pelleting and drying; irrigation equipment; seeding machinery; fruit harvesting equipment; harvesting and wet fractionation of terrestrial and aquatic vegetation; spontaneous ignition of agricultural crops. *Mailing Add:* 5418 Lake Mendota Dr Madison WI 53705

BRUHN, JOHN G, PUBLIC HEALTH, EPIDEMIOLOGY. *Current Pos:* VPRES ACAD AFFAIRS & RES & PROF NURSING & HEALTH SCI, UNIV TEX, EL PASO, 91-, ADJ PROF MGT & POL SCI, SCH PUB HEALTH, HOUSTON, 91- *Personal Data:* b Norfolk, Nebr, Apr 27, 34. *Educ:* Univ Nebr, BA, 56, MA, 58; Yale Univ, PhD(med sociol), 61. *Prof Exp:* Res sociologist, Dept Psychol Med, Univ Edinburg, 61-62; instr, med sociol, Sch Health, Univ Okla Med Ctr, 62-63, asst prof, Dept Psychiat & Behav Scis, 63-64, asst prof, 64-67, assoc prof med, prev med & pub health, 67-70, prof & chmn, Dept Human Ecol, 69-72; assoc dean, community affairs, Univ Tex Med Br, Galveston, 72-81, dean, Sch Allied Health Scis & spec asst to the pres, 81-91. *Concurrent Pos:* Res, Conn Dept Ment Health, 58-59; instr social, Southern Coun Col, 60-61; res sociologist, Grace New Haven Community Hosp, 60-61; USPHS fel, 60-61, US Fulbright fel, 61-62, John E Fogarty Health Scientist Exchange fel, 89 & WHO fel, 91; consult, Am Soc Anesthesiologists, 66-71; assoc prof sociol, Univ Okla, Norman, 67-72; career develop award, Nat Heart Inst, 68-69; mem, Task Force on Funding, Am Pub Health Asn, 73-74; Danforth Found assoc, 73-86. *Mem:* Fel Am Pub Health Asn; fel Am Orthopsychiat Asn; Am Psychosom Soc; Pavlovian Soc N Am; fel Royal Soc Health; Am Psychosomatic Soc. *Res:* Study of the psychological and social factors that influence the etiology and clinical course of coronary heart disease; published numerous articles in various journals. *Mailing Add:* 601 Firedale Ln El Paso TX 79912. *Fax:* 915-747-5068; *E-Mail:* bitnet: im11@utep

BRUHWEILER, FREDERICK CARLTON, JR, ASTRONOMY, ASTROPHYSICS. *Current Pos:* MEM STAFF, LAB ASTRON & SOLAR PHYSICS, NASA GODDARD SPACE FLIGHT CTR, 77-; PROF PHYSICS, CATHOLIC UNIV, 93-, DIR, ASTROPHYS & COMPUTATIONAL SCI, 96- *Personal Data:* b Quincy, Ill, Dec 4, 46; m 77. *Educ:* Coe Col, BA, 68; Univ Tex, Austin, MA, 73, PhD(astron), 77. *Concurrent Pos:* Assoc, Nat Acad Sci-Nat Res Coun, 77-; res prof, Cath Univ, 83-92, prof, 92- *Mem:* Am Astron Soc. *Res:* Ultraviolet astronomy, early type stars and the interstellar medium. *Mailing Add:* 228 Mowbray Rd Silver Spring MD 20904

BRUICE, THOMAS CHARLES, BIO-ORGANIC CHEMISTRY. *Current Pos:* PROF CHEM, UNIV CALIF, SANTA BARBARA, 64- *Personal Data:* b Los Angeles, Calif, Aug 25, 25; m; c 3. *Educ:* Univ Southern Calif, BA, 50, PhD(biochem), 54. *Prof Exp:* Lilly fel, Univ Calif, Los Angeles, 54-55; from instr to asst prof, Yale Univ, 55-58; asst prof, Sch Med, Johns Hopkins Univ, 58-60; prof chem, Cornell Univ, 60-64. *Concurrent Pos:* USPHS sr fel, 57-58; career investr, NIH, 62- *Mem:* Nat Acad Sci; Am Chem Soc; Royal Soc Chem; Am Soc Biochem; Am Acad Arts & Sci. *Res:* Physical organics; bioorganics. *Mailing Add:* Dept Chem Univ Calif Santa Barbara CA 93106

BRUINS, PAUL F(ASTENAU), chemical engineering; deceased, see previous edition for last biography

BRULEY, DUANE FREDERICK, PROCESS CONTROL & BIOPROCESS ENGINEERING, SYSTEMS PHYSIOLOGY. *Current Pos:* dean eng, 91-95, PROF CHEM & BIOCHEM ENG, UNIV MD, 95-, DIR DEPT GRAD PROG, 95- *Personal Data:* b Chippewa Falls, Wis, Aug 3, 33; m 59, Suzanne Bigler; c Scott, Randy & Mark. *Educ:* Univ Wis, BS, 56; Stanford Univ, MS, 59; Univ Tenn, PhD(chem eng), 62. *Honors & Awards:* Outstanding Contribution to Res Award, Am Soc Eng Educ, 67; Chem Eng Educator Award, Chem Eng Educ Mag, 70; Charls M Kerr Award, 83; Teeter Award, 85. *Prof Exp:* Assoc develop engr, Oak Ridge Nat Labs, Union Carbide Co, 56-59; from asst prof to prof chem eng, Clemson Univ, 62-72; prof chem eng & head dept, Tulane Univ, 72-76; vpres acad affairs & dean fac, Rose-Hulman Inst Technol, 76-81; prof & head biomed eng, La Tech Univ, 81-84; dean eng, Calif Polytech State Univ, 84-87, prof eng, 87-91. *Concurrent Pos:* NSF grant, 64-65; consult, WVa Pulp & Paper Co, 64-, Am Enka, Med Univ SC, E I DuPont de Nemours & Co, 73-, Exxon Corp, 78- & El Paso Polyolifens Co, 81-82; NIH res grant, 67-73; vis prof, Princeton Univ, 70- & Univ Yamagata, Japan, 75; adj prof, Dept Physiol & Dept Anat, Tulane Univ, 73-78; prog dir & sect head, bioeng & environ systs, NSF, 87-90; spec opportunity award biomed eng, Witaker Found, 94-97. *Mem:* Fel Am Inst Chem Engrs; Biomed Eng Soc; Int Soc Oxygen Transp Tissue (pres, 82); Nat Soc Prof Engrs; Am Soc Mech Engrs; Am Soc Eng Educ; fel Int Asn Med & Biol Environ. *Res:* Process dynamics and control; biomedical and bioprocess engineering; downstream processing to separate and purify protein c, a powerful anti-coagulant and anti-thrombotic. *Mailing Add:* 7345 Swan Point Way Columbia MD 21045. *Fax:* 410-455-1049; *E-Mail:* bruley@umbcz.umbc.edu

BRUMAGE, WILLIAM HARRY, SOLID STATE PHYSICS. *Current Pos:* from asst prof to assoc prof, 52-64, PROF PHYSICS, LA TECH UNIV, 64-, CHMN DEPT, 65- *Personal Data:* b Slick, Okla, Nov 18, 23; m 47; c 1. *Educ:* Okla State Univ, BS, 48, MS, 49; Univ Okla, PhD(physics), 64. *Prof Exp:* Instr physics, Ark Agr & Mech Col, 49-52. *Mem:* Am Phys Soc; Am Asn Physics Teachers; Sigma Xi; Optical Soc Am. *Res:* Paramagnetic susceptibilities of ions in host crystals; laser induced chemistry. *Mailing Add:* 1802 Saddleback Blvd Norman OK 73072

BRUMBAUGH, DONALD VERWEY, PHYSICAL CHEMISTRY, MOLECULAR SPECTROSCOPY. *Current Pos:* RES CHEMIST, PHOTOG RES LAB, EASTMAN KODAK CO, 81- *Personal Data:* b Rochester, NY, Sept 18, 52. *Educ:* Williams Col, AB, 74; State Univ NY, Binghamton, PhD(chem), 80. *Prof Exp:* Res assoc spectros, Dept Chem, James Franck Inst, Univ Chicago, 79-81. *Concurrent Pos:* Mem, Ctr Photoinduced Charge Transfer, Univ Rochester, 91- *Mem:* Am Chem Soc; Sigma Xi. *Res:* Laser induced fluorescence spectra of molecules; spectral sensitization of photographic emulsions. *Mailing Add:* 155 Haskins Lane S Hilton NY 14468-9003

BRUMBAUGH, JOE H, MARINE BIOLOGY, MARINE & FRESHWATER INVERTEBRATES. *Current Pos:* from asst prof to assoc prof biol, 64-71, chmn, Div Natural Sci, 71-74, PROF BIOL, SONOMA STATE COL, 71- *Personal Data:* b Eldorado, Ohio, Sept 14, 30; m 61; c 3. *Educ:* Miami Univ, BSEd, 52; Purdue Univ, MS, 56; Stanford Univ, PhD(biol), 65. *Prof Exp:* High sch teacher, Ohio, 52-54; instr biol & bot, Wabash Col, 56-59. *Mem:* Am Soc Zoologists; AAAS; Western Soc Naturalists; Sigma Xi. *Res:* Anatomy, diet and feeding mechanisms in marine invertebrates, particularly holothurian echinoderms; functional morphology of marine and freshwater invertebrates; natural history of marine and freshwater invertebrates. *Mailing Add:* 5815 Yerba Buena Rd Santa Rosa CA 95409

BRUMBAUGH, JOHN (ALBERT), GENETIC CONTROL GENE EXPRESSION. *Current Pos:* from asst prof to assoc prof, 64-73, PROF GENETICS, SCH BIOL SCI, UNIV NEBR, LINCOLN, 73- *Personal Data:* b Buffalo, NY, May 3, 35; m 58; c 3. *Educ:* Cedarville Col, BS, 58; Iowa State Univ, PhD(develop genetics), 63. *Prof Exp:* From instr to assoc prof biol, Cedarville Col, 59-64. *Concurrent Pos:* Attend, NSF Col Teachers Res Partic Prog, Purdue Univ, 64; Nat Inst Gen Med Sci res career develop award, 69-74; Lasby vis prof human & oral genetics, Univ Minn, 77-78; Prog dir eukaryotic genetics, NSF, 89-90. *Mem:* Am Genetic Asn; Am Soc Cell Biol; Genetics Soc Am; Int Pigment & Cell Soc; Poultry Sci Asn. *Res:* Melanocyte differentiation in the fowl; genetic regulation in higher organisms; somatic cell genetics of melanocytes in culture including melanoma; molecular biology of tyrosinase; automated DNA sequencing. *Mailing Add:* 8335 Karl Ridge Rd Lincoln NE 68506. *Fax:* 402-472-2083

BRUMBAUGH, PHILIP, quality control, industrial engineering; deceased, see previous edition for last biography

BRUMBERGER, HARRY, CATALYSIS, MATERIALS SCIENCE. *Current Pos:* from asst prof to prof, Syracuse Univ, 57-95, dir grad biophys prog, 77-83, dir, Solid State Sci & Tech Prog, 87-93, EMER PROF PHYS CHEM, SYRACUSE UNIV, 95- *Personal Data:* b Vienna, Austria, Aug 28, 26; nat US; m 50, Vilma Musry; c Jesse & Eva. *Educ:* Polytech Inst Brooklyn, BS, 49, MS, 52, PhD(chem), 55. *Prof Exp:* Res assoc chem, Cornell Univ, 54-57. *Concurrent Pos:* Res leave, Graz Univ & Nat Bur Stand 62-63, Weizmann Inst Sci, 74, Univ Cambridge, 83-84 & Swiss Fed Inst Technol, 90-91; mem policy comt, Nat Ctr Small-Angle Scattering Res, Oak Ridge Nat Lab, 78-81. *Mem:* AAAS; Am Crystallog Asn; Mat Res Soc. *Res:* Supported-metal catalysts, structure-property correlations, sintering and redispersion phenomena, small-angle x-ray scattering, scattering models; application and theory of small-angle scattering for multicomponent systems. *Mailing Add:* Dept Chem Syracuse Univ Syracuse NY 13244-1200

BRUMER, MILTON, CIVIL ENGINEERING. *Current Pos:* RETIRED. *Personal Data:* b Philadelphia, Pa, Jan 21, 02; m 26; c 2. *Educ:* Rensselaer Polytech Inst, ME, 23; Univ Ala, MS, 24. *Hon Degrees:* DE, Rensselaer Polytech Inst, 70. *Prof Exp:* Asst engr, Port NY Auth, 25-38; chief engr tunnel design, Pa Turnpike Comn, 38-40; prin engr, O H Ammann & Ammann & Whitney, 40-50, pres, Ammann & Whitney, Inc & Ammann & Whitney Int, Ltd, 50-75, partner & prin engr, Ammann & Whitney, Inc, 75-79. *Concurrent Pos:* Lectr, numerous cols & univs. *Mem:* Nat Acad Eng; fel NY Acad Sci; Am Inst Consult Engrs; fel am Soc Civil Engrs. *Res:* Suspension bridge design; structural steel bridges; highways; turnpikes; hangars; vehicular tunnels. *Mailing Add:* 6750 Entrada Pl Boca Raton FL 33433

BRUMER, PAUL WILLIAM, THEORETICAL CHEMISTRY, CHEMICAL PHYSICS. *Current Pos:* from asst prof to assoc prof, 75-83, PROF CHEM, UNIV TORONTO, 83- *Personal Data:* b New York, NY, June 8, 45; m 68, Abbey Pohrille; c Deborah, Jeremy, Eric & Sharon. *Educ:* Brooklyn Col, BS, 66; Harvard Univ, PhD(chem physics), 72. *Honors & Awards:* Hudnall lectr Award, Univ Chicago, 83; Noranda Award, CIC, 85; Palladium Medal, Chem Inst Can, 93. *Prof Exp:* Fel chem physics, Weizmann Inst Sci, 72-73 & molecular physics, Harvard Col Observ, 73-74, lectr astron, 74-75. *Concurrent Pos:* Alfred P Sloan Found fel, 77-81; Killam res fel, 81-83; prof leader, Ont Laser & Lightwave Res Ctr, 89- *Mem:* Fel Am Phys Soc; Sigma Xi; fel Chem Inst Can. *Res:* Theories of intermolecular and intramolecular nonlinear mechanics and chemical dynamics; classical quantum correspondence; laser induced chemistry; control of molecular dynamics with lasers. *Mailing Add:* Dept Chem Univ Toronto Toronto ON M5S 1A1 Can. *Fax:* 416-978-8775; *E-Mail:* pbrumer@tikva.chem.utoronto.ca

BRUMLEVE, STANLEY JOHN, PHYSIOLOGY. *Current Pos:* from asst prof to assoc prof, 57-73, actg chmn, dept, 64-65, PROF PHYSIOL & PHARMACOL, MED SCH, UNIV NDAK, 73-, CHMN DEPT, 72- *Personal Data:* b Teutopolis, Ill, July 3, 24; m 55; c 4. *Educ:* St Louis Univ, BS, 50, MS, 54, PhD(physiol, biochem), 57. *Prof Exp:* Asst physiol, St Louis

Univ, 54; instr biol, Webster Col, 55-57. *Concurrent Pos:* Asst, Univ Alaska, 54. *Mem:* Am Physiol Soc. *Res:* Environmental physiology; temperature regulation; high pressure and other stresses. *Mailing Add:* 749 S 30th St No 226 Grand Forks ND 58201

BRUMM, DOUGLAS B(RUCE), ELECTRONICS, INSTRUMENTATION. *Current Pos:* asst prof, 70-81, ASSOC PROF ELEC ENG, MICH TECHNOL UNIV, 81- *Personal Data:* b Nashville, Mich, Aug 4, 40; m 65, Phyllis Orthner; c Bruce D & Dawn M. *Educ:* Mich Technol Univ, BS, 62; Univ Mich, MSE, 64, PhD(elec eng), 70. *Honors & Awards:* Teetor Award, Soc Automotive Engrs, 84. *Prof Exp:* Assoc eng, Wayland Lab, Raytheon Co, 62-63; teaching fel elec eng, Univ Mich, 63-64, res asst holography, Radar & Optics Lab, 64, res asst, Electro-Optical Sci Lab, 65-66, res assoc, 66-70. *Concurrent Pos:* Res engr, USDA, 75-91; consult, InfraRed Telemetrics, 92- *Mem:* Inst Elec & Electronics Engrs; Inst Elec & Electronics Engrs Indust Electronics Soc. *Res:* Electronics; microprocessor applications; instrumentation for automotive research; electronic applications to the wood products industry; laser applications; fiber optics; holography. *Mailing Add:* MTU/EE Dept 122 EERC 1400 Townsend Dr Houghton MI 49931-1295. *Fax:* 906-487-2949; *E-Mail:* dbbrumm@mtu.edu

BRUMMER, ELMER, MEDICAL RESEARCH, FUNGAL INFECTIONS. *Current Pos:* SR RES ASSOC, SANTA CLARA VALLEY MED CTR, 79-; SR LECTR, STANFORD UNIV MED SCH, 79- *Personal Data:* b Litchfield, Ill, May 11, 26. *Educ:* Univ Notre Dame, BS, 48; NMex Highlands Univ, MS, 62; Clemson Univ, PhD(microbiol), 72. *Prof Exp:* Fel, Baylor Col Med, 72-75, NY Univ Med Sch, 75-79. *Mem:* Am Soc Microbiol; Am Asn Immunologists. *Mailing Add:* Dept Med Santa Clara Valley Med Ctr 751 S Bascom Ave San Jose CA 95128-2699

BRUMMER, JOHANNES J, ECONOMIC GEOLOGY, EXPLORATION GEOLOGY. *Current Pos:* CONSULT, GEOLOGIST MINERALS EXPLOR, 84- *Personal Data:* b Graaff Reinet, SAfrica, Sept 2, 21; Can citizen; m 58, Eva Andersen; c Douglas A & William D. *Educ:* Univ Witwatersrand, c, 44 & 45, MSc, 51; McGill Univ, PhD(geol), 55. *Honors & Awards:* Duncan R Derry Medal, Geol Asn Can, 84. *Prof Exp:* Mine surveyor, E Geduld Mines Ltd, SAfrica, 45-47; mine geologist, Roan Antelope Copper Mines Ltd, Zambia, 47-49; chief geologist, Mufulira Copper Mines Ltd, 49-51 & Rhodesian Selection Trust Serv Ltd, 51-53; sr geologist, Kennco Explor Ltd, Que, 55-57, Vancouver, 57-58 & Toronto, 58-61; resident geologist, Cent Can, Falconbridge Nickel Mines Ltd, 61-68, explor mgr, Cent Div, 68-70; vpres explor, Occidental Minerals Corp Can, 70-72, explor mgr, Minerals Div, Can Occidental Petrol Ltd, Toronto, Ont, 72-83. *Concurrent Pos:* J J Brummer Mgt, Inc, 84- *Mem:* Soc Econ Geologists; Geol Soc Am; Can Inst Mining & Metall & Petrol; Geol Asn Can; Geol Soc SAfrica. *Res:* Exploration for economic deposits of nickel in ultramafic rocks; sedimentary copper and porphyry copper deposits; volcanic sulfide and pyrometasomatic copper deposits; unconformity controlled (Saskatchewan-type) uranium deposits; gold deposits associated with Precambrian volcanic belts; platinum group elements in layered mafic complexes; diamonds in kimberlite diatremes. *Mailing Add:* 6 Wilgar Rd Toronto ON M8X 1J4 Can

BRUMMETT, ROBERT E, PHARMACOLOGY, OTOLARYNGOLOGY. *Current Pos:* from asst to assoc prof otolaryngol, 64-80, assoc prof pharmacol, 64-80, PROF OTOLARYNGOL & PHARMACOL, SCH MED, UNIV ORE, 81- *Personal Data:* b Concordia, Kans, Feb 11, 34; m 54, Naomi D Weaver; c Randall, Wendy, Robin & Philip. *Educ:* Ore State Univ, BS, 59, MS, 60; Univ Ore, PhD, 64. *Prof Exp:* Asst prof pharmacog & pharmacol, Sch Pharm, Ore State Univ, 61-62. *Mem:* AAAS; Soc Exp Biol & Med; Am Acad Otolaryngol; Soc Toxicol; Soc Neurosci; Sigma Xi; Asn Res Otolaryngol. *Res:* Effect of drugs on hearing, ototoxicity; cochlear function; clinical pharmacology of drugs used in otolaryngology. *Mailing Add:* 2366 N Menzies Ct Portland OR 97217-8219. *Fax:* 503-494-5656

BRUMMOND, DEWEY OTTO, BIOCHEMISTRY. *Current Pos:* RETIRED. *Personal Data:* b Towner, NDak, July 28, 25; m 54; c 2. *Educ:* NDak State Univ, BS, 50; Univ Wis, MS, 52, PhD(biochem), 54. *Prof Exp:* Fel, Nat Found Infantile Paralysis, 54-56; prin scientist, Radioisotope Serv, Vet Admin Hosp, Cleveland, Ohio, 56-64; assoc prof biochem, NDak State Univ, 65-66; prof chem, Moorhead State Univ, 66-91. *Concurrent Pos:* Sr instr, Western Res Univ, 56-64. *Mem:* Am Soc Biol Chemists; Sigma Xi. *Res:* Enzymatic synthesis of cellulose. *Mailing Add:* 215 Palmer Dr Franklin NC 28734-2819

BRUMUND, WILLIAM FRANK, CIVIL ENGINEERING, SOIL MECHANICS. *Current Pos:* PRES, GOLDEN ASSOCS INC, 74- *Personal Data:* b Joliet, Ill, June 12, 42; m 64; c 2. *Educ:* Purdue Univ, BSCE, 64, MSCE, 65, PhD(civil eng, soil mech), 69. *Prof Exp:* Asst prof civil eng, Ga Inst Technol, 69-74, assoc prof, 74-75. *Mem:* Am Soc Civil Engrs. *Res:* Soil dynamics of granular systems. *Mailing Add:* 2809 Woodland Park Dr NE Atlanta GA 30345

BRUN, MILIVOJ KONSTANTIN, CERAMICS ENGINEERING. *Current Pos:* STAFF SCIENTIST CERAMICS, RES & DEVELOP, GEN ELEC CORP, 79- *Personal Data:* b Novi Sad, Yugoslavia, Jan 8, 48; US citizen; m 80, Cathie-Jo Master; c Christina & Sonja Nicole. *Educ:* Pa State Univ, BSc, 70, PhD(ceramic sci), 74. *Prof Exp:* Asst inorg chem, Tech Univ Norway, Trondheim, 76-77; res assoc ceramics, Mat Res Lab, Pa State Univ, 79. *Mem:* Am Ceramic Soc; AAAS. *Res:* Processing and characterization of structural ceramics; hot isostatic pressing; ceramic composites. *Mailing Add:* Charlton Rd Ballston Lake NY 12019

BRUN, WILLIAM ALEXANDER, CROP PHYSIOLOGY. *Current Pos:* RETIRED. *Personal Data:* b NJ, Sept 10, 25; m 50; c 3. *Educ:* Univ Miami, BS, 50; Univ Ill, MS, 51, PhD(bot), 54. *Prof Exp:* Asst bot & plant physiol, Univ Ill, 50-54; asst prof bot, NC State Col, 54-57; plant physiologist, Agr Res Serv, USDA, 57-59 & United Fruit Co, 59-65; from asst prof to prof agron & plant genetics, Univ Minn, St Paul, 65-87. *Mem:* Am Soc Plant Physiol; Scand Soc Plant Physiol. *Res:* Growth and reproduction; photosynthesis; water relations; nitrogen fixation. *Mailing Add:* 8285 SW Rogue Ln Wilsonville OR 97070

BRUNDA, MICHAEL J, CYTOKINES, MACROPHAGES. *Current Pos:* sr scientist, 82-86, res investr, 86-91, RES LEADER, DEPT ONCOL, HOFFMANN LA-ROCHE, INC, 91- *Personal Data:* b Passaic, NJ, Dec 16, 50; m 79, Patricia Mongini; c Nicole & John. *Educ:* Univ Rochester, AB, 71; Stanford Univ, PhD(med microbiol), 75. *Prof Exp:* Fel, Nat Jewish Hosp & Res Ctr, 75-78; immunologist, Nat Cancer Inst, 78-81. *Mem:* Am Asn Immunologists; Am Asn Cancer Res; Soc Leukocyte Biol; AAAS. *Res:* Antitumor effects of interferon and other cytokines, especially interleukin-12. *Mailing Add:* Dept Oncol Hoffmann-La Roche Inc Nutley NJ 07110. *Fax:* 973-235-3093; *E-Mail:* michael.brundar@roche.com

BRUNDAGE, ARTHUR LAIN, DAIRY HUSBANDRY. *Current Pos:* Prof, 68-85, EMER PROF ANIMAL SCI, UNIV ALASKA, 85- *Personal Data:* b Wallkill, NY, Dec 19, 27; m 51, Helen E Harvey; c William H, Carolin E (Dec), Richard T & Rodney A. *Educ:* Cornell Univ, BS, 50; Univ Minn, MS, 52, PhD, 55. *Concurrent Pos:* Animal husbandman, USDA, Univ Alaska. *Mem:* AAAS; Am Dairy Sci Asn; Am Inst Biol Sci. *Mailing Add:* PO Box 616 Palmer AK 99645-0616

BRUNDAGE, DONALD KEITH, ORGANIC CHEMISTRY. *Current Pos:* from assoc prof to prof, 46-78, EMER PROF CHEM, UNIV TOLEDO, 78- *Personal Data:* b Traverse City, Mich, Oct 24, 13; m 38; c 5. *Educ:* Eastern Mich Univ, AB, 33; Univ Mich, PhD(phys org chem), 40. *Prof Exp:* Asst chem, Univ Mich, 35-38; chemist, Bendix Aviation Corp, Mich, 41; instr chem, St Cloud State Col, 41-46. *Concurrent Pos:* Res assoc, Univ Calif, Irvine, 67-68. *Mem:* Fel AAAS; Am Chem Soc; fel Am Inst Chemists. *Res:* Equilibrium; kinetics. *Mailing Add:* 2532 Glenwood Ave Toledo OH 43610-1327

BRUNDEN, KURT RUSSELL, ALZHEIMERS DISEASE, GLIAL RESEARCH. *Current Pos:* head biomolecular res, 91-92, from dir to sr dir discovery res, 92-96, VPRES RES, GLIATECH, INC, 97- *Personal Data:* b East Lansing, Mich, Mar 19, 58; m 88, Sherry Beecher. *Educ:* Western Mich Univ, BS, 80; Purdue Univ, PhD(biochem), 85. *Prof Exp:* Fel neurosci, Dept Neurol & Biochem, Mayo Clin, 85-87, res assoc & instr, 88; asst prof biochem, Univ Miss Med Ctr, 88-91. *Mem:* Am Soc Cell Biol; Am Soc Neurochem; Am Soc Neurosci. *Res:* Biomolecular research; development of proprietary products based on glial cell properties; role of glia in Alzheimer's disease. *Mailing Add:* Gliatech Inc 23420 Commerce Park Rd Beachwood OH 44122. *Fax:* 216-831-4220

BRUNDEN, MARSHALL NILS, biostatistics, for more information see previous edition

BRUNDLE, CHRISTOPHER RICHARD, CHARACTERIZATION OF MATERIAL SURFACES & INTERFACES, SURFACE SCIENCE. *Current Pos:* res staff mgr, IBM Res, San Jose, 75-93, proj mgr, 84-86, dept mgr, 86-89, proj mgr, 89-93, EMER RES STAFF MEM, IBM RES, ALMADEN RES CTR, 93- *Personal Data:* b Stoke-on-Trent, UK, Aug 7, 44. *Educ:* Manchester Univ, UK, BSc, 65; Imp Col, UK, PhD(phys chem), 68. *Honors & Awards:* W F Meggares Award, Soc Appl Spectros, 69; Peter Mark Award, Am Vacuum Soc, 80. *Prof Exp:* Lectr phys chem, Bradford Univ, UK, 70-75. *Concurrent Pos:* Ed, J Electron Spectros, 72-; chmn, Surface Sci Div, Am Vacuum Soc, 79; consult prof chem eng, Stanford Univ, 80-88; vis prof, Univ Hawaii, 84 & Univ Heidelberg, Ger, 92-93. *Mem:* Am Chem Soc; fel Am Phys Soc; Am Vacuum Soc. *Res:* Surface elemental, chemical composition and structural analysis and characterization; reactions at surfaces and interfaces, including catalysis related, oxidation and corrosion and electronic device materials. *Mailing Add:* IBM Res Almaden Res Ctr Dept K32 650 Harry Rd San Jose CA 95120. *Fax:* 408-294-3353; *E-Mail:* brundle@almaden

BRUNE, JAMES N, SEISMOLOGY, GEOPHYSICS. *Current Pos:* DIR, SEISMOL LAB, UNIV NEV, RENO, 87- *Personal Data:* b Modesto, Calif, Nov 23, 34; m 57, Karla Whituey; c Richard, Karla, Lawrence & Rebecca. *Educ:* Univ Nev, BS, 56; Columbia Univ, PhD(seismol), 61. *Honors & Awards:* Macelwane Award, Am Geophys Union, 62, Karl Gilbert Award, 67. *Prof Exp:* Res scientist, Lamont Geol Observ, Columbia Univ, 58-64; geophysicist, US Coast & Geod Surv, 64; assoc prof geophys, Calif Inst Technol, 65-69; prof, Scripps Inst Oceanog, Univ Calif, San Diego, 69-92, assoc dir, Inst Geophys & Planetary Physics, 71-76, chmn, Geol Res Div, 74-76. *Concurrent Pos:* Adj assoc prof geol, Columbia Univ, 64. *Mem:* Fel Geol Soc Am; fel Am Geophys Union; Seismol Soc Am (pres, 70). *Res:* Earthquake hazard; seismology; earth structure; earth quake source mechanism; heat flow; geology. *Mailing Add:* Dept Geol Univ Nev Reno NV 89557-0901. *Fax:* 702-784-1833; *E-Mail:* brune@seismo.unr.edu

BRUNEAU, ANGUS A, ELECTRICAL ENGINEERING. *Current Pos:* DIR, MARITIME ELECTRIC CO LTD, 90-, SNC GROUP INC, 91- *Personal Data:* b Toronto, Ont, Dec 12, 35; m 59, Jean McInnis; c Peter, Ian & Stephen. *Educ:* Univ Toronto, BA, 58; Univ London, DIC & PhD, 62.

Honors & Awards: Julian C Smith Medal, Eng Inst Can, 92; Gold Medal, Can Acad Eng, 88. *Concurrent Pos:* Lectr math, Univ Waterloo, 58-59, lectr, res mat engr & mat sci group leader, 62-68, dir gen eng, 66-68; dean eng, Mem Univ, 68-74. *Mem:* Fel Can Acad Eng. *Mailing Add:* 53 Tupper St St John's NF A1A 2T6 Can

BRUNEAU, LESLIE HERBERT, GENETICS. *Current Pos:* From asst prof to assoc prof, 55-66, chmn biol sci, 60-74, PROF ZOOL, OKLA STATE UNIV, 66- *Personal Data:* b Cornwall, Ont, Nov 28, 28; nat US; m 53; c 2. *Educ:* McGill Univ, BSc, 50; Univ Tex, MA, 52, PhD(cytogenetics), 56. *Mailing Add:* 2140 W Admiral Rd Stillwater OK 74074

BRUNEL, PIERRE, MARINE ECOLOGY. *Current Pos:* sr lectr, 66-68, from asst prof to assoc prof, 68-79, PROF BIOL SCI, UNIV MONTREAL, 79- *Personal Data:* b Montreal, Que, Mar 21, 31; m 55, Monique Parant; c Simon, Lucie, Fabien & Frederic. *Educ:* Univ Montreal, BSc, 53; Univ Toronto, MA, 57; McGill Univ, PhD, 68. *Prof Exp:* Asst invertebrates, Royal Ont Mus Zool, 53-55; zoologist, Marine Biol Sta Grande-Riviere, 55-66. *Concurrent Pos:* Vpres, Que Interuniv Oceanog Res Group, 70-88; pres, Mus Coord Comt, Dept Biol Sci, Univ Montreal, 83-; mem, In house & liaison comts, Joint MA Prog Museology, Univ Montreal & Univ Que, Montreal, 86- *Mem:* Am Inst Biol Sci; Can Soc Zool; Sigma Xi; Sci Res Soc; Soc Preserv Natural Hist Collections; Int Oceanog Found. *Res:* Ecology of marine bottom invertebrates and communities of northern seas; carcinology; taxonomy; zoogeography, ecology of Peracarid Crustacea, Amphipoda. *Mailing Add:* Dept Biol Sci Univ Montreal PO Box 6128 Montreal PQ H3C 3J7 Can. *Fax:* 514-343-2293

BRUNELL, KARL, MECHANICAL ENGINEERING. *Current Pos:* SR TECH ADV, JOHN DUSENBERY CO, CLIFTON, 69- *Personal Data:* b Cologne, Ger, Oct 7, 22; US citizen; m 47; c 2. *Educ:* City Col NY, BME, 58. *Prof Exp:* Plant engr graphic arts, A A Watts Co, Inc, 51-54; sr proj engr, Mergenthaler Linotype Co, 54-59; asst to dir res, Bell & Howell Co, Ill, 59-61; proj consult optics, Mech Res Div, Am Mach & Foundry Co, 61-62; mgr res & develop mech eng, Universal Box Mach Corp, 62-64; sr res assoc eng sci, Princeton Lab, Am Can Co, 64-69. *Mem:* Am Soc Mech Engrs. *Res:* Cams; optics; graphic arts; high speed machines; engineering management. *Mailing Add:* 25 Scarsdale Dr Livingston NJ 07039

BRUNELL, PHILIP ALFRED, PEDIATRICS, VIROLOGY. *Current Pos:* PROF PEDIAT, UNIV CALIF, LOS ANGELES, 87- *Personal Data:* b New York, NY, Feb 1, 31; m 52; c Wayne, Robert & Rhonda. *Educ:* City Col New York, BS, 50; Univ Ill, MS, 52; Univ Buffalo, MD, 57. *Prof Exp:* Asst physiol, Univ Ill, 51-53; intern pediat, Meyer Mem Hosp, Buffalo, NY, 57-58; resident, Children's Hosp, Buffalo, 58-60; med off in chg, Virus Reference Unit, Nat Commun Dis Ctr, 63-64; from asst prof to assoc prof pediat, Sch Med, NY Univ, 69-75; prof pediat & chmn dept, Univ Tex Health Sci Ctr, San Antonio, 75-81; prof pediat & head pediat infectious dis, Cedars Sinai Med Ctr, 81-87, dir infectious dis & vchair, 87-96. *Concurrent Pos:* Mem adv comt, Human Resources Admin, Head Start, New York, 64-; res grants, NIH, 64-, Nat Commun Dis Ctr, 68- & WHO, 69-78 & 80-; consult, Am Acad Pediat, 66-, US Mil Acad, 69- & Northwick Park Hosp, Harrow, Eng, 71-72; vis scientist, Clin Res Ctr, Harrow, 71-72; dir pediat, Bexar Co Hosp, San Antonio, 75-81; chair, Comn Infectious Dis, Am Acad Pediat, 83-87; chief med ed, Infectious Dis Child, 87-. *Mem:* Am Acad Pediat; Sigma Xi; Soc Pediat Res; Infectious Dis Soc Am; fel Am Pediat Soc; Pediat Dis Soc (pres, 87-89); fel Am Acad Microbiol; World Pediat Infectious Dis Soc (secy, 96). *Res:* Viral immunology; first to describe passive immunizations against chickenpox; acquired immune deficiency syndrome; developed a serologic marker for follicular dendritic cell function; clinical virology; infectious diseases of infants and children; varicellazoster virus; passive immunization. *Mailing Add:* Dept Pediat Cedars Sinai Med Ctr 8700 Beverly Blvd Los Angeles CA 90048. *Fax:* 310-967-0145; *E-Mail:* pbrunell@ucla.edu

BRUNELLE, EUGENE JOHN, JR, AERONAUTICS. *Current Pos:* ASSOC PROF AERONAUT, RENSSELAER POLYTECH INST, 64- *Personal Data:* b Montpelier, Vt, Mar 17, 32; m 55; c 3. *Educ:* Univ Mich, BSE, 54, MSE, 55; Mass Inst Technol, ScD(aerothermoelasticity), 62. *Prof Exp:* Asst prof aeronaut, Princeton Univ, 60-64. *Concurrent Pos:* Vis prof mech, USAF Inst Technol, 83-85. *Mem:* Am Inst Aeronaut & Astronaut; Am Soc Mech Engrs; Am Acad Mech; Soc Indust & Appl Math; Math Asn Am. *Res:* Solid mechanics; effects of transverse isotropy on beams and plates; non-linear beam and plate theory; theory of joined shells; higher order beam, plate, and shell theories; initially stressed and deformed solids; aeroelastic effects of composite material structures; mechanics of composite plates and shells; fluid flow in affine spaces; computational productivity. *Mailing Add:* 66 Thimbleberry Rd Ballston Spa NY 12020-4302

BRUNELLE, PAUL-EDOUARD, HYDRAULICS. *Current Pos:* Lectr civil eng, 58-62, from asst prof to assoc prof, 62-76, head, Dept Hydraul, 65-70, PROF CIVIL ENG & CHIEF HYDRAUL, SECT FLUID MECH, UNIV SHERBROOKE, 76-, CHMN, DEPT CIVIL ENG, 68- *Personal Data:* b Sherbrooke, Que, May 27, 36; m 55; c 2. *Educ:* Univ Montreal, BASc, 58; Laval Univ, MASc, 63; Univ Toulouse, CES, 65, Dr Ing(hydraul), 68. *Concurrent Pos:* Fels, Nat Res Coun, 64, Asn Stages Tech France, 65 & Defense Res Bd, 67-69; consult, Rajasthan Power Proj, 65-66, Pickering Hydro, Ont, 66-67, Karachi Power Proj, 66-67, Hydro-Que, 67-70 & Sherbrooke Hydro Syst, 68-69; partic, Int Asn Hydraul Res Conf, Ft Collins, 67 & Kyoto, 69. *Mem:* Eng Inst Can; Int Asn Hydraul Res. *Res:* Stability of surge tanks and hydroelectric systems; optimal control and use of hydraulic resources; analog and numerical simulation of power systems. *Mailing Add:* Dept Civil Eng Univ Sherbrooke 2500 Univ Blvd Sherbrooke PQ J1K 2R1 Can

BRUNELLE, RICHARD LEON, FORENSIC SCIENCE, INK DATING CHEMISTRY. *Current Pos:* OWNER, BRUNELLE FORENSIC LAB, 88- *Personal Data:* b Littleton, Mass, May 9, 37; m 58; c 2. *Educ:* Clark Univ, BA, 60; George Washington Univ, MS, 72. *Honors & Awards:* John A Dondero Mem Award, Int Asn Identification, 71. *Prof Exp:* Res chemist, Worcester Found Exp Biol, 60-61; analytical chemist, US Food & Drug Admin, 61-63; forensic & regulatory chemist, Bur Alcohol, Tobacco & Firearms, US Dept Treas, 63-74, chief, Identification Lab, 74-78, Forensic Sci Br, 78-85, dep dir, Lab Serv, 85-87, dir, Forensic Sci Lab, 87-88. *Concurrent Pos:* Mem fac, George Washington Univ, 74-82, Antioch Sch Law, 78-82 & Northeastern Univ; ed, J Forensic Sci. *Mem:* Int Asn Identification (pres, 81); fel Asn Off Analytical Chemists; Fel Am Acad Forensic Sci. *Res:* Forensic science: methods for analysis and dating documents, ink and paper. *Mailing Add:* 81 E River Bend Rd Fredericksburg VA 22407

BRUNELLE, THOMAS E, BIOCHEMISTRY, ORGANIC CHEMISTRY. *Current Pos:* Chemist, 57-60, group leader org chem, 60-64, asst mgr org & biol res, 67-69, MGR CORP RES SECT, RES & DEVELOP DEPT, ECON LAB, INC, 69-, VPRES CORP SCI & TECHNOL, 75- *Personal Data:* b Crookston, Minn, Feb 12, 35; m 58; c 3. *Educ:* Col St Thomas, BS, 57; Univ Minn, MS, 62, PhD(biochem), 68. *Mem:* AAAS; Am Chem Soc; Am Oil Chemists' Soc. *Res:* Acid polysaccharide chemistry; surface active agents. *Mailing Add:* 1252 Ohio St West St Paul MN 55118-2053

BRUNENGRABER, HENRI, METABOLISM. *Current Pos:* PROF & CHMN DEPT NUTRIT, CASE WESTERN RES UNIV, CLEVELAND, OHIO, 90- *Personal Data:* b Apr 2, 1940. *Educ:* Univ Brussels, Belg, MD, 68, PhD(metab), 76. *Prof Exp:* Prof physiol chem, Univ Montreal, 84-90. *Mem:* Am Soc Biochem & Molecular Biol; Biochem Soc; Am Diabetes Asn. *Res:* Design and testing of artificial nutrients; cardiac metabolism; metabolic regulation; ketone body metabolism. *Mailing Add:* Div Nutrit Case Western Univ One Mt Sinai Dr Cleveland OH 44106-4198

BRUNER, BARBARA STEPHENSON, PEDIATRICS. *Current Pos:* RETIRED. *Personal Data:* b Pittsburgh, Pa, Dec 10, 31; m 60; c 2. *Educ:* Chatham Col, BS, 52; Emory Univ, MD, 56. *Prof Exp:* Instr, Sch Med, Emory Univ, 59-61, assoc, 61-69, from asst prof to assoc prof pediat, 69-91. *Concurrent Pos:* Asst dir pediat, Ambulatory Care, Grady Mem Hosp, 68-84, asst dir, Poison Control Ctr, 68-, dir, Pediat Emergency Clin, 85- *Mem:* Am Acad Pediat; AMA; Ambulatory Pediat Asn. *Mailing Add:* 1328 Hanover W Dr NW Atlanta GA 30327

BRUNER, DORSEY WILLIAM, MICROBIOLOGY. *Current Pos:* vet bacteriologist, Dept Path & Bact, 49-65, vet microbiologist & chmn, Dept Vet Microbiol, 65-72, EMER PROF VET MICROBIOL, STATE UNIV NY VET COL, CORNELL UNIV, 72- *Personal Data:* b Windber, Pa, Dec 25, 06; m 40. *Educ:* Albright Col, BS, 29; Cornell Univ, PhD(bact), 33, DVM, 37. *Honors & Awards:* 12th Int Vet Cong Prize, Am Vet Med Asn, 72. *Prof Exp:* Teacher high sch, Pa, 29-30; instr res, Dept Path & Bact, State Univ NY Vet Col, Cornell Univ, 31-37; asst bacteriologist, Dept Animal Path, Exp Sta, Univ Ky, 41-42, virologist, 46-48, bacteriologist, 48-49. *Mem:* Soc Exp Biol & Med; Am Soc Microbiol; Am Vet Med Asn. *Res:* Genus Salmonella; equine virus abortion; neonatal isoerythrolysis; acidfast bacteria. *Mailing Add:* 40 Horizon Dr Ithaca NY 14850

BRUNER, LEON JAMES, BIOPHYSICS. *Current Pos:* from asst prof to assoc prof, 62-73, PROF PHYSICS, UNIV CALIF, RIVERSIDE, 73- *Personal Data:* b Ponca City, Okla, Dec 28, 31; m 60; c 3. *Educ:* Univ Chicago, AB, 52, MS, 55, PhD(physics), 59. *Prof Exp:* Staff mem physics, Watson Sci Comput Lab, Int Bus Mach Corp, 59-62. *Mem:* AAAS; Biophys Soc; Am Phys Soc. *Res:* Bioelectric phenomena; structure and transport properties of membranes. *Mailing Add:* Dept Physics Univ Calif Riverside CA 92521. *Fax:* 909-787-4529; *E-Mail:* bruner@ucrac1.ucr.edu

BRUNER, LEONARD BRETZ, JR, CHEMISTRY. *Current Pos:* RETIRED. *Personal Data:* b Wichita Falls, Tex, Oct 12, 21; m 47; c 1. *Educ:* Univ Tulsa, ChB, 43; Univ Mich, MS, 49, PhD(chem), 57. *Prof Exp:* Jr chemist, Phillips Petrol Co, 43-44; instr chem, Univ Tulsa, 46-47; res chemist, Dow Corning Corp, 55-59; sr scientist, Trionics Corp, 59-61; assoc prof, Eureka Col, 61-65; tech dir, Stauffer-Wacker Silicone Corp, 66-75, vpres & gen mgr, SWS Silicone Corp, 75-84. *Concurrent Pos:* Consult, Stauffer Chem Co, 63-65. *Mem:* Am Chem Soc. *Res:* Grignard reactions; organic azides; siloxane chemistry; polymerization; properties of siloxane polymers; electrical properties of ceramics. *Mailing Add:* 11233 Bemis Rd Manchester MI 48158

BRUNER, MARILYN E, SPACE PHYSICS. *Current Pos:* MEM STAFF, RES LAB, LOCKHEED MISSILE & SPACE CO, 76- *Personal Data:* b Oklahoma City, Okla, July 27, 34; div; c 3. *Educ:* Univ Ariz, BS, 57, MS, 59; Univ Colo, PhD(physics), 64. *Prof Exp:* Phys sci aide, Naval Ord Test Sta, China Lake, Calif, 55; teaching asst, Univ Ariz, 57-58; physicist, US Naval Ord Test Sta, China Lake, 58-60; teaching asst, Lab Atmospheric & Space Physics, Univ Colo, 60-62, res asst, 62-64, res assoc, 64-76. *Concurrent Pos:* Consult, Los Alamos Sci Lab, 75-76; prin investr, numerous NASA prog, 70- *Mem:* Am Astron Soc; Soc Photo-Optical Instrumentation Eng; Am Geophys Union. *Res:* High resolution ultraviolet and x-ray spectroscopy of the sun; structure and dynamics of the solar chromosphere and transition zone; design of space instrumentation; absolute ultraviolet spectroradiometry. *Mailing Add:* Lockheed Martin Missiles & Space, Adv Technol Ctr Orgn H1-12 Bldg 252 3251 Hanover St Palo Alto CA 94304. *Fax:* 650-424-3994; *E-Mail:* bruner@sag.space.lockheed.com

BRUNETT, EMERY W, MEDICINAL CHEMISTRY, PHARMACY. *Current Pos:* asst prof, 69-75, assoc prof pharm, 75-93, EMER ASSOC PROF, UNIV WYO, 93- *Personal Data:* b Ovando, Mont, Dec 3, 27; m 60, Iris Stephens; c Emery Jr, Katherine, Stephenie & Barbara. *Educ:* Univ Mont, BS, 53, MS, 56; Univ Wash, PhD(pharmaceut chem), 66. *Prof Exp:* Instr pharm, Univ Mont, 57-58, vis asst prof, 64-65; instr pharm, Univ Wash, 61-62; asst prof pharmaceut chem, Drake Univ, 66-69. *Mem:* AAAS; Am Asn Cols Pharm; fel Pharaceut Mfrs Asn. *Res:* Aminothiophene chemistry; vitamin A analogs; hay fever pollens; home remedies; microelements; tableting. *Mailing Add:* 315 S 11th St Laramie WY 82070

BRUNETTE, DONALD MAXWELL, CELL BIOLOGY. *Current Pos:* assoc prof, 79-85, PROF & HEAD DEPT ORAL BIOL, FAC DENT, UNIV BC, 85- *Personal Data:* b Hamilton, Ont, Aug 4, 44; m 71; c 1. *Educ:* Univ Toronto, BSc, 66, MSc, 68, PhD(med biophys), 72. *Prof Exp:* Fel cell biol, York Univ, 72-74; asst prof, Fac Dent, 74-78, assoc prof cell biol, Med Res Coun Group, Univ Toronto, 78-79. *Mem:* Int Asn Dent Res; Bromeliad Soc; Can Soc Cell Biol; Sigma Xi. *Res:* In vitro studies of cell function in epithelial and fibroblast-like cells derived from periodontal ligament; effects of surface topography on cell behavior in vitro & in vivo. *Mailing Add:* 4134 W Tenth Ave Vancouver BC V6R 2H3 Can

BRUNGRABER, ROBERT J, CIVIL ENGINEERING, STRUCTURAL ENGINEERING. *Current Pos:* PRESIDENTIAL PROF CIVIL ENG, BUCKNELL UNIV, 76-; PRES, SLIP-TEST, 76- *Personal Data:* b Birmingham, Mich, Dec 20, 29; m 51; c 2. *Educ:* Univ Mich, BSE, 51; Cornell Univ, MS, 56; Carnegie Inst Technol, PhD(civil eng), 63. *Prof Exp:* Field engr, Porter-Urquhart, Skidmore, Owings & Merrill, 51-53; instr civil eng, Cornell Univ, 53-56; res engr, Alcoa Res Labs, 56-60; res asst civil eng, Carnegie Inst Technol, 60-62; asst prof, Princeton Univ, 62-66; assoc prof, Union Col, NY, 66-68; prof & chmn dept, Bucknell Univ, 68-74; intergovt personnel act appointee, Nat Bur Stand, 74-76. *Concurrent Pos:* Dir & treas, Nat Inst Bldg Sci, 76-80. *Mem:* Am Soc Civil Engrs; Am Soc Test & Mat. *Res:* Welded aluminum structures; flow of low density detergent foam; shear strength of reinforced concrete structures; behavior of pile foundations; slip-resistance of walkway surfaces; reinforcement of steel and iron through truss bridges. *Mailing Add:* PO Box 387 Spring Lake NJ 07762

BRUNGS, ROBERT ANTHONY, SOLID STATE PHYSICS. *Current Pos:* Fel & res assoc physics, 66-70, asst prof physics, 70-75, asst prof dogmatic & syst theol, 72-75, assoc prof physics, 75-85, counr, Med Ctr, 70-73, ASSOC PROF THEOL STUDIES, ST LOUIS UNIV, 75-, ADJ PROF PHYSICS, 85- *Personal Data:* b Cincinnati, Ohio, July 7, 31. *Educ:* Bellarmine Col, NY, AB, 55; Loyola Sem, PhL, 56; St Louis Univ, PhD(physics), 62; Woodstock Col, Md, STL, 65. *Concurrent Pos:* Consult, US Cath Bishops Comt on Sci, Technol & Human Values, 85- *Mem:* Am Phys Soc; AAAS. *Res:* Experimental investigation of semiconductor properties of crystalline beta-rhombohedral boron. *Mailing Add:* St Louis Univ Dept Physics 221 N Grand Blvd St Louis MO 63103. *Fax:* 314-977-7264; *E-Mail:* brungsr@wpogate.slu.edu

BRUNGS, WILLIAM ALOYSIUS, POLLUTION BIOLOGY. *Current Pos:* CONSULT, 87- *Personal Data:* b Covington, Ky, Aug 10, 32; m 62; c 2. *Educ:* Ohio State Univ, BSc, 58, MSc, 59, PhD(aquatic toxicol), 63. *Prof Exp:* Aquatic biologist, USPHS, 61-64; mem staff, Cincinnati Water Res lab, Fed Water Pollution Control Admin, Narragansett, US Environ Protection Agency, 64-68, chief, Newtown Fish Toxicol Lab, 68-71, asst dir water qual criteria, Environ Res Lab, Duluth, 71-80, dep dir, 80-83, dir Environ Res Lab, 83-86. *Concurrent Pos:* NSF fels, 59 & 61. *Mem:* Soc Environ Toxicol & Chem. *Res:* Distribution of radionuclides in fresh-water environments; determination of acute and chronic effects of water pollution on fish and the relationship of environmental variables on these effects. *Mailing Add:* 391 Yawgoo Valley Rd Exeter RI 02822

BRUNING, DONALD FRANCIS, ORNITHOLOGY. *Current Pos:* Curatorial trainee ornith, 67-69, from asst cur to assoc cur, 69-74, CUR ORNITH, NEW YORK ZOOL SOC, 75-, CHMN, 87- *Personal Data:* b Boulder, Colo, Dec 18, 42; m 69; c 3. *Educ:* Univ Colo, BA, 66, MA, 67, PhD(zool), 74. *Concurrent Pos:* Res assoc, Ctr Field Biol & Conserv, New York Zool Soc, 73-; consult, Time/Life Bks, 73-; adj assoc prof, Fordham Univ, 74-; bd dirs, Am Asn Zool Parks & Aquaria, 82-85; tour leader, NY Zool Soc; chmn, Parrot Specialist Group, Int Comt Bird Preserv & Int Union Conserv Nature. *Mem:* AAAS; Am Ornithologists Union; Wilson Ornith Soc; Am Asn Zool Parks & Aquaria; Nat Audubon Soc; Nat Geog Soc. *Res:* Conducting captive and field research on birds of paradise and parrots while encouraging their conservation and establishing parks and reserves in Papua New Guinea and Indonesia. *Mailing Add:* 34 Revere Rd Ardsley NY 10502. *Fax:* 718-733-7300; *E-Mail:* dbruning.wcs@mcimail.com

BRUNJES, A(USTIN) S, chemical engineering; deceased, see previous edition for last biography

BRUNJES, PETER CRAWFORD, NEUROBIOLOGY. *Current Pos:* PROF PSYCHOL, UNIV VA, 81- *Personal Data:* b Columbus, Ohio, June 19, 53; m 76; c Benjamin, Lee & Samuel. *Educ:* Mich State Univ, BS, 74; Ind Univ, PhD(psychol), 79. *Prof Exp:* Fel, Univ Ill, Champaign, 79-80. *Concurrent Pos:* Prin investr grants, NIH, 81- *Mem:* AAAS; Soc Neurosci; Int Soc Develop Psychobiol. *Res:* Investigations of the development of the brain and behavior; sensory development; neuroanatomical maturation; the role of experience during early life. *Mailing Add:* Dept Psychol 102 Gilmer Hall Univ Va Charlottesville VA 22903. *E-Mail:* brunjles@virginia.edu

BRUNK, CLIFFORD FRANKLIN, MOLECULAR EVOLUTION. *Current Pos:* from asst prof to assoc prof, 67-92, PROF & CHMN BIOL, UNIV CALIF, LOS ANGELES, 92- *Personal Data:* b Detroit, Mich, Feb 11, 40; m 62, Judith Lembke; c Clifford A, Natasha & Lytha. *Educ:* Mich State Univ, BS, 61; Stanford Univ, MS, 62, PhD(biophys), 67. *Concurrent Pos:* USPHS fel, Carlsberg Biol Inst, Copenhagen, Denmark, 67-68; vis prof, Weismann Inst, 74-75, York Univ, Toronto, Can, 80-81, Univ Copenhagen, 86-87. *Mem:* Soc Study Evolution; Am Soc Cell Biol; Sigma Xi; Molecular Biol Evolution Soc. *Res:* Genome reorganization in tetrahymena; DNA sequence elimination in somatic cell lines; molecular phylogenics of protists. *Mailing Add:* Dept Biol Univ Calif Los Angeles CA 90024-1606. *Fax:* 310-206-0484; *E-Mail:* brunk@uclabio.bitnet

BRUNK, HUGH DANIEL, STATISTICS, MATHEMATICS. *Current Pos:* RETIRED. *Personal Data:* b Manteca, Calif, Aug 22, 19; m 42; c 3. *Educ:* Univ Calif, AB, 40; Rice Inst, MA, 42, PhD(math), 44. *Prof Exp:* Asst math, Rice Inst, 40-44, from instr to asst prof, 46-51; mathematician, Sandia Corp, 51-52; from assoc prof to prof math, Univ Mo, 52-61; prof, Univ Calif, Riverside, 61-63; prof statist, Univ Mo, 63-69, Ore State Univ, 69-88. *Concurrent Pos:* Fulbright lectr, Univ Copenhagen, 58-59; vis sr lectr, Univ Col Wales, 66-67; hon res assoc statist, Univ Col London, 71. *Mem:* Fel Am Statist Asn; Am Math Soc; Math Asn Am; fel Inst Math Statist; Int Statist Inst. *Res:* Analysis; mathematical statistics; probability. *Mailing Add:* 28087 Ewelty Way Corvallis OR 97330

BRUNK, WILLIAM EDWARD, ASTRONOMY. *Current Pos:* RETIRED. *Personal Data:* b Cleveland, Ohio, Nov 24, 28; div, Anna Kathryn; c 1. *Educ:* Case Inst Technol, BS, 52, MS, 54, PhD(astron), 63. *Honors & Awards:* Harold Mazursky Moritorios Serv Award, Am Astron Soc, 95- *Prof Exp:* Res scientist, Lewis Flight Propulsion Lab, Nat Adv Comt, Aeronaut, 54-58; aerospace res engr, Lewis Res Ctr, NASA, 58-64, staff scientist, 64-65, actg chief, 65, prog chief, Planetary Astron, 65-82, chief, Planetary Sci Br, NASA HQS, 82-85; prog chief cometary sci, Univ Space Res Asn, 85-94. *Mem:* Am Astron Soc; Int Astron Union; fel AAAS. *Res:* Stellar and planetary astronomy; aerodynamics; heat transfer; trajectory analysis. *Mailing Add:* PO Box 3466 Annapolis MD 21403

BRUNKARD, KATHLEEN MARIE, MEMBRANE BIOLOGY, ELECTROPHYSIOLOGY. *Current Pos:* ASSOC PROF BIOL, EAST STROUDSBURG UNIV, 84- *Personal Data:* b New Haven, Conn, June 21, 53; m 83, James; c Jacob & Molly. *Educ:* Southern Conn State Col, BS, 77; Syracuse Univ, MS, 79; Univ Mass, PhD(plant & soil sci), 82. *Prof Exp:* Postdoctoral res assoc, Wash Univ, 82-84. *Mem:* Am Soc Plant Physiologists; Bot Soc Am; Am Inst Biol Sci; Sigma Xi. *Res:* Effects of environmental factors on membranes and membrane transport systems; effects of environmental stress on plant growth and development. *Mailing Add:* Biol Sci Dept E Stroudsburg Univ East Stroudsburg PA 18301. *E-Mail:* brunkard@esu.edu

BRUNKE, KAREN J, gene regulation, promoter research, for more information see previous edition

BRUNNER, CARL ALAN, CHEMICAL ENGINEERING, HAZARDOUS WASTE TREATMENT. *Current Pos:* RETIRED. *Personal Data:* b Cincinnati, Ohio, Feb 21, 34; m 59, Janet Kraemer; c Robert & Thomas. *Educ:* Univ Cincinnati, ChemE, 57, MS, 59, PhD(chem eng), 63. *Prof Exp:* Instr chem eng, Univ Cincinnati, 58-59; chem eng, USPHS, 63-67; chem engr, US Environ Protection Agency, 67-95. *Mem:* Am Inst Chem Engrs; Water Environ Fedn. *Res:* Wastewater treatment; wastewater reuse; storm and combined sewer discharges; hazardous wastes; pollution prevention. *Mailing Add:* 6674 Hitching Post Lane Cincinnati OH 45230

BRUNNER, CHARLOTTE, MARINE MICROPALEONTOLOGY. *Current Pos:* ASSOC PROF MARINE SCI, UNIV SOUTHERN MISS, 88- *Personal Data:* b Helena, Mont, Oct 9, 48. *Educ:* Univ RI, BA, 70; Grad Sch Oceanog, PhD(oceanog), 78. *Prof Exp:* Res asst, Grad Sch Oceanog, Univ RI, 70-73; asst prof micropaleont, Univ Calif, Berkeley, 79-87; lectr, Calif State Univ, Hayward, 87-88. *Mem:* Geol Soc Am; Soc Econ Paleontologists & Mineralogists; AAAS. *Res:* Paleoceanography, taphonomy and marine stratigraphy of the neogene, based on quantitative analyses of microfossils, principally foraminifer. *Mailing Add:* Inst Marine Sci Bldg 1103 Rm 105 Univ Southern Miss Stennis Space Center MS 39529

BRUNNER, EDWARD A, PHARMACOLOGY, ANESTHESIOLOGY. *Current Pos:* from asst prof to assoc prof anesthesia, 66-71, PROF ANESTHESIA & CHMN DEPT, MED SCH, NORTHWESTERN UNIV, 71- *Personal Data:* b Erie, Pa, July 18, 29; m 55; c 4. *Educ:* Villanova Univ, BS, 52; Hahnemann Med Col & Hosp, MD, 59, PhD(pharmacol), 62. *Prof Exp:* Instr pharmacol, Hahnemann Med Col & Hosp, 60-62, instr anesthesia, Sch Med, Univ Pa, 62-65, instr pharmacol, 64-65. *Mem:* Sigma Xi. *Res:* Carbohydrate metabolism in liver, brain and muscle; effects of anesthetic agents on metabolism; muscle relaxants; medical education. *Mailing Add:* Dept Anesthesia Northwestern Univ Med Sch 303 E Chicago Ave Chicago IL 60611-3008

BRUNNER, GORDON FRANCIS, RESEARCH ADMINISTRATION. *Current Pos:* engr, Procter & Gamble Co, 61-71, assoc dir, 71-77, mgr prod coordr, Europe, 77-83, mgr res & develop, 83-85, vpres, 85-87, SR VPRES, PROCTER & GAMBLE CO, 87-, BD DIRS, 91- *Personal Data:* b Des Plaines, Ill, Nov 6, 38; m 63, Nadine M Slosar; c Christine (Conselyea), Pamela A & Meggan T. *Educ:* Univ Wis, BS, 61; Xavier Univ, MBA, 65. *Prof*

Exp: Eng asst, Universal Oil Prods Co, 59-61. *Concurrent Pos:* Trustee, Christ Hosp, Cincinnati Mus Natural Hist & Xavier Univ; mem, Govt-Univ-Indust Res Roundtable. *Mem:* Am Chem Soc; Am Oil Chemists Soc. *Res:* Management of research and development of consumer goods and health care technologies; patentee in field. *Mailing Add:* Procter & Gamble Co One Procter & Gamble Plaza Cincinnati OH 45202-3315

BRUNNER, JAY ROBERT, FOOD SCIENCE, DAIRY CHEMISTRY. *Current Pos:* from instr to assoc prof, 46-59, prof, 59-87, EMER PROF FOOD SCI & HUMAN NUTRIT, MICH STATE UNIV, 87- *Personal Data:* b Royersford, Pa, Sept 17, 18; m 47, Jeane Adams; c Thomas, Barbara (Sharpe) & Kathryn (Juhas). *Educ:* Pa State Univ, BS, 40; Univ Calif, MS, 42; Mich State Univ, PhD(dairy & phys chem), 52. *Honors & Awards:* Borden Award, Am Chem Soc, 64. *Prof Exp:* Asst, Univ Calif, 40-42; US Navy Serv, 42-46. *Concurrent Pos:* Mem EBC study sect, USPHS; Sigma Xi sr res award, Mich State Univ, 79; vis prof, Dept Food Sci, Univ Fla, 79-80. *Mem:* Am Dairy Sci Asn; Inst Food Technol; Am Chem Soc; AAAS; Sigma Xi. *Res:* Physical and chemical properties of milkfat and milk proteins; dairy products processing; chemistry of milk. *Mailing Add:* Dept Food Sci & Human Nutrit 3940 Zimmer Rd Rte 2 Williamston MI 48895

BRUNNER, MATHIAS J, MECHANICAL, AEROSPACE & GAS TURBINE ENGINEERING. *Current Pos:* PRES & CONSULT ENGR, BRUNNER ASSOCS, INC, 82- *Personal Data:* b Brooklyn, NY, May 28, 22; m 51, Lillian A Sholtis; c Douglas M, Carol B (Burns) & Janet C (Cramer). *Educ:* Pratt Inst, BME, 43; Univ Pa, MSME, 47. *Prof Exp:* Jr design engr, Steam Div, Westinghouse Elec Corp, Pa, 43-50, design engr, 50-54, sr design engr, 54-56, fel engr, 56-57; specialist advan studies, Gen Elec Co, 57-68, consult engr, 68-79, sr aerothermodynamics engr, Re-entry Systs Div, 79-82. *Concurrent Pos:* Lectr, exten, Pa State Univ, 48-50; mem, Nat Tech Comt Thermophysics, Am Inst Aeronaut & Astronaut. *Mem:* Am Soc Mech Engrs; assoc fel Am Inst Aeronaut & Astronaut; NY Acad Sci; Nat Soc Prof Engrs. *Res:* Fluid mechanics; internal aerodynamics; aerothermodynamics; heat transfer; aerothermophysics; space and re-entry vehicle research and development; axial flow compressor research and development design for wind tunnel and gas turbine applications. *Mailing Add:* 645 Willow Valley Sq J411 Lancaster PA 17602-4871

BRUNNER, MICHAEL, molecular biology, for more information see previous edition

BRUNNER, ROBERT LEE, NEUROPSYCHOLOGY, PHYSIOLOGICAL PSYCHOLOGY. *Current Pos:* asst prof, 75-80, ASSOC PROF, COL MED, UNIV CINCINNATI & CHILDREN'S MED CTR, 80- *Personal Data:* b Chicago, Ill, Sept 11, 45. *Educ:* Univ Calif, Los Angeles, BA, 67; Univ Cincinnati, MA, 69, PhD(psychol), 71. *Prof Exp:* Fel & res assoc, Dept Biol Sci, Purdue Univ, 71-74; res scholar, Inst Develop Res, 74-75. *Concurrent Pos:* Prof consult, Cincinnati Ctr Develop Dis, 75- *Mem:* Am Psychol Asn; Int Neuropsychol Soc; Nat Acad Neuropsychologists. *Res:* Neuropsychological aspects of central nervous system related disorders in children, with emphasis on recovery over time; metabolic diseases; anorexia nervosa. *Mailing Add:* 4392 Airymont Ct Cincinnati OH 45211

BRUNNING, RICHARD DALE, HEMATOLOGY, PATHOLOGY. *Current Pos:* from instr to assoc prof lab med & assoc dir hemat labs, 65-74, PROF LAB MED & DIR HEMAT LABS, UNIV MINN, MINNEAPOLIS, 74- *Personal Data:* b Grand Forks, NDak, Mar 5, 32. *Educ:* Univ NDak, BSc, 57; McGill Univ, MD, 59. *Prof Exp:* Intern, Ancker Hosp, St Paul, Minn, 59-60; fel path, Univ Minn, Minneapolis, 60-62, fel lab med, 63-64. *Concurrent Pos:* Am Cancer Soc fel, 63-64. *Mem:* Am Soc Hemat; Am Asn Cancer Res; Am Soc Clin Oncol; Soc Hematopath; Europ Soc Hematopath. *Res:* Morphologic, ultrastructural and cytochemical characteristics of peripheral blood and bone marrow cells in inherited disorders; cytochemical and morphologic features of blast cells in leukemic disorders; enyelodysplastic syndromes. *Mailing Add:* Dept Lab Med Univ Minn Health Sci Ctr Minneapolis MN 55455

BRUNO, CHARLES FRANK, BIOCHEMISTRY, BACTERIOLOGY. *Current Pos:* DIR, BURROUGHS WELLCOME MFG, 91- *Personal Data:* b Westerly, RI, June 23, 36; m 58, Margaret; c James, Jennifer, JoAnne, Charles, Joyce & Judith. *Educ:* Roanoke Col, BS, 58; Va Polytech Inst, MS, 61, PhD(biochem), 63. *Prof Exp:* Sr res scientist microbiol & biochem, Squibb Inst Med Res, 63-71, process develop mgr fermentation, 71-75, dept head, 75-80, dir fermentation, 80-82; vpres opers, Cell Prod Inc, 82-87; dir mfg, Wel Gen, 87-91. *Concurrent Pos:* Sr Vpres Environ Technol. *Mem:* Am Chem Soc; Am Soc Microbiol; AAAS. *Res:* Fermentation, especially antibiotics from fungi and actinomyces; production and isolation of bacterial and fungal enzymes; production and purification of polysaccharide vaccine; currently involved in developing and designing Bioremediation systems; previously involved in biotechnology industry in the design and operation of facility to manufacture genetically engineered products. *Mailing Add:* 11 Westwood Rd East Brunswick NJ 08816-1311. *Fax:* 732-821-1551

BRUNO, DAVID JOSEPH, PROCESS DEVELOPMENT, NEW TECHNOLOGIES FOR FOODS. *Current Pos:* Sect head shortening & oils, Foods Div, 79-81, soy protein analog technol, 81-84, salted snacks, 84-85, new products Crisco, Crisco Oil & Puritan, Edible Oils Div, 85-87, ASSOC DIR, OLESTRA DIV, PROCTER & GAMBLE, 87- *Personal Data:* b Martins Ferry, Ohio, Sept 6, 51; m 88; c 2. *Educ:* Case Inst Technol, BS, 73; Univ Cincinnati, MS, 79. *Mem:* Am Inst Chem Engrs; Am Oil Chemist Soc; Inst Food Technologists. *Res:* Development of new technologies to satisfy consumer needs; soy analogs; shortening and oil products; savory snacks; fat substitutes such as olestra. *Mailing Add:* 6959 Rock Springs Dr Hamilton OH 45011

BRUNO, MARIA SOLEDAD, FORMULATIONS SCALE-UP, GENE THERAPY. *Current Pos:* Sr Scientist gene delivery, 95-96, SR SCIENTIST FURMULATIONS SCALE-UP, GENE MED INC, 95- *Personal Data:* b San Juan, PR, Sept 16, 66; m 90, Marshall L Orris; c Joshua M Orris, Nicole L Orris & Natalia L Orris. *Educ:* Univ PR, BS, 88; Univ Wis-Madison, MS, 92, PhD(pharmaceut), 95. *Mem:* Am Asn Pharmaceut Sci. *Res:* Drug delivery; use of lipid-based systems for drug delivery and gene therapy; formulation scale-up of gene medicine for phase I clinical trials. *Mailing Add:* 831 New Trails Dr The Woodlands TX 77381. *Fax:* 281-364-0858

BRUNO, MERLE SANFORD, SENSORY PHYSIOLOGY, SCIENCE EDUCATION. *Current Pos:* asst prof, 71-77, dean natural sci, 85-89, ASSOC PROF BIOL, HAMPSHIRE COL, 77- *Personal Data:* b Schenectady, NY, Jan 30, 39; m 82. *Educ:* Syracuse Univ, BS, 60; Harvard Univ, MA, 63, PhD(biol), 71. *Prof Exp:* Staff developer, Educ Develop Ctr, 66-69; res assoc biol, Yale Univ, 71. *Concurrent Pos:* Consult, Workshop for Learning Things, 69-71; mem bd dirs, Yurt Found, 73-; NSF sch systs grant, 74-75; mem bd trustees, Hampshire Col, 80-82; mem adv bd, Mass Turning Points Proj, Proj Spark; proj dir, Partners Elem Sci, 87-90, Five Col Pub Sch Partnership Steering Comt, 87- *Mem:* Sigma Xi. *Res:* Comparative biochemistry of invertebrate visual systems; implementation of innovative science programs in elementary schools and middle schools; adult science education; recruiting women and minorities into science. *Mailing Add:* Sch Natural Sci Hampshire Col 893 West St Amherst MA 01002-3372

BRUNO, MICHAEL STEPHEN, COASTAL ENGINEERING, COASTAL WATER QUALITY. *Current Pos:* ASSOC PROF CIVIL & OCEANOG ENG & DIR, DAVIDSON LAB, STEVENS INST TECHNOL, 89- *Personal Data:* b Newark, NJ, Apr 16, 58; m 88. *Educ:* NJ Inst Technol, BS, 80; Univ Calif, Berkeley, MS, 81; Mass Inst Technol, PhD(civil & oceanog eng), 86. *Prof Exp:* Prin engr coastal eng, NJ Dept Environ Protection, 81-82; asst prof civil eng, NJ Inst Technol, 86-89. *Concurrent Pos:* Mem sci & tech adv comt, Del Estuary Prog, Environ Protection Agency, 88-89; young investr, Off Naval Res, 91; mem US deleg, NSF Workshop US-Arg Res Marine Sci, 91- *Mem:* Am Geophys Union; Am Soc Civil Eng; Am Soc Mech Eng; Oceanog Soc; Soc Naval Architects & Marine Eng. *Res:* Hydrodynamics, with emphasis on problems in coastal engineering, including the computer modeling of coastal circulation and pollution transport, wave transformation, sediment transport and beach erosion. *Mailing Add:* Davidson Lab Stevens Inst Tech Castle Point NJ 07030. *Fax:* 201-420-5714

BRUNO, RONALD C, PHYSICS, ENERGY TECHNOLOGY. *Current Pos:* PROJ MGR, STANFORD TELECOM, 83- *Personal Data:* b New York, NY, Nov 25, 46; m 77; c 2. *Educ:* City Col New York, BS, 67; Mass Inst Technol, PhD(physics), 72. *Prof Exp:* Asst prof physics, Southern Ill Univ, 72-77, assoc prof, 77-80; consult, 80-83. *Concurrent Pos:* Am Phys Soc Cong Sci fel, US Cong, 76-77. *Mem:* Am Phys Soc; AAAS; Inst Elec & Electronics Engrs. *Res:* Behavior of superconductors in high magnetic fields; applications of superconductivity; energy technology and policy; electrical and communications engineering. *Mailing Add:* 3203 N Fourth St N Arlington VA 22201. *Fax:* 703-523-1411

BRUNO, STEPHEN FRANCIS, MARINE ECOLOGY, PLANT PHYSIOLOGY. *Current Pos:* CONSULT, 80- *Personal Data:* b New York, NY, Jan 1, 48; m 71; c 2. *Educ:* St John's Univ, BS, 69; Fordham Univ, MS, 71, PhD(biol), 75. *Prof Exp:* Instr biol, Col Mt St Vincent, 73-75; asst res scientist marine sci, NY Ocean Sci Lab, Affil Col & Univ Inc, 75-80. *Mem:* Am Soc Limnol & Oceanog; Phycol Soc Am; Sigma Xi. *Res:* Environmental regulation of phytoplankton productivity in estuaries and coastal waters; role of vitamins in marine phytoplankton ecology; nutritional physiology of marine phytoplankton in culture and in situ. *Mailing Add:* 36 Holland Lane Colts Neck NJ 07722-1632

BRUNO, THOMAS J, INSTRUMENT DESIGN, EQUATIONS OF STATE. *Current Pos:* Res assoc, 81-83, SCIENTIST, NAT INST STAND & TECHNOL, 83-; ADJ PROF INSTRUMENTATION, COLO SCH MINES, 85- *Personal Data:* b New York, NY, Oct 12, 54; m 87, Clare Cronin; c Kelly A. *Educ:* Polytech Inst Brooklyn, BS, 76; Georgetown Univ, MS, 78, PhD (phys chem), 81. *Honors & Awards:* Eugene Hult Award, Eugene Holt Found Award, 76; Bronze Medal, Dept Com, 86. *Concurrent Pos:* Pres, Bd Dir, Mamie Doud Eisenhower Libr, 87-; vis prof, Inst Super Tech, Lisbon, Port. *Mem:* Am Chem Soc; Am Inst Chem Engrs; Am Soc Testing & Mat. *Res:* Experimental thermophysics of fluids, including phase equilibria and transport properties; methods in analytical chemistry, component design. *Mailing Add:* Thermophys Div Nat Inst Stand & Technol Boulder CO 80303-3328. *Fax:* 303-497-5927; *E-Mail:* thomas.bruno@boulder.nist.gov

BRUNS, CHARLES ALAN, PHYSICS. *Current Pos:* asst prof, 64-69, ASSOC PROF PHYSICS, FRANKLIN & MARSHALL COL, 69- *Personal Data:* b Baltimore, Md, Nov 1, 30; m 53; c 3. *Educ:* Tufts Univ, BS, 52; Johns Hopkins Univ, PhD(physics), 61. *Prof Exp:* From instr to asst prof physics, Univ Mich, 61-64. *Mem:* Am Phys Soc; Optical Soc Am; Sigma Xi. *Res:* Holography; lasers. *Mailing Add:* 1123 Spring Grove Ave Lancaster PA 17603-4908

BRUNS, DAVID EUGENE, CLINICAL CHEMISTRY. *Current Pos:* From asst prof to assoc prof, 77-90, PROF PATH, UNIV VA, 90- *Personal Data:* b St Louis, Mo; c 2. *Educ:* Wash Univ, St Louis, BS, 63 & AB, 65; St Louis Univ, MD, 73. *Honors & Awards:* Roche Res Award, Am Asn Clin Chem, 87; Sunderman Award, Asn Clin Sci, 87. *Concurrent Pos:* assoc dir clin chem, Univ Va Hosp, 77-; Prin investr, NIH, 78-81, Am Cancer Soc, 82-85 & Nat Dairy Coun, 88-90; co-prin investr, NIH,78; vis prof, Wash Univ, 85-86;

chmn, Lab Utilization Comt, Asn Am Clin Chem, 86-88; ed, Clin Chem, 90. *Mem:* Am Asn Clin Chem; Asn Clin Scientists (pres, 80); Acad Clin Lab Physicians & Scientists; Endocrine Soc; Am Soc Bone Mineral Res. *Res:* Calciotropic hormones in mammalian reproduction; new methods in clinical chemistry. *Mailing Add:* Dept Path Univ Va Med Ctr Charlottesville VA 22908. *Fax:* 804-924-2574; *E-Mail:* dbruns@virginia.edu

BRUNS, DONALD GENE, lasers, adaptive optics, for more information see previous edition

BRUNS, HERBERT ARNOLD, crop physiology, crop ecology, for more information see previous edition

BRUNS, LESTER GEORGE, PHARMACY, BIOCHEMISTRY. *Current Pos:* grad fel, 62-65, from asst prof to assoc prof, 65-78, PROF BIOCHEM, ST LOUIS COL PHARM, 78- *Personal Data:* b Robertsville, Mo, Feb 11, 33; m 54, Juanita Carter; c Mark S & Michael G. *Educ:* St Louis Col Pharm, BS, 55, MS, 57; St Louis Univ, PhD, 72. *Prof Exp:* From instr to asst prof pharmaceut chem, St Louis Col Pharm, 57-62. *Concurrent Pos:* Biopharmaceut chemist, Norcliff Thayer Co, St Louis, Mo, 77-89. *Mem:* Am Asn Cols Pharm; Nutrit Today Soc; Am Chem Soc. *Res:* Bile acid metabolism and nutritional biochemistry. *Mailing Add:* St Louis Col Pharm Dept Chem 4588 Parkview Pl St Louis MO 63110. *Fax:* 314-367-8132; *E-Mail:* lbruns@slcop.stleop.edu

BRUNS, PAUL DONALD, obstetrics & gynecology; deceased, see previous edition for last biography

BRUNS, PAUL ERIC, FORESTRY. *Current Pos:* chmn dept, 59-68, prof, 59-80, EMER PROF FOREST RESOURCES, UNIV NH, 80- *Personal Data:* b New York, NY, July 30, 15; m 44, Patricia Byrne; c Pamela (Brayton), Eric W, Robert T & Susan J. *Educ:* NY Univ, AB, 37; Yale Univ, MF, 40; Univ Wash, PhD(forestry), 56. *Prof Exp:* Timber cruiser, Hamilton Veneer Co, SC, 41-42; instr aircraft engines & aerodyn, Southeastern Air Serv, 42-44, asst dir acads, 43 & dir, 44; assoc forester, Northeastern Forest Exp Sta, US Forest Serv, 44-45; woodlands mgr, N Troy Div, Blair Veneer Co, Vt, 45-47; assoc prof forestry, Univ Mont, 46-55; consult, 55-58. *Concurrent Pos:* Vis prof forest mgt, Univ Minn, 57-58; mem adv comt, Northeastern Forest Exp Sta, US Forest, 59-68, chmn 65-66; mem, Nat Coun Forestry Sch Exec, 58-68, chmn 64-65; consult, Glastenbury Timberlands, Bennington, Vt, 69-83; vis scientist remote sensing, Univ Ariz, 72. *Mem:* Golden mem Soc Am Foresters; emer mem Am Soc Photogram; emer mem Sigma Xi. *Res:* Forest management; remote sensing. *Mailing Add:* 4930 Squires Dr Titusville FL 32796-1067

BRUNS, PETER JOHN, GENETICS, DEVELOPMENTAL BIOLOGY. *Current Pos:* From asst prof to assoc prof genetics, chmn sect genetics & develop, 80-85, PROF GENETICS, CORNELL UNIV, 82- *Personal Data:* b Syracuse, NY, May 2, 42; m 85, Jennifer H Shea; c Elizabeth B & Nicholas E. *Educ:* Syracuse Univ, AB, 63; Univ Ill, PhD(cell biol), 69. *Concurrent Pos:* Fel John Guggenhiem Mem Found, 77-78; vis scientist, Biol Inst Carlsberg Found, Copenhagen, 77-78; mem, Biomed Sci Study Sect, NIH, 83-87; assoc dir, Cornell Biotech Prog, 84- & dir, Div Biol Sci, Cornell Univ, 87-; consult examr, Genetics & Biotech, Charter Oak Col, 86-88. *Mem:* AAAS; Genetics Soc Am; Soc Protozoologists. *Res:* Developmental genetics of tetrahymena thermophila; germinal and somatic genetic organization; genetic and molecular studies of conjugation. *Mailing Add:* Div Biol Sci Cornell Univ 169 Biotechnol Bldg Ithaca NY 14853. *Fax:* 607-255-2428; *E-Mail:* pjb4@cornell.edu

BRUNS, ROBERT FREDERICK, NEUROPHARMACOLOGY, COMPUTATIONAL CHEMISTRY. *Current Pos:* res scientist, 88-95, SR RES SCIENTIST, LILLY RES LABS, LILLY RES CTR, 96- *Personal Data:* b 1950; m; c 4. *Educ:* Univ Calif, San Diego, PhD(neurosci), 78. *Prof Exp:* Group leader, Warner-Lambert Parke-Davis, 85-88. *Mem:* Am Soc Pharmacol Exp Therapeut; Soc Neurosci; Am Soc Biochem Molecular Biol. *Res:* Receptor biochemistry; screening; molecular diversity; adenosine, neuropeptides, acetylcholine, melatonin. *Mailing Add:* Dept Molecular Diversity Lilly Res Lab Lilly Res Ctr Indianapolis IN 46285

BRUNS, THOMAS DICKINSON, BOTANY, PHYTOPATHOLOGY. *Current Pos:* postdoctoral fel, Dept Bot, 87-89, ASST PROF DEPT PLANT PATH, UNIV CALIF, BERKELEY, 89- *Personal Data:* b Blue Island, Ill, Apr 13, 53; m 79, Barbara Jean Brown; c Emily L, Patricia J & Samuel P. *Educ:* Univ Minn, BS, 78, MS, 82; Univ Mich, PhD(bot), 87. *Honors & Awards:* Alexopoulos Prize, Mycol Soc Am, 94. *Prof Exp:* Teaching asst, Dept Bot, Univ Minn, St Paul, 79-82, Univ Mich, Ann Arbor, 82-85, res asst, 86-87. *Concurrent Pos:* Grad fel, Mycol Soc Am, 84-85; NSF grantee, 87-90 & 90- *Mem:* Fel AAAS; Am Phytopath Soc; Am Soc Study Evolution; Mycol Soc Am. *Res:* Contributed articles to professional journals. *Mailing Add:* Dept Plant Path Univ Calif Berkeley CA 94720

BRUNSCHWIG, BRUCE SAMUEL, PHYSICAL INORGANIC CHEMISTRY, PHOTOCHEMISTRY & KINETICS. *Current Pos:* res collabr, Brookhaven Nat Labs, 74-77, vis chemist, 77-79, assoc chemist, 79-84, CHEMIST, BROOKHAVEN NAT LAB, 84- *Personal Data:* b Philadelphia, Pa, July 29, 44; m 66, Karen Spencer; c Felisa & Anya. *Educ:* Univ Rochester, BA, 66; Polytech Inst NY, PhD(chem physics), 72. *Prof Exp:* Asst prof chem, Hofstra Univ, 72-79, chmn dept, 75-78. *Concurrent Pos:* Res collabr, Brookhaven Nat Labs, 74-77, vis chemist, 77-79; vis fac, Calif Inst Technol, 91-92. *Mem:* Am Chem Soc; AAAS; Sigma Xi. *Res:* Study of photochemical and thermal electron-transfer reactions of transition metals in inorganic complexes and metalloproteins; modelling of electron-transfer reactions; chemical kinetics. *Mailing Add:* Brookhaven Nat Lab Dept Chem Bldg 555 Upton NY 11973. *Fax:* 516-344-5815; *E-Mail:* bsb@bnl.gov

BRUNSER, OSCAR, PEDIATRIC GASTROENTEROLOGY. *Current Pos:* asst prof pediat, Sch Med, 69-76, assoc prof, 76-78, PROF PEDIAT, INST NUTRIT FOOD TECH, UNIV CHILE, 78- *Personal Data:* b Buenos Aires, Arg, Nov 24, 35; Chilean citizen; m 64, Norma I Rabovich; c Gustavo, Alejandro & Nicole. *Educ:* Univ Chile, Baccalaureate, 53, MD, 61; State Univ NY, Albany, MD, 75. *Prof Exp:* Instr Dept Pediat, Sch Med Univ Chile, 61-66, Internal Med, Sch Med, Univ Wash, Seattle, 67-69. *Concurrent Pos:* John Simon Guggenheim Mem Found fel, 65 & 67; fel anat, Dept Biol Struct, Univ Wash, Seattle, 66-69; Williams Waterman Fund Res Corp fel, 68-69; asst prof pediat, Albert Einstein Sch Med, Bronx, 73-76. *Mem:* Am Inst Nutrit; Am Soc Clin Nutrit; Soc Res Int Nutrit; Am Acad Pediat. *Res:* Reaction of the intestine of children living in a less developed country to food deprivation and the microbiological contamination of the environment, developing chronic environmental enteropathy, malabsorption of nutrients and diarrhea. *Mailing Add:* Inst Nutrit & Food Technol Univ Chile Casilla 138-11 Santiago 11 Chile. *Fax:* 56 2-221-4030; *E-Mail:* obrunser@reund.cl

BRUNSKI, JOHN BEYER, BIOMATERIALS, BIOMECHANICS. *Current Pos:* PROF, DEPT BIOMED ENG, RENSSELAER POLYTECH INST, 77- *Personal Data:* b Philadelphia, Pa, June 10, 49; m 79, Betsy Sachter; c Jeff & Leah. *Educ:* Univ Pa, BS, 70, PhD(metall, mat sci), 77; Stanford Univ, MS, 72. *Concurrent Pos:* Sect Ed, Int J Oral & Maxillofacial Implants; consult, Dent Prod Panel, Food & Drug Admin. *Mem:* Sigma Xi; Soc Biomat; Int Asn Dent Res; Am Soc Mech Engrs; Orthop Res Soc; Acad Osseointegration. *Res:* Dental implants, especially engineering aspects of their design and use; physiology and mechanical properties of bone. *Mailing Add:* Jonsson Eng Ctr Rensselaer Polytech Inst Rm 7040 Troy NY 12180-3590. *Fax:* 518-276-3035; *E-Mail:* brunsj@rpi.edu

BRUNSKILL, GREGG JOHN, LIMNOLOGY, ENVIRONMENTAL SCIENCES. *Current Pos:* PRIN RES SCIENTIST, AUSTRALIAN INST MARINE SCI, 92- *Personal Data:* b Kansas City, Kans, Sept 10, 41; m 70; c 2. *Educ:* Augustana Col, SDak, 63; Cornell Univ, PhD(biogeochem), 68. *Prof Exp:* Res scientist, Freshwater Inst Environ Can, Fisheries & Oceans Can, 67-91. *Concurrent Pos:* Adj prof earth sci, Univ Man, 71-74 & 80-86; vis scientist, Lamont-Doherty Geol Observ, Columbia Univ, 77. *Mem:* AAAS; Geochem Soc; Am Soc Limnol & Oceanog; Int Soc Limnol; Int Asn Gt Lakes Res; Arctic Inst N Am. *Res:* Aqueous and recent sediment geochemistry and radiochemistry of fresh and estuarine waters; lakes; aquatic ecology of arctic and subarctic ecosystems. *Mailing Add:* Australian Inst Marine Sci PMB No 3 Townsville MC Townsville Qld 4810 Australia. *E-Mail:* g.brunskill@aims.gov.au

BRUNSON, CLAYTON (CODY), poultry husbandry, for more information see previous edition

BRUNSON, JOHN TAYLOR, PHYSIOLOGY. *Current Pos:* asst prof, 71-80, ASSOC PROF ZOOL, STATE UNIV NY COL OSWEGO, 81- *Personal Data:* b Kalamazoo, Mich, June 4, 40; m 71; c 2. *Educ:* Hope Col, AB, 62; Univ Mich, Ann Arbor, MS, 64; Colo State Univ, PhD(zool), 73. *Prof Exp:* Instr biol & chem, State Univ NY Col Oneonta, 65-68; instr, Children's Sch Sci, Woods Hole, Mass, 66, 67 & 81. *Mem:* Am Soc Zoologists; AAAS; Sigma Xi. *Res:* Physiological ecology, particularly respiratory physiology at low oxygen tension or high altitude; history of biology; insect physiology; voltage clamping studies of epithelial tissues. *Mailing Add:* Dept Biol State Univ NY Col Oswego Oswego NY 13126

BRUNSON, KENNETH W, CANCER AND PRECLINICAL RESEARCH, DRUG RECOVERY. *Current Pos:* MEM, CANCER METASTASIS & CELL BIOL PROG, UNIV PITTSBURGH CANCER INST, 91-; ASSOC PROF, DEPT PATH, UNIV PITTSBURGH SCH MED. *Personal Data:* b Chico, Tex, 1936; m 63, Myrna Lapre'; c Gregory & Geoffrey. *Educ:* Univ NTex, BA, 64, MA, 66; Univ Minn, PhD(microbiol & biochem), 73. *Prof Exp:* Sr res scientist, Cancer Biol Group, Pharmacol Div, Pfizer Pharmaceut Co, 84-91; asst prof, Ind Univ Sch Med, Dept Microbiol & Immunol, 79-84, Dept Path, 80-84. *Concurrent Pos:* Dir, UPCI Tumor Model Labs, 95- & In Vivo Preclin Res, Health Sci, Univ Pittsburgh, 96- *Mem:* Am Asn Cancer Res; Am Soc Cell Biol; Am Asn Immunologists; Am Inst Biol Sci; NY Acad Sci; Sigma Xi. *Res:* Immunobiology and therapy of cancer metastasis; cancer immunosuppression; cellular systems for drug discovery of novel therapeutic agents; bacterial toxin interx with mammalian cells. *Mailing Add:* Univ Pittsburgh Cancer Inst 200 Lothrop St BST Suite E1040 Pittsburgh PA 15213. *Fax:* 412-624-7737; *E-Mail:* brunsont@pitt.edu

BRUNSON, ROYAL BRUCE, ZOOLOGY. *Current Pos:* RETIRED. *Personal Data:* b DeKalb, Ill, Feb 16, 14; m 36; c 2. *Educ:* Western Mich Col Educ, BS, 38; Univ Mich, MS, 45, PhD(zool), 47. *Prof Exp:* Teaching fel zool, Univ Mich, 42-46; from instr to prof zool, Univ Mont, 46-80. *Mem:* Am Malacol Union; Am Soc Ichthyologists & Herpetologists; Am Soc Limnol & Oceanog; Am Micros Soc; Soc Syst Zool. *Res:* Taxonomy and natural history of North American Gastrotricha; taxonomy and distribution of Western Montana invertebrates; limnology of Western Montana lakes. *Mailing Add:* 1522 34th St Missoula MT 59801

BRUNSTING, ELMER H(ENRY), CHEMICAL ENGINEERING. *Current Pos:* RETIRED. *Personal Data:* b Hull, Iowa, Sept 29, 21; m 50, Nelva Rensink; c Candace (Curtis), Carole, Carl, Amy (Tschirhart) & Anita (Riley). *Educ:* Cent Col, Iowa, BS, 44; Iowa State Col, PhD(chem eng), 50. *Prof Exp:* Process engr, Vulcan Copper & Supply Co, 50-53; sr process engr, Mathieson Chem Corp, 53-54; chief process engr, John Deere Chem Co, 54-65; sr process engr, Eng Dept, Gulf Oil Chem Co, 65-67, dir process eng, 67-72, mgr, specialty chem, 72-83; pres, Graff Eng, 83-86; sr staff specialist, Stubbs Overbeck, 87-90. *Mem:* Am Chem Soc; Am Inst Chem Engrs. *Res:* Acidulation characteristics of various rock phosphates. *Mailing Add:* 13630 Pinerock Houston TX 77079

BRUNSWICK, MARK, CELL BIOLOGY, IMMUNOLOGY. *Current Pos:* SR STAFF FEL IMMUNOL & CELL BIOLOGY, FOOD & DRUG ADMIN, 91- *Personal Data:* b London, Eng, 1957. *Educ:* Univ Col London, BSc, 79, PhD(immunol), 86. *Prof Exp:* asst prof, Dept Med, Uniformed Servs Univ Health Sci, 85-91. *Mem:* Brit Soc Immunol; Am Asn Immunologists. *Mailing Add:* Food & Drug Admin DMA 1401 Rockville Pike Bldg 29 Rm 231 Bethesda MD 20852

BRUNTON, GEORGE DELBERT, GEOLOGY, MINERALOGY. *Current Pos:* AT DEPT GEOL & GEOL ENG, UNIV MISS. *Personal Data:* b McGill, Nev, Dec 20, 24. *Educ:* Univ Nev, BS, 50; Univ NMex, MS, 52; Ind Univ, PhD, 57. *Prof Exp:* Res asst, Pa State Univ, 52-53; geologist, Res Explor & Prod Res Lab, Shell Develop Co, 53-57, Pure Oil Res Ctr, 57-63 & US Gypsum Co, 63-64; geologist, Oak Ridge Nat Lab, 64-80; tech mgr, Battelle Mem Inst, 80- *Mem:* Mineral Soc Am; Soc Mining Engrs. *Res:* Clay mineralogy; carbonate mineralogy; crystal structures; phase equilibria. *Mailing Add:* Dept Geol & Geol Eng Univ Miss University MS 38677

BRUNTON, LAURENCE, CELLULAR PHYSIOLOGY, MOLECULAR PHARMACOLOGY. *Current Pos:* scholar, 76-78, asst res pharmacologist & lectr med, 78-80, ASST PROF MED, DIV PHARMACOL & CARDIOL, SCH MED, UNIV CALIF, SAN DIEGO, 81- *Personal Data:* b Charlottesville, Va, Mar 26, 47; c 1. *Educ:* Harvard Col, BA, 69; Univ Va, PhD(pharmacol), 76. *Prof Exp:* Instr math & sci, Windsor Sch, 70-71. *Concurrent Pos:* Nat Res Serv Award fel, NIH, 76-78, Res Career Develop Award, 81-86. *Mem:* Am Soc Pharmacol & Exp Therapeut; Am Fedn Clin Res. *Res:* Cyclic nucleotide metabolism and transport; mechanisms of specifically of cyclic nucleotide action; regulation of cell growth; interactions of drugs and hormones with the cell membrane. *Mailing Add:* Dept Med Civ Pharmacol 0636 Univ Calif San Diego 9500 Gilman Dr La Jolla CA 92093-0636. *Fax:* 619-534-6833

BRUNZELL, JOHN D, METABOLISM, INTERNAL MEDICINE. *Current Pos:* resident internal med, 66-69, fel endocrinol & metab, 69-71, PROF MED, DEPT MED, DIV METAB, UNIV WASH, 71- *Personal Data:* b Lewiston, Idaho, May 10, 37. *Educ:* Whitman Col, BA, 59; Univ Wash, MD, 63. *Prof Exp:* Med officer, US Army, 64-66. *Mem:* Am Heart Asn; Am Soc Clin Invest. *Mailing Add:* Dept Med Div Metab RG-26 Univ Wash Seattle WA 98195-0001

BRUS, LOUIS EUGENE, CHEMICAL PHYSICS & CLUSTERS. *Current Pos:* mem tech staff, 73-80, DISTINGUISHED MEM STAFF, AT&T BELL LABS, 80- *Personal Data:* b Cleveland, Ohio, Aug 10, 43; m 70; c 3. *Educ:* Rice Univ, BA, 65; Columbia Univ, PhD(chem physics), 69. *Prof Exp:* Sci staff officer physics & chem, US Naval Res Lab, 69-73. *Mem:* Fel Am Phys Soc; Am Chem Soc. *Res:* Molecular radiationless transitions and condensed phase kinetics; photochemistry near surfaces and semiconductor nanocrystals. *Mailing Add:* AT&T Bell Labs 1T 202 600 Mountain Ave Murray Hill NJ 07974. *Fax:* 908-582-3958; *E-Mail:* leb@allwise.att.com

BRUSCA, GARY J, ZOOLOGY, BIOLOGY. *Current Pos:* from asst prof to assoc prof, 67-74, PROF BIOL, HUMBOLDT STATE UNIV, 74- *Personal Data:* b Bell, Calif, Oct 10, 39; m 62; c 5. *Educ:* Calif State Polytech Col, BS, 60; Univ of the Pac, MA, 61; Univ Southern Calif, PhD(biol), 65. *Prof Exp:* Asst prof biol & asst dir Pac Marine Sta, Univ of the Pac, 64-67. *Concurrent Pos:* Dir, Humboldt State Marine Lab, Trinidad, Calif, 70- *Res:* Crustacean systematics. *Mailing Add:* Dept Biol Humboldt State Univ 1 Harpe St Arcata CA 95521-8299

BRUSCA, RICHARD CHARLES, INVERTEBRATE ZOOLOGY, MARINE ECOLOGY. *Current Pos:* JOSHUA L BAILY CUR & CHMN, DEPT MARINE INVERT, SAN DIEGO NATURAL HIST MUS, 87- *Personal Data:* b Los Angeles, Calif, Jan 25, 45; div; c 2. *Educ:* Calif State Polytech Univ, San Luis Obispo, BS, 67; Calif State Univ, Los Angeles, MS, 70; Univ Ariz, PhD(biol), 75. *Honors & Awards:* Cong Medal, Serv Antarctica, 68. *Prof Exp:* Res biochemist, CalBioChem, Los Angeles, 69; teaching asst zool & cur insects & asst investr, Aquatic Insect Labs, Calif State Univ, Los Angeles, 69-70; resident dir, Univ Ariz-Univ Sonora Coop Marine Sta, Puerto Penasco, Mex, 70-72; marine biologist, Biol Educ Exped, Vista, Calif, 74-75; from asst prof to assoc prof biol, Univ Southern Calif, Los Angeles, 75-84, cur crustacea, Allan Hancock Found, 75-84; cur & head invert zool sect, Los Angeles Co Mus Natural Hist, 84-87. *Concurrent Pos:* Vpres, Panamic Environ Consult, Ariz, 73-75; sci ed, Allan Hancock Found Publ, 76-84; consult shallow water trop ecosystems, Univ Costa Rica, 79-81; dir acad progs, Catalina Marine Sci Ctr, Univ Southern Calif, 81-83; mem bd dirs, Orgn Trop Biol, 84-86; field reviewer, Inst Mus Serv, 85-; biol syst prog, NSF, 86-89, ad hoc mem adv panel, numerous res grants; adj prof biol, Calif State Univ, Long Beach, 86-, San Diego, 87-; res assoc, Scripps Inst Oceanog, 90-; panel mem, Nat Acad Sci & Charles Lindberg Fund. *Mem:* Am Soc Zool; AAAS; Sigma Xi; Soc Syst Zool; Willig Hennig Soc; Crustacean Soc; Western Soc Naturalists. *Res:* Evolutionary biology of invertebrates; crustacean biology; shallow water marine ecology; tropical marine ecosystems; marine symbiosis; parasites of marine fishes; biogeography. *Mailing Add:* Univ Charleston 205 Ft Johnson Rd Charleston SC 29412

BRUSENBACK, ROBERT A(LLEN), CHEMICAL ENGINEERING. *Current Pos:* process develop engr, 59-63, ANALOG COMPUT SPECIALIST, ABBOTT LABS, 63- *Personal Data:* b Chicago, Ill, Sept 24, 27; m 51; c 3. *Educ:* Northwestern Univ, BS, 50, MS, 53, PhD(chem eng), 63. *Prof Exp:* Process develop engr, Houdry Process Corp, 53-56; instr chem eng, Northwestern Univ, 56-59. *Mem:* Am Inst Chem Engrs; Instrument Soc Am; Sigma Xi. *Res:* Microscopic analysis of fluidized bed heat transfer; application of analog computation to problems in the pharmaceutical industry. *Mailing Add:* 15429 W Cherrywood Lane Libertyville IL 60048

BRUSEWITZ, GERALD HENRY, AGRICULTURAL ENGINEERING. *Current Pos:* From asst prof to prof, 69-92, REGENTS PROF AGR ENG, OKLA STATE UNIV, 92- *Personal Data:* b Green Bay, Wis, June 1, 42; m 90, Glenna Williams; c Kelly & Nicole. *Educ:* Univ Wis, BS, 64 & 65, MS, 67; Mich State Univ, PhD(agr eng), 69. *Concurrent Pos:* Vis prof, Univ Calif, Davis, 79, Cornell Univ, 88; eng consult, Solar Energy Dept, Kuwait Inst Sci Res, 80. *Mem:* Am Asn Cereal Chemists; Am Soc Eng Educ; fel Am Soc Agr Engrs; Inst Food Technol. *Res:* Physical and mechanical properties of biological materials; food process engineering. *Mailing Add:* Dept Biosysts Agr Eng Okla State Univ Stillwater OK 74078-0497. *Fax:* 405-744-6059; *E-Mail:* jbrusew@agen.okstate.edu

BRUSH, ALAN HOWARD, ZOOLOGY. *Current Pos:* asst prof zool, 65-69, assoc prof biol sci group, 69-76, PROF BIOL SCI GROUP, UNIV CONN, 76- *Personal Data:* b Rochester, NY, Sept 29, 34; div; c 2. *Educ:* Univ Southern Calif, BA, 56; Univ Calif, Los Angeles, MA, 57, PhD(zool), 64. *Prof Exp:* Res technician nuclear med & biophys, Univ Calif, Los Angeles, 56-61; postdoctoral fel zool, Cornell Univ, 64-65. *Concurrent Pos:* NIH spec fel, Univ Calif, Berkeley, 71-72; NSF int fel, Commonwealth Sci & Indust Res Orgn, Melbourne, Australia; ed, The Auk, 84- *Mem:* AAAS; Cooper Ornith Soc; Am Soc Zool; Am Physiol Soc; fel Am Ornith Union. *Res:* Comparative biochemistry and physiology; biochemical evolution; functional morphology. *Mailing Add:* Physiol & Neurobiol Univ Conn N Eagleville Rd Storrs CT 06268

BRUSH, F(RANKLIN) ROBERT, PSYCHOBIOLOGY, PSYCHONEUROENDOCRINOLOGY. *Current Pos:* head, Dept Psychol, 81-83, PROF, PURDUE UNIV, 81- *Personal Data:* b Phoenixville, Pa, Nov 24, 29; c Robert C & Elizabeth. *Educ:* Princeton Univ, BA, 51; Harvard Univ, MA, 53, PhD(social psychol), 56. *Prof Exp:* Asst prof psychol, Univ Md, 56-59 & Univ Pa, 59-65; assoc prof med psychol, Med Sch, Univ Ore, 65-67, prof, 67-71; prof psychol, Syracuse Univ, 71-80. *Concurrent Pos:* Vis asst prof & vis scientist, Dept Psychol & Regional Primate Res Ctr, Univ Wis, 64-65; res scientist develop award, NIMH, 67-71; vis prof, Sherrington Sch Physiol, St Thomas Hosp Med Sch, London, 76, Univ Hawaii, 82; vis prof, Genetics & Neurogenetics Lab, Univ Rene Descarte, Paris, 93. *Mem:* Behav Genetics Asn; Sigma Xi. *Res:* Psychobiology of stress and aversively motivated behaviors, focusing especially on behavioral effects of pituitary adrenocortical hormones and genetic determinants of individual differences in animal learning. *Mailing Add:* Dept Psychol Sci Purdue Univ West Lafayette IN 47907. *Fax:* 765-496-1264

BRUSH, GRACE SOMERS, FOREST ECOLOGY, PALYNOLOGY. *Current Pos:* res scientist, 70-75 & 78-81, PROF & PRIN RES SCIENTIST, DEPT GEOG & ENVIRON ENG, JOHNS HOPKINS UNIV, 81- *Personal Data:* b Antigonish, NS, Jan 18, 31; US citizen; m 53; c 3. *Educ:* St Francis Xavier Univ, BA, 49; Univ Ill, Urbana-Champaign, MS, 51; Radcliffe Col, PhD(biol), 56. *Prof Exp:* Technician, Geol Surv Can, 49-50, 51-52 & US Geol Surv, 56-57; lectr bot, George Washington Univ, 57-58; asst prof, Univ Iowa, 59-63; res assoc geol, Princeton Univ, 64-66, res staff mem, 66-70. *Concurrent Pos:* Asst prof, Rutgers Univ, 64-66. *Mem:* AAAS; Am Soc Limnol & Oceanog; Am Quaternary Asn; Ecol Soc Am; Am Asn Stratig Palynologists; Am Inst Biol Sci. *Res:* Relations between modern pollen distributions in water and surface sediments and vegetation; settling properties of pollen in water; mapping terrestrial vegetation; forest patterns; estuarine biostratigraphy. *Mailing Add:* Dept Environ Eng Johns Hopkins Univ 3400 N Charles St Baltimore MD 21218-2608

BRUSH, JAMES S, BIOCHEMISTRY. *Current Pos:* RETIRED. *Personal Data:* b Mankato, Minn, Mar 21, 29; m 58; c 4. *Educ:* Univ Chicago, PhD(biochem), 56. *Prof Exp:* Res assoc biochem, Univ Chicago, 56-57; clin chemist, Hurley Hosp, Flint, Mich, 58-60; fel biochem, Okla Med Res Inst, Oklahoma City, 60-63; biochemist, US Vet Admin, Wood, Wis, 63-69; from asst prof to assoc prof biochem, Col Basic Med Sci, Univ Tenn, Memphis, 69-74; assoc prof, Fac Med, Univ PR Med Sci Campus, San Juan, 75-83, prof, Dept Biochem & Nutrit, 83-91; vis scientist, NIH, Phoenix, 88-90. *Concurrent Pos:* Instr biochem, Sch Med, Marquette Univ, 64-69; prin investr Vet Admin grants, 69-72 & NIH, NSF grants, 74-77, 78-80; biochemist, US Vet Admin, Memphis, 69-74. *Mem:* AAAS; Am Soc Biochem & Molecular Biol; Endocrine Soc. *Res:* Protein sulfhydryl chemistry; enzyme kinetic mechanism of gulonolactone oxidase; insulin metabolism and mechanism of action; mechanisms of cyclic nucleotide action; cosmology of Swedenborg's Principia. *Mailing Add:* 7665 E Rancho Vista Dr Scottsdale AZ 85251-1518

BRUSH, JOHN (BURKE), MECHANICAL ENGINEERING, CHEMICAL PROCESS DESIGN. *Current Pos:* PRES, BRUSH AUTOBOAT CO, 58- *Personal Data:* b New York, NY, Nov 25, 12; m 41, 71, Marian E Natorp; c Deborah, Jay, Burke, Randal & Gary. *Educ:* Cornell Univ, ME, 34. *Prof Exp:* Trainee, Procter & Gamble, Inc, 34, engr packaging mach, 36; chief engr, Philippine Mfg Co, 41; assoc chief engr packaging mach, Procter & Gamble Co, 49, assoc chief engr opers & planning, 51-56, mgr airplane opers, 53-57, head, Mech Dept, Overseas Eng Div, 55-68, Patent Div, 69-70, Eng Develop Div, 70-77. *Mem:* Am Soc Mech Engrs; Soc Automotive Engrs. *Res:* Automatic packaging machinery; pneumatic conveying; materials handling; converting standard autos for amphibious operation; auto cooling; fuel systems cooling; increased reliability; reduced emissions and increased air conditioning capacity; vehicle fire prevention; 6 patents. *Mailing Add:* 2 Beech Knoll Dr Cincinnati OH 45224

BRUSH, LUCIEN M(UNSON), JR, civil & geological engineering; deceased, see previous edition for last biography

BRUSH, MIRIAM KELLY, NUTRITION. *Current Pos:* RETIRED. *Personal Data:* b Boston, Mass, Nov 9, 15; m 42; c 4. *Educ:* Mt Holyoke Col, AB, 37; Oberlin Col, AM, 39; Iowa State Col, PhD(nutrit), 46. *Prof Exp:* Assoc nutrit, Iowa State Col, 46-47; assoc cancer res, McArdle Mem Lab, Med Sch, Univ Wis, 47-50; assoc geront, Med Sch, Washington Univ, 51; lectr nutrit, Col Nursing, Rutgers Univ, 56-69, prof nutrit, 69-86. *Mem:* AAAS; Am Inst Nutrit; Am Home Econ Asn; Am Dietetic Asn; Am Pub Health Asn; Sigma Xi. *Res:* Protein and amino acid metabolism; nutrition and the aging process; protein-vitamin B6 inter-relationships; vitamin C nutrition in school children; nutrition in infancy and early childhood. *Mailing Add:* 58 Braine Rd Mt Holly NJ 08060

BRUSH, STEPHEN GEORGE, HISTORY OF SCIENCE. *Current Pos:* assoc prof hist & res assoc prof, Inst Fluid Dynamics & Appl Math, 68-71, prof, 71-95, DISTINGUISHED UNIV PROF HIST SCI, UNIV MD, COLLEGE PARK, 95- *Personal Data:* b Bangor, Maine; m 60; c 2. *Educ:* Harvard Univ, AB, 55; Oxford Univ, DPhil(phys sci), 58. *Honors & Awards:* Pfizer Award, Hist Sci Soc, 77; Pollock Award, Dudley Observ, 87. *Prof Exp:* NSF fel, 58-59; physicist, Lawrence Radiation Lab, Univ Calif, 59-65; res assoc physics & ed, Harvard Proj Physics, 65-68, lectr physics & hist of sci, Harvard Univ, 66-68. *Concurrent Pos:* Mem, Inst Advan Study, Princeton, 92-93. *Mem:* Acad Int Hist Sci; Am Phys Soc; Hist of Sci Soc (vpres, 88, pres, 90-91). *Res:* History of physical science in 19th and 20th centuries, especially geophysics, astrophysics, kinetic theory and statistical mechanics; use of historical case studies to test philosophical theses about science. *Mailing Add:* Inst Phys Sci & Technol Univ Md College Park MD 20742-2431. *Fax:* 301-314-9363

BRUSIE, JAMES POWERS, PHYSICAL CHEMISTRY. *Current Pos:* RETIRED. *Personal Data:* b North Egremont, Mass, July 3, 18; m 47; c 3. *Educ:* Lafayette Col, BS, 40; Yale Univ, PhD(phys chem), 43. *Prof Exp:* Res chemist, Manhattan Proj & Off Sci Res & Develop contract, Div War Res, Yale Univ, 42-43 & Columbia Univ, 43-44; sect supvr, Carbide & Carbon Chem Corp, Oak Ridge, 44-46; res chemist, Gen Aniline & Film Corp, 46-50, group leader, 50-52, res assoc, 52-55, prog mgr, 55-62, sr tech assoc, 62-64; tech dir, Girdler Catalysts Dept, Chemetron Corp, 64-68; prod mgr, Alrac Corp, 69-74; res assoc, Pullman Kellogg, 74-76, res supur, M W Kellogg, 76-80. *Mem:* Am Chem Soc. *Res:* Catalysis, pressure acetylene reactions; polymerization of alpha-halo-acrylic esters; polymerization of 2-pyrrolidone to nylon-4; catalysis and coal conversion; flue gas desulfurization. *Mailing Add:* 10546 Idlebrook Houston TX 77070-2921

BRUSILOW, SAUL W, PEDIATRICS, PHYSIOLOGY. *Current Pos:* asst resident, Johns Hopkins Hosp, 56-57, Nat Found Infantile Paralysis fel, Johns Hopkins Sch Med, 57-59, from instr to assoc prof, 59-74, PROF PEDIAT, SCH MED, JOHNS HOPKINS UNIV, 74- *Personal Data:* b Brooklyn, NY, June 7, 27; wid; c 2. *Educ:* Princeton Univ, AB, 50; Yale Univ, MD, 54. *Honors & Awards:* Joseph P Kennedy Jr Foundation Award, 95. *Prof Exp:* Intern, Grace-New Haven Hosp, Conn, 54-55, asst resident, 55-56. *Mem:* Am Pediat Soc; Am Physiol Soc; Soc Pediat Res. *Res:* Inborn errors of metabolism; nephrology. *Mailing Add:* Dept Pediat Johns Hopkins Univ Sch Med 600 N Wolfe St Baltimore MD 21205-2182. *Fax:* 410-955-0761

BRUSSARD, PETER FRANS, POPULATION BIOLOGY, CONSERVATION BIOLOGY. *Current Pos:* prof & chair Biol Dept, 89-97, dir, Biodiversity Res Ctr, 93-96, PROF BIOL, UNIV NEV, RENO, 96- *Personal Data:* b Reno, Nev, June 20, 38; m 69, Trudy Byers; c William R & Peter H. *Educ:* Stanford Univ, AB, 60, PhD(biol), 69; Univ Nev, Reno, MS, 66. *Honors & Awards:* Silver Eagle Award, US Fish & Wildlife Serv. *Prof Exp:* From asst prof to assoc prof ecol, Cornell Univ, 75-85; dir, Rocky Mountain Biol Lab, 78-82; prof & head biol dept, Mont State Univ, 85-89. *Concurrent Pos:* Vis prof, Univ Tex, 77, Univ Dunedin, Otago NZ, 89; vis scholar, Univ Ariz, 84. *Mem:* Fel AAAS; Ecol Soc Am; Am Soc Naturalists (treas, 80-83); Soc Study Evolution; Soc Conservation Biol (secy-treas, 85-90, pres-elect, 90-93, pres, 93-95). *Res:* Relations between genetic variation, distribution and ecology of natural populations; conservation biology. *Mailing Add:* Dept Biol Univ Nev Reno NV 89557-0050. *Fax:* 702-784-1302; *E-Mail:* brussard@scs.unr.edu

BRUSSEAU, MARK LEWIS, TRANSPORT & FATE OF CONTAMINANTS IN THE SUBSURFACE, CLEAN UP OF CONTAMINATED SUBSURFACE ENVIRONMENTS. *Current Pos:* Asst prof, 89-93, ASSOC PROF SUBSURFACE HYDROL & ENVIRON CHEM, UNIV ARIZ, 93- *Personal Data:* b Pontiac, Mich, June 17, 58. *Educ:* Univ Nev, Reno, BS & BA, 82; Univ Iowa, MS, 84; Univ Fla, PhD(hydrol & environ chem), 89. *Honors & Awards:* Young Investr, Nat Acad Sci, 93. *Concurrent Pos:* Vis scientist, Tech Univ Denmark, 89; res fel, USAF Off Res, 90, US Dept Energy, 92; assoc ed, J Contaminant Hydrol; deleg, Univ Coun Water Resources; mem, Comt Pesticides & Other Toxic Organics in Soil & Their Potential for Groundwater Contamination, USDA. *Mem:* Am Chem Soc; Am Geophys Union; Asn Groundwater Scientists & Engrs; Int Asn Hydrogeologists; Soil Sci Soc Am. *Res:* Investigating the factors that influence the transport and fate of contaminants in the subsurface. *Mailing Add:* 429 Shantz Bldg 38 Univ Ariz Tucson AZ 85721-0002. *Fax:* 520-621-1647; *E-Mail:* nonequil@ccit.arizona.edu

BRUSSEL, MORTON KREMEN, PHYSICS. *Current Pos:* res asst prof, 60-64, from assoc prof to prof, 64-95, EMER PROF PHYSICS, UNIV ILL, URBANA-CHAMPAIGN, 95- *Personal Data:* b New Haven, Conn, Mar 31, 29; m 57, Phyllis Lobdell; c Jeffrey Kremen & Eric Saxton. *Educ:* Yale Univ, BS, 51; Univ Minn, PhD(physics), 57. *Prof Exp:* Res assoc fel physics, Brookhaven Nat Lab, 57-59, asst physicist, 59-60. *Concurrent Pos:* Assoc prog dir nuclear physics, Physics Sect, NSF, 72-73; sabbatical leaves, Inst of Nuclear Physics, Orsay, France, 68-69, Div de Physique Nucleaire-High Energy, Centre D'Etudes Nucleaire, Saclay, France, 78-79, 87-88. *Mem:* Am Phys Soc; Fedn Am Scientists; Am Asn Univ Profs; Sigma Xi; Europ Phys Soc. *Res:* Experimental nuclear physics; nuclear structure studies; electron and photon induced reactions especially from light nuclei. *Mailing Add:* Dept Physics Univ Ill 1110 W Green St Urbana IL 61801. *E-Mail:* brussel@uiuc.edu

BRUST, DAVID PHILIP, PHOTOGRAPHIC CHEMISTRY, MAGNETIC MEDIA CHEMISTRY. *Current Pos:* RETIRED. *Personal Data:* b Albion, NY, Aug 13, 34; m 59, Beverly Brownell; c Thomas, Daniel & David Jr. *Educ:* State Univ NY Buffalo, BA, 55; Univ Rochester, PhD(org chem), 65. *Honors & Awards:* Kodak Sci Achievement Award. *Prof Exp:* Res chemist polymer chem, Color Hardcopy, 58-61, sr res chemist, 65-72, res assoc photog chem, 72-83, res assoc, magnetic formulations, 83-87, res assoc Color Hardcopy, 88-92. *Mem:* Am Chem Soc; AAAS; Soc Photog Scientists & Engrs. *Res:* Polymers in photographic systems. *Mailing Add:* 239 Southridge Dr Rochester NY 14626-4222

BRUST, HARRY FRANCIS, ORGANIC CHEMISTRY. *Current Pos:* RETIRED. *Personal Data:* b Milwaukee, Wis, Jan 2, 14; m 39; c 3. *Educ:* Univ Wis, BS, 38; Univ Pa, MS, 40, PhD(chem), 43. *Prof Exp:* Asst instr chem, Univ Pa, 38-43; chemist & group leader, Dow Chem Co, 43-68, sr res chemist, 68-73, sr res specialist, 73-79. *Mem:* Am Chem Soc; Sigma Xi. *Res:* Chlorination; bromination of a variety of organic chemicals; agricultural chemicals, chiefly herbicides; new process development and reaction kinetics. *Mailing Add:* 601 Hillcrest St Midland MI 48640-3337

BRUST, MANFRED, PHYSIOLOGY. *Current Pos:* from asst prof to assoc prof rehab med, 63-70, ASSOC PROF PHYSIOL, STATE UNIV NY DOWNSTATE MED CTR, 70- *Personal Data:* b Chemnitz, Ger, Oct 22, 23; nat US; m 57; c 3. *Educ:* NY Univ, BA, 44, MSc, 46; Univ Ill, PhD(physiol), 54. *Prof Exp:* Asst physiol, Univ Chicago, 46-48; asst entom, Univ Ill, 50-53; res assoc zool, Syracuse Univ, 53-55; res assoc biol, Wash Sq Col, NY Univ, 55-59; res assoc, Div Physiol, Inst Muscle Dis, Inc, New York, 59-61, asst mem, 61-63. *Concurrent Pos:* Asst, Babies Hosp, Columbia-Presby Med Ctr, 57. *Mem:* AAAS; Am Physiol Soc; NY Acad Sci; Biophys Soc. *Res:* Basic physiology of muscle contraction; excitation and muscle pharmacology in both normal and diseased conditions; muscular dystrophy; physiology of neuromuscular disease; fast and slow muscle; fatigue; ultrasound; atherosclerosis; cardiovascular control. *Mailing Add:* 245 E 87th St Apt No 14B New York NY 10128

BRUST, REINHART A, ENTOMOLOGY, INSECT ECOLOGY. *Current Pos:* From asst prof to assoc prof, 64-72, PROF ENTOM, UNIV MAN, 73- *Personal Data:* b Sibbald, Alta, Feb 7, 34; m 59; c 2. *Educ:* Univ Man, BSc, 59, MSc, 60; Univ Ill, Urbana, PhD(entom), 64. *Mem:* Entom Soc Am; fel, Entom Soc Can. *Res:* Ecology of North American species of mosquitoes, pathogen transmission, biology and systematics of mosquitoes. *Mailing Add:* Dept Entomol Univ Man Winnipeg MB R3T 2N2 Can

BRUSVEN, MERLYN ARDEL, ENTOMOLOGY. *Current Pos:* PROF ENTOM, UNIV IDAHO, 65- *Personal Data:* b Powers Lake, NDak, Mar 23, 37; m 59; c 3. *Educ:* NDak State Univ, BS, 59, MS, 61; Kans State Univ, PhD(entom), 65. *Prof Exp:* Instr biol, Friends Univ, 61-63. *Mem:* Am Soc Limnol & Oceanog; Entom Soc Am. *Res:* Insect ecology, especially grasshopper taxonomy and aquatic entomology; pollution; population and community dynamics. *Mailing Add:* Dept Plant Sci Univ Idaho 375 S Line St Moscow ID 83843-4140

BRUTCHER, FREDERICK VINCENT, JR, ORGANIC CHEMISTRY. *Current Pos:* from asst prof to assoc prof, 59-, EMER PROF CHEM, UNIV PA. *Personal Data:* b Dorchester, Mass, Dec 5, 22. *Educ:* Univ Mass, BS, 47; Yale Univ, MS, 49, PhD(org chem), 51. *Prof Exp:* Fel, Harvard Univ, 51-53. *Mem:* Am Chem Soc. *Res:* Conformational analysis of substituted cyclopentanes; mathematics of organic chemistry; synthesis of indole and alicyclic compounds. *Mailing Add:* Dept Chem Univ Pa Philadelphia PA 19104-6323

BRUTLAG, DOUGLAS LEE, MOLECULAR BIOLOGY. *Current Pos:* asst prof, 74-81, ASSOC PROF BIOCHEM, STANFORD UNIV, 81- *Personal Data:* b Alexandria, Minn, Dec 19, 46; m 75, Simone Mantevil; c Benjamin B & Pauline B. *Educ:* Calif Inst Technol, BS, 68; Stanford Univ, PhD(biochem), 72. *Honors & Awards:* Computerworld-Smithsonian Award, 92. *Prof Exp:* Res scientist genetics, Commonwealth Sci & Indust Res Orgn, 72-74; dir, Intellicorp, 80-85 & Intelligenetics, 85-92. *Concurrent Pos:* Genetics study sect, NIH, 82-86; mem Bd Sci Counr, Nat Libr Med, 89-93; consult, Intelligenetics, 92-95. *Mem:* Fedn Am Soc Exp Biol; fel Am Soc Biol Chemists; Int Soc Comput Biol. *Res:* Application of computer science methods to molecular biology; bioinformatics. *Mailing Add:* Dept Biochem Beckman Ctr B400 Stanford Med Sch Stanford CA 94305-5307. *Fax:* 415-713-6783; *E-Mail:* brutlag@stanford.edu

BRUTSAERT, WILFRIED, HYDROLOGY. *Current Pos:* From asst prof to assoc prof, 62-74, PROF HYDROL, CORNELL UNIV, 74- *Personal Data:* b Ghent, Belg, May 28, 34; nat US; m 71, Toyo Konari; c Siska M, Rik C, Erika F & Karl M. *Educ:* State Univ Ghent, BEng, 58; Univ Calif, MSc, 60, PhD(eng), 62. *Honors & Awards:* Horton Award, Am Geophys Union, 88, Walter B Langbein Award, 97; Horton lectr, Am Meteorol Soc, 93; Linsley Award, Am Inst Hydrol, 93; Eng Award, Nat Acad Engrs, 94. *Concurrent Pos:* Vis scholar, Tohoku Univ, Japan, 69-70 & 83-84; Am Soc Civil Engrs Freeman fel, 75; Fulbright-Hays vis prof, Wageningen, Neth, 76-77, Univ Ghent, Belg, 90-91; pres-elect, Hydrol Sect, Am Geophys Union, 90-92, pres, 92-94. *Mem:* Nat Acad Eng; fel Am Geophys Union; fel Am Meteorol Soc; Sigma Xi; Am Soc Civil Engrs; Am Inst Hydrol. *Res:* Flow through porous media; permeability; infiltration and drainage; microclimatology; evaporation; surface water hydrology; hydrologic systems. *Mailing Add:* Sch Civil & Environ Eng Hollister Hall Cornell Univ Ithaca NY 14853. *Fax:* 607-255-9004; *E-Mail:* whb2@cornell.edu

BRUTTEN, GENE J, COMMUNICATION DISORDERS, STUTTERING. *Current Pos:* from asst prof to prof, 57-93, chair, 87-92, EMER PROF, DEPT COMMUN DIS, SOUTHERN ILL UNIV, 93- *Personal Data:* b New York, NY, May 28, 28; m 55, 93, Martine Vanryckeghem; c Lori & Mark. *Educ:* Kent State Univ, BA, 51; Brooklyn Col, MA, 52; Univ Ill, PhD, 57. *Prof Exp:* Asst prof, NY State Univ, 54-56. *Concurrent Pos:* Coord, Speech & Hearing Serv, Southern Ill Univ, 61-65; vis prof, Univ Minn, 64, City Univ New York, Grad Ctr, 66-67; vis dir, Hunter Col, City Univ, New York, 66-67; Fulbright vis prof, Acad Med Sch, Holland, 71-72, res prof, 78-79; ed-in-chief, J Fluency Dis, 91-; guest prof, Dept Ear, Nose & Throat, Acad Hosp, Univ Gent, Belgium, 92-93. *Mem:* Am Speech & Hearing Asn; Am Psychol Asn; Am Asn Behav Ther; Int Fluency Asn. *Res:* Molecular analysis of the fluency failures of stutterers and nonstutterers so as to improve differential diagnosis and to enhance the strategy and tactics of therapy. *Mailing Add:* Dept Commun Dis & Sci Southern Ill Univ Carbondale IL 62901. *Fax:* 407-384-2119; *E-Mail:* gbrutten@pegasus.cc.ucf.edu

BRUTTIG, STEPHEN PHILIP, CARDIOVASCULAR & MICROVASCULAR PHYSIOLOGY, TRAUMA & RESUSCITATION. *Current Pos:* staff scientist, Cold Res Div, Res Inst Environ Med, US Army, 81-86, br chief, Mil Trauma Res Div, Letterman Inst Res, 86-92, div dir, 91-92, dep dir, 92-96, DIR COMBAT CASUALTY CARE RES PROG, MED RES & MAT COMMAND, US ARMY, 97- *Personal Data:* b Los Angeles, Calif, Mar 3, 44; m 67, Bonnie Jean Stock; c Stephanie & Andrew. *Educ:* Loyola/Marymount Univ, Los Angeles, BS, 70; Colo State Univ, MS, 76; Univ Nebr, PhD(physiol), 80. *Prof Exp:* Postdoctoral fel, Col Med, Univ Va, 78-81. *Mem:* Am Physiol Soc; Microcirculatory; AAAS; Sigma Xi; Am Heart Asn. *Res:* Uncontrolled hemorrhage models, characterizing traumatic injury and hemorrhage; developing appropriate life-sustaining resuscitative strategies; role of vascular cell's metabolism in controlling local blood flow. *Mailing Add:* 6945 Fox Chase Rd New Market MD 21774. *Fax:* 301-619-7067; *E-Mail:* maj.stephen.bruttig@ftdetrck-ccmail.army.mil

BRUTVAN, DONALD RICHARD, CHEMICAL ENGINEERING. *Current Pos:* asst dean, Millard Fillmore Col, 65-69, actg univ dean, 68-69 & 75-78, assoc dean, Div Continuing Educ, 70-78, ASSOC PROF CHEM ENG, STATE UNIV NY BUFFALO, 61- *Personal Data:* b Johnson City, NY, Oct 14, 24; m 50; c 4. *Educ:* Rensselaer Polytech Inst, BChE, 50, MChE, 54, PhD(chem eng), 58. *Honors & Awards:* Prof Achievement Award, Am Inst Chem Engrs, 67-68. *Prof Exp:* Asst res engr, Behr Manning, Norton Abrasives, NY, 50-53; instr chem eng, Rensselaer Polytech Inst, 53-57; res engr, Metals Res Labs, Union Carbide Metals Co, 57-61. *Mem:* Am Inst Chem Engrs; Am Soc Eng Educ; Sigma Xi. *Res:* Phase equilibria and staged operations; economics and process design. *Mailing Add:* 149 Somerton Ave Buffalo NY 14217

BRYAN, ASHLEY MONROE, plant biochemistry; deceased, see previous edition for last biography

BRYAN, BILLY BIRD, AGRICULTURAL ENGINEERING. *Current Pos:* from asst prof to prof, 53-91, from actg dept head to dept head, 64-85, EMER PROF AGR ENG, UNIV ARK, FAYETTEVILLE, 91- *Personal Data:* b Forrest City, Ark, Aug 8, 21; m 42; c 2. *Educ:* Univ Nebr, BS, 50, MS, 54. *Prof Exp:* Exten agr engr, Kans State Univ, 51-53. *Mem:* Am Soc Agr Engrs. *Res:* Soil and water, especially hydraulic applications in agriculture and water resources; machinery and mechanization of cotton production. *Mailing Add:* Dept Biol & Agr Eng Univ Ark AGRI 101 Fayetteville AR 72701-1202. *E-Mail:* awhin99a@prodigy.com

BRYAN, CARL EDDINGTON, ORGANIC CHEMISTRY, POLYMER CHEMISTRY. *Current Pos:* RETIRED. *Personal Data:* b West Point, Miss, Jan 12, 17; m 42; c 2. *Educ:* Univ Miss, BA, 37; Univ Minn, PhD(org chem), 42. *Prof Exp:* Instr chem, Delta Jr Col, 37-38; asst chem, Univ Minn, 38-42; asst, Univ Ill, 42-44; res chemist, E I du Pont de Nemours & Co, 44-46, res chemist, Southern Res Inst, 46-50, head org sect, 48-50; res chemist, Res Ctr, US Rubber Co, 50-59, res scientist, 59-61; sr res chemist, Chemstrand Res Ctr, Monsanto Co, 61-67; res chemist, Mallinckrodt Chem Works, Mo, 67-68; res assoc textiles chem, NC State Univ, 68-76, lectr & lab supvr org chem, 76-84. *Concurrent Pos:* With Off Sci Res & Develop; with Off Rubber Reserve; prin investr res projs, Water Resources Res Inst, US Environ Protection Agency & Am Dye Mfrs Inst, NC State Univ. *Mem:* AAAS; NY Acad Sci; Am Chem Soc; Am Inst Chem; Am Asn Textile Chemists & Colorists. *Res:* Organic synthesis and structure determinations; polymers and polymerization; textile chemistry and waste control. *Mailing Add:* 2631 St Mary's St Raleigh NC 27609-7670

BRYAN, CHARLES F, ICHTHYOLOGY, LIMNOLOGY. *Current Pos:* LEADER, LA COOP FISH & WILDLIFE RES UNIT, 70- *Personal Data:* b Louisville, Ky, Jan 17, 37; m 62. *Educ:* Bellarmine Col, Ky, BA, 60; Univ Louisville, PhD(zool), 64. *Prof Exp:* Asst cur fish, John G Shedd Aquarium, 64-65; fishery biologist, Marion Inserv Training Sch, US Bur Sport Fisheries, 65-67; asst leader, Calif Coop Fishery Unit, 67-71. *Concurrent Pos:* Adj prof, La State Univ; sr scientist, Am Fisheries Soc. *Mem:* Am Soc Limnol & Oceanog; Am Soc Ichthyologists & Herpetologists; Am Fisheries Soc; Int Asn Theoret & Appl Limnol; fel Am Fisheries Res Biol; fel Am Inst Fisheries Res Biol. *Res:* Stream and swamp limnology; water quality; ecology of fishes. *Mailing Add:* Sch Forestry & Wildlife La State Univ Baton Rouge LA 70803-6202. *Fax:* 504-388-4144

BRYAN, CHARLES STONE, INFECTIOUS DISEASES, MEDICAL HISTORY. *Current Pos:* Dir, Div Infectious Dis, 77-93, HEYWARD GIBBES DISTINGUISHED PROF INTERNAL MED & CHAIR, DEPT MED, UNIV SC SCH MED, 92- *Personal Data:* b Columbia, SC, Jan 15, 42; m 82, Donna Hennessee; c Eleanor C & Emily S. *Educ:* Johns Hopkins Univ, BA, 64, MD, 67. *Honors & Awards:* William Osler Medal, Am Asn Hist Med, 67; Advan Achievement Internal Med, Am Bd Internal Med, 87; Laureate Award, Am Col Physicians, 93. *Concurrent Pos:* Adj prof microbiol & immunol, Univ SC Sch Med, 77-, adj prof path, 92- *Mem:* Fel Am Col Physicians; fel Infectious Dis Soc Am; Am Asn Hist Med; Am Soc Microbiol; Asn Profs Med; Am Osler Soc. *Res:* Clinical infectious diseases with particular interest in bloodstream infections and hospital epidemiology; history of medicine with particular interest in nineteenth century medicine and in Sir William Osler. *Mailing Add:* Dept Med & Infectious Dis Univ SC Sch Med Columbia SC 29208-0001

BRYAN, CHRISTOPHER F, ORGAN TRANSPLANTATION, IMMUNOLOGY. *Current Pos:* LAB DIR, MIDWEST ORGAN BANK, 89- *Personal Data:* b Augusta, Ga, Apr 10, 51. *Educ:* Baylor Univ, BS, 73; Tex A&M Univ, MS, 75, PhD(immunogenetics), 78. *Prof Exp:* Supvr, Immunogenetics Lab, Med Sch, La State Univ, 80-84; lab dir, Transplantation-Immunol Lab, Baylor Univ Med Ctr, 84-87; dir histocompatibility, Iowa Methodist Med Ctr, 87-89. *Mem:* Transplantation Soc; Am Soc Histocompatibility & Immunogenetics; Clin Immunol Soc. *Mailing Add:* Midwest Organ Bank 1900 W 47th Pl Suite 400 Westwood KS 66205-1801

BRYAN, DAVID A, SOLID-STATE LASERS, OPTICAL WAVEGUIDES. *Current Pos:* RES ENGR, LASER DIODE, INC, EARTH CITY, 89- *Personal Data:* b Austin, Tex, July 29, 46; m 74; c 5. *Educ:* Rice Univ, BA, 68; Univ Mo, Rolla, MS, 73, PhD(physics), 76. *Prof Exp:* Tech specialist, McDonnell Douglas Corp, 76-89. *Concurrent Pos:* Reviewer, Appl Physics Lett, 85- *Mem:* Optical Soc Am; Int Laser Commun Soc. *Res:* Developed optical waveguide components for integrated optic wavelength demultiplexer; magnesium-doped lithium niobate for improved optical damage resistance; semiconductor waveguide components and coupling to fibers; analysis and experiment on laser beam combining with fibers; compact, high-energy Nd:YAG laser with unstable resonator; one US patent. *Mailing Add:* 4901 McKenna Ct Columbia MO 65203

BRYAN, EDWARD H, WATER SUPPLY, WASTEWATER TREATMENT MANAGEMENT. *Current Pos:* prog mgr, Environ Systs & Resources, NSF, 72-74, Systs Integration & Anal, 74-75, Regional Environ Mgt, 76-77, Comm Water Mgt, 78-79 & Appropriate Technol, 79-81, prog dir, Water Resources & Environ Eng, 81-82, Environ & Water Qual Eng, 82-84, Environ Eng, 84-88, prog dir, environ & ocean systs, 88-92, PROG DIR, ENVIRON ENG, NSF, 93- *Personal Data:* b Milwaukee, Wis, Oct 30, 24; m 49, Dolores Lepak; c James, Nancy & Elizabeth. *Educ:* Univ Wis, BS, 49, MS, 50, PhD(civil & sanit eng), 54. *Prof Exp:* Res assoc sanit eng, Univ Wis, 49-50, instr civil eng, 50-53; sanit engr, Dow Chem Co, 53-54, develop engr, plastics tech serv, 54-57, mkt res specialist, 57-58, develop engr tech serv & develop, 58-59, environ eng consult, Chem Dept, 59-60; assoc prof civil & environ eng, Duke Univ, 60-64, prof & dir undergrad studies civil eng, 64-70; mgr, Process Systs Sect, Rex Chainbelt Inc, 70, mgr environ projs group, Ecol Div, 70-71, mgr tech mkt & environ projs, 71-72. *Concurrent Pos:* Prof engr, Wis, 54-; diplomate, Am Acad Environ Eng, 75-; mem, Coun Pub Health Consults, Nat Sanit Found, 89-96. *Mem:* Am Water Works Asn; Water Environ Fedn; Am Soc Civil Engrs; Int Asn Water Quality; Fed Water Qual Asn; Fed Con Environ Engr; Am Acad Environ Engr. *Res:* Water supply and treatment; pollution control; industrial and municipal waste control and treatment; water resources; radiological health; public health engineering; bacteriology of water and wastes; urban storm and sanitary drainage; spills of hazardous substances; residuals. *Mailing Add:* 4006 Thornapple St Chevy Chase MD 20815. *Fax:* 702-306-0312

BRYAN, FRANK LEON, BACTERIOLOGY, FOOD MICROBIOLOGY. *Current Pos:* training, Off Pub Health, New Eng Field Training Sta, USPHS, 56-58, environ health, Nat Commun Dis Ctr, 58-63, scientist dir & chief, Foodborne Dis Training, Ctr Dis Control, 65-85, DIR, FOOD SAFETY CONSULT & TRAINING, USPHS, 85- *Personal Data:* b Indianapolis, Ind, Aug 29, 30; m 52, Ruth Ann McDonald; c Steven & Sharryl. *Educ:* Ind Univ, BS, 53; Univ Mich, MPH, 56; Iowa State Univ, PhD(bact), 65. *Honors & Awards:* Sherman Res Awards. *Prof Exp:* Pub health aide milk & environ sanit, USPHS, Durham & Chapel Hill Local Health Dept, NC, 53; sanitarian, Ind State Bd Health, 55. *Concurrent Pos:* Lectr, Univ Mass, 56-58; consult, WHO, UN Food & Agr Orgn, Pan Am Health Orgn; adj fac, Emory Univ, 85 & 87. *Mem:* Am Soc Microbiol; Inst Food Technol; Sigma Xi; Int Comn Microbiol Spec Foods; Am Pub Health Asn; Int Asn Milk, Food & Environ Sanitarians; World Asn Vet Food Hyg. *Res:* Salmonella in turkey products; time-temperature factors in thawing, cooking, chilling and reheating turkey products rice, oriental foods and beef; clostridium perfringens in beef; staphylococcal intoxication; foodborne infections and intoxications and miscellaneous foodborne diseases; hazard analysis food service and catering operations; hazard analyses of street vended foods and homes in developing countries. *Mailing Add:* 8233 Pleasant Hill Rd Lithonia GA 30058

BRYAN, GEORGE TERRELL, MEDICINE, PHARMACOLOGY. *Current Pos:* instr cancer res, 61-63, from asst prof to prof clin oncol & surg, 63-75, PROF HUMAN ONCOL, SCH MED, UNIV WIS-MADISON, 75- *Personal Data:* b Antigo, Wis, July 29, 32; m 54; c 5. *Educ:* Univ Wis, BS, 54, MD, 57, PhD(oncol, biochem), 63. *Prof Exp:* Intern med, NC Baptist Hosp, Winston-Salem, 57-58. *Concurrent Pos:* Consult, Food & Drug Admin, Environ Protection Agency & Nat Cancer Inst. *Mem:* fel Am Col Physicians; Am Asn Cancer Res; Soc Surg Oncol; Am Soc Exp Path; Am Soc Biol Chemists. *Res:* Chemical carcinogenesis; clinical and experimental cancer chemotherapy; metabolic disorders and normal human metabolism; nutrition. *Mailing Add:* K/4 Rm 528 Clin Cancer Ctr Univ Wis 600 Highland Ave Madison WI 53792-0001. *Fax:* 608-263-8613

BRYAN, GEORGE THOMAS, MEDICAL EDUCATION. *Current Pos:* from asst prof to assoc prof, Univ Tex, 63-73, asst dir, Clin Study Ctr & dir, Div Endocrinol, Dept Pediat, 63-70, assoc dean curric affairs, 74-77, PROF PEDIAT, UNIV TEX MED BR, GALVESTON, 73-, DEAN MED, 77-, VPRES ACAD AFFAIRS, 83- *Personal Data:* b Sewanee, Tenn, Nov 19, 30; m 52; c 2. *Educ:* Univ Tenn, MD, 55; Am Bd Pediat, dipl, 69. *Prof Exp:* Intern, DC Gen Hosp, 55-56; resident pediat, State Univ Iowa Hosps, 56-58, fel pediat endocrinol, 58-59; clin assoc pediat, Nat Inst Allergy & Infectious Dis, 59-60, pediatrician, Clin Endocrinol Br, 61-63. *Concurrent Pos:* Markle Found scholar acad med, 67-72. *Mem:* AMA; Am Pediat Soc; Soc Pediat Res; Endocrine Soc; Am Fedn Clin Res. *Res:* Adrenal steroid biosynthesis; carcadian periodicity; hypertension; hypopituitarism. *Mailing Add:* Off Dean Emer Univ Tex Med Br Rt 1011 Galveston TX 77550-1011

BRYAN, GORDON HENRY, PHARMACOLOGY. *Current Pos:* Instr pharm, 47-49, from asst prof to prof, 50-80, EMER PROF PHARMACOL, UNIV MONT, 80- *Personal Data:* b Ashton, Idaho, Oct 22, 15; m 46; c 2. *Educ:* Mont State Univ, BS, 42, MS, 47; Univ Md, PhD(pharmacol), 56. *Concurrent Pos:* NIH fel, 64-65; vis lectr med, Univ Utah, 57. *Mem:* AAAS; Am Pharmaceut Asn. *Res:* Cardiology. *Mailing Add:* 515 Dickinson St Missoula MT 59802

BRYAN, HERBERT HARRIS, HORTICULTURE, PLANT PHYSIOLOGY. *Current Pos:* Asst prof hort, NFla Exp Sta, Univ Fla, 64-66, asst prof, Agr Res & Educ Ctr, 67-74, assoc prof hort & assoc horticulturist, 74-80, PROF HORT, 80- *Personal Data:* b Brunswick, Ga, Jan 25, 32; m 56; c 2. *Educ:* Univ Fla, BSA, 53; Cornell Univ, MS, 61, PhD(veg crops), 64. *Mem:* Am Soc Hort Sci; Int Soc Hort Sci. *Res:* Nutrition and herbicides of vegetables and peaches; mechanical harvesting of tomatoes for fresh market; cultural practices; mulches; pole bean breeding; cover crops rotation with potatoes; bean and tomato growth regulators and plant populations. *Mailing Add:* 187 NW 20th St Homestead FL 33030

BRYAN, HORACE ALDEN, INORGANIC CHEMISTRY. *Current Pos:* from asst prof to assoc prof, 55-67, PROF CHEM, DAVIDSON COL, 67- *Personal Data:* b Bluff City, Tenn, Jan 1, 28. *Educ:* King Col, BS, 50; Univ Tenn, PhD, 55. *Prof Exp:* Asst inorg chem, Univ Tenn, 51-55. *Concurrent Pos:* Vis prof chem, Univ Hawaii, 85. *Mem:* Am Chem Soc. *Res:* Polarography of azo compounds; extraction of metal-containing anions; cation-ligand equilibria. *Mailing Add:* PO Box 503 Davidson NC 28036-0503

BRYAN, JAMES BEVAN, precision engineering, for more information see previous edition

BRYAN, JAMES CLARENCE, CHEMICAL ENGINEERING. *Current Pos:* RETIRED. *Personal Data:* b Tenn, Jan 26, 23; m 48, Helen L Sehorn; c James C (deceased) & James F. *Educ:* Univ Tenn, BS, 48, MS, 52, PhD(chem eng), 54. *Prof Exp:* Process engr, Phillips Petrol Co, 48-50; sr engr nylon, E I du Pont de Nemours & Co, Inc, 54-62, sr res engr, 62-65 & 70-84, process supvr, 65-70. *Concurrent Pos:* Chmn, Palmetto Sect, Am Inst Chem Engrs. *Mem:* Am Chem Soc; fel Am Inst Chem Engrs; Sigma Xi. *Res:* Polymerization technology; process control analysis; chemical process analysis; mathematical statistics; probability. *Mailing Add:* 1900 Brook Dr Camden SC 29020

BRYAN, JOHN HENRY DONALD, GENETIC DISEASES, MALE STERILITY & HYDROCEPHALUS. *Current Pos:* PROF ZOOL, UNIV GA, 67- *Personal Data:* b London, Eng, Sept 18, 26; nat US; m 52; c 2. *Educ:* Univ Sheffield, BSc, 47; Columbia Univ, AM, 49, PhD(zool), 52. *Honors & Awards:* Paxton lectr, Int Asn Torch Clubs, 86. *Prof Exp:* Lectr zool, Columbia Univ, 49-50; instr biol, Mass Inst Technol, 51-54; asst prof genetics, Iowa State Univ, 54-60, from asst prof to assoc prof zool, 60-67, chmn comt cell biol, 61-67. *Concurrent Pos:* Consult, NSF-AID Indian Educ Prog, 68. *Mem:* Fel AAAS; Am Soc Cell Biol; Am Soc Zool; Genetics Soc Am; Sigma Xi. *Res:* Cell structure and function, especially the nucleus; cytochemistry; chromosome ultrastructure; genetic control of cell differentiation, especially gametogenesis; use of mutations as probes of cell function, including male infertility and neurological development. *Mailing Add:* Dept Zool Univ Ga Biol Sci Bldg Athens GA 30602-0001. *Fax:* 706-542-4271

BRYAN, JOHN KENT, PLANT PHYSIOLOGY, BIOCHEMISTRY. *Current Pos:* asst prof bot, 64-69, assoc prof biol, 70-76, PROF BIOL, SYRACUSE UNIV, 77-, ASSOC CHAIR, 91- *Personal Data:* b Indianapolis, Ind, Mar 20, 36; m 58, Patricia A Karius. *Educ:* Butler Univ, BS, 58; Univ Tex, PhD(cellular physiol), 62. *Prof Exp:* Res asst biochem, Inst Psychiat Res, Sch Med, Ind Univ, 58-59; res asst electron micros, Plant Res Inst, Univ Tex, 62; res assoc molecular biol, Wash Univ, 62-64. *Mem:* AAAS; Am Soc Plant Physiol; Am Soc Biol Chem & Molecualr Biol; Int Soc Plant Molecular Biol; Am Inst Biol Sci. *Res:* Biochemistry of plant growth and development; control mechanisms of amino acid biosynthesis. *Mailing Add:* Dept Biol Biol Res Labs Syracuse Univ 130 College Pl Syracuse NY 13244-1220. *Fax:* 315-443-2012; *E-Mail:* jkbryan@cyr.edu

BRYAN, JOSEPH, BIOCHEMISTRY, CELL BIOLOGY. *Current Pos:* assoc prof, 78-80, PROF CELL BIOL, BAYLOR COL MED, 80- *Personal Data:* b Pittsburgh, Pa. *Educ:* Rensselaer Polytech Inst, BS, 63, Univ Pa, PhD(anat), 67. *Prof Exp:* Instr med, Univ Pa, 63-64; fel cell biol, Univ Calif, Berkeley, 67-71, actg asst prof zool, 70-71; from asst prof to assoc prof biol, Univ Pa, 71-78. *Concurrent Pos:* Mem bd, NIH Ad Hoc Cell Biol Study Sect, 78-79, Molecular Biol Study Sect, 80-81 & 81-83 & Cell Biol Study Sect, 83-85. *Mem:* Am Soc Cell Biol; AAAS. *Res:* Biochemistry and cell biology of actin and actin associated proteins. *Mailing Add:* Dept Cell Biol Baylor Col Med One Baylor Plaza Houston TX 77030. *Fax:* 713-790-0545

BRYAN, KIRK, (JR), METEOROLOGY. *Current Pos:* oceanogr, Geophys Fluid Dynamics Lab, Nat Oceanog & Atmospheric Admin, 68-94, SR RES SCHOLAR, PRINCETON UNIV, 94- *Personal Data:* b Albuquerque, NMex, July 21, 29; m 56; c Samuel & Elizabeth (Kohnstamm). *Educ:* Yale Univ, BS, 51; Mass Inst Technol, PhD(meteorol), 57. *Honors & Awards:* Sverdrup Gold Medal, Am Meteorol Soc, 70; Maurice Ewing Medal, Am Geophys Union, 93. *Prof Exp:* Res assoc meteorol, Woods Hole Oceanog Inst, 58-61; res meteorologist, Gen Circulation Res Lab, US Weather Bur, 61-68. *Concurrent Pos:* Vis lectr, Princeton Univ, 68-78; mem, Panel Climatic Variation, Global Atmos Res Prog, Nat Acad Sci, 72-74; chmn working group numerical models, Sci Comt Ocean Res, 75-77; pres, Oceanog Sect, Am Geophys Union, 76-78. *Mem:* Fel Am Meteorol Soc; Am Geophys Union; fel Am Geophys Soc; foreign mem Russ Acad Sci. *Res:* Dynamic meteorology; physical oceanography; general circulation of the atmosphere and the oceans. *Mailing Add:* Dept Geol Sci Princeton Univ Princeton NJ 08544-1003

BRYAN, PHILIP STEVEN, INORGANIC CHEMISTRY. *Current Pos:* res chemist, 77-79, SR RES CHEMIST, EASTMAN KODAK CO, 80- *Personal Data:* b Lima, Ohio, Oct 5, 44; m 67; c 2. *Educ:* Ohio State Univ, BS, 66; Univ Mich, PhD(chem), 70. *Prof Exp:* Asst prof chem, Macalester Col, 71-72; asst prof chem, Colgate Univ, 72-77. *Mem:* Am Chem Soc. *Res:* Synthesis and characterization of transition metal complexes containing multidentate ligands; polymer-bound ligands and complexes and other new inorganic materials. *Mailing Add:* Eastman Kodak Co Res Labs B-81 Rochester NY 14650-2033

BRYAN, RICHARD D S, CONSERVATIONIST. *Honors & Awards:* Oak Leaf Award, Nature Conservancy, 93. *Mem:* Nature Conservancy. *Mailing Add:* 10 Buttonwood Lane E Rumson NJ 07760-1010

BRYAN, ROBERT FINLAY, CRYSTALLOGRAPHY. *Current Pos:* assoc prof, 67-82, PROF CHEM, UNIV VA, 82- *Personal Data:* b Rhu, Scotland, May 15, 33. *Educ:* Glasgow Univ, BSc, 54, PhD(chem), 57. *Prof Exp:* Res assoc chem, Fed Inst Technol, Zurich, 57-59; res assoc biol, Mass Inst Technol, 59-61; asst prof biophysics, Sch Med, Johns Hopkins Univ, 61-67. *Concurrent Pos:* Fel, Battelle, 57-59, Sloane, 59-60 & NIH, 60-61. *Mem:* Am Crystallog Asn. *Res:* X-ray diffraction studies of molecular and crystal structure, especially of materials showing liquid-crystalline behavior. *Mailing Add:* Dept Chem Univ Va Charlottesville VA 22901. *Fax:* 804-924-3710; *E-Mail:* rfb6w@virginia.edu

BRYAN, ROBERT H(OWELL), MATERIALS SCIENCE, NUCLEAR ENGINEERING. *Current Pos:* CONSULT, 89- *Personal Data:* b Hendersonville, Tenn, May 19, 24; m 46, Dorothy Oakley; c 4. *Educ:* US Mil Acad, BS, 46; NC State Col, MS, 53, PhD(nuclear eng), 54. *Prof Exp:* Spec sci employee, Argonne Nat Lab, 54-56; tech analyst, US Atomic Energy Comn, 56-58, reactor engr, 58-61, chief, Res & Power Reactor Safety Br, 61-64, chief, Facilities Standards Br, 64-67; asst dir nuclear safety prog, Oak Ridge Nat Lab, 67-74, asst dir heavy-sect steel technol prog, 74-82, struct testing & analytical group leader, 82-89. *Mem:* Am Phys Soc. *Res:* Physics of fast nuclear reactors; neutron production by fission; reactor safety; fracture mechanics; large vessel testing. *Mailing Add:* 5424 Yosemite Trail Knoxville TN 37909

BRYAN, ROBERT NEFF, LINEAR ALGEBRA. *Current Pos:* asst prof, 69-70, ASSOC PROF MATH, UNIV WESTERN ONT, 70- *Personal Data:* b Salt Lake City, Utah, Mar 18, 39; m 88, Teresa A Stoyle; c Lindsay W, Allison W & Michael R. *Educ:* Univ Utah, BA, 61, MA, 62, PhD(differential equations), 65. *Prof Exp:* Asst prof math, Ithaca Col, 65-69. *Concurrent Pos:* Vis prof, Univ Ulm, WGer, 78-79; vis scholar, Univ Utah, 85-86. *Mem:* Math Asn Am; Can Math Soc. *Res:* Linear differential systems with general boundary conditions; unbounded linear operators. *Mailing Add:* Dept Math Univ Western Ont London ON N6A 5B7 Can

BRYAN, ROBERT NICK, NEURORADIOLOGY & NEUROSURGERY, OTOLARYNGOLOGY. *Current Pos:* PROF RADIOL & NEUROSURG, JOHNS HOPKINS UNIV SCH MED, 88-, PROF OTOLARYNGOL, 90-, VCHMN, DEPT RADIOL, 96- *Personal Data:* b Stamford, Tex, Feb 5, 44. *Educ:* Univ Tex, MD, 69, PhD(anat), 73; Am Bd Radiol, cert, 73. *Prof Exp:* Instr anat, Univ Tex Med Br, 66-68, intern rotating radiologist, 69-70, residency, 71-73; radiologist & chief spec procedures lab, Nat Med Ctr, USNR, 74-76; assoc prof clin radiol, Colombia Univ, 76-77; asst prof, Dept Radiol, Baylor Col Med, 77-78, Neurobiol Fel Prog, 77-88, assoc prof & assoc chmn, 78-83, dir biomed, NMR Ctr, 81-88, prof radiol, 83-88, prof, Ctr Biotechnol, 86-88. *Concurrent Pos:* NIH post doctoral fel, 70-71, spec fel, 73-74; assoc attend radiologist, Baylor Col Med, 77-78; dir neuroradiol, Methodist Hosp, 77-85, attend radiologist, 77-88, dir, MRI, 85-88; assoc attend radiologist, Bentaub Gen Hosp, 79-88; consult radiologist, Tex Children's Hosp; grantee, NIH, 83-; Fulbright sr scholar, Marseilles, France, 94-95. *Mem:* Soc Neurosci; Am Col Radiol; Am Soc Neuroradiol; Am Soc Head & Neck Radiol; Radiol Soc NAm; AAAS; Am Roentgen Ray Soc; Soc Magnetic Resonance Imaging; Soc Magnetic Resonance Med. *Res:* Double midline intracranial atypical teratomas: a recognizable neuroendocrinologic syndrome; locating and somatotopic organization of the cells of origin of the spinocervical tract; infantile hydrocephalus and cerebral angiography; published 11 articles. *Mailing Add:* Dept Radiol Johns Hopkins Hosp Baltimore MD 21287-2182

BRYAN, RONALD ARTHUR, NUCLEAR & PARTICLE THEORY. *Current Pos:* vis lectr, 68-69, assoc prof, 69-73, PROF PHYSICS, TEX A&M UNIV, 73- *Personal Data:* b Portland, Ore, June 16, 32; m 53, 63, Mary Lind; c William, Scott, Phoebe & Jennifer. *Educ:* Yale Univ, BS, 54; Univ Rochester, PhD(theoret physics), 61. *Prof Exp:* Res assoc theoret physics, Univ Calif, Los Angeles, 60-63; physicist, Lab Nuclear Physics, Univ Paris, 63-64; physicist, Lawrence Radiation Lab, 64-67. *Concurrent Pos:* NATO fel, France, 63-64; long term vis staff mem, Los Alamos Sci Lab, 73-74; Nordic Inst Theoret Atomic Physics fel, Univ Helsinki, Finland, 74-75; vis prof, Univ Nijmegen, Netherlands, 79-80. *Mem:* Fel Am Phys Soc; AAAS. *Res:* Scattering theory; two-nucleon interaction; elementary particles in higher-dimensional space. *Mailing Add:* Dept Physics Tex A&M Univ College Station TX 77843. *Fax:* 409-693-5554; *E-Mail:* bryan@phys.tamu.edu

BRYAN, SARA E, biochemistry, for more information see previous edition

BRYAN, THOMAS T, PHYSICAL CHEMISTRY, BIOMATERIALS. *Current Pos:* RES SPECIALIST BIOMAT, 3M CO, 61- *Personal Data:* b Yugoslavia, Sept 27, 25; US citizen; m 49; c 4. *Educ:* Univ Belgrade, MS, 52. *Prof Exp:* Res chemist photochem, Lindy Ain, 54-56; res chemist crystal growth, Carborundum, 56-58; res chemist photochem, Am Photog Equip Co, 58-61. *Mem:* Am Chem Soc; Soc Biomat. *Res:* Biomaterials as artificial prosthetic devices; particularly hard tissue replacement and dental applications; surface and interface reactions to biomedical systems; dental materials. *Mailing Add:* 212 Edgecumbe Dr St Paul MN 55115

BRYAN, WILBUR LOWELL, PHARMACEUTICAL CHEMISTRY. *Current Pos:* chemist, 45-61, res investr, 61-69, SR RES INVESTR PHARMACEUT, E R SQUIBB & SONS, 69- *Personal Data:* b South River, NJ, Feb 20, 21; m 47. *Educ:* Lafayette Col, BA, 42. *Prof Exp:* Chemist explosives, Hercules Powder Co, 42-43. *Mem:* Am Chem Soc; NY Acad Sci. *Res:* Isolation techniques of natural products, particularly antibiotics. *Mailing Add:* 611 Canal Rd Somerset NJ 08873-7325

BRYAN, WILFRED BOTTRILL, MARINE GEOLOGY, PLANETARY GEOLOGY. *Current Pos:* assoc scientist, 70-82, SR SCIENTIST, DEPT GEOL & GEOPHYS, WOODS HOLE OCEANOG INST, 82- *Personal Data:* b Waterbury, Conn, Feb 18, 32; m 53; c 3. *Educ:* Dartmouth Col, BA, 54; Univ Wis-Madison, MA, 56, PhD(petrol), 59. *Prof Exp:* Geologist, M A Hanna Co, 59-61; sr lectr petrol, Univ Queensland, 61-67; sr fel, Carnegie Inst, Geophys Lab, 67-70. *Concurrent Pos:* Field asst, US Geol Survey, 53-59; consult, Exoil Proprietary Ltd & Magellan Petrol Co, 63-65 & Tennant Mineral Develop Co Proprietary Ltd, 65-67; mem subcomt volcanology, Australian Acad Sci, 66-67; leader, Nat Geog-Smithsonian Exped, Tonga Islands, 69; chief scientist oceanog expeds, 71-88; mem team 5, Planetary Basaltic Volcanism Proj, NASA, 76-79; vis prof, Dept Oceanog, Univ Wash, 80, Dept Earth Planetary Sci, McDonnell Ctr, 83, Dept Geol, Univ Hawaii, 89. *Mem:* Geol Soc Australia; Geol Soc Am; Am Geophys Union; Int Asn Volcanology; Mineral Soc Gt Brit & Ireland; Sigma Xi; Math Asn Am. *Res:* Lunar and planetary volcanology; distribution and geological relationships of volcanic rocks in and around the ocean basins; compositional relationships and fractionation effects within genetically related rock suites; relations between geophysical phenomena and igneous activity; seafloor structure and morphology. *Mailing Add:* 50 Stowers St Eat Falmouth MA 02543-6758

BRYAN, WILLIAM L, BIOTECHNOLOGY. *Current Pos:* RETIRED. *Personal Data:* b Gainesville, Fla, Sept 25, 28; m 57; c 3. *Educ:* Univ Fla, BChE, 49; Yale Univ, DEng, 59. *Prof Exp:* Develop engr, Rohm & Haas Co, 54-59, res engr ballistics, Redstone Arsenal Res Div, 59; res engr, E I du Pont de Nemours & Co, Inc, 59-63, staff engr film dept, 63-65, sr res engr textile fibers dept, 65-71; res chem engr, US Citrus & Subtrop Prod Lab, USDA, 71-79, res chem engr, Southern Agr Energy Ctr, 80-85, chem engr, Northern Regional Res Ctr, 85-90, chem engr, Nat Ctr Agr Utilization Res, 91. *Mem:* Am Inst Chem Engrs; Am Chem Soc; AAAS. *Res:* Research and development for manufacture of agricultural chemicals, ion exchange resins, rocket propellants, industrial films and fibers, processing of citrus fruit, sweet sorghum processing, solid substrate fermentation, viscosity measurement, manufacture of acetate road deicers. *Mailing Add:* 61614-1015 Peoria IL 61614

BRYAN, WILLIAM PHELAN, biochemistry, biophysics, for more information see previous edition

BRYANS, ALEXANDER (MCKELVEY), MEDICINE, PEDIATRICS. *Current Pos:* from assoc prof to prof, 59-71, dir, Health Sci Off Educ, 71-87, EMER PROF PEDIAT, QUEEN'S UNIV, ONT, 87- *Personal Data:* b Toronto, Ont, Sept 16, 21; m 54; c 3. *Educ:* Univ Toronto, MD, 44; Mich State Univ, MA, 71; FRCP, 52. *Prof Exp:* McLaughlin traveling fel, 56-57. *Mem:* Fel Am Acad Pediat; Can Med Asn; Can Pediat Soc; Physicians Global Survival Can; Int Physicians Prev Nuclear War. *Res:* Medical education. *Mailing Add:* 31 Lakeland Pt Dr Kingston ON K7M 4E8 Can

BRYANS, CHARLES IVERSON, JR, obstetrics & gynecology; deceased, see previous edition for last biography

BRYANS, JOHN THOMAS, ANIMAL VIROLOGY. *Current Pos:* Virologist, Univ Ky, 54-60, chmn dept, 74-87, prof vet sci, Agr Exp Sta, 60-91, distinguished alumni prof, 87-91, EMER PROF VET SCI, UNIV KY, 91- *Personal Data:* b Paterson, NJ, June 1, 24; m 59; c 2. *Educ:* Fla Southern Col, BS, 49; Univ Ky, MS, 51; Cornell Univ, PhD(vet bact & path), 54. *Hon Degrees:* DMV, Univ Bern, Switz, 78. *Mem:* AAAS; Am Soc Microbiol; Am Vet Med Asn. *Res:* Etiology, immunology and epizootiology of infectious diseases of domestic animals; pathogenesis and immunology of herpesviral infection. *Mailing Add:* 1158 Athenia Dr Lexington KY 40504

BRYANS, TRABUE DALEY, MICROBIOLOGY, BIOLOGY. *Current Pos:* CONSULT, 93- *Personal Data:* b Atlanta, Ga, Mar 20, 52. *Educ:* Univ Ga, BS, 75. *Prof Exp:* Chief microbiologist, MacMillan Res Ltd, 75-76; med technologist microbiol, Med Col Ga, 77-78; dir microbiol, MacMillan Res, Ltd, 78-85, vpres, 85-93. *Mem:* Am Soc Clin Pathologists; Am Soc Micro Biol. *Res:* Sterility testing of medical products, microbiology of foods and water. *Mailing Add:* 1400 Pine Springs Dr Kennesaw GA 30152

BRYANT, BARBARA EVERITT, SURVEY RESEARCH. *Current Pos:* RES SCIENTIST, SCH BUS ADMIN, UNIV MICH, 93- *Personal Data:* b Ann Arbor, Mich, Apr 5, 26; m 48, John H; c Linda (Valentine), Randal E & Lois (Chen). *Educ:* Cornell Univ, BA, 47; Mich State Univ, MA, 67, PhD(commun), 70. *Hon Degrees:* LHD, Univ Ill, Urbana-Champaign, 94. *Prof Exp:* Art ed, Chem Eng Mag, McGraw-Hill Publ Co, NY, 47-48; ed res asst, Grad Col, Univ Ill, 48-49; freelance ed, 50-61; dir pub rels & sci course coordr, Div Continuing Educ, Oakland Univ, Rochester, Mich, 61-65; res asst, Mich State Univ, 65-70; sr res analyst & sr vpres, Mkt Opinion Res, Detroit, 70-89; dir, Bur Census, US Dept Com, US Dept Com, Washington, DC, 89-93. *Concurrent Pos:* Mem, Job Develop Auth, State Mich, 80-85; mem adv comt, US Census Bur, 80-86; adj prof, Grad Sch Bus Admin, Univ Mich, 84-85; nat headliner, Women Commun, Inc, 80; mem nat bd, Am Mkt Asn; vpres, Anjoy QSP Co, 94- *Mem:* Am Mkt Asn; Women Commun; Am Statist Asn; Am Asn Pub Opinion Res; Pop Asn Am; Am Soc Qual Control. *Res:* Combining attitudes, interests and behaviors with traditional demographics to segment populations into life style clusters; administering 1990 census, adjustment research and survey modernization at Bureau of the Census; operationalization and administration of American Customer Satisfaction Index (ACSI). *Mailing Add:* Sch Bus Admin Univ Mich Ann Arbor MI 48109-1234. *Fax:* 313-668-0474; *E-Mail:* barbara_bryant.@ccmail.bus.umich.edu

BRYANT, BEN S, WOOD TECHNOLOGY. *Current Pos:* From instr to prof, 49-88, dir, Inst Forest Prod, 60-64, EMER PROF WOOD SCI & TECHNOL, COL FOREST RESOURCES, UNIV WASH, 88- *Personal Data:* b Seattle, Wash, Mar 28, 23; m 47; c 3. *Educ:* Univ Wash, BS, 47, MS, 48; Yale Univ, DFor(wood technol), 51. *Concurrent Pos:* Consult, forest prod industs, asn, chem & mach co, US & foreign govts in forest prod develop, adhesive develop, forest prod industs develop & surv, 51- *Mem:* Soc Am Foresters; Forest Prod Res Soc; Tech Asn Pulp & Paper Indust; Soc Wood Sci & Technol. *Res:* Structural utilization of wood; adhesion and gluing process technology; product development methods; forest utilization. *Mailing Add:* 4102 51st Ave NE Seattle WA 98105

BRYANT, BILLY FINNEY, MATHEMATICS. *Current Pos:* From instr to prof, 48-86, chmn dept, 70-76, EMER PROF MATH, VANDERBILT UNIV, 86- *Personal Data:* b McKenzie, Tenn, Nov 29, 22; m 46, Mary N Park; c Robert, David & Elizabeth. *Educ:* Univ SC, BS, 45; Peabody Col, BA, 48; Vanderbilt Univ, PhD(math), 54. *Honors & Awards:* Meritorious Serv Award, Math Asn Am. *Concurrent Pos:* Ford Found fac fel, Princeton Univ, 55-56; sci fac fel, Univ Calif, Berkeley, 67-68. *Mem:* Am Math Soc; Math Asn Am. *Res:* Point set topology. *Mailing Add:* 6020 Sherwood Dr Nashville TN 37215-5733

BRYANT, BRUCE HAZELTON, REGIONAL GEOLOGY. *Current Pos:* Geologist, 55-63, res geologist, 63-69, GEOLOGIST, US GEOL SURV, 69- *Personal Data:* b New York, NY, Sept 25, 30; m 55, Dolores Becker; c Lisa, Ross, Keith & Mark. *Educ:* Dartmouth Col, AB, 51; Univ Wash, PhD(geol), 55. *Mem:* Fel Mineral Soc Am; fel Geol Soc Am; Am Geophys Union. *Res:* Geologic mapping; structure; petrology of igneous and metamorphic rocks; boundary between the basin and range and Colorado plateau provinces in West Central Arizona. *Mailing Add:* 26553 Columbine Glen Ave Golden CO 80401. *Fax:* 303-236-0214

BRYANT, DAVID, HYDROFORMYLATION CHEMISTRY, ORGANIC CHEMISTRY. *Current Pos:* res scientist, Union Carbide Corp, 67-75, sr res scientist, 75-79, corp fel, 84-87, SR CORP FEL, UNION CARBIDE CORP, 87- *Personal Data:* b Greensboro, NC, May 8, 36. *Educ:* Wake Forest Univ, BS, 58; Duke Univ, PhD(org chem), 61. *Hon Degrees:* DSc, Wake Forest Univ, 90. *Honors & Awards:* Chem Pioneer Award, Am Inst Chemists, 89; Indust Chem Award, Am Chem Soc, 92, Carothers Award, 93. *Mem:* Am Chem Soc; Am Inst Chemists. *Mailing Add:* Union Carbide Corp Tech Ctr PO Box 8361 South Charleston WV 25303. *Fax:* 304-747-4123; *E-Mail:* adrbrd1@peabody.sct.ucarb.com

BRYANT, DONALD G, MINING. *Current Pos:* DESIGNING ENGR, MARTIN MARIETTA, 86- *Personal Data:* b Hollywood, Calif, June 21, 27. *Educ:* Univ Ariz, BA, 54; Calif Tech Inst, MA, 55; Stanford Univ, PhD(geol), 64. *Prof Exp:* Chief explor geologist, Molybdenum Corp, 64-70; pres, Donald G Bryant Inc, 70-87. *Mem:* Fel Geol Soc Am; Soc Econ Geologists. *Mailing Add:* 714 S Filmore St Denver CO 80209

BRYANT, EDWARD CLARK, STATISTICS. *Current Pos:* pres, 61-78, chmn, 78-85, EMER CHMN STATIST & MGT, WESTAT INC, 85- *Personal Data:* b Hat Creek, Wyo, June 28, 15; m 41; c 2. *Educ:* Univ Wyo, BS, 38, MS, 40; Iowa State Univ, PhD(statist), 55. *Prof Exp:* Jr statistician & economist, Interstate Com Comn, 40-42; statistician, War Prod Bd, 42-43; chief statistician, Armed Forces, Mid Pac, 46-47; from asst prof to prof statist, Univ Wyo, 47-61. *Concurrent Pos:* Vis prof math, Ariz State Univ, 61-63. *Mem:* Fel Am Statist Asn; fel AAAS; Int Asn Surv Statisticians; Prof Servs Coun; Am Soc Qual Control. *Res:* Efficiency of sample survey designs; statistical analysis; evaluation of government programs; information retrieval; statistical process control. *Mailing Add:* 9000 Rouen Lane Potomac MD 20854

BRYANT, ERNEST ATHERTON, NUCLEAR CHEMISTRY, GEOCHEMISTRY. *Current Pos:* mem staff radiochem, Los Alamos Nat Lab, Univ Calif, 57-71, alt group leader radiochem, 71-80, group leader isotope geochem, 80-87, STAFF MEM ISOTOPE GEOCHEM, LOS ALAMOS NAT LAB, UNIV CALIF, 87- *Personal Data:* b Brewster, Mass, Oct 13, 31; m 53; c 2. *Educ:* Univ NMex, BS, 53; Washington Univ, PhD(radiochem), 56. *Prof Exp:* Instr chem, Washington Univ, 56-57. *Mem:* AAAS; Am Chem Soc. *Res:* High temperature chemistry; nuclear chemistry; radiochemical analysis; reactor technology; geologic behavior of radioactive waste; atmospheric chemistry; mass spectrometry; photo acoustic spectroscopy. *Mailing Add:* 125 La Senda Rd Los Alamos NM 87544

BRYANT, GEORGE MACON, FIBER SCIENCE, TEXTILE & PAPER TECHNOLOGY. *Current Pos:* CONSULT, 86- *Personal Data:* b Anniston, Ala, Aug 3, 26; m 50, Merrilee Miles; c Fred B II & George M Jr. *Educ:* Auburn Univ, BS, 48; Inst Textile Technol, MS, 50; Princeton Univ, MA, 52, PhD(chem), 54. *Honors & Awards:* Award, Fiber Soc, 64; Henry Milson Award, Am Inst Textile Chemists & Colorists, 82; Sci Achievement Award, Am Chem Soc, 79. *Prof Exp:* Res chemist, Chem Div, Union Carbide Corp, 54-58, group leader, 58-63, res & develop mgr textile prod, 63-66, technol mgr, Fibers & Fabrics Div, 66-71, develop assoc res & develop, 71-75, corp res fel, 75-86. *Concurrent Pos:* Lectr, Fiber Soc, 66 & 81; consult, fiber, textile & paper fields, 86- *Mem:* Am Chem Soc; Sigma Xi; Fiber Soc (pres, 68). *Res:* Physical chemistry of textile fibers; chemicals and polymers for oil recovery; foam finishing and dyeing of fabrics and paper; mechanical behavior of polymers; textile and paper chemicals. *Mailing Add:* 1204 Williamsburg Way Charleston WV 25314

BRYANT, GLENN D(ONALD), aeronautics, marine engineering; deceased, see previous edition for last biography

BRYANT, HENRY UHLMAN, PHARMACOLOGY. *Current Pos:* sr pharmacologist, 88-93, RES SCIENTIST, ELI LILLY & CO, 93- *Personal Data:* b Indianapolis, Inc, Mar 21, 58. *Educ:* Purdue Univ, BPharm, 81, MS, 84, PhD(pharmacol), 86. *Honors & Awards:* Glen L Jenkins Award, Purdue Univ, 85; Nat Res Coun Award, 86; Mead-Johnson Travel Award, Am Col Neuropsychopharmacol, 87. *Prof Exp:* Res assoc immunopharmacol, Walter Reed Army Inst Res, 86-88. *Mem:* Am Soc Bone & Mineral Res; Soc Neurosci; Am Soc Pharmacol & Exp Therapeut. *Res:* Pharmacology. *Mailing Add:* Div Skeletal Dis Res Eli Lilly & Co Lilly Corp Ctr Indianapolis IN 46285-0001

BRYANT, HOWARD CARNES, HIGH ENERGY ATOMIC PHYSICS. *Current Pos:* from asst prof to assoc prof, 60-71, PROF PHYSICS, UNIV NMEX, 71- *Personal Data:* b Fresno, Calif, July 9, 33; m 60, Mona Jordan; c Matthew, Clifford & Susannah. *Educ:* Univ Calif, Berkeley, BA, 55; Univ Mich, MS, 57, PhD(physics), 61. *Concurrent Pos:* Vis scientist, Stanford Linear Accelerator Ctr, 67-69; consult, Los Alamos Sci Lab, 61-; sr vis fel, Queen Mary Col, Univ London, 75-76; Fulbright guest prof, Univ Innsbruck, Austria, 83-84; fac res lectr, 85. *Mem:* Optical Soc Am; fel Am Phys Soc; Am Asn Physics Teachers. *Res:* Experimental particle and atomic physics; physical optics. *Mailing Add:* Dept Physics & Astromony Univ NMex 800 Yale Blvd NE Albuquerque NM 87131-1156. *Fax:* 505-277-1520; *E-Mail:* hzero@bootes.unm.edu

BRYANT, JOHN H(AROLD), PHYSICAL ELECTRONICS. *Current Pos:* vis scholar, 78-85, ADJ RES SCIENTIST, ELEC ENG & COMPUT SCI DEPT, UNIV MICH, 85- *Personal Data:* b Baird, Tex, Apr 15, 20; m 48, Barbara Everitt; c Linda B (Valentine), Randal E & Lois B (Chen). *Educ:* Tex A&M Univ, BS, 42; Univ Ill, MS, 46, PhD(elec eng), 49. *Honors & Awards:* Microwave Career Award, Inst Elec & Electronics Engrs, 96. *Prof Exp:* Staff, IT&T Res Labs, 49-55, Bendix Corp, Res Labs, 55-62; pres, Omni Spectra, Inc, 62-80. *Concurrent Pos:* Mem numerous comts, Inst Elec & Electronics Engrs, 65- *Mem:* Am Phys Soc; fel Inst Elec & Electronics Engrs; Sigma Xi. *Res:* History of electromagnetics; history of radar and allied systems and technology; electron tubes; author of numerous publications; granted 14 patents. *Mailing Add:* 1505 Sheridan Dr Ann Arbor MI 48104

BRYANT, JOHN LOGAN, MATHEMATICS. *Current Pos:* from asst prof to assoc prof, 66-74, chmn, Dept Math & Comput Sci, 80-84, PROF MATH, FLA STATE UNIV, 74- *Personal Data:* b Corinth, Miss, Aug, 27, 40; m 58; c 2. *Educ:* Univ Miss, BS & MS, 62; Univ Ga, PhD(math), 65. *Prof Exp:* Asst prof math, Univ Miss, 65-66. *Mem:* Am Math Soc; Math Asn Am. *Res:* Geometric topology; properties of topological embeddings of polyhedra. *Mailing Add:* Dept Math Fla State Univ 600 W College Ave Tallahassee FL 32306-1096

BRYANT, LAWRENCE E, JR, MECHANICAL ENGINEERING, NUCLEAR ENGINEERING. *Current Pos:* SUPVR NONDESTRUCTIVE TESTING, LOS ALAMOS NAT LAB, 61- *Personal Data:* b Nashville, Tenn, Mar 9, 36; m 71; c 2. *Educ:* Vanderbilt Univ, BS, 58, MS, 59. *Prof Exp:* Naval officer mech & nuclear eng, Naval Res Lab, Washington, DC, 59-61. *Mem:* Fel Am Soc Nondestructive Testing. *Res:* Industrial radiography; ranging from low energy, microradiography to high energy radiography; flash (high speed) radiography and cine radiography, infrared imaging, high speed videography. *Mailing Add:* 1034A 48th St Los Alamos NM 87544

BRYANT, LESTER RICHARD, MEDICINE, THORACIC SURGERY. *Current Pos:* PROF SURG & DEAN, SCH MED, UNIV MO, COLUMBIA, MO, 89- *Personal Data:* b Louisville, Ky, Sept 8, 30; m 84, Linda; c 2. *Educ:* Univ Ky, BS, 51; Univ Cincinnati, MD, 55, DSc(surg), 62; Am Bd Surg, dipl, 62; Am Bd Thoracic Surg, dipl, 63. *Prof Exp:* Fel physiol, Col Med, Baylor Univ, 61; instr, Univ Cincinnati, 61-62; from instr to prof surg, Med Ctr, Univ Ky, 62-73; prof surg & chief thoracic & cardiovasc surg, La State Univ Med Ctr, New Orleans, 73-77; prof surg & chmn dept, Col Med, ETenn State Univ, 77-85; prof surg, dean & vpres, Sch Med, Marshall Univ, Huntington, WVa, 85-88. *Concurrent Pos:* Resident coordr, Surg Adjuvant Breast Proj, Nat Coop Study, 61-62; responsible investr coop study on coronary artery dis & coop study of cirrhosis & esophago-gastric varices, Vet Admin, 62-63, consult, 63-; consult, USPHS, 65-, Charity Hosp of La & Vet Admin Hosp, New Orleans, 73-77; mem assoc staff, Southern Baptist Hosp, New Orleans & Hotel Dieu Hosp, New Orleans, 74-77. *Mem:* Am Asn Thoracic Surg; Am Col Surg; AMA; Asn Acad Surg; Int Soc Surg. *Res:* Cardiothoracic surgery; development of primate smoking model; evaluation of prophylactic antibiotics in thoracic trauma; comparison of incisions for tracheostomy; study of bacterial colonization profile in patients with tracheostomy. *Mailing Add:* Univ Mo Columbia Med Sch One Hospital Dr Columbia MO 65201-5276. *Fax:* 573-884-4808

BRYANT, MARVIN PIERCE, MICROBIAL ECOLOGY. *Current Pos:* assoc prof bact, 64-66, prof, 66-94, EMER PROF MICROBIOL, UNIV ILL, URBANA-CHAMPAIGN, 94- *Personal Data:* b Boise, Idaho, July 4, 25; m 46, Margaret Betabemner; c Peggy, Susan (Kouidencer), Katherine C (Smith), Robert M & Steven E. *Educ:* State Col Wash, BS, 49, MS, 50; Univ Md, PhD(bact), 55. *Honors & Awards:* Superior Serv Award, USDA, 59; Borden Award, Am Dairy Sci Asn, 78; Fisher Award in Appl & Environ Microbiol, Am Soc Microbiol, 86. *Prof Exp:* Res asst, State Col Wash, 49-51; bacteriologist, Agr Res Serv, USDA, 51-64. *Concurrent Pos:* Ed, Appl Environ Microbiol, 68-71, ed-in-chief, 71-80; trustee, Bergey's Manual of Determinative Bact, 75-81, vchmn trust, 76-80; vis scientist, Inst Microbiol, Gottingen, Ger, 76-77. *Mem:* Nat Acad Sci; fel AAAS; Am Soc Microbiol; Am Dairy Sci Asn; Brit Soc Gen Microbiol. *Res:* Ruminal bacteriology; systematics; nutrition; physiology; ecology; nonsporeforming anaerobic bacteria and ciliate protozoa; methanogenic bacteria. *Mailing Add:* 902 Ramblewood Ct Savoy IL 61874

BRYANT, MICHAEL DAVID, TRIBOLOGY, ELECTROMECHANICS. *Current Pos:* assoc prof, 88-95, PROF MECH ENG, UNIV TEX, AUSTIN, 95- *Personal Data:* b Danville, Ill, Feb 8, 51; m 78, Eugenia Sturino; c David, Daniella, Christina, Andrea & Michael. *Educ:* Univ Ill, BS, 72; Northwestern Univ, MS, 80, PhD(eng sci), 81. *Prof Exp:* Asst prof, 81-85, assoc prof mech & aerospace eng, NC State Univ, 85-88. *Concurrent Pos:* Consult, 85-; presidential young investr award, NSF, 85; Lybarger fel, 90-; chair, Cent Tex Chap, Am Soc Mech Engrs, 96- *Mem:* Am Soc Mech Engrs; Soc Mfg Engrs; Inst Elec & Electronics Engrs; Sigma Xi. *Res:* Electro-mechanics; wear of sliding contacts; active control of structures; precision positioning systems; precision machining systems; physics of electrical contacts; maintenance science; mechatronics. *Mailing Add:* Dept Mech Eng Univ Tex Austin TX 78712-1063. *Fax:* 512-471-7682; *E-Mail:* mbryant@mail.utexas.edu

BRYANT, PATRICIA SAND, SCIENCE POLICY, PSYCHOLOGY. *Current Pos:* HEALTH SCIENTIST ADMIN, CRANIOFACIAL ANOMALIES PAIN CONTROL & BEHAV RES BR, NAT INST DENT RES, NIH, 76- *Personal Data:* b Minot, NDak, July 18, 40; m 75; c 2. *Educ:* Univ Wash, BS, 61, MS, 63, PhD(psychol), 64. *Honors & Awards:* Merit Award, NIH, 85. *Prof Exp:* Res asst psychol, Univ Wash, 61-64, Sch Med, 64-66, asst prof, Sch Nursing, 66-67, from asst prof to assoc prof, Dept Rehab Med, 68-75. *Concurrent Pos:* Consult, Seattle Artificial Kidney Ctr, 65-67; SRS grant, 73-75; adj assoc prof, Uniformed Serv Univ Health Sci, Betheseda, Md, 81-84. *Mem:* Am Psychol Asn; Am Asn Dent Res; Int Asn Dent Res; Am Cong Rehab Med; Behav Sci Dent Res (pres, 85-86); Int Asn Study Pain. *Res:* Behavioral research relating to oral health; psychological aspects of illness-health; rehabilitation; behavioral factors in chronic pain; behavioral factors in oral health and dental care. *Mailing Add:* Nat Inst Health 45 Ctr Dr NTCHER 4AN24E Bethesda MD 20892

BRYANT, PAUL JAMES, SOLID STATE PHYSICS. *Current Pos:* RETIRED. *Personal Data:* b Kansas City, Mo, May 11, 29; m 60. *Educ:* Rockhurst Col, BS, 51; St Louis Univ, MS, 53, PhD(physics), 57. *Prof Exp:* Prin physicist, Midwest Res Inst, 58-68; assoc prof, 68-74, prof physics, Univ Mo, Kansas City, 74-92. *Mem:* Am Phys Soc; Am Vacuum Soc. *Res:* Solid state structure studies; surface physics; field emission microscopy; friction of solids; ultra high vacuum technology. *Mailing Add:* 7217 Canterbury Shawnee Mission MO 66708

BRYANT, PETER JAMES, DROSOPHILA GENETICS, MOLECULAR GENETICS. *Current Pos:* from lectr to assoc prof, 70-77, PROF GENETICS, DEPT DEVELOP & CELL BIOL, UNIV CALIF, IRVINE, 77-, DIR, DEVELOP BIOL CTR, 79- *Personal Data:* Brit citizen. *Educ:* Kings Col, London, BSc, 64; Univ Col, London, MSc, 65; Univ Sussex, Falmer, DPhil, 67. *Prof Exp:* Scholar, Case Western Univ & Univ Calif, Irvine, 67-70. *Concurrent Pos:* Prin investr, NIH grants, 74-; dir, NIH Training grant, 79-; consult, NSF, 83-85; ed-in-chief, Develop Biol, 85- *Mem:* Soc Develop Biol; Genetics Soc Am; AAAS; Int Soc Develop Biol; Soc Exp Biol; Am Cetacean Soc (pres, 82). *Res:* Analysis of pattern formation and growth control during organ development in animals, using molecular genetic approaches in the fruitfly Drosophila melanogaster; tumor suppressor genes. *Mailing Add:* Dept Develop & Cell Biol Univ Calif Irvine CA 92717-0001

BRYANT, REBECCA SMITH, MICROBIAL ENHANCED OIL RECOVERY. *Current Pos:* MGR, PROD TECHNOL, BDM PETROL TECHNOL, 83- *Personal Data:* b Checotah, Okla, May 23, 55; m 84, Richard M Jr; c 1. *Educ:* Okla State Univ, BS, 76, MS, 79, PhD(microbiol), 82. *Prof Exp:* Vis asst prof microbiol, Univ Tulsa, 82-83. *Concurrent Pos:* Adj instr cell biol, Univ Ctr Tulsa, 83 & adj prof, Univ Tulsa, 84-; consult, Biotechnol Res Workshop, 85-91. *Mem:* Am Soc Microbiol; Soc Indust Microbiol; Soc Petrol Engrs; Am Asn Univ Women; Sigma Xi; Am Soc Testing & Mat. *Res:* Use of micro-organisms for petroleum production and environmental pollutant degradation for government agencies and industry; directing microbial research and writing proposals relating to above topics. *Mailing Add:* BDM-Petrol Technol PO Box 2543 Bartlesville OK 74005

BRYANT, RHYS, ORGANIC CHEMISTRY. *Current Pos:* PRES, RHYS BRYANT LTD CONSULT SERV, 91- *Personal Data:* b Swansea, Wales, Nov 28, 36; m 60; c 3. *Educ:* Univ Wales, BSc, 57, PhD(org chem), 60. *Prof Exp:* Fulbright res scholar chem, Yale Univ, 60-61; fel org chem, Mellon Inst, 61; res chemist, Unilever Res Lab, Eng, 61-63; asst lectr chem, Univ Manchester, 63-65; group leader instrumentation & methods develop, Res Ctr, Mead Johnson & Co, 65-67, sect leader, 67-68, dir pharmaceut qual control, 68-76; vpres qual control, Plough Div, Schering-Plough Corp, Memphis, 76-78; group dir qual assurance, Pharmaceut Prod Group, Searle Worldwide Pharmaceut, G D Searle & Co, 78-79, vpres qual assurance, NAm Region, 79-80, group dir qual assurance, Searle Pharmaceut Inc, 81-86, sr dir, Tech Opers, 87-89, vpres sci affairs, Bausch & Lomb Pharmaceut Div, 89-91. *Mem:* Am Chem Soc; Sigma Xi; Chem Soc; Royal Inst Chem. *Res:* Synthesis of oxygen heterocyclic compounds; sesquiterpenoids; analysis of experimental drug products; author of Pharmaceutical Quality Control Handbook. *Mailing Add:* 15 Whitby Circle Lincolnshire IL 60069-3405

BRYANT, ROBERT EMORY, CELL BIOLOGY, GENETICS. *Current Pos:* ASST PROF BIOCHEM, UNIV TENN, 77- *Personal Data:* b Charleston, SC, Feb 26, 42; m 68; c 1. *Educ:* Univ Ala, BS, 64; Purdue Univ, MS, 66; Univ Ill, PhD (microbiol), 73. *Prof Exp:* Fel cell biol, Sch Med, Yale Univ, 73-76. *Concurrent Pos:* Jane Coffin Childs Fund Med Res fel, 73-75. *Mem:* Am Soc Microbiol; AAAS. *Res:* Genetics of cultured animal cells; nucleotide metabolism. *Mailing Add:* 1200 Foxcrolf Dr Knoxville TN 37923

BRYANT, ROBERT GEORGE, BIOPHYSICAL CHEMISTRY. *Current Pos:* UNIV ROCHESTER MED CTR, DEPT BIOPHYS, 88- *Personal Data:* b Mineola, NY, Sept 13, 43; m 65; c 3. *Educ:* Colgate Univ, AB, 65; Stanford Univ, PhD(chem), 69. *Prof Exp:* From asst prof to assoc prof, Univ Minn, Minneapolis, 69-78, prof chem, 78-87. *Concurrent Pos:* Teacher-scholar grant, Dreyfus Found, 74. *Mem:* AAAS; Am Chem Soc; Biophys Soc; Sigma Xi. *Res:* Application of nuclear magnetic resonance spectroscopy to investigation of metal ion protein interactions, water macromolecule interactions, metalloenzymes, and macromolecule dynamics. *Mailing Add:* Dept Chem Univ Va McCormick Rd Charlottsville VA 22901. *Fax:* 804-924-3710

BRYANT, ROBERT L, FORESTRY. *Current Pos:* RETIRED. *Personal Data:* b New York, NY, Jan 3, 28; m 49, Nadine Wheeler; c 3. *Educ:* La State Univ, BS, 53, MS, 54; Mich State Univ, PhD(forestry), 63. *Prof Exp:* Biologist wildlife invest, La Wildlife & Fisheries Comn, 52-53, res biologist refuge mgt, 53-54; asst prof forestry, McNeese State Col, 54-59; asst, Mich State Univ, 59-62; from asst prof to prof forestry, McNeese State Univ, 62-76; forest & biol consult, 76-91; Agt, Erwin Heirs Inc, Property Mgt, 78-94. *Concurrent Pos:* Collabr, Lake States Forest Exp Sta, 59-62. *Mem:* Soc Am Foresters; Am Forestry Asn; Ecol Soc Am. *Res:* Forest ecology; ecology of lowland hardwood forests, soils and ground-water; remote sensing of environment within forest structures. *Mailing Add:* 111 Orchard Dr Lake Charles LA 70605

BRYANT, ROBERT LEAMON, MATHEMATICS. *Current Pos:* arts & sci prof, 87-88, J M KREPS PROF, DUKE UNIV, DURHAM, NC, 88- *Personal Data:* b Harnett Co, NC, Aug 30, 53. *Educ:* NC State Univ, BS, 74; Univ NC, PhD, 79. *Prof Exp:* From asst prof to assoc prof, Rice Univ, Houston, 79-82, prof, 82-85, Noah Harding prof, 85-87. *Concurrent Pos:* A P Sloan fel, 83; Presidential Young Investr Award, NSF, 84. *Res:* Mathematics. *Mailing Add:* Dept Math Duke Univ PO Box 90320 Durham NC 27708-0320

BRYANT, ROBERT WESLEY, LEUKOTRIENE, PROSTAGLANDIN. *Current Pos:* SR PRIN SCIENTIST, SCHERING-PLOUGH CORP, 83- *Educ:* Fla State Univ, PhD(biochem), 73. *Mailing Add:* K15-4 MS4800 Schering-Plough Corp 2015 Galloping Hills Rd Kenilworth NJ 07033-5039. *Fax:* 908-298-7115

BRYANT, ROBERT WILLIAM, APPLIED MATHEMATICS. *Current Pos:* INSTR MATH, SHEPHERD COL, 80- *Personal Data:* b Oxford, Ohio, June 8, 25; m 46, Betty L Whitney; c Rebecca (Fleck), Bonnie L, Barbara (Zingg) & Elizabeth (Burkholder). *Educ:* Miami Univ, AB, 47; Univ Ala, MA, 48. *Prof Exp:* Instr math, Miami Univ, 48-51; rating exam sci & tech personnel, Potomac River Naval Command, 51-52; mathematician, Underwater Sound Propagation, US Naval Res Lab, 52-56, supvry mathematician, 58-59; mathematician, Celestial Mech & Appl Orbit Anal, Goddard Space Flight Ctr, NASA, 59-66; mathematician, Systs Anal Staff, Anti-Submarine Warfare Spec Proj Off, HQS, Washington, DC, 66-72, systs analyst, Anti-Submarine Warfare Systs Proj Off, 72-80. *Mem:* Fel AAAS. *Res:* Celestial mechanics; density of upper atmosphere; solar radiation pressure effects on echo type satellites; density interference from drag; signal processing; cosmology. *Mailing Add:* Rte 1 Box 106 Steamboat Run Shepherdstown WV 25443

BRYANT, SHIRLEY HILLS, PHARMACOLOGY, PHYSIOLOGY. *Current Pos:* from instr to assoc prof pharmacol, 55-69, PROF PHARMACOL, COL MED, UNIV CINCINNATI, 69- *Personal Data:* b Pittsfield, Mass, Dec 28, 24; m 46, 63, 87; c 3. *Educ:* Aurora Col, BS, 48; Univ Chicago, PhD(physiol), 54. *Prof Exp:* Asst physiol, Univ Chicago, 50-54. *Concurrent Pos:* USPHS career develop award, Univ Cincinnati, 59-69; vis prof, Univ PR, 65-66 & Cambridge Univ, 72-73. *Mem:* AAAS; Soc Neurosci; Biophys Soc; Am Physiol Soc. *Res:* Physiology and pharmacology of excitation, conduction and synaptic transmission in excitable tissues; biophysics nerve and muscle; abnormal repetitive impulse production and excitation-contraction coupling mechanisms in skeletal muscle; myotonia in goats. *Mailing Add:* Dept Pharmacol & Cell Biophysics Univ Cincinnati Col Med 231 Bethesda Ave ML 575 Cincinnati OH 45267-0575. *Fax:* 513-558-1169

BRYANT, STEPHEN G, POSTMARKETING DRUG SURVEILLANCE. *Current Pos:* ASSOC PROF PSYCHIAT & PSYCHOPHARMACOL, UNIV TEX MED BR, GALVESTON, 82- *Personal Data:* b New York, NY, Nov 15, 51. *Educ:* St Johns Univ, BS, 75; Univ Tex, Austin, Pharm D, 79. *Prof Exp:* Fel psychopharmacol, Tex Dept Mental Health, 78-79; clin coordr psychopharmacol, NY Hosp-Cornell Med Ctr, 79-82. *Concurrent Pos:* Prin investr, Food & Drug Admin Psychopharmacol Violence Study, 82-; mem, Credentials Comt, Am Col Clin Pharm, 85-87; mem, Med Adv Comt, Tex Bd Mental Health, 85- *Mem:* Sigma Xi; AAAS; Am Col Clin Pharmacol; Am Col Clin Pharm; Am Soc Hosp Pharmacists. *Res:* Clinical psychopharmacology of violence and depression; postmarketing drug surveillance. *Mailing Add:* Dept Psychiat Univ Tex Med Sch 301 University Blvd Galveston TX 77550-2708

BRYANT, SUSAN VICTORIA, DEVELOPMENTAL BIOLOGY, CELL BIOLOGY. *Current Pos:* from lectr to assoc prof, 69-81, PROF BIOL, UNIV CALIF, IRVINE, 81- *Personal Data:* b Sheffield, Eng, May 24, 43. *Educ:* Univ London, BSc, 64, PhD(zool), 67. *Prof Exp:* Res fel zool, Case Western Reserve Univ, 67-69. *Concurrent Pos:* Prog dir, develop biol, NSF, 81-82. *Mem:* Am Soc Zool; Soc Develop Biol; Asn Women Sci; Int Soc Develop Biologists. *Res:* Regeneration in vertebrates. *Mailing Add:* Dept Develop Cell Biol 5205 Biol Sci II Univ Calif Irvine CA 92697-2300. *Fax:* 714-856-5385

BRYANT, THOMAS EDWARD, PUBLIC HEALTH. *Current Pos:* PRES, FRIENDS NAT LIBR MED, 86- *Personal Data:* b Bellamy, Ala, Jan 17, 36; m 61; c 2. *Educ:* Emory Univ, AB, 58, MD, 62, JD, 67. *Prof Exp:* Intern, Grady Mem Hosp, Atlanta, Ga, 62-63; dir health affairs, Off Econ Opportunity, 69-71; pres, Nat Drug Abuse Coun, 71-77; chmn & dir, Pres Comn Ment Health, 77-79; chmn, Pub Comt Ment Health, 79-87. *Concurrent Pos:* Vis lectr, Georgetown Univ. *Mem:* Inst Med-Nat Acad Sci; Am Pub Health Asn. *Mailing Add:* 1555 Connecticut Ave NW Suite 200 Washington DC 20036

BRYANT, VAUGHN MOTLEY, JR, ANTHROPOLOGY, BOTANY. *Current Pos:* from asst prof to prof, 71-80, HEAD, DEPT ANTHROP, TEX A&M UNIV, 75-, DIR PALYNOLOGY LAB, 90- *Personal Data:* b Dallas, Tex, Oct 5, 40; m 64; c 3. *Educ:* Univ Tex, Austin, BA, 64, MA, 66, PhD(bot), 69. *Prof Exp:* Asst prof anthrop & dir palynology lab, Wash State Univ, 69-71. *Concurrent Pos:* Managing ed, Am Asn Stratig Palynologists, 79-83, pres, 85, trustee, 90- *Mem:* Am Asn Stratig Palynologists; Soc Am Archaeol; Am Quaternary Asn; Am Phytolith Soc. *Res:* Pollen analytical studies of Quaternary paleoenvironments with special emphasis on areas in the American Southwest; prehistoric diets, pollen and macrofossil analysis of fossil human coprolites; pollen analytical and paleoethnobotanical studies of archaeological deposits; forensic palynology. *Mailing Add:* Dept Anthrop Tex A&M Univ College Station TX 77843. *Fax:* 409-845-4070; *E-Mail:* vbryant@tamu.edu

BRYANT, WILLIAM RICHARDS, MARINE GEOLOGY, OCEANOGRAPHY. *Current Pos:* res scientist, 62-64, from asst prof to assoc prof oceanog, 64-71, PROF OCEANOG, TEX A&M UNIV, 71- *Personal Data:* b Chicago, Ill, Feb 12, 30; m 65; c 3. *Educ:* Univ Chicago, MS, 60, PhD(geol), 66. *Prof Exp:* Oceanogr, Off Naval Res, 60-62. *Concurrent Pos:* Proj supvr, Off Naval Res grant, 66-; NSF grant, 69- *Mem:* AAAS; Sigma Xi. *Res:* Marine geotechnique; geology and geophysics of the Gulf of Mexico and Caribbean; acoustic characteristics of marine sediments; sediment transport. *Mailing Add:* 2811 Cherry Creek Bryan TX 77802-2927

BRYANT, WILLIAM STANLEY, FOREST ECOLOGY, GRASSLAND ECOLOGY. *Current Pos:* from instr to assoc prof biol, 71-80, PROF BIOL & CHMN DEPT, THOMAS MORE COL, 80- *Personal Data:* b Frankfort, Ky, Nov 9, 43; m 69; c 2. *Educ:* Tenn Technol Univ, BS, 66; Southern Ill Univ, MS, 69, PhD(bot), 73. *Prof Exp:* Evening instr ecol, Ky State Univ, 70-72. *Mem:* Ecol Soc Am; Sigma Xi. *Res:* Structure and dynamics of forest and grassland systems in the Midwest and Upper South. *Mailing Add:* Dept Biol Thomas More Col Ft Mitchell KY 41017

BRYANT-GREENWOOD, GILLIAN DOREEN, ENDOCRINOLGOY, REPRODUCTIVE BIOLOGY. *Current Pos:* asst researcher, Dept Biochem & Biophys, 68-72, asst prof reproductive endocrinol, 72-75, assoc prof, 75-81, PROF, DEPT ANAT & REPROD BIOL, UNIV HAWAII, 81- *Personal Data:* b Oxfordshire, Eng, July 20, 42; m 76; c 2. *Educ:* Brunel Univ, BSc, 65, PhD(biol, endocrinol), 68. *Prof Exp:* Res staff, Imperial Cancer Res Fund, London, 65-68. *Concurrent Pos:* Res career develop award, NIH, 72-78, grants, 72 & 81-; sr Fogarty Int fel, 85-86. *Mem:* Endocrine Soc; Soc Endocrinol; Soc Study Reprod & Fertility; Asn Women Sci. *Res:* The hormone relaxin, its isolation from ovaries and uteri of different species, its chemical structure; the development of radioimmunoassays and elucidation of its biological and reproductive functions. *Mailing Add:* Dept Anat Univ Hawaii Burns Med Sch 1960 East-West Rd Honolulu HI 96822-2319

BRYCE, GALE REX, QUALITY IMPROVEMENT. *Current Pos:* asst prof, 72-75, assoc prof, 75-80, PROF STATIST, BRIGHAM YOUNG UNIV, 80-, DEPT CHAIR, 94- *Personal Data:* b Safford, Ariz, Nov 18, 39; m 63; c 9. *Educ:* Ariz State Univ, BS, 67; Brigham Young Univ, MS, 70; Univ Ky, PhD(exp statist), 74. *Prof Exp:* Math programmer, Semiconductor Prod Div, Motorola Inc, 63-68. *Concurrent Pos:* Mgr qual technol, Intel Corp, 86-88. *Mem:* Fel Am Statist Asn; Sigma Xi; Am Soc Qual Control. *Res:* Linear models with special emphasis in the analysis of unbalanced designs where a mixed model is appropriate; quality management, quality improvement, industrial applications of statistics. *Mailing Add:* Dept Statist Brigham Young Univ 230 Tmcb Provo UT 84602-1044

BRYCE, HUGH GLENDINNING, PHYSICAL CHEMISTRY. *Current Pos:* RETIRED. *Personal Data:* b Melville, Sask, Nov 30, 17; m 43, Laverne Maggs; c James D & Warren H. *Educ:* Univ Sask, BA, 38, MA, 40; Columbia Univ, PhD(chem), 43. *Prof Exp:* Res chemist, Off Sci Res & Develop contract, Columbia Univ, 42-43; res chemist, Los Alamos Lab, Univ Calif, 43-46; res chemist, Res Labs, Sharples Corp, Philadelphia, 46-49; head prod develop, Fluorochems Dept, 3M Co, 49-59, develop mgr, 59-61, asst tech dir, 61-66, tech dir, Chem Div, 66-73, exec dir, Cent Res Labs, 73-75, staff vpres, Cent Res Labs, 75-82. *Mem:* AAAS; Am Chem Soc; Indust Res Inst; Sigma Xi. *Res:* Ultracentrifuge; low temperatures; ion exchange resins; ultracentrifugal behavior of starch and its triacetate and trimethyl derivatives; chemistry of carbon fluorine compounds. *Mailing Add:* 1327 Heggens St Hudson WI 54016-9224

BRYDEN, JOHN HEILNER, X-RAY CRYSTALLOGRAPHY. *Current Pos:* RETIRED. *Personal Data:* b Nampa, Idaho, Sept 9, 20; m 45, Mary Evelyn Estus; c Linda Diane & David. *Educ:* Col Idaho, BS, 42; Calif Inst Technol, MS, 45; Univ Calif, Los Angeles, PhD(chem), 51. *Prof Exp:* Chemist, Hercules Powder Co, 42-43; fel, Calif Inst Technol, 43-45; chemist, E I du Pont de Nemours & Co, 45-46; asst, Univ Calif, Los Angeles, 47-51; chemist, Res Dept, US Naval Ord Test Sta, 51-59; mem tech staff, Hughes Aircraft Co, 59-61; prof chem, Calif State Univ, Fullerton, 61-86. *Mem:* AAAS; Am Crystallog Asn; Am Chem Soc. *Res:* Crystal structures of organic and inorganic substances by x-ray diffraction. *Mailing Add:* 1416 Vista Del Mar Dr Fullerton CA 92831-1125

BRYDEN, ROBERT RICHMOND, ANIMAL ECOLOGY. *Current Pos:* Dana prof biol & head dept, 61-83, EMER DANA PROF BIOL, GUILFORD COL, 83- *Personal Data:* b Erie, Pa, July 19, 16; m 43; c 4. *Educ:* Mt Union Col, BS, 38; Ohio State Univ, MS, 41; Vanderbilt Univ, PhD(zool), 51. *Prof Exp:* Instr biol, Univ Akron, 40-41; asst sci, Goodyear Aircraft Corp, 41-43; assoc prof biol, Mid Tenn State Univ, 46-51; biologist, AEC, 51-54; head biol dept & chmn sci div, Union Col, 54-58; prof biol, High Point Col, 58-61. *Concurrent Pos:* AAAS & Tenn Acad res grant, 49; Am Acad Arts & Sci res grant, 58; Sigma Xi res grant, 59. *Mem:* AAAS; Am Soc Zoologists. *Res:* Limnology; physiology; invertebrate zoology. *Mailing Add:* 1805 Evans St Morehead City NC 28557

BRYDEN, WAYNE A, WIDE BANDGAP SEMICONDUCTOR PHYSICS, PHYSICAL VAPOR DEPOSITION. *Current Pos:* Fel, Johns Hopkins Univ, 82-83, sr staff chemist, 83-90, PROG SUPVR, APPL PHYSICS LAB, JOHNS HOPKINS UNIV, 90-, PRIN PROF STAFF CHEMIST, 93- *Personal Data:* b Chestertown, Md, Aug 18, 55; m 79, Noella Auerbach; c Matthew, Daniel & Benjamin. *Educ:* Frostburg State Univ, BS, 77; Johns Hopkins Univ, MS, 82, PhD(chem), 83. *Concurrent Pos:* Fac mem, Continuing Prof Progs, Eng Sch, 86-, lectr, Interdisciplinary Courses, Johns Hopkins Univ, 87- *Mem:* Am Phys Soc; Am Vacuum Soc; Mat Res Soc; Am Chem Soc; Sigma Xi. *Res:* Physical vapor deposition of wide bandgap semiconductors; electrical, optical and morphological characterization of semiconductor thin films; applications of magnetic resonance imaging technique to damage characterization of solids; electron paramagnetic resonance spectroscopy; cryogenic technology. *Mailing Add:* 4652 Pinto Ct Ellicott City MD 21043-6416. *Fax:* 301-953-6904; *E-Mail:* bryden@aplcomm.jhuapl.edu

BRYGIDER, BRANDON RONALD, ENERGY & ENVIRONMENTAL TECHNOLOGIES, ENERGY & ENVIRONMENTAL REGULATORY COMPLIANCE. *Current Pos:* ASST PROF, ENVIRON TECHNOL DEPT, NY INST TECHNOL, 93- *Personal Data:* b Lynbrook, NY, Oct 2, 55. *Educ:* Colo Sch Mines, BS, 78, MS, 80; St Johns Law Sch, JD, 85. *Prof Exp:* Res asst, Colo Sch Mines, 78-81; geophysicist, Group Seven Inc, 80-82; law assoc, Mendes & Mount, 85-93. *Mem:* Soc Explor Geophysicists. *Res:* Environmental issues concerning groundwater protection; surface water pollution control; alternative energies. *Mailing Add:* NY Inst Technol Old Westbury NY 11568-8000

BRYMAN, DOUGLAS ANDREW, PHYSICS. *Current Pos:* SR RES SCIENTIST PHYSICS, TRI-UNIV, MESON FACIL, 75- *Personal Data:* b Brooklyn, NY, June 12, 45; m 68; c 2. *Educ:* Syracuse Univ, BS, 66; Rutgers Univ, MS, 69; Va Polytech Inst & State Univ, PhD(physics), 72. *Prof Exp:* Res fel, Univ Victoria, BC, 72-75. *Concurrent Pos:* Prog dir intermediate energy physics, NSF, 77-78; adj prof, Univ Victoria, 80- *Mem:* Fel Am Phys Soc; Can Asn Physics; Inst Particle Physics. *Res:* Elementary particle physics. *Mailing Add:* 4454 W Seventh Ave 4004 Wesbrook Mall Vancouver BC V6R 1W9 Can

BRYNER, CHARLES LESLIE, BOTANY, TAXONOMIC BOTANY. *Current Pos:* RETIRED. *Personal Data:* b Dunbar, Pa, Oct 15, 14; m 47, Anna M Wilson; c Lisbeth A & Bryner L. *Educ:* Waynesburg Col, BS, 40; Univ WVa, MS, 48, PhD(bot), 57. *Hon Degrees:* DSc, Waynesburg Col, 82. *Prof Exp:* Teacher & supvry prin, Pub Schs, Pa, 40-42; from assoc prof to prof bot, Waynesburg Col, 46-81, dean men, 53-58, chmn, Div Sci, 58-71, asst acad vpres, 59-81. *Res:* Genus Helianthus in West Virginia; taxonomic botany; author of one publication. *Mailing Add:* RR 3 Waynesburg PA 15370

BRYNER, JOSEPH S(ANSON), METALLURGY. *Current Pos:* RETIRED. *Personal Data:* b Pittsburgh, Pa, Dec 15, 20; m 49, Audrey Rantsch; c Margaret (Saunders), Ellen (Stafford) & Lucinda (Glenday). *Educ:* Washington & Jefferson Col, AB, 42; Carnegie Inst Technol, BS, 42; Pa State Univ, MS, 49, PhD(metall), 57. *Prof Exp:* Res metallurgist magnesium alloys, Dow Chem Co, 43-44; res metallurgist nickel alloys, Int Nickel Co, 46-47, asst, Pa State Univ, 48-50, assoc metallurgist liquid metals, Brookhaven Nat Lab, 51-59, metallurgist, 59-69; sr engr, Bettis Atomic Power Lab, Westinghouse Elec Corp, 70-86. *Mem:* Am Soc Metals. *Res:* Electron microscopy of magnesium alloys; development of inconel arc-welding electrodes; production and behavior of dispersions in liquid metals; electron microscopy of radiation damage, corrosion and stress corrosion. *Mailing Add:* 114 Telstar Dr Pleasant Hills PA 15236-4557

BRYNILDSON, OSCAR MARIUS, ZOOLOGY. *Current Pos:* CONSULT, 78- *Personal Data:* b Wis, Mar 5, 16. *Educ:* Univ Wis, BA, 47, MA, 50, PhD(zool), 58. *Prof Exp:* Asst fishery biol, Univ Wis, 48-52; fishery biologist, Wis Conserv Dept, 52-57, group leader cold water res, 57-69; limnologist, Wis Dept Natural Resources, 69-78. *Mem:* Am Soc Limnol & Oceanog; Am Fisheries Soc. *Res:* Ecology of trout and other cold water fishes in lakes and streams. *Mailing Add:* Rte 2 Box 25-A-5 Black River Falls WI 54615-9606

BRYNJOLFSSON, ARI, IRRADIATION TECHNOLOGY. *Current Pos:* DIR, APPL RADIATION INDUSTS, 92- *Personal Data:* b Akureyri, Iceland, Dec 7, 26; US citizen; m 50, Marguerite S Reman; c Ariane, Olaf, Erik, John & Alan. *Educ:* Univ Iceland, BSc, 48; Univ Copenhagen, Cand Phil, 49, Cand Mag & Mag Sci, 54; Niels Bohr Inst, Dr Phil(theoret nuclear physics), 73; Harvard Univ, AMP, 71. *Honors & Awards:* Radiation Sci & Technol Award, Am Nuclear Soc, 88. *Prof Exp:* Res physicist, Danish AEC Res Estab, Riso, Denmark, 57-58, head, Radiation Res Group, 57-59, dir, Radiation Res Labs, 59-62 & 63-65; consult, US Army Natick Labs, 62-63; chief, Radiation Sources Div, US Army, 65-72, actg dir food irradiation, 72-74, chief radiation preserve, Food Div & dir, Radiation Lab, 74-80, chief, Physics & Math Sci Advan Technol Lab, 80-83, res chemist, Natick Res & Develop Lab, 83-88; proj dir, Int Facil Food Irradiation Technol, Joint Div Int Atomic Energy Agency & Food & Agr Orgn Div, Vienna, Austria, 88-92. *Concurrent Pos:* Consult, Int Atomic Energy Agency Panels, 70- & Iranian

Govt, 72-; vis lectr, Mass Inst Technol, Cambridge, 81-86; consult, USDA-NAL Washington DC, Int Atomic Energy Agency, Vienna, Austria, WHO, Geneva Switz. *Mem:* Am Phys Soc; Radiation Res Soc. *Res:* Theory of stopping of charged particles and degradation of radiation; basic radiation physics and effects of radiation on biological systems; design and operation of isotopes and electron accelerator irradiation facilities; irradiation of foods and medical products; research and industrial application; astrophysics; theory of general relativity; redshift. *Mailing Add:* 7 Bridle Path Wayland MA 01778. *Fax:* 508-358-5518; *E-Mail:* abrynjolfs@aol.com

BRYSK, MIRIAM MASON, BIOLOGICAL CHEMISTRY. *Current Pos:* from asst prof to assoc prof, 80-88, DIR, DERMAT RES LAB, UNIV TEX MED BR, 80-, PROF DERMAT, MICROBIOL HUMAN BIOL CHEM & GENETICS, GALVESTON, 88- *Personal Data:* b Warsaw, Poland, Mar 10, 35; US citizen; m 55; c 2. *Educ:* NY Univ, BA, 55; Univ Mich, MS, 58; Columbia Univ, PhD(biol sci), 67. *Prof Exp:* Lectr biol, Queens Col, NY, 60-61; fel protein chem, Inst Muscle Dis, 67-69; res biologist, Dept Biol, Univ Calif, San Diego, 79-71; NIH fel cellular chem, Univ Mich, 74-77; res asst prof biochem & med & res scientist, Cancer Res & Treatment Ctr, Sch Med, Univ NMex, 77-80. *Mem:* Am Soc Microbiol; Soc Invest Dermat; affil mem Am Acad Dermat; Sigma Xi; Am Soc Biochem & Molecular Biol; Am Soc Cell Biol. *Res:* Amino acid and cyanide metabolism in microorganisms; synthesis of cell walls in plants; differentiation and carcinogenesis of the epidermis; biochemistry of epidermis. *Mailing Add:* Dept Dermat Univ Tex Med Br Galveston TX 77555-0783. *Fax:* 409-772-1943

BRYSON, ARTHUR E(ARL), JR, CONTROL SYSTEMS. *Current Pos:* chmn, Dept Appl Mech, 69-71, chmn, Dept Aeronaut & Astronaut, 71-79, PROF APPL MECH, AERONAUT & ASTRONAUT, STANFORD UNIV, 68-, PAUL PIGOTT PROF ENG, 72- *Personal Data:* b Evanston, Ill, Oct 7, 25; m 46; c 4. *Educ:* Iowa State Col, BS, 46; Calif Inst Technol, PhD(aeronaut), 51. *Honors & Awards:* Pendray Award, Am Inst Aeronaut & Astronaut, 68, Mech & Control Flight Award, 80; Westinghouse Award, Am Soc Eng Educ, 69; Rufus Oldenburger Medal, Am Soc Mech Engrs, 80; Control Systs Sci & Eng Award, Inst Elec & Electronics Engrs, 86; Control Heritage Award, Am Control Coun, 90. *Prof Exp:* Aerodyn engr, Hughes Res & Develop Labs, 50-53; from asst prof to prof mech eng, Harvard Univ, 53-68. *Concurrent Pos:* Chmn, Aeronaut & Space Eng Bd, Nat Res Coun, 76-78. *Mem:* Nat Acad Sci; Nat Acad Eng; Am Soc Eng Educ; hon fel Am Inst Aeronaut & Astronaut; Am Acad Arts & Sci. *Res:* Automatic control; flight mechanics; systems engineering; fluid mechanics. *Mailing Add:* Dept Aeronaut & Astronaut Sch Eng Stanford Univ Stanford CA 94305

BRYSON, GEORGE GARDNER, PHYSIOLOGY, PSYCHOPHYSIOLOGY. *Current Pos:* RETIRED. *Personal Data:* b Santa Barbara, Calif, Dec 16, 35. *Educ:* Univ Calif, Santa Barbara, BA, 57, PhD, 81; San Francisco State Col, MA, 71. *Prof Exp:* Zoologist, Santa Barbara Cottage Hosp Res Inst, 57-71, physiologist, 71-87. *Mem:* Am Asn Cancer Res. *Res:* Psychophysiology of steroid hormones and catecholamines, pituitary-adrenal-gonadal function in aggression and reproductive behavior, carcinogenic mechanisms, solid state carcinogenesis; biologic transport of steroids. *Mailing Add:* 2412 Chapala St Santa Barbara CA 93105

BRYSON, MELVIN JOSEPH, CLINICAL BIOCHEMISTRY. *Current Pos:* RETIRED. *Personal Data:* b Providence, Utah, June 7, 16; m 42; c 2. *Educ:* Utah State Agr Univ, BS, 46; Univ Utah, MS, 48; Agr & Mech Tex State Univ, PhD(biochem & nutrit), 52. *Prof Exp:* Asst, Utah State Agr Col, 48-49; res biochemist & head drug enzym unit, Eaton Labs, 52-57; res assoc, Univ Utah, 57-64, asst res prof, 65-70, assoc res prof obstet & gynec, 71-83, adj assoc prof pathol, Col Med, 81-83. *Concurrent Pos:* Dir, Intermountain Perinatal Res & Serv Lab, 70-83; Interwest Endocrine Lab, 84-91. *Mem:* Endocrine Soc. *Res:* Synthesis and metabolism of steroid hormones and relation to intermediary metabolism; affect of drugs on enzymes systems; intestinal absorption; clinical endocrinology; clinical chemistry. *Mailing Add:* 5262 Woodcrest Dr Salt Lake City UT 84117

BRYSON, REID ALLEN, CLIMATOLOGY, PALEOCLIMATOLOGY. *Current Pos:* prof, Univ Wis-Madison, 57-68, chmn dept, 57-61, prof meteorol & geog, 68-86, dir, Inst Environ Studies, 70-85, SR SCIENTIST, CTR CLIM RES, UNIV WIS-MADISON, 86- *Personal Data:* b Detroit, Mich, June 7, 20; m 42; c 4. *Educ:* Denison Univ, BA, 41, Univ Chicago, PhD(meteorol), 48. *Hon Degrees:* DSc, Denison Univ, 71. *Prof Exp:* Asst prof meteorol & geol, Univ Wis, 46-48, from asst prof to assoc prof meteorol, 48-56, chmn dept, 48-50 & 52-54; prof, Univ Ariz, 56-57. *Concurrent Pos:* Trustee, Univ Corp Atmospheric Res, 59-66; mem environ studies bd, Nat Acad Sci-Nat Acad Eng, 70-73; sci adv comt, Arctic & Alpine Res Inst. *Mem:* Soc Am Archaeol; Am Meteorol Soc; Am Quaternary Assn (pres, 88-90); fel AAAS. *Res:* Physical limnology; paleoclimatology; dynamic climatology; interdisciplinary environmental studies; climate modeling. *Mailing Add:* 11 Rosewood Circle Madison WI 53711. *E-Mail:* rabryson@facstaff.wisc.edu

BRYSON, THOMAS ALLAN, ORGANIC BIOCHEMISTRY. *Current Pos:* asst prof, 71-75, ASSOC PROF ORG CHEM, UNIV SC, 75- *Personal Data:* b Pittsburgh, Pa, July 24, 44; m 66; c 2. *Educ:* Washington & Jefferson Col, BA, 66; Univ Pittsburgh, PhD(org chem), 70. *Prof Exp:* NIH fel synthetic org chem, Stanford Univ, 70-71. *Concurrent Pos:* NSF trainee, 66-76. *Mem:* Am Chem Soc; Sigma Xi. *Res:* Synthetic organic chemistry; natural products chemistry; key biological compounds, particularly cortisone, juvenile hormone and nicotinamide-adenine dinucleotide. *Mailing Add:* Dept Chem Univ SC Columbia SC 29208

BRYTCZUK, WALTER L(UCAS), EXTRACTIVE METALLURGY, ENVIRONMENTAL ENGINEERING. *Current Pos:* RETIRED. *Personal Data:* b Carteret, NJ, Oct 18, 07; m 40, Jean Bujko; c Roberta (Williams), Gary & Janina (Birtolo). *Educ:* NY Univ, BS, 36; Polytech Inst Brooklyn, MS, 42. *Prof Exp:* Asst supt electrolytic ref, US Metals Ref Co, 29-36, supt, 36-47, ref metallurgist, 47-52, dir res, 52-56; assoc dir res non-ferrous metals, Am Metal Climax, Inc, 56-62; plant metallurgist, US Metals Ref Co, 62-69, metall asst to plant mgr, 69-74; consult, 74-82. *Concurrent Pos:* Adj prof, Polytech Inst Brooklyn, 53-56 & Grad Sch, Newark Col Eng, 56-66; consult, Electrolytic Copper Ref Powder Metall; mem, LAN Assoc, 68-85; vol, Int Exec Serv Corp, 77-80. *Mem:* Am Soc Metals; Am Inst Mining, Metall & Petrol Engrs; assoc mem Sigma Xi; Am Acad Environ Engrs. *Res:* Production of metals powders; germanium and semiconductors; extractive metallurgy of non-ferrous metals; electrolytic refining of copper; air and water pollution control; granted three patents in field. *Mailing Add:* 430 Galloping Hill Rd Roselle Park NJ 07204-2134

BRZAKOVIC, DRAGANA, IMAGE PROCESSING, PATTERN RECOGNITION. *Current Pos:* ASSOC PROF ELEC ENG, LEHIGH UNIV, 92- *Personal Data:* b Belgrade, Yugoslavia, July 18, 52. *Educ:* Univ Belgrade, Yugoslavia, BS, 76; Univ Fla, ME, 79, PhD(elec eng), 84. *Prof Exp:* Asst prof elec eng, Univ Tenn, 84-90, assoc prof, 90-95. *Concurrent Pos:* Fulbright scholar, Int Inst Educ, 78-79; prin investr, 84-; consult, Martin Marietta Energy Systs & Martin Marietta Aerospace, 88-92. *Mem:* Inst Elec & Electronics Engrs; Asn Comput Mach. *Res:* Novel algorithms for texture analysis in application to digital mammography, industrial inspection and document authentication. *Mailing Add:* Dept Elec Eng Lehigh Univ Bethlehem PA 18015. *E-Mail:* dbo9@lehigh.edu

BRZENK, RONALD MICHAEL, NUMBER THEORY. *Current Pos:* Asst prof, 74-80, ASSOC PROF MATH, HARTWICK COL, 80- *Personal Data:* b Jersey City, NJ, Jan 30, 49; m 71; c 2. *Educ:* St Peter's Col, NJ, BS, 69; Univ Notre Dame, PhD(math), 74. *Mem:* Am Math Soc; Math Asn Am. *Res:* Axiomatic approaches to class field theory; computer applications in number theory and algebra. *Mailing Add:* Dept Math Hartwick Col PO Box 4020 Oneonta NY 13820-4020

BRZOZOWSKI, JANUSZ ANTONI, HARDWARE SYSTEMS. *Current Pos:* chmn dept, 78-83 & 87-89, PROF COMPUT SCI, UNIV WATERLOO, 67-96, EMER DISTINGUISHED PROF, 96- *Personal Data:* b Warsaw, Poland, May 10, 35; Can citizen; m 59; c 2. *Educ:* Univ Toronto, BASc, 57, MASc, 59; Princeton Univ, MA & PhD(elec eng), 62. *Prof Exp:* Asst prof elec eng, Univ Ottawa, 62-65, assoc prof, 65-67. *Mem:* Inst Elec & Electronics Engrs; Asn Comput Mach. *Res:* Asynchronous circuits; testing. *Mailing Add:* Dept Comput Sci Univ Waterloo Waterloo ON N2L 3G1 Can

BRZUSTOWSKI, THOMAS ANTHONY, MECHANICAL ENGINEERING. *Current Pos:* From asst prof to assoc prof, 62-66, chmn dept, 67-70, assoc dean eng grad studies, 70-77, PROF MECH ENG, UNIV WATERLOO, 66-, VPRES ACAD, 75- *Personal Data:* b Warsaw, Poland, Apr 4, 37; Can citizen; m 64; c 3. *Educ:* Univ Toronto, BASc, 58; Princeton Univ, AM, 60, PhD(aeronaut eng), 63. *Concurrent Pos:* Am Soc Eng Educ-Ford Found resident prof, environ control & safety dir, Esso Res & Eng Co, 70-71. *Mem:* Am Soc Mech Engrs; Am Inst Aeronaut & Astronaut; Am Soc Eng Educ; Sigma Xi; fel Inst Energy UK; fel Eng Inst Can; Can Soc Mech Eng. *Res:* Combustion of liquid fuels; flaring; applied thermodynamics-second law analysis. *Mailing Add:* Pres Nat Sci & Eng Res Counc 350 Albert St Ottawa ON K1A 1H5 Can

BUBAR, JOHN STEPHEN, AGRONOMY. *Current Pos:* RETIRED. *Personal Data:* b NB, Sept 13, 29; m 54, Margaret H Dickson; c Donald S & Carol J. *Educ:* McGill Univ, BSc, 52, PhD(genetics), 57; Pa State Univ, MS, 54. *Prof Exp:* Asst agron, Pa State Univ, 52-53; asst, Macdonald Col, McGill Univ, 53-54, lectr, 54-59, asst prof, 59-67; assoc prof, 67-71, head dept, 67-83, prof agron, NS Agr Col, 71-92. *Concurrent Pos:* Mem, Expert Comt Forage Crops Breeding, 74-77; AK Publications Comt, 85- *Mem:* Agr Inst Can; Can Soc Agron (pres, 71-72); hon mem Can Seed Growers Asn. *Res:* Crops production and breeding, specifically red clover alfalfa and birdsfoot trefoil breeding and genetics; adaptation of cultivars to Atlantic provinces of Canada. *Mailing Add:* RR 1 Tatamagouche NS B0K 1V0 Can

BUBE, RICHARD HOWARD, PHOTOELECTRONIC, PROPERTIES OF SEMICONDUCTORS. *Current Pos:* from assoc prof to prof, Stanford Univ, 62-92, chmn dept, 75-86, assoc chmn dept, 90 & 91, EMER PROF MAT SCI & ELEC ENG, STANFORD UNIV, 92- *Personal Data:* b Providence, RI, Aug 10, 27; m 48, Betty J Meeker; c Mark T, Kenneth P, Sharon E & Meryl L. *Educ:* Brown Univ, ScB, 46; Princeton Univ, MA, 48, PhD(physics), 50. *Prof Exp:* Res physicist, Labs Div, Radio Corp Am, 48-62. *Concurrent Pos:* Ed, J Am Sci Affil, 69-83; assoc ed, Ann Rev Mat Sci, 69-83,; consult ed, Mat Lett, 82-89. *Mem:* Fel AAAS; fel Am Phys Soc; fel Am Sci Affil; Am Soc Eng Educ; Sigma Xi; Am Div Int Solar Energy Soc. *Res:* Luminescence; photoconductivity; trapping in solids; phosphors; electronic crystal defect phenomena; semiconductors; photoelectronic properties of materials and devices; photovoltaics; amorphous materials. *Mailing Add:* Dept Mat Sci & Eng Stanford Univ Stanford CA 94305-2205. *Fax:* 650-725-4034; *E-Mail:* bube@leland.stanford.edu

BUBECK, ROBERT CLAYTON, PHYSICAL & CHEMICAL LIMNOLOGY. *Current Pos:* SUPVR HYDROLOGIST GEOCHEM, WATER RESOURCES DIV, US GEOL SURV, 81- *Personal Data:* b Wilkes-Barre, Pa, Mar 20, 37; m 65; c 2. *Educ:* Univ Rochester, BA, 60,

PhD(geol sci), 72; Pa State Univ, MS, 65. *Prof Exp:* Asst prof chem geol, Chem Dept, US Naval Acad, 65-67; estuarine oceanographer chem, Fed Water Pollution Control Admin, US Dept Interior, 67-69; res asst, Dept Geol Sci, Univ Rochester, 69-73; hydrologist geochem & limnol, Water Resources Div, US Geol Surv, 73-76; chief inorg chem unit & staff hydrologist, Region III Lab, US Environ Protection Agency, 76-81. *Concurrent Pos:* Res assoc sea grant, Dept Geol Sci, Univ Rochester, Nat Oceanic & Atmospheric Admin, 72-73; adj prof, Dept Biol & Ctr Marine Studies, Am Univ, 80- *Mem:* Am Soc Limnol & Oceanog; Int Soc Theoret & Appl Limnol; AAAS; Sigma Xi; Am Water Resources Asn. *Res:* Limnology of lakes and reservoirs; geochemistry of estuaries, rivers and streams; chemical characteristics of ground water. *Mailing Add:* 2577 Park Blvd V101 Palo Alto CA 94306

BUBEL, HANS CURT, MEDICAL BACTERIOLOGY. *Current Pos:* from asst prof to assoc prof, 58-70, PROF MICROBIOL, UNIV CINCINNATI, 70- *Personal Data:* b Mannheim, Ger, Oct 3, 25; nat US; m 58; c 2. *Educ:* Univ Utah, BS, 50, MS, 53, PhD(bact), 58. *Prof Exp:* Res assoc virol, Univ Utah, 53-58. *Mem:* NY Acad Sci; Am Soc Microbiol. *Res:* Host-cell virus interactions; polio-virus and herpes simplex virus; vaccinia virus; host resistance to virus infection; biology of the macrophage; antiviral immunity. *Mailing Add:* Dept Microbiol Univ Cincinnati Col Med 231 Bethesda Ave Cincinnati OH 45267-0001

BUBENZER, GARY DEAN, SOIL & WATER CONSERVATION, EROSION CONTROL. *Current Pos:* from asst prof to assoc prof, 69-78, chmn, 83-88, PROF AGR ENG, UNIV WIS-MADISON, 78- *Personal Data:* b Bicknell, Ind, Aug 21, 40; m 62, Sandra L Capehort; c Nathan E & Brian P. *Educ:* Purdue Univ, BS, 62, MS, 64; Univ Ill, PhD(agr eng), 70. *Prof Exp:* Instr conserv eng & surv, Univ Ill, 64-69. *Concurrent Pos:* Vis assoc prof, Univ Idaho, 77-78; vis lectr, Kyoto Univ, Japan, 81. *Mem:* Fel Am Soc Agr Engrs. *Res:* Rainfall simulation; soil erosion mechanics and small watershed hydrology. *Mailing Add:* Agr Eng 115 Agr Eng Univ Wis 460 Henry Mall Madison WI 53706-1533

BUBLITZ, CLARK, BIOCHEMISTRY. *Current Pos:* asst prof biochem, 60-71, ASSOC PROF BIOCHEM, UNIV COLO MED CTR, 71- *Personal Data:* b Merrill, Wis, Dec 8, 27; m 58; c 5. *Educ:* Univ Chicago, PhB, 49, PhD(biochem), 55. *Prof Exp:* Am Cancer Soc fel, 55-58; sr instr pharmacol, Sch Med, St Louis Univ, 59-60. *Mem:* AAAS; Am Chem Soc; Am Soc Biol Chemists. *Res:* Enzymology. *Mailing Add:* Dept Biochem Univ Colo Med Ctr 4200 E Ninth Ave B121 Denver CO 80262-0001. *Fax:* 303-270-8215

BUBLITZ, DONALD EDWARD, ORGANIC CHEMISTRY. *Current Pos:* CONSULT, 82- *Personal Data:* b Chicago, Ill, Dec 6, 35; m 57; c 2. *Educ:* Univ Calif, Riverside, AB, 57; Univ Kans, PhD(chem), 61. *Prof Exp:* Res assoc chem, Univ Ill, 61-62; res chemist, Dow Chem USA, 62-70, sr res chemist, 70-72, res specialist, Western Div, Dow Chem USA, 72-82. *Mem:* Am Chem Soc; NY Acad Sci. *Res:* Synthesis of agricultural and pharmaceutical chemicals; organometallic compounds. *Mailing Add:* 1592 Hoytt Dr Concord CA 94521-1817

BUBLITZ, WALTER JOHN, JR, PULP CHEMISTRY, PAPER CHEMISTRY. *Current Pos:* RETIRED. *Personal Data:* b Kansas City, Mo, Sept 26, 20; m 54, Mary H Chase; c Philip (deceased) & David L. *Educ:* Univ Ariz, BS, 41; Lawrence Col, PhD(paper chem), 49. *Honors & Awards:* Richter Prize, Tech Asn Pulp & Paper Indust, 91. *Prof Exp:* Res chemist, Lithographic Tech Found, 49-50; chemist, Munising Paper Co, 50-52; res chemist, Kimberly Clark Corp, 52-59; res chemist, Duplicating Prod Div, Minn Mining & Mfg Co, 59-60 & Paper Prod Div, 60-66; prof pulp & paper res, Ore State Univ, 66-83. *Concurrent Pos:* Guest lectr, SChina Inst Technol, Canton, China, 84; Tasman fel, Univ Canterbury, Christ Church, NZ, 85. *Mem:* Fel Tech Asn Pulp & Paper Indust; Can Pulp & Paper Asn. *Res:* Research and development of specialty paper products; technical problems of lithography; 3M Brand Action paper; pulping research. *Mailing Add:* 1430 NW 14th Pl Corvallis OR 97330-4624

BUCALA, RICHARD, BIOCHEMISTRY. *Current Pos:* assoc prof, 91-93, PROF & HEAD, LAB MED BIOCHEM, PICOWER INST MED RES, 94- *Personal Data:* m, Anne; c 2. *Educ:* Yale Univ, BS & MS, 79; Rockefeller Univ, PhD(biochem), 85; Cornell Univ, MD, 86. *Prof Exp:* Assoc physician, Rockefeller Univ Hosp, 88-90, asst prof, Rockefeller Univ, 90-91. *Concurrent Pos:* Adj physician, N Shore Univ Hosp, 91-; scholar award, Am Found AIDS Res, 92. *Mem:* Molecular Med Soc(sec/treas, 95-); Am Soc Biochem; NY Acad Sci; Am Diabetes Asn; AAAS. *Mailing Add:* Med Biochem Lab Picower Inst Med Res 350 Community Dr Manhasset NY 11030. *E-Mail:* rbucala@picower.edu

BUCCAFUSCO, JERRY JOSEPH, NEUROPHARMACOLOGY. *Current Pos:* asst prof pharmacol & toxicol, 79-85, asst prof psychiat, 82-85, ASSOC PROF PHARMACOL, TOXICOL & PSYCHIAT, MED COL GA, 85- *Personal Data:* b Jersey City, NJ, Aug 20, 49; m 73; c 2. *Educ:* St Peter's Col, BS, 71; Canisius Col, MS, 73; Univ Med & Dent, NJ, PhD(pharmacol), 78. *Prof Exp:* Fel pharmacol, Roche Inst Molecular Biol, Roche Pharmaceut, 77-79. *Concurrent Pos:* Dir, neuropharmacol lab, Vet Admin Med Ctr, 82-; mem, Int Adv Bd, Giornale Italiano D I Pathologia Clinica; Pharmacol II Study Sect, Nat Inst Drug Abuse. *Mem:* Am Soc Pharmacol & Exp Therapeut; Soc Neurosci; Soc Exp Biol & Med; Sigma Xi; AAAS; Am Soc Hypertension. *Res:* Neuropharmacology and neurochemical studies on central cardiovascular regulation and the role of the brain in hypertensive disease; brain mechanisms mediating the symptoms of narcotic withdrawal syndrome; protection against the toxic effects of agricultural insecticides; learning and memory in non-human primates. *Mailing Add:* Dept Pharmacol & Toxicol Med Col Ga Augusta GA 30912-2300. *Fax:* 706-721-2347

BUCCI, ENRICO, PHYSICAL BIOCHEMISTRY. *Current Pos:* assoc prof, 69-74, PROF BIOCHEM, SCH MED, UNIV MD, 74- *Personal Data:* b Este, Italy, May 27, 32; US citizen; m 59; c 4. *Educ:* Univ Rome, MD, 56, PhD(biochem), 62. *Prof Exp:* From vol asst to asst biochem, Univ Rome, 56-65; asst prof, Med Sch, Ind Univ, 65-69. *Mem:* Am Soc Biol Chemists; Am Chem Soc; NY Acad Sci; Biophys Soc; Am Soc Photobiol; Sigma Xi. *Res:* Structure function relationships and protein folding of hemoglobin and membrane proteins systems as seen in the physico-biochemical behavior of the entire molecules, their subunits and large peptides obtained from them. *Mailing Add:* Dept Biochem Univ Md Sch Med 108 N Greene St Baltimore MD 21201-1503. *Fax:* 410-706-7390

BUCCI, ROBERT JAMES, STRUCTURAL MATERIALS & ASSOCIATED CHARACTERIZATION & DESIGN METHODOLOGIES. *Current Pos:* staff engr, Alcoa Res Labs, 73-80, tech supvr fatigue & fracture, 80-85, tech specialist, 85-87, sr tech specialist, 87-90, TECH CONSULT, ALCOA RES LABS, 90- *Personal Data:* b Cambridge, Mass, Aug 18, 41; m 69; c 1. *Educ:* Northeastern Univ, BS, 64; Brown Univ, MS, 67; Lehigh Univ, PhD(appl mech), 70. *Prof Exp:* Vpres res fracture mech, Del Res Corp, 69-73. *Concurrent Pos:* Chmn task group fatigue crack growth testing, Am Soc Testing & Mat, 73-80, chmn subcomt on subcritical crack growth, 80- *Mem:* Am Soc Testing & Mat; Mineral, Metals & Mat Soc; Am Soc Metals Int; Soc Advan Mat & Process Eng; Sigma Xi; Am Inst Aeronaut & Astronaut. *Res:* Fatigue and fracture mechanics; test method development; aluminum aerospace materials; design; failure analysis; structural integrity. *Mailing Add:* Alcoa Tech Ctr Aluminum Co Am 100 Technical Dr Alcoa Center PA 15069

BUCCI, THOMAS JOSEPH, COMPARATIVE PATHOLOGY. *Current Pos:* DIR PATH SERV, NAT CTR TOXICOL RES, DEPT HEALTH & HUMAN SERV, JEFFERSON, ARK, 81- *Personal Data:* b Smithfield, RI, July 21, 34; m 57, Clara E Holiday; c 4. *Educ:* Univ Pa, VMD, 59; Univ Rochester, MS, 62; Univ Colo Med Ctr, PhD(path), 74. *Prof Exp:* Chief, Vet Div, 5th US Army Med Lab, 59-61, vet pathologist, Div Nuclear Med, Walter Reed Army Inst Res, 65-66, chief, Path Div, US Army Med Res & Nutrit Lab, 66-69, chief, Dept Comp Med, Letterman Army Inst Res, 74-78; head, Vet Med Dept, Med Res Unit, US Navy, Cairo, Egypt, 78-81. *Concurrent Pos:* Assoc prof, Pharmacol Dept, Univ Ark Med Scis, Little Rock, Ark. *Mem:* Am Col Vet Pathologists; Int Acad Pathologists; Am Asn Exp Pathologists; Am Vet Med Asn; Soc Toxicol Pathologists. *Res:* Radiation pathology; exercise physiology; comparative nutrition; vitamin metabolism; reproduction of nonhuman primates; infectious disease; toxicologic pathology. *Mailing Add:* Path Serv Path Assoc Inc PO Box 26 Jefferson AR 72079-0026

BUCCINO, ALPHONSE, SCIENCE ADMINISTRATION, MATHEMATICS. *Current Pos:* CONSULT & CO-DIR, VITA MATH FOUND, 95- *Personal Data:* b New York, NY, Mar 14, 31; m 53, Estelle M Ambrose; c Daniel Laurence. *Educ:* Univ Chicago, BS, 58, MS, 59, PhD(math), 67. *Prof Exp:* Dept head, Univ Math, 63-70; sci educ adminr, Sr Exec Serv, NSF, 70-84; dean, Col Educ, Univ Ga, 84-94. *Concurrent Pos:* Consult sci & technol policy, educ & prog develop. *Mem:* Fel AAAS; Nat Coun Teachers Math; Am Math Soc; Math Asn Am. *Res:* Historical and contextual studies of mathematics, science and technology policy analysis; research administration. *Mailing Add:* Contemporary Commun Inc 5615 Glenwood Rd Bethesda MD 20817-6727. *Fax:* 301-718-6136; *E-Mail:* abuccino@aol.com

BUCCINO, SALVATORE GEORGE, NUCLEAR PHYSICS. *Current Pos:* from asst prof to assoc prof, 65-70, PROF PHYSICS, TULANE UNIV, 70- *Personal Data:* b New Haven, Conn, Dec 23, 33; m 69, Victoria A Milliken; c Tracy A & Alexander K. *Educ:* Yale Univ, BS, 56; Duke Univ, PhD(nuclear physics), 63. *Prof Exp:* Res assoc nuclear physics, Duke Univ, 62-63; asst physicist, Argonne Nat Lab, 63-65. *Concurrent Pos:* Consult, Radiation Lab, Aberdeen Proving Grounds, 73 & 74; vis scholar physics, Duke Univ, 74-75. *Mem:* Am Phys Soc; Sigma Xi. *Res:* Coulomb excitation; fast time-of-flight techniques; gamma ray spectroscopy, particularly high spin systems. *Mailing Add:* Dept Physics Tulane Univ New Orleans LA 70118. *Fax:* 504-862-8702; *E-Mail:* salb@mailhost.tcs.tulane.edu

BUCCOLA, STEVEN THOMAS, AGRICULTURAL MARKETS. *Current Pos:* from asst prof to assoc prof, 80-88, PROF AGR ECON, ORE STATE UNIV, 88- *Personal Data:* b Pasadena, Calif, Dec 30, 44; m 73, Amy Hess; c Matthew & Vincent. *Educ:* Saint Mary's Col Calif, BA, 66; Univ Calif, Davis, MS, 72, PhD(agr econ), 76. *Prof Exp:* Asst prof, Va Polytech Inst & State Univ, 76-80. *Concurrent Pos:* Co-ed, Am J Agr Econ, 91-94. *Mem:* Am Agr Econ Asn; West Agr Econ Asn. *Res:* Application of decision theory to farmer and food processor decisions under risk; analysis of pricing mechanisms and contractual arrangements with a view to evaluating market performance. *Mailing Add:* Dept Agr & Resource Econ Ore State Univ 213 Bakkard Ext Hall Corvallis OR 97331-3601

BUCH, ROBERT MICHAEL, NON-INVASIVE CHEMICAL ANALYSIS TECHNIQUES, BIOSENSORS & MICROANALYSIS. *Current Pos:* scientist, 90-91, sr scientist, 91-93, RES ASSOC, WARNER-LAMBERT CO, 93- *Personal Data:* m 91, Karen Fisher. *Educ:* Franklin & Marshall Col, BA, 84; Univ Del, MS, 87, PhD(anal chem), 91. *Prof Exp:* Researcher, Hawaii Biosensor Lab, Univ Hawaii, 89-90. *Mem:* Am Chem Soc. *Res:* Application of non-invasive chemical analyses to the development of novel health-care products, ranging from diagnostic devices to oral health medications to upper respiratory and gastrointestinal drugs. *Mailing Add:* Smithkline Beecham 1500 Littleton Rd Parsippany NJ 07054. *Fax:* 973-540-4300

BUCHAL, ROBERT NORMAN, APPLIED MATHEMATICS. *Current Pos:* MATHEMATICIAN, AIR FORCE OFF SCI RES, 75- *Personal Data:* b Passaic, NJ, Apr 14, 30; m 57; c 3. *Educ:* St Lawrence Univ, BS, 51; Univ Conn, MA, 52; NY Univ, PhD(math), 59. *Prof Exp:* Analytical engr, Bendix Aviation Corp, 52-54; res asst, Inst Math Sci, NY Univ, 54-58; asst prof, Math Res Ctr, US Army, Univ Wis, 58-60; assoc mathematician, Argonne Nat Lab, 60-70; mathematician, Off Naval Res, 70-75. *Mem:* Soc Indust & Appl Math. *Res:* Asymptotic solutions and generalized solutions of differential equations; wave equations; mathematical biology. *Mailing Add:* 8707 Highgate Rd Alexandria VA 22308-2325

BUCHAN, GEORGE COLIN, MEDICINE, NEUROPATHOLOGY. *Current Pos:* RETIRED. *Personal Data:* b Seattle, Wash, Aug 30, 27; m 62; c 2. *Educ:* McGill Univ, MD, CM, 58. *Prof Exp:* From asst prof to assoc prof, Ore Health Sci, Univ Ore, 67-68, prof path & head, Div Neuropath, 68-90. *Concurrent Pos:* Fel neuropath, Univ Wash, 63-65. *Mem:* Am Asn Neuropath. *Res:* Factors influencing myelination in the nervous system. *Mailing Add:* Div Neuropath Ore Health Sci Univ 3181 SW Sam Jackson Park Rd Portland OR 97201-3011

BUCHANAN, BERNARD J, ENDOCRINOLOGY. *Current Pos:* PVT PRACT, INTERNAL MED, 82- *Personal Data:* b Elmhurst, Ill, 1947. *Educ:* Elmhurst Col, BA, 70; Loyola Univ, PhD(physiol), 75, MD, 77. *Prof Exp:* Med researcher, Northwestern Univ, 77-81; fel, Vet Admin Hosp, Hines, Ill, 81-82. *Concurrent Pos:* Group practr, Trover Clin, Madisonville, KY, 82-92. *Mem:* Am Diabetes Asn. *Mailing Add:* Physicians Affilate Care 1020 Hathaway St PO Box 1919 Owensboro KY 42303

BUCHANAN, BOB BRANCH, BIOCHEMISTRY, MICROBIOLOGY. *Current Pos:* NIH fel biochem, 62-63, chair, Div Plant Biol, 82-88, PROF PLANT & MICRIOBIAL BIOL, UNIV CALIF, BERKELEY, 63- *Personal Data:* b Richmond, Va, Aug 7, 37; m 65; c 4. *Educ:* Emory & Henry Col, AB, 58; Duke Univ, PhD(microbiol), 62. *Honors & Awards:* Spec Creativity Award, NSF, 82, Sr Scientist Award, 84; Bessenyei Medal, Hungary, 87. *Concurrent Pos:* Guggenheim Found fel, 74, Off Comprehensive Employment fel, 84; vis prof, Univ Paris-Sud, Orsay, 84 & 91. *Mem:* Nat Acad Sci; Am Soc Biol Chemists; Am Soc Microbiol; NY Acad Sci; Am Soc Plant Physiol; AAAS. *Res:* Plant biochemistry; photosynthesis; enzymology; bacterial metabolism. *Mailing Add:* Dept Plant & Microbial Biol Univ Calif 111 Koshland Hall Berkeley CA 94720-0001. *Fax:* 510-642-4995

BUCHANAN, BRUCE G, COMPUTER SCIENCE. *Current Pos:* PROF COMPUT SCI & PROF PHILOS & MED, UNIV PITTSBURGH. *Personal Data:* b St Louis, Mo, July 7, 40; m 61; c 2. *Educ:* Ohio Wesleyan Univ, AB, 61; Mich State Univ, MA & PhD(philos), 66. *Prof Exp:* Res assoc comput sci, Stanford Univ, 66-71, res comput scientist, 72-76, adj prof comput sci, 76- *Concurrent Pos:* NIH career develop award, 71-76; prog chmn, Int Joint Conf Artificial Intel, 79. *Mem:* Inst Med-Nat Acad Sci; Philos Sci Asn; AAAS; Am Asn Artificial Intel. *Res:* Application of artificial intelligence to scientific inference. *Mailing Add:* Dept Comput Sci Univ Pittsburgh 322 Alumni Hall Pittsburgh PA 15260-3803

BUCHANAN, BRYANT W, EVOLUTION OF REPRODUCTIVE TACTICS, SENSORY ECOLOGY. *Current Pos:* INSTRUCTOR BIOL, UNIV MO, 93- *Personal Data:* b Jackson, Miss, July 1, 60; m 92, Sharon Wise. *Educ:* Univ Southern Miss, BS, 86; Univ Southwestern La, MS, 88, PhD(environ & evolutionary biol), 93. *Prof Exp:* Teach asst biol, Univ Southwestern La, 86-88 & 92-93, fel, 88-92. *Concurrent Pos:* Pratt fel, Mountain Lake Biol Sta, Univ Va, 93 & 94; vis asst prof biol, Univ Mo, 96- *Mem:* Sigma Xi; Am Soc Naturalists; Soc Study Evolution; Animal Behav Soc; Int Soc Behav Ecol; Am Soc Ichthyol & Herpet; Nat Ctr Sci Educ. *Res:* Evolution and expression of alternative reproductive tactics; satellite behavior using hylid frogs as a model system; sensory constraints on visual communication in nocturnal amphibians. *Mailing Add:* 204 Tucker Hall Univ Mo Columbia MO 65211. *Fax:* 573-882-0123; *E-Mail:* bbryant@biosci.mbp.missouri.edu

BUCHANAN, C RICHARD, DENTISTRY. *Current Pos:* ACTG ASST CHIEF MED DIR DENT & DIR DENT EDUC & RES, DEPT VET AFFAIRS, 96- *Personal Data:* b Kansas City, Mo, May 13, 44; m 66, Sandra L Buchanan; c Michael S & Jeffrey T. *Educ:* Univ Ore, BS, 66; Sch Dent, Portland, DMD, 70. *Prof Exp:* Staff dentist, Vet Admin Med Ctr, 76-83, from asst chief to chief dent serv, 83-96, actg chief staff, 92-93. *Concurrent Pos:* Instr, Ore Health Sci Ctr Sch Dent, 73-76, Diablo Valley Col, 86-93; pvt pract, Aloha, Ore, 73-74, St Helens, Ore, 74-76; instr, Hosp Dent Prog, Vet Admin Med Ctr, 84-93, dir, Gen Pract Residency Prog, 85-93; adj asst prof, Univ Pac Sch Dent, 85-93. *Mem:* Fel Int Col Dentists; Am Dent Asn; Am Asn Dent Schs; Asn Mil Surgeons US. *Mailing Add:* Off Dent Dept Vet Affairs 112D 810 Vermont NW Washington DC 20420. *Fax:* 202-273-9105

BUCHANAN, CHRISTINE ELIZABETH, MICROBIAL PHYSIOLOGY, MICROBIAL GENETICS. *Current Pos:* from asst prof to assoc prof, 77-89, dept chair, 88-90, PROF BIOL SCI, SOUTHERN METHODIST UNIV, 89- *Personal Data:* b St Louis, Mo, July 5, 46; m 69. *Educ:* Drake Univ, BA, 68; Univ Chicago, PhD(microbiol), 73. *Prof Exp:* Postdoctoral biochem & molecular biol, Harvard Univ, 73-77. *Concurrent Pos:* Prin investr, funded res proj, NSF, 80-82, NIH, 83-; mem, Study Sect Microbial, Physiol & Genetics, NIH, 85-89; chair, Div K, Am Soc Microbiol, 88-89; from alt counr to counr, Am Soc Microbiol Div K, 94- *Mem:* Am Soc Microbiol; AAAS; Sigma Xi. *Res:* Role of penicillin-binding proteins in bacterial cell division, morphogenesis, and sporulation. *Mailing Add:* 6324 Lafayette Way Dallas TX 75230-1820

BUCHANAN, DAVID HAMILTON, PHYSICAL ORGANIC CHEMISTRY, COAL CHEMISTRY. *Current Pos:* from asst prof to assoc prof, 71-81, PROF CHEM, EASTERN ILL UNIV, 81-, CHMN CHEM, 89- *Personal Data:* b Indiana, Pa, July 4, 42; m 67, Susanna Forbes; c Jeannette & Rebecca. *Educ:* Case Inst Technol, BS, 64; Univ Wis-Madison, PhD(org chem), 69. *Prof Exp:* NIH fel organometallic chem, Univ Calif, Berkeley, 68-71. *Concurrent Pos:* Vis scientist, SRI, Inc, 78-79; secy, Fuel Chem Div, Am Chem Soc, 90-92. *Mem:* Am Chem Soc; AAAS. *Res:* Organic chemistry of coal and coal liquefaction; mechanisms of SN2 reactions; chemistry of ethers; coal desulfurization. *Mailing Add:* Col Arts & Sci Westchester Univ West Chester PA 19383. *Fax:* 217-581-2722; *E-Mail:* cfdhb01@eiu.edu

BUCHANAN, DAVID ROYAL, TEXTILE PHYSICS. *Current Pos:* prof textile mat & mgt & head dept, 78-83, PROF TEXTILE ENG & SCI, NC STATE UNIV, 83-, ASSOC DEAN, COL TEXTILES, 88- *Personal Data:* b Mansfield, Ohio, Mar 28, 34; m 57; c 4. *Educ:* Capital Univ, BSc, 56; Ohio State Univ, PhD(chem), 62. *Prof Exp:* Res chemist, Chemstrand Res Ctr, Inc, NC, 62-68; sr res chemist, Phillips Petrol Co, Okla, 68-70, proj mgr, Phillips Fibers Corp, SC, 70-72, mgr textile testing, 72-75; assoc prof design & environ anal, Cornell Univ, 75-78. *Concurrent Pos:* Consult; gov coun, Fiber Soc, 80-83. *Mem:* Am Phys Soc; Am Chem Soc; Fiber Soc; Nat Coun Textile Educ; Sigma Xi; Soc Mfg Engr, Robotics Int. *Res:* Structure and properties of polymers, fibers and textiles; nonwoven processes and products; fiber extrusion processes and products; process automation in the textile and allied industries; applications of machine vision and robotics to process automation. *Mailing Add:* Dept Textile Eng & Sci NC State Univ Raleigh NC 27695-0001

BUCHANAN, DAVID SHANE, ANIMAL BREEDING, BEEF CATTLE GENETICS. *Current Pos:* From asst prof to assoc prof, 80-88, PROF ANIMAL SCI, OKLA STATE UNIV, 88- *Personal Data:* b Fargo, NDak, Mar 20, 53; m 75; c 3. *Educ:* NDak State Univ, BS, 75; Univ Nebr-Lincoln, MS, 77, PhD(animal sci), 79. *Concurrent Pos:* Ed, Am Soc Am Sci, 84-86; res comt, Nat Pork Producer's Coun, 85-; dir, Nat Swine Improvement Fedr, 87. *Mem:* Am Soc Animal Sci; Am Genetic Asn; Coun Agr Sci & Technol; Am Registry Prof Animal Scientists; Sigma Xi. *Res:* Animal breeding and genetics; beef cattle; swine and sheep; author of 34 articles in refereed journals and over 170 reports, abstracts and articles. *Mailing Add:* Dept Animal Sci Okla State Univ Stillwater OK 74078-0001

BUCHANAN, EDWARD BRACY, JR, ANALYTICAL CHEMISTRY. *Current Pos:* from asst prof to assoc prof, 60-88, PROF CHEM, UNIV IOWA, 67- *Personal Data:* b Detroit, Mich, Sept 12, 27. *Educ:* Univ Detroit, BS, 50, MS, 54; Iowa State Univ, PhD, 59. *Prof Exp:* Instr chem, Iowa State Univ, 59-60. *Mem:* Am Chem Soc; Soc Electroanal Chem. *Res:* Electrochemistry; design of instrumentation; hardware and software systems. *Mailing Add:* 4008 Stewart Rd NE Iowa City IA 52240

BUCHANAN, GEORGE DALE, SCIENCE EDUCATION, ANATOMY. *Current Pos:* assoc prof nursing & anat, 75-84, prof nursing & anat, 84-88, PROF BIOMED SCI, MCMASTER UNIV, 88- *Personal Data:* b Wichita Falls, Tex, Oct 1, 28. *Educ:* Rice Inst, BA, 50, MA, 54, PhD(biol), 56. *Prof Exp:* From asst prof to assoc prof biol, Houston State Col, 56-58; res assoc, Rice Inst, 58-59; from instr to assoc prof anat, Med Units, Univ Tenn, 59-68; assoc prof anat, Med Col Ohio, 68-75. *Concurrent Pos:* Vis prof morphol & biol, Univ Valle, Colombia, 66-67. *Mem:* AAAS; Am Asn Anat; Am Soc Mammalogists; Brit Soc Study Fertil; Soc Study Reproduction; Sigma Xi. *Res:* Reproductive biology; blastocyst implantation; reproductive asymmetry; reproduction in bats. *Mailing Add:* McMaster Univ 1200 Main St Rm 4N79 Hamilton ON L8S 4J9 Can

BUCHANAN, GEORGE R(ICHARD), ENGINEERING, ENGINEERING MECHANICS. *Current Pos:* From asst prof to assoc prof, 65-76, PROF ENG SCI, TENN TECHNOL UNIV, 76-, CHMN DEPT, 78- *Personal Data:* b Campbellsville, Ky, June 29, 39; m 61; c 3. *Educ:* Univ Ky, BS, 61, MS, 62; Va Polytech Inst, PhD(civil eng), 66. *Mem:* Assoc Am Soc Civil Engrs; Soc Eng Sci. *Res:* Structural mechanics; nonlinear analysis; wave propagation; finite elements. *Mailing Add:* Dept Civil Eng Tenn Technol Univ 900 N Dixie Ave Cookeville TN 38501-2684

BUCHANAN, GERALD WALLACE, ORGANIC CHEMISTRY. *Current Pos:* PROF, CARLETON UNIV, 80- *Personal Data:* b London, Ont, Mar 1, 43; m 67; c 1. *Educ:* Univ Western Ont, BSc, 65, PhD(org chem), 69. *Prof Exp:* Nat Res Coun Can fel, 69-70; vis asst prof chem, Univ Windsor, 70-71; from asst prof to assoc prof chem, Carleton Univ, 71-79; assoc prof, Louis Pasteur Univ, Strasbourg, France, 79-80. *Mem:* Am Chem Soc; Chem Inst Can. *Res:* Conformational analysis of organic molecules; multinuclear magnetic resonance; organic reaction mechanisms; nuclear magnetic resonance spectroscopy. *Mailing Add:* Dept Chem Carleton Univ Ottawa ON K1S 5B6 Can

BUCHANAN, HAYLE, PLANT ECOLOGY. *Current Pos:* from asst prof to assoc prof, 65-71, PROF BOT, WEBER STATE COL, 71- *Personal Data:* b Teasdale, Utah, Apr 3, 25; m 53; c 4. *Educ:* Brigham Young Univ, BA, 51, MA, 53; Univ Utah, PhD(bot), 60. *Prof Exp:* Teacher & prin, Tabiona & Hurricane Latter-Day Saints Sem, 53-56; teacher high sch, 58-60; asst prof bot, Church Col Hawaii, 60-62; instr life sci & bot, Am River Jr Col, 62-65. *Concurrent Pos:* Partic range mgt res, US Forest Serv, 66- *Mem:* Ecol Soc Am; Nat Parks Asn; Sigma Xi. *Res:* Ecological study of an area for outdoor education; management of forests in national parks; ecological life history studies. *Mailing Add:* 3068 N 1050 E Ogden UT 84414

BUCHANAN, J ROBERT, MEDICINE. *Current Pos:* PROF MED, HARVARD MED SCH, 82- *Personal Data:* b Newark, NJ, Mar 8, 28. *Educ:* Amherst Col, AB, 50; Cornell Univ Med Sch, MD, 54; Nat Bd Med Examr & Am Bd Int Med, dipl. *Prof Exp:* Intern med, NY Hosp, 54-55, asst resident physician, 57-58, res fel endocrinol, 56-57; res fel, Cornell Univ Med Col, 60-61, from instr to asst prof med, 61-67, assoc dean, 65-69, assoc prof, 69-71, dean, 69-76; prof, Univ Chicago, 77-82; gen dir, Mass Gen Hosp. *Concurrent Pos:* Fel, WHO, 63; asst to chmn, Dept Med, Cornell Univ Med Col, 64-65, clin assoc prof med, 67-69; assoc dean, Pritzker Sch Med, 78-82; physician, NY Hosp, 56-57 & 60-62, Michael Reese Hosp & Med Ctr, 77-82 & Mass Gen Hosp, 83-; asst chief & chief med, APO 20 Korea Patterson Army Hosp, 58-59; from asst attend physician to attend physician, NY Hosp, 58-59; pres, Michael Reese Hosp & Med Ctr, 77-82, Spaulding Rehab Hosp & Prof Serv Corp, Mass Gen Hosp, 84 & gen dir 82, assoc med sch, NY & NJ, 72-76; consult endocrinol & metab dis, Riverview Hosp, 60-68; asst dir, Comprehensive Care & Teaching Prog, Cornell Univ Med Sch, 61-65; assoc dir, Welfare Med Care Proj, NY Hosp, 61-64, asst dir, Eugene F DuBois Clin Res Ctr, 63-65; mem, Comt Sci Policy, mem, Sloan-Kettering Cancer Ctr, 69-76, Coun Deans, Asn Med Col, 69-76 & chmn, 75-76, bd dirs, Winifred Masterson Burke Relief Found, 72 & 80, Pub Health Res Inst NY City, 69-76, Psychiat Comt, NY Hosp Bd Gov, 69, Cornell Med Ctr Affil Comt, Hosp Spec Surg, NY Hosp, 69-76, bd dirs, Marie & John Zimmerman Fund, 72, vpres, 84-, Conf Jewish Hosp Dirs, 77, Comt Review Inst Med-Nat Acad Sci & pres, Search Comt, Asn Am Med Cols, 83-86, Spec Comt Mission & Priorities, Am Hosp Asn, 86-, bd dirs, Charles River Labs, 87, Priv Ind Coun Bostin, 88-; vchmn bd dirs, Asn Mgt Resources, 78-82, Ill Hosp Res & Educ Found, 78-79; chmn, Coun Teaching Hosp, Admin Bd, Asn Am Med Col, 88- *Mem:* Nat Acad Sci; fel Am Col Physicians; Sigma Xi. *Res:* Author of over 30 publications. *Mailing Add:* World Care Inc One Cambridge Ctr Cambridge MA 02114

BUCHANAN, JAMES WESLEY, PHYSICAL CHEMISTRY, INORGANIC CHEMISTRY. *Current Pos:* chmn dept, 77-, PROF CHEM, APPALACHIAN STATE UNIV, 77- *Personal Data:* b Union Mills, NC, May 5, 37; m 59; c 2. *Educ:* Univ NC, AB, 59; Univ Fla, MS, 62, PhD(radiation chem), 68. *Prof Exp:* Instr chem, Ga Col Milledgeville, 62-63; head dept, Gaston Jr Col, 64-66; from asst prof to assoc prof, Salem Col, NC, 70-75, chmn, Dept Chem & Physics, 71-75; sr chemist, Environ Measurements Dept, Res Triangle Inst, NC, 75-77. *Mem:* Am Chem Soc. *Res:* Radiation chemistry of both liquid and gas phase; radiolysis of ammonia-carbon tetrachloride solutions; radiolysis of phosphine and phosphine-containing gas mixtures. *Mailing Add:* 254 Eastview Dr Boone NC 28607

BUCHANAN, JOHN DONALD, RADIOCHEMISTRY. *Current Pos:* RETIRED. *Personal Data:* b Mesa, Ariz, Oct 1, 27; m 55; c Margaret M, John M, Andrew T & David B. *Educ:* Univ Ariz, BS, 49; Am Bd Health Physics, cert, 70. *Honors & Awards:* Meritorious Serv, High Qual Serv & Spec Achievement Awards, US Nuclear Regulatory Comn. *Prof Exp:* Radiochemist, Tracerlab, Inc, 50-56, sr chemist & sect head, 56-59; sr chemist, Gen Atomic, Inc, 59-62; sr radiochemist, Hazelton-Nuclear Sci Corp, 62-67, mgr nuclear measurements dept, 65-67, mgr nuclear prod, appln & measurements, Palo Alto Labs, Teledyne-Isotopes, Inc, 67-71; mgr appl res & radiation safety officer, Int Nutronics, Inc, 71-73; supvr, Radiol Monitoring Progs & Radiol Serv, NUS Corp, 73-75; radiochemist & health physicist & sr health physicist, US Nuclear Regulatory Comn, 75-94. *Mem:* Fel Health Physics Soc; Am Chem Soc; Am Nuclear Soc; Soc Risk Anal; Am Acad Health Physics; fel AAAS. *Res:* Radiation protection standards, nuclear regulatory standards; environmental radiation and radioactivity, radioassay, radiological monitoring; radiochemical analysis. *Mailing Add:* 7508 Dew Wood Dr Derwood MD 20855

BUCHANAN, JOHN MACHLIN, BIOCHEMISTRY. *Current Pos:* prof & head div, 53-67, Wilson prof, 67-88, WILSON EMER PROF BIOCHEM, MASS INST TECHNOL, 88- *Personal Data:* b Winamac, Ind, Sept 29, 17; m 48; c 4. *Educ:* DePauw Univ, BS, 38; Univ Mich, MS, 39; Harvard Univ, PhD(biochem), 43. *Hon Degrees:* DSc, Univ Mich, 61, DePauw Univ, 75. *Honors & Awards:* Eli Lilly Award Biol Chem, Am Chem Soc, 51. *Prof Exp:* Instr biochem, Univ Pa, 43-46; Nat Res Coun fel med, Nobel Inst, Stockholm, 46-48; from asst to prof biochem, Univ Pa, 48-53. *Concurrent Pos:* Sabbatical leave, Salk Inst Biol Studies, 64-65; mem, Fel Comt, Div Med Sci, Nat Res Coun, 54-63, mem, Subcomt Nomenclature Biochem, 60-66; mem, Biochem Study Sect, NIH, 59-63, chmn, 61-63; mem nat comt, Int Union Biochemists, 57-60, 63-69, secy-treas, 63-65, vchmn, 65-66; mem bd, Fedn Am Socs Exp Biol, 64-67; mem, Biochem Training Grant Comt, 65-69. *Mem:* Nat Acad Sci; Am Soc Biol Chemists (secy, 69-72); Am Chem Soc; Am Acad Arts & Sci; Sigma Xi. *Res:* Synthesis of glycogen; oxidation of fatty acids and ketone bodies; synthesis of purines; isolation and purification of enzymes; metabolism of bacteriophage infected bacteria; metabolic responses of eukaryotic cells to growth factors and oncogenic viruses. *Mailing Add:* 56 Meriam St Lexington MA 02173

BUCHANAN, RELVA CHESTER, CERAMIC SCIENCE. *Current Pos:* assoc prof ceramic eng, 74-84, PROF CERAMIC SCI ENG, DEPT MATS SCI & ENG, UNIV ILL, URBANA-CHAMPAIGN, 84- *Personal Data:* b Port Antonio, Jamaica, WI, Apr 10, 36; m 57; c 1. *Educ:* Alfred Univ, BS, 60; Mass Inst Technol, ScD(ceramic sci), 64. *Prof Exp:* Sr assoc engr, IBM Corp, 64-66, staff engr, 66-70, adv engr, 71-73. *Concurrent Pos:* Vis prof, Dept Ceramic Eng, Univ Ill, Urbana, 71-72; consult, Ctr Prof Advan, East Brunswick, NJ; adj prof Dept Mats Sci & Engr, Purdue Univ, 83; mem, Comt Appln Ferroelectrics, Inst Elec & Electronics Engrs. *Mem:* Fel Am Ceramic Soc; Nat Inst Ceramic Engrs; found mem Int Soc Hybrid Microelectronics; NAm Thermal Anal Soc; Electrochem Soc; Mat Res Soc; AAAS. *Res:* Electrical properties of glass and ceramic materials; ceramic substrate, glass-metal and electronic ceramic components; surface properties of ceramics and glasses; low temperature densification of refractory oxides; high TC superconductors; thin films; thick films; packaging; co-authored and edited two books; published over 60 technical works. *Mailing Add:* Dept Mat Sci Univ Cincinnati 2600 Clifton Ave Cincinnati OH 45220-2872

BUCHANAN, ROBERT ALEXANDER, PEDIATRICS, PHARMACOLOGY. *Current Pos:* RETIRED. *Personal Data:* b Detroit, Mich, Sept 8, 32; m 62, Jeannine Duffell; c Lawrence, Elizabeth & Gregory. *Educ:* Univ Mich, MD, 57; Am Bd Pediat, dipl, 64. *Prof Exp:* Intern, Philadelphia Gen Hosp, Pa, 57-58; resident pediat, Med Ctr, Univ Mich, 60-62; pvt pract, 62-66; investr, Park, Davis & Co, 66-67, asst dir, 67-68, assoc dir, 69-74, dir, 74-83, vpres, Clin Res Dept, 83-88, vpres, Sci Liaison, 89-91. *Concurrent Pos:* Sr exam, Fed Aviation Agency, 63-; dir, Guthrie Clin Res Found, 68-; clin assoc prof pediat, Med Sch, Univ Mich, 68- *Mem:* AMA; fel Am Acad Pediat; Am Therapeut Soc; Am Epilepsy Soc. *Res:* Pediatric pharmacology, especially new drug development in anticonvulsants and antibiotics; medical electronic diagnostic instrument development. *Mailing Add:* 3045 Foxcroft Ann Arbor MI 48104. *Fax:* 313-971-5617

BUCHANAN, ROBERT LESTER, MICROBIAL FOOD SAFETY, MYCOTOXICOLOGY. *Current Pos:* RES LEADER, RES ADMIN, USDA, 82- *Personal Data:* b Seattle, Wash, July 3, 46; m 74; c 3. *Educ:* Rutgers Univ, BS, 69, MS, 71, MPhil, 72, PhD(food sci), 74. *Prof Exp:* Res assoc, Univ Ga, 74-75; from asst prof to assoc prof res, Drexel Univ, 75-82. *Concurrent Pos:* Am Soc Microbiol; Inst Food Technologists. *Mem:* Fel Am Acad Microbiol. *Res:* Conducted research on the microbiology of foods and food safety including work with pathogenic bacteria and mycotoxigenic fungi. *Mailing Add:* USDA 600 E Mermaid Lane Glenside PA 19038-8598

BUCHANAN, ROBERT MARTIN, ELECTROANALYTICAL, CATALYSIS. *Current Pos:* PROF INORG CHEM, UNIV LOUISVILLE, 82- *Personal Data:* b Baltimore, Md, May 29, 51; m 75. *Educ:* Western Md Col, BA, 73; WVa Univ, MS, 75; Univ Colo, PhD(chem), 80. *Honors & Awards:* Davoe Raynolds Chem Award. *Prof Exp:* Res assoc, Solar Energy Res Inst, Univ Colo, 80-81, Mass Inst Technol, 81-82. *Mem:* Am Chem Soc; Sigma Xi; Am Asn Univ Prof. *Res:* Synthesis, characterization nuclear magnetic and electron spin resonance spectroscopy of organo-transition metal complexes; electrocatalytic reactions at chemically modified electrode surfaces; electroanalytical investigations of biologically important compounds; transition metal chemistry; bioinorganic; organometallic chemistry; electrocatalysis; synthesis of multifunctional ligands; activation of small molecules; magnetic exchange interactions and EPR; binuclear Cu, Fe and Mn complexes as models of protein active sites. *Mailing Add:* Dept Chem Univ Louisville 2301 S Third St Louisville KY 40292-0001

BUCHANAN, RONALD LESLIE, PHARMACEUTICAL LICENSING. *Current Pos:* PHARMACEUT CONSULT, INT LICENSING, 93- *Personal Data:* b Kirkland Lake, Ont, May 15, 37; m 61; c 3. *Educ:* Univ Western Ont, BSc, 59, PhD(org chem), 63. *Prof Exp:* Res fel, Univ BC, 63-64; sr res chemist, Bristol-Myers Co, 64-76, from asst dir to assoc dir res planning & licensing, 76-82, assoc dir licensing, 82-89; dir licensing, Bristol-Myers Squibb Co, 89-91, sr dir, licensing, 91-93. *Mem:* Am Chem Soc; NY Acad Sci; AAAS; Am Soc Microbiol. *Res:* Synthesis of biologically interesting monfluorinated compounds; biogenetic-type synthesis of natural products; synthesis of general medicinal agents. *Mailing Add:* 285 Highcrest Rd Wethersfield CT 06109. *Fax:* 860-563-1548

BUCHANAN, RONNIE JOE, RADIATION PHYSICS, HEALTH PHYSICS. *Current Pos:* RES PHYSICIST, HALLIBURTON SERV, 85- *Personal Data:* b Mulberry, Kans, July 14, 41; m 64, Marilyn K Rhuems; c Shelli L. *Educ:* Univ Kans, Lawrence, BA, 73, PhD(radiation physics), 76; Am Bd Health Physics, cert. *Prof Exp:* Technician health physics, US Navy, Antarctica, 69-70; radiation physicist, Los Alamos Nat Lab, 77-81; mem staff, Nuclear Sci Ctr, Tex A&M Univ, 81-84. *Concurrent Pos:* Radiation physicist, Univ Kans, Lawrence, 70-74, res asst, 74-77. *Mem:* Health Physics Soc; Am Acad Health Physics. *Res:* Neutron detection and reactions; methods of determining neutron dose; developing new and better methods of determining neutron spectrums; determining pulsed neutron flux and dose; gamma-ray detection and radiation instrumentation. *Mailing Add:* Halliburton Res Group PO Box 1431 Duncan OK 73536-0450. *Fax:* 580-251-3218; *E-Mail:* rjbuchanan@halnet.com

BUCHANAN, RUSSELL ALLEN, POLYMER CHEMISTRY, NATURAL PRODUCTS. *Current Pos:* ENVIRON CHEMIST, MARION CO HEALTH DEPT, 85- *Personal Data:* b Indianapolis, Ind, Aug 24, 28; m 50; c 10. *Educ:* Ind Univ, BS, 50. *Prof Exp:* Res chemist food oils & fats, Stand Brands Inc, 50-56; chief chemist prod, Com Solvents Corp, 56-60; res chemist chemurgy, Northern Regional Res Ctr, USDA, 60-79; sr chem, Soil & Land Use Technol, Inc, 79-84. *Mem:* Am Chem Soc; Soc Econ Bot. *Res:* Food products; industrial uses for starch; hydrocarbon producing plants; processing of multi-use crops; botanochemicals and biomass conversions. *Mailing Add:* 702 Willow Ct Danville IN 46122-1477

BUCHANAN, THOMAS JOSEPH, WATER RESOURCES ENGINEERING. *Current Pos:* Jr engr, Water Resources Div, US Geol Surv, NY, 51-52, asst engr, 52-55, assoc engr, 55-56, off engr, 56-58, engr-in-charge, 58-61, staff engr, Washington DC, 62-64, asst dist engr, NJ, 64-66, asst dist chief, 67-68, subdist chief, Fla, 68-76, ASST CHIEF HYDROLOGIST OPERS, US GEOL SURV, 76- *Personal Data:* b Albany, NY, Oct 26, 29; m 51; c 6. *Educ:* Rensselaer Polytech Inst, BSCE, 51;

Princeton Univ, MSCE, 67. *Concurrent Pos:* Chmn, Interagency Task Force on Water Policy-Instream Flows, 78-79. *Mem:* Am Soc Civil Engrs; Am Water Works Asn; Am Water Resources Asn; Nat Soc Prof Engrs. *Res:* Updated techniques used in measurement of stream discharge; developed techniques for use in time of travel studies in streams using fluorescent tracers; longitudinal dispersion in streams. *Mailing Add:* 1834 St Boniface St Vienna VA 22182

BUCHANAN-DAVIDSON, DOROTHY JEAN, BIOCHEMISTRY. *Current Pos:* RETIRED. *Personal Data:* b Monmouth, Ill, Dec 22, 25; m 57, Max A Davidson; c Scott A, Janet D (Gildner) & Nancy D (Purdy). *Educ:* Wash State Col, BS, 47; Univ Cincinnati, MS, 49, PhD(biochem), 51. *Prof Exp:* Instr biochem, Sch Med, Vanderbilt Univ, 50-53; Nat Res Coun fel, Lister Inst, London, 53-55; USPHS fel immunochem, Pasteur Inst, Paris, 55-56; proj assoc biochem, Univ Wis, 56-60, prog coordr, Ctr Affective Disorders, 83-86, ed, Sch Nursing, 86-90; abstractor, Chem Abstr, 60-76. *Concurrent Pos:* Consult ed, Mother's Manual, 64-69; instr, Madison Area Tech Col, 74-76; proj specialist, Water Resources Ctr, Univ Wis, 75-76, sci writer, Wis Clin Cancer Ctr, 76-80; ed, Admin Med Prog, Univ Wis, 80-83. *Mem:* Am Med Writers Asn; Soc Tech Commun; Anciens Eleves Inst Pasteur; Sigma Xi. *Res:* Immunochemistry; chemistry of blood-group-specific substances and meconium; phosphorous poisoning; x-irradiation; immunochemical agar-gel diffusion techniques; immunochemistry and biological properties of synthetic polypeptides and modified proteins; immunochemistry of plant proteins; cancer; administrative medicine; writing on chemistry, biochemistry, cancer, and psychiatry. *Mailing Add:* 335 Waterman St Oregon WI 53575

BUCHANAN-SMITH, JOCK GORDON, ANIMAL SCIENCE, ANIMAL NUTRITION. *Current Pos:* from asst prof to assoc prof, 69-84, PROF ANIMAL SCI, UNIV GUELPH, 85- *Personal Data:* b Edinburgh, Scotland, Mar 9, 40; m 64, Virginia Maxson; c Peter & Rachel. *Educ:* Aberdeen Univ, BSc, 62; Iowa State Univ, BS, 63; Tex Tech Col, MS, 65; Okla State Univ, PhD(animal sci), 69. *Honors & Awards:* Excellence in Res in Nutrit & Meat Sci, Can Soc Animal Sci. *Prof Exp:* Res asst animal sci, Tex Tech Col, 64-65; res asst, Okla State Univ, 65-69. *Concurrent Pos:* Nat Res Coun Can operating grants, 69-88; Agr Can operating grant, 75-78; ed, Can J Animal Sci, 85-87, Animal Feed Sci & Technol. *Mem:* AAAS; Am Soc Animal Sci; Am Dairy Sci Asn; Agr Inst Can; Sigma Xi. *Res:* Utilization of forages by ruminants; pasture and silage; ruminant animal ecology. *Mailing Add:* Dept Animal & Poultry Sci Univ Guelph Guelph ON N1G 2W1 Can. *Fax:* 519-836-9873; *E-Mail:* jbs@aps.uoguelph.ca

BUCHBERG, HARRY, ENGINEERING. *Current Pos:* res engr, 47-57, PROF ENG, UNIV CALIF, LOS ANGELES, 57- *Personal Data:* b Detroit, Mich, Oct 17, 17; m 43; c 3. *Educ:* Univ Calif, Berkeley, BS, 41; Univ Calif, Los Angeles, MS, 54. *Prof Exp:* Res & design engr, Lockheed Aircraft Corp, 41-47. *Concurrent Pos:* Consult thermal & solar design & anal, 55-; Fulbright scholar, 62 & 72; vis prof, Technion, Israel, 62 & Bogagici Univ, Turkey 71-72. *Mem:* Am Soc Mech Engrs; Am Soc Eng Educ; Am Soc Heating, Refrig & Air-Conditioning Engrs; Solar Energy Soc. *Res:* Thermal and solar engineering; solar energy collectors and energy conversion; published numerous scientific paper and reports. *Mailing Add:* 9833 Vicar St Los Angeles CA 90034

BUCHEL, JOHANNES A, FLAVOR CHEMISTRY. *Current Pos:* RETIRED. *Personal Data:* b Neth, July 31, 26; m 71. *Educ:* Hogere Tech Sch, Neth, BSc, 46. *Prof Exp:* Tech dir, Naardeh, SAfrica, 56-64, vpres tech dir, USA, 64-71, tech dir, Eng, 72-73; vpres int res & develop, Pepsi-Cola Inc, 74-91; pres, Perlarom Inc, 94-97. *Concurrent Pos:* Pres, Flavor & Extract Mfg Asn, 90. *Mem:* Am Chem Soc; Inst Food Technologists; Soc Flavor Chemists. *Res:* Management of soft drink research and development, including materials research, flavor research and flavor creation. *Mailing Add:* 13618 N Pima Spring Way Tucson AZ 85737-7199

BUCHELE, W(ESLEY) F(ISHER), AGRICULTURAL ENGINEERING, MACHINERY DESIGN & SAFETY. *Current Pos:* prof, 68-89, EMER PROF AGR ENG, IOWA STATE UNIV, 89- *Personal Data:* b Cedar Vale, Kans, Mar 18, 20; m 45, Mary Jagger; c Rodney, Mary E, Sheron & Steven. *Educ:* Kans State Univ, BS, 43; Univ Ark, MS, 51; Iowa State Univ, PhD(soil physics, agr eng), 54. *Honors & Awards:* Cyrus Hall McCormick-Jerome Increase Case Medalist, 88. *Prof Exp:* Student engr, John Deere Waterloo Tractor Works, 46-48, jr engr, 48; asst prof agr eng, Univ Ark, 48-51; asst prof & agr engr, Res Br, Agr Res Serv, USDA, Iowa State Univ, 54-56; assoc prof, Mich State Univ, 56-63. *Concurrent Pos:* Consult various cos, 53-90; mem numerous comts, Am Soc Agr Engrs, 57-; deleg numerous int confs, 61-88; vis lectr, Manila, 63, WGer, 64, Moscow, 68, Ghana, 69, Philippines, 79 & 91, NZ, 79, Australia, 79, 87 & 88, Africa, 79, Hungary, 80, Japan, 83, China, 83, Peru, 86, Zambia, 88,Tanzania, 90 & Mex, 93; vis prof & head div, Univ Ghana, 68-69; res engr, IITA, Ibadan, Nigeria, 79; vis scientist, CSIRO, Melbourne, Australia, 79; vis prof, Beijing Inst Agr Mechanization, 83, Nat Agrarian Univ, La Molina, Peru, 86 & 88; exec engr, special purpose vehicles, Sydney, Australia, 87, JAC Tractor Co, Sydney, 88. *Mem:* Am Soc Agron; fel Am Soc Agr Engrs; Soc Automotive Eng; Int Asn Mechanization Field Exp; Int Soc Terrain-Vehicle Systs; Osborne Asn; fel Nat Inst Agr Engrs; Int Platform Asn; AAAS; Sigma Xi. *Res:* Tillage; soil compaction; vehicular mechanics; torque meters; threshing cylinders and undisturbed soil samplers; agricultural safety; harvesting of grain and hay; energy conversion systems; biomass furnaces; producer gas generators; alcohol distillation; design of slot and punch planters for conservation production system of farming; vegetable-oil expelling and use; author or co-author of approximately 220 technical articles, 19 books and recipient of numerous patents. *Mailing Add:* 239 Parkridge Circle Ames IA 50010. *Fax:* 515-292-5011

BUCHENAU, GEORGE WILLIAM, PLANT PATHOLOGY. *Current Pos:* From asst prof to assoc prof plant sci, 59-80, PROF PLANT PATH, SDAK STATE UNIV, 80- *Personal Data:* b Amarillo, Tex, May 23, 32; m 55, 72; c 2. *Educ:* NMex State Univ, BS, 54, MS, 55; Iowa State Univ, PhD(plant path), 60. *Mem:* Am Phytopath Soc. *Res:* Wheat disease; resistance, chemical control and biological control. *Mailing Add:* 1215 Third St Brookings SD 57006

BUCHER, JOHN HENRY, STEEL RESEARCH & DEVELOPMENT, QUALITY CONTROL. *Current Pos:* DIR, RES & QUAL CONTROL, LUKENS STEEL CO, 84- *Personal Data:* b Newport, Ky, June 23, 39. *Educ:* Univ Cincinnati, BEng, 61; Ohio State Univ, MS, 62, PhD(metall eng), 64. *Honors & Awards:* Sigma Xi. *Prof Exp:* Res eng, Jones & Laughlin Steel Corp, 64-65, sr res eng, 65-66, res supvr, 66-72, chief metall, 72-73, mgr quality control, 73-74, staff engr, 74-76, supvr prod develop, Jones & Laughlin Steel Corp, 76-84. *Concurrent Pos:* Instr, mat eng, Carnegie-Mellon Univ, 67-70; pres, J H Bucher & Assoc Metall Consults Inc, 81- *Mem:* Am Soc Metals; Am Inst Mining; Metall & Petrol Eng; Am Iron & Steel Inst; Am Iron & Steel Engr. *Res:* Invented and developed steels with uniquely valuable properties such as improved motor lamination steels, high strength low alloy flat rolled and bar steels as well as new steelmaking practice. *Mailing Add:* 143 Barton Dr Spring City PA 19475

BUCHER, NANCY L R, MEDICINE. *Current Pos:* res fel & assoc med, 45-59, clin assoc, 59-68, asst clin prof med, 68-72, assoc prof med, 72-80, ASSOC PROF SURG, HARVARD MED SCH, 80-, ASSOC BIOLOGIST, MASS GEN HOSP, 52- *Personal Data:* b Baltimore, Md, May 4, 13. *Educ:* Bryn Mawr Col, AB, 35; Johns Hopkins Univ, MD, 43. *Prof Exp:* Intern, Mass Mem Hosp, Boston, 43-44, clin fel, 44-45. *Mem:* Am Asn Study Liver Dis; Am Soc Biol Chemists; Int Asn Study Liver; Tissue Culture Asn; Am Soc Cell Biol; Sigma Xi. *Res:* Cancer; growth regulation; cholesterol biosynthesis; liver regeneration. *Mailing Add:* Dept Path Boston Univ Sch Med 80 E Concord St Boston MA 02118-2394. *Fax:* 617-638-4085

BUCHER, T(HOMAS) T(ALBOT) NELSON, RADIO COMMUNICATIONS & SYSTEMS ENGINEERING. *Current Pos:* RETIRED. *Personal Data:* b Philadelphia, Pa, June 29, 19; m 46, Margaret F Summer; c Anne W B (Ertel), Elizabeth B (Lucas) & Victoria M (Gariffo). *Educ:* Drexel Inst Technol, BS, 41; Univ Pa, MS, 47, PhD(elec eng), 58. *Prof Exp:* Patent engr, Proctor Elec Co, 41-42; engr, Spec Apparatus Div, RCA Corp, 42-46, eng leader, Surface Commun Div, 46-47, eng mgr, 57-63, staff engr, Commun Systs Div, 63-84; consult eng, 84-94. *Concurrent Pos:* Lectr, Grad Sch, Villanova Univ, 59-63. *Mem:* Inst Elec & Electronics Engrs. *Res:* Communications equipment and system design; communication theory. *Mailing Add:* 309 Bridgeboro Rd Apt 3238 Moorestown NJ 08057-1429

BUCHHEIM, H PAUL, PALEOENVIRONMENTS, PALEOLIMNOLOGY. *Current Pos:* From asst prof to assoc prof, 79-88, PROF, LOMA LINDA UNIV, 89- *Personal Data:* b Vallejo, Calif, Apr 21, 47; m 72, Carole; c Hans, Ivan & Heather. *Educ:* Pac Union Col, BA, 71, MA, 72; Univ Wyo, PhD(geol), 78. *Honors & Awards:* President's Award, Am Asn Petrol Geologists. *Concurrent Pos:* Fel geol, Johns Hopkins Univ, 78-79. *Mem:* Geol Soc Am; Soc Econ Paleontologists & Mineralogists; Am Asn Petrol Geologists. *Res:* Lacustrine deposits and their sedimentology, paleontology and geochemistry, both ancient and modern; taphonomy and sediment-organism relationships; sedimentary petrology of laminated rocks. *Mailing Add:* 27876 Vista Rd Nuevo CA 92567. *Fax:* 909-824-4859

BUCHHEIT, RICHARD D(ALE), metallurgy, for more information see previous edition

BUCHHOLTZ, LOUIS J, PHYSICS. *Current Pos:* assoc prof, 86-91, PROF PHYSICS, CALIF STATE UNIV, 91- *Personal Data:* b Madison, Wis, June 23, 51; m, Barbara E Janzen. *Educ:* Oberlin Col, BA, 73; Stanford Univ, MS, 75, PhD(physics), 77. *Prof Exp:* Alexander von Humboldt Stiftung res fel, 77-80; res fel, Los Alamos Nat Lab, 80-82; asst prof physics, St Olaf Col, 82-86. *Concurrent Pos:* J William Fulbright res fel, 94-95. *Mem:* Am Asn Physics Teachers; Am Phys Soc; Sigma Xi. *Res:* Effect of a diffuse surface on an anisotopically paired superconductor; thermodynamics of a d-wave superconductor near a surface; superfluid 3He-B in a realistic thin film: current on a rough substrate; published 19 articles. *Mailing Add:* Dept Physics Calif State Univ Chico CA 95929-0202

BUCHHOLZ, ALLAN C, physical organic chemistry, polymer chemistry, for more information see previous edition

BUCHHOLZ, JEFFREY CARL, SURFACE PHYSICS. *Current Pos:* STAFF RES SCIENTIST, GEN MOTORS RES LABS, 76- *Personal Data:* b Sheboygan, Wis, June 10, 47; m 70. *Educ:* Univ Wis, Eau Claire, BS, 69; Univ Wis-Madison, MS, 71 & 73, PhD(mat sci), 74. *Prof Exp:* Res assoc chem, Univ Calif, Berkeley, 74-76. *Mem:* Am Vacuum Soc; Am Phys Soc; Sigma Xi; Mat Res Soc; Soc Photo Optical Instrumentation Engrs. *Res:* Study of the solid-gas and solid-liquid interface; modification of surface properties using ion beams and laser treatment; thin film materials. *Mailing Add:* Micro-Opt Tech Inc PO Box 620377 Middleton WI 53562

BUCHHOLZ, ROBERT HENRY, PHYSIOLOGY. *Current Pos:* Asst prof zool, 50-57, assoc prof biol, 57-63, PROF BIOL, MONMOUTH COL, ILL, 63- *Personal Data:* b Wakeeney, Kans, Aug 26, 24; m 47; c 3. *Educ:* Ft Hays Kans State Col, BS, 49; Kans State Col, MS, 50; Univ Mo, PhD, 57. *Concurrent Pos:* Mem staff, Argonne Nat Lab, 62-63; NIH fel, Dept Physiol, Univ Edinburgh, 63-64. *Mem:* AAAS; Am Soc Zoologists; Am Soc Mammal; assoc mem Am Physiol Soc; Sigma Xi. *Res:* Gastrointestinal physiology; digestive enzymes in bat, rat and mole; pancreatic lipase in the mole and rat. *Mailing Add:* Dept Biol Monmouth Col 700 E Broadway Monmouth IL 61462-1998

BUCHHOLZ SHAW, DONNA MARIE, PHARMACEUTICAL RESEARCH & DEVELOPMENT, TECHNOLOGY TRANSFER. *Current Pos:* res info scientist, Abbott Labs, 80-82, sr proj mgr, 82-87, opers mgr, Thrombolytics Venture, 87-89, mgr, In-Licensing, 89-90, dir, technol assessment & licensing, 90-94, DIR STRATEGIC ASSESSMENT, ABBOTT LABS, 94- *Personal Data:* b Chicago, Ill, May 27, 50; m 87, H Laurence Shaw; c David. *Educ:* Quincy Col, BS, 72; Univ Ill, MS, 75, PhD(microbiol), 78. *Honors & Awards:* Res Award, Sigma Xi, 78. *Prof Exp:* Res assoc immunol, Argonne Nat Lab, 78-80. *Concurrent Pos:* Guest scientist, Argonne Nat Lab, 80-93; part-time fac, NEastern Ill Univ, 85-93. *Mem:* Am Soc Microbiol; fel Am Acad Microbiol; Am Asn Immunologists; Sigma Xi; Licensing Execs Soc. *Res:* Discovery, development and clinical appraisal of new thrombolytic agents; licensing; immunological responses to cancer and immunological approaches to treatment of metastatic disease; strategic assessment; competitive analysis. *Mailing Add:* 86 Druid Hill Rd Summit NJ 07901-3225. *Fax:* 847-938-5852

BUCHI, GEORGE, ORGANIC CHEMISTRY. *Current Pos:* RETIRED. *Personal Data:* b Baden, Switz, Aug 1, 21. *Educ:* Swiss Fed Inst Technol, DSc, 47. *Hon Degrees:* Dr, Univ Heidelberg, 84, Switz Fed Inst Technol, 87. *Honors & Awards:* Ruzicka Award, 57; Fritzche Award, 58; Am Chem Soc Award, 73. *Prof Exp:* Firestone fel chem, Univ Chicago, 48-49, instr, 49-51; from asst prof to prof, Mass Inst Technol, 51-71, Camille Dreyfus prof chem, 71-92. *Mem:* Nat Acad Sci; fel Chem Soc London; Am Chem Soc; Swiss Chem Soc; Ger Chem Soc; Japanese Chem Soc; hon foreign mem Pharmaceut Soc Japan. *Res:* Synthetic organic chemistry; natural products; free radical reactions. *Mailing Add:* Dept Chem Mass Inst Technol 77 Massachusetts Ave Cambridge MA 02139

BUCHLER, EDWARD RAYMOND, ETHOLOGY. *Current Pos:* AT ORI INC. *Personal Data:* b Chicago, Ill, Sept 6, 42; m 65; c 3. *Educ:* Calif State Polytech Col, BS, 64; Univ Calif, Santa Barbara, MA, 66; Univ Mont, PhD(zool), 72. *Honors & Awards:* Original Res Contribs Achievement Award, US Army, 68. *Prof Exp:* Res zoologist, US Army, Ft Detrick, MD, 66-68; res assoc ethology, Rockefeller Univ, 72-75; asst prof ethology, Univ Md, Col Park, 75- *Concurrent Pos:* NSF grant; consult bat conserv & control. *Mem:* AAAS; Animal Behav Soc; Am Soc Mammalogists; Am Asn Zool Parks & Aquaria; Sigma Xi. *Res:* Acoustic communication systems in animals; echolocation in small mammals; hunting strategies, prey selection and communication in insectivorous bats; environmental cues used by migrating and foraging bats. *Mailing Add:* 3595 Sky Harbor Dr Coeur D'Alene ID 83814

BUCHLER, JEAN-ROBERT, STELLAR EVOLUTION & PULSATION. *Current Pos:* assoc prof, 74-80, PROF PHYSICS, UNIV FLA, 80- *Personal Data:* b Luxembourg City, Luxembourg, Apr 4, 42; US citizen; m 73, Daniele Cros; c Nicolas, Norbou & Yasha. *Educ:* Univ Liege, Belg, Licence, 65; Univ Calif, San Diego, MS, 67, PhD(physics), 69. *Prof Exp:* Res fel physics, Calif Inst Technol, 69-71; asst prof physics, Belfer Grad Sch, Yeshiva Univ, 71-74. *Concurrent Pos:* Consult, Los Alamos Nat Lab, 77-; guest prof, Niels Bohr Inst, Copenhagen, Denmark, 78-79 & Univ Paris VI, France; vis scientist, Observ Nice, France, 82, 84, 86 & Inst Astropys, Univ Liege, Belg. *Mem:* Int Astron Union; Am Astron Union; NY Acad Sci. *Res:* Theoretical astrophysics; stellar evolution; variable stars; nonlinear dynamics; chaotic behavior; supernovae; equation of state of dense matter; radiative transfer; hydrodynamics. *Mailing Add:* Physics Dept Univ Fla Gainesville FL 32611. *Fax:* 352-392-0524; *E-Mail:* buchler@phys.ufl.edu

BUCHMAN, ELWOOD, INTERNAL MEDICINE, GASTROENTEROLOGY. *Current Pos:* MED DIR, CINTEST, 80- *Personal Data:* b Iowa City, Iowa, June 10, 23; m 44; c 2. *Educ:* Univ Iowa, BA, 40, MD, 43. *Prof Exp:* Set chief gastroenterol, Vet Admin Hosp, Dearborn, Mich, 48-52; asst chief med, Vet Admin Hosp, Iowa City, 52-69; chief med serv, Vet Admin Hosp, Des Moines, 69-73; dir gastroenterol, Eaton Labs, Norwich, NY, 73-78; assoc group dir gastroenterol, Merrell Nat Labs, 78-80. *Concurrent Pos:* Asst prof gastroenterol, Wayne State Univ, 48-52; assoc prof med, Univ Iowa, 73-78. *Mem:* Fel Am Col Physicians; Am Col Gastroenterol; Am Col Clin Pharmacol; Sigma Xi; Am Soc Clin Pharm & Therapeut. *Res:* Gastrointestinal drugs; clinical pharmacology. *Mailing Add:* 6080 Miami Rd Cincinnati OH 45243

BUCHMAN, RUSSELL, PROCESS DEVELOPMENT, PROCESS CHEMISTRY. *Current Pos:* MGR, CONTRACT SYNTHESIS, G D SEARLE & CO, 93- *Personal Data:* b New York, NY, Dec 19, 47; m 70, Diane D Dorfman; c Joshua & Matthew. *Educ:* State Univ NY, Buffalo, BA, 69; Purdue Univ, PhD(med chem), 73. *Prof Exp:* Res assoc med chem, Univ Kans, 73-75; res chemist agr chem & pharmaceut chem, Diamond Shamrock Corp, 75-78, sr res chemist agr chem, 78-79, res supvr process develop, 79-82, group leader, 82-85, group leader anal serv, SDS Biotech Corp, 85-86; group leader chem & formulations, Ricerca Inc, 86-90; dir res & develop, Q O Chem Inc, 90-92. *Mem:* Am Chem Soc. *Res:* Scale-up of intermediates for analog synthesis programs and final products for biological evaluations; process scouting activities evaluate different synthetic approaches to target compounds; process development activities define and optimize selected synthetic routes. *Mailing Add:* G D Searle & Co 4901 Searle Pkwy Skokie IL 60077. *Fax:* 847-982-7465; *E-Mail:* rrbuch@searle.monsanto.com

BUCHMEIER, MICHAEL J, PATHOLOGY. *Current Pos:* Res fel immunopathol, Scripps Res Inst, 77-78, res assoc immunopathol, 78-79, asst mem I immunopathol, 79-80, asst mem II immunopathol, 80-82, ASSOC MEM NEUROPHARMACOL, SCRIPPS RES INST, 82-; ASSOC ADJ PROF PATHOL, UNIV CALIF, SAN DIEGO, 84- *Personal Data:* b Sedro-Woolley, Wash, Mar 19, 48; M, Nancy A Niederkorn; c Joshua & Michelle. *Educ:* Wash State Univ, BS, 70, MS, 72; McMaster Univ, PhD, 76. *Honors & Awards:* Established Invstr Award, Am Heart Asn, 79-84; Lectr, Am Soc Microbiol Found, 92-93. *Concurrent Pos:* Asst adj prof pathol, Univ Calif, San Diego, 80-84. *Mem:* Am Soc Immunol; Am Soc Virol; Am Soc Microbiol; Soc Gen Microbiol; AAAS; Pluto Soc. *Res:* Virology and immunobiology of lymphocytic choriomeningitis virus infection; pathogenesis of infection by the neurotropic murine corona viruses. *Mailing Add:* Dept Neuropharmacol Scripps Clin & Res Found 10666 N Torrey Pines Rd La Jolla CA 92037-1092

BUCHNEA, ALEX, ENVIRONMENTAL SCIENCE, HEALTH PHYSICS. *Current Pos:* PRES, SCIMUS INC, 83- *Personal Data:* m 72, Wendy Colwill; c Christopher, Danniel, Adam & David. *Educ:* Univ Toronto, BSc, 68, MSc, 69, PhD (nuclear physics), 76. *Prof Exp:* Nuclear sensor designer, Sentrol Systs, 74-77; nuclear design engr-specialist, Ont Hydro, 77-81; mgr nuclear sci, McLaren Plansearch Inc, 81-83. *Mem:* Can Nuclear soc; Can Radiaiton Protection Asn; Air & Waste Mgt Asn. *Res:* Application of novel technologies to the remediation of soils and ground water on contaminated sites, landfills and mine and industrial tailings; environmental impact analysis of these applications. *Mailing Add:* 18 Aneta Circle North York ON M2M 3J2 Can

BUCHNER, MORGAN M(ALLORY), JR, ELECTRICAL ENGINEERING. *Current Pos:* Mem tech staff, Bell Tel Labs, 65-69, supvr traffic res, 69-72, head, Performance Measurement Dept, 72-75, dir, Traffic Network Planning, 75-77, DIR, OPERS SYSTS PLANNING, BELL TEL LABS, 77- *Personal Data:* b Baltimore, Md, Mar 5, 39; m 63; c 2. *Educ:* Johns Hopkins Univ, BES, 61, PhD(elec eng), 65. *Mem:* Inst Elec & Electronics Engrs. *Mailing Add:* 635 Prospect Ave Little Silver NJ 07739

BUCHNER, STEPHEN PETER, SOLID STATE PHYSICS. *Current Pos:* RES SCIENTIST PHYSICS, MARTIN MARIETTA LABS, 77- *Personal Data:* b Cape Town, SAfrica, Sept 20, 45; m 76. *Educ:* Princeton Univ, BA, 68; Univ Pa, MS, 70, PhD(physics), 75. *Prof Exp:* Res assoc physics, Univ Md, 76-77. *Mem:* Am Phys Soc. *Res:* Semiconductor infrared detectors; metal oxide semiconductor devices for charge coupled device; surface physics; Raman scattering. *Mailing Add:* 4205 Bright Bay Way Ellicot City MD 21042. *Fax:* 410-204-2100

BUCHOLTZ, DENNIS LEE, AGRONOMY, PLANT PHYSIOLOGY. *Current Pos:* Fel, Agron Dept, 78-79, FEL, BOT & PLANT PATH DEPT, PURDUE UNIV, 80-, GRANTS ADMINR, MIDWEST PLANT BIOTECHNOL CONSORTIUM, 90- *Personal Data:* b Greenville, Ohio, Jan 23, 51. *Educ:* Manchester Col, BS, 73; Univ Nebr, Lincoln, MS, 75, PhD(agron), 78. *Mem:* Weed Sci Soc Am. *Res:* Effects of herbicides on the physiology and biochemistry of plants; processes involved in the absorption of herbicides into plants; biosynthesis of lignin in normal and mutant sorghum. *Mailing Add:* 819 Vine St West Lafayette IN 47906

BUCHSBAUM, DAVID ALVIN, MATHEMATICS. *Current Pos:* assoc prof, 60-63, PROF MATH, BRANDEIS UNIV, 63- *Personal Data:* b New York, NY, Nov 6, 29; m 49; c 3. *Educ:* Columbia Col, NY, AB, 49; Columbia Univ, PhD, 54. *Prof Exp:* Instr math, Princeton, 53-54, NSF fel, 54-55; instr math, Univ Chicago, 55-56; asst prof, Brown Univ, 56-59, assoc prof, 59-60. *Concurrent Pos:* NSF fel, 60-61; Guggenheim fel, 64-65. *Mem:* Am Math Soc. *Res:* Foundations and applications to commutative ring theory of homological algebra. *Mailing Add:* 3 Victoria Circle Newton Center MA 02159-1016

BUCHSBAUM, GERSHON, VISION & COLOR, IMAGE ANALYSIS. *Current Pos:* From asst prof to assoc prof, 79-93, grad group chmn, 87-91, PROF BIOENG, UNIV PA, 93-, CHAIR, DEPT BIOENG, 96- *Personal Data:* b Tel Aviv, Israel, July 24, 49; US citizen; m 76, Maya Y Hecht; c 3. *Educ:* Tel-Aviv Univ, BSc, 74, MSc, 75, PhD(eng sci), 79. *Hon Degrees:* MA, Univ Pa, 86. *Concurrent Pos:* NSF presidential young investr, 84; prin investr, NSF, 84-90, NIH, 86-89 & AFOSR, 90- *Mem:* Fel Inst Elec & Electronics Engrs; fel Optical Soc Am; Asn Res Vision Ophthal; Biomed Eng Soc; fel Am Inst Med & Biol Eng. *Res:* Image coding and analysis by the visual system. *Mailing Add:* Dept Bioeng Univ Pa Philadelphia PA 19104-6392

BUCHSBAUM, MONTE STUART, MEDICINE. *Current Pos:* sr asst surg, USPHS, 66-68, med officer, 68-75, actg chief, Sect Perceptual & Cognitive Studies, 70-75, chief, 75-78, CHIEF, SECT CLIN PSYCHOPHYSIOL, USPHS, 78-; PROF PSYCHIAT, UNIV CALIF, IRVINE. *Personal Data:* b Chicago, Ill, Apr 15, 40; m 68; c 2. *Educ:* Univ Pittsburgh, BS, 61; Univ Calif, San Francisco, MD, 65. *Honors & Awards:* Borden Award, 65. *Prof Exp:* Res asst, Univ Pittsburgh, 61-62, Langley Porter Neuropsychiat Inst, San Francisco, 63-65; intern, Univ Calif Med Ctr, 65-66. *Concurrent Pos:* Co-ed-in-chief, Psychiat Res. *Mem:* Soc Psychiat Res; Soc Psychophysiol Res. *Res:* Clinical studies of the psychophysiology of psychiatric patients and electrophysiological correlates of pharmacological treatment; positron emission tomography. *Mailing Add:* Dept Psychiat & Human Develop Univ Calif Irvine CA 92697

BUCHSBAUM, RALPH, INVERTEBRATE ZOOLOGY, CELL BIOLOGY. *Current Pos:* prof, 50-71, EMER PROF BIOL, UNIV PITTSBURGH, 71- *Personal Data:* b Chickasha, Okla, Jan 2, 07; m 33, Mildred B Shaffer; c Vicki (Pearse) & Monte S. *Educ:* Univ Chicago, BS, 28, PhD(zool), 32. *Honors & Awards:* Univ Chicago Prize, 40; Condon Lectr, 54. *Prof Exp:* Asst zool, Univ Wis, 28-29; from instr biol to asst prof zool, Univ Chicago, 31-42, asst prof, 45-47, res assoc, Inst Radiobiol Biophys, 47-50. *Concurrent Pos:* Instr, Gary Col, 33-35; cur, Mus Sci & Indust, Univ Chicago, 45-47; hon res assoc, Carnegie Mus, 55-; chief adv biol, Encycl Britannica Films, 59-; Fulbright award, Thailand, 59-60; dir, Ctr Studies Learning, 62; mem staff, Educ Mission, India, UNESCO, 64, chief consult biol teaching, Africa, 65-66; US AID-Univ Pittsburgh Ecuador Educ Proj, 65-67; ed, Boxwood Press, 72- *Mem:* Am Soc Zoologists; Ecol Soc Am; NY Acad Sci; AAAS; Biol Photog Asn. *Res:* Invertebrate biology; ecology of invertebrates; effects of irradiating living cells with various radiations in tissue cultures; cellular physiology; perfusion techniques in tissue culture; invertebrate physiology; ecology; environmental sciences. *Mailing Add:* 183 Ocean View Blvd Pacific Grove CA 93950-3093. *Fax:* 408-375-0430

BUCHTA, JOHN C(HARLES), ELECTRICAL ENGINEERING. *Current Pos:* ENGR, JDR SYSTS CORP, 90- *Personal Data:* b Minneapolis, Minn, Apr 13, 27; m 53; c 3. *Educ:* Univ Minn, BA, 49; Univ Ill, MS, 51 & 55, PhD(elec eng), 59. *Prof Exp:* Res assoc, Control Syst Lab, Univ Ill, 51-53; proj engr, Electronics Lab, 57-66, consult engr, 66-74, mgr, Eng Underseas Electronics Prod Dept, 74-76, mgr advan develop eng, Heavy Mil Electronics Dept, 76-80, mgr electronics technol, Turbine Bus Group, Gen Elec Co, Schenectady, NY, 80-86; mgr adv technol prog, Ocean Systs Div, Gen Elec, Syracuse, NY, 86-90. *Mem:* Inst Elec & Electronics Engrs; Sigma Xi; AAAS. *Res:* Computer science; electrical apparatus; digital equipment; electrical power systems. *Mailing Add:* 113 Hiawatha Trail Liverpool NY 13088-4432

BUCHTA, RAYMOND CHARLES, ANALYTICAL CHEMISTRY. *Current Pos:* res chemist, E I Du Pont de Nemours & Co, Inc, 69-75, sr res chemist, 75-80, res assoc, 80-93, SR RES ASSOC, EXP STA, E I DU PONT DE NEMOURS & CO, INC, 93- *Personal Data:* b Philadelphia, Pa, Dec 17, 42; m 68, Margrit Nagel; c Raymond & Daniel. *Educ:* Pa State Univ, BS, 65; Univ Wis-Madison, PhD(anal chem), 69. *Prof Exp:* Technician, Rohm and Haas Co, 62-63, chemist, 65. *Mem:* Am Chem Soc. *Res:* Electroanalytical chemistry; electrochemical detection in liquid chromatography; general trace analysis; gas chromatography; liquid chromatogaphy. *Mailing Add:* 2415 Allendale Rd Wilmington DE 19803

BUCHTEL, HENRY AUGUSTUS, IV, NEUROPSYCHOLOGY, PSYCHOLOGY. *Current Pos:* staff psychologist, 80-85, ACTG CHIEF, PSYCHOL SERV, VET ADMIN MED CTR, ANN ARBOR, 85-; ASSOC PROF PSYCHOL & NEUROPSYCHOL, UNIV MICH, ANN ARBOR, 80- *Personal Data:* b Denver, Colo, Nov 29, 42; m 75, E Margaret Evans; c Emma & Henry. *Educ:* Dartmouth Col, BA, 64; McGill Univ, MA, 65, PhD(psychol), 69. *Prof Exp:* Res fel, Inst Physiol, Univ Pisa, Italy, 69-72; clin neuropsychologist & res assoc, Dept Psychol, Nat Hosp Nervous Dis, London, 72-75; res assoc & vis prof psychol, Inst Human Physiol, Univ Parma, Italy, 75-78; clin neuropsychologist & res assoc, Psycol Dept, Montreal Neurol Inst & Hosp, 78-80. *Concurrent Pos:* Vis prof, Scuola Normale Superiore & Univ Pisa, Italy, 71-72; Am Acad Sci fel, Prague, Czech, 73; vis prof, Sch Specialization Neurol & Psychiat, Univ Parma, Italy, 75-78; vis prof, Peking Univ, China, 96. *Mem:* Am Psychol Asn; Neurosci Soc; Sigma Xi; Int Brain Res Orgn; Am Epilepsy Soc. *Res:* Biological basis of mind, especially the brain mechanisms of perception and attention; cerbral localization of functions and the nature of hemispheric dominance. *Mailing Add:* Dept Psychiat 480 Med Inn Univ Mich Med Campus Ann Arbor MI 48109-0840

BUCHTHAL, DAVID C, MATHEMATICS, GROUP THEORY. *Current Pos:* From asst prof to assoc prof, Univ Akron, Ohio, 71-85, asst dept head, 85-90, act dept head, 90-92, dept head math sci, 92-94, dept chair, 94-96, PROF MATH, UNIV AKRON, OHIO, 85-, ASSOC DEAN, ARTS & SCIS, 96- *Personal Data:* b Chicago, Ill Oct 10, 43; m 66, Janice L Schneider; c David M, Daniel T & Mark W. *Educ:* Loyola Univ, BS, 66; Purdue Univ, MS, 68, PhD(math), 71. *Concurrent Pos:* Lewis res grant, NASA, 95- *Mem:* Am Math Soc; Math Asn Am. *Res:* Sylow theory of finite groups; group factorizations; finite group theory products of groups and generalizations. *Mailing Add:* Col Arts & Sci Univ Akron Akron OH 44325-1901. *Fax:* 330-972-7222; *E-Mail:* dbuchthal@uakron.edu

BUCHWALD, CARYL EDWARD, ENVIRONMENTAL GEOLOGY. *Current Pos:* from asst prof to assoc prof, 67-77, PROF GEOL, CARLETON COL, 77-, LLOYD MCBRIDE PROF ENVIRON STUDIES, 85- *Personal Data:* b Medford, Mass, Oct 15, 37; m 59, Cynthia M Greene; c Charles E, Julia G & Adam R. *Educ:* Union Col, BS, 60; Syracuse Univ, MS, 63; Univ Kans, PhD(geol), 66. *Prof Exp:* Teaching fel geol, McMaster Univ, 66-67. *Concurrent Pos:* Mem, Minn Environ Qual Bd, 79-89; dir & supv naturalist, Carleton Arboretum, 78-87; bd mem, Sch Nature Area Proj, 93-; bd chmn, Minn Environ Sci Found, Inc, 94- *Mem:* Fel Geol Soc Am; Sigma Xi; Paleont Soc; Nat Asn Col Sci Teachers. *Res:* River hydrology; land use planning; geological limnology. *Mailing Add:* Dept Geol Carleton Col One N College St Northfield MN 55057. *E-Mail:* ebuchwal@carleton.edu

BUCHWALD, HENRY, GENERAL SURGERY. *Current Pos:* from instr to assoc prof, 65-77, PROF SURG & BIOMED ENG, UNIV MINN, MINNEAPOLIS, 77- *Personal Data:* b Vienna, Austria, June 21, 32; US citizen; m 54, Emilie D Bix; c Jane N, Amy E, Claire G & Dana A. *Educ:* Columbia Univ, BA, 54, MD, 57; Univ Minn, Minneapolis, MS & PhD(surg), 66. *Honors & Awards:* Schering Award, 57; Sam D Gross Award, 67; Cine Clins Award, Am Col Surg, 69; Distinguished Serv Award, Asn Acad Surg, 76. *Prof Exp:* Intern, Columbia Presby Med Ctr, 57-58. *Concurrent Pos:* Helen Hay Whitney fel, 63-65; estab investr, Am Heart Asn, 65-70; treas & prog comt chair, Cent Surg Asn, 84-93, secy-gen & chmn, Int Study Group Diabetes Treat Implantable Insulin Delivery Devices, 84-; Minn Gov Bd Invention, 93- *Mem:* Am Surg Asn; Am Col Surg; Soc Univ Surg; Am Heart Asn; Am Soc Artificial Internal Organs; Cent Surg Asn(pres, 97-98). *Res:* Atherosclerosis and the hyperlipidemias; development of surgical procedures for lipid reduction; cholesterol and bile acid metabolism; implantable infusion devices; hemodynamic rheology; morbid obesity. *Mailing Add:* Box 290 Univ Minn Hosp Minneapolis MN 55455. *Fax:* 612-625-3206

BUCHWALD, JED ZACHARY, PHYSICS. *Current Pos:* BERN DIBNER PROF & DIR DIBNER INST HIST, SCI & TECHNOL, MASS INST TECHNOL, 92- *Personal Data:* b Apr 25, 49. *Educ:* Princeton Univ, BA, 71; Harvard Univ, MA, 73, PhD, 74. *Prof Exp:* From lectr to assoc prof, Inst Hist, Philos, Sci & Technol, Univ Toronto, 74-89, prof, 89-92, dir, 91-92. *Concurrent Pos:* Res grantee & leave fel, Soc Sci & Humanities Res Coun, Can, 85-86, grantee, 88-89, 90-91 & 92-95; Killiam fel, 90-92; MacArthur fel, 95-; Sloan Found grantee, 97- *Mem:* Int Acad Hist Sci. *Res:* Contributed numerous publications to professional journals. *Mailing Add:* Dibner Inst Mass Inst Technol 77 Massachusetts Ave Cambridge MA 02139

BUCHWALD, JENNIFER S, NEUROPHYSIOLOGY, HUMAN-ELECTROPHYSIOLOGY. *Current Pos:* From asst prof to assoc prof physiol, 65-73, assoc dir, Brain Res Inst, 78-89, PROF PHYSIOL, UNIV CALIF, SCH MED, LOS ANGELES, 73- *Personal Data:* b Okmulgee, Okla, Oct 20, 30; m 52; c 3. *Educ:* Lindenwood Col, AB, 51; Tulane Univ, PhD(neuroanat), 59. *Hon Degrees:* LLD, Lindenwood Col, 70. *Concurrent Pos:* Consult, NIH, NSF & NIMH; Ment Health Training Prog fel, 61; Parkinsonism Found sr fel, 63-66; USPHS res career develop grant, 64-69, spec fel award, 64-66; assoc dir, Brain Res Inst, Univ Calif, Los Angeles, 78-89, mem, Ment Retardation Res Ctr; vchair, Dept Physiol, Univ Calif, Los Angeles, 85-87. *Mem:* Asn Women Sci; Neurosci Soc; Am Physiol Soc; Am Asn Anat. *Res:* Mechanisms of acoustic communication; auditory physiology; natural and synthesized vocalizations; animal and human subjects. *Mailing Add:* 3201 Birdsall Ave Oakland CA 94619

BUCHWALD, MANUEL, HUMAN MOLECULAR GENETICS, SOMATIC CELL GENETICS. *Current Pos:* From asst prof to assoc prof, 73-86, PROF MOLECULAR & MED GENETICS, UNIV TORONTO, 86-; SR SCIENTIST, RES INST, HOSP SICK CHILDREN, 70- *Personal Data:* b Lima, Peru, June 7, 40; Can citizen; m 85, Cheryl A Cowan. *Educ:* Dartmouth Col, AB, 62; Brandeis Univ, PhD(biochem), 67. *Concurrent Pos:* Vis scientist, Univ Calif, San Francisco, 78-79, Inst Pasteur, 93; asst dir res, Hosp for Sick Children, 82-86, actg dir, 86-87, assoc dir, 87-91. *Mem:* Am Soc Human Genetics; Can Genetics Soc; Human Genome Orgn; AAAS. *Res:* Analysis of the basic defect and treatment of human genetic disorders, in particular, cystic fibrosis and Fanconi anemia. *Mailing Add:* Dept Genetics Hosp Sick Children 555 University Ave Toronto ON M5G 1X8 Can. *Fax:* 416-813-4931; *E-Mail:* buchwald@sickkids.on.ca

BUCHWALD, NATHANIEL AVROM, NEUROPHYSIOLOGY, NEUROANATOMY. *Current Pos:* from asst res anatomist to assoc res anatomist, 57-61, from assoc prof to prof anat, 61-69, assoc dir res, Ment Retardation Res Ctr, 71-74, PROF ANAT & PSYCHIAT, UNIV CALIF, LOS ANGELES, 69-, DIR, MENT RETARDATION RES CTR, 74- *Personal Data:* b Brooklyn, NY, July 19, 25. *Educ:* Univ Minn, Minneapolis, PhD(neuroanat, neurophysiol), 53. *Prof Exp:* Instr anat, Sch Med, Tulane Univ, 53-57. *Concurrent Pos:* Consult, Fed and state agencies, 57-; USPHS career develop award, 58-67. *Mem:* AAAS; Am Physiol Soc; Soc Neurosci; Am Asn Anat. *Res:* Brain function with relation to behavior and mental retardation. *Mailing Add:* Dept Psychiat Neruopsychiat Inst Univ Calif 760 Westwood Plaza Los Angeles CA 90024-1759

BUCK, ALAN CHARLES, SAMPLING & ANALYSIS OF TOXIC & HAZARDOUS MATERIALS, CIVIL & CRIMINAL FORENSICS. *Current Pos:* PRES & SR INVESTR, ENVIRON FORENSICS, 89- *Personal Data:* b Chicago, Ill, Oct 26, 34; m 91, Kay Collins. *Educ:* Univ Ill, BS, 54, MS 59; Univ Hawaii, PhD(environ physiol), 67. *Prof Exp:* Sr lectr physiol, Makerere Univ Med Sch, London Univ, 68; sr scientist, NASA MSC, 69-75; mgr regulatory & environ affairs, Gulf Interstate Eng Co, 75-78; proj mgr & mgr environ affairs, D'Appolonia, 81-83; pres & prod mgr, Chem Applns Technologies, 81-86; pres & researcher, Practical Sci, Inc, 86-89. *Concurrent Pos:* Sr proj mgr, Practical Sci, Inc, 82-; dir qual assurance & standards coordr, Nat Nutrit Foods Asn 84-86; sr researcher, Chem Applns Technologies, Inc, 85- *Mem:* EAfrican Vet Med Soc; Am Chem Soc. *Res:* Five patents in electro-chemistry and food additives; etiology of various pulmonary disease syndromes evident in workers exposed to workplace/office hazards; innovative methods of hazards measurement; support for tort/criminal attorneys involved in environmental accidents. *Mailing Add:* 6073 Nauru St Cypress CA 90630. *Fax:* 714-898-1157

BUCK, ALFRED A, EPIDEMIOLOGY, TROPICAL MEDICINE. *Current Pos:* ADJ PROF, INT HEALTH & MOLECULAR MICROBIOL & IMMUNOL, JOHNS HOPKINS UNIV, 86-, SR ASSOC EPIDEMIOL 86- *Personal Data:* b Hamburg, WGer, Mar 9, 21; m 62, Kay Amann; c Suzanne & Andy. *Educ:* Univ Hamburg, MD, 45; Johns Hopkins Univ, MPH, 59, PhD(epidemiol), 61. *Honors & Awards:* Nat Award, Repub Korea, 58; Craig Lectr, Am Soc Trop Med & Hyg, 79; Meritorious Honor Award, USAID, 80, 86, Supr Unit Citation, 91; Bernard Nocht Medal, 81; Donald Mackay Medal,

Am Soc Trop Med & Royal Brit STM, 95. *Prof Exp:* Resident internal med, Hamburg City Hosp Altona, Ger, 46-52; physician in chg internal & trop med, Gen Hosp, Makassar-Celebes, Repub Indonesia, 52-55; chief, Dept Med, Ger Red Cross Hosp, Pusan, Korea, 56-58; asst prof epidemiol & pub health admin, Sch Hyg & Pub Health, Johns Hopkins Univ, 61-63, from assoc prof to prof epidemiol & int health, 63-71, res dir geog epidemiol, 64-71, dir, Div Bact & Mycol, 67-71; sr med officer & chief epidemiol method & clin path, Div Malaria & Other Parasitic Dis, WHO, Geneva, 71-74, chief med officer, Res Coord Epidemiol & Training, 74-78; trop med adv, Dept State, Agency for Int Develop, 78-85. *Concurrent Pos:* Consult, US Agency Int Develop, Ethiopia, 62, Cent & WAfrica & WHO, Geneva, 71 & Sci & Technol Bur, 85; sr assoc immunol, infectious dis, epidemiol & int health, Johns Hopkins Univ, 80-; adj prof trop med, Tulane Univ, 81-; lectr trop pub health, Harvard Univ, 82-; mem sci working group & steering comt on epidemiol & appl field res on malaria, WHO, 82-; assoc ed, Trop Med & Parasitol, 82-; hon fel trop med, Liverpool Sch Trop Med & Hyg, 83; consult, Sci & Tech Bur, 85-; res scientist, Nat Inst Allergy & Infectious Dis, NIH, Regional Proj Vector-Borne Dis, Cairo, Egypt, 90-92; vis prof, Ain Shams Univ, Cairo, 90-, Univ Hannover, Ger, 91- *Mem:* Fel Am Col Epidemiol; Am Soc Trop Med & Hyg; fel Am Pub Health Asn; Ger Soc Trop Med; Int Soc Epidemiol; Am Soc Epidemiol Res. *Res:* International health; prevalence and interaction of diseases in Peru, Chad, Afghanistan and Cameroon by comprehensive epidemiologic investigations and laboratory studies; epidemiology and control of onchocerciasis and treponematoses; disease control and primary health care; environmental health and global warming. *Mailing Add:* Sch Pub Health Johns Hopkins Univ 1603 East Ave McLean VA 22101. *E-Mail:* abuck1603@aol.com

BUCK, CARL JOHN, POLYMER CHEMISTRY & POLYMER SYNTHESIS FOR DENTAL APPLICATIONS, NEW BIS-CYANOACRULATE MONOIMERS. *Current Pos:* res chemist org & polymer synthesis, 70-90, CONSULT, JOHNSON & JOHNSON RES CTR, 90- *Personal Data:* b Philadelphia, Pa, Mar 6, 29; m 53, Audrey McGuinness; c 3. *Educ:* Temple Univ, BA, 50, MA, 54; Cornell Univ, PhD(org chem), 58. *Honors & Awards:* Distinguished Scientist Award, Johnson & Johnson, 77. *Prof Exp:* Instr biochem & dent mat, Sch Dent, Temple Univ, 50-51; anal chemist petrol, Sinclair Refining Co, 51-54; res chemist org synthesis, Pfizer Inc, 57-63, Shell Chem, 63-70. *Mem:* Sigma Xi; Am Chem Soc. *Res:* Organic synthesis of antibiotics; medicinal agents; industrial chemicals; monomers and polymers for dental, orthopedic and wound care applications. *Mailing Add:* 58 Greenbriar Dr Berkeley Heights NJ 07922-1244

BUCK, CAROL WHITLOW, PUBLIC HEALTH & EPIDEMIOLOGY. *Current Pos:* From asst prof to prof, Dept Psychiat & Prev Med, Univ Western Ont, 52-67, chmn, Dept Epidemiol & Prev Med, 67-77, prof epidemiol, 67-90, EMER PROF EPIDEMIOL, UNIV WESTERN ONT, 90- *Personal Data:* b London, Ont, Apr 2, 25; m 46, Robert C; c Lucy A & Effie L. *Educ:* Univ Western Ont, MD, 47, PhD, 50; London Sch Trop Med, DPH, 51. *Hon Degrees:* LLD, Dalhousie Univ, Can, 89. *Honors & Awards:* Defries Award, Can Pub Health Asn, 87. *Concurrent Pos:* Mem, Sci Coun Can, 70-73; fel, Royal Soc Can, 88. *Mem:* Soc Epidemiol Res; Int Epidemiol Asn (pres, 81-84); Can Pub Health Asn; fel Am Col Epidemiol. *Res:* Epidemiology; medical statistics. *Mailing Add:* Dept Epidemiol Univ Western Ont Fac Med London ON N6A 5C1 Can

BUCK, CHARLES (CARPENTER), MATHEMATICS. *Current Pos:* RETIRED. *Personal Data:* b Metamora, Ohio, June 28, 15; m 51; c 2. *Educ:* Univ Mich, BS, 40, MS, 47, PhD, 54. *Prof Exp:* Instr math, Univ Nebr, 49-52 & Wayne Univ, 53; from asst prof to assoc prof, Univ Ala, 53-61; res assoc, Educ Res Coun, 61-67; assoc prof math, Cleveland State Univ, 67- *Concurrent Pos:* Consult, Educ Res Coun, 71- *Mem:* AAAS; Am Math Soc; Math Asn Am. *Res:* Foundations, non-Euclidean and differential geometry. *Mailing Add:* 1803 Wilton Rd Cleveland Heights OH 44118-1628

BUCK, CHARLES ELON, BACTERIOLOGY. *Current Pos:* RETIRED. *Personal Data:* b Linton, NDak, Jan 5, 19; m 48; c 3. *Educ:* NDak State Col, BS, 42, MS, 47; Ohio State Univ, PhD(bact), 51. *Prof Exp:* From asst prof to assoc prof bact, Univ Maine, Orono, 51-74, prof microbiol, 74-82, emer prof, 82. *Mem:* Am Soc Microbiol. *Res:* Virology and tissue culture. *Mailing Add:* 191 Bennoch Rd Orono ME 04473

BUCK, CHARLES FRANK, animal husbandry, for more information see previous edition

BUCK, CLAYTON ARTHUR, BIOCHEMISTRY, CANCER. *Current Pos:* PROF, WISTAR INST, 75- *Personal Data:* b Lyons, Kans, Mar 2, 37; m 61; c 2. *Educ:* Kans State Univ, BS, 59; Mont State Univ, PhD(bact), 64. *Prof Exp:* NIH fel, Univ Calif, Irvine, 64-67; asst prof therapeut res, Univ Pa, 67-70; assoc prof biol, Kans State Univ, 70-75. *Mem:* Am Soc Biol Chemists; Am Soc Microbiol. *Res:* Virology, protein biosynthesis and animal cell membranes; tRNA in mitochondria and glycoproteins from the surface of virus-transformed and normal animal cells and their role in controlling cellular adhesion and morphology. *Mailing Add:* Wistar Inst 3601 Spruce St Rm 385 Philadelphia PA 19104-4268. *Fax:* 215-573-2097

BUCK, DAVID HOMER, FISHERIES. *Current Pos:* RETIRED. *Personal Data:* b Clifton, Ariz, Dec 31, 20; m 53; c 4. *Educ:* Agr & Mech Col, Tex, BS, 43; Okla State Univ, PhD(zool), 51. *Prof Exp:* Aquatic biologist, State Game & Fish Comn, Tex, 46-48; dist biologist, Corps Engrs, Ft Worth Dist, 51-52; fisheries investr, State Game & Fish Dept, Okla, 54-56; assoc aquatic biologist, 56-68, aquatic biologist, Ill Natural Hist Surv, 68-90; assoc prof, Dept Animal Sci, Univ Ill, 80-87. *Concurrent Pos:* Mem, Int Comt Prod Use Wastes Develop Countries & chmn, Sect Aquacult, Nat Acad Sci, 80-; mem task force, UN Food & Agr Org, China, 81-; consult, USAID/Aquacult, Rwanda, 88. *Mem:* Am Fisheries Soc; Am Soc Limnol & Oceanog; World Aquacult Soc. *Res:* Productivity and population dynamics of freshwater fisheries; effects of turbidity on fish production; species interrelationships of pond fishes; culture of channel catfish; use of specialized fishes for control of eutrophication; recycling of animal wastes for polyculture of fishes. *Mailing Add:* 220 W Porter St Salem IL 62881

BUCK, DOUGLAS EARL, chemistry, for more information see previous edition

BUCK, DOUGLAS L, DENTISTRY. *Current Pos:* from asst prof to assoc prof, 62-71, PROF ORTHOD, DENT SCH, UNIV ORE, 71-, CHMN DEPT, 73- *Personal Data:* b Frederic, Wis, May 9, 31; m 54; c 2. *Educ:* Univ Minn, BS, 54, DDS, 60, MSD, 62. *Prof Exp:* Asst orthod, Sch Dent, Univ Minn, 61-62. *Concurrent Pos:* Fulbright lectr, Ecuador, 68-69; vis prof, Sch Dent, Hokkaido Univ, 75. *Mem:* Am Asn Orthod; Int Asn Dent Res; Am Cleft Palate Asn; Sigma Xi. *Res:* Histology of tooth movement. *Mailing Add:* M/C-CDRC 3181 SW Sam Jackson Park Rd Portland OR 97201

BUCK, ERNEST MAURO, MEAT SCIENCE. *Current Pos:* RETIRED. *Personal Data:* b Hartford, Conn, Apr 21, 30; m 54; c 4. *Educ:* Univ Conn, BS, 55; NC State Col, MS, 57; Univ Mass, Amherst, PhD(food sci & technol), 66. *Prof Exp:* Assoc dean, Univ Mass, Amherst, 69-76, prof food sci & nutrit, 76-89. *Mem:* Am Meat Sci Asn; Inst Food Technol. *Res:* Meats; physico-chemical changes in muscle after death; seafood analogs. *Mailing Add:* 12 Mash Pee Dr North Attleboro MA 02760

BUCK, F(RANK) A(LAN) MACKINNON, CHEMICAL ENGINEERING. *Current Pos:* managing partner, 79-80, MANAGING PRIN, KING, BUCK & ASSOCS, INC, 81- *Personal Data:* b Ottawa, Ont, June 26, 20; nat US; m 45; c 2. *Educ:* Univ BC, BApSc, 43, MApSc, 44; Purdue Univ, PhD(phys chem), 48. *Prof Exp:* Develop engr, Powell River Co, Can, 44-45; sessional lectr chem, McGill Univ, 45-46; instr chem eng, Univ Wash, 48-49; chem engr exec, Shell Chem Co, 49-68; tech specialist, Off Oil & Gas, US Dept Interior, Washington, DC, 68-69; chem engr exec, Shell Chem Co, 69-76, bus rep, 76-79. *Concurrent Pos:* Vchmn, San Diego Co, Air Pollution hearing bd, 86- *Mem:* Am Chem Soc; Am Inst Chem Engrs. *Res:* Electron diffraction of gases; synthesis of fuels by Fischer-Tropsch process; petroleum research and plant operations. *Mailing Add:* 5058 Southview Dr San Diego CA 92117-5347

BUCK, GEORGE SUMNER, JR, CHEMICAL ENGINEERING. *Current Pos:* PRES, RAMCON, INC, 70-, CHMN RAMCON ENVIRON CORP, 70-; PRES, FIBERLOK, INC, 70- *Personal Data:* b Hartford, Conn, Sept 12, 14; m 42; c 4. *Educ:* Johns Hopkins Univ, BS, 35. *Hon Degrees:* DTextileSci, Philadelphia Col Textiles Sci, 63. *Prof Exp:* Asst chemist, William Hooper & Sons, Md, 35-37, overseer, Finishing Plant, 37-41, supt, 41-46; tech supt, Tech Serv Dept, Nat Cotton Coun Am, 46-47, tech serv dir, 47-49, tech dir, 49-57, asst to exec vpres, 57-68, dir res, 68-70. *Concurrent Pos:* Res consult, Cotton Producers Inst, 62-70; pres, Mid-South Res Assoc, 68-70; exec vpres, Oscar Johnston Cotton Found & Cotton Found, 68-73. *Mem:* Textile Res Inst; AAAS; Am Chem Soc; Am Soc Testing & Mat; Am Asn Textile Chemists & Colorists. *Res:* Textile fire-resistance and flammability; textile finishes; market research; consumer surveys; management research. *Mailing Add:* 6707 Fletcher Creek CV Memphis TN 38133-7055. *Fax:* 901-387-0400

BUCK, JAMES R, HUMAN FACTORS-ERGONOMICS, ENGINEER ECONOMICS. *Current Pos:* PROF INDUST ENG, UNIV IOWA, 81- *Personal Data:* b Big Rapids, Mich, Feb 22, 30; m 62; c 3. *Educ:* Mich Technol Univ, BS, 52, MS, 53; Univ Mich, PhD(indust eng), 64. *Honors & Awards:* Eugene Grant Award, Am Soc Eng Educ, 79 & 87. *Prof Exp:* Struct engr, Austin Engrs Ltd, Detroit, 56-57; field engr, Cabinet Flexicore Corp, 57-58; instr math, Ferris State Col, 58-59; asst prof indust eng, Univ Mich, Ann Arbor & Dearborn, 60-66; from assoc prof to prof, Purdue Univ, 66-81. *Concurrent Pos:* Consult, 76- *Mem:* Fel Inst Indust Engrs; Am Soc Eng Educ; Inst Mgt Sci; Human Factors Soc; Ergonomics Soc. *Res:* Development of techniques to facilitate design or analysis such as sampling, simulation, visual abilities, inspection, economic analysis, risk measurement; human performance prediction. *Mailing Add:* Dept Indust Eng Univ Iowa 4131 Engineering Blvd Iowa City IA 52242-1527

BUCK, JEAN COBERG, POLYMER CHEMISTRY, ANALYTICAL CHEMISTRY. *Current Pos:* mgr, Qual Control Tech Servs Lab, 85-91, ASSOC DIR, QUAL ASSURANCE PLANNING, MERCK & CO, INC, 91- *Personal Data:* b Schenectady, NY; m 68, Warren H; c Allison Jean. *Educ:* Philadelphia Col Pharm & Sci, BSc, 57; Univ Del, PhD(chem), 68. *Prof Exp:* Jr analytical res chemist, Rohm & Haas Co, Philadelphia, 57-61, sr res chemist polymer chem, 67-71; teacher, Booth Sch, Rosemont, Pa, 71-74; sr analytical res chemist, Betz Labs Inc, 74-85. *Mem:* Am Chem Soc; NAm Thermal Anal Soc. *Res:* Organic analysis of proprietary materials; characterization of aqueous polymer systems. *Mailing Add:* Qual Planning MMD 38M2 Merck & Co Inc West Point PA 19486. *Fax:* 215-661-3573

BUCK, JOHN BONNER, EVOLUTION. *Current Pos:* cytologist, 45-47, sr biologist, 47-56, prin physiologist, 56-62, chief, Lab Phys Biol, 62-75, chief, Sect Comp Physiol, 75-85, EMER SCIENTIST, NIH 85- *Personal Data:* b Hartford, Conn, Sept 26, 12; m 39, Elisabeth T Mast; c 4. *Educ:* Johns

Hopkins Univ, AB, 33, PhD(zool), 36. *Prof Exp:* Asst zool, Johns Hopkins Univ, 33-36; Nat Res fel, Calif Inst Technol, 36-37; res assoc embryol, Carnegie Inst Washington, 37-39; from instr to asst prof zool, Univ Rochester, 39-45. *Concurrent Pos:* Mem, Hopkins Exped, Jamaica, 36, 41 & 63; mem corp, Marine Biol Lab, Woods Hole, 37-, instr, 42-44 & 57-59, trustee, 63-80; vis prof, Univ Wash, 51, Calif Inst Technol, 53 & Cambridge Univ, 63; chief scientist, Alpha Helix Exped, New Guinea, 69. *Mem:* Am Soc Zool (vpres, 56); Soc Gen Physiol (secy-treas, 53-55, pres, 60). *Res:* Physiology and behavior of fireflies; chromosome and physiological cytology; biochemistry and physiology of insect blood; insect respiration; bioluminescence in invertebrates. *Mailing Add:* 7200 Third Ave Sykesville MD 21784

BUCK, JOHN DAVID, MARINE MICROBIOLOGY. *Current Pos:* asst prof bact, Univ Conn, 65-71, assoc prof biol, 71-80, prof marine sci, 80-92, EMER PROF MARINE SCI, UNIV CONN, 92- *Personal Data:* b Hartford, Conn, Oct 3, 35; m 60, Patricia Jones; c Bethany, Kristin & John (Tanner). *Educ:* Univ Conn, BA, 57, MS, 60; Univ Miami, PhD(marine sci), 65. *Prof Exp:* Asst instr bact, Univ Conn, 60-61; res instr marine microbiol, Univ Miami, 61-62 & 64-65. *Concurrent Pos:* Sr scientist, Mote Marine Lab, Sarasota, Fla. *Mem:* Am Soc Microbiol. *Res:* Enumeration and sampling methods in marine microbiology; diseases of marine mammals. *Mailing Add:* Marine Res Lab Univ Conn Noank CT 06340

BUCK, JOHN HENRY, NUCLEAR POWER DEVELOPMENT. *Current Pos:* RETIRED. *Personal Data:* b London, Eng, Sept 22, 12; US citizen; m 40, Carolyn F Wilcox; c John A & Barbara C. *Educ:* Univ Sask, BSc, 33, MSc, 35; Univ Rochester, PhD(nuclear physics), 38. *Prof Exp:* Teaching fel physics, Univ Rochester, 36-38; instr physics, Mass Inst Technol, 38-41; staff mem, Mass Inst Technol Radiation Lab, 41-46; mgr, Mobil Oil Co, 46-50; proj mgr, Oak Ridge Nat Lab, 50-53; vpres & gen mgr, Well Surveys Inc, 53-59; vpres & gen mgr, Instruments Div, Budd Co, 59-69; vchmn, Appeal Panel, AEC, 69-74; vchmn, Appeal Panel, Nuclear Regulatory Comn, 74-82; consult, Nuclear Power, 84-91. *Concurrent Pos:* Mem, sr rev team, Commanche Peak Nuclear Power Plants, 83-91. *Mem:* Fel Am Phys Soc; Am Nuclear Soc; Sigma Xi. *Res:* Early nuclear physics investigations with cyclotrons; molten salt reactor and material testing reactor. *Mailing Add:* 5606 Marengo Rd Bethesda MD 20816-3313

BUCK, KEITH TAYLOR, FLAVOR CHEMICALS, PROCESS DESIGN. *Current Pos:* MGR ORG SYNTHESIS, FRIES & FRIES DIV, MALLINCKRODT, INC, 79-, SR RES FEL, 85- *Personal Data:* b Norwalk, Conn, Aug 1, 40; m 80. *Educ:* Univ Mich, BS, 61; Ohio State Univ, PhD(organ chem), 66. *Prof Exp:* Fel chem, Pa State Univ, 65-66; asst prof org chem, Dickinson Col, 66-68; fel & asst prof, Univ Idaho, 68-70; fel chem, Univ Pa, 71-74; dir res, Frankincense Co, 75-77; dir aroma chem, Northville Labs, 77-79. *Mem:* Am Chem Soc. *Res:* Synthesis of flavor chemicals; isoquinoline alkaloids. *Mailing Add:* 10629 Convo Ct Cincinnati OH 45242-3218

BUCK, MARION GILMOUR, ENZYMES, CELL MEDIATORS. *Current Pos:* assoc res scientist biochem, Yale Univ, 70-91, CONSULT, 91- *Personal Data:* b New Hope, Pa, May 24, 36; m 69, Donald T; c Marianne E & Elizabeth A. *Educ:* Wilmington Col, Ohio, BS, 58; Rutgers Univ, PhD(biochem), 65. *Prof Exp:* Fel biochem, Royal North Shore Hosp, Sydney, Australia, 65-66; fel, Univ Pa, 66-67; asst prof, Sch Med, Univ Louisville, 67-70. *Concurrent Pos:* Muscular Dystrophy Asn Am fel, 65-67; vis sr res fac, Univ Utrecht, 79; prin investr, 80-86. *Mem:* Am Chem Soc; AAAS. *Res:* Mechanisms of cell to cell communication including cell mediators and effects of toxic inhalants; isolation, purification and identification of pharmacologically active plant compounds; effect of ascorbic acid on c-AMP phosphodiesterase; characterization of cytochrome oxidase and cytochrome b-5. *Mailing Add:* Old Town St Hadlyme CT 06439

BUCK, OTTO, METAL PHYSICS. *Current Pos:* SR SCIENTIST & PROF, AMES LAB, IOWA STATE UNIV, 80-, PROG DIR, 89- *Personal Data:* b Ger, May 14, 33; m 61, 85, Martha L Hoffer; c Bettina & Stefanie. *Educ:* Univ Stuttgart, BS, 56, MS, 59, PhD(physics), 61. *Prof Exp:* Asst metal physics, Univ Stuttgart, 61-64; mem tech staff, sci ctr, NAm Aviation Inc, 64-66 & Siemens Co, Ger, 66-68; mem tech staff, Sci Ctr Rockwell Int, 68-75, group leader, 75-80. *Mem:* Fel Am Soc Metals; Am Soc Testing & Mat; Am Inst Mining, Metall & Petrol Engrs; Mat Res Soc. *Res:* Plasticity of metals; dislocation theory; nonlinear theory of elasticity; internal friction; point-defect migration; fracture mechanics; surface properties; fatigue; nondestructive evaluation. *Mailing Add:* Ames Lab Iowa State Univ Ames IA 50011. *Fax:* 515-294-8727; *E-Mail:* buck@ameslab.gov

BUCK, PAUL, PLANT ECOLOGY, AEROBIOLOGY. *Current Pos:* RETIRED. *Personal Data:* b Highland Park, Mich, Sept 9, 27; m 50; c 2. *Educ:* Univ Tulsa, BS, 58, MS, 59; Univ Okla, PhD(bot), 62. *Prof Exp:* From asst prof to assoc prof bot, Univ Tulsa, 62-88. *Concurrent Pos:* Summer instr & sr researcher, Rocky Mountain Biol Lab, 79-; instr, Tulsa Jr Col & Univ Ctr, Tulsa. *Mem:* AAAS; Ecol Soc Am. *Res:* Airborne allergenic pollen and mold spores in Oklahoma; sub-alpine habitats of Colorado; plant systematics with primary focus on woody vegetation of Oklahoma. *Mailing Add:* Dept Life Sci Univ Tulsa Tulsa OK 74104-3189. *Fax:* 918-631-2762

BUCK, RAYMOND WILBUR, JR, CYTOGENETICS. *Current Pos:* RETIRED. *Personal Data:* b Monticello, Maine, Apr 20, 19. *Educ:* Univ Maine, BS, 41; Univ Md, MS, 50, PhD(bot), 52. *Prof Exp:* Instr bot, Univ Maine, 46-48; geneticist, bur plant indust, soils & agr eng, USDA, 52-53 & hort crops res br, Agr Res Serv, 53-68; from assoc prof to prof biol, 68-84, Montgomery Col, chmn dept, 70-76. *Mem:* AAAS; Bot Soc Am; Am Genetic Asn; Am Inst Biol Sci; Sigma Xi. *Res:* Cytogenetics of tuber-bearing Solanum species. *Mailing Add:* 4902 Laguna Rd College Park MD 20740-1444

BUCK, RICHARD F, ATMOSPHERIC PHYSICS. *Current Pos:* res physicist, Okla State Univ, 48-53, from asst proj dir to proj dir, Electronics Lab, 53-60, proj dir res found & instr physics, 60-67, dir, Electronics Lab, Res Found & asst prof physics, Sch Arts & Sci, 67-76, dir, Electronics Lab-CEAT & assoc prof eng res, 76-84, EMER ENG TECH, OKLA STATE UNIV, 84- *Personal Data:* b Enterprise, Kans, Dec 8, 21; m 95, Patsy Poskey Summers; c David R, Janet H, Paul S, Bryan T, Neal A, Daniel C. *Educ:* Univ Kans, BS, 43; Okla State Univ, MS, 60. *Prof Exp:* Appl engr, Radio Tube Dept, Tung Sol Lamp Works, Inc, 46-48. *Concurrent Pos:* Consult electronic eng, 63- *Mem:* Inst Elec & Electronics Engrs; Nat Soc Prof Engrs; AAAS; Sigma Xi. *Res:* Electronic instrumentation of rockets and satellites for measurement of physical parameters of space. *Mailing Add:* 1016 Oak Ridge Dr Stillwater OK 74074-1108

BUCK, RICHARD PIERSON, PHYSICAL CHEMISTRY, ANALYTICAL CHEMISTRY. *Current Pos:* assoc prof, 67-75, PROF CHEM, UNIV NC, CHAPEL HILL, 75- *Personal Data:* b Los Angeles, Calif, July 29, 29; m 59; c 3. *Educ:* Calif Inst Technol, BS, 50, MS, 51; Mass Inst Technol, PhD(chem), 54. *Honors & Awards:* Von Humboldt Preis, WGer, 89; Achievement Award, Sensor Dir, Electrochem Soc, 96. *Prof Exp:* Res chemist polarography & electrochem, Calif Res Corp, 54-56, asst to gen mgr, 56-58, res chemist combustion & high temperature inorg chem, 58-60, electrochem fuel cells, 60-61; prin res chemist, electrochem, electroanal chem & instrumentation, Bell & Howell Res Ctr, 61-65; sr scientist, Beckman Instruments, Inc, 65-67. *Concurrent Pos:* VChmn, Gordon Res Conf Electrochem, 64, chmn, 65; vis prof, Bristol Univ, Eng, 76-77, Imp Col, London, Eng, 87-88, Bundeswehr Univ, Munich, Ger, 89 & 91; organizer symp, Ion-Selective Electrodes Biol & Med, Dortmund, 80 & Erlangen, Ger, 83, Electrochem Soc, Hollywood Fla, 80, Neutral Carrier Mechan, NY, 85, Kinetics Liquid & Liquid Interfaces, Boston, Mass, 86, fundamental processes sensors, Hollywood, Fla, 89, invivo sensors, Montreal, 90, sensor mechanisms, New Orleans, 93, impedance Symp, San Francisco, 94; mem rev panels & site visit teams, NIH; exec bd, Int Soc Electrochem, 90-91; adj prof biomed eng, Univ NC, Chapel Hill, 90-; chmn, Sensors Group, Electrochem Soc, 91-92; titular mem, Int Union Pure & Appl Chem, 90-95. *Mem:* Int Soc Electrochem; Am Chem Soc; fel Electrochem Soc; Soc Electroanal Chem. *Res:* Electrochemistry; electrode processes; electroanalysis; chemical instrumentation; bioelectrochemistry and biosensors; trace analysis; solid state transport; membrane electrochemistry; cardiovascular sensors; vaginal sensors. *Mailing Add:* Dept Chem Univ NC Chapel Hill NC 27599-3290. *E-Mail:* richard_buck@unc.edu

BUCK, ROBERT CRAWFORTH, ANATOMY, HISTOLOGY. *Current Pos:* From asst prof to assoc prof, 53-62, chmn dept, 67-73, PROF ANAT, UNIV WESTERN ONT, 62- *Personal Data:* b London, Ont, Sept 23, 23; m 46; c 2. *Educ:* Univ Western Ont, MD, 47, MSc, 50; Univ London, PhD(path), 52. *Mem:* Am Asn Anat; Can Asn Anat; Anat Soc Gt Brit & Ireland; Path Soc Gt Brit. *Res:* Cytology; electron microscopy in fields of blood vascular pathology and tumor pathology. *Mailing Add:* 181 Elmwood E London ON N6C 1K1 Can

BUCK, ROBERT CREIGHTON, MATHEMATICAL ANALYSIS. *Current Pos:* from assoc prof to prof, Univ Wis-Madison, 50-80, chmn dept, 64-66, dir, Math Res Ctr, 73-75, HILLDALE PROF MATH, UNIV WIS-MADISON, 80- *Personal Data:* b Cincinnati, Ohio, Aug 30, 20; m 44; c 2. *Educ:* Univ Cincinnati, BA, 41, MA, 42; Harvard Univ, PhD(math), 47. *Honors & Awards:* Piedmont lectr, 70; Ford Award, 81. *Prof Exp:* Jr fel, Soc Fels, 42-43 & 45-47; asst prof math, Brown Univ, 47-49. *Concurrent Pos:* Ed, Proc, Am Math Soc, 53-55, 64-67; Guggenheim fel, 58-59; vis prof, Stanford Univ, 58-59; mem staff proj focus, Inst Defense Anal, 59-60; mem math div, Nat Res Coun, 61-64, travelling lectr, Math Asn Am, 62-63; mem, Nat Security Agency Adv Bd, 63-71; mem, US Comn Math Instruct, 63-67; mem math adv panel, NSF, 65-70; adv bd, Sch Math Study Group, 66-69; Nat Adv Coun Educ Prof Develop, 70-71, 73-76; trustee, Soc Indust & Appl Math, 73-74; mem panel to evaluate, Nat Bur Stand Appl Math Prog, 74-77. *Mem:* Fel AAAS; Am Math Soc (vpres, 72-74); Math Asn Am (vpres, 75-77); Soc Indust & Appl Math. *Res:* Complex variable theory; algebraic analysis; number theory; approximation theory; mathematics education; history of mathematics. *Mailing Add:* 3601 Sunset Dr Madison WI 53705-1432

BUCK, STEPHEN HENDERSON, neuropeptides, neuropharmacology, for more information see previous edition

BUCK, THOMAS M, SURFACE PHYSICS & CHEMISTRY, ION SCATTERING. *Current Pos:* RETIRED. *Personal Data:* b Elizabeth, Pa, June 29, 20; m 44, Mary Jo Haines; c David A, Lucinda A (Alwa), Sarah J & Marian (Murray). *Educ:* Muskingum Col, BS, 42; Univ Pittsburgh, MS, 48, PhD(chem), 50. *Prof Exp:* Asst, Univ Pittsburgh, 46-50; res chemist, Nat Lead Co, 50-52; mem tech staff, Bell Tel Labs, 52-63, supvr, Surface Studies Group, Semiconductor Device Technol Dept, 63-68, mem tech staff, Chem Electronics Res Dept, 68-71, distinguished mem tech staff, Bell Labs, 71-84 & Radiation Physics Res Dept, 84-89; adj prof, Dept Mat Sci & Eng, Univ Pa, Philadelphia, 89-92. *Concurrent Pos:* Adj prof, Mat Sci & Eng Dept, Univ Pa, Philadelphia, 89-92. *Mem:* Sigma Xi. *Res:* Composition and atomic arrangement of single-crystal alloy surfaces, using low energy ion scattering, low energy electron diffraction and Auger electron spectroscopy; neutralization behavior in low energy ion scattering. *Mailing Add:* 50 Edgewood Rd Bedminster NJ 07921

BUCK, WARREN HOWARD, PHYSICAL CHEMISTRY, POLYMER CHEMISTRY. *Current Pos:* res chemist, Polymer Prod Dept, 69-80, sr res chemist, 80-87, RES ASSOC, E I DUPONT DE NEMOURS & CO INC, 87- *Personal Data:* b Neptune, NJ, June 22, 42; m 68, Jean Coberg; c Allison J. *Educ:* Lehigh Univ, BA, 64; Univ Del, PhD(phys chem), 70. *Mem:* Am Chem Soc; NAm Thermal Anal Soc. *Res:* Physical chemistry of macromolecules; morphology of thermoplastic elastomers, polyurethane foams and elastomers, polymer blends, ethylene copolymers, fire retardance, fluoropolymer characterization; perfluorodioxole polymers; perfluorinated ion-exchange membranes. *Mailing Add:* DuPont Fluoroproducts E I DuPont de Nemours & Co Exp Sta PO Box 80323 Wilmington DE 19880-0323

BUCK, WARREN LOUIS, RADIATION PHYSICS. *Current Pos:* RETIRED. *Personal Data:* b Normal, Ill, Jan 20, 21; m 44; c 2. *Educ:* Ill State Norm Univ, BS, 46; Univ Ill, MS, 47. *Prof Exp:* Asst physics, Univ Ill, 46-50; assoc physicist, Argonne Nat Lab, 50-72, physicist, 72-82. *Mem:* Am Phys Soc; Sigma Xi. *Res:* Scintillation counters; luminescent materials; effects of radiation on materials; neutron flux monitors. *Mailing Add:* 453 Lakewood Blvd Park Forest IL 60466-1626

BUCK, WARREN W, III, RELATAVISTIC INTERMEDIATE ENERGY & NUCLEAR PHYSICS, QUARK MODELS. *Current Pos:* assoc prof, 84-88, FULL PROF PHYSICS, HAMPTON UNIV, 89- *Personal Data:* b Washington, DC, Feb 16, 46; m 77; c 2. *Educ:* Morgan State Univ, BS, 68; Col William & Mary, MS, 70, PhD(theoret physics), 76. *Honors & Awards:* Outstanding Serv Award, Continious Electron Beam Accelerator Facil Users Group; Hon Super Accomplishment Award, NASA. *Prof Exp:* Fel, State Univ NY, Stony Brook, 76-79; res assoc physics, Inst Nuclear Physics, Orsay, France, 79-80; vis asst prof, Col William & Mary, 84. *Concurrent Pos:* Vis staff mem, Los Alamos Nat Lab, 77-80; prin investr, NASA, 84-, NSF, 87-, US Dept Energy, 87-; dir, NuHep Ctr Excellence, 91-; consult, Va Union Univ, 93- *Mem:* Life mem Am Phys Soc; AAAS; NY Acad Sci; Nat Soc Black Physicists. *Res:* Theoretical studies of few body systems including nucleon-nucleon and nucleon-antinucleon systems as well as multiquark interactions. *Mailing Add:* Dept Physics Hampton Univ Hampton VA 23668

BUCK, WILLIAM R, BRYOLOGY. *Current Pos:* Assoc cur, 79-86, CUR BRYOPHYTES, NY BOT GARDEN, 86- *Personal Data:* b Jacksonville, Fla, Dec 27, 50. *Educ:* Univ Fla, BS, 72, MS, 74; Univ Mich, PhD, 79. *Honors & Awards:* Greenman Award, 81. *Mem:* Am Bryological & Lichenological Soc; Am Fern Soc; Am Soc Plant Taxonomists; Brit Bryological Soc; Brit Pteridological Soc; Sigma Xi. *Res:* Family concepts in the large moss order Hypnobryales and Isobryales and monographic studies on many of the genera traditionally placed in these orders. *Mailing Add:* NY Bot Garden Bronx NY 10458-5126. *Fax:* 718-562-6780; *E-Mail:* bbuck@nybg.org

BUCKALEW, LOUIS WALTER, HUMAN ENGINEERING, RESEARCH DESIGN. *Current Pos:* SR RES PSYCHOLOGIST & CHIEF, US ARMY RES LAB, FT GORDON, GA, 93- *Personal Data:* b Bloomsburg, Pa, Apr 21, 44; m 85, Nancy Maits; c Louis W IV. *Educ:* Ga Southern Col, BA, 67; Univ Southern Miss, MS, 69; Howard Univ, PhD, 89. *Prof Exp:* Admin specialist, US Army, Vietnam, 69-70; instr psychol, SC State Col, 70-73; managing partner, Buckalew & Davis Assocs, 73-75; assoc prof psychol, Ala A&M Univ, 75-85; sr res psychologist, US Army Res Inst, Ft Hood, Tex, 85-93; dir res, Univ Cent Tex, 86-91. *Concurrent Pos:* Reviewer Psychol Reports-Perceptual & Motor Skills, 79-, J Alcohol & Drug Educ, 84-; asst prof, Univ Ala, Huntsville, 80-85; res assoc, Aerospace Med Res Lab-Sch, USAF, 81-84; reviewer, Sociological Inquiry, 89-94. *Mem:* Sigma Xi; Psychonomic Soc. *Res:* Psychopharmacology; medication, physical properties of drugs, patient compliance, placebo effects and methodology,; consumer psychology and human engineering; author of over 90 journal articles and books. *Mailing Add:* 1834 Valleybrook Dr Grovetown GA 30813-8524

BUCKALEW, VARDAMAN M, JR, NEPHROLOGY, HYPERTENSION. *Current Pos:* PROF MED & PHYSIOL, BOWMAN-GRAY SCH MED, FOREST UNIV, 73-, CHIEF NEPHROLOGY SECT, 74- *Personal Data:* b Mobile, Ala, Mar 19, 33. *Educ:* Univ Pa, MD, 58. *Mem:* Royal Soc Med; Am Fedn Clin Res; Am Soc Nephrology; Am Soc Hypertension. *Mailing Add:* Dept Med & Nephrol Bowman-Gray Sch Med Wake Forest Univ Med Ctr Blvd Winston-Salem NC 27157. *Fax:* 919-716-4318

BUCKARDT, HENRY LLOYD, AGRONOMY. *Current Pos:* PRES, PAEONIAN SPRINGS COUN, 86- *Personal Data:* b Leland, Ill, Oct 24, 04; m 37. *Educ:* Univ Ill, BS, 26, MS, 29, PhD(agron), 32. *Prof Exp:* Asst prin & instr high sch, Ill, 26-27; asst crop prod, Dept Agron, Univ Ill, 28-33, Standard Oil Co fel, 33, erosion exten specialist coordr, 35-36; agronomist, Soil Conserv Serv, USDA, 34, Iowa, 37, DC, 38-40; head admin off, US Civil Serv Comn, 40-46; civil serv adminr & adv, Civil Affairs Div, US War Dept, Korea, 46; personnel policy specialist, Off Secy Defense, Nat Mil Estab, 48-50, staff mem personnel policy bd, US Dept Defense, 50-52, spec asst to Asst Secy Defense, Manpower & Personnel, 52-55; agr attache, Seoul, Korea, 56-57, Far Eastern are off, Foreign Agr Serv, USDA, Washington, DC, 58, agr attache, Montevideo, Uruguay, 58-69; pres, Am Work Horse Mus, 70- *Concurrent Pos:* Hon mem, Asn Intensification Com Uruguay, Montevideo, 69. *Mem:* AAAS; Am Soc Agron; Assoc Soc Personnel Admin. *Res:* Crop productions; physiological botany; soil conservation; weed eradication; personnel administration and training; civil service systems. *Mailing Add:* 20503 Falcons Landing Circle Apt 3004 Sterling VA 20165-7595

BUCKELEW, ALBERT RHOADES, JR, MICROBIOLOGY. *Current Pos:* From asst prof to assoc prof, 69-84, PROF BIOL, BETHANY COL, WVA, 84- *Personal Data:* b Washington, DC, Oct 22, 42; m 65, Susan Cooper; c Dana & Sara. *Educ:* Fairleigh Dickinson Univ, BS, 64; Univ NH, PhD(microbiol), 68. *Concurrent Pos:* Ed, Redstart. *Mem:* AAAS; Am Soc Microbiol; Wilson Ornith Soc; Am Ornith Union. *Res:* Interaction of staphylococcal alpha toxin with monolayer films; properties of pulmonary surfactants; distribution of West Virginia birds. *Mailing Add:* Dept Biol Bethany Col Bethany WV 26032

BUCKELEW, THOMAS PAUL, PARASITOLOGY, ELECTRON MICROSCOPY. *Current Pos:* PROF BIOL, CALIF UNIV PA, 69- *Personal Data:* b Easton, Pa, Aug 2, 43; m 71; c Chelsea, Meghan & Colin. *Educ:* Muhlenberg Col, BS, 65; Univ SC, MS, 67, PhD(biol), 71. *Honors & Awards:* Darbaker Award, 81. *Concurrent Pos:* Consult inst teaching electron micros, Asn Pa State Col & Univ Biologists, 78-80; consult inst training in-serv teachers molecular biol, NSF, 78-79; fel, Commonwealth Pa, 78, teaching chair, 79. *Res:* Histology and ultrastructure of hypothalamic nuclei; ultrastructural changes induced by anaboloic steroids; Physiology. *Mailing Add:* Dept Biol Calif Univ Pa California PA 15419

BUCKER, HOMER PARK, JR, ACOUSTICS, SPECTROSCOPY. *Current Pos:* head sound propagation br,69-70, RES PHYSICIST, NAVAL RES LAB, NAVAL UNDERSEA CTR, 70-; AT NAVAL OCEAN SYSTS CTR. *Personal Data:* b Ponca City, Okla, July 23, 33; m 55; c 2. *Educ:* Univ Okla, BS, 55, PhD(physics), 62. *Prof Exp:* Engr, Univ Okla, 55-60; physicist, US Navy Electronics Lab, 62-67; res physicist, Tracor, Inc, Tex, 67-69. *Mem:* Acoust Soc Am. *Res:* Propagation of sound in the ocean; infrared and Raman molecular spectroscopy. *Mailing Add:* 808 Moana Dr San Diego CA 92106

BUCKEYE, DONALD ANDREW, MATHEMATICS. *Current Pos:* PROF MATH, EASTERN MICH UNIV, 68- *Personal Data:* b Lakewood, Ohio, Mar 12, 30; m 62, Nancy; c Pam & Karen. *Educ:* Ashland Col, BS, 53; Ind Univ, MA, 61, EdD(math), 68. *Prof Exp:* Teacher, high sch, 53-54 & 56-66; instr math, Army Educ Ctr, Sendai, Japan, 54-56; teaching assoc, Ind Univ, 66-68. *Concurrent Pos:* Assoc instr, Ohio State Univ, Cleveland, 64-66. *Mem:* Nat Coun Teachers Math; Math Asn Am. *Res:* Ways of increasing the creative ability of students in mathematics; use of a laboratory approach to the teaching of mathematics and its effects on attitude, creativity and achievement. *Mailing Add:* 1823 Witmire Blvd Ypsilanti MI 48197

BUCKHAM, JAMES A(NDREW), chemical engineering, for more information see previous edition

BUCKHEIT, ROBERT WALTER, JR, VIROLOGY, ANTIVIRAL RESEARCH. *Current Pos:* DIR VIROL, RES DIV, FREDERICK RES CTR, 92- *Personal Data:* b Baltimore, Apr 10, 60; m 84, Elizabeth Kendrick; c 3. *Educ:* Lehigh Univ, BS, 82; Duke Univ, PhD(microbiol/immunol), 86. *Prof Exp:* Fel, Univ NC, Chapel Hill, 86-89; sect head, Southern Res Inst, 89-92. *Mem:* Int Soc Antiviral Res; AAAS; Am Soc Microbiol. *Res:* Microbiology. *Mailing Add:* Frederick Res Ctr 431 Aviation Way Frederick MD 21701. *Fax:* 301-694-7223; *E-Mail:* buckheit@sri.org

BUCKHOLTZ, EMILY ANN, VERTEBRATE PALEONTOLOGY, PALEONEUROLOGY. *Current Pos:* asst prof geol, 77-80, asst prof, 88-95, ASSOC PROF BIOL SCI, WELLESLEY COL, 95- *Personal Data:* b Madison, Wis, Sept 9, 47; m 69; c Daniel & Hannah. *Educ:* Col Wooster, BA, 69; Univ Wis, MS, 71; George Washington Univ, PhD(biol sci), 74. *Prof Exp:* Cur paleont, Pa State Mus, 74-76; asst prof geol, Univ Wis, Milwaukee, 80-88. *Mem:* Soc Vert Paleont; Soc Integrative & Comp Biol; Paleont Soc; Geol Soc Am; Sigma Xi; AAAS. *Res:* Paleontology; vertebrate paleontology and paleoneurology; comparative vertebrate anatomy; functional morphology of the vertebral column. *Mailing Add:* Dept Biol Sci Wellesley MA 02181. *Fax:* 781-283-3642; *E-Mail:* ebuchholtz@wellesley.edu

BUCKHOLTZ, JAMES DONNELL, MATHEMATICAL ANALYSIS. *Current Pos:* assoc prof, 64-69, PROF MATH, UNIV KY, 69- *Personal Data:* b Little Rock, Ark, Feb 25, 35; m 59; c 2. *Educ:* Univ Tex, BA, 57, PhD(math), 60. *Prof Exp:* Instr math, Univ NC, 60-61, asst prof, 61-62; vis asst prof, Univ Wis, 62-63; asst prof math, Univ NC, 63-64. *Mem:* Am Math Soc. *Res:* Analytic functions; zeros of polynomials; polynomial expansions. *Mailing Add:* 685 Providence Rd Lexington KY 40502

BUCKHOUSE, JOHN CHAPPLE, RANGE HYDROLOGY. *Current Pos:* ASST & ASSOC PROF RANGE WATERSHED MGT, ORE STATE UNIV, 74-, RES SCIENTIST RANGE HYDROL, 74- *Personal Data:* b Billings, Mont, Feb 23, 44. *Educ:* Univ Calif, Davis, BS, 66; Utah State Univ, MS, 68, PhD(watershed sci), 74. *Concurrent Pos:* Consult, Nat Acad Sci, 80-81 & Off Tech Assessment for Cong. *Mem:* Soc Range Mgt; Soil & Water Conserv Soc Am; Sigma Xi. *Res:* Natural resource and watershed valves associated with land uses and water quality; effects of livestock grazing in riparian zones. *Mailing Add:* Rangeland Res Ore State Univ 202 Strand Agr Hall Corvallis OR 97331-2208

BUCKINGHAM, ALFRED CARMICHAEL, FLUID PHYSICS, THEORETICAL MECHANICS. *Current Pos:* physicist, fluid dynamics, computational physics, 74-93, prog leader, turbulent flow & erosion, 79-84, prog leader, turbulent drug reduction, 83-88, prin investr, compressible turbulent flow, 85-93, EMER GUEST SCIENTIST FLUID DYNAMICS,

LAWRENCE LIVERMORE NAT LAB, UNIV CALIF, 93- *Personal Data:* b New York City, NY, June 10, 31; m 60, Nora Lee F Hayter. *Educ:* Univ Okla, BSc, 58, MSc, 59; Univ Calif, PhD(eng physics), 63. *Prof Exp:* Teaching asst & res asst eng sci & thermodyn, Univ Okla, 58-59; aerodynamicist re-entry gasdynamics, Douglas Aircraft Co, Santa Monica, Calif, 59-61; res scientist fluid physics, Lockheed Aircraft Corp, Palo Alto, Calif, 61-69; sr physicist, Physics Int Co, San Leandro, Calif, 69-73; staff engr & scientist gasdynamics, Aerotherm/Acurex Corp, Mountain View, Calif, 73-74. *Concurrent Pos:* Organizer, Ctr Compressible Turbulence, Lawrence Livermore Nat Lab, 88-; assoc ed, Int J Numerical Methods in Heat & Fluid Flow, 90-; organizer, Int Workshop Whys Comp Turb Mix, 88, 90, 92 & 95; NASA, 88-90; Multiphase Flow, Am Soc Mech Engrs, 88-; J Wiley Int Publ, 90. *Mem:* Fel Am Inst Aeronaut & Astronaut; Sigma Xi; Am Rocket Soc; Combustion Inst Am; Am Phys Soc. *Res:* Fluid physics; computational (numerical) fluid dynamics; turbulent flow; theoretical transport processes; three-dimensional viscous flow. *Mailing Add:* 630 Huntleigh Dr Lafayette CA 94549. *Fax:* 510-422-2644; *E-Mail:* alfredcb@unl.gov

BUCKINGHAM, AMYAND DAVID, OPTICAL ELECTRIC & MAGNETIC PROPERTIES OF MOLECULES, INTERMOLECULAR FORCES. *Current Pos:* PROF CHEM, UNIV CAMBRIDGE, 69- *Personal Data:* b Sydney, Australia, Jan 28, 30; m 65, Jillian Bowles; c Lucy E, Mark V & Alice S. *Educ:* Univ Sydney, BSc, 51, MSc, 53; Cambridge Univ, PhD(theoret chem), 56, ScD, 85. *Hon Degrees:* DSc, Univ Nancy I, 79, Univ Sydney, 93. *Prof Exp:* Univ lectr, Inorg Chem Lab, Oxford Univ, 58-65; prof theoret chem, Univ Bristol, UK, 65-69. *Concurrent Pos:* Vis prof, Harvard Univ, 61, Princeton Univ, 65, Western Ont Univ, 74, Univ Calif, Los Angeles, 75, Univ Ill, Urbana, 76, Univ Wis-Madison, 78, Univ Copenhagen, 81; fel, Pembroke Col, Cambridge, 70-; vis fel, Australian Nat Univ, 79 & 82, Univ Canterbury, NZ, 90. *Mem:* Foreign assoc Nat Acad Sci; fel Royal Soc Chem; foreign hon mem Am Acad Arts & Sci; fel Optical Soc Am; fel Am Phys Soc; Am Chem Soc. *Res:* Measurement and interpretation of optical, electric and magnetic properties of matter. *Mailing Add:* Chem Lab Cambridge Univ Lensfield Rd Cambridge CB2 1EW England

BUCKINGHAM, WILLIAM THOMAS, COMMUNICATIONS SCIENCE, PLANT BREEDING. *Current Pos:* PRES, BUCKINGHAM ELECTRONIC DIV, BUCKINGHAM PROD, PRES & GEN MGR, BUCKINGHAM ORCHARDS, 68- *Personal Data:* b Lancaster, Ohio, Dec 21, 21; m 55; c 3. *Educ:* Otterbein Col, BA, 45, BS, 46; Ohio Univ, MBA, 79. *Prof Exp:* Prin chemist, Battelle Mem Inst, 42-46; asst prof metall chem, Ohio State Univ, 47-54; prin chemist, Battelle Mem Inst, 54-56; lab mgr & spec proj off, Foseco, Inc, 56-68. *Concurrent Pos:* Consult, Metall/Chem & Commun, 68-; consult & assoc sponsor, Dale Carnegie Courses, 68-85; asst prof, Emerson E Evans Sch Bus, Univ Rio Grande. *Mem:* Am Chem Soc. *Res:* Laboratory and general management; chemical treatment of metals; exothermics and explosives; development and growth of new fruit cultivars from origination to full scale commercial production. *Mailing Add:* 8803 Cheshire Rd Sunbury OH 43074-9276

BUCKLAND, BARRY C, BIOTECHNOLOGY. *Current Pos:* dir, Fermentation Pilot Plant, Mercks & Co Inc, 80-86, Biochem Process Res & Develop, 86-90, sr dir, 90-93, exec dir, 93-96, VPRES BIO PROCESS RES & DEVELOP, MERCK & CO INC, 96- *Personal Data:* b London, Eng, Jan 6, 48. *Educ:* Manchester Univ, Eng, BSc, 70, Univ Col, London, MSc, 71, PhD(biochem eng), 74. *Prof Exp:* Biochem engr, Abbott Lab, Chicago, 74-77; sr engr, Lederle Lab, NY, 77-80. *Concurrent Pos:* Vis prof, Univ Col, London, Eng, 89-, Rutgers Univ, 90-; dir, Food, Pharmaceut & Bioeng Div, Am Inst Chem Engrs, 93-95; lectr, Am Chem Soc, 94, Int Inst Biotechnol, London, 95. *Mem:* Nat Acad Eng; Am Inst Chem Engrs; fel Am Inst Med & Biol Eng; fel Int Inst Biotechnol; Am Chem Soc; Am Inst Chem Engrs. *Mailing Add:* Merck & Co Inc PO Box 2000 RY80Y-11D Rahway NJ 07065-0900

BUCKLAND, PETER GRAHAM, STRUCTURAL ENGINEERING. *Current Pos:* PRES, BUCKLAND & TAYLOR LTD, N VANCOUVER, BC, 70- *Personal Data:* b London, Eng, Sept 7, 38; m 74, Aralee Buckland; c 3. *Educ:* Cambridge Univ, BA, 60, MA, 72. *Hon Degrees:* LLD(hon), Univ BC, 92. *Honors & Awards:* Le Priv PL Pratley Award, 91 & 92. *Prof Exp:* Engr & proj mgr, Canron Inc, Vancouver, BC, 63-68; engr, Swan Wooster-CBA, Vancouver, 68-70. *Mem:* Inst Civil Engrs; Am Soc Civil Engrs. *Res:* Derivation of loading for long span bridges; contributed to seismic upgrading of Golden Gate Bridge in San Francisco; independent engineer for 13 km-long Northumberland Strait crossing bridge. *Mailing Add:* Buckland & Taylor Ltd 1591 Bowser Ave North Vancouver BC V7P 2Y4 Can

BUCKLAND, ROGER BASIL, POULTRY GENETICS, REPRODUCTIVE PHYSIOLOGY. *Current Pos:* from asst prof to assoc prof, McGill Univ, 71-81, chmn, 79-85, dean, fac agr, 85-90, PROF ANIMAL SCI, MACDONALD COL, MCGILL UNIV, 81-, VPRIN, 85-, DEAN, FAC AGR & ENVIRON SCI, 90- *Personal Data:* b Jemseg, NB, May 18, 42; m 65; c 2. *Educ:* McGill Univ, BSc, 63, MSc, 65; Univ Md, PhD(physiol genetics), 68. *Honors & Awards:* Poultry Sci Res Award, Poultry Sci Asn, 72. *Prof Exp:* Res scientist poultry physiol, Can Dept Agr, 67-71. *Mem:* Can Soc Animal Sci; Poultry Sci Asn; World Poultry Sci Asn; Genetics Soc Can. *Res:* Genetics of reproduction, metabolism of chicken sperm; resistance to stress in poultry. *Mailing Add:* Dept Animal Sci McGill Univ Macdonald Col 21111 Lakeshore Rd Ste Anne de Belle PQ H9X 1C0 Can

BUCKLER, ERNEST JACK, CHEMISTRY, POLYMER CHEMISTRY. *Current Pos:* RETIRED. *Personal Data:* b Birmingham, Eng, June 3, 14; m 42, Brough Maclean. *Educ:* Cambridge Univ, MA, 35, PhD(phys chem), 38. *Hon Degrees:* LLD, Queens Univ, Ont, 59. *Honors & Awards:* Tech Award, Int Inst Synthetic Rubber Producers, 80; R S Jane Mem Award, Chem Inst Can, 83. *Prof Exp:* Res chemist, Trinidad Leaseholds, BWI, 38-41 & Imp Oil, Sarnia, 41-42; prod controller, St Clair Processing Corp, 42-45, tech supt, 45-48; mgr res, Polymer Corp, 48-53, vpres res & develop, 53-79; consult, Polysar Ltd, 79-91. *Mem:* Fel Chem Inst Can; Am Chem Soc; Soc Chem Indust. *Res:* Chemical kinetics, gas phase; petroleum refining and petrochemicals; polymer synthesis and characterization; research management. *Mailing Add:* 139 Wellington St Sarnia ON N7T 1G4 Can

BUCKLER, SHELDON A, THERMODYNAMICS & MATERIAL PROPERTIES, TECHNICAL MANAGEMENT. *Current Pos:* mgr chem develop, 64-66, dir chem res & develop div, 66-69, asst vpres res, 69-72, vpres res, 72-75, group vpres, 75-77, sr vpres, 77-80, EXEC VPRES, POLAROID CORP, 80- *Personal Data:* b New York, NY, May 18, 31; m 52, 78; c 3. *Educ:* NY Univ, BA, 51; Columbia Univ, MA, 52, PhD(chem), 54. *Prof Exp:* Asst, Columbia Univ, 51-53; res fel, Univ Md, 55-56; res chemist & group leader basic res dept, Am Cyanamid Co, 56-62; mgr org res, Am Mach & Foundry Co, 62-64. *Concurrent Pos:* Dir, Advan Color technol, Lord Corp. *Mem:* Am Chem Soc; Soc Photog Sci & Eng. *Res:* Technical management; process research and development; synthetic and theoretical organophosphorus chemistry; photographic chemicals; carbohydrates; organometallics; organic peroxides. *Mailing Add:* 200 Dudley Rd Newton MA 02159

BUCKLES, ROBERT EDWIN, PHYSICAL ORGANIC CHEMISTRY. *Current Pos:* from instr to assoc prof, 45-59, PROF ORG CHEM, UNIV IOWA, 59- *Personal Data:* b Fallon, Nev, Aug 11, 17; m 44; c 2. *Educ:* Univ Calif, BS, 39, MS, 40; Univ Calif, Los Angeles, PhD(phys-org chem), 42. *Prof Exp:* Asst, Ill Inst Technol, 40-41 & Univ Calif, Los Angeles, 41-42; du Pont fel & instr org chem, Univ Minn, 43-45. *Mem:* Am Chem Soc. *Res:* Molecular structure; addition reactions; replacement reactions; reaction mechanisms; halogen chemistry; chemistry education. *Mailing Add:* 3113 Cambridge Rd Cameron Pk Shingle Springs CA 95682-9140

BUCKLEY, CHARLES EDWARD, INTERNAL MEDICINE, ALLERGY. *Current Pos:* Assoc med & immunol, Duke Univ, 58-67, assoc immunol, 67-70, asst prof microbiol & immunol, 70-74, asst prof med to assoc prof med, 67-78, PROF MED, DUKE UNIV MED CTR, 78-, DIR ALLERGY & CLLIN, IMMUNOL LAB, 70- *Personal Data:* b Charleston, WVa, Sept 2, 29; m 55; c 4. *Educ:* Va Polytech Inst, BS, 50; Duke Univ, MD, 54. *Concurrent Pos:* USPHS res career develop award, 61-69; mem adv coun, Nat Inst Allergy & Infectious Dis, 75-79. *Mem:* Am Fedn Clin Res; Am Thoracic Soc; Am Acad Allergy; Am Col Physicians; Am Asn Immunol; Sigma Xi. *Res:* Allergy, clinical immunology; immunochemistry; biochemical and immunochemical characterization of antigens important in human disease; genetics and epidemiology of immunity. *Mailing Add:* 3621 Westover Rd Durham NC 27707

BUCKLEY, DALE ELIOT, GEOCHEMISTRY, MARINE GEOLOGY. *Current Pos:* sci officer marine geol, Atlantic Oceanog Lab, Bedford Inst Oceanog, 62-69, phys scientist environ marine geol, Atlantic Geosci Ctr, 70-79, res scientist, 79-90, SR RES SCIENTIST, BEDFORD INST OCEANOG, 90- *Personal Data:* b Wolfville, NS, May 3, 36; m 64; c 3. *Educ:* Acadia Univ, BSc, 59; Univ Western Ont, MSc, 63; Univ Alaska, PhD(marine sci), 69. *Honors & Awards:* Merit Award, Giol Surv Can, 92. *Prof Exp:* Tech officer, Can Hydrographic Surv, Dept Mines & Tech Surv, 60-61 & Oceanog Res Div, 61-62. *Concurrent Pos:* Lectr, Calif State Col, Los Angeles, 65-66; prof geol, St Mary's Univ, Halifax, NS, 91-93; hon res assoc environ sci, Dalhousie Univ, Halifax, NS, 92- *Mem:* Prof Inst Pub Serv Can; fel Geol Asn Can; Can Meteorol & Oceanog Soc; Am Chem Soc. *Res:* Marine inorganic geochemistry, particularly processes of chemical exchange between natural sediments and ionic metals in seawater, research to be applied to problems of coastal pollution and waste disposal, including deep sea disposal of nuclear waste. *Mailing Add:* 21 Dumbarton Ave Dartmouth NS B2X 1Z7 Can

BUCKLEY, DENIS NOEL, OPTOELECTRONIC MATERIALS, ELECTROCHEMISTRY. *Current Pos:* MEM TECH STAFF, AT&T BELL LABS, 79- *Personal Data:* b Cork, Ireland, Dec 26, 49; m 84, Melody; c Sonia & Michelle. *Educ:* Nat Univ Ireland, BS, 71, PhD(chem), 75. *Prof Exp:* Res assoc & lectr chem, Nat Univ Ireland, 75-76; res assoc, Univ Pa, 76-79. *Concurrent Pos:* Lectr chem, Col St Elizabeth Morristown, NJ, 87-; adj prof chem, Cooper Union Advan Art & Sci, New York, 92- *Mem:* Electrochem Soc; Am Chem Soc; Am Asn Crystal Growth. *Res:* Thermodynamics and kinetics of interfacial processes; epitaxial crystal growth of compound semiconductor materials; development of precursors and growth chemistries for chemical vapor deposition; in situ electrochemical generation of precursor materials. *Mailing Add:* Lucent Technols Murray Hill NJ 07974. *Fax:* 908-668-0427

BUCKLEY, EDWARD HARLAND, DEVELOPMENTAL BIOLOGY, STRESS PHYSIOLOGY. *Current Pos:* RETIRED. *Personal Data:* b Brandon, Man, Jan 30, 31; m 56; c 3. *Educ:* Ont Agr Col, BSA, 54; Columbia Univ, MA, 56, PhD(plant physiol), 59. *Prof Exp:* Plant physiologist, Cent Res Labs, United Fruit Co, 58-60, plant biochemist, 61-65; plant biochemist, Boyce Thompson Inst Plant Res, Cornell Univ, 65- *Concurrent Pos:* Prin investr, ecol zoning proj estuary Hudson River, 68-74. *Mem:* NY Acad Sci; Am Soc Plant Physiol; Can Soc Plant Physiol; Soc Wetland Scientist; Am Soc Cell Biol. *Res:* Host-parasite relationships in plants; biosynthesis of flavor and aroma compounds and of phenolic compounds in banana; biochemical aspects of plant gametogenesis; development of fungi; estuarine ecology; ecotoxicology. *Mailing Add:* 165 Iradell Rd Ithaca NY 14850

BUCKLEY, FRED THOMAS, MATHEMATICS, GRAPH THEORY. *Current Pos:* from asst prof to assoc prof, 82-88, PROF MATH, BARUCH COL, NY, 88- *Personal Data:* b Newark, NJ, Feb 4, 51; m 75. *Educ:* Pace Univ, BA, 73; City Univ New York, PhD(math), 78. *Prof Exp:* Asst prof math, St John's Univ, 78-82. *Concurrent Pos:* Vchmn math, NY Acad Sci, 90-91. *Mem:* Math Asn Am; NY Acad Sci. *Res:* Ramsey theory; graph operations; line graphs; distance in graphs; Ramsey-type matrix problems; centrality in graphs. *Mailing Add:* Dept Math City Univ NY Bernard Baruch 17 Lexington Ave New York NY 10010-5526

BUCKLEY, JAMES THOMAS, BIOCHEMISTRY. *Current Pos:* From asst prof to assoc prof, 72-82, PROF BIOCHEM, UNIV VICTORIA, 82- *Personal Data:* b Ottawa, Ont, Oct 3, 42; div; c 2. *Educ:* McGill Univ, BSc, 65, PhD(biochem), 69. *Mem:* Can Biochem Soc. *Res:* Protein lipid interactions; mechanism of protein export by gram negative bacteria; mechanism action of hole-forming toxins. *Mailing Add:* Dept Biochem Univ Victoria Box 3055 Victoria BC V8W 3P6 Can

BUCKLEY, JAY SELLECK, JR, INFORMATION SCIENCE. *Current Pos:* DIR TECH INFO, PFIZER, INC, 74- *Personal Data:* b Ansonia, Conn, Feb 16, 24; m 48; c 4. *Educ:* Williams Col, BS, 44; Univ Minn, PhD(org chem), 49. *Prof Exp:* Res chemist, Winthrop Chem Co, 45-46; res chemist, Comput Based Info Serv, 49-51, res supvr, 51-54, res mgr, 54-68, mgr, 68-74. *Mem:* Am Chem Soc. *Res:* Organic chemistry; mechanisms of organic reactions and medicinal products; systems for encoding and retrieval of chemical and biological information; methods for efficient and economical utilization of information resources available to research organizations. *Mailing Add:* 16 Birch Lane Groton CT 06340-6003

BUCKLEY, JOHN DENNIS, MATERIALS SCIENCE, SPACE SCIENCES. *Current Pos:* Aerospace technologist mat sci, Langley Res Ctr, NASA, 59-70, supvr aerospace eng & thermodyn, 70-71, supvr mat eng, 71-73, TECH ASST MAT PROCESSING, FABRICATION DIV, LANGLEY RES CTR, NASA, 73- *Personal Data:* b Saranac Lake, NY, Oct 28, 28; m 59; c 3. *Educ:* St Lawrence Univ, BS, 50; Clemson Univ, BS, 59, MS, 61; Iowa State Univ, PhD(eng), 68. *Honors & Awards:* Exceptional Serv Medal, NASA, 77 & Technol Utilization Award, 78; IR-100 Award, 79. *Concurrent Pos:* Assoc prof eng, George Washington Univ, 68-, assoc prof gen studies, 70-; fac mem, NASA- Langley-George Washington Univ Joint Inst Advan Flight Sci, 71-; mem, Va State Bd Health, 72-76; mem, City Newport News Planning Comn; lectr eng, Thomas Nelson Community Col, 75-; lectr mat sci, Old Dom Univ, 80-; lectr physics, Christopher Newport Col, 81- *Mem:* Am Inst Aeronaut & Astronaut; fel Am Ceramic Soc; Am Soc Metals; Soc Mfg Engrs; Nat Inst Ceramic Engrs. *Res:* Physical and thermal properties of materials, metals, ceramics, polymers; design and fabrication of composite materials. *Mailing Add:* 23 E Governor Dr Newport News VA 23602

BUCKLEY, JOSEPH J, ANESTHESIOLOGY. *Current Pos:* From instr to assoc prof, 54-61, PROF ANESTHESIOL, MED COL, UNIV MINN, MINNEAPOLIS, 61-, HEAD DEPT, 79- *Personal Data:* b Methuen, Mass, Sept 11, 22; m 45; c 4. *Educ:* Dartmouth Col, AB, 44; NY Med Col, MD, 46; Univ Minn, MS, 58. *Concurrent Pos:* Consult, US Vet Admin, 58-; vis prof, Col Physicians & Surgeons, Columbia Univ, 62, Univ Man, 76, Univ Tex, San Antonio, 77, Wash Univ, 85. *Mem:* AMA; Am Soc Anesthesiol; Acad Anesthesiol. *Res:* Cardiac and pulmonary physiology; mass spectrometry. *Mailing Add:* 10919 Glen Wilding Pl Minneapolis MN 55431

BUCKLEY, JOSEPH THADDEUS, MATHEMATICS. *Current Pos:* asst prof, 70-74, assoc prof, 74-80, PROF MATH, WESTERN MICH UNIV, 80- *Personal Data:* b Boston, Mass, Apr 13, 37; m 61, Ann L Thompson; c Anne (Dueweke), John, Paul & Timothy. *Educ:* Boston Col, BS, 58; Ind Univ, PhD(math), 64. *Prof Exp:* Young res instr math, Dartmouth Col, 64-67; asst prof, Univ Mass, 67-70. *Mem:* Am Math Soc; Math Asn Am. *Res:* Group theory; group rings; cohomology of groups; extensions; nilpotent groups; homological algebra. *Mailing Add:* Dept Math Western Mich Univ Kalamazoo MI 49008-5152

BUCKLEY, NANCY MARGARET, CARDIOVASCULAR PHYSIOLOGY. *Current Pos:* RETIRED. *Personal Data:* b Philadelphia, Pa, Dec 2, 24; m 84, John H E Fried; c Jaqueline. *Educ:* Univ Pa, AB, 45, MD, 50. *Prof Exp:* Asst med dir, Columbus Blood Prog, Am Red Cross, 51-52; res assoc med, Ohio State Univ, 52, asst prof & res assoc physiol, 52-55; from asst prof to prof physiol, Albert Einstein Col, 55-89, prof biophys, 81-89. *Concurrent Pos:* Consult physiol, Div Pediat Cardiol, Long Island Jewish Med Ctr, 75-89. *Mem:* AAAS; Am Physiol Soc; NY Acad Sci; Am Heart Asn. *Res:* Cardiodynamics; cardiovascular development. *Mailing Add:* 372 Central Park W Apt 2-Y New York NY 10025-8203

BUCKLEY, PAGE SCOTT, systems design & systems science; deceased, see previous edition for last biography

BUCKLEY, R RUSS, CORPORATE MANAGEMENT, TECHNICAL MANAGEMENT. *Current Pos:* EXEC VPRES, PROCESS SYSTS, BALZERS, LTD, 93- *Personal Data:* b Jackson, Miss, May 7, 39; m 60, Ann Adams; c Lisa (Mohan), Karen (Irwin) & Suzanne (Klein). *Educ:* Millsaps Col, BS, 61; Univ SC, PhD(inorg chem), 66. *Prof Exp:* Tech supvr, Bell Tel Labs, 65-85; co-founder & vpres, Gain Electronics Corp, 85-88, corp secy, 86-88; vpres & gen mgr, Mat Res Corp, 89-92. *Mem:* Am Mgt Asn; Sigma Xi. *Res:* Management of research, development, and improvement of process equipment, materials and processes of interest to the semiconductor and electronics industry. *Mailing Add:* 2 Gilboa Lane Nashua NH 03062. *Fax:* 908-273-8391

BUCKLEY, REBECCA HATCHER, PEDIATRICS, ALLERGY AND IMMUNOLOGY. *Current Pos:* Intern pediat, Duke Univ, 58-59, from asst resident to resident, 59-61, from instr to prof pediat, 61-79, from asst prof to assoc prof immunol, 69-79, J BUREN SIDBURY PROF PEDIAT & PROF IMMUNOL, SCH MED, DUKE UNIV, 79-, CHIEF, DIV ALLERGY & IMMUNOL, 74-, DIST PROF, 79- *Personal Data:* b Hamlet, NC, Apr 1, 33; m 55; c Charles E IV, Elizabeth A, Rebecca K & Sarah M. *Educ:* Duke Univ, AB, 54; Univ NC, MD, 58. *Honors & Awards:* Allergic Dis Acad Award; Gen Clin Res Ctr Excellence Award, NIH, 90; Bret Ratner Award, 92. *Concurrent Pos:* Fel allergy, Sch Med, Duke Univ, 61-63, fel immunol, 63-65; dir, Am Bd Allergy & Immunol, 71-73 & 82-87; mem, Immunol Sci Study Sect, NIH, 76-79, chmn, 79-80; Merit Res Award, NIH, 87- *Mem:* Am Acad Allergy & Immunol (pres 79-80); Am Acad Pediat; Soc Pediat Res; Am Asn Immunologists; Sigma Xi (pres 80-81); Am Pediat Soc. *Res:* Cellular and molecular bases of human primary immunodeficiency; cell-mediated immune responsiveness in the atopic diseases; regulation of human IgE synthesis; bone marrow transplantation; stem cell education in the human thymus. *Mailing Add:* Duke Univ Box 2898 Durham NC 27710-0001. *Fax:* 919-681-7979; *E-Mail:* buckloo3@mc.duke.edu

BUCKLIN, ROBERT VAN ZANDT, LEGAL MEDICINE. *Current Pos:* CONSULT, LEGAL MED & FORENSIC PATH, 87-; DEP MED EXAMR, CLARY CO, LOS VEGAS, NEV, 95- *Personal Data:* b Chicago, Ill, June 25, 16; m 67, Patricia Lynch; c Barbara, Jay, James, Rik & Garry. *Educ:* Loyola Univ, Ill, BSM, 38, MD, 41; STex Col Law, JD, 69; Am Bd Path, dipl path anat, clin & forensic path. *Prof Exp:* Intern, St Josephs Hosp, Tacoma, Wash, 40-41; resident path, Tacoma Gen Hosp, 41-42; chief lab serv path, St Mary's Hosp & Saginaw Gen Hosp, Mich, 46-63; assoc med examr, Harris Co, Tex, 64-68; chief med examr, Galveston Co, Tex, 69-71, dir med legal affairs, Health Commun, Inc, 72-74; dep med examr, Los Angeles Co, 74-77; chief med examr, Travis Co, Tex, 77-78; dep chief med examr, Harris Co, Tex, 78-80; dep med examr, Los Angeles Co, Calif, 80-83; pathologist, San Diego Co Coroner, 83-87. *Concurrent Pos:* Forensic path consult, 69-; prof fath, Univ Tex Med Br, Galveston, 69-71; clin prof path, Univ Southern Calif, 80-86. *Mem:* Am Col Physicians; Am Soc Clin Path; Am Col Legal Med; Am Acad Forensic Sci; Nat Asn Med Examrs. *Res:* Medical and legal aspects of the Crucifixion; aging and dating of traumatic lesions. *Mailing Add:* 3255 Lindell Rd Las Vegas NV 89102-6926. *Fax:* 702-247-9084

BUCKMAN, ALVIN BRUCE, ELECTROOPTICS, OPTICAL PHYSICS. *Current Pos:* ASSOC PROF ELEC ENG, UNIV TEX, AUSTIN, 74- *Personal Data:* b Omaha, Nebr, Dec 7, 41; m 66. *Educ:* Mass Inst Technol, BS, 64; Univ Nebr, MS, 66, PhD(elec eng), 68. *Prof Exp:* Instr elec eng, Univ Nebr, Lincoln, 66-68, from asst prof to assoc prof, 68-74, assoc prof elec eng, 73-74. *Concurrent Pos:* Consult, 74- *Mem:* Am Phys Soc; Optical Soc Am. *Res:* Optical properties and electronic structure of solids; especially surface and thin film effects; integrated optical devices. *Mailing Add:* 1800 Brookhaven Dr Austin TX 78704

BUCKMAN, ROBERT W, LEGAL MEDICINE, PHARMACEUTICAL COMMUNICATIONS. *Current Pos:* PRES & CHIEF EXEC OFFICER, MED SCI INFO RESOURCES, 88- *Personal Data:* b Detroit, Mich, Dec 23, 38. *Educ:* Univ Detroit, BS(chem) & BS(biol), 61; Loyola Univ Chicago, PhD(pharmacol & toxicol), 74; Loyola Univ, PhD(clin pharmacol), 74. *Prof Exp:* Health officer, Village Bellwood, Ill, 68-72; comn med officer, lieutenant comdr, USN, 75-77; sr vpres & dir med affairs, McCann Brickson Worldwide, 77-88. *Concurrent Pos:* Lectr pharmacol, Loyola Univ Chicago, 72, clin pharmacol, Univ Calif, San Francisco, 75-77, Berkeley, 76-77; vis clin fac, Univ Calif, 75-77; consult clin pharmacol, Health Care Indust, 75-, Pain Control in Cancer, Northwestern, 79-82 & clin pharmacol, Ill State Med Soc-Drug & Therapeut, 80-; sr scientist, Sch Pub Health, Univ Calif, 75-77. *Mem:* Am Col Clin Pharmacol; Am Col Legal Med; Am Soc Clin Oncol; Am Soc Clin Pharmacol & Therapeut; Am Soc Law & Med; Drug Info Asn. *Res:* Ethical support of issues in legal medicine and healthcare communications. *Mailing Add:* 1325 Heatherton Dr Naperville IL 60563-2230. *Fax:* 630-357-1277

BUCKMAN, WILLIAM GORDON, SOLID STATE PHYSICS. *Current Pos:* from asst prof to assoc prof, 67-73, PROF PHYSICS, WESTERN KY UNIV, 73- *Personal Data:* b Morganfield, Ky, Dec 1, 34; m 59; c William G Jr, Charles R & John M. *Educ:* Western Ky Univ, BS, 60; Vanderbilt Univ, MS, 62; Univ NC, PhD(pub health, radiation physics), 67. *Prof Exp:* Instr radiation hyg, Univ NC, 62-64; chmn, Dept Physics & Math, Ky Wesleyan Col, 66-67. *Concurrent Pos:* Consult environ radioactivity & dosimetry. *Mem:* Am Phys Soc; Health Physics Soc. *Res:* Luminescence; solid state radiation dosimetry. *Mailing Add:* 504 Memphis Junction Rd Bowling Green KY 42101

BUCKMASTER, HARVEY ALLEN, ELECTRON PARAMAGNETIC RESONANCE, MICROWAVE COMPLEX PERMITTIVITY. *Current Pos:* from asst prof to prof, 60-93, EMER PROF PHYSICS, UNIV CALGARY, 93- *Personal Data:* b Calgary, Alta, Apr 8, 29; m 56, 68, Margaret R Lynett. *Educ:* Univ Alta, BSc, 50; Univ BC, MA, 52, PhD(physics), 56. *Honors & Awards:* Queen Elizabeth II Can Silver Jubilee Medal 78; Harvey & Margaret Buckmaster Park Award, 91. *Prof Exp:* Nat Res Coun Can Overseas fel, Cavendish Lab, Cambridge Univ, 56-57; asst prof physics, Univ Alta, 57-60. *Concurrent Pos:* Leverhulme vis res fel, Univ Keele, 64-65; mem, Sci Adv Comt, Environ Conserv Authority, Prov Alta, 71-77; trustee, Univ Alta Pension Plan, 72-78, Alta Univs Pension Plan, 78-86; mem bd gov, Univ Calgary, 75-78; chmn, Sci Adv Comt, Environ Coun Alta, 77-79, mem, 77-88; mem Nat Sci & Eng Res Coun Can Mainline Phys Grant Selection Comt, 82-85; mem, Can Scholar & Fel Comt, Nat Sci & Eng Res Coun, 93-; adj prof elec & comput eng, Univ Victoria, 93-94, adj prof physics & astron, 94-; Acad Res Comt, Dept Nat Defense, Can, 95- *Mem:* Sr mem Inst Elec & Electronics Engrs; Can Asn Physicists; Fel Brit Inst Physics; Am Asn Physics Teachers; fel AAAS; Int Soc Magnetic Resonance; Int Electron Paramagnetic Resonance Soc; Sigma Xi. *Res:* Electronic paramagnetic resonance and endor lanthanide elements in hydrated, deuterated and anhydrous lattices; application determinations in biophysics; dielectric properties of biological tissue at millimeter wave lengths; electron paramagnetic resonance; energy consumption and climate change studies; energy scenarios; dielectric properties of high loss liquids (water, deuterium); electron paramagnetic resonance instrumentation development; microwave complex permittivity spectroscopy instrumentation development; fossil fuel studies using electron paramagnetic resonance; application of pulsed electron paramagnetic resonance to fossil fuel and biophysics studies; electron paramagnetic resonance spin-label studies of biological tissue. *Mailing Add:* Dept Physics Astron Univ Victoria PO Box 3055 Victoria BC V8W 3P6 Can. *Fax:* 250-721-7715; *E-Mail:* buckmast@uvic.ca

BUCKMASTER, JOHN DAVID, FLUID MECHANICS, APPLIED MATHEMATICS. *Current Pos:* assoc prof, 74-78, PROF MATH & MECH, UNIV ILL, URBANA, 78- *Personal Data:* b Belfast, Northern Ireland, Feb 2, 41; m 66; c 1. *Educ:* Univ London, BSc, 62; Cornell Univ, PhD(appl math), 69. *Prof Exp:* Res engr fluids, Cornell Aeronaut Lab, Buffalo, NY, 62-65; lectr, Univ London, 68-69; asst prof, NY Univ, 69-72; asst prof eng & appl sci, Yale Univ, 72-74. *Mem:* Am Phys Soc; Soc Indust & Appl Math. *Mailing Add:* AAE Dept Univ Ill 104 S Wright St Urbana IL 61801

BUCKMIRE, REGINALD EUGENE, FOOD CHEMISTRY, TROPICAL AGRICULTURE. *Current Pos:* indust develop expert, 87-95, CONSULT, GRENADA DEVELOP BANK, 95-; MANAGING DIR, PARRIS PHARM, 95- *Personal Data:* b Oct 3, 38; Brit citizen; m 75; c Ron, Regina & Rae. *Educ:* Univ WI, BS, 61; Univ Mass, Amherst, MS, 71, PhD(food sci & nutrit), 74. *Prof Exp:* Agr exten officer, USDA, 61-68; asst soils, Univ Mass, 68-74; group leader foods, Quaker Oats Co, Ill, 74-78; proj leader, Foremost Foods, Calif, 78; proj appraisal & food consult, Caribbean Develop Bank, 78-81, proj leader, 81-83, food consult, Technol Transfer & Tech Serv, 84-87. *Concurrent Pos:* Dir, Agro-Indust Prog, Grenada, 81-82; agro-indust consult, feasibility studies & food mfg, 81-83; chief exec officer, Superior Foods Ltd, 83-84; Caribbean tech consult & serv network coordr, technol networking, 83-84; vis lectr food & nutrit, Barbados Polytech, 84-; assoc consult, Redma Consult Ltd, Can, 84-, Indust Develop, 87- *Mem:* Inst Food Technologists. *Res:* Food product development; food program development for lesser developed countries; applied research in the use of tropical fruits and vegetables. *Mailing Add:* Parris Pharm Ltd St Andrew's PO Box 904 Grenville Grenada

BUCKNAM, ROBERT CAMPBELL, GEOLOGY. *Current Pos:* GEOLOGIST, US GEOL SURV, 68- *Personal Data:* b Lander, Wyo, Sept 29, 40; m 63; c 3. *Educ:* Colo Sch Mines, Geol Eng, 62; Univ Colo, PhD(geol), 69. *Mem:* Fel Geol Soc Am; Seismol Soc Am; Am Geophys Union. *Res:* Structural geology; geology of earthquakes. *Mailing Add:* 14550 W 70th Dr Arvada CO 80004

BUCKNER, CARL KENNETH, AUTONOMIC-PHARMACOLOGY, IMMUNO-PHARMACOLOGY. *Current Pos:* AT ICI AMERICAS INC. *Educ:* Ohio State Univ, PhD(pharmacol), 70. *Prof Exp:* prof pharmacol, Univ Wis, Madison, 81- *Mailing Add:* Am Coun Pharmaceut Educ 311 Superior Chicago IL 61610

BUCKNER, CHARLES HENRY, WILDLIFE ECOLOGY. *Current Pos:* RETIRED. *Personal Data:* b Toronto, Ont, Oct 8, 28; m 53; c 2. *Educ:* Univ Toronto, BA, 52; Univ Man, MSc, 54; Univ Western Ont, PhD(zool), 59. *Prof Exp:* Res officer mammal, Can Dept Agr, 52-60 & Can Dept Fisheries & Forestry, 60-66; head vert biol, Chem Control Res Inst, 66-70, dep dir, 75-76, dir, 76-78, head ecol impact, 70-87. *Concurrent Pos:* Prog mgr, Int Spruce Budworms Agreement, 78- *Mem:* Am Soc Mammal; Entom Soc Can. *Res:* Impact of pesticides on non-target organisms; vertebrate damage to forests; populations feeding and behavior; ornithology; population dynamics; vertebrate predation on forest insects. *Mailing Add:* 54 Moorcroft Rd Nepean ON K2G 0M7 Can

BUCKNER, DAVID LEE, PLANT ECOLOGY, SOIL SCIENCE. *Current Pos:* CONSULT PLANT ECOL & SOIL SCI, ENVIRON SCI DIV, CAMP DRESSER & MCKEE, 77- *Personal Data:* b Boulder, Colo, Feb 4, 48; m 73; c 1. *Educ:* Univ Colo, BA, 70, MA, 73, PhD(plant ecol), 77. *Prof Exp:* Consult plant ecol & soil sci, Genge Environ Consults, 75-77. *Mem:* Ecol Soc Am; Soc Range Mgt; Sigma Xi. *Res:* Recovery of alpine tundra following disturbance; recovery rates of semi-desert to subalpine ecosystems following pipeline construction; dynamics of high elevation forest-meadow ecosystems. *Mailing Add:* 1077 S Cherryvale Rd Boulder CO 80303

BUCKNER, JAMES STEWART, BIOCHEMISTRY. *Current Pos:* RES BIOCHEMIST, BIOSCI RES LAB, AGR RES SERV, FED RES, USDA, 76- *Personal Data:* b Portland, Ore, June 26, 42; m 66; c 1. *Educ:* Univ Idaho, BS, 64; NDak State Univ, MS, 69, PhD(chem), 71. *Prof Exp:* Res scientist, Dept Agr Chem, Wash State Univ, 71-76. *Mem:* Am Soc Biochem & Molecular Biol. *Res:* Elucidation and description of essential physiological processes in insects, such as nitrogen metabolism and surface lipid metabolism, which are controlled by the neuroendocrine system. *Mailing Add:* Biosci Res Lab USDA Agr Res Serv-Fed Res Fargo ND 58105. *Fax:* 701-237-1202; *E-Mail:* nu065528@ndsuvm1

BUCKNER, RALPH GUPTON, VETERINARY MEDICINE. *Current Pos:* SELF-EMPLOYED VET PRACTR. *Personal Data:* b Casper, Wyo, May 12, 21; m 49, Jacqueline Gleason; c Katherine & Kenneth. *Educ:* Westminster Col, AB, 47; Kans State Univ, BS, DVM, 56; Univ Okla, MS, 66. *Honors & Awards:* Am Animal Hosp Outstanding Practr Award, 90. *Prof Exp:* Inst vet med & surg, Okla State Univ, 56-58, from asst prof to assoc prof vet path, 58-67, assoc prof vet med & surg, 67-69, prof vet path, 69-73, prof vet med & chief small animal med, 74-86. *Concurrent Pos:* Consult. *Mem:* Am Vet Med Asn; Am Soc Vet Clin Path; Am Col Vet Int Med; Sigma Xi. *Res:* Clinical pathology, especially hematology and blood coagulation diseases; canine hemophilia; theriogenology. *Mailing Add:* 65 University Circle Stillwater OK 74074

BUCKNER, RICHARD LEE, PARASITOLOGY. *Current Pos:* asst prof, 78-84, ASSOC PROF BIOL, LIVINGSTON UNIV, 84- *Personal Data:* b Owensboro, Ky, Jan 9, 47; m 73; c 1. *Educ:* Western Ky Univ, BS, 70, MS, 72; Univ Nebr-Lincoln, PhD(zool), 76. *Prof Exp:* Vis asst prof, Ind State Univ, Evansville, 76-78. *Mem:* Am Soc Parasitologists; Am Inst Biol Sci. *Res:* Taxonomy and host-parasite relationships of the acanthocephalans. *Mailing Add:* Div Math & Sci Univ W Ala Livingston AL 35470

BUCKPITT, ALAN R, PULMONARY TOXICOLOGY, XENOBIOTIC METABOLISM. *Current Pos:* assoc prof, 85-90, PROF PHARMACOL & TOXICOL, VET MED SCH, UNIV CALIF, DAVIS, 90- *Personal Data:* b Cambridge, Mass, July 28, 48. *Educ:* William & Mary Col, BS, 70; Ind Univ, MS, 73, PhD(pharmacol), 75. *Prof Exp:* From asst prof to assoc prof pharmacol, Univ Calif, Irvine. 79-85. *Mem:* Soc Toxicol; Am Soc Pharmacol & Exp Therapeut. *Mailing Add:* Dept Pharmacol & Toxicol Sch Vet Med Univ Calif Davis CA 95616-5224

BUCKS, DALE A, ENVIRONMENTAL SCIENCES. *Current Pos:* NAT PROG LEADER WATER QUAL & MGT, US DEPT AGR, 90- *Personal Data:* b Davenport, Iowa, Nov 28, 43. *Educ:* Univ Ariz, PhD(soil & water sci), 79. *Mailing Add:* US Dept Agr Nat Prog Staff BARC-West Bldg 005 Rm 233 Beltsville MD 20705

BUCKSBAUM, PHILIP HOWARD, ATOMIC PHYSICS. *Current Pos:* PROF PHYSICS, UNIV MICH, 90- *Personal Data:* b Grinnell, Iowa, Jan 14, 53; m 85, Roberta J Morris. *Educ:* Harvard Col, AB, 75; Univ Calif, Berkeley, PhD(physics), 80. *Prof Exp:* Res fel, Lawrence Berkeley Lab, 80-81, AT&T Bell Labs, 81-82; prin investr mem tech staff, Physics Res Div, AT&T Bell Labs, 82-90. *Concurrent Pos:* Adj assoc prof appl physics, Columbia Univ, 89-90. *Mem:* Fel Am Phys Soc. *Res:* Atomic physics, nonlinear optics and fundamental light matter interactions; above-threshold ionization of atoms and molecules in ultra intense laser radiation fields; laser induced ponderomotive forces on atoms, free electrons and low density plasmas and fundamental tests of T-violations in atoms. *Mailing Add:* Dept Physics Univ Mich Ann Arbor MI 48109-1120

BUCKWALTER, GARY LEE, PHYSICS. *Current Pos:* INSTR, DAYTONA BEACH COMMUNITY COL, 87- *Personal Data:* b Kittanning, Pa, June 29, 34; m 57; c 2. *Educ:* Pa State Univ, BS, 56; Cath Univ Am, MS, 61, PhD(physics), 66. *Prof Exp:* From instr to asst prof, US Naval Acad, 59-65; fel, Cath Univ Am, 66; from assoc prof to prof physics, Ind Univ Pa, 66-87, chmn dept, 75-83. *Concurrent Pos:* Res Corp Am res grant, 67- *Mem:* Am Asn Physics Teachers; Am Phys Soc. *Res:* High energy cosmic ray physics. *Mailing Add:* 2919 N Peninsula Dr Daytona Beach FL 32118

BUCKWALTER, JOSEPH ADDISON, SURGERY. *Current Pos:* PROF SURG, SCH MED, UNIV NC, CHAPEL HILL, 70- *Personal Data:* b Royersford, Pa, Jan 4, 20; m 46; c 4. *Educ:* Colgate Univ, AB, 41; Univ Pa, MD, 44; Am Bd Surg, dipl. *Prof Exp:* Intern, Col Med, Univ Iowa, 44-45, resident gen surg, 45-46 & 49-52, assoc surg, 52-54, from asst prof to prof, 54-70. *Concurrent Pos:* Fel anat, Sch Med, Univ NC, 48, fel path, 48-49; sr registr, Postgrad Med Sch, Univ London, 53-54; dir surg, Dorothea Dix Hosp, Raleigh, NC. *Mem:* Soc Exp Biol & Med; AMA; Am Col Surg; Soc Univ Surg; Int Soc Surg. *Res:* Clinical and basic studies of thyroid disorders, gastroenterology, blood groups, human genetics, parathyroid physiology and disease, blood volume dynamics. *Mailing Add:* 608 Sugarberry Rd Chapel Hill NC 27514

BUCKWOLD, SIDNEY JOSHUA, analytical chemistry, soil chemistry, for more information see previous edition

BUCOVAZ, EDSEL TONY, BIOCHEMISTRY & ORGANIC CHEMISTRY, MOLECULAR BIOLOGY. *Current Pos:* from assoc prof to prof biochem, 69-75, ASSOC DIR BASIC RES, MEMPHIS REGIONAL CANCER CTR, 74- *Personal Data:* b Eldorado, Ill, May 8, 28; m 53, Alma R Hankla; c 2. *Educ:* Southern Ill Univ, BA, 55, MA, 57; St Louis Univ, PhD(biochem), 62. *Honors & Awards:* Res Award, Cent Asn Obstets & Gynec, 77. *Prof Exp:* Control & res chemist, US Chem Co, 53-54; asst prof biochem, Ctr Health Sci, Univ Tenn, Memphis, 64-69. *Concurrent Pos:* Res assoc fel biochem, Sch Med, Univ Tenn, 62-64; ed-in-chief, Cancer Res, Ther & Control, 87-92, emer consult ed, 92- *Mem:* Sigma Xi; AAAS; Am Chem Soc; Am Asn Cancer Res; Am Asn Clin Chem; Am Soc Biochem & Molecular Biol. *Res:* Protein biosynthesis; cancer research; chemical carcinogenesis; human research related to fetal maturity and respiratory depression caused by analgesics; developer of B-protein assay for the detection of cancer; discover coenzyme A-synthesizing protein complex of bakers' yeast. *Mailing Add:* 6935 Deerfield Rd Bartlett TN 38135

BUCY, J FRED, SEMICONDUCTORS, GEOPHYSICS. *Current Pos:* RETIRED. *Personal Data:* b Tahoka, Tex, July 29, 28; m 47, Odetta Greer; c Diane, Roxanne & Fred. *Educ:* Tex Tech Univ, BA, 51; Univ Tex, Austin, MA, 53. *Hon Degrees:* DSc, Tex Tech Univ, 94. *Honors & Awards:* Distinguished Engr Award, Tex Tech Univ, Lubbock. *Prof Exp:* Res physicist, Defense Res Lab, Tex, 53; design engr, Ctr Res Librs, Tex Instruments Inc, 53-54, proj engr, 54-58, prog mgr, 58-59, proj engr, VenSun Flow Sta in Maracaibo, 59-61, dept head, Petrol Div, 59-61, group mgr, Indust Prod Div, 61-63, vpres, Mil Equip Div, 63-67, vpres, Semiconductor-Components Div, 67, group vpres, Components, 67-72, exec vpres, 72-76, mem bd dirs, 74-85, chief opers officer, Tex Instruments Inc, 75-84, pres, 76-85, chief exec officer, 84-85. *Concurrent Pos:* Mem, Defense Sci Bd, Dept Defense, 70-83; mem, Brazil/US Bus Coun; mem, Adv Coun, Nat Strategy Info Ctr; mem, Subcomt Export Admin, Pres Export Coun; mem, Technol Assessment Adv Coun, Off Technol Assessment US Cong, 77-83; consult, US Army Mat Systs Anal Activ, Aberdeen Proving Ground, Md & Tex Instruments Inc, Dallas; mem bd dirs & trustee, SW Res Inst, San Antonio, Tex; bd mem, Alliant Techsysts Inc, Edina, Minn, Thomas Group Inc, Irving, Tex & Optical Data Systs Inc, Richardson, Tex; chmn, Tex Nat Res Comn, 95. *Mem:* Nat Acad Eng; fel Inst Elec & Electronics Engrs; Soc Explor Geophysicists; Am Phys Soc. *Res:* Integrated circuit design and development; data processing systems-research, design, technology and engineering; author and co-author of technical reports and publications; holder of patents for data processing equipment. *Mailing Add:* PO Box 780929 Dallas TX 75378-0929

BUCY, RICHARD SNOWDEN, APPLIED MATHEMATICS. *Current Pos:* assoc prof aerospace & math, 67-70, PROF AEROSPACE ENG & MATH, UNIV SOUTHERN CALIF, 70- *Personal Data:* b Washington, DC, July 20, 35; m 61, Ofelia; c Erwin & Phillip. *Educ:* Mass Inst Technol, BS, 57; Univ Calif, Berkeley, PhD(probability), 63. *Honors & Awards:* Humboldt Prize, WGer Govt, 75. *Prof Exp:* Assoc mathematician, Appl Physics Lab, Johns Hopkins Univ, 57-60; mathematician, Res Inst Advan Studies, 60-61 & 63-64; asst prof math, Univ Md, College Park, 64-65; assoc prof, Univ Colo, Boulder, 65-67. *Concurrent Pos:* Consult math dept, Rand Corp, Thompson Ramo Wooldridge Corp, Mass Inst Technol Lincoln Lab, Aerospace Corp & Electrac Inc; ed & founder, J Stochastics, 71-77; vis prof, Univ Paul Sabitier, Toulouse, France, 72-73, French Govt, 73, 83 & 91, Tech Univ Berlin, 75-76, Univ Nice, France, 83-84 & 90-91; deleg, Inst Elec & Electronics Engrs Soviet Acad Info Theory Meeting, Moscow, 75; dir, advan study prog nonlinear stochastic probs, NATO, Algarve, Portugal, 83; ed, J Info Scis, 86- & J Math Modelling & Sci Comput, 93- *Mem:* Am Math Soc; fel Inst Elec & Electronics Engrs. *Res:* Probability and control theory; optimum control and filtering theory; adaptive control; Markov processes; discrete potential theory; analysis and synthesis of optimal devices to separate signal from noise, with emphasis on direction finding; author of 3 books and over 100 papers. *Mailing Add:* Aerospace Eng & Math Dept Univ Southern Calif Los Angeles CA 90089-0192. *Fax:* 213-740-7774; *E-Mail:* bucy@spock.usc.edu

BUDAI, JOHN DAVID, CONDENSED MATTER PHYSICS, X-RAY DIFFRACTION. *Current Pos:* PHYSICIST, OAK RIDGE NAT LAB, 84- *Personal Data:* b Poughkeepsie, NY, Dec 2, 52; m 82; c 2. *Educ:* Dartmouth Col, BA, 74; Cornell Univ, MS, 79, PhD(physics), 82. *Prof Exp:* Assoc, AT&T Bell Labs, 82-84. *Mem:* Am Phys Soc; Am Soc Metals; Mat Res Soc. *Res:* X-ray diffraction studies of the structure of condensed matter systems with emphasis on the areas of crystal interfaces, epitaxial thin films, superconductors and nanocrystals. *Mailing Add:* Oak Ridge Nat Lab PO Box 2008 Bldg 3025 Oak Ridge TN 37831-6030

BUDAY, PAUL VINCENT, PHARMACOLOGY. *Current Pos:* DIR, REGULATORY AFFAIRS, PORTON INT, 88- *Personal Data:* b Jersey City, NJ, Aug 19, 31; m 56, Jeanette I Hosgood; c Gene, Mark, Stephen, Helene, Roberta & Kathleen. *Educ:* Fordham Univ, BS, 53; Temple Univ, MS, 55; Purdue Univ, PhD(pharmacol), 58, Seton Hall Sch Law, JD, 77. *Prof Exp:* Asst chem, Temple Univ, 53-55; asst pharmacol, Purdue Univ, 55-56; asst prof biol sci, Fordham Univ, 58-59; asst prof pharmacol, Col Pharm, Univ RI, 59-61; pharmacol ed, Lederle Labs, NY, 61-63; head sci info, Vick Div Res & Develop, Richardson-Merrell Inc, 63-65; med res assoc, Warner-Chilcott Labs, NJ, 65-66, asst to dir med serv, Warner-Lambert Res Inst, 66-67; head drug regulatory affairs, Sandoz, 67-69; dir regulatory affairs, Ethicon, Inc, 69-77; dir extramural affairs, Block Drug Co, 77-78; corp dir regulatory affairs, G D Searle, 78-80; dir int regulatory affairs, Warner-Lambert Co, 80-84; mgr regulatory/clin affairs, Novametrix Med Syst, 84-86; dir regulatory affairs, QA Lukens Corp, 86-88. *Concurrent Pos:* Gustavus A Pfeiffer Mem res fel, Am Found Pharmaceut Ed, 58-59. *Mem:* Fel AAAS; Sigma Xi; Drug Info Asn; Regulatory Affairs Prof Soc. *Res:* Pharmacology of neurohormones; interrelationships between endocrine hormones and drug action; drug interactions and preclinical toxicity; medical writing; clinical testing of drugs; food and drug law. *Mailing Add:* 7114 Springbrook Terr Spotsylvania VA 22553. *Fax:* 540-891-4058

BUDD, ANN FREEMAN, SYSTEMATICS OF SCLERACTINIAN REEF CORALS, GEOLOGIC HISTORY OF CARIBBEAN REEFS. *Current Pos:* Asst prof, 88-89, ASSOC PROF GEOL, UNIV IOWA, 89- *Educ:* Lawrence Univ, BA, 73; Johns Hopkins Univ, MA, 75, PhD(earth & planetary sci), 78. *Mem:* Paleont Soc Am; Int Soc Reef Studies; Soc Econ Paleontologists & Mineralogists; Sigma Xi; AAAS. *Res:* Patterns of change in the Caribbean reef coral fauna over the past 22 million years and their association with the regional changes in climate and oceanographic circulation. *Mailing Add:* Geol Dept Univ Iowa Iowa City IA 52242

BUDD, GEOFFREY COLIN, CELL BIOLOGY, PHYSIOLOGY. *Current Pos:* from asst prof to assoc prof, 69-74, PROF PHYSIOL, MED COL OHIO, 74- *Personal Data:* b London, Eng, Dec 2, 35; m 59; c 4. *Educ:* Chelsea Col Sci & Technol, Univ London, BSc, 58; Birkbeck Col, Univ London, BSc, 61; Royal Free Hosp Med, Univ London, PhD(zool), 66. *Prof Exp:* Tech officer, Med Res Coun Biophys Res Unit, Kings Col, Univ London, 58-61; asst lectr biol & radiation biol, Royal Free Hosp Sch Med, Univ London, 61-62, lectr, 62-66; res assoc appl physics, neurobiol & behav, Cornell Univ, 66-68, vis asst prof, 68-69. *Mem:* Fel AAAS; Am Soc Cell Biol; Electron Micros Soc Am; Tissue Cult Asn; Histochem Soc; Sigma Xi. *Res:* Extra pancreatic insulin synthesis; development and application of quantitative electron microscope autoradiography. *Mailing Add:* Physiol PO Box 10008 Med Col Ohio Toledo OH 43699-0008. *Fax:* 419-382-7395

BUDD, THOMAS WAYNE, PLANT PHYSIOLOGY, MOLECULAR BIOLOGY. *Current Pos:* ASSOC PROF BIOL, ST LAWRENCE UNIV, 72- *Personal Data:* b Pittsburgh, Pa, Oct 1, 46. *Educ:* NDak State Univ, BS, 68, PhD(bot), 72. *Concurrent Pos:* Vis asst prof, Dept Med, Univ Tenn Ctr Health Sci, 81-82. *Mem:* AAAS; Am Soc Plant Physiologists; Sigma Xi; NY Acad Sci; Int Asn Aerobiol. *Res:* Cancer immunology - tumor escape mechanisms, cell tumor surveillance; allergy immunology - mold allergen identification; electron microscopist. *Mailing Add:* Dept Biol St Lawrence Univ Canton NY 13617

BUDDE, MARY LAURENCE, ZOOLOGY, MICROBIOLOGY. *Current Pos:* RETIRED. *Personal Data:* b Covington, Ky, May 17, 29. *Educ:* Villa Madonna Col, AB, 53; Cath Univ Am, MS, 55, PhD(zool), 58. *Prof Exp:* Instr, Thomas More Col, KY, 58-61, from asst prof to prof biol, 61-96, acad dean, 81-85. *Concurrent Pos:* Dir, Fresh-Water Biol Sta. *Mem:* AAAS; Sigma Xi. *Res:* Endocrinology: regulation of calcium and phosphorus metabolism in bony fish; aquatic biology: power plant operations and microorganisms and fish population effects; medical technology education. *Mailing Add:* Thomas More Col Crestview Hills KY 41017

BUDDE, PAUL BERNARD, AGRICULTURAL CHEMISTRY. *Current Pos:* RETIRED. *Personal Data:* b Covington, Ky, June 24, 26; m 59; c 6. *Educ:* Xavier Univ, Ohio, BS, 50, MS, 51. *Prof Exp:* Chemist, Agr Prod Dept, Dow Chem Co, 59-62, from res chemist to sr res chemist, 62-86. *Mem:* Am Chem Soc. *Res:* Agricultural formulations. *Mailing Add:* 3803 Ridgeway Pl Traverse City MI 49684-8955

BUDDE, WILLIAM L, ANALYTICAL CHEMISTRY. *Current Pos:* sect chief advan instrumentation, Off Res & Develop, 71-88, DIR, CHEM RES DIV, US ENVIRON PROTECTION AGENCY, 88- *Personal Data:* b Cincinnati, Ohio, Dec 18, 34; m 59; c 6. *Educ:* Xavier Univ, BS, 57, MS, 59; Univ Cincinnati, PhD(chem), 63. *Prof Exp:* Fel, Univ Calif, Riverside, 63-64; vis asst prof chem, Univ Kans, 64-65; assoc to sr chemist, Midwest Res Inst, 65-69; assoc dir, Mass Spectrometry Ctr, Purdue Univ, 69-71. *Mem:* Am Chem Soc; Am Soc Mass Spectrometry. *Res:* Mass spectrometry: trace organic analysis by computerized gas chromatography; laboratory automation with digital computers. *Mailing Add:* Environ Protection Agency Monit & Support Lab 26 W Martin Luther King Dr Cincinnati OH 45268

BUDDENHAGEN, IVAN WILLIAM, PLANT PATHOLOGY. *Current Pos:* MEM STAFF CEREAL IMPROV PROG, INT INST TROP AGR, 75- *Personal Data:* b Ventura, Calif, Apr 26, 30; m 50; c 4. *Educ:* Ore State Col, BS, 53, MS, 54, PhD, 57. *Prof Exp:* Plant pathologist, United Fruit Co, Honduras, 57-64; prof plant path, Univ Hawaii, 64-75. *Mem:* Am Phytopath Soc. *Res:* Bacterial plant diseases; international plant path; host-parasite interaction; wilt diseases. *Mailing Add:* 1012 Plum Lane Davis CA 95616

BUDDING, ANTONIUS JACOB, GEOLOGY. *Current Pos:* from asst prof to assoc prof, NMex Inst Mining & Technol, 56-72, chmn, Dept Geosci, 81-84, prof, 72-89, EMER PROF GEOL, NMEX INST MINING & TECHNOL, 89- *Personal Data:* b Amsterdam, Neth, Jan 30, 22; m 53; c 2. *Educ:* Univ Amsterdam, BSc, 42, MSc, 48, PhD(geol), 51. *Prof Exp:* Instr geol & petrol, Geol Inst, Amsterdam, 46-51; geologist, Geol Surv, Sask, 51-52, prin geologist, 52-56. *Concurrent Pos:* Consult, Los Alamos Sci Lab, 72-81. *Mem:* Fel Geol Soc Am; Ger Geol Soc; Am Geophys Union; fel AAAS; Sigma Xi. *Res:* Metamorphic and igneous petrology; structural geology. *Mailing Add:* 277 Spruce Ct Boulder CO 80302-4962

BUDDINGTON, RANDAL K, ONTOGENIC DEVELOPMENT OF PHYSIOLOGIC PROCESSES, INTEGRATIVE & REGULATORY PHYSIOLOGY. *Current Pos:* ASSOC PROF BIOL, MISS STATE UNIV, 88-, ASSOC PROF VET MED, 89- *Personal Data:* b Fresno, Calif, Aug 21, 54; m 90, Cynthia A Moncreiff. *Educ:* Univ Calif, Riverside, BS, 76; Ariz State Univ, MS, 78; Univ Calif, Davis, PhD(ecol & physiol), 83. *Honors & Awards:* Douglas-Walker Award, Miss Acad Sci, 89 & 91; Magnolia Award, Miss Dietetics Asn, 93. *Prof Exp:* Res physiologist, Univ Calif Los Angeles Med Ctr, 83-88. *Mem:* Am Physiol Soc; Am Inst Nutrit. *Res:* Understanding how events early in development influence physiological processes late in life; impact of nutrition during infancy. *Mailing Add:* Dept Biol Sci Miss State Univ PO Box GY Mississippi State University MS 39762-5759

BUDEN, ROSEMARY V, GEOCHEMISTRY, MINERALOGY-PETROLOGY. *Personal Data:* b New Haven, Conn, Mar 27, 31; m 51, 84, David; c 6. *Educ:* Oberlin Col, BA, 52; Univ Mich, MS, 54; Yale Univ, PhD(geol), 68. *Prof Exp:* From asst prof to assoc prof geol, State Univ NY, Binghamton, 68-75; res fel, Carnegie Inst, Washington, DC, 74-75;

staff mem, Los Alamos Nat Lab, 75-77, assoc group leader nuclear chem, 78-80, assoc group leader isotope geochem, 80-85, consult, 85-88; prog dir exp & theoret geochem, NSF, 88-90; prin scientist, Idaho Nat Eng Lab, 90-92. *Concurrent Pos:* Consult. *Mem:* Fel AAAS; Geochem Soc; fel Am Mineral Soc; Sigma Xi; fel Geol Soc Am. *Res:* Experimental element transport and retention; geothermal systems. *Mailing Add:* 12108 Holly Ave Albuquerque NM 87122

BUDENSTEIN, PAUL PHILIP, PHYSICS. *Current Pos:* asst prof, 59-62, ASSOC PROF PHYSICS, AUBURN UNIV, 63- *Personal Data:* b Philadelphia, Pa, June 27, 28; m 57; c 5. *Educ:* Temple Univ, BA, 49; Lehigh Univ, MS, 51, PhD(physics), 57. *Prof Exp:* Instr physics, Lehigh Univ, 52-56; mem, Tech Staff, Bell Tel Labs, 57-58. *Concurrent Pos:* Consult, US Army Missile Command, 69-77. *Mem:* Am Vacuum Soc; Electrochem Soc; Am Phys Soc; Am Asn Physics Teachers. *Res:* Dielectric breakdown in solids; current filamentation in solids. *Mailing Add:* 370 Bowden Dr Auburn AL 36830

BUDERER, MELVIN CHARLES, PHYSIOLOGY. *Current Pos:* Nat res coun resident res assoc, L B Johnson Space Ctr, 70-72, res physiologist, Technol Inc, 72-79, mgr, sci support & mission opers, gen elect, 79-84, PROJ SCIENTIST, L B JOHNSON SPACE CTR, NASA, 84-, CHIEF, PAYLOAD ENG BR, 88- *Personal Data:* b Sacramento, Calif, May 12, 41; m 84, Jeannie McLain; c Christian H & Suzanne L. *Educ:* Univ Calif, Berkeley, AB, 63, PhD(physiol), 70. *Mem:* Aerospace Med Asn; Sigma Xi; AAAS. *Res:* Environmental physiology; space physiology. *Mailing Add:* 1814 Linfield Way Houston TX 77058

BUDGE, LARRY D, ECONOMICS. *Current Pos:* STAFF, INST DEFENSE ANALYSES. *Personal Data:* b Logan, Utah, July 24, 39. *Educ:* US Military Acad, BS, 61; Oxford Univ, MA. *Prof Exp:* Nat intel officer gen purpose forces, Cent Intel Agency, US Army, asst div comdr, Ninth Infantry Div, dep dir opers, readiness & mobilization, Off Dep Chief Staff Opers & Plans, brigade comdr chief staff, First Armored Div, Europe, asst dep chief staff personnel, 92. *Concurrent Pos:* Asst dir simulation, Defense Advan Res Proj Agency. *Res:* Simulation. *Mailing Add:* Inst Defense Analyses 1801 N Beauregard St Alexandria VA 22311-1772

BUDGE, WALLACE DON, CIVIL ENGINEERING. *Current Pos:* assoc prof, 64-77, PROF CIVIL ENG, BRIGHAM YOUNG UNIV, 77- *Personal Data:* b Pleasant View, Utah, Apr 25, 33; m 57; c 2. *Educ:* Utah State Univ, BS, 59, MS, 61; Univ Colo, PhD(civil eng), 64. *Prof Exp:* Instr civil eng, Utah State Univ, 59-61; res assoc, Univ Colo, 63-64. *Concurrent Pos:* Univ liaison rep, Hwy Res Bd, Nat Acad Sci-Nat Res Coun, 65- *Mem:* Am Soc Civil Engrs; Am Soc Eng Educ; Am Soc Testing & Mat. *Res:* Concrete; swelling soils. *Mailing Add:* Dept Civil Eng Brigham Young Univ 368 Cb Provo UT 84602-1021

BUDGOR, AARON BERNARD, STATISTICAL PHYSICS, LASER PHYSICS. *Current Pos:* VPRES INFO SYSTS, SCI APPLN INT CORP, 92- *Personal Data:* b Munich, Ger, July 6, 48; US citizen; m 77, Karen Luria; c Adam & Mindy. *Educ:* Univ Calif, Los Angeles, BS, 69; Univ Rochester, MS, 71, PhD(phys chem), 74. *Prof Exp:* Statist physics, Univ Calif, San Diego, 74-76; staff laser physicist, Lawrence Livermore Lab, Univ Calif, 76-80; laser physicist & prog mgr, Rocketdyne Corp, 80-82; dept mgr, Allied Corp, 82-84; sect mgr, Northrop Electron Div, 84-87; prog mgr optical discrimination, Dept Navy, 87-91; dep dir off, secy defense, 91-92. *Concurrent Pos:* Vis prof, Univ Mex, 73-76; res consult, Phys Dynamics Inc, 75-87; prof, Dept Appl Sci, Univ Calif, Davis, 78-79; appointee, Strategic Defense Initiative Orgn, interactive discrimination study, 86, laser radar study, 88, midcourse & terminal tier rev, 90. *Mem:* Am Phys Soc. *Res:* Nonlinear deterministic and stochastic processes; laser systems design; electronic and vibrational structure of solids and amorphous materials; critical phenomena in liquids. *Mailing Add:* 7804 Laurel Leaf Dr Potomac MD 20854

BUDIANSKY, BERNARD, SOLID MECHANICS, STRUCTURAL MECHANICS. *Current Pos:* from assoc prof to prof, 55-95, GORDON MCKAY EMER PROF STRUCT MECHS, ABBOTT & JAMES LAWRENCE EMER PROF ENG, HARVARD UNIV, 95- *Personal Data:* b New York, NY, Mar 8, 25; m 52, Nancy Cromer; c Michael & Stephen. *Educ:* City Col, BCE, 44; Brown Univ, PhD(appl math), 50. *Hon Degrees:* DSc, Northwestern Univ, 86, Technion, 95. *Honors & Awards:* Von Karman Medal, Am Soc Civil Engrs, 82; Eringen Medal, Soc Eng Sci, 85; Timoshenko Medal, Am Soc Mech Engrs, 89. *Prof Exp:* Aeronaut res scientist, Nat Adv Comt Aeronaut, Va, 44-52, head, Struct Mech Br, 52-55. *Concurrent Pos:* Consult, Avco Corp, 58-70 & Gen Motors Res Lab, 63-78; Guggenheim fel, Tech Univ Denmark, 61; mem, Mat Res Coun, Defense Advan Res Proj Agency, 68-, US Nat Comt Theoret & Appl Mech, 70-80, NASA Space Systs & Technol Adv Comt, 78-84 & Aeronaut & Space Eng Bd, Nat Res Coun, 85-90, Advan Space Technol Comt, 92-; vis prof, Technion, Haifa, 76; Sackler fel, Tel Aviv Univ, 83. *Mem:* Nat Acad Sci; Nat Acad Eng; fel Am Acad Arts & Sci; fel Am Soc Mech Engrs; fel Am Inst Aeronaut & Astronaut; Am Geophys Union. *Res:* Elastic stability; plasticity; shell theory; fracture mechanics; composite materials. *Mailing Add:* Div Appl Sci Harvard Univ Cambridge MA 02138

BUDICK, BURTON, NUCLEAR PHYSICS, ATOMIC PHYSICS. *Current Pos:* from asst prof to assoc prof, 68-81, PROF PHYSICS, NY UNIV, 81- *Personal Data:* b Bronx, NY, May 22, 38; m 64, Cynthia Cherner; c Ariella & Seth. *Educ:* Harvard Univ, AB, 59; Univ Calif, Berkeley, PhD(physics), 62. *Prof Exp:* Res assoc, Radiation Lab, Columbia Univ, 62-63, instr, 63-64; lectr, Hebrew Univ, Jerusalem, 64-67, sr lectr, 67-68. *Concurrent Pos:* NSF fel Hebrew Univ, 65-67. *Mem:* Am Phys Soc. *Res:* Experimental nuclear physics; muonic and pionic atoms; atomic hyperfine structure; beta-decay. *Mailing Add:* 156 W 86th St New York NY 10024. *Fax:* 212-995-4016; *E-Mail:* budick@acfcluster.nyu.edu

BUDINGER, THOMAS FRANCIS, MEDICAL PHYSICS, NUCLEAR MEDICINE. *Current Pos:* physicist, Lawrence Livermore Lab, Univ Calif, 66-67, res physician, Donner Lab & Lawrence Berkeley Lab, 67-76, H MILLER PROF MED RES & GROUP LEADER RES MED, DONNER LAB, & PROF ELEC ENG & COMPUT SCI, UNIV CALIF, 76-, SR STAFF SCIENTIST, LAWRENCE BERKELEY LAB, 80- & PROF RADIOL, UNIV CALIF, SAN FRANCISCO, 84- *Personal Data:* b Evanston, Ill, Oct 25, 32; m 65; c 3. *Educ:* Regis Col, Colo, BS, 54; Univ Wash, MS, 57; Univ Colo, MD, 64; Univ Calif, Berkeley, PhD, 71. *Honors & Awards:* Special Award, Am Nuclear Soc, 84. *Prof Exp:* Asst chem, Regis Col, Colo, 53-54; anal chemist, Indust Labs, 54; sr oceanogr, Univ Wash, 61-66. *Concurrent Pos:* Peter Bent Brigham Hosp, Boston, 64; dir med serv, Lawrence Berkeley Lab, 68-76; chmn, Study Sect, NIH, 81-84. *Mem:* Nat Acad Eng; Inst Med-Nat Acad Sci; NY Acad Sci; Soc Nuclear Med; Soc Magnetic Res Med (pres, 84-85); AAAS; Am Geophys Union. *Res:* Imaging body functions; electrical, magnetic, sound and photon radiation fields; electron microscopy; mathematics and computers in biology; polar oceanography; nuclear magnetic resonance; reconstruction tomography and instrument development; cardiology. *Mailing Add:* Lawrence Berkeley Lab Univ Calif Bldg 55 Berkeley CA 94720

BUDINSKI, KENNETH GERARD, TRIBOLOGY, MACHINE DESIGN. *Current Pos:* metallurgist, 64-68, sr metallurgist, 68-85, TECH ASSOC, KODAK PARK DIV, EASTMAN KODAK CO, 85- *Personal Data:* b Rochester, NY, June 29, 39; m 62; c 3. *Educ:* Gen Motors Inst, BS, 61; Mich Technol Univ, MS,63. *Prof Exp:* Develop engr, Rochester Prod Div, GMC, 60-62. *Concurrent Pos:* Consult, Mat Technol Inc, 65-70; instr, Rochester Inst Technol, 70-72; chmn, Rochester Chap, Am Soc Metals, 73; assoc prof, Monroe Community Col, 72-74; chmn, hardace ed comt, Welding Res Coun, 85, 62 comt wear & erosion, Am Soc Testing & Mat, 86-88; ed, Welding Inst, Surface Eng Soc. *Mem:* Fel Am Soc Metals; fel Am Soc Testing & Mat; Soc Automotive Engrs; Surface Eng Soc; fel Am Soc Metals Int. *Res:* Tribological properties of engineering materials, particularly tool material and engineering plastics. *Mailing Add:* 3177 Latta Rd Suite 146 Rochester NY 14612-3092

BUDKE, CLIFFORD CHARLES, ANALYTICAL CHEMISTRY. *Current Pos:* RETIRED. *Personal Data:* b Cincinnati, Ohio, Apr 3, 32; m 63, Patsy E Henson; c Clifford C III, Joelle (Sickler) & Michelle (Terry). *Educ:* Univ Cincinnati, BS, 54, MS, 67. *Prof Exp:* Analytical chemist, US Indust Chem Co, Div Nat Distillers & Chem Corp, 56-68, res supvr, 68-78, res assoc, 78-84, sr res assoc, 84-87; sr proj leader, USI Div, Quantum Chem Corp, 87-89, assoc scientist, 89-92. *Concurrent Pos:* Adj instr, Ohio Col Appl Sci, 92- *Mem:* Am Chem Soc; hon fel Am Soc Testing & Mat. *Res:* Chemical and instrumental methods of analysis, especially trace analysis, functional group analysis, electrometric methods of analysis, and liquid chromatography. *Mailing Add:* 5715 Scarborough Dr Cincinnati OH 45238. *E-Mail:* hnho39a@prodigy.com

BUDKER, DMITRY, ATOMIC PHYSICS, LASER SPECTROSCOPY. *Current Pos:* ASST PROF PHYSICS, UNIV CALIF, BERKELEY, 95- *Personal Data:* b Sept 6, 63; m 85, Olga; c 2. *Educ:* Novosibirsk State Univ, USSR, MS, 85; Univ Calif, Berkeley, PhD(physics), 93. *Prof Exp:* Jr researcher, Inst Nuclear Physics, Novosibirsk, USSR, 85-88. *Concurrent Pos:* Fac scientist, Nuclear Sci Div, Lawrence Berkeley Nat Lab. *Mem:* Am Phys Soc. *Res:* Parity violation in rare earth atoms and Stark-effect measurements in atomic thallium; laser spectroscopy of atoms and its application to experiments on parity and time-reversal invariance violation; author of 22 publications. *Mailing Add:* Dept Physics Univ Calif Berkeley CA 94720-7300. *E-Mail:* budker@physics.berkeley.edu

BUDNICK, JOSEPH IGNATIUS, PHYSICS. *Current Pos:* PROF PHYSICS, UNIV CONN, 74-, HEAD DEPT, 77- *Personal Data:* b Jersey City, NJ, July 9, 29. *Educ:* St Peters Col, BS, 51; Rutgers Univ, PhD(physics), 55. *Prof Exp:* Asst physics lab, Rutgers Univ, 51-52, asst atomic & nuclear lab, 52-53; proj physicist superconductivity, Res Ctr, IBM, NY, 55; from assoc prof to prof, Fordham Univ, 55-74. *Concurrent Pos:* Instr, IBM Gen Educ, 57-58. *Mem:* AAAS; Am Phys Soc. *Res:* Superconductivity; low temperature solid state physics of metals. *Mailing Add:* Dept Physics U46 Univ Conn 2152 Hillside Rd Rm 107 Storrs CT 06269

BUDNITZ, ROBERT JAY, ENVIRONMENTAL SYSTEMS & TECHNOLOGY, NUCLEAR REACTOR SAFETY. *Current Pos:* PRES, FUTURE RESOURCES ASSOC, INC, 81- *Personal Data:* b Pittsfield, Mass, Oct 12, 40; m 61, Barbara Paresky; c Paul, Benjamin & Elizabeth. *Educ:* Yale Univ, BA, 61; Harvard Univ, MA, 62, PhD(physics), 68. *Prof Exp:* Physicist, Lawrence Berkeley Lab, Univ Calif, 67-71, coordr, Environ Prog, 74-75, head, Energy & Environ Div, 74-75, assoc dir, 75-78, sr staff scientist environ sci, 71-78. *Concurrent Pos:* Mem, Reactor Safety Study Group, Am Phys Soc, 74-75, reactor hazards comt, Berkeley Res Reactor, Univ Calif, Berkeley, 74-78; ed-in-chief, CRC Forums Energy, CRC Press, West Palm Beach, Fla, 76-80; US rep, Comt on the Safety Nuclear Installations, Nuclear Energy Agency, Orgn Economic Coop & Develop, Paris, 79-80; tech coord, Spec Inquiry Group into the Three Mile Island, US Nuclear Regulatory Comn, 79-80, dir res, 79-80; chmn, Peer Review Group, Dept Energy Off Crystalline Repository Develop, Battelle Prog Mgt Div, 83-86, Expert Panel Seismic Design Margins, Peer Review Expert Panel Plant Aging, Battelle Pac NW Lab, US Nuclear Regulatory Comn, 87-88; chmn, Peer Review Group, Off

Crystalline Respository Develop, Batelle Proj Mgt Div, Dept Energy, 83-86; mem, explor comt future nuclear power generation, Nat Acad Sci, 84 & Energy Eng Bd, 83-86; mem, sr comt environ, safety & econ aspects fusion energy, US Dept Energy, 85-87; mem, Chernobyl Adv Panel, Elec Power Res Inst, 86-87, bd dirs, Pac Energy & Resources Ctr, 85-, Adv Group Treatment Hazards Probabilistic Safety Assessment, Int Atomic Energy Agency, Vienna, 86-; mem, US Army Chem Munitions Disposal Risk Assessment Rev Panel, GA Technol, Inc, 87-88 & Performance Assessment Peer Rev Panel, Dept Energy, Waste Isolation Pilot Plant, Sandia Nat Labs, 87-; chmn, Buried & Tank Waste Comt, Nat Acad Sci, 93. *Mem:* AAAS; Am Phys Soc; Am Nuclear Soc; Soc Risk Analysis. *Res:* Instrumentation for measuring radiation in the environment; nuclear reactor environmental impact and safety analysis; radioactive waste disposal technology. *Mailing Add:* 734 Alameda Berkeley CA 94707

BUDNY, JOHN ARNOLD, TOXICOLOGY. *Current Pos:* PRES, PHARMACAL LTD, 87- *Personal Data:* b Chicago, Ill, Apr 9, 43; m 68, Mary C Madonich; c Matthew, Hallie & Lindsey. *Educ:* Lewis Univ, BS, 65; Ohio State Univ, PhD(physiol chem), 70; Pepperdine Univ, MBA, 83. *Prof Exp:* Instr chem, Sacred Heart Acad, 64-65, Mich Tech Univ, 65-66; instr biochem, Ohio State Univ Col Med, 66-68, res asst, 68-70; res scientist, Procter & Gamble Co, 70-75; chief toxicologist, Diamond Shamrock Corp, 75-79; mgr health sci, Atlantic Richfield, 79-87. *Concurrent Pos:* Res assoc, Dept Surg, Ohio State Univ Col Med, 66; res fel, NIH, 69-70; guest lectr, Mt St Mary's Col, 93-; assoc prof, I P Pavlov First Med Inst. *Mem:* AAAS; NY Acad Sci; Soc Toxicol; Am Chem Soc; fel Am Inst Chemists. *Res:* Medical, dental and biological sciences covering toxicology, chemistry, biochemistry, food, nutrition and industrial and therapeutic applications of enzymes. *Mailing Add:* Pharmacal Ltd 31308 Via Colinas Suite 107 Westlake Village CA 91362. *Fax:* 818-706-2413; *E-Mail:* jabudny@earthlink.net

BUDNY, ROBERT VIERLING, PLASMA PHYSICS, CONTROLLED THERMONUCLEAR FUSION. *Current Pos:* instr physics, 77-78, RES PHYSICIST PLASMA PHYSICS, PRINCETON UNIV, 79- *Personal Data:* b Honolulu, Hawaii, July 27, 42. *Educ:* Mass Inst Technol, BS, 63; Univ Paris, CES, 65; Univ Md, PhD(physics), 71. *Prof Exp:* Fel physics, Oxford Univ, 71-73 & Stanford Univ, 73-75; res assoc, Rockefeller Univ, 75-77. *Concurrent Pos:* Consult, US Dept Defense, 67; vis physicist, Aspen Inst Theoret Physics, 71, 76 & Conseil Europ Rescherche Nucleaire, 78; tutorial fel, Worcester Col, Oxford Univ, 72-73. *Mem:* Am Phys Soc; Am Vacuum Soc. *Res:* Limiter design observation and modeling of edge plasmas in Tokamaks unified theories of weak and electromagnetic interactions of elementary particles; electron-positron annihilations; neutrino scattering; observation and modeling of edge plasmas in Tokamaks. *Mailing Add:* Plasma Physics Lab Princeton Univ PO Box 451 Princeton NJ 08543

BUDRYS, RIMGAUDAS S, SURFACE CHEMISTRY. *Current Pos:* sr res scientist, 82-93, CONSULT, NALCO CHEM CO, 93- *Personal Data:* b Kaunas, Lithuania, Aug 2, 25; m 65, Aldona Wingendorf; c 1. *Educ:* Univ Queensland, BSc, 59; Ill Inst Technol, PhD(phys chem), 64. *Prof Exp:* Chief chemist, Brisbane City Coun, Tennyson Power Sta, Queensland, Australia, 59-60; sr res chemist, res & develop ctr, Swift & Co, 63-65; sr res chemist, Continental Group, Inc, 65-67, adv scientist, 67-81. *Mem:* AAAS; Am Chem Soc; Am Inst Physics; Sigma Xi. *Res:* Intermolecular bonding conformations and structural rearrangements in high polymers; characterization of metal surfaces; adhesion of polymers to metals; infrared spectroscopy of interfaces; physical chemistry of high polymers, coatings and surfaces. *Mailing Add:* 9200 S Meade Oak Lawn IL 60453

BUDWIG, RALPH S, FLUID DYNAMICS CONVECTION. *Current Pos:* ASSOC PROF MECH ENG, UNIV IDAHO, 88- *Res:* Fluid dynamics convection. *Mailing Add:* Mech Eng Dept Univ Idaho 375 S Line St Moscow ID 83843-4140

BUDYKO, MIKHAIL I, GEOPHYSICS. *Honors & Awards:* Robert E Horton Award, Am Geophys Union, 94. *Mailing Add:* State Hydrol Inst V O 2-ya Liniya 23 St Petersburg 19905 Russia

BUDZIK, GERALD P, IMMUNOSCIENCE RESEARCH, CARDIOVASCULAR RESEARCH. *Current Pos:* RES INVESTR, IMMUNOL SCI DIV, ABBOTT LABS, 84- *Personal Data:* b Chicago, Ill, Nov 4, 49; m 90, Linda M Langebartels. *Educ:* Ill Inst Technol, BS, 71; Mass Inst Technol, PhD(biochem), 76; Lake Forest Sch Mgt, MBA,, 88. *Prof Exp:* Res fel, Harvard Med Sch, 76-79, asst prof, dept surg, 79-84. *Mem:* AAAS; NY Acad Sci; Am Chem Soc; Sigma Xi; Am Soc Cell Biol; Am Mgt Soc. *Res:* Membrane receptor mechanisms; signal transduction; cell-cell adhesion; assay development; molecular endocrinology; protein purification and characterization. *Mailing Add:* Abbott Lab Immunol Res Div D-UNA AP-10 One Abbott Park Rd Abbott Park IL 60064

BUDZILOVICH, GLEB NICHOLAS, PATHOLOGY, NEUROPATHOLOGY. *Current Pos:* asst prof, 64-67, ASSOC PROF PATH & NEUROPATH, NY UNIV MED CTR, 67- *Personal Data:* b Zlobin, Russia, Sept 7, 23; US citizen; m 50; c 1. *Educ:* Univ Munich, MD, 53. *Prof Exp:* Provisional asst pathologist, Med Ctr, Cornell Univ, 55-57; resident, Manhattan Vet Admin Hosp, 57-58, pathologist, 60-61; fel, NY Univ Med Ctr, 61-64. *Concurrent Pos:* Am Cancer Soc fel, Francis Delafield Hosp, NY, 58-60, resident, 58-60; consult path, Manhattan Vet Admin Hosp, 63-; vis pathologist, Bellevue Hosp Med Ctr, New York, 65-; attend pathologist, Univ Hosp, NY Univ Med Ctr, 65-; neuropath consult, Off Med Examr, Suffolk Co, NY, 67-; off chief med examr, NY. *Mem:* Am Asn Neuropathologists. *Res:* General pathology of peripheral sensory and sympathetic ganglia; pathology of sympathetic nervous system in diabetes mellitus; role of diabetic neuropathy in pathogenesis of peripheral vascular disease. *Mailing Add:* 234 Villard Ave Hastings-on-Hudson NY 10706

BUDZINSKI, WALTER VALERIAN, EXPERIMENTAL SOLID STATE PHYSICS, SUPERCONDUCTIVITY. *Current Pos:* Asst prof, 67-70, ASSOC PROF PHYSICS, ST BONAVENTURE UNIV, 70- *Personal Data:* b Buffalo, NY, Aug 12, 37; m 65, Elizabeth Bieranowski; c Ann, Susan & Joseph. *Educ:* Canisius Col, BS, 59; Univ Pittsburgh, MS, 64, PhD(physics), 67. *Concurrent Pos:* Vis assoc prof physics, Univ Pittsburgh, 74-75. *Mem:* Am Phys Soc; Sigma Xi; Am Asn Physics Teachers. *Res:* Tunneling into metals; microwave absorption by superconductors; thermal and optical properties of matter. *Mailing Add:* Physics Dept St Bonaventure Univ St Bonaventure NY 14778. *Fax:* 716-375-2389; *E-Mail:* wbudzins@sbu.edu

BUDZYNSKI, ANDREI Z, BIOCHEMISTRY. *Current Pos:* BIOCHEMIST, DEPT BIOCHEM, TEMPLE UNIV SCH MED, 71- *Personal Data:* b Warsaw, Poland, July 21, 26. *Educ:* Univ Warsaw, MS, 50; Polish Acad Sci, PhD(biochem), 62. *Prof Exp:* Fel biochem, Univ Calif, Berkeley, 68-71. *Mem:* Am Chem Soc; Am Soc Biochem & Molecular Biol. *Mailing Add:* Dept Biochem Temple Univ Sch Med 3400 N Broad St Philadelphia PA 19140

BUECH, RICHARD REED, BEHAVIOR, ECOLOGY & SOCIOBIOLOGY OF BEAVERS. *Current Pos:* res forester, Forest Serv, 64-69, res wildlife biologist, 69-81, proj leader, 81-84, prin wildlife biologist, 84-96, PROJ LEADER, FOREST SERV, USDA, 96- *Personal Data:* b Milwaukee, Wis, April 13, 40; m 68, Mary Kopecky; c Heidi, Stephanie & Sarah. *Educ:* Univ Mont, BS, 62; Yale Univ, MFS, 68; Univ Minn, PhD(wildlife), 88. *Mem:* Am Soc Mammologists; Soc Study Amphibians & Reptiles; Wildlife Soc; Chelonian Res Found. *Res:* Behavior, ecology and sociobiology of beavers modeling wildlife-habitat relations; study of the spatial and temperal aspects of wildlife-habitat management; natural history of wood turtles; ecology of amphibians in ephemeral ponds. *Mailing Add:* 800 N Shoal Lake Rd Grand Rapids MN 55744. *E-Mail:* buech002@maroon.tc.umn.edu

BUECHE, FREDERICK JOSEPH, SCIENCE EDUCATION. *Current Pos:* PROF PHYSICS, UNIV DAYTON, 61- *Personal Data:* b Flushing, Mich, Aug 12, 23; m; c 2. *Educ:* Univ Mich, BS, 44; Cornell Univ, PhD(physics), 48. *Prof Exp:* Asst eng physics, Cornell Univ, 44-48, res assoc phys chem, 48-52; from asst prof to prof physics, Univ Wyo, 52-59; physicist, Rohm and Haas Co, 53-54; prof physics, Univ Akron, 59-61. *Concurrent Pos:* Peace Corps, 64-66. *Mem:* Am Phys Soc. *Res:* Physical properties of polymers; properties of liquids and gases; author of physics texts. *Mailing Add:* 541 Oakbrook Ctr Flushing MI 48433

BUEGE, DENNIS RICHARD, MEAT SCIENCE. *Current Pos:* EXTEN SPECIALIST MEATS, UNIV WIS, 77- *Personal Data:* b Juneau, Wis, Apr 2, 45; m 66; c 2. *Educ:* Univ Wis-Madison, BS, 67, PhD(meat & animal sci), 75; Cornell Univ, MS, 69. *Prof Exp:* Sr food technologist, George A Hormel & Co, 75-77. *Concurrent Pos:* Military food inspector. 70-72. *Mem:* Inst Food Technologists; Am Meat Sci Asn. *Res:* Meat tenderness; basic causes and practical methods of improving; carry out extension education programs in meat technology aimed at meat processors, livestock producers and consumers; special interest in processed meats. *Mailing Add:* Dept Animal Sci 256 Animal Sci Univ Wis 1675 Observatory Dr Madison WI 53706-1205

BUEHLER, EDWIN VERNON, TOXICOLOGY. *Current Pos:* dir toxicol, 84-87, VPRES SCI AFFAIRS, HILLTOP BIOLABS INC, 87- *Personal Data:* b Alliance, Ohio, Sept 23, 29; m 50, Mary L Morrison; c Cynthia A, Mary B, Robert E & Edwin D. *Educ:* Ohio State Univ, BA, 51, MSc, 56, PhD(bact), 58; Am Bd Toxicol, dipl, 80; Acad Toxicol Sci, dipl, 84. *Prof Exp:* Bacteriologist, Res Div, Miami Valley Labs, Procter & Gamble Co, 58-61, res toxicologist, 61-63, group leader, 64-70, head toxicol, 70-78, head immunotoxicol, 78-84. *Mem:* Soc Toxicol; Soc Cosmetic Chem; Am Col Toxicol; fel Acad Toxicol Sci. *Res:* Immunology; toxicology; immediate hypersensitivity; contact sensitization. *Mailing Add:* Hill Top Biolabs Inc PO Box 429501 Cincinnati OH 45242

BUEHRING, GERTRUDE CASE, CANCER. *Current Pos:* asst prof, 73-80, ASSOC PROF MED MICROBIOL & TUMOR BIOL, SCH PUB HEALTH, UNIV CALIF, BERKELEY, 80- *Personal Data:* b Chicago, Ill, May 28, 40; m 62; c 2. *Educ:* Stanford Univ, BA, 62; Univ Calif, Berkeley, PhD(genetics), 72. *Prof Exp:* Fel breast cancer, Nat Cancer Inst, 72-73. *Concurrent Pos:* Recipient grants, Nat Cancer Inst. *Mem:* Sigma Xi; Am Asn Cancer Res; Soc In Vitro Biol; Am Soc Microbiol; AAAS. *Res:* Human breast cancer-cell biology, virology and molecular biology; bovine leukemia; virus-pathogenesis. *Mailing Add:* Sch Pub Health Warren Hall Univ Calif Berkeley CA 94720

BUELL, DUNCAN ALAN, NUMBER THEORY, COMPUTER SCIENCE. *Current Pos:* res staff mem, 86-87, dir, algorithms res, 87-91, SR RES SCI, CTR COMPUT SCI, BOWIE, MD, 91- *Personal Data:* b Detroit, Mich, Oct 17, 50. *Educ:* Univ Ariz, BS, 71; Univ Mich, MA, 72; Univ Ill, Chicago, PhD(math), 76. *Prof Exp:* Res assoc math, Carleton Univ, Ottawa, 76-77; asst prof comput sci, Bowling Green State Univ, 77-79; from asst prof to assoc prof, La State Univ, Baton Rouge, 79-85. *Mem:* Asn Comput Mach; Am Math Soc; Inst Elec & Electronics Engrs; AAAS. *Res:* Computational number theory, parallel computations and computers, and document retrieval systems. *Mailing Add:* Ctr Comput Sci 17100 Sci Dr Bowie MD 20715. *E-Mail:* duncan@super.org

BUELL, GLEN R, CHEMICAL EDUCATION. *Current Pos:* assoc prof, 88-93, EMER PROF CHEM, WRIGHT STATE LAB, LAKE CAMPUS, 93- *Personal Data:* b Lee's Summit, Mo, Jan 10, 31; m 61, Pat Verbich; c Christopher & Mark. *Educ:* Univ Mo, BS, 53, MA, 55; Univ Kans, PhD(chem), 61. *Prof Exp:* Res chemist, Pittsburgh Plate Glass Co, 61-62; vis res assoc organo-silicon, Ohio State Res Found, 62-63; res chemist, Aerospace Res Labs, Wright-Patterson AFB, Ohio, 63-75, res chemist, Lubricants Br, 75-79, mat engr, Mfg Technol Div, Mat Lab, 79-84, systs mgt engr, Off Aerospace Indust Modernization, 84-88. *Concurrent Pos:* Assoc prof chem, Ball State Univ, Muncie, Ind. *Mem:* Am Chem Soc; Sigma Xi. *Res:* Use of learning theory to improve chemical education. *Mailing Add:* 3548 Eastern Dr Beavercreek OH 45432-2206. *E-Mail:* gbuell@desire.wright.edu

BUELOW, FREDERICK H(ENRY), AGRICULTURAL ENGINEERING. *Current Pos:* RETIRED. *Personal Data:* b Minot, NDak, Mar 13, 29; m 54, S Lois Eia; c David, Diane, Darci & Darin. *Educ:* NDak Agr Col, BS, 51; Purdue Univ, MSE, 52; Mich State Univ, PhD(agr eng), 56. *Prof Exp:* From asst prof to prof agr eng, Mich State Univ, 56-66; chmn dept, Univ Wis-Madison, 66-83, prof agr eng, 66-94. *Concurrent Pos:* Mem Eng Accreditation Comt, Accreditation Bd Eng & Technol, 80-85. *Mem:* Fel Am Soc Agr Engrs. *Res:* Agricultural building environment research; instrumentation for agricultural engineering research; agricultural materials handling. *Mailing Add:* Dept Biol Syst Engr 460 Henry Mall Univ Wis Madison WI 53706

BUENING, GERALD MATTHEW, VETERINARY IMMUNOLOGY, VETERINARY VIROLOGY. *Current Pos:* from asst prof to assoc prof, 69-81, PROF VET MICROBIOL, UNIV MO-COLUMBIA, 81- *Personal Data:* b Decatur Co, Ind, Sept 14, 40; m 64; c 2. *Educ:* Iowa State Univ, MS, 66; Purdue Univ, DVM, 64, PhD(vet virol), 69; Am Col Vet Microbiologists, dipl, 70. *Honors & Awards:* Beecham Award for Res Excellence, Mo Vet Med, 87. *Prof Exp:* Instr vet microbiol, Purdue Univ, 66-69. *Mem:* Am Vet Med Asn; Conf Res Workers Animal Dis; Am Soc Microbiol; Asn Am Vet Cols. *Res:* Cell-mediated immunity of domestic animals; in vitro methods are utilized to follow the cell-mediated immunity response during disease processes and recovery; bovine hemotrophic diseases; biotechnology. *Mailing Add:* 1003 Hickory Hill Dr Columbia MO 65203

BUERK, DONALD GENE, ELECTROCHEMICAL MICROSENSORS FOR PHYSIOLOGICAL MEASUREMENTS, BIOTRANSPORT PHENOMENA. *Current Pos:* RES ASST PROF, DEPT OPHTHAL & BIOENG, UNIV PA, 90- *Personal Data:* b St Louis, Mo, Jan 28, 46; m 68, Steffie Greif; c Jesse N & Daniel J. *Educ:* Case Western Res Univ, BS, 69, MS, 76; Northwestern Univ, PhD(chem eng), 80. *Prof Exp:* Assoc prof biomed eng, La Tech Univ, 82-87; res assoc prof, Biomed Eng & Sci Inst, Drexel Univ, 87-90. *Mem:* Biomed Eng Soc; Am Physiol Soc; Inst Elec & Electronics Engrs; Int Soc Oxygen Transport Tissue; Microcirculatory Soc; Sigma Xi. *Res:* Electrochemical microsensors for oxygen, dopamine, hydrogen peroxide and nitric oxide are being used to study chemoreception by the carotid body and blood flow regulation in the retina and optic nerve of the eye. *Mailing Add:* Inst Environ Med One John Morgan Bldg Philadelphia PA 19104-6068. *Fax:* 215-898-0868

BUESCHER, BRENT J, NUCLEAR REACTOR SAFETY RESEARCH. *Current Pos:* SR ENG SPECIALIST, IDAHO NAT ENG LAB, LOCKHEED MARTIN IDAHO TECHNOLOGIES CO, 79- *Personal Data:* b Galesburg, Ill, Sept 15, 40; m 65, Katherine L Christy; c Brent J Jr & Andrew E. *Educ:* Univ NC, BS, 62; Univ Ariz, PhD(physics), 69. *Prof Exp:* Asst, Univ NC, 61-62 & Univ Ariz, 62-69; res assoc physics, Rensselaer Polytech Inst, 69-71; assoc, Argonne Nat Lab, 71-73; prin engr, Power Generation Group, Babcock & Wilcox Co, 73-79. *Concurrent Pos:* US Nuclear Res Ctr deleg, Karlsruhe Nuclear Res Ctr; mem, ANS 5-4 subcomt Plenum Gas, ANS 5-3 subcomt Fission Prod Release, AERO Subcomt Nuclear Reactor Safety Anal Reports. *Mem:* Am Phys Soc; Am Nuclear Soc. *Res:* Performance of nuclear reactor fuel under various conditions; normal (non-accident) reactor operation and behavior during accidents; radiation effects on ceramic and metal reactor fuel components; reactor safety and nuclear plant aging. *Mailing Add:* Lockheed Martin Idaho Technologies Co PO Box 1625 Idaho Falls ID 83415-7136. *Fax:* 208-533-4173

BUESKING, CLARENCE W, MATHEMATICS. *Current Pos:* prof math & dir comput ctr, 57-78, head comput sci dept, 70-78, ASSOC PROF MATH, UNIV EVANSVILLE, 78- *Personal Data:* b Ft Wayne, Ind, Apr 10, 19; m 43; c 4. *Educ:* Ball State Univ, BA, 47; Purdue Univ, MS, 52. *Prof Exp:* Teacher math, Tri-State Col, 47, teacher math & sci, Burris Lab Sch, Ball State Univ, 47-49 & pub schs, Ind, 50-57. *Mem:* Math Asn Am; Asn Comput Mach. *Res:* Undergraduate mathematics; computer programming. *Mailing Add:* 4617 Taylor Ave Evansville IN 47714

BUESSOW, SCOTT, IMMUNOLOGY. *Current Pos:* mgr esoteric immunol, 87-89, TECH DIR LABS, SMITH-KLINE BEECHAM LABS, 89- *Personal Data:* b Mt Vernon, NY, Dec 18, 52. *Educ:* Univ Miami, Fla, BS, 73, PhD(immunol), 82. *Prof Exp:* Res fel tumor immunol, Univ NC Cancer Res Ctr, 82-84; asst prof med tech, Tex Tech Health & Sci Ctr, 84-87. *Mem:* Am Asn Clin Chem; Am Asn Immunol; Am Soc Clin Pathologists. *Res:* Immunology. *Mailing Add:* Smith-Kline Beecham Labs 1737 Airport Way S No 200 Seattle WA 98134-1600

BUETOW, DENNIS EDWARD, CELL BIOLOGY. *Current Pos:* assoc prof, 65-70, head, Dept Physiol & Biophys, 83-88, PROF PHYSIOL, UNIV ILL, URBANA-CHAMPAIGN, 70-, PROF, DEPT PLANT BIOL & COL MED, 83- *Personal Data:* b Chicago, Ill, June 20, 32; m 60, Mary K Carney; c Katherine, Thomas (deceased), Michael & Ellen. *Educ:* Univ Calif, Los Angeles, AB, 54, MA, 57, PhD(zool), 59. *Prof Exp:* Biochemist, Baltimore City Hosps & biologist, biophys lab, NIH, Md, 59-65. *Mem:* Fel AAAS; Am Inst Biol Sci; Am Soc Cell Biol; Am Physiol Soc; fel Geront Soc; Sigma Xi. *Res:* Molecular biology of subcellular organelles; cardiovascular physiology; biology of aging. *Mailing Add:* Dept Molecular & Integrative Physiol Univ Ill 407 S Goodwin Urbana IL 61801. *Fax:* 217-333-1133

BUETOW, KENNETH H, GENETICS. *Current Pos:* trainee, 86-87, res geneticist, 87-88, assoc mem, 88-92, MEM FOX CHASE CANCER CTR, 92- *Personal Data:* b Chicago, Ill, Dec 12, 56. *Educ:* Ind Univ, BA, 80; Univ Pittsburgh, MS, 83, PhD(human genetics), 85. *Concurrent Pos:* Adj asst prof pediat, Univ Penn Sch Med, 92- *Mem:* Human Gerome Orgn; Am Soc Human Genetics; Genetics Soc Am; Am Soc Prev Onocol; Sigma Xi. *Res:* Construction of human genetics maps; molecular genetic epidemiology of primary liver cancer; mendelian disease gene mapping; candidate locus susceptibility studies of common US cancers; descriptive genetic epidemiology of congenital anolmalies. *Mailing Add:* Fox Chase Cancer Ctr 7701 Burholme Ave Philadelphia PA 19111. *Fax:* 215-728-5574

BUETTNER, GARRY RICHARD, PHYSICAL CHEMISTRY, PHOTOBIOLOGY. *Current Pos:* EXPERT, NAT INST ENVIRON HEALTH SCI & NIH, RES TRIANGLE PARK, 87- *Personal Data:* b Vinton, Iowa, Oct 11, 45; m 69; c 4. *Educ:* Univ Northern Iowa, BA, 67; Univ Iowa, MS, 69, PhD(chem), 76. *Prof Exp:* Fel radiation biol, Radiation Res Lab, Univ Iowa, 76-78; asst prof chem, Wabash Col, 78-83; Fulbright fel, Neuherberg, WGer, 85-87. *Concurrent Pos:* Vis prof, Med Col Wis, 81. *Mem:* Am Chem Soc; Sigma Xi; Am Soc Photobiol; Soc Free Radical Res; Oxygen Soc. *Res:* Superoxide and superoxide dismutase in human health. *Mailing Add:* EMRB 68/ESR Circle Univ Iowa Col Med Iowa City IA 52242

BUETTNER, MARK ROLAND, AGRONOMY, ANIMAL SCIENCE. *Current Pos:* AGRONOMIST, BRANDT CONSOL. *Personal Data:* b Cottonwood, Idaho, Sept 9, 49; m 78; c 3. *Educ:* Univ Idaho, BS, 72, MS, 75; Purdue Univ, PhD(agron), 78. *Prof Exp:* Asst prof agron, Mountain Meadow Res Ctr, Colo State Univ, 78-79; asst prof agron, Klamath Exp Sta, Ore State Univ, 79- *Concurrent Pos:* From asst dir to dir limnol, Student Originated Studies, NSF, 71-72. *Mem:* Am Soc Agron; Crop Sci Soc Am. *Res:* Legume establishment and production; grass production; meadow and range species; forage physiology; digestion coefficients; total N content; cell wall; lignin; lignin-hemicellulose; infra-red absorbance; nuclear magnetic resonance. *Mailing Add:* RR 2 Petersburg IL 62675

BUFE, CHARLES GLENN, SEISMOLOGY, TECTONICS. *Current Pos:* GEOPHYSICIST, US GEOL SURV, 73- *Personal Data:* b Duluth, Minn, Jan 2, 38; c Glennica, Sierra & Nathaniel. *Educ:* Mich Tech Univ, BS, 60, MS, 62; Univ Mich, PhD(geol), 69. *Prof Exp:* Res asst geophys, Willow Run Labs, Univ Mich, 64, res assoc, 67-69, assoc res geophysicist, 69; geophysicist, US Earthquake Mech Lab, Nat Oceanic & Atmospheric Admin, 69-73. *Concurrent Pos:* Vis asst prof, Univ Wis, Milwaukee, 73; geothermal liaison, Dept Energy, Washington, DC, 80-83; tech adv to Kingdom Saudi Arabia, Riyadh, 85-86; prin investr seismicity, Yucca Mountain Proj, Nev, 88-89. *Mem:* Seismol Soc Am; Am Geophys Union; Soc Explor Geophys; Earthquake Eng & Res Inst. *Res:* Seismicity of geothermal areas; micro-earthquake and fault-creep studies; earthquake recurrence, prediction and control; induced seismicity and earthquake triggering; global seismology; nonlinear dynamics of tectonic processes. *Mailing Add:* US Geol Surv MS 967 Box 25046 DFC Denver CO 80225. *Fax:* 303-273-8450; *E-Mail:* cbufe@gldfs.cr.usgs.gov

BUFF, FRANK PAUL, PHYSICAL CHEMISTRY, STATISTICAL MECHANICS. *Current Pos:* from instr to assoc prof chem, 50-61, PROF CHEM, UNIV ROCHESTER, 61- *Personal Data:* b Munich, Ger, Feb 13, 24; nat US; m 56; c 2. *Educ:* Univ Calif, BA, 44; Calif Inst Technol, PhD(chem), 49. *Concurrent Pos:* AEC fel, Calif Inst Technol, 49-50; NSF sr fel, Inst Theoret Physcis, Utrecht, Netherlands, 59-60; consult, Scony mobil Co, Inc, Mobil Oil Corp. *Mem:* AAAS; Am Chem Soc; fel Am Phys Soc; Sigma Xi. *Res:* Molecular theories of fluids; surface phenomena; solutions and chemical kinetics; nucleation processes; electrochemistry. *Mailing Add:* 90 Roby Dr Rochester NY 14618

BUFFALOE, NEAL DOLLISON, BIOLOGY. *Current Pos:* prof, 57-87, EMER PROF BIOL, UNIV CENT ARK, 87- *Personal Data:* b Leachville, Ark, Nov 15, 24; m 47, Inez Owens; c Bonnie, Robert, Anne, Laurie, Don. *Educ:* David Lipscomb Col, BS, 49; Vanderbilt Univ, MS, 52, PhD(biol), 57. *Prof Exp:* Instr biol, David Lipscomb Col, 49-54 & Vanderbilt Univ, 54-56. *Concurrent Pos:* Instr biol, George Peabody Col, 55. *Mem:* AAAS. *Res:* Cytology and cytogenetics. *Mailing Add:* 3610 Irby Dr Conway AR 72032

BUFFETT, RITA FRANCES, BIOLOGY, PHYSIOLOGY. *Current Pos:* RETIRED. *Personal Data:* b Beverly, Mass, Jan 18, 17. *Educ:* Boston Univ, AB, 47, AM, 48, PhD(biol), 54. *Prof Exp:* Instr biol, Boston Univ, 50-54; res asst exp path, Children's Cancer Res Found, Mass, 54-59; res scientist exp path, 59-61, res scientist viral oncol, 61-69, asst & assoc res prof microbiol, Roswell Park Mem Inst, 69-80. *Mem:* AAAS; Am Soc Microbiol; Am Asn Cancer Res; NY Acad Sci; Sigma Xi. *Res:* Oncogenesis; radiation, hormonal and viral. *Mailing Add:* 1782 Sharon Dr Concord CA 94519-1453

BUFFINGTON, ANDREW, ASTROPHYSICS. *Current Pos:* RES PHYSICIST, UNIV CALIF, SAN DIEGO, 84- *Personal Data:* b Fall River, Mass, Dec 25, 38; m 68; c 2. *Educ:* Mass Inst Technol, BS, 61, PhD(physics), 66. *Prof Exp:* Res asst physics, Mass Inst Technol, 66-68; res physicist, Space Sci Lab & Lawrence Berkeley Lab, Univ Calif, Berkeley, 68-79; res assoc, Calif Inst Technol, Pasadena, 79-84. *Mem:* Sigma Xi; Am Phys Soc; Am Astronaut Soc. *Res:* Measurement of cosmic-ray, nuclear and isotopic abundances; interpretation of these to deduce cosmic-ray history; search for cosmic ray antimatter and measurement of antiproton flux; development of flexible telescope techniques to restore atmospherically perturbed images from astronomical telescopes; development of photoelectric astrometric telescopes. *Mailing Add:* 3166 Bremerton Pl La Jolla CA 92037-2211

BUFFINGTON, DENNIS ELVIN, AGRICULTURAL ENGINEERING. *Current Pos:* PROF & HEAD, AGR ENG DEPT, PA STATE UNIV, UNIVERSITY PARK, 85- *Personal Data:* b Elizabethville, Pa, Aug 11, 44; m 68, Anna C Stafford; c Kristen & Melanie. *Educ:* Pa State Univ, BS, 66, MS, 70; Univ Minn, PhD, 71. *Prof Exp:* From asst prof to assoc prof agr eng, Univ Fla, Gainesville, 71-82, prof, 82-85. *Mem:* Am Soc Agr Engrs; Am Soc Eng Educ; Am Soc Heating Refrig & Air Conditioning Engrs. *Res:* Agricultural engineering; published 110 technical articles. *Mailing Add:* 250 Agr Eng Pa State Univ University Park PA 16802-1909

BUFFINGTON, EDWIN CONGER, MARINE GEOLOGY. *Current Pos:* RETIRED. *Personal Data:* b Ontario, Calif, Aug 21, 20; m 43; c 4. *Educ:* Carleton Col, BA, 41; Calif Inst Technol, MSc, 47; Univ Southern Calif, PhD, 73. *Prof Exp:* Marine geologist, USN Electronics Lab, 48-69; head, Marine Geol Br, Navy Undersea Res & Develop Ctr, 69-74; assoc chief, Marine Geol Br, US Geol Surv, 74-80. *Concurrent Pos:* Dir, Gen Oceanog, Inc. *Mem:* Fel Geol Soc Am; Soc Econ Paleontologists & Mineralogists; Am Asn Petrol Geologists; Asn Eng Geol; Am Geophys Union; Sigma Xi; fel AAAS. *Res:* Bathymetry; sea floor geomorphology; plate tectonics. *Mailing Add:* 1015 Devonshire Dr San Diego CA 92107-4003

BUFFINGTON, JOHN DOUGLAS, ECOLOGY, FISH & WILDLIFE SCIENCES. *Current Pos:* dir, Alaska Sci Ctr, 94-97, REGIONAL CHIEF BIOLOGIST, US GEOL SURV, 97- *Personal Data:* b Jersey City, NJ, Nov 26, 41; m 65; c 2. *Educ:* St Peter's Col, NJ, BS, 63; Univ Ill, Urbana-Champaign, MS, 65, PhD(zool), 67. *Prof Exp:* Asst prof, dept biol sci, Ill State Univ, 69-72; biologist, Argonne Nat Lab, 72-77, asst div dir, 76-77; sr staff, Coun Environ Qual, Washington, DC, 77-80; chief, Off Biol Serv, Nat Biol Serv, 80-82, dep assoc dir res & develop, 82-89, regional dir res & develop, US Fish & Wildlife Serv, 89-92, actg regional dir, 92-94. *Concurrent Pos:* Adj assoc prof, Northern Ill Univ, 75-77; dir, WAEPA, 83- *Mem:* AAAS; Ecol Soc Am. *Res:* Fish and wildlife management. *Mailing Add:* US Geol Surv 909 First Ave Suite 800 Seattle WA 98104

BUFFLER, CHARLES ROGERS, MICROWAVE PROCESSING. *Current Pos:* VPRES, MICROWAVE RES CTR, 94- *Personal Data:* b Bryn Mawr, Pa, Apr 8, 34; m 56, Nancy Walker; c Susan, J Robert & John. *Educ:* Univ Tex, BS, 55; Harvard Univ, MS, 56, PhD(eng & appl physics), 60. *Prof Exp:* Res scientist, Varian Assocs, 59-66; mgr, Ferrite Eng, Microwave Assocs, 66-68; pres, Microwave Magnetics, 68-73; assoc dir, Advan Eng Resources, Leeds & Northrop, 73-75; dir res & develop, Litton Microwave Cooking, 75-85; pres, Assoc Sci Res Found, Inc, 85-94. *Concurrent Pos:* Dir, Int Microwave Power Inst, 77-82; expert witness, Litton Microwave Cooking, 85-90; consult, Assoc Sci Res Found, 85-94. *Mem:* Fel Int Microwave Power Inst; Bioelectromagnetics Soc; sr mem Inst Elec & Electronics Engrs. *Res:* Microwave processing, oven design and microwave interaction with foods. *Mailing Add:* Microwave Res Ctr 126 Water St Marlborough NH 03455-9701. *Fax:* 603-876-4079; *E-Mail:* cbuff@monad.net

BUFFLER, PATRICIA ANN HAPP, EPIDEMIOLOGY, PUBLIC HEALTH. *Current Pos:* DEAN, PUB HEALTH DEPT, UNIV CALIF, BERKELEY, 91- *Personal Data:* b Doylestown, Pa, Aug 1, 38; m 62, Richard T; c Martyn & Monique. *Educ:* Cath Univ Am, BSN, 60; Univ Calif, Berkeley, MPH, 65, PhD(epidemiol), 73. *Honors & Awards:* Lilienfeld Award, Am Col Epidemiol. *Prof Exp:* Asst prof epidemiol, Sch Pub Health, Univ Tex, 70-72; dir, Ctr Health Sci & asst prof health sci, Alaska Methodist Univ, 73-74; dir, Epidemiol Res Unit & asst prof, Dept Prev Med & Community Health, Univ Tex Med Br, 74-78; prof epidemiol, Sch Pub Health, Univ Tex Health Sci Ctr, 79-91. *Concurrent Pos:* Consult to various pvt, pub & govt agencies, 73-79; mem, Med Adv Bd, Tex Air Qual Control Bd, 77-79. *Mem:* Inst Med-Nat Acad Sci; Am Pub Health Asn; Am Col Epidemiol; Am Acad Epidemiol Soc; AAAS; Soc Epidemiol Res. *Res:* Chronic disease epidemiology; cancer; environmental and occupational diseases; mental illness and occupational diseases. *Mailing Add:* 85 El Camino Rd Berkeley CA 94705

BUFFLER, RICHARD THURMAN, MARINE GEOLOGY, MARINE GEOPHYSICS. *Current Pos:* RES SCIENTIST MARINE GEOL & GEOPHYS, UNIV TEX INST GEOPHYS, 75- *Personal Data:* b Troy, NY, Nov 4, 37; m 62, Patricia Happ; c Martyn & Monique. *Educ:* Univ Tex, Austin, BS, 59; Univ Calif, Berkeley, PhD(geol), 67. *Prof Exp:* Geologist explor res, Shell Oil Co, 67-71; assoc prof geol, Univ Alaska, 71-74. *Mem:* Am Asn Petrol Geologists; Geol Soc Am; Am Geophys Union; Soc Sedimenntol Geol. *Res:* Sedimentology; stratigraphy; depositional environments; petroleum geology; seismic (sequence) stratigraphy. *Mailing Add:* Inst Geophys Univ Tex 8701 Mopac Blvd Austin TX 78759-8345. *Fax:* 512-471-8844; *E-Mail:* dick@utig.ig.utexas.edu

BUFFONE, GREGORY J, CLINICAL PATHOLOGY, MEDICAL RESEARCH. *Current Pos:* PROF PATH, BAYLOR COL MED & TEX CHILDRENS HOSP, 79- *Personal Data:* b Steubenville, Ohio, 1948. *Educ:* Jacksonville Univ, BS, 70; Univ Fla, MS, 72; Univ NC, PhD(biochem & path), 75. *Prof Exp:* Assoc prof path, George Washington Univ, 75-79; dir clin chem, Childrens Hosp Nat Med Ctr, 75-79. *Mem:* Am Asn Clin Chemists; Am Informatics Asn. *Mailing Add:* Dept Path Baylor Col Med 1 Baylor Plaza Houston TX 77030-3411

BUFFORD, RODGER K, CLINICAL PSYCHOLOGY, BEHAVIORAL PSYCHOLOGY. *Current Pos:* DIR, RES & INTEGRETION, GEORGE FOX COL, 95- *Personal Data:* b Dec 23, 44; m 68, Kathleen A Parson; c Heather & Brett. *Educ:* King's Col, BA, 66; Univ Ill, Urbana, MA, 70, PhD(clin psychol), 71. *Honors & Awards:* Tempteton Found Humility Theol Award, 93. *Prof Exp:* Psychol intern, Adolf Meyer Zone Ctr, 69-70; asst prof psychol, Am Univ, 71-76; chair psychol, Huntington Col, 76-77; assoc prof & dir training, Psychol Studies Inst, 77-81; prof & chair clin psychol, Western Conservative Baptist, 82-90. *Concurrent Pos:* Psychologist, Atlanta Coun Ctr, 80-82 & Western Psychol & Coun Serv, 82- *Mem:* Am Psychol Asn; Am Sci Affil; Soc Sci Study Relig; Christian Asn Psychol Studies; Western Psychol Asn. *Res:* Spiritual well-being as a factor in social-emotional health and subjective well-being; religious factors in the process and outcome of psychotherapy. *Mailing Add:* George Fox Col 6146 414 N Meridian St Newberg OR 97132-2697. *Fax:* 503-537-3834; *E-Mail:* rbufford@georgefox.edu

BUFFUM, C(HARLES) EMERY, ELECTRICAL ENGINEERING. *Current Pos:* RETIRED. *Personal Data:* b Toulon, Ill, June 14, 10; wid; c 4. *Educ:* Calif Inst Technol, BS, 31, MS, 32. *Prof Exp:* Asst test engr, Consol Steel Corp, Calif, 33-34; computer, Western Geophys Co, 34-35, party chief in charge seismog field party, 35-38; seismog party chief, Pan Am Petrol Corp, 38-41, res engr, Amoco Prod Co, 41-44, tech group supvr, 44-46, supvr design, Construct & Tech Serv Sect, 46-49, res group supvr, 49-50, res sect supvr, 50-52, lab serv supt, 53-72. *Res:* Design of seismograph amplifiers, oscillography, radio transmitters and auxiliary equipment. *Mailing Add:* 9524 E 71st St Tulsa OK 74133

BUFFUM, DONALD C, PHYSICAL METALLURGY. *Current Pos:* RETIRED. *Personal Data:* b Narberth, Pa, Apr 13, 18; m 43, Dorothea M Hollis; c Donald C Jr & Barbara H (Pedersen). *Educ:* Tufts Univ, BS, 39. *Prof Exp:* Phys sci aide, Army Mat & Mech Res Ctr, 40-42, jr metall engr, 42, metall engr, 42-44, physicist, 46-51, phys metallurgist, 51-55, supvry phys metallurgist, 55-78. *Mem:* Am Inst Mech Engrs; Am Soc Metals; Am Welding Soc; Am Vacuum Soc. *Res:* Metals joining; alloy development of ferrous and titanium alloys; the temper brittleness of steel and welding of metals and alloys. *Mailing Add:* 7 Ivy Circle Arlington MA 02174

BUFKIN, BILLY GEORGE, POLYMER SCIENCE & TECHNOLOGY. *Current Pos:* VPRES RES, CONSUMER DIV, SHERWIN-WILLIAMS CO. *Personal Data:* b Columbia, Miss, Oct 8, 46; m 66; c 3. *Educ:* Univ Southern Miss, BS, 68, PhD(org chem), 72. *Prof Exp:* from asst prof to assoc prof polymer sci, Univ Southern Miss, 71-80, dept chmn, 76-80; SR VPRES SCI AFFAIRS, DAP, INC, 81- *Concurrent Pos:* Consult, Tenn Eastman Co, 73-76. *Mem:* Am Chem Soc; Fedn Soc Coatings Technol; Soc Plastics Engrs. *Res:* Crosslinkable emulsions; emulsion polymerization; antifouling materials which function by controllable release mechanisms; utilization of renewable resources; organic chemistry. *Mailing Add:* Sherwin-Williams Co 601 Canal Rd Cleveland OH 44113-2424

BUGENHAGEN, THOMAS GORDON, QUEUEING THEORY, TECHNICAL MANAGEMENT. *Current Pos:* RETIRED. *Personal Data:* b Derby, NY, Dec, 16, 32; m 56, Katherine Leeth; c Karl, Jeffrey & John. *Educ:* Maryville Col, BA, 56; Univ Tenn, MA, 59. *Honors & Awards:* David Rist Prize, Mil Opers Res Soc, 76. *Prof Exp:* Instr math, Maryville Col, 57-58, Univ Tenn, 58-59; mathematician opers anal, Johns Hopkins Univ, 59-81, group supvr opers anal, Appl Physics Lab, 81-95. *Concurrent Pos:* Prin staff mem, Appl Physics Lab, Johns Hopkins Univ, 80. *Mem:* Fel AAAS; Opers Res Soc Am; Mil Opers Res Soc. *Res:* Application of operations research technique, queueing theory, to the solution of operational problems for anti-air warfare, Kalman filters; for ship tracking algorithms and simulations for determining requirements. *Mailing Add:* 5341 Trailway Dr Rockville MD 20853

BUGG, CHARLES EDWARD, PHYSICAL CHEMISTRY. *Current Pos:* asst prof biochem, 68-74, assoc prof biochem, 74-77, PROF BIOCHEM, UNIV ALA MED CTR, 77-, ASSOC DIR, UNIV ALA COMPREHENSIVE CANCER CTR, 76- *Personal Data:* b Durham, NC, June 5, 41; m 62. *Educ:* Duke Univ, AB, 62; Rice Univ, PhD(phys chem), 65. *Prof Exp:* Res fel, Calif Inst Technol, 65-66; res chemist, Dacron Res Lab, E I du Pont de Nemours & Co, 66-67; res fel, Calif Inst Technol, 67-68. *Mem:* Am Crystallog Asn; Sigma Xi. *Res:* Crystal structures of compounds of biological interest. *Mailing Add:* BioCryt Pharmaceut Inc 2190 Pkwy Lake Dr Birmingham AL 35244-2812

BUGG, STERLING L(OWE), CIVIL ENGINEERING. *Current Pos:* RETIRED. *Personal Data:* b Harrodsburg, Ky, June 12, 20; m 47, Elizabeth A Brauer; c Nancy L (Miller), Robert L & R Dale. *Educ:* Univ Ky, BS, 44; Purdue Univ, MS, 48. *Prof Exp:* Eng aide, Ky Hwy Dept, 42; mat engr, Dept Hwys, 45-46; asst, Purdue Univ, 46-48; asst prof civil eng, Univ Fla, 48-52; struct engr, US Naval Civil Eng Lab, 52-55, supvr struct res engr, 55-63, head, Dept Civil Eng, 63-69, head, Dept Ocean Eng, 69-75, head, Dept Civil Eng,

75- *Concurrent Pos:* Regist prof engr Fla, 52-90; chmn, Ventura Co, Transp Adv Comt, Calif, 75-88; eng consult, 75-81. *Mem:* Am Soc Civil Engrs (pres, 58); Am Concrete Inst; Sigma Xi. *Res:* Engineering materials; highway design; research structure. *Mailing Add:* 600 Janetwood Dr Oxnard CA 93030

BUGG, WILLIAM MAURICE, PHYSICS. *Current Pos:* From asst prof to assoc prof, 59-69, PROF PHYSICS & HEAD DEPT, UNIV TENN, KNOXVILLE, 69- *Personal Data:* b St Louis, Mo, Jan 23, 31; m 54, Marian Sly; c Susan T (Ward), Thomas M, Linda A (Brogdan) & David W. *Educ:* Washington Univ, AB, 52; Univ Tenn, PhD(physics), 59. *Concurrent Pos:* Consult, Oak Ridge Nat Lab, 59-79 & Danforth Assocs, 69-70. *Mem:* Fel Am Phys Soc; Inst Elec & Electronics Engrs. *Res:* Silicon detectors; electron positron interactions at high energy; photon electron interactions; QED tests; radiation damage. *Mailing Add:* Dept Physics Univ Tenn Knoxville TN 37996-1200. *Fax:* 423-974-7843

BUGLIARELLO, GEORGE, SCIENCE ADMINISTRATION. *Current Pos:* pres, 73-94, CHANCELLOR, POLYTECHNIC UNIV, 94- *Personal Data:* b Trieste, Italy, May 20, 27; US citizen; m, Virginia Harding; c Federico David & Nicholas Luigi. *Educ:* Univ Padua, Dott Ing BS, 51; Univ Minn, MS, 54; Mass Inst Technol, ScD, 59. *Hon Degrees:* LLD, Carnegie-Mellon Univ, 86; Dr, Univ Trieste, 89; DE, Milwaukee Sch Eng, 91; LHD & DSC, Ill Inst Technol, 93; LHD, Pace Univ, 94. *Honors & Awards:* Huber Res Prize, Am Soc Civil Engrs, 67; Alza lectr, Biomed Eng Soc, 76; Golden San Giusto Award, Trieste, Italy, 78; Centennial Award, Am Soc Mech Engrs, 80. *Prof Exp:* Fulbright scholar, Univ Minn, 52-54; asst to chair, Hydraul Proj, Univ Padua, 54-55; res asst, Hydrodynamics Lab, Mass Inst Technol, 56-59, res asst, 59; from asst prof to assoc prof civil eng, Carnegie-Mellon Univ, 59-66, chmn, Biotech Prog, 64-69, prof biotechnol & civil eng, 66-69; dean eng & prof civil eng & biotechnol, Dept Systs Eng, Univ Ill, Chicago Circle, 69-73. *Concurrent Pos:* Chmn, Comt Fluid Dynamics, Am Soc Civil Engrs, 66-68, Task Comt Biol Flows, 67-71, Task Comt Prob-Oriented Lang, 67-72, Task Comt Civil Eng Biomed & Health Care Systs, 69-73, mem, Res Comt, 69-73, Adv Bd & Res Coun Comput Pract, 72-76; mem, Bio Med Eng Training Comt, Nat Inst Gen Med Sci, 66-70 & Proj Comt, Gen Med Res Prog, 71-74; NATO sr fel, Tech Univ Berlin, 68; pub health serv spec fel sci policy res, Harvard Univ, 68; sci adv panel, Armed Forces Safety Explosives Bd, Dept Defense, 68-69; mem, Comn Educ, Nat Acad Eng, 70-73 & chmn, Comt Educ Systs, 71-73, Joint Nat Acad Eng & Nat Acad Sci Comt Role US Eng Sch Tech Foreign Assistance, 71-74, Steering Comt Modern Technol Methods Improving Qual Educ, 78, Int Affairs Adv Comt, 88-; consult, State Univ NY, Buffalo, 71; mem, Eng Design Comt, Am Soc Eng Educ, 72-73, Conf Theme Comt, 73 & Comt Govt Rel, 72-75; consult, Chemother Prog, Nat Cancer Inst, 72-74; mem Mayor's Coun Environ, 74-77, Comn Sci & Technol, 84-, chair, 87-, Task Force, Water Conserv, 85-88; mem, Comt Sci & Pub Policy, NY Acad Sci, 75; secy, Coun Sci & Technol Develop, 77-82; mem, Adv Comt Sci Educ, NSF, 79-80 & chair, 80-81; mem, US Panel Joint Comt Coop Prog Sci & Technol Planning, Nat Res Coun, 82 & Comn Int Rel, 81-82; univ prog panel, Energy Res Adv Bd, Dept Energy, 82-83; chair, Adv Panel Technol Transfer Mid E, Off Technol Assessment, 82-84; co-chair, Prog Planning & Agenda Subcomt, Comt Sci, Eng & Pub Policy & Conf Prog & Tours Comt, AAAS, 84, Review Panel Philip Hauge Abelsm Prize, 85, chair, Panel Phys Sci & Eng, Carnegie & AAAS Proj 2061, 85- & Comt Sci, Eng & Pub Policy, 86-; US rep, Prog Sci Stability, NAtlantic Treaty Orgn, 84-; eval comt, Nat Med Technol Nomination, Dept Com, 87-; chair bd, Infrastructure & Constructed Environ, Nat Res Coun. *Mem:* Nat Acad Sci; Nat Acad Eng; fel Am Soc Eng Educ; Int Asn Hydraul Res; fel NY Acad Sci; fel AAAS; Am Arbitration Asn; Cardiovasc Syst Dynamics Soc; Asn Independent Technol Univ (pres, 86-88); Acad Educ Develop; fel Am Inst Med Biol Eng; Int Soc Hemorheol (secy, 66-69); Int Water Resources Asn; Ital Hydrotech Asn; Sigma Xi (pres-elect, 90); Soc Natural Philos; Soc Rheology; Soc Col & Univ Planning; fel Am Soc Civil Engrs. *Res:* Author of 10 books on engineering; over 200 publications on engineering and related subjects. *Mailing Add:* Polytech Univ 6 Metrotech Ctr Brooklyn NY 11201. *Fax:* 718-260-3974; *E-Mail:* gbugliar@poly.edu

BUGNOLO, DIMITRI SPARTACO, STOCHASTIC WAVE PROPAGATION, BALLISTIC MISSILE DEFENSE. *Current Pos:* RETIRED. *Personal Data:* b Atlantic City, NJ, Feb 3, 29; m 58; c 3. *Educ:* Univ Pa, BSEE, 52; Yale Univ, MEng, 55; Columbia Univ, ScD(elec eng), 60. *Prof Exp:* Comput components res, Burroughs Res Lab, 52-54; res asst, Yale Univ, 54-56; instr elec eng, Columbia Univ, 56-60; consult to lab dir & mem tech staff, Bell Tel Labs, 60-61 & 63-66; asst prof elec eng, Columbia Univ, 61-63, sr res scientist, Hudson Labs, 66-67; prin engr adv res, Submarine Signal Div, Raytheon Corp, 67-69; consult engr & physicist, 69-80; assoc prof elec & comput eng, Fla Inst Technol, 80-83 & Univ Ala, Huntsville, 83-87; Mitre Corp, 87-89. *Concurrent Pos:* Mem comn, Int Sci Radio Union, 64-68; consult & full prof, Nat Inst Sci Res, Univ Quebec, 71-73. *Mem:* Am Phys Soc; sr mem Inst Elec & Electronics Engrs; Sigma Xi; Optical Soc Am. *Res:* Applied plasma physics; wave propagation in random media; plasma turbulence; propagation theory; electromagnetic theory and practice; antenna theory and practice; atmospheric turbulence; computer simulation; ballistic missile defense research. *Mailing Add:* 16 Laurie Lane Westminster MA 01473. *E-Mail:* bugnolo@net1plus.com

BUGOSH, JOHN, PHYSICAL CHEMISTRY, COLLOID CHEMISTRY. *Current Pos:* res supvr, Del, 50-68, planning consult, Pa, 68-72, DEVELOP MGR, E I DU PONT DE NEMOURS & CO, INC, 72-, CONSULT, 89-; PRES, TRAKON, INC, 89- *Personal Data:* b Cleveland, Ohio, July 1, 24; m 52, Nancy A Perron; c Nancy J, Pamela M & John A. *Educ:* Heidelberg Col & Adelbert Col, BS, 45; Western Reserve Univ, MS, 47, PhD(chem), 49; Escuela Interamericana de Verano, dipl, 48. *Honors & Awards:* Award, Am Chem Soc, 62. *Prof Exp:* Res assoc ultrasonics, Western Reserve Univ, 48-49, lectr physics, 49-50. *Mem:* AAAS; Am Chem Soc; Sigma Xi. *Res:* Ultrasonic transducers; electrolytic solutions, inorganic colloids; determination of masses of ions by ultrasonics; new form of film forming fibrous boehmite. *Mailing Add:* 622 Khyber Lane Venice FL 34293-4423

BUHAC, IVO, GASTROENTEROLOGY, INTERNAL MEDICINE. *Current Pos:* PVT PRACT. *Personal Data:* b Dubrovnik, Yugoslavia, Sept 4, 26; m 62; c 1. *Educ:* Univ Zagreb, MD, 52, ScD, 64; Univ Erlangen, MD, 62. *Prof Exp:* Intern med, Zagreb, Yugoslavia, 52-53; resident, 57-60, staff physician med & gastroenterol, 62-68; instr med, Med Col Va, 69-70; chief gastroenterol, Albany Vet Admin Hosp, 70- *Concurrent Pos:* Alexander von Humboldt fel, Med Sch, Univ Hamburg, 64-65; fel gastroenterol, Vet Admin Hosp, Richmond, Va, 68-70; from asst prof to prof med, Albany Med Col, 82- *Mem:* Am Gastroenterol Asn; Am Asn Study Liver Dis; fel Am Col Physicians; NY Acad Sci; Am Soc Gastrointestinal Endoscopy. *Res:* Peritoneal permeability; portal hypertension; albumin distribution. *Mailing Add:* 330 Pomfert St Suite 1 Putnam CT 06260

BUHKS, EPHRAIM, EDUCATIONAL ADMINISTRATION. *Current Pos:* ASST DIR COL ADMIN, ORT OPERS USA, ORT TECH INSTS, 90- *Personal Data:* b Kishinev, USSR, Apr 30, 49; m 83; c 2. *Educ:* Kishinev Univ, USSR, BS, 71; Tel-Aviv Univ, Israel, PhD(chem), 80. *Honors & Awards:* Von Humboldt Found Award, 80. *Prof Exp:* Res fel photoelectrochem, Physics Dept, Univ Del, 80-81; proj leader photovoltaics, Solavolt Int, Shell Oil Co, 81-83; proj mgr opto-electronic mat, B F Goodrich Res & Develop Ctr, 83-87; tech dir IR imaging & detectors, Sunstone Inc, 87-89. *Concurrent Pos:* Consult biophys, Johnson Res Found, Univ Pa, 80-83, IR detectors, Belor Technol Co, Inc, 87-89, fiber-optics, Kingston Technol, Inc, 89, SBIR, Energia Inc, 90. *Mem:* Optical Soc Am; Phys Soc Am; Int Soc Optical Eng. *Res:* Electron transfer processes; photosynthesis; photoelectrochemistry; opto-electronic materials; solar cells; luminescent materials; IR imaging; IR detectors; fiber-optics; organic electronic materials; conducting polymers; photoresists; electrochromics; photochromics; optical data storage. *Mailing Add:* 33 Thoreau Dr Plainsboro NJ 08536-3018

BUHL, ALLEN EDWIN, ZOOLOGY, PHYSIOLOGY. *Current Pos:* res scientist reprod physiol res, 81-87, sr res scientist dermat, 87-92, SR SCIENTIST BIOCHEM, UPJOHN CO, 92- *Personal Data:* b Evanston, Ill, Nov 10, 47. *Educ:* Carthage Col, BA, 69; Univ Ill, MS, 71, PhD(zool), 76. *Prof Exp:* Res assoc reprod physiol, Ore Regional Primate Res Ctr, 77-78, asst scientist, 78-80. *Mem:* Soc Investigative Dermat; Soc Study Reprod; AAAS. *Res:* Male fertility and reproductive physiology; mensenchymal-epithelial interactions in organ development and function; control of growth and differentiation of cutaneous structures especially hair; drug discovery and development. *Mailing Add:* 5120 Brennerton Dr Portage MI 49002

BUHL, DAVID, radio astronomy, for more information see previous edition

BUHL, ROBERT FRANK, CORROSION, PHYSICS. *Current Pos:* res physicist, Unocal Corp, 66-67, sr res physicist, 67-75, res assoc, Res Ctr, 75-84, SR RES ASSOC, SCI & TECHNOL DIV, UNOCAL CORP, 84- *Personal Data:* b Utica, NY, Apr 20, 22; m 45; c 5. *Educ:* Ohio State Univ, BS, 43. *Prof Exp:* Res asst, Ohio State Univ Res Found, Off Sci & Res Develop, Nat Defense Res Comt, 44-45; res assoc, Pure Oil Co, Ill, 45-61, group supvr, 62-66. *Mem:* Nat Asn Corrosion Eng; Inst Noise Control Eng. *Res:* Analytical instrument design and construction; spectro- metric analysis method development for lubes, fuels and petro-chemicals; infrared and ultraviolet analysis; corrosion control and coatings evaluation; industrial noise control; nondestructive testing. *Mailing Add:* 1141 N Richman Ave Fullerton CA 92835

BUHLE, EMMETT LOREN, INDUSTRIAL ORGANIC CHEMISTRY. *Current Pos:* RETIRED. *Personal Data:* b Moline, Ill, May 7, 18; m 47, Elsie Smith; c Christopher, Warren, Loren & Gordon. *Educ:* Johns Hopkins Univ, AB, 41, MA, 42, PhD(chem), 48. *Prof Exp:* Res assoc, Mass Inst Technol, 48-50; res asst pharmacol, Johns Hopkins Univ, 50-54, instr, 52-54; chemist, Exp Sta, E I du Pont de Nemours & Co, 54-58; sr res chemist, Wyeth Lab, 58-82, prod develop coordr, 82-84. *Concurrent Pos:* Mem surv antimalarial drugs, Nat Res Coun, 42-46. *Mem:* Am Chem Soc; AAAS. *Res:* Antimalarial drugs; synthetic steroids; semisynthetic penicillins; prostaglandins; development of chemical processes. *Mailing Add:* 714 Hemlock Rd Media PA 19063

BUHLER, DONALD RAYMOND, BIOCHEMICAL PHARMACOLOGY. *Current Pos:* assoc prof, 68-74, PROF, DEPT AGR CHEM, ENVIRON HEALTH SCI CTR, ORE STATE UNIV, 74-, CHMN TOXICOL PROG, 83- *Personal Data:* b San Francisco, Calif, Oct 11, 25; m 76. *Educ:* Ore State Col, BA & BS, 50, Ore State Univ, PhD(biochem), 56. *Prof Exp:* Asst, Ore State Col, 51-55; staff biochemist, div exp med, Med Sch, Univ Ore, 55-56, USPHS fel, 56-58; biochemist, western fish nutrit lab, US Fish & Wildlife Serv, 58-59, Upjohn Co, Mich, 59-64, western fish nutrit lab, US Fish & Wildlife Serv, 64-66 & Pac Northwest Labs, Battelle Mem Inst, 66-68. *Concurrent Pos:* Mem, Toxicol Study Sect, NIH, 77-81. *Mem:* Am Chem Soc; Am Soc Biol Chemists; Soc Toxicol; Am Soc Pharm Exp Therapeut. *Res:* Biochemical mechanisms for toxicity; drug metabolism and pharmacokinetics; synthesis of radioactive compounds; fate of chemicals in the environment; heavy metal toxicity; biochemistry of fishes. *Mailing Add:* Dept Agr Chem Ore State Univ Agr & Life Sci 1107 Corvallis OR 97331-7301. *Fax:* 541-737-0497

BUHR, ROBERT K, METALLURGY. *Current Pos:* RETIRED. *Educ:* McGill Univ, BS, 51. *Prof Exp:* Head, Foundry Sect, Metals Technol Labs, Can Met, 53-89. *Mem:* Fel Am Soc Metals. *Mailing Add:* 7 Tiffany Crescent Kanata ON K2K 1W1 Can

BUHRMAN, ROBERT ALAN, ELECTRON DEVICES, SUPERCONDUCTIVITY. *Current Pos:* From asst prof to prof appl & eng physics, 73-93, assoc dir, Nat Res & Resource Facil, Submicron Struct, 80-83, JOHN ELSON SWEET PROF ENG, CORNELL UNIV, 93- *Personal Data:* b Waynesboro, Pa, Apr 24, 45; m 72, Karen Fimbel; c Kristina, Susannah & John. *Educ:* Johns Hopkins Univ, BES, 67; Cornell Univ, MS, 70, PhD(appl physics), 73. *Concurrent Pos:* Dir, Sch Appl & Eng Physics, 88- *Mem:* Am Phys Soc; fel Mat Res Soc. *Res:* Superconducting quantum devices; low temperature properties of metals; size effects in metals; optical properties of composite materials; high temperature superconductivity; defects states in semiconductors and insulators; nanolithography and nanotechnology; thin film science. *Mailing Add:* Sch Appl & Eng Physics Clark Hall Cornell Univ Ithaca NY 14853. *Fax:* 607-255-7658; *E-Mail:* rab8@cornell.edu

BUHSE, HOWARD EDWARD, JR, ZOOLOGY. *Current Pos:* asst prof biol sci, 65-68, assoc prof, 68-77, PROF BIOL SCI, UNIV ILL, CHICAGO CIRCLE, 77- *Personal Data:* b Chicago, Ill, July 22, 34; m 57; c 3. *Educ:* Grinnell Col, AB, 57; Univ Iowa, MS, 60, PhD(zool), 63. *Prof Exp:* Res fel microbiol, State Univ NY Upstate Med Ctr, 63-65. *Concurrent Pos:* NIH fel, 63-65; NSF develop biol grant, 67-69. *Mem:* Soc Protozool; Sigma Xi. *Res:* Morphogenesis in the ciliated protozoa. *Mailing Add:* 1524 Thornwood Dr Downers Grove IL 60516

BUHSMER, CHARLES P, CERAMICS, PHYSICAL CHEMISTRY. *Current Pos:* OWNER & PRES, BUFFALO BATT & FELT CORP, 83- *Personal Data:* b Wilkes-Barre, Pa, Sept 4, 37; m 65, Annette Unfried; c 2. *Educ:* Kings Col, Pa, BS, 59; Pa State Univ, MS, 62; State Univ NY Col Ceramics, Alfred, PhD(ceramic sci), 68. *Honors & Awards:* Medal, Am Chem Soc, 59. *Prof Exp:* Res scientist, Airco-Speer Res Labs, Niagara Falls, 62-64, 67-70, mgr carbon & graphite res, 70-71; assoc scientist, Dexter Hysol, 71-73; new venture mgr, Horizons Res Inc, 73-75; dir, Abrasivee Tech Ctr, Carborundum Co, 76-83. *Mem:* Am Ceramic Soc; NY Acad Sci; Am Chem Soc. *Res:* Kinetics of solid state reactions; diffusion in the solid state; high temperature composite materials; thick film microelectronics; carbon and graphite; abrasive components and systems. *Mailing Add:* 46 Olde Stone Lane Lancaster NY 14086

BUI, ANTON, MATHEMATICAL ANALYSIS. *Current Pos:* assoc prof, 67-71, PROF MATH, UNIV BC, 71- *Personal Data:* b Hanoi, Vietnam, Jan 23, 37; m 63; c 3. *Educ:* Saigon Univ, BSc, 59; Mass Inst Technol, PhD(math), 64. *Prof Exp:* Res staff mathematician, Yale Univ, 63-64; vis asst prof, Math Res Ctr, Univ Wis, 64-65; Nat Res Coun Can fel, 65-66; asst prof math, Univ Montreal, 66-67. *Mem:* Can Math Cong. *Res:* Partial differential equations. *Mailing Add:* Dept Math 121 1984 Mathematics Rd Vancouver BC V6T 1Z2 Can

BUI, TIEN DAI, COMPUTER SCIENCE. *Current Pos:* from asst prof to assoc prof, 74-85, chmn, 86-90, PROF COMPUT SCI, CONCORDIA UNIV, 85-, ASSOC VRECTOR ACAD, 92- *Personal Data:* b Bac Ninh, Vietnam, Mar 22, 45; Can citizen; m 69, Thuy; c Don, Helen & Dan. *Educ:* Univ Saigon, BSc, 64; Univ Ottawa, BASc, 69; Carleton Univ, MEng, 69; York Univ, PhD(space sci), 71. *Prof Exp:* Res engr, Inst Aerospace Studies, Univ Toronto, 68-69; res assoc & asst prof lasers & comput, Dept Mech Eng, McGill Univ, 71-74. *Concurrent Pos:* Prof Asn Res & Develop Fund assoc, McGill Univ, 71-74; vis prof, Inst Appln Calcolo, Romo, 78-79, Univ Calif Berkeley, 83-84. *Mem:* Brit Inst Physics; Soc Comput Simul; Asn Comput Mach; Soc Indust Appl Math; Am Math Soc. *Res:* Computational methods for analysis of complex systems, numerical modeling; optimization and simulation of various physical phenomena; numerical analysis; large scale scientific computation. *Mailing Add:* Dept Comput Sci Concordia Univ 1455 De Maisonneuve St W Montreal PQ H3G 1M8 Can. *Fax:* 514-848-4504; *E-Mail:* bui@cs.concordia.ca

BUI, TIEN RUNG, CONTROL SYSTEMS. *Current Pos:* CHAIR PROF, NATURAL SCI & ENG-RES COUN CAN, ALCAN, 90- *Personal Data:* b Hanoi, Vietnam, Feb 18, 35; Can citizen; m 80, Tuan Pham; c Huy, Tiu, Beba, Betu & Kim. *Educ:* Ecole Navale, Brest, France, Eng, 56; Naval Postgrad Sch, PhD, 64. *Prof Exp:* Prof eng, Naval Acad, Nhatrang, Vietnam, 64-67 & Nat Tech Ctr, Saigon, Vietnam, 67-70; rep, Econ Comn Asia & Far East, Bangkok, Thailand, 70-74; prof eng, Univ Que, 75-90. *Concurrent Pos:* Louis Beauchamp sci res award, Que, 90. *Mem:* Metall Soc; Sigma Xi; Inst Elec & Electronics Engrs; Can Inst Mining & Metall. *Res:* Mathematical modeling of industrial thermophysical processes; industrial process control. *Mailing Add:* Dept Appl Sci Univ Que Chicoutimi PQ G7H 2B1 Can. *E-Mail:* rtbui@uqac.uquebec.ca; Internet Home Page: http://dsaing.uquc.uquebec.ca/chip

BUICK, FRED, JR, PHYSIOLOGY, MEDICAL SCIENCE. *Current Pos:* DEFENSE SCIENTIST AEROSPACE PHYSIOL, DEFENSE & CIVIL INST ENVIRON MED, NORTH YORK, ONT, 83- *Personal Data:* b July 16, 51. *Educ:* York Univ, Toronto, BS, 74, MS, 79; McMaster Univ, Ont, PhD(med sci), 85. *Hon Degrees:* Dr, State Sci Res Inst Aerospace Med, Russia, 95. *Honors & Awards:* Eric J Liljencrantz Award, Aerospace Med Asn, 93. *Concurrent Pos:* Proj officer aerospace med, life support & aircrew syst, Air Stand Coord Comt, Washington, 84-; mem, Adv Group Aerospace Res & Develop NATO, Paris, 88-91; adj mem fac, Grad Prog Excercise & Health Sci, York Univ, 88-, Grad Prog Community Health, Univ Toronto, 92- *Mem:* Aerospace Med Asn. *Res:* Physiology of hypoxia and altitude life support equipment; chemical defense protection; physiological responses to high G-forces; human factors in CF-18 pilot environment. *Mailing Add:* Defense Civil Inst Environ Med PO Box 2000 1133 Sheppard Ave W North York ON M3M 3B9 Can

BUICK, RONALD N, medical research, cancer research; deceased, see previous edition for last biography

BUIE, BENNETT FRANK, economic geology; deceased, see previous edition for last biography

BUIKEMA, ARTHUR L, JR, AQUATIC TOXICOLOGY, ECOLOGY. *Current Pos:* from asst to assoc prof, 71-80, asst dir, Univ Ctr Environ Studies, 78-83, PROF ZOOL, VA POLYTECH INST & STATE UNIV, 80- *Personal Data:* b Evergreen Park, Ill, Feb 4, 41; m 92, Alison Galway; c Ami, Jill, Jane, Eric, Matthew, Sarah, Rachel, Andrew, Arthur III, David & Jessie. *Educ:* Elmhurst Col, BS, 62; Univ Kans, MA, 65, PhD(zool), 70. *Honors & Awards:* G Burke Johnson "Renaissance Man" Award. *Prof Exp:* Asst prof biol, St Olaf Col, 67-71. *Concurrent Pos:* Sr ecologist, Ecol Soc Am. *Mem:* Am Soc Environ Toxicol & Chem; Ecol Soc Am; NAm Benthol Soc. *Res:* Pollution biology; ecology and physiology of invertebrates; bioassay technique development; environmental physiology. *Mailing Add:* Dept Biol Va Polytech Inst Blacksburg VA 24061-0406. *Fax:* 540-231-9307

BUIKSTRA, JANE ELLEN, BIOLOGICAL ANTHROPOLOGY, ARCHAEOLOGY. *Current Pos:* DISTINGUISHED PROF ANTHROP, UNIV NMEX, 95- *Personal Data:* b Evansville, Ind, Nov 2, 45. *Educ:* DePauw Univ, BA, 67; Univ Chicago, MA, 69, PhD(anthrop), 72. *Honors & Awards:* Nat Asn Stud Anthropologists, Serv Award, Am Anthrop Asn, 91; 20th Ann Mildred Trotter Lectr, Wash Univ, 96. *Prof Exp:* Teaching asst, Dept Anthrop, Univ Chicago, 68-69, prof, 86-95, Harold H Swift distinguished serv prof anthrop, 89-95, res assoc, 95-; from instr to prof anthrop, Northwestern Univ, Evanston, 70-86, assoc dean, Col Arts & Sci, 81-84. *Concurrent Pos:* NIH bio-med sci res grant, Northwestern Univ, 71; NSF res grants, 74-76, 77-79, 83-85, 88-89, 90-97; bd dirs, Ill Archaeol Surv, 75-79, Soc Prof Archaeologists, 76, Found Ill Archaeol/Ctr Am Archaeol, 80-, Archaeol Caonserv, 86-91; Wenner-Gren Found grant, 78-79 & 83; assoc ed, Am J Phys Anthrop, 78-81, 91-; res assoc, Field Mus Natural Hist, 81-86, 93-98, Mus Am Indian, 83-86; resident scholar, Sch Am Res, 84-85; adj prof anthrop, Wash Univ, 86-; Nat Geog Soc grant, 86-89; Nat Endowment humanities, 87-89. *Mem:* Nat Acad Sci; Am Anthrop Asn (pres, 89-91); Am Asn Phys Anthropologists (secy-treas, 81-85, pres, 85-87); fel Am Acad Forensic Sci; Soc Prof Archaeologists; fel AAAS; Sigma Xi; Soc Am Archaeol; Soc Archaeol Sci; Paleopath Asn; Soc Latin Am Bioanthropolgists. *Res:* Intensive regional approach to the study of prehistoric skeletal populations emphasizing micro-evolutionary change and biological response to environmental stress; bone microstructure; author of numerous technical publications. *Mailing Add:* Dept Anthrop Univ NMex Albuquerque NM 87131-1086

BUIS, OTTO J, GEOLOGY, GEOPHYSICS. *Current Pos:* PRES & CHIEF EXEC OFFICER, POZO RESOURCES, INC, 90- *Personal Data:* b St Joseph, Mo, June 9, 31; m, Lavonne Mayhugh; c Al, Chris, Marie & Julie. *Educ:* Southwestern La Inst, BS, 53; La State Univ, MS; 58. *Prof Exp:* Geophysicist, La Oil Explor Co, 53-54; dist geologist, Texaco Inc, Houston & Bogota, Colombia, 59-68; vpres & bd dir, Shenandoah Oil Corp, Ft Worth & Quito, Ecuador, 68-79; pres & bd dir, OKC Corp, 79-81 & CBK Assoc, 81-89; pres & chief exec officer, MSR Explor Ltd, 89-90. *Mem:* Ecuadorian Geol & Geophys Soc (founder & pres, 69); Colombian Soc Geologists & Geophysicists (pres, 67); Am Asn Petrol Geologists; fel Geol Soc Am. *Mailing Add:* 3800 Encanto Dr Ft Worth TX 76109. *Fax:* 817-877-1709

BUIS, PATRICIA FRANCES, coal geochemistry, bioremediation, for more information see previous edition

BUIST, A(LINE) SONIA, PULMONARY EPIDEMIOLOGY. *Current Pos:* PROF MED & HEAD, PULMONARY & CRITICAL CARE DIV, ORE HEALTH SCI UNIV, 66- *Personal Data:* b June 27, 40; m, Neil R; c Catrina, Alison & Diana. *Educ:* Univ St Andrews, Scotland, MD, 64; McGill Univ, Montreal, dipl epidemiol & biostatist, 78. *Mem:* Am Thoracic Soc (pres); Am Physiol Soc; Am Fedn Clin Res; Am Col Epidemiol. *Res:* Pulmonary epidemiology with major emphasis on asthma and tobacco-related disorders. *Mailing Add:* Dept Med & Physiol MCL334A Ore Health Sci Univ 3181 SW Sam Jackson Park Rd Portland OR 97201. *Fax:* 503-494-5407; *E-Mail:* buists@ohsu.edu

BUIST, NEIL R M, AMINO ACID DISORDERS, MUSCLE DISEASES. *Current Pos:* assoc prof, 70-76, PROF PEDIAT & MED GENETICS, ORE HEALTH SCI UNIV, 76- *Personal Data:* b Karachi, India, July 11, 32; UK citizen; c 3. *Educ:* Univ St Andrews, Scotland, MB & ChB, 56; Inst Child Health, London, DCH, 60; Royal Col Physicians, Edinburgh, MRCPE, 61; FRCP(Edinburgh), 77. *Prof Exp:* House officer internal med, St Andrews Univ, 56-57, resident, 60-62, lectr child health, 62-64; fel metab, Med Sch, Univ Colo, 64-66; asst prof pediat, Med Sch, Univ Ore, 66-70. *Concurrent Pos:* House officer pediat, Royal Hosp Sick Children, Edinburgh, 57; vis scientist, Univ Montreal, 77-78; overseas adv, Soc Study Inborn Errors of Metab, 76-; ed, Kellys Pract Pediat, 80-; travelling pediatrician, Int relief work with Refugees, Kampuchea, 80, Ethiopia & Sudan, 85. *Mem:* Soc Inherited Metab Dis (treas, 78-); Soc Study Inborn Errors of Metab; Soc Pediat Res;

Am Pediat Soc; Brit Med Asn. *Res:* Recognition, diagnosis, evaluation and treatment of inherited or acquired metabolic diseases; pediatrics; metabolism; inborn errors of metabolism. *Mailing Add:* Biochem Genetics Lab Ore Health Sci Univ 3181 SW Sam Jackson Park Rd Portland OR 97201-3098

BUITING, FRANCIS P, ELECTRONICS ENGINEERING, INDUSTRIAL CONTROLS. *Current Pos:* RETIRED. *Personal Data:* b Belfeld, Neth, Jan 25, 24; nat US; m 52; c 3. *Educ:* Technol Univ Delft, Engr, 52. *Prof Exp:* Engr, Philips Telecommun Indust, Neth, 50-55, dept chief elec mech & instrumentation, 55-56; proj engr, AMP, Inc, Pa, 56-58; prin engr, Fenwal, Inc, Mass, 58-60, chief develop engr, 60-61, chief electronics engr, 61-64; mgr res & develop, Metals & Controls Inc, Div Tex Instruments, Inc, 64-69; vpres & gen mgr, Matrix Res & Develop Corp, 69-71; vpres & gen mgr, Europe for Transitron Electronic Corp, 72-75 & Transitron Electronics Corp, 75-77; vpres & gen mgr, Com Prod Sparton Electronics Div, Sparton Corp, 77-80; vpres bus planning & res & develop, Thomas & Betts Corp, 80-, vpres Europe, Thomas & Betts Int. *Mem:* Inst Elec & Electronics Engrs; Neth Royal Inst Eng. *Res:* Development and design of automatic test equipment; development of temperature monitoring, indicating and control equipment; infrared sensing and flame and explosion protection equipment; aerospace power supplies; semiconductor manufacturing; electronic sensing systems; interconnect systems. *Mailing Add:* 15 Mountain Spring Dr Hendersonville NC 28739

BUJAKE, JOHN EDWARD, JR, PHYSICAL CHEMISTRY, FOOD SCIENCE. *Current Pos:* VPRES RES & DEVELOP, BROWN-FORMAN BEVERAGE CO, 87- *Personal Data:* b New York, NY, May 23, 33; m 64, Gail Cruise; c John III, Laura, Jacquelyn & William. *Educ:* Manhattan Col, BS, 54; Col Holy Cross, MS, 55; Columbia Univ, PhD(phys chem), 59; NY Univ, MBA, 63. *Prof Exp:* Res assoc phys chem & new prod develop, Lever Brothers Co, NY, 59-68; develop assoc, Foods Div, Coca-Cola Co, 68-69, mgr tech serv, 69-71, dir, Res & Develop, 71-72; dir res & develop technol, Quaker Oats Co, 72-75, dir res & develop, Foods Div, 75-77; dir, Seven Up Co, 77-78, vpres res & develop, 78-87. *Mem:* Am Chem Soc; Inst Food Technol; Indust Res Inst; Int Soc Beverage Technologists. *Res:* Alcoholic beverages, soft drinks, cereal, citrus, coffee, frozen foods, baked goods, snack protein food product development; processing and packaging; colloid chemistry; rheology, reaction kinetics. *Mailing Add:* Brown Forman Beverage Co PO Box 1080 Louisville KY 40201-1080

BUJARSKI, JOZEF JULIAN, PLANT RNA VIRUSES. *Current Pos:* PROF MOLECULAR VIROL, BIOL SCI/PLANT MOLECULAR BIOL CTR, NORTHERN ILL UNIV, 94- *Personal Data:* b Poznan, Poland, Mar 19, 48. *Educ:* Adam Mickiewicz Univ, MS, PhD(bioorg chem), 76. *Concurrent Pos:* Fulbright scholar, Scottish Crop Res Inst, UK, 97. *Res:* Genetic recombination between pea early browning and tobacco rattle tobaviruses. *Mailing Add:* Plant Molecular Biol Ctr Montgomery Hall Northern Ill Univ DeKalb IL 60115

BUKACEK, RICHARD F, CHEMICAL ENGINEERING. *Current Pos:* CONSULT, 87- *Personal Data:* b Cedar Rapids, Iowa, Nov 3, 27; m 52; c 7. *Educ:* Univ Iowa, BS, 49; Ill Inst Technol, MS & MGasTechnol, 51, PhD(chem eng), 60. *Prof Exp:* Engr, North Shore Gas Co, 51-52; res supvr, Inst Gas Technol, Ill Inst Technol, 53-57, instr chem eng, 57-60; asst prof, 60-62; sr engr, Air Prod & Chem, Inc, 62-63; chmn educ prog, Inst Gas Technol, Ill Inst Technol, 63-65, adj assoc prof gas technol & dir educ, 65-87. *Mem:* Am Inst Chem Engrs. *Res:* Fluid mechanics; thermodynamics; systems analysis. *Mailing Add:* 9235 S Winchester Ave Chicago IL 60620

BUKANTZ, SAMUEL CHARLES, CLINICAL MEDICINE. *Current Pos:* PROF MED, UNIV SFLA, 72- *Personal Data:* b New York, NY, Sept 12, 11; m 41; c 2. *Educ:* NY Univ, BS, 30, MD, 34; Am Bd Int Med, dipl; Am Bd Allergy, dipl. *Prof Exp:* From instr to assoc prof med, Sch Med, Wash Univ, 47-54, assoc prof clin med, 54-58, asst dean, Sch Med, 48-54; med & res dir, Jewish Nat Home Asthmatic Children & Children's Asthma Res Inst & Hosp, Denver & assoc prof clin med, Med Ctr, Univ Colo, 58-63; assoc prof clin med, Sch Med, NY Univ, 64-72; chief, 72-84, emer chief sect allergy, med serv, Vet Admin Hosp, Tampa, 84- *Concurrent Pos:* Baruch fel, Harlem Hosp, NY, 38-40; fel allergy, Internal Med Dept, Sch Med, Wash Univ, 46-47; sr attend physician, Jefferson Barracks Vet Hosp, 46-48; chmn res comt, Vet Admin Hosp, St Louis, 52-54, secy dean's comt, 51-54; consult, Beth Israel Hosp, Newark, NJ, 63- & Clara Maass Hosp, Belleville, 63-; assoc dir med res clin invest, Schering Corp, 63-65; assoc vis physician, Bellevue Med Ctr, NY, 64-72; dir dept clin res, Hoffmann-La Roche Inc, NJ, 65-67; ed, Hosp Pract, 69- *Mem:* Am Soc Exp Biol; AMA; fel Am Col Physicians; Am Col Chest Physicians; Am Asn Immunol; fel Am Acad Allergy & Immunol. *Res:* Clinical investigation with new drugs; experimental hyper-sensitive states; pathogenesis and therapy of bronchial asthma; immunochemistry. *Mailing Add:* 4940 W San Rafael St Tampa FL 33629-5435

BUKAVECKAS, PAUL A, ENVIRONMENTAL SCIENCES. *Current Pos:* ASST PROF BIOL, UNIV LOUISVILLE, 93. *Personal Data:* b Decorah, Iowa, Dec 4, 46. *Educ:* DePaul Univ, BS, 81; Ind Univ, PhD, 89. *Prof Exp:* Post doctoral assoc, Inst Ecosyst Studies, 90-93. *Concurrent Pos:* Assoc ed, J Environ Pollution, 94-; grantee, US Geol Sur, 94-96, US Environ Protection Agency, 94-96; Fulbright scholar, Klaipeda Univ, Lithuania, 96-97. *Res:* Ecosystems Ecology; aquatic ecology; ecological effects of pollutants; author of numerous publications in field. *Mailing Add:* Univ Louisville Belknap Campus 139 Life Sci Bldg Louisville KY 40292

BUKER, ROBERT JOSEPH, PLANT BREEDING. *Current Pos:* RETIRED. *Personal Data:* b Vancouver, Wash, June 2, 30; m; c 5. *Educ:* Wash State Univ, BS, 53; Purdue Univ, MS, 59, PhD(plant breeding, genetics), 63. *Prof Exp:* Instr agron, Purdue Univ, 56-61; dir res, Farmers Forge Res Coop, FFR Coop, 61-73, exec vpres & gen mgr, 73-85; res dir & prof, Univ Wyo, Baidoa Somalia, 85-87; plant breeder, Int Prog Agr, Ohio State Univ, Kampala, Uganda, 89-92. *Mem:* Fel Am Soc Agron; Am Forage & Grassland Coun (pres); Nat Coun Com Plant Breeders (pres); Sigma Xi. *Res:* Breeding forage crop varieties; directing forage, turf, soybean and corn breeding programs; improving field plot techniques and equipment. *Mailing Add:* 5808 NW Alki Rd Vancouver WA 98663

BUKO, ALEXANDER MICHAEL, PROTEIN SEQUENCING USING MASS SPECTROMETRY. *Current Pos:* SR RES CHEMIST, ABBOTT LABS, 84- *Personal Data:* b Poughkeepsie, NY, Oct 20, 53; m, Anna White; c Elizabeth, Anna & Andrew. *Educ:* Univ Va, BA, 75, PhD(chem), 80. *Prof Exp:* Staff fel, Bur Biologics, Food & Drug Admin, 80-84. *Concurrent Pos:* Staff instr org chem, Col Lake Co, 89- *Mem:* Am Soc Mass Spectrometry. *Res:* Biopolymers such as carbohydrates and proteins; determine the structure of unknown biopolymers through state-of-the-art analytical biochemical tools. *Mailing Add:* Dept 418 Bldg AP31 One Abbott Park Rd Abbott Park IL 60064. *Fax:* 847-938-9226

BUKOVAC, MARTIN JOHN, HORTICULTURE, PLANT PHYSIOLOGY. *Current Pos:* From res asst to res assoc, 54-57, from asst prof to prof, 57-92, DISTINGUISHED PROF HORT, MICH STATE UNIV, 92- *Personal Data:* b Johnston City, Ill, Nov 12, 29; m 56, Judith A Kelley; c Janice L. *Educ:* Mich State Univ, BS, 51, MS, 54, PhD, 57. *Hon Degrees:* Hon Dr Agri, Univ Bonn, Ger, 95. *Honors & Awards:* Joseph Harvey Gourley Award, Am Soc Hort Sci, 69 & 76, M A Blake Award & Marion W Meadows Award, 75, Carrol R Miller Award, 80 & Outstanding Res Award, 88; Hatch Centennial Medallion, Nat Asn State Univ & Land Grant Col, 87; Dennis R Hoagland Award, Am Soc Plant Physiologists, 88, Humbolot Res Prize, 95. *Concurrent Pos:* Lectr, Japan Atomic Energy Res Inst, Tokyo, 58; adv, Int AEC, Vienna, 61; mem, Subcomt Effect Pesticides Physiol Fruits & Veg, Nat Acad Sci-Nat Res Coun, 64-68; NSF sr fel, Oxford Univ & Univ Bristol, 65-66; Nat Acad Sci exchange visitor, Coun Acad, Yugoslavia, 71; mem, US Nat Comn, Int Union Biol Sci, 71-76, Agr Res Adv Comt, Eli Lilly, 71-88; distinguished vis prof, NMex State Univ, Las Cruces, 76; vis prof, Japan Soc Prom Sci, Univ Osaka, 77 & Univ Guelph, Ont, Can, 82, Ohio State Univ, 90; US rep, Coun Int Soc Hort Sci, 77-78; guest lectr, Polish Acad Sci, Warsaw & Servian Sci Coun, Fruit Res Inst, Cacak, Yugoslavia, 79; guest res, Hort Res Inst, Budapest, Hungary, 83; vis lectr, Inst Hort, Univ Zagreb, Yugoslavia; distinguished lectr, Dept Sci & Technol, Min Agr, Animal Husb & Fisheries, People's Repub China, 84; Humboldt res prize, 95. *Mem:* Nat Acad Sci; fel AAAS; fel Am Soc Hort Sci (pres, 74-75); Am Hort Soc; Am Soc Plant Physiol; Bot Soc Am; Am Chem Soc. *Res:* Plant growth and development; plant growth substances; mechanisms of foliar penetration. *Mailing Add:* Dept Hort 390 PSSB Mich State Univ East Lansing MI 48823. *Fax:* 517-353-0890; *E-Mail:* bukovacm@pilot.msu.edu

BUKOVSAN, LAURA A, GENETICS, MICROBIOLOGY. *Current Pos:* from asst prof to assoc prof, 80-90, PROF MICROBIOL, STATE UNIV NY, ONEONTA, 90- *Personal Data:* b Norfolk, Va, Jan 2, 40; m 64; c 2. *Educ:* Univ Richmond, BS, 61; Ind Univ, MA, 63, PhD(genetics), 69. *Prof Exp:* Teaching asst zool, Ind Univ, 62-63; lectr genetics, State Univ NY, Oneota, 74-78; lectr biol, Hartwick Col, 78-80. *Mem:* Genetics Soc Am; AAAS; Am Soc Microbiol; Soc Protozoologists. *Res:* Cytology of conjugation in Tokophrya lemnarum; genetics of mating type inheritance in the suctorian Tokophrya lemnarum; biology of aging in Tokophrya lemnarum. *Mailing Add:* One Hyatt St Otego NY 13825

BUKOVSAN, WILLIAM, ENDOCRINOLOGY. *Current Pos:* PROF BIOL, STATE UNIV NY COL ONEONTA, 67- *Personal Data:* b Chicago, Ill, June 4, 29; m 64; c 2. *Educ:* Univ Ill, BS, 54, MS, 58; Ind Univ, PhD(zool), 67. *Mem:* AAAS; Am Soc Zool; NY Acad Sci; Sigma Xi. *Res:* Adrenal phosphorus metabolism of the newly hatched chick. *Mailing Add:* One Hyatt St Otego NY 13825

BUKOWIECKI, LUDWIK J, PHYSIOLOGY, BIOCHEMSTRY. *Current Pos:* PROF CELL BIOLOGY, LAVAL UNIV FAC MED SCH, 76- *Personal Data:* b Poland, June 10, 41. *Educ:* Univ Brussels, BS, 62, MS, 64; Univ Ottowa, PhD(biochem), 72. *Prof Exp:* Fel, Gren Inst Biochem, Univ Stockholm, 73-74, Ctr Endocrinol, Metab & Nutrit, Northwestern Univ-Chicago Med Sch, 74-76. *Mem:* Am Physiol Soc; Endocrine Soc. *Mailing Add:* Dept Physiol Laval Univ Fac Med Sch Quebec City PQ G1K 7P4 Can

BUKOWINSKI, MARK S T, MINERAL PHYSICS AT HIGH PRESSURES, STRUCTURE OF THE EARTH AND ITS EVOLUTION. *Current Pos:* from asst prof to assoc prof, 78-89, PROF GEOPHYS, UNIV CALIF, BERKELEY, 89- *Personal Data:* b Trani, Italy, Oct 17, 46; m 70, Halina V Mudy; c Katherine, Anna, John & Christopher. *Educ:* Univ Calif, Los Angeles, BS, 69, PhD(physics), 75. *Prof Exp:* Asst res geophysicist, Univ Calif, Los Angeles, 75-78. *Concurrent Pos:* Mem, Mineral Physicist Comt, Am Geophys Union, 88-90, assoc ed, J Geophys Res, 88-91, chair, Theoret Equation State Working Group, 88; prin investr, numerous NSF res grants; mem, Publ Comt, Mineral Soc Am, 88-92, chmn, 91-92; vis prof geol sci, Va Polytechnic Inst & State Univ, 89-90. *Mem:* Am Geophys Union; Am Mineral Soc; AAAS; fel Mineral Soc Am. *Res:* Theoretical investigations of mineral stability and properties under extreme pressure and temperature conditions inside planets; developed methods for accurate theoretical predictions of mineral structures, bonding and thermodynamic properties, and how these might affect planetary properties. *Mailing Add:* Dept Geol & Geophys Univ Calif Berkeley CA 94720. *Fax:* 510-643-9980; *E-Mail:* markb@garnet.berkeley.edu

BUKOWSKI, JULIA VICTORIA, SYSTEMS RELIABILITY. *Current Pos:* ASSOC PROF ELEC & COMPUT ENG, VILLANOVA UNIV, 85- *Personal Data:* b Philadelphia, Pa, Jan 24, 53; m, Lawrence Eisenberg; c Seth & Adam. *Educ:* Univ Pa, BS, 74, PhD(systs eng), 79; Imp Col Sci & Technol, DIC, 75. *Prof Exp:* Asst prof systs eng, Univ Pa, 79-85. *Concurrent Pos:* Consult, Naval Air Develop Ctr, 82-84; Fulbright sr lectr, US Govt, 92-93; vis assoc prof indust eng, Techion Israel Inst Technol, 92-93; adj assoc prof systs, Univ Pa, 94-96. *Res:* Hardware, software and network reliability. *Mailing Add:* Dept Elec & Comput Eng Villanova Univ Villanova PA 19085. *Fax:* 610-519-4336; *E-Mail:* bukowski@vu.vlsi.ee.vill.edu

BUKOWSKI, RICHARD WILLIAM, FIRE PROTECTION ENGINEERING. *Current Pos:* res engr, Nat Bur Stand, 75-80, head hazard anal, 80-89, MGR TECHNOL TRANSFER, CTR FIRE RES, NAT INST STAND & TECHNOL 89- *Personal Data:* b Chicago, Ill, July 4, 47; m 68; c 1. *Educ:* Ill Inst Technol, BS, 70. *Honors & Awards:* Silver Medal, Dept Com, 90. *Prof Exp:* Sr proj engr, Underwriters Labs, Inc, 70-75. *Mem:* Soc Fire Protection Engrs; Int Asn Fire Safety Sci; Nat Fire Protection Asn. *Res:* Assessment of the hazards to building occupants from fires. *Mailing Add:* 20135 Laurel Hill Way Germantown MD 20874

BUKREY, RICHARD ROBERT, SOLID STATE PHYSICS. *Current Pos:* Asst prof, 72-76, chmn dept 76-85, ASSOC PROF PHYSICS, LOYOLA UNIV, 76- *Personal Data:* b St Paul, Minn, June 26, 41; m 64; c 2. *Educ:* St Mary's Col, Minn, BA, 63; Marquette Univ, MS, 65; Wayne State Univ, PhD(physics), 72. *Concurrent Pos:* Undergrad res partic prog dir, NSF, 76-77, instrnl sci equip prog proj dir, 77-79. *Mem:* Am Phys Soc. *Res:* Structure and properties of amorphus magnetic materials, studies by Mossbauer effect; x-ray diffraction; magnetic susceptibility; electron spin resonance. *Mailing Add:* Dept Physics Loyola Univ 6525 N Sheridan Rd Chicago IL 60626. *Fax:* 773-508-3534

BUKRY, JOHN DAVID, MICROPALEONTOLOGY. *Current Pos:* geologist, US Geol Surv, La Jolla, 67-84, geologist, US Minerals Mgt Serv, 84-86, GEOLOGIST, US GEOL SURV, MENLO PARK, 86- *Personal Data:* b Baltimore, Md, May 17, 41. *Educ:* Johns Hopkins Univ, AB, 63; Princeton Univ, AM, 65, PhD(geol), 67. *Prof Exp:* Geologist, US Army CEngr, 63; res asst micropaleont, Socony-Mobil Oil Co, 65. *Concurrent Pos:* Biostratig consult, Deep Sea Drilling Proj, 68-87; res assoc, Scripps Inst Oceanog, 70-; ed, Marine Micropaleont, 76-83, Micropaleont, 85-90. *Mem:* Fel AAAS; fel Geol Soc Am; Am Asn Petrol Geologists; fel Explorers Club; Sigma Xi; Int Nannoplankton Asn. *Res:* Phytoplankton micropaleontology and ocean stratigraphy; evolutionary trends, paleoecology, and taxonomy of calcareous nannoplankton and silicoflagellates (300 new species described). *Mailing Add:* Res Assoc & Res Geol Scripps Inst Oceanography Univ Calif San Diego 0231 9500 Gilmar Dr La Jolla CA 92093-0231

BULA, RAYMOND J, PLANT PHYSIOLOGY, ECOLOGY & SPACE BIOLOGY. *Current Pos:* SR SCIENTIST & EXEC DIR, WIS CTR SPACE AUTOMATION & ROBOTICS, UNIV WIS-MADISON, 86- *Personal Data:* b Antigo, Wis, Aug 3, 27; m 52; c 8. *Educ:* Univ Wis, BS, 49, MS, 50, PhD(agron, bot), 52. *Prof Exp:* Asst prof, seed analyst & agronomist, NY Agr Exp Sta, Geneva, 52-53; agronomist, Agr Res Serv, Agr Exp Sta, USDA, Alaska, 53-56 & Crops Res Div, Purdue Univ, 56-74; area dir, Agr Res Serv, USDA, 74-79, dir, US Dairy Forage Res Ctr, Agr Res Serv, Univ Wis-Madison, 79-84; dir res, Phytofarms Am, Dekalb, Ill, 84-86. *Mem:* Fel AAAS; fel Crop Sci Soc Am; fel Am Soc Agron; Am Soc Plant Physiol; Am Soc Space & Gravitation Biol; Inst Aeronaut & Astronaut. *Res:* Forage crop production; weed control; physiology of cold resistance; forage crop physiology; influence of environment on genetic stability and plant growth and development; controlled environment growth of plants; hydroponics; space biology. *Mailing Add:* 7872 Deer Run Rd Cross Plains WI 53528. *Fax:* 608-262-9458; *E-Mail:* bula@engr.wise.edu

BULANI, WALTER, PHYSICAL CHEMISTRY, CHEMICAL ENGINEERING. *Current Pos:* RETIRED. *Personal Data:* b Sask, July 7, 28; m 51; c 5. *Educ:* Univ Sask, BScChEng, 49, MSc, 50; McGill Univ, PhD(phys chem), 55. *Prof Exp:* Res officer chem, Can Chem Co, 55-56 & E I du Pont de Nemours & Co, Inc, 56-59; asst prof eng sci, Univ Western Ont, 59-64, from assoc prof to prof chem eng, 64-87, chmn dept, 64-70. *Concurrent Pos:* Mem, Air Pollution Comt, Can Stand Asn, 70-; secy, treas & vchmn develop, Can Nat Comt, Int Asn Water Pollution Res & Control, 72-84. *Mem:* Am Inst Chem Engrs; Chem Inst Can; Can Soc Chem Engrs; Am Soc Eng Educ; NY Acad Sci; Can Asn Water Pollution Res & Control (pres, 85-); Int Asn Water Pollution Res & Control. *Res:* Wastewater treatment; fluidization; froth flotation; mineral recovery from oil-sand tailings. *Mailing Add:* 22 Regency Rd London ON N6H 4A8 Can

BULAS, ROMUALD, PHYSICAL CHEMISTRY. *Current Pos:* RES ASSOC, CENT RES LABS, BASF CORP, CLIFTON, 51- *Personal Data:* b Chabno, Russia, Feb 2, 22; US citizen; m 50; c 3. *Educ:* Univ Heidelburg, BS, 49; Polytech Inst Brooklyn, MS, 63. *Mem:* Am Chem Soc; Soc Rheology. *Res:* Colloid chemistry; rheology; mass spectrometry. *Mailing Add:* 388 Beechspring Rd South Orange NJ 07079

BULGER, ROGER JAMES, INFECTIOUS DISEASES, INTERNAL MEDICINE. *Current Pos:* PRES & CHIEF EXEC OFFICER, ASN ACAD HEALTH CTRS, 88- *Personal Data:* b New York, NY, May 18, 33; m 60; c 2. *Educ:* Harvard Univ, AB, 55, MD, 60. *Hon Degrees:* LHD, Thomas Jefferson Univ, 95, Univ Md, 96. *Prof Exp:* From asst prof to assoc prof med, Sch Med, Univ Wash, 66-70; prof community health sci & assoc dean, Sch Med, Duke Univ, 70-72; exec officer health policy, Inst Med, Nat Acad Sci, 72-76; chancellor-dean med, Univ Mass Med Ctr, 76-78; pres, Health Sci Ctr, Univ Tex, 78-88. *Concurrent Pos:* Clin investr, US Vet Admin, 67-; mem adv comt, Allied Health Prof, NC State Bd Educ & Higher Educ, 70-71; mem consortium bd, NC Health Manpower Develop Comt, 70-71; consult, Inst Human Values Med, 72-74; mem adv panel, Nat Health Insurance, Subcomt Health, Comt & Means, US House Rep, 75-76; Burroughs-Welcome vis prof; clin investr, US Vet Admin. *Mem:* Inst Med-Nat Acad Sci; Am Soc Microbiol; Am Soc Nephrology; Infectious Dis Soc Am; fel Am Col Physicians; distinguished fel Asn health Serv Res (pres, 93-94). *Res:* Clinical pharmacology; antibiotics; bacterial resistance; hospital epidemiology and clinical infectious disease; health and science policy. *Mailing Add:* 1400 16th St NW Suite 410 Washington DC 20036

BULGER, RUTH ELLEN, ANATOMY, PATHOLOGY. *Current Pos:* DIR, DIV HEALTH SCI POLICY, INST MED-NAT ACAD SCI, 88- *Personal Data:* b Kansas City, Mo, 36; m 60; c 2. *Educ:* Vassar Col, AB, 58; Radcliffe Col, AM, 59; Univ Wash, PhD(anat), 62. *Honors & Awards:* Minnie Stevens Piper Award, 85; John Freeman Award, 85. *Prof Exp:* Asst prof path, Med Sch, Univ Wash, 67-70; assoc prof anat, Univ NC, 70-72; from assoc prof to prof, Univ Md, Baltimore City, 72-76; prof path, Med Sch, Univ Mass, 76-77, prof anat, 77-78, chmn dept, 77-78; prof path & lab med, depts neurobiol & anat, Sch Med, Univ Tex Health Sci Ctr Houston, 78-88. *Concurrent Pos:* Fel anat, Harvard Med Sch, 63-64; fel path, Univ Wash, 64-67. *Mem:* Am Soc Nephrology; Fedn Am Soc Exp Path; Electron Micros Soc Am; Int Soc Nephrology; Am Asn Anatomists; Am Soc Cell Biol. *Res:* Kidney morphology and function. *Mailing Add:* Uniformed Serv Univ Health Sci 4301 Jones Bridge Rd Bethesda MD 20814. *Fax:* 202-334-1385

BULGREN, WILLIAM GERALD, computer science, statistics; deceased, see previous edition for last biography

BULGRIN, VERNON CARL, PHYSICAL CHEMISTRY. *Current Pos:* instr, 53-56, from asst prof to prof, 56-85, head dept, 62-67, EMER PROF CHEM, UNIV WYO, 85- *Personal Data:* b Cuyahoga Falls, Ohio, May 10, 23; m 54, Dorothy Littig; c Thomas F & Anne L. *Educ:* Univ Akron, BS, 48; Iowa State Univ, PhD(chem), 53. *Prof Exp:* Asst, Iowa State Univ, 48-53. *Concurrent Pos:* Res Corp grant, 56, 58; vis prof, Purdue Univ, 67-68. *Mem:* Fel AAAS; Am Chem Soc. *Res:* Kinetics of specific oxidation reactions; homogeneous equilibria. *Mailing Add:* 2311 Twin Lakes Dr Uniontown OH 44685-9717

BULICH, ANTHONY ANDREW, MICROBIOLOGY. *Current Pos:* sr develop microbiologist, 76-77, mgr appln develop, 77-81, prin develop microbiologist, 77-86, vpres sci & technol, 86-96, CHIEF OPERATING OFFICER, AZUR ENVIRON CORP, 96- *Personal Data:* b San Pedro, Calif, Feb 16, 44; m 67; c 2. *Educ:* Univ Southern Calif, BA, 66; Iowa State Univ, MS, 68, PhD(microbiol), 72. *Prof Exp:* Res microbiologist, A E Staley Mfg Co, 72-75, sr res microbiologist fermentation res, 75-76. *Mem:* AAAS; Am Soc Microbiol; Soc Indust Microbiol; Am Chem Soc. *Res:* Isolation and characterization of carbohydrase producing microorganism; strain improvement thru genetic manipulation and fermentation optimization; use of luminescent bacteria for environmental monitoring; characterization of thermophilic and acidophilic amylase producing microorganisms. *Mailing Add:* 14019 Mercado Dr Del Mar CA 92014

BULKIN, BERNARD JOSEPH, PHYSICAL & ANALYTICAL CHEMISTRY, FUELS & REFINING. *Current Pos:* mgr, Prod Div, 89-90, head oil technol, 93, DIR, MFG & SUPPLY, CHIEF TECHNOL OFFICER, BRIT PETROL CO, 94- *Personal Data:* b Trenton, NJ, Mar 9, 42; m 66, 75, Susan H Lees; c Anna, Noah & David. *Educ:* Polytech Inst Brooklyn, BS, 62; Purdue Univ, PhD(phys chem), 66. *Honors & Awards:* Coblentz Award, 75; Oscar Foster Award, 78. *Prof Exp:* NSF fel, Swiss Fed Inst Technol, 66-67; from asst prof to prof chem, Hunter Col, 67-75, chmn dept, 73-75; prof & dean arts & sci, Polytech Inst NY, 75-82; vpres, Res & Grad Affairs & dir, Inst Imaging Sci, 82-85; dir, Anal Sci Lab, Stand Oil Co, Ohio, 85-88; dir, Downstream Oil Res & Develop, 88. *Concurrent Pos:* Petrol Res Fund grant, 67-69; Am Cancer Soc res grant, 68-75; Army Res Off-Durham res grant, 69-75; dir, NSF High Sch Inst, 70-71 & NSF Women in Sci career facilitation grant, 76-78; mem, NSF Comt Equal Opportunity Sci & Technol, 83-86; bd dir, Optronics Int, 84-87, Spex Group Inc, 84-88; prin investr, NSF res grant, 84-87, Corn Refiners Asn res grant, 85-86. *Mem:* Soc Appl Spectros; Coblentz Soc (pres, 79-81); Am Chem Soc; fel Royal Soc Chem. *Res:* Oil products and processes. *Mailing Add:* 37 Glenmore Rd London NW3 4DA England. *Fax:* 441-71-496-4970; *E-Mail:* bulkinbj@bp.com

BULKLEY, GEORGE, MEDICINE, UROLOGY. *Current Pos:* Assoc, 51-55, from asst prof to prof, 56-87, EMER PROF UROL, MED SCH, NORTHWESTERN UNIV, 87- *Personal Data:* b Pa, Apr 16, 17; m 41, Patricia Bartlett; c Gregory B, Peter T, Paige & George B. *Educ:* Northwestern Univ, BS, 38, MD, 42. *Concurrent Pos:* From assoc attend to sr attend urologist, Chicago Wesley Mem Hosp, 53-; consult urologist, Passavant Mem Hosp, 70-; sr attend urologist, Northwestern Mem Hosp, 80- *Mem:* AMA; Am Urol Asn; Am Col Surg; Int Soc Urol; Am Asn Genitourinary Surgeons. *Res:* Urologic clinical research; use of radioactive materials in treatment of carcinoma of the prostate. *Mailing Add:* 251 E Chicago Ave Chicago IL 60611. *Fax:* 312-908-0376

BULKLEY, JONATHAN WILLIAM, WATER RESOURCE POLICY, CIVIL ENGINEERING. *Current Pos:* from asst prof to assoc prof nat resources, 68-77, from asst prof to assoc prof civil eng, 68-77, PROF, SCH NAT RESOURCES & COL ENG, UNIV MICH, ANN ARBOR, 77- *Personal Data:* b Kansas City, Mo, May 17, 38; m 62; c 2. *Educ:* Mass Inst Technol, SB(polit sci) & SB(civil eng), 61, SM, 63, PhD(polit sci), 66. *Prof Exp:* Res asst civil eng, Mass Inst Technol, 61-63, instr, 63-66. *Concurrent Pos:* VChmn, Mich Environ Rev Bd, 76-79. *Mem:* Am Soc Civil Engrs; Inst Asn Great Lakes Res; Sigma Xi; Water Pollution Cent Fed. *Res:* Water policy; risk analysis; institutional arrangements; water planning and management. *Mailing Add:* Dept Civil Eng Univ Mich Ann Arbor MI 48109

BULKOWSKI, JOHN EDMUND, CATALYSIS, BIOINORGANIC. *Current Pos:* ASST PROF INORG CHEM, CHEM DEPT, UNIV DEL, 75- *Personal Data:* b Weymouth, Mass, Sept 7, 42; m 66; c 2. *Educ:* Brown Univ, ScB, 65; Carnegie-Mellon Univ, MS, 71, PhD(chem), 74. *Prof Exp:* Officer, USN Nuclear Prog, 65-67; engr, Westinghouse Elec Corp, 67-69; res fel, Harvard Univ, 73-75. *Mem:* Am Chem Soc; Sigma Xi. *Res:* Inorganic and organometallic chemistry: specifically the use of binuclear transition metal compounds as catalysts and biological models; and the use of photosensitive arrays for light assisted catalysis and solar energy conversion. *Mailing Add:* Dept Chem Univ Del Newark DE 19717-0001

BULL, ALICE LOUISE, DEVELOPMENTAL BIOLOGY. *Current Pos:* assoc prof zool, 64-76, from assoc prof to prof biol, 76-90, EMER PROF BIOL, HOLLINS COL, 90- *Personal Data:* b White Plains, NY, May 16, 24. *Educ:* Middlebury Col, AB, 46; Mt Holyoke Col, MA, 48; Yale Univ, PhD(zool), 53. *Prof Exp:* Asst zool, Yale Univ, 48-50; asst, Mt Holyoke Col, 46-48, instr, 53-55; from instr to asst prof, Wellesley Col, 55-64. *Concurrent Pos:* Am Asn Univ Women fel, Univ Zurich, 52-53. *Mem:* AAAS; Genetics Soc Am; Am Soc Zoologists; Soc Develop Biol; Sigma Xi. *Res:* Oogenesis, fertility regulation and developmental genetics in Drosophila; embryogenesis in Mormoniella. *Mailing Add:* Dept Biol Hollins Col PO Box 9633 Roanoke VA 24020

BULL, BRIAN S, PATHOLOGY. *Current Pos:* from asst prof to assoc prof, 68-72, PROF PATH & CHMN DEPT, LOMA LINDA UNIV, 73-, ASSOC DEAN ACAD AFFAIRS, SCH MED. *Personal Data:* b London, Eng, Sept 14, 37; US citizen; m 63, Maureen H Huse; c Beverly V & Beryl H. *Educ:* Walla Walla Col, BS, 57; Loma Linda Univ, MD, 61. *Honors & Awards:* Merk Manual Award, 61; E B Cotlove Mem lectr, 72. *Prof Exp:* Intern, Grace New Haven Med Ctr, 61-62, resident, 62-63; resident, NIH, 63-65, staff hematologist, 66-67. *Concurrent Pos:* Fel lab med, NIH, 65-66, spec fel hemat, Nat Inst Arthritis & Metab Dis, 67-68; vis prof, Inst Cellular Path, Paris, 72, Royal Postgrad Med Sch, London, 72, Univ Wis-Madison, 73, Univ Ohio, Columbus, 74, Univ Minn, Minneapolis, 79, Univ Hawaii, Honolulu, 81, St Thomas Hosp & Med Sch, Londen, 81, Mayo Clin & Med Sch, Rochester, Minn, 85; ed-in-chief, Blood Cells, 85- *Mem:* Am Soc Clin Path; AMA; Soc Acad Clin Lab Physicians & Scientists; Col Am Path; Am Soc Hemat. *Res:* Physiology of blood cells, particularly erythrocytes and platelets; clinical laboratory test development and automation; quality control of clinical laboratory tests. *Mailing Add:* Dept Path & Human Anat Loma Linda Univ Med Ctr Loma Linda CA 92354-2870. *Fax:* 909-824-4189

BULL, COLIN BRUCE BRADLEY, GEOPHYSICS, GLACIOLOGY. *Current Pos:* vis asst prof, Ohio State Univ, 61-62, assoc prof, 62-65, dir inst polar studies, 65-69, chmn dept geol, 69-72, dean col math & phys sci, 72-85, PROF GEOL, OHIO STATE UNIV, 65-, EDUC & SCI CONSULT, 85- *Personal Data:* b Birmingham, Eng, June 13, 28; m 56; c 3. *Educ:* Univ Birmingham, BS, 48, PhD(physics), 51. *Honors & Awards:* Polar Medal, 55; Antarctic Serv Award, US Cong, 74. *Prof Exp:* Geophysicist, Cambridge Univ, 52-55; Imp Chem Industs res fel geophys, Univ Birmingham, 55-56; sr lectr physics, Victoria Univ, NZ, 56-61. *Concurrent Pos:* Geophysicist & chief scientist, Brit N Greenland Exped, 52-55; mem, Ross Dependency Res Comt, NZ Govt, 59-61; mem panels glaciol, geol & geophys & comt polar res, Nat Acad Sci; US rep, Sci Comt Antarctic Res, 78; consult & lectr, Antarctic Peninsula Area, Abercrombie & Kent, 92- *Mem:* Am Geophys Union; Arctic Inst NAm; Glaciol Soc; Geol Soc Am; Royal Soc Arts. *Res:* Geophysical and glaciological investigations in polar regions, particularly Greenland and Antarctica. *Mailing Add:* PO Box 4675 Rollingbay WA 98061-0675

BULL, DANIEL NEWELL, CHEMICAL ENGINEERING. *Current Pos:* DIR ENG, HENDERSON INDUSTS, WEST CALDWELL, NJ, 90- *Personal Data:* b Highland Park, Mich, July 5, 39; m 67. *Educ:* Univ Mich, BSE, 62, MSE, 64, PhD(chem eng), 68. *Prof Exp:* Res chem engr, Continental Oil Co, Okla, 69-71; sr chem engr, Hoffmann-La Roche Inc, 71-77, res chem engr, 77-80; vpres & tech dir, New Brunswick Sci Co, 80-82; pres, Sartori Corp, NJ, 82-90. *Res:* Mass transfer; fermentation kinetics; hydrocarbon dermentations; continuous fermentations; separation of biologicals; tissue culture. *Mailing Add:* 403 N Fullerton Ave Montclair NJ 07043-2231

BULL, DON LEE, ENTOMOLOGY. *Current Pos:* RES ENTOMOLOGIST TOXICOL, AGR RES SERV, USDA, 61- *Personal Data:* b Raymondville, Tex, Sept 3, 29; m 54, Betty A Moore; c Constance D (Spjut). *Educ:* Tex A&M Univ, BS, 53, MS, 60, PhD(entom), 62. *Prof Exp:* Analyst, Amoco Chem Corp, 56-57 & Shell Chem Co, 57-58. *Mem:* Entom Soc Am; Am Chem Soc. *Res:* Insect toxicology and physiology. *Mailing Add:* 10523 Normant Dr Houston TX 77070

BULL, EVERETT L, JR, PROGRAMMING LANGUAGE SEMANTICS & VERIFICATION, ALGORITHM ANALYSIS. *Current Pos:* vis asst prof, 78-80, from asst prof to assoc prof, 81-90, PROF MATH, POMONA COL, 90- *Personal Data:* b Stockton, Calif, Aug 12, 49. *Educ:* Pomona Col, BA, 71; Mass Inst Technol, PhD(math), 76. *Prof Exp:* Adj asst prof math, Univ Calif, Los Angeles, 76-78. *Concurrent Pos:* Res fel, Stanford Univ, 80-81; vis assoc prof, Cornell Univ, 85-86. *Mem:* Am Math Soc; Asn Comput Mach; Inst Elec & Electronics Engrs Comput Soc. *Res:* Application of logic to computer science. *Mailing Add:* Dept Math Pomona Col Claremont CA 91711. *E-Mail:* rbull@pomona.claremont.edu

BULL, LEONARD SETH, ANIMAL NUTRITION, PHYSIOLOGY. *Current Pos:* PROF & HEAD, DEPT ANIMAL SCI, UNIV VT, 81- *Personal Data:* b Westfield, Mass, Jan 31, 41; m 71; c 3. *Educ:* Okla State Univ, BSc, 63, MSc, 64; Cornell Univ, PhD(nutrit), 69. *Prof Exp:* NASA fel physiol, Med Sch Univ Va, 68-70; from asst prof to assoc prof, Univ Md, 70-75; assoc prof nutrit, Univ Ky, 75-79; prof nutrit, Univ Maine, 79-81. *Mem:* Am Dairy Sci Asn; Am Soc Animal Sci; Am Reg Prof Animal Sci. *Res:* Animal nutrition with special interest in energy metabolism, digestive physiology and trace element interactions on metabolism; body compositon and animal calorimetry plus regulation of energy balance. *Mailing Add:* Dept Animal Sci NC State Univ Box 7621 Raleigh NC 27695-0001

BULL, RICHARD C, ANIMAL NUTRITION, BIOCHEMISTRY. *Current Pos:* AT TOXICOL & MICROBIOL DIV, ENVIRON PROTECTION AGENCY. *Personal Data:* b Cedaredge, Colo, Nov 25, 34; m 59; c 2. *Educ:* Colo State Univ, BS, 57, MS, 60; Ore State Univ, PhD(animal nutrit, biochem), 66. *Prof Exp:* Res assoc animal nutrit, Ore State Univ, 63-67; asst prof, Univ Idaho, 67-72, assoc prof animal sci & assoc animal scientist, 72- *Mem:* Am Inst Biol Sci; Am Soc Animal Sci. *Res:* Nutritional biochemistry, especially vitamin E and selenium. *Mailing Add:* Animal & Vet Sci Univ Idaho Agr Sci Bldg Moscow ID 83843-2230

BULL, RICHARD J, PHARMACOLOGY, TOXICOLOGY. *Current Pos:* PROF PHARMACOL & TOXICOL, WASH STATE UNIV, COL PHARM, 87- *Personal Data:* b Stillwater, Okla, Oct 25, 40. *Res:* Pharmacology; toxicology. *Mailing Add:* Battelle Pac Northwest Lab PO Box 999-P7-56 Richland WA 99352

BULL, STANLEY R(AYMOND), RESEARCH ADMINISTRATION. *Current Pos:* sr eng, acad & univ prog, Solar Energy Inst, Golden, Colo, 80-81, sr sci adv, 81-82, mgr, planning & eval off, 82-84, dep dir, Solar Fuels Res Div, 84-86, div dir, Fuels & Chem Res & Eng Div, 86-91, TECH DIR, TRANSP PROGS, NAT RENEWABLE ENERGY LAB, GOLDEN, COLO, 91- *Personal Data:* b Montezuma, Iowa, May 15, 41; m 63; c Melanie J, Julia D & Jeffrey D. *Educ:* Univ Mo, BS, 63; Stanford Univ, MS, 64, PhD(mech eng), 67. *Honors & Awards:* Francis Van Morriss Award, 93. *Prof Exp:* From asst prof to prof eng, Univ Mo Columbia, 67-80. *Concurrent Pos:* Vis scientist, Argonne Nat Lab, Ill, 69, consult, 69 & 71; consult, Ellis Fischel State Cancer Hosp, 72-80; sr Fulbright-Hays prof, Int Educ & Cult Exchange Prog, 73; vis scientist, Ctr d'Etudes Nucleaires, Grenoble, France, 73-74. *Mem:* Am Inst Chem Engrs; Am Soc Mech Engrs; Int Solar Energy Soc; Soc Automotive Engrs. *Res:* Energy systems and resources; renewable fuel options and processes; evaluation renewable energy technology; alternative fuels and vehicle evaluation and testing; research and development resource allocations; advanced vehicle systems and integration. *Mailing Add:* 7577 Parkview Mountian Littleton CO 80127

BULL, W(ILLIAM) REX, MINERAL PROCESSING. *Current Pos:* ASSOC PROF METALL ENG, COLO SCH MINES, 67- *Personal Data:* b Hull, Eng, Oct 27, 29; m 56; c 4. *Educ:* Univ Leeds, BSc, 51, Grad Dipl mineral processing, 52; Univ Queensland, PhD(mineral processing), 66. *Prof Exp:* Sci officer mineral processing, Can Dept Mines & Technol Surv, 52-56; from lectr to sr lectr, Univ Queensland, 56-67. *Concurrent Pos:* Vis lectr, McGill Univ, 62-63; consult to mining & metall co, 64- *Mem:* Am Inst Mining, Metall & Petrol Engrs; Australian Inst Mining & Metall. *Res:* Mathematical modelling; control of mineral treatment processes. *Mailing Add:* 205 Ford St Golden CO 80403

BULL, WILLIAM BENHAM, CLIMATIC GEOMORPHOLOGY, TECTONIC GEOMORPHOLOGY. *Current Pos:* from asst prof to PROF GEOSCI, UNIV ARIZ, 68- *Personal Data:* b San Francisco, Calif, Apr 19, 30; m 53, Mary J Pierson; c Roger P & Kathy B (Mackey). *Educ:* Univ Colo, BA, 53; Stanford Univ, MS, 57, PhD(geol), 60. *Honors & Awards:* Neil Miner Award, Nat Asn Geol Teachers, 91; Kirk Bryan Award, Geol Soc Am, 93. *Prof Exp:* Geologist & res hydrologist, Water Resources Div, US Geol Surv, 56-76. *Mem:* Am Geophys Union; Geol Soc Am; Nat Asn Geol Teachers; Sigma Xi. *Res:* Effects of climate change and tectonic uplift on geomorphic processes and landscape evolution of arid and humid regions; lichen and tree-ring dating and locating of prehistorical plate-boundary earthquakes. *Mailing Add:* 6550 N Camino Katrina Tucson AZ 85718. *Fax:* 520-621-2672; *E-Mail:* wbbull@ccit.arizona.edu

BULL, WILLIAM EARNEST, INORGANIC CHEMISTRY. *Current Pos:* From asst prof to assoc prof, 57-70, PROF CHEM, UNIV TENN, KNOXVILLE, 70-, DIR GEN CHEM, 74-, ASSOC HEAD, 79- *Personal Data:* b Franklin Co, Mo, Jan 17, 33; m 55; c 3. *Educ:* Southern Ill Univ, AB, 54; Univ Ill, AM, 55, PhD(chem), 57. *Concurrent Pos:* Fulbright-Hayes award, Univ Col, Dublin, 70-71. *Mem:* AAAS; Am Chem Soc; Sigma Xi. *Res:* Nonaqueous solvents; coordination compounds; photoelectron spectroscopy. *Mailing Add:* 5400 Shenandoah Dr Knoxville TN 37909-1821

BULLA, LEE AUSTIN, JR, MICROBIOLOGY, BIOCHEMISTRY. *Current Pos:* PROF DEPT MICROBIOL & BIOCHEM & DEAN, COL AGR, UNIV WYO, 84- *Personal Data:* b Oklahoma City, Okla, May 1, 41; m 62; c 3. *Educ:* Midwestern Univ, BS, 65; Ore State Univ, PhD(microbiol), 68. *Prof Exp:* Bacteriologist & chemist water purification, City of Wichita Falls, Tex, 65; microbiologist, Northern Regional Res Lab, USDA, 68-73, microbiologist, US Grain Mkt Res Ctr, 73-81; prof, div biol, Kans State Univ, 77-81; prof dept basteriology & biochem & dir, Inst Molecular & Agr Genetic Eng, Univ Idaho, Moscow, 81-84. *Concurrent Pos:* Assoc dean Col Agr & dir Idaho Agr Exp Sta, 81-84. *Mem:* AAAS; Am Soc Microbiol; Soc Invertebrate Path; NY Acad Sci. *Res:* Molecular biology of bacterial sporulation; biochemical and biophysical characterization of baculoviruses. *Mailing Add:* Dept Molecular Biol Univ Wyo PO Box 3944 Laramie WY 82071-3944. *Fax:* 307-766-5098

BULLARD, CLARK W, TECHNOLOGY POLICY ANALYSIS. *Current Pos:* prof mech eng & dir, Off Energy Res, 80-90, AFFIL NUCLEAR ENG, UNIV ILL, URBANA-CHAMPAIGN, 84-, DIR, AIR CONDITIONING & REFRIG CTR, 90- *Personal Data:* b Springfield, Ill, Mar 22, 44; m 70; c 3. *Educ:* Univ Ill, Urbana-Champaign, BS, 66, MS, 67, PhD(aeronaut & astronaut eng), 71. *Honors & Awards:* Chevron Nat Conserv Award, 90. *Prof Exp:* Assoc engr-scientist, Flight Kinetics Dept, Missile & Space Systs Div, Douglas Aircraft Co, Santa Monica, 66; engr-scientist specialist, Advan Aerothermodyn Dept, McDonnell Douglas Astronaut Co, Huntington Beach, 67-69; teaching & res asst aeronaut & astronaut eng, Univ Ill, Urbana-Champaign, 69-71, res assoc prof, Ctr Advan Comput, 71-77; dir, Off Conserv & Advan Energy Systs Policy, US Dept Energy, Washington, DC, 77-79; sr analyst, Off Technol Assessment, US Cong, Washington, DC, 79-80. *Concurrent Pos:* Mem, Comt Nuclear & Alternative Energy Systs, Demand-Conserv Panel, Nat Acad Sci, 76-80; chmn adv panel, Workshop Solar Power Satellite & Alternatives, Off Technol Assessment, US Cong, 80, Workshop Nuclear Power, 82; consult, Off Technol Assessment, US Cong, SAIC, Radian Corp, ETA, Inc, GRI, 80; deleg, Midwest Univs Energy Consortium, 80-89; mem, Orgn Econ Coop & Develop, Int Energy Agency Res Adv Bd, 82-83 & Gov's Task Force Utility Reform, State Ill, 82-84; chmn & mem, Cent Midwest Compact Comn Low Level Radioactive Waste Mgt, 84-; mem, Am Coun Energy Efficient Econ; Fulbright scholar, Sussex Univ, 86. *Mem:* Am Soc Mech Engrs; Am Soc Heating, Refrig & Air Conditioning Engrs; Fedn Am Scientist; AAAS; Int Inst Refrig. *Res:* Thermal systems analysis; simulation and optimization of cogeneration, heating, refrigeration and air conditioning systems; design and siting of radioactive waste disposal technologies; acid emission reduction strategies for electric utilities. *Mailing Add:* Dept Mech Eng Univ Ill 1206 W Green St Urbana IL 61801

BULLARD, EDWIN ROSCOE, JR, GEOPHYSICS, ACOUSTICS. *Current Pos:* PRIN, CHAPARRAL PHYSICS CONSULTS, 85- *Personal Data:* b El Paso, Tex, Dec 15, 21; m 49, Norma E Holford; c 1. *Educ:* Univ Tex, El Paso, BS, 49 & 63. *Prof Exp:* Subsurface geologist, Kerr-McGee Oil Indust, Inc, 49-51, Tex Gulf Prod Co, 51-56, Ambassador Oil Corp, 56-60 & Ralph Lowe of Midland, Tex, 60-62; proj physicist, Schellenger Res Lab, Univ Tex, El Paso, 63-64; res geophysicist, Water Resources Div, US Geol Surv, 64-66; res geophysicist, Globe Explor Co, 66-69, dir, Globe Universal Sci, Advan Proj Div, Shell Oil Co, 69-70, Atlantic Richfield, 70-83 & Tex Eastern, 83-85. *Concurrent Pos:* Geophys petrol grant, Gus Mfg. *Mem:* Am Asn Petrol Geologists; Am Inst Prof Geologists. *Res:* Bringing the state of the art to seismic and borehole geophysics for oil exploration; very low frequency acoustics. *Mailing Add:* 7405 Capulin Rd NE Albuquerque NM 87109-4907. *E-Mail:* bullard@alb.com

BULLARD, ERVIN TROWBRIDGE, HORTICULTURE, TROPICAL HORTICULTURE. *Current Pos:* RETIRED. *Personal Data:* b New York, NY, May 25, 20; m, Marie G; c John M, Carol (Rice) & Ellen (Schedin). *Educ:* NC State Col, BS, 43; Cornell Univ, MS, 46; Purdue Univ, PhD(hort), 50. *Prof Exp:* Asst prof veg crops, Univ RI, 46-47; asst horticulturist, Purdue Univ, 50. Prof Exp: Asst prof veg crops, Univ RI, 46-47; asst horticulturist, Purdue Univ, 48-50; assoc prof veg res, Univ Idaho, 50-54; agr res adv, USAID, 54-64, agr prod adv, Brazil, 64-68, dep rural develop off, Repub Panama, 69-72, chief, Agr Div, India, 72-74, chief agr prod, Pakistan, 74-77, dep rural develop off, Honduras, 77-79, Chief of Party, Burma, 84-86; consult trop horticulturist, Dominican Repub & Pakistan, 86-93. *Concurrent Pos:* Fulbright res scholar, Univ Cairo, 51-52; vis prof, UNESCO Israel & Turkey, 52, Dept Hort, Ohio State Univ, 68-69. *Mem:* Am Soc Hort Sci; Interam Soc Trop Hort; Sigma Xi. *Res:* Cacao; coffee; vegetable crops; breeding and nutritional problems of tropical crops. *Mailing Add:* 129 Cimmaron Dr Palm Coast FL 32137

BULLARD, FRED MASON, geology, volcanology; deceased, see previous edition for last biography

BULLARD, TRUMAN ROBERT, PHYSIOLOGY, SCIENCE EDUCATION. *Current Pos:* EDUC CONSULT MIDAS REX INST, FT WORTH, TEX, 85- & INT SERV COORDR, 89- *Personal Data:* b Miami, Fla, Jan 15, 39; m 60; c 2. *Educ:* Asbury Col, AB, 61; WVa Univ, MS, 63, PhD(physiol), 66. *Prof Exp:* Fel physiol, Sch Med, Univ Va, 65-68; asst prof physiol, Christian Med Col, Ludhiana, Punjab, India, 68-69 & Rutgers Univ, 69-71; reader physiol, Christian Med Col, Vellore, India, 71-84. *Concurrent Pos:* Vis assoc prof pharmacol, Sch Med, Tex Tech Univ, 80-81 & 84-85; mem bd, Ludhiana Christian Med Col, 89- *Mem:* Am Chem Soc; Am Soc Bone & Mineral Res; Am Hosp Asn; Asn Advan Med Instrumentation. *Res:* Effects of exercise on body composition and energy metabolism; interaction of endocrines and atrophy of disuse in bone; vitamin D metabolism. *Mailing Add:* 1408 Navaho St Arlington TX 76012-4341

BULLAS, LEONARD RAYMOND, MICROBIAL GENETICS. *Current Pos:* from instr to assoc prof, 62-80, PROF MICROBIOL, SCH MED, LOMA LINDA UNIV, 80- *Personal Data:* b Lismore, NSW, Dec 8, 29; wid; c 2. *Educ:* Univ Adelaide, BSc, 53, MSc, 57; Mont State Col, PhD(genetics), 63. *Prof Exp:* Instr bact, Univ Adelaide, 53-58. *Concurrent Pos:* Vis prof, Univ Louvain, Belg, 73-74 & Europ Molecular Biol Lab, Ger, 81-82; MacPherson Soc investr basic sci, 75 & 81; invited prof, Univ Louvain, Belg, 89. *Mem:* Am Soc Microbiol; Genetics Soc Am; Sigma Xi. *Res:* Genetics and molecular biology of the genes for modification and restriction of DNA in salmonella. *Mailing Add:* Microbiol Dept Loma Linda Univ Loma Linda CA 92354. *Fax:* 909-824-4035; *E-Mail:* lbullas@ccmail.llu.edu

BULLEN, ALLAN GRAHAM ROBERT, TRANSPORTATION ENGINEERING. *Current Pos:* ASSOC PROF CIVIL ENG & ENVIRON SYST ENG, UNIV PITTSBURGH, 70- *Personal Data:* b Wellington, NZ, Dec 8, 36. *Educ:* Univ NZ, BSc, 60; Univ Wellington, MSc, 62; Northwestern Univ, MS Eng, 65, PhD(transp), 69. *Honors & Awards:* O'Farrill Hwy Award, Int Road Fedn, 64. *Prof Exp:* Traffic eng cadet, NZ Govt Transp Dept, 55-60, traffic engr, 60-66; res engr traffic flow, Northwestern Univ, 67-69; asst prof civil eng & res asst prof, Coord Sci Lab, Univ Ill, Urbana-Champaign, 69-70; civil engr traffic control, Ill Div Hwys, 70. *Concurrent Pos:* NZ Govt rep, World Traffic Eng Conf, London, 64; mem, Hwy Res Bd, Nat Acad Sci-Nat Res Coun. *Mem:* Inst Transp Eng; Am Soc Civil Engrs; Transp Res Forum; Sigma Xi. *Res:* Multi-lane models of traffic flow, traffic flow theory; traffic control, expressway control systems; impact of new urban transportation facilities; travel structure. *Mailing Add:* 4626 Hidden Pond Dr Allison PA 15101-2520

BULLEN, PETER SOUTHCOTT, MATHEMATICS. *Current Pos:* from instr to assoc prof math, 56-70, PROF MATH, UNIV BC, 70- *Personal Data:* b Portsmouth, Eng, Jan 19, 28; m 52; c 4. *Educ:* Univ Natal, MSc, 49; Univ Cambridge, PhD(math), 55. *Prof Exp:* Lectr, Dept Pure & Appl Math, Univ Natal, 47-50, 53-56. *Res:* Non-absolute integration. *Mailing Add:* Dept Math Univ BC 121 1984 Math Rd Vancouver BC V6T 1Z2 Can. *Fax:* 604-822-6074

BULLER, CLARENCE S, MICROBIOLOGY. *Current Pos:* res fel, 66-73, from asst prof to assoc prof, 66-77, PROF MICROBIOL, UNIV KANS, 77- *Personal Data:* b McPherson, Kans, June 21, 32; m 59; c 2. *Educ:* Univ Kans, BA, 58, MA, 60, PhD(bact), 63. *Prof Exp:* Res fel microbiol, Western Res Univ, 63-66. *Mem:* Am Soc Microbiol. *Res:* Physiology of bacteriophage infected coliforms; function of phospholipases; virus induced changes in cell surfaces. *Mailing Add:* Dept Microbiol Univ Kans Lawrence KS 66045-0001

BULLERMAN, LLOYD BERNARD, FOOD MICROBIOLOGY, MYCOLOGY. *Current Pos:* from asst prof to assoc prof, 70-79 acting dept head, 80-81, PROF, FOOD SCI & TECHNOL, UNIV NEBR, LINCOLN, 79- *Personal Data:* b Adrian, Minn, June 20, 39; m 60; c 4. *Educ:* SDak State Univ, BS, 61, MS, 65; Iowa State Univ, PhD(bact, food technol), 68. *Prof Exp:* Lab technician qual control, Dairy Prod, Inc, SDak, 61-63; food scientist prod develop, Green Giant Co, Minn, 68-70. *Mem:* Inst Food Technol; Am Soc Microbiol; Int Asn Milk, Food & Environ Sanit; Am Asn Cereal Chemists; Sigma Xi. *Res:* Food microbiology, food safety and toxicology, mycology and mycotoxins, particularly food-borne microorganisms that may be toxic or pathogenic to humans; food product development; waste disposal; biotechnology of solid state fungal fermentations. *Mailing Add:* Dept Food Sci & Technol Univ Nebr 349 FIB East Campus Lincoln NE 68583-0919

BULLIS, GEORGE LEROY, MATHEMATICS. *Current Pos:* RETIRED. *Personal Data:* b Eau Claire, Wis, Apr 26, 22; m 45; c 4. *Educ:* Wis State Univ, Eau Claire, BS, 41; Univ Wis, MA, 42. *Prof Exp:* Instr math, Univ Wis, 43-45; assoc prof, Univ Wis, Platteville, 45-68, from actg dean to dean, Sch Arts & Sci, 68-77, prof math, 77-86. *Mem:* Math Asn Am. *Mailing Add:* 405 Feltham Trail Sun City Center FL 33573

BULLIS, HARVEY RAYMOND, JR, MARINE BIOLOGY. *Current Pos:* RETIRED. *Personal Data:* b Milwaukee, Wis, June 14, 24; m 44; c 4. *Educ:* Wis State Col, BS, 49; Univ Miami, MS, 51. *Honors & Awards:* Award, US Dept Interior, 54. *Prof Exp:* Asst zool, Univ Miami, 49-50; marine biologist, US Fish & Wildlife Serv, 50-70; assoc dir, Marine Fisheries Serv, Nat Oceanic & Atmospheric Admin, US Dept Com, 70-71, dir, 71-78, sr scientist, Southeast Fisheries Ctr, Nat Marine Fisheries Serv, 78-79; Bromeliad Hort Develop Prog, collecting in Costa Rica, Panama, Brazil, Trinidad, 79-88; fishery surv, Red Sea, Egyptian Acad Sci, 81-83; Fishery Develop Prog, Quintana Roo, Mex, 83-85. *Concurrent Pos:* Dir, Bur Com Fisheries Explor Fishing Base, 55-56; consult, USAID, surv WAfrican fisheries, 61; mem, Nat Acad Sci Comt Technol & Sci Base Puerto Rican econ, 66-67, Sino-Am colloquium ocean resources, 71; US asst nat coordr fisheries, Coop Invests Caribbean & Adjacent Regions, 71-76, asst int coordr, 75-76; US deleg, WCent Atlantic Fisheries Comn, 75; consult trop marine fisheries, 79-91. *Mem:* Fel Am Inst Fishery Res Biologists. *Res:* Zoogeography of tropical West Atlantic; fishery exploration and resource analysis. *Mailing Add:* 12400 SW 248th St Homestead FL 33032

BULLIS, WILLIAM MURRAY, SEMICONDUCTOR ELECTRONICS. *Current Pos:* PRIN MAT & METROL, 91- *Personal Data:* b Cincinnati, Ohio, Aug 29, 30; m 53, Kathleen; c Keith, Bruce & Claire. *Educ:* Miami Univ, AB, 51; Mass Inst Technol, PhD(physics), 56. *Honors & Awards:* Standards Honor Award, Semiconductor Equip & Mat Inst, 87; Thurber Award, Am Soc Testing Mat Comt F-1, 84, Award of Merit, 79; Rosa Award, Nat Bur Stand, 80; Silver Medal, US Dept Com, 79. *Prof Exp:* Asst physics, Mass Inst Technol, 52-54; staff mem solid state physics, Lincoln Lab, 54 &

Los Alamos Sci Lab, 56-57; sr engr, Farnsworth Electronics, 57-59; mem tech staff, Tex Instruments Inc, Dallas, 59-65; res physicist, Nat Bur Stand, 65-68, chief, Semiconductor Characterization Sect, 68-75, prog mgr semiconductor technol, Electronic Technol Div, 75-78, chief Electron Devices Div, 78-81; mgr, semiconductor mat, Fairchild Adv, Res & Develop Lab, 81-83; dir technol, Siltec Silicon, 83-88, vpres res & develop, 88-91. *Concurrent Pos:* Lectr elec eng, Univ Md, 66-70; chmn, Electronics Div, Electrochem Soc, 87-89; hon mem, Am Soc Testing Mat Comt F-1, 87. *Mem:* Am Phys Soc; Electrochem Soc; fel Am Soc Testing & Mat; sr mem Inst Elec & Electronics Engrs. *Res:* Transport and defect phenomena in silicon and other high-punity crystalline semiconducting materials; transport phenomena in solids and fluids; semiconductor measurement technology. *Mailing Add:* Mat & Metrol 1477 Enderby Way Sunnyvale CA 94087-4015

BULLOCK, FRANCIS JEREMIAH, PHARMACY. *Current Pos:* vpres new drug discovery 79-81, SR VPRES RES OPERS, SCHERING-PLOUGH, 81- *Personal Data:* b Brookline, Mass, Jan 14, 37; m 61; c 2. *Educ:* Mass Col Pharm, BS, 58; Harvard Univ, AM, 61, PhD(chem), 63. *Prof Exp:* Res assoc, Dept Pharmacol, Harvard Med Sch, 63-64 & chem biodynamics, Univ Calif, Berkeley, 64-65; proj staff, Arthur D Little, Inc, 65-72; mgr med chem, Abbott Labs, 72-79. *Concurrent Pos:* Instr, Dept Food & Nutrit Sci, Mass Inst Technol & Sch Pharm, Northeastern Univ, 71-72; vpres, DNAX Res Inst Molecular Biol & Immunol, 82- *Mem:* Am Chem Soc; Am Soc Microbiol; Am Soc Pharmacol & Exp Therapeut; Royal Soc Chem. *Res:* New drug discovery research; drug safety evaluation. *Mailing Add:* A D Little 25 Acorn Pk Cambridge MA 02140

BULLOCK, GRAHAM LAMBERT, BACTERIOLOGY, FISH PATHOLOGY. *Current Pos:* SR RES SCIENTIST, CONSERVATION FUND, FRESHWATER INST, 90- *Personal Data:* b Martinsburg, WVa, Mar 6, 35; m 55, Anna C Dunbar; c Jane, Jeffry, Daniel, Keith & David. *Educ:* Shepherd Col, WVa, BS, 57; Univ Wis-Madison, MS, 59; Fordham Univ, PhD(biol sci), 70. *Prof Exp:* Bacteriologist qual control, Thomas J Lipton Inc, NJ, 59-60; researcher bact fish dis, Eastern Fish Dis Lab, Fish & Wildlife Serv, Dept Interior, 60-81, actg dir, 81, dir, 81-90. *Concurrent Pos:* Vis prof, Ore State Univ, 73-74. *Mem:* Am Soc Microbiol; Am Fisheries Soc; Sigma Xi. *Res:* Nature and control of bacterial infections of fish including the role of environmental factors, chemotherapy and serological methods for detection and identification of bacterial pathogens; microbiology of fluidized biofilters control of disease in fish recycle systems. *Mailing Add:* Leetown Kearneysville WV 25430. *Fax:* 304-876-0739

BULLOCK, J BRUCE, AGRICULTURAL FINANCE. *Current Pos:* dept chair, Dept Agr Econ, 82-88, ASSOC DEAN RES, COL AGR, UNIV MO, 88- *Personal Data:* b Lindsay, Okla, June 23, 40; m 59; c 3. *Educ:* Okla State Univ, BS, 62, MS, 64; Univ Calif, Berkeley, PhD(agr econ), 68. *Prof Exp:* From asst prof to assoc prof agr econ, NC State Univ, 69-76; res dir, Farmbank Serv, 76-80; assoc prof, Okla State Univ, 80-82. *Mem:* Am Agr Econ Asn. *Res:* Economics of information; agricultural finance; agricultural commodity markets. *Mailing Add:* Dept Agr Econ 200 Mumford Hall Univ Mo Columbia MO 65211

BULLOCK, JOHN, ENDOCRINOLOGY. *Current Pos:* res asst, 57-61, staff mem & res assoc, 61-62, asst prof, 65-75, ASSOC PROF PHYSIOL, COL MED & DENT NJ, NEWARK, 75- *Personal Data:* b Orange, NJ, Apr 24, 32; m 58; c 3. *Educ:* Seton Hall Univ, BS, 57; Rutgers Univ, MS, 62; Colo State Univ, PhD(physiol), 65. *Prof Exp:* Res technician, Merck Inst Therapeut Res, 56-57. *Mem:* Microcirculatory Soc; Am Physiol Soc; Sigma Xi. *Res:* Androgenic control of connective tissue; biochemistry of tumors; mechanism of action of androgenic esters; connective tissue physiology; biochemistry of cancer; physiology of aging; bile acid metabolism. *Mailing Add:* Dept Physiol Univ Med & Dent NJ Med Sch 185 S Orange St Newark NJ 07103-2714. *Fax:* 973-982-7950

BULLOCK, JONATHAN S, IV, ELECTRO CHEMISTRY, INORGANIC CHEMISTRY. *Current Pos:* mem develop staff, Martin Marietta Energy Systs, 84-94, SR DEVELOP STAFF MEM, LOCKHEED MARTIN ENERGY SYSTS, 94- *Personal Data:* b Mobile, Ala, Dec 8, 42; m 69, Nora Marie Duncan; c Julia C & Arwyn M. *Educ:* Ala Col, BS, 64; Tulane Univ, PhD(phys chem), 69. *Prof Exp:* Develop chemist, Union Carbide Corp, 68-76, mem develop staff, Nuclear Div, 76-84; mem develop staff, Martin Marietta Energy Systs, 84-94. *Mem:* Am Chem Soc; Sigma Xi; AAAS. *Res:* Solvent effect in kinetics; electrochemistry of fluid-electrode and solid-electrode systems; gas-solid interface reactions; corrosion; electrochemical energy systems; electrochemical machining; high-temperature thermochemistry; electrodeposition; fused-salt processes; chaos. *Mailing Add:* 120 Euclid Circle Oak Ridge TN 37830

BULLOCK, KATHRYN RICE, electrochemistry, battery technology, for more information see previous edition

BULLOCK, KENNETH C, GEOLOGY. *Current Pos:* RETIRED. *Personal Data:* b Pleasant Grove, Utah, Sept 8, 18; m 38; c 4. *Educ:* Brigham Young Univ, BS, 40, MA, 42; Univ Wis, PhD(geol), 49. *Prof Exp:* From instr to prof geol, Brigham Young Univ, 43-83, chmn dept, 56-62. *Concurrent Pos:* Geol engr, US Steel Corp, 53-54; res geologist, Columbia Iron Mining Co, 60 & US Bur Mines, 75; geologist, Utah Geol & Mineral Surv, 67, 74. *Mem:* Fel Geol Soc Am; Am Inst Mining Metall & Petrol Engrs; Nat Asn Geol Teachers. Mineral Soc Am. *Res:* Economic geology; mineralogy; petrology; iron and fluorite deposits of Utah. *Mailing Add:* 1035 N 900 East Provo UT 84604

BULLOCK, LESLIE PATRICIA, ENDOCRINOLOGY, LABORATORY ANIMAL MEDICINE. *Current Pos:* CAMPUS VET, BOYDEN LAB, UNIV CALIF, RIVERSIDE, 90- *Personal Data:* b Los Angeles, Calif, May 20, 36. *Educ:* Pomona Col, BA, 57; Univ Calif, Davis, DVM, 63. *Prof Exp:* Res fel endocrinol, Nat Cancer Inst, 68-70 & Med Col, Cornell Univ, 67-68; intern & mem staff, Angell Mem Hosp, Boston, 63-67; from asst prof to assoc prof comp med, Milton S Hershey Med Ctr, Pa State Univ, 71-82; prof depts med & physiol, Sch Vet Med, Tufts Univ, 82-88; dir, Lab Animal Sci Prog, Nat Ctr Resource Recovery & NIH, 88-90. *Mem:* AAAS; Am Asn Lab Animal Sci; Am Soc Lab Animal Practrs; Am Vet Med Asn. *Res:* Interaction of androgens and other steroid and protein hormones at the biologic and molecular level; molecular mechanism of androgen action. *Mailing Add:* Dept Biol Univ Calif 900 University Ave Riverside CA 92521

BULLOCK, NORMA KATHRYN RICE, ELECTROCHEMICAL SCIENCE & TECHNOLOGY, BATTERIES. *Current Pos:* PROD DEVELOP MGR POWER SOURCES, MEDTRONIC, INC, 96- *Personal Data:* m 67, Kenneth Richard; c Kerry R & Kevin R. *Educ:* Univ Colo, BA, 67; Northwestern Univ, MS, 69, PhD(phys chem), 72. *Honors & Awards:* Battery Res Award, Electrochem Soc, 80; Plante Medal, Bulgarian Acad Sci, 96. *Prof Exp:* Res chemist, Gates Co, 72-76; sr electrochemist, Johnson Controls, Inc, 77-80, dept mgr chem res, 80-91; tech mgr battery develop, AT&T Bell Labs, 91-96. *Concurrent Pos:* Adj asst prof, Univ Wis-Milwaukee, 79. *Mem:* Electrochem Soc (vpres, 92-95, pres, 95-96); fel Royal Soc Chem; fel Am Inst Chemists; Am Chem Soc; Int Soc Electrochem. *Res:* Development of materials, processes and designs for batteries and capacitors. *Mailing Add:* Power Sources Medtronic Inc 6700 Shingle Creek Pkwy Brooklyn Center MN 55430. *Fax:* 612-514-1163; *E-Mail:* kathryn.bullock@medtronic.com

BULLOCK, R MORRIS, MECHANISTIC ORGANOMETALLIC CHEMISTRY, HOMOGENEOUS CATALYSIS. *Current Pos:* from asst chemist to assoc chemist, 85-89, CHEMIST, CHEM DEPT, BROOKHAVEN NAT LAB, 89- *Personal Data:* b Greensboro, NC, Apr 18, 57; m 83, Cindy Blenke; c Claude G III & Lindsay B. *Educ:* Univ NC, Chapel Hill, BS, 79; Univ Wis-Madison, PhD(chem), 84. *Prof Exp:* Res assoc, Colo State Univ, 84-85. *Mem:* Am Chem Soc. *Res:* Mechanistic and synthetic transition metal organometallic chemistry; reactions of metal hydrides with unsaturated substrates; intrinsic barriers to atom transfer reactions; hydrogen atom transfer reactions of metal hydrides. *Mailing Add:* Chem Dept Brookhaven Nat Lab Upton NY 11973-5000. *Fax:* 516-282-5815; *E-Mail:* rmb@bnl.gov

BULLOCK, RICHARD MELVIN, HORTICULTURE, RESEARCH ADMINISTRATION. *Current Pos:* RETIRED. *Personal Data:* b Glasco, Kans, July 8, 18; m 47, Frances Witting; c Richard P & Barclay D. *Educ:* Kans State Univ, BS, 40; Wash State Univ, MS, 42, PhD, 50. *Prof Exp:* Asst hort, Wash State Univ, 40-42, asst & assoc horticulturist, Tree Fruit Exp Sta, 46-52; prof & head dept hort, Utah State Agr Col, 52-53; supt & horticulturist, Southwestern Wash Exp Sta, 53-58, North Willamette Exp Sta, Ore State Univ, 58-69; horticulturist, 69-72, asst dir, Hawaii Agr Exp Sta, 69-75, agronomist, 72-75, prof hort, 72-81, prof agron, 74-75, horticulturist, 75-81, emer prof hort, Univ Hawaii, Manoa, 81-; consult horticulturist, 81; courtesy emer prof hort, Ore State Univ. *Mem:* Fel AAAS; Am Soc Plant Physiol; fel Am Soc Hort Sci; Sigma Xi; Int Plant Propagators Soc. *Res:* Nutrition, production, culture and management of horticultural crops, flower and fruit cycling; plant physiology; plant growth regulation; herbicides; research administration. *Mailing Add:* 1151 Upper Devon Lane Lake Oswego OR 97034

BULLOCK, ROBERT CROSSLEY, ENTOMOLOGY. *Current Pos:* ASSOC ENTOMOLOGIST, AGR RES CTR, UNIV FLA, 61- *Personal Data:* b New York, NY, Oct 16, 24; m 52, Jean Gronwoldt; c David & Susan. *Educ:* St Lawrence Univ, BS, 48; Univ Conn, MS, 50, PhD(entom), 54. *Prof Exp:* Entomologist, Trop Res Dept, Tela RR Co, Repub Honduras, 54-61. *Mem:* Entom Soc Am. *Res:* Biology and control of insect pests of citrus. *Mailing Add:* Indian River Res & Educ Ctr 2199 S Rock Rd Ft Pierce FL 34945

BULLOCK, ROBERT M, III, AUDIO APPLICATIONS. *Current Pos:* asst prof, 66-82, ASSOC PROF MATH & STATIST, MIAMI UNIV, 82- *Personal Data:* b Cincinnati, Ohio, June 30, 37; m 63; c 2. *Educ:* Univ Cincinnati, BS, 61, MA, 62, PhD(math), 66. *Prof Exp:* Teacher pvt sch, Ohio, 62-63; instr math, Univ Cincinnati, 63-66. *Mem:* Inst Elec & Electronics Engrs; Soc Indust & Appl Math; Audio Eng Soc. *Res:* Mathematical models of loudspeaker and loudspeaker-crossover systems; design and construction methods based on the models. *Mailing Add:* Dept Math & Statist Miami Univ Oxford OH 45056

BULLOCK, RONALD ELVIN, NUCLEAR ENGINEERING, MATERIALS SCIENCE. *Current Pos:* SR TECH STAFF, GEN ATOMICS, 92- *Personal Data:* b Camden, Ark, June 17, 34; m 64; c 1. *Educ:* La Polytech Inst, BS, 56; Tex Christian Univ, MA, 63, MS, 69. *Prof Exp:* From nuclear engr to sr nuclear engr, Gen Dynamics Corp, 56-72, sr design engr mat, 72-73; staff nuclear scientist, Gen Atomic Co, 73-86; sr eng specialist, Convair Div, Gen Dynamics, Inc, 86-92. *Mem:* Am Ceramics Soc; Am Carbon Soc. *Res:* Irradiation effects on materials; nuclear fuel performance; fracture mechanics; brittle materials design; advanced composite structures; high-temperature materials. *Mailing Add:* 1127 Sea Village Dr Cardiff by the Sea CA 92007

BULLOCK, THEODORE HOLMES, NEUROBIOLOGY. *Current Pos:* prof, 66-83, EMER PROF NEUROSCI, UNIV CALIF, SAN DIEGO, 83- *Personal Data:* b Nanking, China, May 16, 15; m 37; c 2. *Educ:* Univ Calif, AB, 36, PhD(zool), 40. *Hon Degrees:* Doctorate, Univ Frankfurt, Ger, 88. *Honors & Awards:* Gerard Prize, Soc Neurosci, 84. *Prof Exp:* Sterling fel, Yale Univ, 40-41, Rockefeller fel, 41-42, res asst pharmacol & neuroanat, 42-43, instr neuroanat, 43-44; asst prof anat, Sch Med, Univ Mo, 44-46; from asst prof to prof zool, Univ Calif, Los Angeles, 46-66. *Concurrent Pos:* Mem corp, Marine Biol Lab, Woods Hole, 44-, trustee, 56-58; fel, Ctr Advan Study Behav Sci, 59-60; mem exec comt, Assembly of Life Sci, 73-76. *Mem:* Nat Acad Sci; Am Soc Zool (pres, 65); Am Philos Soc; Soc Neurosci (pres, 75); Int Soc Neuroethology (pres, 84-86); Am Acad Arts & Sci; Am Physiol Soc; Int Brain Res Orgn. *Res:* Comparative neurophysiology. *Mailing Add:* Dept Neurosci Univ Calif San Diego La Jolla CA 92093-0201

BULLOCK, THOMAS EDWARD, JR, ELECTRICAL ENGINEERING. *Current Pos:* from asst prof to assoc prof, 66-74, PROF ELEC ENG, UNIV FLA, 74- *Personal Data:* b Abilene, Tex, July 21, 38; m 80; c 5. *Educ:* Rice Univ, BA, 60, BSEE, 61; Stanford Univ, MSEE, 62, PhD(elec eng), 66. *Prof Exp:* Res assoc elec eng, Stanford Univ, 62-63. *Mem:* Inst Elec & Electronics Engrs; Soc Indust & Appl Math. *Res:* Mathematical systems theory; digital control; applications of microprocessors in control. *Mailing Add:* Dept Elec Eng 216 Larsen Hall Univ Fla Gainesville FL 32611-2044

BULLOCK, WARD ERVIN, JR, MEDICINE, IMMUNOLOGY & MICROBIOLOGY. *Current Pos:* dean, Sch Med, 94-95, PROF MED, UNIV CONN, FARMINGTON, CONN, 94- *Personal Data:* b Cincinnati, Ohio, June 21, 31. *Educ:* State Univ NY, Buffalo, BA, 54; Temple Univ, MS & MD, 59; Am Bd Internal Med, dipl, 66. *Prof Exp:* Med intern, Univ Minn Hosp, 59-60, fel internal med, 60-62; sr resident internal med, Yale Univ Med Ctr, 62-63, advan res fel immunol, 63-64; dir, Clin Res Ward, US Naval Med Res Unit No 2, Taipei, Taiwan, Repub China, 64-66, vis lectr, Infectious Dis & Clin Immunol, Nat Defense Med Ctr Hosp, Taiwan, 64-66; sr instr internal med, Univ Rochester Col Med, 66-67, asst prof microbiol, 66-68; from assoc prof to prof med & dir, Div Infectious Dis, Univ Ky Col Med, 70-80; dir, Infectious Dis Div, Arthur Russell Morgan prof med & adj prof, Dept Molecular Genetics, Biochem & Microbiol, Univ Cincinnati Col Med, 80-94, assoc chmn res, Dept Med, 88-89, sr assoc dean, Col Med, 89-91, assoc chmn res, 93-94. *Concurrent Pos:* Grantee, USPHS & WHO, 67-95; mem, US Leprosy Panel, US-Japan Coop Med Sci Prog, NIH, 72-77 & 83-85, Bacterial & Mycotic Dis Study Sect, US Army Res & Develop Command, 75-79, Bact & Mycol Study Sect, Nat Inst Allergy & Infectious Dis, NIH, 76-80, Sci Adv Bd, Am Leprosy Found, 81-84; mem consult staff, Cincinnati Children's Hosp Med Ctr, 80-94; mem, Microbiol & Infectious Dis Res Comt, Nat Inst Allergy & Infectious Dis, NIH, 88-92, chmn, 90-92; coun, Infectious Dis Soc Am, 90-93; NIH Reviewers Res, 94- *Mem:* Sigma Xi; Am Fedn Clin Res; Am Soc Clin Invest; Asn Am Physicians; Am Asn Immunologists; fel Am Col Physicians; fel Infectious Dis Soc Am; AAAS; Am Soc Microbiol; Int Leprosy Asn. *Res:* Microbiology; immunology; medical mycology; infectious diseases; leprosy. *Mailing Add:* Dept Med Univ Conn Health Ctr 263 Farmington Ave MC3212 Farmington CT 06030. *Fax:* 860-679-4701; *E-Mail:* bullock@nso.uchc.edu

BULLOCK, WILBUR LEWIS, PARASITOLOGY. *Current Pos:* from instr to assoc prof, Univ NH, 48-61, actg chmn dept, 58-59, prof zool, 61-87, EMER PROF ZOOL, UNIV NH, 87- *Personal Data:* b New York, NY, Mar 8, 22; m 44, Cecilia Groenewold; c Walter A, Robert C, Clifford A & Judith B (Blanchard). *Educ:* Queen's Col, NY, BS, 42; Univ Ill, MS, 47, PhD(zool), 48. *Prof Exp:* Univ Va fel, Mountain Lake Biol Sta, 48. *Concurrent Pos:* Asst instr, US Army Univ, France, 45; res fel biol, Rice Inst, 55-56; vis res prof, Fla Presby Col, 62-63; res affil, Harold W Manter Lab, Univ Nebr State Mus, 72- *Mem:* Am Soc Parasitol; Am Sci Affil. *Res:* Morphology and taxonomy of Acanthocephala; fish intestinal histology and histopathology; blood and intestinal protozoa of marine fish. *Mailing Add:* 13 Thompson Lane Durham NH 03824

BULLOFF, JACK JOHN, CHEMICAL & ENVIRONMENTAL SAFETY & HEALTH, IMAGE-WISE PHOTO PROCESSING MATERIALS & METHODS. *Current Pos:* OWNER, PRIN CHEM & ENVIRON CONSULT & EXPERT WITNESS, J BULLOFF, CONSULT, SCHENECTADY, NY, 68- *Personal Data:* b New York, NY, Dec 9, 14; m 42, 52, Gertrude S Pollock; c Dorie L, Eric D (deceased), Aaron H & Steven M. *Educ:* City Col New York, BS, 39; Rensselaer Polytech Inst, PhD, 53. *Prof Exp:* Jr chemist, Los Alamos Nat Lab, 46; asst prof chem, assoc Col Upper NY State, 46-50; asst, Rensselaer Polytech Inst, 50-52; proj supvr, Commonwealth Eng Co, 53-56; prin chemist & assoc fel, Battelle Mem Inst, 56-68; prof hist sci & dir, Sci & Technol Studies, State Univ NY, Albany, 68-76; res assoc, Fla State Univ, Tallahassee, 77-78; safety & wastes consult, JT Baker Chem Co, US & Can, 78-85; chief consult scientist, NY State Legis Comn Sci & Technol, 85-92. *Concurrent Pos:* Consult, Graphic Arts & Photoprod Patents, 68-; chair, Safety Chemists Workplace Comt, Am Inst Chemists, 93-95; co-chair, Environ Concerns & Govt Affairs Comts, 95-96. *Mem:* Fel AAAS; Am Chem Soc; NY Acad Sci; fel Am Inst Chemists; Sigma Xi. *Res:* Actinides; metallic soaps; polyoxyions; graphic arts; image-wise photopolymerization; technological forecasting; science and technology assessment; research and development planning; oil and chemical spill amelioration; environmental chemistry; science policy; science education; history of chemistry; chemical safety; hazardous wastes management; science and technology legislation; technology transfer; superconductor synthesis; photoultramicrominiaturization and diazophotosensitization. *Mailing Add:* 399 Ridge Hill Rd Schenectady NY 12303-5716

BULLOUGH, VERN L, SEX & HISTORY, NURSING. *Current Pos:* VIS PROF NURSING, UNIV SOUTHERN CALIF. *Personal Data:* b Salt Lake City, Utah, July 24, 28; wid; c David C (deceased), James, Steven, Susan & Michael. *Educ:* Univ Utah, BA, 51; Univ Chicago, MA, 51, PhD(hist & hist sci), 54; Calif State Univ, Long Beach, BSN, 81. *Honors & Awards:* Garrison Lectr, Am Asn Hist Med, 88; Distinguished Sci Achievement Award, Soc Sci Study Sex, 90. *Prof Exp:* Assoc prof hist & social sci, Youngstown Univ, 54-59; from asst prof to prof, Calif State Univ, Northridge, 59-80; prof, State Univ Col NY, Buffalo, 80-87, dean col, 80-89, distinguished prof hist & hist sci, 87-93. *Concurrent Pos:* Co-prin investr, Proj Michaelson grant, USN, 61-64; adj prof, Calif Col Med, 61-68; Fulbright prof, Ain Shams Univ, Cairo, Egypt, 66-67; prin investr, US Off Educ grant, 66-69, Erickson Found grant, 69-76; vis prof, Univ Southern Calif, 69; lectr, Sch Pub Health, Univ Calif, Los Angeles, 70-79; comnr bldg & safety, City Los Angeles, 74-77; adj prof nursing, State Univ NY, Buffalo, 80-93. *Mem:* Soc Sci Study Sex (pres, 81-83); Am Asn Hist Med; Hist Sci Soc; Am Asn Hist Nursing; Am Hist Asn; AAAS; fel Am Acad Nursing. *Res:* Human sexuality (history & sociology); history of intellectual and creative, achievement, sex research and medicine and nursing; influences of biological factors upon history. *Mailing Add:* 17434 Mayall St Northridge CA 91325. *E-Mail:* vbullough@csun.edu

BULOW, FRANK JOSEPH, FISH BIOLOGY. *Current Pos:* From asst prof to assoc prof, 69-80, PROF BIOL, TENN TECHNOL UNIV, 80- *Personal Data:* b Oaklawn, Ill, July 11, 41; m 63; c 4. *Educ:* Southern Ill Univ, BA, 64, MA, 66; Iowa State Univ, PhD(fisheries biol), 69. *Honors & Awards:* Sigma Xi Res Award, 79. *Concurrent Pos:* Res grants, Sport Fishing Inst, 68-69, Tenn Technol Univ, 69-80, Bur Sport Fisheries & Wildlife Dingell-Johnson grant, 69-75 & US Army CEngr, 81-85 & 85-87; pres, Tenn chap, Am Fisheries Soc, 79-80; cert fisheries scientist. *Mem:* Am Fisheries Soc; Sigma Xi. *Res:* Propagation and rearing of channel catfish; relationship between nucleic acid concentrations and growth rate of fishes; water pollution biology; factors limiting fish production in reservoirs, streams and ponds. *Mailing Add:* Dept Biol Tenn Technol Univ 900 N Dixie Ave Cookeville TN 38501-2684

BULTMAN, JOHN D, CHEMISTRY, MARINE BIOLOGY. *Current Pos:* chemist, Bur Mines, US Dept Interior, 50, RES CHEMIST, NAVAL RES LAB, 50- *Personal Data:* b Chicago, Ill, Apr 11, 24; m 52, Elizabeth Dean; c Patricia L. *Educ:* George Washington Univ, BS, 50, MS, 54; Georgetown Univ, PhD(chem), 62. *Prof Exp:* Mem staff, E I du Pont de Nemours & Co, 42-43. *Concurrent Pos:* Assoc Ed, Biotropica; assoc ed, Naval Res Rev. *Mem:* Am Chem Soc; Am Wood Preserv Asn; Asn Trop Biol; Asn Advan Indust Corps. *Res:* Biological deterioration of materials in the terrestrial and marine environments; utilization of non-rubber-producing components of the guayule (parthenium argentatum) plant. *Mailing Add:* US Naval Res Lab Code 6127 Washington DC 20375-5342

BULUSU, DUTT V, FIBER OPTIC SOURCES & DETECTORS, FIBER OPTIC LANS, LOCAL AREA NETWORKS. *Current Pos:* DIR COMPONENT ENG, CODENOLL TECHNOL CORP, 85- *Personal Data:* b Pradesh, India, Apr 18, 39; US citizen, m; c Adity A & Sudha. *Educ:* Andhra Univ, BE, 61; Indian Sci, ME, 63; Univ Southern Calif, PhD(mat sci), 74. *Prof Exp:* Fel, Univ Southern Calif, 73-76; sr res engr, Honeywell, 76-78; mem tech staff, AT&T Bell Labs, 78-85. *Concurrent Pos:* Lectr elec eng, Regional Eng Col, 63-65, Ind Inst Technol, 68-69; develop engr, Seshasayee Indust Ltd, 65-68. *Mem:* Inst Elec & Electronics Engrs; Sigma Xi. *Res:* Primary research activity is in III-V & II-VI alloy semi conductor materials and devices; activity in fiber optic local area networks. *Mailing Add:* 1324 Mekeel St Yorktown Heights NY 10598. *Fax:* 914-965-9811; *E-Mail:* codenoll@panix.com

BULUSU, SURYANARAYANA, ORGANIC & PHYSICAL CHEMISTRY, RADIATION CHEMISTRY. *Current Pos:* RES CHEMIST, EXPLOSIVES LAB, ARMAMENT RES, DEVELOP & ENG CTR, PICATINNY ARSENAL, US ARMY, 60- *Personal Data:* b Ellore, India, Aug 22, 27; US citizen. *Educ:* Andhra Univ, India, BSc, 48; Univ Bombay, BSc, 50, PhD(org chem), 54. *Prof Exp:* J N Tata Endowment Higher Educ Indians overseas fel chem, Yale Univ, 54, univ fel, 54-56; res assoc, Brookhaven Nat Lab, 56-59 & Univ Wis-Madison, 59-60. *Concurrent Pos:* Vis scientist, Sandia Nat Labs, Livermore, Calif. *Mem:* AAAS; Am Chem Soc; Sigma Xi; Am Soc Mass Spectrometry; hon mem High Energy Mat Soc India. *Res:* Organic mass spectrometry; applications to study of structural chemistry of explosives; nuclear magnetic resonance spectroscopy; decomposition chemistry of energetic materials; spectroscopy of energetic materials. *Mailing Add:* 22 Skyview Terr Morris Plains NJ 07950

BUMBY, RICHARD THOMAS, NUMBER THEORY. *Current Pos:* PROF MATH, RUTGERS UNIV, 77- *Personal Data:* b Brooklyn, NY. *Educ:* Mass Inst Technol, SB, 57; Princeton Univ, MA, 59, PhD(math), 62. *Prof Exp:* From instr to asst prof, 60-68, assoc prof, 68-77. *Concurrent Pos:* Problem sect ed, Am Math Monthly, 92-96. *Mem:* Am Math Soc; Am Asn Univ Professors; Math Asn Am. *Res:* Number theory, especially diophantine problems; analogs of Littlewood's approximation problem; the Markoff spectrum; algebraic and combinatorial problems in number theory. *Mailing Add:* Dept Math Rutgers Univ Brunswick NJ 08903-2101. *E-Mail:* bumby@math.rutgers.edu

BUMCROT, ROBERT J, MATHEMATICS. *Current Pos:* assoc prof, 68-74, chmn dept, 69-75, PROF MATH, HOFSTRA UNIV, 74- *Personal Data:* b Kansas City, Mo, Nov 24, 36; m 60, 75, Francesca Turchiano; c Christopher & David. *Educ:* Univ Chicago, BS, 59, MS, 60; Univ Mo, PhD(math), 62. *Prof Exp:* Asst prof math, Ohio State Univ, 62-66; lectr, Univ Sussex, 66-67; asst prof, Ohio State Univ, 67-68. *Mem:* Am Math Soc; Math Asn Am; NY Acad Sci. *Res:* Geometry; abstract structures; combinatorics. *Mailing Add:* Dept Math Hofstra Univ Hempstead NY 11550

BUMGARDNER, CARL LEE, ORGANIC CHEMISTRY. *Current Pos:* assoc prof chem, 64-67, PROF CHEM, NC STATE UNIV, 67-, HEAD DEPT, 76- *Personal Data:* b Belmont, NC, Jan 8, 25; m 56; c 5. *Educ:* Univ Toronto, BASc, 52; Mass Inst Technol, PhD(org chem), 56. *Prof Exp:* Res assoc, Mass Inst Technol, 56; res chemist, Redstone Res Div, Rohm & Haas Co, 56-64. *Mem:* Am Chem Soc. *Res:* Elimination reactions; photochemistry; nitrenes. *Mailing Add:* 4113 Glen Laurel Dr Raleigh NC 27612

BUMOL, THOMAS F, CARDIOVASCULAR RESEARCH, CELL BIOLOGY. *Current Pos:* DIR CARDIOVASC RES, LILLY RES LABS, 91- *Personal Data:* b Detriot, Mich, April 13, 53. *Res:* Cardiovascular research; cell biology. *Mailing Add:* 12006 Eden Glen Dr Carmel IN 46033

BUMP, CHARLES KILBOURNE, CHEMISTRY. *Current Pos:* RETIRED. *Personal Data:* b Pittsfield, Mass, June 1, 07; m 34; c 2. *Educ:* Amherst Col, AB, 29; Cornell Univ, PhD(phys chem), 33. *Prof Exp:* Fel chem, Amherst Col, 34-35; teacher sci, Dorland-Bell Sch, NC, 35-36; inspector, Food & Drug Admin, USDA, 36-37; res chemist, plastics div, Monsanto Chem Co, 37-38, group leader, 38-46, asst dir res, 46-57, res personnel mgr, Monsanto Co, 58-70, res specialist, plastics prod & resins div, 70-72. *Mem:* Am Chem Soc. *Res:* Industrial problems dealing with plastics; resins for surface coatings. *Mailing Add:* 78 North Rd Hampden MA 01036

BUMPUS, JOHN ARTHUR, HEMEPROTEINS, MYCOLOGY. *Current Pos:* ASSOC FAC FEL, NOTRE DAME, 90- *Personal Data:* b Syracuse, NY, Apr 25, 48; m 79, Nancy K Von Bukel; c 1. *Educ:* State Univ NY, Oswego, BS, 71, MS, 73, Binghamton, MA, 77; St Louis Univ, PhD(biochem), 80. *Prof Exp:* Fel biochem, St Louis Univ, 80-81; asst prof chem, Lake Superior State Col, 81-84; vis asst prof, Mich State Univ, 84-87; res assoc prof, Utah State Univ, 87-90. *Mem:* AAAS; Am Chem Soc; Am Soc Microbiol; Brit Mycol Soc; AAAS; Soc Toxicol. *Res:* Structure and function of hemeproteins, especially peroxidases and cytochrome P-450 containing monooxygenases; biodegradation of environmental pollutants by micro-organisms. *Mailing Add:* Dept Chem Univ Northern Iowa Cedar Falls IA 50614-0423. *Fax:* 219-631-6652

BUNAG, RUBEN DAVID, CARDIOVASCULAR PHYSIOLOGY, PHARMACOLOGY. *Current Pos:* assoc prof, 70-75, PROF PHARMACOL, MED CTR, UNIV KANS, 75- *Personal Data:* b Manila, Philippines, June 3, 31; m 56; c 2. *Educ:* Univ Philippines, MD, 55; Univ Kans, MA, 62. *Prof Exp:* Instr physiol, Univ Philippines, 55-57; from asst prof to assoc prof pharmacol, Med Ctr, Univ of the East, Manila, 57-60; USPHS int res fel, 60-62; Life Ins Med Res Fund res fel, Med Sch, Case Western Res Univ, 62-63; res fel, Cleveland Clin Res Div, 63-69, assoc res staff, 69-70. *Concurrent Pos:* Res pharmacologist, Vet Admin Hosp, Kansas City, Kans, 70-72; Chancellor's Club res award, Univ Kans, 92. *Mem:* Sigma Xi; Soc Exp Biol & Med; Neurosci Soc; Am Physiol Soc; Coun High Blood Pressure Res. *Res:* Cardiovascular pharmacology; experimental hypertension; central neural mechanisms for cardiovascular regulation; autonomic pharmacology; experimental diabetes, obesity and aging. *Mailing Add:* Dept Pharmacol Univ Kans Med Ctr 39th & Rainbow Kansas City KS 66103

BUNBURY, DAVID LESLIE, PHYSICAL ORGANIC CHEMISTRY. *Current Pos:* asst prof, 58-65, ASSOC PROF CHEM, ST FRANCIS XAVIER UNIV, 65- *Personal Data:* b Georgetown, Brit Guiana, Feb 12, 33; m 57; c 4. *Educ:* Berea Col, BA, 52; Univ Notre Dame, PhD(phys chem), 56. *Prof Exp:* Fel chem, Univ Colo, 56-58. *Concurrent Pos:* Nat Res Coun Can grant, 59-71. *Mem:* Am Chem Soc; Chem Inst Can; Royal Soc Chem. *Res:* The photochemical decomposition of some ketones. *Mailing Add:* Dept Chem St Francis Xavier Univ Antigonish NS B2G 2W5 Can

BUNCE, ELIZABETH THOMPSON, GEOPHYSICS. *Current Pos:* res asst, 51-52, form assoc scientist to sr scientist, 52-80, EMER SCIENTIST, WOODS HOLE OCEANOG INST, 80- *Personal Data:* b Mineola, NY, Apr 25, 15. *Educ:* Smith Col, AB, 37, MA, 49. *Hon Degrees:* ScD, Smith Col, 71. *Prof Exp:* Instr physics, Smith Col, 49-51. *Mem:* Fel Geol Soc Am; Soc Explor Geophys; Am Geophys Union; Am Asn Petrol Geologists. *Res:* Marine seismology; underwater acoustics. *Mailing Add:* PO Box 623 West Falmouth MA 02574

BUNCE, GEORGE EDWIN, NUTRITION, BIOCHEMISTRY. *Current Pos:* asst prof, 65-70, assoc prof, 70-78, PROF BIOCHEM, VA POLYTECH INST & STATE UNIV, 78- *Personal Data:* b Nashville, Tenn, Dec 13, 32; m 55; c 3. *Educ:* Va Polytech Inst, BS, 54, MS, 56; Univ Wis, PhD(biochem), 61. *Prof Exp:* Biochemist, US Army Med Res & Nutrit Lab, Fitzsimons Gen Hosp, Denver, Colo, 61-63; chief clin chem, Tripler Gen Hosps, Honolulu, Hawaii, 63-65. *Concurrent Pos:* Vis scientist, chem physiol lab, Cath Univ Louvain, 70-71, Rowett Inst, Aberdeen, 81-82. *Mem:* Am Inst Nutrit. *Res:* Mineral nutrition, particularly magnesium and its relation to soft tissue calcinosis and urolithiasis; nutritional effects on cataract; zinc and steroids. *Mailing Add:* Dept Biochem Hillcrest Hall Va Polytech Inst & State Univ Blacksburg VA 24061-0427. *Fax:* 540-231-9070

BUNCE, GERRY MICHAEL, HIGH ENERGY PHYSICS. *Current Pos:* assoc physicist, 77-80, PHYSICIST, BROOKHAVEN NAT LAB, 80- *Personal Data:* b Pontiac, Mich; m; c 2. *Educ:* Mass Inst Technol, BS, 67; Univ Mich, PhD(physics), 71. *Prof Exp:* Res assoc physics, Univ Mich, 71; vis scientist, Centre d'Etudes l'Energie Nucleaire, Saclay, France, 71-73; res assoc, Univ Wis-Madison, 73-77. *Concurrent Pos:* Vis physicist, Lab d' Annecy-Le-Vieux, France, 85-86, Univ Marseille, France, 86. *Mem:* Am Phys Soc. *Res:* Weak interactions; strong interaction dynamics; study of color transparency and dynamics of large angle scattering of protons; precise measurement of the moun g-2; experiments colliding polarized protons at RHIC. *Mailing Add:* Accelerator Dept Bldg 911B Brookhaven Nat Lab Upton NY 11973

BUNCE, HUBERT WILLIAM, FOREST MANAGEMENT INVENTORY-SILVICULTURE, AIR POLLUTANT IMPACT ON FOREST GROWTH. *Current Pos:* CONSULTING FORESTER, SIMONS, REID, COLLINS, 72- *Personal Data:* b London, Eng, Oct 26, 32; Can & Brit citizen; m 60, Jill Gooden; c Hubert, Christopher & Sarah. *Educ:* Univ Wales, UK, BSc Hons, 55; Univ BC, MF, 60; Syracuse Univ, PhD(forest mgt & econ), 67. *Prof Exp:* Asst forester, Can Forest Prods Ltd, 55-60; forester staff, Columbia Cellulose Co Ltd, 60-71. *Concurrent Pos:* Res assoc, State Univ NY, 65-67. *Mem:* Fel Inst Chartered Foresters; Commonwealth Forestry Asn. *Res:* Impact of air pollutants on forest growth, reproduction, ecology and environment; effects of logging on biomass. *Mailing Add:* 111 Dunsmuir St Suite 400 Vancouver BC V6B 5W3 Can. *Fax:* 604-664-5433

BUNCE, JAMES ARTHUR, PHYSIOLOGICAL ECOLOGY. *Current Pos:* PLANT PHYSIOLOGIST, USDA, 77- *Personal Data:* b Troy, NY, June 19, 49; m 75; c 2. *Educ:* Bates Col, BS, 71; Cornell Univ, PhD(phys ecol), 75. *Prof Exp:* Res assoc crop physiol, Duke Univ, 75-77. *Mem:* Sigma Xi; Ecol Soc Am; Am Soc Plant Physiologists. *Res:* Analysis of plant adaptations and responses to environmental factors, especially water, and consequences of these in determining distribution patterns and productivity. *Mailing Add:* 3270 Bottner Rd Gambrills MD 21054

BUNCE, NIGEL JAMES, ORGANIC CHEMISTRY, ENVIRONMENTAL CHEMISTRY & TOXICOLOGY. *Current Pos:* From asst prof to assoc prof, 69-80, PROF CHEM, UNIV GUELPH, 80-, COORDR TOXICOL PROG, 89- *Personal Data:* b Sutton Coldfield, Eng, June 10, 43; m 91, Michelle Normandin; c Charles. *Educ:* Oxford Univ, BA, 64, DPhil(chem), 69. *Honors & Awards:* Union Carbide Award, Chem Inst Can, 92. *Concurrent Pos:* Killam Mem fel, Univ Alta, 67-69. *Mem:* Chem Inst Can; Air & Waste Mgt Asn; Soc Toxicol Can. *Res:* Mechanisms of free radical and photochemical reactions; photochemistry of aromatic compounds; environmental chemistry and toxicology of chlorinated aromatic compounds; tropospheric chemistry. *Mailing Add:* Dept Chem & Biochem Univ Guelph Guelph ON N1G 2W1 Can. *E-Mail:* bunce@chemblo.uoguelph.ca

BUNCE, PAUL LESLIE, MEDICINE. *Current Pos:* RETIRED. *Personal Data:* b Fargo, NDak, Sept 24, 16; m 45; c 2. *Educ:* Oberlin Col, AB, 38; Univ Chicago, MD, 42. *Prof Exp:* Asst instr pharmacol, Univ Pa, 46-48; house officer & resident urol, Johns Hopkins Univ, 48-51, instr, 50-52; from asst prof to prof surg, Univ NC, Chapel Hill, 52-81. *Mem:* AMA; Am Urol Asn. *Res:* Urology. *Mailing Add:* 970 Fairfield Dr Chapel Hill NC 27514-7770

BUNCE, RICHARD ALAN, SYNTHETIC METHODS DEVELOPMENT, MECHANISTIC & SYNTHETIC PHOTOCHEMISTRY. *Current Pos:* asst prof to assoc prof, 83-97, PROF CHEM, OKLA STATE UNIV, STILLWATER, 97- *Personal Data:* b Hartford, Conn, Oct 31, 53. *Educ:* Marietta Col, BS, 75; Univ Wis-Madison, PhD(org chem), 81. *Prof Exp:* NIH fel, Univ Calif, Berkeley, 81-83. *Concurrent Pos:* Prin investr, NIH, Am Chem Soc & other state agencies, 83-; consult, Koch Industs, Kans, 85-88; distinguished vis scientist, Kerr-McGee Corp, 89. *Mem:* Am Chem Soc; AAAS; Sigma Xi; Inter-Am Photochem Soc; Royal Chem Soc London. *Res:* Development of new synthetic methods, mechanistic and synthetic organic photochemistry, mechanistic and synthetic organic chemistry at high pressures. *Mailing Add:* Dept Chem Okla State Univ Stillwater OK 74078-3071

BUNCE, STANLEY CHALMERS, ORGANIC CHEMISTRY, SCIENCE EDUCATION. *Current Pos:* RETIRED. *Personal Data:* b Bayonne, NJ, Aug 21, 17; m 43, Lillis Jackson; c Gale (Schmidt), Judi (Turner) & James. *Educ:* Lehigh Univ, BS, 38, MA, 42; Rensselaer Polytech Inst, PhD(chem), 51. *Prof Exp:* Teacher, high sch, Pa, 39-41 & NJ, 41-43; res chemist, Johns-Manville Corp, 43-46; from instr to prof, Rensselaer Polytech Inst, 46-84, emer prof chem, 84- *Concurrent Pos:* Vis prof, Univ Oslo, 74. *Mem:* Fel AAAS; Am Chem Soc. *Res:* Organic reaction mechanisms; synthetic organic chemistry; medicinal chemistry. *Mailing Add:* Dept Chem Rensselaer Polytech Inst Troy NY 12180-3590. *E-Mail:* bunces@rpi.edu

BUNCEL, ERWIN, PHYSICAL ORGANIC CHEMISTRY. *Current Pos:* from asst prof to assoc prof, 62-66, PROF CHEM, QUEEN'S UNIV, ONT, 70- *Personal Data:* b Presov, Czech, May 31, 31; Can citizen; m 56, Henny Bienenfeld; c Irene & Jacqueline. *Educ:* Univ London, BSc, 54, PhD(chem), 57. *Hon Degrees:* DSc, Univ London, 70. *Honors & Awards:* Syntex Award Phys Org Chem, Chem Inst Can, 85. *Prof Exp:* Res assoc chem & fel, Univ NC, 57-58; Nat Res Coun Can fel, McMaster Univ, 58-61; res chemist, Am Cyanamid Co, 61-62. *Concurrent Pos:* Ed, Can J Chem, Isotopes Org Chem, Comprehensive Carbanion Chem, Isotopes in the Phys & Biomed Sci, J Labelled Compounds & Radiopharmaceut. *Mem:* Am Chem Soc; Chem Inst Can; Royal Soc Chem; Int Isotope Soc. *Res:* Isotope effects in organic reaction mechanisms; aromatic substitution; carbanion mechanisms; dynamics of nitroaromatic-base interactions; cyclodextrim enzyme models, organosulfur and organophosphorus reactivity, solvatochromism and photochromism; metal ion-biomolecule interactions; organometallic chemistry; environmental chemistry; author of over 250 publications; reviews, chapters, books and edited monographs. *Mailing Add:* Dept Chem Queen's Univ Kingston ON K7L 3N6 Can. *Fax:* 613-545-6669

BUNCH, DAVID WILLIAM, CHEMICAL ENGINEERING. *Current Pos:* process design engr, Ethyl Corp, 64-66, sr chem engr, 66-69, supvr, 69-79, prod mgr, 79-82, mkt mgr, 82-87, MKT DEVELOP DIR, ETHYL CORP, 87- *Personal Data:* b Eldon, Mo, Jan 20, 36; m 56; c 2. *Educ:* Mo Sch Mines, BS, 57, MS, 60, PhD(chem eng), 64. *Prof Exp:* Instr chem eng, Mo Sch Mines, 57-64. *Mem:* Am Inst Chem Engrs. *Res:* Mass transfer; vaporliquid equilibria; process dynamics; mathematical simulation. *Mailing Add:* 10086 Byrnes Rd St Francisville LA 77075

BUNCH, HARRY DEAN, AGRONOMY. *Current Pos:* RETIRED. *Personal Data:* b Yukon, Okla, Oct 3, 15; m 41; c 3. *Educ:* Okla State Univ, BS, 41; Univ Tenn, MS, 42, PhD(agron, seed technol), 59. *Prof Exp:* Instr agron, Univ Ky, 42-43; asst agronomist, Agr Exp Sta, Miss State Univ, 46-55, assoc agronomist & supvr, Seed Technol Lab, 55-64, prof agron, 64-85, dir, Int Progs Agr & Forestry, 67-85. *Mem:* Am Soc Agron. *Res:* Seed storage; mechanical injury of seeds; electrostatic separation of seeds; magnetic seed cleaning. *Mailing Add:* 1145 Blackjack Rd Starkville MS 39759. *Fax:* 601-323-6028

BUNCH, JAMES R, NUMERICAL ANALYSIS. *Current Pos:* assoc prof, 74-79, PROF MATH, UNIV CALIF, SAN DIEGO, 79- *Personal Data:* b Globe, Ariz, Sept 23, 40. *Educ:* Univ Ariz, BS, 62; Univ Calif, Berkeley, MA, 65, PhD(appl math), 69. *Prof Exp:* Asst mathematician, Argonne Nat Lab, 69-70; instr math, Univ Chicago, 70-71; asst prof comput sci, Cornell Univ, 71-74. *Concurrent Pos:* Consult, Argonne Nat Lab, 74-, Los Alamos Nat Lab, 80- *Mem:* Am Math Soc; Soc Indust & Appl Math; Asn Comput Mach. *Res:* Numerical linear algebra; linear equations, inertia, sparse matrics, Toeplitz matrices, eigenproblems, signal processing. *Mailing Add:* Dept Math Univ Calif San Diego La Jolla CA 92093-0112

BUNCH, KYLE, ELECTROMAGNETICS, COMPUTATIONAL PHYSICS. *Current Pos:* fel, 90, RES ASST PROF ELEC ENG, UNIV UTAH, 91- *Personal Data:* b Pueblo, Colo, May 5, 60; m 90, Magdalena Gniazdowska. *Educ:* Univ Colo BS, 82; Univ Utah, ME, 85, EE, 87, PhD(elec eng), 90. *Prof Exp:* Engr, TRW Inc, 82-83, Hughes Aircraft, 84-87. *Concurrent Pos:* Fel, TRW Inc, 83; consult, Sci Dynamics, 90-94; Fulbright fel & vis prof, Coun Int Exchange Scholars, Tech Univ Lodz, Poland, 94. *Mem:* Inst Elec & Electronics Engrs. *Res:* Computational electromagnetics including numerical simulations into wave phenomena within electron beams and solid state/superconducting devices. *Mailing Add:* 128 S St Salt Lake City UT 84103. *Fax:* 801-355-8128; *E-Mail:* bunch@ee.utah.edu

BUNCH, PHILLIP CARTER, MEDICAL PHYSICS. *Current Pos:* res physicist, 75-80, SR RES PHYSICIST, RES LABS, EASTMAN KODAK CO, 80-, RES ASSOC, 85- *Personal Data:* b Maryville, Tenn, Sept 14, 46; m 67, Margaret Tyler; c Jonathan & Jessica. *Educ:* Univ Chicago, AB, 69, MS, 71, PhD(med physics), 75. *Mem:* Inst Elec & Electronics Engrs; Am Asn Physicists in Med; Radiol Soc NAm. *Res:* Radiologic image analysis; Monte Carlo simulation of the optical characteristics of radiographic screen-film systems; objective measurement of optical and noise properties of radiologic imaging systems; application of visual psychophysics to radiography. *Mailing Add:* 1999 Lake Ave Health Sci Res Div Bldg 81 R1/BSMT Rochester NY 14650-2035. *Fax:* 716-477-9537

BUNCH, ROBERT MAXWELL, SOLID STATE PHYSICS. *Current Pos:* from asst prof to assoc prof, 83-93, PROF ROSE-HULMAN INST, 93- *Personal Data:* b Natchez, Miss, Oct 29, 53; m 83; c Samuel D & Luke L. *Educ:* La State Univ, BS, 75; Kans Univ, PhD(physics), 81. *Prof Exp:* Res assoc, Kans Univ, 81; asst res prof & lectr, San Diego State Univ, 81- *Concurrent Pos:* Asst dir, Tech Assistance & Serv Ctr; res scientist, Ctr Appl Optics Studies. *Mem:* Am Phys Soc; Soc Photo-Optical Instrumentation Engrs; Optical Soc Am; Am Asn Physics Teachers. *Res:* Light scattering in solids; fiber optics; fiber optic components and systems, optical instrument design and prototypes; optical inspection systems. *Mailing Add:* Dept Physics & Appl Optics Rose-Hulman Inst Technol 5500 Wabash Ave Terre Haute IN 47803-3999. *E-Mail:* robert.m.bunch@rose-hulman.edu

BUNCH, THEODORE EUGENE, ASTROGEOLOGY, GEOLOGY. *Current Pos:* NSF-Nat Res Coun fel, 66-69, RES SCIENTIST PLANETARY SCI & METEORITES, NASA-AMES RES CTR, 69- *Personal Data:* b Huntsville, Ohio, Mar 1, 36; m 63; c 2. *Educ:* Miami Univ, BA, 59, MS, 62; Univ Pittsburgh, PhD(geol), 66. *Honors & Awards:* H J Allen Award, NASA, 81. *Prof Exp:* Res asst geosci, Mellon Inst Sci, 61-64; res asst impact craters & meteorites, Univ Pittsburgh, 64-66. *Concurrent Pos:* Vis prof, Univ Cologne, 71 & Sonoma State Col, 74-; res assoc, Scripps Inst Oceanog, Univ Calif, San Diego, 74- *Mem:* Fel Mineral Soc Am; fel Meteoritical Soc (secy, 70-75). *Res:* Geological research on the moon, earth, Mars, asteroids, meteorites, interplanetary and interstellar dust. *Mailing Add:* 932 Arlington Ct Sunnyvale CA 94087

BUNCH, WILBUR LYLE, PHYSICS. *Current Pos:* RETIRED. *Personal Data:* b Pine Bluffs, Wyo, Apr 24, 25; m 46, Margaret May; c 5. *Educ:* Univ Wyo, BS, 49, MS, 51. *Prof Exp:* Engr, Gen Elec Co, 51-62, sr physicist, 62-64; res assoc reactor shielding, Battelle Mem Inst, 65-66, mgr, 67-70; mgr radiation & shielding analysis, Wadco, 70-72; mgr radiation & shield anal, Westinghouse Hanford Co, 72-88. *Mem:* Am Nuclear Soc. *Res:* Nuclear reactor shielding; nuclear instrumentation; reactor design; granted five US patents. *Mailing Add:* 2403 Pullen St Richland WA 99352

BUNCH, WILTON HERBERT, orthopedic surgery, for more information see previous edition

BUNCHER, CHARLES RALPH, BIOSTATISTICS, EPIDEMIOLOGY. *Current Pos:* asst prof statist, 70-73, PROF & DIR, DIV EPIDEMIOL & BIOSTATIST, MED COL, UNIV CINCINNATI, 73- *Personal Data:* b Dover, NJ, Jan 9, 38. *Educ:* Mass Inst Technol, BS, 60; Harvard Univ, MS, 64, ScD, 67. *Prof Exp:* Statistician, Atomic Bomb Casualty Comn, Nat Acad Sci, 67-70; chief biostatistician, Merrell-Nat Labs, 70-73. *Mem:* AAAS; Am Pub Health Asn; Am Statist Asn; Biomet Soc; Soc Epidemiol Res. *Res:* Cancer epidemiology; screening, diagnosis, and treatment, as well as occupational and environmental epidemiology; statistical research; clinical trials; design of experiments; pharmaceutical research; biostatistical analysis, pharmaceutical statistics; ALS epidemiology; risk analysis. *Mailing Add:* Environ Health Univ Cincinnati Col Med 231 Bethesda Ave Cincinnati OH 45267-0001

BUNDE, DARYL E, ZOOLOGY, PHYSIOLOGY. *Current Pos:* asst prof, 65-74, ASSOC PROF ZOOL, IDAHO STATE UNIV, 74- *Personal Data:* b Sioux Falls, SDak, Oct 29, 37; m 59; c 3. *Educ:* Augustana Col, SDak, BA, 59; Univ Tex, MA, 62; Mont State Univ, PhD(zool), 65. *Prof Exp:* Assoc Rocky Mountain Univs fac orientation grant, Los Alamos Sci Lab, 65. *Mem:* Am Soc Zoologists. *Res:* Amino acid metabolism of an insect; metabolism of radioactive elements in mammals. *Mailing Add:* Dept Biol Idaho State Univ 921 S Eighth Ave Pocatello ID 83209-0001

BUNDSCHUH, JAMES EDWARD, PHYSICAL CHEMISTRY. *Current Pos:* VPRES ACAD AFFAIRS, XAVIER UNIV, 93- *Personal Data:* b St Louis, Mo, Nov 13, 41; m 65, Lois Ottenad; c 4. *Educ:* St Louis Univ, BS, 63; Duquesne Univ, PhD(phys chem), 67. *Prof Exp:* Fel, Univ Ill, Chicago Circle, 67-68; asst prof chem, Western Ill Univ, 68-75, assoc prof & chmn dept, 75-80, prof, 80; mem staff, Dept Chem & Dean, Sch Sci & Humanities, Ind Univ-Purdue Univ, Ft Wayne, 80-86; dean, Col Arts & Sci, St Louis Univ, 86-93. *Concurrent Pos:* Guest lectr, Univ Stuttgart, 73-74. *Mem:* Am Chem Soc; Sigma Xi. *Res:* Surface chemistry; atmospheric chemistry; nuclear magnetic resonance. *Mailing Add:* Xavier Univ 3800 Victory Pkwy Cincinnati OH 45207-1092. *Fax:* 513-745-3341

BUNDY, FRANCIS P, EARTH SCIENCES. *Current Pos:* CONSULT, 86- *Personal Data:* b Columbus, Ohio, Sept 1, 10; m 36, Hazel Forwood; c John F, Suzanne B (Moffat), Freda B (Hofland) & David S. *Educ:* Otterbein Col, BS, 31; Ohio State Univ, MS, 33, PhD(physics), 37. *Hon Degrees:* Otterbein Col, DSci(physics), 59. *Honors & Awards:* Roozeboom Gold Medal, Neth Acad Arts & Sci, 69; Bridgman Gold Medal, Int Asn Adv High Pressure Sci & Technol, 87. *Prof Exp:* Instr & asst prof physics, Ohio Univ, Athens, 37-42; res assoc physics, Harvard Underwater Sound Lab, 42-45, Gen Elec Res & Develop Ctr, 46-86. *Mem:* Am Phys Soc; AAAS; Sigma Xi. *Res:* Fields of spectroscopy, electro-mechanical transducers, vacuum thermal insulation, high pressure science and technology; diamond synthesis by high pressure and temperature; behavior of matter at ultra-high pressure. *Mailing Add:* 4607 Swallow Ct Lebanon OH 45036

BUNDY, GORDON LEONARD, ORGANIC CHEMISTRY. *Current Pos:* RES CHEMIST, UPJOHN CO, 68- *Personal Data:* b Akron, Ohio, Nov 27, 42; m 66; c 3. *Educ:* Col Wooster, BA, 64; Northwestern Univ, PhD(org chem), 68. *Mem:* Am Chem Soc; The Chem Soc. *Res:* Chemistry and synthesis of naturally occurring materials, especially sesquiterpenes, steroids and prostaglandins; new synthetic methods; arachidonic acid cascade modulation; quinolone antibacterials; renin inhibitors. *Mailing Add:* Dept Discovey Chem 7254-209-605 Pharmacin & Upjohn Inc 7000 Portage Rd Kalamazoo MI 49001

BUNDY, HALLIE FLOWERS, BIOCHEMISTRY. *Current Pos:* from asst prof to prof, 60-90, EMER PROF BIOCHEM, MT ST MARY'S COL, CALIF, 90- *Personal Data:* b Los Angeles, Calif, Apr 2, 25. *Educ:* Mt St Mary's Col, BA, 47; Univ Southern Calif, MS, 55, PhD, 58. *Prof Exp:* Instr, Univ Southern Calif, 58-60. *Concurrent Pos:* Asst prog dir, undergrad res participation, NSF, Washington DC, 65-66; sci fac fel, NSF; Grant-in-Aid, Grad Women in Sci, 75. *Mem:* Am Chem Soc; Sigma Xi. *Res:* Chemistry of proteins; proteolytic enzymes; zymogens and inhibitors; carbonic anhydrase; comparative biochemistry. *Mailing Add:* PO Box 4338 Sunriver OR 97707

BUNDY, KIRK JON, BIOMATERIALS, CORROSION SCIENCE & ENGINEERING. *Current Pos:* assoc prof, 83-92, PROF BIOMAT, BIOMED ENG DEPT, TULANE UNIV, 92- *Personal Data:* b Highland Park, Mich, May 21, 47. *Educ:* Mich State Univ, BS, 68; Stanford Univ, MS, 70, PhD(mat sci & eng), 75. *Prof Exp:* Res asst, Dept Aeronaut & Astron, Stanford Univ, 71; sci assoc, Biomed Eng Inst, Swiss Fed Inst Technol, 71-75; teaching fel biomat & metall, Metall Prog, Ga Inst Technol, 75-78; asst prof biomat, mat sci & eng, Biomed Eng Dept & Mat Sci & Eng Dept, Johns Hopkins Univ, 78-83. *Concurrent Pos:* Consult, Metall Div, Nat Bur Stand, 81-83; sabbatical, Lab Exp Surg, Davos, Switz, 90; Fogarty sr int fel, 90. *Mem:* Soc Biomat; Biomed Eng Soc; Acad Dent Mat; Am Soc Testing & Mat; Soc Environ Geochem & Health; Nat Asn Corrosion Eng. *Res:* Interaction of applied stresses and corrosion processes as related to surgical implant materials; application of composite theory to bone; environmental sample analysis; polarographic analysis; corrosion and electrochemistry. *Mailing Add:* Biomed Eng Dept Tulane Univ 6823 St Charles Ave New Orleans LA 70118-5665

BUNDY, LARRY GENE, CORN NITROGEN MANAGEMENT, NITROGEN CYCLING IN CROPPING SYSTEMS. *Current Pos:* asst prof to assoc prof, 82-92, PROF SOIL FERTIL, UNIV WIS- MADISON, 92- *Personal Data:* b Red Bud, Ill, Dec 21, 43; m 66; c 2. *Educ:* Univ Ill, Urbana,

BS, 66, MS, 67; Iowa State Univ, PhD(soil chem), 73. *Prof Exp:* Soil specialist, Libby, McNeil & Libby, 73-77, Nestle Enterprises, Inc, 77-82. *Concurrent Pos:* Exten soil scientist, Univ Wis Exten, 82- *Mem:* Fel Am Soc Agron; Soil Sci Soc Am. *Res:* Improvement of nitrogen management in corn production; evaluation of diagnostic tests to predict corn nitrogen needs and development of nitrogen management techniques for improved agronomic efficiency and reduced environmental risks. *Mailing Add:* Dept Soil Sci 1525 Observatory Dr Madison WI 53706-1298

BUNDY, ROBERT W(ENDEL), ENGINEERING MECHANICS. *Current Pos:* PRES, SECURITY ELECTRONICS, INC, 71- *Personal Data:* b Passaic, NY, Jan 25, 24; m 52; c 3. *Educ:* Va Polytech Inst, BS, 47, MS, 48; Pa State Univ, PhD(eng mech), 54. *Prof Exp:* Asst, Pa State Univ, 48-52, instr, 52-53; engr, Am Flexible Coupling Co, 51-52; res physicist, E I du Pont de Nemours & Co, 54-61, res supvr, 61-71. *Concurrent Pos:* Consult eng & security; chmn bd, PSA Security Network, 77- *Mem:* Soc Exp Stress Anal; Am Soc Indust Security. *Res:* Design and installation of closed circuit television and access control systems. *Mailing Add:* 2836 Logan St Nashville TN 37211

BUNDY, ROY ELTON, PHYSIOLOGY. *Current Pos:* PROF & CHMN DEPT BIOL, OKALOOSA-WALTON COMMUNITY COL, 68- *Personal Data:* b Zanesville, Ohio, July 8, 24; c 2. *Educ:* Ohio State Univ, BS, 46, MS, 48; Univ Wis, PhD(zool), 55. *Prof Exp:* Teacher pub sch & instr physics, Ohio State Univ, 46-47; instr biol, Transylvania Col, 48-51; asst, Univ Wis, 51-55; asst prof biol, Wagner Col, 55-57; asst prof biol & physiol, Sch Dent, Fairleigh Dickinson Univ, 57-61, assoc prof physiol & chmn dept, 61-68. *Mem:* AAAS. *Mailing Add:* 370 Brian Circle Mary Esther Niceville FL 32569

BUNGAY, HENRY ROBERT, III, MICROBIAL BIOENGINEERING. *Current Pos:* PROF CHEM & ENVIRON ENG, RENSSELAER POLYTECH INST, 76- *Personal Data:* b Cleveland, Ohio, Jan 22, 28; m 52; c 3. *Educ:* Cornell Univ, BChE, 49; Syracuse Univ, PhD(biochem), 54. *Honors & Awards:* James Van Lanen Award, Am Chem Soc; Marvin Johnson Award, Am Chem Soc. *Prof Exp:* Biochemist, Eli Lilly & Co, Ind, 54-62; prof sanit eng, Va Polytech Inst, 62-67, prof bioeng, Clemson Univ, 67-73; vpres, Worthington Biochem Corp, 73-76. *Mem:* Am Chem Soc; fel Am Inst Chem Engrs; Am Soc Microbiol; Sigma Xi. *Res:* Bioengineering; fermentation processes; biological waste treatment. *Mailing Add:* Dept Chem Eng Rensselaer Polytech Inst Troy NY 12180-3590

BUNGAY, PETER M, SUSPENSION HYDRODYNAMICS. *Current Pos:* grants assoc, Div Res Grants, 73-74, spec asst, Off Dir, 74-75, CHEM ENGR, NAT CTR RES RESOURCES, NIH, 75- *Personal Data:* b Brooklyn, NY, June 17, 41; m 67, Janet Duvall. *Educ:* Cooper Union, BChE, 63; Carnegie-Mellon Univ, PhD(chem eng & biotechnol), 71. *Prof Exp:* Res fel, Montreal Gen Hosp, Univ Med Clin, McGill Univ, 71-73. *Mem:* Am Inst Chem Engrs; AAAS; NAm Membrane Soc; Europ Soc Membrane Sci & Technol. *Res:* Physiological pharmacokinetics of drugs and environmental agents; low-Reynolds-number hydrodynamics of suspensions; biomedical research applications of synthetic membranes; transport phenomena in the microcirculation; microdialysis. *Mailing Add:* Biomed Eng & Instrumentation Prog NIH Bldg 13 Rm 3N-17 Bethesda MD 20892. *E-Mail:* bungay@box_b.nih.gov

BUNGE, CARLOS FEDERICO, atomic spectroscopy, electronic structure calculations, for more information see previous edition

BUNGE, MARIO AUGUSTO, THEORETICAL PHYSICS, PHILOSOPHY & SOCIOLOGY. *Current Pos:* PROF PHILOS, MCGILL UNIV, 66- *Personal Data:* b Buenos Aires, Arg, Sept 21, 19; Arg & Can citizen; m 40, 59, Marta Cavallo; c Carlos, Mario, Eric & Silvia. *Educ:* Univ La Plata, PhD(physics), 52. *Hon Degrees:* LLD, Simon Fraser Univ, 81, Univ Rosario, 85, Univ La Plata, 87, Univ Fed Santa Caterina, 91, Univ Cardoba, 95, Univ del Sur, 96, Univ Imca Garcilaso dela Vega, 96, Univ Cagetano Heredia, 96. *Honors & Awards:* Prince of Asturias Prize, 82; Humanist Laureate, Acad Humanism, 85. *Prof Exp:* Prof physics, Univ Buenos Aires, 56-58, prof philos, 57-63. *Concurrent Pos:* Ed, Minerva, 44-45, Arg Physics Asn, 53-63, Episteme, D Reidel Publ Co, 74- & Found & Philos Sci & Technol, Pergamon Press, 79-; prof physics, Univ La Plata, 56-59; vis prof philos, Univ Pa, 60-61, physics & philos, Temple Univ, 63-64, Univ Del, 64-65, Univ Freiburg, 65-66 & ETH Zurich, 73; res prof philos, Univ Mex, 75-76, Univ Geneva, 86-87; nat lectr, Sigma Xi, 80-82, Univ Geneva, 86-87, Univ Genoa, 93-94; Guggenheim fel. *Mem:* Int Acad Philos Sci; Int Inst Philos; fel AAAS; Brit Soc Philos Sci; Can Philos Asn; fel Royal Soc Can. *Res:* Theoretical physics; foundations and philosophy of physics, psychology and social science; semantics, ontology, epistemology, sytems theory, value theory and ethics. *Mailing Add:* 29 Bellevue Ave Montreal PQ H3Y 1G4 Can

BUNGE, MARY BARTLETT, CYTOLOGY. *Current Pos:* PROF CELL BIOL ANAT & NEUROSURG SURG, UNIV MIAMI, 89- *Personal Data:* b New Haven, Conn, Apr 3, 31; m 56; c 2. *Educ:* Simmons Col, BS, 53; Univ Wis, MS, 55, PhD(zool, cytol), 60. *Prof Exp:* Asst med, Univ Wis, 53-56, asst zool, 56-60; res assoc anat, Col Physicians & Surgeons, Columbia Univ, 62-70; from res asst prof to res assoc prof, Sch Med, Wash Univ, 70-74, assoc prof anat, 74-78, prof anat neurobiol, 78-89. *Concurrent Pos:* Nat Inst Neurol Dis & Blindness fel, Col Physicians & Surgeons, Columbia Univ, 60-62; res assoc, Harvard Med Sch, 68-69; mem, Neurol Dis Prog Proj Rev Comt, Nat Inst Neurol & Commun Dis & Stroke, NIH, 83-87; Nat Adv Neurol & Commun Dis & Stroke Coun, NIH, 87- *Mem:* Soc Neurosci; Am Soc Cell Biol; Am Asn Anat; Electron Micros Soc Am. *Res:* Growth, differentiation, injury and repair of nervous tissue; normal and pathological nervous tissue; tissue culture and cell fine structure; cell to cell and cell to extra cellular matrix interaction in developing and regenerating nervous tissue. *Mailing Add:* Miami Proj Univ Miami Sch Med 1600 NW Tenth Ave R-48 Miami FL 33136. *Fax:* 305-548-4427

BUNGE, RICHARD PAUL, ANATOMY, CELL BIOLOGY. *Current Pos:* SCI DIR, MIAMI PROJ/PARALYSIS DIV & PROF NEUROSURG CELL BIOL ANAT, MIAMI UNIV, 89- *Personal Data:* b Madison, SDak, Apr 15, 32; m 56; c 2. *Educ:* Univ Wis, BA, 54, MS, 56, MD, 60. *Prof Exp:* Asst anat, Univ Wis, 54-57, instr, 57-58; from asst prof to assoc prof anat, Col Physicians & Surgeons, Columbia Univ, 62-70; prof anat, Sch Med, Wash Univ, 70-89. *Concurrent Pos:* Nat Multiple Sclerosis Soc fel surg, Col Physicians & Surgeons, Columbia Univ, 60-62; Lederle med fac award, 64-67; vis Auburn Univ prof, Harvard Med Sch, 68-69. *Mem:* Am Asn Anat; Am Soc Cell Biol; Tissue Cult Asn; Am Asn Neuropath; Soc Neurosci. *Res:* Biology of cells of the nervous system in vivo and in vitro. *Mailing Add:* Miami Proj Univ Miami Med Sch 1600 NW Tenth Ave R-48 Miami FL 33136. *Fax:* 305-362-9862

BUNGER, JAMES WALTER, FUELS ENGINEERING, ANALYTICAL CHEMISTRY. *Current Pos:* res assoc fuels eng, 75-79, RES ASST PROF FUELS ENG & SCI ADV, UNIV UTAH, 79- *Personal Data:* b Orange City, Iowa, Apr 7, 45; c 2. *Educ:* Univ Wyo, BSc, 68; Univ Utah, PhD(fuels eng), 79. *Prof Exp:* Lab technician chem, Laramie Energy Technol Ctr, Dept Energy, 67-68, chemist, 68-75. *Mem:* Am Chem Soc; Am Inst Chem Engrs. *Res:* Characterization, processing and utilization research and development of tar sand, oil shale and coal resources. *Mailing Add:* Dept Chem Eng Univ Utah 3290 Merrill Eng Salt Lake City UT 84112-1107

BUNGER, ROLF, METABOLIC HEART & CORONARY RESEARCH, BIOENERGETICS OF THE HEART. *Current Pos:* from asst prof to assoc prof, 79-92, PROF PHYSIOL, UNIFORMED SERV UNIV HEALTH SCI, BETHESDA, MD, 92-, PROF MOLECULAR/CELL BIOL, 94- *Personal Data:* b Hamburg, Ger, Oct 19, 41; m 73, Margriet Akkerman; c Nils & Frank. *Educ:* Univ Heidelberg, Dr med, 70; Univ Hamburg, MD, 71; Univ Munich, Dr med habil(physiol), 79. *Prof Exp:* Intern clin med, Heidberg Hosp, Hamburg, 70; sci asst physiol, Tech Univ Aachen, Ger, 70-74 & Univ Munich, 74-79. *Concurrent Pos:* Reviewer sci manuscripts Am & Europ journals physiol & related fields, 78-; vis prof, Uniformed Serv Univ Health Sci, Bethesda, Md, 78, prin investr, 79-; travel awards, Ger Res Asn, 78 & NSF, 83; NIH res grant, 82-99; vis prof, Erasmus Univ, Rotterdam, Neth, 92. *Mem:* Ger Physiol Soc; Am Physiol Soc; Am Heart Asn; AAAS. *Res:* Metabolic regulation of coronary flow in relation to cellular compartments of cardiac adenine nucleotides; energy and redox metabolism in normal and oxygen-deficient hearts; regulation of pyruvate metabolism and transport; metabolic regulation of cardiac contractility; patentee in field since 1996. *Mailing Add:* Dept Physiol Uniformed Serv Univ 4301 Jones Bridge Rd Bethesda MD 20814-4799. *Fax:* 301-295-3566

BUNGO, MICHAEL WILLIAM, CARDIOVASCULAR MEDICINE, AEROSPACE MEDICINE. *Current Pos:* PROF MED & MED DIR, HEART STA, UNIV TEX MED BR, GALVESTON. *Personal Data:* b Passaic, NJ, July 18, 50. *Educ:* Rensselaer Polytech Inst, BS, 71; NJ Med Sch, MD, 75. *Honors & Awards:* Louis H Bauer Founders Award, Aerospace Med Asn, 87. *Prof Exp:* Resident med, New Eng Deaconess Hosp, Boston, Mass, 75-78, fel cardiol, 78-80; head cardiovasc res, Johnson Space Ctr, NASA, Houston, 80-86, dir, Space Biomed Res Inst, 86-90, chief scientist, Med Sci Div, 90-91. *Concurrent Pos:* Clin asst prof med, Health Sci Ctr, Univ Tex, Houston, 84. *Mem:* Fel Am Col Cardiol; Am Heart Asn; Aerospace Med Asn. *Res:* Aerospace medicine, particularly the cardiovascular changes occurring in humans exposed to space flight. *Mailing Add:* PO Box 580431 Houston TX 77258. *Fax:* 409-772-4982; *E-Mail:* mbungo@cardiology.utmb.edu

BUNICK, GERARD JOHN, PROTEIN CRYSTALLOGRAPHY, NEUTRON SCATTERING. *Current Pos:* RES ASST PROF, OAK RIDGE GRAD SCH BIOMED SCI, UNIV TENN, 82- *Personal Data:* b Boston, Mass, May 27, 47; m 73; c 2. *Educ:* Univ Mass, BS, 69; Univ Pa, PhD(biol chem), 75. *Prof Exp:* Asst scientist, Anal Div, Silver Lab, Polaroid Corp, 69; res assoc, Dept Chem, Univ Pa, 74-77; res chemist, Oak Ridge Nat Lab, 77-81. *Concurrent Pos:* Lectr, Oak Ridge Grad Sch Biomed Sci, Univ Tenn, 79- *Mem:* Am Chem Soc; Am Crystallog Asn; AAAS; Am Inst Physics. *Res:* Application of biophysical techniques, especially x-ray diffraction and small angle neutron scattering, to elucidate the structure of biologically important macromolecules. *Mailing Add:* Dept Biol Oak Ridge Nat Lab PO Box 2009 MS 8077 Oak Ridge TN 37831-8077. *Fax:* 423-574-1274

BUNIMOVICH, LEONID A, NONLINEAR DYNAMICS & CHAOS THEORY, STATISTICAL MECHANICS. *Current Pos:* PROF, SCH MATH, GA INST TECHNOL, 91-, DIR, SOUTHEAST APPL ANALYTICAL CTR, 96- *Personal Data:* b Moscow, USSR, Aug 1, 47; US permanent resident; m 72, Lorissa; c Yulia & Yuri. *Educ:* Moscow Univ, MS, 69, PhD(probability theory), 73; Inst Theoret Physics Kiev, DrSci(theoret & math physics), 86. *Prof Exp:* Jr scientist, Inst Psychiat, USSR Acad Med Sci, 72-77; sr scientist, Res Inst Paper, 77-78; leading scientist, Inst Oceanog, USSR Acad Sci, 78-92. *Concurrent Pos:* Vis prof, Courant Inst, NY Univ, 89-90 & Rutgers Univ, 90-91; prof, Physics Dept, Univ Bielefeld, 90-91; lectr, Newton Inst, Cambridge Univ, 95. *Mem:* Am Math Soc; Soc Indust & Appl Math; Int Asn Math Physics; Moscow Math Soc. *Res:* Time and/or space chaotic motion; space-time chaos; ergodic theory; spatially extended dynamical systems; mechanisms of chaos, order-chaos transitions; mathematical biology; foundations of statistical mechanics; dynamics of ocean; industrial mathematics. *Mailing Add:* 5102 Nicolet Ct Marietta GA 30062. *Fax:* 404-894-4409; *E-Mail:* buhimovh@math.gatech.edu

BUNKER, BRUCE ALAN, XRAY SPECTROSCOPY. *Current Pos:* asst prof, 83-87, ASSOC PROF PHYSICS, UNIV NOTRE DAME, 87- *Personal Data:* b Pasadena, Calif, Apr 20, 52. *Educ:* Univ Wash, BSc, 74, PhD(physics), 80. *Prof Exp:* Res assoc, Univ Wash, 80 & NC State Univ, 81; IBM fel physics, Univ Ill, 81-83. *Mem:* Am Phys Soc. *Res:* X-ray and ultraviolet spectroscopy using synchrotron radiation sources. *Mailing Add:* Dept Phys Univ Notre Dame Col Sci Notre Dame IN 46556. *Fax:* 219-631-5952

BUNKER, JAMES EDWARD, medicinal chemistry, for more information see previous edition

BUNKER, JOHN PHILIP, MEDICINE. *Current Pos:* PROF ANESTHESIA, SCH MED, STANFORD UNIV, 60-, PROF FAMILY, COMMUNITY & PREV MED, 75-, DIR HEALTH SERV RES, 76- *Personal Data:* b Boston, Mass, Feb 13, 20; m 44; c 4. *Educ:* Harvard Univ, BA, 42, MD, 45; Am Bd Anesthesiol, dipl. *Prof Exp:* Instr anesthesia, Harvard Med Sch, 50-52, assoc, 52-55, asst clin prof, 55-60. *Concurrent Pos:* Anesthetist, Mass Gen Hosp, Boston, 50-60. *Mem:* Am Soc Anesthesiol; Am Soc Pharmacol & Exp Therapeut. *Res:* Health services research; technology assessment. *Mailing Add:* Anesthesia & Health Res & Policy 13 The Green Twickenham Middlesex TW2 5TU England. *Fax:* 44-72-326-3497

BUNKER, MERLE E, NUCLEAR PHYSICS. *Current Pos:* RETIRED. *Personal Data:* b Kansas City, Mo, Feb 8, 23; m 43, Wilma J Horine; c Bruce C & Paul G. *Educ:* Purdue Univ, BS, 46; Ind Univ, PhD(physics), 50. *Prof Exp:* Mem staff, Physics Div, Los Alamos Nat Lab, Univ Calif, 50-65, alt group leader, Group P-2, 65-74, group leader, Group P-2, 74-81, Group Inc-5, 81-90. *Concurrent Pos:* NSF sr fel, 64-65; supvr res reactor, 54-90; adv, Nuclear Data Group, Oak Ridge Nat Lab, 67-78; lab assoc, Los Alamos Nat Lab, Univ Calif, 90- *Mem:* Fel Am Phys Soc. *Res:* Gamma-ray spectroscopy; nuclear structure; neutron activation analysis. *Mailing Add:* 2218 46th St Los Alamos NM 87544

BUNN, CLIVE LEIGHTON, CELL BIOLOGY, BIOTECHNOLOGY. *Current Pos:* PRIN RES SCIENTIST, BIOTECH AUSTRALIA, 87- *Personal Data:* b Melbourne, Australia, May 25, 45; m 76, Kay Plymat. *Educ:* Monash Univ, BSc Hons, 69, PhD(biochem), 75. *Prof Exp:* Assoc res, Dept Human Genetics, Yale Univ, 72-76; vis scientist, Genetics Div, Nat Inst Med Res, UK, 76-79; asst prof, Dept Biol, Univ SC, 80-87. *Concurrent Pos:* Beit fel, 76-79. *Mem:* Am Soc Cell Biol; Soc In Vitro Biol; Australian Biotechnol Asn; Australian NZ Soc Cell Biol. *Res:* Biology of cultured animal cells, and their applications in biotechnology, toxicology, aging studies, and therapeutics. *Mailing Add:* Biotech Australia 28 Barcoo St PO Box 20 Roseville NSW 2069 Australia. *Fax:* 61-2-9928-8899; *E-Mail:* clive_bunn@bioaust.com.au

BUNN, HOWARD FRANKLIN, HEMATOLOGY, BIOCHEMISTRY. *Current Pos:* from asst prof to assoc prof, 73-79, PROF MED, SCH MED, HARVARD UNIV, 79; DIR HEMAT RES, PETER BENT BRIGHAM HOSP, 75- *Personal Data:* b Morristown, NJ, July 7, 35; m 62, Elizabeth Godard; c George, Emory & Andrew. *Educ:* Harvard Univ, AB, 57; Univ Pa, MD, 61. *Honors & Awards:* Merit Award, NIH, 90. *Prof Exp:* Asst prof med, Albert Einstein Col Med, 68-69. *Concurrent Pos:* Res career develop award, Nat Heart & Lung Inst, NIH, 69-74; scholar in residence, Fogarty Int Ctr, NIH, 82-84. *Mem:* Am Soc Biol Chemists; Am Soc Clin Invest; Asn Am Physicians; Am Soc Hemat (pres, 93). *Res:* Erythropoiesis; hemoglobinopathies; sickle cell anemia; red cell metabolism; hemoglobin structure and function; erythropoietin. *Mailing Add:* Div Hemat 721 Huntington Ave Boston MA 02115. *Fax:* 617-739-0748

BUNN, JOE M(ILLARD), AGRICULTURAL ENGINEERING. *Current Pos:* PROF AGR ENG, CLEMSON UNIV, 78- *Personal Data:* b Goldsboro, NC, Jan 20, 32; m 55, Marie Gaben; c Ronnie & Kenneth. *Educ:* NC State Col, BS, 55, MS, 57; Iowa State Univ, PhD(agr eng, math), 60. *Prof Exp:* From asst prof to assoc prof agr eng, Univ Ky, 60-78. *Concurrent Pos:* Engr, Univ Ky-Agency Int Develop contract team, Thailand, 68-69. *Mem:* Fel Am Soc Agr Engrs; Coun Agr Sci & Technol. *Res:* Engineering aspects of agricultural and food processing and materials handling; food eng with emphasis on edible films. *Mailing Add:* Agr Eng Dept Clemson Univ Clemson SC 29634-0357. *Fax:* 864-656-0338; *E-Mail:* jbunn@clust1.clemson.edu

BUNN, PAUL A, JR, MEDICAL ONCOLOGY. *Current Pos:* fel, Med Br, 73-76, sr investr, Med Oncol Br, 76-81, CHIEF MED ONCOL, CELLULAR KINETIC SECT, NAVY MED ONCOL BR, NAT CANCER INST, 81- *Personal Data:* b New York, NY, Mar 16, 45; m 68; c 3. *Educ:* Amherst Col, BA, 67; Cornell Univ, MD, 71. *Prof Exp:* Intern med, H C Moffitt Hosp, Univ Calif, San Francisco, 71-72, resident, 72-73. *Concurrent Pos:* Asst prof med, Med Col, Georgetown Univ, 77-81; assoc prof med, Uniformed Serv Univ Health Sci, 81- *Mem:* Am Soc Hemat; Am Soc Clin Oncol; Am Asn Cancer Res; Cell Kinetic Soc; Am Fedn Clin Res; fel Am Col Physicians. *Res:* Growth and characterization of malignant tritium cell disorders; cell biology of malignant tritium cell disorders; clinical studies of malignant lymplomas and small cell lung cancer. *Mailing Add:* Univ Colo Cancer Ctr 4200 E Ninth Ave Box B 188 Denver CO 80262

BUNN, WILLIAM BERNICE, III, OCCUPATIONAL CARCINOGENS. *Current Pos:* STAFF MEM, NAVISTAR INT TRANSPORT CORP, CHICAGO, ILL, 95- *Personal Data:* b Raleigh, NC, June 28, 52; m 83; c 1. *Educ:* Duke Univ, AB, 74, MD & JD, 79; Univ NC, MPH, 83. *Prof Exp:* Intern & resident internal med, Duke Univ Med Ctr, 81-83, from asst prof to assoc prof, Dept Community & Family Med, Div Occup Med, 84-85, dir res, 85; asst clin prof, Dept Epidemiol, Sch Med, Yale Univ, 86; dir occup health & environ affairs, Pharmaceut Res & Develop Div, Bristol-Myers Co, 86, sr dir, 87; vpres & corp med dir, Manville Sales Corp, 88-95, vpres & sr dir health safety & environ, 89-95. *Concurrent Pos:* Occup Safety & Health Admin fel, 73, Mercury Res fel, 78-80, NIH cancer res fel, 82-83, Nat Inst Occup Safety & Health training fel, 83-84. *Mem:* Am Col Physicians; Am Acad Occup Med; Am Occup Med Asn; AMA; Am Col Occup Med. *Res:* Cancer epidemiology; nasal carcinogens; toxic effects of mercury; legal research; author of over 40 technical publication; fiber toxicity and carcinogenicity. *Mailing Add:* Navistar Int Trans Corp 455 N Cityfront Plaza Dr Chicago IL 60611

BUNNELL, FREDERICK LINDSLEY, WILDLIFE ECOLOGY, CONSERVATION BIOLOGY. *Current Pos:* PROF WILDLIFE, UNIV BC, 80-, DIR, CTR APPL CONSERV BIOL & FOREST RENEWAL PROF, 96- *Personal Data:* b Vancouver, BC, May 8, 42; m 78; c 1. *Educ:* Univ BC, BSF, 65; Univ Calif, Berkeley, PhD(wildland resource sci), 73. *Honors & Awards:* Gold Medal, Can Inst Forestry, Can Forestry Sci Award, 89; Outstanding Scientist, NWest Sci Asn, 94. *Prof Exp:* Res assoc forestry, Univ Calif, Berkeley, 66-69, from instr II to assoc prof wildlife, 71-79. *Concurrent Pos:* Consult, BC Fish & Wildlife Br, 75-; hon consult, Int Union Conserv Nature & Natural Resources, 76-80; Nuffield Found fel, 78-79; Natural Sci & Eng Res Coun sr indust fel, 85-86; assoc ed, Forestry Chronicle, 91-; independent chair, Claroquot Sci Panel, 93-96; adj prof, Univ Idaho. *Mem:* Can Wildlife Soc (vpres, 81-83); Can Inst Forestry; Int Union Forest Res Orgn; Wildlife Soc; Soc Conserv Biol. *Res:* Wildlife habitat relationships, particularly impacts of forestry practices upon terrestrial vertebrates; planning models of vertebrate-forest relations at standard forest level. *Mailing Add:* Fac Forestry Univ BC Vancouver BC V6T 1Z4 Can

BUNNER, ALAN NEWTON, HIGH ENERGY ASTROPHYSICS, X-RAY ASTRONOMY. *Current Pos:* br chief astrophys, 86-96, SCI PROG DIR, NASA HQ, 96- *Personal Data:* b St Catharines, Ont, Jan 11, 38; US citizen; m 73; c Andrew A & Anne E. *Educ:* Univ Toronto, BA, 60; Cornell Univ, MS, 64, PhD(physics), 67. *Prof Exp:* Instr physics, Cornell Univ, 66-67; assoc scientist space physics, Univ Wis, 67-79; sr scientist, Perkin-Elmer Corp, 79-85. *Mem:* Am Astron Soc; Int Astron Union; Soc Photo-Optical Instrumentation Engrs; Am Inst Aeronaut & Astronaut. *Res:* Advanced x-ray astrophysics. *Mailing Add:* 7200 Burtonwood Dr Alexandria VA 22307. *Fax:* 202-358-3098; *E-Mail:* alan.bunner@hq.nasa.gov

BUNNETT, JOSEPH FREDERICK, REACTION MECHANISMS. *Current Pos:* prof, 66-91, EMER PROF CHEM, UNIV CALIF, SANTA CRUZ, 91- *Personal Data:* b Portland, Ore, Nov 26, 21; m 42, Sara A Telfer; c Alfred, David & Peter (deceased). *Educ:* Reed Col, BA, 42; Univ Rochester, PhD(org chem), 45; Brown Univ, MA, 59. *Honors & Awards:* James Flack Norris Award, Am Chem Soc, 92. *Prof Exp:* Res chemist, Western Pine Asn, Portland, 45-46; instr org chem, Reed Col, 46-48, asst prof chem, 48-52; from asst prof to assoc prof chem, Univ NC, 52-58; from assoc prof to prof, Brown Univ, 58-66, chmn dept, 61-64. *Concurrent Pos:* Fulbright fel, Univ London, 49-50; res grants, Res Corp, NSF Petrol Res Fund, Am Chem Soc & NIH; Fulbright & Guggenheim fels, Univ Munich, 60-61; ed, Accounts Chem Res, 66-86, trustee, Reed Col; chmn, Comn on Phys Org Chem, Int Union Pure & Appl Chem, 78-83, pres, Org Chem Div, 85-87; chmn, Task Force Sci Aspects Destruction Chem Warfare Agents, 91-; mem, Nat Res Coun Comt on Alternative Chem Demilitarization Technol, 92-93. *Mem:* Am Acad Arts & Sci; Am Chem Soc; Royal Soc Chem UK; hon mem Chem Soc Italy; hon mem Pharmaceut Soc Japan; fel Japan Soc Prom Sci; hon Accademia Gioenia di Catania Italy. *Res:* Mechanisms of reactions of aromatic compounds with basic or nucleophilic reagents, of reactions of diazonium salts, of olefin-forming elimination reactions, of reactions involving electron transfer steps. *Mailing Add:* Thimann Labs Univ Calif Santa Cruz CA 95064. *Fax:* 408-459-2935

BUNNEY, BENJAMIN STEPHENSON, PHARMACOLOGY, NEUROSCIENCE. *Current Pos:* fel psychiat, Yale Univ, 68-71, from asst prof to assoc prof, 71-84, from asst prof to assoc prof pharmacol, 74-84, PROF PSYCHIAT & PHARMACOL, SCH MED, YALE UNIV, 84-, CHMN, DEPT PSYCHIAT & CHARLES B G MURPHY PROF, 88- *Personal Data:* b Lansing, Mich, Sept 27, 38; m 60; c 3. *Educ:* NY Univ, BA, 60, MD, 64. *Honors & Awards:* Daniel H Efron Res Award, Am Col Neuropsychopharmacol; Leiber Prize, Nat Alliance Res Schizophrenia & Depression. *Prof Exp:* Intern internal med, Bellevue Hosp, 64-65, resident, 65-66; with USAF, 66-68. *Concurrent Pos:* Mem, Basic Psychopharmacol Res Rev Subcomt, 77-81, Res Scientists Develop Rev Comt, 82-86; psychiatrist-in-chief, Yale-New Haven Hosp. *Mem:* Inst Med-Nat Acad Sci; Psychiat Res Soc; Am Col Neuropsychopharmacol; Soc Neurosci; Am Psychiat Asn; NY Acad Sci. *Res:* Electrophysiological and anatomical techniques to study the central site and mechanism of action of psychoactive drugs and central nervous system circuitry and function. *Mailing Add:* Dept Psychiat Yale Univ 25 Park St New Haven CT 06519-1189

BUNSHAH, ROINTAN F(RAMROZE), METALLURGY. *Current Pos:* metallurgist, Lawrence Radiation Lab, Univ Calif, Livermore, 60-69, prof, 69-91, EMER PROF ENG, UNIV CALIF, LOS ANGELES, 91- *Personal Data:* b Bombay, India, Dec 18, 27; US citizen; m 91, Zohreh Firovzabodi. *Educ:* Benares Hindu Univ, BSc, 48; Carnegie Inst Technol, MS, 51, DSc(metall), 52. *Honors & Awards:* Hadfield Medal, Geol, Mining & Metall Inst India, 48; Gaede-Langmuir Prize, Am Vac Soc, 86. *Prof Exp:* Res metallurgist & instr metall, Metals Res Lab, Carnegie Inst Technol, 52-54; res scientist & adj prof, Res Div, Col Eng, NY Univ, 54-60. *Mem:* Fel Am Soc Metals; fel Am Vacuum Soc (pres, 70-71); Indian Vacuum Soc. *Res:* Vacuum metallurgy; ultra-high vacuum techniques; high rate physical vapor deposition processes; space processing of materials; materials synthesis, plasma-assisted vapor deposition techniques; electronic and opto-electronic materials, super hard coatings for wear resistance; biomaterials; diamond films; high technetium super conducting films. *Mailing Add:* Dept Mat Sci Univ Calif 5732 Boelter Hall Los Angeles CA 90024-1595. *Fax:* 310-206-7353

BUNTINAS, MARTIN GEORGE, TOPOLOGICAL SEQUENCE SPACES WITH APPLICATIONS TO FOURIER ANALYSIS. *Current Pos:* from asst prof to assoc prof, 70-80, PROF MATH, LOYOLA UNIV, CHICAGO, 80- *Personal Data:* b Klaipeda, Lithuania, Sept 1, 41; US citizen; m 66, Ruta Laisvenas; c Rimas M, Darius T & Aras A. *Educ:* Univ Chicago, AB, 64; Ill Inst Technol, MS, 67, PhD(math), 70. *Prof Exp:* Instr math, Ill Inst Technol, 67-70. *Concurrent Pos:* Res fel, Alexander von Humboldt Found, 71-72 & 77-78, Fulbright Prog, 77-78. *Mem:* Am Math Soc; Math Asn Am; Am Statist Asn. *Res:* Functional analysis and topological sequence spaces. *Mailing Add:* Dept Math & Comput Sci Loyola Univ 6525 N Sheridan Rd Chicago IL 60626-5385. *Fax:* 773-508-2123; *E-Mail:* mgb@math.lluc.edu

BUNTING, BRIAN TALBOT, ENVIRONMENTAL SCIENCES. *Current Pos:* assoc prof, McMaster Univ, 68-74, mem, Arctic Res Group, 69-76, prof geog & pedology, 75-96, EMER PROF, MCMASTER UNIV, 97- *Personal Data:* b Sheffield, Eng, Oct 15, 32; m 58; c 2. *Educ:* Univ Sheffield, BA, 53, MA, 57; Univ London, PhD, 70. *Prof Exp:* Demonstr geog, Univ Keele, Eng, 54-55; lectr, Birkbeck Col, London, 57-68. *Concurrent Pos:* Kemsley fel, Copenhagen Univ, 53-54; instr, Field Studies Coun, UK, 64-68; Brit Coun Interchange, Sorbonne, Paris, 65; vis lectr, Univ Ibadan, 65-66; guest prof, Univ Montana, 69, Aarhus Univ, 74-75 & Lakehead Univ, 78. *Mem:* Soil Sci Soc Am; Can Soc Soil Sci; Int Soc Soil Sci; Asn Scand Studies Can. *Res:* Studies of soil genesis and soil amelioration; geography of soils, especially factorial influences on microfabrics of soils; impact of forest fire on soils; soil pollution from landfill sites, land zoning analysis. *Mailing Add:* Dept Geog BS 313 McMaster Univ Hamilton ON L8S 4K1 Can

BUNTING, BRUCE GORDON, INTERNAL COMBUSTION ENGINES, TRIBOLOGY. *Current Pos:* TECH ADV, CUMMINS ENGINE CO, 96- *Personal Data:* b Detroit, Mich, Feb, 22, 48; m 73, Barbra Gula. *Educ:* Mich State Univ, BS, 70; Mich Technol Univ, MS, 75; Rensselaer Polytech Inst, PhD(mech eng), 87. *Prof Exp:* Res engr, Mich Technol Univ, 75-78; tech specialist, Cummins Engine Co, 78-81; sr engr, United Technologies Diesel Systs, 81-85; sr scientist, MRC Bearings, SKF USA Inc, 87-89; staff engr, Amoco Oil Co, 89-96. *Mem:* Soc Automotive Engrs; Am Soc Mech Engrs. *Res:* Development of emission control catalysts and control strategies for diesel engines. *Mailing Add:* 3470 W Carr Hill Rd Columbus IN 47201. *Fax:* 812-377-7226; *E-Mail:* b.g.bunting@ctc.cummins.com

BUNTING, CHRISTOPHER DAVID, ELECTRICAL ENGINEERING. *Current Pos:* DIR ENG, HUNTER ASSOCS LAB INC, 84- *Personal Data:* b Lytham, Gt Brit, Oct 2, 44; m 88. *Educ:* Cambridge Univ, BA, 66, MA, 70, PhD(elec eng), 71. *Prof Exp:* Sr electronics engr elec eng, Eurotherm Ltd, UK, 73-75, vpres, 77-84, dir res & develop elec eng, Eurotherm Corp, 75- *Concurrent Pos:* Fel, Trinity Col, Cambridge Univ, 70-74. *Res:* Application of advanced electronics to the control of processes in industry and research. *Mailing Add:* 9924 Browns Mill Rd Vienna VA 22182

BUNTING, DEWEY LEE, II, RESEARCH ADMINISTRATION. *Current Pos:* From asst prof to assoc prof, 68-74, PROF ZOOL, UNIV TENN, 74-, DIR, ECOL PROG, 81- *Personal Data:* b Louisville, Ky, Sept 1, 32; m 57; c 3. *Educ:* Univ Louisville, BA, 57, MS, 59; Okla State Univ, PhD(zool), 63. *Concurrent Pos:* USPHS res grant, 66-69; Fed Water Pollution Control Admin res grants, 67-69; res grants, Off Water Resources Res, 69-74, Ecol Prog Subcontract Admin, 81- *Mem:* Am Soc Limnol & Oceanog; Int Asn Theoret & Appl Limnol; Ecol Soc Am. *Res:* Ecological effects of water pollution; systematics of fresh-water invertebrates. *Mailing Add:* Ecol Prog Univ Tenn 1345 Circle Park Knoxville TN 37996-0001

BUNTING, JACKIE ONDRA, AERONAUTICAL & ASTRONAUTICAL ENGINEERING. *Current Pos:* res scientist, Martin Marietta Corp, 69-76, sr group engr, 76-80, dir eng opers, 81-88, dir launch vehicle technol, 88-94, PROG MGR, RLV SYSTS, DENVER DIV, MARTIN MARIETTA CORP, 94- *Personal Data:* b Poquoson, Va, Jan 27, 38; m 61; c 2. *Educ:* Univ Va, BS, 60, MS, 62; Stanford Univ, PhD(aeronaut, astronaut), 67. *Prof Exp:* Asst, Stanford Univ, 62-67; asst prof aerodyn, Univ Va, 67-69. *Mem:* Am Inst Aeronaut & Astronaut. *Res:* Experimental measurements of transport properties of high temperature gases; measurement of velocity distributions for aerodynamic molecular beams. *Mailing Add:* 10722 W Dakan Mountain Littleton CO 80127

BUNTING, JOHN WILLIAM, physical organic chemistry; deceased, see previous edition for last biography

BUNTING, ROGER KENT, INORGANIC CHEMISTRY. *Current Pos:* from asst prof to assoc prof, 66-85, chmn dept, 80-81, PROF CHEM, ILL STATE UNIV, 85- *Personal Data:* b Creston, Ill, Nov 27, 35; m 58, Sheila McGuire; c Bryan, Rachel, Laura & Stephen. *Educ:* Univ Ill, BS, 58, MS, 61; Pa State Univ, PhD(chem), 65. *Prof Exp:* Vis res assoc chem, Ohio State Univ, 65-66. *Concurrent Pos:* Hon res fel, Birkbeck Col, Univ London, 74-75; Air Sci Eng fel, USAF Academy, 78; consult, Advan Sci Div, Eureka Co, 76-; res fel, Univ Florence, Italy, 82; vis prof, Ohio State Univ, 83; distinguished vis prof, US Air Force Acad, 87-88; fac res assoc, Air Force Armament Lab, 89; resident res affil, Jet Propulsion Lab, 92; res assoc, Univ del Pais Vasco, Spain, 93. *Mem:* Am Chem Soc; Royal Soc Chem; Sigma Xi; Royal Photographic Soc. *Res:* Electronically conducting polymers; inorganic polymers and heterocycles; chemistry of photographic imaging systems. *Mailing Add:* Dept Chem Ill State Univ Normal IL 61761. *Fax:* 309-438-5538; *E-Mail:* bunting@xenon.che.ilstu.edu

BUNTLEY, GEORGE JULE, SOIL MORPHOLOGY. *Current Pos:* assoc prof agron, 68-81, PROF PLANT & SOIL SCI, UNIV TENN, KNOXVILLE, 81- *Personal Data:* b Sheldon, Iowa, Feb 20, 24; m 47; c 2. *Educ:* SDak State Univ, BS, 49, MS, 50, PhD(soils), 62. *Prof Exp:* From asst prof to assoc prof agron, SDak State Univ, 50-68. *Concurrent Pos:* Vis prof agron, Univ Tenn, 66-67. *Mem:* Am Soc Agron; Soil Sci Soc Am; Int Soil Sci Soc; Soil Conserv Soc Am; Coun Agr Sci & Technol. *Res:* Relationships between the physical and chemical properties of soils and specific land use alternatives. *Mailing Add:* 516 Gila Trail Knoxville TN 37919-6973

BUNTON, CLIFFORD A, ORGANIC CHEMISTRY, CHEMICAL DYNAMICS. *Current Pos:* prof, 63-90, chmn dept, 67-72, EMER PROF CHEM, UNIV CALIF, SANTA BARBARA, 90- *Personal Data:* b Chesterfield, Eng, Jan 4, 20; US citizen; m 45, Ethel M Clayton; c Julia M & Claire J. *Educ:* Univ London, BSc, 42, PhD(org chem), 45. *Hon Degrees:* DSc, Univ Perugia, 86. *Honors & Awards:* Tolman Medal, 87. *Prof Exp:* Lectr, Univ London, 45-58, reader, 58-63. *Concurrent Pos:* Commonwealth Fund fel, Columbia Univ, 48-49; Brit Coun vis lectr, Chile & Arg, 60; vis lectr, Univ Calif, Los Angeles, 61 & Univ Toronto, 62; mem policy comt, Univ Chile-Univ Calif Coop Prog; vis prof, Univ Lausanne, Switz, 76-79; adj prof, Univ Chile, 88. *Mem:* Fel Am Chem Soc; Brit Chem Soc; fel AAAS; corresp mem Chilean Acad Sci. *Res:* Mechanisms of organic and inorganic reactions; colloid chemistry. *Mailing Add:* Dept Chem Univ Calif Santa Barbara CA 93106. *Fax:* 805-893-4120

BUNTROCK, ROBERT EDWARD, INFORMATION SCIENCE, ORGANIC CHEMISTRY. *Current Pos:* RES ASSOC, AMOCO CORP, 85- *Personal Data:* b Minneapolis, Minn, Nov 19, 40; m 61, Gloria F Kral; c Stephen R & Christine L. *Educ:* Univ Minn, Minneapolis, BChem, 62; Princeton Univ, MA, 64, PhD(org chem), 67. *Prof Exp:* Asst org chem, Princeton Univ, 62-63; res chemist pesticide chem, Air Prod & Chem, Inc, 67-70; proj chemist, Am Oil Co, 70-71; res info scientist, Stand Oil Co, 71-81, sr res info scientist, 81-85. *Concurrent Pos:* Chmn, Div Chem Info, Am Chem Soc, 81. *Mem:* Asn Ind Info Prof; Am Chem Soc; Am Soc Info Sci; Sigma Xi. *Res:* Information retrieval; evaluation of information systems; selective dissemination of information; end-user training; amide hemiaminals; 1,2,4-oxadiazetidines; cyclization reactions of 2,2-disubstituted biphenyls; syntheses of pesticides; heterocyclic chemistry. *Mailing Add:* 670 N Eagle St Naperville IL 60563-3024. *Fax:* 630-961-7992, 420-2314; *E-Mail:* rebuntrock@amoco.com

BUNYAN, ELLEN LACKEY SPOTZ, THEORETICAL CHEMISTRY, SCIENCE EDUCATION. *Current Pos:* from asst prof to assoc prof chem, 72-91, adj prof, continuing educ, 91-94, ADJ PROF, UNIV DC AT WALTER REED ARMY MED CTR, 95- *Personal Data:* b Clarks Mills, Pa, Aug 14, 21; wid; c Mark S, Leslie C & Elizabeth (O'Rourke). *Educ:* Univ Pittsburgh, BS, 42; Univ Wis-Madison, PhD(chem), 50. *Prof Exp:* Chemist, Eastman Kodak Co, 42-44; instr chem, Univ Wis-Milwaukee, 46-47, res asst, Univ Wis-Madison, 47-50, proj assoc, 50-52; instr physics, St Agnes Acad, Houston, Tex, 65; Welch fel chem, Rice Univ, 68-69; lectr, Montgomery Col, 70-72. *Concurrent Pos:* Guest worker, Nat Bur Stand, 76; fel Nat Urban League, Eastman Kodak, 76. *Mem:* Am Chem Soc; Sigma Xi. *Res:* Molecular theory of gases; transport properties gases; intermolecular forces; theory of mass spectra-translational energy of fragments of ion decomposition of hydrocarbons; curriculum development reentering students and allied health. *Mailing Add:* 8215 Roanoke Ave Takoma Park MD 20912-6226

BUOL, STANLEY WALTER, SOIL SCIENCE, SOIL GENESIS & CLASSIFICATION. *Current Pos:* from assoc prof to assoc prof, 66-92, WILLIAM NEAL REYNOLDS PROF SOIL SCI, NC STATE UNIV, 92- *Personal Data:* b Madison, Wis, June 14, 34; m 60, Joan Showers; c Gregory & Glenda. *Educ:* Univ Wis, BS, 56, MS, 58, PhD(soils), 60. *Honors & Awards:* Int Soil Sci Award, Am Soc Agron. *Prof Exp:* Asst prof agr chem & soils, Univ Ariz, 60-64, assoc prof, 64-66. *Concurrent Pos:* Consult, Sensory Systs Lab, 63-65, West Va Co, 80 , Int Paper, 81 & World Bank, 93; mem, Scope Comm Nat Res Coun, 93-94. *Mem:* Fel Am Soc Agron; fel Soil Sci Soc Am. *Res:* Micromorphology of soil profiles with related work in soil genesis and classification; studies of soil formation and classification with related land use in intertropical areas of America, Asia and Africa; soil functions in sustainable food production. *Mailing Add:* Dept Soil Sci NC State Univ Raleigh NC 27695-7619. *Fax:* 919-515-2167; *E-Mail:* stanley__buol@ncsu.edu

BUONAMICI, RINO, MECHANICAL ENGINEERING. *Current Pos:* PRIN ENGR, WESTINGHOUSE HANFORD CO, 74- *Personal Data:* b Italy, Jan 13, 29; US citizen; m 54; c 2. *Educ:* Univ Nev, BSME, 55. *Prof Exp:* Engr, Douglas Aircraft Co, 55-56; engr, Martin Co, 56-57; engr specialist & mgr, Aerojet Rocket Co, 57-63; fluidic engr, Naval Ammunition Depot, 73-74. *Concurrent Pos:* Prin investr, Aerojet Liquid Rocket Co & Hanford Engr Develop Lab; consult, Williams & Lane Co. *Mem:* Am Soc Mech Engrs. *Res:* Thermodynamic, fluid and heat transfer fields for materials in a cryogenic and high temperature environments; sophisticated rotating machinery for aerospace and nuclear applications; analysis and design, structural and dynamic testing of complex structures, deployment and actuation systems for engine/space vehicles; design and development of complex nuclear power plant systems; in the fluidic engineering field designed sophisticated hydraulic, pneumatic and mechanical systems including remote control operation; extensive analysis and design of major components: steam generators, boiler systems for steam power. *Mailing Add:* 507 S Taft St Kennewick WA 99336

BUONGIORNO, JOSEPH, FOREST ECONOMICS. *Current Pos:* from asst prof to assoc prof forest econ, 75-82, PROF FORESTRY, UNIV WIS-MADISON, 82- *Personal Data:* b Golfech, France, Jan 15, 44; m 72; c 2. *Educ:* Advan Sch Forestry, Paris, Ingenieur, 67; State Univ NY, Syracuse, MS, 69; Univ Calif, Berkeley, PhD(forest econ), 71. *Honors & Awards:* Carl Schenk Award, Soc Am Foresters, 88. *Prof Exp:* Forestry officer, Food & Agr Orgn, UN, 71-75. *Concurrent Pos:* Consult, Food & Agr Orgn, UN, World Bank, Int Trop Timber Orgn. *Mem:* Am Econ Asn; Soc Am Forestry; Am Agr Econ Asn; Inst Mgt Sci. *Res:* Forestry and forest products economics; forestry sector planning; international trade of forest products; computer models. *Mailing Add:* 38 S Eau Claire Ave Madison WI 53705

BUONI, FREDERICK BUELL, DECISION ANALYSIS, EXPERT SYSTEMS. *Current Pos:* assoc prof, 78-79, chmn, Opers Res Prog, 79-95, PROF OPERS RES & COMPUT SCI, FLA INST TECHNOL, 79-, ASSOC DEAN, COL ENG, 95- *Personal Data:* b Brooklyn, NY, July 15, 34; m 58, 80, Dorothy W. Culpepper; c Frederick B II & Gregory P. *Educ:* Rutgers Univ, AB, 57; Ohio State Univ, MS, 67, PhD(nuclear eng), 71. *Prof Exp:* Chief, reactor eng br, Air Force Inst Technol, 65-68; chief, atmospheric br, Air Force Tech Appln Ctr, Patrick AFB, Fla, 71-76, dep dir advan technol, 76-78. *Concurrent Pos:* Adj prof, Fla Inst Technol, 72-79; pres, Fla Acad Scis, 90-91, treas, 94-96; vis prof, E I S T I, Cergy, France, 92-93. *Mem:* Inst Elec & Electronics Engrs; Int Ref Orgn Forensic Med & Sci; Asn Comput Mach. *Res:* Development and use of computer-based decision aids for decision analysis and decision making; artificial intelligence; expert systems; decision support systems; multiobjective decision theory. *Mailing Add:* Col Eng Fla Inst Technol 150 W University Blvd Melbourne FL 32901-6988. *Fax:* 407-676-0883; *E-Mail:* buoni@zach.fit.edu

BUONI, JOHN J, COMPUTATIONAL MATHEMATICS. *Current Pos:* From asst prof to assoc prof, 70-80, PROF MATH, YOUNGSTOWN STATE UNIV, 80- *Personal Data:* b Philadelphia, Pa, Apr 25, 43; m 70; c 2. *Educ:* St Joseph's Col, Pa, BS, 65; Univ Pittsburgh, MS, 68, PhD(math), 70. *Concurrent Pos:* Vis prof, Kent State Univ, 78-79. *Mem:* Am Math Soc; Soc Indust & Appl Math; Sigma Xi. *Res:* Numerical linear algebra; micro-computer software; operators on Banach spaces. *Mailing Add:* 79 Green Bay Dr Youngstown OH 44512

BUONO, JOHN ARTHUR, SURFACE SCIENCE, FAILURE ANALYSIS. *Current Pos:* DIR, PHOTOMETRICS INC, 77-, VPRES TECH DIV, 81- *Personal Data:* b Cambridge, Mass, Apr 29, 47. *Educ:* Merrimack Col, BS, 69; Univ RI, PhD(anal chem), 75. *Prof Exp:* Lab mgr, Fisher Anal Inst Div, 73-77. *Mem:* Am Chem Soc; Int Soc Hybrid Microelectronics; Soc Appl Spectros; Am Soc Qual Control. *Res:* Application of surface analysis techniques to research and development problems in microelectronics and materials. *Mailing Add:* Analytical Answers 4 Arrow Dr Woburn MA 01801-2087

BUONO, RUSSELL JOSEPH, DEVELOPMENT & FUNCTION OF VERTEBRATE RETINA, GENE EXPRESSION & FUNCTION DURING DEVELOPMENT. *Current Pos:* ASST PROF PSYCHOL, SCH MED, UNIV PA, 97- *Personal Data:* b Philadelphia, Pa, May 21, 61; m 85, Michelle R Zimmerman; c Michael S. *Educ:* Temple Univ, BA, 84, MA, 86, PhD(cell & develop biol), 89. *Prof Exp:* Fel, March of Dimes, NIH, 89-90, Univ Fla, 90-92; asst prof anat & develop biol, Jefferson Med Col, Thomas Jefferson Univ, 93-97. *Concurrent Pos:* Biomatrix travel fel, Fifth Int Eye Cong, Stressa, Italy, 92. *Mem:* AAAS; Am Soc Cell Biol; Asn Res Vision & Ophthal. *Res:* Development of the vertebrate retina examining the processes of differential gene expression, signal transduction and cell proliferation. *Mailing Add:* Psychol Univ Pa Sch Med Philadelphia PA 19104. *Fax:* 215-923-3808; *E-Mail:* rbuono@tjuvm.tju.edu

BUONOMO, FRANCES CATHERINE, ENDOCRINOLOGY, ANIMAL PHYSIOLOGY. *Current Pos:* Res biologist, 81-89, ASSOC RES FEL, ANIMAL SCI DIV, MONSANTO CO, 89- *Personal Data:* b Brooklyn, NY, June 29, 55; m 79, Thomas Komar; c Deborah. *Educ:* Cook Col Agr & Environ Sci, BS, 77; Rutgers Univ, PhD(physiol), 81. *Concurrent Pos:* Adj prof, Dept Food Sci & Nutrit, Univ Mo, Columbia. *Mem:* Am Soc Animal Sci; Poultry Sci Asn; Endocrine Soc; Am Soc Zoologists. *Res:* Endocrine physiology of growth and metabolism in food-producing and companion animal species. *Mailing Add:* Monsanto Co-BB3F 700 Chesterfield Pkwy N Chesterfield MO 63198. *Fax:* 314-537-7002; *E-Mail:* fcbuon@monsanto.com

BUONOPANE, RALPH A(NTHONY), CHEMICAL ENGINEERING, HEAT TRANSFER. *Current Pos:* Teaching asst, 61-63, instr chem eng, 63-64, asst prof, 66-71, actg dept chmn, 81-82, ASSOC PROF CHEM ENG, NORTHEASTERN UNIV, 71-, DEPT CHMN, 86- *Personal Data:* b Boston, Mass, Dec 5, 38; m 65; c 2. *Educ:* Northeastern Univ, BS, 61, MS, 63, PhD(chem eng), 67. *Concurrent Pos:* Consult, Jet-Vac Corp, Mass, 63 & 66, Polaroid Corp, 69-81, Kendall Corp, 81, YTL Eng, Inc, 82-84, Off Energy Related Inventions & US Nat Bur Stand, 82-84; lectr, Lincoln Col, Northeastern Univ Eve Div, 64-77. *Mem:* fel Am Inst Chem Engrs; Am Soc Eng Educ; Sigma Xi. *Res:* Heat transfer equipment research; plate and spiral heat exchangers; evaporators. *Mailing Add:* 443 Oak St Westwood MA 02090-3222

BUR, ANTHONY J, OPTICS, POLYMER PHYSICS. *Current Pos:* physicist polymer dielectrics, 63-71, physicist dent res, 72-77, physicist polymer res, 77-86, PHYSICIST POLYMER PROCESSING, NAT BUR STAND, 87- *Personal Data:* b Phildelphia, Pa, Dec 4, 35; m 63, Margaret O'Brien; c 6. *Educ:* St Joseph's Col, Pa, BS, 57; Pa State Univ, PhD(physics), 62. *Prof Exp:* Fel mech, Johns Hopkins Univ, 62-63. *Mem:* Am Chem Soc; Am Phys Soc; Soc Plastics Engr. *Res:* Electrical properties of insulators; polymer dielectrics and physics; solution properties of polymers; piezoelectric effect; thermodynamics; physical properties of teeth, bone and skin; fluorescence properties of polymers; polymer processing. *Mailing Add:* Polymer Bldg B 210 Nat Inst Stand & Technol Gaithersburg MD 20899. *E-Mail:* abur@enh.nist.gov

BURACK, WALTER RICHARD, INTERNAL MEDICINE, EPIDEMIOLOGY. *Current Pos:* RETIRED. *Educ:* Wake Forest Univ, MD, 51. *Prof Exp:* Dir med serv, Allied Signal, Inc, 77-89. *Res:* Occupational medicine. *Mailing Add:* PO Box 5 Jackson NH 03840

BURAS, EDMUND MAURICE, ORGANIC CHEMISTRY. *Current Pos:* PRIN SCIENTIST, GILLETTE RES INST, 69- *Personal Data:* b New Orleans, La, Oct 24, 21; m 43; c 3. *Educ:* Tulane Univ, BS, 41, MS, 47. *Prof Exp:* Chemist, southern regional res lab, Bur Agr & Indust Chem, USDA, 42-57; group leader, Harris Res Labs, 57-69. *Mem:* Am Chem Soc; Fiber Soc; Am Inst Chemists; Am Asn Textile Chemists & Colorists; Brit Textile Inst. *Res:* Physics and chemistry of cutting and shaving; absorbency; chemical modification of natural and synthetic fibers; highway marking materials; instrumentation. *Mailing Add:* 824 Burnt Mills Ave Silver Spring MD 20901

BURAS, NATHAN, DESIGN OF WATER RESOURCES SYSTEMS, OPERATION OF REGIONAL WATER RESOURCES SYSTEMS. *Current Pos:* head, 81-89, PROF HYDROL & WATER RES, UNIV ARIZ, 81- *Personal Data:* b Barlad, Romania, Aug 23, 21; US citizen; m 51, Netty Stivel; c Nir H. *Educ:* Univ Calif, Berkeley, BS, 49; Technion, Israel Inst Technol, MS, 58; UCLA, PhD(eng), 62. *Honors & Awards:* A Blanc Medal, Sixth Int Congress of Agr Eng, 64; Cert of Appreciation for Res Achievements, USDA, 70. *Prof Exp:* Soil survr soil mapping, Israel Ministry Agr, 51-52; dist engr drainage, Water Planning Corp Israel, 54-57; jr res engr water resources, Univ Calif, Los Angeles, 59-62; prof agr eng, Technion, Israel Inst Technol, 62-80; vis prof opers res, Stanford, 80-81. *Concurrent Pos:* Consult, Water Planning Corp Israel, 63-79, World Bank, Mex Nat Water Plan, 72-76, World Bank, Narmada River Proj, India, 80-82, Waterloo Regional Munic, Ontario, Can, 90-92, Great Northern Paper, 92-; dean agr eng, Technion, Israel Inst Technol, 66-68; vis prof, Dept Opers Res, Stanford, 76-80; mem, Comt Terminol, Int Glossary Hydrology, UNESCO, 96- *Mem:* Am Geophys Union; fel Am Soc Civil Engrs; Am Water Resources Asn; fel Int Water Resources Asn; AAAS. *Res:* Conjunctive management of surface and ground water resources with multiple decision makers; environmental effects of irrigated agriculture and its long term sustainability; global climatic change and its effect on regional water resources. *Mailing Add:* Dept Hydrol & Water Resources Univ Ariz Tucson AZ 85721. *Fax:* 520-621-1422; *E-Mail:* nburas@ccit.arizona.edu

BURATTI, BONNIE J, PLANETARY ASTRONOMY. *Current Pos:* MEM TECH STAFF PLANETARY ASTRON, JET PROPULSION LAB, CALIF INST TECNOL, 83- *Personal Data:* b Bethlehem, Pa; c 3. *Educ:* Mass Inst Technol, MS, 77; Cornell Univ, MS, 80, PhD(astron & space sci), 83. *Prof Exp:* Teaching & res asst astron, Cornell Univ, 77-83. *Mem:* Am Astron Soc; Asn Women Sci. *Res:* Telescopic and spacecraft observation of planetary surfaces; modeling and interpretation of results; laboratory measurements of planetary surface analogues. *Mailing Add:* Jet Propulsion Lab 4800 Oak Grove Dr MS 183-501 Bldg 183 Rm 501 Pasadena CA 91109

BURATTO, STEVEN K, CHEMISTRY, EDUCATION. *Current Pos:* ASST PROF CHEM, UNIV CALIF SANTA BARBARA, 94- *Personal Data:* b Clarkston, Wash, Dec 3, 64; m 90, Laura Oliver; c William R. *Educ:* Univ Puget Sound, BS, 87; Calif Inst Technol, PhD, 92. *Honors & Awards:* Henry & Camille Dreyfus New Fac Award, Henry & Camille Dreyfus Found, 94. *Prof Exp:* Scholar, AT&T Bell Labs, 89-92, mem tech staff, 92-94. *Mem:* AAAS; Am Phys Soc. *Res:* Contributed articles to science journals. *Mailing Add:* 7693 Bradford Dr Goleta CA 93117-1972

BURBA, JOHN VYTAUTAS, RADIOBIOLOGY, PHARMACOLOGY. *Current Pos:* RETIRED. *Personal Data:* b Lithuania, Oct 1, 26; Can citizen; m 55; c 2. *Educ:* Loyola Col Montreal, BSc, 51; Univ Ottawa, PhD(biochem), 63. *Prof Exp:* Control chemist, Merck & Co, Montreal, 51-52; tech sales rep, Can Lab Supplies, 52-54; tech sales rep, Mallinckrodt Chem Works, 54-57; med detail man, Frank W Horner, Ltd, 57-58; asst prof pharmacol, Univ Ottawa, 62-65; res scientist, Radiation Protection Bur, 65-69, sci adv, Bur Drugs, 69-73, head, Radiopharmacol Sect, 73-84, radiopharmacol adv, 84-88. *Concurrent Pos:* Fel, Dept Pharmacol, Yale Univ, 66-67. *Mem:* Soc Toxicol Can; Pharmacol Soc Can. *Res:* Toxicity of drugs and their metabolites; drug metabolizing activity of human placenta; stereospecificity in enzymic reactions; effect of drugs on hepatic azo reductase activity; effect of stannous ion on hepatic azo reductase and aromatic hydroxylase activity; effect of molybdenum-99 on sulfite and xanthine oxidase. *Mailing Add:* 1357 Fontenay Cresent Ottawa ON K1V 7K5 Can

BURBAGE, JOSEPH JAMES, inorganic chemistry; deceased, see previous edition for last biography

BURBANCK, MADELINE PALMER, BOTANY, ECOLOGY. *Current Pos:* RETIRED. *Personal Data:* b Moorestown, NJ, Oct 27, 14; m 40, William D; c Melinda & George. *Educ:* Wellesley Col, AB, 35, AM, 38; Univ Chicago, PhD, 41. *Prof Exp:* Asst bot, Wellesley Col, 36-39 & Univ Chicago, 40; guest, Columbia Univ, 41-42; special instr, Drury Col, 42-46, asst prof, 46-50; herbarium asst, 56-65; res assoc biol, Emory Univ, 50-83. *Concurrent Pos:* Mem corp, Marine Biol Lab, Woods Hole, Mass. *Mem:* Ecol Soc Am; Estuarine Res Fedn. *Res:* Cytology and morphology of Cyathura polita; plant succession on granite outcrops. *Mailing Add:* 1164 Clifton Rd NE Atlanta GA 30307

BURBANCK, WILLIAM DUDLEY, PROTOZOOLOGY, ANIMAL & ESTUARINE ECOLOGY. *Current Pos:* prof, 50-80, chmn dept, 52-57, EMER PROF BIOL, EMORY UNIV, 80- *Personal Data:* b Indianapolis, Ind, Aug 20, 13; m 40, Madeline Palmer; c Melinda A (Miller) & George P. *Educ:* Earlham Col, AB, 35; Haverford Col, MS, 36; Univ Chicago, PhD(zool), 41. *Prof Exp:* Instr biol, Earlham Col, 36-38, City Col NY, 41-42; guest, Dept Zool, Columbia Univ, 41-42; from asst prof to assoc prof, Drury Col, 42-45, prof, 45-50, chmn dept, 42-50. *Concurrent Pos:* Vis prof, Emory Univ, 49-50; Assoc ed, Estuaries, 77-83; mem corp, Marine Biol Lab, Woods Hole, Mass. *Mem:* Soc Protozool (vpres, 56-57); Int Asn Theoret & Appl Limnol; Ecol Soc Am; Marine Biol Asn UK; Estuarine Res Fedn. *Res:* Competition among protozoological populations; estuarine ecology, physiology and zoogeography of species of the isopod Cyathura. *Mailing Add:* 1164 Clifton Rd NE Atlanta GA 30307

BURBANK, NATHAN C, JR, civil & sanitary engineering; deceased, see previous edition for last biography

BURBAUM, BEVERLY WOLGAST, CHIRAL PRODUCTS, MEDICINAL CHEMISTRY. *Current Pos:* RES SCI, FMC CORP, 96- *Personal Data:* b Cambridge, Mass, Nov 18, 59; m 81, Jonathan; c Matthew & Nicholas. *Educ:* Rensselaer Polytech Inst, BS, 81; Brandeis Univ, MA, 84, PhD(org chem), 86. *Prof Exp:* Res scientist, Duracell Res Ctr, 86, Harvard Univ, 87-89 & Alkermes, Inc, 89-91; sr res scientist, Celgene Corp, 92-96. *Mem:* Am Chem Soc. *Res:* Chiral syntheses of small organic molecules which are pharmaceutical intermediates or end-products; medicinal chemistry especially in areas of anti-hypertensive (angiotension converting enzyme inhibitors) and neuropharmacology (anti-Alzheimer's, nerve growth factor). *Mailing Add:* 11 Adams Dr Cranbury NJ 08512-2708

BURBECK, CHRISTINA ANDERSON, VISUAL PSYCHOPHYSICS. *Current Pos:* RES ASSOC PROF PSYCHOL, UNIV NC, CHAPEL HILL, 90-, RES ASSOC PROF COMPUT SCI, 94- *Personal Data:* b Los Angeles, Calif, Sept 2, 48; m 79, Stephen; c Daniel & Michael. *Educ:* Univ Calif, San Diego, BA, 70, MA, 74; Univ Calif, Irvine, PhD(psychol), 80. *Prof Exp:* res psychologist, SRI Int, 79-86, dir, Vis Sci Prog, 86-90. *Mem:* Optical Soc Am; Asn Res Vision & Ophthal; Psychonomic Soc. *Res:* Human visual processing: perception of shape and spatial relations. *Mailing Add:* Dept Comput Sci Univ NC Chapel Hill NC 27599-3175

BURBIDGE, ELEANOR MARGARET, OBSERVATIONAL ASTROPHYSICS. *Current Pos:* assoc res prof, Univ Calif, 62-64, prof, 64-90, dir Ctr Astrophys & Space Sci, 79-88, univ prof, 84-90, RES PROF, 90- *Personal Data:* b Davenport, Eng, Aug 12, 19; US citizen; m 48; c 1. *Educ:* Univ London, BSc, 39, PhD(astrophys), 43. *Hon Degrees:* DSc, Smith Col, 63, Univ Sussex, 70, Univ Bristol, 72, Univ Leicester, 72, City Univ, London, 74, Univ Mich, 78, Univ Mass, 78, Williams Col, 79, SUNY, Stony Brook, 85, Univ Notre Dame, 86, Rensselaer Poly Inst, 86, Univ Notre Dame, 86, Univ Chicago, 91. *Honors & Awards:* Warner Prize, Am Astron Soc, 59, Russell Prize, 84; Bruce Medal, Astron Soc Pacific, 82; Nat Medal Sci, 85; David Elder lectr, Univ Strathclyde, 72; V Gildersleeve lectr, Barhard Col, 74; Jansky lectr, Nat Radio Astron Observ, 77; Henry Norris Russel lectr, 84; Lindsay Mem Lectr, NASA, 85; Brode Lectr, Whitman Col, 86; Albert Einstein World Award Sci, World Cult Coun, 88; DeVaucouleurs Lectr, Univ Tex, 91. *Prof Exp:* Actg dir, Univ London Observ, 43-51; res assoc astron, Yerkes Observ, 51-53; res fel astrophys, Calif Inst Technol, 55-57; Shirley Farr fel astron, Yerkes Observ, 57-59; assoc prof, Univ Chicago, 59-62. *Concurrent Pos:* Abby Mauze Rockefeller prof, Mass Inst Technol, 68; mem, Space Sci Bd, Nat Acad Sci-Nat Res Coun, 71-74 & Astron Comt, 73-75, NSF Astron Adv Panel, 72-74, Steering Group for Large Space Telescope, 73-77 & Assoc Univs for Res Astron Bd, 74-79; dir, Royal Greenwich Observ, 72-73; Virginia Gildersleeve prof, Barnard Col, NY, 74; chmn bd, AAAS, 83; chair, Sect 12, Nat Acad Sci, 86-89. *Mem:* Nat Acad Sci; Am Astron Soc (vpres, 72-74, pres, 76-78); Royal Astron Soc; fel Am Acad Arts & Sci; Int Astron Union; fel AAAS (pres, 82); Am Philos Soc; fel Royal Soc London; NY Acad Sci. *Res:* Astronomical spectroscopy; quasi-stellar objects; radio galaxies; masses and evolution of normal galaxies; nucleosynthesis; chemical evolution of the universe; chemical compo; Hubble Space Telescope; approximately 300 research articles including encyclopedia and review articles. *Mailing Add:* Ctr Astrophysics & Space Sci Univ Calif San Diego 0424 La Jolla CA 92093-0424. *Fax:* 619-534-7051; *E-Mail:* mburbidge@ucsd.edu

BURBIDGE, GEOFFREY, ASTRONOMY. *Current Pos:* from assoc prof to emer prof, 62-88, PROF PHYSICS, UNIV CALIF SAN DIEGO, 88- *Personal Data:* b Chipping Norton, Eng; m 48; c 1. *Educ:* Univ Bristol, BSc Hons, 46; Univ Col, London, PhD(theoret physics), 51. *Honors & Awards:* Warner Prize, Am Astron Soc, 58; Bappu Prize, Indian Acad Scis, 91. *Prof Exp:* Lectr astron, Univ London, 50-51; Agassiz fel, Harvard Univ, 51-52; res fel, Univ Chicago, 52-53, from asst prof to assoc prof, 57-62. *Concurrent Pos:* Res fel physics, Cavendish Lab, Cambridge Univ, 53-55; Carnegie fel, Mt Wilson & Palomar Observ, 55-57; sr res fel, Calif Inst Technol, 58-62; Phillips vis prof, Harvard Univ, 68; mem coun, Am Astron Soc, 68-71; fel, Royal Soc London, 68, Univ Col London, 70; bd dirs, Astron Soc Pac, 69-75, pres, 74-76; dir, Kitt Peak Nat Observ, 78-84. *Mem:* Am Astron Soc; Astron Soc Pac; fel Am Phys Soc; Royal Astron Soc; fel Am Acad Arts & Sci; fel Royal Soc London. *Res:* Research in extragalactic astronomy and high energy astrophysics. *Mailing Add:* Cass Mail Code 011 Univ Calif San Diego La Jolla CA 92093

BURBUTIS, PAUL PHILIP, PLANT PATHOLOGYENTOMOLOGY. *Current Pos:* from asst prof to prof, entom, 58-87, chmn, Entom & Appl Ecol Dept, 81-82 & 84-87, EMER PROF ENTOM, UNIV DEL, 87- *Personal Data:* b Haverhill, Mass, Nov 1, 27; m 52, Constance L Williams; c Phillip & Daniel. *Educ:* Univ Mass, BS, 50; Rutgers Univ, MS, 52, PhD, 54. *Prof Exp:* Asst entom, Rutgers Univ, 50-54, asst res specialist, 54-58. *Mem:* Entom Soc Am; Sigma Xi; Am Entom Soc; Am Asn Univ Prof. *Res:* Economic entomology; biological insect control; Plant Pathology and biological control of pests. *Mailing Add:* PO Box 111 Nobleboro ME 04555-0111

BURCH, BENJAMIN CLAY, MATHEMATICS. *Current Pos:* PRES, RTR SOFTWARE, RALEIGH, NC, 82- *Personal Data:* b Wilson, NC, Oct 23, 48; m 85, Deborah Friia. *Educ:* NC State Univ, BS, 70; Tulane Univ, MS, 73, PhD(math), 75. *Prof Exp:* Asst prof math, Northwestern Univ, Evanston, 75-76; from asst prof to assoc prof, Univ Tex, El Paso, 76-83. *Res:* Initial value, boundary value and free boundary problems for nonlinear partial differential equations. *Mailing Add:* 513 Watauga St Raleigh NC 27604

BURCH, CLARK WAYNE, VETERINARY MEDICINE. *Current Pos:* RETIRED. *Personal Data:* b Harrisonville, Mo, Sept 8, 07; m 35. *Educ:* Kans State Univ, BS, 32, DVM, 37. *Prof Exp:* With livestock sanit, State Dept Agr, Wis, 37-38; practicing vet, 38-42, 46-52; from prof to emer prof vet sci, Col Agr, Univ Wis-Madison, 52-73. *Mailing Add:* 10419 High Dr Shawnee Mission KS 66206

BURCH, DAVID STEWART, PHYSICS. *Current Pos:* RETIRED. *Personal Data:* b Sapulpa, Okla, Oct 9, 26; m 49. *Educ:* Univ Wash, BS, 50, MS, 54, PhD(physics), 56. *Prof Exp:* Physicist, Atomic Physics Lab, Nat Bur Stand, 56-58; from asst prof to assoc prof, Ore State Univ, 58-67, prof physics, 68-89. *Res:* Electronic, ionic, atomic and molecular collisions; gaseous electronics; upper atmosphere physics; atomic and molecular structure; spectroscopy. *Mailing Add:* PO Box 338 Yamhill OR 97148. *E-Mail:* dburch1@ix.netcom.com

BURCH, DEREK GEORGE, TROPICAL ORNAMENTAL PLANTS, TAXONOMY. *Current Pos:* state specialist & assoc prof ornamental hort, 79-86, VIS PROF, UNIV FLA, 86-; CONSULT. *Personal Data:* b Caerphilly, UK, June 26, 33; m 61, Nancy Hudgins; c David & Laura. *Educ:* Univ Col Wales, BSc, 54, MSc, 57; Univ Fla, PhD(plant taxon), 65. *Prof Exp:* Asst prof bot, Wash Univ, 65-69; assoc prof biol, Univ SFla, 69-74. *Concurrent Pos:* Chief horticulturist, Mo Bot Garden, 65-69; dir, Bot Gardens, Univ SFla, 69-74; Bot & Hort consult, 86. *Mem:* Int Plant Propagators Soc; Asn Trop Biol; Int Asn Plant Taxon; Am Soc Hort Sci. *Res:* Taxonomy and biology of new world Euphorbieae; taxonomy of horticultural plants (tropical); propagation and cultural techniques for tropical ornamentals. *Mailing Add:* 4044 SW Fourth St Plantation FL 33317-4007

BURCH, GEORGE NELSON BLAIR, POLYMER CHEMISTRY. *Current Pos:* RETIRED. *Personal Data:* b Charlottetown, PEI, Sept 22, 21; nat US; m 44, 92, Laura J Macleod; c Penelope, Jocelyn, Jean & Melissa. *Educ:* Mt Allison, BSc, 43; McGill Univ, MSc, 46; Ohio State Univ, PhD(chem), 49. *Prof Exp:* Asst anal chem, Ohio State Univ, 46-48; res chemist, Hercules Powder Co, 49-56, res supvr, 56-57, lab supvr, 57-62, sr res chemist, 62-68, mgr auxiliary group, 68-75, mgr upholstery develop, 75-79, mgr, Tech Serv Labs, 79-82, mem fiber fundamental group, Hercules, Inc, 82-90. *Mem:* Am Chem Soc. *Res:* Tall oil; organic fluorides; polyhydric alcohols; polymers; fibers, fiber design, processing and application in home furnishings; design and formation of non-woven fabrics. *Mailing Add:* 20 Lansdowne Ave Charlottetown PE C1A 3J2 Can

BURCH, JAMES LEO, MAGNETOSPHERIC PHYSICS. *Current Pos:* mgr, Space Physics Sect, 77-80, dir, Space Sci Dept, 80-85, VPRES, INSTRUMENTATION & SPACE RES DIV, SOUTHWEST RES INST, 85- *Personal Data:* b San Antonio, Tex, Nov 28, 42; m 65; c 3. *Educ:* St Mary's Univ, Tex, BS, 64; Rice Univ, PhD(space sci), 68; George Wash Univ, MSA, 73. *Prof Exp:* Physicist, Redstone Arsenal, Ala, 68-69, Sci Res Lab, US Mil Acad, 70-71, NASA-Goddard Space Flight Ctr, 71-74, NASA-Marshall Space Flight Ctr, 74-77. *Concurrent Pos:* Assoc ed, J Geophys Res & Geophys Res Lett; ed-in-chief, J Geophys Res Lett, 89-93; mem, Space Sci & Appln Adv Comt, NASA, 90-93. *Mem:* Am Geophys Union; Sigma Xi. *Res:* Experimental study of the geophysics and plasma physics of the earth's magnetosphere, particularly those processes that couple the magnetosphere, ionosphere and upper atmosphere. *Mailing Add:* Southwest Res Inst PO Drawer 28510 San Antonio TX 78228-0510. *Fax:* 210-647-4325; *E-Mail:* jim@swri.span.nasa.gov

BURCH, JOHN BAYARD, MALACOLOGY. *Current Pos:* Res assoc, 58-62, from asst prof to prof zool, 62-70, PROF BIOL, UNIV MICH, 70-, PROF NATURAL RESOURCES, 80-, CUR, MOLLUSKS, MUS, 62- *Personal Data:* b Charlottesville, Va, Aug 12, 29; m 51, Margaret E Smith; c Jo E (Sherman), John B Jr & Judith K (Jones). *Educ:* Randolph-Macon Col, BS,

52; Univ Richmond, MS, 54; Univ Mich, PhD, 59. *Concurrent Pos:* Res awards, Va Acad, 53 & NSF, 54; exec secy-treas, Inst Malacol, 61-62; USPHS res career develop award, 64-69; res career develop award, USPHS, 64-69; regents fel, Smithsonian Inst, 83-84. *Mem:* Inst Malacol (treas, 63-67, pres, 76-78 & 92-94); Soc Exp & Descriptive Malacol (pres, 68-80, exec secy-treas, 81-); French Soc Malacol; Malacol Soc Philippines; Unitas Malacologica; Int Soc Med & Appl Malacol (pres, 85); Am Malacol Union (vpres, 75). *Res:* Cytology, comparative biochemistry and systematics of mollusks; medical malacology; Protozoa of mollusks. *Mailing Add:* 1630 Northbrook Dr Ann Arbor MI 48103-6191

BURCH, MARY KAPPEL, MATERIAL SCIENCE COMPOSITES. *Current Pos:* res chemist, 86-89, RES DEPT MGR, ROHM & HAAS CO, 89- *Personal Data:* b St Paul, Minn, Mar 27, 57; m 83; c 1. *Educ:* Col St Catherine, BA, 79; Univ Calif, Berkeley, PhD(chem), 83. *Prof Exp:* Teaching asst, Chem Lab, Col St Catherine, 78-79; student fel chem, Univ Minn, 78, 3M Central Labs, 78-79; res assoc gen chem & inorg, Univ Calif, Berkeley, 79-83; NIH postdoctorate biochem, La State Med Sch, New Orleans, 83-85; asst prof gen chem & thermo, Loyola Col, Baltimore, MD, 85-86. *Mem:* Am Chem Soc; Am Ceramic Soc. *Res:* Inorganic-organic solid state composite materials-physical characterization including polymer interactions with cementitious materials as well as interactions with refractory materials; inorganic solution thermodynamics and bioinorganics chemistry. *Mailing Add:* Rohm & Haas Co 727 Norristown Rd Bldg 2 Spring House PA 19477

BURCH, ROBERT EMMETT, INTERNAL MEDICINE, NUTRITION. *Current Pos:* PRICE-GOLDSMITH PROF CLIN NUTRIT, MED SCH, TULANE UNIV, 80- *Personal Data:* b St Louis, Mo, Oct 9, 33; m 56; c 2. *Educ:* St Louis Univ, BS, 55, MD, 59. *Prof Exp:* Intern med & surg, Jewish Hosp, St Louis, 59-60; resident med, Firmin Desloge Hosp, St Louis Univ, 60-62; asst vis physician, Goldwater Mem Hosp, Columbia Univ, 65-68, assoc med, Univ, 65-69, asst prof, Col Physicians & Surgeons, 69-71; from assoc prof to prof med, Sch Med, Creighton Univ, 71-77; prof med & assoc chmn dept, Sch Med, Marshall Univ, 77-80. *Concurrent Pos:* Fel biochem, Western Reserve Univ, 62-65; asst vis physician, Francis Delafield Hosp, 68-70, assoc vis physician, 70-71; asst physician, Presby Hosp, 70; staff physician, Vet Admin Hosp, Omaha, 71-77; chief, Med Serv, Huntington, WVa, 77-; mem coun arteriosclerosis, Am Heart Asn; assoc chmn dept med, Sch Med, Marshall Univ, 77-80; chief sect clin nutrit, Tulane Univ Med Sch, 80-; assoc chief staff, New Orleans Vet Admin Hosp, 80- *Mem:* Am Physiol Soc; Am Inst Nutrit; Am Soc Clin Nutrit; Cent Soc Clin Res; Am Fedn Clin Res. *Res:* Trace element metabolism; zinc deficiency; role of zinc deficiency in ethanol metabolism. *Mailing Add:* Sch Med Tulane Univ 1430 Tulane Ave New Orleans LA 70112

BURCH, ROBERT RAY, MEDICINE. *Current Pos:* from instr to assoc prof clin & prev med, 54-73, clin prof med, 73-91, EMER CLIN PROF MED, SCH MED, TULANE UNIV, 91- *Personal Data:* b Edgard, La, May 28, 24; m 56, Lillie M Daves; c Robert R Jr & Carle A. *Educ:* Tulane Univ, BS, 48, MD, 51; Am Bd Internal Med, dipl, 58. *Prof Exp:* Intern med, Philadelphia Gen Hosp, 51-52; asst resident, Duke Univ Hosp, 52-53. *Concurrent Pos:* Fel internal med, Sch Med, Tulane Univ, 53-54; Nat Heart Inst trainee, 54-55, fel internal med, 55-56; pvt pract, 56- *Mem:* AMA; Am Heart Asn; Am Geriat Soc; fel Am Col Physicians; NY Acad Sci. *Res:* Cardio-renal diseases. *Mailing Add:* 14152 Tulane Ave New Orleans LA 70112

BURCH, ROBERT RAY, JR, INORGANIC & ORGANOMETALLIC CHEMISTRY, POLYMER CHEMISTRY. *Current Pos:* Vis scientist, 84-85, RES CHEMIST, E I DU PONT DE NEMOURS & CO, 85- *Personal Data:* b New Orleans, La, Oct 18, 56; m 83; c 1. *Educ:* Tulane Univ, BS, 78; Univ Calif, Berkeley, PhD(chem), 82. *Mem:* Am Chem Soc. *Res:* Inorganic and organometallic chemistry; catalysis; polymer synthesis; fine chemical synthesis. *Mailing Add:* DuPont Exp Sta Rte 141 & Henry Clay 328/232 Wilmington DE 19880

BURCH, RONALD MARTIN, PHARMACOLOGY, PATHOLOGY. *Current Pos:* staff scientist, 87-88, group leader, 88-90, DIR, NOVA PHARMACEUT CORP, 91- *Personal Data:* b Annapolis, Md, Jan 16, 55; m 80; c 2. *Educ:* Col Charleston, BS(marine biol) & BS(chem), 77; Med Univ SC, PhD(pharmacol), 81, MD, 85. *Prof Exp:* Med staff fel, NIH, 85-87. *Concurrent Pos:* Guest researcher, Lab Cell Biol, NIMH, 87- *Mem:* Am Soc Pharmacol & Exp Therapeut; Am Fedn Clin Res; Inflammation Res Asn. *Res:* Pharmacology of inflammatory mediators; cell biology of fibroblasts and neutrophils. *Mailing Add:* Purdue Fredrick 100 Connecticut Ave Norwalk CT 06850. *Fax:* 302-886-2766

BURCH, THADDEUS JOSEPH, SOLID STATE PHYSICS. *Current Pos:* assoc prof, Marquette Univ, 76-80, chmn dept, 76-86, actg dean grad sch, 85-86, dean grad sch, 86, PROF PHYSICS, MARQUETTE UNIV, 80- *Personal Data:* b Baltimore, Md, June 4, 30. *Educ:* Bellarmine Col, NY, AB, 54, PhL, 55; Fordham Univ, MA, 56, MS, 65, PhD(physics), 67; Woodstock Col, Md, STB, 60, STL, 62. *Prof Exp:* Asst prof physics, St Joseph's Col, Pa, 69-72; asst prof, Fordham Univ, New York, 72-74; assoc prof, Univ Conn, 74-76. *Concurrent Pos:* Res collab, Brookhaven Nat Lab, 68-75. *Mem:* Am Phys Soc; Am Asn Physics Teachers. *Res:* Study of magnetic and crystallographic phase transitions in ferromagnetic alloys and magnetic semiconductors by nuclear magnetic resonance, Mossbauer effect, specific heat and resistivity measurements. *Mailing Add:* Physics Dept Marquette Univ Milwaukee WI 53233

BURCHALL, JAMES J, MOLECULAR BIOLOGY. *Current Pos:* HEAD, MICROBIOL DEPT, BURROUGHS WELLCOME & CO, 68-, DIR DIV MOLECULAR GENETICS & MICROBIOL, 89-; PRES, NC BR, AM SOC MICROBIOL, 86- *Personal Data:* b Brooklyn, NY, Feb 25, 32; m 60; c 3. *Educ:* St John's Univ, BS, 54; Brooklyn Col, MA, 59; Univ Ill, PhD(bact), 63. *Prof Exp:* Sr res microbiologist, Wellcome Res Labs, Burroughs Wellcome, 62-68. *Concurrent Pos:* Adj prof, Duke Univ & Univ NC, 74-; mem, Bd Dirs, NC Biotechnol, 86- *Mem:* Am Soc Biol Chemists; AAAS; Am Soc Microbiol. *Res:* Molecular genetics; chemotherapy; recombinant DNA. *Mailing Add:* 1325 Kershaw Dr Raleigh NC 27609. *Fax:* 919-248-8375

BURCHAM, PAUL BAKER, MATHEMATICS. *Current Pos:* asst prof, 46-54, PROF MATH, UNIV MO-COLUMBIA, 54- *Personal Data:* b Fayette, Mo, Feb 22, 16; m 41; c 2. *Educ:* Cent Col, Mo, BS, 35; Northwestern Univ, MA & PhD(math), 41. *Prof Exp:* Asst math, Northwestern Univ, 39-41; asst instr math, Cent Col, Mo, 41-42. *Mem:* Am Math Soc; Math Asn Am. *Res:* Some inclusion relations in the domain of Hausdorff matrices; summability of series. *Mailing Add:* 401 Westmount Ave Columbia MO 65203

BURCHARD, HERMANN GEORG, MATHEMATICS. *Current Pos:* assoc prof, 72-77, PROF MATH, OKLA STATE UNIV, 77- *Personal Data:* b Wurzburg, Ger, Dec 9, 34; m 61; c 4. *Educ:* Univ Hamburg, Dipl-math, 63; Purdue Univ, PhD(comput sci), 68. *Prof Exp:* Res mathematician, Gen Motors Res Labs, Mich, 63-66; vis asst prof, Math Res Ctr, US Army, Univ Wis Madison, 68-69; asst prof, Ind Univ, Bloomington, 69-72. *Concurrent Pos:* Consult, Phillips Petroleum Co, 75- *Mem:* Am Math Soc; Soc Indust & Appl Math; Math Asn Am. *Res:* Approximation theory; numerical analysis; applied mathematics. *Mailing Add:* Dept Math Okla State Univ Stillwater OK 74078-0613

BURCHARD, JEANETTE, microbiology, serology, for more information see previous edition

BURCHARD, JOHN KENNETH, TECHNICAL MANAGEMENT. *Current Pos:* environ engr specialist, Dept Environ Qual, 90-94, MGR, SPEC PROJ UNIT, STATE ARIZ, 94- *Personal Data:* b St Louis, Mo, May 12, 36; m 58, Elizabeth Shesserott; c Christopher & Gregory. *Educ:* Carnegie-Mellon Univ, BS, 57, MS, 59, PhD(chem eng), 62. *Prof Exp:* Staff scientist, United Technol Ctr, 61-68; chief scientist, Combustion Power Co, 68-70; lab dir, Environ Protection Agency, 70-80; div dir, Res Triangle Inst, 80-83; pres, Search Assocs, 83-85; dir res & sponsored progs, Univ Cent Ark, 85-87; asst dir, Res Admin, Ariz State Univ, 87-90. *Mem:* Am Inst Chem Engrs; Sigma Xi. *Res:* Pollution control technology; aerosol physics; synthetic fuels technology; catalysis; chemical kinetics; combustion; environmental assessments. *Mailing Add:* 2101 E Redmon Dr Tempe AR 85283-2250

BURCHARD, ROBERT P, BACTERIOLOGY. *Current Pos:* from asst prof to assoc prof, 67-77, PROF BIOL SCI, UNIV MD, BALTIMORE CO, 77- *Personal Data:* b New York, NY, Nov 7, 38; m 67, Ann Cihac; c Rachel & Robert. *Educ:* Brown Univ, BA, 60, MSc, 62; Univ Minn, Minneapolis, PhD(microbiol), 65. *Prof Exp:* Lectr microbiol, Univ Ife, Nigeria, 65-66. *Concurrent Pos:* NSF res grants, 68-70, 71-73, 75-77, 78-79 & 80-82; Off Naval Res, grant, 88-90, UK Sci Res Coun vis fel, Dept Biochem, Univ Leeds, 73-74; vis prof, Univ Md, Sch Med; Md Seq Grant, 91-94; prog off, metab biochem, NSF, 91-92, interim dean arts/scis, 94-96. *Mem:* Am Soc Microbiol; AAAS. *Res:* Behavior and mechanisms of motility and adhesion of gliding bacteria. *Mailing Add:* Dept Biol Univ Md Baltimore Co Baltimore MD 21250

BURCHELL, HOWARD BERTRAM, MEDICINE, CARDIOLOGY. *Current Pos:* EMER PROF MED, UNIV MINN, MINNEAPOLIS, 74- *Personal Data:* b Athens, Ont, Nov 28, 07; nat US; m 42, Margaret Helmholz; c Susan, Judith, Cynthia & Rebecca. *Educ:* Univ Toronto, MD, 32; Univ Minn, PhD(med), 40. *Prof Exp:* Instr med, Univ Pittsburgh, 36; from instr to prof, Mayo Found, 41-67, chief, Sect Cardiol, 67-74, prof med, Univ Hosp, Univ Minn, Minneapolis, 67-74; sr cardiologist, Northwestern Hosp, Minneapolis, 74-78. *Concurrent Pos:* Ed, Circulation, 66-70; vis prof, Stanford Univ, 75-80. *Mem:* Am Physiol Soc; Am Fedn Clin; Asn Am Physicians; Am Heart Asn. *Res:* Clinical investigation; physiology of circulation. *Mailing Add:* 260 Woodlawn Ave St Paul MN 55105. *E-Mail:* 103157.177@compuserve.com

BURCHENAL, JOSEPH HOLLAND, MEDICINE. *Current Pos:* mem, 52-, Head Appl Ther Lab & Field Coordr Human Cancer, 73-, EMER MEM, SLOAN-KETTERING INST CANCER RES. *Personal Data:* b Milford, Del, Dec 21, 12; m 48; c 7. *Educ:* Princeton Educ: Univ Pa, MD, 37. *Honors & Awards:* Alfred P Sloan Award, 63; Albert Lasker Award Clin Cancer Chemother, 72; Prix Leopold Griffuel, 70; David A Kamoksky Mem Award, Am Soc Clin Oncol, 74; John Phillips Award, 74; James Ewing Soc Award, 75. *Prof Exp:* Intern, Union Mem Hosp, Baltimore, 37-38; resident dept pediat, NY Hosp, Cornell Univ, 38-39; asst resident, Boston City Hosp, 40-42; assoc, Sloan-Kettering Inst Cancer Res, 48-52, vpres, 64-72; asst prof clin med, Med Col, Cornell Univ, 49-50, asst prof med, 50-51, assoc prof, Sloan-Kettering Div, 51-52, prof, 52-55, prof med, med col, Cornell Univ, 55- *Concurrent Pos:* Res fel med, Harvard Med Sch, 40-42; spec fel, Mem Hosp, NY, 46-49; intern, NY Hosp, 38-39; asst attend physician, Med Serv, Mem Hosp, NY, 49-52, attend physician, 52-, chief chemother serv, 52-64, assoc dir clin invest, 64-66, dir clin invest, 66-; consult, USPHS, Am Cancer Soc & Div Med Sci, Nat Res Coun, 54-56; mem, Nat Panel Consult Conquest of Cancer, US Senate Comt Labor & Pub

Welfare, 70; chmn, Chemother Adv Comt, Nat Cancer Inst, 70-71; vpres med & sci affairs & chmn, Med & Sci Adv Comt, Leukemia Soc Am, 70-75. *Mem:* Am Soc Cli; Soc Exp Biol & Med; Asn Cancer Res (vpres, 64-65, pres, 65-66); Am Soc Trop Med & Hyg; Am Fedn Clin Res. *Res:* Chemotherapy of cancer and leukemia. *Mailing Add:* 18 Juniper Rd Darien CT 06820

BURCHETT, O NEILL J, MECHANICAL ENGINEERING. *Current Pos:* PROF, NMEX STATE UNIV, 93- *Personal Data:* b Seiling, Okla, June 11, 35; m 61; c 2. *Educ:* Okla State Univ, BS, 58, MS, 60, PhD(mech eng), 66. *Prof Exp:* From instr to asst prof mech eng, Okla State Univ, 59-66; assoc prof, Ariz State Univ, 67-68; staff mem tech, Sandia Labs, 68-69, div supvr, 69-90, adj prof, 90-93. *Mem:* Am Soc Mech Engrs. *Res:* Nondestructive testing; materials characterization; nonlinear vibrations. *Mailing Add:* Dept Mech Eng NMex State Univ Main Campus Las Cruces NM 88003

BURCHFIEL, BURRELL CLARK, GEOLOGY. *Current Pos:* prof, 77-84, SCHLUMBERGER PROF GEOL, MASS INST TECHNOL, 84- *Personal Data:* b Stockton, Calif, Mar 21, 34; m 83, Leigh Royden; c Brian E, Brook E, Benjamin C & Halsey R. *Educ:* Stanford Univ, BS, 57, MS, 58; Yale Univ, PhD(geol), 61. *Prof Exp:* Geologist, US Geol Surv, 61; from asst prof to prof geol, Rice Univ, 61-75, Carey Croneis prof, 74-76. *Concurrent Pos:* Exchange prof, Geol Inst Belgrade, Yugoslavia, 68 & Geol Inst Bucharest, Romania, 70; vis prof, Australian Nat Univ, 76; Guggenheim fel, 85-86; vis scientist, Univ Athens, 86, Inst Geol, Bulgarian Acad Sci, 90, Univ Lund, 92. *Mem:* Nat Acad Sci; fel Geol Soc Am; Am Asn Petrol Geologists; Geol Soc Australia; fel Am Geophys Union; Am Acad Arts & Sci; hon foreign fel Europ Union Geologists. *Res:* Tectonics of the western United States, China, Eastern Europe; regional tectonics; orogenesis and its relation to plate boundary activity; structural geology; regional geology. *Mailing Add:* Dept Earth & Planetary Sci Mass Inst Technol Cambridge MA 02139. *Fax:* 617-252-1800; *E-Mail:* burch@mit.edu

BURCHFIEL, JAMES LEE, EPILEPSY, NEUROPHYSIOLOGY. *Current Pos:* assoc prof neurol, 89-93, CO-DIR, COMPREHENSIVE EPILEPSY PROG, STRONG MEM HOSP, UNIV ROCHESTER, 89-, DIR, NEUROPHYSIOL LABS, 89-, PROF NEUROL, 93- *Personal Data:* b Los Angeles, Calif, Mar 16, 41; m 63, Rae Demler; c Corin & Kendra. *Educ:* Stanford Univ, BS, 63, PhD(pharmacol), 69. *Prof Exp:* From res assoc to prin res assoc neurol, Sch Med, Harvard Univ, 70-89. *Concurrent Pos:* Prin investr, NIH, 79-; mem, Comt Tech Matters, Long-Term Monitoring, Am EEG Soc, 83-85, Childhood Epilepsy Comt, Am Epilepsy Soc, 90-93, Med Instrumentation Comt, Am EEG Soc, 93-, Investrs Workshop Comt, Am Epilepsy Soc, 93- *Mem:* Soc Neurosci; fel Am Epilepsy Soc; Am EEG Soc; fel Eastern Asn Electroencephalographers (secy-treas, 83-86, pres-elect to pres, 86-89). *Res:* Neurophysiology and neuropharmacology of epilepsy, especially neuronal mechanisms associated with the development of focal (kindled) epilepsy; diagnosis of central nervous system pathology through computer analysis of electrophysiological data. *Mailing Add:* Dept Neurol Strong Mem Hosp Univ Rochester 601 Elmswood Ave Box 673 Rochester NY 14642-8673. *Fax:* 716-275-8113; *E-Mail:* leif@troi.cc.rochester.edu

BURCHFIELD, HARRY P, BIOCHEMISTRY. *Current Pos:* PRIN SCIENTIST, RES ASSOC, 76- *Personal Data:* b Pittsburgh, Pa, Dec 22, 15; m 42, 63; c 5. *Educ:* Columbia Univ, AB & MA, 38, PhD, 56. *Honors & Awards:* Prize, Chicago Rubber Group, 46. *Prof Exp:* Analyst, Nat Oil Prod Co, NJ, 38-40; res chemist, 40-41, group leader, 41-50, dir plantations res dept, Naugatuck Chem Div, US Rubber Co, 50-51; assoc dir, Boyce Thompson Inst Plant Res, 51-61; inst scientist & mgr anal & biochem, Southwest Res Inst, 61-65; officer-in-charge, pesticides res lab, USPHS, 65-67; sci dir & dir biol sci, Gulf South Res Inst, 67-76; res prof & head, Div Molecular Biol, Med Res Inst, Fla Inst Technol, 77-82. *Concurrent Pos:* Adj prof, Univ Southwestern La, 67-; consult, Environ Protection Agency, 76- *Mem:* Am Inst Biol Sci; Soc Toxicol; Am Chem Soc. *Res:* Biochemical applications of gas chromatography; metabolism and analysis of drugs, pesticides and natural products; mechanism of action of biocides; chemical carcinogenesis and mutagenesis; armadillo biochemistry. *Mailing Add:* 72 Riverview Terr Indialantic FL 32903-4640

BURCHFIELD, THOMAS ELWOOD, SOLUTION THERMODYNAMICS. *Current Pos:* sr chemist, 83-84, mgr, recovery processes res, 84-89, DIR, ENERGY PROD RES, NAT INST PETROL & ENERGY RES, 89- *Personal Data:* b Marshfield, Mo, Aug 6, 51; m 73; c 1. *Educ:* Univ Mo, Rolla, BSc, 73, MSc, 75, PhD(phys chem), 77. *Honors & Awards:* Sumner Award, 86. *Prof Exp:* Res assoc, dept chem, Univ Lethbridge, Can, 77-79; res chemist, Bartlesville Energy Technol Ctr, US Dept Energy, 79-83. *Concurrent Pos:* Mem, Calorimetry Conf; mem adv bd, Found Chem Res. *Mem:* Am Chem Soc; Sigma Xi; Soc Petrol Engrs; Calorimetry Conf; Int Union Pure & Appl Chem. *Res:* Thermodynamics properties of surfactant systems; experimental thermodynamics and solution calorimetry; understanding the thermodynamics of micellization, solubilization, and microemulsion formation by measuring the thermodynamics properties of surfactant systems; enhanced oil recovery; colloid chemistry. *Mailing Add:* 2705 SE Kensington Way Bartlesville OK 74006-9410

BURCHILL, BROWER RENE, CELL BIOLOGY. *Current Pos:* RETIRED. *Personal Data:* b El Dorado, Kans, Dec 29, 38; m 60; c 2. *Educ:* Phillips Univ, BA, 60; Fla State Univ, MS, 63; Western Res Univ, PhD(biol), 66. *Prof Exp:* NIH trainee, Fla State Univ, 63; postdoctoral appointee, Los Alamos Sci Lab, Univ Calif, 66-68; asst prof zool, Univ Kans, 68-69, from asst to assoc prof physiol & cell biol, 69-76, chmn, Div Biol Sci, 73-79, assoc vchmn acad affairs, 76-95, prof physiol & cell biol, 84-95. *Mem:* AAAS; Am Soc Cell Biol; Soc Protozool (treas, 78-). *Res:* Nucleocytoplasmic interactions essential to oral differentiation in the ciliate protozoan Stentor coeruleus. *Mailing Add:* 1612 St Andrews Dr Lawrence KS 66047. *Fax:* 785-864-4463

BURCHILL, CHARLES EUGENE, PHYSICAL CHEMISTRY. *Current Pos:* asst prof, 66-68, ASSOC PROF CHEM, UNIV MAN, 68- *Personal Data:* b Makwa, Sask, Dec 12, 32; m 57; c 4. *Educ:* Univ Sask, BA, 55, MA, 61; Univ Leeds, PhD(phys chem), 68. *Prof Exp:* Instr chem, Victoria Col, 56-63, demonstr phys chem, Univ Leeds, 63-66. *Res:* Kinetics and mechanisms of free-radical reactions in solution; radiation chemistry and photochemistry of aqueous solutions. *Mailing Add:* Dept Chem Univ Man Winnipeg MB R3T 2N2 Can

BURCK, LARRY HAROLD, FAILURE ANALYSIS, FRACTURE MECHANICS. *Current Pos:* CONSULT & VPRES, WEISS & BURCK CONSULT ENGRS, 84- *Personal Data:* b Detroit, Mich, Sept 25, 45; m 67; c 3. *Educ:* Mich State Univ, BS, 67; Rensselaer Polytech Inst, MS, 71; Northwestern Univ, PhD(mat sci), 75. *Prof Exp:* Res engr, Advan Mat Res & Develop Lab, Pratt & Whitney Aircraft, 67-72; from asst prof to assoc prof mat sci, Univ Wis-Milwaukee, 75-84. *Mem:* Am Soc Metals; Am Inst Mining Metall & Petrol Engrs; Am Soc Mech Engrs. *Res:* Fracture, fatigue and mechanical behavior of materials; analytical and experimental fracture mechanics; failure analysis; machine guarding. *Mailing Add:* Weiss & Burck, Ltd 744 N Fourth St Suite 580 Milwaukee WI 53203

BURCK, PHILIP JOHN, BIOCHEMISTRY. *Current Pos:* RES SCIENTIST BIOCHEM, LILLY RES LABS, ELI LILLY & CO, 62- *Personal Data:* b Milwaukee, Wis, Sept 21, 36; m 68; c 1. *Educ:* Lawrence Univ, AB, 58; Univ Ill, MS, 60, PhD(biochem), 62. *Mem:* AAAS; Am Chem Soc. *Res:* Enzyme and enzyme inhibitor purification and characterization; physiological role of proteases and protease inhibitors. *Mailing Add:* 8954 Bay Breeze Lane Indianapolis IN 46236

BURCKEL, ROBERT BRUCE, MATHEMATICS. *Current Pos:* actg chmn dept, 74-75, assoc prof, 71-80, PROF MATH, KANS STATE UNIV, 81- *Personal Data:* b Louisville, Ky, Dec 15, 39; m 67, Glenna Ferris. *Educ:* Univ Notre Dame, BS, 61; Yale Univ, MA, 63, PhD(math), 68. *Prof Exp:* From instr to asst prof, Univ Ore, 66-70. *Concurrent Pos:* Asst prof, Univ Saarland, 77-78; guest prof, Univ Erlangen-Nuremburg, 84-85, 92-93. *Mem:* Am Math Soc; Ger Math Soc. *Res:* Harmonic analysis, classical and abstract; function algebras; hardy spaces, classical and abstract; Banach algebra; classical complex analysis. *Mailing Add:* Dept Math Kans State Univ Cardwell Hall Manhattan KS 66506-2602

BURCKHARDT, CHRISTOPH B, ELECTRICAL ENGINEERING. *Current Pos:* SCIENTIST, KONTRON INSTRUMENTS, 92- *Personal Data:* b Zurich, Switz, Apr 25, 35; nat US; m 64; c 2. *Educ:* Swiss Fed Inst Technol, MS, 59, PhD(elec eng), 63. *Prof Exp:* Asst, Swiss Fed Inst Technol, 60-63; mem tech staff, Bell Tel Labs, 63-70, Hoffman-La Roche, Inc, 70-92. *Mem:* Fel Inst Elec & Electronics Engrs. *Res:* Hall-effect, varactor diode applications; optical and acoustical holography; ultrasonic imaging for medical diagnosis. *Mailing Add:* Kontron Instruments AG Reinacherstrasse Basel PB 4002 Switzerland

BURD, LAURENCE IRA, OBSTETRICS & GYNECOLOGY. *Current Pos:* co-dir, Perinatal Ctr & assoc prof obstet & gynec, 76-83, CLIN ASSOC PROF, UNIV CHICAGO, 83- *Personal Data:* b New York, NY. *Educ:* Univ Rochester, AB, 62; Chicago Med Sch, MD, 66. *Prof Exp:* Res fel, Div Perinatal Med, Univ Colo, 73-75; dir obstet, Michael Reese Hosp, 76-83. *Concurrent Pos:* NIH res fel, 74-75; Basil O'Connor grant, Nat Found March of Dimes, 76-; attending physician obstet & gynec, Michael Reese Hosp, 76- & attending physician pediat, 78-83. *Mem:* Soc Gynec Invest; Perinatal Res Soc. *Res:* Maternal and fetal physiologic changes at the time of parturition; fetal and maternal pathophysiology. *Mailing Add:* Dept Obstet & Gynec Michael Reese Hosp 31st & Lake Shore Dr Chicago IL 60616

BURDE, RONALD MARSHALL, OPHTHALMOLOGY, NEURO-OPHTHALMOLOGY. *Current Pos:* PROF & CHMN, DEPT OPHTHAL, ALBERT EINSTEIN COL MED, 88-, PROF NEUROL & NEUROL SURG, 88- *Personal Data:* b New York, NY, Dec 24, 38; m, Sharon Kaplan; c Howard, Bradley & Jeffrey. *Educ:* Mass Inst Technol, BS, 60; Jefferson Med Col, Philadelphia, MD, 64. *Prof Exp:* From asst prof to prof ophthal, Sch Med, Wash Univ, 70-88, prof neurol & neurol surg, 75-88. *Concurrent Pos:* Vis prof ophthal, Hadassah Med Orgn, 77; ed, J Neuroopthal. *Mem:* Am Neurol Asn; NAm Neuroophthal Soc; Am Acad Ophthal; Am Asn Neurol Surgeons; Asn Univ Prof Ophthal; Am Ophthal Soc. *Res:* Immunohistochemistry of thyroid orbitopathy. *Mailing Add:* Dept Ophthal Albert Einstein Col Med 1300 Morris Park Ave Bronx NY 10461-1926. *Fax:* 718-515-3734

BURDEN, HARVEY WORTH, AERONAUTICS, MECHANICAL ENGINEERING. *Current Pos:* ADJ PROF AERONAUT, US NAVAL POSTGRAD SCH, MONTEREY, CALIF, 81- *Personal Data:* b Glendale, Calif, Nov 20, 33; m 61; c 2. *Educ:* US Naval Acad, BS, 55; US Naval Postgrad Sch, BS, 63; Calif Inst Technol, AeE, 64; Univ Pa, PhD(mech eng), 69. *Prof Exp:* Sr scientist, Teledyne McCormick Seiph, 75-78; prin staff mem, BDM Corp, 78-81. *Mem:* Sigma Xi; Am Inst Aeronaut & Astronaut; Am Soc Mech Engrs. *Res:* Heat and mass transfer in fluid flows; boundary layer flows. *Mailing Add:* 1013 Sombrero Rd Pebble Beach CA 93953-2724

BURDEN, HUBERT WHITE, REPRODUCTIVE ENDOCRINOLOGY. *Current Pos:* from asst prof to assoc prof, 71-79, PROF ANAT, E CAROLINA UNIV, 80- *Personal Data:* b Elizabeth City, NC, Sept 12, 43; m 67; c 2. *Educ:* Atlantic Christian Col, AB, 65; ECarolina Univ, MA, 67;

Tulane Univ, PhD(anat), 71. *Prof Exp:* Instr biol, ECarolina Univ, 67-68; teaching asst anat, Med Sch, Tulane Univ, 68-71. *Concurrent Pos:* USPHS res grants, 75 & 79. *Mem:* Soc Study Reproduction; Soc Develop Biol; Am Asn Anatomists; Am Soc Zoologists; Pan Am Asn Anatomists; Sigma Xi. *Res:* Research on the role of the peripheral autonomic nervous system in reproductive function. *Mailing Add:* Dept Anat & Cell Biol E Carolina Univ Sch Med Greenville NC 27858-4354

BURDEN, RICHARD L, MATHEMATICS. *Current Pos:* PROF MATH, YOUNGSTOWN STATE UNIV, 70- *Educ:* Albion Col, BA, 66; Case Inst Technol, MS, 68; Case Western Res Univ, PhD(math), 71; Univ Pittsburgh, MS, 81. *Mem:* Soc Indust & Appl Math; Asn Comput Mach; Math Asn Am. *Res:* Numerical solution of partial differential equations, numerical algebra & programming languages. *Mailing Add:* Dept Math Youngstown State Univ Youngstown OH 44503

BURDEN, STANLEY LEE, JR, CHEMICAL INSTRUMENTATION, ANALYTICAL CHEMISTRY. *Current Pos:* from instr to assoc prof, 66-74, chmn sci div, 85-89, PROF CHEM, TAYLOR UNIV, 75-, CHMN DEPT, 78-, ASSOC DEAN, DIV NATURAL SCI, 90- *Personal Data:* b Aurora, Ill, Mar 9, 39; m 62; c 2. *Educ:* Taylor Univ, BS, 61; Ind Univ, PhD(anal chem) 66. *Prof Exp:* Teacher, high sch, Ind, 61-62. *Concurrent Pos:* NASA res fel, Manned Spacecraft Ctr, 69. *Mem:* Am Chem Soc; Am Sci Affil. *Res:* Instrumentation of analytical methods of analysis; environmental analysis and on-line computer applications in chemical instrumentation. *Mailing Add:* Dept Chem Taylor Univ Upland IN 46989-1001. *Fax:* 765-998-4940; *E-Mail:* stburden@tayloru.edu

BURDETT, JEREMY KEITH, PHYSICAL INORGANIC CHEMISTRY. *Current Pos:* from asst prof to assoc prof, Univ Chicago, 78-86, assoc dean phys sci div, 87-91, PROF CHEM, UNIV CHICAGO, 86-, CHMN, DEPT CHEM, 92- *Personal Data:* b London, Eng, July 1, 47; m 72; c 2. *Educ:* Cambridge Univ, BA, 68, MS & PhD(chem), 72; Univ Mich, Ann Arbor, MS, 70; Univ Cambridge, ScD, 90. *Honors & Awards:* Meldola Medal & Prize, Soc Maccabeans & Royal Inst Chem, 77. *Prof Exp:* Bye fel chem, Magdalene Col, Eng, 71-72; sr res officer chem, Univ Newcastle, Eng, 72-78. *Concurrent Pos:* Fel Alfred P Sloan Found, 79-84, teacher scholar, Camille & Henry Dreyfus Found, 79-84; Wilsmore fel, Univ Melbourne, Australia, 85; Guggenheim fel, 90. *Mem:* Am Chem Soc; Royal Inst Chem. *Res:* Theoretical studies on structural, electronic and kinetic properties of molecules and solids. *Mailing Add:* Searle Chem Lab Univ Chicago Chicago IL 60637

BURDETT, LORENZO WORTH, ANALYTICAL CHEMISTRY. *Current Pos:* RETIRED. *Personal Data:* b Pocatello, Idaho, Aug 9, 16; m 45; c 7. *Educ:* Univ Idaho, BS, 43; Univ Ill, PhD(anal chem), 49. *Prof Exp:* Jr chemist, Shell Develop Co, 43-46; res chemist, Standard Oil Co Ind, 49-52; res chemist, Union Oil Co Calif, 52-55, sect leader chem, 55-58, sr sect leader, 58-65, supvr res dept, 65-83. *Mem:* Am Chem Soc; Am Soc Testing Mat. *Res:* Method development and analytical research in electrochemical and chemical area. *Mailing Add:* 1607 N Mountain Oaks Dr Orem UT 84057-2309

BURDETTE, WALTER JAMES, GENERAL & THORACIC SURGERY, GENETICS. *Current Pos:* CHIEF THORACIC & CARDIOVASC SURG, PARK PLAZA HOSP. *Personal Data:* b Hillsboro, Tex, Feb 5, 15; m 47, Kathryn Lynch; c Susan B (Radoux) & William J. *Educ:* Baylor Univ, AB, 35; Univ Tex, AM, 36, PhD(zool), 38; Yale Univ, MD, 42; Am Bd Surg, dipl, 50; Am Bd Thoracic Surg, dipl, 53. *Prof Exp:* Intern, Johns Hopkins Hosp, 42-43; Cushing fel surg, Yale Univ, 43-44; resident, New Haven Hosp, Conn, 44-46; from instr to assoc prof, Sch Med, La State Univ, 46-55, coordr cancer res & teaching, 48-55; prof surg & chmn dept, Sch Med, Univ Mo, 55-56, prof clin surg, Sch Med, St Louis Univ, 56-57; prof surg & head dept, Col Med, Univ Utah, 57-65; prof surg & assoc dir, Univ Tex M D Anderson Hosp & Tumor Inst, 65-75. *Concurrent Pos:* Asst vis surgeon, Charity Hosp of La, New Orleans, 46-47, vis surgeon, 47-55; vis surgeon, Southern Baptist Hosp, 53-55; vis investr, Chester Beatty Inst Cancer Res, London, Eng, 53 & Univ Tubingeng, W Germany, 57; surgeon-in-chief, Univ Hosp, Univ Mo, 55-56; dir, St Louis Univ Surg Serv, Vet Admin Hosp, 56-57; dir, Lab Clin Biol, 57-; surgeon-in-chief, Salt Lake Gen Hosp, 57-65; Gibson lectr advan surg, Oxford Univ, 66; vis prof, Off Univ Congo, 68; lectr, Hosp Martinez, PR, 69, Univ Sendai, Japan, 70, Univ Melbourne, 70 & Univ Freiburg, 70. Consult, Oak Ridge Inst Nuclear Studies, 51 & Touro Infirmary, New Orleans, 53-55; chief surg consult, Vet Admin Hosp, Salt Lake City, 57-65, Mem morphol & genetics study sect, NIH, 55-58, chmn genetics study sect, 57-61, mem nat adv cancer coun, 61-65, mem nat adv heart coun, 65, dir working cadre on carcinoma of large intestine, Nat Cancer Inst; chmn res adv coun, Am Cancer Soc, 57-67; mem adv comt smoking & health, Surgeon Gen US, 62-64; chmn Nat Acad Sci comt, Int Union Against Cancer, 62-; mem transplantation comt, Nat Acad Sci; pvt pract gen & thoracic surg, 76- *Mem:* Am Asn Cancer Res; Soc Exp Biol & Med; Am Col Surgeons; Soc Clin Surgeons (treas, 63-64); Am Surg Asn; Am Soc Clin Oncol. *Res:* Genetics and cancer; metabolism of cardiac muscle; cardiovascular and thoracic surgery; invertebrate hormones. *Mailing Add:* 239 Chimney Rock Rd Houston TX 77024

BURDG, DONALD EUGENE, MATHEMATICS. *Current Pos:* RETIRED. *Personal Data:* b Milford, Nebr, Aug 12, 29; m 52; c 2. *Educ:* Colo State Univ, BS, 51; Univ Northern Colo, MA, 52; Ore State Univ, MS, 66. *Prof Exp:* Asst prof math, Cent Ore Community Col, 56-67; prof math, SWestern Ore Community Col, 67-94. *Mem:* Nat Coun Teachers Math; Math Asn Am; Am Math Asn Two Yr Cols. *Mailing Add:* 1160 Oakway Dr Coos Bay OR 97420

BURDGE, DAVID NEWMAN, FUEL TECHNOLOGY & PETROLEUM ENGINEERING. *Current Pos:* RETIRED. *Personal Data:* b Sullivan, Ind, May 1, 31; m 53; c 2. *Educ:* Purdue Univ, BS, 52, MS, 56, PhD(org chem), 59. *Prof Exp:* Res chemist, Marathon Oil Co, 59-67, mgr, Org Chem Dept, 67-70, mgr, Ref Sci & Eng Dept, 70-72, mgr, Petrol Chem Dept, 72-77, sr staff engr, 77-80, mgr, Tech Projs, Offshore Technol Div, 80-86, assoc dir, technol serv, 86-92. *Concurrent Pos:* Res chemist, Eastman Kodak Co, 61-62. *Mem:* Am Chem Soc; Soc Petroleum Engrs; Sigma Xi. *Res:* Organic sulfur chemistry; oxidation of alkyl aromatics; petroleum and refining chemistry; petroleum production chemistry; enhanced recovery chemicals and techniques. *Mailing Add:* 2118 Gunwale Circle Willis TX 77378-8488

BURDGE, GEOFFREY LYNN, NON-LINEAR OPTICS, QUANTUM ELECTRONICS. *Current Pos:* MEM TECH STAFF, LAB PHYS SCI, 80- *Personal Data:* b Munich, Ger, Sept 20, 47; US citizen; m 71. *Educ:* Univ Md, BS, 70, MS, 74, PhD(electronics eng), 81. *Prof Exp:* Mem tech staff, US Dept Defense, 70-80. *Mem:* Optical Soc Am; Inst Elec & Electronics Engrs. *Res:* Nonlinear optics; phase conjugation and its application to optical processing; modelocked semiconductor lasers; high intensity, near resonant excitation of sodium vapor. *Mailing Add:* Lab Phys Sci 8050 Greenmead Dr College Park MD 20740

BURDI, ALPHONSE R, DENTAL RESEARCH, CHILD GROWTH. *Current Pos:* USPHS res trainee, 60-61, from instr to assoc prof, 62-74, PROF ANAT, UNIV MICH, 74-, DIR INTEGRATED PREMED-PROG, 82- *Personal Data:* b Chicago, Ill, Aug 28, 35; m 69; c 2. *Educ:* Northern Ill Univ, BSEd, 57; Univ Ill, MS, 59; Univ Mich, MS, 61, PhD(anat), 63. *Concurrent Pos:* Fel Inst Advan Educ Dent Res, 64. *Mem:* AAAS; Am Asn Anat; Am Asn Phys Anthrop; Am Cleft Palate Asn; Tissue Cult Asn; Int Asn Dent Res. *Res:* Embryology and prenatal craniofacial growth; biomechanics of the facial skeleton; developmental craniofacial biology; birth defects; mechanisms of seven orofacial tissue interactions; cephalometrics; human teratology. *Mailing Add:* Dept Anat Univ Mich 5815 Med Sci Bldg II Ann Arbor MI 48109-0616

BURDICK, ALLAN BERNARD, GENETICS, CYTOGENETICS. *Current Pos:* chmn, Dept Genetics, Univ Mo Columbia, 69-70, group leader cytol & genetical sci, 70-75, prof, 69-86, EMER PROF GENETICS, UNIV MO, COLUMBIA, 86- *Personal Data:* b Cincinnati, Ohio, Aug 16, 20; m 43, 83, Elizabeth Wolfman; c Michael Allen, Nancy Cecilia, Stephen Franklin & Lindy Lou. *Educ:* Iowa State Col, BS, 45, MS, 47; Univ Calif, Berkeley, PhD, 49. *Prof Exp:* Asst prof genetics & plant breeding, Univ Ark, 49-52; from asst prof to prof genetics, Purdue Univ, 52-63; prof & assoc dean sci, Am Univ Beirut, 63-66; prof biol & chmn dept, Adelphi Univ, 66-69, actg dir, Adelphi Inst Marine Sci, 67-68. *Concurrent Pos:* Res collabr, Brookhaven Nat Lab, 55, 57; Fulbright res prof, Kyoto Univ, 59-60; Guggenheim fel, 59-60; vis prof, Sch Med, Ind Univ, 82, Peking Univ, 86. *Mem:* Fel AAAS; Genetics Soc Am; Soc Craniofacial Genetics; Am Soc Human Genetics; Am Soc Cell Biol; Am Bd Med Genetics. *Res:* Quantitative inheritance; human genetics; Drosophila gene structure; tomato genetics; mutation; mammalian meiotic cytogenetics; clinical genetics. *Mailing Add:* 3000 Woodkirk Dr Columbia MO 65203

BURDICK, DANIEL, SURGERY. *Current Pos:* RETIRED. *Personal Data:* b Syracuse, NY, Oct 21, 15; m 49; c 5. *Educ:* Syracuse Univ, AB, 37, MD, 50; Am Bd Surg, dipl. *Prof Exp:* Clin dir tumor clin & attend surgeon, Univ Hops, Upstate Med Ctr, State Univ NY, 54-97. *Concurrent Pos:* Attend, Syracuse Crouse-Irving Mem Hosp, 54-; surgeon, Community Gen Hosp. *Mem:* Am Col Surgeons; Soc Surg Oncol; Am Soc Clin Oncol. *Res:* Cancer research. *Mailing Add:* 119 Janet Dr Syracuse NY 13224

BURDICK, DONALD SMILEY, MATHEMATICAL STATISTICS. *Current Pos:* from asst prof to assoc prof math, 62-77, assoc prof, 77-88, ASSOC PROF STATIST & MATH & BIOMED ENG, DUKE UNIV, 88- *Personal Data:* b Newark, NJ, Feb 8, 37; m 58; c 3. *Educ:* Duke Univ, BS, 58; Princeton Univ, MA, 60, PhD(math statist), 61. *Prof Exp:* Instr, Princeton Univ, 61-62. *Concurrent Pos:* Consult, Army Res Off, 62-66, Res Triangle Inst, 85- & Metametrics Corp, 86-; vis asst prof statist, Univ Wis, 65-66; statist ed, J Parapsychol, 81; vis assoc prof, Va Polytech Inst & State Univ, 85-86. *Mem:* Am Statist Asn; Royal Statist Soc. *Res:* Linear statistical models; multivariate statistics; application of statistical methods in chemometrics and psychometrics, including measurement of reading comprehension. *Mailing Add:* Inst Statist Duke Univ Durham NC 27706-8001

BURDICK, GLENN ARTHUR, DEVICE PHYSICS, ACCIDENT RECONSTRUCTION. *Current Pos:* from assoc prof to prof elec eng, 65-86, dean, 79-86, DISTINGUISHED PROF ENG, UNIV S FLA, 86- *Personal Data:* b Pavillion, Wyo, Sept 9, 32; m 51, Joyce Huggett; c Stephen & Randy. *Educ:* Ga Inst Technol, BS, 58, MS, 59; Mass Inst Technol, PhD(physics), 61. *Honors & Awards:* Wiliam K Pursley Award. *Prof Exp:* Mem staff & spec tools design, Ga Technol Inst, 54-57, instr physics, 57-59; researcher, Div Sponsored Res, Mass Inst Technol, 59-61; sr mem res staff, Sperry Microwave, 61-65. *Concurrent Pos:* Prof, Univ Fla, 62-65; accident reconstruction expert, 65-; consult, Sperry Rand, 65-69, Fla Power Co, 67-, Los Alamos Sci Labs, 71; pres, Burdick Eng & Sci, Inc; dir, Mus Sci & Indust, Tampa. *Mem:* Int Soc Hybrid Microelectrons (pres, 74); Inst Elec & Electronics Engrs; Am Soc Eng Educ; NY Acad Sci; Am Acad Forensic Scientists. *Res:* Solid state physics; electromagnetic device physics; microelectronics; ferroelectrics; pyroelectrics; theoretical determination of energy bands and Fermi surface of copper. *Mailing Add:* 18728 Lake Iola Rd Dade City FL 33523. *Fax:* 352-588-5239

BURDINE, HOWARD WILLIAM, plant nutrition, physiology, for more information see previous edition

BURDINE, JOHN ALTON, NUCLEAR MEDICINE. *Current Pos:* instr nuclear med, Dept Radiol, 65-66, from asst prof to assoc prof radiol, 66-74, actg chmn dept, 68-71, PROF RADIOL, BAYLOR COL MED, 74-, CHIEF NUCLEAR MED SECT, 65- *Personal Data:* b Austin, Tex, Feb 7, 36; m 59; c 3. *Educ:* Univ Tex, Austin, BA, 59; Univ Tex Med Br Galveston, MD, 61. *Prof Exp:* Intern med, Med Ctr, Ind Univ, Indianapolis, 61-62; resident internal med, Univ Tex Med Br Galveston, 62-65. *Concurrent Pos:* Consult, US Army, 66; chief nuclear med serv, St Luke's Episcopal-Tex Children's Hosps, 69-85, pres & chief exec officer, 84-90, vchmn & chief exec officer, 85. *Mem:* Soc Nuclear Med. *Res:* Development and evaluation of new radiopharmaceuticals; design and implementation of a computer system for processing scintillation camera data, including development of radionuclide techniques for quantification of regional pulmonary function, bone densitometric studies. *Mailing Add:* Dept Radiol Baylor Col Med 1 Baylor Plaza Houston TX 77030-3411

BURDITT, ARTHUR KENDALL, JR, ENTOMOLOGY. *Current Pos:* RETIRED. *Personal Data:* b Elizabeth, NJ, Feb 12, 28; m 52; c 4. *Educ:* Rutgers Univ, BS, 50; Univ Minn, MS, 53, PhD(entom), 55. *Prof Exp:* Asst prof, Univ Mo, 55-57; res entomologist, fruit fly lab, US Dept Agr, 57-60, invest leader, citrus insect invest, 60-64, asst chief, fruit fly res br, 64-68, asst dir, entom res div, 68-71, staff asst, plant sci & entom, 71-72, res leader, subtrop hort res, 72-80, dir, Yakima Agr Res Lab, 80-83, res leader, Quarantine Treatment Res Unit, Agr Res Serv, Yakima, Wash, 83-89. *Concurrent Pos:* Affil prof, Univ Hawaii, 60; adj prof, Univ Fla, 72-81; courtesy prof, Univ Miami, Fla, 78-80; courtesy entomologist, Wash State Univ, 81-; consult, Agency Int Develop, 84-85, Int Atomic Energy Agency, 81- *Mem:* Fel AAAS; Entom Soc Am. *Res:* Treatments for pests infesting commodities of quarantine treatments, including fumigation, refrigeration and gamma radiation; techniques for detection of pests of quarantine importance. *Mailing Add:* 9068 C SW 82nd Terr Ocala FL 34481

BURDSALL, HAROLD HUGH, JR, MYCOLOGY. *Current Pos:* Botanist, Forest Dis Lab, Laurel, Md, 67-71, botanist, 71-82, SUPVR BOTANIST & PROJ LEADER, FOREST PROD LAB, CTR FOREST MYCOL RES, FOREST SERV, USDA, 82- *Personal Data:* b Hamilton, Ohio, Nov 18, 40; div; c 2. *Educ:* Miami Univ, BA, 62; Cornell Univ, PhD(mycol), 67. *Concurrent Pos:* Lectr, Dept Forest Prod, Univ Wis-Madison, 71-74, from adj asst prof to adj assoc prof, Dept Plant Path, 74-88, adj prof, 88- *Mem:* Mycol Soc Am (secy, 83-86); Brit Mycol Soc; Am Inst Biol Sci; Int Asn Plant Taxon. *Res:* Systematics of Armillaria, and other Basidiomycetous root rot and decay fungi, including culture studies, genetics, morphology and ecology. *Mailing Add:* 9350 Union Valley Rd Black Earth WI 53515

BUREK, ANTHONY JOHN, SOLAR PHYSICS, X-RAY ASTRONOMY. *Current Pos:* MEM STAFF, NAT BUR STANDARDS, 77- *Personal Data:* b Rockville Ctr, NY, June 14, 46. *Educ:* Princeton Univ, AB, 68; Univ Chicago, MS, 69, PhD(physics), 75. *Prof Exp:* Fel physics, Los Alamos Sci Lab, 75-77. *Mem:* Am Phys Soc; Sigma Xi. *Res:* Solar x-ray spectroscopy; theory and evaluation of x-ray diffracting properties of crystals. *Mailing Add:* PO Box 742 Upton NY 11973

BURES, DONALD JOHN (CHARLES), MATHEMATICS. *Current Pos:* RETIRED. *Personal Data:* b Winnipeg, Man, Jan 23, 38; m 76. *Educ:* Queen's Univ, Ont, BA, 58; Princeton Univ, PhD(math), 61. *Prof Exp:* Asst prof math, Queen's Univ, Ont, 61-62; from asst prof to prof math, Univ BC, 62-97, head dept, 73-78. *Mem:* Am Math Soc; Can Math Cong; Royal Soc Can. *Res:* Abstract analysis; von Neumann algebras. *Mailing Add:* Dept Math Univ BC Rm 121 1984 Mathematics Rd Vancouver BC V6T 1Z2 Can

BURES, JAN, PHYSIOLOGY. *Current Pos:* Lab head, 60-80, SR RES SCIENTIST, INST PHYSIOL, CZECH ACAD SCI, 81- *Personal Data:* b Ctyrl Dvory, Czech Repub, June 13, 26. *Educ:* Charles Univ Prague, MD, 50; Czech Acad Sci, PhD, 55, DSc, 63. *Hon Degrees:* Dr, Univ Lethbridge, Can, 92. *Mem:* Foreign assoc Nat Acad Sci; Europ Acad Sci. *Mailing Add:* Inst Physiol Czech Acad Sci Videnska 1083 Prague 14220 Czech Republic. *Fax:* 420-2-471-9517; *E-Mail:* bures@biomed.cas.cz

BURES, MILAN F, epidemiology, public health, for more information see previous edition

BURFENING, PETER J, REPRODUCTIVE PHYSIOLOGY, GENETICS. *Current Pos:* PROF ANIMAL PHYSIOL, MONT STATE UNIV, 60- *Personal Data:* b Reno, Nev, Nov 8, 42; m 64; c 1. *Educ:* Colo State Univ, BS, 64; NC State Univ, MS, 66, PhD(animal physiol), 68. *Mem:* Am Soc Animal Sci. *Res:* Reproductive physiology of domestic animals with special emphasis on the relationship between genotype and the environment as it relates to reproductive events. *Mailing Add:* Dept Animal Sci Mont State Univ Bozeman MT 59717-0001

BURFORD, ARTHUR EDGAR, PETROLEUM GEOLOGY, ECONOMIC GEOLOGY. *Current Pos:* prof geol, 68-89, from actg head dept to head dept, 70-82, EMER PROF GEOL, UNIV AKRON, 90-; PRES, GEOCONCEPTS, INC, 90- *Personal Data:* b Olean, NY, Mar 5, 28; m 53, Dhreoma Reed; c Karen, Cheryl, Patricia, Arthur, Dhreoma, Elizabeth & Paul. *Educ:* Cornell Univ, AB, 52; Univ Tulsa, MS, 54; Univ Mich, PhD(geol), 60. *Prof Exp:* Geologist, Pan Am Petrol Corp, Utah & Colo, 58-60; from asst prof to assoc prof, WVa Univ, 60-68. *Concurrent Pos:* Geologist, US Geol Surv, 52, 53, 54, 79 & 80; fel, NSF, 55-58; coop geologist, WVa Geol & Econ Surv, 62-69; chmn, N Cent Sect, Geol Soc Am, 87-88. *Mem:* Fel Geol Soc Am; Am Asn Petrol Geol; Am Soc Photogram & Remote Sensing; Am Geophys Union; Ger Geol Union; Am Inst Prof Geologists; N Cent Sect Geol Soc Am. *Res:* Geology of Rocky Mountains and Appalachians; geologic interpretation of remote sensing imagery; structural analysis of joints; geologic exploration for petroleum; cementation history and porosity-permeability development of well-cemented sandstones. *Mailing Add:* 180 Atterbury Blvd Hudson OH 44236-1644

BURFORD, HUGH JONATHAN, MEDICOLEGAL ALCOHOL IMPAIRMENT, MEASUREMENT. *Current Pos:* RETIRED. *Personal Data:* b Memphis, Tenn, Aug 5, 31; m 57, Dorothy M Moffett; c Jonathan Mark & Jennifer Lynn. *Educ:* Millsaps Col, BS, 54; Univ Miss, MS, 56; Univ Kans, PhD(pharmacol), 62. *Prof Exp:* Asst chem, Univ Miss, 54-56; asst pharmacol, Univ Kans, 57-60; asst prof, Bowman Gray Sch Med, 63-68; assoc prof pharmacol & dir, MDL Labs, Med Sch, Northwestern Univ, 68-71; assoc prof pharmacol & teaching assoc med sci, Univ NC, Chapel Hill, 71-93, assoc prof pharm, Pharm Sch, 73-93. *Concurrent Pos:* USPHS fel, Tulane Univ, 62-63; Am Heart Asn, USPHS & Nat Fund Med Educ grants, 64-; mem, Asn Multidisc Educ in H H Sci, 69, health prof, Educ Spec Interest Group, Am Educ Res Asn, 70; fac fel, Kellogg Ctr Teaching Professions, 70-71; consult, Am Soc Pharmacol & Exp Therapeut & Nat Lib Med, 80-86; NC Comt Blood Alcohol Adv Comm, 49-80; Fund Advan ... Div H H Servs, 84-91; chair teaching & eval mat, Educ Affairs Comm, Am Soc Pharm Exp Therapeut, 86-91; mem, Responsible Beverage Serv Coun, 88-91. *Mem:* AAAS; Am Soc Pharmacol & Exp Therapeut; Am Educ Res Asn. *Res:* Optimizing education in pharmacology; production and evaluation of pharmacology teaching materials for health profession students including textual, visual and electronic media formatted for individualized and group learning; research on alcohol and health policy which focuses on server intervention and highway safety; software for alcohol pharmacokinetics. *Mailing Add:* PO Box 1287 Waynesville NC 28786. *Fax:* 704-452-7985

BURFORD, M GILBERT, PHYSICAL CHEMISTRY. *Current Pos:* from instr to assoc prof, 36-47, E B Nye Prof Chem, 47-77, assoc provost, 69-76, chmn, Col Sci Soc, 78-79, EMER PROF CHEM, WESLEYAN UNIV, 77-, ADMIN CONSULT, 77- *Personal Data:* b Brooklyn, NY, Oct 27, 10; m 34. *Educ:* Wesleyan Univ, AB, 32; Princeton Univ, AM, 33, PhD(chem), 35. *Prof Exp:* Asst chem, Princeton Univ, 33-34; instr, Cornell Univ, 35-36. *Concurrent Pos:* Consult & supvr, Conn State Dept Environ Protection, 42-80 & New Eng Interstate Water Pollution Control Comn, 49-80; Fund Advan of Educ fac fel, 55-56; chmn bd dirs, Univ Res Inst Conn, 74-77. *Mem:* Fel AAAS; Am Chem Soc; fel Am Inst Chemists. *Res:* Chemical reactions of hydriodic acid and ammonium iodide; analytical chemistry of difficulty soluble compounds; spectrophotometric methods of analysis; industrial trade waste disposal; chemical kinetics. *Mailing Add:* PO Box 119 Haddam CT 06438-0119

BURFORD, NEIL, NON-METAL SYNTHETIC CHEMISTRY, CHEMISTRY OF PHOSPHORUS & ARSENIC. *Current Pos:* asst prof, 87-91, ASSOC PROF INORG CHEM, DALHOUSIE UNIV, HALIFAX, NS, 91- *Personal Data:* b Liverpool, Eng, Apr 29, 58; m 80; c 2. *Educ:* Univ Wales Col, Cardiff, BSc, 79; Univ Calgary, Alta, PhD(inorg chem), 83. *Prof Exp:* Postdoctoral fel inorg chem, Univ Alta, Edmonton, 83-84; res assoc inorg chem, Univ NB, Fredericton, 84-86. *Concurrent Pos:* Jour referee, Can J Chem, J Chem Soc, Dalton Trans, J Am Chem Soc. *Mem:* Am Chem Soc; Chem Inst Can. *Mailing Add:* Dept Chem Dalhousie Univ Halifax NS B3H 4J3 Can

BURFORD, ROGER LEWIS, STATISTICS, ECONOMICS. *Current Pos:* from assoc prof to prof, 63-90, EMER PROF STATIST, LA STATE UNIV, 90- *Personal Data:* b Independence, Miss, Jan 19, 30; m 48, Bettye Marshall; c Pamela & Roger. *Educ:* Univ Miss, BBA, 56, MA, 57; Ind Univ, PhD(econ, statist), 61. *Prof Exp:* Lectr econ & statist, Ind Univ, 59-60; asst prof, Ga State Univ, 60-63. *Concurrent Pos:* Ford fac fel, Carnegie Inst Technol, 62; Fulbright prof, Nat Taiwan Univ, 67-68; dir bus res econ, La State Univ, 69-74; exec vpres statist & econ, Econ & Issues Res Inc, 69-; chmn, La Gov's Coun Econ Advan, 73-75, mem, 73-79. *Mem:* Am Statist Asn; Econometric Soc; Regional Sci Asn. *Res:* Random variate generation; input-output multipliers; mathematical methods and models in regional economic and demographic research. *Mailing Add:* 1282 E Stanwick Pl Baton Rouge LA 70810. *Fax:* 504-923-0823; *E-Mail:* rogerbur@msn.com

BURG, ANTON BEHME, INORGANIC CHEMISTRY. *Current Pos:* from asst prof to prof, 39-74, head dept, 40-50, EMER PROF CHEM, UNIV SOUTHERN CALIF, 74- *Personal Data:* b Dallas City, Ill, Oct 18, 04. *Educ:* Univ Chicago, BS, 27, MS, 28, PhD(chem), 31. *Honors & Awards:* Tolman Medal, Am Chem Soc, 61, Award Distinguished Serv Advan Inorg Chem, 69. *Prof Exp:* Instr inorg chem, Univ Chicago, 31-39. *Concurrent Pos:* Consult var govt agencies, 47- *Mem:* Fel AAAS; Am Chem Soc; Sigma Xi. *Res:* Boron and silicon hydrides; fluorine compounds; vacuum technique; non-aqueous solvents and addition compounds; organo-phosphorus and inorganic polymers; metal-carbonyl analogues; fluorocarbon phosphines; study of new syntheses and compound-types in both fields. *Mailing Add:* Dept Chem Univ Southern Calif Univ Pk MC 1062 Los Angeles CA 90089

BURG, JOHN PARKER, DEVELOPMENT OF ENTROPIC CONCEPTS, DIGITAL SIGNAL PROCESSING. *Current Pos:* CHMN, ENTROPIC PROCESSING INC, 83-; CHMN, ENTROPIC SPEECH INC, 86- *Personal Data:* b Great Bend, Kans, Dec 17, 31; div; c 5. *Educ:* Univ Tex, Austin, BA, 53, BS, 53; Mass Inst Technol, MS, 60; Stanford Univ, PhD(geophys), 75. *Honors & Awards:* Best Presentation Award, Soc Explor Geophysicists, 67; Naval Res Lab Res Publ Award, 84. *Prof Exp:* Eng, Tex Instruments Inc,

56-60, geophysicist, 60-62, sr res geophysicist, 62-73; pres, Time & Space Processing, Inc, 73-78, chmn, 78-83. *Concurrent Pos:* Chmn, Entropic Res Lab, Inc, 90- *Mem:* Fel Inst Elec & Electronics Engrs. *Res:* Development of new signal processing methods and entropic processing concepts with applications to speech compression to low bit rates (2400 bps), to geophysical seismic data processing as well as to other fields such as anti submarine warfare. *Mailing Add:* 20990 Valley Green Dr Apt 703 Cupertino CA 95014-1846. *Fax:* 408-252-4893

BURG, MARION, ORGANIC CHEMISTRY. *Current Pos:* RETIRED. *Personal Data:* b Bridgeport, Conn, May 25, 21. *Educ:* Queens Col, BS, 42; Cornell Univ, PhD(org chem), 47. *Prof Exp:* Asst instr chem, Queens 42-44; res assoc org chem, Mass Inst Technol, 47-51; with E I du Pont de Nemours Co, Inc, 51-86. *Mem:* Am Chem Soc. *Res:* Synthetic organic chemistry; photochemistry. *Mailing Add:* 2300 Riddle Ave Apt 6 Wilmington DE 19806-2161

BURG, MAURICE B, NEPHROLOGY. *Current Pos:* res assoc, 57-75, CHIEF, LAB KIDNEY & ELECTROLYTE METAB, NIH, 75- *Personal Data:* b Boston, Mass, Apr 9, 31; m 66; c 4. *Educ:* Harvard Univ, BA, 52, MD, 55. *Mem:* Nat Acad Sci; Am Soc Clin Invest; Am Fedn Clin Res; Biophys Soc; Soc Gen Physiol; Am Physiol Soc. *Res:* Renal and electrolyte physiology. *Mailing Add:* 3106 Q St NW Washington DC 20007

BURG, RICHARD WILLIAM, MICROBIAL BIOCHEMISTRY. *Current Pos:* RETIRED. *Personal Data:* b Ft Wayne, Ind, June 22, 32; m 61, Helene W Schenker; c Stephen P & Suzanne M. *Educ:* Wabash Col, AB, 54; Univ Ill, PhD(biochem), 58. *Prof Exp:* NSF res fel, Univ Calif, Berkeley, 58-60; sr res microbiol, Merck Res Labs, 60-69, from res fel to sr res fel, 70-81, sr investr, 82-93. *Mem:* AAAS; Am Chem Soc; Am Soc Microbiol; Am Soc Pharmacog. *Res:* Biochemistry of viruses; antibiotics and physiologically active products of microorganisms. *Mailing Add:* 38151 Grand Oaks Ave Palm Desert CA 92211

BURG, WILLIAM ROBERT, industrial hygiene, analytical chemistry, for more information see previous edition

BURGAUER, PAUL DAVID, ORGANIC CHEMISTRY, PHARMACEUTICAL CHEMISTRY. *Current Pos:* RETIRED. *Personal Data:* b St Gallen, Switz, May 21, 26; nat US; m 51, Margaret Roos; c Steven & James. *Educ:* Swiss Fed Inst Technol, dipl ing, PhD(org & pharmaceut chem), 52. *Prof Exp:* Res chemist, Hilton-Davis Chem Co, 53-54; patent liaison, E I du Pont de Nemours & Co, 54-59; mem staff, Patent Dept, Abbott Labs, 59-72, int patent mgr, 72-81. *Concurrent Pos:* Patent agent, 61- *Res:* Polymer chemistry; natural and synthetic drugs and polymers. *Mailing Add:* 813 Hayes Libertyville IL 60048. *E-Mail:* pdb@lnd.com

BURGE, DENNIS KNIGHT, HIGH TECHNICAL MIRRORS & WINDOWS. *Current Pos:* physicist, 57-63, RES PHYSICIST, NAVAL AIR WARFARE CTR, WEAPONS DIV, 63- *Personal Data:* b Ogden, Utah, Dec 8, 35; div; c 2. *Educ:* Univ Nev, Reno, BS, 56, MS, 61. *Mem:* Optical Soc Am; Sigma Xi. *Res:* Optical properties of solids; thin films; reflectometry; high energy laser optics. *Mailing Add:* 624 Randall St Ridgecrest CA 93555-3308. *Fax:* 760-939-1409

BURGE, JEAN C, RENAL DISEASE. *Current Pos:* ASST PROF NUTRIT, UNIV NC, 80- *Personal Data:* b Detroit, MI, Mar 10, 47; m; c 2. *Educ:* Mich State Univ, PhD(nutrit), 79. *Honors & Awards:* Mary P Huddleson Award, Am Dietetic Found. *Mem:* Am Inst Nutrit; Am Pediat Asn; Am Pub Health Asn; Am Dietetic Asn. *Mailing Add:* Dept Gen Surg Ohio State Univ N737 Doan Hall 410 W Tenth Ave Columbus OH 43210

BURGE, ROBERT ERNEST, JR, ORGANIC CHEMISTRY. *Current Pos:* RETIRED. *Personal Data:* b Kansas City, Mo, Aug 21, 25; m 50. *Educ:* Univ Ill, BS, 48; Cornell Univ, PhD(chem), 52; Bernard M Baruch Col, MBA, 69. *Prof Exp:* Asst org chem, Cornell Univ, 48-51; res chemist, Shell Chem Corp, 51-54, group leader, 54-58, sr chemist, 57-59, sr technologist, 59-60, sr chemist, 60-63, supvr, 63-68; from asst prof to prof chem, Suffolk Co Community Col, 68-90. *Mem:* Soc Invest Recurring Events; Mkt Technicians Asn. *Res:* Organic chemical synthesis; macrocyclic carbon compounds; epoxy resins. *Mailing Add:* RR1 Box 342-1 Waitsfield VT 05673-9722. *E-Mail:* bobburge@madriver.com

BURGE, WYLIE D, MICROBIOLOGY, BIOCHEMISTRY. *Current Pos:* RETIRED. *Personal Data:* b Denver, Colo, June 2, 25; m 58; c 2. *Educ:* Colo State Univ, BS, 50, MS, 56; Univ Calif, Davis, PhD(soil microbiol), 58. *Prof Exp:* Jr soil scientist soil microbiol, Univ Calif, Berkeley, 58-60; assoc specialist soils res & sta supt, Antelope Valley Field Sta, Univ Calif, Riverside, 60-66; res soil scientist, Agr Res Serv, USDA, 66-73, microbiologist, Agr Environ Qual Inst Sci & Educ Admin, 73-86. *Mem:* Soil Sci Soc Am; Am Soc Microbiol; Sigma Xi. *Res:* Ammonium fixation by soil organic matter; biochemistry of nitrification; chemistry of ammonium potassium fixation by soils; microbiology of pesticide degradation in soils; fate of pathogens during land application and composting of sewage sludges; fate in the soil mutagens derived from hazardous wastes in farmed land; molecular processes in the infection of plants by microorganisms. *Mailing Add:* 1106 Edgevale Rd Silver Spring MD 20910-1638

BURGEE, JOHN HENRY, ARCHITECTURE. *Current Pos:* PARTNER, JOHN BURGEE ARCHITECTS, NEW YORK, 82- *Personal Data:* b Chicago, Ill, Aug 28, 33; m 56, Gwendolyn Mary Henson; c John Gerard. *Educ:* Univ Notre Dame, BArch, 56. *Hon Degrees:* DEngr, Univ Notre Dame, 83. *Honors & Awards:* Reynolds Aluminum Prize, 78. *Prof Exp:* Proj mgr, Naess & Murphy, Chicago, 58-61; admin design & proj architect, C F Murphy Assocs, Chicago, 61-65, assoc partner, 65-67, partner, 67; assoc, Philip Johnson Architects, New York, 67-68; partner, Johnson/Burgee, New York, 68-82. *Concurrent Pos:* Chmn, Bldg Mat Sect, Metrop Crusade Mercy, Chicago, 66-67; chmn, Archit Rev Bd, Bronxville, NY, 74-75; chmn, Bronxville Planning Comn, 75-77; chmn archit comt, Statue of Liberty/Ellis Island Centennial Comn; bd dirs, Lenox Hill Hosp, 82-91, Parsons Sch Design, 85-92, Univ Notre Dame, 88-, Chicago Athenaeum, 89-92. *Mem:* Fel Am Inst Architects; fel Urban Design Inst; Inst Archit & Urban Studies (pres, 84). *Mailing Add:* Perelandra Farm Skunks Misery Rd Millerton NY 12546

BURGENER, FRANCIS ANDRE, RADIOLOGY. *Current Pos:* from asst prof to assoc prof, 71-81, PROF RADIOL, UNIV ROCHESTER, 82- *Personal Data:* b Visp, Switz, May 21, 42; m 70, Therese Christen; c Philipp & Michele. *Educ:* Univ Bern, MD, 67, Diss, 69; Am Bd Radiol, dipl & cert diag radiol, 72. *Prof Exp:* Resident radiol, Univ Bern, 67-68; fel exp med, Univ Zurich, 68-69; resident radiol, Univ Bern, 69-70; instr, Univ Mich, 70-71. *Concurrent Pos:* Panelist, US Pharmacopeia Adv Panel, 75-80; mem bd investr radiol, 77-90; ed, J Med Imaging, 87-90. *Mem:* AAAS; NY Acad Sci. *Res:* Radiological and MRI contrast media; liver imaging portal hypertension; bone imaging; radiation biology. *Mailing Add:* Dept Radiol Univ Rochester Med Sch 601 Elmwood Ave Rochester NY 14642-0001. *Fax:* 716-273-1033

BURGER, ALFRED, MEDICINAL CHEMISTRY. *Current Pos:* res assoc, Drug Addiction Lab, Nat Res Coun, 29-38, actg asst prof, 38-39, from asst prof to prof, 39-70, chmn dept, 62-63, EMER PROF CHEM, UNIV VA, 70- *Personal Data:* b Vienna, Austria, Sept 6, 05; nat US; m 36; c 1. *Educ:* Univ Vienna, PhD(chem), 28. *Hon Degrees:* DSc, Col Pharm & Sci, Philadelphia, 71. *Honors & Awards:* Pasteur Medal, 53; Smissman Award, Am Chem Soc, 77; Am Pharm Soc Found Award, 71. *Prof Exp:* Chemist, Hoffmann-La Roche Co, 28-29. *Concurrent Pos:* Chmn, Med Chem Div, Am Chem Soc, 54; USPHS, 56-59; mem chem panel, Cancer Chemother Nat Serv Ctr, 56-59, med chem, 60-64; vchmn, Gordon Res Conf Med Chem, 58, chmn, 59; mem study sect on exp ther & pharmacol; vis lectr, Univ Calif, 63; NIH spec fel biochem, Univ Hawaii, 65; consult, Smith Kline & French Labs & Philip Morris Res Ctr, Dept Health, Mex; ed, J Med Chem; mem psychopharmacol study comt, Nat Inst Ment Health, 67-71 & 76-80. *Mem:* Am Chem Soc; Am Pharmacol Soc; AAAS. *Res:* General organic chemistry; chemistry of opium alkaloids; syntheses of morphine substitutes; chemotherapy; antimalarials; antituberculous drugs; organic phosphorus compounds; antimetabolites; psychopharmacological drugs; synthesis and design of drugs. *Mailing Add:* 2600 Barracks Rd Apt 439 The Collonades Charlottesville VA 22901-2100

BURGER, AMBROSE WILLIAM, AGRONOMY, SCIENCE EDUCATION. *Current Pos:* prof agron, 53-86, EMER PROF AGRON, UNIV ILL, URBANA-CHAMPAIGN, 86- *Personal Data:* b Jasper, Ind, Nov 27, 23; m 46, 67, Phyllis Jacob Voorhees; c Kathreine S (Christiansen, Marie C, Patricia A (Bennett), Carol J & Judy A (Haselhorst). *Educ:* Purdue Univ, BSA, 47; Univ Wis, MSA, 48, PhD(agron & plant physiol), 50. *Honors & Awards:* Agron Educ Award, Am Soc Agron, 64. *Prof Exp:* Asst prof agron, Univ Md, 50-53. *Mem:* Crop Sci Soc Am; AAAS; fel Nat Asn Col Teachers Agr; fel Am Soc Agron; Sigma Xi. *Res:* Forage crop production; pasture investigations; field crop science. *Mailing Add:* 2010 Eagle Ridge Ct No B Urbana IL 61801

BURGER, CAROL J, EXPERIMENTAL BIOLOGY *Current Pos:* grad res asst, NIH, Biol Dept, Va Tech, 81-83, res assoc, Div Vet Biol, Col Vet Med, 84-85, Dept Vet Biosci, 86-87, vis asst prof, Dept Biol, 87-88, ASST PROF MICROBIOL & IMMUNOL, DEPT BIOL, VA TECH & DIR, WOMEN'S RES INST, 89-; ED-IN-CHIEF, J WOMEN & MINORITIES SCI & ENG, 93- *Personal Data:* b Flushing, NY, Jan 3, 44; m 73, James; c Catherine, John & Julia. *Educ:* Rosary Col, BA, 65; Va Polytech Inst & State Univ, PhD(immunol), 83. *Prof Exp:* Med technologist, St Francis Hosp, Peoria, Ill, 65-66, pediat hemato/oncol, Riley Hosp Children, Indianapolis, Ind, 71-73; res tech, Animal Sci Dept, Purdue Univ, 74; med technologist, Patterson-Coleman Labs, Gainesville, Fla, 76-77, pediat hemat/oncol, Shands Teaching Hosp, Gainesville, 77-79. *Concurrent Pos:* Grants, var orgns & corps, 80-92. *Mem:* Sigma Xi; Am Soc Microbiol; Am Asn Immunologists; Soc Leukocyte Biol. *Res:* Biology; immunology; pediatric hematology/oncology. *Mailing Add:* Ctr Interdisciplinary Studies Va Tech Lane Hall Blacksburg VA 24061-0227. *Fax:* 540-231-7669; *E-Mail:* wri@vtvm1.cc.vt.edu

BURGER, CHRISTIAN P, EXPERIMENTAL MECHANICS & PHOTOMECHANICS, ELECTRO OPTICS. *Current Pos:* PROF MECH ENG, TEX A&M UNIV, COLLEGE STATION, 86- *Personal Data:* b George, SAfrica, Dec 30, 29; US citizen; m 56, Marie M Kenyon; c Marie, Christian & Robert. *Educ:* Univ Stellenbosch, BSc, 52; Univ Cape Town, PhD(eng), 67. *Honors & Awards:* Peterson Award, Soc Exp Stress Anal, 74 & 75, Hetenyi Award, 84, Frocht Award, 84. *Prof Exp:* Engr, Vacuum Oil Co, SAfrica, 55-62; sr lectr eng, Univ Cape Town, 62-71; prof eng mech, Iowa State Univ, 71-86. *Mem:* Fel Soc Exp Stress Analysis; Am Soc Nondestructive Testing; Am Soc Mech Eng; Soc Photo-Optical Instrumentation Engrs; Am Soc Testing Mat; Brit Soc Strain Measurement; fel AAAS. *Res:* Thermal stress analysis; experimental mechanics; nondestructive evaluation; fracture mechanics; fiber optic sensors; high temperature and severe environment testing; design methodology. *Mailing Add:* 9204 Waterford Dr College Station TX 77845

BURGER, DIONYS, FOREST ECOLOGY, SOILS. *Current Pos:* RETIRED. *Personal Data:* b Ambarawa, Indonesia, May 29, 23; Can citizen; m 52, Johanna F Prins; c Dionys H & John A. *Educ:* State Agr Univ Wageningen, MF, 52; Univ Toronto, PhD(bot), 65. *Prof Exp:* Forester, Ont Ministry Natural Resources, 53-61, res scientist forest soil, Res Br, 61-77, head, Ont Forest Res Ctr, 77-81, prin scientist, Ecol & Silvicult, Ont Tree Improvement & Forest Biomass Inst, 81-88. *Concurrent Pos:* Leader, Working Group Site Classification, Int Union Forest Res Orgn, 70-80; mem, Ont Joint Forest Res Comn, 75-; mem, Can Nat Res Coun, Assoc Comn Univ Res, 78-80; adv, forest site classification & evaluation, Forestry Fac, Agr Univ Malaysia, Serdang, 80; adj prof land classification, Forestry Fac, Univ Toronto, 81-87; forest soil specialist, F A O prof, Forest Res Inst, Yezin, Burma, 82; consult forest soil & ecosystems, Can Int Develop Agency, Lanxiang, Heilongjang, People's Repub China; consult forest ecologist, 88- *Mem:* Can Inst Forestry; Int Soc Trop Foresters; Int Soc Soil Sci; Ger Soc Forest Site Sci & Tree Breeding. *Res:* Physiographic site classification; ecological regions; mapping on aerial photographs; surface geology. *Mailing Add:* Forest Ecologist RR 1 Gilford ON L0L 1R0 Can

BURGER, EDWARD JAMES, JR, MEDICINE, HEALTH POLICY. *Current Pos:* clin asst prof, 76-81, assoc prof prev med, 81-88, DIR, INST HEALTH POLICY ANAL, 81-, PROF PREV MED, GEORGETOWN UNIV, 88- *Personal Data:* b Cleveland, Ohio, Feb 23, 33; m 60, Sarah Greene; c Heidi & Hilary. *Educ:* McGill Univ, BSc, 54, MDCM, 58; Harvard Univ, MIH, 60, ScD(physiol), 66. *Prof Exp:* Intern med, Royal Victoria Hosp, Montreal, Que, 58-59; res assoc physiol, Sch Pub Health, Harvard Univ, 66-69; staff asst, Off Sci & Technol, Exec Off of the President, 69-76. *Concurrent Pos:* Consult, President's Adv Comn, 67; assoc, J F Kennedy Sch Pub Admin, 67-68; mem, Nat Cancer Adv Bd & Nat Heart, Lung & Blood Inst Adv Coun, NIH, 73-76; deleg, Orgn Econ Coop & Develop, Paris, 73-76; sr sci adv, Econ Comn Europe, UN, 74. *Mem:* Am Col Prev Med; AAAS. *Res:* Oxygen toxicity and its effects on the lung; effects of environmental contaminants on human health; public policy issues concerning health. *Mailing Add:* 3403 Woodley Rd NW Washington DC 20007-2292

BURGER, GEORGE VANDERKARR, WILDLIFE CONSERVATION. *Current Pos:* RETIRED. *Personal Data:* b Woodstock, Ill, Jan 22, 27; m 49, Jeannine Willis; c Suzanne (Campbell), Christine (Rice) & Nancy (Smith). *Educ:* Beloit Col, BS, 50; Univ Calif, MA, 52; Univ Wis, PhD(wildlife mgt), 59. *Honors & Awards:* Leopold Award, Green Tree Club, 58; Nature Conservancy Nat Award, 54. *Prof Exp:* Asst zool & wildlife mgt, Univ Calif, 50-52; instr zool, bot & conserv, Contra Costa Jr Col, 52-54; asst wildlife mgt, Univ Wis, 54-58; field rep, Sportsmen's Serv Bur, NY, 58-62; mgr wildlife mgt, Remington Arms Co, 62-66; gen mgr, McGraw Wildlife Found, 66-88, dir res, 88-92. *Concurrent Pos:* Ed, Wildlife Soc Bull, Wildlife Soc, 72-75; mem, Ill Surface Mining Adv Coun, 91-; pvt consult. *Mem:* Hon mem Wildlife Soc; Am Fisheries Soc; Outdoor Writers Asn Am; Audobon Soc. *Res:* Waterfowl and upland game bird management and ecology; shooting preserve and game farm management; wildlife and general conservation education. *Mailing Add:* 650 N Airlite St Elgin IL 60123-2675

BURGER, HAROLD, HIV INFECTION, INFECTIONS DISEASES. *Current Pos:* CO-DIR HIV RES, WADSWORTH CTR, NY STATE DEPT HEALTH, 91- *Personal Data:* b New York, NY, Sept 29, 47; m 73, Barbara Weiser; c 2. *Educ:* Univ Chicago, BS, 69; Rockefeller Univ, PhD(virol), 76; Albert Einstein Col Med, MD. *Prof Exp:* Asst prof med & microbiol, State Univ NY, Stony Brook, 85-91. *Concurrent Pos:* Assoc prof med, Albany Med Col, 91-97. *Mem:* Am Soc Microbiol; Infectious Dis Soc Am. *Res:* HIV pathogenesis; viral and molecular determinants of pathogenesis. *Mailing Add:* Wadsworth Ctr 120 New Scotland Ave Albany NY 12208

BURGER, HENRY ROBERT, III, STRUCTURAL GEOLOGY, GEOPHYSICS. *Current Pos:* From asst prof to assoc prof, 66-75, PROF GEOL, SMITH COL, 75- *Personal Data:* b Pittsburgh, Pa, Aug 2, 40; m 63; c 2. *Educ:* Yale Univ, BS, 62; Ind Univ, AM, 64, PhD(geol), 66. *Mem:* AAAS; Am Geophys Union; Geol Soc Am; Nat Asn Geol Teachers (pres, 85-86); Sigma Xi. *Res:* Gravity and magnetics of rifts; fracture analysis; petrofabrics; computer assisted instruction. *Mailing Add:* Dept Geol Smith Col Northampton MA 01063-0001

BURGER, JOANNA, ETHOLOGY, ECOLOGY. *Current Pos:* asst prof, 73-76, assoc prof, 76-81, PROF BIOL, RUTGERS UNIV, 81-, DISTINGUISHED PROF, 91- *Personal Data:* b Schenectady, NY, Jan 18, 41; m 81, Michael Gochfeld; c Deborah & David. *Educ:* State Univ NY Albany, BS, 63; Cornell Univ, MS, 64; Univ Minn, PhD(ecol & behav), 72. *Prof Exp:* Instr biol, State Univ NY Buffalo, 64-68; asst, Univ Minn, 68-72; res assoc ethology, Rutgers Inst Animal Behav, 72-73. *Concurrent Pos:* Mem, BEST, Nat Res Coun, 89-92, SCOPE, 92-; bd dirs, Off Toxic Substance; Endocrine Disruptor Comt, Nat Res Coun. *Mem:* Fel Am Ornith Union; Animal Behav Soc; Ecol Soc; AAAS; Soc Toxicol. *Res:* Examination of the relationship between an animal's environment and its behavior, particularly in the ways animals partition the environment, such as food resources and nesting habitat; effects of heavy metal on behavioral development; effects of incubation behavior on behavioral development. *Mailing Add:* Div Life Sci Rutgers Univ Piscataway NJ 08855-1059. *E-Mail:* burger@biology.rutgers.edu

BURGER, LELAND LEONARD, PHYSICAL INORGANIC CHEMISTRY. *Current Pos:* res assoc chem, 65-77, STAFF SCIENTIST, PAC NORTHWEST LAB, BATTELLE MEM INST, 77- *Personal Data:* b Buffalo, Wyo, Nov 5, 17; m 42, Eleanor McMorris; c Harold, Virginia & James. *Educ:* Univ Wyo, BA, 39; Univ Wash, PhD(chem), 48. *Prof Exp:* Res chemist, Div War Res, Columbia Univ, 42-45 & Hanford Labs, Gen Elec Co, 48-64. *Concurrent Pos:* Adj prof chem, Wash State Univ, 73- *Mem:* Fel AAAS; Am Chem Soc; Am Inst Physics; Am Nuclear Soc. *Res:* Solvent extraction mechanisms, absorption spectroscopy; chemistry and control volatile fission products; nuclear fuel reprocessing; fluorine chemistry; radiation chemistry. *Mailing Add:* 1925 Howell Ave Richland WA 99352-2319

BURGER, RICHARD MELTON, MOLECULAR PHARMACOLOGY. *Current Pos:* assoc, 86-93, ASSOC INVESTR, PUB HEALTH RES INST, 93- *Personal Data:* b New York, NY, Mar 23, 41; m 77, Deborah Mellis; c Claudia & Abigail. *Educ:* Adelphi Col, BA, 62; Princeton Univ, PhD(biol), 69. *Honors & Awards:* Stohlman Mem Scholar, Leukemia Soc Am, 87. *Prof Exp:* Spec trainee microbiol, Harvard Med Sch, 64-65, spec trainee biochem, Brandeis Univ, 65-68; Nat Cancer Inst trainee, Univ Calif, Berkeley, 68-71; asst prof biol, Mid E Tech Univ, Turkey, 71-72; assoc, Sloan-Kettering Inst Caner Res, 72-77; assoc molecular pharmacol, Albert Einstein Col Med, 77-82, prin assoc, 82-86. *Concurrent Pos:* Res assoc, Haskins Labs, New York, 59-; asst prof biochem, Sloan-Kettering Div, Cornell Univ, 73-77; assoc biol sci, Columbia Univ, 76-77; adj assoc prof biol sci, Lehman Col, City Univ New York, 80-81; adj assoc prof pharmacol, NY Univ Sch Med, 86-91, adj prof biol, 91-92, adj prof chem, 91 & vis res prof biol, 92-91; sr scientist, Redox Pharmaceut Corp, 94-96, chief scientist, 96-; vis prof chem, City Col NY, 97- *Mem:* Soc Biol Chem; Harvey Soc; Am Chem Soc; Asn Res Vision & Ophthal. *Res:* Drug-induced DNA damage; metal-oxygen interactions; metal-organic antiviral agents. *Mailing Add:* Pub Health Res Inst 455 First Ave New York NY 10016. *Fax:* 212-578-0804; *E-Mail:* burger@phri.nyu.edu

BURGER, ROBERT M, TECHNOLOGY POLICY, COOPERATIVE RESEARCH. *Current Pos:* VPRES, SEMICONDUCTOR RES CORP, 82- *Personal Data:* b Frederick, Md, Feb 14, 27; m 49, Marian Abbott; c Sharon (Milikowsky), Lisa (Gurganus) & Robert M Jr. *Educ:* Col William & Mary, BS, 49; Brown Univ, ScM, 52, PhD(physics), 55. *Prof Exp:* Physicist, US Dept Defense, 55-59; fel eng, Solid State Lab, Air Arm Div, Westinghouse Elec Corp, 59-62; dir solid state lab, Res Triangle Inst, 62-67, dir eng & environ sci div, 67-71, chief scientist, 71-82. *Concurrent Pos:* Res affil, Univ Md, 56-61; adj assoc prof elec eng, Duke Univ, 62-69; chmn scientific rev comt, Dent Res Ctr, Univ NC, 74-81; consult mem, Adv Group Electron Devices, Dept Dent, 83- *Mem:* AAAS; Am Phys Soc; fel Inst Elec & Electronics Engrs; Electrochem Soc. *Res:* Technology policy; semiconductor research; cooperative research; solid state electronics and physics; electronic systems; materials; public policy; technology management; instrumentation; research utilization and analysis; sensors. *Mailing Add:* 107 Links End Dr Cary NC 27513. *Fax:* 919-541-9450; *E-Mail:* burger@src.org

BURGER, WARREN CLARK, PLANT SCIENCE. *Current Pos:* RETIRED. *Personal Data:* b Ripon, Wis, Feb 11, 23; m 44; c 2. *Educ:* Univ Wis, BS, 48, MS, 50, PhD(biochem), 52. *Prof Exp:* Res chemist, 52-73, DIR, BARLEY & MALT LAB, AGR RES SERV, USDA, 73-; prof agron, Univ Wis-Madison, 79-84. *Concurrent Pos:* Adj assoc prof agron, Univ Wis-Madison, 74-79. *Mem:* Am Soc Plant Physiol; Am Chem Soc; Am Soc Brewing Chemists. *Res:* Plant proteolytic enzymes; malting and brewing biochemistry; barley nutritional quality. *Mailing Add:* 1928 Lewis Rd Mt Horeb WI 53572

BURGERT, BILL E, ORGANIC CHEMISTRY. *Current Pos:* RETIRED. *Personal Data:* b Horton, Kans, Aug 9, 29; m 72. *Educ:* Kans State Teachers Col, AB, 51; Kans State Col, MS, 52; Northwestern Univ, PhD(chem), 55. *Prof Exp:* Res chemist, Dow Chem Co, 55-58, proj leader, 58-60, group leader, 60-64, div leader, 64-68, dir, Phys Res Lab, 68-79, tech dir, saran & converted prod res, 79-84, proj dir, Mich Div Res, 84-86. *Mem:* Am Chem Soc; Sigma Xi. *Res:* Polymer chemistry. *Mailing Add:* 1920 Sylvan Lane Midland MI 48640-6788

BURGES, STEPHEN JOHN, SURFACE WATER HYDROLOGY. *Current Pos:* from asst prof to assoc prof, 70-79, PROF CIVIL ENG, UNIV WASH, 79- *Personal Data:* b Newcastle, Australia, Aug 26, 44; m 70, Sylvia Tregidga. *Educ:* Univ Newcastle, Australia, BSc & BE Hons, 67; Stanford Univ, MS, 68, PhD(civil eng), 70. *Prof Exp:* Res asst civil eng, Stanford Univ, 67-70. *Concurrent Pos:* Co-ed, Water Resources Res, Am Geophys Union, 81-84, guest ed, 85-86, ed, Water Resources Monogr, 85-87; mem, Water Sci & Technol Bd, US Nat Res Coun, 85-89; chmn, WSTB Steering Comt Climate Change & Water Resource Mgt, Nat Res Coun, 89-90, 90-92; pres-elect, Hydrology Sect, Am Geophys Union, 92-94; pres, Hydrol Sect, Am Geophys Union, 94-96; prof hydrologist, Am Inst Hydrol. *Mem:* Fel Am Soc Civil Engrs; fel Am Geophys Union; fel AAAS; Am Water Resources Asn; Sigma Xi; Int Asn Hydraul Res. *Res:* Surface water hydrology; hydrologic process representation; rainfall-runoff modeling; stochastic hydrology; water resource system analysis, design and operation; urban hydrology; integrated learning systems. *Mailing Add:* Dept Civil Eng 160 Wilcox Hall Box 352700 Univ Wash Seattle WA 98195-2700. *Fax:* 206-685-3836; *E-Mail:* sburges@u.washinton.edu

BURGESON, ROBERT EUGENE, BIOCHEMISTRY, CELL BIOLOGY. *Current Pos:* PROF, BIOCHEM & MOLECULAR BIOL, CELL BIOL & ANAT & DERMAT, ORE HEALTH SCI UNIV, 88- *Personal Data:* b Newhall, Calif, Aug 5, 45. *Educ:* Univ Calif, Irvine, BS, 68; Univ Calif, Los Angeles, PhD(molecular biol), 74. *Prof Exp:* Res biochemist molecular biol, Sch Dent, Univ Calif, Los Angeles, 73-74, asst res biochemist med genetics, assoc prof pediat, Harbor Med Ctr, 76-87; assoc res dir, Shriners Hosp, 86-88. *Concurrent Pos:* NIH fel, 74-76. *Mem:* AAAS; Am Soc Cell Biol. *Res:* Investigations of the structure and function of connective tissue macromolecules with regard to human growth, development and inheritable disease. *Mailing Add:* Cutaneous Biol Res Ctr Mass Gen Hosp E Bldg 149 3rd Fl 13th St Charleston MA 02129-2060

BURGESS, ANN BAKER, CELLULAR BIOLOGY. *Current Pos:* fel, McArdle Lab, Univ Wis-Madison, 71-72, asst scientist, 72-73, lectr biol core curric, 73-87, assoc chmn, 80-90, SR LECTR, UNIV WIS-MADISON, 87-, DIR, 90- *Personal Data:* b Madison, Wis, Sept 20, 42; m 67, Richard R; c 2. *Educ:* Univ Wis-Madison, BS, 64; Harvard Univ, PhD(molecular biol), 69. *Prof Exp:* Fel, Inst Molecular Biol, Univ Geneva, Switz, 69-71. *Concurrent Pos:* Adv, Fac Adv Serv, Univ Wis-Madison, 78-93; vis scientist, Dept Genetics, Univ Wash-Seattle, 83-84. *Mem:* Asn Biol Lab Educ. *Mailing Add:* Biol Core Curric Univ Wis 361 Noland Hall Madison WI 53706. *E-Mail:* aburgess@macc.wisc.edu

BURGESS, ANN WOLBERT, NURSING. *Current Pos:* VAN AMERIGEN PROF PSYCHIAT & MENT HEALTH NURSING, UNIV PA SCH NURSING, 83-, CHAIRPERSON, DIV PSYCHIAT MENT HEALTH NURSING, 90- *Educ:* Boston Univ, BS, 58; Univ Md, MS, 59; Boston Univ, DNSc, 66. *Honors & Awards:* Stephen Shafer Award, Nat Orgn Victim Assistance, 78; Current Impact Res & Scholar Award, Am Nurses Asn, 79, Hon Nursing Practice Award, 82, Hilegard Peplan Award, 96; Outstanding Prof Award, Am Prof Soc, 92; Pioneer Award, Int Soc Traumatic Stress Studies, 93. *Prof Exp:* Clin nursing instr, Spring Grove State Hosp, Baltimore, 59-61; instr, Boston Univ Sch Nursing, 61-62, prof & dir nursing res, 79-82; res nursing supvr, Metabolic Depression Unit, Mass Ment Health Ctr, 65-66; prof nursing, Boston Col, 76-79. *Concurrent Pos:* Adj asst prof, Boston Univ Sch Nursing, 66-69 & Boston Col, 69-71; individual & couples psychother, 66-; mem, Sci Comt Ment Health Needs of Victims, World Fedn Ment Health, 81-83; mem, US Atty Gen's Task Force Family Violence, 83-84; mem, Study Sect HIV & Related Res, NIH, 89-92, chair, 92-94; distinguished fel award, Int Asn Forensic Nurses, 95. *Mem:* Inst Med-Nat Acad Sci; Am Nurses Asn; fel Am Orthopsychiat Asn; Nat Orgn Victim Assistance; Am Acad Nursing. *Res:* Rape trauma; child pornography; child sexual abuse; post-traumatic stress disorder; contributor of numerous publications. *Mailing Add:* Sch Nursing Univ Pa Nursing Educ Bldg 420 Guardian Dr Philadelphia PA 19104. *Fax:* 215-573-7483

BURGESS, CECIL EDMUND, MATHEMATICS. *Current Pos:* from instr to assoc prof, 51-61, chmn dept, 67-77, PROF MATH, UNIV UTAH, 61- *Personal Data:* b Happy, Tex, Jan 21, 20; m 48, Charlotte J Stevenson; c Grant & Carol. *Educ:* WTex State Univ, BS, 41; Univ Tex, PhD(math), 51. *Honors & Awards:* Cert of Meritorious Serv, Math Asn Am, 85. *Prof Exp:* Instr math, Univ Tex, 41-42; with Naval Ord Lab, 42-43; instr math, Univ Tex, 46-51. *Concurrent Pos:* Vis lectr, Univ Wis, 56-57; vis mem, Inst Advan Study, 62-63; vis prof, Univ Tex, Austin, 77-78; vis mem, Math Inst, Univ Warwick, Eng, 78, comt undergrad prog math, 65-67. *Mem:* Am Math Soc; Math Asn Am. *Res:* Geometric topology; embeddings of surfaces in Euclidean 3-dimensional space. *Mailing Add:* 900 Donner Way No 202 Salt Lake City UT 84108

BURGESS, DAVID RAY, CELL BIOLOGY. *Current Pos:* PROF & CHMN, DEPT BIOL SCI, UNIV PITTSBURGH, 90- *Personal Data:* b Hobbs, NMex, Nov 21, 47; c 4. *Educ:* Calif Polytech State Univ, BS, 69, MS, 71; Univ Calif, Davis, PhD(zool), 74. *Prof Exp:* Res assoc zool, Univ Wash, 74-76; asst prof, Dartmouth Col, 76-82; from assoc prof to prof, Sch Med, Univ Miami, 82-90. *Concurrent Pos:* NIH fel, Univ Wash, 74-76; NIH career develop award, 81-86; mem, Cell Biol Study Sect, NIH, 82-86, mem, Cell & Molecular Basis Dis Study Sect, 89-94; instr physiol, Marine Biol Lab, Woods Hole, Mass, 87-88. *Mem:* AAAS; Am Soc Cell Biol; Soc Develop Biol. *Res:* Cellular morphogenesis; biochemistry of actin-based motility in single cells and in organ development. *Mailing Add:* Dept Biol Sci Univ Pittsburgh 234 Langley Hall Pittsburgh PA 15260-0001. *Fax:* 412-624-0563; *E-Mail:* dburg@vms.cis.pitt.edu

BURGESS, DONALD WAYNE, ATMOSPHERIC SCIENCE, RADAR METEOROLOGY. *Current Pos:* RES METEOROLOGIST RADAR METEOROL, NAT SEVERE STORMS LAB, ENVIRON RES LAB, NAT OCEANIC & ATMOSPHERIC ADMIN, DEPT COM, 70- *Personal Data:* b Okmulgee, Okla, July 11, 47; m 72; c 2. *Educ:* Univ Okla, BS, 71, MS, 74. *Honors & Awards:* Special Achievement Award, Nat Oceanic & Atmospheric Admin, 76; Silver Medal Award, Dept Com, 79; Outstanding Proj, Nat Soc Prof Engrs, 80; Distinguished Authorship Award, Dept Com, 87. *Mem:* Am Meteorol Soc; Nat Weather Asn. *Res:* Radar, particularly Doppler, applied to detection of and further understanding of severe local storms and tornados. *Mailing Add:* 3318 Pheasant Run Rd Norman OK 73072

BURGESS, EDWARD MEREDITH, ORGANIC CHEMISTRY. *Current Pos:* from asst prof to assoc prof, 64-74, PROF CHEM, GA INST TECHNOL, 74- *Personal Data:* b Birmingham, Ala, June 8, 34; m 57; c 2. *Educ:* Auburn Univ, BS, 56; Mass Inst Technol, PhD(org chem), 62. *Prof Exp:* Instr chem, Yale Univ, 62-64. *Mem:* Am Chem Soc; The Chem Soc. *Res:* Organic photochemistry; small ring heterocycle synthesis; new functional groups. *Mailing Add:* Sch Chem Ga Inst Technol 225 N Ave NW Atlanta GA 30332-0001

BURGESS, FRED J, CIVIL & SANITARY ENGINEERING. *Current Pos:* RETIRED. *Personal Data:* b La Grande, Ore, June 7, 26; m 49; c 3. *Educ:* Ore State Univ, BS, 50; Harvard Univ, MS, 55. *Honors & Awards:* Clemens Award, Harvard Univ, 55. *Prof Exp:* From instr to assoc prof, Ore State Univ, 53-62, head dept, 66-74, prof civil eng, 62-, dean eng, 70- *Concurrent Pos:* Consult, USPHS, 63-; mem, Am Environ Eng Intersoc Bd, Gov Capitol Planning Comn, Univ-Gov Environ Sci Adv Comt & Univ Marine Sci Coun; chmn nat environ sci training comt, USPHS, 62-63, mem training & demonstration grants comt, 62- *Mem:* Am Soc Civil Engrs; Am Water Works Asn; Nat Soc Prof Eng; Water Pollution Control Fedn; Sigma Xi. *Res:* Water supply and waste disposal; water resources engineering. *Mailing Add:* 32399 SW Lake Dr Wilsonville OR 97070-7408

BURGESS, JACK D, geology, botany, for more information see previous edition

BURGESS, JAMES HARLAND, MAGNETIC RESONANCE. *Current Pos:* from instr to assoc prof, 57-73, PROF PHYSICS, WASHINGTON UNIV, 73- *Personal Data:* b Portland, Ore, May 11, 29; m 51, Dorothy R Crosby; c Karen, Donald & Joanne. *Educ:* State Col Washington, BS, 49, MS, 51; Washington Univ, PhD(physics), 55. *Prof Exp:* Sr engr, Sylvania Elec Prod, Inc, 55-56; res assoc physics, Stanford Univ, 56-57, asst prof, 58-62. *Mem:* Am Phys Soc; Am Asn Physics Teachers; Sigma Xi. *Res:* Nuclear magnetic resonance; paramagnetic resonance; magnetic cooperative phenomena; molecular dynamics. *Mailing Add:* Dept Physics Washington Univ St Louis MO 63130. *E-Mail:* jhb@howdy.wustl.edu

BURGESS, JOHN C(ARGILL), ACOUSTICS. *Current Pos:* chmn dept, 66-68, PROF MECH ENG, UNIV HAWAII, 66- *Personal Data:* b Providence, RI, Oct 29, 23; m 53; c 3. *Educ:* Brown Univ, BS, 44; Stanford Univ, MS, 49, PhD(eng mech), 55. *Honors & Awards:* Distinguished Serv Award, Acoust Soc Japan, 78 & Medal of Special Merit, 88. *Prof Exp:* Instr eng drawing & descriptive geom, Brown Univ, 46-48; asst, Stanford Univ, 48-49 & 50-51, res asst, 51-53; instr eng mech, Univ PR, 49-50; mech engr, Stanford Res Inst, 53-61; head, Appl Mech Dept, United Tech Ctr, 61-62, asst mgr, Eng Sci Br, 62-64, mgr, 64-66. *Concurrent Pos:* US Int Educ Exchange Serv lectr, Cordoba Nat Univ, 56; pres, Univ Hawaii Col Eng fac senate, 69-71; chmn, Adv Comt Noise Control, Hawaii State Dept Health, 70-72; inv researcher, Nat Res Coun Can, 73, 87 & 90-91; resident visitor, Bell Labs, 79-80. *Mem:* Am Soc Eng Educ; Am Soc Mech Engrs; Acoust Soc Am; Inst Elec & Electronics Engrs. *Res:* Dynamics of rigid and flexible bodies; vibration, stress waves, acoustics; structural dynamics; automatic control; signal processing; computer modelling of dynamic systems; adaptive sound control. *Mailing Add:* 1269 Mokulua Dr Kailua HI 96734

BURGESS, JOHN HERBERT, PULMONARY CIRCULATION, CARDIAC FAILURE. *Current Pos:* dir, cardiol, 73-94, SR CARDIOLOGIST, MONTREAL GEN HOSP, 94-; PROF MED, MCGILL UNIV, 75- *Personal Data:* b Montreal, Que, May 24, 33; m 58; c 4. *Educ:* McGill Univ, BSc, 54, MD, 58. *Honors & Awards:* Gold Medal, McGill Univ, 58; Order of Can, 87. *Prof Exp:* Med resident, McGill Univ, 58-60 & 62-64, from asst to assoc prof, 66-75; res fel, Univ Birmingham, Eng, 60-62; res fel, Cardiovasc Res Inst, Univ Calif, San Francisco, 64-66. *Concurrent Pos:* Nuffield Found fel, 60-62; R S McLaughlin Found fel, 64-66; Med Res Coun Scholar, 66-71; gov, Am Col Physicians, 79-83; pres, Royal Col of Physicians & Surgeons Can, 90-92. *Mem:* Am Col Physicians; Royal Col Can; Am Physiol Soc; AAAS; Am Heart Asn; Can Heart Found. *Res:* Pulmonary circulation; pulmonary diffusive capacity; pulmonary capillary blood volume; nor-epinephrine extraction in normal and failing heart; cardiomyoplasty. *Mailing Add:* Montreal Gen Hosp 1650 Cedar Ave Montreal PQ H3G 1A4 Can

BURGESS, JOHN S(TANLEY), PHYSICS, ELECTRONICS. *Current Pos:* RETIRED. *Personal Data:* b Milwaukee, Wis, May 1, 18; m 48, Delma Frelick; c Leslie, Michael & Robert. *Educ:* St Lawrence Univ, BS, 40; Univ Notre Dame, MS, 42; Ohio State Univ, PhD(physics), 49. *Prof Exp:* Asst microwaves, Res Lab, Gen Elec Co, 42-46; asst prof physics, St Lawrence Univ, 49-51; proj engr, Rome Air Develop Ctr, 51-53, sect chief radar lab, 53-56, chief, 56-57, tech dir control & guid, 57-60, chief scientist ground electronics, 60-71, dep dir, Shape Tech Ctr, 71-76, chief scientist, 76-80. *Concurrent Pos:* Mem adv comt electron tubes, US Dept Defense, 52-58; mem tech mgt coun, USAF Systs Command, 60-65 & USAF Coun Scientists, 61-64. *Mem:* Fel Inst Elec & Electronics Engrs; Am Phys Soc. *Res:* Thermionic and secondary electron emission; infrared spectrum of methane and deutero-ammonia; microwave tubes; radar technology. *Mailing Add:* 36 Julie Lane Newark DE 19711-2671

BURGESS, KATHRYN HOY, PLANT & INSECT ECOLOGY & EVOLUTION, MOLECULAR SYSTEMATICS. *Current Pos:* RES ASSOC, CTR FOR INSECT SCI, 91- *Educ:* Dartmouth Col, AB, 83; Harvard Univ, AM, 85, PhD(biol), 91. *Concurrent Pos:* Dir, Nat Youth Sci Camp, WVa, 90-92. *Res:* Ecology of flower feeding; theory and field experiments with insect-plant systems; field and laboratory work to create a molecular phylogeny for the Heliothinae (Noctuidae-Lepidoptera), a major group of agricultural pests. *Mailing Add:* 6021 Princeton Ave NE Seattle WA 98115-7763

BURGESS, PAUL RICHARDS, NEUROBIOLOGY. *Current Pos:* assoc prof, 72-75, PROF PHYSIOL, MED SCH, UNIV UTAH, 75- *Personal Data:* b Logan, Utah, May 2, 34; m 63. *Educ:* Reed Col, BA, 56; Oxford Univ, BA, 59; Rockefeller Inst, PhD(physiol), 65. *Prof Exp:* From instr to assoc prof, Univ Utah, 67-72. *Concurrent Pos:* Fel physiol, Univ Utah, 65-67. *Mem:* Soc Neurosci; Am Physiol Soc. *Res:* Somatic sensation; nerve growth. *Mailing Add:* Dept Physiol Univ Utah Sch Med 50 N Medical Dr Salt Lake City UT 84132-0001

BURGESS, RICHARD RAY, SCIENCE EDUCATION, PROTEIN BIOCHEMISTRY. *Current Pos:* from asst prof to assoc prof, 71-82, dir, Biotechnol Ctr, 84-96, PROF ONCOL, MCARDLE LAB CANCER RES, UNIV WIS-MADISON, 82- *Personal Data:* b Mt Vernon, Wash, Sept 8, 42; m 67, Ann Baker; c Kristin & Andreas. *Educ:* Calif Inst Technol, BS, 64; Harvard Univ, PhD(molecular biol & biochem), 69. *Honors & Awards:* Pfizer Award for Enzyme Chem, 82. *Prof Exp:* Helen Hay Whitney Found fel, Inst Molecular Biol, Geneva, Switz, 69-71. *Concurrent Pos:* Mem, Molecular Biol

Study Sect, NSF, 81-84; Guggenheim fel, 83-84; chmn bd dirs, Consortium Plant Biotechnol Res Inc, 93-96. *Mem:* Am Soc Biochem & Molecular Biol; Am Chem Soc; Am Asn Cancer Res; Protein Soc; Am Soc Microbiol. *Res:* RNA polymerase and the regulation of gene expression; purification, subunit structure, physical and enzymatic properties, and regulation of the DNA-dependent RNA polymerases from prokaryotic and eukaryotic cells; protein biotechnology, immunoaffinity purification. *Mailing Add:* McArdle Lab Cancer Res Univ Wis 1400 University Ave Madison WI 53706. *Fax:* 608-262-2824; *E-Mail:* burgess@oncology.wisc.edu

BURGESS, ROBERT LEWIS, PLANT ECOLOGY, BOTANY. *Current Pos:* PROF & CHMN, DEPT ENVIRON & FOREST BIOL, STATE UNIV NY COL ENVIRON SCI & FORESTRY, 81- *Personal Data:* b Kalamazoo, Mich, Sept 12, 31; m 55, Vera T Ballegoin; c Karen, Steven, Susan, Ellen & Jonathan. *Educ:* Univ Wis-Milwaukee, BS, 57; Univ Wis-Madison, MS, 59, PhD(plant ecol), 61. *Honors & Awards:* Distinguished Serv Citation, Ecol Soc Am, 88. *Prof Exp:* Asst prof bot, Ariz State Univ, 60-63, dir desert inst, 63; from asst prof to assoc prof bot, NDak State Univ, 63-71; dep dir, Eastern Deciduous Forest Biome, Int Biol Prog, Oak Ridge Nat Lab, 71-77, prog dir, sect head & sr res ecologist, Environ Sci Div, 72-81. *Concurrent Pos:* res collab, Nat Park Serv, Dept Interior, 64; vis prof bot, Pahlavi Univ, Iran, 65-66; consult, NSF, 74-75, EPA, 85-87; mem bd govd, Am Inst Biol Sci, 81-84, bd dir, 91-93. *Mem:* Ecol Soc Am; Wilderness Soc; fel AAAS; Am Inst Biol Sci; Nature Conservancy; Brit Ecol Soc. *Res:* Regional vegetation studies on composition, structure and dynamics of native plant communities in Wisconsin, Arizona, New York and North Dakota; application of statistical methods to community analysis and interpretation; vegetation mapping; landscape dynamics; history of ecology. *Mailing Add:* Dept Environ & Forest Biol State Univ NY Col Environ Sci & Forestry Syracuse NY 13210

BURGESS, TERESA LYNN, CELL BIOLOGY, MEMBRANE TRAFFICKING. *Current Pos:* fel, Neurosci Res Inst, 88-90, RESEARCHER, DEPT BIOL SCI, UNIV CALIF, SANTA BARBARA, 90- *Personal Data:* b San Francisco, Calif, Apr 12, 57; m 83; c 1. *Educ:* Univ Calif, Berkeley, BA, 80; Univ Calif, San Francisco, PhD(biochem), 87. *Prof Exp:* Fel, Dept Cell Biol, Yale Univ, 87. *Mem:* Am Soc Cell Biol; AAAS. *Res:* Interaction of the microtubular cytoskeleton with membrane bound organelles; post-translational modifications of tubulin on the structure/organization of the Golgi apparatus. *Mailing Add:* Amgen Inc 1840 DeHavilland Dr Thousand Oaks CA 93120-1789. *Fax:* 805-499-1140

BURGESS, THOMAS EDWARD, INORGANIC CHEMISTRY. *Current Pos:* TECH DIR, BURGESS ANALYTICAL LAB, 71- *Personal Data:* b Pontiac, RI, Nov 19, 23; m 49. *Educ:* RI State Col, BS, 49; Syracuse Univ, MS, 52; Univ Conn, PhD(chem), 59. *Prof Exp:* Chemist, Am Optical Co, 52-54; chemist, Sprague Elec Co, North Adams, 59-71. *Mem:* Am Soc Test & Mat; Am Ind Hygiene Asn; Am Ceramic Soc. *Res:* Analytical chemistry of semiconductor thin films; radiotracer studies of diffusion in solids; atomic absorption spectroscopy; optical emission spectroscopy. *Mailing Add:* 47 Grandview Dr Williamstown MA 01267-2546

BURGESS, WILLIAM HOWARD, APPLIED CHEMISTRY. *Current Pos:* Res asst food sci, Cornell Univ, 49-50, dairy chem, 50-53, nutrit & biochem, 53-54, from asst prof to prof, 54-89, EMER PROF CHEM ENG, UNIV TORONTO, 89- *Personal Data:* b Boston, Mass, Mar 13, 24; m 49, Mary R Bond; c Ellen & Ruth. *Educ:* Cornell Univ, BChE, 49, MFS, 50, PhD(dairy chem), 54. *Res:* Reaction kinetics; photo chemistry. *Mailing Add:* Dept Chem Eng 200 College St Rm 217 Toronto ON M5S 1A4 Can

BURGESS, WILSON HALES, PROTEIN FUNCTION. *Current Pos:* SR SCIENTIST, MOLECULAR BIOL LAB, AM RED CROSS, JEROME HOLLAND LAB BIOMED SCI, ROCKVILLE, MD, 87- *Personal Data:* b Alexandria, Va, Sept 29, 54. *Educ:* Univ Va, BA, 76, PhD(biol), 81. *Prof Exp:* Teaching asst biol, Univ Va, 76-77, Governors fel, 77-78, res asst, 78-81; res assoc, Dept Pharmacol, Sch Med, Vanderbilt Univ, Nashville, Tenn & assoc, Howard Hughes Med Inst, 81-84; sr scientist, Div Cell Biol, Revlon Biotechnel Res Ctr, Rockville, Md, 84-86; sect mgr, Protein Biochem Div, Rorer Biotechnol Inc, Rockville, Md, 86-87. *Concurrent Pos:* Lectr cell biol, Univ Va, 80; mem ad hoc rev, NSF, peer rev subcomt, Am Cancer Soc & Am Heart Asn. *Mem:* Am Soc Cell Biol; AAAS. *Res:* Molecular biology; author of numerous publications. *Mailing Add:* Dept Molecular Biol Am Red Cross 15601 Crabbs Branch Way Rockville MD 20855-2743. *Fax:* 301-738-0794

BURGETT, MICHAEL, orthopedic diagnostics, for more information see previous edition

BURGGRAF, ODUS R, AERONAUTICAL ENGINEERING, COMPUTATIONAL FLUID DYNAMICS. *Current Pos:* from assoc prof to prof, 64-88, EMER PROF AERONAUT & ASTRONAUT ENG, OHIO STATE UNIV, 89- *Personal Data:* b Ft Wayne, Ind, Feb 27, 29; m 50, Helen C Rapp; c Lisa A (McCauley), Donna L (Wenndt) & Susan K (Caughran). *Educ:* Ohio State Univ, BAeroE & MSc, 52; Calif Inst Technol, PhD(aeronaut, physics), 55. *Prof Exp:* Aerodynamicist, Douglas Aircraft Corp, 52; asst prof mech eng, USAF Inst Technol, 54-56; eng specialist, Curtiss-Wright Corp, 56-59; staff scientist, Lockheed Missiles & Space Co, 60-64. *Concurrent Pos:* Consult, Astro Res Corp, Calif, 59-69 & Lockheed Missiles & Space Co, 64-65; hon res fel, Math Dept, Univ Col London, 72, spec lectr, 78; sr fel, Nat Center Atmospheric Res, 77; mem, Nat Tech Comt Fluid Dynamics, Am Inst Aeronaut & Astronaut, 78-80. *Mem:* Assoc fel Am Inst Aeronaut & Astronaut. *Res:* Boundary layer stability theory, separated flows; turbulent boundary layers; vortex flows; ducted-propeller theory; stall propagation in axial compressors, optimum filamentary structures; trajectory statistical analysis. *Mailing Add:* 1370 Stoneygate Lane Columbus OH 43221. *E-Mail:* orb@steinbek.eng.ohio-state.edu

BURGGREN, WARREN WILLIAM, COMPARATIVE PHYSIOLOGY, EVOLUTIONARY & DEVELOPMENTAL BIOLOGY. *Current Pos:* From asst prof to assoc prof, 78-87, PROF ZOOL, UNIV MASS, 87- *Personal Data:* b Edmonton, Alta, Aug 14, 51; m 85; c 3. *Educ:* Univ Calgary, BSc, 73; Univ East Anglia, Eng, PhD(physiol), 76. *Concurrent Pos:* Prin investr, NSF, 79-; ed, Physiol Zoo, 88- *Mem:* Can Soc Zoologists; Soc Exp Biol; Am Soc Zoologists. *Res:* Comparative animal physiology; evolution of respiratory and cardiovascular physiology; growth of regulatory processes during development from embryo to adult. *Mailing Add:* Dept Biol Sci Univ Nev 4505 Maryland Pkwy Las Vegas NV 89154

BURGHARDT, GORDON MARTIN, CHEMORECEPTION, BIOPSYCHOLOGY. *Current Pos:* from asst prof to assoc prof psychol, Univ Tenn, 68-74, prof ecol, 77-95, prof zool, 80-95, dir, Grad Prog Ethology Life Sci, 81-91, PROF PSYCHOL, UNIV TENN, KNOXVILLE, 74-, PROF ECOL & EVOLUTION BIOL, 96- *Personal Data:* b Milwaukee, Wis, Oct 11, 41; m 83, Sandra L Twardosz; c Niko, Karin & Liana. *Educ:* Univ Chicago, BS, 63, PhD(biopsychol), 66. *Prof Exp:* Instr biol, Univ Chicago, 66-67. *Concurrent Pos:* Res grants, NIMH, 67-75 & NSF, 75-; J S Guggenheim fel, 76-77; ed, Ethology, 81-87. *Mem:* Am Soc Ichthyol & Herpet; Animal Behav Soc (2nd pres-elect, 84-85, 1st pres-elect, 85-86, pres, 86-87; Am Psychol Asn; Psychonomic Soc; Soc Study Amphibians & Reptiles; Am Psychol Soc. *Res:* Chemical and visual perception; theoretical and historical issues; ontogeny and evolution of behavior; behavior of reptiles; precocial behavior, growth and play. *Mailing Add:* Dept Psychol Univ Tenn Knoxville TN 37996-0900. *Fax:* 423-974-3330; *E-Mail:* gburghar@utk.edu

BURGHARDT, ROBERT CASEY, CELL BIOLOGY, REPRODUCTIVE BIOLOGY. *Current Pos:* from asst prof biol to assoc prof vet anat, Tex A&M Univ, 78-91, dir, Electron Micros Ctr, 82-87, assoc prof med physiol, 90-91, DIR, IMAGE ANALYSIS LAB, COL VET MED, TEX A&M UNIV, 87-, PROF VET ANAT, PUB HEALTH, 91-, PROF MED PHYSIOL, 91- *Personal Data:* b Detroit, Mich, Apr 15, 47; m, Rebecca Lawrence; c 3. *Educ:* Univ Mich, BS, 69; Wayne State Univ, MS, 73, PhD(biol), 76. *Prof Exp:* Fel anat, Lab Human Reproduction & Reproductive Biol, Harvard Med Sch, 76-78. *Mem:* Sigma Xi; Am Soc Cell Biol; Soc Study Reproduction; Am Asn Cancer Res. *Res:* Development and application of vital analytical imaging methods to study intercellular communication, signal transduction and mechanisms of cytotoxicity in normal and transformed reproductive tissues. *Mailing Add:* Dept Vet Anat Tex A&M Univ Col Vet Med College Station TX 77843-4458. *Fax:* 409-847-8981; *E-Mail:* rburghardt@uthvax.tamu.edu

BURGHART, JAMES H(ENRY), CONTROL SYSTEMS, ELECTRICAL ENGINEERING. *Current Pos:* chmn, 75-85, PROF ELEC ENG, CLEVELAND STATE UNIV, 75-, CHMN DEPT, 89- *Personal Data:* b Erie, Pa, July 18, 38; m 61, Judy Hoff; c Jill (Lemke) & Mark A. *Educ:* Case Western Res Univ, BS, 60, MS, 62, PhD(eng), 65. *Prof Exp:* Asst prof elec eng, USAF Inst Technol, 65-68; from asst prof to assoc prof, State Univ NY, Buffalo, 68-75, dir grad studies, 70-75. *Concurrent Pos:* Chmn, Student Activ Comt, Indust Appln Soc, 78-88; secy, Region 2, Inst Elec & Electronics Engrs, 88-96, Chmn Prof Activities Comt, 97- *Mem:* Inst Elec & Electronics Engrs; Am Soc Eng Educ. *Res:* Control systems; optimization; artificial intelligence, knowledge-based control systems; artifical intelligence. *Mailing Add:* Dept Elec Eng Cleveland State Univ Cleveland OH 44115-2440. *E-Mail:* j.burghart@ieee.org

BURGHOFF, HENRY L, physical metallurgy & physical metallurgical engineering; deceased, see previous edition for last biography

BURGI, ERNEST, JR, AUDIOLOGY, SPEECH PATHOLOGY. *Current Pos:* assoc prof, 62-69, PROF SPEECH & THEATRE ARTS, UNIV PITTSBURGH, 69- *Personal Data:* b Salt Lake City, Utah, Mar 22, 24; m 47; c 2. *Educ:* Ariz State Univ, BA, 50; Univ Denver, MA, 51; Univ Pittsburgh, PhD(audiol), 57. *Prof Exp:* Instr speech & speech path, Univ Nebr, 51-55; res assoc speech & hearing dis, Univ Pittsburgh, 55-57; asst prof audiol, Bowling Green State Univ, 57-58; assoc prof audiol & speech path, Univ Nebr, 59-62. *Concurrent Pos:* Consult, Cleft Palate Proj, Univ Pittsburgh, 58. *Mem:* Am Speech & Hearing Asn; Speech Asn Am. *Mailing Add:* RR 2 Cheswick PA 15024

BURGIN, GEORGE HANS, APPLIED MATHEMATICS, ELECTRICAL ENGINEERING. *Current Pos:* CHIEF SCIENTIST, TITAN SYSTS, INC, 83- *Personal Data:* b Switz, Feb 13, 30; US citizen; m 60; c 3. *Educ:* Swiss Fed Inst Technol, Dipl EEng, 54, PhD(elec eng), 60. *Prof Exp:* Mgr comput prog, Omni Ray, Switz, 60-62; design specialist, Gen Dynamics/Convair, 62-66; sr scientist, Decision Sci Inc, 66-83. *Concurrent Pos:* Consult, Narmco Res & Develop Div, Whittaker Corp, 64-66; instr, Exten Div, Univ Calif, San Diego, 66-88; lectr, Dept Math, San Diego State Univ, 79- *Mem:* Asn Comput Mach; Simulation Coun; Inst Elec & Electronics Engrs; Int Soc Neural Networks. *Res:* Application of modern control theory to the design of aircraft stability; augmentation system; systems engineering; computer simulation; neural networks. *Mailing Add:* Titan Syst Inc Science Park Rd San Diego CA 92121

BURGINYON, GARY ALFRED, NUCLEAR PHYSICS. *Current Pos:* RETIRED. *Personal Data:* b Spokane, Wash, June 29, 35; m 58; c 2. *Educ:* Wash State Univ, BS, 58; Yale Univ, MS, 61, PhD(physics), 66. *Prof Exp:* Physicist, Naval Res Lab, 61-62; res staff physicist, Yale Univ, 66-68; physicist, Lawrence Livermore Lab, 68-93. *Mem:* Am Phys Soc; Am Astron Soc. *Res:* Collective nuclear structure studies among rare earth nuclei; x-ray astronomy; x-ray plasma diagnostics. *Mailing Add:* 721 Canterbury Ave Livermore CA 94550

BURGMAIER, GEORGE JOHN, ORGANIC CHEMISTRY, PHOTOGRAPHY. *Current Pos:* SR RES CHEMIST, EASTMAN KODAK CO, 70- *Personal Data:* b Utica, NY, Jan 28, 44; m 68; c 2. *Educ:* Univ Toronto, BSc, 66; Yale Univ, PhD(org chem), 70. *Mem:* Am Chem Soc; Sigma Xi. *Res:* Chemistry of highly strained small ring hydrocarbons; preparation of chemicals with photographic applications. *Mailing Add:* 74 Stuyvesant Rd Pittsford NY 14534

BURGNER, ROBERT LOUIS, FISH BIOLOGY. *Current Pos:* Fishery biologist, Univ Wash, 46-54, asst dir, 55, res assoc prof, 57-64, assoc prof, 64-69, asst dir, 57-67, prof fisheries, Res Inst, 67-84, EMER PROF FISHERIES, UNIV WASH, 85- *Personal Data:* b Yakima, Wash, Jan 16, 19; wid; c R Peter & Ronald L. *Educ:* Univ Wash, BS, 42, PhD(fisheries), 58. *Honors & Awards:* Outstanding Achievement Award, Am Inst Fishery Biologists, 91; Award of Excellence, Western Div, Am Fisheries Soc, 94. *Mem:* Am Fisheries Soc; Am Inst Fisheries Res Biol. *Res:* Life history and survival of salmonid; lake ecology and limnology; ocean distribution and migrations of salmonids; fisheries management. *Mailing Add:* 14370 Edgewater Lane NE Seattle WA 98125

BURGOA, BENALI, water movement & chemical transport, soil-solute interaction, for more information see previous edition

BURGOYNE, EDWARD EYNON, ORGANIC CHEMISTRY. *Current Pos:* from asst prof to prof, 51-83, EMER PROF CHEM, ARIZ STATE UNIV, 84- *Personal Data:* b Montpelier, Idaho, Sept 26, 18; m 50, Mary I Ream; c Mary A (Wood), Elaine B (LeVan), Edward R & Bryce W. *Educ:* Utah State Univ, BS, 41; Univ Chicago, cert, 43; Univ Wis, MS, 47, PhD(chem), 49. *Prof Exp:* Alumni Res Found asst org chem, Univ Wis, 46-48; res chemist, Phillips Petrol Co, 49-51. *Mem:* Fel AAAS; Am Chem Soc. *Mailing Add:* 223 E 15th St Tempe AZ 85281-6609

BURGOYNE, GEORGE HARVEY, MICROBIOLOGY. *Current Pos:* chief, Tuberculosis Unit, Diag Microbiol Sect, 72-76, CHIEF VIROL VACCINES SECT, MICH DEPT PUB HEALTH, BUR LAB SERV & DIS CONTROL, 76- *Personal Data:* b Flint, Mich, June 5, 39; m 83; c 8. *Educ:* Mich State Univ, BS, 63, MS, 66, PhD(virol), 72. *Prof Exp:* Res microbiologist virol, Regional Poultry Res Lab, USDA, 63-72. *Mem:* Am Soc Microbiol. *Res:* Development for human use of an inactivated rabies virus vaccine of tissue culture origin and of a live attenuated vaccine for influenza using temperature sensitive mutants. *Mailing Add:* 6615 Lyons Rd Portland MI 48875

BURGOYNE, PETER NICHOLAS, MATHEMATICAL PHYSICS. *Current Pos:* assoc prof, 68-74, PROF MATH, UNIV CALIF, SANTA CRUZ, 74- *Personal Data:* b Bracknell, Eng, Oct 8, 32; Can citizen; m 62. *Educ:* McGill Univ, BSc, 55, MSc, 56; Princeton Univ, PhD(math physics), 61. *Prof Exp:* Instr math, Princeton Univ, 59-61; asst prof, Univ Calif, Berkeley, 61-66; assoc prof, Univ Ill, Chicago, 66-68. *Concurrent Pos:* Sloan Found fel, 63-65. *Res:* Theoretical physics, particularly problems in the theory of elementary particles; pure mathematics, particulary finite group theory and number theory. *Mailing Add:* 2525-B Canning Way No 593 Berkeley CA 94704

BURGSTAHLER, ALBERT WILLIAM, ORGANIC CHEMISTRY. *Current Pos:* instr & res assoc, 56-57, from asst prof to assoc prof chem, 57-65, PROF CHEM, UNIV KANS, 65- *Personal Data:* b Grand Rapids, Mich, July 10, 28; m 57, Patricia L Bokor; c Judith M, Albert P, Janet L, Jennifer A & David F. *Educ:* Univ Notre Dame, BS, 49; Harvard Univ, MA, 50, PhD(chem), 53. *Honors & Awards:* Notre Dame Centennial Sci Award, 65. *Prof Exp:* Instr org chem, Univ Notre Dame, 53-54; proj assoc, Univ Wis, 55-56. *Concurrent Pos:* Sloan fel, 61-64. *Mem:* Am Chem Soc; Int Soc Fluoride Res (pres, 70-73). *Res:* Environmental chemistry; reactions and synthesis of natural products; newer synthetic methods and applications; stereochemistry and circular dichroism. *Mailing Add:* Dept Chem Malott Hall Univ Kans Lawrence KS 66045. *Fax:* 785-864-5396; *E-Mail:* chemists@caco3.chem.ukans.edu

BURGSTAHLER, SYLVAN, MATHEMATICS. *Current Pos:* Asst prof, 61-70, head dept, 64-72, assoc prof, 74-77, PROF MATH, UNIV MINN, DULUTH, 77- *Personal Data:* b Corvuso, Minn, Nov 7, 28; m 61; c 3. *Educ:* Univ Minn, BS, 51, MS, 53, PhD(math), 63. *Mem:* Math Asn Am; Am Math Soc. *Res:* Flow of heat between materials having different physical constants; solution of polynomial equations. *Mailing Add:* Univ Minn Duluth MN 55812

BURGUS, ROGER CECIL, biochemistry, neuroendocrinology; deceased, see previous edition for last biography

BURGUS, WARREN HAROLD, RADIOCHEMISTRY. *Current Pos:* RETIRED. *Personal Data:* b Burlington, Iowa, Oct 28, 19; m 51; c 2. *Educ:* Univ Iowa, BS, 41; Wash Univ, PhD(chem), 49. *Prof Exp:* Asst metall lab, Univ Chicago, 42-43; res assoc, Oak Ridge Nat Lab, 43-46; mem staff, Los Alamos Nat Lab, 48-54; head, Mat Testing Reactor Chem Sect, Atomic Energy Div, Phillips Petrol Co, 54-68, sr tech consult, Water Reactor Safety Prog Off, Atomic Energy Div, 68-69; sr scientist, Aerojet Nuclear Co, 71-76; sr scientist, Earth & Life Sci Div, EG&G, Idaho, Inc, 76-82. *Mem:* Fel AAAS; Am Chem Soc. *Res:* Radiochemical procedures; hot atom chemistry; radioactive decay schemes; fission products; chemical processing of reactor fuels; cross sections. *Mailing Add:* 13027 Ballad Dr Sun City West AZ 85375

BURHANS, RALPH W(ELLMAN), ELECTRICAL ENGINEERING. *Current Pos:* CONSULT, 85- *Personal Data:* b Cleveland, Ohio, May 30, 22; m 54; c 2. *Educ:* Oberlin Col, AB, 47. *Prof Exp:* Res assoc, Standard Oil Co, Ohio, 47-65; res assoc, Ohio Univ, 65-66; sta mgr, Nat Radio Astron Observ, Kitt Peak, Ariz, 66-67; res engr, Dept Elec Eng, Ohio Univ, 67-85, lectr, 70-85. *Mem:* Inst Elec & Electronics Engrs; Audio Eng Soc; Am Inst Navigation; Int OMEGA Asn; Sigma Xi. *Res:* Instrumentation; avionics; time and phase measurements; electronic music; VLF and Loran-C navigation. *Mailing Add:* 161 Grosvenor St Athens OH 45701-1717

BURHOLT, DENNIS ROBERT, CELL BIOLOGY, CANCER. *Current Pos:* from res asst cancer res to res assoc cancer res, 73-82, sr res scientist, Cancer Res Ctr, 82-89, DIR REPRODUCTION SCI RES, DEPT OBSTET & GYNEC, ALLEGHENY GEN HOSP, 89- *Personal Data:* b New York, NY, Sept 22, 42; m 64; c 2. *Educ:* Adelphi Col, BA, 63; Univ Fla, PhD(bot, zool), 68. *Prof Exp:* Asst prof biol, Southampton Col, 68-69; NIH fel, Brookhaven Nat Lab, 69-71; res asst, Inst Med Radiation Sci, Wurzburg, WGer, 71-73. *Mem:* Radiation Res Soc; Am Asn Cancer Res. *Res:* Influence of radiation and chemotherapeutic agents on gastrointestinal epithelial cell proliferation. *Mailing Add:* 502 Kerrwood Dr Pittsburgh PA 15215

BURHOP, KENNETH EUGENE, CARDIOPULMONARY PHYSIOLOGY, ARTIFICIAL BLOOD RESEARCH. *Current Pos:* postdoctoral physiol & pharm, Dept Appl Sci, Baxter Healthcare Corp, 86-87, mgr res sci, 87-90, mgr res sci, Dept Blood Substitutes, 90-93, DIR BIOL SCIS, BAXTER HEALTHCARE CORP, 93- *Personal Data:* b Port Washington, Wis, May 7, 53; m 77, Christine Krueger; c Ryan, Kelly & James. *Educ:* Univ Wis, Milwaukee, BA, 75; Univ Wis-Madison, MS, 79, PhD(vet sci & physiol), 84. *Prof Exp:* Res asst physiol, Dept Vet Sci, Univ Wis-Madison, 76-79, res specialist, Dept Prev Med, 79-80, res asst, Dept Vet Sci, 80-84; NIH pulmonary res fel physiol, Dept Physiol, Albany Med Col, 84-86. *Concurrent Pos:* Co-investr, Lung Prog Proj, Dept Physiol, Albany Med Col, 84-86. *Mem:* Am Physiol Soc; NY Acad Sci; Shock Soc; Am Soc Artificial Organs; Soc Critical Care Med. *Res:* Biocompatibility assessment of materials and compounds, especially as it relates to acute lung injury; shock and the development and evaluation of modified hemoglobin solutions and other blood substitute solutions. *Mailing Add:* 1230 Regent Dr Mundelein IL 60060. *Fax:* 847-270-5306

BURIAN, RICHARD M, RELATIONS BETWEEN GENETICS & EVOLUTIONARY BIOLOGY, DEVELOPMENTAL BIOLOGY & GENETICS. *Current Pos:* PROF & DEPT HEAD PHILOS, VA POLYTECH INST, 83- *Personal Data:* b Hanover, NH, Sept 14, 41; m 63, 89; c 3. *Educ:* Reed Col, Portland, Ore, BA, 63; Univ Pittsburgh, PhD(philos), 71. *Prof Exp:* From instr to assoc dean, Col Philos, Brandeis Univ, 67-76; res assoc, Mus Comp Zool, Harvard Univ, 76-77; assoc prof philos, Drexel Univ, 77-83. *Concurrent Pos:* Vis asst prof, Fla A&M Univ, 68-69; vis assoc prof, Univ Pittsburg, 78, Univ Calif, Davis, 82; adj prof sci studies, Va Polytech Inst & State Univ, 83-; NSF grants, 84-85, 85-87 & 89; res fel, Nat Humanities Ctr, Research Triangle Park, 91-92. *Mem:* AAAS; Am Philos Asn; Am Soc Zool; Philos Sci Asn; Hist Sci Soc; Int Soc Hist, Philos & Soc Studies Biol. *Res:* History and philosophy of biology, especially developmental and evolutionary biology plus genetics; relations of embryology, evolution, genetics; French treatments of heredity; interdisciplinary relations, epistemological evaluation of experiments, and of evidence for biological theories. *Mailing Add:* Sceonce Studies Va Polytech Inst Blacksburg VA 24061-0247

BURICK, RICHARD JOSEPH, CHEMICAL ENGINEERING, NUCLEAR ENGINEERING. *Current Pos:* staff & group leader, 75-80, prog mgr, 80-84, dep assoc dir, 84-93, DIV DIR ENG SCI, LOS ALAMOS NAT LAB, 93- *Personal Data:* b Pueblo, Colo, Aug 10, 39; m 61; c 3. *Educ:* Colo State Univ, BS, 61; Purdue Univ, MS, 64, PhD(mech eng), 67. *Prof Exp:* Res asst, Purdue Univ, 62-67; res scientist, Martin-Marietta, 67-69; staff tech mgt, Rockwell Int, 69-75. *Mem:* AAAS; Laser Inst Am. *Res:* High energy lasers; laser isotope separation; neutral particle beams; combustion; fluid dynamics. *Mailing Add:* 1600 Camino Redondo Los Alamos NM 87544

BURIOK, GERALD MICHAEL, FINITE MATHEMATICS, APPLIED PROGRAM LANGUAGE. *Current Pos:* prof math, Indiana Univ, Pa, 71-77, dept chmn & prof comput sci, 79-84, actg dean, Col Natural Sci & Math, 84-85, PROF MATH, INDIANA UNIV PA, 85-, DEPT CHMN, 91- *Personal Data:* b Heilwood, Pa, Nov 6, 43; m 66; c 2. *Educ:* Ind State Col, BS, 65; Pa State Univ, MA, 67, DEd(math), 71. *Prof Exp:* Asst prof math, State Univ Col, Oneonta, NY, 67-70. *Mem:* Math Asn Am; Nat Coun Teachers Math. *Res:* use of computer in teaching math; developing advance program language tools for mathematics educ. *Mailing Add:* 986 Barclay Rd Indiana PA 15701

BURISH, THOMAS GERARD, BEHAVIORAL MEDICINE, CLINICAL PSYCHOLOGY. *Current Pos:* from asst prof to assoc prof, Vanderbilt Univ, 76-86, chmn, 84-86, assoc provost, 86-93, PROF, VANDERBILT UNIV, 86-, PROVOST, 93- *Personal Data:* b Menominee, Mich, May 4, 50; m 76, Pamela J Zebrasky; c Mark & Brent. *Educ:* Univ Notre Dame, AB, 72; Univ Kans, MA, 75, PhD, 76. *Honors & Awards:* David Shulman Award for Clinical Psychol. *Prof Exp:* Asst instr, Univ Kans, 75-76. *Concurrent Pos:* consult, 83- *Mem:* Am Psychol Asn; Am Psychol Soc; Acad Behav Med Res. *Res:* Stress and coping; etiology and chemotherapy. *Mailing Add:* Vanderbilt Univ 2201 W End Ave Nashville TN 37240-0001

BURK, CARL JOHN, PLANT SYSTEMATICS, BIOGEOGRAPHY. *Current Pos:* from instr to assoc prof bot, 61-73, actg chmn dept biol sci, 70-71, chmn, 72-75 & 83-86, PROF BIOL SCI, SMITH COL, 73-, GATES PROF, 82- *Personal Data:* b Troy, Ohio, Dec 30, 35; m 66, Lale Aka; c John S & Nicholas M. *Educ:* Miami Univ, AB, 57; Univ NC, MA, 59, PhD(bot), 61. *Honors & Awards:* Katherine Asher Engel lectr, 87. *Prof Exp:* Asst bot, Univ NC, 58-59, part-time instr, 60-61. *Mem:* Int Asn Plant Taxon; New Eng Bot Club; Am Soc Plant Taxonomists; Sigma Xi; Ecol Soc Am; AAAS; Am Inst Biol Sci. *Res:* Biosystematics of Quercus, Hepatica, Heterotheca; ecology, biogeography and floristics of coastal and freshwater ecosystems. *Mailing Add:* Clark Sci Ctr Smith Col Northampton MA 01063

BURK, CORNELIUS FRANKLIN, JR, INFORMATION MANAGEMENT, AUDITING. *Current Pos:* ASSOC, IMTC, 92. *Personal Data:* b Sarnia, Ont, Jan 8, 33; m 59; c 2. *Educ:* Univ Western Ont, BSc, 56; Northwestern Univ, PhD(geol), 59. *Prof Exp:* Explor geologist, Texaco, Inc, 59-60; geologist, Geol Surv Can, Dept Energy, Mines & Resources, 60-70, res scientist, 67-68, nat coordr, Secretariat Geosci Data, 68-70, dir, Can Ctr Geosci Data, 70-81, adv, Info Resources, 81-82, dir, Off Auditor Gen, 82-88; assoc dir, DMR Group Inc, 88-92. *Concurrent Pos:* Mem, Ad Hoc Comt Storage & Retrieval Geol Data, Nat Adv Comt Res Geol Sci, Can, 65-68, mem, Subcomt Comput Appln, 68-73, mem, Comt Storage, Automatic Processing & Retrieval Geol Data, Comt Geol Data for Sci & Technol, secy, 73-76, ed, 75- 80; ed, Bull Can Petrol Geol & Cogeodata News; chmn, Can Nat Comt for Comt Data for Sci & Technol, 77-82, chmn, Cogeodata Task Group, Geol Data Sources, 78- *Mem:* Asn Fed Info Resources Mgt; Info Res Mgt Asn Can. *Res:* Regional stratigraphy, especially Silurian of eastern Canada and Upper Cretaceous of Western Canada; computer-based storage and retrieval of geoscience data and national information systems for science; information management; development and management of science information services; information management. *Mailing Add:* IMTC Inc 331 Cooper St Suite 600 Ottawa ON K2P 0G5 Can

BURK, DAVID LAWRENCE, quality assurance, industrial & manufacturing engineering; deceased, see previous edition for last biography

BURK, LAWRENCE G, genetics, for more information see previous edition

BURK, RAYMOND FRANKLIN, JR, LIVER DISEASES. *Current Pos:* PROF MED & DIR GASTROENTEROL, VANDERBILT UNIV SCH MED, NASHVILLE, 87- *Personal Data:* b Kosciusko, Miss, Dec 9, 42; m 67, Enikoe Vikor; c Teresa M & Stephen M (deceased). *Educ:* Univ Miss, BA, 63; Vanderbilt Univ, MD, 68. *Honors & Awards:* Osborne & Mendel Award, Am Inst Nutrit, 93. *Prof Exp:* Res internist nutrit, US Army Med Res & Nutrit Lab, 70-73; teaching fel liver dis, Southwestern Med Sch, Dallas, Tex, 73-74, asst prof med, 75-78, asst prof biochem, 77-78; assoc prof med & biochem, Sch Med, La State Univ, Shreveport, 78-80; assoc prof med, Health Sci Ctr, Univ Tex, San Antonio, 80-82, prof med, 82-87. *Mem:* Am Inst Nutrit; Am Soc Biol Chemists; Am Soc Clin Invest. *Res:* Selenium metabolism; role of lipid peroxidation in cell injury. *Mailing Add:* C-2104 MCN Vanderbilt Univ 1161 21st Ave S Nashville TN 37232-2279. *Fax:* 615-343-6229

BURKA, MARIA KARPATI, ENGINEERING. *Current Pos:* PROG DIR, NSF, 84- *Personal Data:* b Budapest, Hungary, June 24, 48; m 68, Robert; c Jacqueline, Michael & Jennifer. *Educ:* Mass Inst Technol, BS, 69 & MS, 70; Princeton Univ, MA, 73 & PhD(chem eng), 78. *Prof Exp:* Process design engr, Sci Design Co, 70-71; asst prof chem eng, Univ Md, 78-81; environ scientist, Environ Protection Agency, 81-82. *Mem:* Sigma Xi; Am Inst Chem Eng (secy & treas, 88-); Am Asn Univ Women; AAAS. *Res:* Process design; process control; reaction engineering; polymerization. *Mailing Add:* 5056 Macomb St NW Washington DC 20016-2673. *Fax:* 703-306-0319; *E-Mail:* mburka@nsf.gov

BURKART, BURKE, GEOLOGY, TECTONICS GEOCHEMISTRY. *Current Pos:* from asst prof to assoc prof, 70-82, PROF GEOL, UNIV TEX, ARLINGTON, 82- *Personal Data:* b Feb 23, 33; US citizen; m 66; c 2. *Educ:* Univ Tex, BS, 54, MA, 60; Rice Univ, PhD(geol), 65. *Prof Exp:* Fel geol, Univ Tex, 65; asst prof, Temple Univ, 65-70. *Concurrent Pos:* Consult geologist, 81- *Mem:* Sigma Xi; fel Geol Soc Am; Am Geophys Union; Am Asn Petrol Geol. *Res:* Regional tectonics of Central America primarily the major transform faults; neogene tectonics of Guatemala and southern Mexico; geomorphological aspects of strike-slip faults. *Mailing Add:* Univ Arlington Tex Box 19049 Arlington TX 76019-0049

BURKART, LEONARD F, WOOD CHEMISTRY, WOOD TECHNOLOGY. *Current Pos:* RETIRED. *Personal Data:* b Mosier, Ore, Oct 8, 20; m 49; c 3. *Educ:* Univ Wash, BSF, 49, MF, 50; Univ Minn, MS, 61, PhD(wood chem), 63. *Prof Exp:* Technologist, Wash Veneer Corp, 50-52; staff missionary, Student Missionary Coun, Ore, 52-54; asst prof wood technol, Stephen F Austin State Col, 63-66, from assoc prof to prof forestry, 66-87. *Mem:* Tech Asn Pulp & Paper Indust; Soc Am Foresters; Forest Prod Res Soc; Sigma Xi. *Res:* Utilization of currently unused ligno-cellulosic materials from landfills, low grade forest trees, logging and agricultural residues etc. for the production of alternate fuels and organic chemicals. *Mailing Add:* 2743 Fifth St SW Loveand CO 80537

BURKART, MILTON W(ALTER), PHYSICAL METALLURGY. *Current Pos:* RETIRED. *Personal Data:* b Chicago, Ill, Sept 1, 22; m 80, Patricia Crumrine. *Educ:* Ill Inst Technol, BS, 44, MS, 48; Columbia Univ, PhD(metall), 53. *Prof Exp:* Lectr, City Col New York, 49; res assoc, Columbia Univ, 50-53; sr scientist, Westinghouse Elec Corp, 53-55, fel, 55-58, supvr irradiations, 58-63, mgr naval reactor mat irradiation, 63-67, mgr mat irradiation, 67-72, mgr, Fuel Element Develop Labs, Bettis Atomic Power Lab, 72-82, adv scientist, 82-95. *Concurrent Pos:* Lectr, Carnegie Inst Technol, 56. *Mem:* Am Soc Metals; Am Inst Mining, Metall & Petrol Engrs; NY Acad Sci; Sigma Xi. *Res:* Diffusionless transformations in metals; corrosion; radiation damage. *Mailing Add:* 7444 Ben Hur St Pittsburgh PA 15208. *E-Mail:* mibsttl8t@pitt.ed

BURKE, BERNARD FLOOD, PHYSICS, ASTROPHYSICS. *Current Pos:* Asst physics, Mass Inst Technol, 50-53, chmn & prof, 65-81, chmn, Astrophys Dir, 70-83, WILLIAM BURDEN PROF PHYSICS, MASS INST TECHNOL, 81- *Personal Data:* b Boston, Mass, June 7, 28; m 53; c 4. *Educ:* Mass Inst Technol, SB, 50, PhD, 53. *Honors & Awards:* Warner Prize, Am Astron Soc, 63; Rumford Prize, Am Acad Arts & Sci, 71. *Concurrent Pos:* Jr res assoc, Brookhaven Nat Lab, 52-53; staff mem, Carnegie Inst Wash, 53-65; mem, Nat Radio Astron Observ Adv Comt, 58-62; astron adv comt, NSF, 58-63, 73-76, consult, Found, 63-, NASA, 68-; assoc ed, Astron J, 62-64; vis prof, Univ Leiden, 71-72; trustee, Assoc Univs Inc, 72-90; trustee & chmn, Northeast Radio Observ Corp, 73-92, chmn, 82-; Sherman Fairchild Scholar, Calif Inst Technol, 84-85; Smithsonian Regents fel, 85; mem Nat Sci Bd, 90-96; vis prof & Royal Soc Scholar, Univ Manchester, 92-93; sr fel, Carnegie Inst Wash, 97. *Mem:* Nat Acad Sci; fel AAAS; Am Acad Arts & Sci; Am Phys Soc; Am Astron Soc (pres, 86); Royal Astron Soc; Int Sci Radio Union; Int Astronom Union. *Res:* Radio astronomy; galactic structure; microwave interferometry; microwave spectroscopy; antenna arrays; low-noise electronic circuitry. *Mailing Add:* Mass Inst Technol Room 26-335 Cambridge MA 02139

BURKE, DAVID H, PHARMACOLOGY, TOXICOLOGY. *Current Pos:* asst prof, 75-80, ASSOC PROF & HEAD, DEPT PHARMACOL, SCH DENT, MARQUETTE UNIV, 80- *Personal Data:* b Philadelphia, Pa, Feb 16, 39; m 64; c 2. *Educ:* Temple Univ, BS, 68, MS, 70, PhD(pharmacol), 72. *Prof Exp:* Asst prof pharmacol, Sch Pharm, Univ Mont, 72-74 & Kansas City Osteop Col Med, 74-75. *Mem:* Am Pharmaceut Asn. *Res:* Thermoregulatory and fetal pharmacology. *Mailing Add:* Dept Dent Careers Marquette Univ PO Box 1881 Milwaukee WI 53201-1881

BURKE, DENNIS GARTH, PHYSICS. *Current Pos:* from asst prof to assoc prof, 65-74, PROF PHYSICS, MCMASTER UNIV, 74- *Personal Data:* b Bracken, Sask, June 4, 35; m 60; c 3. *Educ:* Univ Sask, BE, 57, MS, 58; McMaster Univ, PhD(physics), 63. *Prof Exp:* Sci officer upper atmosphere physics, Defence Res Bd, 58-60; fel, Niels Bohr Inst, Copenhagen, 63-65. *Concurrent Pos:* Alfred P Sloan Found fel, 66-70. *Mem:* Can Asn Physicists. *Res:* Instrumentation of rocket nose cones for upper atmosphere studies; nuclear spectroscopy using decay scheme studies; nuclear structure studies using nuclear reactions. *Mailing Add:* Dept Physics McMaster Univ 1280 Main St West Hamilton ON L8S 4M1 Can

BURKE, DENNIS KEITH, SET-THEORETIC TOPOLOGY. *Current Pos:* From asst prof to assoc prof, 69-79, PROF MATH, MIAMI UNIV, 79- *Personal Data:* b Omaha, Nebr, June 29, 43; m 63; c 3. *Educ:* Univ Wyo, BA, 64, MS, 66; Wash State Univ, PhD(math), 69. *Concurrent Pos:* Ed, Proceedings of the Am Math Soc, 84- *Mem:* Math Asn Am; Am Math Soc; Sigma Xi. *Res:* Study of covering properties; metrization theorems, continuous mappings, counter examples and base axioms for topological spaces. *Mailing Add:* 7783 Fairfield Rd Oxford OH 45056-9704

BURKE, EDMUND C, PEDIATRICS. *Current Pos:* Consult, Mayo Clin, 52, from instr to asst prof, Mayo Found, 53-64, assoc prof clin pediat, Mayo Grad Sch Med, Univ Minn, 64-72, prof pediat, 72-86, EMER PROF PEDIAT, MAYO MED SCH, 86- *Personal Data:* b Fargo, NDak, Nov 23, 19; m 45; c 9. *Educ:* St Thomas Col, BS, 41; Univ Minn, MB, 44, MD, 45, MS, 51. *Honors & Awards:* Abraham Jacobi Award, Am Asn Pediat, 97. *Concurrent Pos:* Fel pediat, Mayo Found, Univ Minn, 48-51; prof pediat & adolescent med, Sch Med, Univ SDak, 86-88. *Mem:* Sigma Xi. *Res:* Renal disease; salt and electrolyte disturbance; migraine in children. *Mailing Add:* Mayo Clin Rochester MN 55905

BURKE, EDMUND C(HARLES), PHYSICAL METALLURGY. *Current Pos:* RETIRED. *Personal Data:* b Bridgeport, Conn, June 21, 21; m 47, Peggy Williams. *Educ:* Mo Sch Mines, BS, 43; Case Western Res Univ, MS, 48; Yale Univ, PhD(phys metall), 51. *Prof Exp:* Res metallographer, Aluminum Co Am, Ohio, 43-48; res metallurgist, Dow Chem Co, 51-56; mgr res lab, Hunter Eng Co, 56-58; res scientist, Lockheed Aircraft Corp, 58-67, dir mat sci lab, Lockheed Palo Alto Res Lab, 67-77, dir mat & struct, Res & Develop Dept, Lockheed Missiles & Space Co, 77-84. *Concurrent Pos:* Mem light aluminium alloys, Mat Adv Bd, Nat Acad Sci, 59-68 & high temp mat comt, 65-66. *Mem:* Am Inst Mining, Metall & Petrol Engrs; fel Am Soc Metalls. *Res:* Plastic deformation of metals; physical metallurgy of aluminum, magnesium, and beryllium alloys; high temperature materials; composite materials; materials science. *Mailing Add:* 241 Ferne Ave Palo Alto CA 94306-4602

BURKE, EDMUND R, ATHLETIC PERFORMANCE, EXERCISE PHYSIOLOGY. *Current Pos:* DIR SPORTS SCI & TECHNOL, US CYCLING FEDN, 82- *Personal Data:* b New York, NY, Aug, 23, 49. *Educ:* Ball State Univ, MA, 76; Ohio State Univ, PhD(exercise physiol), 79. *Prof Exp:* Fel, Univ Iowa Hosp, 79-81, res scientist, 81-82. *Mem:* Fel Am Col Sports Med; Am Alliance Health Phys Educ. *Mailing Add:* 3240 Wade Ct Colorado Springs CO 80917

BURKE, EDWARD ALOYSIUS, THEORETICAL PHYSICS. *Current Pos:* assoc prof, 66-69, dir space related sci, 66-70, PROF PHYSICS, ADELPHI UNIV, 69- *Personal Data:* b White Plains, NY, Oct 21, 29; m 55; c 7. *Educ:* NY Univ, BA, 54; Fordham Univ, MS, 55, PhD(physics), 59. *Prof Exp:* Electronics engr, Raytheon Mfg Co, 54; instr physics, US Maritime Acad, 55; asst, Fordham Univ, 55-58; asst prof phys sci, Montclair State Col, 58-59; from asst prof to assoc prof physics, St John's Univ, NY, 59-66, chmn dept, 62-65. *Concurrent Pos:* Vis prof, Univ Del, 80-81. *Mem:* Am Asn Physics Teachers; Am Phys Soc; Am Asn Univ Professors; Sigma Xi. *Res:* Theoretical atomic physics. *Mailing Add:* 11 Indian Hill Rd Woburn MA 01801-5419

BURKE, EDWARD RAYMOND, MAGNETISM, RECORDING SCIENCE. *Current Pos:* SR PHYSICIST, LAB PHYS SCI, 68- *Personal Data:* b Brooklyn, NY, Oct 25, 35; m 70, Peggy Markwood; c Cynthia & Mary E. *Educ:* St Joseph's Col, Philadelphia, BS, 57; Univ Md, PhD(physics), 68. *Mem:* Inst Elec & Electronics Engrs Magnetics Soc. *Res:* Physics research in magnetism; magnetic recording. *Mailing Add:* LPS 8050 Greenmead Dr College Park MD 20740

BURKE, EDWARD WALTER, JR, PHYSICS. *Current Pos:* RETIRED. *Personal Data:* b Macon, Ga, Sept 16, 24; m 46, Julia Struby; c Edward W III & Julia R. *Educ:* Presby Col, BS, 47; Univ Wis, MS, 49, PhD(physics), 54. *Honors & Awards:* Pegram Award, Am Phys Soc. *Prof Exp:* Vpres acad affairs, King Col, 77-79, Mary Reynolds Babcock prof physics, 49-91, chmn Div Natural Sci & Math, 61-91. *Concurrent Pos:* Fulbright lectr, Univ Chile, 59. *Mem:* Sigma Xi; Am Astron Soc; Am Asn Physics Teachers; Astron Soc Pac. *Res:* Spectroscopy; isotope shift in the atomic spectra of boron; astrophysics; photoelectric study of variable stars. *Mailing Add:* King Col Bristol TN 37620. *E-Mail:* king.physics@applelink.apple.com

BURKE, G THOMPSON, biochemistry, protein science, for more information see previous edition

BURKE, GEORGE WILLIAM, III, transplantation of liver, pancreas & kidney, for more information see previous edition

BURKE, HANNA SUSS, ORGANIC CHEMISTRY. *Current Pos:* RETIRED. *Personal Data:* b Karlsruhe, Ger, Oct 5, 26; nat US; m 65. *Educ:* Goucher Col, BA, 48; Univ Pa, MS, 52, PhD(org chem), 56. *Prof Exp:* Chemist, Johns Hopkins Univ, 48-51 & Rohm & Haas Co, 55-63; tech info specialist, Fibers & Plastics Co, Allied Chem Corp, 63-90. *Mem:* Am Chem Soc; Am Inst Chemists. *Res:* Separation of amino acids; isolation and synthesis of natural products; water soluble polymers; literature and patent searching; surveillance and indexing of literature and patents in fields of fiber technology and related subjects; registered patent agent. *Mailing Add:* 1805 Briardale Lane Richmond VA 23229

BURKE, J ANTHONY, ASTRONOMY, ASTROPHYSICS. *Current Pos:* ASSOC PROF ASTRON, UNIV VICTORIA, 68- *Personal Data:* b New York, NY, Jan 29, 37. *Educ:* Harvard Univ, AB, 58, AM, 59, PhD(astron), 65. *Prof Exp:* Res assoc astrophys, Brandeis Univ, 64-67; lectr & res assoc, Dept Astron, Boston Univ, 67-68. *Mem:* AAAS; Am Astron Soc; Can Astron Soc; Royal Astron Soc; Int Astron Union. *Res:* Cosmogony; interstellar medium. *Mailing Add:* Dept Physics & Astron Univ Victoria Victoria BC V8W 3P6 Can. *Fax:* 250-721-7715

BURKE, J(OSEPH) E(LDRID), MICROSTRUCTURE & PROPERTIES OF MATERIALS. *Current Pos:* CONSULT MAT SCI & ENG, 79- *Personal Data:* b Berkeley, Calif, Sept 1, 14; wid, Mary Wilson; c Charles R & Margaret (van Decar). *Educ:* McMaster Univ, BA, 35; Cornell Univ, PhD(chem), 40. *Honors & Awards:* Jeppson Medal, Am Ceramic Soc, 81; Frenkel Prize, Int Inst Sintering, 81. *Prof Exp:* Chemist, Int Nickel Co, NJ, 40-41; chemist, Norton Co, Mass, 41-43, metallurgist & group leader, Manhattan dist, Los Alamos, 43-46; assoc prof metall inst study metals, Univ Chicago, 46-49; res assoc, Knolls Atomic Power Lab, 49-52, mgr metall, 52-54, mgr, Ceramic Br, Gen Elec Co Res & Develop Ctr, 54-72, mgr spec projs, 72-79. *Concurrent Pos:* Adj prof mat sci, Renssalaer Polytech Inst, 79-84. *Mem:* Nat Acad Eng; fel Am Soc Metals; fel Am Ceramic Soc (pres, 74-75); fel Am Nuclear Soc. *Res:* Grain growth and recrystallization; metallography; metallurgy of uranium; materials for nuclear reactors; sintering; structure and properties of ceramics. *Mailing Add:* 2463 Nott St E Schenectady NY 12309. *E-Mail:* joeeburk@aol.com

BURKE, JAMES DAVID, ORGANIC CHEMISTRY. *Current Pos:* sr res scientist, 66-72, placement supvr, 72-79, sr scientist, 79-81, mgr res security, 81-83, RECRUITMENT SUPVR, ROHM & HAAS CO, 84- *Personal Data:* b Darby, Pa, June 30, 37; m 68; c 4. *Educ:* Spring Hill Col, BS, 61; Univ Calif, Berkeley, PhD(org chem), 65; Univ Pa, dipl, 77. *Prof Exp:* NIH fel, Columbia Univ, 65-66. *Mem:* Am Chem Soc. *Res:* Surface active agents for aqueous and non-aqueous systems; acrylate polymers; technology evaluation; dispersants; technology security. *Mailing Add:* ROHM/HAAS Co Independence Mall W Philadelphia PA 19105

BURKE, JAMES EDWARD, APPLIED MATHEMATICS, MATHEMATICAL PHYSICS. *Current Pos:* LAB MGR, ELECTROMAGNETIC SYST LABS, INC, 69- *Personal Data:* b Los Angeles, Calif, Oct 8, 31; m 54; c 3. *Educ:* San Jose State Col, BA, 53; Stanford Univ, MS, 55, PhD(math), 58. *Prof Exp:* Mathematician, Edwards AFB, 53-54; aeronaut res scientist syst anal, Ames Lab, NASA, 54-55; asst, Stanford Univ, 54-57; scattering specialist, Sylvania Electronics Defense Lab, Gen Tel & Electronics Co, 58-69. *Mem:* Sigma Xi; Am Math Soc; Soc Indust & Appl Math; Optical Soc Am; fel Acoust Soc Am. *Res:* Scattering of electromagnetic and acoustic waves by single and many objects. *Mailing Add:* 19960 Angus Ct Saratoga CA 95070-4406

BURKE, JAMES JOSEPH, POLYMER PHYSICS, MEMBRANE SCIENCE. *Current Pos:* PRIN RES ASSOC, PERMEA, INC, 91- *Personal Data:* b Northampton, Mass, June 11, 37; m 57, Louise M Souther. *Educ:* Univ Mass, BS, 58; Mass Inst Technol, PhD(phys chem), 62. *Prof Exp:* Res assoc phys chem, Mass Inst Technol, 62-63; res chemist, Chemstrand Res Ctr, Inc, 63-66, sr res chemist, 66-67, res specialist, 67-68, res group leader, 68-72, sr res group leader, 72-74; sr res group leader, Monsanto Co, Triangle Park, 74-77, Monsanto fel, 77-89, Monsanto sr fel, 89-91. *Mem:* AAAS; Am Chem Soc; Am Soc Testing & Mat; NY Acad Sci; Fiber Soc; NAm Membrane Soc. *Res:* Membrane science; hollow fiber membrane spinning; membranes for gas separations; membrane separation; new product development; membranes in biological applications; bioseparations; controlled delivery; polymer and fiber characterization. *Mailing Add:* 11444 Lackland Rd St Louis MO 63146-3523. *Fax:* 314-995-3500

BURKE, JAMES JOSEPH, JR, OPTICAL WAVEGUIDES. *Current Pos:* res assoc, Univ Ariz, 67-74, staff scientist & lectr, 74-82, prof, Optical Sci Ctr, 82-96, dir, Optical Data Storage Ctr, 87-96, EMER PROF, UNIV ARIZ, 96- *Personal Data:* b Chicago, Ill, July 26, 31; m 63; c 1. *Educ:* Univ Chicago, MS, 59; Univ Ariz, PhD(optics), 72. *Prof Exp:* Asst physicist optics, Ill Inst Technol Res Inst, 59-61; from res physicist to sr physicist, Optics Technol, Inc, 61-67. *Mem:* Fel Optical Soc Am; fel Soc Photo-Optical Instrumentation Engrs. *Res:* Optical waveguides and integrated optics, image analysis and processing; optical recording. *Mailing Add:* Optical Sci Ctr Univ Ariz Tucson AZ 85721. *Fax:* 520-621-4358

BURKE, JAMES L(EE), SYSTEMS INTEGRATION. *Current Pos:* DIR, RESOURCES DEVELOP, BISBEE, ARIZ. *Personal Data:* b Jamestown, NY, Sept 25, 18; m 42, Mary E Dromgoole; c 4. *Educ:* Univ Ariz, BS, 72, MA, 78. *Prof Exp:* Regular serv positions, US Army, 41-50, comdr, Res & Develop Procedurement Off, Ft Monmouth, NJ, 50-54, signal off, Allied Land Forces, Denmark, 55-58, chief, Mutual Security Div, Off of Chief Signal Officer, 58-61, chief, Instrumentation & Range Develop & Combat Surveillance Dept, Electronic Proving Ground, 62-65, chief, Logistics-Commun Div, Army Concept Team, Vietnam, 65, asst to commanding gen, Aviation & Aviation Electronics, Army Electronics Command, 66-69, dir, Prof Study Groups, 64-69, asst commandant, Electronic Warfare Sch, 69-70; vpres, Systs Eng Inc, Ariz, 70-75. *Concurrent Pos:* Consult & dir systs planning, Mentic Corp, Calif, 70-; mil com pilot; dir bus finance, Univ Hosp, Univ Ariz, 74. *Mem:* Sr mem Inst Elec & Electronics Engrs; assoc fel Am Inst Aeronaut & Astronaut; Army Aviation Asn Am. *Res:* Research and development, test and evaluation in electronic, surveillance, avionics and optics; development and evaluation in electromagnetic compatibility and radio intelligibility; human engineering and resources research and application; specialization in systems integration. *Mailing Add:* Box BB Bisbee AZ 85603

BURKE, JAMES OTEY, medicine, for more information see previous edition

BURKE, JAMES PATRICK, BIOCHEMISTRY, ZINC DEFICIENCY. *Current Pos:* ASSOC PROF PHYSIOL SCI, PA COL PODIATRIC MED, 75- *Educ:* Mt Sinai Sch Med, PhD(biochem), 74. *Mailing Add:* Dept Physiol Sci Pa Col Podiatric Med Eighth St at Race Philadelphia PA 19107

BURKE, JANICE MARIE, RETINAL CELL BIOLOGY, OCULAR PATHOLOGY. *Current Pos:* ASSOC PROF OPHTHAL, ANAT & CELL BIOL, MED COL WIS, 82- *Educ:* Univ Mass, PhD(cell & develop biol), 72. *Res:* Cell proliferation. *Mailing Add:* Dept Ophthal Med Col Wis 8700 W Wisconsin Ave Milwaukee WI 53226-3512. *Fax:* 414-257-7353

BURKE, JOHN A, INORGANIC CHEMISTRY. *Current Pos:* From asst prof to assoc prof chem, Trinity Univ, 63-74, chmn dept, 69-76, dean, Div Sci Math & Eng, 76-86, chmn dept, 88-89, PROF CHEM, TRINITY UNIV, 74- *Personal Data:* b Eastland, Tex, Dec 14, 36; m 62; c 3. *Educ:* Tex Tech Col, BS, 59; Ohio State Univ, MSc, 61, PhD(inorg chem), 63. *Mem:* Coun Undergrad Res; Am Chem Soc. *Res:* Inorganic chemistry, especially coordination compounds. *Mailing Add:* Dept Chem Trinity Univ 715 Stadium Dr San Antonio TX 78284

BURKE, JOHN FRANCIS, SURGERY. *Current Pos:* prof surg, 75-93, Helen Andrus Benedict prof, 76-93, EMER PROF SURG, HARVARD MED SCH, 93- *Personal Data:* b Chicago, Ill, July 22, 22; m 50; c 4. *Educ:* Univ Ill, BS, 47; Harvard Med Sch, MD, 51. *Prof Exp:* Intern surg, Mass Gen Hosp, Boston, 51-52, resident, 52-56, resident surgeon, 57; instr surg, Harvard Med Sch, 58-60, tudor med sci, 60-65, clin assoc surg, 60-66, asst clin prof, 66-69, assoc prof surg, 69-75; chief staff, 69-81, chief surg, Shriners Burns Inst, Boston Unit, 68-69. *Concurrent Pos:* Asst surg, Mass Gen Hosp, 58-60, asst surgeon, 61-63, assoc vis surgeon, 64-68, vis surgeon, 68-, chief, Trauma Serv, 81. *Mem:* Am Thoracic Soc; Soc Univ Surg; Infectious Dis Soc Am; Am Surg Asn; Am Asn Surg Trauma. *Res:* Host defense against infection and the treatment of traumatic injury and thermal injury. *Mailing Add:* Mass Gen Hosp Rm Warren 941 Boston MA 02114

BURKE, KENNETH B S, GEOPHYSICS. *Current Pos:* GEOPHYS CONSULT, 95- *Personal Data:* b Willenhall, Eng, Dec 28, 35; m 61, Elizabeth Kidd; c Helen & David. *Educ:* Univ Leeds, BSc, 58, dipl, 59, PhD(appl geophys), 61. *Prof Exp:* Mining geophysicist, Henry Krumb Sch Mines, Columbia Univ, 61-62; asst prof appl geophys, Univ Sask, 62-68; vis prof, Univ Man, 68-69; from assoc prof to prof geol, Univ NB, 69-95. *Mem:* Fel Geol Asn Can; Soc Explor Geophys; Asn Prof Eng; Seismol Soc Am; Environ & Eng Geophys Soc. *Res:* Earthquake seismology; historical seismicity studies; intraplate seismicity; environmental geophysics; mining geophysics. *Mailing Add:* Adler Geophys & Admin Serv 378 Oxford St Fredericton NB E3B 2W7 Can. *Fax:* 506-455-0533; *E-Mail:* kbsb@nbnet.nb.ca

BURKE, KEVIN CHARLES, GEOLOGY. *Current Pos:* DEPT GEOSCI, UNIV HOUSTON. *Personal Data:* b London, Eng, Nov 13, 29; m 61, Angela Phipps; c Nick, Matt & Jane. *Educ:* Univ London, BSc, 51, PhD(geol), 53. *Honors & Awards:* Du Toit Mem Lectr, Geol Soc SAfrica, 95. *Prof Exp:* Lectr geol, Univ Ghana, 53-56; geologist nuclear raw mat, Geol Surv, Gt Brit, 56-60; adv, Govt Korea, Int Atomic Energy Agency, 60-61; sr lectr geol, Univ West Indies, 61-65; prof, Univ Ibadan, 65-71; vis prof, Univ Toronto, 71-72; prof geol, State Univ NY Albany, 72-87; Lunar & Planetary Inst, Houston, TX, 83-88. *Concurrent Pos:* Vis prof, Calif Inst Technol, 76, Univ Minn, 78 & Univ Calgary, 79; consult, Oil Indust & NASA; scholar in residence, Nat Res Coun, Washington, DC, 89-92. *Mem:* Geol Soc Am; Am Geophys Union; Nigerian Mining, Geol & Metall Soc. *Res:* Application of the findings of plate tectonics to interpretation of the geological history of the earth. *Mailing Add:* 1110 Camino Village Dr Apt 2527 Houston TX 77058. *Fax:* 713-748-7906; *E-Mail:* kburke@uh.edu

BURKE, MEGHAN ANNE, MATHEMATICS. *Current Pos:* ASST PROF MATH, KENNESAW STATE COL, 95- *Personal Data:* b Park Ridge, Ill, Jan 24, 66; m, Gregory Abowd. *Educ:* Brown Univ, ScB, 87; Oxford Univ, DPhil(math), 92. *Prof Exp:* Postdoctoral res asst, Univ Pittsburgh, 92-94; postdoctoral res assoc, Emory Univ, 94-95. *Mem:* Am Math Soc; Math Asn Am; Asn Women Math; Soc Math Biol. *Res:* Mathematical models arising from applications in biology, chemistry and medicine; technology in teaching. *Mailing Add:* Math Dept Kennesaw State Col 1000 Chastain Rd Kennesaw GA 30144. *Fax:* 770-423-6629; *E-Mail:* mburke@ksumail.kennesaw.edu

BURKE, MICHAEL FRANCIS, ANALYTICAL CHEMISTRY. *Current Pos:* asst prof, 67-74, ASSOC PROF CHEM, UNIV ARIZ, 74- *Personal Data:* b Gallup, NMex, Jan 29, 39; m 60; c 4. *Educ:* Regis Col, BS, 60; Va Polytech Inst, PhD, 65. *Prof Exp:* Teacher, New Orleans, La, 60-61; fel, Purdue Univ, 65-66, asst prof, 66-67. *Mem:* Am Chem Soc. *Res:* Digital data handling and control of analytical instrumentation by means of small high speed computers; chromatographic separations; pyrolysis-gas chromatography; thermodynamics of gas-solid chromatography; high pressure chromatography. *Mailing Add:* Dept Chem Univ Ariz 1600 E University Blvd Tucson AZ 85721-0001

BURKE, MICHAEL JOHN, BIOPHYSICS. *Current Pos:* ASSOC DEAN, COL AGR SCI, ORE STATE UNIV, 84- *Personal Data:* b Westchester, Ill, July 7, 42; m 64, Mary E Mueller; c John E & Mara J. *Educ:* Blackburn Col, BA, 64; Iowa State Univ, PhD(biophys), 69. *Honors & Awards:* Darrow Award, Am Soc Hort Sci. *Prof Exp:* Res asst biophys, Iowa State Univ, 64-69; fel chem, Univ Minn, 69-71, fel bot, 71-72, from res assoc to asst prof hort, 72-76; assoc prof hort, Colo State Univ, 76-79; prof & chmn, dept fruit crops, Univ Fla, 79-84. *Mem:* Am Soc Hort Sci; AAAS; Am Chem Soc; Am Soc Plant Physiologists; Cryobiol Soc. *Res:* Plant stress physiology and physiological ecology; emphasis on biophysical properties of plants which allow them to survive low temperature and drought. *Mailing Add:* Col Agr Sci Ore State Univ Corvallis OR 97331-2201. *Fax:* 541-737-2256; *E-Mail:* burkem@ccmail.orst.edu

BURKE, MORRIS, PROTEIN CHEMISTRY, ORGANIC CHEMISTRY. *Current Pos:* asst prof, 78-82, ASSOC PROF BIOL, CASE WESTERN RESERVE UNIV, 82- *Personal Data:* b Hong Kong, Oct 25, 38; m 64; c 2. *Educ:* Univ Sydney, BSc, 60; Univ New South Wales, MSc, 63, PhD(wool chem), 66. *Prof Exp:* Res assoc radiation biochem, Mich State Univ, 66-67; res assoc phys biochem, Johns Hopkins Univ, 67-74, fel biol, 68-74; asst prof physiol, Sch Dent, Univ Md, 74-78. *Mem:* Am Chem Soc; Biophys Soc; Protein Soc. *Res:* Molecular basis of muscle contraction; mechanism of myosin and actomyosin Mg ATPase; selective chemical modification of proteins; peptide fractionation; associating macromolecules. *Mailing Add:* Dept Biol Case Western Reserve Univ Cleveland OH 44106. *Fax:* 216-368-4672

BURKE, PAUL J, OPERATIONS RESEARCH. *Current Pos:* MEM TECH STAFF PROBABILITY & STATIST, BELL LABS, 53- *Personal Data:* b New York, NY, Apr 21, 20. *Educ:* City Col New York, BS, 40; Harvard Univ, EdM, 50; Columbia Univ, PhD(math statist), 66. *Mem:* Fel AAAS; Opers Res Soc Am. *Res:* Telephone traffic theory; queuing theory. *Mailing Add:* 430 W 24th St Apt 1F New York NY 10011-1342

BURKE, RICHARD LERDA, ORGANIC CHEMISTRY. *Current Pos:* RETIRED. *Personal Data:* b San Francisco, Calif, Aug 30, 25; m 50; c 4. *Educ:* Univ San Francisco, BS, 44, MS, 48; Mich State Univ, PhD(org chem), 52. *Prof Exp:* Asst chem, Univ San Francisco, 47-48 & Mich State Univ, 48-52; chemist, Calif Res Corp, 52-57; tech rep prod develop, Oronite Chem Co, 57-60, prod specialist indust chem, Oronite Div, Calif Chem Co, 60-63; sr res chemist, Res & Develop Dept, Colgate Palmolive Co, 64-69; tech dir, Pac Soap Co, 69-88. *Mem:* Am Chem Soc. *Res:* Detergents and bleaches. *Mailing Add:* 5322 Soledad Rancho Ct San Diego CA 92109

BURKE, ROBERT D, MORPHOGENESIS. *Current Pos:* NSERC univ res fel, 80-85, asst prof 85-87, ASSOC PROF EMBRYOL, DEPT BIOL, UNIV VICTORIA, CAN, 87- *Personal Data:* b Swift Current, Sask, July, 31, 51; m 81; c 2. *Educ:* Univ Alberta, BSc, 74, PhD(embryol), 78. *Prof Exp:* Nat Oceanic & Atmospheric Admin Sea Grant fel, dept zool, Univ Md, 78-79; Smithsonian Inst fel, Washington, DC, 79-80. *Concurrent Pos:* Vis asst prof, Bamfield Marine Sta, BC, 83 & 84 & Friday Harbor Labs, Univ Wash, 84. *Mem:* AAAS; Am Soc Zool; Soc Develop Biol. *Res:* Developmental and cell biology; morphogenetic mechanisms involved in embryonic and larval development of sea urchins; application of immunological techniques to problems of differentiation of cell surface molecules, metamorphosis and evolution. *Mailing Add:* Dept Biol Univ Victoria Box 1700 Victoria BC V8W 2Y2 Can

BURKE, ROBERT EMMETT, NEUROPHYSIOLOGY. *Current Pos:* staff scientist, 68-75, LAB CHIEF, LAB NEURAL CONTROL, NIH, 75- *Personal Data:* b New York, NY, July 26, 34; m 60; c Mary K, David W, Jean E & Christina E. *Educ:* St Bonaventure Univ, BS, 56; Univ Rochester, MD, 61. *Prof Exp:* Intern & asst resident internal med, Mass Gen Hosp, 61-63, asst resident neurol, 63-64; res assoc spinal cord sect, Lab Neurophysiol, Nat Inst Neurol & Commun Disorders & Stroke, NIH, 64-67; vis scientist, Dept Physiol, Univ Goteborg, Sweden, 67-68. *Mem:* Am Physiol Soc; Soc for Neurosci; Int Brain Res Orgn. *Res:* Structure and function of spinal cord; neural control of movement; synaptic transmission; cellular biology of neurons; neurobiology of motor units; computational models of neuron structure and function. *Mailing Add:* Lab Neural Control Bldg 49 Rm 3A50 NINDS NIH Bethesda MD 20892. *Fax:* 301-402-4836; *E-Mail:* reburke@helix.nih.gov

BURKE, ROBERT F, CHEMICAL ENGINEERING, PROCESS DESIGN. *Current Pos:* sr chem engr, 67-75, CHEM ENGR CONSULT, HOFFMANN-LA ROCHE, INC, 75- *Personal Data:* b Joliet, Ill, June 13, 25; m 57; c 2. *Educ:* Carnegie Inst Technol, BS & MS, 49, DSc(chem eng), 52. *Prof Exp:* Design engr, Foster Wheeler Corp, NY, 51-55; res engr, Esso Res & Eng Co, NJ, 55-59; sr res staff mem, Raytheon Co, Mass, 59-60; sr res engr, T J Lipton Inc, NJ, 60-64; sr process design engr, Lummus Co, 64-67. *Mem:* Am Chem Soc; Sigma Xi. *Res:* Food dehydration; freeze drying; high temperature decomposition and deposition; chemical process design and research; fluidization; reaction kinetics; vitamin plant design and operation. *Mailing Add:* 530 Brook Ave Hillsdale NJ 07642

BURKE, ROBERT WAYNE, NP COMPLETENESS, ALGORITHM DEVELOPMENT. *Current Pos:* HEAD INFO SYSTS, NAVAL RES LAB, STENNIS SPACE CENTER, 91- *Personal Data:* b Ridgecrest, Calif, Feb 2, 58; m 91, JoAnn Goodner; c Sarah & John. *Educ:* Univ Calif, Santa Barbara, BS & BA, 82; Calif State Univ, Chico, CA, MS, 97. *Prof Exp:* Head, Sci Appl Br & Electronics engr, Naval Weapons Ctr, China Lake, 82-91. *Concurrent Pos:* Mem, Subcomt Parallel & Heterogeneous Distrib Comput, Defense Acquisition Bd, 90-91, Navy Lab/Ctr Comput Comt, 91-, Navy Adv Group, High Perform Comput, 91- *Mem:* Inst Elec & Electronics Engrs Comput Soc; Soc Comput Simulation. *Res:* Parallel and heterogeneous distributed computing; theoretical computer science, particularly The Knapsack Problem. *Mailing Add:* 1000 Buckingham Ct Slidell LA 70460-5321. *E-Mail:* burke@nrlssc.navy.mil

BURKE, SHAWN EDMUND, DISTRIBUTED PARAMETER CONTROL SYSTEMS, SONAR TRANSDUCTION. *Current Pos:* Instr mech eng, 84-85, fel, 85-89, MEM TECH STAFF, C S DRAPER LAB, 89- *Personal Data:* b Waterville, Maine, Oct 28, 59; m 85. *Educ:* Princeton Univ, BSE, 81; Mass Inst Technol, MS, 83, PhD(mech eng), 89. *Concurrent Pos:* Sr engr, Chase Inc, 84-86; consult scientist, Technol Integration & Develop Group, 85-86. *Mem:* Sigma Xi; Int Soc Optical Eng. *Res:* Application of distributed transducer technology for structural vibration and shape control; sonar; hydrodynamics; hydroacoustics. *Mailing Add:* 39 Kathleen Dr Andover MA 01810

BURKE, STEVEN DOUGLAS, SYNTHETIC ORGANIC & NATURAL PRODUCTS CHEMISTRY. *Current Pos:* PROF CHEM, UNIV WIS-MADISON, 87- *Personal Data:* b Eau Claire, Wis, June 29, 51. *Educ:* Univ Wis, BS, 73; Univ Pittsburgh, PhD(chem), 78. *Prof Exp:* From asst prof to Carolina res prof chem, Univ SC, 78-87. *Concurrent Pos:* Vis assoc prof chem, Univ Wis-Madison, 84; consult, Wyeth-Ayerst Pharmaceut, 85-; reviewer, Biomed Sci Study Sect, NIH, 80-86, Biorg & Natural Prod Study Sect, 87; Alfred P Sloan res fel, 84. *Mem:* Am Chem Soc; Royal Chem Soc. *Res:* Total synthesis of biologically active natural products; organometallics; asymmetric synthesis; structure-activity relationships; molecular modeling; ion recognition; transport by synthetic macrocydic ligands; pharmaceutical chemistry. *Mailing Add:* Dept Chem 1101 Univ A Univ Wis Madison WI 53706

BURKE, THOMAS J, BIOCHEMISTRY, BIOLOGY RESEARCH. *Current Pos:* BIOMED RESEARCHER, PAN VERA CORP, 92- *Personal Data:* b Madison, Wis, Feb 15, 55. *Educ:* Edgewood Col, BS, 77; Marquette Univ, PhD(biol), 86. *Prof Exp:* Dir mfg, Promega Corp, 87-92. *Mem:* Am Soc Microbiol; Am Soc Biochem & Molecular Biol. *Mailing Add:* Pan Vera Corp 565 Science Dr Madison WI 53711

BURKE, THOMAS JOSEPH, PHYSIOLOGY. *Current Pos:* ASST PROF PHYSIOL, MED SCH, UNIV COLO MED CTR, DENVER, 73- *Personal Data:* b Baltimore, Md, Mar 15, 38; m 65; c 2. *Educ:* Niagara Univ, BS, 61; Adelphi Univ, MS, 66; Univ Houston, PhD(physiol), 70. *Concurrent Pos:* Nat

Heat & Lung Inst fel, Med Sch, Duke Univ, 69-73. *Mem:* Am Soc Nephrol; Int Soc Nephrol; Am Fedn Clin Res. *Res:* Renal autoregulation of blood flow and filtration rate; micropuncture techniques; nephron function; sodium balance; renin-angiotensin system. *Mailing Add:* Dept Renal Med & Med C281 Univ Colo Med Ctr 4200 E Ninth Ave Denver CO 80262

BURKE, WILLIAM HENRY, GEOPHYSICS. *Current Pos:* RETIRED. *Personal Data:* b Dallas, Tex, Sept 1, 24; m 53; c 3. *Educ:* Rice Inst, PhD(physics), 51. *Prof Exp:* Sr res physicist, Mobil Res & Develop Corp, 51-56, res assoc, Field Res Labs, 65-85. *Concurrent Pos:* Consult, Grad Res Ctr, 64-65. *Mem:* Am Phys Soc; Am Soc Mass Spectrometry. *Res:* Isotope geology; nuclear reactions induced by proton, deuteron and neutron bombardment; extremely low level radioactivity measurements; mass spectrometry; geochronometry; terrestrial heat flow; geochemistry. *Mailing Add:* 3226 Tower Trail Dallas TX 75229

BURKE, WILLIAM J, AURORAL PHYSICS, WAVE PLASMA INTERACTIONS. *Current Pos:* res physicist, 80-84, PHYSICIST, AIR FORCE GEOPHYS LABS, SPACE PHYSICS DIV, HANSCOM AFB, MASS, 84- *Personal Data:* b Newton, Mass, June 9, 35; m 73; c 3. *Educ:* Boston Col, BS, 60; Mass Inst Technol, PhD(physics), 71. *Prof Exp:* Postdoctoral fel, dept physics & astron, Rice Univ, 71-73; fel, Earth Resources Div, Nat Res Coun, Johnson Space Ctr, Houston, 73-75; res physicist, Regis Col, 75-78; res physicist, physics dept, Boston Col, 78-80. *Mem:* Am Geophys Union; AAAS; Am Phys Soc. *Res:* Electrodynamics of coupling between the ionosphere and magnetosphere at equatorial and high magnetic latitudes. *Mailing Add:* 12 Vanderbelt Rd Acton MA 01720-4305

BURKE, WILLIAM JAMES, polymer chemistry; deceased, see previous edition for last biography

BURKE, WILLIAM JOSEPH, NEUROLOGY. *Current Pos:* Intern med, St Louis Univ, 72-73, resident neurol, 73-76, asst prof, 76-83, assoc prof, 83-93, PROF NEUROL, MED SCH, ST LOUIS UNIV, 93- *Personal Data:* b Milwaukee, Wis, July, 24, 40; m 77, Mary Rowe; c Cathrine, Christine, Erin & Joseph. *Educ:* Marquette Univ, BS, 62; St Louis Univ, MD & PhD(biochem), 72. *Concurrent Pos:* Prin investr, Vet Admin Med Ctr, St Louis, 77-; merit rev grant, Vet Admin, 77-; NIH grant, 91-94. *Mem:* Am Soc Biol Chemists; Am Acad Neurol; Soc Neurosci. *Res:* Aging; biochemical mechanisms regulating catecholamine synthesizing enzymes; pathogenic mechanisms in Alzheimer's disease. *Mailing Add:* Vet Admin Med Ctr Jefferson Barracks 11G JB St Louis MO 63125

BURKE, WILLIAM L, theoretical physics; deceased, see previous edition for last biography

BURKE, WILLIAM THOMAS, JR, biology, biochemistry, for more information see previous edition

BURKEL, WILLIAM E, ANATOMY, CELL BIOLOGY. *Current Pos:* from asst prof to assoc prof, 66-82, PROF ANAT & CELL BIOL, UNIV MICH, 82- *Personal Data:* b Mankato, Minn, Oct 4, 38; m 66; c 7. *Educ:* St John's Univ, Minn, BA, 60; Univ NDak, MS, 62, PhD(anat), 64. *Prof Exp:* NIH fel anat, Lab Electron Micros, Univ NDak, 64-66. *Mem:* AAAS; Electron Micros Soc Am; Am Soc Cell Biol; Am Asn Anat; Am Soc Artificial Internal Organs; Am Asn Clin Anat. *Res:* Electron microscopy; development of artificial blood vessels. *Mailing Add:* Dept Anat & Cell Biol 4643 Med Sci 2 Univ Mich Med Sch 1301 Catherine Rd Ann Arbor MI 48109-0616. *Fax:* 313-763-1166; *E-Mail:* wburkel@umich.edu

BURKET, GEORGE EDWARD, FAMILY MEDICINE. *Current Pos:* RETIRED. *Personal Data:* b Kingman, Kans, Dec 10, 12; m 38; c 3. *Educ:* Univ Kans, MD, 37. *Honors & Awards:* John Walsh Founders Award, Am Acad Family Physicians, 79. *Prof Exp:* Pvt pract med, 40-73; prof family med, Univ Kans, 73-78, clin prof, 78-88. *Mem:* Inst Med-Nat Acad Sci; Am Acad Family Physicians (pres, 68); Am Bd Family Pract (pres, 75-77); Asn Am Med Cols. *Res:* Health care delivery. *Mailing Add:* Larksfield Plv-208 7373 E29th St N Wichita KS 67226

BURKETT, GERALD RAY, BIOLOGY, ENTOMOLOGY. *Current Pos:* asst prof biol, 84-89, assoc prof & chair biol, Div Nat Sci & Math, 89-97, PROF BIOL, HANNIBAL-LA GRANGE COL, 97- *Personal Data:* b Aiken, SC, Sept 9, 47; m 70, Mary Toney; c Joseph Henry & Jonathan Burkett. *Educ:* Mars Hill Col, BS, 71; Clemson Univ, MAg, 72; Miss State Univ, PhD(entom), 81. *Prof Exp:* Entomologist, SC Dept Health & Environ Control, 73-78; instr biol, Wood Jr Col, 83-84. *Mem:* Entom Soc Am; Human Anat & Physiol Soc; Am Orchid Soc. *Res:* Host plant resistance studies with the tomato fruitworm, Heliothis zea and the tobacco budworm, Heliothis virescens; established rearing program for Heliothis virescens so that biology students can carry out independent research involving the life cycle of this insect. *Mailing Add:* Dept Nat Sci Hannibal La Grange Col 2800 Palmyra Rd Hannibal MO 63401-1940. *E-Mail:* gburkett@hlg.edu

BURKETT, HOWARD (BENTON), ORGANIC CHEMISTRY. *Current Pos:* from asst prof to prof chem, 54-81, rotating head dept, 64-81, EMER PROF CHEM, DEPAUW UNIV, 81- *Personal Data:* b Putnam Co, Ind, Feb 26, 16; m 36; c 4. *Educ:* DePauw Univ, BA, 38; Univ Wis, PhD(org chem), 42. *Prof Exp:* Asst, Univ Wis, 38-40; res chemist, Eli Lilly & Co, Ind, 42-45. *Concurrent Pos:* Fel, Univ Wash, 53-54, Petrol Res Fund grant, 62-63; sr eng assoc, Naka Works, Hitachi, Ltd, Japan, 70-71; org chem sect, Nat Inst Arthritis & Metab & Digestive Dis, NIH, Bethesda, Md, 77-78. *Mem:* Am Chem Soc. *Res:* Organic synthesis; barbituric acid derivatives; aliphatic nitro-compounds, basic condensations, physical-organic; acid catalysis. *Mailing Add:* PO Box 37 DePauw Univ Greencastle IN 46135-0037

BURKEY, BRUCE CURTISS, TECHNICAL MANAGEMENT. *Current Pos:* PHYSICIST, EASTMAN KODAK CO, 67- *Personal Data:* b Ravenna, Ohio, Nov 29, 38. *Educ:* Hiram Col, BA, 61; Mich State Univ, MS, 63, PhD(physics), 67. *Mem:* Am Phys Soc; Sigma Xi; Inst Elec & Electronics Engrs. *Res:* Device physics and solid state image sensor research and development. *Mailing Add:* 37 Berkshire Dr Rochester NY 14626-3814

BURKEY, RONALD STEVEN, ENGINEERING. *Current Pos:* SR ENGR, HEADS-UP TECHNOL, 86- *Personal Data:* b Columbis, Ohio, March 24, 57. *Educ:* Ohio State Univ, BA, 78; Univ Tex, Dallas, MS, 83. *Mem:* Am Phys Soc; Inst Elec & Electronics Engrs; Sigma Xi. *Mailing Add:* Heads Up Technol 2033 Chenault Dr 100 Carrollton TX 75006

BURKHALTER, ALAN, PHARMACOLOGY. *Current Pos:* PROF PHARMACOL, MED CTR, UNIV CALIF, SAN FRANCISCO, 59- *Personal Data:* b Bloomington, Ind, Aug 11, 32; m 54; c 4. *Educ:* DePauw Univ, BA, 54; Univ Iowa, MS, 56, PhD(pharmacol), 57. *Prof Exp:* Sr asst scientist, Lab Chem Pharmacol, Nat Heart Inst, 57-59. *Concurrent Pos:* USPHS grants, 60-63, 64-67; NIH spec fel, 63-64; consult, State of Calif, 60-62. *Mem:* AAAS; Am Soc Pharmacol & Exp Therapeut; Tissue Cult Asn. *Res:* Biochemical pharmacology; effect of drugs on enzyme regulation; histamine metabolism; effect of drugs during fetal and neonatal development; use of cell and organ culture in pharmacologic research. *Mailing Add:* Dept Pharmacol Box 0450 Univ Calif Med Ctr San Francisco CA 94143-0001. *Fax:* 415-476-5292

BURKHALTER, BARTON R, OPERATIONS RESEARCH & EVALUATION, INTERNATIONAL PUBLIC HEALTH. *Current Pos:* TECH OFFICER, ACAD EDUC DEVELOP. *Personal Data:* b Toledo, Ohio, July 22, 38; m 63, 78, Eliana Godoy; c 5. *Educ:* Univ Mich, BS, 61, MS, 62, PhD(indust eng), 64. *Prof Exp:* Res asst regional develop, Inst Sci & Technol, Univ Mich, 61-62, res asst systs eng, 63-64, teaching fel, Indust Eng Univ, 63, instr, 64; lectr mgt sci, Wayne State Univ Exten, 62-63; exec dir, Community Systs Found, 64-69, pres, 69-73, chmn & sr scientist, CSF Ltd, 73-76, assoc & sr scientist, 75-88; res prof, Univ Ariz, 80-96; prin, Performance Inst, 81-85; vpres, Zana Int Inc, 83-84, WV Int Indust Inc, 84-85; pres, Winch Inst Am Inc, 84-87; assoc dir, Wellstart, 86-88; dir, Ctr Int Health Info, 88-91. *Concurrent Pos:* Adj prof, PhD Prog Urban & Regional Planning, Univ Mich, 70-77; ed, Nutrit Planning, 77-80; consult, Papago Tribe Ariz, 78-79 & Hopi Tribe, 81-82. *Mem:* Hosp Mgt Systs Soc (pres, 72-73); Opers Res Soc Am; Am Pub Health Asn; AAAS. *Res:* Planning; public health; science and American Indian communities; measurement of system performance; nutrition policy simulation. *Mailing Add:* 10310 Gary Rd Potomac MD 20854

BURKHALTER, PHILIP GARY, PHYSICS. *Current Pos:* RETIRED. *Personal Data:* b Ft Wayne, Ind, July 20, 37; m 59; c 4. *Educ:* Purdue Univ, BS, 59; Drexel Inst Technol, MS, 65. *Prof Exp:* Assoc engr x-ray diffraction, Martin-Marietta Corp, 59-61; scientist x-ray anal, US Bur Mines, 61-70, res physicist atomic physics, Naval Res Lab, 70-96. *Concurrent Pos:* Group leader extreme ultraviolet spectros, Naval Res Lab, prog mgr, Systs/Prog Off, Strategic Defense Initiative, 87. *Mem:* Optical Soc Am; Am Phys Soc. *Res:* X-ray diagnostics of high-temperature plasmas; atomic spectroscopy of highly-ionized atoms, x-ray detection devices. *Mailing Add:* 408 Vistaway Ft Washington MD 20744

BURKHARD, DONALD GEORGE, PHYSICS. *Current Pos:* RES DIR, PHYSICS, ENG & CHEM RES ASSOCS, INC, 56-; PROF PHYSICS & ASTRON, UNIV GA, 65- *Personal Data:* b NJ, Feb 10, 18; m 48; c 3. *Educ:* Univ Calif, AB, 41; Univ Mich, MS, 47, PhD(physics), 50. *Prof Exp:* Physicist, Radiation Lab, Univ Calif, 44; res physicist, Carter Oil Co, Okla, 44-45; res assoc, Ohio State Univ, 49-50; from asst prof to prof physics, Univ Colo, 50-64. *Mem:* AAAS; Am Phys Soc; Optical Soc Am; Am Acoustical Soc; Am Asn Physics Teachers; Sigma Xi. *Res:* Theoretical physics; theoretical atomic and molecular structure; infrared and microwave spectroscopy; psychometrics; solid state physics; physical and geometrical optics. *Mailing Add:* Physic Dept Univ GA Athens GA 30601

BURKHARD, MAHLON DANIEL, ACOUSTICS. *Current Pos:* PRES, SONIC PERCEPTIONS, INC, 90- *Personal Data:* b Seward, Nebr, Jan 14, 23; m 45; c 4. *Educ:* Nebr Wesleyan Univ, AB, 46; Pa State Col, MS, 50. *Prof Exp:* Teacher high sch, Nebr, 46-47; asst acoustics, Dept Physics, Pa State Univ, 47-50; physicist, Nat Bur Stand, 50-57; supvr, Acoustics Sect, IIT Res Inst, 57-60; mgr acoust res, Indust Res Prod, Inc, 60-75, mgr res, 75-87, vpres & gen mgr, Prof Sound Prod, 87-89. *Concurrent Pos:* Cert Superior Accomplishment, US Dept Com, 54; chmn stand working group, Am Nat Stand Inst, 58-; exec coun, Acoustical Soc Am, 83-86. *Mem:* Sr mem Inst Elec & Electronics Engr; fel Acoust Soc Am; fel Audio Eng Soc; Nat Soc Prof Engrs; Sigma Xi. *Res:* Atmospheric sound propagation; edge tone and whistle sound sources; calibration and standardization of audiometric instruments and microphones; acoustic impedance measurements; ultrasonic phenomena in gases, liquids, and solids; electro mechanical transducers; sound and noise control; hearing and hearing aids; auditorium acoustics; Sound reproduction; digital processing of sound and speech. *Mailing Add:* Sonic Perceptions Inc 114A Washington St Norwalk CT 06854

BURKHARD, RAYMOND KENNETH, BIOCHEMISTRY. *Current Pos:* From instr to prof, 50-89, EMER PROF BIOCHEM, KANS STATE UNIV, 89- *Personal Data:* b Tempe, Ariz, Aug 6, 24; m 48; c 4. *Educ:* Ariz State Univ, AB, 47; Northwestern Univ, PhD(chem), 50. *Concurrent Pos:* Res fel, Inst Enzyme Res, Wis, 59-60; vis prof, Yale Univ, 77. *Mem:* Am Soc Biochem & Molecular Biol; Am Chem Soc. *Res:* Protein interactions; microcalorimetry. *Mailing Add:* Dept Biochem Kans State Univ Willard Hall Manhattan KS 66506-3700

BURKHARDT, ALAN ELMER, BIOCHEMISTRY, CHEMISTRY. *Current Pos:* DIR, CHIRON DIAG. *Personal Data:* b Buffalo, NY, Jan 19, 47; m 71. *Educ:* Clarkson Col Technol, BS, 68; Cornell Univ, MS, 73, PhD(chem), 75. *Prof Exp:* Fel biochem, NIH, 75-77; res scientist, Miles Labs, 77-80, supvr, 80-83, mgr, 83-85, dir, Dry Reagent chem Lab, Ames Div, 85- *Mem:* Am Chem Soc; AAAS; Am Asn Clin Chem; fel Nat Acad Clin Biochem. *Res:* Clinical chemistry, biochemistry; rapid diagnostic tests. *Mailing Add:* Chiron Diag 333 Coney St East Walpole MA 02032-1516

BURKHARDT, CHRISTIAN CARL, entomology, for more information see previous edition

BURKHARDT, KENNETH J, MICROCOMPUTER & WORKSTATION DESIGN, INTEGRATION OF VOICE & COMPUTERS. *Current Pos:* EXEC VPRES, DIALOGIC CORP, 87- *Personal Data:* b Elizabeth, NJ, Mar 30, 45; m 81; c 3. *Educ:* Cornell Univ, AB, 67; Rutgers Univ, MS, 70; Univ Wash, PhC, 72, PhD(comp sci), 75. *Prof Exp:* Systs programmer, Am Cyanamid Co, 67-70; res assoc comp sci, Univ Wash, 71-76; vpres systs, Intec Inc, 75-78; asst prof elec eng, Rutgers Univ, 76-82; pres, KJ Burkhardt & Co, Inc, 78-90; syst architect, Burroughs Corp, 81-87. *Concurrent Pos:* Res award, Am Cyanamid Co, 71-72; res assoc, NIH, 73-74. *Mem:* Inst Elec & Electronics Engrs; Asn Comput Mach. *Res:* Computer systems design; microcomputer system design; computer architecture. *Mailing Add:* Quaker Lane Farm Quakertown NJ 08868

BURKHARDT, THEODORE W, PHYSICS. *Current Pos:* assoc prof, 81, PROF PHYSICS, TEMPLE UNIV, 87- *Personal Data:* b July 12, 40. *Educ:* Vanderbilt Univ, BA, 62; Stanford Univ, MA, PhD(physics), 67. *Prof Exp:* NATO res fel, Max Planck Inst, WGer, 67-69; asst prof, Lincoln Univ, 69-73; res scientist, Kernforschungsanlage, WGer, 73-76, 78-80, Inst Laue-Langevin, France, 76-78, 80-81. *Concurrent Pos:* Lectr, Univ Essen, WGer, 79, Curtis Inst Music, 88; vis prof, Univ Wash, Seattle, 88-89, L M Univ, Ger, 93. *Res:* Ground-state and low-excited properties of liquid helium calculated with a two-body potential. *Mailing Add:* Dept Physics Temple Univ Philadelphia PA 19122

BURKHARDT, WALTER H, COMPUTER SCIENCE, HARDWARE & SOFTWARE SYSTEMS. *Current Pos:* CHMN & EMER PROF HARDWARE, DIR, INST INFOMATICS, UNIV STUTTGART, 74- *Personal Data:* b Stuttgart, Ger; US citizen; m 77, Ursula Gross; c Barbara & Susan. *Educ:* Univ Stuttgart, Vordiplom, 51, Dipl Phys, 54, Dr rer nat(physics), 58. *Prof Exp:* Sr asst programmer, World Trade Co & Data Syst Div, IBM Corp, 61-64; prin systs programmer, Univac Div, Sperry Rand Co, 64-66; sr staff res & develop, Comput Control Div, Honeywell, Inc, 65-66; staff prog mgr advan systs, Info Systs Div, RCA Corp, 66-69; assoc prof comput sci, Univ Pittsburgh, 69-74. *Concurrent Pos:* Reviewer, Comput Rev, 66; dir, DPM Comput Leasing Co, 69; mem exec comt, Comput Ctr, Univ Pittsburgh, 72-74. *Mem:* Asn Comput Mach; Inst Elec & Electronics Engrs. *Res:* Microcomputer systems; micro-programming and micro-implementation; multi-processor systems; design automation. *Mailing Add:* 20 Breitwiesen St 70565 Stuttgart Germany. *Fax:* 49-711-781-6370; *E-Mail:* burkhardt@informatik.uni_stuttgart.de

BURKHART, HAROLD EUGENE, FOREST BIOMETRY. *Current Pos:* From asst prof to prof, 69-81, THOMAS M BROOKS PROF FOREST BIOMET, VA POLYTECH INST & STATE UNIV, 81- *Personal Data:* b Wellington, Kans, Feb 29, 44; m 71, Katherine West; c Anna K. *Educ:* Okla State Univ, BS, 65; Univ Ga, MS, 67, PhD(forest biomet), 69. *Honors & Awards:* J Shelton Horsley Res Award; Sci Achievement Award, Int Union Forestry Res Orgn; Barrington Moore Mem Award, Soc Am Forsters; Distinguished Statist Ecol Award, Int Asn Ecol. *Concurrent Pos:* Sr res fel, Forest Res Inst, Rotorua, NZ, 76-77. *Mem:* Fel AAAS; fel Soc Am Foresters; Biomet Soc; Sigma Xi. *Res:* Forest growth and yield. *Mailing Add:* Dept Forestry Va Polytech Inst & State Univ Blacksburg VA 24061-0324. *Fax:* 540-231-3698; *E-Mail:* burkhart@vt.edu

BURKHART, JAMES GAYLORD, MOLECULAR APPROACHES TO ENVIRONMENTAL MUTAGENESIS, HAZARD ASSESSMENTS FOR ECOTOXICOLOGY & HUMAN HEALTH. *Current Pos:* RES CHEMIST, NAT INST ENVIRON HEALTH SCI, 76-; ASST PROF, DUKE UNIV, 91- *Personal Data:* b Urbanna, Ill, Dec 19, 46; c 2. *Educ:* Univ Mo, BS, 69, MS, 75; NC State Univ, PhD(biochem-genetics), 89. *Prof Exp:* Res chemist, Nat Ctr Toxicol Res, 75-76. *Mem:* Environ Mutagen Soc; AAAS. *Res:* Mechanisms and biological significance of somatic and germinal mutagenesis in vivo in animals as a result of exposure to environmental agents; development and characterization of new models for genetic hypersensitive cohorts. *Mailing Add:* 7713 Jenks Rd Apex NC 27502

BURKHART, RICHARD DELMAR, PHYSICAL CHEMISTRY. *Current Pos:* from asst prof to assoc prof, 65-71, PROF PHYS CHEM, UNIV NEV, RENO, 71- *Personal Data:* b Kersey, Colo, June 26, 34; m 58; c 3. *Educ:* Dartmouth Col, AB, 56; Univ Colo, PhD(phys chem), 60. *Prof Exp:* Res chemist, Chem Div, Union Carbide Corp, 60-63; res assoc chem kinetics, Univ Ore, 63-65. *Mem:* Am Chem Soc; Sigma Xi. *Res:* Energy migration in amorphous solids; diffusion of excited species; photochemistry. *Mailing Add:* Dept Chem MS 216 Univ Nev Reno NV 89557

BURKHART, RICHARD HENRY, APPLIED OPTIMIZATION, STOCHASTIC PROCESSES. *Current Pos:* APPL MATHEMATICIAN, BOEING COMPUT SERV, 81- *Personal Data:* b Tacoma, Wash, Dec 17, 46; m 71; c 3. *Educ:* Reed Col, BA, 69; Dartmouth Col, AM, 74, PhD(math), 76. *Prof Exp:* Asst prof math, Univ NC, Wilmington, 76-80. *Mem:* Am Math Soc; Math Asn Am; Soc Indust & Appl Math; Asn Comput Mach. *Res:* Numerical analysis; linear algebra; a symptotic analysis and optimization methods applied to the numerical solution of partial differential equations especially in aerodynamics and acoustics. *Mailing Add:* Info Support Serv Boeing PO Box 3707 MS-7L-21 Seattle WA 98124-2207

BURKHEAD, MARTIN SAMUEL, ASTROPHYSICS. *Current Pos:* asst prof, 64-71, ASSOC PROF ASTRON, IND UNIV, BLOOMINGTON, 71-, ASSOC DIR, GOETHE LINK OBSERV, 74- *Personal Data:* b Ogden, Utah, May 23, 33; m 56; c 2. *Educ:* Tex A&M Univ, BS, 55; Univ Calif, Los Angeles, MS, 57, PhD(astron), 64. *Prof Exp:* Sta chief, Smithsonian Satellite Tracking Prog, 57-60; res assoc astron, Univ Wis, 61-64. *Concurrent Pos:* Vis prof USAID, Seoul Nat Univ, Korea, 77-78. *Res:* Photoelectric photometry. *Mailing Add:* 618 S Eastside Dr Ind Univ Bloomington IN 47401

BURKHOFF, DANIEL, CIRCULATORY PHYSIOLOGY. *Current Pos:* ASST PROF CARDIAC PHYSIOL, COLUMBIA PRESBY HOSP, 91- *Personal Data:* b Newark, NJ, Jan 30, 58. *Res:* Circulatory physiology. *Mailing Add:* Dept Med Columbia Presby Hosp 630 W 168th St New York NY 10032

BURKHOLDER, DONALD LYMAN, MATHEMATICAL PROBABILITY & ANALYSIS. *Current Pos:* From asst prof to assoc prof, 55-64, PROF MATH, UNIV ILL, URBANA, 64-, PROF, CTR ADVAN STUDY, 78- *Personal Data:* b Octavia, Nebr, Jan 19, 27; m 50, Jean A Fox; c Kathleen, Peter & William. *Educ:* Earlham Col, BA, 50; Univ Wis, MS, 53; Univ NC, PhD(math statist), 55. *Mem:* Nat Acad Sci; fel Inst Math Statist (pres, 75-76); AAAS; Soc Indust & Appl Maths; London Math Soc; Am Acad Arts & Scis; Am Math Soc. *Res:* Probability and its applications to analysis. *Mailing Add:* Dept Math Univ Ill Urbana IL 61801. *E-Mail:* donburk@math.uiuc.edu

BURKHOLDER, JOHN HENRY, ZOOLOGY. *Current Pos:* Head dept, McPherson Col, 54-70, prof biol, 53-91, chmn div natural sci, 67-74, head dept, 74-91, EMER PROF BIOL, MCPHERSON COL, 91- *Personal Data:* b Octavia, Nebr, July 11, 25; m 50, Donna Bowman; c David, Philip, Doug & Debra. *Educ:* McPherson Col, AB, 49; Univ Chicago, PhD(zool), 54. *Honors & Awards:* Burkholder Res Award. *Mem:* Sigma Xi. *Res:* Genetics; position effects in Drosophila melanogaster. *Mailing Add:* 127 N Charles St McPherson KS 67460

BURKHOLDER, PETER M, PATHOLOGY, HEALTH CARE MANAGEMENT. *Current Pos:* CLIN PROF, UNIV ARIZ SCH MED, 82-, CHMN, DEPT PATH, 89-; PRES, MARICOPA PATHOLOGISTS, LTD, 93- *Personal Data:* b Cambridge, Mass, May 7, 33; m 56, Barbara Beers; c Kristen R & Lisanne R. *Educ:* Yale Univ, BS, 55; Cornell Univ, MD, 59; Am Bd Path, dipl, 64. *Prof Exp:* Intern path, NY Hosp-Cornell Med Ctr, 59-60; asst, Med Col, Cornell Univ, 60-62, from instr to asst prof, 62-65; asst prof, Med Ctr, Duke Univ, 65-70; assoc prof, Sch Med, Univ Wis-Madison, 70-72, chmn dept, 72-74, prof path, 72-79; dir, Kidney Disease Inst, 79-81; actg dir, NY State Dept Health, Lab Med Inst, 80, dep dir, Div Lab, 81-82; chief of staff, Univ Mich Med Sch, 82-84, prof path, 82-89, staff pathologist, Vet Admin Med Ctr, 84-89. *Concurrent Pos:* USPHS trainee, 60-63; asst pathologist, NY Hosp, 60-63, asst attend pathologist, 63-65; consult pathologist, Nat Nephrotic Sydrome Study & Adult Glomerula Dis Study. *Mem:* Renal Path Soc; Am Col Physician Execs; Am Soc Nephrol; Int Soc Path; Int Soc Nephrol; Am Soc Clin Path; Col Am Path; Am Soc Investigative Path; AMA. *Res:* Experimental pathology; immunochemistry of serum complement; immunohistochemistry and electron microscopy of renal disease. *Mailing Add:* 7248 N Red Ledge Dr 2601 E Roosevelt PO Box 5099 Paradise Valley AZ 85253. *Fax:* 602-267-5406

BURKHOLDER, TIMOTHY JAY, VERTEBRATE PHYSIOLOGY. *Current Pos:* PROF BIOL, TAYLOR UNIV, 70- *Personal Data:* b Orrville, Ohio, Jan 15, 41; m 64, Carolyn Williamson; c Joleen, Alison & Andrew. *Educ:* Taylor Univ, BA, 63; Ohio State Univ, MS, 65, PhD(biol sci), 70. *Prof Exp:* Instr biol, Wooster High Sch, 65-67. *Mem:* Sigma Xi; Am Sci Affiliation; Nat Asn Biol Teachers; Creation Res Soc. *Res:* Comparative anatomic innervation of the mammalian heart; relation of serum calcium levels to the reproductive cycle and egg production of the red-winged blackbird, Agelaius Phoeniceus. *Mailing Add:* Dept Biol Taylor Univ 500 W Reade Ave Upland IN 46989-1001. *Fax:* 765-998-4940

BURKHOLDER, WENDELL EUGENE, ENTOMOLOGY. *Current Pos:* from asst prof to assoc prof, 67-70, prof entom, 75-96, EMER PROF, UNIV WIS-MADISON, 96- *Personal Data:* b Octavia, Nebr, June 24, 28; m 51, Leona Flory; c Paul, Anne, Joseph & Stephen. *Educ:* McPherson Col, AB, 50;

Univ Nebr, MSc, 56; Univ Wis, PhD(entom), 67. *Honors & Awards:* C V Riley Achievement Award in Entomol, 88. *Prof Exp:* Entomologist, USDA, 56-96. *Mem:* Entom Soc Am; Soc Invert Path; AAAS; Sigma Xi; Int Soc Chem Ecol. *Res:* Insect pheromones; reproductive biology; sex attractants; insect behavior; dermestid beetles, stored grain insects and other stored product insects; insect management technology. *Mailing Add:* Dept Entom Univ Wis Madison WI 53706. *E-Mail:* burkhold@entomolgy.wisc.edu

BURKI, NAUSHERWAN KHAN, INTERNAL MEDICINE, PHYSIOLOGY & PULMONARY MEDICINE. *Current Pos:* PROF INTERNAL MED & CHIEF PULMONARY DIV, KY MED CTR. *Educ:* Univ Pakistan, MD; London Univ, Eng, PhD(med). *Concurrent Pos:* Chief exec officer, SKM Cancer Hosp & Res Ctr, Lohore, Pakistan, 95-96. *Mem:* Am Thoracic Soc; Am Col Chest Physicians; Med Res Soc Eng; Cent Soc Clin Res; Am Physiol Soc; Am Col Physicians; fel Col Physicians & Surgeons Pakistan. *Res:* High altitude studies. *Mailing Add:* Pulmonary Div Ky Med Ctr 800 Rose St Lexington KY 40536. *Fax:* 606-323-1020

BURKLE, JOSEPH S, NUCLEAR MEDICINE. *Current Pos:* RETIRED. *Personal Data:* b Philadelphia, Pa, July 28, 19; m 44; c 3. *Educ:* Univ Pa, AB, 40, MD, 43; Am Bd Internal Med, dipl, 55 & 77; Am Bd Nuclear Med, dipl, 72. *Prof Exp:* Intern, US Naval Hosp, Pa, US Navy, 44, resident med, Pa Hosp, 47-48, resident med, US Naval Hosp, Pa, 50-51, clin & lab instr, Radioisotope Lab, St Albans, NY, 56-60, mem staff, Bethesda, Md, 60-63, & US Naval Sta Hosp, 63-66, cmndg officer, Armed Forces Radiobiol Res Inst, Defense Atomic Support Agency, 66-67; chmn, Dept Nuclear Med, York Hosp, 67-; asst clin prof med, Univ Md, 70- *Concurrent Pos:* Adj prof, Millersville State Col & Harrisburg Community Col; staff, Dept Nuclear Med, Harrisburg Hosp; pres, Am Col Nuclear Med, 87-88, Penna Col Nuclear Med, site visitor, Joint Rev Comt; radiation mgt consult, 87- *Mem:* AMA; fel Am Col Physicians; Soc Nuclear Med; fel Am Col Nuclear Med. *Res:* Internal medicine; nuclear medicine; ultrasound. *Mailing Add:* 75 Bridlewood Way York PA 17402

BURKLEY, RICHARD M, RESEARCH ADMINISTRATION. *Current Pos:* dir, 81-86, VPRES, AUTO-TROL, 86- *Personal Data:* b Pittsburgh, Pa, Sept 5, 41; m 65; c 5. *Educ:* Georgetown Univ, BS, 61; Ohio State Univ, MS, 63. *Prof Exp:* Physicist, David Taylor Model Basin, US Navy, 60-63; programmer, IBM, 64-68, mgr, 68-81. *Concurrent Pos:* Lectr, Univ Calif, Los Angeles, 69-70. *Mem:* Asn Comput Mach; Nat Comput Graphic Asn; Am Inst Maintenance. *Mailing Add:* 1333 Marble Dr Boulder CO 80303

BURKMAN, ALLAN MAURICE, TOXICOLOGY, PHARMACY. *Current Pos:* from assoc prof to prof, 66-95, chmn div, 78-87 & 94-95, EMER PROF PHARMACOL, OHIO STATE UNIV, 95- *Personal Data:* b Waterbury, Conn, Apr 23, 32; m 65, Katherine Horween; c David Eric & Deborah Rae. *Educ:* Univ Conn, BS, 54; Ohio State Univ, MSc, 55, PhD(pharmacol), 58. *Honors & Awards:* Mead Johnson Award for Undergrad Res Direction, 65. *Prof Exp:* Teaching asst pharmacol, Ohio State Univ, 54-57; asst prof, Univ Ill, 58-63; assoc prof, Butler Univ, 63-66. *Concurrent Pos:* Fel, Am Found Pharmaceut Educ, 57-58; vis prof, Univ Utah, 81-82, Univ Cent Venezuela, 94. *Mem:* Am Pharmaceut Asn; Soc Exp Biol & Med; Am Soc Pharmacol & Exp Therapeut. *Res:* Bioassay and drug screening methods development; emetic and antiemetic mechanism; drug-receptor theory. *Mailing Add:* Div Pharmacol Col Pharm Ohio State Univ Columbus OH 43210-1214

BURKMAN, ERNEST, SCHOOL IMPROVEMENT, TEXTBOOK DESIGN. *Current Pos:* from asst prof to assoc prof, 60-67, head dept, 65-67, PROF SCI EDUC & INST SYST, FLA STATE UNIV, 66- *Personal Data:* b Detroit, Mich, Oct 4, 29; m 54; c 4. *Educ:* Eastern Mich Univ, BS, 52; Univ Mich, MS, 56, MA, 59, EdD(ed), 62. *Honors & Awards:* Fulbright lectr, Uruguay, 75. *Prof Exp:* Teacher high sch, Mich, 55-60. *Concurrent Pos:* Consult sci curric develop, var sch systs, 60-90; co-dir, Turkish Nat High Sch Sci Proj, Ford, 62-65; regional consult, Biol Sci Curric Study, 62-63; consult, Ministries Educ Turkey, 62-65, Philippines, 67-68, Uruguay, 75, Saudi Arabia, 78, Botswana, 87-89, Egypt, 94, US Dept Defense, 69, 71, 77, Arthur Andersen & Co, 85; dir, NSF Intermediate Sci Curric Study, 66-71; dir, Educ Res Inst, Fla State Univ, 70-72 & Div Instrnl Design, 72-74; dir, NSF Individualized Sci Instrnl Syst Proj, 72-85. *Mem:* Fel AAAS; Nat Asn Biol Teachers; Nat Sci Teachers Asn; Nat Asn Res Sci Teaching. *Res:* Science curriculum development; science education; school improvement; textbook design. *Mailing Add:* 865 Maderia Circle Tallahassee FL 32312

BURKS, CHRISTIAN, BIOINFORMATICS, COMPUTATIONAL BIOLOGY. *Current Pos:* DIR BIOINFORMATICS, EXELIXIS PHARMACEUT INC, 97- *Personal Data:* b Wash, DC, Mar 23, 54; m 76, Janet Moody; c Caitlin & Marcail. *Educ:* St Johns Col, Santa Fe, BA, 76; Yale Univ, PhD(molecular biol), 82. *Prof Exp:* Postdoctoral fel, Los Alamos Nat Lab, 82-84, staff mem, 84-90, group leader theoret biol & biophys, 90-93, prog mgr computational biol, 93-97. *Mem:* AAAS; Biophys Soc. *Res:* Pattern recognition in nucleotide sequences; development of databases pertinent to molecular biology; assembly of genomic maps and sequences. *Mailing Add:* Los Alamos Nat Lab PO Box 1663 T-10 MS K710 Los Alamos NM 87545. *E-Mail:* cb@t10.lanl.gov

BURKS, JAMES KENNETH, endocrinology, biochemistry, for more information see previous edition

BURKS, STERLING LEON, ECOLOGY, LIMNOLOGY. *Current Pos:* Res assoc water pollution, 69-70, from asst prof to assoc prof, 71-83, PROF ZOOL, OKLA STATE UNIV, 83-, DIR ANALYTICAL LAB RESERVOIR RES CTR, 70-, DIR, OKLA STATE UNIV WATER QUAL RES LAB, 80- *Personal Data:* b Reydon, Okla, Mar 3, 38. *Educ:* Southwestern State Col, Okla, BS, 63; Okla State Univ, MS, 65, PhD(zool), 69. *Concurrent Pos:* Fel, Fed Water Pollution Control Admin, US Dept Interior, 68-70, proj dir, Off Water Resources Res, 70-72. *Mem:* Water Pollution Control Fedn; Am Chem Soc; Soc Environ Toxicol & Anal Chem. *Res:* Identification of fish toxicants in surface waters with gas chromatography, mass spectrometry and atomic absorption spectrophotometry; determination of effects of chemical contaminants upon aquatic organisms. *Mailing Add:* Dept Zool Okla State Univ Stillwater OK 74078-0001

BURKS, THOMAS F, PHARMACOLOGY. *Current Pos:* prof & head, Pharmacol, 77-84, ASSOC DEAN RES, COL MED, UNIV ARIZ, 84- *Personal Data:* b Houston, Tex, Apr 3, 38; m 62; c 2. *Educ:* Univ Tex, BS, 62, MS, 64; Univ Iowa, PhD(pharmacol), 67. *Prof Exp:* From instr to assoc prof pharmacol, Sch Med, Univ NMex, 67-71; from assoc prof to prof pharmacol, Univ Tex Med Sch, Houston, 74-77. *Concurrent Pos:* USPHS fel, Nat Inst Med Res, Eng, 67-68; USPHS res grant, 69- *Mem:* Am Soc Pharmacol & Exp Therapeut; Am Fedn Clin Res; Soc Exp Biol & Med; AAAS; Am Heart Asn. *Res:* Pharmacology of peripheral and central neuro transmission; mode of action of narcotic analgesic agents. *Mailing Add:* Univ Tex Health Sci Ctr PO Box 20036 DCT17015 Houston TX 77225. *Fax:* 713-792-4908

BURKSTRAND, JAMES MICHAEL, SURFACE PHYSICS. *Current Pos:* staff scientist, 81-82, DIR MKT, PHYS ELECTRONICS DIV, PERKIN-ELMER CORP, 82- *Personal Data:* b Philadelphia, Pa, Jan 29, 46; m 67; c 2. *Educ:* Rensselaer Polytech Inst, BS, 67; Univ Ill, Urbana, MS, 69, PhD(physics), 72. *Prof Exp:* Staff res physicist, Gen Motors Res Labs, 72-81. *Mem:* Am Vacuum Soc; Am Phys Soc; Sigma Xi. *Res:* Experimental investigation of chemical and electronic properties of solid surfaces and interfaces and the application of this information to the solution of technological problems. *Mailing Add:* Phys Electron 6509 Flying Cloud Dr Eden Prairie MN 55344. *Fax:* 612-828-6322

BURKWALL, MORRIS PATON, JR, FOOD CHEMISTRY, FOOD SCIENCE & TECHNOLOGY. *Current Pos:* Group leader food chem, Quaker Oats Co, 66-70, sr group leader, 70-71, sect mgr semi-moist pet foods, 71-72, sect mgr dog food res, 72-75, mgr, 75-77, sr mgr, explor pet foods, 77-90, SR MGR, TECHNOL DEVELOP, JOHN STUART RES LAB, QUAKER OATS CO, 90- *Personal Data:* b Kansas City, Mo, May 16, 39; m 63, Mary K Bayfield; c Karen (Johnson), Katherine (Ciscon) & John. *Educ:* Fla State Univ, BS, 61; Univ Minn, MS, 63, PhD(biochem), 66. *Honors & Awards:* Sherwood Award, Am Asn Cereal Chem, 64. *Concurrent Pos:* Facilitator, Off Innovation, 91- *Mem:* Am Chem Soc; Inst Food Technol; Am Asn Cereal Chem; Asn Mgrs Innovation. *Res:* Biochemical modification of meat and cereal byproducts; theory of flavor and palatability; microstability of semi-moist foods and pet foods; toxicology of food ingredients; founded office of Innovation-turn raw ideas into sponsored new product entities; awarded 13 US patents and many international patents. *Mailing Add:* 456 W Oakwood Dr Barrington IL 60010. *Fax:* 847-304-2392

BURKY, ALBERT JOHN, PHYSIOLOGICAL ECOLOGY. *Current Pos:* from asst prof to assoc prof, 73-90, PROF BIOL, UNIV DAYTON, 91- *Personal Data:* b Utica, NY, June 30, 42; m 70; c 4. *Educ:* Hartwick Col, BA, 64; Syracuse Univ, PhD(zool), 69. *Prof Exp:* Vis asst prof zool, Syracuse Univ, 69; fel, Cent Univ Venezuela, 69-70; instr biol, Case Western Reserve Univ, 71-73. *Mem:* AAAS; Am Soc Zoologists; Ecol Soc Am; Am Malacol Union; Malacol Soc London. *Res:* Physiological ecology of freshwater clams, snails and terrestrial snails; energy budgets of natural populations, especially growth, reproduction and metabolism, and the physiological metabolic adaptations to environmental conditions. *Mailing Add:* Dept Biol Univ Dayton 300 College Park Dayton OH 45469-0001

BURLAGA, LEONARD F, PHYSICS, ASTROPHYSICS. *Current Pos:* Nat Acad Sci-Nat Res Coun res assoc, 66-68, ASTROPHYSICIST, GODDARD SPACE FLIGHT CTR, NASA, 68- *Personal Data:* b Superior, Wis, Oct 1, 38; m, Catherine M McDonough; c 2. *Educ:* Univ Chicago, BS, 60; Univ Minn, MS, 62, PhD(physics), 66. *Honors & Awards:* Except Sci Achievement Medal, NASA, 79; Lindsay Award, 88. *Prof Exp:* From teaching asst to teaching assoc physics, Univ Minn, 60-63 res assoc, 63-66. *Concurrent Pos:* Goddard sr fel, 88. *Mem:* Am Geophys Union; Int Astron Union. *Res:* Interplanetary medium; propagation of cosmic rays. *Mailing Add:* Code 692 NASA Goddard Space Flight Ctr Greenbelt MD 20771

BURLAND, DONALD MAXWELL, ORGANIC OPTICAL MATERIALS. *Current Pos:* res staff mem chem, IBM Almaden Res Ctr, 71-80, mgr optical mat physics, 80-82, mgr rec media, 82-83, mgr electrophotography, IBM Res Lab, 83-89, MGR NONLINEAR OPTICAL MAT, IBM ALMADEN RES CTR, SAN JOSE, CALIF, 89- *Personal Data:* b La Jolla, Calif, Sept 14, 43; m 68, Jan E Leary; c 1. *Educ:* Dartmouth Col, AB, 65; Calif Inst Technol, PhD(chem & physics), 70. *Prof Exp:* Asst physics, Univ Leiden, Neth, 70-71. *Mem:* Fel Am Phys Soc; Am Chem Soc; Optical Soc Am; AAAS. *Res:* Physics of energy and charge transport in molecular crystals and amorphous solids; holographic techniques to investigate solid state photochemistry; materials for electrophotography; organic nonlinear optical materials; slow relaxation processes in polymers. *Mailing Add:* IBM Almaden Res Ctr Dept K13/E1 650 Harry Rd San Jose CA 95120-6099. *Fax:* 408-927-3310; *E-Mail:* burland@almaden.ibm.com

BURLANT, WILLIAM JACK, ORGANIC CHEMISTRY. *Current Pos:* AT GAF CORP. *Personal Data:* b Chicago, Ill, Oct 20, 28; m 55; c 2. *Educ:* City Col New York, BS, 49; Brooklyn Col, MA, 51; Polytech Inst Brooklyn, PhD(chem), 55. *Prof Exp:* USPHS asst, Brooklyn Col, 50-52, instr org & gen chem, 53-54; Res Corp asst, Polytech Inst Brooklyn, 52-53; instr org & gen chem, Cooper Union, 54-55; chemist, Sci Lab, Ford Motor Co, 55, mgr res staff, Mat Applications Dept, 55-69, asst dir chem sci, 69-79, exec engr, 72-79; mgr technol opers, Gen Elec Co, 79-; tech dir, Kendall Co, 81- *Mem:* Am Chem Soc. *Res:* Radiation chemistry of organic systems; structure and properties of polymers; plastic applications; composites. *Mailing Add:* 38 Lockly Ct Wayne NJ 07470

BURLEIGH, BRUCE DANIEL, JR, BIOCHEMISTRY, PROTEIN CHEMISTRY. *Current Pos:* RES MGR/SR RES SCIENTIST, MALLINCKRODT INC, 92- *Personal Data:* b Augusta, Ga, June 23, 42; div; c Michael E. *Educ:* Carnegie-Mellon Univ, BS, 64; Univ Mich, MS, 67, PhD(biochem), 70. *Prof Exp:* Vis scholar molecular biol, Med Res Coun Lab, Cambridge, Eng, 70-72, res staff, 72-73; asst prof biochem, M D Anderson Hosp & Tumor Inst, Univ Tex Systs Cancer Ctr & Grad Sch Biomed Sci, 73-79, assoc biochemist, 80-81; res scientist, Int Minerals & Chem Corp, 81-83, sr res scientist, 83-87; prin res scientist, Pitman-Moore Inc, 88-92. *Concurrent Pos:* Am Cancer Soc fel, 70-72; adj assoc prof biochem, Sch Med, Ind Univ, 88- *Mem:* AAAS; Am Chem Soc; Am Soc Biochem & Molecular Biol; Endocrine Soc; Sigma Xi. *Res:* Structure and function of peptide hormones; hormonal control of cell states; animal growth regulation; hormone-receptor studies; medical imaging. *Mailing Add:* Discovery Res Mallinckrodt Med Inc 675 McDonnell Blvd Box 5840 St Louis MO 63134. *Fax:* 314-895-8938; *E-Mail:* bdburle@mkg.com

BURLEIGH, JAMES REYNOLDS, PLANT PATHOLOGY, GENETICS. *Current Pos:* RES PLANT PATHOLOGIST, SCI & EDUC ADMIN-AGR RES, USDA, 64-; ASSOC PROF PLANT SIC, CALIF STATE UNIV, CHICO, 71- *Personal Data:* b Fresno, Calif, Sept 6, 36; m 59; c 4. *Educ:* Fresno State Col, BS, 58; Wash State Univ, MS, 62, PhD(plant path), 65. *Prof Exp:* Res asst agron, Wash State Univ, 59-61, res asst plant path, 61-64; res plant pathologist, sci & educ admin-agr res, USDA, 64- *Concurrent Pos:* Asst prof plant physiol, Kans State Univ, 64-71. *Mem:* Am Phytopath Soc; Am Mycol Soc. *Res:* Epidemiology of cereal rust diseases. *Mailing Add:* Sch Agr Calif State Univ 101 Orange St Chico CA 95929-0001

BURLEIGH, JOSEPH GAYNOR, INSECT ECOLOGY, PSYCHOLOGY. *Current Pos:* PROF ENTOM, UNIV ARK, PINE BLUFF, 72- *Personal Data:* b Crowley, La, Jan 20, 42; m 69; c Michael R & Glenn T. *Educ:* Univ Southwestern La, BS, 64; La State Univ, MS, 66, PhD(entom), 70; Univ Cent Ark, MS, 79. *Prof Exp:* Mem planning & recreation dept, La State Parks Comn, 66-68; res assoc entom, Okla State Univ, 70-72. *Concurrent Pos:* Psychotherapist, 80-97. *Mem:* Entom Soc Am. *Res:* Ecology and population dynamics of the bollworm and tobacco budworm; effects of cultural practices on soybean insects, sunflower insects; aquatic insect populations in minnow production ponds. *Mailing Add:* Dept Agr Univ Ark Pine Bluff AR 71611. *E-Mail:* burleigh_j@vx.4500.uapb.edu

BURLESON, GARY R, VIRAL IMMUNOLOGY, PULMONARY IMMUNOLOGY. *Current Pos:* IMMUNOLOGIST, MIAMI VALLEY LABS, PROCTER & GAMBLE. *Educ:* Med Col Wis, PhD(microbiol), 72. *Res:* Microbiology. *Mailing Add:* 7602 Wetherington Dr West Chester OH 45069

BURLESON, GEORGE ROBERT, EXPERIMENTAL NUCLEAR PHYSICS. *Current Pos:* assoc prof, 71-78, PROF PHYSICS, NMEX STATE UNIV, 78-, DEPT HEAD, 95- *Personal Data:* b Baton Rouge, La, Oct 12, 33; m 60, Carol Yowell; c Geoffrey & Christopher. *Educ:* La State Univ, BS, 55; Stanford Univ, MS, 57, PhD(physics), 60. *Prof Exp:* Res assoc high energy physics, Argonne Nat Lab, 60-62, asst scientist, 62-64; asst prof physics, Northwestern Univ, 64-71. *Concurrent Pos:* Vis staff mem, Los Alamos Sci Lab, 72, 73 & 74. *Mem:* Am Phys Soc; Sigma Xi. *Res:* Electron scattering at medium energies; hyperon polarization; mesonic x-rays; polarization in hadron-nucleon scattering; pion-nucleus scattering at medium energies, nucleon-nucleon interactions. *Mailing Add:* Dept Physics Box 30001 Dept 3D NMex State Univ Las Cruces NM 88003

BURLETT, DONALD JAMES, POLYMER CHEMISTRY. *Current Pos:* sr res chemist, 77-89, ASSOC SCIENTIST, RES & DEVELOP ASSOC, GOODYEAR TIRE & RUBBER CO, 89- *Personal Data:* b Orange, NJ, Dec 20, 49; m 73, Margaret. *Educ:* State Univ NY Col Oswego, BS, 71; Univ Cincinnati, PhD(org chem), 76. *Prof Exp:* Res asst org chem, Mass Inst Technol, 76-77. *Mem:* Am Chem Soc; NAm Thermal Anal Soc; Tire Soc. *Res:* Synthetic organic chemistry; polymer bound reagents; thermal analysis; heterocyclic chemistry; vulcanization chemistry; oxidation and antioxidants for polymers; reactive processing; polymer alloys. *Mailing Add:* Goodyear Tire & Rubber Co 142 Goodyear Blvd Akron OH 44305. *Fax:* 330-796-3304; *E-Mail:* djburlett@goodyear.com

BURLEY, CARLTON EDWIN, PHYSICS, NONDESTRUCTIVE EVALUATION. *Current Pos:* res scientist, 53-56, supvr physics & elec, 56-65, DIR PHYSICS & INSTRUMENTATION, METALL RES DIV, REYNOLDS METALS CO, 65- *Personal Data:* b Auburn, NY. *Educ:* Syracuse Univ, AB, 41, MS, 42, MS, 49. *Prof Exp:* Instr physics, Utica Col, Syracuse Univ, 49-53. *Concurrent Pos:* Adj fac math, Va Commonwealth Univ, 59- *Mem:* Am Phys Soc; Am Soc Metals; Am Soc Testing & Mat; fel Am Soc Non Destructive Testing; Inst Elec & Electronics Engrs. *Res:* Materials physical properties; applied mechanics; electrical and thermal properties; vacuum techniques; non destructive test development and operator training. *Mailing Add:* 8207 Metcalf Dr Richmond VA 23227

BURLEY, DAVID RICHARD, PHYSICAL CHEMISTRY, COMPUTER SCIENCE. *Current Pos:* PRES, TECHLINE, INC, 89- *Personal Data:* b Crooksville, Ohio, Nov 1, 42; m 66; c 2. *Educ:* Ohio State Univ, BS, 64; Univ Calif, PhD(phys chem), 69; Rider Col, MBA, 78. *Prof Exp:* Fel photochem, Univ Col Swansea, Wales, 69-71; head chem res, Tile Coun Am, 71-75; sr chemist, Am Cyanamid Co, 75-76, group leader, 76-78, bus planner, 78-79, mkt mgr, 79-81, bus mgr, 81-89. *Mem:* Am Chem Soc; Int Soc Pharmaceut Engrs. *Res:* Photochemistry; surface chemistry; chemical technology; management. *Mailing Add:* 652 Beechwood Lane Butler NJ 07405

BURLEY, GORDON, ENVIRONMENTAL CHEMISTRY, SCIENCE ADMINISTRATION. *Current Pos:* RETIRED. *Personal Data:* b Giessen, Ger, Feb 15, 25; nat US; m 57, 72, Cynthia Stafford. *Educ:* Temple Univ, AB, 48; Univ Md, MS, 52; Georgetown Univ, PhD, 62. *Prof Exp:* Res assoc, Geophys Lab, Carnegie Inst Wash, 50-52; phys chemist, Nat Bur Stand, 52-67; sr scientist, Div Reactor Licensing, US AEC, 67-72; br chief, US Environ Protection Agency, 72-79, dep div dir, 79-81, actg dir, 81-82, sci adv, Off Radiation Progs, 82-94; consult, 94-96. *Mem:* Am Chem Soc. *Res:* Solid state chemistry; environmental radiation standards; mathematical models; transuranium elements; science policy. *Mailing Add:* 4620 N Park Ave Apt 807W Chevy Chase MD 20815-4553

BURLEY, J WILLIAM ATKINSON, plant physiology, agricultural research, for more information see previous edition

BURLEY, NANCY, EVOLUTION OF BEHAVIOR, SEXUAL SELECTION. *Current Pos:* PROF ECOL, UNIV CALIF, IRVINE, 92- *Personal Data:* b Syracuse, NY, July 5, 49. *Educ:* Syracuse Univ, BS, 71; Univ Cincinnati, MS, 73; Univ Tex, Austin, PhD(zool), 77. *Prof Exp:* Asst prof biol, McGill Univ, 77-79; asst prof, 79-84, assoc prof ecol, Ethology & Evolution, Univ Ill, Urbana-Champaign, 84-91. *Concurrent Pos:* Assoc prof scientist, Ill Nat Hist Surv, 85- *Mem:* AAAS; Animal Behav Soc; Soc Study Evolution; Am Soc Naturalists; Am Ornithologists Union. *Res:* Evolution of behavior; sexual selection theory; experimental investigation of male choice in monogamous species of birds; sex-ratio manipulation. *Mailing Add:* Dept Ecol Univ Calif Irvine CA 92717-0001

BURLEY, STEPHEN KEVIN, BIOPHYSICS. *Current Pos:* from asst prof to assoc prof, 90-94, PROF HEAD LAB, ROCKEFELLER UNIV, 94-; INVESTR, HOWARD HUGHES MED INST, 94- *Personal Data:* b London, Eng, Nov 13, 57. *Educ:* Univ Western Ont, BSc, 80; Harvard Med Sch, MD, 87; Univ Oxford, PhD, 83. *Prof Exp:* Postdoctoral res fel protein crystallog, Dept Chem, Harvard Univ, 87-90; intern internal med, Brigham & Women's Hosp, Harvard Med Sch, 87-88, resident, 88-90. *Concurrent Pos:* Rhodes scholar, 80; Nat Sci & Eng Res Coun Can res fel, 80 & 84-86; W R Grace Found Res fel, 86-90; Medical Found Inc res fel, 88-87; chair elect, Synchrotron Radiation Spec Interest Group, Am Crystallog Asn, 96. *Mem:* Am Crystallog Asn; Biophys Soc; NY Acad Sci; Can Soc Biochemists; fel Royal Soc Can. *Res:* Author numerous publications. *Mailing Add:* Lab Molecular Biophysics Howard Hughes Med Inst Rockefeller Univ 1230 York Ave Box 78 New York NY 10021-6399. *Fax:* 212-327-8337; *E-Mail:* burley@rockvax.rockefeller.edu

BURLING, JAMES P, MATHEMATICS. *Current Pos:* PROF MATH, STATE UNIV NY, COL OSWEGO, 65- *Personal Data:* b Baltimore, Md, May 29, 30; m 61; c 2. *Educ:* Grinnell Col, BA, 52; State Univ NY, Albany, MA, 57; Univ Colo, PhD(math), 65. *Prof Exp:* High sch teacher, NY, 55-56; asst prof math, State Univ NY, Col Oneonta, 57-60. *Mem:* AAAS; Math Asn Am; Am Math Soc. *Res:* Coloring problems of families of convex bodies. *Mailing Add:* Dept Math State Univ NY Col Oswego NY 13126

BURLING, RONALD WILLIAM, OCEANOGRAPHY. *Current Pos:* RETIRED. *Personal Data:* b Masterton, NZ, Aug 4, 20; m 48; c 1. *Educ:* Univ NZ, BSc, 49, MSc, 50; Univ London, PhD(meteorol), 55. *Prof Exp:* Scientist, Oceanog Observ, Dept Sci & Indust Res, NZ, 49-51; mem staff, Nat Inst Oceanog, Eng, 53-55; scientist, Oceanog Observ, Dept Sci & Indust Res, NZ, 55-60; from asst prof to assoc prof phys & dynamical oceanog, Univ BC, 60-67, prof oceanog, Dept Oceanog, 67-85. *Res:* Physical and dynamical oceanography; air sea interaction; transfer of momentum, energy, heat and water vapor across the sea surface; inlet studies; carbon dioxide in the ocean. *Mailing Add:* 1881 Allison Rd Vancouver BC V6T 1T1 Can

BURLINGAME, ALMA L, PHYSICAL CHEMISTRY, BIOCHEMISTRY. *Current Pos:* Res chemist, Space Sci Lab, 63-84, DIR, BIOMED & ENVIRON MASS SPECTROMETRY RESOURCE, UNIV CALIF, BERKELEY, 73- *Personal Data:* b Cranston, RI, Apr 29, 37; div; c 2. *Educ:* Univ RI, BS, 59; Mass Inst Technol, PhD(chem), 62. *Concurrent Pos:* Mem, Lunar Sample Anal Planning Team & Lunar Sample Preliminary Exam Team, NASA Johnson Space Ctr, 69-73; Guggenheim fel, 70-71; prof pharmaceut chem & chem, Univ Calif, San Francisco, 78- *Mem:* Fel AAAS; Am Chem Soc; Am Soc Mass Spectrometry; Am Soc Biochem & Molecular Biol. *Res:* Development of mass spectrometry; elucidation of organic molecular structures and biological macromolecules; applications to biomedical and environmental problems; molecular basis of xenobiotic substances toxicity; sequencing of proteins and study of post-translational modifications; structures of glycoconjugates. *Mailing Add:* Dept Pharmaceut Chem Univ Calif San Francisco CA 94143-0446

BURLINGTON, D BRUCE, HEALTH SCIENCES. *Current Pos:* res fel biol prog, Food & Drug Admin, chief, Respiratory Virus Lab, dir, Div Biol Invest New Drugs, dep dir, Off Drug Eval II, Ctr Drug Eval & Res, 88-93, DIR, CTR DEVICES & RADIOL HEALTH, FOOD & DRUG ADMIN, 93- *Educ:* La State Univ, MD, 75. *Prof Exp:* Intern internal med & infectious dis, Univ Colo. *Concurrent Pos:* Actg dir, Off Generic Drugs, Food & Drug Admin, dep dir, Med Affairs Ctr. *Mailing Add:* Ctr Devices & Radiol Health Dept Health & Human Serv 12720 Twinbrook Pkwy Rockville MD 20857

BURLINGTON, HAROLD, PHYSIOLOGY. *Current Pos:* PROF PHYSIOL & BIOPHYS, MT SINAI SCH MED, 68- *Personal Data:* b Yonkers, NY, June 26, 25. *Educ:* Franklin & Marshall Col, BS, 48; Syracuse Univ, MS, 49, PhD(physiol), 51. *Prof Exp:* Asst zool, Syracuse Univ, 48-51; instr physiol, NY State Col Med, Syracuse, 51-55; from asst prof to prof, Col Med, Univ Cincinnati, 55-68. *Mem:* AAAS; Am Physiol Soc; NY Acad Sci. *Res:* Cellular metabolism; regulation of growth and function. *Mailing Add:* Dept Physiol Mt Sinai Sch Med One Gustave Levy Plaza New York NY 10029-6504

BURLINGTON, ROY FREDERICK, ENVIRONMENTAL PHYSIOLOGY. *Current Pos:* PROF BIOL, CENT MICH UNIV, 70- *Personal Data:* b South Bend, Ind, Oct 2, 36; m 59; c 3. *Educ:* Purdue Univ, BS, 59, MS, 61, PhD(environ physiol), 64. *Prof Exp:* Res physiologist, US Army Res Inst Environ Med, 66-70. *Mem:* Am Soc Zoologists; Am Physiol Soc. *Res:* Effects of pollution on aquatic invertebrate populations; hypoxic tolerance in and cellular physiology of hibernating mammals; effects of starvation on intermediary metabolism; myocardial metabolism and nutrition at high altitude. *Mailing Add:* Dept Biol Cent Mich Univ Mt Pleasant MI 48859-0001

BURLITCH, JAMES MICHAEL, MATERIALS CHEMISTRY, CERAMIC PRECURSORS. *Current Pos:* from asst prof to assoc prof, 65-94, PROF INORG CHEM, CORNELL UNIV, 94- *Personal Data:* b Wheeling, WVa. *Educ:* Wheeling Col, BS, 60; Mass Inst Technol, PhD(inorg chem), 65. *Prof Exp:* Postdoctoral assoc, Mass Inst Technol, 64-65. *Concurrent Pos:* Alfred P Sloan found fel, 70-72. *Mem:* Am Chem Soc. *Res:* Inorganic chemistry of materials; syntheses of ceramics with geological value and technological interest; metal-ceramic adhesion; metal-ceramic composites; optical ceramics; nanophase materials. *Mailing Add:* Dept Chem Baker Lab Cornell Univ Ithaca NY 14853-1301

BURMAN, KENNETH DALE, MEDICINE. *Current Pos:* RETIRED. *Personal Data:* b St Louis, Mo, Aug 9, 44; m 72; c 5. *Educ:* Wash Univ, AB, 66; Univ Mo, MD, 70. *Honors & Awards:* Van Meter Award, Am Thyroid Asn, 75; Young Investr Award, Am Fedn Clin Res, 75. *Prof Exp:* House officer internal med, Barnes Hosp, Washington Univ Med Ctr, St Louis, Mo, 70-72; endocrine fel, Walter Reed Army Med Ctr, 72-74, staff endocrine, 74-91, chief endocrine, 91-94c. *Concurrent Pos:* Consult nutrit, Surgeon Gen US Army, 75-; prof, Uniformed Serv Univ Health Sci, Bethesda, Md, 77-; chmn, Future Meetings Comt, Endocrine Soc, 88- *Mem:* Endocrine Soc; Am Thyroid Asn; Am Soc Clin Invest. *Res:* Clinical immunology and molecular biology processes involved in the genesis and propogation of thyroid diseases. *Mailing Add:* Sect Endocrinol Wash Hosp Ctr 110 Irving St NW Washington DC 20010

BURMAN, ROBERT L, NUCLEAR PHYSICS. *Current Pos:* staff mem, 68-81, FEL, LOS ALAMOS NAT LAB, 81- *Personal Data:* b Chicago, Ill, June 13, 33; m 56; c 3. *Educ:* Mass Inst Technol, BS, 55; Univ Ill, MS, 57, PhD(physics), 61. *Prof Exp:* NSF fel, Bohr Inst Theoret Physics, Copenhagen, Denmark, 61-62, Ford Found fel, 62-63; asst prof physics, Univ Rochester, 63-68. *Mem:* Fel Am Phys Soc. *Res:* Beta decay; nucleon-nucleon forces; pion-nucleus interactions; neutrino physics; gamma ray astrophysics. *Mailing Add:* Los Alamos Nat Lab P-Div MS 846 Los Alamos NM 87545. *E-Mail:* burman@lanl.gov

BURMAN, SUDHIR, HIGH PERFORMANCE LIQUID CHROMATOGRAPHY, PROTEIN SCIENCE. *Current Pos:* assoc sr investr, 88-93, sr investr, 93-97, ASST DIR, SMITH KLINE BEECHAM PHARMACEUT, 97- *Personal Data:* b Farrukhabad, India, July 17, 55; m 82, Sneh; c Bharat & Deeya. *Educ:* Univ Delhi, BS, 74; Indian Inst Technol, Delhi, MS, 76; Indian Inst Sci, Bangalore, PhD(chem), 81. *Prof Exp:* Fel chem, Drexel Univ, Philadelphia, 80-82; res assoc, Univ Va, Charlottesville, 82-85 & Cornell Univ Med Col, NY, 85-88. *Concurrent Pos:* Instr, Drexel Univ, 80-82. *Mem:* Am Soc Biochem & Molecular Biol; Am Chem Soc; Protein Soc. *Res:* Development of high performance liquid chromatography based analytical methods for the characterization of biopharmaceuticals from recombinant sources; solution properties-aggregation and degradation of proteins; elucidation of primary structure of proteins. *Mailing Add:* Smith Kline Beecham Pharmaceut PO Box 1539 King of Prussia PA 19406. *Fax:* 610-270-6727

BURMEISTER, HARLAND RENO, microbiology, for more information see previous edition

BURMEISTER, JOHN LUTHER, INORGANIC CHEMISTRY. *Current Pos:* from asst prof to assoc prof, Univ Del, 64-69, assoc dir, Ctr Catalytic Sci & Technol, 77-79, prof chem, 73-93, ASSOC CHMN, DEPT CHEM & BIOCHEM, UNIV DEL, 74-, ALUMNI DISTINGUISHED PROF, 93- *Personal Data:* b Fountain Springs, Pa, Feb 20, 38; m 60, Doris A Crawford; c Lisa A & Jeffrey S. *Educ:* Franklin & Marshall Col, BS, 59; Northwestern Univ, PhD(coord chem), 64. *Honors & Awards:* Catalyst Award, Chem Mfrs Asn, 81. *Prof Exp:* Instr inorg chem, Univ Ill, 63-64. *Concurrent Pos:* Mem ed bd, Inorganica Chimica Acta & Synthesis & Reactivity in Inorg & Metalorg Chem; exec secy, Intercollegiate Student Chemists, 68-71; consult, Sun Oil Co, 69-74, AMP, Inc, 71-73 & Control Data Corp, 81-85; secy-treas, Inorg Chem Div, Am Chem Soc, 75-77. *Mem:* Am Chem Soc; Sigma Xi. *Res:* Coordination chemistry of ambidentate ligands; inorganic linkage isomerism; generation and stabilization of unusual oxidation states; synthesis of metal-ylide complexes. *Mailing Add:* Dept Chem & Biochem Univ Del Newark DE 19716. *Fax:* 302-831-6335; *E-Mail:* john.burmeister@mvs.udel.edu

BURMEISTER, LOUIS C, MECHANICAL ENGINEERING, HEAT TRANSFER. *Current Pos:* from asst prof to assoc prof, 66-76, PROF MECH ENG, UNIV KANS, 76- *Personal Data:* b Great Bend, Kans, July 20, 35; m 59; c 1. *Educ:* Kans State Univ, BS, 57, MS, 59; Purdue Univ, PhD(mech eng), 66. *Prof Exp:* Mech engr, Sandia Corp, NMex, 59-62. *Mem:* Am Soc Mech Engrs; Sigma Xi. *Res:* Effect of pressure fluctuations on film boiling; spray production through use of strong, nonuniform electric fields; transient pressure effects on convective heat transfer in a cylinder. *Mailing Add:* 2604 Stratford Rd Lawrence KS 66049-2844

BURMEISTER, ROBERT ALFRED, MATERIALS SCIENCE, SOLID STATE PHYSICS. *Current Pos:* HEAD MAT RES DEPT, HEWLETT-PACKARD LABS, 65- *Personal Data:* b Milwaukee, Wis, Dec 28, 39; m 66. *Educ:* Univ Wis, BS, 61; Stanford Univ, MS, 62, PhD(mat sci), 65. *Prof Exp:* Asst mat res, Stanford Univ, 61-65. *Concurrent Pos:* Mem tech staff, Bell Tel Labs, NJ, 63; lectr, Stanford Univ & Univ Calif; mem, Solid State Sci Adv Panel, Nat Res Coun. *Mem:* Am Phys Soc; Am Inst Mining, Metall & Petrol Engrs; Inst Elec & Electronics Engrs; Electrochem Soc. *Res:* Electronic materials of elemental and compound semiconductors, optical and magnetic materials; measurement of optical and electrical transport properties; physical property measurements; solid state devices. *Mailing Add:* Saratoga Tech Assoc 12520 Saratoga Creek Dr Saratoga CA 95070

BURN, IAN, CERAMICS. *Current Pos:* SR RES ASSOC, DUPONT CO, 83- *Personal Data:* b Dewsbury, Eng, Nov 25, 37; US citizen; m 61; c 2. *Educ:* Durham Univ, BSc, 60; Leeds Univ, PhD(ceramics), 66. *Prof Exp:* Physicist, Brit Oxygen Co Ltd, 60-62; res asst ceramics, Univ Leeds, 62-66; sr scientist, Pilkington Brothers Ltd, 66-67; sr tech staff ceramics, Sprague Elec Co, 67-83. *Concurrent Pos:* Assoc prof, North Adams State Col, 68-80. *Mem:* Brit Inst Physics; fel Am Ceramic Soc; Int Soc Hybrid Microelectronics. *Res:* Ceramic dielectrics, including interactions with base metals and glass-ceramic systems. *Mailing Add:* 9 Pierson Dr Hockessin DE 19810

BURNELL, EDWIN ELLIOTT, CHEMICAL PHYSICS, NUCLEAR MAGNETIC RESONANCE. *Current Pos:* from asst prof to assoc prof, 72-84, PROF CHEM, UNIV BC, 84- *Personal Data:* b St John's, Nfld, Dec 4, 43; m 71, C Bonnie McKnight; c Tara K, Fima J & Kevin E. *Educ:* Mem Univ Nfld, BSc, 65, MSc, 68; Bristol Univ, PhD(chem), 70. *Prof Exp:* Fel physics, Univ BC, 69-71 & Univ Basel, 71-72. *Concurrent Pos:* Sabbatical leave, Univ Utrecht, 78-79. *Mem:* Chem Inst Can. *Res:* Nuclear magnetic resonance studies of liquid crystals and of molecules partially oriented in liquid crystal solvents; understanding the intermolecular forces leading to orientational order in liquids. *Mailing Add:* Dept Chem 2036 Main Mall Univ BC Vancouver BC V6T 1Z1 Can. *Fax:* 604-822-2847; *E-Mail:* bur@nematic.chem.ubc.ca

BURNELL, JAMES MCINDOE, medicine, physiology, for more information see previous edition

BURNELL, LOUIS A, THEORETICAL CHEMISTRY. *Current Pos:* ASSOC PROF CHEM, NY UNIV, 66- *Personal Data:* b Belg, Sept 15, 28; m 55; c 2. *Educ:* Univ Liege, BSc, 50, PhD(chem), 55. *Honors & Awards:* Stas-Spring Prize, Royal Acad Belg, 55. *Prof Exp:* Researcher molecular physics, Univ Liege, 55-60, lectr, 60-63; res physicist, Res Inst Advan Study, 63-66. *Concurrent Pos:* Belg govt travel grant, 55; Brit Coun scholar, Oxford Univ, 56-57; Nat Acad Sci grant, Ind Univ & Mass Inst Technol, 59-60; expert, UNESCO, Colombia, 74- *Mem:* Am Chem Soc. *Res:* Quantum chemistry; interpretation of the electronic spectra of polyatomic molecules; theoretical problems concerned with the nature of the chemical bonds and molecular reactivity; history of science. *Mailing Add:* Casilla 8551 Guayaquil Ecuador

BURNELL, ROBERT H, ORGANIC CHEMISTRY. *Current Pos:* PROF CHEM, LAVAL UNIV, 64- *Personal Data:* b Tondu, Wales, Nov 23, 29; m 50; c 3. *Educ:* Sir George Williams Univ, BSc, 52; Univ NB, PhD(org chem), 55. *Prof Exp:* Lectr org chem, Univ West Indies, 55-62; investr nat prod, Venezuelan Inst Sci Res, 62-64. *Mem:* Chem Inst Can; The Chem Soc; Am Soc Pharmacog. *Res:* Extraction and isolation of alkaloids from plants; structure elucidation of alkaloids; synthesis of natural products, particularly the group of polyhydroxylated diterpenes. *Mailing Add:* Dept Chem Laval Univ Quebec PQ G1K 7P4 Can

BURNER, ALPHEUS WILSON, JR, FLOW VISUALIZATION, CAMERA CALIBRATION. *Current Pos:* PHYSICIST, LANGLEY RES CTR, NASA, 69- *Personal Data:* b Jacksonville, Fla, Dec 4, 47; m 68; c 2. *Educ:* Univ SC, BS, 69; Univ Rochester, MS, 76. *Mem:* Optical Soc Am. *Res:* Holographic flow visualization; video photogrammetry; video camera calibration. *Mailing Add:* Hwy 1314 Hayes VA 23072. *E-Mail:* a.w.burner@larc.nasa.gov

BURNESS, JAMES HUBERT, BIOINORGANIC CHEMISTRY. *Current Pos:* asst prof, 76-92, ASSOC PROF CHEM, PA STATE UNIV, YORK CAMPUS, 92- *Personal Data:* b Philadelphia, Pa, Nov 20, 49; m 71, Mary Regel; c Monika L & Allison N. *Educ:* Rutgers Univ, BA, 71; Va Polytech Inst & State Univ, PhD(inorg chem), 75. *Honors & Awards:* J Shelton Horsley Res Award, Va Acad Sci; Sigma Xi Res Award, 75. *Prof Exp:* Fel biophys, Mich State Univ, 75-76. *Concurrent Pos:* Vis prof, Univ Md, Munich Campus, 83-85; guest researcher, Tech Univ Munich, 83-85. *Mem:* Am Chem Soc; Sigma Xi. *Res:* Model systems for vitamin B-12 and hemoglobin; binding of oxygen to metals; x-ray photoelectron spectroscopy of transition metal complexes; platinum complexes in cancer chemotherapy; inverse gas chromatography. *Mailing Add:* Pa State Univ 1031 Edgecomb Ave York PA 17403. *Fax:* 717-771-4062; *E-Mail:* jhb3@psu.edu

BURNET, GEORGE, CHEMICAL ENGINEERING. *Current Pos:* chmn, Nuclear Eng Dept, 78-83, coordr, Eng Educ Projs Off, 78-90, ASSOC DEAN ENG, IOWA STATE UNIV, 90- *Personal Data:* b Ft Dodge, Iowa, Jan 30, 24; m 44; c 6. *Educ:* Iowa State Univ, BS, 48, MS, 49, PhD(chem eng), 51. *Honors & Awards:* Iowa Citizen Chemical Engr Award, Iowa Sect, Am Inst Chem Engrs, 70; Founders Award, Am Inst Chem Engrs, 81; Mikol Schmitz Award & Lamme Medal, Am Soc Eng Educ, 82; Grinter Award, Accreditation Bd Eng & Technol, 84. *Prof Exp:* Instr chem eng, Iowa State Univ, 50-51; process engr, Commercial Sovents Corp, Ind, 52-56; prof chem eng, Iowa State Univ, 56-61, chmn dept, 61-78; assoc eng, Ames Lab, Dept Energy, 56-61, chief chem eng div, 61-78, sr engr, 78-90. *Concurrent Pos:* Consult, Frye Mfg Co, Iowa, 57-60, Int Minerals & Chem Corp, Ill, 63-65 & Agency Int Develop higher educ prog, India, 67; Phillips lectr, Okla State Univ, 70; mem educ & accreditation comt, Engrs Coun Prof Develop, 70-77, chmn, 76-77; mem bd dirs, Engrs Joint Coun, 76-77; chmn, Educ Affairs Coun, Am Asn Eng Soc, 80-82; bd dirs, Accreditation Bd Eng & Technol, 77-83, exec comt, 81-83; US Rep Comt Educ & Training, World Fedn Eng Socs, 84-88. *Mem:* Am Chem Soc; fel Am Inst Chem Engrs; hon mem Am Soc Eng Educ (pres, 76-77); Nat Soc Prof Eng; AAAS. *Res:* Fertilizer technology; coal waste utilization; separations chemistry. *Mailing Add:* Col Eng 104 Marston Hall Iowa State Ames IA 50014

BURNETT, BRUCE BURTON, analytical chemistry, polymer physics; deceased, see previous edition for last biography

BURNETT, BRYAN REEDER, MARINE ECOLOGY, CRUSTACEAN CIRCULATORY MORPHOLOGY. *Current Pos:* FORENSIC CONSULT, 82- *Personal Data:* b Bethlehem, Pa, Aug 10, 45; m 75; c 2. *Educ:* San Diego State Univ, BS, 68, MS, 71; Scripps Inst Oceanog, Univ Calif, San Diego, MS, 75. *Prof Exp:* Sr res analyst, Univ Calif, San Diego, 75-82. *Mem:* Am Acad Forensic Sci; Am Micros Soc. *Res:* Analysis of inorganic particulates in lung tissue; analysis of gunshot residue; forensic applications of scanning electron microscopy; energy dispersive x-ray analysis. *Mailing Add:* Meixa Tech PO Box 844 Cardiff CA 92007

BURNETT, CLYDE RAY, PHYSICS. *Current Pos:* assoc prof & chmn dept, 64-70, PROF PHYSICS, FLA ATLANTIC UNIV, 70- *Personal Data:* b Nora Springs, Iowa, Dec 23, 23; m 47; c 5. *Educ:* Univ Upper Iowa, BS, 46; Univ Wis, MS, 48, PhD(physics), 51. *Prof Exp:* Asst prof physics, SDak State Col, 50-53 & Pa State Univ, 53-57; physicist, Proj Matterhorn, Princeton Univ, 57-58; assoc prof physics, Pa State Univ, 58-63; res assoc & lectr, Univ Wis, 63-64. *Mem:* Am Phys Soc; Optical Soc Am; Am Meteorol Soc; Am Asn Physics Teachers. *Res:* Atomic spectroscopy; aeronomy. *Mailing Add:* PO Box 426 Rollinsville CO 80474-0426. *Fax:* 303-467-5518

BURNETT, DONALD STACY, GEOCHEMISTRY. *Current Pos:* NSF res fel physics, Calif Inst Technol, 63-65, asst prof nuclear geochem, 65-68, assoc prof, 68-77, PROF NUCLEAR GEOCHEM, CALIF INST TECHNOL, 77- *Personal Data:* b Dayton, Ohio, June 25, 37; m 59; c 2. *Educ:* Univ Chicago, BS, 59; Univ Calif, Berkeley, PhD(chem), 63. *Res:* Origin and abundances of the elements; nuclear chemistry. *Mailing Add:* Geol & Planetary Sci 170-25 Calif Inst Technol 1201 E California Pasadena CA 91125-0001

BURNETT, JAMES R, SYSTEM ENGINEERING. *Current Pos:* RETIRED. *Personal Data:* b Eldorado, Ill, Nov 27, 25; m 47, Anne K Knox; c James W, Karen B (Cofer), Susan B (Hicks) & Janice B (Clark). *Educ:* Purdue Univ, BS, 46, MS, 47, PhD, 49. *Hon Degrees:* DEng, Purdue Univ, 69. *Honors & Awards:* Charles A Coffin Award. *Prof Exp:* Mem fac, Purdue Univ, 49-56; mem staff, TRW Inc, 56-75, vpres & asst gen mgr, Defense & Space Systs Group, 75-82, vpres & gen mgr, Defense Systs Group, 82-85, exec vpres & dep gen mgr, Space & Defense Sector, 85-91. *Concurrent Pos:* Mem selection bd, NSF; consult, Argonne Nat Lab, Dept Defense, other govt agencies & Lawrence Livermore Nat Lab. *Mem:* Nat Acad Eng; fel Am Inst Aeronaut & Astronaut; Sigma Xi. *Res:* Early work in servomechanisms and digital computers; later work in system engineering and technical direction of minuteman ICBM. *Mailing Add:* 7136 Avenida Altisima Rancho Palos Verdes CA 90275. *Fax:* 310-265-1267; *E-Mail:* rburnett@aol.com

BURNETT, JEAN BULLARD, BIOLOGICAL CHEMISTRY, HISTOPATHOLOGY & ANATOMY. *Current Pos:* assoc prof & asst to chmn dept biochem, Col Osteop Med, 73-82, prof dept anat, 82-84, PROF DEPT ZOOL, COL NATURAL SCI, MICH STATE UNIV, 84- *Personal Data:* b Flint, Mich, Feb 19, 24; m 47. *Educ:* Mich State Univ, 44, MS, 45, PhD(chem & math), 52. *Prof Exp:* Instr math, Mich State Univ, 46-49, 50-52, natural sci, 52-54, res assoc zool, 54-59, asst prof res, Biol Chem, 59-62; vis prof dermat, Harvard Univ, 62-64, assoc biol chem & dermat, 64-70, prin assoc biol chem & dermat, 70-73, mem fac med, 64-73; assoc biochemist, Mass Gen Hosp, 70-73. *Concurrent Pos:* Vis prof, Dept Biol, Univ Ariz, Tucson, 79-80. *Mem:* AAAS; Am Chem Soc; Genetics Soc Am; Am Inst Biol Sci; Soc Invest Dermat; Sigma Xi. *Res:* Biochemical genetics; genetic control of protein synthesis; enzymes; biology of melanin; detection, diagnosis, prognosis and treatment of malignant melanoma; identification, physiological role, and mode of action of neurotrophic factors. *Mailing Add:* PO Box 805 Okemos MI 48805

BURNETT, JERROLD J, RADIATION DETECTION, SCIENCE ADMINISTRATION. *Current Pos:* from asst prof to assoc prof, 66-75, prof physics, 75-86, EMER PROF, COLO SCH MINES, 86-; MGR, MEASUREMENT STAND LAB, KING FAHD UNIV PETROL & MINERALS, DHAHRAN, SAUDI ARABIA, 89- *Personal Data:* b Mt Pleasant, Tex, May 31, 31; m 53; c 2. *Educ:* Tex A&M Univ, BA, 53; Tex A&I Univ, MS, 59; Univ Okla, PhD(eng sci), 66. *Prof Exp:* Equip engr, Southwest Bell Tel Co, Tex, 55-57; instr physics & math, Univ Dallas, 58-59; res physicist, NMex Inst Mining & Tech, 59-61; assoc prof physics & head dept, Northwestern State Col, Okla, 61-64. *Concurrent Pos:* Prog mgr, Grad & Postdoctoral Progs, NSF, 77-78; lab mgr, Optics & Radiation, Measurement Standards, Univ Petrol & Minerals, Dhahran, Saudi Arabia, 82-84; sr engr, Los Alamos Tech Assoc, Hanford, WA, 87-88. *Mem:* AAAS; Am Asn Physics Teachers; Nat Sci Supvrs Asn; Nat Sci Teachers Asn; Sigma Xi. *Res:* Neutron radiography; activation analysis in bore-holes; radiological health; uranium and tritium in water analysis; low energy radiation detection; equipment and system design; metrology; quality assurance. *Mailing Add:* 13590 Colfax Ave Golden CO 80401-3578

BURNETT, JOHN L, EXPLORATION & DEVELOPMENT OF ORE DEPOSITS. *Current Pos:* Geologist, 58-95, CONSULT GEOLOGIST, CALIF DIV MINES & GEOL, 96- *Personal Data:* b Wichita, Kans, Aug 28, 32; div; c John F & Laurence G. *Educ:* Univ Calif, Berkeley, AB, 57, MS, 60. *Concurrent Pos:* Lectr, Univ Calif Exten, 67-73; instr, Cosumnes River Col, 81- *Mem:* Fel Geol Soc Am. *Res:* Exploration and development of ore deposits using geochemical and other techniques; development of industrial mineral deposits; geological research in northern and eastern California. *Mailing Add:* 8227 Union House Way Sacramento CA 95823. *Fax:* 916-689-4830

BURNETT, JOHN LAMBE, INORGANIC CHEMISTRY, PHYSICAL CHEMISTRY. *Current Pos:* RETIRED. *Personal Data:* b Bismarck, NDak, Dec 1, 34; m 57; c 3. *Educ:* NDak State Univ, BS, 56; Univ Calif, PhD(chem), 64. *Prof Exp:* Chemist, Isotopes Div, Oak Ridge Nat Lab, 65-66 & Chem Div, 66-69; chemist, Div Phys Res, US AEC, 69-75 & Div Phys Res, US Energy Res & Develop Admin, 75-77; nuclear & heavy element chemist, Div Nuclear Sci/BES, Dept Energy, 77-79, chemist, Div Chem Sci/BES, 79-95. *Res:* Lanthanide and actinide thermodynamics and inorganic chemistry; nuclear chemistry. *Mailing Add:* 18429 Kingshill Rd Germantown MD 20874

BURNETT, JOHN NICHOLAS, ANALYTICAL CHEMISTRY. *Current Pos:* from asst prof to prof chem, Davidson Col, 68-80, chmn dept, 72-85, assoc dean fac res & develop, 80-85, dir, Lib Arts Prog Technol, 82-85, MAXWELL CHAMBERS PROF CHEM, DAVIDSON COL, 81- *Personal Data:* b Atlanta, Ga, Aug 19, 39. *Educ:* Emory Univ, BA, 61, MS, 63, PhD(chem), 65. *Honors & Awards:* Thomas Jefferson Award, 80- *Prof Exp:* Res chemist, Org Chem Dept, E I du Pont de Nemours & Co, Del, 65-66; res assoc chem, Univ NC, Chapel Hill, 66-68. *Concurrent Pos:* Vis fel, Civil Eng Dept, Princeton Univ, 85-86; secy-treas, Int Ctr Disarmament & Conversion, 93- *Mem:* Soc Hist Technol; Am Chem Soc; Royal Chem Soc; Hist Sci Soc; Am Asn Univ Prof; Am Inst Chem Engrs. *Res:* Oxidation reduction processes in biologically important compounds, organometallic complexes and electro-spectrochemical techniques; history of chemical technology. *Mailing Add:* Dept Chem Davidson Col PO Box 238 Davidson NC 28036-0238

BURNETT, JOSEPH W, DERMATOLOGY. *Current Pos:* asst prof, 65-69, assoc prof med, 69-76, PROF INTERNAL MED, SCH MED, UNIV MD, BALTIMORE CITY, 76- *Personal Data:* b Oil City, Pa, Mar 21, 33; m 60; c 3. *Educ:* Yale Univ, AB, 54; Harvard Med Sch, MD, 58. *Prof Exp:* Intern & asst resident, Johns Hopkins Univ, 58-61; resident dermat, Harvard Med Sch, 61-63. *Concurrent Pos:* Fel med, Johns Hopkins Univ, 58; fel dermat, Mass Gen Hosp, Boston, 61-63; fel trop pub health, Harvard Med Sch, 63-65. *Mem:* Am Soc Exp Path; Soc Invest Dermat; Am Fedn Clin Res; AMA; Am Acad Dermat. *Res:* Toxins and pathogens of skin. *Mailing Add:* Univ Md Sch Med 655 W Baltimore St Baltimore MD 21201-1559

BURNETT, LOUIS E, PHYSIOLOGY. *Current Pos:* PROF BIOL, COL CHARLESTON, 91-, CHAIR BIOL SCI, 91- *Personal Data:* b Richmond, Va, Sept 12, 51. *Res:* Physiology. *Mailing Add:* Grice Marine Biol Lab Col Charleston 205 Ft Johnson Rd Charleston SC 29424

BURNETT, LOWELL JAY, INSTRUMENTATION DEVELOPMENT, SYNTHETIC MEMBRANES. *Current Pos:* pres, 88-94, CHIEF EXEC OFFICER, QUANTUM MAGNETICS, 94- *Personal Data:* b Portland, Ore, June 15, 41; m 61, Joan S Merk; c David A & Craig M. *Educ:* Portland State Univ, BS, 64; Univ Wyo, MS, 67, PhD(physics), 70. *Honors & Awards:* R & D 100 Award Devel Package Scanner, 95. *Prof Exp:* Presidential fel chem, Los Alamos Nat Lab, 70-72; from asst prof to assoc prof, 72-78, chmn physics dept, 79- 87, prof physics, San Diego State Univ, 78- *Concurrent Pos:* Prin investr numerous grants and contracts, 73-; fac fel, Assoc Western Univs, 73 & 74; mem, int adv panel, Electronics, McGraw-Hill, 74; consult, UOP Inc, 74-85, Gillette Co, 75-76, Los Alamos Nat Lab, 78-85, IRT Corp, 82-83, Sci Applns Inc, 82- & Nat Inst Petrol & Energy Res, 85-86, Quantum Design, 87-

Mem: AAAS; Am Chem Soc; Am Phys Soc; Sigma Xi. *Res:* Design of nuclear magnetic resonance and microwave instrumentation for expolsives and narcotics detection applications; development of synthetic polymer membranes for the separation of mixed gas streams. *Mailing Add:* 10937 Quail Canyon Rd El Cajon CA 92021. *E-Mail:* lowell.burnett@sdsu.edu

BURNETT, MARGARET MYERS, VISUAL PROGRAMMING LANGUAGES, SOFTWARE VISUALIZATION & STEERING. *Current Pos:* asst prof, 93-96, ASSOC PROF COMPUT SCI, ORE STATE UNIV, 96- *Personal Data:* b Springfield, Ill, June 3, 49; m 70. *Educ:* Miami Univ, Ohio, BS, 71; Univ Kans, MS, 81, PhD(comput sci), 91. *Prof Exp:* Systs engr, Proctor & Gamble, 71-72; partner, Acct Systs & Mgt, 72-74; software consult, 74-81; pres, Bulgren & Burnett Inc, 81-87; asst prof comput sci, Mich Technol Univ, 91-92. *Concurrent Pos:* Lectr comput sci, Univ Kans, 81-87; young investr award, NSF, 94. *Mem:* Asn Comput Mach; Inst Elec & Electronics Engrs. *Res:* Scalability and understandability issues for declarative visual programming languages; principal architect of the Forms3 visual programming language. *Mailing Add:* Dept Comput Sci Ore State Univ Corvallis OR 97331

BURNETT, ROBERT WALTER, CLINICAL CHEMISTRY, PATHOLOGY INFORMATICS. *Current Pos:* ASSOC DIR CLIN CHEM LAB, HARTFORD HOSP, 69-, DIR LAB INFO SYSTS, 80-; ASST PROF LAB MED, SCH MED, UNIV CONN, 74- *Personal Data:* b Lima, Ohio, Aug 5, 44. *Educ:* Purdue Univ, BS, 66; Emory Univ, PhD(chem), 69; Rensselaer Polytech Inst, MS, 85. *Concurrent Pos:* Mem, Expert Panel on Blood PH & gases, Int Fedn Clin Chemists, 82- *Mem:* Am Asn Clin Chem; Sigma Xi. *Res:* Reference methods and materials for clinical analyses; high accuracy spectrophotometry; blood pH and gas analysis; applied mathematics; computer applications in laboratory medicine. *Mailing Add:* Dept Path Hartford Hosp Hartford CT 06102-5037

BURNETT, ROGER MACDONALD, PROTEIN CRYSTALLOGRAPHY, VIRUS STRUCTURE. *Current Pos:* PROF CHEM, UNIV PA, 88-, PROF BIOCHEM & BIOPHYS, 89-; PROF, WISTAR INST, 88-, ASSOC DIR SCI DEVELOP, 96- *Personal Data:* b London, Eng, Jan 10, 41; m, Ingrid K Schuller; c Stephanie & Daniel V. *Educ:* Univ London, BSc, 64; Purdue Univ, PhD(protein crystallog), 70; Univ Basel, Habilitation, 75. *Prof Exp:* Assoc res biophysicist, Biophys Res Div, Univ Mich, 70-73; vollassistent Biozentrum, Univ Basel, Switz, 73-75, privatdozent, 75-80, projektleiter, 77-80; assoc prof biochem, Col Physicians & Surgeons, Columbia Univ, 80-88. *Concurrent Pos:* Prin investr, Nat Inst Allergy & Infectious Dis, 80-, NSF, 85-; mem adv panel, Biophys Prog, Div Molecular Biosci, NSF, 86-90; chmn, Struct Biol Prog, Wistar Inst, 91-95. *Mem:* Am Crystallog Soc; Biophys Soc; Am Asn Advan Sci; Harvey Soc. *Res:* Use of x-ray crystallography and electron microscopy to determine the molecular structure of proteins; definition of architecture, principles of construction, and manner of assembly of viruses, in particular adenovirus. *Mailing Add:* Wistar Inst 3601 Spruce St Philadelphia PA 19104-4268

BURNETT, THOMPSON HUMPHREY, EXPERIMENTAL HIGH ENERGY PHYSICS. *Current Pos:* from asst prof to assoc prof, 76-85, PROF PHYSICS, UNIV WASH, 85- *Personal Data:* b Bethlehem, Pa, July 25, 41; m 64; c 3. *Educ:* Univ Calif, Berkeley, AB, 63; Univ Calif, San Diego, PhD(physics), 68. *Prof Exp:* NSF fel, 69; res assoc physics, Princeton Univ, 68-70 & Univ Calif, San Diego, 70-76. *Concurrent Pos:* Alfred P Sloan Found fel, 77-79. *Mem:* Am Phys Soc. *Mailing Add:* Dept Physics Univ Wash PO Box 351560 Seattle WA 98195

BURNETT, WILLIAM CRAIG, MARINE GEOCHEMISTRY, CHEMICAL OCEANOGRAPHY. *Current Pos:* asst prof, 77-81, ASSOC PROF CHEM OCEANOG, FLA STATE UNIV, 81- *Personal Data:* b Lynn, Mass, Sept 20, 45; m 75; c 1. *Educ:* Upsala Col, BS, 68; Univ Hawaii, MS, 71, PhD(geol, geophys), 74. *Prof Exp:* Fel geochem, Dept Earth & Space Sci, State Univ NY, Stony Brook, 74-76; vis scientist, Inst Fisica, Univ Fed Bahia, Salvador, Brazil, 76-77. *Concurrent Pos:* Res fel, E-W Ctr Resources Systs Inst, 79; Co-proj leader, UNESCO Phosphate Proj, Int Geol Correlation Proj 156, 84-; various res grants from fed & state agencies. *Mem:* Geochem Soc; Am Geophys Union; Geol Soc Am; AAAS. *Res:* Uranium-series isotopes in authigenic mineral deposits of the sea floor and natural waters; origin and geochemistry of phosphate deposits; water quality studies in marine and fresh water systems. *Mailing Add:* Dept Oceanog Fla State Univ 600 W College Ave Tallahassee FL 32306-1096

BURNETTE, MAHLON ADMIRE, III, FOOD SCIENCE, NUTRITION. *Current Pos:* PRES, ARNON FOOD POLICY, 83- *Personal Data:* b Lynchburg, Va, May 18, 46; m 84, Mary Hurff; c Joshua & Brett. *Educ:* Va Polytech Inst, BS, 68; Rutgers Univ, MPhil, 73, PhD(nutrit & food sci), 74. *Prof Exp:* Dir sci affairs, Grocery Mfrs Am, Inc, 74-80; exec officer, Nat Nutrit Consortium, 80-81, League Int Food Educ, 82-83. *Mem:* Inst Food Technologists; AAAS; Coun Agr Sci & Technol; Sigma Xi. *Res:* Population nutrition; food safety; federal food and drug regulations; protein metabolism; food safety, labeling and nutrition legislation. *Mailing Add:* 631 Walker Rd Great Falls VA 22066-3406. *Fax:* 703-759-5984

BURNETTE, WALTER NEAL, DEVELOPMENT OF RECOMBINANT VACCINES, BIOMEDICAL CONSULTING. *Current Pos:* PRES & CHIEF EXEC OFFICER, MOLECULAR PHARMACEUT CORP, 93- *Personal Data:* b Mitchell Army Airfield, NY, Aug 14, 44; m 68, Judith Byrd; c Rosemary B & Ashlee M. *Educ:* Tex Christian Univ, BA, 68; Vanderbilt Univ, PhD(microbiol), 75. *Prof Exp:* Postdoctoral fel, Albert Einstein Col Med, 75-77; res assoc, Fred Hutchinson Cancer Res Ctr, 77-79; sr res assoc, Salk Inst Biol Studies, 79-81; dir virol & vaccine develop, Amgen Inc, 81-92. *Concurrent Pos:* Med serv corps officer, USAR, 70-; bd dirs, Photogenesis Inc, 94- *Mem:* AAAS; Am Soc Microbiol; Fedn Am Soc Exp Biol. *Res:* Molecular biology of microbial pathogens; recombinant DNA derived vaccines; immunological assays; biomedical business development. *Mailing Add:* Molecular Pharmaceut Corp 1553 Falling Star Westlake Village CA 91362-5280. *Fax:* 818-991-5184; *E-Mail:* burnetten@inam.com

BURNEY, CURTIS MICHAEL, CHEMICAL ECOLOGY, MICROBIAL ECOLOGY. *Current Pos:* res assoc, 80-81, asst prof, 81-90, ASSOC PROF, OCEANOG CTR, NOVA SOUTHEASTERN UNIV, 90- *Personal Data:* b Beatrice, Nebr, Sept 26, 47; m 72; c 3. *Educ:* Nebr Wesleyan Univ, BS, 69; Univ RI, MS, 76, PhD(oceanog), 80. *Prof Exp:* Res asst, Grad Sch Oceanog, Univ RI, 74-80. *Concurrent Pos:* Prog co-dir, Inst Marine & Coastal Studies, Nova Southeastern Univ. *Mem:* Am Soc Microbiol; Am Soc Limnol & Oceanog; Sigma Xi. *Res:* Dissolved organic matter in natural waters, its nature, dynamics and interactions with the biota. *Mailing Add:* Oceanog Ctr Nova Southeastern Univ 8000 N Ocean Dr Dania FL 33004. *E-Mail:* burney@ocean.nova.edu

BURNEY, DONALD EUGENE, INDUSTRIAL ORGANIC CHEMISTRY. *Current Pos:* RETIRED. *Personal Data:* b Hartington, Nebr, Oct 17, 15; m 42; c 4. *Educ:* Univ SDak, BA, 37; Univ Ill, PhD(org chem), 41. *Prof Exp:* Res chemist, Amoco Chem Corp, 41-47, group leader, 47-57, sect leader, 57-65, div dir, 65-69, mgr org chem res & develop, 69-71, exec dir, Amoco Found, Inc, 71-80. *Mem:* Am Chem Soc. *Res:* Chemicals from petroleum; propylene polymerization to make synthetic lubricating oils; synthetic detergents; reactions of 2, 8-dihydoxynaphtaldehyde; oxidation of hydrocarbons-production of aromatic polybasic acids; polymerization of olefins to thermoplastics. *Mailing Add:* 1005 Anne Rd Naperville IL 60540-5503

BURNHAM, ALAN KENT, PHYSICAL CHEMISTRY. *Current Pos:* CHEMIST, LAWRENCE LIVERMORE NAT LAB, UNIV CALIF, 77- *Personal Data:* b Decorah, Iowa, Oct 10, 50; m 70, Mary; c 3. *Educ:* Iowa State Univ, BS, 72; Univ Ill, Urbana, PhD(phys chem), 77. *Prof Exp:* Jr chemist, Ames Lab, 72. *Concurrent Pos:* Ed Bd, Energy & Fuels, 87-; sci ed, Energy & Technol Rev, 89-90. *Mem:* Am Phys Soc; Am Chem Soc, Geochem Div (secy, 91-93). *Res:* Petroleum formation; chemistry of oil-shale retorting; electro-optics; dielectric properties of liquids; analysis of trace organics in water; kinetics of organic pyrolysis; fabrication of laser fusion targets. *Mailing Add:* Lawrence Livermore Nat Lab Univ Calif PO Box L207 Livermore CA 94551. *E-Mail:* burnham1@llnl.gov

BURNHAM, BRUCE FRANKLIN, biochemistry; deceased, see previous edition for last biography

BURNHAM, CHARLES WILSON, MINERALOGY. *Current Pos:* from assoc prof to prof, 66-96, EMER PROF MINERAL, HARVARD UNIV, 96- *Personal Data:* b Detroit, Mich, Apr 6, 33; m 58, Mary S Morgan; c Jeffrey W & David W. *Educ:* Mass Inst Technol, SB, 54, PhD(mineral, petrol), 61. *Hon Degrees:* AM, Harvard Univ, 66. *Prof Exp:* Fel, Geophys Lab, Carnegie Inst, 61-63, petrologist, 63-66. *Concurrent Pos:* Assoc ed, Am Mineralogist, 74-76; vis scientist, Los Alamos Nat Lab, 81, 88, 90; vis fel, Clare Hall, Univ Cambridge, 87-88. *Mem:* AAAS; fel Mineral Soc Am (vpres, 88, pres, 89); Am Geophys Union. *Res:* Determination and refinement of the crystal structures of minerals; theoretical and experimental aspects of relationships between crystal structures, crystal chemistry and phase relations of minerals in natural systems. *Mailing Add:* Harvard Univ Hoffman Lab 20 Oxford St Cambridge MA 02138

BURNHAM, DONALD C, MECHANICAL, INDUSTRIAL & MANUFACTURING ENGINEERING. *Current Pos:* RETIRED. *Personal Data:* b Athol, Mass, Jan 28, 15; m 37; c 5. *Educ:* Purdue Univ, BS, 36. *Hon Degrees:* DEng, Purdue Univ, 59, Ind Inst Technol, 52, 63, Drexel Inst Technol, 64 & Polytech Inst Brooklyn, 67. *Honors & Awards:* Richards Mem Award, Am Soc Mech Engrs, 58; Outstanding Achievement in Mgt Award, Am Inst Indust Engrs, 64; Hoover Medal, 78; Nat Engr Award, Am Asn Engrs Soc, 81. *Prof Exp:* Staff mem, Gen Motors Corp, 36-54, asst chief engr, Oldsmobile Div, 53-54; vpres mfg, Westinghouse Elec Corp, 54-62, head, Div Indust Prod, 62-63, pres, 63-69, chmn, 69-75, dir officer, 76-80. *Concurrent Pos:* Dir, Mellon Nat Bank & Trust Co & Logistics Mgt Inst; vchmn, Nat Comt Productivity & Work Qual, 74-75; dir, Am Productivity & Work Qual, 74-75, Nat Ctr Productivity & Qual Work Life, 75-76. *Mem:* Nat Acad Eng; Am Soc Mech Engrs; Soc Automotive Eng; Inst Elec & Electronics Engrs; Am Soc Metals; Inst Indust Engrs. *Res:* Industrial production; productivity improvement. *Mailing Add:* 1290 Boyce Rd Apt C233 Pittsburgh PA 15241

BURNHAM, DONALD LOVE, PSYCHIATRY. *Current Pos:* RETIRED. *Personal Data:* b Lebanon, NH, Dec 6, 22; m 46; c 3. *Educ:* Dartmouth Col, BA, 43; Cornell Univ, MD, 46. *Prof Exp:* From resident psychiat to dir res, Chestnut Lodge, Md, 50-63, Ford Found grant, 57-63; res psychiatrist, Div Clin & Behav Res, HIMH, 63-82. *Concurrent Pos:* From instr to pres, Wash Psychoanal Inst, 56-; trustee, William Alanson White Psychiat Found, 62-; ed, J Psychiat, 62-85. *Mem:* Am Psychoanal Asn; fel Am Psychiat Asn. *Res:* Personality development and mental illness, particularly schizophrenia, thought and language, and psychotherapy; psycho-biographic study of August Strindberg. *Mailing Add:* 5003 Edgemoor Lane Bethesda MD 20814

BURNHAM, DUANE LEE, ACCOUNTING. *Current Pos:* Sr vpres finance & chief financial officer, Abbott Labs, 82-84, exec vpres, chief financial officer & dir, 85-87, vchmn & chief financial officer, 87-89, CHMN & CHIEF EXEC OFFICER, ABBOTT LABS, CHICAGO, 90- *Personal Data:* b Excelsior, Minn, Jan 22, 42; m 63, Susan Elizabeth Klinner; c David Lee & Matthew Beckwith. *Educ:* Univ Minn, BS, 63, MBA, 72. *Concurrent Pos:* Bd dirs, Sara Lee Corp, Evanston Hosp Corp, Mus Sci & Indust, Chicago & Healthcare Leadership Coun; trustee, Northwestern Univ; chmn, Emergency Comt Am Trade. *Mailing Add:* Abbott Labs 100 Abbott Park Rd Abbott Park IL 60064-3500

BURNHAM, DWIGHT COMBER, ELECTROGRAPHIC TECHNOLOGY, INVESTMENT MANAGEMENT. *Current Pos:* RETIRED. *Personal Data:* b Macomb, Ill, Mar 17, 22; m 47; c Dianne B (Bewley), Kenneth C & Nancy A. *Educ:* Iowa State Univ, BS, 43; US Mil Acad, BS, 46; Univ Ill, MS, 56, PhD(physics), 60. *Prof Exp:* Teaching & res asst physics, Univ Ill, 54-59; physicist, Mil Photog Dept, Kodak Res Labs, Eastman Kodak Co, NY, 59-61 & Solid State Phys Dept, 61-67, prod planning specialist, Bus Systs Mkt Div, 67-73, prod planning coordr, Bus Systs Mkt Div, 73-81, res assoc develop, Electrographic Technol Div, 81-86. *Concurrent Pos:* investment mgt, Burney Co, 86-88. *Mem:* Am Phys Soc. *Res:* Ionic crystals; emphasis on magnetic resonance techniques and problems; computer-microfilm information systems; electrographic technology. *Mailing Add:* 42 Creek Ridge Pittsford NY 14534-4404

BURNHAM, JEFFREY C, MICROBIOLOGY. *Current Pos:* from asst prof to assoc prof, 69-84, actg chmn dept, 77-78, PROF MICROBIOL, MED COL OHIO, 85- *Personal Data:* b Beverly, Mass, Aug 6, 42; m 64; c 2. *Educ:* Dartmouth Col, AB, 64; Univ NH, PhD(microbiol), 67. *Honors & Awards:* Pres Award, Ohio Pub Health Asn. *Prof Exp:* USPHS fel, Univ Ky, 67-69. *Concurrent Pos:* Adj prof biol, Bowling Green State Univ, 72- *Mem:* AAAS; Am Soc Microbiol; Electron Micros Soc Am; Phycol Soc Am; Can Soc Microbiol. *Res:* Relationship between microbial cell function and structure; bacterial control of algae populations; microbiol adherence to epithelial cells; water pollution microbiology; electron cytochemistry; infectious diseases. *Mailing Add:* Dept Microbiol Med Col Ohio PO Box 10008 Toledo OH 43699-0008

BURNHAM, MARVIN WILLIAM, ENGINEERING MECHANICS, MANUFACTURING PRODUCTIVITY. *Current Pos:* CONSULT, 87- *Personal Data:* b Wichita, Kans, May 15, 25; m 54; c 2. *Educ:* Univ Kans, BS, 50; Univ Ark, MS, 57; Univ Colo, PhD(mech eng), 66. *Honors & Awards:* Citation Prof Achievement, Soc Mfg Engrs, 77, Award of Merit, 85; Award of Merit, Calif Coun Bus Prof Asn, 87. *Prof Exp:* Instr mech eng, Univ Ark, 54-57; asst prof, Univ Denver & res engr, Denver Res Inst, 57-62; sr res engr, Falcon Res & Develop Co, 62-67; sr res engr, Dow Chem Co, 67-75; sr res engr, Rockwell Int, 75-80, assoc scientist, 80-87. *Concurrent Pos:* Chmn, Soc Mfg Engrs Nat Mat Removal Coun, 77-80; chmn, Rockwell Corp Task Group, 84-87. *Mem:* Soc Exp Stress Anal; NY Acad Sci; fel Soc Mfg Engrs; Sigma Xi. *Res:* Solid mechanics; elasticity; shell theory, energy conversion; experimental mechanics; mechanics of metal cutting; high accuracy manufacturing and metrology; manufacturing automation; product design innovation and improvement; remote manufacturing. *Mailing Add:* 4705 Ricara Dr Boulder CO 80303

BURNHAM, ROBERT DANNER, SEMICONDUCTORS. *Current Pos:* VPRES & CHIEF TECH OFFICER, PHOENIX PHOTONIX INC, 94- *Personal Data:* b Havre de Grace, Md, Mar 21, 44; m 65, Kyungsoon Kim; c Jennifer W, Benjamin R & Kimberly M. *Educ:* Univ Ill, BS, 66, MS, 68, PhD(elec eng), 71. *Honors & Awards:* Jack A Morton Award, Inst Elec & Electronics Engrs, 85. *Prof Exp:* Res staff, Palo Alto Res Ctr, Xerox, Calif, 71-77, mat res specialist, 77-80, prin scientist, 80-83, res fel, 83-86; sr res assoc, Amoco Technol Co, Naperville, Ill, 86-89, TECH DIR, 89-94. *Concurrent Pos:* Edward J James Scholar, 62-66, NDEA fel, 66-69, Gen Tel & Electronics, 69-71. *Mem:* Nat Acad Eng; fel Inst Elec & Electronics Engrs; Metall Soc; fel Optical Soc Am. *Res:* Growth and fabrication of gallium aluminum arsenide; quantum well heterostructures with emphasis on lasers for optoelectronic integration, using growth technique of metalorganic chemical vapor deposition; author or co-author of over 379 publications and holder of 76 patents; high power cw diode laser. *Mailing Add:* Phoenix Photonix Inc 1180 Briarcliffe Blvd Wheaton IL 60187. *E-Mail:* phoenixrdbe@aol.com

BURNHAM, ROBYN JEANETTE, SYSTEMATICS & ECOLOGY OF CLIMBING PLANTS, PLANT MORPHOLOGY. *Current Pos:* CUR PALEONT & BOT, MUS PALEONT & ASST PROF BIOL, UNIV MICH, 92- *Personal Data:* b Corona, Calif, Dec 12, 56. *Educ:* Univ Calif, Berkeley, AB, 80; Univ Wash, MS, 83, PhD(bot), 87. *Prof Exp:* Researcher, Smithsonian Inst, 88-89; cur bot & paleobot, NMex Mus Natural Hist, 90-92. *Concurrent Pos:* Asst prof, Dept Biol, Univ NMex, 90-; assoc researcher, Smithsonian Inst, 90- *Mem:* Bot Soc Am; Asn Trop Biol; Paleont Soc; Int Asn Wood Anatomists; Int Orgn Paleobot. *Res:* Evolutionary history and paleoecology of climbing plants of tropical and subtropical forests; Cretaceous and Early Tertiary paleoecology of the intermountain west of North America. *Mailing Add:* Mus Paleont Univ Mich Ann Arbor MI 48109-1079. *Fax:* 313-936-1380; *E-Mail:* robyn.burnham@um.cc.umich.edu

BURNHAM, THOMAS K, DERMATOLOGY, IMMUNOLOGY. *Current Pos:* RETIRED. *Personal Data:* b Berlin, Ger, June 6, 27; m 52, Marie McGenn; c Susan, Jane, Miranda & Terence. *Educ:* Univ London, MB, BS, 52; Am Bd Dermat, dipl, 63. *Honors & Awards:* Gold Medal, Am Acad Dermat, 66. *Prof Exp:* Staff physician dermat, Henry Ford Hosp, 62-86, dir dermat res lab, 68-86. *Mem:* Am Acad Dermat; AMA; Am Dermat Asn. *Res:* Auto-immunity; antinuclear factors; fluorescent antibody; evaluation of the diagnostic and prognostic aspects of antinuclear antibodies detected by indirect immunofluorescence, being analyzed now immunologically by other immunologic techniques to determine responsible nuclear antigens; discovered Lupus "Band", which resulted in the lupus band test. *Mailing Add:* 962 Santa Helena Park Ct Solana Beach CA 92075

BURNISON, BRYAN KENT, DISSOLVED ORGANIC MATTER, TOXICITY IDENTIFICATION & EVALUATION. *Current Pos:* Head, Nutrient Pathways Sect, 79-86, RES SCIENTIST, CAN CTR INLAND WATERS, 73- *Personal Data:* b Great Falls, Mont, Feb 26, 43; m 71, Gayle Beierwaltes; c Gregory, Kevin & Laura. *Educ:* Mont State Col, BS, 65; Ore State Univ, MS, 68, PhD(microbiol), 71. *Concurrent Pos:* Fel, Univ BC, 71-73; assoc prof, Univ Guelph. *Mem:* Int Humic Substances Soc. *Res:* Organic colloid chemistry in lake waters - isolation, purification and chemical composition; pulp mill MFO inducing substances for fish; dissolved organic matter; PAHs; toxicity identification and evaluation. *Mailing Add:* Aquatic Ecosystems Protection Br Nat Wat Res Inst 867 Lakeshore Rd Burlington ON L7R 4A6 Can. *Fax:* 905-336-4420; *E-Mail:* kent.burnison@cciw.ca

BURNISTON, ERNEST EDMUND, APPLIED MATHEMATICS. *Current Pos:* from asst prof to assoc prof, 65-72, PROF MATH, NC STATE UNIV, 72-, HEAD DEPT, 80- *Personal Data:* b Sheffield, Eng, Oct 26, 37; m 59; c 3. *Educ:* Univ London, BSc, 60, PhD(math), 62. *Prof Exp:* Lectr math, Univ London, 62-65. *Mem:* Soc Indust & Appl Math; Math Asn Am. *Res:* Fracture mechanics; transport theory. *Mailing Add:* Dept Math NC State Univ PO Box 8205 Raleigh NC 27695-8205

BURNS, ALASTAIR H, PHYSIOLOGY. *Current Pos:* PROF PHYSIOL, LA STATE UNIV MED CTR, 78- *Personal Data:* b Spokane, Wash, Nov 10, 41. *Educ:* Parsons Col, BS, 64; Univ Fla, MS, 66, PhD(physiol), 72. *Prof Exp:* Asst prof physiol, Univ Ala, Birmingham, 72-78. *Mem:* Am Physiol Soc. *Mailing Add:* Dept Physiol La State Univ Med Ctr 1901 Perdido St New Orleans LA 70122-2865

BURNS, ALLAN FIELDING, SILICAS, SILICATES. *Current Pos:* RETIRED. *Personal Data:* b Washington, DC, Nov 22, 36; m 58, Asenath E Payne; c John, Robert, Thomas & Laurie. *Educ:* Cornell Univ, BS, 58; Purdue Univ, MS, 60, PhD(soil chem), 62. *Prof Exp:* Res chemist silicates, Johns-Manville Res & Eng Ctr, Johns-Manville Corp, 62-66, sr res chemist, 66-69, sect chief basic chem, 69-71; chemist pollution abatement, US Army Picatinny Arsenal, 72-73; tech mgr silica & silicates, Philadelphia Quartz Co, 73-77, tech mgr specialty chem, 77-78, mgr corp planning, 78-82, mgr mkt develop, 82-85, mkt mgr, 85-89, assoc dir res & develop, 89-91, tech dir res & develop, 91-93. *Mem:* Am Chem Soc; Indust Res Inst. *Res:* Clay chemistry; structural and surface modification of clays; chemistry of soluble alkali and organic ammonium silicates; amorphous synthetic and natural silicas; synthetic insoluble silicates; zeolites. *Mailing Add:* 2140 Bayview Point Lane Cape Charles VA 23310

BURNS, BRUCE PETER, COMPOSITE MATERIALS & APPLICATIONS, TRANSIENT STRUCTURAL ANALYSIS. *Current Pos:* officer, US Army Ballistic Res Lab, 70-72, mech engr, 72-77, asst to dir, 77-78, mech engr & team leader, 78-82, SUPV GEN ENGR, US ARMY BALLISTIC RES LAB, 82- *Personal Data:* b Mt Vernon, NY, Feb 11, 42; m, Bonnie F Dubel; c Rebecca L, Bethany J & Thomas T Jr. *Educ:* Drexel Inst Technol, BS, 64, MS, 66; Drexel Univ, PhD(appl mech), 69. *Honors & Awards:* R H Kent Award. *Prof Exp:* Postdoctoral, Drexel Univ, 69-70. *Concurrent Pos:* Adj prof mech eng & short course coordr, Drexel Univ, 90-; mem, Exec Comt, Ballistics Div, Am Defense Preparedness Asn; founding mem, Int Ballistics Comt. *Mem:* Am Soc Composites; Am Soc Composites. *Res:* Basic and applied research pertaining to the structural performance of projectiles and guns subjected to launch forces; structural behavior of complicated projectiles; author of more than 60 publications; awarded ten patents. *Mailing Add:* PO Box 443 Churchville MD 21028

BURNS, C(HARLES) M(ICHAEL), CHEMICAL ENGINEERING, POLYMER SCIENCE. *Current Pos:* From asst prof to assoc prof, 67-84, assoc chmn undergrad studies chem eng, 84-87, PROF CHEM ENG, UNIV WATERLOO, 84- *Personal Data:* b Detroit, Mich, June 7, 38; Can citizen; m 63; c 2. *Educ:* Univ Toronto, BASc, 61, MASc, 62; Polytech Inst Brooklyn, PhD(chem), 67. *Concurrent Pos:* Consult, Steel Co Can, 69-75 & Dominion Chain Co, 80-82. *Mem:* Am Chem Soc; Chem Inst Can; Can Soc Chem Eng; Assoc Prof Engrs Ont. *Res:* Correlation of polymer structure and properties; synthesis and characterization of new monomers and polymers; characterization of copolymers and mixed polymer systems; polymer-polymer compatability; adhesion of polymers; gas permeation; polyblends. *Mailing Add:* Dept Chem Eng Univ Waterloo Waterloo ON N2L 3G1 Can. *Fax:* 519-746-4979; *E-Mail:* cburns@chemical.watstar.uwaterloo.ca

BURNS, CHESTER RAY, HISTORY OF MEDICINE. *Current Pos:* Asst prof hist, 69-71, from James Wade Rockwell asst prof to assoc prof, 71-79, asst prof to assoc prof, Dept Prev Med & Community Health, 74-79, JAMES WADE ROCKWELL PROF HIST MED & PROF, DEPT PREV MED & COMMUNITY HEALTH, UNIV TEX MED BR, GALVESTON, 79-, MEM INST MED HUMANITIES, 74- *Personal Data:* b Nashville, Tenn, Dec 5, 37; m 62, Ann Griffey; c Christine & Derek. *Educ:* Vanderbilt Univ, BA, 59, MD, 63; Johns Hopkins Univ, PhD(hist med), 69. *Concurrent Pos:* Dir, Hist Med Div, Univ Tex Med Br, Galveston, 69-74, assoc dir, Inst Med

Humanities, 74-80, assoc, Grad Sch Biomed Sci, 74-77, mem, 79- *Mem:* Am Asn Hist Med; Soc Health & Human Values (pres, 75-76); Int Soc Hist Med (treas, 91-); Hist Sci Soc; Am Hist Asn. *Res:* History of medicine, especially medical education, medical science, medical ethics and medical jurisprudence. *Mailing Add:* Dept Prev Med-Pub Health Univ Tex Med Sch 301 University Blvd Galveston TX 77555-1050. *Fax:* 409-772-5640

BURNS, DANIEL ROBERT, SEISMIC WAVE PROPAGATION, BOREHOLE GEOPHYSICS. *Current Pos:* ACAD ADMIN, MIT, 93- *Personal Data:* b Boston, Mass, Sept 25, 55; m 78; c 2. *Educ:* Bridgewater State Col, BA, 77; Colo Sch Mines, MS, 79; Mass Inst Technol, PhD, 86. *Prof Exp:* Geophysicist, Union Oil Co Calif, 79-83; sr res geophysicist, Unocal Sci & Technol Div, 87-88; exec vpres, New Eng Res, Inc, 89-93. *Concurrent Pos:* Staff scientist, Arthur D Little Inc, 80-81; vis scientist, Mass Inst Technol, 88-; asst scientist, Woods Hole Oceanog Inst, 88-; prin investr, NSF, 89-91, Off Naval Res & Off Naval Technol, 89-; mem assoc panel, Nat Res Coun, 91- *Mem:* Soc Explor Geophysicists; Am Geophys Union. *Res:* Numerical modeling of elastic wave propagation; borehole acoustics; property estimation from geophysical data; in-situ permeability estimation; subsurface characterization for energy, environmental and engineering applications. *Mailing Add:* 100 Screenhouse Lane Duxbury MA 02332

BURNS, DAVID JEROME, AGRICULTURAL ECONOMICS, RESOURCE ECONOMICS. *Current Pos:* assoc prof, 56-60, PROF AGR ECON, RUTGERS UNIV, NEW BRUNSWICK, 60-, ACAD ADMINR, 80- *Personal Data:* b Hobart, La, July 13, 22; m 46; c 2. *Educ:* Univ Md, BS, 48, MS, 49, PhD(agr econ), 54. *Prof Exp:* From instr to asst prof agr econ, Univ Md, 51-56. *Mem:* Am Agr Econ Asn. *Res:* Marketing of fruits and vegetables and land use planning. *Mailing Add:* 21 Hale St New Brunswick NJ 08901

BURNS, DAVID JOHN, PROTEIN EXPRESSION. *Current Pos:* AT ABBOTT LABS, 94- *Personal Data:* b Altoona, Pa, June 2, 59. *Educ:* Univ Scranton, BS, 81; Ind Univ, PhD(biochem), 87. *Prof Exp:* Fel, Duke Univ, 87-90; scientist I, Sphinx Pharmaceut Corp, 90-91, mgr, 91-92, sr mgr molecular biol, 92-94. *Mem:* Am Asn Cancer Res; Am Soc Microbiol; Am Soc Biochem & Molecular Biol. *Res:* Isolation, cloning, expression and characterization of signal transduction enzymes; large scale production of recombinant proteins in insect cells and Escherichia coli; development and characterization of cell-based reporter assays. *Mailing Add:* Abbot Labs Dept 4CP Bldg AP10 100 Abbott Park Rd Abbott Park IL 60064-3500

BURNS, DENVER P, RESEARCH ADMINISTRATION. *Current Pos:* DIR, ROCKY MOUNTAIN FOREST & RANGE EXP STA, 92- *Personal Data:* b Bryan, Ohio, Oct 27, 40; m 65; c 1. *Educ:* Ohio State Univ, BSc, 62, MSc, 64, PhD(entom), 67; Harvard Univ, MPA, 81. *Prof Exp:* From asst entomologist, US forest serv, 62-68, res entomologist, 68-72, asst dir, Southern Forest Exp Sta, 72-74, staff asst dep chief res, 74-76, dep dir, NCent Exp Sta, 76-81, dir, Northeastern Forest Exp Sta, 81-92. *Mem:* AAAS. *Res:* Research administration; insect-host tree interactions; biology and bionomics of insects; biology, ecology and behavior of borers attacking living hardwoods. *Mailing Add:* Rocky Mountain Forest & Range Exp Sta 240 W Prospect Rd Ft Collins CO 80526

BURNS, DONAL JOSEPH, EXPERIMENTAL ATOMIC PHYSICS. *Current Pos:* res assoc, Univ Nebr, Lincoln, 68, jr fac fel, Univ Res Coun, 69, from asst prof to assoc prof, 68-76, assoc dean arts & sci, 77-82, dir, Univ Studies Prog, 80-86, asst exec vpres & provost, 86-89, PROF PHYSICS, UNIV NEBR, LINCOLN, 76-, ASSOC EXEC VPRES & PROVOST, 89- *Personal Data:* b Belfast, Ireland, Mar 5, 41, m 72, Ileana M Beller; c 2. *Educ:* Queen's Univ, Belfast, BSc, 62, PhD(physics), 65. *Prof Exp:* Lectr physics, Queen's Univ, Belfast, 65-68. *Concurrent Pos:* Vis scientist, Meudon Observ, France, 64. *Mem:* Am Phys Soc; fel Inst Physics & Phys Soc. *Res:* Observations on forbidden transitions; measurement of atomic and molecular excitation cross sections; lifetimes of excited states; coherent beam foil spectroscopy; atomic alignment and orientation in coincidence experiments. *Mailing Add:* 111 Varner Hall Univ Nebr 3835 Holdrege St Lincoln NE 68583-0743

BURNS, DRUSILLA LORENE, BIOCHEMISTRY. *Current Pos:* sr staff fel, 84-87, res chemist, 87-94, CHIEF, LAB PERTUSSIS, CTR BIOLOGICS EVAL RES, FOOD & DRUG ADMIN, 94- *Personal Data:* b Manhattan, Kans, Feb 14, 53. *Educ:* Tulane Univ, BS, 75; Univ Calif, Berkeley, PhD(biochem), 80. *Honors & Awards:* Am Inst Chemists Award, 75. *Prof Exp:* Staff fel, Lab Cellular Metab, Nat Heart Lung & Blood Inst, NIH, 80-84. *Concurrent Pos:* Mem, Int Activ Comt, Pub Sci Affairs Bd, Am Soc Microbiol, 89-92, Petussis Subcomt, Nat Vaccine Prog, 90-92, Inst Biosafety Comt, NIH, 90-95. *Mem:* AAAS; Am Soc Microbiol. *Res:* Bordetella pertussis, pertussis toxin, bacterial protein toxins and bacterial pathogenesis; granted two US patents; contributed to several professional publications. *Mailing Add:* CBER FDA Bldg 29 Rm 418 8800 Rockville Pike Bethesda MD 20892. *Fax:* 301-402-2776; *E-Mail:* burns@1.cber.fda.gov

BURNS, EDWARD EUGENE, FOOD SCIENCE. *Current Pos:* RETIRED. *Personal Data:* b Ft Wayne, Ind, Apr 13, 26; m 48; c 4. *Educ:* Purdue Univ, BS, 50, MS, 52, PhD(food technol), 56. *Honors & Awards:* Cruess Award, Inst Food Technol, 72. *Prof Exp:* Asst, Purdue Univ, 47-50, instr, 52-56; prof hort, Tex A&M Univ, 56- *Mem:* Am Hort Soc; Sigma Xi; Inst Food Technol; Am Soc Hort Sci. *Res:* Quality control techniques and methods; chemical and physiological indicators of quality; human foods of plant origin. *Mailing Add:* 1203 Park College Station TX 77840

BURNS, EDWARD ROBERT, MICROSCOPIC ANATOMY, EXPERIMENTAL EMBRYOLOGY. *Current Pos:* From instr to assoc prof, 68-79, PROF ANAT, MED COL, UNIV ARK, LITTLE ROCK, 79- *Personal Data:* b Catskill, NY, Nov 6, 39; m 60; c 2. *Educ:* Hartwick Col, BA, 61; Univ Maine, MS, 63; Tulane Univ, PhD(anat), 67. *Concurrent Pos:* NIH fel exp path, George Washington Univ, 67-68; NIH res career develop award, 74-79. *Mem:* AAAS; Am Asn Anatomists; Am Soc Zoologists; Int Soc Chronobiol; Am Asn Cancer Res; Sigma Xi. *Res:* Experimental oncology; control of growth and differentiation in normal and neoplastic tissues; chronochemotherapy; chronobiology of neoplasia. *Mailing Add:* Dept Anat Univ Ark 4301 W Markham Little Rock AR 72205

BURNS, ELIZABETH MARY, neuroscience, aging, for more information see previous edition

BURNS, ERSKINE JOHN THOMAS, NUCLEAR PHYSICS. *Current Pos:* MEM TECH STAFF, SANDIA LABS, 76- *Personal Data:* b Calgary, Alta, Oct 23, 44; m 82. *Educ:* Occidental Col, BA, 66; Calif State Univ, Los Angeles, MS, 68; Univ Calif, Davis, PhD(physics), 71. *Prof Exp:* Res physicist, 71-75, chief, X-ray Diag Group, Air Force Weapons Lab, 75-76. *Mem:* Am Phys Soc. *Res:* Ion sources for nuclear fusion. *Mailing Add:* Orgn 2564 MS 0516 Sandia Labs Albuquerque NM 87185

BURNS, FRANK BERNARD, analytical chemistry, physical organic chemistry, for more information see previous edition

BURNS, FREDRIC JAY, TOXICOLOGY. *Current Pos:* Asst prof, 69-74, assoc prof, 75-80, PROF ENVIRON MED, MED CTR, NY UNIV, 80- *Personal Data:* b Wilmington, Del, Apr 20, 37; m 62; c 2. *Educ:* Harvard Col, AB, 59; Columbia Univ, MA, 61; NY Univ, PhD(biol), 67. *Concurrent Pos:* NIH fel, Inst Cancer Res, Sutton, Eng, 67-69. *Mem:* Radiation Res Soc; Am Asn Cancer Res. *Res:* Cell population kinetics; radiation and chemical carcinogenesis in skin and liver; control of cell division; cell cycle models. *Mailing Add:* Inst Environ Med NY Univ Sch Med 550 First Ave New York NY 10016-6481

BURNS, GEORGE, THEORETICAL CHEMISTRY, ENVIRONMENTAL ARCHAEOLGICAL CHEMISTRY. *Current Pos:* from asst prof to prof, 62-71, assoc chmn dept, 74-75, prof chem, 71-90, EMER PROF CHEM, UNIV TORONTO, 90- *Personal Data:* b Russia, Apr 6, 25; US citizen; c 2. *Educ:* Columbia Univ, BS, 51; Princeton Univ, PhD(chem), 61. *Prof Exp:* Chemist, Gen Elec Co, 52-56; Nat Acad Sci-Nat Res Coun fel phys chem, Cambridge Univ, 61-62. *Mem:* Am Phys Soc; Am Chem Soc. *Res:* Theoretical and experimental gas phase chemical kinetics; recombination-dissociation reactions, theory and experiment; environmental archaeological chemistry. *Mailing Add:* Dept Chem Lash Miller Chem Lab Univ Toronto Toronto ON M5S 3H6 Can. *Fax:* 416-978-8775

BURNS, GEORGE ROBERT, SOIL FERTILITY. *Current Pos:* Res soil scientist, US Soil Lab, USDA, 62-64, asst to dir agr res, Sulpher Inst, 64-67, br chief, Soil & Water Conserv Res Div, 67-72, AREA DIR, SOUTHERN REGION, USDA, 72- *Personal Data:* b Lineville, Ala, Nov 12, 31; m 54; c 3. *Educ:* Auburn Univ, BS, 54; NC State Univ, MS, 56; Iowa State Univ, PhD(soil fertil), 61. *Mem:* Am Soc Agron; Soil Sci Soc Am; Soil Conserv Soc Am; Sigma Xi. *Res:* Chemistry of soil and plant interaction; chemistry of nitrogen and phosphorous in soil. *Mailing Add:* 125 Twinlakes Rd Athens GA 30605

BURNS, GEORGE W, genetics; deceased, see previous edition for last biography

BURNS, GROVER PRESTON, applied mechanics, theoretical physics, for more information see previous edition

BURNS, H DONALD, ORGANIC CHEMISTRY, NUCLEAR MEDICINE & RADIOPHARMACOLOGY. *Current Pos:* sr res fel, Dept Res Imaging, 87-90, head, Dept radiopharmacol, 90-92, SR INVESTR, MERCK RES LABS, 96- *Personal Data:* b Scranton, Pa, Apr 17, 46; m 69; c 2. *Educ:* Univ Scranton, BS, 68; Lehigh Univ, MS, 72, PhD(org chem), 74. *Honors & Awards:* Nat Res Serv Award, Nat Heart & Lung Inst, 75. *Prof Exp:* NIH fel, Johns Hopkins Med Inst, 74-75, asst prof nuclear med, Div Nuclear Med, 75-76; from asst prof to assoc prof radiol, environ health sci & radiol, 76-87. *Concurrent Pos:* Assoc prof, Dept Radiation Therapy & Nuclear Med, Hahnemann Univ, 78-79; assoc dir res, Div Radiation Health Sci, Johns Hopkins Univ, 82-87. *Mem:* Soc Nuclear Med; Am Chem Soc; Sigma Xi; AAAS; Am Asn Pharmaceut Scientists; Soc Nuclear Imaging & Drug Develop. *Res:* Application of nuclear imaging to drug discovery, development and approval; radiopharmacology. *Mailing Add:* Merck Res Labs WP-44C-2 West Point PA 19486

BURNS, JACK O'NEAL, RADIO ASTRONOMY. *Current Pos:* from asst prof to assoc prof, 80-90, PROF ASTRON & DEPT HEAD, NMEX STATE UNIV, 89- *Personal Data:* b Ayer, Mass, Jan 2, 53; m 80; c 2. *Educ:* Univ Mass, BS, 74; Ind Univ, MA, 76, PhD(astron), 78. *Prof Exp:* Res asst radio astron, Nat Radio Astron Observ, 77-78, res assoc, 78-80. *Concurrent Pos:* Consult, Sandia Nat Labs, 82-89, Los Alamos Nat Labs, 86- *Mem:* Royal Astron Soc; Am Astron Soc; Int Astron Union; Sigma Xi; AAAS. *Res:* Radio interferometry; extended extragalactic radio sources; study of radio galaxies and clusters of galaxies at radio, optical and x-ray frequencies. *Mailing Add:* Dept Astron NMex State Univ Box 30001 Dept 4500 Las Cruces NM 88003-0001

BURNS, JAY, III, PHYSICS. *Current Pos:* prof physics & head dept physics & space sci, 76-87, prof, 87-94, EMER PROF PHYSICS & SPACE SCI, FLA INST TECHNOL, 94- *Personal Data:* b Lake Wales, Fla, Mar 22, 24; m 48, Dulcie Evans; c Jay IV, William Scott & Wendy. *Educ:* Northwestern Univ, BS, 47; Univ Chicago, MS, 51, PhD, 59. *Prof Exp:* Physicist, Chicago Midway Labs, 51-57; sr physicist, Labs Appl Sci, Univ Chicago, 57-63, dir, 63-65; assoc prof astron, Northwestern Univ, 65-67; assoc dir res, Rauland Div, Zenith Radio Corp, 67-68; assoc prof astron & head lab exp astrophys, Northwestern Univ, 68-71, dir, Astro-Sci Workshops. *Concurrent Pos:* Vis prof physics, Univ Ill, Chicago Circle & sr res consult, Zenith Radio Corp, 71-76. *Mem:* Am Phys Soc; Am Phys Soc. *Res:* Secondary electron emission; photoelectric emission; solid state; surface physics; astronomical image tubes; atomic and molecular transition probabilities; electron emission from solids; solid surface physics; polymer physics; biophysics. *Mailing Add:* Dept Physics & Space Sci Fla Inst Technol Melbourne FL 32901

BURNS, JOHN ALLEN, APPLIED MATHEMATICS. *Current Pos:* ASSOC PROF MATH, VA POLYTECH INST & STATE UNIV, 74- *Personal Data:* b Little Rock, Ark, Aug 15, 45; m 65; c 1. *Educ:* Ark State Univ, BSE, 67, MSE, 68; Univ Okla, MA, 70, PhD(math), 73. *Prof Exp:* Spec instr math, Univ Okla, 72-73; asst prof, Lefschetz Ctr Dynamical Syst, Brown Univ, 73-74. *Mem:* Soc Indust & Appl Math. *Res:* Control theory; ordinary differential equations; functional differential equations. *Mailing Add:* Dept Math Va Polytech Inst & State Univ Blacksburg VA 24061

BURNS, JOHN HOWARD, XRAY DIFFRACTION. *Current Pos:* ADJ ASSOC PROF, UNIV NC, ASHEVILLE, 93- *Personal Data:* b Kilgore, Tex, Oct 8, 30; m 52, 76 & 93, Nancy Shaw; c Julia & Austin. *Educ:* Rice Inst, BA, 51, MA, 53, PhD(chem), 55. *Prof Exp:* Res assoc chem, Oak Ridge Nat Lab, 55-56; asst prof, Univ Ky, 56-57; asst chemist, Argonne Nat Lab, 57-59, assoc chemist, 59-60; chemist, Oak Ridge Nat Lab, 60-78, sr res staff, 78-93. *Mem:* Am Chem Soc; Am Crystallog Asn. *Res:* X-ray and neutron diffraction; chemistry of actinide elements and of crown ethers. *Mailing Add:* Chem Dept Univ NC 1 University Heights Asheville NC 28804-3299. *E-Mail:* jburnsavl@aol.com

BURNS, JOHN J, BIOCHEMISTRY. *Current Pos:* ADJ PROF PHARMACOL, MED COL, CORNELL UNIV, 96- *Personal Data:* b Flushing, NY, Oct 8, 20. *Educ:* Queens Col, BS, 42; Columbia Univ, AM, 48, PhD(chem), 50. *Hon Degrees:* DSc, Queens Col, City Univ New York. *Prof Exp:* Dep chief, Lab Chem Pharmacol, NIH, 58-60; dir, Res Pharmacodynamics Div, Wellcome Res Labs, 60-66; vpres res, Hoffmann-La Roche Inc, 67-84, adj mem, Roche Inst Molecular Biol, 84-96. *Concurrent Pos:* Mem, Pharmacol & Exp Therapeut Study Sect, NIH, 58-62 & Drug Res Bd, Nat Acad Sci-Nat Res Coun, 64-; vis prof, Albert Einstein Sch Med, 60-68 & Cornell Univ Med Col, 68-; adj prof, Rockefeller Univ, 84-94. *Mem:* Nat Acad Sci; Inst Med-Nat Acad Sci; Am Soc Pharmacol & Exp Therapeut; Am Soc Biol Chem; NY Acad Sci (vpres, 64); AAAS; Am Chem Soc. *Res:* Metabolism of vitamin C, pentoses, uronic acids; antirheumatic drugs; muscular relaxants; barbiturates; anticoagulants; local anesthetics; mechanism of action of adrenergic blocking drugs. *Mailing Add:* 331 Landsdowne Westport CT 06880. *Fax:* 203-255-5508

BURNS, JOHN JOSEPH, JR, SOLID MECHANICS, ENGINEERING. *Current Pos:* RETIRED. *Personal Data:* b Chicago, Ill, Dec 16, 25; m 50; c 4. *Educ:* Ill Inst Technol, BS, 45; Drexel Inst Technol, MS, 53 & 55; Univ Colo, Boulder, PhD(appl mech), 67. *Prof Exp:* Engr, Bell Aircraft Corp, 45-46; sr engr, Fairchild Engine & Airplane Corp, 47-51; chief struct engr, Aerospace Div, Kaiser Metal Prod Co, 51-55; tech specialist, Missile Syst Div, Repub Aviation Corp, 55-59; sect head, Denver Div, Martin-Marietta Corp, 59-66; staff engr, Lockheed-Ga Corp, 66-67; assoc prof eng sci & mech, Univ Fla, 67-72; prof mech & engr, Univ Ill, Champaign, 72-76. *Concurrent Pos:* Indust mem, Mil Spec 25 Comt on Composite Mat, 50-67; consult, Gen Elec Co, 67-, Martin-Marietta Corp, 68- & US Navy, 68-; head struct res, US Nuclear Regulatory Comn, 73-; assoc ed, J Mech Design, Am Soc Mech Engrs. *Mem:* AAAS; Am Inst Aeronaut & Astronaut; Am Soc Eng Educ; Sigma Xi; Am Soc Mech Engrs; Am Acad Mech; Am Asn Eng Educ. *Res:* Effects of load, dynamics, thermal environment on civil, mechanical and aerospace structures; shell stability and deformation process, mechanical and structural reliability; fracture mechanics; fatigue and shock load failures of materials and components; high speed aerodynamics. *Mailing Add:* 12304 Pueblo Rd Gaithersburg MD 02878-2062

BURNS, JOHN M(CLAUREN), SYSTEMATICS, EVOLUTION. *Current Pos:* assoc cur, 75-77, CUR ENTOM, NAT MUS NATURAL HIST, SMITHSONIAN INST, 78- *Personal Data:* b Rochester, NY, June 6, 32; m 54, Sarah Nance; c Laura, Karen & Colin Douglas. *Educ:* Johns Hopkins Univ, AB, 54; Univ Calif, Berkeley, MA, 57, PhD(zool), 61. *Prof Exp:* Asst zool, Univ Calif, Berkeley, 54-57, asst entom, 57-58; asst prof biol, Wesleyan Univ, 61-69; assoc cur lepidoptera, Mus Comp Zool, Harvard Univ, 69-75, assoc prof biol, 72-75. *Mem:* Fel AAAS; Soc Study Evolution; Am Soc Naturalists; Soc Syst Biologists; Lepidopterists' Soc (pres, 95-96). *Res:* Population differentiation and speciation in sexually reproducing animals; genetics and ecology of polymorphism, including electrophoretically detectable protein polymorphisms; systematics and behavior of Lepidoptera, primarily skipper butterflies (Hesperiidae), with special attention to genitalia; biological poetry. *Mailing Add:* Dept Entom Smithsonian Inst Washington DC 20560

BURNS, JOHN MITCHELL, PHYSIOLOGY, ENDOCRINOLOGY. *Current Pos:* from asst prof to assoc prof biol sci, 69-80, PROF BIOL SCI, TEX TECH UNIV, 80- *Personal Data:* b Hobbs, NMex, Dec 18, 40; m 63; c 2. *Educ:* NMex State Univ, BS, 63, MS, 66; Ind Univ, PhD(zool), 69. *Prof Exp:* Sci aide & comput programmer, Phys Sci Lab, NMex State Univ, 63-65, res asst microbial physiol, 65-66; teaching assoc zool, Ind Univ, 66-69. *Mem:* AAAS; Am Soc Zoologists; Am Chem Soc; Endocrine Soc; Soc Develop Biol. *Res:* Steroid mechanism of action. *Mailing Add:* Dept Biol Tex Tech Univ Lubbock TX 79409-0001

BURNS, JOHN THOMAS, CHRONOBIOLOGY. *Current Pos:* PROF BIOL, BETHANY COL, 85- *Personal Data:* b Richmond, Ind, Feb 22, 43; m 75, Anne E Ramsey; c 2. *Educ:* Wabash Col, Crawfordsville, Ind, BA, 65; La State Univ, MS, 68, PhD(zool), 77. *Prof Exp:* Asst prof biol, Baker Univ, 68-77; asst prof anat, WVa Sch Osteop Med, 77-79; exec dir, Found Study Cycles, 79-85. *Mem:* AAAS; Found Study Cycles (secy, 85-); Int Soc Chronobiol; Soc Biol Rhythm Res; Europ Soc Chronobiol. *Res:* Biological rhythms in the physiology of vertebrates; hormonal and neurochemical regulation of seasonal physiological and behavioral changes in migrating birds and hibernating mammals. *Mailing Add:* Dept Biol Bethany Col Bethany WV 26032

BURNS, JOHN W, ACCELERATION PHYSIOLOGY. *Current Pos:* res physiologist, 71-91, Armstrong Lab, USAF, chief acceleration function, 91-93, chief, Flight Motion Effects Br, 93-95, SR SCIENTIST, AL/CFT, ARMSTRONG LAB, USAF, 95- *Personal Data:* b Alton, Ill, Nov 2, 36; m 93, Sandra A Wanke; c Laure E, Elizabeth A, Margaret E & Paul A. *Educ:* Southern Ill Univ, AB, 59; Georgetown Univ, PhD, 68. *Honors & Awards:* Arnold D Tuttle Award, Aerospace Med Asn, 86; Paul Bert Award, Aerospace Physiologist Soc. *Prof Exp:* Postdoct fel, Dept Med, Univ Calif, San Diego, 68-71. *Mem:* Am Physiol Soc; Aerospace Med Asn; Sigma Xi. *Res:* Physiology; investigation of the cardiopulmonary effects of high sustained (plus 96z) acceleration and high onset plus 6z (66/sec); develop techniques and equipment to protect pilots in the high (plus 6z) environment. *Mailing Add:* Armstrong Lab/CFT 2504 Gillingham Dr Brooks AFB TX 78235-5104

BURNS, JOHN WILLIAM, PATENT & BIO-TECHNOLOGY LAW. *Current Pos:* RES VIROLOGIST, PALO ALTO VET ADMIN MED CTR, 91- *Personal Data:* b Tooele, Utah, Aug 28, 53. *Educ:* Ohio State Univ, BS, 75; San Diego State Univ, MS, 82; Baylor Col Med, PhD(virol & epidemiol), 88. *Prof Exp:* Fel, Scripps Clin & Res Found, 88-91. *Mem:* Am Asn Immunologists; Am Soc Microbiol; Am Soc Virol. *Mailing Add:* Fenwick West 2 Palo Alto Square Palo Alto CA 94306

BURNS, JOSEPH A, PLANETARY SCIENCE, CELESTIAL MECHANICS. *Current Pos:* Asst prof mech, Cornell Univ, 66-75, assoc prof, 75-81, chmn dept, 87-93, PROF MECH & ASTRON, CORNELL UNIV, 81-, IP CHURCH PROF, 94- *Personal Data:* b New York, NY, Mar 22, 41; m 67, Judith Klein; c Patrick & Caitlin. *Educ:* Webb Inst Naval Archit, BS, 62; Cornell Univ, PhD(space mech), 66. *Honors & Awards:* Laus Nixon Prize, Russian Acad Sci, 62; Masursky Prize, Am Astron Soc, Int Acad Astron, 94. *Concurrent Pos:* Nat Acad Sci-Nat Res Coun res assoc theoret div, Goddard Space Flight Ctr, NASA, 67-68; prin investr, NY Coun Arts, 72, NY Sci Found, 74, NASA, 74-, NSF, 83-86; Nat Acad Sci exchange fel, Schmidt Inst, Moscow & Astron Inst, Prague, 73; sr scientist, Space Sci Div, NASA Ames Res Ctr, 75-76, 82-83; ed, Icarus, 79-; prof astron, Paris Observ, 80, Univ Calif, Berkeley, 82-83, Univ Ariz, 89-90; adv comt, Space & Earth Sci, NASA, 83-87; mem, Space Studies Bd, Nat Res Coun, 89-95, chair, Comt Planet & Lunar Explor, 92-95. *Mem:* AAAS; fel Am Geophys Union; Am Astron Soc; Int Astron Union. *Res:* Mechanics of solar system; celestial rotation; asteroid collisions; origin of solar system; orbital evolution; planetary satellites, dust dynamics; Saturn's rings celestial mechanics; teaching methods; space policy. *Mailing Add:* Dept Theoret & Appl Mech 209 Kimball Hall Cornell Univ Ithaca NY 14853

BURNS, JOSEPH CHARLES, FORAGE QUALITY, SECONDARY COMPOUNDS. *Current Pos:* from asst prof to assoc prof, 67-76, PROF CROP SCI & ANIMAL SCI, NC STATE UNIV, 76-; RES PLANT PHYSIOLOGIST, AGR RES SERV, USDA, 67- *Personal Data:* b Iowa City, Iowa, Feb 16, 37; m 56, Marijane L Connell; c Joan T, Dann M, Patricia L, Leah M, Ann K & Shawn P. *Educ:* Iowa State Univ, BS, 60, MS, 63; Purdue Univ, PhD(plant physiol, ecol), 66. *Prof Exp:* Dist sales mgr, Boeke Feed Co, Iowa, 61; res asst forage crop prod, Iowa State Univ, 61-63; res asst plant physiol & ruminant nutrit, Purdue Univ, 63-66; prof forage physiol, Tex A&M Univ, 66. *Mem:* Fel Am Soc Agron; Am Forage & Grassland Coun; Fel Crop Sci Soc Am. *Res:* Initiation and accumulation of secondary plant products from primary plant metabolite induced through management, environment and genetic control and relationship of these constituents to animal acceptance, intake and conversion and utilization of forages by grazing ruminants. *Mailing Add:* Dept Crop Sci 1119 Williams Hall NC State Univ Raleigh NC 27695-7620. *Fax:* 919-515-7959; *E-Mail:* jburns@cropserv1.cropsci.ncsu.edu

BURNS, KENNETH FRANKLIN, VIROLOGY. *Current Pos:* prof comp med & chmn Dept Vivarial Sci & Res, 62-76, PROF & CHMN COMP MED, SCH MED, TULANE MED CTR, TULANE UNIV, 76- *Personal Data:* b Lebanon, Ind, June 6, 16; m 39. *Educ:* Ont Vet Col, DVM, 40; Univ Toronto, DVSc, 50; Univ Tokyo, PhD(microbiol), 52; Am Bd Vet Pub Health, dipl, 55; Am Col Lab Animal Med, dipl, 61. *Prof Exp:* Chief, Virol & Vet Br, Army Med Lab, Ft McPherson, Ga, 41-43, chief, Virol & Vet Br, 4th Army Med Lab, Ft Sam Houston, Tex, 46-47, chief, Dept Virus & Rickettsial Dis, 406th

Med Gen Lab, Japan, 47-51, dep chief, Vet Microbiol Div, Chem Corps Biol Warfare Labs, Ft Detrick, Md, 51-53, chief vet & virol br, 4th Army Area Med Lab, Brooke Army Med Ctr, Tex, 53-58, chief, Animal Colonies Div, Directorate Med Res, US Army Chem Warfare Labs, Army Chem Ctr, Md, 59-61, chief pub health officer, Civil Affairs Group & Lab & consult High Comnr, Ryukyu Islands, 61-62. *Concurrent Pos:* Consult, US Ord Command, 59-61. *Mem:* Am Vet Med Asn; Animal Care Panel. *Res:* Laboratory animal medicine. *Mailing Add:* 2344 Killdear St New Orleans LA 70122

BURNS, LAWRENCE ANTHONY, SYSTEMS ECOLOGY, ECOTOXICOLOGY. *Current Pos:* RES ECOLOGIST, ATHENS ERD, US ENVIRON PROTECTION AGENCY, 77- *Personal Data:* b Washington, DC, Aug 12, 40; m 75, Karen J Ramey; c Liisa, Lara & Alexander. *Educ:* NY Univ, BA, 68; Univ NC, Chapel Hill, PhD(ecol), 78. *Honors & Awards:* Civil Serv Silver Medal, US Environ Protection Agency, 73, Sci Achievement Award, 85. *Prof Exp:* Lab technician microbiol, NY Univ, 66-68; res asst ecol, Univ NC, Chapel Hill, 68-71; res aquatic biologist, Region IV Surveillance & Anal Div, US Environ Protection Agency, 71-73; res asst, Ctr Wetlands, Phelps Lab, Univ Fla, 73-76. *Mem:* Ecol Soc Am; Int Soc Ecol Model; AAAS; Am Inst Biol Sci; Soc Environ Toxicol Chem. *Res:* Mathematical and computer modeling of ecosystem dynamics; transport, fate, and effects of nutrients and toxic chemicals in aquatic systems; ecological risk assessment of synthetic organic chemicals. *Mailing Add:* US EPA-NERL 960 College Station Rd Athens GA 30605-2700. *Fax:* 706-355-8104; *E-Mail:* burns.lawrence@epamail.epa.gov

BURNS, MARCELLINE, PSYCHOLOGY. *Current Pos:* COFOUNDER, CALIF RES INST, LOS ANGELES, 73- *Educ:* San Diego State Univ, BS, 55; Calif State Univ, Los Angeles, MA, 69; Calif State Univ, Irvine, PhD, 72. *Concurrent Pos:* Consult & lectr. *Res:* Development of software for a databacs of drug evaluations; alcohol and drug effects on boating skills; field soberity tests for the boating environment. *Mailing Add:* Southern Calif Res Inst 11914 W Washington Blvd Los Angeles CA 90066

BURNS, MICHAEL J, SURFACE SCIENCE, ELECTRONIC TRANSPORT. *Current Pos:* PROF PHYSICS, UNIV FLA, 87- *Personal Data:* b Hollywood, Calif, Oct 6, 56. *Educ:* Univ Calif, Los Angeles, BS, 78, MS, 80, PhD(physics), 84. *Prof Exp:* MTS engr, Hughes Aircraft Co, 78-80; res physicist, Univ Pa, 83-85; postdoctoral fel, Harvard Univ, 85-87. *Mem:* Am Physical Soc; Mat Res Soc. *Res:* Magnetic field induced metal-insulator transitions in semiconductors; magnetic flux quantization in aperiodic superconducting structures; electronic and magnetic properties of monolayer films and organic molecule formation in deep space. *Mailing Add:* Conductus 969 W Maude Ave Sunnyvale CA 94086

BURNS, MOORE J, biochemistry, physiology, for more information see previous edition

BURNS, NANCY A, RURAL HEALTH, HOSPICES. *Current Pos:* dir, Rural Hosp Outreach Prog, Univ Tex, Arlington, 75-81, dir continuing educ, 75-81, from asst prof to assoc prof, 78-86, PROF NURSING, UNIV TEX, ARLINGTON, 86-, DIR, CTR NURSING RES, 87- *Personal Data:* b Ft Worth, Tex, Aug 21, 36; m 56; c 2. *Educ:* Tex Christian Univ, BS, 57; Tex Women's Univ, MS, 74, PhD(nursing), 81. *Honors & Awards:* Sword of Hope Award, Am Cancer Soc, 83. *Prof Exp:* Pub health nurse, Ft Worth Health Dept, 57-59; nurse, All Saints Hosp, Ft Worth, 61-68; instr, All Saints Voc Nursing Sch, 68-72, dir, 72-74; instr, Syst Sch Nursing, Univ Tex, Ft Worth, 74-76. *Concurrent Pos:* Consult, var hosps, 74-; area chmn, Cancer Prev Study, Am Cancer Soc, 82-88. *Mem:* Am Nurses Asn; Nat League Nursing; Oncol Nursing Soc; Nat Rural Health Asn. *Res:* Rural health; health service; hospice care; oncology; smoking among nurses; author of two books and numerous publications. *Mailing Add:* Box 19407 Nurse/Grad Prog Univ Tex Arlington TX 76019-0407

BURNS, NED HAMILTON, CIVIL ENGINEERING. *Current Pos:* from asst prof to prof civil eng, Univ Tex, 62-80, grad adv, 63-77, 80-86, prof, 80-86, ZARROW CENTENNIAL PROF ENG, UNIV TEX, 86- *Personal Data:* b Magnolia, Ark, Nov 25, 32; m 55, Martha A Fontaine; c Kathryn J, Stephanie A (Wechsler) & Michael B. *Educ:* Univ Tex, BS, 54, MS, 58; Univ Ill, PhD(civil eng), 62. *Honors & Awards:* Martin Korn Award, Prestressed Concrete Inst, 93; T Y Lin Award, Am Soc Civil Engrs, 94. *Prof Exp:* Engr, Mosher Steel Co, Tex, 54-55; instr civil eng, Univ Tex, 57-59, res engr struct mech, Balcones Res Ctr, 59; asst civil eng, Univ Ill, 59-62. *Concurrent Pos:* Res reinforced concrete, USAF Spec Weapons Ctr, 63-; NSF res grant, 64-65; Tex Hwy Dept Res, 67-; consult, struct eng prods on reinforced & prestressed concrete. *Mem:* Am Concrete Inst; Am Soc Civil Engrs; Nat Soc Prof Engrs; Sigma Xi. *Res:* Prestressed concrete flat slabs with unbonded tendons; long-span prestressed concrete bridges with segmental construction and other research in prestressed concrete. *Mailing Add:* Dept Civil Eng Univ Tex Austin TX 78712-1076

BURNS, PAUL YODER, FORESTRY. *Current Pos:* prof, 55-86, EMER PROF FORESTRY, LA STATE UNIV, BATON ROUGE, 86- *Personal Data:* b Tulsa, Okla, July 4, 20; m 42, Kathleen Chase; c Virginia B (Belland), Margaret B (Feierabend) & Nancy B (McNeill). *Educ:* Univ Tulsa, BS, 41; Yale Univ, MF, 46, PhD, 49. *Prof Exp:* From asst prof to assoc prof forestry, Univ Mo, 48-55. *Mem:* Fel Soc Am Foresters; Sigma Xi. *Res:* Silvics; silviculture; mensuration. *Mailing Add:* Sch Forestry La State Univ Baton Rouge LA 70803-6200

BURNS, RICHARD CHARLES, biochemistry, for more information see previous edition

BURNS, RICHARD PRICE, PHYSICAL CHEMISTRY, INORGANIC CHEMISTRY. *Current Pos:* asst prof, 65-70, ASSOC PROF CHEM, UNIV ILL, CHICAGO CIRCLE, 70- *Personal Data:* b Bartlesville, Okla, Sept 19, 32; m 59; c 2. *Educ:* Okla Baptist Univ, AB, 54; Univ Chicago, PhD(chem), 65. *Prof Exp:* Jr chemist, Lawrence Radiation Lab, Univ Calif, 55-58; res asst physics, Univ Chicago, 59-65. *Mem:* Am Chem Soc; Am Phys Soc. *Res:* Applications of the mass spectrometer and thermal imaging techniques to high temperature chemistry, thermodynamics, kinetics and materials. *Mailing Add:* 1478 E 56th St Chicago IL 60637

BURNS, ROBERT ALEXANDER, MINERAL METABOLISM, INFANT & PROTEIN NUTRITION. *Current Pos:* sr scientist, Mead Johnson Nutrit, 82-85, sr res scientist, 85-89, mgr, 89-92, ASSOC DIR, NUTRIT BIOCHEM, MEAD JOHNSON NUTRIT, 92- *Personal Data:* b June 3, 50; m 74, Cecelia McCann; c Owen R & Katie A. *Educ:* Queen's Univ, Belfast, Northern Ireland, BS(Hons), 72, PhD(nutrit), 76. *Prof Exp:* Res assoc, Univ Nottingham, 76-79, Univ Ill, 79-82. *Mem:* Am Inst Nutrit; Am Soc Clin Nutrit; Am Chem Soc; Int Soc Res Human Milk & Lactation; Nutrit Soc. *Res:* Major research activities involve investigations of nutrietns and food substances regarding their roles in growth and treatment of disease states. *Mailing Add:* 1046 Pine Gate Rd Evansville IN 47711. *Fax:* 812-429-5925

BURNS, ROBERT DAVID, ZOOLOGY. *Current Pos:* RETIRED. *Personal Data:* b Detroit, Mich, Feb 28, 29; m 60, Jeanette Pearson; c Robert & Cynthia. *Educ:* Mich State Univ, BS, 51, MS, 54, PhD(zool), 58. *Hon Degrees:* DSc, Kenyon Coll, 92. *Prof Exp:* Asst prof zool, Univ Okla, 58-63; from asst prof to prof biol, Kenyon Col, 63-92, chmn dept, 69-71 & 79-84. *Concurrent Pos:* Vis prof, Biol Sta, Mich State Univ, 61; vpres, Ohio Acad Sci, 74-75. *Mem:* AAAS; Ecol Soc Am; Am Soc Mammal; Am Ornith Union; Wilson Ornith Soc. *Res:* Feeding and behavior in kangaroo rats; reproductive behavior in birds and mammals; physiology of the vestibular portion of the inner ear in kangaroo rats. *Mailing Add:* PO Box 204 Gambier OH 43022

BURNS, ROBERT EARLE, OCEANOGRAPHY. *Current Pos:* RETIRED. *Personal Data:* b New York, NY, May 1, 25; m 51; c 2. *Educ:* Col Wooster, AB, 47; Lehigh Univ, MS, 50; Univ Wash, PhD(oceanog), 62. *Prof Exp:* Instr geol, Bucknell Univ, 49-51; oceanogr, div oceanog, US Navy Hydrographic Off, 51, head tides & currents unit, 51-52, dep head regional sect, 52-53, tech asst, 53-54, head geol oceanog unit, 54-56, supv oceanogr, 56-57; assoc oceanog, Univ Wash, 57-62; res oceanogr, Off Res & Develop, US Coast & Geod Surv, 62-65; chief environ sci serv admin complement, Joint Oceanog Res Group, Univ Wash, 65-69; res oceanogr, Pac Oceanog Labs, Nat Oceanic & Atmospheric Admin, 70-73, actg dir, Pac Marine Environ Lab, 73-76, proj mgr, deep ocean mining environ studies, 76-79, mgr, long range effects studies, Off Marine Pollution Assessment, 80-83, mgr, marine resources res div, Pac Marine Environ Lab, 84-85. *Concurrent Pos:* Chmn, Fed Interagency Subcomt Sedimentation, 63-64; vis geoscientist prog, Am Geol Inst, 64-65 & Am Geophys Union, 66-67, 70; chmn, Joint Oceanog Insts Deep Earth Sampling Pac Adv Panel, 68-73. *Mem:* Geophys Union; Marine Technol Soc. *Res:* Assessment of potential impact of man's activities on the marine environment. *Mailing Add:* 3602 47th Ave NE Seattle WA 98105

BURNS, ROBERT EMMETT, PLANT PHYSIOLOGY. *Current Pos:* RETIRED. *Personal Data:* b Oxford, Iowa, May 9, 18; m 52; c 4. *Educ:* Univ Iowa, BA, 40, MS, 47, PhD(plant physiol), 49. *Prof Exp:* Instr, Univ Calif, Santa Barbara, 49-50; plant physiologist, USDA, Univ Ga, 50-64, assoc plant physiologist, 64-84, emer assoc prof, Exp Sta, Agr Res Serv, 84. *Mem:* Am Soc Plant Physiol. *Res:* Seed physiology; turf physiology. *Mailing Add:* 1010 E McIntosh Rd Griffin GA 30223

BURNS, ROBERT WARD, MICROELECTRONIC PACKAGING & ASSEMBLY PROCESSES, FIBER OPTIC SENSING MANUFACTURING EQUIPMENT. *Current Pos:* DIR, ELECTRONIC PROCESS ENG, PRIMEX CORP, 92- *Personal Data:* b Fresno, Calif, Nov 30, 41; m 67, Sylvia Greybeck; c 2. *Educ:* Univ Calif, Berkeley, BS, 64, MS, 66; Univ Wash, Seattle, PhD(ceramic eng), 72. *Prof Exp:* Sr engr, Tektronix Inc, 74-80; opers mgr, PM Industs, 80-81; develop mgr, Brush Wellman, 81-82; eng sect mgr, John Fluke Mfg, 82-86; prin engr, Boeing Electronics Co, 86-87; mfg mgr, Metricor, 87-92. *Mem:* Fel Int Soc Hybrid Microelectronics; Am Ceramic Soc; Am Electronics Asn. *Res:* Processing of advanced materials for electronic applications; thick and thin film hybrids; ceramic substrates; surface mount technology; integrated circuit packaging; polymer thick film; electronic process development. *Mailing Add:* Primex Corp PO Box 97009 Redmond WA 98073. *Fax:* 425-882-5812

BURNS, ROGER GEORGE, geochemistry, mineralogy; deceased, see previous edition for last biography

BURNS, RUSSELL MACBAIN, SILVICULTURE, PLANT PHYSIOLOGY. *Current Pos:* RETIRED. *Personal Data:* b New York, NY, Aug 25, 26; m 48; c 3. *Educ:* Mich State Univ, BS, 50; Univ Miss, MS, 59; Univ Fla, PhD, 71. *Prof Exp:* Res forester, US Forest Serv, 51-67, silviculturist, 67-77, prin conifer silviculturist, US Forest Serv, 77-91. *Concurrent Pos:* Res consult, Arg govt; US rep to USSR, US Man & Biosphere Prog, UNESCO; USDA Forest Serv rep to India, US-INDO Agr Coop; chmn, Nat Capital Soc Am Foresters, 91-92. *Mem:* Soc Am Foresters; Am Soc Plant Physiol; Soil Conserv Soc Am. *Res:* Silviculture problems; tree physiology and soil chemistry. *Mailing Add:* 1205 S Frederick St Arlington VA 22204

BURNS, SCOTT FRIMOTH, SOIL RESEARCH, QUATERNARY GEOLOGY. *Current Pos:* assoc prof, 90-96, PROF, DEPT GEOL, PORTLAND STATE UNIV, 97- *Personal Data:* b Portland, Ore, Oct 7, 47; m 74, Glenda Stemmler; c Lisa, Doug & Tracy. *Educ:* Stanford Univ, BS, 69, MS, 70; Univ Colo, Boulder, PhD(geol), 80. *Prof Exp:* Asst prof, Am Col Switz, 70-75, Lincoln Col, NZ, 80-81, Western Washington Univ, 81-82; assoc prof, La Tech Univ, 82-90. *Concurrent Pos:* Kellogg Nat fel, Nat Leadership Prog, Kellogg Found, 90; pres, Ore Soil Sci Soc, 94-95; secy, Eng Geol Div, Geol Soc Am, 96-97, vpres, 97-98; pres, Ore Soc, Asn Eng Geol, 96-98. *Mem:* Geol Soc Am; Asn Eng Geol; Nat Asn Geol Teachers; Soil Sci Soc Am. *Res:* Using geology to solve human problems such as landslides, radon gas in homes, heavy metals and trace elements in soils, flood and earthquake hazards; soils; quaternary history of sediments; geomorphology. *Mailing Add:* Dept Geol Portland State Univ PO Box 751 Portland OR 97207

BURNS, STEPHEN JAMES, FRACTURE MECHANICS, PHASE TRANSFORMATIONS. *Current Pos:* assoc prof, 72-79, PROF, DEPT MECH ENG, UNIV ROCHESTER, 79-, DIR MAT SCI, 95- *Personal Data:* b New York, NY, Jan 31, 39; m 64, Violanda Oliverio; c Sean, Brian & Stephen. *Educ:* Pratt Inst, BS, 61; Cornell Univ, MS, 65, PhD(mat sci), 67. *Prof Exp:* Res assoc eng, Brown Univ, 66-67, res & teaching fel, 67-68, asst prof, 68-72. *Concurrent Pos:* Vis prof, Stanford Univ, 77-78. *Mem:* Mat Res Soc; Am Ceramic Soc; Am Soc Mech Engrs. *Res:* X-ray diffraction topography; mechanical properties of solids; fracture mechanics for tough materials; phase transformations in ceramics, metals and polymers. *Mailing Add:* Dept Mech Eng Univ Rochester Rochester NY 14627-0133. *Fax:* 716-256-2509; *E-Mail:* burns@me.vodiester.edu

BURNS, THOMAS WADE, INTERNAL MEDICINE, ENDOCRINOLOGY. *Current Pos:* asst prof, 55-57, assoc prof, 57-65, PROF MED, SCH MED, UNIV MO, COLUMBIA, 65-, PHYSICIAN, MED CTR, 55-, DIR DIV ENDOCRINOL & METAB, 69- *Personal Data:* b Dayton, Ohio, July 29, 24; m 52; c 4. *Educ:* Univ Utah, BA, 45, MD, 47, MS, 48; Am Bd Internal Med, dipl, 55. *Prof Exp:* Intern, Boston City Hosp, 48-49; asst resident, Harvard Med Sch, 49-50; clin investr, US Naval Hosp, Calif, 51-52; clin investr, US Naval Med Res Unit, Egypt, 52-54; res physician, Med Ctr, Univ Calif, 55. *Concurrent Pos:* Fel, Harvard Med Sch, 49-50; fel med, Sch Med, Duke Univ, 50-51. *Mem:* AAAS; Endocrine Soc; Am Diabetes Asn; AMA; Am Col Physicians; Am Fedn Clin Res; Am Soc Internal Med. *Res:* Endocrine and metabolic disorders. *Mailing Add:* Univ Mo Columbia Med Ctr D110 A Columbia MO 65212

BURNS, TIMOTHY JOHN, ORDINARY & PARTIAL DIFFERENTIAL EQUATIONS, ASYMPTOTIC METHODS. *Current Pos:* MATHEMATICIAN APPL MATH, COMPUT & APPL MATH LAB, NAT INST STANDARDS & TECHNOL, 86- *Personal Data:* b Ames, Iowa, June 28, 49; m 78, Gretchen Erzinger; c Hannah. *Educ:* Univ NMex, BS, 70, MA, 72, PhD(math), 77. *Prof Exp:* Mem tech staff appl math, Solid Dynamics Res Dept, Sandia Nat Labs, 77-86. *Mem:* Soc Indust & Appl Math; Am Soc Mech Engrs. *Res:* Asymptotic, numerical methods and mathematical modeling for problems in applied and classical mechanics. *Mailing Add:* Nat Inst Stand & Technol Bldg 820 Rm 365 Gaithersburg MD 20899. *Fax:* 301-990-4127; *E-Mail:* burns@cam.nist.gov

BURNS, VICTOR WILL, BIOPHYSICS, CELL PHYSIOLOGY. *Current Pos:* from assoc prof to prof, 64-90, EMER PROF BIOPHYS, UNIV CALIF, DAVIS, 90- *Personal Data:* b Los Angeles, Calif, Nov 16, 25; m 50; c 3. *Educ:* Univ Calif, PhD(biophys), 55. *Prof Exp:* Assoc med physics, Univ Calif, 53-55; dir high energy proton biophys, Royal Univ Uppsala, 55-56; from res assoc to lectr, Stanford Univ, 56-64. *Mem:* Radiation Res Soc; Biophys Soc. *Res:* Cell division and intracellular coordination; biological and physical effects of ionizing radiation; fluorescence analysis of cells and nucleic acids. *Mailing Add:* 638 Elmwood Dr Davis CA 95616

BURNS, WILLIAM, JR, TECHNICAL MANAGEMENT, HARDWARE SYSTEMS. *Current Pos:* CONSULT, 93- *Personal Data:* b New Castle, Pa, Dec 18, 38; m 66, Charlotte F Williams; c Gary R & Evonne M. *Educ:* Carnegie Mellon Univ, BS, 61, MS, 62, PhD(elec eng), 65. *Prof Exp:* Res geophysicist, Gulf Res & Develop Ctr, 65-66; sr researcher astrophys, Observ Paris, 66-67; asst scientist radio astron, Nat Radio Astron Observ, 67-68, assoc scientist radio astron, 68-69, head, Comput Div, 69-91, dep asst dir comput, 91-93. *Concurrent Pos:* Fel, Nat Ctr Sci Res, France, 66-67; bd dirs, Delphian Signals, 79-85; mem, Site Vis Comt, NSF, 85, bd dirs, R-Tech Inc, 85-91; consult, var co, 83-91. *Mem:* Inst Elec & Electronics Engrs. *Res:* Signal processing; investigations of computer hardware systems; communications networking; computer management both from applied and research consideration; general business management. *Mailing Add:* 2320 Westover Dr Charlottesville VA 22901. *E-Mail:* bburns@nrao.edu

BURNS, WILLIAM CHANDLER, PARASITOLOGY. *Current Pos:* teaching asst, 52-57, actg instr, 57-58, from instr to assoc prof, 58-68, PROF ZOOL, UNIV WIS-MADISON, 68- *Personal Data:* b Fargo, NDak, Jan 5, 26; m 56; c 4. *Educ:* Ore State Col, BS, 50, MA, 52; Univ Wis-Madison, PhD(zool), 58. *Prof Exp:* Teaching asst zool, Ore State Col, 50-52. *Concurrent Pos:* NSF fel, Ore State Col, 59-61. *Mem:* Am Soc Parasitol. *Res:* Ecology of helminths; coccidiosis; host-parasite relationships. *Mailing Add:* Dept Zool Univ Wis 250 N Mills Noland Hall Madison WI 53706

BURNSIDE, EDWARD BLAIR, population genetics, animal breeding, for more information see previous edition

BURNSIDE, JOAN, ANIMAL SCIENCE & NUTRITION. *Current Pos:* ASSOC PROF MOLECULAR ENDOCRINOL, DEPT ANIMAL & FOOD SCI, UNIV DEL, 89- *Personal Data:* b New York, NY, May 23, 51. *Educ:* Univ Md, BS, 72; Univ Mass, MS, 76; Dartmouth Col, PhD(biochem), 81. *Prof Exp:* Staff fel, Nat Inst Diabetes Digestive & Kidney Dis, NIH, 83-85; res assoc, Howard Hughes Med Inst, Harvard Med Sch, 85-89. *Concurrent Pos:* Fulbright scholar, Natl Inst Health & Med Res, 95. *Mem:* Endocrine Soc; AAAS; Poultry Sci Asn. *Mailing Add:* Univ Del 4010 Townsend Hall Newark DE 19717. *Fax:* 302-831-3651; *E-Mail:* joan@strauss.udel.edu

BURNSIDE, MARY BETH, CELL BIOLOGY, NEUROBIOLOGY. *Current Pos:* from asst prof to assoc prof, 75-82, dean biol sci, 83-90, PROF CELL & DEVELOP BIOL, UNIV CALIF, BERKELEY, 82-; CHANCELLOR PROF, 96. *Personal Data:* b San Antonio, Tex, Apr 23, 43. *Educ:* Univ Tex, Austin, BA, 65, MA, 67, PhD(zool), 68. *Honors & Awards:* Merit Award, Nat Eye Inst, NIH. *Prof Exp:* Instr anat, Harvard Med Sch, 71-72; asst prof anat, Univ Pa, 72-75. *Concurrent Pos:* Am Asn Univ Women fel, Hubrecht Lab, Utrecht, Holland, 68-69; NIH fels, Harvard Univ Biolabs, Cambridge, 69-70 & Harvard Med Sch, Boston, 70-71; vis scholar, Harvard Univ, 80-81; Miller prof, Univ Calif, Berkeley. *Mem:* Fel AAAS; Am Soc Cell Biol; Asn Res Vision & Ophthal. *Res:* Roles of molecular motors in morphogenesis and nitracellular transport in photoreceptors and retinal pigment epithelial cells; techniques are electron microscopy, biochemistry, molecular biology and immunocytochemistry. *Mailing Add:* Dept Molecular & Cell Biol 335 Life Sci Annex Univ Calif Berkeley CA 94720. *Fax:* 510-643-6791; *E-Mail:* burnside@violet.berkeley.edu

BURNSIDE, ORVIN C, WEED SCIENCE, AGRONOMY. *Current Pos:* head, Dept Agron & Plant Genetics, 85-90, PROF WEED SCI, UNIV MINN, 91- *Personal Data:* b Hawley, Minn, June 9, 32; m 54, 91, Clarice Hanson; c Bruce D & Kristi L (Shoemaker). *Educ:* NDak State Univ, BS, 54; Univ Minn, MS, 58, PhD(weed sci), 59. *Honors & Awards:* Outstanding Scientist & Spokesman Award, Nat Agr Chem Asn, 70; Res Award, Weed Sci Soc Am, 79; Outstanding Contributor to Agr Award, Ciba-Geigy, 79; Res Award, Am Soybean Asn, 84; Outstanding Serv to Weed Sci & Nebr Agr Award, 85; Award in Appreciation of Serv to Soybean Indust, 85. *Prof Exp:* From asst prof to prof agron, Univ Nebr, Lincoln, 59-85. *Mem:* Fel Weed Sci Soc Am; Int Weed Sci Soc; fel Am Soc Agron; Crop Sci Soc Am; Coun Agr Sci Technol; Int Cong Plant Protection; hon mem Am Soybean Asn. *Res:* Weed control in agronomic crops; phenology and life history of weeds; integrated weed management; cultural and biological weed management technologies; weed competitiveness in crop cultivare. *Mailing Add:* Dept Agron & Plant Genetics Univ Minn 1991 Buford Circle 308 Hayes Hall St Paul MN 55108-6026. *Fax:* 612-625-1268; *E-Mail:* burns004@maroon.tc.umn.edu

BURNSIDE, PHILLIPS BROOKS, CONTEMPORARY AMERICAN PHILOSOPHY. *Current Pos:* from asst prof to prof, 59-94, ELLA FULTON DUNHAM UNIV PROF PHYSICS, OHIO WESLEYAN UNIV, 94- *Personal Data:* b Columbus, Ohio, July 20, 27; m 54, Christel Rossmann; c Thomas B, Paul & John. *Educ:* Ohio State Univ, BSc, 51, MSc, 54, PhD(physics), 58. *Prof Exp:* Instr physics, Ohio State Univ, 58-59. *Mem:* AAAS; Optical Soc Am; Am Asn Physics Teachers; Hist Sci Soc. *Res:* Foundations of physics; optical physics; philosophy of science. *Mailing Add:* Dept Physics Ohio Wesleyan Univ Delaware OH 43015

BURNSTEIN, RAY A, ELEMENTARY PARTICLE PHYSICS. *Current Pos:* assoc prof, 66-73, PROF PHYSICS, ILL INST TECHNOL, 73- *Personal Data:* b Harrisburg, Pa, Oct 5, 30; m 63, Ilene Gitlin; c Kenneth & Jonathan. *Educ:* Univ Chicago, BS, 52; Univ Wash, MS, 56; Univ Mich, PhD(physics), 60. *Prof Exp:* Asst prof physics, Univ Md, 60-66, vis assoc prof, 72-73. *Concurrent Pos:* Guest scientist, Physics Dept, Fermilab, 80-81, 86-87. *Mem:* Fel Am Phys Soc. *Res:* Experiments using visual detectors and counter techniques at high energy; neutrino interactions. *Mailing Add:* Dept Physics Ill Inst Technol Chicago IL 60616. *Fax:* 312-567-3396; *E-Mail:* hepburnstein@iitvax

BURNSTEIN, THEODORE, virology; deceased, see previous edition for last biography

BURNSWORTH, RANDY JAMES, VIDEO IMPROVEMENT PROCESSING, MACHINE TECHNOLOGY. *Current Pos:* SR SCIENTIST & TECHNOL OFFICER, RAVE ENG CORP, 89- *Personal Data:* b Portland, Ore, Aug 1, 49; m 67, Carolyn Ruth Bowers; c James, Darrin & Deanna. *Prof Exp:* Owner & designer, Randy's Mic & Mach Eng, Calif, 60-70; chief exec officer, Video Ventures, 78-89. *Mailing Add:* Rave Eng Corp 9411 Pipilo St San Diego CA 92129-3563

BUROW, KENNETH WAYNE, JR, synthetic organic chemistry, for more information see previous edition

BURR, ALEXANDER FULLER, X-RAY PHYSICS, PHYSICS EDUCATION. *Current Pos:* asst prof, 66-69, assoc prof, 69-77, PROF PHYSICS, NMEX STATE UNIV, 77- *Personal Data:* b Cambridge, Mass, July 18, 31; m 62, Marjorie McKinstry; c Margaret, Catherine & Susan. *Educ:* Jamestown Col, BS, 53; Univ Edinburgh, MS, 58; Johns Hopkins Univ, PhD(physics), 66. *Prof Exp:* Res asst, Univ NDak, 50 & 53; physicist, Ballistics Res Lab, Aberdeen Proving Ground, Md, 54; res physicist, US Naval Res Lab, 65-66. *Concurrent Pos:* Nat Acad Sci-Nat Res Coun res assoc, 65-66; sr vis fel, Univ Strathclyde, Scotland, 73; chief scientist, Duntech

Indust, 79-80; consult, Int Atomic Energy Agency, 81, 83, 85 & 88-91. *Mem:* Fel AAAS; Am Asn Physics Teachers; Am Phys Soc. *Res:* X-ray wavelengths and the x-ray wavelength scale; determination of electron binding energies; physics of soft x-rays; application of computers to physics education. *Mailing Add:* Dept Physics NMex State Univ Las Cruces NM 88003-0001. *Fax:* 505-646-1934; *E-Mail:* aburr@nmsu.edu

BURR, ARTHUR ALBERT, PHYSICAL METALLURGY. *Current Pos:* RETIRED. *Personal Data:* b Manor, Can, Aug 23, 13; nat US; m 41; c 2. *Educ:* Univ Sask, BS, 38, MS, 40; Pa State Col, PhD(physics), 43. *Honors & Awards:* Outstanding Teacher Award, Am Soc Metals, 52. *Prof Exp:* Instr physics, Univ Sask, 38-40 & Pa State Col, 40-43; res physicist, Armstrong Cork Co, 43-46; from asst prof to prof metall eng, Rensselaer Polytechnic Inst, 46-78, head dept, 55-62, dean, Sch Eng, 62-74, chair, Rensselaer prof, 74-78, emer prof & emer dean, 78. *Mem:* Am Soc Metals; Am Soc Eng Educ; Am Inst Mining, Metall & Petrol Engrs. *Res:* Properties of thin films; physical metallurgy of alloys; thermodynamics and kinetics of metallurgical reactions; nondestructive testing; applications of x-rays; instrumentation. *Mailing Add:* 17 Mallard Way Wynantskill NY 12198

BURR, BROOKS MILO, ICHTHYOLOGY, SYSTEMATICS. *Current Pos:* from asst prof to assoc prof, 77-87, PROF ZOOL, SOUTHERN ILL UNIV, CARBONDALE, 87- *Personal Data:* b Toledo, Ohio, Aug 15, 49; div; c Jordan B. *Educ:* Greenville Col, BA, 71; Univ Ill, Urbana-Champaign, MS, 74, PhD(zool), 77. *Honors & Awards:* Leo Kaplan Mem Res Award, Sigma Xi, 90. *Prof Exp:* Lab instr biol, Greenville Col, 71-72; res asst ichthyol, Ill Natural Hist Surv, 72-77. *Concurrent Pos:* Res assoc & vis prof ichthyol, Inst Marine Sci, Univ NC, Chapel Hill, 83-84; dir grad studies zool, Southern Ill Univ, Carbondale, 84-88 & 94-; res assoc, Ill Nat Hist Surv, 88-; vis prof & res assoc, Dept Biol, Univ NMex, Albuquerque, 90-91; adj prof, Dept Ecol, Ethol & Evolution, Univ Ill, 94- *Mem:* Am Soc Ichthyologists & Herpetologists (secy, 90-94); Soc Syst Zool; Am Fish Soc; AAAS; Asn Syst Collections. *Res:* Systematics, ecology, geography, and conservation biology of North American and Neotropical freshwater fishes; fishes of Kentucky; biology of Ictalurid catfishes. *Mailing Add:* 203 S Wedgwood Carbondale IL 62901. *Fax:* 618-453-2806; *E-Mail:* burr@zoology.siu.edu

BURR, DAVID BENTLEY, SKELETAL BIOLOGY, BIOMECHANICS. *Current Pos:* PROF & CHMN ANAT, IND UNIV, 90-, PROF ORTHOP SURG, 90-, ADJ PROF ANTHROP, 91- *Personal Data:* b Findlay, Ohio, June 28, 51; m 73, Alice M Moore; c Kathryn L & Michael D. *Educ:* Beloit Col, BA, 73; Univ Colo, MA, 74, PhD(anthrop), 77. *Prof Exp:* From instr to asst prof anat, Univ Kans Med Ctr, 77-80; from asst prof to prof anat & orthop surg, WVa Univ Sch Med, 80-90. *Concurrent Pos:* Res grantee, NIH, 88-; consult, Am Inst Biol Sci, Nat Acad Sci, 90-, US Cong Off Technol Assessment, 90 & NASA, 90-91. *Mem:* Orthop Res Soc; Am Asn Anatomists; Am Asn Phys Anthropologists; Am Soc Biomech; Am Soc Gravitiational & Space Biol; Sigma Xi. *Res:* Biological & mechanical aspects of age-related bone & cartilage changes including mechanical usage effects on the health and degeneration of joints, bone remodeling physiology and sports medicine; causes, prevention and treatment of osteoporosis, arthritis and related musculoskeletal diseases. *Mailing Add:* 4910 Melbourne Rd Indianapolis IN 46208. *Fax:* 317-278-2040; *E-Mail:* dburr@indyvax.iupui.edu

BURR, JOHN GREEN, PHOTOCHEMISTRY, PHOTOBIOLOGY. *Current Pos:* prof, 69-86, EMER PROF CHEM & RADIOL SCI, UNIV OKLA, 86- *Personal Data:* b Ft Sill, Okla, Mar 12, 18; m 43; c 7. *Educ:* Mass Inst Technol, BS & MS, 40; Northwestern Univ, PhD(org chem), 48. *Honors & Awards:* Rosetta Brigel Bartin lectr, Univ Okla, 68. *Prof Exp:* Chemist, Jackson Lab, E I du Pont de Nemours & Co, Inc, 40-41, 42, asst, Manhattan Dist, Chicago, 43-44; asst prof chem, Miami Univ, 47-48; sr chemist, Oak Ridge Nat Lab, 48-57; supvr, Atomics Int, 57-62; group leader, NAm Sci Ctr, 62-69. *Concurrent Pos:* USPHS spec fel, Univ London, Eng, 53-54; Guggenheim fel, Cambridge Univ, 65-66; USPHS serv fel, 75-76; vis prof, Hebrew Univ & Max Planck Inst Radiation Chem, 75; NIH Serv fel, Nat Cancer Inst, 75-76. *Mem:* AAAS; Am Chem Soc; Radiation Res Soc; fel Am Inst Chem; Am Photobiol Asn. *Res:* Isotope tracers; organic radiation chemistry; organic reaction mechanisms; nucleic acid photochemistry; aqueous photochemistry; energy transfer; coal chemistry and properties; chemiluminescence. *Mailing Add:* 1101 Woodland Dr Norman OK 73072-6350

BURR, WILLIAM WESLEY, JR, BIOCHEMISTRY, MEDICINE. *Current Pos:* chmn, Med & Health Scis Div, 84-90, EMER CHMN, MED SCIS DIV, OAK RIDGE ASSOC UNIV, 90- *Personal Data:* b Lincoln, Nebr, Mar 12, 23; m 50, Cornelia Clary; c William, Cornelia A, George, Mamie, Linda & Scott. *Educ:* Univ Nebr, AB, 47; Univ Ill, MS, 48, PhD(chem), 51; Univ Tex, MD, 60. *Prof Exp:* From asst prof biochem to prof, Southwestern Med Sch, Tex, 51-63; chief, Med Res Br, US AEC, 61-69, asst dir med & health res, Div Biol & Med, 70-72, dep dir, Div Biomed & Environ Res, 72-75; dep dir, Div Biomed & Environ Res, US Energy Res & Develop Admin, 75-77; dep dir, Div Biomed & Environ Res, US Dept Energy, 77-78, actg dir, 78-79, dir, 79-80, dep asst secy res, Off Environ, 80-81. *Mem:* Fel AAAS; Am Inst Nutrit; Am Chem Soc; Am Soc Biochem & Molecular Biol; AMA. *Res:* Protein and lipid metabolism. *Mailing Add:* PO Box 3567 Gaithersburg MD 20885

BURRAGE, LAWRENCE MINOTT, ELECTRICAL ENGINEERING, PHYSICS. *Current Pos:* VPRES, VAN BURR ASSOC, 90- *Personal Data:* b Cleveland, Ohio, Nov 18, 25; m 50, Ruth Van Derwerken; c Margery, David, Paul & Cathleen. *Educ:* Rensselaer Polytech Inst, BEE, 51; Marquette Univ, MS, 68. *Honors & Awards:* Centennial Medal, Inst Elec & Electronics Engrs, 84. *Prof Exp:* Jr engr, Line Mat Industs, 51-52, asst engr test, 52-55, engr, 55-59, engr design, 59-61; sr engr res & develop, Cooper Power Systs, 61-69, chief engr, 69-78, prog mgr, 78-80, sr staff engr, 80-92. *Mem:* Sr mem & fel Inst Elec & Electronics Engrs; Am Vacuum Soc; Gaseous Electronics Conf; Am Phys Soc; Nuclear & Plasma Sci Soc (secy, 80). *Res:* Electric arc; electrical insulation; arc interruption phenomena. *Mailing Add:* 1221 Columbia Ave South Milwaukee WI 53172-3619

BURRELL, DAVID COLIN, CHEMICAL OCEANOGRAPHY. *Current Pos:* RETIRED. *Personal Data:* b Eng. *Educ:* Univ Nottingham, BS, 61, PhD(geochem), 64. *Prof Exp:* From asst prof to assoc prof, Univ Alaska, 65-76, prof marine sci, 76- *Mem:* Geochem Soc; Am Geophys Union; Arctic Inst NAm. *Res:* Marine trace metal chemistry. *Mailing Add:* 1005 Gilmore St Fairbanks AK 99701

BURRELL, ELLIOTT JOSEPH, JR, PHYSICAL CHEMISTRY. *Current Pos:* from asst dean to assoc dean sci, Col Arts & Sci, 70-74, asst prof, 63-65, ASSOC PROF CHEM, LOYOLA UNIV, CHICAGO, 65- *Personal Data:* b Phoenix, Ariz, Feb 3, 29; m 50, Alicia Swiderski; c Patricia, Michael, Marcia & Stephen. *Educ:* Univ Notre Dame, BS, 50, MS, 51; Pa State Univ, PhD(phys chem), 54. *Prof Exp:* Res chemist, Fabrics & Finishes Div, E I du Pont de Nemours & Co, Inc, 54-58, from res chemist to sr res chemist, Radiation Physics Lab, 58-63. *Concurrent Pos:* Lectr, Temple Univ, 55-57, 58-63 & Univ Pa, 57-58; consult, Commonwealth Edison, 78-82. *Mem:* Am Chem Soc. *Res:* Nuclear and radiation chemistry; pulse radiolysis; photochemistry; kinetics; physical-organic chemistry; magnetic resonance spectroscopy; flash photolysis. *Mailing Add:* Dept Chem Loyola Univ 6525 N Sheridan Rd Chicago IL 60626

BURRELL, KEITH H, PLASMA PHYSICS. *Current Pos:* coordr, 82-86, sr tech adv to mgr, 86-91, SR TECH ADV, BOUNDRY PHYSICS & TECHNOL DIV, GEN ATOMICS, 91- *Educ:* Stanford Univ, BS, 68; Calif Inst Technol, MS, 70, PhD(physics appl math & history), 74. *Prof Exp:* Group leader, Oak Ridge Nat Lab, 76-82. *Mem:* Fel Am Phys Soc. *Res:* Theoretical and experimental plasma physics; author of 11 publications. *Mailing Add:* 13595 Mira Montana Dr Del Mar CA 92014

BURRELL, ROBERT, IMMUNOLOGY, MICROBIOLOGY. *Current Pos:* RETIRED. *Personal Data:* b Springfield, Ohio, Aug 26, 33; m 55; c 2. *Educ:* Ohio State Univ, BS, 55, MS, 56, PhD(bact), 58. *Prof Exp:* Asst prof biol sci, Carnegie Inst Technol, 58-61; asst prof, Sch Med, WVa Univ, 61-69, prof microbiol, 69- *Mem:* Am Asn Immunol; fel Am Acad Microbiol; Am Acad Allergy & Clin Immunol. *Res:* Immune injury in pulmonary diseases; tissue antigens; responses to inhaled microbial antigens. *Mailing Add:* 357 Soundview Dr Kill Devil Hills NC 27948. *Fax:* 304-293-7823

BURRELL, VICTOR GREGORY, JR, MARINE SCIENCES. *Current Pos:* assoc marine scientist, Marine Resources Res Inst, 72-73, asst dir, 73-74, dir, 74-91, EMER DIR, MARINE RESOURCES RES INST, SC, 91- *Personal Data:* b Wilmington, NC, Sept 12, 25; m 56, Katherine; c Cheri (Oulla), Cathey (Farley), Charlene (Burroughs) & Sarah. *Educ:* Col Charleston, BS, 49; Col William & Mary, MA, 68, PhD(marine sci), 72. *Prof Exp:* Res assoc, Va Inst Marine Sci, 66-68, from asst marine scientist to assoc marine scientist, 68-72. *Concurrent Pos:* Adj prof biol, Col Charleston, 74-; mem, Outer Continental Shelf Tech Adv Comt Fisheries & adj assoc prof marine biol med, Univ SC, 81- *Mem:* Am Inst Fishery Res Biologists; Estuarine Res Fedn (secy, 77-79); hon mem Nat Shellfish Asn (pres, 82-83); Gulf & Caribbean Fisheries Inst; World Mariculture Soc; hon mem SEastern Estuarine Res Soc (pres, 86-88). *Res:* Estuarine and marine zooplankton dynamics; copepod taxonomy; marine fisheries science; shellfish biology. *Mailing Add:* Marine Resources Res Inst PO Box 12559 Charleston SC 29412

BURRESON, EUGENE M, PROTOZOOLOGY, FISH DISEASES. *Current Pos:* SR MARINE SCIENTIST PARASITOL & ASST PROF, VA INST MARINE SCI, COL WILLIAM & MARY, 77- *Personal Data:* b Seattle, Wash, July 25, 44; m 66; c 2. *Educ:* Eastern Ore State Col, BS, 66; Ore State Univ, MS, 73, PhD(zool), 75. *Prof Exp:* Proj dir, Normandeau Assoc, Inc, 75-77. *Mem:* Am Soc Parasitologists; Soc Protozoologists; Soc Syst Zool. *Mailing Add:* Dept Marine Sci William & Mary Sch Marine Sci Gloucester Point VA 23062

BURRI, BETTY JANE, ANTIOXIDANTS, VITAMINS. *Current Pos:* res chemist GS, 85-91, RES CHEMIST GM NUTRIT, WESTERN HUMAN NUTRIT RES CTR, 91- *Personal Data:* b San Francisco, Calif, Jan 23, 55; m 84, Kurt R Annweiler. *Educ:* San Francisco State Univ, BA, 76; Calif State Univ, Long Beach, MS, 78; Univ Calif, San Diego, PhD(chem), 82. *Prof Exp:* Res assoc molecular immunol, Res Inst Scripps Clin, 82-85. *Concurrent Pos:* Adj prof nutrit, Univ Nev, Reno, 93-; ed, Carotenoid News, 95- *Mem:* Am Soc Clin Nutrit; Asn Women Sci; Am Soc Nutrit Sci. *Res:* Determining whether carotenoids, such as beta-carotene, are essential nutrients for humans; identify the major factors determining the conversion of beta-carotene to vitamin A; identify people with marginal antioxidant nutrition and develop appropriate nutrient guidelines. *Mailing Add:* ARS Western Human Nutrit Ctr PO Box 29997 San Francisco CA 94129-0602. *Fax:* 415-556-1432

BURRIDGE, MICHAEL JOHN, PEST CONTROL, BIOTECHNOLOGY. *Current Pos:* assoc prof, 76-82, chmn, Dept Infectious Dis, 84-93, PROF EPIDEMIOL, UNIV FLA, 82- *Personal Data:* b St Albans, Eng, Apr 27, 42; m 83, Karen M Bengtsson; c Christina M. *Educ:* Univ Edinburgh, BVM&S, 66; Univ Calif, Davis, MPVM, 74, PhD(epidemiol), 76. *Prof Exp:* Res asst, EAfrican Trypanosomiasis Res Org, Uganda, 66; vet, Grant & Arnold, Woking, UK, 67-68; animal health officer, Food & Agr Org UN, Kenya, 68-73; grad res asst, Univ Calif, Davis, 73-76. *Concurrent Pos:* Mem, Nat Acad Sci Comt Animal Health, 80-83; dir, Ctr Trop Animal Health, 82-93. *Mem:* Fel Am Col Epidemiol; Royal Col Vet Surgeons; Am Vet Med Asn. *Res:* Development using biotechnology of improved vaccines for tropical animal diseases that form important constraints to food production in developing countries; development of innovative, non-polluting methods for pest control. *Mailing Add:* Dept Pathobiol Univ Fla PO Box 110880 Gainesville FL 32611-0880. *Fax:* 352-846-0246; *E-Mail:* burridge.vetmed1@mail.health.ufl.edu

BURRIDGE, ROBERT, ASYMPTOTIC ANALYSIS, WAVE MOTION. *Current Pos:* SCI ADV, SCHLUMBERGER-DOLL RES, 86- *Personal Data:* b Westcliff-on-Sea, Essex, UK, Dec 6, 37; m 87, Marylyn Sexton; c Rosalind Kate, Lucinda Clare & Robert Raven. *Educ:* Univ Cambridge, BA, 59, PhD(math), 63, ScD, 80. *Honors & Awards:* Adams Prize, Cambridge Univ, 71. *Prof Exp:* Res fel seismol, Calif Inst Technol, 63-64; res geophysicist, Univ Calif, Los Angeles, 64-65; asst lectr math, Univ Cambridge, 65-67; res fel math, UK Atomic Energy Authority, 67-71; from assoc prof to prof math, Courant Inst, NY Univ, 71-86. *Concurrent Pos:* Fel, King's Col, Cambridge, 65-71; prin investr, NSF, 71-86; consult, Gulf Oil, Pittsburgh, Pa, 78-80 & Exxon, Clinton, NJ, 80-86. *Mem:* Soc Indust & Appl Math; Soc Explor Geophysicists. *Res:* Wave propagation; high frequency asymptotics; caustics; waves in finely layered and heterogeneous media; seismology; earthquake mechanisms; fracture mechanics; mechanics of fluid-filled porous media and other types of media with microstructure. *Mailing Add:* Schlumberger-Doll Res Old Quarry Rd Ridgefield CT 06877-4120

BURRIER, ROBERT E, BIOCHEMISTRY. *Current Pos:* sr scientist, 87-88, prin scientist, 88-89, SR PRIN SCIENTIST, SCHERING-PLOUGH, BLOOMFIELD, NJ, 89- *Personal Data:* b York, Pa, Oct 2, 57; m. *Educ:* Univ Mass, BS, 79; Boston Univ, PhD(biochem), 83. *Prof Exp:* Postdoctoral fel, Lipoprotein Res Lab, Wake Forest Univ, Winston-Salem, NC, 83-85; postdoctoral fel, Cardiovasc Res Inst, Boston Univ Sch Med, 85-86, asst res prof biochem, 86-87. *Concurrent Pos:* NIH training grants, 80-83, 83-85 & 85-86. *Mem:* Am Heart Asn; assoc mem Am Soc Biol Chemists. *Res:* Effect of cholestyramine and a ACAT inhibitor on cholesterol metabolism in the hamster; circulation; author of several articles. *Mailing Add:* Dept Pharmacol Schering-Plough 2015 Galloping Hill Rd Kenilworth NJ 07033-0539. *Fax:* 908-298-3294

BURRILL, CLAUDE WESLEY, SOFTWARE QUALITY ASSURANCE, MATHEMATICS. *Current Pos:* CONSULT, 87- *Personal Data:* b Akron, Iowa, Feb 19, 25; m 93, Shew-Hui Leong; c 3. *Educ:* Univ Iowa, BS, 48, MS, 50, PhD(math), 52. *Hon Degrees:* LHD, William Paterson Col NJ, 79. *Prof Exp:* Instr math, Univ Iowa, 48-52; asst prof, NY Univ, 53-56; mathematician, IBM Corp, 56-57; assoc prof math, NY Univ, 57-67; consult, IBM Systs Res Syst, 57-67, sr staff mem, 67-72, IBM Systs Sci Inst, 72-81, sr staff mem, 81-87. *Concurrent Pos:* Fulbright scholar, 52-53; chmn, Bd Trustees, William Paterson Col, NJ, 74-76, actg pres, 76-77; sr teaching fel, Nat Univ Singapore, 87-89. *Mem:* Am Math Soc; Am Soc Qual Control. *Res:* Financial model building; project methodology; software quality assurance; statistical analysis. *Mailing Add:* 27 E Dovetail Pl Coralville IA 52241

BURRILL, MELINDA JANE, GENETICS, ANIMAL BREEDING. *Current Pos:* from asst prof to assoc prof 76-85, dir, 76-89, PROF & GRAD STUDIES COORDR, SMALL ANIMAL RES LAB, CALIF STATE POLYTECH UNIV, 85- *Personal Data:* b Washington, DC, Mar 31, 47. *Educ:* Univ Ariz, BS, 69; Ore State Univ, PhD(genetics), 74. *Prof Exp:* Lab technologist toxicity, Indust Bio-Test Inc, 69; teaching asst animal sci, Ore State Univ, 70-74. *Concurrent Pos:* Res fel, Univ Minn, 75-76; CIES, res fel, INRA, Jouy-en-Josas, France, 80-; Women in Develop fel, The Gambia, 84. *Mem:* Am Soc Animal Sci; Brit Soc Animal Prod; Can Soc Animal Sci; Am Genetics Asn; Sigma Xi; Am Statist Asn. *Res:* Large animal breeding; selection theory and breed evaluation; sheep and goat semen evaluation and storage; evaluation of various dairy cattle rations. *Mailing Add:* Dept Animal & Vet Sci Calif State Polytech Univ Pomona CA 91768. *Fax:* 909-869-4454; *E-Mail:* mjburrill@csupomona.edu

BURRILL, ROBERT MEREDITH, BIOGEOGRAPHY, PHYSICAL GEOGRAPHY. *Current Pos:* ADJ PROF, TROY STATE UNIV, FLA REGION, 84- *Personal Data:* b Oklahoma City, Okla, Oct 23, 33; m 73, Terry Oshita. *Educ:* Wesleyan Univ, BA, 56; Univ Chicago, MS, 61; Univ Kans, PhD(geog), 70. *Prof Exp:* Instr geog, Ohio Univ, 61-63; asst prof geog, Univ Ga, 66-79; vis assoc prof, Univ WFla, 80-82. *Mem:* Am Geog Soc; Asn Am Geogrs; Ecol Soc Am. *Res:* Investigation of weather effects upon honeybee activity using an invention which makes measure of honeybee activity possible; geographic analysis of animal behavior; environmental resource management (coastal zone). *Mailing Add:* 541 Woodbine Dr Pensacola FL 32503

BURRIS, CONRAD TIMOTHY, CHEMICAL ENGINEERING, PHYSICAL CHEMISTRY. *Current Pos:* Instr chem, Manhattan Col, 55-58, dir chem eng, 58-61, head dept, 61-71, dean eng, 71-80, prof chem eng, 80-89, head dept, 83-89, PROF LECTR, MANHATTAN COL, 89- *Personal Data:* b Edmonton, Alta, May 17, 24; US citizen. *Educ:* Univ Alta, BChE, 46, MChE, 48; Cath Univ Am, PhD(phys chem), 55. *Mem:* Fel Am Inst Chem Engrs; Am Chem Soc; Am Soc Eng Educ; Sigma Xi. *Res:* Pressure effects on liquid phase reactions; dissolved oxygen analysis by polarography; factors influencing oxygen uptake rate in aqueous systems. *Mailing Add:* 4415 Post Rd Bronx NY 10471-3408

BURRIS, JAMES F, HYPERTENSION, PREVENTIVE CARDIOLOGY. *Current Pos:* from asst prof to assoc prof internal med, Georgetown Univ Med Sch, 81-91, asst dean sponsored res, 87-90, ASSOC PROF PHARMACOL, GEORGETOWN UNIV MED CTR, 86-, ATTEND PHYSICIAN MED, 87-, ASSOC DEAN RES OPERS, 90- & PROF INTERNAL MED, 91- *Personal Data:* b Mauston, Wis, Apr 15, 47; m 71, Christine Tuve; c Cameron W. *Educ:* Brown Univ, BA & BSc, 70; Col Physicians & Surgeons, Columbia Univ, MD, 74; Am Bd Internal Med, dipl, 79, dipl geriat med, 88; Am Bd Clin Pharmacol, dipl, 91. *Honors & Awards:* Physicians Recognition Award, Am Med Asn, 82, 85, 88, 91 & 94. *Prof Exp:* Intern, Roosevelt Hosp, 74-75; gen med officer, USPHS, 75-77; resident, Georgetown Univ Med Ctr, 77-79; fel hypertension, Vet Admin Med Ctr, 79-81. *Concurrent Pos:* Res assoc, Hypertension Res Unit, Vet Admin Med Ctr, Washington, DC, 81-92; attending physician, Georgetown Univ Med Ctr, 81-85 & 87-; vis investr, div nephrol & hypertension, Univ Vaudois Med Ctr, Lausanne, Switz, 82-83; consult hypertension, Cardiovasc Ctr, Northern, Va, 84-94; staff physician, Geriat Unit, Vet Admin Med Ctr, Washington, DC, 85-87; mem, Bd Dirs, Nations Capital Affil, Am Heart Asn, Washington, DC, 87-93 & Metrop Wash Chap, Am Geriat Soc, 89-92; bd regents, Am Col Clin Pharmacol, 90-95, Am Bd Clin Pharmacol, 92- *Mem:* Fel Am Col Cardiol; fel Am Col Physicians; fel Am Geriat Soc; Am Soc Clin Pharmacol & Therapeut; Am Soc Hypertension; Nat Coun Univ Res Adminrs. *Res:* Administer medical center research programs, technology transfer, and environmental health and safety; investigator for clinical trials (specifically hypertension, hyperlipidemia, angina) and basic research on glucocorticoid-induced hypertension in rats and sodium-potassium pump in human hypertension; geriatrics; clinical pharmacology. *Mailing Add:* Off Dean Res & Grad Educ NE 120 Med-Dent Georgetown Univ Med Sch 3900 Reservoir Rd NW Washington DC 20007. *Fax:* 202-687-2585; *E-Mail:* burrisj@odrge.odr.georgetown.edu

BURRIS, JOHN EDWARD, MARINE BIOLOGY, PLANT PHYSIOLOGY. *Current Pos:* DIR & CHIEF OFFICER, MARINE BIOL LAB, 92- *Personal Data:* b Madison, Wis, Feb 1, 49; m 74, Sally Sandermann; c Jennifer, Margaret & Mary. *Educ:* Harvard Univ, AB, 71; Univ Calif, San Diego, PhD(marine biol), 76. *Prof Exp:* From asst prof to assoc prof biol, Pa State Univ, 76-85; dir, Bd Biol, Nat Res Coun, 84-89, exec dir, Comn Life Sci, 88-92. *Concurrent Pos:* Adj assoc prof biol, Pa State Univ, 85-89, adj prof, 89-; Mem, Comn Life Sci, 93-97. *Mem:* Am Inst Biol Sci (pres, 96); AAAS. *Res:* Science policy and administration; plant ecology and physiology; photosynthesis and photo-respiration in aquatic and terrestrial plants; coral reef biology. *Mailing Add:* Marine Biol Lab Woods Hole MA 02543. *E-Mail:* jburris@mbl.edu

BURRIS, JOSEPH STEPHEN, PLANT PHYSIOLOGY. *Current Pos:* SEED PHYSIOLOGIST, SEED SCI CTR, IOWA STATE UNIV, 68- *Personal Data:* b Cleveland, Ohio, Apr 18, 42; m 63, Judith Bunkley; c 4. *Educ:* Iowa State Univ, BSc, 64; Va Polytech Inst, MSc, 66, PhD(agron), 68. *Prof Exp:* Instr agron, Va Polytech Inst, 67. *Mem:* Am Soc Agron; Crop Sci Soc Am; Asn Official Seed Analysts; Int Seed Testing Asn. *Res:* Seed quality, production and technology with emphasis on the drying management of seed corn and the production of soybean seed and subsequent quality assurance programs; consultant to development programs. *Mailing Add:* 2727 Meadow Glen Rd Ames IA 50014

BURRIS, LESLIE, NUCLEAR ENGINEERING. *Current Pos:* RETIRED. *Personal Data:* b Carmi, Ill, Sept 1, 22; m 44, Mary E Bush; c Susan (Madeira), James L & Kathryn (Turner). *Educ:* Univ Colo, BS, 43; Ill Inst Technol, MS, 56. *Honors & Awards:* Robert E Wilson Award, nuclear chem eng, 84; Glenn T Seaborg Actinide Separtations Award, 94. *Prof Exp:* Chem engr, Monsanto Chem Co, 43-48; spec assignment, Tracerlab, 48; assoc chem eng, Argonne Nat Lab, 48-62, group leader, sect head, prog mgr & div dir, 48-88, sr chem engr, 62-89, assoc div dir, 69-73, div dir, 73-84, prog mgr, 84-89. *Mem:* Am Nuclear Soc; fel Am Inst Chem Engrs; Sigma Xi. *Res:* Atomic energy; development of processes for recovery and decontamination of nuclear fuels discharged from nuclear power reactors. *Mailing Add:* 206 Douglas Naperville IL 60540

BURRIS, MARTIN JOE, GENETICS, ANIMAL HUSBANDRY. *Current Pos:* RETIRED. *Personal Data:* b Hebron, Nebr, Mar 30, 27; wid; c 4. *Educ:* Univ Nebr, BS, 49, MS, 51; Ore State Col, PhD(genetics), 53. *Prof Exp:* Asst animal breeding, Univ Nebr, 49-51; asst prof, Univ Ark, 53-54; assoc prof, Va Agr Exp Sta, 54-57; animal geneticist, Coop State Res Serv, USDA, 57-58, prin animal geneticist, 58-66, asst dir, Mont Agr Exp Sta, Mont State Univ, 66-67, assoc dir, 67-80, prof, Animal & Range Sci Dept, 80- *Concurrent Pos:* Vis prof animal sci, Purdue Univ, 64-65. *Mem:* Am Soc Animal Sci; Genetics Soc Am. *Res:* Beef cattle breeding; hormone physiology; meat processing; growth in domestic animals; livestock breeding and genetics; research administration. *Mailing Add:* 2503 Springcreek Dr Bozeman MT 59715

BURRIS, ROBERT HARZA, BIOCHEMISTRY, MICROBIOLOGY. *Current Pos:* Asst agr bact, Univ Wis-Madison, 36-40, from instr to prof biochem, 41-84, chmn dept, 58-70, EMER PROF BIOCHEM, UNIV WIS-MADISON, 84- *Personal Data:* b Brookings, SDak, Apr 13, 14; m 45, Katherine B Brusse; c Jean, John & Ellen. *Educ:* SDak State Univ, BS, 36; Univ Wis, MS, 38, PhD(agr bact), 40. *Hon Degrees:* DSc, SDak State Univ, 66. *Honors & Awards:* Stephen Hales Award & Charles Reid Barnes Award,

Am Soc Plant Physiol; Thom Award, Soc Indust Microbiol; Browning Award, Am Soc Agron; Carty Award, Nat Acad Sci; Wolf Award; Spencer Award, Am Chem Soc; Nat Medal Sci. *Concurrent Pos:* Nat Res Coun fel, Columbia Univ, 40-41; consult, NSF, 53-57 & NIH, 61-71; Guggenheim fel, 54; chmn bot sect, Nat Acad Sci, 71; Indo-US Sci Technol Initiative, NASA-CELSS, Bd Sci Tech Int Develop. *Mem:* Nat Acad Sci; Am Soc Biochem & Molecular Biol; Am Chem Soc; Soc Plant Physiol (pres, 60); Am Acad Arts & Sci; Am Philos Soc; foreign fel Indian Nat Sci Acad. *Res:* Biological nitrogen fixation; respiration of plants; nitrogen metabolism of plants; photosynthesis; biological oxidations; cytochromes; hydrobiology. *Mailing Add:* Dept Biochem 420 Henry Mall Univ Wis Madison WI 53706-1569. *Fax:* 608-262-3453; *E-Mail:* burris@biochem.wisc.edu

BURROS, RAYMOND HERBERT, BAYESIAN STATISTICS. *Current Pos:* RETIRED. *Personal Data:* b Scranton, Pa, Sept 24, 22; m 50, Helen Klenetsky; c Jonathan I & Deborah. *Educ:* Trinity Col, BS, 45; Yale Univ, MA, 46, PhD(psychol), 49. *Prof Exp:* Asst prof psychol, Univ Ark, 49-51 & Univ Ill, 51-54; vis assoc prof, Univ Houston, 54-55; dir statist controls, Inst Motivational Res Inc, 55; sr opers res analyst, Tech Opers Inc, 55-61; indust design specialist human factors, Gen Elec Co, 61-62; opers res scientist sr, Syst Develop Corp, 62-66; sr opers res analyst, Sanders Assoc Inc, 67-68; sr engr, Sperry Rand Corp, 68-69; res engr, Port Authority NY & NJ, 69-79; staff engr, Lockheed Elec Co Inc, 80-81, eng sect head & staff engr, Harris Corp, 81-84, sr engr, Eaton Corp, 84-90. *Mem:* Am Statist Asn; Sigma Xi. *Res:* Application theory of stochastic processes to structural engineering, including spectral analysis and fire protection; logical foundations of statistical decision theory; application of Bayesian statistics to electronic warfare. *Mailing Add:* 55 Fleets Cove Rd Huntington NY 11743

BURROUGHS, RICHARD, COASTAL RESOURCE MANAGEMENT. *Current Pos:* ASST/ASSOC PROF, GRAD PROG MARINE AFFAIRS, UNIV RI, KINGSTON, 83- *Personal Data:* b New Haven, Conn, July 5, 46; m 84, Nancy Rowe; c 2. *Educ:* Princeton Univ, AB, 69; Mass Inst Technol, PhD(oceanog & marine geol), 75. *Prof Exp:* Staff off, Nat Res Coun, Nat Acad Sci, 74-77; sr fel, Marine Biol Lab, 77-79, 81, sci adv to dir, Bur Land Mgt, US Dept Interior, 79-81; res scientist, John E Gray Inst, Lamar Univ, 82-83. *Concurrent Pos:* vis lectr, Sch Forestry & Environ Studies, Yale Univ, 78-79; vis prof, Col Atlantic, 88-90; vis assoc prof, Sch Forestry & Environ Studies, Yale Univ, 90-91, adj prof, 94. *Mem:* AAAS; Am Geophys Union; Geol Soc Am; Sigma Xi; Estuarine Res Fedn. *Res:* Management of marine resources. *Mailing Add:* Dept Marine Affairs Univ RI Kingston RI 02881-0817

BURROUGHS, RICHARD LEE, PETROLEUM GEOLOGY. *Current Pos:* prof geol & head dept, 63-85, EMER PROF GEOL, ADAMS STATE COL, 88- *Personal Data:* b Detroit, Mich, Aug 30, 32; m 60, Ruth Williams; c Pamela Elizabeth & Eric Lee. *Educ:* Okla State Univ, BS, 55; Univ Ariz, MS, 59; Univ NMex, PhD(geol), 72. *Prof Exp:* Explor geologist, Pure Oil Co, 56-58 & Monsanto Chem Co, 60-63. *Concurrent Pos:* Consult geol, 73-; sr consult geologist, Bangladesh Oil, Gas & Mineral Resources, Dhaka, 85-86. *Mem:* Geol Soc Am. *Res:* Subsurface geology of the San Luis Basin and Rio Grande rift; geothermal hydrocarbons. *Mailing Add:* 1008 Douglas Dr Alamosa CO 81101

BURROUS, STANLEY EMERSON, BIOCHEMISTRY. *Current Pos:* RETIRED. *Personal Data:* b Elkhart, Ind, Mar 14, 28; m 56, 90, M J Canne Whallon; c Beth A, Mary R & Sarah E. *Educ:* Manchester Col, BA, 50; Ind Univ, MA, 53; Univ Ill, PhD(microbiol), 62. *Prof Exp:* Res asst virol, Upjohn Co, 58-60; asst prof bioeng, Okla State Univ, 62-63; sr res scientist, E R Squibb Div, Olin Mathieson Chem Corp, 63-65; sr biochemist, Smith Kline & French Labs, Pa, 65-67; unit leader, Eaton Labs Div, Norwich Pharmacal Co, 67-75; pres, Burrous Enterprises, 75-77; sci res admin, NIH, 77-90, referral officer, Div Res Grants, 88-90. *Mem:* AAAS; Am Soc Microbiol; Am Chem Soc. *Res:* New drug development; animal models; selection and management of scientific peer review groups. *Mailing Add:* 243 Red Oak Trail Boone NC 28607-9539

BURROW, GERARD N, INTERNAL MEDICINE. *Current Pos:* RETIRED. *Personal Data:* b Boston, Mass, Jan 9, 33; m 56; c 3. *Educ:* Brown Univ, AB, 54; Yale Univ, MD, 58; FRCPS(C); Am Bd Internal Med, cert, 65 & 74. *Prof Exp:* Intern internal med, Yale New Haven Hosp, 58-59, resident med, 61-63; instr, 65-66, from asst prof to assoc prof internal med, Sch Med, Yale Univ, 70-75; prof med, Univ Toronto, 75-81, Sir John & Lady Eaton prof & chmn, Dept Med, 81-87; vchancellor health sci & dean, Sch Med, Univ Calif, San Diego, 88-92, prof, Dept Med, 88-92. *Concurrent Pos:* Fel metab, Yale New Haven Hosp, 63-65; res career develop award, 68-73; chief med res, Yale New Haven Hosp, 65-66; vis scientist, Fac Med, Univ Marseille, 72-73; dir, Endocrinol Sect & sr physician, Toronto Gen Hosp, 76-81, physician-in-chief, 81-87. *Mem:* Inst Med-Nat Acad Sci; Can Asn Professors Med (vpres, 85, pres, 86); Asn Am Physicians; Can Soc Clin Invest; Endocrine Soc; fel Am Col Physicians; Am Thyroid Asn (pres-elect, 85, pres, 86); Am Fedn Clin Res; AMA; Am Soc Cell Biol. *Res:* Thyroid gland. *Mailing Add:* Off Dean Yale Univ Sch Med 333 Cedar St New Haven CT 06510

BURROW, PAUL DAVID, ELECTRON SCATTERING. *Current Pos:* assoc prof, 76-78, PROF PHYSICS, UNIV NEBR, 78- *Personal Data:* b Okla City, Okla, Aug 3, 38; m 65, Mary L Gwynne; c David I & Gillian A. *Educ:* Mass Inst Technol, BS, 60; Univ Calif, PhD(physics), 66. *Prof Exp:* From asst prof to assoc prof eng & appl sci, Yale Univ, 67-76. *Concurrent Pos:* Exchange prof, Univ Paris-Sud, Orsay, France, 82. *Mem:* Fel Am Phys Soc; Am Indian Sci & Eng Soc. *Res:* Low energy electron scattering studies particularly temporary negative ion formation in complex molecules. *Mailing Add:* Behlen Lab Univ Nebr Lincoln NE 68588. *Fax:* 402-472-2879; *E-Mail:* pburrow@unlinfo.unl.edu

BURROWS, ADAM SETH, HYDRODYNAMICS, RADIATIVE TRANSFER. *Current Pos:* ASSOC PROF PHYSICS & ASTRON, UNIV ARIZ, 86- *Personal Data:* b Salt Lake City, Utah. *Educ:* Princeton Univ, AB, 75; Mass Inst Technol, PhD(physics), 79. *Honors & Awards:* Alfred Sloan Found award, 87. *Prof Exp:* Lectr, physics, Univ Mich, Ann Arbor, 79-80; fel, State Univ NY, Stony Brook, 80-83, asst prof physics, 83-86. *Mem:* Am Astron Soc; Int Astron Union; Am Phys Soc; AAAS; NY Acad Sci; Sigma Xi. *Res:* Supernova theory, neutron stars, neutrino astronomy, brown dwarf theory, nuclear astrophysics; published articles in various journals. *Mailing Add:* Dept Physics Univ Ariz Stewart Observ Tucson AZ 85721

BURROWS, BENJAMIN, INTERNAL MEDICINE, PULMONARY DISEASE. *Current Pos:* PROF MED & DIR RESPIRATORY SCI CTR, UNIV ARIZ, 68- *Personal Data:* b New York, NY, Dec 16, 27; m 49, Nancy A Kreiter; c Jan, Susan (Theobald), Lynn (Evans) & Steven. *Educ:* Johns Hopkins Univ, MD, 49. *Prof Exp:* Instr med, Univ Chicago Clins, 55-56, from asst prof to assoc prof, 56-68. *Concurrent Pos:* Consult, Tucson Vet Admin Hosp. *Mem:* Am Physiol Soc; Am Fedn Clin Res; Am Thoracic Soc; fel Am Col Chest Physicians; fel Am Col Physicians; Asn Am Physicians; emer mem Am Soc Clin Invest. *Res:* Pulmonary disease; pulmonary physiology; diffusion; epidemiology of airways; obstructive diseases. *Mailing Add:* 6840 N Table Mountain Rd Tucson AZ 85718

BURROWS, BRIAN WILLIAM, MANUFACTURING TECHNOLOGY. *Current Pos:* VPRES RES & DEVELOP, USG CORP, 86- *Personal Data:* b Burnie, Tasmania, Australia, Nov 15, 39; div; c Karin. *Educ:* Univ Tasmania, BSc, 60, BSc Hons, 62; Southampton Univ, PhD, 66. *Prof Exp:* Staff scientist, Tyco Labs Inc, Waltham, 66-68; lectr, Macquarie Univ, Sydney, 69-71; chef de sect, Battelle-Geneva, Switz, 71-75; group leader, Inco Ltd, Mississauga, 76-77; mgr prog & lab dir, Gould Inc, Rolling Meadows, 77-86. *Concurrent Pos:* Mem bd dirs, Ibacos Inc, Pittsburgh; co rep, Indust Res Inst, Washington. *Mem:* AAAS; Am Chem Soc; Mat Res Soc; Inst Elec & Electronics Engrs. *Res:* Product and process development in building materials; contributed articles to technical journals and patentee in field. *Mailing Add:* USG Res Ctr 700 N US Hwy 45 Libertyville IL 60048-1296. *Fax:* 847-362-4871

BURROWS, CYNTHIA JANE, PHYSICAL ORGANIC CHEMISTRY, BIO-ORGANIC CHEMISTRY. *Current Pos:* ASSOC PROF CHEM, STATE UNIV NY, STONY BROOK, 83- *Personal Data:* b St Paul, Minn, Sept 23, 53. *Educ:* Univ Colo, Boulder, BA, 75; Cornell Univ, MS, 78, PhD(chem), 82. *Prof Exp:* Res assoc org chem, Univ Louis Pasteur, Strasbourg, France, 81-83. *Mem:* Am Chem Soc; Sigma Xi; AAAS. *Res:* Synthetic macrocyclic compounds for formation of molecular complexes; enzyme mimetic chemistry; reaction mechanisms. *Mailing Add:* Dept Chem Univ Utah Salt Lake City UT 84112

BURROWS, ELIZABETH PARKER, MASS SPECTROMETRY. *Current Pos:* res chemist, Biomed Res & Develop Lab, 80-95, RES CHEMIST, CTR PREV MED, US ARMY, 96- *Personal Data:* b Pittsburgh, Pa, Nov 5, 30; m 58, Dickinson. *Educ:* Middlebury Col, AB, 52; Stanford Univ, MS, 54, PhD(chem), 57. *Prof Exp:* Res assoc pharmacol, Stanford Univ, 56-57; fel chem, Wayne State Univ, 57-58; fel, Mass Inst Technol, 58-61, res assoc, 62-66; res assoc, Children's Cancer Res Found, Mass, 66-67; staff scientist, Worcester Found Exp Biol, 67-70; res assoc chem, Oakland Univ, 70-71; from res assoc to res asst prof, Vanderbilt Univ, 71-76; res assoc, Johns Hopkins Univ, 76-79; lectr, Univ Md, 79-80. *Mem:* Am Chem Soc; Am Inst Chemists; Sigma Xi. *Res:* Mechanistic and analytical problems associated with trace organics in the environment; organic structural determination by spectroscopic methods; ion-molecule reactions in mass spectrometry. *Mailing Add:* 5111 Valley Pine Ct Frederick MD 21703-7432

BURROWS, ENID LORETTA REEDER, MATHEMATICS EDUCATION, MATHEMATICS TECHNOLOGY & CURRICULUM. *Current Pos:* PROF MATH & DEPT CHAIR, PLYMOUTH STATE COL, 70- *Personal Data:* b San Diego, Calif, Sept 5, 42; m 69, wid; c Robin & Lanette. *Educ:* Univ Nebr, Lincoln, BS, 64; Univ Southern Ill, Carbondale, MS, 66; Univ NH, PhD(math), 78. *Honors & Awards:* Balomenos Math Educ Serv Award, 94. *Prof Exp:* Asst prof math, Nebr Wesleyan Univ, 66-70. *Concurrent Pos:* Vis prof math, Hollins Col, 84-85; Am Coun Educ fel, 95-96; inst fel, Bates Col, 96-97. *Mem:* Math Asn Am; Nat Coun Teachers Math; Consortium Math & Appln; Asn Women Math. *Res:* Collegiate mathematics education, development of curriculum; use of technology to teach mathematics. *Mailing Add:* Math Dept Plymouth State Col Plymouth NH 03264. *E-Mail:* enidb@psc.plymouth.edu

BURROWS, GEORGE EDWARD, VETERINARY PHARMACOLOGY, VETERINARY TOXICOLOGY. *Current Pos:* PROF CLIN PHARMACOL & TOXICOL, OKLA STATE UNIV, 78- *Personal Data:* b Seattle, Wash, Feb 17, 35; m 55; c 6. *Educ:* Univ Calif, Davis, BS, 64, DVM, 66; Wash State Univ, MS, 69, PhD(pharmacol, toxicol), 72. *Prof Exp:* From instr to asst prof vet med, Col Vet Med, Wash State Univ, 66-72; vis lectr, Univ Nairobi & Colo State Univ, 72-74; asst prof, Col Vet Med, Wash State Univ, 74-75; assoc prof vet pharmacol & toxicol, Univ Idaho & Northwest Col Vet Med, 75-78. *Concurrent Pos:* Vis prof, Univ Zimbabwe, 86-87. *Mem:* Am Vet Med Asn; Am Col Vet Toxicologists. *Res:* Cyanide intoxication and its therapy and prevention; plants toxic to domestic animals; diet and its effects on xenobiotic disposition in animals; clinical pharmacology of antibiotics in domestic animals. *Mailing Add:* Dept Anat Pathol & Pharmacol Okla State Univ Stillwater OK 74078

BURROWS, JAMES H, MATHEMATICS. *Current Pos:* DIR, COMPUT SYSTS LAB, NAT INST STAND & TECHNOL, 79- *Personal Data:* b Williamsport, Pa. *Educ:* Mass Inst Technol, BS, 49; Univ Chicago, MS, 51. *Concurrent Pos:* Chmn, Info Systs Stand Bd, Am Nat Stand Inst; mem, Comt Comput Res & Applns, Fed Coord Coun Sci Eng & Technol; mem, Fed Info Resources Mgt Policy Coun. *Mem:* Inst Elec & Electronics Engrs; AAAS; Asn Comput Mach; Data Processing Mgrs Asn. *Res:* Computer sciences. *Mailing Add:* 6101 Edsall Rd Apt 206 Alexandria VA 22304

BURROWS, KERILYN CHRISTINE, POLAROGRAPHY, VOLTAMETRY. *Current Pos:* ASST PROF CHEM, MADONNA COL, 78- *Personal Data:* b Catasauqua, Pa, Jan 15, 51; m 79. *Educ:* Muhlenberg Col, BS, 72; Lehigh Univ, PhD(chem), 79. *Prof Exp:* Instr chem, Muhlenberg Col, 76-78. *Mem:* Am Chem Soc; Nat Wildlife Fedn. *Res:* Linear sweep differential pulse voltametry; analysis of metals in environmental systems. *Mailing Add:* 4202 Hart Rd Richfield OH 44286-9782

BURROWS, MICHAEL L(EONARD), ELECTRICAL ENGINEERING. *Current Pos:* STAFF MEM, LINCOLN LAB, MASS INST TECHNOL, 64- *Personal Data:* b London, Eng, July 30, 34; m 60; c 3. *Educ:* Univ London, BSc, 56; Univ Mich, MS, 59, PhD(elec eng), 64. *Prof Exp:* Apprentice elec eng, Brit Insulated Callenders Cables, 56-58, sci off electronics, 59-60. *Mem:* Sr mem Inst Elec & Electronics Engrs; Brit Inst Elec Engrs. *Res:* Antennas, electromagnetic scattering and propagation; eddy-current testing; communications. *Mailing Add:* Mass Inst Technol Lincoln Lab PO Box 73 Lexington MA 02173

BURROWS, ROBERT BECK, parasitology; deceased, see previous edition for last biography

BURROWS, THOMAS WESLEY, NUCLEAR PHYSICS, COMPUTER PROGRAMMING. *Current Pos:* asst physicist, Nat Neutron Cross Sect Ctr, 74-76, assoc physicist nuclear physics, 76-78, PHYSICIST, NAT NUCLEAR DATA CTR, BROOKHAVEN NAT LAB, 78- *Personal Data:* b Janesville, Wis, May 17, 43; m 68; c 2. *Educ:* Univ Wis-Madison, BS, 65, PhD(physics), 72. *Prof Exp:* Nuclear Info Res assoc, Univ Ky, 72-74. *Concurrent Pos:* Secy, Panel Ref Nuclear Data, 76-81; file mgr, Evaluated Nuclear Struct Data File, 81-82; secy & ed, NEANDC Specialists Meeting on Yields & Decay Data Fission Prod Nuclides, 83-84. *Mem:* Am Phys Soc; Inst Physics; affil mem Am Chem Soc; AAAS. *Res:* Nuclear structure; neutron physics; evaluating nuclear structure and decay data for publication in nuclear data sheets; supervise other evaluators; develop, modify and write analysis programs for these activities. *Mailing Add:* Nat Nuclear Data Ctr Bldg 197D Brookhaven Nat Lab PO Box 5000 Upton NY 11923

BURROWS, VERNON DOUGLAS, PLANT BREEDING. *Current Pos:* Plant physiologist, 58-69, head, 69-97, EMER HEAD, CEREAL SECT, RES STA, AGR CAN, 97- *Personal Data:* b Winnipeg, Man, Jan 9, 30; m 54; c 2. *Educ:* Univ Man, BSA, 51, MSc, 53; Calif Inst Technol, PhD, 58. *Honors & Awards:* Grindley Medal, Agr Inst Can, 75. *Res:* Plant breeding in general and oats breeding in particular. *Mailing Add:* 32 Scholar Ct Nepean ON K2E 7S2 Can

BURROWS, WALTER HERBERT, INDUSTRIAL CHEMISTRY. *Current Pos:* RETIRED. *Personal Data:* b Columbia, SC, Oct 23, 11; m 35; c 2. *Educ:* Emory Univ, AB, 33, MS, 38. *Prof Exp:* Prof sci & math, Spartanburg Jr Col, SC, 38-41; from instr to asst prof chem, Ga Inst Technol, 41-56, res assoc prof & head, Indust Prod Br, Eng Exp Sta, 56-67, prin res chemist & head, Spec Projs Br, 67-73, head, Indust Chem Lab, Eng Exp Sta, 73-76. *Concurrent Pos:* Pres, W H Burrows, Consult, 72- *Mem:* AAAS; Am Chem Soc; Am Inst Chemists; Am Inst Chem Engrs; Nat Fire Protection Asn; Am Soc Testing & Mat. *Res:* Surface chemistry, lubricant, coatings, adhesives sealants, detergents, corrosion; fire and combustion technology; nomography, graphical and mechanical computation; bioconversion of energy, anaerobic fermentation, waste utilization. *Mailing Add:* 3007 Northbrook Dr Atlanta GA 30340-4317

BURROWS, WILLIAM DICKINSON, ENVIRONMENTAL CHEMISTRY. *Current Pos:* environ engr, Biomed Res & Develop Lab, 74-94, ENVIRON ENGR, CTR HEALTH PROM & PREV MED, US ARMY, 94- *Personal Data:* b Saginaw, Mich, Dec; m 58, Elizabeth Parker. *Educ:* Cornell Univ, BA, 53; Stanford Univ, PhD(chem), 56; Vanderbilt Univ, MS, 73. *Prof Exp:* Res assoc chem, Mass Inst Technol, 58-61; asst prof, Clarkson Col Technol, 61-62; res assoc, Mass Inst Technol, 62-66; sr vis scientist, US Army Natick Labs, 66-68; sr chemist, Garrett Res & Develop Co, Occidental Petrol Corp, 68-69; sr engr, Assoc Water & Air Resources Engrs Inc, 73-75. *Concurrent Pos:* Adj prof, George Washington Univ, 82-87; vpres, Schaub Burrows Assoc, Ltd, 85- *Mem:* Am Acad Environ Engrs; Water Environ Fed; Sigma Xi; Am Water Works Asn. *Res:* Aquatic chemistry and treatment of munitions production wastes; military water supply and sanitation. *Mailing Add:* US Army Ctr Health Prom & Prev Med Aberdeen Proving Ground MD 21010-5422. *E-Mail:* william_burrows@chppm-ccmail.apgea.army.mil

BURRUS, CHARLES ANDREW, JR, OPTOELECTRONICS. *Current Pos:* mem tech staff, AT&T Bell Labs, 55-96, CONSULT LUCENT BELL LABS, 96- *Personal Data:* b Shelby, NC, July 16, 27; m 57, Barbara Dunlevy; c 3. *Educ:* Davidson Col, BS, 50; Emory Univ, MS, 51; Duke Univ, PhD, 55. *Honors & Awards:* David Richardson Medal, Optical Soc Am, 82. *Prof Exp:* Res assoc physics, Duke Univ, 54-55. *Concurrent Pos:* Distinguished mem tech staff, AT&T Bell Labs, 82, fel, 88. *Mem:* Fel AAAS; fel Inst Elec & Electronics Engrs; fel Am Phys Soc; fel Optical Soc Am. *Res:* Microwave spectroscopy in the shorter millimeter and sub-millimeter wave region; millimeter-wave diodes; semiconductor lasers, electroluminescent diodes and high speed photodetectors; optical communications; optical-fiber devices; single-crystal fibers; photonic and opto-electronic integrated circuits. *Mailing Add:* Crawford Hill Lab Lucent Bell Labs 791 Holmdel-Keyport Rd Holmdel NJ 07733-0400. *Fax:* 732-888-7074; *E-Mail:* cburrus@lucent.com

BURRUS, CHARLES SIDNEY, ELECTRICAL ENGINEERING. *Current Pos:* from asst prof to assoc prof, 65-74, PROF ELEC ENG, RICE UNIV, 74- *Personal Data:* b Abilene, Tex, Oct 9, 34; m 58; c 2. *Educ:* Rice Univ, BA & BS, 58, MS, 60; Stanford Univ, PhD(elec eng), 65. *Honors & Awards:* Tech Achievement Award, Inst Elec & Electronics Engrs, 85. *Prof Exp:* Res asst elec eng, Stanford Univ, 62-65. *Concurrent Pos:* Grants, Ford Found, 62-66, NSF, 66-68, 70-85; sr award, Alexander von Humboldt Found, 75; vis prof, Univ Erlangen, Ger, 75-76 & 79-80; Fulbright fel, 79; vis fel, Trinity Col, Cambridge, 84; chmn, ECE dept, Rice Univ, 84-; vis prof, Mass Inst Technol, 89-90. *Mem:* Fel Inst Elec & Electronics Engrs. *Res:* System theory, especially signal theory; optimization theory; digital signal processing. *Mailing Add:* Dept Elec Eng Rice Univ Box 1892 Houston TX 77251

BURRUS, ROBERT TILDEN, INORGANIC & PHYSICAL CHEMISTRY, FIBER & POLYMER PROCESSING. *Current Pos:* res chemist, Fiber Surface Res Sect, 62-69, sr res chemist, 69-89, RES ASSOC, DACRON STAPLE & YARN, EI DUPONT DE NEMOURS & CO, 89- *Personal Data:* b High Point, NC, July 15, 35; m 64, Patricia A Newman; c Robert T Jr & Sarah N. *Educ:* Univ NC, BS, 57; Univ Tenn, PhD(Chem), 62. *Prof Exp:* Trainee, Westinghouse Elec Corp, 57-58; asst chem, Univ Tenn, 58-62. *Mem:* Am Chem Soc. *Res:* Physical inorganic chemistry; electrochemistry in nonaqueous media; friction and surface chemistry of polymers; finish development for synthetic fibers; fiber and polymer chemistry; physics of fiber formation and quenching; fiber spinning and processing; texturing of continous filament yarns; process waste minimization; new fiber development. *Mailing Add:* 1601 Sabra Dr Kinston NC 28501-1414. *Fax:* 919-522-6597

BURRY, JOHN HENRY WILLIAM, MATHEMATICS, FRACTALS & CHAOS THEORY. *Current Pos:* Lectr, 61-63, from asst prof to assoc prof, 63-75, head, Dept Math Statist & Comput Sci, 76-85, PROF MATH & STATIST, MEM UNIV NFLD, 86- *Personal Data:* b Nfld, June 10, 38; m 65, Myrtle Tucker; c Brett & Dana. *Educ:* Mem Univ Nfld, BAEd, 58; Dalhousie Univ, MSc, 61; Queen's Univ, Ont, PhD(math), 71. *Concurrent Pos:* Chmn, Nat Can Olympiad Comt, 78-80. *Mem:* Can Math Soc; Can Asn Univ Teachers; Am Math Soc; Nat Coun Teachers Math; Math Asn Am. *Res:* Radon measures in Euclidian spaces; measure theory; information theory; fractals and chaos theory. *Mailing Add:* Dept Math Mem Univ Nfld Prince Philip Dr St John's NF A1C 5S7 Can. *E-Mail:* jburry@riemann.math.mun.ca

BURRY, KENNETH A, REPRODUCTIVE ENDOCRINOLOGY, INFERTILITY. *Current Pos:* from asst prof to assoc prof, obstet & gynec, Ore Health Sci Univ, 76-89, co-dir infertil serv, 85-89, dir, Ore Reproduction Res & Fertil Prog, 82-89, PROF & ASST CHMN OBSTET & GYNEC, ORE HEALTH SCI UNIV, 89- *Personal Data:* b Monterey Park, Calif, Oct 2, 42; m 82, Katherine Johnson; c Michael C & Lisa B. *Educ:* Whittier Col, BA, 64; Univ Calif, Irvine, MD, 68. *Honors & Awards:* Lange Award, Univ Calif, 66. *Prof Exp:* Fel reprod endocrinol, Univ Wash, 74-76. *Concurrent Pos:* Dir, fel training reprod endocrinol & infertil, Ore Health Sci Univ, 84- *Mem:* Fel Am Col Obstet & Gynec; Endocrine Soc; Am Soc Reprod Med; Soc Reprod Endocrinologists; Soc Reprod Surgeons; Am Fedn Clin Res; Soc Assisted Reprod Technol. *Res:* Evaluation of endocrine and physical causes of reproductive failure; emotional sequence of infertility specifically ovulation induction, in vitro fertilization and endometriosis. *Mailing Add:* 3181 SW Sam Jackson Park Rd Portland OR 97201. *Fax:* 503-494-3708; *E-Mail:* burryk@ohsu.edu

BURSCHKA, MARTIN A, STATISTICAL PHYSICS. *Current Pos:* RES ASSOC, ROCKEFELLER UNIV, 85- *Personal Data:* b Troisdors, WGer, May 11, 52. *Educ:* Univ Aachen, MD, 81, MS, 78; Rikks Univ, Utrecht, PhD(math), 85. *Mem:* AAAS; Am Phys Soc; NY Acad Sci. *Mailing Add:* Elsterweg 10 47229 Duisburg Germany

BURSE, RICHARD LUCK, ENVIRONMENTAL PHYSIOLOGY, ENGINEERING PSYCHOLOGY. *Current Pos:* PHYSIOLOGIST ENVIRON PHYSIOL, US ARMY RES INST ENVIRON MED, 74- *Personal Data:* b Boston, Mass, Feb 6, 36; c 1. *Educ:* Mass Inst Technol, BS, 58; Harvard Univ, MAT, 62; Univ Pittsburgh, MSc, 70. *Hon Degrees:* ScD, Univ Pittsburgh, 72. *Prof Exp:* Sci teacher biol & chem, Newton High Sch, Mass, 62-63; eng psychol human factors, US Army Natick Labs, Mass, 63-69; asst prof physiol, Sch Med, St Louis Univ, 73. *Concurrent Pos:* Mallinkrodt vis prof, Sch Med, St Louis Univ, 73; guest lectr, Sch Allied Health Prof, Boston Univ, 75-80, adj asst prof, 81-; res & develop coordr, Hq US Army Mat Command, Alexandria, Va, 79- *Mem:* Am Physiol Soc; Human Factors Soc; Sigma Xi. *Res:* Environmental and work physiology; human thermoregulatory and altitude adaptation; control of breathing; human strength capabilities. *Mailing Add:* 147 Jackson Rd Newton MA 02158-1406. *Fax:* 508-651-5298

BURSEY, CHARLES ROBERT, HERPTILE PARASITOLOGY, HELMINTHOLOGY. *Current Pos:* from asst prof to assoc prof, 70-83, PROF BIOL, PA STATE UNIV, 83- *Personal Data:* b Paris, Tenn, Feb 13, 40; m 64, Shirley Wright; c Brent & Laura. *Educ:* Kalamazoo Col, BA, 62; Mich State Univ, MS, 65, PhD(zool), 69. *Prof Exp:* NIH fel, Inst Marine Sci, Univ Miami, 69-70. *Concurrent Pos:* Partic, Univ Miami Deep Sea Exped to PR Trench, R/V Pillsbury, 70; chief scientist student training cruises R/V Annandale, Marine Sci Consortium, Millersville, 72-75; instr NSF Sci Student Training Prog Coastal Biol, Marine Sci Consortium, Wallops Island, Va, 77. *Mem:* Wildlife Dis Asn; Am Micros Soc; Am Soc Zoologists. *Res:* Cestode and nematode infections of amphibians and reptiles; pathologies; taxomony. *Mailing Add:* Dept Biol Pa State Univ 147 Shenango Sharon PA 16146-1537

BURSEY, JOAN TESAREK, MASS SPECTROMETRY, ENVIRONMENTAL ANALYSIS. *Current Pos:* sr scientist, 84-87, SR STAFF SCIENTIST, RADIAN CORP, 87- *Personal Data:* b Omaha, Nebr, Mar 25, 43; m 70, Maurice Moyer; c John & Sara. *Educ:* Creighton Univ, BSChem, 65; Univ Calif, Berkeley, PhD(chem), 69. *Prof Exp:* Res assoc chem, Univ NC, Chapel Hill, 69-71; jr chemist, Res Triangle Inst, 71-74, chemist, 74-78, sr chemist, 78-81, mgr, Mass Spectrometry Lab, 81-84. *Mem:* Am Soc Mass Spectrometry; Am Chem Soc; Royal Soc Chem. *Res:* Gas chromatography-mass spectrometry; environmental and biomedical analysis; organic mass spectrometry. *Mailing Add:* 101 Longwood Pl Chapel Hill NC 27514-9584. *Fax:* 919-460-1631

BURSEY, MAURICE MOYER, ANALYTICAL CHEMISTRY. *Current Pos:* from asst prof to assoc prof, 66-74, dir undergrad studies chem, 85-88, PROF CHEM, UNIV NC, CHAPEL HILL, 74- *Personal Data:* b Baltimore, Md, July 27, 39; m 70, Joan Tesarek; c John & Sara. *Educ:* Johns Hopkins Univ, BA, 59, MA, 60, PhD(chem), 63. *Prof Exp:* Lectr chem, Johns Hopkins Univ, 63-64; asst prof, Purdue Univ, 64-66. *Concurrent Pos:* Sloan fel, 69-71; vis scientist, Nato Inst Environ Health Sci, 77-78, sr vis scientist, 84-85. *Mem:* Am Chem Soc; Am Soc Mass Spectrometry; Royal Soc Chem; Japanese Soc Mass Spectros. *Res:* Mass spectrometry; chemistry of gaseous ions by mass spectrometry; chemistry of formation of gaseous ions from condensed phases. *Mailing Add:* 101 Longwood Pl Chapel Hill NC 27514-9584. *Fax:* 919-962-2388

BURSH, TALMAGE POUTAU, PHYSICAL CHEMISTRY. *Current Pos:* Asst instr phys sci, 57, from assoc prof to prof chem, 68-80, AT SOUTHERN UNIV. *Personal Data:* b Leesville, La, Dec 24, 32; m 54; c 3. *Educ:* Southern Univ, BS, 56; Alfred Univ, PhD(chem), 63. *Res:* Interaction of water with silica, alumina and silica alumina co-oxide surfaces and the relationship of these interactions to catalytic activities of these oxides. *Mailing Add:* Dept Chem Southern Univ A&M Col Main Campus PO Box 9200 Baton Rouge LA 70813-9998

BURSIAN, STEVEN JOHN, TOXICOLOGY. *Current Pos:* from asst prof to assoc prof, 79-90, PROF, DEPT ANIMAL SCI, MICH STATE UNIV, 90- *Personal Data:* b Petoskey, Mich, Sept 7, 47; div; c 2. *Educ:* Univ Mich, BS, 69; Univ Minn, MS, 71; NC State Univ, PhD(physiol), 78. *Prof Exp:* Res biologist, US Environ Protection Agency, 71-79. *Mem:* AAAS; Sigma Xi; Soc Toxicol; Soc Neurosci; Soc Exp Biol & Med. *Res:* Examine the neurotoxicological effects of environmental pollutants in various species of animals. *Mailing Add:* Dept Animal Sci Mich State Univ East Lansing MI 48824

BURSNALL, JOHN TREHARNE, ARCHEAN GEOLOGY. *Current Pos:* ASSOC PROF MINERAL & PETROL, ST LAWRENCE UNIV, 89- *Personal Data:* b Neath, UK, May 9, 40; m 66, 85, Catherine Shrady; c Katren & Jon. *Educ:* Univ London, BSc, 68; Univ Cambridge, PhD(geol), 75. *Prof Exp:* Demonstr-tutor geol, Univ Cambridge, 68-72; tutor-organizer natural sci, Workers' Educ Asn, UK, 72-75; asst prof struct geol, Syracuse Univ, 75-82 & St Lawrence Univ, 82-83; prof struct geol, Southampton Col, 83-86, Univ Mass, 86-87 & Univ Idaho, 87-88; prof struct geol, Univ Mass, 86-87 & Univ Idaho, 87-88; res fel geophys, Univ Toronto, 89. *Concurrent Pos:* Vis lectr geol, Cambridgeshire Col Arts & Technol, 68-72. *Mem:* Geol Soc Can; Sigma Xi; Geol Soc Am. *Res:* Geological structure of parts of the northern Appalachians, central Maine, northwest Newfoundland; ophiolite emplacement and deformation history within orogenic belts, shear zones in foliated rocks; mid to lower Archean crust, Kapukasing structual zone, Ontario; fault rocks, Ivanhoe Lake fault zone, Ontario. *Mailing Add:* Dept Geol St Lawrence Univ Canton NY 13617. *Fax:* 315-379-5804; *E-Mail:* jbur@music.stlawu.edu

BURSON, BYRON LYNN, PLANT CYTOGENETICS, PLANT GENETICS. *Current Pos:* RES GENETICIST, SOUTHERN CROP GERMPLASM LAB, AGR RES SERV, USDA, COLLEGE STATION, TEX, 93- *Personal Data:* b Hobart, Okla, Feb 24, 40; m 61, Sharon Conrad; c Laura A & Byron L II. *Educ:* Okla State Univ, BS, 62; Tex A&M Univ, MS, 65, PhD(plant breeding, cytogenetics), 67. *Prof Exp:* Asst prof grass cytogenetics & asst agronomist, Miss State Univ, 67-71, assoc prof grass cytogenetics & assoc agronomist, 71-75; res geneticist, Grassland, Soil & Water Res Lab, Agr Res Serv, USDA, Temple, Tex, 75-93. *Mem:* Fel Am Soc Agron; fel Crop Sci Soc Am; Am Genetic Asn; AAAS. *Res:* Cytogenetics of grasses; reproductive systems, especially apomixis; species relationships within genus paspalum; cell and tissue culture. interspecific hybridization. *Mailing Add:* Dept Soil & Crop Sci USDA Agr Res Serv Tex A&M Univ College Station TX 77843-2474. *Fax:* 409-845-0456; *E-Mail:* b-burson@tamu.edu

BURSON, SHERMAN LEROY, JR, ORGANIC CHEMISTRY. *Current Pos:* RETIRED. *Personal Data:* b Pittsburgh, Pa, Dec 24, 23; m 44; c 4. *Educ:* Univ Pittsburgh, BS, 47, PhD(org chem), 53. *Prof Exp:* Asst chem, Univ Pittsburgh, 47-48, 52; chemist, Lederle Lab Div, Am Cyanamid Co, 52-57; assoc prof chem, Pfeiffer Col, 57-60, prof & chmn dept, 60-63; prof chem, Univ NC, Charlotte, 63-67, chmn dept, 63-75, Charles H Stone prof chem, 67-85, dean, Col Sci & Math, 75-80, dean, Col Arts & Sci, 80-85. *Mem:* Am Chem Soc. *Res:* Biotin analogues; polysaccharides; natural products. *Mailing Add:* 52 Dusty Miller Lane South Chatham MA 02659

BURST, JOHN FREDERICK, CLAY MINERALOGY. *Current Pos:* PRES, TRIANGLE ENVIRON SCI & ENG, 90- *Personal Data:* b St Louis, Mo, Oct 16, 23; m 56; c 4. *Educ:* Univ Mo-Rolla, MS, 47; Univ Mo-Columbia, PhD(geol), 50. *Prof Exp:* Mem staff geol, Shell Develop Co, Tex, 50-65; dir res & develop, Gen Refractories Co, 65, dir res, 65-70, tech dir, 70-73; tech adv, Certain-Teed Prods Co, 73-75; tech dir, Dresser Minerals, 75-80, dir planning, Harbison-Walker Group, 80-82, vpres resource develop, Dresser Minerals Div, Dresser Indust, 82-85; exec dir, Mo Inc Found, 86-88; prin, Immi Consult Group, 85- *Mem:* Fel Geol Soc Am; fel Mineral Soc Am; Clay Minerals Soc (pres, 71); Soc Petrol Geol; Am Ceramic Soc; distinguished mem, Soc Mining Engrs; Mineral Soc London. *Res:* Chemistry minerals and ceramics. *Mailing Add:* 1605 Lincoln Lane Rolla MO 65401-2613

BURSTEIN, DAVID, COSMOLOGY, STRUCTURE OF GALAXIES. *Current Pos:* from asst prof to assoc prof, 82-94, PROF PHYSICS DEPT, ARIZ STATE UNIV, 94- *Personal Data:* b Englewood, NJ, May 19, 47; m 71, Gail Kelly; c Jonathan & Elizabeth. *Educ:* Wesleyan Univ, BA, 69; Univ Calif, Santa Cruz, PhD(astron), 78. *Prof Exp:* Res fel astron, Dept Terrestrial Magnetism, Carnegie Inst Washington, 77-79; res assoc, Nat Radio Astron Observ, 79-82. *Concurrent Pos:* Vis sr astronr, Univ Padova, Italy, Univ Munich, Ger, Beijing Astron Observ, China Nat Cent Univ, Chung-Lin, Roc. *Mem:* Am Astron Soc; Sigma Xi; Int Astron Union. *Res:* Stellar content, structure and dynamics of galaxies; galactic structure; large scale structure of universe cosmology. *Mailing Add:* Dept Physics & Astron Ariz State Univ Box 871504 Tempe AZ 85287-1504. *Fax:* 602-965-7954; *E-Mail:* burstein@samuri.la.asu.edu

BURSTEIN, ELIAS, CONDENSED MATTER PHYSICS. *Current Pos:* prof, 58-82, Mary Amanda Wood prof, 82-88, EMER MARY AMANDA WOOD PROF PHYSICS, UNIV PA, 88- *Personal Data:* b New York, NY, Sept 30, 17; m 43, Rena; c Joanna B, Sandra J & Miriam S. *Educ:* Brooklyn Col, AB, 38; Univ Kans, AM, 41. *Hon Degrees:* DTech, Chalmers Univ Technol, Gothenburg, Sweden, 82; DSc, Brooklyn Col, 85, Emory Univ, 94. *Honors & Awards:* Res Soc Am Pure Sci Award, 58; John Price Wetherill Medal, Franklin Inst, 79; Isakson Prize, Am Phys Soc, 86. *Prof Exp:* Assoc, Nat Defense Res Comt Proj, Mass Inst Technol, 42-44; res & develop proj engr, White Res Assocs Mass, 44-45; physicist, Crystal Br, Naval Res Lab, 45-57, head, Semiconductor Br, 58. *Concurrent Pos:* Chmn, Solid State Sci Comt, Nat Res Coun-Nat Acad Sci, 77-78; ed-in-chief, Solid State Commun; consult, Thomas J Watson Res Ctr, IBM, 71-95; co-ed, Comments on Solid State Physics, 72-; vis Jubilee prof physics, Chalmers Univ Technol, Sweden, 81; Guggenheim fel, 80-81; Alexander von Humboldt sr US scientist award, 88-89. *Mem:* Nat Acad Sci; fel Optical Soc Am; fel Am Phys Soc. *Res:* Dielectrics; electromagnetic phenomena at metal surfaces; surface enhanced Raman scattering; Raman scattering and photoluminescence of adsorbates on metal surfaces; nonlinear optical properties of metal and semiconductor surfaces and interfaces; photophysics of fullerene molecules. *Mailing Add:* Dept Physics Univ Pa Philadelphia PA 19104. *E-Mail:* burstein@dept.physics.upenn.edu

BURSTEIN, SAMUEL Z, APPLIED MATHEMATICS. *Current Pos:* ASSOC PROF APPL MATH, COURANT INST MATH SCI, NY UNIV, 62- *Personal Data:* b Brooklyn, NY, Oct 4, 35; m 59; c 2. *Educ:* Polytech Inst Brooklyn, BME, 57, MME, 58, PhD(mech eng), 62. *Prof Exp:* Instr mech eng, Polytech Inst Brooklyn, 57-62. *Concurrent Pos:* Assoc ed, J Comput Physics, 68-74. *Mem:* Soc Indust & Appl Math. *Res:* Combustion instability in rocket motors; numerical methods in hydrodynamics; computation of shock waves and hypersonic flow; transonic flow; biomechanics; reactive gas dynamics; deformation of nonlinear elastic-plastic materials. *Mailing Add:* Eight Bay Ave Larchmont NY 10538

BURSTEIN, SOL, NUCLEAR & MECHANICAL ENGINEERING. *Current Pos:* CONSULT, 87- *Personal Data:* b Chelsea, Mass, Dec 25, 22; m 45; c Paul H & Nadine A (Hubbell). *Educ:* Northeastern Univ, BS, 44. *Hon Degrees:* DSc, Univ Wis, 87. *Prof Exp:* Chief power plants, Wis Elec Power Co, 65-66, vpres, 66-69, sr vpres, 69-73, dir & exec vpres, 83-84, vchmn bd, 84-87. *Mem:* Nat Acad Eng; fel Am Soc Mech Eng; Am Soc Metals; Am Soc Testing & Mat; Inst Elec & Electronics Engrs. *Mailing Add:* 7475 N Crossway Rd Milwaukee WI 53217. *Fax:* 414-351-0664; *E-Mail:* sburstein@nas.edu; sburstein@nas.bitnet

BURSTEIN, SUMNER, MECHANISM DRUG ACTION. *Current Pos:* ASSOC PROF BIOCHEM, SCH MED, UNIV MASS, 76- *Personal Data:* b Boston, Mass, Feb 22, 32. *Educ:* Wayne State Univ, PhD(chem), 59. *Mem:* AAAS; Am Chem Soc; Am Soc Pharmacol & Exp Therapeut. *Mailing Add:* Dept Biochem Sch Med Univ Mass 55 Lake Ave N Worcester MA 01655-0001. *Fax:* 508-856-6231

BURSTEN, BRUCE EDWARD, INORGANIC CHEMISTRY. *Current Pos:* from asst prof to assoc prof, 80-90, PROF CHEM, OHIO STATE UNIV, 90- *Personal Data:* b Chicago, Ill, Mar 8, 54; m 77, Marian Stager; c Julia. *Educ:* Univ Chicago, SB, 74; Univ Wis, PhD(chem), 78. *Prof Exp:* NSF fel chem, Tex A&M Univ, 78-80. *Concurrent Pos:* Sloan Found fel; teacher-scholar, Dreyfus Found. *Mem:* Am Chem Soc. *Res:* Bonding and electronic structural studies of transition metal complexes, particularly organometallic, organoactinide, and metal cluster systems; molecular orbital theory; organometallic photochemistry. *Mailing Add:* Dept Chem Ohio State Univ 100 W 18th Ave Columbus OH 43210-1173. *Fax:* 614-292-1685; *E-Mail:* bursten.1@osu.edu

BURSTONE, CHARLES JUSTIN, ORTHODONTICS. *Current Pos:* head, Dept Orthod, Sch Dent Med, 70-93, prof, 93-95, EMER PROF, UNIV CONN, 95- *Personal Data:* b Kansas City, Mo, Apr 4, 28. *Educ:* Wash Univ, DDS, 50; Ind Univ, MS, 55. *Hon Degrees:* PhD, Royal Deutol Col. *Prof Exp:* From asst prof to assoc prof orthod, Sch Dent, Ind Univ, 55-70. *Mem:* AAAS; Am Asn Orthod; Am Dent Asn. *Res:* Application of biophysics to orthodontics; soft tissue morphology of the face; segmented arch therapy; growth and development; biomaterials. *Mailing Add:* 252 Old Mountain Rd Farmington CT 06032

BURSUKER, ISIA, TUMOR IMMUNOLOGY, IMMUNOREGULATION. *Current Pos:* sr res scientist, Bristol-Myers Squibb Co, 84-90, sr res investr II, Tumor Immunol, 90-92, sr res investr II, Natural Prods Br, 92-96, GROUP LEADER, BIOMOLECULAR SCREENING, BRISTOL-MYERS SQUIBB CO, 96- *Personal Data:* b USSR, Sept 15, 41; Israel citizen; m 67, Veronika Trubkina; c Moshe. *Educ:* Czernowitz State Univ, USSR, MSc, 68; Weizmann Inst Sci, Israel, PhD(biol), 82. *Prof Exp:* Engr membrane res, Weizmann Inst Sci, 73-78; res assoc tumor immunol, Trudeau Inst, Saranac Lake, NY, 82-84. *Concurrent Pos:* Adj assoc prof, Univ Conn, Storrs, 88- *Mem:* Am Asn Immunologists; Soc Leukocyte Biol; AAAS. *Res:* Research in tumor immunology; down-regulation of antitumor immunity by suppressor cells; immunomodulation; immunotherapy of cancer; modulation of hemopoiesis; biomolecular screening. *Mailing Add:* Natural Prods Res Bristol-Myers Squibb Co 5 Res Pkwy Wallingford CT 06492

BURSZTAJN, SHERRY, NEUROBIOLOGY, TRANSPORT OF SYNAPTIC PROTEINS. *Current Pos:* ASSOC PROF PSYCHIAT NEUROSCI, HARVARD MED SCH, 94- *Personal Data:* b Poland, Feb 19, 46; US citizen; m 84. *Educ:* Fairleigh Dickinson Univ, BS, 69; Syracuse Univ, PhD(develop biol), 74. *Honors & Awards:* Res Career Develop Award. *Prof Exp:* Teaching fel neurobiol, Med Col, Cornell Univ, 74-76; teaching fel immunol, Med Sch, Yale Univ, 76-77; res assoc neurobiol, Med Sch, Harvard Univ, 77-80; asst prof neurobiol, Baylor Col Med, 80-90, asst prof psychiat neurosci, 90-93. *Concurrent Pos:* Corp mem, Marine Biol Lab, Woods Hole, Mass, 81-; adv, Mult Sclerosis Soc, 85-; vis scholar, Harvard Univ, 87-88; mem, Study Sect, NIH, 93- *Mem:* Am Soc Cell Biol; Soc Neurosci; AAAS. *Res:* Mechanisms involved in the organization of the postsynaptic membrane during early stages of synapse formation; excito toxicity. *Mailing Add:* Mailman Res Ctr McLean Hosp 115 Mill St Belmont MA 02178-1048. *Fax:* 617-855-3570; *E-Mail:* bursztajn@helix.mgh.harvard.edu

BURT, ALVIN MILLER, III, NEUROCHEMISTRY, NEUROANATOMY. *Current Pos:* from asst prof to prof anat, 66-85, PROF CELL BIOL, VANDERBILT UNIV, MED SCH, 85- *Personal Data:* b Bridgeport, Conn, Aug 14, 35; m 61,91, Judith Nath; c Constance (Walker), Carolyn M & Stephen J Nath. *Educ:* Amherst Col, BA, 57; Univ Kans, PhD(anat), 62. *Prof Exp:* Asst prof anat, Med Col Va, Richmond, 62-63; instr, Sch Med, Yale Univ, 63-66. *Concurrent Pos:* USPHS res career develop award, Vanderbilt Univ, 68-73; vis scientist neurochem, Agr Res Coun, Inst Animal Physiol, Babraham, Cambridge, Eng, 72-73; prof cell biol, 94- *Mem:* AAAS; Am Soc Neurochem; Am Asn Anat; Soc Neurosci; Int Soc Neurochem; Int Brain Res Orgn; Sigma Xi. *Res:* Developmental neurochemistry with particular reference to neurotransmitter systems and intermediary metabolism; author of various publications. *Mailing Add:* Dept Cell Biol Vanderbilt Univ Nashville TN 37232. *Fax:* 615-343-7711; *E-Mail:* alvin.burt@mcmail.vanderbilt.edu

BURT, BRIAN AUBREY, DENTAL EPIDEMIOLOGY. *Current Pos:* assoc prof, 74-81, PROF, DENT PUB HEALTH, SCH PUB HEALTH & DENT, UNIV MICH, ANN ARBOR, 81- *Personal Data:* b Melbourne, Australia, Jan 14, 39; m 65; c 2. *Educ:* Univ Western Australia, BDSc, 60; Univ Mich, Ann Arbor, MPH, 66; Univ London, PhD(dent epidemiol), 73. *Prof Exp:* Sr clin dentist, Perth Dent Hosp, Western Australia, 60-65; pub health adv dent, Div Dent Health, USPHS, 66-67; lectr, London Hosp Dent Sch, 68-74. *Concurrent Pos:* Chmn, Dept Community Health Progs, Sch Pub Health, Univ Mich. *Mem:* Am Pub Health Asn; Int Asn Dent Res; Am Asn Pub Health Dentists. *Res:* Epidemiology of dental disease; prevention of dental disease; delivery of dental care. *Mailing Add:* Sch Pub Health Univ Mich Main Campus 109 Observatory St Ann Arbor MI 48109-2029

BURT, CHARLES TYLER, BIOPHYSICAL CHEMISTRY, PHYSIOLOGY. *Current Pos:* CTB CONSULT, 95- *Personal Data:* b Tampa, Fla, Dec 20, 42; m 68. *Educ:* Carnegie Inst Technol, BS, 64; Univ Chicago, MS, 67; Fla State Univ, PhD(phys chem), 72. *Prof Exp:* Fel biochem, Inst Muscle Dis, 72-74; fel, dept biol chem, Med Ctr Univ Ill, 74-75, res assoc, 75-76, asst prof 76-79; asst prof, Reed Col, 79-80; asst prof, dept radiol, Harvard Med Sch, Mass Gen Hosp, 81-83; vis scientist, Mass Inst Technol, 83-85; nuclear magnetic resonance expert, Nat Inst Environ Health Sci, 85-89; Dept Radiol, Col Med, Univ Ill, 90-94; Dept Chem, NC State, 95. *Mem:* Am Chem Soc; Soc Magnetic Resonance Med. *Res:* Mechanisms of contraction and diseases that effect them; nuclear magnetic resonance and its application to biological processes from the molecular level to intact organs; nuclear magnetic resonance imaging. *Mailing Add:* 7601 Humie Olive Rd Apex NC 27502

BURT, DAVID REED, MOLECULAR PHARMACOLOGY, NEUROSCIENCE. *Current Pos:* from asst prof to assoc prof, 76-96, PROF PHARMACOL, SCH MED, UNIV MD, 96- *Personal Data:* b East Orange, NJ, Oct 28, 43; m 91, Mary E Holmes. *Educ:* Amherst Col, AB, 65; Johns Hopkins Univ, PhD(biophys), 72. *Prof Exp:* Assoc res scientist biophys, Johns Hopkins Univ, 72-73, fel pharmacol, Sch Med, 73-76. *Concurrent Pos:* Sr Fogarty int fel, MRC molecular neurobiol unit, Univ Cambridge Med Sch, Eng, 85-86. *Mem:* Am Soc Neurochem; Am Soc Pharmacol & Exp Therapeut; Soc Neurosci; Endocrine Soc. *Res:* Neuropharmacology; neuroendocrinology; peptide neurotransmitters; molecular pharmacology and molecular biology of neurotransmitter receptors. *Mailing Add:* Dept Pharmacol & Exp Therapeut Univ Md Sch Med Baltimore MD 21201. *Fax:* 410-706-0032; *E-Mail:* dburt@umabnet.ab.umd.edu

BURT, DONALD MCLAIN, MINERALOGY, ORE DEPOSITS. *Current Pos:* from asst prof to assoc prof, 75-83, PROF, ARIZ STATE UNIV, 83- *Personal Data:* b East Orange, NJ, Oct 27, 43; m 72; c 2. *Educ:* Princeton Univ, AB, 65; Harvard Univ, AM, 68, PhD(geol), 72. *Prof Exp:* Lectr geochem, State Univ Utrecht, 72-73; Gibbs instr, Yale Univ, 73-75. *Concurrent Pos:* Assoc ed, Am Mineralogist, 77-80; distinguished lectr, Can Inst Mining & Metall, 81; vis scientist, Lunar & Planetary Inst, Houston, 87-88. *Mem:* Mineral Soc Am; Mineral Asn Can; Geol Soc Am; Am Geophys Union; Soc Econ Geologists; Geochem Soc; Am Ceramic Soc. *Res:* Mineralogy and petrology of skarn, greisen, pegmatite and volcanogenic ore deposits; phase equilibria; geochemistry of acid-base processes; crystal chemistry; new mineral named "Burtite". *Mailing Add:* Dept Geol Ariz State Univ Box 871404 Tempe AZ 85287-1404

BURT, GERALD DENNIS, ORGANIC CHEMISTRY. *Current Pos:* sr res chemist, 66-76, RES ASSOC, HARSHAW CHEM CO DIV, GULF OIL CO, 76- *Personal Data:* b Dovray, Minn, Jan 3, 36. *Educ:* Luther Col, BA, 57; Univ Iowa, MS, 60, PhD(org chem), 61. *Prof Exp:* Asst proj chemist, Am Oil Co, Ind, 61-64; res fel chem, Univ Tex, Austin, 64-65. *Mem:* AAAS; Am Chem Soc; Sigma Xi; Coblentz Soc. *Res:* Synthetic organic chemistry; flame retardants; organometallic chemistry; surface modified resin fillers; rheology; pryolysis-IR; plastics additives. *Mailing Add:* 877 Ridge Rd Lewiston NY 14092-9730

BURT, HELEN MARY, DRUG DELIVERY SYSTEMS, CELL SIGNALING. *Current Pos:* From asst prof to assoc prof, 80-95, PROF PHARMACEUT, UNIV BC, 95- *Personal Data:* b Manchester, Eng, Apr 17, 54; m 81, Anthony; c Jennifer M & William J. *Educ:* Univ Bath, Eng, BPharm, 75; Univ BC, Can, PhD(pharmaceut), 80. *Concurrent Pos:* Mem, Pharm Sci Comt, Med Res Coun, Can, 91-94; panel examiners, Pharm Exam Bd, Can, 92-; consult, Stanley Pharm Inc, Ironwood Clay Co & Angiotech, 92-; dir res, Angiotech Pharmaceut, 96-97. *Mem:* Royal Pharm Soc Gt Brit; Asn fac Pharm Can (pres, 90-92); Am Asn Pharmaceut Scientists; Soc Can Women Sci & Technol. *Res:* Solid state pharmaceutics; signal transduction in neutrophils stimulated by inflammatory microcrystals; polymeric drug delivery systems for paclitaxel and other hydrophobic drugs. *Mailing Add:* Fac Pharm Sci Univ BC Vancouver BC V6T 1Z3 Can. *E-Mail:* burg@unixg.ubc.ca

BURT, JAMES KAY, VETERINARY RADIOLOGY. *Current Pos:* RETIRED. *Personal Data:* b Des Moines, Mar 5, 34; m 54; c 5. *Educ:* Iowa State Univ, DVM, 62, MS, 67; Am Col Vet Radiol, dipl. *Prof Exp:* Instr obstet & radiol, Iowa State Univ, 62-65, vet clin sci, 65-66, asst prof, 66-67; asst prof vet surg & radiol, Ohio State Univ, 67-70, from assoc prof to emer prof vet clin sci, 70-87. *Mem:* Am Vet Med Asn; Am Col Vet Radiol. *Res:* Teratologic effects of drugs on the embryo-fetus; dynamics of bone metabolism in eosinophilic panosteitis. *Mailing Add:* 6633 Guyer St Worthington OH 43085

BURT, JANIS MAE, EXCITATION CONTRACTION COUPLING. *Current Pos:* Asst prof cardiac-physiol, 82-89, ASSOC PROF PHYSIOL, UNIV ARIZ, 89- *Educ:* Univ Calif, Irvine, PhD(cell-physiol), 80. *Mem:* Am Physiol Soc; Am Soc Cell Biologists; Biophys Soc; Microcirculatory Soc; Am Heart Asn. *Res:* Cardiac physiology; intercelluar communication; regulation of gap junction channel function and expression as related to heart and fascular physiology and pathophysiology. *Mailing Add:* Dept Physiol Col Med Univ Ariz 1501 N Campbell Tucson AZ 85724-0001. *Fax:* 520-626-2383

BURT, MICHAEL DAVID BRUNSKILL, BIOLOGY, PARASITOLOGY. *Current Pos:* RETIRED. *Personal Data:* b Colombo, Ceylon, Jan 19, 38; m 60; c 4. *Educ:* Univ St Andrews, BSc, 61, PhD(parasitol), 67. *Honors & Awards:* W A Wardle Award in Parasitol, Can Soc Zool. *Prof Exp:* From asst prof to assoc prof, Univ NB, 61-75, chmn dept, 74-85, prof biol, 85-95. *Concurrent Pos:* Brit Coun scholar, Inst Zool, Univ Neuchatel, 63. *Mem:* Am Soc Parasitol; Can Soc Zool; Brit Soc Parasitol; World Fedn Parasitologists; Sci Coun Can. *Res:* Cestode and Platyhelminth biology with reference to functional morphology and developmental changes using light and electron microscopy, life cycles, seasonal variation, and geographical distribution and systematics, host specificity, and evolution. *Mailing Add:* Huntsman Marine Sci Ctr St Andrews NB E0G 2X0 Can

BURT, MICHAEL E, THORACIC SURGERY, SURGICAL METABOLISM. *Current Pos:* ATTEND SURG, MEM SLOAN-KETTERING CANCER CTR, 92-; ASSOC PROF SURG, CORNELL MED CTR, 92- *Res:* Thoracic surgery; surgical metabolism. *Mailing Add:* Thoracic Surg Dept Mem Sloan-Kettering Cancer Ctr 1275 York Ave New York NY 10021-6007

BURT, PHILIP BARNES, THEORETICAL PHYSICS. *Current Pos:* from asst prof to assoc prof, 65-73, head, Dept Physics & Astron, 82-85, PROF PHYSICS, CLEMSON UNIV, 73- *Personal Data:* b Memphis, Tenn, July 1, 34; m 55, Harriet Clack; c Elizabeth L, Sydney F, Konni N & Timothy. *Educ:* Univ Tenn, AB, 56, MS, 58, PhD(physics), 61. *Prof Exp:* Sr scientist, Jet Propulsion Lab, Pasadena, Calif, 61-65. *Concurrent Pos:* Vis asst prof, Univ Southern Calif, 62; consult, Oak Ridge Nat Lab, assoc physicist, 60, res partic, 66; vis, Stanford Linear Accelerator Ctr, 75-76; bd trustees, Southeastern Univ Res Asn, 89- *Mem:* Am Math Soc; Am Phys Soc; Sigma Xi. *Res:* Plasma quantum and field theories; quantum mechanics and nonlinear waves; scattering; theoretical high energy physics; non perturbative quantum electrodynamics. *Mailing Add:* Dept Physics Clemson Univ Clemson SC 29634-1911. *E-Mail:* philb@clemson or philb@clemson.edu

BURT, ROBERT NORCROSS, CHEMICAL ENGINEERING, DEFENSE. *Current Pos:* dir corp planning, FMC Corp, 73-76, vpres agr chem group, 76-83, vpres defense group, 83-88, exec vpres, 88-90, pres, 90-91, CHMN & CHIEF EXEC OFFICER, FMC CORP, 91- *Personal Data:* b Lakewood, Ohio, May 24, 37; m 69, Lynn Chilton; c Tracy, Randy & Charlie. *Educ:* Princeton Univ, BSChemE, 59; Harvard Univ, MBA, 64. *Prof Exp:* Staff, Mobil Oil Corp, NY & Tokyo, 64-68; dir corp planning & acquistions, Chemetron Corp, 68-70, mgr int div, 70-73. *Concurrent Pos:* Mem vis comt, Col Arts & Sci, Northwestern Univ, 90-, leadership coun, Princeton Univ, Sch Eng & Appl Sci, 91-, Defense Policy Adv Comt Trade, 92-; bd dirs, Rehab Inst Chicago, 91-, Phelps Dodge, 93-, World Resources Inst, 94-, Warner-Lambert, 95- & Evanston Hosp, Ill, 95- *Mem:* Mfrs Alliance Productivity & Innovation. *Mailing Add:* FMC Corp 200 E Randolph St Chicago IL 60601-6436

BURT, WAYNE VINCENT, oceanography; deceased, see previous edition for last biography

BURTE, HARRIS M(ERL), MATERIALS SCIENCE, BEHAVIOR OF BIOLOGIC MATERIALS. *Current Pos:* proj engr res & develop, USAF, 53-55, consult, Mat Lab, Wright Air Develop Ctr, 55-56, chief, Prog Br, Mat Lab, 56-59, adv, Metall Studies Br, 59-60, chief engr mat, Dept Systs Eng, Aeronaut Systs Div, 60-61, chief, Metals & Ceramic Div, 61-77, chief scientist, Air Force Mat Lab, 77-78, dir, Metals & Ceramics Div, 78-81, chief scientist, 81-94, EMER CHIEF SCIENTIST, AERONAUT SYSTS DIV, AIR FORCE MAT LAB, WRIGHT AIR DEVELOP CTR, USAF, 95- *Personal Data:* b New York, NY, Nov 14, 27; m 55, Miriam Rose; c Lorin, Kerrin & Paul. *Educ:* NY Univ, BS, 46; Mass Inst Technol, MS, 47; Princeton Univ, PhD(chem eng), 50. *Prof Exp:* Sr res engr, Textile Res Inst, 47-53. *Concurrent Pos:* Mem, Nat Acad Sci/Nat Acad Eng/Nat Res Coun panels adv Nat Bur Stand, 67-73, NASA subcomt mat processing in space, 76-78 & NATO adv group aerospace res & develop struct & mat panel, 79-84; adj prof, Univ Cincinnati, 69-78, Wright State Univ, 80-86; chmn, Comt Eng Mgt, 71-72, comt govt, energy & mat, Metall Soc, 77-80 & dir Metall Soc, Am Inst Mining, Metall & Petrol Engrs, 81-84. *Mem:* Am Chem Soc; Fiber Soc; Am Inst Mining, Metall & Petrol Engrs; fel Am Soc Metals. *Res:* Properties of materials; textiles; plastics; metals; ceramics; technology and societal issues; behavior of elastic and contractile biological materials, nondestructive evaluation. *Mailing Add:* 3006 Hedge Run Ct Dayton OH 45415-2808. *E-Mail:* burtehm@ml.wpafb.af.mil

BURTIS, CARL A, JR, BIOCHEMISTRY, ANALYTICAL CHEMISTRY. *Current Pos:* CHIEF CLIN CHEM, OAK RIDGE NAT LAB, 79- *Personal Data:* b Flagstaff, Ariz, July 3, 37; m 59; c 3. *Educ:* Colo State Univ, BS, 59; Purdue Univ, MS, 64, PhD(biochem), 67. *Prof Exp:* Chemist, Ind State Control Labs, 63-66; fel bioanal, Oak Ridge Nat Lab, 66-67, res assoc molecular anat, 67-69; sr chemist, Varian Aerograph, 69-70; group leader gemsaec fast analyzer proj, Molecular Anat Prog, Oak Ridge Nat Lab, 70-76, coordr biotechnol prog, 73-77; chief, Anal Biochem Br, Ctr Dis Control, 76-79. *Mem:* Am Asn Clin Chemists; Am Soc Biol Chemists; AAAS; Am Chem Soc. *Res:* Chemical inducement of ovine ketosis; separation and quantitation of body fluid constituents by liquid chromatography; separation of nucleic acid constituents by high efficiency liquid chromatography; rapid clinical analysis; reference methods and materials. *Mailing Add:* Chem Tech Div Bldg 4500N Oak Ridge Nat Lab PO Box 2008 MS 6194 Oak Ridge TN 37831

BURTNER, DALE CHARLES, ANALYTICAL CHEMISTRY. *Current Pos:* from asst prof to assoc prof, 58-67, chmn dept, 65-67, dean sch arts & sci, 67-69, PROF CHEM, CALIF STATE UNIV, 67- *Personal Data:* b Portland, Ore, Oct 20, 26; m 50; c 2. *Educ:* Reed Col, BA, 48; Univ Wash, Seattle, MS, 51, PhD(chem), 54. *Prof Exp:* Chemist, Shell Develop Co, 54-58. *Mem:* Am Chem Soc. *Res:* Trace metal analysis; coordination compounds; spectrophotometry; flame photometry; microchemistry. *Mailing Add:* 1309 N Coventry Fresno CA 93727-9439

BURTNER, ROGER LEE, SEDIMENTARY PETROLOGY & CLAY MINERALOGY, INORGANIC GEOCHEMISTRY. *Current Pos:* PRES, R L BURTNER & ASSOCS, 92-, VPRES, REMOTE SENSING TECHNOL, 96- *Personal Data:* b Hershey, Pa, Mar 31, 36; m 65, Carol A Spitzer; c Pamela S. *Educ:* Franklin & Marshall Col, BS, 58; Stanford Univ, MS, 59; Harvard Univ, PhD(geol), 65. *Prof Exp:* From assoc res geologist to res geologist, Calif Res Corp Div, 63; explor geologist, Chevron Oil Field Res Co, Stand Oil Co Tex, 68-69, from res geologist to sr res geologist, 69-77, sr res assoc, Calif, 77-92. *Concurrent Pos:* Chmn, res proj adv comt, Am Petrol Inst, 72-75; petrol group proj leader, Chevron Oil Field Res Co, 75-80, supvr, Electron Micros Lab, 77-82; counr, Clay Minerals Soc, 81-84; adj prof, Case Western Res Univ, 92- *Mem:* Geol Soc Am; Geochem Soc; Soc Sedimentary Geol; Am Asn Petrol Geol; Clay Minerals Soc; Int Asn Geochem & Cosmochem; Sigma Xi. *Res:* Origin and evolution of formation waters; thermochronology of thrust belts; basin evaluation; diagenesis of sandstones and shales; isotope geochemistry of authigenic minerals processing; geochemistry of 129 iodine & 127 iodine; interpretation of Landsat TM images for mineral industry. *Mailing Add:* 721 E Harmony Lane Fullerton CA 92613. *E-Mail:* rockdoc2@aol.com, rockdoc@pacbell.net

BURTNESS, ROGER WILLIAM, ELECTRICAL ENGINEERING. *Current Pos:* assoc prof, 59-87, EMER ASSOC PROF ELEC ENG, UNIV ILL, URBANA, 87- *Personal Data:* b Chicago, Ill, May 13, 25; m 47, Kathryn Cobb; c Roger W Jr, Kathryn (Blomker) & Thomas H. *Educ:* Univ Ill, BS, 46, MS, 51, PhD(elec eng), 53; St Olaf Col, BA, 47. *Prof Exp:* Test engr, Gen Elec Co, 47-48, field engr, 48-49; asst elec eng, Univ Ill, 49-52, instr, 52-53; sect engr, Electro-Motive Div, Gen Motors Corp, 53-56; proj engr radar & digital control, Stewart Warner Electronics, 56-58, mgr eng & res mil electronics, 58-59. *Concurrent Pos:* Consult, Trionics, Wis, 59-62, Control Systs Inc, Ill, 59-62, Borg Warner Res Ctr, 62-65 & Electro-Motive Div, Gen Motors Corp, 65-70. *Mem:* Sr mem Inst Elec & Electronics Engrs. *Res:* Linear integrated circuits; solid state power conversion. *Mailing Add:* 2113 Zuppke Dr Urbana IL 61801

BURTON, ALBERT FREDERICK, BIOCHEMISTRY, CANCER. *Current Pos:* Asst prof, 62-67, ASSOC PROF BIOCHEM, UNIV BC, 67- *Personal Data:* b Brandon, Man, Feb 7, 29; m 53; c 2. *Educ:* Brandon Col, BSc, 53; Univ Western Ont, MSc, 56; Univ Sask, PhD, 58. *Concurrent Pos:* Nat Cancer Inst Can res fel biochem, Univ BC, 59-62. *Mem:* Soc Exp Biol & Med; Can Biochem Soc; Can Investrs Reproduction; Sigma Xi. *Res:* Metabolism of corticosteroids and their biological action, especially in fetal tissues and in relation to cancer. *Mailing Add:* 297 Rodello St Comox BC V9N 4Z9 Can

BURTON, ALEXIS LUCIEN, HISTOLOGY, CYTOLOGY. *Current Pos:* RETIRED. *Personal Data:* b Paris, France, Feb 4, 22; US citizen; m 52, G Claustres; c Odile, Patricia & Sophia. *Educ:* Univ Geneva, BMSc, 43; Univ Strasbourg, MD, 46. *Prof Exp:* Surgeon, Dept Pub Health, Morocco, 51-56; asst prof microanat, Fac Med, Univ Montreal, 57-63; from asst prof to prof anat, Med Sch, Univ Tex, San Antonio, 64- *Concurrent Pos:* Fel anat, Univ Tex Med Sch San Antonio, 63-64; vis prof anat, Nat Yang Ming Med Col, Taipei, Repub China. *Mem:* Am Asn Anat; Tissue Cult Asn; Soc Motion Picture & TV Eng. *Res:* Scientific cinematography; cytology of the connective tissue; tissue culture and cinemicrography. *Mailing Add:* 100 W El Prado #304 San Antonio TX 78212

BURTON, ALICE JEAN, BIOCHEMISTRY, MICROBIOLOGY. *Current Pos:* ASSOC PROF BIOL, ST OLAF COL, 70- *Personal Data:* b Peiping, China, May 19, 34; US citizen. *Educ:* Univ Mich, BS, 57; Univ Ill, PhD(biol). *Prof Exp:* NIH res fel, Calif Inst Technol, 61-63, res fel biol, 63-64; from asst biochemist to biochemist, Brookhaven Nat Lab, 64-70. *Concurrent Pos:* Mem US nat comt, Int Union Pure & Appl Biophys, 75-78. *Mem:* Biophys Soc; Am Chem Soc; AAAS; Sigma Xi. *Res:* Biochemistry of nucleic acids, particularly the replication of bacteriophages and host modification of the replicative process. *Mailing Add:* Dept Biol St Olaf Col 1520 T Olaf Ave Northfield MN 55057-1098. *Fax:* 507-663-3549

BURTON, BENJAMIN THEODORE, NUTRITION, NEPHROLOGY. *Current Pos:* assoc dir & chief artificial kidney prog, Nat Inst Diabetes, Digestive & Kidney Dis, 67-83, assoc dir dis pres & technol, transfer, EMER PROF SCI, NAT INST DIABETES, DIGESTIVE & KIDNEY DIS. *Personal Data:* b Wiesbaden, Ger, Aug 29, 19; nat US; m 52, Cynthia D Taylor; c David A B & Audrey J. *Educ:* Univ Calif, BS, 41, MS, 43, PhD(microbiol, biochem), 47. *Honors & Awards:* Superior Serv Award, US Dept Health, Educ & Welfare, 70; NIH Dir Award, 79. *Prof Exp:* Res chemist, Mills Orchards Corp, 41-42; outside supvr & tech consult, Rosenberg Bros & Co, 42-48; vpres & tech dir, Pac States Labs, Inc, 52-55; staff consult nutrit, H J Heinz Co, 55-60; from nutritionist & spec asst to dir, 60-67. *Mem:* Am Inst Nutrit; Europ Dialysis & Transplant Asn; Int Soc Nephrol; Am Soc Artificial Internal Organs; Am Soc Nephrology; hon mem Am Soc Extracorporeal Technol. *Res:* Human nutrition; intermediate metabolism; nutritional and metabolic diseases; malnutrition; chronic kidney failure and uremia; artificial kidney development; dialysis. *Mailing Add:* 8311 Whiteman Dr Bethesda MD 20817

BURTON, CLYDE LEAON, plant pathology, horticulture, for more information see previous edition

BURTON, DANIEL FREDERICK, botany; deceased, see previous edition for last biography

BURTON, DAVID NORMAN, BIOCHEMISTRY, MICROBIOLOGY. *Current Pos:* fel, Univ Man, 68-69, from asst prof to assoc prof, 69-77, assoc dean sci, 87-97, asst vpres, 97, PROF MICROBIOL, UNIV MAN, 77- *Personal Data:* b Birkenhead, Eng, Feb 3, 41; m 65; c 3. *Educ:* Univ Liverpool,

BSc, 62, PhD(biochem), 65. *Prof Exp:* Fel biochem, Univ Calif, Davis, 65-66; chemist, Lipid Metab Lab, Vet Admin Hosp, Madison, Wis, 66-68. *Concurrent Pos:* Nat Res Coun Can res operating grant, 69- *Mem:* Can Biochem Soc. *Res:* Mechanisms and control of lipid metabolism in microorganisms and animals; membrane and surface properties of cultured mammalian cells. *Mailing Add:* Dept Microbiol Univ Man Winnipeg MB R3T 2N2 Can

BURTON, DENNIS THORPE, AQUATIC ECOLOGY, PHYSIOLOGICAL ECOLOGY. *Current Pos:* SR RES SCIENTIST, WYE RES & EDUC CTR, UNIV MD SYST, 91- *Personal Data:* b Richmond, Va, Apr 16, 41; m 69; c 3. *Educ:* Va Commonwealth Univ, BS, 65; Va Polytech Inst & State Univ, PhD(zool), 70. *Honors & Awards:* Prof Fisheries Scientist Cert, Am Fishery Soc, 71. *Prof Exp:* Res assoc aquatic ecol, Va Polytech Inst & State Univ, 70-71; asst cur, Acad Natural Sci, Philadelphia, 71-77, assoc cur limnol & ecol, 77-80; sr prof staff biologist, Johns Hopkins Univ, 80-85, prin prof staff biologist, appl physics lab, 85-91. *Concurrent Pos:* Fel, Va Polytech Inst & State Univ, 70-71; consult, utility & indust corp, 71-; mem, Environ Res Guidance Comt, State Md Power Plant Siting Prog, 73-78 & 84-87, chmn, 78-80, mem, Power Plant Siting Adv Comt, 78-; assoc ed, Chesapeake Sci, 74-78; adj res assoc, Ctr Environ & Estuarine Studies, Univ Md, 76-77, adj assoc prof, Dept Path, Sch Med, 79-85; adj res scientist, Chesapeake Bay Inst, Johns Hopkins Univ, 84-; mem Environ Biol Rev Panel, US Environ Protection Agency, 86-; vchmn, exec comt sci adv bd, Md Dept Nat Res, 87-89. *Mem:* AAAS; Am Fisheries Soc; Am Soc Zoologists; Sigma Xi; fel Am Inst Fishery Res Bd; Soc Environ Toxicol Chem; Estuarine Res Fedn. *Res:* Physiological responses of aquatic organisms exposed to temperature changes; low dissolved oxygen conditions; biocides and organic compounds; heavy metals; as well as multifactorial combinations of these variables; effects of low oxygen on anaerobic metabolism of fishes; biofouling control at industrial facilities; bioluminescence in marine organisms; toxicity evaluation of industrial and municipal discharges; toxicity evaluation of groundwater; toxicity evaluation of nitrated organic compounds. *Mailing Add:* Wye Res & Educ Ctr Univ Md Systs PO Box 169 Queenstown MD 21658

BURTON, DONALD EUGENE, NUMERICAL HYDRODYNAMICS, NUMERICAL ANALYSIS. *Current Pos:* dep leader, Geotech Group, Earth Sci Div, Univ Calif, 82-85, leader, Grok Design Code Group, 85-93, flag proj leader, A-Div, Defense Sci Dept, Lawrence Livermore Nat Lab, 93-96, STAFF MEM, LOS ALAMOS NAT LAB, UNIV CALIF, 96- *Personal Data:* b Kansas City, Mo, Apr 24, 41; m 70, Chong S Im; c Michael C & Jennifer K. *Educ:* Univ Mo, Rolla, BS, 62; Kans State Univ, PhD(theoret nuclear physics), 69. *Honors & Awards:* US Army Commendation Medal Res, 73. *Prof Exp:* Res & develop coordr, radiol safety, Nuclear Cratering Group, 68-69, nuclear cratering, Eng Explosive Excavation Res Lab, US Army CEngrs, 70-73; physicist, 73-77, proj leader, Earth Sci Div, 80-85, group leader, Geomechan Code Develop, Lawrence Livermore Nat Lab, Univ Calif, 77-82. *Mem:* Am Geophys Union; Int Soc Rock Mech. *Res:* Development of large multidimensional computer code systems used principally for geoscience applications; develop constitutive model for earth materials; energy coupling from nuclear explosions; development of nuclear weapons design codes. *Mailing Add:* Group XHM MS-F663 Los Alamos Nat Lab Los Alamos NM 87544. *E-Mail:* burton@land.gov

BURTON, DONALD JOSEPH, ORGANIC CHEMISTRY. *Current Pos:* from asst prof to assoc prof, 62-70, PROF CHEM, UNIV IOWA, 70- *Personal Data:* b Baltimore, Md, July 16, 34; m 58, Margaret Billing; c Andrew, Jennifer, David, Julie & Elizabeth. *Educ:* Loyola Col, Md, BS, 56; Cornell Univ, PhD(org chem), 61. *Honors & Awards:* Am Chem Soc Award, Fluorine Div, 84. *Prof Exp:* Fel, Purdue Univ, 61-62. *Concurrent Pos:* Carver-Shriner prof, 89. *Mem:* Am Chem Soc; The Chem Soc. *Res:* Synthesis and chemistry of polyfluorinated compounds; chemistry of polyhalogenated organoboranes; metal halide catalysis of halogenated olefins; preparation and reactions of halogenated ylides, polyfluorinated organ metallics. *Mailing Add:* Dept Chem Univ Iowa Iowa City IA 52242. *Fax:* 319-335-2951; *E-Mail:* donald-burton@uiowa.edu

BURTON, ELIZABETH ANN, AQUEOUS GEOCHEMISTRY, ENVIRONMENTAL GEOCHEMISTRY. *Current Pos:* Asst prof, 88-94, ASSOC PROF GEOL, NORTHERN ILL UNIV, 94- *Personal Data:* b San Francisco, Calif, July 25, 58. *Educ:* Bryn Mawr Col, BA, 80; Univ Miami, MS, 84; Washington Univ, St Louis, PhD(earth & planetary sci), 88. *Mem:* Am Chem Soc; Am Asn Petrol Geologists; Am Asn Univ Woman. *Res:* Fate and transport of dissolved chemicals in natural waters, in particular, the interactions of these with minerals and their effects on mineral kinetics and stability. *Mailing Add:* Dept Geol Northern Ill Univ DeKalb IL 60115-2854

BURTON, FREDERICK GLENN, ANALYTICAL CHEMISTRY, ORGANOPHOSPHORUS CHEMISTRY. *Current Pos:* res scientist controlled release, Battelle Mem Inst, 74-76, sr res scientist bioanal chem, Pac Northwest Div, 76-85, proj mgr surety agent res, 85-89, LAB DIR, BATTELLE TOOELE OPERS, BATTELLE MEM INST, 90- *Personal Data:* b Greensburg, Pa, Nov 30, 39; m 68, Jeanne Nesper. *Educ:* Col Wooster, BA, 62; Wesleyan Univ, MA, 66; Univ Rochester, PhD(biophys), 71. *Honors & Awards:* Spec Award for Excellence in Technol Transfer, Fed Lab Consortium, 86. *Prof Exp:* Instr dairy sci, Ohio Agr Exp Sta, 62-64; fel origins of life, Salk Inst Biol Studies, 71-73. *Concurrent Pos:* Consult, Immunodiag Inc, 73-74. *Mem:* AAAS; Sigma Xi; Int Soc Study Origins Life; Controlled Release Soc; Am Chem Soc. *Res:* Sustained release devices; bioanalytical applications of toxicology; surface chemistry; chemical surety agents. *Mailing Add:* PO Box 1179 Tooele UT 84074-1179

BURTON, GILBERT W, ORGANIC CHEMISTRY, POLYMER CHEMISTRY. *Current Pos:* staff chemist, 75-84, SR STAFF CHEMIST, EXXON CHEM CO, 84- *Personal Data:* b Covington, Va, Mar 2, 36; m 64, Velta Eichvalds; c Steven. *Educ:* Univ Calif, BS, 58; Univ Ill, PhD(org chem), 64. *Prof Exp:* Res Prof Exp: From res chemist to sr res chemist, Esso Res & Eng Co, 64-75. *Mem:* AAAS; Am Chem Soc; Sigma Xi. *Res:* Organic photochemistry; chemistry of ozonization of organic compounds; anionic coordination polymerization; elastomer chemistry; environmental affairs. *Mailing Add:* 1179 Puddingstone Rd Mountainside NJ 07092-2007

BURTON, GLENN WILLARD, AGRONOMY. *Current Pos:* from agent to sr geneticist, Div Forage Crops & Dis, Bur Plant Indust, 36-53, RES GENETICIST & LEADER, AGR RES SERV, US DEPT AGR, 53- *Personal Data:* b Clatonia, Nebr, May 5, 10; m 34; c 5. *Educ:* Univ Nebr, BA, 32; Rutgers Univ, MS, 33, PhD(agron), 36. *Hon Degrees:* ScD, Rutgers Univ, 55; ScD, Univ Nebr, 62. *Honors & Awards:* Stevenson Award & S Seedman Asn Award, 49; Sears Roebuck Award, 53, 61; John Scott Award, 57; Edward W Browning Award, Am Soc Agron, 75; Nat Medal of Sci, 83; Alexander von Humboldt Found Award, 88; Fred V Grau Turfgrass Sci Award, 91; Serv to Am & World Agr Award, Nat Asn County Agr Agents, 96. *Prof Exp:* Asst agron, Rutgers Univ, 32-36. *Concurrent Pos:* Chmn, Agron Div, Univ Ga, 50-64. *Mem:* Nat Acad Sci; fel Am Soc Agron (vpres, 61, pres, 62); Am Genetic Asn; Range Soc Am; fel Crop Sci Soc Am; hon mem Grassland Soc SAfr; Sigma Xi; Am Forage & Grassland Soc; Coun Agr Sci & Technol. *Res:* Grass breeding and genetics; grass cytology; grass seed production; grass fertilization and management; revegetation of native ranges; inheritance of significant characters including apomixis; propagation and management of superior varieties; development of improved plant breeding methods. *Mailing Add:* Ga Coastal Plain Exp Sta Tifton GA 05794

BURTON, GRAHAM WILLIAM, BIO-ORGANIC CHEMISTRY, FREE RADICAL BIOLOGY. *Current Pos:* res assoc, 78-82, assoc res officer, 82-87, SR RES OFFICER, NAT RES COUN CAN, 88- *Personal Data:* b Lower Hutt, NZ, Dec 12, 46; m 69, Hedy McFarland; c Matthew, Jolyon & Nicholas. *Educ:* Univ Auckland, NZ, BSc, 68, MSc, 69, PhD(chem), 74. *Prof Exp:* Fel, Univ Ark, 74-75, Univ Calif, 76-78. *Concurrent Pos:* Lectr, Univ Auckland, 72-73; mem, Panel Review Comt, Nat Cancer Inst Can, 87-88; adj prof, Dept Biochem, Univ Ottawa, 89-; assoc ed, Free Radical Biol & Med, 92-93. *Mem:* AAAS; Am Inst Nutrit; fel Can Soc Chem. *Res:* Free radical biology with regard to disease and its control by antioxidants; mechanisms of action of vitamin E and betacarotene; molecular recognition phenomena. *Mailing Add:* Steacie Inst Molecular Sci Nat Res Coun Can 100 Sussex Dr Ottawa ON K1A 0R6 Can

BURTON, HAROLD, NEUROPHYSIOLOGY. *Current Pos:* asst prof neurobiol & physiol, 70-76, assoc prof anat neurobiol & physiol, 76-83, PROF ANAT & NEUROBIOL, MED SCH, WASHINGTON UNIV, 83- *Personal Data:* b New York, NY, Jan 19, 43; m 63; c 1. *Educ:* Univ Mich, BA, 64; Univ Wis, PhD(physiol), 68. *Prof Exp:* Nat Inst Neurol Dis & Blindness trainee neurophysiol, Med Sch, Univ Wis, 68-70. *Mem:* Soc Neurosci. *Res:* Somato sensory system physiology and anatomy. *Mailing Add:* Dept Anat Wash Univ Sch Med 660 S Euclid Ave St Louis MO 63110-1010

BURTON, IAN, RISK ASSESSMENT, NATURAL HAZARDS. *Current Pos:* dir, Environ Adaptation Res, 91-96, EMER SCIENTIST, ENVIRON CAN, 91-; ADJ PROF, UNIV TORONTO. *Educ:* Univ Birmingham, UK, BA, 56, MA, 57; Univ Chicago, PhD(geog), 62. *Honors & Awards:* Mitchell Prize, Houston Advan Res Ctr, 89. *Prof Exp:* Prof geog, Univ Toronto, 61-90, dir, Inst Environ Studies, 79-84. *Concurrent Pos:* Consult water mgt, Ford Found, 64-66; sr adv, Int Develop Res Ctr, 70-73; vis prof, Univ EAnglia, 72-73; consult, Royal Comn Ocean Ranger Marine Disaster, 82-84; sr Connaught fel, Univ Toronto, 85; dir, Int Fedn Insts Advan Study, 86-91. *Mem:* Fel Royal Soc Can; Sigma Xi; fel World Acad Arts & Sci; Asn Am Geogrs. *Res:* Environmental risk assessment, human adjustment to natural hazards, adaption to climate and atmospheric change, environmental perception and behavior, environmental theory, environmental policy. *Mailing Add:* 72 Coolmine Rd Toronto ON M6J 3E9 Can. *Fax:* 416-739-4297

BURTON, JAMES S, WATER RESOURCES. *Current Pos:* water res prog mgr, 83-89, CHIEF, NAT WATER DATA EXCHANGE, US GEOL SUPV, 89- *Personal Data:* b Richmond, Ky, Aug 1, 36. *Educ:* Berea Col, AB, 58; Howard Univ, MS, 62, PhD(phys chem), 64. *Prof Exp:* Sr chemist, Melpar Inc, Va, 63-66; sr chemist, Gen Technol Corp, 66-67, div, Environ Sci Res, 67-69; tech staff, MITRE Corp, Va, 69-73, dir, Solar Energy Prog, 73-74; dir, Water Resources Res Ctr, Univ DC, 74-75; asst dir res, Off Water Res & Technol, Dept Interior, 75-79, staff asst, Off Asst Secy Land & Water Resources, 79-81, spec asst-res prog, Bur Reclamation, 81-82, spec asst-res prog mgr, Off Water Policy, 82-83. *Concurrent Pos:* Lectr, Northern Va Community Col, 71-72 & George Mason Univ, 87-88. *Mem:* Am Water Resources Asn; Sigma Xi; Am Soc Testing & Mat; Am Chem Soc. *Res:* Applications of client-server systems and nucrocomputers in information processing. *Mailing Add:* PO Box 3408 Reston VA 20195-1408. *Fax:* 703-648-5295; *E-Mail:* jburton@usgs.gov

BURTON, JOHN HESLOP, ANIMAL NUTRITION. *Current Pos:* Res assoc, 69-70, from asst prof to assoc prof, 71-90, PROF ANIMAL NUTRIT, UNIV GUELPH, 90- *Personal Data:* b Ottawa, Can, Aug 27, 38; m 69; c 2. *Educ:* Univ Toronto, BSc, 62; Cornell Univ, MSc, 67, PhD(nutrit), 70. *Mem:* Can Nutrit Soc; Agr Inst Can; Am Dairy Sci Asn; Am Soc Animal Sci; NY Acad Sci; Sigma Xi. *Res:* Role of metabolic hormones in controlling milk synthesis and production in dairy cattle and growth in the bovine; growth and energy metabolism in the equine. *Mailing Add:* Dept Animal & Poultry Sci Univ Guelph Guelph ON N1G 2W1 Can. *E-Mail:* jburton@aps.uoguelph.ca

BURTON, JOHN WILLIAMS, COMPUTER SCIENCES, EXPERIMENTAL NUCLEAR PHYSICS. *Current Pos:* assoc prof & head dept, 64-81, dir, Comput Ctr, 81-89, PROF PHYSICS, CARSON-NEWMAN COL, 66- *Personal Data:* b Atlanta, Ga, Apr 15, 37; m 59, Patricia A Wilson; c Rebecca L, Timothy W, Amy R & John M. *Educ:* Carson-Newman Col, BS, 59; Univ Ill, MS, 61, PhD(physics), 65; Univ Tenn, MS, 77. *Prof Exp:* Asst physics, Univ Ill, 61-64. *Concurrent Pos:* Consult, Oak Ridge Nat Lab, 65-75. *Mem:* Am Phys Soc; Am Asn Physics Teachers. *Res:* Mossbauer effect on the surface of tungsten, involving ultra high vacuum techniques; Mossbauer spectroscopy; computer programming for data analysis; computer assisted instruction. *Mailing Add:* Carson-Newman Col PO Box 71917 Jefferson City TN 37760. *Fax:* 423-471-3502; *E-Mail:* burton@cncacc.cn.edu

BURTON, KAREN POLINER, CARDIOLOGY, ULTRASTRUCTURE. *Current Pos:* asst prof physiol, 83-88, asst prof radiol, 89-90, ASSOC PROF RADIOL, SOUTHWESTERN MED CTR, UNIV TEX, DALLAS, 90- *Personal Data:* b Albuquerque, NMex, Feb 18, 52; m 74, M David; c Christopher & Kevin. *Educ:* Southern Methodist Univ, BS, 74; Univ Tex Health Sci Ctr, PhD(physiol), 78. *Honors & Awards:* New Invest Res Award, NIH, 82-85. *Prof Exp:* Fel physiol, Univ Tex Health Sci Ctr, Dallas, 78-79, fac assoc, 79, instr, 79-82; asst prof pharmacol & physiol, Col Med, Univ SAla, 81-82. *Concurrent Pos:* Investr, NIH Res Award, 82-85, & res career develop award, 86-91; prin investr, NIH Grant, 85-88, 88-93. *Mem:* Am Physiol Soc; Am Soc Heart Res; AAAS; Electron Micros Soc Am; Sigma Xi; Am Heart Asn; Oxygen Soc. *Res:* Cardiovascular pathophysiology, role of calcium and electrolyte alterations in the development of ischemic myocardial damage; role of oxygen-derived free radicals in heart damage; fluorescent indicators for calcium measurements. *Mailing Add:* Dept Radiol Univ Tex Southwestern Med Ctr 4904 Ellensburg Dr Dallas TX 75244

BURTON, LARRY C(LARK), PHYSICAL ELECTRONICS, SEMICONDUCTOR & SURFACE PHYSICS. *Current Pos:* ASSOC PROF ELEC ENG, VA POLYTECH INST & STATE UNIV, 77- *Personal Data:* b Neola, Utah, Nov 2, 39; m 62; c 2. *Educ:* Temple Univ, BA, 62, MS, 66; Pa State Univ, PhD(physics), 70. *Prof Exp:* Engr advan develop group, Philco Corp, Pa, 63-65; scientist res & develop div, Leeds & Northrup Co, 65-66; asst prof elec eng, Tex Tech Univ, 70-73; mem staff, Inst Energy Conversion, Univ Del, 73-77. *Mem:* AAAS; Inst Elec & Electronics Engrs; Am Phys Soc; Am Soc Eng Educ. *Res:* Thermionic, photoelectric and field emission of electrons from semiconductor surfaces; semiconductor surface preparation and evaluation; electronic transport in solids; analyses of ultra-high frequency semiconductor devices and switching circuits. *Mailing Add:* Dept Elec Eng Pa State Univ University Park PA 16802

BURTON, LEONARD PATTILLO, MATHEMATICS. *Current Pos:* from asst prof to prof, 54-65, head prof, 65-77, PROF MATH, AUBURN UNIV, 77- *Personal Data:* b Jasper, Ala, June 8, 18; m 42; c 3. *Educ:* Univ Ala, AB, 39, MA, 40; Univ NC, PhD(math), 51. *Prof Exp:* Instr math, Univ Ala, 46-48; from instr to asst prof, Univ Calif, 51-54. *Mem:* Am Math Soc; Math Asn Am; Sigma Xi. *Res:* Ordinary differential equations. *Mailing Add:* Dept Math Auburn Univ Auburn AL 36830

BURTON, LESTER PERCY JOSEPH, POLYMER STABILIZATION. *Current Pos:* SR MGR, MONTELL USA, 88- *Personal Data:* b Sudbury, Ont, Mar 5, 53; m 78; c 1. *Educ:* Univ Western Ont, BSc, 76; Ore State Univ, PhD(org chem), 81. *Prof Exp:* Sr res scientist, Ethyl Corp, 81-88. *Res:* Design and synthesis of stabilizers for polymers. *Mailing Add:* Montell USA Res & Develop Ctr 912 Appleton Rd Elkton MD 21921-3920

BURTON, LLOYD EDWARD, pharmacy, public health; deceased, see previous edition for last biography

BURTON, LOUIS, BIOCHEMISTRY. *Current Pos:* Scientist, protein & biochem, 82-85, SR SCIENTIST, PROCESS RES & DEVELOP, GENENTECH INC, 85- *Personal Data:* b Ft Riley, Kans, June 15, 49; c 2. *Educ:* Mich State Univ, PhD(biochem), 76. *Mem:* Am Soc Biochem & Molecular Biol. *Res:* Biotechnology; recovery of recombinant proteins. *Mailing Add:* Genentech Inc 460 Pt San Bruno Blvd South San Francisco CA 94080-4918

BURTON, PAUL RAY, ZOOLOGY, CELL BIOLOGY. *Current Pos:* RETIRED. *Personal Data:* b Burnsville, NC, Dec 7, 31; m 59; c 2. *Educ:* Western Carolina Col, BS, 54; Univ Miami, MS, 56; Univ NC, PhD(zool), 60. *Prof Exp:* Asst prof biol, St Olaf Col, 60-63; NIH fel anat, Sch Med, Univ Wis, 63-64; from asst prof to assoc prof, Univ Kans, 64-69, prof physiol & cell biol, 69-91, chmn, Dept Physiol & Cell Biol, 73-76. *Concurrent Pos:* USPHS Career Develop Award, 68-73. *Mem:* Am Micros Soc; Electron Micros Soc Am; Am Soc Parasitol; AAAS; Am Soc Cell Biol. *Res:* Electron microscopy; studies on the structure and function of microtubular elements, particularly in neuronal systems. *Mailing Add:* PO Box 250 Ephraim WI 54211

BURTON, RALPH A(SHBY), MECHANICAL ENGINEERING. *Current Pos:* PVT RESEARCHER, BURTON TECHNOL, INC, 85-; ADJ PROF MECH ENG, DUKE UNIV; EMER PROF, NC STATE UNIV. *Personal Data:* b Shreveport, La, Oct 31, 25; m 48; c R Gaines. *Educ:* Univ Ark, BS, 47; Univ Tex, MS, 51, PhD(mech eng), 52. *Honors & Awards:* Centennial Medal, Am Soc Mech Engrs. *Prof Exp:* Instr, Univ Ark, 47-49; asst prof mech eng, Mass Inst Technol, 52-54; assoc prof, Univ Mo, 54-58; sr res engr, SW Res Inst, 58-61, staff scientist & mgr, Lubrication Res Sect, 61-67; physicist on leave, Off Naval Res London, 67, liaison scientist, 67-69; prof mech eng & astronaut sci, Northwestern Univ, 69-80; prof mech & aerospace eng & head dept, NC State Univ, 80-85. *Concurrent Pos:* Consult, Westinghouse Labs, 77-78; on leave, US Off Naval Res, Arlington, 78-79. *Mem:* Fel Am Soc Mech Engrs. *Res:* Surface mechanics; wear mechanisms; thermoelastic effects; applied mechanics; liquid metal current collectors; ultralow wear materials; carbon composite materials; carbon metal composite materials. *Mailing Add:* Burton Technologies Inc PO Box 33809 Raleigh NC 27636. *Fax:* 919-783-0035; *E-Mail:* rburton@me1.egr.duke.edu

BURTON, RALPH GAINES, CARBON-METAL COMPOSITES, TRIBOLOGY. *Current Pos:* vpres, 84-94, PRES, BURTON TECHNOLOGIES INC, 94- *Personal Data:* b Columbia, Mo, Jan 3, 55; m 78, Carol D Elden. *Educ:* Northwestern Univ, BS, 78. *Prof Exp:* Sr engr, Newport News Shipbuilding, 79-80, sr shift test engr, 80-84. *Concurrent Pos:* Co-prin investr, Burton Technologies Inc, 88-97. *Mem:* Am Soc Metals; AAAS. *Res:* Liquid-metal electrical contacts; active, feed forward and feedback, control of gas bearings and metrology systems; development of a family of vitreous carbon based composite materials for seals, bearings, electrical, and structural applications. *Mailing Add:* Burton Technologies Inc PO Box 33809 Raleigh NC 27636-0809. *Fax:* 919-783-0035

BURTON, RALPH P, ENTOMOLOGY, PESTICIDE REGISTRATION. *Current Pos:* Tech rep, 68-79, MGR PROD REGIST, ISK BIOSCI CORP, 79- *Personal Data:* b Afton, Wyo, Mar 20, 36; m 60, Beth Hoopes; c Blair, Brent, Lance, Wade, Bruce, Myrna, Marsha & Wynn. *Educ:* Va Polytech Inst, DEntom. *Mem:* Sigma Xi; Am Phytopath Soc; Weed Sci Soc Am; Agr Res Inst; Entom Soc Am. *Res:* Commercial development; coordinate research to support registration of pesticide products. *Mailing Add:* ISK Biosci Corp 5966 Heisley Rd PO Box 8000 Mentor OH 44061

BURTON, ROBERT CLYDE, GEOLOGY, CONODONT BIOSTRATIGRAPHY. *Current Pos:* assoc prof, WTex State Univ, 65-66, head dept, 66-76, prof, 66-89, adj prof geol, 89-96, EMER PROF GEOL, WTEX STATE UNIV, 96- *Personal Data:* b Borger, Tex, Feb 27, 29; m 51, Jean Hill; c Randall, Roger, Jana & Jill. *Educ:* Tex Tech Col, BA, 57, MSc, 59; Univ NMex, PhD(geol), 65. *Prof Exp:* Instr geol, Tex Tech Col, 58-59; from instr to asst prof, WTex State Univ, 59-63; vis lectr, Univ NMex, 65. *Concurrent Pos:* Petrol Res Fund grant, Am Chem Soc, 69-71; owner, Geomag Surv; prof geol (dean's app), Temple Univ, Japan, 90-91. *Mem:* Nat Asn Geol Teachers (secy, 68, vpres, 69, pres, 70). *Res:* Biostratigraphy; conodont biostratigraphy in New Mexico; exploration magnetics; geomagnetics. *Mailing Add:* 711 Taylor Lane Canyon TX 79015

BURTON, ROBERT LEE, PROPULSION SYSTEMS, GAS DYNAMICS. *Current Pos:* MGR ENG, BOEING AEROSPACE & ELECTRONICS, OAK RIDGE, 89- *Personal Data:* b Bluefield, Va, May 29, 43; m 65; c 1. *Educ:* Va Polytechnic Inst & State Univ, BS, 66; George Washington Univ, MS, 73. *Prof Exp:* Res engr Saturn V/Apollo, Boeing Aerospace, NASA Hq Consult, 66-72; lead engr jet eng controls, Boeing Com Airplane, 747, 72-79; eng supvr gas centrifuge, Boeing Eng Co SE, 79-85; technol mgr gas centrifuge, Boeing Tenn, Inc, 85-89. *Concurrent Pos:* Recorder, NASA Apollo Exp, Photog Team, 70-72; Boeing rep, NASA Apollo Mission Readiness Rev, 70-72, Indust/FAA/EPA Jet Engine Emissions Controls, 77-79, Dept Energy Gas Centrifuge Gas Dynamics Working Group, 81-85; moderator, NASA, Indust Post-Apollo Mission Study Team, 72; prin investr, Nat Aerospace Plane Hypersonic Wind Tunnel, 85-88; consult, Dept Energy, Indust Centrifuge Chem Separation, 87-88; bd dirs, WATTec, Inc, 90-91. *Mem:* Nat Space Soc. *Res:* High speed gas dynamics analysis and design associated with aircraft, jet engines, rockets, spacecraft and gas centrifuges; avenger missile launcher engineering; thermal design for laser isotope separation systems; gas dynamic lasers; composite materials; granted one patent. *Mailing Add:* Boeing Aerospace & Electronics 767 Boeing Rd Oak Ridge TN 37830

BURTON, ROBERT M, JR, MATHEMATICS. *Current Pos:* From asst prof to assoc prof, 78-88, PROF MATH, ORE STATE UNIV, 88- *Personal Data:* b Bethesda, Md, Aug 4, 48. *Educ:* Washington Univ, BA, 72; Stanford Univ, PhD(math), 77. *Concurrent Pos:* Vis asst prof math, Univ Colo, Boulder, 77-78; NSF res grant, 79, 80-83, 82-85, 86-87, 86-88, 87, 91-93; Humboldt res fel, Inst Stochastic Math, Univ Gotlingen, Ger, 84-85, vis prof, 88, 92; guest prof, Tech Univ Delft, 91-92. *Mem:* Am Math Soc; Inst Math Statist; Math Asn Am. *Res:* Probability and dynamics. *Mailing Add:* Dept Math 368 Kidder Hall Ore State Univ Corvallis OR 97331-4605

BURTON, ROBERT MAIN, BIOCHEMISTRY, PHARMACOLOGY. *Current Pos:* CONSULT, BURTON INT, 79- *Personal Data:* b Oklahoma City, Okla, Mar 5, 27; m 47; c 5. *Educ:* Univ Md, BS, 50; Georgetown Univ, MS, 52; Johns Hopkins Univ, PhD(biol, biochem), 55. *Prof Exp:* Chemist, USDA, Md, 50; chemist, Nat Heart Inst, 50-52; chemist, Nat Inst Neurol Dis & Blindness, 55-57; from asst prof to assoc prof pharmacol, Sch Med, Wash Univ, 57-78; prof & chmn, Dept Pharmacol, Sch Med, Oral Roberts Univ, 78-79. *Concurrent Pos:* Lectr, Georgetown Univ, 56-57; Am Chem Soc & Am Soc Biol Chemists travel award, Int Biochem Cong, Vienna, 58, Moscow, 61 & Tokyo, 67; NSF sr fel, Inst Phys Chem, Univ Cologne, 63; mem child health & human develop prog comt, NIH, 68-69, mem pop res & training comt, 69-70, chmn, 70-72; sci adv, Ctr Biochem Studies, Portugal, 65-; assoc ed, Lipids, 65-; mem med adv bd, Nat Tay-Sachs & Allied Dis, Inc, 75-; mem genetic dis rev and adv comt, Health Serv Admin, USPHS, 81-; Fulbright res scholar, Univ Porto, Port, 81- *Mem:* Am Soc Pharmacol & Exp Therapeut; Am Chem Soc; Am Soc Biol Chemists; Am Soc Neurochem; fel Am Inst Chemists; Sigma Xi. *Res:* Biochemistry of nervous system; lipid and glycolipid metabolism; biochemical basis for neuropharmacological activity of drugs; hyperlipoproteinemias in children. *Mailing Add:* Burton Int Biomed Box 190280 St Louis MO 63119-6280. *Fax:* 314-961-3506

BURTON, RUSSELL ROHAN, PHYSIOLOGY, MANAGEMENT. *Current Pos:* chief scientist, Crew Systs Directorate, 90-95, CHIEF SCIENTIST, ARMSTRONG LAB, BROOKS AFB, 95- *Personal Data:* b Chico, Calif, Jan 15, 32; m 83, Sharon L Milton; c Robert P, Russell P, Jennifer P (Wetz) & Heather L (Regnault). *Educ:* Univ Calif, Davis, BS, 54, DVM, 56, MS, 65, PhD, 70. *Honors & Awards:* Paul Bert Award, Aerospace Med Asn, 75, Arnold D Tuttle Award, 76, Environ Sci Award, 80 & Eric Liljencrantz Award, 88. *Prof Exp:* Pvt pract, 56-62; from assoc res specialist to res specialist, Univ Calif, Davis, 62-71; res physiologist, USAF, 71-80, br chief, 80-88, chief scientist, Sch Aerospace Med, 88-90. *Concurrent Pos:* Prof, Univ Tex, San Antonio, 84- & USAF Sch Aerospace Med; panel mem, Adv Group Aerospace Res & Develop, 93-; ed, Safe J, 93- *Mem:* AAAS; Sigma Xi; fel Aerospace Med Asn; Am Physiol Soc; Survival & Flight Equip Asn; Aerospace Human Factors Asn. *Res:* Pathophysiologic effects of high-levels of sustained acceleration and microgravity resulting in methods to protect aircrew and astronauts. *Mailing Add:* 2509 Kennedy Circle Armstrong Lab Brooks AFB TX 78235-5118

BURTON, SHERIL DALE, microbiology, biochemistry, for more information see previous edition

BURTON, THEODORE ALLEN, MATHEMATICS. *Current Pos:* assoc prof, 66-71, PROF MATH, SOUTHERN ILL UNIV, CARBONDALE, 71- *Personal Data:* b Longton, Kans, Sept 7, 35; m 61. *Educ:* Wash State Univ, BS, 59, MA, 62, PhD(math), 64. *Prof Exp:* Asst prof math, Univ Alta, 64-66. *Concurrent Pos:* Fulbright Scholar. *Mem:* Am Math Soc; Math Asn Am; Soc Indust Appl Math. *Res:* Stability theory of ordinary differential equations and integral equations. *Mailing Add:* Dept Math Southern Ill Univ Carbondale IL 62901-4408

BURTON, THOMAS MAXIE, AQUATIC ECOLOGY. *Current Pos:* asst prof, Inst Water Res, 75-79, assoc prof, Fisheries & Wildlife, 79-84, PROF AQUATIC ECOL, DEPT ZOOL, FISHERIES & WILDLIFE, MICH STATE UNIV, 84- *Personal Data:* b West Carroll Parish, La, Nov 24, 41; m; c 1. *Educ:* Northeast La Univ, BS, 63, MS, 65; Cornell Univ, PhD(ecol), 73. *Prof Exp:* Teacher sci, Winnsboro High Sch, 65-66; instr biol, Univ NC, Charlotte, 66-67; res technician, US Army Res Inst Environ Med, Mass, 67-69; ecol consult, Eng-Sci, Cincinnati, 73; res assoc aquatic ecol, Fla State Univ, 74-75. *Concurrent Pos:* Indo-Am fel, 88-89. *Mem:* Ecol Soc Am; Am Soc Limnol & Oceanog; Sigma Xi; AAAS; NAm Benthological Soc; Int Soc Limnol; Wetlands Soc. *Res:* Studies of stream and marsh biota at the community and ecosystem level; acidification effects on stream biota; logging effects on stream biota; intrasystem nutrient cycles in streams and marshes. *Mailing Add:* Dept Zool Mich State Univ East Lansing MI 48824

BURTON, VERONA DEVINE, BOTANY. *Current Pos:* from asst prof to prof, 48-86, EMER PROF BIOL SCI, MANKATO STATE UNIV, 86- *Personal Data:* b Reading, Pa, Nov 23, 22; m 50, Daniel F; c John. *Educ:* Hunter Col, AB, 44; State Univ Iowa, MS, 46, PhD(plant anat), 48. *Prof Exp:* Asst, State Univ Iowa, 44-48. *Mem:* AAAS; Bot Soc Am; Am Fern Soc; Int Soc Plant Morphol; Sigma Xi. *Res:* Floral abscission and plant embryology. *Mailing Add:* 512 Hickory St Mankato MN 56001

BURTON, WILLARD WHITE, ORGANIC CHEMISTRY. *Current Pos:* RETIRED. *Personal Data:* b Richmond, Va, Feb 24, 22; m 48, Anabel Spillman; c Raymond M, Julia B (Beaton) & Ellen B (Bumgardner). *Educ:* Univ Richmond, BS, 43. *Prof Exp:* From jr res assoc to res assoc, Am Tobacco Co, 46-68, supvr org chem sect, 68-70, supvr chem develop, Process Develop Lab, 70-71, supvr res, 71-81, asst res mgr, Dept Res & Develop, 81-87. *Mem:* Am Chem Soc; fel Am Inst Chem. *Res:* Tobacco chemical composition; browning reaction pigments; phenols; amino acids; carbohydrates and organic acids; analytical methods development. *Mailing Add:* 6808 Greenvale Dr Richmond VA 23225

BURTS, EVERETT C, ENTOMOLOGY. *Current Pos:* ENTOMOLOGIST, WASH STATE UNIV, 58- *Personal Data:* b Mae, Wash, Sept 25, 31; m 54; c 2. *Educ:* State Col Wash, BS, 54; Ore State Col, MS, 57, PhD(entom), 59. *Prof Exp:* Jr entomologist, Ore State Col & agt, Div Entom, Agr Res Serv, USDA, 54-58. *Mem:* AAAS; Entom Soc Am. *Res:* Biology and control of insects and mites of tree fruits; insect vectors of plant viruses; deciduous fruit insect pest management. *Mailing Add:* 912 N Surry Rd Wenatchee WA 98801

BURTT, BENJAMIN PICKERING, PHYSICAL CHEMISTRY, RADIATION CHEMISTRY. *Current Pos:* instr, 46-48, from instr to prof, 49-91, EMER PROF CHEM, SYRACUSE UNIV, 92 - *Personal Data:* b Newburyport, Mass, June 7, 21; m 45, Dorothy Watson; c Ruth, Ben & Mary. *Educ:* Ohio State Univ, BA, 42, PhD(chem), 46. *Prof Exp:* Asst chem & instr physics, Ohio State Univ, 42-45, instr chem, 45-46. *Concurrent Pos:* Assoc scientist, Brookhaven Nat Lab, 48-49. *Mem:* Am Chem Soc. *Res:* Mass spectrometric studies of electron impact phenomena; ion-molecule reactions. *Mailing Add:* Smokey Hollow Rd Jamesville NY 13078. *E-Mail:* bpburtt@ suvm

BURTT, EDWARD HOWLAND, JR, BIOMECHANICS, ELECTRON MICROSCOPY. *Current Pos:* from asst to assoc prof, 77-87, dept chmn, 91-93, PROF ZOOL, OHIO WESLEYAN UNIV, 87- *Personal Data:* b Waltham, Mass, Apr 22, 48; m 72, Pam Young; c Michelle & Jeremy. *Educ:* Bowdoin Col, AB, 70; Univ Wis-Madison, MS, 73, PhD(zool), 77. *Prof Exp:* Vis instr psychol, Univ Tenn, 76-77. *Concurrent Pos:* Rev ed, J Field Ornith, 78-85; res fel zool, Ohio State Univ, 81-82; first elect parliamentarian, Animal Behav Soc, 83-89; ed, J Field Ornithol, 85-90; exec coun, Wilson Ornith Soc, 89-91. *Mem:* Fel Am Ornithologists Union; Brit Ornithologists Union; Wilson Ornith Soc; Animal Behav Soc; Soc Am Naturalists; Cooper Orinth Soc; Asn Field Ornithologists (vpres, 89-91, pres, 91-93). *Res:* Evolution and function of color and pattern in animals; avian reproductive ecology; maintenance behavior; bacteria living on feathers. *Mailing Add:* Dept Zool Ohio Wesleyan Univ Delaware OH 43015. *Fax:* 614-368-3299

BURWASH, RONALD ALLAN, PRECAMBRIAN GEOLOGY. *Current Pos:* from asst prof to prof, 56-91, EMER PROF GEOL, UNIV ALTA, 91- *Personal Data:* b Edmonton, Alta, Sept 20, 25; m 52, Ruth W Moore; c Susan C, Brock M & Elizabeth J. *Educ:* Univ Alta, BSc, 45, BEd, 47, MSc, 51; Univ Minn, PhD(geol), 55. *Prof Exp:* Geologist, Sullivan Mines, BC, 51-52; petrogr, Shell Oil Co, Alta, 55-56. *Concurrent Pos:* Vis prof, Univ Aberdeen, Scotland, 63-64, Univ WAustralia, 70; vis scientist, Geol Surv Can, Ottawa, 77-78. *Mem:* Geol Asn Can; Can Soc Petrol Geologists; Mineral Asn Can; Asn Prof Engrs. *Res:* Geologic evolution of the precambrian shield of northwestern North America; Precambrian geology; geochemistry of Continental crust. *Mailing Add:* Dept Earth & Atmosphere Sci Univ Alta Edmonton AB T6G 2E3 Can

BURWASSER, HERMAN, PHYSICAL CHEMISTRY. *Current Pos:* CONSULT, 85- *Personal Data:* b New York, NY, June 21, 27; m 54; c 3. *Educ:* Rutgers Univ, BS, 50; NY Univ, PhD(phys chem), 54. *Prof Exp:* Asst combustion chem, Princeton Univ, 54-56; res chemist, Atlantic Refining Co, 56-59; res scientist, AeroChem Res Labs, Inc, 59-60; proj chemist, Thiokol Chem Corp, 60-68; tech assoc, GAF Corp, 66-82; tech assoc, Transcopy Inc, 82-85. *Mem:* Am Chem Soc. *Res:* Photo and radiation chemistry of organic materials, especially reversible photochemical reactions; organic photoconductors; electrophotography. *Mailing Add:* 21 Dogwood Lane Rd 1 Boonton NJ 07005

BURWELL, CALVIN C, ENERGY ANALYSIS, ELECTRICAL TECHNOLOGY. *Current Pos:* PVT CONSULT, 89- *Personal Data:* b Lafayette, Ind, Sept 20, 30; m 51, 76, Nancy Newgent; c Bronnen G, Shawn, Andrea, Carter & Lee D. *Educ:* Purdue Univ, BS, 52; Univ NMex, MS, 60. *Prof Exp:* Tech engr, Procter & Gamble Mfg Co, 52-55, prod mgr, 55-57; staff mem mat studies, Los Alamos Sci Lab, Calif, 57-63, eng design, 63-65; asst dir nuclear desalination, Oak Ridge Nat Lab, 65-69, tech dir Mid East studies, 69-72, lab prog planning & analysis, 72-78, res engr, Oak Ridge Assoc Univs, 78-88. *Concurrent Pos:* Traveling lectr, Oak Ridge Nat Lab, 66-67. *Res:* Nuclear desalination; liquid metal containment; remote equipment design; nuclear siting policy; national energy policy; solar biomass energy; electricity end-use efficiency. *Mailing Add:* 441 Peach Orchard Rd Clinton TN 37716

BURWELL, JAMES ROBERT, ELEMENTARY PARTICLE PHYSICS, HIGH ENERGY PHYSICS. *Current Pos:* from asst prof to prof physics, Univ Okla, 59-85, chmn dept, 64-65, from asst dean to dean, Col Arts & Sci, 66-84, Regents prof, 85-88, EMER REGENTS PROF PHYSICS, UNIV OKLA, 88- *Personal Data:* b Anderson, Ind, Mar 28, 29; m 51, Joyce E Wilson; c Anthony D, David C & Donald E. *Educ:* Ind Univ, BS, 52, MS, 54, PhD(physics), 57. *Prof Exp:* Res assoc high energy physics, Ind Univ, 57-58 & nuclear physics, 58-59. *Mailing Add:* 708 Cedarbrook Dr Norman OK 73072

BURWELL, ROBERT LEMMON, JR, CATALYSIS, SURFACE CHEMISTRY. *Current Pos:* from instr to prof, Northwestern Univ, 39-70, chmn dept, 52-57, Ipatieff prof, 70-80, EMER IPATIEFF PROF CHEM, NORTHWESTERN UNIV, 80- *Personal Data:* b Baltimore, Md, May 6, 12; m 39, Elise Frank; c Polly & Augusta. *Educ:* St John's Col, Md, AB, 32; Princeton Univ, AM, 34, PhD(phys chem), 36. *Honors & Awards:* Kendall Award, Am Chem Soc, 73, Lubrizol Award Petrol Chem, 83; Alexander von Humboldt Found sr US scientist award, 81; Robert Burwell Award, Catalysis Soc, 83; Langmuir Distinguished Lectr Award, 85. *Prof Exp:* Instr chem, Trinity Col, Conn, 36-39. *Concurrent Pos:* Chemist, Naval Res Lab, 43-45; mem bd dirs, Int Cong Catalysis, 56-64, mem coun, 64-80, secy, 68-72, vpres, 72-76, pres-elect, 76-80, pres, 80-84; chmn, Gordon Res Conf Catalysis, 57; mem subcomt heterogeneous catalysis, Int Union Pure & Appl Chem, 62-67, assoc mem comn colloid & surface chem, 67-69, mem, 69-77; mem chem adv panel, NSF, 68-71; vis prof, Univ Pierre & Marie Curie, Paris, 82. *Mem:* Am Chem Soc; Catalysis Soc (vpres, 68-73, pres, 73-77); Royal Soc Chem. *Res:* Heterogeneous catalysis and surface chemistry. *Mailing Add:* 5700 Williamsburg Landing Dr Apt 302 Williamsburg VA 23185. *Fax:* 757-565-6537

BURWELL, WAYNE GREGORY, COMBUSTION SCIENCE, LASERS. *Current Pos:* sr res scientist, United Technologies Res Ctr, 62-67, chief kinetics & thermal sci, 67-72, mgr kinetics & gas lasers, 72-74, mgr energy res, 74-77, asst dir, 77-81, dep dir res, 81-82, DIR RES, UNITED TECHNOLOGIES RES CTR, 82- *Personal Data:* b New Haven, Conn, Feb 21, 33; m 55; c 4. *Educ:* Yale Univ, BEng, 55, MEng, 56, DEng, 62; Harvard Univ, AMP, 78. *Prof Exp:* Res engr, Gen Motors Corp, 56-59. *Concurrent Pos:* Lectr, Yale Univ, 60-61 & Univ Conn, 63-68; consult, Lycoming Div, Avco Corp, 60-61. *Mem:* Fel Am Inst Aeronaut & Astronaut; Combustion Inst; Asn Res Dir; Indust Res Inst (vpres); Software Productivity Consortium; Res & Develop Coun Am Mgt Asn (vpres). *Res:* Propulsion technology; combustion processes; gas lasers, energy conversion systems; systems analysis. *Mailing Add:* 36 Old Pepperidge Lane No C3 Wethersfield CT 06109

BURWEN, SUSAN JO, CELL BIOLOGY, PHYSIOLOGY. *Current Pos:* FREELANCE MED WRITER, 93- *Personal Data:* b New York, NY, Nov 9, 46; m 68. *Educ:* Brandeis Univ, AB, 68; Harvard Univ, PhD(physiol), 72. *Prof Exp:* Fel molecular biol, Syntex Res, 72-73, fel cell biol, Univ Calif, Berkeley, 73-80; mem staff, Vet Admin Med Ctr, 80-93. *Mem:* Am Soc Cell Biol; Women Cell Biol; AAAS; Sigma Xi. *Res:* Cell physiology: hepatocyte protein transport function, including endocytosis, intracellular processing and biliary secretion. *Mailing Add:* 1114 Blue Lake Sq Mountain View CA 94040

BURZYNSKI, NORBERT J, EXPERIMENTAL PATHOLOGY, CLINICAL GENETICS. *Current Pos:* RETIRED. *Personal Data:* b South Bend, Ind, July 7, 29; m 61; c 3. *Educ:* Ind Univ, AB, 52; St Louis Univ, DDS, 60, MS, 63. *Prof Exp:* USPHS fel oral path, St Louis Univ, 60-62; from asst prof to assoc prof, Sch Dent, Univ Louisville, 65-73, prof oral diag & oral med & chmn dept, 73-90, prof & chmn diag sci, 83-93. *Concurrent Pos:* Fel med genetics, Ind Univ, 70-72; consult, Nat Cancer Inst, 78-80. *Mem:* Fel AAAS; Am Soc Human Genetics; Int Asn Dent; fel Am Col Dentists; Am Dent Asn. *Res:* Chemistry of mucous membrane; genetics and neoplasia; salivary gland metabolism. *Mailing Add:* Sch Dent E-4 Univ Louisville Louisville KY 40292

BURZYNSKI, STANISLAW RAJMUND, ONCOLOGY, PROTEIN CHEMISTRY. *Current Pos:* PRES, BURZYNSKI RES INST, 77- *Personal Data:* b Lublin, Poland, Jan 23, 43; m 79, Barbara Sadlej; c Gregory, Monika & Kinga. *Educ:* Med Acad, Lublin, Poland, MD, 67, PhD(biochem), 68. *Honors & Awards:* Medal Cancer Res, Inst Drug Res & Control, Poland. *Prof Exp:* Teaching asst chem, Med Acad, Lublin, Poland, 62-67, from intern to resident internal med, 67-70; res assoc biochem, Baylor Col Med, 70-72, asst prof, 72-77. *Concurrent Pos:* Nat Cancer Inst grantee, 74; West Found grantee, 75. *Mem:* AAAS; AMA; World Med Asn; Soc Neurosci; Sigma Xi; Am Chem Soc; NY Acad Sci. *Res:* Discovery of antineoplastons-components of biochemical defense system against cancer; elucidation of the structure of Ameletin-first substance known to be responsible for remembering sound in animal's brain; discovery of antiviral and anti-AIDS drugs. *Mailing Add:* 12000 Richmond Ave Houston TX 77082. *Fax:* 713-596-1166

BUS, JAMES STANLEY, TOXICOLOGY, PHARMACOLOGY. *Current Pos:* TECH DIR, HEALTH & ENVIRON RES LAB, DOW CHEMICAL CO, 89- *Personal Data:* b Kalamazoo, Mich, June 27, 49; m 74; c 3. *Educ:* Univ Mich, Ann Arbor, BS, 71; Mich State Univ, PhD(pharmacol), 75. *Honors & Awards:* Achievement Award, Soc Toxicol. *Prof Exp:* Asst prof environ health toxicol, Univ Cincinnati, 75-76; scientist biochem toxicol, Chem Indust Inst Toxicol, 77-86; assoc dir toxicol & dir drug metab res, UpJohn Co, 86-89. *Concurrent Pos:* Adj prof, Dept Pharmacol & Toxicol, Mich State Univ. *Mem:* Sigma Xi; AAAS; Teratology Soc; Soc Toxicol; Am Thoracic Soc; Am Soc Pharmacol & Exp Therapeut. *Res:* Biochemical and developmental toxicology; disposition of industrial chemicals after parenteral or inhalation dosing. *Mailing Add:* Toxicol Res Lab Dow Chem Co 1803 Bldg Midland MI 48674. *Fax:* 517-638-9863

BUSALACCHI, ANTONIO JAMES, JR, EQUATORIAL OCEANOGRAPHY, SHORT TERM COUPLED CLIMATE VARIABILITY. *Current Pos:* Oceanographer, Oceans & Ice Br, Goddard Lab Atmospheric Sci, NASA, 82-88, head, Lab Hydrospheric Processes, 88-90, asst chief, 90-91, CHIEF RES, LAB HYDROSPHERIC PROCESSES, NASA GODDARD SPACE FLIGHT CTR, 91- *Personal Data:* b Milwaukee, Wis, July 20, 56; m 77, Connie J Leland; c Antonio J III. *Educ:* Fla State Univ, BS, 77, MS, 80, PhD(oceanog), 82. *Honors & Awards:* J R Fisher Award, Sigma Xi, 82; Arthur S Flemming Award, Nat Jaycees, 91. *Concurrent Pos:* Adj assoc prof, Dept Aerospace Eng Sci, Univ Colo, 82-90; H Burr Steinbach vis scholar, Woods Hole Oceanograph Inst, 97 *Mem:* Am Geophys Union; Am Meteorol Soc; Oceanog Soc; Sigma Xi. *Res:* Ocean modelling studies of tropical ocean circulation and El Mino phenomena; study of the coupled ocean-atmosphere system; application remotely-sensed ocean data to studies of tropical ocean circulation. *Mailing Add:* Lab Hydrospheric Processes Goddard Space Ctr NASA Greenbelt MD 20771. *Fax:* 301-286-1761

BUSBEE, DAVID L, GENETICS & CELL BIOLOGY, RESEARCH ENVIRONMENTAL TOXICOLOGY- HUMAN AGING. *Current Pos:* PROF GENETICS & CELL BIOL, TEX A&M UNIV, 83- *Personal Data:* b Okla, July 23, 41; m 68, Donna J Cloy. *Educ:* Univ Wichita, BS, 65; Wichita State Univ, MS, 68; Univ Tex, Austin, PhD(genetics & biochem), 71. *Honors & Awards:* Beecham Award, 87; Carrington Award, 90; Fisher Found Award Res, 96. *Prof Exp:* Nat Cancer Inst fel, Cancer Ctr, Univ Tex, Houston, 71-72; prof biol, Univ NTex, 72-82. *Mem:* Am Soc Biochem & Molecular Biol; Am Aging Asn (pres, 92-93). *Mailing Add:* Dept Anat & Pub Health Col Vet Med Tex A&M Univ College Station TX 77843

BUSBY, EDWARD OLIVER, TRANSPORTATION & CONCRETE, BITUMINOUS PAVEMENT. *Current Pos:* assoc prof, Col Eng, Univ Wis-Platteville, 66-68, dean, 66-84, prof civil eng, 68-88, EMER DEAN, COL ENG, UNIV WIS-PLATTEVILLE, 88-; PRES, BUSBY & ASSOC, 88- *Personal Data:* b Macomb, Ill, June 22, 26; m 50, Lois Teham; c Thomas, John & Paula. *Educ:* Univ Wis, BS, 50, MS, 62 & PhD, 71. *Prof Exp:* Engr, State Hwy Comn, Wis, 50-51; asst engr, City La Crosse, 51-53; sales engr, Wis Culvert Co, 53-59; lectr civil eng, Univ Wis-Madison, 59-66. *Concurrent Pos:* Engrs sect, Wis Exam Bd Architects & Prof Engrs; vis prof, Univ Tenn, 84-85. *Mem:* Nat Soc Prof Engrs; fel Am Soc Civil Engrs; Am Soc Eng Educ; Nat Coun Exam Engrs & Surveyors. *Res:* Hardening of asphaltic concrete; flexural properties of bituminous paving mixture, including modulus of rupture and modulus of elasticity in flexure at low temperatures. *Mailing Add:* 7628 Widgeon Way Madison WI 53717

BUSBY, HUBBARD TAYLOR, JR, ORGANIC CHEMISTRY, INDUSTRIAL ORGANIC CHEMISTRY. *Current Pos:* GEN MGR, SANDOZ CHEM CORP, 85- *Personal Data:* b Birmingham, Ala, May 20, 41; m 63; c 3. *Educ:* Miss Col, BS, 63; Univ NC, PhD(org chem), 68. *Prof Exp:* Res chemist, Southern Dyestuff Co, 67-73; group leader, Martin Marietta Chem Co, 73-76, area prod mgr, Disperse Dyes & Chem Intermediates, 76-81, gen mgr, 81-84. *Mem:* Am Chem Soc; Am Asn Textile Chem & Colorists; Com Develop Asn. *Res:* Interannular substituent effects in ferrocene; synthesis and development of marketable dye stuff; organic chemical process development. *Mailing Add:* Sandoz Agro Inc 12200 Denton Dr Dallas TX 75234-7239

BUSBY, ROBERT CLARK, MATHEMATICS. *Current Pos:* from asst prof to assoc prof, 69-81, PROF MATH, DREXEL UNIV, 82- *Personal Data:* b Darby, Pa, July 1, 40; m 64; c 2. *Educ:* Drexel Inst, BS, 63; Univ Pa, AM, 64, PhD(math), 66. *Prof Exp:* Instr math, Drexel Inst, 65-67; asst prof, Oakland Univ, 67-69. *Concurrent Pos:* Consult math, Off Emergency Preparedness, Exec Off Pres, 68-71. *Mem:* Am Math Soc; Soc Indust & Appl Math. *Res:* Modern analysis and applications; algebras of operators on a Hilbert space and group representations; mathematical demography; integral operators. *Mailing Add:* Dept Math Drexel Univ 3141 Chestnut St Philadelphia PA 19104-6395

BUSBY, WILLIAM FISHER, JR, CARCINOGENESIS. *Current Pos:* SR STAFF SCIENTIST, HEALTH EFFECTS INST, 90- *Personal Data:* b Pawtucket, RI, Oct 29, 39; m 62; c 1. *Educ:* Univ RI, BS, 61; Univ Calif, San Diego, PhD(marine biol), 66. *Prof Exp:* Res assoc biochem, Worcester Found Exp Biol, 66-71; res assoc toxicol, Mass Inst Technol, 71-81, res scientist toxicol, 81-90. *Mem:* Am Asn Cancer Res; Soc Toxicol. *Res:* Development of short-term animal bioassays for carcinogenicity testing; toxicokinetics of xenobiotics; molecular epidemiology; mycotoxins; limited-term animal bioassays for testing polynuclear aromatic hydrocarbons and their derivatives; carcinogenic interactions of components of combustion-derived complex mixtures. *Mailing Add:* Redstone Hill Rd Sterling MA 01564

BUSCEMI, PHILIP AUGUSTUS, limnology, environmental management, for more information see previous edition

BUSCH, DANIEL ADOLPH, GEOLOGY. *Current Pos:* RETIRED. *Personal Data:* b St Paul, Minn, May 31, 12; m 39, Emilie Finch; c Daniel A & David A. *Educ:* Capital Univ, BS, 34; Ohio State Univ, AM, 36, PhD(geol), 39. *Hon Degrees:* DSc, Capital Univ, 60. *Honors & Awards:* Orton Award, Ohio State Univ, 59, 60; Matson Award, Am Asn Petrol Geol, 59, Levorsen Award, 71; President's Award, Am Asn Petrol Geol, 76, Sidney Powers Mem Medal, 82. *Prof Exp:* Asst geol, State Geol Surv, Ohio, 35-36; instr, Univ Pittsburgh, 38-43; petrol geologist, State Topog & Geol Surv, Pa, 43-44; consult geologist, Huntley & Huntley, Pittsburgh, 44-46; sr res geologist, Carter Res Lab, 46-49; staff geologist, Carter Oil Co, 49-51; explor mgr, Zephyr Petrol Co, 51-54; consult geologist, 54-91. *Concurrent Pos:* Carnegie Mus field exped, 41; vis prof, Ohio State Univ, 63, Univ Tulsa, 63-64 & Univ Okla, 64-74; world-wide lectr, Oil & Gas Consults Int, Inc, 69-91. *Mem:* Hon mem Am Asn Petrol Geol (vpres, 66-67, pres, 73-74); fel Geol Soc Am; Sigma Xi. *Res:* Silurian and Devonian stratigraphy of Appalachian Basin; Pennsylvania stratigraphy and sedimentology; subsurface stratigraphy of mid-continent; stratigraphy and structure of Mexican Gulf Coast. *Mailing Add:* 3757 S Wheeling Ave Tulsa OK 74105

BUSCH, DARYLE HADLEY, INORGANIC CHEMISTRY, COORDINATION CHEMISTRY. *Current Pos:* ROY A ROBERTS DISTINGUISHED PROF, UNIV KANS, 88- *Personal Data:* b Carterville, Ill, Mar 30, 28; m 51, Geraldine Barnes; c Derek H, Michael C, Steven J, Cheryl A (Rome) & Kristina M (Rodriguez). *Educ:* Southern Ill Univ, BA, 51; Univ Ill, MS, 52, PhD, 54. *Honors & Awards:* Inorg Chem Award, Am Chem Soc, 63, Morley Medal, 75 & Distinguished Serv in Advan of Inorg Chem, 76; Dwyer Medal, Australia, 78; Bailar Medal; Izatt-Christensen Award in Macrocyclic Chemistry, 94. *Prof Exp:* From asst prof to presidential prof chem, Ohio State Univ, 54-87. *Concurrent Pos:* Consult, E I du Pont de Nemours & Co, 56-, Div Res Grants, NIH, 61-65, Div Res Grants, NSF, 65-68, Beaunit Fibers, 66-68 & Chem Abstr Serv, 67-87; consult ed, Allyn & Bacon, Inc, 63-, Air Prod & Chem Corp, 82-86, 3M Co, 87-92, Monsanto Co, 89-; vis prof, Univ Calif, Los Angeles, 75, Kyushu Univ, 78; Guggenheim fel, 81-82; consult, Procter & Gamble Co, 93- Praxair, 96-; chair, chem sect, AAAS, 95. *Mem:* Am Chem Soc; fel AAAS; Sigma Xi; Int Union Pure & Appl Chem. *Res:* Transition metal complexes, including original synthesis, structure, reactions, catalysis and biomimics; subjects in supramolecular chemistry, focusing on heteromultisited receptors and orderly molecular entanglements. *Mailing Add:* Dept Chem Univ Kans Malott Hall Lawrence KS 66045. *Fax:* 785-864-5747; *E-Mail:* dbusch@eureka.chem.ukans.edu

BUSCH, GEORGE JACOB, IMMUNO-PATHOLOGY, TRANSPLANTATION PATHOLOGY. *Current Pos:* ASSOC PROF PATH, MED SCH, HARVARD UNIV, 65-, CHIEF PATH, VET ADMIN MED CTR, 81- *Educ:* Johns Hopkins Univ, MD, 62. *Mailing Add:* 43 Glenridge Dr Bedford MA 01730-2009

BUSCH, HARRIS, PHARMACOLOGY, BIOCHEMISTRY. *Current Pos:* prof biochem & chmn dept, 60-62, PROF PHARMACOL & CHMN DEPT, BAYLOR COL MED, 60- *Personal Data:* b Chicago, Ill, May 23, 23; m 45; c 4. *Educ:* Univ Ill, MD, 46; Univ Wis, PhD(biochem), 52. *Prof Exp:* Asst & sr asst surgeon, USPHS, 47-49; asst prof biochem, Yale Univ, 52-54, asst prof med & biochem, 54-55; assoc prof pharmacol, Univ Ill, 55-59, prof, 59-60.

Concurrent Pos: Baldwin scholar oncol, Sch Med, Yale Univ, 51-55, scholar cancer res, 54-55; vis prof, Univ Chicago, 68, Northwestern Univ, Ore State Univ, Ind Univ, Vet Hosp & Methodist Hosp, Houston; dir, Cancer Res Ctr; mem consult bd, Eli Lilly Co; mem pathogenesis panel, Am Cancer Soc; mem cancer chemother study sect, USPHS; consult, Uniformed Servs Univ, Bethesda, Md, 75; mem bd sci counrs, Div Cancer Treatment, Nat Cancer Inst, 75; vis prof, Univ Toronto, 75. *Mem:* AAAS; Biochem Soc; Am Chem Soc; Am Asn Cancer Res; Am Soc Biol Chemists. *Res:* Metabolism of nuclear proteins in tumor nuclei; isolation and metabolism of tumor nucleoli. *Mailing Add:* Dept Pharmacol Baylor Col Med Houston TX 77030-3498

BUSCH, KENNETH LOUIS, ANALYTICAL CHEMISTRY, BIOENGINEERING & BIOMEDICAL ENGINEERING. *Current Pos:* ASST PROF, IND UNIV, BLOOMINGTON, 83- *Personal Data:* b New York, NY, Oct 26, 53. *Educ:* Univ Md, BS, 75; Univ NC, PhD(chem), 79. *Prof Exp:* Asst res scientist, Purdue Univ, W Lafayette, Ind, 81-83. *Concurrent Pos:* Secy anal chem div, Am Chem Soc, 88- *Mem:* Am Chem Soc; Am Soc Mass Spectrometry; AAAS; Sigma Xi. *Res:* Analytical mass spectrometry; fast atom bombardment; the coupling of chromatography with secondary ion mass spectrometry. *Mailing Add:* 3861 W Clinton Ct Marietta GA 30062-5856

BUSCH, KENNETH WALTER, INFRARED SPECTROSCOPY, COLLOID CHEMISTRY. *Current Pos:* from asst prof to assoc prof, 74-88, PROF CHEM, BAYLOR UNIV, 88- *Personal Data:* b Mt Vernon, NY, Mar 29, 44; m 68, Marianna Anderson. *Educ:* Fla Atlantic Univ, BS, 66; Fla State Univ, PhD(anal chem), 71. *Prof Exp:* Teaching fel chem, Fla State Univ, 71-72; res assoc, Cornell Univ, 72-74. *Concurrent Pos:* Vis assoc, Calif Inst Technol, 83; vis scientist, Cornell Univ, 85, 86, 87 & 88. *Mem:* Am Chem Soc; Soc Appl Spectros; Int Soc Optical Eng; fel Am Inst Chemists; Am Water Works Asn; AAAS. *Res:* Design of spectroscopic instrumentation; infrared systems design; infrared physics; applications of infrared emission; analytical chemistry. *Mailing Add:* Dept Chem Baylor Univ PO Box 97348 Waco TX 76798-7348. *Fax:* 254-755-2403; *E-Mail:* kenneth_busch@baylor.edu

BUSCH, LLOYD VICTOR, PHYTOPATHOLOGY. *Current Pos:* RETIRED. *Personal Data:* b London, Ont, Nov 15, 18; m 43; c 4. *Educ:* Ont Agr Col, BSA, 42; Univ Toronto, MSA, 48; Univ Wis, PhD(plant path), 55. *Prof Exp:* From lectr to assoc prof, Univ Guelph, 46-71, prof environ biol, Ont Agr Col, 72-83. *Mem:* Can Phytopath Soc (pres, 74-75); Am Phytopath Soc. *Res:* Physiology of broad leafed plants and alfalfa wilt; physiology and histology of wilting; fusarium stock and cob rot of corn mycotoxins; diseases of greenhouse ornamentals. *Mailing Add:* 55 Mary St Guelph ON N1G 2A9 Can

BUSCH, MARIANNA ANDERSON, ANALYTICAL SPECTROSCOPY, COLLOID CHEMISTRY. *Current Pos:* lectr, 75 & 77, from asst prof to assoc prof, 77-91, PROF CHEM, BAYLOR UNIV, 91-, DEPT CHMN, 93- *Personal Data:* b Pittsburgh, Pa, Oct 28, 43; m 68, Kenneth W. *Educ:* Randolph-Macon Woman's Col, BA, 65; Fla State Univ, PhD(inorg chem), 72. *Honors & Awards:* James Lewis Howe Award, Am Chem Soc, 65. *Prof Exp:* Lectr chem, Cornell Univ, 72, res assoc, 73-74. *Concurrent Pos:* Robert A Welch fel, 74-75 & 77, NSF energy-related fel, 76-77; vis assoc, Dept Environ & Eng Sci, Calif Inst Technol, 83, vis scientist, Chem Dept, Cornell Univ, 85-88; consult scientist, Nat Bur Standards, 84-; Fulbright fel, Victoria Univ, Wellington, NZ, 66; vis scientist, DuPont, Wilmington, Del, 86. *Mem:* Am Chem Soc; Sigma Xi; fel Am Inst Chemists; Soc Appl Spectros; Int Soc Optical Eng. *Res:* Design and application of spectroscopic instrumentation; infrared emission spectrometry; colloid chemistry. *Mailing Add:* Dept Chem Baylor Univ PO Box 97348 Waco TX 76798-7348. *Fax:* 254-755-2403; *E-Mail:* marianna_busch@baylor.edu

BUSCH, PAUL L, ENVIRONMENTAL ENGINEERING. *Current Pos:* CHMN, PRES & CHIEF EXEC OFFICER, MALCOM PIRNIE INC, 88- *Personal Data:* b New York, NY, Oct 31, 37. *Educ:* Mass Inst Technol, BS, MS; Harvard Univ, PhD(eng). *Honors & Awards:* Kappe Distinguished Lectr, Am Acad Environ Engrs, 90; Gordon Maskew Fair Award, 91. *Concurrent Pos:* Vis prof, Univ NC. *Mem:* Nat Acad Eng; Am Soc Civil Engrs; Am Water Works Asn; Water Environ Fedn; AAAS; Am Chem Soc; NY Acad Sci. *Res:* Development of drinking water and wastewater technology; feasibility/treatability of toxic and complex wastewaters. *Mailing Add:* Malcolm Pirnie Inc 104 Corporate Park Dr White Plains NY 10602

BUSCH, ROBERT EDWARD, ANIMAL GENETICS. *Current Pos:* assoc prof, 63-77, PROF ANIMAL SCI, CALIF STATE UNIV, CHICO, 77- *Personal Data:* b Independence, Mo, May 13, 24; m 54; c 2. *Educ:* Univ Mo, BS, 45, MEd, 55; Ore State Univ, PhD(genetics), 63. *Prof Exp:* Instr high schs, Mo, 45-59; res geneticist, US Fish & Wildlife Serv, 62-63. *Mem:* Am Soc Animal Sci; Int Embryo Transfer Soc. *Res:* Sheep genetics; genetics of fish; swine genetics and nutrition. *Mailing Add:* Dept Agr Calif State Univ Chico CA 95929-0130

BUSCH, ROBERT HENRY, GENETICS, STATISTICS. *Current Pos:* AT DEPT AGRON, UNIV MINN. *Personal Data:* b Jefferson, Iowa, Oct 22, 37; m 58; c Shari & Todd. *Educ:* Iowa State Univ, BS, 59, MS, 63; Purdue Univ, PhD(genetics, plant breeding), 67. *Prof Exp:* Technician, Iowa State Univ, 59-61, res assoc agron, 61-63; instr, Purdue Univ, 66-67; from asst prof to assoc prof agron, NDak State Univ, 67-77, prof, 77- *Concurrent Pos:* Res geneticist agron & plant genetics, Sci & Educ Admin-Agr Res, USDA, Univ Minn, 78. *Mem:* Fel Am Soc Agron; fel Crop Sci Soc Am. *Res:* Quantitative inheritance of economic characteristics of spring wheat and more effective methods of effecting genetic control and selection; premier seedsman. *Mailing Add:* Dept Agron Univ Minn 411 Borlaug Hall 1991 Upper Buford Circle St Paul MN 55108-6024. *Fax:* 612-625-1268

BUSCHBACH, THOMAS CHARLES, TECTONICS. *Current Pos:* RETIRED. *Personal Data:* b Cicero, Ill, May 12, 23; m 47; c 3. *Educ:* Univ Ill, BS, 50, MS, 51, PhD, 59. *Prof Exp:* From asst geologist to geologist, Ill State Geol Surv, 51-78; res prof geol, St Louis Univ, 78-85. *Concurrent Pos:* Consult, US Nuclear Regulatory Comn, 75-85; geol consult, 78- *Mem:* fel Geol Soc Am; Am Asn Petrol Geol. *Res:* Cambrian and Ordovician stratigraphy; underground gas storage; siting of nuclear facilities; tectonics of midcontinent-US. *Mailing Add:* 604 Park Lane Dr Champaign IL 61820

BUSCHE, ROBERT M(ARION), RESEARCH PLANNING, TECHNOL ECONOMIC ANALYSIS. *Current Pos:* PRES, BIO EN-GENE-ER ASSOCS, INC, 85- *Personal Data:* b St Louis, Mo, June 14, 26; m 80, Emma R Ruch; c Robert E, David C, Kristin A & Amy E. *Educ:* Washington Univ, St Louis, BS, 48, MS, 49, DSc(chem eng), 52. *Prof Exp:* Chem engr, Coal to Oil Demonstr Plant, Bur Mines, 50-53; asst tech supt, Belle Works, E I Du Pont de Nemours & Co, Inc, 53-56 & Sabine River Works, 56-59, res & develop supvr, Exp Sta Labs, 59-62, tech serv supvr, Chestnut Run Labs, 62-64, prod develop mgr, Newport Labs, 64-66, tech mgr, Heat Transfer Prod Div, 66-67, staff consult, Mgt Serv Div, 67-70, res planning consult life sci, Cent Res & Develop Dept, 70-85. *Concurrent Pos:* Res Found fel; adj prof chem eng, Univ Pa; consult biotechnol. *Mem:* Am Chem Soc; Am Inst Chem Engrs; Bio-Energy Coun; Sigma Xi. *Res:* Chemicals from renewable resources via biotechnology; high-temperature reaction systems; coal gasification; spray drying; nylon intermediates; hydrocarbon polymers; plastics fabrication; business analysis; new venture development; single-cell protein; renewable resource utilization. *Mailing Add:* Bio En-Gene-Er Assoc Inc 533 Rothbury Rd Wilmington DE 19803-2439. *Fax:* 302-571-1150

BUSCHERT, ROBERT CECIL, SOLID STATE PHYSICS. *Current Pos:* PROF PHYSICS, GOSHEN COL, 65- *Personal Data:* b Preston, Ont, Nov 28, 24; m 48; c 3. *Educ:* Goshen Col, BA, 48; Purdue Univ, MS, 52, PhD(physics), 57. *Prof Exp:* Instr physics & math, Goshen Col, 48-50; mem tech staff, Bell Tel Labs, 56-58; asst prof physics, Purdue Univ, 58-65. *Mem:* Am Phys Soc. *Res:* Structure of semiconductors; germanium and silicon. *Mailing Add:* Dept Physics Goshen Col S Main St Goshen IN 46526. *Fax:* 219-535-7509

BUSCHKE, HERMAN, NEUROLOGY, NEUROPSYCHOLOGY. *Current Pos:* assoc prof, 69-74, PROF NEUROL & NEUROSCI, ALBERT EINSTEIN COL MED, 74-, GLUCK DISTINGUISHED SCHOLAR NEUROL, 73- *Personal Data:* b Berlin, Ger, Oct 15, 32; US citizen; div. *Educ:* Reed Col, BA, 54; Western Reserve Univ, MD, 58; Am Bd Psychiat & Neurol, dipl, 66. *Prof Exp:* Intern med, Bronx Munic Hosp Ctr, NY, 58-59, resident neurol, 59-62; from instr to asst prof, Sch Med, Stanford Univ, 62-69, res assoc, Inst Math Studies in Soc Sci, 68-69. *Concurrent Pos:* USPHS fel, Albert Einstein Col Med, 59-62, res scientist develop award, 64-69; consult, Vet Admin Hosp, Palo Alto, Calif, 63-69; sr investr, Rose F Kennedy Ctr Res Ment Retardation & Human Develop, 69- *Mem:* Fel AAAS; Cognitive Sci Soc; Int Neuropsychol Soc; fel Am Acad Neurol; fel Am Psychol Asn; Soc Neurosci. *Res:* Human memory; learning; cognition; neuropsychology. *Mailing Add:* Dept Neurol 1300 Morris Park Ave Albert Einstein Col Med Bronx NY 10461. *Fax:* 718-824-3058; *E-Mail:* buschke@aecom.yu.edu

BUSCHMANN, MARYBETH TANK, GERONTOLOGY, NEUROBIOLOGY. *Current Pos:* teaching asst anat, Univ Ill Med Ctr, 71-74, from asst prof to prof gen nursing, 75-85, asst prof anat, 75-93, PROF MED-SURG NURSING, UNIV ILL MED CTR, 85- *Personal Data:* b Evanston, Ill, Oct 10, 42; m 70. *Educ:* Augustana Col, BSN, 65; Univ Ill, MS, 68, PhD(anat), 75. *Prof Exp:* Staff regist nurse med surg, McKinley Univ Hosp & Mercy Hosp, 66-67; res asst zool, Univ Ill, Urbana, 68, teaching asst, 68-69; res dir, Renal Lab, Univ Wis, 69-70. *Concurrent Pos:* NIH fel, 75-76; prin investr, Univ Ill, 75-79 & Am Nurses Found, 76-78; Am Nurses Found scholar, 79. *Mem:* AAAS; Nat Geront Nursing Asn; Soc Neurosci; Am Soc on Aging; Geront Soc; Sigma Xi. *Res:* Gerontological nursing; neurobiology of aging and depression in the elderly employing the intervention of touch; neurobiology of Alzheimer's disease and the effects of milieu on these victims. *Mailing Add:* Univ Ill M/C 845 S Damen Chicago IL 60612. *Fax:* 312-996-4979; *E-Mail:* u2641z@vicvm

BUSCHMANN, ROBERT J, ULTRASTRUCTURAL PATHOLOGY, MORPHOMETRY. *Current Pos:* Physiologist, 69-72, DIR ELECTRON MICROS PROG, VET ADMIN WEST SIDE MED CTR, 72- *Personal Data:* b Chicago, Ill, July 30, 42; m 70. *Educ:* Loyola Univ, Ill, BS, 64; Univ Ill, Urbana, MS, 66, PhD(physiol), 69. *Mem:* AAAS; Int Soc Stereology; Am Soc Cell Biol; Electron Micros Soc Am; Am Asn Pathol; AAAS. *Res:* Liver cirrhosis. *Mailing Add:* Dept Path MP113 Vet Affairs West Side Med Ctr 820 S Damen Ave Chicago IL 60612-3740. *Fax:* 312-633-2110

BUSCOMBE, WILLIAM, ASTROPHYSICS. *Current Pos:* PROF ASTRON, NORTHWESTERN UNIV, EVANSTON, 68- *Personal Data:* b Hamilton, Ont, Feb 12, 18; m 42; c 8. *Educ:* Univ Toronto, BA, 40, MA, 48; Princeton Univ, PhD(astron), 50. *Prof Exp:* Meteorologist, Dept Transp, Govt Can, 41-45; instr math & astron, Univ Sask, 45-48; res fel, Mt Wilson & Palomar Observ, 50-52; astronr, Mt Stromlo Observ, Australian Nat Univ, 52-68. *Concurrent Pos:* Vis prof, Univ Pa, 64-65, Northern Ill Univ, 70-73; nat lectr, Am Astron Soc, 84-93. *Mem:* Am Astron Soc; Royal Astron Soc Can; Int Astron Union. *Res:* Stellar spectra; radial velocities; binary orbits; galactic kinematics; interstellar gas; variable stars; compiler catalogs of stellar data. *Mailing Add:* Dearborn Observ Northwestern Univ Evanston IL 60208. *E-Mail:* buscombe@nwu.edu

BUSE, JOHN FREDERICK, INTERNAL MEDICINE. *Current Pos:* assoc prof, 56-70, PROF MED, MED UNIV SC, 70- *Personal Data:* b Charleston, SC, Oct 17, 21; m 56; c 1. *Educ:* Univ SC, BS, 44, MD, 50. *Prof Exp:* Intern, Roper Hosp, 50-51, asst resident med, 51-52; asst resident, Univ Va, 52-53. *Concurrent Pos:* Fel, Med Col SC, 53-54 & Cox Inst, Univ Pa, 54-56. *Mem:* Am Fedn Clin Res; Endocrine Soc; Am Diabetes Asn. *Res:* Diabetes mellitus; influence of muscular activity on insulin requirement. *Mailing Add:* Dept Med Endocrinol Med Univ SC 171 Ashley Ave Charleston SC 29425-0001

BUSE, MARIA F GORDON, MEDICINE. *Current Pos:* res assoc med, 56-59, instr biochem, 59-61, assoc, 61-62, from asst prof to assoc prof res med, 62-72, PROF MED, MED UNIV SC, 72-, PROF BIOCHEM, 74- *Personal Data:* b Budapest, Hungary, July 17, 27; m 56; c 3. *Educ:* Univ Buenos Aires, MD, 54. *Prof Exp:* Res fel physiol, Inst Exp Biol & Med, Univ Buenos Aires, 54-55; fel med, Univ Pa, 55-56. *Concurrent Pos:* NIH res career develop award, 63. *Mem:* AMA; Am Fedn Clin Res; Soc Nuclear Med; Am Phys Soc; Am Soc Biol Chemists; Am Diabetes Asn; Endocrine Soc. *Res:* Diabetes; action of insulin; intermediary metabolism. *Mailing Add:* Med Univ SC Dept Med 171 Ashley Ave Charleston SC 29425-0002

BUSE, REUBEN CHARLES, AGRICULTURAL ECONOMICS. *Current Pos:* from asst prof to assoc prof, 59-69, PROF AGR ECON, UNIV WIS, 69- *Personal Data:* b Fergus Falls, Minn, July 8, 32; div; c 2. *Educ:* Univ Minn, BS, 54, MS, 56; Pa State Univ, PhD(agr econ), 59. *Honors & Awards:* Qual of Commun Award, Am Agr Econ Asn. *Prof Exp:* Res asst agr econ, Univ Minn, 54-56; instr, Pa State Univ, 56-59. *Concurrent Pos:* Consult, Brazilian & Peruvian Ministry of Planning, USDA, AID & several private firms. *Mem:* Am Agr Econ Asn; Am Econ Asn; Int Asn Agr Economists. *Res:* Quantitative methods in agricultural economics; consumer expenditure behavior. *Mailing Add:* 3436 Valley Creek Circle Middleton WI 53562

BUSECK, PETER R, GEOCHEMISTRY, MINERALOGY. *Current Pos:* REGENTS' PROF GEOL & CHEM, ARIZ STATE UNIV, 63- *Personal Data:* b Sept 30, 35; US citizen; m 60, Alice Bien; c 4. *Educ:* Antioch Col, AB, 57; Columbia Univ, MA, 59, PhD(geol), 62. *Prof Exp:* Fel, Geophys Lab, Carnegie Inst Washington, 61-63. *Concurrent Pos:* Vis prof, Oxford Univ, 70-71, Stanford Univ, 79-80, Univ Paris, 86-87; distinguished res prof, Ariz State Univ, 78-79; spec asst to dir, NSF, 94-95; sci staff, White House Off Sci & Technol Policy, 94-95. *Mem:* Geochem Soc (secy, 76-79); fel Meteoritical Soc; Am Geophys Union; fel Geol Soc Am; fel AAAS; fel Mineral Soc Am. *Res:* Electron microscopy and diffraction of minerals; electron microprobe analysis of air pollutants and minerals; scanning electron microscopy; meteoritics. *Mailing Add:* Dept Chem Ariz State Univ PSF 648 Dept Geol Tempe AZ 85287-1404

BUSENBERG, EURYBIADES, GEOCHEMISTRY. *Current Pos:* HYDROLOGIST, US GEOL SURV, 78- *Personal Data:* b Jerusalem, Israel, Nov 13, 39; m 74. *Educ:* NY Univ, BA, 61, MS, 67; State Univ NY Buffalo, PhD(geochem), 75. *Prof Exp:* Chemist, Am Petrol Inst, 65-67; petrol geologist, Texaco Inc, 69-71; vis asst prof, 74-75, asst prof geochem, State Univ NY Buffalo, 75-78. *Mem:* Sigma Xi; Clay Minerals Soc. *Res:* The dissolutions kinetics of aluminosilicate minerals; natural weathering reactions of aluminosilicates and their products; the aquatic chemistry of natural waters. *Mailing Add:* 11628 Quail Ridge Ct Reston VA 22094-1112

BUSENBERG, STAVROS NICHOLAS, differential equations, mathematical modelling; deceased, see previous edition for last biography

BUSER, KENNETH RENE, ORGANIC CHEMISTRY. *Current Pos:* res chemist, Exp Sta, 54-69, staff chemist, Fabrics & Finishes Dept, 69-85, RES ASSOC, E I DU PONT DE NEMOURS & CO, INC, 85- *Personal Data:* b Bloomington, Ind, Apr 13, 25; m 46; c 3. *Educ:* Wabash Col, BA, 50; Purdue Univ, MS, 52, PhD(chem), 54. *Prof Exp:* Asst, Purdue Univ, 50-54. *Mem:* Am Chem Soc. *Res:* Organic chemistry of sulfur, polymer chemistry, finishes. *Mailing Add:* 2813 Ambler Ct Wilmington DE 19808

BUSER, MARY PAUL, mathematics, computer science, for more information see previous edition

BUSEY, RICHARD HOOVER, PHYSICAL CHEMISTRY, THERMODYNAMICS. *Current Pos:* RETIRED. *Personal Data:* b Cairo, Ill, Apr 6, 19; m 42; c 4. *Educ:* Southern Methodist Univ, BS, 41; Univ Calif, PhD(chem), 50. *Prof Exp:* Res anal chemist, Magnolia Petrol Co, 41-45; assoc, Univ Calif, 50-52; res chemist, Oak Ridge Nat Lab, 52-84. *Mem:* AAAS; Am Chem Soc. *Res:* Low temperature calorimetry; spectroscopy; chemistry of Technetium and Rhenium; high temperature aqueous inorganic species equilibria; high temperature and pressure calorimetry on aqueous solutions. *Mailing Add:* 106 S Tampa Oak Ridge TN 37830

BUSH, ALFRED LERNER, ECONOMIC GEOLOGY, ENVIRONMENTAL GEOLOGY. *Current Pos:* From jr geologist to sr geologist, 46-87, EMER GEOLOGIST, US GEOL SURV, 87- *Personal Data:* b Rochester, NY, Dec 21, 19; m 42, 65, JoAnn Gilstrap; c Caroline L (Miller), Martha E (Poland), John E, Amy E (Calkins), James A, David R Heath, Margaret A (Retting) & Diane D (Peifer). *Educ:* Univ Rochester, AB, 41, MS, 46. *Concurrent Pos:* Sci secy mineral resources, US deleg, UN Conf Sci & Technol, Switz, 63. *Mem:* Fel Geol Soc Am; fel Soc Econ Geol; Int Asn Genesis Ore Deposits. *Res:* Uranium deposits of the Colorado Plateau; geology of the western San Juan Mountains, Colorado; economic geology of lightweight aggregates, United States and worldwide. *Mailing Add:* US Geol Surv MS 941 Denver Fed Ctr Box 25046 Denver CO 80225. *Fax:* 303-236-5348; *E-Mail:* abush@usgs.gov

BUSH, C ALLEN, BIOPHYSICAL CHEMISTRY. *Current Pos:* PROF CHEM, UNIV MD, 81- *Personal Data:* b Rochester, NY, Aug 2, 38. *Educ:* Cornell Univ, BA, 61; Univ Calif, Berkeley, PhD(chem), 65. *Prof Exp:* Res assoc chem, Cornell Univ, 66-68; from asst prof to assoc prof, Ill Inst Tech, 68-81. *Concurrent Pos:* Mem staff, Ctr Marine Biotechnol, Baltimore. *Mem:* Am Soc Biol Chemists; Am Chem Soc; Biophys Soc. *Res:* Circular dichroism; oligosaccharide structure and conformation glycoproteins; nuclear magnetic resonance; bacterial polysaccharides. *Mailing Add:* Dept Chem Univ Md 5401 Wilkens Ave Baltimore MD 21228-5398. *E-Mail:* bush@umbc.edu

BUSH, CHARLES EDWARD, FUSION ENERGY RESEARCH, BOLOMETRIC & INFRARED DIAGNOSTICS. *Current Pos:* RES STAFF FUSION, OAK RIDGE NAT LAB, 72- *Personal Data:* b Miami, Fla, Aug 21, 38; m 66; c 2. *Educ:* Knoxville & Lafayette Col, BS, 62; Univ Wis, Madison, MS, PhD (nuclear eng), 72. *Prof Exp:* Proj engr, US Army, Edgewood Arsenal, Md, 62-64. *Concurrent Pos:* Vis fac fusion res, Princeton Plasma Physics Lab, Princeton Univ, 83-; chmn comt minorities in physics, Am Phys Soc, 78-82. *Mem:* Am Phys Soc; Am Nuclear Soc; Sigma Xi; NY Acad Sci; Am Asn Advan Sci. *Res:* Energy and power balance and confinement of high temperature plasma in tokamaks; bolometric and infrared diagnostics in fusion. *Mailing Add:* 192 Loomis Ct Princeton Univ C-Site LOB B233 PO Box 451 Princeton NJ 08540-3439

BUSH, DAVID CLAIR, ORGANIC CHEMISTRY. *Current Pos:* RETIRED. *Personal Data:* b Malad City, Idaho, Nov 6, 22; m 44; c 4. *Educ:* Univ Idaho, BS, 48; Ore State Col, MS, 50, PhD(org chem), 53. *Prof Exp:* Res chemist, Pittsburgh Plate Glass Co, 52-54; vpres, Idaho Chem Industs, 54-86. *Mem:* Am Chem Soc. *Res:* Metal pyridine salts; Mannich reaction; synthetic polymers; polyesters and epoxy resins. *Mailing Add:* 6820 McMullen Boise ID 83709

BUSH, DAVID E, CARDIOLOGY, HEMODYNAMICS. *Current Pos:* Intern med, Johns Hopkins Univ Sch Med, 77-78, resident med, 78-80, cardiol fel, 80-83, asst med, 83-85, instr med, 85-87, ASST PROF MED, JOHNS HOPKINS UNIV SCH MED, 87- *Personal Data:* b Washington, DC, Feb 24, 52. *Educ:* Univ Calif, San Francisco, MD, 77. *Mem:* Am Heart Asn. *Res:* Effects of drugs and aging on cardiovascular (ventricular-vascular) couplings; cardiac magnetic resonances imaging; human atherosclerosis, pathogenesis and drug effects. *Mailing Add:* Johns Hopkins Bay View Med Ctr 4940 Eastern Ave Baltimore MD 21224. *Fax:* 410-550-1183; *E-Mail:* dbush@welchlink.welch.jhu.edu

BUSH, DAVID GRAVES, ENVIRONMENTAL ANALYSIS, INDUSTRIAL HYGIENE. *Current Pos:* OCCUP HEALTH CONSULT, DAVID G BUSH ASSOCS, 84- *Personal Data:* b Westfield, Mass, Apr 21, 22; m 45, Lila Weaver; c David L, Stuart G & Melissa L. *Educ:* Univ Mass, BS, 47; Univ Minn, MS, 50. *Honors & Awards:* Rochester Sect Award, Am Chem Soc, 87. *Prof Exp:* Asst synthetic rubber res, Univ Minn, 52; from res chemist to sr res chemist, Eastern Kodak Co, 52-64, res assoc anal res & develop, 64-75, lab head, Res Labs, 75-78, anal consult, Health & Environ Lab, 79-84. *Mem:* Am Chem Soc; AAAS; Am Indust Hyg Asn; Am Soc Safety Eng. *Res:* Gas chromatography; functional group analysis; liquid chromatography; polymer identification and analysis; light microscopy; atomic absorption spectroscopy. *Mailing Add:* 147 Landing Park Rochester NY 14625-1717. *Fax:* 716-288-2394

BUSH, FRANCIS M, ZOOLOGY. *Current Pos:* from asst prof to assoc prof, 69-92, PROF GEN DENT, MED COL VA, VA COMMONWEALTH UNIV, 69- *Personal Data:* b Bloomfield, Ky, Sept 5, 33; m 59. *Educ:* Univ Ky, BS, 55, MS, 57, DMD, 75; Univ Ga, PhD(zool), 62. *Prof Exp:* From asst prof to assoc prof biol, Stanford Univ, 60-64. *Concurrent Pos:* Mary Glide Goethe travel awards, 59-60; Sigma Xi res grant, 63; Am Philos Soc grant, 64; USPHS grant, 65-68. *Mem:* Am Dent Soc; Int Asn Dent Res. *Res:* Epidemiology of mandibular dysfunction; facial pain; effect of local anesthetics on skeletal muscle. *Mailing Add:* 13411 Torrington Dr Midlothian VA 23113

BUSH, GARY GRAHAM, MAGNETICS, INSTRUMENTATION DESIGN. *Current Pos:* res specialist, 85-89, STAFF SCIENTIST, LOCKHEED PALO ALTO RES LABS, 89-, PRIN SCIENTIST, MICROMAGNETICS LAB, 89-, SR STAFF SCIENTIST, 91- *Personal Data:* b Atlanta, Ga, Dec 29, 50; m 82, Freeda C Leach; c Joseph D & Deborah G. *Educ:* Ga Inst Technol, BSNE, 72, MS, 73, MS(physics) & MS(elec eng), 76, PhD(elec eng), 83. *Prof Exp:* Sr engr, Intel Magnetics, 84-85. *Concurrent Pos:* Chief engr & owner, DosTek, Comput Systs Integrator, 87- *Mem:* Sr mem Inst Elec & Electronics Engrs; assoc mem Sigma Xi. *Res:* Artificial magnetodielectric materials and their modeling and measurement; electromagnetic applications of materials and design and analysis of thin film materials and bulk materials for EM applications. *Mailing Add:* 5505 Castle Manor Dr San Jose CA 95129. *E-Mail:* gary@maglab.com

BUSH, GEORGE CLARK, ALGEBRA, DATA STRUCTURES. *Current Pos:* RETIRED. *Personal Data:* b St Catharines, Ont, Oct 18, 30; m 60; c 2. *Educ:* McMaster Univ, BA, 54; Mass Inst Technol, SM, 56; Queen's Univ, Ont, PhD(math), 61; Inst Retraining Comput Sci, cert, 85. *Prof Exp:* Asst prof math, Queen's Univ, Ont, 61-66; assoc prof, Beirut Univ Col, 67-71; spec lectr, Queen's Univ, Ont, 71-73; assoc prof, Col Arts & Sci, Univ Shiraz, 73-76; assoc prof, Acadia Univ, 76-78; from asst prof to assoc prof math, Univ Col Cape Breton, 78-88; assoc prof, Mid E Tech Univ, Turkey, 88-92. *Mem:* Math Asn Am; Am Math Soc; Can Math Soc. *Res:* Algebra; numerical analysis; data structures. *Mailing Add:* 66 Meadowbrook Dr Bedford NS B4A 1R1 Can

BUSH, GEORGE F(RANKLIN), BIOMEDICAL & MECHANICAL ENGINEERING. *Current Pos:* FOUNDER, OWNER & DIR, G F BUSH ASSOCS, 47- *Personal Data:* b Philadelphia, Pa, July 1, 09; m 39; c 3. *Educ:* Lafayette Col, BS, 32; Univ Pa, MS, 47. *Prof Exp:* From instr to assoc prof mech & asst dean, George Washington Univ, 39-42; asst prof eng, Princeton Univ, 42-45. *Concurrent Pos:* Mem, Bioinstrumentation Adv Coun, USN. *Mem:* AAAS; Sigma Xi. *Res:* New scientific instrument creation and design; mechanical, electromechanical, electrochemical and biomedical devices. *Mailing Add:* Oceanville 1 Stonington ME 04681

BUSH, GLENN W, METALLURGY. *Current Pos:* PRES, BUSH & ASSOCS, 88- *Personal Data:* b Bellwood, Pa, Sept 9, 33; m 56; c Glenn Jr, John & Kelley. *Educ:* Pa State Univ, BS, 55, MS, 58, PhD(metall), 60. *Prof Exp:* Metallurgist, Allegheny Ludlum Steel Corp, 55-56; res metallurgist, Nat Steel Corp, 60-63, sr res metallurgist, 63-65, supvr coated prod res, 65-69, asst div chief, 69-78, div chief, 78-84, sr res consult, 85, mgr coated prod/process, 85-87, mgr, finished prod/processes, 87-88. *Mem:* Am Soc Metals; Am Inst Mining, Metall & Petrol Engrs; Metall Soc; Sigma Xi. *Res:* Physical metallurgy; effect of a residual element on properties of steel; measurement of residual stress in electrodeposited metals; relationship of micro-structure of properties of metals; production and application of coated products. *Mailing Add:* 213 Timberyoke Rd Moon Township PA 15108

BUSH, GUY L, EVOLUTIONARY BIOLOGY. *Current Pos:* HANNAH PROF, DISTINGUISHED PROF, EVOLUTIONARY BIOL, MICH STATE UNIV, 82- *Personal Data:* b Greenfield, Iowa, July 9, 29; m 59; c 3. *Educ:* Iowa State Col, BS, 53; Va Polytech Inst, MS, 60; Harvard Univ, PhD(biol), 64. *Honors & Awards:* Founders Mem Award, Entom Soc Am, 87. *Prof Exp:* Entomologist, USDA, 55-57; NIH fel, Univ Melbourne, 64-66; asst prof, 66-73, assoc prof, 73-76, prof zool, Univ Tex, Austin, 76-82. *Concurrent Pos:* Guggenheim fel, Univ Calif, Berkeley, 77; vis res scientist, Swiss Fed Res Sta Arboracultur, Hort & Viticulture, W-deuswil, 71; vis prof, Dept Biol Sci, Univ Sao Paulo, 77; vis fel, Oxford Univ, 90-91. *Mem:* Fel AAAS; Soc Study Evolution (vpres, 80, pres, 81); Genetics Soc Am; Entom Soc Am; Soc Syst Zool; Sigma Xi; Am Soc Naturalists (vpres, 80). *Res:* Modes of speciation; systematics of higher Diptera; evolutionary cytogenetics; genetics of host-parasite interactions. *Mailing Add:* Dept Zool Mich State Univ East Lansing MI 48824-1115

BUSH, JOHN BURCHARD, JR, CONSUMER PRODUCTS. *Current Pos:* VPRES RES & DEVELOP, GILLETTE CO, BOSTON, 80- *Personal Data:* b Lake Charles, La, Sept 3, 33; m 55, Yasuko Tsuchiya; c Catherine, Carolyn & John. *Educ:* Univ Calif, Berkeley, BS, 57, PhD, 63. *Prof Exp:* Asst prof, Univ Ore, Eugene, 60-63; chemist, Gen Elec Co, Schenectady, NY, 63-68, mgr, Polymer Unit, 68-70, Technol Admin, 70-73, Electrochem Br, 73-76, Energy Progs, 77-78, res & develop mgr mat sci & eng, 78-79. *Mem:* NY Acad Sci; Am Chem Soc; Electrochem Soc; Sigma Xi. *Res:* Consumer products. *Mailing Add:* Gillette Co Prudential Tower Bldg Boston MA 02199-8001

BUSH, KAREN JEAN, microbiology, for more information see previous edition

BUSH, LEON F, ANIMAL NUTRITION. *Current Pos:* ASSOC PROF ANIMAL SCI, S DAK STATE UNIV, 54- *Personal Data:* b Brooksville, Ky, Jan 28, 24; m 49; c 4. *Educ:* Univ Ky, BS, 50, MS, 51; Cornell Univ, PhD(nutrit & physiol), 54. *Mem:* Am Soc Animal Sci. *Res:* Sheep management and nutrition; physiology of reproduction studies with sheep. *Mailing Add:* RR 3 No 33 Brookings SD 57006

BUSH, LINVILLE JOHN, DAIRY NUTRITION. *Current Pos:* assoc prof, 58-77, prof dairy sci, 77-88, EMER PROF, OKLA STATE UNIV, 88- *Personal Data:* b Winchester, Ky, May 7, 28; m 52, Clara P Sigle; c John E, Susan H, Mark E & Peggy L. *Educ:* Univ Ky, BSc, 48; Ohio State Univ, MSc, 49; Iowa State Univ, PhD(dairy nutrit), 58. *Honors & Awards:* Tyler Prof Distinction, 78. *Prof Exp:* Field agent, Dairying, Ky, 53-55. *Concurrent Pos:* Consult, US Feed Grains Coun, Mexico & Venezuela. *Mem:* Am Dairy Sci Asn; Prof Animal Scientists; Coun Agricult Sci & Technol. *Res:* Nutrition of young dairy calf; dietary requirements of lactating dairy cows; factors affecting rumen function. *Mailing Add:* Dept Animal Sci Okla State Univ Stillwater OK 74078

BUSH, LOWELL PALMER, AGRONOMY, PLANT PHYSIOLOGY. *Current Pos:* assoc prof, 66-75, PROF AGRON, UNIV KY, 75- *Personal Data:* b Tyler, Minn, Mar 31, 39; m 62, Joan Thompson; c 3. *Educ:* Macalester Col, BA, 61; Iowa State Univ, MS, 63, PhD(plant physiol), 64. *Honors & Awards:* Philip Morris Distinguished Sci Award. *Prof Exp:* Fel plant path, Univ Minn, 64-66. *Concurrent Pos:* Fulbright res scholar, Agr Inst, Repub Ireland, 87; Philip Morris Prof, 87- *Mem:* Am Soc Plant Physiol; Phytochem Soc; fel Am Soc Agron; fel Crop Sci Soc Am. *Res:* Alkaloid metabolism in plants. *Mailing Add:* Dept Agron Univ Ky Lexington KY 40546-0091. *Fax:* 606-257-7125; *E-Mail:* lpbush@ca.uky.edu

BUSH, MAURICE E, cellular immunology, for more information see previous edition

BUSH, NORMAN, STATISTICS. *Current Pos:* PRES, ENSCO, INC, VA, 72- *Personal Data:* b New York, NY, Dec 10, 29; m 52; c 3. *Educ:* City Col New York, BBA, 51, MBA, 52; NC State Col, PhD, 62. *Prof Exp:* Statistician, Army Chem Ctr, Md, 52-56, Patrick AFB, Fla, 56-61 & Instrument Corp, Fla, 61-63; res dir statist, D Brown Assocs, Fla, 63-64; prin engr, Pan Am World Airways, 64-72. *Concurrent Pos:* Statistician, Comput Ctr, Univ NC, 59-62; adj asst prof, Grad Eng Educ Syst, Univ Fla, Cape Kennedy, 67-70. *Mem:* Am Statist Asn. *Res:* Technometrics; regression analysis; experimental design; computers. *Mailing Add:* 1300 Crystal Dr Arlington VA 22202

BUSH, RICHARD WAYNE, POLYMER CHEMISTRY. *Current Pos:* Res chemist, 60-64, sr res chemist, 64-69, res supvr, 69-72, RES ASSOC, W R GRACE & CO, 72- *Personal Data:* b Cleveland, Ohio, Nov 5, 34; m 69; c 2. *Educ:* Mass Inst Technol, SB, 56; Univ Ill, PhD(org chem), 60; Johns Hopkins Univ, MAS, 78. *Mem:* Am Chem Soc; Soc Plastics Engrs. *Res:* Photopolymers; adhesives. *Mailing Add:* 5478 Treefrog Pl Columbia MD 21045

BUSH, ROY SIDNEY, ANIMAL SCIENCE & NUTRITION, BIOCHEMISTRY. *Current Pos:* res scientist, 77-93, SUPT, EXP FARM, AGR CAN, 93- *Personal Data:* b Aug 31, 46; Can citizen; m 73; c 1. *Educ:* Univ Alta, BSA, 68, MSc, 70; Univ Man, PhD(animal biochem), 75. *Concurrent Pos:* Fel, Animal Res Inst, Agr Can, 74-77; sabbatical, Lab du Jeune Ruminants, INRA, Rennes, 88-89. *Mem:* Am Dairy Sci Asn; Am Soc Animal Sci; Can Soc Animal Sci; Agr Inst Can. *Res:* Development of the preruminant calf and lamb into a functional ruminant; feed additives for the young ruminant; digestive immune reactions. *Mailing Add:* Ex Farm Nappan NS B0L 1C0 Can. *Fax:* 902-667-2361; *E-Mail:* bushv@em.agr.ca

BUSH, S(PENCER) H(ARRISON), CODES & STANDARDS, SAFETY. *Current Pos:* PRES, REV & SYNTHESIS ASSOCS, 82-; SR STAFF SCIENTIST, BATTELLE MEM INST, 87- *Personal Data:* b Flint, Mich, Apr 4, 20; m 48, Roberta L Warren; c David S & Carl E. *Educ:* Univ Mich, BS(chem eng), 48, BS, 48, MS, 50, PhD(metall eng), 53. *Honors & Awards:* Gillett Lectr, Am Soc Testing & Mat, 74; Mehl Lectr, Am Soc Nondestructive Testing, 81; Bernard Langer Nuclear Codes & Stands Award, Am Soc Mech Eng, 83; TJ Thompson Award, Am Nuclear Soc, 87. *Prof Exp:* Assoc, Eng Res Inst, Univ Mich, 47-53, res asst, Off Naval Res, 50-53, instr dent mat, 51-53; metallurgist, Hanford Atomic Prods Oper, Gen Elec Co, 53-54, supvr phys metall, 54-57, fuels fabrication develop, 57-60, metall specialist, 60-63, consult metallurgist, 63-65; consult to dir, Pac Northwest Lab, Battelle Mem Inst, 65-70, sr staff consult, 70-81. *Concurrent Pos:* Adj prof metall, Joint Ctr Grad Study, Richland, Wash; mem, Reactor Safeguards Adv Comt, US AEC, 66-67, vchmn, 70, chmn, 71; regents prof metall eng, Univ Calif, Berkeley, 73-74. *Mem:* Nat Acad Eng; fel Am Soc Mech Engrs; fel Am Soc Metals; Am Inst Mining, Metall & Petrol Engrs; fel Am Nuclear Soc. *Res:* Temper embrittlement, stress corrosion of steels; metallurgy of reactor metals; safety of nuclear reactor systems. *Mailing Add:* 630 Cedar Ave Richland WA 99352. *Fax:* 509-943-6755; *E-Mail:* sh_bush@pnl.gov

BUSH, STEWART FOWLER, PHYSICAL CHEMISTRY, SPECTROSCOPY. *Current Pos:* from asst prof to assoc prof, 69-80, PROF CHEM, UNIV NC, CHARLOTTE, 81- *Personal Data:* b Charlotte, NC, Jan 8, 41; m 65, Jennie Alexander; c Benjamin A & Daniel F. *Educ:* Erskine Col, AB, 63; Univ SC, PhD(phys chem), 67. *Honors & Awards:* NSF Prof Develop Award, 78; Intergovt Personal Act Award, NIH, 79; NSF Injection Laser Illuminator Award, 73, 93. *Prof Exp:* Asst prof chem, Erskine Col, 67-69. *Concurrent Pos:* NSF prof develop award, 78; vis scientist, NIH, Washington, DC, 78-79. *Mem:* Am Chem Soc; Coblentz Soc. *Res:* Infrared, far-infrared and Raman spectroscopy as applied to vibrational analysis and molecular structure determination; mechanisms of interaction between cell membrane componets. *Mailing Add:* Dept Chem Univ NC Charlotte NC 28223-0002. *Fax:* 704-547-3151; *E-Mail:* sfbush@email.uncc.edu

BUSH, WARREN VAN NESS, PETROLEUM CHEMISTRY, ENVIRONMENTAL SCIENCE. *Current Pos:* INDEPENDENT CONSULT PETROL & SULFUR CHEM & PROCESS TECHNOL, 92- *Personal Data:* b Montclair, NJ, June 10, 31; m 57, Dorothy H Hendrickson; c 3. *Educ:* Princeton Univ, BS, 53; Calif Inst Technol, PhD, 58. *Prof Exp:* Chemist, Shell Develop Co, Calif, 57-65, engr, Shell Oil Co, NY, 65-67, chemist, Shell Develop Co, 67-68, supvr, 68, group leader, Shell Oil, Martinez Refinery, 68-72, sr res engr, Shell Develop Co, 72-74, supvr staff, 74-76, staff res engr, 76-77, sr staff res engr, 77-89, res assoc, 89-92. *Concurrent Pos:* Career consult, Am Chem Soc, 89- *Mem:* AAAS; Am Chem Soc; Am Inst Chem Engrs; Sigma Xi. *Res:* Organic chemistry and chemical engineering, principally as applied to petroleum refining, petrochemical manufacture, gas treating, sulfur manufacture, and air pollution control; environmental engineering. *Mailing Add:* 11407 Valley Spring Dr Houston TX 77043-4622

BUSHAW, DONALD (WAYNE), MATHEMATICS. *Current Pos:* from instr to assoc prof, Wash State Univ, 52-62, actg chmn dept, 66-68, actg dir libr, 84-85 & 89-90, PROF MATH, WASH STATE UNIV, 62-, VPROVOST INSTRUCTION, 86- *Personal Data:* b Anacortes, Wash, May 5, 26; m 46; c 5. *Educ:* State Col Wash, BA, 49; Princeton Univ, PhD(math), 52. *Prof Exp:* Instr math, State Col Wash, 48-49; asst, Princeton Univ, 49-51; math consult, Stevens Inst Technol, 51-52. *Concurrent Pos:* Vis scientist, Res Inst Advan Study, 62-63; NAS-PAN exchangee, Jagiellonian Univ, Cracow, Poland, 72-73. *Mem:* Math Asn Am; Polish Math Soc. *Res:* Qualitative theory of ordinary differential equations; general topology; mathematical economics; history of mathematics; postsecondary mathematics education. *Mailing Add:* Wash State Univ PO Box 124 Pullman WA 99164-0124

BUSHEY, ALBERT HENRY, physical chemistry, analytical chemistry; deceased, see previous edition for last biography

BUSHEY, DEAN FRANKLIN, SYNTHETIC ORGANIC CHEMISTRY. *Current Pos:* biochemist, 86-90, MGR BIOCHEM & BIOTECHNOL, RHxNE POULENC AGR CO, 90- *Personal Data:* b Gettysburg, Pa, Oct 27, 50; m 73; c 2. *Educ:* Gettysburg Col, BA, 72; Univ SC, PhD(org chem), 76. *Prof Exp:* NIH fel, Mass Inst Technol, 76-77; res chemist, Union Carbide Corp, 77-84. *Concurrent Pos:* Vis scientist, Cornell Biotechnol Inst, 84-86. *Mem:* Sigma Xi; Am Chem Soc. *Res:* Synthesis of natural products and small ring heterocycles; pesticide metabolism. *Mailing Add:* 5336 Cherry Crest Ct Raleigh NC 27609-4620

BUSHEY, GORDON LAKE, PHYSICAL CHEMISTRY, CHEMICAL ENGINEERING. *Current Pos:* RETIRED. *Personal Data:* b Mission, Tex, Jan 13, 22; m 50, Phyliss Howard; c David, Sarah & Anne. *Educ:* Rice Univ, BS, 43, MA, 44, PhD(chem), 48. *Prof Exp:* Instr chem, Univ Ill, 48-51; sci asst, Off Chief Chem Officer, US Army, 51-62, asst sci affairs, US Defense Off NAtlantic & Medit Areas, Paris, 62-64, asst chief scientist, US Army Mat Command, 64-70, sci asst, Dept, 70-75, phys sci adminr, Off Asst Dep Sci & Technol, 75-85. *Concurrent Pos:* Exec officer, Div Chem & Chem Technol, Nat Res Coun, 51-53 & Nat War Col, 59-60. *Mem:* Am Inst Chem; AAAS; Am Chem Soc; NY Acad Sci. *Res:* Absorption by hydrous oxides; physical chemistry of soap crystals; x-ray diffraction studies of colloids and mixed crystals; arms control; international science organizations; technical information; physical sciences of military interest. *Mailing Add:* T-3 3364 Woodburn Rd Annandale VA 22003

BUSHEY, MICHELLE MARIE, BIOTECHNOLOGY, BIOANALYTICAL CHEMISTRY. *Current Pos:* Asst prof, 90-96, ASSOC PROF CHEM ANALYTICAL CHEM, TRINITY UNIV, 96- *Personal Data:* b Boston, Mass, Apr 26, 60; m 83, Dennis Kelley; c Erin & Sean. *Educ:* Oberlin Col, BA, 82; Univ NC, PhD(anal chem), 90. *Mem:* Am Chem Soc; Coun Undergrad Res; Am Asn Univ Prof. *Res:* Protein structure and properties by capillary electrophoresis; optimal separation strategies in micellar electrokinetic capillary chromatography; application of capillary electrophoresis to biologically significant problems such as investigation of bilirubin-bile salt interactions by MEKC techniques. *Mailing Add:* Dept Chem Trinity Univ 715 Stadium Dr San Antonio TX 78212

BUSHINSKY, DAVID ALLEN, MEDICINE, PHYSIOLOGY. *Current Pos:* assoc prof, 89-92, PROF MED & PHYSIOL, UNIV ROCHESTER, 92-; CHIEF NEPHROLOGY UNIT, STRONG MEM HOSP, 89- *Personal Data:* b Elizabeth, NJ, Mar 16, 49; m 78, Nancy Kriegen; c Joshua & Seth. *Educ:* Lehigh Univ, BS, 71; Tufts Univ, MD, 75. *Prof Exp:* Intern med, Tufts-New Eng Med Ctr, 75-76, resident med, 76-77, clin fel nephrology, 77-78, res fel nephrology, 78-79; instr med, Sch Med, Tufts Univ, 79-80; from asst prof to assoc prof med, Univ Chicago, 80-89. *Concurrent Pos:* Attend physician, Michael Reese Hosp & Med Ctr, 80- & Univ Chicago Hosp, 82-89. *Mem:* Am Soc Nephrology; Int Soc Nephrology; Am Fed Clin Res; Am Soc Bone & Mineral Res; Central Soc Clin Res; Am Physiol Soc; Am Soc Clin Invest. *Res:* The effects of hydrogen ions on bone and the mechanism of hypercalciuric in genetic hypercalciuric, stone forming rats. *Mailing Add:* Unit Chief Nephrol Univ Rochester 601 Elmwood Ave Box 675 Rochester NY 14642-0001. *Fax:* 716-442-9201; *E-Mail:* dbushi@medicine.rochester.edu

BUSHKIN, YURI, MOLECULAR IMMUNOLOGY. *Current Pos:* assoc, Dept Retroviral Biol, Pub Health Res Inst, 86-88, asst mem, 88-96, Lab Molecular Immunol, 88-96, HEAD, LAB MOLECULAR IMMUNOL, PUB HEALTH RES INST, 88-, ASSOC MEM, 96-; RES ASSOC PROF PATH, DEPT PATH, NY UNIV MED CTR, 89- *Personal Data:* b Riga, USSR, Oct 22, 49. *Educ:* Latvian State Univ & Inst Cytol, USSR, MSc, 71; Weizmann Inst Sci, Israel, PhD(genetics), 78. *Prof Exp:* Vis res fel immunogenetics, Lab Cell Surface Immunogenetics, Sloan-Kettering Inst Cancer Res, 77-81, res assoc immunol, Lab Molecular Immunol, 81-86. *Concurrent Pos:* Cancer res award, Milberg Women's Cancer Res Fund, 85; prin investr grantee, NIH, 84-91, Nat Cancer Cytol Ctr, 86-87, Am Cancer Soc, 87, Coun Tobacco Res, 92-95, Elsa U Pardee Found, 95-96. *Res:* Elucidation of structures and specific molecular interactions of the T cell surface receptors and medium soluble factors and role of these interactions in functional activities of T cells. *Mailing Add:* Pub Health Res Inst 455 First Ave New York NY 10016. *Fax:* 212-578-0804; *E-Mail:* yuri@phri.nyu.edu

BUSHMAN, JESS RICHARD, GEOLOGY. *Current Pos:* From asst prof to assoc prof, 55-70, PROF GEOL, BRIGHAM YOUNG UNIV, 70- *Personal Data:* b American Fork, Utah, May 12, 21; c 5. *Educ:* Brigham Young Univ, BA, 49; Princeton Univ, PhD, 58. *Concurrent Pos:* Consult-geologist, Ministry Mines & Hydrocarbons, Venezuela, 53-55, 58 & 59-60; vis lectr, Ministry Coal Ind, Peoples Repub China. *Mem:* Geol Soc Am; Am Asn Petrol Geol; Asn Mining & Petrol Geol Venezuela; Nat Asn Geol Teachers; Am Asn Stratig Palynologists. *Res:* Sedimentation; palynology; stratigraphy; history of geology; science education. *Mailing Add:* 1238 E 640 S Provo UT 84606

BUSHMAN, JOHN BRANSON, ECOLOGY, VERTEBRATE ZOOLOGY. *Current Pos:* zoologist, US Army Desert Test Ctr, Salt Lake City, Utah, 62-72, ECOLOGIST, US ARMY CORPS ENGRS, WASHINGTON, DC, 72- *Personal Data:* b Farmington, NMex, Aug 26, 26; m 51; c 5. *Educ:* Univ Utah, BS, 52, MS, 55, PhD, 83. *Prof Exp:* Asst cur birds, Univ Utah, 46 & 49-52; from asst ecologist to ecologist, Univ Utah, 54-62. *Mem:* Wilson Ornith Soc; Cooper Ornith Soc; Am Ornith Union; Am Soc Mammal; Wildlife Soc. *Res:* Endangered species; avian and mammalian ecology; life histories; distribution and population dynamics. *Mailing Add:* US Army Corps Engrs Civil Works 20 Massachusetts Ave NW Washington DC 20314-1000

BUSHNELL, DAVID L, PHYSICS. *Current Pos:* assoc prof, 61-75, PROF PHYSICS, NORTHERN ILL UNIV, 75- *Personal Data:* b Platteville, Wis, Apr 14, 29; m; c 3. *Educ:* Univ Wis, BS, 51, MS, 53; Va Polytech Inst, PhD(physics), 61. *Prof Exp:* Instr physics, Mankato State Col, 53-55; from instr to asst prof, Va Polytech Inst, 56-61. *Mem:* Am Phys Soc; Am Asn Physics Teachers; Int Solar Energy Soc. *Res:* Neutron capture gamma-ray studies; gamma-ray spectroscopy and nuclear level schemes; solar energy applications; high temperature solar oven with heat storage. *Mailing Add:* Dept Physics Northern Ill Univ DeKalb IL 60115-2853

BUSHNELL, DENNIS MEYER, FLUID MECHANICS, GAS MECHANICS. *Current Pos:* Res engr, NASA, Langley Res Ctr, Hampton, Va, 63-68, sect head, 69-72, br chief viscous flows, 73-88, assoc chief, Fluid Mech Div, 89-93, ASSOC CHIEF, GAS DYNAMICS DIV, NASA, LANGLEY RES CTR, 94- *Personal Data:* b New Haven, Conn, May 10, 41; m 63, Judith A Simoni; c Matthew G. *Educ:* Univ Conn, BSME, 63; Univ Va, MSME, 67. *Honors & Awards:* Sperry Award, Am Inst Aeronaut & Astronaut, 75; Zara Award, USAF, 89; Fluid & Plasma Dynamics Award, 91; Lancaster lectr, Royal Aeronaut Soc, 92. *Concurrent Pos:* External vpres, Jaycees, Gloucester Co, Va, , 67-69; emergency med technician Abingdon Rescue Squad, 69-75; Consult, Off Sci Res, USAF, Washington, 80-, Nat Aerospace Plane, Dayton, Ohio, 86-, Defense Advan Res Proj Agency, Washington, 88- *Mem:* Fel Am Inst Aeronat & Astronaut; fel Am Soc Mech Eng; Sigma Xi. *Res:* Patent on transonic wing passive boundary layer control device; submicron high pressure particle generator; riblets technique to reduce turbulent drag; high speed quiet tunnel device; transition estimation approach; author of over 200 research papers. *Mailing Add:* NASA Langley Res Ctr M/S 197 Hampton VA 23665. *Fax:* 757-864-7923

BUSHNELL, GORDON WILLIAM, STRUCTURAL CHEMISTRY, CRYSTALLOGRAPHY. *Current Pos:* assoc prof, 67-87, PROF CHEM, UNIV VICTORIA, 87- *Personal Data:* b Oxford, Eng, June 17, 36; m 59; c 2. *Educ:* Oxford Univ, MA, 59, BSc, 63; Univ Wisc, PhD(chem), 66. *Prof Exp:* Sci officer, UK Atomic Energy Auth, 59-63; lectr chem, Univ WI, 63-67. *Mem:* Chem Inst Can; Am Crystallog Asn. *Res:* X-ray crystallography of coordination compounds; structure determination by single crystal x-ray diffraction of proteins. *Mailing Add:* Dept Chem Univ Victoria Box 3065 Victoria BC V8W 3V6 Can

BUSHNELL, JAMES JUDSON, AIR CONDITIONING & REFRIGERATION SYSTEM DESIGN, VEHICLE DESIGN. *Current Pos:* SR STAFF ENGR, ALLIEDSIGNAL AEROSPACE SYST & EQUIP, 91- *Personal Data:* b Madison, Wis, Nov 13, 34; m 55, Mary Wallace; c Carla, Beverly & G Roxanne. *Educ:* Univ Wis-Madison, BSME, 57. *Prof Exp:* Designer, Hamilton Standard Div, United Technol, 57-59; sr engr, Lockheed Aircraft, 69-70 & Rohr Industs, 70-77; supvr, RMI Inc, 77-82; sr engr, Gen Dynamics, 59-69, eng specialist, Convair Div, 82-91. *Concurrent Pos:* Mem, Tech Comts, Am Soc Heating Refrig & Air Conditioning Engrs, 83-, chmn, Transp Air Conditioning Comt, 85-87 & Transp Refrig Comt, 89-93; consult, Teltech Inc, 91- *Mem:* Am Soc Heating Refrig & Air Conditioning Engrs; Soc Automotive Engrs. *Res:* Human comfort related to transportation environments. *Mailing Add:* 215 Carmelita Pl Solana Beach CA 92075. *E-Mail:* 75500.716@compuserve.com

BUSHNELL, JOHN HORACE, INVERTEBRATE ZOOLOGY, HYDROBIOLOGY. *Current Pos:* from asst prof to assoc prof, 64-71, PROF ENVIRON, POP & ORGANISMIC BIOL, UNIV COLO, BOULDER, 71- *Personal Data:* b Grand Rapids, Mich, Mar 17, 25; m 51, 86, Bambi Haney; c John, Jeffrey, Romney, Heather, Hadley, Madeleine & Rose. *Educ:* Vanderbilt Univ, BA, 48; Mich State Univ, MS, 56, PhD(zool), 61. *Prof Exp:* US State Dept spec lectr biol & English, Habibia Col, Kabul, Afghanistan, 48-50; asst secy & sales mgr, Wagemaker Boat Co & US Molded Shapes, Inc, 50-55; instr zool, Mich State Univ, 59-60; asst prof biol, Washington & Jefferson Col, 60-64; vis prof, Harvard Univ, 66-67. *Concurrent Pos:* AEC summer study & continuing isotopes res grant, 63-; assoc ed, Am Midland Naturalist, 67-74; consult ed, Barnes & Noble Publ House, 70-; NSF alpine flowage system grant; exec comt mem, Am Soc Zool, 73-76, Am Microsci Soc, 78-82; vpres, Hydrobiol Soc, India, 87-97, Rocky Flats Nuclear Fac, 92-93. *Mem:* Sigma Xi; Am Soc Zool; Am Micros Soc (prog chmn, 73-74, vpres,75-76, pres, 76-77); Int Bryozool Asn; NY Acad Sci. *Res:* Ecology, zoogeography and systematics of Ectoprocta and other aquatic published studies on invertebrates include crustacea, oligochaetes, sponges oribatid mites hydrozoans; phenotypic plasticity, adaptation and physiological ecology of aquatic invertebrates; nutritional and pollution studies and life cycle studies on Ectoprocta and other invertebrates; Ectoproct population studies. *Mailing Add:* Dept Environ Pop & Organic Biol Univ Colo Boulder Box 334 Boulder CO 80309-0002

BUSHNELL, KENT O, ENVIRONMENTAL GEOLOGY, GEOPHYSICS. *Current Pos:* assoc prof, 68-74, PROF GEOL, SLIPPERY ROCK STATE COL, 74-, CHAIRPERSON DEPT, 76- *Personal Data:* b Tolland, Conn, Dec 12, 29; m 55. *Educ:* Univ Conn, BA, 51; Yale Univ, MS, 52, PhD(geol), 55. *Prof Exp:* Geologist, Stand Oil Co Calif, 55-68. *Concurrent Pos:* Dir, NSF seismic equip grant, 70-72. *Mem:* Am Asn Petrol Geol; Geol Soc Am; Soc Explor Geophys; Sigma Xi. *Res:* Gravity surveys for buried valleys; Pleistocene history of western Pennsylvania. *Mailing Add:* Dept Geol Slippery Rock Univ Slippery Rock PA 16057

BUSHNELL, ROBERT HEMPSTEAD, ATMOSPHERIC PHYSICS, USE OF METRIC MEASURES. *Current Pos:* RETIRED. *Personal Data:* b Wooster, Ohio, May 11, 24; m 65, Martha Dicks; c Helen & Orson. *Educ:* Ohio State Univ, BSc, 47, MSc, 48; Univ Wis, PhD(meteorol), 62. *Prof Exp:*

Physicist, Hoover Co, 48-50, Goodyear Aircraft Co, 50-56, Radio Corp Am, 57-58, Univ Wis, 58-62 & Nat Ctr Atmospheric Res, Boulder, Colo, 62-74; consult, 74-85; consult, Nat Oceanic Atmospheric Admin, US Dept Com, 86-96. *Concurrent Pos:* Univ Corp Atmospheric Res fel, 61. *Mem:* AAAS; Sigma Xi; Am Meteorol Soc; Am Soc Testing & Mat; Int Solar Energy Soc. *Res:* Climatology and statistics of sunshine and temperature related to solar heating; thunderstorm structure; weather radar. *Mailing Add:* 502 Ord Dr Boulder CO 80303-4732

BUSHNELL, WILLIAM RODGERS, PHYSIOLOGY OF PLANT DISEASE. *Current Pos:* PLANT PHYSIOLOGIST, USDA, 60- *Personal Data:* b Wooster, Ohio, Aug 19, 31; m 52, Ann Holcomb; c Mary, John & Thomas. *Educ:* Univ Chicago, AB, 51; Ohio State Univ, BS, 53, MS, 55; Univ Wis, PhD(bot), 60. *Honors & Awards:* Alexander Von Humboldt Sr US Scientist Award, 84. *Concurrent Pos:* From asst prof to prof, Dept Plant Path, Univ Minn, 66-73. *Mem:* Am Soc Plant Physiol; fel Am Phytopath Soc; AAAS. *Res:* Physiology of parasitism, especially rust and mildew diseases of cereals. *Mailing Add:* Cereal Rust Lab Univ Minn 1551 Lindis St St Paul MN 55108. *Fax:* 612-649-5054

BUSHONG, JEROLD WARD, PLANT PATHOLOGY. *Current Pos:* sr agr chem scientist, 67-69, supvr agr eval, 69-70, mgr agr chem, 70-73, mgr biol & field develop, 73-75, mgr int mkt & prod develop, Minn Mining & Mfg Co, 75-80, mgr int mkt & prod develop, 3M DO Brazil, 80-83, prod mgr, hearing health prods, 84-86, INT MKT MGR, MICROBIOL PROD, 3M EUROPE, 87- *Personal Data:* b Dayton, Ohio, Sept 22, 35; m 55; c 2. *Educ:* Miami Univ, BA, 57; Univ Ill, MS, 59, PhD(plant path), 61. *Prof Exp:* Sr plant pathologist, Fungicide Res, Niagara Chem Div, FMC Corp, 61-66; asst dir pesticide res, W R Grace & Co, 66-67. *Concurrent Pos:* Ed staff, Plant Dis Reporter, 74-76. *Mem:* Am Chem Soc; Int Weed Sci Soc; Am Phytopath Soc; Weed Sci Soc Am. *Res:* Fungicide chemistry; legume and fruit pathology; mycology; entomology. *Mailing Add:* 322 Floral Dr W St Paul MN 55126

BUSHONG, STEWART CARLYLE, RADIOLOGICAL HEALTH. *Current Pos:* asst prof to assoc prof, 66-76, PROF RADIOL SCI, BAYLOR COL MED, 76- *Personal Data:* b Washington, DC, Nov 25, 36; m 58; c 3. *Educ:* Univ Md, BS, 59; Univ Pittsburgh, MS, 63, ScD(radiol health), 67. *Prof Exp:* Health serv officer, USPHS, Washington, DC, 59-61; health physicist, Univ Pittsburgh, 62-64. *Concurrent Pos:* Assoc prof radiol, Univ Tex Dent Br, 70-; assoc prof radiol sci, Houston Community Col, 71- *Mem:* Am Asn Physicists Med; Health Physics Soc; Soc Nuclear Med; Am Indust Hyg Asn; Radiation Res Soc. *Res:* Investigations of radiation dose and dose distribution in patients receiving radiologic examination for medical diagnosis. *Mailing Add:* 3001 Carnegie St Houston TX 77005

BUSHUK, WALTER, CEREAL CHEMISTRY. *Current Pos:* provost, 80-84, PROF PLANT SCI, UNIV MAN, 66-, EMER PROF FOOD SCI, 84- *Personal Data:* b Pruzana, Poland, Jan 2, 29; Can citizen; m 55; c 2. *Educ:* Univ Man, BSc, 52, MSc, 53; McGill Univ, PhD(phys chem), 56. *Hon Degrees:* Dr, Agr Acad, Poznan, Poland. *Honors & Awards:* Osborne Medal; Neumann Medal. *Prof Exp:* Chemist, Grain Res Lab, Man, Can, 53-61, sect head, 61-62; dir, Ogilvie Flour Mills Co, Ltd, 62-64; res chemist, Grain Res Lab, 64, head wheat sect, 64-66. *Concurrent Pos:* Nat Res Coun Can overseas fel, Macromolecule Res Ctr, France, 57-58. *Mem:* Am Asn Cereal Chem; fel Chem Inst Can; Can Inst Food Technol; fel Royal Soc Can; Sigma Xi; fel Agr Inst Can. *Res:* Enzyme kinetics; surface properties of flour; physicochemical properties of polymers; mechanism of flour quality improvement; wheat proteins. *Mailing Add:* Dept Food Sci Univ Man Winnipeg MB R3T 2N2 Can. *Fax:* 204-261-1488

BUSHWAY, RODNEY JOHN, METHODS DEVELOPMENT OF NATURAL TOXICANTS, PESTICIDE RESIDUES & VITAMINS IN FOOD, FOOD CHEMISTRY & FOOD ANALYSIS. *Current Pos:* from asst prof to assoc prof, 78-86, PROF FOOD SCI, UNIV MAINE, 86- *Personal Data:* b Milo, Maine, June 23, 49; m 84, Sandra Carlson; c Nicholas & Meghan. *Educ:* Univ Maine, BS, 71; Tex A&M Univ, MS, 73, PhD(biochem),77. *Prof Exp:* Res asst, Tex A&M Univ, 71-77; res anal chemist, Phillips Petrol, 77-78. *Concurrent Pos:* Consult, Millipore, Calgene Fresh, Celex Corp & All Jack Corp, 80-; prin investr numerous grants, 80- *Mem:* Am Potato Asn; Am Chem Soc; Inst Food Technologists; Asn Off Anal Chemists. *Res:* Development of analytical methods for the analysis of natural toxicants, pesticides and vitamins in water, soil and/or foods using gas chromatography, high performance liquid chromatography, gas chromatography advanced electronic design, enzyme link-immunosorbent assay; developed an official method for roterone in pesticide formulations and a tomatine method for tomatoes in order for bioengineered tomatoes to get FDA approval. *Mailing Add:* 102 B Holmes Hall Univ Maine Orono ME 04469. *Fax:* 207-581-1636

BUSHWELLER, CHARLES HACKETT, PHYSICAL ORGANIC CHEMISTRY, STRUCTURAL CHEMISTRY. *Current Pos:* PROF CHEM & CHMN DEPT, UNIV VT, 78- *Personal Data:* b Port Jervis, NY, June 21, 39; m 61; c 3. *Educ:* Hamilton Col, AB, 61; Middlebury Col, MS, 63; Univ Calif, Berkeley, PhD(org chem), 66. *Prof Exp:* Sr chemist, Mobil Chem Co, 66-68; asst prof, 68-72, assoc prof chem, Worcester Polytech Inst, 72-76; prof chem, State Univ NY Albany, 76-78. *Concurrent Pos:* Alfred P Sloan res fel, 71-73; Camille & Henry Dreyfus teacher scholar, 72-75. *Mem:* Am Chem Soc. *Res:* Nuclear magnetic resonance spectroscopy; stereodynamics of organic and inorganic systems. *Mailing Add:* Chem Cept Cook Bldg Univ Vt Burlington VT 05405-0125

BUSING, WILLIAM RICHARD, PHYSICAL CHEMISTRY. *Current Pos:* chemist, 54-90, CONSULT, OAK RIDGE NAT LABS, 90- *Personal Data:* b Brooklyn, NY, June 21, 23; m 51; c 3. *Educ:* Swarthmore Col, BA, 43; Princeton Univ, MA, 48, PhD(chem), 49. *Honors & Awards:* Martin J Buerger Award, Am Crystallog Asn, 85; Mat Sci Award, Dept Energy, 88. *Prof Exp:* Res assoc chem, Brown Univ, 49-51; instr, Yale Univ, 51-54. *Concurrent Pos:* Mem, US Nat Comt Crystallog, Nat Res Coun, 70-76 & 79-81, secy-treas, 74-76; US deleg, Int Cong Crystallog, Kyoto, 72 & Amsterdam, 75. *Mem:* Am Crystallog Asn (pres, 71). *Res:* Molecular structure and spectroscopy; neutron diffraction; crystallographic computation; interionic and intermolecular forces in crystals; fiber crystallography. *Mailing Add:* 317 Louisiana Ave Oak Ridge TN 37830-8514

BUSINGER, JOOST ALOIS, METEOROLOGY. *Current Pos:* EMER PROF METEROL, UNIV WASH, 83- *Personal Data:* b Haarlem, Neth, Mar 29, 24; m 49, 87, Marianne Koolman; c Ferdi, Steven & Margaret A. *Educ:* State Univ Utrecht, BS, 47, MSc, 50, PhD(meteorol), 54. *Honors & Awards:* Second Half Century Award, Am Meteorol Soc, 78. *Prof Exp:* Technician, Inst Heating Eng, Neth, 48-51 & Inst Hort Eng, 51-56; assoc & proj dir, Dept Meteorol, Univ Wis, 56-58; from asst prof to prof meteorol, Univ Wash, 58-83, chmn geophys exec comt, 63-65, chmn fac sen, 76-77; sr scientist, Nat Ctr Atmospheric Res, 86-89. *Concurrent Pos:* Corresp mem, Royal Neth Acad Sci, 80; vis scientist, Nat Ctr Atmospheric Res, 83-86. *Mem:* Fel Am Meteorol Soc; Am Geophys Union; fel AAAS. *Res:* Energy transfer in atmosphere; turbulence; radiation; micro and physical meteorology; air-sea interaction. *Mailing Add:* Businger Box 351640 Univ Wash Seattle WA 98195-1640

BUSK, GRANT CURTIS, JR, product & process development, food research management, for more information see previous edition

BUSKE, NORMAN L, alternative methodologies, for more information see previous edition

BUSKIRK, ELSWORTH ROBERT, HUMAN APPLIED PHYSIOLOGY, ENVIRONMENTAL PHYSIOLOGY. *Current Pos:* prof appl physiol, Pa State Univ, 63-88, dir, Lab Human Performance, chmn grad physiol prog, 63-92, Marie A Noll prof, 88-92, EMER PROF HUMAN PERFORMANCE RES, PA STATE UNIV, 92- *Personal Data:* b Beloit, Wis, Aug 11, 25; m 48, Mable Heen; c Laurel A (Wiegand) & Kristine J (Hallett). *Educ:* St Olaf Col, BA, 50; Univ Minn, MA, 51, PhD(physiol hyg), 54. *Honors & Awards:* Res Citation, Am Col Sports Med, 73, Honor Award, 84; Honor Award, Am Physiol Soc, 93. *Prof Exp:* Res assoc physiol, Lab Physiol Hyg, Univ Minn, 54; physiologist, Environ Protection Res Div, Q Res & Develop Ctr, Mass, 54-56, chief, Environ Physiol Sect, 56-57; physiologist, Metab Dis Br, Inst Arthritis & Metab Dis, NIH, 57-63. *Concurrent Pos:* Mem coun, Sci Adv Comt, President's Coun Phys Fitness, 59-61, thermal factors subcomt, Nat Acad Sci, 63-64, human adaptability subcomt, Int Biol Prog, 68-72, comt interaction eng with biol & med, Nat Acad Eng-Nat Acad Sci, 68-75, Educ Mat Rev Comt, Asn Am Med Cols, 76-84 & epidemiol sect, Am Heart Asn; chmn, study sect appl physiol & bioeng, NIH, 64-68 & appl physiol & orthop, 76-80; mem, subcomt calories, food & nutrit bd, Nat Acad Sci-Nat Res Coun, 68-70, comt personnel protection, 71-74 & comt mil nutrit res, 79-92; sect ed, J Appl Physiol, Am Physiol Soc, 73-84, assoc ed, 76-84; NATO sr fel sci, NSF, 77; mem nutrit res coun, Nat Acad Sci Nat Res Coun, 79-80; ed-in-chief, Med & Sci in Sports & Exercise, 85-89, consult ed, 89-; mem res comt, Am Heart Asn, 89-94; mem, Clin Sci Study Sect, NIH, 89-93; mem, Comt Defense Women's Health Res, Inst Med-Nat Acad Sci/Nat Res Coun, 95. *Mem:* AAAS; Am Physiol Soc; Aerospace Med Soc; Am Inst Nutrit; Am Soc Heating, Refrig & Air-Conditioning Engrs; Am Heart Asn; Am Col Sports Med (pres, 64-65); Sigma Xi; Am Soc Clin Nutrit; NY Acad Sci; Am Heart Asn; hon mem Am Acad Phys Educ. *Res:* Human applied physiology with an emphasis on exercise and environmental physiology; the effects of age, gender, physical condition and fitness, body composition and life style; metabolism; growth, development and aging; epidemiology of coronary heart disease and obesity. *Mailing Add:* 216 Hunter Ave State College PA 16801

BUSKIRK, FRED RAMON, THEORETICAL PHYSICS, EXPERIMENTAL PHYSICS. *Current Pos:* from asst prof to assoc prof, 60-74, PROF PHYSICS, US NAVAL POSTGRAD SCH, 74- *Personal Data:* b Indianapolis, Ind, Dec 29, 28; m 58. *Educ:* Western Res Univ, BS, 51, MS, 55, PhD(physics), 58. *Prof Exp:* Proj assoc physics, Univ Wis, 58-59; instr, Case Western Res Univ, 59-60. *Res:* Nuclear and field theory; nuclear and accelerator experiments. *Mailing Add:* Code 61 BS Physics Dept Naval Postgrad Sch Monterey CA 93943. *Fax:* 408-656-2834

BUSKIRK, RUTH ELIZABETH, ANIMAL BEHAVIOR, ANIMAL ECOLOGY. *Current Pos:* lectr, 78-90, RES SCIENTIST, UNIV TEX, 78-, SR LECTR, BIOL SCI, 90- *Personal Data:* b Indianapolis, Ind, Mar 9, 44; c 3. *Educ:* Earlham Col, AB, 65; Harvard Univ, MAT, 66; Univ Calif, Davis, PhD(zool), 72. *Prof Exp:* Instr biol, Southern Univ, 66-68; fel, Univ Calif, Davis, 72-74; asst prof behav, Cornell Univ, 74-78. *Concurrent Pos:* Mem, Orgn Trop Studies, 75-; mem, NSF Animal Behav Adv Panel, 90-93. *Mem:* Animal Behav Soc; Ecol Soc Am; Am Geophys Union; Am Soc Arachnologists; Asn Trop Biol. *Res:* Animal social behavior; behavioral ecology of predators; animal response to geophysical phenomena; text and software material for college biology courses. *Mailing Add:* Dept Microbiol Univ Tex Austin TX 78712-1026. *Fax:* 512-471-7088; *E-Mail:* rbuskirk@utxvms.cc.utexas.edu

BUSLIG, BELA STEPHEN, BIOCHEMISTRY, PLANT PHYSIOLOGY. *Current Pos:* Chemist, 67-69, res biochemist, 69-77, RES SCIENTIST BIOCHEM CITRUS, FLA DEPT CITRUS, 77- *Personal Data:* b Budapest, Hungary, Aug 27, 38; US citizen; m 64, Bertha Horafall; c Aileen & Bela. *Educ:* Queen's Univ, BA, 62; Fla State Univ, MS, 67; Univ Fla, PhD(plant biochem), 70. *Concurrent Pos:* Res assoc, Univ Fla, 67-71, adj asst prof, 71-84, adj assoc prof, 84- *Mem:* Am Chem Soc; Can Soc Plant Physiologists; Inst Food Technologists; Genetics Soc Am; AAAS; fel Am Inst Chemists. *Res:* Metabolism of citrus plants; organic acids and energetics of respiration; enzymic regulation of metabolites; constituents of processed citrus products; process control instruments; color measurements. *Mailing Add:* Fla Dept Citrus USDA PO Box 1909 Winter Haven FL 33883. *E-Mail:* buslig@concentric.net

BUSLIK, ARTHUR J, REACTOR PHYSICS. *Current Pos:* assoc physicist, 79-80, PHYSICIST, BROOKHAVEN NAT LAB, 80- *Personal Data:* b Philadelphia, Pa, Mar 7, 33. *Educ:* Univ Pa, BA, 54; Columbia Univ, MA, 56; Univ Pittsburgh, PhD(physics), 62. *Prof Exp:* From assoc scientist to sr scientist, Bettis Atomic Power Lab, Westinghouse Elec Corp, 58-72; adv nuclear engr, Gulf United Nuclear Fuels Corp, 72-74. *Concurrent Pos:* Vis prof nuclear eng, Ben Gurion Univ Negev, Israel, 78-79. *Mem:* Am Phys Soc; Am Nuclear Soc. *Res:* Theoretical solid state physics; magnetic resonance line width; kinetics and stability; neutron resonance absorption; variational principles in reactor physics. *Mailing Add:* 4701 Willard Ave Apt 226 Chevy Chase MD 20815

BUSNAINA, AHMED A, MICRO CONTAMINATION CONTROL, COMPUTATIONAL FLUID DYNAMICS. *Current Pos:* asst prof, 84-88, assoc prof, 88-96, PROF ENG, CLARKSON UNIV, 96- *Personal Data:* b Sept 2, 53; US citizen; m 77; c 3. *Educ:* Univ Tripoli, BSc hons, 76; Okla State Univ, MS, 79, PhD(mech eng), 83. *Honors & Awards:* John W Graham Jr Award, Clarkson Univ, 90. *Prof Exp:* Engr, Gen Elec Co, 76, Esso Oil Co, 77; instr eng, Univ Garyounis, 77; teaching & res asst eng, Okla State Univ, 78-79, teaching & res assoc, 80-83; vis asst prof eng, San Diego State Univ, 83-84. *Concurrent Pos:* Consult, IBM, 85-, Du Pont, 88-89 & Motorola, 89-90; pres, Advan Comput Sci, 86-; dir, Microcontamination Lab, 87-, Ctr Particulate Control, 90-; mem exec comt, Fine Particle Soc, 88-; mem, Comput Eng Comt, Am Soc Mech Engrs, 88-; mem adv bd, Inst Environ Sci, 89-; Fulbright sr scholar award, 93-94. *Mem:* Am Inst Aeronaut & Astronaut; Am Soc Mech Engrs; Am Soc Eng Educ; Inst Environ Sci; Fine Particle Soc; Am Phys Soc. *Res:* Numerical computation of fluid flow phenomena with turbulence, diffusion and swirl, with applications to combustion; microcontamination control; microcontaminant particle adhesion, removal and deposition. *Mailing Add:* Mech Eng Dept Clarkson Univ Potsdam NY 13699-5725. *Fax:* 315-268-6438; *E-Mail:* aab@decaab.mic.clarkson.edu

BUSS, DARYL DEAN, CARDIOVASCULAR PHYSIOLOGY, CORONARY PHYSIOLOGY. *Current Pos:* assoc prof, 76-80, PROF & CHMN, DEPT PHYSIOL SCI, COL VET MED, UNIV FLA, 80- *Personal Data:* b Rock Rapids, Iowa, Sept 20, 45; m 68; c 1. *Educ:* Univ Minn, St Paul, BS, 66, DVM, 68; Univ Wis-Madison, MS, 74, PhD(vet sci), 75. *Prof Exp:* Intern vet med, Animal Med Ctr, NY, 68-69; assoc, Hillcrest Animal Hosp, Whitebear Lake, Minn, 69-70; instr, Col Vet Med, Univ Minn, 70-71; instr, Sch Vet Med, Univ Pa, 71-72; NIH fel physiol, Univ Wis, 72-75. *Concurrent Pos:* Fel physiol, Max Planck Inst Physiol & Clin Res, 75-76; prin investr, Am Heart Asn-NIH, 76-; mem, sci adv bd, Morris Animal Found, 84-87; mem, coun basic sci, Am Heart Asn; mem, Res Peer Rev Comt, Am Heart Asn, Fla Affil, 87-88. *Mem:* Am Vet Med Asn; Am Heart Asn; Am Physiol Soc. *Res:* Regulation of coronary blood flow to the heart, transitional physiological changes in the coronary circulation in the newborn, and tolerance of the newborn heart to global ischemia. *Mailing Add:* Univ Wis Sch Vet Med Madison WI 53706-1102

BUSS, DAVID R(ICHARD), CHEMICAL ENGINEERING, CHEMISTRY. *Current Pos:* Chem eng Res & Develop, Upjohn Co, 66-71, mkt develop, 71-73, res scientist, 73-77, prod mgt, 77-78, Res & Develop mgt, 78-80, dir mat planning, 80-89, DIR ADMIN SERV, UPJOHN CO, 89- *Personal Data:* b Chicago, Ill, May 6, 39; m 62, Carleen Leahy; c Daniel, Michael & Matthew. *Educ:* Harvey Mudd Col, BS, 62; Univ Calif, Berkeley, PhD(chem eng), 66. *Honors & Awards:* UpJohn Award, 84. *Mem:* Am Chem Soc; Am Inst Chem Engrs. *Res:* Resolution of optical isomers; chemical process research and development; fermentation research and development. *Mailing Add:* 6346 Applewood St Portage MI 49024-3184

BUSS, DENNIS DARCY, SOLID STATE ELECTRONICS, SEMICONDUCTORS. *Current Pos:* VPRES TECHNOL, ANALOG DEVICES, 87- *Personal Data:* b Gainesville, Fla, July 11, 42; m 64; c 2. *Educ:* Mass Inst Technol, SB, 63, SM, 64, PhD(solid state physics), 68. *Prof Exp:* Asst prof elec eng, Mass Inst Technol, 68-69; res staff theoret physics, Tex Instruments Inc, 69-74; vis assoc prof elec eng, Mass Inst Technol, 75; br mgr solid state res, Tex Instruments Inc, 75-87, vpres, Semiconductor Process & Design Ctr. *Concurrent Pos:* Mem prog comts, Int Electron Device Meeting & Int Solid State Circuits Conf, 75-77; assoc ed, Inst Elec & Electronics Engrs Trans Electron Devices, 76 & J Solid State Circuits, 77-87; Tex Instruments fel, 78. *Mem:* Inst Elec & Electronics Engrs. *Res:* Development of advanced, charge-coupled solid state structures for digital memory and analog signal processing. *Mailing Add:* 804 Woburn St Wilmington MA 01887

BUSS, EDWARD GEORGE, POULTRY GENETICS. *Current Pos:* from assoc prof to prof poultry sci, 56-83, chmn grad sch interdept prog genetics, 69-74, prof agr, 83-86, EMER PROF AGR, PA STATE UNIV, 87- *Personal Data:* b Concordia, Kans, Aug 28, 21; m 49, Dorothy Arvidson; c Ellen & Norman. *Educ:* Kans State Col, BS, 43; Purdue Univ, MS, 49, PhD(poultry genetics), 56. *Honors & Awards:* Corrispondente Award, Ital Soc Zootechnol, 72; Fulbright lectr, Sierra Leone, WAfrica, 88. *Prof Exp:* Asst prof poultry husb, Colo State Univ, 49-55, actg head dept, 50-55; instr, Purdue Univ, 55-56. *Concurrent Pos:* Prin investr, NIH Res Grant, 61-80 & Small Bus Innovation Res; mem, Comn Undergrad Educ Biol Sci panel, 65-67; mem exec comt, Am Inst Biol Sci, 73-75; rep gov bd, Am Inst Biol Sci, 65-73 & 77-78, rep, Coun Agr & Sci Technol, 78-80; coun mem, Am Genetic Asn, 74-76; assoc ed, Breeding & Genetics, 81-83; consult, poultry breeding, Indonesia & India, 86; sr scientist, Biopore, Inc, 86-94. *Mem:* Am Soc Zool; fel Poultry Sci Asn; Am Genetic Asn; Genetics Soc Am; Am Inst Biol Sci; Soc Study Reproduction; fel AAAS; Sigma Xi. *Res:* Poultry genetics and physiology of reproduction; parthenogenesis in turkeys; biochemical nature of gene action (riboflavin, chondrodystrophy, diabetes insipidus), infertility, obesity and eggshell quality. *Mailing Add:* 1420 S Garner St State College PA 16801-6330. *Fax:* 814-234-2025

BUSS, GLENN RICHARD, SOYBEAN BREEDING, PLANT GENETICS. *Current Pos:* From asst prof to assoc prof, 67-90, PROF AGRON, VA POLYTECH INST & STATE UNIV, 90- *Personal Data:* b Easton, Pa, Apr 12, 40; m 61; c Paula & Gary. *Educ:* Pa State Univ, BS, 62, MS, 64, PhD(genetics), 67. *Mem:* Am Soc Agron; Crop Sci Soc Am; Am Genetic Asn; Coun Agr Sci & Tech. *Res:* Qualitative genetics and cultivar development in soybeans; genetics of host-pathogen interactions among soybean genotypes and soybean mosaic virus strains. *Mailing Add:* Crop & Soil Environ Sci Dept Va Polytech Inst & State Univ Blacksburg VA 24061. *Fax:* 540-231-3431

BUSS, JACK THEODORE, VERTEBRATE PHYSIOLOGY. *Current Pos:* from asst prof to assoc prof, 75-85, PROF BIOL, FERRIS STATE UNIV, 85- *Personal Data:* b Benton Harbor, Mich, Oct 2, 43; m 65; c 2. *Educ:* Bethel Col, BA, 65; Wayne State Univ, MS, 68; Univ Minn, PhD(zool), 71. *Prof Exp:* Instr biol, Bethel Col, 66-68; assoc prof biol, William Jewell Col, 71-75. *Concurrent Pos:* Dir res, Antigen Labs, Inc, 72-75. *Mem:* AAAS; Asn Res Vision Ophthal. *Res:* Ocular development; corneal neovascularization. *Mailing Add:* Dept Biol Sci Ferris State Univ 901 S State St Big Rapids MI 49307-2251

BUSS, LEO WILLIAM, EVOLUTIONARY BIOLOGY. *Current Pos:* From asst prof to assoc prof biol, 79-90, assoc prof geol, 89-90, prof biol & Geol, Yale Univ, 90-96, CUR, PEABODY MUS NATURAL HIST, 79- *Personal Data:* b Alexandria, Va, Sept 27, 53; m, Jane Moore; c Evan & Blake. *Educ:* Johns Hopkins Univ, BA, 75, MA, 77, PhD(geol), 79. *Hon Degrees:* MA, Yale Univ, 91. *Concurrent Pos:* Fel, John Simon Guggenheim Found, 84; prize fel, John T & Catherine B MacArthur Found, 89; dir, Yale Inst Biospheric Studies, 91- & Sears Found Marine Res, 91- *Mem:* AAAS. *Res:* Structure and confirmation of evolutionary theory, with particular reference to expanding current theory to accommodate multiple units of selection. *Mailing Add:* Dept Biol Yale Univ New Haven CT 06511

BUSS, WILLIAM CHARLES, ANTIBIOTICS, TRANSLATION & CYCLOSPORIN. *Current Pos:* from asst prof to assoc prof, 73-89, actg chmn dept, 89-92 & 92-96, PROF PHARMACOL, SCH MED, UNIV NMEX, 89- *Personal Data:* b Bremerton, Wash, Aug 13, 38; m 65, 79, Arian L Pregenzer; c William D. *Educ:* Portland State Univ, BSc, 65; Univ Alta, MSc, 67; Univ Ore, PhD(pharmacol), 71. *Prof Exp:* Fel biochem, Univ Calif, San Francisco, 72. *Concurrent Pos:* Vis assoc prof molecular biol, Sch Med, Univ Calif, San Diego, 83; vis prof pharmacol, Sch Med, Georgetown Univ, 92. *Mem:* Am Soc Pharmacol & Exp Therapeut; AAAS; Am Soc Biochem & Molecular Biol. *Res:* Effects of chemical agents on eukaryotic transcription and translation; mechanisms of action and toxicity of antibiotics; cyclosporin. *Mailing Add:* Dept Pharmacol BMSB Rm 143 Sch Med Univ NMex Albuquerque NM 87131-5316

BUSSARD, ROBERT W, NON-EQUILIBRIUM DYNAMICAL PLASMAS, GASEOUS ELECTRONICS & ELECTROSTATICS. *Current Pos:* FOUNDER & TECH DIR, ENERGY/MATTER CONVERSION CORP, MANASSAS, VA, 84- *Personal Data:* b Washington, DC, Aug 11, 28; m 81, Dolly H Gray; c Elise M (Bright), William J, Robert L & Virginia L (Barauski). *Educ:* Univ Calif, Los Angeles, BS, 50, MS, 52; Princeton Univ, AM, 59, PhD(physics), 61. *Prof Exp:* Design engr, Falcon Prog, Hughes Aircraft Co, 49-51; mech engr, Aircraft Nuclear Propulsion Prog, Oak Ridge Nat Lab, 52-55; alt group leader, Nuclear Rocket Prog, Los Alamos Sci Lab, 55-62, alt leader, Laser Div, 71-73; dir nuclear systs staff, asst dir, Mech Div, Space Tech Labs, TRW Inc, Redondo Beach, Calif, 62-64; assoc mgr res & eng, corp chief scientist, Electro-Optical Systs Div, Xerox Corp, Pasadena, Calif, 64-69; CSI Corp, Los Angeles, 69-70; mgr, Cherokee Assocs, Pasadena, Calif, 70-74; founder, pres & chmn, Energy Resources Group, Inc, Arlington, Va, 74-86, Int Nuclear Energy Systs Co, Inc, La Jolla, Calif & McLean, Va, 76-84; asst dir, Div Controlled Thermonuclear Res, USAEC, 73-74; founder & pres, Energy Resources Group, Inc, 74-84; pres, Inesco Inc, 76-83, chmn, 76-84. *Concurrent Pos:* Lectr, Univ Calif, Los Angeles, 60-69, Univ Fla, 62-64; consult, NATO, 60-64, US Dept Energy, 74-78; mem bd dirs, Am Inst Aeronaut & Astronaut, 62-68, vpres tech activ, 65-66; asst dir, Div Controlled Thermonuclear Res, USAEC, Washington, 73-74; sr scientist, PSR Corp, Arlington, Va, 85-88. *Mem:* Fel Am Inst Aeronaut & Astronaut; Am Phys Soc; Int Acad Astronaut. *Res:* Electro-optical systems; nuclear space power and propulsion; nuclear weapon effects; high density plasma physics and application; rocket propulsion systems; fusion plasmas and fusion power systems; laser physics; energy conversion; technical economic parametric analysis of advanced energy conversion systems; author of 2 publications and numerous articles; granted several patents. *Mailing Add:* 8505 Euclid Ave No 3 1200 N Nash St Manassas Park VA 20111-2407. *E-Mail:* 76234.3303@compuserve.com

BUSSE, EWALD WILLIAM, PSYCHIATRY, GERIATRICS. *Current Pos:* prof psychiat & chmn dept, 53-74, assoc provost & dean, 74-82, EMER DEAN MED & ALLIED HEALTH EDUC, SCH MED, DUKE UNIV, 82-, EMER DEAN & EMER PROF PSYCHIAT, 87- *Personal Data:* b St Louis, Mo, Aug 18, 17; m 41; c 4. *Educ:* Westminster Col, AB, 38; Wash Univ, MD, 42; Am Bd Psychiat & Neurol, dipl. *Hon Degrees:* ScD, Westminster Col, 60. *Honors & Awards:* Strecker Award, Pa Hosp Inst, 67; Robert W Kleemeier Award, Geront Soc, 68,; William C Menninger Award, 71; Mod Med Award, 72; Seltzer Award, 75; Malford W Thewlis Award, Am Geriat Soc, 79; Sandoz Prize Gerontol, 83; Brookdale Found Award, Geront Soc Am, 82; Jack Weinberg Mem Award, Am Psychiat Asn, 83, Distinguished Serv Award, 88; Awards named in honor, Busse Res Award & Ewald Busse Award, 90. *Prof Exp:* From instr to prof psychiat, Med Ctr, Univ Colo, 46-53; pres & chief exec officer, NC Inst Med, 87-94. *Concurrent Pos:* Dir, EEG Lab, Colo Psychopath Hosp, 46-53; lectr, Sch Grad Educ, Univ Denver, 47-53; head, Div Psychosom Med, Colo Gen Hosp, 50-53; actg head, Ment Hyg & Child Guid Clin, Univ Colo, 52-53; dir, Ctr Study Aging, Duke Univ, 57-70; dir, Am Bd Psychiat & Neurol, 61-69; chmn, Sect Psychogeriat, WHO, 69-72; consult, US Navy, US Army, Vet Admin & NIH; mem, President's Biomed Res Panel, 75-76; chmn, Comt Geriat & Geront, Vet Admin, 81-85; recipient res awards, numerous insts & socs. *Mem:* Inst Med-Nat Acad Sci; fel Am Psychiat Asn (pres, 71-72); fel Am Col Physicians; fel Am Geriat Soc (pres, 75-76); fel Geront Soc (pres, 67-68); Int Asn Geront (pres, 83-89); Sigma Xi. *Res:* Electroencephalography; gerontology; author of numerous articles and publications. *Mailing Add:* 1132 Woodburn Rd Durham NC 27705

BUSSE, FRIEDRICH HERMANN, GEOPHYSICS, FLUID DYNAMICS. *Current Pos:* PROF GEOPHYS, UNIV CALIF, LOS ANGELES, 70-; PROF PHYSICS, UNIV BAYREUTH, GER, 70- *Personal Data:* b Berlin, Ger, Sept 30, 36; m 76, Cordula Braun; c Claudia, Angela & Martin. *Educ:* Univ Munich, Dr rer nat, 62. *Prof Exp:* Sci asst physics, Univ Munich, 61-65; res fel math, Mass Inst Technol, 65-66; assoc res geophysicist, Univ Calif, Los Angeles, 66-67; sr scientist astrophys, Max Planck Inst Physics, 67-70. *Concurrent Pos:* Guggenheim Mem Found fel, 72. *Mem:* Foreign assoc Nat Acad Sci; fel Am Geophys Union; hon foreign mem Am Acad Arts & Sci; fel Am Phys Soc. *Res:* Theory of rotating fluids; bounds on properties of turbulent flows; origin of planetary magnetism and dynamo theory; theory and experiments of thermal convection. *Mailing Add:* Inst Geophys & Planetary Physics Univ Calif Los Angeles CA 90024

BUSSE, ROBERT FRANKLYN, biochemistry, organic chemistry, for more information see previous edition

BUSSELL, BERTRAM, COMPUTER SCIENCE. *Current Pos:* Jr engr, Univ Calif, 50-55, assoc res engr, 55-63, from asst prof to assoc prof eng, 63-70, assoc prof comput sci & vchmn dept, 70-76, PROF ENG & APPL SCI, UNIV CALIF, LOS ANGELES, 76- *Personal Data:* b New York, NY, Sept 30, 23; m 52, 70; c 3. *Educ:* Univ Calif, Los Angeles, BS, 50, MS, 52, PhD(eng), 62. *Mem:* Inst Elec & Electronics Engrs; Asn Comput Mach. *Res:* Optimized design of digital computer systems for the optimal solution of important classes of scientific and nonscientific problems. *Mailing Add:* West Coast Univ 440 Shatto Pl Los Angeles CA 90020

BUSSELL, WILLIAM HARRISON, MECHANICAL ENGINEERING. *Current Pos:* RETIRED. *Personal Data:* b Rochelle, Ga, Jan 29, 23; m 50; c 4. *Educ:* Univ Fla, BME, 48, MS, 53; Mich State Univ, PhD(mech eng), 64. *Prof Exp:* Instr & asst res, Univ Fla, 48-52, asst prof, 53-57; mech engr, Southeastern Forest Exp Sta, US Forest Serv, 52-53; assoc prof mech eng, La Polytech Inst, 57-65; prof mech eng, Auburn Univ, 65-89. *Mem:* Am Soc Mech Engrs; Sigma Xi. *Res:* Design; mechanisms; levered vehicles; lubrication. *Mailing Add:* 230 Singleton St Auburn AL 36830-6316

BUSSERT, JACK FRANCIS, organic chemistry, for more information see previous edition

BUSSEY, ARTHUR HOWARD, BIOLOGY. *Current Pos:* asst prof, 69-73, assoc prof biol, 73-, PROF, MCGILL UNIV, 73- *Personal Data:* Can citizen. *Educ:* Univ Bristol, BSc, 63, PhD(microbiol), 66. *Prof Exp:* Fulbright fel microbial regulation & travel scholar, Dept Biol Sci, Purdue Univ, Lafayette, 66-69. *Mem:* Can Genetics Soc; Am Soc Microbiol; AAAS. *Res:* Eukaryotic cell surface; energy coupling; yeast killer factor; cell-cell recognition; regulatory switching. *Mailing Add:* Dept Biol McGill Univ Sherbrooke St W Montreal PQ H3G 2M5 Can

BUSSEY, HOWARD EMERSON, ELECTROMAGNETISM. *Current Pos:* RETIRED. *Personal Data:* b Yankton, SDak, Sept 14, 17; m 46; c 4. *Educ:* George Washington Univ, BA, 43, MS, 51; Univ Colo, PhD(physics), 64. *Prof Exp:* Sci aide physics, Nat Bur Stand, 41-42, meteorologist, synoptic & radar, 43-46, phys scientist, 46-49, physicist, 50-80. *Concurrent Pos:* Guest worker, Nat Bur Stand, 80- *Mem:* Am Phys Soc; Inst Elec & Electronics Eng; Sigma Xi; Int Sci Radio Union. *Res:* Microwave measurements; dielectric and ferrimagnetic measurements; antenna theory; electromagnetic wave scattering theory and experiment. *Mailing Add:* 1860 Bluebell Ave Boulder CO 80302-8022

BUSSGANG, J(ULIAN) J(AKOB), ELECTRICAL ENGINEERING. *Current Pos:* CONSULT, 87- *Personal Data:* b Lwow, Poland, Mar 26, 25; nat US; m 60, Fay Vogel; c Jessica E, Julia C & Jeffrey J. *Educ:* Univ London, BSc, 49; Mass Inst Technol, MSEE, 51; Harvard Univ, PhD(appl physics), 55. *Prof Exp:* Asst res lab electronics, Mass Inst Technol, 50-52; mem staff, Lincoln Lab, 52-53; asst, Gordon McKay Lab, Harvard Univ, 54-55; mgr radar develop & appl res, RCA, 55-62; pres, Signatron, Inc, 62-87. *Concurrent Pos:* Consult, Lincoln Lab, 53-55, Mitre Corp, 62-65 & Rand Corp, 62-69; lectr, Northeastern Univ, 61-65 & Harvard Univ, 64; mem, Comn C, Int Sci Radio Union; assoc ed, Radio Sci, 76-78; mem bd, Overseers, Boston Mus Sci, 89-95; volunteer exec, Int Exec Serv Corp, 93-95; chmn, Boston Sect, Int Elec & Electronics Engrs, 95. *Mem:* Fel Inst Elec & Electronics Engrs. *Res:* Electronic systems; radar; statistical theory of communications; random processes; sequential analysis. *Mailing Add:* Two Forest St Lexington MA 02173

BUSSIAN, ALFRED ERICH, geophysics, petroleum engineering, for more information see previous edition

BUSSMAN, JOHN W, PEDIATRICS. *Current Pos:* MED DIR, ORE MED PROF REV ORGN, 91- *Personal Data:* b Mankato, Minn, 1924; m; c 6. *Educ:* Univ Minn, MD, 47; Am Bd Pediat, dipl, 53; Am Bd Pediat Cardiol, dipl, 62. *Prof Exp:* Intern, Sioux Valley Hosp, 48; assoc staff, St Vincent Hosp, 51-53; from asst prof to prof pediat, Univ Ore, 63-91. *Concurrent Pos:* Mem bd dirs, Am Asn Found Med Care, 73-86; mem, Nat Health Care Technol Coun, 79-80 & Conf Health Care Cost Containment, 83; consult, Rand Corp. *Mem:* Inst Med-Nat Acad Sci; Am Acad Pediat Dent; Am Col Clin Pharm; fel Am Acad Pediat; fel Am Col Chest Physicians; fel Am Col Cardiol. *Mailing Add:* Ore Med Prof Rev Orgn 1220 SW Morrison Suite 200 Portland OR 97205

BUSTA, FRANCIS FREDRICK, FOOD MICROBIOLOGY. *Current Pos:* from assoc prof to prof 67-84, PROF & HEAD DEPT FOOD SCI & NUTRIT, UNIV MINN, 87- *Personal Data:* b Faribault, Minn, Sept 25, 35; m 57; c 2. *Educ:* Univ Minn, Minneapolis, BA, 57; Univ Minn, St Paul, MS, 61; Univ Ill, PhD(food sci), 63. *Honors & Awards:* Educator Award, Int Asn Milk Food & Environ Sanit. *Prof Exp:* From asst prof to assoc prof food sci, NC State Univ, 63-67; prof & head dept food sci & nutrit, Univ Fla, 84-87. *Concurrent Pos:* Vis scientist, Commonwealth Sci & Indust Res Orgn, Sydney, Australia, 74-75; educ res grant, Campbell Soup Co Res Inst, 74; mgr, Int Mkt Res Capsule Labs, St Paul, Minn, 81-82. *Mem:* Am Meat Sci Asn; Int Asn Milk, Food & Environ Sanit; Am Soc Microbiol; fel Inst Food Technologists; Brit Soc Appl Bact; fel Am Acad Microbiol; Am Asn Cereal Chemists. *Res:* Microbiological aspects of food processing; environmental stress on microorganisms; microbiological quality of food; food substances inhibitory or stimulative to microorganisms; bacterial spore physiology. *Mailing Add:* Dept Food Sci & Nutrit Univ Minn 1334 Eckles Ave St Paul MN 55108-6099. *Fax:* 612-625-5272

BUSTAD, LEO KENNETH, ANIMAL ASSISTED THERAPY. *Current Pos:* prof physiol & dean, Col Vet Med, 73-83, EMER PROF & EMER DEAN, COL VET MED, WASH STATE UNIV, 84- *Personal Data:* b Stanwood, Wash, Jan 10, 20; m 42, Signe Byrd; c Leo B, Karen A (deceased) & Rebecca L (Henson). *Educ:* Wash State Univ, BS, 41, MS, 48, DVM, 49; Univ Wash, PhD, 60. *Honors & Awards:* John G Rutherford Mem Lectr, 79; Wesley Spink Lectr, 79; LaCroix Mem Lectr, 80; Award of Merit, Am Animal Hosp Asn, 84; Prof Larry Smith & John O'Donaghue Mem Lectr, 85; Prof Mark Allam Lectr, 86; Int Award for Serv to Prof, World Small Animal Vet Asn, 91. *Prof Exp:* Mgr, Exp Farm, Biol Labs, Hanford Labs, Gen Elec Co, 49-64; scientist, Battelle Pac NW Lab, 64-65; prof radiation biol & dir, Radiobiol & Comp Oncol Labs, Univ Calif, Davis, 65-73. *Concurrent Pos:* Consult, USAF-AEC, 58-63; guest fac, Univ Wash, 60-65; mem subcomt, Adv Comt Civil Defense, Nat Res Coun-Nat Acad Sci, 60-65, Comt Prof Educ, Inst Lab Animal Resources, 66-68, Subcomt Stand Large Animals, 67-70, adv coun, 69-74, Subcomt Radioactivity Food, 67-70, Food Protection Comt, 67-75; consult scientist, Biol Dept, Battelle Mem Inst, 65; assoc ed, Lab Animal Care, 67-77; mem, Nat Coun Radiation Protection & Measurements, 69-75; mem, Panel Consult, Nev Opers Off, AEC, 69-78; mem, Bd Regents, Calif Lutheran Col, 70-73; mem, Bd Gov, Found Human Ecol, 70-76; mem, Adv Res Resources Coun, NIH, 75-78; chmn, Comt Vet Med Sci, Nat Res Coun-Nat Acad Sci, 75-79; nat consult vet med, Surgeon Gen, USAF, 75-, consult, Lovelace Biomed & Environ Res Inst, 77-89; exec dean, Wash, Ore, Idaho, Regional Prog Vet Med; vis prof, Murdoch Univ, 83, Sch Med, Univ Wash, 83; distinguished vis bicentennial prof, Univ Ga, 84; vis lectr, Univ Tenn, Knoxville, 86 & 88, Pac Lutheran Univ, 86 & La State Univ, 88; Miller vis prof, Univ Ill, 87. *Mem:* Sr mem Inst Med-Nat Acad Sci; Am Asn Lab Animal Sci; Am Vet Med Asn; Am Physiol Soc; Am Inst Biol Sci; Delta Soc (pres, 81-88). *Res:* Veterinary medical education; cooperative regional curriculum; carcinogenesis and aging; health sciences education; human companion animal bond; animal assisted therapy; ethics and values in animal-oriented professions; reverence for life. *Mailing Add:* Peyle Pet Partnership Col Vet Med Wash State Univ Box 647010 Pullman WA 99164-7010. *Fax:* 509-335-6094

BUSTAMANTE, CARLOS JOSE, MOLECULAR BIOLOGY. *Current Pos:* PROF CHEM & MEM INST MOLECULAR BIOL, UNIV ORE, 91- *Personal Data:* b Lima, Peru, May 6, 51; US citizen; c 2. *Educ:* Univ Peruana Cayetano Heredia, BS, 73; Univ Nat Mayor de San Marcos, MS, 75; Univ Calif, Berkeley, PhD(biophys), 81. *Prof Exp:* Fel, Lawrence Berkeley Lab, Univ Calif, 81-82; from asst prof to prof chem, Univ NMex, 82-90. *Concurrent Pos:* Fulbright Comn & Inst Int Educ fel, 75-76; Alfred P Sloan fel, 85; presidential lectr chem, Univ NMex, 86. *Mem:* AAAS; Biophys Soc; Am Chem Soc; Am Phys Soc. *Res:* Molecular biology; author of over 100 publications. *Mailing Add:* Inst Molecular Biol Univ Ore Eugene OR 97403-1229

BUSTARD, THOMAS STRATTON, NUCLEAR ENGINEERING, ENERGY CONVERSION. *Current Pos:* PRES, ENERGETICS, INC, 80- *Personal Data:* b Baltimore, Md, Feb 18, 34; m 57, Debra Schoew; c Cara L(Clark) & Richard T. *Educ:* Johns Hopkins Univ, BES, 55; Drexel Inst Technol, MSME, 61; Univ Md, PhD(chem eng), 65. *Prof Exp:* Technologist, E I du Pont de Nemours & Co, 55-56; process engr, Davison Chem Co, 56-57; staff engr, Martin-Marietta Corp, 57-65; vpres, Hittman Assocs, Inc, 65-78; consult, US Dept Energy, 78-80. *Mem:* Am Nuclear Soc; Am Soc Mech Engrs; Sigma Xi; Health Physics Soc; Asn Advan Med Instrumentation. *Res:* Systems for nuclear auxiliary power devices; production of electricity from radioisotopes by advanced energy conversion methods; radioactive waste disposal; industrial energy conservation; cogeneration; fuel switching; energy conservation; environmental technologies. *Mailing Add:* 11205 Shadowmere Mews Columbia MD 21044-5714

BUSTEAD, RONALD LORIMA, JR, FOOD TECHNOLOGY, FOOD CHEMISTRY. *Current Pos:* RETIRED. *Personal Data:* b Woburn, Mass, Mar 29, 30; m 61. *Educ:* Mass Inst Technol, BS, 52; Northeastern Univ, MS, 66. *Prof Exp:* Dairy technologist, H P Hood & Sons, 56-57; chemist, Nat Lead Co, Mass, 57-58; food technologist, Schroeder Industs, Inc, 58-59, vending machine engr, 59-62; food technologist, H A Johnson Co, 62; qual control specialist, Armed Forces Food & Container Inst, 62-64, food technologist, 64-70, opers res analyst, US Army Natick Labs, 70-85. *Mem:* Inst Food Technol; Am Chem Soc. *Res:* Feeding systems; military rations; space foods; new convenience foods; quality assurance for foods; application of operations research, systems analysis and computer sciences to feeding situations. *Mailing Add:* 124 Winter St Framingham MA 01702

BUSTER, JOHN EDMOND, GYNECOLOGY. *Current Pos:* Intern, Harbor-Univ Calif, Los Angeles, Med Ctr, Torrance, 66-67, resident, 67-71, res fel, 71-73, FAC MEM, HARBOR UNIV CALIF, LOS ANGELES, MED CTR, TORRANCE, 75-; PROF OBSTET & GYNEC, UNIV TENN, MEMPHIS, 87- *Personal Data:* b Oxnard, Calif, July 18, 41; wid. *Educ:* Univ Calif, Los Angeles, MD, 66; Am Bd Gynec, dipl. *Concurrent Pos:* Prof obstet & gynec, Univ Calif Los Angeles Sch Med, 83, dir div endocrinol, dir res group human embryo transplants; examr, Am Bd Obstet & Gynec. *Mem:* Am Gynec & Obstet Soc; Soc Gynec Invest. *Res:* Obstetrics and gynecology. *Mailing Add:* Dept Obstet/Gynec Baylor Col Med 1 Baylor Plaza Houston TX 77030-3411

BUSTIN, MICHAEL, MOLECULAR BIOLOGY, BIOCHEMISTRY. *Current Pos:* vis scientist biochem, 75-85, SUPVRY CHEMIST BIOCHEM, NIH, 85-, SECT HEAD BIOCHEM, 85- *Personal Data:* b Bucharest, Romania, Apr 19, 37; US citizen; m 67; c 2. *Educ:* Univ Denver, BS, 64; Univ Calif, Berkeley, PhD(biochem), 68. *Honors & Awards:* Lubell Prize, Weizmann Inst, 75; Tosse Prize Child Rhematology, Berlin, 94. *Prof Exp:* Res assoc biochem, Rockefeller Univ, 68-69; res assoc, Weizmann Inst, 69-73, jr scientist immunochem, 74-76, assoc prof, 76-78. *Concurrent Pos:* Adj prof, Sch Dent, Georgetown Univ, 84-95. *Mem:* Am Soc Biol Chemists; Am Soc Cell Biol. *Res:* Gene structure and function; chromatin; chromosomal proteins and the manner in which they regulate gene expression; use of immunochemical techniques for studies on chromatin and chromosomes. *Mailing Add:* Nat Cancer Inst NIH Bldg 37 Rm 3D 12 Bethesda MD 20892. *Fax:* 301-496-8419; *E-Mail:* bustin@helix.nih.gov

BUSTIN, ROBERT MARC, COAL GEOLOGY. *Current Pos:* ASSOC PROF GEOL, UNIV BC, 85- *Personal Data:* b Sask, Can, July 29, 52. *Educ:* Univ Calgary, BSc, 75, MSc, 77; Univ BC, PhD(geol), 80. *Prof Exp:* Geologist explor, Mobil Oil Can, 76, Gulf Oil Can, 77-78. *Concurrent Pos:* Consult, Coal & Oil Explor, 79- *Mem:* Can Soc Petrol Geologists; Soc Econ Paleontologists & Mineralogists; Geol Asn Can; Int Coal Petrol Asn; Am Asn Petrol Geologists. *Res:* Sedimentology, structure and petrology of coal and coal measures. *Mailing Add:* Dept Geol Sci Univ BC 2329 West Mall Vancouver BC V6T 1W5 Can

BUSTOS-VALDES, SERGIO ENRIQUE, BIOCHEMISTRY & CELL BIOLOGY. *Current Pos:* assoc prof, 71-74, chmn, Biochem Sect, 79-96, PROF BIOCHEM, DEPT ORAL BIOL, MED COL GA, 74-, PROF, SCH GRAD STUDIES, 74- *Personal Data:* b Constitucion, Chile, July 6, 32; m 63, Roxann Reddick; c Rodrigo A, Gabriela E & Susana V. *Educ:* Univ Concepcion, Chile, DDS, 58; Univ Rochester, PhD(biochem), 68. *Prof Exp:* From instr to asst prof physiol, Sch Med, Univ Concepcion, Chile, 58-67, from assoc prof to prof, Inst Biomed Sci, 67-71. *Concurrent Pos:* Fulbright scholar & US State Dept grant, Univ Rochester, 62-63; vis prof, Univ Concepcion, Chile, 75, 83; consult, 79. *Mem:* Sigma Xi; Int Asn Dent Res; Am Soc Cell Biol. *Res:* Cell surface and extracellular matrix proteins which are involved in cell to cell communication and cell adhesion. *Mailing Add:* Dept Oral Biol Biochem Med Col Ga 1120 15th St Augusta GA 30912. *Fax:* 706-721-6276; *E-Mail:* sbustos@mailgw.mcg.edu

BUSZA, WIT, EDUCATION, ELEMENTARY PARTICLE PHYSICS. *Current Pos:* from asst prof to assoc prof, 69-79, PROF PHYSICS, MASS INST TECHNOL, 79- *Personal Data:* b Ploesti, Romania, Jan 14, 40; m 64; c 2. *Educ:* Univ London, BSc, 60, PhD(nuclear physics), 64. *Prof Exp:* Res assoc physics, Univ Col, Univ London, 63-66 & Stanford Linear Accelerator Ctr, 66-69. *Mem:* Am Inst Physics. *Res:* Study of elementary particles by observing their interactions with nuclei at high energies; study of nucleon structure and fundamental interactions using muon as a probe. *Mailing Add:* Rm 24-518 Mass Inst Technol Cambridge MA 02139

BUSZARD, DEBORAH, HORTICULTURE, FRUIT CROP MANAGEMENT & STRAWBERRY BREEDING. *Current Pos:* Assoc dean, Fac Agr & Environ Sci, 91-96, PROF HORT, MCGILL UNIV, 80-, DEAN, 96- *Personal Data:* b Ripon, Eng, Mar 29, 52; m 74, John; c Henry & Simon. *Educ:* Univ Bath, UK, BSc, 76; Univ London, UK, PhD(hort), 83. *Mem:* Am Soc Hort Sci; Can Soc Hort Sci (pres, 86-87); Int Soc Hort Sci. *Res:* Strawberry breeding; cold hardness of fruit crops. *Mailing Add:* 21111 Lakeshore Ste Anne De Bellevue PQ H9W 3Z6 Can

BUTA, RONALD JAMES, OBSERVATIONAL EXTRAGALACTIC ASTRONOMY. *Current Pos:* ASSOC PROF ASTRON, UNIV ALA, 89- *Personal Data:* b Lorain, Ohio, May 10, 52; m 88, Debra A Crocker; c Sarah P. *Educ:* Case Western Res Univ, BS, 74; Mich State Univ, MS, 76; Univ Tex, Austin, MS, 78, PhD(astron), 84. *Prof Exp:* Fel, Australian Nat Univ, 84-86; res assoc, Univ Tex, Austin, 86-88. *Concurrent Pos:* Prin investr, NASA, 91-92 & NSF, 91-94. *Mem:* Am Astron Soc. *Res:* Morphology and dynamics of normal galaxies; measure surface brightness distribution and velocity fields for certain types of galaxies; produce catalogues of basic data on galaxies of all types; resonance phenomena in barred galaxies. *Mailing Add:* 2139 Brandon Pkwy Tuscaloosa AL 35406

BUTCHBAKER, ALLEN F, AGRICULTURAL ENGINEERING. *Current Pos:* CONSULT, 80- *Personal Data:* b Three Rivers, Mich, May 22, 35; m 84, Patricia McGovern; c Barbara, Bruce, Karen & James. *Educ:* Mich State Univ, BS, 57, MS, 60; Univ Mo, PhD(agr eng), 64. *Prof Exp:* Asst agr eng, Mich State Univ, 58-60; instr, Univ Mo, 60-63; from asst prof to assoc prof, NDak State Univ, 63-70; assoc prof, Okla State Univ, 70-75; pres, B&C Irrig, Inc, 75-80. *Concurrent Pos:* Consult engr; comnr, Drain Comn, Cass Co, Mich, 88, 92 & 96. *Mem:* Am Soc Agr Engrs. *Res:* Livestock facilities with emphasis on environment and animal waste management; irrigation system design; electrical applications. *Mailing Add:* 57865 Kaylor Rd Jones MI 49061

BUTCHER, BRIAN T, IMMUNOLOGY, ALLERGY. *Current Pos:* GROUP VPRES RES, ARTHRITIS FOUND, 88- *Personal Data:* b Guildford, Eng, Dec 28, 40; m 62, Carol A Mudie; c Douglas. *Educ:* Inst Med Lab Technol, London, FIMLT, 64; Univ NC, Chapel Hill, MS, 68; La State Univ, New Orleans, PhD(microbiolimmunol), 73. *Prof Exp:* Lab technician clin lab, King George V Hosp, 57-63; lab supvr clin lab, St Thomas Hosp, 63-64; lab supvr epidemiol, Sch Pub Health, Univ NC, 64-68; instr epidemiol, Med Ctr, Tulane Univ, 68-71; res assoc med, Med Ctr, La State Univ, 73-75; from asst prof to prof med, Med Ctr, Tulane Univ, 75-88. *Concurrent Pos:* Adj prof med, Tulane & Med Col Ga; asst prof pediat, Emory Univ. *Mem:* Am Acad Allergy; Orthop Res Soc; Am Soc Microbiol; AAAS; Soc Exp Biol & Med; Am Col Rheumatology. *Res:* Pathogenesis of occupational asthma; immunopharmacology; arthritis. *Mailing Add:* Arthritis Found 1330 W Peachtree St Atlanta GA 30309. *Fax:* 404-872-9559; *E-Mail:* bbutcher@arthritis.org

BUTCHER, FRED RAY, BIOCHEMISTRY. *Current Pos:* chmn, 81-84, assoc dean res & grad studies, 84-90, PROF BIOCHEM, WVA UNIV, 78-, CANCER CTR DIR, 89-, SR ASSOC VPRES HEALTH SCI, 93- *Personal Data:* b Rochester, Pa, Aug 11, 43; m 65, Letty J Lytton; c Allen R & Amy J. *Educ:* Ohio State Univ, BSc, 65, PhD(biochem), 69. *Prof Exp:* NIH fel oncol, Univ Wis, 69-71; from asst prof to assoc prof biochem, Brown Univ, 71-78. *Mem:* Am Soc Biol Chemists. *Res:* Role of cyclic nucleotides and calcium in the regulation of target tissue physiology and biochemistry by regulatory agents; the rat parotid gland, primary culture of liver cells, and tissue culture cell lines HL-60 and friend cells are used as models. *Mailing Add:* MBR Cancer Ctr Wva Univ Box 9300 Mary Babb Randolph Cancer Ctr Morgantown WV 26506-9300. *Fax:* 304-293-4667; *E-Mail:* fred@wvuohsr.hsc.wvu.edu

BUTCHER, HARVEY RAYMOND, III, ASTRONOMY. *Current Pos:* DIR GEN, NETH FOUND RES ASTRON, 91- *Personal Data:* b Salem, Mass, Aug 3, 47; m 71, Phillipa Ruth Newton; c 2. *Educ:* Calif Inst Technol, BS, 69; Australian Nat Univ, PhD(astron), 74. *Prof Exp:* Bart Bok fel, Steward Observ, Univ Ariz, 74-76; asst astronr, Kitt Peak Nat Observ, Asn Univs Res Astron, 76-79, assoc astronr, 79-81, astronr, 81-83; prof astron & dir, Kapteyn Observ, Univ Groningen, Neth, 83-91. *Mem:* Am Astron Soc; Int Astron Soc; Royal Astron Soc. *Res:* Elucidation of the evolution of galaxies over cosmological time. *Mailing Add:* Floralaan 8 Roden 9301 KE Netherlands

BUTCHER, HENRY CLAY, IV, PLANT PHYSIOLOGY, BIOCHEMISTRY. *Current Pos:* from asst prof to assoc prof, 69-77, chmn dept, 71-75, 78-83, EMER PROF BIOL, LOYOLA COL, MD, 77- *Personal Data:* b Newton, Mass, July 31, 33; m 58; c 3. *Educ:* Tufts Univ, BSc, 55; Ohio State Univ, MS, 61, PhD(plant physiol), 64. *Prof Exp:* Fel, Res Inst Advan Studies, Md, 64-65. *Concurrent Pos:* Guest plant physiologist, Brookhaven Nat Lab, 75-76; vis sr scientist, Johns Hopkins Univ, 83-84. *Mem:* AAAS; Am Soc Plant Physiol; Am Inst Biol Sci; Plant Molecular Biol Soc; Sigma Xi. *Res:* Biochemistry of plant cell vacuoles; translocation of organic solutes in plants; photosynthesis; tissue culture; differentiation; molecular biology of aging. *Mailing Add:* Dept Biol Loyola Univ 4501 N Charles St Baltimore MD 21210. *E-Mail:* butcher@loyola.edu

BUTCHER, JOHN EDWARD, ANIMAL PRODUCTION. *Current Pos:* CONSULT, 86- *Personal Data:* b Belle Fourche, SDak, Aug 4, 23; m 51; c 3. *Educ:* Mont State Col, BS, 50, MS, 52; Utah State Univ, PhD(animal prod), 56. *Prof Exp:* Instr animal indust, Mont State Col, 49-50, range mgt, 52-53; from asst prof to prof animal sci, Utah State Univ, 55-86. *Concurrent Pos:*

Mem subcomt sheep nutrit, Nat Res Coun, 75; mem, Nat Pub Land Adv Coun, Bur Land Mgt, US Dept Interior, 82-84. *Mem:* Fel AAAS; fel Am Soc Animal Sci; Soc Range Mgt; Am Soc Farm Mgr & Rural Appraisers. *Res:* Ruminant nutrition and environment. *Mailing Add:* 1703 E 1030 N Logan UT 84321

BUTCHER, LARRY L, BRAIN HISTOCHEMISTRY. *Current Pos:* PROF PSYCHOL, UNIV CALIF, LOS ANGELES, 80- *Personal Data:* b Richmond, Ind, Feb 21, 40. *Educ:* Univ Mich, PhD(psychol), 66. *Mem:* Soc Neurosci; Western Pharmacol Soc; Am Soc Pharmacol & Exp Therapeut. *Mailing Add:* Dept Psychol Univ Calif 405 Hilgard Ave Los Angeles CA 90024-1563. *Fax:* 310-206-5895

BUTCHER, RAYMOND JOHN, X-RAY CRYSTALLOGRAPHY, BIOINORGANIC CHEMISTRY. *Current Pos:* asst prof, 77-83, ASSOC PROF CHEM, HOWARD UNIV, WASHINGTON, DC, 83- *Personal Data:* b Greymouth, NZ, Oct 11, 45; US citizen; m 79, Arona Mahan; c Arun & Anand. *Educ:* Univ Canterbury, NZ, BSc Hons, 68, PhD(chem), 74, Christchurch Teachers Col, NZ, dipl physics & math, 70. *Prof Exp:* Instr chem, Univ Va, Charlottesville, 74-76; postdoctoral fel inorg chem, Georgetown Univ, Wash, DC, 76-77. *Concurrent Pos:* Vis assoc prof, Univ Va, Charlottesville, 85-86, Univ Canterbury, NZ, 93; fac fel, Goddard Space Flight Ctr, 87 & 88; adj prof, Hampton Univ, 87-90; sr scientist, Naval Res Lab, Washington, DC, 89, 90, 91 & 93-96; int Fulbright fel, Univ Poona, India, 89; vis scientist, Los Alamos Nat Lab, 94. *Mem:* Am Chem Soc; Sigma Xi; NY Acad Sci; AAAS; Am Crystallog Asn. *Res:* Magneto-structural correlations in exchange-coupled systems; bioinorganic chemistry of manganese, iron, copper and molybdenum; promotion of electrophilic and nucleophilic substitution reactions by use of coordinated exchange inert metal complexes. *Mailing Add:* Dept Chem Howard Univ Washington DC 20059. *E-Mail:* rbutcher@fac.chem.howard.edu

BUTCHER, REGINALD WILLIAM, BIOCHEMISTRY, PHYSIOLOGY. *Current Pos:* DEAN, GRAD SCH BIOMED SCI, UNIV TEX HEALTH DCI CTR, HOUSTON, 79-, PROF BIOCHEM & MOLECULAR BIOL, MED SCH, 79- DIR, INST TECHNOL DEVELOP & ASSESSMENT, 84- *Personal Data:* b Bayshore, NY, May 4, 30; m 53; c 3. *Educ:* US Naval Acad, BS, 53; Western Reserve Univ, PhD(pharmacol), 63. *Prof Exp:* From instr to assoc prof physiol, Vanderbilt Univ, 63-69, investr, Howard Hughes Med Inst, 66-69; prof biochem & chmn dept, Med Sch, Univ Mass, 69-79, assoc dean sci affairs, 76-79. *Concurrent Pos:* Vis prof, Univ Libre de Bruxelles, Belgium, 77-; Fulbright Sr Res Scholar, 77-78; dir, Speech & Hearing Inst, Univ Tex Health Sci Ctr, Houston, 82-, actg dir, Position Diag & Res Ctr,87- *Mem:* Endocrine Soc; NY Acad Sci; Am Physiol Soc; Am Soc Biol Chemists; Sigma Xi. *Res:* Mechanism of hormone action at the molecular level; control of cyclic adenosinemonophosphate levels by adenyl cyclase and phosphodiesterase activities and effects of cyclic AMP on cellular processes. *Mailing Add:* GSBS Univ Tex Health Sci Ctr PO Box 20334 Houston TX 77225-0334. *Fax:* 713-794-1601

BUTCHER, ROY LOVELL, REPRODUCTIVE PHYSIOLOGY. *Current Pos:* From instr to assoc prof, 62-78, PROF OBSTET & GYNEC, WVA UNIV, 78- *Personal Data:* b Reedy, WVa, Dec 15, 30; m 55; c 3. *Educ:* WVa Univ, BS, 53, MS, 59; Iowa State Univ, PhD(animal reproduction), 62. *Mem:* Endocrine Soc; Soc Study Reproduction; Am Soc Animal Sci; Soc Gynec Invest; Brit Soc Study Fertil. *Res:* Control of luteal function; effects of delayed ovulation on congenital anomalies. *Mailing Add:* Dept Obstet & Gynec WVa Univ Sch Med Morgantown WV 26506-0002

BUTCHER, SAMUEL SHIPP, PHYSICAL CHEMISTRY. *Current Pos:* from asst prof to assoc prof, 64-74, PROF CHEM, BOWDOIN COL, 74- *Personal Data:* b Gaylord, Mich, Nov 12, 36; m 61; c 2. *Educ:* Albion Col, AB, 58; Harvard Univ, AM, 61, PhD(chem), 63. *Prof Exp:* Fel spectros, Nat Res Coun Can, 62-64. *Mem:* AAAS; Am Chem Soc; Am Meteorol Soc. *Res:* Atmospheric chemistry. *Mailing Add:* Dept Chem Bowdoin Col Brunswick ME 04011

BUTEAU, L(EON) J, MATERIALS SCIENCE, THERMODYNAMICS. *Current Pos:* PROF PHYSICS, NJ INST TECHNOL, 65-; ASSOC DEAN, COL SCI & LIBERAL ARTS. *Personal Data:* b Teaneck, NJ, Nov 19, 32. *Educ:* Newark Col Eng, BS, 58; Stanford Univ, MS, 59; Univ Fla, PhD(mat eng), 63. *Prof Exp:* Mem tech staff systs eng, Bell Tel Labs, 63-65. *Mem:* Sigma Xi. *Res:* Topology of powder metallurgy, the neuron networks in the brain and the law of supply and demand; twinning systems in zirconium; cycle theories in economics. *Mailing Add:* Dept Physics NJ Inst Technol 323 High St Newark NJ 07102

BUTEL, JANET SUSAN, VIROLOGY, CELL BIOLOGY. *Current Pos:* Fel, 66-68, from asst prof to assoc prof, 68-76, PROF VIROL, BAYLOR COL MED, 76-, HEAD, DIV MOLECULAR VIROL, 89- *Personal Data:* b Overbrook, Kans, May 24, 41; m 67; c 2. *Educ:* Kans State Univ, BS, 63; Baylor Univ, PhD(virol), 66. *Honors & Awards:* Am Cancer Soc Fac Res Award, 72; Joseph L Melnick Prof Virol, 86. *Concurrent Pos:* Exp virol study sect, NIH, 80-84; bd scientific counr, Div Cancer Etiol, Nat Cancer Inst, 85-89; co-ed, Med Microbiol, Lange Med Pub, 89- *Mem:* Fel AAAS; Am Soc Microbiol; Am Soc Virol; Sigma Xi; Am Asn Cell Biol; Int Asn Breast Cancer Res. *Res:* Tumor viruses; oncogenes; transformation of cells. *Mailing Add:* 3031 Albans Rd Houston TX 77005-2145. *Fax:* 713-798-5075

BUTENSKY, IRWIN, COSMETIC CHEMISTRY, PHARMACEUTICAL CHEMISTRY. *Current Pos:* vpres res & develop, Int Playtex Inc, 79-90, SR VPRES, PLAYTEX FAMILY PRODS CORP, 90- *Personal Data:* b New York, NY, Jan 27, 36; m 69. *Educ:* Columbia Univ, BS, 56; Univ Mich, MS, 59, PhD(pharmaceut chem), 61. *Prof Exp:* Develop chemist, Lederle Labs, Am Cyanamid Co, NY, 61-66, group leader process improve lab, 66-67; develop chemist pharmaceut res & develop, Vicks Div Res & Develop, Richardson-Merrell, Inc. 67-69, sect head, Vicks Div Res, 69-71, asst dir pharmaceut develop, 71-72, dir skin care & toiletries, 72-79. *Mem:* AAAS; Am Pharmaceut Asn; Am Chem Soc; Soc Cosmetic Chem. *Res:* Tablet coating technology; spraying techniques; fine particle technology; suspensions of natural product; proprietary drug development; aerosols, creams and all other dosage forms; plastics; development of new cosmetic and dermatological products. *Mailing Add:* 533 Winthrop Rd Teaneck NJ 07666-2817

BUTENSKY, MARTIN SAMUEL, CHEMICAL ENGINEERING. *Current Pos:* tech mgr, 88-89, mfg & tech mgr, 89-92, MFG COORDR, CYTEC INDUSTS, 92- *Personal Data:* b Brooklyn, NY, Nov 28, 37; m 60, Pat Meyers; c Gregg, Susan & Ellen. *Educ:* Columbia Col, BA, 57; Columbia Sch Eng, BS, 58; Mass Inst Technol, ScD(chem eng), 63. *Prof Exp:* From res engr to sr res chem engr, Chem Res Div, Am Cyanamid Co, 62-75, res group leader process develop, 75-86, projs mgr process technol, 86-88. *Mem:* Am Inst Chem Engrs. *Mailing Add:* 90 Nutmeg Lane Stamford CT 06905

BUTERA, RICHARD ANTHONY, SOLID STATE CHEMISTRY, PHYSICAL CHEMISTRY. *Current Pos:* asst prof to assoc prof, 63-79, PROF PHYS CHEM, UNIV PITTSBURGH, 79- *Personal Data:* b Carnegie, Pa, Nov 30, 34; m; c 2. *Educ:* Univ Pittsburgh, BS, 60; Univ Calif, Berkeley, PhD(phys chem), 63. *Prof Exp:* Res assoc phys chem, Univ Pittsburgh, 57-60; res asst low temperature chem, Univ Calif, Berkeley, 60-63. *Mem:* Am Phys Soc; Am Chem Soc; AAAS; NY Acad Sci; fel Am Inst Chem. *Res:* Magneto-thermo-dynamic studies of magnetic phase transitions; heat capacity studies of intermetallic compounds and high temp superconductors; computer controlled experimentation; metal/semiconductor interfaces; high temperature superconductors. *Mailing Add:* 230 Elbe Dr Pittsburgh PA 15209

BUTH, CARL EUGENE, CIVIL ENGINEERING. *Current Pos:* Res asst, Tex Transp Inst, 63-66, engr res assoc, 66-68, asst res engr, 68-74, head fabrication & testing sect, Tech Support Servs, 69-70, head eng & construct, Proving Ground Res Prog, 70-73, head, 73-78, from instr to asst prof civil eng, Tex A&M Univ, assoc res engr, Tex Transp Inst, 74-79, ASSOC PROF CIVIL ENG, TEX A&M UNIV, 77-, HEAD, SAFETY DIV, TEX TRANSP INST, 78-, RES ENGR, 79- *Personal Data:* b Gatesville, Tex, June 17, 40; m 61; c 3. *Educ:* Tex A&M Univ, BS, 63, ME, 64, PhD(civil eng), 72. *Mem:* Nat Soc Prof Engrs; Am Soc Civil Engrs; Am Soc Eng Educ; Sigma Xi. *Res:* Structural analysis and design; highway safety. *Mailing Add:* Dept Civil Eng Tex A&M Univ College Station TX 77843-3136

BUTH, DONALD GEORGE, PHYLOGENETIC SYSTEMATICS, ICHTHYOLOGY. *Current Pos:* res fel systematics, Univ Calif, 78-79, lectr pop genetics, 80, from asst prof to assoc prof, 80-92, PROF BIOL, UNIV CALIF, LOS ANGELES, 92- *Personal Data:* b Chicago, Ill, Feb 23, 49; m 89, Karen F Gustafson; c Erik & Jessie. *Educ:* Univ Ill, BS, 71, AB, 72, MS, 74, PhD(ecol, ethology & evolution), 78. *Concurrent Pos:* Consult, endangered species recovery team, 79-; sectional ed, Copeia, 85-93; ed, Isozyme Bulletin, 90-93. *Mem:* Am Soc Ichthyologists & Herpetologists; Soc Systematic Biol; Am Fisheries Soc; Soc Study Evolution; fel AAAS; fel Willi Hennig Soc. *Res:* Biochemical systematics of reptiles, gasterosteiform, cypriniform and perciform fishes; polyploid gene expression in fishes. *Mailing Add:* Dept Biol Univ Calif Los Angeles CA 90095-1606. *Fax:* 310-206-3987; *E-Mail:* dbuth@ucla.edu

BUTKOV, EUGENE, THEORETICAL PHYSICS. *Current Pos:* asst prof, 65-68, chmn dept, 74-80, ASSOC PROF PHYSICS, ST JOHN'S UNIV, NY, 68- *Personal Data:* b Pancevo, Yugoslavia, Sept 16, 28; US citizen. *Educ:* Univ BC, BASc, 54, MA, 56; McGill Univ, PhD(theoret physics), 60. *Prof Exp:* Asst prof physics, St John's Univ, NY, 59-62 & Hunter Col, 62-65. *Mem:* Am Phys Soc; Math Asn Am; Soc Ind Appl Math. *Res:* Theory of non-linear differential equations; quantum field theory. *Mailing Add:* Dept Physics St Albert Hall St John's Univ Grand Central & Utopia Jamaica NY 11439

BUTKOWSKI, RALPH J, PROTEIN CHEMISTRY. *Current Pos:* CONSULT, INC STAR, 92- *Personal Data:* b Melrose, Minn, Jan 6, 48. *Educ:* Univ Minn, PhD(biochem), 78. *Res:* Protein chemistry. *Mailing Add:* Inc Star PO Box 285 Stillwater MN 55082

BUTKUS, ANTANAS, ANALYTICAL CHEMISTRY, CARDIOVASCULAR DISEASES. *Current Pos:* asst staff mem lipids, Cleveland Clin, 62-67, assoc staff mem, 67-69, STAFF MEM, CLEVELAND CLIN FOUND, 69- *Personal Data:* b Lithuania, June 20, 18; US citizen; m 43; c 2. *Educ:* Univ Halle, BAgrSci, 43; Univ Bonn, DrAgrSci, 47. *Prof Exp:* Chief chemist, Processing Lab, Southland Frozen Meat, NZ, 54-62; chemist, Water Control Comn, Md, 62. *Mem:* AAAS; Am Chem Soc; Am Oil Chem Soc; Am Soc Exp Path. *Res:* Disorders of lipid metabolism and arteriosclerosis. *Mailing Add:* 19406 Van Aken Blvd Beachwood OH 44122

BUTLER, ALISON, BIOINORGANIC CHEMISTRY, METALLOBIOCHEMISTRY. *Current Pos:* PROF CHEM, UNIV CALIF, SANTA BARBARA, 86- *Personal Data:* b Chicago, Ill, Nov 19, 54. *Educ:* Reed Col, BA, 77; Univ Calif, San Diego, PhD(chem), 82. *Prof Exp:* Fel, Univ Calif, Los Angeles, 82-84, Calif Inst Tech, 84-86. *Concurrent Pos:* Jr fac res award, Am Cancer Soc, 88-91; alt counr, Am Chem Soc, 93-95; A P Sloan Found fel, 93- *Mem:* Am Chem Soc; AAAS. *Res:* Metallobiochemistry and bioinorganic chemistry; marine environment; vanadium bromoperoxidase and new marine siderophores. *Mailing Add:* Dept Chem Univ Calif Santa Barbara CA 93106

BUTLER, ANN BENEDICT, NEUROANATOMY. *Current Pos:* INDEPENDENT NEURO & ANAT RES SCIENTIST, 86- *Personal Data:* b Wilmington, Del, Dec 2, 45; m 68, Thomas; c Whitney. *Educ:* Oberlin Col, BA, 67; Case Western Reserve Univ, PhD(anat), 71. *Prof Exp:* NIH fel neuroanat, Brown Univ, 71-72 & Univ Va, 72-73; asst prof anat, George Washington Univ, 73-75; from asst prof to assoc prof anat, Georgetown Univ, 74-84. *Mem:* Soc Neurosci. *Res:* Comparative neuroanatomy of the visual system; evolution of sensory system organization in the thalamus and telencephalon; evolution of neocortex and of limbic system. *Mailing Add:* ITNI 4433 N 33rd St Arlington VA 22207. *Fax:* 703-533-3028

BUTLER, ARTHUR P, RESOURCES. *Current Pos:* RETIRED. *Personal Data:* b Morristown, NJ, June 23, 08; m 48, Josephine Mendenhall; c Priscilla, A Emery, Sarah B (Watson) & Warren T. *Educ:* Harvard Univ, BA, 30, MA, 37, PhD(geol), 46. *Prof Exp:* Geologist, US Geol Surv, 41. *Mem:* Soc Econ Geologist; Sigma Xi; Geol Soc Am. *Mailing Add:* 9625 W 36th Ave Wheat Ridge CO 80033-5708

BUTLER, BLAINE R(AYMOND), JR, ASTRONAUTICAL & AERONAUTICAL ENGINEERING. *Current Pos:* RETIRED. *Personal Data:* b Johnstown, NY, Aug 11, 25; m 48; c 3. *Educ:* US Mil Acad, BS, 48; Purdue Univ, MS, 61, PhD(aeronaut eng), 65. *Prof Exp:* USAF, 48-72, from instr to asst prof aeronaut, USAF Acad, 63-66, prof & head dept, 66-69, dep comdr, Space Defense Ctr, NAm Air Defense Command, 70-71, analyst, Joint Strategic Planning Staff & Joint Chiefs of Staff, Washington, DC, 71-72; prof eng, Purdue Univ, 72-83; prof & dept head, Aerospace Eng, Embry-Riddle Aeronaut Univ, 83-88. *Mem:* Am Inst Aeronaut & Astronaut; Am Soc Eng Educ; assoc fel Can Aeronaut & Space Inst; fel Brit Interplanetary Soc. *Mailing Add:* 2242 Loma Rica Circle Prescott AZ 86303

BUTLER, BRUCE DAVID, PULMONARY PHYSIOLOGY, SPACE MEDICINE. *Current Pos:* Fel, Dept Anesthesiol, 81-82, from instr to asst prof, 82-89, ASSOC PROF ANESTHESIOL, UNIV TEX MED SCH, 89- *Personal Data:* b Houston, Tx, Jan 27, 53. *Educ:* Univ Tex, BA, 75, PhD(physiol & biophys), 80. *Concurrent Pos:* Mem, Sch Biomed Sci, 84-, adj asst prof, Univ Tex Health Sci Ctr, 87- *Mem:* Undersea Med Soc; Am Physiol Soc; Aerospace Med Asn; Sigma Xi; Int Union Physiol Scientists. *Res:* Pulmonary pathophysiology & decompression biology; studies in physiology, biochemistry, & biophysical indicies in decompression sickness experience by commercial deep sea divers or astronauts; pulmonary pathophysiological studies related to surfactant molecules and their role in lungs. *Mailing Add:* Dept Anesthesiol Univ Tex Health Sci Ctr 6431 Fannin 5-020 MSMB Houston TX 77030. *Fax:* 713-794-4157

BUTLER, BYRON C, GEMOLOGY, GYNECOLOGY. *Current Pos:* DIR, 53-86, PRES, BUTLER RES FOUND, PHOENIX, 70- *Personal Data:* b Carroll, Iowa, Aug 10, 18; m 75, JoAnn Nicolls; c 5. *Educ:* Columbia Univ, MD, 43, ScD, 51; Gemological Inst Am, GG, 87. *Prof Exp:* Instr path, Col Physicians & Surgeons, Columbia Univ, 41-42, instr obstet & gynec, 50-53. *Concurrent Pos:* Am Cancer Soc grant, 51 & NIH grant, 52-53. *Mem:* Fel AAAS; Am Gemological Trade Asn. *Res:* Hypnosis in relation to relief of pain in cancer; fibrinolysin enzyme system in relation to blood clotting defects in pregnancy; bacterial vaginal flora; magnetic field inhibition of cancer cells in tissue culture; infertility; diagnosis and treatment of cancer of cervix and early detection; diagnosis of cancer and viral diseases in gynecology; laser surgery in treatment of cancer and viral disease in gynecology; gemologic research in color, inclusions and identification; computer science; exploration by hypnotic regression of experiences by UFO contactees; study of historical concepts of the origin of the universe and present day concepts. *Mailing Add:* 77 E Missouri Ave No 20 Phoenix AZ 85012. *Fax:* 602-423-5717

BUTLER, CALVIN CHARLES, MATHEMATICAL STATISTICS. *Current Pos:* PROF MATH, COL SOUTHERN IDAHO, 71- *Personal Data:* b Fowler, Colo, Nov 8, 37; m 59; c 4. *Educ:* Colo State Univ, BS, 62, MS, 63, PhD(math statist), 66. *Prof Exp:* Asst prof math, Univ Colo, Boulder, 66-71. *Mem:* Am Statist Asn. *Res:* Applied probability theory; stochastic processes. *Mailing Add:* Dept Math Col Southern Idaho PO Box 1238 Twin Falls ID 83303-1238

BUTLER, CHARLES MORGAN, STATISTICS, OPERATIONS RESEARCH. *Current Pos:* RETIRED. *Personal Data:* b Columbia, Tenn, Dec 16, 29; m 58; c 3. *Educ:* US Mil Acad, BS, 53; Mass Inst Technol, SM, 62; Univ Ala, MA, 66, PhD(math), 70. *Prof Exp:* Asst prof indust eng, Univ Ala, 68-70; from assoc prof to prof statist, Miss State Univ, 70-96. *Res:* Application of statistical and other quantitative techniques for the solution of business and industrial problems; air pollution data processing. *Mailing Add:* Dept Mkt Miss State Univ Drawer N Mississippi State MS 39762-5513

BUTLER, CHARLES THOMAS, NEURAL NETWORKS. *Current Pos:* RETIRED. *Personal Data:* b Muskogee, Okla, Nov 30, 32; m 81, Mary Odell; c Elizabeth, Deborah & David. *Educ:* Iowa State Univ, BS, 54; Tex A&M Univ, MS, 57; Okla State Univ, PhD(physics), 72. *Prof Exp:* Sr scientist, Jet Propulsion Lab, Calif Inst Technol, 56-60; physicist, Oak Ridge Nat Lab, 60-70; mem fac, Dept Physics, Okla State Univ, 70-78; mem fac, Dept Physics, Va Commonwealth Univ, 78-84; prin staff mem, BDM Int, 84-89; prin res scientist, Phys Sci, Inc, 89-96. *Mem:* Am Phys Soc; AAAS; Sigma Xi; Inst Elec & Electronics Engrs; Int Neurol Network Soc. *Res:* Metal hydrides; radiation damage in insulators; crystal growth; neural network applications. *Mailing Add:* 11641 Newbridge Ct Reston VA 20191

BUTLER, DIXON MATLOCK, ASTRONOMY. *Current Pos:* Nat Res Coun resident res assoc, NASA Goddard Space Flight Ctr, 76-77, res scientist, 77-79, chief, Advan Missions & Interdisciplinary Sci Br, NASA Hq, 80-89, dir, Modeling Data & Info Systs Prog Off, 89-93, DIR OPERS, DATA & INFO SYSTS DIV, OFF MISSION TO PLANET EARTH, NASA HQ, 93- *Personal Data:* b Winston-Salem, NC, July 15, 49; m, Susan Lewis; c William, Evora, Isaac & Lillian. *Educ:* Harvard Univ, AM & AB, 71; Rice Univ, MS, 74, PhD(space physics & astron), 75. *Prof Exp:* Res fel, Rice Univ, 75-76. *Concurrent Pos:* Cong sci fel, Am Phys Soc, 79-80; dir, Va Environ Endowment. *Res:* Conducts ozone depletion modeling research; data analysis. *Mailing Add:* 1920 Quincy St NW Washington DC 20011

BUTLER, DON, EXPLOSION BONDING. *Personal Data:* b Camden, NJ, July 2, 60. *Educ:* Tulane Univ, BS, 82. *Prof Exp:* Sr proj engr, Northwest Tech Industs, 84-97. *Mem:* Am Soc Mech Engrs. *Res:* Explosion bonding and forming materials which have low ductility. *Mailing Add:* 71 Garden Lane Sequim WA 98382

BUTLER, DONALD EUGENE, ORGANIC CHEMISTRY, PHARMACEUTICAL CHEMISTRY. *Current Pos:* From assoc res chemist to sr res chemist, Warner Lambert-Parke Davis, 58-77, res assoc, 77-81, sect dir, 91-92, assoc res fel, 92-94, SR RES ASSOC & SR GROUP MGR, WARNER LAMBERT-PARKE DAVIS PHARMACEUT RES DIV, 77-, RES FEL, 94- *Personal Data:* b Detroit, Mich, Dec 1, 33; m 62, Mary E Shrehan; c 3. *Educ:* Wayne State Univ, BS, 55; Univ Fla, PhD(chem), 58. *Mem:* Am Chem Soc; AAAS. *Res:* Piperazine derivatives; synthetic organic medicinals; gastrointestinal and central nervous system pharmacology; heterocyclic chemistry, pyrrollidines and pyrazoles; learning and memory; new routes to known compounds and large scale syntheses. *Mailing Add:* Warner Lambert-Parke Davis 188 Howard Holland MI 49424-6596

BUTLER, DONALD J(OSEPH), civil engineering, for more information see previous edition

BUTLER, DOUGLAS NEVE, STRUCTURAL CHEMISTRY, ORGANIC CHEMISTRY. *Current Pos:* Asst prof, 68-71, ASSOC PROF, CHEM DEPT, YORK UNIV, 71- *Personal Data:* b Melbourne, Victoria, Australia, Mar 30, 36; m 73; c 1. *Educ:* Univ NSW, BSc, 58; Univ Manchester, Victoria, PhD(chem), 63. *Concurrent Pos:* Vis prof, Chem Dept, Univ Capetown, SAfrica, 71 & Bond Univ, Queensland, Australia, 89; vis fel, Chem Dept, Australia Nat Univ, 74-75 & 81-82. *Res:* Design and synthesis of rigid polycyclic organic chemical frameworks bearing fixed or flexibly attached functional groups as specific binding agents on catalysts. *Mailing Add:* Ctr Molecular Archit Central Queensland Univ Rockhampton Qld 4702 Australia. *Fax:* 61-79-30-9917; *E-Mail:* d.butler@cqu.edu.au

BUTLER, DWAIN KENT, GEOPHYSICS, GEOSCIENCE ENGINEERING. *Current Pos:* Res physicist, Naval Ord Lab, 68-71, res physicist & geophysicist, Mo River Div Lab, 71-73, RES GEOPHYSICIST, WATERWAYS EXP STA, CORPS ENGRS, 73- *Personal Data:* b Stamford, Tex, Jan 6, 46; m 68, Fay E Agnew; c Tasha & Tamara. *Educ:* Tex Tech Univ, BS, 68; Univ Md, MS, 71; Texas A&M Univ, PhD, 83. *Honors & Awards:* Herbert D Vogel Award, Outstanding Scientist, Waterways Exp Sta, 85, Outstanding Tech Presentation Award, 85. *Concurrent Pos:* Instr physics, St Aloysius High Sch, Vicksburg, 75-76; advan study sabbatical, Waterways Exp Sta, Tex A&M Univ, 77-78; adj prof geosci, Univ Southern Miss & Miss State Univ, 80-88; prof, Geophys, Tex A&M Univ, 89- *Mem:* Am Phys Soc; Soc Explor Geophysicists; Am Inst Prof Geologists; Int Soc Rock Mech; Am Geophys Union; Soc Am Mil Engrs. *Res:* Engineering geophysics; microgravimetry for site investigations; water resources; global plate tectonics, global gravity field. *Mailing Add:* 6109 Lancelot Lane Vicksburg MS 39180-8509. *Fax:* 601-634-3139

BUTLER, EDWARD EUGENE, PHYTOPATHOLOGY, MYCOLOGY. *Current Pos:* jr plant pathologist, Univ Calif, Davis, 55-56, lectr plant path & asst plant pathologist, 57-61, from assoc prof to prof, 61-90, EMER PROF PLANT PATH, UNIV CALIF, DAVIS, 90- *Personal Data:* b Wilmington, Del, Dec 8, 19; m 47; c 5. *Educ:* Univ Del, BS, 43; Mich State Univ, MS, 48; Univ Minn, PhD(plant path), 54. *Honors & Awards:* WH Weston Award, Mycol Soc Am. *Prof Exp:* Asst bot, Mich State Univ, 46-49; instr plant path, Univ Minn, 51-54. *Concurrent Pos:* Vis prof, Univ PR, 66-67; assoc ed, Phytopath, 73-76; vis mycologist, Rancho Santa Ana Bot Garden, 83-84. *Mem:* Fel AAAS; Am Phytopath Soc; Mycol Soc Am; Brit Mycol Soc. *Res:* Ecology and taxonomy of plant pathogenic fungi especially soil borne species causing root diseases; mycoparasitisan. *Mailing Add:* Plant Path Univ Calif Davis CA 95616

BUTLER, ELIOT ANDREW, analytical chemistry, for more information see previous edition

BUTLER, G(ERARD), chemical engineering, for more information see previous edition

BUTLER, GEORGE BERGEN, ORGANIC CHEMISTRY, POLYMER SCIENCE. *Current Pos:* from instr to assoc prof, Univ Fla, 46-57, dir, Ctr Macromolecular Sci, 70, res prof, 57-90, EMER PROF CHEM, UNIV FLA, 90- *Personal Data:* b Liberty, Miss, Apr 15, 16; m 44, Claudia Eldridge; c George B Jr & Barbara B (Ward). *Educ:* Miss Col, BA, 38; Univ NC, PhD(org chem), 42. *Hon Degrees:* DSc, Miss Col, 86. *Honors & Awards:* Polymer Award, Am Chem Soc, 80. *Prof Exp:* Res chemist, Rohm & Haas Co, Philadelphia, 42-46. *Concurrent Pos:* Past vpres, Peninsular Chem Res, Inc; consult, TRW, Inc, IMC, Inc, Allied Chem Co, Chemstrand, Proctor & Gamble & Atlantic Richfield; co-ed, J Macromolecular Sci Rev & Rev Macromolecular Chem. *Mem:* AAAS; Am Chem Soc; Sigma Xi; Am Inst Chemists. *Res:* Biologically active polymers; pharmaceutical chemicals; water-soluble polymers, polymer modification; polyelectrolytes; ion exchange resins; reaction mechanisms; cyclopolymerization, triazolinedione polymers, quaternary ammonium compounds and polymers; polymerization mechanisms. *Mailing Add:* 1906 NW 24th St Gainesville FL 32605. *Fax:* 904-392-9741

BUTLER, GEORGE DANIEL, JR, ENTOMOLOGY. *Current Pos:* RETIRED. *Personal Data:* b Newark, NJ, Apr 13, 23; m 49; c 3. *Educ:* Univ Mass, BS, 48; Cornell Univ, PhD(entom), 51. *Prof Exp:* Asst prof entom, Univ Ariz, 51-59, assoc prof, 59-66; res entomologist, Cotton Insects Br, USDA, 66-72, res entomologist, Western Cotton Res Lab, 72-86, collabr, 87- *Mem:* Am Entom Soc; Ecol Soc Am. *Res:* Biological control of insects; biology and control of emisia tabaci. *Mailing Add:* USDA Cotton Res Lab 4135 E Broadway Phoenix AZ 85040

BUTLER, GILBERT W, NUCLEAR CHEMISTRY. *Current Pos:* STAFF MEM & CHEMIST, LOS ALAMOS SCI LAB, 72- *Personal Data:* b Ft Collins, Colo, Feb 22, 41; m 78. *Educ:* Ore State Univ, BS, 63; Univ Calif, Berkeley, PhD(nuclear chem), 67. *Prof Exp:* Res nuclear chemist, Lawrence Radiation Lab, 67-70 & Argonne Nat Lab, 70-72. *Mem:* Am Phys Soc; Am Chem Soc. *Res:* Study of high energy nuclear reactions using solid state detectors; high resolution gamma ray spectroscopy. *Mailing Add:* 522 Canyon Rd Los Alamos NM 87544. *Fax:* 505-665-4955

BUTLER, GORDON CECIL, biochemistry, for more information see previous edition

BUTLER, HARRY, embryology, for more information see previous edition

BUTLER, HERBERT I, PHYSICS, ELECTRICAL ENINEERING. *Current Pos:* RETIRED. *Personal Data:* b New York, NY, July 24, 14; m 40, Kathleen Sweeney; c Alan C & David E. *Educ:* Monmouth Col, BS, 59, MAT, 76. *Prof Exp:* Chief engr, Bruno Labs, Inc, NY, 38-41; proj & equip develop engr, US Army Signal Res & Develop Labs, 41-54, chief data processing sect, 54-57, mem spec task force, Proj Cyclops, 57-58, Signal Corps tech rep, US Army Satellite Prog, 58-60, Tiros Proj mgr, 60, chief aoc chief projs, Aeronomy & Meteorol Div, Goddard Space Flight Ctr, NASA, 61-65, chief oper satellites off, 66-69, staff asst meteorol planning, 69-72; consult, Herbert Butler-Aerospace, 72- *Concurrent Pos:* Chmn subcomt meteorol satellites, Intdept Comt Appl Meteorol Res, 63- *Mem:* AAAS; Am Inst Aeronaut & Astronaut; sr mem Inst Elec & Electronics Engrs; Planetary Soc; Union Concerned Scientists. *Res:* Development of meteorological satellite systems and radio direction finding equipment. *Mailing Add:* Meadow Lakes No 501-L Hightstown NJ 08520

BUTLER, HOWARD W(ALLACE), MECHANICAL ENGINEERING. *Current Pos:* RETIRED. *Personal Data:* b Cranston, RI, Oct 14, 16; m 41; c 4. *Educ:* Univ RI, BS, 40; Yale Univ, MEng, 52, DEng, 58. *Prof Exp:* Instr mech eng, Univ Conn, 41-44; asst dir res, New Britain Mach Co, 44-47; from asst prof to assoc prof, Univ Conn, 47-57; prof, Rensselaer Polytech Inst, 57-65; prof & chem dept, WVa Univ, 65-78; prof mech eng, Brown Univ, 77. *Concurrent Pos:* Consult, New Britain Mach Co, 47-50, Am Thermos Bottle Co & Raymond Eng Labs, 49, Whiton Mach Co, 51-53, Eastern Indust, Inc, 52-53, Terry Stream Turbine Co, 55 & 58-59, Liberty Mutual Life Ins Co, 61, 66, 69 & 71, Sikorsky Aircraft Div, 63, Kaman Aircraft, 64 & FMC Corp, 68. *Mem:* AAAS; Am Soc Mech Engrs; Am Soc Eng Educ; Sigma Xi. *Res:* Irreversible thermodynamics; turbulence; gas dynamics; underground coal gasification. *Mailing Add:* 3 Quartz Dr Westerly RI 02891

BUTLER, HUGH C, SURGERY, PHYSIOLOGY. *Current Pos:* RETIRED. *Personal Data:* b Helena, Mont, Jan 7, 25; m 48; c 3. *Educ:* Mont State Col, BS, 50; Wash State Univ, DVM, 54, MS, 68; Am Col Vet Surgeons, dipl. *Honors & Awards:* McLean Mem Award. *Prof Exp:* Asst state vet, Livestock Sanit Bd, Mont, 54-55; from instr to assoc prof clin med & surg, Wash State Univ, 55-64, assoc prof physiol & pharmacol, 64-66; head, Dept Surg, Animal Med Ctr, NY, 66-68; prof surg, Kans State Univ, 68-86. *Concurrent Pos:* Vis scientist exp surg, Mayo Clin, 63. *Mem:* Am Vet Med Asn; Am Col Vet Surgeons. *Res:* Experimental surgery with emphasis on cardiovascular orthopedic and tissue transplantation. *Mailing Add:* 290 N Many Lakes Dr Kalispell MT 59901

BUTLER, IAN SYDNEY, INORGANIC CHEMISTRY. *Current Pos:* from asst prof to assoc prof, 66-75, PROF CHEM, McGILL UNIV, 75-, DIR GRAD STUDIES, 85- *Personal Data:* b Newhaven, Eng, Aug 22, 39; m 66; c 4. *Educ:* Bristol Univ, BSc, 61, PhD(inorg chem), 65. *Prof Exp:* Res assoc, Ind Univ, 64-65 & Northwestern Univ, 65-66. *Concurrent Pos:* Co-ed, Can J Spectros, 72-86, sr ed, 86-; vis prof, CNRS Lab Chem Coord, 84 & Univ Montreal, 77. *Mem:* Am Chem Soc; Fel Chem Inst Can; Spectros Soc Can; The Chem Soc; Sigma Xi. *Res:* Synthesis and studies of the physical properties of transition metal organometallic compounds, particularly metal carbonyls; infrared, nuclear magnetic resonance and laser Raman spectroscopy. *Mailing Add:* Dept Chem McGill Univ 801 Sherbrooke St W Montreal PQ H3A 2K6 Can

BUTLER, JACK F, SOLID STATE PHYSICS, ELECTRICAL ENGINEERING. *Current Pos:* PRES, AURORA TECHNOL CORP, 91- *Personal Data:* b El Centro, Calif, July 18, 33; m 59, Colette Guerard; c Jack, Alice, Michael & Patricia. *Educ:* Univ Calif, BS, 59, MS, 60, PhD(elec eng), 63. *Prof Exp:* Assoc elec eng, Univ Calif, 61-62; staff mem solid state physics, Lincoln Lab, Mass Inst Technol, 62-68; staff scientist, Gen Dynamics Pomona Div, 68-71; sr scientist, Arthur D Little, Inc, 71-74; pres, Laser Analytics, Inc, 74-80; pres, Butler Res & Eng, Inc, 80-85, San Diego Semiconductors, Inc, 85-95. *Concurrent Pos:* Chief tech officer, Digirad, 95- *Mem:* Am Phys Soc; Inst Elec & Electronics Engrs; AAAS; Health Physics Soc. *Res:* Applied research in the optical and electronic properties of semiconductors; lead-tin-chalcogenide tunable infrared lasers; photodetectors; nuclear radiation detectors; II-VI compounds. *Mailing Add:* PO Box 1333 Rancho Santa Fe CA 92067

BUTLER, JACKIE DEAN, horticulture; deceased, see previous edition for last biography

BUTLER, JAMES EHRICH, CHEMICAL PHYSICS, DIAMOND CHEMICAL VAPOR DEPOSITION. *Current Pos:* RES CHEMIST, CHEM DIV, US NAVAL RES LAB, 75- *Personal Data:* b Tenafly, NJ, Nov 29, 44; m 69. *Educ:* Mass Inst Technol, BS, 66; Univ Chicago, PhD(chem physics), 72. *Prof Exp:* Fel chem physics, NIH, Univ Chicago, 72-74; res assoc, James Franck Inst, Univ Chicago, 74-75. *Concurrent Pos:* Distinguished lectr, Mech Eng Dept, Univ Minn, 96; Benjamin Meeker vis prof physics & chem, Univ Bristol, 97. *Mem:* Am Phys Soc; Optical Soc Am; Coblentz Soc; Mat Res Soc; Sigma Xi. *Res:* Photochemistry; chemical kinetics; chemical vapor reposition; surface vibrational spectroscopy; diamond film growth; in situ diagnostics. *Mailing Add:* Chem Div Code 6174 Naval Res Lab Washington DC 20375. *E-Mail:* butler@ccf.nrl.navy.mil

BUTLER, JAMES HANSEL, DENTISTRY, PERIODONTICS. *Current Pos:* assoc prof occlusion & chmn dept, 74-81, prof gen dent & chmn dept, 81-88, PROF PERIODONT, SCH DENT, VA COMMONWEALTH UNIV-MED COL VA, 88- *Personal Data:* b Canton, Ohio, Dec 7, 36; m 61, Carol Teegardin; c Catherine J, Matthew T & Sarah A. *Educ:* Denison Univ, BA, 58; Ohio State Univ, DDS, 62; Univ Rochester, MS, 67; Eastman Dent Ctr, Rochester, NY, cert periodont, 67. *Prof Exp:* Assoc prof periodont, assoc mem grad fac & mem hosp staff, Univ Minn, 67-74. *Concurrent Pos:* Consult, US Army, Ft Meade, Md, 75-82, Vet Admin Hosp, Richmond, 75-, J Am Dent Asn, 76-, Asn Am Med Cols, 76-80, J Prosthetics Dent, 78-83 & J Dent Educ, 80-85. *Mem:* Am Dent Asn; Am Acad Periodont; Int Asn Dent Res; Am Asn Dent Schs; fel Int Col Dentists; fel Am Col Dentists. *Res:* Occlusion; mandibular dysfunction; clinical periodontics. *Mailing Add:* Dept Periodont Va Commonwealth Univ Sch Dent 520 N 12th St Richmond VA 23298

BUTLER, JAMES JOHNSON, PATHOLOGY. *Current Pos:* RETIRED. *Personal Data:* b Jackson, Tenn, May 5, 26; m 52; c 2. *Educ:* Univ Mich, MD, 52. *Prof Exp:* Intern, Cincinnati Gen Hosp, Ohio, 52-53; resident path, Univ Iowa & Univ Cincinnati, 53-57; from jr pathologist to assoc pathologist, Armed Forces Inst Path, 57-61; asst pathologist, M D Anderson Hosp & Tumor Inst, Univ Tex, Houston, 59-60 & 62-64, assoc pathologist, 64-74, pathologist, 74-94, prof path, 75-94. *Concurrent Pos:* Mem path panel, Lymphoma Clin Trials. *Mem:* AAAS; AMA; Am Soc Hemat; Int Acad Path. *Res:* Path-physiology of the reticuloendothelial system; cancer research. *Mailing Add:* 10023 Pine Forest Rd Houston TX 77042

BUTLER, JAMES KEITH, HOLOCRINE SECRETION, HISTOTECHNIQUE. *Current Pos:* RETIRED. *Personal Data:* b Temple, Tex, Sept 26, 26; m 49; c 1. *Educ:* Univ Tex, BS, 50, MA, 52, PhD(zool), 61. *Prof Exp:* Asst anat, Med Br, Univ Tex, 52-53, res assoc orthop surg, 53-55; assoc prof cell biol, Univ Tex, Arlington, 60- *Concurrent Pos:* Genetics Found fel, Univ Tex, Austin, 65; vis assoc prof anat, Univ Tex Southwestern Med Sch, Dallas, 67; vis scientist, Harvard Sch Pub Health, 74. *Mem:* AAAS. *Res:* Holocrine secretory mechanisms in invertebrate endocrine and reproductive systems; invention and development of an instrument system for preparing specimens for high resolution light microscopical histochemistry. *Mailing Add:* 1412 Woodbine Ct Arlington TX 76012

BUTLER, JAMES LEE, agricultural engineering, for more information see previous edition

BUTLER, JAMES NEWTON, PHYSICAL CHEMISTRY, ENVIRONMENTAL & MARINE SCIENCES. *Current Pos:* GORDON McKAY PROF APPL CHEM, HARVARD UNIV, 71-, MEM FAC EARTH & PLANETARY SCI, 72- *Personal Data:* b Cleveland, Ohio, Mar 27, 34; m 57, 66, Rosamond Alden Hatch; c Christopher James, Kenneth MacRobert Bee & Alden Garner Bee. *Educ:* Rensselaer Polytech Inst, BSc, 55; Harvard Univ, PhD(chem physics), 59. *Prof Exp:* Fel chem, Harvard Univ, 59; from instr to assoc prof, Univ BC, 59-63; sr scientist chem physics, Tyco Labs, Inc, 63-66, head phys chem dept, 66-71. *Concurrent Pos:* Lectr, Harvard Univ, 70-71, mem comt oceanog, 72-90; trustee, Bermuda Biol Sta, 72-, vpres, 85-86, pres, 86-89; consult various companies & agencies, 68-; mem comt, Petrol Marine Environ, Nat Res Coun-Nat Acad Sci, 73-75,

Environ Decision Making, 75-76 & Petrol Marine Environ, 80-82; NSF fac sci fel, 77; chmn, Comt on Effectiveness of Oil spill Dispersants, Nat Res Coun-Nat Acad Sci, 85-88. *Mem:* Am Soc Limnol & Oceanog; AAAS; Am Chem Soc. *Res:* chemical oceanography, oil pollution; environmental quality. *Mailing Add:* Div Eng & Appl Sci Harvard Univ Pierce Hall Rm 123 29 Oxford St Cambridge MA 02138-4993. *E-Mail:* butler@deas.harvard.edu

BUTLER, JAMES PRESTON, BIOMECHANICS, STEREOLOGY. *Current Pos:* From asst prof to assoc prof, 78-89, ADJ ASSOC PROF BIOMATH, HARVARD UNIV SCH PUB HEALTH, BOSTON 89-; SR SCIENTIST, BIOMECH INST, BOSTON, 89- *Personal Data:* b Boston, Mass, Aug 19, 45; m 73; c 2. *Educ:* Pomona Col, BA, 67; Harvard Univ, MA, 68, PhD(physics), 74. *Concurrent Pos:* Henry Luce Found scholar, 74. *Mem:* Math Asn Am. *Res:* Biomechanics of airflow in mammalian and avian lungs; light scattering; stereology; intracellular magnetometry; applied mathematics; endocrinology. *Mailing Add:* Harvard Sch Pub Health 665 Huntington Boston MA 02115

BUTLER, JAMES ROBERT, geology, petrology; deceased, see previous edition for last biography

BUTLER, JERRY FRANK, VETERINARY ENTOMOLOGY, MEDICAL ENTOMOLOGY. *Current Pos:* asst prof, 68-74, assoc prof, 74-79, PROF ENTOM, UNIV FLA, 79- *Personal Data:* b Lingle, Wyo, Apr 17, 38; m 61, Marilyn Kay Shoemaker; c Kelly Elane & Scott Allen. *Educ:* Univ Wyo, BS, 62, MS, 64; Cornell Univ, PhD(entom), 68. *Prof Exp:* Res asst entom, Univ Wyo, 62-64; res asst, Cornell Univ, 64-68, res technician, 68. *Mem:* Entom Soc Am; Acarology Soc Am; Soc Vector Ecol Am. *Res:* Bionomics and control of arthropods of veterinary importance; special interest in population dynamics of ectoparasites and host parasite interaction; granted 63 US and foreign patents. *Mailing Add:* Dept Entom & Nematol Univ Fla 1 Melab Bldg 970 Gainesville FL 32611. *Fax:* 352-392-0190; *E-Mail:* jfb@gnv.ifas.ufl.edu

BUTLER, JOHN BEN, JR, MATHEMATICS. *Current Pos:* assoc prof, 61-65, PROF MATH, PORTLAND STATE UNIV, 66- *Personal Data:* b New York, NY, Aug 26, 23; m 46; c 2. *Educ:* Swarthmore Col, BS, 45; NY Univ, MS, 47; Univ Calif, PhD, 54. *Honors & Awards:* Fulbright lectr, Robert Col, Istanbul, 65. *Prof Exp:* Instr math, Univ Calif, 55-56; asst prof, Univ Wash, 57-59 & Univ Ariz, 59-60. *Concurrent Pos:* AID prof, Middle East Tech Univ, Ankara, 69-70. *Mem:* Soc Indust & Appl Math; Am Math Soc. *Res:* Abstract analysis; differential equations. *Mailing Add:* 6815 SW 14th Ave Portland OR 97219-2019

BUTLER, JOHN C, INTERNET, MINERALOGY. *Current Pos:* from asst prof to assoc prof, Univ Houston, 68-80, chmn dept, 85-88, assoc dean, 88-91, PROF GEOL, UNIV HOUSTON, 80-, DEAN, 92- *Personal Data:* b Port Clinton, Ohio, Oct 31, 41; m 91; c John, Jill, Jennifer, Neal, Michael & Aaron. *Educ:* Miami Univ, BA, 63, MS, 65; Ohio State Univ, PhD(mineral), 68. *Prof Exp:* Instr geol, Miami Univ, 66-68. *Mem:* Mineral Soc Am. *Res:* Structural states of alkali feldspars; mineralogy of contact metamorphosed marbles; size analysis of lunar regolith. *Mailing Add:* Dept Geol Univ Houston Houston TX 77204-0001. *E-Mail:* jbutler@uh.edu

BUTLER, JOHN EARL, botany; deceased, see previous edition for last biography

BUTLER, JOHN EDWARD, IMMUNOLOGY & BIOCHEMISTRY. *Current Pos:* from asst prof to assoc prof, 71-80, dir, Iowa Biotechnol Training Prog, 84-90, PROF MICROBIOL, UNIV IOWA, 80- *Personal Data:* b Rice Lake, Wis, Jan 10, 38; div; c Kirsten D. *Educ:* Univ Wis-River Falls, BS, 61; Univ Kans, PhD(zool), 66. *Prof Exp:* Actg asst prof zool, Univ Kans, 65-66, res assoc immunobiol, 66-67; res biologist, Agr Res Serv, USDA, 67-71. *Concurrent Pos:* USPHS fel & NSF fel, 64-66; vis prof, Max Planck Inst, WGer, 73-74; Fogarty Int Sr fel, WGer, 82-83. *Mem:* Am Asn Immunologists; NY Acad Sci. *Res:* Enzyme-linked immunosorbent assay; immunochemistry; maternal-neonatal immune regulation; immunoglobulin genes and antibody repertoire development. *Mailing Add:* Dept Microbiol Univ Iowa Sch Med Iowa City IA 52241. *Fax:* 319-335-9006; *E-Mail:* jebutler@blue.weeg.uiowa.edu

BUTLER, JOHN F(RANCIS), PHYSICAL METALLURGY. *Current Pos:* DIR, PROD DEVELOP, LTV STEEL CORP, 84- *Personal Data:* b McKeesport, Pa, June 26, 32; m 61; c 4. *Educ:* Carnegie Inst Technol, BS, 54, MS, 57, PhD(metall eng), 58. *Prof Exp:* Sr res engr, Jones & Laughlin Steel Corp, 58-63, res assoc phys metall & vacuum coating, 63-69, res supvr vacuum vapor coating, 69-72, res supvr alloy design, 72-73, dir, Prod Metall, Graham Res Lab, 73-84. *Concurrent Pos:* Vis scientist, Fr Iron & Steel Res Inst, 62-63; instr, Carnegie Inst Technol, 63-64. *Mem:* Am Soc Metals; Am Inst Mining Metall & Petrol Engrs; Soc Automotive Engrs. *Res:* Ferrous physical metallurgical research in the areas of yielding, strain aging and quench aging; development work in vacuum metallic, inorganic and organic coating of continuous sheet material; alloy design of high strength and corrosion resistant steels; management of steel product research and development programs. *Mailing Add:* LTV Steel Technol Ctr 6801 Brecksville Rd Independence OH 44131

BUTLER, JOHN JOSEPH, HEMATOLOGY, MEDICAL ONCOLOGY. *Current Pos:* ASSOC CLIN PROF MED, NYU MED SCH, 74- *Personal Data:* b Rochester, NY, Oct 18, 20; m 48; c 5. *Educ:* Univ Toronto, BA, 42; Univ Rochester, MD, 44; Am Bd Internal Med, dipl, 51, dipl hemat, 76, dipl med oncol, 81. *Prof Exp:* From instr to asst prof med, Georgetown Univ, 52-59; assoc prof, Seton Hall Col Med & Dent, 59-66; CHIEF HEMAT, CATH MED CTR BROOKLYN & QUEENS, 66- *Mem:* Am Col Physicians; Am Fedn Clin Res; Am Soc Hemat; Int Soc Hemat; Am Soc Clin Oncol. *Res:* Red and white cell metabolism. *Mailing Add:* 152-11 89th Ave Jamaica NY 11432

BUTLER, JOHN LOUIS, PHYSICS. *Current Pos:* PRES, IMAGE ACOUST, INC, 75- *Personal Data:* b Brockton, Mass, Aug 23, 34; m 59; c 5. *Educ:* Northeastern Univ, BS, 57, PhD(acoust), 67; Brown Univ, ScM, 62. *Prof Exp:* Res engr, Melpar Inc, 61-62; sr engr, Harris ASW Div, Gen Instrument Corp, 62-66; res assoc physics & acoust, Parke Math Labs, Inc, 66-70; develop engr acoust, Massa Div Dynamics Corp of Am, 70-72; sr engr, Raytheon Co, Submarine Signal Div, 72-75. *Concurrent Pos:* Lectr, Northeastern Univ, 68, 70, 73 & 75. *Mem:* Fel Acoust Soc Am; Audio Eng Soc. *Res:* Acoustical radiation from underwater sound sources and arrays; acoustic transducers and arrays. *Mailing Add:* Image Acoust Inc 97 Elm St Cohasset MA 02025

BUTLER, JON TERRY, DIGITAL LOGIC DESIGN, SYSTEM DIAGNOSIS. *Current Pos:* PROF COMPUT ENG, NAVAL POSTGRAD SCH, 87- *Personal Data:* b Baltimore, Md, Dec 26, 43; m 68; c 1. *Educ:* Rensselaer Polytech Inst, BEE, 66, MEng, 67; Ohio State Univ, PhD(elec eng), 73. *Honors & Awards:* Meritorious Serv, Inst Elec & Electronics Engrs, Comput Soc, 88 & 92, TAB Pioneer Award, 89. *Prof Exp:* USAF capt, Comput Eng, Air Force Avionics Lab, Wright-Patterson AFB, Ohio, 67-70, Nat Res Coun postdoctoral, 73-74; assoc prof, Northwestern Univ, Evanston, 74-87. *Concurrent Pos:* Chmn, Mult-Valued Logic Tech Comt, Inst Elec & Electronics Engrs, Comput Soc, 80-81, mem, distinguished vis, 82-85, vchair, Tech Activ Bd, 87-88, chmn, Mag Adv Comt, 90-91; ed, Inst Elec & Electronics Engrs Trans Comput, 82-86, ed-in-chief, Comput, 91-; Navalex chair prof, Naval Postgrad Sch, 85-87; prin investr, NSF, USN, USAF, NATO & Sigma Xi. *Mem:* Fel Inst Elec & Electronics Engrs; Inst Elec & Electronics Engrs Comput Soc. *Res:* Computer hardware; multiple-valued logic and reliable computing; development of the first multiple-valued programmable logic array, the first computer-aided design tool for multiple-valued logic, and discovery of a flaw in almost all commercially available programmable logic arrays; reliable multiprocessing systems; binary logic design; cellular automata; analysis of computer programs. *Mailing Add:* Dept Elec & Comput Eng Naval Postgrad Sch Code EC/BU Monterey CA 93943

BUTLER, KARL DOUGLAS, SR, AGRICULTURE. *Current Pos:* BUS & AGR CONSULT, 67- *Personal Data:* b Douglas, Ariz, Feb 4, 10; m; c 5. *Educ:* Univ Ariz, BS, 31, MS, 33; Cornell Univ, PhD(plant sci), 40. *Honors & Awards:* Am Meat Inst Award, 63. *Prof Exp:* Asst plant path, Iowa State Col, 33-34; jr forest pathologist, Div Forest Path, USDA, 34; res asst & instr plant path, Univ Ariz, 34-36, asst plant pathologist, 37-40; agt rubber dis invests, Bur Plant Indust, USDA, 40-43, dir res agr chem, Coop Grange League Fedn Exchange, Inc, 43-45, dir educ & res, 45-47; pres, Am Inst Coop, Washington, DC, 47-50; farm counr, 50-67. *Concurrent Pos:* Mem, Am Rubber Surv, Bolivia & Brazil, 40-41; exec secy, Nat Inst Animal Agr, Purdue Univ, 49-59; columnist & consult, Syracuse Post Stand, 51-; pres, Comn Increased Industs Use Agr Prods, 56-57; USDA farm mech exchange deleg to USSR, 58; agr specialist, Peace Corps, Latin Am Countries, 63-64, US AID, Taiwan & India, 64 & WAfrican Studies for Afro-Am Labor Ctr, New York, 66; chmn exec comt & mem res comt, Chemurgic Coun; mem farmers exchange progs, Italy, India, Ireland & Latin Am; consult to Chief of Staff, USAF. *Mem:* Fel AAAS; Am Inst Animal Agr (secy); Am Soc Agr Engrs. *Res:* Farmer cooperatives; diseases of cotton, dates, lettuce, trees, cereal crops and watermelons. *Mailing Add:* 1583 E Shore Dr Ithaca NY 14850

BUTLER, KATHARINE GORRELL, SPEECH & LANGUAGE PATHOLOGY. *Current Pos:* dir Div Spec Educ & Rehab, 79-83, DIR CTR RES, SYRACUSE UNIV, 83- *Personal Data:* b Chicago Heights, Ill, March 15, 25; m 44; c 3. *Educ:* Western Mich Univ, BA, 50, MA, 53; Mich State Univ, PhD(speech & hearing sci), 67. *Prof Exp:* Asst prof psychol, Western Mich Univ, 61-64; asst prof speech path & audiol, San Jose State Univ, 64-68, assoc prof, 68-69, chmn, Dept Spec Educ, 69-74, prof & dir, Speech & Hearing Ctr, 69-77, assoc dean grad studies & res, 75-77, actg dean, 77-79. *Concurrent Pos:* Ed, Topics Lang Dis, 79-; chair, Joint Nat Comt Learning Disabilities, 81. *Mem:* Fel Am Speech-Lang-Hearing Asn (pres, 77-78); Am Psychol Asn; Int Asn Logopedics & Phoniatrics (pres, 83-86, 86-89); Nat Asn Hearing & Speech Action (pres, 79-87). *Res:* Language processing of children and adults suffering from language disorders, including children 3 to 6 who exhibit semantic processing disorders. *Mailing Add:* Commun Sci & Disorders Syracuse Univ 200 Hoople Blvd Syracuse NY 13244

BUTLER, KEITH WINSTON, BIOPHYSICS. *Current Pos:* SCI EVALUATOR, HEALTH CAN, 94- *Personal Data:* b St Boniface, Man, Apr 12, 41; m 66, Cynthia Klopp; c Katherine Ellen & Samuel Leonard. *Educ:* Univ Toronto, BSA, 63; Duke Univ, PhD(physiol), 68. *Prof Exp:* Univ fel, Aarhus Univ, 68-69; Nat Res Coun Can fel, 69-71, vis scientist, 71-72, asst res officer biophys, 72-77, asst res officer, 77-86, sr res officer, Nat Res Coun Can, 86-93. *Res:* Electron spin resonance and nuclear magnetic resonance studies of metabolism. *Mailing Add:* 43 Dunuegan Ottawa ON K1K 3G1 Can

BUTLER, LARRY G, international agriculture, chemical ecology; deceased, see previous edition for last biography

BUTLER, LEWIS CLARK, MATHEMATICS. *Current Pos:* instr math, 47-49, dean grad sch, 63-89, EMER PROF & DEAN, ALFRED UNIV, 89- *Personal Data:* b Hornell, NY, July 11, 23; m 48; c 4. *Educ:* Alfred Univ, BA, 44; Rutgers Univ, MS, 48; Univ Ill, PhD(math), 57. *Prof Exp:* Asst, Univ Ill, 49-54; instr, Pa State Univ, 54-57; from asst prof to assoc prof, Col Ceramics, State Univ NY, Alfred Univ, 57-62. *Concurrent Pos:* Dir, Cent Inst Math, Concepcion Univ, 61-63. *Mem:* Am Math Soc. *Res:* Algebraic topology; fiber spaces. *Mailing Add:* Eight Terrace St Alfred NY 14802

BUTLER, LILLIAN CATHERINE, interrelationship of vitamins & hormones, endocrinology; deceased, see previous edition for last biography

BUTLER, LILLIAN IDA, ANALYTICAL CHEMISTRY, BIOLOGICAL CHEMISTRY. *Current Pos:* RETIRED. *Personal Data:* b Saginaw, Mich, Jan 31, 10. *Educ:* Univ Mich, BS, 29, MS, 30. *Prof Exp:* Asst chem, Mich State Col, 30-42; assoc human nutrit & home econ, USDA, 42-43, chemist, 43-47, Div Bee Cult, 47-51, pesticides chem res, 51-53, asst head chemist, 53-58, actg in charge, 57-68, res chemist & asst head, 58-81. *Concurrent Pos:* Mem, Gov Status of Women Comn, Wash, 63-65; collabr, USDA, Agr Res Serv. *Mem:* Fel AAAS; Am Chem Soc; fel Am Inst Chem; Entom Soc Am. *Res:* Analytical methods, primarily in foods and crops; inorganic minerals; vitamins; insecticides; antibiotics and virus; development of methods; use of attractants of insects in monitoring of flights in field for insect control; isolation of sex attractants from insects. *Mailing Add:* 2804 W Arlington Yakima WA 98902-4050

BUTLER, LINDA, ENTOMOLOGY. *Current Pos:* From asst prof to assoc prof, 68-75, PROF ENTOM, WVA UNIV, 75- *Personal Data:* b Martin, Tenn, Nov 11, 43. *Educ:* Univ Ga, BS, 65, MS, 66, PhD(entom), 68. *Honors & Awards:* J Everett Bussart Mem Award, Entom Soc Am, 74. *Mem:* AAAS; Entom Soc Am; Lepidopterists Soc. *Res:* Insect pest management; lepidoptera; forest entomology; nontarget impact of gypsy moth defoliation, impact of bacillus thuringiensis and dimilin. *Mailing Add:* Dept Plant Sci Box 6108 WVa Univ Morgantown WV 26506-6108. *Fax:* 304-293-2960; *E-Mail:* lbutler@wvu.edu

BUTLER, LOUIS PETER, RADAR SYSTEMS DESIGN, ELECTRONIC WARFARE SOFTWARE SYSTEMS DESIGN. *Current Pos:* STAFF, NORTHROP GRUMMAN ESSD, 96- *Personal Data:* b Baltimore, Md, Oct 9, 53; m 77, Betty A Cave; c William J. *Educ:* Univ Md, College Park, BS, 75; George Washington Univ, MS, 81. *Prof Exp:* Apprentice engr, ILSD, Westinghouse Elec, 74, engr, 75-88, supvry engr, ESG-BWI, 88-93, fel engr, 93-96. *Concurrent Pos:* Consult, Onal's Agency, 81-88. *Mem:* Am Inst Aeronaut & Astronaut; Asn Old Crows. *Res:* Software systems and public safety systems with a transition of these software systems into defense and commercial venues for application and production utilization in national and international programs. *Mailing Add:* PO Box 746 MS 432 Baltimore MD 21203-0746

BUTLER, MARGARET K, MATHEMATICS. *Current Pos:* dir, 60-92, SR COMPUT SCIENTIST, NAT ENERGY SOFTWARE CTR, 80-; SPEC APPOINTEE, ARGONNE NAT LAB, 93- *Personal Data:* b Evansville, Ind, Mar 7, 24; m 51, James W; c Jay. *Educ:* Ind Univ, AB, 44. *Honors & Awards:* Spec Award, Math & Comput Div, Am Nuclear Soc, 92. *Prof Exp:* Statistician, US Bur Labor Statist, 45-46 & US Air Forces in Europe, 46-48; mathematician, Argonne Nat Lab, 48-49; statistician, US Bur Labor Statist, 49-51; mathematician, Argonne Nat Lab, 51-80, dir, Nat Energy Software Ctr, 60-93, sr comput scientist, 80-93. *Concurrent Pos:* Consult, AMF Corp, 56-57, Orgn Econ Coop & Develop, 64, Poole Bros, 67, ed, Comput Physics Comm, 69-80; adv comt comput info systs, Col DuPage, 87-; chair, Prog Comt Nat Comput Conf, 87; indust adv bd comput sci, Bradley Univ. *Mem:* Fel Am Nuclear Soc; Asn Comput Mach; AAAS; Asn Women Sci. *Res:* Information systems; computer program interchange; computer system performance; documentation standards; scientific and engineering computer applications; image processing. *Mailing Add:* PO Box 277 Lemont IL 60439. *Fax:* 630-252-5230; *E-Mail:* mkbutler@anl.gov

BUTLER, MICHAEL ALFRED, SOLID STATE PHYSICS. *Current Pos:* MEM TECH STAFF, SANDIA LABS, 75- *Personal Data:* b Chesterfield, Eng, Nov 24, 43; m 66; c 2. *Educ:* Rensselaer Polytech Inst, BS, 64; Univ Calif, Santa Barbara, MA, 66, PhD(physics), 69. *Prof Exp:* Res fel, Univ Calif, Santa Barbara, 69-70; mem tech staff, Bell Tel Labs, Inc, NJ, 70-75. *Mem:* Am Phys Soc; Electrochem Soc. *Res:* Development of new sensor technology based on the interaction of light with matter. *Mailing Add:* Div 1315 Sandia Nat Labs Albuquerque NM 87185. *Fax:* 505-844-1198

BUTLER, OGBOURNE DUKE, JR, MEATS RESEARCH, DIET-HEALTH ISSUE. *Current Pos:* RETIRED. *Personal Data:* b Orange, Tex, Sept 29, 18; m 43; c 3. *Educ:* Agr & Mech Col Tex, BS, 39, MS, 47; Mich State Univ, PhD(animal husb), 53. *Prof Exp:* From instr to assoc prof, Tex A&M Univ, 47-57, prof animal sci & head dept, 57-78, assoc vpres agr & renewable resources, 78-80, assoc dep chancellor agr, 80-86. *Concurrent Pos:* Tech adv, Am Nat Cattlemen's Asn, 61; mem, Coun Agr Sci & Technol, pres, 80. *Mem:* Fel Am Soc Animal Sci (pres, 71); Am Inst Food Technologists; Am Meat Sci Asn; Am Dairy Sci Asn. *Res:* Meats; microbiology; biochemistry; statistics; nutrition and its effects on the diet-health issue. *Mailing Add:* 700 Thomas St College Station TX 77840

BUTLER, PHILIP ALAN, MARINE BIOLOGY. *Current Pos:* RETIRED. *Personal Data:* b Upper Montclair, NJ, May 15, 14; m 41; c 2. *Educ:* Northwestern Univ, BS, 35, PhD(zool), 40. *Prof Exp:* Fishery res biologist, US Fish & Wildlife Serv, 46-58, dir biol lab, 58-68, res consult, 68-70; res consult, Environ Protection Agency, 71-79. *Mem:* AAAS; Am Soc Limnol & Oceanog; Nat Shellfisheries Asn (secy-treas, 57-59, vpres, 59-61, pres, 61-63); Am Fisheries Soc. *Res:* Biology and economics of shellfish; effects of pesticides in estuaries. *Mailing Add:* 106 Matamoros Dr Gulf Breeze FL 32561

BUTLER, R(OGER) M(OORE), CHEMICAL ENGINEERING & HEAVY OIL RECOVERY. *Current Pos:* endowed chmn petrol eng, 83-96, EMER PROF CHEM ENG, UNIV CALGARY, 96-; PRES, GRAVDRAIN INC, CALGARY, 95- *Personal Data:* b London, Eng, Oct 14, 27; m 54, C Joyce Allen; c Allen, Peter & Mary (Douglas). *Educ:* Univ London, BSc, 48, PhD(eng), 51, DIC, 51. *Honors & Awards:* R S Jane Award, Can Soc Chem Eng, 87; Distinguished lectr, Soc Petrol Engrs, 87-88. *Prof Exp:* Asst prof chem eng, Queen's Univ, Ont, 51-55; res chemist, Imp Oil Enterprises, Ltd, 55-64, sr res chemist, New Proj, 64-68, res adv, 68-69, asst to refinery mgr, 69-70, mgr bus & tech serv, Sarnia Refinery, 70-71; planning adv, Exxon Corp, 71-73; new technol mgr, Logistics Dept, Imp Oil Enterprises, Ltd, 73-74, sci adv, New Energy Resources Dept, Imp Oil Ltd, 74-75; mgr, heavy crude recovery res, Esso Resources Can, 75-82 & dir tech progs, Alta Oil Sands Technol Res Authority, 82-83. *Mem:* Fel Inst Chem Engrs UK; fel Chem Inst Can; fel Am Inst Chem Engrs; Sigma Xi; Soc Petrol Engrs; fel Can Inst Mining & Metall. *Res:* In-situ recovery of heavy crudes. *Mailing Add:* 7 Bayview Dr SW Calgary AB T2V 3N7 Can. *Fax:* 403-238-1985

BUTLER, RICHARD GORDON, ANIMAL PHYSIOLOGY. *Current Pos:* asst prof, 74-80, ASSOC PROF ANAT, MCMASTER UNIV, 80- *Personal Data:* b Toronto, Can, Mar 17, 43. *Educ:* Univ Toronto, BSc, 65, MSc, 68; Australian Nat Univ, PhD(neurobiol), 72. *Prof Exp:* Fel physiol, Oxford Univ, 72-74. *Mem:* Can Asn Anatomists; Am Asn Anatomists; Can Phyisol Soc; Soc Neurosci. *Res:* Competitive reinnervation of mammalian muscle spindles following injury, by appropriate and inappropriate fusimotor neurones; development of muscle spindles in fetal and neonatal animals. *Mailing Add:* Dept Biomed Sci 1R1 McMaster Univ 1200 Main St W Hamilton ON L8N 3Z5 Can

BUTLER, ROBERT ALLAN, PSYCHOACOUSTICS. *Current Pos:* res assoc biopsychol, Univ Chicago, 57-65, assoc prof surg & psychol, 65-72, prof, 72-, chmn, Dept Behav Sci, 79-82, actg chmn, Sect Otolaryngol, 83-84, EMER PROF SURG & BEHAV SCI, UNIV CHICAGO. *Personal Data:* b Pittsfield, Mass, Mar 29, 23; m 52; c 4. *Educ:* Univ Fla, BA, 47; Univ Chicago, PhD(psychol), 51. *Prof Exp:* Instr psychol, Univ Wis, 51-53; res psychologist, Walter Reed Army Hosp, 53-57. *Concurrent Pos:* Div fel, Univ Chicago, 92- *Mem:* Am Otol Soc; fel Acoustical Soc Am; Asn Res Otolaryngol (pres, 75-76). *Res:* Psychophysics of hearing. *Mailing Add:* 5542 Kimbark Ave Chicago IL 60637

BUTLER, ROBERT FRANKLIN, PALEOMAGNETISM. *Current Pos:* from asst prof to assoc prof, 74-83, PROF GEOPHYS, UNIV ARIZ, 83- *Personal Data:* b Eugene, Ore, July 6, 46; m 67; c 1. *Educ:* Ore State Univ, BS, 68; Stanford Univ, MS, 70, PhD(geophys), 72. *Prof Exp:* Fel geophys, Univ Minn, Minneapolis, 72-74. *Concurrent Pos:* Assoc ed, J Geophys Res, 78-81, Geol Soc Am Bull, 90-92. *Mem:* Am Geophys Union; AAAS; Geol Soc Am. *Res:* Paleomagnetic polarity stratigraphy of Cretaceous-lower Tertiary deposits; Mesozoic and Cenozoic apparent polar wander, plate tectonics and microplate tectonics. *Mailing Add:* Dept Geosci Gould Simpson Bldg Univ Ariz Tucson AZ 85721-0001

BUTLER, ROBERT NEIL, GERONTOLOGY, PSYCHIATRY. *Current Pos:* CHMN, BROOK DALES LONGEVITY CTR, 95- *Personal Data:* b New York, NY, Jan 21, 27; m 50, 75, Myrna Lewis; c Christine, Cynthia, Carole & Alexander. *Educ:* Columbia Univ, BA, 49, MD, 53. *Hon Degrees:* DSc, Univ Southern Calif & Univ Gothenberg, Sweden, 81. *Honors & Awards:* Pulitzer Prize, 76; Leo Laks Award, 76; Sander Award, 93. *Prof Exp:* Intern med, St Luke's Hosp, NY, 53-54; resident psychiat, Univ Calif, 54-55; res psychiatrist, NIMH, 55-62; clin prof, Sch Med, George Washington Univ, 62-82; Brookdale prof geriat & adult development & chmn dept, Mt Sinai Med Ctr, NY, 82-95. *Concurrent Pos:* Resident psychiat, NIMH, Chestnut Lodge, Md, 57-58, clin adminr psychother aged, 58-59, consult, 59-68; lectr, Washington Psychoanal Inst, 62-76; res psychiatrist, Washington Sch Psychiat, 62-; consult, St Elizabeth's Hosp, Washington, DC, 64-76, US Senate Comt Aging, 71-76 & NIMH; chmn, Adv Comt Aging, Washington, DC; mem bd, Nat Coun Aging; chmn, Comt Aging, Group Advan Psychiat; dir, Nat Inst Aging, NIH, 76-82. *Mem:* Inst Med-Nat Acad Sci; fel Am Psychiat Asn; fel Am Geriat Soc; Geront Soc. *Res:* Psychotherapy theory and technique; nature of health and disorder in the aged; aging; methods in psychiatry; creativity; Alzheimers disease; social policy. *Mailing Add:* Interut Longevity Ctr NY Acad Med 1216 Fifth Ave Suite 552 New York NY 10029

BUTLER, RONALD GEORGE, AVIAN ECOLOGY, VERTEBRATE BEHAVIORAL ECOLOGY. *Current Pos:* ASSOC PROF ANIMAL ECOL, DEPT BIOL, UNIV MAINE, FARMINGTON, 86- *Personal Data:* b Oswego, NY, Feb 21, 51. *Educ:* State Univ NY, Oswego, BA, 73; Syracuse Univ & State Univ NY, Syracuse, PhD(zool), 78. *Prof Exp:* Res assoc behav ecol, State Univ NY Res Found, 77-78; assoc res scientist ecol & toxicol, Mt Desert Island Biol Lab, Maine, 77-81; asst prof, 81-85, assoc prof animal ecol, Dept Biol, Duquesne Univ, 85-86. *Concurrent Pos:* Vis scientist, Polish Acad Sci, Antarctica, 80-81; res fel, Mem Univ, St John's, Nfld, 83-84. *Mem:* Am Ornithologists Union; Animal Behav Soc; Cooper Ornith Soc; Sigma Xi;

Wilson Ornith Soc. *Res:* Ecology of marine birds; evolution and ecology of vertebrate behavior; effects of environmental pollutants on animal populations. *Mailing Add:* Dept Math & Sci Univ Maine 86 Main St Farmington ME 04938-1991

BUTLER, THOMAS ARTHUR, CHEMISTRY. *Current Pos:* SUPT, OAK RIDGE NAT LAB, 51- *Personal Data:* b Farmington, Ark, May 14, 19; m 45, 53; c 3. *Educ:* Southwest Mo State Col, AB, 41; Iowa State Col, MS, 51. *Prof Exp:* Asst chem, Iowa State Col, 41-42, jr res chemist, 42-51. *Mem:* Am Chem Soc. *Res:* Preparation of uranium compounds; separation of rare earth elements; radioisotope research and development. *Mailing Add:* 119 Dana Dr Oak Ridge TN 37830-7728

BUTLER, THOMAS DANIEL, FLUID DYNAMICS. *Current Pos:* Staff mem group T-3, Los Alamos Nat Lab, 60-72, assoc group leader T-3, 72-73, alt group leader T-3, 73-79, group leader T-3 Fluid Dynamics, 80-84, DEP GROUP LEADER T-3, LOS ALAMOS NAT LAB, 85- *Personal Data:* b Oklahoma City, Okla, Apr 19, 38; m 58; c 3. *Educ:* NMex Inst Mining & Technol, BS, 60; Univ NMex, MS, 64. *Concurrent Pos:* Consult, Battelle Columbus Labs, Durham Opers Off, 75-80. *Mem:* Inst Liquid Atomization & Spray Systs N & SAm. *Res:* Development of numerical methods to solve a wide variety of multidimensional, transient fluid dynamics problems; emphasis in spray combustion and multi-phase flows. *Mailing Add:* Theoret Div Los Alamos Nat Lab Mail Stop B 216 Group T-3 Los Alamos NM 87545

BUTLER, THOMAS MICHAEL, PHYSIOLOGY, BIOCHEMISTRY. *Current Pos:* asst prof, 76-81, ASSOC PROF PHYSIOL, THOMAS JEFFERSON UNIV, 81- *Personal Data:* b Pittsburgh, Pa, May 17, 48. *Educ:* La Salle Col, BA, 70; Univ Pa, PhD(molecular biol), 74. *Prof Exp:* Fel, Univ Pa, 74-76. *Mem:* Am Physiol Soc; Biophys Soc. *Res:* Muscle energetics. *Mailing Add:* Dept Physiol Rm 425 Thomas Jefferson Univ 1020 Locust St Philadelphia PA 19107-6731. *Fax:* 215-955-2073

BUTLER, THOMAS W(ESLEY), APPLIED MECHANICS, MATERIALS SCIENCE. *Current Pos:* from asst prof to assoc prof, 68-77, dept chmn, 80-82, PROF MECH ENG, US NAVAL ACAD, 77- *Personal Data:* b Baltimore, Md, Oct 22, 38; m 61; c 2. *Educ:* Johns Hopkins Univ, BES, 61; George Washington Univ, MSE, 65; Brown Univ, PhD(mech, mat), 69. *Prof Exp:* Mech engr, eng mech sect, Nat Bur Stand, 61-65. *Concurrent Pos:* Lectr, Johns Hopkins Univ, 69-; consult mat failures, 70- *Mem:* Am Soc Testing Mat; Am Soc Metals; Sigma Xi. *Res:* Analysis of materials failures; experimental stress analysis and continuum plasticity; fracture mechanics. *Mailing Add:* Dept Mech Eng US Naval Acad 590 Holloway Rd Annapolis MD 21402-5042

BUTLER, VINCENT PAUL, JR, INTERNAL MEDICINE, IMMUNOCHEMISTRY. *Current Pos:* vis fel, Dept Microbiol, 61-63, from asst prof to assoc prof, 63-74, PROF MED, COL PHYSICIANS & SURGEONS, COLUMBIA UNIV, 74-, ATTEND PHYSICIAN, PRESBY HOSP, NEW YORK, 74- *Personal Data:* b Jersey City, NJ, Feb 16, 29. *Educ:* St Peter's Col, AB, 49; Columbia Univ, MD, 54. *Honors & Awards:* Joseph Mather Smith Prize, Col Physicians & Surgeons, Columbia Univ, 73. *Prof Exp:* Intern med, Presby Hosp, New York, 54-55, asst resident, 55-56 & 58-59; asst med & microbiol, Sch Med & Dent, Univ Rochester, 59-60, instr med, 60-61. *Concurrent Pos:* Helen Hay Whitney Found fel, 60-63; vis res fel microbiol, Col Physicians & Surgeons, Columbia Univ, 61-63; asst attend physician, First Med Div, Bellevue Hosp, 63-68; sr investr, Arthritis Found, 63-68; from asst to assoc attend physician, Presby Hosp, New York, 68 74; asst vis physician, Harlem Hosp, 68-88; res career develop award, Nat Heart, Lung & Blood Inst, 68-73; career scientist, Irma T Hirschl Found, 73-78; vis fel, Tumour Immunol Unit, Univ Col London, 79-80; mem, Immunol Sci Study Sect, NIH, 79-83, chmn, 80-83; mem, Res Comt, Arthritis Found, 86-91, Chmn, 89-91, mem bd trustees, 88-90. *Mem:* Asn Am Physicians; Am Asn Immunol; Am Heart Asn; Am Soc Clin Invest; Am Soc Pharmacol & Exp Therapeut; fel AAAS. *Res:* Immunochemical studies of rheumatoid factor; purine specific antibodies and their cross reactions with DNA; digoxin-specific antibodies; immunochemical studies of fibrinogen. *Mailing Add:* Dept Med Columbia Univ Col Phys & Surg New York NY 10032. *Fax:* 212-305-8466; *E-Mail:* butlerv@cpmc3.cls.columbia.edu

BUTLER, WALTER CASSIUS, mathematics; deceased, see previous edition for last biography

BUTLER, WALTER JOHN, electrical engineering, solid state physics, for more information see previous edition

BUTLER, WILLIAM ALBERT, PHYSICS. *Current Pos:* RETIRED. *Personal Data:* b Independence, Kans, Jan 4, 22; m 44, Virginia Ann Christine; c Elizabeth Earlyne (Gaulke), Dorothy Diane (Whalin) & Carol Christine (Vaughan). *Educ:* Univ Kansas City, BA, 42; Univ Ill, MS, 47, PhD(physics), 52. *Prof Exp:* Asst physics, Univ Ill, 46-52; from asst prof to prof, Carleton Col, 52-70; prof & head dept, Eastern Ill Univ, 70-87. *Concurrent Pos:* Vis assoc prof, Univ Calif, Berkeley, 60-61; vis scientist, Univ Ill, 67-68; res assoc, Alliance Save Energy, Washington, DC, 78; vis prof, Nat Kaohsiung Normal Univ, Taiwan, 89-90. *Mem:* Am Phys Soc. *Res:* Nuclear and solid state physics. *Mailing Add:* 13771 E Marina Dr Unit B Aurora CO 80014

BUTLER, WILLIAM BARKLEY, BREAST CANCER, STEROID HORMONES. *Current Pos:* PROF, BIOL DEPT, INDIANA UNIV, PA, 88- *Personal Data:* b Ithaca, NY, Feb 10, 43; m 64, 86, Christine Damon; c Sarah & Amy (Hendry). *Educ:* Miami Univ, BA, 64; Univ Wis-Madison, MS, 68, PhD(biochem), 69. *Prof Exp:* Fel oncol, McArdle Lab Cancer Res, Med Sch, Univ Wis-Madison, 69-74; res scientist biochem, Mich Cancer Found, 74-80; asst mem, Mich Cancer Found, 80-88. *Concurrent Pos:* Asst prof, Dept Biochem, Sch Med, Wayne State Univ, 80-88. *Mem:* Am Asn Cancer Res. *Res:* Mechanisms of steroid hormone action on breast cancer with a special emphasis on the effects of the antiestrogen tamoxifen and retinoic acid on Michigan Cancer Found-Seventh Sample breast cancer cells. *Mailing Add:* Dept Biol Indiana Univ Pa Indiana PA 15705-0001. *Fax:* 412-357-5700

BUTLER, WILLIAM H, SOLID STATE PHYSICS, THEORY OF MATERIALS. *Current Pos:* mgr comput planning, 84-85, MEM RES STAFF, OAK RIDGE NAT LAB, 72-, GROUP LEADER, 85- *Personal Data:* b Tallassee, Ala, Aug 13, 43; m 67, Jamie F; c William S & Susanna F. *Educ:* Univ Calif, San Diego, PhD(physics), 69. *Honors & Awards:* Award for Outstanding Res, Dept Energy. *Prof Exp:* Asst prof physics, Auburn Univ, 69-72. *Mem:* AAAS; fel Am Phys Soc; Mat Res Soc. *Res:* Theory of electronic states in metals and alloys; theory of disordered alloys; electron phonon interaction in transition metals; transport and superconductivity in metals; transport in magnetic multilayers. *Mailing Add:* Metals & Ceramic Div MS 6114 Bldg 45005 Oak Ridge Nat Lab Oak Ridge TN 37831-6114. *Fax:* 423-574-7659; *E-Mail:* bhb@ornd.gov

BUTLER, WILLIAM T, MEDICINE. *Current Pos:* pres, 79-96, CHANCELLOR, BAYLOR COL MED, HOUSTON, TEX, 96- *Personal Data:* b Boston, Mass, Aug 10, 32. *Mem:* Inst Med-Nat Acad Sci. *Mailing Add:* Baylor Col Med One Baylor Plaza Houston TX 77030

BUTLER, WILLIAM THOMAS, biochemistry, for more information see previous edition

BUTMAN, BRYAN TIMOTHY, BIOTECHNOLOGY, IMMUNOCHEMISTRY. *Current Pos:* SR SCIENTIST, BIOTECHNOL RES INST, 85- *Personal Data:* b Massilon, Ohio, May 25, 52; m 74; c 3. *Educ:* Univ Detroit, BS, 74; Wayne State Univ, MS, 77, PhD(biol sci), 81. *Prof Exp:* Scientist, Warner-Lambert Co, 83-85. *Mem:* Am Asn Clin Chem; Am Soc Microbiol; Inst Food Technologists; Am Soc Cell Biol; AAAS. *Res:* Hybridoma; immunoassay development; infectious disease; oncology; development and characterization of monoclonal antibodies with diagnostic significance; antigens as diverse as infectious agents (listeria, chlamydia, human immunodeficiency virus), cancer markers (carcinoembryonic antigen, alpha-fetoprotein), coagulation factors, cardiovascular disease markers and toxins; several monoclonal antibodies have been used for diagnostic immunoassays. *Mailing Add:* Invitro Diag Prod Per Immune 1330A Piccard Dr Rockville MD 20850-4373. *Fax:* 301-840-2161

BUTMAN, CHERYL ANN, BIOLOGICAL-PHYSICAL INTERACTIONS, MARINE BENTHIC ECOLOGY. *Current Pos:* grad res fel, Woods Hole Oceanog Inst, 78-84, fel investr, 84-86, asst scientist, 86-89, ASSOC SCIENTIST, APPL OCEAN PHYSICS & ENG DEPT, WOODS HOLE OCEANOG INST, 89- *Personal Data:* b Albany, Calif, Nov 26, 54; m 84, Bradford; c Dylan C. *Educ:* San Jose State Univ, BA, 76, MA, 80; Mass Inst Technol, PhD(biol oceanog), 84. *Honors & Awards:* Young Investr Award, Office Naval Res, 86; Walter A & Hope Noves Smith, Special Studies Award, Woods Hole Oceanog Inst, 86-87. *Prof Exp:* Invert mus cur, San Jose Univ, 75-76. *Concurrent Pos:* Res asst, Moss Landing Marine Lab, 75; proj coord & grad res asst, Moss Landing Marine Lab, 76-78; teaching asst gen biol, Mass Inst Technol, 79; vis instr & guest fel gen marine ecol, Ezra Stiles Col, Yale Univ, 81; young investr award, Off Naval Res, 86; Walter A & Hope Noves Smith spec studies award, Woods Hole Oceanog Inst, 86-87; mem adv comt Ocean Sci, NSF, 88-92; co-chair comt, Biol Diversity Marine Syst, Nat Res Coun, 93- *Mem:* AAAS; Am Soc Limnol & Oceanog; Am Soc Zoologists; Asn Women Sci; Ecol Soc Am; Oceanog Soc. *Res:* Near-bottom flow regime on organisms that live on or in bottom sediments as adults, especially studies of the planktonic larval stages. *Mailing Add:* Woods Hole Oceanog Inst Woods Hole MA 02543. *Fax:* 508-457-2194; *E-Mail:* cbutman@whoi.edu

BUTOW, RONALD A, BIOCHEMISTRY. *Current Pos:* PROF BIOCHEM, UNIV TEX HEALTH SCI CTR DALLAS, 71- *Personal Data:* b Aug 1, 36; US citizen; m 58, Virginia Edwards; c David. *Educ:* Hobart Col, BS, 58; Cornell Univ, MNS, 60, PhD(biochem), 63. *Prof Exp:* NSF res fel biochem, Pub Health Res Inst New York, 63-65; asst prof, Princeton Univ, 65-71. *Concurrent Pos:* USPHS res grant, 66. *Mem:* AAAS; Am Soc Biol Chemists; Genetics Soc Am. *Res:* Biological electron transport systems; oxidative phosphorylation bioenergetic reactions; structure; function and biogenesis of membranes. *Mailing Add:* Dept Biochem Univ Tex Southwestern Med Ctr 5323 Harry Hines Blvd Dallas TX 72535-9038. *Fax:* 214-648-8537; *E-Mail:* butow@utsw

BUTRUM, RITVA RAUANHEIMO, FOOD SCIENCE. *Current Pos:* ACTG CHIEF, DIET & CANCER BR, DIV CANCER PREV & CONTROL, NAT CANCER INST, NIH, 83- *Personal Data:* b Helsinki, Finland, Oct 30, 27; US citizen; m 55; c 4. *Educ:* Col Home Econ, Univ Helsinki, BS, 51; Univ Calif, Los Angeles, MS, 56; Univ Md, PhD(food sci), 77. *Prof Exp:* Nutritionist, NIH, 66-69 & Fedn Am Soc Exp Biol, 70-73; nutrit analyst, Consumer & Food Econ Inst, USDA, 73-77, res nutritionist, Nutrient Compos Lab, 77-78, assoc prog mgr, Competitive Res Grants Off, 78-83. *Concurrent Pos:* Fulbright scholarship, Univ Calif, Los Angeles, 54-56;

Fulbright lectr grant, Univ Helsinki, Finland, 82. *Mem:* Am Inst Nutrit; Inst Food Technologists; Am Chem Soc; Soc Nutrit Educ; Asn Consumer Res. *Res:* Protein quality; zinc and copper nutrition; folacin methodology and content in foods; food sampling designs for nutrient analysis; data management systems for nutrients and contaminants; nomenclature of foods, parts and processes; diet and cancer; fat and breast cancer; fiber and colon cancer. *Mailing Add:* 4082 Norbeck Sq Rockville MD 20853-1861. *Fax:* 301-460-4083

BUTSCH, ROBERT STEARNS, MAMMALOGY. *Current Pos:* RETIRED. *Personal Data:* b Owatonna, Minn, July 10, 14; m 41, Miriam Palmer; c Elizabeth A (Cardinal). *Educ:* Univ Iowa, BA, 36, MA, 41; Univ Mich, PhD(zool), 54. *Prof Exp:* Cur, Arrowhead Mus, 36-37; chief preparator marine zool, Barbados Mus & Hist Soc, Barbados, BWI, 38-39; asst to dir, Univ Mich, 51-55, assoc cur, 56-64, cur exhibits, 64-74, actg dir, 74-75, dir exhibit mus, 75-85. *Mem:* Am Soc Mammal; Am Asn Mus. *Res:* Ecology of vertebrates; design and construction of natural history exhibits; teaching of museum methods. *Mailing Add:* 1219 S Forest Ann Arbor MI 48104

BUTSON, ALTON THOMAS, MATHEMATICS. *Current Pos:* PROF MATH, UNIV MIAMI, 61- *Personal Data:* b Pa, Feb 18, 26; wid; c 4. *Educ:* Franklin & Marshall Col, BS, 50; Mich State Univ, MS, 51, PhD(math), 55. *Prof Exp:* Asst math, Mich State Univ, 50-54, instr, 54-55; from asst prof to assoc prof, Univ Fla, 55-59; res specialist, Boeing Co, Wash, 59-61. *Mem:* Am Math Soc; Math Asn Am. *Res:* Lattice, group and number theory; combinatorial analysis. *Mailing Add:* 4751 Exeter Estate Lane Lake Worth FL 33467

BUTT, HUGH ROLAND, GASTROENTEROLOGY, NUTRITION. *Current Pos:* RETIRED. *Educ:* Univ Va, MD, 33. *Prof Exp:* Chmn sci adv comt, Lugwid Inst Cancer Res, 79. *Res:* Liver disease. *Mailing Add:* Dept Gastrol Mayo Sch Med Rochester MN 55902

BUTT, JOHN B(AECHER), CHEMICAL ENGINEERING. *Current Pos:* prof chem eng, 70-81, WALTER P MURPHY PROF CHEM ENG, TECHNOL INST, NORTHWESTERN UNIV, 81- *Personal Data:* b Norfolk, Va, Sept 10, 35; m 63, Regina Roche; c 1. *Educ:* Clemson Univ, BChE, 56; Yale Univ, MEng, 58, DEng(chem eng), 60. *Honors & Awards:* Alan P Colburn Award, 68 & Prof Prog Award, 78, Am Inst Chem Engrs; Alexander von Humboldt Sr US Scientist Award, 86. *Prof Exp:* Instr chem eng, Yale Univ, 59-60, from asst prof to assoc prof chem eng & appl sci, 60-70. *Concurrent Pos:* Asst master, Calhoun Col, 60-64; vis prof chem eng, Univ Brussels, 71; assoc ed, Indust & Eng Chem Process Design & Develop, 78-87. *Mem:* AAAS; Am Inst Chem Engrs; Am Chem Soc; Catalysis Soc; Sigma Xi. *Res:* Catalysis and kinetics of chemical reactions; simultaneous mass and heat transport in reacting systems. *Mailing Add:* Dept Chem Eng Northwestern Univ Evanston IL 60201

BUTT, TAUSEEF RASHID, REGULATION OF GENE EXPRESSION, STEROID HORMONE ACTION. *Current Pos:* assoc sr investr, 82-86, sr investr, 86-88, ASST DIR, SMITH KLINE BEECHAM PHARMACEUT, 88- *Personal Data:* b Lahore, Pakistan, Nov 1, 52; US citizen; m 88, Varsha; c Samir & Sabrina. *Educ:* Univ Dundee, Scotland, BSc, 72, MSc, 73; Univ Glasgow, PhD(biochem), 77. *Prof Exp:* Res assoc, Biochem Dept, Georgetown Univ Med Sch, 77-80; staff fel, NIH, 80-82. *Concurrent Pos:* Adj prof, Dept Biochem & Biophys, Univ Pa Med Sch, 88- *Mem:* Am Soc Biochem & Molecular Biol; AAAS; Am Soc Microbiol. *Res:* Study mechanisms of gene transcriptions using human steroid hormone receptors; role of human steroid hormone receptors in pathophysiology; drug discovery programs on injection and immunity; development of methods to overexpress genes in heterologous systems. *Mailing Add:* Gene Transcription Technol Inc PO Box 1752 Southeastern PA 19399-1752. *Fax:* 610-270-5381; *E-Mail:* butt%phvax.dnet@rdpharm.na.sb.com

BUTTAR, HARPAL SINGH, PHARMACOLOGY, TOXICOLOGY. *Current Pos:* RES SCIENTIST & HEAD, REPRODUCTIVE TOXICOL SECT, BUR DRUG RES, HEALTH PROTECTION BR, HEALTH & WELFARE CAN, 71- *Personal Data:* b Nanonkee, India, Nov 2, 39; Can citizen; m 62; c 3. *Educ:* Col Vet Med, India, BVSc, 61; Univ Alta, MSc, 66, PhD(pharmacol), 71. *Prof Exp:* Lectr pharmacol, Col Vet Med, India, 61-64; teaching asst, Univ Alta, 64-70; res fel med, Sch Med, Wayne State Univ, 70-71. *Mem:* NY Acad Sci; Chem Inst Can; Soc Toxicol Can; Soc Toxicol; Teratology Soc; Can Col Neuropsychopharmacol. *Res:* Toxicological assessment of drugs, drug metabolites and cosmetics with reference to their absorption, distribution, biotransformation and excretion as well as drug interactions and embryotoxicity/teratogenicity; author & co-author of 50 scientific publications and three book chapters. *Mailing Add:* Bur Drug Res Health Protection Br Health & Welfare Can Ottawa ON K1A 0L2 Can

BUTTEMER, WILLIAM ASHLEY, PHYSIOLOGICAL ECOLOGY, BIOPHYSICAL ECOLOGY. *Current Pos:* lectr, 86-88, LECTR HUMAN & ANIMAL PHYSIOL, DEPT PHYSIOL, UNIV TASMANIA, 91- *Personal Data:* b San Diego, Calif, Jan 9, 47. *Educ:* San Diego State Univ, AB, 71; Univ Mich, PhD(biol), 81. *Prof Exp:* Postdoctor researcher avian sci, Univ Calif, Davis, 81-83; asst prof comp physiol, Dept Biol, Rutgers Univ, 83-85; lectr avian energetics, Sch Biol Sci, Univ NSW, 85-86; res assoc avian endocrinol, Dept Zool, Univ Wash, 88-91. *Concurrent Pos:* Consult, Orca Seafarms, Inc, 85-; lectr, Dept Zool, Univ Wash, 90-91; vis scholar, Ocean Sci Ctr, Mem Univ Nfld, 91- *Mem:* Sigma Xi; Am Soc Zool; Am Ornith Soc. *Res:* Renal physiology; endocrinology; thermoregulation. *Mailing Add:* Dept Biol sci Univ Wollongong Wollongong NSW 2500 Australia

BUTTER, STEPHEN ALLAN, INORGANIC CHEMISTRY. *Current Pos:* RETIRED. *Personal Data:* b New York, NY, May 15, 37; m 63; c 1. *Educ:* Brooklyn Col, BS, 59; Univ Del, PhD(inorg chem), 65. *Honors & Awards:* Excellence Catalysis Award, Catalysis Soc, 84. *Prof Exp:* Teaching asst, Univ Md, 59-60; chemist, Thiokol Chem Corp, 63; res chemist, Indust & Biochem Dept, E I du Pont de Nemours & Co, 64-66; res fel, Univ Sussex, 66-67; sr res chemist, Mobil Chem Co, 67-76, mem staff, Res Dept, Paulsburo Lab, Mobil Res & Develop Corp, 76-80; prog mgr, US Dept Energy, 80-81; mgr chem res, Corp Res Dept, Air Prod & Chem Inc, 81-86; prog mgr, Div Chem Sci, Off Basic Energy Sci, US Dept Energy, 86-97. *Mem:* AAAS; Catalysis Soc; NY Acad Sci; Am Chem Soc. *Res:* Basic research in chemical sciences: fossil chemistry, synthesis-gas chemistry, homogeneous and heterogeneous catalysis involving transitional metals and zeolites; energy and synthetic fuels; boron chemistry; coordination complexes; zeolites; homogeneous and heterogeneous catalysis. *Mailing Add:* 2 Klakring Ct Annapolis MD 21403

BUTTERFIELD, DAVID ALLAN, BIOPHYSICAL CHEMISTRY. *Current Pos:* from asst prof to assoc prof, 75-83, PROF CHEM, UNIV KY, 83-, DIR, CTR MEMBRANE SCI, 86- *Personal Data:* b Milo, Maine, Jan 14, 46; m 68; c 1. *Educ:* Univ Maine, BA, 68; Duke Univ, PhD(phys chem), 74. *Prof Exp:* Teacher chem high sch, United Methodist Church, Rhodesia, 68-71; NIH fel neurosci, Med Sch, Duke Univ, 74-75. *Concurrent Pos:* Vis scientist, St Jude Children's Res Hosp. *Mem:* Am Chem Soc; Sigma Xi; Biophys Soc; Am Soc Biochem & Molecular Biol. *Res:* Biological applications of electron spin resonance, with particular emphasis on membrane systems; effects of neurotoxins, environmental pollutants and pharmacological agents on membrane structure and function; muscular dystrophy; Huntington's disease; Alzheimer's disease; relationships between skeletal membrane proteins and cell surface carbohydrates; transmembrane signaling; biofunctional membranes. *Mailing Add:* Dept Chem & Ctr Memb Sci Univ Ky Lexington KY 40506-0055. *Fax:* 606-323-1069

BUTTERFIELD, EARLE JAMES, PLANT PATHOLOGY. *Current Pos:* fel, 76-78, ASST PLANT PATHOLOGIST, BOYCE THOMPSON INST, 78- *Personal Data:* b Gilroy, Calif, Feb 11, 49; m 69; c 3. *Educ:* Univ Calif, Davis, BS, 71, PhD(plant path), 75. *Prof Exp:* Fel plant path, Univ Calif, Davis, 75-76. *Mem:* Am Phytopath Soc; Sigma Xi. *Res:* Soil microbiology; epidemiology; chemical control of pathogens. *Mailing Add:* 6123 Farmington Rd Apt G6 Chapel Hill NC 27514

BUTTERFIELD, VELOY HANSEN, JR, COMPUTER SCIENCES. *Current Pos:* SALES MGR, ALTA TECHNOLOGIES, 91- *Personal Data:* b Fillmore, Utah, Sept 24, 42; m 66; c 4. *Educ:* Univ Utah, BSEE, 67, MEA, 73. *Honors & Awards:* Res Award, Kennecott Copper Corp, 74. *Prof Exp:* Electronic engr, Design Div, Mare Island Naval Shipyard, 68-70; assoc scientist, Res Ctr, Kennecott Minerals Co, 70-80, sect head process instrumentation, control & technol, 80-83; prog mgr, Leeds & Northrup Systs, 83-85. *Mem:* Inst Elec & Electronics Engrs; Instrument Soc Am. *Res:* Computer applications; cybernetics; microelectronics applications. *Mailing Add:* 4876 Colony Dr Salt Lake City UT 84117

BUTTERWORTH, BERNARD BERT, ANATOMY. *Current Pos:* from assoc prof to prof anat, Sch Dent, Univ Mo, Kansas City, 64-86, dir admis, 73-80, chmn dept, 75-86, EMER PROF ANAT, SCH DENT, UNIV MO, KANSAS CITY, 90- *Personal Data:* b Woodbine, Iowa, May 2, 23. *Educ:* Univ Mich, BS, 52, MS, 54; Univ Southern Calif, PhD(zool), 60. *Prof Exp:* Asst biol, Univ Southern Calif, 55-58; lectr, Los Angeles State Col, 58-59; asst prof, Univ Wichita, 60-62, Sch Dent, Univ Southern Calif, 62-64 & Univ Ariz, 64. *Concurrent Pos:* Res partic, Inst Trop Biol, Costa Rica, 62. *Mem:* Soc Study Evolution; Ecol Soc Am; Soc Syst Zool; Am Soc Mammal; Am Asn Anatomists. *Res:* Mammalian behavior and reproduction; Heteromyidae; growth and development human, head and neck. *Mailing Add:* 6501 E 55th Terr Kansas City MO 64129

BUTTERWORTH, BYRON EDWIN, GENETIC TOXICOLOGY, VIROLOGY. *Current Pos:* CHIEF GENETIC TOXICOL, CHEM INDUST INST TOXICOL, 77- *Personal Data:* b Salt Lake City, Utah, Dec 9, 41; m 96, Amy R Johnson; c 4. *Educ:* Brigham Young Univ, BS, 68; Univ Wis-Madison, PhD(biochem), 72. *Prof Exp:* Mem res staff virol, E I du Pont de Nemours & Co, 72-75; chief molecular biol, Haskell Lab Toxicol & Indust Med, 75-77. *Concurrent Pos:* Adj assoc prof path, Univ NC, Chapel Hill, 78; adj prof toxicol, Duke Univ, NC. *Mem:* Environ Mutagen Soc; Am Asn Cancer Res; Soc Toxicol; Genotoxicity & Environ Mutagen Soc (pres, 97). *Res:* Mechanism of action of antiviral agents; short-term tests for predicting the mutagenic-carciogenic potential of chemicals; nongenotoxic mechanisms in carcinogenesis; chemical carcinogenesis. *Mailing Add:* Chem Indust Inst Toxicol PO Box 12137 Research Triangle Park NC 27709

BUTTERWORTH, CHARLES E, JR, INTERNAL MEDICINE. *Current Pos:* from instr to assoc prof internal med, 58-66, prof & chmn, Dept Nutrit Sci, 76, PROF INTERNAL MED, SCH MED, UNIV ALA, 66- *Personal Data:* b Lynchburg, Va, Mar 11, 23; m 46; c 3. *Educ:* Univ Va, BA, 44, MD, 48. *Honors & Awards:* Goldberger Award, AMA, 76; McCollum Award, Am Soc Clin Nutrit, 77; Lederle Award, Am Inst Nutrit, 83. *Prof Exp:* Intern, Med Col Ala, 48-49, resident hemat, 49-50, resident internal med, 51-53; mem staff, Trop Res Med Lab, San Juan, PR, 55-57; mem staff, Walter Reed Army Inst Res, Washington, DC, 57-58. *Concurrent Pos:* Consult, NIH, 69- & WHO, 71; mem, Food & Nutrit Bd, Nat Res Coun, Nat Acad Sci, 77-80. *Mem:* Am Fedn Clin Res; Am Clin & Climat Asn; hon mem Am Dietetic Asn; Am Col Physicians; Am Soc Clin Nutrit (pres, 74-75). *Res:* Hematology; nutrition support of hospitalized patients; studies of nutritional anemia; studies on nutrition and the chemoprevention of cancer. *Mailing Add:* Dept Nutrit Sci Univ Ala Sch Med UAB Sta Birmingham AL 35294-3360. *Fax:* 205-934-7049

BUTTERWORTH, FRANCIS M, CELL BIOLOGY, GENOTOXICITY. *Current Pos:* from asst prof to assoc prof, 66-74, PROF GENETICS, OAKLAND UNIV, 74- *Personal Data:* b Philadelphia, Pa, Mar 29, 35; m 61; c 2. *Educ:* Columbia Univ, BA, 57; Northwestern Univ, PhD(genetics), 65. *Prof Exp:* USPHS fel, Univ Va, 65-66. *Concurrent Pos:* Guest prof, Univ Nijmegen, Holland, 73-74; adj prof, Mich State Univ, 79-, Wayne State Univ, 82-88; vis prof, Wayne State Univ, 85; grants from NSF, NIH, Res Corp, Environ Protection Agency. *Mem:* AAAS; Environ Mutagen Soc; Genetics Soc Am; Sigma Xi; Am Soc Cell Biol. *Res:* Genetic, cellular, and molecular control of development, aging, and protein folding; genotoxicity of toxic waste metabolites. *Mailing Add:* Inst River Int 672 Sandstone Dr Rochester MI 48309. *Fax:* 313-370-2286

BUTTERWORTH, GEORGE A M, PHYSICS, MECHANICAL ENGINEERING. *Current Pos:* dir Prod Div & vpres fibers, 91-93, vpres, Mat Technol, 93-95, VPRES, ADVAN TECHNOL, TAMBRANDS, INC, 95- *Personal Data:* b Bramhall, Eng, Sept 3, 35; m 60, Nancy N Towner; c Craig & Neil. *Educ:* Univ Manchester, BSc, 58; Mass Inst Technol, SM, 61. *Honors & Awards:* McKay Mem Award, 57; Distinguished Achievement Award, Fiber Soc, 79. *Prof Exp:* Res assoc, Fabric Res Labs, Inc, Dedham, 60-61, sr res assoc, 61-64, asst dir, 64-69, vpres, 69-72; mgr res & develop, Johnson & Johnson, 72-78; dir prod develop, Am Hosp Supply, 79-82. *Concurrent Pos:* Trustee, Textile Res Inst, Princeton, NJ. *Mem:* AAAS; Fiber Soc (pres, 80-81); fel Brit Textile Inst; Sigma Xi. *Res:* Materials technology and engineering, especially structural and interactive behavior of fibrous, organic and related materials; physical and mechanical properties of high polymers; biomedical materials; tire cord reinforcements and non-woven structures; disposable medical products; fibers and fibrous structures. *Mailing Add:* Tambrands Inc Bridge & Springfield St PO Box 271 Palmer MA 01069. *Fax:* 413-846-3433; *E-Mail:* buttert@tambrands.com

BUTTERWORTH, THOMAS AUSTIN, FOOD ENGINEERING, CHEMICAL ENGINEERING. *Current Pos:* AUSTIN FOOD TECH INC. *Personal Data:* b Los Angeles, Calif, Apr 30, 44; m 68; c 2. *Educ:* Univ Calif, Berkeley, BS, 67; Mass Inst Technol, PhD(biochem eng), 73. *Prof Exp:* Res engr chem eng, Western Regional Res Lab, USDA, 68; assoc dir & res develop, Beatrice/Hunt-Wesson Inc, 73-88. *Mem:* Inst Food Technologists; Am Inst Chem Engrs; AAAS. *Res:* Food engineering topics related to industrial application. *Mailing Add:* 114 Pearl Ave Newport Beach CA 92662

BUTTIKER, MARKUS, theoretical physics, for more information see previous edition

BUTTKE, THOMAS MARTIN, LIPID METABOLISM, MEMBRANE STRUCTURE FUNCTION. *Current Pos:* ASSOC PROF MICROBIOL, E CAROLINA UNIV SCH MED, 86- *Personal Data:* b Bay Shore, NY, Dec 5, 52; m 77; c 2. *Educ:* Univ NC, Wilmington, BA, 74; Univ Fla, MS, 75, PhD(microbiol), 78. *Prof Exp:* Fel chem, Harvard Univ, 78-80; from asst prof to assoc prof microbiol, Med Ctr, Univ Miss, 85-86. *Mem:* Am Asn Immunologists; Am Soc Microbiol; Am Chem Soc; AAAS. *Res:* Lipid metabolism and function, with particular emphasis on the role of lipids in cells associated with the immune system; regulation of membrane lipid composition in yeast. *Mailing Add:* Dept Microbiol & Immunol ECarolina Univ Sch Med Greenville NC 27858. *Fax:* 919-816-3104

BUTTLAIRE, DANIEL HOWARD, BIOCHEMISTRY, BIOPHYSICS. *Current Pos:* from asst prof to prof, 75-83, chmn, Dept Chem, 80-97, ASSOC DEAN SCI & ENG, SAN FRANCISCO STATE UNIV, 97- *Personal Data:* b New York, NY, Sept 5, 41; m 63, Barbara Sosin; c Lori & Roni (Raposo). *Educ:* Univ Denver, BA, 63; Univ Kans, PhD(biochem), 70. *Prof Exp:* Res assoc biochem, Univ Kans, 70-71; res fel biophys, Johnson Res Found, Sch Med, Univ Pa, 71-74. *Concurrent Pos.* USPHS fel, 71-73; Cottrell res grant, Res Corp, 77-79; NASA-Univ Consortium res grant, Ames Res Ctr, 78-79; bridges to future grants, NIH, 92-94 & 93- *Mem:* Am Chem Soc; Sigma Xi; Int Soc Magnetic Resonance; Am Soc Biochem & Molecular Biol. *Res:* Structure-function relationships in macromolecular systems; mechanisms of enzyme action; roles of metal ions in biological systems. *Mailing Add:* Dept Chem & Biochem San Francisco State Univ San Francisco CA 94132. *Fax:* 415-338-2384; *E-Mail:* db@sfsu.edu

BUTTLAR, RUDOLPH O, INORGANIC CHEMISTRY. *Current Pos:* Asst prof chem, 62-71, asst dean col arts & sci, 67-70, assoc dean, 70-74, actg dean, 74-75, ASSOC PROF CHEM, KENT STATE UNIV, 71-, DEAN COL ARTS & SCI, 75- *Personal Data:* b Chicago, Ill, Dec 31, 34; m 55; c 3. *Educ:* Wheaton Col, BS, 56; Ind Univ, PhD(inorg chem), 62. *Mem:* Am Chem Soc. *Res:* Boron hydride and boron-nitrogen chemistry, especially cyclic boron-nitrogen compounds. *Mailing Add:* 5936 Horning Rd Kent OH 44240

BUTTLES, H SUNNY, PROBLEM SOLVING, COGNITION IN GENETICS. *Current Pos:* ASSOC PROF BIOL-GENETICS, OUR LADY OF THE LAKE UNIV, 78- *Personal Data:* b Milwaukee, Wis, May 2, 47; m 66, Lewis. *Educ:* Univ Cincinnati, BS, 70; Wayne State Univ, MS, 77; Univ Tex, Austin, PhD, 95. *Concurrent Pos:* Asst res scientist, SW Found Biomed Res, 80-82, sr res scientist, 87-89; NSF vis scientist, Lawrence Livermore Labs, 80; chair, Title III Grant Proposal Eval Team, NSF, 82-; prin investr, NSF/ILI, 93-95. *Mem:* Nat Asn Res Sci Educ; Nat Asn Biol Teachers; Am Educ Res Asn; AAAS; Am Inst Biol Sci; Asn Educ Teachers Sci. *Res:* Content domain of genetics; role of group interaction, individual goal orientation and prior knowledge in developing problem solving skills in the undergraduate genetics student. *Mailing Add:* 411 SW 24th St San Antonio TX 78207-4689. *E-Mail:* butth@lake.ollusa.edu

BUTTNER, F(REDERICK) H(OWARD), PHYSICAL METALLURGY, MECHANICAL ENGINEERING. *Current Pos:* CONSULT, 88- *Personal Data:* b Cleveland, Ohio, Oct 11, 20; m, Phebe Powell; c Charles H & Janet E (Patterson). *Educ:* Mich State Univ, BS, 44; Mass Inst Technol, MS, 49, ScD, 51. *Prof Exp:* Asst prof chem & math, Muskegon Community Col, 46-47; instr & res assoc, Mass Inst Technol, 47-51; staff metallurgist, Nat Acad Sci-Nat Res Coun, 51-53; staff metallurgist tech serv & develop, Union Carbide Metals, 53-57, mgr new prod eng, 57-62; res assoc, Battelle Mem Inst, 62-66, fel, 66-88. *Concurrent Pos:* Consult, Saudi Arabian Standards Orgn. *Mem:* AAAS; Am Chem Soc; Am Soc Metals; Am Inst Mining, Metall & Petrol Engrs; Sigma Xi. *Res:* Advanced construction and manufacturing practices; corporate investigations and profitability analyses of new venture options, leading to long term implementation plans and monitoring of them; metal commodity analyses to forecast supply/demand/price relationships; technology assessment; technology forecasting; technology transfer; insation. *Mailing Add:* 4153 Rowanne Columbus OH 43214

BUTTON, DON K, BIOCHEMISTRY, MARINE MICROBIOLOGY. *Current Pos:* From asst prof marine biochem to assoc prof marine sci, 64-74, PROF MARINE SCI, INST MARINE SCI, UNIV ALASKA, 74- *Personal Data:* b Kenosha, Wis, Oct 2, 33; m 61; c 5. *Educ:* Wis State Col, Superior, BS, 55; Univ Wis, MS, 61, PhD(biochem), 64. *Concurrent Pos:* Res assoc, Dept Biophys, Univ Colo Med Ctr, 69-70; consult, continuous cult oper & design, oil slick biodegradation. *Mem:* Am Soc Microbiol; Am Soc Limnol & Oceanog; Am Chem Soc; Sigma Xi. *Res:* Microbial biochemistry; metabolism kinetics of marine heterotrophs. *Mailing Add:* 2730 Goldstream Rd Fairbanks AK 99709

BUTTON-SHAFER, JANICE, EXPERIMENTAL HIGH ENERGY PHYSICS, NUCLEAR STRUCTURE. *Current Pos:* assoc prof, 66-70, PROF PHYSICS, UNIV MASS, AMHERST, 70- *Personal Data:* b Cincinnati, Ohio, Sept 13, 31; m 62, John; c Christina, Charles & John. *Educ:* Cornell Univ, BEngPhys, 54; Univ Goettingen, Ger, Vordiplom, 55; Univ Calif, Berkeley, PhD(physics), 59. *Prof Exp:* Physicist, Lawrence Radiation Lab, Univ Calif, 59-66, lectr physics, Univ Calif, Berkeley, 62-64. *Concurrent Pos:* Fulbright fel, Ger, 54-55; G E Coffin fel, Berkeley, 56-57; prin investr, High Energy Physics, Dept Energy, Univ Mass, 66-85; vis scholar, Harvard Univ, 79; Dept Energy fel, Assoc Western Univs, 90; vis prof, Univ Calif, Berkeley, 92. *Mem:* Fel Am Phys Soc; AAAS; Sigma Xi. *Res:* High-energy and nuclear experimental physics. *Mailing Add:* Dept Physics Univ Mass Amherst MA 01003. *Fax:* 413-545-0648; *E-Mail:* jbs@phast.umass.edu

BUTTREY, BENTON WILSON, PROTOZOOLOGY. *Current Pos:* RETIRED. *Personal Data:* b Craigmont, Idaho, Mar 25, 19; m 61. *Educ:* Univ Idaho, BS, 47, MS, 49; Univ Pa, PhD(zool), 53. *Prof Exp:* Asst zool, Univ Idaho, 47-49; asst instr, Univ Pa, 49-52; from asst prof to prof, Univ SDak, 53-61; prof entom, Iowa State Univ, 61-76, prof zool, 61-88. *Mem:* AAAS; Soc Protozool; Am Soc Zool; Am Soc Parasitol. *Res:* Morphology; taxonomy and host-parasite relationships of the protozoa from amphibia and swine; morphological variations in trichomonad protozoa. *Mailing Add:* 2020 Country Club Blvd Ames IA 50014

BUTTRILL, SIDNEY EUGENE, JR, ANALYTICAL CHEMISTRY. *Current Pos:* AT CHARLES EVANS & ASSOC. *Personal Data:* b Corpus Christi, Tex, July 21, 44; m 65; c 3. *Educ:* Mass Inst Technol, BS, 66; Stanford Univ, PhD(chem), 70. *Honors & Awards:* Robert H Carleson Award, 79. *Prof Exp:* Asst prof chem, Univ Minn, Minneapolis, 69-76; sr scientist mass spectros, SRI Int, 76-85, mgr, Mass Spectros Develop, 78-85; prof & chmn dept, 74-85, Aderhold distinguished prof sci educ, Univ Ga, 85- *Mem:* AAAS; Am Chem Soc; Am Soc Mass Spectrometry. *Res:* Field ionization mass spectrometry; chemical ionization mass spectrometry; ion-molecule chemistry; fossil fuels analysis by field ionization mass spectrometry; drug analysis by gas chromatography and field ionization mass spectrometry. *Mailing Add:* 1417 Parkinson Palo Alto CA 94301-3455

BUTTS, DAVID, BIOLOGY, SCIENCE EDUCATION. *Current Pos:* prof & chmn dept, 74-85, Aderhold distinguished prof, 85-96, EMER PROF SCI EDUC, UNIV GA, 96- *Personal Data:* b Rochester, NY, May 9, 32; m 58, Velma Walton; c 2. *Educ:* Butler Univ, BS, 54; Univ Ill, MS, 60, PhD(bot, sci educ), 62. *Honors & Awards:* Robert Carleton Award, Nat Sci Teachers Asn, 79. *Prof Exp:* Asst prof sci educ, Olivet Nazarene Col, 61-62; from asst prof to assoc prof, Univ Tex, Austin, 62-71, prof curric & instr, 71-74. *Concurrent Pos:* Consult, Robert E Lee Sci Curric Proj, 62-63; consult, Eval Ctr & mem, Stanford Writing Conf, AAAS Elem Sci Proj, 63 & 64; dir, Sci In-Serv Proj, 65-66, TAB Sci Test Proj, 65-69 & Elem Process-Oriented Curric Proj; proj dir, Personalized Teacher Educ Prog, 66-74. *Mem:* AAAS; Nat Asn Res Sci Teaching. *Res:* Curriculum materials in sciences for elementary and junior high students. *Mailing Add:* Dept Sci Educ Univ Ga Athens GA 30602. *Fax:* 706-549-0582

BUTTS, HUBERT S, MATHEMATICS. *Current Pos:* RETIRED. *Personal Data:* b Burkburnett, Tex, Nov 7, 23; m 47; c 3. *Educ:* NTex State Univ, BS, 47, MS, 48; Ohio State Univ, PhD(math), 53. *Prof Exp:* Instr math, NTex State Univ, 47-48; from asst prof to assoc prof, La State Univ, Baton Rouge, 53-62, prof math, 62- *Mem:* Am Math Soc. *Res:* Algebraic number theory; ideal theory in commutative rings. *Mailing Add:* 610 Louray Baton Rouge LA 70808

BUTTS, JEFFREY A, PARASITOLOGY. *Current Pos:* assoc prof, 81-84, PROF BIOL, APPALACHIAN STATE UNIV, 84-, CHAIR DEPT, 81- *Personal Data:* b Lansing, Mich, May 25, 47; m 69; c 3. *Educ:* Albion Col, AB, 69; Bowling Green State Univ, MS, 71, PhD(biol), 73. *Prof Exp:* From asst prof to assoc prof biol, Univ NC, Charlotte, 73-81. *Concurrent Pos:* Pres, NC conf, Am Asn Univ Prof, 86-87. *Mem:* AAAS; Am Soc Parasitologists; Am Asn Univ Profs; Sigma Xi. *Res:* Filiariasis specifically heartworm (Dirofilaria immitis) and toxoplasmosis; coccidia of amphibians. *Mailing Add:* Biol Dept Applachian State Univ Boone NC 28608-0001

BUTTS, SUSAN BEDA, CHROMATOGRAPHY, CATALYSIS. *Current Pos:* sr res chemist, Dow Chem Co, 79-83, safety & regulatory affairs coordr, 83-86, res leader, 86-87, tech placement mgr, 87-89, group leader, 89-94, res mgr, 94-95, sr res mgr, 95-96, GLOBAL RES & DEVELOP MGR, DOW CHEM CO, 96- *Personal Data:* b Muskegon, Mich, Feb 5, 53; m 76, Bertie N; c Robert & William. *Educ:* Univ Mich, BS, 75, Northwestern, MS, 78, PhD(inorg chem), 80. *Mem:* Am Chem Soc; Sigma Xi. *Res:* Development of homogeneous and heterogeneous catalysts for chemical synthesis; mechanisms of reaction of organometal carbonyl compounds. *Mailing Add:* 3907 Westbrier Terr Midland MI 48642

BUTTS, WILLIAM CUNNINGHAM, LABORATORY MEDICINE. *Current Pos:* DIR CLIN CHEM, GROUP HEALTH OF PUGET SOUND, 75- *Personal Data:* b Evanston, Ill, Jan 13, 42; m 63; c 2. *Educ:* Purdue Univ, BS, 63; Iowa State Univ, PhD(anal chem), 68. *Prof Exp:* Res chemist, Oak Ridge Nat Lab, 68-71; fel clin chem, Univ Wash, 71-73; sr clin chemist, Insts Med Sci, San Francisco, 73-75. *Concurrent Pos:* Clin asst prof, Univ Wash, 76- *Mem:* Am Asn Clin Chem; Am Chem Soc; AAAS. *Res:* Identification of constituents isolated from physiologic fluids; development of separation techniques for biochemical systems; gas chromatography of inorganic species; individual biochemical profiles. *Mailing Add:* Chem Lab Group Health 12400 E Marginal Way S Seattle WA 98124

BUTTS, WILLIAM LESTER, ENTOMOLOGY, ORNITHOLOGY. *Current Pos:* assoc prof, 66-69, PROF BIOL, STATE UNIV NY COL ONEONTA, 69- *Personal Data:* b Reynoldsburg, Ohio, Dec 7, 31; m 54; c 3. *Educ:* Wilmington Col, Ohio, BSc, 53; Ohio State Univ, MSc, 54, PhD(entom), 64. *Prof Exp:* From instr to assoc prof entom, Purdue Univ, 57-66. *Mem:* Am Mosquito Control Asn; Sigma Xi; NY Acad Sci. *Res:* Medical and public health entomology. *Mailing Add:* HC 87 Box 7 Franklin NY 13775

BUTZ, ANDREW, INSECT PHYSIOLOGY. *Current Pos:* asst prof, 58-64, ASSOC PROF ZOOL, UNIV CINCINNATI, 64- *Personal Data:* b Perth Amboy, NJ, Feb 15, 31. *Educ:* St Peter's Col, BS, 52; Fordham Univ, MS, 54, PhD, 56. *Honors & Awards:* Barbour Distinguished Serv, 90. *Prof Exp:* Asst physiol, Fordham Univ, 52-56. *Mem:* AAAS; Am Soc Zoologists; Entom Soc Am; Am Inst Biol Sci; Sigma Xi. *Res:* Circadian rhythm; RNA studies; protein studies; pheromones; metabolism; insect ecology; soil arthropods; insecticidal relationships; insect immunology and toxicology; plant/extracts and their development and or metamorphosis; factors which influence vitellogensis. *Mailing Add:* 882 Old Ludlow Ave Cincinnati OH 45220

BUTZ, DONALD JOSEF, EXPLOSIVE ORDNANCE DISPOSAL, ARMOR DEVELOPMENT. *Current Pos:* researcher ord eng, Battelle Mem Inst, 81-83, from res scientist to Prin res scientist ord eng, 83-88, sr res scientist ord eng, 88-92, assoc dept mgr ord applin, 92-95, dept mgr ord systs, 94-96, RES LEADER ORD SYSTS, BATTELLE MEM INST, 96- *Personal Data:* b Marion, Ohio, Oct 3, 58; m 82, Therese R Burger. *Educ:* Ohio State Univ, BS, 81. *Prof Exp:* Student res assoc aeronaut eng, Aeronaut & Astronaut Res Lab, Ohio State Univ, 79-81. *Mem:* Sigma Xi; Am Inst Aeronaut & Astronaut; Am Defense Preparedness Asn; Soc Explosives Engrs; Int Asn Bomb Technicians & Investigators; Am Phys Soc; Int Asn Counter Terrorism Prof. *Res:* Applications of explosives and other high energy density phenomena to defense and civilian requirements. *Mailing Add:* Battelle Mem Inst 505 King Ave Columbus OH 43201. *Fax:* 614-424-3776; *E-Mail:* butz@battelle.org

BUTZER, KARL W(ILHELM), ARCHAEOLOGY, HUMAN GEOGRAPHY. *Current Pos:* DICKSON CENTENNIAL PROF LIB ARTS, UNIV TEX, AUSTIN, 84- *Personal Data:* b Ger. *Educ:* McGill Univ, BSc, 54, MSc, 55; Univ Bonn, Dr rer nat(geog), 57. *Honors & Awards:* Meritorious Contrib Award, Asn Am Geogr, 68; Busk Medal, Royal Geog Soc, 79; Fryxell Medal, Soc Am Archeol, 81; Stopes Medal, Geologists Asn London, 82. *Prof Exp:* Ger Acad grant, Univ Bonn, 57-59; from asst prof to assoc prof geog, Univ Wis, 59-66; prof anthrop & geog, Univ Chicago, 66-80, Henry Schultz prof environ archeol, 80-84. *Concurrent Pos:* NSF grants, 64-; Wenner-Gren grants, 65-; chair prof human geog, Swiss Fed Inst Technol, Zurich, 81-82. *Mem:* Nat Acad Sci; Am Quaternary Asn; Asn Am Geogr; fel Am Acad Arts & Sci; Asn Field Archeol. *Res:* Environmental archaeology; cultural ecology; environmental geomorphology. *Mailing Add:* Dept Geog Univ Tex Austin TX 78712-1098

BUTZOW, JAMES J, BIOCHEMISTRY, STRUCTURAL MOLECULAR BIOLOGY. *Current Pos:* Res chemist, Geront Br, Nat Heart Inst, 62-65, res chemist, Geront Res Ctr, Nat Inst Child Health & Human Develop, 67-75, RES CHEMIST, GERONT RES CTR, NAT INST AGING, 75- *Personal Data:* b Chicago, Ill, Oct 17, 35; m 80, Sandra T Watson. *Educ:* St Bonaventure Univ, BS, 57; Stanford Univ, PhD(biochem), 63. *Concurrent Pos:* Fel, Dept Biochem, Univ Goteborg, Sweden, 65-67; mem, Carroll House Found (res in med ethics), Baltimore, 73- *Mem:* Am Chem Soc. *Res:* Physical chemistry of nucleic acids and proteins; interaction of metals with nucleic acids; RNA polymerase. *Mailing Add:* 6626 Walnutwood Circle Baltimore MD 21212. *Fax:* 410-558-8173

BUURMAN, CLARENCE HAROLD, INDUSTRIAL ORGANIC CHEMISTRY. *Current Pos:* RETIRED. *Personal Data:* b Orange City, Iowa, July 31, 15; m 43; c 4. *Educ:* Univ Iowa, AB, 36, MS, 38, PhD(org chem), 41. *Prof Exp:* Semi works chemist, Iowa State Dept Health, 39-41; chief chemist, GAF Corp, 41-52, chief chemist surfactants sulfur color & chlorine area, 52-56, prod mgr vats-intermediates & org chem dept, 56-65, plant mgr, 67-70; vpres & gen mgr, Mauldin Oper, Emery Indust, Inc, 70-84. *Mem:* Am Chem Soc; Am Inst Chemists. *Res:* Organic research chemistry; photographic products; dye and pigment chemistry; surface active agents; agricultural chemistry; textile chemistry. *Mailing Add:* 19 Red Fox Trail Greenville SC 29615-3737

BUXBAUM, JOEL N, IMMUNOGLOBULINS AMYLOIDOSIS & IMMUNOGLOBULIN GENES. *Current Pos:* from asst prof to assoc prof, 71-81, PROF MED, NY UNIV MED SCH, 81- *Personal Data:* b New York, NY, Feb 22, 38; m 61; c 2. *Educ:* Union Col, BS, 58; Tufts Med Sch, MD, 62. *Prof Exp:* Instr cell biol, Albert Einstein Sch Med, 69-71. *Concurrent Pos:* Chief, Cell Biol Res Lab, NY Dept Vet Affairs Med Ctr, 71- *Mem:* Am Soc Clin Invest; AAAS; Am Asn Immunologists; Am Col Rheumatology; Asn Am Physicians. *Res:* Molecular mechanisms responsible for diseases in which abnormal proteins plan a role in the pathogenesis; human immunoglobulin heavy chain disease; light chain amyloidosis; familial amyloidotic poly-neuropathy. *Mailing Add:* Res Serv Dept Vet Affairs Med Ctr 423 E 23rd St New York NY 10010

BUXSER, STEPHEN EARL, CELL BIOLOGY, MICROBIOLOGY. *Current Pos:* res scientist, 84-90, SR RES SCIENTIST, UPJOHN CO, 90- *Personal Data:* b Massillon, Ohio, 1951. *Educ:* Ohio State Univ, BS, 74; Univ Wis-Madison, MS, 76; Univ Cincinnati, PhD(microbiol), 80. *Prof Exp:* Fel, Univ Mass Med Sch, 80-84. *Mem:* AAAS; Fedn Am Socs Exp Biol. *Res:* Kinetics of biochemical and cellular processes; pharmaceutical evaluation and design; drug delivery. *Mailing Add:* Upjohn & Co 301 Henrietta St Kalamazoo MI 49007-4940

BUXTON, DWAYNE REVERE, CROP PHYSIOLOGY & PRODUCTION. *Current Pos:* PLANT PHYSIOLOGIST, AGR RES SERV, USDA & PROF AGRON, IOWA STATE UNIV, 81- *Personal Data:* b Tremonton, Utah, Apr 14, 39; m 64, Mary B Cowan; c Robert, Brent, Lynda, Angela, Mark, Aleece & Scott. *Educ:* Utah State Univ, BS, 64, MS, 66; Iowa State Univ, PhD(agron), 69. *Prof Exp:* From asst prof to prof agron & plant genetics, Univ Ariz, 69-77; supt, Malheur Exp Sta & prof agron, Ore State Univ, 77-81. *Mem:* Fel AAAS; fel Am Soc Agron; fel Crop Sci Soc Am; Am Forage & Grassland Coun; Coun Agr Sci & Technol. *Res:* Ecological and physiological factors responsible for variation in nutritive value of forages with special emphasis on all wall carbohydrate and ligmin deposition and chemical composition. *Mailing Add:* 1505 Curtiss Ave Ames IA 50010. *Fax:* 515-294-9359; *E-Mail:* drbuxton@iastate.edu

BUXTON, IAIN LAURIE OFFORD, CYCLIC NUCLEOTIDES, RECEPTOR-EFFECTOR COUPLING. *Current Pos:* ASST PROF PHARMACOL, SCH MED, UNIV NEV, 85- *Personal Data:* b Haulton, Eng, Oct 1, 50; nat US; m 81; c 1. *Educ:* Univ Calif, San Diego, BA, 73; Univ Pac, DPh(pharmaceut sci), 78. *Honors & Awards:* New Investr Res Award, NIH, 84. *Prof Exp:* Res assoc biochem, Univ NC, Raleigh, 73-74 & res assoc cell biol, Salk Inst, La Jolla, Calif, 74-75; clin instr, clin pharm, Univ Southern Calif, Los Angeles, 78-80; resident clin pharm & therapeut, Vet Admin Med Ctr, San Diego, 78-81; teaching fel pharmacol, Sch Med, Univ Calif, San Diego, 81-84, asst res pharmacologist, 84-85. *Concurrent Pos:* Lectr, cardiovasc drug ther, Clin Clerkship Prog, Univ Pac, 78-80 & drug abuse pharmacol, Nat Univ, San Diego, 80-81; teaching fel, NIH, 81-84; prin investr, NIH, 84-87. *Mem:* Am Heart Asn; AAAS; Am Col Clin Pharm; Am Soc Pharmacol & Exp Therapeut. *Res:* Investigation of the mechanisms of action of adrenergic receptors in mammalian cells; regulation of cyclic adrenosine monophosphate compartmentation in cardiac tissue; hormonal control of adrenylate cyclase and inositol-phospholipid metabolism in mammalian cells. *Mailing Add:* Dept Pharmacol 340 Univ Nev Sch Med Reno NV 89557-0046. *Fax:* 702-784-1620

BUXTON, JAY A, ENTOMOLOGY. *Current Pos:* prof & chmn dept, 67-87, EMER PROF, CATAWBACOL, 87- *Personal Data:* b Carrara, Italy, May 29, 19; m 74, Elda Iverson; c John T, Rebecca (Leonard) & Cynthia (Voth). *Educ:* Southwest Tex State Teachers Col, BS, 48; Univ Tex, MA, 50; Ohio State Univ, PhD(entom), 57. *Honors & Awards:* Algernon Sidney Sullivan Award. *Prof Exp:* Tech res asst entom, Ohio State Res Found, 50-52; entomologist, Battelle Mem Inst, 52-57; assoc prof biol, Tex Col Art & Indust, 57-61; asst prof entom, Clemson Univ & asst entomologist, Exp Sta, 61-67. *Mem:* AAAS; Entom Soc Am; Am Inst Biol Sci; Sigma Xi. *Res:* Taxonomy of immature Orthoptera and genus Melanoplus; fruit insects. *Mailing Add:* 2425 N Jake Alex Blvd N Salisbury NC 28147

BUYERS, WILLIAM JAMES LESLIE, SOLID STATE PHYSICS. *Current Pos:* fel, Atomic Energy Can, Ltd, 65-66, assoc res officer, 66-75, sr res officer physics, 75-85, mgr, Neutron & Solid State Phyics, 85-91, SR SCIENTIST AECL RES, 91- *Personal Data:* b Aboyne, Scotland, Apr 10, 37; Can citizen; m 66; c 3. *Educ:* Aberdeen Univ, BSc, 59, PhD(physics), 63. *Honors & Awards:* Rutherford Gold Medal, Royal Soc Can, 86. *Prof Exp:* From asst lectr to lectr physics, Aberdeen Univ, 62-65. *Concurrent Pos:* Sr res fel, Oxford Univ, 71-72; vis scientist, Oak Ridge Nat Lab, 72, Riso Nat Lab, Denmark, 75, Inst Theoret Physics, Santa Barbara, 80-81, Riso Nat Lab, Denmark, 84, Univ Lausanne, 85; chmn, Can Nat Comt, Int Union Crystallog, 82-85; dir, NATO Advan Studies Inst, Vancouver Island, 83; mem, Can Nat Comt, Int Union Pure & Appl Physics; secy, Comn

Magnetism, Int Union Pure & Appl Physics, 84-96. *Mem:* Can Asn Physicists; fel Am Phys Soc; fel Inst Physics; fel Royal Soc Can. *Res:* Neutron scattering from spin waves, phonons in solids and liquids; crystal fields, soft modes, phase transitions, defects and random alloys, quantum spins, haldanegap one-dimensional magnetism, actinide magnetism, heavy-fermions. *Mailing Add:* AECL Res Chalk River ON K0J 1J0 Can. *Fax:* 613-584-4040; *E-Mail:* buyersw@aecl.ca

BUYNISKI, JOSEPH P, PHARMACOLOGY. *Current Pos:* head cardiovasc res, 69-72, asst dir, 72-74, DIR, DEPT PHARMACOL, BRISTOL LABS, 75-, PROJ DIR CARDIOVASC DRUGS, 79- *Personal Data:* b Worcester, Mass, July 18, 41; m 73; c 2. *Educ:* Univ Cincinnati, BS, 63, PhD(pharmacol), 67. *Prof Exp:* NIH cardiovasc res fel, Bowman Gray Sch Med, 67-69, instr, 68-69. *Concurrent Pos:* NC Heart Asn grants, 68 & 69. *Mem:* Am Soc Pharmacol & Exp Therapeut; assoc Am Physiol Soc; Am Heart Asn; NY Acad Sci. *Res:* Antidysrhythmic, antithrombotic and antihypertensive drug research; myocardial infarction and lethal arrhythmias; tissue catecholamine levels and cardiovascular hemodynamics; endotoxemia and platelet function; control mechanisms affecting cerebral blood flow. *Mailing Add:* Pharmaceut Res Inst Bristol-Myers Squibb Co Five Res Pkwy PO Box 5100 Wallingford CT 06492-7660. *Fax:* 203-284-7750

BUYSKE, STEVE GEORGE, DIFFERENTIAL GEOMETRY OF SUBMANIFOLDS, INNOVATIONS IN MATHEMATICS TEACHING. *Current Pos:* ASST PROF MATH, LAFAYETTE COL, 88- *Personal Data:* b New York, NY, July 19, 61; m 88, Ann Jurecic; c Quinta. *Educ:* Haverford Col, BA, 83; Brown Univ, MSc, 86, PhD(math), 88. *Mem:* AAAS; Sigma Xi; Am Math Soc; Math Asn Am; Asn Women Math. *Res:* Modern approaches to old problems and concepts in the differential geometry of submanifolds and surfaces; Lie Sphere geometry, Baecklund transformations, and the differential geometry of affine spaces. *Mailing Add:* 75 Bonnell St Flemington NJ 08822. *E-Mail:* buyskes@lafvax.lafayette.edu

BUZACOTT, J(OHN) A(LAN), OPERATIONS RESEARCH, INDUSTRIAL ENGINEERING. *Current Pos:* PROF DEPT MGT SCI, YORK UNIV, 91. *Personal Data:* b Burwood, Australia, May 21, 37; m 63, Ursula Schulmerich; c Alan J & Kimberly A. *Educ:* Univ Sydney, BSc, 57, BE, 59; Univ Birmingham, MSc, 62, PhD(eng prod), 67. *Prof Exp:* Engr, Assoc Elec Indust Ltd, 59-61 & Opers Res Off, Hotpoint Ltd, 63-64; from asst prof to prof indust eng, Univ Toronto, 67-83; prof mgt sci, Univ Waterloo, 84-91. *Concurrent Pos:* Assoc ed, Int J Prod Res, 70-81, Naval Res Logistics Quart, 84-88, Transactions, Inst Indust Engrs, 84-88, Queueing Syst Theory & Appln, 86-; res scientist, IIASA, Laxenburg, Austria, 79-80; mem, NATO Adv Comt, Adv Study Inst & Adv Res Workshops, 82-85. *Mem:* Opers Res Soc Am; Can Opers Res Soc (pres, 84-85). *Res:* Production and inventory control; reliability; manufacturing system modeling; technological innovation and productivity. *Mailing Add:* Schulich Sch Bus Rm 332 York Univ 4700 Keele St North York ON M3J 1P3 Can. *Fax:* 416-736-5687; *E-Mail:* jbuzacot@ronserver.mgts.yorku.ca

BUZARD, JAMES ALBERT, BIOCHEMISTRY. *Current Pos:* RETIRED. *Personal Data:* b Warren, Ohio, Nov 2, 27; m 51; c 2. *Educ:* Kent State Univ, BS, 49; Univ Buffalo, MA, 51, PhD(biochem), 54. *Prof Exp:* Sr res biochemist, Sect Biol, Eaton Labs, Norwich Pharmacal Co, 54-55, unit head, 55-58, group leader, 58-59, chief biochem sect, 59-62, from asst dir to dir biol res, 62-65, dir res, 65-68; dir develop, Searle Labs, 68-69, dir res, 69-70, vpres res & develop, 70-72, pres, Searle Labs, 72-75, vpres, 72-75, exec vpres opers, G D Searle & Co, 75-79; exec vpres, Merrell Dow Pharmaceut, Inc, 9-90. *Mem:* Am Chem Soc; Am Soc Biol Chem. *Res:* Intermediary metabolism; drug metabolism and mode of action; chemotherapy; analytical biochemistry; research management; commercial management worldwide. *Mailing Add:* 5575 Graydon Meadow Cincinnati OH 45243

BUZAS, MARTIN A, PALEOECOLOGY. *Current Pos:* CUR INVERT PALEONT, SMITHSONIAN INST, 63- *Personal Data:* b Bridgeport, Conn, Jan 30, 34; m 58; c 3. *Educ:* Univ Conn, BA, 58; Brown Univ, MSc, 60; Yale Univ, PhD(geol), 63. *Mem:* AAAS; Cushman Found; Paleont Soc. *Res:* Quantitative ecology, paleoeoclogy; Benthonic Forminifera. *Mailing Add:* 13508 Keating St Rockville MD 20853

BUZBEE, BILLY LEWIS, NUMERICAL ANALYSIS, MATHEMATICS. *Current Pos:* DIR, SCI COMPUTING DIV, NAT CTR ATMOSPHERIC RES, 87- *Personal Data:* b Gorman, Tex, Sept 12, 36; div; c 3. *Educ:* Univ Tex, Austin, BA, 61, MA, 62; Univ NMex, PhD(math), 72. *Prof Exp:* Staff mem, Los Alamos Sci Lab, 62-67 & 68-73; analyst, Esso Prod Res Co, 67-68; vis prof comput sci, Chalmers Inst Technol, 73-74; group leader, Los Alamos Nat Lab, 74-80, asst computer div leader, 80-84, dep leader, 84-87. *Concurrent Pos:* Dir, Sci Comput Div, Nat Ctr Atmospheric Res. *Mem:* Asn Comput Mach; Sigma Xi; IEEE Comput Soc; Soc Indust & Applied Math. *Res:* Numerical solution of elliptic and parabolic difference approximations. *Mailing Add:* Sci Computer Div Nat Ctr Atmospheric Res PO Box 3000 Boulder CO 80307

BUZEN, JEFFREY PETER, COMPUTER SCIENCE, QUEUEING THEORY. *Current Pos:* VPRES, BGS SYSTS INC, 75- *Personal Data:* b Brooklyn, NY, May 28, 43. *Educ:* Brown Univ, ScB, 65; Harvard Univ, ScM, 66, PhD(appl math), 71. *Honors & Awards:* A A Michelson Award, 79. *Prof Exp:* Tech staff, Honeywell, 71-75. *Concurrent Pos:* Adj fac, Harvard Univ, Brown Univ. *Mem:* Sigmetrics; Asn Comput Mach; Comput Measurement Group. *Res:* Mathematical models of computer system performance; stochastic and operational analysis; queueing network models; capacity planning. *Mailing Add:* BGS Systs Inc 1 First Ave Waltham MA 02254. *Fax:* 781-890-0000

BUZIN, CAROLYN HATTOX, BIOCHEMISTRY. *Current Pos:* ASST RES SCIENTIST, CITY OF HOPE MED CTR, DUARTE, CALIF, 75- *Educ:* Univ Tex, Austin, PhD(biochem), 67. *Res:* Differentiation of Drosophila embryonic cells; heat shock protein. *Mailing Add:* 2219 Canyon Rd Arcadia CA 91006

BUZINA, RATKO, ENDEMIC GOITRE, CORONARY HEART DISEASE. *Current Pos:* head, Dept Nutrit, 72-85, RES CONSULT NUTRIT, INST PUB HEALTH, ZAGREB, 86-; PROF NUTRIT, SCH PUB HEALTH, ZAGREB, 63- *Personal Data:* b Samobor, Croatia, Yugoslavia, Nov 27, 20; m 80, Kornelija; c Ratko & Kristina. *Educ:* Univ Zagreb, MD, 44, Dipl, 53, ScD, 62. *Prof Exp:* Res asst biochem, Inst Biochem, Univ Basel, 50-51; chief physiol nutrit, Inst Pub Health, Zagreb, 52-54; res assoc, Lab Physiol Hyg, Univ Minn, 55-56; assoc prof nutrit, Sch Pub Health, Univ Zagreb, 56-63. *Concurrent Pos:* Vis researcher, Dept Nutrit, Vanderbilt Univ, Nashville, 56; prin investr, Epidemiol Coronary Heart Dis, Yugoslavia, 59-66. *Mem:* Am Soc Clin Nutrit; fel Am Inst Nutrit; Am Pub Health Asn; Int Union Nutrit Sci; Int Soc & Fedn Cardiol. *Res:* Pathophysiology of endemic goitre including the role of goitrogenic factors; epidemiology of coronary heart disease (seven country study) and effects of subclinical micronutrient deficiencies on functional status of the body, primarily physical activity, immunity and cognitive functions. *Mailing Add:* Nutrit Unit WHO Geneva 27 Switzerland. *Fax:* 41-22-791-4156; *E-Mail:* buzinar@ccm.who.ch

BUZYNA, GEORGE, FLUID DYNAMICS, HEAT TRANSFER. *Current Pos:* asst prof meteorol, 74-75, RES ASSOC, GEOPHYS FLUID DYNAMICS, FLA STATE UNIV, 69-, ASSOC PROF & ASSOC CHMN, DEPT MECH ENG, FAMU/FSU COL ENG, 89- *Personal Data:* b Kovel, Poland, Apr 25, 38; m 65; c 2. *Educ:* Ill Inst Technol, BS, 60, MS, 62; Yale Univ, PhD(eng & appl sci), 67. *Prof Exp:* Res staff, Yale Univ, 67-69. *Mem:* Sigma Xi; Am Soc Mech Engrs; Am Phys Soc; Am Geophys Union. *Res:* Experimental gas dynamics; geophysical fluid dynamics; rotating differentially heated fluid convection; large-scale atmospheric circulation. *Mailing Add:* FAMU/FSU Col Eng 2525 Pottsdamer St Tallahassee FL 32310-0646

BUZZELL, JOHN GIBSON, POLYMER CHEMISTRY. *Current Pos:* res chemist, 55-67, SR RES CHEMIST, E I DU PONT DE NEMOURS & CO, INC, 67- *Personal Data:* b Delavan, Wis, Apr 29, 22; m 50; c 3. *Educ:* Univ Wis, BS, 48; Univ Iowa, PhD(chem), 55. *Prof Exp:* Chemist, Sherwin-Williams, 48-51. *Mem:* Am Chem Soc; Sigma Xi. *Res:* Photo polymer process research. *Mailing Add:* 1708 Woodledge Circle State College PA 16803-1844

BUZZELL, RICHARD IRVING, PLANT BREEDING, PLANT GENETICS. *Current Pos:* Head, Crop Sci Sect, Harrow Res Sta, 76-91, RES SCIENTIST BREEDING & GENETICS, CAN DEPT AGR, 62- *Personal Data:* b Lincolnville, Maine, May 1, 29; m 56; c Richard, David, Mary & Susan. *Educ:* Univ Maine, BS, 58; Iowa State Univ, MS, 60, PhD(plant breeding), 62. *Concurrent Pos:* Mem assoc grad fac, crop sci dept, Univ Guelph; ed, Can J Plant Sci, 89-91. *Mem:* Can Soc Agron; hon mem Can Seed Growers Asn. *Res:* Genetics of soybeans and corn; variety development. *Mailing Add:* Box 373 Harrow ON N0R 1G0 Can. *Fax:* 519-738-2929

BUZZELLI, DONALD EDWARD, MISCONDUCT IN SCIENCE-ENGINEERING RESEARCH & EDUCATION, SCIENCE TECHNOLOGY STATISTICS. *Current Pos:* RETIRED. *Personal Data:* b Detroit, Mich, July 24, 36. *Educ:* Cornell Univ, BChE, 59, Mass Inst Technol, ScD(chem eng), 64; Fordham Univ, MA, 71, PhD(philos), 74. *Prof Exp:* From res engr to sr res engr chem eng, Chevron Res Co, 64-69; prog analyst, NSF, 75-89, staff assoc for oversight & sr scientist, Off Inspector Gen, 89-93, dep asst inspector gen oversight, 93-97. *Mem:* AAAS. *Mailing Add:* 2400 Pennsylvania Ave NW Washington DC 20037. *E-Mail:* dbuzzell@nsf.gov

BUZZELLI, EDWARD S, PHYSICS, ELECTROCHEMISTRY. *Current Pos:* CONSULT ELECTROCHEM & ENERGY STORAGE, 96- *Personal Data:* b Cleveland, Ohio, July 31, 39; m 60, Rosemary C Dobrzeniecki; c Edward Jr, Anthony, Michael & Karen. *Educ:* John Carroll Univ, BS, 62, MS, 65. *Prof Exp:* From jr physicist to physicist, Res & Develop Lab, Stand Oil Co, Ohio, 62-65, sr physicist & proj leader, 65-67, sr res physicist, 67-70; sr engr, Westinghouse Elec Corp, 70-73, proj mgr, 73-80, mgr, Spec Projs Venture, 84-90, mgr electrochem technol, Res & Develop Ctr, 80-92, mgr advan batteries, 90-92; mgr electrochem, AER Energy Resources, 92-96. *Mem:* Electrochem Soc; Marine Tech Soc; Am Defense Preparedness Asn. *Res:* Fused salt electrochemistry; secondary batteries; reactions in fused salt media; solid state reactions and devices; air electrode and metal-air battery development; alkaline and lithium batteries; fuel cells; hydrogen production; metal-air electrochemistry; zinc batteries. *Mailing Add:* 3013 Braxton Ct Kennesaw GA 30152. *Fax:* 770-425-3931; *E-Mail:* esbuzzi@worldnet.att.net

BYALL, ELLIOTT BRUCE, FORENSIC SCIENCE. *Current Pos:* forensic chemist, 71-80, forensic br chief, 81-, LAB CHIEF, SAN FRANCISCO LAB CTR, BUR ALCOHOL, TOBACCO & FIREARMS. *Personal Data:* b Fall River, Mass, May 31, 40; m 62; c 4. *Educ:* Sterling Col, BS, 62; Ore State Univ, PhD(org chem), 67. *Prof Exp:* Res chemist, E I Du Pont de Nemours & Co, Inc, 67-71. *Mem:* Int Asn Identification. *Res:* New methods for forensic analysis; explosive and gunshot residue examinations. *Mailing Add:* San Francisco Lab Ctr Bur Alcohol Tobacco & Firearms 355 N Wiget Lane Walnut Creek CA 94598

BYARD, JAMES LEONARD, TOXICOLOGY, BIOCHEMISTRY. *Current Pos:* CONSULT TOXICOLOGIST, 84- *Personal Data:* b Hartwick, NY, Dec 1, 41; c 2. *Educ:* Cornell Univ, BS, 64; Univ Wis, MS, 66, PhD(biochem), 68; Am Bd Toxicol, dipl. *Prof Exp:* Arthritis fel, Harvard Med Sch, 68-70; asst prof toxicol & biochem, Albany Med Col, 70-74; from asst prof to assoc prof environ toxicol, Univ Calif, Davis, 74-84. *Mem:* Soc Toxicol; Soc Environ Toxicol & Chem; AAAS. *Res:* Metabolism and molecular mechanism of toxic action of environmental chemicals; primary hepatocyte culture; chemical carcinogenesis. *Mailing Add:* PO Box 2556 El Macero CA 95618

BYARD, PAMELA JOY, POPULATION GENETICS, HUMAN GROWTH. *Current Pos:* Asst prof anthrop, 83-86, ASSOC PROF PEDIAT & ASST PROF EPIDEMIOL & BIOSTATIST, CASE WESTERN RES UNIV, 86- *Personal Data:* b Rochester, NY, Sept 16, 51; m 93, Jerry W Davison. *Educ:* State Univ NY, Albany, BA, 75, MA, 77; Univ Kans, PhD(biol anthrop), 81. *Prof Exp:* Res assoc growth & genetics, Fels Res Inst, Sch Med, Wright State Univ, 81-82; fel, Div Biostatist, Wash Univ, St Louis MD, 82-83. *Mem:* Am Asn Phys Anthrop; Human Biol Coun. *Res:* Genetic control of human growth, growth retardation in cystic fibrosis; segregation analysis of complex human traits. *Mailing Add:* Dept Pediat Univ Hosp Cleveland 11100 Eclid Ave Cleveland OH 44106

BYARS, EDWARD F(ORD), MECHANICAL ENGINEERING & ENGINEERING MECHANICS. *Current Pos:* RETIRED. *Personal Data:* b Lincolnton, NC, Mar 22, 25; m 50; c 4. *Educ:* Clemson Univ, BME, 46, MCE, 53; Univ Ill, PhD(appl mech), 57. *Prof Exp:* From asst prof to assoc prof eng mech, Clemson Univ, 47-60; prof mech eng & chmn dept, WVa Univ, 60-80; exec asst to pres, Clemson Univ, 80-85. *Concurrent Pos:* Consult, biomech & exp mech. *Mem:* Am Soc Eng Educ; Soc Exp Stress Anal; Sigma Xi. *Res:* Author engineering mechanics textbooks. *Mailing Add:* 126 Elm St Clemson SC 29631

BYATT, JOHN CHRISTOPHER, MAMMARY BIOLOGY, PLACENTAL LACTOGENS. *Current Pos:* sr res biochemist, New Prod ID Group, Monsanto Co, 85-88, res specialist, Dairy Res Group, 88-90, sr res specialist, 90-93, ASSOC FEL, MONSANTO CO, 93- *Personal Data:* b London, Eng, July 25, 58; m 85; c 2. *Educ:* Univ London, BSc, 79; Univ Reading, PhD(physiol), 83. *Prof Exp:* Fel, Dept Dairy Sci, Univ Wis-Madison, 83-85. *Mem:* Am Dairy Sci Asn; Endocrine Soc. *Res:* Investigation of the factors responsible for regulating mammary growth and differentiation in cattle; bovine placental lactogen and bovine somatot ropin. *Mailing Add:* 214 Country Creek Ct Ballwin MO 63011

BYATT, PAMELA HILDA, VIROLOGY. *Current Pos:* RETIRED. *Personal Data:* b Cape Town, SAfrica, Nov 28, 16; nat US. *Educ:* Univ Calif, Los Angeles, BA, 43, MA, 47, PhD(microbiol), 50. *Prof Exp:* Asst microbiol, Univ Wash, 50-52; virologist, Dept Med Microbiol & Immunol & Clin Labs, Univ Calif, Los Angeles, 53-73, chief Virol Lab, Microbiol Sect, Clin, Ctr Health Sci, 73-80. *Mem:* AAAS; Am Soc Microbiol; Tissue Cult Asn; NY Acad Sci. *Res:* Staphylococci; antibiotics; viruses; microbiology. *Mailing Add:* 1223 19th St No B Santa Monica CA 90404

BYBEE, RODGER W, SCIENCE EDUCATION, PSYCHOLOGY. *Current Pos:* assoc dir, Biol Sci Curric Study, 85-92, chair, Working Group, Nat Sci Educ Stand, 93-95, EXEC DIR, CTR SCI MATH ENG EDUC, NAT RES COUN, 95- *Educ:* Univ Northern Colo, BA, MA; NY Univ, PhD(sci educ & psychol). *Prof Exp:* Prof educ, Carleton Col, 72-85. *Mailing Add:* Nat Res Coun 2101 Const Ave NW Harris 450 Washington DC 20007

BYCK, ROBERT, PHARMACOLOGY, PSYCHIATRY. *Current Pos:* fel psychiat & lectr pharmacol, 69-72, assoc prof, 72-77, PROF PSYCHIAT & PHARMACOL, YALE UNIV, 77- *Personal Data:* b Newark, NJ, Apr 26, 33; m 76; c 4. *Educ:* Univ Pa, AB, 54, MD, 59. *Hon Degrees:* MA, Yale Univ, 77. *Prof Exp:* Res assoc, NIH, 60-62; sr fel pharm, Yeshiva Univ, 62-64, asst prof rehab med & pharmacol, 64-69. *Concurrent Pos:* NIMH sr fel & res career develop award, Dept Pharmacol, Albert Einstein Col Med, 67-69; Burroughs Wellcome Fund scholar clin pharmacol, 72-; dir psychiat consult & assoc physician, Yale New Haven Hosp, 72-; mem adv bd, Med Letter on Drugs & Therapeut, 75-90; resident fel, Pierson Col, 76-80. *Mem:* Am Soc Pharmacol & Exp Therapeut; AAAS; Am Soc Clin Pharmacol & Therapeut; Am Col Neuropsychopharmacol. *Res:* Neuropharmacology; clinical pharmacology; psychopharmacology; magnetic resonance imaging; biological basis of positive mood using pharmacological probes and magnetic resonance imaging. *Mailing Add:* Dept Pharmacol Yale Univ Sch Med 333 Cedar St New Haven CT 06510-3219

BYDAL, BRUCE A, MATH MODELING. *Current Pos:* Res engr, Eng Res Lab, E I Du Pont de Nemours & Co Inc, Del, 62-63, from res engr to sr res engr, Textile Fibers Dept, Va, 63-73, from sr engr to sr consult, Appl Math Group, 73-94, sr res assoc, Process Modeling & Simulation, 94-96, SR RES ASSOC, PROCESS UNDERSTANDING & CONTROL TECHNOL, E I DU PONT DE NEMOURS & CO, INC, 96- *Personal Data:* b Chicago, Ill, Mar 2, 37; m 64, Karen Miesner; c Dawn, Stephen & Mark. *Educ:* Univ Ill, BS, 59; Univ Minn, PhD(chem eng), 62. *Res:* Math modeling; initiating explosives; metal working/machining. *Mailing Add:* 2912 Jaffe Rd Wilmington DE 19808-1918. *E-Mail:* b4dol@e.svax.dnet.dupont.com

BYDALEK, THOMAS JOSEPH, ANALYTICAL CHEMISTRY, INORGANIC CHEMISTRY. *Current Pos:* assoc prof, 65-68, PROF CHEM, UNIV MINN, DULUTH, 68- *Personal Data:* b Grand Rapids, Mich, Apr 22, 35; m 57; c 4. *Educ:* Aquinas Col, BS, 57; Purdue Univ, PhD(anal chem), 61. *Prof Exp:* From instr to asst prof chem, Univ Wis, 61-65. *Mem:* Am Chem Soc. *Res:* Electrochemical methods development for analysis of metal ions at trace levels in natural waters; computer interfacing of analytical instrumentation; kinetics of multidentate Ligand complexes of the transition metals and their application in analysis. *Mailing Add:* Dept Chem Univ Minn 10 Univ Dr Duluth MN 55812-2496

BYE, ROBERT ARTHUR, evolution & ecology of useful plants, biology & ethnopharmacology of medicinal & edible plants, for more information see previous edition

BYER, NORMAN ELLIS, SOLID STATE PHYSICS. *Current Pos:* res scientist infrared quantum counter detector res, Res Inst Advan Studies, 69-74, sr res scientist infrared detector develop, 74-79, MGR, SEMICONDUCTOR PHYSIC DEPT, MARTIN MARIETTA LABS, 79- *Personal Data:* b Brooklyn, NY, July 17, 40; m 64; c 3. *Educ:* Cooper Union, BEE, 62; Princeton Univ, MSE, 63; Cornell Univ, PhD(appl physics), 67. *Honors & Awards:* Indust Res 100 Award, 78. *Prof Exp:* Res assoc appl physics, Cornell Univ, 66-67; mem, Sci Staff Injection Laser Studies, RCA Labs, 67-69. *Mem:* Am Phys Soc; Inst Elec & Electronics Engrs. *Res:* Research and development of infrared and microwave detection including narrow bandgap semiconductor detectors; pyroelectric detectors and millimeter wave devices such as impatt's and mixers; optically active defects in infrared detection materials; studies of pyroelectric and other infrared detectors. *Mailing Add:* 31 Louise Dr Hollis NH 03049-6008

BYER, PHILIP HOWARD, ENVIRONMENTAL ASSESSMENT, ENVIRONMENTAL PLANNING. *Current Pos:* From asst prof to assoc prof, 75-93, PROF CIVIL ENG, UNIV TORONTO, 93-, CHAIR, DIV ENVIRON ENG, 95- *Personal Data:* b Washington, DC, Jan 16, 48; m 70; c 2. *Educ:* Mass Inst Technol, SB, 72, SM, 72, PhD(civil eng), 75. *Concurrent Pos:* Chmn, Ont Environ Assessment Adv Comt, 86-95. *Mem:* Am Soc Civil Eng; Int Asn Impact Assessment; Air & Waste Mgt Asn. *Res:* Development and application of environmental impact assessment, risk assessment and multiobjective evaluation techniques for public projects; solid waste management, transportation and water resources planning; environmental planning. *Mailing Add:* Dept Civil Eng Univ Toronto Toronto ON M5S 1A4 Can. *Fax:* 416-978-3674; *E-Mail:* byer@civ.utoronto.ca

BYER, ROBERT L, RESEARCH ADMINISTRATION. *Current Pos:* from asst prof to assoc prof appl physics, Stanford Univ, 69-79, dept chair, 80-83, assoc dean humanities & sci, 84-86, vprovost & dean res, 87-92, PROF APPL PHYSICS, STANFORD UNIV, 79-, DIR, CTR NONLINEAR OPTICAL MAT, 92- *Personal Data:* b Glendale, Calif, May 9, 42; m, Eva M Guzsella; c 4. *Educ:* Univ Calif, Berkeley, BA, 64; Stanford Univ, MS, 67, PhD(appl physics), 69. *Honors & Awards:* Adolph Lomb Medal, Optical Soc Am, 72; R V Pole Mem Lectr, Conf Lasers & Electrooptics, 87; Quantum Electronics Award, Inst Elec & Electronics Engrs Lasers & Electrooptics Soc, 96. *Prof Exp:* Mem, Spectra Physics, Mountain View, Calif, 64-65. *Concurrent Pos:* Sloan fel, 74-77; co-founder, Quanta Ray Inc, 75; mem, Educ Comt, Optical Soc Am, 83-86, bd dirs, 86-89; co-founder & mem bd dirs, Lightwave Electronics Corp, 84-; guest prof, Tshinghua Univ, Beijing, China, 86; mem bd dirs, ILC Technol, 87-89; mem, Calif Coun Sci & Technol, 89-, chair, 95-; mem, Eng Adv Comn, NSF, 90-91; consult lasers & nonlinear optics; mem, Dir Res & Develop Prog Comt, Lawrence Livermore Nat Lab, 92-93; mem, Comt Optical Sci & Eng, Nat Res Coun, 95-96, Comt Inertial Confinement Fusion, 96- *Mem:* Nat Acad Eng; fel AAAS; fel Am Phys Soc; fel Inst Elec & Electronics Engrs; fel Inst Elec & Electronics Engrs Lasers & Electrooptics Soc (pres, 84-85); fel Optical Soc Am (pres, 94-95). *Res:* Diode pumped solid state lasers; nonlinear optics; nonlinear materials; optical parametric oscillators; coherent antistokes raman spectroscopy; laser remote sensing; optical tomography; slab lasers; soft x-ray lithography and microscopy; single crystal fiber growth and applications; laser diode pumped solid state laser sources; laser interferometry gravitational wave detection; laser driven particle acceleration; author more than 300 technical publications; granted more than 30 patents. *Mailing Add:* Stanford Univ Ginzton Lab Stanford CA 94305-4085

BYERLEY, LAURI OLSON, TUMOR METABOLISM, SEPSIS CYTOKINES. *Current Pos:* res dietitian, Clin Study Ctr, 81-83, res assoc, Res & Educ Inst, 83-87, POSTDOCTORAL FEL, DEPT ENDOCRINOL, NUTRIT & METAB, HARBOR-UNIV CALIF LOS ANGELES MED CTR, TORRANCE, 89-, INSTR, DEPT PEDIAT, 90- *Personal Data:* b Peoria, Ill, Mar 25, 57; m 81. *Educ:* Iowa State Univ, BS, 79; Purdue Univ, MS, 81; Univ Calif, Los Angeles, PhD(pub health & nutrit sci), 87. *Prof Exp:* Clin dietitian specialist, Nutrit Dept, Stanford Univ Hosp, Calif, 88-89. *Concurrent Pos:* Chief dietitian, Div Clin Nutrit, Sch Med, Univ Calif, Los Angeles, 84-88; postdoctoral fel, Div Gen Surg, Stanford Med Ctr, Calif, 88-89; lectr nutrit, Dept Home Econ, Calif State Univ, Long Beach, 90-91; prin investr, individual NRSA, Nat Cancer Inst, NIH, 91- *Mem:* Am Soc Clin Nutrit; Am Inst Nutrit; Am Dietetic Asn; Sigma Xi. *Res:* Stable isotopes to trace cellular metabolism; tumor cell metabolism; cytokines effects on cellular metabolism. *Mailing Add:* Dept Human Ecol Univ Tex GEA 117 Austin TX 78712-1097. *Fax:* 512-471-5630

BYERLY, DON WAYNE, GEOLOGY. *Current Pos:* asst prof, 67-81, ASSOC PROF GEOL, UNIV TENN, KNOXVILLE, 82- *Personal Data:* b Wilmington, Del, Mar 8, 33; m 55; c 4. *Educ:* Col Wooster, AB, 55; Univ Tenn, MS, 57, PhD(geol), 66. *Prof Exp:* Instr geol, Univ Tenn, 56-66; asst prof, Murray State Univ, 66-67. *Concurrent Pos:* Consult, Tenn Div Geol, 63-65 & Oak Ridge Nat Lab, 73-82. *Mem:* Sigma Xi; Geol Soc Am; Nat Asn Geol Teachers; Am Asn Prof Geologists; Asn Ground Water Scientists & Engrs; Asn Eng Geol. *Res:* Areal and environmental geological mapping; high and low nuclear waste disposal in geological media; abandoned mine sealing; strip mine reclamation; acid drainage related to mining and highway construction. *Mailing Add:* Dept Geol Univ Tenn Knoxville TN 37996-1410

BYERLY, GARY RAY, PETROLOGY, ELECTRON & OPTICAL MICROSCOPY. *Current Pos:* from asst prof to assoc prof, 77-87, PROF PETROL & MICROS, LA STATE UNIV, BATON ROUGE, 88-, SUPVR MICROS LAB, CHMN, DEPT GEOL & GEOPHYS. *Personal Data:* b Paducah, Ky, Apr 13, 48; m 81, Maud Walsh; c Zachary & Benjamin. *Educ:* Mich State Univ, BS, 70, MS, 72, PhD(geol), 74. *Prof Exp:* Fel geol, Smithsonian Inst, 74-75; res fel, US Geol Surv, 75-76. *Mem:* Geol Soc Am; Am Geophys Union; Sigma Xi. *Res:* Chemical and mineralogical variation of basalts and formation of ocean floor; the textures of igneous and metamorphic rocks; early evolution of the earth's crust, particularly the Archean of South Africa and Australia; effects of large meteorite impacts. *Mailing Add:* 7113 Joliet Ave Baton Rouge LA 70806-8124. *Fax:* 504-388-2302; *E-Mail:* glbyer@lsuvm.sncc.lsu.edu

BYERLY, PAUL ROBERTSON, JR, PHYSICS. *Current Pos:* RETIRED. *Personal Data:* b Lancaster, Pa, Sept 4, 22; m 47; c 5. *Educ:* Washington & Jefferson Col, AB, 43; Univ Pa, PhD, 51. *Prof Exp:* Instr physics, Washington & Jefferson Col, 43-44; jr physicist, Tenn Eastman Corp, 44-45; instr physics, Univ Pa, 45-50; physicist, Radiation Lab, Univ Calif, 50-58; educ adv physics, Govt Philippines, 58-63; assoc prof physics, Univ Nebr, Lincoln, 63-82. *Concurrent Pos:* Regional counr, physics, Nebr, 65-71. *Mem:* Am Phys Soc; Am Asn Physics Teachers. *Res:* Mass spectroscopy; nuclear physics; Mossbauer effect; computer graphics; computer assisted instruction. *Mailing Add:* 2685 Woodsdale Blvd Lincoln NE 68502. *Fax:* 402-423-5041

BYERLY, PERRY EDWARD, GEOPHYSICS. *Current Pos:* SR RES SCIENTIST, CONTINENTAL OIL CO, 70- *Personal Data:* b Berkeley, Calif, Feb 2, 26; m 59; c 1. *Educ:* Univ Calif, AB, 49; Harvard Univ, AM, 51, PhD(geophys), 54. *Prof Exp:* From geophysicist to sr res geophysicist, US Geol Surv, 52-63; geophys rep, Calif Res Corp, Houston, 64-66; sr geophysicist, Chevron Explor Co, 67-69, sr res geophysicist, Chevron Oilfield Res Co, 69-70. *Concurrent Pos:* Asst prof, Johns Hopkins Univ, 54-55. *Mem:* Am Geophys Union; Seismol Soc Am; Soc Explor Geophys. *Res:* Explosion seismology; gravity and magnetics; geothermal problems; general geophysics. *Mailing Add:* Byerly PE Tulsa OK 74119

BYERLY, RADFORD, JR, SCIENCE POLICY. *Current Pos:* VPRES PUB POLICY, UNION, CORP ATMOSPHERE RES, BOULDER, 93-; DIR, ROBERTS INST, 93- *Personal Data:* b Houston, Tex, May 22, 36; m 60, 87, Carol A Ries; c Laura, Hamilton & Charles. *Educ:* Williams Col, BA, 58, MA, 60; Rice Univ, PhD, 67. *Prof Exp:* Sr engr, N Res & Eng Co, Mass, 61-63; NSF fel, 63-67; fel, Univ Colo, Boulder, 67-69, dir, Ctr Space & Geosci Policy, 87-91. *Concurrent Pos:* Physicist & mgr, Nat Bur Stands, 69-75; mem, Prof Staff Comt Sci & Technol, US House of Rep, Washington, 75-87, chief of staff, 91-93, hon lectr, Mid-Am State Univs Asn, 88-89. *Mem:* AAAS; Am Soc Testing & Mats; Am Inst Aeronaut & Astronaut; Am Phys Soc; Am Astronaut Soc; Sigma Xi. *Res:* Science policy; public policy. *Mailing Add:* 3870 Birchwood Dr Boulder CO 80304

BYERRUM, RICHARD UGLOW, BIOCHEMISTRY. *Current Pos:* From instr to prof chem, Mich State Univ, 47-59, asst provost, 59-62, actg dir biol & med, 61-62, dean, Col Natural Sci, 62-86, prof, 57-92, EMER PROF BIOCHEM, MICH STATE UNIV, 92- *Personal Data:* b Aurora, Ill, Sept 22, 20; m 45, Claire Somers; c Elizabeth, Mary & Carey. *Educ:* Wabash Col, AB, 42; Univ Ill, Urbana, PhD(biochem, org chem), 47. *Hon Degrees:* DSc, Wabash Col, 67. *Concurrent Pos:* Sabbatical leave, Calif Polytech Inst, 56 & Scripts Inst Oceanog, 73; travel awards, Int Cong Biochem, Vienna, 58 & Montreal, 59; consult, Am Chem Soc, 58-62; vis scientist, 62-64; mem bd, Mich Health Coun, 61-; consult, NCent Asn Sec Schs & Cols, 62- & Nat Acad Sci, 72-74. *Mem:* AAAS; Am Chem Soc; Am Soc Plant Physiol; Soc Exp Biol & Med; Am Soc Biochem Molecular Biol. *Res:* Metabolism in plants with special emphasis on the production of glycerol; glycerol phosphate during photosynthesis. *Mailing Add:* 522 Biochem Bldg Mich State Univ East Lansing MI 48824

BYERS, BENJAMIN ROWE, MICROBIOLOGY. *Current Pos:* from asst prof to assoc prof, 67-73, PROF MICROBIOL, MED CTR, UNIV MISS, 73- *Personal Data:* b Austin, Tex, Nov 7, 36; m 57; c 2. *Educ:* Univ Tex, Austin, BA, 58, MA, 60, PhD(microbiol), 65. *Prof Exp:* Bacteriologist, Stand Brands05137779x-62; NIH fel, Univ Tex, Austin, 65-66, asst prof microbiol, 66. *Concurrent Pos:* NIH res career develop award, Med Ctr, Univ Miss, 71-75, NIH res grant, 71-, NIH contract, 74-78; Cooley's Anemia Found res grant, 78-82; Am Heart Asn res grant, 83-85. *Mem:* AAAS; Am Soc Microbiol. *Res:* Iron and trace metal metabolism; mechanisms of iron and trace metal transport; iron chelating agents in treatment of iron storage disease; iron and infection. *Mailing Add:* Dept Microbiol Univ Miss Sch Med 2500 N State St Jackson MS 39216-4505

BYERS, BRECK EDWARD, GENETICS OF YEAST CELL CYCLE & MEIOSIS. *Current Pos:* PROF GENETICS & ADJ PROF BIOCHEM, UNIV WASH, 71-, CHAIR, 91- *Personal Data:* b St Louis, Mo, July 4, 39; m 64, Margaret Read; c 2. *Educ:* Univ Colo, BS, 61; Harvard Univ, PhD(biol), 67. *Honors & Awards:* Merit Award, NIH, 92. *Mem:* Am Soc Cell Biol; Am Soc Microbiol; Genetics Soc Am. *Res:* Employ molecular genetics and cytological methods in yeast to analyze mechanisms that control microtubule; distribution and cell cycle progression in mitosis and that regulate chromosomal organization and recombination in meiosis. *Mailing Add:* Dept Genetics Univ Wash Box 357360 Seattle WA 98195-7360. *Fax:* 206-543-0754; *E-Mail:* byers@genetics.washington.edu

BYERS, CHARLES HARRY, CHEMICAL ENGINEERING. *Current Pos:* GROUP LEADER, OAK RIDGE NAT LAB, 80-; PROF CHEM ENG, UNIV TENN, 84- *Personal Data:* b Buckingham, Que, Feb 29, 40; m 93, Rosemary Barrett; c 3. *Educ:* McGill Univ, BEng, 62; Univ Calif, Berkeley, PhD(chem eng), 66. *Prof Exp:* Asst prof chem eng, Univ Rochester, 66-70; res chem engr, Merichem Co, 70-77; prin engr, Polaroid Corp, 77-80. *Concurrent Pos:* Pres, Syst Designs Inc & Isopro Int Inc. *Mem:* Am Inst Chem Engrs; Am Chem Soc. *Res:* Heat and mass transport; interfacial phenomena; laser light scattering. *Mailing Add:* Oak Ridge Nat Lab PO Box 2008 Oak Ridge TN 37831. *Fax:* 423-481-0919; *E-Mail:* kdb@ornl.gov

BYERS, CHARLES WESLEY, GEOLOGY. *Current Pos:* PROF GEOL & GEOPHYS, UNIV WIS-MADISON, 73- *Personal Data:* b Philadelphia, Pa, Aug 23, 46; m 82; c 2. *Educ:* Marietta Col, BS, 68; Yale Univ, MPh, 71, PhD(geol), 73. *Mem:* Geol Soc Am; Paleont Soc; Soc Econ Paleontologists & Mineralogists; Sigma Xi; AAAS. *Res:* Stratigraphy and paleoecology of cretaceous rocks; deposition of shales; cambrian paleoenvironments; trace fossils. *Mailing Add:* Dept Geol & Geophys Univ Wis-Madison 1215 W Dayton St Madison WI 53706

BYERS, DAVID M, MEDICAL RESEARCH, BIOCHEMISTRY. *Current Pos:* MED RESEARCHER & BIOCHEMIST, ATLANTIC RES CTR, DALHOUSIE UNIV, 85- *Personal Data:* b Kingston, Ont, Nov 14, 54. *Educ:* Dalhousie Univ, BS, 76, MS, 78; Univ Alta, Edmonton, PhD(biochem), 83. *Prof Exp:* Fel biochem, McGill Univ, Montreal, 83-85. *Concurrent Pos:* Med Res Coun scholar, 86-91. *Mem:* Am Soc Biochem & Molecular Biol. *Res:* Membrane biochemistry; cell signaling; disorders of cholesterol metabolism; bacterial fatty acid metabolism. *Mailing Add:* Clin Res Ctr Rm C-202 Dalhousie Univ 5849 University Ave Halifax NS B3H 4H7 Can. *Fax:* 902-494-1394; *E-Mail:* byersd@tupdean1.med.dal.ca

BYERS, FLOYD MICHAEL, ANIMAL NUTRITION. *Current Pos:* assoc prof, 80-86, PROF BEEF CATTLE NUTRIT & GROWTH, TEX A&M UNIV, 86- *Personal Data:* b Rush City, Minn, Feb 8, 47; m 67; c 3. *Educ:* Univ Minn, BS, 69; SDak State Univ, MS, 72; Colo State Univ, PhD(ruminant nutrit), 74. *Prof Exp:* Lab technician plant res, Univ Minn, 65-67, nutrit res, 67-69; feedlot mgr, SDak State Univ, 70-71, dir, Ruminant Nutrit Lab, 71-72; res asst energy metab, Colo State Univ, 72-73, NDEA res fel, 73-74; asst prof beef cattle nutrit, Ohio Agr Res & Develop Ctr, 75-80. *Concurrent Pos:* Consult, Food Safety Inspection Serv, USDA, 87. *Mem:* Am Soc Animal Sci; Am Inst Nutrit; Animal Nutrit Res Coun; Sigma Xi. *Res:* Investigations concerning protein and energy requirements and efficiency of protein and energy utilization for maintenance and production of cattle, varying in mature size, fed rations varying in available energy *Mailing Add:* 4969 Schehin Rd College Station TX 77845

BYERS, FRANK MILTON, JR, PETROGRAPHY OF IGNEOUS ROCKS, GEOCHEMISTRY OF IGNEOUS ROCKS. *Current Pos:* EMER SCIENTIST, US GEOL SURV, 93- *Personal Data:* b Moline, Ill, Mar 5, 16; m 45, Virginia Pratt; c John A, Carol L, H Randolph & Ardath E. *Educ:* Augustana Col, AB, 38; Univ Chicago, PhD(geol), 55. *Prof Exp:* Geologist, US Geol Surv, 41-81; petrologist, Los Alamos Nat Lab, 82-88, lab assoc, 88-93. *Concurrent Pos:* Guest assoc ed, J Geophys Res, 87-88. *Mem:* Fel Geol Soc Am; Am Geophys Union. *Res:* Mineralogy, petrology and geochemistry of silicic volcanic rocks; geological characterization of potential underground nuclear waste repository at Yucca Mountain, Nevada. *Mailing Add:* 125 Everett St Lakewood CO 80226. *Fax:* 303-236-4930; *E-Mail:* fmbyers@usgs.gov

BYERS, GEORGE WILLIAM, ENTOMOLOGY, SYSTEMATICS & BIOLOGY OF TIPULIDAE DIPTERA & MECOPTERA. *Current Pos:* from asst prof to prof entom, 56-88, chmn, Dept Entom, 69-72 & 84-87, EMER PROF ENTOM, UNIV KANS, 88- *Personal Data:* b Washington, DC, May 16, 23; m 55, Gloria B. *Educ:* Purdue Univ, BS, 47; Univ Mich, MS, 48, PhD, 52. *Prof Exp:* Rackham fel zool, Univ Mich, 52-53; res med entomologist, US Army, Korea & Japan, 53-56; asst cur, Snow Entom Mus, Univ Kans, 56-73, cur, 74-88, dir, 83-88. *Concurrent Pos:* Ed, Syst Zool, Soc Syst Zool, 63-66; vis prof, Biol Sta, Univ Va, 61-92 & Univ Minn, 70. *Mem:* Soc Study Evolution; Soc Syst Biol; Entom Soc Am; Am Soc Naturalists; Entom Soc Can. *Res:* Biology and classification of Tipulidae and Mecoptera. *Mailing Add:* Dept Entom Univ Kans Lawrence KS 66045-2119

BYERS, HORACE ROBERT, METEOROLOGY, CLOUD PHYSICS. *Current Pos:* dean, Col Geosci, Tex A&M Univ, 65-68, distinguished prof, 65-74, acad vpres, 68-71, EMER PROF METEOROL, TEX A&M UNIV, 74- *Personal Data:* b Seattle, Wash, Mar 12, 06; m 27; c 1. *Educ:* Univ Calif, AB, 29; Mass Inst Technol, MS, 32, ScD(meteorol), 35. *Honors & Awards:* Losey Award, Am Inst Aeronaut & Astronaut, 41; Brooks Award, Am Meteorol Soc, 60, Cleveland Abbe Award, 78. *Prof Exp:* Asst, Mass Inst

Technol, 30-32 & Scripps Inst, Univ Calif, 32-33; instr meteorol, Transcontinental & Western Air, 33-35; meteorologist, US Weather Bur, 35-40; from assoc prof to prof meteorol, Univ Chicago, 40-65, chmn dept, 48-60. *Concurrent Pos:* Dir, US Interdept Thunderstorm Proj, 46-50; vpres, Int Asn Meteorol & Atmospheric Physics, 54-60, pres, 60-63; chmn bd, Univ Corp Atmospheric Res, 63-65 & Gulf Univ Res Corp, 66-69; vis prof, Univ Clermont-Ferrand, France, 75. *Mem:* Nat Acad Sci; Am Meteorol Soc (pres, 52-53). *Res:* Thunderstorms; physical and dynamic meteorology. *Mailing Add:* 300 Hot Springs Rd No 178 Santa Barbara CA 93108

BYERS, HUGH RANDOLPH, CANCER RESEARCH, CELL BIOLOGY. *Current Pos:* ASSOC PROF DERMAT, BOSTON UNIV MED SCH, 94- *Personal Data:* b Pomona, Calif, Sept 14, 53; m 80, Danielle Levi Alvares; c Johnathan & Julie. *Educ:* Harvard Med Sch, MD, 83; Harvard Univ, PhD(anat), 83. *Prof Exp:* From instr to asst prof path, Harvard Med Sch, 87-94. *Concurrent Pos:* Prin investr, Boston Univ Med Ctr. *Mem:* Am Soc Cell Biol; Soc Invest Dermat. *Res:* Study molecular mechanism of melanoma cell motility and metastasis. *Mailing Add:* Dept Dermat Boston Univ Sch Med 609 Albany St Boston MA 02118-2394. *Fax:* 617-726-2365

BYERS, JOHN ROBERT, ENTOMOLOGY. *Current Pos:* RES SCIENTIST, CAN DEPT AGR, 68- *Personal Data:* b Stoughton, Sask, July 27, 37; m 63; c 2. *Educ:* Univ Sask, BSA, 62, MSc, 63, PhD(entom, physiol), 66. *Prof Exp:* Nat Res Coun Can overseas fel, 66-67; asst prof biol, Univ Sask, 67-68. *Mem:* Can Soc Zoologists; Entom Soc Can; Entom Soc Am. *Res:* Behavior and ecology of noctuid moths; agricultural entomology. *Mailing Add:* Res Sta Agr Can Lethbridge AB T1J 4B1 Can

BYERS, LARRY DOUGLAS, BIOCHEMISTRY. *Current Pos:* from asst prof to assoc prof chem, 75-86, PROF CHEM, TULANE UNIV, 86- *Personal Data:* b Los Angeles, Calif, Feb 18, 47. *Educ:* Univ Calif, Los Angeles, BS, 68; Princeton Univ, MS, 70, PhD(biochem), 72. *Prof Exp:* Fel enzym, Univ Calif, Berkeley, 72-75. *Concurrent Pos:* NIH fel, 73-75. *Mem:* Am Chem Soc; Am Soc Biochemists & Molecular Biol. *Res:* Mechanism of action of enzymes; design of enzyme inhibitors. *Mailing Add:* Dept Chem Tulane Univ New Orleans LA 70118. *Fax:* 504-865-5596

BYERS, LAWRENCE WALLACE, BIOCHEMISTRY, NUTRITION. *Current Pos:* RETIRED. *Personal Data:* b Pulaski, Pa, Nov 12, 16; m 56, Mary Burrier; c Christina L (Voeiker) & Clayton H. *Educ:* Westminster Col, Pa, BS, 38; Oberlin Col, MA, 40; Univ Ill, PhD(biochem), 48. *Prof Exp:* Teaching asst chem, Oberlin Col, 38-40; res asst, Exp Sta, Mich State Univ, 40-42; org res, Dow Chem Co, Mich, 42-45; teaching asst, Univ Ill, 45-46; res biochemist, Bristol Labs, 48-52, Ft Detrick, Md, 52-56; res biochemist, Dept Psychiat & Neurol, Sch Med, Tulane Univ, 56-66, asst prof biochem, 60-66; res biochemist, Dept Path, Baptist Mem Hosp, Memphis, 66-85; from asst prof to res prof biochem, Ctr Health Sci, Univ Tenn, Memphis, 85-94. *Concurrent Pos:* Biochem consult, Vet Hosp, Gulfport, Miss, 64-66 & USPHS grant; res biochemist, Dept Path, Baptist Mem Hosp, Memphis, 66-85, Univ Tenn, Memphis, 85- *Mem:* AAAS; NY Acad Sci; Am Asn Clin Chemists; Sigma Xi. *Res:* Carotenoids; fatty acids; silicones; phospholipids; antibiotics; nutrition; intermediary metabolism, biochemical aspects of mental illness; antihypertensive factors of kidney medulla. *Mailing Add:* 3138 Dumbarton Rd Memphis TN 38128

BYERS, NINA, PARTICLE & THEORETICAL PHYSICS, HISTORY OF TWENTIETH CENTURY PHYSICS. *Current Pos:* from asst prof to assoc prof, 61-67, PROF PHYSICS, UNIV CALIF, LOS ANGELES, 67- *Personal Data:* b Los Angeles, Calif, Jan 19, 30; m 74, Arthur Milhaiyst; c Gretchen, Marrinee (Rendr), Tony, Charles & Ann (Bottinelli). *Educ:* Univ Calif, BA, 50; Univ Chicago, MS, 53, PhD(physics), 56. *Hon Degrees:* MA, Oxford Univ, 67. *Prof Exp:* Res fel math physics, Univ Birmingham, 56-58; res assoc, Stanford Univ, 58-59, asst prof, 59-61. *Concurrent Pos:* Guggenheim fel & vis mem, Inst Advan Study, 63-64; fac lectr, Oxford Univ, 67-68; Janet Watson vis fel, Univ Calif, Los Angeles & Oxford, 68-74, vis scientist, 69-74 & 77-78, off tutor physics, 67-78, vis res scientist, 69-74 & 77-78, sci res fel, 78; counr-at-large, Am Phys Soc, 77-81, comt mem on opportunities in physics 80-83, panel on pub affairs, 80-82, vchmn forum on physics, 81, chmn forum on physics, 82; comt mem, Sect Physics, AAAS, 83-87; comt mem sci freedom & res possibility, AAAS, 92-95. *Mem:* Fel Am Phys Soc; Fedn Am Scientists; fel AAAS. *Res:* Superconductivity, theoritical particle physics; history of 20th century physics with particular attention to contributions of women. *Mailing Add:* Dept Physics Univ Calif Los Angeles CA 90024. *E-Mail:* byers@physics.ucla.edu

BYERS, R LEE, CHEMICAL ENGINEERING, AIR POLLUTION. *Personal Data:* b Hagerstown, Md, Dec 20, 35; m 57; c 4. *Educ:* Juniata Col, BA, 58; Carnegie-Mellon Univ, BS, 58; Univ Rochester, MS, 60; Pa State Univ, PhD(chem eng), 67. *Prof Exp:* From instr to asst prof physics & pre-eng, Elizabethtown Col, 59-63; asst prof mech eng, Pa State Univ, 68-70; assoc prof chem eng, Univ NH, 70-72; mem eng staff, Environ Control & Safety Div, Exxon Res & Eng Co, 72-80. *Mem:* Sigma Xi; Am Inst Chem Engrs; Air Pollution Control Asn. *Res:* Gas purification; small particle dynamics; ambient air quality evaluation. *Mailing Add:* 6 Laurel Ridge Rd East Stroudsburg PA 18301

BYERS, ROBERT ALLAN, ENTOMOLOGY. *Current Pos:* Res entomologist, Entom Res Div, Tifton, Ga, 61-66, Lafayette, Ind, 66-70, RES ENTOMOLOGIST, US REGIONAL PASTURE RES LAB, AGR RES SERV, USDA, UNIVERSITY PARK, PA, 70- *Personal Data:* b Latrobe, Pa, Dec 6, 36; m 60; c 2. *Educ:* Pa State Univ, BSc, 60; Ohio State Univ, MSc, 61; Purdue Univ, PhD(entom), 71. *Mem:* Entom Soc Am. *Res:* Biology and control of the two-lined spittlebug on Coastal bermuda grass; effect of a complex of insects on the yield of Coastal bermuda grass; ability of the Hessian fly to stunt winter wheat; host plant resistance to alfalfa blotch leafminer, and clover root curculio in alfalfa; invertebrate control on legumes in conservation-tillage systems. *Mailing Add:* 205 Homestead Lane Boalsburg PA 16827

BYERS, ROLAND O, INDUSTRIAL TECHNOLOGY, ENGINEERING GRAPHICS. *Current Pos:* RETIRED. *Personal Data:* b Boston, Ohio, Sept 9, 19; m 44; c 2. *Educ:* Ohio Univ, BS, 46, MS, 49. *Prof Exp:* Assoc prof eng graphics, Univ Wichita, 46-51, head dept, 53-54; prof gen eng & chmn dept, Univ Idaho, 54-81. *Mem:* Am Soc Eng Educ. *Res:* Engineering descriptive geometry. *Mailing Add:* 821 Nez Perce St Moscow ID 83843

BYERS, RONALD ELNER, THEORETICAL PHYSICS. *Current Pos:* teacher, 70-77, ASSOC PROF PHYSICS, CENT COL, 78- *Personal Data:* b Everett, Wash, Nov 8, 36; m 60; c 2. *Educ:* Wash State Univ, BS, 66, PhD(physics), 74. *Prof Exp:* Mathematician, Strategy & Tactics-Anal Group, US Army, 60-62; technologist, Battelle Northwest Lab, 62-65. *Mem:* Am Asn Physics Teachers. *Res:* Quantum hidden variables theory unifying essentials of quantum mechanics and general relativity; evolution processes in scientific theory making; philosophical grounding of scientific theories. *Mailing Add:* RR 3 Pella IA 50219

BYERS, SANFORD OSCAR, BIOCHEMISTRY. *Current Pos:* RETIRED. *Personal Data:* b New York, NY, May 1, 18; m 42; c 5. *Educ:* Rensselaer Polytech Inst, BSc, 39; Univ Cincinnati, PhD(biochem), 44. *Prof Exp:* Instr biochem & physiol, Washington Univ, 44-45; res biochemist, Nat Drug Co, Philadelphia, 45-46; res biochemist, Harold Brunn Inst, Mt Zion Hosp, 46-78. *Concurrent Pos:* Fel coun arteriosclerosis, Am Heart Asn. *Mem:* AAAS; Reticuloendothelial Soc; Am Chem Soc; Am Soc Exp Biol & Med; Am Physiol Soc. *Res:* Atherosclerosis; metabolism of digitalis, cholesterol, and lipids; catecholamines. *Mailing Add:* 40 Newhall Dr San Rafael CA 94901-1319

BYERS, STANLEY A, CERAMICS. *Current Pos:* RETIRED. *Personal Data:* b Ashland, Ohio, Jan 9, 31; m 66; c 2. *Educ:* Antioch Col, BA, 55; Mich State Univ, BS, 57; Case Western Res Univ, PhD(mat sci), 74. *Prof Exp:* Metall & ceramics engr, Ohio Brass Co, 58-63; ceramic engr, Am Stand Inc, 63-69 & Carborundum Co, 69-70; res scientist mat, Res Exp Sta, Ga Inst Technol, 72-75; mem staff, Ball Corp, 75-80, mgr mat res & assoc prof indust & technol, 80-96. *Mem:* Am Ceramic Soc; Am Soc Metals. *Res:* Glass processing and formulation; glass coatings. *Mailing Add:* 2000 N Nebo Rd Muncie IN 47304

BYERS, THOMAS JONES, GENETICS. *Current Pos:* asst prof zool & entom, Ohio State Univ, 64-68, dir develop biol prog, 72-75, assoc prof microbiol & cell biol, 68-77, prof microbiol, 77-87, PROF MOLECULAR GENETICS, OHIO STATE UNIV, 87-, ASSOC DEAN BIOL SCI, 90- *Personal Data:* b Philadelphia, Pa, Oct 12, 35; m 60, Sandra A Roberts; c Stephen A & Linda M (Fontana). *Educ:* Cornell Univ, AB, 58; Univ Pa, PhD(zool), 62. *Prof Exp:* USPHS fel biophys, Carnegie Inst Dept Terrestrial Magnetism, 62-64. *Concurrent Pos:* Vis prof, Dept Biochem, Univ Ala, Birmingham, 87. *Mem:* Soc Protozool. *Res:* Developmental biology of protoza; molecular biology and phylogeny of pathogenic amoebas; development of DNA-based diagnostic reagents for the detection and identification of amoebas associated with human disease. *Mailing Add:* Dept Molecular Genetics Ohio State Univ 484 W 12th Ave Columbus OH 43210-1214

BYERS, VERA STEINBERGER, IMMUNOBIOLOGY. *Current Pos:* DIR CORP DEVELOP IMMUNOL, VILMA XOMA CORP. *Personal Data:* b Houston, Tex, Nov 18, 42; m 73. *Educ:* Univ Calif, Los Angeles, BA, 65, MS, 67, PhD(immunobiol), 69; Univ Calif, San Francisco, MD, 81. *Prof Exp:* Bench chemist, Res Div, Abbott Labs, 69-71; res immunologist, Dept Med, Univ Calif, San Francisco, 71-74, asst prof dermat, 75- *Concurrent Pos:* Nat Inst Allergy & Infectious Dis fels, 68 & 72; Arthritis Found fel, 72. *Res:* Human cellular immunology; lymphocyte regulation and maturation; cancer immunobiology. *Mailing Add:* Allergene Inc 1650 Borel Pl Suite 234 San Mateo CA 94402

BYERS, WALTER HAYDEN, PHYSICS. *Current Pos:* RETIRED. *Personal Data:* b Johnstown, Pa, July 6, 14; m 45; c 3. *Educ:* Univ Fla, BS, 36, MS, 38; Pa State Col, PhD(physics), 42. *Prof Exp:* Physicist, USAF, 43-46; asst prof physics, Univ Okla, 46-47; asst prof elec eng, Univ Ill, 46-51; physicist, USAF, 51-54; weapon syst analyst, Sandia Corp, 54-56; physicist, USAF, 56-71; asst prof eng, Clark Tech Col, 71-73, assoc prof eng & natural sci, 73-84. *Mem:* Sigma Xi. *Res:* Ultrasonics; astronautics; space system engineering. *Mailing Add:* 3155 Meadow Wood Dr Springfield OH 45505

BYFIELD, JOHN ERIC, RADIOTHERAPY, ONCOLOGY. *Current Pos:* DIR, RADIATION THER ASN, BAKERSFIELD, CALIF, 86- *Personal Data:* b Toronto, Ont, Nov 26, 36; US citizen; m 73; c 4. *Educ:* Univ Calif, Los Angeles, BA, 60, MD, 65, PhD(physiol), 70. *Prof Exp:* Intern path, Lab Nuclear Med & Radiation Biol, Sch Med, Univ Calif, Los Angeles, 66-67, radiation therapist, 67-70, instr radiol, 69-70, from asst prof & asst res physician to assoc prof & assoc res physician, 70-75; assoc prof radiol & chief radiation ther, Univ San Diego, 76-82, prof radiol & med, 76-83. *Concurrent Pos:* Chief radiation ther, Harbor Gen Hosp, Torrance, Calif, 70-75. *Mem:* Am Soc Clin Oncol; fel Am Col Radiol; Am Soc Therapeut Radiol; Am Soc Cell Biologists; Am Asn Cancer Res. *Res:* Biochemistry of anticancer drugs; clinical chemotherapy; radiation biology; clinical radiation therapy. *Mailing Add:* 3550 Q St Bakersfield CA 93301

BYINGTON, KEITH H, BIOCHEMICAL PHARMACOLOGY, PHARMACOLOGY. *Current Pos:* asst prof, 68-74, ASSOC PROF PHARMACOL, SCH MED, UNIV MO, COLUMBIA, 74- *Personal Data:* b Plymouth, Iowa, Mar 14, 35; m 55; c 4. *Educ:* Univ Iowa, BS, 58; Univ SDak, PhD(pharmacol), 64. *Prof Exp:* Org chemist, 58-60; instr pharmacol, Univ SDak, 63-64; fel, Univ Fla, 64-65; fel biochem, Inst Enzyme Res, Univ Wis, 65-68. *Mem:* Am Soc Pharmacol & Exp Therapeut. *Res:* Drug metabolism; drug enzyme interaction; drug-membrane interactions; toxicology. *Mailing Add:* Dept Pharmacol M617 Med Sci Bldg Univ Mo Sch Med Columbia MO 65212-0001

BYL, JOHN, ASTRONOMY, ASTRODYNAMICS. *Current Pos:* fac, 78-86, PROF & CHAIR MATH, TRINITY WESTERN UNIV, 86- *Personal Data:* b Hague, Neth, Jan 1, 49; Can citizen; m 72, Margaret Hoogland; c 6. *Educ:* Univ BC, BSc, 69, PhD(astron), 73. *Prof Exp:* Postdoctoral fel astron, Univ BC, 73-75, lectr, 76-77; vis prof physics, Dordt Col, Iowa, 77-78. *Res:* Interactions between cosmology, theology and philosophy; effects of the galaxy on comet orbits. *Mailing Add:* 7600 Glover Rd Langley BC V2Y 1Y1 Can. *E-Mail:* byl@twu.ca

BYLANDER, EREST GERALD, WIDE ANGLE OPTICAL MODULATOR & THIN FILM PLZT LENS FOR OPHTHALMOLOGY, PACKAGING & TESTING OF BRAIN PROBES FOR CENTRAL NERVOUS SYSTEM STUDIES. *Current Pos:* PRES, BYLANDER ASSOCS INC, 93- *Personal Data:* b Farmington, Ariz, May 22, 31; m 53, 75, Jane Ests; c 5. *Educ:* Univ Ariz, BS, 54, MS, 62; Southern Methodist Univ, MS, 86, PhD(elec eng), 88. *Prof Exp:* Engr, Convair Div, Gen Dynamics, 55-59; sr engr, Tex Instruments Inc, 59-63; res physicist, Melpar, 62-63, US Naval Ordinance Lab/WO, 63-66; mem tech staff, Tex Instruments, 66-83, group mem tech staff, 83-86; instr electronics, Grayson County Col, 86-93. *Concurrent Pos:* Instr math, Univ Mo, Rolla, 56-57; adj instr physics, Montgomery County Jr Col, 64-65; adj instr electronics, Grayson County Col, 74-76; adj instr chem, Austin Col, 76. *Mem:* Sr mem Inst Elec & Electronics Engrs. *Res:* Research and development of terroelectric plzt variable density lens and spectacle systems for ophthalmological diagnosis and treatment; central nervous system (brain) probes and headstages; microelectronics packaging and flex circuits. *Mailing Add:* Bylander Assocs Inc 1501 Ridgeway Dr Sherman TX 75092-3211

BYLER, DAVID MICHAEL, INFRARED & RAMAN SPECTROSCOPY. *Current Pos:* ASSOC PROF, & ASST DEAN CHEM, SCH SCI & HEALTH, PHILADELPHIA COL TEXTILES & SCI, 90- *Personal Data:* b Mishawaka, Ind, Dec 23, 45; m 92, Penelope A Hamilton; c D Andrew & Jonathan E. *Educ:* Univ NC, Chapel Hill, AB, 68; Northwestern Univ, Evanston, MS, 69, PhD(inorg chem), 74. *Honors & Awards:* Sigma Xi, 74. *Prof Exp:* Instr chem, Dept Phys Sci, Wilbur Wright Col, Kennedy-King Col & Chicago City Cols, 70 & 73; instr, dept chem, Drexel Univ, 73-75; vis asst prof, dept chem, Temple Univ, 75-78; Nat Res Coun res fel, 78-79, res chemist, Eastern Regional Res Ctr, USDA, 79-90. *Concurrent Pos:* Vis Scientist & Consult, SmithKline Beecham Pharmaceut, King of Prussia, Pa, 93- *Mem:* Soc Appl Spectros; Can Spectros Soc; Am Chem Soc; The Chem Soc; Sigma Xi; Coblentz Soc. *Res:* Estimation of protein conformation by resolution-enhanced infrared spectroscopy; vibrational spectroscopy of amino acids, polypeptides, and other biomolecules; vibrational spectroscopic characterization of clays and their intercalates with small molecules and ions. *Mailing Add:* Sch Sci & Health Philadelphia Col Textile & Sci Philadelphia PA 19144-5497. *Fax:* 215-951-2615; *E-Mail:* michael_byler-1@sbphrd.com

BYLES, PETER HENRY, anesthesiology, for more information see previous edition

BYLUND, DAVID BRUCE, NEUROPHARMACOLOGY, BIOCHEMICAL PHARMACOLOGY. *Current Pos:* PROF & CHAIR, DEPT PHARMACOL, UNIV NEBR MED CTR, 89- *Personal Data:* b Spanish Fork, UT, Apr 16, 46; m 70, Elaine C Thurman; c Carma, Eric, Michelle, Kevin, Jennie, Kristen & Emily. *Educ:* Univ Calif, PhD(biochem), 74. *Prof Exp:* Prof pharmacol, Sch Med, Univ Mo, 77-89. *Concurrent Pos:* Ed, Pharmacol Rev. *Mem:* Soc Neurosci; Am Soc Pharmacol & Exp Therapeut. *Res:* Regulation classification and mechanism of action of adrenergic receptors. *Mailing Add:* Dept Pharmacol Univ NE Med Ctr 600 42nd St Omaha NE 68198-6260. *E-Mail:* dbylund@mail.unmc.edu

BYNUM, BARBARA S, SCIENCE ADMINISTRATION. *Current Pos:* RETIRED. *Personal Data:* b Washington, DC, June 13, 36. *Prof Exp:* Sci Adminr & Dir, Extramural Activ, Nat Cancer Inst, NIH, 81-94. *Mailing Add:* 4624 Norbeck Rd Rockville MD 20853

BYNUM, T E, CLINICAL GASTROENTEROLOGY. *Current Pos:* CHIEF INTERNAL MED & GASTROENTEROL, MARLBOROUGH HOSP, 93- *Personal Data:* b Chickasha, Okla, Sept 13, 39. *Educ:* Univ Okla, MD. *Prof Exp:* Chief clin gastroenterol, Brigham & Women's Hosp, Harvard Med Sch, 79-92. *Mailing Add:* 65 Fremont St Marlborough MA 01752

BYNUM, WILLIAM LEE, MATHEMATICS. *Current Pos:* asst prof, 69-74, assoc prof math, 74-83, PROF COMPUT SCI, COL WILLIAM & MARY, 83- *Personal Data:* b Carlsbad, NMex, June 28, 36; m 65. *Educ:* Tex Technol Col, BS, 57; Univ NC, MA, 64, PhD(math), 66. *Prof Exp:* Engr, Bell Helicopter Corp, Tex, 57-61; instr math, Univ NC, 65-66; asst prof, La State Univ, 66-69. *Mem:* Asn Comput Mach; Inst Elec & Electronics Engrs; Inst Elec & Electronics Engrs Comput Sci. *Mailing Add:* Dept Comput Sci Col William & Mary PO Box 8795 Williamsburg VA 23187-8795

BYRAM, GEORGE WAYNE, INSTRUMENTATION, ELECTRICAL ENGINEERING. *Current Pos:* ELECTRONIC ENGR, NAVAL COMMAND, CONTROL & OCEAN SURVEILLANCE CTR RDT & E DIV, SAN DIEGO, 70- *Personal Data:* b Asheville, NC, Nov 25, 38; m 91, Judith Krusemark; c Mark. *Educ:* Ga Inst Technol, BEE, 61, MSEE, 62; Mass Inst Technol, SM, 64, ScD(instrumentation), 67. *Prof Exp:* Electronic engr, Naval Undersea Res & Develop Ctr, Pasadena, 61-68; res engr, Naval Res Lab, 68-70. *Res:* Signal processing algorithms and implementations; parallel computation. *Mailing Add:* 3250 McCall St San Diego CA 92106-3305. *E-Mail:* byram@nose.mil

BYRD, BENJAMIN FRANKLIN, JR, SURGERY, ONCOLOGY. *Current Pos:* CLIN PROF SURG, MEHARRY MED COL, 69- & SCH MED, VANDERBILT UNIV, 71- *Personal Data:* b Nashville, Tenn, May 18, 18; m 50; c 6. *Educ:* Vanderbilt Univ, AB, 37, MD, 41. *Concurrent Pos:* Surg, Pvt Pract, 48-; chmn breast cancer task force, Am Cancer Soc, 71-; chmn cancer adv comt, Joint Comn Accreditation of Hosp, 72-76; cancer control community activ rev comt, Div Cancer Control & Rehab, Nat Cancer Inst, 76-77. *Mem:* Am Cancer Soc (pres, 75-76); Sigma Xi; Soc Surg Oncol; AAAS; Am Col Surgeons; Am Surg Asn. *Res:* Diagnosis and management of breast cancer; long-term effects of estrogen administration. *Mailing Add:* 4230 Harding Rd Suite 609 Nashville TN 37205

BYRD, DANIEL MADISON, III, SAFETY EVALUATION, BIOLOGICAL MODELING. *Current Pos:* PRES, CTRAPS, 88- *Personal Data:* b Detroit, Mich, Dec 30, 40; div; c Mary, Laura & Dan. *Educ:* Yale Univ, BA, 63, PhD(pharmacol), 71; Am Bd Toxicol, dipl, 82. *Prof Exp:* Res assoc cell biol, Sch Med, Univ Md, 70; vis scientist pharmacol, Nat Cancer Inst, 71; res assoc oncol, Med Sch, Johns Hopkins Univ, 71-72; from asst cancer res scientist to cancer res scientist, Roswell Park Mem Inst, 72-75; asst prof, pharmacol, Col Med, Univ Okla, 75-79; sci adv premanufacture rev, Off Toxic Substances, US Environ Protection Agency, pharmacologist hazard eval, Off Pesticides & toxologist, carcinogen assessment group, Off Res Develop, 80-81 & exec secy adv bd, 84-87; sci adv, Am Petrol Inst, 82-83; dir sci affairs, Cammer Assoc, 87-88. *Concurrent Pos:* Liaison, Soc Risk Anal & Am Col Toxicol; assoc ed, Toxicol Indust Health. *Mem:* Soc Risk Anal; Soc Toxicol; Am Col Toxicol; Soc Epidemiol Res; Am Chem Soc; Am Asn Cancer Res. *Res:* Toxicology; risk assessment, uncertainty analysis, chronic disease mechanics (cancer, develop, immunol, mutation, neurol & reproductive); biological simulation models. *Mailing Add:* 1425 Fourth St SW Suite A-211 Washington DC 20024. *Fax:* 202-484-6019; *E-Mail:* ctraps@radix.net

BYRD, DAVID LAMAR, DENTISTRY, ORAL & MAXILLOFACIAL SURGURY. *Current Pos:* PVT PRACT, 85- *Personal Data:* b Houston, Tex, June 3, 22; m 50, Carobeth Weeber; c 1. *Educ:* Univ Tex, DDS, 46; Northwestern Univ, MSD, 49. *Prof Exp:* Resident oral surg, Jackson Mem Hosp, Fla, 49-50; intern, Charity Hosp La, 50-51; prof oral surg & chmn dept, Baylor Col Dent, 51-84, chief dent, Baylor Med Ctr, 64-84, dir, Ann Oral Surg Sem, Col Dent, 77-84. *Concurrent Pos:* Consult, Attend Staff, Baylor Med Ctr, Parkland Mem Hosp; ed, Current Ther Dent, Vols I-III; past mem, Am Bd Oral Surg. *Mem:* Am Soc Oral Surg; Sigma Xi; fel Am Col Dent. *Res:* Clinical oral pathology; diseases of soft tissue of bone of head and neck; research in facial and oral pain. *Mailing Add:* 3409 Worth St Suite 610 Sammons Tower Dallas TX 75246. *Fax:* 214-824-3440

BYRD, DAVID SHELTON, ORGANIC CHEMISTRY, PHYSICAL CHEMISTRY. *Current Pos:* from asst prof to assoc prof, 60-69, PROF CHEM, NORTHEAST LA UNIV, 69- *Personal Data:* b Stephens, Ark, May 28, 30; m 53; c 2. *Educ:* Southern State Col, BS, 52; Univ Ky, MS, 55; Univ Louisville, PhD(org chem), 60. *Prof Exp:* Instr chem, Univ Louisville, 57-60. *Mem:* Am Chem Soc; Sigma Xi. *Res:* Trace metal analysis of soil and water. *Mailing Add:* 2314 Whitney Dr Monroe LA 71201

BYRD, EARL WILLIAM, JR, DEVELOPMENTAL BIOLOGY. *Current Pos:* asst prof, 84-90, ASSOC PROF, DEPT OBSTET & GYNEC, SOUTHWESTERN MED SCH, 90- *Personal Data:* b Pomona, Calif, Mar 17, 46; m, Kelly Leyard; c Adrienne. *Educ:* San Francisco State Univ, BA, 68, MA, 70; Univ BC, PhD(zool), 73. *Prof Exp:* Fel develop biol, Scripps Inst Oceanog, 73-75; asst prof embryol, La State Univ, Baton Rouge, 76-82; res scientist, Univ Tex-Houston Sci Ctr, 82-84. *Concurrent Pos:* Chair, Reproductive Biol SIG, Am Fertil Soc, 90-92. *Mem:* Soc Develop Biol; Am Soc Cell Biol; Am Asn Clin Chemists; AAAS; Soc Study Reprod; Am Fertility Soc. *Res:* Human sperm maturation and capacitation in vitro. *Mailing Add:* Dept Obstet & Gynec Southwestern Med Sch 5323 Harry Hines Blvd Dallas TX 75235. *Fax:* 214-648-7604; *E-Mail:* ebyrd@mednet.swmed.edu

BYRD, ISAAC BURLIN, FISHERIES MANAGEMENT, MARINE BIOLOGY. *Current Pos:* RETIRED. *Personal Data:* b Canoe, Ala, Mar 14, 25; m 49, Maljorie Elmore; c Cathy Ann, Teresa Carol & Galy Curtis. *Educ:* Auburn Univ, BS, 48, MS, 50. *Honors & Awards:* Ala Gov Conserv Award, 64; Ala Fisheries Asn Freshwater Div Award, 65. *Prof Exp:* Fisheries res asst, Auburn Univ, 49-51; chief fisheries sect, Ala Dept Conserv, 51-65; chief div fed aid, Fisheries Res & Develop, Nat Marine Fisheries Serv, 65-74, chief, Fisheries Mgt Div, 74-76, chief, Grants Admin Br, 76-84, asst red dir, 84-91. *Concurrent Pos:* Chmn, Gulf of Mex, State/Fed Fisheries Mgt Bd, 85-86; mem, S Atlantic State/Fed Fisheries mgt Bd. *Mem:* Am Fisheries Soc (pres, 65); Gulf & Caribbean Fisheries Inst; World Maricult Soc; fel Am Inst Fishery Res Biol; Int Asn Fish & Wildlife Agencies. *Res:* Marine and freshwater fisheries; estuarine waters; fish population dynamics; reservoir management; aquaculture; aquatic botany and biology; ecology; water pollution; oceanography; public fishing lakes; hydrology. *Mailing Add:* 11105 Seventh St E Treasure Island FL 33706

BYRD, J ROGERS, cytogenetics, genetics, for more information see previous edition

BYRD, JAMES DOTSON, ORGANIC POLYMER CHEMISTRY, MANAGEMENT. *Current Pos:* sr res chemist, 67-74, MAT GROUP SUPVR, HUNTSVILLE DIV, THIOKOL CORP, 74- *Personal Data:* b Jackson, Miss, July 9, 32; m 54; c 3. *Educ:* Miss Col, BS, 54; Univ Ala, MS, 74. *Honors & Awards:* NASA Awards, 54-67. *Prof Exp:* Res asst chem, Purdue Univ, 54-55; chemist, Ethyl Corp, 55-61; sr chemist, Geigy Chem Corp, 61-63; unit chief polymer chem, George C Marshall Space Flight Ctr, NASA, 63-67. *Mem:* Am Chem Soc; fel Am Inst Chem; Soc Aerospace Mat & Process Eng; Am Mgt Asn. *Res:* New adhesive and insulation materials used in a rocket motor environment, such as high and low temperature, vacuum and radiation, including the development of new formulations. *Mailing Add:* 35802-2910 Huntsville AL 35802

BYRD, JAMES WILLIAM, ENERGY. *Current Pos:* EXEC VPRES, MT OLIVE COL, 92- *Personal Data:* b Mt Olive, NC, Dec 4, 36; m 59, Marvis Edwards; c James W Jr, John E & Jennifer A. *Educ:* NC State Univ, BS, 59, MS, 61; Pa State Univ, PhD(physics), 63. *Prof Exp:* From assoc prof to prof physics, ECarolina Univ, 62-84, chmn dept, 65-84; dean, Col Arts & Sci, Appalachian State Univ, 84-90, prof physics, 84-92. *Mem:* Am Phys Soc; Am Asn Physics Teachers; Sigma Xi; Am Asn Higher Educ. *Res:* Plasma and fluid physics; mathematical methods; energy. *Mailing Add:* 634 Hender St Mt Olive Col Mt Olive NC 28365. *Fax:* 919-658-7180

BYRD, KENNETH ALFRED, ALGEBRA. *Current Pos:* ASST PROF MATH, UNIV NC, GREENSBORO, 69- *Personal Data:* b Erwin, NC, Sept 17, 40; m 64; c 2. *Educ:* Duke Univ, BS, 62; NC State Univ, PhD(math), 69. *Mem:* Am Math Soc; Math Asn Am. *Res:* Non-commutative ring theory; quotient rings; homological algebra as it applies to the module category of a ring. *Mailing Add:* Dept Math Univ NC Greensboro NC 27412-0001

BYRD, LARRY DONALD, BEHAVIORAL PHARMACOLOGY, PSYCHOBIOLOGY. *Current Pos:* psychobiologist & chmn, Div Primate Behav, Yerkes Ctr, Emory Univ, 74-80, assoc prof, & chief, 80-82, assoc prof pharmacol, 81-94, RES PROF & CHIEF, DIV BEHAV BIOL, YERKES REGIONAL PRIMATE RES CTR, EMORY UNIV, 82-, PROF PHARMACOL, 95- *Personal Data:* b Salisbury, NC, July 14, 36; m 61, Corrinne Williams; c Kay, Lynn, Renee & Andrew. *Educ:* ECarolina Univ, AB, 62, MA, 64; Univ NC, Chapel Hill, PhD(exp psychol), 68. *Prof Exp:* Instr psychol, E Carolina Univ, 63-64; res asst, Univ NC, Chapel Hill, 65-67; USPHS res fel pharmacol, Med Sch, Harvard Univ, 67-70, instr psychiat, 70-73, prin assoc psychiat, 73-74. *Concurrent Pos:* Assoc scientist, NEng Regional Primate Res Ctr, 69-74, prin assoc psychobiology, 74; Assoc ed, J Exp Anal Behav, 70-76; prin investr, Nat Inst Drug Abuse res grant, 75-; consult, Univ Chicago, 73, Mass Inst Technol press, 75, US Food & Drug Admin, 76-77, Southwest Found Res & Educ, 77, US Navy, 77, Nat Inst Drug Abuse, 79-, Neurobehav Toxicity Test Standards Comn, Am Psychol Asn, 80-84, US Vet Admin, 83, NIH, 83-84, NSF, 84, Fed Am Socs Exp Biol, 84 & Int Study Group Investigating Drugs and Reinforcers; adj prof psychol, Ga Inst Technol, 75- & Emory Univ, 81-; mem, Spec Rev Comt, Nat Inst Drug Abuse, 79-81 & 84, Spec Study Sect, NIH, 84; consult ed, Am J Primatol, 80-83. *Mem:* Am Soc Pharmacol & Exp Therapeut; Behav Pharmacol Soc (pres, 84-86); fel Am Psychol Asn (pres, 82-83); Soc Exp Anal Behav (vpres, 75-76); fel AAAS; fel Am Psychol Soc. *Res:* Behavioral effects of drugs; drug effects on the central nervous system; conditioned behavior; experimental analysis of behavior; behavior of primates; effects of prenatal drug exposure. *Mailing Add:* Yerkes Regional Primate Res Ctr Emory Univ Atlanta GA 30322. *Fax:* 404-727-1266; *E-Mail:* byrd@rmy.emory.ed

BYRD, LLOYD G, SCIENCE ADMINISTRATION, TECHNICAL MANAGEMENT. *Current Pos:* CONSULT ENGR, 86- *Personal Data:* m 43, Jeanne M Parkhurst; c Gary D, Jeffrey A, Donna (Anderson) & Julie (Burke). *Educ:* Ohio State Univ, BCE, 50. *Honors & Awards:* Wilbur S Smith Award, Am Soc Civil Engrs, 85; Roy W Crum Distinguished Serv Award, Transp Res Bd, 87; P D McLean Award, Road Gang, Washington, DC, 89; Francis C Turner Lectr, Am Soc Civil Engrs, 95. *Prof Exp:* Engr, Geomet Design Sect, Ohio Dept Hwys, 49-52; field engr, Ohio Turnpike Comn, 52-56, maintenance engr, 55-60; assoc ed, Pub Works Publ, Ridgewood, NJ, 60-63; partner, Byrd, Tallamy, MacDonald & Lewis, consult engrs, 63-72; sr vpres & dir, Wilbur Smith & Assocs, 72-84; interim dir, Strategic Hwy Res Prog, Am Asn State Hwy & Transp Officials, 84-86. *Concurrent Pos:* Mgr, Byrd, Tallamy, MacDonald & Lewis, 72-84; chmn, Nat Transp Policy Comt, Am Soc Civil Engrs, mem, Nat Comt Govt Affairs, Hwy Div Res Comt; gov bd, Nat Res Coun; pres, Fairfax County, Va Chamber Commerce 75-76; chmn, Human Rights Cmn, 78-79; nat bd direction, Am Soc Civil Engrs, 79-82. *Mem:* Nat Acad Eng; Am Soc Civil Engrs; Transp Res Bd; Am Pub Works Asn. *Res:* Policy studies in the field of transportation and transportation research. *Mailing Add:* 3904 Rive Dr Alexandria VA 22309

BYRD, MITCHELL AGEE, ZOOLOGY. *Current Pos:* From asst prof to prof, 56-92, head dept, 62-92, EMER PROF BIOL, COL WILLIAM & MARY, 92- *Personal Data:* b Franklin, Va, Aug 16, 28; m 54. *Educ:* Va Polytech Inst, BS, 49, MS, 51, PhD(biol), 54. *Mem:* Am Soc Parasitol; Am Soc Mammal; Am Ornith Union. *Res:* Mammalogy; ecology; taxonomy; wildlife diseases and parasites; avian ecology. *Mailing Add:* 115 Copse Way Williamsburg VA 23185

BYRD, NORMAN ROBERT, ORGANIC POLYMER CHEMISTRY. *Current Pos:* head org-polymer sect, Astropower Labs, Douglas Aircraft Co, 62-69, STAFF MGR-MCDONNEL DOUGLAS CORP FEL, CHEM RES, DOUGLAS AIRCRAFT DIV, MCDONNEL DOUGLAS CORP, 69-, fel, 84- *Personal Data:* b New York, NY, Mar 10, 21; m 95, Chris Sorensen; c Lauri Anne & Geoffrey Norman. *Educ:* Polytech Inst Brooklyn, BS, 49, PhD(org chem), 55. *Prof Exp:* Res chemist, Nat Starch Prod, NY, 48-51; asst, Polytech Inst Brooklyn, 51-52 & US Navy Proj, 52-54; res chemist, E I Du Pont de Nemours & Co, Inc, 54-55; sr res chemist, Goodyear Tire & Rubber Co, 55-58; head fundamental sect, Rayonier, Inc, 58-60; res scientist, Aeronutronic, Calif, 61-62. *Mem:* AAAS; Am Chem Soc; Am Inst Chem; The Chem Soc; NY Acad Sci. *Res:* Starch and cellulose chemistry; synthetic resins; elastomers; graft and block polymers; organic reactions macromolecules; electrical properties of organic polymers; semiconductor; adhesion studies; fire-resistant materials; icephobics. *Mailing Add:* 17991 Athens Ave Villa Park CA 92861. *E-Mail:* 04226@mdcpo202.ib.mdc.com

BYRD, RICHARD DOWELL, MATHEMATICS. *Current Pos:* from asst prof to assoc prof, 67-72, PROF MATH, UNIV HOUSTON, 72- *Personal Data:* b Newport, Ark, Mar 14, 33; m 64; c 1. *Educ:* Hendrix Col, BA, 58; Univ Ark, MS, 59; Tulane Univ, PhD(math), 66. *Prof Exp:* Instr math, La State Univ, New Orleans, 60-64; asst prof, Lehigh Univ, 66-67. *Mem:* Am Math Soc; Math Asn Am. *Res:* Lattice-ordered groups. *Mailing Add:* Univ Houston Houston TX 77204-3476

BYRD, ROGER CARL, NUCLEAR PHYSICS. *Current Pos:* staff mem, medium energy physics, 86-89, space plasma physics, 89-93, STAFF MEM, ASTROPHYS & RADIATION MEASUREMENTS, LOS ALAMOS NAT LAB, 93- *Personal Data:* b Nov 24, 50; m 83, Jill Blacharsh. *Educ:* Ga Inst Technol, BS, 72; Duke Univ, PhD(physics), 78. *Prof Exp:* Instr & res assoc, Duke Univ & Triangle Univ Nuclear Lab, 78-79, asst prof & res assoc, 80-83; sr res assoc, Ind Univ Cyclotron Fac, 84-86, staff physicist, 86. *Mem:* Am Nuclear Soc; Am Phys Soc; Inst Flec Electronics Engrs. *Res:* Detector development for arms control applications. *Mailing Add:* Astrophys & Radiation Measurements Group MS D436 Los Alamos Nat Lab Los Alamos NM 87545. *E-Mail:* rbyrd@lanl.gov

BYRKIT, DONALD RAYMOND, MATHEMATICS, APPLIED STATISTICS. *Current Pos:* From asst prof to assoc prof, 67-75, PROF MATH & STATIST, UNIV WFLA, 75- *Personal Data:* b Indianapolis, Ind, March 19, 33; m 58, 75, Marnette Cook; c Steven & Linda. *Educ:* Ill Inst Technol, BS, 55; Ill State Univ, MS, 58; Fla State Univ, PhD(math educ), 68. *Concurrent Pos:* Vis prof, Kaohsiung Teachers Col, Taiwan, 78-79; chmn, Univ WFla, 72-76 & 87-91, assoc dean, 91-92. *Mem:* Am Statist Asn; Math Asn Am; Nat Coun Teachers Math Sch Sci & Math Asn. *Res:* Writer on topics of statistics, business calculus, number theory. *Mailing Add:* 4995 Woodcliff Dr Pensacola FL 32504. *E-Mail:* dbyrkit@math-stat.math.uwf.edu

BYRN, ERNEST EDWARD, PHYSICAL CHEMISTRY, ANALYTICAL CHEMISTRY. *Current Pos:* chmn dept, 66-70, prof, 66-86, EMER PROF CHEM, EASTERN KY UNIV, 86- *Personal Data:* b Frederick, Okla, Apr 4, 24; m 52, Doris Cooper; c Judson & Ann. *Educ:* Univ Tenn, BS, 50, PhD, 54. *Prof Exp:* Res chemist, Buckeye Cellulose Corp, 54-55; asst prof chem, Univ Okla, 55-61; asst res dir, MacDermid, Inc, 61-62, res dir, 62-64; prof, George Peabody Col, 64-66. *Mem:* AAAS; Am Chem Soc; Sigma Xi. *Res:* Organic reagents for inorganic analysis; titrations in nonaqueous solvents; liquid-liquid extractions; surface activity and detergency; chemical education. *Mailing Add:* 125 Buckwood Dr Richmond KY 40475

BYRN, STEPHEN ROBERT, BIOPHYSICAL CHEMISTRY, SOLID STATE CHEMISTRY. *Current Pos:* from asst prof to assoc prof, 72-81, assoc dept head, 79-88, PROF MED CHEM, PURDUE UNIV, 81-, DEPT HEAD, 88-, CHARLES B JORDAN PROF MED CHEM, 92- *Personal Data:* b New Albany, Ind, Oct 7, 44; m 69, Sarah Rushmore; c Elizabeth, Robert, John, Mary, David, Rebecca, Sarah & Daniel. *Educ:* DePauw Univ, BA, 66; Univ Ill, Urbana, PhD(chem), 70. *Prof Exp:* Scholar, Univ Calif, Los Angeles, 71-72; fel, NSF & NIH. *Concurrent Pos:* From asst dean to assoc dean, Grad Sch, Purdue Univ, 85-88. *Mem:* Am Chem Soc; Am Crystallog Asn; Am Asn Pharm Sci. *Res:* Solid state reactions of organic crystals, particularly drugs; interaction of drugs with DNA; design and synthesis of anti-AIDS agents; solid state NMR spectroscopy. *Mailing Add:* Dept Med Sch Pharm Purdue Univ Sch Pharm Lafayette IN 47907-0702. *Fax:* 765-494-6790

BYRNE, BARBARA JEAN MCMANAMY, SURFACE PROTEINS OF PARAMECIUM, PARAMECIUM BEHAVIOR. *Current Pos:* DEAN NATURAL SCI & MATH, RICHARD STOCKTON COL NJ, 90- *Personal Data:* b Baraboo, Wis, Aug 9, 41; m 68, Bruce C; c Joshua & Jenny. *Educ:* Blackburn Col, BA, 62; Ind Univ, Bloomington, MA, 63, PhD(genetics), 69. *Prof Exp:* Lectr biol, Ind Univ, 71-72; res specialist genetics, Cornell Univ, 72-74; from asst prof to assoc prof, Wells Col, 74-87, assoc dean & registrar, 84-87, prof biol, 87-90. *Concurrent Pos:* Vis scholar, Ind Univ, 81-82; NIH area grant, PI, 87-89; NIH Extramural Assoc, 89. *Mem:* Sigma Xi; Genetics Soc Am; AAAS. *Res:* Behavioral genetics of Paramecium aurelia; ciliary antigens of paramecium; molecular investigations of the structure of surface protein genes and their control regions; emphasis on comparison of stocks with different frequency of expression of selected genes. *Mailing Add:* Dean Natural Sci & Math Richard Stockton Col NJ Pomona NJ 08240-9988. *Fax:* 609-748-5515; *E-Mail:* iaprod573@vax003.stockton.edu

BYRNE, BRUCE CAMPBELL, MOLECULAR BIOLOGY, MEDICINE. *Current Pos:* ADJ PROJ MED, ROBERT WOOD JOHNSON MED SCH, CAMDEN, 89-; ASSOC PROF, CORIELL INST MED RES, CAMDEN, 89- *Personal Data:* b Hammond, Ind, May 13, 45; m 68, Barbara McManamy; c Joshua & Jenny. *Educ:* Ind Univ, Bloomington, AB, 67, PhD(genetics), 72. *Prof Exp:* USPHS trainee genetics, Cornell Univ, 72-74; from asst prof to prof biol, Wells Col, 74-89. *Concurrent Pos:* Vis scientist, State Univ NY, HSC at Syracuse, 87-89; mgr acad support comput, Univ Med & Dent NJ. *Mem:*

AAAS. *Res:* Development of new molecular probes for human immunodeficiency virus; oncogene expression; applications of computer technologies to molecular biology and medicine. *Mailing Add:* Dept Med Univ Med & Dent NJ R W Johnson Med Sch 401 Haddon Ave Camden NJ 08103. *E-Mail:* byrne@umdnj.edu

BYRNE, FRANCIS PATRICK, ANALYTICAL CHEMISTRY. *Current Pos:* ADJ PROF, DEPT CHEM, WESTERN KY UNIV, 78- *Personal Data:* b Kansas City, Mo, July 25, 13; m 42; c 6. *Educ:* Rockhurst Col, BS, 35; Creighton Univ, MS, 38; Univ Tenn, PhD(chem), 49. *Honors & Awards:* Lundel-Bright Award, Am Soc Testing & Mat, 74. *Prof Exp:* Instr chem, St Joseph Col, 40-42; res chemist, Westvaco Chlorine Prods, 42-46; instr chem, Univ Tenn, 46-49; mgr, Analytical Chem Dept, Westinghouse Res & Develop Labs, 49-78. *Concurrent Pos:* Pres, Pittsburgh Conf Analytical Chem & Appl Spectros, 64; mem, NSF Adv Panel to Analytical Div, Nat Inst Standards & Technol, 72-75; adj prof, Western Ky Univ, 78- *Mem:* Am Chem Soc; Am Soc Testing & Mat. *Res:* Detection and determination of pertinent materials in environmental situations. *Mailing Add:* 78 Nightsong Ct The Woodlands TX 77380

BYRNE, GEORGE D, numerical analysis, for more information see previous edition

BYRNE, GERALD I, MICROBIOLOGY, SEXUALLY TRANSMITTED DISEASES. *Current Pos:* PROF, DEPT MED MICROBIOL, UNIV WIS MED SCH, 82- *Personal Data:* Quincy, Mass, 1947. *Educ:* NMex State Univ, BS, 70; Miami Univ, MS, 72, PhD(microbiol), 77. *Prof Exp:* Fel & asst prof, Cornell Univ Med Sch, 77-82. *Concurrent Pos:* Romnes scholar, 88-93. *Mem:* Am Soc Microbiol; Am Asn Immunologists. *Mailing Add:* Dept Med Microbiol Univ Wisc Med Sch 1300 University Ave Madison WI 53706-1532

BYRNE, J(OSEPH) GERALD, PHYSICAL METALLURGY. *Current Pos:* assoc prof metall, 66-69, prof mat sci & eng, 69-85, PROF METALL, UNIV UTAH, 85-, CHAIR, 86-, IVOR D THOMAS PROF PHYS METALL, 87- *Personal Data:* b New York, NY, July 15, 30; m 57, Joan O'Brian; c Beth, Maura, Dan & Noreen. *Educ:* Stevens Inst Technol, ME, 53, MS, 57; Northwestern Univ, PhD(metall), 60. *Prof Exp:* Mech engr, Heat-X-Changer Corp, 53-54; metallurgist, Crucible Steel Co, 54-55 & Am Brake Shoe Co, 55-57; res asst metall, Northwestern Univ, 57-60; res engr, Dow Chem Co, 60-62; from asst prof to assoc prof, Stevens Inst Technol, 62-66. *Concurrent Pos:* Mem, Nat Mat Adv Bd, Nat Acad Sci, 72; vis prof, Cent Univ Venezuela, 72-73; mem, Exec Comt, Int Confs Mat Technol, 77-; assoc ed, Mat Sci & Eng. *Mem:* Am Inst Mining, Metall & Petrol Engrs; Am Soc Testing & Mat; Acad Metals & Mats; Am Powder Metall Inst; fel Am Soc Metals Int. *Res:* Strengthening of solids; phase transformations; recrystallization; dislocation theory; position annihilation applied to damage in solids. *Mailing Add:* 1159 First Ave Salt Lake City UT 84103. *Fax:* 801-581-4937; *E-Mail:* jgbyrne@mines.utah.edu

BYRNE, JEFFREY EDWARD, PHARMACOLOGY, CARDIOVASCULAR RESEARCH. *Current Pos:* SR RES SCIENTIST II, BRISTOL-MYERS PROD, 87- *Personal Data:* b Minneapolis, Minn, July 15, 39; m 78; c 3. *Educ:* Univ NDak, BA, 62; Univ SDak, MA, 64, PhD(physiol & pharmacol), 66. *Prof Exp:* Fel & lectr pharmacol & exp therapeut, Univ Man, 66-69; sr scientist cardiovasc pharmacol, 69-73, sr investr, 73-81, prin res scientist, Mead Johnson & Co, 81-87. *Concurrent Pos:* Adj fac mem, Sch Nursing, Evansville Univ & Sch Med, Ind Univ, 72-87. *Mem:* AAAS; NY Acad Sci; Sigma Xi; Am Heart Asn; Am Soc Pharmacol & Exp Therapeut. *Res:* Cardiovascular pharmacology; cardiac arrhythmia, antiarrhythmic drugs; myocardial ischemia; electrophysiology. *Mailing Add:* 590 Atkinson Lane Langhorne PA 19047. *Fax:* 609-683-6609

BYRNE, JOHN HOWARD, NEUROBIOLOGY. *Current Pos:* PROF PHYSIOL & CELL BIOL, UNIV TEX HEALTH SCI CTR, HOUSTON, 82- *Educ:* Polytech Inst Brooklyn, PhD(bioeng), 73. *Res:* Learning and memory; synaptic transmission. *Mailing Add:* Dept Neurobiol Univ Tex Health Sci Ctr 6431 Fannin St Suite 7 046 PO Box 20708 Houston TX 77225-9964. *Fax:* 713-792-5795

BYRNE, JOHN JOSEPH, SURGERY. *Current Pos:* RETIRED. *Personal Data:* b Morristown, NJ, Aug 30, 16. *Educ:* Princeton Univ, AB, 37; Harvard Univ, MD, 41. *Prof Exp:* Mem staff, Sch Med, Boston Univ, 47-57, prof surg, 57-73, prof sociol-med sci, 73; chief surg, Framingham Union Hosp, 73-78. *Concurrent Pos:* Asst chief, Neurosurg Sect, May Gen Hosp, Ill; dir hand serv & vis surgeon, Boston City Hosp; chief surg, Framingham Union Hosp; mem staff, Boston Univ Hosp. *Mem:* AAAS; Am Surg Asn; Am Soc Surg Hand; Am Asn Surg Trauma; Am Col Surgeons; Sigma Xi. *Res:* Physiology of pulmonary embolism; serum amylase activity in intestinal obstruction; diseases of the hand; phlebitis; medical history; shock; pancreatitis. *Mailing Add:* 3300 Gulfshore Blvd No 206 Maple FL 02313

BYRNE, JOHN RICHARD, mathematics, for more information see previous edition

BYRNE, JOHN VINCENT, OCEANOGRAPHY. *Current Pos:* pres, 84-95, EMER PROF, ORE STATE UNIV, 96- *Personal Data:* b Hempstead, NY, May 9, 28; m 54, Shirley O'Connor; c Donna, Lisa, Karen & Steven. *Educ:* Hamilton Col, AB, 51; Columbia Univ, MA, 53; Univ Southern Calif, PhD(geol), 57. *Hon Degrees:* Dr, Hamilton Col, 94. *Prof Exp:* Field asst, Newell Reef Study, Am Mus, 51 & Raroia Exped, Pac Sci Bd, 52; lab assoc, Univ Southern Calif, 53-55; geologist, Res Sect, Humble Oil & Refining Co, Tex, 57-60; from assoc prof to prof oceanog, Ore State Univ, 60-81, chmn dept, 68-81, dean, Sch Oceanog, 72-77, dean res, 77-80, vpres res & grad studies, 80-81; admin, Nat Oceanic & Atmospheric Admin, US Dept Com, 81-84. *Concurrent Pos:* Dir, Oceanog Prog, NSF, 66-67. *Mem:* AAAS; Am Geophys Union; Geol Soc Am; Am Asn Petrol Geologists; Soc Econ Paleontologists & Mineralogists. *Res:* Marine geology. *Mailing Add:* Autzen House Ore State Univ 811 SW Jefferson Corvallis OR 97333. *E-Mail:* byrnej@ccmail.orst.edu

BYRNE, KEVIN J, BEVERAGE PRODUCTION & ANALYSIS. *Current Pos:* SR RES SCIENTIST, RES, E & J GALLO WINERY, 96- *Personal Data:* b Philadelphia, Pa, Mar 23, 44; m 81, Linda Ball; c Annan, Brandon & Caitlin. *Educ:* La Salle Col, BA, 66; Villanova Univ, MS, 69, PhD(chem), 73. *Prof Exp:* Res assoc chem, Col Environ Sci & Forestry, State Univ NY, 73-74 & Monell Chem Senses Ctr, Univ Pa, 74-76; res scientist, Joseph E Seagram & Sons, Inc, 76-83, sr res scientist, Res & Develop, 83-96. *Mem:* Am Chem Soc; Asn Official Anal Chemists. *Res:* Identification and evaluation of sensory compounds in alcoholic beverages; development of analysis for regulated compounds in alcoholic beverages; study changes in beverages during maturation. *Mailing Add:* 1760 Palmer Dr Turlock CA 95353. *Fax:* 209-579-4541

BYRNE, KEVIN M, FERMENTATION MICROBIOL, BIOCHEMISTRY. *Current Pos:* res fel fermentation microbiol, 85-92, SR RES FEL, NATURAL PROD DRUG DISCOVERY, MERCK SHARP & DOHME RES LABS, MERCK & CO, INC, 92- *Personal Data:* b Aug 6, 48; m 76, Patricia Repik; c Kimberly & Kristen. *Educ:* Fairfield Univ, BS, 71; Rutgers Univ, PhD(biochem), 76. *Prof Exp:* Res assoc, Sch Chem Sci, Univ Ill, Urbana, 76-78; scientist I, microbiol sect, fermentation prog, Frederick Cancer Res Facil, Nat Cancer Inst, 78-80, scientist II, 80-85. *Mem:* Am Soc Microbiol; Am Chem Soc; Am Soc Biochem Molecular Biol; Soc Indust Microbiol; Am Soc Pharmacol. *Res:* Discovery, biosynthesis, mechanism of action and regulation of natural products. *Mailing Add:* Merck Sharp & Dohme Res Labs R80Y-210 PO Box 2000 Rahway NJ 07065-0900. *Fax:* 732-594-1399; *E-Mail:* kevin_byrne@merck.com

BYRNE, NELSON, PLASMA PHYSICS, COMPUTATIONAL PHYSICS. *Current Pos:* mem staff transport & diffusion, 71-74, ASST DIR PLASMA PHYSICS LABS, SCI APPLN INC, 74-, SR SCIENTIST. *Personal Data:* b Pittsfield, Mass, Sept 23, 37; m; c 2. *Educ:* Calif Inst Technol, BS, 59; Stanford Univ, PhD(physics), 65. *Prof Exp:* Group leader transport & diffusion, Lawrence Livermore Labs, 65-71. *Mem:* Am Phys Soc. *Res:* Applications of numerical models to analysis of physical systems. *Mailing Add:* MS No 32 SAIC 10260 Campus Pt Dr San Diego CA 92121

BYRNE, PETER M, GEOTECHNICAL ENGINEERING. *Current Pos:* asst prof civil eng, 67, PROF, UNIV BC. *Personal Data:* b Dublin, Ireland, Mar 3, 36; Can citizen; m 62; c 2. *Educ:* Nat Univ Ireland, BE, 59; Univ BC, MASc, 66, PhD(soil mech), 69. *Prof Exp:* Design engr, George Wimpey, Eng, 59-60 & CBA Eng, BC, 60-63. *Concurrent Pos:* Nat Res Coun Can study grant earth sci; partner, Peacs Eng, Comput & Eng Serv. *Mem:* Eng Inst Can. *Res:* Application of the finite element method of analysis to the solution of both static and dynamic problems in porous media such as soil, concrete and rock. *Mailing Add:* Dept Civil Eng Univ BC 2324 Main Mall Vancouver BC V6T 1Z4 Can

BYRNE, ROBERT HOWARD, OCEANOGRAPHY. *Current Pos:* PROF CHEM, UNIV S FLA, ST PETERSBURG. *Personal Data:* b Omaha, Nebr, Apr 15, 41; m 67; c 1. *Educ:* Univ Chicago, BS, 64; DePaul Univ, MS, 67; Boston Univ, MA, 70; Univ RI, PhD(oceanog), 74. *Prof Exp:* Res assoc oceanog, Univ RI, 74- *Res:* Investigation of the physical chemistry of seawater; trace metal speciation in seawater with special emphasis on the speciation of ferric ions. *Mailing Add:* Marine Sci Dept Univ S Fla 140 Seventh Ave St Petersburg FL 33701-5001

BYRNE, ROBERT JOHN, OCEANOGRAPHY. *Current Pos:* assoc prof marine sci, 69-72, SR MARINE SCIENTIST, VA INST MARINE SCI, 72-, PROF MARINE SCI & ASSOC DIR RES. *Personal Data:* b Chicago, Ill, Sept 17, 32; m 56; c 2. *Educ:* Univ Chicago, MS, 61, PhD(geophys sci), 64. *Prof Exp:* Ford Found fel, Woods Hole Oceanog Inst, 64-65, asst scientist, Dept Geophys & Geol, 65-67; res oceanogr, Land & Sea Interaction Lab, Environ Sci Serv Admin, 67-69. *Concurrent Pos:* Assoc prof, Sch Marine Sci, Col William & Mary, 72- *Mem:* Am Geophys Union. *Res:* Geological oceanography; coastal engineering; mechanics of sediment transport; coastal fluid and sediment processes; coastal zone planning. *Mailing Add:* Sch Marine Sci Inst Res William & Mary Gloucester Point VA 23062

BYRNES, CHRISTOPHER IAN, ACADEMIC RESEARCH IN DYNAMICAL SYSTEMS, AUTOMATIC CONTROL. *Current Pos:* prof & chmn, Dept Systs Sci & Math, 89-91, DEAN ENG & APPL SCI, WASH UNIV, ST LOUIS, 91- *Personal Data:* b New York City, NY, June 28, 49; m 84, Catherine Morris; c Kathleen, Alison & Christopher. *Educ:* Manhattan Col, BS, 71; Univ Mass, MS, 73, PhD, 75. *Honors & Awards:* George Axelby Award, Inst Elect & Electronics Engrs, 91. *Prof Exp:* Instr, Univ Utah, Salt Lake City, 75-78, asst prof, Harvard Univ, Mass, 78-81, assoc prof, 81-85; res prof, Ariz State Univ Tempe, 85-89. *Concurrent Pos:* Consult, Sci Syst, Inc Cambridge, 80-84, Syst Eng Inc, Greenbelt, Md, 86; adj prof, Royal Inst Technol, Stockholm, 85-90; mem, Bd Dirs, Belden, Inc; chmn bd, Ctr Emerging Technol. *Mem:* AAAS; fel Inst Elec & Electronics Engrs; Soc

BYRNES, EUGENE WILLIAM, ORGANIC CHEMISTRY. *Current Pos:* from asst prof to assoc prof, 68-85, chem div natural sci & math, 72-77, PROF CHEM, ASSUMPTION COL, MASS, 85- *Personal Data:* b Roselle, NJ, July 3, 33; m 62; c 2. *Educ:* Rensselaer Polytech Inst, BS, 56; Univ NH, PhD(org chem), 64. *Honors & Awards:* C P Snow Lectr, Ithaca Col, 64. *Prof Exp:* Prod chemist, Schering Corp, 56; instr chem, Ohio Northern Univ, 62-63; NIH fel biochem, Mich State Univ, 63-65; asst prof chem, Liberty State Col, 65-66 & Alliance Col, 66-68. *Concurrent Pos:* Vis scientist, AB Hassie, Molndal, Sweden, 76. *Mem:* Sigma Xi; Am Chem Soc. *Res:* Synthesis of antiarrhythmic and local anesthetic drugs; antiarrhythmic drugs. *Mailing Add:* 191 Nola Dr Holden MA 01520-2633

BYRNES, WILLIAM RICHARD, FORESTRY. *Current Pos:* from assoc prof to prof, 62-75, asst head & dir res, 75-85, HEAD DEPT FORESTRY, PURDUE UNIV, 85- *Personal Data:* b Barnesboro, Pa, Oct 12, 24; m 47; c 5. *Educ:* Pa State Univ, BS, 50, MF, 51, PhD(agron, soils), 61. *Prof Exp:* Asst forestry, Pa State Univ, 50-51; soil scientist, Soil Conserv Serv, USDA, 51-52; instr forestry, Pa State Univ, 52-61, assoc prof, 61-62. *Mem:* Soc Am Foresters; Am Soc Agron; Weed Sci Soc Am; Soil Sci Soc Am; Nat Walnut Coun. *Res:* Forest soils; watershed management; ecology; silviculture; physiology. *Mailing Add:* 2208 Huron Rd West Lafayette IN 47906

BYRON, FREDERICK WILLIAM, JR, PHYSICS. *Current Pos:* from asst prof to assoc prof, 66-74, PROF PHYSICS, UNIV MASS, 74- *Personal Data:* b Manchester, NH, July 8, 38; m, Edith Iselin; c 2. *Educ:* Harvard Col, AB, 59; Columbia Univ, PhD(physics), 63. *Honors & Awards:* Chancellor's Medal, Univ Mass, 93. *Prof Exp:* Actg asst prof, Univ Calif, 63-65, asst prof, 65-66. *Concurrent Pos:* Pfister fel, Columbia Univ, 61-62, Raytheon fel, 62-63, Alfred P Sloan Found, 65-67; vis prof, Univ Brussels, 73-74; Fulbright res scholar, Belg, 73-74; head, Dept Physics & Astron, Univ Mass, 75-79, dean nat sci & math, 79-93. *Mem:* Fel Am Phys Soc. *Res:* Contributed numerous articles to professional publications. *Mailing Add:* Dept Physics GR Tower C Univ Mass Amherst MA 01003

BYRON, JOSEPH WINSTON, pharmacology; deceased, see previous edition for last biography

BYSTROFF, ROMAN IVAN, ANALYTICAL CHEMISTRY. *Current Pos:* SR CHEMIST, LAWRENCE LIVERMORE LAB, 58- *Personal Data:* b San Francisco, Calif, Nov 6, 31; m 56; c 4. *Educ:* Univ Calif, Berkeley, BS, 53; Iowa State Univ, PhD(chem), 59. *Mem:* Am Chem Soc. *Res:* Stability of coordination compounds in solution; inorganic analysis by solution chemistry; ultraviolet and visible spectrophotometry; flame spectroscopy, both emission and atomic absorption. *Mailing Add:* 330 Scott St Livermore CA 94550

BYSTRYN, JEAN-CLAUDE, DERMATOLOGY, IMMUNODERMATOPATHOLOGY. *Current Pos:* PROF DERMATOL, NY UNIV, 70-, DIR, IMMUNOFLUORESCENCE LAB, 72- *Personal Data:* b Paris, France, May 8, 38; m, Marcia Hammill; c Annie & Alex. *Educ:* Univ Chicago, BS, 58; NY Univ, MD, 62. *Honors & Awards:* Irma T Hirschl Career Scientist Award, 79; Annual Award, Skin Cancer Found, 85. *Concurrent Pos:* Dir, Melanoma Prog, Kaplan Cancer Ctr, 83- *Mem:* Am Dermatol Asn; Am Asn Immunologist; Am Asn Cancer Res; Soc Investigative Dermatol; Am Soc Cell Biol. *Res:* Cancer vaccines; melanoma immunology; vitiligo; autoimmune bullous skin diseases. *Mailing Add:* NY Univ Med Ctr 560 First Ave New York NY 10016. *Fax:* 212-263-8561; *E-Mail:* bystryn@is.nyu.edu

BYVIK, CHARLES EDWARD, SOLID STATE PHYSICS. *Current Pos:* SR SCIENTIST, W J SCHAFER ASSOC, 88- *Personal Data:* b Ladd, Ill, Mar 26, 40; m 64; c 3. *Educ:* Ill Inst Technol, BS, 63; Univ Mo, Rolla, MS, 64; Va Polytech Inst & State Univ, PhD(physics), 72. *Prof Exp:* Physicist, NASA, Hampton, Va, 64-88. *Mem:* Sigma Xi; AAAS. *Res:* Identification and characterization of tunable solid state laser materials; spectroscopy of laser ions in solid state hosts and modeling of ion-host interactions. *Mailing Add:* 1014 Emerald Dr Alexandria VA 23308

BZOCH, KENNETH R, SPEECH PATHOLOGY, AUDIOLOGY. *Current Pos:* assoc prof, 64-80, PROF COMMUN DIS, COL HEALTH RELATED PROFESSIONS, UNIV FLA, 80-, CHMN DEPT, 64- *Personal Data:* b Chicago, Ill, Nov 6, 27; m 50; c 2. *Educ:* DePaul Univ, BA, 50; Northwestern Univ, MA & PhD(speech path), 56. *Prof Exp:* Instr, DePaul Acad, Ill, 50; lectr speech, Univ Col, Northwestern Univ, 51; asst prof, Grad Sch, Loyola Univ Ill, 53-57; prof grad fac & coordr, Cleft Lip & Palate Inst, Northwestern Univ, Chicago, 57-59 & 60-64. *Concurrent Pos:* Consult, St Francis Hosp, Evanston, Ill, 53-58, Vet Res Hosp, Chicago, 57-59, Nat Inst Dent Res, 64, 66-70 & 80-84, HEW Div, Hosp & Med Facil, 64 & Vet Hops, Gainesville, 70-; HEW dir, Hosp & Med Fac, Nat Inst Dent Res, 80-84. *Mem:* Fel Am Speech & Hearing Asn; Speech Asn Am; Am Cleft Palate Asn (pres, 76). *Res:* Cineflurographic studies of co-articulation in normal and abnormal speech; efficacy of cleft palate habilitation procedures; normal and abnormal language development in infancy; physiological phonetics. *Mailing Add:* 640 NW 57th St Gainesville FL 32607

BZOCH, RONALD CHARLES, MATHEMATICS. *Current Pos:* RETIRED. *Personal Data:* b Chicago, Ill, Mar 16, 30; m 51; c 2. *Educ:* DePaul Univ, AB, 53, MS, 54; Ill Inst Technol, PhD(math), 57. *Prof Exp:* Asst math, Ill Inst Technol, 54-57; asst prof math, Univ Minn, 57-60 & Univ Utah, 60-61; assoc prof math, La State Univ, 61-66, assoc chmn dept, 64-66; prof math & chmn dept, Univ NDak, 66-92. *Mem:* Math Asn Am. *Res:* Real variables; integration theory. *Mailing Add:* Univ NDak Box 8162 Univ Sta Grand Forks ND 58202